This volume is part of
THE ARTSCROLL® SERIES
an ongoing project of
translations, commentaries and expositions on
Scripture, Mishnah, Talmud, Midrash, Halachah,
liturgy, history, the classic Rabbinic writings,
biographies and thought.

For a brochure of current publications visit your local
Hebrew bookseller or contact the publisher:

Mesorah Publications, ltd

313 Regina Avenue / Rahway, New Jersey 07065
(718) 921-9000 / www.artscroll.com

# Scriptural Index

**Tanna** [pl. **Tannaim**] – Sage of the Mishnaic period whose view is recorded in a **Mishnah** or **Baraisa.**

**Tanna Kamma** – anonymous first opinion of a **Mishnah** or **Baraisa.**

**Targum** – lit. translation. The Aramaic interpretive translation of Scripture.

**techum** [pl. **techumim**] – Sabbath bounadry; the distance of 2,000 **amos** from a perso's place of residence which he is permitted to travel on th **Sabbath** or **Yom Tov.**

**tefach** [pl. **tefachim**] – handbreadth; a measure of length equal to the width of four thumbs.

**tefillah** – (a) prayer, specifically the daily prayer services and the additions added on the Sabbath and Festivals; (b) in Talmudic usage, tefillah invariably refers to **Shemoneh Esrei.**

**tefillin** – phylacteries. Two black leather casings, each of which contains Torah passages written on parchment. It is a **mitzvah** for adult males to wear one on the head and one on the arm.

**Temple** – See **Beis HaMikdash.**

**Temple Mount** – site of the Holy Temple. See **Beis HaMikdash.**

**terumah** [pl. **terumos**] – the portion of the crop separated and given to the **Kohen,** usually between $^1/_{40}$ and $^1/_{60}$ of the total crop. **Terumah** may not be eaten by a non-Kohen, or by a **Kohen** in a state of **tumah.**

**terumas maaser** – the tithe portion separated by the **Levite** from **maaser rishon** and given to a **Kohen.**

**tevel** – produce of **Eretz Yisrael** that has become subject to the obligation of **terumah** and **tithes;** forbidden for consumption until *terumah* and all tithes have been designated.

**Teves** – tenth month of the Hebrew calendar.

**tevilah** – immersion in a **mikveh** for the purpose of cleansing of their **tumah**-contamination.

**tevul yom** – people or utensils that were **tamei** and underwent immersion in a **mikveh** but still retain a vestige of their **tumah** until nightfall.

**Tishah B'Av** – lit. the Ninth of Av; the fast day that commemorates the destruction of the First and Second **Beis HaMikdash** and other national tragedies.

**Tishrei** – seventh month of the Hebrew calendar.

**todah** – thanksgiving offering brought when a person survives a potentially life-threatening situation.

**tofes** – see **toref.**

**toladah** [pl. **tolados**] – subcategory of an **av** (pl. **avos**), a main category.

**Torah** – the five books of Moses; the **Chumash** or Pentateuch.

**toref** – a document's essence, specifying its date, the names of the principals and the pertinent facts particular to the document. The document's form – the **tofes** – contains the rest of the document's text including a summary of all the significant information contained in the *toref* except for the document's date.

**Tosefta** – a written collection of **Baraisos**.

**treifah** – (a) a person, animal, or bird possessing one of a well-defined group of life-threatening body defects.

**tumah** – legally defined state of impurity inherent in certain people (e.g. a **niddah**) or objects (e.g. a corpse). Under specific conditions, this contamination can be transmitted to other people or objects, with the degree of **tumah** generally declining with each transmission. People or utensils in a state of **tumah** are restricted from contact and certain other forms of interaction with holy objects by a body of intricate and complex laws. People or utensils that are **tamei** can remove their contamination and become **tahor** by being immersed in a **mikveh.**

**tumas meis** – the **tumah** of a human corpse.

**tumas ohel** – lit. roof *tumah*; certain **tamei** objects or persons convey **tumah** to others under the same roof.

**tzaraas** – (a) various skin afflictions described in *Lev.* ch. 13 that render a person **tamei**. *Tzaraas* is often, though erroneously, described as leprosy. The individual inflicted with *tzaraas* is known as a **metzora.**

**tzitzis** – the fringes that by Torah law must be placed on a four-cornered garment.

**tzon-barzel** – lit. iron-sheep; the portion of a woman's dowry assessed prior to the marriage whose value is recorded in the *kesubah.* Should the marriage end, reimbursement is made to the woman at the property's assessed value, even if in the interim it was lost or damaged. Thus, the property's value remains preserved for the wife like *iron.*

**unpaid custodian** – a **shomer** who receives no remuneration for his services.

**yavam** – see **yibum.**

**ye'ush** – abandoning hope, despair – generally used regarding lost or stolen property.

**yevamah** – see **yibum.**

**yibum** – levirate marriage. When a man dies childless, the Torah provides for one of his brothers to marry the widow. This marriage is called *yibum*. The surviving brother, upon whom the obligation to perform the mitzvah of *yibum* falls, is called the **yavam.** The widow is called the **yevamah.** *Yibum* is effected only through cohabitation. See **chalitzah.**

**Yisrael** [pl. **Yisraelim**] – (a) Jew; (b) Israelite (in contradistinction to **Kohen** or **Levi**).

**yiud** – lit. designation; a Hebrew maidservant may be released from servitude through *yiud,* marriage to her master or his son.

**Yom Kippur** – Day of Atonement; a day of prayer, penitence, fasting and abstention from **melachah.**

**Yom Tov** [pl. **Yamim Tovim**] – holiday; the festival days on which the Torah prohibits **melachah.** Specifically, it refers to the first and last days of **Pesach,** the first day of **Succos, Shemini Atzeres, Shavuos, Yom Kippur** and two days of **Rosh Hashanah.** Outside of **Eretz Yisrael,** a second day of Yom Tov is added to each of these festivals, except Yom Kippur and Rosh Hashanah.

**Yovel** – fiftieth year [Jubilee]; the year following the conclusion of seven **shemittah** cycles. On **Yom Kippur** of that year, the **shofar** is sounded to proclaim freedom for the Jewish servants, and to signal the return of any field sold during the previous forty-nine years to its original owner. **Yovel** is only observed at times when most of the Jewish nation resides in Eretz Yisrael.

**zav** [pl. **zavim**] – a man who has become **tamei** because of a specific type of seminal emission. If three emissions were experienced during a three-day period, the man must bring offerings upon his purification.

**zavah** – After a woman concludes her seven days of **niddah,** there is an eleven-day period during which any evidence of vaginal bleeding renders her a *minor zavah.* If the menstruation lasts for three consecutive days, she is a *major zavah* and must bring offerings upon her purification.

**zechiyah** – rule which states one can act as a person's agent without his prior knowledge or consent if the act is clearly advantageous to the beneficiary.

**zechus** – unqualified benefit.

**zerikah** – throwing; applying the blood of an offering to the Altar. It is one of the four essential blood **avodos.**

**zivah** – the type of discharge which causes one to be a **zavah** or **zav.**

**zomeim** [pl. **zomemim**] – witnesses prove false through **hazamah.**

**zuz** – (a) monetary unit equal to a **dinar;** (b) a coin of that value; (c) the weight of a **zuz** coin.

**reshus hayachid** – lit. private domain: any area measuring at least four **tefachim** by four *tefachim* and enclosed by partitions at least ten *tefachim* high. According to most opinions, it needs to be enclosed only on three sides to qualify as a *reshus hayachid*. Private ownership is not a prerequisite.

**retushim** – willfully abandoned property.

**Rishon** – [pl. **Rishonim**] – a Torah authority of the period following the **Geonim** (approx. 1000-1500 C.E.).

**rishon l'tumah** – a **tamei** of the first degree. He can transmit **tumah** to food and drink but not to other people or utensils.

**Rosh Chodesh** – (a) festival celebrating the new month; (b) the first of the month.

**Rosh Hashanah** – the **Yom Tov** which is celebrated at the beginning of the new year. It falls on the first and second days in **Tishrei.**

**Sadducees** – heretical sect during the Second Temple era named after Tzaddok, a disciple of Antigonas of Socho. They denied the validity of the Oral Law and refused to accept the Sages' interpretation of the Torah.

**Sages** – (a) the collective body of Torah authorities in the Mishnaic era; (b) the anonymous majority opinion in a **Mishnah** or **Baraisa.**

**Sanctuary** – a term applied to the **Temple** edifice, consisting of the **Holy** and the **Holy of Holies.**

**Sanhedrin** – (a) the High Court of Israel; the Supreme Court consisting of seventy-one judges whose decisions on questions of Torah law are definitive and binding on all courts; (b) a lesser High Court of twenty-three judges authorized to inflict capital and corporal punishment.

**saris** – (a) a male who is incapable of maturing sexually; (b) a person who was castrated.

**se'ah** – a Mishnaic measure of volume; six **kav.**

**Seder** – lit. order. The Mishnah is divided into six **Sedarim: Zeraim** (Plants), **Moed** (Festivals), **Nashim** (Women), **Nezikim** (Damages), **Kodashim** (Sacred Things) and **Tohoros** (Ritual Purities).

**sela** – a silver coin having the weight of 384 barleycorns. This is the equivalent of four **dinars.**

**semichah** – (a) Rabbinical ordination empowering one to serve as a judge; (b) a rite performed with almost all personal sacrificial offerings. The owner of the offering places both his hands on the animal's head and presses down with all his might upon it. In the case of a **chatas,** or an **asham,** he makes his confession during *semichah*. In the case of a **shelamim** or **todah** offering, he praises and thanks God.

**shaatnez** – a garment containing both linen and wool. See **kilayim.**

**Seventeenth of Tammuz** – a fast day.

**Shabbos** – (a) the Sabbath; (b) the Talmudic tractate that deals with the laws of the Sabbath.

**Shacharis** – the morning prayer service.

**Shavuos** – Pentecost; the festival that celebrates the giving of the Torah to the Jewish nation on Mount Sinai.

**Shechinah** – Divine Presence.

**shechitah** – (a) ritual slaughter; the method prescribed by the Torah for killing a kosher animal so that it may be consumed; it consists of cutting through most of the esophagus and windpipe from the front of the neck with a specially sharpened knife that is free of nicks; (b) one of the four essential blood **avodos.**

**shekel** – Scriptural coin equivalent to the Aramaic **sela,** or four **dinars.** In Mishnaic terminology the Scriptural half-*shekel* is called a *shekel,* and the Scriptural *shekel* is called by its Aramaic name, **sela.**

**shelamim** – peace offering; generally brought by an individual on a voluntary basis. Part of it is burnt on the **Altar,** part is eaten by a **Kohen** (and the members of his household) and part is eaten by the owner. It is one of the **kodashim kalim.**

**shelichus** – see **agency.**

**shelichus yad** – (partial) misappropriation. The theft by a **shomer** of part of an item that was entrusted to him.

**Shemini Atzeres** – the eighth and concluding day of the **Succos** celebration. In many respects, it is a **Yom Tov** in its own right.

**shemittah** – the Sabbatical year, occurring every seventh year, during which the land of **Eretz Yisrael** may not be cultivated. See also **prosbul.**

**Shemoneh Esrei** – the silent, standing prayer, one of the main feature of the daily prayer services.

**sheretz** [pl. **sheratzim**] – one of eight rodents or reptiles, listed by the Torah, whose carcasses are a source of **tumah.**

**Shevat** – eleventh month of the Hebrew calendar.

**Sheviis** – see **shemittah.**

**shich'chah** – forgotten sheaves. One of the various portions of the harvest which the Torah grants to the poor. See **leket, peah.**

**shituf** – see **shitufei mevo'os.**

**shitufei mevo'os** – incorporation of the alleys; a provision similar to **eruvei chatzeiros,** instituted to permit carrying from a courtyard into an alley. It merges the different courtyards in a common ownership of a **mavoi.**

**shliach tzibur** – lit. messenger of the congregation. The individual leading the prayer service.

**shofar** – trumpet formed from the horn of a ram or certain other animals. It is a Biblical obligation to hear the blowing of a *shofar* on **Rosh Hashanah.**

**shomer** – One that has assumed custodial responsibility for another's property.

**shtar** [pl. **shtaros**] – legal document(s).

**Shulchan** – literally, table; the golden Table for the **lechem hapanim,** located in the **Holy.**

**shuman** – those parts of the fats of an animal that are permitted for consumption (as opposed to **cheilev** which is prohibited).

**Sifra** – lit. the book; the primary collection of Tannaic exegesis, mainly halachic in nature, on the Book of *Leviticus.* It is also known as *Toras Kohanim.*

**Sifri (or Sifrei)** – lit. the books; the counterpart of the **Sifra,** it expounds on the Books of *Numbers* and *Deuteronomy.*

**siman** [pl. **simanim**] – identifying mark; the mark or feature by which a lost object may be identified and reclaimed..

**Sivan** – third month of the Hebrew calendar.

**sotah** – an adulteress, or a woman whose suspicious behavior has established her as a suspected adulteress. The Torah prescribes, under specific circumstances, that her guilt or innocence be established by having her drink specially prepared water on the grounds of the **Beis HaMikdash.**

**sprinkling** – see **haza'ah.**

**succah** – (a) the temporary dwelling in which one must live during the festival of **Succos;** (b) [cap.] the Talmudic tractate that deals with the laws that pertain to the festival of **Succos.**

**Succos** – one of the three **pilgrimage festivals,** during which one must dwell in a ***succah.***

**Tabernacle** – a portable **Sanctuary** for the sacrificial service during the forty years of national wandering in the Wilderness and the first fourteen years after entry into Eretz Yisrael.

**taharah** – a halachically defined state of ritual purity; the absence of **tumah**-contamination.

**tahor** – person or object in a state of **taharah.**

**tamei** – person or object that has been contaminated by **tumah.**

**tamid** – communal **olah** offering that is offered twice daily.

**Tammuz** – fourth month of the Hebrew calendar.

**mi'un** – By Rabbinic enactment, an underaged orphan girl may be given in marriage by her mother or brothers. She may annul the marriage anytime before reaching majority by declaring, before a **beis din** of three judges, her unwillingness to continue in the marriage. This declaration and process is called *mi'un.*

**monetary law** – law dealing with financial matters rather than matters of prohibition.

**movables, movable property** – property that is transportable; in contrast to real estate.

**muchzak** – one who has the assumed legal possession of an object.

**muktzeh** – a class of objects which, in the normal course of events, do not stand to be used on the Sabbath or **Yom Tov.** The Rabbis prohibited moving such objects on the Sabbath or Yom Tov.

**mussaf** – (a) additional sacrifices offered on the Sabbath, Rosh Chodesh, or **Yom Tov;** (b) [cap.] the prayer service which is recited in lieu of these sacrifices.

**naarah** – a girl at least 12 years old who has sprouted at least two pubic hairs. This marks her coming of age as an adult.

**naarus** – term which refers to the state of being a ***naarah.***

**nasi** – the prince. He served as the head of the **Sanhedrin** and de facto as the spiritual leader of the people.

**nazir** – a person who takes the vow of **nezirus,** which prohibits him to drink wine, eat grapes, cut his hair or contaminate himself with the **tumah** of a corpse.

**negaim** – **tzaraas** spots.

**nesachim** – a libation, generally of wine which is poured upon the Altar.

**nesech wine** – wine poured as a libation in idolatrous service; a Jew is prohibited to drink or derive any benefit from it. The Rabbis added to this a decree regarding wine touched or poured by a gentile, even not as an idolatrous libation.

**nesin** [pl. **nesinim**] – descendant of the Gibeonites, who deceptively concluded a peace treaty with Joshua (*Josh.* 9:3-27) and converted to Judaism.

**netushim** – property which is involuntarily abandoned by its owner due to circumstances beyond his control.

**neveilah** – the carcass of an animal that was not slaughtered according to procedure prescribed by the Torah. A *neveilah* may not be eaten. It is an **av hatumah.** The term *neveilah* is sometimes used generically for forbidden food.

**nezirah** – female **nazir.**

**nezirus** – the state of being a **nazir.**

**niddah** – a woman who has menstruated but has not yet completed her purification process, which concludes with immersion in a **mikveh.**

**Nissan** – first month of the Hebrew calendar

**nisuin** – second stage of marriage. It is effected by a procedure called **chuppah.** See **kiddushin.**

**Noahide laws** – the seven commandments given to Noah and his sons, which are binding upon all gentiles. These laws include the obligation to have a body of civil law, and the prohibitions against idolatry, immorality, bloodshed, blasphemy, stealing and robbing, and eating limbs from a live animal.

**nossar** – part of a **korban** left over after the time to be eaten has passed.

**olah** [pl. **olos**] – burnt or elevation offering; an offering which is consumed in its entirety by the **Altar** fire. It is one of the **kodshei kodashim.**

**omer** – an obligatory **minchah** offering brought on the sixteeth of Nissan. It was forbidden to eat from the new grain crop (*chadash*) before this offering was brought.

**onein** [f. **onenes**] – a person on the day of the death of a close relative, to whom special laws of bereavement apply.

**Oral Sinaitic Law** – **Halachah LeMoshe MiSinai.**

**orlah** – fruit that grows on a tree during its first three years. The Torah prohibits any benefit from such fruit.

**Outer Altar** – the great **Altar** built of stone which stands in the Courtyard of the **Beis HaMikdash**, to which the blood of most offerings is applied, and on which the offerings are burned.

**paid custodian** – a **shomer** who receives remuneration for his services.

**parah adumah** – lit. red cow. The ashes of the *parah adumah* are mixed with **mayim chaim.** The resulting mixture is known as **mei chatas** and is used in the purification process of people or objects who have contracted **tumah** from a human corpse.

**parsah** [pl. **parsaos**] – measure of length equal to eight thousand **amos**.

**peace offering** – see **shelamim.**

**pe'ah** – the portion of the crop that must be left unreaped as a gift to the poor. See *Leviticus* 19:9, 23:22. See **shichachah, leket, peret, olelos.**

**peret** – individual grapes which fell during harvesting one of the various portions of the harvest which the Torah grants to the poor.

**perutah** – smallest coin used in Talmudic times. In most cases its value is the minimum that is legally significant.

**Pesach** – Passover. The **Yom Tov** that celebrates the Exodus of the Jewish nation from Egypt.

**pesach offering** – sacrifice offered on the afternoon of the 14th day of Nissan to be eaten after nightfall. It is one of the **kodashim kalim.**

**piggul** – an offering which was made unfit by means of incorrect intent during one of the four *avodos*. The intention was expressed to eat of it or place it on the Altar after the allotted time.

**pikadon** – An object deposited with a custodian for safekeeping.

**pilgrimage** – a title designated for the holidays of **Pesach, Shavuos** and **Succos,** when all Jewish males were obligated to appear at the **Beis HaMikdash** in Jerusalem.

**positive commandment** – a Torah commandment expressed as a requirement *to do.*

**poskim** – authoritative decisors of Torah law.

**Priestly Blessing** – the blessing the **Kohanim** are obligated to confer upon the congregation. It contains the Scriptural verses designated for the blessing in the Torah (*Numbers* 6:24-26), and is recited aloud by the Kohanim, while they keep their hands raised, toward the conclusion of the **Shemoneh Esrei.**

**prohibition** – a negative commandment, which the Torah expresses as a command *not to do.*

**prohibitory law** – **[issura]** refers to the category of Torah law which deals with questions of permissible or forbidden status, as opposed to questions of monetary law.

**prosbul** – the Torah requires all loans to be canceled by **shemittah.** The Rabbis enacted a law allowing for loans to be collected after the Sabbatical year through a process whereby the lender authorizes the court to collect all his debts. The document which authorizes that court to assume responsibility for the collection of those debts is called a *prosbul.*

**pundyon** – a coin.

**purification waters** – See **mei chatas.**

**R'** – Rabbi; specifically a **Tanna,** or **Amora** of **Eretz Yisrael.**

**Rebbi** – R' Yehudah HaNasi; prince or president of the Supreme **Sanhedrin.** He was the redactor of the **Mishnah.**

**Red cow** – see **parah adumah.**

**reshus harabim** – lit. public domain: any unroofed, commonly used street, public area or highway at least sixteen **amos** wide and open at both ends. According to some, it must be used by at least 600,000 people.

**kor** – large dry measure; a measure of volume consisting of thirty **se'ah.**

**kri u'ksiv** – a word *written one way but read differently* by special directive to Moses at Sinai.

**lashes** – see **malkus** and **makkas mardus.**

**lavud** – a Halachah **Le Moshe MiSinai** that allows a gap of less than three **tefachim** (as between two sections of a wall) to be viewed as if it were actually closed.

**leaning** – see **semichah.**

**lechatchilah** – (a) before the fact; (b) performance of a **mitzvah** or procedure in the proper manner.

**leket** – gleanings. One of the various portions of the harvest which the Torah grants to the poor. This refers to one or two stalks of grain that fall from within the sickle or the reaper's hand when he gathers the harvest. See ***shichchah, pe'ah.***

**Levi** – [pl. **Leviim**] – descendant of the tribe of Levi in the male line, who is sanctified for auxiliary services in the **Beis HaMikdash**. The **Leviim** were the recipients of **maaser rishon.**

**log** – [pl. **luggin**] – a liquid measure equal to volume of six eggs.

**lulav** – the branch of a date palm tree. One of the **four species** used on the festival of **Succos.**

**ma'ah** – the smallest silver unit in Talmudic coinage. Thirty-two **perutah** equal one *ma'ah* and six *ma'ah* equal a silver **dinar.**

**Maariv** – the evening prayer service.

**maaser** [pl. **maaseros**] – tithe; it is a Biblical obligation to give two tithes, each known as *maaser,* from one's crop. The first tithe (**maaser rishon**) is given to a **Levi.** The second tithe (**maaser sheni**) is taken to Jerusalem and eaten there or else redeemed with coins which are then taken to Jerusalem for the purchase of food to be eaten there. In the third and sixth years of the **shemittah** cycle, the *maaser sheni* obligation is replaced with **maaser ani,** the tithe for the poor.

**maaser ani** – the tithe for the poor.

**maaser beheimah** – the animal tithe. The newborn kosher animals (specifically oxen, sheep, goats) born to one's herds and flocks are gathered into a pen and made to pass through one at a time. Every tenth animal is designated as ***maaser.*** It is brought as an offering in the Temple and is eaten there by its owner.

**maaser rishon** – first tithe (after **terumah**) from produce of the Land of Israel. It is given to a **Levi.**

**maaser sheni** – second tithe from produce of the Land of Israel; taken in the first, second, fourth and fifth years of each seven-year **shemittah** cycle. It must be brought to Jerusalem and eaten there, or else redeemed for coins which are then taken to Jerusalem for the purchase of food to be eaten there.

**mah matzinu** – a **binyan av** from one verse. Just as one particular law possesses aspect A and aspect B, so any other law that possesses aspect A should also possess aspect B.

**makkas mardus** – lashes for rebelliousness. This is the term used for Rabbinically authorized lashes.

**malkus** – the thirty-nine lashes imposed by the court for violations of Biblical prohibitions.

**mamzer** [pl. **mamzerim**] – (a) offspring of illicit relationships punishable by **kares** or capital punishment; (b) offspring of a *mamzer* or *mamzeress.*

**mamzeress** – female **mamzer.**

**maneh** – (a) equivalent to 100 **zuz** or ***dinar***; (b) a measure of weight, equal to 17 ounces.

**Marcheshvan** – see **Cheshvan.**

**matanos [or matnos kehunah]** – lit: gifts. The Torah commands that we give the right forceps, jaws and maw of an ox, sheep or goat that are slaughtered (for non-sacrifical purposes) to the **Kohen.** These are referred to as the "gifts."

**matzah** – unleavened bread; any loaf made from dough that has not been allowed to ferment or rise. One is Biblically obligated to eat matzah on the night of the 15th of Nissan.

**mavoi** – alley; specifically an alley into which courtyards open. See **shitufei mevo'os.**

**mazal** – fortune.

**mei chatas** – springwater consecrated by the addition of ashes of a **parah adumah.** This was used to cleanse individuals or objects of **tumas meis.**

**me'ilah** – unlawfully benefiting from Temple property or removing such property from the Temple ownership.

**melachah** [pl. **melachos**] – labor; specifically, one of the 39 labor categories whose performance is forbidden by the Torah on the Sabbath and **Yom Tov.**

**melikah** – the unique manner in which bird offerings were slaughtered. The **Kohen** pierces the back of a bird's neck with his right thumbnail and cuts through the neck. *Melikah* differs from **shechitah** in two respects: (a) The cut is done with the Kohen's thumbnail rather than with a knife. (b) The neck is cut from the back rather than the throat. Birds for non-sacrificial purposes must have **shechitah.**

**melog** – a married woman's property in which she retains ownership of the property itself, but her husband enjoys the right of usufruct, i.e. he owns the yield of that property.

**menachos** – see **minchah.**

**Men of the Great Assembly** – a group of 120 sages active at the end of the Babylonian exile and during the early years of the Second Temple. They were responsible for the formulation of our prayers and many other enactments.

**Menorah** – the seven-branched gold candelabrum which stood in the **Holy**.

**meshichah** – pulling, or otherwise causing an object to move. One of the methods of acquisition.

**mesirah** – handing over; transferring the animal to a buyer by handing him its reins or mane; a means of acquisition used for articles too heavy to be acquired via **meshichah** or **hagbahah.**

**metzora** – a person afflicted with any of a number of skin conditions called **tzaraas** (decribed in *Lev.* ch. 13) that render a person **tamei** and upon healing must undergo the purification process outlined in *Lev.* ch. 14 and bring offering.

**mezuzah** [pl. **mezuzos**] – small scroll containing the passages *Deut.* 6:4-9 and 11:13-21, that is affixed to the right doorpost.

**migo** – literally: since. A rule of procedure. If one makes a claim that seems improbable, it nonetheless must be accepted, "since" had he wished to tell an untruth he would have chosen a more probable claim that is certainly acceptable to the court.

**mikveh** – ritualarium; a body of standing water containing at least forty **se'ah.** It is used to cleanse (by immersion) peple and utensils of their **tumah**-contamination. A **mikveh** consists of waters naturally collected, without direct human intervention. Water drawn in a vessel is not valid for a *mikveh.*

**minchah** – (a) [cap.] the afternoon prayer service; (b) [pl. **menachos**] a flour offering, generally consisting of fine wheat flour, oil and frankincense, part of which is burnt on the **Altar.** See **kemitzah.**

**minyan** – quorum of ten adult Jewish males necessary for the communal prayer service and other matters.

**mishmar** [pl. **mishmaros**] – lit. watches; one of the twenty-four watches of **Kohanim** and **Leviim** who served in the Temple for a week at a time on a rotating basis.

**Mishnah** [pl. **Mishnahs**] – (a) the organized teachings of the **Tannaim** compiled by **R' Yehudah HaNasi;** (b) a paragraph of that work.

**Hebrew maidservant** – girl up to the age of twelve sold by her father into servitude. See **yiud.**

**Hebrew servant** – Jewish man sold as an indentured servant, generally for a period of six years, for reasons of poverty or because he was convicted of stealing and lacks the funds to repay his theft.

**hechsher l'tumah** – rendering a food susceptible to **tumah** contamination by contact with one of seven liquids – water, dew, milk, date honey, olive oil, wine or blood.

**hefker** – ownerless

**heilach** – lit. behold [it is] for you. A claim that the defendant admits and is prepared to pay immediately. There is a dispute in the Gemara whether such a claim is already deemed paid.

**hekdesh** – (a) items consecrated to the Temple treasury or as offerings; (b) the state of consecration; (c) the Temple treasury.

**hekeish** – Scriptural analogy. Two subjects that are juxtaposed in one Scriptural verse are compared to each other in the manner of a *gezeirah shavah*. This rule of exegesis is termed **hekeish.**

**henpeik** – statement of certification issued by ***beis din.*** This statement states that *beis din* examined a document and confirmed the authenticity of the signatures that appear on it.

**hesess** – a special oath imposed by the post-Mishnaic Rabbis on one who denies the entire claim made against him, on the assumption that a plaintiff would not make a totally frivolous claim.

**holachah** – one of the four essential blood **avodos.** It involves carrying the blood of the offering to the Altar.

**Holy** – anterior chamber of the **Temple** edifice containing the **Shulchan, Inner Altar** and **Menorah.**

**Holy Ark** – the Ark in which rested the Tablets of the Ten Commandments and the **Torah** Scroll written by Moses; it stood in the **Holy of Holies.**

**Holy of Holies** – interior chamber of the **Temple** edifice. During most of the First Temple era, it contained the **Holy Ark;** later it was empty of any utensil. Even the **Kohen Gadol** is prohibited from entering it except on **Yom Kippur.**

**Hoshanah Rabbah** – the seventh day of *Succos*. It is the custom to take a willow branch in hand and beat it against the ground on this day.

**Inner Altar** – the gold-plated Altar which stood in the **Sanctuary.** It was used for the daily incense service and for the blood applications of inner **chataos.**

**Israelites' Courtyard** – an area in the Temple Courtyard, extending eleven **amah** from the eastern Courtyard wall inward into the Courtyard, and abutted on its west side by the **Kohanim's Courtyard.** It reached across the entire width of the Courtyard from north to south.

**issaron** – a dry measure which equals one-tenth of an **ephah** or approximately (depending on the conversion factor) eleven or twenty-one cups.

**Iyar** – second month of the Hebrew calendar.

**Jubilee** – see **Yovel.**

**kabbalah** – (a) term used throughout the Talmud to refer to the Books of the Prophets; (b) receiving the blood of a sacrificial animal that is slaughtered; one of the four blood **avodos.**

**kal vachomer** – lit. light and heavy, or lenient and stringent; an a fortiori argument. One of the thirteen principles of hermeneutics by which the Torah is expounded. It involves the following reasoning: If a particular stringency applies in a usually lenient case, it must certainly apply in a more serious case; the converse of this argument is also a *kal vachomer.*

**kares** – excision. Divinely imposed premature death decreed by the Torah for certain classes of transgression.

**kav** [pl. **kabim**] – a Talmudic measure equal to four ***luggin.***

**keifel** – see **double payment.**

**Kehunah** – priesthood; the state of being a Kohen.

**kemitzah** – the first of the four essential services of a **minchah** offering, in which the **Kohen,** using the three middle fingers of his hand, scoops out flour from the **minchah** to burn on the **Altar.**

**kesubah** – (a) marriage contract; the legal commitments of a husband to his wife upon their marriage, the foremost feature of which is the payment awarded her in the event of their divorce or his death; (b) document in which this agreement is recorded.

**kezayis** – an olive's volume [lit. as an olive]. Minimum amount of food whose consumption is legally considered "eating."

**kiddush** – the benediction recited over wine before the evening and morning meals on the **Sabbath** and **Yom Tov.**

**kiddushin** [**betrothal**] – Jewish marriage consists of two stages – **erusin** and **nisuin.** Kiddushin is the procedure which establishes the first stage of marriage [*erusin*].

**kilayim** – various forbidden mixtures, including: **shaatnez** (cloth made from a blend of wool and linen); cross-breeding of animals; cross-breeding (or side-by-side planting) of certain food crops; working with different species of animals yoked together; and mixtures of the vineyard.

**kilei hakerem** – forbidden mixtures of the vineyard; see **kilayim.**

**kinyan** – [pl. **kinyanim**] formal act of acquisition. An action which causes an agreement (exchange) to be legally binding.

**kinyan agav** – lit. acquisition by dint of; the term for the acquisition of movable property by means of the acquisition of land.

**kinyan chalifin** – (a) Even exchange: an exchange of two items of comparable value, in which each item serves as payment for the other. The acquisition of any of the items automatically effects the acquisition of the other. (b) Uneven exchange: An item of relatively negligible value is given in order to effect the acquisition of the item for sale. A handkerchief or the like is traditionally used.

**kinyan chatzeir** – The acquisition of movable property by virtue of it being in the premises of the person acquiring it.

**kinyan chazakah** – See **chazakah** (definition b).

**Kislev** – ninth month of the Hebrew calendar.

**kodashim kalim** – offerings of lesser holiness (one of the two classifications of sacrificial offerings). They include the **todah, shelamim, bechor, masser** and **pesach offerings.** This category of offerings are not subject to the stringencies applied to **kodshei kodashim.**

**kodesh** – (a) any consecrated object; (b) the anterior chamber of the **Temple** – the **Holy;** (c) portions of sacrificial offerings.

**kodshei kodashim** – most-holy offerings – one of the two classifications of sacrificial offerings. They include the **chatas, olah, asham,** and communal *shelamim*. These are subject to greater stringencies than **kodashim kalim** and may be eaten in the Temple Courtyard only by the **Kohanim** on the day it is offered and the following night.

**Kohanim's Courtyard** – eleven-**amah**-wide area in the Courtyard of the **Beis HaMikdash** abutting the Israelites' Courtyard on its east side, and the **Altar** on its west side. It reached across the entire width of the Courtyard from north to south.

**Kohen** [pl. **Kohanim**] – member of the priestly family descended in the male line from Aaron. The **Kohen** is accorded the special priestly duties and privileges associated with the **Temple** service and is bound by special laws of sanctity.

**Kohen Gadol** – High Priest.

**kometz** – see **kemitzah.**

**korban** – an offering which is brought on the **Altar** in the **Beis HaMikdash** in Jerusalem.

**chayah** – wild animal. See **beheimah.**

**chazakah** – (a) legal presumption that conditions remain unchanged unless proven otherwise; (b) a proprietary act by which land can be acquired.

**cheilev** – (a) animal fats forbidden for human consumption. See **shuman.**

**Cheshvan** – eighth month of the Hebrew calendar.

**Chol HaMoed** – the Intermediate Days of the Festivals of **Pesach** and **Succos,** which enjoy a quasi-**Yom Tov** status.

**chullin** – any substance that is not sanctified. See **kodesh.**

**chuppah** – (a) the bridal canopy; (b) a procedure for effecting **nisuin,** the final stage of marriage.

**Cuthites** – a non-Jewish tribe brought by the Assyrians to settle the part of Eretz Yisrael left vacant by the exile of the Ten Tribes; their subsequent conversion to Judaism was considered questionable and their observance of many laws was lax.

**daf** – one **leaf** in the Gemara.

**daitiki** – sickbed will.

**decapitated calf** – If a person is found murdered between two cities and his murderer is not known, the elders of the Sanhedrin must measure the distance to the surrounding cities to determine the city closest to the corpse. The elders of that city must then bring a female calf and decapitate it in a valley, in accordance with the procedure outlined in *Deuteronomy* 21:1-9.

**demai** – produce of Eretz Yisrael that is obtained from an unlearned person; its status regarding the separation of **maaser** is uncertain, and by Rabbinic law it must be tithed.

**dinar** – a coin. The silver content of the coin was equivalent to ninety-six grains of barley. It was worth 1/25 the value of a *gold dinar.*

**double payment** – the fine a thief must pay to the owner. He must return the stolen property and pay a fine equal to the value of the stolen object.

**eglah arufah** – see **decapitated calf.**

**Elul** – sixth month of the Hebrew calendar.

**emurin** – the portions of an animal offering burnt on the Altar.

**encumbered property** – land owned by a debtor at the time he incurred a debt, but which he later sold or gave to a third party. Such land is encumbered by the debt; for the creditor can collect it from the current owner to satisfy the debt, if the debtor defaults.

**ephah** [pl. **ephos**] – a measure of volume equal to three **se'ah.**

**Eretz Yisrael** – **Land of Israel.**

**erev Pesach** – the day before the Passover holiday. It is the day on which the **pesach offering** is sacrificed in order to be eaten that night.

**erusin** – betrothal, the first stage of marriage. This is effected by the man giving the woman an object of value, in the presence of witnesses, to betroth her. At this point the couple is not yet permitted to have conjugal relations, but is nonetheless considered legally married in most respects.

**eruv** – popular contraction of **eruvei tavshilin, eruvei techumin** or **eruvei chatzeiros.**

**eruvei chatzeiros** – a legal device which merges several separate ownerships **(reshus hayachid)** into a single joint ownership. This procedure allows us to view all the houses opening into the courtyard as the property of a single consortium (composed of all the residents of the courtyard). This permits all the contributing residents of the *chatzeir* to carry items during the Sabbath from the houses into the *chatzeir* and from one house to another.

**eruvei tavshilin** – food set aside prior to a Yom Tov that falls on Friday to serve as a token food for the Sabbath that follows. Once this token food has been set aside, the person is allowed to complete his preparations for the Sabbath on Yom Tov.

**eruvei techumin** – a legal device which allows a person to shift his Sabbath residence from which the 2,000-**amah techum** is measured. This is accomplished by placing a specific amount of food at the desired location before the start of the Sabbath. The place where the food has been placed is then viewed as his Sabbath residence, and his **techum**-limit is measured from there.

**ervah** [pl. **arayos**] – sexual relationships forbidden under penalty of *kares* or death, as enumerated in *Leviticus* ch. 18.

**esrog** – citron; one of the **four species** that one is commanded to hold on **Succos.**

**extension of oath** – literally: rolling of the oath. Once an obligation to swear is established in regard to a specific claim, the defendant can be made to swear in regard to other claims the plaintiff has against him as well, even if those other claims would not in themselves create an obligation for the defendant to swear. This rule is Biblical in origin.

**five grains** – wheat, barley, oats, spelt and rye.

**forbidden labors of the Sabbath** – see **avos melachah.**

**four species** – (a) **lulav** – palm branch; (b) **hadasim** – myrtle branches; (c) **aravos** – willow branches; (d) **esrog** – citron. We are commanded to hold these *four species* in hand on the Festival of **Succos.**

**Gaon** [pl. **Geonim**] – (a) title accorded the heads of the academies in Sura and Pumbedisa, the two Babylonian seats of Jewish learning, from the late 6th to mid-11th centuries C.E. They served as the link in the chain of Torah tradition that joined the **Rishonim** to the **Amoraim;** (b) later used to describe any brilliant Torah scholar.

**Gemara** – portion of the Talmud which discusses the **Mishnah;** also, loosely, a synonym for the Talmud as a whole.

**gematria** – the numeric valuation of the Hebrew alphabet.

**get** – (a) bill of divorce. The document that effects the dissolution of a marriage when it is handed to the wife; (b) any document.

**gezeirah shavah** – one of the thirteen principles of hermeneutical exposition. If a similar word or phrase occurs in two otherwise unrelated passages in the Torah, the principle of *gezeirah shavah* teaches that these passages are linked to one another, and the laws of one passage are applied to the other. Only those words which are designated by the Oral Law for this purpose may serve as a basis for a *gezeirah shavah.*

**gid hanasheh** – sciatic nerve. This portion of an animal is prohibited even if the animal has undergone valid ritual slaughter.

**gifts to the poor** – these include **leket, shichah pe'ah, peret, olelos. Maaser ani** is also a *gift to the poor.*

**Golden Altar** – see **Inner Altar**.

**Great Court** – see **Sanhedrin**.

**hadas** – myrtle branch. One of the **four species** that one is commanded to hold in hand on **Succos.**

**hagbahah** – lifting. One of the methods of acquisition.

**halachah** [pl. **halachos**] – (a) a Torah law; (b) [cap.] the body of Torah law; (c) in cases of dispute, the position accepted as definitive by the later authorities and followed in practice; (d) a **Halachah LeMoshe MiSinai.**

**Halachah LeMoshe MiSinai** – laws taught orally to Moses at Sinai, which cannot be derived from the Written Torah.

**Hashem** – lit. the Name; an expression used to refer to God without pronouncing His Ineffable Name.

**Havdalah** – lit. distinction; the blessing recited at the conclusion of the Sabbath.

**hazamah** – the process by which witnesses are proven false by testimony that places them elsewhere at the time of the alleged incident. Such witnesses are punished with the consequences they had planned to inflict upon their intended victim.

# Glossary

**Adar** – twelfth month of the Hebrew calendar.

**Adar Sheni** – lit. the second *Adar*. When it is deemed necessary for a leap year to be designated, an extra month is added. This thirteenth month is placed between **Adar** and **Nissan** and is called *Adar Sheni.*

**agav** – see **kinyan agav.**

**agency** – the principle that an agent may act as proxy of a principal and have his actions legally accepted on behalf of the principal.

**Aggadah, aggadata** – the homiletical teachings of the Sages and all non-halachic Rabbinic literature found in the Talmud.

**ailonis** – an adult woman who never developed the physical signs of female maturity; she is therefore assumed to be incapable of bearing children.

**akum** – idolater.

**Altar** – the great Altar, which stands in the Courtyard of the **Beis HaMikdash.** Certain portions of every offering are burnt on the Altar. The blood of most offerings is applied to the walls of the Altar.

**amah** [pl. **amos**] – cubit; a linear measure equaling six **tefachim.** Opinions regarding its modern equivalent range between 18 and 24 inches.

**am haaretz** [pl. **amei haaretz**] – common, ignorant person.

**Amora** [pl. **Amoraim**] – sage of the Gemara; cf. **Tanna.**

**amud** – one side (column) of the **daf** in Gemara.

**Anshei Knesses HaGedolah** – see **Men of the Great Assembly.**

**aravos** – willow branches. One of the **four species** that one is commanded to hold in hand on **Succos.**

**arusah** – a woman who is only betrothed and not yet fully married. See **erusin.**

**asham** [pl. **ashamos**] – guilt offering, an offering brought to atone for one of several specific sins, as well as a part of certain purification offerings. It is one of the **kodshei kodashim.**

**asham gezeilos** – **asham** of theft. If a defendant denies under oath a monetary claim against him and then admits that he perjured himself, he must pay the debt plus a fifth to the plaintiff and offer an *asham* sacrifice. This *asham* is known as *asham gezeilos.*

**Av** – fifth month of the Hebrew calendar.

**av beis din** – chief of the court. This position was second in importance to the **nasi** who served as head of the **Sanhedrin.**

**av** [pl. **avos**] – see **melachah.**

**av** [pl. **avos**] **hatumah** – primary source of **tumah;** an object possessing a degree of *tumah* sufficient to contaminate a person or utensil. Usually, an *av hatumah* is a person or substance from which *tumah* originates, such as **metzora, neveilah,** et al.

**avi avos hatumah** – a human corpse, which is the most severe source of **tumah.**

**avodah** [pl. **avodos**] – the sacrificial service, or any facet of it. There are four critical *avodos* to the sacrificial service. They are **shechitah, kabbalah, holachah** and **zerikah.**

**avodah zarah** – idol worship, idolatry.

**Baraisa** [pl. **Baraisos**] – the statement(s) of **Tannaim** that were not included by **Rebbi** in the Mishnah. R' Chiya and R' Oshaya, the students of Rebbi, researched and reviewed the Baraisos and compiled an authoritative collection of them, based on the teachings of Rebbi.

**bechor** – (a) firstborn male child; (b) a firstborn male kosher animal. Such an animal is born with sacrificial sanctity, as a result of which it is to be offered as a *bechor* sacrifice in the Temple. Unlike other sacrifices, the **bechor** is automatically sacred from birth even without being designated as such by a person.

**bedi'avad** – after the fact. See **lechatchilah.**

**beheimah** – domestic species, livestock. In regard to various laws, the Torah distinguishes between two categories of animals: (a) *beheimah* – domestic species; e.g. cattle, sheep, goats. (b) **chayah:** wild species; e.g. deer, antelope.

**bein hashemashos** – the twilight period preceding night. The legal status of *bein hashemashos* as day or night is uncertain.

**beis din** – court, Rabbinical court. See also **Sanhedrin.**

**beis hamidrash** – a Torah study hall.

**Beis HaMikdash** – Holy Temple in Jerusalem. The Temple edifice was comprised of (a) the Antechamber; (b) the **Holy** or *heichal;* and (c) the **Holy of Holies.**

**bikkurim** – The first-ripening fruits of any of the seven species (wheat, barley, grapes, figs, pomegranates, olives, dates), with which the Torah praises Eretz Yisrael. They are brought to the Temple and given to the **Kohanim.**

**bill of emancipation** – Document given to a slave, which frees him from his servitude.

**binyan av** – one of the thirteen principles of Biblical hermeneutics. This principle dictates that whenever a commonality of law or essence is found in two separate areas of Torah law, analogies may be drawn from one area to the other, and the laws that apply to one can be applied to the other as well.

**Bircas Kohanim** – see **Priestly Blessing.**

**bris milah** – circumcision.

**chadash** – new crop of any of the **five grains;** *chadash* may not be eaten until the **omer** offering is brought on the second day of **Pesach**, the sixteenth of **Nissan.**

**chagigah offering** – festival offering. Every adult Jewish male is required to bring a *chagigah* offering on the first day of the festivals of **Pesach, Shavuos** and **Succos.** It is one of the **kodashim kalim**, specifically a type of **shelamim** offering.

**chalifin** – see **kinyan chalifin.**

**chalitzah** – (a) procedure [taking off the shoe] by which a **yevamah** can be released from her attachment to her brothers-in-law. See **yibum.**

**challah** – (a) portion removed from a dough of the **five grains,** given to a **Kohen;** if *challah* is not taken, the dough is **tevel** and may not be eaten. The minimum amount of dough from which *challah* must be separated is the volume of 43.2 eggs which is one **issaron.** Nowadays the *challah* is removed and burned. (b) One of the three special **mitzvos** for women.

**chametz** – leaven. *Chametz* is forbidden on **Pesach.**

**Chanukah** – Festival of Lights. The holiday that commemorates the Maccabean victory over the Greeks. It begins on the 25th of **Kislev** for eight days.

**chatas** [pl. **chataos**] – sin offering; an offering generally brought in atonement for the inadvertent transgression of a **kares**-bearing sin. A **chatas** is also brought as one of various purification offerings. It is one of the **kodshei kodashim.**

**chatzitzah** – lit. an interposition; foreign matter attached or adhering to the person or object to be immersed in the **mikveh,** which prevents the water from coming in contact with the whole of their surface; this invalidates the *tevilah.*

**chaver** [pl. **chaverim**] – lit. colleague. *Chaver* is a technical term that applies to one who observes the laws of ritual purity. In everyday life, it commonly connotes a Torah scholar who is scrupulous in his observance of **mitzvos.**

# Glossary

# Scriptural Index

גמ' מנהני מילי [א] דתנו רבנן (א) על כל דבר פשע בית שמאי אומרים מלמד שחייב על המחשבה כמעשה ובית הלל אומרים אינו חייב עד שישלח בו יד שנאמר (ב) אם לא שלח ידו במלאכת רעהו אמרו להן ב"ש לב"ה והלא כבר נאמר על כל דבר פשע אמרו להן ב"ה לב"ש והלא כבר נאמר אם לא שלח ידו במלאכת רעהו א"כ מה תלמוד לומר על כל דבר פשע שיכול אין לי אלא הוא [א] אמר לעבדו ולשלוחו מנין תלמוד לומר על כל דבר פשע: הטה את החבית כו': אמר רבה לא שנו אלא נשברה [ב] אבל החמיצה משלם את כולה מאי טעמא גירי דידיה הוא דאהנו לה: הגביהה ונטל הימנה כו': אמר שמואל לא נטל ממש אלא [ג] כיון שהגביהה ליטול אע"פ שלא נטל לימא קא סבר שמואל שליחות יד אינה צריכה חסרון אמרי לא שאני הכא דניחא ליה דתיהוי הא חבית כולה בסיס להא רביעית [ד] בעי רב אשי הגביה ארנקי ליטול הימנה דינר מהו חמרא הוא דלא מינטר אלא אגב חמרא אבל זוזא מינטר או דלמא שאני נטירותא דארנקי מנטירותא דדינר תיקו:

## הדרן עלך המפקיד

הזהב [ה] קונה את הכסף הכסף אינו קונה את הזהב [ו] הנחשת קונה את הכסף והכסף אינו קונה את הנחשת [ז] מעות הרעות קונות את היפות והיפות אינן קונות את הרעות [ח] אסימון קונה את המטבע והמטבע אינו קונה את אסימון מטלטלין קונין את המטבע מטבע אינו קונה את המטלטלין [א] [ט] (ג) (זה הכלל) כל המטלטלים קונין זה את זה [י] כיצד משך הימנו פירות ולא נתן לו מעות אינו יכול לחזור בו (ו) [כ] נתן לו מעות ולא משך הימנו פירות יכול לחזור בו [ל] אבל אמרו מי שפרע מאנשי דור המבול ומדור הפלגה הוא עתיד להפרע ממי שאינו עומד בדבורו (ז) רבי שמעון אומר כל שהכסף בידו ידו על העליונה: גמ' מתני ליה רבי לרבי שמעון בריה הזהב קונה את הכסף א"ל רבי שנית לנו בילדותיך הכסף קונה את הזהב ותחזור ותשנה לנו בזקנותיך הזהב קונה את הכסף (ח) בילדותיה מאי סבר ובזקנותיה מאי סבר בילדותיה סבר דהבא דחשיב הוי טבעא כספא דלא חשיב הוי פירא וקני ליה פירא לטבעא בזקנותיה סבר כספא דחריף

**רש"י**

גמ' אמר לעבדו. שישלח יד וכן עשה: מנין. שהוא חייב: לא שנו. דהיכא דנטל ולא הגביה כל החבית פטור: אלא נשברה. דאונס הוא והרי לא קנאה שיתחייב באונסין: אבל החמיצה. פשיעה היא ומזיק בידים הוא דבשביל שחיסרה התחילה שכן דרך יין להחמיץ בכלי חסר: גירי דידיה אהנו לה. חצים שלו גרמו לה להחמיץ: דניחא ליה דתיהוי כולה חבית בסיס להאי רביעית. שתשמר אותה רביעית ולא תחמיץ ולעולם שליחות יד בדבר אחר צריכה חסרון והנוטל פקדון ומגביהו על מנת לשלוח בו יד כל זמן שלא חסרו אינו מתחייב בהגבהתו הואיל ולא נטלו ע"מ לגזול את כולו אלא לשלוח בו יד ושליחות יד בלא חסרון ליתיה אבל יין שאינו משתמר אלא בכלי מלא הוה ליה כמי שנטל והניחו עם השאר להשתמר ונעשה שואל על כל שאר החבית: הגביה ארנקי ליטול דינר. ולא נטל לשמואל מהו: אבל זוזא מינטר. לבדו ולא ניחא ליה דלהוי אינך בסיס להאי ולא הוי כנוטל ומניח: שאני נטירותא דארנקי. כיס מלא נראה ומשתמר ואין נוח להיות נאבד כדינר יחידי:

הדרן עלך המפקיד

הזהב קונה את הכסף. הלוקח דינרי זהב טבועים בדינרי כסף ונתן לו דינרי זהב משיכת הזהב קונה את הכסף לבעל הזהב ונתחייב לו זה משקיבל דינרי זהב לתת לו דינרי הכסף ואינו יכול לחזור בו אבל הכסף אינו קונה את הזהב שאם נתן לו דינרי הכסף תחילה לא קנה ויכולין שניהם לחזור דמטבע כסף הוי מעות משום דחריפי ליתנן בהוצאה ודינר זהב אינו אלא כשאר מטלטלין ופירות ומעות אין קונות עד שימשוך המטלטלין אבל משיכת המטלטלין קונה ואין אחד מהם יכול לחזור בו ובגמ' מפרש טעמא איכא דיליף משיכה מן התורה ואיכא דמוקי לה בתקנתא דרבנן: הנחושת. פרוטות של נחושת: קונה את הכסף. דינרי של כסף או כל מטבע של כסף כולן טעם אחד להם מי שטבעו חשוב לטבוע הוי מעות ואינו קונה ומי שאין טבעו חשוב וחריף הוי כפירות ומשיכתן הוא קיום דבר: מעות הרעות. שנפסלו: אסימון. שאין עליו צורה פלדו"ן בלעז זוזים עגולין ומוכנים לצור עליהם את הצורה בחותם שקורין קוי"ן: כל המטלטלין קונין זה את זה. בין בתורת חליפין שהחליף אלו באלו כיון שמשך האחד קנה חבירו את שלו בין בתורת דמים בכמה תתן לי את שלך בכך וכך חזה חוזר ואומר לו בכמה תתן לי שלך בכך וכך ונתרצו ומשך האחד נתקיימו הדברים והאי כל לאתויי אפי' כיס מלא מעות בכיס מלא מעות כדריש לקיש בגמרא (י): יכול לחזור בו. זה וזה: כל שהכסף בידו כו'. פליג אדרבנן דאמרי נתן לו מעות יכול לחזור בו אפילו לוקח ואתא ר"ש למימר מוכר שהכל בידו הוא דיכול לחזור בו אבל לוקח אין יכול לחזור בו ובגמ' מפרש טעמא: גמ' דחריף

**תוספות**

הזהב. הנחושת קונה את הכסף. האי איצטריך דאע"ג דבאתרא דמסגי פריטי חריפין טפי (ז) [מכספא] הוו פירא משום דאיכא אתרא דלא מסגי כדאמר בגמרא (עמוד ב) אך תימה אמאי איצטריך למיתני דמעות הרעות שנפסלו דמקרו פירי השתא נחשת דסגי טובא הוי פירי כל שכן מעות שנפסלו ותו דכל המטלטלים קונין זה את זה מוקי בגמ' (ח) במעות חד פסלתו מלכות וחד פסלתו מדינה כל שכן דמעות שנפסלו דמקרו פירי לגבי כסף לכך נראה דמעות הרעות היינו שיוצאות קצת ואסימון אצטריך לפרש"י דמפרש אסימון הוי שעשוי כתקון המטבע היוצאת בעיר ואין חסר רק צורה אשמועינן דאפילו הכי הוי פירי אע"ג דאינו חסר כ"א מעט דבדבר מועט יטביעו הרבה מהם ולרבינו תם דמפרש אסימון שיש עליו צורה ואינה יוצאה בהוצאה צ"ל שיוצאת בדוחק אך לא כל כך בדוחק כמו מעות הרעות ומטלטלין קונין מטבע אשמועינן דקונין אפילו מטבע כמו מעות הרעות ואסימון דמקרי פירי לגבי כספא ולגבי מטלטלין מקרי טבעא:

אסימון. פרש"י שאין בו צורה כלל וקשה לרבינו תם דבפרק במה אשה (שבת דף סה. ושם ד"ה ליעבד) אמרו יוצאין בסלע שעל גבי הצינית אי משום צורתא ליעביד ליה פולסא משמע דפולסא יש עליו צורה ובגמרא מפרש לקמן (ט) מאי אסימון פולסא וי"ל לפרש"י דכל דבר שאינו כתקונו קרי אסימון או שאין בו צורה או שיש בו צורה שאינה חשובה וא"ת מה בין אסימון שאין עליו צורה למעות הניתנין לסימן בבית המרחץ דאמרי' בגמ' (שם) ושוין רבי דוסא דאמר מחללין על אסימון מודה שאין מחללין על מעות הניתנין כו' ויש לומר דאסימון הם מעות שנעשו ברוחב ובעובי ובמשקל המטבע היוצא בעיר ובדבר מועט יטביעו הרבה מהם ולכך מחללין על אסימון ור"ת מפרש דאסימון יש בה צורה ואינה יוצאה בהוצאה וא"ת בגמרא קאמר רבי דוסא דאמר מחללין על אסימון ורבי ישמעאל אמרו דבר אחד דתניא וצרת הכסף לרבות כל דבר הנצרר ביד דברי רבי ישמעאל ר"ע אומר לרבות דבר שיש בו צורה משמע דרבי ישמעאל לא בעי צורה ואסימון יש בו צורה וא"כ היאך אמרו דבר אחד ויש לומר לרבות כל דבר הנצרר ביד אע"פ שאינו יוצא בהוצאה אך שיהיה בו צורה כל דהו ור"ע בעי צורה חשובה שתלא בהוצאה אך יוצאה לגמרי לא בעי מדאיצטריך לרבוי ולפי' רש"י אתי שפיר: נעשה

**מסורת הש"ס**

א) [קדושין דף מב:], ב) [ברי"ף והרא"ש ל"ג זה הכלל וכן נכון עי' מי"ט], ג) גיטין ל., ד) [לקמן מז:, עד:], ה) [עבודה זרה נב:], ו) [לקמן מו:], ז) מהר"ם, ח) [דף מו:], ט) [דף מז:].

**הגהות הגר"א**

[א] במשנה (זה הכלל) תא"מ:

**תורה אור השלם**

א) עַל כָּל דְּבַר פֶּשַׁע עַל שׁוֹר עַל חֲמוֹר עַל שֶׂה עַל שַׂלְמָה עַל כָּל אֲבֵדָה אֲשֶׁר יֹאמַר כִּי הוּא זֶה עַד הָאֱלֹהִים יָבֹא דְּבַר שְׁנֵיהֶם אֲשֶׁר יַרְשִׁיעֻן אֱלֹהִים יְשַׁלֵּם שְׁנַיִם לְרֵעֵהוּ: [שמות כב, ח]

ב) אִם לֹא יִמָּצֵא הַגַּנָּב וְנִקְרַב בַּעַל הַבַּיִת אֶל הָאֱלֹהִים אִם לֹא שָׁלַח יָדוֹ בִּמְלֶאכֶת רֵעֵהוּ: [שמות כב, ז]

**לעזי רש"י**

פלדו"ן. פירוש כסף שלא נקבע בו צורה (רש"י ברכות דף מז ע"ב ד"ה אסימון), חתיכת מתכת שלא טבעו עליה צורת מטבע. קוי"ן. פירוש חותם (שבו טובעים מטבעות) (עיין רש"י גיטין דף כ ע"א ד"ה מיתכך תריך).

**ליקוטי רש"י**

על כל דבר פשע. בתר אם לא שלח ידו כתיב. אין לי אלא הוא. שנתחייב באונסין בשליחות יד אלא בזמן ששלח בה יד הוא עצמו [קידושין מב:].

אסימון. כסף שלא נקבע בו צורה וקורין לו פלו"ן בלע"ז [ברכות מז:].

**עין משפט נר מצוה**

קז א מיי' פ"ג מהל' גזילה הל' יא טוש"ע ח"מ סי' רלב סעי' ה:

קח ב מיי' שם הל' יג סמג עשין עג טוש"ע ח"מ שם סעי' ג:

קט ג ד מיי' שם הלכה יב ועיין בהשגות ובמגיד משנה טוש"ע שם סעי' ב:

א ה מיי' פ"ו מהל' מכירה הל' ג סמג עשין פב טוש"ע ח"מ סי' רג סעי' ד:

ב ו מיי' שם טוש"ע שם סעי' ה:

ג ז ח מיי' שם הל' ה טוש"ע שם סעי' ח:

ד ט מיי' שם פ"ה הל' א סמג שם טוש"ע שם סעי' א:

ה י מיי' שם פ"ג הל' א סמג שם טוש"ע ח"מ סי' קצח סעי' א:

ו כ מיי' שם טוש"ע שם וסעי' ה:

ז ל מיי' שם פ"ז הל' א סמג שם טוש"ע ח"מ סי' רד סעי' א וסעי' ד:

**רבינו חננאל**

אין לי אלא הוא אמר לעבדו או לשלוחו ושלחו בו יד מניין ת"ל על כל דבר פשע אפי' בדיבור חייב וקיימא לן כב"ה דב"ש במקום ב"ה אינה משנה. היטה את החבית ונטל ממנה רביעית ונשברה אינו משלם אלא [רביעית] פי' כגון שהיטה את החבית ונטל ממנה רביעית והושיבה כמו שהיתה יושבת ואחר כך נשברה ודוקא היטה ולא טילטלה ולא נטלה הוא שמשלם הרביעית בלבד ודוקא נשברה אבל החמיצה משלם כולה שהוא גרם לה להחמיץ שכל זמן שהיא מליאה אינה מחמצת ואם מפחית מעט ממנה ממהרת להחמיץ. וזה פי' גיריה דידיה אהנו ליה. הגביה ונטל ממנה רביעית ונשברה משלם כולה. אוקמה שמואל כיון שהגביה ליטול ממנה אע"פ שלא נטל משלם כולה דניחא ליה דתיהוי הא חבית כולה בסיס לרביעית זו כי בהיות זו הרביעית בתוך החבית משתמרת ואינה מפיגה טעמה ולא ריחה. אבל המגביה ארנקי ליטול ממנה דינר ולא נטל ונגנב או נאבד עלתה בתיקו:

הדרן עלך המפקיד

הזהב קונה את הכסף והכסף אינו קונה את הזהב כך היה רבי שונה בזקנותו מאי טעמא איידי דכסף הוא חריף הוי טיבעא דהבא דליתיה חריף הוי פירא. וקני ליה פירא לטיבעא וכן הלכה. ובילדותיה היה שונה הכסף קונה את הזהב.

הֵימֶנָּה דִּינָר – **in order to take a coin from it** for himself, מַהוּ – **what is [the law]** according to Shmuel? Does he assume responsibility for the entire purse immediately, or not until he removes the coin?[10]

Rav Ashi explains the two sides of the inquiry:

חַמְרָא הוּא דְּלָא מִינַּטַר אֶלָּא אַגַּב חַמְרָא – Perhaps **it is** only with regard to **wine, which is not secure except** together **with** other **wine** (in a full keg), that the *shomer* is presumed to want the portion he is misappropriating to be stored in the keg. אֲבָל זוּזָא מִינַּטַר – **But** with regard to **a coin,** since it **is secure** by itself, there are no grounds for presuming that the *shomer* wants the coin he is misappropriating to be stored in the purse. Therefore, he is not responsible for the entire purse until he removes the coin. אוֹ דִּלְמָא – **Or perhaps,** we say שָׁאנִי נְטִירוּתָא דְּאַרְנָקִי מִנְּטִירוּתָא דְּדִינָר – that **the security of a purse** full of coins **is different than the security of a** single **coin.** Since a coin is more secure when it is in a full purse,[11] perhaps the *shomer* deliberately wants the coin he is misappropriating to be stored in the purse. Therefore, he should be responsible for the entire purse, even if he did not remove the coin.

The Gemara concludes:

תֵּיקוּ – **Let [the question] stand** unresolved.

## הדרן עלך המפקיד

## WE SHALL RETURN TO YOU, HAMAFKID

NOTES

10. This inquiry assumes that misappropriation is dependent upon a loss. According to the position that misappropriation is *not* dependent upon a loss, he is certainly liable for the entire purse (*Raavad,* cited by *Shitah Mekubetzes*; *Ritva*; cf. *Rambam, Hil. Gezeilah VaAveidah* 3:12, *Meiri*).

11. A full purse is noticeable and secure, and less likely to be lost than a single loose coin (*Rashi*).

גמ' מנהני מילי [א] דתנו רבנן [א] על כל דבר פשע בית שמאי אומרים מלמד שחייב על המחשבה כמעשה ובית הלל אומרים אינו חייב עד שישלח בו יד שנאמר [ב] אם לא שלח ידו במלאכת רעהו אמרו להן ב"ש לב"ה והלא כבר נאמר על כל דבר פשע אמרו להן ב"ה לב"ש והלא כבר נאמר אם לא שלח ידו במלאכת רעהו א"כ מה תלמוד לומר על כל דבר פשע שיכול אין לי אלא הוא [א]אמר לעבדו ולשלוחו מנין תלמוד לומר על כל דבר פשע: הטה את החבית כו': אמר רבה לא שנו אלא נשברה [ב]אבל החמיצה משלם את כולה מאי טעמא גירי דידיה הוא דאהנו לה: הגביהה ונטל הימנה כו': אמר שמואל לא נטל נטל ממש אלא [ג]כיון שהגביהה ליטול אע"פ שלא נטל לימא קא סבר שמואל שליחות יד אינה צריכה חסרון אמרי לא שאני הכא דניחא ליה דתיהוי הא חבית כולה בסיס להא רביעית [ד]בעי רב אשי הגביה ארנקי ליטול הימנה דינר מהו חמרא הוא דלא מינטר אלא אגב חמרא אבל זוזא מינטר או דלמא שאני נטירותא דארנקי מנטירותא דדינר תיקו:

## הדרן עלך המפקיד

**הזהב** [ה]קונה את הכסף הכסף אינו קונה את הזהב [ו]הנחשת קונה את הכסף והכסף אינו קונה את הנחשת [ז]מעות הרעות קונות את היפות והיפות אינן קונות את הרעות [ח]אסימון קונה את המטבע והמטבע אינו קונה את אסימון מטלטלין קונין את המטבע מטבע אינו קונה את המטלטלין [א] [ט](ג) (זה הכלל) כל המטלטלים קונין זה את זה [י]כיצד משך הימנו פירות ולא נתן לו מעות אינו יכול לחזור בו (ג) [כ]נתן לו מעות ולא משך הימנו פירות יכול לחזור בו [ל]אבל אמרו מי שפרע מאנשי דור המבול ומדור הפלגה הוא עתיד להפרע ממי שאינו עומד בדבורו (ד) רבי שמעון אומר כל שהכסף בידו ידו על העליונה: גמ' מתני ליה רבי לרבי שמעון בריה הזהב קונה את הכסף א"ל רבי שנית לנו בילדותיך הכסף קונה את הזהב ותחזור ותשנה לנו בזקנותיך הזהב קונה את הכסף (ה) בילדותיה מאי סבר ובזקנותיה מאי סבר בילדותיה סבר דהבא דחשיב הוי טבעא כספא דלא חשיב הוי פירא וקני ליה פירא לטבעא בזקנותיה סבר כספא דחריף

רש"י

גמ' אמר לעבדו. שישלח יד וכן עשה: מנין. שהוא חייב: לא שנו. דהיכא דנטל ולא הגביה כל החבית פטור: אלא נשברה. דאונס הוא והרי לא קנאה שיתחייב באונסין: אבל החמיצה. פשיעה היא ומזיק בידים הוא דבשביל שחסרה התחילה שכן דרך יין להחמיץ בכלי חסר: גירי דידיה אהנו לה. חלים שלו גרמו לה להחמיץ: דניחא ליה דתיהוי כולה חבית בסיס להאי רביעית. שתשמר אותה רביעית ולא תחמיץ ולעולם שליחות יד בדבר אחר צריכה חסרון והנוטל פקדון ומגביהו על מנת לשלוח בו יד כל זמן שלא חסרו אינו מתחייב בהגבהתו הואיל ולא נטלו ע"מ לגזול את כולו אלא לשלוח בו יד ושליחות יד בלא חסרון ליתיה אבל יין שאינו משתמר אלא בכלי מלא הוה ליה כמי שנטל והניחו עם השאר להשתמר ונעשה שואל על כל שאר החבית: הגביה ארנקי ליטול דינר. ולא נטל לשמואל מהו: אבל זוזא מינטר. לבדו ולא ניחא ליה דלהוי אינך בסיס להאי ולא הוי כנוטל ומניח: שאני נטירותא דארנקי. כיס מלא נראה ומשתמר ואין נוח להיות נאבד כדינר יחידי:

הדרן עלך המפקיד

**הזהב** קונה את הכסף. הלוקח דינרי זהב טבועים בדינרי כסף ונתן לו דינרי זהב משיכת הזהב קונה את הכסף לבעל הזהב ונתחייב לו זה משקיבל דינרי זהב לתת לו דינרי הכסף ואינו יכול לחזור בו אבל הכסף אינו קונה את הזהב שאם נתן לו דינרי הכסף תחילה לא קנה ויכולין שניהם לחזור דמטבע כסף הוי מעות משום דחריפי ליתנן בהוצאה ודינר זהב אינו אלא כשאר מטלטלין ופירות ומעות אין קונות עד שימשוך המטלטלין אבל משיכת המטלטלין קונה ואין אחד מהם יכול לחזור בו ובגמ' מפרש טעמא איכא דיליף משיכה מן התורה ואיכא דמוקי לה בתקנתא דרבנן: הנחושת. פרוטות של נחושת: קונה את הכסף. דינרי של כסף או כל מטבע של כסף כולן טעם אחד להם מי שטבעו חשוב לטבוע הוי מעות ואינו קונה ומי שאין טבעו חשוב וחריף הוי כפירות ומשיכתן הוא קיום דבר: מעות הרעות. שנפסלו: אסימון. שאין עליו צורה פלדו"ן בלעז זוזים עגולין ומוכנים לצור עליהם את הצורה בחותם שקורין קוי"ן: כל המטלטלין קונין זה את זה. בין בתורת חליפין שהחליף אלו באלו כיון שמשך האחד קנה חבירו את שלו בין בתורת דמים בכמה תתן לי את שלך בכך וכך וזה חוזר ואומר לו בכמה תתן לי שלך בכך וכך ונתרצו ומשך האחד נתקיימו הדברים והאי כל לאתויי אפי' כיס מלא מעות בכיס מלא מעות כדרים לקים בגמרא (י): יכול לחזור בו. זה וזה: כל שהכסף בידו כו'. פליג אדרבנן דאמרי נתן לו מעות יכול לחזור בו אפילו לוקח ואתא ר"ש למימר מוכר שהכל בידו הוא דיכול לחזור בו אבל לוקח אין יכול לחזור בו ובגמ' מפרש טעמא: גמ' דחריף

תוספות

**הזהב.** הנחושת קונה את הכסף. הא איצטריך לאע"ג דבאתרא דמסגי פריטי חריפין טפי (ו) [מכספא] הוו פירא משום דאיכא אתרא דלא מסגי כדאמר בגמרא (עמוד ב) אך תימה אמאי איצטריך למיתני דמעות הרעות שנפסלו דמקרו פירי השתא נחשת דסגי טובא הוי פירי כל שכן מעות שנפסלו ותו דכל המטלטלים קונין זה את זה מוקי בגמ' (ח) במעות חד פסלתו מלכות וחד פסלתו מדינה כל שכן דמעות שנפסלו דמקרו פירי לגבי כסף לכך נראה דמעות הרעות היינו שיוצאות קצת ואסימון אצטריך לפרש"י דמפרש אסימון הוי שעשוי כתקון המטבע היוצאת בעיר ואין חסר רק צורה אשמועינן דאפילו הכי הוי פירי אע"ג דאינו חסר כ"א מעט דבדבר מועט יטביעו הרבה מהם ולרבינו תם דמפרש אסימון שיש עליו צורה ואינה יוצאה בהוצאה צ"ל שיוצאת בדוחק אך לא כל כך בדוחק כמו מעות הרעות ומטלטלין קונין מטבע אשמועינן דקונין אפילו מטבע כמו מעות הרעות ואסימון דמקרי פירי לגבי כספא ולגבי מטלטלין מקרי טבעא:

**אסימון.** פרש"י שאין בו צורה כלל וקשה לרבינו תם דבפרק במה אשה (שבת דף סה. ושם ד"ה ליעבד) אמרו יוצאין בסלע שעל גבי הנינית אי משום צורתא ליעביד ליה פולסא משמע דפולסא יש עליו צורה ובגמרא מפרש לקמן (ט) מאי אסימון פולסא וי"ל לפרש"י דכל דבר שאינו כתקונו קרי אסימון או שאין בו צורה או שיש בו צורה שאינה חשובה וא"ת מה בין אסימון שאין עליו צורה למעות הניתנין לסימן בבית המרחץ דאמרי' בגמ' (שם) ושוין רבי דוסא דאמר מחללין על אסימון מודה שאין מחללין על מעות הניתנין כו' ויש לומר דאסימון הם מעות שנעשו ברוחב ובעובי ובמשקל המטבע היוצא בעיר ובדבר מועט יטביעו הרבה מהם ולכך מחללין על אסימון ור"ת מפרש דאסימון יש בה צורה ואינה יוצאה בהוצאה וא"ת בגמרא קאמר רבי דוסא דאמר מחללין על אסימון ורבי ישמעאל אמרו דבר אחד דתניא וגרת הכסף לרבות כל דבר הנגרר ביד דברי רבי ישמעאל ר"ע אומר לרבות דבר שיש בו צורה משמע דרבי ישמעאל לא בעי צורה ואסימון יש בו צורה וא"כ היאך אמרו דבר אחד ויש לומר לרבות כל דבר הנגרר ביד אע"פ שאינו יוצא בהוצאה אך שיהיה בו צורה כל דהו ור"ע בעי צורה חשובה שתצא בהוצאה אך יוצאה לגמרי לא בעי מדאיצטריך לרבוי ולפי' רש"י אתי שפיר:

נעשה



מסורת הש"ס

א) [קדושין דף מב:], ב) [ברי"ף והרא"ש ל"ג זה הכלל וכן נכון עי' תי"ט], ג) גיטין ל., ד) [לקמן מז:, עד:], ה) [עבודה זרה נב:], ו) [לקמן מו:], ז) מהר"ם, ח) [דף מו:], ט) [דף מז:].

הגהות הגר"א

[א] במשנה (זה הכלל) תא"מ:

תורה אור השלם

א) עַל כָּל דְּבַר פֶּשַׁע עַל שׁוֹר עַל חֲמוֹר עַל שֶׂה עַל שַׂלְמָה עַל כָּל אֲבֵדָה אֲשֶׁר יֹאמַר כִּי הוּא זֶה עַד הָאֱלֹהִים יָבֹא דְּבַר שְׁנֵיהֶם אֲשֶׁר יַרְשִׁיעֻן אֱלֹהִים יְשַׁלֵּם שְׁנַיִם לְרֵעֵהוּ: [שמות כב, ח]

ב) אִם לֹא יִמָּצֵא הַגַּנָּב וְנִקְרַב בַּעַל הַבַּיִת אֶל הָאֱלֹהִים אִם לֹא שָׁלַח יָדוֹ בִּמְלֶאכֶת רֵעֵהוּ: [שמות כב, ז]

לעזי רש"י

פלדו"ן. פירוש כסף שלא נקבע בו צורה (רש"י ברכות דף מז ע"ב ד"ה אסימון), חתיכת מתכת שלא טבעו עליה צורת מטבע. קוי"ן. פירוש חותם (שבו טובעים מטבעות) (עיין רש"י גיטין דף כ ע"א ד"ה מיחרך חריך).

ליקוטי רש"י

**על כל דבר פשע.** בתר אם לא שלח ידו כתיב. **אין לי אלא הוא.** שנתחייב באונסין בשליחות יד אלא בזמן ששלח בה יד הוא עצמו [קידושין מב:].

**אסימון.** כסף שלא נקבע בו צורה וקורין לו פלז"ון בלע"ז [ברכות מז:].

עין משפט נר מצוה

קז א מיי' פ"ג מהל' גזילה הל' יא טוש"ע ח"מ סי' רלב סעי' ה:

קח ב מיי' שם הל' יג סמג עשין עג טוש"ע ח"מ שם סעי' ג:

קט ג ד מיי' שם הלכה יב ועיין בהשגות ובמגיד משנה טוש"ע שם סעי' ב:

א ה מיי' פ"ו מהל' מכירה הל' ג סמג עשין פב טוש"ע ח"מ סי' רג סעי' ד:

ב ו מיי' שם טוש"ע שם סעי' ה:

ג ז ח מיי' שם הל' ה טוש"ע שם סעי' א:

ד ט מיי' שם פ"ה הל' א סמג שם טוש"ע שם סעי' א:

ה י מיי' שם פ"ג הל' א סמג שם טוש"ע ח"מ סי' קצא סעי' א:

ו כ מיי' שם טוש"ע שם וסעי' ה:

ז ל מיי' שם פ"ז הל' א סמג שם טוש"ע ח"מ סי' רד סעי' א וסעי' ד:

רבינו חננאל

אין לי אלא הוא אמר לעבדו או לשלוחו ושלחו בו יד מניין ת"ל על כל דבר פשע אפי' בדיבור חייב וקיימא לן כב"ה דב"ש במקום ב"ה אינה משנה. היטה את החבית ונטל ממנה רביעית ונשברה אינו משלם אלא [רביעית] פי' כגון שהיטה את החבית ונטל ממנה רביעית והושיבה כמו שהיתה יושבת ואחר כך נשברה ודוקא היטה ולא טילטלה ולא נטלה הוא שמשלם הרביעית בלבד ודוקא נשברה אבל החמיצה משלם כולה שהוא גרם לה להחמיץ שכל זמן שהיא מליאה אינה מחמצת ואם מפחית מעט ממנה ממהרת להחמיץ. וזה פי' גיריה דידיה אהנו ליה. הגביה ונטל ממנה רביעית ונשברה משלם כולה. אוקמה שמואל כיון שהגביה ליטול ממנה אע"פ שלא נטל משלם כולה דניחא ליה דתיהוי הא חבית כולה בסיס לרביעית זו כי בהיות זו הרביעית בתוך החבית משתמרת ואינה מפיגה טעמה ולא ריחה. אבל המגביה ארנקי ליטול ממנה דינר ולא נטל ונגנב או נאבד עלתה בתיקו:

הדרן עלך המפקיד

**הזהב** קונה את הכסף והכסף אינו קונה את הזהב כך היה רבי שונה בזקנותו מאי טעמא אידי דכסף הוא חריף הוי טיבעא דהבא דליתיה חריף הוי פירא. וקני ליה פירא לטיבעא וכן הלכה. ובילדותיה היה שונה הכסף קונה את הזהב.

**Gemara** The Mishnah recorded a dispute between Beis Shammai and Beis Hillel as to whether intent for misappropriation causes liability immediately, even if the misappropriation did not yet take place. The Gemara seeks the Scriptural sources for each of their views:

מְנָהָנֵי מִילֵּי – **From where are these rulings** derived? דְּתָנוּ רַבָּנָן – **As the Rabbis taught in a Baraisa:** "עַל־כָּל־דְּבַר־פֶּשַׁע" – Scripture states: *FOR EVERY MATTER OF NEGLIGENCE.*[1] בֵּית שַׁמַּאי אוֹמְרִים – BEIS SHAMMAI SAY: מְלַמֵּד שֶׁחַיָּיב עַל הַמַּחֲשָׁבָה כְּמַעֲשֶׂה – [THIS VERSE] TEACHES THAT [A *SHOMER*] IS LIABLE FOR INTENT to misappropriate just AS he is liable for AN ACT of misappropriation.[2] וּבֵית הִלֵּל אוֹמְרִים – BUT BEIS HILLEL SAY: אֵינוֹ חַיָּיב עַד שֶׁיִּשְׁלַח בּוֹ יָד – [A *SHOMER*] IS NOT LIABLE UNTIL HE actually MISAPPROPRIATES [THE DEPOSIT], שֶׁנֶּאֱמַר: "אִם־לֹא שָׁלַח יָדוֹ בִּמְלֶאכֶת רֵעֵהוּ" – AS IT IS SAID: *IF HE DID NOT LAY HIS HAND UPON* (i.e. misappropriate) *THE GOODS OF HIS FELLOW.*[3]

The Baraisa continues:

אָמְרוּ לָהֶן בֵּית שַׁמַּאי לְבֵית הִלֵּל – BEIS SHAMMAI SAID TO BEIS HILLEL: וַהֲלֹא כְּבָר נֶאֱמַר – BUT IS IT NOT ALREADY STATED: "עַל־כָּל־דְּבַר־פֶּשַׁע" – *FOR EVERY MATTER OF NEGLIGENCE,* which implies that even intent for misappropriation creates liability?

Beis Hillel responded:

אָמְרוּ לָהֶן בֵּית הִלֵּל לְבֵית שַׁמַּאי – BEIS HILLEL SAID TO BEIS SHAMMAI: וַהֲלֹא כְּבָר נֶאֱמַר – BUT IS IT NOT ALREADY STATED: "אִם־לֹא שָׁלַח יָדוֹ בִּמְלֶאכֶת רֵעֵהוּ" – *IF HE DID NOT LAY A HAND UPON* (i.e. misappropriate) *THE GOODS OF HIS FELLOW,* which implies that he is not liable unless he actually misappropriated the deposit? אִם כֵּן מָה תַּלְמוּד לוֹמַר: "עַל־כָּל־דְּבַר־פֶּשַׁע" – IF SO, Beis Hillel continue, WHY DOES SCRIPTURE STATE: *FOR EVERY MATTER OF NEGLIGENCE?* שֶׁיָּכוֹל – FOR IT WOULD HAVE BEEN POSSIBLE to say: אֵין לִי אֶלָּא הוּא – I WOULD ONLY KNOW that a *shomer* is liable for misappropriation if HE performed the deed himself. אָמַר לְעַבְדּוֹ וְלִשְׁלוּחוֹ מִנַּיִן – FROM WHERE do I know that if [A *SHOMER*] TOLD HIS SERVANT OR AGENT to misappropriate the deposit that he is liable for *their* deed?[4] תַּלְמוּד לוֹמַר – SCRIPTURE therefore STATES: "עַל־כָּל־דְּבַר־פֶּשַׁע" – FOR EVERY MATTER OF NEGLIGENCE, to teach that a *shomer* is liable even for the deed of his agent.[5]

The Gemara discusses the second part of our Mishnah:

הִטָּה אֶת הֶחָבִית כו׳ – If [A *SHOMER*] TILTED a KEG of wine that had been entrusted to him **etc.** and took a *reviis* of wine from it, and later it broke as a result of an unavoidable accident, he is liable to compensate the owner for only a *reviis* of wine.

This ruling is qualified:

אָמַר רַבָּה – **Rabbah said:** לֹא שָׁנוּ אֶלָּא נִשְׁבְּרָה – **They taught** this ruling **only** in reference to a situation where **[the keg] was broken.** אֲבָל הֶחֱמִיצָה – **But if** the wine in **[the keg] turned to vinegar,** מְשַׁלֵּם אֶת כּוּלָּהּ – **he pays for it all.** מַאי טַעְמָא – **Why** is he liable to pay for more than he took?[6] גִּירֵי דִּידֵיהּ הוּא דְּאַהֲנוּ לָהּ – Because **his "arrows" caused [the wine]** to sour. I.e. it was his removal of the *reviis* of wine that caused the rest of the wine to become vinegar.[7]

The Mishnah stated:

הִגְבִּיהָהּ וְנָטַל הֵימֶנָּה כו׳ – But if [THE *SHOMER*] RAISED [THE KEG] AND then TOOK a *revi'is* of wine FROM IT, **etc.** and later it broke through an unavoidable accident, he pays its entire value.

The Gemara comments:

אָמַר שְׁמוּאֵל – **Shmuel said:** לֹא נָטַל נָטַל מַמָּשׁ – When the Mishnah says **"he took,"** it does **not** mean that **he actually took** the *reviis.* אֶלָּא כֵּיוָן שֶׁהִגְבִּיהָהּ לִיטּוֹל – **Rather,** the Mishnah means that **as soon as he lifted [the keg]** with intent **to take** from its wine, אַף עַל פִּי שֶׁלֹּא נָטַל – **even though he did not** yet **take** any wine, he is liable as if he had taken some.

The Gemara asks:

לֵימָא קָא סָבַר שְׁמוּאֵל – Are we **to say** that **Shmuel holds that** שְׁלִיחוּת יָד אֵינָהּ צְרִיכָה חִסָּרוֹן – **misappropriation is not dependent upon a loss,** and that is why he rules that the *shomer* assumes liability even before he causes any loss to the wine in the keg?

The Gemara answers:

אָמְרִי לֹא – **One could say** that this is **not** necessarily the reason for Shmuel's explanation of the Mishnah. Perhaps, Shmuel holds that misappropriation *is* dependent upon a loss. שָׁאנֵי הָכָא – Yet **here it is different,** דְּנִיחָא לֵיהּ דְּתֶיהֱוֵי הָא חָבִית כּוּלָּהּ בָּסִיס לְהָא רְבִיעִית – **because [the *shomer*] wants the entire keg** of wine **to be a holder for the *reviis*** of wine he intends to eventually remove. He wants the *reviis* to be stored with the rest of the wine in the keg (until he is ready to remove it), for it is better preserved in a full container.[8] Therefore, this situation is essentially no different from one in which a *shomer* removed a *reviis* of wine from the keg and then put it back there for storage.[9]

In the light of this explanation of Shmuel's teaching, the Gemara raises an inquiry:

בָּעֵי רַב אַשִׁי – **Rav Ashi asked:** הִגְבִּיהַּ אַרְנְקִי לִיטּוֹל – If [a *shomer*] **lifted a purse** that had been entrusted to his safekeeping

NOTES

1. *Exodus* 22:8. This verse discusses the responsibilities of an unpaid *shomer.* It immediately follows the phrase, אִם־לֹא שָׁלַח יָדוֹ בִּמְלֶאכֶת רֵעֵהוּ, *if he did not lay his hand upon* (i.e. misappropriate) *the goods of his fellow,* from which the law of *shelichus yad* is derived.

2. The word דְּבַר (matter) can be expounded as a derivative of the root דבר, *speak.* Beis Shammai infer from this that even a *declaration* of intent is enough to create liability (see *Ritva*).

3. Ibid. vv. 7 and 10.

4. The general rule is that if one person orders another to commit a sin, the agent, rather than the principal, is responsible for the deed. Therefore, a Scriptural reference is required to teach that with regard to *shelichus yad* the principal is liable (*Ritva*; see *Kiddushin* 42b-43a). [Some authorities say that the agent is also liable (see *Shach* 292:4, *Ketzos HaChoshen* ibid. §1, *Nesivos* ibid. §5).]

5. The word דְּבַר *(matter)* – which can be seen as a derivative of the root דבר, *speak* – teaches that a *shomer* can become liable for an act of misappropriation merely by *telling* someone else to do it (*Ritva*).

6. Since he did not perform an act of acquisition upon the remaining wine, he should not be liable for its unavoidable loss (see 43b note 29).

7. Wine tends to sour if the container in which it is stored is not full. Hence, by removing some of the wine from the keg, the *shomer* caused the rest of the wine to sour. He is liable, therefore, for damaging the rest of the wine (*Rashi*; see *Maayan HaChachmah,* cited by *Otzar Mefarshei HaTalmud,* n. 27).

8. See previous note.

9. And he is considered a borrower with regard to the rest of the wine [for he is using it to preserve the *reviis* of wine he intends to take for himself] (*Rashi*).There are several explanations as to why *Rashi* added this point: (1) As already mentioned, the law of *shelichus yad* dictates that a *shomer* who misappropriates part of the deposit is responsible for all of it. But, according to the view that *shelichus yad* is dependent upon a loss, if he did not cause a loss to the deposit, he has not committed an act of *shelichus yad.* He is, however, liable for stealing the portion he intended for himself. *Rashi* adds that he is a borrower to explain why he is responsible for the rest of the deposit (*Terumas HaKri* 292:2; see 41a note 12). (2) Alternatively: The reason why *shelichus yad* is dependent on a loss is that if the portion the *shomer* intended for himself is not removed or consumed, it cannot be deemed to have entered his possession as a stolen object, because it is mixed with the rest of the deposit that is still in the owner's possession. In our case, however, since he is a borrower with regard to the rest of the wine (and thus all the wine is considered to be in his possession to some extent), the portion he intends for himself *does* enter his possession as a stolen object. As a result, he is responsible for the entire deposit, in accordance with the law of *shelichus yad* (*Chidushei R' Meir Simchah;* see 41a note 12).

A variant view regarding the opinion of R' Akiva:

אָמַר לֵיהּ רַבִּי אוֹשַׁעְיָא לְרַב יְהוּדָה – **R' Oshaya said to Rav Yehudah:** רַבִּי אַתָּה אוֹמֵר כֵּן – **My teacher!** Is **that** what **you say?!** הָכִי אָמַר רַבִּי אַסִּי אָמַר רַבִּי יוֹחָנָן – But **this** is what **R' Assi said in the name of R' Yochanan:** חָלוּק הָיָה רַבִּי עֲקִיבָא – **R' Akiva disagreed** with his colleagues אֲפִילּוּ בִּמְקוֹם שֶׁיֵּשׁ עֵדִים – **even with regard to a case where there are witnesses** to the theft. מַאי טַעְמָא – **What is the reason** for this position? דְּאָמַר קְרָא – **For Scripture states:** "לַאֲשֶׁר הוּא לוֹ יִתְּנֶנּוּ בְּיוֹם אַשְׁמָתוֹ" – ***To whom it belongs he shall give it on the day of his guilt.*** A thief pays according to the value of the stolen property on the day he is declared guilty. וּבֵי דִינָא הוּא דְּקָא מְחַיְּיבֵי לֵיהּ אַשְׁמָה – **And** even where there are witnesses to the theft, **it is the court that declares him guilty!** Hence, regardless of whether there are witnesses, R' Akiva holds that a thief pays according to the value on the day of his judgment in court.

Further discussion about the view of R' Akiva:

אָמַר לֵיהּ רַבִּי זֵירָא לְרַבִּי אַבָּא בַּר פַּפָּא – **R' Zeira said to R' Abba bar Pappa:** כִּי אָזְלַתְּ לְהָתָם – **"When you go there** [Eretz Yisrael], אַקִּיף אַסּוּלְמָא דְּצוֹר – **make a detour to the ascent of** Mount **Tzor.** וְעוּל לְגַבֵּיהּ דְּרַבִּי יַעֲקֹב בַּר אִידִי – **Visit R' Yaakov bar Iddi** (who lives there) וּבְעֵי מִינֵּיהּ – **and ask him** אִי שְׁמִיעָא לֵיהּ לְרַבִּי יוֹחָנָן – **whether he has heard from** his teacher **R' Yochanan** הֲלָכָה כְּרַבִּי עֲקִיבָא – that **the law accords with** the view of **R' Akiva,** אוֹ אֵין הֲלָכָה כְּרַבִּי עֲקִיבָא – **or** that **the law does not accord with** the view of **R' Akiva."** R' Abba bar Pappa went to R' Yaakov bar Iddi, אָמַר לֵיהּ – and **[R' Yaakov bar Iddi] said to him:** הָכִי אָמַר רַבִּי יוֹחָנָן – **"This** is what **R' Yochanan said:** הֲלָכָה כְּרַבִּי עֲקִיבָא לְעוֹלָם – **The law always accords with** the view of **R' Akiva."**

The Gemara asks:

מַאי לְעוֹלָם – **What** did R' Yochanan mean by saying that the law **"always"** accords with the view of R' Akiva?

Rav Ashi offers two interpretations:

אָמַר רַב אַשִׁי – **Rav Ashi said:** שֶׁלֹּא תֹּאמַר – R' Yochanan put it that way so **that you should not say,** הָנֵי מִילֵּי הֵיכָא דְּלֵיכָּא עֵדִים – **"This ruling** of R' Akiva (that the thief pays according to the value at the time of the claim) applies **where there are no witnesses** to the theft, אֲבָל הֵיכָא דְּאִיכָּא עֵדִים – **but where there are witnesses** to the theft, לֹא – it does **not** apply (rather, the thief pays according to the value at the time of the theft)." To reject this notion, R' Yochanan said "always," thereby indicating that R' Akiva's ruling applies even where there are witnesses.

וְאִי נַמִּי – **Alternatively,** R' Yochanan used the word "always" to teach דְּאַהְדְּרָהּ לְדוּכְתָּהּ וְאִיתַּבְרָא – **that** even if **[a *shomer*] put a deposit back in its place** after having misappropriated it, **and** then **it broke** through an unavoidable accident, he is liable to compensate the owner. לְאַפּוּקֵי מִדְּרַבִּי יִשְׁמָעֵאל – According to this interpretation, the point of R' Yochanan's statement is **to preclude [the view] of R' Yishmael,** דְּאָמַר לֹא בְּעִינַן דַּעַת בְּעָלִים – **who said** that **the owner's knowledge** of the return of stolen property **is not required** to release the thief from liability. קָא מַשְׁמַע לָן – **[R' Yochanan] informs us** that here too the law accords with R' Akiva's view; דִּבְעִינַן דַּעַת בְּעָלִים – namely, **that the owner's knowledge** of the return of a stolen item **is required** to absolve the thief from liability.[24]

The Gemara above cited Shmuel's opinion that the law accords with the view of R' Akiva. The Gemara now presents a dissenting opinion:

וְרָבָא אָמַר – **But Rava said:** הֲלָכָה כְּבֵית הִלֵּל – **The law accords with** the view of **Beis Hillel,** who rule that a *shomer* who misappropriated a deposit pays what it was worth when he removed it from the owner's possession.[25]

**Mishnah** The Mishnah continues its discussion about misappropriation:

הַחוֹשֵׁב לִשְׁלוֹחַ יָד בְּפִקָּדוֹן – If **[a *shomer*] intends to misappropriate a deposit,** i.e. he declared[26] that he intended to misappropriate it, בֵּית שַׁמַּאי אוֹמְרִים – **Beis Shammai say:** חַיָּיב – From the moment of the declaration **he is liable** for any mishap that might befall the deposit. וּבֵית הִלֵּל אוֹמְרִים – **But Beis Hillel say:** אֵינוֹ חַיָּיב עַד שֶׁיִּשְׁלַח בּוֹ יָד – **He does not assume liability until he** actually **misappropriates it;** שֶׁנֶּאֱמַר: "אִם־לֹא שָׁלַח יָדוֹ בִּמְלֶאכֶת רֵעֵהוּ" – **as it is said:** ***If he did not lay his hand upon*** (i.e. misappropriate) ***the goods of his fellow,***[27] which implies actual misappropriation as opposed to mere intent.

Another law about misappropriation:

הִטָּה אֶת הֶחָבִית – If **[a *shomer*] tilted a barrel** of wine that had been entrusted to him, וְנָטַל הֵימֶנָּה רְבִיעִית – **and took a *reviis***[28] of wine **from it,** וְנִשְׁבְּרָה – **and** later **it broke** through an unavoidable accident, אֵינוֹ מְשַׁלֵּם אֶלָּא רְבִיעִית – **he pays for only a *reviis*** of wine. He is not responsible for the rest of the barrel, because he never performed an act of acquisition upon it.[29]

הִגְבִּיהָהּ וְנָטַל הֵימֶנָּה רְבִיעִית – But if **he lifed [the barrel] up,** which is an act of acquisition, **and** then **took a *reviis*** of wine **from it,** וְנִשְׁבְּרָה – **and** later **it broke** through an unavoidable accident, מְשַׁלֵּם דְּמֵי כוּלָּהּ – **he pays for its entire value.**[30]

NOTES

24. This dispute between R' Akiva and R' Yishmael was discussed above, 40b-41a.

25. [Beis Hillel's position is explained above, in notes 16 and 18.]

We follow the view of Rava, as opposed to that of Shmuel, because Rava lived after Shmuel (*Rashi*). [As a rule, in a dispute between two Amoraim, the halachah follows the view of the later scholar. There are different opinions regarding the application of this rule (see *Yad Malachi* 167, 168).]

26. In the presence of witnesses (*Rashi;* cf. *Ritva*).

The commentators ask why *Rashi* says that witnesses are required. Some explain, based on *Sanhedrin* 29a, that such a statement is not taken seriously unless it was made before witnesses (*Nachalas Moshe, Bircas Avraham;* see the alternative explanations cited by *Otzar Mefarshei HaTalmud*).

27. *Exodus* 22:7 and 10. The law of *shelichus yad* is derived from this verse; see 41a note 10.

28. A *reviis* (which means quarter) is a quarter of a *log.*

29. One is not liable for theft or *shelichus yad* unless he performs a *kinyan* (see 41a note 22). Since he performed a *kinyan* upon only a *reviis,* that is all he is responsible for (*Ritva*).

30. Even though he took only a *reviis,* he is responsible for the entire barrel. According to the law of *shelichus yad,* a *shomer* who misappropriates part of a deposit assumes responsibility for all of it (see 41a note 10).

אלא פשיטא כשעת הוצאה מבית בעלים לימא רבה דאמר כבית שמאי אמר לך רבה ביתר כולי עלמא לא פליגי כי פליגי בחסר ב"ש סברי שליחות יד אינה צריכה חסרון וכי חסר ברשותא דידיה חסר וב"ה סברי שליחות יד צריכה חסרון וכי חסר ברשותא דמריה חסר אלא הא דאמר רבא א) שליחות יד אינה צריכה חסרון לימא רבא דאמר כב"ש אלא הכא במאי עסקינן ב) כגון שטלטלה להביא עליה גוזלות ובשואל שלא מדעת קא מיפלגי ב"ש סברי ג) שואל שלא מדעת גזלן הוי וכי חסר ברשותא דידיה חסר וב"ה סברי שואל שלא מדעת שואל הוי וכי חסר ברשותא דמרה חסר אלא הא ד) דאמר רבא א שואל שלא מדעת לרבנן גזלן הוי לימא רבא דאמר כב"ש אלא הכא בשבח של גזילה קמיפלגי ב"ש סברי ב שבח גזילה דנגזל הוי ובית הלל סברי שבח גזילה דגזלן הוי ובפלוגתא דהני תנאי דתניא ה) הגוזל את הרחל גזזה וילדה משלם אותה ואת גיזותיה ואת ולדותיה דברי ר"מ ר' יהודה אומר ג גזילה חוזרת בעיניה דיקא נמי דקתני ב"ש אומרים ילקה בחסר וביתר וב"ה אומרים כשעת הוצאה ש"מ: ר"ע אומר כשעת התביעה: אמר רב יהודה אמר שמואל הלכה כר' עקיבא ומודה ר"ע במקום שיש עדים מ"ט דאמר קרא א) לאשר הוא לו יתננו ביום אשמתו וכיון דאיכא עדים מההוא שעתא הוא דאיחייב ליה אשמה א"ל ר' אושעיא לרב יהודה ר' אתה אומר כן הכי א"ר אסי אמר ר' יוחנן חלוק היה ר"ע אפי' במקום שיש עדים מ"ט דאמר קרא לאשר הוא לו יתננו ביום אשמתו ובי דינא הוא דקא מחייבי ליה אשמה א"ל ר' זירא לר' אבא בר פפא כי אזלת להתם אקיף אסולמא דצור ועול לגביה דר' יעקב בר אידי ובעי מיניה אי שמיעא ליה לר' יוחנן הלכה כר"ע או אין הלכה כר"ע א"ל הכי אמר ר' יוחנן הלכה כרבי עקיבא לעולם מאי לעולם אמר רב אשי שלא תאמר הני מילי היכא דליכא עדים אבל היכא דאיכא עדים לא ואי נמי דאהדרה לדוכתה ואיתברא לאפוקי מדרבי ישמעאל דאמר ו) לא בעינן דעת בעלים קא משמע לן דבעינן דעת בעלים ורבא אמר הלכה כבית הלל: **מתני'** החושב לשלוח יד בפקדון בית שמאי אומרים חייב ובית הלל אומרים ד אינו חייב עד שישלח בו יד שנאמר ב) אם לא שלח ידו במלאכת רעהו ה הטה את החבית ונטל הימנה רביעית ונשברה אינו משלם אלא רביעית ו הגביהה ונטל הימנה רביעית ונשברה משלם דמי כולה: גמ'

## רש"י

**אלא פשיטא כשעת הוצאה מבית בעלים.** כשעת הגזילה וביתר פליגי דקאמרי ב"ש אם הוקרה ילקה לשלם כשעת הוצאה מן העולם ובית הלל אמרי כשעת הוצאה מבית הבעלים: **כי פליגי בחסר.** וקאמרי ב"ה כשעת הוצאה מן העולם ודקא קשיא לך כל הגזלנין משלמים כשעת הגזילה הי בגזילה ממש דגזלה מעיקרא ה"נ אבל הכא דבהיתרא אתא לידי' ומשום שליחות יד קמחייבת ליה בהא פליגי: **ב"ש סברי שליחות יד אינה צריכה חסרון.** ומשלח בה יד אע"פ שלא חסרה הויא גזילה וקמה ברשותיה וכשהחולה ברשותו הוזלה ואם היתה בעין אומר לו הרי שלך לפניך עכשיו שהוציאה משלם כשעת שליחות יד: **אלא הא דאמר רבא.** לעיל בשמעתין (דף מא:): **שליחות יד אינה צריכה חסרון.** דקאמר שלא תאמר שליחות יד כו': **הא דאמר רבא.** בהמוכר את הספינה (ב"ב דף פח.): **שואל שלא מדעת לרבנן גזלן הוא.** גבי שולח את בנו אצל חנוני דפליגי רבנן ור' יהודה ואוקי רבא פלוגתייהו בשואל שלא מדעת ואמר דלרבנן גזלן הוי ומדאוקי רבא לרבנן בהכי סבירא ליה לדידיה גזלן הוי ואהדר לאוקמי מילתיה כרבנן דהלכתא כרבים: **לימא כב"ש.** אמרה: **אלא הכא בשבח גזילה פליגי.** והאי חסר ויתר דמתני' לאו ביוקרא וזולא אלא במאי דחסרה דהיינו גיזות ובמאי שהותירה כגון אם נתעברה אצלו דב"ש סברי הכל ישלם כר"מ דברייתא וב"ה כרבי יהוד' כשעת הוצאה מבית הבעלים: **דיקא נמי.** דבגיזות וולדות פליגי דקתני לשון חסר ויתר ולא קתני לשון זול ויוקר: **ומודה ר"ע במקום שיש עדי'.** כמה היתה שוה ביום שגזלה וראו שגזלה הימנו דמשלם כשעת הגזילה: **מאי טעמא דרבי עקיבא.** דאמר כשעת התביעה: **דאמר קרא ביום אשמתו.** בדמים של אותו יום שהוא מתחייב לו והיכא דתבעו והודה דעל פיו הוא מתחייב העמדתו בדין והודאתו הוא יום אשמתו אבל אם יש עדים משעה שראוהו שגזלה הוא אשם לו: **להתם.** לארץ ישראל: **אקיף.** הרבה את הדרך וסבב דרך ארוכה על דבר זה ללכת דרך מעלת של הר צור מקום שר' יעקב שם ובעי מיניה מה שמע מר' יוחנן רבו על כך כל מהלך דרך ארוכה במקום שיש קצרה מקיף הוא: **אי נמי דאהדרה לדוכתה.** להכי אשמועינן לעולם לומר שאם החזירה למקומה לאחר ששלח בה יד ונשברה באונס אף בזו הלכה כר"ע דאמר לעיל גבי גנב טלה מן העדר צריך דעת בעלי': **ורבא אמר הלכה כב"ה.** כשעת גזילה ואנן כרבא עבדינן דהוה ליה בתרא: **מתני' החושב לשלוח יד.** (א) אמר בפני עדים אטול פקדונו של פלוני לעצמי: **חייב.** באונסים מהיום והלאה אם נאנס חייב באחריות: **הטה את החבית.** מלתא באנפי נפשה היא: **ונשברה.** לאחר זמן: **אינו משלם אלא רביעית.** דשליחות יד אינו מתחייב באונסין עד שימשוך או יגביה דהוי קנייה: **הגביהה ונטל.** דהוי קנייה בהגבהתה וחסרון מנטילת רביעית חייב באונסיה:

## תוספות

**לימא** רבה דאמר כב"ש. וא"ת לוקי פלוגתייהו באתבר ממילא ורבה כב"ה וי"ל דא"כ לא הוו פליגי בית שמאי: **בית** שמאי סברי שליחות יד אינה צריכה חסרון. וא"ת א"כ תרי בבי הך דהכא וסיפא דהחושב לשלוח יד למה לי וי"ל דסיפא אשמועי' דלב"ש אפילו דבור בלא משיכה חייב והך דהכא אשמועינן דלב"ה צריכה חסרון: **אלא** הא דאמר רבא שואל שלא מדעת גזלן הוי. אומר ר"ת דגרסינן בכל הני רבא דהך דשואל ע"כ רבא הוי דקאמר בתר רבה ורב יוסף בהמוכר הספינה (ב"ב דף פח.) ומדהאי רבא כולהו נמי רבא דאי לאו הכי לא פריך מידי דמאי דלאוקומה פלוגתיה כחד מהנך פלוגתי' דלעיל: **משלם** אותה ואת גיזותיה ואת ולדותיה דברי ר"מ רבי יהודה אומר גזלה חוזרת בעיניה. וא"ת הא דתנן בפרק הגוזל קמא (ב"ק דף ק:) הנותן צמר לצבע לצבוע לו אדום וצבעו שחור אם השבח יתר על הוצאה נותן לו היציאה ואם הוצאה יתירה על השבח נותן לו השבח דברי רבי יהודה ר"מ אומר אין נותן לו אלא דמי צמרו בלבד אלמא סברתם הפוכות ותירץ ר"ת דהכא גבי גזילה סבר ר"מ שינוי אינו קונה משום דקנסא קנים במזיד אבל בלצבוע לו אדום דשוגג לא קנים והכי איתא בהגוזל ור' יהודה דסבר הכא דשינוי קונה היינו משום דמתכוין לקנות בשינוי אבל צבעו שחור אין מתכוין לקנותו בכך: **ר"ע** אומר כשעת התביעה. תימה מאי קסבר אי קסבר שינוי קונה למה ישלם השבח כשעת התביעה הלא בשעת גזיזה קנאה ואם הגדילה רחל או הגזיזה ונתייקרה לא ישלם אלא כמו ששוה רחל בשעת גזיזה ואי קסבר שינוי אינו קונה א"כ כשגוזה אחר התביעה נמי יהא הכל לנגזל דבמאי קנה ועוד דקאמר ומודה ר"ע במקום שיש עדים בשעת שליחות יד שישלם כאותה שעה במאי קנה והלא אכתי אפילו שינוי ליכא וגם כי יגוזנה שינוי לא יקנה ועוד למאן מודה הלא בין לב"ש בין לב"ה לא קנאה בשעת שליחות יד עד שעת שינוי ועוד דשמואל ור' יוחנן פסקו כר"ע בשמעתין ובהגוזל קמא (ב"ק דף צד:) אית להו דשינוי קונה לכך נראה לב"ש דאמרי ילקה בחסר ויתר מיירי אף ביוקרא וזולא דאם הוקרה משלם כשעת הוצאה מן העולם ואם הוזלה משלם כשעת הגזלה וב"ה לא פליגי נמי בהא והיינו כרבה אלא ב"ש מיירי נמי בשינוי כדקאמר דיקא נמי מדלא קתני בזול וביוקר ובהא פליגי ב"ה דשינוי קונה ור"ע פליג אזול ויוקר דאמר משלם כשעת התביעה בין הזל ובין הוקר: **החושב** לשלוח יד. ° הך מחשבה הוי דבור כדיליף מעל כל דבר וכן מחשבת פגול נמי הוי בדבור ולא בלב כדמוכח בפרק ב' דזבחים (דף ל.) ובפ"ק דמנחות (דף ג:) ובפרק תמיד נשחט (פסחים דף סג.) ובפרק הנזקין (גיטין דף נד:) ובמקומות אחרים פירשתי ז):

הדרן עלך המפקיד

## עין משפט נר מצוה

קב א מיי' פ"ג מהל' גזילה ואבידה הל' טו סמג עשין עג טוש"ע ח"מ סי' שנט סעי' ה:
קג ב מיי' שם פ"ב הל' ג ועיין בהשגות ובמ"מ סמג עשין שם טוש"ע ח"מ סי' שסב סעי' ב ז:
קד ג מיי' שם טוש"ע שם סעי' ז:
קה ד מיי' פ"ג שם הל' יא סמג שם טוש"ע ח"מ סי' רלב סעי' ד:
קו ה ו מיי' שם הל' יב ועיין בהשגות ובמ"מ טוש"ע שם סעי' ב:

## תורה אור השלם

א) אוֹ מִכֹּל אֲשֶׁר יִשָּׁבַע עָלָיו לַשֶּׁקֶר וְשִׁלַּם אֹתוֹ בְּרֹאשׁוֹ וַחֲמִשִׁתָיו יֹסֵף עָלָיו לַאֲשֶׁר הוּא לוֹ יִתְּנֶנּוּ בְּיוֹם אַשְׁמָתוֹ: [ויקרא ה, כד]

ב) אִם לֹא יִמָּצֵא הַגַּנָּב וְנִקְרַב בַּעַל הַבַּיִת אֶל הָאֱלֹהִים אִם לֹא שָׁלַח יָדוֹ בִּמְלֶאכֶת רֵעֵהוּ: [שמות כב, ז]

## רבינו חננאל

אלא פשיטא טעמא דבית הלל כשעת הוצאה מבית בעלים היא והיא שעת הגזילה והיתה שוה באותה שעה זוז ובשעה ששתאה שוה ד' בזה חלקו בית הלל ובית שמאי ב"ש סברי ד' משלם כי השתא וב"ה סברי [דמשלם] כשעת הגזילה והוא זוזא לימא רבה דאמר משלם [ד'] כב"ש דהא בית הלל זוזא חדא קאמרי. ופריק רבה ביותר כלומ' אם עת ששתאה היתה שוה יותר ממה שהיתה שוה בשעת גזילתה דברי הכל ד' כי השתא משלם כטעמא דידי שפירשנו למעלה כי פליגי בחסר כגון שהיתה שוה עת ששלח ידו בפקדון של חבירו ד' ועכשיו שוה זוז בית שמאי סברי שליחות יד אינה צריכא חסרון ומשעה דשלח בה יד איחייב בה. וב"ה סברי שליחות יד צריכא חסרון וכ"ז [דלא] חסרה ברשותיה דמריה קאי ובעידנא דתברה או שתיא וחיסרה בההיא שעתא מיחייב עלה וההיא שעתא זוזא הוא דשויא. ואלא רבה דאמר שליחות יד אינה צריכא חסרון כב"ש וכו'. ואוקימנא למתני' חלוקת ב"ש וב"ה בשבח גזילה ב"ש סברי דנגזל הוי וב"ה סברי דגזלן הוי וכי הני תנאי דתניא הגוזל רחל גזזה וילדה משלם אותה ואת גיזותיה וולדותיה דברי ר' מאיר ר' יהודה אומר גזלה חוזרת בעיניה. ר' מאיר כב"ש ר' יהודה כב"ה וקיימא לן כר' יהודה דבית הלל קיימי כותיה. וקיימא לן הא דאוקימנא אליבא דב"ה שבח גזילה דגזלן הוא בשבח שהשביחה בגופה אבל שבח שהשביחה בדמים דנגזל הוי כדרבה דאמר ביתר כולי עלמא לא פליגי דודאי לנגזל הוי כי פליגי בחסר. וקיימא לן כרבא וכן הלכה. ר' עקיבא אומר כשעת התביעה. ואע"ג דאמר רב יהודה אמר שמואל הלכה כר' עקיבא. ובתלמוד ארץ ישראל פסקו כר' עקיבא אנן לא סמכינן אלא בהא דאמר רבא דהוא בתרא ופסק הלכה כב"ה וכיון דסלקא שמעתא הכי ש"מ דשבח גזילה דגזלן הוי ומדחזינן רבה דפריק שליחות יד אינה צריכא חסרון ושואל שלא מדעת גזלן הוי ש"מ דהלכתא אינון. א) פי' כיון דאיכא עדים מההיא שעתא דגזל נתחייב לשלם אבל אם אין עדים אין חייב לשלם אלא בעת תביעתו בב"ד והל' המפקיד אצל חבירו בעדים ואפי' בשטר אין צריך להחזיר לו בעדים אלא כי אמר החזרתיו לך נאמן וכן אם אמר נאנסו נאמן ובתרויהו אינו חייב אלא שבועה שנאנסו או החזרתים לך: מתני' החושב לשלוח יד בפקדון בית שמאי מחייבין ובית הלל אומרים אינו חייב עד שישלח בו יד כו' שנאמר אם לא שלח ידו במלאכת רעהו מלמד שאינו חייב עד שישלח ידו בו

חשק שלמה על ר"ח א) נראה דחסר כאן וצ"ל ומודה ר"ע במקום שיש עדים פי' כיון דאיכא עדים וכו'.

## מסורת הש"ס

א) לעיל מא:, ב) [לעיל מא.], ג) [שם], ד) בבא בתרא פח., ה) בבא קמא צה. ע"ש, ו) [לעיל מ:], ז) [וע"ע תוספות פסחים סג. ד"ה ר' מאיר, ותוס' זבחים ד: ד"ה מחשבה, ותוס' בכורות נט. ד"ה במחשבה, ותוס' חולין לט. ד"ה אלא זביחה].

## הגהות הב"ח

(א) רש"י ד"ה החושב לשלוח יד אמר. נ"ב ובקדושין סוף דף מב [ע"ב] פרש"י דלאו דוקא אמר אלא חשב:

## גליון הש"ם

תוס' ד"ה החושב וכו' הך מחשבה. עיין בהרא"ש ריש הלכות ס"ת:

## ליקוטי רש"י

**שליחות יד.** שחייבו הכתוב עליו אפילו נאנסה כדכתיב [שמות כב] ומת או נשבר או נשבה וגו' שבועת ה' תהיה בין שניהם אם לא שלח ידו וגו' דמשמע הא שלח נתחייב שוב במיתתה ובשבייתה. **צריכה חסרון.** לא הוי שליחות יד להעמידה ברשותו אלא א"כ חסרה. וכל זמן שלא חסרה לא קמה ברשותיה להתחייב באונסיה. **שטלטלה להביא עליה גוזלות.** לעלות עליה כדרך סולם ליטול גוזלות מקן גבוה [לעיל מא.]. **שואל שלא מדעת שואל הוי.** וכי מחזירו למקום שנטלו משם די. **שואל שלא מדעת גזלן הוי.** וקנייה להתחייב בה עד שתבא ליד בעלים דבעינן והשיב את הגזילה [רשב"ם ב"ב פח.]. **משלם אותה ואת גיזותיה.** כל מה שנטל ממנה ומה שהשביחה. **גזילה חוזרת בעיניה.** כמות שהיא עכשיו ריקנית יחזירנה והדר משלם דמי גיזות ועובר כמו שהיה בשעת הגזילה ולא שבח הגיזה שהשביחה אצלו ולא שבח הולד [ב"ק צה.]. **אסולמא דצור.** סלע הר גבוה סביב [לעלות בו לא"י] [עירובין כב.]. **דבעינן דעת בעלים.** ואם לא הודיעם חייב באחריותם אם מת או נגנב דמדסלקיה קם ליה ברשותיה והשבה בלא ידיעה לאו השבה היא [לעיל מא.]. **החושב לשלוח יד בפקדון בש"א חייב.** שאם אמר או חשב לשלוח יד בפקדון הרי הוא ברשותו מאותה שעה ואילך להתחייב בכל אונסין שיעלו בו אפילו הוי שומר חנם שלא היה חייב עד עכשיו אלא בפשיעה [קדושין מב:]. הך מחשבה הואלת דיבור בפה הוא כדאמרי' בבבא מציעא על כל דבר פשע לחייב על המחשבה כמעשה דאי לא מוליאו בפה מחשבתו למאי נחייב לה [מנחות ב: רש"י ד"ה אבל מחשבה].

that **Rava rules in accordance with Beis Shammai** as opposed to Beis Hillel?![14]

To avoid this difficulty, the Gemara presents a totally different interpretation of the dispute between Beis Shammai and Beis Hillel. According to this interpretation, when the Mishnah says that the deposit "increased" or "decreased," it refers not to fluctuations in market value, but to physical changes in the deposit: **אֶלָּא הָכָא בְּשֶׁבַח שֶׁל גְּזֵילָה קָמִיפַּלְגֵי – Rather, they disagree about** physical **improvements in stolen property. בֵּית שַׁמַּאי סָבְרֵי – Beis Shammai hold: שֶׁבַח גְּזֵילָה דְנִגְזָל הָוֵי** – Physical **improvements in stolen property belong to the owner. וּבֵית הִלֵּל סָבְרֵי – Beis Hillel hold: שֶׁבַח גְּזֵילָה דְגַזְלָן הָוֵי** – Physical **improvements in stolen property belong to the thief. וּבִפְלוּגְתָּא דְהָנֵי תַּנָּאֵי – And** their dispute is the same **as the dispute between these Tannaim, דְּתַנְיָא – as it was taught in a Baraisa:** הַגּוֹזֵל אֶת הָרָחֵל – IF SOMEONE STOLE A EWE גְּזָזָהּ – and HE SHEARED IT of its wool, וְיָלְדָה – OR IT GAVE BIRTH, מְשַׁלֵּם אוֹתָהּ וְאֶת גִּיזוֹתֶיהָ וְאֶת וְלָדוֹתֶיהָ – HE RETURNS[15] not only [THE EWE] but also ITS FLEECE AND ITS OFFSPRING; דִּבְרֵי רַבִּי מֵאִיר – these are THE WORDS OF R' MEIR. רַבִּי יְהוּדָה אוֹמֵר – But R' YEHUDAH SAYS: גְּזֵילָה חוֹזֶרֶת בְּעֵינֶיהָ – THE STOLEN PROPERTY GOES BACK AS IT IS. I.e. only the ewe itself is returned to the owner; its fleece and offspring are acquired by the thief.[16]

Beis Shammai, who said in our Mishnah that the *shomer* suffers the loss whether the deposit "increased" or "decreased," hold (as does R' Meir) that a thief is liable to give any physical improvements to the owner.[17] Beis Hillel, who said that the *shomer* returns the deposit as it was at the time of its "removal [from the owner's possession]," hold (as does R' Yehudah) that a thief keeps the physical improvements.[18]

The Gemara provides support for this interpretation of our Mishnah:

**דַּיְקָא נַמִּי – This** interpretation **is also** borne out **by a precise** reading of our Mishnah: **דְּקָתָנֵי – For the Mishnah says:** בֵּית שַׁמַּאי אוֹמְרִים – BEIS SHAMMAI SAY: יִלְקֶה בְּחָסֵר וּבְיָתֵר – [THE *SHOMER*] SUFFERS the loss WHETHER IT "DECREASED" OR "INCREASED." וּבֵית הִלֵּל אוֹמְרִים – BUT BEIS HILLEL SAY: כִּשְׁעַת הוֹצָאָה – He pays ACCORDING TO its value at THE TIME OF its REMOVAL [from the owner's possession]. Since the Mishnah speaks of "decrease" and "increase" (as opposed to "depreciation" and "appreciation"), this implies physical, rather than market-value, change. **שְׁמַע מִינָּהּ – Indeed, one can learn from this** that our Mishnah refers to physical change.

The Gemara quotes the third opinion recorded in our Mishnah: רַבִּי עֲקִיבָא אוֹמֵר – R' AKIVA SAYS: כִּשְׁעַת הַתְּבִיעָה – The *shomer* pays ACCORDING TO the value of the deposit at THE TIME OF THE CLAIM.[19]

Regarding our Mishnah's three-way dispute between Beis Shammai, Beis Hillel, and R' Akiva, the Gemara cites a halachic ruling:

**אָמַר רַב יְהוּדָה אָמַר שְׁמוּאֵל – Rav Yehudah[20] said in the name of Shmuel: הֲלָכָה כְּרַבִּי עֲקִיבָא – The law accords with** the view of **R' Akiva.**

Rav Yehudah continues in the name of Shmuel: **וּמוֹדֶה רַבִּי עֲקִיבָא – And R' Akiva concedes** בְּמָקוֹם שֶׁיֵּשׁ עֵדִים – that **where there are witnesses** who saw the *shomer* misappropriate the deposit,[21] the *shomer* pays what the deposit was worth when he misappropriated it. **מַאי טַעְמָא – For what is the reason** behind R' Akiva's position that the *shomer* pays according to the value at the time of the claim? **דְּאָמַר קְרָא: ,,לַאֲשֶׁר הוּא לוֹ יִתְּנֶנּוּ בְּיוֹם אַשְׁמָתוֹ" – From that** which **Scripture states:** ***To whom it belongs he shall give it on the day of his guilt,***[22] R' Akiva infers that one who is liable to pay compensation for property he has stolen pays according to its value on the day he is deemed guilty. So in the event that his guilt is established only by his admission in court, he pays according to the value on the day of his judgment in court. **וְכֵיוָן דְּאִיכָּא עֵדִים – But where there are witnesses** to the theft, he pays according to the value at the time of the theft, **מֵהַהוּא שַׁעְתָּא הוּא דְּאִיחַיַּיב לֵיהּ אַשְׁמָה – for it is from that time that he is deemed guilty.**[23]

NOTES

14. See note 2.

15. Literally: he pays.

16. This dispute applies regardless of whether the animal was laden with wool when it was stolen, or it grew wool while in the possession of the thief. Similarly, in the second case, it makes no difference whether the animal conceived before or after it was stolen (see *Rashi, Baal HaMaor, Maharsha*). However, in the case that the ewe was laden with wool or pregnant when it was stolen, R' Yehudah would agree that the thief must also pay back the difference between the current value of the ewe and its value at the time of the theft, for a thief cannot return *less* than what he stole.

R' Yehudah's position is based on the concept of שִׁנּוּי, [acquisition through] *change.* That is, if a thief steals something which then undergoes a significant physical change, the stolen property becomes his. He need not return the stolen item itself, but pays according to what it was worth when he stole it. [In the present case, the birth and shearing (or conception and growth of wool) are not considered changes in the body of the ewe. Therefore, the thief acquires only the fleece and offspring, and returns the ewe itself.] R' Meir agrees with the concept of שִׁנּוּי, *change*, on the Biblical level, but he holds that the Rabbis imposed a penalty on the thief requiring him to return the fleece or offspring, so that he does not benefit from his crime (see *Rashi* to *Bava Kamma* 95a ד״ה גזילה חוזרת בעיניה; cf. *Rosh* ibid.).

[It is a matter of dispute whether, according to R' Yehudah, a thief may keep improvements that developed in his possession and are still attached to the animal (e.g. if a sheep grew wool after it was stolen, and was not yet shorn of it) (see *Bava Kamma* 95b).]

17. According to this interpretation, the word "decreased" refers to a case such as that of a ewe that was laden with wool when it was stolen and was then shorn by the thief. The word "increased" refers to a case such as an animal that conceived (and gave birth) after it was stolen (*Rashi;* see *Maharsha* and *Pnei Yehoshua*).

18. Beis Hillel hold that the *shomer* returns only the deposited object itself and keeps any physical improvements. [However, where necessary, he must also pay the difference between the current value of the deposited item and its value when he misappropriated it (see note 16).]

19. According to R' Akiva, a *shomer* who misappropriated a deposit is not considered a thief (to acquire physical improvements) until he is found guilty in court. Hence, he acquires only those improvements that developed after his sentencing in court. For example, if a *shomer* misappropriated an animal and it gave birth after the misappropriation but before the sentencing, he must return the offspring to the owner. But if it gave birth *after* the sentencing, he acquires the offspring (*Baal HaMaor;* cf. *Rif; Ritva,* cited by *Shitah Mekubetzes,* writes that *Rashi* takes the approach of *Baal HaMaor*).

[From *Rashi's* commentary it seems that R' Akiva refers not only to *shelichus yad,* but to regular theft as well. According to R' Akiva, even a regular thief acquires only those physical improvements that developed *after* his sentencing in court.]

20. [This is Rav Yehudah, the Amora, not Rabbi Yehudah (abbreviated to R' Yehudah), the Tanna.]

21. And they know how much [the deposit] was worth at that time (*Rashi*).

22. *Leviticus* 5:24.

23. [I.e. that which establishes him as guilty (viz. the witnesses) is at hand from that time; the court sentencing is only a question of legal process revealing what is already known (*Rif*).]

אלא פשיטא כשעת הוצאה מבית בעלים לימא רבה דאמר כבית שמאי אמר לך רבה ביתר כולי עלמא לא פליגי כי פליגי בחסר ב"ש סברי שליחות יד אינה צריכה חסרון וכי חסר ברשותא דידיה חסר וב"ה סברי שליחות יד צריכה חסרון וכי חסר ברשותא דמריה חסר אלא הא דאמר רבא [א] שליחות יד אינה צריכה חסרון לימא רבא דאמר כב"ש אלא הכא במאי עסקינן [ב] כגון שטלטלה להביא עליה גזולות ובשואל שלא מדעת קא מיפלגי ב"ש סברי [ג] שואל שלא מדעת גזלן הוי וכי חסר ברשותא דידיה חסר וב"ה סברי שואל שלא מדעת שואל הוי וכי חסר ברשותא דמרה חסר אלא הא [ד] דאמר רבא [א] שואל שלא מדעת לרבנן גזלן הוי לימא רבא דאמר כב"ש אלא הכא בשבח של גזילה קמיפלגי ב"ש סברי [ב] שבח גזילה דנגזל הוי ובית הלל סברי שבח גזילה דגזלן הוי ובפלוגתא דהני תנאי דתניא [ה] הגוזל את הרחל גזזה וילדה משלם אותה ואת גיזותיה ואת ולדותיה דברי ר"מ ר' יהודה אומר [ג] גזילה חוזרת בעיניה דיקא נמי דקתני ב"ש אומרים ילקה בחסר וביתר וב"ה אומרים כשעת הוצאה ש"מ: ר"ע אומר כשעת התביעה: אמר רב יהודה אמר שמואל הלכה כר' עקיבא ומודה ר"ע במקום שיש עדים מ"ט דאמר קרא [א] לאשר הוא לו יתננו ביום אשמתו וכיון דאיכא עדים מההוא שעתא הוא דאיחייב ליה אשמה א"ל ר' אושעיא לרב יהודה ר' אתה אומר כן הכי א"ר אסי אמר ר' יוחנן חלוק היה ר"ע אפי' במקום שיש עדים מ"ט דאמר קרא לאשר הוא לו יתננו ביום אשמתו ובי דינא הוא דקא מחייבי ליה אשמה א"ל ר' זירא לר' אבא בר פפא כי אזלת להתם אקיף אסולמא דצור ועול לגביה דר' יעקב בר אידי ובעי מיניה אי שמיע ליה לר' יוחנן הלכה כר"ע או אין הלכה כר"ע א"ל הכי אמר ר' יוחנן הלכה כרבי עקיבא לעולם מאי לעולם אמר רב אשי שלא תאמר הני מילי היכא דליכא עדים אבל היכא דאיכא עדים לא ואי נמי דאהדרה לדוכתה ואיתברא לאפוקי מדרבי ישמעאל דאמר [ו] לא בעינן דעת בעלים קא משמע לן דבעינן דעת בעלים ורבא אמר הלכה כבית הלל: **מתני'** החושב לשלוח יד בפקדון בית שמאי אומרים חייב ובית הלל אומרים [ד] אינו חייב עד שישלח בו יד שנאמר [ב] אם לא שלח ידו במלאכת רעהו [ה] הטה את החבית ונטל הימנה רביעית ונשברה אינו משלם אלא רביעית [ו] הגביהה ונטל הימנה רביעית ונשברה משלם דמי כולה:

גמ'

---

אלא פשיטא כשעת הוצאה מבית בעלים. כשעת הגזילה וביתר פליגי דקאמרי ב"ש אם הוקרה ילקה לשלם כשעת הוצאה מן העולם ובית הלל אמרי כשעת הוצאה מבית הבעלים: כי פליגי בחסר. וקאמרי ב"ה כשעת הוצאה מן העולם ודקא קשיא לך כל הגזלנין משלמים כשעת הגזילה הני מילי בגזילה ממש דגזלה מעיקרא ה"נ אבל הכא דבהיתרא אתא לידי' ומשום שליחות יד קמחייבת ליה בהא פליגי: ב"ש סברי שליחות יד אינה צריכה חסרון. ומשלח בה יד אע"פ שלא חסרה הויא גזילה וקמה ברשותיה וכשהוזלה ברשותו הוזלה ואם היתה בעין אומר לו הרי שלך לפניך עכשיו שהוציאה משלם כשעת שליחות יד: אלא הא דאמר רבא. לעיל בשמעתין (דף מא:): שליחות יד אינה צריכה חסרון. דקאמר שלא תאמר שליחות יד כו': הא דאמר רבא. בהמוכר את הספינה (ב"ב דף פח.): שואל שלא מדעת לרבנן גזלן הוא. גבי שולח את בנו אצל חנוני דפליגי רבנן ור' יהודה ואוקי רבא פלוגתייהו בשואל שלא מדעת ואמר דלרבנן גזלן הוי ומדאוקי רבא לרבנן בהכי סבירא ליה לדידיה גזלן הוי ואהדר לאוקמי מילתיה כרבנן דהלכתא כרבים: לימא כב"ש. אמרה: אלא הכא בשבח גזילה פליגי. והאי חסר ויתר דמתני' לאו ביוקרא וזולא אלא במאי דחסרה דהיינו גיזות ובמאי שהותירה כגון אם נתעברה אצלו דב"ש סברי הכל ישלם כר"מ דברייתא וב"ה כרבי יהוד' כשעת הוצאה מבית הבעלים: דיקא נמי. דבגיזות וולדות פליגי דקתני לשון חסר ויתר ולא קתני לשון זול ויוקר: ומודה ר"ע במקום שיש עדי'. כמה היתה שוה ביום שגזלה ורואו שגזלה הימנו דמשלם כשעת הגזילה: מאי טעמא דרבי עקיבא. דאמר כשעת התביעה: דאמר קרא ביום אשמתו. בדמים של אותו יום שהוא מתחייב לו והיכא דתבעו והודה דעל פיו הוא מתחייב העמדתו בדין והודאתו הוא יום אשמתו אבל אם יש עדים משעה שראוהו שגזלה הוא אשם לו: להתם. לארץ ישראל: אקיף. הרבה את הדרך וסבב דרך ארוכה על דבר זה ללכת דרך מעלת של הר צור מקום שר' יעקב שם ובעי מיניה מה שמע מר' יוחנן רבו על כן כל מהלך דרך ארוכה במקום שיש קצרה מקיף הוא: אי נמי דהדרה לדוכתה. להכי אשמועינן לעולם לומר שאם החזירה למקומה לאחר ששלח בה יד ונשברה באונס אף בזו הלכה כר"ע דאמר לעיל גבי גנב טלה מן העדר צריך דעת בעלי': ורבא אמר הלכה כב"ה. כשעת גזילה ואנן כרבא עבדינן דהוה ליה בתראה: **מתני'** החושב לשלוח יד. (א) אמר בפני עדים אטול פקדונו של פלוני לעצמי: חייב. באונסים מהיום והלאה אם נאנס חייב באחריות: הטה את החבית. מלתא באנפי נפשה היא: ונשברה. לאחר זמן: אינו משלם אלא רביעית. דשליחות יד אינו מתחייב באונסין עד שימשוך או יגביה דהוי קנייה: הגביהה ונטל. דהוי קנייה בהגבהתה וחסרון מנטילת רביעית חייב באונסיה:

---

**לימא** רבה דאמר כב"ש. וא"ת לוקי פלוגתייהו באתבר ממילא ורבה כב"ה וי"ל דא"כ לא הוו פליגי בית שמאי:

**בית** שמאי סברי שליחות יד אינה צריכה חסרון. וא"ת א"כ תרי בבי הך דהכא וסיפא דהחושב לשלוח יד למה לי וי"ל דסיפא אשמועי' דלב"ש אפילו דבור בלא משיכה חייב והך דהכא אשמועינן דלב"ה צריכה חסרון:

**אלא** הא דאמר רבא שואל שלא מדעת גזלן הוי. אומר ר"ת דגרסינן בכל הני רבא דהך דשואל ע"כ רבא הוי דקאמר בתר רבה ורב יוסף בהמוכר הספינה (ב"ב דף פח.) ומדהאי רבא כולהו נמי רבא דאי לאו הכי לא פריך מידי דמצי לאוקומה פלוגתיה כחד מהנך פלוגתי' דלעיל:

**משלם** אותה ואת גיזותיה ואת ולדותיה דברי ר"מ רבי יהודה אומר גזלה חוזרת בעיניה. וא"ת הא דתנן בפרק הגוזל קמא (ב"ק דף ק:) הנותן למר לצבע לצבוע לו אדום וצבעו שחור אם השבח יתר על הוצאה נותן לו היציאה ואם הוצאה יתירה על השבח נותן לו השבח דברי רבי יהודה ר"מ אומר אין נותן לו אלא דמי צמרו בלבד אלמא סברתם הפוכות ותירץ ר"ת דהכא גבי גזילה סבר ר"מ שינוי אינו קונה משום דקנסא קניס במזיד אבל בלצבוע לו אדום דשוגג לא קניס והכי איתא בהגוזל ור' יהודה דסבר הכא דשינוי קונה היינו משום דמתכוין לקנות בשינוי אבל לצבעו שחור אין מתכוין לקנותו בכך:

**ר"ע** אומר כשעת התביעה. תימה מאי קסבר אי קסבר שינוי קונה למה ישלם השבח כשעת התביעה הלא בשעת גזיזה קנאה ואם הגדילה רחל או הגזיזה ונתייקרה לא ישלם אלא כמו ששוה רחל בשעת גזיזה ואי קסבר שינוי אינו קונה א"כ כשגוזזה אחר התביעה נמי יהא הכל לנגזל דבמאי קנה ועוד דקאמר ומודה ר"ע במקום שיש עדים בשעת שליחות יד שישלם כאותה שעה במאי קנה הא אכתי אפילו שינוי ליכא וגם כי יגזזנה שינוי לא יקנה ועוד למאן מודה הלא בין לב"ש בין לב"ה לא קנאה בשעת שליחות יד עד שעת שינוי ועוד דשמואל ור' יוחנן פסקו כר"ע בשמעתין ובהגוזל קמא (ב"ק דף צד:) אית להו דשינוי קונה לכך נראה לב"ש דאמרי ילקה בחסר ויתר מיירי אף ביוקרא וזולא דאם הוקרה משלם כשעת הוצאה מן העולם ואם הוזלה משלם כשעת הגזלה וב"ה לא פליגי נמי בהא והיינו כרבה אלא ב"ש מיירי נמי בשינוי כדקאמר דיקא נמי מדלא קתני בזול וביוקר ובהא פליגי ב"ה דשינוי קונה ור"ע פליג אזול ויוקר דאמר משלם כשעת התביעה בין הזול ובין הוקר:

**החושב** לשלוח יד. [ט] הך מחשבה הוי דבור כדיליף מעל כל דבר וכן מחשבת פגול נמי הוי בדבור ולא בלב כדמוכח בפרק ב' דזבחים (דף ל.) ובפ"ק דמנחות (דף ג:) ובפרק תמיד נשחט (פסחים דף סג.) ובפרק הנזקין (גיטין דף נד:) ובמקומות אחרים פירשתי [ז]:

**הדרן עלך המפקיד**

---

עין משפט נר מצוה

קב א מיי' פ"ג מהל' גזלה ואבידה הל' טו סמג עשין עג טוש"ע ח"מ סי' שנט סעי' ה:

קג ב מיי' שם פ"ב הל' ג ועיין בהשגות ובמ"מ סמג עשין שם טוש"ע ח"מ סי' שסב סעי' ג ז:

קד ג מיי' שם טוש"ע שם סעי' ז:

קה ד מיי' פ"ג שם הל' יא סמג שם טוש"ע ח"מ סי' רצב סעי' ד:

קו ה ו מיי' שם הל' יב ועיין בהשגות ובמ"מ טוש"ע שם סעי' ב:

תורה אור השלם

א) אוֹ מִכֹּל אֲשֶׁר יִשָּׁבַע עָלָיו לַשֶּׁקֶר וְשִׁלַּם אֹתוֹ בְּרֹאשׁוֹ וַחֲמִשִׁתָיו יֹסֵף עָלָיו לַאֲשֶׁר הוּא לוֹ יִתְּנֶנּוּ בְּיוֹם אַשְׁמָתוֹ: [ויקרא ה, כד]

ב) אִם לֹא יִמָּצֵא הַגַּנָּב וְנִקְרַב בַּעַל הַבַּיִת אֶל הָאֱלֹהִים אִם לֹא שָׁלַח יָדוֹ בִּמְלֶאכֶת רֵעֵהוּ: [שמות כב, ז]

רבינו חננאל

אלא פשיטא טעמא דבית הלל כשעת הוצאה מבית בעלים היא והיא שעת הגזילה והיתה שוה באותה שעה זוז ובשעה ששתאה שוה ד' בזה חלקו בית הלל ובית שמאי ב"ש סברי ד' משלם כי השתא וב"ה סברי [משלם] כשעת הגזילה והוא זוזא לימא רבה דאמר משלם [ד'] כב"ש דהא בית הלל זוזא חדא קאמרי. ופריק רבה ביותר כלום' אם עת ששתאה היתה שוה יותר ממה שהיתה שוה בשעת גזילתה דברי הכל ד' כי השתא משלם כטעמא דידי שפירשנו למעלה כי פליגי בחסר כגון שהיתה שוה עת ששלח ידו בפקדון של חבירו ד' ועכשיו שוה זוז בית שמאי סברי שליחות יד אינה צריכא חסרון ומשעה דשלח בה יד איחייב בה. וב"ה סברי שליחות יד צריכא חסרון וכ"ז [דלא] חסרה ברשותיה דמריה קאי ובעידנא דחברה או שתיא וחיסרה בההיא שעתא מיחייב עלה וההיא שעתא זוזא הוא דשויא. ואלא רבה דאמר שליחות יד אינה צריכה חסרון כב"ש וכו'. ואוקימנא למתני' חלוקת ב"ש וב"ה בשבח גזילה ב"ש סברי דגזלן הוי וכי הני תנאי דתניא הגוזל רחל גזזה וילדה משלם אותה ואת גיזותיה וולדותיה דברי ר' מאיר ר' יהודה אומר גזלה חוזרת בעיניה. ר' מאיר כב"ש ור' יהודה כב"ה וקיימא לן כר' יהודה דבית הלל קיימי כוותיה. וקיימא לן הא דאוקימנא אליבא דב"ה שבח גזילה דגזלן הוא בשבח שהשביחה בגופה אבל שבח שהשביחה בדמים דנגזל הוי כדרבה דאמר ביותר כולי עלמא לא פליגי דודאי לנגזל הוי כי פליגי בחסר. וקיימא לן כרבא וכן הלכה. ר' עקיבא אומר כשעת התביעה. ואע"ג דאמר רב יהודה אמר שמואל הלכה כר' עקיבא. ובתלמוד ארץ ישראל פסקו כר' עקיבא אנן לא סמכינן אלא בהא דאמר רבא דהוא בתרא ופסק הלכה כב"ה וכיון דסלקא שמעתא הכי ש"מ דשבח גזילה דגזלן הוי ומדחזינן רבה דפריק שליחות יד אינה צריכא חסרון ושואל שלא מדעת גזלן הוי ש"מ דהלכתא אינון. א) פי' כיון דאיכא עדים מההיא שעתא דגזל נתחייב לשלם אבל אם אין עדים אין חייב לשלם אלא בעת תביעתו בב"ד והל' המפקיד אצל חבירו בעדים ואפי' בשטר אין צריך להחזיר לו בעדים אלא כי אמר החזרתיו לך נאמן וכן אם אמר נאנסו נאמן ובתרויהו אינו חייב אלא שבועה שנאנסו או החזרתים לך: מתני' החושב לשלוח יד בפקדון בית שמאי מחייבין ובית הלל אומרים אינו חייב עד שישלח בו יד כו' שנאמר אם לא שלח ידו במלאכת רעהו מלמד שאינו חייב עד שישלח ידו בו

חשק שלמה על ר"ח א) נראה דחסר כאן וצ"ל ומודה ר"ע במקום שיש עדים פי' כיון דאיכא עדים וכו'.

---

מסורת הש"ס

א) לעיל מא., ב) [לעיל מא.], ג) [שם], ד) בבא בתרא פח., ה) בבא קמא צה. ע"ש, ו) [לעיל מ:], ז) [וע"ע תוספות פסחים סג. ד"ה ר' מאיר, ותוס' זבחים ד: ד"ה מחשבה, ותוס' בכורות נט. ד"ה במחשבה, ותוס' חולין לט. ד"ה אלא זביחה].

הגהות הב"ח

(א) רש"י ד"ה החושב לשלוח יד אמר. נ"ב ובקדושין סוף דף מב [ע"ב] פרש"י דלאו דוקא אמר אלא חשב:

גליון הש"ס

תוס' ד"ה החושב וכו' הך מחשבה. עיין בהרא"ש ריש הלכות ס"ת:

ליקוטי רש"י

שליחות יד. שחייבו הכתוב עליו אפילו נאנסה כדכתיב [שמות כב] ומת או נשבר או נשבה וגו' שבועת ה' תהיה בין שניהם אם לא שלח ידו וגו' דמשמע הא שלח נתחייב שוב במיתתה ובשבייתה. צריכה חסרון. לא הוי שליחות יד להעמידה ברשותו אלא א"כ חסרה. וכל זמן שלא חסרה לא קמה ברשותיה להתחייב באונסיה. שטלטלה להביא עליה גזולות. לעלות עליה כדרך כולם ליטול גחלת ממקום גבוה [לעיל מא.]. שואל שלא מדעת שואל הוי. וכי מחזירו למקום שנטלו משם. שואל שלא מדעת גזלן הוי. וקנייה להתחייב בה עד שתבא ליד בעלים [רשב"ם ב"ב פח.]. משלם אותה ואת גיזותיה. כל מה שנטל ממנה ומה שהשביחה. גזילה חוזרת בעיניה. כמות שהיא עכשיו יחזירנה והדר משלם דמי גיזות וולדות כמו שהיה בשעת הגזילה ולא שבח הגיזה שהשביחה אצלו ולא שבח הולד [ב"ק צה.]. אסולמא דצור. סולם של הר גבוה סביב [לעולם כו'] [עירובין כב.]. דבעינן דעת בעלים. [illegible] [לעיל מא.]. החושב לשלוח יד בפקדון בש"א חייב. [illegible] [קידושין מב:]. הך מחשבה. [illegible] [מנחות ב:]. רש"י ד"ה אבל מחשבה.

Having demonstrated that Beis Hillel cannot mean removal from the world, the Gemara now turns to the only other possible explanation of Beis Hillel's words:

**אֶלָּא פְּשִׁיטָא – Rather, it is obvious** that when Beis Hillel say "removal," they mean **כִּשְׁעַת הוֹצָאָה מִבֵּית בְּעָלִים – "according to the time of** its **removal from the owner's possession,"** i.e. the *shomer* pays what the deposit was worth when he misappropriated it (regardless of whether it later increased or decreased in value).

According to this explanation, the dispute between Beis Hillel and Beis Shammai is as follows: If the value of the deposit increased after the *shomer* misappropriated it, Beis Shammai rule that the *shomer* pays what it was worth when he destroyed it, while Beis Hillel rule that he pays what it was worth when he misappropriated it.

The Gemara challenges this interpretation:

**לֵימָא רַבָּה דְּאָמַר כְּבֵית שַׁמַּאי** – Are we **to say** that **Rabbah** (who holds that where the value of the stolen property increased, the thief pays what it was worth when he destroyed it)[1] **rules in accordance with Beis Shammai,** as opposed to Beis Hillel?![2]

Because of this difficulty, the Gemara returns to its first explanation of Beis Hillel's words; namely, that "removal" means removal from the world (i.e. the *shomer* pays what the deposit was worth when he destroyed it, regardless of whether its value had increased or decreased):

**אָמַר לָךְ רַבָּה – Rabbah will respond to you: בְּיָתֵר – Where [the deposit] increased** in value, **כּוּלֵּי עָלְמָא לֹא פְּלִיגֵי – no one disputes** that the *shomer* pays what it was worth when he destroyed it.[3] **כִּי פְּלִיגֵי – In which case do they disagree? בְּחָסֵר** – They disagree **where [the deposit] decreased** in value. **בֵּית שַׁמַּאי סָבְרֵי – Beis Shammai hold: שְׁלִיחוּת יָד אֵינָהּ צְרִיכָה חִסָּרוֹן – Misappropriation is not dependent upon a loss.**[4] Thus, as soon as the *shomer* took the deposit, even before he caused a loss in it, it entered his possession as a stolen object,[5] **וְכִי חָסַר – and when it** subsequently **decreased** in value **בִּרְשׁוּתָא דִּידֵיהּ חָסַר – it decreased** while **in his possession.** Therefore, he is liable to pay what the deposit was worth when he took it (rather than when he destroyed it).[6] **וּבֵית הִלֵּל סָבְרֵי – But Beis Hillel hold: שְׁלִיחוּת יָד צְרִיכָה חִסָּרוֹן – Misappropriation is dependent upon a loss.** Thus, when the *shomer* took the deposit, it did not yet enter his possession as a stolen object, **וְכִי חָסַר – and when it** subsequently **decreased** in value, **בִּרְשׁוּתָא דְּמָרֵיהּ חָסַר – it decreased** while still **in the owner's possession.** Therefore, the *shomer* pays only what it was worth when he destroyed it.[7]

The Gemara challenges this interpretation as well:

**אֶלָּא הָא דְּאָמַר רָבָא – But** what about **that which Rava said: שְׁלִיחוּת יָד אֵינָהּ צְרִיכָה חִסָּרוֹן – Misappropriation is not dependent upon a loss?**[8] **לֵימָא רָבָא דְּאָמַר כְּבֵית שַׁמַּאי** – Are we **to say** that **Rava rules in accordance with Beis Shammai** as opposed to Beis Hillel?![9]

To avoid this difficulty, the Gemara (although still understanding Beis Hillel's mention of "removal" as referring to removal from the world) suggests a different explanation of the dispute between Beis Shammai and Beis Hillel:

**אֶלָּא הָכָא בְּמַאי עָסְקִינַן – Rather, what are we dealing with here?** We are dealing with a case where the *shomer* did not misappropriate the deposit, but merely borrowed it before he destroyed it. **כְּגוֹן שֶׁטִּלְטְלָהּ לְהָבִיא עָלֶיהָ גּוֹזָלוֹת – For example, [a *shomer*]** who had been entrusted with a barrel **moved it** to use as a platform **on which to** stand and **fetch** some **young birds** from a dovecote. **וּבְשׁוֹאֵל שֶׁלֹּא מִדַּעַת קָא מִיפַּלְגֵי – And they** (Beis Shammai and Beis Hillel) **disagree about** the legal status of **one who borrows** an article **without** its owner's **permission. בֵּית שַׁמַּאי סָבְרֵי – Beis Shammai hold: שׁוֹאֵל שֶׁלֹּא מִדַּעַת גַּזְלָן הָוֵי – One who borrows** something **without** its owner's **permission is** considered **a thief.**[10] Thus, as soon as the *shomer* unlawfully borrowed the deposit, it entered his possession as a stolen object, **וְכִי חָסַר – and when it** subsequently **decreased** in value, **בִּרְשׁוּתָא דִּידֵיהּ חָסַר – it decreased** while **in his possession.** Therefore, he pays what the deposit was worth when he borrowed it (rather than when he destroyed it).[11] **וּבֵית הִלֵּל סָבְרֵי – And Beis Hillel hold: שׁוֹאֵל שֶׁלֹּא מִדַּעַת שׁוֹאֵל הָוֵי – One who borrows** something **without** its owner's **permission is** considered **a borrower** rather than a thief. Thus, when the *shomer* unlawfully borrowed the deposit, it did not enter his possession as a stolen object, **וְכִי חָסַר – and when it** subsequently **decreased** in value, **בִּרְשׁוּתָא דְּמָרֵיהּ חָסַר – it decreased** while still **in its owner's possession.** Therefore, the *shomer* pays only what it was worth when he destroyed it.[12]

The Gemara challenges this interpretation:

**אֶלָּא הָא דְּאָמַר רָבָא – But** what about **that which Rava said: שׁוֹאֵל שֶׁלֹּא מִדַּעַת לְרַבָּנָן גַּזְלָן הָוֵי – One who borrows** an object **without** its owner's **permission is** considered **a thief according to the Rabbis?**[13] **לֵימָא רָבָא דְּאָמַר כְּבֵית שַׁמַּאי** – Are we **to say**

NOTES

1. See 43a with note 26.

2. In disputes between Beis Shammai and Beis Hillel, the halachah almost invariably follows the view of Beis Hillel (see *Eruvin* 13b).

3. This accords with Rabbah's ruling.

4. See 41a with note 11. According to this explanation, Beis Shammai and Beis Hillel refer to a case where the *shomer* performed a *kinyan* upon the deposit with intent to use it, but did not carry out this intent until it decreased in value.

5. Ordinarily, a deposit is considered to be in the possession of the depositor. But if the *shomer* misappropriates the deposit, it enters his possession in the same way that any stolen property enters the possession of the thief (see 40b note 23).

6. Since, according to Beis Shammai, the very taking of the deposit is considered theft, he must pay what it was worth at that time, in accordance with the rule cited above (43a): כָּל הַגַּזְלָנִין מְשַׁלְּמִין כִּשְׁעַת הַגְּזֵילָה, *all thieves pay according to* [the stolen object's value at] *the time of the theft.*

7. According to this explanation, the dispute between Beis Shammai and Beis Hillel applies only to a *shomer.* As far as a regular thief is concerned, both would agree that if he stole something and destroyed it after its value decreased, he pays only what it was worth when he stole it (see note 6). But with regard to a *shomer,* Beis Hillel hold that he pays what the deposit was worth when he depleted it, for a *shomer* is not considered to have misappropriated the deposit until that point (*Rashi*).

8. It is evident that this is Rava's view from his Scriptural derivation recorded above (41b): ...חֲדָא לוֹמַר לָךְ שְׁלִיחוּת יָד אֵין צְרִיכָה חִסָּרוֹן וכו׳, *...one* [reference to the law of misappropriation serves] *to teach you* [that] *misappropriation is not dependent upon a loss etc.* (see *Rashi*).

9. See note 2.

10. See 41a note 14.

11. See note 6.

12. Unlike a thief, whose liability to pay is in effect from the moment he takes the object, a borrower does not become liable to pay until the object is damaged.

13. Rava interpreted a dispute between R' Yehudah and the Rabbis (recorded in the Mishnah, *Bava Basra* 87b) as concerning the question of whether one who borrows without permission is considered a thief or a borrower. Rava explained that the Rabbis maintain that he is a thief, while R' Yehudah maintains that he is a borrower. From the fact that Rava wished to align the majority view (which is generally adopted as law) with the position that one who borrows without permission is a thief, it is evident that Rava himself follows this view (*Rashi*).

עין משפט נר מצוה

קב א מיי' פ"ג מהל' גזלה ואבידה הל' טו סמג עשין עג טוש"ע ח"מ סי' שנט סעי' ה:
קג ב מיי' שם פ"ב הל' ג ועיין בהשגות ובמ"מ סמג עשין שם טוש"ע ח"מ סי' שסב סעי' ג ז:
קד ג מיי' שם טוש"ע שם סעי' ז:
קה ד מיי' פ"ג שם הל' יא סמג שם טוש"ע ח"מ סי' רצב סעי' ד:
קו ה ו מיי' שם הל' יב ועיין בהשגות ובמ"מ טוש"ע שם סעי' ג:

תורה אור השלם

א) אוֹ מִכֹּל אֲשֶׁר יִשָּׁבַע עָלָיו לַשֶּׁקֶר וְשִׁלַּם אֹתוֹ בְּרֹאשׁוֹ וַחֲמִשִׁתָיו יֹסֵף עָלָיו לַאֲשֶׁר הוּא לוֹ יִתְּנֶנּוּ בְּיוֹם אַשְׁמָתוֹ: [ויקרא ה, כד]

ב) אִם לֹא יִמָּצֵא הַגַּנָּב וְנִקְרַב בַּעַל הַבַּיִת אֶל הָאֱלֹהִים אִם לֹא שָׁלַח יָדוֹ בִּמְלֶאכֶת רֵעֵהוּ: [שמות כב, ז]

אלא פשיטא כשעת הוצאה מבית בעלים לימא רבה דאמר כבית שמאי אמר לך רבה ביתר כולי עלמא לא פליגי כי פליגי בחסר ב"ש סברי שליחות יד אינה צריכה חסרון וכי חסר ברשותא דידיה חסר וב"ה סברי שליחות יד צריכה חסרון וכי חסר ברשותא דמריה חסר אלא הא דאמר רבא [א] שליחות יד אינה צריכה חסרון לימא רבא דאמר כב"ש אלא הכא במאי עסקינן [ג] כגון שטלטלה להביא עליה גוזלות ובשואל שלא מדעת קא מיפלגי ב"ש סברי [ג] שואל שלא מדעת גזלן הוי וכי חסר ברשותא דידיה חסר וב"ה סברי שואל שלא מדעת שואל הוי וכי חסר ברשותא דמרה חסר אלא הא [ד] דאמר רבא א שואל שלא מדעת לרבנן גזלן הוי לימא רבא דאמר כב"ש אלא הכא בשבח של גזילה קמיפלגי ב"ש סברי ב שבח גזילה דנגזל הוי ובית הלל סברי שבח גזילה דגזלן הוי ובפלוגתא דהני תנאי דתניא [ה] הגוזל את הרחל גזזה וילדה משלם אותה ואת גיזותיה ואת ולדותיה דברי ר"מ ר' יהודה אומר ג גזילה חוזרת בעיניה דיקא נמי דקתני ב"ש אומרים ילקה בחסר וביתר וב"ה אומרים כשעת הוצאה ש"מ: ר"ע אומר כשעת התביעה: אמר רב יהודה אמר שמואל הלכה כר' עקיבא ומודה ר"ע במקום שיש עדים מ"ט דאמר קרא א) לאשר הוא לו יתננו ביום אשמתו וכיון דאיכא עדים מההוא שעתא הוא דאיחייב ליה אשמה א"ל ר' אושעיא לרב יהודה ר' אתה אומר כן הכי א"ר אסי אמר ר' יוחנן חלוק היה ר"ע אפי' במקום שיש עדים מ"ט דאמר קרא לאשר הוא לו יתננו ביום אשמתו ובי דינא הוא דקא מחייבי ליה אשמה א"ל ר' זירא לר' אבא בר פפא כי אזלת להתם אקיף אסולמא דצור ועול לגביה דר' יעקב בר אידי ובעי מיניה אי שמיעא ליה לר' יוחנן הלכה כר"ע או אין הלכה כר"ע א"ל הכי אמר ר' יוחנן הלכה כרבי עקיבא לעולם מאי לעולם אמר רב אשי שלא תאמר הני מילי היכא דליכא עדים אבל היכא דאיכא עדים לא ואי נמי דאהדרה לדוכתה ואיתברא לאפוקי מדרבי ישמעאל דאמר [ו] לא בעינן דעת בעלים קא משמע לן דבעינן דעת בעלים ורבא אמר הלכה כבית הלל:

מתני' החושב לשלוח יד בפקדון בית שמאי אומרים חייב ובית הלל אומרים ד אינו חייב עד שישלח בו יד שנאמר ב) אם לא שלח ידו במלאכת רעהו ה הטה את החבית ונטל הימנה רביעית ונשברה אינו משלם אלא רביעית ו הגביהה ונטל הימנה רביעית ונשברה משלם דמי כולה:

גמ'

רש"י

אלא פשיטא כשעת הוצאה מבית בעלים. כשעת הגזילה וביתר פליגי דקאמרי ב"ש אם הוקרה ילקה לשלם כשעת הוצאה מן העולם ובית הלל אמרי כשעת הוצאה מבית הבעלים: כי פליגי בחסר. וקאמרי ב"ה כשעת הוצאה מן העולם ודקא קשיא לך כל הגזלנין משלמים כשעת הגזילה הי בגזילה ממש דגזלה מעיקרא ה"נ אבל הכא דבהיתרא אתא לידי' ומשום שליחות יד קמחייבת ליה בהא פליגי: ב"ש סברי שליחות יד אינה צריכה חסרון. ומשלח בה יד אע"פ שלא חסרה הויא גזילה וקמה ברשותיה וכשהוזלה ברשותו הוזלה ואם היתה בעין אומר לו הרי שלך לפניך עכשיו שהוציאה משלם כשעת שליחות יד: אלא הא דאמר רבא. לעיל בשמעתין (דף מא:): שליחות יד אינה צריכה חסרון. דקאמר שלא תאמר שליחות יד כו': הא דאמר רבא. בהמוכר את הספינה (ב"ב דף פח.): שואל שלא מדעת לרבנן גזלן הוא. גבי שולח את בנו אצל חנוני דפליגי רבנן ור' יהודה ואוקי רבא פלוגתייהו בשואל שלא מדעת ואמר דלרבנן גזלן הוי ומדאוקי רבא לרבנן בהכי סבירא ליה לדידיה גזלן הוי ואהדר לאוקמי מילתיה כרבנן דהלכתא כרבים: לימא כב"ש. אמרה: אלא הכא בשבח גזילה פליגי. והאי חסר ויתר דמתני' לאו ביוקרא וזולא אלא במאי דחסרה דהיינו גיזות ובמאי שהותירה כגון אם נתעברה אצלו דב"ש סברי הכל ישלם כר"מ דברייתא וב"ה כרבי יהוד' כשעת הוצאה מבית הבעלים: דיקא נמי. דבגיזות וולדות פליגי דקתני לשון חסר ויתר ולא קתני לשון זול ויוקר: ומודה ר"ע במקום שיש עדי'. כמה היתה שוה ביום שגזלה וראו שגזלה הימנו דמשלם כשעת הגזילה: מאי טעמא דרבי עקיבא. דאמר כשעת התביעה: דאמר קרא ביום אשמתו. בדמים של אותו יום שהוא מתחייב לו והיכא דתבעו והודה דעל פיו הוא מתחייב העמדתו בדין והודאתו הוא יום אשמתו אבל אם יש עדים משעה שראוהו שגזלה הוא אשם לו: להתם. לארץ ישראל: אקיף. הרבה את הדרך וסבב דרך ארוכה על דבר זה ללכת דרך מעלת של הר צור מקום שר' יעקב שם ובעי מיניה מה שמע מר' יוחנן רבו על כך כל מהלך דרך ארוכה במקום שיש קצרה מקיף הוא: אי נמי דהדרה לדוכתה. להכי אשמועינן לעולם לומר שאם החזירה למקומה לאחר ששלח בה יד ונשברה באונס אף בזו הלכה כר"ע דאמר לעיל גבי גנב טלה מן העדר צריך דעת בעלי': ורבא אמר הלכה כב"ה. כשעת גזילה ואנן כרבא עבדינן דהוה ליה בתראה: מתני' החושב לשלוח יד. (א) אמר בפני עדים אטול פקדונו של פלוני לעצמי: חייב. באונסים מהיום והלאה אם נאנס חייב באחריות: הטה את החבית. מלתא באנפי נפשה היא: ונשברה. לאחר זמן: אינו משלם אלא רביעית. דשליחות יד אינו מתחייב באונסין עד שימשוך או יגביה דהוי קנייה: הגביהה ונטל. דהוי קנייה בהגבהתה וחסרון מנטילת רביעית חייב באונסיה:

תוספות

לימא רבה דאמר כב"ש. וא"ת לוקי פלוגתייהו באתבר ממילא ורבה כב"ה וי"ל דא"כ לא הוו פליגי בית שמאי: בית שמאי סברי שליחות יד אינה צריכה חסרון. וא"ת א"כ תרי זמני הך דהכא וסיפא דהחושב לשלוח יד למה לי וי"ל דסיפא אשמועי' דלב"ש אפילו דבור בלא משיכה חייב והך דהכא אשמועינן דלב"ה צריכה חסרון: אלא הא דאמר רבא שואל שלא מדעת גזלן הוי. אומר ר"ת דגרסינן בכל הני רבא דהך דשואל ע"כ רבא הוי דקאמר בתר רבה ורב יוסף בהמוכר הספינה (ב"ב דף פח.) ומדהאי רבא כולהו נמי רבא דאי לאו הכי לא פריך מידי דמצי לאוקומה פלוגתיה כחד מהנך פלוגתי' דלעיל: משלם אותה ואת גיזותיה ואת ולדותיה דברי ר"מ רבי יהודה אומר גזלה חוזרת בעיניה. וא"ת הא דתנן בפרק הגוזל קמא (ב"ק דף ק:) הנותן צמר לצבע לצבוע לו אדום וצבעו שחור אם השבח יתר על הוצאה נותן לו היציאה ואם הוצאה יתירה על השבח נותן לו השבח דברי רבי יהודה ר"מ אומר אין נותן לו אלא דמי צמרו בלבד אלמא סברתם הפוכות ותירץ ר"ת דהכא גבי גזילה סבר ר"מ שינוי אינו קונה משום דקנסא קנים במזיד אבל בלצבוע לו אדום דשוגג לא קניס והכי איתא בהגוזל ור' יהודה דסבר הכא דשינוי קונה היינו משום דמתכוין לקנות בשינוי אבל צבעו שחור אין מתכוין לקנותו בכך: ר"ע אומר כשעת התביעה. תימה מאי קסבר אי קסבר שינוי קונה למה ישלם השבח כשעת התביעה הלא בשעת גזיזה קנאה ואם הגדילה רחל או הגזיזה ונתייקרה לא ישלם אלא כמו ששוה רחל בשעת גזיזה ואי קסבר שינוי אינו קונה א"כ כשגזזה אחר התביעה נמי יהא הכל לנגזל דמאי קנה ועוד דקאמר ומודה ר"ע במקום שיש עדים בשעת שליחות יד שישלם כאותה שעה במאי קנה והלא אכתי אפילו שינוי ליכא וגם כי יגזזנה שינוי לא יקנה ועוד למאן מודה הלא בין לב"ש בין לב"ה לא קנאה בשעת שליחות יד עד שעת שינוי ועוד דשמואל ור' יוחנן פסקו כר"ע בשמעתין ובהגוזל קמא (ב"ק דף צד:) אית להו דשינוי קונה לכך נראה לב"ש דאמרי ילקה בחסר ויתר איירי אף ביוקרא וזולא דאם הוקרה משלם כשעת הוצאה מן העולם ואם הוזלה משלם כשעת הגזלה וב"ה לא פליגי נמי בהא והיינו כרבה אלא ב"ש איירי נמי בשינוי כדקאמר דיקא נמי מדלא קתני בזול וביוקר ובהא פליגי ב"ה דשינוי קונה ור"ע פליג אזול ויוקר דאמר משלם כשעת התביעה בין הוזל ובין הוקר: החושב לשלוח יד. [ט] הך מחשבה הוי דבור כדיליף מעל כל דבר וכן מחשבת פגול נמי הוי בדבור ולא בלב כדמוכח בפרק ב' דזבחים (דף ל.) ובפ"ק דמנחות (דף ג:) ובפרק תמיד נשחט (פסחים דף סג.) ובפרק הנזקין (גיטין דף נד:) ובמקומות אחרים פירשתי [ז]:

הדרן עלך המפקיד

רבינו חננאל

אלא פשיטא טעמא דבית הלל כשעת הוצאה מבית בעלים היא והיא שעת הגזילה והיתה שוה באותה שעה זוז ובשעה ששתאה שוה ד' בזה חלקו בית הלל ובית שמאי ב"ש סברי ד' משלם כי השתא וב"ה סברי [דמשלם] כשעת הגזילה והוא זוזא לימא רבה דאמר משלם [ד'] כב"ש דהא בית הלל זוזא חדא קאמרי. ופריק רבה ביותר כלומ' אם עת ששתאה היתה שוה יותר ממה שהיתה שוה בשעת גזילתה דברי הכל ד' כי השתא משלם כטעמא דידי שפירשנו למעלה כי פליגי בחסר כגון שהיתה שוה עת ששלח ידו בפקדון של חבירו ד' ועכשיו שוה זוז בית שמאי סברי שליחות יד אינה צריכא חסרון ומשעה דשלח בה יד איחייב בה. וב"ה סברי שליחות יד צריכא חסרון וכ"ז [דלא] חסרה ברשותיה דמריה קאי ובעידנא דתברה או שתיא וחיסרה בההיא שעתא מיחייב עלה וההיא שעתא זוזא הוא דשויא. ואלא רבה דאמר שליחות יד אינה צריכא חסרון כב"ש וכו'. ואוקימנא למתני' חלוקת ב"ש וב"ה בשבח גזילה ב"ש סברי דנגזל הוי וב"ה סברי דגזלן הוי וכי הני תנאי דתניא הגוזל רחל גזזה וילדה משלם אותה ואת גיזותיה וולדותיה דברי ר' מאיר ר' יהודה אומר גזלה חוזרת בעיניה. ר' מאיר כב"ש ר' יהודה כב"ה וקיימא לן כר' יהודה דבית הלל קיימי כותיה. וקיימא לן הא דאוקימנא אליבא דב"ה שבח גזילה דגזלן הוא בשבח שהשביחה בגופה אבל שבח שהשביחה בדמים דנגזל הוי כדרבה דאמר ביתר כולי עלמא לא פליגי דודאי לנגזל הוי כי פליגי בחסר. וקיימא לן כרבא וכן הלכה. ר' עקיבא אומר כשעת התביעה. ואע"ג דאמר רב יהודה אמר שמואל הלכה כר' עקיבא. ובתלמוד ארץ ישראל פסקו כר' עקיבא אנן לא סמכינן אלא בהא דאמר רבא דהוא בתרא ופסק הלכה כב"ה וכיון דסלקא שמעתא הכי ש"מ דשבח גזילה דגזלן הוי ומדחזינן רבה דפריק שליחות יד אינה צריכא חסרון ושואל שלא מדעת גזלן הוי ש"מ דהלכתא אינון. א) פי' כיון דאיכא עדים מההיא שעתא דגזל נתחייב לשלם אבל אם אין עדים אין חייב לשלם אלא בעת תביעתו בב"ד והל' המפקיד אצל חבירו בעדים ואפי' בשטר אין צריך להחזיר לו בעדים אלא כי אמר החזרתיו לך נאמן וכן אם אמר נאנסו נאמן ובתרויהו אינו חייב אלא שבועה שנאנסו או החזרתים לך: מתני' החושב לשלוח יד בפקדון בית שמאי מחייבין ובית הלל אומרים אינו חייב עד שישלח בו יד כו' שנאמר אם לא שלח ידו במלאכת רעהו מלמד שאינו חייב עד שישלח ידו בו

חשק שלמה על ר"ח א) נראה דחסר כאן וצ"ל ומודה ר"ע במקום שיש עדים פי' כיון דאיכא עדים וכו'.

מסורת הש"ס

א) לעיל מא., ב) [לעיל מא.], ג) [שם], ד) בבא בתרא פח., ה) בבא קמא צה. ע"ש, ו) [לעיל מא:], ז) [וע"ע תוספות פסחים סג. ד"ה ר' מאיר, ותוס' זבחים ד: ד"ה מחשבה, ותוס' בכורות נט. ד"ה במחשבה, ותוס' חולין לט. ד"ה אלא זביחה].

הגהות הב"ח

(א) רש"י ד"ה החושב לשלוח יד אמר. נ"ב ובקדושין סוף דף מב [ע"ב] פרש"י דלאו דוקא אמר אלא חשב:

גליון הש"ס

תוס' ד"ה החושב וכו' הך מחשבה. עיין בהרא"ש ריש הלכות ק"ש:

ליקוטי רש"י

שליחות יד. שחייבו הכתוב עליו אפילו נאנסה לבסוף [שמות כב] ומת או נשבר או נשבה וגו' שבועת ה' תהיה בין שניהם אם לא שלח ידו וגו' מכאן שאם שלח בה יד חייב שוב במיתתה ובגניבתה. צריכה חסרון. לא הוי שליחות יד לאחייביה באונסים עד שיחסרנה. וכל זמן שלא חסרה לא קמה ברשותיה באונסיה. שטלטלה להביא עליה גוזלות. לעלות עליה כדרך בני אדם שעולין עליה ליטול גוזלות מקן גבוה [לעיל מא.]. שואל שלא מדעת שואל הוי. וכי מחזירו למקום שנטלו משם די. שואל שלא מדעת גזלן הוי. וקנייה להתחייב בה עד שתבא ליד בעלים לדעתן וכשיודע בעל הגזלה [רשב"ם ב"ב פח.]. משלם אותה ואת גיזותיה. כל מה שגזז ממנה ומה שהשביחה. גזילה חוזרת בעיניה. כמות שהיא עכשיו ריקנית יחזירנה והגיזות והולדות משלם דמי גיזות וולדות כמו שהיה בשעת הגזילה ולא שבח הגיזה שהשביחה אצלו [ב"ק צה.]. אסולמא דצור. שם הר גבוה סביב [עירובין כב:]. דעת בעלים. ואם לא הודיעם חייב באחריותם. החושב לשלוח יד בפקדון. בש"א חייב. שאם אמר לשלוח יד בפקדון או אמר הריני שולח יד בפקדון חייב באונסין אף על פי שלא שלח בו יד [קידושין מב:]. הך מחשבה הואיל ודיבור בפה הוא כל המחשבה כמעשה דאי לא מוליאו בפה מחשבתו למאי נחייב לה [מנחות ב:]. רש"י ד"ה אבל מחשבה.

מסורת הש"ס

א) קדושין נג., [מעילה כא:], ב) לעיל כט., לקמן נח., ג) [תוספתא דמעילה סוף פרק ב], מעילה כא: [וע"ש בתוס'], ד) בבא קמא סה., ה) [גירסת רי"ף רבא, ועיין תוס' ע"ב ד"ה אלא], ו) [בבא קמא לג., צו., קג., פסחים לב.], ז) מהרש"ל.

הגהות הב"ח

(א) גמ' דהואיל ונהנה מהנה. נ"ב ע"ל דף פא ע"א: (ב) תוס' ד"ה מאי וכו' דמייתי אפלוגתא. נ"ב דף מח: (ג) בא"ד פוסק עמו על הגדים. נ"ב לקמן דף עב ע"ב:

ליקוטי רש"י

אצל בעל הבית. בין צרורין ובין מותרין לא ישתמש בהן דלהכי הפקידן אצל בעה"ב שהוא יודע שבעה"ב אין דרכו לפרוט ולהחליף ולא חשש אם צרורין אם מותרין [מעילה כא:]. חנוני כבעל הבית דברי ר"מ. שאינו צריך תמיד למעות שנותנים לו פירות וכל מכר חנותו באשראי ודי לו במיעוט מעות שבידו [קדושין נג:]. שאינו רגיל במילופין כשולחני ובין כך ובין כך לא יגע בהן. ר' יהודה אומר חנוני כשולחני. דלפעמים נמי הוא רגיל להחליף כשולחני לפיכך דינו כשולחני [מעילה שם]. בלסטין מזויין. דאונס הוא [לקמן נח.]. המפקיד מעות. של הקדש אצל שולחני. אם צרורין לא ישתמש בהן. דלהכי הפקידן אצלו צרורין דלא הוה בעי לישתמש בהו לפיכך אם הוציא השולחני מעל. מותרין ישתמש בהן. שלדעת כן הפקידן אצלו שיתעסק בהן שיחליפם לפיכך אם הוציא לא מעל השולחני אלא המפקיד. דאי איתה הדרא למרה בעינא. דהא בעי לאהדורה הלכך כדשויא למרה הוקרה והשתא שעתא דתברה ושתייה הוא דקא גזיל לה [ב"ק סה.]. בעינא. כמו שהיתה [לעיל טו.].

עין משפט נר מצוה

צז א ב ג ד ה מיי' פ"ז מהל' שאלה ופקדון הל' ו סמג עשין פח טוש"ע ח"מ סי' רלב סעי' ז:

צח ו מיי' פ"ז מהל' מעילה הל' ט והל' י:

צט ז מיי' פ"ג מהל' גזילה הל' א סמג עשין עא עב טוש"ע ח"מ סי' רלב סעי' ה:

ק ח מיי' שם הל' א ב ופ"א מה' גניבה הל' יד סמג שם טוש"ע ח"מ סי' שנד סעי' ג וסי' שסב סעי' י:

קא ט מיי' פ"ג מהל' גזילה הל' ב טוש"ע ח"מ סי' שסב סעי' ב וסעי' יא וסעי' יב וסי' שה סעי' ה:

ומשלם ליה דמי כיסי: **מתני'** [א]המפקיד מעות אצל שולחני אם צרורין לא ישתמש בהן לפיכך אם אבדו אינו חייב באחריותן מותרין ישתמש בהן לפיכך אם אבדו חייב באחריותן אצל בעל הבית בין צרורין ובין מותרין לא ישתמש בהן לפיכך אם אבדו אינו חייב באחריותן (א) חנוני כבעל הבית דברי ר"מ ר' יהודה אומר [ב]חנוני כשולחני: **גמ'** משום דצרורין לא ישתמש בהן אמר רב אסי אמר רב יהודה [ג]בצרורין וחתומין שנו רב מרי אמר [ד]בקשר משונה איכא דאמרי בעי רב מרי קשר משונה מאי תיקו: מותרין ישתמש בהן כו': אמר רב הונא ואפילו נאנסו והא אבדו קתני כדרבה (ב) דאמר רבה נגנבו בלסטין מזויין אבדו שטבעה ספינתו בים ורב נחמן אמר [ה]נאנסו לא אמר ליה רבא לר"נ לדידך דאמרת נאנסו לא אלמא לא הוי שואל עלייהו אי שואל לא הוי שומר שכר נמי לא הוי א"ל בהא מודינא לך (א) דהואיל ונהנה מהנה בההוא הנאה דאי מיתרמי ליה זבינא דאית בה רווחא זבן בהו הוי עלייהו שומר שכר איתיביה רב נחמן לרב הונא (ג) [ו]המפקיד מעות אצל שולחני אם צרורין לא ישתמש בהן לפיכך אם הוציא לא מעל הגזבר ואם מותרין ישתמש בהן לפיכך אם הוציא מעל הגזבר ואי אמרת אפילו נאנסו מאי איריא הוציא אפילו לא הוציא נמי אמר ליה הוא הדין אע"ג דלא הוציא ואיידי דתנא רישא הוציא תנא סיפא נמי הוציא: **מתני'** השולח יד בפקדון בית שמאי אומרים ילקה בחסר וביתר ובית הלל אומרים [ז]כשעת הוצאה ר"ע אומר כשעת התביעה: **גמ'** (ד) אמר (ה) רבה [ח]האי מאן דגזל חביתא דחמרא מחבריה מעיקרא שויא זוזא השתא שויא ארבעה תברה או שתייה משלם ארבעה איתבר ממילא משלם זוזא מאי טעמא כיון דאי איתה הדרא למרה בעינא ההיא שעתא דקא שתי ליה או דקא תבר לה קא גזל מיניה ותנן (ו) [ט]כל הגזלנין משלמין כשעת הגזילה איתבר ממילא משלם זוזא מ"ט השתא לא עביד לה ולא מידי אמאי קא מחייבת ליה אההיא שעתא דגזלה ההיא שעתא זוזא הוא דשויא תנן בית הלל אומרים כשעת הוצאה מאי כשעת הוצאה אילימא כשעת הוצאה מן העולם ובמאי אי בחסר מי איכא למ"ד והא תנן כל הגזלנין משלמין כשעת הגזילה ואי ביתר היינו ב"ש

אלא

ומשלם לו דמי כיסי. דמי כשות של קוליס לפי מה שהשביח: גמ' משום דצרורין לא ישתמש בהן. בתמיה ומה גילוי דעת יש כאן שאין חפץ שישתמש בהם מאחר שאם הן מותרין קאמרת ישתמש בהן דהמפקיד אצלו יודע שהוא צריך תדיר למעות צרורין נמי ישתמש דדרך כל אדם לצור מעותיו: ואפילו נאנסו. קאמר מתני' דחייב באחריותן ואפילו לא נשתמש בהן דמהשתא הוי שואל עלייהו: נאנסו לא. כל זמן שלא נשתמש לא הוי שואל אלא אבדו דוקא חייב כשומר שכר: ואי שואל לא הוי שומר שכר נמי לא הוי. מה שכר נטל על שמירתם אלא על שסמך עליהם להחליפן ולהשתכר אם יבא לידו אתה מחייבו ושאלה היא זו שהרי כל הנאה שלו: בהא מודינא. אע"ג דאמינא לא הוי שואל מהשתא עד שישתמש מודינא דשומר שכר הוי: דהואיל ונהנה מהנה. לבעלים: המפקיד מעות. גזבר שהפקיד מעות הקדש כסבור שהן שלו: לא מעל גזבר. שהרי לא ברשות הוציאן ואינו שלוחו: מותרין. דהוה ליה כנותן רשות והוה ליה שלוחו: לפיכך אם הוציא. שולחני מעל גזבר: ואי אמרת אפילו נאנסו. תנא מתני' דחייב שולחני באחריותן נמצא משעה שהפקידו אצלו יצאו מרשות הקדש ובאו לרשות שולחני ונעשה כמו שלוה לו ואין הוצאה גדולה מזו מאי איריא הוציא: איידי דתנא רישא הוציא. לאשמועינן רבותא דאפילו הוציא לא מעל תנא סיפא הוציא: מתני' ילקה בחסר וביתר. אם חסרו דמיה שהוזלה בשוק ישלם דמיה כמו שהיתה שוה בשעה ששלח בה יד שהיא שעת הגזילה וכן כל הגזלנין משלמין כשעת הגזילה וכגון שהוציאה שאינה בעין אבל אם ישנה בעין כמות שגזלה אומר לו הרי שלך לפניך כדאמרינן גבי מטבע ונפסל תרומה ונטמאת בפ' הגוזל [קמא] (ב"ק דף צו:): וביתר. אם השבחה בידו משלח בה יד ונתייקרה ואח"כ הוציאה לוקה ביתר דמיה לשלם כשעת הוצאה: ובית הלל אומרים כו'. בגמרא מפרש מאי קאמרי: כשעת התביעה. כשעת שיתבעו לדין ובגמרא מפרש טעמא: גמ' מעיקרא. כשגזלה: ולבסוף. כשילתה מן העולם: תברה. בידים: או שתייה. אחר שהוקרה: דאי איתה. כאן בשעת התביעה הוה מהדרנא בעינא דכי אמרינן משלם כשעת הגזילה היכא דליתה בעין אבל ישנה בעין בין שהוקרה בין שהוזלה חוזרת כמות שהיא הלכך הואיל ואם תבעה בעודה קיימת לאחר שהוקרה היתה חוזרת בעין אשתכח דההיא שעתא דקא שתי לה הוא דגזיל לה: ובמאי. אהייא פליגי בית הלל: אי בחסר. כשהוזלה דקאמרי ב"ש ילקה לשלם כדמים שהיתה בשעת הגזילה וקאמרי בית הלל כשעת הוצאה: ומי איכא למאן דאמר. היכא דליתיה בעין דכל הגזלנין לאו כשעת הגזילה משלמין:

אלא

**מאי** איריא הוציא כי לא הוציא נמי. כיון דהיתר תשמיש מחייב באונסין וא"ת הא דתנן לקמן בהזהב (דף מד. מז: מח.) נתן לו מעות ולא משך ממנו פירות יכול לחזור בו לרב הונא דאית ליה דהיתר תשמיש מחייב באונסין וכן לרב יוסף בפרק אלו מציאות (לעיל דף כט.) המוכר אסור להשתמש במעות שקבל שאם היה מותר להשתמש תקשה להו הך ברייתא (ב) דמייתי אפלוגתא דרבי יוחנן ור"ל נתן לבלן מעל דוקא בלן דלא מחסרא משיכה כדקתני סיפא הרי מרחץ לפניך הכנס ורחוץ אבל ספר לא מעל עד דמשיך ולדידהו כי נתנה לספר נמי למעול אע"ג דלא משיך כיון דספר מותר להשתמש בהן בין מיירי בספר נכרי כר' יוחנן בין בספר ישראל כר"ל וכמו שאסור להשתמש בהם לרב הונא ולרב יוסף ה"נ לר"ל ולר' יוחנן דבהא לא פליגי ולא הוה המוכר על אותם מעות כי אם שומר חנם לכ"ע וא"כ לרבי יוחנן מה הועילו במה שתקנו דאין מעות קונות דאי מעות קונות יאמר מוכר נשרפו חטיך בעליה השתא דלא קני יאמר נשרפו מעותיך בעליה ועוד דרב הונא גופיה סבר בפ' הזהב (לקמן דף מו:) דבר תורה מעות קונות כרבי יוחנן דאמר רב הונא מכור לי באלו קנה וי"ל דאע"ג דלא הוי על המעות כי אם שומר חנם לא מצי א"ל נשרפו מעותיך בעליה דכספים אין להם שמירה אלא בקרקע וא"ת כיון דהיכא שלא משך אסור להשתמש במעות א"כ הא דאמר (ג) פוסק עמו על הגדים או על שער שבשוק מה מרויח בהקדמת מעות וי"ל כגון שפירש ע"מ להשתמש בהם א"נ אפילו בסתמ' כיון שהוא פוסק ומקדים לו מעות חצי שנה מן הגדים עד ימות הקיץ אדעתא דהכי נותן שישתמש בהן ועוד י"ל דלרבי יוחנן ולרב הונא דאית להו דבר תורה מעות קונות לא הפקיעו כח שיש לו למוכר במעות שיכול להשתמש בהם כיון דקונות מן התורה והוי שואל עלייהו ולא מצי א"ל נשרפו מעותיך בעליה ולא תקנו משיכה אלא כדי שלא יאמר לו נשרפו חטיך בעליה אבל לר"ל ודאי כיון דמעות אינם קונות אסור להשתמש במעות ולא הוי שואל עלייהו ולכך נתנה לספר לא מעל עד שימשוך וכן לרבי יוחנן ולרב הונא בספר נכרי לא מעל עד שימשוך דמעות בנכרי אינם קונות:

**והתנן** כל הגזלנים משלמין כשעת הגזלה. ואע"ג דבפ' הגוזל [קמא] (ב"ק דף צו:) אמרי' זה הכלל כל הגזלנים משלמין כשעת הגזלה לאתויי דרבי אלעאי דאמר גנב טלה ונעשה איל עגל ונעשה שור נעשה שינוי בידו וקנאה משמע דלא איירי ביוקרא וזולא אלא בשינוי כדמיירי ברישא דמתני' הגוזל עצים ועשה כלים למר ועשה בגדים היינו דוקא יתורא דזה הכלל אבל פשטא דמתניתין דמשלמין כשעת הגזילה מיירי ביוקרא וזולא והתם בהגוזל (דף קג.) נמי מייתי לענין יוקרא וזולא גבי אייקר כתנא דרב כהנא ובפרק כל שעה (פסחים דף לב.) גבי לפי דמים משלם וא"ת רב דאמר במרובה (ב"ק דף סה. ושם ד"ה גופא) קרן כעין שגנב [ז][כפל וכו'] ואוקמה כגון דמעיקרא שויא ד' ולבסוף שויא זוזא מאי קמ"ל מתני' היא ועוד מאי בעי התם מאי טעמא דרב ליבעי מאי טעמא דמתניתין וי"ל דרב קמ"ל דאע"ג דקרן כעין שגנב כפל לא הוי כמו קרן אלא כשעת העמדה בדין ובעינן מאי טעמא דרב דמחלק כפל מדין קרן ומשני גנבה וחיים אחייה לקרן כעין שגנב דוקא קרן ולא כפל:

לימא

רבינו חננאל

דמישתרשי ליה ואי הוה חלא ולא אישתרשי ליה מידי משלם ליה דמי כיסי פי' כיסי כשותא שאינה מתוקנת שעדיין צריכא תיקון: **[מתני'] המפקיד מעות אצל שולחני אם צרורין לא ישתמש בהן לפיכך אם אבדו אין חייב באחריותן.** אוקמה ר' אמי בצרורין וחתומים. קשר משונה איבעיא ועלתה בתיקו. הלכך לא ישתמש בהן: **פיסקא מותרין ישתמש בהן לפיכך אם אבדו חייב באחריותן.** אמר רב הונא ואפי' נאנסו והאי דקתני במתני' אבדו כדרבא דאמר בפרק הזהב נגנבו בליסטים מזויין. אבדו שטבעה ספינתו בים. ורב נחמן אמר נאנסו לא אלא בההוא הנאה דאי מתרמי ליה זבינא דאית ליה רווחא זבין בהו הוי עלייהו שומר שכר. וקיימא לן כרב נחמן: המפקיד אצל בעל הבית בין צרורין בין מותרין אל ישתמש בהן לפיכך אם אבדו אין חייב באחריותן חנווני כבעל הבית דברי ר' מאיר ר' יהודה אומר כשולחני וקיימא לן כר' יהודה. ומותיב רב נחמן לרב הונא דאמר בשולחני אפי' נאנסו חייב הא דתנן במסכת מעילה המפקיד מעות אצל שולחני מותרין ישתמש בהם לפיכך אם הוציא מעל הגזבר. ואי אמרת אפי' נאנסו חייב הני מעות הקדש כיון דמסרינהו הגיזבר לשולחני אי חייב בהו באונסין הוו להו כמלוה ואע"ג דלא אפקינהו עדיין השולחני למעול הגזבר דהא הוא אפקינהו. ופריק רב הונא הוא הדין אע"ג דאכתי לא אפקינהו מעל הגזבר ולא הוה בעי למיתנא הוציא אלא איידי דתנא רישא הוציא תנא נמי סיפא הוציא: **מתני' השולח יד בפיקדון ילקה בחסר וביתר** תנא א) כיצד הפקיד לו משתי סאין בסלע ועמדו מארבע משלם משתי סאין בסלע. הפקיד לו מארבע ועמדו משתים נותן לו משתים. בית הלל אומרים כשעת ההוצאה פי' כשיעור שהיה שוה בעת ששלח בו ידו והוציאו לצרכיו. אמר רבה מאן דגזל חביתא דחמרא מחבריה מעיקרא שויא זוזא ולבסוף שויא ד' שתיא או תברא משלם ד' מאי טעמא דכל זמן דאיתא הדרא למרא בעינא בעידנא דתברא או שתיא בההיא שעתא קא גזיל ליה ותנן כל הגזלנין משלמין כשעת הגזילה וההיא שעתא ד' הוא דשויא. איתבר ממילא משלם זוזא מאי טעמא השתא לא גזיל אמאי קא מחייבת ליה אההיא שעתא דגזל ב) זוזא הויא שויא. ואקשי' עליה תנן בית הלל אומרים כשעת ההוצאה מאי היא אילימא בעת ההוצאה מן העולם כלומר בעידנא דתברא או שתיא. ובחסר מי איכא מאן דאמר כלומר אם בשעת הגזילה היתה שוה ד' ובעת ההוצאה מן העולם שוה זוז כי האי גוונא יש מי שאמר משלם זוז. וכי חולק אדם על משנתינו דתנן כל הגזלנים משלמין כשעת הגזילה

חשק שלמה על ר"ח א) הוא תוספתא דמכלתין פ"ג ע"ש. ב) נ"ל וההיא שעתא זוזא הויא שויא.

A dissenting view:

וּבֵית הִלֵּל אוֹמְרִים – **But Beis Hillel say:** בִּשְׁעַת הוֹצָאָה – He pays **according to** the value of the deposit at **the time of** its **removal.**[23]

A third view:

רַבִּי עֲקִיבָא אוֹמֵר – **R' Akiva says:** בִּשְׁעַת הַתְּבִיעָה – He pays **according to** the value of the deposit at **the time of the claim.**[24]

**Gemara** The Gemara begins its analysis of the Mishnah with a teaching about how much an ordinary thief must pay for property that was stolen and then destroyed:

אָמַר רַבָּה – **Rabbah said:** הַאי מַאן דְּגָזַל חָבִיתָא דְּחַמְרָא מֵחַבְרֵיהּ – Concerning **one who stole a barrel of wine from another** מֵעִיקָּרָא שָׁוְיָא זוּזָא – that **originally** (i.e. when he stole it) **was worth a** ***zuz,*** הַשְׁתָּא שָׁוְיָא אַרְבָּעָה – and **now** (i.e. when it was destroyed) **is worth four** *zuz,* the amount that the thief must pay is determined according to the following rules: תַּבְרָהּ אוֹ שַׁתְיֵיהּ – If he destroyed it actively, e.g. **he broke [the barrel] or drank [its wine],** מְשַׁלֵּם אַרְבָּעָה – **he pays four** *zuz* (its value at the time of destruction). אִיתְּבַר מִמֵּילָא – But if it was destroyed without the active involvement of the thief, e.g. **it broke as a result of** external **circumstances,** מְשַׁלֵּם זוּזָא – **he pays** only **a** ***zuz*** (its value at the time of the theft).

Rabbah gives the reason for the first part of his teaching:

מַאי טַעְמָא – **What is the reason** for the ruling that where the thief actively destroyed the stolen property, he must pay what it was worth when he destroyed it? כֵּיוָן דְּאִי אִיתַהּ – **Since, if [the barrel]** of wine **was still here,** הֲדָרָא לְמָרָהּ בְּעֵינָא – **it would have been returned to its owner as it is,**[25] הַהִיא שַׁעְתָּא דְּקָא שָׁתֵי לֵיהּ – it comes out that **when [the thief] drank [the wine]** אוֹ דְּקָא תָּבַר לַהּ – **or broke [the barrel],** קָא גָּזֵיל מִינֵּיהּ – **he,** in effect, **stole it from [its owner]** at that time.[26] וּתְנַן – **And we learned in a Mishnah,**[27] concerning stolen property for which a thief is liable to pay: כָּל הַגַּזְלָנִין מְשַׁלְּמִין כִּשְׁעַת הַגְּזֵילָה – **ALL THIEVES PAY ACCORDING TO** the value of the stolen property at **THE TIME OF THE THEFT.**

Rabbah gives the reason for the second part of his teaching:

אִיתְּבַר מִמֵּילָא מְשַׁלֵּם זוּזָא – **If [the barrel] broke as a result of circumstances, he pays** only **a** ***zuz*** (its value at the time of the theft). מַאי טַעְמָא – **What is the reason** for this ruling? הַשְׁתָּא לָא עֲבִיד לַהּ וְלָא מִידֵּי – **Now** (i.e. when the barrel broke), **he did not do anything to it at all!** אַמַּאי קָא מְחַיְּיבַתְּ לֵיהּ – So **on what** basis **do you deem him liable** to compensate the owner? אַהַהִיא שַׁעְתָּא דְּגַזְלָהּ – He became liable **when he** originally **stole**[28] **[the barrel],** הַהִיא שַׁעְתָּא זוּזָא הוּא דְּשָׁוְיָא – and **at that time it was worth a** ***zuz.*** Therefore, he pays only a *zuz.*

The Gemara analyzes Beis Hillel's ruling in our Mishnah:

תְּנַן – **We learned in our Mishnah:** בֵּית הִלֵּל אוֹמְרִים – **BEIS HILLEL SAY:** בִּשְׁעַת הוֹצָאָה – The *shomer* pays **ACCORDING TO** the value of the deposit at **THE TIME OF** its **REMOVAL.** מַאי בִּשְׁעַת הוֹצָאָה – **What** is meant by **"according to the time of** its **removal"?** אִילֵימָא בִּשְׁעַת הוֹצָאָה מִן הָעוֹלָם – **Perhaps you will say** that it means **"according to the time of** its **removal from the world,"** i.e. when he destroyed it. וּבְמַאי – **And to which** of the two possible cases do Beis Hillel refer: where the value of the deposit decreased, or where it increased? אִי בְּחָסֵר – **If** you say that they refer to the case **where it decreased** in value (i.e. they rule that the *shomer* pays what the deposit was worth when he destroyed it even though its value had decreased in the meantime), the following difficulty arises: מִי אִיכָּא לְמַאן דְּאָמַר – **Is there anyone who says** that if a thief has to pay for property that *decreased* in value after he stole it, he does not pay what it was worth when he stole it? וְהָא תְּנַן – **Why, we have learned otherwise in the Mishnah:** כָּל הַגַּזְלָנִין מְשַׁלְּמִין כִּשְׁעַת הַגְּזֵילָה – **ALL THIEVES PAY ACCORDING TO** the value of the stolen property at **THE TIME OF THE THEFT.**[29] Evidently, therefore, Beis Hillel do not refer to the case where the deposit decreased in value. וְאִי בְּיָתֵר – **But if** you say that Beis Hillel refer to the case **where it increased** in value (i.e. they rule that since the deposit's value increased, the *shomer* must pay what it was worth when he destroyed it),[30] הַיְינוּ בֵּית שַׁמַּאי – then **[their opinion] is** identical to that of **Beis Shammai!** Both would be saying that, in such a case, the *shomer* pays what the deposit was worth when he destroyed it.

Thus, either way, Beis Hillel's statement cannot be explained as meaning "removal from the world."

NOTES

whether its value changed in the meantime. But if the property has been destroyed (or sold) and the thief has to pay money, he pays what the item was worth at the time of the theft [*Bava Kamma* 93b, 96b] (*Rashi*). [The Gemara explains why, in the event that the value of the misappropriated deposit increased, Beis Shammai rule that the *shomer* pays what it was worth when he destroyed it, rather than what it was worth when he stole it (as a thief would).]

23. The Gemara will explain the meaning of this statement.

24. I.e. the time when the *shomer* appeared in court and was sentenced to pay (*Ritva;* see *Rashi* to 43b ד"ה דאמר קרא).

25. See note 22.

26. If the owner had demanded the return of his property while it was still in existence, the object itself would have been returned to him. Now that the object has been destroyed, he receives only monetary compensation. Thus, the destruction of the object is considered a new act of theft, inasmuch as it prevents the return of the actual object to the owner (see *Rashi*).

27. *Bava Kamma* 93b.

28. [Even though the Gemara says that he "stole" the keg, several commentators contend that he is liable for הֶזֵּק, *causing damage,* rather than גְּזֵלָה, *theft* (see *Ran, Tos. R' Akiva Eiger* to the Mishnah in *Bava Kamma* §29, *Ketzos HaChoshen* 34:3; cf. *Nesivos* 34:5; see *Imrei Moshe* §32).]

29. [Although we learned above that where the thief actively destroyed the stolen article, he is liable to pay its worth at the time of its destruction, that ruling applies only where the value of the article had increased in the meantime. If its value had decreased, the thief pays what it was worth when he originally stole it. Since both acts are crimes for which he is liable, he always pays the higher value.]

30. As Rabbah ruled above (see note 26).

ומשלם ליה דמי כיסי: **מתני'** [א]המפקיד מעות אצל שולחני אם צרורין לא ישתמש בהן לפיכך אם אבדו אינו חייב באחריותן מותרין ישתמש בהן לפיכך אם אבדו חייב באחריותן אצל בעל הבית בין צרורין ובין מותרין לא ישתמש בהן לפיכך אם אבדו אינו חייב באחריותן (א) חנוני כבעל הבית דברי ר"מ ר' יהודה אומר [ב]חנוני כשולחני: **גמ'** משום דצרורין לא ישתמש בהן אמר רב אסי אמר רב יהודה [ג]בצרורין וחתומין שנו רב מרי אמר [ד]בקשר משונה איכא דאמרי בעי רב מרי קשר משונה מאי תיקו: מותרין ישתמש בהן כו': אמר רב הונא ואפילו נאנסו והא אבדו קתני כדרבה (ב) דאמר רבה נגנבו בלסטין מזויין אבדו שטבעה ספינתו בים ורב נחמן אמר [ה]נאנסו לא אמר ליה רבא לר"נ לדידך דאמרת נאנסו לא אלמא לא הוי שואל עלייהו אי שואל לא הוי שומר שכר נמי לא הוי א"ל בהא מודינא לך (א) דהואיל ונהנה מהנה בההוא הנאה דאי מיתרמי ליה זבינא דאית בה רווחא זבן בהו הוי עלייהו שומר שכר איתיביה רב נחמן לרב הונא (ג) [ו]המפקיד מעות אצל שולחני אם צרורין לא ישתמש בהן לפיכך אם הוציא לא מעל הגזבר ואם מותרין ישתמש בהן לפיכך אם הוציא מעל הגזבר ואי אמרת אפילו נאנסו מאי איריא הוציא אפילו לא הוציא נמי אמר ליה הוא הדין אע"ג דלא הוציא ואיידי דתנא רישא הוציא תנא סיפא נמי הוציא: **מתני'** השולח יד בפקדון בית שמאי אומרים ילקה בחסר וביתר ובית הלל אומרים [ז]כשעת הוצאה ר"ע אומר כשעת התביעה: **גמ'** (ד) אמר (ה) רבה [ח]האי מאן דגזל חביתא דחמרא מחבריה מעיקרא שויא זוזא השתא שויא ארבעה תברה או שתייה משלם ארבעה איתבר ממילא משלם זוזא מאי טעמא כיון דאי איתה הדרא למרה בעינא ההיא שעתא דקא שתי ליה או דקא תבר לה קא גזל מיניה ותנן (ו) [ט]כל הגזלנין משלמין כשעת הגזילה איתבר ממילא משלם זוזא מ"ט השתא לא עביד לה ולא מידי אמאי קא מחייבת ליה אההיא שעתא דגזלה ההיא שעתא זוזא הוא דשויא תנן בית הלל אומרים כשעת הוצאה מאי כשעת הוצאה אילימא כשעת הוצאה מן העולם ובמאי אי בחסר מי איכא למ"ד והא תנן כל הגזלנין משלמין כשעת הגזילה ואי ביתר היינו ב"ש אלא

ומשלם לו דמי כיסי. דמי כסות של קוליס לפי מה שהשביח: גמ' משום דצרורין לא ישתמש בהן. בתמיה ומה גילוי דעת יש כאן שאין חפץ שישתמש בהם מאחר שאם הן מותרין קאמרת ישתמש בהן דהמפקיד אלו יודע שהוא צריך תדיר למעות לצורין נמי ישתמש דדרך כל אדם לצור מעותיו: ואפילו נאנסו. קאמר מתני' דחייב באחריותן ואפילו לא נשתמש בהן דמהשתא הוי שואל עלייהו: נאנסו לא. כל זמן שלא נשתמש לא הוי שואל אלא אבדו דוקא חייב כשומר שכר: ואי שואל לא הוי שומר שכר נמי לא הוי. מה שכר נטל על שמירתם אלא על שסמך עליהם להחליפן ולהשתכר אם יבא לידו אתה מחייבו ושאלה היא זו שהרי כל הנאה שלו: בהדיא מודינא. אע"ג דאמינא לא הוי שואל מהשתא עד שישתמש מודינא דשומר שכר הוי: דהואיל ונהנה מהנה. לבעלים: המפקיד מעות. גזבר שהפקיד מעות הקדש כסבור שהן שלו: לא מעל גזבר. שהרי לא ברשות הוציאן ואינו שלוחו: מותרין. דהוה ליה כנותן רשות והוה ליה שלוחו: לפיכך אם הוציא. שולחני מעל גזבר: ואי אמרת אפילו נאנסו. תנא מתני' דחייב שולחני באחריותן נמלא משעה שהפקידו אלו יצאו מרשות הקדש ובאו לרשות שולחני ונעשה כמו שלוה לו ואין הולאה גדולה מזו מאי איריא הוליא: איידי דתנא רישא הוציא. לאשמועינן רבותא דאפילו הוליא לא מעל תנא סיפא הוליא: מתני' ילקה בחסר וביתר. אם חסרו דמיה שהוזלה בשוק ישלם דמיה כמו שהיתה שוה בשעה ששלח בה יד שהיא שעת הגזילה וכן כל הגזלנין משלמין כשעת הגזילה וכגון שהוליאה שאינה בעין אבל אם ישנה בעין כמות שגזלה אומר לו הרי שלך לפניך כדאמרינן גבי מטבע ונפסל תרומה ונטמאת בפ' הגוזל [קמא] (ב"ק דף נו:): וביתר. אם שהתה בידו משנשלח בה יד ונתייקרה ואח"כ הוליאה לוקה ביתר דמיה לשלם כשעת הולאה: ובית הלל אומרים כו'. בגמרא מפרש מאי קאמרי: כשעת התביעה. כשעת שיתבעו לדין ובגמרא מפרש טעמא: גמ' מעיקרא. כשגזלה: ולבסוף. כשילתה מן העולם: תברה. בידים: או שתייה. אחר שהוקרה: דאי איתה. כאן בשעת התביעה הוה מהדרנא בעינא דכי אמרינן משלם כשעת הגזילה היכא דליתה בעין אבל ישנה בעין בין שהוקרה בין שהוזלה חוזרת כמות שהיא הלכך הואיל ואם תבעה בעודה קיימת לאחר שהוקרה היתה חוזרת בעין אשתכח דההיא שעתא דקא שתי לה הוא דגזיל לה: ובמאי. אהייא פליגי בית הלל: אי בחסר. כשהוזלה דקאמרי ב"ש ילקה לשלם כדמים שהיתה בשעת הגזילה וקאמרי בית הלל כשעת הולאה: ומי איכא למאן דאמר. היכא דליתיה בעין דכל הגזלנין לאו כשעת הגזילה משלמין: אלא

מאי אירא הוציא כי לא הוציא נמי. כיון דהיתר תשמיש מחייב באונסין וא"ת הא דתנן לקמן בהזהב (דף מד. מז: מח.) נתן לו מעות ולא משך ממנו פירות יכול לחזור בו לרב הונא דאית ליה דהיתר תשמיש מחייב באונסין וכן לרב יוסף בפרק אלו מליאות (לעיל דף כט.) המוכר אסור להשתמש במעות שקבל שאם היה מותר להשתמש תקשה להו הך ברייתא (ב) דמייתי אפלוגתא דרבי יוחנן ור"ל נתן לבלן מעל דוקא בלן דלא מחסרא משיכה כדקתני סיפא הרי מרחץ לפניך הכנס ורחוץ אבל ספר לא מעל עד דמשיך ולדידהו כי נתנה לספר נמי למעול אע"ג דלא משיך כיון דספר מותר להשתמש בהן בין מיירי בספר נכרי כר' יוחנן בין בספר ישראל כר"ל וכמו שאסור להשתמש בהם לרב הונא ולרב יוסף ה"נ לר"ל ולר' יוחנן דבהא לא פליגי ולא הוה המוכר על אותם מעות כי אם שומר חנם לכ"ע וא"כ לרבי יוחנן מה הועילו במה שתקנו דאין מעות קונות דאי מעות קונות יאמר מוכר נשרפו חטיך בעליה השתא דלא קני יאמר נשרפו מעותיך בעליה ועוד דרב הונא גופיה סבר בפ' הזהב (לקמן דף מו:) דבר תורה מעות קונות כרבי יוחנן דאמר רב הונא מכור לי באלו קנה וי"ל דאע"ג דלא הוי על המעות כי אם שומר חנם לא מצי א"ל נשרפו מעותיך בעליה דכספים אין להם שמירה אלא בקרקע וא"ת כיון דהיכא שלא משך אסור להשתמש במעות א"כ הא דאמר (ג) פוסק עמו על הגדיש או על שער שבשוק מה מרויח בהקדמת מעות וי"ל כגון שפירש ע"מ להשתמש בהם א"נ אפילו בסתמ' כיון שהוא פוסק ומקדים לו מעות חצי שנה מן הגדיש עד ימות הקיץ אדעתא דהכי נותן שישתמש בהן ועוד י"ל דלרבי יוחנן ולרב הונא דאית להו דבר תורה מעות קונות לא הפקיעו כח שיש לו למוכר במעות שיכול להשתמש בהם כיון דקונות מן התורה והוי שואל עלייהו ולא מצי א"ל נשרפו מעותיך בעליה ולא תקנו משיכה אלא כדי שלא יאמר לו נשרפו חטיך בעליה אבל לר"ל ודאי כיון דמעות אינם קונות אסור להשתמש במעות ולא הוי שואל עלייהו ולכך נתנה לספר לא מעל עד שימשוך וכן לרבי יוחנן ולרב הונא בספר נכרי לא מעל עד שימשוך דמעות בנכרי אינם קונות:

**והתנן** כל הגזלנים משלמין כשעת הגזלה. ואע"ג דבפ' הגוזל [קמא] (ב"ק דף נו:) אמרי' זה הכלל כל הגזלנים משלמין כשעת הגזלה לאתויי דרבי אלעאי דאמר גנב טלה ונעשה איל עגל ונעשה שור נעשה שינוי בידו וקנאו משמע דלא מיירי ביוקרא וזולא אלא בשינוי כדמיירי ברישא דמתני' הגוזל עלים ועשה כלים למר ועשה בגדים היינו דוקא יתורא דזה הכלל אבל פשטא דמתניתין דמשלמין כשעת הגזלה מיירי ביוקרא וזולא והתם בהגוזל (דף קג.) נמי מייתי לענין יוקרא וזולא גבי אייקר כתנא דרב כהנא ובפרק כל שעה (פסחים דף לב.) גבי לפי דמים משלם וא"ת רב דאמר במרובה (ב"ק דף סה. ושם ד"ה גופא) קרן כעין שגנב [ז][כפל וכו'] ואוקמה כגון דמעיקרא שויא ד' ולבסוף שויא זוזא מאי קמ"ל מתני' היא ועוד מאי בעי התם מאי טעמא דרב ליבעי מאי טעמא דמתניתין וי"ל דרב קמ"ל דאע"ג דקרן כעין שגנב כפל לא הוי כמו קרן אלא כשעת העמדה בדין ובעינן מאי טעמא דרב דמחלק כפל מדין קרן ומשני גנבה וחייס אחייה לקרן כעין שגנב דוקא קרן ולא כפל:

לימא

## עין משפט נר מצוה

צז א ב ג ד ה מיי' פ"ז מהל' שאלה ופקדון הל' ו סמג עשין פח טוש"ע ח"מ סי' רלב סעי' ז:
צח ו מיי' פ"ז מהל' מעילה הל' ט והל' י:
צט ז מיי' פ"ג מהל' גזילה הל' א סמג עשין עא עב טוש"ע ח"מ סי' רלב סעי' ה:
ק ח מיי' שם הל' א ב ופ"א מה' גניבה הל' יד סמג שם טוש"ע ח"מ סי' שנד סעי' ג וסי' שסב סעי' י:
קא ט מיי' פ"ג מהל' גזילה הל' ב טוש"ע ח"מ סי' שסב סעי' ב וסעי' יא וסעי' יב וסי' שה סעי' ה:

## רבינו חננאל

דמישתרשי ליה ואי הוה חלא ולא אישתרשי ליה מידי משלם ליה דמי כיסי פי' כיסי כשותא שאינה מתוקנת שעדיין צריכא תיקון: **[מתני'] המפקיד מעות אצל שולחני אם צרורין לא ישתמש בהן לפיכך אם אבדו אין חייב באחריותן.** אוקמה ר' אמי בצרורין וחתומים. קשר משונה איבעיא ועלתה בתיקו. הלכך לא ישתמש בהן: **פיסקא מותרין ישתמש בהן לפיכך אם אבדו חייב באחריותן.** אמר רב הונא ואפי' נאנסו והאי דקתני במתני' אבדו כדרבא דאמר בפרק הזהב נגנבו בליסטים מזויין. אבדו שטבעה ספינתו בים. ורב נחמן אמר נאנסו לא אלא בההוא הנאה דאי מתרמי ליה זבינא דאית ליה רווחא זבין בהו הוי עלייהו שומר שכר. וקיימא לן כרב נחמן: המפקיד אצל בעל הבית בין צרורין בין מותרין אל ישתמש בהן לפיכך אם אבדו אין חייב באחריותן חנווני כבעל הבית דברי ר' מאיר ר' יהודה אומר כשולחני וקיימא לן כר' יהודה. ומותיב רב נחמן לרב הונא דאמר בשולחני אפי' נאנסו חייב הא דתנן במסכת מעילה המפקיד מעות אצל שולחני מותרין ישתמש בהם לפיכך אם הוציא מעל הגזבר. ואי אמרת אפי' נאנסו חייב הני מעות הקדש כיון דמסרינהו הגיזבר לשולחני אי חייב בהו באונסין הוו להו כמלוה ואע"ג דלא אפקינהו עדיין השולחני למעול הגזבר דהא הוא אפקינהו. ופריק רב הונא הוא הדין אע"ג דאכתי לא אפקינהו מעל הגזבר ולא הוה בעי למיתנא הוציא אלא איידי דתנא רישא הוציא תנא נמי סיפא הוציא: **מתני'** השולח יד בפיקדון ילקה בחסר וביתר תנא א) כיצד הפקיד לו משתי סאין בסלע ועמדו מארבע משלם משתי סאין בסלע. הפקיד לו מארבע ועמדו משתים נותן לו משתים. בית הלל אומרים כשעת ההוצאה פי' כשיעור שהיה שוה בעת ששלח בו ידו והוציאו לצרכיו. אמר רבה מאן דגזל חביתא דחמרא מחבריה מעיקרא שויא זוזא ולבסוף שויא ד' שתיא או תברא משלם ד' מאי טעמא דכל זמן דאיתא הדרא למרא בעינא בעידנא דתברא או שתיא בההיא שעתא קא גזיל ליה ותנן כל הגזלנין משלמין כשעת הגזילה וההיא שעתא ד' הוא דשויא. איתבר ממילא משלם זוזא מאי טעמא השתא לא גזיל אמאי קא מחייבת ליה אההיא שעתא דגזל ב) זוזא הויא שויא. ואקשי' עליה תנן בית הלל אומרים כשעת ההוצאה מאי היא אילימא בעת ההוצאה מן העולם כלומר בעידנא דתברא או שתיא. ובחסר מי איכא מאן דאמר כלומר אם בשעת הגזילה היתה שוה ד' ובעת ההוצאה מן העולם שוה זוז כי האי גוונא יש מי שאמר משלם זוז. וכי חולק אדם על משנתינו דתנן כל הגזלנים משלמין כשעת הגזילה

## מסורת הש"ס

א) קדושין נג:, [מעילה כא:], ב) לעיל כט:, לקמן מח., ג) [תוספתא דמעילה סוף פרק ב], מעילה כא: וע"ש בתוס'], ד) בבא קמא סה., ה) [גירסת רי"ף רבא, ועיין תוס' ב"ב ד"ה אלא], ו) [בבא קמא נג:, נו:, קג., פסחים לב.], ז) מהרש"ל.

## הגהות הב"ח

(א) גמ' דהואיל ונהנה מהנה. נ"ב ע"ל דף פא ע"א: (ב) תום' ד"ה מאי כו' דמייתי אפלוגתא. נ"ב דף מח: (ג) בא"ד פוסק עמו על הגדיש. נ"ב לקמן דף עב ע"ב:

## ליקוטי רש"י

אצל בעל הבית. בין צרורין ובין מותרין לא ישתמש בהן דלהכי הפקידן אצל בעה"ב שהוא יודע שבעה"ב אין דרכו לפרוט ולהחליף ולא חשש אם צרורין אם מותרין [מעילה כא:]. חנוני כבעל הבית דברי ר"מ. שאינו צריך תמיד למעות שנותנים לו פירות בכל מכר מנותם באשראי די לו במיעוט מעות שבידו [קדושין נג:]. שאינו רגיל בחילופין כשולחני בין כך ובין כך לא יגע בהן. ר' יהודה אומר חנוני כשולחני. לפעמים נמי הוא רגיל להחליף כשולחני לפיכך דינו כשולחני [מעילה שם]. בלסטין מזויין. דאונס הוא [לקמן נח.]. המפקיד מעות. של הקדש אצל שולחני. אם צרורין לא ישתמש בהן. דלהכי הפקידן אלו צרורין דלא הוה בעי דלישתמש בהו לפיכך אם הוציאן השולחני מעל. מותרין ישתמש בהן. שלדעת כן הפקידן אלו מותרין שיתעסק בהן שיחליפם לפיכך לא מעל השולחני אלא המפקיד. דאי איתה הדרא למרה בעינא. דהא בעי לאהדורה הלכך ברשותא דמרה הוקרה וההיא שעתא דתברה ושתייה הוא דקא גזיל לה [ב"ק סה.]. בעינא. כמו שהיתה [לעיל טו.].

This view is challenged:

אָמַר לֵיהּ רָבָא לְרַב נַחְמָן – **Rava said to Rav Nachman:** לְדִידָךְ דְּאָמְרַתְּ נֶאֱנְסוּ לֹא – **According to you, who said** that if [the money] **is lost through an unavoidable accident** the moneychanger is **not** liable, אַלְמָא לֹא הָוֵי שׁוֹאֵל עֲלַיְיהוּ – **evidently, [the moneychanger] is not** considered **a borrower of [the money].** אִי שׁוֹאֵל לֹא הָוֵי – But **if he is not a borrower,** שׁוֹמֵר שָׂכָר נַמֵּי לֹא – **he should not be** regarded as **a paid *shomer*** either, for he did not receive any payment. Therefore, he should not be liable even for ordinary loss![14] – ? –

Rav Nachman answers:

אָמַר לֵיהּ – **[Rav Nachman] said to [Rava]:** בְּהָא מוֹדֵינָא לָךְ – Although I maintain that he is not considered a borrower, **this much I concede to you,** that he is considered a paid *shomer.* דְּהוֹאִיל וְנֶהֱנֶה מֵהֶן – **For since he derives** a degree of **benefit** from the deposited money, **he provides** a degree of **benefit** to its owner. That is to say: בְּהַהוּא הֲנָאָה – **By virtue of the benefit** he derives from the money, דְּאִי מִיתְרַמֵּי לֵיהּ זְבִינָא דְּאִית בָּהּ רַוְוחָא זָבֵן בְּהוּ – namely, **that if a purchase that has** a potential **for profit comes his way, he can buy** it **with [the entrusted money],** הָוֵי עֲלַיְיהוּ שׁוֹמֵר שָׂכָר – **he is** considered **a paid *shomer* with regard to [the money],** and he is therefore liable to pay the owner for theft and loss.[15]

Rav Nachman challenges his disputant, Rav Huna:

אֵיתִיבֵיהּ רַב נַחְמָן לְרַב הוּנָא – **Rav Nachman challenged Rav Huna** on the basis of the following Mishnah:[16] הַמַּפְקִיד מָעוֹת אֵצֶל שׁוּלְחָנִי – Concerning [A TREASURER OF TEMPLE FUNDS] WHO DEPOSITS Temple MONEY WITH A MONEYCHANGER, mistakenly believing that the money is his own, the law is as follows: אִם צְרוּרִין – IF [THE MONEY] IS TIED UP in a bundle, לֹא יִשְׁתַּמֵּשׁ בָּהֶן – [THE MONEYCHANGER] MAY NOT USE IT. לְפִיכָךְ אִם הוֹצִיא – THEREFORE, IF [THE MONEYCHANGER] SPENT the money, לֹא מָעַל הַגִּזְבָּר – THE TREASURER IS NOT GUILTY OF *ME'ILAH.*[17] וְאִם מוּתָּרִין – BUT IF [THE MONEY] IS LOOSE, יִשְׁתַּמֵּשׁ בָּהֶן – [THE MONEYCHANGER] MAY USE IT. לְפִיכָךְ אִם הוֹצִיא – THEREFORE, IF [THE MONEYCHANGER] SPENT the money, מָעַל הַגִּזְבָּר – THE TREASURER IS GUILTY OF *ME'ILAH,* for the moneychanger is regarded as his agent.[18]

Rav Nachman concludes his challenge to Rav Huna:

וְאִי אָמְרַתְּ אֲפִילוּ נֶאֱנְסוּ – **Now, if you say** that a moneychanger who was given loose money to watch is liable to pay the owner **even** if it was **lost through an unavoidable accident,** מַאי אִירְיָא הוֹצִיא – **why** did the Mishnah **state,** in the latter clause, that **[the moneychanger] spent** the money? אֲפִילוּ לֹא הוֹצִיא נַמֵּי – **Even if he did not spend** the money, the treasurer should still be guilty of *me'ilah,* for the very transfer of the money to the moneychanger should be considered a removal of the money from the Temple's ownership.[19] – ? –

Rav Huna answers:

אָמַר לֵיהּ – **[Rav Huna] said to [Rav Nachman]:** הוּא הַדִּין – In fact, **the same law** (namely, that the treasurer is guilty of *me'ilah)* indeed applies אַף עַל גַּב דְּלֹא הוֹצִיא – **even where [the moneychanger] did not spend** the money. וְאַיְּידֵי דְּתָנָא רֵישָׁא הוֹצִיא – **But since the first part** of the Mishnah **says** that **[the moneychanger] spent** the money,[20] תָּנָא סֵיפָא נַמֵּי הוֹצִיא – for the sake of stylistic symmetry[21] **the last part** of the Mishnah **also says** that **[the moneychanger] spent** the money.

**Mishnah** The following Mishnah discusses a *shomer* who misappropriated the deposit and destroyed (or sold) it some time later. Specifically, it deals with the question of how much compensation he must pay in the event that there was a change in the value of the deposit:

הַשּׁוֹלֵחַ יָד בְּפִקָּדוֹן – If [**a *shomer***] **misappropriated a deposit,** and later destroyed it, בֵּית שַׁמַּאי אוֹמְרִים – **Beis Shammai say:** יִלְקֶה בְּחָסֵר וּבְיָתֵר – **[The *shomer*] suffers** the loss **whether it decreased or increased** in value. I.e. he always pays the greater amount – if its value decreased after the misappropriation, he pays what the deposit was worth when he misappropriated it; if its value increased, he pays what it was worth when he destroyed it.[22]

NOTES

status of a borrower until he actually uses the money. Until then, he is considered a paid *shomer,* who is liable only for standard (avoidable) loss (*Rashi*).

14. His liability is based *solely* on his right to use the coins [for he did not receive any other payment] (*Rashi;* see note 8). Hence, if this right does not render him a borrower, he should not assume the responsibilities of even a paid *shomer*!

15. Since the benefit is only potential, the moneychanger is essentially a *shomer* who has the option to borrow the money should the opportunity arise. This right to borrow the money is considered payment for his custodianship. Therefore, he assumes the responsibilities of a paid *shomer.* It is only when the benefit is realized (i.e. he uses the money) that he becomes a borrower.

16. *Me'ilah* 21b. See *Pnei Yehoshua* here.

17. מְעִילָה, *me'ilah,* is defined as unlawfully benefiting from Temple property or removing such property from the Temple's ownership. One who commits this crime inadvertently (e.g. he did not realize that he was using Temple property, as in our case) must bring an *asham* offering and pay the principal plus a quarter to the Temple treasury (*Leviticus* 5:14-16; verse 16 refers to the added quarter as a "fifth" because it is a fifth of the *total* payment).

In the present case, the treasurer is not guilty of *me'ilah,* because he merely deposited the money with a *shomer,* and did not remove it from the Temple's ownership. Although the *shomer* subsequently spent the money (thereby removing it from the Temple's ownership), the treasurer is not responsible for this, because the *shomer* acted without his consent (see *Rashi*). [The *shomer,* however, is indeed liable for inadvertently removing the money from the Temple's ownership (*Rashi* to *Me'ilah* 21b ד״ה אם).]

18. Since one who gives loose money to a moneychanger for safekeeping presumably permits him to use it (see note 6), the moneychanger is regarded as if he were the agent of the treasurer. Therefore, when the moneychanger spends the money, it is the treasurer [and not the moneychanger – *Rashi* to *Me'ilah* 21b] who is guilty of *me'ilah* (*Rashi*).

As a rule, if someone orders another to commit a sin, the agent, and not the principal, is responsible for the deed. This concept is referred to as אֵין שָׁלִיחַ לִדְבַר עֲבֵרָה, *there is no* [liability on the part of a principal for the actions of his] *agent in a matter of sin.* However, it is derived from Scripture that *me'ilah* is an exception to this rule. Therefore, if someone committed an act of *me'ilah* on behalf of another, it is the principal who is responsible (see *Kiddushin* 42b-43a).

19. When one lends an article to another, it is considered as if one has transferred it to his possession. Therefore, according to Rav Huna, who holds that entrusting loose money to a moneychanger is the equivalent of a loan (see note 9), the Temple treasurer should be liable for *me'ilah* as soon as he gave over the money to the moneychanger, even before it was used (*Rashi*).

20. The Mishnah's first clause (which refers to tied-up money, whose use is forbidden) deliberately specifies that the moneychanger *spent* the money, in order to teach that the treasurer is not guilty of *me'ilah* in that case, even where the Temple funds were indeed transferred to private ownership (*Rashi*).

21. [Originally, the Mishnah was taught orally and memorized. It was composed in a manner that would make this easier.]

22. As we learned above (41a note 10), *shelichus yad* (misappropriation) is a form of stealing. With regard to stealing, the law is that if the stolen property is undamaged, the thief returns it as it is, regardless of

ומשלם ליה דמי כיסי: **מתני׳** א) המפקיד מעות אצל שולחני אם צרורין לא ישתמש בהן לפיכך אם אבדו אינו חייב באחריותן מותרין ישתמש בהן לפיכך אם אבדו חייב באחריותן אצל בעל הבית בין צרורין ובין מותרין לא ישתמש בהן לפיכך אם אבדו אינו חייב באחריותן א) חנוני כבעל הבית דברי ר״מ ר׳ יהודה אומר ב) חנוני כשולחני: **גמ׳** משום דצרורין לא ישתמש בהן אמר רב אסי אמר רב יהודה ג) בצרורין וחתומין שנו רב מרי אמר ד) בקשר משונה איכא דאמרי בעי רב מרי קשר משונה מאי תיקו: מותרין ישתמש בהן כו׳: אמר רב הונא ואפילו נאנסו והא אבדו קתני כדרבה ג) דאמר רבה נגנבו בלסטין מזויין אבדו שטבעה ספינתו בים ורב נחמן אמר ה) נאנסו לא אמר ליה רבא לר״נ לדידך דאמרת נאנסו לא אלמא לא הוי שואל עלייהו אי שואל לא הוי שומר שכר נמי לא הוי א״ל בהא מודינא לך (א) דהואיל ונהנה מהנה בההוא הנאה דאי מיתרמי ליה זבינא דאית בה רווחא זבן בהו הוי עלייהו שומר שכר איתיביה רב נחמן לרב הונא ג) ו) המפקיד מעות אצל שולחני אם צרורין לא ישתמש בהן לפיכך אם הוציא לא מעל הגזבר ואם מותרין ישתמש בהן לפיכך אם הוציא מעל הגזבר ואי אמרת אפילו נאנסו מאי איריא הוציא אפילו לא הוציא נמי אמר ליה הוא הדין אע״ג דלא הוציא ואיידי דתנא רישא הוציא תנא סיפא נמי הוציא: **מתני׳** השולח יד בפקדון בית שמאי אומרים ילקה בחסר וביתר ובית הלל אומרים ז) כשעת הוצאה ר״ע אומר כשעת התביעה: **גמ׳** ד) אמר ה) רבה ח) האי מאן דגזל חביתא דחמרא מחבריה מעיקרא שויא זוזא השתא שויא ארבעה תברה או שתייה משלם ארבעה איתבר ממילא משלם זוזא מאי טעמא כיון דאי איתה הדרא למרה בעינא ההיא שעתא דקא שתי ליה או דקא תבר לה קא גזל מיניה ותנן ו) ט) כל הגזלנין משלמין כשעת הגזילה איתבר ממילא משלם זוזא מ״ט השתא לא עביד לה ולא מידי אמאי קא מחייבת ליה אההיא שעתא דגזלה ההיא שעתא זוזא הוא דשויא תנן בית הלל אומרים כשעת הוצאה מאי כשעת הוצאה אילימא כשעת הוצאה מן העולם ובמאי אי בחסר מי איכא למ״ד והא תנן כל הגזלנין משלמין כשעת הגזילה ואי ביתר היינו ב״ש
אלא

## רש״י

ומשלם לו דמי כיסו. דמי כשות של קוליס לפי מה שהשביח: **גמ׳ משום דצרורין לא ישתמש בהן.** בתמיה ומה גילוי דעת יש כאן שאין חפץ שישתמש בהם מאחר שאם הן מותרין קאמרת ישתמש בהן דהמפקיד אללו יודע שהוא לריך תדיר למעות לרורין נמי ישתמש דדרך כל אדם לצור מעותיו: **ואפילו נאנסו.** קאמר מתני׳ דחייב באחריותן ואפילו לא נשתמש בהן דמהשתא הוי שואל עלייהו: **נאנסו לא.** כל זמן שלא נשתמש לא הוי שואל אלא אבדו דוקא חייב כשומר שכר: **ואי שואל לא הוי שומר שכר נמי לא הוי.** מה שכר נטל על שמירתם אלא על שסמך עליהם להחליפן ולהשתכר אם יבא לידו אתה מחייבו ושאלה היא זו שהרי כל הנאה שלו: **בהדיא מודינא.** אע״ג דאמינא לא הוי שואל מהשתא עד שישתמש מודינא דשומר שכר הוי: **דהואיל ונהנה מהנה.** לבעלים: **המפקיד מעות.** גזבר שהפקיד מעות הקדש כסבור שהן שלו: **לא מעל גזבר.** שהרי לא ברשות הוליאן ואינו שלוחו: **מותרין.** דהוה ליה כנותן רשות והוה ליה שלוחו: **לפיכך אם הוציא.** שולחני מעל גזבר: **ואי אמרת אפילו נאנסו.** תנא מתני׳ דחייב שולחני באחריותן נמלא משעה שהפקידו אללו יצאו מרשות הקדש ובאו לרשות שולחני ונעשה כמו שלוה לו ואין הולאה גדולה מזו מאי איריא הוליא: **איידי דתנא רישא הוציא.** לאשמועינן רבותא דאפילו הוליא לא מעל תנא סיפא הוליא: **מתני׳ ילקה בחסר וביתר.** אם חסרו דמיה שהוזלה בשוק ישלם דמיה כמו שהיתה שוה בשעה ששלח בה יד שהיא שעת הגזילה וכן כל הגזלנין משלמין כשעת הגזילה וכגון שהוליאה שאינה בעין אבל אם ישנה בעין כמות שגזלה אומר לו הרי שלך לפניך כדאמרינן גבי מטבע ונפסל תרומה ונטמאת בפ׳ הגוזל [קמא] (ב״ק דף נו:): **וביתר.** אם שהתה בידו משסלח בה יד ונתייקרה ואח״כ הוליאה לוקה ביתר דמיה לשלם כשעת הולאה: **ובית הלל אומרים כו׳.** בגמרא מפרש מאי קאמרי: **כשעת התביעה.** כשעת שיתבעו לדין ובגמרא מפרש טעמא: **גמ׳ מעיקרא.** כשגזלה: **ולבסוף.** כשילתה מן העולם: **תברה.** בידים: **או שתייה.** אחר שהוקרה: **דאי איתה.** כאן בשעת התביעה הוה מהדרנא בעינא דכי אמרינן משלם כשעת הגזילה היכא דליתה בעין אבל ישנה בעין בין שהוקרה בין שהוזלה חוזרת כמות שהיא הלכך הואיל ואם תבעה בעודה קיימת לאחר שהוקרה היתה חוזרת בעין אשתכח דההיא שעתא דקא שתי לה הוא דגזיל לה: **ובמאי.** אהייא פליגי בית הלל: **אי בחסר.** כשהוזלה דקאמרי ב״ש ילקה לשלם כדמים שהיתה בשעת הגזילה וקאמרי בית הלל כשעת הולאה: **ומי איכא למאן דאמר.** היכא דליתיה בעין דכל הגזלנין לאו כשעת הגזילה משלמין: אלא

## תוספות

**מאי** איריא הוציא כי לא הוציא נמי. כיון דהיתר תשמיש מחייב באונסין וא״ת הא דתנן לקמן בהזהב (דף מד. מז: מח.) נתן לו מעות ולא משך ממנו פירות יכול לחזור בו לרב הונא דאית ליה דהיתר תשמיש מחייב באונסין וכן לרב יוסף בפרק אלו מציאות (לעיל דף כט.) המוכר אסור להשתמש במעות שקבל שאם היה מותר להשתמש תקשה להו הך ברייתא (ב) דמייתי אפלוגתא דרבי יוחנן ור״ל נתן לבנך מעל דוקא בנך דלא מחסרא משיכה כדקתני סיפא הרי מרחץ לפניך הכנס ורחוץ אבל ספר לא מעל עד דמשיך ולדידהו כי נתנה לספר נמי למעול אע״ג דלא משיך כיון דספר מותר להשתמש בהן בין מיירי בספר נכרי כר׳ יוחנן בין בספר ישראל כר״ל וכמו שאסור להשתמש בהם לרב הונא ולרב יוסף ה״נ לר״ל ולר׳ יוחנן דבהא לא פליגי ולא הוה המוכר על אותם מעות כי אם שומר חנם לכ״ע וא״כ לרבי יוחנן מה הועילו במה שתקנו דאין מעות קונות דאי מעות קונות יאמר מוכר נשרפו חטיך בעליה השתא דלא קני יאמר נשרפו מעותיך בעליה ועוד דרב הונא גופיה סבר בפ׳ הזהב (לקמן דף מו:) דבר תורה מעות קונות כרבי יוחנן דאמר רב הונא מכור לי באלו קנה וי״ל דאע״ג דלא הוי על המעות כי אם שומר חנם לא מצי א״ל נשרפו מעותיך בעליה דכספים אין להם שמירה אלא בקרקע וא״ת כיון דהיכא שלא משך אסור להשתמש במעות א״כ הא דאמר (ג) פוסק עמו על הגדים או על שער שבשוק מה מרויח בהקדמת מעות וי״ל כגון שפירש ע״מ להשתמש בהם א״נ אפילו בסתמ׳ כיון שהוא פוסק ומקדים לו מעות אגב שנה מן הגדים עד ימות הקיץ אדעתא דהכי נותן שישתמש בהן ועוד י״ל דלרבי יוחנן ולרב הונא דאית להו דבר תורה מעות קונות לא הפקיעו כח שיש לו למוכר במעות שיכול להשתמש בהם כיון דקונות מן התורה והוי שואל עלייהו ולא מצי א״ל נשרפו מעותיך בעליה ולא תקנו משיכה אלא כדי שלא יאמר לו נשרפו חטיך בעליה אבל לר״ל ודאי כיון דמעות אינם קונות אסור להשתמש במעות ולא הוי שואל עלייהו ולכך נתנה לספר לא מעל עד שימשוך וכן לרבי יוחנן ולרב הונא בספר נכרי לא מעל עד שימשוך דמעות בנכרי אינם קונות:

**והתנן** כל הגזלנים משלמין כשעת הגזלה. ואע״ג דבפ׳ הגוזל [קמא] (ב״ק דף נו:) אמרי׳ זה הכלל כל הגזלנים משלמין כשעת הגזלה לאתויי דרבי אלעאי דאמר גנב טלה ונעשה איל עגל ונעשה שור נעשה שינוי בידו וקנאה משמע דלא מיירי ביוקרא וזולא אלא בשינוי כדמיירי ברישא דמתני׳ הגוזל עלים ועשה כלים למר ועשה בגדים היינו דוקא יתורא דזה הכלל אבל פשטא דמתניתין דמשלמין כשעת הגזילה מיירי ביוקרא וזולא והתם בהגוזל (דף קג.) נמי מייתי לענין יוקרא וזולא גבי אייקר כתנא דרב כהנא ובפרק כל שעה (פסחים דף לב.) גבי לפי דמים משלם וא״ת רב דאמר במרובה (ב״ק דף סה. ושם ד״ה גופא) קרן כעין שגנב ז) [כפל וכו׳] ואוקמה כגון דמעיקרא שויא ד׳ ולבסוף שויא זוזא מאי קמ״ל מתני׳ היא ועוד מאי בעי התם מאי טעמא דרב ליבעי מאי טעמא דמתניתין וי״ל דרב קמ״ל דאע״ג דקרן כעין שגנב כפל לא הוי כמו קרן אלא כשעת העמדה בדין ובעינן מאי טעמא דרב דמחלק כפל מדין קרן ומשני גנבה וחייס אחייה לקרן כעין שגנב דוקא קרן ולא כפל:

לימא

## עין משפט נר מצוה

צז א ב ג ד ה מיי׳ פ״ז מהל׳ שאלה ופקדון הל׳ ו סמג עשין פח טוש״ע ח״מ סי׳ רלב סעי׳ ז:

צח ו מיי׳ פ״ז מהל׳ מעילה הל׳ ט והל׳ י:

צט ז מיי׳ פ״ג מהל׳ גזילה הל׳ א סמג עשין עא עב טוש״ע ח״מ סי׳ רלב סעי׳ ה:

ק ח מיי׳ שם הל׳ א ב ופ״א מה׳ גניבה הל׳ יד סמג שם טוש״ע ח״מ סי׳ שנד סעי׳ ג וסי׳ שסב סעי׳ י:

קא ט מיי׳ פ״ג מהל׳ גזילה הל׳ ב טוש״ע ח״מ סי׳ שסב סעי׳ ב וסעי׳ יא וסעי׳ יב וסי׳ שה סעי׳ ה:

## רבינו חננאל

דמישתרשי ליה ואי הוה חלא ולא אישתרשי ליה מידי משלם ליה דמי כיסי פי׳ כיסי כשותא שאינה מתוקנת שעדיין צריכא תיקון: [מתני׳] המפקיד מעות אצל שולחני אם צרורין לא ישתמש בהן לפיכך אם אבדו אין חייב באחריותן. אוקמה ר׳ אמי בצרורין וחתומים. קשר משונה איבעיא ועלתה בתיקו. הלכך לא ישתמש בהן: **פיסקא מותרין ישתמש בהן לפיכך אם אבדו חייב באחריותן.** אמר רב הונא ואפי׳ נאנסו והאי דקתני במתני׳ אבדו כדרבא דאמר בפרק הזהב נגנבו בליסטים מזויין. אבדו שטבעה ספינתו בים. ורב נחמן אמר נאנסו לא אלא בההוא הנאה דאי מתרמי ליה זבינא דאית ליה רווחא זבין בהו הוי עלייהו שומר שכר. וקיימא לן כרב נחמן: המפקיד אצל בעל הבית בין צרורין בין מותרין אל ישתמש בהן לפיכך אם אבדו אין חייב באחריותן חנוני כבעל הבית דברי ר׳ מאיר ר׳ יהודה אומר כשולחני וקיימא לן כר׳ יהודה. ומותיב רב נחמן לרב הונא דאמר בשולחני אפי׳ נאנסו חייב הא דתנן במסכת מעילה המפקיד מעות אצל שולחני מותרין ישתמש בהם לפיכך אם הוציא מעל הגזבר. ואי אמרת אפי׳ נאנסו חייב הני מעות הקדש כיון דמסרינהו הגיזבר לשולחני אי חייב בהו באונסין הוו להו כמלוה ואע״ג דלא אפקינהו עדיין השולחני למעול הגזבר דהא הוא אפקינהו. ופריק רב הונא הוא הדין אע״ג דאכתי לא אפקינהו מעל הגזבר ולא הוה בעי למיתנא הוציא אלא איידי דתנא רישא הוציא תנא נמי סיפא הוציא: **מתני׳ השולח יד בפיקדון ילקה בחסר וביתר** תנא א) כיצד הפקיד לו משתי סאין בסלע ועמדו מארבע משלם משתי סאין בסלע. הפקיד לו מארבע ועמדו משתים נותן לו משתים. בית הלל אומרים כשעת ההוצאה פי׳ כשיעור שהיה שוה בעת ששלח בו ידו והוציאו לצרכיו. אמר רבה מאן דגזל חביתא דחמרא מחבריה מעיקרא שויא זוזא ולבסוף שויא ד׳ שתיא או תברא משלם ד׳ מאי טעמא דכל זמן דאיתא הדרא למרא בעינא

בעידנא דתברא או שתיא בההיא שעתא קא גזיל ליה ותנן כל הגזלנין משלמין כשעת הגזילה וההיא שעתא ד׳ הוא דשויא. איתבר ממילא משלם זוזא מאי טעמא השתא לא גזיל אמאי קא מחייבת ליה אההיא שעתא דגזל ב) זוזא הויא שויא. ואקשי׳ עליה תנן בית הלל אומרים כשעת ההוצאה מאי היא אילימא בעת ההוצאה מן העולם כלומר בעידנא דתברא או שתיא. ובחסר מי איכא מאן דאמר כלומר אם בשעת הגזילה היתה שוה ד׳ ובעת ההוצאה מן העולם שוה זוז כי האי גוונא יש מי שאמר משלם זוז. וכי חולק אדם על משנתינו דתנן כל הגזלנים משלמין כשעת הגזילה

## מסורת הש״ס

א) קדושין נג:, [מעילה כא:], ב) לעיל כט:, לקמן מח., ג) [תוספתא דמעילה סוף פרק ב], מעילה כא: ע״ש בתוס׳], ד) בבא קמא סה., ה) [גירסת הרי״ף רבא, ועיין תוס׳ ב״ב ד״ה אלא], ו) [בבא קמא לג:, לו:, קג., פסחים לב.], ז) מהרש״ל.

## הגהות הב״ח

(א) גמ׳ דהואיל ונהנה מהנה. נ״ב ע״ל דף פא ע״א: (ב) תוס׳ ד״ה מאי וכו׳ דמייתי אפלוגתא. נ״ב דף מח: (ג) בא״ד פוסק עמו על הגדים. נ״ב לקמן דף עב ע״ב:

## ליקוטי רש״י

**אצל בעל הבית.** בין צרורין ובין מותרין לא ישתמש בהן דלהכי הפקידן אצל בעה״ב שהוא יודע שבעה״ב אין דרכו לפרוט ולהחליף ולא חשש אם צרורין אם מותרין [מעילה כא:]. **חנוני כבעל הבית דברי ר״מ.** שאינו צריך תמיד למעות שנותנים לו פירות וכל מכר חנותו באשראי ודי לו במיעוט מעות שבידו [קדושין נג:]. שאינו רגיל בחילופין כשולחני ובין כך ובין כך לא יגע בהן. **ר׳ יהודה אומר חנוני כשולחני.** לפעמים נמי הוא רגיל להחליף כשולחני לפיכך דינו כשולחני [מעילה שם]. **בלסטין מזויין.** דאונס הוא [לקמן נח.]. **המפקיד מעות.** של הקדש אצל שולחני. **אם צרורין לא ישתמש בהן.** דלהכי הפקידן אללו צרורין דלא הוה בעי דלישתמש בהו לפיכך אם הוציאן השולחני מעל. **מותרין ישתמש בהן.** שלדעת כן הפקידן אללו מותרין שיתעסק בהן שיחליפם לפיכך לא מעל השולחני אלא המפקיד. **דאי איתה הדרא למרה בעינא.** דהא בעי לאהדורה הלכך ברשותא דמרה הוקרה וההיא שעתא דתברה ושתייה הוא דקא גזיל לה [ב״ק סה.]. **בעינא.** כמו שהיתה [לעיל טו.].

**חשק שלמה על ר״ח** א) הוא תוספתא דמכלתין פ״ג ע״ש. ב) נ״ל וההיא שעתא זוזא הויא שויא.

וּמְשַׁלֵּם לֵיהּ דְּמֵי כִּיסֵי – and in this case, **[the *shomer*] must** indeed **pay [the owner] the value of** inferior hops that are mixed with **thorns;** i.e. he pays the amount by which the value of the beer increased due to the deposited hops.[1]

**Mishnah** The Mishnah teaches other laws that apply to a *shomer* who was given money for safekeeping: הַמַּפְקִיד מָעוֹת אֵצֶל שׁוּלְחָנִי – Concerning **one who deposits money with a moneychanger,**[2] the law is: אִם צְרוּרִין – **If [the money] is tied up** in a bundle, לֹא יִשְׁתַּמֵּשׁ בָּהֶן – **[the moneychanger] may not use it.** לְפִיכָךְ – **Therefore,** אִם אָבְדוּ – **if it is lost,** אֵינוֹ חַיָּיב בְּאַחֲרָיוּתָן – **he is not liable** to pay the owner **for it.**[3] מוּתָּרִין – If, however, **[the money] is loose,** יִשְׁתַּמֵּשׁ בָּהֶן – **he may use it.** לְפִיכָךְ אִם אָבְדוּ – **Therefore, if it is lost,** חַיָּיב בְּאַחֲרָיוּתָן – **he is liable** to pay the owner **for it.**[4]

אֵצֶל בַּעַל הַבַּיִת – But if someone deposits money **with a** private **householder,** בֵּין צְרוּרִין וּבֵין מוּתָּרִין – **whether [the money] is tied up or loose,** לֹא יִשְׁתַּמֵּשׁ בָּהֶן – **[the householder] may not use it.**[5] לְפִיכָךְ אִם אָבְדוּ – **Therefore, if it is lost,** אֵינוֹ חַיָּיב בְּאַחֲרָיוּתָן – **he is not liable** to pay the owner **for it.**

Having distinguished between a moneychanger and a private householder, the Mishnah now discusses the status of a storekeeper with regard to this law:

חֶנְוָנִי כְּבַעַל הַבַּיִת – **A storekeeper is** treated **like a householder;** דִּבְרֵי רַבִּי מֵאִיר – these are **the words of R' Meir.** רַבִּי יְהוּדָה אוֹמֵר – **R' Yehudah says:** חֶנְוָנִי כְּשׁוּלְחָנִי – **A storekeeper is** treated **like a moneychanger.**

**Gemara** The Gemara raises a difficulty with the Mishnah's ruling that a moneychanger who is given tied-up money for safekeeping may not use it:

מִשּׁוּם דִּצְרוּרִין לֹא יִשְׁתַּמֵּשׁ בָּהֶן – **He may not use it because it is tied up?!** What difference does it make whether the money is tied up or not? Since a moneychanger may use money that is *not* tied up, he should be permitted to use tied-up money as well![6] – ? –

The Gemara gives two answers:

אָמַר רַב אַסִּי אָמַר רַב יְהוּדָה – **Rav Assi answered in the name of Rav Yehudah:** בִּצְרוּרִין וַחֲתוּמִין שָׁנוּ – It was **in reference to** a bundle of **[money]** that was not only **tied** but also **sealed as well** that **they taught** this ruling.[7]

The second answer:

רַב מָרִי אָמַר – **Rav Mari answered:** בְּקֶשֶׁר מְשׁוּנֶּה – The Mishnah discusses **a case where** the bundle of money was tied **with an unusual knot.**

An alternative version of Rav Mari's statement:

אִיכָּא דְּאָמְרֵי – **There are those who cite** the following version of R' Mari's statement: בָּעֵי רַב מָרִי – **Rav Mari inquired:** קֶשֶׁר מְשׁוּנֶּה מַאי – **What** is the law concerning a bundle of money tied **with an unusual knot?** Is a moneychanger allowed to use such money?

The Gemara responds to this inquiry:

תֵּיקוּ – **Let [the question] stand** unresolved.[8]

The Gemara quotes from the Mishnah:

מוּתָּרִין יִשְׁתַּמֵּשׁ בָּהֶן כו׳ – If [THE MONEY] IS LOOSE, [THE MONEYCHANGER] MAY USE IT **etc.** Therefore, if the money is lost, he is liable to repay the owner.

Rav Huna defines the extent of the moneychanger's liability:

אָמַר רַב הוּנָא – **Rav Huna said:** וַאֲפִילּוּ נֶאֱנְסוּ – He is liable to repay the owner **even if [the money] was lost through an unavoidable accident.**[9]

The Gemara challenges Rav Huna's view:

וְהָא אָבְדוּ קָתָנֵי – **But the Mishnah says,** "if **it is lost,** he is liable etc." The word "lost" signifies ordinary loss, as opposed to unavoidable loss.[10] – ? –

The Gemara answers:

כִּדְרַבָּה – Our Mishnah may be explained in **the same way as Rabbah** explained a different Mishnah:[11] דְּאָמַר רַבָּה – **For Rabbah said:** נִגְנְבוּ בְּלִסְטִין מְזוּיָּין – When the Mishnah there says **"they were stolen,"** it refers **to** theft by **an armed bandit,** which is an unavoidable loss. אָבְדוּ שֶׁטָּבְעָה סְפִינָתוֹ בַּיָּם – And when the Mishnah there says **"they were lost,"** it refers to a case **where his ship sunk in the sea,** which is an unavoidable loss. Thus, we see that the word "lost" can refer even to unavoidable loss.[12]

The Gemara presents a different view regarding the moneychanger's liability:

וְרַב נַחְמָן אָמַר – **But Rav Nachman said:** נֶאֱנְסוּ לֹא – **If [the money] was lost through an unavoidable accident,** the moneychanger is **not** liable.[13]

NOTES

1. *Rashi.* [The beer improved to a small extent from the addition of the deposited hops. Since the *shomer* benefited by that amount, he must pay it (see 42b note 17).]

2. The word שׁוּלְחָנִי, *moneychanger,* is derived from שֻׁלְחָן, *table.* A moneychanger had a table before him, on which he and his customers would put their money (*Rashi* to 26b ד״ה שולחני).

3. The moneychanger was not paid for watching the money. Therefore, as long as the loss of the deposit did not occur as a result of his negligence, he is not liable to repay the owner.

4. Since he is allowed to use the money, he has the status of either a paid *shomer* or a borrower (this matter is discussed in the Gemara). Either way, he is liable for theft and loss.

5. The reason why a moneychanger is different from a private householder is given in the following note.

6. A moneychanger may use loose money that is given to him for safekeeping, even though the owner did not expressly give him permission to do so. This is because it is assumed that one who gives money to a moneychanger to watch does so with the understanding that the moneychanger will use it, for a moneychanger is constantly in need of money for his work. If the owner does *not* want his money to be used, he is the one who must tell this to the moneychanger. The Gemara argues that since people usually tie up their money, the mere fact that the deposited money was tied up should not be enough to indicate that the owner does not want the money to be used (*Rashi*).

7. A seal is a sure indication that the owner does not want the moneychanger to use his money.

8. For an explanation of the term תֵּיקוּ, see 34b note 17.

9. While the money is in the possession of the moneychanger, since he is allowed to use it, all the benefit that can be derived from it is available to him alone. Therefore, he is considered a borrower (who is liable for unavoidable accidents) from the moment he receives the money, even before he actually uses it (*Rashi* ד״ה ואפילו and ד״ה ואי).

10. At this point, the Gemara assumes that if the Mishnah was referring to unavoidable loss as well, it would have used the word נֶאֱנְסוּ (literally: forced), rather than אָבְדוּ, *lost.* Therefore, from the Mishnah's use of the word אָבְדוּ, *lost,* it seems that the moneychanger's liability is limited to ordinary, avoidable loss.

11. Rabbah's statement was made in reference to *Shekalim* 2:1; it is recorded in the Gemara below, 58a.

12. And this is how Rav Huna interprets this word in our Mishnah as well.

13. According to Rav Nachman, the moneychanger does not assume the

Another incident:

הַהוּא גַּבְרָא דְּאַפְקִיד כְּשׁוּתָא גַּבֵּי חַבְרֵיהּ – **A certain man deposited** some **hops with his fellow,** הֲוָה לֵיהּ לְדִידֵיהּ נַמִּי כַּרְיָא דִּכְשׁוּתָא – **who also had his own pile of hops.** אֲמַר לֵיהּ לְסַרְסֵיהּ – While pointing out his own pile of hops, **[the *shomer*] told his attendant:** מֵהַאי רְמֵי – **"Cast** hops **from this** pile into the beer you are brewing for me." אָזַל רָמָא מֵאִידָךְ – **[His attendant] went and cast** hops **from the other** pile (i.e. the deposited hops) into the beer by mistake. אָמַר רַב עַמְרָם – **Rav Amram said:** הֵיכִי נִדַיְינוּ דַּיָּינֵי לְהַאי דִּינָא – **How should judges rule in this case?** נֵימָא לֵיהּ לְדִידֵיהּ זִיל שַׁלֵּים – If **we tell [the *shomer*]** to **go** and **pay,** אָמַר – **he can say:** אֲנָא אָמְרִי לֵיהּ מֵהַאי רְמֵי – **I said to [my attendant]: "Cast** hops **from this** pile into the beer." I indicated that he should take *my* hops. It was not my mistake![13] נֵימָא לֵיהּ לְסַרְסֵיהּ זִיל שַׁלֵּים – If **we tell his attendant** to **go** and **pay,**[14] אָמַר – **he can say:** לֹא אָמַר לִי – **[The *shomer*] did not say to me,** מֵהַאי רְמֵי – **"Cast** hops **from this** pile, וּמֵהַאי לֹא תִּירְמֵי – **but do not cast** hops **from that** pile!"[15]

The Gemara asks why Rav Amram found it difficult to rule in this case. If the entrusted hops were farther away than the *shomer's,* there is a simple method of ascertaining whether the *shomer* is liable:

וְאִי דְּשָׁהָא שִׁיעוּר לְאַיְתוּיֵי לֵיהּ – **But if [the attendant] waited the amount** of time that it would have taken **to bring [the *shomer*]** his own hops, וְלֹא אַיְיתֵי לֵיהּ – **and did not bring** them **to him** within that time, גָּלֵי אַדַּעְתֵּיהּ דְּנִיחָא לֵיהּ – **[the *shomer*] has shown that it is acceptable to him** that the deposited hops be used. For he knew that the attendant must have taken from the deposited hops, and yet did not rebuke him. – ? –

The Gemara answers:

בְּדְלָא שָׁהָא – We are dealing with a case **where [the attendant] did not wait** any longer than it takes to bring hops from the *shomer's* pile before adding the hops. Therefore, the *shomer* cannot be blamed for the use of the deposited hops.

Again, the Gemara questions why Rav Amram was unsure how to rule in this case:

סוֹף סוֹף – **In the final analysis,** מַאי פְּסֵידָא אִיכָּא – **what loss is there?** וְהָא קָא מִשְׁתַּרְשֵׁי לֵיהּ – **[The *shomer*] gained** from the deposited hops that were cast into his beer.[16] Thus, he should simply replace the owner's hops with his own.[17] – ? –

The Gemara presents two answers:

אָמַר רַב סָמָא בְּרֵיהּ דְּרָבָא – **Rav Sama son of Rava answered:** דַּהֲוָה שִׁיכְרָא חַלָּא – We are dealing with a case **where the** *shomer's* **beer** spoiled and **turned into vinegar.** Since the *shomer* gained no benefit from the entrusted hops, he does not have to pay the owner because of the benefit he received.

The second answer:

רַב אַשִׁי אָמַר – **Rav Ashi answered:** בְּכִיסֵי – The deposited hops were of an inferior type, mixed **with thorns,** and as a result the beer did not turn out as well as the *shomer* had wanted;[18]

NOTES

prerequisite of such a compromise] cannot be assumed when it comes to orphans [who are minors] (*Rashi;* see *Ritva*).

Alternatively: This ruling was not a compromise. For even if the administrator would have told the broker immediately that the ox was toothless, he would not have recouped its full value. [Since it is difficult to keep such an animal alive,] he would have slaughtered it right away and sold its meat cheaply, rather than wait until the next market day, when merchandise is sold for its full value (*Tosafos*). [According to this approach, the "cheap rate" does not necessarily mean two-thirds of the full value. Rather, it means whatever amount the broker would have ended up with had the ox been returned to him right away. Thus, if the herdsman received the ox on a market day, he would have to pay the full value.]

An apparent difficulty: Why is the herdsman liable to pay the broker at all? He was a *shomer* for the orphans, not for the broker! The answer is that this case is comparable to that of the Mishnah above (35b): The owner of a cow leased it to someone who lent it to a third party, and then the cow died while in the borrower's possession. Although the owner has no legal relationship with the borrower, R' Yose rules (and the halachah follows his view) that since the renter has a claim upon the borrower (although the renter did not suffer any loss, for he is not liable for the cow's death), the owner may "take the place" of the renter and litigate against the borrower. Likewise, in our case, since the orphans have a claim against the herdsman, the broker "takes their place" and collects from the herdsman whom they had hired (*Rashi;* see *Tosafos, Ritva*).

13. Since the *shomer* was not paid, he was not expected to take the extra effort to expressly instruct the attendant *not* to take from the entrusted hops (*Ritva*).

14. [Because he actively destroyed the property of another (see *Nachalas Moshe*).]

15. The attendant can claim that he thought that his master was just pointing out one pile merely as an example (*Ritva*).

16. The fact that the deposited hops were used means that the *shomer* still has an equal amount of his own hops (see *Rashi*).

17. *Rashi.* One who benefits from the use of another's property, which is used up as a result, must pay what he benefited (see *Bava Kamma* 20a-21a).

18. The *shomer* was upset that these hops were cast into his beer (*Rashi*). [Therefore, he would not be liable to pay the owner for their full value by replacing them; see Gemara further, top of 43a.]

[א] כל המפקיד על דעת אשתו ובניו הוא מפקיד נימא לה לאימיה זילי שלימי אמרה לא אמר לי דלאו דידיה נינהו דאקברינהו נימא ליה אמאי לא אמרת לה אמר כ"ש דכי אמינא לה דדידי נינהו טפי מזדהרא בהו אלא אמר רבא [א]משתבע איהו דהנהו זוזי אשלמינהו לאימיה ומשתבעא אימיה דהנהו זוזי אותבינהו בקרטליתא ואיגנוב ופטור ההוא אפוטרופא דיתמי דזבן להו תורא ליתמי ומסריה לבקרא לא הוו ליה [ג]ככי ושיני למיכל ומית אמר רמי בר חמא היכי נדיינו דייני להאי דינא נימא ליה לאפוטרופא זיל שלים אמר אנא לבקרא מסרתיה נימא ליה לבקרא זיל שלים אמר אנא בהדי תורי אוקימתיה אוכלא שדאי ליה לא הוה ידעינן דלא אכל מכדי בקרא שומר שכר דיתמי הוא איבעי ליה לעיוני אי איכא פסידא דיתמי הכי נמי והכא במאי עסקינן דליכא פסידא דיתמי דאשכחוהו למריה דתורא ושקול יתמי זוזי מיניה אלא מאן קא טעין מריה דתורא קטעין איבעי ליה לאודוען מאי מודעינן ליה מידע ידע [ב]דמקח טעות הוי [ג]בספסירא דזבן מהכא ומזבין להכא [ד]הלכך מישתבע איהו דלא הוה ידע ומשלם בקרא [ג]דמי בשר בזול [ה]ההוא גברא דאפקיד כשותא גבי חבריה הוה ליה לדידיה נמי כריא דכשותא א"ל לסרסיה מהאי רמי אזל רמא מאידך אמר רב עמרם היכי נדיינו דייני להאי דינא נימא ליה לדידיה זיל שלים אמר אנא אמרי ליה מהאי רמי נימא ליה לסרסיה זיל שלים אמר לא א"ל מהאי רמי ומהאי לא תירמי [ו]ואי דשהא שיעור לאיתויי ליה ולא אייתי ליה גלי אדעתיה דניחא ליה בדלא שהא סוף סוף מאי פסידא איכא והא קא משתרשי ליה א"ר סמא בריה דרבא [ז]דהוה שיכרא חלא רב אשי אמר [ח]בכיסי ומשלם

**רש"י**

כל המפקיד כו'. על דעת שלא יהא שומר נמנע מלמוסרן לאנשי ביתו הגדולים ונאמנים לו הוא דמפקיד: נימא לה לאימיה. שתשלם בשביל שלא קברתו: לבקרא מסרתיה. היה לו להודיעני שאינו אוכל: איבעי ליה לעיוני. אם אוכל אם לאו: אי איכא פסידא ליתמי כו'. תירוצא הוא: דאשכחיה למריה דתורא. המוכר: ושקול דמייהו. דאמרי ליה מקח טעות הוא: אלא מאן טעין. מי תובע כלום דקאמר [ז](רבא) היכי נידיינו: מריה דתורא טעין. ושואל שמתה בהמתו אצלך ותובע את האפוטרופוס: ספסירא. קונה ומוכר בהמות בשוק ביום שקנה מוכר: משתבע ספסירא. דלא הוה ידע: ומשלם בקרא דמי בשר בזול. ותמיה אני מנין לרמי בר חמא דין זה מה לו לספסירא עם הרועה לא שומר שלו הוא ונראה לי דמתניתין (לעיל דף לה:) דהשוכר (א) הפרה לחבירו והשאילה לאחר ומתה כדרכה דקאמר ר' יוסי יחזיר פרה לבעלים ואוקימנא הלכה כר' יוסי אלמא אע"פ שאין הבעלים בעלי דברים של שואל והשוכר שהוא לו בעל דברים אינו חסר כלום שהרי פטור באונסין אפי' הכי הואיל ויש לו דין על השואל לגבות יעמדו הבעלים הראשונים במקומו וגובין מן השואל ה"נ הואיל ויש ליתומים לגבות מן הרועה שהוא שומר שכר שלהם יעמדו בעלים במקום היתומים וגובין ומיהו אי הוה מפסדי יתומים לא היה עושה פשרה בממון יתומים לשלם בזול דיתמי לאו בני מחילה נינהו אבל עכשיו שהוא מגבה לבעלים וכאן אין פשיעה כל כך דאמר בהדי תוראי אוקימתיה כו' הטיל פשרה ביניהם ולא ישלם כל דמי השור כמות שהוא חי אלא העור יחזיר לבעלים והבשר שמין וישלם שני שלישים דהיכא דאמרינן בגמרא משלם בזול כל זוזא שהוא שוה מעה כסף חשבינן בארבעה דנקי [ט] בפרק מי שמת (ב"ב דף קמו:): כשותא. הומלון שמטילין לתוך השכר: כריא. כרי: אמר ליה. בעל הבית: לסרסיה. לאשר על ביתו העושה שכר שלו: מהא רמי. הראהו הכרי שלו וא"ל מזה תטיל [ה]לשכר: מאידך. של פקדון: ואי דשהא שיעור כו'. גמ' פריך אם היה כרי שלו קרוב ושל פקדון רחוק ושהא השליח שיעור מהלך דרך הקרוב ולא אייתי: גלי דעתיה. דבעל הבית דניחא ליה שהרי ידע שמשל פקדון הוי ולא מיחה בידו: והא קמשתרשי ליה. והלא הוא נשכר הכשות של פקדון שהטילו בשכר ושלו עומד וישלם משלו: חלא. החמיץ: בכיסי. שהיתה כישות (ג) גרועה וקוצים מעורבין בה ולא השביח השכר כרצונו וקשה בעיניו שהטילוהו בתוכו:

ומשלם

**תוספות**

כל המפקיד על דעת אשתו ובניו הוא מפקיד. אומר ר"ת דהיינו לענין שאינו יכול לומר את מהמנת לי בשבועה ולא האיך אבל אם פשעו אפי' אין להם מה לשלם ישלם הנפקד דאם לא כן כל מה שהופקד אצל בעה"ב תבא אשתו ותאכל ותפטר ולכך נמי הכא משתבעא אמיה דהנהו זוזי אותבינהו בקרטליתא שלא פשעה והא דקאמר נימא לה לאימי' לישלמא לאו משום דאם לא היה לה מה לשלם שיפטר הנפקד אלא תשלם לבנה כשיהיה לה:

נימא ליה לאפוטרופוס זיל שלים אמר [אנא] לבקרא מסרתיה. משמע דאם לא היתה זאת הטענה הוי פושע וחייב וקשה דבפ' ד' וה' (ב"ק דף לט. ושם ד"ה דאי) אמרינן מעליית מאן מעליית יתומים דאי אמרת מעליית אפוטרופוס ממנעי ולא עבדי אלמא פטורים מן הפשיעה וממתני' דהנזקין (גיטין דף נב.) דקתני מינהו ב"ד לא ישבע מינהו אבי יתומים ישבע אבל שאול אומר חילוף הדברים אין להוכיח דחייב בפשיעה די"ל דהשבועה לא הויא שלא פשע אלא שלא עכב כלום משלהם משום דמורי היתירא דטרח קמייהו וי"ל דודאי אפוטרופוס חייב בפשיעה כדמשמע הכא ולא ממנע כיון שהחזיקוהו בנאמן אבל התם שלא מנוהו לצורך היתומים אלא לתקנת העולם שלא יוזקו משורם התם דוקא חיישינן דלמא ממנעי והכי איתא בירושלמי פרק הנזקין דקאמר אתיא דר' יוחנן כרבנן בתמיה פירוש כרבנן דאמרי מנוהו ב"ד לא ישבע אפילו סבר כאבא שאול בעי ההוא בר נש מיתן בגין דמתקרי מהימן פי' רוצה ליתן אם יפשע ולא ימנע כיון שנקרא נאמן אבל הכא שלא הועמד אלא לתקנת העולם חיישינן דלמא ממנע אתיא דרבי יוסי בר חנינא כאבא שאול בתמיה אפילו סבר כרבנן אדם מבריח עצמו מן השבועה ואין מבריח עצמו מן התשלומין פירוש כשיודע שפשע רוצה לשלם אבל אם נאבד אינו חפץ לשבע שלא פשע דא"כ חושדין אותו [י]:

הכא בספסירא דזבן מהכא וזבן להכא. ומספקא ליה בהא דינא אליבא דר' יוסי דאמר תחזור פרה לבעלים הראשונים אלמא משכיר במקום שוכר קאי ואית ליה דינא בהדי שואל והכא נמי ספסירא במקום יתמי קאי ואית ליה דינא בהדי בקרא כאילו הוי שומר שלו או דלמא לא דמי דהתם ודאי קאי משכיר במקום שוכר דשוכר שייך בגוף הפרה שהרי שכרה אבל גבי יתמי כיון דמקח טעות הוא אין להם בגוף השור מאומה איך יעמוד הספסירא במקומם ומיהו אי לאו דטעין בקרא אנא בהדי תוראי אוקימתיה הוה פשיטא ליה דמיחייב בקרא אע"ג דמקח טעות הוא ולית ליה דינא בהדי ספסירא כיון דפשע חייב דספסירא תובע ליתמי שורו שמת בפשיעה והם שומרים חנם עליו והיתומים יחזרו על הבקרא שיפטרם מן הספסירא כי פושע הוא:

דמי בשר בזול. פרש"י הטיל פשרה ביניהם ורבינו תם פירש דדין גמור הוא דאם היה מודיעו היה הספסירא שוחטו מיד ומוכרו בזול ולא היה יכול להשהותו עד יום השוק שהיה מת קודם: מי אמר לי מהאי רמי מהאי לא תרמי. ואם תאמר דבפ' התקבל (גיטין דף סה: ושם ד"ה הא) תני חדא ערב לי בתמרים ועירב לו בגרוגרות עירובו עירוב ותניא אידך אין עירובו עירוב כאן בשלו כאן בשל חבירו וקמפרש דשלו הוי קפידא ואע"ג דלא אמר ליה מהא לא תערב ויש לומר דבשני מינין הוי קפידא אע"ג דלא א"ל מהאי לא תערב וגבי הבא לי מן החלון והביא מן הדלוסקמא (מעילה כא.) דשליח מעל אע"ג דמין אחד הוא התם מיירי שלא היו במקום אחד והכא מיירי שהיו בבית אחד ולא היה לו לידע שאמר דוקא מהאי רמי [ז]:

בכיסי. פרש"י שהיה הכשות מלא קוצים ולא השביח בשכר כ"א מעט וא"ת פשיטא שלא יתן יותר אלא כמו ששוה להטיל בשכר וי"ל דאע"פ שהיו שוים יותר למאכל בהמה לא ישלם אלא מה ששוה לשכר דראוין הם לבהמה כדאמר בהמוליא [יין] (שבת דף עז:) דגמלא זוטרא גנובתיה משום דאכלה כיסי כי היכי דלא לישתרבו בה ור"ת פירש כיסי הוא שם כשות שצריך ריכוך ובלא ריכוך אין שוה להטיל בשכר ולכך לא היה שכר טוב וקמ"ל שלא ישלם אלא כמו ששוה השכר אע"פ שהיו שוים הרבה יותר שבדבר מועט היה נעשה הריכוך:

מאי

**עין משפט נר מצוה**

צד א מיי' פ"ד מהל' שאלה ופקדון הל' ח סמג עשין פח טוש"ע ח"מ סי' רלא סעי' כג:

צה ב ג ד מיי' פט"ז מהלכות מכירה הל' ט י יא סמג לאוין קע טוש"ע ח"מ סי' רלב סעי' יח:

צו ה ו ז ח מיי' פ"ד מהל' שאל' ופקדון הל' ט סמג עשין פח טוש"ע ח"מ סי' רלא סעי' כה:

**רבינו חננאל**

אמרה אימיה לא אמר לי בני דפקדון נינהו דאטמרינהו בקרקע וברא אמר כל שכן דכי אמינא דידי אינון טפי אזדהרה בהו אמר רבא דמישתבע איהו דהני זוזי אשלמינהו לאימיה דלא יכול למימר ליה אין רצוני שיהא פקדוני ביד אחר דקי"ל כל המפקיד על דעת אשתו ובניו הוא מפקיד ואמו כיוצא בהן ומישתבעא אימיה דהני זוזי אותבינהו בקרטליתא ואיגנוב. וכן הלכה. גרסי' בפרק הכותב לאשתו דין ודברים אין לי בנכסיך ההוא דאפקיד כסא דכספא בי חסא שכיב חסא ולא פקיד אתו לקמיה דרב נחמן אמר ידענא ביה בחסא דלא אמיד ועוד הא קא יהיב סימנא ולא אמרנא אלא דלא רגיל דעייל ונפיק לגביה אבל אי רגיל דעייל ונפיק לגביה אימור איניש אחרינא אפקיד גביה וחזייה האי לסימניה. וקיימא לן כרב נחמן דהא עבדו רבנן עובדא בההוא דאפקיד שב מרגניתא ציירי בסדינא בי ר' מיאשא וביההוא דאפקיד מיטכסא בי רב דימי כרב נחמן. ש"מ דאי אפקיד חד גבי חבריה מידי ושכיב ואיכא סהדי דהאי גברא הוא דאפקיד גביה הדין א) מדלא (בענייניה) שקיל ליה ואפי' מיתמי ולא יכלי למיטען דלמא בתר הכי זבניה אבונן מינך ומה"נ כדאיתיה בחיים נמי לא יכיל למיטען זבינתיה. וראייה אחריתי נמי הא דגרסי' בחזקת הבתים מתיב רב נחמן בר יצחק אומן אין לו חזקה הא אחר יש לו חזקה היכי דמי אי דאיכא עדים אחר אמאי יש לו חזקה ש"מ היכא דאיכא עדים דאפקדיה גביה מעיקרא ליכא חזקה וכן הלכה בתלמוד א"י בשקלים [פ"ד] הלכה מותר שירי לישכה. אדא בר זבינא איתפקד גבי מדלא דיתמי אתא שאיל לר' מני אמר ליה אין בעית ליהוי פסידא עלך ואגרא דתרווייהו שרי. ר' חייה בר אדא איתפקיד גביה מדלא דיתמי עבד כן אגרא ביני וליתמי והפסידא עליה. ההוא אפטרופא דיתמי דזבן תורא ליתמי ומסרה לבקרא לא הוו ליה ככי ושיני למיכל שערי וכיוצא בהן אלא כד הוה גביה מריה הוה ספי ליה גבול השתא לא ספי ליה ומית. אמר רמי בר חמא היכי דינא נימא לאפטרופא שלים אמר אנא לבקרא מסרתיה נימא לבקרא שלים אמר אנא בהדי תורא אוקימתיה אוכלא שדיי ליה לא הוינא ידע דלא מצי למיכל ואמרי' בקרא שומר שכר דיתמי הוא איבעי ליה לעיוני אי איכא פסידא ליתמי ואסיק' אי המוכר בעל הבית הוא מקח טעות הוא וחייב המוכר לשלם ואם המוכר ספסירא הוא דזבין מהכא וזבין להכא מישתבע ספסירא דלא הוינא ידע דלית ליה ככי ושיני ומשלם בקרא דמי בשר בזול. תוספתא [דמכילתין פ"א] המפקיד שטרות אצל חבירו אע"פ שאין כתובין על שמו הרי זה מחזיר לו את שלו מת יתן ליורשיו ואם אמר בשעת מיתתו ינתנו לפלוני שהן שלו יעשה מפורש כפירושו. ההוא דאפקיד כשותא גביה חבריה והוה ליה לדידיה נמי כריא דכשותא אחריתי אמר ליה לסרסיה מיהא כשותא רמי אזל סרסיא רמא מכשותא דהוה פקדון גביה אמר רב עמרם היכי דינא נימא לבעל הפקדון שלים אמר אמרי לסרסיא מכשותא דידי רמי סרסיא אמר לא אודעין מיהא רמי מיהא לא תרמי. חזינן אי שהא סרסיא שיעור לאיתויי מכשותא דידיה ולא אייתי גליא דעתיה דניחא ליה ואי לא שהא משלם למריה דכשותא שיעור מאי

**מסורת הש"ס**

א) לעיל לו., ב) [עי' פירוש בתוס' דע"ז כח. ד"ה ככי] ג) [בבא קמא כ., קיב. כתובות לד:, בבא בתרא קמו:], ד) [נ"ל רמי בר חמא], ה) נ"א בשכר מהרש"ל, ו) [ועי' תוס' גיטין נב: ד"ה הלכה] ז) [ועי' תוס' גיטין סה ד"ה הא והא].

**הגהות הב"ח**

(א) רש"י ד"ה ומשלם וכו' דהשוכר פרה מחבירו וכו' ר' יוסי תחזור (ב) שם ד"ה בכיסי שהיתה כישות זרועה בקוצים וקוצים מעורבין:

**גליון הש"ס**

רש"י ד"ה ומשלם בקרא דמי בשר בזול כו' בפרק מי שמת. עי' בב"ק כ ע"א רש"י ד"ה דמי שעורין:

**לעזי רש"י**

הומלו"ן. פירוש כשות (צמח שמשתמשים בו להכין שכר שעורים ושכר תמרים וכדומה).

**ליקוטי רש"י**

כל המפקיד על דעת אשתו ובניו וכו'. על דעת שהנפקד מוסר לאשתו ובניו הגדולים ואי יכולין לומר אין רצוני וכו' [לעיל לו:]. אפוטרופא. מכניס ומוליא נכסיו [ברכות סג.]. כשותא. כשות [ע"ז לא:]. לסרסיה. שמעיו [בכורות לא:]. עושה שכר מתמרים של בעל הבית למלאכת שכר [קדושין נב:].

חשק שלמה על ר"ח א) אולי נ"ל דאפקיד גביה הדין האי מידי בעיניה שקיל להו אפי' מיתמי וכ"ה הלשון ברי"ף ז"ל כאן וכל לשון הרי"ף ז"ל שם הוא מתורתו של רבינו ז"ל כאן ע"ש.

עַל כָּל הַמַּפְקִיד – **Whoever deposits** something with another דַּעַת אִשְׁתּוֹ וּבָנָיו הוּא מַפְקִיד – **deposits** it **with the understanding** that the *shomer* may give it to **his wife,** grown **children,** or any other member of his household whom he trusts, for safekeeping. In our case, therefore, the *shomer's* transfer of the coins to his mother's safekeeping should not be considered negligence. נֵימָא לָהּ לְאִימֵּיהּ זִילִי שַׁלֵּימִי – If **we tell his mother** to **go and pay,** because she was negligent in that she did not bury the coins,[1] אָמְרָה – **she may say:** לֹא אָמַר לִי דְּלָאו דִּידֵיהּ נִינְהוּ – **[My son] did not tell me that [the coins] were not his,** דְּאֶקְבְּרִינְהוּ – **so that I would** have known to **bury them.**[2] נֵימָא לֵיהּ – **Shall we tell [the *shomer*]:** אַמַּאי לֹא אָמַרְתְּ לָהּ – **Why did you not tell [your mother]** that the coins were not yours? אָמַר – **He can say:** כָּל שֶׁכֵּן דְּכִי אֲמִינָא לָהּ דְּדִידִי נִינְהוּ טְפֵי מִזְדַּהֲרָא בְּהוּ – I thought that **if I would tell her that they were mine, she certainly would take better care of them!**

Rava decides the halachah:

אֶלָּא אָמַר רָבָא – **Rather, Rava said:** מִשְׁתַּבַּע אִיהוּ דְּהָנְהוּ זוּזֵי אַשְׁלְמִינְהוּ לְאִימֵּיהּ – **[The *shomer*] swears that he gave over these coins to his mother,** וּמִשְׁתַּבְּעָא אִימֵּיהּ דְּהָנְהוּ זוּזֵי אוֹתְבִינְהוּ בְּקַרְטַלִיתָא וְאִיגְּנוּב – **and his mother swears that she put these coins in a chest and they were stolen.** וּפָטוּר – **And** then **[the *shomer*] is not liable** to pay compensation.[3]

Another incident:

הַהוּא אַפּוֹטְרוֹפָּא דְיַתְמֵי – **A certain administrator of** property that belonged to **orphans** דְּזָבַן לְהוּ תּוֹרָא לְיַתְמֵי – **bought an ox for the orphans** וּמַסְרֵיהּ לְבַקָּרָא – **and gave it over to a herdsman** for safekeeping. לֹא הֲוּ לֵיהּ כַּבֵּי וְשִׁינֵּי לְמֵיכַל – **[The ox] did not have molars or** front **teeth** with which **to eat,** וּמִית – **and it died** of starvation as a result. אָמַר רָמִי בַּר חָמָא – **Rami bar Chama said:** הֵיכִי נִדַיְינוּ דַּיָּינֵי לְהַאי דִּינָא – **How should judges rule in this case?** נֵימָא לֵיהּ לְאַפּוֹטְרוֹפָּא זִיל שַׁלֵּים – If **we tell [the administrator]** to **go** and **pay** the orphans,[4] אָמַר – **he can say:** אֲנָא לְבַקָּרָא מְסַרְתֵּיהּ – **I entrusted [the ox] to a herdsman.** It was his responsibility to inform me that the ox was not eating![5] נֵימָא לֵיהּ לְבַקָּרָא זִיל שַׁלֵּים – **If we tell the herdsman** to **go** and **pay,** אָמַר – **he can say:** אֲנָא בַּהֲדֵי תּוֹרֵי אוֹקִימְתֵּיהּ – **I put [the ox] together with the** other **oxen** אוּכְלָא שְׁדַאי לֵיהּ – **and I threw food to it.** לֹא הֲוָה יָדְעִינַן דְּלֹא אָכַל – **I was not aware that it was not eating!**[6]

The Gemara challenges this plea:

מִכְּדִי – **Let us see:** בַּקָּרָא שׁוֹמֵר שָׂכָר דְּיַתְמֵי הוּא – **The herdsman is a paid *shomer*,** as he was hired to work **for the orphans.** אִיבָּעֵי לֵיהּ לְעַיּוּנֵי – Therefore, **he should have paid attention** as to whether or not the ox was eating.[7] Since he failed to do so, he should be liable to pay the orphans. – ? –

The Gemara answers:

אִי אִיכָּא פְּסֵידָא דְיַתְמֵי – **If there would have been a loss to the orphans,** הָכִי נָמִי – **indeed,** the herdsman would have been obligated to pay them. וְהָכָא בְּמַאי עַסְקִינַן – **However, what are we dealing with here?** דְּלֵיכָּא פְּסֵידָא דְיַתְמֵי – We are dealing with a case **where there is no loss to the orphans,** דְּאַשְׁכְּחוּהוּ לְמָרֵיהּ דְּתוֹרָא – **for they had found the** previous **owner of the ox,** וְשָׁקוּל יַתְמֵי זוּזֵי מִינֵּיהּ – **and,** since the sale was invalid,[8] **the orphans had taken** their **money** back **from him.**

Since the orphans did not suffer a loss, the Gemara asks:

אֶלָּא מַאן קָא טָעֵין – **But** then **who is demanding** payment?[9] מָרֵיהּ דְּתוֹרָא קָטָעֵין – **The** original **owner of the ox is demanding** payment from the administrator, claiming: אִיבָּעֵי לֵיהּ לְאוֹדוּעַן – **He should have notified me** that the animal had no teeth![10]

The Gemara rejects this claim:

מַאי מוֹדְעִינַן לֵיהּ – **What should [the administrator] have told him?** מֵידַע יָדַע דְּמִקָּח טָעוּת הֲוֵי – **[The owner] himself knew that it was a mistaken purchase.** Surely he was aware that his ox was toothless! – ? –

The Gemara explains why the owner's claim is valid:

בְּסַפְסִירָא – Here we are dealing **with a broker,** דְּזָבֵן מֵהָכָא וּמְזַבֵּין לְהָכָא – **who buys** from **here and sells** to **there** on the same day. Since the animal was in his possession for only a short time, he might not have been aware that it had no teeth; and it is the broker who is demanding payment from the administrator.

Rami bar Chama decided the law as follows:

הִלְכָּךְ מִישְׁתַּבַּע אִיהוּ דְּלֹא הֲוָה יָדַע – **Therefore,**[11] **[the owner] swears that he did not know** that the ox was toothless, מְשַׁלֵּם בַּקָּרָא דְּמֵי בָשָׂר בְּזוֹל – **and the herdsman pays** the broker **the value of** the ox's **meat** when sold **at the cheap rate.**[12]

NOTES

1. Since the mother was negligent, she pays her son (for whom she was appointed as a *shomer*), and the son pays the owner. If the mother has no money with which to pay, the son must pay the owner regardless (see *Tosafos, Rosh;* cf. *Ritva* and *Rambam, Hil. She'eilah U'Fikadon* 4:9).

The mother's failure to bury the money is considered negligence on her part. This incident took place in a time when people would keep their money in the ground, and thus a *shomer* who was entrusted with money, even if he was unpaid, was required to bury it (*Ritva*; see 42a note 21).

2. Since the mother thought that the coins were her son's, her failure to bury the coins does not constitute negligence, because she can claim that she thought that her son wanted the coins to be readily available to him (see *Ramban*). [This claim, however, is valid only with regard to her son. A son might entrust coins to his mother and yet want them to be readily available. Had she known that the coins belonged to an outside party, she would have been expected to bury them, for an outside party would not deposit coins with another person if he thinks that he might need them back quickly (see 42a note 7).]

3. The mother certainly is not liable.

[The Rishonim differ as to whether these oaths are required only Rabbinically or even Biblically (see *Ketzos HaChoshen*) 291:8 for discussion).]

4. Because he was negligent, in that he bought an ox without checking whether it had teeth (*Ritva*).

5. The administrator can claim that it was not his responsibility to inspect the animal, as he gave it over to a herdsman for that purpose (*Ritva*).

6. [The herdsman can claim that he is not required to check that each and every animal in his herd is eating (as most animals will eat on their own), and his failure to do so does not constitute negligence.]

7. [Since he was a paid *shomer*, he was obligated to take extra measures to safeguard the ox (see 42a note 2).]

8. *Rashi*. [For there was a severe deficiency in the animal that the seller did not inform the buyer about, and this causes the sale to be invalid.]

9. From Rami bar Chama's question, "How should judges rule in this case," it is evident that someone was making a claim (*Rashi*).

10. [Since the sale was invalid, the ox is still the property of the seller.] He therefore made a claim against the administrator for allowing his ox to die (*Rashi*).

11. [I.e. since the orphans themselves were repaid by the broker, so they suffered no loss; see following note.]

12. The cheap rate is two-thirds of the normal market value (see *Bava Basra* 146b). The herdsman must also return the ox's hide to the broker.

This represents a compromise settlement. In truth, since the herdsman was a paid *shomer,* he should have been liable to pay the full value. However, Rami bar Chama had compassion on him, for his claim (viz. "I put it with the other oxen etc.") does have some validity.

Had the loss been borne by the orphans, Rami bar Chama would not have imposed a compromise on them, for a waiver of rights [which is a

עין משפט
נר מצוה

צד א מיי' פ"ד מהל' שאלה ופקדון הל' ח סמג עשין פח טוש"ע ח"מ סי' רצא סעי' כג:

צה ב ג ד מיי' פט"ו מהלכות מכירה הל' ט י יא סמג לאוין קע טוש"ע ח"מ סי' רלב סעי' יח:

צו ה ו ז ח מיי' פ"ד מהל' שאל' ופקדון הל' ט סמג עשין פח טוש"ע ח"מ סי' רצא סעי' כה:

מסורת הש"ס

א) לעיל לו., ב) [עי' פירושו בתוס' דע"ז כח. ד"ה כיון], ג) [בבא קמא כ., קיב., כתובות לד:, בבא בתרא קמו:], ד) [נ"ל רמי בר חמא], ה) נ"א בשכר, מהרש"ל, ו) [ועי' תוס' גיטין נג: ד"ה הלכה], ז) [ועי' תוס' גיטין סה: ד"ה הא והא].

א) כל המפקיד על דעת אשתו ובניו הוא מפקיד נימא לה לאימיה זילי שלימי אמרה לא אמר לי דלאו דידיה נינהו דאקברינהו נימא ליה אמאי לא אמרת לה אמר כ"ש דכי אמינא לה דדידי נינהו טפי מזדהרא בהו אלא אמר רבא א משתבע איהו דהנהו זוזי אשלמינהו לאימיה ומשתבעא אימיה דהנהו זוזי אותבינהו בקרטליתא ואיגנוב ופטור ההוא אפוטרופא דיתמי דזבן להו תורא ליתמי ומסריה לבקרא לא הוו ליה ב) ככי ושיני למיכל ומית אמר רמי בר חמא היכי נדיינו דייני להאי דינא נימא ליה לאפוטרופא זיל שלים אמר אנא לבקרא מסרתיה נימא ליה לבקרא זיל שלים אמר אנא בהדי תורי אוקימתיה אוכלא שדאי ליה לא הוה ידעינן דלא אכל מכדי בקרא שומר שכר דיתמי הוא איבעי ליה לעיוני אי איכא פסידא דיתמי הכי נמי והכא במאי עסקינן דליכא פסידא דיתמי דאשכחוהו למריה דתורא ושקול יתמי זוזי מיניה אלא מאן קא טעין מריה דתורא קטעין איבעי ליה לאודוען מאי מודעינן ליה מידע ידע ב דמקח טעות הוי ג בספסירא דזבן מהכא ומזבין להכא ד הלכך מישתבע איהו דלא הוה ידע ומשלם בקרא ג) דמי בשר בזול ה ההוא גברא דאפקיד כשותא גבי חבריה הוה ליה לדידיה נמי כריא דכשותא א"ל לסרסיה מהאי רמי אזל רמא מאידך אמר רב עמרם היכי נדיינו דייני להאי דינא נימא ליה לדידיה זיל שלים אמר אנא אמרי ליה מהאי רמי נימא ליה לסרסיה זיל שלים אמר לא א"ל מהאי רמי ומהאי לא תירמי ו ואי דשהא שיעור לאיתויי ליה ולא אייתי ליה גלי אדעתיה דניחא ליה בדלא שהא סוף סוף מאי פסידא איכא והא קא משתרשי ליה א"ר סמא בריה דרבא ז דהוה שיכרא חלא רב אשי אמר ח בכיסי ומשלם

רש"י

כל המפקיד כו'. על דעת שלא יהא שומר נמנע מלמוסרן לאנשי ביתו הגדולים ונאמנים לו הוא דמפקיד: נימא לה לאימיה. שתשלם בשביל שלא קברתו: לבקרא מסרתיה. היה לו להודיעני שאינו אוכל: איבעי ליה לעיוני. אם אוכל אם לאו: אי איכא פסידא ליתמי כו'. תירוצא הוא: דאשכחיה למריה דתורא. המוכר: ושקול דמיהו. דאמרי ליה מקח טעות הוא: אלא מאן טעין. מי תובע כלום דקאמר ד) (רבא) היכי נידיינו: מריה דתורא טעין. ושואל שמתה בהמתו אצלך ותובע את האפוטרופוס: ספסירא. קונה ומוכר בהמות בשוק ביום שקנה מוכר: משתבע ספסירא. דלא הוה ידע: ומשלם בקרא דמי בשר בזול. ותמיה אני מנין לרמי בר חמא דין זה מה לו לספסירא עם הרועה לא שומר שלו הוא ונראה לי דמתניתין (לעיל דף לה:) דהשוכר (א) הפרה לחבירו והשאילה לאחר ומתה כדרכה דקאמר ר' יוסי יחזיר פרה לבעלים ואוקימנא הלכה כר' יוסי אלמא אע"פ שאין הבעלים בעלי דברים של שואל והשוכר שהוא לו בעל דברים אינו חסר כלום שהרי פטור באונסין אפי' הכי הואיל ויש לו דין על השואל לגבות יעמדו הבעלים הראשונים במקומו וגובין מן השואל ה"נ הואיל ויש ליתומים לגבות מן הרועה שהוא שומר שכר שלהם יעמדו בעלים במקום היתומים וגובין ומיהו אי הוה מפסדי יתומים לא היה עושה פשרה בממון יתומים לשלם בזול דיתמי לאו בני מחילה נינהו אבל עכשיו שהוא מגבה לבעלים וכאן אין פשיעה כל כך דאמר בהדי תוראי אוקימתיה כו' הטיל פשרה ביניהם ולא ישלם כל דמי השור כמות שהוא חי אלא העור יחזיר לבעלים והבשר שמין וישלם שני שלישים דהיכא דאמרינן בגמרא משלם בזול כל זוזא שהוא שש מעה כסף חשבינן בארבעה דנקי ט בפרק מי שמת (ב"ב דף קמו:): כשותא. הומלון שמטילין לתוך השכר: כריא. כרי: אמר ליה. בעל הבית: לסרסיה. לאשר על ביתו העושה שכר שלו: מהא רמי. הראהו הכרי שלו וא"ל מזה תטיל ה) לשכר: מאידך. של פקדון: ואי דשהא שיעור כו'. גמ' פריך אם היה כרי שלו קרוב ושל פקדון רחוק ושהא השליח שיעור מהלך דרך הקרוב ולא אייתי: גלי דעתיה. דבעל הבית דניחא ליה שהרי ידע שמשל פקדון הוי ולא מיחה בידו: והא קמשתרשי ליה. והלא הוא נשכר הכשות של פקדון שהטילו בשכר ושלו עומד וישלם משלו: חלא. החמיץ: בכיסי. שהיתה כישות (ב) גרועה וקוצים מעורבין בה ולא השביח השכר כרצונו וקשה בעיניו שהטילוהו בתוכו:

תוספות

כל המפקיד על דעת אשתו ובניו הוא מפקיד. אומר ר"ת דהיינו לענין שאינו יכול לומר את מהמנת לי בשבועה ולא האיך אבל אם פשעו אפי' אין להם מה לשלם ישלם הנפקד דאם לא כן כל מה שהופקד אצל בעה"ב תבא אשתו ותאכל ותפטר ולכך נמי הכא משתבעא אמיה דהנהו זוזי אותבינהו בקרטליתא שלא פשעה והא דקאמר נימא לה לאימי' דלישלמא לאו משום דאם לא היה לה מה לשלם שיפטר הנפקד אלא תשלם לבנה כשיהיה לה:

נימא ליה לאפוטרופוס זיל שלים אמר [אנא] לבקרא מסרתיה. משמע דאם לא היתה זאת הטענה הוי פושע וחייב וקשה דבפ' ד' וה' (ב"ק דף לט. ושם ד"ה דאי) אמרינן מעליית מאן מעליית יתומים דאי אמרת מעליית אפוטרופוס ממנעי ולא עבדי אלמא פטורים מן הפשיעה וממתני' דהנזקין (גיטין דף נב.) דקתני מינהו ב"ד לא ישבע מינהו אבי יתומים ישבע אבא שאול אומר חילוף הדברים אין להוכיח דחייב בפשיעה די"ל דהשבועה לא הויא שלא פשע אלא שלא עכב כלום משלהם משום דמורי היתירא דטרח קמייהו וי"ל דודאי אפוטרופוס חייב בפשיעה כדמשמע הכא ולא ממנע כיון שהחזיקוהו בנאמן אבל התם שלא מנוהו לצורך היתומים אלא לתקנת העולם שלא יוזקו משורם התם דוקא חיישינן דלמא ממנעי והכי איתא בירושלמי פרק הנזקין דקאמר אתיא דר' יוחנן כרבנן בתמיה פירוש כרבנן דאמרי מנוהו ב"ד לא ישבע אפילו סבר כאבא שאול בעי ההוא בר נש מיתן בגין דמתקרי מהימן פי' רוצה ליתן אם יפשע ולא ימנע כיון שנקרא נאמן אבל הכא שלא הועמד אלא לתקנת העולם חיישינן דלמא ממנע אתיא דרבי יוסי בר חנינא כאבא שאול בתמיה אפילו סבר כרבנן אדם מבריח עצמו מן השבועה ואין מבריח עצמו מן התשלומין פירוש כשיודע שפשע רוצה לשלם אבל אם נאבד אינו חפץ לשבע שלא פשע דא"כ חושדין אותו ו):

הכא בספסירא דזבן מהכא וזבן להכא. ומספקא ליה בהא דינא אליבא דר' יוסי דאמר תחזור פרה לבעלים הראשונים אלמא משכיר במקום שוכר קאי ואית ליה דינא בהדי שואל והכא נמי ספסירא במקום יתמי קאי ואית ליה דינא בהדי בקרא כאילו הוי שומר שלו או דלמא לא דמי דהתם ודאי קאי משכיר במקום שוכר דשוכר שייך בגוף הפרה שהרי שכרה אבל גבי יתמי כיון דמקח טעות הוא אין להם בגוף השור מאומה איך יעמוד הספסירא במקומם ומיהו אי לאו דטעין בקרא אנא בהדי תוראי אוקימתיה הוה פשיטא ליה דמיחייב בקרא אע"ג דמקח טעות הוא ולית ליה דינא בהדי ספסירא כיון דפשע חייב דספסירא תובע ליתמי שורו שמת בפשיעה והם שומרים חנם עליו והיתומים יחזרו על הבקרא שיפטרם מן הספסירא כי פושע הוא:

דמי בשר בזול. פרש"י הטיל פשרה ביניהם ורבינו תם פירש דדין גמור הוא דאם היה מודיעו היה הספסירא שוחטו מיד ומוכרו בזול ולא היה יכול להשהותו עד יום השוק שהיה מת קודם: מי אמר לי מהאי רמי מהאי לא תרמי. ואם תאמר דבפ' התקבל (גיטין דף סה: ושם ד"ה הא) תני חדא ערב לי בתמרים ועירב לו בגרוגרות עירובו עירוב ותניא אידך אין עירובו עירוב כאן בשלו כאן בשל חבירו וקמפרש דשלו הוי קפידא ואע"ג דלא אמר ליה מהא לא תערב ויש לומר דבשני מינין הוי קפידא אע"ג דלא א"ל מהאי לא תערב וגבי הבא לי מן החלון והביא מן הדלוסקמא (מעילה כא.) דשליח מעל אע"ג דמין אחד הוא התם מיירי שלא היו במקום אחד והכא מיירי שהיו בבית אחד ולא היה לו לידע שאמר דוקא מהאי רמי ז):

בכיסי. פרש"י שהיה הכשות מלא קוצים ולא השביח בשכר כ"א מעט וא"ת פשיטא שלא יתן יותר אלא כמו ששוה להטיל בשכר וי"ל דאע"פ שהיו שוים יותר למאכל בהמה לא ישלם אלא מה ששוה לשכר דראוין הם לבהמה כדאמר בהמוליא [יין] (שבת דף עז:) דגמלא זוטרא גנובתיה משום דאכלה כיסי כי היכי דלא ליסתרבו בה ור"ת פירש כיסי הוא שם כשות שצריך ריכוך ובלא ריכוך אין שוה להטיל בשכר ולכך לא היה שכר טוב וקמ"ל שלא ישלם אלא כמו ששוה השכר אע"פ שהיו שוים הרבה יותר שבדבר מועט היה נעשה הריכוך:

מאי

רבינו חננאל

אמרה אימיה לא אמר לי בני דפקדון נינהו דאטמרינהו בקרקע וברא אמר כל שכן דכי אמינא דידי אינון טפי אזדהרה בהו אלא אמר רבא דמישתבע איהו דהני זוזי אשלמינהו לאימיה דלא יכול למימר ליה אין רצוני שיהא פקדוני ביד אחר דקי"ל כל המפקיד על דעת אשתו ובניו הוא מפקיד ואמו כיוצא בהן ומישתבעא אימיה דהני זוזי אותבינהו בקרטליתא ואיגנוב. וכן הלכה. גרסי' בפרק הכותב לאשתו דין ודברים אין לי בנכסיך ההוא דאפקיד כסא דכספא בי חסא שכיב חסא ולא פקיד אתו לקמיה דרב נחמן אמר ידענא ביה בחסא דלא אמיד ועוד הא קא יהיב סימנא ולא אמרנא אלא דלא רגיל דעייל ונפיק לגביה אבל אי רגיל דעייל ונפיק לגביה אימור איניש אחרינא אפקיד גביה וחזייה האי לסימניה. וקיימא לן כרב נחמן דהא עבדו רבנן עובדא בההוא דאפקיד שב מרגניתא ציירי בסדינא בי ר' מיאשא ובההוא דאפקיד מיטכסא בי רב דימי כרב נחמן. ש"מ דאי אפקיד חד גבי חבריה מידי ושכיב ואיכא סהדי דהאי גברא הוא דאפקיד גביה חדין א) מדלא (בעניניה) שקיל ליה ואפי' מיתמי ולא יכלי למיטען דלמא בתר הכי זבניה אבונן מינך ומה"נ כדאיתיה בחיים נמי לא יכיל למיטען זבינתיה. וראייה אחריתי נמי הא דגרסי' בחזקת הבתים מתיב רב נחמן בר יצחק אומן אין לו חזקה הא אחר יש לו חזקה היכי דמי אי דאיכא עדים אחר אמאי יש לו חזקה ש"מ היכא דאיכא עדים דאפקדיה גביה מעיקרא ליכא חזקה וכן הלכה בתלמוד א"י בשקלים [פ"ד] הלכה מותר שירי לישכה. אדא בר זבינא איתפקד גבי מדלא דיתמי אתא שאיל לר' מני אמר ליה אין בעית ליהוי פסידא עלך ואגרא דתרווייהו שרי. ר' חייה בר אדא איתפקיד גביה מדלא דיתמי עבד כן אגרא ביני וליתמי והפסידא עליה. ההוא אפטרופא דיתמי דזבן תורא ליתמי ומסרה לבקרא לא הוו ליה ככי ושיני למיכל שערי וכיוצא בהן אלא כד הוה גביה מריה הוה ספי ליה גבול השתא לא ספי ליה ומית. אמר רמי בר חמא היכי דינא נימא לאפטרופא שלים אמר אנא לבקרא מסרתיה נימא לבקרא שלים אמר אנא בהדי תורא אוקימתיה אוכלא שדיי ליה לא הוינא ידע דלא מצי למיכל ואמרי' בקרא שומר שכר דיתמי הוא איבעי ליה לעיוני אי איכא פסידא ליתמי ואסיק' אי המוכר בעל הבית הוא מקח טעות הוא וחייב המוכר לשלם ואם המוכר ספסירא הוא דזבין מהכא וזבין להכא מישתבע ספסירא דלא הוינא ידע דלית ליה ככי ושיני ומשלם בקרא דמי בשר בזול. תוספתא [דמכילתין פ"א] המפקיד שטרות אצל חבירו אע"פ שאין כתובין על שמו הרי זה מחזיר לו את שלו מת יתן ליורשיו ואם אמר בשעת מיתתו ינתנו לפלוני שהן שלו יעשה מפורש כפירושו. ההוא דאפקיד כשותא גביה חבריה והוה ליה לדידיה נמי כריא דכשותא אחריתי אמר ליה לסרסיה מיהא כשותא רמי אזל סרסיא רמא מכשותא דהוה פקדון גביה אמר רב עמרם היכי דינא נימא לבעל הפקדון שלים אמר אמרי לסרסיא מכשותא דידי רמי סרסיא אמר לא אודעין מיהא רמי מיהא לא תרמי. חזינן אי שהא סרסיא שיעור לאייתויי מכשותא דידיה ולא אייתי גליא דעתיה דניחא ליה ואי לא שהא משלם למריה דכשותא שיעור מאי

חשק שלמה על ר"ח א) אולי צ"ל דאפקיד גביה הדין האי מידי בעיניה שקיל להו אפי' מיתמי וכ"ה הלשון ברי"ף ז"ל כאן וכל לשון הרי"ף ז"ל שם הוא מתורתו של רבינו ז"ל כאן ע"ש.

הגהות הב"ח

(א) רש"י ד"ה ומשלם וכו' דהשוכר פרה מחבירו וכו' ר' יוסי תחזור: (ב) שם ד"ה בכיסי שהיתה כישות זרועה בקוצים וקוצים מעורבין:

גליון הש"ס

רש"י ד"ה ומשלם בקרא דמי בשר בזול כו' בפרק מי שמת. עי' בב"ק כ ע"א רש"י ד"ה דמי שעורין:

לעזי רש"י

הומלו"ן. פירוש כשות (צמח שמשתמשים בו להכין שכר שעורים ושכר תמרים וכדומה).

ליקוטי רש"י

כל המפקיד על דעת אשתו ובניו וכו'. על דעת שהנפקד מוסרו לאשתו ובניו הגדולים ואין יכולין לומר אין רצוננו וכו' [לעיל לו:]. אפוטרופא. מכניס ומוציא נכסיו [ברכות סג.]. כשותא. כשות [ע"ז לא:]. לסרסיה. שמעיה [בכורות לא:]. עושה שכר מתמרים של בעל הבית למתלים שכר [קדושין נב:].

מתני' א המפקיד מעות אצל חברו צררן והפשילן לאחוריו ב או שמסרם לבנו ולבתו הקטנים ג ונעל בפניהם שלא כראוי חייב שלא שימר כדרך השומרים ואם שימר כדרך השומרים פטור: גמ' בשלמא כולהו שלא שימר כדרך השומרים אלא צררן והפשילן לאחוריו מאי הוה ליה למיעבד אמר רבא א"ר יצחק אמר קרא א) וצרת הכסף בידך ג אע"פ שצרורין יהיו בידך וא"ר יצחק לעולם יהא כספו של אדם מצוי בידו שנאמר וצרת הכסף בידך וא"ר יצחק לעולם ישליש אדם את מעותיו שליש בקרקע ושליש בפרקמטיא ושליש תחת ידו ד וא"ר יצחק אין הברכה מצוייה אלא בדבר הסמוי מן העין שנאמר ב) יצו ה' אתך את הברכה באסמיך תנא דבי רבי ישמעאל אין הברכה מצויה אלא בדבר שאין העין שולטת בו שנאמר יצו ה' אתך את הברכה באסמיך ת"ר ד ההולך למוד את גורנו אומר יהי רצון מלפניך ה' אלהינו שתשלח ברכה במעשה ידינו התחיל למוד אומר ברוך השולח ברכה בכרי הזה מדד ואח"כ בירך הרי זה תפילת שוא ה לפי שאין הברכה מצוייה לא בדבר השקול ולא בדבר המדוד ולא בדבר המנוי אלא בדבר הסמוי מן העין שנאמר יצו ה' אתך את הברכה באסמיך אמר שמואל ו כספים אין להם שמירה אלא בקרקע אמר רבא ומודי שמואל ז בערב שבת בין השמשות דלא אטרחוהו רבנן ח ואי שהא למוצאי שבת שיעור למקברינהו ולא קברינהו מחייב ט ואי צורבא מרבנן הוא סבר דלמא מיבעי ליה זוזי לאבדלתא והאידנא דשכיחי גשושאי אין להן שמירה אלא בשמי קורה והאידנא דשכיחי פרומאי אין להם שמירה אלא ביני אורבי אמר רבא ומודה שמואל בכותל י (אי נמי בין הקרנות) י והאידנא דשכיחי טפוחאי אין להן שמירה אלא בטפח הסמוך לקרקע או בטפח הסמוך לשמי קורה א"ל רב אחא בריה דרב יוסף לרב אשי התם תנן ז כ חמץ שנפלה עליו מפולת הרי הוא כמבוער רשב"ג אומר כל שאין הכלב יכול לחפש אחריו ותנא כמה חפישת הכלב ג' טפחים הכא מאי מי בעינן שלשה טפחים או לא אמר ליה התם משום ריחא בעינן ג' טפחים הכא משום איכסויי מעינא לא בעינן ג' טפחים וכמה אמר רפרם מסיכרא ל טפח ההוא גברא דאפקיד זוזי גבי חבריה אותבינהו בצריפא דאורבני איגנוב אמר רב יוסף מ אע"ג דלענין גנבי נטירותא היא לענין נורא פשיעותא היא הוה ט תחלתו בפשיעה וסופו באונס חייב ואיכא דאמרי אע"ג דלענין נורא פשיעותא היא לענין גנבי נטירותא היא ותחלתו בפשיעה וסופו באונס פטור והילכתא תחלתו בפשיעה וסופו באונס חייב ההוא גברא דאפקיד זוזי גבי חבריה א"ל הב לי זוזאי א"ל לא ידענא היכא אותבינהו אתא לקמיה דרבא א"ל י נ כל לא ידענא פשיעותא היא זיל שלים ס ההוא גברא דאפקיד זוזי גבי חבריה אשלמינהו לאימיה ואותבינהו בקרטליתא ואיגנוב אמר רבא היכי נדיינו דייני להאי דינא נימא ליה לדידיה זיל שלים אמר

כל

**רש"י**

מתני' צררן. בסודרו והפשילן לאחוריו: גמ' מאי הוה ליה למיעבד. הרי צררן: מצוי בידו. לא יפקידנו לאחרים במקום אחר שאם תזדמן לו סחורה לשכר יהא מזומן לו: תחת ידו. להיות מזומן לו לצורך ריוח הבא פתאום: אין הברכה. שמתברך ורבה מאליו פויישו"ן בלעז: באסמיך. דריש ליה לשון דבר הסמוי מן העין: שאין העין שולטת בו. שנאמר באסמיך לשון גנזים: אין להם שמירה כו'. דאם לא טמנן ונגנבו פשיעה היא: ואם צורבא מרבנן הוא. המפקיד שהוא חרד על מצות הבדלה על הכוס אמר השומר דלמא מיבעי ליה זוזי לאבדלתא להכי לא קברינהו ופטור: גשושאי. מגששין בקרקע בשפודין של ברזל להכיר מקום שתחתיו חלל: בשמי קורה. בגג מתחתיו: פרומאי. סותרי התקרה: ביני אורבי. בין שורות הבנין בכותל: טפוחאי. מטפחים בכותל לידע אם יש שם חלל: או בטפח הסמוך כו'. וכולן בכותל: הרי הוא כמבוער. ואין צריך לבערו דאין כאן עוד בל יראה: הכא מאי. לענין שמירת כספים: משום ריחא. שהכלב מריח וחופש אחריו והרי הוא מוציאו ונראה: מסיכרא. שם מקום: צריפא דאורבני. בית קטן עגול כמין כובע שעושין ליידי עופות לארוב: דאורבני. של ערבה היה: אע"ג דלענין גנבי נטירותא היא. אפי' בלא קבורה שאין גנבי' הולכין שם לגנוב שאין ממון מצוי שם: תחלתו בפשיעה. שמא תפול שם דליקה ונמצא פשע שלא קברן: וסופו באונס. שהרי נגנבו וגניבה לשומר חנם אונס הוא: אשלמינהו. מסרן לאמו: קרטליתא. ארגז אשקר"א בלע"ז: נימא ליה לדידיה [זיל] שלים. דשומר שמסר לשומר חייב:

כל

**תוספות**

אמר שמואל כספים אין להם שמירה כו'. צריך עיון אם שמרס בקרקע (א) ונגנבו משם אם שומר שכר חייב ובפרק הכונס (ב"ק דף מ. ושם ד"ה כגון) משמע דחייב דפריך אביי לרב יוסף והאמר ר' יוחנן הטוען טוענת גנב באבידה משלם תשלומי כפל ואי שומר אבידה שומר שכר הוי קרנא בעי לשלומי ומאי פריך דלוקמא בטוען שנגנבה באונס כגון שהעמיק בקרקע ק' אמות או שתקפתו שינה או חולי אלמא כל גניבה לא הויא אונס אלא לסטים מזויין וכן בתר הכי דמייתי לא אי אמרת בשומר חנם שכן משלם כפל ואי לסטים מזויין גנב הוא שומר שכר נמי משלם כפל משמע דמשום גניבה לא מפטר שומר שכר אם לא בטענת גניבת ליסטים מזויין מיהו הנהו יש לדחות דה"מ למימר וליטעמיך דבלאו הכי נמי מצי למימר וליטעמיך אפי' גזלן הוא תמלא שומר שכר משלם כפל בבעלים ויש להביא ראיה מפ' השואל (לקמן דף צה. ושם) דכי יליף גניבה ואבידה בשואל משומר שכר פריך מה לשומר שכר שכן משלם כפל בטענת ליסטין מזויין ומשני אי בעית אימא גזלן הוא משמע שאין שום גניבה שיפטר בה שומר שכר אך תמהון גדול הוא למה לא יהא אונס אם העמיק בקרקע ק' אמות דמאי ה"ל תו למיעבד או אם תקפתו שינה או חולי גדול ואיך יתכן שמום גניבה לא נמלא שתהא אונס גמור כליסטין מזויין ולרבה אית ליה בסוף הפועלים (לקמן דף צג:) דאי על בעידנא דעיילי אינשי פטור א"כ תמלא גניבת אונס בשומר שכר ומיהו יש לדחות דרבה יסבור כאידך שינויא דקרנא עדיף כרב יוסף בהכונס (ב"ק דף מ:) ומ"מ אין סברא כלל שלא נמלא גניבת אונס שיפטר בה שומר שכר ואין לתרץ דהואיל וחייב רחמנא שומר שכר בגניבה אע"פ שהיא קרובה לאונס כדאמר בהשואל (לקמן ד' לד:) חייב אף בכל גניבת אונס דהא בליסטין מזויין הוא פטור אע"ג דגנב הוא לרב יוסף א"כ מאי משני בהשואל (דף נה.) לסטין מזויין גזלן הוא אכתי איכא למיפרך מה לשומר שכר שכן משלם כפל בטענת גניבת אונס תאמר בשואל דכי נילף שחייב בגניבה ואבידה לא ישלם כפל אפילו בטענת גניבת אונס דמסתמא הוא חייב קרן בכל אונסין ט דכעין זה פריך פ"ק דמנחות (דף ה:) גבי הלאן להוליא הטרפה ובפרק שור שנגח ד' וה' (ב"ק דף מ:) גבי שור האלטדין מהו לגבי מזבח ונראה דכיון דאתי שואל מק"ו דשומר שכר אין לחייבו בגניבת אונס בקרן ודיו לבא מן הדין להיות כנדון דשומר שכר פטור מגניבת אונס אף שואל כן וא"ת וגניבת אונס בשואל לפי האמת מנ"ל דלא מלינו ששואל פטור אלא במתה מחמת מלאכה דמשומר שכר לא אתי כדפי' וי"ל דנפקא לן מוכי ישאל איש וי"ו מוסיף על ענין ראשון והוי כאילו כתיב גניבה ואבידה להדיא בשואל וכיון דכתיב ביה גניבה ואבידה ואונסין ליכא למפטריה בגניבת אונס והא דיליף בברייתא מק"ו היינו אילו לא נאמר קרא הייתי אומר ק"ו:

שאין הכלב יכול לחפש אחריו. ואם תאמר והלא פטור לבדוק חור מפני סכנת עקרב ז וי"ל דהכא יכול לפנות המפולת א"נ הכא שיש שם חמץ בודאי אינו פטור משום חששת עקרב דהא מבעיא לן בפסחים (דף י:) ככר בפי נחש צריך חבר להוליאו או לאו: ה"ג ר"ח הילכתא תחלתו בפשיעה וסופו באונס חייב. ל וכן מוכח בשלהי הפועלים (לקמן דף צג:) דהלכתא דחייב דפריך אביי אי הכי תחלתו בפשיעה וסופו באונס הוא וחייב וכן מוכח ריש פרק הכונס (ב"ק דף נ.) ודוקא היכא שיכול להיות שהאונס לא היה נארע אם לא פשע בתחלה אבל פשע בה ויצאת לאגם ומתה פטור דמלאך המות מה לי וכו' וצריך לומר דצריפא דאורבני הוי שמירה מעליא לזוזי לענין גנבי כמו קרקע להכי קרי ליה לענין גנבי אונס:

כל

עין משפט נר מצוה

פב א מיי' פ"ד מהל' שאלה ופקדון הל' ו סמג עשין פח טוש"ע ח"מ סי' רצא סעיף כ:
פג ב מיי' שם הל' ח טוש"ע שם סעי' כא:
פד ג מיי' שם הל' ו טוש"ע שם סעי' כ:
פה ד ה מיי' פ"י מהל' ברכות הל' כב סמג עשין כז טוש"ע א"ח סי' רל סעי' ב [רב אלפס ברכות פ"ט דף מח.]:
פו ו מיי' פ"ד מהל' שאלה ופקדון הל' ד סמג עשין פח טוש"ע ח"מ סי' רצא סעי' טו [רב אלפס כאן ועוד לעיל בפירקין דף פ:]:
פז ז ח ט מיי' שם הל' ה ועיין בהשגות ובמ"מ טוש"ע שם סעי' טז:
פח י מיי' שם הל' ד טוש"ע שם סעי' טו:
פט כ מיי' פ"ג מהל' חמץ הל' יא סמג עשין לט טוש"ע א"ח סי' תלג סעי' ח:
צ ל מיי' פ"ד מהל' שאלה ופקדון הל' ד סמג עשין פח טוש"ע ח"מ סי' רצא סעי' טו:
צא מ מיי' שם הל' ו טוש"ע שם סעי' ו:
צב נ מיי' שם הל' ז טוש"ע שם סעי' ז:
צג ס מיי' שם הל' ח טוש"ע שם סעי' כג:

**רבינו חננאל**

מתניתין המפקיד מעות אצל חבירו צררן והפשילן לאחוריו מסרן לבניו הקטנים נעל בפניהן שלא כראוי חייב שלא שימר כדרך השומרים ואם שימר כדרך השומרים פטור. צררן והפשילן לאחוריו חייב כדר' יצחק דאמר כתיב וצרת הכסף בידך אע"פ שהוא צרור יהיה בידך. אמר שמואל כספין אין להן שמירה אלא בקרקע ובערב שבת לא אטרחוה רבנן. ואסיקנא משום איכסוי מעינא הילכך בטפח סגי ליה. והשתא דשכיחי גשושי פי' שמגששין בקרקע ומגלין הטמונות אין לה שמירה אלא בשמי קורה. פי' פרומאי מלשון בגדיו יהיו פרומים. טיט שנותן הבנאי בין ארחא לארחא בעובי הכותל נקרא ביני אורבי. כדגרסי' בגמ' דהשותפין כותל כפיסין ד' טפחים אריח מכאן שהוא טפח ומחצה שיעור חצי לבינה ואריח מכאן כנגדו הרי ג' טפחים נשאר טפח בין שני אריחין ממלאו באבנים קטנים וטיט ונקרא ביני אורבי. פי' טפוחאי שמנקשין בטפח שלהן ומרגישין אם יש בכותל כספין או זולתן: ההוא דאפקיד זוזי גביה חבריה אותבינהו בצריפא דאורבני פי' נתנם בבית המסוכך בעצי ערבה ונגנבו סבר רב יוסף למיפטריה משום דהוא שומר חנם וכו' איכא דאמרי אמר רב יוסף אע"ג דלענין גנבי נטירותא היא לענין נורא פשיעותא היא תחלתו בפשיעה וסופו באונס חייב וכן הלכה למעשה תחלתו בפשיעה וסופו באונס חייב. ההוא דאפקיד זוזי גביה חבריה אמר ליה הב לי זוזיי אמר ליה לא ידענא היכא איתנחתינהו. אמר רבא כל לא ידענא פשיעותא היא וכן הלכה. ההוא דאפקיד זוזי גביה חבריה אשלימינהו לאימיה ואותבינהו בקרטליתא ואיגנוב

מסורת הש"ס

א) לעיל לו. ב) ועיין ברש"י לו. משמע דל"ג או אלא מסרן, ג) והרי"ף והרא"ש גרסי או נעל וכו', ד) תענית ח:, ה) [פסחים לא:], ו) מהרש"ל מ"ז, ז) שם לא:, ח) [שם], ט) [לעיל לו:, וש"נ], י) [לעיל לה.], כ) [כדאיתא בפסחים ח. וע"ש בתוס' ד"ה הכא], ל) [ועי' היטיב תוס' קדושין נב. ד"ה ביע"ל].

**הגהות הב"ח**

(א) תוס' ד"ה אמר וכו' שמרס בקרקע מאה אמה ונגנבו משם:

**גליון הש"ס**

תוס' ד"ה אמר וכו' דכעין זה פריך פ"ק דמנחות. עיין יבמות דף מז ע"ב תוס' ד"ה רב אמר:

**תורה אור השלם**

א) וְנָתַתָּה בַּכָּסֶף וְצַרְתָּ הַכֶּסֶף בְּיָדְךָ וְהָלַכְתָּ אֶל הַמָּקוֹם אֲשֶׁר יִבְחַר יְיָ אֱלֹהֶיךָ בּוֹ: [דברים יד, כה]

ב) יְצַו יְיָ אִתְּךָ אֶת הַבְּרָכָה בַּאֲסָמֶיךָ וּבְכֹל מִשְׁלַח יָדֶךָ וּבֵרַכְךָ בָּאָרֶץ אֲשֶׁר יְיָ אֱלֹהֶיךָ נֹתֵן לָךְ: [דברים כח, ח]

**לעזי רש"י**

פויישו"ן. פירוש שובע (רש"י סוטה דף י ע"א ד"ה במה בירכו), שפע. אשקר"א. פירוש ארגז (עיין רש"י יחזקאל כז, כד).

**ליקוטי רש"י**

ונעל בפניהם. בפני אותם הקטנים שלא יצאו לחוץ ויאבדו המעות [לעיל לו.]. הסמוי מן העין. שאינו יודע הסכום. ברוך השולח ברכה. ושפע ומזכיר בה מלכות ואזכרה ככל הברכות כולן. הרי זו תפלת שוא. דשוב אין ברכה נכנסת בה [תענית ח:]. כספים אין להם שמירה וכו'. של פיקדון אין להם שמירה אלא בקרקע ואם לא נתנן בקרקע ואבדו פשיעה היא אצלו [פסחים לא:]. צורבא מרבנן. תלמיד חכם [שבת קיט.]. בחור חריף כמו ביעי דלריבן במסכת ביצה (ז.) תלמיד חכם זקן לא קרי צורבא אלא ההוא מרבנן קרי ליה [תענית ד.]. ביני אורבי. בין דימוס שמכאן ובין דימוס שמכאן ונותן טיט באמצע [ב"ב ג.]. צריפא. כמין כוך עגול ככובע ונחבאים בתוכו ליידי עופות. דאורבני. עשוי מענפי ערבות וגודלין אותו מתחתיו פיו רחב ולמעלה קושרין ראשי הנלרים בחבל קשר אחד כעין כלי מצודות שצדין דגים קטנים שעושין בגומא שקורין יונק"ש אבל אין בצריף שלשה וארבעה בתי אריגה כמו שיש למצודה [סוכה יג:]. נורא. אש [שבת קנו.].

OVER some *CHAMETZ,* הֲרֵי הוּא כִּמְבוֹעָר – [THE *CHAMETZ*] IS regarded AS having been REMOVED from its owner's possession.[23] רַבָּן שִׁמְעוֹן בֶּן גַּמְלִיאֵל אוֹמֵר – RABBAN SHIMON BEN GAMLIEL SAYS:[24] כָּל שֶׁאֵין הַכֶּלֶב יָכוֹל לְחַפֵּשׂ אַחֲרָיו – That is so AS LONG AS the leaven is buried so deeply that A DOG CANNOT SEARCH AFTER IT and dig it up. וְתָנָא – **And a Tanna taught** the following Baraisa, which defines Rabban Shimon ben Gamliel's statement: כַּמָּה חֲפִישַׁת הַכֶּלֶב – TO WHAT [DEPTH] DOES A DOG SEARCH? שְׁלֹשָׁה טְפָחִים – THREE *TEFACHIM.*

Rav Acha concludes his inquiry:

הָכָא מַאי – **Here,** regarding the safekeeping of money, **what** is the law? מִי בְּעֵינַן שְׁלֹשָׁה טְפָחִים אוֹ לֹא – **Do we require** burial to a depth of **three *tefachim,*** as in the case of *chametz,* **or not?**

Rav Ashi answers:

אָמַר לֵיהּ – **[Rav Ashi] said to [Rav Acha]:** הָתָם מִשּׁוּם רֵיחָא בְּעֵינַן שְׁלֹשָׁה טְפָחִים – **There,** in the Mishnah about *chametz,* **we require** that the *chametz* be at least **three *tefachim*** below the surface **because** otherwise a dog will detect its **smell** and dig it up.[25] הָכָא מִשּׁוּם אִיכַּסּוּיֵי מֵעֵינָא – **Here,** however, regarding the safekeeping of money, burial is necessary only **for the sake of hiding** it **from** the **sight** of thieves; לֹא בְּעֵינַן שְׁלֹשָׁה טְפָחִים – therefore, **we do not require three *tefachim.***

The Gemara concludes:

וְכַמָּה – **And how much** depth is required for the proper safeguarding of money? אָמַר רַפְרָם מִסִּיכְרָא – **Rafram of Sichra said:** טֶפַח – **One *tefach.***

The Gemara records several incidents about the safekeeping of money:

הַהוּא גַּבְרָא דְּאַפְקִיד זוּזֵי גַּבֵּי חַבְרֵיהּ – **A certain man deposited money with his fellow** for safekeeping. אוֹתְבִינְהוּ בִּצְרִיפָא דְּאוּרְבָּנֵי – **[The *shomer*] put it in a hut** made **of willow branches.**[26] אִיגְּנוּב – **[The money] was stolen** from the hut. אָמַר רַב יוֹסֵף – **Rav Yosef said:** אַף עַל גַּב דִּלְעִנְיַן גַּנָּבֵי נְטִירוּתָא הִיא – **Although it** [storing the money in such a hut] **is** considered adequate **protection** with regard to **thieves,**[27] לְעִנְיַן נוּרָא פְּשִׁיעוּתָא הִיא – **it is** considered **negligence with regard to fire.**[28] הָוֵה תְּחִלָּתוֹ בִּפְשִׁיעָה וְסוֹפוֹ בְּאוֹנֶס חַיָּיב – Thus, **this is [a situation] that began with** the *shomer's* **negligence and ended with an unavoidable mishap,**[29] in which case the law is that **[the *shomer*] is liable.**[30]

The Gemara reports an opposite version of Rav Yosef's ruling:

וְאִיכָּא דְּאָמְרֵי – **But there are those who say** that Rav Yosef responded as follows: אַף עַל גַּב דִּלְעִנְיַן נוּרָא פְּשִׁיעוּתָא הִיא – **Although it** [storing the money in such a hut] **is** considered **negligence with regard to fire,** לְעִנְיַן גַּנָּבֵי נְטִירוּתָא הִיא – **it is** considered adequate **protection with regard to thieves.** וּתְחִלָּתוֹ בִּפְשִׁיעָה וְסוֹפוֹ בְּאוֹנֶס פָּטוּר – **And** regarding **[a situation] that began with negligence but ended with an unavoidable mishap,** the law is that **[the custodian] is not liable.**[31]

The Gemara decides the law:

וְהִילְכְתָא – **And the law is** תְּחִלָּתוֹ בִּפְשִׁיעָה וְסוֹפוֹ בְּאוֹנֶס – that in **[a situation] that began with negligence but ended with an unavoidable mishap,** חַיָּיב – **[the custodian] is liable.**

Another incident:

הַהוּא גַּבְרָא דְּאַפְקִיד זוּזֵי גַּבֵּי חַבְרֵיהּ – **A certain man deposited money with his fellow** for safekeeping. אָמַר לֵיהּ – When **he said to [the** *shomer***]:** הַב לִי זוּזַאי – **"Give me my money,"** אָמַר לֵיהּ – **[the *shomer*] answered him:** לֹא יָדַעְנָא הֵיכָא אוֹתְבִינְהוּ – **"I do not know where I put it."** אֲתָא לְקַמֵּיהּ דְּרָבָא – **[The custodian] appeared before Rava** for a ruling on the matter. אָמַר לֵיהּ – **[Rava] said to him:** כָּל לֹא יָדַעְנָא פְּשִׁיעוּתָא הִיא – **"Whenever** a custodian says, **'I do not know,' it is** considered **negligence** on his part. זִיל שַׁלֵּים – **Go and pay!"**

Another incident:

הַהוּא גַּבְרָא דְּאַפְקִיד זוּזֵי גַּבֵּי חַבְרֵיהּ – **A certain man deposited money with his fellow** for safekeeping. אַשְׁלְמִינְהוּ לְאִימֵּיהּ – **[The *shomer*] gave it over to his mother** for her to safeguard, וְאוֹתְבִינְהוּ בְּקַרְטַלִיתָא – **and she put it in a chest.**[32] וְאִיגְּנוּב – **[The money] was stolen.** אָמַר רָבָא – **Rava said:** הֵיכִי נַדַיְינוּ דַּיָּינֵי לְהַאי דִּינָא – **How should judges rule in this case?** נֵימָא לֵיהּ לְדִידֵיהּ זִיל שַׁלֵּים – **If we tell [the *shomer*]** to **go and pay,**[33] אָמַר – **he can say:**

NOTES

23. The Torah states that during the festival of Pesach, וְלֹא־יֵרָאֶה לְךָ חָמֵץ, *chametz shall not be seen in your possession* (*Exodus* 13:7). In the present case, since the *chametz* cannot be seen, this prohibition does not apply. Hence, it is not necessary to remove the debris in order to find and destroy the *chametz* (*Rashi*). [In addition, the Torah states (ibid. 12:19): שְׂאֹר לֹא יִמָּצֵא בְּבָתֵּיכֶם, *leaven shall not be found in your homes.* However, this prohibition is not relevant to our case, for it applies only to *chametz* that was actively hidden, not to *chametz* that became hidden through circumstances (see *Rashi* to *Pesachim* 5b ד״ה יכול, *Mishnah Berurah* 433:38).]

24. Rabban Shimon ben Gamliel is explaining the Tanna Kamma's view (*Rambam, Commentary to the Mishnah*; see *Tos. Yom Tov* ibid.).

25. The *chametz* will thereby be uncovered [and the owner will be in violation of the Torah law: וְלֹא־יֵרָאֶה לְךָ חָמֵץ, *chametz shall not be seen in your possession*; see note 23] (*Rashi*).

26. A small round hut (called a blind) in which bird hunters lie in wait for their prey (*Rashi*).

27. Even though the money was not buried, this is considered adequate protection. Since money is generally not found in such a place, thieves do not go there to look for money to steal (*Rashi*).

28. He should have buried the money to protect it from fire (*Rashi*).

29. The case concerned an unpaid *shomer,* regarding whom theft is considered an unavoidable mishap (*Rashi*).

30. Although the deposit was lost through an unforeseeable mishap, the *shomer* is liable because his storage of the deposit was negligent.

This ruling applies only where the unforeseeable mishap was made possible by the act of negligence (as in this instance, where the money might not have been stolen were it not in the hut). If there is no connection between the act of negligence and the subsequent mishap, as in the case where the mishap would have happened anyway, the *shomer* is not liable (*Tosafos*; see 36b note 15).

31. For, in relation to the theft, the *shomer* was not negligent.

32. As will become clear from the Gemara below, the son led his mother to believe that the coins were his own.

33. Although the *shomer* was not paid, he is liable for the theft (even if no negligence was involved on the part of the mother) for Rava holds that a *shomer* who entrusts a deposit to another *shomer* assumes liability for *all* subsequent mishaps (see *Rashi;* see Gemara above, 36a).

מתני' (א) א המפקיד מעות אצל חברו צררן והפשילן לאחוריו (ב) ב או שמסרם לבנו ולבתו הקטנים (ג) ונעל בפניהם שלא כראוי חייב שלא שימר כדרך השומרים ואם שימר כדרך השומרים פטור: גמ' בשלמא כולהו שלא שימר כדרך השומרים אלא צררן והפשילן לאחוריו מאי הוה ליה למיעבד אמר רבא א"ר יצחק אמר קרא א) וצרת הכסף בידך ג אע"פ שצרורין יהיו בידך וא"ר יצחק לעולם יהא כספו של אדם מצוי בידו שנאמר וצרת הכסף בידך וא"ר יצחק לעולם ישליש אדם את מעותיו שליש בקרקע ושליש בפרקמטיא ושליש תחת ידו (ד) וא"ר יצחק אין הברכה מצוייה אלא בדבר הסמוי מן העין שנאמר ב) יצו ה' אתך את הברכה באסמיך תנא דבי רבי ישמעאל אין הברכה מצויה אלא בדבר שאין העין שולטת בו שנאמר יצו ה' אתך את הברכה באסמיך ת"ר ד ההולך למוד את גורנו אומר יהי רצון מלפניך ה' אלהינו שתשלח ברכה במעשה ידינו התחיל למוד אומר ברוך השולח ברכה בכרי הזה מדד ואח"כ בירך הרי זה תפילת שוא ה לפי שאין הברכה מצוייה לא בדבר השקול ולא בדבר המדוד ולא בדבר המנוי אלא בדבר הסמוי מן העין שנאמר יצו ה' אתך את הברכה באסמיך אמר שמואל (ה) ו כספים אין להם שמירה אלא בקרקע אמר רבא ומודי שמואל ז בערב שבת בין השמשות דלא אטרחוהו רבנן ח ואי שהא למוצאי שבת שיעור למקברינהו ולא קברינהו מחייב ט ואי צורבא מרבנן הוא סבר דלמא מיבעי ליה זוזי לאבדלתא והאידנא דשכיחי גשושאי אין להן שמירה אלא בשמי קורה והאידנא דשכיחי פרומאי אין להם שמירה אלא ביני אורבי אמר רבא ומודה שמואל בכותל (ו) (אי נמי בין הקרנות) י והאידנא דשכיחי טפוחאי אין להן שמירה אלא בטפח הסמוך לקרקע או בטפח הסמוך לשמי קורה א"ל רב אחא בריה דרב יוסף לרב אשי התם תנן (ז) כ חמץ שנפלה עליו מפולת הרי הוא כמבוער רשב"ג אומר כל שאין הכלב יכול לחפש אחריו ותנא כמה חפישת הכלב ג' טפחים הכא מאי בעינן שלשה טפחים או לא אמר ליה התם משום ריחא בעינן ג' טפחים הכא משום איכסויי מעינא לא בעינן ג' טפחים וכמה אמר רפרם מסיכרא (ח) ל טפח ההוא גברא דאפקיד זוזי גבי חבריה אותבינהו בצריפא דאורבני איגנוב אמר רב יוסף מ אע"ג דלענין גנבי נטירותא היא לענין נורא פשיעותא היא (ט) תחלתו בפשיעה וסופו באונס חייב ואיכא דאמרי אע"ג דלענין נורא פשיעותא היא לענין גנבי נטירותא היא ותחלתו בפשיעה וסופו באונס פטור והילכתא תחלתו בפשיעה וסופו באונס חייב ההוא גברא דאפקיד זוזי גבי חבריה א"ל הב לי זוזאי א"ל לא ידענא היכא אותבינהו אתא לקמיה דרבא א"ל (י) נ כל לא ידענא פשיעותא היא זיל שלים ס ההוא גברא דאפקיד זוזי גבי חבריה אשלמינהו לאימיה ואותבינהו בקרטליתא ואיגנוב אמר רבא היכי נדיינו דייני להאי דינא נימא ליה לדידיה זיל שלים אמר

כל

**רש"י**

מתני' צררן. בסודרו והפשילן לאחוריו: גמ' מאי הוה ליה למיעבד. הרי צררן: מצוי בידו. לא יפקידנו לאחרים במקום אחר שאם תזדמן לו סחורה לשכר יהא מזומן לו: תחת ידו. להיות מזומן לו לצורך ריוח הבא פתאום: אין הברכה. שמתברך ורבה מאליו פויישו"ן בלעז: באסמיך. דריש ליה לשון דבר הסמוי מן העין: שאין העין שולטת בו. שנאמר באסמיך לשון גנזים: אין להם שמירה כו'. דאם לא טמנן ונגנבו פשיעה היא: ואם צורבא מרבנן הוא. המפקיד שהוא חרד על מצות הבדלה על הכוס אמר השומר דלמא מיבעי ליה זוזי לאבדלתא להכי לא קברינהו ופטור: גשושאי. מגששין בקרקע בשפודין של ברזל להכיר מקום שתחתיו חלל: בשמי קורה. בגג מתחתיו: פרומאי. שוברי התקרה: ביני אורבי. בין שורות הבנין בכותל: טפוחאי. מטפחים בכותל לידע אם יש שם חלל: או בטפח הסמוך כו'. וכולן בכותל: הרי הוא כמבוער. ואין צריך לבערו דאין כאן עוד בל יראה: הכא מאי. לענין שמירת כספים: משום ריחא. שהכלב מריח וחופש אחריו והרי הוא מוציאו ונראה: מסיכרא. שם מקום: צריפא דאורבני. בית קטן עגול כמין כובע שעושין ליידי עופות לארוב: דאורבני. של ערבה היה: אע"ג דלענין גנבי נטירותא היא. אפי' בלא קבורה שאין גנבי' הולכין שם לגנוב שאין ממון מצוי שם: תחלתו בפשיעה. שמא תפול שם דליקה ונמצא פשע שלא קברן: וסופו באונס. שהרי נגנבו וגניבה לשומר חנם אונס הוא: אשלמינהו. מסרן לאמו: קרטליתא. ארגז אשקר"א בלע"ז: נימא ליה לדידיה [זיל] שלים. דשומר שמסר לשומר חייב:

כל

**תוספות**

אמר שמואל כספים אין להם שמירה כו'. לריך עיון אם שמרס בקרקע (א) ונגנבו משם אם שומר שכר חייב ובפרק הכונס (ב"ק דף נז. ושם ד"ה כגון) משמע דחייב דפריך אביי לרב יוסף והאמר ר' יוחנן הטוען טענת גנב באבידה משלם תשלומי כפל ואי שומר אבידה שומר שכר הוי קרנא בעי לשלומי ומאי פריך דלוקמא בטוען שנגנבה באונס כגון שהעמיק בקרקע ק' אמות או שתקפתו שינה או חולי אלמא כל גניבה לא הויא אונס אלא לסטים מזוין וכן בתר הכי דמייתי לא אי אמרת בשומר חנם שכן משלם כפל ואי לסטים מזוין גנב הוא שומר שכר נמי משלם כפל משמע דמשום גניבה לא מפטר שומר שכר אם לא בטענת גניבת ליסטים מזוין מיהו הנהו יש לדחות דה"מ למימר וליטעמיך דבלאו הכי נמי מצי למימר וליטעמיך אפי' גזלן הוא תמצא שומר שכר משלם כפל בבעלים ויש להביא ראיה מפ' השואל (לקמן דף צה. ושם) דכי יליף גניבה ואבידה בשואל משומר שכר פריך מה לשומר שכר שכן משלם כפל בטענת ליסטין מזוין ומשני אי בעית אימא גזלן הוא משמע שאין שום גניבה שיפטר בה שומר שכר אך תמהון גדול הוא למה לא יהא אונס אם העמיק בקרקע ק' אמות דמאי ה"ל תו למיעבד או אם תקפתו שינה או חולי גדול ואיך יתכן שום גניבה לא נמצא שתהא אונס גמור כליסטין מזוין ולרבה אית ליה בסוף הפועלים (לקמן דף צג:) דאי על בעידנא דעיילי אינשי פטור א"כ תמצא גניבת אונס בשומר שכר ומיהו יש לדחות דרבה יסבור כאידך שינויא דקרנא עדיף כרב יוסף בהכונס (ב"ק דף נז:) ומ"מ אין סברא כלל שלא נמצא גניבת אונס שיפטר בה שומר שכר ואין לתרץ דהואיל וחייב רחמנא שומר שכר בגניבה אע"פ שהיא קרובה לאונס כדאמר בהשואל (לקמן ד' צד:) חייב אף בכל גניבת אונס דהא בליסטין מזוין הוא פטור אע"ג דגנב הוא לרב יוסף א"כ מאי משני בהשואל (דף צה.) לסטין מזוין גזלן הוא הכתי איכא למיפרך מה לשומר שכר שכן משלם כפל בטענת גניבת אונס תאמר בשואל דכי נילף שחייב בגניבה ואבידה לא ישלם כפל אפילו בטענת גניבת אונס דמסתמא הוא חייב קרן בכל אונסין (ב) דכעין זה פריך פ"ק דמנחות (דף ה:) גבי הלכך להוציא הטרפה ובפרק שור שנגח ד' וה' (ב"ק דף מ:) גבי שור האצטדין מהו לגבי מזבח ונראה דכיון דאתי שואל מק"ו דשומר שכר אין לחייבו בגניבת אונס בקרן ודיו לבא מן הדין להיות כנדון דשומר שכר פטור מגניבת אונס אף שואל כן וא"ת וגניבת אונס בשואל לפי האמת מנ"ל דלא מלינו ששואל פטור אלא במתה מחמת מלאכה דמשומר שכר לא אתי כדפי' וי"ל דנפקא לן מוכי ישאל איש וי"ו מוסיף על ענין ראשון והוי כאילו כתיב ביה גניבה ואבידה להדיא בשואל וכיון דכתיב ביה גניבה ואבידה ואונסין ליכא למפטריה בגניבת אונס והא דיליף בברייתא מק"ו היינו אילו לא נאמר קרא הייתי אומר ק"ו:

שאין הכלב יכול לחפש אחריו. ואם תאמר והלא פטור לבדוק חור מפני סכנת עקרב (ג) וי"ל דהכא יכול לפנות המפולת א"נ הכא שיש שם חמץ בודאי אינו פטור משום חששת עקרב דהא מבעיא לן בפסחים (דף י:) ככר בפי נחש צריך חבר להוציאו או לאו: ה"ג ר"ח הילכתא תחלתו בפשיעה וסופו באונס חייב. (ד) וכן מוכח בשלהי הפועלים (לקמן דף צג:) דהלכתא דחייב דפריך אביי אי הכי תחלתו בפשיעה וסופו באונס הוא וחייב וכן מוכח ריש פרק הכונס (ב"ק דף נו.) ודוקא היכא שיכול להיות שהאונס לא היה נארע אם לא פשע בתחלה אבל פשע בה ויצאת לאגם ומתה פטור דמלאך המות מה לי וכו' וצריך לומר דצריפא דאורבני הוי שמירה מעליא לזוזי לענין גנבי כמו קרקע להכי קרי ליה לענין גנבי אונס:

כל

**עין משפט נר מצוה**

פב א מיי' פ"ד מהל' שאלה ופקדון הל' ו סמג עשין פח טוש"ע ח"מ סי' רצא סעיף כ:
פג ב מיי' שם הל' ח טוש"ע שם סעי' כא:
פד ג מיי' שם הל' ו טוש"ע שם סעי' כ:
פה ד ה מיי' פ"י מהל' ברכות הל' כב סמג עשין כז טוש"ע א"ח סי' רל סעי' ב [רב אלפס ברכות פ"ט דף מח.]:
פו ו מיי' פ"ד מהל' שאלה ופקדון הל' ד סמג עשין פח טוש"ע ח"מ סי' רצא סעי' טו [רב אלפס כאן ועוד לעיל בפירקין דף פ:]:
פז ז ח ט מיי' שם הל' ה ועיין בהשגות ובמ"מ טוש"ע שם סעי' טז:
פח י מיי' שם הל' ד טוש"ע שם סעי' טו:
פט כ מיי' פ"ג מהל' חמץ הל' יא סמג עשין לט טוש"ע א"ח סי' תלג סעי' ח:
צ ל מיי' פ"ד מהל' שאלה ופקדון הל' ד סמג עשין פח טוש"ע ח"מ סי' רצא סעי' טו:
צא מ מיי' שם הל' ו טוש"ע שם סעי' ו:
צב נ מיי' שם הל' ז טוש"ע שם סעי' ז:
צג ס מיי' שם הל' ח טוש"ע שם סעי' כג:

**רבינו חננאל**

מתניתין המפקיד מעות אצל חבירו צררן והפשילן לאחוריו מסרן לבניו הקטנים נעל בפניהן שלא כראוי חייב שלא שימר כדרך השומרים ואם שימר כדרך השומרים פטור. צררן והפשילן לאחוריו חייב כדר' יצחק דאמר כתיב וצרת הכסף בידך אע"פ שהוא צרור יהיה בידך. אמר שמואל כספין אין להן שמירה אלא בקרקע ובערב שבת לא אטרחוה רבנן. ואסיקנא משום איכסוי מעינא הילכך בטפח סגי ליה. והשתא דשכיחי גשושי פי' שמגששין בקרקע ומגלין הטמונות אין לה שמירה אלא בשמי קורה. פי' פרומאי מלשון בגדיו יהיו פרומים. טיט שנותן הבנאי בין ארחא לארחא בעובי הכותל נקרא ביני אורבי. כדגרסי' בגמ' דהשותפין כותל כפיסין ד' טפחים אריח מכאן שהוא טפח ומחצה שיעור חצי לבינה ואריח מכאן כנגדו הרי ג' טפחים נשאר טפח בין שני אריחין ממלאו באבנים קטנים וטיט ונקרא ביני אורבי. פי' טפוחאי שמנקשין בטפח שלהן ומרגישין אם יש בכותל כספין או זולתן: ההוא דאפקיד זוזי גביה חבריה אותבינהו בצריפא דאורבני פי' נתנם בבית המסוכך בעצי ערבה ונגנבו סבר רב יוסף למיפטריה משום דהוא שומר חנם וכו' איכא דאמרי אמר רב יוסף אע"ג דלענין גנבי נטירותא היא לענין נורא פשיעותא היא תחלתו בפשיעה וסופו באונס חייב וכן הלכה למעשה תחלתו בפשיעה וסופו באונס חייב. ההוא דאפקיד זוזי גביה חבריה אמר ליה הב לי זוזי אמר ליה לא ידענא היכא איתנחתינהו. אמר רבא כל לא ידענא פשיעותא היא וכן הלכה. ההוא דאפקיד זוזי גביה חבריה אשלימינהו לאימיה ואותבינהו בקרטליתא ואיגנוב

**מסורת הש"ס**

א) לעיל לו., ב) ועיין ברש"י לו. משמע דל"ג או אלא מסרן, ג) והרי"ף והרא"ש גרסי או נעל וכו', ד) תענית ח:, ה) [פסחים לא:], ו) מהרש"ל מ"ז, ז) שם לא:, ח) [שם], ט) [לעיל לו:, וש"נ], י) [לעיל לה.], כ) [כדאיתא בפסחים ח. וע"ש בתוס' ד"ה הכא], ל) [ועי' היטיב תוס' קדושין נג. ד"ה ביע"ל].

**הגהות הב"ח**

(א) תוס' ד"ה אמר וכו' שמרס בקרקע מאה אמה ונגנבו משם:

**גליון הש"ס**

תוס' ד"ה אמר וכו' דכעין זה פריך פ"ק דמנחות. עיין יבמות דף נז ע"ב תוס' ד"ה רב אמר:

**תורה אור השלם**

א) וְנָתַתָּה בַּכָּסֶף וְצַרְתָּ הַכֶּסֶף בְּיָדְךָ וְהָלַכְתָּ אֶל הַמָּקוֹם אֲשֶׁר יִבְחַר יְיָ אֱלֹהֶיךָ בּוֹ: [דברים יד, כה]

ב) יְצַו יְיָ אִתְּךָ אֶת הַבְּרָכָה בַּאֲסָמֶיךָ וּבְכֹל מִשְׁלַח יָדֶךָ וּבֵרַכְךָ בָּאָרֶץ אֲשֶׁר יְיָ אֱלֹהֶיךָ נֹתֵן לָךְ: [דברים כח, ח]

**לעזי רש"י**

פויישו"ן. פירוש שובע (רש"י סוטה דף י ע"א ד"ה במה בירכו), שפע. אשקר"א. פירוש ארגז (עיין רש"י יחזקאל כז, כד).

**ליקוטי רש"י**

ונעל בפניהם. בפני אותם הקטנים שלא יצאו לחוץ ויאבדו המעות [לעיל לו.]. הסמוי מן העין. שאינו יודע השכום. ברוך השולח ברכה. ושפע ומזכיר בה מלכות ואזכרה ככל הברכות כולן. הרי זו תפלת שוא. דשוב אין ברכה נכנסת בה [תענית ח:]. כספים אין להם שמירה וכו'. של פיקדון אין להם שמירה אלא בקרקע ואם לא נתנן בקרקע ואבדו פשיעה היא אללו [פסחים לא:]. צורבא מרבנן. תלמיד חכם [שבת קיט.]. בחור חריף כמו ביעי דלריבן במסכת ביצה (ז.) תלמיד חכם זקן לא קרי צורבא אלא ההוא מרבנן קרי ליה [תענית ד.]. ביני אורבי. בין דימוס שמכאן ובין דימוס שמכאן ונותן טיט באמצע [ב"ב ג.]. צריפא. כמין כוך עגול ככובע ונתבאים בתוכו ליידי עופות. דאורבני. עשוי מענפי ערבות וגודלין אותו מתמתיו פיו רחב ולמעלה קושרין ראשי הנגרים בחבל קשר אחד כעין כלי מצודות שצדין דגים קטנים שעושין בגומא שקורין יונק"ש אבל אין בצריף שלשה וארבעה בתי אריגה כמו שיש למצודה [סוכה יג:]. נורא. אש [שבת קנו.].

"BLESSED IS THE ONE WHO BESTOWS BLESSING UPON THIS PILE."[14] מָדַד וְאַחַר כָּךְ בֵּירַךְ – If HE first MEASURED the pile of grain AND THEN RECITED THE BLESSING, הֲרֵי זֶה תְּפִילַּת שָׁוְא – THIS PRAYER IS IN VAIN. At that point, it is too late for the blessing to take effect, לְפִי שֶׁאֵין הַבְּרָכָה מְצוּיָה – FOR BLESSING IS NOT FOUND לֹא בְּדָבָר הַשָּׁקוּל – IN SOMETHING THAT already HAS BEEN WEIGHED, וְלֹא בְּדָבָר הַמָּדוּד – NOR IN SOMETHING THAT already HAS BEEN MEASURED, וְלֹא בְּדָבָר הַמָּנוּי – NOR IN SOMETHING THAT already HAS BEEN COUNTED. אֶלָּא בְּדָבָר הַסָּמוּי מִן הָעַיִן – Blessing is found ONLY IN SOMETHING THAT IS HIDDEN FROM THE EYE, i.e. its quantity is unknown, שֶׁנֶּאֱמַר – AS IT IS SAID: "יְצַו ה׳ אִתְּךָ אֶת־הַבְּרָכָה בַּאֲסָמֶיךָ" – *HASHEM WILL COMMAND THE BLESSING to be WITH YOU IN YOUR SILOS.*[15]

The Gemara returns to the subject of safeguarding deposited money:

אָמַר שְׁמוּאֵל – **Shmuel said:** כְּסָפִים אֵין לָהֶם שְׁמִירָה אֶלָּא בְּקַרְקַע – **There is no** acceptable method for **safeguarding money other than** to bury it **in the ground.**[16]

This ruling is qualified:

אָמַר רָבָא – **Rava said:** וּמוֹדֵי שְׁמוּאֵל בְּעֶרֶב שַׁבָּת בֵּין הַשְּׁמָשׁוֹת – **And Shmuel concedes** that if money was entrusted to a *shomer* **on Friday** afternoon, **close to sunset,**[17] it need not be buried, דְּלֹא אַטְרְחוּהוּ רַבָּנָן – **for the Sages did not burden him** with this chore so close to the Sabbath. וְאִי שְׁהָא לְמוֹצָאֵי שַׁבָּת – **But if he waited after the Sabbath** שִׁיעוּר לְמִקְבְּרִינְהוּ – **the amount** of time that it takes **to bury [the money]** וְלֹא קְבָרִינְהוּ – **and he did not bury it,** מִחַיֵּיב – **he is liable** for theft if it is then stolen. וְאִי צוּרְבָא מֵרַבָּנָן הוּא – **If, however, [the owner]** of the money **is a Rabbinic student,** the *shomer* is not liable even if he did not bury the money immediately after the Sabbath, סָבַר דִּלְמָא מִיבְּעֵי לֵיהּ זוּזֵי לְאַבְדַּלְתָּא – for he may claim that **he thought** that **[the owner] might require** the **money** right after the Sabbath to purchase wine **for** the **Havdalah** ceremony.[18]

Shmuel's ruling is qualified further:

וְהָאִידְנָא דִּשְׁכִיחֵי גַּשּׁוֹשָׁאֵי – **And nowadays, when there are many [thieves] who strike** the ground with metal rods to try to find any hollows beneath the ground in which valuables might be stored, אֵין לָהֶן שְׁמִירָה אֶלָּא בִּשְׁמֵי קוֹרָה – **there is no** acceptable method for **safeguarding [money] other than** to hide it **above the beams** that are beneath the ceiling of the *shomer's* house.

During a later era, that method too was considered inadequate:

וְהָאִידְנָא דִּשְׁכִיחֵי פְּרוֹמָאֵי – **And nowadays, when there are many [thieves] who break** roofs to look for hidden money, אֵין לָהֶם שְׁמִירָה אֶלָּא בֵּינֵי אוּרְבֵי – **there is no** acceptable method for **safeguarding [money] other than** to insert it **between the rows** of bricks in a wall.[19] אָמַר רָבָא וּמוֹדֶה שְׁמוּאֵל בְּכוֹתֶל (אִי נַמִּי בֵּין הקרנות) – **Rava said: Shmuel concedes** that money may be stored anywhere **in a wall.**[20]

However, at a later time, even that method became ineffective:

וְהָאִידְנָא דִּשְׁכִיחֵי טַפּוּחָאֵי – **And nowadays, when there are many [thieves] who tap** on walls to find hollows in which valuables might be stored, אֵין לָהֶן שְׁמִירָה אֶלָּא – **there is no** acceptable method of **safeguarding money other than** to insert it in a wall, בְּטֶפַח הַסָּמוּךְ לְקַרְקַע – either **within one *tefach* of the floor** אוֹ בְּטֶפַח הַסָּמוּךְ לִשְׁמֵי קוֹרָה – **or within one *tefach* of the ceiling.**[21]

Shmuel ruled that a *shomer* who has been entrusted with money must bury it in the ground. The Gemara discusses how deeply it must be buried:

אָמַר לֵיהּ רַב אַחָא בְּרֵיהּ דְּרַב יוֹסֵף לְרַב אַשִׁי – **Rav Acha son of Rav Yosef asked Rav Ashi:** הָתָם תְּנַן – **We learned there in a Mishnah:**[22] חָמֵץ שֶׁנָּפְלָה עָלָיו מַפּוֹלֶת – If A RUIN COLLAPSED

NOTES

14. Like all other blessings, this one must include God's Name and a mention of His kingdom; that is, one says: בָּרוּךְ אַתָּה ה׳ אֱלֹהֵינוּ מֶלֶךְ הָעוֹלָם הַשּׁוֹלֵחַ בְּרָכָה בִּכְרִי הַזֶּה, *Blessed are You, Hashem, our God, King of the Universe, Who bestows blessing on this pile* (*Ritva; Rashi* to *Taanis* 8b).

This blessing is recited only by one who is measuring his pile of grain for the purpose of taking *terumos* and *maasros*. In such a case, his blessing will not be in vain, because one is guaranteed Divine blessing for separating *terumos* and *maasros*, as it is said (*Malachi* 3:10): הָבִיאוּ אֶת־כָּל־הַמַּעֲשֵׂר...וַהֲרִיקֹתִי לָכֶם בְּרָכָה עַד־בְּלִי־דָי, *Bring all the maaser... and I will pour out blessing to you without limit* (*Ritva*, in the name of *Ramban*; see *Maharsha*).

*Eliyah Rabbah* (*Orach Chaim* 230:7) rules that when measuring for the purpose of taking *terumos* and *maasros,* one recites the blessing with the mention of God's Name and His kingdom; otherwise, one recites the blessing without these expressions (*Mishnah Berurah* ibid. §4).

15. See note 12.

16. If the deposit was not safeguarded in this way, the *shomer* is considered to have acted negligently, and therefore [even if he is an unpaid *shomer*] he is liable if the deposit is stolen (*Rashi*).

The ruling taught above, that a *shomer* is required to keep money in his hand, applies only to a *shomer* who is traveling. [The verse cited in support of that ruling refers to the taking of *maaser sheni* coins to Jerusalem.] The ruling given here applies to a *shomer* who is at home (*Rav* to *Mishnah;* see *Rambam, Hil. She'eilah U'Fikadon* 4:6).

17. The term בֵּין הַשְּׁמָשׁוֹת, *bein hashmashos,* usually refers to the time of day between sunset and the appearance of stars (nightfall). In this case, however, it refers to the time of day that immediately *precedes* sunset (*Rosh*; see *Pilpula Charifta; cf. Mordechai*).

18. [הַבְדָּלָה, Havdalah, is the blessing recited after the Sabbath has ended, which gives praise to God for making the distinction between the Sabbath and the other days of the week.]

Scholars [who are conscientious in their performance of mitzvos] will endeavor to recite the Havdalah blessing over a cup of wine (*Rashi*).

Actually, it is an *obligation* for *everyone* to recite the Havdalah blessing over wine. However, this law applies specifically to a scholar, because wine was expensive, and other people might fulfill their obligation by hearing someone else recite the Havdalah blessing for them. A scholar, however, will make every effort to procure wine so that he can fulfill the mitzvah in a superior fashion by reciting the blessing himself (*Maggid Mishneh, Hil. She'eilah U'Fikadon* 4:5, in explanation of *Rashi*).

19. The words in parentheses are deleted by *Maharam.*

20. I.e. according to Shmuel, storing money in a wall is sufficient *without* inserting it between the rows of bricks (*Rosh,* end of §22; see *Ritva* [old] and *Lechem Mishneh, Hil. She'eilah U'Fikadon* 4:4).

21. [Hollows in these places do not reverberate to a significant degree when tapped, and thus they cannot be easily detected.]

An apparent difficulty: Our Mishnah, which states that a *shomer* who locked up money inadequately is liable, implies that locking up money adequately is sufficient. This seems to contradict Shmuel's ruling: "There is no acceptable method for safeguarding money other than burying it in the ground."

Many Rishonim answer that Shmuel's statement was not intended as an absolute requirement. Rather, the method a *shomer* must use to safeguard money is dependent upon the circumstances, which change according to the time and place. This point is borne out by the present passage of Gemara: "But nowadays, when there are many [thieves] who strike [the ground] etc." Indeed, *Yerushalmi* states: In what circumstances did they say that an unpaid *shomer* ... is not liable [to pay the owner for the loss or theft of money that had been entrusted to him]? Where he guarded it in the normal manner of *shomrim.* If he put it in a house and locked the door adequately, or tied it up adequately, or put it in his belt, or bundled it up in a sheet and put it in front of himself, or put it in a chest or closet, and then it was stolen or lost, he is not liable... In the event that he put it in a place where he puts his own money, if that place is safe, he is not liable; otherwise, he is liable (*Rosh, Ritva, Nimukei Yosef; cf. Hagahos Asheri*).

22. *Pesachim* 31b.

מתני' א) [א] המפקיד מעות אצל חברו צררן והפשילן לאחוריו ב) [ב] או שמסרם לבנו ולבתו הקטנים ג) ונעל בפניהם שלא כראוי חייב שלא שימר כדרך השומרים ואם שימר כדרך השומרים פטור: גמ' בשלמא כולהו שלא שימר כדרך השומרים אלא צררן והפשילן לאחוריו מאי הוה ליה למיעבד אמר רבא א"ר יצחק אמר קרא א) וצרת הכסף בידך [ג] אע"פ שצרורין יהיו בידך וא"ר יצחק לעולם יהא כספו של אדם מצוי בידו שנאמר וצרת הכסף בידך וא"ר יצחק לעולם ישליש אדם את מעותיו שליש בקרקע ושליש בפרקמטיא ושליש תחת ידו ד) וא"ר יצחק אין הברכה מצויה אלא בדבר הסמוי מן העין שנאמר ב) יצו ה' אתך את הברכה באסמיך תנא דבי רבי ישמעאל אין הברכה מצויה אלא בדבר שאין העין שולטת בו שנאמר יצו ה' אתך את הברכה באסמיך ת"ר [ד] ההולך למוד את גורנו אומר יהי רצון מלפניך ה' אלהינו שתשלח ברכה במעשה ידינו התחיל למוד אומר ברוך השולח ברכה בכרי הזה מדד ואח"כ בירך הרי זה תפילת שוא [ה] לפי שאין הברכה מצויה לא בדבר השקול ולא בדבר המדוד ולא בדבר המנוי אלא בדבר הסמוי מן העין שנאמר יצו ה' אתך את הברכה באסמיך אמר שמואל ה) [ו] כספים אין להם שמירה אלא בקרקע אמר רבא ומודי שמואל [ז] בערב שבת בין השמשות דלא אטרחוהו רבנן [ח] ואי שהא למוצאי שבת שיעור למקברינהו ולא קברינהו מחייב [ט] ואי צורבא מרבנן הוא סבר דלמא מיבעי ליה זוזי לאבדלתא והאידנא דשכיחי גשושאי אין להן שמירה אלא בשמי קורה והאידנא דשכיחי פרומאי אין להם שמירה אלא ביני אורבי אמר רבא ומודה שמואל בכותל ו) (אי נמי בין הקרנות) [י] והאידנא דשכיחי טפוחאי אין להן שמירה אלא בטפח הסמוך לקרקע או בטפח הסמוך לשמי קורה א"ל רב אחא בריה דרב יוסף לרב אשי התם תנן ז) [כ] חמץ שנפלה עליו מפולת הרי הוא כמבוער רשב"ג אומר כל שאין הכלב יכול לחפש אחריו ותנא כמה חפישת הכלב ג' טפחים הכא מאי מי בעינן שלשה טפחים או לא אמר ליה התם משום ריחא בעינן ג' טפחים הכא משום איכסויי מעינא לא בעינן ג' טפחים וכמה אמר רפרם מסיכרא ח) [ל] טפח ההוא גברא דאפקיד זוזי גבי חבריה אותבינהו בצריפא דאורבני איגנוב אמר רב יוסף [מ] אע"ג דלענין גנבי נטירותא היא לענין נורא פשיעותא היא הוה ט) תחלתו בפשיעה וסופו באונס חייב ואיכא דאמרי אע"ג דלענין נורא פשיעותא היא לענין גנבי נטירותא היא ותחלתו בפשיעה וסופו באונס פטור והילכתא תחלתו בפשיעה וסופו באונס חייב ההוא גברא דאפקיד זוזי גבי חבריה א"ל הב לי זוזאי א"ל לא ידענא היכא אותבינהו אתא לקמיה דרבא א"ל י) [נ] כל לא ידענא פשיעותא היא זיל שלים [ס] ההוא גברא דאפקיד זוזי גבי חבריה אשלמינהו לאימיה ואותבינהו בקרטליתא ואיגנוב אמר רבא היכי נדיינו דייני להאי דינא נימא ליה לדידיה זיל שלים אמר

כל

## רש"י

מתני' צררן. בסודרו והפשילן לאחוריו: גמ' מאי הוה ליה למיעבד. הרי צררן: מצוי בידו. לא יפקידנו לאחרים במקום אחר שאם תזדמן לו סחורה לשכר יהא מזומן לו: תחת ידו. להיות מזומן לו לצורך ריוח הבא פתאום: אין הברכה. שמתברך ורבה מאליו פוייסו"ן בלעז: באסמיך. דריש ליה לשון דבר הסמוי מן העין: שאין העין שולטת בו. שנאמר באסמיך לשון גנזים: אין להם שמירה כו'. דאם לא טמנן ונגנבו פשיעה היא: ואם צורבא מרבנן הוא. המפקיד שהוא חרד על מלות הבדלה על הכוס אמר השומר דלמא מיבעי ליה זוזי לאבדלתא להכי לא קברינהו ופטור: גשושאי. מגששין בקרקע בשפודין של ברזל להכיר מקום שתחתיו חלל: בשמי קורה. בגג מתחתיו: פרומאי. שוברי התקרה: ביני אורבי. בין שורות הבנין בכותל: טפוחאי. מטפחים בכותל לידע אם יש שם חלל: או בטפח הסמוך כו'. וכולן בכותל: הרי הוא כמבוער. ואין צריך לבערו דאין כאן עוד בל יראה: הכא מאי. לענין שמירת כספים: משום ריחא. שהכלב מריח וחופש אחריו והרי הוא מוליאו ונראה: מסיכרא. שם מקום: צריפא דאורבני. בית קטן עגול כמין כובע שעושין ליידי עופות לארוב: דאורבני. של ערבה היה: אע"ג דלענין גנבי נטירותא היא. אפי' בלא קבורה שאין גנבי' הולכין שם לגנוב שאין ממון מלוי שם: תחלתו בפשיעה. שמא תפול שם דליקה ונמצא פשע שלא קברן: וסופו באונס. שהרי נגנבו וגניבה לשומר חנם אונס הוא: אשלמינהו. מסרן לאמו: קרטליתא. ארגז אשקר"א בלע"ז: נימא ליה לדידיה [זיל] שלים. דשומר שמסר לשומר חייב:

כל

## תוספות

אמר שמואל כספים אין להם שמירה כו'. צריך עיון אם שמרס בקרקע (א) ונגנבו משם אם שומר שכר חייב ובפרק הכונס (ב"ק דף נו. ושם ד"ה כגון) משמע דחייב דפריך אביי לרב יוסף והאמר ר' יוחנן הטוען טענת גנב באבידה משלם תשלומי כפל ואי שומר אבידה שומר שכר הוי קרנא בעי לשלומי ומאי פריך דלוקמא בטוען שנגנבה באונס כגון שהעמיק בקרקע ק' אמות או שתקפתו שינה או חולי אלמא כל גניבה לא הויא אונס אלא לסטים מזוין וכן בתר הכי דמייתי לא אי אמרת בשומר חנם שכן משלם כפל ואי לסטים מזוין גנב הוא שומר שכר נמי משלם כפל משמע דמשום גניבה לא מפטר שומר שכר אם לא בטענת גניבת ליסטים מזוין מיהו הנהו יש לדחות דה"מ למימר וליטעמיך דבלאו הכי נמי מצי למימר וליטעמיך אפי' גזלן הוא תמצא שומר שכר משלם כפל בבעלים ויש להביא ראיה מפ' השואל (לקמן דף צה. ושם) דכי יליף גניבה ואבידה בשואל משומר שכר פריך מה לשומר שכר שכן משלם כפל בטענת ליסטין מזוין ומשני אי בעית אימא גזלן הוא משמע שאין שום גניבה שיפטר בה שומר שכר אך תמהון גדול הוא למה לא יהא אונס אם העמיק בקרקע ק' אמות דמאי ה"ל תו למיעבד או אם תקפתו שינה או חולי גדול ואיך יתכן ששום גניבה לא נמצא שתהא אונס גמור כליסטין מזויין ולרבה אית ליה בסוף הפועלים (לקמן דף צג:) דאי על בעידנא דעיילי אינשי פטור א"כ תמצא גניבת אונס בשומר שכר ומיהו יש לדחות דרבה יסבור כאידך שינויא דקרנא עדיף כרב יוסף בהכונס (ב"ק דף נז:) ומ"מ אין סברא כלל שלא נמצא גניבת אונס שיפטר בה שומר שכר ואין לתרץ דהואיל וחייב רחמנא שומר שכר בגניבה אע"פ שהיא קרובה לאונס כדאמר בהשואל (לקמן ד' צד:) חייב אף בכל גניבת אונס דהא בליסטין מזוין הוא פטור אע"ג דגנב הוא לרב יוסף א"כ מאי משני בהשואל (דף צה.) לסטין מזויין גזלן הוא אכתי איכא למיפרך מה לשומר שכר שכן משלם כפל בטענת גניבת אונס תאמר בשואל דכי נילף שחייב בגניבה ואבידה לא ישלם כפל אפילו בטענת גניבת אונס דמסתמא הוא חייב קרן בכל אונסין ° דכעין זה פריך פ"ק דמנחות (דף ה:) גבי הלאן להוליא הטרפה ובפרק שור שנגח ד' וה' (ב"ק דף מ:) גבי שור האצטדין מהו לגבי מזבח ונראה דכיון דאתי שואל מק"ו דשומר שכר אין לחייבו בגניבת אונס בקרן ודיו לבא מן הדין להיות כנדון דשומר שכר פטור מגניבת אונס אף שואל כן וא"ת וגניבת אונס בשואל לפי האמת מנ"ל דלא מלינו ששואל פטור אלא במתה מחמת מלאכה דמשומר שכר לא אתי כדפי' וי"ל דנפקא לן מוכי ישאל איש וי"ו מוסיף על ענין ראשון והוי כאילו כתיב גניבה ואבידה להדיא בשואל וכיון דכתיב ביה גניבה ואבידה ואונסין ליכא למפטריה בגניבת אונס והא דיליף בברייתא מק"ו היינו אילו לא נאמר קרא הייתי אומר ק"ו:

שאין הכלב יכול לחפש אחריו. ואם תאמר והלא פטור לבדוק חור מפני סכנת עקרב ° וי"ל דהכא יכול לפנות המפולת א"נ הכא שיש שם חמץ בודאי אינו פטור משום חששת עקרב דהא מבעיא לן בפסחים (דף י:) ככר בפי נחש צריך חבר להוליאו או לאו: ה"ג ר"ח הילכתא תחלתו בפשיעה וסופו באונס חייב. ° וכן מוכח בשלהי הפועלים (לקמן דף צג:) דהלכתא דחייב דפריך אביי אי הכי תחלתו בפשיעה וסופו באונס הוא וחייב וכן מוכח ריש פרק הכונס (ב"ק דף נו.) ודוקא היכא שיכול להיות שהאונס לא היה נארע אם לא פשע בתחלה אבל פשע בה ויצאת לאגם ומתה פטור דמלאך המות מה לי וכו' וצריך לומר דצריפא דאורבני הוי שמירה מעליא לזוזי לענין גנבי כמו קרקע להכי קרי ליה לענין גנבי אונס:

כל

## מסורת הש"ס

א) לעיל לו., ב) ועיין ברש"י לו. משמע דל"ג או אלא מסרן, ג) והרי"ף והרא"ש גרסי או נעל וכו', ד) תענית ח:, ה) [פסחים לא:], ו) מהרש"ל מ"ז, ז) שם לא:, ח) [שם], ט) [לעיל לו: וש"נ], י) [לעיל לה.], כ) [כדאיתא בפסחים ח. וע"ש בתוס' ד"ה הכא], ל) [ועי' היטיב תוס' קדושין נב. ד"ה ביע"ל].

## הגהות הב"ח

(א) תוס' ד"ה אמר וכו' שמרס בקרקע מאה אמה ונגנבו משם:

## גליון הש"ס

תוס' ד"ה אמר וכו' דכעין זה פריך פ"ק דמנחות. עיין יבמות דף נז ע"ב תוס' ד"ה רב אמר:

## תורה אור השלם

א) וְנָתַתָּה בַּכָּסֶף וְצַרְתָּ הַכֶּסֶף בְּיָדְךָ וְהָלַכְתָּ אֶל הַמָּקוֹם אֲשֶׁר יִבְחַר יְיָ אֱלֹהֶיךָ בּוֹ: [דברים יד, כה]

ב) יְצַו יְיָ אִתְּךָ אֶת הַבְּרָכָה בַּאֲסָמֶיךָ וּבְכֹל מִשְׁלַח יָדֶךָ וּבֵרַכְךָ בָּאָרֶץ אֲשֶׁר יְיָ אֱלֹהֶיךָ נֹתֵן לָךְ: [דברים כח, ח]

## לעזי רש"י

פויישו"ן. פירוש שובע (רש"י סוטה דף י ע"א ד"ה כמה בירכו), שפע. אשקר"א. פירוש ארגז (עיין רש"י יחזקאל כז, כד).

## ליקוטי רש"י

ונעל בפניהם. בפני אותם הקטנים שלא יצאו לחוץ ויאבדו המעות [לעיל לו.]. הסמוי מן העין. שאינו יודע השכום. ברוך השולח ברכה. ושפע ומזכיר בה מלכות ואזכרה ככל הברכות כולן. הרי זו תפלת שוא. דשוב אין ברכה נכנסת בה [תענית ח:]. כספים אין להם שמירה וכו'. של פיקדון אין להם שמירה אלא בקרקע ואם לא נתנן בקרקע ואבדו פשיעה היא אצלו [פסחים לא:]. צורבא מרבנן. תלמיד חכם [שבת קיט.]. בחור חריף כמו ביעי דצריכן במסכת ביצה (ז.) תלמיד חכם זקן לא קרי צורבא אלא ההוא מרבנן קרי ליה [תענית ד.]. ביני אורבי. בין דימוס שמכאן ובין דימוס שמכאן ונותן טיט באמצע [ב"ב ג.]. צריפא. כמין כוך עגול ככובע ונחבאים בתוכו ליידי עופות. דאורבני. עשוי מענפי ערבות וגודלין אותו מתחתיו פיו רחב ולמעלה קושרין ראשי הנצרים בחבל קשר אחד כעין כלי מצודות שצדין דגים קטנים שעושין בגומא שקורין יונק"ש אבל אין בנציף שלשה וארבעה בתי אריגה כמו שיש למצודה [סוכה יג:]. נורא. אש [שבת קנו.].

## עין משפט נר מצוה

פב א מיי' פ"ד מהל' שאלה ופקדון הל' ו סמג עשין פח טוש"ע ח"מ סי' רצא סעיף כ:
פג ב מיי' שם הל' ח טוש"ע שם סעי' כא:
פד ג מיי' שם הל' ו טוש"ע שם סעי' כ:
פה ד ה מיי' פ"י מהל' ברכות הל' כב סמג עשין כז טוש"ע א"ח סי' רל סעי' ב [רב אלפס ברכות פ"ט דף מח.]:
פו ו מיי' פ"ד מהל' שאלה ופקדון הל' ד סמג עשין פח טוש"ע ח"מ סי' רצא סעי' טו [רב אלפס כאן ועוד לעיל בפירקין דף פ:]:
פז ז ח ט מיי' שם הל' ה ועיין בהשגות ובמ"מ טוש"ע שם סעי' טז:
פח י מיי' שם הל' ד טוש"ע שם סעי' טו:
פט כ מיי' פ"ג מהל' חמץ הל' יא סמג עשין לט טוש"ע א"ח סי' תלג סעי' ח:
צ ל מיי' פ"ד מהל' שאלה ופקדון הל' ד סמג עשין פח טוש"ע ח"מ סי' רצא סעי' טו:
צא מ מיי' שם הל' ו טוש"ע שם סעי' ו:
צב נ מיי' שם הל' ז טוש"ע שם סעי' ז:
צג ס מיי' שם הל' ח טוש"ע שם סעי' כג:

## רבינו חננאל

מתניתין המפקיד מעות אצל חבירו צררן והפשילן לאחוריו מסרן לבניו הקטנים נעל בפניהן שלא כראוי חייב שלא שימר כדרך השומרים ואם שימר כדרך השומרים פטור. צררן והפשילן לאחוריו חייב כדר' יצחק דאמר כתיב וצרת הכסף בידך אע"פ שהוא צרור יהיה בידך. אמר שמואל כספין אין להן שמירה אלא בקרקע ובערב שבת לא אטרחוה רבנן. ואסיקנא משום איכסוי מעינא הילכך בטפח סגי ליה. והשתא דשכיחי גשושי פי' שמגששין בקרקע ומגלין הטמונות אין לה שמירה אלא בשמי קורה. פי' פרומאי מלשון בגדיו יהיו פרומים. טיט שנותן הבנאי בין ארחא לארחא בעובי הכותל נקרא ביני אורבי. כדגרסי' בגמ' דהשותפין כותל כפיסין ד' טפחים אריח מכאן שהוא טפח ומחצה שיעור חצי לבינה ואריח מכאן כנגדו הרי ג' טפחים נשאר טפח בין שני אריחין ממלאו באבנים קטנים וטיט ונקרא ביני אורבי. פי' טפוחאי שמנקשין בטפח שלהן ומרגישין אם יש בכותל כספין או זולתן: ההוא דאפקיד זוזי גביה חבריה אותבינהו בצריפא דאורבני פי' נתנם בבית המסוכך בעצי ערבה ונגנבו סבר רב יוסף למיפטריה משום דהוא שומר חנם וכו' איכא דאמרי אמר רב יוסף אע"ג דלענין גנבי נטירותא היא לענין נורא פשיעותא היא תחלתו בפשיעה וסופו באונס חייב וכן הלכה למעשה תחלתו בפשיעה וסופו באונס חייב. ההוא דאפקיד זוזי גביה חבריה אמר ליה הב לי זוזיי אמר ליה לא ידענא היכא איתנחתינהו. אמר רבא כל לא ידענא פשיעותא היא וכן הלכה. ההוא דאפקיד זוזי גביה חבריה אשלימינהו לאימיה ואותבינהו בקרטליתא ואיגנוב

**Mishnah** This Mishnah discusses the concept of פְּשִׁיעָה, *negligence,* for which even an unpaid *shomer* is liable: הַמַּפְקִיד מָעוֹת אֵצֶל חֲבֵרוֹ — If **one deposited coins with his fellow** for safekeeping צְרָרָן — and **he** either **bundled them up** in a cloth וְהִפְשִׁילָן לַאֲחוֹרָיו — **and hung them over his back,** אוֹ שֶׁמְּסָרָם לִבְנוֹ וּלְבִתּוֹ הַקְּטַנִּים — **or he transferred them to his young son or daughter** וְנָעַל בִּפְנֵיהֶם שֶׁלֹּא כָּרָאוּי — **and** then **locked** the door **before them improperly,**[1] חַיָּיב — **[the** ***shomer*****] is liable** for loss and damage, שֶׁלֹּא שִׁימֵּר כְּדֶרֶךְ הַשּׁוֹמְרִים — **because he did not guard** the money **in the** normal **manner of** responsible ***shomrim.*** וְאִם שִׁימֵּר כְּדֶרֶךְ הַשּׁוֹמְרִים — **But if he did guard** the money **in the** normal **manner of** ***shomrim,*** פָּטוּר — **he is not liable.**[2]

**Gemara** The Gemara raises a difficulty with the first case of the Mishnah:

בִּשְׁלָמָא כּוּלְּהוּ — **It is understandable** why the *shomer* is liable in **all [the cases]** of the Mishnah besides the first one, שֶׁלֹּא שִׁימֵּר כְּדֶרֶךְ הַשּׁוֹמְרִים — **for he did not guard** the money **in the** normal **manner of** ***shomrim.***[3] אֶלָּא צְרָרָן וְהִפְשִׁילָן לַאֲחוֹרָיו — **But** in the first case, where **he bundled up [the money]** in a kerchief **and slung it behind him,** why is he liable? מַאי הֲוָה לֵיהּ לְמֶיעֱבַד — **What** more **should he have done?**[4]

The Gemara answers:

אָמַר רָבָא אָמַר רַב יִצְחָק — **Rava said in the name of Rav Yitzchak:** אָמַר קְרָא — **The verse states:**[5] "וְצַרְתָּ הַכֶּסֶף בְּיָדְךָ" — ***And you shall bundle up the money in your hand.*** This verse teaches that when you take *maaser sheni* money to Jerusalem, אַף עַל פִּי שֶׁצְּרוּרִין — **even though it is bundled up,** יְהִיוּ בְּיָדְךָ — **it should** still **be in your hand.** From this it is evident that the proper safeguarding of money requires that it be kept in one's hand.[6]

Since the previous teaching was authored by Rav Yitzchak, the Gemara cites a series of related teachings by this Amora:

וְאָמַר רַב יִצְחָק — **And Rav Yitzchak said:** לְעוֹלָם יְהֵא כַּסְפּוֹ שֶׁל אָדָם מָצוּי בְּיָדוֹ — **A person's money should always be readily available to him;**[7] שֶׁנֶּאֱמַר — **as it is stated:** "וְצַרְתָּ הַכֶּסֶף בְּיָדְךָ" — ***And you shall bundle up the money in your hand.***[8]

Another teaching by Rav Yitzchak:

וְאָמַר רַב יִצְחָק — **And Rav Yitzchak said:** לְעוֹלָם יְשַׁלֵּשׁ אָדָם אֶת מָעוֹתָיו — **A person should always divide his money into three parts:** שְׁלִישׁ בְּקַרְקַע — **one-third** should be invested **in land,**[9] וּשְׁלִישׁ בִּפְרַקְמַטְיָא — **one-third in merchandise,** וּשְׁלִישׁ תַּחַת יָדוֹ — **and one-third** should be **readily available to him.**[10]

Another teaching of Rav Yitzchak:

וְאָמַר רַב יִצְחָק — **And Rav Yitzchak said:** אֵין הַבְּרָכָה מְצוּיָה — **Blessing**[11] **is not found** אֶלָּא בְּדָבָר הַסָּמוּי מִן הָעַיִן — **except in something that is hidden from the eye,** שֶׁנֶּאֱמַר — **as it is said:** "יְצַו ה׳ אִתְּךָ אֶת־הַבְּרָכָה בַּאֲסָמֶיךָ" — ***Hashem will command the blessing** to be **with you in your silos.***[12]

A similar teaching:

תָּנָא דְּבֵי רַבִּי יִשְׁמָעֵאל — **A Baraisa was taught in the academy of R' Yishmael:** אֵין הַבְּרָכָה מְצוּיָה — BLESSING IS NOT FOUND אֶלָּא בְּדָבָר שֶׁאֵין הָעַיִן שׁוֹלֶטֶת בּוֹ — EXCEPT IN SOMETHING AT WHICH THE EYE CANNOT GAZE, שֶׁנֶּאֱמַר — AS IT IS SAID: "יְצַו ה׳ אִתְּךָ אֶת־הַבְּרָכָה בַּאֲסָמֶיךָ" — *HASHEM WILL COMMAND THE BLESSING to be WITH YOU IN YOUR HIDDEN STORAGE PLACES.*[13]

The Gemara cites a related Baraisa:

תָּנוּ רַבָּנָן — **The Rabbis taught in a Baraisa:** הַהוֹלֵךְ לָמוֹד אֶת גּוֹרְנוֹ — ONE WHO IS ABOUT TO MEASURE the pile of grain in HIS SILO אוֹמֵר יְהִי רָצוֹן מִלְּפָנֶיךָ ה׳ אֱלֹהֵינוּ — SHOULD RECITE the following prayer: "MAY IT BE YOUR WILL, HASHEM, OUR GOD, שֶׁתִּשְׁלַח בְּרָכָה בְּמַעֲשֵׂה יָדֵינוּ — THAT YOU BESTOW BLESSING UPON THE WORK OF OUR HANDS." הִתְחִיל לָמוֹד — When HE BEGINS TO MEASURE the pile of grain, אוֹמֵר בָּרוּךְ הַשּׁוֹלֵחַ בְּרָכָה בִּכְרִי הַזֶּה — HE SAYS:

NOTES

1. The lock was not strong enough to prevent the children from taking the money outside and losing it (*Rashi* to 36a ד״ה בפניהם; see note 3).

2. An unpaid *shomer* is required to safeguard the deposit in a manner that is usually effective under the prevailing circumstances (see Gemara below and note 21). Provided that he did this, he is not liable to pay the owner for any loss to the deposit.

The preceding applies to an unpaid *shomer.* A paid *shomer,* however, is expected to safeguard the deposit in a manner that is better than the norm. As stated in the Gemara below (93a), the owner may claim to a paid *shomer:* "That is why I paid you — so that you would safeguard the deposit in a superior fashion."

In fact, some Rishonim hold that a paid *shomer* must personally watch the deposit at all times. According to this view, the only instance in which a paid *shomer* is not liable is where the deposit was forcibly taken away from him *while* he was watching it (*Ritva* et al.). But others say that even a paid *shomer* is not expected to go to such extremes. Provided that he safeguarded the deposit in a superior fashion (e.g. he buried it deeply in the ground), he is not liable for theft or loss (*Tosafos* et al.). See *Tosafos* to *Bava Kamma* 57a ד״ה כגון, *Rosh* ibid. §5, and *Shulchan Aruch, Choshen Mishpat* 303:2.

3. The Gemara refers to the second case of the Mishnah, where the *shomer* gave the money over to his young children and failed to lock the door adequately.

[According to *Rashi,* there are only two cases in the first part of the Mishnah, so the word כּוּלְּהוּ, *all of them,* is not precise. Others explain that giving the money to minor children and failing to lock the door properly are two separate cases [see 36a note 27] (see *Ritva*).]

4. Surely, just to bundle up the money would be sufficient. The fact that he slung the bundle behind his back should not make a difference (see *Rashi*).

5. *Deuteronomy* 14:25. The verse discusses one who redeems his *maaser sheni* (second tithe) produce with coins and takes those coins to Jerusalem.

6. In fact, the bundle of money need not be actually kept in his hand. As long as it is in a position where the *shomer* can see it at all times, he is not liable (*Rosh;* see *Ritva*; *Rambam, Hil. Sh'eilah U'Fikadon* 4:6, and *Yerushalmi* quoted in note 21).

7. Literally: found in his hand. A person should not entrust his money to someone else, because if he does, it will not be available to him should an opportunity for profit suddenly come up (*Rashi*).

8. See note 5.

9. *Maharsha,* second explanation.

10. Each of these three has an advantage not found in the others. Real estate is secure, but investment in merchandise yields higher profits. The advantage of having money readily available is that one can benefit from business opportunities that might suddenly arise (*Maharsha;* see *Maharam Schif*).

[This teaching of Rav Yitzchak qualifies the previous one; it is enough for only one-third of one's money to be readily available.]

11. This refers to produce that is "blessed" and increases in quantity, [apparently] of its own accord (*Rashi*).

12. *Deuteronomy* 28:8. This exposition is based on the similarity between the words אֲסָמֶיךָ, *your silos,* and סָמוּי, *hidden* (*Rashi*).

13. This exposition is based on the literal translation of אֲסָמֶיךָ as *your hidden storage places* (*Rashi*).

As far as their messages are concerned, this teaching is the same as the previous one. The difference between them is only how to derive the lesson from the word אֲסָמֶיךָ, *your silos* (*Maharsha*; cf. *Riaf* to *Ein Yaakov, Taanis* 8b; *Nachalas Yisrael, Ben Yehoyada,* and *Iyun Yaakov*).

לֹא כָּל שֶׁכֵּן – **is it not certain** that they are liable for all mishaps if they misappropriate it?[9]

Rava continues:

לָמָּה נֶאֱמַר – Given that this is so, **why is it** [the law of misappropriation] **stated** in connection with a paid *shomer* and an unpaid *shomer*? Since this law can be derived from the laws of a borrower, *both* of these references are apparently superfluous! The answer is: חֲדָא לוֹמַר לָךְ – **One** reference serves **to teach you** שְׁלִיחוּת יָד אֵין צְרִיכָה חִסָּרוֹן – that **misappropriation is not dependent upon a loss.** וְאִידָךְ – **And the other** reference teaches שֶׁלֹּא תֹּאמַר – **that you should not say,** דַּיּוֹ לָבֹא מִן הַדִּין לִהְיוֹת כַּנִּדּוֹן – **"It is sufficient that the derived law** [misappropriation] **is the same as the source law** [borrowing]";[10] i.e. this extra reference teaches that we should not say מַה שּׁוֹאֵל בִּבְעָלִים פָּטוּר – that **just as a borrower [who had] the owner** in his employ **is not liable** for unavoidable mishaps,[11] אַף שׁוֹמֵר חִנָּם וְשׁוֹמֵר שָׂכָר בִּבְעָלִים פָּטוּר – **so too an unpaid *shomer* or a paid *shomer* [who had] the owner** in his employ and later misappropriated the deposit **is not liable** for unavoidable mishaps.[12]

The Gemara now shows how this view (that the law of misappropriation is derived from the laws of borrowing) can be reconciled even with the view of Rav that misappropriation *is* dependent upon a loss:[13]

וּלְמַאן דְּאָמַר שְׁלִיחוּת יָד צְרִיכָה חִסָּרוֹן – **And according to the one who said** that **misappropriation is dependent upon a loss,** הָנֵי תַּרְתֵּי שְׁלִיחוּת יָד לָמָּה לִי – **why do I need these two** references to the law of **misappropriation?** חֲדָא שֶׁלֹּא תֹּאמַר – **One** reference teaches **that you should not say:** דַּיּוֹ לָבֹא מִן הַדִּין לִהְיוֹת כַּנִּדּוֹן – **"It is sufficient that the derived law** [misappropriation] **is the same as the source law** [borrowing]."[14] וְאִידָךְ לִכְדְתַנְיָא – **And the other** reference[15] is the source **for that which is taught in the** following **Baraisa:** "וְנִקְרַב בַּעַל־הַבַּיִת אֶל־הָאֱלֹהִים" – When Scripture states, ***THE HOUSEHOLDER*** [an unpaid *shomer* who claims that the deposit was stolen] ***SHALL BE BROUGHT BEFORE THE JUDGES,***[16] לִשְׁבוּעָה – it means that he is brought before the judges FOR the purpose of taking AN OATH.[17]

The Baraisa proves that the verse refers to an oath:

אַתָּה אוֹמֵר לִשְׁבוּעָה – Now YOU SAY that the verse means that he is brought before the judges FOR the purpose of taking AN OATH. אוֹ אֵינוֹ אֶלָּא לְדִין – But PERHAPS it means that he is brought before the judges ONLY FOR the sake of JUDGMENT? How do you know that the verse teaches that he must have made an oath? [18] נֶאֶמְרָה שְׁלִיחוּת יָד לְמַטָּה – The proof is that since MISAPPROPRIATION IS MENTIONED BELOW (in the passage about a paid *shomer*) וְנֶאֶמְרָה שְׁלִיחוּת יָד לְמַעְלָה – AND MISAPPROPRIATION IS MENTIONED ABOVE (in our passage about an unpaid *shomer*), the two passages are considered linked.[19] From this linkage, we infer: מַה לְּהַלָּן לִשְׁבוּעָה – JUST AS THERE (in the passage about a paid *shomer*) the Torah requires AN OATH,[20] אַף כָּאן לִשְׁבוּעָה – HERE TOO (in the passage about an unpaid *shomer*), the Torah requires AN OATH.[21]

NOTES

9. [The basis for comparing misappropriation and borrowing is as follows:] A borrower is totally liable for the borrowed article because, while it is in his possession, he is the sole recipient of all of its benefit. Similarly, a *shomer* who misappropriates a deposit is the sole recipient of its benefit (*Rashi*).

10. A *kal vachomer* argument can only put the derived law on the same footing as the source law; it cannot be used to derive greater stringencies or leniencies than those of the source law. This limitation is expressed by the formula: דַּיּוֹ לָבֹא מִן הַדִּין לִהְיוֹת כַּנִּדּוֹן, *it is sufficient that the derived law is the same as the source law* (see *Bava Kamma* 25a).

11. The verse (*Exodus* 22:14): אִם־בְּעָלָיו עִמּוֹ לֹא יְשַׁלֵּם, *if the owner is with him, he need not pay,* teaches that a borrower is not liable for unavoidable mishaps if the owner was working for him (*Rashi*). [This exemption applies where the owner was working for the borrower at the time the article was first borrowed (*Shulchan Aruch, Choshen Mishpat* 346:2; see Gemara below, 95b-96a).]

12. The reference to the law of misappropriation in the passage about a paid *shomer* teaches that although this law is derived from the laws of borrowing, it is more stringent than its source, in that it applies even where the owner was working for the *shomer*.

This teaching is derived from the passage about a paid *shomer;* however, it is equally applicable to both a paid and an unpaid *shomer* (*Rashi*).

According to Rava's approach, the meaning of R' Elazar's statement, "*This* [reference] *is the same as the other* [reference]," is that *neither* reference is required to teach the basic law of misappropriation; rather, each one is available to teach a detail of this law (*Tosafos*, second approach).

13. According to this view, both of the Torah's references to the law of misappropriation are apparently superfluous. Rava explained that one of these references teaches that misappropriation is not dependent upon a loss. The Gemara now explains what Rav, who holds that misappropriation *is* dependent on a loss, would derive from these two references.

14. See notes 10-12.

15. I.e. the one from which Rava derived that misappropriation is not dependent upon a loss.

16. *Exodus* 22:7.

17. Thus, the verse teaches that if an unpaid *shomer* took an oath that the deposit was stolen from him and witnesses then testify that the deposit is in his possession, he must pay a double payment (see note 5).

The verse is interpreted as follows: אִם לֹא יִמָּצֵא הַגַּנָּב וְנִקְרַב בַּעַל־הַבַּיִת אֶל־הָאֱלֹהִים...אֲשֶׁר יַרְשִׁיעֻן אֱלֹהִים יְשַׁלֵּם שְׁנַיִם לְרֵעֵהוּ, *If it is not found* to be as the *shomer* claimed – but rather witnesses testify that he is *the thief,* after *the householder* [the *shomer*] *had been brought before the judges* and sworn falsely that the deposit was stolen from him – (v. 8) *the judges shall declare him guilty, and he shall pay double to his fellow* [the owner] (*Rashi*, from *Bava Kamma* 63b).

18. That is, one might have thought that an unpaid *shomer* who falsely claimed in court that the deposit was stolen from him and then was found to have stolen it himself is liable to a double payment even if he had not made a false oath to back up his claim (*Rashi*).

19. *Exodus* 22:6-8 is the passage about an unpaid *shomer*. Ibid. vv. 9-12 is the passage about a paid *shomer.* In both passages, misappropriation is mentioned: אִם־לֹא שָׁלַח יָדוֹ בִּמְלֶאכֶת רֵעֵהוּ, *if he did not misappropriate his fellow's goods* (vv. 7 and 10). Since both passages contain the same phrase, they are considered linked to one another, and the laws of one are applied to the subject of the other. This method of exegesis is known as *gezeirah shavah*. [Only words or phrases that are known by Sinaitic tradition to have been designated for the purpose may serve as a basis for a *gezeirah shavah.*]

The Torah added one of these two references to the law of misappropriation for the sake of this *gezeirah shavah*. [A *gezeirah shavah* cannot be expounded unless at least one of the two terms on which it is based is available for that purpose [i.e. it is otherwise superfluous] (see *Niddah* 22b).]

20. As it is said (*Exodus* 22:10): שְׁבֻעַת ה׳ תִּהְיֶה בֵּין שְׁנֵיהֶם, *an oath of Hashem shall be between them.* [The verse teaches that a paid *shomer* must pay unless he takes an oath that the loss of the deposit was due to circumstances beyond his control.]

21. According to the Baraisa's conclusion, an unpaid *shomer* is not liable to a double payment unless he had taken an oath (that the deposit was stolen from him). From this it is also derived that an unpaid *shomer* must take an oath to support a claim of loss or theft (*Rashi*; see *Rashi* to *Bava Kamma* 63b and *Maharsha* ibid.).

ואני אומר אינה משונה ומאי משונה לא תאמר שליחות יד בשומר שכר ותיתי משומר חנם ומה שומר חנם שפטור בגנבה ואבדה שלח בה יד חייב שומר שכר שחייב בגנבה ואבידה לא כל שכן למאי הלכתא כתבינהו רחמנא לומר לך שליחות יד אינה צריכה חסרון ואני אומר אינה משונה כר' אלעזר דאמר דא ודא אחת היא מאי דא ודא אחת (א) משום דאיכא למפרך מה לשומר חנם שכן משלם תשלומי כפל בטוען טענת גנב ומאן דלא פריך סבר [א] קרנא בלא שבועה עדיפא מכפילא בשבועה רבא אמר לא תאמר שליחות יד לא בשומר חנם ולא בשומר שכר ותיתי משואל ומה שואל דלדעת בעלים קא עביד (ב) שלח בה יד חייב שומר חנם ושומר שכר לא כל שכן למה נאמר חדא לומר לך שליחות יד אין צריכה חסרון ואידך שלא תאמר דיו לבא מן הדין להיות כנדון מה שואל בבעלים פטור אף שומר חנם ושומר שכר בבעלים פטור ולמאן דאמר שליחות יד צריכה חסרון הני תרתי שליחות יד למה לי חדא שלא תאמר דיו לבא מן הדין להיות כנדון ואידך לכדתניא [ג] א ונקרב בעל הבית אל האלהים [א] לשבועה אתה אומר לשבועה או אינו אלא לדין נאמרה שליחות יד למטה ונאמרה שליחות יד למעלה מה להלן לשבועה אף כאן א לשבועה:

מתני'

**רש"י**

**ואני אומר.** ר' יוחנן פליג אדרבי יוסי בן נהוראי רביה ואמר אף היא לצורך נאמרה ולוי ס"ל כרבי יוסי בן נהוראי למידרש מיניה דאין צריכה חסרון דאי מקרא קמא לא תיסק אדעתין לחיוביה עד דמחסר ליה: **בשומר חנם נאמר** ונקרב בעל הבית וגו' בשומר שכר כתיב שבועת ה' תהיה וגו' ואמרינן בהשואל (לקמן דף צד:) פרשה ראשונה נאמרה בשומר חנם שניה בשומר שכר וכתיב בתרוייהו אם לא שלח הא אם שלח נתחייב בדברים שהוא פטור עליהם כגון שומר חנם בין בגנבה בין באונסין דמשלח בה יד קנאה וקמה ברשותו ושומר שכר פטור במת או נשבר או נשבה דהיינו אונסין: **שומר חנם שפטור.** כל זמן שלא שלח בה יד כדכתיב אם לא ימצא הגנב ונקרב בעה"ב דנשבע שלא שלח בה יד ולא פשע בשמירתו ופטור כדאמרינן לקמן בשמעתין דהאי ונקרב שבועה הוא: **שומר שכר שחייב בגנבה ואבדה.** דפרשה שניה בו נאמרה וכתיב בה אם גנב יגנב כו': **לא כ"ש.** שאם שלח בה יד חייב באונסין: **דא ודא אחת היא.** כמשמעה של זו כך משמעה של זו לפי ששתיהן הוצרכו ואין כאן מקרא יתר: **מאי דא ודא אחת היא.** למה שתיהן שוות הלא לא הוצרכה השניה: **שומר חנם שפוטר עצמו בטענת גנב.** כלומר גנב גנבה ממני ובאו עדים שהיא אצלו משלם תשלומי כפל דכתיב אם לא ימצא הגנב וגו' ודרשינן בבבא קמא (דף סג:) אם לא ימצא כמה שאמר אלא שהוא עצמו גנבו מה כתיב אחריו אשר ירשיעון אלהים ישלם שנים אבל שומר שכר אינו משלם כפל שאם טען נגנבה משלם קרן שהרי הוא חייב בגניבה וטענה אחרת אינה מביאה אותו לידי כפל: **קרנא בלא שבועה עדיפא מכפילא בשבועה.** חמור שומר שכר שחייב בקרן עד שלא נשבע לשקר במקום ששומר חנם פטור דהיינו גניבה ואבידה משומר חנם שמשלם כפל ומדה זו אינה אלא לאחר שנשבע לשקר שנגנבה ובאו עדים שהוא גנבה דכי אתרבי כפל בטוען טענת גנב לאחר שבועה אתרבי כדלקמן בשמעתין: **רבא אמר.** אפילו לרבי אלעזר נמי אתיא דלא תימא כו': **ותיתי משואל.** שחייבו הכתוב באונסין בשביל שכל הנאה שלו ושולח יד נמי כל הנאה שלו: (ג) (ומה שואל) **שלדעת בעלים.** שלח בה יד לעשות מלאכתו חייב באונסין: **שומר חנם ושומר שכר.** השולחין יד שעושין מלאכתן שלא לדעת בעלים לא כ"ש דחייב שוב באונסיה: **למה נאמרה.** בשתיהן: **חדא לומר לך** שליחות יד אינה צריכה חסרון: **ואידך.** האמורה בשומר שכר: **שלא תאמר דיו לבא כו'.** אם לא נאמרה בשאר שומרין ולמדה משואל הייתי אומר דיו לשליחות יד דשומרין שבא מדין שואל להיות כנדון: **מה שואל.** אם בעליו עמו כתיב לא ישלם אונסין אף שומרין ששלחו יד אם בעליו עמו יפטר כתב קרא יתירא לחייבו אפילו בבעלים וגלי רחמנא בחדא והוא הדין בכולהו: **לשבועה.** והכי קאמר אם לא ימצא כמה שאמר שנגנבה אלא הוא גנבה והוא כבר נקרב אל הדיינין לשבועה ונשבע לשקר ואח"כ באו עדים אשר ירשיעון הדיינין ישלם כפל: **אתה אומר.** קריבה לשבועה או אינו אלא קריבה לדין שמשעה שטען בב"ד נגנבה אע"פ שלא נשבע ישלם כפל אם באו עדים: **נאמר שליחות יד למטה.** אצל שומר שכר שבועת ה' תהיה בין שניהם אם לא שלח: **ונאמר שליחות יד למעלה.** ונקרב בעל הבית אל האלהים אם לא שלח: **אף כאן לשבועה.** למדנו שאין משלמין כפל ע"י טענת גנב אלא לאחר שבועה וגם למדנו שנפטר מגנבה ואבדה בשבועה:

**תוספות**

**לומר** לך שליחות יד אינה צריכה חסרון. וא"ת התינח שומר שכר דאייתר קרא להכי אלא בשומר חנם מנ"ל אי משומר שכר מה לשומר שכר שכן חייב בגנבה ואבדה וי"ל כיון דשליחות יד חייב בתרוייהו אין זה אלא גילוי מילתא למילף דין של זה בזה:

**קרנא** בלא שבועה. וא"ת ורבי יוחנן ור' אלעזר דלית להו הך סברא מנ"ל דפ' ראשונה בשומר חנם ושניה בשומר שכר דבריש השואל (לקמן דף צד:) לא קים לן אלא מהך סברא דקרנא עדיפא ופי' רבינו שמואל דמסברא ידעינן דבפרשה ראשונה כתיב כסף או כלים ורגילות הוא לשמרם בחנם דליכא בהו טרחא ובפרשה שניה כתיב בהמה דאיכא טרחא ורגילות לשמרה בשכר אי נמי דלכ"ע אית להו דקרנא עדיפא מכפילא בשבועה ומ"מ סבירא להו לר' יוחנן ולרבי אלעזר דאין ללמוד שומר שכר משומר חנם הקל כיון שיש בו חומרא שמשלם כפל מה שאין כן בשומר שכר ואע"ג דשומר שכר ודאי חמור שחייב בגנבה ואבדה ומאן דלא פריך סבר דמכפל אפילו פירכא לא עבדינן משום דמה דמשלם כפל הוא מחמת קולא שהוא פוטר עצמו בגנבה כדמפרש בריש מכלתין (דף ד. ושם) גבי תורת הזמה לא פריך והשתא אתי שפיר הא דריש השואל (לקמן דף לה.) גבי הא דגמר גנבה בשואל מק"ו דשומר שכר דפטור באונס וחייב בגנבה ואבדה שואל לא כל שכן ופריך מה לשומר שכר דחייב בכפל ד) [בטוען טענת לסטים מזויין] והשתא תימה לפי מה דסבר דכפל הוי חומרא מאי פריך אדרבה כיון שהוא חמור הוה לו ליפטר מגנבה כדי שיתחייב כפל וע"ק ברייתא גופה שואל שחייב בשבורה ומתה כו' אדרבה היא הנותנת דמפני שהוא חמור פטר בו הגנבה כדי לחייבו בכפל ולפי מה דפרישית אתי שפיר וא"ת לר' יוחנן דסבר הכא דמכפל עבדינן פירכא וגם סבר רב יוסף בפרק הכונס (ב"ק דף נז. ושם) גבי שומר אבדה לר' יוחנן דלסטים מזויין גנב הוא אם כן גנבה ואבדה בשואל מנ"ל דכי פריך בהשואל מה לשומר שכר שכן משלם כפל בלסטים מזויין ה) ומשני לסטים מזויין גזלן הוא איבעית אימא קרנא בלא שבועה עדיפא וי"ל דלר' יוחנן נפקא ליה מוכי ישאל וי"ו מוסיף על ענין ראשון וכה"ג יליף התם לעניין פטור בבעלים ואע"ג דרבי יוסי ברבי נהוראי הוא תנא וסבר דקרנא עדיפא וכן ברייתא דהשואל (לקמן דף לה.) סבר דקרנא עדיפא או לסטים מזויין גזלן הוא ור' יוחנן פליג בתרוייהו הא לא קשיא דר' יוחנן סבר כתנא דהכונס (ב"ק דף נז:) דקאמר לא אם אמרת בשומר חנם שכן משלם כפל לכך שלח בה יד חייב דקאי אמילתיה דרבי יוסי בר' נהוראי:

**רבא** אמר לא תימא שליחות יד כו'. פרש"י דסבר אפילו כרבי אלעזר ואין להקשות לפירושו הא דקאמר ואידך שלא תאמר דיו והא תרוייהו צריכי לאינה צריכה חסרון לר' אלעזר דהא לא יליף שומר שכר משומר חנם דהא בתר הכי פריך ולמ"ד ו) [שליחות יד] צריכה חסרון תרתי למה לי ולדידיה לא ילפינן חד מחבריה אפילו הכי לא מוקמינן תרוייהו לדיו והיינו משום כדפי"ל דכיון דשליחות יד חייב בתרוייהו גלוי מלתא בעלמא למילף דין של זה בזה ועוד יש לומר דרבא בא לפרש דהא דאמר ר"א דא ודא אחת היא לא שניהם צריכי לגופייהו כדאמרינן אלא שניהם מיותרין דגמר להו משואל וסבר רבא קרנא עדיפא ושפיר גמר שומר שכר משומר חנם לכולי עלמא זה מזה מיהו ברייתא דהכונס (שם) סברה דלא ילפינן זה מזה דקתני לא אם אמרת בשומר חנם כו':

**חדא** לומר [לך שליחות יד] אין צריכה חסרון. וא"ת ונילף משואל דאינה צריכה חסרון דמשעת משיכה חייב באונסיה אע"ג דלא נשתמש כדאמר בפ' השואל (לקמן דף צט.) גבי שואל קורדום מחבירו כ"ש שומרין שמושכין להשתמש שלא מדעת בעלים שחייבים וי"ל בשואל דין הוא כיון דמושך לדעת בעלים חשיב כאילו נשתמש בה דלדעת כן שאלה ולאו לאוקמה בכילתא אבל שלא לדעת אינו חשיב כאילו כבר נשתמש בשביל משיכה לבדה לכך לא ילפינן משואל אלא משיכה שיש בה חסרון: **חדא** לדיו וחדא לכדתניא. ולמ"ד נמי אינה צריכה חסרון דצריכי תרוייהו יליף שפיר ג"ש לכדתניא לפי שיש כל כך תיבות בזה כמו בזה אם לא שלח ידו במלאכת רעהו:

אמר

**עין משפט נר מצוה**

[פ א מיי' פ"א מהלכות שכירות הל' ג סמג עשין פט טוש"ע ח"מ סי' רלא סעיף א]:
פא א מיי' פ"ד מהל' גניבה הלכה א טוש"מ סי' שנב:

**רבינו חננאל**

עוד שליחות יד בשומר שכר אלא ללמד שאפי' שליחות יד בלא חסרון חייב. ורבי יוחנן דידיה אמר ואני אומר אינה משונה כלומר אין זה יכול ללמד מזה שאין שומר חנם קל משומר שכר שהרי חייבה תורה בשומר חנם שטען כי נגנב ונמצא שהוא גנבו שהוא משלם תשלומי כפל ושומר שכר שטוען טענת גנב ונמצא שהוא גנבו פטור מכפל מפני שחייב בשומר שכר בגניבה כך הייתי אומר כי שלח בו יד פטור א) מכפל ועוד אם יש לומר אי הכי נכתוב שליחות יד בשומר שכר וילמד שומר חנם ממנו איכא למיפרך הכי כי שומר חנם ושומר שכר שגנבו הפקדון שהיה בידם וטענו שנגנב שומר שכר חייב לשלם מיד שהרי חייב בגניבה ואבידה ושומר חנם אינו חייב אלא עד שישבע שנגנב ואחר כך באו עדים שהוא גנבו הלכך לא זה לומד מזה ולא זה מזה הלכך לגופיה בא בתרוייהו ולעולם שליחות יד צריכה חסרון לטעמיה דר' יוחנן. ורבא דהוא בתרא אמר אינה צריכה [חסרון]. הא דאמר רבא לא תאמר שליחות יד לא בשומר חנם ולא בשומר שכר ותיתי משואל והא לא כתיבא שליחות יד בשואל כלל. כך פירושה לא תאמר שליחות יד אלא בשואל בלבד ולא היה צריך לכתוב לא בשומר חנם ולא בשומר שכר ויבואו וילמדו מן השואל ולמה נאמר בהן ללמד שאין צריכה חסרון ושלא תאמר דיו לבא מן הדין להיות כנדון כו' ופשוטה היא. שליחות יד דכתיבא בשומר חנם ובשומר שכר ואפי' אשואל וכי ישאל ו' מוסיף על ענין ראשון וכאילו בשלשתם כתיבא שליחות יד הני כולהו למה לי וכו'.

**חשק שלמה על ר"ח**

א) נראה דצ"ל פטור מאונסין.

**תורה אור השלם**

א) אִם לֹא יִמָּצֵא הַגַּנָּב וְנִקְרַב בַּעַל הַבַּיִת אֶל הָאֱלֹהִים אִם לֹא שָׁלַח יָדוֹ בִּמְלֶאכֶת רֵעֵהוּ: [שמות כב, ז]

**מסורת הש"ס**

א) [לקמן לד:, בבא קמא נז:], ב) בבא קמא סג:, ג) מהרש"ל מ"ז, ד) מהרש"ס, ה) נ"ל משני בלא וא"ו, מהרש"ס. ו) מהרש"ס.

**הגהות הב"ח**

(א) גמ' אחת היא משום דאיכא: (ב) שם דשלח בה יד:

**ליקוטי רש"י**

**בטוען טענת גנב.** טוען שנגנבה הימנו ונמצא שהוא עצמו גנבה חייב בה כפל בפרשה ראשונה דכתיב אם לא ימצא הגנב וסמיך ליה על כל דבר פשע ישלם שנים ואוקימנא בפ' מרובה (ב"ק דף סג:) אם לא ימצא כמו שאומר אלא הוא עצמו גנבו ישלם שנים וכגון שנשבע תחילה לשקר שנגנב אבל באו עדים קודם שנשבע תחלה לשקר אינו משלם כפל דהכי כתיב אם לא ימצא הגנב וכבר נשבע ונקרב בעל הבית אל האלהים לשבועה על כל דבר פשע אשר ירשיעון דיינין בעדים ישלם שנים. **קרנא בלא שבועה עדיפא מכפילא בשבועה.** מחייבתו לשלם קרן משאמר נגנבה ואפילו לא נשבע לשקר זה חמורה מן הראשונה שפוטרתו מלשלם קרן אם לא באו עדים שהוא גנבה אע"פ שמחייבתו כפל לאחר שנשבע לשקר ובאו עדים ובלא שבועה אין שם כפל [לקמן צד:]. **לשבועה.** שכיון שטוען וגונב מביא האיש ישבע שנגנבה ויפטר [ב"ק סג:]. ונקרב אל הדיינין לדון עם זה ולישבע לו שלא שלח ידו בשלו [שמות כב, ז]. **או אינו אלא לדין.** לפרעון דשומר חנם שטוען נגנבה ישלם דהאי קרא בש"ח כתיב כדאמרי' בהשואל [ב"ק שם].

R' Yochanan then added his own opinion: וַאֲנִי אוֹמֵר – **But I say** אֵינָהּ מְשׁוּנָּה – that **it is not different.**

The Gemara first explains the opinion of R' Yose ben Nehorai: וּמַאי מְשׁוּנָּה – **What** does R' Yose ben Nehorai mean by saying that the Torah's reference to the law of misappropriation written by a paid *shomer* is **different** from the one written by an unpaid *shomer*? He reasons as follows: לֹא תֵּאָמֵר שְׁלִיחוּת יָד בְּשׁוֹמֵר שָׂכָר – The law of **misappropriation need not have been stated in connection with a paid *shomer*,** וְתֵיתֵי מִשּׁוֹמֵר חִנָּם – because **it could have been** logically **derived from** its mention in connection with **an unpaid *shomer*,** through a *kal vachomer* argument: וּמַה שׁוֹמֵר חִנָּם שֶׁפָּטוּר בִּגְנֵבָה וַאֲבֵדָה – **If an unpaid *shomer*, who is not obligated** to pay the owner **for theft or loss** of the deposit, שָׁלַח בָּהּ יָד חַיָּיב – **is** nevertheless **obligated** to pay even for unavoidable mishaps if **he misappropriated it,**[1] שׁוֹמֵר שָׂכָר שֶׁחַיָּיב בִּגְנֵבָה וַאֲבֵדָה – **a paid *shomer*, who *is* obligated** to pay the owner **for theft and loss** of the deposit, לֹא כָּל שֶׁכֵּן – **is it not certain** that he is liable for unavoidable mishaps if he misappropriated it? לְמַאי הִלְכְתָא כְּתָבִינְהוּ רַחֲמָנָא – So **for** the sake of teaching **which law did the Merciful One write [this twice]** in the Torah, when writing it just in connection with an unpaid *shomer* would have sufficed? לוֹמַר לָךְ – We can say that the law was repeated in the passage of a paid *shomer* **to teach you** שְׁלִיחוּת יָד אֵינָהּ צְרִיכָה חֶסְרוֹן – that **misappropriation is not dependent upon a loss.**[2]

The Gemara now turns to R' Yochanan's view: וַאֲנִי אוֹמֵר – **But I** [R' Yochanan] **say** אֵינָהּ מְשׁוּנָּה – that the Torah's reference to the law of misappropriation by a paid *shomer* is **not different** from the reference to this law by an unpaid *shomer*. כְּרַבִּי אֶלְעָזָר – R' Yochanan's statement **accords with** the opinion of **R' Elazar,** דְּאָמַר דָּא וְדָא אַחַת הִיא – **who said** that **one** reference to the law of misappropriation **is the same as the other.** I.e. both are required to teach the basic law of misappropriation; neither is extra to teach that misappropriation is not dependent upon a loss.

The Gemara questions this approach: מַאי דָּא וְדָא אַחַת – **What** does R' Elazar mean by saying that **one** reference **is the same as the other?** But the reference to the law of misappropriation in the passage about a paid *shomer* is not necessary in its own right,[3] for the application of this law to a paid *shomer* can be inferred by a *kal vachomer* argument from an unpaid *shomer*, as was explained above.[4] —?—

The Gemara answers that R' Elazar finds fault with the *kal vachomer* argument: מִשּׁוּם דְּאִיכָּא לְמִפְרַךְ – According to R' Elazar, the *kal vachomer* argument is flawed, **because there are** grounds **for refuting** it, as follows: מַה לְשׁוֹמֵר חִנָּם – **What** can you prove **from an unpaid *shomer*,** שֶׁכֵּן מְשַׁלֵּם תַּשְׁלוּמֵי כֶפֶל – **who pays a double payment** בְּטוֹעֵן טַעֲנַת גַּנָּב – **when he claims** that the deposit was **stolen,** and witnesses then testify that he had stolen it himself?[5] A paid *shomer*, on the other hand, never makes a double payment.[6] Since there is an instance in which an unpaid *shomer* is treated more stringently than a paid *shomer*, the law of misappropriation cannot be derived from the former to the latter.[7]

The Gemara now turns back to the opinion of R' Yose ben Nehorai, and explains why he does not consider the preceding point a refutation of the *kal vachomer* argument: וּמַאן דְּלָא פָּרִיךְ סָבַר – **And the one** [R' Yose ben Nehorai] **who does not refute** the *kal vachomer* argument in this manner **holds** קַרְנָא בְּלָא שְׁבוּעָה – that a paid *shomer's* obligation to pay the **principal** if the deposit was lost or stolen, even **without** taking **a** false **oath,** עֲדִיפָא מִכְּפֵילָא בִּשְׁבוּעָה – **is greater** in severity **than** an unpaid *shomer's* obligation to make **a double payment,** which applies only **after** he has taken **a** false **oath.** Therefore, overall, a paid *shomer* is treated more stringently than an unpaid *shomer*. Consequently, it is possible to derive the law of misappropriation from an unpaid *shomer* to a paid *shomer*, and the Torah's repetition of the law can teach that misappropriation does not require a loss.

The Gemara above cited R' Elazar's statement that the two Scriptural references to the law of misappropriation [the one in the passage about an unpaid *shomer* and the one in the passage about a paid *shomer*] are the same. Initially, this was understood to mean that each reference is required to teach the basic law of misappropriation, and neither is available to teach the law that misappropriation is not dependent upon a loss. The Gemara now presents a different understanding of R' Elazar's words, according to which R' Elazar agrees that one of the references *is* available to teach this point:

רָבָא אָמַר – **Rava said:** לֹא תֵּאָמֵר שְׁלִיחוּת יָד לֹא בְּשׁוֹמֵר חִנָּם – The law of **misappropriation need not have been mentioned neither in** the passage of **an unpaid *shomer*** וְלֹא בְּשׁוֹמֵר שָׂכָר – **nor in** the passage about **a paid *shomer*,** וְתֵיתֵי מִשּׁוֹאֵל – for **it can be derived from** the law that **a borrower** is liable for unavoidable mishaps, as follows: וּמַה שּׁוֹאֵל דִּלְדַעַת בְּעָלִים קָא עָבֵיד – **If a borrower, who acts with the consent of the owner** when he uses the item, שָׁלַח בָּהּ יָד חַיָּיב – **is liable** for all mishaps as soon as **he takes [the article]** to use,[8] שׁוֹמֵר חִנָּם וְשׁוֹמֵר שָׂכָר – **an unpaid *shomer* and a paid *shomer*,** who violate the will of the owner should they use the deposit for their own purposes,

NOTES

1. The Gemara assumes that if a *shomer* misappropriates a deposit, the Torah places it in his possession – as is the case with stealing – and thus he assumes liability for *all* mishaps (see *Rashi*). [Therefore, from the reference to the law of misappropriation in the passage about an unpaid *shomer*, it can be derived that liability for misappropriation includes liability for unavoidable mishaps, even though unavoidable mishaps are not mentioned in that passage.]

2. This is the source for Levi's ruling (see 41a note 17).

Although it is only the reference to misappropriation written in connection with an unpaid *shomer* that is apparently superfluous, the law that misappropriation is not dependent upon a loss applies equally to both a paid and an unpaid *shomer*, because a derivation is not necessary to say that the definition of what is considered misappropriation is the same in both cases (*Tosafos*).

3. And so it can be expounded to teach that misappropriation is not dependent upon a loss.

4. As the Gemara stated above in explanation of the opinion of R' Yose ben Nehorai, the *kal vachomer* argument is: An unpaid *shomer* is treated more stringently than a paid *shomer*, for he is not liable for theft and loss, whereas a paid *shomer* is; therefore, if the law of misappropriation applies to an unpaid *shomer*, it certainly applies to a paid *shomer*.

5. If an unpaid *shomer* swore (falsely) that the deposit was stolen from him, and then witnesses testify that it is still in his possession, the Torah mandates that in addition to returning the deposit to the owner, he is fined an amount equal to the value of the deposit. The Scriptural source for this law is given below, in note 17.

6. The Torah imposes a double payment on a *shomer* only where he attempted to exempt himself by claiming that the object had been stolen. Since a paid *shomer* is liable to pay for the deposit if he claims that it had been stolen, there is no case in which a paid *shomer* is fined a double payment (see *Rashi*).

7. Therefore, the reference to the law of misappropriation in the passage about a paid *shomer* is necessary in its own right, and is not available to teach that misappropriation is not dependent upon a loss.

8. I.e. when he takes it from the owner, even before he actually uses it (*Tosafos* ד״ה חדא לומר, from Gemara below, 99a).

ואני אומר אינה משונה ומאי משונה לא תאמר שליחות יד בשומר שכר ותיתי משומר חנם ומה שומר חנם שפטור בגנבה ואבדה שלח בה יד חייב שומר שכר שחייב בגנבה ואבידה לא כל שכן למאי הלכתא כתבינהו רחמנא לומר לך שליחות יד אינה צריכה חסרון ואני אומר אינה משונה כר' אלעזר דאמר דא ודא אחת היא מאי דא ודא אחת (א) משום דאיכא למפרך מה לשומר חנם שכן משלם תשלומי כפל בטוען טענת גנב ומאן דלא פריך סבר [א] קרנא בלא שבועה עדיפא מכפילא בשבועה רבא אמר לא תאמר שליחות יד לא בשומר חנם ולא בשומר שכר ותיתי משואל ומה שואל דלדעת בעלים קא עביד (ב) שלח בה יד חייב שומר חנם ושומר שכר לא כל שכן למה נאמר חדא לומר לך שליחות יד אין צריכה חסרון ואידך שלא תאמר דיו לבא מן הדין להיות כנדון מה שואל בבעלים פטור אף שומר חנם ושומר שכר בבעלים פטור ולמאן דאמר שליחות יד צריכה חסרון הני תרתי שליחות יד למה לי חדא שלא תאמר דיו לבא מן הדין להיות כנדון ואידך לכדתניא [ג] א) ונקרב בעל הבית אל האלהים [א] לשבועה אתה אומר לשבועה או אינו אלא לדין נאמרה שליחות יד למטה ונאמרה שליחות יד למעלה מה להלן לשבועה אף כאן [א] לשבועה:

מתני'

**לומר** לך שליחות יד אינה צריכה חסרון. וא"ת התינח שומר שכר דאייתר קרא להכי אלא בשומר חנם מנ"ל אי משומר שכר מה לשומר שכר שכן חייב בגנבה ואבדה וי"ל כיון דשליחות יד חייב בתרוייהו אין זה אלא גילוי מילתא למילף דין של זה בזה:

**קרנא** בלא שבועה. וא"ת ורבי יוחנן ור' אלעזר דלית להו הך סברא מנ"ל דפ' ראשונה בשומר חנם ושניה בשומר שכר דבריש השואל (לקמן דף צד:) לא קים לן אלא מהך סברא דקרנא עדיפא ופי' רבינו שמואל דמסברא ידעינן דפרשה ראשונה כתיב כסף או כלים ורגילות הוא לשמרם בחנם דליכא בהו טרחא ובפרשה שניה כתיב בהמה דאיכא טרחא ורגילות לשמרה בשכר אי נמי דלכ"ע אית להו דקרנא עדיפא מכפילא בשבועה ומ"מ סבירא להו לר' יוחנן ולרבי אלעזר דאין ללמוד שומר שכר משומר חנם הקל כיון שיש בו חומרא שמשלם כפל מה שאין כן בשומר שכר ואע"ג דשומר שכר ודאי חמור שחייב בגנבה ואבדה ומאן דלא פריך סבר דמכפל אפילו פירכא לא עבדינן משום דמה דמשלם כפל הוא מחמת קולא שהוא פוטר עצמו בגנבה כדמפרש בריש מכלתין (דף ד. ושם) גבי תורת הזמה לא פריך והשתא אתי שפיר הא דריש השואל (לקמן דף צה.) גבי הא דגמר גנבה בשואל מק"ו דשומר שכר דפטור באונס וחייב בגנבה ואבדה שואל לא כל שכן ופריך מה לשומר שכר דחייב בכפל [ד] [בטוען טענת לסטים מזוין] והשתא תימה לפי מה דסבר דכפל הוי חומרא מאי פריך אדרבה כיון שהוא חמור הוה לו ליפטר מגנבה כדי שיתחייב כפל וע"ק ברייתא גופה שואל שחייב בשבורה ומתה כו' אדרבה היא הנותנת דמפני שהוא חמור פטר בו הגנבה כדי לחייבו בכפל ולפי מה דפרישית אתי שפיר וא"ת לר' יוחנן דסבר הכא דמכפל עבדינן פירכא וגם סבר רב יוסף בפרק הכונס (ב"ק דף נז. ושם) גבי שומר אבדה לר' יוחנן דלסטים מזוין גנב הוא אם כן גנבה ואבדה בשואל מנ"ל דכי פריך בהשואל מה לשומר שכר שכן משלם כפל בלסטים מזוין [ה] ומשני לסטים מזוין גזלן הוא איבעית אימא קרנא בלא שבועה עדיפא וי"ל דלר' יוחנן נפקא ליה מוכי ישאל וי"ו מוסיף על ענין ראשון וכה"ג יליף התם לעניין פטור בבעלים ואע"ג דרבי יוסי ברבי נהוראי הוא תנא וסבר דקרנא עדיפא וכן ברייתא דהשואל (לקמן דף צה.) סבר דקרנא עדיפא או לסטים מזוין גזלן הוא ור' יוחנן פליג בתרוייהו הא לא קשיא דר' יוחנן סבר כתנא דהכונס (ב"ק דף נז:) דקאמר לא אם אמרת בשומר חנם שכן משלם כפל לכך שלח בה יד חייב דקאי אמילתיה דרבי יוסי בר' נהוראי:

**רבא** אמר לא תימא שליחות יד כו'. פרש"י דסבר אפילו כרבי אלעזר ואין להקשות לפירושו הא דקאמר ואידך שלא תאמר דיו והא תרוייהו צריכי לאינה צריכה חסרון לר' אלעזר דהא לא יליף שומר שכר משומר חנם דהא בתר הכי פריך ולמ"ד [ו] [שליחות יד] צריכה חסרון תרתי למה לי ולדידיה לא ילפינן חד מחבריה אפילו הכי לא מוקמינן תרוייהו לדיו והיינו משום כדפ"ל דכיון דשליחות יד חייב בתרוייהו גלוי מלתא בעלמא למילף דין של זה בזה ועוד יש לומר דרבא בא לפרש דהא דאמר ר"א דא ודא אחת היא לא שניהם צריכי לגופייהו כדאמרינן אלא שניהם מיותרין דגמר להו משואל וסבר רבא קרנא עדיפא ושפיר גמר שומר שכר משומר חנם לכולי עלמא זה מזה מיהו ברייתא דהכונס (שם) סברה דלא ילפינן זה מזה דקתני לא אם אמרת בשומר חנם כו':

**חדא** לומר [לך שליחות יד] אין צריכה חסרון. וא"ת ונילף משואל דאינה צריכה חסרון דמשעת משיכה חייב באונסיה אע"ג דלא נשתמש כדאמר בפ' השואל (לקמן דף צט.) גבי שואל קורדום מחבירו כ"ש שומרין שמושכין להשתמש שלא מדעת בעלים שחייבים וי"ל בשואל דין הוא כיון דמושך לדעת בעלים חשיב כאילו נשתמש בה דלדעת כן שאלה ולאו לאוקמה בכילתא אבל שלא לדעת אינו חשיב כאילו כבר נשתמש בשביל משיכה לבדה לכך לא ילפינן משואל אלא משיכה שיש בה חסרון: **חדא** לדיו וחדא לכדתניא. ולמ"ד נמי אינה צריכה חסרון דצריכי תרוייהו יליף שפיר ג"ש לכדתניא לפי שיש כל כך תיבות בזה כמו בזה אם לא שלח ידו במלאכת רעהו:

**ואני אומר.** ר' יוחנן פליג אדרבי יוסי בן נהוראי רביה ואמר אף היא לצורך נאמרה ולוי ס"ל כרבי יוסי בן נהוראי למידרש מיניה דאין צריכה חסרון דאי מקרא קמא לא תיסק אדעתין לחיוביה עד דמחסר ליה: בשומר חנם נאמר ונקרב בעל הבית וגו' בשומר שכר כתיב שבועת ה' תהיה וגו' ואמרינן בהשואל (לקמן דף צד:) פרשה ראשונה נאמרה בשומר חנם שניה בשומר שכר וכתיב בתרוייהו אם לא שלח הא אם שלח נתחייב בדברים שהוא פטור עליהם כגון שומר חנם בין בגנבה בין באונסין דמדשלח בה יד קנאה וקמה ברשותו ושומר שכר פטור במת או נשבר או נשבה דהיינו אונסין: **שומר חנם שפטור.** כל זמן שלא שלח בה יד כדכתיב אם לא ימצא הגנב ונקרב בעה"ב דנשבע שלא שלח בה יד ולא פשע בשמירתו ופטור כדאמרינן לקמן בשמעתין דהאי ונקרב שבועה הוא: **שומר שכר שחייב בגנבה ואבדה.** דפרשה שניה בו נאמרה וכתיב בה אם גנב יגנב כו': **לא כ"ש.** שאם שלח בה יד חייב באונסין: **דא ודא אחת היא.** כמשמעה של זו כך משמעה של זו לפי ששתיהן הוצרכו ואין כאן מקרא יתר: **מאי דא ודא אחת היא.** למה שתיהן שוות הלא לא הוצרכה השניה: **שומר חנם שפוטר עצמו בטענת גנב.** כלומר גנב גנבה ממני ובאו עדים שהיא אצלו משלם תשלומי כפל דכתיב אם לא ימצא הגנב וגו' ודרשינן בבבא קמא (דף סג:) אם לא ימצא כמה שאמר אלא שהוא עצמו גנבו מה כתיב אחריו אשר ירשיעון אלהים ישלם שנים אבל שומר שכר אינו משלם כפל שאם טען נגנבה משלם קרן שהרי הוא חייב בגניבה וטענה אחרת אינה מביאה אותו לידי כפל: **קרנא בלא שבועה עדיפא מכפילא בשבועה.** חמור שומר שכר שחייב בקרן עד שלא נשבע לשקר במקום ששומר חנם פטור דהיינו גניבה ואבידה משומר חנם שמשלם כפל ומדה זו אינה אלא לאחר שנשבע לשקר שנגנבה ובאו עדים שהוא גנבה דכי אתרבי כפל בטוען טענת גנב לאחר שבועה אתרבי כדלקמן בשמעתין: **רבא אמר.** אפילו לרבי אלעזר נמי אתיא דלא תימא כו': **ותיתי משואל.** שחייבו הכתוב באונסין בשביל שכל הנאה שלו ושולח יד נמי כל הנאה שלו: (ג) ומה שואל) **שלדעת בעלים.** שלח בה יד לעשות מלאכתו חייב באונסין: **שומר חנם ושומר שכר.** השולחין יד שעושין מלאכתן שלא לדעת בעלים לא כ"ש דחייב שוב באונסיה: **למה נאמרה.** בשתיהן: **חדא לומר לך** שליחות יד אינה צריכה חסרון: **ואידך.** האמורה בשומר שכר: **שלא תאמר דיו לבא כו'.** אם לא נאמרה בשאר שומרין ולמדה משואל הייתי אומר דיו לשליחות יד דשומרין שבא מדין שואל להיות כנדון: **מה שואל.** אם בעליו עמו כתיב לא ישלם אונסין אף שומרין ששלחו יד אם בעליו עמו יפטר כתב קרא יתירא לחייבו אפילו בבעלים וגלי רחמנא בחדא והוא הדין בכולהו: **לשבועה.** והכי קאמר אם לא ימצא כמה שאמר שנגנבה אלא הוא גנבה והוא כבר נקרב אל הדיינין לשבועה ונשבע לשקר ואח"כ באו עדים אשר ירשיעון הדיינין ישלם כפל: **אתה אומר.** קריבה לשבועה או אינו אלא קריבה לדין שמשעה שטען בב"ד נגנבה אע"פ שלא נשבע ישלם כפל אם באו עדים: **נאמר שליחות יד למטה.** אצל שומר שכר שבועת ה' תהיה בין שניהם אם לא שלח: **ונאמר שליחות יד למעלה.** ונקרב בעל הבית אל האלהים אם לא שלח: **אף כאן לשבועה.** למדנו שאין משלמין כפל ע"י טענת גנב אלא לאחר שבועה וגם למדנו שנפטר מגנבה ואבדה בשבועה:

עין משפט
נר מצוה

[פ א מיי' פ"א מהלכות שכירות הל' ג סמג עשין פט טוש"ע ח"מ סי' רצא סעיף א]:

פא א מיי' פ"ד מהל' גניבה הלכה א טוש"מ סי' שנב:

## רבינו חננאל

עוד שליחות יד בשומר שכר אלא ללמד שאפי' שליחות יד בלא חסרון חייב. ורבי יוחנן דידיה אמר ואני אומר אינה משונה כלומר אין זה יכול ללמד מזה שאין שומר חנם קל משומר שכר שהרי חייבה תורה בשומר חנם שטען כי נגנב ונמצא שהוא גנבו שהוא משלם תשלומי כפל ושומר שכר שטוען טענת גנב ונמצא שהוא גנבו פטור מכפל מפני שחייב בשומר שכר בגניבה כך הייתי אומר כי שלח בו יד פטור א) מכפל ועוד אם יש לומר אי הכי נכתוב שליחות יד בשומר שכר וילמד שומר חנם ממנו איכא למיפרך הכי כי שומר חנם ושומר שכר שגנבו הפקדון שהיה בידם וטענו שנגנב שומר שכר חייב לשלם מיד שהרי חייב בגניבה ואבידה ושומר חנם אינו חייב אלא עד שישבע שנגנב ואחר כך באו עדים שהוא גנבו הלכך לא זה לומד מזה ולא זה מזה הלכך לגופיה בא בתרוייהו ולעולם שליחות יד צריכה חסרון לטעמיה דר' יוחנן. ורבא דהוא בתרא אמר אינה צריכה [חסרון]. הא דאמר רבא לא תאמר שליחות יד לא בשומר חנם ולא בשומר שכר ותיתי משואל והא לא כתיבא שליחות יד בשואל כלל. כך פירושה לא תאמר שליחות יד אלא בשואל בלבד ולא היה צריך לכתוב לא בשומר חנם ולא בשומר שכר ויבואו וילמדו מן השואל ולמה נאמר בהן ללמד שאין צריכה חסרון ושלא תאמר דיו לבא מן הדין להיות כנדון כו' ופשוטה היא. שליחות יד דכתיבא בשומר חנם ובשומר שכר ואפי' אשואל וכי ישאל ו' מוסיף על ענין ראשון וכאילו בשלשתם כתיבא שליחות יד הני כולהו למה לי וכו'.

חשק שלמה על ר"ח

א) נראה דל"ל פטור מאונסין.

תורה אור השלם

א) אִם לֹא יִמָּצֵא הַגַּנָּב וְנִקְרַב בַּעַל הַבַּיִת אֶל הָאֱלֹהִים אִם לֹא שָׁלַח יָדוֹ בִּמְלֶאכֶת רֵעֵהוּ: [שמות כב, ז]

מסורת הש"ס

א) [לקמן לד:, בבא קמא מז:], ב) בבא קמא סג:, ג) מהרש"ל מ"ז, ד) מהר"ם, ה) ל"ל משני בלא וא"ו, מהר"ם. ו) מהר"ם.

הגהות הב"ח

(א) גמ' אחת היא משום דאיכא: (ב) שם דשלח בה יד:

ליקוטי רש"י

**בטוען טענת גנב.** טוען שנגנבה הימנו ונמצא שהוא עצמו גנבה חייב בה כפל בפרשה ראשונה דכתיב אם לא ימצא הגנב וסמיך ליה על כל דבר פשע ישלם שנים ואוקימנא בפ' מרובה (ב"ק דף סג:) אם לא ימצא כמו שאומר אלא הוא עצמו גנבו ישלם שנים וכגון שנשבע תחילה לשקר שנגנב אבל באו עדים קודם שנשבע תחלה לשקר אינו משלם כפל דהכי כתיב אם לא ימצא הגנב וכבר נשבע ונקרב בעל הבית אל האלהים לשבועה על כל דבר פשע אשר ירשיעון דיינין בעדים ישלם שנים. **קרנא בלא שבועה עדיפא מכפילא בשבועה.** מחייבתו לשלם קרן משאמר נגנבה ואפילו לא נשבע לשקר זה חמורה מן הראשונה שפוטרתו מלשלם קרן אם לא באו עדים שהוא גנבה אע"פ שמחייבתו כפל לאחר שנשבע לשקר ובאו עדים ובלא שבועה אין שם כפל [לקמן צד:]. **לשבועה.** שכיון שטוען וגונב מבית האיש ישבע שנגנבה ויפטר [ב"ק סג:]. ונקרב אל הדיינין לדון עם זה ולישבע לו שלא שלח ידו בשלו [שמות כב, ז]. **או אינו אלא לדין.** לפרעון דשומר חנם שטוען נגנבה ישלם דהאי קרא בש"ח כתיב כדאמרי' בהשואל [ב"ק שם].

**צריך** דעת בעלים אי רבי ישמעאל מאי איריא לא יחדו אפילו יחדו נמי לא מיבעיא קאמר לא מיבעיא יחדו דמקומה הוא אלא אפילו לא יחדו דלאו מקומה הוא לא בעינן דעת בעלים אימא סיפא יחדו לה הבעלים מקום וטלטלה ונשברה בין מתוך ידו בין משהניחה לצרכו חייב לצרכה פטור אתאן לר"ע דאמר בעינן דעת בעלים אי ר"ע מאי איריא יחדו אפילו לא יחדו נמי לא מיבעיא קאמר לא מיבעיא לא יחדו דלאו מקומה הוא אלא אפילו יחדו נמי דמקומה הוא בעינן דעת בעלים רישא רבי ישמעאל וסיפא ר"ע ° אין (א) דא"ר יוחנן מאן דמתרגם לי חבית אליבא דחד תנא מובלנא מאניה בתריה לבי מסותא תרגמה רבי יעקב בר אבא קמיה דרב שנטלה על מנת לגוזלה תרגמה ר' נתן בר אבא קמיה דרב שנטלה ע"מ לשלוח בה יד במאי קמיפלגי בשליחות יד צריכה חסרון מאן דאמר לגוזלה קסבר שליחות יד צריכה חסרון ומ"ד לשלוח בה יד קסבר שליחות יד אינה צריכה חסרון מתקיף לה רב ששת מידי נטלה קתני טלטלה קתני אלא אמר רב ששת הכא במאי עסקינן כגון שטלטלה להביא עליה גוזלות וקא סבר שואל שלא מדעת גזלן הוי וכולה רבי ישמעאל היא וסיפא שהניחה במקום שאינה מקומה ור' יוחנן הניחה במקומה משמע איתמר רב ולוי חד אמר שליחות יד צריכה חסרון וחד אמר שליחות יד אינה צריכה חסרון תסתיים דרב הוא דאמר שליחות יד אינה צריכה חסרון דתניא רועה שהיה רועה עדרו והניח עדרו ובא לעיר ובא זאב וטרף ובא ארי ודרס פטור הניח מקלו ותרמילו עליה חייב והוינן בה משום דהניח מקלו ותרמילו עליה חייב הא שקלינהו (א) אמר ר"נ אמר רבה בר אבוה אמר רב בעודן עליה וכי עודן עליה מאי הוי הא לא משכה ואמר רב שמואל בר רב יצחק אמר רב שהכישה במקל ורצתה לפניו והא לא חסרה אלא לאו ש"מ קסבר שליחות יד אינה צריכה חסרון אימא שהכחישה במקל דיקא נמי דקתני שהכישה במקל ש"מ ומדרב סבר שליחות יד צריכה חסרון לוי סבר שליחות יד אינה צריכה חסרון מאי טעמא דלוי א"ר יוחנן משום ר' יוסי בן נהוראי משונה שליחות יד האמורה בשומר שכר משליחות יד האמורה בשומר חנם

ואני

---

**רש"י**

צריך דעת בעלים. ואם לא הודיעם חייב באחריותם אם מת או נגנב דמדשקליה קם ליה ברשותיה והשבה בלא ידיעה לאו השבה היא: דמקומה היא. וכיון דבאותו מקום החזירה חזרה גמורה היא: אתאן לר"ע. תירוצא הוא: תרגמה רבי יעקב. דתיקו כולה כחד תנא ובתרי טעמי רישא שהחזירה למקומה דכל מקום שהחזירה מקומה היא דהא לא יחדו לה מקום וסיפא שהחזירה למקום שאינה מקומה כדמסיים במסקנא דהא דמסקינן בסיומא וסיפא שהניחה במקום שאינה מקומה אתרגמא דכולהו קאי אדר' יעקב ואדר' נתן ואדרב ששת ומשום דהניחה חוץ למקומה לא הויא חזרה וכגון שנטלו מתחלה על מנת לגוזלה והיינו לצרכו דמתניתין דאילו לשאלה בעלמא ולתשמיש כיון דלאו גזילה הוא סגי לה בהשבה כל דהו וכל מקום שהניחה פטור באונסין אבל משום דגזולה הואי ובגזילה כתיב והשיב וזה שהניחה למקום שלא יחדו לה בעלים לא הויא השבה: ור' נתן תרגמה. דאפילו לא נטלה על מנת לגוזלה כו' אלא על מנת לשלוח בה יד וליטול מקצתה ולא נטל אפ"ה קמה ליה ברשותיה כולה והויא לה גזילה ובעי' השבה ובמקום שאינו מקומה לאו השבה היא ורב ששת לא שביק דליסיימו לתירוצייהו ואתקיף מידי נטלה קתני כו' ומיהו סיומא דמילתא דמסקנא וסיפא שהניחה במקום שאינו מקומה אכולהו קאי: שליחות יד. שחייבו הכתוב עליו אפילו נאנסה כדכתיב (שמות כב) ומת או נשבר או נשבה [וגו'] שבועת ה' תהיה בין שניהם אם לא שלח ידו וגו' דמשמע הא שלח נתחייב שוב במיתתה ובשבייתה: צריכה חסרון. לא הוי שליחות יד להעמידה ברשותו אלא א"כ חסרה: מידי נטלה קתני. דמשמע שנטלה לעצמו: טלטלה קתני. לתשמיש בעלמא משמע לצרכו דמתני': אלא כגון שטלטלה להביא עליה גוזלות. לעלות עליה כדרך סולם ליטול גוזלות מקן גבוה ואפ"ה הויא גזילה למיקם ברשותיה עד דעביד השבה דקסבר שואל שלא מדעת בעלים גזלן הוא: וכולה ר' ישמעאל היא. אשינויא דכולהו קאי אדר' יעקב ואדר' נתן ואדרב ששת: וסיפא שהניחה במקום שאינה מקומה. אבל רישא כל מקום שהניחה מקומה היא: ור' יוחנן. דאמר לעיל מאן דמתרגם לי כו': הניחה במקומה משמע. הלכך לא מיתוקמא ° כרבי ישמעאל: שליחות יד. שחייבו הכתוב עליו ואפי' נאנסה כדכתיב או נשבר או נשבה וגו' שבועת ה' תהיה אם לא שלח דמשמע הא אם שלח נתחייב שוב במיתתה ובשבייתה: צריכה חסרון. וכל זמן שלא חסרה לא קמה ברשותיה להתחייב באונסיה: זאב. טורף נושא הטרף לחורו: ארי. אינו טורפה אלא דורסה במקומה ואוכלה: פטור. דאונסין ניהו ולאו משום דהניח עדרו ופשיעה היא מוקמינן לה לעיל בעידנא דעיילי אינשי כדאמרינן בהשוכר את הפועלים (לקמן צג:) א"נ דשמע קול אריה ועל: הא שקלינהו. ואי נמי שליחות יד חשיבא הא הדר אהדרה כשנטלו הימנו ואנן מוקמינן לעיל סתם מתני' כרבי ישמעאל דאין צריך דעת בעלים: הא לא משכה. בשליחות יד כדי לקנותה ומטלטלין אין נקנין אלא במשיכה לא במקח ולא לענין גזל ולא לענין שליחות יד כדתנן במתני' (לקמן דף מג.) הטה את החבית ונטל ממנה רביעית אין משלם אלא רביעית אלמא בעינן דליקנייה כו': ואמר רב שמואל. גרסינן: שהכישה במקל. כשנתנו עליה ורצתה זו היא משיכה משעקרה יד ורגל על ידו: והא לא חסרה. לאו פירכא היא אלא מסקנא וסיומא הוא למילתיה דאמר תסתיים דרב הוא דאמר אין צריכה חסרון מדשני רב למתניתין משום הכישה ורצתה לפניו ואי קשיא דלמא הא דהניח מקלו ותרמילו חוייב לאו משום שליחות יד הוא לאיבעי חסרון אלא משום שואל שלא מדעת הוא כי ההוא דלעיל דחבית לא היא דהא דכי אמרינן שואל שלא מדעת בדבר שאינו מכחיש וחיסר מחמת מלאכה אבל בעלי חיים המכחישים מחמת מלאכה מתחלתו שליחות יד היא: שהכחישה. בהכאתו דהיינו חסרון: דיקא נמי. דהכחישה קאמר רב מדנקט הכאת מקל דמכה חזקה היא: ומדרב סבר צריכה חסרון. דהא דייקינן מדנקט מקל: לוי. בר פלוגתיה סבר אין צריכה חסרון: משונה שליחות יד כו'. כלומר אינה דומה לו שזו נאמרה לצורך ולא משמע אלא של שומר שכר נאמרה שלא לצורך אלא לדרשה ללמד שאינה צריכה חסרון:

ואני

---

**תוספות**

**אי** רבי ישמעאל אפילו יחדו נמי. וא"ת מנ"ל י"ל מדנקט טלה וסלע דסתם טלה לא יחד לו מקום אלא הולך ממרעה למרעה וסתם סלע יחדו לו מקום בכיס וגם כיס יחדו לו מקום בתיבה ולכך פריך נמי בסמוך לר"ע אפילו לא יחדו נמי:

**שנטלה** והגביהה ע"מ לגוזלה כו'. והיינו חסרון שהכל גוזל ונוטל לצורך עצמו:

**שנטלה** ע"מ לשלוח בה יד. פי' ליטול מקצת אע"פ שלא נטל אותה מקצת חייב בכולה כדאמר בשלהי פרקין (דף מד.) לא נטל נטל ממש אלא כיון שהגביה ליטול אע"פ שלא נטל אבל למ"ד ע"מ לגוזלה דבעי חסרון אם הגביה ליטול קצת אינו חייב עד שיטול המקצת כיון דבעי חסרון וקשה דבשלהי פרקין קאמר אפי' למ"ד בעי חסרון מודה בחבית אם הגביהה אע"פ שלא נטל חייב דניחא ליה דתיהוי כולה בסיס להאי רביעית ומתני' בחבית איירי ויש לומר דמתני' איירי אפילו בשמן דלא מנטר פורתא אגב האחר:

**ובא** זאב וטרף. בשעת משלחת זאבים ורבי יהודה היא דאמר זאב אחד אונס בפ' הפועלים (לקמן דף צג:):

**הא** שקלינהו. לרבי ישמעאל פריך דאמר לא בעינן דעת בעלים כפרש"י:

**הא** לא משכה. דאע"ג דעודן עליה לא קיימא ברשותיה להתחייב באונסיה עד שימשוך כדאמר במתני' (לקמן דף מג.) הטה את החבית ונטל ממנה רביעית אינו חייב אלא דמי רביעית כיון דלא הגביה את החבית ומשני שהניח מקלו ותרמילו עליה כל כך בחוזק עד שרצתה לפניו:

**דיקא** נמי דקתני שהכישה. וא"ת בפ"ק דקדושין (דף כב:) תניא או שהכישה במקל ורצתה לפניו דאקרי משיכה ולא הויא הכחשה וי"ל דהתם דאדם נכרי לקחה ואינה מכירתו בדבורו שייך למיתני הכישה אבל הכא דאיירי ברועה שהבהמה מכירתו ואזלה מחמת דבורו לא שייך למיתני שהכישה:

לומר

---

**מסורת הש"ס**

א) סנהדרין דף סב., ב) [ערכין דף ל:], ג) [לקמן מג.], ד) [שם], ה) [לקמן מג., בבא בתרא פח.], ו) [קדושין מב.], ז) [לקמן צג: [ע"ש], קו. [ע"ש], ח) גירסת מהרש"ם דאמר.

**הגהות הב"ח**

(א) גמ' הא שקלינהו ואמר ר"נ:

**גליון הש"ס**

גמ' אין דאר"י. עי' שבת דף פו ע"ב קידושין דף סג ע"ב מנחות דף נה ע"א: רש"י ד"ה הניחה במקומה כו' כרבי ישמעאל. עי' שבת דף פו ע"א ברש"י ד"ה ומאן מוקי:

**ליקוטי רש"י**

מאן דמתרגם לי חבית אליבא דחד תנא. דקתני התם המפקיד חבית אצל חבירו ולא יחדו לה הבעלים מקום וטלטלה ונשברה אם מתוך ידו נשברה לצרכו חייב לצרכה פטור אם משהניחה בין לצרכו בין לצרכה פטור יחדו לה הבעלים מקום וטלטלה ונשברה בין מתוך ידו בין משהניחה לצרכו חייב לצרכה פטור ופריך התם מני אי ר' ישמעאל דאמר לא צריך דעת בעלים דתניא הגונב טלה מן העדר וסלע מן הכיס ממקום שגנב יחזיר ר' ישמעאל ור' עקיבא אומר צריך דעת בעלים אי ר' ישמעאל מאי איריא יחדו אפילו לא יחדו נמי לא מבעיא קאמר לא מבעיא יחדו דמקומה הוא אלא אפילו לא יחדו דלאו מקומה הוא לא בעינן דעת בעלים אימא סיפא ר' עקיבא ואי ר' עקיבא מאי איריא לא יחדו אפילו יחדו נמי לא מבעיא קאמר לא מבעיא לא יחדו דלאו מקומה הוא אלא אפילו יחדו נמי דמקומה הוא בעינן דעת בעלים רישא ר' ישמעאל וסיפא ר' עקיבא ואוקמה ר' יוחנן רישא בשהניחה במקומה וסיפא בשהניחה במקום שאינו מקומה כר' ישמעאל ומוקי כולה כחד תנא [שבת פו.]. מובלנא מאניה. כגדין [יומא נב.]. מסותא. מרחץ [סנהדרין סב.]. ואפשר ... [סוטה ח.]. שליחות יד אינה צריכה חסרון. ומשלחת בה יד ע"פ שלא חסרה חייב באונסיה ...

**עין משפט נר מצוה**

עז א מיי' פ"ד מהלכות גניבה הל' י ועי' בהשגות ובמ"מ סמג עשין עא טוש"ע ח"מ סי' שנה סעיף א וסעיף ב וע"ש:
עח ב מיי' פ"ז מהל' שאלה ופקדון הלכה ט סמג עשין פח טוש"ע ח"מ סי' רצב סעיף ו:
עט ג מיי' פ"ג מהל' גזילה הל' יא סמג עשין עג טוש"ע ח"מ סי' רלב סעיף א:
פ ד מיי' פ"ד מהל' שכירות הל' ח סמג עשין פט טוש"ע ח"מ סי' שג סעיף י:

**רבינו חננאל**

ומקשי' אי הכי יחדו להאי חבית הבעלים מקום [נמי] דהא שמעינן ליה לר' ישמעאל דאומר הגונב סלע מן הכיס והנה יחדו הבעלים להאי סלע מקום בכיס ואמר ר' ישמעאל יחזיר למקום שגנב ואין צריך דעת בעלים ואי מתני' ר' ישמעאל היא אמאי קתני ולא יחדו לה בעלים דשמעינן מינה דדוקא לא יחדו הא יחדו לא. ופרקי' לא מיבעיא קאמר לא מיבעיא יחדו לה הבעלים מקום והחזירה באותו מקום דודאי פטור הא החזירה במקומה וכיון שהחזירה במקומה כלא טלטלה דמי אלא אפי' לא יחדו לה בעלים מקום כיון דלאו במקומה מחזירה פטור. אוקימנא אליבא דר' ישמעאל אם יחדו לה הבעלים מקום בין לא יחדו לה הבעלים מקום כיון שהחזירה למקומה אם נשברה פטור הוא. אי הכי אימא סיפא יחדו לה בעלים מקום וטלטלה ונשברה בין מתוך ידו בין משהניחה לצרכה פטור לצרכו חייב אמאי חייב והא משהניחה קתני ויש מי שמפרק בשהניחה במקום שאינו מקומה. ור' יוחנן אמר הניחה במקומה משמע. ופרקי' סיפא אתאן לר' עקיבא דאמר צריך דעת בעלים הלכך לצרכו חייב. ומקשינן אי מתני' רבי עקיבא היא למה ליה יחדו לה בעלים מקום אפי' לא יחדו אמר ר' עקיבא צריך דעת בעלים דתניא הגונב טלה מן העדר וכו' הנה לא יחדו בעלים מקום לטלה והצריך ר' עקיבא בהחזרה דעת בעלים כו'. ועמדה רישא כר' ישמעאל וסיפא כר' עקיבא. אמר ר' יוחנן מאן דמתרגם ליה חבית אליבא דחד תנא וכו' פי' אמר ר' יוחנן מי שיפרש לי משנתנו זו המפקיד חבית אצל חבירו וכו' ויעמידה אי אליבא דר' ישמעאל אי אליבא דר' עקיבא סיפא ורישא בחד תנא אני מוליך לו כליו אחריו לבית המרחץ כי הוא כמו רב ואני תלמיד שמשמש כתלמיד לרב. ובא רב יעקב בר אבא לאוקמה למתני' בנוטלה על מנת לגוזלה. ורב נתן בר יעקב מוקמה בנוטלה על מנת לשלח בה יד וכולה ר' ישמעאל. ורב ששת טעם שניהם ואמר מידי במתני' קתני נטלה דלישמעינן נטלה לגזלה או לשלח בה יד טלטלה קתני ואין בלשון טלטול לא לשון גזילה ולא שילוח בה יד. אלא אמר רב ששת כגון שטלטלה

---

**הגהות וציונים**

לעמוד עליה ולפשוט ידו בתוך הקן ליטול גוזלות וסבר האי תנא שואל שלא מדעת בעלים גזלן הוי וכולה ר' ישמעאל היא וסיפא שהניחה במקום שאינה מקומה לפיכך חייב. ור' יוחנן אמר סיפא ר' עקיבא היא כי הניחה במקומה משמע. ואעפ"כ צריך דעת בעלים כר' עקיבא וכיון שלא ידעו בה הבעלים שהחזירה לפיכך לצרכו חייב. איתמר רב ולוי חד אמר שליחות יד צריכה חסרון. מדתניא רועה שהיה רועה עדרו ובא זאב וטרף ארי ודרס פטור פי' פטור הוא כי שומר שכר הוא והשוכר פטור מן האונסין. הא הניח מקלו או תרמילו עליה פי' כיון שנשתמש בה כאילו גזלה וחייב באונסיה. ואקשי' עלה. ואוקמה רב בעודן עליה בעודו עליה הא לא משכה ופריק רב כגון שהכישה במקלו ורצתה לפניו. דייקי' מדלא קתני

שואל שלא מדעת גזלן הוי. וקנייה להתחייב בה באונסים כאילו גזלה ומדעת גזלן הוי וכולה כ' ישמעאל היא ... בנוטלה בה יד אע"פ שלא חסרה הויא גזילה וקמה ברשותיה [לקמן מג.]. שואל שלא מדעת בעלים ... שליחות יד צריכה חסרון. ... ובא זאב וטרף ובא ארי ודרס. ... ותרמילו. ... חמת של עור שנותן בה פתו ותולה בצוארו [יבמות פו:].

ההנהגה בקול אלא הכישה במקל ש"מ שהכישה במקל והכחשה דהיינו חסירה ולפיכך חייב ש"מ דרב הוא דאמר שליחות יד צריכה חסרון ואם אין שם חסרון פטור באונסיה ולוי אמר שליחות יד אינה צריכה חסרון מאי טעמא. אמר ר' יוחנן משום ר' יוסי בר נהוראי משונה שליחות יד האמורה בשומר שכר משליחות יד האמורה בשומר חנם שדינו קל חייב בו שליחות יד שומר שכר לא כל שכן למה כתב

removal should be tantamount to the return of the sheep.[21] Why, then, is the shepherd liable?

The following answer was given:

אָמַר רַב נַחְמָן אָמַר רַבָּה בַּר אֲבוּהּ אָמַר רַב – And **Rav Nachman answered in the name of Rabbah bar Avuha, who said** this answer **in the name of Rav:** בְּעוֹדָן עָלֶיהָ – The Baraisa discusses a case **where [the shepherd's articles] were still on [the sheep]** at the time of the attack. Thus, the sheep was never returned, and the shepherd remained liable, since he had misappropriated it.

The following difficulty was then raised:

וְכִי עוֹדָן עָלֶיהָ מַאי הָוֵי – **But even if [the articles] were still on [the sheep], what** difference **does this** make? הָא לֹא מְשָׁכָהּ – **Why, [the shepherd] did not** perform an act of acquisition on the sheep by **drawing it** (*meshichah*) into his legal domain. Hence, he should not be held liable for having misappropriated the sheep, for it never entered his possession as a stolen object.[22] – ? –

And the following answer was given:

וְאָמַר רַב שְׁמוּאֵל בַּר רַב יִצְחָק אָמַר רַב – **And Rav Shmuel bar Rav Yitzchak answered in the name of Rav:** שֶׁהִכִּישָׁהּ בְּמַקֵּל – The Baraisa refers to a case **where [the shepherd] hit [the sheep] with** his **staff**[23] when he put it on the sheep, וְרָצְתָה לְפָנָיו – **and it ran before him** from the force of the blow. In this way, he indeed drew it into his legal domain.[24]

Basing itself on the fact that it was Rav who gave this answer, the Gemara concludes its proof regarding Rav's opinion about misappropriation:

וְהָא לֹא חִסְּרָהּ – **But,** according to Rav, **[the shepherd] did not cause a loss in [the sheep],** for Rav said that the shepherd merely hit the sheep.[25] אֶלָּא לָאו שְׁמַע מִינָּהּ – **Surely then,** one can **learn from this** קָסָבַר שְׁלִיחוּת יָד אֵינָהּ צְרִיכָה חִסָּרוֹן – that **[Rav] holds** that **misappropriation is not dependent upon a loss.**[26] – ? –

The Gemara rejects this proof, and asserts that, in fact, Rav holds the opposite view:

אֵימָא שֶׁהִכְחִישָׁהּ בְּמַקֵּל – But one could **say** that Rav means **that [the shepherd] weakened [the sheep]** when he hit it **with** his **staff,** which is considered a loss. דַּיְקָא נַמִי דְּקָתָנֵי – **Indeed,** this interpretation is **also** borne out **by** a **precise** reading of **what [Rav] said:** שֶׁהִכִּישָׁהּ בְּמַקֵּל – **"**The Baraisa refers to a case **where [the shepherd] hit [the sheep] with** his **staff."** Rav deliberately mentioned the staff,[27] which delivers a strong blow. שְׁמַע מִינָּהּ – **Learn from this** that according to Rav, misappropriation is dependent upon a loss.

Having decided which opinion is held by Rav, the Gemara seeks to show that the other view is held by Levi:

וּמִדְּרַב סָבַר שְׁלִיחוּת יָד צְרִיכָה חִסָּרוֹן – **And since Rav holds** that **misappropriation is dependent upon a loss,** as we just concluded, לֵוִי סָבַר שְׁלִיחוּת יָד אֵינָהּ צְרִיכָה חִסָּרוֹן – this would mean that it is **Levi** who **holds** that **misappropriation is not dependent upon a loss.**

The Gemara seeks the basis for Levi's opinion:[28]

מַאי טַעְמָא דְּלֵוִי – **What is Levi's reasoning?** אָמַר רַבִּי יוֹחָנָן מִשּׁוּם רַבִּי יוֹסֵי בֶּן נְהוֹרַאי – **R' Yochanan said in the name of R' Yose ben Nehorai:** מְשׁוּנָּה שְׁלִיחוּת יָד הָאֲמוּרָה בְּשׁוֹמֵר שָׂכָר – The Torah's reference to the law of **misappropriation mentioned in connection with a paid *shomer* is different** מִשְּׁלִיחוּת יָד הָאֲמוּרָה בְּשׁוֹמֵר חִנָּם – **from** the Torah's reference to the law of **misappropriation mentioned in connection with an unpaid *shomer*.**[29]

NOTES

21. The Gemara established above (according to R' Yaakov, R' Nassan, and R' Sheishess) that our anonymous Mishnah follows the view of R' Yishmael, who rules that a thief is no longer liable for mishaps once he returns a stolen item, even if the owner is not notified of his property's return. The ruling of an anonymous Mishnah is often adopted as halachah (see above, 33a). Therefore, the Gemara assumes that the Baraisa, too, follows this view (see *Rashi*).

22. In order to acquire something, one must perform an act of acquisition (*kinyan*) upon it. This rule applies both to stealing and to *shelichus yad.* Someone who steals or misappropriates an object does not "acquire" it (see 40b note 23) unless he performs an appropriate *kinyan.* With regard to movable property [as opposed to real property], one can acquire it by performing the *kinyan* known as *meshichah, drawing [it] near* [that is, he moves it into his legal domain; see note 24] (*Rashi*).

23. Or his pouch (*Tosafos*).

24. *Meshichah* [drawing near] is accomplished by pulling or drawing the animal (see above, 8b) from the public domain (or from an area belonging to the owner) into the domain of the one who is acquiring it, or into a סִימְטָא, *simta* [a public area set aside for temporary use by individuals; see *Rashi* to *Kiddushin* 25b ד״ה בסימטא]. It is not necessary to actually physically pull the animal in order to acquire it. One can effect the *kinyan* by calling the animal and having it come to him, or by prodding it with a stick to drive it into his domain (*Kiddushin* 22b). [As soon as the animal raises a front and a hind leg because of him, he has acquired it (*Rashi* here; see *Bava Basra* 75b).]

25. Rav did not say that the shepherd caused a loss to the sheep by weakening it with the blow [thereby damaging it] (see *Rashi*).

26. An apparent difficulty: How can the Gemara derive from here that *shelichus yad* is not dependent upon a loss? Perhaps the reason the shepherd is liable to pay for the sheep is not that he misappropriated it, but because he borrowed it without the owner's permission (as Rav Sheishess interpreted our Mishnah), and thus he is liable even though he did *not* cause a loss!

The answer is that a *shomer* is held liable for borrowing a deposit without permission only if the deposit is an item that does not deteriorate with use. If a *shomer* illicitly used an item that *does* deteriorate with use (such as an animal), he is liable for *shelichus yad* rather than improper borrowing (*Rashi*). [Such use is considered *shelichus yad,* for it is as if he took the animal with intent to deplete it.]

Several commentators object strongly to the answer given by *Rashi,* arguing that it is not logical, and suggest answers of their own (see *Ramban, Baal HaMoar, Tosefos HaRosh, Maharam,* and *Beur HaGra* to *Choshen Mishpat* 292:2).

[From *Rashi's* question and answer, it is evident that where a *shomer* intended to use a deposit in such a way that it will *not* be depleted, he is not liable for misappropriation, but for borrowing without permission. According to *Rashi,* misappropriation involves intent to cause some sort of loss to the deposit. Thus, the case of our Mishnah as interpreted by Rav Sheishess above (that the *shomer* took the barrel in order to stand on it) is not a case of misappropriation. *Nimukei Yosef, Tur* and *Shulchan Aruch* (*Choshen Mishpat* 292:1) all concur with this view (cf. *Baal HaMaor;* see *Beur HaGra* ibid. and *Chazon Ish, Likkutim* §2).]

27. Rav need not have mentioned the staff. He could simply have said that the shepherd hit the sheep (see *Rashi;* cf. *Tosafos*).

28. The Gemara seeks a source for Levi's position but not for that of Rav, because Rav's position, that misappropriation *is* dependent upon a loss, is based on logic (see *Rashi* below, 41b ד״ה ואני). [*Ritva* 44a ד״ה דשאני, however, does provide a reason for Rav's position, as follows: If, after performing an act of acquisition upon a deposit with intent to take some of it for himself, the *shomer* did not consume or even remove any of the deposit, we can assume that he has changed his mind and no longer wishes to misappropriate it.]

29. As explained above (note 10), the source for the law of misappropriation is the phrase: אִם־לֹא שָׁלַח יָדוֹ בִּמְלֶאכֶת רֵעֵהוּ, *if he did not lay his hand upon* (i.e. misappropriate) *his fellow's goods.* This phrase appears twice in the Torah: once in the passage about an unpaid *shomer (Exodus* 22:6-8), and once in the passage about a paid *shomer* (ibid. vv. 9-12).

The Gemara below (41b) will explain what R' Yose ben Nehorai means by saying that the two references to this law are different, and how this serves as a basis for Levi's ruling.

צריך דעת בעלים אי רבי ישמעאל מאי איריא לא יחדו אפילו יחדו נמי לא מיבעיא קאמר לא מיבעיא יחדו דמקומה הוא אלא אפילו לא יחדו דלאו מקומה הוא לא בעינן דעת בעלים אימא סיפא יחדו לה הבעלים מקום וטלטלה ונשברה בין מתוך ידו בין משהניחה לצרכו חייב לצרכה פטור אתאן לר"ע דאמר בעינן דעת בעלים אי ר"ע מאי איריא יחדו אפילו לא יחדו נמי לא מיבעיא קאמר לא מיבעיא לא יחדו דלאו מקומה הוא אלא אפילו יחדו נמי דמקומה הוא בעינן דעת בעלים רישא רבי ישמעאל וסיפא ר"ע אין דא"ר יוחנן מאן דמתרגם לי חבית אליבא דחד תנא מובלנא מאניה בתריה לבי מסותא תרגמה רבי יעקב בר אבא קמיה דרב שנטלה על מנת לגוזלה תרגמה ר' נתן בר אבא קמיה דרב שנטלה ע"מ לשלוח בה יד במאי קמיפלגי בשליחות יד צריכה חסרון מאן דאמר לגוזלה קסבר שליחות יד צריכה חסרון ומ"ד לשלוח בה יד קסבר שליחות יד אינה צריכה חסרון מתקיף לה רב ששת מידי נטלה קתני טלטלה קתני אלא אמר רב ששת הכא במאי עסקינן כגון שטלטלה להביא עליה גוזלות וקא סבר שואל שלא מדעת גזלן הוי וכולה רבי ישמעאל היא וסיפא שהניחה במקום שאינה מקומה ור' יוחנן הניחה במקומה משמע איתמר רב ולוי חד אמר שליחות יד צריכה חסרון וחד אמר שליחות יד אינה צריכה חסרון תסתיים דרב הוא דאמר שליחות יד אינה צריכה חסרון דתניא רועה שהיה רועה עדרו והניח עדרו ובא לעיר ובא זאב וטרף ובא ארי ודרס פטור הניח מקלו ותרמילו עליה חייב והוינן בה משום דהניח מקלו ותרמילו עליה חייב הא שקלינהו (א) אמר ר"נ אמר רבה בר אבוה אמר רב בעודן עליה וכי עודן עליה מאי הוי הא לא משכה ואמר רב שמואל בר רב יצחק אמר רב שהכישה במקל ורצתה לפניו והא לא חסרה אלא לאו ש"מ קסבר שליחות יד אינה צריכה חסרון אימא שהכחישה במקל דיקא נמי דקתני שהכישה במקל ש"מ ומדרב סבר שליחות יד צריכה חסרון לוי סבר שליחות יד אינה צריכה חסרון מאי טעמא דלוי א"ר יוחנן משום ר' יוסי בן נהוראי משונה שליחות יד האמורה בשומר שכר משליחות יד האמורה בשומר חנם

ואני

## רש"י

צריך דעת בעלים. ואם לא הודיעם חייב באחריותם אם מת או נגנב דמדשקליה קם ליה ברשותיה והשבה בלא ידיעה לאו השבה היא: דמקומה היא. וכיון דבאותו מקום החזירה חזרה גמורה היא: אתאן לר"ע. תירוצא הוא: תרגמה רבי יעקב. דתיקו כולה כחד תנא ובתרי טעמי רישא שהחזירה למקומה דכל מקום שהחזירה מקומה היא דהא לא יחדו לה מקום וסיפא שהחזירה למקום שאינה מקומה כדמסיים במסקנא דהא דמסקינן בסיומא וסיפא שהניחה במקום שאינה מקומה אתרצתא דכולהו קאי אדר' יעקב ואדר' נתן ואדרב ששת ומשום דהניחה חוץ למקומה לא הויא חזרה וכגון שנטלו מתחלה על מנת לגוזלה והיינו לצרכו דמתניתין דאילו לשאלה בעלמא ולתשמיש כיון דלאו גזילה הוא סגי לה בהשבה כל דהו וכל מקום שהניחה פטור באונסין אבל משום דגזולה הואי ובגזילה כתיב והשיב וזה שהניחה למקום שלא יחדו לה בעלים לא הויא השבה: ור' נתן תרגמה. דאפילו לא נטלה על מנת לגוזלה כו' אלא על מנת לשלוח בה יד וליטול מקצתה ולא נטל אפ"ה קמה ליה ברשותיה כולה והויא לה גזילה ובעי' השבה ובמקום שאינו מקומה לאו השבה היא ורב ששת לא שביק דליסיימו לתירולייהו ואתקיף מידי נטלה קתני כו' ומיהו סיומא דמילתא דמסקנא וסיפא שהניחה במקום שאינו מקומה אכולהו קאי: שליחות יד. שחייבו הכתוב עליו אפילו אונסה כדכתיב (שמות כב) ומת או נשבר או נשבה [וגו'] שבועת ה' תהיה בין שניהם אם לא שלח ידו וגו' דמשמע הא שלח נתחייב שוב במיתתה ובשבייתה: צריכה חסרון. לא הוי שליחות יד להעמידה ברשותו אלא א"כ חסרה: מידי נטלה קתני. דמשמע שנטלה לעצמו: טלטלה קתני. לתשמיש בעלמא משמע לצרכו דמתני': אלא כגון שטלטלה להביא עליה גוזלות. לעלות עליה כדרך סולם ליטול גוזלות מקן גבוה ואפ"ה הויא גזילה למיקם ברשותיה עד דעביד השבה דקסבר שואל שלא מדעת בעלים גזלן הוא: וכולה ר' ישמעאל היא. אשינויא דכולהו קאי אדר' יעקב ואדר' נתן ואדרב ששת: וסיפא שהניחה במקום שאינה מקומה. אבל רישא כל מקום שהניחה מקומה היא: ור' יוחנן. דאמר לעיל מאן דמתרגם לי כו': הניחה במקומה משמע. הלכך לא מיתוקמא כרבי ישמעאל: שליחות יד. שחייבו הכתוב עליו ואפי' נאנסה כדכתיב או נשבר או נשבה וגו' שבועת ה' תהיה אם לא שלח דמשמע הא אם שלח נתחייב שוב במיתתה ובשבייתה: צריכה חסרון. וכל זמן שלא חסרה לא קמה ברשותיה להתחייב באונסיה: זאב. טורף נושא הטרף לחורו: ארי. אינו טורפה אלא דורסה במקומה ואוכלה: פטור. דאונסין נינהו ואי משום דהניח עדרו ופשיעה היא מוקמינן לה דעל בעידנא דעיילי אינשי כדאמרינן בהשוכר את הפועלים (לקמן צג:) א"נ דשמע קול אריה ועל: הא שקלינהו. ואי נמי שליחות יד חשיבא הא הדר אהדרה כשנטלו הימנו ואנן מוקמינן לעיל סתם מתני' כרבי ישמעאל דאין צריך דעת בעלים: הא לא משכה. בשליחות יד כדי לקנותה ומטלטלין אין נקנין אלא במשיכה לא במקח ולא לענין גזל ולא לענין שליחות יד כדתנן במתני' (לקמן דף מג.) הטה את החבית ונטל ממנה רביעית יין אין משלם אלא רביעית אלמא בעינן דליקנייה כו': ואמר רב שמואל. גרסינן: שהכישה במקל. כשנתנו עליה ורצתה זו היא משיכה משעקרה יד ורגל על ידו: והא לא חסרה. לאו פירכא היא אלא מסקנא וסיומא הוא למילתיה דאמר תסתיים דרב הוא דאמר אין צריכה חסרון מדשני רב למתניתין משום דהכישה ורצתה לפניו ואי קשיא דלמא הא דהניח מקלו ותרמילו חיוביה לאו משום שליחות יד הוא דליבעי חסרון אלא משום שואל שלא מדעת הוא כי ההוא דלעיל דחבית לא היא דכי אמרינן בשומרין שאלה שלא מדעת בדבר שאינו כיחש וחיסר מחמת מלאכה אבל בעלי חיים המכחישים מחמת מלאכה תחלתו שליחות יד היא: שהכחישה. בהכאתו דהיינו חסרון: דיקא נמי. דהכחישה קאמר רב מדנקט הכשת מקל דמכה חזקה היא: ומדרב סבר צריכה חסרון. דהא דייקינן מדנקט מקל: לוי. בר פלוגתיה סבר אין צריכה חסרון: משונה שליחות יד כו'. כלומר אינה דומה לזו שזו נאמרה לצורך ולא משתמע אלא בחסרון אבל של שומר שכר נאמרה שלא לצורך משמעות שבה אלא לדרשה וללמד שאינה צריכה חסרון:

ואי

## תוספות

אי רבי ישמעאל אפילו יחדו נמי. וא"ת מנ"ל י"ל מדנקט טלה וסלע דסתם טלה לא יחד לו מקום אלא הולך ממרעה למרעה וסתם סלע יחדו לו מקום בכיס וגם כיס יחדו לו מקום בתיבה ולכך פריך נמי בסמוך לר"ע אפילו לא יחדו נמי: שנטלה והגביהה ע"מ לגוזלה כו'. והיינו חסרון שהכל גוזל ונטל לצורך עצמו: שנטלה ע"מ לשלוח בה יד. פי' ליטול מקצת אע"פ שלא נטל אותה מקצת חייב בכולה כדאמר בשלהי פרקין (דף מד.) לא נטל נטל ממש אלא כיון שהגביה ליטול אע"פ שלא נטל אבל למ"ד ע"מ לגוזלה דבעי חסרון אם הגביה ליטול קצת אינו חייב עד שיטול המקצת כיון דבעי חסרון וקשה דבשלהי פרקין קאמר אפי' למ"ד בעי חסרון מודה בחבית אם הגביהה אע"פ שלא נטל חייב דניחא ליה דתיהוי כולה בסים להאי רביעית ומתני' בחבית איירי ויש לומר דמתני' איירי אפילו בשמן דלא מנטר פורתא אגב האחר: ובא זאב וטרף. בשעת משלחת זאבים ורבי יהודה היא דאמר זאב אחד אונס בפ' הפועלים (לקמן דף צג:): הא שקלינהו. לרבי ישמעאל פריך דאמר לא בעינן דעת בעלים כפרש"י: הא לא משכה. דאע"ג דעודן עליה לא קיימא ברשותיה להתחייב באונסיה עד שימשוך כדאמר במתני' (לקמן דף מג.) הטה את החבית ונטל ממנה רביעית אינו חייב אלא דמי רביעית כיון דלא הגביה את החבית ומשני שהניח מקלו ותרמילו עליה כל כך בחוזק עד שרצתה לפניו: דיקא נמי דקתני שהכישה. וא"ת בפ"ק דקדושין (דף כב:) תניא או שהכישה במקל ורצתה לפניו דאקרי משיכה ולא הויא הכחשה וי"ל דהתם דאדם נכרי לקחה ואינה מכירתו בדבורו שייך למיתני הכישה אבל הכא דאיירי ברועה שהבהמה מכירתו ואזלה מחמת דבורו לא שייך למיתני שהכישה:

לומר

## עין משפט נר מצוה

עז א מיי' פ"ד מהלכות גניבה הל' י ועי' בהשגות ובמ"מ סמג עשין עא טור ש"ע ח"מ סי' שנה סעיף א וסעיף ג וע"ש:

עח ב מיי' פ"ז מהל' שאלה ופקדון הלכה ט סמג עשין פח טוש"ע ח"מ סי' רצב סעיף ו:

עט ג מיי' פ"ג מהל' גזילה הל' יא סמג עשין עג טוש"ע ח"מ סי' רצב סעיף א:

פ ד מיי' פ"ג מהל' שכירות הל' ח סמג עשין פט טוש"ע ח"מ סי' שג סעיף י:

## רבינו חננאל

ומקשי' אי הכי יחדו להאי חבית הבעלים מקום [נמי] דהא שמעינן ליה לר' ישמעאל דאומר הגונב סלע מן הכיס והנה יחדו הבעלים להאי סלע מקום בכיס ואמר ר' ישמעאל יחזיר למקום שגנב ואין צריך דעת בעלים ואי מתני' ר' ישמעאל היא אמאי קתני ולא יחדו לה בעלים דשמעינן מינה דדוקא לא יחדו הא יחדו לא. ופרקי' לא מיבעיא קאמר לא מיבעיא יחדו לה הבעלים מקום והחזירה באותו מקום דודאי פטור דהא החזירה במקומה וכיון שהחזירה במקומה כלא טלטלה דמי אלא אפי' לא יחדו לה בעלים מקום דלאו במקומה מחזירה פטור. אוקימנא אליבא דר' ישמעאל בין יחדו לה הבעלים מקום בין לא יחדו לה הבעלים מקום כיון שהחזירה למקומה אם נשברה פטור הוא. אי הכי אימא סיפא יחדו לה בעלים מקום וטלטלה ונשברה בין מתוך ידו בין משהניחה לצרכה פטור לצרכו חייב אמאי חייב והא משהניחה קתני ויש מי שמפרק בשהניחה במקום שאינו מקומה. ור' יוחנן אמר הניחה במקומה משמע. ופרקי' סיפא אתאן לר' עקיבא דאמר צריך דעת בעלים הלכך לצרכו חייב. ומקשינן אי מתני' רבי עקיבא היא למה ליה יחדו לה בעלים מקום אפי' לא יחדו אמר ר' עקיבא צריך דעת בעלים דתניא הגונב טלה מן העדר וכו' הנה לא יחדו בעלים מקום לטלה והצריך ר' עקיבא בהחזרה דעת בעלים כו'. ועמדה רישא ר' ישמעאל וסיפא ר' עקיבא. אמר ר' יוחנן מאן דמתרגם ליה חבית אליבא דחד תנא וכו' פי' אמר ר' יוחנן מי שיפרש לי משנתינו זו המפקיד חבית אצל חבירו וכו' ויעמידה אי אליבא דר' ישמעאל אי אליבא דר' עקיבא סיפא ורישא בחד תנא אני מוליך לו כליו אחריו לבית המרחץ כי הוא כמו רב ואני תלמיד שנמצאתי משמשו כתלמיד לרב. ובא רב יעקב בר אבא לאוקמה למתני' בנוטלה על מנת לגוזלה. ורב נתן בר יעקב מוקמה בנוטלה על מנת לשלח בה יד וכולה ר' ישמעאל. ודחה רב ששת טעם שניהם ואמר מידי במתני' קתני נטלה דלישמעינן נטלה לגזלה או לשלח בה יד טלטלה קתני ואין בלשון טלטול לא לשון גזילה ולא שילוח בה יד. אלא אמר רב ששת כגון שטלטלה לעמוד עליה ולפשוט ידו בתוך הקן ליטול גוזלות וסבר האי תנא שואל שלא מדעת בעלים גזלן הוי וכולה ר' ישמעאל היא וסיפא שהניחה במקום שאינה מקומה לפיכך תנן לצרכו חייב. ור' יוחנן אמר סיפא ר' עקיבא היא כי הניחה במקום שנטלה משמע. ואעפ"כ צריך דעת בעלים כר' עקיבא וכיון שלא ידעו בה הבעלים שהחזירה למקומה לפיכך לצרכו חייב. איתמר רב אמר שליחות יד צריכה חסרון. מדתניא רועה שהיה רועה עדרו ובא זאב וטרף ארי ודרס פטור פי' פטור הוא כי שוכר הוא והשוכר פטור מן האונסין. ואם הניח מקלו או תרמילו עליה פי' כיון שנשתמש בה כאילו גזלה וחייב באונסיה. ואקשי' עלה. ואוקמה רב בעודו עליה מקלו ותרמילו. ואמרי' והא לא משכה ופריק רב כגון שהכישה במקלו ורצתה לפניו. דייקי' מדלא קתני הנהיגה בקול אלא הכישה במקל ש"מ שהכישה במקל והוכחשה דהיינו חיסרה ולפיכך חייב ש"מ דרב הוא דאמר שליחות יד צריכה חסרון ואם אין שם חסרון פטור באונסיה ולוי אמר שליחות יד אינה צריכה חסרון מאי טעמא. אמר ר' יוחנן משום ר' יוסי בר נהוראי משנה שליחות יד האמורה בשומר חנם משליחות יד האמורה בשומר שכר כלומר שומר חנם דינו קל ושומר שכר דינו חמור שחייב בגניבה ואבידה ואם שומר חנם שדינו קל חייב בו בשליחות יד שומר שכר לא כל שכן שחייב אם שלח בו יד למה כתב

## מסורת הש"ס

א) סנהדרין דף סב:, ב) [עירובין דף ס:], ג) [לקמן מג:], ד) [שם], ה) [לקמן מג:, בבא בתרא פח.], ו) [קדושין מב], ז) לקמן צג: [ע"ש], קו. [ע"ש], ח) גירסת מהר"ם דאמר.

## הגהות הב"ח

(א) גמ' הא שקלינהו ואמר ר"נ:

## גליון הש"ס

גמ' אין דאר"י. עי' שבת דף פו ע"א קידושין דף סג ע"ב מנחות דף נה ע"א: רש"י ד"ה הניחה במקומה כו' כרבי ישמעאל. עי' שבת דף פו ע"א ברש"י ד"ה ומאן דמוקי:

## ליקוטי רש"י

מאן דמתרגם לי חבית אליבא דחד תנא. דקתני התם המפקיד חבית אצל חברו ולא יחדו לה הבעלים מקום וטלטלה ונשברה אם מתוך ידו נשברה לצרכו חייב לצרכה פטור אם משהניחה נשברה בין לצרכו בין לצרכה פטור יחדו לה הבעלים מקום וטלטלה ונשברה בין מתוך ידו בין משהניחה לצרכו חייב לצרכה פטור ופריך התם מני ר' ישמעאל היא דאמר לא בעינן דעת בעלים דתניא הגונב טלה מן העדר וסלע מן הכיס למקום שגנב יחזיר דברי ר' ישמעאל ר' עקיבא אומר צריך דעת בעלים אי ר' ישמעאל מאי איריא לא יחדו אפילו יחדו נמי לא מבעיא קאמר לא מיבעיא יחדו דמקומה הוא אלא אפילו לא יחדו דלאו מקומה הוא לא בעיא דעת בעלים סיפא אתאן לר' עקיבא אי ר' עקיבא מאי איריא יחדו אפילו לא יחדו נמי לא מבעיא קאמר לא מבעיא לא יחדו דלאו מקומה הוא אלא אפילו יחדו נמי דמקומה הוא בעינן דעת בעלים רישא ר' ישמעאל וסיפא ר' עקיבא ואילו הוה בעי לאוקמא רישא בשהניחה במקומה הראשון וסיפא בשהניחה במקום שאינה מקומה כדמוקי לה אמוראי ה"מ לאוקמיה כולה כר' ישמעאל ור"י מאן דמתרגם כו' דלא הוה בעי לאוקמיה רישא כחד טעמא וסיפא כחד טעמא [סנהדרין סב:]. אליבא דחד תנא וכו'. דניחא ליה לאוקומי כתנא מלאוקמי משבשתא היא ולמלאכת בתרי טעמי. ופלוגתא היא בהמפקיד גבי חבית דאמר ר' יוחנן מאן דמתרגם לי חבית אליבא דחד תנא מובילנא ליה מאני לבי מסותא ומוקי רישא ר' ישמעאל וסיפא רבי עקיבא ולא הוה בעי הוה מצי לאוקמי בתרי טעמי ובחד תנא ואיכא דמוקי לה התם בחד תנא ומוקי סיפא בשהניחה במקום שאינו מקומה [שבת פו.]. מאניה. בגדיו [יומא נב.]. מסותא. מרחץ כמו מסחותה וירחץ מתרגמינן ואסחי [סנהדרין סב:]. תרגמה. פרש אותה [סוטה ח:]. שליחות יד אינה צריכה חסרון. ומשלח בה יד אע"פ שלא חסרה הויא גזילה וקמה ברשותיה [לקמן מג:]. שואל שלא מדעת גזלן הוי. וקנייה להתחייב בה עד שתבא ליד בעלים דבעינן והשיב את הגזילה [רשב"ם ב"ב פח.]. תסתיים. תתפרש אמיתו של דבר [מגילה יד:]. תיאמר בשם אומרה [ע"ז טז:]. ובא זאב וטרף ובא ארי ודרס. ארי דרכו לדרוס הבהמה במקום שמוצאה ודרך זאב לטורפה חיה ולהוליכה במקום שהוא בטוח ושם הורגה [לקמן צג:]. דרס שלא הרגה אלא מחיים אכלה דאורחיה הוא [ב"ק טז:]. ותרמילו. חמת של עור בשטייל"א בלע"ז ורועה נותן בה פתו וכלי מלאכתו [יבמות פו:].

R' Yaakov and R' Nassan: מִידִי נְטָלָהּ קָתָנֵי – **Does the Mishnah say, "he took it,"** which would indicate that the *shomer* intended to take all or some of the barrel's contents for himself? טִלְטְלָהּ קָתָנֵי – All **it says is, "he moved it,"** which indicates that the *shomer* merely moved the barrel in order to use it temporarily, not to take it permanently for himself. – ? –

Rav Sheishess offers his own interpretation of the Mishnah: אֶלָּא אָמַר רַב שֵׁשֶׁת – **Rather, Rav Sheishess said:** הָכָא בְּמַאי עַסְקִינַן – **What are we dealing with here?** We are dealing with a case where the *shomer* moved the barrel with intent to use it for a while and then return it to safekeeping. כְּגוֹן שֶׁטִּלְטְלָהּ לְהָבִיא עָלֶיהָ גּוֹזָלוֹת – **For example, he moved [the barrel]** to use it as a support **on which to** stand and **bring** some **young birds** from a dovecote.

The Gemara explains Rav Sheishess' view: וְקָא סָבַר – **And [Rav Sheishess] holds** שׁוֹאֵל שֶׁלֹּא מִדַּעַת – that **one who borrows** an article **without** its owner's **permission** גַּזְלָן הָוֵי – **is** considered **a thief.**[14]

The Gemara now explains how these three Amoraim (R' Yaakov, R' Nassan, and Rav Sheishess) understand the Mishnah: וְכוּלָּהּ רַבִּי יִשְׁמָעֵאל הִיא – **And the entire [Mishnah] follows** the view of **R' Yishmael** that the owner's knowledge of the return of a stolen item is not required to release the thief from liability. The Gemara explained above that the first ruling in the Mishnah follows the view of R' Yishmael. וְסֵיפָא – **And the second part** of the Mishnah, which rules that the *shomer* is responsible for the barrel even after he returned it to safekeeping, also follows his view, שֶׁהֱנִיחָהּ בְּמָקוֹם שֶׁאֵינָהּ מְקוֹמָהּ – for it speaks of a case **where [the *shomer*] put the barrel in a place other than its** designated **place.**[15]

The Gemara now explains the opinion of R' Yochanan, who could not find an interpretation of the Mishnah that reconciled both of its clauses with the viewpoint of a single Tanna: וְרַבִּי יוֹחָנָן – **And R' Yochanan,** why did he not accept this interpretation of the Mishnah, according to which both of its clauses are consistent with the view of R' Yishmael? הֱנִיחָהּ – He holds that the Mishnah's statement, **"he put it down,"** בִּמְקוֹמָהּ מַשְׁמַע – **implies** that he returned it **to its** rightful **place.**[16]

The Gemara returns to the question mentioned above: If a *shomer* picked up a deposit with intent to take some of it for himself, does he assume responsibility immediately, or not until he actually uses it?

אִיתְּמַר – **It was stated:** רַב וְלֵוִי – **Rav and Levi** disputed this matter. חַד אָמַר – **One** of them **said:** שְׁלִיחוּת יָד צְרִיכָה חֶסְרוֹן – **Misappropriation is dependent upon a loss.** וְחַד אָמַר – **And** the other **one said:** שְׁלִיחוּת יָד אֵינָהּ צְרִיכָה חֶסְרוֹן – **Misappropriation is not dependent upon a loss.**

The Gemara attempts to identify who holds each opinion: תִּסְתַּיֵּים דְּרַב הוּא דְּאָמַר – **It can be determined that Rav is the one who said** שְׁלִיחוּת יָד אֵינָהּ צְרִיכָה חֶסְרוֹן – that **misappropriation is not dependent upon a loss.** דְּתַנְיָא – **For it was taught in a Baraisa:** רוֹעֶה שֶׁהָיָה רוֹעֶה עֶדְרוֹ – If A SHEPHERD WAS TENDING HIS FLOCK, וְהִנִּיחַ עֶדְרוֹ וּבָא לָעִיר – AND then HE LEFT HIS FLOCK AND WENT INTO THE TOWN, וּבָא זְאֵב וְטָרַף – AND in his absence A WOLF CAME AND TORE a sheep, וּבָא אֲרִי וְדָרַס – OR A LION CAME AND CLAWED a sheep,[17] פָּטוּר – HE IS NOT LIABLE to pay the owner for the sheep, for such an attack is considered an unavoidable mishap.[18] הִנִּיחַ מַקְלוֹ וְתַרְמִילוֹ עָלֶיהָ – If, however, prior to the attack, HE HAD PUT HIS STAFF OR HIS POUCH ON [THE SHEEP] that was later attacked, חַיָּיב – HE IS LIABLE to pay for it, for by doing so he had misappropriated that animal.[19]

Rav's opinion regarding whether misappropriation requires a loss is derived from the following discussion of the Baraisa's last ruling: וְהַוִינַן בָּהּ – **And we had raised the** following **difficulty concerning [this ruling]:** מִשּׁוּם דְּהִנִּיחַ מַקְלוֹ וְתַרְמִילוֹ עָלֶיהָ חַיָּיב – **[The shepherd] is liable** to pay damages merely **because he put his staff or his pouch on [the sheep]!?** הָא שַׁקְלִינְהוּ – **But he removed them** before the attack occurred![20] Even if the placement of the articles on the sheep was an act of misappropriation, their

NOTES

14. It is a matter of dispute whether one who borrows something without the owner's permission is treated as a borrower or as a thief (*Bava Basra* 88a). (Either way, borrowing without permission is forbidden, and one who does so is liable for unavoidable mishaps; but a thief is under the special obligation mandated by the verse [*Leviticus* 5:23]: וְהֵשִׁיב אֶת־הַגְּזֵלָה, *and he shall return the stolen property*.) The following note will explain the Gemara's reason for stating that Rav Sheishess takes the view that he is considered a thief (see also note 26).

15. When the latter part of the Mishnah states, "he put [the keg] down," it means that he put it down in a place that was *not* the place designated for it by the owner. Hence, he has not fulfilled his obligation of returning the keg, as required by the verse (*Leviticus* 5:23): וְהֵשִׁיב אֶת־הַגְּזֵלָה, *and he shall return the stolen property*. Therefore, the article remains in his possession and he continues to be responsible for any damage that might occur to it.

In the first part of the Mishnah, however, no particular place had been designated for the keg's storage, and thus the *shomer* fulfills his obligation of returning the stolen keg merely by putting it in any safe place. Once he has done so, he is no longer liable for unavoidable mishaps (even though he did not notify the owner, according to R' Yishmael), but reverts to his status as a *shomer*. [According to these Amoraim, the Mishnah's first ruling speaks *specifically* of a case where the owner did *not* designate a place for the barrel, unlike the Gemara's position above.]

The dispute between R' Yaakov and R' Nassan (who explained the Mishnah as referring to a *shomer* who stole all or part of the deposit) and Rav Sheishess (who explained the Mishnah as referring to a *shomer* who merely borrowed the deposit) can now be understood, as follows:

Rav Sheishess regards one who borrows without permission as a thief, who is not released from liability until he restores the barrel to its *rightful* place, as mandated by the verse (*Leviticus* 5:23), וְהֵשִׁיב אֶת־הַגְּזֵלָה, *and he shall return the stolen property*. But according to R' Yaakov and R' Nassan, one who borrows without permission is not considered a thief. Hence, in their view, were the *shomer* to have merely borrowed the barrel, it would have been sufficient for him to return it to *any* safe place, not necessarily the one designated by the owner. Thus, the latter clause of the Mishnah, which teaches that the *shomer* remains liable if he did not return the deposit to its designated place, cannot refer to a case of borrowing (*Rashi*).

16. According to R' Yochanan's understanding, the latter part of the Mishnah, which rules that the *shomer* is liable, cannot be attributed to R' Yishmael [for according to R' Yishmael, once a thief has returned the stolen item to its rightful place, he is released from liability even if he did not notify the owner of its return] (*Rashi*).

17. A lion kills and devours its prey out in the field immediately without fear; whereas a wolf, since it is afraid of other creatures, first drags its prey to its lair, and then kills it and consumes it there (see *Rashi* below, 93b, and to *Taanis* 8a; see also *Rashi* to *Bava Kamma* 16b).

18. [A shepherd is a paid *shomer*, and as such is not liable for unavoidable mishaps.] The fact that the shepherd left the flock before the attack is not regarded as negligence on his part, for he left the flock and entered the town at the time of day when it is customary to do so. Alternatively, the shepherd left his flock [out of fear] when he heard the roar of the lion [which is also not considered negligence] (*Rashi,* from Gemara below, 93b).

19. It is explained below (in note 26) why this is considered *shelichus yad,* as opposed to borrowing the sheep.

20. The Gemara assumes that this was so, for the Baraisa uses the word הִנִּיחַ, *he put* [past tense], as opposed to מוּנָחִים, *they are lying* [present tense] (*Ramban*).

**מסורת הש"ס**

א) סנהדרין דף סב., ב) [עירובין דף מ:], ג) [לקמן מג:], ד) [שם], ה) [לקמן מג:, ב"ב בתרא פח.], ו) (קדושין מג), ז) לקמן לג: [ע"ש], קו. [ע"ש], ח) גירסת מהר"ס דאמר.

[א]צריך דעת בעלים אי רבי ישמעאל מאי איריא לא יחדו אפילו יחדו נמי לא מיבעיא קאמר לא מיבעיא יחדו דמקומה הוא אלא אפילו לא יחדו דלאו מקומה הוא לא בעינן דעת בעלים אימא סיפא יחדו לה הבעלים מקום וטלטלה ונשברה בין מתוך ידו בין משהניחה לצרכו חייב לצרכה פטור אתאן לר"ע דאמר בעינן דעת בעלים אי ר"ע מאי איריא יחדו אפילו לא יחדו נמי [ב]לא מיבעיא קאמר לא מיבעיא לא יחדו דלאו מקומה הוא אלא אפילו יחדו נמי דמקומה הוא בעינן דעת בעלים רישא רבי ישמעאל וסיפא ר"ע ° אין (א) דא"ר יוחנן מאן דמתרגם לי חבית אליבא דחד תנא (ג) מובלנא מאניה בתריה לבי מסותא תרגמה רבי יעקב בר אבא קמיה דרב שנטלה על מנת לגוזלה תרגמה ר' נתן בר אבא קמיה דרב שנטלה ע"מ לשלוח בה יד במאי קמיפלגי (ג)בשליחות יד צריכה חסרון מאן דאמר לגוזלה קסבר שליחות יד צריכה חסרון ומ"ד לשלוח בה יד קסבר שליחות יד אינה צריכה חסרון מתקיף לה רב ששת מידי נטלה קתני טלטלה קתני אלא אמר רב ששת הכא במאי עסקינן (ד)כגון שטלטלה להביא עליה גוזלות וקא סבר (ה)שואל שלא מדעת גזלן הוי וכולה רבי ישמעאל היא וסיפא שהניחה במקום שאינה מקומה ור' יוחנן הניחה במקומה משמע (ו)איתמר רב ולוי חד אמר שליחות יד צריכה חסרון וחד אמר [ג]שליחות יד אינה צריכה חסרון תסתיים דרב הוא דאמר שליחות יד אינה צריכה חסרון דתניא (ז)[ד]רועה שהיה רועה עדרו והניח עדרו ובא לעיר ובא זאב וטרף ובא ארי ודרס פטור הניח מקלו ותרמילו עליה חייב והוינן בה משום דהניח מקלו ותרמילו עליה חייב הא שקלינהו (א) אמר ר"נ אמר רבה בר אבוה אמר רב בעודן עליה וכי עודן עליה מאי הוי הא לא משכה ואמר רב שמואל בר רב יצחק אמר רב שהכישה במקל ורצתה לפניו והא לא חסרה אלא לאו ש"מ קסבר שליחות יד אינה צריכה חסרון אימא שהכחישה במקל דיקא נמי (ח)דקתני שהכישה במקל ש"מ ומדרב סבר שליחות יד צריכה חסרון לוי סבר שליחות יד אינה צריכה חסרון מאי טעמא דלוי א"ר יוחנן משום ר' יוסי בן נהוראי משונה שליחות יד האמורה בשומר שכר משליחות יד האמורה בשומר חנם ואני

**רש"י**

צריך דעת בעלים. ואם לא הודיעם חייב באחריותם אם מת או נגנב דמדשקליה קם ליה ברשותיה והשבה בלא ידיעה לאו השבה היא: דמקומה היא. וכיון דבאותו מקום החזירה חזרה גמורה היא: אתאן לר"ע. תירוצא הוא: תרגמה רבי יעקב. דתיקו כולה כחד תנא ובתרי טעמי רישא שהחזירה למקומה דכל מקום שהחזירה מקומה היא דהא לא יחדו לה מקום וסיפא שהחזירה למקום שאינה מקומה כדמסיים במסקנא דהא דמסקינן בסיומא וסיפא שהניחה במקום שאינה מקומה אתרלתא דכולהו קאי אדר' יעקב ואדר' נתן ואדרב ששת ומשום דהניחה חוץ למקומה לא הויא חזרה וכגון שנטלו מתחלה על מנת לגוזלה והיינו לצרכו דמתניתין דאילו לשאלה בעלמא ולתשמיש כיון דלאו גזילה הוא סגי לה בהשבה כל דהו וכל מקום שהניחה פטור באונסין אבל משום דגזולה הואי ובגזילה כתיב והשיב וזה שהניחה למקום שלא יחדו לה בעלים לא הויא השבה: ור' נתן תרגמה. דאפילו לא נטלה על מנת לגוזלה כו' אלא על מנת לשלוח בה יד וליטול מקצתה ולא נטל אפ"ה קמה ליה ברשותיה כולה והויא לה גזילה ובעי' השבה ובמקום שאינו מקומה לאו השבה היא ורב ששת לא שביק דליסיימו לתירולייהו ואתקיף מידי נטלה קתני כו' ומיהו סיומא דמילתא דמסקנא וסיפא שהניחה במקום שאינו מקומה אכולהו קאי: שליחות יד. שחייבו הכתוב עליו אפילו נאנסה כדכתיב (שמות כב) ומת או נשבר או נשבה [וגו'] שבועת ה' תהיה בין שניהם אם לא שלח ידו וגו' דמשמע הא שלח נתחייב שוב במיתתה ובשבייתה: צריכה חסרון. לא הוי שליחות יד להעמידה ברשותו אלא א"כ חסרה: מידי נטלה קתני. דמשמע שנטלה לעצמו: טלטלה קתני. לתשמיש בעלמא משמע לצרכו דמתני': אלא כגון שטלטלה להביא עליה גוזלות. לעלות עליה כדרך סולם ליטול גוזלות מקן גבוה ואפ"ה הויא גזילה למיקם ברשותיה עד דעביד השבה דקסבר שואל שלא מדעת בעלים גזלן הוא: וכולה ר' ישמעאל היא. אשינויא דכולהו קאי אדר' יעקב ואדר' נתן ואדרב ששת: וסיפא שהניחה במקום שאינה מקומה. אבל רישא כל מקום שהניחה מקומה היא: ור' יוחנן. דאמר לעיל מאן דמתרגם לי כו': הניחה במקומה משמע. הלכך לא מיתוקמא ° כרבי ישמעאל: שליחות יד. שחייבו הכתוב עליו ואפי' נאנסה כדכתיב או נשבר או נשבה וגו' שבועת ה' תהיה אם לא שלח דמשמע הא אם שלח נתחייב שוב במיתתה ובשבייתה: צריכה חסרון. וכל זמן שלא חסרה לא קמה ברשותיה להתחייב באונסיה: זאב. טורף נושא הטרף לחורו: ארי. אינו טורפה אלא דורסה במקומה ואוכלה: פטור. דאונסין נינהו ואי משום דהניח עדרו ופשיעה היא מוקמינן לה דעל בעידנא דעיילי אינשי כדאמרינן בהשוכר את הפועלים (לקמן צג:) א"נ דשמע קול אריה ועל: הא שקלינהו. ואי נמי שליחות יד חשיבא הא הדר אהדרה כשנטלו הימנו ואנן מוקמינן לעיל סתם מתני' כרבי ישמעאל דאין צריך דעת בעלים: הא לא משכה. בשליחות יד כדי לקנותה ומטלטלין אין נקנין אלא במשיכה לא במקח ולא לענין גזל ולא לענין שליחות יד כדתנן במתני' (לקמן דף מג:) הטה את החבית ונטל ממנה רביעית יין אין אין משלם אלא רביעית אלמא בעינן דליקנייה כו': ואמר רב שמואל. גרסינן: שהכישה במקל. כשנתנו עליה ורצתה זו היא משיכה משעקרה יד ורגל על ידו: והא לא חסרה. לאו פירכא היא אלא מסקנא וסיומא הוא למילתיה דאמר תסתיים דרב הוא דאמר אין צריכה חסרון מדשני רב למתניתין משום דהכישה ורצתה לפניו ואי קשיא דלמא הא דהניח מקלו ותרמילו חיוביה לאו משום שליחות יד הוא דליבעי חסרון אלא משום שואל שלא מדעת הוא כי ההוא דלעיל דחבית לא היא דכי אמרינן בשומרין שאלה שלא מדעת בדבר שאינו כיחש וחיסר מחמת מלאכה אבל בעלי חיים המכחישים מחמת מלאכה תחלתו שליחות יד היא: שהכחישה. בהכאתו דהיינו חסרון: דיקא נמי. דהכחישה קאמר רב מדנקט הכשת מקל דמכה חזקה היא: ומדרב סבר צריכה חסרון. דהא דייקין מדנקט מקל: לוי. בר פלוגתיה סבר אין צריכה חסרון: משונה שליחות יד כו'. כלומר אינה דומה לזו שזו נאמרה לצורך ולא משתמע אלא בחסרון אבל של שומר שכר נאמרה שלא לצורך משמעות שבה אלא לדרשה וללמד שאינה צריכה חסרון:

**תוספות**

**אי** רבי ישמעאל אפילו יחדו נמי. וא"ת מנ"ל י"ל מדנקט טלה וסלע דסתם טלה לא יחד לו מקום אלא הולך ממרעה למרעה וסתם סלע יחדו לו מקום בכיס וגם כיס יחדו לו מקום בתיבה ולכך פריך נמי בסמוך לר"ע אפילו לא יחדו נמי:

**שנטלה** והגביהה ע"מ לגוזלה כו'. והיינו חסרון שהכל גוזל ונטל לצורך עצמו:

**שנטלה** ע"מ לשלוח בה יד. פי' ליטול מקצת אע"פ שלא נטל אותה מקצת חייב בכולה כדאמר בשלהי פרקין (דף מד.) לא נטל נטל ממש אלא כיון שהגביה ליטול אע"פ שלא נטל אבל למ"ד ע"מ לגוזלה דבעי חסרון אם הגביה ליטול קצת אינו חייב עד שיטול המקצת כיון דבעי חסרון וקשה דבשלהי פרקין קאמר אפי' למ"ד בעי חסרון מודה בחבית אם הגביהה אע"פ שלא נטל חייב דניחא ליה דתיהוי כולה בסים להאי רביעית ומתני' בחבית איירי ויש לומר דמתני' איירי אפילו בשמן דלא מנטר פורתא אגב האחר:

**ובא** זאב וטרף. בשעת משלחת זאבים ורבי יהודה היא דאמר זאב אחד אונס בפ' הפועלים (לקמן דף צג:):

**הא** שקלינהו. לרבי ישמעאל פריך דאמר לא בעינן דעת בעלים כפרש"י:

**הא** לא משכה. דאע"ג דעודן עליה לא קיימא ברשותיה להתחייב באונסיה עד שימשוך כדאמר במתני' (לקמן דף מג:) הטה את החבית ונטל ממנה רביעית אינו חייב אלא דמי רביעית כיון דלא הגביה את החבית ומשני שהניח מקלו ותרמילו עליה כל כך בחוזק עד שרצתה לפניו:

**דיקא** נמי דקתני שהכישה. וא"ת בפ"ק דקדושין (דף כב:) תניא או שהכישה במקל ורצתה לפניו דאקרי משיכה ולא הויא הכחשה וי"ל דהתם דאדם נכרי לקחה ואינה מכירתו בדבורו שייך למיתני הכישה אבל הכא דאיירי ברועה שהבהמה מכירתו ואזלה מחמת דבורו לא שייך למיתני שהכישה:

לומר

**עין משפט נר מצוה**

עז א מיי' פ"ד מהלכות גניבה הל' י ועי' בהשגות וכמ"מ סמג עשין עא טור ש"ע ח"מ סי' שנה סעיף א וסעיף ג וע"ש:
עח ב מיי' פ"ז מהל' שאלה ופקדון הלכה ט סמג עשין פח טוש"ע ח"מ סי' רצב סעיף ו:
עט ג מיי' פ"ג מהל' גזילה הל' יא סמג עשין עג טוש"ע ח"מ סי' רצב סעיף א:
פ ד מיי' פ"ג מהל' שכירות הל' ח סמג עשין פט טוש"ע ח"מ סי' שג סעיף י:

**רבינו חננאל**

ומקשי' אי הכי יחדו להאי חבית הבעלים מקום [נמי] דהא שמעינן ליה לר' ישמעאל דאומר הגונב סלע מן הכיס והנה יחדו הבעלים להאי סלע מקום בכיס ואמר ר' ישמעאל יחזיר למקום שגנב ואין צריך דעת בעלים ואי מתני' ר' ישמעאל היא אמאי קתני ולא יחדו לה בעלים דשמעינן מינה דדוקא לא יחדו הא יחדו לא. ופרקי' לא מיבעיא קאמר לא מיבעיא יחדו לה הבעלים מקום והחזירה באותו מקום דודאי פטור דהא החזירה במקומה וכיון שהחזירה במקומה כלא טלטלה דמי אלא אפי' לא יחדו לה בעלים מקום דלאו במקומה מחזירה פטור. אוקימנא אליבא דר' ישמעאל בין יחדו לה הבעלים מקום בין לא יחדו לה הבעלים מקום כיון שהחזירה למקומה אם נשברה פטור הוא. אי הכי אימא סיפא יחדו לה בעלים מקום וטלטלה ונשברה בין מתוך ידו בין משהניחה לצרכה פטור לצרכו חייב אמאי חייב והא משהניחה קתני ויש מי שמפרק בשהניחה במקום שאינו מקומה. ור' יוחנן אמר הניחה במקומה משמע. ופרקי' סיפא אתאן לר' עקיבא דאמר צריך דעת בעלים הלכך לצרכו חייב. ומקשינן אי מתני' רבי עקיבא היא למה ליה יחדו לה בעלים מקום אפי' לא יחדו אמר ר' עקיבא צריך דעת בעלים דתניא הגונב טלה מן העדר וכו' הנה לא יחדו בעלים מקום לטלה והצריך ר' עקיבא בהחזרה דעת בעלים כו'. ועמדה רישא ר' ישמעאל וסיפא ר' עקיבא. אמר ר' יוחנן מאן דמתרגם ליה חבית אליבא דחד תנא וכו' פי' אמר ר' יוחנן מי שיפרש לי משנתינו זו המפקיד חבית אצל חבירו וכו' ויעמידה אי אליבא דר' ישמעאל אי אליבא דר' עקיבא סיפא ורישא בחד תנא אני מוליך לו כליו אחריו לבית המרחץ כי הוא כמו רב ואני תלמיד שנמצאתי משמשו כתלמיד לרב. ובא רב יעקב בר אבא לאוקמה למתני' בנוטלה על מנת לגוזלה. ורב נתן בר יעקב מוקמה בנוטלה על מנת לשלח בה יד וכולה ר' ישמעאל. ודחה רב ששת טעם שניהם ואמר מידי במתני' קתני נטלה דלישמעינן נטלה לגזלה או לשלח בה יד טלטלה קתני ואין בלשון טלטול לא לשון גזילה ולא שילוח בה יד. אלא אמר רב ששת כגון שטלטלה לעמוד עליה ולפשוט ידו בתוך הקן ליטול גוזלות וסבר האי תנא שואל שלא מדעת בעלים גזלן הוי וכולה ר' ישמעאל היא וסיפא שהניחה במקום שאינה מקומה לפיכך תנן לצרכו חייב. ור' יוחנן אמר סיפא ר' עקיבא היא כי הניחה במקום שנטלה משמע. ואעפ"כ צריך דעת בעלים כר' עקיבא וכיון שלא ידעו בה הבעלים שהחזירה למקומה לפיכך לצרכו חייב. איתמר רב אמר שליחות יד צריכה חסרון. מדתניא רועה שהיה רועה עדרו ובא זאב וטרף ארי ודרס פטור פי' פטור הוא כי שוכר הוא והשוכר פטור מן האונסין. ואם הניח מקלו או תרמילו עליה פי' כיון שנשתמש בה כאילו גזלה וחייב באונסיה. ואקשי' עלה. ואוקמה רב בעודו עליה מקלו ותרמילו. ואמרי' והא לא משכה ומפרק ר' בכגון שהכישה במקל ורצתה לפניו. דייק' מדלא קתני הנהיגה בקול אלא הכישה במקל ש"מ שהכישה במקל והוכחשה דהיינו חסירה ולפיכך חייב ש"מ דרב הוא דאמר שליחות יד צריכה חסרון ואם אין שם חסרון פטור באונסיה ולוי אמר שליחות יד אינה צריכה חסרון מאי טעמא. אמר ר' יוחנן משום ר' יוסי בר נהוראי משונה שליחות יד האמורה בשומר חנם משליחות יד האמורה בשומר שכר כלומר שומר חנם שדינו קל חייב בו בשליחות יד שומר שכר לא כל שכן שחייב אם שלח בו יד למה כתב

**הגהות הב"ח**

(א) גמ' הא שקלינהו ואמר ר"נ:

**גליון הש"ס**

גמ' אין דאר"י. עי' שבת דף פו ע"א קידושין דף סג ע"ב מנחות דף נה ע"א: רש"י ד"ה הניחה במקומה כו' כרבי ישמעאל. עי' שבת דף פו ע"א ברש"י ד"ה ומאן דמוקי:

**ליקוטי רש"י**

מאן דמתרגם לי חבית **אליבא** דחד **תנא.** דקתני התם המפקיד חבית אצל חברו ולא ייחדו לה הבעלים מקום וטלטלה ונשברה אם מתוך ידו נשברה לצרכו חייב לצרכה פטור אם משהניחה נשברה בין לצרכה בין לצרכו פטור ייחדו לה הבעלים מקום וטלטלה ונשברה בין מתוך ידו בין משהניחה לצרכו חייב לצרכה פטור ופריך התם מני ר' ישמעאל היא דאמר לא בעינן דעת בעלים דתניא הגונב טלה מן העדר וסלע מן הכיס למקום שגנב יחזיר דברי ר' ישמעאל ר' עקיבא אומר צריך דעת בעלים אי ר' ישמעאל מאי איריא לא ייחדו אפילו ייחדו נמי לא מבעיא קאמר לא מיבעיא ייחדו דמקומה הוא אלא אפילו לא ייחדו דלאו מקומה הוא לא בעיא דעת בעלים סיפא אתאן לר' עקיבא אי ר' עקיבא מאי איריא ייחדו אפילו לא ייחדו נמי לא מבעיא קאמר לא מבעיא לא ייחדו דלאו מקומה הוא אלא אפילו ייחדו נמי דמקומה הוא בעינן דעת בעלים רישא ר' ישמעאל וסיפא ר' עקיבא ואילו הוה בעי לאוקמא רישא בשהניחה במקומה הראשון וסיפא בשהניחה במקום שאינה מקומה כדמוקי לה אמוראי ה"מ לאוקמיה כולה כר' ישמעאל ואר"י מאן דמתרגם כו' דלא הוה בעי לאוקמיה רישא בחד טעמא וסיפא בחד טעמא [סנהדרין סב:]. **אליבא** **דחד** **תנא** וכו'. דניחא ליה לאוקומי כתנאי מלמימר משבשתא היא ולאוקמי בתרי טעמי. ופלוגתא היא בהמפקיד גבי חבית דאמר ר' יוחנן מאן דמתרגם לי חבית אליבא דחד תנא מובילנא ליה מאני לבי מסותא ומוקי רישא ר' ישמעאל וסיפא רבי עקיבא ולא הוה בעי הוה מצי לאוקמי בתרי טעמי ובחד תנא ואיכא דמוקי לה התם בחד תנא ומוקי סיפא בשהניחה במקום שאינו מקומה [שבת פו.]. **מאניה.** בגדיו [יומא נב.]. **מסותא.** מרחץ כמו מסחותא וירחץ מתרגמינן ואסחי [סנהדרין סב:]. **תרגמה.** פרש אותה [סוטה ח:]. **שליחות** **יד** **אינה** **צריכה** **חסרון.** ומשלח בה יד אע"פ שלא חסרה הוא גזילה וקמה ברשותיה [לקמן מג:]. **שואל** **שלא** **מדעת** **גזלן** **הוי.** וקנייה להתחייב בה עד שתבא ליד בעלים דבעינן והשיב את הגזילה [רשב"ם ב"ב פח.]. **תסתיים.** תתפרש אמיתו של דבר [מגילה יד:]. איאמר בשם אומרה [ע"ז טז:]. **ובא** **זאב** **וטרף** **ובא** **ארי** **ודרס.** ארי דרכו לדרוס הבהמה במקום שמוצאה ודרך זאב לטורפה חיה ולהוליכה במקום שהוא בטוח ושם הורגה [לקמן צג:]. דרס שלא הרגה אלא מחיים אכלה דאורחיה הוא [ב"ק טז:]. **ותרמילו.** חמת של עור בטיי"ל בלע"ז ורועה נותן בה פתו ותולה בצוארו [יבמות פו:].

[the barrel] **was not** put back **in its** designated **place,** and thus the owner's knowledge of the barrel's return is more likely to be required. אֶלָּא אֲפִילוּ יִחֲדוּ נַמִּי – **Rather,** the Tanna teaches the more novel ruling that **even if [the owner] did designate a place,** דִּמְקוֹמָהּ הוּא – **in which case, [the barrel] is** back **in its** designated **place** of storage, בְּעִינַן דַּעַת בְּעָלִים – R' Akiva still holds that **the owner's knowledge** of the barrel's return **is** nevertheless **required.**[7]

The Gemara exclaims:

רֵישָׁא רַבִּי יִשְׁמָעֵאל – But then **the former clause** of the Mishnah follows the opinion of **R' Yishmael,** וְסֵיפָא רַבִּי עֲקִיבָא – **and the latter clause** follows the opinion of **R' Akiva.** How is it possible that a single anonymous Mishnah follows two opposing viewpoints?

The Gemara responds:

אִין – **Yes,** this is the explanation of the Mishnah, דְּאָמַר רַבִּי יוֹחָנָן – **for R' Yochanan said:** מַאן דִּמְתַרְגֵּם לִי חָבִית – **If someone explains to me** both rulings of the Mishnah about **a barrel** (i.e. our Mishnah), אַלִּיבָא דְּחַד תַּנָּא – **in accordance with** only **one Tanna,** מוֹבַלְנָא מָאנֵיהּ בַּתְרֵיהּ לְבֵי מַסּוּתָא – **I will carry his clothing after him to the bathhouse!**[8]

The Gemara now quotes two Amoraim who both resolve the Mishnah's internal contradiction in the same way. Both their approaches are based on the premise that when the Mishnah says that the *shomer* took the barrel "for his benefit," it means that he stole it. However, they argue as to what form of stealing was involved. The Gemara explores their differences regarding this point before it explains how they understood the Mishnah:[9]

תַּרְגְּמָהּ רַבִּי יַעֲקֹב בַּר אַבָּא קַמֵּיהּ דְּרַב – **R' Yaakov bar Abba explained [the Mishnah] before Rav,** as follows: When the Mishnah says that the *shomer* took the barrel "for his own benefit," שֶׁנְּטָלָהּ עַל מְנָת לְגוֹזְלָהּ – it means **that he took it in order to steal** all **of it.** תַּרְגְּמָהּ רַבִּי נָתָן בַּר אַבָּא קַמֵּיהּ דְּרַב – **R' Nassan bar Abba explained [the Mishnah] before Rav** as follows: When the Mishnah says that the *shomer* took the barrel "for his own benefit," שֶׁנְּטָלָהּ עַל מְנָת לִשְׁלוֹחַ בָּהּ יָד – it means **that he took it in order to misappropriate it,** i.e. to steal only some of it.[10]

The Gemara explains the basis of this dispute:

בְּמַאי קָמִיפַּלְגֵי – **Regarding what** point of law **do they** [R' Yaakov and R' Nassan] **disagree?** בִּשְׁלִיחוּת יָד צְרִיכָה חִסָּרוֹן – The difference between them is **whether** a *shomer's* liability for **misappropriating** a deposit **is dependent upon** his having caused **a loss** to it.[11] מַאן דְּאָמַר לְגוֹזְלָהּ – **The one** [R' Yaakov] **who said** that the Mishnah refers to a *shomer* who took the barrel in order **to steal** all of **it** קָסָבַר שְׁלִיחוּת יָד צְרִיכָה חִסָּרוֹן – **holds** that liability for **misappropriation is dependent upon a loss,** and therefore our Mishnah, which speaks of a case where the *shomer* did not actually take anything from the barrel, cannot refer to a case of misappropriation.[12] וּמַאן דְּאָמַר לִשְׁלוֹחַ בָּהּ יָד – **And the one** [R' Nassan] **who said** that the Mishnah refers to a *shomer* who took the barrel in order **to misappropriate it** קָסָבַר שְׁלִיחוּת יָד אֵינָהּ צְרִיכָה חִסָּרוֹן – **holds** that **misappropriation is not dependent upon a loss,** and thus our Mishnah may well refer to a case of misappropriation.[13]

Before R' Yaakov and R' Nassan were able to conclude their statements and explain how they understand the Mishnah, Rav Sheishess interrupted with an objection:

מַתְקִיף לָהּ רַב שֵׁשֶׁת – **Rav Sheishess challenged** the opinions of

NOTES

7. [Returning the keg to its designated place is a superior form of returning than simply putting it back in any safe place. Therefore, the Gemara concludes that, in fact, R' Akiva's stringency is more likely to apply in the event that no place was designated than in the event a place was designated.]

8. That is, I will acknowledge him as my master (see *Rashi* to *Leviticus* 25:39).

9. [In truth, the premise that our Mishnah refers to stealing has been assumed by the Gemara all along. The commentators ask why the Gemara chooses to delve into this issue at this particular point (see *Maharam Schif, Pnei Yehoshua* et al., cited by *Otzar Mefarshei HaTalmud).*]

10. *Shelichus yad* (misappropriation) is the theft by a *shomer* of *part* of an item that was entrusted to him. As is the case with regular theft, a *shomer* who misappropriates a deposit is liable even for unavoidable mishaps. However, a *shomer* who performs *shelichus yad* differs from a regular thief in the following way:

In the case of a regular thief who performs an act of acquisition on the property of another with intent to remove only part of it from the owner's possession, the thief assumes responsibility *for that part only.* [For example, if someone picked up a jug of oil that belongs to another with intent to remove some of the oil from the jug for his own use and return the rest, and then, through an unavoidable mishap, the jug broke and all the oil was ruined, he pays only for the amount of oil that he intended to keep.] The law of *shelichus yad,* however, teaches that a *shomer* who performs an act of acquisition upon a deposit with intent to remove only some of it for himself assumes responsibility for *the entire object.* He is therefore liable for mishaps that befall any part of it (*Rashi;* cf. *Ritva*).

The law of *shelichus yad* is derived from the verses in *Exodus* (22:9,10) that discuss the liability of a *shomer* for an animal that was entrusted to him: ...וּמֵת אוֹ־נִשְׁבַּר אוֹ־נִשְׁבָּה אֵין רֹאֶה. שְׁבֻעַת ה׳ תִּהְיֶה בֵּין שְׁנֵיהֶם אִם־לֹא שָׁלַח יָדוֹ בִּמְלֶאכֶת רֵעֵהוּ,... *and it dies, or* [its limb] *is fractured, or it is captured without anyone seeing. Hashem's oath shall be between them that he* [the custodian] *did not lay his hand upon* (i.e. misappropriate) *the goods of his fellow.* [If the *shomer* takes this oath, he is not liable to pay for the loss of the animal.] We learn from this verse that if the *shomer did* "lay his hand" upon the animal, he is liable to pay for its loss even if it dies, fractures a limb, or is captured, although these are unavoidable accidents (*Rashi*). [This verse is found in the passage about a paid *shomer.* The Torah makes reference to the law of *shelichus yad* in the passage about an unpaid *shomer* as well. The Gemara below, 41a-b, discusses why both references are necessary.]

11. The question they debate is as follows: If a *shomer* performed an act of acquisition upon a deposit with intent to remove part of it for himself, is he liable as a thief immediately, or not until he actually takes some of the deposit?

12. [Rather, it refers to a *shomer* who wished to steal the entire deposit.] The theft by a *shomer* of the entire deposit is treated as regular theft, as opposed to *shelichus yad.* Thus, regarding such a case, all agree that the *shomer* is liable even though he did not cause any actual loss to the deposit (from *Rashi;* cf. *Tosafos*).

[According to the opinion that *shelichus yad* is dependent upon a loss, if a *shomer* performed an act of acquisition upon a deposit with intent to remove some of it for himself but did not yet do so, there is no question that he is not responsible for the *entire* deposit. However, it is a matter of dispute whether [according to this view, as explained by *Rashi*] he is responsible for that part which he *did* intend to remove for himself. Some Acharonim argue that, in effect, he stole that portion, and therefore he is responsible for it (*Terumas HaKri;* see *Chazon Ish, Likkutim*). But others contend that from *Rashi's* commentary it seems that if none of the deposit was actually taken, the *shomer* is not responsible for any part of it. They explain that the part he intended to take for himself cannot be deemed to have entered his possession (as a stolen object), because it is mixed with the rest of the deposited item, which is still in the owner's possession (*Chidushei R' Meir Simchah*). According to the first of these two approaches, the proof that our Mishnah does not refer to *shelichus yad* is derived from the fact that the Mishnah rules, without qualification, that the *shomer* is liable, implying that he is responsible for the *entire* deposit. According to the latter approach, the proof is simply from the Mishnah's ruling that he is liable.]

13. According to this opinion, the Mishnah could refer either to stealing or to *shelichus yad.* However, R' Nassan says that the Mishnah is referring to *shelichus yad,* for that is the lesser of the two crimes (see *Ritva*).

**מסורת הש"ס**

א) סנהדרין דף סב., ב) [עירובין דף סו:], ג) [לקמן מג:] [שם], ד) [לקמן מג:, בבא קמא פה.], ה) [קדושין מג.], ו) [לקמן צג: ע"ש], קו. [ע"ש], ח) גירסת מהרש"ל דאמר.

**עין משפט נר מצוה**

עז א מיי' פ"ד מהלכות גניבה הל' י ועי' בהשגות וכמ"מ סמג עשין עא טור ש"ע ח"מ סי' שנח סעיף ו וסעיף ז וע"ש:
עח ב מיי' פ"ז מהל' שאלה ופקדון הלכה ט סמג עשין פח טוש"ע ח"מ סי' רצב סעיף ו:
עט ג מיי' פ"ג מהל' גזילה הל' יא סמג עשין עג טוש"ע ח"מ סי' רצב סעיף ח:
פ ד מיי' פ"ד מהל' שכירות הל' ח סמג עשין פט טוש"ע ח"מ סי' שג סעיף י:

**גמרא**

א צריך דעת בעלים אי רבי ישמעאל מאי איריא לא יחדו אפילו יחדו נמי לא מיבעיא קאמר לא מיבעיא יחדו דמקומה הוא אלא אפילו לא יחדו דלאו מקומה הוא לא בעינן דעת בעלים אימא סיפא יחדו לה הבעלים מקום וטלטלה ונשברה בין מתוך ידו בין משהניחה לצרכו חייב לצרכה פטור אתאן לר"ע דאמר בעינן דעת בעלים אי ר"ע מאי איריא יחדו אפילו לא יחדו נמי ב לא מיבעיא קאמר לא מיבעיא לא יחדו דלאו מקומה הוא אלא אפילו יחדו נמי דמקומה הוא בעינן דעת בעלים רישא רבי ישמעאל וסיפא ר"ע ° אין (א) דא"ר יוחנן מאן דמתרגם לי חבית אליבא דחד תנא ג) מובלנא מאניה בתריה לבי מסותא תרגמה רבי יעקב בר אבא קמיה דרב שנטלה על מנת לגוזלה תרגמה ר' נתן בר אבא קמיה דרב שנטלה ע"מ לשלוח בה יד במאי קמיפלגי ג) בשליחות יד צריכה חסרון מאן דאמר לגוזלה קסבר שליחות יד צריכה חסרון ומ"ד לשלוח בה יד קסבר שליחות יד אינה צריכה חסרון מתקיף לה רב ששת מידי נטלה קתני טלטלה קתני אלא אמר רב ששת הכא במאי עסקינן ד) כגון שטלטלה להביא עליה גוזלות וקא סבר ה) שואל שלא מדעת גזלן הוי וכולה רבי ישמעאל היא וסיפא שהניחה במקום שאינה מקומה ור' יוחנן הניחה במקומה משמע ו) איתמר רב ולוי חד אמר שליחות יד צריכה חסרון וחד אמר ג שליחות יד אינה צריכה חסרון תסתיים דרב הוא דאמר שליחות יד אינה צריכה חסרון דתניא ז) ד רועה שהיה רועה עדרו והניח עדרו ובא לעיר ובא זאב וטרף ובא ארי ודרס פטור הניח מקלו ותרמילו עליה חייב והוינן בה משום דהניח מקלו ותרמילו עליה חייב הא שקלינהו (א) אמר ר"נ אמר רבה בר אבוה אמר רב בעודן עליה וכי עודן עליה מאי הוי הא לא משכה ואמר רב שמואל בר רב יצחק אמר רב שהכישה במקל ורצתה לפניו והא לא חסרה אלא לאו ש"מ קסבר שליחות יד אינה צריכה חסרון אימא שהכחישה במקל דיקא נמי ח) דקתני שהכישה במקל ש"מ ומדרב סבר שליחות יד צריכה חסרון לוי סבר שליחות יד אינה צריכה חסרון מאי טעמא דלוי א"ר יוחנן משום ר' יוסי בן נהוראי משונה שליחות יד האמורה בשומר שכר משליחות יד האמורה בשומר חנם

ואני

**רש"י**

צריך דעת בעלים. ואם לא הודיעם חייב באחריותם אם מת או נגנב דמדשקליה קם ליה ברשותיה והשבה בלא ידיעה לאו השבה היא: דמקומה היא. וכיון דלאותו מקום החזירה חזרה גמורה היא: אתאן לר"ע. תירוצא הוא: תרגמה רבי יעקב. דתיקו כולה כחד תנא ובתרי טעמי רישא שהחזירה למקומה דכל מקום שהחזירה מקומה היא דהא לא יחדו לה מקום וסיפא שהחזירה למקום שאינה מקומה כדמסיים במסקנא דהא דמסקינן בסיומא וסיפא שהניחה במקום שאינה מקומה אתרצתא דכולהו קאי אדר' יעקב ואדר' נתן ואדרב ששת ומשום דהניחה חוץ למקומה לא הויא חזרה וכגון שנטלו מתחלה על מנת לגוזלה והיינו לצרכו דמתניתין דאילו לשאלה בעלמא ולתשמיש כיון דלאו גזילה הוא סגי לה בהשבה כל דהו וכל מקום שהניחה פטור באונסין אבל משום דגזולה הואי ובגזילה כתיב והשיב וזה שהניחה למקום שלא יחדו לה בעלים לא הויא השבה: ור' נתן תרגמה. דאפילו לא נטלה על מנת לגוזלה כו' אלא על מנת לשלוח בה יד וליטול מקצתה ולא נטל אפ"ה קמה ליה ברשותיה כולה והויא לה גזילה ובעי' השבה ובמקום שאינו מקומה לאו השבה היא ורב ששת לא שביק דליסיימו לתירוצייהו ואתקיף מידי נטלה קתני כו' ומיהו סיומא דמילתא דמסקנא וסיפא שהניחה במקום שאינו מקומה אכולהו קאי: שליחות יד. שחייבו הכתוב עליו אפילו נאנסה כדכתיב (שמות כב) ומת או נשבר או נשבה [וגו'] שבועת ה' תהיה בין שניהם אם לא שלח ידו וגו' דמשמע הא שלח נתחייב שוב במיתתה ובשבייתה: צריכה חסרון. לא הוי שליחות יד להעמידה ברשותו אלא א"כ חסרה: מידי נטלה קתני. דמשמע שנטלה לעצמו: טלטלה קתני. לתשמיש בעלמא משמע לצרכו דמתני': אלא כגון שטלטלה להביא עליה גוזלות. לעלות עליה כדרך סולם ליטול גוזלות מקן גבוה ואפ"ה הויא גזילה למיקם ברשותיה עד דעביד השבה דקסבר שואל שלא מדעת בעלים גזלן הוא: וכולה ר' ישמעאל היא. אשינויא דכולהו קאי אדר' יעקב ואדר' נתן ואדרב ששת: וסיפא שהניחה במקום שאינה מקומה. אבל רישא כל מקום שהניחה מקומה היא: ור' יוחנן. דאמר לעיל מאן דמתרגם לי כו': הניחה במקומה משמע. הלכך לא מיתוקמא ° כרבי ישמעאל: שליחות יד. שחייבו הכתוב עליו ואפי' נאנסה כדכתיב או נשבר או נשבה וגו' שבועת ה' תהיה אם לא שלח דמשמע הא אם שלח נתחייב שוב במיתתה ובשבייתה: צריכה חסרון. וכל זמן שלא חסרה לא קמה ברשותיה להתחייב באונסיה: זאב. טורף נושא הטרף לחורו: ארי. אינו טורפה אלא דורסה במקומה ואוכלה: פטור. דאונסין נינהו ולאו משום דהניח עדרו ופשיעה היא מוקמינן לה דעל בעידנא דעיילי אינשי כדאמרינן בהשוכר את הפועלים (לקמן צג:) א"נ דשמע קול אריה ועל: הא שקלינהו. ולאו נמי שליחות יד חשיבא הא הדר אהדרה כשנטלו הימנו ואנן מוקמינן לעיל סתם מתני' כרבי ישמעאל דאין צריך דעת בעלים: הא לא משכה. בשליחות יד כדי לקנותה ומטלטלין אין נקנין אלא במשיכה לא במקח ולא לענין גזל ולא לענין שליחות יד כדתנן במתני' (לקמן דף מג:) הטה את החבית ונטל ממנה רביעית יין אין משלם אלא רביעית אלמא בעינן דליקנייה כו': ואמר רב שמואל. גרסינן: שהכישה במקל. כשנתנו עליה ורצתה זו היא משיכה משעקרה יד ורגל על ידו: והא לא חסרה. לאו פירכא היא אלא מסקנא וסיומא הוא למילתיה דאמר תסתיים דרב הוא דאמר אין צריכה חסרון מדשני רב למתניתין משום דהכישה ורצתה לפניו ואי קשיא דלמא הא דהניח מקלו ותרמילו חיוביה לאו משום שליחות יד הוא דליבעי חסרון אלא משום שואל שלא מדעת הוא כי ההוא דלעיל דחבית לא היא דכי אמרינן בשומרין שאלה שלא מדעת בדבר שאינו כיחש וחיסר מחמת מלאכה אבל בעלי חיים המכחישים מחמת מלאכה תחלתו שליחות יד היא: שהכחישה. בהכאתו דהיינו חסרון: דיקא נמי. דהכחישה קאמר רב מדנקט הכשת מקל דמכה חזקה היא: ומדרב סבר צריכה חסרון. דהא דייקינן מדנקט מקל: לוי. בר פלוגתיה סבר אין צריכה חסרון: משונה שליחות יד כו'. כלומר אינה דומה לזו שזו נאמרה לצורך ולא משתמע אלא בחסרון אבל של שומר שכר נאמרה שלא לצורך משמעות שבה אלא לדרשה וללמד שאינה צריכה חסרון:

ואי

**תוספות**

אי רבי ישמעאל אפילו יחדו נמי. וא"ת מנ"ל י"ל מדנקט טלה וסלע דסתם טלה לא יחד לו מקום אלא הולך ממרעה למרעה וסתם סלע יחדו לו מקום בכיס וגם כיס יחדו לו מקום בתיבה ולכך פריך נמי בסמוך לר"ע אפילו לא יחדו נמי:

שנטלה והגביהה ע"מ לגוזלה כו'. והיינו חסרון שהכל גזל ונטל לצורך עצמו:

שנטלה ע"מ לשלוח בה יד. פי' ליטול מקצת אע"פ שלא נטל אותה מקצת חייב בכולה כדאמר בשלהי פרקין (דף מד.) לא נטל נטל ממש אלא כיון שהגביה ליטול אע"פ שלא נטל אבל למ"ד ע"מ לגוזלה דבעי חסרון אם הגביה ליטול קצת אינו חייב עד שיטול המקצת כיון דבעי חסרון וקשה דבשלהי פרקין קאמר אפי' למ"ד בעי חסרון מודה בחבית אם הגביהה אע"פ שלא נטל חייב דניחא ליה דתיהוי כולה בסים להאי רביעית ומתני' בחבית איירי ויש לומר דמתני' איירי אפילו בשמן דלא מנטר פורתא אגב האחר:

ובא זאב וטרף. בשעת משלחת זאבים ורבי יהודה היא דאמר זאב אחד אונס בפ' הפועלים (לקמן דף צג:):

הא שקלינהו. לרבי ישמעאל פריך דאמר לא בעינן דעת בעלים כפרש"י:

הא לא משכה. דאע"ג דעודן עליה לא קיימא ברשותיה להתחייב באונסיה עד שימשוך כדאמר במתני' (לקמן דף מג:) הטה את החבית ונטל ממנה רביעית אינו חייב אלא דמי רביעית כיון דלא הגביה את החבית ומשני שהניח מקלו ותרמילו עליה כל כך בחוזק עד שרצתה לפניו:

דיקא נמי דקתני שהכישה. וא"ת בפ"ק דקדושין (דף כב:) תניא או שהכישה במקל ורצתה לפניו דאקרי משיכה ולא הויא הכחשה וי"ל דהתם דאדם נכרי לקחה ואינה מכירתו בדבורו שייך למיתני הכישה אבל הכא דאיירי ברועה שהבהמה מכירתו ואזלה מחמת דבורו לא שייך למיתני שהכישה:

לומר

**רבינו חננאל**

ומקשי' אי הכי יחדו להאי חבית הבעלים מקום [נמי] דהא שמעינן ליה לר' ישמעאל דאומר הגונב סלע מן הכיס והנה יחדו הבעלים להאי סלע מקום בכיס ואמר ר' ישמעאל יחזיר למקום שגנב ואין צריך דעת בעלים ואי מתני' ר' ישמעאל היא אמאי קתני לא יחדו לה בעלים דשמעינן מינה דדוקא לא יחדו הא יחדו לא. ופרקי' לא מיבעיא קאמר לא מיבעיא היכא דיחדו לה הבעלים מקום והחזירה באותו מקום דודאי פטור הא החזירה במקומה וכיון שהחזירה במקומה כלא טלטלה דמי אלא אפי' לא יחדו לה הבעלים מקום דלאו במקומה מחזירה פטור. אוקימנא אליבא דר' ישמעאל בין יחדו לה הבעלים מקום בין לא יחדו לה הבעלים מקום כיון שהחזירה למקומה אם נשברה פטור הוא. אי הכי אימא סיפא יחדו לה בעלים מקום וטלטלה ונשברה בין מתוך ידו בין משהניחה לצרכו חייב אמאי חייב והא משהניחה לצרכו ויש מי שמפרש בשהניחה במקום שאינו מקומה. ור' יוחנן אמר הניחה במקומה משמע. ופרקי' סיפא אתאן לר' עקיבא דאמר צריך דעת בעלים הלכך לצרכו חייב. ומקשינן אי מתני' רבי עקיבא היא למה ליה יחדו לה בעלים מקום אפי' לא יחדו אמר ר' עקיבא צריך דעת בעלים דתניא הגונב טלה מן העדר וכו' והנה לא יחדו בעלים מקום לטלה והצריך ר' עקיבא בהחזרה דעת בעלים כו'. ועמדה רישא ר' ישמעאל וסיפא ר' עקיבא. אמר ר' יוחנן מאן דמתרגם ליה חבית אליבא דחד תנא וכו' פי' אמר ר' יוחנן מי שיפרש לי משנתנו זו המפקיד חבית אצל חבירו וכו' ויעמידה אי אליבא דר' ישמעאל אי אליבא דר' עקיבא סיפא ורישא בחד תנא אני מוליך לו כליו אחריו לבית המרחץ כי הוא כמו רב ואני תלמיד שנמצאתי משמשו כתלמיד לרב. ובא רב יעקב בר אבא לאוקמה למתני' בנוטלה על מנת לגוזלה. ורב נתן בר יעקב מוקמה בנוטלה על מנת לשלח בה יד וכולה ר' ישמעאל. ודחה רב ששת טעם שניהם ואמר מידי במתני' קתני נטלה דלישמעינן נטלה לגוזלה או לשלח בה יד טלטלה קתני ואין בלשון טלטול לא לשון גזילה ולא שילוח בה יד. אלא אמר רב ששת כגון שטלטלה

**הגהות הב"ח**

(א) גמ' הא שקלינהו ואמר ר"נ:

**גליון הש"ס**

גמ' אין דא"ר. ע' שבת דף פו ע"א קידושין דף סג ע"ב מנחות דף נו ע"א: רש"י ד"ה הניחה במקומה כו' כרבי ישמעאל. ע' שבת דף פו ע"א ברש"י ד"ה ומאן דמוקי:

**ליקוטי רש"י**

מאן דמתרגם לי חבית אליבא דחד תנא. דקתני התם המפקיד חבית אצל חברו ולא ייחדו לה הבעלים מקום וטלטלה ונשברה אם מתוך ידו נשברה לצרכו חייב לצרכה פטור אם משהניחה נשברה בין לצרכו בין לצרכה פטור ייחדו לה הבעלים מקום וטלטלה ונשברה בין מתוך ידו בין משהניחה לצרכו חייב לצרכה פטור ופריך התם מני אי ר' ישמעאל היא אפילו לא יחדו נמי ... וכו'. דניחא ליה לאוקמי כתנאי מלמימר משבשתא היא ולאוקמי בתרי טעמי. ופלוגתא היא בהמפקיד גבי חבית דאמר ר' יוחנן מאן דמתרגם לי חבית אליבא דחד תנא מובילנא ליה מאני לבי מסותא ומוקי רישא ר' ישמעאל וסיפא רבי עקיבא ואי הוה בעי הוה מצי לאוקמי בתרי טעמי ובחד תנא ואיכא דמוקי לה התם בחד תנא ומוקי סיפא בשהניחה במקום שאינו מקומה [שבת פו.]. מאניה. בגדיו [יומא נב.]. מסותא. מרחץ כמו מסחותא וירקן מתרגמינן ואסחי [סנהדרין סב.]. תרגמה. פרש אותה [סוטה ח:]. שליחות יד אינה צריכה חסרון. ומשלח בה יד אע"פ שלא חסרה הויא גזילה וקמה ברשותיה [לקמן מג:]. שואל שלא מדעת גזלן הוי. וקנייה להתחייב בה עד שתבא ליד בעלים דבעינן והשיב את הגזלה [רשב"ם ב"ב פח.]. תסתיים. תתפרש אמיתו של דבר [מגילה יד:]. מיאמר בשם אומרה [ע"ז טז:]. ובא זאב וטרף ובא ארי ודרס. ארי דרכו לדרוס הבהמה במקום שמוצאה ודרך זאב לטורפה חיה ולהוליכה במקום שהוא בטוח ושם טורפה [לקמן צג:]. דרס שלא הרגה אלא מתיים אכלה לאורחיה הוא [ב"ק טז:]. ותרמילו. חמת של עור בשטיי"א בלע"ז ורועה נותן בה פתו ותולה בצוארו [יבמות פו:].

**רבינו חננאל (המשך)**

לעמוד עליה ולפשוט ידו בתוך הקן ליטול גוזלות וסבר האי תנא שואל שלא מדעת בעלים גזלן הוי וכולה ר' ישמעאל היא וסיפא שהניחה במקום שאינה מקומה לפיכך תנן לצרכו חייב. ור' יוחנן אמר סיפא ר' עקיבא היא כי הניחה במקום שנטלה משמע. ואעפ"כ צריך דעת בעלים כר' עקיבא וכיון שלא ידעו בה הבעלים שהחזירה למקומה לפיכך לצרכו חייב. איתמר רב אמר שליחות יד צריכה חסרון. מדתניא רועה שהיה רועה עדרו ובא זאב וטרף ארי ודרס פטור פי' פטור הוא כי שוכר הוא והשוכר פטור מן האונסין. ואם הניח מקלו או תרמילו עליה פי' כיון שנשתמש בה כאילו גזלה וחייב באונסיה. ואקשי' עלה. ואוקמה רב בעודו עליה מקלו ותרמילו. ואמרי' והא לא משכה ופריק רב כגון שהכישה במקלו ורצתה לפניו. דייקי' מדלא קתני הנהיגה בקול אלא הכישה במקל ש"מ שהכישה במקל והכחשה דהיינו חיסרה ולפיכך חייב ש"מ דרב הוא דאמר שליחות יד צריכה חסרון ואם אין שם חסרון פטור באונסיה ולוי אמר שליחות יד אינה צריכה חסרון מאי טעמא. אמר ר' יוחנן משום ר' יוסי בר נהוראי משונה שליחות יד האמורה בשומר חנם משליחות יד האמורה בשומר שכר כלומר שומר חנם שדינו קל ושומר שכר דינו חמור שחייב בגניבה ואבידה ואם שומר חנם שדינו קל חייב בו בשליחות יד שומר שכר לא כל שכן שחייב אם שלח בו יד למה כתב

צָרִיךְ דַּעַת בְּעָלִים — **HE REQUIRES THE OWNER'S KNOWLEDGE;** i.e. the thief remains liable until he notifies the owner that the stolen object has been returned.[1]

The Gemara asks:

אִי רַבִּי יִשְׁמָעֵאל — **If** our Mishnah follows the view of **R' Yishmael,** מַאי אִירְיָא לֹא יִחֲדוּ — **why** does it **teach** in its first ruling that the *shomer* is exempt once he returns the stolen barrel to a safe place only where **[the owner] did not designate** a place for the storage of the barrel? אֲפִילוּ יִחֲדוּ נַמִּי — According to R' Yishmael, **even if [the owner] did designate** such a place, the *shomer* should not be liable once he returns the barrel there.[2] **— ? —**

The Gemara answers:

לֹא מִיבַּעְיָא קָאָמַר — **[The Tanna],** by choosing in its first ruling to speak of a case where the owner did not designate a place for the barrel, **is using** the style of "it is **not necessary** to say ..." (that is, he teaches only the most novel ruling, and other rulings can be derived from it without it being necessary to mention them). The Gemara explains: לֹא מִיבַּעְיָא יִחֲדוּ — **It is not necessary** to teach that the *shomer* is exempt according to R' Yishmael once he replaces the stolen barrel in a case where **[the owner] designated** a place for the barrel's storage, דִּמְקוֹמָהּ הוּא — **because,** in such a case, **[the barrel] is** now in **its** original **place** of storage, and thus the owner's knowledge of the barrel's return is less likely to be required.[3] אֶלָּא אֲפִילוּ לֹא יִחֲדוּ — **Rather,** the Tanna teaches the more novel ruling, that **even** if **[the owner] did not designate** a place, דְּלָאו מְקוֹמָהּ הוּא — **in which case,** [the barrel] **is not** back in **its** designated **place** of storage, לֹא בְּעֵינַן דַּעַת בְּעָלִים — R' Yishmael still holds that **the owner's knowledge** of the barrel's return **is** nevertheless **not required.**[4]

The Gemara asks that this conclusion does not fit with the Mishnah's second ruling:

אֵימָא סֵיפָא — But **look at the latter clause** of the Mishnah, which stated: יִחֲדוּ לָהּ הַבְּעָלִים מָקוֹם — If **THE OWNER DESIGNATED A PLACE** in the *shomer's* domain **FOR** the storage of **[THE BARREL]** וְטִלְטְלָהּ וְנִשְׁבְּרָה — **AND [THE** ***SHOMER*****] MOVED IT AND IT BROKE,** בֵּין מִתּוֹךְ יָדוֹ בֵּין מִשֶּׁהֱנִיחָהּ — then it makes no difference **WHETHER** it broke while falling **FROM HIS HAND OR AFTER HE PUT IT DOWN** in a safe place. לְצָרְכּוֹ חַיָּיב — Either way, if his purpose in moving it was **FOR HIS** own **BENEFIT, HE IS LIABLE** to pay for it, לְצָרְכָּהּ פָּטוּר — and if he moved it **FOR ITS BENEFIT, HE IS NOT LIABLE.** Here, the Mishnah teaches that if the custodian moved the keg from a designated place "for his benefit" (i.e. he stole it), he is liable for all mishaps even after he put it back in safekeeping. This contradicts the Gemara's conclusion above that the return of stolen property to the owner's designated place without notifying the owner releases the thief from liability. **— ? —**

The Gemara answers:

אֲתָאן לְרַבִּי עֲקִיבָא — In the Mishnah's second ruling, **we have come to** the opinion of **R' Akiva,** דְּאָמַר בְּעֵינַן דַּעַת בְּעָלִים — **who said** that the **owner's knowledge** of the return of stolen property **is required** to release the thief from liability.[5]

The Gemara asks:

אִי רַבִּי עֲקִיבָא — **If** the Mishnah's second ruling follows the opinion of **R' Akiva,** מַאי אִירְיָא יִחֲדוּ — **why** does it **teach** that the *shomer* is liable once he returns the barrel only in a case where **[the owner] designated** a place for the barrel's storage? אֲפִילוּ לֹא יִחֲדוּ נַמִּי — According to R' Akiva, **even** if **[the owner] did not designate** a place, the *shomer* should **also** be liable, because he did not notify the owner of the barrel's return.[6] **— ? —**

The Gemara answers:

לֹא מִיבַּעְיָא קָאָמַר — **[The Tanna],** by choosing in its second ruling to speak of a case where the owner designated a place for the barrel, **is using** the style of "it is **not necessary** to say ..." (that is, he teaches only the most novel ruling, and other rulings can be derived from it without it being necessary to mention them). לֹא מִיבַּעְיָא לֹא יִחֲדוּ — **It is not necessary** to teach that the *shomer* is liable according to R' Akiva even after he returns the barrel in a case where **[the owner] did not designate** a place for the barrel's storage, דְּלָאו מְקוֹמָהּ הוּא — **because** in such a case,

NOTES

1. R' Akiva holds that stolen property that is returned without telling the owner is not considered returned in the legal sense. Therefore, it remains in the thief's "possession" (see 40b note 23), and he continues to be responsible for it (*Rashi*).

[The Gemara in *Bava Kamma* (118b) concludes that the dispute between R' Yishmael and R' Akiva applies to the same type of case as that of our Mishnah; namely, a *shomer* who stole the object that was entrusted to him (see ibid., and *Pnei Yehoshua* here).]

2. [The Gemara here is asking about the Mishnah's *first* ruling. The fact that the Mishnah's *second* ruling clearly states that the *shomer* is liable even after he returns the barrel to a place that was designated by the owner will be discussed by the Gemara below.] The language of the Gemara ("*even* if the owner did designate etc.") implies that there is less reason to exempt the *shomer* if a place had been designated for the barrel's storage than in a case where no such place had been designated. The reason for this distinction is that if a place had been designated, when the *shomer* stole the barrel, he removed it from where it was supposed to be. [In fact, according to *Rashi,* who explained that the designated place is an area borrowed from the *shomer* by the owner (see 40b note 24), when the *shomer* stole the object he removed it from the owner's "domain."] His act of stealing is therefore more severe than if the owner had not designated an area. For this reason, one might have thought that if a place had been designated, even R' Yishmael would agree that the owner must be notified (*Maharsha*).

[Indeed, *Tosafos* ask why the Gemara assumes that R' Yishmael's leniency would apply even where a place had been designated for the article! *Tosafos* answer that this is derived from the Baraisa's mention of both a sheep and a coin. Normally, a sheep is not confined to a particular place; it is moved from one grazing ground to another. A coin, however, is kept in a purse, which is usually stored in a particular chest. Thus, it is evident from the Baraisa that R' Yishmael's leniency applies even in a case such as that of a coin, where the stolen article was taken from its designated place.]

3. For the barrel was returned to the place reserved for the owner, which is a "perfect" return (*Rashi*).

4. Although the return was not "perfect," the *shomer* still has fulfilled his responsibility, and is no longer deemed a thief. [Taking a deposit from its designated place is a more severe form of stealing (see note 2). But, by the same token, putting it back in that place is a superior form of returning. The Gemara's question focused on the *shomer's* act of stealing, and thus assumed that R' Yishmael's leniency is *less* likely to apply where a place had been designated. The Gemara's answer, however, is that the primary issue here is not the stealing of the article, but its return. That is why, in conclusion, the Gemara takes the opposite view; namely, that R' Yishmael's leniency is *more* likely to apply where a place had been designated.]

5. R' Akiva disputes the view of R' Yishmael in the Baraisa cited above (40b-41a). [The Gemara will ask below how it is possible that a single anonymous Mishnah follows two opposing viewpoints.]

6. Therefore, he should still be deemed a thief. [The language of the Gemara ("*even* if the owner did not designate etc.") implies that R' Akiva's stringency is less likely to apply in the event a place was not designated than in the event that a place was designated. The reason for this distinction is that the *shomer's* stealing of the barrel is considered less severe in the event that no place was designated; see above, note 2 (from *Maharsha* ibid.).]

The Gemara derives that R' Akiva's stringency does in fact apply even where a place was not designated for the item by the owner, from the mention in the Baraisa (above, 40b-41a) of a sheep. A sheep is not confined to a particular place, yet R' Akiva ruled that the owner's knowledge of the sheep's return is required (see *Tosafos;* see note 2).

**Gemara** The Mishnah first rules that if the *shomer* moved the barrel "for his benefit" (i.e. he stole it) and it broke after he put it back in a safe place, he is not liable to pay for it. Evidently, our Tanna holds that by putting the barrel back in safekeeping, the *shomer* has effectively returned it, even though he did not notify the owner. On this basis, the Gemara identifies the Tanna of our Mishnah:

הָא מַנִּי – **Whose** view **is this?** רַבִּי יִשְׁמָעֵאל הִיא – **It is** the view of **R' Yishmael,** דְּאָמַר לֹא בְּעִינַן דַּעַת בְּעָלִים – **who said** that **the owner's knowledge** of the return of a stolen object **is not required** to release the thief from liability.

The Gemara cites a Baraisa in which R' Yishmael's vie
appears:

דְּתַנְיָא – **For it was taught in a Baraisa:** גּוֹנֵב טָלֶה מִן הָעֵדֶר – If ONE STEALS A SHEEP FROM A FLOCK, וְסֶלַע מִן הַכִּיס – OR COIN FROM A PURSE, לְמָקוֹם שֶׁגָּנַב יַחֲזִיר – HE SHOULD RETURN I TO THE PLACE FROM WHICH HE STOLE it, and, having done so, he i released from liability, even though he did not notify the owne דִּבְרֵי רַבִּי יִשְׁמָעֵאל – these are THE WORDS OF R' YISHMAEL. בִּי עֲקִיבָא אוֹמֵר – R' AKIVA, however, SAYS:

דל תלתין ושיתא בשיתא פשו ליה תריסר דל תמניא שתותי פשו להו ארבעה [א] והאמר שמואל [א]המשתכר אל ישתכר יותר על שתות איכא גולפי [ב] ושמריא אי הכי נפיש ליה טפי משתות איכא טרחיה ודמי ברזנייתא: אם היה שמן מזוקק אינו יוציא לו שמרים [וכו']: והא אי אפשר דלא בלע אמר רב נחמן במזופפין שנו אביי אמר אפילו תימא שלא במזופפין כיון דטעון טעון: ר"י אומר אף המוכר שמן מזוקק לחבירו כל ימות השנה הרי זה מקבל עליו לוג ומחצה שמרים למאה: אמר אביי כשתמצא לומר לדברי ר"י מותר לערב שמרים לדברי חכמים [ב]אסור לערב שמרים לדברי רבי יהודה מותר לערב שמרים והיינו טעמא דמקבל דאמר ליה אי בעי לערובי לך מי לא ערבי לך השתא נמי קביל ולימא ליה אי ערבת ליה הוה מזדבן לי השתא מאי אעביד ליה לחודיה לא מזדבן לי בבעל הבית עסקינן דניחא ליה בצילא ולימא ליה מדלא ערבית לי אחולי אחלת לי רבי יהודה לטעמיה דלית ליה מחילה דתנן [ג] [ג]מכר לו את הצמד לא מכר לו את הבקר מכר לו את הבקר לא מכר לו את הצמד ר"י אומר הדמים מודיעין כיצד אמר לו מכור לי צמדך במאתים זוז הדבר ידוע שאין הצמד במאתים זוז וחכ"א אין הדמים ראיה לדברי חכמים אסור לערב שמרים והיינו טעמא דלא מקבל דא"ל אי בעית לערובי מי הוה שרי לך השתא נמי לא מקבילנא א"ל רב פפא לאביי אדרבה איפכא מסתברא לדברי חכמים מותר לערב שמרים והיינו טעמא דלא מקבל דא"ל מדלא ערבת לי אחולי אחלית לי לדברי רבי יהודה אסור לערב שמרים והיינו טעמא דמקבל דאמר ליה אי בעי לערובי לא שרי לי לערובי לך קבולי לא מקבלת [ד] זבון וזבין תגרא איקרי תנא אחד הלוקח ואחד המפקיד לפקטים מאי לפקטים אילימא כי היכי דלוקח לא מקבל פקטים מפקיד נמי לא מקבל פקטים ולימא ליה פקטך מאי איעביד להו אלא כי היכי דמפקיד מקבל פקטים [ד]לוקח נמי מקבל פקטים ומי מקבל לוקח פקטים והתניא ר"י אומר לא אמרו שמן עכור אלא למוכר בלבד שהרי לוקח מקבל עליו לוג ומחצה שמרים בלא פקטים לא קשיא [ה]הא דיהיב ליה זוזי בתשרי וקא שקיל מיניה בניסן כי מדה דתשרי הא דיהיב ליה זוזי בניסן וקא שקיל מיניה בניסן כי מדה דניסן:

**מתני'** [ו]המפקיד חבית אצל חבירו ולא יחדו לה בעלים מקום וטלטלה ונשתברה אם מתוך ידו נשברה לצורכו חייב לצורכה פטור אם משהניחה נשברה בין לצורכו בין לצורכה פטור יחדו לה הבעלים מקום וטלטלה ונשברה בין מתוך ידו ובין משהניחה לצורכו חייב לצורכה פטור: **גמ'** הא מני רבי ישמעאל היא דאמר [ה] לא בעינן דעת בעלים [ז]דתניא הגונב טלה מן העדר וסלע מן הכיס למקום שגנב יחזיר דברי רבי ישמעאל רבי עקיבא אומר

צריך

**רש"י**

דל תלתין ושיתא. כוזי בשיתא זוזי שקנאה פשו תריסר: דל תמניא שתותי. של מ"ח שדרך הוא לחסר בבליעת הקנקן כדתנן יוציא לו שתות ליין פשו לו לשכרו ארבע: והאמר שמואל המשתכר. בדברים שיש בהם חיי נפש: אל ישתכר יותר על השתות. הא שתות ישתכר ולמה לא ישתכר רב יהודה עד שתות: איכא גולפי ושמריא. משתכר הוא הקנקן והשמרים שלקח הכל בו' זוז: דמי ברזנייתא. שנותן דמים לחנווני למוכר' ומוליאן ומכריז עליו בחוצות. כרזנייתא לשון כרוז לשון אחר (א) אומנות יש בנקיבת ברזא בחבית של חרס וצריך ליתן שכר: במזופפין. דכיון דישנים הם ונתבלעו בלעותם תו לא בלעי: כיון דטעון טעון. תו לא בלע: כשתמצא לומר. כשתדקדק ותדע מילוי הדברים: מותר לערב שמרים. המוכר שמן לחבירו סתם בעת שהוא מזוקק ששקעו ושקטו שמריו מותר לו לערב ולבלבל שמרים המשוקעות שיחזרו ויתערבו ויצאו עם השמן בתוך המדה: אסור לערב שמרים. שבחזקת מזוקק לוקחו ממנו וזה מקלקלו: והיינו טעמא דמקבל עליו. לוקח לוג ומחצה שמרים בשלא ערבו ונתנו לו מזוקק: דא"ל. מוכר אי בעי לערובי כו': הוה מזדבן. כשהייתי מוכרו בחנות היה נמכר שמרים עם השמן: בבעה"ב עסקינן. שהלוקח בעה"ב הוא ולקחו למאכל ביתו: צמד. העול שהוא מוטל על שני השוורים ומלמידם: הדבר ידוע. שאין צמד נמכר במאתים זוז אלא כמות שהוא עם הבקר מכרו לו: וחכמים אומרים אין הדמים ראיה. אע"ג דלא שוה כולי האי אחולי אחליה לוקח זה יתר הדמים ור"י לית ליה שיהא מוחל מן הסתם אלא אם כן פירש: קבולי נמי לא מקבלת. עלך חסרון השמרים א"כ מה משתכר הרי השכר כולו בשמרים: זבון וזבין תגרא איקרי. בתמיה משל הוא לאמר לשוטה לקח בדמים וחזור ומכור בלא שכר ותיקרי תגר: אחד הלוקח ואחד המפקיד לפקטים. לוקח ומפקיד אחד הן לענין פקטים תורה אחת לשניהם: פקטים. פסולת הגרעינים הצפין על פני השמן: לוקח מקבל פקטים. אם מכר לו שמן סתם יקבל ממנו שמן עם פקטים: לא אמרו שמן עכור אלא למוכר. לא אמרו הפסד עכירת השמן אלא למוכר: שהרי הלוקח מקבל עליו. לפחות ממאה לוגין לוג ומחצה מחמת שמרים לפיכך צריך ליתן לו שמן מזוקק בלא פקטים: כי מדה דתשרי. כשער הדמים של תשרי שהוא בזול וסתם שמנים עכורים וקיבל עליו פקטים: הא דשקל מיניה בניסן כשער של ניסן. ביוקר דלכך כל השמנים להיות מזוקקין בניסן והלוקח סתם והמוכר סתם אין מוכר אלא מזוקק: מתני' לא יחדו לו הבעלים מקום. בבית שומר לאמר לו זוית זו השאילני: לצורכו. להשתמש בה: לצורכה. שהיתה במקום התורפה וקרובה להשתבר: אם משהניחה. שכלה תשמישו הושיבה במקום משתמר בין שטלטלה מתחלה לצורכה בין שטלטלה לצורכו פטור ובגמרא פריך מאי שנא לא יחדו מיחדו: גמ' (ב) מני. הא דקתני רישא דאם משהניחה נשברה אף על פי שלצורכו נטלה מתחלה פטור דאמר משהחזירה הרי היא ברשות הבעלים כבתחלה ואינו עליה אלא כשומר חנם ופטור על אונסיה ואף על פי שלא הודיע לבעלים לומר נטלתיה והחזרתיה הויא השבה רבי ישמעאל היא כו':

**תוספות**

**אל** ישתכר יותר על שתות. הא עד שתות משתכר ומסתמא רב יהודה היה מולא שיתנו לו יותר ולמה הניח מלהרויח עד שתות: **במזופפין** שנו. וא"ת כל שכן דבלע טפי כדאמרינן לעיל באתרא דמר חפו בכופרא דמייץ טפי וי"ל דהיינו חדש אבל ישן שכבר בלע אינו בולע יותר אי נמי התם ביין אבל הכא בשמן לא בלע כיון שהוא ישן:

**לחודיה** לא מזדבן. וא"ת ויתן לו מוכר ללוקח לוג ומחלה שמרים שיערב עדיין וימכור וי"ל דמיירי מתני' אפי' אין השמן בעין שלקחו מעט מעט ומכרו או אכלו:

**לדברי** חכמים אסור לערב. וא"ת ונימא משום דאית ליה מחילה ולעולם מותר לערב וי"ל דמתניתין נמי מיירי אפי' כשהשמן עדיין בעין והתם אין שייך מחילה כיון שיכול לתקן כי יאמר לו קח השמרים וערב בשמן ולרב פפא דאמר דטעמייהו משום מחילה סבר דהשמן אינו בעין דאילו הוה בעין לא שייך ביה מחילה אי נמי סבר דאף ע"פ שהוא בעין שייך ביה מחילה כיון דמדדו מזוקק:

**לדברי** ר"י אסור. וא"ת ולימא מותר וטעמא דמקבל משום דלית ליה מחילה וי"ל דרב פפא סבר דלמד ובקר איכא הוכחה דלאו מחילה דמסתמא לא רלה ליתן מאתים זוז על הצמד בלא בקר אבל הכא לוג ומחלה שהוא דבר מועט מדלא עירב אחולי אחיל:

**זבון** וזבין תגרא איקרי. מיירי שלא היה מולא למכור ביוקר יותר משלקחו לכך א"ל אדעתא דהכי קנית ממני שהיית יודע שאעכב לוג ומחלה כדי שארויח קלת:

**לא** אמרו שמן עכור אלא למוכר. פי' לא אמרו הפסד של עכירת פקטים אלא למוכר דכשנותן ללוקח שמן מזוקק אינו מחסר לו כלום ממאה לוג בשביל הפקטים כי אם לוג ומחלה בשביל השמרים מיהו עכירה לא שייכא כל כך בפקטים אלא בדבר המתערב כמו שמרים וי"ל דלא אמרינן הפסד של עכירת השמרים אלא למוכר שאם מוכר כשהוא מזוקק מקבל עליו לוקח בשביל השמרים לוג ומחלה והמוכר מרויח השמרים וכשהוא מוכר שמן עכור נותן מאה לוגין שלמים שמן עכור ומפסיד השמרים ע"י מה שמכר כשהוא עכור וכשמוכר מזוקק לא קרי הפסד לוקח אע"פ שמפסיד שמרים משום דבעה"ב ניחא ליה בצילא:

אי

**עין משפט נר מצוה**

עב א מיי' פי"ד מהל' מכירה הל' א סמג לאוין קע טוש"ע ח"מ סי' רלא סעיף כ:

עג ב מיי' שם פי"ח הלכה ח סמג עשין שם טוש"ע ח"מ סי' רכח סעיף יט:

עד ג מיי' שם פכ"ז הל' ג ועיין בהשגות ובמ"מ סמג עשין פב טוש"ע ח"מ סי' רכ סעיף ד:

עה ד ה מיי' שם פי"ח הל' ט י סמג לאוין קע טוש"ע ח"מ סי' רכח סעיף כ:

עו ו מיי' פ"ז מהלכות שאלה ופקדון הל' ט סמג עשין פח טוש"ע ח"מ סי' רלב סעיף ו:

**רבינו חננאל**

טפיחין יצאו ח' שהן שתות לכל החבית בחסרונות כדתנן יוציא לו שתות ליין נשארו ד' טפיחין ריוח. ומקשי' היכי עביד רב יהודה הכי והאמר שמואל לא ישתכר אדם יותר משתות ולא פחות משתות והשתות הוא זוז ועוד וזה לא נשתייר לו אלא ד' טפיחין. ופרקי' נשתייר החבית והשמרין שבתוכו ואיכא גולפי ושדריא למלאת השתות. ומקשי' אי הכי הני כולהו טפי משתות נינהו. ופרקי' נשאר לו לקונה ליטול זולת הריוח אגר טירחיה שמודד לו לקונה לכל אחד ואחד לזה עכשיו ולחבירו למחר ומתבטל ממלאכתו והדמים למי שנוקב לו הנקבים בחבית להוציא היין בהן מן החבית וזה פי' דמי ברזניתיה. פי' ברזא נקב החבית כדגרסי' א) דעד ברזא. נוטל אלו כולן בריוח שלו וגם בשכרו. יוציא לו ג' לוג שמן לק' לוג כו' אם היו קנקנים ישנים אין מוציא לו בלע. ואוקמה רב פפא במזופפין. אמר אביי כיון דטעון טעון כלומר מאחר שהיה בהן שמן ומצצי ושבעי שוב. אין מוציאין לעולם: פיסקא ר' יהודה אומר אף המוכר שמן מזוקק לחבירו כל השנה הרי זה מקבל עליו לוג ומחצה שמרין לק'. אמר אביי אם תמצא לומר לדברי ר' יהודה מותר לערב שמרין. לדברי חכמים אסור לערב שמרין כו' אמר ליה רב פפא אדרבה איפכא מסתברא לדברי חכמים מותר לערב שמרין והיינו טעמא דלא מקבל דאמר ליה מדלא ערבית אחולי אחלת לי. לדברי ר' יהודה אסור לערב והיינו טעמא דמקבל דאמר לערובי לך אסור קבולי לא תקבל זבון חבין תגרא איקרי וכי לא בעינא לאישתכורי הלכך מקבל וקיימא לן כתנא קמא: מתני' המפקיד אצל חבירו חבית ולא יחדו לה הבעלים מקום וטלטלה ונשברה וכו' עד אם משהניחה בין לצרכה בין לצרכו פטור. פי' לצרכה כדי שלא תשבר וכיוצא בה. אוקימנא לר' ישמעאל דאמר כשמחזירה אין צריך דעת בעלים דתניא הגונב טלה מן העדר וסלע מן הכיס למקום שגנב יחזיר דברי ר' ישמעאל ר' עקיבא אומר צריך דעת בעלים

ומקשי'

**מסורת הש"ס**

א) בבא בתרא צ., מנחות עז., ב) נ"א ושדריא ג) בבא בתרא עז:, ד) [בבא בתרא צ., מנחות עז.] ה) [לקמן מג:], ו) בבא קמא קיח.:

**הגהות הב"ח**

(א) רש"י ד"ה דמי כרזנייתא וכו' לשון אחר ברזנייתא אומנות. נ"ב עיין פרק השואל סוף דף לט (ב) ד"ה אם וכו' מיהו הס"ד ואח"כ מ"ה הא מני דקתני:

**ליקוטי רש"י**

אל ישתכר יותר על שתות. כגון חנווני הקונה יין ופירות מן הסיטון הרבה ביחד כדי למכור מעט מעט אל ישתכר יותר משתות [רשב"ם ב"ב צ.]. איכא גולפי. דרך למוכר חביות של יין ליתן גם החביות ללוקחין והכא אמרינן בהמפקיד איכא גולפי ושדריה שהלוקח מוכרו בחנות משתכר בהם לבד מה שהוא משתכר ביין [ע"ז סה:]. גולפי קנקן של חרס [מגילה כו.]. ודמי ברזנייתא שנותנין למכריז בעיר על היין בשווקים וברחובות יש בבית פלוני יין למכור ברזנייתא לשון ברזא דיישי"ר בלע"ז כלומר יוצא היין הנמכר בברזא בפרוטות וי"מ שהיו צריכין לשכור אומן לנקב נקב בחביות מפני שהוא של חרס ולתקן ברזא הנך דמי מנהו להו [לקמן צט:]. כשתמצא לומר כשתעמוד לסוף דבר [כתובות כ:]. כשתדקדק בדבריהם תמצא [עירובין פט.]. כשתדקדק בדבריהם ותעמוד על מכונו תמצא [פסחים יא:]. הצמד. הוא העול וכן העגלה קטנה והעגל עצמה המחברין את השוורים יחד. לא מכר לו את הצמד. דכל הכל היא אלא דפליגי רבי יהודה ורבנן בפירוש דה מילתא דלרבי יהודה זימנין מכר זימנין לא מכר ולרבנן לעולם לא מכר אין הדמים ראיה אלא במתנה ביקש ליתן המותר אי נמי ליהוי מקח טעות כדאמרינן בגמרא ויחזיר לו מעותיו ויטול למדו [רשב"ם ב"ב עז:]. זבון וזבין תגרא איקרי. בתמיה משל הוא וכי לכך קנה התבואה רחוק ממקום שיתננה כל בלותן דמים כדי שיקנו תגר ולהרויח אינו חוש [רשב"ם ב"ב צ.].

**חשק שלמה על ר"ח**

א) נראה דצ"ל מדגרסי' בע"ז (דף ס ע"ב) דעד ברזא וכו' ועי' בערוך ער' נטל אלו וכו'.

The Gemara therefore explains the Baraisa in the opposite way: אֶלָּא – **Rather,** this is what the Baraisa means: כִּי הֵיכִי דְּמַפְקִיד מְקַבֵּל פְּקָטִים – **Just as a depositor must accept** the **scum** as part of his oil when it is returned to him, לוֹקֵחַ נַמִּי מְקַבֵּל פְּקָטִים – **so too, a purchaser must accept** the **scum** as part of his purchase.[18]

The Gemara raises a difficulty with this explanation:

וּמִי מְקַבֵּל לוֹקֵחַ פְּקָטִים – **But** is it so that **a purchaser** must **accept** the **scum?** וְהַתַּנְיָא – **Why, it has been taught in a Baraisa:** רַבִּי יְהוּדָה אוֹמֵר – R' YEHUDAH SAYS: לֹא אָמְרוּ שֶׁמֶן עָכוּר אֶלָּא לְמוֹכֵר בִּלְבַד – THEY DID NOT SAY that the loss for CLOUDY OIL (i.e. the loss caused by the presence of scum) is borne EXCEPT BY THE SELLER ALONE, שֶׁהֲרֵי לוֹקֵחַ מְקַבֵּל עָלָיו – for SINCE THE BUYER ACCEPTS UPON HIMSELF לוֹג וּמֶחֱצָה שְׁמָרִים – a reduction of ONE-AND-A-HALF *LOGS* for each hundred *logs* of oil he buys to compensate for the SEDIMENT, he can expect that the remaining oil will be pure, בְּלֹא פְּקָטִים – WITHOUT any SCUM in it. This contradicts the Baraisa cited above, which ruled that the purchaser must accept the scum.[19] – ? –

The Gemara resolves the contradiction:

לֹא קַשְׁיָא – There is **no difficulty.** הָא דְיָהִיב לֵיהּ זוּזֵי בְּתִשְׁרֵי – **This** Baraisa (the first one) speaks of a case **where [the purchaser] paid** for the oil **in** the month of **Tishrei,** soon after the olive harvest, when oil is cloudy and inexpensive, וְקָא שָׁקִיל מִינֵּיהּ בְּנִיסָן כִּי מִדָּה דְּתִשְׁרֵי – **and he took** his oil **from [the seller] in Nissan** when oil is refined, **according to the price of Tishrei.**[20] Since in Tishrei, oil usually contains scum, R' Yehudah rules that the buyer must accept the scum as part of his purchase. הָא דְיָהִיב לֵיהּ זוּזֵי בְּנִיסָן – **The other** Baraisa (the second one) refers to a case **where [the buyer] paid in Nissan,** when oil is pure and more expensive, וְקָא שָׁקִיל מִינֵּיהּ בְּנִיסָן כִּי מִדָּה דְּנִיסָן – **and he took** his oil **from [the seller] in Nissan,**[21] **according to the prices of Nissan.** Since, in Nissan, oil is generally pure, and neither the buyer nor the seller specified anything, we assume that the purchase is of pure oil, without any scum in it.[22]

## Mishnah

The following Mishnah discusses the laws that apply to a *shomer* who stole the article that was entrusted to him. Normally, a *shomer* is not liable for unavoidable mishaps. If, however, he stole the deposit, he then assumes the status of a thief, who is liable for any mishap that might occur to the stolen property before he returns it to its owner:[23]

הַמַּפְקִיד חָבִית אֵצֶל חֲבֵירוֹ – If **someone deposited a barrel with his fellow** for safekeeping וְלֹא יִחֲדוּ לָהּ בְּעָלִים מָקוֹם – **and the owner did not designate a place** in the *shomer's* domain **for** the storage of **[the barrel],**[24] וְטִלְטְלָהּ וְנִשְׁתַּבְּרָה – **and [the *shomer*] moved [the barrel] and it broke** through an unavoidable accident, the law is as follows: אִם מִתּוֹךְ יָדוֹ נִשְׁבְּרָה – **In the event that [the barrel] broke** by falling **from [the custodian's] hand,** before he returned it to safekeeping, then לְצוֹרְכּוֹ חַיָּיב – if his purpose in moving the barrel was **for his own benefit,** that is to take it for himself, **he is liable** to pay for the barrel, because he was stealing the barrel when it broke; לְצוֹרְכָּהּ פָּטוּר – but if he moved it **for its benefit,**[25] **he is not liable.**

אִם מִשֶּׁהֱנִיחָהּ נִשְׁבְּרָה – **But if [the barrel] broke after [the *shomer*] put it down** in a safe place, בֵּין לְצוֹרְכּוֹ בֵּין לְצוֹרְכָּהּ – then regardless of **whether** he moved the barrel **for his benefit or for its benefit,** פָּטוּר – **he is not liable.**[26]

The Mishnah now discusses the laws that apply if the owner *did* designate a place for the barrel's storage:

יִחֲדוּ לָהּ הַבְּעָלִים מָקוֹם – **If the owner designated a place** in the *shomer's* property **for** the storage of **[the barrel]** וְטִלְטְלָהּ וְנִשְׁבְּרָה – **and [the *shomer*] moved it and it broke,** בֵּין מִתּוֹךְ יָדוֹ וּבֵין מִשֶּׁהֱנִיחָהּ – then it makes no difference **whether** it broke while falling **from his hand or after he put it down** in a safe place. לְצוֹרְכּוֹ חַיָּיב – Either way, if his purpose in moving the barrel was **for his own benefit, he is liable** to pay for it, לְצוֹרְכָּהּ פָּטוּר – and if he moved it **for its benefit, he is not liable.**[27]

NOTES

18. Unless pure oil was specified at the time of the sale (*Rashi*).

19. The Gemara assumes that the previous Baraisa, too, follows the view of R' Yehudah (see *Ritva*).

20. [It makes no difference whether the buyer took the oil in Nissan or Tishrei. The Gemara specifies Nissan in order to teach a more novel ruling; namely, that even though he took the oil in Nissan, he must accept the scum, since he paid for the oil in Tishrei.]

21. The same would apply were the buyer to receive the oil in Tishrei. The Gemara specifies Nissan merely because oil without any scum in it is not common in Tishrei (*Ritva*).

22. Since the Gemara has explained the second Baraisa as referring to a purchase made in Nissan, it is evident that, according to R' Yehudah, the ruling that a buyer of oil must accept a reduction for sediment applies even if he bought the oil in Nissan, when oil is usually pure. [The reason for R' Yehudah's view was disputed above by Abaye and Rav Pappa.] Scum, however, is regarded as an independent entity; therefore, once the scum has accumulated on the oil's surface (in Nissan), the buyer does not have to accept it as part of his purchase (see *Maharam Schif* with *Beur*).

23. Regarding a thief, the Torah states (*Leviticus* 5:23): וְהֵשִׁיב אֶת־הַגְּזֵלָה, *and he shall return the stolen property.* From here we learn that the Torah places stolen property in the "possession" of a thief until he returns it to its owner. This means that any loss to the stolen object is paid for by the thief. If the object is destroyed or damaged, even because of factors beyond his control, the thief must pay the owner for the object.

24. I.e. the owner did not borrow an area in the *shomer's* domain for the storage of the barrel (*Rashi*). The Gemara will explain what difference this makes.

25. [For example,] he was moving it from an unsafe place, where it was likely to break (*Rashi*).

26. For once he put it back in a safe place, he has fulfilled his obligation of returning the barrel to the owner, even if he took it improperly (see note 23). From that point in time, he reverts to his status as a *shomer* who is not liable for unavoidable mishaps.

The *shomer* is not required to put the barrel back in the owner's domain. Since the owner had deposited the barrel with him for safekeeping, all the *shomer* has to do is put it in a safe place in his own domain and he is once again treated as a *shomer* (see *Bava Kamma* 118b).

27. The rules set forth in the Mishnah may be summarized and explained as follows:

(1) If the *shomer* moved the barrel for its benefit and then it broke – whether before or after he put it down – he is not liable to pay compensation. [He did not steal the barrel. He remains a *shomer,* who is not liable for unavoidable mishaps.]

(2) If the *shomer* moved the barrel for his benefit and it broke *before* he put it back in safekeeping, he is liable to pay for it. [The *shomer* stole the barrel, and therefore is liable for any mishap that occurs before he returns it (see note 23).]

(3) If the *shomer* moved the barrel for his benefit and it broke *after* he put it back in safekeeping, it seems from the Mishnah that if the owner had designated a place for the barrel's storage, the *shomer* is liable; otherwise, he is not liable. [The *shomer* certainly stole the barrel; hence, the question of his liablity is dependent on whether his act of putting the barrel back in safekeeping is considered a fulfillment of his obligation to return it. The Gemara will explain why this is so.]

דל תלתין ושיתא בשיתא פשו ליה תריסר דל תמניא שתותי פשו להו ארבעה (א) והאמר שמואל המשתכר אל ישתכר יותר על שתות איכא גולפי ושמריא אי הכי נפיש ליה טפי משתות איכא טרחיה ודמי ברזנייתא: אם היה שמן מזוקק אינו יוצא לו שמרים [וכו']: והא אי אפשר דלא בלע אמר רב נחמן במזופפין שנו אביי אמר אפילו תימא שלא במזופפין כיון דטעין טעון: ר"י אומר אף המוכר שמן מזוקק לחבירו כל ימות השנה הרי זה מקבל עליו לוג ומחצה שמרים למאה: אמר אביי כשתמצא לומר לדברי ר"י מותר לערב שמרים לדברי חכמים אסור לערב שמרים לדברי רבי יהודה מותר לערב שמרים והיינו טעמא דמקבל דאמר ליה אי בעי לערובי לך מי לא ערבי לך השתא נמי קביל ולימא ליה אי ערבת ליה הוה מזדבן לי השתא מאי אעביד ליה לחודיה לא מזדבן לי בבעל הבית עסקינן דניחא ליה בצילא ולימא ליה מדלא ערבית לי אחולי אחלת לי רבי יהודה לטעמיה דלית ליה מחילה דתנן מכר לו את הצמד לא מכר לו את הבקר מכר לו את הבקר לא מכר לו את הצמד ר"י אומר הדמים מודיעין כיצד אמר לו מכור לי צמדך במאתים זוז הדבר ידוע שאין הצמד במאתים זוז וחכ"א אין הדמים ראיה לדברי חכמים אסור לערב שמרים והיינו טעמא דלא מקבל דא"ל אי בעית לערובי מי הוה שרי לך השתא נמי לא מקבילנא א"ל רב פפא לאביי אדרבה איפכא מסתברא לדברי חכמים מותר לערב שמרים והיינו טעמא דלא מקבל דא"ל מדלא ערבת לי אחולי אחלית לי לדברי רבי יהודה אסור לערב שמרים והיינו טעמא דמקבל דאמר ליה בעי לערובי לא שרי לי לערובי לך קבולי לא מקבלת זבון וזבין תגרא איקרי תנא אחד הלוקח ואחד המפקיד לפקטים מאי לפקטים אילימא כי היכי דלוקח לא מקבל פקטים מפקיד נמי לא מקבל פקטים ולימא ליה פקטך מאי איעביד להו אלא כי היכי דמפקיד מקבל פקטים לוקח נמי מקבל פקטים ומי מקבל לוקח פקטים והתניא ר"י אומר לא אמרו שמן עכור אלא למוכר בלבד שהרי לוקח מקבל עליו לוג ומחצה שמרים בלא פקטים לא קשיא הא דיהיב ליה זוזי בתשרי וקא שקיל מיניה בניסן כי מדה דתשרי הא דיהיב ליה זוזי בניסן וקא שקיל מיניה בניסן כי מדה דניסן: **מתני'** המפקיד חבית אצל חבירו ולא יחדו לה בעלים מקום וטלטלה ונשתברה אם מתוך ידו נשברה לצורכו חייב לצורכה פטור אם משהניחה נשברה בין לצורכו בין לצורכה פטור יחדו לה הבעלים מקום וטלטלה ונשברה בין מתוך ידו ובין משהניחה לצורכו חייב לצורכה פטור: **גמ'** הא מני רבי ישמעאל היא דאמר לא בעינן דעת בעלים דתניא הגונב טלה מן העדר וסלע מן הכיס למקום שגנב יחזיר דברי רבי ישמעאל רבי עקיבא אומר

## רש"י

דל תלתין ושיתא. כוזי בשיתא זוזי שקנאה פשו תריסר: דל תמניא שתותי. של מ"ח שדרך הוא לחסר בבליעת הקנקן כדתנן יוצא לו שתות ליין פשו לו לשכרו ארבע: והאמר שמואל המשתכר. בדברים שיש בהם חיי נפש: אל ישתכר יותר על השתות. הא שתות ישתכר ולמה לא ישתכר רב יהודה עד שתות: איכא גולפי ושמריא. משתכר הוא הקנקן והשמרים שלקח הכל בו' זוז: דמי ברזנייתא. שנותן דמים לחנוני למוכר' ומוליאן ומכריז עליו בחוצות. כרזנייתא לשון כרוז לשון אחר (א) אומנות יש בנקיבת ברזא בחבית של חרס וצריך ליתן שכר: במזופפין. דכיון דישנים הם ונתבלעו בלעוסם תו לא בלעי: כיון דטעון טעון. תו לא בלע: כשתמצא לומר. כשתדקדק ותדע מילוי הדברים: מותר לערב שמרים. המוכר שמן לחבירו סתם בעת שהוא מזוקק ששקעו ושקטו שמריו מותר לו לערב ולבלבל שמרים המשוקעות שיחזרו ויתערבו ויצאו עם השמן בתוך המדה: אסור לערב שמרים. שבחזקת מזוקק לוקחו ממנו וזה מקלקלו: והיינו טעמא דמקבל עליו. לוקח לוג ומחצה שמרים בשלא ערבו ונתנו לו מזוקק: דא"ל. מוכר אי בעי לערובי כו': הוה מזדבן. כשהייתי מוכרו בחנות היה נמכר שמרים עם השמן: בבעה"ב עסקינן. שהלוקח בעה"ב הוא ולקחו למאכל ביתו: צמד. העול שהוא מוטל על שני השוורים ומלמדם: הדבר ידוע. שאין צמד נמכר במאתים זוז אלא כמות שהוא עם הבקר מכרו לו: וחכמים אומרים אין הדמים ראיה. אע"ג דלא שוה כולי האי אחולי אחליה לוקח זה יתר הדמים ור"י לית ליה שיהא מוחל מן הסתם אלא אם כן פירש: קבולי נמי לא מקבלת. עלך חסרון השמרים א"כ מה משתכר הרי השכר כולו בשמרים: זבון וזבין תגרא איקרי. בתמיה משל הוא לאמר לשוטה לקח בדמים וחזור ומכור בלא שכר ותיקרי תגר: אחד הלוקח ואחד המפקיד לפקטים. לוקח ומפקיד אחד הן לענין פקטים תורה אחת לשניהם: פקטים. פסולת הגרעינים הצפין על פני השמן: לוקח מקבל פקטים. אם מכר לו שמן סתם יקבל ממנו שמן עם פקטים: לא אמרו שמן עכור אלא למוכר. לא אמרו הפסד עכירת השמן אלא למוכר: שהרי הלוקח מקבל עליו. לפחות ממאה לוגין לוג ומחצה מחמת שמרים לפיכך צריך ליתן לו שמן מזוקק בלא פקטים: כי מדה דתשרי. כשער הדמים של תשרי שהוא בזול וסתם שמנים עכורים וקיבל עליו פקטים: הא דשקל מיניה בניסן כשער של ניסן. ביוקר דדרך כל השמנים להיות מזוקקין בניסן והלוקח סתם והמוכר סתם אין מוכר אלא מזוקק: מתני' לא יחדו לו הבעלים מקום. בבית שומר לאמר לו זוית זו השאילני: לצורכו. להשתמש בה: לצורכה. שהיתה במקום התורפה וקרובה להשתבר: אם משהניחה. שכלה תשמישו הושיבה במקום משתמר בין שטלטלה מתחלה לצורכה בין שטלטלה לצורכו פטור ובגמרא פריך מאי שנא לא יחדו מיחדו: גמ' (ב) מני. הא דקתני רישא דאם משהניחה נשברה אף על פי שלצורכו נטלה מתחלה פטור דאמר משהחזירה הרי היא ברשות הבעלים כבתחלה ואינו עליה אלא כשומר חנם ופטור על אונסיה ואף על פי שלא הודיע לבעלים לומר נטלתיה והחזרתיה הויא השבה רבי ישמעאל היא כו':

צריך

## תוספות

**אל** ישתכר יותר על שתות. הא עד שתות משתכר ומשמע דרב יהודה היה רוצה שיתנו לו יותר ולמה הניח מלהרויח עד שתות:

**במזופפין** שנו. וא"ת כל שכן דבלע טפי כדאמרינן לעיל באתרא דמר חפו בכופרא דמייץ טפי וי"ל דהיינו חדש אבל ישן שכבר בלע אינו בולע יותר אי נמי התם ביין אבל הכא בשמן לא בלע כיון שהוא ישן:

**לחודיה** לא מזדבן. וא"ת ויתן לו מוכר ללוקח לוג ומחצה שמרים שיערב עדיין וימכור וי"ל דמיירי מתני' אפי' אין השמן בעין שלקחו מעט מעט ומכרו או אכלו:

**לדברי** חכמים אסור לערב. וא"ת ונימא משום דאית ליה מחילה ולעולם מותר לערב וי"ל דמתניתין נמי איירי אפי' כשהשמן עדיין בעין והתם אין שייך מחילה כיון שיכול לתקן כי יאמר לו קח השמרים וערב בשמן ולרב פפא דאמר דטעמייהו משום מחילה סבר דהשמן אינו בעין דאילו הוה בעין לא שייך ביה מחילה אי נמי סבר דאף ע"פ שהוא בעין שייך ביה מחילה כיון דמדדו מזוקק:

**לדברי** ר"י אסור. וא"ת ולימא מותר וטעמא דמקבל משום דלית ליה מחילה וי"ל דרב פפא סבר דצמד ובקר איכא הוכחה דלאו מחילה דמסתמא לא רצה ליתן מאתים זוז על הצמד בלא בקר אבל הכא לוג ומחצה שהוא דבר מועט מדלא עירב אחולי אחיל:

**זבון** וזבין תגרא איקרי. מיירי שלא היה רוצה למכור ביוקר יותר משלקחו לכך א"ל אדעתא דהכי קנית ממני שהיית יודע שאעכב לוג ומחצה כדי שתרויח קצת:

**לא** אמרו שמן עכור אלא למוכר. פי' לא אמרו הפסד של עכירת פקטים אלא למוכר דכשנותן ללוקח שמן מזוקק אינו מחסר לו כלום ממאה לוג בשביל הפקטים כי אם לוג ומחצה בשביל השמרים מיהו עכירה לא שייכא כל כך בפקטים אלא בדבר המתערב כמו שמרים וי"ל דלא אמרינן הפסד של עכירת השמרים אלא למוכר שאם מוכר כשהוא מזוקק מקבל עליו לוקח בשביל השמרים לוג ומחצה והמוכר מרויח השמרים וכשהוא מוכר שמן עכור נותן מאה לוגין שלמים שמן עכור ומפסיד השמרים ע"י מה שמכר כשהוא עכור וכשמוכר מזוקק לא קרי הפסד לוקח אע"פ שמפסיד שמרים משום דבעה"ב ניחא ליה בצילא:

אי

## עין משפט נר מצוה

עב א מיי' פי"ד מהל' מכירה הל' א סמג לאוין קע טוש"ע ח"מ סי' רלא סעיף כ:

עג ב מיי' שם פי"ח הלכה ח סמג עשין שם טוש"ע ח"מ סי' רכח סעיף יט:

עד ג מיי' שם פכ"ז הל' ב ועיין בהשגות ובמ"מ סמג עשין פב טוש"ע ח"מ סי' רכ סעיף ד:

עה ד ה מיי' שם פי"ח הל' ט י סמג לאוין קע טוש"ע ח"מ סי' רכח סעיף כ:

עו ו מיי' פ"ז מהלכות שאלה ופקדון הל' ט סמג עשין פח טוש"ע ח"מ סי' רלב סעיף ו:

## רבינו חננאל

טפיחין יצאו ח' שהן שתות לכל החבית בחסרונות כדתנן יוציא לו שתות ליין נשארו ד' טפיחין ריוח. ומקשי' היכי עביד רב יהודה הכי והאמר שמואל לא ישתכר אדם יותר משתות ולא פחות משתות והשתות הוא זוז ועוד וזה לא נשתייר לו אלא ד' טפיחין. ופרקי' נשתייר החבית והשמרין שבתוכו ואיכא גולפי ושדריא למלאת השתות. ומקשי' אי הכי הני כולהו טפי משתות נינהו. ופרקי' נשאר לו לקונה ליטול זולת הריוח אגר טירחיה שמודד לו לקונה לכל אחד ואחד לזה עכשיו ולחבירו למחר ומתבטל ממלאכתו והדמים למי שנוקב לו הנקבים בחבית להוציא היין בהן מן החבית וזה פי' דמי ברזניתיה. פי' ברזא נקב החבית כדגרסי' א) דעד ברזא. נוטל אלו כולן בריוח שלו וגם בשכרו. יוציא לו ג' לוג שמן לק' לוג כו' אם היו קנקנים ישנים אין מוציא לו בלע. ואוקמה רב פפא במזופפין. אמר אביי כיון דטעון טעון כלומר מאחר שהיה בהן שמן ומצצי ושבעי שוב. אין מוציאין לעולם: פיסקא ר' יהודה אומר אף המוכר שמן מזוקק לחבירו כל השנה הרי זה מקבל עליו לוג ומחצה שמרין לק'. אמר אביי אם תמצא לומר לדברי ר' יהודה מותר לערב שמרין. לדברי חכמים אסור לערב שמרין כו' אמר ליה רב פפא אדרבה איפכא מסתברא לדברי חכמים מותר לערב שמרין והיינו טעמא דלא מקבל דאמר ליה מדלא ערבית אחולי אחלת לי. לדברי ר' יהודה אסור לערב והיינו טעמא דמקבל דאמר לערובי לך אסור קבולי לא תקבל זבון וזבין תגרא איקרי וכי לא בעינא לאישתכורי הלכך מקבל וקיימא לן כתנא קמא: מתני' המפקיד אצל חבירו חבית ולא יחדו לה הבעלים מקום וטלטלה ונשברה וכו' עד אם משהניחה בין לצרכה בין לצרכו פטור. פי' לצרכה כדי שלא תשבר וכיוצא בה. אוקימנא לר' ישמעאל דאמר כשמחזירה אין צריך דעת בעלים דתניא הגונב טלה מן העדר וסלע מן הכיס למקום שגנב יחזיר דברי ר' ישמעאל ר' עקיבא אומר צריך דעת בעלים

ומקשי'

## מסורת הש"ס

א) בבא בתרא צ., מנו[ת] טז., ב) נ"א ושדרי[א], ג) בבא בתרא עז:, ד) [ב]בא בתרא צ., מנחות ע[...], ה) [לקמן מג:], ו) ב[בא] קמא קיח:.

## הגהות הב"ח

(א) רש"י ד"ה ד[מי] כרזנייתא וכו' לשון א[חר] ברזנייתא אומנות. נ"ב ע[יין] פרק השואל סוף דף [...] (ב) ד"ה אם וכו' מי[...] הס"ד ואח"כ מ"ה הא [...] דקתני:

## ליקוטי רש"י

אל ישתכר יותר [על] שתות. כגון ה[...] הקונה יין ופירות [...] הסיטון הרבה ביחד [...] למכור מעט מעט [...] ישתכר יותר משת[ות] [רשב"ם ב"ב צ.]. איכ[א] גולפי. דרך למו[כר] חביות של יין ליתן [...] החביות ללוקחין ו[...] אמרינן בהמפקיד אי[כא] גולפי ושדריה שהלו[קח] מוכרו בחנות משתכר [...] לבד מה שהוא משתכ[ר] ביין [ע"ז סה:]. גולפ[י] קנקן של חרס [מגילה כו] ודמי ברזניית[א] שנותנין למכריז בעיר היין בשווקים וברחוב[ות] יש בבית פלוני יין למכ[ור] ברזנייתא לשון ברזא דיי[...] בלע"ז כלומר יציאת ה[...] הנמכר בברזא בפרוטו[ת] וי"מ שהיו צריכין לשכ[ור] אומן לנקב נקב בחב[ית] מפני שהוא של ח[רס] ולתקן ברזא הנך דמי מ[...] להו [לקמן צט]. כשתמצא לומ[ר] כשתעמוד לסוף דב[ר] [כתובות כ:]. כשתדק[דק] בדבריהם תמצא [עירובין פט.]. כשתדק[דק] בדבריהם ותעמוד מכונו תמצא [פסחים יא]. הצמד. הוא העול ו[...] העגלה קטנה והעג[לה] עלמה המחברין [...] השוורים יחד. לא מכ[ר] לו את הצמד. ד[...] הכל היא אלא דפליגי ר[בי] יהודה ורבנן בפירוש ד[...] מילתא דלרבי יהו[דה] זימנין מכר זימנין לא מ[כר] ולרבנן לעולם לא מכ[ר]. אין הדמים ראי[ה] אלא במתנה ביקש ליתן המותר אי נמי ליהוי מ[...] טעות כדאמרינן בגמ[...] ויחזיר לו מעותיו ויט[...] למדו [רשב"ם ב"ב עז]. זבון וזבין תגר[א] איקרי. בתמיה משל ה[וא] וכי לכך קנה התבו[אה] רחוק מכאן שיתננה כ[...] באותן דמים כדי שיקר[א] תגר ולהרויח אינו חו[...] [רשב"ם ב"ב צ.].

## חשק שלמה על ר"ח

א) נראה דל"ל כדגרסי' בע[...] (דף ס ע"א) דעד ברזא ו[...] נוטל אלו וכו' ועי' בערוך ע[רך] ברז.

Therefore, you must give me the full amount of oil I purchased, although you gave me pure oil." — ? —

The Gemara answers:

בְּבַעַל הַבַּיִת עַסְקִינַן — Here, **we are dealing with** a buyer who is **a homeowner,** דְּנִיחָא לֵיהּ בְּצִילָא — **who prefers** a reduced amount of **pure** oil to a full volume of impure oil, because he is buying it for his own use, not for resale.

The Gemara raises another difficulty with Abaye's explanation of R' Yehudah's opinion:

וְלֵימָא לֵיהּ — **But let [the buyer] say to [the merchant]:** מִדְּלָא עָרְבִית לִי — **"Since you did not mix** the sediment into the oil, אַחוּלֵי אַחֲלִית לִי — **you waived** your right to do so." — ? —

The Gemara answers:

רַבִּי יְהוּדָה לְטַעְמֵיהּ — In this matter, **R' Yehudah follows his own reasoning** in a different context, דְּלֵית לֵיהּ מְחִילָה — **for** we find elsewhere that **[R' Yehudah] does not** assume that a person **waived** his rights unless that person does so explicitly.

The Gemara cites the source for R' Yehudah's view with respect to this issue:

דִּתְנַן — **As we learned in a Mishnah:**[12] מָכַר לוֹ אֶת הַצֶּמֶד — IF SOMEONE SOLD A YOKE (a bar that is used to attach a team of oxen in a row so that they can work together to plow a field) TO [ANOTHER PERSON], לֹא מָכַר לוֹ אֶת הַבָּקָר — HE HAS NOT SOLD HIM THE team of OXEN that use it. מָכַר לוֹ אֶת הַבָּקָר — Likewise, IF HE SOLD HIM THE team of OXEN, לֹא מָכַר לוֹ אֶת הַצֶּמֶד — HE HAS NOT SOLD HIM THE YOKE. רַבִּי יְהוּדָה אוֹמֵר — R' YEHUDAH, however, SAYS: הַדָּמִים מוֹדִיעִין — THE purchase PRICE TELLS us what was included in the sale. כֵּיצַד — HOW SO? אָמַר לוֹ — If [THE BUYER] SAID TO [THE OWNER], מְכוֹר לִי צִמְדְּךָ בְּמָאתַיִם זוּז — "SELL ME YOUR YOKE FOR TWO HUNDRED *ZUZ*," he could not have meant to buy only the yoke, הַדָּבָר יָדוּעַ — because EVERYBODY KNOWS שֶׁאֵין הַצֶּמֶד בְּמָאתַיִם זוּז — THAT A YOKE alone IS NOT sold FOR TWO HUNDRED *ZUZ*. Therefore, the oxen are included in the sale. We do not assume that the buyer intended the extra money to be a gift to the seller.[13] וַחֲכָמִים אוֹמְרִים — BUT THE SAGES SAY: אֵין הַדָּמִים רְאָיָה — THE purchase PRICE IS NOT a PROOF of what is included in the sale, for although a yoke is not worth two hundred *zuz*, we assume that the purchaser waived his right to the additional money, and wanted it to be a gift to the seller.

From this Mishnah, it is evident that R' Yehudah does not assume a person to have waived his rights to money unless he states this explicitly. According to R' Yehudah, in our case as well, the oil merchant's failure to mix in the sediment does not mean that he has waived his right to do so; therefore, he may deduct the value of the sediment if he delivers pure oil.

Abaye now explains the view of the Sages:

לְדִבְרֵי חֲכָמִים — According to **the Sages,** אָסוּר לְעָרֵב שְׁמָרִים — **it is forbidden to mix sediment** back into the oil, וְהַיְינוּ טַעְמָא דְּלָא מְקַבֵּל — **and this is the reason** that the Sages rule **that [a purchaser] does not** have to **accept** a reduction in the amount of oil he receives. דְּאָמַר לֵיהּ — **Since [the buyer] can say to [the seller]:** אִי בָּעֵית לְעָרוּבֵי — **"If you wanted to mix** the sett[...] sediment back into the oil, מִי הֲוָה שָׁרֵי לָךְ — **would you ha[ve] been allowed** to? No! הַשְׁתָּא נַמִּי — So **now,** even though y[ou] gave me refined oil, לָא מְקַבֵּילְנָא — **I am not** required to **acce[pt]** any reduction."

The Gemara challenges Abaye's explanation of the dispu[te] between R' Yehudah and the Sages:

אֲמַר לֵיהּ רַב פָּפָּא לְאַבָּיֵי — **Rav Pappa said to Abaye:** אַדְּרַבָּה — **On the contrary,** אִיפְּכָא מִסְתַּבְּרָא — **the reverse** of what y[ou] say **is** more **logical,** as follows: לְדִבְרֵי חֲכָמִים — **In the opini[on] of the Sages,** מוּתָּר לְעָרֵב שְׁמָרִים — **it is** *permitted* **to mix** t[he] **sediment** into the oil. וְהַיְינוּ טַעְמָא דְּלָא מְקַבֵּל — **And the reas[on] that [a buyer] does not** have to **accept** a reduction in the amou[nt] of pure oil he receives **is** דְּאָמַר לֵיהּ — **because [the buyer] m[ay] say to [the seller]:** מִדְּלָא עָרַבְתְּ לִי — **"Since you did not m[ix]** in the sediment, אַחוּלֵי אַחֲלִית לִי — **you waived** your right [to] do so."

לְדִבְרֵי רַבִּי יְהוּדָה — But **according to R' Yehudah,** [אָס]וּר לְעָרֵב שְׁמָרִים — **it is forbidden to mix** in the **sediment.** [וְהַ]יְינוּ טַעְמָא דִּמְקַבֵּל — **And the reason** for his ruling, that **[a buyer] must a[c]cept** a reduction in the amount of pure oil he receives **is** [דְּאָ]מַר לֵיהּ — **that [the seller] may say to him:** אִי בָּעֵי לְעָרוּבֵי — **"I[f I] had wanted to mix in** the sediment, לָא שָׁרֵי לִי לְעָרוּבֵי לָךְ — **would not have been allowed to do so** — [אַח]וּלֵי לָא מְקַבְּלַתְּ — and now you tell me that **you will not accept** a reduction [in] the amount of pure oil I dispense to you?! But if I am allow[ed] neither to mix in sediment nor to give you less pure oil, I will n[ot] make any profit![14] Am I a fool, about whom the following sayi[ng] is stated: זְבוֹן וְזַבֵּין תַּגְרָא אִיקְרִי — **'Buy and sell** without prof[it] **and be called a merchant?!'** "[15]

Having discussed whether a purchaser must accept the sed[i]ment that sinks to the bottom of the oil, the Gemara now discuss[es] whether he must accept the scum[16] that floats on the oil's surfac[e]:

תָּנָא — **A Tanna taught the** following **Baraisa:** [אֶ]חָד הַלּוֹקֵחַ וְאֶחָד הַמַּפְקִיד — The same law applies to BOTH A BUYER AND DEPOSITOR לְפִקְטִים — WITH REGARD TO the SCUM.

The Gemara discusses the meaning of this ruling:

מַאי לְפִקְטִים — **What** is meant by, "The same law applies t[o] both a purchaser and a depositor **with regard to the scum"** אִילֵימָא — **Perhaps you will say** that it means: [כִּ]י הֵיכִי דְּלוֹקֵחַ לָא מְקַבֵּל פִּקְטִים — **Just as a buyer** who bought a fixed amou[nt] of oil **does not** have to **accept** the **scum** as part of his purchas[e], מַפְקִיד נַמִּי לָא מְקַבֵּל פִּקְטִים — so **too a depositor,** who had entruste[d] oil to a *shomer,* **does not** have to **accept** the **scum** when the oil i[s] returned to him.[17] But such an explanation of the Baraisa seem[s] incorrect, וְלֵימָא לֵיהּ — because **[the *shomer*] could say to [th]e depositor]:** פִּקְטָךְ מַאי אֵיעֱבִיד לְהוּ — **"What should *I* do wit[h] your scum?** Since this scum is clearly from the oil you gave m[e] to safeguard, you must take it back along with the oil I return t[o] you!" — ? —

NOTES

12. *Bava Basra* 77b.

13. The Mishnah speaks of a place where most of the people generally refer to a yoke and oxen separately, but a minority of people use the term צֶמֶד, *yoke*, to refer to both the yoke and the oxen together (*Bava Basra* 77b). [According to R' Yehudah, since the purchaser did not expressly state that the extra money was a gift, it is assumed that he is from the minority group.]

14. The value of the sediment represented the merchant's entire profit (*Rashi*). In this case, the seller had not been able to find anyone who would buy the oil at a higher price than he had paid for it (and the buyer was aware of this). Therefore, the seller may say to the buye[r] "You bought the oil with the knowledge that I would retain 1.5 pe[r]cent of the amount you bought (the equivalent of the sediment), so would make at least some profit" (*Tosafos;* cf. *Ritva,* cited by *Shita[h] Mekubetzes*).

15. One who makes no profit at all is a merchant in name only (*Rash[i]* see also *Rashbam* to *Bava Basra* 90a ד״ה זבן).

16. [Formed by] the residue of olive seeds (*Rashi*).

17. That is, he can demand that the full amount of oil he had deposite[d] be returned to him as pure oil.

דל תלתין ושיתא בשיתא פשו ליה תריסר דל תמניא שתותי פשו להו ארבעה (א) והאמר שמואל (א) המשתכר אל ישתכר יותר על שתות איכא גולפי (ג) ושמריא אי הכי נפיש ליה טפי משתות איכא טרחיה ודמי ברזנייתא: אם היה שמן מזוקק אינו יוציא לו שמרים [וכו']: והא אי אפשר דלא בלע אמר רב נחמן במזופפין שנו אביי אמר אפילו תימא שלא במזופפין כיון דטעון טעון: ר"י אומר אף המוכר שמן מזוקק לחבירו כל ימות השנה הרי זה מקבל עליו לוג ומחצה שמרים למאה: אמר אביי כשתמצא לומר לדברי ר"י מותר לערב שמרים לדברי חכמים (ב) אסור לערב שמרים לדברי רבי יהודה מותר לערב שמרים והיינו טעמא דמקבל דאמר ליה אי בעי לערובי לך מי לא ערבי לך השתא נמי קביל ולימא ליה אי ערבת ליה הוה מזדבן לי השתא מאי אעביד ליה לחודיה לא מזדבן לי בבעל הבית עסקינן דניחא ליה בצילא ולימא ליה מדלא ערבית לי אחולי אחלת לי רבי יהודה לטעמיה דלית ליה מחילה דתנן (ז) (ג) מכר לו את הצמד לא מכר לו את הבקר מכר לו את הבקר לא מכר לו את הצמד ר"י אומר הדמים מודיעין כיצד אמר לו מכור לי צמדך במאתים זוז הדבר ידוע שאין הצמד במאתים זוז וחכ"א אין הדמים ראיה לדברי חכמים אסור לערב שמרים והיינו טעמא דלא מקבל דא"ל אי בעית לערובי מי הוה שרי לך השתא נמי לא מקבילנא א"ל רב פפא לאביי אדרבה איפכא מסתברא לדברי חכמים מותר לערב שמרים והיינו טעמא דלא מקבל דא"ל מדלא ערבת לי אחולי אחלית לי לדברי רבי יהודה אסור לערב שמרים והיינו טעמא דמקבל דאמר ליה אי בעי לערובי לא שרי לי לערובי לך קבולי לא מקבלת (ד) זבון וזבין תגרא איקרי תנא אחד הלוקח ואחד המפקיד לפקטים מאי לפקטים אילימא כי היכי דלוקח לא מקבל פקטים מפקיד נמי לא מקבל פקטים ולימא ליה פקטך מאי איעביד להו אלא כי היכי דמפקיד מקבל פקטים (ד) לוקח נמי מקבל פקטים ומי מקבל לוקח פקטים והתניא ר"י אומר לא אמרו שמן עבור אלא למוכר בלבד שהרי לוקח מקבל עליו לוג ומחצה שמרים בלא פקטים לא קשיא (ה) הא דיהיב ליה זוזי בתשרי וקא שקיל מיניה בניסן כי מדה דתשרי הא דיהיב ליה זוזי בניסן וקא שקיל מיניה בניסן כי מדה דניסן:

**מתני'** (ו) המפקיד חבית אצל חבירו ולא יחדו לה בעלים מקום וטלטלה ונשתברה אם מתוך ידו נשברה לצורכו חייב לצורכה פטור אם משהניחה נשברה בין לצורכו בין לצורכה פטור יחדו לה הבעלים מקום וטלטלה ונשברה בין מתוך ידו ובין משהניחה לצורכו חייב לצורכה פטור:

**גמ'** הא מני רבי ישמעאל היא דאמר (ה) לא בעינן דעת בעלים (י) דתניא הגונב טלה מן העדר וסלע מן הכיס למקום שגנב יחזיר דברי רבי ישמעאל רבי עקיבא אומר

---

**רש"י**

דל תלתין ושיתא. כוזי בשיתא זוזי שקנאה פשו תריסר: דל תמניא שתותי. של מ"ח שדרך הוא לחסר בבליעת הקנקן כדתנן יוציא לו שתות ליין פשו לו לשכרו ארבע: והאמר שמואל המשתכר. בדברים שיש בהם חיי נפש: אל ישתכר יותר על השתות. הא שתות ישתכר ולמה לא ישתכר רב יהודה עד שתות: איכא גולפי ושמריא. משתכר הוא הקנקן והשמרים שלקח הכל בו' זוז: דמי ברזנייתא. שנותן דמים לחנווני למוכר' ומוליכן ומכריז עליו בחוצות. כרזנייתא לשון כרוז לשון אחר (א) אומנות יש בנקיבת ברזא בחבית של חרס וצריך ליתן שכר: במזופפין. דכיון דישנים הם ונתבלעו בלעותם תו לא בלעי: כיון דטעון טעון. תו לא בלע: כשתמצא לומר. כשתדקדק ותדע מילוי הדברים: מותר לערב שמרים. המוכר שמן לחבירו סתם בעת שהוא מזוקק ששקעו ושקטו שמריו מותר לו לערב ולבלבל שמרים המשוקעות שיחזרו ויתערבו ויצאו עם השמן בתוך המדה: אסור לערב שמרים. שבחזקת מזוקק לוקחו ממנו וזה מקלקלו: והיינו טעמא דמקבל עליו. לוקח לוג ומחצה שמרים בשלא ערבו ונתנו לו מזוקק: דא"ל. מוכר אי בעי לערובי כו': הוה מזדבן. כשהייתי מוכרו בחנות היה נמכר שמרים עם השמן: בבעה"ב עסקינן. שהלוקח בעה"ב הוא ולקחו למאכל ביתו: צמד. העול שהוא מוטל על שני השוורים ומלמדם: הדבר ידוע. שאין צמד נמכר במאתים זוז אלא כמות שהוא עם הבקר מכרו לו: וחכמים אומרים אין הדמים ראיה. אע"ג דלא שוה כולי האי אחולי אחליה לוקח זה יתר הדמים ור"י לית ליה שיהא מוחל מן הסתם אלא אם כן פירש: קבולי נמי לא מקבלת. עלך חסרון השמרים א"כ מה משתכר הרי השכר כולו בשמרים: זבון וזבין תגרא איקרי. בתמיה משל הוא לאמר לשוטה לקח בדמים וחזור ומכור בלא שכר ותיקרי תגר: אחד הלוקח ואחד המפקיד לפקטים. לוקח ומפקיד אחד הן לענין פקטים תורה אחת לשניהם: פקטים. פסולת הגרעינים הצפין על פני השמן: לוקח מקבל פקטים. אם מכר לו שמן סתם יקבל ממנו שמן עם פקטים: לא אמרו שמן עבור אלא למוכר. לא אמרו הפסד עכירת השמן אלא למוכר: שהרי הלוקח מקבל עליו. לפחות ממאה לוגין לוג ומחצה מחמת שמרים לפיכך צריך ליתן לו שמן מזוקק בלא פקטים: כי מדה דתשרי. כשער הדמים של תשרי שהוא בזול וסתם שמנים עכורים וקיבל עליו פקטים: הא דשקל מיניה בניסן כשער של ניסן. ביוקר דדרך כל השמנים להיות מזוקקין בניסן והלוקח סתם והמוכר סתם אין מוכר אלא מזוקק: מתני' לא יחדו לו הבעלים מקום. בבית שומר לאמר לו זוית זו השאילני: לצורכו. להשתמש בה: לצורכה. שהיתה במקום התורפה וקרובה להשבר: אם משהניחה. שכלה תשמישו הושיבה במקום משתמר בין שטלטלה מתחלה לצורכה בין שטלטלה לצורכו פטור ובגמרא פריך מאי שנא לא יחדו מיחדו: גמ' (ג) מני. הא דקתני רישא דאם משהניחה נשברה אף על פי שלצורכו נטלה מתחלה פטור דאמר משהחזירה הרי היא ברשות הבעלים כבתחלה ואינו עליה אלא כשומר חנם ופטור על אונסיה ואף על פי שלא הודיע לבעלים לומר נטלתיה והחזרתיה הויא השבה רבי ישמעאל היא כו':

---

**תוספות**

אל ישתכר יותר על שתות. הא עד שתות משתכר ומסתמא רב יהודה היה מולא שיתנו לו יותר ולמה הניח מלהרויח עד שתות:

במזופפין שנו. וא"ת כל שכן דבלע טפי כדאמרינן לעיל באתרא דמר חפו בכופרא דמייץ טפי וי"ל דהיינו חדש אבל ישן שכבר בלע אינו בולע יותר אי נמי התם ביין אבל הכא בשמן לא בלע כיון שהוא ישן:

לחודיה לא מזדבן. וא"ת ויתן לו מוכר ללוקח לוג ומחלה שמרים שיערב עדיין וימכור וי"ל דמיירי מתני' אפי' אין השמן בעין שלקחו מעט מעט ומכרו או אכלו:

לדברי חכמים אסור לערב. וא"ת ונימא משום דאית ליה מחילה ולעולם מותר לערב וי"ל דמתניתין נמי מיירי אפי' כשהשמן עדיין בעין והתם אין שייך מחילה כיון שיכול לתקן כי יאמר לו קח השמרים וערב בשמן ולרב פפא דאמר דטעמייהו משום מחילה סבר דהשמן אינו בעין דאילו הוה בעין לא שייך ביה מחילה אי נמי סבר דאף ע"פ שהוא בעין שייך ביה מחילה כיון דמדדו מזוקק:

לדברי ר"י אסור. וא"ת ולימא מותר וטעמא דמקבל משום דלית ליה מחילה וי"ל דרב פפא סבר דצמד ובקר איכא הוכחה דלאו מחילה דמסתמא לא רצה ליתן מאתים זוז על הצמד בלא בקר אבל הכא לוג ומחלה שהוא דבר מועט מדלא עירב אחולי אחיל:

זבון וזבין תגרא איקרי. מיירי שלא היה מולא למכור ביוקר יותר משלקחו לכך א"ל אדעתא דהכי קנית ממני שהיית יודע שאעכב לוג ומחלה כדי שארויח קצת:

לא אמרו שמן עבור אלא למוכר. פי' לא אמרו הפסד של עכירת פקטים אלא למוכר דכשנותן ללוקח שמן מזוקק אינו מחסר לו כלום ממאה לוג בשביל הפקטים כי אם לוג ומחלה בשביל השמרים מיהו עכירה לא שייכא כל כך בפקטים אלא בדבר המתערב כמו שמרים וי"ל דלא אמרינן הפסד של עכירת השמרים אלא למוכר שאם מוכר כשהוא מזוקק מקבל עליו לוקח בשביל השמרים לוג ומחלה והמוכר מרויח השמרים וכשהוא מוכר שמן עכור נותן מאה לוגין שלמים שמן עכור ומפסיד השמרים ע"י מה שמכר כשהוא עכור וכשמוכר מזוקק לא קרי הפסד לוקח אע"פ שמפסיד שמרים משום דבעה"ב ניחא ליה בצילא:

אי

---



עב א מיי' פי"ד מהל' מכירה הל' א סמג לאוין קע טוש"ע ח"מ סי' רלא סעיף כ:

עג ב מיי' שם פי"ח הלכה ח סמג עשין שם טוש"ע ח"מ סי' רכח סעיף יט:

עד ג מיי' שם פכ"ז הל' ב ועיין בהשגות ובמ"מ סמג עשין פב טוש"ע ח"מ סי' רכ סעיף ד:

עה ד ה מיי' שם פי"ח הל' ט י סמג לאוין קע טוש"ע ח"מ סי' רכח סעיף כ:

עו ו מיי' פ"ז מהלכות שאלה ופקדון הל' ט סמג עשין פח טוש"ע ח"מ סי' רלב סעיף ו:

**רבינו חננאל**

טפיחין יצאו ח' שהן שתות לכל החבית בחסרונות כדתנן יוציא לו שתות ליין נשארו ד' טפיחין ריוח. ומקשי' היכי עביד רב יהודה הכי והאמר שמואל לא ישתכר אדם יותר משתות ולא פחות משתות והשתות הוא זוז ועוד וזה לא נשתייר לו אלא ד' טפיחין. ופרקי' נשתייר החבית והשמרין שבתוכו ואיכא גולפי ושדריא למלאת השתות. ומקשי' אי הכי הני כולהו טפי משתות נינהו. ופרקי' נשאר לו לקונה ליטול זולת הריוח אגר טירחיה שמודד לו לקונה לכל אחד ואחד לזה עכשיו ולחבירו למחר ומתבטל ממלאכתו והדמים למי שנוקב לו הנקבים בחבית להוציא היין בהן מן החבית וזה פי' דמי ברזניתיה. פי' ברזא נקב החבית כדגרסי' (א) דעד ברזא. נוטל אלו כולן בריוח שלו וגם בשכרו. יוציא לו ג' לוג שמן לק' לוג כו' אם היו קנקנים ישנים אין מוציא לו בלע. ואוקמה רב פפא במזופפין. אמר אביי כיון דטעון טעון כלומר מאחר שהיה בהן שמן ומצצי ושבעי שוב. אין מוציאין לעולם: **פיסקא** ר' יהודה אומר אף המוכר שמן מזוקק לחבירו כל השנה הרי זה מקבל עליו לוג ומחצה שמרין לק'. אמר אביי אם תמצא לומר לדברי ר' יהודה מותר לערב שמרין. לדברי חכמים אסור לערב שמרין כו' אמר ליה רב פפא אדרבה איפכא מסתברא לדברי חכמים מותר לערב שמרין והיינו טעמא דלא מקבל דאמר ליה מדלא ערבית אחולי אחלת לי. לדברי ר' יהודה אסור לערב והיינו טעמא דמקבל דאמר לערובי לך אסור קבולי לא תקבל זבון וזבין תגרא איקרי וכי לא בעינא לאישתכורי הלכך מקבל וקיימא לן כתנא קמא: **מתני'** המפקיד אצל חבירו חבית ולא יחדו לה הבעלים מקום וטלטלה ונשברה וכו' עד אם משהניחה בין לצרכה בין לצרכו פטור. פי' לצרכה כדי שלא תשבר וכיוצא בה. אוקימנא לר' ישמעאל דאמר כשמחזירה אין צריך דעת בעלים דתניא הגונב טלה מן העדר וסלע מן הכיס למקום שגנב יחזיר דברי ר' ישמעאל ר' עקיבא אומר צריך דעת בעלים ומקשי'

---



א) בבא בתרא צ., מנחות עז., ב) נ"א ושדריא ג) בבא בתרא עז:, ד) [בבא בתרא צ., מנחות עז.] ה) [לקמן מג:], ו) בבא קמא קיח.:

**הגהות הב"ח**

(א) רש"י ד"ה דמי כרזנייתא וכו' לשון אחר ברזנייתא אומנות. נ"ב עי' פרק השואל סוף דף צט (ב) ד"ה אם וכו' מיחד הס"ד ואח"כ מ"ה הא מני דקתני:

**ליקוטי רש"י**

אל ישתכר יותר על שתות. כגון חנוני הקונה יין ופירות מן הסיטון הרבה ביחד כדי למכור מעט מעט לא ישתכר יותר משתות [רשב"ם ב"ב צ.]. איכא גולפי. דרך למוכר חביות של יין ליתן גם החביות ללוקחין והכי אמרינן בהמפקיד איכא גולפי ושדריה שהלוקח מוכרו בחנות משתכר בהן לבד מה שהוא משתכר ביין [ע"ז סה:]. גולפי. קנקן של חרס [מגילה כו.] ודמי ברזנייתא. שנותנין למכריז בעיר על היין בשווקים וברחובות יש בבית פלוני יין למכור ברזנייתא לשון ברזא דייש"ר בלע"ז כלומר יציאת היין הנמכר בברזא בפרוטות וי"מ שהיו צריכין לשכור אומן לנקב נקב בחבית מפני שהוא של חרס ולתקן ברזא הנך דמי מנכי להו [לקמן צט:] כשתמצא לומר. כשתעמוד לסוף דברי [כתובות כ:]. כשתדקדק בדבריהם תמצא כ [עירובין פט.]. כשתדקדק בדבריהם ותעמוד על מכונו תמצא [פסחים יא:] הצמד. הוא העול וכל העגלה קטנה והעגלה עצמה המחברין את השוורים יחד. לא מכר לו את הצמד. דבר הכל היא אלא דפליגי רב יהודה ורבנן בפירוש דהך מילתא דלרבי יהודה זימנין מכר זימנין לא מכר ולרבנן לעולם לא מכר אין הדמים ראיה. אלא במתנה ביקש ליתן ל המותר אי נמי ליהוי מקח טעות כדאמרינן בגמרא ויחזיר לו מעותיו ויטול למדו [רשב"ם ב"ב עז:] זבון וזבין תגרא איקרי. בתמיה משל הוא וכי לכך קנה התבואה רחוק מכאן שיתננה כאן באותן דמים כדי שיקרא תגר ולהרויח אינו חושש [רשב"ם ב"ב צ.].

**חשק שלמה על ר"ח**

א) נראה דל"ל כדגרסי' בע"ז (דף ס ע"א) דעד ברזא וכו נוטל אלו וכו' ועי' בערוך ערך בזח.

The Gemara calculates the profit Rav Yehudah would make on each barrel he bought:

דַּל תְּלָתִין וְשִׁיתָּא בְּשִׁיתָּא – **Subtract thirty-six** *kuz* of wine (from the total of forty-eight *kuz*), **for** which Rav Yehudah would receive his original purchase price of **six** *zuz*, פָּשׁוּ לֵיהּ תְּרֵיסַר – **and there will remain twelve** *kuz* of wine to be sold for profit. דַּל תְּמַנְיָא שְׁתוּתֵי – But from these twelve *kuz,* we must **subtract** another **eight** *kuz*, which is **a sixth** of the original forty-eight *kuz,* for a sixth of the wine is absorbed by the barrel,[1] פָּשׁוּ לְהוּ אַרְבָּעָה – **and** therefore, **there remain four** *kuz* of wine as his profit. Thus, one-twelfth of the wine (four *kuz* out of forty-eight) was sold for profit.

The Gemara asks:

וְהָאָמַר שְׁמוּאֵל – **But Shmuel has said:** הַמִּשְׂתַּכֵּר – **One who profits** from selling staple commodities such as grain, wine, or oil אַל יִשְׂתַּכֵּר יוֹתֵר עַל שְׁתוּת – **may not profit by more than a sixth.** A sixth, however, is permitted. Why, then, did Rav Yehudah limit his profit to one-twelfth?[2]

The Gemara answers:

אִיכָּא גּוּלְפֵי וּשְׁמָרַיָּא – **There are the barrel and the sediment,** which Rav Yehudah also kept. Their value must be included in the profit, for they were part of the initial purchase.

The Gemara asks:

אִי הָכִי – **If** this is **so,** נְפִישׁ לֵיהּ טְפֵי מִשְׁתוּת – **he is left with more than a sixth** as profit,[3] and this should be forbidden! – ? –

The Gemara answers:

אִיכָּא טִרְחֵיהּ – **There is** the cost of **his labor,**[4] וּדְמֵי בְּרָזְנַיְיתָא – **and the cost of** hiring **a tapper** to open the barrel properly.[5] When these factors are taken into account, Rav Yehudah's profit margin was not more than a sixth, even including the barrel and sediment.

The Mishnah stated regarding the deductions that a *shomer* makes from oil:

אִם הָיָה שֶׁמֶן מְזוּקָּק – IF THE OIL WAS REFINED, אֵינוֹ מוֹצִיא לוֹ שְׁמָרִים וכו׳ – [THE *SHOMER*] DOES NOT DEDUCT anything FOR SEDIMENT **etc.** Also, if the jugs in which the oil was stored were old, he does not deduct anything for absorption.

The Gemara asks:

וְהָא אִי אֶפְשָׁר דְּלֹא בָּלַע – **But** even if an old jug is used, **it is impossible that it will not absorb** at least some oil. – ? –

The Gemara gives two answers:

אָמַר רַב נַחְמָן – **Rav Nachman said:** בִּמְזוּפָּפִין שָׁנוּ – It was **regarding [jugs] lined with pitch** that **they taught** this ruling. Such jugs, when they are old and their sides are saturated, indeed do not absorb any more oil at all.[6]

אַבַּיֵי אָמַר – **Abaye said:** אֲפִילוּ תֵּימָא שֶׁלֹּא בִּמְזוּפָּפִין – **You ma[y] say** that our Mishnah refers **even** to **[jugs] that are not line[d] with pitch,** כֵּיוָן דִּטְעוּן טְעוּן – for **once [a jug] is saturated, it** [is] fully **saturated,** and indeed does not absorb any more.

The Mishnah stated:

רַבִּי יְהוּדָה אוֹמֵר – R' YEHUDAH SAYS: [הַ]מּוֹכֵר שֶׁמֶן מְזוּקָּק לַחֲבֵירוֹ כָּל יְמוֹת הַשָּׁנָה – ALSO, IF SOMEONE SELLS REFINED OIL TO H[IS] FELLOW, and agrees to provide him with oil a little at a tim[e] THROUGHOUT THE YEAR, הֲרֵי זֶה מְקַבֵּל עָלָיו – in such a case, [TH[E] BUYER] ACCEPTS UPON HIMSELF לוֹג וּמֶחֱצָה שְׁמָרִים לְמֵאָה – ON[E]-AND-A-HALF *LOGS* OF SEDIMENT FOR each one HUNDRED *logs* [o]f oil he purchased. That is, the buyer cannot demand 100 *logs* [o]f refined oil, but must accept a total of 98 ½ *logs* of refined oil; th[e] rest of the purchase is made up with sediment.[7]

The Sages, however, disagree with R' Yehudah. In their view the buyer does not have to accept a reduction in the amount of o[il] he receives, even though all of the oil he is getting is refined.

The Gemara analyzes this dispute:

אָמַר אַבַּיֵי – **Abaye said:** כְּשֶׁתִּמְצָא לוֹמַר – **When you wish t[o]** explain this dispute, **you will** have the following **to say:** דִּבְרֵי רַבִּי יְהוּדָה – **According to R' Yehudah,** מוּתָּר לְעָרֵב שְׁמָרִים – **it is permitted** for one who sells oil **to mix sediment** from th[e] bottom of the container back into the pure oil on top, even afte[r] the sediment has settled on the bottom.[8] לְדִבְרֵי חֲכָמִים – **I[n] the opinion of the Sages,** however, אָסוּר לְעָרֵב שְׁמָרִים – **it i[s] prohibited to mix** the **sediment** back into the pure oil.[9]

Abaye explains R' Yehudah's opinion according to his under[-]standing of the dispute:

לְדִבְרֵי רַבִּי יְהוּדָה – According to **R' Yehudah,** [מ]וּתָּר לְעָרֵב שְׁמָרִים – **it is permitted to mix sediment** into the pure oil, [וְ]הַיְינוּ טַעְמָא דִּמְקַבֵּל – and **this is the reason** that R' Yehudah rule[s] in our Mishnah **that [a purchaser] accepts** a reduction of 1.[5] percent if all of the oil he receives is pure. דְּאָמַר לֵיהּ – **Fo[r] [the merchant] can say to him:** אִי בָּעֵי לְעָרוּבֵי לָךְ – **"If I ha[d] wanted to mix** the sediment into the pure oil, [מִ]י לֹא עָרְבֵי לָךְ – **could I not have mixed it in for you?** הַשְׁתָּא נַמִּי קַבֵּיל – **S[o] now** that I did not do so, **accept** less pure oil, for it contains n[o] sediment."

The Gemara questions this explanation:

וְלֵימָא לֵיהּ – **But let [the purchaser] say to [the merchant]:** [אִ]י עָרְבַתְּ לֵיהּ – **"If you would have mixed** the sediment into th[e] oil, הֲוָה מִזְדַּבַּן לִי – **I would have been able to sell [the sedi-ment]** together with the oil![10] הַשְׁתָּא מַאי אֶעֱבִיד לֵיהּ – **Now** tha[t] you have given me pure oil, **what can I do with [the sediment]?** לְחוּדֵיהּ לֹא מִזְדַּבַּן לִי – **I cannot sell [the sediment] by itself!**[11]

NOTES

1. In accordance with the opinion of the Tanna Kamma of our Mishnah.

2. Presumably, Rav Yehudah could have found customers for his wine even if he would have sold it at a higher price (*Tosafos*).

3. [The Gemara assumes that the barrel and the sediment are worth more than one-twelfth of the value of the wine.]

4. Measuring out small amounts of wine to customers all day is considered an expense to a shopkeeper, for while he is doing this he cannot engage in his other work (*R' Chananel*). [Had he been selling large quantities, his time would have been spent more profitably.]

5. Wine barrels were made of earthenware; thus, boring a hole into a barrel to make a spigot required an expert, who had to be paid.

An alternative version of the text reads: כָּרוֹזְנַיְיתָא, *announcer.* This refers to a crier, who was paid to take the wine out into the streets and find people willing to buy it (*Rashi;* see *Hagahos HaBach* §1).

6. When the Gemara said above (40a) that pitch-lined kegs are very absorbent, it was referring to *new* kegs. Here, the reference is to *old* jugs that are already saturated (*Tosafos,* first approach).

7. See 40a note 34.

8. The purchaser did not specify that he was buying refined oil. [Thus,] although at the time of purchase the sediment had already settled, the merchant would be permitted to stir up the sediment and include it in the measure of oil he is committed to sell (*Rashi*). Therefore, if he did not do so, he may deduct an amount equal to the sediment from the amount he must deliver.

9. The Sages hold that although the purchaser did not *specify* refined oil, we assume that he bought the oil on the presumption that it was refined, for the sediment in the barrels of oil had already settled; see previous note. Therefore, the merchant is not allowed to stir up the sediment and thereby ruin the oil (*Rashi*). Accordingly, he may not deduct anything from the amount he agreed to deliver.

10. The Gemara assumes that the buyer is a retailer, who buys the oil to sell at a profit.

11. Since the buyer received the oil a bit at a time, he has no oil left to mix the sediment into (*Tosafos;* cf. *Ritva*); and sediment on its own is worthless.

דל תלתין ושיתא בשיתא פשו ליה תריסר דל תמניא שתותי פשו להו ארבעה [א] והאמר שמואל [א]המשתכר אל ישתכר יותר על שתות איכא גולפי [ב] ושמריא אי הכי נפיש ליה טפי משתות איכא טרחיה ודמי ברזנייתא: אם היה שמן מזוקק אינו יוציא לו שמרים [וכו']: והא אי אפשר דלא בלע אמר רב נחמן במזופפין שנו אביי אמר אפילו תימא שלא במזופפין כיון דטעון טעון: ר"י אומר אף המוכר שמן מזוקק לחבירו כל ימות השנה הרי זה מקבל עליו לוג ומחצה שמרים למאה: אמר אביי כשתמצא לומר לדברי ר"י מותר לערב שמרים לדברי חכמים [ב]אסור לערב שמרים לדברי רבי יהודה מותר לערב שמרים והיינו טעמא דמקבל דאמר ליה אי בעי לערובי לך מי לא ערבי לך השתא נמי קביל ולימא ליה אי ערבת ליה הוה מזדבן לי השתא מאי אעביד ליה לחודיה לא מזדבן לי בבעל הבית עסקינן דניחא ליה בצילא ולימא ליה מדלא ערבית לי אחולי אחלת לי רבי יהודה לטעמיה דלית ליה מחילה דתנן [ג] [ג]מכר לו את הצמד לא מכר לו את הבקר מכר לו את הבקר לא מכר לו את הצמד ר"י אומר הדמים מודיעין כיצד אמר לו מכור לי צמדך במאתים זוז הדבר ידוע שאין הצמד במאתים זוז וחכ"א אין הדמים ראיה לדברי חכמים אסור לערב שמרים והיינו טעמא דלא מקבל דא"ל אי בעית לערובי מי הוה שרי לך השתא נמי לא מקבילנא א"ל רב פפא לאביי אדרבה איפכא מסתברא לדברי חכמים מותר לערב שמרים והיינו טעמא דלא מקבל דא"ל מדלא ערבת לי אחולי אחלית לי לדברי רבי יהודה אסור לערב שמרים והיינו טעמא דמקבל דאמר ליה אי בעי לערובי לא שרי לי לערובי לך קבולי לא מקבלת [ד] זבון וזבין תגרא איקרי תנא אחד הלוקח ואחד המפקיד לפקטים מאי לפקטים אילימא כי היכי דלוקח לא מקבל פקטים מפקיד נמי לא מקבל פקטים ולימא ליה פקטך מאי איעביד להו אלא כי היכי דמפקיד מקבל פקטים [ד]לוקח נמי מקבל פקטים ומי מקבל לוקח פקטים והתניא ר"י אומר לא אמרו שמן עכור אלא למוכר בלבד שהרי לוקח מקבל עליו לוג ומחצה שמרים בלא פקטים לא קשיא [ה]הא דיהיב ליה זוזי בתשרי וקא שקיל מיניה בניסן כי מדה דתשרי הא דיהיב ליה זוזי בניסן וקא שקיל מיניה בניסן כי מדה דניסן:

**מתני'** [ו]המפקיד חבית אצל חבירו ולא יחדו לה בעלים מקום וטלטלה ונשתברה אם מתוך ידו נשברה לצורכו חייב לצורכה פטור אם משהניחה נשברה בין לצורכו בין לצורכה פטור יחדו לה הבעלים מקום וטלטלה ונשברה בין מתוך ידו ובין משהניחה לצורכו חייב לצורכה פטור:

**גמ'** הא מני רבי ישמעאל היא דאמר [ה] לא בעינן דעת בעלים [ו]דתניא הגונב טלה מן העדר וסלע מן הכיס למקום שגנב יחזיר דברי רבי ישמעאל רבי עקיבא אומר

---

**רש"י**

דל תלתין ושיתא. כוזי בשיתא זוזי שקנאה פשו תריסר: דל תמניא שתותי. של מ"ח שדרך הוא לחסר בבליעת הקנקן כדתנן יוציא לו שתות ליין פשו לו לשכרו ארבע: והאמר שמואל המשתכר. בדברים שיש בהם חיי נפש: אל ישתכר יותר על השתות. הא שתות ישתכר ולמה לא ישתכר רב יהודה עד שתות: איכא גולפי ושמריא. משתכר הוא הקנקן והשמרים שלקח הכל בו' זוז: דמי ברזנייתא. שנותן דמים לחנווני למוכר' ומוליכן ומכריז עליו בחוצות. כרזנייתא לשון כרזא לשון אחר (א) אומנות יש בנקיבת ברזא בחבית של חרס וצריך ליתן שכר: במזופפין. דכיון דישנים הם ונתבלעו בלעותם תו לא בלעי: כיון דטעון טעון. תו לא בלע: כשתמצא לומר. כשתדקדק ותדע מילוי הדברים: מותר לערב שמרים. המוכר שמן לחבירו סתם בעת שהוא מזוקק ששקעו ושקטו שמריו מותר לו לערב ולבלבל שמרים המשוקעות שיחזרו ויתערבו ויצאו עם השמן בתוך המדה: אסור לערב שמרים. שבחזקת מזוקק לוקחו ממנו וזה מקלקלו: והיינו טעמא דמקבל עליו. לוקח לוג ומחצה שמרים בשלא ערבו ונתנו לו מזוקק: דא"ל. מוכר אי בעי לערובי כו': הוה מזדבן. כשהייתי מוכרו בחנות היה נמכר שמרים עם השמן: בבעה"ב עסקינן. שהלוקח בעה"ב הוא ולקחו למאכל ביתו: צמד. העול שהוא מוטל על שני השוורים ומלמידם: הדבר ידוע. שאין למד נמכר במאתים זוז אלא כמות שהוא עם הבקר מכרו לו: וחכמים אומרים אין הדמים ראיה. אע"ג דלא שוה כולי האי אחולי אחליה לוקח זה יתר הדמים ור"י לית ליה שיהא מוחל מן הסתם אלא אם כן פירש: קבולי נמי לא מקבלת. עלך חסרון השמרים א"כ מה משתכר הרי השכר כולו בשמרים: זבון וזבין תגרא איקרי. בתמיה משל הוא לאמר לשוטה לקח בדמים וחזור ומכור בלא שכר ותיקרי תגר: אחד הלוקח ואחד המפקיד לפקטים. לוקח ומפקיד אחד הן לענין פקטים תורה אחת לשניהם: פקטים. פסולת הגרעינים הצפין על פני השמן: לוקח מקבל פקטים. אם מכר לו שמן סתם יקבל ממנו שמן עם פקטים: לא אמרו שמן עכור אלא למוכר. לא אמרו הפסד עכירת השמן אלא למוכר: שהרי הלוקח מקבל עליו. לפחות ממאה לוגין לוג ומחצה מחמת שמרים לפיכך צריך ליתן לו שמן מזוקק בלא פקטים: כי מדה דתשרי. כשער הדמים של תשרי שהוא בזול וסתם שמנים עכורים וקיבל עליו פקטים: הא דשקל מיניה בניסן כשער של ניסן. ביוקר דדרך כל השמנים להיות מזוקקין בניסן והלוקח סתם והמוכר סתם אין מוכר אלא מזוקק: מתני' לא יחדו לו הבעלים מקום. בבית שומר לאמר לו זווית זו השאילני: לצורכו. להשתמש בה: לצורכה. שהיתה במקום התורפה וקרובה להשתבר: אם משהניחה. שכלה תשמישו הושיבה במקום משתמר בין שטלטלה מתחלה לצורכה בין שטלטלה לצורכו פטור ובגמרא פריך מאי שנא לא יחדו מיחדו: גמ' (ג) מני. הא דקתני רישא דאם משהניחה נשברה אף על פי שלצורכו נטלה מתחלה פטור דאמר משהחזירה הרי היא ברשות הבעלים כבתחלה ואינו עליה אלא כשומר חנם ופטור על אונסיה ואף על פי שלא הודיע לבעלים לומר נטלתיה והחזרתיה הויא השבה רבי ישמעאל היא כו':

צריך

---

**תוספות**

אל ישתכר יותר על שתות. הא עד שתות משתכר ומסתמא רב יהודה היה מולא שיתנו לו יותר ולמה הניח מלהרויח עד שתות:

במזופפין שנו. וא"ת כל שכן דבלע טפי כדאמרינן לעיל באתרא דמר חפו בכופרא דמייך טפי וי"ל דהיינו חדש אבל ישן שכבר בלע אינו בולע יותר אי נמי התם ביין אבל הכא בשמן לא בלע כיון שהוא ישן:

לחודיה לא מזדבן. וא"ת ויתן לו מוכר ללוקח לוג ומחצה שמרים שיערב עדיין וימכור וי"ל דמיירי מתני' אפי' אין השמן בעין שלקחו מעט מעט ומכרו או אכלו:

לדברי חכמים אסור לערב. וא"ת ונימא משום דאית ליה מחילה ולעולם מותר לערב וי"ל דמתניתין נמי מיירי אפי' כשהשמן עדיין בעין והתם אין שייך מחילה כיון שיכול לתקן כי יאמר לו קח השמרים וערב בשמן ולרב פפא דאמר דטעמייהו משום מחילה סבר דהשמן אינו בעין דאילו הוה בעין לא שייך ביה מחילה אי נמי סבר דאף ע"פ שהוא בעין שייך ביה מחילה כיון דמדלו מזוקק:

לדברי ר"י אסור. וא"ת ולימא מותר וטעמא דמקבל משום דלית ליה מחילה וי"ל דרב פפא סבר דצמד ובקר איכא הוכחה דלאו מחילה דמסתמא לא רצה ליתן מאתים זוז על הצמד בלא בקר אבל הכא לוג ומחצה שהוא דבר מועט מדלא עירב אחולי אחיל:

זבון וזבין תגרא איקרי. מיירי שלא היה מולא למכור ביוקר יותר משלקחו לכך א"ל אדעתא דהכי קנית ממני שהיית יודע שאעכב לוג ומחצה כדי שארויח קצת:

לא אמרו שמן עכור אלא למוכר. פי' לא אמרו הפסד של עכירת פקטים אלא למוכר דכשנותן ללוקח שמן מזוקק אינו מחסר לו כלום ממאה לוג בשביל הפקטים כי אם לוג ומחצה בשביל השמרים מיהו עכירה לא שייכא כל כך בפקטים אלא בדבר המתערב כמו שמרים וי"ל דלא אמרינן הפסד של עכירת השמרים אלא למוכר שאם מוכר כשהוא מזוקק מקבל עליו לוקח בשביל השמרים לוג ומחצה והמוכר מרויח השמרים וכשהוא מוכר שמן עכור נותן מאה לוגין שלמים שמן עכור ומפסיד השמרים ע"י מה שמכר כשהוא עכור וכשמוכר מזוקק לא קרי הפסד לוקח אע"פ שמפסיד שמרים משום דבעה"ב ניחא ליה בצילא:

אי

---

**עין משפט נר מצוה**

עב א מיי' פי"ד מהל' מכירה הל' א סמג לאוין קע טוש"ע ח"מ סי' רלא סעיף כ:

עג ב מיי' שם פי"ח הלכה ח סמג עשין שם טוש"ע ח"מ סי' רכח סעיף יט:

עד ג מיי' שם פכ"ז הל' ב ועיין בהשגות ובמ"מ סמג עשין פב טוש"ע ח"מ סי' רכ סעיף ד:

עה ד ה מיי' שם פי"ח הל' ט י סמג לאוין קע טוש"ע ח"מ סי' רכח סעיף כ:

עו ו מיי' פ"ז מהלכות שאלה ופקדון הל' ט סמג עשין פח טוש"ע ח"מ סי' רלב סעיף ו:

---

**רבינו חננאל**

טפיחין יצאו ח' שהן שתות לכל החבית בחסרונות כדתנן יוציא לו שתות ליין נשארו ד' טפיחין ריוח. ומקשי' היכי עביד רב יהודה הכי והאמר שמואל לא ישתכר אדם יותר משתות ולא פחות משתות והשתות הוא זוז ועוד וזה לא נשתייר לו אלא ד' טפיחין. ופרקי' נשתייר החבית והשמרין שבתוכו ואיכא גולפי ושדריא למלאת השתות. ומקשי' אי הכי הני כולהו טפי משתות נינהו. ופרקי' נשאר לו לקונה ליטול זולת הריוח אגר טירחיה שמודד לו לקונה לכל אחד ואחד לזה עכשיו ולחבירו למחר ומתבטל ממלאכתו והדמים למי שנוקב לו הנקבים בחבית להוציא היין בהן מן החבית וזה פי' דמי ברזניתיה. פי' ברזא נקב החבית כדגרסי' א) דעד ברזא. נוטל אלו כולן בריוח שלו וגם בשכרו. יוציא לו ג' לוג שמן לק' לוג כו' אם היו קנקנים ישנים אין מוציא לו בלע. ואוקמה רב פפא במזופפין. אמר אביי כיון דטעון טעון כלומר מאחר שהיה בהן שמן ומצצי ושבעי שוב. אין מוציאין לעולם: פיסקא ר' יהודה אומר אף המוכר שמן מזוקק לחבירו כל השנה הרי זה מקבל עליו לוג ומחצה שמרין לק'. אמר אביי אם תמצא לומר לדברי ר' יהודה מותר לערב שמרין. לדברי חכמים אסור לערב שמרין כו' אמר ליה רב פפא אדרבה איפכא מסתברא לדברי חכמים מותר לערב שמרין והיינו טעמא דלא מקבל דאמר ליה מדלא ערבית אחולי אחלת לי. לדברי ר' יהודה אסור לערב והיינו טעמא דמקבל דאמר לערובי לך אסור קבולי לא תקבל זבון חבין תגרא איקרי וכי לא בעינא לאישתכורי הלכך מקבל וקיימא לן כתנא קמא: מתני' המפקיד אצל חבירו חבית ולא יחדו לה הבעלים מקום וטלטלה ונשברה וכו' עד אם משהניחה בין לצרכה בין לצרכו פטור. פי' לצרכה כדי שלא תשבר וכיוצא בה. אוקימנא לר' ישמעאל דאמר כשמחזירה אין צריך דעת בעלים דתניא הגונב טלה מן העדר וסלע מן הכיס למקום שגנב יחזיר דברי ר' ישמעאל ר' עקיבא אומר צריך דעת בעלים ומקשי'

---

**מסורת הש"ס**

א) בבא בתרא צ., מנחות עז., ב) נ"א ושדריא ג) בבא בתרא עז: ד) [בבא בתרא צ., מנחות עז.] ה) [לקמן מג:], ו) בבא קמא קיח.:

---

**הגהות הב"ח**

(א) רש"י ד"ה דמי ברזנייתא וכו' לשון אחר ברזנייתא אומנות. נ"ב עיין פרק השואל סוף דף לט: (ב) ד"ה אם וכו' מיחדו הס"ד ואח"כ מ"ה הא מני דקתני:

---

**ליקוטי רש"י**

אל ישתכר יותר על שתות. כגון חנוני הקונה יין ופירות מן הסיטון הרבה ביחד כדי למכור מעט מעט אל ישתכר יותר משתות [רשב"ם ב"ב צ.]. איכא גולפי. דרך למוכרי חביות של יין ליתן גם החביות ללוקחין והכי אמרינן בהמפקיד איכא גולפי ושדריה שהלוקח מוכרו בחנות משתכר בהן לבד מה שהוא משתכר ביין [ע"ז סה:]. גולפי. קנקן של חרס [מגילה כו.]. ודמי ברזנייתא. שנותנין למכריז בעיר על היין בשווקים וברחובות יש בבית פלוני יין למכור, ברזנייתא לשון ברזא דייש"י בלע"ז כלומר יציאת היין הנמכר בברזא בפרוטות. וי"מ שהיו צריכין לשכור אומן לנקב נקב בחבית מפני שהוא של חרס ולתקן ברזא הנך דמי מנכי להו [לקמן צט:]. כשתמצא לומר. כשתעמוד לסוף דבריו [כתובות כ:]. כשתדקדק בדבריהם תמצא כן [עירובין פט.]. כשתדקדק בדבריהם ותעמוד על מכונו תמצא [פסחים יא:]. הצמד. הוא העול וכלי העגלה קטנה והעגלה עצמה המחברין את השוורים יחד. לא מכר לו את הצמד. דברי הכל היא אלא דפליגי רבי יהודה ורבנן בפירושא דהך מילתא דלרבי יהודה זימנין מכר זימנין נמי לא מכר ולרבנן לעולם לא מכר. אין הדמים ראיה. אלא במתנה ביוקר ליתן לו המותר או נמי ליהוי מקח טעות ויחזיר לו מעותיו ויטול למלו [רשב"ם ב"ב עז:]. זבון וזבין תגרא איקרי. בתמיה משל הוא וכי לכך קנה התבואה רחוק מכאן שיתנה כאן באותו המקח כדי שיקרא תגר ולהרויח אינו חושש [רשב"ם ב"ב צ.].

---

**חשק שלמה על ר"ח**

א) נראה דצ"ל כדגרסי' בע"ז (דף ס ע"ב) דעד ברזא וכו' טוטל אלו וכו' וער' ערוך ערך כח.

וכן אמר רבה השביחו לאמצע א"ל אביי מי דמי התם גדולים גבי קטנים ידעי וקא מחלי הכא מי ידע דליחיל אגלגל מלתא ומטא לקמיה דרבי אמי [א]אמר להו גדולה מזו אמרו שמין להם כארים השתא דידיה לא יהבינן ליה אהדרוה [א]הא לקמיה דרב חסדא אמר להו מי דמי התם ברשות נחית הכא לאו ברשות נחית ועוד קטן הוא ואין מורידין קרוב לנכסי קטן [ב]אהדרוה לקמיה דרבי אמי אמר להו לא סיימוה קמי דקטן הוא:

**מתני'** [ג]המפקיד פירות אצל חבירו הרי זה יוציא לו חסרונות לחטים ולאורז תשעה חצאי קבין לכור לשעורין ולדוחן תשעה קבין לכור לכוסמין ולזרע פשתן שלש סאין לכור הכל לפי המדה והכל לפי הזמן א"ר יוחנן בן נורי וכי מה אכפת להן לעכברין והלא אוכלות בין מהרבה ובין מקמעא אלא אינו יוציא לו חסרונות אלא לכור אחד בלבד רבי יהודה אומר אם היתה מדה מרובה אינו מוציא לו חסרונות מפני שמותירות:

**גמ'** אורז טובא חסר אמר רבה בר בר חנה א"ר יוחנן [ד]באורז קלוף שנו: לכוסמין ולזרע פשתן ג' סאין לכור (וכו'): א"ר יוחנן א"ר חייא זרע [ה]פשתן בגבעולין שנו תניא נמי הכי לכוסמין ולזרע פשתן בגבעולין [ו]ולאורז שאינו קלוף שלשה סאין לכור: הכל לפי המדה וכו': [ז]תנא כן לכל כור וכור וכן לכל שנה ושנה: א"ר יוחנן בן נורי וכו': תניא אמרו לו לרבי יוחנן הרבה אובדות מהן הרבה מתפזרות מהן תנא בד"א שעירבן עם פירותיו אבל יחד לו קרן זוית אומר לו הרי שלך לפניך וכי עירבן עם פירותיו מאי הוי ליחזי לדידיה כמה הויין במסתפק מהם וליחזי כמה אסתפק [ח]דלא [ג]ידעי כמה אסתפק: ר"י אומר אם היתה וכו': כמה מדה מרובה אמר רבה בר בר חנה א"ר יוחנן עשרה כורין תניא נמי הכי כמה מדה מרובה עשרה כורין תני תנא קמיה דרב נחמן בד"א שמדד לו מתוך גורנו והחזיר לו מתוך גורנו אבל מדד לו מתוך גורנו והחזיר לו מתוך ביתו אינו יוציא לו חסרונות מפני שמותירות א"ל וכי בשופטני עסקינן דיהבי בביילא רבא ושקלי בביילא זוטא דלמא בימות הגורן קאמרת [ט]בד"א שמדד לו בימות הגורן והחזיר לו בימות הגורן אבל מדד לו בימות הגורן והחזיר לו בימות הגשמים אינו יוציא לו חסרון מפני שמותירות א"ל רב פפא לאביי א"כ לפקע כדא הוה עובדא ופקע כדא אבע"א משום איצצא:

**מתני'** [י]יוציא לו שתות ליין ר"י אומר חומש [כ]יוציא לו שלשה לוגין שמן למאה לוג ומחצה שמרים לוג ומחצה בלע אם היה שמן מזוקק אינו יוציא לו שמרים אם היו קנקנים ישנים אינו יוציא לו בלע ר"י אומר אף [ל]המוכר [ג]שמן מזוקק לחבירו כל ימות השנה הרי זה מקבל עליו לוג ומחצה שמרים למאה:

**גמ'** ולא פליגי [ד]מר כי אתריה ומר כי אתריה באתריה דמר חפו בקירא ולא מייץ טפי באתריה דמר חפו בכופרא ומייץ טפי איבעית אימא משום גרגישתא הא מייצא טפי והא לא מייצא טפי באתריה דרב יהודה רמו ארבעים ותמני כוזי בדנא אזיל דנא בשיתא זוזי פרים רב יהודה שיתא שיתא בזוזא

---

**רש"י**

וכן אמר רבה השביחו לאמצע. לא גרסינן שאין זה לשון גמרא להביא דברי האמוראים סיוע למשנה ועוד רבה תלמידיה דרב חסדא הוה והיכי אמר רב חסדא שמעתא משמיה ואי גרס ליה וכן אמר רב גרסינן שהיה רבו של רב חסדא משום דאיכא למ"ד בבבא בתרא (דף קמג:) לא שנו אלא ששבחו נכסים מחמת נכסים אבל שבחו מחמת עלמן של אחים השביחו לעלמן אמרה רב חסדא להא דרב הכא למימר דלית לן ההיא שמעתא אלא אפילו השביחו מחמת טורחן של משביחין כי הכא דשתל פרדס השביחו לאמלע: ידעי. אלו שיטלו חלקם: מי ידע. שיש לו אחים: גדולה מזו. קרוב היורד לנכסי שבוי שאם יבאו הבעלים יטלו שלהם: אמרו שמין להם כארים הכא דידיה לא יהבינן ליה. בתמיה זה שעשה והשביחן לדעת עלמו לא יהבי' ליה כארים בחלק השני: ברשות ב"ד נחתי. דמורידין קרוב לנכסי שבוי: הכא לא ברשות נחית. כשירד זה לתוכו לא נמלך בב"ד: ועוד. אם בא לימלך לא היו מורידין אותו דהא אחיו קטן הוה ואין מורידין קרוב לנכסי קטן: **מתני'** הרי זה יוציא לו חסרונות. כשיחזירם לו יפחות כמה הם רגילים לחסור ובגמ' מוקי לה בשעירבן עם פירותיו: אורז. מי"ל: [ה]דוחן. פטי"ל ודומה לאורז: הכל לפי המדה. וכן לכל כור וכור: הכל לפי הזמן. שהניחן בידו לכל שנה ושנה יניח לו כך: ר' יוחנן בן נורי אמר. אהכל לפי המדה פליג: אם היתה מדה מרובה. שהפקיד אללו הרבה ובגמרא מפרש י' כורים לא יוליא לו חסרונות מפני שהם מותירות שבימות הגורן כשמפקיד החיטין יבשין ובימות הגשמים כשמחזיר נופחות ובאכילת עכברים אינן נחסרים כל כך לכל כור וכור דכולי האי לא אכלי עכברים מי' כורין הלכך נפיחתו משלמת חסרון המגיע לשני כורים או שלשה שהעכברים אוכלין: **גמ'** זרע פשתן בגבעולין. חסר כל כך לפי שהגבעולין מתייבשין ונופלים והרוח מנשבתן אבל זרע פשתן נקי אינו חסר כ"כ: לכל כור וכור. פירוש דמתניתין הוא: ליחזי דידיה כמה הוו כו'. ויראה כמה חסרו ויטול על של חברו כפי חשבון: מדת הגורן. היתה יתירה על של בתים: בשופטני. שוטים: בביילא. במדה: בימות הגורן. סמוך ליובשן שנתיבשו בחמה: והחזיר לו בימות הגשמים. חזרו ונתפחו מלחלוחית הגשם והקור: א"כ. שדרכו לתפוח: לפקע כדא. כשממלאין כד חיטין או שעורין בימות הגורן וגפין את הכד יפקע בימות הגשמים מחמת תפיחת התבואה: איצצא. דוחק מתוך שהם במקום צר נדחקו יחד ואין תפוחין: **מתני'** ליין. אם הפקיד אללו יין ועירבו עם יינו הקנקנים בולעין שתות: אף המוכר כו'. כשם שאמרו במפקיד כן אמרו במוכר שהמוכר שמן לחבירו ונותן לו מתוך חביותיו כשהוא מסתפק תמיד והוא מזוקק הרי הלוקח מקבל עליו לפחות לו לוג ומחצה מחמת שמרים: למאה. למאה לוג: **גמ'** חפו בקירא. טחו החביות מבפנים בשעוה כדרך שעושין אנו בזפת: זפת: כופרא. גרגישתא. קרקע שעושין ממנה החביות ארדלי"א בלע"ז: הא. באתריה דר"י מייץ טפי מההיא דאתריה דתנא קמא: באתריה דרב יהודה. מילתא באפי נפשיה היא ולאו אמתניתין קאי: רמו ארבעין ותמניא כוזי בדנא. מדה קטנה היתה במקומו שארבעים ושמונה ממלאין את החבית: אזיל דנא בשיתא. בששה זוזים היתה נמכרת ביחד בימות הבציר: פרים ליה רב יהודה שיתא בזוזא. נעשה רב יהודה חנווני והיה מוכרן שש כוזי בזוז:

---

**תוספות**

**וכן** אמר רבה: גרס. רש"י גרס וכן אמר רב ופליג אמ"ד בפ' מי שמת (ב"ב דף קמג: ושם ד"ה לא) נכסים ששבחו מחמת עלמן של אחין השבח לעלמן וקאמר דאפי' שבחו מחמת טרחם של משביחין כי הכא דשתל פרדיסא השביחו לאמלע וזהו תימה שחולק רבא על רב דהתם רבא קאמר ולא מייתי התם מילתיה דרב ונראה דגרס רבה וכן בספר ר"ת ולא מדברי רב חסדא הוא (א) שהגמ' מביא שמעשה כיולא בזה בא לפני רבה ופסק דהשביחו לאמלע כמו רב חסדא והביאו הגמרא משום קושית אביי דא"ל אביי לרבה מי דמי כו' ולא חשש רבה מקושיותיו ודן דהשביחו לאמלע: **אגלגל** מלתא. פסק של רב חסדא ומטא לקמיה דרבי אמי: **וכי** מה אכפת להו לעכברים. וטעמייהו דרבנן מפרש בירושלמי הני עכברי רשיעי נינהו כד חמיין עיבור לא מסתייהו דאכלי אלא קריין לחבריהון דאכלי עמהון והא דאמרינן בגמרא אמרו לו הרבה אובדות מהם הרבה מתפזרות מהם י"ל דלדבריו דרבי יוחנן קאמר אפילו לית [ו]לך טעמא דמפרש בירושלמי מ"מ הרבה אובדות מהם:

**אלא** לכור בלבד. וא"ת אם כן בפחות מכור נמי יוליא כמו לכור וי"ל דאין להם ריוח להטמן [ז]בתוכה ומ"מ לפי חשבון הראוי להתחסר יוליא דאי אפשר שלא יתחסרו: **ולאורז** שאינו קלוף ג' סאין לכור. וא"ת ואמאי לא חשיב במתניתין אורז שאינו קלוף עם זרע פשתן כיון דאית להו חד שיעורא וי"ל דפשוט לו דבאורז תתחסר כל כך וברישא גבי אורז קלוף לא חשיב זרע פשתן קלוף דשמא דינם חלוק:

**מדה** מרובה י' כורין. וא"ת אפי' ב' כורין או ג' מתנפחין לפי חשבון החסרונות העולה להם וי"ל דבי' כורין עולה להם הנפוח חסרון של כור אחד ולא יוליא להם חסרונות היינו כל החסרון דחסרון של כור אחד לא יוליא ולהכי נקט י' כורים לאפוקי פחות:

אל

---

**מסורת הש"ס**

א) [תו"ג, יעב"ץ], ב) [נ"ל דע, יעב"ץ], ג) מהרש"ל שמן לחבירו מזוקק בל, ד) [פסחים ג. וש"נ], ה) [עי' פירש"י ברכות לז.], ו) נ"א לן, ז) נ"א בתיבה.

**הגהות הב"ח**

(א) תום' ד"ה וכן וכו' מדברי רב חסדא הוא אלא שהגמרא:

**לעזי רש"י**

מי"ל. פירוש "הירוש". פטי"ל. פירוש "פענכעל הירוש". ארדלי"א. פירוש טיט אדום (רמב"ם שבת פ"ח מ"ה), קרקע שעושין ממנה החביות.

**ליקוטי רש"י**

שמין להם כארים. אם יבואו הבעלים יטלו אלו בשבח קרקעות ופירות כמנהג אריסי המקום [לעיל לט.]. ולדוחן. פנ"ך [ברכות לז.]. לכוסמין. איספילטא בלע"ז [פסחים לה.]. בגבעולין. גבעול הוא קנה האמלעי שהזרע בראשו כקנבוס ופשתן [סוכה יג.]. ומייץ. ויונק [שבת קלד.]. גרגישתא. ארזיל"א במעבה האדמה (מלכים א ז) מתרגמינן בגרגישתא דארעא [יבמות קו:]. אדמה [כתובות ס:].

**עין משפט נר מצוה**

סז א ב מיי' פ"ט מהל' נחלות הל' ד ועיין בהשגות ובמגיד משנה סמג עשין לג טוש"ע ח"מ סי' רפז סעיף ג וע"ש:

סח ג ד ה ו ז ח מיי' פ"ה מהל' שאלה ופקדון הל' ה סמג עשין פח טוש"ע ח"מ סי' רלב סעיף יא:

סט ט מיי' שם טוש"ע שם סעיף יב:

ע י כ מיי' שם טוש"ע שם סעיף יג:

עא ל מיי' פי"ח מהל' מכירה הל' ט סמג לאוין קע טוש"ע ח"מ סי' רכח סעיף כ [ודלא כר"ן]:

**רבינו חננאל**

מתני' המפקיד פירות אצל חבירו הרי זה יוציא לו חסרונות לחטים ולאורז ט' חצאי קבין לכור. ואוקימנא באורז קלוף תנא וכן לכל כור וכור וכן לכל שנה ושנה. וקיימא לן כתנא קמא דמתני' והוא שעירבן בין פירותיו ומסתפק מהן ואינו יודע כמה הוציא לברר החסרון אבל יחד לו קרן זוית אומר לו הרי שלך לפניך: **פיס' ר' יהודה אומר אם היתה מדה מרובה לא יוציא לו חסרונות מפני שמותירות** ותני עלה בד"א שמדד לו בימי הגרנות שהפירות יבשין מאד שהחום מייבשן ומחזירן לו בימות הגרנות זהו שמוציא לו חסרונות אבל אם מחזירן לו בימות הגשמים אין מוציא לו חסרונות מפני שאויר הגשמים מלחלחן ומתנפחות ונמצאו מותירות. הוה עובדא שמילאו כדא בימות הגרנות חטים וכשהגיעו ימות הגשמים נתנפחו בכדא והיה פי הכדא סתום ונתבקעה הכדא איבעית אימא משום איצצא: **מתני' יוציא לו שתות ליין ר' יהודה אומר חומש.** ולא פליגי במקומו של ת"ק היו מכסין פי הדנא בשעוה ולא היה א) מוצין לפיכך מוציא לו שתות בחסרון. ב) פי' גרגישתא שם העפר שעושין ממנו כלי חרס כגון הדנא וכיוצא בה. יש עפר מוצין ויש עפר שאינו מוצין. באתריה דרב יהודה רמו [מ' ותמני] כוזי בדנא וכו' פי' במקומו של רב יהודה היו נותנין ג) טפיחין של יין בחבית והיו קונין החבית והיין שבתוכו ו' זוזים וכאשר היה היין מתיישן ושוקעין שמריו בתחתיתו היה מצוה רב יהודה לקונים למכור ו' טפיחין לזוז ל"ו טפיחים בו' זוזין והן דמי כל החבית נשארו י'

**חשק שלמה על ר"ח**

א) קלת נראה מזה דרבינו לא גרס ולא מייץ טפי רק ולא מייץ והא דמוליא לו שתות לאו משום דבלע ועי' בחדושי הריטב"א ובשמ"ק ודו"ק. ב) נראה דחסר כאן ול"ל אבע"א בגרגישתא פי' גרגישתא וכו'. ג) נ"ל היו טמנין מ"ח טפיחין של יין בחבית וכו' והיין שבתוכו בששה זוזים וכאשר וכו' למכור ששה טפיחין בזוז ל"ו טפיחים בששה זוזים והן דמי כל החביות נשארו י"ב טפיחים כצ"ל וכ"ה בשמ"ק כאן בהעתקת לשון רבינו.

דל

*SHOMER*] RETURNED it TO HIM IN "THE SEASON OF THE GRANARY." אֲבָל מָדַד לוֹ בִּימוֹת הַגּוֹרֶן – BUT if [THE OWNER] MEASURED OUT the produce TO [THE *SHOMER*] IN "THE SEASON OF THE GRANARY," וְהֶחֱזִיר לוֹ בִּימוֹת הַגְּשָׁמִים – AND [THE *SHOMER*] RETURNED it TO HIM IN THE RAINY SEASON, אֵינוֹ יוֹצִיא לוֹ חִסָּרוֹן – HE DOES NOT DEDUCT anything for DEPLETION, מִפְּנֵי שֶׁמּוֹתִירוֹת – BECAUSE IT EXPANDS by absorbing moisture in the rainy season, and this added volume makes up for the decrease.[29]

The Gemara questions this explanation:

אָמַר לֵיהּ רַב פָּפָּא לְאַבַּיֵי – **Rav Pappa said to Abaye:** אִם כֵּן – **If** this is **so,** that produce expands to such an extent in the rainy season, לִפְקַע כַּדָּא – **a** sealed **barrel** that was filled with dried grain **should burst** in the rainy season as the grain expands!

The Gemara gives two answers:

הֲוָה עוּבְדָא וּפְקַע כַּדָּא – Indeed, **there was a case in which** such **a barrel burst!**

אִיבָּעֵית אֵימָא – Or, **if you prefer, answer** that such barrels do not burst מִשּׁוּם אִיצְצָא – **because they are pressed** together. Since the grains are packed together tightly, they do not absorb moisture and swell.

## Mishnah

This Mishnah continues the discussion begun in the previous Mishnah, listing the amounts that a *shomer* may deduct from stored wine and oil:[30]

יוֹצִיא לוֹ שְׁתוּת לַיַּיִן – **With regard to wine, [a** ***shomer*****] deducts a sixth,** for this proportion of wine is absorbed by the barrels over time.[31] רַבִּי יְהוּדָה אוֹמֵר – **R' Yehudah says:** חוֹמֶשׁ – **A fifth** is deducted from wine.[32]

The Mishnah now discusses oil:

יוֹצִיא לוֹ שְׁלֹשָׁה לוּגִּין שֶׁמֶן לְמֵאָה – **[A** ***shomer*****] deducts three** ***logs*** **of oil** from **each hundred:** לוֹג וּמֶחֱצָה שְׁמָרִים – **one-and-a-half** ***logs*** to account for the **sediment** that has settled out of the deposited oil, לוֹג וּמֶחֱצָה בֶּלַע – **and one-and-a-half** ***logs*** to account for the oil **that was absorbed** into the walls of its container. אִם הָיָה שֶׁמֶן מְזוּקָק – **If the** deposited **oil was refined,** i.e. pure, אֵינוֹ יוֹצִיא לוֹ שְׁמָרִים – **[the** ***shomer*****] does not deduct anything for sediment,** because pure oil contains no sediment. אִם הָיוּ קַנְקַנִּים יְשָׁנִים – **Also, if the jugs** in which the oil was stored **were old,** אֵינוֹ יוֹצִיא לוֹ בֶּלַע – **he does not deduct anything for absorption,** because such jugs are already saturated, and do not absorb more oil.[33]

According to the next view, the rule that 1.5 percent of standard, unrefined oil is sediment also applies to sales: רַבִּי יְהוּדָה אוֹמֵר – **R' Yehudah says:** אַף הַמּוֹכֵר שֶׁמֶן מְזוּקָק לַחֲבֵירוֹ כָּל יְמוֹת הַשָּׁנָה – **Also, if someone sells refined oil to his fellow,** and agrees to provide him with oil a little at a time **throughout the year,**[34] הֲרֵי זֶה מְקַבֵּל עָלָיו – in such a case, **[the buyer] accepts upon himself** לוֹג וּמֶחֱצָה שְׁמָרִים לְמֵאָה – **one-and-a-half** ***logs*** **of sediment for** each **one hundred** *logs* of oil he purchased. That is, the buyer cannot demand 100 *logs* of refined oil, but must accept a total of only 98 ½ *logs* of refined oil; and the rest of the purchase is made up with sediment.[35]

## Gemara

The Gemara explains the difference between the opinions of the Tanna Kamma and R' Yehudah concerning the deduction for wine:

וְלֹא פְּלִיגֵי – In fact, **they do not disagree.** מַר כִּי אַתְרֵיהּ – The opinion of one **master reflects** the circumstances present in **his locale,** וּמַר כִּי אַתְרֵיהּ – **and** the opinion of the other **master reflects** the custom of **his locale.**

The Gemara explains:

בְּאַתְרֵיהּ דְּמַר – **In the locale of** this **master** [the Tanna Kamma], חָפוּ בְּקִירָא – **they coated** the insides of their barrels **with wax,** וְלָא מָיְיץ טְפֵי – **and they did not absorb so much.** In such barrels, the wine suffers a loss of only one-sixth through absorption. בְּאַתְרֵיהּ דְּמַר – But **in the locale of** the other **master** [R' Yehudah], חָפוּ בְּכוּפְרָא – **they coated** the insides of their barrels **with pitch,** וּמָיְיץ טְפֵי – **which absorbs more.** In such barrels, one-fifth of the wine is absorbed.

The Gemara offers an alternative explanation of the difference between the Tanna Kamma and R' Yehudah:

אִיבָּעֵית אֵימָא – Or, **if you prefer, say** מִשּׁוּם גַּרְגִּישְׁתָּא – that the difference between them was **due to the** different types of **clay** used for making barrels in their respective locales. הָא מָיְיצָא טְפֵי – **This** type of clay, the type used in R' Yehudah's locale, **absorbs a lot;** וְהָא לָא מָיְיצָא טְפֵי – **but the other** type of clay, i.e. the type used in the Tanna Kamma's locale, **does not absorb** so **much.**

The Gemara cites a related incident:

בְּאַתְרֵיהּ דְּרַב יְהוּדָה – **In the locale of Rav Yehudah,**[36] רָמוּ אַרְבְּעִים וְתַמְנֵי כּוּזֵי בְּדַנָּא – **they would pour forty-eight** ***kuz***[37] of wine **into** such **a barrel,** אָזִיל דַּנָּא בְּשִׁיתָּא זוּזֵי – **and** at harvest time **a barrel sold for six** ***zuz.*** פָּרֵיס רַב יְהוּדָה – **Rav Yehudah,** who was a storekeeper, bought such barrels for six *zuz* each, and then **sold** the wine from the barrel שִׁיתָּא שִׁיתָּא בְּזוּזָא – at the price of each **six** ***kuz*** **for a** ***zuz.***

NOTES

29. If the *shomer* returns what appears to be the same amount he received, he is actually returning less, because the volume of moistened grain has increased. Therefore, he is not entitled to deduct anything more.

30. [As in the previous Mishnah,] these deductions are made only if the *shomer* mixed the wine or oil with his own (*Rashi*). If the produce was stored separately, the *shomer* simply returns it as it is.

31. *Rashi; see Rashash.*

32. The reason for the difference between the Tanna and R' Yehudah's views is given in the Gemara.

33. Unlike the deductions discussed in the previous Mishnah, which are made per year, the deductions for wine and oil are made only once. The reason is that once the sediment has settled and the walls of the container have absorbed enough to become saturated, no more wine or oil will be lost. The commentators discuss how long the wine and oil must be in storage for these one-time deductions to apply (see *Maharam Schif* et al., cited by *Otzar Mefarshei HaTalmud*).

34. In this case, neither party specified that the sale would consist of refined oil (*Shitah Mekubetzes;* see *Rashi* here and to 40b ד״ה הא דשקל and ד״ה מותר לערב). However, as the seller dispenses the oil, he takes it from the top of his barrels, where the oil is pure (see *Rashi* here). So, as a practical matter, the seller is *delivering* refined oil.

35. Since the seller did not say that he was selling refined oil, he is entitled to supply oil that is mixed with the standard amount of sediment (1.5 percent). But since the oil he is supplying is in fact sediment-free, he has to provide only 98.5 percent of the agreed amount. [See below, 40b, for the Sages' dissenting view.]

36. This refers to Rav Yehudah the Amora, not Rabbi Yehudah (abbreviated to R' Yehudah) the Tanna.

37. A *kuz* is a small measure that was used in Rav Yehudah's locale (*Rashi*).

וכן אמר רבה השביחו לאמצע א"ל אביי מי דמי התם גדולים גבי קטנים ידעי וקא מחלי הכא מי ידע דליחיל אגלגל מלתא ומטא לקמיה דרבי אמי [א]אמר להו גדולה מזו אמרו שמין להם כארים השתא דידיה לא יהבינן ליה אהדרוה [ה]הא לקמיה דרב חסדא אמר להו מי דמי התם ברשות נחית הכא לאו ברשות נחית ועוד קטן הוא ואין מורידין קרוב לנכסי קטן [ב]אהדרוה לקמיה דרבי אמי אמר להו לא סיימוה קמי דקטן הוא:

מתני' [ג]המפקיד פירות אצל חבירו הרי זה יוציא לו חסרונות לחטים ולאורז תשעה חצאי קבין לכור לשעורין ולדוחן תשעה קבין לכור לכוסמין ולזרע פשתן שלש סאין לכור הכל לפי המדה והכל לפי הזמן א"ר יוחנן בן נורי וכי מה אכפת להן לעכברין והלא אוכלות בין מהרבה ובין מקמעא אלא אינו יוציא לו חסרונות אלא לכור אחד בלבד רבי יהודה אומר אם היתה מדה מרובה אינו מוציא לו חסרונות מפני שמותירות: גמ' אורז טובא חסר אמר רבה בר בר חנה א"ר יוחנן [ד]באורז קלוף שנו: לכוסמין ולזרע פשתן ג' סאין לכור (וכו'): א"ר יוחנן א"ר חייא זרע [ה]פשתן בגבעולין שנו תניא נמי הכי לכוסמין ולזרע פשתן בגבעולין [ו]ולאורז שאינו קלוף שלשה סאין לכור: הכל לפי המדה וכו': [ז]תנא כן לכל כור וכור וכן לכל שנה ושנה: א"ר יוחנן בן נורי וכו': תניא אמרו לו לרבי יוחנן הרבה אובדות מהן הרבה מתפזרות מהן תנא בד"א שעירבן עם פירותיו אבל יחד לו קרן זוית אומר לו הרי שלך לפניך וכי עירבן עם פירותיו מאי הוי ליחזי לדידיה כמה הויין במסתפק מהם וליחזי כמה אסתפק [ח]דלא [ג]ידעי כמה אסתפק: ר"י אומר אם היתה וכו': כמה מדה מרובה אמר רבה בר בר חנה א"ר יוחנן עשרה כורין תניא נמי הכי כמה מדה מרובה עשרה כורין תני תנא קמיה דרב נחמן בד"א שמדד לו מתוך גורנו והחזיר לו מתוך גורנו אבל מדד לו מתוך גורנו והחזיר לו מתוך ביתו אינו יוציא לו חסרונות מפני שמותירות א"ל וכי בשופטני עסקינן דיהבי בביילא רבא ושקלי בביילא זוטא דלמא בימות הגורן קאמרת [ט]בד"א שמדד לו בימות הגורן והחזיר לו בימות הגורן אבל מדד לו בימות הגורן והחזיר לו בימות הגשמים אינו יוציא לו חסרון מפני שמותירות א"ל רב פפא לאביי א"כ לפקע כדא הוה עובדא ופקע כדא אבע"א משום איצצא: מתני' [י]יוציא לו שתות ליין ר"י אומר חומש [כ]יוציא לו שלשה לוגין שמן למאה לוג ומחצה שמרים לוג ומחצה בלע אם היה שמן מזוקק אינו יוציא לו שמרים אם היו קנקנים ישנים אינו יוציא לו בלע ר"י אומר אף [ל]המוכר [ג]שמן מזוקק לחבירו כל ימות השנה הרי זה מקבל עליו לוג ומחצה שמרים למאה: גמ' ולא פליגי [ד]מר כי אתריה ומר כי אתריה באתריה דמר חפו בקירא ולא מייץ טפי באתריה דמר חפו בכופרא ומייץ טפי איבעית אימא משום גרגישתא הא מייצא טפי והא לא מייצא טפי באתריה דרב יהודה רמו ארבעים ותמני כוזי בדנא אזיל דנא בשיתא זוזי פרים רב יהודה שיתא שיתא בזוזא

## רש"י

וכן אמר רבה השביחו לאמצע. לא גרסינן שאין זה לשון גמרא להביא דברי האמוראים סיוע למשנה ועוד רבה תלמידיה דרב חסדא הוה והיכי אמר רב חסדא שמעתא משמיה ואי גרס ליה וכן אמר רב גרסינן שהיה רבו של רב חסדא משום דאיכא למ"ד בבבא בתרא (דף קמג.) לא שנו אלא ששבחו נכסים מחמת נכסים אבל שבחו מחמת עצמן של אחים השביחו לעצמן אמרה רב חסדא להא דרב הכא למימר דלית לן בהיא שמעתא אלא אפילו השביחו מחמת טורחן של משביחין כי הכא דשתל פרדס השביחו לאמצע: ידעו. אלו שיטלו חלקם: מי ידע. שיש לו אחים: גדולה מזו. קרוב היורד לנכסי שבוי שאם יבאו הבעלים יטלו שלהם: אמרו שמין להם כאריס הכא דידיה לא יהבינן ליה. בתמיה זה שעשה והשביחן לדעת עצמו לא יהבי' ליה כאריס בחלק השני: ברשות ב"ד נחית. דמורידין קרוב לנכסי שבוי: הכא לא ברשות נחית. כשירד זה לתוכו לא נמלך בב"ד: ועוד. אם בא לימלך לא היו מורידין אותו דהאי אחיו קטן הוה ואין מורידין קרוב לנכסי קטן: מתני' הרי זה יוציא לו חסרונות. כשמחזירם לו יפחות כמה הם רגילים לחסור ובגמ' מוקי לה בשעירבן עם פירותיו: אורז. מי"ל: [ט]דוחן. פטי"ל ודומה לאורז: הכל לפי המדה. וכן לכל כור וכור: הכל לפי הזמן. שמניחן בידו לכל שנה ושנה יניח לו כך: ר' יוחנן בן נורי אמר. אהכל לפי המדה פליג: אם היתה מדה מרובה. שהפקיד אצלו הרבה ובגמרא מפרש י' כורים לא יוציא לו חסרונות מפני שהם מותירות שבימות הגורן כשמפקיד החטין יבשין ובימות הגשמים כשמחזיר נופחות ובאכילת עכברים אינן נחסרים כל כך לכל כור וכור דכולי האי לא אכלי עכברים מי' כורין הלכך נפיחתו משלמת חסרון המגיע לשני כורים או שלשה שהעכברים אוכלין: גמ' זרע פשתן בגבעולין. חסר כל כך לפי שהגבעולין מתייבשין ונופלים והרוח מנשבתן אבל זרע פשתן נקי אינו חסר כ"כ: לכל כור וכור. פירוש דמתניתין הוא: ליחזי דידיה כמה הוו כו'. וידע כמה חסרו ויטול על של חבירו כפי חשבון: מדת הגורן. היתה יתירה על של בתים: בשופטני. שוטים: בביילא. במדה: בימות הגורן. סמוך לגורן שנתייבשו בחמה: והחזיר לו בימות הגשמים. חזרו ונתפחו מלחלוחית הגשם והקור: א"כ. שדרכו לתפוח: לפקע כדא. כשממלאין כד חיטין או שעורין בימות הגורן וגפין את הכד יפקע בימות הגשמים מחמת תפיחת התבואה: איצצא. דוחק מתוך שהם במקום צר נדחקו יחד ואין תפוחין: מתני' ליין. אם הפקיד אצלו יין ועירבו עם יינו הקנקנים בולעין שתות: אף המוכר כו'. כשם שאמרו במפקיד כן אמרו במוכר שהמוכר שמן לחבירו ונותן לו מתוך חביותיו כשהוא מסתפק תמיד והוא מזוקק הרי הלוקח מקבל עליו לפחות לו לוג ומחצה מחמת שמרים: למאה. למאה לוג: גמ' חפו בקירא. טחו החביות מבפנים בשעוה כדרך שעושין אנו בזפת: כופרא. זפת: גרגישתא. קרקע שעושין ממנה החביות ארזיל"א בלע"ז: הא. באתריה דר"י מייץ טפי מהאי דאתריה דתנא קמא: באתריה דרב יהודה. מילתא באפי נפשיה היא ולאו אמתניתין קאי: רמו ארבעין ותמניא כוזי בדנא. מדה קטנה היתה במקומו שארבעים ושמונה ממלאין את החבית: אזיל דנא בשיתא. בששה זוזים היתה נמכרת ביחד בימות הבציר: פרים ליה רב יהודה שיתא שיתא בזוזא. נעשה רב יהודה חנווני והיה מוכרן שש כוזי בזוז:

## תוספות

וכן אמר רבה: גרס. רש"י גרס וכן אמר רב ופליג אמ"ד בפ' מי שמת (ב"ב דף קמג: ושם ד"ה לא) נכסים ששבחו מחמת עצמן של אחין השבח לעצמן וקאמר דאפי' שבחו מחמת טרחם של משביחין כי הכא דשתל פרדיסא השביחו לאמצע והוי תימה שחולק רבא על רב דהתם רבא קאמר ולא מייתי התם מילתיה דרב ונראה דגרס רבה וכן בספר ר"ת ולא מדברי רב חסדא הוא (א) שהגמ' מביא שמעשה כיוצא בזה בא לפני רבה ופסק דהשביחו לאמצע כמו רב חסדא והביאו הגמרא משום קושית אביי דא"ל אביי לרבה מי דמי כו' ולא חשש רבה מקושיותיו ודן דהשביחו לאמצע: אגלגל מלתא. פסק של רב חסדא ומטא לקמיה דרבי אמי: וכי מה אכפת להו לעכברים. וטעמייהו דרבנן מפרש בירושלמי הני עכברי רשיעי ניהו כד חמיין עיבור לא מסתפייהו דאכלי אלא קריין לחברייהו דאכלי עמהון והא דאמרינן בגמרא אמרו לו הרבה אובדות מהם הרבה מתפזרות מהם י"ל דלדבריו דרבי יוחנן קאמר אפילו לית לך טעמא דמפרש בירושלמי מ"מ הרבה אובדות מהם: אלא לכור בלבד. וא"ת אם כן בפחות מכור נמי יוציא כמו לכור וי"ל דאין להם ריוח להטמן בתוכה ומ"מ לפי חשבון הראוי להתחסר יוציא דאי אפשר שלא יתחסרו: ולאורז שאינו קלוף ג' סאין לכור. וא"ת ולמאי לא חשיב במתניתין אורז שאינו קלוף עם זרע פשתן כיון דאית להו חד שיעורא וי"ל דפשוט לו דבאורז מתחסר כל כך וברישא גבי אורז קלוף לא חשיב זרע פשתן קלוף דשמא לינס חלוק: מדה מרובה י' כורין. וא"ת אפי' ב' כורין או ג' מתנפחין לפי חשבון החסרונות העולה להם וי"ל דבי' כורין עולה להם הנפוח חסרון של כור אחד ולא יוציא להם חסרונות היינו כל החסרון דחסרון של כור אחד לא יוציא והכי נקט י' כורים לאפוקי פחות: אל

דל

## מסורת הש"ס

א) [תוי"ט, יעב"ץ], ב) [צ"ל ידע, יעב"ץ]. ג) מהרש"ל שמן לחבירו מזוקק כל, ד) [פסחים ג. וש"נ], ה) [עי' פירש"י ברכות לז.], ו) נ"א לן, ז) נ"א בחיבה.

## הגהות הב"ח

(א) תוס' ד"ה וכן וכו' מדברי רב חסדא הוא אלא שהגמרא:

## לעזי רש"י

מי"ל. פירוש "הירזש". פטי"ל. פירוש "פענכעל הירזש". ארדלי"א. פירוש טיט אדום (רמב"ם שבת פ"ח מ"ה), קרקע שעושין ממנה החביות.

## ליקוטי רש"י

שמין להם כארים. אם יבואו הבעלים יטלו אלו בשבח קרקעות ופירות כמנהג אריסי המקום [לעיל לט.]. ולדוחן. פנ"ך [ברכות לז.]. לכוסמין. איספילטא בלע"ז [פסחים לה.]. בגבעולין. גבעול הוא קנה האמצעי שהזרע בראשו כקנבוס ופשתן [סוכה יג.]. ומייץ. ויונק [שבת קלד.]. גרגישתא. ארזיל"א במעבה האדמה (מלכים א ז) מתרגמינן בגרגישתא דארעא [יבמות קו:]. אדמה [כתובות ס:].

## עין משפט נר מצוה

סז א ב מיי' פ"ט מהל' נחלות הל' ד ועיין בהשגות ובמגיד משנה סמג עשין לז טוש"ע ח"מ סי' רפז סעיף ג וע"ש:

סח ג ד ה ו ז ח מיי' פ"ה מהל' שאלה ופקדון הל' ה סמג עשין פח טוש"ע ח"מ סי' רלב סעיף יא:

סט ט מיי' שם טוש"ע שם סעיף יב:

ע י כ מיי' שם טוש"ע שם סעיף יג:

עא ל מיי' פי"ח מהל' מכירה הל' ט סמג לאוין קט טוש"ע ח"מ סי' רכח סעיף כ [ודלא כר"ין]:

## רבינו חננאל

מתני' המפקיד פירות אצל חבירו הרי זה יוציא לו חסרונות לחטים ולאורז ט' חצאי קבין לכור. ואוקימנא באורז קלוף תנא וכן לכל כור וכור וכן לכל שנה ושנה. וקיימא לן כתנא קמא דמתני' והוא שעירבן בין פירותיו ומסתפק מהן ואינו יודע כמה הוציא לברר החסרון אבל יחד לו קרן זוית אומר לו הרי שלך לפניך: פיס' ר' יהודה אומר אם היתה מדה מרובה לא יוציא לו חסרונות מפני שמותירות ותני עלה בד"א שמדד לו בימי הגרנות שהפירות יבשין מאד שהחום מייבשן ומחזירן לו בימות הגרנות זהו שמוציא לו חסרונות אבל אם מחזירן לו בימות הגשמים אין מוציא לו חסרונות מפני שאויר הגשמים מלחלחן ומתנפחות ונמצאו מותירות. הוה עובדא שמילאו כדא בימות הגרנות חטים וכשהגיעו ימות הגשמים נתנפחו בכדא והיה פי הכדא סתום ונתבקעה הכדא איבעית אימא משום איצצא: מתני' יוציא לו שתות ליין ר' יהודה אומר חומש. ולא פליגי במקומו של ת"ק היו מכסין פי הדנא בשעוה ולא היה א) מוצין לפיכך מוציא לו שתות בחסרון. ב) פי' גרגישתא שם העפר שעושין ממנו כלי חרס כגון הדנא וכיוצא בה. יש עפר מוצין ויש עפר שאינו מוצין. באתריה דרב יהודה רמו [מ' ותמני] כוזי בדנא וכו' פי' במקומו של רב יהודה היו נותנין ג) טפיחין של יין בחבית והיו קונין החבית והיין שבתוכו ו' זוזים וכאשר היה היין מתיישן ושוקעין שמריו בתחתיתו היה מצוה רב יהודה לקונים למכור ו' טפיחין לזוז ל"ו טפיחים בו' זוזין והן דמי כל החבית נשארו י"

## חשק שלמה על ר"ח

א) קצת נראה מזה דרבינו לא גרס ולא מייץ טפי רק ולא מייץ והא דמוציא לו שתות לאו משום דבלע ועי' בחדושי הריטב"א ובשמ"ק ודו"ק. ב) נראה דחסר כאן וצ"ל אבע"א בגרגישתא פי' גרגישתא וכו'. ג) צ"ל היו נותנין מ"ח טפיחין של יין בחבית וכו' והיין שבתוכו בששה זוזים וכאשר וכו' ולמכור בששה טפיחין לזוז ל"ו טפיחים בששה זוזים והן דמי כל החבית ונשארו י"ב טפיחים לאו וכ"ה בשמ"ק כאן בהעתקת לשון רבינו.

hange based on the amount of produce given to the *shomer.* The 'ollowing Baraisa teaches the Tanna Kamma's response to R' Yochanan ben Nuri's argument:

תַּנְיָא – **A Baraisa taught:** אָמְרוּ לוֹ לְרַבִּי יוֹחָנָן – [THE SAGES] RESPONDED TO R' YOCHANAN ben Nuri: הַרְבֵּה אוֹבְדוֹת מֵהֶן – In addition to the amount eaten by mice, MUCH [OF THE PRODUCE] IS RUINED (by spoilage), הַרְבֵּה מִתְפַּזְּרוֹת מֵהֶן – and MUCH OF IT IS SCATTERED (by wind or storms). The amount of produce lost due to these factors will certainly increase if a larger total amount of produce was deposited.[22]

The following Baraisa qualifies our Mishnah's basic law that when a *shomer* returns produce that was entrusted to him, he may return less than he received:

תָּנָא – **A Tanna taught** in a Baraisa: בַּמֶּה דְּבָרִים אֲמוּרִים – WHEN WAS THIS RULING STATED? שֶׁעֵירְבָן עִם פֵּירוֹתָיו – It applies WHERE [THE *SHOMER*] MIXED [THE PRODUCE HE WAS GIVEN TO GUARD] together WITH HIS OWN PRODUCE, and we do not know which produce belongs to the *shomer* and which to the depositor.[23] אֲבָל יִחֵד לוֹ קֶרֶן זָוִית – BUT IF THE [*SHOMER*] DESIGNATED A CORNER specifically FOR the produce of [THE DEPOSITOR], אוֹמֵר לוֹ – HE SAYS TO [THE DEPOSITOR], הֲרֵי שֶׁלְּךָ לְפָנֶיךָ – "BEHOLD, WHAT IS YOURS IS BEFORE YOU!" That is, he returns the produce as it is, without deducting anything from it.

The Gemara asks:

וְכִי עֵירְבָן עִם פֵּירוֹתָיו מַאי הָוֵי – **But if he did mix [the entrusted produce] with his** own **produce, what** difference should that make? לֵיחֱזֵי לְדִידֵיהּ כַּמָּה הֲוַיִין – **Let him see how much of his** own produce **was** originally present! On the basis of that information, he can calculate the proportion of the mixture that belonged to the depositor. That proportion of whatever is left should then be returned to the depositor, and there should be no need to make any other calculations.[24] – ? –

The Gemara answers:

בְּמִסְתַּפֵּק מֵהֶם – The Mishnah refers to a case **where [the custodian] was supplying himself from [the produce]** while it was stored there. Therefore, there is no way to know how much of the *shomer's* own produce remains, for his proportion of the amount that is there now is not the same as his proportion of the original amount.

The Gemara persists:

וְלֵיחֱזֵי כַּמָּה אִסְתַּפַּק – **Then let him see how much he took for himself!** Adding that quantity to the amount that remains will tell us what the current total would have been had the *shomer* not taken anything. The depositor's portion of what remains can then be calculated as a fraction of this total, without any deductions necessary. – ? –

The Gemara answers:

דְּלָא יָדְעֵי כַּמָּה אִסְתַּפַּק – The Mishnah speaks of a case **where [the *shomer*] does not know how much he used for himself.** In such a case, there is no way to calculate the owner's portion of what remains, and the only way we can determine what to give the depositor is by deducting the typical amount of decrease from the quantity that the *shomer* received.

The Gemara discusses R' Yehudah's opinion:

רַבִּי יְהוּדָה אוֹמֵר – R' YEHUDAH SAYS: אִם הָיְתָה וכו' – IF the amount of produce given to the *shomer* WAS large **etc.,** the *shomer* does not deduct anything at all for depletion, because a large quantity expands by an amount that is equal to the amount that is lost.

The Gemara defines what is considered "a large quantity" in this context:

כַּמָּה מִדָּה מְרוּבָּה – **How much is "a large quantity"?** אָמַר רַבָּה בַּר בַּר חָנָה אָמַר רַבִּי יוֹחָנָן – **Rabbah bar bar Chanah said in the name of R' Yochanan:** עֲשָׂרָה כּוֹרִין – **Ten** ***kors.***[25] תַּנְיָא נַמִּי הָכִי – **This was also taught in a Baraisa:** כַּמָּה מִדָּה מְרוּבָּה – HOW MUCH IS "A LARGE QUANTITY"? עֲשָׂרָה כּוֹרִין – TEN *KORS.*

The following Baraisa clarifies R' Yehudah's position:

תָּנֵי תַּנָּא קַמֵּיהּ דְּרַב נַחְמָן – **A teacher of Baraisos taught** the following Baraisa **in the presence of Rav Nachman:** בַּמֶּה דְּבָרִים אֲמוּרִים – WHEN WAS THE Mishnah's RULING, that a *shomer* makes deductions from produce, STATED? שֶׁמָּדַד לוֹ מִתּוֹךְ גּוֹרְנוֹ – It applies in a case WHERE [THE OWNER] MEASURED OUT the produce TO [THE *SHOMER*] FROM HIS GRANARY, using the measures that are normally used in a granary, וְהֶחֱזִיר לוֹ מִתּוֹךְ גּוֹרְנוֹ – AND [THE *SHOMER*] RETURNED it TO HIM FROM HIS GRANARY, using the same type of measures. אֲבָל מָדַד לוֹ מִתּוֹךְ גּוֹרְנוֹ – BUT if [THE OWNER] MEASURED OUT the produce TO [THE *SHOMER*] FROM HIS GRANARY, using the type of measures that are normally used in a granary, וְהֶחֱזִיר לוֹ מִתּוֹךְ בֵּיתוֹ – AND [THE *SHOMER*] RETURNED it TO HIM FROM HIS HOUSE, using the type of measures that are normally used in a house, which are smaller than those used in a granary,[26] אֵינוֹ יוֹצִיא לוֹ חֶסְרוֹנוֹת – HE DOES NOT DEDUCT anything for DEPLETION, מִפְּנֵי שֶׁמּוֹתִירוֹת – BECAUSE when smaller measures are used, the measure of the produce INCREASES.[27] This increase makes up for the depletion.[28]

This understanding of the Baraisa is questioned:

אָמַר לֵיהּ – **Rav Nachman said to him** [the teacher of Baraisos]: וְכִי בְּשׁוּפְטָנֵי עָסְקִינַן – **Are we dealing with fools,** דְּיָהֲבֵי בְּבַיְילָא רַבָּא – **who give** produce to a *shomer* **in big measures,** וְשָׁקְלֵי בְּבַיְילָא זוּטָא – **and take** it back **in small measures?!** Why would any depositor agree to this?

Rav Nachman suggests a different understanding of the Baraisa:

דִּלְמָא בִּימוֹת הַגּוֹרֶן קָאָמְרַתְּ – **Perhaps you mean "in the season of the granary."** That is, when the Baraisa says that the *shomer* returned the produce "from the granary," it refers not to the *measures* used in a granary, but to the *season* when produce is put in the granary (that is, at the end of the summer, after the produce has been dried by the sun). Accordingly, the Baraisa is to be understood as follows: בַּמֶּה דְּבָרִים אֲמוּרִים – WHEN WAS THE MISHNAH'S RULING, that a *shomer* makes deductions from produce, STATED? שֶׁמָּדַד לוֹ בִּימוֹת הַגּוֹרֶן – It applies in a case WHERE [THE OWNER] MEASURED OUT the produce TO [THE *SHOMER*] IN "THE SEASON OF THE GRANARY," וְהֶחֱזִיר לוֹ בִּימוֹת הַגּוֹרֶן – AND [THE

NOTES

22. Thus, the Sages agree that mice eat only a certain amount; they increase the amount the *shomer* may deduct when he received more produce because the amount lost through other factors will increase.

23. A *shomer* is not allowed to mix his own produce with the depositor's. Our Mishnah discusses the law that applies in the case of a *shomer* who violated this prohibition (*Rambam, Hil. She'eilah* 5:5).

24. For example, if he accepted 3 *kors* of produce for safekeeping and 1 *kor* of his own was mixed with them, three-quarters of the total belongs to the depositor; therefore, the *shomer* should simply return three-quarters of whatever produce is left to the depositor.

25. See note 18.

26. The household measures were known by the same names as the granary measures (*kor, kav,* etc.), but they were actually smaller.

27. Obviously, produce that is a certain number of granary-*kors* will be a larger number of the smaller household-*kors.*

28. If, for example, a *shomer* who has been entrusted with ten granary-*kors* were to return ten household-*kors*, he will have returned less than the original volume (see previous note). Therefore, any further reduction would be uncalled for. [The Gemara will immediately wonder why the depositor would consent to such an arrangement.]

וכן אמר רבה השביחו לאמצע א"ל אביי מי דמי התם גדולים גבי קטנים ידעי וקא מחלי הכא מי ידע דליחיל אגלגל מלתא ומטא לקמיה דרבי אמי [א]אמר להו גדולה מזו אמרו שמין להם כארים השתא דידיה לא יהבינן ליה אהדרוה [א)]הא לקמיה דרב חסדא אמר להו מי דמי התם ברשות נחית הכא לאו ברשות נחית ועוד קטן הוא ואין מורידין קרוב לנכסי קטן [ב]אהדרוה לקמיה דרבי אמי אמר להו לא סיימוה קמי דקטן הוא: **מתני'** [ג]המפקיד פירות אצל חבירו הרי זה יוציא לו חסרונות לחטים ולאורז תשעה חצאי קבין לכור לשעורין ולדוחן תשעה קבין לכור לכוסמין ולזרע פשתן שלש סאין לכור הכל לפי המדה והכל לפי הזמן א"ר יוחנן בן נורי וכי מה אכפת להן לעכברין והלא אוכלות בין מהרבה ובין מקמעא אלא אינו יוציא לו חסרונות אלא לכור אחד בלבד רבי יהודה אומר אם היתה מדה מרובה אינו מוציא לו חסרונות מפני שמותירות: **גמ'** אורז טובא חסר אמר רבה בר בר חנה א"ר יוחנן [ד]באורז קלוף שנו: לכוסמין ולזרע פשתן ג' סאין לכור (וכו'): א"ר יוחנן א"ר חייא זרע [ה]פשתן בגבעולין שנו תניא נמי הכי לכוסמין ולזרע פשתן בגבעולין [ו]ולאורז שאינו קלוף שלשה סאין לכור: הכל לפי המדה וכו': [ז]תנא כן לכל כור וכור וכן לכל שנה ושנה: א"ר יוחנן בן נורי וכו': תניא אמרו לו לרבי יוחנן הרבה אובדות מהן הרבה מתפזרות מהן תנא בד"א שעירבן עם פירותיו אבל יחד לו קרן זוית אומר לו הרי שלך לפניך וכי עירבן עם פירותיו מאי הוי ליחזי לדידיה כמה הויין במספק מהם וליחזי כמה אסתפק [ח]דלא [ג)]ידעי כמה אסתפק: ר"י אומר אם היתה וכו': כמה מדה מרובה אמר רבה בר בר חנה א"ר יוחנן עשרה כורין תניא נמי הכי כמה מדה מרובה עשרה כורין תני תנא קמיה דרב נחמן בד"א שמדד לו מתוך גורנו והחזיר לו מתוך גורנו אבל מדד לו מתוך גורנו והחזיר לו מתוך ביתו אינו יוציא לו חסרונות מפני שמותירות א"ל וכי בשופטני עסקינן דיהבי בביילא רבא ושקלי בביילא זוטא דלמא בימות הגורן קאמרת [ט]בד"א שמדד לו בימות הגורן והחזיר לו בימות הגורן אבל מדד לו בימות הגורן והחזיר לו בימות הגשמים אינו יוציא לו חסרון מפני שמותירות א"ל רב פפא לאביי א"כ לפקע כדא הוה עובדא ופקע כדא אבע"א משום איצצא: **מתני'** [י]יוציא לו שתות ליין ר"י אומר חומש [כ]יוציא לו שלשה לוגין שמן למאה לוג ומחצה שמרים לוג ומחצה בלע אם היה שמן מזוקק אינו יוציא לו שמרים אם היו קנקנים ישנים אינו יוציא לו בלע ר"י אומר אף [ל]המוכר [ג)]שמן מזוקק לחבירו כל ימות השנה הרי זה מקבל עליו לוג ומחצה שמרים למאה: **גמ'** ולא פליגי [ד)]מר כי אתריה ומר כי אתריה באתריה דמר חפו בקירא ולא מייץ טפי באתריה דמר חפו בכופרא ומייץ טפי איבעית אימא משום גרגישתא הא מייצא טפי והא לא מייצא טפי באתריה דרב יהודה רמו ארבעים ותמני כוזי בדנא אזיל דנא בשיתא זוזי פרים רב יהודה שיתא שיתא בזוזא

וכן אמר רבה השביחו לאמצע. לא גרסינן שאין זה לשון גמרא להביא דברי האמוראים סיוע למשנה ועוד רבה תלמידיה דרב חסדא הוה והיכי אמר רב חסדא שמעתא משמיה ואי גרס ליה וכן אמר רב גרסינן שהיה רבו של רב חסדא משום דאיכא למ"ד בבבא בתרא (דף קמג:) לא שנו אלא ששבחו נכסים מחמת נכסים אבל שבחו מחמת עצמן של אחים השביחו לעצמן אמרה רב חסדא להא דרב הכא למימר דלית לן ההיא שמעתא אלא אפילו השביחו מחמת טורחן של משביחין כי הכא דשתל פרדס השביחו לאמצע: ידעי. אלו שיטלו חלקם: מי ידע. שיש לו אחים: גדולה מזו. קרוב היורד לנכסי שבוי שאם יבאו הבעלים יטלו שלהם: אמרו שמין להם כארים הכא דידיה לא יהבינן ליה. בתמיה זה שעשה והשביחן לדעת עצמו לא יהבי' ליה כארים בחלק השני: ברשות ב"ד נחתי. דמורידין קרוב לנכסי שבוי: הכא לא ברשות נחית. כשירד זה לתוכו לא נמלך בב"ד: ועוד. אם בא לימלך לא היו מורידין אותו דהא אחיו קטן הוה ואין מורידין קרוב לנכסי קטן: **מתני'** הרי זה יוציא לו חסרונות. כשיחזירם לו יפחות כמה הם רגילים לחסור ובגמ' מוקי לה בשעירבן עם פירותיו: אורז. מי"ל: [ה)]דוחן. פטי"ל ודומה לאורז: הכל לפי המדה. וכן לכל כור וכור: הכל לפי הזמן. שהניחן בידו לכל שנה ושנה יניח לו כך: ר' יוחנן בן נורי אמר. אהכל לפי המדה פליג: אם היתה מדה מרובה. שהפקיד אצלו הרבה ובגמרא מפרש י' כורים לא יוציא לו חסרונות מפני שהם מותירות שבימות הגורן כשמפקיד החיטין יבשין ובימות הגשמים כשמחזיר נופחות ובאכילת עכברים אינן נחסרים כל כך לכל כור וכור דכולי האי לא אכלי עכברים מי' כורין הלכך נפיחתו משלמת חסרון המגיע לשני כורים או שלשה שהעכברים אוכלין: **גמ'** זרע פשתן בגבעולין. חסר כל כך לפי שהגבעולין מתייבשין ונופלים והרוח מנשבתן אבל זרע פשתן נקי אינו חסר כ"כ: לכל כור וכור. פירוש דמתניתין הוא: ליחזי דידיה כמה הוו כו'. ויראה כמה חסרו ויטול על של חברו כפי חשבון: מדת הגורן. היתה יתירה על של בתים: בשופטני. שוטים: בביילא. במדה: בימות הגורן. סמוך ליובשן שנתייבשו בחמה: והחזיר לו בימות הגשמים. חזרו ונתפחו מלחלוחית הגשם והקור: א"כ. שדרכו לתפוח: לפקע כדא. כשממלאין כד חיטין או שעורין בימות הגורן וגפין את הכד יפקע בימות הגשמים מחמת תפיחת התבואה: איצצא. דוחק מתוך שהם במקום צר נדחקו יחד ואין תפוחין: **מתני'** ליין. אם הפקיד אצלו יין ועירבו עם יינו הקנקנים בולעין שתות: אף המוכר כו'. כשם שאמרו במפקיד כן אמרו במוכר שהמוכר שמן לחבירו ונותן לו מתוך חביותיו כשהוא מסתפק תמיד והוא מזוקק הרי הלוקח מקבל עליו לפחות לו לוג ומחצה מחמת שמרים: למאה. למאה לוג: **גמ'** חפו בקירא. טחו החביות מבפנים בשעוה כדרך שעושין או בזפת: כופרא. זפת: גרגישתא. קרקע שעושין ממנה החביות ארדלי"א בלע"ז: הא. באתריה דר"י מייץ טפי מההיא דאתריה דתנא קמא: באתריה דרב יהודה. מילתא באפי נפשיה היא ולאו אמתניתין קאי: רמו ארבעין ותמניא כוזי בדנא. מדה קטנה היתה במקומו שארבעים ושמונה ממלאין את החבית: אזיל דנא בשיתא. בששה זוזים היתה נמכרת ביחד בימות הבציר: פרים ליה רב יהודה שיתא שיתא בזוזא. נעשה רב יהודה חנווני והיה מוכרן שש כוזי בזוז:

וכן אמר רבה: גרס. רש"י גרס וכן אמר רב ופליג אמ"ד בפ' מי שמת (ב"ב דף קמג: ושם ד"ה לא) נכסים ששבחו מחמת עצמן של אחין השבח לעצמן וקאמר דאפי' שבחו מחמת טרחם של משביחין כי הכא דשתל פרדיסא השביחו לאמצע וחהו תימה שחולק רבא על רב דהתם רבא קאמר ולא מייתי התם מילתיה דרב ונראה דגרס רבה וכן בספר ר"ת ולא מדברי רב חסדא הוא (א) שהגמ' מביא שמעשה כיוצא בזה בא לפני רבה ופסק דהשביחו לאמצע כמו רב חסדא והביאו הגמרא משום קושית אביי דא"ל אביי לרבה מי דמי כו' ולא חשש רבה מקושיותיו ודן דהשביחו לאמצע: **אגלגל** מלתא. פסק של רב חסדא ומטא לקמיה דרבי אמי: **וכי** מה אכפת להו לעכברים. וטעמייהו דרבנן מפרש בירושלמי הני עכברי רשיעי ניהו כד חמיין עיבור לא מסתייהו דאכלי אלא קריין לחבריהון דאכלי עמהון והא דאמרינן בגמרא אמרו לו הרבה אובדות מהם הרבה מתפזרות מהם י"ל דלדבריו דרבי יוחנן קאמר אפילו לית [ו)]לך טעמא דמפרש בירושלמי מ"מ הרבה אובדות מהם: **אלא** לכור בלבד. וא"ת אם כן בפחות מכור נמי יוציא כמו לכור וי"ל דאין להם ריוח להטמן [ז)]בתוכה ומ"מ לפי חשבון הראוי להתחסר יוציא דאי אפשר שלא יתחסרו: **ולאורז** שאינו קלוף ג' סאין לכור. וא"ת ואמאי לא חשיב במתניתין אורז שאינו קלוף עם זרע פשתן כיון דאית להו חד שיעורא וי"ל דפשוט לו דבאורז תתחסר כל כך וברישא גבי אורז קלוף לא חשיב זרע פשתן קלוף דשמא דינם חלוק: **מדה** מרובה י' כורין. וא"ת אפי' ב' כורין או ג' מתנפחין לפי חשבון החסרונות העולה להם וי"ל דבי' כורין עולה להם הנפוח חסרון של כור אחד ולא יוציא להם חסרונות היינו כל החסרון דחסרון של כור אחד לא יוציא ולהכי נקט י' כורים לאפוקי פחות:



) [תו"כ, יעב"ץ], ב) [צ"ל רע, יעב"ץ]. ג) מהרש"ל שמן לחבירו מזוקק ל, ד) [פסחים ג. וש"נ], ) [עי' פירש"י ברכות ז.], ו) כ"א לן, ז) כ"א בתיבה.

## הגהות הב"ח

א) תוס' ד"ה וכן וכו' ודברי רב חסדא הוא אלא שהגמרא:

## לעזי רש"י

מי"ל. פירוש "הירוש". פטי"ל. פירוש "פענכעל הירוש". ארדלי"א. פירוש טיט אדום (רמב"ם שבת פ"ח מ"ה), קרקע שעושין ממנה החביות.

## ליקוטי רש"י

שמין להם כארים. אם יבואו הבעלים יטלו אלו כשבח קרקעות ופירות כמנהג אריסי המקום [לעיל לט.]. ולדוחן. פנ"ך [ברכות לז.]. לכוסמין. איספילטא בלע"ז [פסחים לה.]. בגבעולין. גבעול הוא קנה האמצעי שהזרע בראשו כקנבוס ופשתן [סוכה יג.]. ומייץ. ויונק [שבת קלד.]. גרגישתא. ארזיל"א במעבה האדמה (מלכים א ז) מתרגמינן בגרגישתא דארעא [יבמות קו:]. אדמה [כתובות ס:].

## עין משפט נר מצוה

סז א ב מיי' פ"ט מהל' נחלות הל' ד ועיין בהשגות ובמגיד משנה סמג עשין לו טוש"ע ח"מ סי' רפו סעיף ג וע"ש:

סח ג ד ה ו ז ח מיי' פ"ה מהל' שאלה ופקדון הל' ה סמג עשין פח טוש"ע ח"מ סי' רצב סעיף יא:

סט ט מיי' שם טוש"ע שם סעיף יב:

ע י כ מיי' שם טוש"ע שם סעיף יג:

עא ל מיי' פי"ח מהל' מכירה הל' ט סמג לאוין קע טוש"ע ח"מ סי' רכח סעיף כ [ודלא כר"ין]:

## רבינו חננאל

מתני' המפקיד פירות אצל חבירו הרי זה יוציא לו חסרונות לחטים ולאורז ט' חצאי קבין לכור. ואוקימנא באורז קלוף תנא וכן לכל כור וכור וכן לכל שנה ושנה. וקיימא לן כתנא קמא דמתני' והוא שעירבן בין פירותיו ומסתפק מהן ואינו יודע כמה הוציא לברר החסרון אבל יחד לו קרן זוית אומר לו הרי שלך לפניך: פיס' ר' יהודה אומר אם היתה מדה מרובה לא יוציא לו חסרונות מפני שמותירות ותני עלה בד"א שמדד לו בימי הגרנות שהפירות יבשין מאד שהחום מייבשן ומחזירן לו בימות הגרנות זהו שמוציא לו חסרונות אבל אם מחזירן לו בימות הגשמים אין מוציא לו חסרונות מפני שאויר הגשמים מלחלחן ומתנפחות ונמצאו מותירות. הוה עובדא שמילאו כדא בימות הגרנות חטים וכשהגיעו ימות הגשמים נתנפחו בכדא והיה פי הכדא סתום ונתבקעה הכדא איבעית אימא משום איצצא: מתני' יוציא לו שתות ליין ר' יהודה אומר חומש. ולא פליגי במקומו של ת"ק היו מכסין פי הדנא בשעוה ולא היה א) מוצין לפיכך מוציא לו שתות בחסרון. ב) פי' גרגישתא שם העפר שעושין ממנו כלי חרס כגון הדנא וכיוצא בה. יש עפר מוצין ויש עפר שאינו מוצין. באתריה דרב יהודה רמו [מ' ותמני] כוזי בדנא וכו' פי' במקומו של רב יהודה היו נותנין ג) טפיחין של יין בחבית והיו קונין החבית והיין שבתוכו ו' זוזים וכאשר היה היין מתיישן ושוקעין שמריו בתחתיתו היה מצוה רב יהודה לקונים למכור ו' טפיחין לזוז ל"ו טפיחים בו' זוזין והן דמי כל החבית נשארו י'

## חשק שלמה על ר"ח

א) קצת נראה מזה דרבינו לא גרס ולא מייץ טפי רק ולא מיין והא דמוליא לו שתות לאו משום דבלע ועי' בחדושי הריטב"א ובשמ"ק ודו"ק. ב) נראה דחסר כאן וצ"ל אבע"א בגרגישתא פי' גרגישתא וכו'. ג) צ"ל היו נותנין מ"ח טפיחין של יין בחבית וכו' והיין שבתוכו בששה זוזים וכאשר וכו' למכור ששה טפיחין בזוז ל"ו טפיחים בששה זוזים והן דמי כל החביות נשארו י"ב טפיחים כצ"ל וכ"ה בשמ"ק כאן בהעתקת לשון רבינו.

דל

a *kor*.[11] לִשְׂעוֹרִין וּלְדוֹחַן – **With regard to barley and** ***panil*****,**[12] תִּשְׁעָה קַבִּין לְכוֹר – **nine** ***kavs*** are deducted from **a** ***kor***.[13] לְכוּסְמִין וּלְזֶרַע פִּשְׁתָּן – **With regard to spelt and flaxseed,** שָׁלֹשׁ סְאִין לְכוֹר – **three** ***se'ah*** are deducted from **a** ***kor***.[14]

הַכֹּל לְפִי הַמִּדָּה וְהַכֹּל לְפִי הַזְּמַן – In **every** case, the full deduction is calculated **according to the** amount that the *shomer* received,[15] **and the** length of **time** that it was kept in storage.[16]

The following Tanna disputes the previous assertion that the deduction is proportional to the amount entrusted: אָמַר רַבִּי יוֹחָנָן בֶּן נוּרִי – **R' Yochanan ben Nuri said:** וְכִי מָה אִכְפַּת לָהֶן לַעֲכְבָּרִין – **But what do the mice care** how much produce is present? וַהֲלֹא אוֹכְלוֹת – **Do they not eat** the same amount בֵּין מֵהַרְבֵּה וּבֵין מִקְמְעָא – **whether** they eat it **from a large or a small amount** that was given to the *shomer*?! אֶלָּא – **Rather,** the rule is that אֵינוֹ יוֹצִיא לוֹ חֶסְרוֹנוֹת אֶלָּא לְכוֹר אֶחָד בִּלְבַד – [the custodian] **deducts** the **depletion for only one** ***kor*****,** even if more than one *kor* was entrusted to him.[17]

A third view:

רַבִּי יְהוּדָה אוֹמֵר – **R' Yehudah says:** אִם הָיְתָה מִדָּה מְרוּבָּה – **If the amount** of produce given to the *shomer* **was large,** אֵינוֹ מוֹצִיא לוֹ חֶסְרוֹנוֹת – [**the** ***shomer***] **does not deduct** anything at all for **depletion,** מִפְּנֵי שֶׁמּוֹתִירוֹת – **because** a large quantity of produce actually **expands** by an amount that is equal to the amount that is lost.[18]

## Gemara

The Gemara questions the Mishnah's ruling that millet decreases by only nine half-*kavs* per *kor* (2.5 percent) yearly:

אוֹרֶז טוּבָא חָסַר – But the proportion by which **millet decreases** is actually **a lot** more than this!

The Gemara answers:

אָמַר רַבָּה בַּר בַּר חָנָה אָמַר רַבִּי יוֹחָנָן – **Rabbah bar bar Chanah said in the name of R' Yochanan:** בְּאוֹרֶז קָלוּף שָׁנוּ – **They taught** this ruling **in reference to peeled millet,** which does not decrease as much as unpeeled millet.[19]

The Mishnah stated:

לְכוּסְמִין וּלְזֶרַע פִּשְׁתָּן – WITH RESPECT TO SPELT AND FLAXSEED, שָׁלֹשׁ סְאִין לְכוֹר (וכו׳) – THREE *SE'AH* are deducted from A *KOR* **(etc.).**

The Gemara qualifies this ruling:

אָמַר רַבִּי יוֹחָנָן אָמַר רַבִּי חִיָּיא – **R' Yochanan said in the name of R' Chiya:** זֶרַע פִּשְׁתָּן בְּגִבְעוֹלִין שָׁנוּ – It was in reference to **flaxseed** that is still **in its husks** that **they taught** this ruling.[20] תַּנְיָא נַמִּי הָכִי – And **this has also been taught in a Baraisa:** לְכוּסְמִין וּלְזֶרַע פִּשְׁתָּן בְּגִבְעוֹלִין – WITH REGARD TO SPELT, FLAXSEED IN ITS HUSKS, וּלְאוֹרֶז שֶׁאֵינוֹ קָלוּף – AND UNPEELED MILLET, שְׁלֹשָׁה סְאִין לְכוֹר – THREE *SE'AH* per year are deducted from EACH *KOR* of stored produce.[21]

After listing the amounts that are deducted for various types of produce, our Mishnah added:

הַכֹּל לְפִי הַמִּדָּה וכו׳ – IN EVERY case, the full deduction is calculated ACCORDING TO THE AMOUNT that the shomer received **etc.** and the time that it was kept in storage.

This law is elaborated upon in the following Baraisa:

תָּנָא – **A Tanna taught** in a Baraisa: בֵּן לְכָל כּוֹר וְכוֹר – A *shomer* deducts THE SAME amount (i.e. the amount specified in the Mishnah) FOR EACH AND EVERY *KOR* that was given to him, וְכֵן לְכָל שָׁנָה וְשָׁנָה – AND he deducts that amount FOR EACH AND EVERY YEAR that the produce was in his safekeeping.

The Gemara discusses the dispute between R' Yochanan ben Nuri and the Tanna Kamma:

אָמַר רַבִּי יוֹחָנָן בֶּן נוּרִי וכו׳ – R' YOCHANAN BEN NURI SAID, **etc.** But what do the mice care how much produce is present? Do they not eat the same amount whether they eat it from a large or a small amount that was given to the *shomer*?!

In the Tanna Kamma's view, however, the deduction does

NOTES

11. One *kor* equals 180 *kavs*. Therefore, the proportion of 9 half-*kavs* (or 4.5 *kavs*) to a *kor* is 1:40 (2.5 percent).

12. *Rashi*. *Panil* is an Old French word that refers to a certain type of millet (see *Targum HaLaaz al HaShas*).

13. A ratio of 1:20 (5 percent).

14. There are 30 *se'ah* in one *kor*. Hence, this is a ratio of 1:10 (10 percent).

The proportions listed above applied in Eretz Yisrael during the time of the Tannaim. In other countries, and at other times, the *shomer* deducts the proportion by which each type of produce is known to decrease (*Rambam, Commentary to the Mishnah*).

15. The amounts taught in the Mishnah are deducted for each *kor* in the *shomer's* safekeeping (*Rashi*, from a Baraisa cited in the Gemara below).

16. These amounts are deducted for each year the produce was in the care of the *shomer* (*Rashi*, from a Baraisa cited in the Gemara below).

17. For example, if wheat was entrusted to the *shomer*, he may deduct only 9 half-*kavs* per year regardless of how much wheat [in excess of one *kor*] was originally deposited (see *Rashi*).

R' Yochanan specifies the quantity of one *kor*, because if *less* than one *kor* was given to the *shomer*, the mice will eat less than their standard 9.5 *kavs*, since there is not enough room in the produce for them to hide. In such a case, R' Yochanan concedes that less than 9.5 half-*kavs* is deducted [following the proportion of 1:40] (*Tosafos*).

18. If a large amount of produce is entrusted to a *shomer* in dry season and returned in the rainy season, it swells as it absorbs moisture, and the volume by which it increases is equal to the amount consumed by the mice. This applies only to a *large* amount of produce (the Gemara identifies the amount as ten *kors*), for in such a case the portion from which the mice will eat (two or three *kors*) is a relatively small fraction of the total [and the decrease caused by the mice will be offset by the increase due to swelling] (*Rashi*; cf. *Tosafos, Ritva*). [According to *Rashi's* explanation, it seems that R' Yehudah's ruling applies *specifically* to an amount of ten *kors*. If a smaller amount was deposited, the *shomer* may indeed deduct from it. And if *more* than ten *kors* were deposited, the *shomer* might even have to return more than the amount deposited originally (see *Dibros Moshe* 41:34).]

R' Yehudah disagrees with the Tanna Kamma, who holds that the amount eaten by mice is a fixed ratio of the total amount present; he also disagrees with R' Yochanan ben Nuri, who is of the opinion that mice eat from only one *kor*, even if a larger amount is present (*Rashi*, as understood by *Maharsha*).

19. Unpeeled millet decreases at a rate of 10 percent [see Gemara below] per year (see *Shulchan Aruch, Choshen Mishpat* 292:11).

20. The husks of stored flaxseed will dry out, fall off, and be blown away by the wind. This results in a much larger depletion of the original volume. Flaxseeds that have been removed from their husks, however, do not suffer such a great loss (*Rashi*).

21. This Baraisa also supports the distinction made in the Gemara above between peeled and unpeeled millet.

וכן אמר רבה השביחו לאמצע א"ל אביי מי דמי התם גדולים גבי קטנים ידעי וקא מחלי הכא מי ידע דליחיל אגלגל מלתא ומטא לקמיה דרבי אמי [א]אמר להו גדולה מזו אמרו שמין להם כארים השתא דידיה לא יהבינן ליה אהדרוה (א) הא לקמיה דרב חסדא אמר להו מי דמי התם ברשות נחית הכא לאו ברשות נחית ועוד קטן הוא ואין מורידין קרוב לנכסי קטן [ב]אהדרוה לקמיה דרבי אמי אמר להו לא סיימוה קמי דקטן הוא: **מתני'** [ג]המפקיד פירות אצל חבירו הרי זה יוציא לו חסרונות לחטים ולאורז תשעה חצאי קבין לכור לשעורין ולדוחן תשעה קבין לכור לכוסמין ולזרע פשתן שלש סאין לכור הכל לפי המדה והכל לפי הזמן א"ר יוחנן בן נורי וכי מה אכפת להן לעכברין והלא אוכלות בין מהרבה ובין מקמעא אלא אינו יוציא לו חסרונות אלא לכור אחד בלבד רבי יהודה אומר אם היתה מדה מרובה אינו מוציא לו חסרונות מפני שמותירות: **גמ'** אורז טובא חסר אמר רבה בר בר חנה א"ר יוחנן [ד]באורז קלוף שנו: לכוסמין ולזרע פשתן ג' סאין לכור (וכו'): א"ר יוחנן א"ר חייא זרע [ה]פשתן בגבעולין שנו תניא נמי הכי לכוסמין ולזרע פשתן בגבעולין [ו]ולאורז שאינו קלוף שלשה סאין לכור: הכל לפי המדה וכו': [ז]תנא כן לכל כור וכור וכן לכל שנה ושנה: א"ר יוחנן בן נורי וכו': תניא אמרו לו לרבי יוחנן הרבה אובדות מהן הרבה מתפזרות מהן תנא בד"א שעירבן עם פירותיו אבל יחד לו קרן זוית אומר לו הרי שלך לפניך וכי עירבן עם פירותיו מאי הוי ליחזי לדידיה כמה הויין במסתפק מהם וליחזי כמה אסתפק [ח]דלא (ג) ידעי כמה אסתפק: ר"י אומר אם היתה וכו': כמה מדה מרובה אמר רבה בר בר חנה א"ר יוחנן עשרה כורין תניא נמי הכי כמה מדה מרובה עשרה כורין תני תנא קמיה דרב נחמן בד"א שמדד לו מתוך גורנו והחזיר לו מתוך גורנו אבל מדד לו מתוך גורנו והחזיר לו מתוך ביתו אינו יוציא לו חסרונות מפני שמותירות א"ל וכי בשופטני עסקינן דיהבי בביילא רבא ושקלי בביילא זוטא דלמא בימות הגורן קאמרת [ט]בד"א שמדד לו בימות הגורן והחזיר לו בימות הגורן אבל מדד לו בימות הגורן והחזיר לו בימות הגשמים אינו יוציא לו חסרון מפני שמותירות א"ל רב פפא לאביי א"כ לפקע כדא הוה עובדא ופקע כדא אבע"א משום איצצא: **מתני'** [י]יוציא לו שתות ליין ר"י אומר חומש [כ]יוציא לו שלשה לוגין שמן למאה לוג ומחצה שמרים לוג ומחצה בלע אם היה שמן מזוקק אינו יוציא לו שמרים אם היו קנקנים ישנים אינו יוציא לו בלע ר"י אומר אף [ל]המוכר (ג) שמן מזוקק לחבירו כל ימות השנה הרי זה מקבל עליו לוג ומחצה שמרים למאה: **גמ'** ולא פליגי [מ]מר כי אתריה ומר כי אתריה באתריה דמר חפו בקירא ולא מייץ טפי באתריה דמר חפו בכופרא ומייץ טפי איבעית אימא משום גרגישתא הא מייצא טפי והא לא מייצא טפי באתריה דרב יהודה רמו ארבעים ותמני כוזי בדנא אזיל דנא בשיתא זוזי פרים רב יהודה שיתא בזוזא

**רש"י**

וכן אמר רבה השביחו לאמצע. לא גרסינן שאין זה לשון גמרא להביא דברי האמוראים סיוע למשנה ועוד רבה תלמידיה דרב חסדא הוה והיכי אמר רב חסדא שמעתא משמיה ואי גרס ליה וכן אמר רב גרסינן שהיה רבו של רב חסדא משום דאיכא למ"ד בבבא בתרא (דף קמג:) לא שנו אלא ששבחו נכסים מחמת נכסים אבל שבחו מחמת עצמן של אחים השביחו לעצמן אמרה רב חסדא להא דרב הכא למימר דלית לן ההיא שמעתא אלא אפילו השביחו מחמת טורחן של משביחין כי הכא דשתל פרדס השביחו לאמצע: ידעו. אלו שיטלו חלקם: מי ידע. שיש לו אחים: גדולה מזו. קרוב היורד לנכסי שבוי שאם יבאו הבעלים יטלו שלהם: אמרו שמין להם כארים הכא דידיה לא יהבינן ליה. בתמיה זה שעשה והשביחן לדעת עצמו לא יהבי' ליה כארים בחלק השני: ברשות ב"ד נחתי. דמורידין קרוב לנכסי שבוי: הכא לא ברשות נחית. כשירד זה לתוכו לא נמלך בב"ד: ועוד. אם בא לימלך לא היו מורידין אותו דהא אחיו קטן הוה ואין מורידין קרוב לנכסי קטן: **מתני'** הרי זה יוציא לו חסרונות. כשיחזירם לו יפחות כמה הם רגילים לחסור ובגמ' מוקי לה בשעירבן עם פירותיו: אורז. מי"ל: (ה) דוחן. פטי"ל ודומה לאורז: הכל לפי המדה. וכן לכל כור וכור: הכל לפי הזמן. שהניחן בידו לכל שנה ושנה יניח לו כך: ר' יוחנן בן נורי אמר. אהכל לפי המדה פליג: אם היתה מדה מרובה. שהפקיד אצלו הרבה ובגמרא מפרש י' כורים לא יוציא לו חסרונות מפני שהם מותירות שבימות הגורן כשמפקיד החיטין יבשין ובימות הגשמים כשמחזיר נופחות ובאכילת עכברים אינן נחסרים כל כך לכל כור וכור דכולי האי לא אכלי עכברים מי' כורין הלכך נפיחתו משלמת חסרון המגיע לשני כורים או שלשה שהעכברים אוכלין: **גמ'** זרע פשתן בגבעולין. חסר כל כך לפי שהגבעולין מתייבשין ונופלים והרוח מנשבתן אבל זרע פשתן נקי אינו חסר כ"כ: לכל כור וכור. פירוש דמתניתין הוא: ליחזי דידיה כמה הוו כו'. ויראה כמה חסרו ויטול על של חברו כפי חשבון: מדת הגורן. היתה יתירה על של בתים: בשופטני. שוטים: בביילא. במדה: בימות הגורן. סמוך ליובשן שנתייבשו בחמה: והחזיר לו בימות הגשמים. חזרו ונתפחו מלחלוחית הגשם והקור: א"כ. שדרכו לתפוח: לפקע כדא. כשממלאין כד חיטין או שעורין בימות הגורן וגפין את הכד יפקע בימות הגשמים מחמת תפיחת התבואה: איצצא. דוחק מתוך שהם במקום צר נדחקו יחד ואין תפוחין: **מתני'** ליין. אם הפקיד אצלו יין ועירבו עם יינו הקנקנים בולעין שתות: אף המוכר כו'. כשם שאמרו במפקיד כן אמרו במוכר שהמוכר שמן לחבירו ונותן לו מתוך חביותיו כשהוא מסתפק תמיד והוא מזוקק הרי הלוקח מקבל עליו לפחות לו לוג ומחצה מחמת שמרים: למאה. למאה לוג: **גמ'** חפו בקירא. טחו החביות מבפנים בשעוה כדרך שעושין אנו בזפת: כופרא. זפת: גרגישתא. קרקע שעושין ממנה החביות ארדלי"א בלע"ז: הא. באתריה דר"י מייץ טפי מהאי דאתריה דתנא קמא: באתריה דרב יהודה. מילתא באפי נפשיה היא ולאו אמתניתין קאי: רמו ארבעין ותמניא כוזי בדנא. מדה קטנה היתה במקומו שארבעים ושמונה ממלאין את החבית: אזיל דנא בשיתא. בששה זוזים היתה נמכרת ביחד בימות הבציר: פרים ליה רב יהודה שיתא בזוזא. נעשה רב יהודה חנווני והיה מוכרן שש כוזי בזוז:

**תוספות**

**וכן** אמר רבה: גרס. רש"י גרס וכן אמר רב ופליג אמ"ד בפ' מי שמת (ב"ב דף קמג: ושם ד"ה לא) נכסים ששבחו מחמת עצמן של אחין השבח לעצמן וקאמר דאפי' שבחו מחמת טרחם של משביחין כי הכא דשתל פרדיסא השביחו לאמצע וזהו תימה שחולק רבא על רב דהתם רבא קאמר ולא מייתי התם מילתיה דרב ונראה דגרס רבה וכן בספר ר"ת ולא מדברי רב חסדא הוא (א) שהגמ' מביא שמעשה כיוצא בזה בא לפני רבה ופסק דהשביחו לאמצע כמו רב חסדא והביאו הגמרא משום קושית אביי דא"ל אביי לרבה מי דמי כו' ולא חשש רבה מקושיותיו ודן דהשביחו לאמצע: **אגלגל** מלתא. פסק של רב חסדא ומטא לקמיה דרבי אמי: **וכי** מה אכפת להו לעכברים. וטעמייהו דרבנן מפרש בירושלמי הני עכברי רשיעי ניהו כד חמיין עיבור לא מסתייהו דאכלי אלא קריין לחבריהון דאכלי עמהון והא דאמרינן בגמרא אמרו לו הרבה אובדות מהם הרבה מתפזרות מהם י"ל דלדבריו דרבי יוחנן קאמר אפילו לית [י] לך טעמא דמפרש בירושלמי מ"מ הרבה אובדות מהם:

**אלא** לכור בלבד. וא"ת אם כן בפחות מכור נמי יוציא כמו לכור וי"ל דאין להם ריוח להטמן [ז] בתוכה ומ"מ לפי חשבון הראוי להתחסר יוציא דאי אפשר שלא יתחסרו: **ולאורז** שאינו קלוף ג' סאין לכור. וא"ת ואמאי לא חשיב במתניתין אורז שאינו קלוף עם זרע פשתן כיון דאית להו חד שיעורא וי"ל דפשוט לו דבאורז תתחסר כל כך וברישא גבי אורז קלוף לא חשיב זרע פשתן קלוף דשמא דינם חלוק:

**מדה** מרובה י' כורין. וא"ת אפי' ב' כורין או ג' מתנפחין לפי חשבון החסרונות העולה להם וי"ל דבי' כורין עולה להם הנפוח חסרון של כור אחד ולא יוציא להם חסרונות היינו כל החסרון דחסרון של כור אחד לא יוציא ולהכי נקט י' כורים לאפוקי פחות:

אל

**מסורת הש"ס**

[...]תז"ג, יעב"ץ], ב) [נ"ל [...]ג, יעב"ץ]. ג) מהרש"ל [...]ין לחבירו מזוקק [...], ד) [פסחים ג. וש"נ], [...]עי' פירש"י ברכות [...], ו) כ"א לג, ז) כ"א בתיבה.

**הגהות הב"ח**

(א) תוס' ד"ה וכן וכו' [...]ברי רב חסדא הוא אלא שהגמרא:

**לעזי רש"י**

[...]י"ל. פירוש "הירוס". [...]טי"ל. פירוש "פענכעל [...]רוס". ארדלי"א. [...]רוס טיט אדום (רמב"ם [...]ת פ"ח מ"ה), קרקע [...]עושין ממנה החביות.

**ליקוטי רש"י**

[...]מין להם כארים. אם [...]ואו הבעלים יטלו אלו [...]בח קרקעות ופירות [...]מנהג אריסי המקום [...]עיל לט.]. ולדוחן. [...]כ"ן [ברכות לז.]. [...]כוסמין. איספילטא [...]ע"ן [פסחים לה.]. [...]גבעולין. גבעול הוא [...]נה האמצעי שהזרע [...]ראשו כקנבוס ופשתן [...]סוכה יג.]. ומייץ. יונק [...]שבת קלד.]. גרגישתא. [...]רזיל"א במעבה האדמה [...]מלכים א ז) מתרגמינן [...]גרגישתא דארעא [יבמות [...]קו:]. אדמה [כתובות ס:].

**עין משפט נר מצוה**

סז א ב מיי' פ"ט מהל' נחלות הל' ד ועיין בהשגות ובמגיד משנה סמג עשין לג טוש"ע ח"מ סי' רפז סעיף ג וע"ש:

סח ג ד ה ו ז ח מיי' פ"ה מהל' שאלה ופקדון הל' ה סמג עשין פח טוש"ע ח"מ סי' רצב סעיף יא:

סט ט מיי' שם טוש"ע שם סעיף יב:

ע י כ מיי' שם טוש"ע שם סעיף יג:

עא ל מיי' פי"ח מהל' מכירה הל' ט סמג לאוין קע טוש"ע ח"מ סי' רכח סעיף כ [ודלא כר"י]:

**רבינו חננאל**

מתני' המפקיד פירות אצל חבירו הרי זה יוציא לו חסרונות לחטים ולאורז ט' חצאי קבין לכור. ואוקימנא באורז קלוף תנא וכן לכל כור וכור וכן לכל שנה ושנה. וקיימא לן כתנא קמא דמתני' והוא שעירבן בין פירותיו ומסתפק מהן ואינו יודע כמה הוציא לברר החסרון אבל יחד לו קרן זוית אומר לו הרי שלך לפניך: פיס' ר' יהודה אומר אם היתה מדה מרובה לא יוציא לו חסרונות מפני שמותירות ותני עלה בד"א שמדד לו בימי הגרנות שהפירות יבשין מאד שהחום מייבשן ומחזירן לו בימות הגרנות זהו שמוציא לו חסרונות אבל אם מחזירן לו בימות הגשמים אין מוציא לו חסרונות מפני שאויר הגשמים מלחלחן ומתנפחות ונמצאו מותירות. הוה עובדא שמילאו כדא בימות הגרנות חטים וכשהגיעו ימות הגשמים נתנפחו בכדא והיה פי הכדא סתום ונתבקעה הכדא איבעית אימא משום איצצא: מתני' יוציא לו שתות ליין ר' יהודה אומר חומש. ולא פליגי במקומו של ת"ק היו מכסין פי הדנא בשעוה ולא היה א) מוצין לפיכך מוציא לו שתות בחסרון. ב) פי' גרגישתא שם העפר שעושין ממנו כלי חרס כגון הדנא וכיוצא בה. יש עפר מוצין ויש עפר שאינו מוצין. באתריה דרב יהודה רמו [מ' ותמני] כוזי בדנא וכו' פי' במקומו של רב יהודה היו נותנין ג) טפיחין של יין בחבית והיו קונין החבית והיין שבתוכו ר' זוזים וכאשר היה היין מתיישן ושוקעין שמריו בתחתיתו היה מצוה רב יהודה לקונים למכור ר' טפיחין לזוז ל"ו טפיחים בו' זוזין והן דמי כל החבית נשארו י'

**חשק שלמה על ר"ח**

א) קצת נראה מזה דרבינו לא גרס ולא מייץ טפי רק ולא מייץ והא דמוציא לו שתות לאו משום דבלע ועי' בחדושי הריטב"א ובשמ"ק ותו"ק. ב) נראה דחסר כאן ונ"ל אבע"א בגרגישתא פי' גרגישתא וכו'. ג) נ"ל היו טמנין מ"ח טפיחין של יין בחבית וכו' והיין שבתוכו בששה זוזים וכאשר וכו' למכור ששה טפיחין בזוז ל"ו טפיחים בששה זוזים והן דמי כל החבית נשארו י"ב טפיחים כצ"ל וכ"ה בשמ"ק כאן בהעתקת לשון רבינו.

וְכֵן אָמַר רַבָּה – **And so Rabbah said:** הִשְׁבִּיחוּ לָאֶמְצַע – **Whatever they improved goes to the middle.**[1]

Rav Chisda's ruling is disputed:

אָמַר לֵיהּ אַבַּיֵי – **Abaye said to [Rav Chisda]:** מִי דָּמֵי – **But is [this case] comparable** to the case of the Mishnah? הָתָם גְּדוֹלִים גַּבֵּי קְטַנִּים יָדְעֵי – **There, the adult sons know that there are minor sons** who will share in the profits, וְקָא מָחֲלֵי – **and** since they did not state that they were working only for themselves, **they waived** their rights to take all of the profits themselves.[2] הָכָא מִי יָדַע – **But there, did [Mari] know** that he had a brother when he planted vineyards and orchards, דְּלֵיחִיל – so his lack of such a declaration would tell us that **he waived** his rights to keep all of the improvements?[3]

The ruling is rejected for other reasons:

אִגַּלְגַּל מִלְּתָא – **The matter** [i.e. Rav Chisda's ruling] **was debated** back and forth,[4] וּמְטָא לְקַמֵּיהּ דְּרַבִּי אַמִּי – **and** eventually **came before R' Ami.** אָמַר לְהוּ – **He told [the students who had told him about this ruling]:** גְּדוֹלָה מִזּוֹ – In another case, where there is a **greater** reason not to pay the manager of the property **than** in **this** case of Mari – namely, where a relative managed the property of a captive owner and the owner returned – אָמְרוּ שָׁמִין לָהֶם כְּאָרִיס – **[the Sages] said:** WE EVALUATE FOR HIM a share of the profits AS IF he was A SHARECROPPER; הַשְׁתָּא דִּידֵיהּ – if so, **now,** regarding Mari who cultivated and improved **his own** land, לֹא יַהֲבִינַן לֵיהּ – **should we not give him** at least the share of a sharecropper in his brother's half of the improvements?[5]

Rav Chisda replies to R' Ami's challenge:

אַהַדְרוּהָ הָא לְקַמֵּיהּ דְּרַב חִסְדָּא – **[The students] relayed this** objection of R' Ami **back to Rav Chisda.** אָמַר לְהוּ – **[R' Chisda] told them:** מִי דָּמֵי – **Is [the case]** of a captive's property **comparable** to our case? הָתָם בִּרְשׁוּת נָחִית – **There, [the manager] entered** the captive's land **with** the **permission** of *beis din*.[6] הָכָא לָאו בִּרְשׁוּת נָחִית – But **here,** Mari entered his father's property **without** the **permission** of *beis din*.[7] וְעוֹד – **And furthermore,** even if Mari *had* consulted with *beis din* beforehand, *beis din* would not have allowed him to enter the property, קָטָן הוּא – for the brother **was a minor** at the time Mari occupied the property, וְאֵין מוֹרִידִין קָרוֹב לְנִכְסֵי קָטָן – **and** *beis din* **does not appoint a relative to** manage **a minor's property.** Therefore, Mari should not be paid for his improvement of the brother's share, since his occupation was not authorized.

R' Ami withdraws his objection:

אַהַדְרוּהָ לְקַמֵּיהּ דְּרַבִּי אַמִּי – **[The students] relayed [Rav Chisda's reply] back to R' Ami.** אָמַר לְהוּ – **He said to them:** לֹא סַיְּימוּהָ קַמַּי – **You did not tell me the whole** story, דְּקָטָן הוּא – including the information **that [the brother] was a minor** at the time Mari occupied the estate. If I had known that, I would have agreed that Mari should not be paid for his improvement of the brother's share.

## Mishnah

Stored produce tends to decrease in quantity over the course of time.[8] Therefore, if a *shomer* is given produce to safeguard, he does not have to return the total quantity that was deposited with him. He may deduct the amount by which such produce usually decreases over the period of time it was in his safekeeping.[9]

הַמַּפְקִיד פֵּירוֹת אֵצֶל חֲבֵירוֹ – If **one deposits produce with his fellow** for safekeeping, when the *shomer* returns the produce הֲרֵי זֶה יוֹצִיא לוֹ חֶסְרוֹנוֹת – **he may deduct** the expected **depletion** before returning it.

The Mishnah lists various types of produce, and the amounts that may be deducted from each type:

לְחִטִּים וּלְאוֹרֶז – **With regard to wheat and millet,**[10] תִּשְׁעָה חֲצָאֵי קַבִּין לְכוֹר – **nine half-*kavs*** are deducted from

NOTES

1. *Rashi* notes that it is unusual for the Gemara to cite an Amora to support a Tannaic ruling stated in a Mishnah, as seems to be the case here. In addition, Rabbah was Rav Chisda's student, and it is unlikely that Rav Chisda would quote his student to support his own ruling! *Tosafos* therefore explain that it is the Gemara, and not Rav Chisda, that cites Rabbah. *Rashi,* however, emends the name of the author of this ruling to *Rav,* who was Rav Chisda's *teacher. Rashi* explains that Rav Chisda here is citing Rav's ruling to explain that the halachah does not follow the opinion of Rava, who states in *Bava Basra* (143b) that if the adult brothers invested their own money or labor to improve the land, they may keep all the profit for themselves. Rav Chisda obviously did not agree with this ruling of Rava, for he ruled that Mari was not entitled to keep the profit from his own planting; the Gemara therefore cites Rav's ruling to show that the halachah is that even in such a case, the profits are divided equally among the brothers (cf. *Ramban*).

2. See above, 39b note 27.

3. Perhaps, if he had known that he had a brother, he would have declared that he wished to keep the value of the improvements for himself (*Ramban*).

An apparent difficulty: The Gemara here seems to say that Mari did not know that he had a brother. But the Gemara above (39b) implied that Mari was aware that he had a brother, but merely did not recognize the claimant! (see note 16 there). Some commentators explain that Mari either had forgotten about his brother, had heard that he had died, or had not expected him to return. Therefore, since Mari did not think he would have to share the improvements with anyone, his failure to declare this does not show that he waived his rights. Others explain that the discussion recorded in the Gemara above (39b) between Rav Chisda and Mari does not necessarily prove that Mari was ever aware that he had a brother (see *Shitah Mekubetzes, Ritva* [old]).

4. Literally: it rolled.

5. R' Ami asked: We pay the manager of a captive's property for his work, even though he has no rights at all in the captive's property. Certainly, then, Mari should be paid for his improvements, for he actually owns part of the estate, and improved it thinking it was his own (*Shitah Mekubetzes;* see *Rashi;* cf. *Ramban*).

6. As the Baraisa stated above (*Rashi*). [Apparently, *Rashi* understands that a relative must actually receive permission from *beis din* before entering a captive's property to manage it (see following note).]

7. I.e. he did not consult with *beis din* before occupying the property (*Rashi*).

The commentators question why Mari's failure to consult *beis din* before occupying the property should be a valid reason to withhold payment from him, given that his occupation was legal! *Rashba* explains that Rav Chisda mentioned this point only as a partial defense (in combination with the second point the Gemara will next mention), but not as an independent reason to deny Mari additional payment. Indeed, *Ritva* explains Rav Chisda's entire response as a single statement – that the possession was illegal *because* the property was owned in part by a minor (see Gemara below). Although Mari may not have even known that he had a brother, as explained above, *Raavad* explains that Mari's occupation of the estate was still unauthorized, because before his death Mari's father willfully abandoned the property without appointing Mari as administrator. Hence, the estate had already been classified as abandoned *retushim* property, for which no manager is appointed (see above, 38b note 33).

8. This decrease is the result of consumption by mice and possibly other factors as well (see Baraisa cited in the Gemara).

9. The Gemara cites a Baraisa that explains that this applies where the *shomer* mixed his own produce with the depositor's [and we cannot identify the produce that was given to the *shomer*] (*Rashi*). Otherwise, the *shomer* must return the produce as it is, without deducting anything from it.

10. The translation of אוֹרֶז as *millet* follows *Rashi. Tosafos* (*Berachos* 37a), however, translate it as rice. *Mishnah Berurah* (208:25) writes that rice is the generally accepted definition.

אָמַר לֵיהּ – [The brother] told [Rav Chisda]: לִפְלוֹג לִי נַמִּי – Let [Mari] also give me half מִפַּרְדֵּיסֵי וּבוּסְתָּנֵי דִּשְׁתַל – of the vineyards and the orchards that he planted.[25] אָמַר לֵיהּ – [Rav Chisda] told [Mari]: שַׁפִּיר קָאָמַר לָךְ – He has spoken to you properly, דִּתְנַן – for we learned in a Mishnah:[26] הִנִּיחַ בָּנִים גְּדוֹלִים וּקְטַנִּים – If [a man] died and LEFT ADULT SONS AND MINOR SONS, וְהִשְׁבִּיחוּ גְּדוֹלִים אֶת הַנְּכָסִים – AND THE ADULT SONS IMPROVED THE PROPERTIES of the estate, הִשְׁבִּיחוּ לְאֶמְצַע – WHATEVER THEY IMPROVED GOES TO THE MIDDLE; that is, the profits are shared equally by all of the sons.[27]

NOTES

25. The brother demanded half of Mari's improvements to the land (*Rashi*).

26. *Bava Basra* 143b.

27. In the Mishnah's case, the estate had not yet been divided among the brothers, and the older brothers did not declare that they were acting only for themselves (see *Rashi* ad loc. ד״ה השביחו הגדולים). The Gemara below (40a) explains that by failing to make such a declaration, the older brothers waived their rights to keep the profits for themselves.

ואפילו הגדיל ולא אמרן אלא באחי דאבא
אבל באחי דאמא לית לן בה ואחי דאבא
נמי לא אמרן אלא בארעתא אבל בבתי
לית לן בה ובארעתא נמי לא אמרן אלא
דלא עביד עיטדא אבל עביד עיטדא קלא
אית לה [א] ולא היא לא שנא אחי דאבא ולא
שנא אחי דאמא לא שנא ארעתא ולא שנא
בתי ולא שנא עביד עיטדא לא שנא לא
עביד עיטדא לא מחתינן [ב] ההיא סבתא
דהויא לה תלת בנתא אישתבאי איהי וחדא
ברתא אידך תרתי בנתא שכיבא חדא מינייהו
ושבקה ינוקא אמר אביי היכי נעביד
לוקמינהו לנכסי בידא דאחתא דלמא
שכיבא סבתא ואין מורידין קרוב לנכסי
קטן נוקמינהו לנכסיה בידא דינוקא דלמא
לא שכיבא סבתא ואין מורידין קטן לנכסי
שבוי אמר אביי הלכך פלגא יהבינא לה
לאחתא ואידך פלגא מוקמינן ליה אפוטרופא
לינוקא רבא אמר [ג] מגו דמוקמינן אפוטרופא
לפלגא מוקמינן ליה אפוטרופא לאידך פלגא
לסוף שמעו דשכיבא סבתא אמר אביי
תילתא יהבינן לה לאחתא ותילתא יהבינן
ליה לינוקא ואידך תילתא יהבינן דנקא
לאחתא ואידך דנקא מוקמינן ליה אפוטרופא
לינוקא רבא אמר [ד] מגו דמוקמים אפוטרופא
לדנקא מוקמינן נמי אפוטרופא לאידך דנקא
[ה] מרי בר איסק אתא ליה אחא מבי חוזאי
א"ל פלוג לי אמר ליה לא ידענא לך אתא
לקמיה דרב חסדא א"ל [ו] שפיר קאמר לך
שנאמר [ז] ויכר יוסף את אחיו והם לא
הכירוהו מלמד שיצא בלא חתימת זקן ובא
בחתימת זקן א"ל זיל אייתי סהדי דאחוה את
אמר ליה אית לי סהדי ודחלי מיניה דגברא
אלימא הוא א"ל לדידיה זיל אנת אייתי סהדי
דלאו אחוך הוא א"ל דינא הכי המוציא
מחבירו עליו הראיה א"ל [ח] הכי דיינינא לך
ולכל אלימי דחברך אמר ליה סוף סוף
אתו סהדי ולא מסהדי א"ל תרתי לא עבדי
לסוף אתו סהדי דאחוה הוא א"ל לפלוג לי
נמי מפרדיסי ובוסתני דשתל אמר ליה שפיר
קאמר לך [ג] דתנן [ט] הניח בנים גדולים וקטנים
והשביחו גדולים את הנכסים השביחו לאמצע

**רש"י**

ואפי' הגדיל. הקטן משירד לתוכו ואכלו ג' שנים בפניו משהגדיל לא הויא חזקה דהואיל ותחילת ירידתו לתוכו הוה קטן לא ידע כשהגדיל שהן של אביו ולפיכך לא מיחה דאי ס"ל לרב הונא דמחזיקין בהן משהגדיל היכי מחתינן נכרי לנכסי קטן שמא יהא בידו משיגדיל ויטעון אתה מכרת לי משגדלת ואכלתים שני חזקה: ולא אמרן. דאין מורידין קרוב לנכסי קטן: אלא באחי דאבא. אחיו מאביו שיטעון בהן לך ירושה: ארעתא. שדות: אבל בבתי לית לן בה. שהשכנים מעידין עליהם שבאו לחלקו של קטן: עיטדא. שטר חלוקה כשחלקו מתחילה (מלכים ב יב) רק הבמות לא סרו מתרגמינן במתא לא [ז] עטדו לא הפליגו מהם: לא שנא אחי דאמא. פן יאמר של אמי היו נכסי מלוג ואביו של קטן בעל אמי היה מוחזק בהן מחמת שהוא אוכל פירות והוא מת קודם לאמי ולא ירשה ואני יורש חליין מחמת אמי: היכי ליעבד. בנכסי דסבתא שאין אנו יודעין אם קיימת אם מתה: בידא דאחתא. דהילכתא כרשב"ג דקם ליה שמואל כוותיה: דלמא שכיבא סבתא. ויש לקטן חלק בהן שהם שלו מחמת אמו או שמא חליין שלו שמא מתו שתי השבויות: לוקמינהו לפלגא דנכסי בידא דינוקא. איכא למיחש דלמא לא שכיבא סבתא ואין לו חלק בהן ואין מורידין קטן לנכסי שבוי: פלגא יהבינן לאחתא. ממה נפשך אם מתו שתי השבויות הרי זו יורשת חליין ואם לאו מורידין קרוב לנכסי שבוי: מוקמינן אפוטרופוס. ולא מחתינן קטן לגוייהו דלמא לא שכיבא ואין מורידין קטן לנכסי שבוי: שמעו דשכיבא סבתא. לסוף שמעו שמתה הזקנה ועל הבת שנשבית לא שמעו: תילתא יהבינן כו'. דהא ודאי שליש הנכסים לזו ושליש לקטן: דנקא. שתות חצי השליש: יהבינן לאחתא. ממה נפשך אם מתה האחות הרי חצי חלקה לזו ואם לאו מורידין קרוב לנכסי שבוי: ואידך דנקא. לא יהבינן לה שמא של קטן הם ואין מורידין קרוב לנכסי קטן: אתא ליה אחא מבי חוזאי. שהלך אביו לבי חוזאי ונשא שם אשה וילדה לו את זה וחזר מרי לכאן וירד לנכסי אביו ובא זה אחריו לזמן מרובה ותבע חלקו: שפיר קאמר לך. שאינו מכירך ואין זה רמאות שכשיצא מאצלך לא היה לך חתימת זקן ועכשיו באת בחתימת זקן: ויכר יוסף את אחיו. שכשיצא מהם היו כולם חתומי זקן והם לא הכירוהו שיצא מאצלם בלא חתימת זקן ובא בחתימת זקן: דלאו אחוך הוא. אותם עדים שיש לו לזה שבאו משם ומכירין בו מי הוא הביאם אתה ויעידו שאינו בן אביך או בקש עדים אחרים: א"ל. מרי לרב חסדא אי מינאי דחלי מה תועלת: סוף סוף אתו סהדי ולא מסהדי. אלא כמותי ולא כמותך: תרתי לא עבדי. מיראתך יעשו אחת שישתקו אבל שתים לא יעשו לא דיין שישתקו ולא יעידו האמת אלא גם שיעידו שקר: א"ל. ההוא אחא לרב חסדא: לפלוג לי מפרדיסי. כרמים: ובוסתני. בית של אילנות: דשתל. איהו והשביחן ויתן לי חליין כמו שהן משובחין:
וכן

**תוספות**

וכי תימא הא פשיטא ליה דאינו יודע למחות בסוף ג' אף ע"פ שהוא נזכר לשאול עידי מכירה דרגילות הוא טפי לשכוח מחאה בסוף כל ג' א"כ בלא רב הונא פשיטא דאין מחזיקין וי"ל דאי לאו רב הונא ממה שמעמידין אפוטרופוס לנכסי יתומין אין להוכיח דאין מחזיקין דאפילו מחזיקין לא חיישינן שמא יחזיק דב"ד לא יבררו כי אם נאמן או משום דידע למחות בסוף כל ג' כדפרישית אבל מדאמר רב הונא אין מורידין קרוב א"כ חושש לרמאות וגם אית ליה דלא ידע למחות בקרוב ולומר שדה זו של אבי ולא הגיע לחלקך אם כן בנכרי נמי לא ידע למחות ולכך אין מחזיקין וא"ת כמו שיש לו לדעת ולומר לנכרי לשאול עידי מכירה כמו כן יהיה לו דעת לומר לקרובו אייתי ראיה שזה הגיע לחלקך וי"ל דגבי קרוב סבור שאומר אמת שהרי של אביהם היה השדה ולא אסיק אדעתיה לומר אייתי ראייה אבל לנכרי מסיק אדעתיה למימר אייתי ראייה עידי מכירה: **לא שנא עביד עיטדא לא מחתינן.** וא"ת דבח"ה (ב"ב דף כט: ושם ד"ה אבל) אמרינן עטדא קלא אית לה וי"ל ביתומים החמירו יותר [ה]: **דלמא שכיבא סבתא.** וא"ת הא דתנן פרק כל הגט (גיטין דף כח. ושם ד"ה והניחו) המביא גט ממדינת הים והניחו זקן או חולה נותנין לה בחזקת שהוא קיים וי"ל דסבתא הגיעה לגבורות דהתם אמרינן כי הגיע לגבורות חיישינן [ו] אך קשה דבסמוך אמרינן הלכך פלגא יהבינן לאחתא תרי תלתי הוה לה למיתב דאפילו שכיבא סבתא מספקא ברתא לא שכיבא דליכא למימר דברתא נמי הגיעה לגבורות דאם כן סבתא איתפלגא ותו ליכא למיחש דלמא שכיבא כדאמר בגיטין (שם) כיון דפלג פלג וי"ל דגבי גט דוקא אמרינן בחזקת שהוא קיים משום עיגונא וכן בשביל אכילת קרבן ותרומה אבל הכא אדרבה החמירו בנכסי יתומים להחזיק הסבתא וברתא במתה דאמרינן לעיל דאפי' בעביד עיטדא לא מחתינן אע"ג דאית לה קלא אי נמי הכא שנשבו חיישינן טפי דלמא מתו לפי שעשו להם יסורין: **מוקמינן ליה אפוטרופוס.** ואם תאמר והא אין מורידין קטן לנכסי שבוי ומסתמא אפי' על ידי אפוטרופוס דהא משמע דאי ודאי לא שכיבא סבתא הוה יהבינן כל נכסי לאחתא ואמאי נוקי פלגא לינוקא על ידי אפוטרופוס אלא ודאי בכל ענין אין מורידין קטן דכיון שהקטן אדון האפוטרופוס אולי ישמע לקטן שלא לחרוש ושלא לזרוע וי"ל דהא דקאמר פלגא מוקמינן ליה אפוטרופוס לינוקא לא לאכול כל הפירות כדין קרוב היורד לנכסי שבוי אלא שישמור האפוטרופוס כדין אריס בחזקת סבתא ויתפרנס הקטן מזה וזה טוב מלתתם לאחתא שתאכל כל הפירות חנם כדין קרוב היורד לנכסי שבוי: **שיצא בלא חתימת זקן.** הוא הדין אם יצא בחתימת זקן דאין נאמן לומר שהוא אחיו דא"כ לא שבקת חיי לכל בריה העשירים שכל אחד יאמר אני אחיך ועוד דהא תנן בפ' יש נוחלין (ב"ב דף קלד.) האומר זה אחי אינו נאמן אלא הכא מרי בר איסק לא היה טוען ברי אלא לא ידענא לך ולכך אם יצא בחתימת זקן אינו נאמן כיון שאינו מכחישו אלא אמר לא ידענא ליה: **זיל את אייתי סהדי דלאו אחוך הוא.** וא"ת וכי כל אדם עשיר אלם יצטרך להביא עדים שאין התובעו אחיו וי"ל דשאני הכא שאותו אמר שיש לו עדים ויראים להגיד א"ל רב חסדא שיעשה עמהם שיעידו ומרי בר איסק א"ל סוף סוף דהשתא נמי יעידו שקר מיראתי ויאמרו שאינו אחי או יאמרו שאינם יודעים אע"פ שיודעין ומשני תרתי לא עבדי חדא שישתקו מלהעיד וחדא שישקרו ויאמרו אין אנו יודעים או שיאמרו אינו אחיו:
וכן

**עין משפט נר מצוה**

סב א מיי' פ"ח מהל' נחלות הל' ב סמג עשין לו טוש"ע ח"מ סי' רפה סעיף ז:
סג ב ג ד מיי' שם סמג שם טוש"ע שם סעיף ט:
סד ה (מיי' פ"ד מהל' נחלות) סמג עשין לו טוש"ע ח"מ סי' רפ סעיף ו:
סה ו מיי' פ"ג מהל' עדות הל' יב סמג עשין קט טוש"ע ח"מ סי' כח סעיף ה:
סו ז מיי' פ"ט מהלכות נחלות הל' ב ועיין בהשגות ובמגיד משנה סמג עשין לו טוש"ע ח"מ סי' רפו סעיף א:

**רבינו חננאל**

מורידין אמר רבא ש"מ מדרב הונא אין מחזיקין בנכסי קטן ואפי' הגדיל זו השמועה של רב הונא בתחלת פ' האשה שנתאלמנה. ומדקמדייק רבא משמעתיה דרב הונא ש"מ היל' כרב הונא והני מילי במקרקעי אין מורידין קרוב לנכסי קטן אבל מעות ומטלטלי אם היה הקרוב נאמן מורידין אותו וכך אמרו הגאונים דבמטלטלי לא חיישינן לקרוב א). ועוד ממעשה דההיא סבתא דהות לה תלת בנתא אישתבאי סבתא וחדא ברתא ומתה חדא מתרתי בנתא דאישתיירו ושבקא ינוקא. ושמעו דשכיבא סבתא אמרי תילתא יהבינן לברתה דהיא חולקאה ותילתא יהבינן לינוקא דהיא חולקא דאימיה ואידך תילתא אימור ברתה דנשבת בחייה היא והוינן מחתי הני קרובין בחולקא מיהו חד מינייהו הוא ינוקא ואין מורידין קטן לנכסי שבוי הילכך מוקמינן אפוטרופא לדנקא שהוא חצי השליש שהיה ראוי להיות ביד הינוקא ומיגו דמוקמינן אפוטרופא להאי דנקא מוקמינן נמי אאידך דנקא. האי מעשה דייקא כשמואל וכרב הונא: מרי בר איסק אתא ליה אחא מבי חוזאי אמר ליה לא ידענא לך אייתי סהדי דהוא אחוה. אמר ליה רב חסדא זיל פלוג בהדיה אפי' בפרדיסי ובוסתני דשתלת דהאי אחוך הוא ואין מורידין קרוב בנכסי קטן ושלא ברשות ירדת לפיכך אין שמין לך כאריס אבל קרוב לנכסי גדול כי האי גוונא שמין לו כאריס. וכן נמי אי ידע דאית ליה אחי זעירי ומשבח השבח לאמצע דתנן הניח בנים גדולים וקטנים והשביחו הגדולים את הנכסים השביחו לאמצע וכן אמר רבא:
מתני'

**חשק שלמה על ר"ח**

א) וכ"כ הרי"ף כאן בשם רב נמה גאון ז"ל.

**מסורת הש"ס**

א) [יבמות פח.], כתובות כז: [ע"ש], ב) [יבמות פח.], ג) בבא בתרא קמג., ד) [ע"ש בתרגום ותמלא דטעות נפל בספרים וצ"ל עטרא וכן הוא בערוך וכ"כ רש"י בגיטין פו. ד"ה ועטיר], ה) [וע"ע תוספות גיטין כח. ד"ה והניחו].

**גליון הש"ס**

גמ' מרי בר איסק. עיין יבמות דף כא ע"ב תוס' ד"ה ר"א: תוס' ד"ה דלמא וכו' אך קשה. עיין בתשו' מעיל צדקה סי' מח:

**תורה אור השלם**

א) וַיַּכֵּר יוֹסֵף אֶת אֶחָיו וְהֵם לֹא הִכִּרֻהוּ: [בראשית מב, ח]

**ליקוטי רש"י**

ואפילו הגדיל. לאחר מיכן והחזיק זה בפניו כמה שנים אינה חזקה הואיל ותחלתו כשהוא קטן ראהו מוחזק בה לא ידע כשהגדיל שהיתה של אביו עד ששומע מפי אחרים [כתובות יז:]. אתא ליה אחא מבי חוזאי. שהלך אביו שם והוליכו עמו וגדלו שם ומת אביו וחזר לעירו ותבע חלקו בנכסי אביו [שם כז:]. השביחו גדולים את הנכסים. שהם בעודן בתפוסת הבית. השביחו לאמצע. ויטלו קטנים כגדולים [רשב"ם ב"ב קמג:].

לֵיהּ אַפּוֹטְרוֹפָּא לִינוּקָא – **we appoint an administrator,** who is not a relative, to manage it **for the young boy.**[11]

Another Amora disagrees:

רָבָא אָמַר – **Rava said:** מִגּוֹ דְּמוֹקְמִינַן אַפּוֹטְרוֹפָּא לְפַלְגָא – **Since we** must **appoint an administrator** who is not related to the minor **for half of the property,** מוֹקְמִינַן לֵיהּ אַפּוֹטְרוֹפָּא לְאִידָךְ פַּלְגָא – **we appoint him** as **adminstrator for the other half** as well.[12]

The Gemara resumes its narration of the incident:

לְסוֹף שָׁמְעוּ דִּשְׁכִיבָא סַבְתָּא – **Eventually they heard that the elderly woman had died,**[13] but they did not hear anything about the captive daughter. אָמַר אַבַּיֵי – **Abaye said:** תִּילְתָּא יַהֲבִינַן לָהּ לַאֲחָתָא – **We give one-third** of the mother's property **to the** uncaptured **sister,** for she certainly inherits this much from her mother's estate; וְתִילְתָּא יַהֲבִינַן לֵיהּ לִינוּקָא – **and we give one-third to the young boy,** for he certainly inherits this much from his grandmother's estate. וְאִידָךְ תִּילְתָּא – **And** as far as **the other third,** יַהֲבִינַן דַּנְקָא לַאֲחָתָא – **we give one-sixth** of the estate [i.e. one-half of the captive sister's share] **to the** uncaptured **sister,**[14] וְאִידָךְ דַּנְקָא – **and** for **the other sixth,** מוֹקְמִינַן לֵיהּ אַפּוֹטְרוֹפָּא לִינוּקָא – **we appoint a** non-relative to manage it **for the young boy.**[15]

The Gemara again presents Rava's dissenting opinion:

רָבָא אָמַר – **Rava said:** מִגּוֹ דְּמוֹקִים אַפּוֹטְרוֹפָּא לְדַנְקָא – **Since we appoint** a non-relative as **administrator over one-sixth** for the minor מוֹקְמִינַן נַמִּי אַפּוֹטְרוֹפָּא לְאִידָךְ דַּנְקָא – **we also appoint** him as **administrator for the other sixth.**

The Gemara records another related incident:

מָרִי בַּר אִיסַק אֲתָא לֵיהּ אַחָא מִבֵּי חוֹזָאֵי – **A brother came to Mari bar Isak from Bei Chozai,**[16] אָמַר לֵיהּ – and **he said to [Mari]:** פְּלוֹג לִי – **Give me half** of our father's property as my rightful share of the inheritance. אָמַר לֵיהּ – **[Mari] said to him:** לֹא יָדַעְנָא לָךְ – **I do not know you,** i.e. I do not know if you are my brother or not! אֲתָא לְקַמֵּיהּ דְּרַב חִסְדָּא – **[The brother] came before Rav Chisda** for a ruling. אָמַר לֵיהּ – **[Rav Chisda] told him:** שַׁפִּיר קָאָמַר לָךְ – **[Mari] has spoken to you properly,** and there is no reason to suspect him of lying. שֶׁנֶּאֱמַר – **For it is stated** regarding Joseph's meeting with his brothers after twenty-two years of separation:[17] ,,וַיַּכֵּר יוֹסֵף אֶת־אֶחָיו – ***And Joseph recognized his brothers,*** וְהֵם לֹא הִכִּרֻהוּ" – ***but they did not recognize him.*** מְלַמֵּד שֶׁיָּצָא בְּלֹא חֲתִימַת זָקָן – **[This] teaches that [Joseph] departed** from his brothers **without a full beard,** וּבָא בַּחֲתִימַת זָקָן – **and he** now **came** before them **with a full beard,** and for that reason they did not recognize him.[18] So, too, Mari did not recognize his brother, because Mari had last seen him without a beard.[19]

Rav Chisda instructed the brother:

אָמַר לֵיהּ – **[Rav Chisda] told him:** זִיל אַיְיתֵי סַהֲדֵי דַּאֲחוּהַּ אַתְּ – **Go** and **bring witnesses that you are [Mari's] brother.** אָמַר לֵיהּ – **[The brother] told [Rav Chisda]:** אִית לִי סַהֲדֵי – **I have witnesses,** וְדָחֲלֵי מִינֵּיהּ – **but they are afraid of [Mari],** דְּגַבְרָא אַלִּימָא הוּא – **for he is a powerful man.** אָמַר לֵיהּ לְדִידֵיהּ – Thereupon, **[Rav Chisda] told [Mari]:** זִיל אַנְתְּ אַיְיתֵי סַהֲדֵי – **You go** and **bring witnesses** דְּלָאו אָחוּךְ הוּא – **that he is not your brother.**[20] אָמַר לֵיהּ – **[Mari] said to [Rav Chisda]:** דִּינָא הָכִי – **Is this the law?** No! הַמּוֹצִיא מֵחֲבֵירוֹ עָלָיו הָרְאָיָה – Rather, if **one** comes to court to **extract** money **from his fellow, the** burden of **proof is upon him!**[21] Why must I bring witnesses to defend myself against an unsupported claim?

Rav Chisda justifies his unusual ruling:

אָמַר לֵיהּ – **[Rav Chisda] told [Mari]:** הָכִי דַּיְינִינָא לָךְ – **This is how I judge you** וּלְכָל אַלִּימֵי דְּחַבְרָךְ – **and all your powerful friends:** If a claimant says that his witnesses are too afraid to testify, the defendant must indeed bring those witnesses to testify on his own behalf.[22] אָמַר לֵיהּ – **[Mari] said to [Rav Chisda]:** סוֹף סוֹף – But **in the end,** אָתוּ סַהֲדֵי וְלֹא מַסְהֲדֵי – **the witnesses will come and will not testify** truthfully![23] So what is gained by forcing me to get them to testify?

אָמַר לֵיהּ – **[Rav Chisda] told him:** תַּרְתֵּי לֹא עָבְדֵי – **They will not commit two** transgressions. I.e. they might remain silent because of fear, but they will not testify falsely.[24] Therefore, if you ask for their testimony and they refuse to testify, it is an indication that the claimant is really not your brother.

The story takes a new turn:

לְסוֹף – **Eventually,** אָתוּ סַהֲדֵי דַּאֲחוּהַּ הוּא – **witnesses came** and testified **that [the claimant] was indeed [Mari's] brother.**

NOTES

11. We cannot permit the minor himself to manage the other half, for if his grandmother and aunt have not died, he would not be allowed to manage captives' property (*Rashi*). On the other hand, even if both captives have died and half the property indeed belongs to the boy, a non-relative may be appointed as an administrator (see Gemara above, 39a). The administrator is paid as a sharecropper (see *Tosafos*).

12. Although *beis din* generally does not look for a caretaker who is not a relative to manage the property of an adult (see above, 39a), Rava holds that in this case, the one who is managing the child's half of the uncaptured daughter can be persuaded to manage the entire property (see *Sma* 285:36; cf. *Shitah Mekubetzes*).

13. I.e. witnesses testified that she died. If her death was only rumored, the minor could not take possession of any of her property (*Ritva*).

14. This sixth, too, should certainly be put into her hands, for if the captive sister has died, the uncaptured sister is entitled to it as part of her share of the mother's estate; and if the captive sister has *not* died, the uncaptured sister is allowed to manage her property (*Rashi;* see above, note 10).

15. We do not allow the uncaptured sister to manage the other sixth as well, for if the captive sister has died, the minor has inherited it, and *beis din* does not appoint a relative to manage the property of a minor (*Rashi*).

16. Mari traveled with his father to Bei Chozai, where his father remarried and had a son with a new wife. Mari returned to his former home and took possession of his father's property after his father's death. After many years the son from Bei Chozai appeared (*Rashi;* see below, 40a note 3).

17. *Genesis* 42:8.

18. Joseph recognized the brothers, however, because they all had full beards when he left them.

19. If Mari had *denied* that the claimant was his brother, *beis din* would believe him even if he had last seen his brother with a beard. However, since he said only that he was *unsure* whether the claimant was his brother, he is believed only if there is a reason that he would not have recognized the brother (*Tosafos*).

20. Rav Chisda instructed Mari to bring either the very witnesses that had come from Bei Chozai to identify the brother, so they would tell the court what they knew (see Gemara below), or another set of witnesses who would testify that the claimant was, in fact, not his brother (*Rashi*).

21. *Bava Kamma* 46b.

22. Although ordinarily in the case of a powerful defendant the plaintiff is not relieved of the burden of proving his claim, this case is different. For here the claimant produced witnesses, but claimed that they were too frightened to testify against the defendant. Therefore, the burden shifts to the defendant to convince the witnesses to testify (*Tosafos*).

23. Since they are afraid of me, they will falsely testify either that he is not my brother, or that they do not know whether he is my brother (*Tosafos*; see *Rashi*).

24. If they testify falsely they commit a double transgression, for not only do they withhold the truth, but they also lie (*Rashi*).

Even testifying that they do not know whether he is the brother would be considered false testimony, if indeed the witnesses know that he is (see *Tosafos*).

עין משפט
נר מצוה

סב א מיי' פ"ח מהל' נחלות הל' ב סמג עשין לו טוש"ע ח"מ סי' רפה סעיף ז:
סג ב ג ד מיי' שם סמג שם טוש"ע שם סעיף ט:
סד ה (מיי' פ"ד מהל' נחלות) סמג עשין לו טוש"ע ח"מ סי' רפ סעיף ו:
סה ו מיי' פ"ג מהל' עדות הל' יב סמג עשין קט טוש"ע ח"מ סי' כח סעיף ה:
סו ז מיי' פ"ט מהלכות נחלות הל' ב ועיין בהשגות ובמגיד משנה סמג עשין לו טוש"ע ח"מ סי' רפז סעיף א:

## רבינו חננאל

מורידין אמר רבא ש"מ מדרב הונא אין מחזיקין בנכסי קטן ואפי' הגדיל זו השמועה של רב הונא בתחלת פ' האשה שנתאלמנה. ומדקמדייק רבא משמעתיה דרב הונא ש"מ היל' כרב הונא והני מילי במקרקעי אין מורידין קרוב לנכסי קטן אבל מעות ומטלטלי אם היה הקרוב נאמן מורידין אותו וכך אמרו הגאונים דבמטלטלי לא חיישינן לקרוב [א]. ועוד ממעשה דההיא סבתא דהות לה תלת בנתא אישתבאי סבתא וחדא ברתא ומתה חדא מתרתי בנתא דאישתיירו ושבקא ינוקא. ושמעו דשכיבא סבתא אמרי תילתא יהבינן לברתה דהיא חולקאה ותילתא יהבינן לינוקא דהיא חולקא דאימיה ואידך תילתא אימור ברתה דנשבת בחייה היא והוינן מחתי הני קרובין בחולקא מיהו חד מינייהו הוא ינוקא ואין מורידין קטן לנכסי שבוי הילכך מוקמינן אפוטרופא לדנקא שהוא חצי השליש שהיה ראוי להיות ביד הינוקא ומיגו דמוקמינן אפוטרופא להאי דנקא מוקמינן נמי אידך דנקא. האי מעשה דייקא כשמואל וכרב הונא: מרי בר איסק אתא ליה אחא מבי חוזאי אמר ליה לא ידענא לך אייתי סהדי דהוא אחוה. אמר ליה רב חסדא זיל פלוג בהדיה אפי' בפרדיסי ובוסתני דשתלת דהאי אחוך הוא ואין מורידין קרוב בנכסי קטן ושלא ברשות ירדת לפיכך אין שמין לך כאריס אבל קרוב לנכסי גדול כי האי גוונא שמין לו כאריס. וכן נמי אי ידע דאית ליה אחי זעירי ומשבח השבח לאמצע דתנן הניח בנים גדולים וקטנים והשביחו הגדולים את הנכסים השביחו לאמצע וכן אמר רבא:

מתני'

### חשק שלמה על ר"ח

א) וכ"כ הרי"ף כאן בשם רב נמח גאון ז"ל.

---

ואפילו הגדיל ולא אמרן אלא באחי דאבא אבל באחי דאמא לית לן בה ואחי דאבא נמי לא אמרן אלא בארעתא אבל בבתי לית לן בה ובארעתא נמי לא אמרן אלא דלא עביד עיטדא אבל עביד עיטדא קלא אית לה [א]ולא היא לא שנא אחי דאבא ולא שנא אחי דאמא לא שנא ארעתא ולא שנא בתי ולא שנא עביד עיטדא לא שנא לא עביד עיטדא לא מחתינן [ב]ההיא סבתא דהויא לה תלת בנתא אישתבאי איהי וחדא ברתא אידך תרתי בנתא שכיבא חדא מינייהו ושבקה ינוקא אמר אביי היכי נעביד לוקמינהו לנכסי בידא דאחתא דלמא שכיבא סבתא ואין מורידין קרוב לנכסי קטן נוקמינהו לנכסיה בידא דינוקא דלמא לא שכיבא סבתא ואין מורידין קטן לנכסי שבוי אמר אביי הלכך פלגא יהבינא לה לאחתא ואידך פלגא מוקמינן ליה אפוטרופא לינוקא רבא אמר [ג]מגו דמוקמינן אפוטרופא לפלגא מוקמינן ליה אפוטרופא לאידך פלגא לסוף שמעו דשכיבא סבתא אמר אביי תילתא יהבינן לה לאחתא ותילתא יהבינן ליה לינוקא ואידך תילתא יהבינן דנקא לאחתא ואידך דנקא מוקמינן ליה אפוטרופא לינוקא רבא אמר [ד]מגו דמוקים אפוטרופא לדנקא מוקמינן נמי אפוטרופא לאידך דנקא ° [א] מרי בר איסק אתא ליה אחא מבי חוזאי א"ל פלוג לי אמר ליה לא ידענא לך אתא לקמיה דרב חסדא א"ל [ה]שפיר קאמר לך שנאמר [ג] א) ויכר יוסף את אחיו והם לא הכירוהו מלמד שיצא בלא חתימת זקן ובא בחתימת זקן א"ל זיל אייתי סהדי דאחוה את אמר ליה אית לי סהדי ודחלי מיניה דגברא אלימא הוא א"ל לדידיה זיל אנת אייתי סהדי דלאו אחוך הוא א"ל דינא הכי המוציא מחבירו עליו הראיה א"ל [ו]הכי דיינינא לך ולכל אלימי דחברך אמר ליה סוף סוף אתו סהדי ולא מסהדי א"ל תרתי לא עבדי לסוף אתו סהדי דאחוה הוא א"ל לפלוג לי נמי מפרדיסי ובוסתני דשתל אמר ליה שפיר קאמר לך [ג] דתנן [ז]הניח בנים גדולים וקטנים והשביחו גדולים את הנכסים השביחו לאמצע

---

**תוספות**

וכי תימא הא פשיטא ליה דאינו יודע למחות בסוף ג' אף ע"פ שהוא נזכר לשאול עידי מכירה דרגילות הוא טפי לשכוח מחאה בסוף כל ג' א"כ בלא רב הונא פשיטא דאין מחזיקין וי"ל דאי לאו רב הונא ממה שמעמידין אפוטרופוס לנכסי יתומין אין להוכיח דאין מחזיקין דאפילו מחזיקין לא חיישינן שמא יחזיק דב"ד לא יבררו כי אם נאמן או משום דידע למחות בסוף כל ג' כדפרישית אבל מדאמר רב הונא אין מורידין קרוב א"כ חושש לרמאות וגם אית ליה דלא ידע למחות בקרוב ולומר שדה זו של אבי ולא הגיע לחלקך אם כן בנכרי נמי לא ידע למחות ולכך אין מחזיקין וא"ת כמו שיש לו לדעת ולומר לנכרי לשאול עידי מכירה כמו כן יהיה לו דעת לומר לקרובו אייתי ראיה שזה הגיע לחלקך וי"ל דגבי קרוב סבור שאומר אמת שהרי של אביהם היה השדה ולא אסיק אדעתיה לומר אייתי ראייה אבל לנכרי מסיק אדעתיה למימר אייתי ראייה עידי מכירה: **לא** שנא עביד עיטדא לא מחתינן. וא"ת דבה"ב (ב"ב דף כט: ושם ד"ה אבל) אמרינן עטדא קלא אית לה וי"ל ביתומים החמירו יותר [ה]: **דלמא** שכיבא סבתא. וא"ת הא דתנן פרק כל הגט (גיטין דף כח. ושם ד"ה והניחו) המביא גט ממדינת הים והניחו זקן או חולה נותנין לה בחזקת שהוא קיים וי"ל דסבתא הגיעה לגבורות דהתם אמרינן כי הגיע לגבורות חיישינן ° אך קשה דבסמוך אמרינן הלכך פלגא יהבינן לאחתא תרי תלתי הוה לה למיתב דאפילו שכיבא סבתא מסתמא ברתא לא שכיבא דליכא למימר דברתא נמי הגיעה לגבורות דאם כן סבתא איתפלגא ותו ליכא למיחש דלמא שכיבא כדאמר בגיטין (שם) כיון דפלג פלג וי"ל דגבי גט דוקא אמרינן בחזקת שהוא קיים משום עיגונא וכן בשביל אכילת קרבן ותרומה אבל הכא אדרבה החמירו בנכסי יתומים להחזיק הסבתא וברתא במתה דאמרינן לעיל דאפי' בעביד עיטדא לא מחתינן אע"ג דאית לה קלא אי נמי הכא שנשבו חיישינן טפי דלמא מתו לפי שעשו להם יסורין: **מוקמינן** ליה אפוטרופוס. ואם תאמר והא אין מורידין קטן לנכסי שבוי ומסתמא אפי' על ידי אפוטרופוס דהא משמע דאי ודאי לא שכיבא סבתא הוה יהבינן כל נכסי לאחתא ואמאי נוקי פלגא לינוקא על ידי אפוטרופוס אלא ודאי בכל ענין אין מורידין קטן דכיון שהקטן אדון האפוטרופוס אולי ישמע לקטן שלא לחרוש ושלא לזרוע וי"ל דהא דקאמר פלגא מוקמינן ליה אפוטרופוס לינוקא לא לאכול כל הפירות כדין קרוב היורד לנכסי שבוי אלא שישמור האפוטרופוס כדין אריס בחזקת סבתא ויתפרנס הקטן מזה וזה טוב מלתתם לאחתא שתאכל כל הפירות חנם כדין קרוב היורד לנכסי שבוי: **שיצא** בלא חתימת זקן. הוא הדין אם יצא בחתימת זקן דאין נאמן לומר שהוא אחיו דא"כ לא שבקת חיי לכל בריה העשירים שכל אחד יאמר אני אחיך ועוד דהא תנן בפ' יש נוחלין (ב"ב דף קלד.) האומר זה אחי אינו נאמן אלא הכא מרי בר איסק לא היה טוען ברי אלא לא ידענא לך ולכך אם יצא בחתימת זקן אינו נאמן כיון שאינו מכחישו אלא אמר לא ידענא ליה: **זיל** את אייתי סהדי דלאו אחוך הוא. וא"ת וכי כל אדם עשיר אלם יצטרך להביא עדים שאין התובעו אחיו וי"ל דשאני הכא שאותו אמר שיש לו עדים ויראים להגיד א"ל רב חסדא שיעשה עמהם שיעידו ומרי בר איסק א"ל סוף סוף דהשתא נמי יעידו שקר מיראתי ויאמרו שאינו אחי או יאמרו שאינם יודעים אע"פ שיודעין ומשני תרתי לא עבדי חדא שישתקו מלהעיד וחדא שישקרו ויאמרו אין אנו יודעים או שיאמרו אינו אחיו:

וכן

---

**רש"י**

**ואפי' הגדיל.** הקטן משירד לתוכו ואכלו ג' שנים בפניו משהגדיל לא הויא חזקה דהואיל ותחילת ירידתו לתוכו הוה קטן לא ידע כשהגדיל שהן של אביו ולפיכך לא מיחה דאי ס"ל לרב הונא דמחזיקין בהן משהגדיל היכי מחתינן נכרי לנכסי קטן שמא יהא בידו משיגדיל ויטעון אתה מכרת לי משגדלת ואכלתים שני חזקה: **ולא אמרן.** דאין מורידין קרוב לנכסי קטן: **אלא באחי דאבא.** אחיו מאביו שיטעון בהן לך ירושה: **ארעתא.** שדות: **אבל בבתי לית לן בה.** שהשכנים מעידין עליהם שבאו לחלקו של קטן: **עיטדא.** שטר חלוקה כשחלקו מתחילה (מלכים ב יב) רק הבמות לא סרו מתרגמינן במתא לא [ד]עטדו לא הפליגו מהם: **לא שנא אחי דאמא.** פן יאמר של אמי היו נכסי מלוג ואביו של קטן בעל אמי היה מוחזק בהן מחמת שהוא אוכל פירות והוא מת קודם לאמי ולא ירשה ואני יורש חליין מחמת אמי: **היכי ליעבד.** בנכסי דסבתא שאין אנו יודעין אם קיימת אם מתה: **בידא דאחתא.** דהילכתא כרשב"ג דקס ליה שמואל כוותיה: **דלמא שכיבא סבתא.** ויש לקטן חלק בהן שהם שלו מחמת אמו או שמא חליין שלו שמא מתו שתי השבויות: **לוקמינהו לפלגא דנכסי בידא דינוקא.** איכא למיחש דלמא לא שכיבא סבתא ואין לו חלק בהן ואין מורידין קטן לנכסי שבוי: **פלגא יהבינן לאחתא.** ממה נפשך אם מתו שתי השבויות הרי זו יורשת חליין ואם לאו מורידין קרוב לנכסי שבוי: **מוקמינן אפוטרופוס.** ולא מחתינן קטן לגוייהו דלמא לא שכיבא ואין מורידין קטן לנכסי שבוי: **שמעו דשכיבא סבתא.** לסוף שמעו שמתה הזקנה ועל הבת שנשבית לא שמעו: **תילתא יהבינן כו'.** דהא ודאי שליש הנכסים לזו ושליש לקטן: **דנקא.** שתות חצי השליש: **יהבינן לאחתא.** ממה נפשך אם מתה האחות הרי חצי חלקה לזו ואם לאו מורידין קרוב לנכסי שבוי: **ואידך דנקא.** לא יהבינן לה שמא של קטן הם ואין מורידין קרוב לנכסי קטן: **אתא ליה אחא מבי חוזאי.** שהלך אביו לבי חוזאי ונשא שם אשה וילדה לו את זה וחזר מרי לכאן וירד לנכסי אביו ובא זה אחריו לזמן מרובה ותבע חלקו: **שפיר קאמר לך.** שאינו מכירך ואין זה רמאות שכשילא מאצלך לא היה לך חתימת זקן ועכשיו באת בחתימת זקן: **ויכר יוסף את אחיו.** שכשילא מהם היו כולם חתומי זקן והם לא הכירוהו שילא מאצלם בלא חתימת זקן ובא בחתימת זקן: **דלאו אחוך הוא.** אותם עדים שיש לו לזה שבאו משם ומכירין בו מי הוא הביאם אתה ויעידו שאינו בן אביך או בקש עדים אחרים: **א"ל.** מרי לרב חסדא אי מינאי דחלי מה תועלת: **סוף סוף אתו סהדי ולא מסהדי.** אלא כמותי ולא כמותך: **תרתי לא עבדי.** מיראתך יעשו אחת שישתקו אבל שתים לא יעשו לא דיין שישתקו ולא יעידו האמת אלא גם שיעידו שקר: **א"ל.** ההוא אחא לרב חסדא: **לפלוג לי מפרדיסי.** כרמים: **ובוסתני.** גינת של אילנות: **דשתל.** איהו והשביחן ויתן לי חליין כמו שהן משובחין:

וכן

---

מסורת הש"ס

א) (יבמות פח.), כתובות כז: [ע"ש], ב) [יבמות פח.], ג) בבא בתרא קמג., ד) [ע"ש בתרגום ותמלא דטעות נפל בספרים וצ"ל עטרא וכן הוא בערוך וכ"כ רש"י בגיטין פו. ד"ה ועטיר], ה) [וע"ע תוספות גיטין כח. ד"ה והניחו].

גליון הש"ס

גמ' מרי בר איסק. עיין יבמות דף כא ע"ב תוס' ד"ה ר"א: תוס' ד"ה דלמא וכו' אך קשה. עיין בתשו' מעיל לדקה סי' מח:

תורה אור השלם

א) וַיַּכֵּר יוֹסֵף אֶת אֶחָיו וְהֵם לֹא הִכִּרֻהוּ: [בראשית מב, ח]

ליקוטי רש"י

**ואפילו הגדיל.** לאחר מיכן והחזיק זה בפניו כמה שנים אינה חזקה הואיל ותחלתו כשהוא קטן ראהו מוחזק בה לא ידע כשהגדיל שהיתה של אביו עד ששומע מפי אחרים [כתובות יז:]. **אתא ליה אחא מבי חוזאי.** שהלך אביו שם והוליכו עמו וגדלו שם ומת אביו וחזר לעירו ותבע חלקו בנכסי אביו [שם כז:]. **השביחו גדולים את הנכסים.** סתם בעודן בתפוסת הבית. **השביחו לאמצע.** ויטלו קטנים כגדולים [רשב"ם ב"ב קמג:].

וַאֲפִילּוּ הִגְדִּיל – **even if [the child] became an adult** after the occupier entered his property.[1]

The Gemara explains that Rav Huna's ruling, that a relative cannot be appointed as a caretaker over a minor's property, applies only in certain cases:

וְלָא אֲמָרַן אֶלָּא – **And [Rav Huna] did not state** his ruling that a relative may not be appointed as the administrator of a minor's property **only** בְּאַחֵי דְּאַבָּא – **regarding the paternal brothers** of the child, who might eventually claim the administered land as part of their own inheritance. אֲבָל בְּאַחֵי דְּאִמָּא – **However, regarding maternal brothers,** who cannot make such a claim, because they do not inherit along with the child, לֵית לָן בָּהּ – **there is no problem with [their appointment].** וְאַחֵי דְּאַבָּא נַמִי לָא אֲמָרַן אֶלָּא בְּאַרְעָתָא – **And even in the case of paternal brothers, [this ruling] was not stated only with regard to** a minor's **fields,**[2] which are not constantly watched by other people. אֲבָל בְּבָתֵּי – **However, regarding** the appointment of a caretaker for a minor's **houses,** לֵית לָן בָּהּ – **there is no problem with [the appointment]** of a paternal brother, because there are neighbors that will know that the houses were inherited by the child, not the caretaker.

וּבְאַרְעָתָא נַמִי לָא אֲמָרַן אֶלָּא – **And even with respect to** a minor's **fields, [this ruling]** prohibiting the appointment of a paternal brother as caretaker **was not stated only** דְּלָא עֲבִיד עִיטְדָא – **where a document of division** detailing which properties were given to each brother **was not written** when the estate was divided. אֲבָל עֲבִיד עִיטְדָא – **However, if a document of division was written,** which identifies the recipient of each share of the estate, קָלָא אִית לָהּ – **[the document] has a "voice"** – that is, it becomes public knowledge that these fields belong to the child, and no harm will result from the appointment of a paternal brother as an administrator.

Although the Gemara just made three qualifications of Rav Huna's ruling, it now reverses its position, and concludes that Rav Huna forbids *any* relative from becoming a caretaker for a minor's property in all cases:

וְלָא הִיא – **But** in truth **it is not** so! לָא שְׁנָא אַחֵי דְּאַבָּא וְלָא שְׁנָא אַחֵי דְּאִמָּא – **There is no difference between paternal brothers and maternal brothers,** לָא שְׁנָא אַרְעָתָא וְלָא שְׁנָא בָּתֵּי – **and there is no difference between fields and houses,** לָא שְׁנָא עֲבִיד עִיטְדָא לָא שְׁנָא לָא עֲבִיד עִיטְדָא – **and there is no difference whether a document of division was written or whether a document of division was not written.** לָא מַחְתִּינָן – In all of these cases, **we do not appoint** a relative to manage a minor's property.[3]

The Gemara records a related incident:

הַהִיא סַבְתָּא – There was **a certain elderly woman** הֲוְיָא לָהּ תְּלַת בְּנָתָא – **who had three daughters.** אִישְׁתְּבַאי אִיהִי וַחֲדָא בְּרַתָּא – **She and one of the daughters were captured.** אִידָךְ תַּרְתֵּי בְּנָתָא – As far as **the other two daughters,** שְׁכִיבָא חֲדָא מִינַּיְיהוּ – **one of them died** וְשַׁבְקָה יְנוּקָא – **and left a young boy** as her sole heir. Neither the elderly woman, the captive daughter, nor the deceased daughter were married at the time that this occurs.

Abaye analyzes the options:

אָמַר אַבַּיֵי – **Abaye said:** הֵיכִי נַעֲבִיד – **What shall we do** with the elderly woman's property?[4] לוֹקְמִינְהוּ לְנִכְסֵי בְּיָדָא דַּאֲחָתָא – **To place** all of the property in the hands of the surviving uncaptured **sister**[5] would not be right, דִּלְמָא שְׁכִיבָא סַבְתָּא – for **perhaps the elderly woman has died,**[6] and her young grandson is entitled to part of her estate as an inheritance,[7] אֵין מוֹרִידִין קָרוֹב לְנִכְסֵי קָטָן – **and** *beis din* **does not appoint a relative to** manage **a minor's property!** נוֹקְמִינְהוּ לְנִכְסֵי בְּיָדָא דִּינוּקָא – **Shall we instead place** half of **the property in the hands of the young boy,** and the other half in the hands of the uncaptured sister?[8] This, too, is not appropriate, דִּלְמָא לָא שְׁכִיבָא סַבְתָּא – for **perhaps the elderly woman is not dead,**[9] אֵין מוֹרִידִין קָטָן לְנִכְסֵי שְׁבוּי – **and** *beis din* **does not appoint a minor to** manage **a captive's property!**

Abaye decides what should be done:

אָמַר אַבַּיֵי – **Abaye said:** הִלְכָּךְ – **Therefore,** פַּלְגָא יָהֲבִינָא לָהּ לַאֲחָתָא – **we give half** of the property **to the** uncaptured **sister** to manage,[10] וְאִידָךְ פַּלְגָא – **and** for **the other half** מוֹקְמִינַן

NOTES

1. Even if the property is occupied for three years after the child came of legal age, and the occupier claims that the child sold him the property after he became an adult, he does not have a valid *chazakah.* Since he first occupied the property while the child was a minor, the child possibly did not realize – even after he became an adult – that the property belonged to his father. For that reason he did not protest the occupation of the property during the first three years of his adulthood.

Since Rav Huna permits a non-relative to be appointed as administrator of a minor's property, he is clearly not concerned with the possibility that the administrator will occupy the land for three years after the child reaches adulthood. We see from this that Rav Huna would not consider this occupation to be a valid *chazakah* (*Rashi*).

2. Literally: lands (see *Rashi*).

3. Even a maternal brother can falsely claim that the property is his, because he can say that it originally belonged to his mother, but was given to the minor's father as *melog* property. [The minor's father was the mother's second husband.] The maternal brother can therefore claim that the minor's father died, and then his wife (the mother) died. In that case, her property would be inherited by both of *her* sons. Therefore, if we permit a maternal brother to manage the minor's property, he could claim that it is part of his share of their mother's estate (*Rashi*).

In addition, a relative is not appointed even to manage houses, and even if a document of division was written, because we are concerned that, over the course of time, the document will be lost, and the true ownership of the property will be forgotten [despite the presence of neighbors] (*Rambam, Hil. Nachalos* 8:2).

4. They did not know whether she was dead or still alive (*Rashi*).

5. Abaye considered this option because it follows the opinion of Rabban Shimon ben Gamliel, who ruled (above, 38b) that the property of a captive who was not rumored to be dead can be placed in the care of an heir. Since Shmuel agrees with this opinion (above, 39a), it is accepted as the halachah. In this case, the uncaptured sister is the only heir that is capable of managing her mother's property [as her nephew is a minor] (see *Rashi*).

6. Although we are not usually concerned that someone in a distant place (even a captive) has died, this case is an exception, since the elderly woman is subject to torture while in captivity. Alternatively, since even a remote possibility exists that some of the property is now owned by an orphaned child, we must be extra careful to safeguard the property (*Tosafos*).

7. A surviving grandson inherits in the place of his parents after their deaths (see *Bava Basra* 115a). In our case, if only the grandmother died the grandson is entitled to his deceased mother's one-third share. If the captured sister died as well, the grandson is also entitled to half of that aunt's one-third share – so half the estate would be his (see *Rashi*).

8. This would avoid the problem of appointing a relative to manage a minor's property (see *Rashi* and see previous note).

9. That is, we should be concerned that the grandmother has not died and that the minor does not own any part of her property (*Rashi*). If this were the case, he would come to the property only as an administrator.

10. This is certainly a valid course of action; for if the grandmother has not died, *beis din* is required to appoint this daughter to administer the captive grandmother's property. If the grandmother has died but the captured sister is still alive, one-third of the property actually belongs to this daughter as her inheritance, and she is also allowed to manage her captive sister's share. And if both captives have died, the daughter indeed would receive half of the property as her share of the inheritance (*Rashi*).

ואפילו הגדיל ולא אמרן אלא באחי דאבא אבל באחי דאמא לית לן בה ואחי דאבא נמי לא אמרן אלא בארעתא אבל בבתי לית לן בה ובארעתא נמי לא אמרן אלא דלא עביד עיטדא אבל עביד עיטדא קלא אית לה [א]ולא היא לא שנא אחי דאבא ולא שנא אחי דאמא לא שנא ארעתא ולא שנא בתי ולא שנא עביד עיטדא לא שנא לא עביד עיטדא לא מחתינן [ב]ההיא סבתא דהויא לה תלת בנתא אישתבאי איהי וחדא ברתא אידך תרתי בנתא שכיבא חדא מינייהו ושבקה ינוקא אמר אביי היכי נעביד לוקמינהו לנכסי בידא דאחתא דלמא שכיבא סבתא ואין מורידין קרוב לנכסי קטן נוקמינהו לנכסיה בידא דינוקא דלמא לא שכיבא סבתא ואין מורידין קטן לנכסי שבוי אמר אביי הלכך פלגא יהבינא לה לאחתא ואידך פלגא מוקמינן ליה אפוטרופא לינוקא רבא אמר [ג]מגו דמוקמינן אפוטרופא לפלגא מוקמינן ליה אפוטרופא לאידך פלגא לסוף שמעו דשכיבא סבתא אמר אביי תילתא יהבינן לה לאחתא ותילתא יהבינן ליה לינוקא ואידך תילתא יהבינן דנקא לאחתא ואידך דנקא מוקמינן ליה אפוטרופא לינוקא רבא אמר [ד]מגו דמוקים אפוטרופא לדנקא מוקמינן נמי אפוטרופא לאידך דנקא [ה] א) מרי בר איסק אתא ליה אחא מבי חוזאי א"ל פלוג לי אמר ליה לא ידענא לך אתא לקמיה דרב חסדא א"ל [ה]שפיר קאמר לך שנאמר ג) א) ויכר יוסף את אחיו והם לא הכירוהו מלמד שיצא בלא חתימת זקן ובא בחתימת זקן א"ל זיל אייתי סהדי דאחוה את אמר ליה אית לי סהדי ודחלי מיניה דגברא אלימא הוא א"ל לדידיה זיל אנת אייתי סהדי דלאו אחוך הוא א"ל דינא הכי המוציא מחבירו עליו הראיה א"ל [ו]הכי דיינינא לך ולכל אלימי דחברך אמר ליה סוף סוף אתו סהדי ולא מסהדי א"ל תרתי לא עבדי לסוף אתו סהדי דאחוה הוא א"ל לפלוג לי נמי מפרדיסי ובוסתני דשתל אמר ליה שפיר קאמר לך ג) דתנן [ז]הניח בנים גדולים וקטנים והשביחו גדולים את הנכסים השביחו לאמצע

ואפי' הגדיל. הקטן משירד לתוכו ואכלו ג' שנים בפניו משהגדיל לא הויא חזקה דהואיל ותחילת ירידתו לתוכו הוה קטן לא ידע כשהגדיל שהן של אביו ולפיכך לא מיחה דאי ס"ל לרב הונא דמחזיקין בהן משהגדיל היכי מחתינן נכרי לנכסי קטן שמא יהא בידו משיגדיל ויטעון אתה מכרת לי משגדלת ואכלתים שני חזקה: ולא אמרן. דאין מורידין קרוב לנכסי קטן: אלא באחי דאבא. אחיו מאביו שיטעון בהן לד ירושה: ארעתא. שדות: אבל בבתי לית לן בה. שהשכנים מעידין עליהם שבאו לחלקו של קטן: עיטדא. שטר חלוקה כשחלקו מתחילה (מלכים ב יב) רק הבמות לא סרו מתרגמינן במתא לא ד) עטדו לא הפליגו מהם: לא שנא אחי דאמא. פן יאמר של אמי היו נכסי מלוג ואביו של קטן בעל אמי היה מוחזק בהן מחמת שהוא אוכל פירות והוא מת קודם לאמי ולא ירשה ואני יורש אותן מחמת אמי: היכי ליעבד. בנכסי דסבתא שאין אנו יודעין אם קיימת אם מתה: בידא דאחתא. דהילכתא כרשב"ג דקם ליה שמואל כוותיה: דלמא שכיבא סבתא. ויש לקטן חלק בהן שהם שלו מחמת אמו או שמא חציין שלו שמא מתו שתי השבויות: לוקמינהו לפלגא דנכסי בידא דינוקא. איכא למיחש דלמא לא שכיבא סבתא ואין לו חלק בהן ואין מורידין קטן לנכסי שבוי: פלגא יהבינן לאחתא. ממה נפשך אם מתו שתי השבויות הרי זו יורשת חציין ואם לאו מורידין קרוב לנכסי שבוי: מוקמינן אפוטרופוס. ולא מחתינן קטן לגוייהו דלמא לא שכיבא ואין מורידין קטן לנכסי שבוי: שמעו דשכיבא סבתא. לסוף שמעו שמתה הזקנה ועל הבת שנשבית לא שמעו: תילתא יהבינן כו'. דהא ודאי שליש הנכסים לזו ושליש לקטן: דנקא. שתות חצי השליש: יהבינן לאחתא. ממה נפשך אם מתה האחות הרי חצי חלקה לזו ואם לאו מורידין קרוב לנכסי שבוי: ואידך דנקא. לא יהבינן לה שמא של קטן הם ואין מורידין קרוב לנכסי קטן: אתא ליה אחא מבי חוזאי. שהלך אביו לבי חוזאי ונשא שם אשה וילדה לו את זה וחזר מרי לכאן וירד לנכסי אביו ובא זה אחריו לזמן מרובה ותבע חלקו: שפיר קאמר לך. שאינו מכירך ואין זה רמאות שכשילא מאצלך לא היה לך חתימת זקן ועכשיו באת בחתימת זקן: ויכר יוסף את אחיו. שכשילא מהם היו כולם חתומי זקן והם לא הכירוהו שילא מאצלם בלא חתימת זקן ובא בחתימת זקן: דלאו אחוך הוא. אותם עדים שיש לו לזה שבאו משם ומכירין בו מי הוא הביאם אתה ויעידו שאינו בן אביך או בקש עדים אחרים: א"ל. מרי לרב חסדא אי מינאי דחלי מה תועלת: סוף סוף אתו סהדי ולא מסהדי. אלא כמותי ולא כמותך: תרתי לא עבדי. מיראתך יעשו אחת שישתקו אבל שתים לא יעשו לא דיין שישתקו ולא יעידו האמת אלא גם שיעידו שקר: א"ל. ההוא אחא לרב חסדא: לפלוג לי מפרדיסי. כרמים: ובוסתני. ביתן של אילנות: דשתל. איהו והשביחן ויתן לי חציין כמו שהן משובחין:

וכן

וכי תימא הא פשיטא ליה דאינו יודע למחות בסוף ג' אף ע"פ שהוא נזכר לשאול עידי מכירה דרגילות הוא טפי לשכוח מחאה בסוף כל ג' א"כ בלא רב הונא פשיטא דאין מחזיקין וי"ל דאי לאו רב הונא ממה שמעמידין אפוטרופוס לנכסי יתומין אין להוכיח דאין מחזיקין דאפילו מחזיקין לא חיישינן שמא יחזיק דב"ד לא יבררו כי אם נאמן או משום דידע למחות בסוף כל ג' כדפרישית אבל מדאמר רב הונא אין מורידין קרוב א"כ חושש לרמאות וגם אית ליה דלא ידע למחות בקרוב ולומר שדה זו של אבי ולא הגיע לחלקך אם כן בנכרי נמי לא ידע למחות ולכך אין מחזיקין וא"ת כמו שיש לו לדעת ולומר לנכרי לשאול עידי מכירה כמו כן יהיה לו דעת לומר לקרובו אייתי ראיה שזה הגיע לחלקך וי"ל דגבי קרוב סבור שאומר אמת שהרי של אביהם היה השדה ולא אסיק אדעתיה לומר אייתי ראייה אבל לנכרי מסיק אדעתיה למימר אייתי ראייה עידי מכירה: **לא** שנא עביד עיטדא לא מחתינן. וא"ת דבח"ה (ב"ב דף כט: ושם ד"ה אבל) אמרינן עטדא קלא אית לה וי"ל ביתומים החמירו יותר ה): **דלמא** שכיבא סבתא. וא"ת הא דתנן פרק כל הגט (גיטין דף כח. ושם ד"ה והניחו) המביא גט ממדינת הים והניחו זקן או חולה נותנין לה בחזקת שהוא קיים וי"ל דסבתא הגיעה לגבורות דהתם אמרינן כי הגיע לגבורות חיישינן ° אך קשה דבסמוך אמרינן הלכך פלגא יהבינן לאחתא תרי תלתי הוה לה למיתב דאפילו שכיבא סבתא מסתמא ברתא לא שכיבא דליכא למימר דברתא נמי הגיעה לגבורות דאם כן סבתא איתפלגא ותו ליכא למיחש דלמא שכיבא כדאמר בגיטין (שם) כיון דפלג פלג וי"ל דגבי גט דוקא אמרינן בחזקת שהוא קיים משום עיגונא וכן בשביל אכילת קרבן ותרומה אבל הכא אדרבה החמירו בנכסי יתומים להחזיק הסבתא וברתא במתה דאמרינן לעיל דאפי' בעביד עיטדא לא מחתינן אע"ג דאית לה קלא אי נמי הכא שנשבו חיישינן טפי דלמא מתו לפי שעשו להם יסורין: **מוקמינן** ליה אפוטרופוס. ואם תאמר והא אין מורידין קטן לנכסי שבוי ומסתמא אפי' על ידי אפוטרופוס דהא משמע דאי ודאי לא שכיבא סבתא הוה יהבינן כל נכסי לאחתא ואמאי נוקי פלגא לינוקא על ידי אפוטרופוס אלא ודאי בכל ענין אין מורידין קטן דכיון שהקטן אדון האפוטרופוס אולי ישמע לקטן שלא לחרוש ושלא לזרוע וי"ל דהא דקאמר פלגא מוקמינן ליה אפוטרופוס לינוקא לא לאכול כל הפירות כדין קרוב היורד לנכסי שבוי אלא שישמור האפוטרופוס כדין אריס בחזקת סבתא ויתפרנס הקטן מזה וזה טוב מלהתם לאחתא שתאכל כל הפירות חנם כדין קרוב היורד לנכסי שבוי: **שיצא** בלא חתימת זקן. הוא הדין אם יצא בחתימת זקן דאין נאמן לומר שהוא אחיו דא"כ לא שבקת חיי לכל בריה העשירים שכל אחד יאמר אני אחיך ועוד דהא תנן בפ' יש נוחלין (ב"ב דף קלד.) האומר זה אחי אינו נאמן אלא הכא מרי בר איסק לא היה טוען ברי אלא לא ידענא לך ולכך אם יצא בחתימת זקן אינו נאמן כיון שאינו מכחישו אלא אמר לא ידענא ליה: **זיל** את אייתי סהדי דלאו אחוך הוא. וא"ת וכי כל אדם עשיר אלם יצטרך להביא עדים שאין התובעו אחיו וי"ל דשאני הכא שאותו אמר שיש לו עדים ויראים להגיד א"ל רב חסדא שיעשה עמהם שיעידו ומרי בר איסק א"ל סוף סוף דהשתא נמי יעידו שקר מיראתי ויאמרו שאינו אחי או יאמרו שאינם יודעים אע"פ שיודעין ומשני תרתי לא עבדי חדא שישתקו מלהעיד וחדא שישקרו ויאמרו אין אנו יודעים או שיאמרו אינו אחיו:

וכן

## עין משפט נר מצוה

סב א מיי' פ"ח מהל' נחלות הל' ב סמג עשין לב טוש"ע ח"מ סי' רפה סעיף ז:

סג ב ג ד מיי' שם סמג שם טוש"ע שם סעיף ט:

סד ה (מיי' פ"ד מהל' נחלות) סמג עשין לב טוש"ע ח"מ סי' רפ סעיף ו:

סה ו מיי' פ"ג מהל' עדות הל' יב סמג עשין קט טוש"ע ח"מ סי' כח סעיף ה:

סו ז מיי' פ"ט מהלכות נחלות הל' ב ועיין בהשגות ובמגיד משנה סמג עשין לב טוש"ע ח"מ סי' רפו סעיף א:

## רבינו חננאל

מורידין אמר רבא ש"מ מדרב הונא אין מחזיקין בנכסי קטן ואפי' הגדיל זו השמועה של רב הונא בתחלת פ' האשה שנתאלמנה. ומדקמדייק רבא משמעתיה דרב הונא ש"מ היל' כרב הונא והני מילי במקרקעי אין מורידין קרוב לנכסי קטן אבל מעות ומטלטלי אם היה הקרוב נאמן מורידין אותו וכך אמרו הגאונים דבמטלטלי לא חיישינן לקרוב א). ועוד ממעשה דההיא סבתא דהות לה תלת בנתא אישתבאי סבתא וחדא ברתא ומתה חדא מתרתי בנתא דאישתיירו ושבקא ינוקא. ושמעו דשכיבא סבתא אמרי תילתא יהבינן לברתה דהיא חולקאה ותילתא יהבינן לינוקא דהיא חולקא דאימיה ואידך תילתא אימור ברתה דנשבת בחייה היא והוינן מחתי הני קרובין בחולקא מיהו חד מינייהו הוא ינוקא ואין מורידין קטן לנכסי שבוי הילכך מוקמינן אפוטרופא לדנקא שהוא חצי השליש שהיה ראוי להיות ביד הינוקא ומיגו דמוקמינן אפוטרופא להאי דנקא מוקמינן נמי אידך דנקא. האי מעשה דייקא כשמואל וכרב הונא: מרי בר איסק אתא ליה אחא מבי חוזאי אמר ליה לא ידענא לך אייתי סהדי דהוא אחוה. אמר ליה רב חסדא זיל פלוג בהדיה אפי' בפרדיסי ובוסתני דשתלת דהאי אחוך הוא ואין מורידין קרוב בנכסי קטן ושלא ברשות ירדת לפיכך אין שמין לך כאריס אבל קרוב לנכסי גדול כי האי גוונא שמין לו כאריס. וכן נמי אי ידע דאית ליה אחי זעירי ומשבח השבח לאמצע דתנן הניח בנים גדולים וקטנים והשביחו הגדולים את הנכסים השביחו לאמצע וכן אמר רבא:

מתני'

## חשק שלמה על ר"ח

א) וכ"כ הרי"ף כאן בשם רב נטמה גאון ז"ל.

## מסורת הש"ס

א) (יבמות פח.), כתובות כח: [ע"ש], ב) [יבמות פח.], ג) בבא בתרא קמג:, ד) [ע"ש בתרגום ותמלא דטעות נפל בספרים וצ"ל עטרא וכן הוא בערוך וכ"כ רש"י בגיטין פו. ד"ה ועטיר], ה) [וע"ע תוספות גיטין כח. ד"ה והניחו].

## גליון הש"ס

גמ' מרי בר איסק. עיין יבמות דף כא ע"ב תוס' ד"ה ר"א: תוס' ד"ה דלמא וכו' אך קשה. עיין בתשו' מעיל לדקה סי' מח:

## תורה אור השלם

א) וַיַּכֵּר יוֹסֵף אֶת אֶחָיו וְהֵם לֹא הִכִּרֻהוּ: [בראשית מב, ח]

## ליקוטי רש"י

ואפילו הגדיל. לאחר מיכן והחזיק זה בפניו כמה שנים אינה חזקה הואיל ותחלתו כשהוא קטן ראהו מוחזק בה לא ידע כשהגדיל שהיתה של אביו עד ששומע מפי אחרים [כתובות יז:]. אתא ליה אחא מבי חוזאי. שהלך אביו שם והוליכו עמו וגדלו שם ומת אביו וחזר לעירו ותבע חלקו בנכסי אביו [שם כז:]. השביחו גדולים את הנכסים. שהם בעודן בתפוסת הבית. השביחו לאמצע. ויטלו קטנים כגדולים [רשב"ם ב"ב קמג:].

נטושים דבע"כ דכתיב א) והשביעית תשמטנה ונטשתה ה) אפקעתא דמלכא רטושים דמדעתן דכתיב ב) אם על בנים רוטשה תנא א וכולם שמין להם כארים אהייא אילימא אשבויין השתא זריז ונשכר הוה מאי דאשבח מיבעיא אלא ארטושים והא מוציאין אותן מידו קתני אלא אנטושים למאן אילימא לרבנן הא אמרי מוציאין אותו מידו אי רבן שמעון בן גמליאל הא אמר שמעתי שהנטושים כשבויין ולא שבויין כשבויין דאין מוציאין אותן מידו ולא שבויין דאילו התם זריז ונשכר ואילו הכא שיימינן ליה כארים ומאי שנא מהא ג) דתנן ב המוציא הוצאות על נכסי אשתו הוציא הרבה ואכל קימעא ואכל הרבה מה שהוציא הוציא ומה שאכל אכל הא לא דמיא אלא להא (ג) דתנן) ג המוציא הוצאות על נכסי אשתו קטנה כמוציא על נכסי אחר דמי אלמא כיון דלא סמכא דעתיה תקינו ליה רבנן כי היכי דלא לפסדינהו הכא נמי תקינו ליה רבנן כי היכי דלא לפסדינהו וכולן שמין להם כארים וכולן לאיתויי מאי לאיתויי הא דאמר רב נחמן אמר שמואל שבוי שנשבה מורידין קרוב לנכסיו יצא לדעת אין מורידין קרוב לנכסיו ורב נחמן דידיה אמר ד בורח הרי הוא כשבוי בורח מחמת מאי אילימא מחמת כרגא היינו לדעת ה אלא בורח מחמת מרדין אמר רב יהודה אמר שמואל ו שבוי שנשבה והניח קמה לקצור ענבים לבצור תמרים לגדור זיתים למסוק בית דין יורדין לנכסיו ומעמידין אפוטרופוס וקוצר ובוצר וגודר ומוסק ואח"כ מורידין קרוב לנכסיו ולוקים אפוטרופא לעולם ז אפוטרופא לדיקנני לא מוקמינן: אמר רב הונא ח אין מורידין קטן לנכסי שבוי ט ולא קרוב לנכסי קטן י ולא קרוב מחמת קרוב לנכסי קטן אין מורידין קטן לנכסי שבוי דלמא מפסיד להו ולא קרוב מחמת קרוב לנכסי קטן באחי מאימא [ולא קרוב לנכסי קטן] כיון דלא מחי אתי לאחזוקי ביה ד) אמר רבא שמע מיניה מדרב הונא כ אין מחזיקין בנכסי קטן ואפילו

---

**רש"י**

ה"ג נטושים על כרחן דכתיב והשביעית תשמטנה ונטשתה. היינו על כרחו: אפקעתא דמלכא. מלות המלך: רטושים מדעתן דכתיב אם על בנים רוטשה. היינו מדעתו ולא שביה דכתיב רישיה דקרא וקם שאון בעמך היו יראים שלא יבאו אויבים עליהם וכל מבצריך יושד יגלו בגולה מאיליהן וישארו העיירות שדודין מאין איש כשוד שלמן בית ארבאל ביום מלחמה כשודדין הבאין למלחמה על ידי מארב על עם היושב בשלום שלא נזהרו בהם לברוח מפניהם ושודדים את הכל וכמוהו (ירמיה יג) הגלת יהודה כולה הגלת שלומים מתוך ישיבת שלום באין מחריד הגלם נבוכדנצר. בית ארבאל תרגם יהונתן בית מארב אל"ף למ"ד יתרים בו כמו (הושע ב) יענו את יזרעאל שהוא לשון זריעה ולא לשון עיר ומדקא אמר יושד כשוד שלמן בית ארבאל מכלל דההוא יומא לאו בית ארבאל ביום מלחמה הוה אלא מורך בא בלבם והמה עוזבים אם על בנים והולכים להם מדאגת האויב שמא יבא עליהם: רוטשה. נעזבה: וכולן. מפ' לקמיה אהייא קאי וכללא לאתויי מאי: שמין להם כארים. אם יבאו הבעלים יטלו אלו בשבח קרקעות ופירות כמנהג אריסי המקום: השתא זריז ונשכר הוי. [א] ויטול הכל: דאילו התם זריז ונשכר. דכיון ששמעו בו שמת כי נחת לה אדעתא דכולהו פירי נחת אבל הכא דלא שמעו שמת לאו אדעתא דכולה נחית אלא ליטול כארים בכל שנה ושאר פירות יהא מונחין: נכסי אשתו. נכסי מלוג שהוא אוכל פירות והקרן שלה: הוציא הרבה ואכל פירות קימעא. קודם שמת או שגירשה: הא לא דמיא. תרוצא הוא הא דנכסי שבויין להא דאשתו קטנה דמי: קטנה. שהיא יתומה שהשיאוה אמה ואחיה ואין קידושין תופסין בה מן התורה אלא מדברי סופרים לפיכך יוצאה במיאון בע"כ אם תמאן: כמוציא על נכסי אחר דמי. ואם הוציא ולא אכל כדי הוצאתו שמין לו כארים: דלא סמכא דעתיה. שיהא מוחזק בידו דדואג שמא תמאן בו: תקינו ליה רבנן. ליטול כארים: כי היכי דלא ניפסדינהו. שלא יקלקל הקרקעות לזורען תמיד ולא יעבוד ולא יעדור כרמים: לאיתויי הא דרב נחמן. בורח מחמת מרדין: יצא לדעת אין מורידין. דכיון שהיה שפוי בדעתו ולא נוהו בלכתו לירד לנכסיו ש"מ לא ניחא ליה: בורח הרי הוא כשבוי. שאין דעתו מיושבת עליו מחמת שהוא בהול: מחמת כרגא. שאין לו ממה לפרוע כסף גולגלתו למלך וברח לפני בוא הזמן: היינו יוצא לדעת. שאין כאן בהלה: מחמת מרדין. שהרג את הנפש ופרסאי הורגין על שפיכות דמים כדאמרינן בבבא קמא (דף קיז.) מרדין היא רליה בלשון פרסי וכן מפורש בשערים דרב האי גאון (שער מ): מעמידין אפוטרופוס. להכניס דבר המוכן ויהא שמור לבעלים ואח"כ מורידין קרוב להשביח וליטול כארים: ולוקים אפוטרופוס לעולם. שלא יטול כלום: אפוטרופא לדיקנני לא מוקמינן. אין בית דין טורחין לבקש אפוטרופוס לאנשים גדולים שנתמלא זקנם לפי שלא ימלאוהו דבשלמא ליתמי איכא דשמע להו והוי אפוטרופוס לדבר מצוה אבל לדיקנני לא שמעי להו: אין מורידין קטן לנכסי שבוי. ואפילו הוא ראוי ליורשו דקא מפסיד להו ומוטב שיורידו להם איש נכרי: ולא קרוב. הראוי לירש בנכסי קטן לעשות ולאכול כדמפרש טעמיה דכיון דקטן לא ידע למחויי אתא האי קרוב לאחזוקי בהן ולומר לחלק ירושתו בא וטוב להם להוריד איש נכרי דלא מצי למטען בהו ירושה: ולא קרוב מחמת קרוב לנכסי קטן. כגון קטן שיש לו אח מאב ואותו אח מאב יש לו אח מאם דלאיש נכרי הוא אבל קטן אין מורידין אותו אח מאם לנכסי קטן מחמת קורבת אחיו של זה שהוא אח של קטן דאתי לאחזוקי בהו לצורך אחיו ויאמר נכסים הללו של אחי מאמי הם שנפלו לו מאביו ואלו לחלקו באו: באחי מאימא. כדפרישית שזה אח מן האם לאחיו של קטן מן האב: ש"מ מדרב הונא. דאמר אין מורידין קרוב לנכסי קטן שמא יחזיק בהם מחמת ירושה אבל אחר שאין לו טענת ירושה מורידין ולא חיישינן שמא יטעון אביו של קטן מכרם לי ואכלתים שני חזקה ש"מ אין מחזיקין בנכסי קטן אם לא אכל בפני האב שלש שנים אין שלש שנים שאכלן בפני הקטן חזקה:
ואפילו

---

**תוספות**

וכולם שמין להם כארים. אנטושים דרשב"ג קאי כדמפיק פי' רש"י דבשבוי (א) דשמע שמתו אוכל כל הפירות ואם יבואו הבעלים קודם שיאכל הפירות יטול כשאר אריסין ויחזיר השאר ובנטושים דלא שמע שמת לא יאכל כל הפירות אלא שמין הפירות שיאכל כשאר אריסין למחצה לשליש ולרביע ולא יאכל כלום בחנם וקשה דלמאי משני לעיל לירד ולמכור תנן לישני לירד ולאכול תנן דהא אפילו לאכול בחנם אינו יורד ועוד מאי פריך בתר הכי אף בניהם כלל לא הא ודאי אין לו כלל אפילו למ"ד מורידין כיון שאין לו אלא כאריס נכרי ועוד מאי פריך מהמוציא הוצאות על נכסי אשתו דהתם יורד לאכול כל הפירות אבל הכא אינו יורד כי אם בתורת אריסות ותו דאמר שמואל לקמן שבוי שהניח קמה לקצור מעמידין אפוטרופוס וקוצר ובוצר ואח"כ מורידין קרוב לנכסיו ומעיקרא אמאי אין מורידין קרוב כיון שלא יאכל הפירות בחנם לכך נראה דודאי שכל הפירות אוכל בחנם ואם זבל וחרש וזרע ובעלים באו קודם שקצר יטול כאריס שכר טרחו ועמלו ולרב וכן לת"ק אית להו שאין שמין כאריס ולכך אין מורידין דלמא מפסיד להו לפי שירא שיבואו הבעלים קודם שיקצור ויאכל ולא יטול כלום ולא ישביח הקרקע אלא כל מה שימצא יאכל בחנם כדין קרוב היורד לנכסי שבוי והשתא פריך שפיר כיון שאוכל כל הפירות כשיבואו הבעלים קודם שילקט אמאי נוטל כאריס טפי מהמוציא הוצאות על נכסי אשתו כו' והא דקאמר ואילו התם זריז ונשכר פי' כששמע הבעלים ממשמשים ובאין מניחין אותו לקדם ולתלוש אע"פ שהפירות ישוו הרבה מעמלו כיון שאם לא יקדם אין משלמין טרחו אבל הכא בנטושים אם באו בעלים אין מניחין אותו לתלוש כיון דלא מפסיד מידי דשיימי' להו כאריס:

**אמר** שמואל שבוי שנשבה מורידין. וא"ת והאמרה שמואל חדא זימנא וי"ל דה"ק אף על גב דבשבוי מורידין יצא לדעת אין מורידין:

**היינו** לדעת. דמסתמא לא פליג אשמואל מדלא קאמר אף בורח או אף יוצא לדעת:

**ש"מ** מדרב הונא אין מחזיקין בנכסי קטן ואפי' הגדיל. פרש"י מדאמר רב הונא אין מורידין קרוב הא נכרי מורידין וקשה דבלא רב הונא כמה משניות יש שמעמידין אפוטרופוס לנכסי יתומים פרק הניזקין (גיטין דף נב.) מנהו ב"ד לא ישבע וע"ק היכי מוכח מדרב הונא דאין מחזיקין דלמא אי טוען שני חזקה מועיל והא דמורידין נכרי משום דליכא למיחש למידי דע"כ כיון דמורידין א"כ יש לו דעת לומר הבא עדים שלקחת מאבי והכי נמי יש לו לדעת ולמחות בסוף כל שלשה וכי

---

מסורת הש"ס

א) [לקמן קו., קטו.], ב) כתובות עט:, ג) ל"ל דאמר ר"י אמר רב חסדא, וכן הוא בכתובות פ. [ועי' תוס' יבמות קז. ד"ה לפי], ד) כתובות ח: [ע"ש בתוס'].

**הגהות הב"ח**

(א) תוס' ד"ה וכולם וכו' דבשבוי שמעו בו שמת וכו' ובנטושים דלא שמעו בו שמת לא:

**הגהות הגר"א**

[א] רש"י ד"ה השתא כו' ויטול הכל. נ"ב ע' תוס' ד"ה וכולן (ועמ"ש רבינו בח"מ סי' רפ"ה ס"ק ז):

**תורה אור השלם**

א) וְהַשְּׁבִיעִת תִּשְׁמְטֶנָּה וּנְטַשְׁתָּהּ וְאָכְלוּ אֶבְיֹנֵי עַמֶּךָ וְיִתְרָם תֹּאכַל חַיַּת הַשָּׂדֶה כֵּן תַּעֲשֶׂה לְכַרְמְךָ לְזֵיתֶךָ: [שמות כג, יא]

ב) וְקָאם שָׁאוֹן בְּעַמֶּךָ וְכָל מִבְצָרֶיךָ יוּשַּׁד כְּשֹׁד שַׁלְמַן בֵּית אַרְבֵאל בְּיוֹם מִלְחָמָה אֵם עַל בָּנִים רֻטָּשָׁה: [הושע י, יד]

**ליקוטי רש"י**

אפקעתא דמלכא. המלך ביטלו מלזורעה והרי היא כמו שאינה ולא קראה הכתוב לישראל שנת תבואה [לקמן קו.]. אם על בנים רוטשה. רוטשה עזובה כמו נטושה [הושע י, יד]. מה שהוציא הוציא. אם גירשה [כתובות עט:]. אשתו קטנה. יתומה שהשיאוה אמה ואחיה יוצאה למאן. כמוציא על נכסי אחר. ואם מיאנה בו שמין לו שבח ונוטל כמשפט אריסי המדינה [שם פ.]. אין מחזיקין בנכסי קטן. המחזיק בנכסי קטן שלש שנים אינה חזקה דהאי דלא מיחה משום דקטן הוא [כתובות יז:].

---

**עין משפט נר מצוה**

נד א מיי' פ"ז מהלכות נחלות הל' ה סמג עשין לז טוש"ע ח"מ סי' רפה סעיף ב וע"ש:
נה ב מיי' פכ"ג מהל' אישות הל' ח סמג עשין מח טוש"ע אה"ע סי' פח סעיף ז:
נו ג מיי' שם הל' י טוש"ע שם סעיף י:
נז ד ה מיי' פ"ז מהלכות נחלות הל' ה סמג עשין לז טוש"ע ח"מ סי' רפה סעיף ב:
נח ו מיי' שם הלכה ו טוש"ע שם סעיף ג:
נט ז מיי' שם הלכה ה טוש"ע שם סעיף ב:
ס ח ט י מיי' שם פ"ח הל' א ב סמג עשין לז טוש"ע ח"מ סי' רפה סעיף ו:
סא כ מיי' פי"ד מהל' טוען ונטען הל' ז סמג עשין לה טוש"ע ח"מ סי' קמט סעיף יט:

**רבינו חננאל**

תנא וכולן שמין להן כאריס. אוקימנא כרשב"ג דאמר שמעתי שהנטושין כשבויין. וסבר האי תנא כשבויין ולא שבויין כשבויין שאם תפשו דאין מוציאין מידם ולא שבויין דאלו גבי שבויין אם קדם ותלש ואכל הרי זה זריז ונשכר ואלו גבי נטושין שמין להן כאריס. ואקשינן מאי שנא מהא דתנן המוציא הוצאות בנכסי אשתו הוציא הרבה ואוכל קימעא מה שהוציא הוציא ומה שאכל אכל וכו' אסיק' תיקנו להן רבנן לשום להן כאריס כי היכי דלא ניפסדינהו לנכסי. ודייקי' וכולן לאתויי שבוי שנשבה שמורידין קרוב לנכסיו. יצא לדעת אין מורידין קרוב לנכסיו מאי טעמא דאמרי' מכדי לדעת יצא היה לו להוריד קרוביו לנכסיו כיון שלא הוריד הוא גם אנו אין מורידין אבל הבורח מחמת מרדין כלומר הבורח מחמת נפשות מורידין קרוב לנכסיו דאמרי' מחמת טירדא הוא דלא הורידם וקיימא לן כשמואל דהא רב נחמן קאי כותיה הלכך במקרקעי מורידין קרוב לנכסי נטושין וכששמעו בהן שמתו מורידין אפילו א) לנכסי נטושין. ומטלטלי אם תפשו אין מוציאין מידם ואם לא תפשו מפקידין אותן ביד נאמנין. ב) ואם נראין הדברים שמתו אע"פ שאין עדות ברורה במיתתן נותנין אותן ליורשיו. פי' אפוטרופא לדיקנני כלומר לאדם גדול בעל זקן אין מעמידין לו אפוטרופוס. וקיימא לן כשמואל דאמר מורידין קרוב לנכסי שבוי דהא רב הונא תלמיד רב הוא אמר אין מורידין (קרוב) [קטן] לנכסי שבוי דלמא מפסיד להו ולא קרוב לנכסי קטן הא גדול ואפי' קרוב בנכסי שבוי

**חשק שלמה על ר"ח**

א) נראה דצ"ל אפילו לנכסי רטושין ועי' בש"מ בשם הרא"ש. ב) נראה דר"ל כגון שעבר כמה שנים שאין להם סוף ויתבאר בזה ועי' ברמב"ם ובש"ס ח"מ ס"ס רפה.

The Gemara presents a related ruling:

**אָמַר רַב יְהוּדָה אָמַר שְׁמוּאֵל – Rav Yehudah said in the name of Shmuel:** שְׁבוּי שֶׁנִּשְׁבָּה – If **someone was taken captive,** וְהִנִּיחַ קָמָה לִקְצוֹר – **and he left standing grain** that was ready **to be reaped** in his field, עֲנָבִים לִבְצוֹר תְּמָרִים לִגְדּוֹר זֵיתִים לְמְסוֹק – or he left behind **grapes, dates,** or **olives** that were ready **to be harvested,**[24] בֵּית דִּין יוֹרְדִין לִנְכָסָיו – ***beis din* enters his property** וּמַעֲמִידִין אַפּוֹטְרוֹפּוֹס – **and appoints an administrator,** who is not related to the owner, וְקוֹצֵר וּבוֹצֵר וְגוֹדֵר וּמוֹסֵק – **and he harvests** all of the ripe crops, and the proceeds are put aside for the owner. וְאַחַר כָּךְ מוֹרִידִין קָרוֹב לִנְכָסָיו – **After** the crop is harvested, *beis din* **appoints a relative to** manage **[the captive's] property,** and he is then paid the wage of a sharecropper to cultivate and improve the land.

The Gemara questions this ruling:

וְלוֹקִים אַפּוֹטְרוֹפָּא לְעוֹלָם – **But let** *beis din* **appoint the administrator permanently,** who will accomplish all these tasks without being paid!

The Gemara answers:

אַפּוֹטְרוֹפָּא לְדִיקְנָנֵי לֹא מוֹקְמִינַן – **We do not appoint** such **an administrator for bearded people** [i.e. adults], since people generally do not volunteer for such an unpaid post.[25]

The Gemara cites other related rulings:

אָמַר רַב הוּנָא – **Rav Huna said:** אֵין מוֹרִידִין קָטָן לְנִכְסֵי שְׁבוּי – *Beis din* **does not appoint a minor to** manage **a captive's property;**[26] וְלֹא קָרוֹב לְנִכְסֵי קָטָן – **nor** does it install **a relative to** manage **a minor's property;**[27] וְלֹא קָרוֹב מֵחֲמַת קָרוֹב לְנִכְסֵי קָטָן – **nor** does it appoint **the relative of a relative to** manage **a minor's property.**[28]

The Gemara explains Rav Huna's rulings:

אֵין מוֹרִידִין קָטָן לְנִכְסֵי שְׁבוּי – *Beis din* **does not appoint a minor to** manage **a captive's property,** דִּלְמָא מַפְסִיד לְהוּ – because **perhaps he will ruin it** due to his youth and inexperience. וְלֹא קָרוֹב מֵחֲמַת קָרוֹב לְנִכְסֵי קָטָן – **Nor does** *beis din* appoint **the relative of a relative to** manage **a minor's property;** בְּאַחִי מֵאִימָּא – for example, **when** he is **a maternal brother** of the minor's relative.[29] [וְלֹא קָרוֹב לְנִכְסֵי קָטָן] – **Nor** does *beis din* appoint **a relative to** manage **a minor's property,** כֵּיוָן דְּלָא מָחֵי – for **since [the child] does not** know to **protest** a false claim, אָתֵי לְאַחֲזוּקֵי בֵּיהּ – we are concerned **[the relative] will try to take possession of [the property],** falsely claiming that it is his share of their joint inheritance.

The Gemara derives a legal principle from Rav Huna's ruling:

אָמַר רָבָא – **Rava said:** שְׁמַע מִינֵּיהּ מִדְּרַב הוּנָא – **We can learn from Rav Huna's** ruling, which prohibits the appointment of relatives as administrators of minors' property, but permits non-relatives to serve in that capacity,[30] אֵין מַחֲזִיקִין בְּנִכְסֵי קָטָן – that **one cannot establish a *chazakah* upon a minor's property** by consuming the crop for three years,[31]

NOTES

24. The words גָּדַר, בָּצַר, and מָסַק all refer to the act of harvesting, but each is used with respect to the picking of a specific type of fruit (grapes, dates, and olives, respectively).

25. *Beis din* does not trouble itself to find an administrator who will care for an adult's property without pay, since such a person is difficult to find – unlike in the case of an orphan's property, where people will volunteer readily, because they feel they are performing a mitzvah (*Rashi*).

However, *beis din* does appoint an administrator to supervise the *harvest* of an adult's crops, as Shmuel ruled above. For since this limited responsibility is not as hard as general administration, volunteers are easier to find (*Shitah Mekubetzes*).

26. Even if the child is the captive's closest heir, it is preferable to appoint an unrelated adult as a manager, lest the child ruin the property (*Rashi*).

27. I.e. a relative who is the minor's closest heir, and who inherited the estate of a different relative along with the minor [for example, the minor's older brother] (see *Ritva*). We are afraid that the relative will falsely claim that the child's land was part of his share of their joint inheritance. As the Gemara will explain below, a child will not necessarily protest a false claim against his property. It is therefore preferable to appoint as caretaker an adult who is not a relative, who cannot claim that the child's property was his inheritance (*Rashi*).

28. Although the relative (Shimon) of the child's relative (Reuven) is totally unrelated to the child (see Gemara below for the case), he may still falsely claim that the child's property is actually the inheritance of Reuven, their mutual relative (*Rashi*).

29. I.e. the child's relative (Reuven) is the child's paternal brother from a different mother, and the relative's relative (Shimon) is Reuven's maternal brother from a different father. Although Shimon cannot claim the land as his own, he can still claim that Reuven, his maternal brother (the child's paternal brother), inherited the land from the child's father (see *Rashi;* see also *Tos. HaRosh,* who emends *Rashi*).

30. Rav Huna permitted non-relatives to serve as administrators for two reasons: (1) because they cannot claim ownership of the property as inheritance, and (2) we are not concerned that they will claim that they purchased the property from the minor's father and occupied it for the requisite three years of *chazakah* [after the father died] (*Rashi;* see next note). [The Mishnah in *Bava Basra* (28a) teaches that if one occupies land for three years, consuming its crops in the manner of an owner, he is believed to claim that he purchased or otherwise legally acquired it from its previous owner (Gemara ibid. 28b), as long as the owner did not protest his occupancy during the three-year period. The legal term for this three-year possession (and the presumption of ownership that follows from it) is חֲזָקָה, *chazakah* (possession).]

31. If the administrator had claimed that he purchased the property from the minor's father and, in fact, he occupied it for three years without the father protesting, he would become the presumptive owner of the land. But if he claimed that the father died after selling him the property and he occupied it for three years *after the father's death* without *the minor* protesting, a *chazakah* is not established. For since the minor did not realize that the property had belonged to his father, he saw no need to protest the administrator's occupation (*Rashi* here and below, 39b ד״ה ואפי׳ הגדיל).

However, a relative may not serve as an administrator for a minor, because he may falsely claim that the minor's property is actually part of his share of a joint inheritance (see *Tosafos* and *Nimukei Yosef*).

נטושים דבע"כ דכתיב א) והשביעית תשמטנה ונטשתה א) אפקעתא דמלכא רטושים דמדעתן דכתיב ב) אם על בנים רוטשה תנא א וכולם שמין להם כארים אהייא אילימא אשבויין השתא זריז ונשכר הוה מאי דאשבח מיבעיא אלא ארטושים והא מוציאין אותן מידו קתני אלא אנטושים למאן אילימא לרבנן הא אמרי מוציאין אותו מידו אי רבן שמעון בן גמליאל הא אמר שמעתי שהנטושים כשבויין כשבויין ולא שבויין כשבויין דאין מוציאין אותן מידו ולא שבויין דאילו התם זריז ונשכר ואילו הכא שיימינן ליה כארים ומאי שנא מהא ג) דתנן ב המוציא הוצאות על נכסי אשתו הוציא הרבה ואכל קימעא קימעא ואכל הרבה מה שהוציא הוציא ומה שאכל אכל הא לא דמיא אלא להא (ג) דתנן ג המוציא הוצאות על נכסי אשתו קטנה כמוציא על נכסי אחר דמי אלמא כיון דלא סמכא דעתיה תקינו ליה רבנן כי היכי דלא לפסדינהו הכא נמי תקינו ליה רבנן כי היכי דלא לפסדינהו וכולן שמין להם כארים וכולן לאיתויי מאי לאיתויי הא דאמר רב נחמן אמר שמואל שבוי שנשבה מורידין קרוב לנכסיו יצא לדעת אין מורידין קרוב לנכסיו ורב נחמן דידיה אמר ד בורח הרי הוא כשבוי בורח מחמת מאי אילימא מחמת כרגא היינו לדעת ה אלא בורח מחמת מרדין אמר רב יהודה אמר שמואל ו שבוי שנשבה והניח קמה לקצור ענבים לבצור תמרים לגדור זיתים למסוק בית דין יורדין לנכסיו ומעמידין אפוטרופוס וקוצר ובוצר וגודר ומוסק ואח"כ מורידין קרוב לנכסיו ולוקים אפוטרופא לעולם ז אפוטרופא לדיקנני לא מוקמינן: אמר רב הונא ח אין מורידין קטן לנכסי שבוי ט ולא קרוב לנכסי קטן י ולא קרוב מחמת קרוב לנכסי קטן אין מורידין קטן לנכסי שבוי דלמא מפסיד להו ולא קרוב מחמת קרוב לנכסי קטן באחי מאימא [ולא קרוב לנכסי קטן] כיון דלא מחי אתי לאחזוקי ביה ד) אמר רבא שמע מיניה מדרב הונא כ אין מחזיקין בנכסי קטן ואפילו

**רש"י**

ה"ג נטושים על כרחן דכתיב והשביעית תשמטנה ונטשתה. היינו על כרחו: **אפקעתא דמלכא.** מלות המלך: **רטושים מדעתן** דכתיב **אם על בנים רוטשה.** היינו מדעתו ולא שביה דכתיב רישיה דקרא וקם שאון בעמך היו יראים שלא יבאו אויבים עליהם וכל מבצריך יושד יגלו בגולה מאליהן וישארו העיירות שודדין מאין איש כשוד שלמן בית ארבאל ביום מלחמה כשודדין הבאין למלחמה על ידי מארב על עם היושב בשלום שלא נזהרו בהם לברוח מפניהם ושודדים את הכל וכמוהו (ירמיה יג) הגלת יהודה כולה הגלת שלומים מתוך ישיבת שלום באין מחריד הגלם נבוכדנצר. בית ארבאל תרגם יונתן בית מארב אע"פ למ"ד יתרים בו כמו (הושע ב) יענו את יזרעאל שהוא לשון זריעה ולא לשון עיר ומדקא אמר יושד כשוד שלמן בית ארבאל מכלל דההוא יומא לאו בית ארבאל ביום מלחמה הוה אלא מורך בא בלבם והמה עוזבים אם על בנים והולכים להם מדאגת האויב שמא יבא עליהם: **רוטשה.** נעזבה: **וכולן.** מפ' לקמיה אהייא קאי וכללא לאתויי מאי: **שמין להם כארים.** אם יבאו הבעלים יטלו אלו בשבח קרקעות ופירות כמנהג אריסי המקום: **השתא זריז ונשכר הוי.** [א] ויטול הכל: **דאילו התם זריז ונשכר.** דכיון ששמעו בו שמת כי נחת לה אדעתא דכולהו פירי נחת אבל הכא דלא שמעו שמת לאו אדעתא דכולה נחית אלא ליטול כארים בכל שנה ושאר פירות יהא מונחין: **נכסי אשתו.** נכסי מלוג שהוא אוכל פירות והקרן שלה: **הוציא הרבה ואכל פירות קימעא.** קודם שמת או שגירשה: **הא לא דמיא.** תרוצא הוא הא דנכסי שבויין להא דאשתו קטנה דמי: **קטנה.** שהיא יתומה שהשיאוה אמה ואחיה ואין קידושין תופסין בה מן התורה אלא מדברי סופרים לפיכך יוצאה במיאון בע"כ אם תמאן: **כמוציא על נכסי אחר דמי.** ואם הוציא ולא אכל כדי הוצאתו שמין לו כאריס: **דלא סמכא דעתיה.** שיהא מוחזק בידו דדואג שמא תמאן בו: **תקינו ליה רבנן.** ליטול כאריס: **כי היכי דלא ניפסדינהו.** שלא יקלקל הקרקעות לזורען תמיד ולא יעבוד ולא יעדור כרמים: **לאיתויי הא דרב נחמן.** בורח מחמת מרדין: **יצא לדעת אין מורידין.** דכיון שהיה שפוי בדעתו ולא נוהו בלכתו לירד לנכסיו ש"מ לא ניחא ליה: **בורח הרי הוא כשבוי.** שאין דעתו מיושבת עליו מחמת שהוא בהול: **מחמת כרגא.** שאין לו ממה לפרוע כסף גולגלתו למלך ובורח לפני בוא הזמן: **היינו יוצא לדעת.** שאין כאן בהלה: **מחמת מרדין.** שהרג את הנפש ופרסאי הורגין על שפיכות דמים כדאמרינן בבבא קמא (דף קיז.) מרדין היא רציחה בלשון פרסי וכן מפורש בשערים דרב האי גאון (שער מ): **מעמידין אפוטרופוס.** להכניס דבר המוכן ויהא שמור לבעלים ואח"כ מורידין קרוב להשביח וליטול כארים: **ולוקים אפוטרופוס לעולם.** שלא יטול כלום: **אפוטרופא לדיקנני לא מוקמינן.** אין בית דין טורחין לבקש אפוטרופוס לאנשים גדולים שנתמלא זקנם לפי שלא ימלאוהו דבשלמא ליתמי איכא דשמע להו והוי אפוטרופוס לדבר מצוה אבל לדיקנני לא שמעי להו: **אין מורידין קטן לנכסי שבוי.** ואפילו הוא ראוי ליורשו דקא מפסיד להו ומוטב שיורידו להם איש נכרי: **ולא קרוב.** הראוי לירש בנכסי קטן לעשות ולאכול כדמסיים טעמיה דכיון דקטן לא ידע למחויי אתא האי קרוב לאחזוקי בהן ולומר לחלק ירושתו בא וטוב להם להוריד איש נכרי דלא מצי למטען בהו ירושה: **ולא קרוב מחמת קרוב לנכסי קטן.** כגון קטן שיש לו אח מאב ואותו אח מאב יש לו אח מאם דאיש נכרי הוא אצל קטן אין מורידין אותו אח מאם לנכסי קטן מחמת קורבת אחיו של זה שהוא אח של קטן דאתי לאחזוקי בהו לצורך אחיו ויאמר נכסים הללו של אחי מאמי הם שנפלו לו מאביו ואלו לחלקו באו: **באחי מאימא.** כדפרישית שזה אח מן האם לאחיו של קטן מן האב: **ש"מ מרב הונא.** דאמר אין מורידין קרוב לנכסי קטן שמא יחזיק בהם מחמת ירושה אבל אחר שאין לו טענת ירושה מורידין ולא חיישינן שמא יטעון אביו של קטן מכרם לי ואכלתים שני חזקה ש"מ אין מחזיקין בנכסי קטן אם לא אכל בפני האב שלש שנים אין שלש שנים שאכלן בפני הקטן חזקה:

**תוספות**

**וכולם** שמין להם כארים. אנטושים דרשב"ג קאי כדמסיק פי' רש"י דבשבוי (א) שמע שמתו אוכל כל הפירות ואם יבואו הבעלים קודם שיאכל הפירות יטול כשאר אריסין ויחזיר השאר ובנטושים דלא שמע שמת לא יאכל כל הפירות אלא שמין הפירות שיאכל כשאר אריסין למחצה לשליש ולרביע ולא יאכל כלום בחנם וקשה דאמאי משני לעיל לירד ולמכור תנן לישני לירד ולאכול תנן דהא אפילו לאכול בחנם אינו יורד ועוד מאי פריך בתר הכי אף בניהם כלל לא הא ודאי אין לו כלל אפילו למ"ד מורידין כיון שאין לו אלא כאריס נכרי ועוד מאי פריך מהמוציא הוצאות על נכסי אשתו דהתם יורד לאכול כל הפירות אבל הכא אינו יורד כי אם בתורת אריסות ותו דאמר שמואל לקמן שבוי שהניח קמה לקצור מעמידין אפוטרופוס וקוצר ובוצר ואח"כ מורידין קרוב לנכסיו ומעיקרא אמאי אין מורידין קרוב כיון שלא יאכל הפירות בחנם לכך נראה דודאי שכל הפירות אוכל בחנם ואם זבל וחרש וזרע ובעלים באו קודם שקצר יטול כארים שכר טרחו ועמלו ולרב וכן לת"ק אית להו שאין שמין כארים ולכך אין מורידין דלמא מפסיד להו לפי שירא שיבואו הבעלים קודם שיקצור ויאכל ולא יטול כלום ולא ישביח הקרקע אלא כל מה שימצא יאכל בחנם כדין קרוב היורד לנכסי שבוי והשתא פריך שפיר כיון שאוכל כל הפירות כשיבואו הבעלים קודם שילקט אמאי נוטל כארים טפי מהמוציא הוצאות על נכסי אשתו כו' והא דקאמר ואילו התם זריז ונשכר פי' כששמע הבעלים ממשמשים ובאין מניחין אותו לקדם ולתלוש אע"פ שהפירות ישוו הרבה מעמלו כיון שאם לא יקדם אין משלמין טרחו אבל הכא בנטושים אם באו בעלים אין מניחין אותו לתלוש כיון דלא מפסיד מידי דשיימי' להו כארים:

**אמר** שמואל שבוי שנשבה מורידין. וא"ת והאמרה שמואל חדא זימנא וי"ל דה"ק אף על גב דבשבוי מורידין יצא לדעת אין מורידין:

**היינו** לדעת. דמסתמא לא פליג אשמואל מדלא קאמר אף בורח או אף יוצא לדעת:

**ש"מ** מדרב הונא אין מחזיקין בנכסי קטן ואפי' הגדיל. פרש"י מדאמר רב הונא אין מורידין קרוב הא נכרי מורידין וקשה דלא רב הונא כמה משניות יש שמעמידין אפוטרופוס לנכסי יתומים פרק הניזקין (גיטין דף נב.) מנהו ב"ד לא ישבע וע"ק היכי מוכח מדרב הונא דאין מחזיקין דלמא אי טוען שני חזקה מועיל והא דמורידין נכרי משום דליכא למיחש למידי דע"כ כיון דמורידין א"כ יש לו דעת לומר הבא עדים שלקחת מאבי והכי נמי יש לו לדעת ולמחות בסוף כל שלשה וכי

**מסורת הש"ס**

א) [לקמן קו., קט.], ב) כתובות עט:, ג) ל"ל דאמר ר"י אמר רב חסדא, וכן הוא בכתובות פ., [ועי' תוס' יבמות קז. ד"ה דאין], ד) כתובות יח: [ע"ש בתוס'].

**הגהות הב"ח**

(א) תוס' ד"ה וכולם וכו' דבשבוי ששמעו בו שמת וכו' ובנטושים דלא שמעו בו שמת לא:

**הגהות הגר"א**

[א] רש"י ד"ה השתא כו' ויטול הכל. נ"ב ע' תוס' ד"ה וכולן (ועמ"ש רבינו בח"מ סי' רפ"ה ס"ק ז):

**תורה אור השלם**

א) וְהַשְּׁבִיעִת תִּשְׁמְטֶנָּה וּנְטַשְׁתָּהּ וְאָכְלוּ אֶבְיֹנֵי עַמֶּךָ וְיִתְרָם תֹּאכַל חַיַּת הַשָּׂדֶה כֵּן תַּעֲשֶׂה לְכַרְמְךָ לְזֵיתֶךָ: [שמות כג, יא]

ב) וְקָאם שָׁאוֹן בְּעַמֶּךָ וְכָל מִבְצָרֶיךָ יוּשַּׁד כְּשֹׁד שַׁלְמַן בֵּית אַרְבֵאל בְּיוֹם מִלְחָמָה אֵם עַל בָּנִים רֻטָּשָׁה: [הושע י, יד]

**ליקוטי רש"י**

**אפקעתא דמלכא.** המלך ביטלו מלזורעה והרי היא כמו שאינה ולא קראה הכתוב לישראל שנת תבואה [לקמן קו.]. **אם על בנים רוטשה.** רוטשה עזובה כמו נוטשה [הושע י, יד]. **מה שהוציא הוציא.** אם גירשה [כתובות עט:]. **אשתו קטנה.** יתומה שהשיאתה אמה ואחיה יכולה למאן. **כמוציא על נכסי אחר.** ואם מיאנה בו שמין לו שבח שהשביח ונוטל כמשפט אריסי המדינה [שם פ.]. **אין מחזיקין בנכסי קטן.** המחזיק בנכסי קטן שלש שנים אינה חזקה דהאי דלא מיחה משום דקטן הוא [כתובות יז:].

**עין משפט נר מצוה**

נד א מיי' פ"ז מהלכות נחלות הל' ה סמג עשין לו טוש"ע ח"מ סי' רפה סעיף ב וע"ש:

נה ב מיי' פכ"ג מהל' אישות הל' ח סמג עשין מח טוש"ע אה"ע סי' פח סעיף ז:

נו ג מיי' שם הל' י טוש"ע שם סעיף י:

נז ד ה מיי' פ"ז מהלכות נחלות הל' ה סמג עשין לו טוש"ע ח"מ סי' רפה סעיף ב:

נח ו מיי' שם הלכה ו טוש"ע שם סעיף ג:

נט ז מיי' שם הלכה ה טוש"ע שם סעיף ב:

ס ח ט י מיי' שם פ"ח הל' א ב סמג עשין לו טוש"ע ח"מ סי' רפה סעיף ו:

סא כ מיי' פי"ד מהל' טוען ונטען הל' ז סמג עשין לה טוש"ע ח"מ סי' קמט סעיף יט:

**רבינו חננאל**

תנא וכולן שמין להן כאריס. אוקימנא כרשב"ג דאמר שמעתי שהנטושין כשבויין. וסבר האי תנא כשבויין ולא שבויין כשבויין שאם תפשו דאין מוציאין מידם ולא שבויין דאלו גבי שבויין אם קדם ותלש ואכל הרי זה זריז ונשכר ואלו גבי נטושין שמין להן כאריס. ואקשינן מאי שנא מהא דתנן המוציא הוצאות בנכסי אשתו הוציא הרבה ואוכל קימעא מה שהוציא הוציא ומה שאכל אכל וכו' אסיק' תיקנו להן רבנן לשום להן כאריס כי היכי דלא ניפסדינהו לנכסי. ודייקי' וכולן לאתויי שבוי שנשבה שמורידין קרוב לנכסיו. יצא לדעת אין מורידין קרוב לנכסיו מאי טעמא דאמרי' מכדי לדעת יצא היה לו להוריד קרוביו לנכסיו כיון שלא הוריד הוא גם אנו אין מורידין אבל הבורח מחמת מרדין כלומר הבורח מחמת נפשות מורידין קרוב לנכסיו דאמרי' מחמת טירדא הוא דלא הורידם וקיימא לן כשמואל דהא רב נחמן קאי כותיה הלכך במקרקעי מורידין קרוב לנכסי נטושין וכששמעו בהן שמתו מורידין אפילו א) לנכסי נטושין. ומטלטלי אם תפשו אין מוציאין מידם ואם לא תפשו מפקידין אותן ביד נאמנין. ב) ואם נראין הדברים שמתו אע"פ שאין עדות ברורה במיתתן נותנין אותן ליורשין. פי' אפוטרופא לדיקנני כלומר לאדם גדול בעל זקן אין מעמידין לו אפוטרופוס. וקיימא לן כשמואל דאמר מורידין קרוב לנכסי שבוי דהא רב הונא דתלמיד רב הוא אמר אין מורידין (קרוב) [קטן] לנכסי שבוי דלמא מפסיד להו ולא קרוב לנכסי קטן הא גדול ואפי' קרוב בנכסי שבוי

**חשק שלמה על ר"ח**

א) נראה דל"ל אפילו לנכסי רטושין ועי' בש"מ כאן מש"כ בשם הרא"ש ז"ל. ב) נראה דר"ל כגון שטבע במים שאין להם סוף וכיוצא בו ועי' ברמב"ם ובש"ע ח"מ ס"ס רפד.

The Gemara questions this interpretation of the Baraisa: וּמַאי שְׁנָא מֵהָא דִּתְנַן – **And how does** this case **differ from that which we learned in a Mishnah:**[11] הַמּוֹצִיא הוֹצָאוֹת עַל נִכְסֵי אִשְׁתּוֹ – IF SOMEONE SPENDS MONEY ON HIS WIFE'S *MELOG*[12] PROPERTIES to improve them, הוֹצִיא הַרְבֵּה וְאָכַל קִימְעָא – whether HE SPENT A LOT of money AND only CONSUMED A SMALL amount of produce, קִימְעָא וְאָכַל הַרְבֵּה – or whether he spent LITTLE, BUT CONSUMED MUCH (before he died or divorced her), מַה שֶּׁהוֹצִיא הוֹצִיא – WHATEVER HE SPENT HE HAS SPENT, וּמַה שֶּׁאָכַל אָכַל – AND WHATEVER HE ATE, HE ATE. That is, he or his heirs keep only the amount of produce that was actually consumed, and do not receive any compensation, even the share of a sharecropper. Why is the law not the same in the case of *netushim* property, according to Rabban Shimon ben Gamliel?

The Gemara answers:

הָא לֹא דָּמְיָא אֶלָּא לְהָא (דִּתְנַן) – **That** case of *netushim* property **is not comparable** to the case in the Mishnah just cited; **rather,** it is comparable **to this** other case, [דְּאָמַר רַב יַעֲקֹב אָמַר רַב חִסְדָּא] – about **which R' Yaakov said in the name of Rav Chisda:**[13] הַמּוֹצִיא הוֹצָאוֹת עַל נִכְסֵי אִשְׁתּוֹ קְטַנָּה – **Someone who spends money on his minor wife's**[14] **property** כְּמוֹצִיא עַל נִכְסֵי אַחֵר דָּמֵי – **is like one that spends** money **on someone else's property,** and he is repaid for his expenses if he has not consumed an equal amount of produce.[15] אַלְמָא כֵּיוָן דְּלָא סָמְכָא דַּעְתֵּיהּ – **We see** in this case that **since** the husband of a wife who is a minor **does not feel sure** that he would get to keep his wife's property,[16] תַּקִּינוּ לֵיהּ רַבָּנָן – **the Rabbis decreed for his benefit** a requirement that he would be compensated like a sharecropper even if the marriage ends, כִּי הֵיכִי דְּלָא לִפְסְדִינְהוּ – **so that he does not ruin [her property]** by taking whatever he can.[17] הָכָא נַמִּי – **Here, too,** in the case of *netushim* property according to Rabban Shimon, תַּקִּינוּ לֵיהּ רַבָּנָן – **the Rabbis enacted** a requirement for his benefit that he be paid like a sharecropper, כִּי הֵיכִי דְּלָא לִפְסְדִינְהוּ – **so that he does not ruin [the property].**[18]

The Gemara continues to analyze the Baraisa:

וְכוּלָּן שָׁמִין לָהֶם כְּאָרִיס – The Baraisa stated: AND regarding ALL THOSE who enter another's property, WE EVALUATE FOR THEM their share of the profits AS IF THEY WERE A SHARECROPPER.

The Gemara asks:

וְכוּלָּן לְאֵיתוּיֵי מַאי – **What does** the expression AND ALL THOSE come **to include?** לְאֵיתוּיֵי הָא דְּאָמַר רַב נַחְמָן אָמַר שְׁמוּאֵל – **It comes to include that which Rav Nachman said in the name of Shmuel:**[19] שָׁבוּי שֶׁנִּשְׁבָּה – **If someone was taken captive,** מוֹרִידִין קָרוֹב לִנְכָסָיו – *beis din* **appoints a relative to** manage **his property.** יָצָא לְדַעַת – **However, if he departed** and abandoned his property **voluntarily,** אֵין מוֹרִידִין קָרוֹב לִנְכָסָיו – *beis din* **does not appoint a relative to** manage **his property.**[20] וְרַב נַחְמָן דִּידֵיהּ אָמַר – **And Rav Nachman himself said:** בּוֹרֵחַ הֲרֵי הוּא כְּשָׁבוּי – **A fugitive is like a captive,** and we appoint a relative to manage his property.[21] The expression "all those" thus comes to include the case of a fugitive – to teach that even in such a case, the relative is paid like a sharecropper.

The Gemara clarifies Rav Nachman's ruling:

בּוֹרֵחַ מֵחֲמַת מַאי – **For what** reason **did [the owner] flee?** אִילֵימָא מֵחֲמַת כַּרְגָּא – **If we say** that he fled **because** he did not have money to pay his **head-tax,** הַיְינוּ לְדַעַת – then **this is** a case of **willful** abandonment![22] אֶלָּא בּוֹרֵחַ מֵחֲמַת מַרְדִּין – **Rather,** Rav Nachman refers to where **he fled because** he is wanted **for murder.**[23]

NOTES

11. *Kesubos* 79b.

12. A husband manages his wife's *melog* property and is entitled to the fruits of her property, but any increase or decrease in the value of the principal belongs to the wife (*Rashi;* see above, 34b note 14).

13. *Rashi.* Our elucidation follows the emendation of *Mesoras HaShas,* who explains the Gemara to be referring to a ruling cited in *Kesubos* 80a.

Even though *Rashi* here mentions נִכְסֵי שְׁבוּיִין, *captives' property,* the Gemara's question actually concerned *netushim* property, of which captives' property is one example (see *Rashi* above, 38b ד״ה נכסי רטושים). Others, however, interpret *Rashi* differently; see *Otzar Mefarshei HaTalmud,* p. 729 #41.

14. According to Biblical law, a girl whose father died cannot be married until she reaches her legal majority. However, the Sages enacted that a minor female may be betrothed by her mother or brother. Since this marriage is only Rabbinic in nature, the girl may nullify it at any time (through the process of *mi'un,* refusal) before she reaches majority (*Rashi*).

15. The general rule is that if someone improves his friend's field with permission, he is paid at the prevailing rate for such work. If he improves it without permission, he is reimbursed either the value of his improvements or his expenses, whichever is less (see *Bava Metzia* 101a; *Rashi* ad loc. ד״ה גליא).

In this case, since he is authorized to improve his wife's property, the husband receives a sharecropper's compensation (see *Rashi*).

16. For he is worried that his wife will nullify the marriage (*Rashi*).

17. Since he is worried that he will lose the rights to the fruits of his minor wife's property, he may damage her fields through excessive planting in order to maximize his profits, or fail to maintain her vineyards properly (*Rashi*).

18. Since he has not heard that the owner died, the caretaker does not know if he will keep the property as an inheritance. Therefore, unless he is paid for his labors like a sharecropper, he may ruin the property in an attempt to maximize his profits before the owner returns.

*Rashi* and *Ramban* understand that the caretaker is paid as a sharecropper, and then he must return any produce that he has already consumed. *Tosafos,* however, rule that the Gemara's discussion here concerns only compensation for unconsumed produce and appreciation, which the caretaker receives *in addition* to whatever produce he has already consumed (see above, note 10).

*Rosh* (§12) explains, based on the Gemara's statement here, that the Gemara is concluding that whenever a caretaker is convinced that he will keep the property, we are not concerned that he will misuse the land. Therefore, there is no need to pay him for unconsumed produce and improvements. This represents a retraction of the Gemara's previous position (see note 6) that a relative who heard about the captive's death is compensated for unconsumed produce and appreciation *in addition* to any produce that he has consumed.

19. Although the Gemara proceeds to cite Shmuel's ruling as well, the Baraisa comes to include Rav Nachman's *own* ruling, which is stated below.

20. Since the owner was not panicked when he departed, and nevertheless did not appoint a caretaker before he left, we infer that he is not agreeable to the appointment of a caretaker (*Rashi*). This is a case of abandoned *retushim* property, which was discussed above (38b; see note 33 there).

21. One who must flee from his home is upset, and can lack the presence of mind to appoint an administrator for his property (*Rashi*). Thus, *beis din* will do it for him.

22. Since his flight was planned, and his mind was calm (see *Rashi*). Hence, *beis din* would not appoint an administrator for him in this case, since he chose not to do so himself; this would be comparable to the previous ruling that the Gemara cited from Rav Nachman in the name of Shmuel [i.e. in the case of voluntary abandonment] (*Tosafos*).

23. He killed another person, and the Persian government imposed capital punishment for murderers (*Rashi;* see *Bava Kamma* 117a).

One might have thought that the relative need not be compensated in this case, since he is certain that the owner will never return, lest he risk capture and execution (see note 18 above). Rav Nachman thus teaches that even in such a case the relative may not feel confident enough that he will keep the field, and he may overwork the field to take whatever he can unless he knows that he will be paid (see *Shitah Mekubetzes*).

נטושים דבע"כ דכתיב א) והשביעית תשמטנה ונטשתה א) אפקעתא דמלכא רטושים דמדעתן דכתיב ב) אם על בנים רוטשה תנא א וכולם שמין להם כארים אהייא אילימא אשבויין השתא זריז ונשכר הוה מאי דאשבח מיבעיא אלא ארטושים והא מוציאין אותן מידו קתני אלא אנטושים למאן אילימא לרבנן הא אמרי מוציאין אותו מידו אי רבן שמעון בן גמליאל הא אמר שמעתי שהנטושים כשבויין ולא שבויין כשבויין דאין מוציאין אותן מידו ולא שבויין דאילו התם זריז ונשכר ואילו הכא שיימינן ליה כארים ומאי שנא מהא ג) דתנן ב המוציא הוצאות על נכסי אשתו הוציא הרבה ואכל קימעא ואכל הרבה מה שהוציא הוציא ומה שאכל אכל הא לא דמיא אלא להא (ג) דתנן) ג המוציא הוצאות על נכסי אשתו קטנה כמוציא על נכסי אחר דמי אלמא כיון דלא סמכא דעתיה תקינו ליה רבנן כי היכי דלא לפסדינהו הכא נמי תקינו ליה רבנן כי היכי דלא לפסדינהו וכולן שמין להם כארים וכולן לאיתויי מאי לאיתויי הא דאמר רב נחמן אמר שמואל שבוי שנשבה מורידין קרוב לנכסיו יצא לדעת אין מורידין קרוב לנכסיו ורב נחמן דידיה אמר ד בורח הרי הוא כשבוי בורח מחמת מאי אילימא מחמת כרגא היינו לדעת ה אלא בורח מחמת מרדין אמר רב יהודה אמר שמואל ו שבוי שנשבה והניח קמה לקצור ענבים לבצור תמרים לגדור זיתים למסוק בית דין יורדין לנכסיו ומעמידין אפוטרופוס וקוצר ובוצר וגודר ומוסק ואח"כ מורידין קרוב לנכסיו ולוקים אפוטרופא לעולם ז אפוטרופא לדיקנני לא מוקמינן: אמר רב הונא ח אין מורידין קטן לנכסי שבוי ט ולא קרוב לנכסי קטן י ולא קרוב מחמת קרוב לנכסי קטן אין מורידין קטן לנכסי שבוי דלמא מפסיד להו ולא קרוב מחמת קרוב לנכסי קטן באחי מאימא [ולא קרוב לנכסי קטן] כיון דלא מחי אתי לאחזוקי ביה ד) אמר רבא שמע מיניה מדרב הונא כ אין מחזיקין בנכסי קטן ואפילו

## רש"י

ה"ג נטושים על כרחן דכתיב והשביעית תשמטנה ונטשתה. היינו על כרחו: **אפקעתא דמלכא.** מלות המלך: **רטושים מדעתן דכתיב אם על בנים רוטשה.** היינו מדעתו ולא שביה דכתיב רישיה דקרא וקם שאון בעמך היו יראים שלא יבאו אויבים עליהם וכל מבצריך יושד יגלו בגולה מאליהן וישארו העיירות שדודין מאין איש כשוד שלמן בית ארבאל ביום מלחמה כשודדין הבאין למלחמה על ידי מארב על עם היושב בשלום שלא נזהרו בהם לברוח מפניהם ושודדים את הכל וכמוהו (ירמיה יג) הגלת יהודה כולה הגלת שלומים מתוך ישיבת שלום דאין מחריד הגלם נבוכדנצר. בית ארבאל תרגם יהונתן בית מארב אל"ף למ"ד יתרים בו כמו (הושע ב) יענו את יזרעאל שהוא לשון זריעה ולא לשון עיר ומדקא אמר יושד כשוד שלמן בית ארבאל מכלל דההוא יומא לאו בית ארבאל ביום מלחמה הוה אלא מורך בא בלבם והמה עוזבים אם על בניס והולכים להם מדאגת האויב שמא יבא עליהם: **רוטשה.** נעזבה: **וכולן.** מפ' לקמיה אהייא קאי וכללא לאתויי מאי: **שמין להם כארים.** אם יבאו הבעלים יטלו אלו בשבח קרקעות ופירות כמנהג אריסי המקום: **השתא זריז ונשכר הוי.** [א] ויטול הכל: **דאילו התם זריז ונשכר.** דכיון ששמעו בו שמת כי נחת לה אדעתא דכולהו פירי נחת אבל הכא דלא שמעו שמת לאו אדעתא דכולה נחית אלא ליטול כארים בכל שנה ושאר פירות יהא מונחין: **נכסי אשתו.** נכסי מלוג שהוא אוכל פירות והקרן שלה: **הוציא הרבה ואכל פירות קימעא.** קודם שמת או שגירשה: **הא לא דמיא.** תרוצא הוא הא דנכסי שבוין להא דאשתו קטנה דמי: **קטנה.** שהיא יתומה שהשיאוה אמה ואחיה ואין קידושין תופסין בה מן התורה אלא מדברי סופרים לפיכך יוצאה במיאון בע"כ אם תמאן: **כמוציא על נכסי אחר דמי.** ואם הוציא ולא אכל כדי הוצאתו שמין לו כארים: **דלא סמכא דעתיה.** שיהא מוחזק בידו דדואג שמא תמאן בו: **תקינו ליה רבנן.** ליטול כארים: **כי היכי דלא ניפסדינהו.** שלא יקלקל הקרקעות לזורען תמיד ולא יעבוד ולא יעדור כרמים: **לאיתויי הא דרב נחמן.** בורח מחמת מרדין: **יצא לדעת אין מורידין.** דכיון שהיה ספו בדעתו ולא נודע בלכתו לירד לנכסיו ש"מ לא ניחא ליה: **בורח הרי הוא כשבוי.** שאין דעתו מיושבת עליו מחמת שהוא בהול: **מחמת כרגא.** שאין לו ממה לפרוע כסף גולגלתו למלך ובורח לפני בוא הזמן: **היינו יוצא לדעת.** שאין כאן בהלה: **מחמת מרדין.** שהרג את הנפש ופרסאי הורגין על שפיכות דמים כדאמרינן בבבא קמא (דף קיז.) מרדין היא רציחה בלשון פרסי וכן מפורש בשערים דרב האי גאון (שער מ): **מעמידין אפוטרופוס.** להכניס דבר המוכן ויהא שמור לבעלים ואח"כ מורידין קרוב להשביח וליטול כארים: **ולוקים אפוטרופוס לעולם.** שלא יטול כלום: **אפוטרופא לדיקנני לא מוקמינן.** אין בית דין טורחין לבקש אפוטרופוס לאנשים גדולים שנתמלא זקנם לפי שלא ימלאוהו דבשלמא ליתמי איכא דשמע להו והוי אפוטרופוס לדבר מלוה אבל לדיקנני לא שמעי להו: **אין מורידין קטן לנכסי שבוי.** ואפילו הוא ראוי ליורשו דקא מפסיד להו ומוטב שיורידו להם איש נכרי: **ולא קרוב.** הראוי לירש בנכסי קטן לעשות ולאכול כדמסיים טעמיה דכיון דקטן לא ידע למחויי אתא האי קרוב לאחזוקי בהן ולומר לחלק ירושתו בא וטוב להם להוריד איש נכרי דלא מצי למטען בהו ירושה: **ולא קרוב מחמת קרוב לנכסי קטן.** כגון קטן שיש לו אח מאב ואותו אח מאב יש לו אח מאם דאיש נכרי הוא אצל קטן אין מורידין אותו אח מאם לנכסי קטן מחמת קורבת אחיו של זה שהוא אח של קטן דאתי לאחזוקי בהו לצורך אחיו ויאמר נכסים הללו של אחי מאמי הם שנפלו לו מאביו ואלו לחלקו באו: **באחי מאימא.** כדפרישית שזה אח מן האם לאחיו של קטן מן האב: **ש"מ מרב הונא.** דאמר אין מורידין קרוב לנכסי קטן שמא יחזיק בהם מחמת ירושה אבל אחר שאין לו טענת ירושה מורידין ולא חיישינן שמא יטעון אביו של קטן מכרם לי ואכלתים שני חזקה ש"מ אין מחזיקין בנכסי קטן אם לא אכל בפני האב שלש שנים שאכלן בפני הקטן אין חזקה: ואפילו

## תוספות

**וכולם** שמין להם כארים. אנטושים דרשב"ג קאי כדמסיק פי' רש"י דבשבוי (א) שמע שמתו אוכל כל הפירות ואם יבואו הבעלים קודם שיאכל הפירות יטול כשאר אריסין ויחזיר השאר ובנטושים דלא שמע שמת לא יאכל כל הפירות אלא שמין הפירות שיאכל כשאר אריסין למחצה לשליש ולרביע ולא יאכל כלום בחנם וקשה דמאי משני לעיל לירד ולמכור תנן ליסני לירד ולאכול תנן דהא אפילו לאכול בחנם אינו יורד ועוד מאי פריך בתר הכי אף בניהם כלל לא הא ודאי אין לו כלל אפילו למ"ד מורידין כיון שאין לו אלא כארים נכרי ועוד מאי פריך מהמוציא הוצאות על נכסי אשתו דהתם יורד לאכול כל הפירות אבל הכא אינו יורד כי אם בתורת אריסות ותו דאמר שמואל לקמן שבוי שהניח קמה לקצור מעמידין אפוטרופוס וקוצר ובוצר ואח"כ מורידין קרוב לנכסיו ומעיקרא אמאי אין מורידין קרוב כיון שלא יאכל הפירות בחנם לכך נראה דודאי שכל הפירות אוכל בחנם ואם זבל וחרש וזרע ובעלים באו קודם שקצר יטול כארים שכר טרחו ועמלו ולרב וכן לת"ק אית להו שאין שמין כארים ולכך אין מורידין דלמא מפסיד להו לפי שירא שיבואו הבעלים קודם שיקצור ויאכל ולא יטול כלום ולא ישביח הקרקע אלא כל מה שימצא יאכל בחנם כדין קרוב היורד לנכסי שבוי והשתא פריך שפיר כיון שאוכל כל הפירות כשיבואו הבעלים קודם שילקט אמאי נוטל כארים טפי מהמוציא הוצאות על נכסי אשתו כו' והא דקאמר ואילו התם זריז ונשכר פי' כששמע הבעלים ממשמשים ובאין מניחין אותו לקדם ולתלוש אע"פ שהפירות ישוו הרבה מעמלו כיון שאם לא יקדם אין משלמין טרחו אבל הכא בנטושים אם באו בעלים אין מניחין אותו לתלוש כיון דלא מפסיד מידי דשיימי' להו כארים:

**אמר** שמואל שבוי שנשבה מורידין. וא"ת והאמרה שמואל חדא זימנא וי"ל דה"ק אף על גב דבשבוי מורידין יצא לדעת אין מורידין:

**היינו** לדעת. דמסתמא לא פליג אשמואל מדלא קאמר אף בורח או אף יוצא לדעת:

**ש"מ** מדרב הונא אין מחזיקין בנכסי קטן ואפי' הגדיל. פרש"י מדאמר רב הונא אין מורידין קרוב הא נכרי מורידין וקשה דבלא רב הונא כמה משניות יש שמעמידין אפוטרופוס לנכסי יתומים פרק הניזקין (גיטין דף נב.) מנהו ב"ד לא ישבע וע"ק היכי מוכח מדרב הונא דאין מחזיקין דלמא אי טוען שני חזקה מועיל והא דמורידין נכרי משום דליכא למיחש למידי דע"כ כיון דמורידין א"כ יש לו דעת לומר הבא עדים שלקחת מאבי והכי נמי יש לו לדעת ולמחות בסוף כל שלשה וכי

## עין משפט נר מצוה

נד א מיי' פ"ז מהלכות נחלות הל' ה סמג עשין לז טוש"ע ח"מ סי' רפה סעיף ב וע"ש:

נה ב מיי' פכ"ג מהל' אישות הל' ח סמג עשין מח טוש"ע אה"ע סי' פח סעיף ז:

נו ג מיי' שם הל' י טוש"ע שם סעיף י:

נז ד ה מיי' פ"ז מהלכות נחלות הל' ה סמג עשין לז טוש"ע ח"מ סי' רפה סעיף ב:

נח ו מיי' שם הלכה ו טוש"ע שם סעיף ג:

נט ז מיי' שם הלכה ה טוש"ע שם סעיף ב:

ס ח ט י מיי' שם פ"ח הל' א ב סמג עשין לז טוש"ע ח"מ סי' רפה סעיף ו:

סא כ מיי' פי"ד מהל' טוען ונטען הל' ז סמג עשין לה טוש"ע ח"מ סי' קמט סעיף יט:

## רבינו חננאל

תנא וכולן שמין להן כאריס. אוקימנא כרשב"ג דאמר שמעתי שהנטושין כשבויין. וסבר האי תנא כשבויין ולא שבויין כשבויין שאם תפשו דאין מוציאין מידם ולא שבויין דאלו גבי שבויין אם קדם ותלש ואכל הרי זה זריז ונשכר ואלו גבי נטושין שמין להן כאריס. ואקשינן מאי שנא מהא דתנן המוציא הוצאות בנכסי אשתו הוציא הרבה ואוכל קימעא מה שהוציא הוציא ומה שאכל אכל וכו' אסיק' תיקנו להן רבנן לשום להן כאריס כי היכי דלא ניפסדינהו לנכסי. ודייקי' וכולן לאתויי שבוי שנשבה שמורידין קרוב לנכסיו. יצא לדעת אין מורידין קרוב לנכסיו מאי טעמא דאמרי' מכדי לדעת יצא היה לו להוריד קרוביו לנכסיו כיון שלא הוריד הוא גם אנו אין מורידין אבל הבורח מחמת מרדין כלומר הבורח מחמת נפשות מורידין קרוב לנכסיו דאמרי' מחמת טירדא הוא דלא הורידם וקיימא לן כשמואל דהא רב נחמן קאי כותיה הלכך במקרקעי מורידין קרוב לנכסי נטושין וכששמעו בהן שמתו מורידין אפילו א) לנכסי נטושין. ומטלטלי אם תפשו אין מוציאין מידם ואם לא תפשו מפקידין אותן ביד נאמנין. ב) ואם נראין הדברים שמתו אע"פ שאין עדות ברורה במיתתן נותנין אותן ליורשין. פי' אפוטרופא לדיקנני כלומר לאדם גדול בעל זקן אין מעמידין לו אפוטרופוס. וקיימא לן כשמואל דאמר מורידין קרוב לנכסי שבוי דהא רב הונא דתלמיד רב הוא אמר אין מורידין (קרוב) [קטן] לנכסי שבוי דלמא מפסיד להו ולא קרוב לנכסי קטן הא גדול ואפי' קרוב בנכסי שבוי

## חשק שלמה על ר"ח

א) נראה דל"ל אפילו לנכסי רטושין ועי' בש"מ כאן מש"כ בשם הרא"ש ז"ל. ב) נראה דר"ל כגון שטבע במים שאין להם סוף וכיוצא בו ועי' ברמב"ם ובש"ע ח"מ ס"ס רפד.

## מסורת הש"ס

א) [לקמן קו., קט.], ב) כתובות עט:, ג) נ"ל דאמר ר"י אמר רב חסדא, וכן הוא בכתובות פ., [ועי' תוס' יבמות קז. ד"ה דאין], ד) כתובות יח: [ע"ש בתוס'].

## הגהות הב"ח

(א) תוס' ד"ה וכולם וכו' דבשבוי ששמעו בו שמת וכו' ובנטושים דלא שמעו בו שמת לא:

## הגהות הגר"א

[א] רש"י ד"ה השתא כו' ויטול הכל. נ"ב עי' תוס' ד"ה וכולן (ועמ"ש רבינו בח"מ סי' רפ"ה ס"ק ז):

## תורה אור השלם

א) וְהַשְּׁבִיעִת תִּשְׁמְטֶנָּה וּנְטַשְׁתָּהּ וְאָכְלוּ אֶבְיֹנֵי עַמֶּךָ וְיִתְרָם תֹּאכַל חַיַּת הַשָּׂדֶה כֵּן תַּעֲשֶׂה לְכַרְמְךָ לְזֵיתֶךָ: [שמות כג, יא]

ב) וְקָאם שָׁאוֹן בְּעַמֶּךָ וְכָל מִבְצָרֶיךָ יוּשַּׁד כְּשֹׁד שַׁלְמַן בֵּית אַרְבֵאל בְּיוֹם מִלְחָמָה אֵם עַל בָּנִים רֻטָּשָׁה: [הושע י, יד]

## ליקוטי רש"י

**אפקעתא דמלכא.** המלך ביטלו מלזורעה והרי היא כמו שאינה ולא קראה הכתוב לישראל שנת תבואה [לקמן קו.]. **אם על בנים רוטשה.** רוטשה עזובה כמו נוטשה [הושע י, יד]. **מה שהוציא הוציא.** אם גירשה [כתובות עט:]. **אשתו קטנה.** יתומה שהשיאתה אמה ואחיה יכולה למאן. **כמוציא על נכסי אחר.** ואם מיאנה בו שמין לו שבח שהשביח ונוטל כמשפט אריסי המדינה [שם פ.]. **אין מחזיקין בנכסי קטן.** המחזיק בנכסי קטן שלש שנים אינה חזקה דהאי דלא מיחה משום דקטן הוא [כתובות יח:].

נטוּשִׁינ – The term ***netushim*** דִּבְעַל כָּרְחָן – refers to properties hat are abandoned **unwillingly.** דִּכְתִיב – **For it is written** n Scripture concerning the *shemittah* year: ,,וְהַשְּׁבִיעִת תִּשְׁמְטֶנָּה וּנְטַשְׁתָּה" – ***And [on] the seventh year, release it and abandon*** *t* (*netashtah*).[1] אַפְקַעְתָּא דְּמַלְכָּא – The requirement to refrain rom planting during *shemittah* is **a command of the King** [i.e. Iashem], and therefore the word *netashtah* refers to an involuntary abandonment. Similarly, the term *netushim* is used to lescribe property that was abandoned against the owner's will. רטוּשִׁינ – The term ***retushim,*** however, דְּמִדַּעְתָּן – is used to refer to properties **that** were abandoned **willingly.** דִּכְתִיב – For it is written: ,,אֵם עַל־בָּנִים רֻטָּשָׁה" – ***The mother, together vith the children, have been abandoned*** (*rutashah*).[2] Since the word *rutashah* in this verse speaks of a voluntary abandonment, he Tanna uses the similar term *retushim* to refer to property that was abandoned voluntarily.

The Gemara cites the conclusion of the Baraisa:

תָּנָא – **The Baraisa taught:** וְכוּלָּם – AND regarding ALL THOSE who enter another's field,[3] שָׁמִין לָהֶם כְּאָרִיס – WE EVALUATE FOR THEM their share of the profits AS IF they came into the field as A SHARECROPPER.[4]

The Gemara elaborates:

אַהֵיָא – **To which** case of the Baraisa does this ruling apply? אִילֵימָא אַשְּׁבוּיִין – **If we say** that it applies **to captives'** property, he ruling is unnecessary! הַשְׁתָּא זָרִיז וְנִשְׂכָּר הָוֵה – **Now,** if the Baraisa has already ruled that a relative who enters a captive's property and consumes the *entire* crop before the owner's return **is quick and profits** from his speed,[5] מַאי דַּאֲשְׁבַּח מִיבַּעְיָא – **is it necessary** to state that he will receive at least the pay of a sharecropper in the uneaten produce and any improvements he made to the land?[6]

The Gemara rejects a second possibility:

אֶלָּא אַרְטוּשִׁינ – **Rather,** shall we say that the Baraisa's ruling here applies **to *retushim*** property? וְהָא מוֹצִיאִין אוֹתָן מִיָּדוֹ קָתָנֵי – **But** this also cannot be, because **it was taught in the Baraisa** regarding *retushim* property: WE TAKE IT OUT OF HIS HANDS! The caretaker in this case receives nothing at all – so how can the Baraisa then rule that he is treated as a sharecropper?

The Gemara rejects a third possibility:

אֶלָּא אַנְּטוּשִׁים – **Rather,** shall we say that the ruling applies **to *netushim*** property? לְמַאן – But **according to whose** view is the Baraisa's ruling taught? אִילֵימָא לְרַבָּנָן – **If we say** that it is **according to** the opinion of **the Rabbis,** as explained by the Tanna Kamma, that cannot be! הָא אָמְרֵי מוֹצִיאִין אוֹתוֹ מִיָּדוֹ – **For they said** regarding this case: WE TAKE [THE PROPERTY] OUT OF [THE CARETAKER'S] HANDS. אִי רַבָּן שִׁמְעוֹן בֶּן גַּמְלִיאֵל – **And if** we say that it was taught according to the opinion of **Rabban Shimon ben Gamliel,** who permits relatives to care for *netushim* property, the ruling is unnecessary! הָא אָמַר שָׁמַעְתִּי שֶׁהַנְּטוּשִׁים כִּשְׁבוּיִין – **For he said:** I HEARD THAT ABANDONED (*netushim*) property is regarded in law LIKE CAPTIVES' properties whose owners are rumored to have died; and in that case, the caretaker may rightfully consume even *all* of the produce before the owner returns. If so, it would not be necessary to state that the caretaker would receive a sharecropper's share in the unconsumed produce and improvement if the owner returns. – ? –

The Gemara answers:

In fact, the Baraisa's ruling does refer to the case of *netushim* properties according to the opinion of Rabban Shimon ben Gamliel. But the ruling is indeed necessary:

כִּשְׁבוּיִין – For according to Rabban Shimon ben Gamliel, abandoned *netushim* property is **like captives'** property in certain legal aspects, וְלֹא שְׁבוּיִין – **but not** entirely the same as **captives'** property. כִּשְׁבוּיִין – **It is like captives'** property in the sense דְּאֵין מוֹצִיאִין אוֹתָן מִיָּדוֹ – **that we do not take [*netushim* property] out of the hands [of the caretaker].**[7] וְלֹא שְׁבוּיִין – **But it is not** exactly like **captives'** property, דְּאִילּוּ הָתָם זָרִיז וְנִשְׂכָּר – **for there,** in that case, if the relative **is quick** to take what is his, **he profits** from his speed, should he eat all the produce before the captive's return.[8] וְאִילּוּ הָכָא – **But here,** with respect to *netushim* property, שַׁיְימִינַן לֵיהּ כְּאָרִיס – **we evaluate for him** his share of the profits **as if** he was **a sharecropper,** but he may not consume more than this.[9] Thus, the Baraisa teaches us that, according to Rabban Shimon ben Gamliel, the caretaker of abandoned *netushim* property is *not* entitled to the entire current crop like the caretaker of a captive's property.[10]

---

NOTES

1. *Exodus* 23:11. The Gemara in *Moed Katan* (3a) explains that during the *shemittah* year, the owner must "release" his land from being planted, and also "abandon" it by not fertilizing or weeding it (see also *Rashi* to *Exodus* ad loc.).

2. *Hosea* 10:14. The Jews were afraid of a surprise enemy attack, and they voluntarily abandoned their homes and families to avoid being captured (see *Rashi*).

3. The Gemara below will explain precisely which type of abandoned property is referred to here, as well as what case the general term "all" comes to include (*Rashi*).

4. Should the captive owner return, the caretaker is paid the percentage of annual proceeds and improvements to the land that is customarily received by a sharecropper in that locale (*Rashi*), and the rest belongs to the owner.

5. I.e. he is allowed to keep even the entire current crop if he ate it before the owner's return (*Rashi*).

6. According to *Rashi* and *Ramban,* the Gemara indeed concludes here that relatives who care for captives' property whose owners are rumored to be dead receive a share in unconsumed produce and improvements like a sharecropper if the owner returns. *Tosafos* and *Rosh,* however, explain that although *this* is indeed the Gemara's position at this point, it is later retracted (see below, end of note 18); the final ruling is that in such a case, relatives receive no compensation other than whatever produce they already consumed *before* the return of the owner.

7. Indeed, a relative is appointed to enter the property, to manage it until the owner returns.

8. Having heard that the captive died, the relative entered the land with the intent of receiving all of its produce as his inheritance. Therefore, it is appropriate that he should keep whatever he consumed, even if the captive eventually returns (*Rashi*).

9. Since he did not hear that the owner died, the relative never entered the land with the intent of consuming all its produce as his inheritance. He intended only to plant the land in the owner's absence, and to be paid as an ordinary sharecropper (*Rashi*).

10. *Rashi* rules that the caretaker may not consume more produce each year than a sharecropper's portion; the rest is set aside until the owner returns. *Rambam* (*Hil. Nachalos* 7:5) and *Ramban,* however, rule that he may consume all of the produce until the owner returns. At that time, his proper compensation is determined, and he must return the balance to the owner (see *Ramban* for the reason; see also *Beur HaGra, Choshen Mishpat* 285:7).

*Tosafos* disagree with both of the opinions cited above. They rule that even in the case of *netushim* property, the caretaker retains whatever produce he consumed before the owner's return (see below, note 18). However, the law of *netushim* property differs from that of captives' property regarding whether the caretaker may rightfully consume produce if he becomes aware of the owner's imminent return. As the Baraisa stated above, he may quickly consume the produce of a captive's property, since otherwise he will not be paid (see above, note 6). In the case of *netushim* property, however, he may not do so, since he will be paid for his work as a sharecropper.

in order to manage it until the father returns. This conflicts with Shmuel's lenient ruling, which authorizes the court to appoint a relative to manage a captive's property even when there is no rumor of his death! — ? —

The Gemara turns back the challenge:

אָמַר רָבָא – **Rava said:** לֵירֵד וְלִמְכּוֹר תְּנַן – **It was stated** in the text of the Baraisa only that the children are not permitted **to enter** their father's property **and sell** it (that is, to possess it as owners). However, it can still be that they may indeed care for it in his absence; and they may eat its produce and be paid as sharecroppers if their father returns.

The Gemara records a related occurrence:

הֲוָה עוּבְדָא בִּנְהַרְדְּעָא – **There was** once **an incident in Nehardea** involving a relative who entered a captive's property to manage it, וּפַשְׁטָה רַב שֵׁשֶׁת מֵהָא מַתְנִיתָא – **and Rav Sheishess decided [the case] on the basis of this** aforementioned **Baraisa,** ruling that the relative could not remain in the property. אָמַר לֵיהּ רַב עַמְרָם – **Rav Amram said to him:** דִּלְמָא לֵירֵד וְלִמְכּוֹר תְּנַן – But **perhaps** the Tanna **stated** only that the children are not permitted **to enter** their father's property **and sell** it; that would not prevent them from caring for their father's property, eating its produce, and being paid as sharecroppers if the father returns! אָמַר לֵיהּ – Rav Sheishess **replied to [Rav Amram]:** דִּלְמָא מִפּוּמְבְּדִיתָא אַתְּ – **Perhaps you are from Pumbedisa,** דְּמְעַיְּילִין פִּילָא בְּקוֹפָא דְמַחֲטָא – **where they push an elephant through the eye of a needle** (i.e. their arguments can be rather forced). וְהָא דּוּמְיָא דִנְשׁוֹתֵיהֶם [וּבְנֵיהֶם] קָתָנֵי – Why, the case of the children that is **taught in the Baraisa** should be **similar to** the case of **their wives!**[28] מַה הָתָם כְּלָל לֹא – **Just as there,** the wives may **not** remarry **at all** because possibly their husbands are still alive, אַף הָכָא נַמִּי כְּלָל לֹא – **here, too,** the children may **not** enter the property **at all,** even just to care for the property.

The Gemara presents a Tannaic dispute about this matter:

וּמוֹרִידִין קָרוֹב לְנִכְסֵי שְׁבוּי תַּנָּאֵי הִיא – **And it is a Tannaic dispute whether** the court **appoints a relative to** manage **a captive's property** when there has been no rumor that the captive died. דְּתַנְיָא – **For it was taught in a Baraisa:** הַיּוֹרֵד לְנִכְסֵי שָׁבוּי – IF SOMEONE [i.e. a relative] ENTERS THE PROPERTY OF A CAPTIVE, אֵין מוֹצִיאִין אוֹתוֹ מִיָּדוֹ – WE DO NOT TAKE IT OUT OF HIS HANDS.[29] וְלֹא עוֹד – AND NOT ONLY THAT, אֶלָּא אֲפִילּוּ שָׁמַע שֶׁמְּמַשְׁמְשִׁין וּבָאִין – BUT EVEN IF the relative HEARD THAT the captive IS SLOWLY MAKING HIS WAY home, וְקָדַם וְתָלַשׁ וְאָכַל – AND HE QUICKLY PICKED AND CONSUMED all of this year's produce, הֲרֵי זֶה זָרִיז וְנִשְׂכָּר – THIS person IS QUICK to take what is his, AND PROFITS from his speed.[30]

The Baraisa continues:

וְאֵלּוּ הֵן נִכְסֵי שְׁבוּיִין – AND THESE ARE THE cases of PROPERTY OF CAPTIVES that we do not remove from a relative's possession: הֲרֵי שֶׁהָיָה אָבִיו אוֹ אָחִיו אוֹ אֶחָד מִן הַמּוֹרִישִׁין – IF HIS FATHER, HIS BROTHER, OR ONE OF THESE relatives THAT HE WOULD INHERIT should that relative die הָלְכוּ לָהֶם לִמְדִינַת הַיָּם – TRAVELED OVERSEAS, וְשָׁמְעוּ בָּהֶן שֶׁמֵּת – AND [PEOPLE] HEARD ABOUT HIM THAT HE DIED. In such cases, the relative may be appointed to supervise the property.

הַיּוֹרֵד לְנִכְסֵי נְטוּשִׁים – However, IF ONE ENTERS UNWILLINGLY ABANDONED PROPERTY (*netushim*), מוֹצִיאִין אוֹתוֹ מִיָּדוֹ – WE TAKE IT OUT OF HIS HANDS.[31] וְאֵלּוּ הֵן נִכְסֵי נְטוּשִׁים – AND THESE ARE considered cases of UNWILLINGLY ABANDONED PROPERTY (*netushim*): הֲרֵי שֶׁהָיָה אָבִיו אוֹ אָחִיו אוֹ אֶחָד מִן הַמּוֹרִישִׁין – IF HIS FATHER, BROTHER, OR ONE OF THE relatives THAT HE WOULD INHERIT הָלְכוּ לָהֶם לִמְדִינַת הַיָּם – TRAVELED OVERSEAS, לֹא שָׁמְעוּ בָּהֶם שֶׁמֵּת – AND [PEOPLE] DID *NOT* HEAR ABOUT HIM THAT HE DIED. If there was no rumor of the captive's death, the relative has no right to enter the property according to this Tanna. אָמַר רַבָּן שִׁמְעוֹן בֶּן גַּמְלִיאֵל – BUT RABBAN SHIMON BEN GAMLIEL SAID: שָׁמַעְתִּי שֶׁהַנְּטוּשִׁים כִּשְׁבוּיִין – I have HEARD THAT ABANDONED PROPERTY (*netushim*) is regarded in law LIKE CAPTIVES' properties, and we appoint a relative over either type of property to care for it. Thus, the Tannaim dispute the law in this case.[32]

The Baraisa continues:

הַיּוֹרֵד לְנִכְסֵי רְטוּשִׁים – IF ONE ENTERS VOLUNTARILY ABANDONED PROPERTY (*retushim*),[33] מוֹצִיאִין אוֹתוֹ מִיָּדוֹ – WE TAKE IT OUT OF HIS HANDS.[34] וְאֵלּוּ הֵן נִכְסֵי רְטוּשִׁים – AND THESE ARE considered VOLUNTARILY ABANDONED PROPERTIES (*retushim*): הֲרֵי שֶׁהָיָה אָבִיו אוֹ אָחִיו אוֹ אֶחָד מִן הַמּוֹרִישִׁין כָּאן – IF HIS FATHER, BROTHER OR ONE OF THE relatives THAT HE WOULD INHERIT if that relative should die WAS HERE and then he disappeared, וְאֵינוֹ יוֹדֵעַ לְהֵיכָן הָלְכוּ – AND HE DOES NOT KNOW WHERE [THE OWNER] WENT.

The Gemara clarifies the meaning of the two types of property discussed in the Baraisa — *"netushim"* and *"retushim"* properties:

מַאי שְׁנָא הָנָךְ דְּקָרוּ לְהוּ נְטוּשִׁים – **What is the difference between those** abandoned properties, **which are called** ***netushim,*** וּמַאי שְׁנָא הָנֵי דְּקָרוּ לְהוּ רְטוּשִׁים – **and these** abandoned properties, **which are called** ***retushim?***

NOTES

second part of the verse therefore must include a second curse — that such sinners will be taken captive, and their families will never learn whether they are dead or still alive. Hence, their wives will remain "widows" forever, and their children will be permanently "orphaned" and not allowed to inherit their fathers' estates (*Rashi*).

28. I.e. the verse compares the "orphans" who cannot inherit their captive father's property to the "widowed" wives who cannot remarry.

29. *Tosafos* comment that the Tanna Kamma's statement is imprecise; for in fact, not only do we not *remove* the heir from the property, we even allow him to enter the property in the first place. *Rambam (Hil. Nachalos* 7:4), however, understands the ruling in this Baraisa differently (see *Kesef Mishneh* ad loc., *Ritva* [old]; cf. *Raavad* ad loc.).

30. If he would have not acted so quickly, and the captive had returned before he ate or sold the produce, the relative would have been paid only as a sharecropper (see *Rashi*). Now, however, he keeps all of the proceeds.

31. The Gemara below (39a) explains that *"netushim"* property is property that was unwillingly abandoned by its owner, due to circumstances beyond his control (*Rashi*). Since he never had the opportunity to instruct *beis din* to appoint a relative to care for his property, his failure to do so does not reveal his attitude on the matter. The Tanna Kamma holds that even in this case *beis din* makes no such appointment, and removes any heir that enters the property on his own (from *Rashi*).

32. The Gemara above stated that Tannaim dispute whether *beis din* appoints a relative to manage a captive's property when there has been no rumor that the captive has died. Unwillingly abandoned (*netushim*) property is equivalent to such property, for the Baraisa defines it as land whose owner has traveled abroad and "[people] did not hear. . .that he died." Rabban Shimon ben Gamliel rules that *beis din* appoints a relative to manage *netushim* property; hence, he would also rule that they do so for a captive's property (even when there was no rumor that the owner died). The Tanna Kamma ruled, however, that *beis din* does not appoint a relative to manage such property; hence, they would likewise rule that *beis din* does not appoint a relative in a captive's property when there has been no rumor that the owner died.

33. The Gemara below (39a) explains that *retushim* is willfully abandoned property, which the owner left behind voluntarily (*Rashi*).

34. The owner of this property, which was voluntarily abandoned, *had* the opportunity to instruct *beis din* to appoint a relative as caretaker. Since he failed to do so, we may conclude that he clearly does not desire the presence of such a manager (*Rashi*); and all agree that *beis din* does not appoint one, and will remove one who enters the property without permission.

## עין משפט נר מצוה

נ א מיי' פ"ז מהלכות שאלה ופקדון הל' ב סמג עשין פח טוש"ע ח"מ סי' רלב סעיף טח:

נא ב ג מיי' פ"ז מהל' נחלות הלכה ד ה ועיין בהשגות ובמגיד משנה סמג עשין לו טוש"ע ח"מ סי' רפה סעיף ב וסעיף ג וסעיף ה:

נב ד טוש"ע שם סעיף א [ועיין בכ"מ שתמה על הרמב"ם שהשמיט זה]:

נג ה מיי' שם הלכה ח טוש"ע שם סעיף א וסעיף ד:

## רבינו חננאל

אצל חבירו והרקיבו וכו' פי' כיון דקם קם כיון שהחמיץ כך יעמיד בחימוצו לעולם. פי' כתישה מלשון אם תכתש את האויל במכתש. וחכמים אומרים עושה להן תקנה ומוכרן בב"ד. וכשמוכרן מוכרן לאחרים ולא לעצמו. עושה להן תקנה. אסקי' תקנה זו לקנקנים שלא יפסידו לגמרי ואפי' הפסד מועט חששו. והלכה כחכמים וכר' יוחנן. רשב"ג אומר ימכרם בב"ד מפני שהוא כמשיב אבידה. קי"ל דחלוקת חכמים ורשב"ג בכדי חסרונן כר' יוחנן והלכה כחכמים ואע"ג דחכמים דברייתא קיימי כרשב"ג. אבל יותר מכדי חסרונן דברי הכל מוכרן בב"ד לאחרים ולא לעצמו: איתמר רב אמר אין מורידין קרוב לנכסי שבוי חיישינן דלמא מפסדי להו. ושמואל אמר מורידין כיון דאמר מר שמין להם כאריס לא מפסדי להו. בששמעו בו שמת כולי עלמא לא פליגי דמורידין כי פליגי בשלא שמעו בו שמת. וקימא לן כשמואל וכרב נחמן. הוה עובדא בנהרדעא בשבוי שנשבה ופשטה רב ששת דאין מורידין קרוב לנכסיו מהא דתניא ר' אומר ממשמע שנאמר והרגתי אתכם איני יודע כי יהיו נשיכם אלמנות ובניכם יתומים אלא מלמד שהן כאלמנות ולא אלמנות ממש כיצד מבקשות לינשא ואין מניחין אותן. בניהן מבקשין לירד בנכסי אביהן ואין מניחין אותן שעדין לא נתבררה מיתתן בעדות. ואע"ג דאוקמה רבא לירד ולמכור אין מניחין אותם אבל מניחין אותן לירד ולתקן. דחאה רב ששת מדכתב נשיכם ובניהם בניהם דומיא דנשיהם מה נשיהם כלל לא אף בניהם כלל לא. מורידין קרוב בנכסי שבוי אוקימנא כתנאי דתניא היורד לנכסי שבוין אין מוציאין אותן מידו והוא ששמעו בהן שמתו. היורד לנכסי נטושין מוציאין אותן מידו. והן שיצאו למדינת הים ואין ידוע להיכן הלכו א).

## חשק שלמה על ר"ח

א) בגמ' איתא לשון זה גבי נכסי רטושין ואולי דרביט היה לו גי' אחרת.

---

עד כאן לא קאמר רשב"ג כו' אבל (א) הכא אין מורידין. וא"ת והא לקמן מייתי דאית ליה לרשב"ג מורידין וי"ל דמהא ליכא למשמע מינה אבל קשה דמאי מוכיח דחד טעמא הוא מדשמואל דסבר כרשב"ג וסבר מורידין לוכח כן מרשב"ג גופיה וי"ל דלא שמיע ליה ברייתא דלקמן:

בששמעו בו שמת כ"ע ל"פ דמורידין. אין לפרש בששמעו בב' עדים דא"כ פשיטא דמורידין אלא ששמעו היינו בקול ועד אחד אע"ג דשמעו בו שמת דבפ' ב' דייני גזירות (כתובות דף קז.) גבי אין פוסקין מזונות לאשת איש משמע סוגיא דהתם דהוי בעדות גמורה [ח]:

אמר רבא לירד ולמכור תנן. וא"ת ואמאי לא פריך ממתניתין דהאשה שהלכה (יבמות דף קטז: ושם ד"ה שאין) דקתני מלינו שאין אחים נכנסין לנחלה על פיה ולשני נמי לירד ולמכור תנן וי"ל דמהא אלימא ליה לאקשויי משום דדומיא דנשותיהם קתני דמשמע כלל כלל לא:

היורד לנכסי שבוי אין מוציאין אותו מידו. (ב) הוא הדין דאפי' מורידין אותו לכתחילה דהא נטושים מורידין לרשב"ג דאמר הנטושים כשבויין אלא אגב דתנא בסיפא בנטושים מוציאין תנא נמי בשבויין אין מוציאין וא"ת לימא רב הלכה כתנא קמא ושמואל הלכה כרשב"ג וי"ל דלא שמיע להו ברייתא אי נמי איכא דמפכי להו:

וכולם

---

למאי חזו שמן חזי לגלדאי דבש לכתישא דגמלי וחכ"א עושה להם תקנה ומוכרן בב"ד מאי תקנתא עביד להו אמר רב אשי [א]לקנקנים במאי קא מיפלגי דמר סבר להפסד מרובה חששו [א]להפסד מועט לא חששו ומר סבר אפילו להפסד מועט נמי חששו: רשב"ג אומר ימכרם בבית דין מפני שהוא כמשיב אבידה לבעלים: אתמר רבי אבא ברבי יעקב א"ר יוחנן הלכה כרשב"ג ורבא אמר רב נחמן הלכה כדברי חכמים והא אמרה ר' יוחנן חדא זמנא [ג]דאמר רבה בר בר חנה א"ר יוחנן כל מקום ששנה רבן שמעון בן גמליאל במשנתינו הלכה כמותו חוץ מערב וצידן וראיה אחרונה אמוראי נינהו ואליבא דר' יוחנן מדרבן שמעון בן גמליאל נשמע דמורידין קרוב לנכסי שבוי מדרבנן נשמע דאין מורידין קרוב לנכסי שבוי וממאי דלמא עד כאן לא קאמר רבן שמעון בן גמליאל הכא אלא משום דקא כליא קרנא אבל התם הכי נמי דאין מורידין ועד כאן לא קאמרי רבנן הכא אלא אי כרב כהנא אי כרב נחמן בר יצחק אבל התם הכי נמי דמורידין למימרא דתרי טעמי נינהו והאמר רב יהודה אמר שמואל הלכה כרבן שמעון ב"ג ואמר שמואל מורידין קרוב לנכסי שבוי לאו משום דחד טעמא הוא לא תרי טעמי נינהו והכי נמי מסתברא דאמר רבא אמר רב נחמן הלכה כדברי חכמים ואמר רב נחמן מורידין קרוב לנכסי שבוי אלא ש"מ תרי טעמי נינהו שמע מינה אתמר שבוי שנשבה רב אמר אין מורידין קרוב לנכסיו שמואל אמר [ב]מורידין קרוב לנכסיו בששמעו בו שמת כ"ע לא פליגי דמורידין כי פליגי [ג]בשלא שמעו בו שמת רב אמר אין מורידין דלמא מפסיד להו ושמואל אמר מורידין כיון דאמר מר שיימינן להו כאריס לא מפסיד להו מיתיבי ר"א אומר [ג]ממשמע שנאמר [א]וחרה אפי והרגתי אתכם יודע אני שנשותיהם אלמנות ובניהם יתומים אלא מה ת"ל והיו נשיכם וגו' מלמד שנשותיהם מבקשות לינשא ואין מניחין אותן ובניהן רוצים לירד לנכסי אביהן ואין מניחין אותן אמר רבא לירד ולמכור תנן הוה עובדא בנהרדעא ופשטה רב ששת מהא מתני' א"ל רב עמרם דלמא לירד ולמכור תנן א"ל דלמא מפומבדיתא את דמעיילין [ד]פילא בקופא דמחטא והא דומיא דנשותיהם [(ה) ובניהם] קתני מה התם כלל לא אף הכא נמי כלל לא ומורידין קרוב לנכסי שבוי תנאי היא דתניא [ו][ה]היורד לנכסי שבוי אין מוציאין אותו מידו ולא עוד אלא אפי' שמע שממשמשין ובאין וקדם ותלש ואכל הרי זה זריז ונשכר ואלו הן נכסי שבויין הרי שהיה אביו או אחיו או אחד מן המורישין הלכו להם למדינת הים ושמעו בהן שמת היורד לנכסי נטושים מוציאין אותו מידו ואלו הן נכסי נטושים הרי שהיה אביו או אחיו או אחד מן המורישין הלכו להם למדינת הים ולא שמעו בהם שמת ואמר רבן שמעון בן גמליאל שמעתי שהנטושים כשבויין [ה]היורד לנכסי רטושים מוציאין אותו מידו ואלו הן נכסי רטושים הרי שהיה אביו או אחיו או אחד מן המורישין כאן ואינו יודע להיכן הלכו מאי שנא הנך דקרו להו נטושים ומאי שנא הני דקרו להו רטושים

נטושים

---

למאי חזו. דקתני מוכרן: לגלדאי. לסוך עורות: לכתישא דגמלא. לכתישה שעל הגמל שגבו כתוש ומסוכב מחמת משאוי איישר"א בלע"ז: לקנקנין. הכלי שהיה בתוכו יתקלקל אם ישהא בתוכו: במאי קמיפלגי. ר"מ ורבנן מאחר שמודה ר"מ ביתר מכדי חסרונן: להפסד מרובה. כגון יתר מכדי חסרונן: הפסד מועט. כגון בכדי חסרון דריקבון פירות וקילקול הקנקן דיין והחמיץ: ערב. בגט פשוט (ב"ב קעג:): צידן. במסכת גיטין (דף עד.): ראייה. בדיני ממונות השני (סנהדרין לא.) שנחלקו בשני מחלוקות במביא שטר ראיה לסתור את הדין בראשונה הלכה כמותו ובאחרונה אין הלכה כמותו: אמוראי נינהו. רבה אמר בכללא אמר ר' יוחנן ור' אבא אמר לאו בכללא אמר רבי יוחנן אלא יש מהן שהלכה כמותו: מדרבן שמעון נשמע דמורידין קרוב. הראוי לירש: בנכסי שבוי. לקרקעות שבוי לעובדן ולשומרן עד שיבאו הבעלים ולקמן פליגי בה אמוראי: עד כאן לא קאמר רבן שמעון הכא. דמוכרן: אלא משום דקא כליא קרנא. אם יניחם שם אבל גבי קרקעות וכרמים אע"פ שמתקלקלות קלת לא כליא קרנא: אי כרב כהנא. דאמר לעיל רוצה אדם בקב שלו: אי כרב נחמן בר יצחק. דאמר שמא עשאן תרומה ומעשר: דתרי טעמי נינהו. מתני' ונכסי שבוי ואיכא דאית ליה מוכרין פירות האבודין ולית ליה מורידין: קרוב. הראוי ליורשו ואין קרוב ממנו: בששמעו בו שמת כולי עלמא לא פליגי דמורידין. דאם יבאו הבעלים קודם שיאכל זה הפירות יטול זה כשאר אריסין ויחזיר השאר ואם יבאו עדים שמת ירש הכל: מפסיד להו. ולא יזבל הקרקעות ויזרעם תמיד ויכחישם: כיון דאמר מר. לקמן [י]וכולם שמין להם כאריס אם יבאו הבעלים שמין לזה חלקו בכל שנה שעבד בה כמנהג אריסי העיר אם מחצה אם שליש אם רביע: אלא מלמד שנשיהם מבקשות לינשא כו'. שילכו בשבי ולא ידעו בניהם אם חיים אם מתים ויהיו נשיהם אלמנות לעולם שאין ב"ד מניחין אותן לינשא ובניהם כיתומים שלא ירשו נכסיהם ושתי קללות הן אחת של חרב ואחת של שבי שמע מינה אין מורידין: הוה עובדא בנהרדעא. בשבוי שירד יורשו לנכסיו: ופשטה רב ששת מהא מתניתא. דאין מורידין: א"ל רב עמרם דלמא לירד ולמכור תנן. [קתני] תנא דאין מניחין אבל לעשות ולאכול וליטול כאריס שפיר דמי: דמעיילין פילא כו'. ומשני שנויא דחיקא כמבקש להכניס פיל שהוא חיה גדולה בנקב מחט: ותלש. פירות שנה זו: הרי זה זריז. מהיר לזכות בשלו בטרם יפסיד ונשכר בזריזותו: ואלו הן נכסי שבויין. דאמר אין מוציאין אותם מידו: שהנטושים כשבוין. ואין מוציאין מידו: נכסי נטושין. שהנכסים נטושין: נכסי רטושין. שהנכסים רטושים ולקמן מפרש להו רטושין משמע שעזבום בעלים מדעתם והלכו להם דכיון דהיה לו לצוות הורידו יורשיו לנכסיו ולא צוה ש"מ לא ניחא ליה ונטושים שנטשום בעליהם בעל כרחן כגון שנשבו והיינו תנאי דרבן שמעון סבר מורידין ורבנן סברי אין מורידין:

ה"ג

---

## מסורת הש"ס

א) [שבת קכד: וש"נ], ב) כתובות עז., גיטין לח. ודף עה., בבא קמא סט. בבא בתרא קעד., סנהדרין לא., [בכורות כד.], ג) [אבות דר' נתן פרק לח], ד) [ברכות נה:], ה) מהרש"ל, ו) [תוספתא דכתובות פרק ח], ז) [דף לח., ח) [ועיין תוס' יבמות קטז: ד"ה שאין ותוס' כתובות קז. ד"ה ששמעו].

## הגהות הב"ח

(א) תוס' ד"ה עד וכו' אבל התם אין מורידין: (ב) ד"ה היורד וכו'. נ"ב עיין בטו"ת ב"ח סי' ר' תמצא פירוש דיבור זה:

## תורה אור השלם

א) וְחָרָה אַפִּי וְהָרַגְתִּי אֶתְכֶם בֶּחָרֶב וְהָיוּ נְשֵׁיכֶם אַלְמָנוֹת וּבְנֵיכֶם יְתֹמִים: [שמות כב, כג]

## לעזי רש"י

איישר"א. פירוש שפשוף, פלע (על גבן של בהמות משא).

## ליקוטי רש"י

גלדאי. רלענים [לעיל כד: חולין מח.] לכתישא דגמלי. כתי שבגבי הסוסים והגמלים מחמת המשאות [שבת עו:]. במשנתינו. ולא בברייתא [רשב"ם ב"ב קעד.]. שיימינן להו כאריס. אם יבואו הבעלים יטלו אלו בשבח קרקעות ופירות כמנהג אריסי המקום [לקמן לט.] אלא מה ת"ל והיו נשיכם וגו'. אלא הרי זו קללה אחרת שיהיו הנשים צרורות כאלמנות חיות שלא יהיו עדים למיתת בעליהן ותהיינה אסורות להנשא והבנים יהיו יתומים שלא יניחום בית דין לירד לנכסי אביהם לפי שאין יודעים אם מתו או נשבו [שמות כב, כג] קופא דמחטא. נקב המחט [ברכות נה:]. מגב ולא מחודו [עי' סנהדרין צו:]. רטושין. עזובין [ערכין כה:].

in the case of the captive, where neither of these reasons apply,[12] הָכִי נַמִּי דְּמוֹרִידִין – perhaps **they would agree that** the court **does appoint** a relative to manage the captive's property!

The Gemara deflects the challenge:

לְמֵימְרָא דִּתְרֵי טַעְמֵי נִינְהוּ – **Do you mean to say that** the case of the Mishnah and the case of the captive **are** dependent on **two** different **reasons?**[13] וְהָאָמַר רַב יְהוּדָה אָמַר שְׁמוּאֵל – **Why, Rav Yehudah said in the name of Shmuel:** הֲלָכָה כְּרַבָּן שִׁמְעוֹן בֶּן גַּמְלִיאֵל – The **halachah follows** the opinion of **Rabban Shimon ben Gamliel,** that spoiled produce should be sold, וְאָמַר שְׁמוּאֵל – **and Shmuel** also **said:** מוֹרִידִין קָרוֹב לְנִכְסֵי שָׁבוּי – The court **appoints a relative to** manage a **captive's property!** לָאו מִשּׁוּם דְּחַד טַעְמָא הוּא – **Is it not true** that Shmuel issued both of these rulings because they are both based on the same **reasoning** – that *beis din* protects the property of an absentee owner from any possible loss, whether large or small?[14]

The Gemara replies:

לֹא – **No!** תְּרֵי טַעְמֵי נִינְהוּ – Really, **these** cases **are** dependent upon **two** different **reasons,** because there may possibly be a distinction between protecting against a large loss and protecting against a small loss. Nevertheless, Shmuel himself does not make such a distinction, and rules that even in the case of a captive, we appoint a relative to manage the captive's property.[15]

The Gemara provides proof that the two rulings are not linked: הָכִי נַמִּי מִסְתַּבְּרָא – **Indeed,** it **stands to reason** that the two rulings are not dependent on each other, דְּאָמַר רָבָא אָמַר רַב נַחְמָן – **for Rava said in the name of Rav Nachman:** הֲלָכָה כְּדִבְרֵי חֲכָמִים – **The halachah accords with the opinion of the Sages** of the Mishnah, who prohibit the sale of deposited produce, וְאָמַר רַב נַחְמָן – **and** yet **Rav Nachman** also **said:** מוֹרִידִין קָרוֹב לְנִכְסֵי שָׁבוּי – The court **appoints a relative to** manage **a captive's property!**[16] אֶלָּא שְׁמַע מִינָּהּ – **Rather, deduce from this** תְּרֵי טַעְמֵי נִינְהוּ – that **these** rulings **are** dependent upon **two** different **reasons.** שְׁמַע מִינָּהּ – Indeed, you can **deduce** it **from this.**

The Gemara now turns to discuss the laws of caring for a captive's property:

אִתְּמַר – **It was stated:** שָׁבוּי שֶׁנִּשְׁבָּה – If **one** was taken **captive:**[17] רַב אָמַר – **Rav said:** אֵין מוֹרִידִין קָרוֹב לִנְכָסָיו – The court **does not appoint a relative to** manage **his property.** שְׁמוּאֵל אָמַר – But **Shmuel said:** מוֹרִידִין קָרוֹב לִנְכָסָיו – The court **does** appoint **a relative to** manage **his property.**

The Gemara explains exactly when this dispute applies:

בְּשֶׁשָּׁמְעוּ בּוֹ שֶׁמֵּת – **In** a case **where they** had **heard** that [the captive] **died,**[18] כּוּלֵּי עָלְמָא לֹא פְּלִיגֵי דְּמוֹרִידִין – **everyone** [i.e. both Rav and Shmuel] **agrees that** the court **appoints** a relative to manage the captive's property, because this arrangement will certainly not be harmful to the property.[19] כִּי פְּלִיגֵי – **When do they disagree?** בְּשֶׁלֹּא שָׁמְעוּ בּוֹ שֶׁמֵּת – **In** a case **where they did not hear that [the captive] died.** רַב אָמַר אֵין מוֹרִידִין – **Rav said** that the court **does not appoint** a relative to manage the captive's property, דִּלְמָא מַפְסִיד לְהוּ – because we are concerned that **perhaps he will ruin [the land],** since it is not his.[20] וּשְׁמוּאֵל אָמַר מוֹרִידִין – **And Shmuel said** that the court **does appoint** a relative to supervise the captive's property, כֵּיוָן דְּאָמַר מַר – for **since the master said,**[21] concerning those that take care of land for an absentee owner, שֶׁיִּימִינַן לְהוּ כְּאָרִיס – that **we evaluate for them** their share of any profit **as if they were a sharecropper,**[22] לֹא מַפְסִיד לְהוּ – the relative **will not ruin [the land],** because he stands to gain by caring for it well.[23]

The Gemara challenges Shmuel's view:

מֵיתִיבֵי – The scholars **retorted** from the evidence of a Baraisa: רַבִּי אֱלִיעֶזֶר אוֹמֵר – **R' ELAZAR**[24] **SAYS:** מִמַּשְׁמַע שֶׁנֶּאֱמַר – **FROM THE PLAIN MEANING OF WHAT IS STATED** in the verse:[25] "וְחָרָה אַפִּי וְהָרַגְתִּי אֶתְכֶם" – ***AND I [HASHEM] SHALL BECOME ANGERED AND I SHALL KILL YOU,*** יוֹדֵעַ אֲנִי שֶׁנְּשׁוֹתֵיהֶם אַלְמָנוֹת וּבְנֵיהֶם יְתוֹמִים – **I WOULD ALREADY KNOW THAT THEIR WIVES** will become **WIDOWS AND THEIR CHILDREN ORPHANS.**[26] לֹא מַה תַּלְמוּד לוֹמַר: "וְהָיוּ נְשֵׁיכֶם וגו׳ " – **IF SO, WHAT TEACHING DOES** the verse, ***AND YOUR WIVES*** **etc.** [*will be widows and your children orphans*], mean **TO TEACH?** מְלַמֵּד שֶׁנְּשׁוֹתֵיהֶם מְבַקְּשׁוֹת לִינָּשֵׂא – **IT TEACHES THAT THEIR WIVES WILL SEEK TO MARRY** again וְאֵין מַנִּיחִין אוֹתָן – **AND WE WILL NOT ALLOW THEM** to do so, because we will not be sure that the husbands are dead; וּבְנֵיהֶן רוֹצִים לֵירֵד לְנִכְסֵי אֲבִיהֶן – **AND** that **THEIR CHILDREN WILL DESIRE TO ENTER THEIR FATHERS' PROPERTIES** וְאֵין מַנִּיחִין אוֹתָן – **AND WE WILL NOT ALLOW THEM** to do so, for the same reason.[27] Scripture thus teaches that *beis din* is not allowed even to appoint a child over his father's property

NOTES

12. Since we are not speaking of the captive's produce, but of managing his property.

13. I.e. is it possible that one would permit the sale of deposited produce (where the entire principal is in danger), yet prohibit a relative from managing a captive's property to prevent a smaller loss? (*Rashi*).

14. *Shitah Mekubetzes.*

15. I.e. although it is possible, from the standpoint of logic, to distinguish between the Mishnah's case of potential destruction of the entire principal and the case of a captive where the potential loss is minimal, Shmuel did not actually make this distinction (*Shitah Mekubetzes*).

16. Rav Nachman's position demonstrates that it is even possible to rule that we act to prevent a smaller loss (in the case of a captive owner), while we do not allow a *shomer* to sell produce even though there is a possibility that the entire principal will be lost.

17. The case concerns not only a captive, but any person who was unavoidably detained elsewhere and is unable to tend to his fields and/or vineyards (*Ritva* [old]).

18. I.e. a rumor circulated or a single witness testified to that effect. If *two* witnesses testify that the captive died, his heir may certainly take the land, for two witnesses are trusted in all matters [and the land is therefore legally his] (*Tosafos*).

19. If, in fact, the captive has not died and returns before his relative consumes the crop, the relative will still be paid as a sharecropper (see below, 39a note 4); and if witnesses later testify that the captive has died, the relative inherits the entire estate. Thus, since the relative knows that he may inherit the land (and that he will at least be fairly paid if the owner does return), the relative will care for the land in a responsible manner (see *Rashi* and *Ritva* [old]).

20. [Since he has no reason to believe that his relative has died in captivity, he does not expect to inherit the land.] We are therefore concerned that he will not bother to fertilize the soil between plantings, but will simply plant one crop after another to get as much produce as he can, thereby exhausting and ruining the land (*Rashi*).

21. Below, 39a.

22. I.e. they are paid the percentage of annual proceeds customarily earned by a sharecropper in that region – be it a quarter, a third, or half of the crop (*Rashi*).

23. Shmuel holds that as long as the relative will be paid for his work, we are not concerned that he will overwork the land.

24. *Maharam* emends רַבִּי אֱלִיעֶזֶר (R' Eliezer) to read: רַבִּי אֶלְעָזָר (R' Elazar).

25. *Exodus* 22:23, which speaks of the punishment that comes to those who oppress widows and orphans. The full verse reads: וְחָרָה אַפִּי וְהָרַגְתִּי אֶתְכֶם בֶּחָרֶב וְהָיוּ נְשֵׁיכֶם אַלְמָנוֹת וּבְנֵיכֶם יְתֹמִים, *And I shall become angered and I shall kill you by the sword, and your wives will be widows and your children orphans.*

26. I.e. the second half of the verse (*. . .and your wives* etc.) appears superfluous, as it tells us nothing we could not have deduced from the first half.

27. In the first part of this verse, Hashem explicitly decrees the curse of death by sword upon one who oppresses widows and orphans. Th

למאי חזו שמן חזי לגלדאי דבש לכתישא דגמלי וחכ"א עושה להם תקנה ומוכרן בב"ד מאי תקנתא עביד להו אמר רב אשי [א] לקנקנים במאי קא מיפלגי דמר סבר להפסד מרובה חששו [א] להפסד מועט לא חששו ומר סבר אפילו להפסד מועט נמי חששו: רשב"ג אומר ימכרם בבית דין מפני שהוא כמשיב אבידה לבעלים: אתמר רבי אבא ברבי יעקב א"ר יוחנן הלכה כרשב"ג ורבא אמר רב נחמן הלכה כדברי חכמים והא אמרה ר' יוחנן חדא זמנא [ג] דאמר רבה בר בר חנה א"ר יוחנן כל מקום ששנה רבן שמעון בן גמליאל במשנתינו הלכה כמותו חוץ מערב וצידן וראיה אחרונה אמוראי נינהו ואליבא דר' יוחנן מדרבן שמעון בן גמליאל נשמע דמורידין קרוב לנכסי שבוי מדרבנן נשמע דאין מורידין קרוב לנכסי שבוי וממאי דלמא עד כאן לא קאמר רבן שמעון בן גמליאל הכא אלא משום דקא כליא קרנא אבל התם הכי נמי דאין מורידין ועד כאן לא קאמרי רבנן הכא אלא אי כרב כהנא אי כרב נחמן בר יצחק אבל התם הכי נמי דמורידין למימרא דתרי טעמי נינהו והאמר רב יהודה אמר שמואל הלכה כרבן שמעון ב"ג ואמר שמואל מורידין קרוב לנכסי שבוי לאו משום דחד טעמא הוא לא תרי טעמי נינהו הכי נמי מסתברא דאמר רבא אמר רב נחמן הלכה כדברי חכמים ואמר רב נחמן מורידין קרוב לנכסי שבוי אלא ש"מ תרי טעמי נינהו שמע מינה אתמר שבוי שנשבה רב אמר אין מורידין קרוב לנכסיו שמואל אמר [ב] מורידין קרוב לנכסיו בששמעו בו שמת כ"ע לא פליגי דמורידין כי פליגי [ג] בשלא שמעו בו שמת רב אמר אין מורידין דלמא מפסיד להו ושמואל אמר מורידין כיון דאמר מר שיימינן להו כארים לא מפסיד להו מיתיבי ר"א אומר [ג] ממשמע שנאמר [א] וחרה אפי והרגתי אתכם יודע אני שנשותיהם אלמנות ובניהם יתומים אלא מה ת"ל והיו נשיכם וגו' מלמד שנשותיהם מבקשות לינשא ואין מניחין אותן ובניהן רוצים לירד לנכסי אביהן ואין מניחין אותן אמר רבא לירד ולמכור תנן הוה עובדא בנהרדעא ופשטה רב ששת מהא מתני' א"ל רב עמרם דלמא לירד ולמכור תנן א"ל דלמא מפומבדיתא את דמעיילין [ד] פילא בקופא דמחטא והא דומיא דנשותיהם [ה] ובניהם] קתני מה התם כלל לא אף הכא נמי כלל לא ומורידין קרוב לנכסי שבוי תנאי היא דתניא [ו] [ד] היורד לנכסי שבוי אין מוציאין אותו מידו ולא עוד אלא אפי' שמע שממשמשין ובאין וקדם ותלש ואכל הרי זה זריז ונשכר ואלו הן נכסי שבויין הרי שהיה אביו או אחיו או אחד מן המורישין הלכו להם למדינת הים ושמעו בהן שמת היורד לנכסי נטושים מוציאין אותו מידו ואלו הן נכסי נטושים הרי שהיה אביו או אחיו או אחד מן המורישין הלכו להם למדינת הים ולא שמעו בהם שמת ואמר רבן שמעון בן גמליאל שמעתי שהנטושים כשבויין [ה] היורד לנכסי רטושים מוציאין אותו מידו ואלו הן נכסי רטושים הרי שהיה אביו או אחיו או אחד מן המורישין כאן ואינו יודע להיכן הלכו מאי שנא הנך דקרו להו נטושים ומאי שנא הני דקרו להו רטושים

נטושים

**רש"י**

**למאי חזו.** דקתני מוכרן: **לגלדאי.** לסוך עורות: **לכתישא דגמלא.** לכתישה שעל הגמל שגבו כתוש ומסוקב מחמת משאוי איישר"א בלע"ז: **לקנקנים.** הכלי שהיה בתוכו יתקלקל אם ישהא בתוכו: **במאי קמיפלגי.** ר"מ ורבנן מאחר שמודה ר"מ ביתר מכדי חסרונן: **להפסד מרובה.** כגון יתר מכדי חסרונן: **הפסד מועט.** כגון בכדי חסרון דריקבון פירות וקילקול הקנקן דיין והחמיץ: **ערב.** בגט פשוט (ב"ב קעג:): **צידן.** במסכת גיטין (דף עד.): **ראייה.** בדיני ממונות השני (סנהדרין לא.) שנחלקו בשני מחלוקות במביא שטר ראיה לסתור את הדין בראשונה הלכה כמותו ובאחרונה אין הלכה כמותו: **אמוראי נינהו.** רבה אמר בכללא אמר ר' יוחנן ור' אבא אמר לאו בכללא אמר רבי יוחנן אלא יש מהן שהלכה כמותו: **מדרבן שמעון נשמע דמורידין קרוב.** הראוי לירש: **בנכסי שבוי.** לקרקעות שבוי לעובדן ולשומרן עד שיבאו הבעלים ולקמן פליגי בה אמוראי: **עד כאן לא קאמר רבן שמעון הכא.** דמוכרן: **אלא משום דקא כליא קרנא.** אם יניחם שם אבל גבי קרקעות וכרמים אע"פ שמתקלקלות קצת לא כליא קרנא: **אי כרב כהנא.** דאמר לעיל רוצה אדם בקב שלו: **אי כרב נחמן בר יצחק.** דאמר שמא עשאן תרומה ומעשר: **דתרי טעמי נינהו.** מתני' ונכסי שבוי ואיכא דאית ליה מוכרין פירות האבודין ולית ליה מורידין: **קרוב.** הראוי ליורשו ואין קרוב ממנו: **בששמעו בו שמת כולי עלמא לא פליגי דמורידין.** דאם יבאו הבעלים קודם שיאכל זה הפירות יטול זה כשאר אריסין ויחזיר השאר ואם יבאו עדים שמת ירש הכל: **מפסיד להו.** ולא יזבל הקרקעות ויזרעם תמיד ויכחישם: **כיון דאמר מר.** לקמן [ז] וכולם שמין להם כאריס אם יבאו הבעלים שמין לזה חלקו בכל שנה שעבד בה כמנהג אריסי העיר אם מחצה אם שליש אם רביע: **אלא מלמד שנשיהם מבקשות לינשא כו'.** שילכו בשבי ולא ידעו בניהם אם חיים אם מתים ויהיו נשיהם אלמנות לעולם שאין ב"ד מניחין אותן לינשא ובניהם כיתומים שלא ירשו נכסיהם ושתי קללות הן אחת של חרב ואחת של שבי שמע מינה אין מורידין: **הוה עובדא בנהרדעא.** בשבוי שירד יורשו לנכסיו: **ופשטה רב ששת מהא מתניתא.** דאין מורידין: **א"ל רב עמרם דלמא לירד ולמכור תנן.** [קתני] תנא דאין מניחין אבל לעשות ולאכול וליטול כאריס שפיר דמי: **דמעיילין פילא כו'.** ומשני שנויא דחיקא כמבקש להכניס פיל שהוא חיה גדולה בנקב מחט: **ותלש.** פירות שנה זו: **הרי זה זריז.** מהיר לזכות בשלו בטרם יפסיד ונשכר בזריזותו: **ואלו הן נכסי שבויין.** דאמר אין מוציאין אותם מידו: **שהנטושים כשבוין.** ואין מוציאין מידו: **נכסי נטושין.** שהנכסים נטושין: **נכסי רטושין.** שהנכסים רטושים ולקמן מפרש להו רטושין משמע שעזבום בעלים מדעתם והלכו להם דכיון דהיה לו לצוות לא ניחא ליה ונטושים שנטשום בעליהם בעל כרחן כגון שנשבו והיינו תנאי דרבן שמעון סבר מורידין ורבנן סברי אין מורידין:

ה"ג

**תוספות**

**עד** כאן לא קאמר רשב"ג כו' אבל (א) הכא אין מורידין. וא"ת והא לקמן מייתי דאית ליה לרשב"ג מורידין וי"ל דמהא ליכא למשמע מינה אבל קשה דמאי מוכיח דחד טעמא הוא מדשמואל דסבר כרשב"ג וסבר מורידין לוכח כן מרשב"ג גופיה וי"ל דלא שמיע ליה ברייתא דלקמן:

**בששמעו** בו שמת כ"ע ל"פ דמורידין. אין לפרש בששמעו בב' עדים דא"כ פשיטא דמורידין אלא ששמעו היינו בקול ועד אחד אע"ג דשמעו בו שמת דפ' ב' דייני גזירות (כתובות דף קז.) גבי אין פוסקין מזונות לאשת איש משמע סוגיא דהתם דהוי בעדות גמורה [ח]:

**אמר** רבא לירד ולמכור תנן. וא"ת ואמאי לא פריך ממתניתין דהאשה שהלכה (יבמות דף קטז: ושם ד"ה שאין) דקתני מצינו שאין אחים נכנסין לנחלה על פיה ולשני נמי לירד ולמכור תנן וי"ל דמהכא אלימא ליה לאקשויי משום דדומיא דנשותיהם קתני דמשמע כלל לא:

**היורד** לנכסי שבוי אין מוציאין אותו מידו. (ב) הוא הדין דאפי' מורידין אותו לכתחילה דהא נטושים מורידין לרשב"ג דאמר הנטושים כשבויין אלא אגב דתנא בסיפא בנטושים מוציאין תנא נמי בשבויין אין מוציאין וא"ת לימא רב הלכה כתנא קמא ושמואל הלכה כרשב"ג וי"ל דלא שמיע להו ברייתא אי נמי איכא דמפכי להו:

וכולם

**עין משפט נר מצוה**

נ א מיי' פ"ז מהלכות שאלה ופקדון הל' ב סמג עשין פח טוש"ע ח"מ סי' רצב סעיף טו:

נא ב ג מיי' פ"ז מהל' נחלות הלכה ד ה ועיין בהשגות ובמגיד משנה סמג עשין צו טוש"ע ח"מ סי' רפה סעיף ב וסעיף ג וסעיף ה:

נב ד טוש"ע שם סעיף א [ועיין בכ"מ שתמה על הרמב"ם שהשמיט זה]:

נג ה מיי' שם הלכה ח טוש"ע שם סעיף א וסעיף ד:

**רבינו חננאל**

אצל חבירו והרקיבו וכו' פי' כיון דקם קם כיון שהחמיץ כך יעמיד בחימוצו לעולם. פי' כתישה מלשון אם תכתש את האויל במכתש. וחכמים אומרים עושה להן תקנה ומוכרן בב"ד. וכשמוכרן מוכרן לאחרים ולא לעצמו. עושה להן תקנה. אסקי' תקנה זו לקנקנים שלא יפסידו לגמרי ואפי' הפסד מועט חששו. והלכה כחכמים וכר' יוחנן. רשב"ג אומר ימכרם בב"ד מפני שהוא כמשיב אבידה. קי"ל דחלוקת חכמים ורשב"ג בכדי חסרונן כר' יוחנן והלכה כחכמים ואע"ג דחכמים דברייתא קיימי כרשב"ג. אבל יותר מכדי חסרונן דברי הכל מוכרן בב"ד לאחרים ולא לעצמו: איתמר רב אמר אין מורידין קרוב לנכסי שבוי חיישינן דלמא מפסדי להו. ושמואל אמר מורידין כיון דאמר מר שמין להם כאריס לא מפסדי להו. בששמעו בו שמת כולי עלמא לא פליגי דמורידין כי פליגי בשלא שמעו בו שמת. וקיימא לן כשמואל וכרב נחמן. הוה עובדא בנהרדעא בשבוי שנשבה ופשטה רב ששת דאין מורידין קרוב לנכסיו מהא דתניא ר' אומר ממשמע שנאמר והרגתי אתכם איני יודע כי יהיו נשיכם אלמנות ובניכם יתומים אלא מלמד שהן כאלמנות ולא אלמנות ממש כיצד מבקשות לינשא ואין מניחין אותן. בניהן מבקשין לירד בנכסי אביהן ואין מניחין אותן שעדין לא נתבררה מיתתן בעדות. ואע"ג דאוקמה רבא לירד ולמכור אין מניחין אותם אבל מניחין אותן לירד ולתקן. דחאה רב ששת מדכתב נשיכם ובניהם בניהם דומיא דנשיהם מה נשיהם כלל לא אף בניהם כלל לא. מורידין קרוב בנכסי שבוי אוקימנא כתנאי דתניא היורד לנכסי שבוין אין מוציאין אותן מידו והוא ששמעו בהן שמתו. היורד לנכסי נטושין מוציאין אותן מידו. והן שיצאו למדינת הים ואין ידוע להיכן הלכו א).

**חשק שלמה על ר"ח**

א) בגמ' איתא לשון זה גבי נכסי רטושין ואולי דרבינו היה לו גי' אחרת.

**מסורת הש"ס**

א) [שבת קכ: וש"נ], ב) כתובות עז., גיטין לח., ודף עה., בבא קמא סט., בבא בתרא קעד., סנהדרין לא., [בכורות כד.], ג) [אבות דר' נתן פרק לח], ד) [ברכות נה:], ה) מהרש"ל, ו) [תוספתא דכתובות פרק ח], ז) [דף לט.], ח) [ועיין תוס' יבמות קטז: ד"ה שאין ותוס' כתובות קז. ד"ה ששמעו].

**הגהות הב"ח**

(א) תוס' ד"ה עד וכו'. אבל התם אין מורידין: (ב) ד"ה היורד וכו'. נ"ב עיין בשו"ת ב"מ סי' ר"ו תמלא פירוש דיבור זה:

**תורה אור השלם**

א) וְחָרָה אַפִּי וְהָרַגְתִּי אֶתְכֶם בֶּחָרֶב וְהָיוּ נְשֵׁיכֶם אַלְמָנוֹת וּבְנֵיכֶם יְתֹמִים: [שמות כב, כג]

**לעזי רש"י**

אייסר"א. פירוש ספסוף, פלע (על גבן של בהמות משא).

**ליקוטי רש"י**

גלדאי. רלענים [לעיל כד: חולין מח.] לכתישא דגמלי. כתיש שבגבי הסוסים והגמלים מחמת המשאות [שבת עו:]. במשנתינו. ולא בברייתא [רשב"ם ב"ב קעד.]. שיימינן להו כארים. אם יבואו הבעלים יטלו אלו בשבח קרקעות ופירות כמנהג אריסי המקום [לקמן לט.] אלא מה ת"ל והיו נשיכם וגו'. אלא הרי זו קללה אחרת שיהיו הנשים צרורות כאלמנות חיות שלא יהיו עדים למיתת בעליהן ותהיינה אסורות להנשא והבנים יהיו יתומים שלא יניחום בית דין לירד לנכסי אביהם לפי שאין יודעים אם מתו אם נשבו [שמות כב, כג]. קופא דמחטא. נקב המחט [ברכות נה:]. מגב ולא מחודו [עי' סנהדרין צז:]. רטושין. עזובים [ערכין כה:].

לְמַאי חֲזוּ – But for what are these items still fit? Why would anyone buy them?

The Gemara answers:

שֶׁמֶן חֲזֵי לְגַלְדָּאֵי – Rancid oil is still usable for leather workers, who apply it to skins to soften them; דְּבַשׁ לְכַתִּישָׁא דְגַמְלֵי – and spoiled honey can still be used as a salve for a camel's sores, which are caused by loads that rub against the camel's back.

The Gemara continues analyzing the Baraisa, which stated: וַחֲכָמִים אוֹמְרִים – BUT THE SAGES SAY: עוֹשֶׂה לָהֶם תַּקָּנָה – HE SHOULD FIX the situation, וּמוֹכְרָן בְּבֵית דִּין – AND SELL the spoiled produce IN *BEIS DIN*. מַאי תַּקַּנְתָּא עָבֵיד לְהוּ – But how can he fix the [produce] if it is already spoiled? What is the point of selling it now? אָמַר רַב אַשִׁי – Rav Ashi said: לְקַנְקַנִּים – He must act for the sake of the vessels by selling the spoiled liquid in them, so the containers do not become ruined as well.

Since, according to R' Yochanan, R' Meir agrees with the Sages that the deposited produce must be sold when more than the normal percentage has spoiled, the Gemara asks:

בְּמַאי קָא מִיפַּלְגִי – In what issue do R' Meir and the Sages disagree?[1] דְּמַר סָבַר – About the following: One master [i.e. R' Meir] held that לְהֶפְסֵד מְרוּבֶּה חָשְׁשׁוּ – the Rabbis were concerned only about a major loss, such as the loss of produce beyond the normal percentage. לְהֶפְסֵד מוּעָט לֹא חָשְׁשׁוּ – However, they were not concerned about a minor loss,[2] or possible damage to vessels containing spoiled liquids. Therefore, in these cases of minor loss the remaining produce may not be sold. וּמַר סָבַר – And the other master [i.e. the Sages] held that אֲפִילּוּ לְהֶפְסֵד מוּעָט נַמִּי חָשְׁשׁוּ – [the Rabbis] were concerned about even a minor loss. Therefore, rotting produce may be sold even if more than a normal amount of it has not yet spoiled, and spoiled liquid may be sold to prevent damage to its containers.

The Mishnah stated the view of Rabban Shimon ben Gamliel, who disputed the position of the Sages:

רַבָּן שִׁמְעוֹן בֶּן גַּמְלִיאֵל אוֹמֵר – RABBAN SHIMON BEN GAMLIEL SAYS: יִמְכְּרֵם בְּבֵית דִּין – HE SHOULD SELL [THE SPOILED PRODUCE] IN COURT,[3] מִפְּנֵי שֶׁהוּא כְּמֵשִׁיב אֲבֵידָה לַבְּעָלִים – BECAUSE HE IS LIKE ONE THAT RETURNS A LOST ARTICLE TO THE OWNER.

The Gemara decides the halachah:

אִתְּמַר – It was stated: רַבִּי אַבָּא בְּרַבִּי יַעֲקֹב אָמַר רַבִּי יוֹחָנָן – R' Abba the son of R' Yaakov said in the name of R' Yochanan: הֲלָכָה כְּרַבָּן שִׁמְעוֹן בֶּן גַּמְלִיאֵל – The halachah follows the opinion of Rabban Shimon ben Gamliel. וְרָבָא אָמַר רַב נַחְמָן – And Rava said in the name of Rav Nachman: הֲלָכָה כְּדִבְרֵי חֲכָמִים – The halachah follows the opinion of the Sages.

The Gemara questions why it was necessary for R' Abba to teach this:

וְהָא אֲמָרָהּ רַבִּי יוֹחָנָן חֲדָא זִמְנָא – But R' Yochanan has already stated this once before – i.e. that the halachah accords with the view of Rabban Shimon ben Gamliel! דְּאָמַר רַבָּה בַּר בַּר חָנָה אָמַר רַבִּי יוֹחָנָן – For Rabbah bar bar Chanah said in the name of R' Yochanan: כָּל מָקוֹם שֶׁשָּׁנָה רַבָּן שִׁמְעוֹן בֶּן גַּמְלִיאֵל בְּמִשְׁנָתֵינוּ – In every place that Rabban Shimon ben Gamliel has taught a ruling in our Mishnah,[4] הֲלָכָה כְּמוֹתוֹ – the halachah follows his opinion, חוּץ מֵעָרֵב – with the exception of the case of a guarantor,[5] וְצַיְדָּן – and the case of the divorce in Tzaidan,[6] וּרְאָיָה אַחֲרוֹנָה – and the last case of bringing proof.[7] If R' Yochanan already stated this as a general rule, why was it necessary for him to specify that the halachah accords with Rabban Shimon ben Gamliel in our case as well?

The Gemara answers:

אַלִּיבָּא דְּרַבִּי יוֹחָנָן אֲמוֹרָאֵי נִינְהוּ – There is an Amoraic dispute concerning the opinion of R' Yochanan. Rabbah bar bar Chanah held that R' Yochanan ruled that the halachah always follows Rabban Shimon ben Gamliel's ruling in a Mishnah; but R' Abba held that R' Yochanan ruled this way only in specific instances, such as the ruling in our Mishnah.

The Gemara derives another law from our Mishnah's rulings:

מִדְּרַבָּן שִׁמְעוֹן בֶּן גַּמְלִיאֵל – From Rabban Shimon ben Gamliel's ruling, which ordered the sale of deposited produce to protect the owner from possible loss, נִשְׁמַע דְּמוֹרִידִין קָרוֹב לְנִכְסֵי שְׁבוּי – we may derive that the court will appoint a relative[8] as a manager over property of someone that has been taken captive, to care for and cultivate the land until the owner's return. מִדְּרַבָּנָן – While from the Sages' ruling, which prohibits the *shomer* from selling the produce, נִשְׁמַע דְּאֵין מוֹרִידִין קָרוֹב לְנִכְסֵי שְׁבוּי – we may derive the opposite – that the court does not appoint a relative to manage a captive's property.

The Gemara challenges this assumption:

וּמִמַּאי – And from what evidence do you draw these conclusions? דִּלְמָא עַד כָּאן לֹא קָאָמַר רַבָּן שִׁמְעוֹן בֶּן גַּמְלִיאֵל הָכָא אֶלָּא – Perhaps Rabban Shimon ben Gamliel said his ruling here only מִשּׁוּם דְּקָא כַּלְיָא קַרְנָא – because the principal[9] might be destroyed if the *shomer* does not sell it. אֲבָל הָתָם – But there, in the case of the captive, הָכִי נַמִּי דְּאֵין מוֹרִידִין – perhaps he would agree that the court does not appoint a relative to manage his property, for although the fields and vineyards may suffer some damage if they are left untended, the land itself will remain intact. עַד כָּאן לֹא קָאָמְרִי רַבָּנָן הָכָא אֶלָּא – And, on the other hand, perhaps the Sages said here that the deposited produce may not be sold only because of a particular reason that applies only to this specific case – אִי כְּרַב כַּהֲנָא אִי כְּרַב נַחְמָן בַּר יִצְחָק – either that of Rav Kahana,[10] or that of Rav Nachman bar Yitzchak.[11] אֲבָל הָתָם – But there,

NOTES

1. That is, in the case of rotting produce, why does R' Meir forbid its sale until the depletion exceeds the expected normal amount? Additonally, in the case of spoiled liquid, where there exists the possibility that the vessel will be ruined, in addition to the fact that the loss already exceeds the normal amount (see above, 38a note 25), why does R' Meir refuse to allow them to be sold?

2. Apparently, as long as the produce has not spoiled at more than the normal rate, R' Meir is not concerned that a great loss will occur.

3. The Gemara's quotation is slightly different from our version of the Mishnah above (38a).

4. I.e. whenever a ruling of R' Shimon ben Gamliel is cited within a Mishnah (as opposed to a Baraisa).

5. See Mishnah, *Bava Basra* 173b.

6. See Mishnah, *Gittin* 74a.

7. The Mishnah in *Sanhedrin* (31a) presents two cases that discuss whether evidence may be brought into court in certain cases to overturn a judgment issued by the court. In both cases, Rabban Shimon issued a ruling. R' Yochanan states that the halachah does not accord with his decision in the second case (*Rashi*).

8. Specifically, the relative who will inherit the captive's property if he dies (*Rashi*). The appointed relative manages the property, and takes a share of the profits as a sharecropper would. It is not appropriate to appoint someone else to do this work, since – should the property's owner die in captivity – the heir would lose the share of the profits that was paid to the manager (*Ramban*).

9. That is, the deposited produce in its entirety.

10. Who explained above (38a) that since a person prefers the fruits of his own labor, the Sages prohibited the *shomer* from selling the deposited produce (*Rashi*).

11. Who explained (ibid.) that the Sages were concerned that the owner of the produce may have made it into *terumah* or *maaser* without the *shomer's* knowledge (*Rashi*).

למאי חזו שמן חזי לגלדאי דבש לכתישא דגמלי וחכ"א עושה להם תקנה ומוכרן בב"ד מאי תקנתא עביד להו אמר רב אשי א לקנקנים במאי קא מיפלגי דמר סבר להפסד מרובה חששו [א] להפסד מועט לא חששו ומר סבר אפילו להפסד מועט נמי חששו: רשב"ג אומר ימכרם בבית דין מפני שהוא כמשיב אבידה לבעלים: אתמר רבי אבא ברבי יעקב א"ר יוחנן הלכה כרשב"ג ורבא אמר רב נחמן הלכה כדברי חכמים והא אמרה ר' יוחנן חדא זמנא [ג] דאמר רבה בר בר חנה א"ר יוחנן כל מקום ששנה רבן שמעון בן גמליאל במשנתינו הלכה כמותו חוץ מערב וצידן וראיה אחרונה אמוראי נינהו ואליבא דר' יוחנן מדרבן שמעון בן גמליאל נשמע דמורידין קרוב לנכסי שבוי מדרבנן נשמע דאין מורידין קרוב לנכסי שבוי וממאי דלמא עד כאן לא קאמר רבן שמעון בן גמליאל הכא אלא משום דקא כליא קרנא אבל התם הכי נמי דאין מורידין ועד כאן לא קאמרי רבנן הכא אלא אי כרב כהנא אי כרב נחמן בר יצחק אבל התם הכי נמי דמורידין למימרא דתרי טעמי נינהו והאמר רב יהודה אמר שמואל הלכה כרבן שמעון ב"ג ואמר שמואל מורידין קרוב לנכסי שבוי לאו משום דחד טעמא הוא לא תרי טעמי נינהו הכי נמי מסתברא דאמר רבא אמר רב נחמן הלכה כדברי חכמים ואמר רב נחמן מורידין קרוב לנכסי שבוי אלא ש"מ תרי טעמי נינהו שמע מינה אתמר שבוי שנשבה רב אמר אין מורידין קרוב לנכסיו שמואל אמר ב מורידין קרוב לנכסיו בששמעו בו שמת כ"ע לא פליגי דמורידין כי פליגי ג בשלא שמעו בו שמת רב אמר אין מורידין דלמא מפסיד להו ושמואל אמר מורידין כיון דאמר מר שיימינן להו כארים לא מפסיד להו מיתיבי ר"א אומר [ג] ממשמע שנאמר [א] וחרה אפי והרגתי אתכם יודע אני שנשותיהם אלמנות ובניהם יתומים אלא מה ת"ל והיו נשיכם וגו' מלמד שנשותיהם מבקשות לינשא ואין מניחין אותן ובניהן רוצים לירד לנכסי אביהן ואין מניחין אותן אמר רבא לירד ולמכור תנן הוה עובדא בנהרדעא ופשטה רב ששת מהא מתני' א"ל רב עמרם דלמא לירד ולמכור תנן א"ל דלמא מפומבדיתא את דמעיילין [ד] פילא בקופא דמחטא והא דומיא דנשותיהם [ה ובניהם] קתני מה התם כלל לא אף הכא נמי כלל לא ומורידין קרוב לנכסי שבוי תנאי היא דתניא [ו] ד היורד לנכסי שבוי אין מוציאין אותו מידו ולא עוד אלא אפי' שמע שממשמשין ובאין וקדם ותלש ואכל הרי זה זריז ונשכר ואלו הן נכסי שבויין הרי שהיה אביו או אחיו או אחד מן המורישין הלכו להם למדינת הים ושמעו בהן שמת היורד לנכסי נטושים מוציאין אותו מידו ואלו הן נכסי נטושים הרי שהיה אביו או אחיו או אחד מן המורישין הלכו להם למדינת הים ולא שמעו בהם שמת ואמר רבן שמעון בן גמליאל שמעתי שהנטושים כשבויין ה היורד לנכסי רטושים מוציאין אותו מידו ואלו הן נכסי רטושים הרי שהיה אביו או אחיו או אחד מן המורישין כאן ואינו יודע להיכן הלכו מאי שנא הנך דקרו להו נטושים ומאי שנא הני דקרו להו רטושים נטושים

## רש"י

למאי חזו. דקתני מוכרן: לגלדאי. לסוף עורות: לכתישא דגמלא. לכתישה שעל הגמל שגבו כתוש ומסוקב מחמת משאוי איישר"א בלע"ז: לקנקניו. הכלי שהיה בתוכו יתקלקל אם ישהא בתוכו: במאי קמיפלגי. ר"מ ורבנן מאחר שמודה ר"מ ביתר מכדי חסרונן: להפסד מרובה. כגון יתר מכדי חסרונן: הפסד מועט. כגון בכדי חסרון דריקבון פירות וקילקול הקנקן דיין והחמיץ: ערב. בגט פשוט (ב"ב קעג:): צידן. במסכת גיטין (דף עד.): ראייה. בדיני ממונות השני (סנהדרין לא.) שנחלקו בשני מחלוקות במביא שטר ראיה לסתור את הדין בראשונה הלכה כמותו ובאחרונה אין הלכה כמותו: אמוראי נינהו. רבה אמר בכללא אמר ר' יוחנן ור' אבא אמר לאו בכללא אמר רבי יוחנן אלא יש מהן שהלכה כמותו: מדרבן שמעון נשמע דמורידין קרוב. הראוי לירש: בנכסי שבוי. לקרקעות שבוי לעובדן ולשומרן עד שיבאו הבעלים ולקמן פליגי בה אמוראי: עד כאן לא קאמר רבן שמעון הכא. דמוכרן: אלא משום דקא כליא קרנא. אם יניחם שם אבל גבי קרקעות וכרמים אע"פ שמתקלקלות קרנא לא כליא קרנא: אי כרב כהנא. דאמר לעיל רוצה אדם בקב שלו: אי כרב נחמן בר יצחק. דאמר שמא עשאן תרומה ומעשר: דתרי טעמי נינהו. מתני' ונכסי שבוי ואיכא דאית ליה מוכרין פירות האבודין ולית ליה מורידין: קרוב. הראוי ליורשו ואין קרוב ממנו: בששמעו בו שמת כולי עלמא לא פליגי דמורידין. דאם יבאו הבעלים קודם שיאכל זה הפירות יטול זה כשאר אריסין ויחזיר השאר ואם יבאו עדים שמת ירש הכל: מפסיד להו. ולא יזבל הקרקעות ויזרעם תמיד ויכחישם: כיון דאמר מר. לקמן [ז] וכולם שמין להם כארים אם יבאו הבעלים שמין לזה חלקו בכל שנה שעבד בה כמנהג אריסי העיר אם מחצה אם שליש אם רביע: אלא מלמד שנשיהם מבקשות לינשא כו'. שילכו בשבי ולא ידעו בניהם אם חיים אם מתים ויהיו נשיהם אלמנות לעולם שאין ב"ד מניחין אותן לינשא ובניהם כיתומים שלא ירשו נכסיהם ושתי קללות הן אחת של חרב ואחת של שבי שמע מינה אין מורידין: הוה עובדא בנהרדעא. בשבוי שירד יורשו לנכסיו: ופשטה רב ששת מהא מתניתא. דאין מורידין: א"ל רב עמרם דלמא לירד ולמכור תנן. [קתני] תנא דאין מניחין אבל לעשות ולאכול וליטול כארים שפיר דמי: דמעיילין פילא כו'. ומשני שנויא דחיקא כמבקש להכניס פיל שהוא חיה גדולה בנקב מחט: ותלש. פירות שנה זו: הרי זה זריז. מהיר לזכות בשלו בטרם יפסיד ונשכר בזריזותו: ואלו הן נכסי שבויין. דאמר אין מוליאין אותם מידו: שהנטושים כשבוין. ואין מוליאין מידו: נכסי נטושין. שהנכסים נטושים ולקמן מפרש להו רטושין משמע שעזבום בעלים מדעתם והלכו להם דכיון דהיה לו לצוות הורידו יורשיו לנכסי ולא צוה ש"מ לא ניחא ליה ונטושים שנטשום בעליהם בעל כרחן כגון שנשבו והיינו תנאי דרבן שמעון סבר מורידין ורבנן סברי אין מורידין:



## תוספות

עד כאן לא קאמר רשב"ג כו' אבל (א) הכא אין מורידין. וא"ת והא לקמן מייתי דאית ליה לרשב"ג מורידין וי"ל דמהא ליכא למשמע מינה אבל קשה דמאי מוכיח דחד טעמא הוא מדשמואל דסבר כרשב"ג וסבר מורידין לוכח כן מרשב"ג גופיה וי"ל דלא שמיע ליה ברייתא דלקמן:

בששמעו בו שמת כ"ע ל"פ דמורידין. אין לפרש בששמעו בב' עדים דא"כ פשיטא דמורידין אלא ששמעו היינו בקול ועד אחד אע"ג דשמעו בו שמת דבפ' ב' דייני גזירות (כתובות דף קז.) גבי אין פוסקין מזונות לאשת איש משמע סוגיא דהתם דהוי בעדות גמורה [ח]:

אמר רבא לירד ולמכור תנן. וא"ת ואמאי לא פריך ממתניתין דהאשה שהלכה (יבמות דף קטז: ושם ד"ה שאין) דקתני מלינו שאין אחים נכנסין לנחלה על פיה ולשני נמי לירד ולמכור תנן וי"ל דמהכא אלימא ליה לאקשויי משום דדומיא דנשותיהם קתני דמשמע כלל כלל לא:

היורד לנכסי שבוי אין מוציאין אותו מידו. (ב) הוא הדין דאפי' מורידין אותו לכתחילה דהא נטושים מורידין לרשב"ג דאמר הנטושים כשבויין אלא אגב דתנא בסיפא בנטושים מוציאין תנא נמי בשבויין אין מוציאין וא"ת לימא רב הלכה כתנא קמא ושמואל הלכה כרשב"ג וי"ל דלא שמיע להו ברייתא אי נמי איכא דמפכי להו:

וכולם

## עין משפט נר מצוה

נ א מיי' פ"ז מהלכות שאלה ופקדון הל' ב סמג עשין פח טוש"ע ח"מ סי' רצב סעיף טז:

נא ב ג מיי' פ"ז מהל' נחלות הלכה ד ה ועיין בהשגות ובמגיד משנה סמג עשין לג טוש"ע ח"מ סי' רפה סעיף ב וסעיף ג וסעיף ה:

נב ד טוש"ע שם סעיף א [ועיין בכ"מ שתמה על הרמב"ם שהשמיט זה]:

נג ה מיי' שם הלכה ח טוש"ע שם סעיף א וסעיף ד:

## רבינו חננאל

אצל חבירו והרקיבו וכו' פי' כיון דקם קם כיון שהחמיץ כך יעמיד בחימוצו לעולם. פי' כתישה מלשון אם תכתש את האויל במכתש. וחכמים אומרים עושה להן תקנה ומוכרן בב"ד. וכשמוכרן מוכרן לאחרים ולא לעצמו. עושה להן תקנה. אסקי' תקנה זו לקנקנים שלא יפסידו לגמרי ואפי' הפסד מועט חששו. והלכה כחכמים וכר' יוחנן. רשב"ג אומר ימכרם בב"ד מפני שהוא כמשיב אבידה. קי"ל דחלוקת חכמים ורשב"ג בכדי חסרונן כר' יוחנן והלכה כחכמים ואע"ג דחכמים דברייתא קיימי כרשב"ג. אבל יותר מכדי חסרונן דברי הכל מוכרן בב"ד לאחרים ולא לעצמו: איתמר רב אמר אין מורידין קרוב לנכסי שבוי חיישינן דלמא מפסדי להו. ושמואל אמר מורידין כיון דאמר מר שמין להם כאריס לא מפסדי להו. בששמעו בו שמת כולי עלמא לא פליגי דמורידין כי פליגי בשלא שמעו בו שמת. וקיימא לן כשמואל וכרב נחמן. הוה עובדא בנהרדעא בשבוי שנשבה ופשטה רב ששת דאין מורידין קרוב לנכסיו מהא דתניא ר' אומר ממשמע שנאמר והרגתי אתכם איני יודע כי יהיו נשיכם אלמנות ובניכם יתומים אלא מלמד שהן כאלמנות ולא אלמנות ממש כיצד מבקשות לינשא ואין מניחין אותן. בניהן מבקשין לירד בנכסי אביהן ואין מניחין אותן שעדיין לא נתבררה מיתתן בעדות. ואע"ג דאוקמה רבא לירד ולמכור אין מניחין אותם אבל מניחין אותן לירד ולתקן. דחאה רב ששת מדכתב נשיכם ובניהם בניהם דומיא דנשיהם מה נשיהם כלל לא אף בניהם כלל לא. מורידין קרוב בנכסי שבוי אוקימנא כתנאי דתניא היורד לנכסי שבוין אין מוציאין אותן מידו והוא ששמעו בהן שמתו. היורד לנכסי נטושין מוציאין אותן מידו. והן שיצאו למדינת הים ואין ידוע להיכן הלכו א).

## חשק שלמה על ר"ח

א) בגמ' איתא לשון זה גבי נכסי רטושין ואולי דרבינו היה לו גי' אחרת.

## מסורת הש"ס

א) [שבת קנד: וש"נ], ב) כתובות עז., גיטין לח., ודף עה., בבא קמא סט., בבא בתרא קעד., סנהדרין לא., [בכורות כד.], ג) [אבות דר' נתן פרק לח], ד) [ברכות נה:], ה) מהרש"ל, ו) [תוספתא דכתובות פרק ח], ז) [דף לח., ח) [ועיין תוס' יבמות קטז: ד"ה שאין ותוס' כתובות קז. ד"ה ששמעו].

## הגהות הב"ח

(א) תוס' ד"ה עד וכו'. אבל התם אין מורידין: (ב) ד"ה היורד וכו'. נ"ב עיין בשו"ת ב"ח סי' ר"ו תמלא פירוש דיבור זה:

## תורה אור השלם

א) וְחָרָה אַפִּי וְהָרַגְתִּי אֶתְכֶם בֶּחָרֶב וְהָיוּ נְשֵׁיכֶם אַלְמָנוֹת וּבְנֵיכֶם יְתֹמִים: [שמות כב, כג]

## לעזי רש"י

איישר"א. פירוש ספסוף, פלע (על גבן של בהמות משא).

## ליקוטי רש"י

גלדאי. רלענים [לעיל כד: חולין מח.]. לכתישא דגמלי. כתית שבגבי הסוסים והגמלים מחמת המשאות [שבת עז:]. במשנתינו. ולא בברייתא [רשב"ם ב"ב קעד.]. שיימינן להו כארים. אם יבואו הבעלים יטלו אלו בשבח קרקעות ופירות כמנהג אריסי המקום [לקמן לט.]. אלא מה ת"ל והיו נשיכם וגו'. אלא הרי זו קללה אחרת שיהיו הנשים צרורות כאלמנות חיות שלא יהיו עדים למיתת בעליהן ותהיינה אסורות להנשא והבנים יהיו יתומים שלא יניחום בית דין לירד לנכסי אביהם לפי שאין יודעים אם מתו אם נשבו [שמות כב, כג]. קופא דמחטא. נקב המחט [ברכות נה:]. מגבו ולא מתודו [עי' סנהדרין צו:]. רטושין. עזובה [ערכין כה:].

והא טעמא דרבי יוסי משום הפסד הרמאי הוא אלא תרוייהו לרבנן איצטריך [א] ולא זו אף זו קתני: **מתני'** [ב] *א* המפקיד פירות אצל חבירו אפילו הן אבודין לא יגע בהן רשב"ג אומר מוכרן בפני ב"ד מפני שהוא כמשיב אבידה לבעלים: **גמ'** מאי טעמא אמר רב כהנא אדם רוצה בקב שלו מתשעה קבים של חבירו ורב נחמן בר יצחק אמר [ב] חיישינן שמא עשאן המפקיד תרומה ומעשר על מקום אחר מיתיבי המפקיד פירות אצל חבירו הרי זה לא יגע בהן לפיכך בעל הבית עושה אותן תרומה ומעשר על מקום אחר בשלמא לרב כהנא היינו דקתני לפיכך אלא לרב נחמן בר יצחק מאי לפיכך הכי קאמר השתא דאמור רבנן לא נזבין דחיישינן לפיכך בעל הבית עושה אותן תרומה ומעשר על מקום אחר אמר רבה בר בר חנה א"ר יוחנן מחלוקת בכדי חסרונן אבל יותר מכדי חסרונן [ג] דברי הכל מוכרן בב"ד אדרב נחמן בר יצחק ודאי פליגא אדרב כהנא מי לימא פליגא כי קאמר רב כהנא בכדי חסרונן קאמר והא רוצה בקב שלו מתשעה קבין של חבירו קאמר גוזמא בעלמא מיתיבי לפיכך בעה"ב עושה אותן תרומה ומעשר על מקום אחר וליחוש דלמא הוו להו יותר מכדי חסרונן וזבנינהו וקא אכיל טבלים יותר מכדי חסרונן לא שכיח ואי משתכחי מאי מזבנינן להו וליחוש שמא עשאן בעל הבית תרומה ומעשר על מקום אחר כי מזבנינן נמי [ד] לכהנים בדמי תרומה מזבנינן להו ולרב נחמן בר יצחק נמי נזבנינהו לכהנים בדמי תרומה בהא פליגי דרבה בר בר חנה סבר יותר מכדי חסרונן לא שכיח מידי וכי משתכח לקמיה הוא דהויא יתר מכדי חסרונן אי עביד להו בעה"ב תרומה ומעשר על מקום אחר מקמיה דהוו להו יותר מכדי חסרונן עביד להו הלכך כי הוו להו יותר מכדי חסרונן נזבנינהו לכהנים בדמי תרומה ורב נחמן בר יצחק סבר יתר מכדי חסרונן משכח שכיח וכי הוו להו לאלתר הוא דהוו להו ואי אמרת נזבנינהו זימנין דקדים ומזבין להו וכי עביד להו בעל הבית תרומה ומעשר על מקום אחר לא ידע דזבנא וקא אכיל טבלים מיתיבי המפקיד פירות אצל חבירו והרקיבו יין והחמיץ שמן והבאיש דבש [ג] והדביש הרי זה לא יגע בהן דברי ר"מ וחכמים אומרים [ה] עושה להם תקנה ומוכרן בבית דין [ו] וכשהוא מוכרן מוכרן לאחרים ואינו מוכרן לעצמו [ז] כיוצא בו [ד] גבאי צדקה בזמן שאין להם עניים לחלק פורטין לאחרים ואין פורטין לעצמן גבאי תמחוי בזמן שאין להם עניים לחלק מוכרין לאחרים ואין מוכרין לעצמן קתני מיהת פירות והרקיבו מאי לאו אפילו יתר מכדי חסרונן לא בכדי חסרונן והא יין והחמיץ שמן והבאיש דבש והדביש דיתר מכדי חסרונן נינהו שאני הני כיון דקם קם

**רש"י**

והא טעמא דרבי יוסי משום הפסד הרמאי הוא. וכיון לטעמא בהכי מה לי כלי מה לי מעות והיכי תיסק אדעתין למימר דמעות מודה להו לרבנן ומאי אצטריך למתנייה: לרבנן איצטריך. לאשמועינן מילתא דרבנן תנינהו לתרוייהו ואי תנא כליס ברישא הכי נמי דלא אצטריך תו למתני מעות אבל השתא דתני מעות ברישא תני כליס למימר לא זו בלבד דליכא פסידא דשבירת כלי אלא אף זו דאיכא פסידא דגדול אמרינן הכי: **מתני'** אבודין. ע"י עכברים או ריקבון: לא יגע בהן. למוכרן וטעמא מפרש בגמ': **גמ'** קב שלו. חביבה עליו על ידי שעמל בהן וקב שישאר לו מהם הוא רוצה מתשעה קבין של אחרים שיקח בדמיהן אם ימכרם: חיישינן כו'. ואסור להאכילו לזרים: (א) לפיכך. הואיל ואסור למוכרן משום דרוצה אדם בקב שלו הרי הן בחזקת קיימים ומותר בעל הבית לעשותן תרומה ומעשר על פירות שיש לו בביתו: מאי לפיכך. איסור מכירה משום הא הוא והיכי תלי תנא עשייתו באיסור מכירה: השתא דאמור רבנן לא תזבין דחיישינן. שמא עשאן המפקיד תרומה הרי הן בחזקת שלא נמכרו ועושה אותן בעל הבית כו': מחלוקת. דמתני': בכדי חסרונן. כדרך שאר תבואות כמו שמפורש במשנתינו (לקמן דף מ.) לחיטין ולאורז תשעה חצאי קבין לכור: אבל אם אבודין יותר מכדי חסרונן. אפי' רבנן מודו דימכרם בב"ד: ודאי פליגא. הא דרבי יוחנן דאי איכא למיחש לשמא עשאן בעליהן תרומה אפילו ביותר מכדי חסרונן נמי אסור למזבינהו: מי לימא פליגא. דוקא אמר רב כהנא שאם תשעה קבין הן נוח לו שיאבדו עד קב ואל ימכרם דהוה ליה יותר מכדי חסרונן ופליגא הא דר' יוחנן עליה או לאו דוקא ט' קבין נקט אלא נוח לו שיהא נפסד קצת ולעולם כדי חסרונן ותו לא: גוזמא. שפת יתר: מיתיבי. לרבי יוחנן: וקאכיל. בעל הבית טבלים שאין פירותיו מתוקנין שאין אלו קיימין שהוא סומך עליהן: לא שכיחי. ואין לחוש בכך: ופרכינן ואי משתכחי (ב) מי מזבנינן להו. בתמיה: ליחוש שמא עשאן כו'. ונמצא המוכר מאכיל תרומה לזרים: בדמי תרומה. בזול שאין עליה קופצין לקנותה שאינה נאכלת אלא לכהנים וצריכה שימור בטהרה: לקמיה הוא דהויא יתר מכדי חסרונן. לזמן מרובה יש באבודן יתר מכדי חסרונן: מקמי דניהוי כו'. שאין אדם משהא טבלים כל כך זמן מרובה כזה מלתקנן: והדביש. יגא טעם דובשנו והחמיץ אשמלי"ר בלע"ז [ה] (כדאתמר) (איוב לא) ובכל תבואתי תשרש תעקר שרשיה וכמו עד לא ירתק חבל הכסף (קהלת יב) יפתחו רתוקות עבותיה: עושה להם תקנה. לקמיה מפרש מאי תקנה יש עוד הלא כל קילקול העתיד לבא כבר בא הוא: ואין מוכרן לעצמו. שלא יחשדוהו שמא לקחן בזול: פורטין. מחליפין פרוטות נחושת בסלעי כסף מפני שהפרוטות מתעפשות ונפסלות: תמחוי. מאכל שגובין מבעלי בתים לחלק לעניים בכל יום: מאי לאו אפילו יתר מכדי חסרונן. ואיכא למאן דאמר לא יגע ואת אמרת דברי הכל מוכרן: כיון דקם קם. מאחר שעמדו בקלקולם הרי כבר עמדו ולא יתקלקלו מעתה יותר אבל שאר פירות הולכין ומרקיבין תמיד: למאי

**תוספות**

**שמא** עשאן תרומה ומעשר על מקום אחר. הקשה ר"ת וכי נחשדו חבירים לתרום שלא מן המוקף כדאמר בפרק כל הגט (גיטין דף ל:) ופ"ק דחולין (דף ז.) גבי ר"מ שאכל עלה של ירק ואור"ת דהכא גבי פקדון תולין בחששא מועטת שלא יגע בהם וחיישינן שמא בערב שבת תרם שלא מן המוקף דשרי כדאמרינן בהאשה רבה (יבמות דף צג.) אי נמי כדאמרינן פרק בכל מערבין (עירובין דף לב:) ניחא ליה לחבר דליעביד איסורא זוטא דהיינו שלא מן המוקף אבל בחולין (דף ז.) ובפרק כל הגט (גיטין דף ל:) לא חיישינן כיון שאינו פקדון וטפי אמרינן בפרק זה בורר (סנהדרין דף ל.) ראו שאביהם הטמין מעות בשידה תיבה ומגדל ואמר של מעשר שני הם אם כמעריס לא אמר כלום אלמא אזלינן בתר רוב מעות שהם חולין להקל ואע"פ שפירש שהם מעשר ובהאשה שהלכה (יבמות דף קטו:) גבי מצא כלי והיה כתוב עליו קו"ף קרבן תי"ו תרומה הא אין כתוב עליו לא חיישינן והא דאמרינן בהזהב (לקמן דף מט.) ישראל שאמר לבן לוי כור מעשר [ו] לאביך בידי רשאי לעשותו תרומת מעשר על מקום אחר היינו נמי בשבתות וימים טובים וכן הא דקתני בסמוך לפיכך בעל הבית עושה אותו תרומה ומעשר על מקום אחר:

**מחלוקת** בכדי חסרונן. פרש"י כדרך שאר תבואות והקשה ריב"ם וכי פליגי במשהו דבפחות מכדי חסרונן לכ"ע לא ימכור ועוד דא"כ מ"ט דרשב"ג וי"ל דפליגי שנתחסר בחדש או בחדשים יותר משרגילות להתחסר עד אותו הזמן ופליגי עד שיעלה החסרון בחדש או בשני חדשים תשעה חצאי קבין לכור שהוא בכדי חסרונן לשנה שלימה:

**מזבנינן** לכהנים. ולשמא יעשם אחר המכירה ליכא למיחש דיתר מכדי חסרונן לא שכיח וכי עביד להו בעה"ב תרומה ומעשר עביד להו מקמי דליהוו יותר מכדי חסרונן ופריך לרב נחמן נמי דלזבינינהו לכהנים בכדי חסרונן לא פריך דהא איכא למיחש לשמא יעשם אלא ביותר מכדי חסרונם פריך דלזבינינהו וכי תימא הכי נמי והא אמרת דרב נחמן ודאי פליג ומשני דלרב נחמן יותר מכדי חסרונן שכיח והקשה ריב"ם מי דחקו לומר דרב נחמן פליג לימא דביתר מכדי חסרונן לד"ה מוכרן וליכא למיחש לשמא יעשם דלא שכיח כמו לרב כהנא ותי' ר"ת דמתני' מיירי אפילו בפשתן או בפירות מתוקנים והתם מאי טעמא לא יגע בהם ע"כ משום דרב כהנא דרוצה אדם בקב שלו מבתשעה קבין של חבירו אם כן מאי אהני טעמא דשמא עשאן תרומה ומעשר על מקום אחר אי לאו לאשמועינן דאפי' ביתר מכדי חסרונן חיישינן א"כ סבר דאפילו יותר מכדי חסרונן שכיח:

עד

למאי

**עין משפט נר מצוה**

מג א מיי' פ"ז מהל' שאלה ופקדון הל' א ועיין בהשגות ובמ"מ סמג עשין פח טוש"ע ח"מ סי' רלב סעיף טו:
מד ב מיי' שם:
מה ג מיי' שם וסמג שם טוש"ע שם:
מו ד מיי' שם:
מז ה מיי' שם הל' ב וסמג שם טוש"ע שם סעיף טז:
מח ו מיי' שם הל' ה טוש"ע שם סעיף יט:
מט ז מיי' פ"ט מהל' מתנות עניים הל' יא סמג עשין קסב טוש"ע י"ד סי' רנז סעיף ב:

**רבינו חננאל**

מתני' המפקיד פירות אצל חבירו אפי' הן אבודין לא יגע בהן מאי טעמא אמר רב כהנא רוצה אדם בקב שלו מט' קבין של חבירו. רב נחמן בר יצחק אמר חיישינן שמא עשאן תרומה ומעשר על מקום אחר. מיתיבי המפקיד פירות אצל חבירו הרי זה לא יגע בהן לפיכך בעה"ב עושה אותן תרומה ומעשר על מקום אחר. ומקשי' בשלמא לטעמיה דרב כהנא היינו דקתני לפיכך פי' כיון שאין אדם רוצה שיחליף לו פירותיו אלא ישארו לו כמות שהן לפיכך בעל הבית עושה אותן תרומה ומעשר על מקום אחר. אלא לטעמיה דרב נחמן מפני שבעל הבית עושה אותן תרומה מיבעי ליה למימר. ופרקינן כיון דאמור רבנן לא יגע בהן דחיישינן שמא בעליהן עשאום תרומה לפיכך בעל הבית עושה אותן תרומה כו': אמר רבה בר בר חנה אמר ר' יוחנן מחלוקת תנא קמא ורשב"ג דאמר תנא קמא לא יגע בהן בזמן [א] שחסרונן כדתנן במתני' הרי זה יוציא לו חסרונות אבל יותר מכדי חסרונן דברי הכל מוכרן בב"ד ודאי אדרב נחמן [בר יצחק] דהוא אמר חיישינן שמא עשאן תרומה ותרומה אינה נמכרת לשום חולין ור' יוחנן הא אמר מוכרן הלכך ודאי פליגי. לימא דהא דר' יוחנן פליגא נמי אדרב כהנא דהא איהו נמי לא ימכרם קאמר. ודחי' אית לן למימר דלא אמר רב כהנא לא ימכרם אלא היכא דחסרי [ג] פחות מכדי חסרונן והוא כדתנן לקמן לחיטים ולאורז ט' חצאי קבין לכור וכו' אבל בחסרון יותר מזה לא אמר רב כהנא לא ימכור ולא פליגא עליה דר' יוחנן. ומקשי' לר' יוחנן וניחוש דלמא הוה בהן חסרון יתר מכדי חסרונן ששנינו במשנתינו ומכרם על פי ב"ד מי שהיו מופקדין אצלו ולמה שנינו לפיכך בעה"ב עושה אותן תרומה כו'. פי' כגון שהיו לו פירות טבל בביתו אומר הפירות שיש לי פקדון אצל פלוני הרי הן תרומה על הפירות הללו ואוכלם על מנת שפירותיו קיימין וכיון שמכרם נמצא אוכל טבלים למפרע ופרקינן כי מזבינן להו להני פירי לכהנים מזבינן להו בדמי תרומה שאם יבואו בעליהן ויאמרו כי תרומה היו יחזרו דמיהן לכהן והדבר ידוע שאין בעליהן עושין אותן תרומה על מקום אחר אלא בקרוב זמן שדבר ברור הוא שאין בתוך זה הזמן עלה בהן יותר מכדי חסרונן דאמרי' ודאי חל עליהן שם תרומה ונפטרו הפירות שהפרישן עליהן אבל אחר זמן הרבה דאיכא למיחש דלמא הוה בהו יותר מכדי חסרונן לא ועל אורחא דא [ג] דשמעתא הדה. ומקשינן המפקיד פירות אצל

**מסורת הש"ס**

א) [יבמות יט. וש"נ], ב) פסחים יג., ג) עיין סנהדרין קא., ובפירש"י שם ד"ה מדביש ובפירש"י דהכא, ד) בבא בתרא ח:, פסחים יג., ה) [צ"ל כמו], ו) [בגמ' שלפנינו איתא לך וכן העתיקו תוס' גיטין ל: ד"ה וכי].

**הגהות הב"ח**

(א) רש"י ד"ה חיישינן וכו' לזרים הס"ד ואח"כ מ"ה היינו דקתני לפיכך הואיל: (ב) ד"ה ופרכינן ואי משתכחי מאי מזבנינן:

**לעזי רש"י**

אשמלי"ר. פירוש להחמיץ, להפסיד את טעם הדבש (ועיין רש"י סנהדרין דף קא ע"א ד"ה מדביש).

**ליקוטי רש"י**

אפילו הן אבודין. נחסרין והולכין [פסחים יג.]. גוזמא בעלמא. כאדם שרוצה להחזיק דבריו מדבר יותר גוזם ואמר מילתא יתירה [ביצה ד.]. מילתא בעלמא ולאו דווקא [חולין צ:]. והדביש. מתקלקל ונעשה לגלג מחמת חמימות [סנהדרין קא.]. גבאי צדקה. המשתכלים אל כל מהו צריך [ב"ב ח:]. פורטין. פרוטות של נחושת שגבו לצדקה ולמשכנין אותם מתלודות לריך לפורטין בכסף [פסחים יג.]. פרוטות שגבו לוקחין דינרי כסף לפי שהפרוטות של נחושת מתלודות [ב"ב ח:]. תמחוי. מאכל לאכל ומיני מאכל שגובין לחלק [פסחים שם]. קערה גדולה היא וגובין בה גבאים מאכל מבעלי בתים ומחלקין לעניים שתי סעודות ליום מיום ליום [שבת קיח.]. ואין מוכרין לעצמן. שמא יחשדום שלקחום בזול [פסחים שם].

חשק שלמה על ר"ח א) נ"ל בזמן שהם אבודין כדי חסרונן כדתנן וכו'. ב) אולי צ"ל דחסרי כדי חסרונן וכו'. ג) אולי צ"ל ועל אורחא דא אמר מסקנא דשמעתא הדה.

ar Chanah, who rules that everyone agrees that the produce ay be sold to Kohanim, סָבַר יוֹתֵר מִכְּדֵי חֶסְרוֹנָן לָא שְׁכִיחַ מִידִי – eld that it is not at all common for produce to be reduced by ore than its normal percentage of loss. וְכִי מִשְׁתַּכַּח – And hen this does happen, לְקַמֵּיהּ הוּא דְּהָוְיָא יָתֵר מִכְּדֵי חֶסְרוֹנָן – it only after a long time that the produce becomes reduced by ore than its normal percentage of loss. אִי עֲבִיד לְהוּ בַּעַל הַבַּיִת תְּרוּמָה וּמַעֲשֵׂר עַל מָקוֹם אַחֵ – Thus, if the owner, in fact, made he produce] into *terumah* or *maaser* for produce in another lace, מִקַּמֵּיהּ דַּהֲווּ לְהוּ יוֹתֵר מִכְּדֵי חֶסְרוֹנָן עָבִיד לְהוּ – we can asume that he did this before it became reduced by more than e normal percentage of loss.[17] הִלְכָּךְ – Therefore, כִּי הָווּ לְהוּ יוֹתֵר מִכְּדֵי חֶסְרו – if it later became reduced by more than s normal percentage of loss, נְזַבְּנִינְהוּ לְכֹהֲנִים בִּדְמֵי תְרוּמָה – we .e. the *shomer*] sell [the produce] to Kohanim for the price of *rumah.* We do not have to worry that the owner will make the roduce into *terumah* or *maaser after* the sale, because he would ave done it before this time.

The Gemara now explains Rav Nachman's position:

וְרַב נַחְמָן בַּר יִצְחָק – But Rav Nachman bar Yitzchak, who rules hat the Sages prohibit selling the produce to Kohanim, סָבַר יָתֵר מִכְּדֵי חֶסְרוֹנָן מִשְׁכַּח שְׁכִי – holds that it is common for producc to become reduced by more than its normal amount of oss. וְכִי הָווּ לְהוּ – And when it happens, לְאַלְתַּר הוּא דַּהֲווּ לְ – it happens immediately (that is, quickly). וְאִי אָמְרַתְּ נְזַבְּנִינְהוּ – Therefore, if you say that we should sell [the prouce] to Kohanim, זִימְנִין דְּקָדִים וּמְזַבֵּין לְהוּ – occasionally e *shomer* will sell it quickly, וְכִי עָבִיד לְהוּ בַּעַל הַבַּיִת תְּרוּמָה וּמַעֲשֵׂר עַל מָקוֹם אַחֵ – and when the owner later wishes to make he produce] into *terumah* or *maaser* for produce in another lace, לָא יָדַע דְּזַבְּנָא – he will not realize that it was already old, and that his designation did not take effect; וְקָא אָכִיל טְבָלִי – and the owner will then come to eat *tevel.* To protect gainst this possibility, the Sages prohibited any sale of deposited roduce.[18]

The Gemara again asks a question on R' Yochanan's ruling:

מֵיתִיבִ – The scholars challenged it from the evidence of a araisa: הַמַּפְקִיד פֵּירוֹת אֵצֶל חֲבֵירוֹ – IF ONE DEPOSITED PRODUCE ITH HIS FELLOW וְהִרְקִיבוּ – AND IT began ROTTING, יַיִן וְהֶחְמִי – or if he deposited WINE AND IT FERMENTED, turning into inegar, שֶׁמֶן וְהִבְאִישׁ – or if he deposited OIL AND IT BECAME POILED, דְּבַשׁ וְהִדְבִּישׁ – or if he deposited HONEY[19] AND IT OURED, הֲרֵי זֶה לֹא יִגַּע בָּהֶן – in each of these cases THIS *shomer* AY NOT TOUCH THEM (i.e. he may not sell the deposit). דִּבְרֵי רַבִּי מֵאִי – These are THE WORDS OF R' MEIR. וַחֲכָמִים אוֹמְרִים – BUT THE SAGES SAY: עוֹשֶׂה לָהֶם תַּקָּנָה – HE SHOULD FIX the ituation,[20] וּמוֹכְרָן בְּבֵית דִּין – AND SELL the spoiled produce N *BEIS DIN.* וּכְשֶׁהוּא מוֹכְרָן – AND WHEN HE SELLS IT, מוֹכְרָן לַאֲחֵרִים – HE MUST SELL the produce TO OTHERS, וְאֵינוֹ מוֹכְרָן לְעַצְמוֹ – AND MAY NOT SELL IT TO HIMSELF, so people will not suspect him of purchasing the produce at a lower price.

The Baraisa discusses other things that are forbidden for the purpose of avoiding suspicion:

כַּיּוֹצֵא בּוֹ – SIMILARLY, גַּבָּאֵי צְדָקָה – CHARITY ADMINISTRATORS, בִּזְמַן שֶׁאֵין לָהֶם עֲנִיִּים לְחַלֵּק – WHEN THEY HAVE NO POOR PEOPLE to whom TO DISTRIBUTE charity funds, פּוֹרְטִין לַאֲחֵרִים – SHOULD EXCHANGE the copper coins in the charity's coffers for larger silver coins WITH OTHER [PEOPLE],[21] וְאֵין פּוֹרְטִין לְעַצְמָן – BUT THEY SHOULD NOT MAKE THIS EXCHANGE THEMSELVES,[22] so people will not suspect them of paying too little for the coins. גַּבָּאֵי תַמְחוּי – Also, ADMINISTRATORS OF THE *TAMCHUY*,[23] בִּזְמַן שֶׁאֵין לָהֶם עֲנִיִּים לְחַלֵּק – WHEN THEY HAVE NO PAUPERS to whom TO DISTRIBUTE the food, מוֹכְרִין לַאֲחֵרִים – SHOULD SELL it TO OTHERS, וְאֵין מוֹכְרִין לְעַצְמָן – AND SHOULD NOT SELL it TO THEMSELVES, so people will not suspect them of buying the food too cheaply.

The Gemara now explains its question:

קָתָנֵי מִיהַת פֵּירוֹת וְהִרְקִיבוּ – In any case, the Baraisa taught – that if one deposited produce and it began rotting, R' Meir rules that the *shomer* may not sell it. מַאי – Now, in what case does this ruling apply? לָאו אֲפִילּוּ יָתֵר מִכְּדֵי חֶסְרוֹנָן – Does it not apply even when the produce has been reduced by more than its normal percentage of loss? If so, the Baraisa refutes R' Yochanan, who stated that in such a case all Tannaim concede that the deposited produce should be sold!

The Gemara answers:

לֹא – No! The Baraisa is not discussing such a case. בִּכְדֵי חֶסְרוֹנָן – Rather, it refers to where the produce was reduced only to its normal percentage of loss. However, should it be reduced by more than this amount, even R' Meir would require that the produce be sold.[24]

The Gemara counters:

וְהָא יַיִן וְהֶחְמִיץ – But there are the Baraisa's cases of one who deposited wine and it fermented, שֶׁמֶן וְהִבְאִישׁ – oil and it became spoiled, דְּבַשׁ וְהִדְבִּישׁ – and honey and it soured, דְּיָתֵר מִכְּדֵי חֶסְרוֹנָן נִינְהוּ – which are all examples of deposited foods that became reduced by more than their normal percentage of loss,[25] and even so, R' Meir rules that they may not be sold. – ? –

The Gemara answers:

שָׁאנֵי הָנֵי – These cases are different than ordinary instances of excessive loss. כֵּיוָן דְּקָם קָם – For once the food has reached this state, it has reached it, and it will not spoil any further. Therefore, R' Meir holds that there is no reason for the *shomer* to sell the spoiled produce at this point.[26]

The Gemara takes a closer look at the Baraisa it just cited:

שֶׁמֶן וְהִבְאִישׁ דְּבַשׁ וְהִדְבִּישׁ – The Sages require the *shomer* to sell oil that became rancid and honey that soured.

NOTES

7. We can assume that a person would not usually maintain produce in s prohibited *tevel* state for such a long period of time (*Rashi*).

8. According to this explanation, Rav Nachman's explanation is imrecisely worded. He states that the sale is prohibited because the eposited produce might have been made into *terumah* or *maaser.* In act, this would not be a problem, because the produce could be sold to Kohanim, who are allowed to eat *terumah.* Rav Nachman should have aid that the sale is prohibited because the owner might unknowingly ttempt to make the produce into *terumah after it had been sold* (see Ramban).

9. The Baraisa refers to date-honey. Honey from bees may certainly be old without concern, since it is not subject to the laws of *terumah* and *naaser.*

0. The Gemara below will explain how the produce can be fixed once it as spoiled (*Rashi*).

21. After a time, copper coins will grow moldy and lose their value (*Rashi*).

22. I.e. they may not take the copper coins for themselves and replace them with their own silver coins.

23. *Tamchuy* (literally: platter) refers to food that was collected daily for immediate distribution to the hungry poor (*Rashi*).

24. According to this explanation, the Sages of the Baraisa, who say that the items should be sold when the spoilage reaches its expected level, agree with the position of Rabban Shimon ben Gamliel in the Mishnah.

25. The Mishnah below (40a) speaks of a *percentage* of the food that spoils. However, in the cases of the Baraisa, the *entire* quantity of food is affected.

26. In a case where some of the produce has spoiled, however, the possibility exists that the rest of the produce will spoil as well, and therefore R' Meir would agree that it should be sold (see *Rashi*).

והא טעמא דרבי יוסי משום הפסד הרמאי הוא אלא תרווייהו לרבנן איצטריך [א] ולא זו אף זו קתני: **מתני'** [ג] [א] המפקיד פירות אצל חבירו אפילו הן אבודין לא יגע בהן רשב"ג אומר מוכרן בפני ב"ד מפני שהוא כמשיב אבידה לבעלים: **גמ'** מאי טעמא אמר רב כהנא אדם רוצה בקב שלו מתשעה קבים של חבירו ורב נחמן בר יצחק אמר [ב] חיישינן שמא עשאן המפקיד תרומה ומעשר על מקום אחר מיתיבי המפקיד פירות אצל חבירו הרי זה לא יגע בהן לפיכך בעל הבית עושה אותן תרומה ומעשר על מקום אחר בשלמא לרב כהנא היינו דקתני לפיכך אלא לרב נחמן בר יצחק מאי לפיכך הכי קאמר השתא דאמור רבנן לא נזבין דחיישינן לפיכך בעל הבית עושה אותן תרומה ומעשר על מקום אחר אמר רבה בר בר חנה א"ר יוחנן מחלוקת בכדי חסרונן אבל יותר מכדי חסרונן [ג] דברי הכל מוכרן בב"ד אדרב נחמן בר יצחק ודאי פליגא אדרב כהנא מי לימא פליגא כי קאמר רב כהנא בכדי חסרונן קאמר והא רוצה בקב שלו מתשעה קבין של חבירו קאמר גוזמא בעלמא מיתיבי לפיכך בעה"ב עושה אותן תרומה ומעשר על מקום אחר וליחוש דלמא הוו להו יותר מכדי חסרונן וזבנינהו וקא אכיל טבלים יותר מכדי חסרונן לא שכיח ואי משתכחי מאי מזבנינן להו וליחוש שמא עשאן בעל הבית תרומה ומעשר על מקום אחר כי מזבנינן נמי [ד] לכהנים בדמי תרומה מזבנינן להו ולרב נחמן בר יצחק נמי נזבנינהו לכהנים בדמי תרומה בהא פליגי דרבה בר בר חנה סבר יותר מכדי חסרונן לא שכיח מידי וכי משתכח לקמיה הוא דהויא יתר מכדי חסרונן אי עביד להו בעה"ב תרומה ומעשר על מקום אחר מקמיה דהוו להו יותר מכדי חסרונן עביד להו הלכך כי הוו להו יותר מכדי חסרונן נזבנינהו לכהנים בדמי תרומה ורב נחמן בר יצחק סבר יתר מכדי חסרונן משכח שכיח וכי הוו להו לאלתר הוא דהוו להו ואי אמרת נזבנינהו זימנין דקדים ומזבין להו וכי עביד להו בעל הבית תרומה ומעשר על מקום אחר לא ידע דזבנא וקא אכיל טבלים מיתיבי המפקיד פירות אצל חבירו והרקיבו יין והחמיץ שמן והבאיש דבש [ו] והדביש הרי זה לא יגע בהן דברי ר"מ וחכמים אומרים [ה] עושה להם תקנה ומוכרן בבית דין [ו] וכשהוא מוכרן מוכרן לאחרים ואינו מוכרן לעצמו [ז] כיוצא בו [ז] גבאי צדקה בזמן שאין להם עניים לחלק פורטין לאחרים ואין פורטין לעצמן גבאי תמחוי בזמן שאין להם עניים לחלק מוכרין לאחרים ואין מוכרין לעצמן קתני מיהת פירות והרקיבו מאי לאו אפילו יתר מכדי חסרונן לא בכדי חסרונן והא יין והחמיץ שמן והבאיש דבש והדביש דיתר מכדי חסרונן נינהו שאני הני כיון דקם קם

למאי

**רש"י**

והא טעמא דרבי יוסי משום הפסד הרמאי הוא. וכיון דטעמא בהכי מה לי כלי מה לי מעות והיכי תיסק אדעתין למימר דבמעות מודה להו לרבנן ואמאי אצטריך למתנייה: לרבנן איצטריך. לאשמועינן מילתא דרבנן תננהו לתרוייהו ואי תנא כליס ברישא הכי נמי דלא אצטריך תו למתני מעות אבל השתא דתני מעות ברישא תני כליס למימר לא זו בלבד דליכא פסידא דשבירת כלי אלא אף זו דאיכא פסידא דגדול אמרינן הכי: **מתני'** אבודין. ע"י עכברים או ריקבון: לא יגע בהן. למוכרן וטעמא מפרש בגמ': **גמ'** קב שלו. חביבה עליו על ידי שעמל בהן וקב שישאר לו מהם הוא רוצה מתשעה קבין של אחרים שיקח בדמיהן אם ימכרם: חיישינן כו'. ואסור להאכילו לזרים: (א) לפיכך. הואיל ואסור למוכרן משום דרוצה אדם בקב שלו הרי הן בחזקת קיימים ומותר בעל הבית לעשותן תרומה ומעשר על פירות שיש לו בביתו: מאי לפיכך. איסור מכירה משום הא הוא והיכי תלי תנא עשייתו באיסור מכירה: השתא דאמור רבנן לא תזבין דחיישינן. שמא עשאן המפקיד תרומה הרי הן בחזקת שלא נמכרו ועושה אותן בעל הבית כו': מחלוקת. דמתני': בכדי חסרונן. כדרך שאר תבואות כמו שמפורש במשנתינו (לקמן דף מ.) לחיטין ולאורז תשעה חצאי קבין לכור: אבל אם אבודין יותר מכדי חסרונן. אפי' רבנן מודו דימכרם בב"ד: ודאי פליגא. הא דרבי יוחנן דאי איכא למיחש לשמא עשאן בעליהן תרומה אפילו ביותר מכדי חסרונן נמי אסור למזבנינהו: מי לימא פליגא. דוקא אמר רב כהנא שאם תשעה קבין הן נוח לו שיאבדו עד קב ואל ימכרם דהוה ליה יותר מכדי חסרונן ופליגא הא דר' יוחנן עליה או לאו דוקא ט' קבין נקט אלא נוח לו שיהא נפסד קצת ולעולם כדי חסרונן ותו לא: גוזמא. שפת יתר: מיתיבי. לרבי יוחנן: וקאכיל. בעל הבית טבלים שאין פירותיו מתוקנין שאין אלו קיימין שהוא סומך עליהן: לא שכיחי. ואין לחוש בכך: ופרכינן ואי משתכחי (ג) מי מזבנינן להו. בתמיה: ליחוש שמא עשאן כו'. ונמצא המוכר מאכיל תרומה לזרים: בדמי תרומה. בזול שאין עליה קופצין לקנותה שאינה נאכלת אלא לכהנים וצריכה שימור בטהרה: לקמיה הוא דהויא יתר מכדי חסרונן. לזמן מרובה יש באבודן יתר מכדי חסרונן: מקמי דניהוי כו'. שאין אדם משהא טבלים כל כך זמן מרובה כזה מלתקנן: והדביש. יצא טעם דובשנו והחמיץ אשמלי"ר בלע"ז [ה] (כדאמר) (איוב לא) ובכל תבואתי תשרש תעקר שרשיה וכמו עד לא ירתק חבל הכסף (קהלת יב) יפתחו רתוקות עבותיה: עושה להם תקנה. לקמיה מפרש מאי תקנה יש עוד הלא כל קילקול העתיד לבא כבר בא הוא: ואין מוכרן לעצמו. שלא יחשדוהו שמא לקחן בזול: פורטין. מחליפין פרוטות נחושת בסלעי כסף מפני שהפרוטות מתעפשות ונפסלות: תמחוי. מאכל שגובין מבעלי בתים לחלק לעניים בכל יום: מאי לאו אפילו יתר מכדי חסרונן. ואיכא למאן דאמר לא יגע ואת אמרת דברי הכל מוכרן: כיון דקם קם. מאחר שעמדו בקלקולם הרי כבר עמדו ולא יתקלקלו מעתה יותר אבל שאר פירות הולכין ומרקיבין תמיד:

**תוספות**

**שמא** עשאן תרומה ומעשר על מקום אחר. הקשה ר"ת וכי נחשדו חבירים לתרום שלא מן המוקף כדאמר בפרק כל הגט (גיטין דף ל:) ופ"ק דחולין (דף ז.) גבי ר"מ שאכל עלה של ירק ואור"ת דהכא גבי פקדון חולין בחששא מועטת שלא יגע בהם וחיישינן שמא בערב שבת תרם שלא מן המוקף דשרי כדאמרינן בהאשה רבה (יבמות דף לג.) אי נמי כדאמרינן פרק בכל מערבין (עירובין דף לב:) ניחא ליה לחבר דליעביד איסורא זוטא דהיינו שלא מן המוקף אבל בחולין (דף ז.) ובפרק כל הגט (גיטין דף ל:) לא חיישינן כיון שאינו פקדון וטפי אמרינן בפרק זה בורר (סנהדרין דף ל.) ראו שאביהם הטמין מעות בשידה תיבה ומגדל ואמר של מעשר שני הם אם כמעריס לא אמר כלום אלמא אזלינן בתר רוב מעות שהם חולין להקל ואע"פ שפירש שהם מעשר ובהאשה שהלכה (יבמות דף קטו:) גבי מצא כלי והיה כתוב עליו קו"ף קרבן תי"ו תרומה הא אין כתוב עליו לא חיישינן והא דאמרינן בהזהב (לקמן דף מט.) ישראל שאמר לבן לוי כור מעשר [י] לאביך בידי רשאי לעשותו תרומת מעשר על מקום אחר היינו נמי בשבתות וימים טובים וכן הא דקתני בסמוך לפיכך בעל הבית עושה אותו תרומה ומעשר על מקום אחר:

**מחלוקת** בכדי חסרונן. פרש"י כדרך שאר תבואות והקשה ריב"ם וכי פליגי במשהו דבפחות מכדי חסרונן לכ"ע לא ימכור ועוד דא"כ מ"ט דרשב"ג וי"ל דפליגי שנתחסר בחדש או בחדשים יותר משרגילות להתחסר עד אותו הזמן ופליגי עד שיעלה החסרון בחדש או בשני חדשים תשעה חצאי קבין לכור שהוא בכדי חסרון לשנה שלימה:

**מזבנינן** לכהנים. ולשמא יעשם אחר המכירה ליכא למיחש דיתר מכדי חסרון לא שכיח וכי עביד להו בעה"ב תרומה ומעשר עביד להו מקמי דליהוו יותר מכדי חסרון ופריך לרב נחמן נמי דלזבנינהו לכהנים בכדי חסרון לא פריך דהא איכא למיחש לשמא יעשם אלא ביותר מכדי חסרונם פריך דלזבנינהו וכי תימא הכי נמי והא אמרת דרב נחמן ודאי פליג ומשני דלרב נחמן יותר מכדי חסרון שכיח והקשה ריב"ם מי דחקו לומר דרב נחמן פליג לימא דביתר מכדי חסרון לד"ה מוכרן וליכא למיחש לשמא יעשם דלא שכיח כמו לרב כהנא ותי' ר"ת דמתני' מיירי אפילו בפשתן או בפירות מתוקנים והתם מאי טעמא לא יגע בהם ע"כ משום דרב כהנא דרוצה אדם בקב שלו מבתשעה קבין של חבירו אם כן מאי אהני טעמא דשמא עשאן תרומה ומעשר על מקום אחר אי לאו לאשמועינן דאפי' ביתר מכדי חסרון חיישינן א"כ סבר דאפילו יותר מכדי חסרון שכיח:

עד



א) [יבמות יט. וש"נ], ב) פסחים יג., ג) עיין סנהדרין קא., ובפירש"י שם ד"ה מדביש ובפירש"י דהכא, ד) בבא בתרא ח:, פסחים יג., ה) [צ"ל כמו], ו) [בגמ' שלפנינו איתא לך וכן העתיקו תוס' גיטין ל: ד"ה וכי].

**הגהות הב"ח**

(א) רש"י ד"ה חיישינן וכו' לזרים הס"ד ואח"כ מ"ה היינו דקתני לפיכך הואיל: (ב) ד"ה ופרכינן ואי משתכחי מאי מזבנינן:

**לעזי רש"י**

אשמלי"ר. פירוש להחמיץ, להפסיד את טעם הדבש (ועיין רש"י סנהדרין דף קא ע"א ד"ה מדביש).

**ליקוטי רש"י**

**אפילו הן אבודין.** נחסרין והולכין [פסחים יג.]. **גוזמא בעלמא.** כאדם שרוצה להחזיק דבריו מדבר יתר גוזם ואמר מילתא יתירא [ביצה ד.]. מילתא בעלמא ולאו דווקא [חולין צ:]. **והדביש.** מתקלקל ונעשה גלול מחמת חמימות [סנהדרין קא.]. **גבאי צדקה.** המשכילים אל דל מהו לריך [ב"ב ח:]. **פורטין.** פרוטות של נחושת שגבו לצדקה וכשמשהין אותם מחלידות לריך לפורטן בכסף [פסחים יג.]. פרוטות שגבו לוקחין דינרי כסף לפי שהפרוטות של נחושת מחלידות [ב"ב שם]. **תמחוי.** מאכל לחם ומיני מאכל שגובין לחלק [פסחים שם]. קערה גדולה היא וגובין בה גבאים מאכל מבעלי בתים ומחלקין לעניים שתי סעודות ליום מיום ליום [שבת קיח.]. **ואין מוכרין לעצמן.** שמא יחשדום שלקחום בזול [פסחים שם].

**עין משפט נר מצוה**

מג א מיי' פ"ז מהל' שאלה ופקדון הל' א ועיין בהשגות ובמ"מ סמג עשין פח טוש"ע ח"מ סי' רצב סעיף טו:
מד ב מיי' שם:
מה ג מיי' שם וסמג שם טוש"ע שם:
מו ד מיי' שם:
מז ה מיי' שם הל' ב וסמג שם טוש"ע שם סעיף טז:
מח ו מיי' שם הל' ה טוש"ע שם סעיף יט:
מט ז מיי' פ"ט מהל' מתנות עניים הל' יא סמג עשין קסב טוש"ע י"ד סי' רנז סעיף ב:

**רבינו חננאל**

מתני' המפקיד פירות אצל חבירו אפי' הן אבודין לא יגע בהן מאי טעמא אמר רב כהנא רוצה אדם בקב שלו מט' קבין של חבירו. רב נחמן בר יצחק אמר חיישינן שמא עשאן תרומה ומעשר על מקום אחר. מיתיבי המפקיד פירות אצל חבירו הרי זה לא יגע בהן לפיכך בעה"ב עושה אותן תרומה ומעשר על מקום אחר. ומקשי' בשלמא לטעמיה דרב כהנא היינו דקתני לפיכך פי' כיון שאין אדם רוצה שיחליף לו פירותיו אלא ישארו לו כמות שהן לפיכך בעל הבית עושה אותן תרומה ומעשר על מקום אחר. אלא לטעמיה דרב נחמן מפני שבעל הבית עושה אותן תרומה מיבעי ליה למימר. ופרקינן כיון דאמור רבנן לא יגע בהן דחיישינן שמא בעליהן עשאום תרומה לפיכך בעל הבית עושה אותן תרומה כו': אמר רבה בר בר חנה אמר ר' יוחנן מחלוקת תנא קמא ורשב"ג דאמר תנא קמא לא יגע בהן בזמן א) שחסרונן כדתנן במתני' הרי זה יוציא לו חסרונות אבל יותר מכדי חסרונן דברי הכל מוכרן בב"ד ודאי אדרב נחמן [בר יצחק] דהוא אמר חיישינן שמא עשאן תרומה ותרומה אינה נמכרת לשום חולין ור' יוחנן הא אמר מוכרן הלכך ודאי פליגי. לימא דהא דר' יוחנן פליגא נמי אדרב כהנא דהא איהו נמי לא ימכרם קאמר. ודחי' אית לן למימר דלא אמר רב כהנא לא ימכרם אלא היכא דחסרי ב) פחות מכדי חסרונן והוא כדתנן לקמן לחיטים ולאורז ט' חצאי קבין לכור וכו' אבל בחסרון יותר מזה לא אמר רב כהנא לא ימכור ולא פליגא עליה דר' יוחנן. ומקשי' לר' יוחנן וניחוש דלמא הוה בהן חסרון יתר מכדי חסרונן ששנינו במשנתינו ומכרם על פי ב"ד מי שהיו מופקדין אצלו ולמה שנינו לפיכך בעה"ב עושה אותן תרומה כו'. פי' כגון שהיו לו פירות טבל בביתו אומר הפירות שיש לי פקדון אצל פלוני הרי הן תרומה על הפירות הללו ואוכלם על מנת שפירותיו קיימין וכיון שמכרם נמצא אוכל טבלים למפרע ופרקינן כי מזבינן להו להני פירי לכהנים מזבינן להו בדמי תרומה שאם יבואו בעליהן ויאמרו כי תרומה היו יחזרו דמיהן לכהן והדבר ידוע שאין בעליהן עושין אותן תרומה על מקום אחר אלא בקרוב זמן שדבר ברור הוא שאין בתוך זה הזמן עלה בהן יותר מכדי חסרונן דאמרי' ודאי חל עליהן שם תרומה ונפטרו הפירות שהפרישן עליהן אבל אחר זמן הרבה דאיכא למיחש דלמא הוה בהו יותר מכדי חסרונן לא ועל אורחא דא ג) דשמעתא הדה. ומקשינן המפקיד פירות אצל

**חשק שלמה על ר"ח** א) נ"ל בזמן שהם אבודין כדי חסרונן כדתנן וכו'. ב) אולי צ"ל דחסרי כדי חסרונן וכו'. ג) אולי צ"ל ועל אורחא לא אמר מסקנא דשמעתא הדה.

The Gemara limits the extent of the disagreement between the Tannaim in the Mishnah:

אָמַר רַבָּה בַּר בַּר חָנָה אָמַר רַבִּי יוֹחָנָן – **Rabbah bar bar Chanah said in the name of R' Yochanan:** מַחֲלוֹקֶת בִּכְדֵי חֶסְרוֹנָן – **The dispute** between the Sages and Rabban Shimon ben Gamliel **concerns a case where** the produce was not reduced by more than **its** normal **percentage of loss.**[10] אֲבָל יוֹתֵר מִכְּדֵי חֶסְרוֹנָן – **However, if** the produce has been reduced by **more than its** normal **percentage of loss,** דִּבְרֵי הַכֹּל מוֹכְרָן בְּבֵית דִּין – **everyone** (i.e. even the Sages) **agrees that [the *shomer*]** must **sell [the produce] in *beis din*.**

The Gemara discusses how this interpretation of the Mishnah fits with each of the two Amoraic explanations of the Sages' ruling that were cited above:

אַדְּרַב נַחְמָן בַּר יִצְחָק וַדַּאי פְּלִיגָא – R' Yochanan's interpretation **clearly conflicts with** the explanation **of Rav Nachman bar Yitzchak.** For if we must be concerned that the produce may have been made into *terumah* or *maaser,* it surely may not be sold even if the loss is more than the usual amount. אַדְּרַב כַּהֲנָא מִי לֵימָא פְּלִיגָא – But **shall we say that** R' Yochanan's interpretation **conflicts with Rav Kahana's** explanation as well?[11] כִּי קָאָמַר רַב כַּהֲנָא – Or perhaps it does not – for we can say that **when Rav Kahana said** that a person would rather have his own produce, and for that reason the deposited produce may not be sold, בִּכְדֵי חֶסְרוֹנָן קָאָמַר – **he said** this only **if** the produce has not been reduced beyond **its** normal **percentage of loss.**[12] However, he may agree that if the loss is greater than this, the owner would want his produce sold.

The Gemara rejects this suggestion:

וְהָא רוֹצֶה בְּקַב שֶׁלּוֹ מִתִּשְׁעָה קַבִּין שֶׁל חֲבֵירוֹ קָאָמַר – **But [Rav Kahana] stated** clearly that a person **would rather have a *kav* of his own** produce that might remain **than nine *kavs* of his fellow's** produce! Clearly, then, even when his produce has lost far more than the normal amount, the owner does not want it to be sold.[13] – ? –

The Gemara answers:

גּוּזְמָא בְּעָלְמָא – Rav Kahana's statement (which contrasted one *kav* with nine *kavs*) was **only an exaggeration.** In fact, if the produce is reduced by more than its normal amount of loss, Rav Kahana might agree that it should be sold.

The Gemara challenges R' Yochanan's ruling:

מֵיתִיבֵי – The scholars **challenged it** from the Baraisa cited above: לְפִיכָךְ – THEREFORE, בַּעַל הַבַּיִת עוֹשֶׂה אוֹתָן תְּרוּמָה וּמַעֲשֵׂר עַל מָקוֹם אַחֵר – THE OWNER of the produce MAY MAKE IT into *TERUMAH* OR *MAASER* FOR produce in ANOTHER PLACE. But according to R' Yochanan, why is the owner allowed to remove the *tevel* prohibition from his other produce by making the produce into *terumah* or *maaser*? וְלֵיחוּשׁ דִּלְמָא הֲווּ לְהוּ יוֹתֵר מִכְּדֵי חֶסְרוֹנָן – **He should be concerned** that **perhaps** the produce **was** reduced by **more than its** normal **percentage of loss,** וְזַבְּנִינְהוּ – **and** the *shomer* **sold it** before he made it into *terumah* or *maaser;* וְקָא אָכֵיל טְבָלִים – **and if this indeed happened, [the owner] is** now **eating *tevel*!**[14] – ? –

The Gemara answers:

יוֹתֵר מִכְּדֵי חֶסְרוֹנָן לָא שְׁכִיחַ – R' Yochanan holds that for produce to be reduced by **more than its** normal **percentage of loss is uncommon.** Therefore, the owner does not have to worry that the deposited produce was sold, and he may make it into *terumah* or *maaser* at any time.

The Gemara asks another question on R' Yochanan's ruling:

וְאִי מִשְׁתַּכְּחֵי מַאי – **But what** is the law **if it happens** that the deposited produce was reduced beyond its normal percentage of loss? מְזַבְּנִינַן לְהוּ – **Do we sell it,** as R' Yochanan suggests? וְלֵיחוּשׁ שֶׁמָּא עֲשָׂאָן בַּעַל הַבַּיִת תְּרוּמָה וּמַעֲשֵׂר עַל מָקוֹם אַחֵר – **But we should be concerned that perhaps the owner made it** into ***terumah* or *maaser* for** produce in **another place** (for he is allowed to do this, as we have just explained). If a Yisrael purchases the deposited produce, he may be eating *terumah,* which is forbidden to him. – ? –

The Gemara answers:

כִּי מְזַבְּנִינַן נַמִּי – **When we sell** it, לְכֹהֲנִים בִּדְמֵי תְרוּמָה מְזַבְּנִינַן לְהוּ – **we sell it** exclusively **to Kohanim for the** lower **price of *terumah.***[15] Therefore, there is no danger that the sale will result in a non-Kohen eating *terumah.*

The Gemara asks:

וּלְרַב נַחְמָן בַּר יִצְחָק נַמִּי – **But according to Rav Nachman bar Yitzchak too,** who explains that the Sages forbid the *shomer* to sell the produce because it might have been made into *terumah* or *maaser,* נְזַבְּנִינְהוּ לְכֹהֲנִים בִּדְמֵי תְרוּמָה – **let us sell** the produce exclusively **to Kohanim for the price of *terumah*!** Why, according to Rav Nachman, do the Sages not allow any sale, if selling inexpensively to Kohanim is possible?[16]

The Gemara explains:

בְּהָא פְּלִיגֵי – Rabbah bar bar Chanah (who reported R' Yochanan's ruling) and Rav Nachman **argue concerning this** very point. The Gemara explains each Amora's position, beginning with the view of Rabbah bar bar Chanah: דְּרַבָּה בַּר בַּר חָנָה – **For Rabbah bar**

NOTES

people would ignore a Rabbinic prohibition against making the produce into *terumah,* since this is an act done in private, and the Sages had no way to enforce such a prohibition. Thus, having decided to prohibit the *shomer's* sale of such produce, the Sages could allow it to be made into *terumah* (see *Shitah Mekubetzes*).

10. A certain percentage of all produce is ruined when it is kept in storage. The Mishnah below (40a) lists the expected amount of loss for various types of grain (see note 13).

*Rashi* (as interpreted by *Tosafos*) understands that the dispute between the Sages and Rabban Shimon ben Gamliel deals with a case of produce that has been reduced by the normal percentage. If less than that percentage of the produce has spoiled, Rabban Shimon agrees that it may not be sold; if more than that percentage has spoiled, the Sages agree that it should be sold.

11. I.e. must we say that Rav Kahana meant literally that a person would rather lose his entire crop – all except a *kav,* in which case the loss is surely a larger percentage than normal – than have it sold? If so, then R' Yochanan and Rav Kahana clearly understand the Mishnah in two different ways (*Rashi*).

12. I.e. in order to enjoy the fruits of his own labor, a person is willing to lose up to the normal percentage of his produce, but not more (*Rashi*).

13. Depending on the crop, the normal measure of loss is between one-tenth and one-fortieth of the crop (see Mishnah below, 40a). Losing eight out of nine *kavs* is thus far more than the normal percentage of loss.

14. The *tevel* prohibition would not be removed from the owner's other produce if the owner no longer owned the deposited produce when he tried to make it into *terumah* or *maaser* for that produce (see *Rashi*).

15. Since *terumah* may be eaten only by Kohanim and since it must be kept *tahor* (which takes extra effort), it costs much less than ordinary produce (*Rashi*). [And since the deposited produce may have been made into *terumah,* it must be sold only to Kohanim.]

16. The Gemara asks only that according to Rav Nachman the *shomer* should be allowed to sell the produce when it has been reduced by more than its normal percentage of loss. We are not worried that the owner might attempt to make it into *terumah* or *maaser* after the produce has suffered this much spoilage. However, the Gemara has no problem with the fact that it is forbidden to sell the produce if it has *not* spoiled to this extent, for then we must certainly be concerned that the owner may unknowingly attempt to make it into *terumah* or *maaser* after the sale (*Tosafos*).

והא טעמא דרבי יוסי משום הפסד הרמאי הוא אלא תרווייהו לרבנן איצטריך (א) ולא זו אף זו קתני: **מתני'** (ב) א המפקיד פירות אצל חבירו אפילו הן אבודין לא יגע בהן רשב"ג אומר מוכרן בפני ב"ד מפני שהוא כמשיב אבידה לבעלים: **גמ'** מאי טעמא אמר רב כהנא אדם רוצה בקב שלו מתשעה קבים של חבירו ורב נחמן בר יצחק אמר ב חיישינן שמא עשאן המפקיד תרומה ומעשר על מקום אחר מיתיבי המפקיד פירות אצל חבירו הרי זה לא יגע בהן לפיכך בעל הבית עושה אותן תרומה ומעשר על מקום אחר בשלמא לרב כהנא היינו דקתני לפיכך אלא לרב נחמן בר יצחק מאי לפיכך הכי קאמר השתא דאמור רבנן לא נזבין דחיישינן לפיכך בעל הבית עושה אותן תרומה ומעשר על מקום אחר אמר רבה בר בר חנה א"ר יוחנן מחלוקת בכדי חסרונן אבל יותר מכדי חסרונן ג דברי הכל מוכרן בב"ד אדרב נחמן בר יצחק ודאי פליגא אדרב כהנא מי לימא פליגא כי קאמר רב כהנא בכדי חסרונן קאמר והא רוצה בקב שלו מתשעה קבין של חבירו קאמר גוזמא בעלמא מיתיבי לפיכך בעה"ב עושה אותן תרומה ומעשר על מקום אחר וליחוש דלמא הוו להו יותר מכדי חסרונן וזבנינהו וקא אכיל טבלים יותר מכדי חסרונן לא שכיח ואי משתכחי מאי מזבנינן להו וליחוש שמא עשאן בעל הבית תרומה ומעשר על מקום אחר כי מזבנינן נמי ד לכהנים בדמי תרומה מזבנינן להו ולרב נחמן בר יצחק נמי נזבנינהו לכהנים בדמי תרומה בהא פליגי דרבה בר בר חנה סבר יותר מכדי חסרונן לא שכיח מידי וכי משתכח לקמיה הוא דהויא יתר מכדי חסרונן אי עביד להו בעה"ב תרומה ומעשר על מקום אחר מקמיה דהוו להו יותר מכדי חסרונן עביד להו הלכך כי הוו להו יותר מכדי חסרונן נזבנינהו לכהנים בדמי תרומה ורב נחמן בר יצחק סבר יתר מכדי חסרונן משכח שכיח וכי הוו להו לאלתר הוא דהוו להו ואי אמרת נזבנינהו זימנין דקדים ומזבין להו וכי עביד להו בעל הבית תרומה ומעשר על מקום אחר לא ידע דזבנא וקא אכיל טבלים מיתיבי המפקיד פירות אצל חבירו והרקיבו יין והחמיץ שמן והבאיש דבש ג והדביש הרי זה לא יגע בהן דברי ר"מ וחכמים אומרים ה עושה להם תקנה ומוכרן בבית דין ו וכשהוא מוכרן מוכרן לאחרים ואינו מוכרן לעצמו ז כיוצא בו ז גבאי צדקה בזמן שאין להם עניים לחלק פורטין לאחרים ואין פורטין לעצמן גבאי תמחוי בזמן שאין להם עניים לחלק מוכרין לאחרים ואין מוכרין לעצמן קתני מיהת פירות והרקיבו מאי לאו אפילו יתר מכדי חסרונן לא בכדי חסרונן והא יין והחמיץ שמן והבאיש דבש והדביש דיתר מכדי חסרונן נינהו שאני הני כיון דקם קם שמן והבאיש דבש והדביש למאי

---

## רש"י

והא טעמא דרבי יוסי משום הפסד הרמאי הוא. וכיון דטעמא בהכי מה לי כלי מה לי מעות והיכי תיסק אדעתין למימר דבמעות מודה להו לרבנן ואמאי אצטריך למתנייה: **לרבנן איצטריך.** לאשמועינן מילתא דרבנן תננהו לתרוייהו ואי תנא כליס ברישא הכי נמי דלא אצטריך תו למתני מעות אבל השתא דתני מעות ברישא תני כליס למימר לא זו בלבד דליכא פסידא דשבירת כלי אלא אף זו דאיכא פסידא דגדול אמרינן הכי: **מתני' אבודין.** ע"י עכברים או ריקבון: **לא יגע בהן.** למוכרן וטעמא מפרש בגמ': **גמ' קב שלו.** חביבה עליו על ידי שעמל בהן וקב שישאר לו מהם הוא רוצה מתשעה קבין של אחרים שיקח בדמיהן אם ימכרם: **חיישינן כו'.** ואסור להאכילו לזרים: (א) **לפיכך.** הואיל ואסור למוכרן משום דרוצה אדם בקב שלו הרי הן בחזקת קיימים ומותר בעל הבית לעשותן תרומה ומעשר על פירות שיש לו בביתו: **מאי לפיכך.** איסור מכירה משום הא הוא והיכי תלי תנא עשייתו באיסור מכירה: **השתא דאמור רבנן לא תזבין דחיישינן.** שמא עשאן המפקיד תרומה הרי הן בחזקת שלא נמכרו ועושה אותן בעל הבית כו': **מחלוקת.** דמתני': **בכדי חסרונן.** כדרך שאר תבואות כמו שמפורש במשנתינו (לקמן דף מ.) לחיטין ולאורז תשעה חצאי קבין לכור: **אבל אם אבודין יותר מכדי חסרונן.** אפי' רבנן מודו דימכרם בב"ד: **ודאי פליגא.** הא דרבי יוחנן דאי איכא למיחש לשמא עשאן בעליהן תרומה אפילו ביותר מכדי חסרונן נמי אסור למזבנינהו: **מי לימא פליגא.** דוקא אמר רב כהנא שאם תשעה קבין הן נוח לו שיאבדו עד קב ואל ימכרם דהוה ליה יותר מכדי חסרונן ופליגא הא דר' יוחנן עליה או לאו דוקא ט' קבין נקט אלא נוח לו שיהא נפסד קלת ולעולם כדי חסרונן ותו לא: **גוזמא.** שפת יתר: **מיתיבי.** לרבי יוחנן: **וקאכיל.** בעל הבית טבלים שאין פירותיו מתוקנין שאין אלו קיימין שהוא סומך עליהן: **לא שכיחי.** ואין לחוש בכך: **ופרכינן ואי משתכחי** (ב) **מי מזבנינן להו.** בתמיה: **ליחוש שמא עשאן כו'.** ונמצא המוכר מאכיל תרומה לזרים: **בדמי תרומה.** בזול שאין עליה קופצין לקנותה שאינה נאכלת אלא לכהנים וצריכה שימור בטהרה: **לקמיה הוא דהויא יתר מכדי חסרונן.** לזמן מרובה יש באבודן יתר מכדי חסרונן: **מקמי דניהוי כו'.** שאין אדם משהא טבלים כל כך זמן מרובה כזה מלתקנן: **והדביש.** יצא טעם דובשנו והחמיץ אשמלי"ר בלע"ז ה) (כדאמר) (איוב לא) ובכל תבואתי תשרש תעקר שרשיה וכמו עד לא ירתק חבל הכסף (קהלת יב) יפתחו רתוקות עבותיה: **עושה להם תקנה.** לקמיה מפרש מאי תקנה יש עוד הלא כל קילקול העתיד לבא כבר בא הוא: **ואין מוכרן לעצמו.** שלא יחשדוהו שמא לקחן בזול: **פורטין.** מחליפין פרוטות נחושת בסלעי כסף מפני שהפרוטות מתעפשות ונפסלות: **תמחוי.** מאכל שגובין מבעלי בתים לחלק לעניים בכל יום: **מאי לאו אפילו יתר מכדי חסרונן.** ואיכא למאן דאמר לא יגע ואת אמרת דברי הכל מוכרן: **כיון דקם קם.** מאחר שעמדו בקלקולם הרי כבר עמדו ולא יתקלקלו מעתה יותר אבל שאר פירות הולכין ומרקיבין תמיד: **למאי**

---

## תוספות

**שמא** עשאן תרומה ומעשר על מקום אחר. הקשה ר"ת וכי נחשדו חבירים לתרום שלא מן המוקף כדאמר בפרק כל הגט (גיטין דף ל:) ופ"ק דחולין (דף ז.) גבי ר"מ שאכל עלה של ירק ואור"ת דהכא גבי פקדון תולין בחששא מועטת שלא יגע בהם וחיישינן שמא בערב שבת תרם שלא מן המוקף דשרי כדאמרינן בהאשה רבה (יבמות דף לג.) אי נמי כדאמרינן פרק בכל מערבין (עירובין דף לב:) ניחא ליה לחבר דליעביד איסורא זוטא דהיינו שלא מן המוקף אבל בחולין (דף ז.) ובפרק כל הגט (גיטין דף ל:) לא חיישינן כיון שאינו פקדון וטפי אמרינן בפרק זה בורר (סנהדרין דף ל.) ראו שאביהם הטמין מעות בשידה תיבה ומגדל ואמר של מעשר שני הם אם כמעריס לא אמר כלום אלמא אזלינן בתר רוב מעות שהם חולין להקל ואע"פ שפירש שהם מעשר ובהאשה שהלכה (יבמות דף קטו:) גבי מלא כלי והיה כתוב עליו קו"ף קרבן תי"ו תרומה הא אין כתוב עליו לא חיישינן והא דאמרינן בהזהב (לקמן דף מט.) ישראל שאמר לבן לוי כור מעשר ו) לאביך בידי רשאי לעשותו תרומת מעשר על מקום אחר היינו נמי בשבתות וימים טובים וכן הא דקתני בסמוך לפיכך בעל הבית עושה אותו תרומה ומעשר על מקום אחר:

**מחלוקת** בכדי חסרונן. פרש"י כדרך שאר תבואות והקשה ריב"ם וכי פליגי במשהו דבפחות מכדי חסרונן לכ"ע לא ימכור ועוד דא"כ מ"ט דרשב"ג וי"ל דפליגי שנתחסר בחדש או בחדשים יותר משרגילות להתחסר עד אותו הזמן ופליגי עד שיעלה החסרון בחדש או בשני חדשים תשעה חצאי קבין לכור שהוא בכדי חסרונן לשנה שלימה:

**מזבנינן** לכהנים. ולשמא יעשם אחר המכירה ליכא למיחש דיתר מכדי חסרונן לא שכיח וכי עביד להו בעה"ב תרומה ומעשר עביד להו מקמי דליהוו יותר מכדי חסרונן ופריך לרב נחמן נמי דלזבניניהו לכהנים בכדי חסרונן לא פריך דהא איכא למיחש לשמא יעשם אלא ביותר מכדי חסרונם פריך דלזבניניהו וכי תימא הכי נמי והא אמרת דרב נחמן ודאי פליג ומשני דלרב נחמן יותר מכדי חסרונן שכיח והקשה ריב"ם מי דחקו לומר דרב נחמן פליג לימא דביתר מכדי חסרונן לד"ה מוכרן וליכא למיחש לשמא יעשם דלא שכיח כמו לרב כהנא ותי' ר"ת דמתני' מיירי אפילו בפשתן או בפירות מתוקנים והתם מאי טעמא לא יגע בהם ע"כ משום דרב כהנא דרוצה אדם בקב שלו מבתשעה קבין של חבירו אם כן מאי אהני טעמא דשמא עשאן תרומה ומעשר על מקום אחר אי לאו לאשמועינן דאפי' ביתר מכדי חסרונן חיישינן א"כ סבר דאפילו יותר מכדי חסרונן שכיח:

עד

---

## עין משפט נר מצוה

מג א מיי' פ"ז מהל' שאלה ופקדון הל' א ועיין בהשגות ובמ"מ סמג עשין פח טוש"ע ח"מ סי' רלב סעיף טו:
מד ב מיי' שם:
מה ג מיי' שם וסמג שם טוש"ע שם:
מו ד מיי' שם:
מז ה מיי' שם הל' ב וסמג שם טוש"ע שם סעיף טז:
מח ו מיי' שם הל' ה טוש"ע שם סעיף יט:
מט ז מיי' פ"ט מהל' מתנות עניים הל' יא סמג עשין קסב טוש"ע י"ד סי' רנז סעיף ב:

## רבינו חננאל

מתני' המפקיד פירות אצל חבירו אפי' הן אבודין לא יגע בהן מאי טעמא אמר רב כהנא רוצה אדם בקב שלו מט' קבין של חבירו. רב נחמן בר יצחק אמר חיישינן שמא עשאן תרומה ומעשר על מקום אחר. מיתיבי המפקיד פירות אצל חבירו הרי זה לא יגע בהן לפיכך בעה"ב עושה אותן תרומה ומעשר על מקום אחר. ומקשי' בשלמא לטעמיה דרב כהנא היינו דקתני לפיכך פי' כיון שאין אדם רוצה שיחליף לו פירותיו אלא ישארו לו כמות שהן לפיכך בעל הבית עושה אותן תרומה ומעשר על מקום אחר. אלא לטעמיה דרב נחמן מפני שבעל הבית עושה אותן תרומה מיבעי ליה למימר. ופרקינן כיון דאמור רבנן לא יגע בהן דחיישינן שמא בעליהן עשאום תרומה לפיכך בעל הבית עושה אותן תרומה כו': אמר רבה בר בר חנה אמר ר' יוחנן מחלוקת תנא קמא ורשב"ג דאמר תנא קמא לא יגע בהן בזמן א) שחסרונן כדתנן במתני' הרי זה יוציא לו חסרונות אבל יותר מכדי חסרונן דברי הכל מוכרן בב"ד ודאי אדרב נחמן [בר יצחק] דהוא אמר חיישינן שמא עשאן תרומה ותרומה אינה נמכרת לשום חולין ור' יוחנן הא אמר מוכרן הלכך ודאי פליגי. לימא דהא דר' יוחנן פליגא נמי אדרב כהנא דהא איהו נמי לא ימכרם קאמר. ודחי' אית לן למימר דלא אמר רב כהנא לא ימכרם אלא היכא דחסרי ב) פחות מכדי חסרונן והוא כדתנן לקמן לחיטים ולאורז ט' חצאי קבין לכור וכו' אבל בחסרון יותר מזה לא אמר רב כהנא לא ימכור ולא פליגא עליה דר' יוחנן. ומקשי' לר' יוחנן וניחוש דלמא הוה בהן חסרון יתר מכדי חסרונן ששנינו במשנתינו ומכרם על פי ב"ד מי שהיו מופקדין אצלו ולמה שנינו לפיכך בעה"ב עושה אותן תרומה כו'. פי' כגון שהיו לו פירות טבל בביתו אומר הפירות שיש לי פקדון אצל פלוני הרי הן תרומה על הפירות הללו ואוכלם על מנת שפירותיו קיימין וכיון שמכרם נמצא אוכל טבלים למפרע ופרקינן כי מזבינן להו להני פירי לכהנים מזבינן להו בדמי תרומה שאם יבואו בעליהן ויאמרו כי תרומה היו יחזרו דמיהן לכהן והדבר ידוע שאין בעליהן עושין אותן תרומה על מקום אחר אלא בקרוב זמן שדבר ברור הוא שאין בתוך זה הזמן עלה בהן יותר מכדי חסרונן דאמרי' ודאי חל עליהן שם תרומה ונפטרו הפירות שהפרישן עליהן אבל אחר זמן הרבה דאיכא למיחש דלמא הוה בהו יותר מכדי חסרונן לא ועל אורחא דא ג) דשמעתא הדה. ומקשינן המפקיד פירות אצל

## מסורת הש"ס

א) [יבמות יט. וש"נ], ב) פסחים יג., ג) עיין סנהדרין קא., ובפירש"י שם ד"ה מדביש ובפירש"י דהכא, ד) בבא בתרא ח:, פסחים יג., ה) [צ"ל כמו], ו) [בגמ' שלפנינו איתא לך וכן העתיקו תוס' גיטין ל: ד"ה ומי].

## הגהות הב"ח

(א) רש"י ד"ה חיישינן וכו' לזרים הס"ד ואח"כ מ"ה היינו דקתני לפיכך הואיל: (ב) ד"ה ופרכינן ואי משתכחי מאי מזבנינן:

## לעזי רש"י

**אשמלי"ר.** פירוש להחמיץ, להפסיד את טעם הדבש (ועיין רש"י סנהדרין דף קא ע"א ד"ה מדביש).

## ליקוטי רש"י

**אפילו הן אבודין.** נחסרין והולכין [פסחים יג.]. **גוזמא בעלמא.** כאדם שרוצה להחזיק דבריו מדבר יתר גוזם ואמר מילתא יתירה [ביצה ד.]. מילתא בעלמא ולאו דווקא [חולין צ:]. **והדביש.** מתקלקל ונעשה צלול מחמת חמימות [סנהדרין קא.]. **גבאי צדקה.** המשכילים אל דל מהו צריך [ב"ב ח:]. **פורטין.** פרוטות של נחושת שגבו לצדקה וכשמשהין אותם מחלידות צריך לפורטן בכסף [פסחים יג.]. פרוטות שגבו לוקחין דינרי כסף לפי שהפרוטות של נחושת מחלידות [ב"ב שם]. **תמחוי.** מאכל לחם ומיני מאכל שגובין לחלק [פסחים שם]. קערה גדולה היא וגובין בה גבאים מאכל מבעלי בתים ומחלקין לעניים שתי סעודות ליום מיום ליום [שבת קיח.]. **ואין מוכרין לעצמן.** שמא יחשדום שלקחום בזול [פסחים שם].

---

**חשק שלמה על ר"ח** א) נ"ל בזמן שהם אבודין כדי חסרונן כדתנן וכו'. ב) אולי צ"ל דחסרי כדי חסרונן וכו'. ג) אולי צ"ל ועל אורחא דא אמר מסקנא דשמעתא הדה.

The Gemara questions this explanation:

וְהָא טַעֲמָא דְּרַבִּי יוֹסֵי – **But R' Yose's** stated **reason** for ruling as he does מִשּׁוּם הֶפְסֵד הָרַמָּאי הוּא – **is because of the dishonest [person's] loss,** i.e. to cause the dishonest person to lose his deposit so as to get him to admit his lie![1]

The Gemara therefore revises its earlier explanation of the need for both rulings:

אֶלָּא – **Rather,** תַּרְוַויְהוּ לְרַבָּנָן אִיצְטְרִיךְ – **both** cases **are necessary to** explain the opinion of **the Rabbis,** וְלֹא זוֹ אַף זוֹ קָתָנֵי – **and [the Mishnah] taught** both cases in the style of **"not only this** but **even that."**[2]

**Mishnah** הַמַּפְקִיד פֵּירוֹת אֵצֶל חֲבֵירוֹ – If **one deposits produce with his fellow,** אֲפִילוּ הֵן אֲבוּדִין – **even if it is getting ruined** by mice, or it is rotting, לֹא יִגַּע בָּהֶן – **[the *shomer*] may not touch it,** i.e. he may not sell the unspoiled portion so at least some of the value will remain to be returned to the owner.[3] רַבָּן שִׁמְעוֹן בֶּן גַּמְלִיאֵל אוֹמֵר – **Rabban Shimon ben Gamliel says:** מוֹכְרָן בִּפְנֵי בֵית דִּין – **He should sell it in the presence of *beis din*,** מִפְּנֵי שֶׁהוּא כְּמֵשִׁיב אֲבֵידָה לִבְעָלִים – **because** by doing this **he is like one who returns a lost article to its owner.**

**Gemara** The Gemara cites two reasons for the Sages' ruling: מַאי טַעְמָא – **What is the reason** that the Sages do not allow the *shomer* to sell the produce? אָמַר רַב כַּהֲנָא – **Rav Kahana said:** אָדָם רוֹצֶה בְּקַב שֶׁלּוֹ – **A person would rather have a *kav*** (a small measure) **of his own** produce מִתִּשְׁעָה קַבִּים שֶׁל חֲבֵירוֹ – **than nine *kavs* of his fellow's** produce[4] that could be bought with the money from selling his produce. Therefore, the owner does not want the *shomer* to sell the produce, even if more of it will be lost. וְרַב נַחְמָן בַּר יִצְחָק אָמַר – **And Rav Nachman bar Yitzchak said:** חַיְישִׁינַן – The *shomer* cannot sell the produce because **we are concerned** שֶׁמָּא עֲשָׂאָן הַמַּפְקִיד תְּרוּמָה וּמַעֲשֵׂר עַל מָקוֹם אַחֵר – that **perhaps the depositor made it *terumah* or *maaser* for** produce that is in **another place.**[5] Thus, the produce may not be sold, since it may be *terumah,* which is prohibited to a non-Kohen.[6]

The Gemara challenges Rav Nachman's explanation:

מֵיתִיבֵי – The scholars **challenged** this from the following Baraisa: הַמַּפְקִיד פֵּירוֹת אֵצֶל חֲבֵירוֹ – IF ONE DEPOSITED PRODUCE WITH HIS FELLOW, הֲרֵי זֶה לֹא יִגַּע בָּהֶן – THIS *shomer* MAY NOT TOUCH IT, i.e. he may not sell the produce. לְפִיכָךְ – THEREFORE, בַּעַל הַבַּיִת עוֹשֶׂה אוֹתָן תְּרוּמָה וּמַעֲשֵׂר עַל מָקוֹם אַחֵר – THE OWNER of the produce MAY MAKE IT *TERUMAH* OR *MAASER* FOR produce that is in ANOTHER PLACE.

The Gemara explains its question:

בִּשְׁלָמָא לְרַב כַּהֲנָא – **According to Rav Kahana,** who explained that the produce may not be sold because the owner wishes to have his own produce, **this is understandable,** for הַיְינוּ דְּקָתָנֵי לְפִיכָךְ – **that is why the Baraisa taught** THEREFORE. The second statement of the Baraisa, that the owner may make the produce into *terumah* or *maaser,* is the result of the fact that the *shomer* may not sell the produce, which is what the connecting word "therefore" implies.[7] אֶלָּא לְרַב נַחְמָן בַּר יִצְחָק – **But according to Rav Nachman bar Yitzchak,** מַאי לְפִיכָךְ – **what** is the meaning of THEREFORE? In R' Nachman bar Yitzchak's view, the Baraisa's second statement is the *reason* for the first ruling, not its result! Why, then, does the Baraisa introduce its second statement with the word "THEREFORE"?[8]

The Gemara answers:

הָכִי קָאָמַר – **This is what [the Baraisa] means** according to R' Nachman bar Yitzchak: הַשְׁתָּא דְּאָמוּר רַבָּנָן לֹא נְזַבִּין – **Now that the Rabbis have said** that **[*shomrim*] may not sell** the produce to protect it from loss דְּחַיְישִׁינַן – **because we are concerned** that the owner made it into *terumah* or *maaser,* the owner may assume that it remains in the *shomer's* hands; לְפִיכָךְ בַּעַל הַבַּיִת עוֹשֶׂה אוֹתָן תְּרוּמָה וּמַעֲשֵׂר עַל מָקוֹם אַחֵר – and THEREFORE, THE OWNER indeed MAY MAKE IT into *TERUMAH OR MAASER* FOR produce in ANOTHER PLACE, and he need not be worried that it is no longer there.[9]

---

NOTES

1. Since R' Yose says that we hold everything back in order to penalize the liar and get him to confess, it should make no difference whether the deposit consists of money or utensils. Why would we assume that R' Yose would agree with the Rabbis in the case of a monetary deposit? (*Rashi*).

2. In other words, both cases were said in order to demonstrate the scope of the Rabbis' ruling. The Mishnah first teaches the more obvious case (deposits of money) to tell us the basic rule that we divide the money that is not contested between them. The Mishnah then goes on to say that this is the law "not only in this case" where dividing the uncontested money causes no loss to the value of the remaining deposit, "but even in this case" of the utensils, where if we divide the value of the uncontested claims there will be a loss to the value of the deposited item (*Rashi*).

3. The Gemara will explain why the Sages do not allow such a sale.

4. Produce that a person himself worked to get is precious to him (*Rashi*).

5. When produce grows in Eretz Yisrael, it is forbidden to everyone as *tevel.* In order to permit eating of the produce, one must first separate *terumah* (usually about 1/50 of the produce) from the produce and give the *terumah* to a Kohen. [If a non-Kohen eats *terumah,* he is punished with premature death at the hands of Heaven, מִיתָה בִּידֵי שָׁמַיִם (*Sanhedrin* 83b; see *Rashi* there ד"ה לימא מר במיתה).] One then separates one-tenth of the remaining produce as *maaser rishon* (first tithe), and gives it to a Levi. One must then separate another tenth of the remaining produce and, depending on the year of the *shemittah* cycle, designate it either as *maaser sheni* (second tithe), which must be eaten within the walls of Jerusalem, or as *maasar ani,* which must be given to poor people.

Ordinarily, one may separate *terumah* only when both the future *terumah* and the *tevel* produce are in front of him (see *Challah* 1:9; *Shach, Yoreh Deah* 331:49; *Mishneh LaMelech, Terumos* 3:17). However, under certain circumstances one may make even produce that is not in front of him into *terumah.* Here we are concerned that perhaps the owner of the produce made the deposited produce into *terumah* from wherever he was (*Tosafos*).

6. Although the halachah allows a Yisrael (that is, someone who is not a Levi) to eat *maaser,* Rav Nachman mentions *maaser* here according to the opinion of R' Meir, who forbids this (*Meiri;* see *Yevamos* 86a).

7. I.e. since the *shomer* is forbidden to sell the produce for the reason that "a person prefers his own *kav* etc.," the owner can assume that the produce is still in the *shomer's* possession. He may therefore make that produce into *terumah* or *maaser* for other produce that he has (*Rashi*).

8. According to Rav Nachman, the possibility that the owner made the produce into *terumah* is the *reason* that the *shomer* may not sell the produce. However, the Baraisa seems to say the reverse, for it states that the prohibition against selling the produce is the reason that making the produce into *terumah* is permitted (*Rashi*).

9. The Rabbinic prohibition against selling the produce allows us to assume that it was not sold. The owner may *therefore* make the produce into *terumah* or *maaser* (*Rashi*).

According to Rav Nachman, selling deposited produce that has begun to spoil is unwise, because it may have been made into *terumah* by its owner (see above, note 5). The Sages had two choices: either to prohibit making such produce into *terumah,* or to prohibit its sale. They chose the second option, because a *shomer* will not sell a deposit without the permission of *beis din* once this has been forbidden. However, some

וְרָבָא – And did Rava actually say[21] כָּל בִּשְׁתֵּי כְּרִיכוֹת – that anytime deposits are made in two bundles at different times, הֲוָה לֵיהּ לְמֵידַק – [the *shomer*] should have paid attention to who gave him which bundle? וְהָאָמַר רָבָא – But Rava said, וְאִי תֵּימָא רַב פָּפָּא – and others say that it was Rav Pappa who said, in regard to a Mishnah in *Bechoros*:[22] הַכֹּל מוֹדִים – All concede [i.e. both R' Akiva and R' Tarfon of that Mishnah] בִּשְׁנַיִם שֶׁהִפְקִידוּ אֵצֶל רוֹעֶה – regarding two [people] who deposited lambs with a shepherd, one of them giving one lamb and the other giving two, and they later contested who gave the larger deposit, שֶׁמַּנִּיחַ רוֹעֶה בֵּינֵיהֶן וּמִסְתַּלֵּק – that the shepherd places the disputed animal between them and withdraws.[23] There, although the animals are comparable to money deposited in two bundles,[24] the shepherd is not held accountable for failing to note the owner and amount of each deposit.[25] – ? –

Rav Ashi answers:

אָמַר לֵיהּ – He said to [Ravina]: הָתָם – Rava's lenient ruling there (in *Bechoros*) applies כְּשֶׁהִפְקִידוּ בְּעֶדְרוֹ שֶׁל רוֹעֶה שֶׁלֹּא מִדַּעְתּוֹ – when they deposited their animals in the flock of the shepherd without his knowledge, so that he never saw who gave two sheep and who gave one.[26] In such a case the *shomer* need not pay both claimants.

The Mishnah states:

וְכֵן שְׁנֵי כֵלִים – AND SO it is in the case of two people who deposited with one *shomer*, TWO UTENSILS, אֶחָד יָפֶה מָנֶה – ONE WORTH A *MANEH* וְאֶחָד יָפֶה אֶלֶף זוּז כו׳ – AND ONE WORTH ONE THOUSAND *ZUZ*, etc.[27]

The Gemara explains why the Mishnah taught the case of utensils, which parallels and seemingly duplicates the previous case of cash deposits:

וּצְרִיכָא – And both rulings are necessary. דְּאִי אַשְׁמוּעִינַן הָךְ קַמַּיְיתָא – For if the Tanna had taught us only that first ruling on monetary deposits, בְּהַהִיא קָאָמְרִי רַבָּנַן – I might have said that in that case the Rabbis rule that the claimants are given the uncontested amounts מִשּׁוּם דְּלֵיכָּא פְּסֵידָא – because there is no loss of value to the deposit (since money can be divided without any loss of value to each coin). אֲבָל בְּהָא – However in this case of two utensils, דְּאִיכָּא פְּסֵידָא דְּגָדוֹל – where there is a loss of value to the large (i.e. more expensive) utensil when it is broken to give an equivalent share to the second claimant, אֵימָא מוֹדוּ לֵיהּ לְרַבִּי יוֹסֵי – I would say that perhaps the Rabbis concede to R' Yose that both utensils should remain in the possession of the *shomer*.[28] וְאִי אִתְּמַר בְּהָא – And if the ruling was stated only in this case of two utensils, בְּהָא קָאָמַר רַבִּי יוֹסֵי – I might have said that only in this case does R' Yose rule that the uncontested amount is held in escrow, because otherwise the rightful owner will incur a loss when the larger utensil is broken. אֲבָל בְּהָךְ – However, in that case of monetary deposits, where the uncontested money can be divided without causing any loss to the remaining money, אֵימָא מוֹדֵי לְהוּ לְרַבָּנַן – I would say that perhaps R' Yose concedes to the Rabbis who rule that the uncontested amount should be returned to each one.

The Gemara concludes:

צְרִיכָא – Therefore, [both] cases are necessary.

NOTES

21. Above, 37a.

22. The Mishnah in *Bechoros* (17b) discusses a case where an animal giving birth for the first time gave birth to two lambs. One of these is a *bechor* and the other is not. One of the lambs then died but we do not know whether it was the *bechor* or the other one. R' Akiva and R' Tarfon argue whether the Kohen has a right to the remaining lamb. Rava comments there (18b) that R' Akiva and R' Tarfon nonetheless agree in the following case.

23. I.e. he places the disputed animal before the court and demands proof of ownership. He then retains the animal and need not pay both claimants an extra lamb, as Rav Safra explained the Mishnah in *Yevamos* above.

24. Even if they both deposited their lambs at the same time in front of each other [where in the case of bundles he would *not* be held responsible to remember who gave him the larger bundle, as Rava said above (37a with note 14)], the shepherd should still be held accountable in our case. Since it is easy to see who gave one lamb and who gave two, the shepherd should have taken note [unlike the case of bundles of coins, where the difference in size between the two bundles is less obvious; see 37a note 15] (*Rashi;* cf. *Tosafos*).

25. On the face of it, the Gemara's question seems difficult to understand. Our Mishnah, to which Rava's earlier statement (concerning two bundles) refers, speaks of fulfilling one's *Heavenly* obligation, as the Gemara explained above. Rava explained that when a *shomer* receives two bundles at two different times and is not careful to note what he received from each depositor, his negligence makes him responsible to pay the full amount to both in order to meet his *Heavenly* responsibility. The Mishnah in *Bechoros,* however, addresses the matter of a *legal* obligation, and in regard to this Rava says that all agree that the *shomer* has no *legal* obligation to give two sheep to each depositor. Our Mishnah does not say otherwise. What then is the contradiction?

*Tosafos* explain that the Gemara's question is based on its previous conclusion that the ruling of our Mishnah is consistent with the views of both R' Tarfon and R' Akiva. Now according to R' Akiva, the ruling of our Mishnah is valid only in the case where the claimants are not sure of their claim (see note 20). This implies that had they made a definite claim against him, the *shomer* would have been *legally* obligated to give the larger amount to both of them. This contradicts Rava's statement in *Bechoros* that even where both owners claim two lambs, he is under no legal obligation to give each one two sheep.

26. Even if the shepherd later became aware that lambs had been placed in his flock, he is not obligated to ascertain their ownership if he did not actually see them when they were deposited (*Tosafos*). [*Ritva* discusses whether in this case the shepherd is responsible to hold onto the contested animal until its true owner can be identified, or whether he may actually abandon it to the claimants since it was deposited without his knowledge. See *Rambam, Hil. She'eilah U'Fikadon* 5:4, who indicates that it should be kept in the possession of a third party until the matter is resolved.]

27. Subsequently, both depositors claim the more expensive utensil. The Sages rule that one is given the less expensive utensil and the other a piece of equal value broken off from the more expensive utensil, the remainder of which is held in escrow. R' Yose rules that both utensils are held in escrow.

28. Since, when the matter is ultimately resolved, it will turn out that the rightful owner of the more expensive utensil has suffered a loss, in that his utensil has been broken, perhaps the Rabbis agree that both utensils should be held in escrow and neither claimant should receive anything (*Rashi*).

צווח מ"ד הלה צווח אבל שתיקה כהודאה ומ"ד הלה שותק שתיקה דהכא לאו כהודאה הוא מצי אמר ליה האי דשתיקי לכל חד וחד דאמינא דלמא האי הוא אמר מר מניח גזילה ביניהם ומסתלק ושקלי לה כולהו ואזלי [א] והאמר רבי אבא בר זבדא אמר רב כל ספק הינוח לכתחלה לא יטול ואם נטל לא יחזיר אמר רב ספרא ויניח א"ל אביי לרבא מי א"ר עקיבא [ב] לא זו הדרך מוציאתו מידי עבירה עד שישלם גזילה לכל חד וחד אלמא מספיקא מפקינן ממונא ולא אמרי' אוקים ממונא בחזקת מריה ורמינהי [ג] נפל הבית עליו ועל אמו יורשי הבן אומרים האם מתה ראשונה ויורשי האם אומרים הבן מת ראשון אלו ואלו מודים שיחלוקו ואמר ר"ע מודה אני בזו שהנכסים בחזקתן אמר ליה התם שמא ושמא גזל אחד מחמשה ברי ושמא והא מתני' דהכא אמר לשנים גזלתי לאחד מכם מנה דשמא ושמא הוא וקתני נותן לזה מנה ולזה מנה וממאי דר"ע היא [ד] דקתני עלה דההיא [ה] מודה ר' טרפון באומר לשנים גזלתי לאחד מכם מנה ואיני יודע איזה מכם כו' למאן מודה [ו] (לאו) לר"ע בר פלוגתיה וממאי דשמא ושמא הוא חדא דלא קתני תובעין אותו ועוד הא תני ר' חייא זה אומר איני יודע וזה אומר איני יודע הא אוקימנא לה בבא לצאת ידי שמים אמר ליה רבינא לרב אשי ומי אמר רבא כל בשתי כריכות הוה ליה למידק [ז] והאמר רבא ואי תימא רב פפא הכל מודים בשנים שהפקידו אצל רועה שמניח רועה ביניהן ומסתלק א"ל התם כשהפקידו בעדרו של רועה שלא מדעתו: וכן שני כלים אחד יפה מנה ואחד יפה אלף זוז כו': וצריכא דאי אשמועינן הך קמייתא בההיא קאמרי רבנן משום דליכא פסידא אבל בהא דאיכא פסידא דגדול אימא מודו ליה לר' יוסי ואי אתמר בהא בהא קאמר ר' יוסי אבל בהך אימא מודי להו לרבנן צריכא

## רש"י

צווח. אמר לכל אחד איני מכירך: ושקלי ליה כולהו ואזלי. נמלא זה מוליא מידו כדי להפסיד הנגזל עולמית: והא"ר אבא בר זבדא ספק הינוח. מלא דבר שאין בו סימן בלד מקום שמשתמר קלת דלא שכיחי אינשי דאזלי ויש לספוקי שמא מדעת הונח שם לגניזה: לכתחלה לא יטלנו. המולאו שכשיבא בעליו לא ימלאנו וסימן אין בו שיכריז לפיכך יניחנו זה ובעליו יבא ויטלנו וכל שכן לודאי הינוח כדתנן (לעיל דף כה:) מלא כלי באשפה מכוסה לא יגע בו: ואם נטל לא יחזיר. ואם בא אחר ואמר שלי הוא וסימן אינו נותן בו לא יחזירנו שמא אינו שלו וסוף הבעלים לבוא ויביא עדים שהניחו שם לפיכך יהא מונח ביד זה עד שיבא אליהו דהאי לא יחזיר לא שיהא שלו קאמר דהא מעיקרא באיסורא אתא לידיה אם הינוח הוא אלמא מידי דמספקא לן דמאן ניהו לריך להניחו בידו מי שהוא עד שיתברר הדבר: אמר רב ספרא ויניח. הא דקתני מסתלק לאו דלישקלו אינהו וליזלו ולא שיוליאנה מידו אלא תהא מונחת בידו עד שיתברר הדבר והאי מסתלק סילוק הדין הוא ויניח גזילה בפניהם בב"ד ויאמר בררו של מי הוא ויטול ומסתלק מן הדין והגזילה יניח בידו עד שיבא אליהו: לא זו הדרך. סיפא דגזל אחד מחמשה הוא ביבמות (דף קיח:): נפל הבית עליו ועל אמו. ואין ידוע איזה מת ראשון והיו לאמו נכסים מבית אביה: יורשי האם. משפחת בית אביה אומרים לקרובי הבן ממשפחת אביו הבאים לירש את הבן: הבן מת ראשון. ולא ירש את אמו להוריש אתכם נכסים אלא הבן מת ראשון ואח"כ מתה אמו ואנו יורשים אותה (נכסיה): ויורשי הבן אומרים האם מתה ראשונה. וירשה בנה ואחריה מת הבן ואנו יורשין אותו: אלו ואלו. ב"ש וב"ה שנחלקו בנפילות אחרות בפרק מי שמת שב"ש אומרים יחלוקו ובית הלל אומרים נכסים בחזקתן כאן מודים שיחלוקו: אמר ר"ע מודה אני בזה. אע"פ שאני משל ב"ש ואומר בשאר הנפילות יחלוקו בזו אני מודה לב"ה שהנכסים בחזקתן ופליגי אמוראי בחזקת מי והתם מפרש טעמא: שמא ושמא. שניהם מכח שמא באים הלכך נכסים בחזקתן: הכא ברי ושמא. כל אחד ואחד אומר אותי גזל היינו טענת ודאי וזה אומר איני יודע וברי עדיף משמא: עלה דההיא. דגזל אחד מחמשה: חדא דלא קתני. מתני' תובעין אותו דלא קתני אותי גזל: ה"ג ועוד הא תני ר' חייא זה אומר איני יודע וזה אומר איני יודע. ול"ג יחלוקו והכי פירושו ועוד הא תני רבי חייא להך מתניתא דגזלתי את אחד מכם בתוספתא דיליה ותני לה הכי אמר לשנים גזלתי אחד מכם ואיני יודע איזהו זה אומר איני יודע וזה אומר איני יודע נותן לזה מנה כו' כדקתני במתני' אלמא בשמא ושמא עסקינן: הכל מודים בשנים שהפקידו כו'. גבי פלוגתא דר"ט ור"ע איתמר במסכת בכורות (דף יח:) שנים שהפקידו זה טלה אחד וזה שנים זה אומר שנים שלי וזה אומר שנים שלי והתם שתי כריכות נינהו ואפילו הפקידו זה בפני זה דבר הנראה הוא מי מביא אחד ומי מביא שנים דבשלמא גבי כריכות מעות הואיל דאלו ואלו צרורין הוא שוכח מי הפקיד אללו צרור גדול ומי צרור קטן הואיל והפקידו אללו יחד אבל גבי טלאים מילתא מוכחת טפי: פסידא דגדול. של כלי גדול ששברוהו וכשיבא אליהו ויאמר של מי הוא נמצא מפסיד בשבירתו: בהא קאמר ר' יוסי. משום פסידא דגדול:

והא

## תוספות

**מודה** אני בזה. אע"ג דקאמר מודה אני לאו משום דליהוי מתלמידי ב"ש דבפ"ק דיבמות (דף טו.) בלרת הבת סבר כב"ה דקאמר (א) תמיה אני מתי תבא לרת הבת לידי ואשיאנה והיינו כב"ה אלא אגב דשנה לעיל אלו ואלו מודים תנא הכא מודה אני:

**וממאי** דר"ע היא. וא"ת ואלא כמאן דאי כר"ט כ"ש דלר"ע נותן לזה מנה ולזה מנה וי"ל דהכי פי' ממאי דר"ע היא ומדינא דלמא ללאת ידי שמים ומשני מדקאמר מודה ר"ט למאן מודה לאו לר"ע דאמר מדינא משלם לכל אחד ואחד ואמר ר"ט מדינא מניח ביניהם ומסתלק אבל ללאת ידי שמים מודינא דמשלם לכל אחד ואחד וקאמר הא אוקימנא בבא ללאת ידי שמים ומודה דקאמר ר"ט ה"פ כי היכי דאמרת בשמא ושמא משלם לכל אחד ואחד ללאת ידי שמים הכי מודינא לך הכא:

**ומי** אמר רבא כל בשתי כריכות ה"ל למידק והא אמר רבא כו'. וא"ת והא מתני' איירי ללאת ידי שמים וי"ל מדנקט במתני' דאתי נמי כר"ע אביו של אחד מכם משמע משום דהוי שמא ושמא אינו חייב אלא ללאת ידי שמים דוקא כדמשמע לשון הודה (ב) הא הפקידו הן עלמן דמסתמא תבעי ליה והוה ליה ברי ושמא חייב אפי' מדינא אע"ג דלא עבד איסורא כיון דה"ל למידק דאי לאו הכי אמאי נקט אביו דאי לאורויי דאפי' בשמא ושמא חייב ללאת ידי שמים זה אין נראה שום חידוש לר"ע ועוד דר"ע נמי אית לי' בהגוזל קמא (ב"ק דף קג: ושם) בלקח מחמשה בני אדם שמשלם לכל אחד ואחד ואע"ג דלא עבד איסורא ומדינא משלם דללאת ידי שמים אפילו ר"ט מודה שמשלם לכל אחד ואחד אע"ג דלא עבד איסורא דהא מתני' אוקמינן נמי כר"ט וקתני אביו של אחד מכם הפקיד לי מנה נותן לכל אחד ולהכי פריך והאמר רבא הכל מודים כו' דאפי' לר"ע מניח ביניהם אע"ג דה"ל למידק כמו שאפרש משום דלא עביד איסורא וה"ה דבלא רבא ה"מ למיפרך מר"ע דאמר גבי מקח אע"ג דלא עבד איסורא משלם לכל אחד ואחד והתם אמר רבא דאפי' לר"ע מניח רועה ביניהם ומסתלק אלא דניחא ליה למיפרך דרבא אדרבא:

**והאמר** רבא הכל מודים בשנים שהפקידו אצל רועה. פרש"י זה טלה אחד וזה שני טלאים שמניח ביניהם ומסתלק והתם כשני כריכות נינהו אפי' הפקידו זה בפני זה דדבר הנראה מי הביא אחד ומי הביא שנים אבל במעות לא היה לו להבחין בין לרור גדול ללרור קטן וקשה דמתני' מסתמא איירי אפילו זה הפקיד מאתים בב' כיסין וזה מנה בכיס אחד ותו דלמא איירי רבא בב' שהפקידו שני טלאים זה כחוש וזה שמן דהוי כמעות דלא הוה ליה למידק אי נמי בשנים שהפקידו שני טלאים ומת אחד מהם וכל אחד אומר שהמת של חבירו דכי האי גוונא איירי מתניתין דהתם בפרק שני דבכורות (דף יז: ושם) אלא יש לומר דאפי' הפקידו טלאים זה בפני זה הוה ליה למידק דלא שייך למימר אתון לא קפדיתון משום דלא יוכלו לתקן דאפי' הפקידו זה שלא בפני זה יראה חבירו הטלאים כשהולכים במרעה ושואל של מי הם אבל במעות שהיה יכול להפקיד שלא בפני חבירו יכול הנפקד לומר אתון לא קפדיתון כל שכן דלא הוה לי למידק:

**שלא** מדעתו. לאו דוקא שלא מדעתו אלא כלומר שלא ברלייתו של רועה דהשתא לא הוה ליה למידק:

שמא

## עין משפט נר מצוה

מ א מיי' פ"ד מהל' גזלה ואבדה הל' ט סמג עשין עג טוש"ע ח"מ סי' שסה סעי' א:

מא ב מיי' פ"ה מהל' נחלות הל' ו סמג עשין לו טוש"ע ח"מ סי' רפ סעי' י:

מב ג ד מיי' פ"ה מהל' שאלה ופקדון הל' ד סמג עשין פח טוש"ע ח"מ סי' ש סעי' ד:

## רבינו חננאל

שמכל מקום השבתה הגזילה לנגזל עצמו. אמר רב ספק הינוח לכתחילה לא יטול ואם נטל לא יחזיר אמר רב ספרא תני ויניח.

## מסורת הש"ס

א) לעיל כה:, ב) [יבמות קיח:], ג) בבא בתרא קנח: [ע"ש], ד) דלמא ר' טרפון היא ס"א, ה) בבא קמא קג:, ו) ס"א ל"ג, ז) בכורות יח:.

## הגהות הב"ח

(א) תוס' ד"ה מודה וכו' כב"ה דקאמר תמהני מתי תבא לרת: (ב) ד"ה ומי כו' כדמשמע לשון הודה מפי עלמו הא:

## ליקוטי רש"י

ספק הינוח. בדבר שאין בו סימן וכ"ש ודאי הינוח. לכתחלה לא יטול. דאי שקלת לה ליכא למרייהו סימנין למיתב בהו ויפסיד הלכך לא יטול והבעלים יזכרו ויבאו ויטלוס. ואם נטל לא יחזיר. דהא ליכא דיהיב סימנא [לעיל כה:]. נפל הבית עליו ועל אמו. כגון שנפל הבית על רחל אשת יעקב באלמנותה ועל יוסף בנה מיעקב ולא היה לה עוד בן מיעקב ולא מאיש אחר. יורשי הבן. כגון ראובן בן יעקב מלאה טוען כל הנכסים ואומר רחל מתה תחילה וירש יוסף את כל נכסיה ואח"כ מת הוא וירשנו כל הנכסים. ויורשי האם אומרים. כגון אחיה מאביה אומרים הבן מת ראשון והיא מתה אחרונה וירשנו כל נכסיה. ואמר ר"ע מודה אני בזו כו'. משום דנקט תנא קמא לישנא דמודים אמר איהו נמי מודה אני כלומר ואני מודה וחולק עליך לדלדברי ב"ה נמי אמרינן הכא נכסים בחזקתם [רשב"ם ב"ב קנח:].

a case both **THESE AND THOSE,** i.e. both Beis Shammai and Beis Hillel, who disagree about the law in similar cases of inheritance,[10] מוֹדִים שֶׁיַּחֲלוֹקוּ – **CONCEDE THAT [THE TWO GROUPS OF HEIRS] SHOULD DIVIDE** the mother's property. וְאָמַר רַבִּי עֲקִיבָא – **AND R' AKIVA SAID:** מוֹדֶה אֲנִי בָּזוֹ – **I CONCEDE**[11] **IN THIS** case שֶׁהַנְּכָסִים בְּחֶזְקָתָן – **THAT THE PROPERTIES** retain **THEIR** previous **STATUS.**[12] This ruling seemingly contradicts R' Akiva's ruling in *Yevamos,* which requires the thief to compensate each and every claimant.[13] – ? –

Rava answers:

אָמַר לֵיהּ – **He said to [Abaye]:** הָתָם – **There,** regarding the status of the deceased woman's property, שֶׁמָּא וְשֶׁמָּא – the son's heirs claim that the property is **possibly** theirs, **and** the mother's heirs claim that the property is **possibly** theirs. Since neither party is certain of its claim, R' Akiva rules that the property should retain its previous status. גָּזַל אֶחָד מֵחֲמִשָּׁה – In the case of someone who **stole from one of five** people, however, בָּרִי וְשֶׁמָּא – each of the five claims that the thief **definitely** stole from him, **and** the thief can respond to each one only that **possibly** he is not the victim. Since a definite claim is stronger than an uncertain claim, R' Akiva rules that the thief must pay each and every claimant.

The Gemara challenges this answer:[13]

וְהָא מַתְנִיתִין דְּהָכָא – **But there is the Mishnah here,** אָמַר לִשְׁנַיִם גָּזַלְתִּי לְאֶחָד מִכֶּם מָנֶה – which concerns a thief who **TOLD TWO PEOPLE, "I STOLE A *MANEH* FROM ONE OF YOU** but I do not know from whom," דְּשֶׁמָּא וְשֶׁמָּא הוּא – **where** each one claims only that **possibly** the thief stole from him,[14] **and** the thief can respond to each one only that **possibly** he is not the victim, וְקָתָנֵי נוֹתֵן לָזֶה מָנֶה וְלָזֶה מָנֶה – **and** yet **the Tanna taught: HE GIVES THIS ONE A *MANEH* AND THAT ONE A *MANEH*.** From here we see that contested property does not retain its previous status even when neither side is making a definite claim. – ? –

This question assumes that R' Akiva agrees with this ruling of our Mishnah. The Gemara now demonstrates that this is indeed so:

וּמִמַּאי דְּרַבִּי עֲקִיבָא הִיא – **And from what** do you conclude **that [the Mishnah]** here **is** reflective of the opinion of **R' Akiva?**[15] דְּקָתָנֵי עֲלָהּ דְּהַהִיא – **For it was taught in a Baraisa concerning that [Mishnah]** in *Yevamos* about the thief who stole from one of five people:[16] מוֹדֶה רַבִּי טַרְפוֹן – **R' TARFON CONCEDES** בְּאוֹמֵר לִשְׁנַיִם – that **IF [A THIEF] TOLD TWO [PEOPLE],** גָּזַלְתִּי לְאֶחָד מִכֶּם מָנֶה – **"I STOLE A *MANEH* FROM ONE OF YOU,** אֵינִי יוֹדֵעַ אֵיזֶה מִכֶּם כו׳ – **AND I DO NOT KNOW WHICH OF YOU** was the victim," **etc.** [the thief must give a *maneh* to each of them]. לְמַאן מוֹדֶה – **To whom** does R' Tarfon **concede** in this Baraisa? לָאו לְרַבִּי עֲקִיבָא בַּר פְּלוּגְתֵּיהּ – **(Is it not) to R' Akiva, his disputant** in that Mishnah in *Yevamos*? Since the cases of that Baraisa and our Mishnah are identical, we can conclude that R' Akiva also agrees with our Mishnah's ruling, which requires the thief to pay both claimants.[17]

The Gemara now explains how we know that our Mishnah is discussing a case where no one is sure of his claim:

וּמִמַּאי דְּשֶׁמָּא וְשֶׁמָּא הוּא – **And from what** do we conclude **that** the Mishnah here rules on a case where each claimant says only that **possibly** the thief stole from him **and** the thief responds to each one only that **possibly** he is not the victim? חֲדָא – **First of all** דְּלֹא קָתָנֵי תּוֹבְעִין אוֹתוֹ – **because the Mishnah did not teach** that the claimants **sued [the thief]** for payment.[18] וְעוֹד – **And, furthermore,** הָא תָּנֵי רַבִּי חִיָּיא – **R' Chiya taught** in a Baraisa about our Mishnah, as follows: זֶה אוֹמֵר אֵינִי יוֹדֵעַ – **And THIS** one **SAYS, "I DO NOT KNOW** if you stole from me," זֶה אוֹמֵר אֵינִי יוֹדֵעַ – **AND THAT** other one **SAYS, "I DO NOT KNOW** if you stole from me," the thief must pay each claimant.[19] It is evident from this Baraisa that our Mishnah speaks of a case where the two claimants are *not* certain as to their claims, and yet R' Akiva requires the thief to pay them both, and does not rule that the contested money remains in the thief's possession until the rightful owner can be determined. – ? –

The Gemara answers:

הָא אוֹקִימְנָא לָהּ – **We have** already **established** that **[the Mishnah]** here discusses a case בְּבָא לָצֵאת יְדֵי שָׁמַיִם – **where [the thief] comes to fulfill** his **Heavenly obligation.** This is why R' Akiva says he must pay each of them even though neither of them is making a definite claim.[20]

The Gemara questions a distinction made previously by Rava:

אָמַר לֵיהּ רָבִינָא לְרַב אַשִׁי – **Ravina said to Rav Ashi:** מִי אָמַר

NOTES

claim that the son died first, and therefore never inherited his mother's property; thus, the mother's estate fell to them (*Rashi*).

10. The Mishnah there (*Bava Basra* 157a, 158b) discusses other cases of two people being killed in uncertain order by the collapse of a house. In those cases Beis Shammai rule that the property in question is divided between the claimants, while Beis Hillel rule that the property remains with its previous status [see note 12] (*Rashi*).

11. Although R' Akiva was a disciple of Beis Shammai, who rule in the other cases that the property must be divided (see previous note), he concedes that in this case it remains in its previous possession (*Rashi;* cf. *Tosafos*).

12. That is, they go to the one who previously had the greater claim to them. There is an Amoraic dispute in *Bava Basra* (158b) who this is (*Rashi*).

13. The Gemara challenges the premise that R' Akiva agrees that where neither party is sure of its claim ("possibly and possibly"), the property stays where it is.

14. Unlike the Mishnah in *Yevamos,* our Mishnah speaks of a case where the two possible victims do *not* claim with certainty that the thief stole from them. The Gemara will explain below how we know that our Mishnah speaks of such a case.

15. The ruling of our Mishnah is stated anonymously.

16. This is the same Baraisa that was quoted above, at the end of 37a.

17. The case in which R' Tarfon "concedes" that the thief must pay both people is the same as the case of our Mishnah here – where the thief came forward on his own and admitted that he stole money from one of two people. Since R' Tarfon in the Baraisa says this as a concession to R' Akiva, we see that R' Akiva also holds that the thief must pay both people. Thus, the ruling of our Mishnah reflects the opinions of both R' Akiva and R' Tarfon.

[R' Tarfon concedes to R' Akiva that he should pay both of them to fulfill his *Heavenly* obligations, as the Gemara explained at the end of 37a. However, the Gemara assumes at this point that R' Akiva himself requires him to pay both of them as a matter of *law,* and not just to fulfill a Heavenly obligation.]

18. I.e. the Mishnah did not state that each one claimed that the thief definitely stole from him (*Rashi*); rather, it says that he told *them* that he had stolen from one of them.

19. In the *Tosefta* that he compiled, R' Chiya taught a Baraisa that discusses the case of our Mishnah. The Baraisa states: "If a thief told two people, 'I stole from one of you, but I do not know from whom,' and this one says, 'I do not know [if you stole from me],' and that one says, 'I do not know [if you stole from me]' " (*Rashi*).

20. [Although in the case of the collapsed house R' Akiva rules that the mother's property retains its status when the claimants are uncertain, that is because no one has done anything wrong to warrant a Heavenly obligation. In the case of a thief, however, R' Akiva maintains that one must pay all the claimants in order to fulfill one's Heavenly obligation.] Thus, the Gemara concludes that in a case where no one is certain of his claim, even R' Akiva agrees that the thief is obligated to pay both of them only to fulfill his Heavenly obligation (*Rosh;* see *Tosafos*).

צווח מ"ד הלה צווח אבל שתיקה כהודאה ומ"ד הלה שותק שתיקה דהכא לאו כהודאה הוא מצי אמר ליה האי דשתיקי לכל חד וחד דאמינא דלמא האי הוא אמר מר מניח גזילה ביניהם ומסתלק ושקלי לה כולהו ואזלי [א] והאמר רבי אבא בר זבדא אמר רב כל ספק הינוח לכתחלה לא יטול ואם נטל לא יחזיר אמר רב ספרא ויניח א"ל אביי לרבא מי א"ר עקיבא [ב] א לא זו הדרך מוציאתו מידי עבירה עד שישלם גזילה לכל חד וחד אלמא מספיקא מפקינן ממונא ולא אמרי' אוקים ממונא בחזקת מריה ורמינהי [ג] נפל הבית עליו ועל אמו יורשי הבן אומרים האם מתה ראשונה ויורשי האם אומרים הבן מת ראשון אלו ואלו מודים שיחלוקו ואמר ר"ע ב מודה אני בזו שהנכסים בחזקתן אמר ליה התם שמא ושמא גזל אחד מחמשה ברי ושמא והא מתני' דהכא אמר לשנים גזלתי לאחד מכם מנה דשמא ושמא הוא וקתני נותן לזה מנה ולזה מנה וממאי דר"ע היא [ד] דקתני עלה דההיא [ה] מודה ר' טרפון באומר לשנים גזלתי לאחד מכם מנה ואיני יודע איזה מכם כו' למאן מודה [ו] (לאו) לר"ע בר פלוגתיה וממאי דשמא ושמא הוא חדא דלא קתני תובעין אותו ועוד הא תני ר' חייא זה אומר איני יודע וזה אומר איני יודע הא אוקימנא לה בבא לצאת ידי שמים אמר ליה רבינא לרב אשי ומי אמר רבא כל בשתי כריכות הוה ליה למידק [ז] והאמר רבא ואי תימא רב פפא ג הכל מודים בשנים שהפקידו אצל רועה שמניח רועה ביניהן ומסתלק א"ל ד התם כשהפקידו בעדרו של רועה שלא מדעתו: וכן שני כלים אחד יפה מנה ואחד יפה אלף זוז כו': וצריכא דאי אשמועינן הך קמייתא בההיא קאמרי רבנן משום דליכא פסידא אבל בהא דאיכא פסידא דגדול אימא מודו ליה לר' יוסי ואי אתמר בהא בהא קאמר ר' יוסי אבל בהך אימא מודי להו לרבנן צריכא

**רש"י**

צווח. אמר לכל אחד איני מכירך: ושקלי ליה כולהו ואזלי. נמצא זה מוציא מידו כדי להפסיד הנגזל עולמית: והא"ר אבא בר זבדא ספק הינוח. מצא דבר שאין בו סימן בצד מקום שמשתמר קצת דלא שכיחי אינשי דאזלי ויש לספוקי שמא מדעת הונח שם לגניזה: לכתחלה לא יטלנו. המוצאו שכשיבא בעליו לא ימצאנו וסימן אין בו שיכריז לפיכך יניחנו זה ובעליו יבא ויטלנו וכל שכן לודאי הינוח כדתנן (לעיל דף כה:) מצא כלי באשפה מכוסה לא יגע בו: ואם נטל לא יחזיר. ואם בא אחר ואמר שלי הוא וסימן אינו נותן בו לא יחזירנו שמא אינו שלו וסוף הבעלים לבוא ויביא עדים שהניחו שם לפיכך יהא מונח ביד זה עד שיבא אליהו דהאי לא יחזיר לא שיהא שלו קאמר דהא מעיקרא באיסורא אתא לידיה אם הינוח הוא אלמא מידי דמספקא לן דמאן ניהו צריך להניחו בידו מי שהוא עד שיתברר הדבר: אמר רב ספרא ויניח. הא דקתני מסתלק לאו דלישקלו איהו וליזלו ולא שיוציאנה מידו אלא תהא מונחת בידו עד שיתברר הדבר והאי מסתלק סילוק הדין הוא ויניח גזילה בפניהם בב"ד ויאמר בררו של מי הוא ויטול ומסתלק מן הדין והגזילה יניח בידו עד שיבא אליהו: לא זו הדרך. סיפא דגזל אחד מחמשה הוא ביבמות (דף קיח:): נפל הבית עליו ועל אמו. ואין ידוע איזה מת ראשון והיו לאמו נכסים מבית אביה: יורשי האם. משפחת בית אביה אומרים לקרובי הבן ממשפחת אביו הבאים לירש את הבן: הבן מת ראשון. ולא ירש את אמו להוריש אתכם נכסים אלא הבן מת ראשון ואח"כ מתה אמו ואנו יורשים אותה (נכסיה): ויורשי הבן אומרים האם מתה ראשונה. וירשה בנה ואחריה מת הבן ואנו יורשין אותו: אלו ואלו. ב"ש וב"ה שנחלקו בנפילות אחרות בפרק מי שמת שב"ש אומרים יחלוקו ובית הלל אומרים נכסים בחזקתן כאן מודים שיחלוקו: אמר ר"ע מודה אני בזה. אע"פ שאני משל ב"ש ואומר בשאר הנפילות יחלוקו בזו אני מודה לב"ה שהנכסים בחזקתן ופליגי אמוראי בחזקת מי והתם מפרש טעמא: שמא ושמא. שניהם מכח שמא באים הלכך נכסים בחזקתן: הכא ברי ושמא. כל אחד ואחד אומר אותי גזל היינו טענת ודאי וזה אומר איני יודע וברי עדיף משמא: עלה דההיא. דגזל אחד מחמשה: חדא דלא קתני. מתני' תובעין אותו דלא קתני אותי גזל: ה"ג ועוד הא תני ר' חייא זה אומר איני יודע וזה אומר איני יודע. ול"ג יחלוקו והכי פירושו ועוד הא תני רבי חייא להך מתניתא דגזלתי את אחד מכם בתוספתא דיליה ותני לה הכי אמר לשנים גזלתי אחד מכם ואיני יודע איזהו זה אומר איני יודע וזה אומר איני יודע נותן לזה מנה כו' כדקתני במתני' אלמא בשמא ושמא עסקינן: הכל מודים בשנים שהפקידו כו'. גבי פלוגתא דר"ט ור"ע איתמר במסכת בכורות (דף יח:) שנים שהפקידו זה טלה אחד וזה שנים זה אומר שנים שלי וזה אומר שנים שלי והתם שתי כריכות נינהו ואפילו הפקידו זה בפני זה דבר הנראה הוא מי מביא אחד ומי מביא שנים דבשלמא גבי כריכות מעות הואיל דאלו ואלו צרורין הוא שוכח מי הפקיד אצלו צרור גדול ומי צרור קטן הואיל והפקידו אצלו יחד אבל גבי טלאים מילתא מוכחת טפי: פסידא דגדול. של כלי גדול ששברוהו וכשיבא אליהו ויאמר של מי הוא נמצא מפסיד בשבירתו: בהא קאמר ר' יוסי. משום פסידא דגדול:

והא

**תוספות**

**מודה** אני בזה. אע"ג דקאמר מודה אני לאו משום דליהוי מתלמידי ב"ש דבפ"ק דיבמות (דף טו.) בצרת הבת סבר כב"ה דקאמר (א) תמיה אני מתי תבא צרת הבת לידי ואשיאנה והיינו כב"ה אלא אגב דשנה לעיל אלו ואלו מודים תנא הכא מודה אני:

**וממאי** דר"ע היא. וא"ת ואלא כמאן דאי כר"ט כ"ש דלר"ע נותן לזה מנה ולזה מנה וי"ל דהכי פי' ממאי דר"ע היא ומדינא דלמא לצאת ידי שמים ומשני מדקאמר מודה ר"ט למאן מודה לאו לר"ע דאמר מדינא משלם לכל אחד ואחד ואמר ר"ט מדינא מניח ביניהם ומסתלק אבל לצאת ידי שמים מודינא דמשלם לכל אחד ואחד וקאמר הא אוקימנא בבא לצאת ידי שמים ומודה דקאמר ר"ט ה"פ כי היכי דאמרת בשמא ושמא משלם לכל אחד ואחד לצאת ידי שמים הכי מודינא לך הכא:

**ומי** אמר רבא כל בשתי כריכות ה"ל למידק והא אמר רבא כו'. וא"ת והא מתני' איירי לצאת ידי שמים וי"ל מדנקט במתני' דאתי נמי כר"ע אביו של אחד מכם משמע משום דהוי שמא ושמא אינו חייב אלא לצאת ידי שמים דוקא כדמשמע לשון הודה (ב) הא הפקידו הן עצמן דמסתמא תבעי ליה והוה ליה ברי ושמא חייב אפי' מדינא אע"ג דלא עבד איסורא כיון דה"ל למידק דאי לאו הכי אמאי נקט אביו דאי לאורויי דאפי' בשמא ושמא חייב לצאת ידי שמים זה אין נראה שום חידוש לר"ע ועוד דר"ע נמי אית לי' בהגוזל קמא (ב"ק דף קג: ושם) בלקח מחמשה בני אדם שמשלם לכל אחד ואחד ואע"ג דלא עבד איסורא ומדינא משלם דלצאת ידי שמים אפילו ר"ט מודה שמשלם לכל אחד ואחד אע"ג דלא עבד איסורא דהא מתני' אוקמינן נמי כר"ע וקתני אביו של אחד מכם הפקיד לי מנה נותן לכל אחד ולהכי פריך והאמר רבא הכל מודים כו' דאפי' לר"ע מניח ביניהם אע"ג דה"ל למידק כמו שאפרש משום דלא עביד איסורא וה"ה דבלא רבא ה"מ למיפרך מר"ע דאמר גבי מקח אע"ג דלא עבד איסורא משלם לכל אחד ואחד והתם אמר רבא דאפי' לר"ע מניח רועה ביניהם ומסתלק אלא דניחא ליה למיפרך דרבא אדרבא:

**והאמר** רבא הכל מודים בשנים שהפקידו אצל רועה. פרש"י זה טלה אחד וזה שני טלאים שמניח ביניהם ומסתלק והתם כשני כריכות נינהו אפי' הפקידו זה בפני זה דדבר הנראה מי הביא אחד ומי הביא שנים אבל במעות לא היה לו להבחין בין צרור גדול לצרור קטן וקשה דמתני' מסתמא איירי אפילו זה הפקיד מאתים בב' כיסין וזה מנה בכיס אחד ותו דלמא איירי רבא בב' שהפקידו שני טלאים זה כחוש וזה שמן דהוי כמעות דלא הוה ליה למידק אי נמי בשנים שהפקידו שני טלאים ומת אחד מהם וכל אחד אומר שהמת של חבירו דכי האי גוונא איירי מתניתין דהתם בפרק שני דבכורות (דף יז: ושם) אלא יש לומר דאפי' הפקידו טלאים זה בפני זה הוה ליה למידק דלא שייך למימר אתון לא קפידיתון משום דלא יוכלו לתקן דאפי' הפקידו זה שלא בפני זה יראה חבירו הטלאים כשהולכים במרעה וישאל של מי הם אבל במעות שהיה יכול להפקיד שלא בפני חבירו יכול הנפקד לומר אתון לא קפידיתון כל שכן דלא הוה לי למידק:

**שלא** מדעתו. לאו דוקא שלא מדעתו אלא כלומר שלא ברצונו של רועה דהשתא לא הוה ליה למידק:

שמא

**עין משפט נר מצוה**

מ א מיי' פ"ד מהל' גזלה ואבדה הל' ט סמג עשין עג טוש"ע ח"מ סי' שסה סעי' א:

מא ב מיי' פ"ה מהל' נחלות הל' ו סמג עשין צו טוש"ע ח"מ סי' רפ סעי' י:

מב ג ד מיי' פ"ה מהל' שאלה ופקדון הל' ד סמג עשין פח טוש"ע ח"מ סי' ש סעי' ד:

**רבינו חננאל**

שמכל מקום השבתה הגזילה לנגזל עצמו. אמר רב ספק הינוח לכתחילה לא יטול ואם נטל לא יחזיר אמר רב ספרא תני ויניח.

**מסורת הש"ס**

א) לעיל כה:, ב) [יבמות קיח:], ג) בבא בתרא קנח: [ע"ש], ד) דלמא ר' טרפון היא ס"א, ה) בבא קמא קג:, ו) ס"א ל"ג, ז) בכורות יח:.

**הגהות הב"ח**

(א) תוס' ד"ה מודה וכו' כב"ה דקאמר תאבני מתי תבא צרת: (ב) ד"ה ומי כו' כדמשמע לשון הודה מפי עצמו הא:

**ליקוטי רש"י**

ספק הינוח. בדבר שאין בו סימן וכ"ש ודאי הינוח. לכתחלה לא יטול. דאי שקלת לה ליכא למרייהו סימנין למיתב בהו ויפסיד הלכך לא יטול והבעלים יזכרו ויבאו ויטלום. ואם נטל לא יחזיר. דהא ליכא דיהיב סימנא [לעיל כה:]. נפל הבית עליו ועל אמו. כגון שנפל הבית על רחל אשת יעקב באלמנותה ועל יוסף בנה מיעקב ולא היה לה עוד בן מיעקב ולא מאיש אחר. יורשי הבן. כגון ראובן בן יעקב מלאה טוען כל הנכסים ואומר רחל מתה תחילה וירש יוסף את כל נכסיה ואח"כ מת הוא וירשנו כל הנכסים. ויורשי האם אומרים. כגון אחיה מאביה אומרים הבן מת ראשון והיא מתה אחרונה וירשנו כל נכסיה. ואמר ר"ע מודה אני בזו כו'. משום דנקט תנא קמא לישנא דמודים אמר איהו נמי מודה אני כלומר ואני מודה וחולק עליך דלדברי ב"ה נמי אמרינן הכא נכסים בחזקתם [רשב"ם ב"ב קנח:].

צוֹוֵחַ – **cries out** to each claimant, "I do not recognize you."[1]

The Gemara explains:

מַאן דְּאָמַר הָלָה צוֹוֵחַ – **The one who said** that **[the thief] cries out** maintains that it is only for this reason that he is exempt from paying all the claimants; אֲבָל שְׁתִיקָה כְּהוֹדָאָה – **however, silence** on his part would be interpreted **as an admission** to each of the claimants.[2]

The Gemara explains the first opinion:

וּמַאן דְּאָמַר הָלָה שׁוֹתֵק – **And the one who said** that **[the thief] remains silent** and is nonetheless exempt from paying all the claimants שְׁתִיקָה דְּהָכָא לָאו כְּהוֹדָאָה הוּא – maintains that his **silence here is not considered an admission,** מָצֵי אָמַר לֵיהּ – for **[the thief] can tell [the judge]:** הַאי דִּשְׁתִיקִי לְכָל חַד וְחַד – **The reason I was silent to each and every** claimant דַּאֲמִינָא דִּלְמָא הַאי הוּא – is **because I said** to myself, **"Perhaps this one is [the one]** from whom I stole." However, I never meant to admit to any of them that their claim was indeed true.

The Gemara continues to analyze the Mishnah in *Yevamos*:

אָמַר מַר – **The master** [R' Tarfon] **said** there: If five people each claim that it was from them that the thief stole the object, מַנִּיחַ גְּזֵילָה בֵּינֵיהֶם וּמִסְתַּלֵּק – [THE THIEF] PLACES THE STOLEN OBJECT BETWEEN THEM AND WITHDRAWS. וְשָׁקְלֵי לָהּ כּוּלְּהוּ וְאָזְלֵי – Does this mean that **all of them take [the object] and go** on their way, i.e. divide it among themselves? וְהָאָמַר רַבִּי אַבָּא בַּר זַבְדָּא אָמַר רַב – **But** how can we say this when **R' Abba bar Zavda said in the name of Rav:** כָּל סָפֵק הִינּוּחַ – **Any** found object, regarding which a **doubt** exists whether it was deliberately **placed** there for safekeeping,[3] לְכַתְּחִלָּה לֹא יִטּוֹל – **one should not pick up in the first place,**[4] וְאִם נָטַל – **but if he picked it up** in violation of the law, לֹא יַחֲזִיר – **he may not return** it to any claimant.[5] We see from this that someone holding property whose ownership cannot be determined must hold onto it until the identity of the rightful owner is clearly established. If so, why does R' Tarfon (in the Mishnah in *Yevamos*) permit the thief to leave the stolen object to be divided among all five claimants?[6] He should say that he should hold onto it until the rightful owner can be properly identified!

Because of this question, the Gemara reinterprets the Mishnah in *Yevamos*:

אָמַר רַב סַפְרָא – **Rav Safra said:** The Mishnah's ruling that the thief "withdraws" does not mean that he may give the stolen object to the claimants and walk away; וְיַנִּיחַ – rather, it means that **he should "place"** it before them in court and challenge each of them to prove that he is the rightful owner. He may then "withdraw" from any further legal obligation to them, but he must nonetheless hold onto the object and care for it until the question of its ownership is resolved.

Having concluded its analysis of R' Tarfon's view in the Mishnah in *Yevamos,* the Gemara now analyzes the view of R' Akiva in that Mishnah:

אָמַר לֵיהּ אַבָּיֵי לְרָבָא – **Abaye said to Rava:** מִי אָמַר רַבִּי עֲקִיבָא – **And did R' Akiva** actually **say** in the conclusion of that Mishnah, regarding a thief who cannot say which of these five claimants he stole from: לֹא זוֹ הַדֶּרֶךְ מוֹצִיאַתּוֹ מִידֵי עֲבֵירָה – THIS IS NOT THE WAY TO EXTRICATE [THE THIEF] FROM SIN; i.e. R' Tarfon's ruling, that he should hold the stolen object until one of them can prove it is his, is not sufficient to undo his sin of stealing. עַד שֶׁיְּשַׁלֵּם גְּזֵילָה לְכָל חַד וְחַד – Rather, he does not fulfill his obligation UNTIL HE PAYS the value of THE STOLEN OBJECT TO EACH AND EVERY ONE of the claimants. אַלְמָא מְסַפֵּיקָא מַפְּקִינַן מָמוֹנָא – **From here we see** that R' Akiva holds that **we extract money** even **out of doubt,** וְלָא אָמְרִינַן אוֹקִים מָמוֹנָא בְּחֶזְקַת מָרֵיהּ – **and we do not say** that **the money remains in the possession of its** present **owner** (the thief) until it can be determined who really has the right to it.

Abaye presents a contradiction:

וּרְמִינְהִי – **But contrast this** ruling with R' Akiva's ruling in another Mishnah, in *Bava Basra* (158b): נָפַל הַבַּיִת עָלָיו וְעַל אִמּוֹ – IF A HOUSE COLLAPSED UPON [A MAN] AND HIS MOTHER, killing them both,[7] יוֹרְשֵׁי הַבֵּן אוֹמְרִים – and THE HEIRS OF THE SON SAY, הָאֵם מֵתָה רִאשׁוֹנָה – "THE MOTHER DIED FIRST, and therefore we inherit her property";[8] וְיוֹרְשֵׁי הָאֵם אוֹמְרִים – AND THE HEIRS OF THE MOTHER SAY, הַבֵּן מֵת רִאשׁוֹן – "THE SON DIED FIRST, and her property falls to us"[9] – אֵלּוּ וָאֵלּוּ – in such

NOTES

1. That is, I do not recognize any of you as being the person from whom I stole (see *Rashi*). *Raavad* (cited by *Shitah Mekubetzes*) understands this to mean that the thief actively denies their claims because he knows that all but one of them are lying.

2. Had he greeted their claims with silence, the thief would have been obligated to pay all five claimants. Although he clearly does not admit to stealing from them all, each silence is taken as an admission of the current claim and a retraction of the previous admission. Thus, since at one time he "admitted" to each of the claims, he must satisfy them all (*Raavad,* cited by *Shitah Mekubetzes*).

3. R' Abba bar Zavda refers to an object of unknown ownership that lacks any identifying mark (*siman*). It was found in a place where few people pass by and is thus somewhat protected. These circumstances dictate that we should consider the possibility that the owner intentionally placed the object in that spot to conceal it [until he can come back for it] (*Rashi*).

4. Because the owner will not find it if he returns for it, and the finder will not announce its discovery since it does not have a *siman* by which to identify it (see previous note). It is better therefore to leave the object alone and allow the owner to return and recover it, if indeed he left it there to come back for it.

This ruling certainly applies when it is *clear* to the finder that the object was deliberately concealed for safekeeping, as stated in the Mishnah above, 25b (*Rashi*).

5. That is, if someone comes and claims [he left it in that place and] it is his, the finder should not give it to him since he has no *siman* by which to identify it. Thus, we must be concerned that perhaps he is not the owner [despite his having identified the object's resting place] and perhaps another person will come with witnesses to *his* having placed it there. Hence, the finder must hold the object until someone can prove it is his, or until Elijah comes and clarifies the matter of ownership (*Rashi*). [See Gemara above (25b) for why the place is not considered a *siman.*]

[The finder may not, however, keep the object for himself, even though it has no *siman,* for if it had been deliberately concealed there by its owner [and was not abandoned after being lost], the finder was not allowed to take it [and must return it to its owner] (*Rashi*).

6. By doing this, the thief is causing an irretrievable loss to the victim (*Rashi* ד״ה ושקלי להו), and is not fulfilling the mitzvah of returning what he stole to its rightful owner (*Shitah Mekubetzes*). It is therefore better that he should hold onto it until the rightful owner can be identified.

7. The mother was widowed and the son, her only child, had no descendants of his own. However, the son had brothers, born to his father from another wife (see *Rashbam* to *Bava Basra* 158b ד״ה נפל). Since it is not known whether the son or the mother died first, two groups of heirs contend for the mother's property, which she had previously inherited from her father (*Rashi*).

[According to the Biblical law of inheritance, a person's property is inherited by his descendants, according to a specific order. If he has no descendants, his father inherits it. If his father is no longer alive, it goes to his paternal brothers (*Numbers* 27:8,9).]

8. A son inherits his mother's estate, but a mother is never an heir of her son (see *Bava Basra* 108a). Thus, the son's brothers claim that the mother died first, so that her property was inherited by the son just before he died, and then by themselves upon his death (*Rashi*).

9. The mother's relatives (from her father's family, e.g. her brothers)

צווח מ"ד הלה צווח אבל שתיקה כהודאה ומ"ד הלה שותק שתיקה דהכא לאו כהודאה הוא מצי אמר ליה האי דשתיקי לכל חד וחד דאמינא דלמא האי הוא אמר מר מניח גזילה ביניהם ומסתלק ושקלי לה כולהו ואזלי [א] והאמר רבי אבא בר זבדא אמר רב כל ספק הינוח לכתחלה לא יטול ואם נטל לא יחזיר אמר רב ספרא ויניח א"ל אביי לרבא מי א"ר עקיבא [ב] לא זו הדרך מוציאתו מידי עבירה עד שישלם גזילה לכל חד וחד אלמא מספיקא מפקינן ממונא ולא אמרי' אוקים ממונא בחזקת מריה ורמינהי [ג] נפל הבית עליו ועל אמו יורשי הבן אומרים האם מתה ראשונה ויורשי האם אומרים הבן מת ראשון אלו ואלו מודים שיחלוקו ואמר ר"ע [ב] מודה אני בזו שהנכסים בחזקתן אמר ליה התם שמא ושמא הכא ברי ושמא והא מתני' דהכא אמר לשנים גזלתי לאחד מכם מנה דשמא ושמא הוא וקתני נותן לזה מנה ולזה מנה וממאי דר"ע היא [ד] דקתני עלה דההיא [ה] מודה ר' טרפון באומר לשנים גזלתי לאחד מכם מנה ואיני יודע איזה מכם כו' למאן מודה [ו] (לאו) לר"ע בר פלוגתיה וממאי דשמא ושמא הוא חדא דלא קתני תובעין אותו ועוד הא תני ר' חייא זה אומר איני יודע וזה אומר איני יודע הא אוקימנא לה בבא לצאת ידי שמים אמר ליה רבינא לרב אשי ומי אמר רבא כל בשתי כריכות הוה ליה למידק [ז] והאמר רבא ואי תימא רב פפא [ג] הכל מודים בשנים שהפקידו אצל רועה שמניח רועה בינידן ומסתלק א"ל [ד] התם כשהפקידו בעדרו של רועה שלא מדעתו: וכן שני כלים אחד יפה מנה ואחד יפה אלף זוז כו': וצריכא דאי אשמועינן הך קמייתא בההיא קאמרי רבנן משום דליכא פסידא אבל בהא דאיכא פסידא דגדול אימא מודו ליה לר' יוסי ואי אתמר בהא בהא קאמר ר' יוסי אבל בהך אימא מודי להו לרבנן צריכא

**רש"י**

צווח. אמר לכל אחד איני מכירך: ושקלי ליה כולהו ואזלי. נמצא זה מוציא מידו כדי להפסיד הנגזל עולמית: והא"ר אבא בר זבדא ספק הינוח. מלא דבר שאין בו סימן בלד מקום שמשתמר קלת דלא שכיחי אינשי דאזלי ויש לספוקי שמא מדעת הונח שם לגניזה: לכתחלה לא יטלנו. המולאו שכשיבא בעליו לא ימלאנו וסימן אין בו שיכריז לפיכך יניחנו זה ובעליו יבא ויטלנו וכל שכן לודאי הינוח כדתנן (לעיל דף כה:) מלא כלי באשפה מכוסה לא יגע בו: ואם נטל לא יחזיר. ואם בא אחר ואמר שלי הוא וסימן אינו נותן בו לא יחזירנו שמא אינו שלו וסוף הבעלים לבוא ויביא עדים שהניחו שם לפיכך יהא מונח ביד זה עד שיבא אליהו דהאי לא יחזיר לא שיהא שלו קאמר דהא מעיקרא באיסורא אתא לידיה אם הינוח הוא אלמא מידי דמספקא לן דמאן ניהו לריך להניחו בידו מי שהוא עד שיתברר הדבר: אמר רב ספרא ויניח. הא דקתני מסתלק לאו דלישקלו אינהו וליזלו ולא שיוליאנה מידו אלא תהא מונחת בידו עד שיתברר הדבר והאי מסתלק סילוק הדין הוא ויניח גזילה בפניהם בב"ד ויאמר בררו של מי הוא ויטול ומסתלק מן הדין והגזילה יניח בידו עד שיבא אליהו: לא זו הדרך. סיפא דגזל אחד מחמשה הוא ביבמות (דף קיח:): נפל הבית עליו ועל אמו. ואין ידוע איזה מת ראשון והיו לאמו נכסים מבית אביה: יורשי האם. משפחת בית אביה אומרים לקרובי הבן ממשפחת אביו הבאים לירש את הבן: הבן מת ראשון. ולא ירש את אמו להוריש אתכם נכסים אלא הבן מת ראשון ואח"כ מתה אמו ואנו יורשים אותה (נכסיה): ויורשי הבן אומרים האם מתה ראשונה. וירשה בנה ואחריה מת הבן ואנו יורשין אותו: אלו ואלו. ב"ש וב"ה שנחלקו בנפילות אחרות בפרק מי שמת שב"ש אומרים יחלוקו ובית הלל אומרים נכסים בחזקתן כאן מודים שיחלוקו: אמר ר"ע מודה אני בזה. אע"פ שאני משל ב"ש ואומר בשאר הנפילות יחלוקו בזו אני מודה לב"ה שהנכסים בחזקתן ופליגי אמוראי בחזקת מי והתם מפרש טעמא: שמא ושמא. שניהם מכח שמא באים הלכך נכסים בחזקתן: הכא ברי ושמא. כל אחד ואחד אומר אותי גזל היינו טענת ודאי וזה אומר איני יודע וברי עדיף משמא: עלה דההיא. דגזל אחד מחמשה: חדא דלא קתני. מתני' תובעין אותו דלא קתני אותי גזל: ה"ג ועוד הא תני ר' חייא זה אומר איני יודע וזה אומר איני יודע. ול"ג יחלוקו והכי פירושו ועוד הא תני רבי חייא להך מתניתא דגזלתי את אחד מכם בתוספתא דיליה ותני לה הכי אמר לשנים גזלתי אחד מכם ואיני יודע איזהו זה אומר איני יודע וזה אומר איני יודע נותן לזה מנה כו' כדקתני במתני' אלמא בשמא ושמא עסקינן: הכל מודים בשנים שהפקידו כו'. גבי פלוגתא דר"ט ור"ע איתמר במסכת בכורות (דף יח:) שנים שהפקידו זה טלה אחד וזה שנים זה אומר שנים שלי וזה אומר שנים שלי והתם שתי כריכות נינהו ואפילו הפקידו זה בפני זה דבר הנראה הוא מי מביא אחד ומי מביא שנים דבשלמא גבי כריכות מעות הואיל דאלו ואלו צרורין הוא שוכח מי הפקיד אלנו צרור גדול ומי צרור קטן הואיל והפקידו אצלו יחד אבל גבי טלאים מילתא מוכחת טפי: פסידא דגדול. של כלי גדול שמשברוהו וכשיבא אליהו ויאמר של מי הוא נמצא מפסיד בשבירתו: בהא קאמר ר' יוסי. משום פסידא דגדול:

והא

**תוספות**

מודה אני בזה. אע"ג דקאמר מודה אני לאו משום דליהוי מתלמידי ב"ש דבפ"ק דיבמות (דף טו.) בלרת הבת סבר כב"ה דקאמר (א) תמיה אני מתי תבא לרת הבת לידי ואשיאנה והיינו כב"ה אלא אגב דשנה לעיל אלו ואלו מודים תנא הכא מודה אני:

וממאי דר"ע היא. וא"ת ואלא כמאן דאי כר"ט כ"ש דלר"ע נותן לזה מנה ולזה מנה וי"ל דהכי פי' ממאי דר"ע היא ומדינא דלמא לצאת ידי שמים ומשני מדקאמר מודה ר"ט למאן מודה לאו לר"ע דאמר מדינא משלם לכל אחד ואחד ואמר ר"ט מדינא מניח ביניהם ומסתלק אבל לצאת ידי שמים מודינא דמשלם לכל אחד ואחד וקאמר הא אוקימנא בבא לצאת ידי שמים ומודה דקאמר ר"ט ה"פ כי היכי דאמרת בשמא ושמא משלם לכל אחד ואחד לצאת ידי שמים הכי מודינא לך הכא:

ומי אמר רבא כל בשתי כריכות ה"ל למידק והא אמר רבא כו'. וא"ת והא מתני' איירי לצאת ידי שמים וי"ל מדנקט במתני' דאתי נמי כר"ע אביו של אחד מכם משמע משום דהוי שמא ושמא אינו חייב אלא לצאת ידי שמים דוקא כדמשמע לשון הודה (ב) הא הפקידו הן עלמן דמסתמא תבעי ליה והוה ליה ברי ושמא חייב אפי' מדינא אע"ג דלא עבד איסורא כיון דה"ל למידק דאי לאו הכי אמאי נקט אביו דאי לאורויי דאפי' בשמא ושמא חייב לצאת ידי שמים זה אין נראה שום חידוש לר"ע ועוד דר"ע נמי אית לי' בהגוזל קמא (ב"ק דף קג: ושם) בלקח מחמשה בני אדם שמשלם לכל אחד ואחד ואע"ג דלא עבד איסורא ומדינא משלם דלצאת ידי שמים אפילו ר"ט מודה שמשלם לכל אחד ואחד אע"ג דלא עבד איסורא דהא מתני' אוקמינן נמי כר"ט וקתני אביו של אחד מכם הפקיד לי מנה נותן לכל אחד ולהכי פריך והאמר רבא הכל מודים כו' דאפי' לר"ע מניח ביניהם אע"ג דה"ל למידק כמו שאפרש משום דלא עביד איסורא וה"ה דבלא רבא ה"מ למיפרך מר"ע דאמר גבי מקח אע"ג דלא עבד איסורא משלם לכל אחד ואחד והתם אמר רבא דאפי' לר"ע מניח רועה ביניהם ומסתלק אלא דניחא ליה למיפרך דרבא אדרבא:

והאמר רבא הכל מודים בשנים שהפקידו אצל רועה. פרש"י זה טלה אחד וזה שני טלאים שמניח ביניהם ומסתלק והתם כשני כריכות נינהו אפי' הפקידו זה בפני זה דדבר הנראה מי הביא אחד ומי הביא שנים אבל במעות לא היה לו להבחין בין לרור גדול ללרור קטן וקשה דמתני' מסתמא איירי אפילו זה הפקיד מאתים בב' כיסין וזה מנה בכיס אחד ותו דלמא איירי רבא בב' שהפקידו שני טלאים זה כחוש וזה שמן דהוי כמעות דלא הוה ליה למידק אי נמי בשנים שהפקידו שני טלאים ומת אחד מהם וכל אחד אומר שהמת של חבירו דכי האי גוונא איירי מתניתין דהתם בפרק שני דבכורות (דף יז: ושם) אלא יש לומר דאפי' הפקידו טלאים זה בפני זה הוה ליה למידק דלא שייך למימר אתון לא קפידיתון משום דלא יוכלו לתקן דאפי' הפקידו זה שלא בפני זה יראה חבירו הטלאים כשהולכים במרעה ושואל של מי הם אבל במעות שהיה יכול להפקיד שלא בפני חבירו יכול הנפקד לומר אתון לא קפידיתון כל שכן דלא הוה לי למידק:

שלא מדעתו. לאו דוקא שלא מדעתו אלא כלומר שלא בראייתו של רועה דהשתא לא הוה ליה למידק:

שמא



מ א מיי' פ"ד מהל' גזלה ואבדה הל' ט סמג עשין עג טוש"ע ח"מ סי' שסה סעי' א:

מא ב מיי' פ"ה מהל' נחלות הל' ו סמג עשין לו טוש"ע ח"מ סי' רפ סעי' י:

מב ג ד מיי' פ"ה מהל' שאלה ופקדון הל' ד סמג עשין פח טוש"ע ח"מ סי' ש סעי' ד:

**רבינו חננאל**

שמכל מקום השבתה הגזילה לנגזל עצמו. אמר רב ספק הינוח לכתחילה לא יטול ואם נטל לא יחזיר אמר רב ספרא תני ויניח.



א) לעיל כה:, ב) [יבמות קיח:], ג) בבא בתרא קנח: [ע"ש], ד) דלמא ר' טרפון היא ס"א, ה) בבא קמא קג:, ו) ס"א ל"ג, ז) בכורות יח:.

**הגהות הב"ח**

(א) תוס' ד"ה מודה וכו' כב"ה דקאמר תאבני מתי תבא לרת: (ב) ד"ה ומי כו' כדמשמע לשון הודה מפי עלמו הא:

**ליקוטי רש"י**

ספק הינוח. בדבר שאין בו סימן וכ"ש ודאי הינוח. לכתחלה לא יטול. דאי שקלת לה ליכא למרייהו סימנין למיתב בהו ויפסיד הלכך לא יטול והבעלים יזכרו ויבאו ויטלוס. ואם נטל לא יחזיר. דהא ליכא דיהיב סימנא [לעיל כה:]. נפל הבית עליו ועל אמו. כגון שנפל הבית על רחל אשת יעקב באלמנותה ועל יוסף בנה מיעקב ולא היה לה עוד בן מיעקב ולא מאיש אחר. יורשי הבן. כגון ראובן בן יעקב מלאה טוען כל הנכסים ואומר רחל מתה תחילה וירש יוסף את כל נכסיה ואח"כ מת הוא וירשנו כל הנכסים. ויורשי האם אומרים. כגון אחיה מאביה אומרים הבן מת ראשון והיא מתה אחרונה וירשנו כל נכסיה. ואמר ר"ע מודה אני בזו כו'. משום דנקט תנא קמא לישנא דמודים אמר איהו נמי מודה אני כלומר ואני מודה וחולק עליך דלדברי ב"ה נמי אמרינן הכא נכסים בחזקתם [רשב"ם ב"ב קנח:].

אף בראשונה הלכה כמותו או אין הלכה כמותו אמר ליה חלוק היה ר' יוסי אף בראשונה והלכה כמותו אף בראשונה אתמר נמי אמר ר' אלעזר חלוק היה ר' יוסי אף בראשונה והלכה כמותו אף בראשונה ור' יוחנן אמר מודה היה ר' יוסי בראשונה שכבר שילם שילם אין לא שילם לא והאמר (א) ר' חייא בר אבא א"ר יוחנן לא שילם שילם ממש אלא כיון שאמר הריני משלם אע"פ שלא שילם אימא מודה היה ר' יוסי בראשונה שכבר אמר הריני משלם:

**מתני'** [א] אמר לשנים גזלתי לאחד מכם מנה ואיני יודע איזה מכם או אביו של אחד מכם הפקיד לי מנה ואיני יודע איזה הוא נותן לזה מנה ולזה מנה שהודה מפי עצמו (ג) [ב] שנים שהפקידו אצל אחד זה מנה וזה מאתים זה אומר שלי מאתים וזה אומר שלי מאתים נותן לזה מנה ולזה מנה והשאר יהא מונח עד שיבא אליהו (ג) א"ר יוסי א"כ מה הפסיד הרמאי ° אלא הכל יהא מונח עד שיבא אליהו [ג] וכן שני כלים אחד יפה מנה ואחד יפה אלף זוז זה אומר יפה שלי וזה אומר יפה שלי נותן את הקטן לאחד מהן ומתוך הגדול נותן דמי קטן לשני והשאר יהא מונח עד שיבא אליהו א"ר יוסי א"כ מה הפסיד הרמאי אלא הכל יהא מונח עד שיבא אליהו:

**גמ'** אלמא מספיקא מפקינן ממונא ולא אמרינן אוקי ממונא בחזקת מריה ורמינהי שנים שהפקידו אצל אחד זה מנה וזה מאתים זה אומר שלי מאתים וזה אומר שלי מאתים נותן לזה מנה ולזה מנה והשאר יהא מונח עד שיבא אליהו א"ל ° פקדון אגזל קא רמית גזל דעבד איסורא קנסוהו רבנן פקדון דלא עבד איסורא לא קנסוהו רבנן ורמי פקדון אפקדון ורמי גזל אגזל פקדון אפקדון דקתני רישא או אביו של אחד מכם הפקיד אצלי מנה ואיני יודע איזה הוא נותן לזה מנה ולזה מנה ורמינהי שנים שהפקידו וכו' אמר רבא [ד] רישא נעשה כמי שהפקידו לו בשני כריכות דהוה ליה למידק (ה) סיפא נעשה כמי שהפקידו לו בכרך אחד דלא הוה ליה למידק כגון דאפקידו תרוייהו בהדי הדדי בחד זימנא דאמר להו אנת גופייכו לא קפדיתו אהדדי אנא קפידנא ורמי גזל אגזל קתני הכא אמר לשנים גזלתי לאחד מכם מנה ואיני יודע איזה מכם או אביו של אחד מכם הפקיד לי מנה ואיני יודע איזהו נותן לזה מנה ולזה מנה ורמינהי (ד) גזל אחד מחמשה ואינו יודע איזה מהן גזל זה אומר אותי גזל וזה אומר אותי גזל מניח גזילה בינידם ומסתלק דברי ר"ט אלמא מספיקא לא מפקינן ממונא ואמרינן (ה) אוקים ממונא בחזקת מריה וממאי דמתני' דהכא ר"ט היא (ו) דקתני עלה דההיא מודה ר"ט באומר לשנים גזלתי לאחד מכם מנה ואיני יודע איזה מכם שנותן לזה מנה ולזה מנה התם דקא תבעי ליה הכא [ו] בבא לצאת ידי שמים דיקא נמי דקתני שהודה מפי עצמו שמע מינה אמר מר התם דקא תבעי ליה והלה מה טוען רב יהודה אמר רב הלה שותק רב מתנה אמר רב הלה

צווח

---

אף בראשונה. בשילם ולא רצה לישבע כילד זה נותן לתוך כיסו כפילו של זה אלא יחזיר הכפל לבעלים: שכבר שילם. קודם שנמלא הגנב וקנה כפל כדאמר מעיקרא אדעתא דהכי אתאי לידיה: **מתני'** שהודה מפי עצמו. הואיל והודה מפי עלמו ובגמ' מפרש טעמא מה הוא: זה אומר מאתים שלי. לאחר זמן כשבאו ליטול פקדון: מה הפסיד הרמאי. א"כ לא יודה לעולם על האמת: מתוך הגדול. ישברנו: **גמ'** מספיקא מפקי' ממונא. דקתני נותן לזה מנה ולזה מנה: ולא אמרינן. כשזה תובע וזה אומר איני יודע אם לך אם לחברך אוקי ממונא בחזקת נתבע זה שלא נפסידנו ממונו ויהא מונח עד שיבא אליהו: רישא. דחד גברא הפקיד אצלו והוה ליה כשנים שהפקידו אצלו בשני כריכות כלומר זה שלא בפני זה דה"ל למידק מי הפקיד אצלו מנה ומי מאתים: סיפא. שהפקידו לו שניהם זה בפני זה ה"ל כמי שנאמנים זה על זה להפקיד שני פקדונותם בצרור אחד דלית ליה למידק מה יש לזה בתוכו ומה יש לחבירו ואע"ג דלא כרך אחד הוה מיהו כיון שהפקידו זה בפני זה גילו דעתן שלא חשדו זה את זה לומר שמא חבירו יתבע המאתים: ומתני' דהכא ממאי דר"ט היא. דתקשי לך דלמא ר"ע היא דפליג נמי בההיא ואומר לא זו הדרך מוליאתו מידי עבירה עד שישלם גזילה לכל אחד ואחד: דקתני עלה דההיא כו'. אלמא מודה ר"ט בהא ומאי שנא: ומשנינן התם דקתבעי ליה. והוא אין חפץ ליתן אלא מן הדין ומספיקא לית לן לחיוביה לכל חד וחד: הכא בבא לצאת ידי שמים. מאליו בא לימלך מה יעשה ולא יענש דהשתא ודאי אמרינן ידי שמים לא יצאת עד שתתן לשניהם שאם תהא מונחת עד שיבא אליהו נמצא הנגזל מפסיד על ידך: דיקא נמי. דטעמא דמתני' בבא לצאת ידי שמים מן העונש ולא מן הדין מדתלי טעמא בהודה מפי עצמו שלא היה אדם תובעו כלום משמע שהוא בא לימלך: והלה מה טוען. לכל אחד דקתני מניח גזילה ביניהם ומסתלק:

צווח

---

**גזל** מחמשה. לא שייך הך פלוגתא לפלוגתא דרבי יוחנן ורב הונא דפ' השולח (לקמן דף לז:) בברי ושמא דאפי' לר"ט דאמר מניח גזילה ביניהם היינו משום דיודע בודאי שלא גזל לכולם רק לאחד אבל ברי ושמא יודה דברי עדיף ואפי' לר"ע דאמר ישלם לכל אחד ואחד היינו משום שיודע בודאי שהוא חייב לאחד מהם אבל גבי ברי ושמא יודה דפטור שאינו יודע שהוא חייב כלל:

**דקתני** עלה ומודה ר"ט. ° ה"ה דה"מ למפרך מברייתא אמאי מודה אלא ניחא ליה למפרך ממתניתין דיבמות אמתניתין (א) (ז):

**התם** דקא תבעי ליה הכא בבא לצאת ידי שמים. לכאורה נראה דהשתא לא צריך לשינויי קמאי דאין חילוק בין כרך אחד לב' כריכות ורישא דנותן מנה לזה ומנה לזה בבא לצאת ידי שמים וסיפא דקתבעי ליה יהא מונח אך מדלא קאמר אלא התם דקא תבעי ליה משמע דלא הדר משנוייא קמא וכן לקמן (ע"ב) דפריך נמי ומי אמר רבא בב' כריכות ה"ל למידק משמע דלא הדר ביה לכך נראה דכולה מתני' איירי בבא לצאת ידי שמים ולכך ברישא דהוה ליה למידק נותן לזה מנה ולזה מנה בבא לצאת ידי שמים וסיפא דבכרך אחד כיון דלא ה"ל למידק אפילו בבא לצאת ידי שמים אינו חייב ולרבי טרפון נקט ברישא אביו של אחד מכם ולא נקט אחד מכם לרבותא דאפילו שמא ושמא נותן לכל אחד ואחד בבא לצאת ידי שמים ולר"ע נקט אביו דמשמע שמא ושמא לכך אינו חייב אלא לצאת ידי שמים כדאמר לקמן (שם) דבשמא ושמא אינו חייב לכל אחד ואחד לר"ע מדינא ונקט אביו דאי הס עצמן הפקידו אם כן מסתמא תבעי ליה וה"ל ברי ושמא ואפילו מדינא חייבין לר"ע דמתניתין אתיא כר"ע נמי דקאמר לקמן (שם) ממאי דמתני' דהכא ר"ע היא ועוד דהלכה כר"ע מחבירו ובסיפא דלא נקט שני אבותיכם הפקידו לרבותא לא תני הכי דאע"ג דטענו ברי פטור אפילו לצאת ידי שמים ואפי' לר"ע כיון דלא פשע דלא הוה ליה למידק ולא מחייב ר"ע מדינא אלא בברי ושמא והיכא דהוה ליה למידק אבל בשמא ושמא אפי' בשני כריכות אינו חייב אלא לצאת ידי שמים והיכא דלא הוי ליה למידק פטור אפי' לצאת ידי שמים ואפילו בברי ושמא וא"ת דבפרק הגוזל קמא (ב"ק דף קג: ושם קד. ד"ה שכבר) קאמר מעשה בחסיד אחד שבא לפני ר"ט ואמר ליה הנח דמי מקח ביניהם וכי לא בעי חסיד לצאת ידי שמים וי"ל דר"ט אמר ליה שכך הדין (ח) וא"ת התם דפריך אמתניתין דקתני הגוזל מחבירו שוה פרוטה ונשבע לו יוליכנו אחריו אפילו למדי ומוקי כר"ט כו' ומאי איריא נשבע אפי' הודה נמי דתניא מודה ר"ט כו' ומאי פריך והא אוקמי' ברייתא דמודה ר"ט בבא לצאת ידי שמים ומתני' דהתם מיירי מדינא וי"ל דמתני' דהתם מיירי לצאת ידי שמים להביא קרבן וקא אמר אם רוצה להביא קרבן צריך להביא גזלו למדי דתנן הביא אשמו עד שלא הביא גזלו לא יצא לכך פריך דבלא שבועה ולא קרבן צריך להביא גזלו למדי אם רוצה לצאת ידי שמים:

מודה

---

מסורת הש"ס

א) [לעיל לד.], ב) [בבא בתרא לד:], ג) לעיל ג., ד) בבא קמא קג: יבמות קיח:, ה) [קדושין מה: וש"נ], ו) דלמא ר"ע היא. ס"א, ז) [וע"ע תוס' שבת עט: ד"ה והא], ח) [ובתוס' דפרק הגוזל שם כתבו עוד א"כ אפילו לצאת ידי שמים אין חייב לר' טרפון אלא בגזול אבל בפקדון ומקח דלא עשה איסורא לא כו' ע"ש] ועיין מהרש"א.

הגהות הב"ח

(א) תוס' ד"ה דקתני וכו' אמתניתין דהכא הס"ד:

גליון הש"ס

מתני' אלא הכל יהא מונח. עיין גיטין דף מד: תוס' ד"ה נטייבה: גמרא פקדון אגזל קרמית. עיין גיטין דף כח. תוס' ד"ה תרומה: תוס' ד"ה דקתני וכו' ה"ה דהו"מ למפרך. וכזה שבת דף עט: ועיין בתוס' שם ד"ה והא:

ליקוטי רש"י

א"כ מה הפסיד הרמאי. ולמה יודה הרי קיבל את שלו [לעיל ג.]. לא יבא להודות דהא לא מפסיד מידי [רשב"ם ב"ב צד:]. אלא הכל יהא מונח וכו'. ויפסיד הרמאי [לעיל ג.]. מניח גזילה ביניהם ומסתלק. ולא בעי לאמטויי לידיה וסגי במניח לפניו שהרי הבעלים שם הוא [ב"ק קג:]. שהודה מפי עצמו. ובא לצאת ידי שמים ואע"ג דבי דינא לא מלי מחייבי ליה אלא מניח לפניהם מיהו ידי עונש אין יוצא עד שישלם לשניהם דהא לאו לבעלים אהדריה [ב"ק קד.].

---

עין משפט
נר מצוה

לה א מיי' פ"ד מהל' גזלה ואבדה הל' י סמג עשין עג טוש"ע ח"מ סי' שסה סעי' ב:

לו ב מיי' פ"ה מהל' שאלה ופקדון הל' ד ועי' במ"מ סמג עשין פח טוש"ע ח"מ סי' ש סעי' א:

לז ג מיי' שם טוש"ע שם סעי' ב:

לח ד ה מיי' שם טוש"ע שם סעי' א:

לט ו מיי' פ"ד מהל' גזלה ואבדה הל' י סמג עשין עג טוש"ע ח"מ סי' שסה סעי' ב:

רבינו חננאל

ואסיקנא שמואל אמר חלוק ר' יוסי אף בראשונה בהא דתנן למי משלם למי שהפקדון אצלו חולק עליו ר' יוסי ואומר אינו משלם אלא לבעל הפקדון ואין הלכה כשמואל דהא ר' יוחנן פליג עליה דהא בהדיא אמר ר' יוחנן מודה ר' יוסי בראשונה שאינו משלם אלא למי שהפקדון אצלו. וקיימא לן כר' יוחנן דסוגיין בעלמא שמואל ור"י הלכה כר' יוחנן וכל שכן ר' אלעזר דתלמיד קטן הוא לגבי ר' יוחנן: **מתני' אמר לשנים גזלתי אחד מכם מנה ואיני יודע איזהו נותן לזה מנה ולזה מנה.** ומקשי' עלה ומספיקא מפקינן ממונא וכו'. ורמינהי שנים שהפקידו אצל אחד זה מנה וזה מאתים וכו'. ודחי' פקדון אגזל קא רמית. ורמי פקדון אפקדון דתנן (בסיפא) [ברישא] דמתני' דהכא או אביו של אחד מכם הפקיד אצלי מנה נותן לזה מנה ולזה מנה שהודה מפי עצמו אימא סיפא דהא מתני' שנים שהפקידו אצל אחד כו'. ופריק רבא רישא היה לו בעת שהפקיד אצלו לומר לו מה שמך וכיון שלא דקדק לידע איזה מהן הוא המפקיד אצלו איהו אפסיד נפשיה לפיכך משלם לזה ולזה. סיפא כגון ששניהן הפקידו צרורותיהן ביחד וכל אחד רואה כי הצרור אחד גדול שיש בו מאתים והאחד קטן שאין בו אלא ק'. יכול למימר מי שהפקדון אצלו כיון דחזיתי דאין מקפיד בעל הצרור הגדול לומר דע כי הצרור הגדול שלי הוא והקטן לחבירו אמינא כיון דלא דייקי אהדדי מהימני לפיכך לא דקדקתי. תוב רמינן ארישא דמתני' דתנן בסוף יבמות גזל אחד מהן ואינו יודע אי זה מהן גזל מניח גזילה ביניהן ומסתלק דברי ר' טרפון וכו'. אלמא מספיקא לא מפקינן ממונא. ואסיק' מדקתני התם ומודה ר' טרפון באומר לשנים גזלתי לאחד מכם מנה ואיני יודע למי מכם שנותן לזה ק' ולזה ק' ש"מ מתני' דהכא ר' טרפון היא קשיין אהדדי. ופרקי' התם גבי גזל אחד מה' כשתובעין אותו [אמר] שמניח גזילה ביניהן ואומר להן הנה היא מונחת לפניכם מי מכם יברר שהיא שלו יטלנה אבל הכא במשנתינו בבא לצאת ידי שמים דקתני שהודה מפי עצמו ואין תובעין אותו אלא ב"ד (אמר) [אמרינן ליה] אין לך דרך לצאת ידי עבירה אלא אם תתן לזה ק' ולזה ק' שמכל

in a separate bundle, we treat it as if it were a single bundle, כְּגוֹן דְּאַפְקִידוּ תַּרְוַויְהוּ בַּהֲדֵי הֲדָדֵי בְּחַד זִימְנָא – because the Mishnah speaks of **a case in which the two of them deposited** their money **together at one time.**[14] דְּאָמַר לְהוּ – **In such a case [the *shomer*] may tell them,** when confronted with the conflicting claims, אַנְתְּ גּוּפַיְיכוּ לֹא קְפַדִיתוּ אַהֲדָדֵי – **"You yourselves were not particular with each other,** and did not specify who gave the larger bundle in order to protect yourselves from a fraudulent claim, אֲנָא קְפֵידְנָא – **should I have been particular** to notice the size of the bundle you each deposited?"[15] Since in this case the *shomer* was not negligent in failing to note the amount of each deposit, we do not require him to pay each depositor two hundred *zuz.*

The Gemara now explains the other contradiction (regarding theft):

וְרָמֵי גָּזֵל אַגָּזֵל – **And contrast** the case of **stolen property with** the other case of **stolen property.** קָתָנֵי הָכָא – **It was taught here** (in the first case of the Mishnah): אָמַר לִשְׁנַיִם – If [A THIEF] TOLD TWO [PEOPLE], גָּזַלְתִּי לְאֶחָד מִכֶּם מָנֶה – "I STOLE A *MANEH* FROM ONE OF YOU, וְאֵינִי יוֹדֵעַ אֵיזֶה מִכֶּם – BUT I DO NOT KNOW from WHICH OF YOU I stole it"; אוֹ – OR if a *shomer* told two people, אָבִיו שֶׁל אֶחָד מִכֶּם הִפְקִיד לִי מָנֶה – "THE FATHER OF ONE OF YOU DEPOSITED A *MANEH* WITH ME, וְאֵינִי יוֹדֵעַ אֵיזֶהוּ – BUT I DO NOT KNOW WHICH ONE HE WAS," נוֹתֵן לָזֶה מָנֶה וְלָזֶה מָנֶה – HE GIVES THIS ONE A *MANEH* AND THAT ONE A *MANEH.* וּרְמִינְהִי – **But contrast this** ruling with that of a Mishnah in *Yevamos:*[16] גָּזַל אֶחָד מֵחֲמִשָּׁה – IF SOMEONE STOLE from ONE OF FIVE [PEOPLE] וְאֵינוֹ יוֹדֵעַ אֵיזֶה מֵהֶן גָּזַל – AND HE DOES NOT KNOW from WHOM HE STOLE, זֶה אוֹמֵר אוֹתִי גָּזַל – and THIS ONE SAYS, "HE STOLE it FROM ME," וְזֶה אוֹמֵר אוֹתִי גָּזַל – AND THAT ONE SAYS, "HE STOLE it FROM ME," מַנִּיחַ גְּזֵילָה בֵּינֵיהֶם וּמִסְתַּלֵּק – [THE THIEF] PLACES THE STOLEN OBJECT BETWEEN THEM AND WITHDRAWS.[17] דִּבְרֵי רַבִּי טַרְפוֹן – These are THE WORDS OF R' TARFON.

The Gemara infers from this second Mishnah:

אַלְמָא מִסְפֵּיקָא לֹא מַפְּקִינַן מָמוֹנָא – **From that** which the thief need not pay each of the claimants, **it may be derived that we do not extract money out of doubt;** וְאַמְרִינַן אוֹקִים מָמוֹנָא בְּחֶזְקַת מָרֵיהּ – **rather, we say** that **the** contested **money remains in the possession of its** present **owner** (the thief). If so, why in our Mishnah must the thief pay both claimants?

This question assumes that R' Tarfon is in agreement with the ruling of our Mishnah. The Gemara now demonstrates this point:

וּמִמַּאי דְּמַתְנִיתִין דְּהָכָא רַבִּי טַרְפוֹן הִיא – **And from what** do you conclude **that the Mishnah here is** reflective of the opinion of **R' Tarfon?** Perhaps our Mishnah accords with R' Akiva, who disagrees in that Mishnah with R' Tarfon and rules there too that the thief must pay each of the claimants![18]

דְּקָתָנֵי עֲלָהּ דְּהַהִיא – **For it was taught in a Baraisa concerning that** Mishnah in *Yevamos:* מוֹדֶה רַבִּי טַרְפוֹן – R' TARFON CONCEDES בְּאוֹמֵר לִשְׁנַיִם – that WHEN [A THIEF] TELLS TWO [PEOPLE], גָּזַלְתִּי לְאֶחָד מִכֶּם מָנֶה – "I STOLE A *MANEH* FROM ONE OF YOU, וְאֵינִי יוֹדֵעַ אֵיזֶה מִכֶּם – AND I DO NOT KNOW from WHICH OF YOU I stole it," שֶׁנּוֹתֵן לָזֶה מָנֶה וְלָזֶה מָנֶה – THAT HE GIVES THIS ONE A *MANEH* AND THAT ONE A *MANEH.* Thus, we see that R' Tarfon agrees with the ruling of our Mishnah.[19] If so, why does he not require the thief to pay each of the five claimants in the case of the Mishnah in *Yevamos?*[20]

The Gemara answers:

הָתָם – The Mishnah **there** in *Yevamos* refers to דְּקָא תָּבְעֵי לֵיהּ – **where [the claimants] sue [the thief]** for payment, but he wants to pay only the actual victim. Since his obligation to each claimant is doubtful, he need not pay all five. הָכָא – **Here,** however, the Mishnah refers to a case בְּבָא לָצֵאת יְדֵי שָׁמַיִם – **where [the thief] comes** on his own to inquire how **to fulfill his Heavenly obligation** to repay what he stole and avoid punishment. We advise him that he cannot avoid being held accountable in the eyes of Heaven until he pays each claimant.[21]

The Gemara cites support for this answer:

דַּיְקָא נַמִי – **This** explanation **is also** supported **by** a **precise** reading of the Mishnah, דְּקָתָנֵי שֶׁהוֹדָה מִפִּי עַצְמוֹ – **for [the Tanna] teaches** that the thief must pay both parties BECAUSE HE ACKNOWLEDGED the debt HIMSELF. שְׁמַע מִינָּה – We can **infer from this** that the Mishnah is not discussing a case where two people made a claim against him, but rather a case where the thief came voluntarily to inquire how to avoid Heavenly punishment.

The Gemara now analyzes the Mishnah in *Yevamos* in light of the explanation given above:

אָמַר מַר – **The master said:** הָתָם דְּקָא תָּבְעֵי לֵיהּ – The Mishnah **there** refers to **where [the claimants] sue [the thief]** for payment. וְהָלָה מַה טוֹעֵן – **Now what does that** thief **claim** to each of them in response?[22] רַב יְהוּדָה אָמַר רַב – **Rav Yehudah said** in the name of **Rav:** הָלָה שׁוֹתֵק – **That** thief **remains silent.** רַב מַתְּנָה אָמַר רַב – **Rav Masnah said** in the name of **Rav:** הָלָה – **That** thief

NOTES

than his due. Hence, the *shomer* did not have to ascertain the exact amount of each deposit (*Rashi*).

14. Although their money was placed in separate bundles, the two men demonstrated mutual trust by making their deposits with the *shomer* in each other's presence — without asking the *shomer* to take notice of which bundle was larger and write that person's name on it. Since the one with the larger bundle (containing the larger number of coins) was not concerned that the other one would later fraudulently claim it was his, the *shomer* was justified in not ascertaining the amount that each deposited (*Rashi,* as explained by *Rashba*).

15. The difference in size between a bundle containing 100 *zuz* and one containing 200 *zuz* is not that great as to be immediately obvious to anyone who sees them (*Rashba*).

16. *Yevamos* 118b.

17. The Gemara below (37b) will explain that, in fact, the thief must watch the object until the matter is resolved.

18. R' Akiva disputes R' Tarfon in that Mishnah and says, "This is not the way that extricates [him] from sin, until he pays [the value of the stolen object] to each of them."

19. R' Tarfon's ruling in this Baraisa is identical to the ruling of our Mishnah.

20. This question could have been posed directly from this Baraisa to that Mishnah there; it was not necessary to cite our Mishnah (and then prove from the Baraisa that our Mishnah follows R' Tarfon). However, the questioner preferred to point out an inconsistency between two Mishnahs (*Tosafos*).

21. If the thief retains the stolen object until Elijah resolves the matter (see Gemara below, 37b), the rightful claimant will be denied the use of his property until then. For this the thief can be held accountable by Heaven. Only by paying all claimants can he escape Heavenly retribution (*Rashi*).

*Tosafos* explain that according to this answer, the entire Mishnah — even the rulings on deposits — refers to where the *shomer* wants to avoid Heavenly retribution for wrongly withholding another's property; they are not actual statements of the law. Hence, in those cases of deposit where he is expected to note what amount he received and from whom (i.e. in the beginning of the Mishnah), the *shomer* must pay both claimants if he wishes to avoid Heavenly retribution. In those cases where he is not expected to pay particular attention to such details (i.e. the Mishnah's second case, where two depositors came together, one with 100 *zuz* and one with 200), the *shomer* is not held accountable even in the eyes of Heaven, and therefore he makes no payment at all, but holds the money for them until it is determined who deserves it. Cf. *Rosh* with *Pilpula Charifta* §7; *Tur, Choshen Mishpat* 300.

22. I.e. under what circumstances may he "place the stolen object between the claimants and withdraw" — thereby fulfilling his legal obligations? (*Rashi*).

מסורת הש"ס

א) [לעיל לד.], ב) [בבא בתרא לד:], ג) לעיל ג., ד) בבא קמא קג: יבמות קיח., ה) [קדושין מה: וש"נ], ו) דלמא ר"ע היא. ס"א, ז) [וע"ע תוס' שבת עט: ד"ה והא], ח) [ובתוס' דפרק הגוזל שם כתבו עוד א"נ אפילו לצאת ידי שמים אין חייב לר' טרפון אלא בגזול אבל בפקדון ומקח דלא עשה איסורא לא כו' ע"ש] ועיין מהרש"א.

הגהות הב"ח

(א) תוס' ד"ה דקתני וכו' אמתניתין דהכא הס"ד:

גליון הש"ס

מתני' אלא הכל יהא מונח. עיין גיטין דף מד: תוס' ד"ה נטייבה: גמרא פקדון אגזל קרמית. עיין גיטין דף כח. תוס' ד"ה תרומה: תוס' ד"ה דקתני וכו' ה"ה דהו"מ למפרך. וכזה שבת דף עט: ועיין בתוס' שם ד"ה והא:

ליקוטי רש"י

א"כ מה הפסיד הרמאי. ולמה יודה הרי קיבל את שלו [לעיל ג.]. לא יבא להודות דהא לא מפסיד מידי [רשב"ם ב"ב צד:]. אלא הכל יהא מונח וכו'. ויפסיד הרמאי [לעיל ג.]. מניח גזילה ביניהם ומסתלק. ולא בעי לאמטויי לידיה וסגי במניח לפניו שהרי הבעלים שם הוא [ב"ק קג:]. שהודה מפי עצמו. ובא לצאת ידי שמים ועפ"י דבר דינא לא מלי מחייבי ליה אלא מניח לפניהם מיהו ידי עונש אין יוצא עד שישלם לשניהם דהא לגו אהדדיה [ב"ק קד.].

רש"י

אף בראשונה. בשילם ולא רצה לישבע כיצד זה נותן לתוך כיסו כפילו של זה אלא יחזיר הכפל לבעלים: שכבר שילם. קודם שנמצא הגנב וקנה כפל כדאמר מעיקרא אדעתא דהכי אתאי לידיה: מתני' שהודה מפי עצמו. הואיל והודה מפי עצמו ובגמ' מפרש טעמא מה הוא: זה אומר מאתים שלי. לאחר זמן כשבאו ליטול פקדון: מה הפסיד הרמאי. א"כ לא יודה לעולם על האמת: מתוך הגדול. ישברנו: גמ' מספיקא מפקי' ממונא. דקתני נותן לזה מנה ולזה מנה: ולא אמרינן. כשזה תובע וזה אומר איני יודע אם לך אם לחברך אוקי ממונא בחזקת נתבע זה שלא נפסידנו ממונו ויהא מונח עד שיבא אליהו: רישא. דחד גברא הפקיד אצלו והוה ליה כשנים שהפקידו אצלו בשני כריכות כלומר זה שלא בפני זה דה"ל למידק מי הפקיד אצלו מנה ומי מאתים: סיפא. שהפקידו לו שניהם זה בפני זה ה"ל כמי שנאמנים זה על זה להפקיד שני פקדונותם בצרור אחד דלית ליה למידק מה יש לזה בתוכו ומה יש לחבירו ואע"ג דלא כרך אחד הוה מיהו כיון שהפקידו זה בפני זה גילו דעתן שלא חשדו זה את זה לומר שמא חבירו יתבע המאתים: ומתני' דהכא ממאי דר"ט היא. דתקשי לך דלמא ר"ע היא דפליג נמי בההיא ואומר לא זו הדרך מוציאתו מידי עבירה עד שישלם גזילה לכל אחד ואחד: דקתני עלה דההיא כו'. אלמא מודה ר"ט בהא ומאי שנא: ומשנינן התם דקתבעי ליה. והוא אין חפץ ליתן אלא מן הדין ומספיקא לית לן לחיוביה לכל חד וחד: הכא בבא לצאת ידי שמים. מאליו בא לימלך מה יעשה ולא יענש דהשתא ודאי אמרינן ידי שמים לא יצאת עד שתתן לשניהם שאם תהא מונחת עד שיבא אליהו נמצא הנגזל מפסיד על ידך: דיקא נמי. דטעמא דמתני' בבא לצאת ידי שמים מן העונש ולא מן הדין מדתלי טעמא בהודה מפי עצמו שלא היה אדם תובעו כלום משמע שהוא בא לימלך: והלה מה טוען. לכל אחד דקתני מניח גזילה ביניהם ומסתלק: צווח

אף בראשונה הלכה כמותו או אין הלכה כמותו אמר ליה חלוק היה ר' יוסי אף בראשונה והלכה כמותו אף בראשונה אתמר נמי אמר ר' אלעזר חלוק היה ר' יוסי אף בראשונה והלכה כמותו אף בראשונה ור' יוחנן אמר מודה היה ר' יוסי בראשונה שכבר שילם שילם אין לא שילם לא והאמר א) ר' חייא בר אבא א"ר יוחנן לא שילם שילם ממש אלא כיון שאמר הריני משלם אע"פ שלא שילם אימא מודה היה ר' יוסי בראשונה שכבר אמר הריני משלם: מתני' א אמר לשנים גזלתי לאחד מכם מנה ואיני יודע איזה מכם או אביו של אחד מכם הפקיד לי מנה ואיני יודע איזה הוא נותן לזה מנה ולזה מנה שהודה מפי עצמו ג) ב שנים שהפקידו אצל אחד זה מנה וזה מאתים זה אומר שלי מאתים וזה אומר שלי מאתים נותן לזה מנה ולזה מנה והשאר יהא מונח עד שיבא אליהו ג) א"ר יוסי א"כ מה הפסיד הרמאי ° אלא הכל יהא מונח עד שיבא אליהו ג וכן שני כלים אחד יפה מנה ואחד יפה אלף זוז זה אומר יפה שלי וזה אומר יפה שלי נותן את הקטן לאחד מהן ומתוך הגדול נותן דמי קטן לשני והשאר יהא מונח עד שיבא אליהו א"ר יוסי א"כ מה הפסיד הרמאי אלא הכל יהא מונח עד שיבא אליהו: גמ' אלמא מספיקא מפקינן ממונא ולא אמרינן אוקי ממונא בחזקת מריה ורמינהי שנים שהפקידו אצל אחד זה מנה וזה מאתים זה אומר שלי מאתים וזה אומר שלי מאתים נותן לזה מנה ולזה מנה והשאר יהא מונח עד שיבא אליהו א"ל ° פקדון אגזל קא רמית גזל דעבד איסורא קנסוהו רבנן פקדון דלא עבד איסורא לא קנסוהו רבנן ורמי פקדון אפקדון ורמי גזל אגזל פקדון אפקדון דקתני רישא או אביו של אחד מכם הפקיד אצלי מנה ואיני יודע איזה הוא נותן לזה מנה ולזה מנה ורמינהי שנים שהפקידו וכו' אמר רבא ד רישא נעשה כמי שהפקידו לו בשני כריכות דהוה ליה למידק ה סיפא נעשה כמי שהפקידו לו בכרך אחד דלא הוה ליה למידק כגון דאפקידו תרווייהו בהדי הדדי בחד זימנא דאמר להו אנת גופייכו לא קפידיתו אהדדי אנא קפידנא ורמי גזל אגזל קתני הכא אמר לשנים גזלתי לאחד מכם מנה ואיני יודע איזה מכם או אביו של אחד מכם הפקיד לי מנה ואיני יודע איזהו נותן לזה מנה ולזה מנה ורמינהי ד) גזל אחד מחמשה ואינו יודע איזה מהן גזל זה אומר אותי גזל וזה אומר אותי גזל מניח גזילה בינידם ומסתלק דברי ר"ט אלמא מספיקא לא מפקינן ממונא ואמרינן ה) אוקים ממונא בחזקת מריה וממאי דמתני' דהכא ר"ט היא ו) דקתני עלה דההיא מודה ר"ט באומר לשנים גזלתי לאחד מכם מנה ואיני יודע איזה מכם שנותן לזה מנה ולזה מנה התם דקא תבעי ליה הכא ו בבא לצאת ידי שמים דיקא נמי דקתני שהודה מפי עצמו שמע מינה אמר מר התם דקא תבעי ליה והלה מה טוען רב יהודה אמר רב הלה שותק רב מתנה אמר רב הלה צווח

תוספות

גזל מחמשה. לא שייך כאן פלוגתא לפלוגתא דרבי יוחנן ורב הונא דפ' השואל (לקמן דף לז:) בברי ושמא דאפי' לר"ט דאמר מניח גזילה ביניהם היינו משום דיודע בודאי שלא גזל לכולם רק לאחד אבל ברי ושמא יודה דברי עדיף ואפי' לר"ע דאמר ישלם לכל אחד ואחד היינו משום שיודע בודאי שהוא חייב לאחד מהם אבל גבי ברי ושמא יודה דפטור שאינו יודע שהוא חייב כלל:

דקתני עלה ומודה ר"ט. ° ה"ה דה"מ למפרך מברייתא אמאי מודה אלא ניחא ליה למפרך ממתניתין דיבמות אמתניתין (א) ז):

התם דקא תבעי ליה הכא בבא לצאת ידי שמים. לכאורה נראה דהשתא לא צריך לשינויי קמאי דאין חילוק בין כרך אחד לב' כריכות ורישא דנותן מנה לזה ומנה לזה בבא לצאת ידי שמים וסיפא דקתבעי ליה יהא מונח אך מדלא קאמר אלא התם דקא תבעי ליה משמע דלא הדר משנוייא קמא וכן לקמן (ע"ב) דפריך נמי ומי אמר רבא בב' כריכות ה"ל למידק משמע דלא הדר ביה לכך נראה דכולה מתני' איירי בבא לצאת ידי שמים ולכך ברישא דהוה ליה למידק נותן לזה מנה ולזה מנה בבא לצאת ידי שמים וסיפא דבכרך אחד כיון דלא ה"ל למידק אפילו בבא לצאת ידי שמים אינו חייב ולרבי טרפון נקט ברישא אביו של אחד מכם ולא נקט אחד מכם לרבותא דאפילו שמא ושמא נותן לכל אחד ואחד בבא לצאת ידי שמים ולר"ע נקט אביו דמשמע שמא ושמא לכך אינו חייב אלא לצאת ידי שמים כדאמר לקמן (שם) דבשמא ושמא אינו חייב לכל אחד ואחד לר"ע מדינא ונקט אביו דאי הם עצמן הפקידו אם כן מסתמא תבעי ליה וה"ל ברי ושמא ואפילו מדינא חייבין לר"ע דמתניתין אתיא כר"ע נמי דקאמר לקמן (שם) ממאי דמתני' דהכא ר"ע היא ועוד דהלכה כר"ע מחבירו ובסיפא דלא נקט שני אבותיכם הפקידו לרבותא לא תני הכי דאע"ג דטענו ברי פטור אפילו לצאת ידי שמים ואפי' לר"ע כיון דלא פשע דלא הוה ליה למידק ולא מחייב ר"ע מדינא אלא בברי ושמא והיכא דהוה ליה למידק אבל בשמא ושמא אפי' בשני כריכות אינו חייב אלא לצאת ידי שמים והיכא דלא הוי ליה למידק פטור אפי' לצאת ידי שמים ואפילו בברי ושמא וא"ת דבפרק הגוזל קמא (ב"ק דף קג: ושם קד. ד"ה שכבר) קאמר מעשה בחסיד אחד שבא לפני ר"ט ואמר ליה הנח דמי מקחך ביניהם וכי לא בעי חסיד לצאת ידי שמים וי"ל דר"ט אמר ליה שכך הדין ח) וא"ת התם דפריך אמתניתין דקתני הגוזל מחבירו שוה פרוטה ונשבע לו יוליכנו אחריו אפילו למדי ומוקי כר"ט כו' ומאי איריא נשבע אפי' הודה נמי דתניא מודה ר"ט כו' ומאי פריך והא אוקמי' ברייתא דמודה ר"ט בבא לצאת ידי שמים ומתני' דהתם מיירי מדינא וי"ל דמתני' דהתם מיירי לצאת ידי שמים להביא קרבן וקא אמר אם רוצה להביא קרבן צריך להביא גזלו למדי דתנן הביא אשמו עד שלא הביא גזלו לא יצא לכך פריך דבלא שבועה ולא קרבן צריך להביא גזלו למדי אם רוצה לצאת ידי שמים:

מודה

עין משפט נר מצוה

לה א מיי' פ"ד מהל' גזלה ואבדה הל' י סמג עשין עג טוש"ע ח"מ סי' שסה סעי' ב:

לו ב מיי' פ"ה מהל' שאלה ופקדון הל' ד ועי' בה"מ סמג עשין פח טוש"ע ח"מ סי' ש סעי' א:

לז ג מיי' שם טוש"ע שם סעי' ב:

לח ד ה מיי' שם טוש"ע שם סעי' א:

לט ו מיי' פ"ד מהל' גזלה ואבדה הל' י סמג עשין עג טוש"ע ח"מ סי' שסה סעי' ב:

רבינו חננאל

ואסיקנא שמואל אמר חלוק ר' יוסי אף בראשונה בהא דתנן למי משלם למי שהפקדון אצלו חולק עליו ר' יוסי ואומר אינו משלם אלא לבעל הפקדון ואין הלכה כשמואל דהא ר' יוחנן פליג עליה דהא בהדיא אמר ר' יוחנן מודה ר' יוסי בראשונה שאינו משלם אלא למי שהפקדון אצלו. וקיימא לן כר' יוחנן דסוגיין בעלמא שמואל ור"י הלכה כר' יוחנן וכל שכן ר' אלעזר דתלמיד קטן הוא לגבי ר' יוחנן: מתני' אמר לשנים גזלתי אחד מכם מנה ואיני יודע איזהו נותן לזה מנה ולזה מנה. ומקשי' עלה ומספיקא מפקינן ממונא וכו'. ורמינהי שנים שהפקידו אצל אחד זה מנה וזה מאתים וכו'. ודחי' פקדון אגזל קא רמית. ורמי פקדון אפקדון דתנן (בסיפא) [ברישא] דמתני' דהכא או אביו של אחד מכם הפקיד אצלי מנה נותן לזה מנה ולזה מנה שהודה מפי עצמו אימא סיפא דהא מתני' שנים שהפקידו אצל אחד כו'. ופריק רבא רישא היה לו בעת שהפקיד אצלו לומר לו מה שמך וכיון שלא דקדק לידע איזה מהן הוא המפקיד אצלו איהו אפסיד נפשיה לפיכך משלם לזה ולזה. סיפא כגון ששניהן הפקידו צרורותיהן ביחד וכל אחד רואה כי הצרור אחד גדול שיש בו מאתים והאחד קטן שאין בו אלא ק'. יכול למימר מי שהפקדון אצלו כיון דחזיתי דאין מקפיד בעל הצרור הגדול לומר דע כי הצרור הגדול שלי הוא והקטן לחבירו אמינא כיון דלא דייקי אהדדי מהימני לפיכך לא דקדקתי. תוב רמינן ארישא דמתני' דתנן בסוף יבמות גזל אחד מהן ואינו יודע אי זה מהן גזל מניח גזילה ביניהן ומסתלק דברי ר' טרפון וכו'. אלמא מספיקא לא מפקינן ממונא. ואסיק' מדקתני התם ומודה ר' טרפון באומר לשנים גזלתי לאחד מכם מנה ואיני יודע למי מכם שנותן לזה ק' ולזה ק' ש"מ מתני' דהכא ר' טרפון היא קשיין אהדדי. ופרקי' התם גבי גזל אחד מה' כשתובעין אותו [אמר] שמניח גזילה ביניהן ואומר להן הנה היא מונחת לפניכם מי מכם יברר שהיא שלו יטלנה אבל הכא במשנתינו בבא לצאת ידי שמים דקתני שהודה מפי עצמו ואין תובעין אותו אלא ב"ד (אמר) [אמרינן ליה] אין לך דרך לצאת ידי עבירה אלא אם תתן לזה ק' ולזה ק' שמכל

אֵלִיָּהוּ – **and the remainder** of the more expensive utensil **should be put away** in the *shomer's* care **until Elijah arrives.**[8] אָמַר רַבִּי יוֹסֵי – **R' Yose said:** אִם כֵּן – **If it is so** that each claimant receives at least the equivalent of his original deposit, מַה הִפְסִיד הָרַמַּאי – **what has the dishonest [person] lost?** Since he stands to lose nothing, he will never admit the truth! אֶלָּא – **Rather,** הַכֹּל יְהֵא מוּנָּח עַד שֶׁיָּבֹא אֵלִיָּהוּ – **everything** [i.e. both utensils] **should be put away** in the *shomer's* care **until Elijah arrives.**

**Gemara** The Gemara notes an inconsistency between the first and second rulings of the Mishnah. The Gemara begins by pointing out the legal principle implied by the Mishnah's first ruling, that if he is not sure which of two parties he owes the *maneh* to, he pays a *maneh* to each:

אַלְמָא מִסְּפֵיקָא מַפְּקִינָן מָמוֹנָא – **From that** which the thief must pay a *maneh* to each of the possible victims in the first case of the Mishnah, **it may be seen that we extract money** even **out of doubt,** וְלֹא אָמְרִינָן אוֹקִי מָמוֹנָא בְּחֶזְקַת מָרֵיהּ – **and we do not say** that **the money remains in the possession of its** present **owner,** the defendant, until Elijah comes and clarifies the matter.[9]

וּרְמִינְהִי – **But** the scholars **contrasted** this ruling with the ruling in the next case in the Mishnah: שְׁנַיִם שֶׁהִפְקִידוּ אֵצֶל אֶחָד – IF TWO [PEOPLE] DEPOSITED MONEY WITH ONE *shomer,* זֶה מָנֶה – THIS ONE A *MANEH* (one hundred *zuz*) וְזֶה מָאתַיִם – AND THAT ONE TWO HUNDRED *zuz,* זֶה אוֹמֵר שֶׁלִּי מָאתַיִם – and when they later come to claim their money, THIS ONE SAYS, "TWO HUNDRED ARE MINE," וְזֶה אוֹמֵר שֶׁלִּי מָאתַיִם – AND THAT ONE SAYS, "TWO HUNDRED ARE MINE," נוֹתֵן לָזֶה מָנֶה וְלָזֶה מָנֶה – HE GIVES THIS ONE A *MANEH* AND THAT ONE A *MANEH,* וְהַשְּׁאָר יְהֵא מוּנָּח עַד שֶׁיָּבֹא אֵלִיָּהוּ – AND THE REMAINDER SHOULD BE PUT AWAY in the *shomer's* care UNTIL ELIJAH ARRIVES to resolve the doubt. In this case the *shomer* is *not* required to pay the contested one hundred *zuz* to each of the claimants. If so, why in the Mishnah's first case must the thief pay both of the possible victims?

The Gemara answers:

אָמַר לֵיהּ – **One** scholar **said to [another]:** פִּקָּדוֹן אַגָּזֵל קָא רָמֵית – **Are you contrasting** a case of **a deposit with** a case of **stolen property?**[10] גָּזֵל דְּעָבַד אִיסּוּרָא – In a case of **stolen property, where** the thief **committed a transgression,** קָנְסוּהוּ רַבָּנָן – **the Rabbis penalized him** by compelling him to pay both claimants. פִּקָּדוֹן דְּלֹא עָבַד אִיסּוּרָא – But in a case of **a deposit, where [the *shomer*] did not commit a transgression,** לֹא קָנְסוּהוּ רַבָּנָן – **the Rabbis did not penalize him,** and so he is not required to pay the contested money to both claimants.

This explanation does not fully answer the question, because the first ruling of the Mishnah referred not only to someone who admitted stealing from one of two people, but also to someone who received a deposit from one of two people (and does not remember from which one). Yet, the Mishnah said about both of these cases that he gives a *maneh* to each. The Gemara now deals with this question as well as another one:

וּרְמֵי פִּקָּדוֹן אַפִּקָּדוֹן – **But contrast** this case of **deposit with** the other case of **deposit** in the Mishnah, וּרְמֵי גָּזֵל אַגָּזֵל – **and contrast** this case of **stolen property with** the case of **stolen property** in another Mishnah.

The Gemara elaborates:

פִּקָּדוֹן אַפִּקָּדוֹן – Contrast this case of **deposit with** the other case of **deposit,** דְּקָתָנֵי רֵישָׁא – **for it was taught in the beginning** of the Mishnah: אוֹ – OR if a *shomer* told two people, אָבִיו שֶׁל אֶחָד מִכֶּם הִפְקִיד אֶצְלִי מָנֶה – "THE FATHER OF ONE OF YOU DEPOSITED A *MANEH* WITH ME, וְאֵינִי יוֹדֵעַ אֵיזֶה הוּא – BUT I DO NOT KNOW WHICH ONE HE WAS," נוֹתֵן לָזֶה מָנֶה וְלָזֶה מָנֶה – HE GIVES THIS ONE A *MANEH* AND THAT ONE A *MANEH.* וּרְמִינְהִי – **But [the scholars] contrasted** this ruling with the one in the second case of the Mishnah: שְׁנַיִם שֶׁהִפְקִידוּ וכו׳ – IF TWO [PEOPLE] DEPOSITED **etc.** money with one person, this one a *maneh* and that one two hundred *zuz,* and when they came to take back their money, each claimed two hundred *zuz,* he gives each one a *maneh,* and the contested one hundred *zuz* remains with him until Elijah comes. He need not pay that money to each of the claimants.

The Gemara answers:

אָמַר רָבָא – **Rava said:** רֵישָׁא – The *shomer* in **the beginning** of the Mishnah (where only one person deposited money with him) נַעֲשָׂה כְּמִי שֶׁהִפְקִידוּ לוֹ בִּשְׁנֵי כְּרִיכוֹת – **is treated like [a *shomer*] with whom** two people **deposited** money **in two bundles** at two different times, דַּהֲוָה לֵיהּ לְמֵידַק – **in which** case **he should have paid attention** to who gave him what sum.[11] Similarly, the *shomer* in the first case of the Mishnah, who received a deposit from only one depositor, acted negligently by failing to note and remember the identity of that one depositor. Since the reason he cannot return the money to its rightful owner is on account of his own negligence, it is appropriate that he should pay both claimants.[12] סֵיפָא – However, the *shomer* in **the later** (i.e. second) **case** of the Mishnah, where two people deposited different amounts of money with him, נַעֲשָׂה כְּמִי שֶׁהִפְקִידוּ לוֹ בִּכְרֶךְ אֶחָד – **is treated like [a *shomer*] with whom** two people **deposited** money **in one bundle,** דְּלֹא הֲוָה לֵיהּ לְמֵידַק – **who need not have paid attention** to how much each one gave him.[13] Although in the second case of our Mishnah they each deposited their money

NOTES

8. Our elucidation follows *Rashi.* In the same vein, *Meiri* explains that the Mishnah speaks only of an object — such as a piece of cloth, or a bar of silver or gold — whose value will not be excessively diminished by breaking it into pieces. However, the Mishnah does not prescribe breaking a glass or metal vessel, for example, if considerable damage or destruction will result. In those cases the *shomer* must sell the more expensive utensil and from the proceeds give the second depositor the cash equivalent of the less expensive utensil. He holds the remainder of the proceeds in escrow until Elijah arrives. Cf. *Rashba,* who maintains that this second procedure is followed in all cases.

9. That is, if one is sued for money or property, and he admits owing it but is uncertain whether he owes it to the person making the claim or to someone else, we do not say, let it remain with him and be put away in safekeeping until it can be determined who is entitled to it. Rather, we require him to pay the person making the claim (see *Rashi*).

The Gemara infers this from the fact that in the first case of the Mishnah, the thief must pay each of the two people he might have stolen from, and we do not say he should hold the *maneh* until it can be determined who is entitled to it.

10. The first case of the Mishnah dealt with someone who admitted stealing a *maneh* from one of two people but he does not remember from which one.

11. A *shomer* who accepts deposits from different people at different times is expected to remember how much each one gave him [or which bundle each one gave him], so that he can return the proper amount to each one (*Rashi*). His failure to do so is negligence and he must therefore pay both claims.

12. The commentators note that this reasoning does not apply in the case of a thief. Rava agrees that the reason the thief in the first case of the Mishnah must pay both is that he is penalized for committing a transgression (*Rashba*). Rava is merely explaining why a *shomer* — who did not commit any transgression — must pay both claimants in the case of a deposit.

13. Since the depositors displayed such trust in each other that they combined their money into one deposit, there was no reason for the *shomer* to be concerned that one would later fraudulently claim more

## גמרא

אף בראשונה הלכה כמותו או אין הלכה כמותו אמר ליה חלוק היה ר' יוסי אף בראשונה והלכה כמותו אף בראשונה אתמר נמי אמר ר' אלעזר חלוק היה ר' יוסי אף בראשונה והלכה כמותו אף בראשונה ור' יוחנן אמר מודה היה ר' יוסי בראשונה שכבר שילם שילם אין לא שילם לא והאמר [א] ר' חייא בר אבא א"ר יוחנן לא שילם שילם ממש אלא כיון שאמר הריני משלם אע"פ שלא שילם אימא מודה היה ר' יוסי בראשונה שכבר אמר הריני משלם:

**מתני'** [א] אמר לשנים גזלתי לאחד מכם מנה ואיני יודע איזה מכם או אביו של אחד מכם הפקיד לי מנה ואיני יודע איזה הוא נותן לזה מנה ולזה מנה שהודה מפי עצמו [ב] שנים שהפקידו אצל אחד זה מנה וזה מאתים זה אומר שלי מאתים וזה אומר שלי מאתים נותן לזה מנה ולזה מנה והשאר יהא מונח עד שיבא אליהו [ג] א"ר יוסי א"כ מה הפסיד הרמאי • אלא הכל יהא מונח עד שיבא אליהו [ג] וכן שני כלים אחד יפה מנה ואחד יפה אלף זוז זה אומר יפה שלי וזה אומר יפה שלי נותן את הקטן לאחד מהן ומתוך הגדול נותן דמי קטן לשני והשאר יהא מונח עד שיבא אליהו א"ר יוסי א"כ מה הפסיד הרמאי אלא הכל יהא מונח עד שיבא אליהו: **גמ'** אלמא מספיקא מפקינן ממונא ולא אמרינן אוקי ממונא בחזקת מריה ורמינהי שנים שהפקידו אצל אחד זה מנה וזה מאתים זה אומר שלי מאתים וזה אומר שלי מאתים נותן לזה מנה ולזה מנה והשאר יהא מונח עד שיבא אליהו א"ל • פקדון אגזל קא רמית גזל דעבד איסורא קנסוהו רבנן פקדון דלא עבד איסורא לא קנסוהו רבנן ורמי פקדון אפקדון דקתני רישא או אביו של אחד מכם הפקיד אצלי מנה ואיני יודע איזה הוא נותן לזה מנה ולזה מנה ורמינהי שנים שהפקידו וכו' אמר רבא [ד] רישא נעשה כמי שהפקידו לו בשני כריכות דהוה ליה למידק [ה] סיפא נעשה כמי שהפקידו לו בכרך אחד דלא הוה ליה למידק כגון דאפקידו תרווייהו בהדי הדדי בחד זימנא דאמר להו אנת גופייכו לא קפדיתו אהדדי אנא קפידנא ורמי גזל אגזל הכא קתני אמר לשנים גזלתי לאחד מכם מנה ואיני יודע איזה מכם או אביו של אחד מכם הפקיד לי מנה ואיני יודע איזהו נותן לזה מנה ולזה מנה ורמינהי [ו] גזל אחד מחמשה ואינו יודע איזה מהן גזל זה אומר אותי גזל וזה אומר אותי גזל מניח גזילה ביניהם ומסתלק דברי ר"ט אלמא מספיקא לא מפקינן ממונא ואמרינן [ז] אוקים ממונא בחזקת מריה וממאי דמתני' דהכא ר"ט היא [ז] דקתני עלה דההיא מודה ר"ט באומר לשנים גזלתי לאחד מכם מנה ואיני יודע איזה מכם שנותן לזה מנה ולזה מנה התם דקא תבעי ליה הכא [ט] בבא לצאת ידי שמים דיקא נמי דקתני שהודה מפי עצמו שמע מינה אמר מר התם דקא תבעי ליה והלה מה טוען רב הונא אמר רב הלה שותק רב יהודה אמר רב הלה

צווח

## רש"י

**אף בראשונה.** בשלם ולא רצה לישבע כילד זה נותן לתוך כיסו כפילו של זה אלא יחזיר הכפל לבעלים: **שכבר שילם.** קודם שנמצא הגנב וקנה כפל כדאמר מעיקרא אדעתא דהכי אתאי לידיה: **מתני' שהודה מפי עצמו.** הואיל והודה מפי עצמו ובגמ' מפרש טעמא מה הוא: **זה אומר מאתים שלי.** לאחר זמן כשבאו ליטול פקדון: **מה הפסיד הרמאי.** א"כ לא יודה לעולם על האמת: **מתוך הגדול.** ישברנו: **גמ' מספיקא מפקי' ממונא.** דקתני נותן לזה מנה ולזה מנה: **ולא אמרינן.** כשזה תובע וזה אומר איני יודע אם לך אם לחברך אוקי ממונא בחזקת נתבע זה שלא נפסידנו ממונו ויהא מונח עד שיבא אליהו: **רישא.** דחד גברא הפקיד אצלו והוה ליה כשנים שהפקידו אצלו בשני כריכות כלומר זה שלא בפני זה דה"ל למידק מי הפקיד אצלו מנה ומי מאתים: **סיפא.** שהפקידו לו שניהם זה בפני זה ה"ל כמי שנאמנים זה על זה להפקיד שני פקדונותם בצרור אחד דלית ליה למידק מה יש לזה בתוכו ומה יש לחבירו ואע"ג דלא כרך אחד הוה מיהו כיון שהפקידו זה בפני זה גילו דעתן שלא חשדו זה את זה לומר שמא חבירו יתבע המאתים: **ומתני' דהכא ממאי דר"ט היא.** דתקשי לך דלמא ר"ע היא דפליג נמי בההיא ואומר לא זו הדרך מוליאתו מידי עבירה עד שישלם גזילה לכל אחד ואחד: **דקתני עלה דההיא כו'.** אלמא מודה ר"ט בהא ומאי שנא: **ומשנינן התם דקתבעי ליה.** והוא אין חפץ ליתן אלא מן הדין ומספיקא לית לן לחיוביה לכל חד וחד: **הכא בבא לצאת ידי שמים.** מאליו בא לימלך מה יעשה ולא יענש דהשתא ודאי אמרינן ידי שמים לא יצאת עד שתתן לשניהם שאם תהא מונחת עד שיבא אליהו נמצא הנגזל מפסיד על ידך: **דיקא נמי.** דטעמא דמתני' בבא לצאת ידי שמים מן העונש ולא מן הדין מדתלי טעמא בהודה מפי עצמו שלא היה אדם תובעו כלום משמע שהוא בא לימלך: **והלה מה טוען.** לכל אחד דקתני מניח גזילה ביניהם ומסתלק:

לוות

## תוספות

**גזל מחמשה.** לא שייך הך פלוגתא לפלוגתא דרבי יוחנן ורב הונא דפ' השואל (לקמן דף צז:) בברי ושמא דאפי' לר"ט דאמר מניח גזילה ביניהם היינו משום דיודע בודאי שלא גזל לכולם רק לאחד אבל ברי ושמא יודה דברי עדיף ואפי' לר"ע דאמר ישלם לכל אחד ואחד היינו משום שיודע בודאי שהוא חייב לאחד מהם אבל גבי ברי ושמא יודה דפטור שאינו יודע שהוא חייב כלל:

**דקתני** עלה ומודה ר"ט. ט) ה"ה דה"מ למפרך מברייתא אמאי מודה אלא ניחא ליה למפרך ממתניתין דיבמות אמתניתין (א) ז):

**התם** דקא תבעי ליה הכא בבא לצאת ידי שמים. לכאורה נראה דהשתא לא צריך לשינויי קמאי דאין חילוק בין כרך אחד לב' כריכות ורישא דנותן מנה לזה ומנה לזה בבא לצאת ידי שמים וסיפא דקתבעי ליה יהא מונח אך מדלא קאמר אלא התם דקא תבעי ליה משמע דלא הדר משנויא קמא וכן לקמן (ע"ב) דפריך נמי ומי אמר רבא בב' כריכות ה"ל למידק משמע דלא הדר ביה לכך נראה דכולה מתני' איירי בבא לצאת ידי שמים ולכך ברישא דהוה ליה למידק נותן לזה מנה ולזה מנה בבא לצאת ידי שמים וסיפא דבכרך אחד כיון דלא ה"ל למידק אפילו בבא לצאת ידי שמים אינו חייב ולרבי טרפון נקט ברישא אביו של אחד מכם ולא נקט אחד מכם לרבותא דאפילו שמא ושמא נותן לכל אחד ואחד בבא לצאת ידי שמים ולר"ע נקט אביו דמשמע שמא ושמא לכך אינו חייב אלא לצאת ידי שמים כדאמר לקמן (שם) דבשמא ושמא אינו חייב לכל אחד ואחד לר"ע מדינא ונקט אביו דאי הם עצמן הפקידו אם כן מסתמא תבעי ליה וה"ל ברי ושמא ואפילו מדינא חייבין לר"ע דמתניתין אתיא כר"ע נמי דקאמר לקמן (שם) ממאי דמתני' דהכא ר"ע היא ועוד דהלכה כר"ע מחבירו ובסיפא דלא נקט שני אבותיכם הפקידו לרבותא לא תני הכי דאע"ג דטענו ברי פטור אפילו לצאת ידי שמים ואפי' לר"ע כיון דלא פשע דלא הוה ליה למידק ולא מחייב ר"ע מדינא אלא בברי ושמא והיכא דהוה ליה למידק אבל בשמא ושמא אפי' בשני כריכות אינו חייב אלא לצאת ידי שמים והיכא דלא הוי ליה למידק פטור אפי' לצאת ידי שמים ואפילו בברי ושמא וא"ת דבפרק הגוזל קמא (ב"ק דף קג: ושם קד. ד"ה שכבר) קאמר מעשה בחסיד אחד שבא לפני ר"ט ואמר ליה הנח דמי מקח ביניהם וכי לא בעי חסיד לצאת ידי שמים וי"ל דר"ט אמר ליה שכך הדין ח) וא"ת התם דפריך אמתניתין דקתני הגוזל מחבירו שוה פרוטה ונשבע לו יוליכנו אחריו אפילו למדי ומוקי כר"ט כו' ומאי איריא נשבע אפי' הודה נמי דתניא מודה ר"ט כו' ומאי פריך והא אוקמי' בריית' דמודה ר"ט בבא לצאת ידי שמים ומתני' דהתם מיירי מדינא וי"ל דמתני' דהתם מיירי לצאת ידי שמים להביא קרבן וקא אמר אם רוצה להביא קרבן צריך להביא גזלו למדי דתנן הביא אשמו עד שלא הביא גזלו לא יצא לכך פריך דבלא שבועה ולא קרבן צריך להביא גזלו למדי אם רוצה לצאת ידי שמים:

מודה

## עין משפט נר מצוה

לה א מיי' פ"ד מהל' גזלה ואבדה הל' י סמג עשין עג טוש"ע ח"מ סי' שסה סעי' ב:

לו ב מיי' פ"ה מהל' שאלה ופקדון הל' ד ועי' במ"מ סמג עשין פח טוש"ע ח"מ סי' ש סעי' א:

לז ג מיי' שם טוש"ע שם סעי' ב:

לח ד ה מיי' שם טוש"ע שם סעי' א:

לט ו מיי' פ"ד מהל' גזלה ואבדה הל' י סמג עשין עג טוש"ע ח"מ סי' שסה סעי' ב:

## רבינו חננאל

ואסיקנא שמואל אמר חלוק ר' יוסי אף בראשונה בהא דתנן למי משלם למי שהפקדון אצלו חולק עליו ר' יוסי ואומר אינו משלם אלא לבעל הפקדון ואין הלכה כשמואל דהא ר' יוחנן פליג עליה דהא בהדיא אמר ר' יוחנן מודה ר' יוסי בראשונה שאינו משלם אלא למי שהפקדון אצלו. וקיימא לן כר' יוחנן דסוגיין בעלמא שמואל ור"י הלכה כר' יוחנן וכל שכן ר' אלעזר דתלמיד קטן הוא לגבי ר' יוחנן: **מתני' אמר לשנים גזלתי אחד מכם מנה ואיני יודע איזהו נותן לזה מנה ולזה מנה.** ומקשי' עלה ומספיקא מפקינן ממונא וכו'. ורמינהי שנים שהפקידו אצל אחד זה מנה וזה מאתים וכו'. ודחי' פקדון אגזל קא רמית. ורמי פקדון אפקדון דתנן (בסיפא) [ברישא] דמתני' דהכא או אביו של אחד מכם הפקיד אצלי מנה נותן לזה מנה ולזה מנה שהודה מפי עצמו אימא סיפא דהא מתני' שנים שהפקידו אצל אחד כו'. ופריק רבא רישא היה לו בעת שהפקיד אצלו לומר לו מה שמך וכיון שלא דקדק לידע איזה מהן הוא המפקיד אצלו איהו אפסיד נפשיה לפיכך משלם לזה ולזה. סיפא כגון ששניהן הפקידו צרורותיהן ביחד וכל אחד רואה כי הצרור אחד גדול שיש בו מאתים והאחד קטן שאין בו אלא ק'. יכול למימר מי שהפקדון אצלו כיון דחזיתי דאין מקפיד בעל הצרור הגדול לומר דע כי הצרור הגדול שלי הוא והקטן לחבירו אמינא כיון דלא דייקי אהדדי מהימני לפיכך לא דקדקתי. תוב רמינן ארישא דמתני' דתנן בסוף יבמות גזל אחד מהן ואינו יודע אי זה מהן גזל מניח גזילה ביניהן ומסתלק דברי ר' טרפון וכו'. אלמא מספיקא לא מפקינן ממונא. ואסיק' מדקתני התם ומודה ר' טרפון באומר לשנים גזלתי לאחד מכם מנה ואיני יודע למי מכם שנותן לזה ק' ולזה ק' ש"מ מתני' דהכא ר' טרפון היא קשיין אהדדי. ופרקי' התם גבי גזל אחד מה' כשתובעין אותו [אמר] שמניח גזילה ביניהן ואומר להן הנה היא מונחת לפניכם מי מכם יברר שהיא שלו יטלנה אבל הכא במשנתינו בבא לצאת ידי שמים דקתני שהודה מפי עצמו ואין תובעין אותו אלא ב"ד (אמר) [אמרינן ליה] אין לך דרך לצאת ידי עבירה אלא אם תתן לזה ק' ולזה ק' שמכל

## מסורת הש"ס

א) [לעיל לד.], ב) [בבא בתרא לד:], ג) לעיל ג., ד) בבא קמא קג: יבמות קיח:, ה) [קדושין מה: וש"נ], ו) דלמא ר"ע היא. ס"א, ז) [וע"ע תוס' שבת עט: ד"ה והא], ח) [ובתוס' דפרק הגוזל שם כתבו עוד א"נ אפילו לצאת ידי שמים אין חייב לר' טרפון אלא בגוזל אבל בפקדון ומקח דלא עשה איסורא לא כו' ע"ש] ועיין מהרש"א.

## הגהות הב"ח

(א) תוס' ד"ה דקתני וכו' אמתניתין דהכא הס"ד:

## גליון הש"ס

מתני' **אלא הכל יהא מונח.** עיין גיטין דף מד: תוס' ד"ה נטייבה: **גמרא פקדון אגזל קרמית.** עיין גיטין דף כח. תוס' ד"ה תרומה: **תוס' ד"ה דקתני וכו' ה"ה דהו"מ למפרך.** וכזה שבת דף עט: ועיין בתוס' שם ד"ה והא:

## ליקוטי רש"י

**א"כ מה הפסיד הרמאי.** ולמה יודה הרי קיבל את שלו [לעיל ג.]. לא יבא להודות דהא לא מפסיד מידי [רשב"ם ב"ב צד:]. **אלא הכל יהא מונח וכו'.** ויפסיד הרמאי [לעיל ג.]. **מניח גזילה ביניהם ומסתלק.** ולא בעי לאמטויי לידיה וסגי במניח לפניו שהרי הבעלים שם הוא [ב"ק קג:]. **שהודה מפי עצמו.** ובא לצאת ידי שמים ואע"ג דבי דינא לא מצי מחייבי ליה אלא מניח לפניהם מיהו ידי עונש אין יוצא עד שישלם לשניהם דהא לאו לבעלים אהדריה [ב"ק קד.].

אַף בְּרִאשׁוֹנָה – **even in the first** Mishnah of the chapter; i.e. even in the case where the *shomer* agreed to pay for the lost animal and not exempt himself by swearing. Here, too, R' Yose holds that if the thief is later caught he pays both the principal and the penalty payment to the owner and not to the *shomer*.[1] הֲלָכָה כְּמוֹתוֹ – **Does the halachah accord with his** opinion in this case as well, אוֹ אֵין הֲלָכָה כְּמוֹתוֹ – **or does the halachah not accord with his** opinion?

Rav Yehudah responds:

אָמַר לֵיהּ – **[Rav Yehudah] told [Rav Shmuel]:** חָלוּק הָיָה רַבִּי יוֹסֵי אַף בְּרִאשׁוֹנָה – **R' Yose** indeed **disputed** the opinion of the Sages **even in the first** Mishnah of the chapter, וַהֲלָכָה כְּמוֹתוֹ אַף בְּרִאשׁוֹנָה – **and the halachah accords with his** opinion **even in the first** Mishnah.

The Gemara cites a dispute of Amoraim about this issue:

אִתְּמַר נַמִּי – **It was also said** regarding this matter: אָמַר רַבִּי אֶלְעָזָר – **R' Elazar said:** חָלוּק הָיָה רַבִּי יוֹסֵי אַף בְּרִאשׁוֹנָה – **R' Yose disputed** the opinion of the Sages **even in the first** Mishnah of the chapter, וַהֲלָכָה כְּמוֹתוֹ אַף בְּרִאשׁוֹנָה – **and the halachah accords with his** opinion **even in the first** Mishnah. וְרַבִּי יוֹחָנָן אָמַר – **But R' Yochanan said:** מוֹדֶה הָיָה רַבִּי יוֹסֵי בְּרִאשׁוֹנָה – **R' Yose conceded** to the Sages **in the first** Mishnah that the penalty payment goes to the *shomer*, שֶׁכְּבָר שִׁילֵּם – **because [the *shomer*] already paid** for the loss before the thief was caught, and thereby acquired the rights to any future penalty payment.[2]

The Gemara points out that R' Yochanan's statement implicitly contradicts another statement by him:

שִׁילֵּם אִין – From R' Yochanan's statement it may be inferred that **if** the *shomer* in fact **paid** for the loss, he **indeed** receives the penalty payment, לֹא שִׁילֵּם לֹא – but that if **he did not pay,** he does **not** receive it even though he promised to pay. וְהָאָמַר רַבִּי חִיָּיא בַּר אַבָּא אָמַר רַבִּי יוֹחָנָן – **But R' Chiya bar Abba said in the name of R' Yochanan:**[3] לֹא שִׁילֵּם שִׁילֵּם מַמָּשׁ – The Mishnah's statement that the *shomer* **paid** does **not** mean that **he actually paid.** אֶלָּא כֵּיוָן שֶׁאָמַר הֲרֵינִי מְשַׁלֵּם – **Rather, once he said, "I will pay,"** he acquires any future penalty payment, אַף עַל פִּי שֶׁלֹּא שִׁילֵּם – **even though he did not** yet **pay.**

The Gemara therefore revises R' Yochanan's statement here:

אֵימָא – **Say** that his statement reads as follows: מוֹדֶה הָיָה רַבִּי יוֹסֵי בְּרִאשׁוֹנָה – **R' Yose conceded** to the Sages **in the first** Mishnah, שֶׁכְּבָר אָמַר הֲרֵינִי מְשַׁלֵּם – **for [the *shomer*] already said, "I will pay."**

**Mishnah** אָמַר לִשְׁנַיִם – If [a thief] **told two [people],** גָּזַלְתִּי לְאֶחָד מִכֶּם מָנֶה – **"I stole a *maneh*** (one hundred *zuz*) **from one of you** וְאֵינִי יוֹדֵעַ אֵיזֶה מִכֶּם – **but I do not know from which of you** I stole it," אוֹ – **or** if a *shomer* told two people, אָבִיו שֶׁל אֶחָד מִכֶּם הִפְקִיד לִי מָנֶה – **"The father of one of you**[4] **deposited a *maneh* with me** וְאֵינִי יוֹדֵעַ אֵיזֶה הוּא – **but I do not know which one he was,"** נוֹתֵן לָזֶה מָנֶה וְלָזֶה מָנֶה – **he gives this one a *maneh* and that one a *maneh*,** שֶׁהוֹדָה מִפִּי עַצְמוֹ – **because he acknowledged** the debt **himself.**[5]

The second ruling of the Mishnah:

שְׁנַיִם שֶׁהִפְקִידוּ אֵצֶל אֶחָד – If **two [people] deposited** money **with one** *shomer*, זֶה מָנֶה – **this one a *maneh*** (one hundred *zuz*) וְזֶה מָאתַיִם – **and that one two hundred** *zuz*, זֶה אוֹמֵר שֶׁלִּי מָאתַיִם – and when they later come to claim their money **this one says, "Two hundred are mine,"** וְזֶה אוֹמֵר שֶׁלִּי מָאתַיִם – **and that one says, "Two hundred are mine,"** נוֹתֵן לָזֶה מָנֶה וְלָזֶה מָנֶה – **[the *shomer*] gives this one a *maneh*** (one hundred *zuz*) **and that one a *maneh*,** the amounts to which they are certainly entitled, וְהַשְּׁאָר יְהֵא מוּנָּח עַד שֶׁיָּבֹא אֵלִיָּהוּ – **and the remainder** (one hundred *zuz*) **should be put away** in the *shomer's* care **until Elijah** the prophet **arrives** to resolve the doubt.[6] אָמַר רַבִּי יוֹסֵי – **R' Yose said:** אִם כֵּן – **If it is so** that each claimant receives the *maneh* that is definitely his, מַה הִפְסִיד הָרַמַּאי – **what has the dishonest [person] lost?**[7] Since he stands to lose nothing, he will never admit the truth! אֶלָּא – **Rather,** הַכֹּל יְהֵא מוּנָּח עַד שֶׁיָּבֹא אֵלִיָּהוּ – **all** the money **should be put away** in the *shomer's* care **until Elijah arrives.** This will force the liar to admit the truth in order to get back the money he deposited.

The third ruling of the Mishnah:

וְכֵן שְׁנֵי כֵלִים – **And so** it is in the case of two people who deposited **two utensils,** אֶחָד יָפֶה מָנֶה – **one worth a *maneh*** (one hundred *zuz*) וְאֶחָד יָפֶה אֶלֶף זוּז – **and one worth one thousand *zuz*,** with one *shomer*. זֶה אוֹמֵר יָפֶה שֶׁלִּי – If **this one says, "The more expensive one is mine,"** וְזֶה אוֹמֵר יָפֶה שֶׁלִּי – **and that one says, "The more expensive one is mine,"** נוֹתֵן אֶת הַקָּטָן לְאֶחָד מֵהֶן – **[the *shomer*] gives the smaller** (i.e. less expensive) **one to one of them,** וּמִתּוֹךְ הַגָּדוֹל – **and from the larger** (i.e. more expensive) **one,** which he breaks, נוֹתֵן דְּמֵי קָטָן לַשֵּׁנִי – **he gives** a piece worth **the value of the less expensive** one **to the second** claimant, וְהַשְּׁאָר יְהֵא מוּנָּח עַד שֶׁיָּבֹא

NOTES

1. In that situation as well, R' Yose maintains that the *shomer* should not profit from the owner's animal by pocketing the penalty payment of a third party (see *Rashi*).

2. As explained above, 34a.

3. This was cited by the Gemara above, 34a.

4. The commentators discuss why the Mishnah chooses a case in which the deposit was made by one of the fathers rather than by one of the parties to whom he is speaking. See *Tosafos, Rosh,* and *Ritva* [old], and note 18 to 37b below.

5. The Gemara below will explain that this ruling implies that, strictly speaking, he does not have to give a *maneh* to each one, since he stole or received just one *maneh*. However, since he admits the matter on his own and wants to do the right thing, he should give each one a *maneh* to avoid any Heavenly punishment.

6. It is a tradition that Elijah the prophet will return to herald the arrival of the Messiah, and at that time he will settle all unresolved issues and disputes.

The commentators ask why the *shomer* is not obligated to pay 200 *zuz* to each claimant. Since they each claim 200 *zuz* and he admits owing each one at least 100 *zuz*, he is obligated to swear a שְׁבוּעַת מוֹדֶה בְּמִקְצָת, *the oath of one who admits to part of a claim,* about the rest of the claim. Since he cannot make this oath, because he does not know who is entitled to the second 100 *zuz*, he should be considered a person who is obligated to swear an oath and cannot do so, which obligates him to pay the entire claim (see Gemara below, 98a)! *Ramban* explains that in this case the *shomer* does not qualify as one who is obligated to swear and cannot. Since he is willing to surrender all the money entrusted to him or that he stole, just that he does not know whom to give it to, he is, in fact, not obligated to swear. *Rashba,* however, explains that the underlying reason one who cannot take a mandatory oath is required to pay is because he should have been able to swear; hence, he pays because he was negligent. In this case, however, the *shomer* is not required to know the amount entrusted to him by each depositor (see below, note 13). Hence, his inability to deny that he owes each claimant the other 100 *zuz* does not constitute negligence, and so he is not obligated to satisfy the entire claim (200 *zuz*) of each depositor.

7. One of these two claimants is lying. If they each receive 100 *zuz*, the liar (who really gave only 100) will lose nothing, since he will still get back his original deposit of 100 *zuz*. What incentive does he have to admit the truth?

פִּקְדּוֹנִי בְּיַד אַחֵר – "It is not my desire that my deposit should be in someone else's hands," אִיכָּא לְאוֹתְבָה לְהַהִיא – it is possible for R' Abba **to challenge [R' Yochanan's ruling]** from the Mishnah, and for R' Ami to respond in the way he chose to respond. לְדִידִי – However, **according to me,** דַּאֲמִינָא – **who has said** that the reason R' Yochanan considers the first *shomer* liable in the case of an unauthorized transfer is because the owner may tell him, אַנְתְּ מְהֵימַנְתְּ לִי בִּשְׁבוּעָה – **"You are** someone whose word is **believable to me with an oath** that you were not negligent; וְהָאִיךְ לָא מְהֵימַן לִי בִּשְׁבוּעָה – **but that one** [the second *shomer*] **is not** someone whose word is **believable to me** even **with an oath,"** לֵיכָּא לְאוֹתְבָה כְּלָל – **it is not possible to challenge [R' Yochanan's ruling]** from the Mishnah **at all,** because in the Mishnah the first *shomer* (the renter) does in fact swear to absolve himself from liability, in which case R' Yochanan agrees that he is exempt![21]

The Gemara challenges Abaye's ruling:

מְתִיב רָמִי בַּר חָמָא – **Rami bar Chama challenged** Abaye's ruling **from** another **Mishnah:**[22] הֶעֱלָה לְרָאשֵׁי צוּקִין וְנָפְלָה – IF [A SHEPHERD] TOOK [AN ANIMAL] UP TO THE narrow TOPS OF STEEP MOUNTAINS AND IT FELL OFF A MOUNTAIN AND DIED, אֵין זֶה אוֹנֶס וְחַיָּיב – THIS IS NOT AN UNAVOIDABLE ACCIDENT,[23] AND so the shepherd IS OBLIGATED to pay the owner. From the Mishnah we may deduce: הָא מֵתָה כְּדַרְכָּהּ – **But if [the animal] died naturally** on the mountaintop, הֲרֵי זֶה אוֹנֶס וּפָטוּר – **then this is** considered **an unavoidable accident, and** the shepherd **is exempt** from liability.[24] וְאַמַּאי – **But why** should this be so, if according to Abaye the animal's death may be blamed on external factors?[25] לֵימָא לֵיהּ – **Let** the owner **tell [the shepherd]:** אֲוִירָא דְּהַר קַטְלָהּ – **"The** cold **mountain air killed it";** אִי נַמִּי – **or else,** let him say: אוּבְצְנָא דְּהַר קַטְלָהּ – **"The exhaustion** caused by the strain **of** climbing **the mountain killed it."** According to Abaye, then, the shepherd should be held liable even though it died of natural causes![26] – ? –

The Gemara answers:

הָכָא בְּמַאי עַסְקִינַן – **Here,** in that Mishnah, **with what** case **are we dealing?** שֶׁהֶעֱלָה לְמִרְעֶה שָׁמֵן וָטוֹב – With a case **where the [shepherd] took [the animal] up to "a luxurious and excellent pasture"**[27] that was located on the mountaintop. Since the local shepherds customarily take their animals there to graze, this shepherd did not act negligently in taking the animal up the mountain for that purpose.

The Gemara questions this explanation:

אִי הָכִי – **If it is so** that the shepherd was not negligent in bringing the animal to the mountaintop, נָפְלָה נַמִּי – then **even if** it **fell off** and was killed he should not be held liable! – ? –

The Gemara answers:

שֶׁהָיָה לוֹ לְתוֹקְפָהּ – The shepherd's conduct is nonetheless deemed negligent **because he should have held [the animal] firmly,** as shepherds customarily and prudently do, וְלֹא תְּקָפָהּ – **and** yet **he did not hold it firmly.** Therefore, he is liable for the animal's fall, since it resulted from his negligence.[28]

The Gemara persists:

אִי הָכִי – **If it is so** that the shepherd is expected to restrain the animal, אֵימָא רֵישָׁא – **say the first** (i.e. preceding) **case** of that Mishnah, which implies otherwise: עָלְתָה לְרָאשֵׁי צוּקִין וְנָפְלָה – IF [THE ANIMAL] WENT UP by itself TO THE TOPS OF STEEP MOUNTAINS AND FELL OFF, הֲרֵי זֶה אוֹנֶס – THIS IS AN UNAVOIDABLE ACCIDENT, and the shepherd is exempt from liability. ניבָעֵי לֵיהּ לְמִיתְקְפָהּ – But why is he exempt? **He should have held [the animal] firmly** and not let it run off to a dangerous place and fall from there. – ? –

The Gemara answers:

לֹא – **No!** The preceding case is not the same; צְרִיכָא – **it was necessary** for the Mishnah to teach that he is exempt in a case שֶׁתְּקָפַתּוּ וְעָלְתָה – **where** the animal **overpowered [the shepherd] and went up** תְּקָפַתּוּ וְיָרְדָה – and then **overpowered him and went down** [i.e. fell].[29]

The Mishnah stated:

אָמַר רַבִּי יוֹסֵי – R' YOSE SAID: כֵּיצַד הַלָּה עוֹשֶׂה סְחוֹרָה בְּפָרָתוֹ כו׳ – HOW CAN THAT renter DO BUSINESS WITH THE COW OF [HIS FELLOW]? **etc.** Rather, the borrower pays the owner for the loss of the cow.

The Gemara decides between the disputants of our Mishnah:

אָמַר רַב יְהוּדָה אָמַר שְׁמוּאֵל – **Rav Yehudah said in the name of Shmuel:** הֲלָכָה כְּרַבִּי יוֹסֵי – The **halachah accords with the** opinion of **R' Yose,** who rules that a *shomer* is not entitled to the damages paid by the borrower; rather the money goes to the owner.

The Gemara inquires further:

אָמַר לֵיהּ רַב שְׁמוּאֵל בַּר יְהוּדָה לְרַב יְהוּדָה – **Rav Shmuel bar Yehudah said to Rav Yehudah:** אָמְרַתְּ לָן מִשְּׁמֵיהּ דִּשְׁמוּאֵל – **You have told us in the name of Shmuel** חָלוּק הָיָה רַבִּי יוֹסֵי – that **R' Yose disputed** the opinion of the Sages

NOTES

21. The Mishnah states clearly that the renter must swear to the owner that the animal died naturally. Thus, the owner is accepting an oath only from the first *shomer,* whom he trusted. He therefore has no complaint against the first *shomer* (the renter), and there was no basis at all for R' Abba's question and R' Ami's answer!

Rava rejects the premise of both R' Abba's question and R' Ami's response. They, in effect, follow Abaye's understanding of R' Yochanan's position. [Therefore, nothing they said about this matter poses a challenge to Rava's view] (see *Rashi*). *Ramban,* however, explains that Rava maintains that the exchange between R' Abba and R' Ami never happened.

22. Below, 93b.

23. Since the *shomer* acted negligently by bringing the animal to a place from which it could easily fall (*Rashi*).

24. Although the *shomer* acted negligently at the outset [תְּחִלָּתוֹ בִּפְשִׁיעָה], the actual loss was unavoidable [סוֹפוֹ בְּאוֹנֶס] (*Rashi*).

25. Abaye ruled previously (in the case of the marsh air), that if a situation begins with an act of negligence but ends with an unavoidable loss, even the lenient opinion considers the *shomer* liable if the seemingly natural loss can be even slightly linked to the act of negligence.

26. Since the shepherd's negligence in bringing the animal to the mountaintop may have contributed to the animal's death by exposing it to the cold (or by exhausting it with the climb).

27. The expression is from *I Chronicles* 4:40.

28. However, if the animal died naturally, Abaye agrees that the shepherd is not liable. Although it is possible that its exposure to the cold air or the exhaustion from its climb contributed to its death, since he was permitted to bring the animal to the mountaintop to graze he is not considered negligent. But he should have kept a tight rein on it as they climbed and grazed on the mountaintop. Not doing so does constitute negligence, and for that reason the shepherd is liable if the animal fell off the mountain.

29. The animal was stronger than the shepherd and could not be restrained (*Rashi*). In such a case the *shomer* incurs no liability. However, when the *shomer* is able to control the animal and prevent it from going up, and he fails to do so, he is indeed judged to be negligent and must pay.

על דעת אשתו ובניו הוא מפקיד אמרי נהרדעי דיקא נמי דקתני או שמסרן לבנו ובתו הקטנים חייב הא לבנו ולבתו הגדולים פטור מכלל דלאחרים לא שנא גדולים ולא שנא קטנים חייב דאם כן ליתני קטנים סתמא שמע מינה אמר רבא [א] הלכתא שומר שמסר לשומר חייב לא מבעיא שומר שכר שמסר לשומר חנם דגרועי גרעה לשמירתו אלא אפילו שומר חנם שמסר לשומר שכר חייב מאי טעמא דאמר ליה את מהימנת לי בשבועה האיך לא מהימן לי בשבועה: אתמר פשע בה ויצאת לאגם ומתה כדרכה אביי משמיה דרבה אמר חייב רבא משמיה דרבה אמר [א] פטור אביי משמיה דרבה אמר חייב כל דיינא דלא דאין כי האי דינא לאו דיינא הוא לא מבעיא למ"ד תחילתו בפשיעה וסופו באונס חייב דחייב אלא אפילו למ"ד פטור הכא חייב מ"ט דאמרינן הבלא דאגמא קטלה רבא משמיה דרבה אמר פטור כל דיינא דלא דאין כי האי דינא לאו דיינא הוא לא מיבעיא למ"ד [ב] תחילתו בפשיעה וסופו באונס פטור דפטור אלא אפילו למ"ד [ב] חייב הכא פטור מאי טעמא דאמרינן מלאך המות מה לי הכא ומה לי התם ומודי אביי דאי הדרא לבי מרה ומתה דפטור מ"ט דהא הדרא לה וליכא למימר הבלא דאגמא קטלה [ג] ומודי רבא כל היכא [ג] דאיגנבה גנב באגם ומתה כדרכה בי גנב דחייב מאי טעמא דאי שבקה מלאך המות בביתיה דגנבא הוה קיימא אמר ליה אביי לרבא לדידך דאמרת מלאך המות מה לי הכא ומה לי התם האי דאותביה ר' אבא בר ממל לרבי אמי ושני ליה בשנתנו לו בעלים רשות להשאיל ולימא ליה מלאך המות מה לי הכא ומה לי התם א"ל לדידכו דמתניתו אין רצוני שיהא פקדוני ביד אחר איכא לאותבה להההיא לדידי דאמינא אנת מהימנת לי בשבועה והאיך לא מהימן לי בשבועה ליכא לאותבה כלל מתיב רמי בר חמא [ד] [ד] העלה לראשי צוקין ונפלה אין זה אונס וחייב [ה] הא מתה כדרכה הרי זה אונס ופטור ואמאי לימא ליה [ו] אוירא דהר קטלה אי נמי אובצנא דהר קטלה הכא במאי עסקינן שהעלה למרעה שמן וטוב אי הכי נפלה נמי שהיה לו לתוקפה ולא תקפה אי הכי אימא רישא [י] עלתה לראשי צוקין ונפלה הרי זה אונס איבעי ליה למיתקפה לא צריכא שתקפתו ועלתה תקפתו וירדה: אמר רבי יוסי כיצד הלה עושה סחורה בפרתו כו': אמר רב יהודה אמר שמואל הלכה כרבי יוסי אמר ליה רב שמואל בר יהודה לרב יהודה אמרת לן משמיה דשמואל חלוק היה רבי יוסי

אף

**דאם** כן ליתני קטנים סתמא. וא"ת תקשה לרב וי"ל דבניו נקט לרבותא דסד"א דעל דעת בניו הקטנים נמי מפקיד דרגילות הוא שלפעמים מוסר חפציו לבניו קטנים קמ"ל אי נמי לכך נקט בניו ולא נקט קטנים סתמא משום דבעי למידק הא גדולים הוי כדרך השומרים ומותר משום דעל דעת בניו הגדולים מפקיד אבל גדולים דעלמא אסור למסור אע"פ שאינו מתחייב בכך:

**את** מהימנת לי בשבועה. ולכך היכא שהשומר הראשון יכול לישבע על האונס או שהיו עדים בדבר פטור ואפי' מסר לחש"ו ומתה ברשותם כיון דאף בבית שומר הראשון היתה מתה דמלאך המות מה לי הכא מ"ל התם כו' וסובר רבא שזהו טעמו של רבי יוחנן ולא כאביי דאמר משום דאין רצוני כו' וכן הלכה כרבא ° ולא כר"ח דפסיק כאביי:

**שהעלה** למרעה שמן וטוב. דהשתא לא הוי פשיעה בהעלאה: **אי** הכי עלתה נמי. בשלמא לרבא דאמר מלאך המות כו' לא יצטרך להעמיד במרעה שמן וטוב ולכך העלה לראשי צוקין ונפלה חייב משום העלאה אע"פ שנפלה בע"כ שתקפתו וירדה ורישא דקתני אי עלתה פטור מיירי שתקפתו ועלתה וכן הנפילה היתה בתקפתו וירדה כמו בסיפא אבל לאביי דאוקמה במרעה שמן וטוב ולא פשע בהעלאה וחייב משום שפשע בנפילתה דמיירי שהיה יכול לתקפה ולא תקפה א"כ רישא נמי אפי' תקפתו ועלתה אמאי פטור ליחייב משום נפילה שהיה לו לשומרה שלא תפול דמסתמא נפלה דרישא הוי כמו נפלה דסיפא שהיה יכול לתקפה ומשני נפלה דרישא מיירי שתקפתו וירדה דומיא דעלתה דמיירי דתקפתו ועלתה ולא דמיא לנפילה דסיפא וא"ת אמאי נקט ברישא עלתה ובסיפא העלה והלא אין חילוק בין העלה מדעתו לעלתה בעל כרחו ובנפילה לבד הוה ליה לפלוגי דתקפתו וירדה הוה אונס לא תקפתו חייב וי"ל דרישא נקט עלתה לגלויי דנפלה הוי בע"כ וסיפא נקט העלה לגלויי דנפלה הוי שהיה בידו לתקפה ולא תקפה דומיא דהעלה שהיה בידו וא"ת וסיפא כיון דמיירי שהיה יכול לתקפה אמאי אוקמה במרעה שמן וטוב אפילו לא היה מרעה שמן וטוב לא פשע בהעלאה כיון שהיה יכול לשומרה מנפילה וי"ל כיון דאין צורך הבהמה בהעלאה זו פושע הוא שיש לו לחוש שמא ישכח ולא ישמרנה מליפול ולכך אם מתה היה חייב:

גזל

על דעת אשתו ובניו. על דעת שהנפקד מוסרו לאשתו ובניו הגדולים ואין יכולין לומר אין רצוננו כו': **דיקא נמי.** דהאי דגדולים פטורין דוקא בניו נקט ולא אחרים: **דא"כ.** דלאחרים נמי גדולים פטור ליתני או שמסרן לקטנים סתמא: **בשבועה.** שלא פשע בה: **האיך לא מהימן לי.** ואני אומר שישנה בידו או אכלה או פשע בה: **פשע בה.** שלא נעל בפניה כראוי: **ויצאת לאגם.** מקום שאינה משתמרת שם אבל זאבים ולא אבל גנבים ומיהו לא אכלוה לא זאבים ולא גנבים: **ומתה.** דהוי תחילתו בפשיעה שמא יטרפוה זאבים וסופו לא אבדה באותה פשיעה אלא בדבר שהוא אונס: **לא מיבעיא למ"ד.** לקמן בפרקין (דף מב.) גבי ההוא דאותיב זוזי דפקדון בצריפא דאורבני דהויא פשיעותא לגבי נורא ונטירותא לענין גנבי ואיגנוב וגניבה לגבי שומר חנם אונס הוא: **אלא אפילו למ"ד פטור הכא חייב.** דהתם ליכא פשיעותא אלא לענין נורא אבל הכא איכא למימר בפשיעה מתה שאם היתה בבית לא מתה ויציאתה לאגם היא פשיעת מיתתה דשמא הבל המלוי באגם קטלה: **מה לי הכא כו'.** אבל התם גבי זוזי אם שמרם כהלכתם דקי"ל (שם) כספים אין להם שמירה אלא בקרקע לא נגנבו ואע"ג דקי"ל בצריפא דאורבני אין דרך גנבים לבקש שם מעות ואונס הוא מיהו ע"י שלא שמר כדין שמירתם אבדו אבל פרה זו אם היתה בבית נמי היתה מתה: **דאיגנבה גנב מאגם.** שזהו דבר שהוא פשיעה אבל יציאתה לאגם אע"פ שסופה מתה בי גנב חייב ולא אמר אי הוה בבית שומר נמי הוה מתה: **מ"ט.** משעת גניבה היא אבודה מן הבעלים דאי נמי שבקה מלאך המות בי גנב הוה קיימא הלכך החיוב בא לו על שעת הגניבה: **הא דאותביה ר' אבא.** לעיל מהשוכר פרה והשאילה לאחר לימא אין רצוני כו': **ושני ליה בשנתנו לו הבעלים רשות.** מאי דוחקיה לשנויי הכי נימא ליה אם אירע בה אונס אחר דמצינו למימר אם היתה בביתו לא נאנסה היה חייב אבל זו מתה כדרכה מלאך המות נמי בבית שוכר קטיל לה ומדלא שני ליה הכי שמעינן למ"ד תחילתו בפשיעה וסופו באונס חייב לא שנא אונס מלאך המות משאר אונסין: **לדידכו.** דאמריתו טעמא דשומר שמסר לשומר חייב משום אין רצוני איכא לאותובה להיא ותאי דניחא ליה לרבי אמי שני ליה אנא לא סבירא לי לא אתקפתא ולא שינויא דלדידי דאמרי לעיל טעמא משום דלא מהימן ליה בשבועה ליכא לאותובה כלל שהרי שוכר עלמו נשבע לו כדתנן ישבע השוכר שמתה כדרכה: **העלה לראשי צוקין.** שומר שהעלה לראשי הרים חדים ומשופעים ונפלה: **אין זה אונס.** אלא פשיעה דדרכה ליפול: **הא מתה** כדרכה. בראש הצוק: **פטור.** דהוי סופו באונס: **אוירא.** לינה: **אובצנא.** עייפות טורח המעלה: **למרעה שמן וטוב.** דדרך הרועים להעלות שם בהמות לרעות: **לתוקפה.** להחזיק בה שכן דרך הרועים: **עלתה.** מאליה: **שתקפתו.** על כרחו ועלתה ולא יכול להחזיק בה שחזקה היתה ממנו:

אף

עין משפט נר מצוה

ל א מיי' פ"ג מהל' שכירות הל' י סמג עשין פח טוש"ע ח"מ סי' רלא סעי' ט:
לא ב מיי' שם הל' ט טוש"ע שם סעי' ו:
לב ג מיי' שם הל' י טוש"ע שם סעי' ט:
לג ד ה מיי' שם הל' ט טוש"ע שם סעי' י:
לד ו מיי' שם ועיין במ"מ טוש"ע שם סעי' יא:

רבינו חננאל

שיהא פקדוני ביד אחר. ופריק רבא אליבא דאביי כל המפקיד על דעת שימסרם מי שנפקדין אצלו לבניו הגדולים ולאשתו הוא מפקיד דלא עדיף ליה ממונא דחבריה מדידיה וממונא דידיה אשתו ובניו נטרי ליה וכן הלכה דנהרדעאי דייקי מתני' כרבא. אמר רבא הלכת' שומר שמסר לשומר חייב ואפילו שומר חנם שמסר לשומר שכר דעלויי עלייה לשמירתו חייב והני מילי היכא דיכול למימר אנת מהימנת לי בשבועה האיך לא מהימן לי בשבועה ואי מיתבריר דאיהו נמי הוה מפקיד גביה כגון מעשה דגינאי בההיא סבתא פטור. איתמר פשע בה ויצאת לאגם ומתה כדרכה אביי משמיה דרבה אמר חייב. רבא משמיה דרבה אמר פטור. וקיימא לן בהא כאביי דאסיקנא והלכתא תחילתו בפשיעה וסופו באונס חייב. ומודה אביי דאי הדרא גבי מרה פטור דהא הדרא לה. ומודה רבא היכא דגנבה גנב מאגם ומתה כדרכה בי גנב מחייב מאי טעמא אי נמי שבקה מלאך המות בי גנב הוה קיימא. מתיב רמי בר חמא לאביי העלה לראשי צוקין פי' ההרים שעולין האבנים וצורים שלו כסכינים ונפלה אין זה אונס ודייקי' מינה [א] הא מתה הוי אונס ופטור אמאי ונימא אוירא דהר קטלה ופרקי' זו אינה פשיעה שהרי העלה למרעה שמן וטוב אי הכי אפי' נפלה יהא פטור ודחינן התם מפני שהיה לו לתקפה כדי שלא תפול ולא תקפה. אי הכי הא דתנינן עלתה לראשי צוקין ונפלה הרי זה אונס אמאי הכא נמי נימא היה לו לתקפה כיון שלא תקפה מחייב ופרקי' סיפא כגון שנתחזקה עליו שהחזיק בה בכל כחו ומשכתו ועלתה ומשכתו וירדה ונפלה ומאי הוה ליה למיעבד הלכך פטור. ואע"ג דאמר רבא כל דיין דלא דאין כוותי לאו דיינא הוא לית הלכת' כוותיה דסוגיין דשמעתא כולה כאביי הוא דסלקא. אמר ר' יוסי כיצד הלה עושה סחורה בפרתו של חבירו אלא תחזיר פרה לבעליה.

ואסיקנא

חשק שלמה על ר"ח

[א] נ"ל טעמא דנפלה הא כו'.

מסורת הש"ס

[א] [בבא קמא יא., נו:], [ב] [בבא קמא כא:, נו., נח., לקמן מב., לג:], [ג] [נ"ל דגנבה, יעב"ץ], [ד] לקמן לג:, [ה] [לקמן עח.].

גליון הש"ס

תוס' ד"ה את וכו' ולא כר"ח דפסק כאביי. עיין קדושין דף נב ע"א תוס' ד"ה ביע"ל. ועיין בתשו' בנימין זאב סי' שג דף תלג ע"ב:

ליקוטי רש"י

**דאמר ליה את מהימנת לי בשבועה.** דשומר חנם נשבע שלא פשע [ב"ק יא:]. דאמר ליה מפקיד את מהימנת לי בשבועה איהו לא מהימן לי בשבועה שנאנסה בפ' המפקיד (ב"מ לו:) [שם נו:]. **ראשי צוקין.** הרים חדין וגבוהין [לקמן צג:]. הר גבוה וזקוף [יומא סז. בד"ה תשעים]. **אוירא דהר קטלה.** הואיל ושינה בה יכול לומר לו לא מתה זו אלא מחמת אויר לא היתה לימודה ליגדל באויר הר וקשה לה. **אובצנא דהר קטלה.** עייפות ויגיעה ממשאה יכול לומר לו עייפות המעלה שעלתה לראש ההר הועיל לה מתחילה ע"כ עייפה לה לאחר זמן כשהלכה בדרך החלקה ויגעה תחת משאה ומתה [לקמן עח.].

**אֶלָּא אֲפִילּוּ לְמַאן דְּאָמַר פָּטוּר – However, even according to the one who says** that where a situation begins with negligence and ends with an unavoidable loss, the negligent party is **exempt** from paying for the unavoidable loss, **הָכָא חַיָּיב – here,** in the case of the animal that was allowed to escape, **[the *shomer*] is obligated** to pay. **מַאי טַעְמָא – What is the reason? דְּאָמְרִינַן הֲבָלָא דְאַגְמָא קַטְלָהּ – Because we say** that possibly **the foul air of the marsh killed it.**[12]

Rava elaborates on his version of Rabbah's opinion:

**רָבָא מִשְּׁמֵיהּ דְּרַבָּה אָמַר – Rava said in the name of Rabbah: פָּטוּר – [The *shomer*] is exempt** from liability for the animal's death, **כָּל דַּיָּינָא דְּלָא דָאִין כִּי הַאי דִּינָא – and any judge that does not judge in accord with this ruling לָאו דַּיָּינָא הוּא – is not** considered **a judge. לֹא מִיבַּעְיָא לְמַאן דְּאָמַר –** Now **it is not necessary** to say that this is so **according to the one who says: תְּחִילָּתוֹ בִּפְשִׁיעָה וְסוֹפוֹ בְּאוֹנֶס פָּטוּר –** When a situation **begins with** an act of **negligence but ends with an unavoidable loss** the negligent party **is exempt** from paying for the unavoidable loss, **דְּפָטוּר –** because according to him it is clear **that** in our case **[the *shomer*] is** similarly **exempt. אֶלָּא אֲפִילּוּ לְמַאן דְּאָמַר חַיָּיב – However, even according to the one who says** that the negligent party **is obligated** to pay for an unavoidable loss, **הָכָא פָּטוּר – here,** in the case of the animal that was allowed to escape, **[the *shomer*] is exempt** from liability for the death of the animal. **מַאי טַעְמָא – What is the reason? דְּאָמְרִינַן – Because we say** that **מַלְאַךְ הַמָּוֶת –** with respect to **the angel of death, מַה לִּי הָכָא וּמַה לִּי הָתָם – what is** the difference **to me whether the animal is located here or there?** The animal would have died even if it had remained in its barn.[13]

The Gemara qualifies these two statements of Abaye and Rava:

**וּמוֹדֵי אַבַּיֵּי – And Abaye concedes דְּאִי הַדְרָא לְבֵי מָרָהּ וּמֵתָה – that if [the animal] was returned to its owner's possession and died** there,[14] **דְּפָטוּר – [the *shomer*] is exempt** from liability. **מַאי טַעְמָא – What is the reason? דְּהָא הַדְרָא לָהּ – Because [the animal] was returned** before it died, **וְלֵיכָּא לְמֵימַר הֲבָלָא דְאַגְמָא קַטְלָהּ – and there is no** reason **to say that the foul air of the marsh killed it.**[15] **וּמוֹדֵי רָבָא – And Rava concedes כָּל הֵיכָא דְּאִיגַּנְבָה גַּנָּב בְּאַגַם – that if a thief shoul[d] steal**[16] **[the animal]** while it is grazing **in the marsh מֵתָה בְּדַרְכָּהּ בֵּי גַנָּב – and it dies naturally in the thief's possession דְּחַיָּיב – that [the *shomer*] is obligated** to pay, since his negli[gence] resulted in the theft of the animal. **מַאי טַעְמָא – Wha[t] is the reason** he is liable for the animal's death when it woul[d] have occurred even if the animal had not escaped to the marsh? **דְּאִי שְׁבַקָהּ מַלְאַךְ הַמָּוֶת –** He is liable **because** even **if the angel o[f] death had spared [the animal], בְּבֵיתֵיהּ דְּגַנָּבָא הֲוָה קַיְימָא – i[t] would** still **be standing in the thief's house!**[17]

Rava's ruling is challenged:

**אָמַר לֵיהּ אַבַּיֵּי לְרָבָא – Abaye told Rava: לְדִידָךְ דְּאָמְרַתְּ מַלְאַךְ הַמָּוֶת – According to you, who said** with respect to **the ange[l] of death, מַה לִּי הָכָא וּמַה לִּי הָתָם – what is** the difference **t[o] me** whether the animal is located **here or there** (i.e. we do no[t] attribute natural death to a change in location), **אִי דְּאוֹתְבֵיהּ רַבִּי אַבָּא בַּר מָמַל לְרַבִּי אַמִּי –** how do you understand **that whic[h] R' Abba bar Mammal** attempted to **refute R' Ami,**[18] **שַׁנֵּי לֵיהּ בְּשֶׁנָּתְנוּ לוֹ בְּעָלִים רְשׁוּת לְהַשְׁאִיל – and [R' Ami]** was forced to **an[swer] him** that the Mishnah speaks **of where the owner gav[e] [the renter] permission to lend** the animal? R' Ami thus im[plied] that if the renter had not received permission, he would b[e] liable even though the animal died naturally in the borrower'[s] possession. **וְלֵימָא לֵיהּ – But** according to you, Rava, **let th[e]** renter simply **tell [the owner]: מַלְאַךְ הַמָּוֶת מַה לִּי הָכָא וּמַה לִּי הָתָם –** "Regarding **the angel of death, what is** the differenc[e] **to me** whether the animal is **here** in my possession **or** there i[n] the borrower's possession? Although I should not have lent th[e] animal without your permission, I should not be held liable fo[r] the animal's death, which would have occurred regardless of th[e] animal's location."[19] – ? –

Rava deflects the challenge:

**אָמַר לֵיהּ – [Rava] told [Abaye]: לְדִידְכוּ דְּמַתְנִיתוּ – Accordin[g] to you, who teaches** that R' Yochanan imposes liability fo[r] any unauthorized transfer of an object given for safekeeping[20] because the owner may tell the first *shomer*, **אֵין רְצוֹנִי שֶׁיְּהֵא**

NOTES

12. In the case of the hut, although the *shomer* was initially negligent in guarding the money against fire, he was not at all negligent in guarding it against theft, and for that reason some say that he is not liable to pay for the theft. However, in our case, since the *shomer* was initially negligent in protecting the animal against thieves and wolves *and* somewhat negligent in protecting it from the foul air commonly found in marshy areas, he is held liable, for the foul air *may* have caused the animal's death (*Rashi*, as explained by *Tos. HaRosh*).

13. Rava maintains that while fetid marsh air may cause sickness, it cannot kill an animal. Alternatively, he holds that animals customarily graze in marshes and that the foul air does not affect them (*Raavad,* cited in *Shitah Mekubetzes*). Hence, Rava holds that in our case the *shomer's* negligence did *not* contribute to the death of the animal (*Tos. HaRosh*); even if he had done everything he should have done, the animal would have died anyway. In the case of the hut, however, had the *shomer* secured the coins in the manner he should have secured them – by burying them – they would not have been stolen. Thus, although the *shomer* employed an effective method of protecting the coins from thieves, he nonetheless bears responsibility for their loss, since the theft resulted from his failure to discharge his duties in the proper manner (*Rashi*).

14. I.e. when the animal wandered back from the marsh, the *shomer* returned it to the owner's possession, where it subsequently died (*Ritva* in explanation of *Rif;* cf. *Rashba, Meiri,* and *Shitah Mekubetzes* for another explanation; see *Nachalas Moshe*).

15. Since the animal appeared healthy when it was returned [so that it is possible that the cause of death arose after the end of the *shomer's* responsibility], even Abaye does not attribute the animal's death to its exposure to the marsh air [since the *shomer* discharged his obligation[s] before it died].

16. *Hagahos Yavetz* emends אִיגַּנְבָה to גַּנְבָהּ, *[he] stole it.*

17. From the time of the theft, the animal was effectively lost to it[s] owner. Since the *shomer* was responsible for the theft, he bears liabilit[y] for the loss of the animal (*Rashi*).

18. The Gemara refers to the exchange recorded above (36a), in which R Ami related the opinion of R' Yochanan, that a *shomer's* unauthorize[d] transfer of an object given to him for safekeeping to another *shome[r]* constitutes negligence, because the owner can claim that he does no[t] desire his object to be in someone else's possession. R' Abba challenge[d] R' Ami by citing the Mishnah, which exempted the renter from liabilit[y] when the animal died in the borrower's possession. [This shows that a] *shomer* (renter) who transfers an animal given to him to another *shome[r]* (borrower) is *not* considered negligent.]

19. I.e. R' Ami should have answered R' Abba that, indeed, where th[e] loss can be attributed to the change of location, R' Yochanan woul[d] rule the first *shomer* liable. However, in the Mishnah's case the ange[l] of death could just as well have struck the animal while it was in th[e] renter's possession. Since R' Ami did not offer this response, we ma[y] conclude – contrary to Rava's opinion – that regarding a situatio[n] that begins with an act of negligence but ends with an unavoidable los[s] (תְּחִילָּתוֹ בִּפְשִׁיעָה וְסוֹפוֹ בְּאוֹנֶס), the stringent opinion does not make an exception for the case of natural death (*Rashi*).

20. R' Yochanan holds the first *shomer* liable even when he is an unpai[d] *shomer* and he transferred the object entrusted to him to a paid *shomer*, thereby raising the level of watching.

על דעת אשתו ובניו הוא מפקיד אמרי נהרדעי דיקא נמי דקתני או שמסרן לבנו ובתו הקטנים חייב הא לבנו ולבתו הגדולים פטור מכלל דלאחרים לא שנא גדולים ולא שנא קטנים חייב דאם כן ליתני קטנים סתמא שמע מינה אמר רבא [א] הלכתא שומר שמסר לשומר חייב לא מבעיא שומר שכר שמסר לשומר חנם דגרועי גרעה לשמירתו אלא אפילו שומר חנם שמסר לשומר שכר חייב מאי טעמא דאמר ליה את מהימנת לי בשבועה האיך לא מהימן לי בשבועה: איתמר פשע בה ויצאת לאגם ומתה כדרכה אביי משמיה דרבה אמר חייב רבא משמיה דרבה אמר [א] פטור אביי משמיה דרבה אמר חייב כל דיינא דלא דאין כי האי דינא לאו דיינא הוא לא מבעיא למ"ד תחילתו בפשיעה וסופו באונס חייב דחייב אלא אפילו למ"ד פטור הכא חייב מ"ט דאמרינן הבלא דאגמא קטלה רבא משמיה דרבה אמר פטור כל דיינא דלא דאין כי האי דינא לאו דיינא הוא לא מיבעיא למ"ד [ב] תחילתו בפשיעה וסופו באונס פטור דפטור אלא אפילו למ"ד [ב] חייב הכא פטור מאי טעמא דאמרינן מלאך המות מה לי הכא ומה לי התם ומודי אביי דאי הדרא לבי מרה ומתה דפטור מ"ט דהא הדרא לה וליכא למימר הבלא דאגמא קטלה [ג] ומודי רבא כל היכא [ג] דאיגנבה גנב באגם ומתה כדרכה בי גנב דחייב מאי טעמא דאי שבקה מלאך המות בביתיה דגנבא הוה קיימא אמר ליה אביי לרבא לדידך דאמרת מלאך המות מה לי הכא ומה לי התם האי דאותביה ר' אבא בר ממל לרבי אמי ושני ליה בשנתנו לו בעלים רשות להשאיל ולימא ליה מלאך המות מה לי הכא ומה לי התם א"ל לדידכו דמתניתו אין רצוני שיהא פקדוני ביד אחר איכא לאותבה להההיא לדידי דאמינא אנת מהימנת לי בשבועה והאיך לא מהימן לי בשבועה ליכא לאותבה כלל מתיב רמי בר חמא [ד] [ד] העלה לראשי צוקין ונפלה אין זה אונס וחייב [ה] הא מתה כדרכה הרי זה אונס ופטור ואמאי לימא ליה [ו] אוירא דהר קטלה אי נמי אובצנא דהר קטלה הכא במאי עסקינן שהעלה למרעה שמן וטוב אי הכי נפלה נמי שהיה לו לתוקפה ולא תקפה אי הכי אימא רישא [י] עלתה לראשי צוקין ונפלה הרי זה אונס איבעי ליה למיתקפה לא צריכא שתקפתו ועלתה תקפתו וירדה: אמר רבי יוסי כיצד הלה עושה סחורה בפרתו כו': אמר רב יהודה אמר שמואל הלכה כרבי יוסי אמר ליה רב שמואל בר יהודה לרב יהודה אמרת לן משמיה דשמואל חלוק היה רבי יוסי

אף

על דעת אשתו ובניו. על דעת שהנפקד מוסרו לאשתו ובניו הגדולים ואין יכולין לומר אין רצוננו כו': דיקא נמי. דהאי דגדולים פטורין דוקא בניו נקט ולא אחרים: דא"כ. דלאחרים נמי גדולים פטור ליתני או שמסרן לקטנים סתמא: בשבועה. שלא פשע בה: האיך לא מהימן לי. ואני אומר שישנה בידו או אכלה או פשע בה: פשע בה. שלא נעל בפניה כראוי: ויצאת לאגם. מקום שאינה משתמרת שם אלא זאבים ולא אלא גנבים ומיהו לא אכלוה לא זאבים ולא גנבים: ומתה. דהוי תחילתו בפשיעה שמא יטרפוה זאבים וסופו לא אבדה באותה פשיעה אלא בדבר שהוא אונס: לא מיבעיא למ"ד. לקמן בפרקין (דף מב.) גבי ההוא דאותיב זוזי דפקדון בצריפא דאורבני דהויא פשיעותא לגבי נורא ונטירותא לענין גנבי ואיגנוב וגניבה לגבי שומר חנם אונס הוא: אלא אפילו למ"ד פטור הכא חייב. דהתם ליכא פשיעותא אלא לענין נורא אבל הכא איכא למימר בפשיעה מתה שאם היתה בבית לא מתה ויציאתה לאגם היא פשעת מיתתה דשמא הבל המצוי באגם קטלה: מה לי הכא כו'. אבל התם גבי זוזי אם שמרם כהלכתם דקי"ל (שם) כספים אין להם שמירה אלא בקרקע לא נגנבו ואע"ג דקי"ל בצריפא דאורבני אין דרך גנבים לבקש שם מעות ואונס הוא מיהו ע"י שלא שמר כדין שמירתם אבדו אבל פרה זו אם היתה בבית נמי היתה מתה: דאיגנבה גנב מאגם. שזהו דבר שהוא פשיעה אבל יציאתה לאגם אע"פ שסופה מתה בי גנב חייב ולא אמר אי הוה בבית שומר נמי הוה מתה: מ"ט. משעת גניבה היא אבודה מן הבעלים דאי נמי שבקה מלאך המות בי גנב הוה קיימא הלכך החיוב בא לו על שעת הגניבה: הא דאותביה ר' אבא. לעיל מהשוכר פרה והשאילה לאחר לימא אין רצוני כו': ושני ליה בשנתנו לו הבעלים רשות. מאי דוחקיה לשנויי הכי נימא ליה אם אירע בה אונס אחר דמצינו למימר אם היתה בביתו לא נאנסה היה חייב אבל זו מתה כדרכה מלאך המות נמי בבית שוכר קטיל לה ומדלא שני ליה הכי שמעינן למ"ד תחילתו בפשיעה וסופו באונס חייב לא שנא אונס מלאך המות משאר אונסין: לדידכו. דאמריתו טעמא דשומר שמסר לשומר חייב משום אין רצוני איכא לאותובה להאי ומאי דניחא ליה לרבי אמי שני ליה אנא לא סבירא לי לא אתקפתא ולא שינויא דלדידי דאמרי לעיל טעמא משום דלא מהימן ליה בשבועה ליכא לאותובה כלל שהרי שוכר עצמו נשבע לו כדתנן ישבע השוכר שמתה כדרכה: העלה לראשי צוקין. שומר שהעלה לראשי הרים חדים ומשופעים ונפלה: אין זה אונס. אלא פשיעה דדרכה ליפול: הא מתה כדרכה. בראש הצוק: פטור. דהוי סופו באונס: אוירא. לינה: אובצנא. עייפות טורח המעלה: למרעה שמן וטוב. דדרך הרועים להעלות שם בהמות לרעות: לתוקפה. להחזיק בה שכן דרך הרועים: עלתה. מאליה: שתקפתו. על כרחו ועלתה ולא יכול להחזיק בה שחזקה היתה ממנו:

אף

דאם כן ליתני קטנים סתמא. וא"ת תקשה לרב וי"ל דבניו נקט לרבותא דסד"א דעל דעת בניו הקטנים נמי מפקיד דרגילות הוא שלפעמים מוסר חפציו לבניו קטנים קמ"ל אי נמי לכך נקט בניו ולא נקט קטנים סתמא משום דבעי למידק הא גדולים הוי כדרך השומרים ומותר משום דעל דעת בניו הגדולים מפקיד אבל גדולים דעלמא אסור למסור אע"פ שאינו מתחייב בכך:

את מהימנת לי בשבועה. ולכך היכא שהשומר הראשון יכול לישבע על האונס או שהיו עדים בדבר פטור ואפי' מסר לחש"ו ומתה ברשותם כיון דאף בבית שומר הראשון היתה מתה דמלאך המות מה לי הכא מ"ל התם כו' וסובר רבא שזהו טעמו של רבי יוחנן ולא כאביי דאמר משום דאין רצוני כו' וכן הלכה כרבא ולא כר"ח דפסיק כאביי:

שהעלה למרעה שמן וטוב. דהשתא לא הוי פשיעה בהעלאה: אי הכי עלתה נמי. בשלמא לרבא דאמר מלאך המות כו' לא יצטרך להעמיד במרעה שמן וטוב ולכך העלה לראשי צוקין ונפלה חייב משום העלאה אע"פ שנפלה בע"כ שתקפתו וירדה ורישא דקתני אי עלתה פטור מיירי שתקפתו ועלתה וכן הנפילה היתה בתקפתו וירדה כמו בסיפא אבל לאביי דאוקמה במרעה שמן וטוב ולא פשע בהעלאה וחייב משום שפשע בנפילתה דמיירי שהיה יכול לתקפה ולא תקפה א"כ רישא נמי אפי' תקפתו ועלתה אמאי פטור ליחייב משום נפילה שהיה לו לשומרה שלא תפול דמסתמא נפלה דרישא הוי כמו נפלה דסיפא שהיה יכול לתקפה ומשני נפלה דרישא מיירי שתקפתו וירדה דומיא דעלתה דמיירי דתקפתו ועלתה ולא דמיא לנפילה דסיפא וא"ת אמאי נקט ברישא עלתה ובסיפא העלה והלא אין חילוק בין העלה מדעתו לעלתה בעל כרחו ובנפילה לבד הוה ליה לפלוגי דתקפתו וירדה הוה אונס לא תקפתו חייב וי"ל דרישא נקט עלתה לגלויי דנפלה הוי בע"כ וסיפא נקט העלה לגלויי דנפלה הוי שהיה בידו לתקפה ולא תקפה דומיא דהעלה שהיה בידו וא"ת וסיפא כיון דמיירי שהיה יכול לתקפה אמאי אוקמה במרעה שמן וטוב אפילו לא היה מרעה שמן וטוב לא פשע בהעלאה כיון שהיה יכול לשומרה מנפילה וי"ל כיון דאין צורך הבהמה בהעלאה זו פושע הוא שיש לו לחוש שמא ישכח ולא ישמרנה מליפול ולכך אם מתה היה חייב:

גזל

עין משפט נר מצוה

לז א מיי' פ"ג מהל' שכירות הל' י סמג עשין פח טוש"ע ח"מ סי' רלא סעי' ט:

לא ב מיי' שם הל' ט טוש"ע שם סעי' ו:

לב ג מיי' שם הל' י טוש"ע שם סעי' ט:

לג ד ה מיי' שם הל' ט טוש"ע שם סעי' י:

לד ו מיי' שם ועיין במ"מ טוש"ע שם סעי' יא:

רבינו חננאל

שיהא פקדוני ביד אחר. ופריק רבא אליבא דאביי כל המפקיד על דעת שימסרם מי שנפקדין אצלו לבניו הגדולים ולאשתו הוא מפקיד דלא עדיף ליה ממונא דחבריה מדידיה וממונא דידיה אשתו ובניו נטרי ליה וכן הלכה דנהרדעאי דייקי מתני' כרבא. אמר רבא הלכת' שומר שמסר לשומר חייב ואפילו שומר חנם שמסר לשומר שכר דעלויי עלייה לשמירתו חייב והני מילי היכא דיכול למימר אנת מהימנת לי בשבועה האיך לא מהימן לי בשבועה ואי מיתבריר דאיהו נמי הוה מפקיד גביה כגון מעשה דגינאי בההיא סבתא פטור. איתמר פשע בה ויצאת לאגם ומתה כדרכה אביי משמיה דרבה אמר חייב. רבא משמיה דרבה אמר פטור. וקיימא לן בהא כאביי דאסיקנא והלכתא תחילתו בפשיעה וסופו באונס חייב. ומודה אביי דאי הדרא גבי מרה פטור דהא הדרא לה. ומודה רבא היכא דגנבה גנב מאגם ומתה כדרכה בי גנב מחייב מאי טעמא אי נמי שבקה מלאך המות בי גנב הוה קיימא. מתיב רמי בר חמא לאביי העלה לראשי צוקין פי' ההרים שעולין האבנים וצורים שלו כסכינים ונפלה אין זה אונס ודייקי' מינה [א] הא מתה הוי אונס ופטור אמאי ונימא אוירא דהר קטלה ופרקי' זו אינה פשיעה שהרי העלה למרעה שמן וטוב אי הכי אפי' נפלה יהא פטור ודחינן התם מפני שהיה לו לתקפה כדי שלא תפול ולא תקפה. אי הכי הא דתנינן עלתה לראשי צוקין ונפלה הרי זה אונס אמאי הכא נמי נימא היה לו לתקפה כיון שלא תקפה מחייב ופרקי' סיפא כגון שנתחזקה עליו שהחזיק בה בכל כחו ומשכתו ועלתה ומשכתו וירדה ונפלה ומאי הוה ליה למיעבד הלכך פטור. ואע"ג דאמר רבא כל דיין דלא דאין כוותי לאו דיינא הוא לית הלכת' כוותיה דסוגיין דשמעתא כולה כאביי הוא דסלקא. אמר ר' יוסי כיצד הלה עושה סחורה בפרתו של חבירו אלא תחזיר פרה לבעליה.

ואסיקנא

חשק שלמה על ר"ח

א) נ"ל טעמא דנפלה הא סי'.

מסורת הש"ס

א) [בבא קמא יא:, ע:] ב) [בבא קמא כא:, ע. נח., לקמן מב., לג:] ג) [נ"ל דגנבה, יעב"ץ] ד) לקמן לג:, ה) [לקמן עח.].

גליון הש"ס

תוס' ד"ה את וכו' ולא כר"ח דפסק כאביי. עיין קדושין דף נב ע"ל תוס' ד"ה ביע"ל. ועיי בתשו' בנימין זאב סי' ש דף תלב ע"ב:

ליקוטי רש"י

דאמר ליה את מהימנת לי בשבועה. דשומר חנם נשבע שלא פשע [ב"ק יא:]. דאמר ליה מפקיד את מהימנת לי בשבועה איהו לא מהימן לי בשבועה שנאמרה בפ' המפקיד (ב"מ לו:) [שם נו:]. ראשי צוקין. הרים חדין וגבוהין [לקמן צג:]. הר גבוה וזקוף [יומא סז. בד"ה תשעים]. אוירא דהר קטלה. הוא ושינה בה יכול לומר לו לא מתה זו אלא מחמת אויר לא היתה לימודה ליגדל באויר הר וקשה לה. אובצנא דהר קטלה. עייפות ויגיעה ממשא יכול לומר לו עייפו המעלה שעלתה לרא ההר הועיל לה מתחילה ע"כ עייפה לה לאחר זמ כשהלכה בדרך החלקה ויגעה תחת משאה ומתה [לקמן עח.].

עַל דַּעַת אִשְׁתּוֹ וּבָנָיו הוּא מַפְקִיד – **deposits** it **with the understanding** that the *shomer* may entrust it to **his wife and his** adult **children** in his place. Therefore, the owner cannot later claim that he did not want the *shomer's* adult children to watch his property. However, he can rightfully protest an unauthorized transfer to anyone else.

The Gemara offers proof for this explanation:

אָמְרֵי נְהַרְדָּעֵי – **The Nehardean** scholars **said:** דַּיְקָא נַמִּי – **A precise [reading]** of the Mishnah's wording **also** supports Rava's answer. דְּקָתָנֵי – **For [the Mishnah] states:** אוֹ שֶׁמְּסָרָן לִבְנוֹ וּבִתּוֹ הַקְּטַנִּים חַיָּיב – OR IF HE GAVE THEM TO HIS YOUNG SON OR DAUGHTER, HE IS OBLIGATED to pay, הָא לִבְנוֹ וּלְבִתּוֹ הַגְּדוֹלִים פָּטוּר – **which implies** that if he gave the coins **to his adult son or daughter** to watch, **he is exempt.** מִכְּלָל דִּלַאֲחֵרִים – **By implication** it follows **that** concerning an unauthorized transfer **to others**[1] לֹא שְׁנָא גְּדוֹלִים וְלֹא שְׁנָא קְטַנִּים – **there is no difference between adults and youngsters,** חַיָּיב – and **[the *shomer*] is** held **liable** regardless. דְּאִם כֵּן – **For if it is so** that he is not held liable for an unauthorized transfer to *any* adult, לִיתְנֵי קְטַנִּים סְתָמָא – **let the Mishnah state "youngsters" without specifying** whose children they are.[2] שְׁמַע מִינָּהּ – Rather, **learn from this** that a *shomer* avoids liability only if he entrusts the object to his own adult children, since such a transfer is anticipated by the owner.[3]

The Gemara presents a final opinion regarding the unauthorized transfer of an object given for safekeeping:

אָמַר רָבָא – **Rava said:** הִלְכְתָא שׁוֹמֵר שֶׁמָּסַר לְשׁוֹמֵר חַיָּיב – **The halachah is** that **a *shomer* who transferred** the object entrusted to him **to** another ***shomer*** without permission of the owner **– is obligated** to pay for even unavoidable loss. לֹא מִבַּעְיָא שׁוֹמֵר שָׂכָר שֶׁמָּסַר לְשׁוֹמֵר חִנָּם – **It is not necessary** to state that **a paid *shomer* who transferred** the object **to an unpaid *shomer*** is liable for all losses, דִּגְרוּעֵי גָּרְעָה לִשְׁמִירָתוֹ – **since he diminished the level** of **watching for [this object];** לָא אֲפִילוּ שׁוֹמֵר חִנָּם שֶׁמָּסַר לְשׁוֹמֵר שָׂכָר – **but even an unpaid *shomer* who transferred** the object **to a paid *shomer* is obligated** to pay for all losses, even though in doing so he upgraded the level of watching. מַאי טַעְמָא – **What is the reason?** דְּאָמַר לֵיהּ – **Because the** owner **may tell [the first *shomer*]:** אַתְּ מְהֵימְנַתְּ לִי בִּשְׁבוּעָה – **"You are** someone whose word is **believable to me with an oath** that you were not negligent; הָאִיךְ לֹא מְהֵימַן לִי בִּשְׁבוּעָה – **that one** [the second *shomer*] **is not** someone whose word is **believable to me** even **with an oath."**[4] Hence, the first *shomer* may not rely on the second *shomer's* oath for his exemption.[5]

The Gemara introduces a new case concerning a *shomer's* liability and relates it to our previous discussion of unauthorized transfers:

אִתְּמַר – **It was said:** פָּשַׁע בָּהּ – If **[a *shomer*] was negligent in** watching **[an animal],**[6] וְיָצְאת לָאֲגַם וּמֵתָה כִּדְרָכָהּ – **and it escaped to a marsh**[7] **and died** there **naturally,**[8] אַבַּיֵי מִשְּׁמֵיהּ דְּרַבָּה אָמַר – **Abaye said in the name of Rabbah:** חַיָּיב – **[The *shomer*] is obligated** to pay for the loss, even though it was unavoidable. רָבָא מִשְּׁמֵיהּ דְּרַבָּה אָמַר – **Rava said in the name of Rabbah:** פָּטוּר – **He is exempt** from having to pay, since the loss was unavoidable.

The Gemara elaborates:

אַבַּיֵי מִשְּׁמֵיהּ דְּרַבָּה אָמַר – **Abaye said in the name of Rabbah:** חַיָּיב – **He is obligated** to pay, כָּל דַּיָּינָא דְּלָא דָּאִין כִּי הַאי דִּינָא – and **any judge that does not judge in accord with this ruling** לָאו דַּיָּינָא הוּא – **is not** considered **a judge.** לֹא מִבַּעְיָא לְמַאן דְּאָמַר – **It is not necessary** to say that this ruling is correct **according to the one who says:** תְּחִילָּתוֹ בִּפְשִׁיעָה וְסוֹפוֹ בְּאוֹנֶס חַיָּיב – **When** a situation **begins with** an act of **negligence but ends with an unavoidable loss,**[9] the negligent party **is obligated** to pay for the unavoidable loss,[10] דְּחַיָּיב – because according to him it is clear **that** in our case the *shomer* **is** similarly **obligated.**[11]

---

NOTES

1. I.e. to anyone who is not a member of the *shomer's* immediate family.

2. Had the Mishnah stated simply that the *shomer* is liable if he transfers the object he is watching to "youngsters," we would have inferred that he acts properly if he transfers it to *any* responsible adult. By specifying that they were *his* young children, the Mishnah implies that the distinction between youngsters and adults applies only in the case of *his* children.

3. According to Rav, who maintains that a *shomer* is not liable when he transfers the object he is watching to any responsible adult, we must say that the Tanna could indeed have employed the unspecific term "youngsters" to imply Rav's teaching. However, the Tanna chose to specify "the *shomer's* own young children" to emphasize that the owner anticipates the *shomer* giving the object only to his adult children, not to his small children as well. Alternatively, by specifying "the *shomer's* young children" the Tanna wished to imply that transferring to a *shomer's* adult children is a customary practice and thus perfectly permissible, but that transferring to other adults, while it does not make the *shomer* liable, is nevertheless uncommon and therefore forbidden (*Tosafos*).

4. [Since he does not trust the second *shomer's* oath,] the owner can claim that he suspects the second *shomer* of negligence, or of stealing or using the object himself (*Rashi*). Since the first *shomer* does not know what happened and must rely on what the second *shomer* says, he cannot free himself from paying the owner if the owner is unwilling to accept the second *shomer's* oath. [The owner is only obligated to accept the oath of the person to whom he entrusted his property for safekeeping, since his willingness to entrust it to him implies a willingness to accept his oath if the object is lost. But he is not obligated to accept anyone else's oath.]

5. However, if the first *shomer* can swear of his own knowledge that the loss was unavoidable (for example, he saw what happened), he is exempt. Similarly, if witnesses attest to that fact that it was unavoidable, the first *shomer* is exempt. Unlike Abaye (who offers a different interpretation of R' Yochanan's rationale; see above, 36a *Tosafos* ד״ה אין and note 19), Rava does not automatically consider an unauthorized transfer to be an act of negligence. It is just that the owner is not obligated to accept the second *shomer's* oath.

Similarly, if the owner customarily deposited his property with the second *shomer,* he may not refuse to accept the second *shomer's* oath (see *Tosafos, Ritva*).

6. For example, he did not properly lock the barn door (*Rashi*).

This ruling concerns *shomrim* who are not liable for unavoidable loss such as the paid *shomer* and unpaid *shomer*.

7. A place that offers no protection against thieves or preying wolves (*Rashi*).

8. Although *initially* the custodian's negligence exposed the animal to the danger of thieves and wolves, *in the end* it did not die on either score but as a result of another, unavoidable factor (*Rashi*).

9. Abaye refers to the case, discussed below (42a), of an unpaid *shomer* who hid money entrusted to him in a hut made from willow branches. Since this kind of hut served as a blind for trappers, it provided adequate protection against theft, for no thief would expect to find valuables in such a structure. On the other hand, [since the hut was composed of flammable material] it provided no protection against fire, and for that reason the *shomer* was negligent in secreting the money there. In the end, though, the money was stolen, and for an unpaid *shomer* – who is not liable for theft – such a loss is considered in law to be the same as an unavoidable loss (*Rashi* here and to 42a).

10. For if the *shomer* had not concealed the object in a flammable place but had properly protected it from fire by burying it in the ground, the theft would not have occurred (*Ritva;* see also *Tosafos* to 36a above ד״ה אין).

11. For if the *shomer* had properly locked the animal in the barn, it would not have been exposed to the potentially lethal foul air of the marsh (*Ritva*).

עין משפט
נר מצוה

ל א מיי' פ"ג מהל' שכירות הל' י סמג עשין פח טוש"ע ח"מ סי' רלא סעי' ט:
לא ב מיי' שם הל' ט טוש"ע שם סעי' ו:
לב ג מיי' שם הל' י טוש"ע שם סעי' ט:
לג ד ה מיי' שם הל' ט טוש"ע שם סעי' י:
לד ו מיי' שם ועיין במ"מ טוש"ע שם סעי' יא:

על דעת אשתו ובניו הוא מפקיד אמרי נהרדעי דיקא נמי דקתני או שמסרן לבנו ובתו הקטנים חייב הא לבנו ולבתו הגדולים פטור מכלל דלאחרים לא שנא גדולים ולא שנא קטנים חייב דאם כן ליתני קטנים סתמא שמע מינה אמר רבא [א] הלכתא שומר שמסר לשומר חייב לא מבעיא שומר שכר שמסר לשומר חנם דגרועי גרעה לשמירתו אלא אפילו שומר חנם שמסר לשומר שכר חייב מאי טעמא דאמר ליה את מהימנת לי בשבועה האיך לא מהימן לי בשבועה: איתמר פשע בה ויצאת לאגם ומתה כדרכה אביי משמיה דרבה אמר חייב רבא משמיה דרבה אמר [א] פטור אביי משמיה דרבה אמר חייב כל דיינא דלא דאין כי האי דינא לאו דיינא הוא לא מבעיא למ"ד תחילתו בפשיעה וסופו באונס חייב דחייב אלא אפילו למ"ד פטור הכא חייב מ"ט דאמרינן הבלא דאגמא קטלה רבא משמיה דרבה אמר פטור כל דיינא דלא דאין כי האי דינא לאו דיינא הוא לא מיבעיא למ"ד [ב] תחילתו בפשיעה וסופו באונס פטור דפטור אלא אפילו למ"ד [ב] חייב הכא פטור מאי טעמא דאמרינן מלאך המות מה לי הכא ומה לי התם ומודי אביי דאי הדרא לבי מרה ומתה דפטור מ"ט דהא הדרא לה וליכא למימר הבלא דאגמא קטלה [ג] ומודי רבא כל היכא [ג] דאיגנבה גנב באגם ומתה כדרכה בי גנב דחייב מאי טעמא דאי שבקה מלאך המות בביתיה דגנבא הוה קיימא אמר ליה אביי לרבא לדידך דאמרת מלאך המות מה לי הכא ומה לי התם האי דאותביה ר' אבא בר ממל לרבי אמי ושני ליה בשנתנו לו בעלים רשות להשאיל ולימא ליה מלאך המות מה לי הכא ומה לי התם א"ל לדידכו דמתניתו אין רצוני שיהא פקדוני ביד אחר איכא לאותבה להא לדידי דאמינא אנת מהימנת לי בשבועה והאיך לא מהימן לי בשבועה ליכא לאותבה כלל מתיב רמי בר חמא [ד] [ד] העלה לראשי צוקין ונפלה אין זה אונס וחייב [ה] הא מתה כדרכה הרי זה אונס ופטור ואמאי לימא ליה [ה] אוירא דהר קטלה אי נמי אובצנא דהר קטלה הכא במאי עסקינן שהעלה למרעה שמן וטוב אי הכי נפלה נמי שהיה לו לתוקפה ולא תקפה אי הכי אימא רישא [ו] עלתה לראשי צוקין ונפלה הרי זה אונס איבעי ליה למיתקפה לא צריכא שתקפתו ועלתה תקפתו וירדה: אמר רבי יוסי כיצד הלה עושה סחורה בפרתו כו': אמר רב יהודה אמר שמואל הלכה כרבי יוסי אמר ליה רב שמואל בר יהודה לרב יהודה אמרת לן משמיה דשמואל חלוק היה רבי יוסי
אף

דאם כן ליתני קטנים סתמא. וא"ת תקשה לרב וי"ל דבניו נקט לרבותא דסד"א דעל דעת בניו הקטנים נמי מפקיד דרגילות הוא שלפעמים מוסר חפציו לבניו קטנים קמ"ל אי נמי לכך נקט בניו ולא נקט קטנים סתמא משום דבעי למידק הא גדולים הוי כדרך השומרים ומותר משום דעל דעת בניו הגדולים מפקיד אבל גדולים דעלמא אסור למסור אע"פ שאינו מתחייב בכך:

את מהימנת לי בשבועה. ולכך היכא שהשומר הראשון יכול לישבע על האונס או שהיו עדים בדבר פטור ואפי' מסר לחש"ו ומתה ברשותם כיון דאף בבית שומר הראשון היתה מתה דמלאך המות מה לי הכא מ"ל התם כו' וסובר רבא שזהו טעמו של רבי יוחנן ולא כאביי דאמר משום דאין רצוני כו' וכן הלכה כרבא [ה] ולא כר"ח דפסיק כאביי:

שהעלה למרעה שמן וטוב. דהשתא לא הוי פשיעה בהעלאה: אי הכי עלתה נמי. בשלמא לרבא דאמר מלאך המות כו' לא יצטרך להעמיד במרעה שמן וטוב ולכך העלה לראשי צוקין ונפלה חייב משום העלאה אע"פ שנפלה בע"כ שתקפתו וירדה ורישא דקתני אי עלתה פטור מיירי שתקפתו ועלתה וכן הנפילה היתה בתקפתו וירדה כמו בסיפא אבל לאביי דאוקמה במרעה שמן וטוב ולא פשע בהעלאה וחייב משום שפשע בנפילתה דמיירי שהיה יכול לתקפה ולא תקפה א"כ רישא נמי אפי' תקפתו ועלתה אמאי פטור ליחייב משום נפילה שהיה לו לשומרה שלא תפול דמסתמא נפלה דרישא הוי כמו נפלה דסיפא שהיה יכול לתקפה ומשני נפלה דרישא מיירי שתקפתו וירדה דומיא דעלתה דמיירי דתקפתו ועלתה ולא דמיא לנפילה דסיפא וא"ת אמאי נקט ברישא עלתה ובסיפא העלה והלא אין חילוק בין העלה מדעתו לעלתה בעל כרחו ובנפילה לבד הוה ליה לפלוגי דתקפתו וירדה הוה אונס לא תקפתו חייב וי"ל דרישא נקט עלתה לגלויי דנפלה הוי בע"כ וסיפא נקט העלה לגלויי דנפלה הוי שהיה בידו לתקפה ולא תקפה דומיא דהעלה שהיה בידו וא"ת וסיפא כיון דמיירי שהיה יכול לתקפה אמאי אוקמה במרעה שמן וטוב אפילו לא היה מרעה שמן וטוב לא פשע בהעלאה כיון שהיה יכול לשומרה מנפילה וי"ל כיון דאין צורך הבהמה בהעלאה זו פושע הוא שיש לו לחוש שמא ישכח ולא ישמרנה מליפול ולכך אם מתה היה חייב:
גזל

על דעת אשתו ובניו. על דעת שהנפקד מוסרו לאשתו ובניו הגדולים ואין יכולין לומר אין רצונו כו': דיקא נמי. דהאי דגדולים פטורין דוקא בניו נקט ולא אחרים: דא"כ. דלאחרים נמי גדולים פטור ליתני או שמסרן לקטנים סתמא: בשבועה. שלא פשע בה: האיך לא מהימן לי. ואני אומר שישנה בידו או אכלה או פשע בה: פשע בה. שלא נעל בפניה כראוי: ויצאת לאגם. מקום שאינה משתמרת שם אלא זאבים ולא אלא גנבים ומיהו לא אכלוה לא זאבים ולא גנבים: ומתה. דהוי תחילתו בפשיעה שמא יטרפוה זאבים וסופו לא אבדה באותה פשיעה אלא בדבר שהוא אונס: לא מיבעיא למ"ד. לקמן בפרקין (דף מב.) גבי ההוא דאותיב זוזי דפקדון בצריפא דאורבני דהויא פשיעותא לגבי נורא ונטירותא לענין גנבי ואיגנוב וגניבה לגבי שומר חנם אונס הוא: אלא אפילו למ"ד פטור הכא חייב. דהתם ליכא פשיעותא אלא לענין נורא אבל הכא איכא למימר בפשיעה מתה שאם היתה בבית לא מתה ויציאתה לאגם היא פשעת מיתתה דשמא הבל המצוי באגם קטלה: מה לי הכא כו'. אבל התם גבי זוזי אם שמרם כהלכתם דקי"ל (שם) כספים אין להם שמירה אלא בקרקע לא נגנבו ואע"ג דקי"ל בצריפא דאורבני אין דרך גנבים לבקש שם מעות ואונס הוא מיהו ע"י שלא שמר כדין שמירתם אבדו אבל פרה זו אם היתה בבית נמי היתה מתה: דאיגנבה גנב מאגם. שזהו דבר שהוא פשיעה אבל יציאתה לאגם אע"פ שסופה מתה בי גנב חייב ולא אמר אי הוה בבית שומר נמי הוה מתה: מ"ט. משעת גניבה היא אבודה מן הבעלים דאי נמי שבקה מלאך המות בי גנב הוה קיימא הלכך החיוב בא לו על שעת הגניבה: הא דאותביה ר' אבא. לעיל מהשוכר פרה והשאילה לאחר לימא אין רצוני כו': ושני ליה בשנתנו לו הבעלים רשות. מאי דוחקיה לשנויי הכי נימא ליה אם אירע בה אונס אחר דמלינו למימר אם היתה בביתו לא נאנסה היה חייב אבל זו מתה כדרכה מלאך המות נמי בבית שוכר קטיל לה ומדלא שני ליה הכי שמעינן למ"ד תחילתו בפשיעה וסופו באונס חייב לא שנא אונס מלאך המות משאר אונסין: לדידכו. דאמריתו טעמא דשומר שמסר לשומר חייב משום אין רצוני איכא לאותובה להאי ומאי דניחא ליה לרבי אמי שני ליה אנא לא סבירא לי לא אתקפתא ולא שינויא דלדידי דאמרי לעיל טעמא משום דלא מהימן ליה בשבועה ליכא לאותובה כלל שהרי שוכר עצמו נשבע לו כדתנן ישבע השוכר שמתה כדרכה: העלה לראשי צוקין. שומר שהעלה לראשי הרים חדים ומשופעים ונפלה: אין זה אונס. אלא פשיעה דדרכה ליפול: הא מתה כדרכה. בראש הצוק: פטור. דהוי סופו באונס: אוירא. לינה: אובצנא. עייפות טורח המעלה: למרעה שמן וטוב. דדרך הרועים להעלות שם בהמות לרעות: לתוקפה. להחזיק בה שכן דרך הרועים: עלתה. מאליה: שתקפתו. על כרחו ועלתה ולא יכול להחזיק בה שחזקה היתה ממנו:
אף

רבינו חננאל

שיהא פקדוני ביד אחר. ופריק רבא אליבא דאביי כל המפקיד על דעת שימסרם מי שנפקדין אצלו לבניו הגדולים ולאשתו הוא מפקיד דלא עדיף ליה ממונא דחבריה מדידיה וממונא דידיה אשתו ובניו נטרי ליה וכן הלכה דנהרדעאי דייקי מתני' כרבא. אמר רבא הלכת' שומר שמסר לשומר חייב ואפילו שומר חנם שמסר לשומר שכר דעלויי עלייה לשמירתו חייב והני מילי היכא דיכול למימר אנת מהימנת לי בשבועה האיך לא מהימן לי בשבועה ואי מיתבריר דאיהו נמי הוה מפקיד גביה כגון מעשה דגינאי בההיא סבתא פטור. איתמר פשע בה ויצאת לאגם ומתה כדרכה אביי משמיה דרבה אמר חייב. רבא משמיה דרבה אמר פטור. וקיימא לן בהא כאביי דאסיקנא והלכתא תחילתו בפשיעה וסופו באונס חייב. ומודה אביי דאי הדרא גבי מרה פטור דהא הדרא לה. ומודה רבא היכא דגנבה גנב מאגם ומתה כדרכה בי גנב מחייב מאי טעמא אי נמי שבקה מלאך המות בי גנב הוה קיימא. מתיב רמי בר חמא לאביי העלה לראשי צוקין פי' ההרים שעולין האבנים וצורים שלו כסכינים ונפלה אין זה אונס ודייקי' מינה [א] הא מתה הוי אונס ופטור אמאי ונימא אוירא דהר קטלה ופרקי' זו אינה פשיעה שהרי העלה למרעה שמן וטוב אי הכי אפי' נפלה יהא פטור ודחינן התם מפני שהיה לו לתקפה כדי שלא תפול ולא תקפה. אי הכי הא דתנינן עלתה לראשי צוקין ונפלה הרי זה אונס אמאי הכא נמי נימא היה לו לתקפה כיון שלא תקפה מחייב ופרקי' סיפא כגון שנתחזקה עליו שהחזיק בה בכל כחו ומשכתו ועלתה ומשכתו וירדה ונפלה ומאי הוה ליה למיעבד הלכך פטור. ואע"ג דאמר רבא כל דיין דלא דאין כוותי לאו דיינא הוא לית הלכת' כוותיה דסוגיין דשמעתא כולה כאביי הוא דסלקא. אמר ר' יוסי כיצד הלה עושה סחורה בפרתו של חבירו אלא תחזיר פרה לבעליה.
ואסיקנא

חשק שלמה על ר"ח
א) נ"ל טעמא דנפלה הא כו'.

מסורת הש"ס

א) [בבא קמא יא., ט:] ב) [בבא קמא כא:, ע. נח., לקמן מב., לג:] ג) [נ"ל דגנבה, יעב"ץ] ד) לקמן לג:, ה) [לקמן עח.].

גליון הש"ס

תוס' ד"ה את וכו' ולא כר"ח דפסק כאביי. עיין קדושין דף נג ע"ל תוס' ד"ה ביע"ל. ועיין בתשו' בנימין זאב סי' שג דף תלג ע"ב:

ליקוטי רש"י

דאמר ליה את מהימנת לי בשבועה. דשומר חנם נשבע שלא פשע [ב"ק יא:]. דאמר ליה מפקיד את מהימנת לי בשבועה איהו לא מהימן לי בשבועה שנאנסה בפ' המפקיד (ב"מ לו:) [שם נו:]. ראשי צוקין. הרים חדין וגבוהין [לקמן צג:]. הר גבוה וזקוף [יומא סז. בד"ה תשעים]. אוירא דהר קטלה. הואיל ושינה בה יכול לומר לו לא מתה זו אלא מחמת אויר לא היתה לימודה ליגדל באויר הר וקשה לה. אובצנא דהר קטלה. עייפות ויגיעה ממשאך יכול לומר לו עייפות המעלה שעלתה לראש ההר הועיל לה מתחילה ע"כ עייפה לה לאחר זמן כשהלכה בדרך החלקה ויגעה תחת משאה ומתה [לקמן עח.].

פעמים ששניהם באשם פעמים שהשוכר בחטאת והשואל באשם פעמים שהשוכר באשם והשואל בחטאת הא כיצד [א]כפירת ממון אשם [ב]ביטוי שפתים חטאת פעמים ששניהם בחטאת כגון שמתה כדרכה ואמרו נאנסה שוכר דבין כך ובין כך מיפטר פטור בחטאת שואל דבין כך ובין כך חיובי מיחייב בחטאת פעמים ששניהם באשם כגון שנגנבה ואמרו מתה מחמת מלאכה דתרוייהו קא כפרי ממונא דהא מיחייבי וקא פטרי נפשייהו שוכר בחטאת ושואל באשם כגון שמתה כדרכה ואמרו מתה מחמת מלאכה שוכר דבין כך ובין כך מיפטר פטור חייב בחטאת שואל דמיחייב במתה כדרכה וקא פטר נפשיה במתה מחמת מלאכה באשם שוכר באשם ושואל בחטאת כגון שנגנבה ואמרו מתה כדרכה שוכר הוא דמיחייב בגניבה ואבידה וקא פטר נפשיה במתה כדרכה באשם שואל דבין כך ובין כך חיובי מיחייב בחטאת מאי קמ"ל לאפוקי מדרבי אמי [א] דאמר כל שבועה שהדיינים משביעים אותה אין חייבין עליה משום שבועת ביטוי שנאמר [א] או נפש כי תשבע לבטא בשפתים כי תשבע מעצמה קמ"ל [ג]דלא כר' אמי [ג] אתמר שומר שמסר לשומר [ג] רב אמר פטור ור' יוחנן אמר [ד]חייב אמר אביי לטעמיה דרב לא מבעיא שומר חנם שמסר לשומר שכר דעלויי עלייה לשמירתו אלא אפילו שומר שכר שמסר לשומר חנם דגרועי גרעה לשמירתו פטור [ס] מאי טעמא דהא מסרה לבן דעת ולטעמיה דר' יוחנן [ה]לא מיבעיא שומר שכר שמסר לשומר חנם דגרועי גרעה לשמירתו אלא אפי' ש"ח שמסר לשומר שכר דעלויי עלייה לשמירתו חייב דא"ל [ד] אין רצוני שיהא פקדוני ביד אחר אמר רב חסדא הא דרב [ה] לאו בפירוש אתמר אלא מכללא דהנהו גינאי דכל יומא הוו מפקדי מרייהו גבה דההיא סבתא יומא חד אפקדינהו לגבי חד מינייהו שמע קלא בי הלולא נפק אזל אפקדינהו לגבה דההיא סבתא אדאזל ואתא אגנוב מרייהו אתא לקמיה דרב ופטריה מאן דחזא סבר משום שומר שמסר לשומר פטור ולא היא שאני התם [י]דכל יומא נמי אינהו גופייהו גבה דההיא סבתא הוו מפקדי להו יתיב ר' אמי וקאמר לה להא שמעתא איתיביה ר' אבא בר ממל לר' אמי השוכר פרה מחבירו והשאילה לאחר ומתה כדרכה ישבע השוכר שמתה כדרכה והשואל משלם לשוכר ואם איתא לימא ליה אין רצוני שיהא פקדוני ביד אחר א"ל הכא במאי עסקינן בשנתנו לו [י] (רשות הבעלים) להשאיל אי הכי לבעלים בעי לשלומי דאמרו ליה לדעתך מתיב רמי בר חמא [ז] [ז]המפקיד מעות אצל חבירו צררן והפשילן לאחוריו [ח]מסרן לבנו ובתו הקטנים [ח] ונעל בפניהם שלא כראוי חייב שלא שמר כדרך השומרים טעמא דקטנים הא גדולים פטור אמאי נימא ליה אין רצוני שיהא פקדוני ביד אחר אמר רבא [ט] [ט]כל המפקיד

**רש"י**

שניהם באשם. אם נשבעו לשקר והיו נשכרים בשבועתם להקל פרעון מעליהם כפירת ממון היא זו וקרבן שבועה שלהם אשם איל בן ב' שנים דכתיב (ויקרא ה) [י] והביא את אשמו איל תמים בערכך כסף (שני) שקלים והוא אשם גזילות: נאנסה. ע"י לסטים ונשבעו שכך (א) אע"פ שהשואל משלם אונסין משביעין אותו כדרב הונא שבועה שאינה ברשותו דחיישינן שמא נתן עיניו בה ונשבע שנאנסה ואינה ברשותו: שוכר דבין כך ובין כך מיפטר. מתשלומין קאי בחטאת: בין כך ובין כך. בין שנשבע באמת שמתה כדרכה בין שנשבע לשקר שנאנסה פטור עצמו מלשלם הלכך אין בשקר זה כפירת ממון דהא אם הודה על האמת היה פטור שבועת ביטוי היא ובחטאת: שואל דבין כך ובין כך חייב לשלם. נמצא שלא כפר ממון בשיקור שבועתו ושבועת ביטוי קאי בחטאת: כגון שנגנבה. והשוכר חייב לשלם לבעלים והשואל ישלם לשוכר: ואמרו מתה מחמת מלאכה. ופטר שואל עצמו בשקר מלשלם לשוכר והשוכר מלשלם לבעלים: שמתה כדרכה. ואם הודו על האמת שוכר פטור ושואל חייב: שנגנבה. ושניהם חייבין: ואמרו מתה כדרכה. השוכר פוטר עצמו בשקר אבל השואל לא נפטר בכך מלשלם: חיובי מיחייב. לשלם קאי על שבועתו בחטאת: מאי קמ"ל. רבי ירמיה משניות שלימות הן בשבועות המשנה מחובה לחובה ומפטור לפטור ומפטור לחובה פטור מאשם גזילות מחובה לפטור חייב: רב אמר פטור. מכל מה שהיה נפטר אם שמרה הוא עצמו: חייב. אפי' באונסין: ולא מיבעיא כו'. דפטור מן האונסין ואין לך לומר פשיעה היא זו שמסרה לאחר: מרייהו. פושוויי"ר בלע"ז: מאן דחזא. אחד מן התלמידים ששמע מפיו דפטריה סבר שומר שמסר לשומר כו': הוו מפקדי לה. דלא מצו אמרי ליה אין רצוננו שיהא בידה: להא שמעתא. דר' יוחנן רביה: אי הכי לבעלים בעי לשלומי. שואל שהם השאילוהו לו: דאמרי ליה. בעלים לשוכר: לדעתך. כרצונך אם תרצה להשאילה לו ימי שכירותך אין אנו מקפידין הלכך הוא השאילה והבעלים אין יכולין לומר אין רצוננו: מסרן לבנו כו'. או שמסרן לבנו ולבתו הקטנים: בפניהם. בפני אותם הקטנים שלא יצאו לחוץ ויאבדו המעות: על

**תוספות**

שוכר דמיחייב בגניבה ואבידה. מכאן יש להוכיח דהלכה כמ"ד דשוכר כשומר שכר דמי וכן מוכח בריש אלמנה לכ"ג (יבמות סו:) וכן פרק השואל (לקמן דף צז. ושם) גבי מרימר בר חנינא אוגר כודנייתא לבי חוזאי [כ]:

לאפוקי מדר' אמי. ה"ה דהוה מצי למימר לאפוקי מדשמואל דאמר פ"ג דשבועות (דף כה.) דשבועת ביטוי ליתא אלא ביכול להיות להבא אבל שבועה שזרק פלוני צרור ליס פטור שאין יכול לומר שבועה שיזרוק והכא מיחייב שבועה כי נשבע שנאנסה אע"ג דליתא בלהבא: רב אמר פטור. וא"ת והא תנן [ס] פ"ג דגיטין (דף כט.) אם אמר טול הימנה חפץ פלוני לא ישלחנו ביד אחר וי"ל דאע"ג דאסור להפקידו ביד אחר מ"מ בשביל כך אינו חייב לפרוע:

אין רצוני שיהא פקדוני ביד אחר. אין לפרש דטעמא דחייב לר' יוחנן אליבא דאביי משום דשינה מדעת המפקיד ולכך יתחייב בכל האונסין אפי' באונסין שהיו ראוין לבא ברשות שומר הראשון דא"כ מאי פריך אביי לרבא לקמן לימא ליה ר' אמי לר' אבא מלאך המות מה לי הכא מה לי התם כו' והלא כיון דשינה מדעת בעל הפרה הוא חייב אפילו באונסין שהיו באין אפי' אם היתה ברשותו לכך הוצרך לתרץ שהשאיל מדעת בעלים אלא י"ל דהטעם הוא דחשיב כאילו פירש לו שאם ישנה מדעתו כגון שימסרנה לאחר שיהיה כאילו פשע בה וכל אונסין שיארעו לה שנוכל לתלות שאם לא מסרה לאחר שלא היו נארעים חייב בה כגון אם מתה בבית שומר שני דיש לתלות דהבלא דאותו בית קטלה ושמא אם היתה בבית שומר הראשון לא היתה מתה שבריא בית אחד יותר מאחר והוי כפשע בה ויצאה לאגם שהוא מרעה שמן וטוב ומתה דחייב לאביי דאמר דהבלא דאגמא קטלה וכן לרב אם מסרה לחש"ו ומתה ברשותן חייב מהאי טעמא והיכא שלא פשע בה כגון לרב כשמסרה לבן דעת או שנעל בפניה כראוי ויצאה לאגם או שהוליכה בעצמו לאגם ומתה שם פטור אבל אם נעל בפניה שלא כראוי אע"פ שפשע אם מתה שם פטור כיון דאפילו נעל בפניה כראוי היתה מתה שם ואפילו למ"ד תחילתו בפשיעה וסופו באונס חייב היינו דוקא כמו צריפא דאורבני דאפשר אם לא פשע מתחילה לא היה נארע אונס של גניבה וכן מוכח פרק האומנין (לקמן דף עח. ושם ד"ה הוחמה) דתנן השוכר את הפרה להוליכה בהר והוליכה בבקעה והוחלקה פטור הוחמה חייב והשתא למ"ד תחילתו בפשיעה וסופו באונס חייב כי נמי הוחלקה אמאי פטור הלא תחילתה בפשיעה לענין הוחמה וסופה באונס לענין הוחלקה אלא משום דאפילו הוליכה בהר כל שכן דהוחלקה לכך פריך לקמן אביי לרבא שפיר ואפי' למ"ד תחילתו בפשיעה וסופו באונס פטור הכא כשמסר לשומר אחר חייב דהתם בצריפא דאורבני לא היה האונס ראוי להיות נארע עד שבאו גנבים אבל הכא אגלאי מילתא שאותו הבל ואותו מקום היה מסוכן יותר להמית בהמה זו דמיד שבאת שם התחיל החולי וכן קאמר אביי לקמן דאפי' למ"ד פטור הכא חייב:

דאם

**עין משפט נר מצוה**

כג א מיי' פ"א מהל' שבועות הל' ט סמג לאוין רמ:
כד ב מיי' שם הל' ג סמג לאוין רלט:
כה ג מיי' שם פ"ז הל' ב ופ"ח הל' ה והל' ו:
כו ד ה מיי' פ"א מהל' שכירות הל' ו ופ"ד מהל' נזקי ממון הל' יא ועי' בהשגות ובמ"מ ובל"מ סמג עשין פט טוש"ע ח"מ סי' רלא סעי' כו וסי' שה סעי' ה וסימן שלו סעיף ט:
כז ו מיי' פ"א מהל' שכירות הל' ד סמג עשין פט טוש"ע ח"מ סי' רלא סעי' כו:
כח ז מיי' פ"ד מהל' שאלה ופקדון הל' ו סמג עשין פח טוש"ע ח"מ סי' רלא סעי' כ:
כט ח ט מיי' שם הל' ח טוש"ע שם סעי' כא:

**רבינו חננאל**

פעמים ששניהם באשם כגון שנגנבה ושניהן חייבין לשלם ונשבעו שמתה מחמת מלאכה דהיא הנאת ממון דבשבועתייהו פטרי נפשייהו מממונא באשם. שוכר בחטאת ושואל באשם כגון שמתה וכיחשו וטענו שמתה מחמת מלאכה ונשבעו בשקר שוכר דינו בשניהן אחד שפטור בשניהן ולא נהנה ממון בשבועתו בחטאת. שואל שבמתה כדרכה חייב ופטר נפשיה במתה מחמת מלאכה באשם. שוכר באשם ושואל בחטאת כגון שנגנבה וטענו מתה כדרכה ונשבעו בשקר שוכר שחייב בגניבה ממון ובשבועתו נפטר באשם שהרי בשבועתו על שקר נהנה ממון אבל השואל דבין גניבה ובין במתה כדרכה חייב ולא נהנה ממון חייב חטאת שנשבע בשקר. ולאפוקי מדר' יוסי דאמר כל שבועה שהדיינין משביעין אותה אין חייבין עליה משום שבועת ביטוי. איתמר שומר שמסר לשומר רב אמר פטור. ואמר רב חסדא [לאו בפירוש אתמר אלא] מכללא אתמר דהנהו גינאי דהוו מפקדי כל יומא (מפקדי) מרייהו גביה דההיא סבתא ואיגנבו ופטריה רב משום דלא יכלי למיטען אנת מהימנת לי בשבועה וההיא סבתא לא מהימנא לן בשבועה דהא אינהו כל יומא גבה דההיא סבתא הוה מפקדי למרייהו. ור' יוחנן אמר שומר שמסר לשומר חייב. ואמר אביי משום דיכול למימר אין רצוני שיהא פקדוני ביד אחר. ומותבינן עליה המפקיד מעות אצל חבירו צררן והפשילן לאחוריו או שמסרן לבניו הקטנים נעל בפניהם שלא כראוי חייב שלא שימר כדרך השומרין. ודייקי' מינה טעמא דקטנים הא בניו (אבל) גדולים פטור ואמאי נימא אין רצוני שיהא

**מסורת הש"ס**

א) שבועות מט:, ב) בבא קמא יא:, ט:, ג) [עיין תוס' גיטין כט. ד"ה כאן הנה, ותוס' בבא קמא יא: ד"ה אף], ד) [גיטין יד., כט.], ה) [ברכות ע. ש"ג], ו) [הבעלים רשות כצ"ל], ז) לקמן מב., ח) והרי"ף והרא"ש גרסי או נעל בפניהם כו', ט) [לקמן מב: עמ"ש תוס' שם בשם ר"ת], י) בפסוק גבי אשם גזילות כתיב בל"א ועיין שם, כ) [ועיין תוס' בבא קמא מ: ד"ה סברוה].

**הגהות הב"ח**

(א) רש"י ד"ה נאנסה וכו' שכך הוא אע"פ:

**גליון הש"ס**

גמרא מ"ט דהא מסרה לבן דעת. עיין לקמן דף ל"ג ע"ב תוס' ד"ה אי: תוס' ד"ה רב וכו' וא"ת והא תנן. כך הקשה בירושל' בגיטין שם ועיין שם:

**תורה אור השלם**

א) אוֹ נֶפֶשׁ כִּי תִשָּׁבַע לְבַטֵּא בִשְׂפָתַיִם לְהָרַע אוֹ לְהֵיטִיב לְכֹל אֲשֶׁר יְבַטֵּא הָאָדָם בִּשְׁבֻעָה וְנֶעְלַם מִמֶּנּוּ וְהוּא יָדַע וְאָשֵׁם לְאַחַת מֵאֵלֶּה: [ויקרא ה, ד]

**לעזי רש"י**

פושוויי"ר. פירוש מעדר, כלי שמגרדים בו את העפר (עיין רש"י ישעיה ז, כה).

**ליקוטי רש"י**

כי תשבע מעצמה. והאי כי תשבע בלשון אי דרשינן לה אם תשבע דהיינו מעצמו ולא שבועת דיינין שהיא בעל כרחו [שבועות מט:]. שומר שמסר לשומר וכו' פטור. הראשון בכל אותן דינים שהיה פטור אם היתה אצלו פטור נמי השתא ולא אמרינן פשיעה היא זו שמסרה לאיש אחר. לטעמיה דרב לא מבעיא שומר חנם שמסר לשומר שכר. ונגנבה או שאבדה דפטור ש"ח כי היכי דמיפטר אילו הואי גביה דלא פשע. דעלויי עלייה לשמירתו. דשומר שכר מסר נפשיה לנטורי טפי משומר חנם שהרי שומר שכר חייב בגניבה ואבידה. אלא אפילו שומר שכר שמסר לשומר חנם דגרועי גרעה לשמירתו פטור. באונסין ולא מצי א"ל בעל הבית פשעת שמסרת לאחר שהרי מסרה לבן דעת [ב"ק יא:]. צררן. בסודרו והפשילן לאחוריו [לקמן מב.]. אמר רבא כל המפקיד ע"ד אשתו ובניו הוא מפקיד. על דעת שלא יהא שומר נמנע מלמוסרן לאנשי ביתו הגדולים ונאמנים לו הוא דמפקיד [לקמן מב:].

o a second *shomer* in whom the owner has not previously placed .is trust, Rav would agree that the first *shomer* becomes liable ɔr any loss.[21]

The Gemara challenges R' Yochanan's opinion[22] from a ruling n the Mishnah:

יָתִיב רַבִּי אַמִּ – **R' Ami sat** וְקָאָמַר לָהּ לְהָא שְׁמַעְתָּא – **and related his teaching** of his mentor, R' Yochanan. אֵיתִיבֵיהּ רַבִּי אַבָּא בַּר מַמָּל לְרַבִּי אַמִּ – **R' Abba bar Mammal challenged R' Ami from** ur **Mishnah:** הַשּׂוֹכֵר פָּרָה מֵחֲבֵירוֹ – IF SOMEONE RENTS A COW 'ROM HIS FELLOW, וְהִשְׁאִילָהּ לְאַחֵר – AND [THE RENTER] LENT IT 'O ANOTHER person to use during the period of the rental, וּמֵתָה כְּדַרְכָּ – AND IT subsequently DIED A NATURAL DEATH, יִשָּׁבַע הַשּׂוֹכֵר שֶׁמֵּתָה כְּדַרְכָּ – THE RENTER SHOULD SWEAR to the owner 'HAT IT DIED NATURALLY, thereby freeing himself from having o pay for it, וְהַשּׁוֹאֵל מְשַׁלֵּם לַשּׂוֹכֵר – AND THE BORROWER, who s liable for this type of loss, PAYS the value of the cow TO THE RENTER. וְאִם אִיתָא – **And if it is true** that an unauthorized ransfer of the object given to a *shomer* generally constitutes an ıct of negligence, לֵימָא לֵיהּ – **let [the owner] tell [the renter]:** אֵין רְצוֹנִי שֶׁיְּהֵא פִּקְדּוֹנִי בְּיַד אַחֵו – **"It is not my desire that my leposit should be in another's hands,"** and you therefore had no right to lend it to someone else.[23] – ? –

The Gemara answers that the Mishnah refers to a special case: אָמַר לִיו – **[R' Ami] said to [R' Abba]:** הָכָא בְּמַאי עַסְקִינַן – **Here,** n the Mishnah, **with what** situation **are we dealing?** בְּשֶׁנָּתְנוּ לוֹ (רשות הבעלים) [הַבְּעָלִים רְשׁוּת] לְהַשְׁאִי – With a case **where the owner gave [the renter] permission**[24] **to lend** the cow to a hird party. Since the transfer was authorized, the first *shomer* is ıot liable.

The Gemara asks:

אִי הָכִ – **If it is so** that the transfer was authorized, לַבְּעָלִים בָּעֵי לְשַׁלּוּמֵ – the borrower **should pay the owner** and not the lender, for in essence the owner was the one who lent it to the borrower, and the renter merely served as his agent. – ? –

The Gemara deflects the challenge:

דְּאָמְרוּ לֵיהּ לְדַעְתָּךְ – The Mishnah discusses a case **where [the owner] told [the renter]:** "You may lend the cow **at your discretion."** Hence, the owner is not considered the lender.[25]

The Gemara presents another challenge to R' Yochanan's opinion:

מָתִיב רָמִי בַּר חָמָא – **Rami bar Chama challenged** R' Yochanan's opinion **from** another **Mishnah:**[26] הַמַּפְקִיד מָעוֹת אֵצֶל חֲבֵירוֹ – IF ONE DEPOSITS COINS WITH HIS FELLOW for safekeeping, צְרָרָן וְהִפְשִׁילָן לַאֲחוֹרָיו – and the *shomer* BUNDLED THEM UP in a cloth AND HUNG THEM OVER HIS BACK, מְסָרָן לִבְנוֹ וּבִתּוֹ הַקְּטַנִּים – or HE TRANSFERRED THEM TO HIS YOUNG SON OR DAUGHTER וְנָעַל בִּפְנֵיהֶם שֶׁלֹּא כָּרָאוּי – AND then LOCKED the door BEFORE THEM IMPROPERLY,[27] חַיָּיב – if the coins were stolen or lost even through an unavoidable accident, HE IS LIABLE to pay, שֶׁלֹּא שָׁמַר כְּדֶרֶךְ הַשּׁוֹמְרִים – BECAUSE HE DID NOT GUARD the coins IN THE MANNER OF responsible *SHOMRIM.* From this Mishnah we can infer טַעְמָא דִּקְטַנִּים – that **the reason** the *shomer* is considered to have been negligent is that he entrusted the coins to **young [children];** הָא גְּדוֹלִים – **however,** had they been **adults,** פָּטוּר – he would be **exempt** from all liability. Now, if according to R' Yochanan an unauthorized transfer of an object someone is given to watch constitutes an act of negligence, אַמַּאי – **why** does the Mishnah imply that transferring to adults is proper? נֵימָא לֵיהּ – **Let** the owner **tell [the *shomer*]:** אֵין רְצוֹנִי שֶׁיְּהֵא פִּקְדּוֹנִי בְּיַד אַחֵר – **"It is not my desire that my deposit should be in another's hands."** – ? –

The Gemara answers:

אָמַר רָבָא – **Rava said:** כָּל הַמַּפְקִיד – **Whoever deposits** an object with another for safekeeping

NOTES

21. Thus, according to Rav Huna, Rav actually agrees with R' Yochanan hat a *shomer* who transfers the object entrusted to him to another *shomer* without permission from the owner *is* considered negligent and must pay for whatever happens. The only exception is where he transfers it to someone the owner himself has previously trusted to guard his things.

22. That an unauthorized transfer of the object given him to watch generally constitutes an act of negligence by the first *shomer.*

23. Thus, according to R' Yochanan, if the loss can in any way be attributed to the new circumstances of the care or use of the cow, the first *shomer* (the renter) should be liable to pay the owner. Why does the Mishnah rule that he is exempt?

24. Our elucidation follows the emendation of *Mesores HaShas,* who substitutes הַבְּעָלִים רְשׁוּת for רְשׁוּת הַבְּעָלִים.

25. Since the owner did not actually *instruct* him to lend it (but merely gave him permission to do so), he cannot be considered the lender, and so is not entitled to the borrower's payment. However, since he did indicate that he does not object to the renter lending it, he cannot claim, "It is not my desire, etc." Hence, the owner is not entitled to receive any payment from the renter either (*Rashi*).

26. Below, 42a.

27. I.e. the *shomer* attempted to prevent his child from leaving the house with the coins and losing them, but he did not lock the door properly (*Rashi*).

In the text of *Rif* and *Rosh* the Mishnah reads: "*or* he locked. . .improperly," which indicates a third situation. According to this version, the *shomer* placed the coins in a box and failed to lock either the box or the door of his house properly (see *Pilpula Charifta* to *Rosh* §20).

פעמים ששניהם באשם פעמים שהשוכר בחטאת והשואל באשם פעמים שהשוכר באשם והשואל בחטאת הא כיצד [א]כפירת ממון אשם [ב]ביטוי שפתים חטאת פעמים ששניהם בחטאת כגון שמתה כדרכה ואמרו נאנסה שוכר דבין כך ובין כך מיפטר פטור בחטאת שואל דבין כך ובין כך חיובי מיחייב בחטאת פעמים ששניהם באשם כגון שנגנבה ואמרו מתה מחמת מלאכה דתרוייהו קא כפרי ממונא דהא מיחייבי וקא פטרי נפשייהו שוכר בחטאת ושואל באשם כגון שמתה כדרכה ואמרו מתה מחמת מלאכה שוכר דבין כך ובין כך מיפטר פטור חייב בחטאת שואל דמיחייב במתה כדרכה וקא פטר נפשיה במתה מחמת מלאכה באשם שוכר באשם ושואל בחטאת כגון שנגנבה ואמרו מתה כדרכה שוכר הוא דמיחייב בגניבה ואבידה וקא פטר נפשיה במתה כדרכה באשם שואל דבין כך ובין כך חיובי מיחייב בחטאת מאי קמ"ל לאפוקי מדרבי אמי [א]דאמר כל שבועה שהדיינים משביעים אותה אין חייבין עליה משום שבועת ביטוי שנאמר [א]או נפש כי תשבע לבטא בשפתים כי תשבע מעצמה קמ"ל [ג]דלא כר' אמי [ג]אתמר שומר שמסר לשומר [ג]רב אמר פטור ור' יוחנן אמר [ד]חייב אמר אביי לטעמיה דרב לא מבעיא שומר חנם שמסר לשומר שכר דעלויי עלייה לשמירתו אלא אפילו שומר שכר שמסר לשומר חנם דגרועי גרעה לשמירתו פטור [ס]מאי טעמא דהא מסרה לבן דעת ולטעמיה דר' יוחנן [ה]לא מיבעיא שומר שכר שמסר לשומר חנם דגרועי גרעה לשמירתו אלא אפי' ש"ח שמסר לשומר שכר דעלויי עלייה לשמירתו חייב דא"ל [ד]אין רצוני שיהא פקדוני ביד אחר אמר רב חסדא הא דרב [ה]לאו בפירוש אתמר אלא מכללא דהנהו גינאי דכל יומא הוו מפקדי מרייהו גבה דההיא סבתא יומא חד אפקדינהו לגבי חד מינייהו שמע קלא בי הלולא נפק אזל אפקדינהו לגבה דההיא סבתא אדאזל ואתא אגנוב מרייהו אתא לקמיה דרב ופטריה מאן דחזא סבר משום שומר שמסר לשומר פטור ולא היא שאני התם [י]דכל יומא נמי אינהו גופייהו גבה דההיא סבתא הוו מפקדי להו יתיב ר' אמי וקאמר לה להא שמעתא איתיביה ר' אבא בר ממל לר' אמי השוכר פרה מחבירו והשאילה לאחר ומתה כדרכה ישבע השוכר שמתה כדרכה והשואל משלם לשוכר ואם איתא לימא ליה אין רצוני שיהא פקדוני ביד אחר א"ל הכא במאי עסקינן בשנתנו לו [י](רשות הבעלים) להשאיל אי הכי לבעלים בעי לשלומי דאמרו ליה לדעתך מתיב רמי בר חמא [ז][ז]המפקיד מעות אצל חבירו צררן והפשילן לאחוריו [ח]מסרן לבנו ובתו הקטנים [ח]ונעל בפניהם שלא כראוי חייב שלא שמר כדרך השומרים טעמא דקטנים הא גדולים פטור אמאי נימא ליה אין רצוני שיהא פקדוני ביד אחר אמר רבא [ט][ט]כל המפקיד

**רש"י**

שניהם באשם. אם נשבעו לשקר והיו נשכרים בשבועתם להקל פרעון מעליהם כפירת ממון היא זו וקרבן שבועה שלהם אשם איל בן ב' שנים דכתיב (ויקרא ה) [י]והביא את אשמו איל תמים בערכך כסף (שני) שקלים והוא אשם גזילות: נאנסה. ע"י לסטים ונשבעו שכך (א) אע"פ שהשואל משלם אונסין משביעין אותו כדרב הונא שבועה שאינה ברשותו דחיישינן שמא נתן עיניו בה ונשבע שנאנסה ואינה ברשותו: שוכר דבין כך ובין כך מיפטר. מתשלומין קאי בחטאת: בין כך ובין כך. בין שנשבע באמת שמתה כדרכה בין שנשבע לשקר שנאנסה פטר עצמו מלשלם הלכך אין בשקר זה כפירת ממון דהא אם הודה על האמת היה פטור שבועת ביטוי היא ובחטאת: שואל דבין כך ובין כך חייב לשלם. נמצא שלא כפר ממון בשיקור שבועתו ושבועת ביטוי קאי בחטאת: כגון שנגנבה. והשוכר חייב לשלם לבעלים והשואל ישלם לשוכר: ואמרו מתה מחמת מלאכה. ופטר שואל עצמו בשקר מלשלם לשוכר והשוכר מלשלם לבעלים: שמתה כדרכה. ואם הודו על האמת שוכר פטור ושואל חייב: שנגנבה. ושניהם חייבין: ואמרו מתה כדרכה. השוכר פוטר עצמו בשקר אבל השואל לא נפטר בכך מלשלם: חיובי מיחייב. לשלם קאי על שבועתו בחטאת: מאי קמ"ל. רבי ירמיה משניות שלימות הן בשבועות המשנה מחובה לחובה ומפטור לפטור ומפטור לחובה פטור מאשם גזילות מחובה לפטור חייב: רב אמר פטור. מכל מה שהיה נפטר אם שמרה הוא עצמו: חייב. אפי' באונסין: ולא מיבעיא כו'. דפטור מן האונסין ואין לך לומר פשיעה היא זו שמסרה לאחר: מרייהו. פושויי"ר בלע"ז: מאן דחזא. אחד מן התלמידים ששמע מפיו דפטריה סבר שומר שמסר לשומר כו': הוו מפקדי לה. דלא מצו אמרי ליה אין רצוננו שיהא בידה: להא שמעתא. דר' יוחנן רביה: אי הכי לבעלים בעי לשלומי. שואל שהם השאילוהו לו: דאמרי ליה. בעלים לשוכר: לדעתך. כרצונך אם תרצה להשאילה לו ימי שכירותך אין אנו מקפידין הלכך הוא השאילה והבעלים אין יכולין לומר אין רצוננו: מסרן לבנו כו'. או שמסרן לבנו ולבתו הקטנים: בפניהם. בפני אותם הקטנים שלא יצאו לחוץ ויאבדו המעות: על

**תוספות**

שוכר דמיחייב בגניבה ואבידה. מכאן יש להוכיח דהלכה כמ"ד דשוכר כשומר שכר דמי וכן מוכח בריש אלמנה לכ"ג (יבמות סו:) וכן פרק השואל (לקמן דף צז. ושם) גבי מרימר בר חנינא אוגר כודנייתא לבי חוזאי [כ]:

לאפוקי מדר' אמי. ה"ה דהוה מצי למימר לאפוקי מדשמואל דאמר פ"ג דשבועות (דף כה.) דשבועת ביטוי ליתא אלא ביכול להיות להבא אבל שבועה שזרק פלוני צרור לים פטור שאין יכול לומר שבועה שיזרוק והכא מיחייב שבועה כי נשבע שנאנסה אע"ג דליתא בלהבא:

רב אמר פטור. וא"ת והא תנן [ס]פ"ג דגיטין (דף כט.) אם אמר טול הימנה חפץ פלוני לא ישלחנו ביד אחר וי"ל דאע"ג דאסור להפקידו ביד אחר מ"מ בשביל כך אינו חייב לפרוע:

אין רצוני שיהא פקדוני ביד אחר. אין לפרש דטעמא דחייב לר' יוחנן אליבא דאביי משום דשינה מדעת המפקיד ולכך יתחייב בכל האונסין אפי' באונסין שהיו ראוין לבא ברשות שומר הראשון דא"כ מאי פריך אביי לרבא לקמן לימא ליה ר' אמי לר' אבא מלאך המות מה לי הכא מה לי התם כו' והלא כיון דשינה מדעת בעל הפרה הוא חייב אפילו באונסין שהיו באין אפי' אם היתה ברשותו לכך הוצרך לתרץ שהשאיל מדעת בעלים אלא י"ל דהטעם הוא דחשיב כאילו פירש לו שאם ישנה מדעתו כגון שימסרנה לאחר שיהיה כאילו פשע בה וכל אונסין שיארעו לה שנוכל לתלות שאם לא מסרה לאחר שלא היו נארעים חייב בה כגון אם מתה בבית שומר שני דיש לתלות דהבלא דאותו בית קטלה ושמא אם היתה בבית שומר הראשון לא היתה מתה שבריא בית אחד יותר מאחר והוי כפשע בה ויצאה לאגם שהוא מרעה שמן וטוב ומתה דחייב לאביי דאמר הבלא דאגמא קטלה וכן לרב אם מסרה לחש"ו ומתה ברשותן חייב מהאי טעמא והיכא שלא פשע בה כגון לרב כשמסרה לבן דעת או שנעל בפניה כראוי ויצאה לאגם או שהוליכה בעצמו לאגם ומתה שם פטור אבל אם נעל בפניה שלא כראוי אע"פ שפשע אם מתה שם פטור כיון דאפילו נעל בפניה כראוי היתה מתה שם ואפילו למ"ד תחילתו בפשיעה וסופו באונס חייב היינו דוקא כמו גריפא דאורבני דאפשר אם לא פשע מתחילה לא היה נארע אונס של גניבה וכן מוכח פרק האומנין (לקמן דף עח. ושם ד"ה הוחמה) דתנן השוכר את הפרה להוליכה בהר והוליכה בבקעה והוחלקה פטור הוחמה חייב והשתא למ"ד תחילתו בפשיעה וסופו באונס חייב כי נמי הוחלקה אמאי פטור הלא תחילתה בפשיעה לענין הוחמה וסופה באונס לענין הוחלקה אלא משום דאפילו הוליכה בהר כל שכן דהוחלקה לכך פריך לקמן אביי לרבא שפיר ואפי' למ"ד תחילתו בפשיעה וסופו באונס פטור הכא כשמסר לשומר אחר חייב דהתם בגריפא דאורבני לא היה האונס ראוי להיות נארע עד שבאו גנבים אבל הכא אגלאי מילתא שאותו הבל ואותו מקום היה מסוכן יותר להמית בהמה זו דמיד שבאת שם התחיל החולי וכן קאמר אביי לקמן דאפי' למ"ד פטור הכא חייב:

**עין משפט נר מצוה**

כג א מיי' פ"א מהל' שבועות הל' ט סמג לאוין רמ:
כד ב מיי' שם הל' ג סמג לאוין רלט:
כה ג מיי' שם פ"ז הל' ב ופ"ח הל' ה והל' ו:
כו ד ה מיי' פ"א מהל' שכירות הל' ו ופ"ד מהל' נזקי ממון הל' יא ועי' בהשגות ובמ"מ ובל"מ סמג עשין פט סה טוש"ע ח"מ סי' רצא סעי' כו וסי' שה סעי' ה וסימן שלו סעיף ט:
כז ו מיי' פ"א מהל' שכירות הל' ד סמג עשין פט טוש"ע ח"מ סי' רצא סעי' כו:
כח ז מיי' פ"ד מהל' שאלה ופקדון הל' ו סמג עשין פח טוש"ע ח"מ סי' רצא סעי' כ:
כט ח ט מיי' שם הל' ח טוש"ע שם סעי' כא:

**רבינו חננאל**

פעמים ששניהם באשם כגון שנגנבה ושניהן חייבין לשלם ונשבעו שמתה מחמת מלאכה דהיא הנאת ממון דבשבועתייהו פטרי נפשייהו מממונא באשם. שוכר בחטאת ושואל באשם כגון שמתה וכיחשו וטענו שמתה מחמת מלאכה ונשבעו בשקר שוכר דינו בשניהן אחד שפטור בשניהן ולא נהנה ממון בשבועתו בחטאת. שואל שבמתה כדרכה חייב ופטר נפשיה במתה מחמת מלאכה באשם. שוכר באשם ושואל בחטאת כגון שנגנבה וטענו מתה כדרכה ונשבעו בשקר שוכר שחייב בגניבה ממון ובשבועתו נפטר באשם שהרי בשבועתו על שקר נהנה ממון אבל השואל דבין גניבה ובין במתה כדרכה חייב ולא נהנה ממון חייב חטאת שנשבע בשקר. ולאפוקי מדר' יוסי דאמר כל שבועה שהדיינין משביעין אותה אין חייבין עליה משום שבועת ביטוי. איתמר שומר שמסר לשומר רב אמר פטור. ואמר רב חסדא [לאו בפירוש אתמר אלא] מכללא אתמר דהנהו גינאי דהוו מפקדי כל יומא (מפקדי) מרייהו גביה דההיא סבתא ואיגנבו ופטריה רב משום דלא יכלי למיטען אנת מהימנת לי בשבועה וההיא סבתא לא מהימנא לן בשבועה דהא אינהו כל יומא גבה דההיא סבתא הוה מפקדי למרייהו. ור' יוחנן אמר שומר שמסר לשומר חייב. ואמר אביי משום דיכול למימר אין רצוני שיהא פקדוני ביד אחר. ומותבינן עליה המפקיד מעות אצל חבירו צררן והפשילן לאחוריו או שמסרן לבניו הקטנים נעל בפניהם שלא כראוי חייב שלא שימר כדרך השומרין. ודייקי' מינה טעמא דקטנים הא בניו (אבל) גדולים פטור ואמאי נימא אין רצוני שיהא

**מסורת הש"ס**

א) שבועות מט:, ב) בבא מא יא:, ט:, ג) [עיין תוס' גיטין כט. ד"ה כאן נה, ותוס' בבא קמא יא: ד"ה אמ], ד) [גיטין יד., ע.], ה) [ברכות ע. ס"נ], ו) [הבעלים רשות כל"ן], ז) לקמן מב., ח) והרי"ף והרא"ש גרסי או נעל בפניהם וכו', ט) [לקמן מב: עמ"ש תוס' שם בשם ר"ת], י) בפסוק גבי אשם גזילות כתיב בל"א ועיין תוס, כ) [ועיין תוס' בבא קמא מז: ד"ה סברוה].

**הגהות הב"ח**

(א) רש"י ד"ה נאנסה וכו' שכך הוה אע"פ:

**גליון הש"ס**

גמרא מ"ט דהא מסרה לבן דעת. עיין לקמן דף ל"ג ע"ב תוס' ד"ה אי: תוס' ד"ה רב כו' וא"ת והא תנן. כן הקשה בירושל' בגיטין שם ועיין שם:

**תורה אור השלם**

א) אוֹ נֶפֶשׁ כִּי תִשָּׁבַע לְבַטֵּא בִשְׂפָתַיִם לְהָרַע אוֹ לְהֵיטִיב לְכֹל אֲשֶׁר יְבַטֵּא הָאָדָם בִּשְׁבֻעָה וְנֶעְלַם מִמֶּנּוּ וְהוּא יָדַע וְאָשֵׁם לְאַחַת מֵאֵלֶּה: [ויקרא ה, ד]

**לעזי רש"י**

פושויי"ר. פירוש מעדר, כלי שמגרדים בו את העפר (עיין רש"י ישעיה ז, כה).

**ליקוטי רש"י**

כי תשבע מעצמה. והאי כי תשבע בלשון לא דרשינן לה אם תשבע דהיינו מעצמו ולא שבועת דיינין שהיא בעל כרחו [שבועות מט:]. שומר שמסר לשומר וכו' פטור. הראשון בכל אונס דינים שהיה פטור אם השמה ולא אמרינן פשיעה היא זו שמסרה לאיש אחר. לטעמיה דרב לא מבעיא שומר חנם שמסר לשומר שכר. ונגנבה או שאבדה דפטור ש"מ כי היכי דמיפטר אילו הוה גביה דלא פשע. דעלויי עלייה לשמירתו. דשומר שכר מסר נפשיה לנטורי טפי משומר חנם שהרי שומר שכר חייב בגניבה ואבידה. אלא אפילו שומר שכר שמסר לשומר חנם דגרועי גרעה לשמירתו פטור. באונסין ולא מצי א"ל בעל הבית פשעת שמסרת לאחר שהרי שומר לבן דעת [ב"ק יא.]. צררן. בסודרו והפשילן לאחוריו [לקמן מב.]. אמר רבא כל המפקיד ע"ד אשתו ובניו הוא מפקיד. על דעת שלא יהא שומר נמנע מלמסרן לאנשי ביתו הגדולים ונאמנים לו הוא מפקיד [לקמן מב:].

**’ Ami;** rather, even for an oath imposed by *beis din,* one must ring a *chatas* if he swears falsely.

The Gemara now discusses the liability of a *shomer* who gives he object entrusted to him to another *shomer* without authoriza-ion from the owner:

**אִתְּמַ – It was said:** **שׁוֹמֵר שֶׁמָּסַר לְשׁוֹמֵר** – Regarding **a *shomer* who transferred** a deposit **to** another ***shomer*** without obtain-ng permission from the owner, **רַב אָמַר פָּטוּר – Rav said:** The irst *shomer* is **exempt** from liability for any loss for which he vould have been exempt had he guarded the object himself.[13] **וְרַבִּי יוֹחָנָן אָמַר חַיָּ – But R’ Yochanan said: He is obligated** to ay for even unavoidable loss, even though he would have been xempt for this had he guarded the item himself.[14]

The Gemara elaborates:

**אָמַר אַבַּיֵ – Abaye said:** **לְטַעְמֵיהּ דְּרַב – According to Rav’s easoning,** **לֹא מִבַּעְיָא שׁוֹמֵר חִנָּם שֶׁמָּסַר לְשׁוֹמֵר שָׂכָר – it is not ecessary** to state that **an unpaid *shomer* who transferred** he object **to a paid *shomer***[15] is not liable for unavoidable loss, **דְּעַלּוּיֵי עַלְּיֵיהּ לִשְׁמִירָת – for he has** actually **upgraded the** level of **vatching for [this object]!**[16] **אֶלָּא אֲפִילּוּ שׁוֹמֵר שָׂכָר שֶׁמָּסַר לְשׁוֹמֵר חִנָּ – But even a paid *shomer* who transferred** the object **to an npaid *shomer*,** **דְּגָרוּעֵי גָּרְעָה לִשְׁמִירָתוֹ – who diminished the** evel of **watching for [this object],** **פָּטוּר – is** also **exempt** from ability for unavoidable loss. **מַאי טַעְמָא – What is the reason** hat this unauthorized transfer is not considered a negligent act? **דְּהָא מְסָרָהּ לְבֶן דַּעַ – Because he gave it to a mentally compe-ent individual,** who could effectively safeguard the object.[17]

Abaye continues:

**וּלְטַעְמֵיהּ דְּרַבִּי יוֹחָנָ – And according to R’ Yochanan’s reason-ng,** that a *shomer* who transfers the object to another *shomer* is onsidered negligent and must pay for even unavoidable losses, **לֹא מִיבַּעְיָא שׁוֹמֵר שָׂכָר שֶׁמָּסַר לְשׁוֹמֵר חִנָּ – it is not necessary** to tate that **a paid *shomer* who transferred** the object **to an un-aid *shomer*** committed a negligent act and is therefore liable or all losses, **דְּגָרוּעֵי גָּרְעָה לִשְׁמִירָתוֹ – since he diminished he** level **of watching for [this object].**[18] **אֶלָּא אֲפִילּוּ שׁוֹמֵר חִנָּם שֶׁמָּסַר לְשׁוֹמֵר שָׂכָ – But even** if **an unpaid *shomer* transferred** he object **to a paid *shomer*,** **דְּעַלּוּיֵי עַלְּיֵיהּ לִשְׁמִירָתוֹ** – thereby **pgrading the** level of **watching for [the object],** **חַיָּיב – he s** still **obligated** to pay for any loss, **דְּאָמַר לֵיהּ – for** the owner **may tell him:** **אֵין רְצוֹנִי שֶׁיְּהֵא פִּקְדוֹנִי בְּיַד אַחֵר – “It is not my desire that my deposit should be in another person’s hands.”** Therefore, even this transfer is considered a negligent act.[19]

The next Amora argues that the opinion attributed to Rav (that a *shomer* who transfers the object entrusted to him to another *shomer* does *not* become liable for whatever happens to it) was attributed to him in error:

**אָמַר רַב חִסְדָּא – Rav Chisda said:** **הָא דְּרַב לַאו בְּפֵירוּשׁ אִתְּמַר – That** opinion **of Rav was not stated** by him **explicitly;** **אֶלָּא מִכְּלָלָא – rather,** it was learned **by implication** from a ruling he once issued. **דְּהָנְהוּ גִּינָּאֵי – For** there was the case of **these gardeners,** **דְּכָל יוֹמָא הֲווּ מַפְקְדֵי מָרְיֵיהוּ גַּבָּהּ דְּהַהִיא סָבְתָּא – who every day would deposit their hoes with a certain elderly woman** for safekeeping. **יוֹמָא חַד אַפְקְדִינְהוּ לְגַבֵּי חַד מִינַּיְיהוּ – One day they deposited [the hoes] with one of their own** instead. **שָׁמַע קָלָא בֵּי הִלּוּלָא – He** [the gardener who had been given the hoes to watch] later **heard the sounds** of celebration coming **from a wedding hall,** and he wanted to attend. **נְפַק אֲזַל אַפְקְדִינְהוּ לְגַבָּהּ דְּהַהִיא סָבְתָּא – He** therefore **left** his home to go to the hall, and on the way **went** and **deposited [the hoes] with that elderly woman.** **אַדְּאָזֵיל וְאָתָא אִגְּנוּב מָרְיֵיהוּ – By the time he went and came back** from the wedding, he found that **their hoes had been stolen.** **אָתָא לְקַמֵּיהּ דְּרַב וּפַטְרֵיהּ – [The gardener] came before Rav** for a ruling, **and [Rav] exonerated him** (i.e. he ruled that he did not have to pay for the stolen hoes). **מַאן דַּחֲזָא סָבַר – One** of the disciples **that witnessed** these proceedings **thought** that the gardener was exonerated **מִשּׁוּם שׁוֹמֵר שֶׁמָּסַר לְשׁוֹמֵר פָּטוּר – because** Rav held as a general rule that **a *shomer* who transferred** the object given to him **to another *shomer* is exempt** from any additional liability,[20] and it was from this disciple’s understanding of Rav’s ruling that it became known that Rav exempts a *shomer* who gave the deposit to another *shomer* to watch.

Rav Chisda takes issue with the disciple’s interpretation of Rav’s decision:

**וְלֹא הִיא – But it is not so!** **שָׁאנֵי הָתָם – There** the situation **was different,** **דְּכָל יוֹמָא נַמִּי – because every** other **day as well** **אִינְהוּ גּוּפַיְיהוּ גַּבָּהּ דְּהַהִיא סָבְתָּא הֲווּ מַפְקְדֵי לְהוּ – [the other gardeners] would themselves deposit [their hoes] with that elderly woman.** Hence, they cannot claim that they do not want her to watch their hoes. However, when an object is transferred

NOTES

3. Although one *shomer* is not allowed to entrust the item he received o another *shomer* without the owner’s permission, doing so does not utomatically obligate him to pay for its loss (*Tosafos*).

4. R’ Yochanan’s reasoning will be explained by the Gemara below.

5. I.e. the original (unpaid) *shomer* hired a replacement to watch the bject.

6. A paid *shomer* will exert himself to guard the object more than the npaid *shomer* will, since the paid *shomer* is liable for loss and theft, hile the unpaid *shomer* is not (*Shitah Mekubetzes*; *Rashi* and *Tosafos* o *Bava Kamma* 11b ד״ה דעלוייה; see also *Tos. HaRosh* here). Thus, the nauthorized transfer of the object did not constitute a negligent act.

Moreover, in giving the object to a paid *shomer* to watch, the first *homer* did not undermine the owner’s position. For if the object is *un-voidably* damaged, both he and the paid *shomer* are anyway exempt rom paying. And should the object be *lost or stolen,* the owner can collect rom the second *shomer* (according to R’ Yose’s opinion in the Mishnah), hereas had the transfer not occurred he would have received nothing rom the first (unpaid) *shomer* (see *Pnei Yehoshua* here, and *Tosafos* ד״ה ל to *Bava Kamma* ibid.).

7. However, even though this unauthorized transfer is not considered negligent act, the first *shomer* remains primarily liable as before. The econd *shomer* is merely his agent, not his replacement. Thus, if the sec-nd *shomer* failed to watch the object, it is as if the first *shomer* failed to do so; and if the failing was the type for which the first *shomer* is responsible (e.g. theft in the case of a paid *shomer*), he remains liable even though the second *shomer* would not be responsible.

*Rashba* and other Rishonim differ with *Rashi’s* interpretation of the Gemara. They understand Rav to mean that when the first *shomer* transfers the object to another *shomer* of equal or greater standing (for example, a paid *shomer* to a paid *shomer*, or an unpaid *shomer* to a paid *shomer*), the latter replaces the former as the *shomer* of record and the first *shomer* is fully absolved from liability.

18. In the sense that an unpaid *shomer* does not exert himself to guard the object to the same degree that a paid *shomer* will guard it, since the former is not liable for loss and theft, while the latter is.

19. Therefore, it is as if the owner said to the first *shomer* that if he should ignore the owner’s wishes and transfer the object to another *shomer,* the first *shomer* will be held liable for any loss that can be attributed to these new circumstances. Thus, for example, the owner could demand payment for the death of his animal by claiming that the bad air in the second *shomer’s* barn contributed to the animal’s death – a loss that might not have occurred had the animal remained in the healthier atmosphere of the first *shomer’s* barn (see *Tosafos, Tos. HaRosh*).

20. Presumably, the gardener was serving as an unpaid *shomer* for his fellow gardeners. Thus, had the hoes been stolen while he was watching them, he would not have been liable.

פעמים ששניהם באשם פעמים שהשוכר בחטאת והשואל באשם פעמים שהשוכר באשם והשואל בחטאת הא כיצד [א]כפירת ממון אשם [ב]ביטוי שפתים חטאת פעמים ששניהם בחטאת כגון שמתה כדרכה ואמרו נאנסה שוכר דבין כך ובין כך מיפטר פטור בחטאת שואל דבין כך ובין כך חיובי מיחייב בחטאת פעמים ששניהם באשם כגון שנגנבה ואמרו מתה מחמת מלאכה דתרווייהו קא כפרי ממונא דהא מיחייבי וקא פטרי נפשייהו שוכר בחטאת ושואל באשם כגון שמתה כדרכה ואמרו מתה מחמת מלאכה שוכר דבין כך ובין כך מיפטר פטור חייב בחטאת שואל דמיחייב במתה כדרכה וקא פטר נפשיה במתה מחמת מלאכה באשם שוכר באשם ושואל בחטאת כגון שנגנבה ואמרו מתה כדרכה שוכר הוא דמיחייב בגניבה ואבידה וקא פטר נפשיה במתה כדרכה באשם שואל דבין כך ובין כך חיובי מיחייב בחטאת מאי קמ"ל לאפוקי מדרבי אמי (א) דאמר כל שבועה שהדיינים משביעים אותה אין חייבין עליה משום שבועת ביטוי שנאמר (א) או נפש כי תשבע לבטא בשפתים כי תשבע מעצמה קמ"ל [ג]דלא כר' אמי (ב) אתמר שומר שמסר לשומר (ג) רב אמר פטור ור' יוחנן אמר [ד]חייב אמר אביי לטעמיה דרב לא מבעיא שומר חנם שמסר לשומר שכר דעלויי עלייה לשמירתו אלא אפילו שומר שכר שמסר לשומר חנם דגרועי גרעה לשמירתו פטור ° מאי טעמא דהא מסרה לבן דעת ולטעמיה דר' יוחנן [ה]לא מיבעיא שומר שכר שמסר לשומר חנם דגרועי גרעה לשמירתו אלא אפי' ש"ח שמסר לשומר שכר דעלויי עלייה לשמירתו חייב דא"ל (ד) אין רצוני שיהא פקדוני ביד אחר אמר רב חסדא הא דרב (ה) לאו בפירוש אתמר אלא מכללא דהנהו גינאי דכל יומא הוו מפקדי מרייהו גבה דההיא סבתא יומא חד אפקדינהו לגבי חד מינייהו שמע קלא בי הלולא נפק אזל אפקדינהו לגבה דההיא סבתא אדאזל ואתא אגנוב מרייהו אתא לקמיה דרב ופטריה מאן דחזא סבר משום שומר שמסר לשומר פטור ולא היא שאני התם [ו]דכל יומא נמי אינהו גופייהו גבה דההיא סבתא הוו מפקדי להו יתיב ר' אמי וקאמר לה להא שמעתא איתיביה ר' אבא בר ממל לר' אמי השוכר פרה מחבירו והשאילה לאחר ומתה כדרכה ישבע השוכר שמתה כדרכה והשואל משלם לשוכר ואם איתא לימא ליה אין רצוני שיהא פקדוני ביד אחר א"ל הכא במאי עסקינן בשנתנו לו (ו) (רשות הבעלים) להשאיל אי הכי לבעלים בעי לשלומי דאמרו ליה לדעתך מתיב רמי בר חמא (ז) [ז]המפקיד מעות אצל חבירו צררן והפשילן לאחוריו [ח]מסרן לבנו ובתו הקטנים (ח) ונעל בפניהם שלא כראוי חייב שלא שמר כדרך השומרים טעמא דקטנים הא גדולים פטור אמאי נימא ליה אין רצוני שיהא פקדוני ביד אחר אמר רבא (ט) [ט]כל המפקיד

**רש"י**

שניהם באשם. אם נשבעו לשקר והיו נשכרים בשבועתם להקל פרעון מעליהם כפירת ממון היא זו וקרבן שבועה שלהם אשם איל בן ב' שנים דכתיב (ויקרא ה) (י) והביא את אשמו איל תמים בערכך כסף (שני) שקלים והוא אשם גזילות: נאנסה. ע"י לסטים ונשבעו שכך (א) אע"פ שהשואל משלם אונסין משביעין אותו כדרב הונא שבועה שאינה ברשותו דחיישינן שמא נתן עיניו בה ונשבע שנאנסה ואינה ברשותו: שוכר דבין כך ובין כך מיפטר. מתשלומין קאי בחטאת: בין כך ובין כך. בין שנשבע באמת שמתה כדרכה בין שנשבע לשקר שנאנסה פטר עצמו מלשלם הלכך אין בשקר זה כפירת ממון דהא אם הודה על האמת היה פטור שבועת ביטוי היא ובחטאת: שואל דבין כך ובין כך חייב לשלם. נמצא שלא כפר ממון בשיקור שבועתו ושבועת ביטוי קאי בחטאת: כגון שנגנבה. והשוכר חייב לשלם לבעלים והשואל ישלם לשוכר: ואמרו מתה מחמת מלאכה. ופטר שואל עצמו בשקר מלשלם לשוכר והשוכר מלשלם לבעלים: שמתה כדרכה. ואם הודו על האמת שוכר פטור ושואל חייב: שנגנבה. ושניהם חייבין: ואמרו מתה כדרכה. השוכר פוטר עצמו בשקר אבל השואל לא נפטר בכך מלשלם: חיובי מיחייב. לשלם קאי על שבועתו בחטאת: מאי קמ"ל. רבי ירמיה משניות שלימות הן בשבועות המשנה מחובה לחובה ומפטור לפטור ומפטור לחובה פטור מאשם גזילות מחובה לפטור חייב: רב אמר פטור. מכל מה שהיה נפטר אם שמרה הוא עצמו: חייב. אפי' באונסין: ולא מיבעיא כו'. דפטור מן האונסין ואין לך לומר פשיעה היא זו שמסרה לאחר: מרייהו. פושוי"ר בלע"ז: מאן דחזא. אחד מן התלמידים ששמע מפיו דפטריה סבר שומר שמסר לשומר כו': הוו מפקדי לה. דלא מצו אמרי ליה אין רצוננו שיהא בידה: להא שמעתא. דר' יוחנן רביה: אי הכי לבעלים בעי לשלומי. שואל שהם השאילוהו לו: דאמרי ליה. בעלים לשוכר: לדעתך. כרצונך אם תרצה להשאילה לו ימי שכירותך אין אנו מקפידין הלכך הוא השאילה והבעלים אין יכולין לומר אין רצוננו: מסרן לבנו כו'. או שמסרן לבנו ולבתו הקטנים: בפניהם. בפני אותם הקטנים שלא יצאו לחוץ ויאבדו המעות:

על

**תוספות**

שוכר דמחייב בגניבה ואבידה. מכאן יש להוכיח דהלכה כמ"ד דשוכר כשומר שכר דמי וכן מוכח בריש אלמנה לכ"ג (יבמות סו:) וכן פרק השואל (לקמן דף צז. ושם) גבי מרימר בר חנינא אוגר כודנייתא לבי חוזאי (ג):

לאפוקי מדר' אמי. ה"ה דהוה מצי למימר לאפוקי מדשמואל דאמר פ"ג דשבועות (דף כה.) דשבועת ביטוי ליתא אלא ביכול להיות להבא אבל שבועה שזרק פלוני צרור ליס פטור שאין יכול לומר שבועה שיזרוק והכא מיחייב שבועה כי נשבע שנאנסה אע"ג דליתא בלהבא:

רב אמר פטור. וא"ת והא תנן ° פ"ג דגיטין (דף כט.) אם אמר טול הימנה חפץ פלוני לא ישלחנו ביד אחר וי"ל דאע"ג דאסור להפקידו ביד אחר מ"מ בשביל כך אינו חייב לפרוע:

אין רצוני שיהא פקדוני ביד אחר. אין לפרש דטעמא דחייב לר' יוחנן אליבא דאביי משום דשינה מדעת המפקיד ולכך יתחייב בכל האונסין אפי' באונסין שהיו ראוין לבא ברשות שומר הראשון דא"כ מאי פריך אביי לרבא לקמן לימא ליה ר' אמי לר' אבא מלאך המות מה לי הכא מה לי התם כו' והלא כיון דשינה מדעת בעל הפרה הוא חייב אפילו באונסין שהיו בא אפי' אם היתה ברשותו לכך הוצרך לתרץ שהשאיל מדעת בעלים אלא י"ל דהטעם הוא דחשיב כאילו פירש לו שאם ישנה מדעתו כגון שימסרנה לאחר שיהיה כאילו פשע בה וכל אונסין שיארעו לה שנוכל לתלות שאם לא מסרה לאחר שלא היו נארעים חייב בה כגון אם מתה בבית שומר שני דיש לתלות דהבלא דאותו בית קטלה ושמא אם היתה בבית שומר הראשון לא היתה מתה שבריא בית אחד יותר מאחר והוי כפשע בה ויצאה לאגם שהוא מרעה שמן וטוב ומתה דחייב לאביי דאמר דהבלא דאגמא קטלה וכן לרב אם מסרה לחש"ו ומתה ברשותן חייב מהאי טעמא והיכא שלא פשע בה כגון לרב כשמסרה לבן דעת או שנעל בפניה כראוי ויצאה לאגם או שהוליכה בעצמו לאגם ומתה שם פטור אבל אם נעל בפניה שלא כראוי אע"פ שפשע אם מתה שם פטור כיון דאפילו נעל בפניה כראוי היתה מתה שם ואפילו למ"ד תחילתו בפשיעה וסופו באונס חייב היינו דוקא כמו גריפא דאורבני דאפשר אם לא פשע מתחילה לא היה נארע אונס של גניבה וכן מוכח פרק האומנין (לקמן דף עח. ושם ד"ה הוחמה) דתנן השוכר את הפרה להוליכה בהר והוליכה בבקעה והוחלקה פטור הוחמה חייב והשתא למ"ד תחילתו בפשיעה וסופו באונס חייב כי נמי הוחלקה אמאי פטור הלא תחילתה בפשיעה לענין הוחמה וסופה באונס לענין הוחלקה אלא משום דאפילו הוליכה בהר כל שכן דהוחלקה לכך פריך לקמן אביי לרבא שפיר ואפי' למ"ד תחילתו בפשיעה וסופו באונס פטור הכא כשמסר לשומר אחר חייב דהתם בגריפא דאורבני לא היה האונס ראוי להיות נארע עד שבאו גנבים אבל הכא אגלאי מילתא שאותו הבל ואותו מקום היה מסוכן יותר להמית בהמה זו דמיד שבאת שם התחיל החולי וכן קאמר אביי לקמן דאפי' למ"ד פטור הכא חייב:



**עין משפט נר מצוה**

כג א מיי' פ"א מהל' שבועות הל' ט סמג לאוין רמ:

כד ב מיי' שם הל' ג סמג לאוין רלט:

כה ג מיי' שם פ"ז הל' ג ופ"ח הל' ה והל' ו:

כו ד ה מיי' פ"א מהל' שכירות הל' ו ופ"ד מהל' נזקי ממון הל' יא ועי' בהשגות ובמ"מ ובל"מ סמג עשין פט פח טוש"ע ח"מ סי' רלא סעי' כו וסי' שה סעי' ה וסימן שלו סעיף ט:

כז ו מיי' פ"א מהל' שכירות הל' ד סמג עשין פט טוש"ע ח"מ סי' רלא סעי' כו:

כח ז מיי' פ"ד מהל' שאלה ופקדון הל' ו סמג עשין פח טוש"ע ח"מ סי' רלא סעי' כ:

כט ח ט מיי' שם הל' ח טוש"ע שם סעי' כא:

**רבינו חננאל**

פעמים ששניהם באשם כגון שנגנבה ושניהן חייבין לשלם ונשבעו שמתה מחמת מלאכה דהיא הנאת ממון דבשבועתייהו פטרי נפשייהו מממונא באשם. שוכר בחטאת ושואל באשם כגון שמתה וכיחשו וטענו שמתה מחמת מלאכה ונשבעו בשקר שוכר דינו בשניהן אחד שפטור בשניהן ולא נהנה ממון בשבועתו בחטאת. שואל שבמתה כדרכה חייב ופטר נפשיה במתה מחמת מלאכה באשם. שוכר באשם ושואל בחטאת כגון שנגנבה וטענו מתה כדרכה ונשבעו בשקר שוכר שחייב בגניבה ממון ובשבועתו נפטר באשם שהרי בשבועתו על שקר נהנה ממון אבל השואל דבין גניבה ובין במתה כדרכה חייב ולא נהנה ממון חייב חטאת שנשבע בשקר. ולאפוקי מדר' יוסי דאמר כל שבועה שהדיינין משביעין אותה אין חייבין עליה משום שבועת ביטוי. איתמר שומר שמסר לשומר רב אמר פטור. ואמר רב חסדא [לאו בפירוש אתמר אלא] מכללא אתמר דהנהו גינאי דהוו מפקדי כל יומא (מפקדי') מרייהו גביה דההיא סבתא ואיגנבו ופטריה רב משום דלא יכלי למיטען אנת מהימנת לי בשבועה וההיא סבתא לא מהימנא לן בשבועה דהא אינהו כל יומא גבה דההיא סבתא הוה מפקדי למרייהו. ור' יוחנן אמר שומר שמסר לשומר חייב. ואמר אביי משום דיכול למימר אין רצוני שיהא פקדוני ביד אחר. ומותבינן עליה המפקיד מעות אצל חבירו צררן והפשילן לאחוריו או שמסרן לבניו הקטנים נעל בפניהם שלא כראוי חייב שלא שימר כדרך השומרין. ודייקי' מינה טעמא דקטנים הא בניו (אבל) גדולים פטור ואמאי נימא אין רצוני שיהא

**מסורת הש"ס**

א) שבועות מט:, ב) בבא קמא יא:, ט:, ג) [עיין תוס' גיטין כט. ד"ה כאן נה, ותוס' בבא קמא יא: ד"ה אח], ד) [גיטין יד., ע.], ה) [ברכות ע. ש"נ], ו) [הבעלים רשות כצ"ל], ז) לקמן מב., ח) והרי"ף והרא"ש גרסי או נעל בפניהם ..., ט) [לקמן מב: עמ"ש תוס' שם בשם ...], י) בפסוק גבי אשם גזילות כתיב בל"א ועיין תוס', כ) [ועיין תוס' בבא קמא נז: ד"ה סברוה].

**הגהות הב"ח**

(א) רש"י ד"ה נאנסה וכו' שכך הוא אע"פ:

**גליון הש"ס**

גמרא מ"ט דהא מסרה לבן דעת. עיין לקמן דף ל"ג ע"ב תוס' ד"ה אי: תוס' ד"ה רב כו' וא"ת והא תנן. כך הקשה בירושל' בגיטין שם ועיין שם:

**תורה אור השלם**

א) אוֹ נֶפֶשׁ כִּי תִשָּׁבַע לְבַטֵּא בִשְׂפָתַיִם לְהָרַע אוֹ לְהֵיטִיב לְכֹל אֲשֶׁר יְבַטֵּא הָאָדָם בִּשְׁבֻעָה וְנֶעְלַם מִמֶּנּוּ וְהוּא יָדַע וְאָשֵׁם לְאַחַת מֵאֵלֶּה: [ויקרא ה, ד]

**לעזי רש"י**

פושוי"ר. פירוש מעדר, כלי שמגרדים בו את העפר (עיין רש"י ישעיה ז, כה).

**ליקוטי רש"י**

כי תשבע מעצמה. יהאי כי תשבע בלשון אי דרשינן לה אם תשבע דהיינו מעצמו ולא שבועת דיינין שהיא בעל כרחו [שבועות מט:]. שומר שמסר לשומר וכו' פטור. הראשון בכל אותן דינים שהיה פטור אם היתה אצלו פטור נמי השתא ולא אמרינן פשיעה היא זו שמסרה לאיש אחר. לטעמיה דרב לא מבעיא שומר חנם שמסר לשומר שכר. נגנבה או שאבדה דפטור מ"מ כי היכי דמיפטר אילו הואי גביה דלא פשע. דעלויי עלייה לשמירתו. דשומר שכר מסר נפשיה לנטורי טפי משומר חנם שהרי שומר שכר חייב בגניבה ואבידה. אלא אפילו שומר שכר שמסר לשומר חנם דגרועי גרעה לשמירתו פטור. באונסין ולא מצי א"ל בעל הבית פשעת שמסרת לאחר שהרי מסרה לבן דעת [ב"ק יא:]. צררן. בסודרו והפשילן לאחוריו [לקמן מב.]. אמר רבא כל המפקיד ע"ד אשתו ובניו הוא מפקיד. על דעת שלא יהא שומר נמנע מלמוסרן לאנשי ביתו הגדולים הנאמנים לו הוא דמפקיד [לקמן מב:].

פְּעָמִים שֶׁשְּׁנֵיהֶם בְּאָשָׁם – At other **times both of them** are obligated to bring **an** ***asham*** offering for swearing a false oath about what happened to the cow. פְּעָמִים שֶׁהַשּׂוֹכֵר בְּחַטָּאת וְהַשּׁוֹאֵל בְּאָשָׁם – **At times the renter** is obligated to bring **a** ***chatas*** **and the borrower an** ***asham.*** פְּעָמִים שֶׁהַשּׂוֹכֵר בְּאָשָׁם וְהַשּׁוֹאֵל בְּחַטָּאת – **At times the renter** is obligated to bring **an** ***asham*** **and the borrower a** ***chatas.***

The Gemara elaborates:

הָא כֵּיצַד – **How is this** possible? כְּפִירַת מָמוֹן אָשָׁם – Because **the denial of** a claim of **money** with a false oath obligates a person to bring **an** ***asham,*** בִּיטּוּי שְׂפָתַיִם חַטָּאת – and a false **utterance of the lips,** i.e. a false oath made about something that does *not* free a person from a monetary obligation, obligates **a** ***chatas.***

The Gemara now explains each case:

פְּעָמִים שֶׁשְּׁנֵיהֶם בְּחַטָּאת – **At times both of them are** obligated **to** bring **a** ***chatas:*** כְּגוֹן שֶׁמֵּתָה כְּדַרְכָּהּ – **for example, when [the cow] died naturally,** וְאָמְרוּ נֶאֶנְסָה – **and they said** and swore falsely that **it was plundered** by bandits.[1] שׂוֹכֵר – **The renter,** דְּבֵין כָּךְ וּבֵין כָּךְ מִיפְטַר פָּטוּר – **who is exempt** from payment **in either case,**[2] בְּחַטָּאת – **must** bring **a** ***chatas,*** not an *asham,* since the false oath did not release him from a monetary obligation.[3] שׁוֹאֵל – **The borrower,** דְּבֵין כָּךְ וּבֵין כָּךְ חִיּוּבֵי מִיחַיֵּיב – **who is obligated** to pay **in either case,**[4] בְּחַטָּאת – **must** bring **a** ***chatas,*** not an *asham*, since his false oath also did not release him from a monetary obligation.[5]

The second case:

פְּעָמִים שֶׁשְּׁנֵיהֶם בְּאָשָׁם – **At** other **times both of them are** obligated **to** bring **an** ***asham:*** כְּגוֹן שֶׁנִּגְנְבָה – **for example, when [the cow] was stolen,**[6] וְאָמְרוּ מֵתָה מַחֲמַת מְלָאכָה – **and they said** and swore falsely that **it died on account of** its **work.**[7] דְּתַרְוַייהוּ קָא כָּפְרֵי מָמוֹן – **For** here **they both deny a monetary** obligation, דְּהָא מִיחַיְּיבֵי – **since they are obligated** to pay if they admit the truth, וְקָא פָּטְרֵי נַפְשַׁיְיהוּ – **and they exempt themselves** by swearing falsely. Therefore, both are obligated to bring an *asham* offering.

The third case:

שׂוֹכֵר בְּחַטָּאת וְשׁוֹאֵל בְּאָשָׁם – At times **the renter must** bring **a** ***chatas*** **and the borrower an** ***asham:*** כְּגוֹן שֶׁמֵּתָה כְּדַרְכָּהּ – **for example, when [the cow] died naturally,**[8] וְאָמְרוּ מֵתָה מַחֲמַת מְלָאכָה – **and they said** and swore falsely that **it died on account of** its **work.** שׂוֹכֵר – **The renter,** דְּבֵין כָּךְ וּבֵין כָּךְ מִיפְטַר פָּטוּר – **who is exempt** from paying **in either case,** חַיָּיב בְּחַטָּאת – **is obligated** to bring **a** ***chatas,*** not an *asham,* since his false oath did not release him from a monetary obligation. שׁוֹאֵל – However, **the borrower,** דְּמִיחַיֵּיב בְּמֵתָה כְּדַרְכָּהּ – **who is obligated** to pay **if** he admits the truth that **it died naturally,** וְקָא פָּטַר נַפְשֵׁיהּ בְּמֵתָה מַחֲמַת מְלָאכָה – **and** yet **he exempted himself by** swearing falsely that **it died on account of** its **work,** בְּאָשָׁם – **must** bring **an** ***asham,*** since his false oath released him from a monetary obligation.

The fourth and final case:

שׂוֹכֵר בְּאָשָׁם וְשׁוֹאֵל בְּחַטָּאת – At times **the renter must** bring **an** ***asham*** **and the borrower a** ***chatas:*** כְּגוֹן שֶׁנִּגְנְבָה – **for example, when [the cow] was stolen,**[9] וְאָמְרוּ מֵתָה כְּדַרְכָּהּ – **and they said** and swore falsely that **it died naturally.** שׂוֹכֵר – **The renter,** הוּא דְּמִיחַיֵּיב בִּגְנֵיבָה וַאֲבֵידָה – **who is obligated** to pay **for theft and loss,** וְקָא פָּטַר נַפְשֵׁיהּ בְּמֵתָה כְּדַרְכָּהּ – **and** yet he **exempted himself by** swearing falsely that **it died naturally,** בְּאָשָׁם – must therefore bring **an** ***asham,*** since his false oath released him from a monetary obligation. שׁוֹאֵל – **The borrower,** דְּבֵין כָּךְ וּבֵין כָּךְ חִיּוּבֵי מִיחַיֵּיב – **who is obligated** to pay **in either case,** בְּחַטָּאת – **must** bring **a** ***chatas,*** since his false oath did not release him from a monetary obligation.

The Gemara questions the necessity of R' Yirmiyah's ruling:

מַאי קָא מַשְׁמַע לָן – **What** new point is R' Yirmiyah **teaching us?**[10]

The Gemara answers:

לְאַפּוּקֵי מִדְּרַבִּי אַמִּי דְּאָמַר – He comes **to reject** the opinion of **R' Ami, who said:** כָּל שְׁבוּעָה שֶׁהַדַּיָּינִים מַשְׁבִּיעִים אוֹתָהּ – **Any oath imposed by judges** in *beis din,* אֵין חַיָּיבִין עָלֶיהָ מִשּׁוּם שְׁבוּעַת בִּיטּוּי – **a person** who swears it falsely **is not obligated** to offer a *chatas* **on its account for a** false **utterance of the lips.**[11] שֶׁנֶּאֱמַר – **For it is stated** in regard to the *chatas* brought for a false oath of utterance: "אוֹ נֶפֶשׁ כִּי תִשָּׁבַע לְבַטֵּא בִשְׂפָתַיִם" – ***Or if a soul will swear uttering with the lips*** (he must bring a *chatas* offering if he swears falsely).[12] "כִּי תִשָּׁבַע" מֵעַצְמָהּ – The words ***if [he] will swear*** imply that he swears **voluntarily,** and not by order of *beis din.* קָא מַשְׁמַע לָן – R' Yirmiyah's ruling thus **teaches us** דְּלָא כְּרַבִּי אַמִּי – that the law does **not accord with**

NOTES

1. Although a borrower is liable for even unavoidable losses (such as this one), he must nonetheless swear that the animal was plundered and is no longer in his possession, as Rav Huna taught above (34b). The oath ensures that the *shomer* did not decide to take the animal for himself and pay for it (*Rashi*).

[In the case of our Mishnah, the renter must swear an oath to the owner in order to avoid paying for the cow, and the borrower must swear his oath to the renter even though he pays for the cow. In this first of R' Yirmiyah's four cases, both swore falsely that the animal had been taken by bandits when it had actually died a natural death.]

2. Since a renter is not liable for unavoidable loss, he exempts himself from paying regardless of whether he swears truthfully that the animal died naturally or swears falsely that it was plundered (*Rashi*).

3. For if he had admitted the truth, the renter would still be exempt from payment. Hence, his oath is not considered a false oath to deny a monetary obligation (*Rashi*), and the *asham* brought for a false *oath of deposit* is brought only for an oath that frees a person from paying (see Mishnah, *Shevuos* 49a).

4. A borrower is liable for even unavoidable loss. Hence, he must pay regardless of whether he swore truthfully that the cow died naturally or swore falsely that it was plundered by bandits.

5. *Rashi.*

6. In which case the renter is obligated to pay the owner and the borrower must pay the renter (*Rashi*).

7. Even a borrower is not held liable for work-related death or breakage of the object (see above, 34a note 15).

8. In which case the renter is exempt [from paying the owner], but the borrower must pay [the renter] (*Rashi*).

9. In which case the renter must pay the owner, while the borrower must pay the renter (see *Rashi*).

10. The Mishnah in *Shevuos* (49a-b) clearly states that only when the false oath releases someone from a monetary obligation an *asham* is brought for atonement. What, then, is the novelty of R' Yirmiyah's ruling? (see *Rashi*).

11. According to R' Ami, a *chatas* is not brought for a false oath of utterance unless the person swears the oath on his own, but if he swears because *beis din* compels him to swear, there is no *chatas.* [R' Ami learns this from the verse cited below.]

R' Yirmiyah addresses such a case – for even a renter or borrower not claiming an exemption from liability must swear that the object is no longer in his possession (see above, note 1). This is an oath imposed upon him by *beis din,* and yet R' Yirmiyah rules explicitly that the dishonest oathtaker must offer a *chatas* for atonement if he swore it falsely in a way that did not release him from a monetary obligation (*Raavad;* see *Ritva*).

12. *Leviticus* 5:4. The word *if* implies (according to R' Ami) that the person has a choice in the matter; he can either swear or not swear. When the court imposes an oath on him, he has no choice (see *Rashi, Shevuos* 49b ד״ה כי תישבע).

פְּעָמִים שֶׁהַבְּעָלִים מְשַׁלְּמִין כַּמָּה פָּרוֹת — אָמַר רַבִּי זֵירָא — R' Zeira said: לַשּׂוֹכֵר — At times the owner will end up having to pay a number of cows to the renter. הֵיכִי דָּמֵי — What is the case? אַגְרָהּ מִינֵּיהּ מְאָה יוֹמֵי — If someone rented [a cow] from [the owner] for one hundred days, וְהָדַר שַׁיְּילָהּ מִינֵּיהּ תִּשְׁעִין יוֹמֵי — and [the owner] then borrowed it back from him for the first ninety of those one hundred days,[10] הָדַר אַגְרָהּ מִינֵּיהּ תְּמָנָן יוֹמֵי — and [the renter] then rented it again from [the owner/borrower] for eighty of those ninety days,[11] וְהָדַר שַׁיְּילָהּ מִינֵּיהּ שִׁבְעִין יוֹמֵי — and [the owner] then borrowed it back from [the renter] again for the first seventy of those eighty days, וּמֵתָה בְּתוֹךְ יְמֵי שְׁאֵלָתָהּ — and [the cow] died in the midst of these seventy days of borrowing, דְּאַכָּל שְׁאֵלָה וּשְׁאֵלָה מִיחַיַּיב חֲדָא פָּרָה — [the owner] is obligated to pay the renter one cow for each and every borrowing of the cow.[12]

The Gemara challenges this conclusion:

אָמַר לֵיהּ רַב אַחָא מִדִּיפְתִּי לְרָבִינָא — Rav Acha of Difti told Ravina: מִכְּדֵי חֲדָא פָּרָה הִיא — Now, it is only one cow that changed hands; עַיְּילָהּ וְאַפְּקָהּ — it was brought into and removed from different states. אַפְּקָהּ מִשְּׂכִירוּת וְעַיְּילָהּ לִשְׁאֵילָה — It was removed from the state of rental and brought into the state of borrowing; אַפְּקָהּ מִשְּׁאֵילָה וְעַיְּילָהּ לִשְׂכִירוּת — it was removed from a state of borrowing and brought back into a state of rental. Hence, the owner should be held liable only for the final borrowing![13]

The challenge is rebutted:

אָמַר לֵיהּ — [Ravina] told [Rav Acha]: וּמִי אִיתָא לְפָרָה בְּעֵינָא — And is the cow intact, דְּנֵימָא לֵיהּ הָכִי — that [the owner] may make this argument to [the renter]?[14]

The Gemara presents an opinion that concurs with Rav Acha'

מַר בַּר רַב אַשִׁי אָמַר — Mar bar Rav Ashi said: ...ין לוֹ עֲלֵיהֶן אֶלָּא שְׁתֵּי פָּרוֹת — [The renter] has a claim against [the owner] f... only two cows: חֲדָא דִּשְׁאֵלָה — one in payment for the lo... incurred during the final borrowing, וַחֲדָא דִּשְׂכִירוּת — and o... for the remaining twenty days of the rental. ...ם שְׁאֵלָה אַחַת הִיא — For all the borrowing is regarded as one, ...וּם שְׂכִירוּת אַחַת הִיא — and all the renting is regarded as one. I.e. sin... only one cow is involved, the second rental and borrowing are n... viewed as new transactions, but as part of the original transactio... that moves back and forth between states of rental and borrov... ing. The owner therefore pays only two cows; and ...שְׁאֵלָה קָנֵי לְגַמְרֵי — [the renter] permanently acquires the one paid for th... borrowing, דִּשְׂכִירוּת עָבֵד בָּהּ יְמֵי שְׂכִירוּתֵיהּ — and the one pai... for the rental he acquires for the remaining days of the renta... וּמִיהְדַּר לֵיהּ לְמָרָהּ — and then returns it to its owner.

When someone unintentionally makes a false oath for so... purpose other than freeing himself from monetary liability, he ... obligated to bring a *chatas* offering as an atonement.[15] Howeve... if he swears falsely *in order to* avoid monetary liability and h... later admits his guilt, he brings an *asham* offering as an aton... ment.[16] The Gemara discusses some applications of these laws i... reference to the renter and borrower discussed by our Mishnah:

אָמַר רַבִּי יִרְמְיָה — R' Yirmiyah said: פְּעָמִים שֶׁשְּׁנֵיהֶם בְּחַטָּאת — At times both of them [the renter and borrower] are obligate... to bring a *chatas* offering for swearing a false oath about wha... happened to the cow.

NOTES

10. At this point, the case is identical to that of the Mishnah, in which a renter lent the cow to someone else. The fact that he lent it to the owner makes no difference. Thus, had the animal died now, and the renter swore that it died naturally, the owner (who borrowed the cow from the renter) would have had to pay him for the dead cow, according to the Tanna Kamma of our Mishnah (see *Rashi*). [He would also have to provide him with another cow to use for the last ten days of the rental term – days 91-100 (*Rashi*).]

The Gemara speaks of a case where the term of the borrowing ends before the term of the rental, because if the two ended at the same time, the rental would be considered completely nullified. [This would be the equivalent of the owner asking the renter to give up the rental and be free from paying anything] (*Tosafos* ד״ה אגרה פי׳ יום, second explanation).

11. After the owner borrowed the cow back from the renter for ninety days, the renter came back to him and asked him to rent the cow back to him for eighty of those ninety days, for a new rental fee (*Rashi*). The owner/borrower agreed. In doing so, the owner/borrower was acting in his capacity as a borrower to rent the cow to someone else – in this case to the same renter as before.

This second rental changes nothing. If the cow dies naturally at this point, and the renter swears to that fact, the owner must give him two cows – one to pay for the cow he borrowed, and another for the renter to use for the final ten days of the original 100-day rental agreement, as explained in the previous note (*Rashi*). [See *Maharsha*, who discusses why the owner does not also have to provide the renter with a cow to use for the remaining days of the second rental.]

12. I.e. the payment for the second borrowing is subject to the same rules as those of the first (see previous note). Hence, the owner as borrower must pay the renter *two* cows outright, since the death of a twice-borrowed cow is equivalent to the deaths of two borrowed cows. In addition, he must supply the renter with two more cows, which may each be use... for ten days and are then returned.

[If the cow had not died, the owner/borrower would not have to retur... two cows; he would simply return the one cow that he borrowed twic... Nevertheless, when the cow *dies*, he must pay two cows. This is becaus... he is now *paying* for a cow, not *returning* a cow. Since each borrowing ob... ligates him to pay for the borrowed object if it should die, he is require... to pay twice (*Rashi*).]

13. [Rav Acha challenges the distinction made at the end of the previou... note.] He argues that in essence only one cow was rented and borrowe... Thus, the owner as borrower need pay only one cow as compensation fo... its loss, and only one cow for the renter to use for twenty days in order t... comply with the terms of the rental agreements (*Rashi*).

14. In fact, if the cow were intact, the owner would be obligated only t... return the cow to the renter for twenty days' use, in accordance wit... the two rental agreements. However, the death of the cow gives rise t... two separate damage claims by the renter against the owner – eac... demanding payment for loss incurred while the animal was in a "bor... rowed" state (*Rashi*; see above, note 12).

15. This is a special *chatas* known as a קָרְבָּן עוֹלֶה וְיוֹרֵד, *variable chata... offering*, so called because an individual's specific obligation is deter... mined by his financial condition. A well-to-do person brings a femal... lamb or kid, a poor person brings two birds (one as a *chatas* and th... other as an *olah*), and a very poor person brings a *minchah* offering o... flour (*Leviticus* 5:4-13).

16. *Leviticus* 5:20-25; see *Shevuos* 49b. This oath is known as a שְׁבוּעַת הַפִּקָּדוֹן, *oath of deposit*. The *asham* offering, which in this case is know... as the אֲשַׁם גְּזֵילוֹת, *asham for theft,* is a ram worth at least two silve... shekels (*Rashi* 36a ד״ה שניהם באשם).

אגביה איהו בחובו פליגי בה רב אחא ורבינא חד אמר הדרה וחד אמר [א]לא הדרה מאן דאמר לא הדרה סבר האי זביני מעליא היא דהא מדעתא דנפשיה אגביה ומאן דאמר הדרה סבר לא זביני מעליא הוא והאי דאגביה מדעתיה ולא אתא לדינא מחמת כיסופא הוא דאגביה ומאימת אכיל פירי רבה אמר מכי מטיא אדרכתא לידיה [א] אביי אמר עדיו בחתומיו זכין לו רבא אמר [ב]מכי שלימו ימי אכרזתא: **מתני'** השוכר פרה מחבירו והשאילה לאחר ומתה כדרכה ישבע השוכר שמתה כדרכה [ג] והשואל ישלם לשוכר א"ר יוסי [ג]כיצד הלה עושה סחורה בפרתו של חבירו אלא תחזור פרה לבעלים: **גמ'** א"ל רב אידי בר אבין לאביי מכדי שוכר במאי קני להאי פרה בשבועה ונימא ליה משכיר לשוכר דל אנת ודל שבועתך ואנא משתעינא דינא בהדי שואל א"ל מי סברת שוכר בשבועה הוא דקא קני לה משעת מיתה הוא דקני ושבועה כדי להפיס דעתו של בעל הבית א"ר זירא פעמים שהבעלים משלמין כמה פרות לשוכר היכי דמי אגרה מיניה מאה יומי והדר שיילה מיניה תשעין יומי הדר אגרה מיניה תמנן יומי והדר שיילה מיניה שבעין יומי ומתה בתוך ימי שאלתה דאכל שאלה ושאלה מיחייב חדא פרה א"ל רב אחא מדיפתי לרבינא מכדי חדא פרה היא עיילה ואפקה אפקה משכירות ועיילה לשאילה אפקה משאילה ועיילה לשכירות א"ל ומי איתא לפרה בעינא דנימא ליה הכי מר בר רב אשי אמר אין לו עליהן אלא שתי פרות חדא דשאלה וחדא דשכירות שום שאלה אחת היא ושום שכירות אחת היא דשאלה קני לגמרי דשכירות עבד בה ימי שכירותיה ומיהדר ליה למרה אמר ר' ירמיה פעמים ששניהם בחטאת פעמים

**רש"י**

אגביה איהו בחובו. לעיל מיהדר גבי שומא כלומר אם לא שמוה ב"ד למלוה על כרחו של לוה וקם ליה מעצמו ולא הטריחו לדין ואמר לו טול קרקע זה בחובך: מאימתי אוכל פירות. מי ששמו לו ב"ד קרקע בחובו מאימת היא קנויה לו לאכול פירות: אדרכתא. לאחר תשעים יום שנפסק הדין דאמרינן [ג] בפ"ק (דף טו) דב"ד כותבין אדרכתא שטר פסק דין אנכסי לוה שבכל מקום שימצאם משלו יקחם ומוסרין לו השטר: עדיו בחתומיו. מיום שנחתם שטר האדרכתא בב"ד אע"פ שלא בא לידו: מכי שלמו ימי אכרזתא. אע"פ שבאה אדרכתא לידו ולא מצא נכסים ללוה עד לאחר זמן וכשמצא הוזקק לבא לב"ד ומכריזין שיש כאן קרקע למכור כדאמרינן בערכין (דף כא:) ואם בא זה וקיבלה ביותר ממה ששמוה אחרים מוסרין אותה בידו לאחר שכלו ימי הכרזה ובמסכת ערכין מפרש כמה ימים מכריזין בפ' שום היתומים (שם) ועד דשלמו הנך יומי הוי פירי דלוה: מתני' השוכר פרה מחבירו. ועמד שוכר והשאילה לאחר לעשות בה ימי שכירותו: ישבע השוכר. למשכיר: שמתה כדרכה. ופטור שהשוכר אינו חייב באונסין: והשואל. שהוא חייב באונסין משלם לשוכר: גמ' בשבועה. שהוא נשבע למשכיר: להפיס דעתו. שלא יאמר פשעת בה: פעמים שהבעלים. המשכירין הראשונים: משלמין. לשוכר זה כמה פרות על פרה זו לפי דברי משנתנו יש שיהו כולם שלו ויש שיעשה בהם ימי שכירותו ויחזירם: כיצד אגרה מיניה מאה יומי והדר שיילה מיניה תשעין יומי וכו'. ראובן שכר פרה משמעון שיעשה בה מלאכה מאה יום וחזר שמעון ואמר לו עשה עמי טובה והשאילני אותה תשעים יום מן המאה ששכרת ולאחר תשעים אחזירנה לך לעשות אצלך י' ימים להשלים המאה וכן עשה יש כאן דין משנתנו דתנן השוכר פרה מחבירו והשאילה לאחר בתוך ימי שכירותה דמה לי בעלים ומה לי אחר אם מתה אצל שואל הרי שוכר פטור בשבועה והשואל משלם לשוכר חזר ראובן ובא אצלו ואמר לו השכירנה לי מתשעים יום שהיא שאולה בידך ממני ואשתעבד בה שמונים יום וטול שכרך וכן עשה הרי היא בחזקת שאילתו על שמעון כאילו השכירה לאחר שהרי נוטל שכרו וכל הנאה שלו ואם היתה מתה אצל ראובן היה ראובן פטור בשבועה ושמעון משלם לו פרה אחת ששאל ממנו והוא חייב באונסים ופרה אחרת לעשות אצלו עשרה ימים להשלים המאה חזר שמעון ושאלה ממנו שבעים יום מן השמונים ששכרה ממנו על מנת שיחזירנה לו ויעשה בה עשרה ימים להשלים השמונים של שכירות השני ואם היתה מתה בתוך שבעים יום הללו הרי יש כאן דין השני כדין הראשון וישבע ראובן שמתה כדרכה ושמעון השואל משלם לו ד' פרות שתים נחלטות לו בשביל שתי פרות שאולות שהשאילו ראובן ובפעם זה כאילו מתו שתיהן שהרי אין פרתו בעין שהשאילו בראשון דנימא הרי החזיר לו פרתו חו שהוא משלם לו עכשיו בתורת תשלומין באה לידו והרי יש לו עליו שתי תביעות על שתי שאלות ושתי תביעות על שתי שכירות לעשות אצלו עשרים יום: מכדי חדא פרה הואי כו'. ולענין תשלומין נמי לשלם ליה פרה אחת ותעמוד במקום הראשונה תחת שתי השאילות ותהא שלו ואחת ימסור לו לעשות בה עשרים יום: מי איתא לפרה בעינא דנימא הכי. אילו היתה קיימת היה פטור לגמרי אלא שיעשה בה עשרים יום עכשיו שמתה בא עליו בתורת תשלומין שואל לשוכר על שתי תביעות: מר בר רב אשי ס"ל כאתקפתא דרב אחא מדפתי: שום שאלה אחת היא. דכיון דחדא פרה הואי אלא שמחמת שוכר שהשאיל הוא בא עליו שני שאילות פרה אחת אינן אלא אחת: פעמים ששניהם בחטאת. אמתניתין קאי השוכר והשואל נשבעו לשקר ולא כפרו ממון והרי הן בשבועות ביטוי וקרבן שלו חטאת כדכתיב בויקרא או נפש כי תשבע וגו':
שניהם

**תוספות**

רבא אמר מכי שלמו ימי אכרזתא. וא"ת שלהי הנושא (כתובות דף קד: ושם ד"ה ה"ג) דאמר רבא אחוי אדרכתיך והתם רבא גרסינן מדאמר והא מר הוא דאמר אחריות טעות סופר הוא והיינו רבא דפסיק כן לעיל בפ"ק (דף טו: ושם) וי"ל אחוי לי אדרכתיך דאי שפיר כתיבא הוה גבי מיומא דאכרזתא ואית דגרסי בשמעתין רבא אמר מכי מטא אדרכתא לידיה ובתר הכי רבה ולפי זה אתי טפי בפשיטות ההיא דהנושא והקדים רבא לאביי ורבה משום דאדרכתא קודם לאכרזתא ודברי אביי דאמר עדיו בחתומיו זכין לו מיושב טפי לשנות בתר דברי רבא מקודם:

תחזור פרה לבעלים הראשונים. אין לפרש משום דא"ל משכיר לשוכר פרתי גבך דהשואל שילם דמיה דבפ' השואל (לקמן דף צו: ושם) בעי רמי בר חמא בעל בנכסי אשתו שוכר הוי או שואל הוי היכא דאגרה פרה מעלמא ואינסיבא אליבא דרבנן ודאי בעלה פטור משום דאשתו עמו במלאכתו והויא שאלה בבעלים [ד] (ואשה חייבת כדין שוכר) כי תבעי לך אליבא דר' יוסי שואל הוי להתחייב לבעלים הראשונים במתה כדרכה או שוכר הוי ופטור והשתא התם כיון דלרבנן הבעל פטור מן האשה משום דהוי שאלה בבעלים לא יתחייב נמי לר' יוסי לבעלים הראשונים אלא טעמא דרבי יוסי הוי משום דסבר דשוכר לא קני אלא בשבועה ומשכיר יאמר לו דל אנת ודל שבועתך ומשתעינא דינא בהדי שואל ואפילו אם יש עדים שמתה כדרכה דאין השוכר צריך לישבע מ"מ לא קני לה אלא בהבאת עדים ויאמר לו אני פוטרך מהבאת עדים ורבנן סברי דשוכר קני לה במיתה ופליגי בדברי המקשה והמתרץ שבגמ' ונראה אם המשכיר עצמו היה שם בשעת שמתה ביד שואל שר' יוסי יודה לדברי רבנן דהתם ודאי קני לה במיתה גרידא דהשתא אין השוכר צריך לעשות כלום:

(א) אגרה ק' יום ושיילה צ' יום. השתא אם מתה חייב שתי פרות לשוכר אחת שתהא שלו ואחת שיעשה בה מלאכה י' ימים ויחזירנה למשכיר אבל אי שיילוה ק' יום לא יתחייב לו רק אחת של שאלה:

אגרה פ' יום. ה"מ למימר אגרה ל' יום אלא לפי שבשאלה הוצרך לפחות פוחת גם בשכירות ועי"ל דאי אגרה ל' יום דהיינו כל ימי השאלה הוי כאילו נתן לו מעות לבטל השאלה כיון שאינה חוזרת לו לאחר השכירות להשלים ימי השאלה ואי סדר שייליה [ה] ע' יום לא יתחייב רק אחת דשאלה ודשכירות [ו] ק' יום וכן י"ל ברישא דאי שייליה ק' יום בימי השכירות כאילו ביקש שיתבטל השכירות ולא יתחייב כלום ומתני' דהשוכר הוי בעלים דשואל לרבנן אי איירי שלא שאל כל ימי השכירות אתי שפיר דלאחר ימי השאלה תחזור לשוכר ואפילו אם השאילה כל ימי השכירות מ"מ כיון שהיא באחריות השוכר מגניבה ואבידה ופשיעה אם היה עם השואל במלאכתו דאז השואל פטור והשוכר חייב מקרי בעלים אבל הכא אי שייליה ק' יום השוכר פטור מכל דבר:
שוכר

**עין משפט נר מצוה**

כ א מיי' פכ"ב מהל' מלוה ולוה הל' יז סמג עשין צד טוש"ע ח"מ סי' קג סעי' י:

כא ב מיי' שם הל' יג סמג שם טוש"ע ח"מ סי' קג:

כב ג מיי' פ"א מהל' שכירות הל' ו סמג עשין פט טוש"ע ח"מ סי' שז סעי' ה:

**רבינו חננאל**

אגביה הלוה מדעתו ומכרה למלוה פליגי בה רב אחא ורבינא וקיימא לן הלכה כדברי המיקל הלכך לא מיהדר. זה ששמו לו מאימת אכיל הפירות א) רבא אמר מכי מטיא אדרכתא לידיה. סדר הדין מוציא מלוה שטרו בב"ד ומקיימו ומחייבין הלוה לפורעו לא פרע קורעין שטר חוב וכותבין למלוה אדרכתא על נכסי הלוה ומכריזין ואחרי ההכרזה שמין נכסי הלוה ומחליטין למלוה לא מצא נכסין בני חורין כותבין לו טירפא ואחרי שיטרף קורעין הטירפא וכותבין לו אדרכתא על הנכסין הללו ואחר כך קורעין האדרכתא וכותבין לו שומא על שדה זו ומחליטין אותה למלוה. אביי אמר בחתימת העדים על האדרכת' מיד זכה המלוה בשדה. רבא אמר מכי שלמן (אדרכתא) [אכרזתא] וקיי"ל כרבא: **מתני'** השוכר פרה והשאילה לאחר ומתה כדרכה ישבע השוכר שמתה כדרכה והשואל משלם לשוכר. אוקמה ר' אמי [לקמן דף לו] בשנתנו לו הבעלים רשות כגון שאמרו לו לדעתו כלומ' אם רצונך להשאילה לו הרשות בידך. עכשיו אם ראה אותה השוכר שמתה ברשות השואל כדרכה ישבע ויפטר. וישלם השואל לשוכר. אמר ר' זירא פעמים שמשלמים הבעלים כמה פרות לשוכר כו' ודברים פשוטין הן. אמר ר' ירמיה פעמים שהשוכר והשואל שניהן בחטאת פעמים ששניהן באשם. פעמים שהשוכר בחטאת והשואל באשם. פעמים שהשואל בחטאת והשוכר באשם. תפוש האי כללא בידך כפירת ממון באשם. אין שם כפירת ממון אלא ביטוי שפתים כלומר נשבע בשקר על דבר שאין לו בו הנאת ממון חייב חטאת. וקיימא לן שומר חנם נשבע על הכל. שואל משלם את הכל חוץ ממתה מחמת מלאכה. נושא שכר והשוכר נשבעין על השבורה ועל השבויה ועל המתה ומשלמין הגניבה והאבידה וכבר פירשנום. שניהן בחטאת ב) כגון שמתה מחמת מלאכה דתרווייהו פטורין מלשלם וכחשו ונשבעו שנאנסה אין אחד מהן נהנה לפיכך שניהן בחטאת.

**חשק שלמה על ר"ח**

א) נראה דצ"ל רבה ועי' בתוס' ד"ה רבא. ב) לפניו בגמ' הגי' כגון שמתה כדרכה ואמרו נאנסה וכו' ואולי דרבינו הי' לו גי' אחרת בגמ' וצ"ע.

**מסורת הש"ס**

א) לעיל יג. [וש"נ], ב) [לקמן לו:], ג) [צ"ל בבבא קמא קיב:], ד) עיין מהרש"א, ה) צ"ל פ', מהרש"ל, ו) צ"ל כ', מהרש"ל.

**הגהות הב"ח**

(א) תוס' ד"ה אגרה ק' וד"ה אגרה פ' הד"א:

**ליקוטי רש"י**

אדרכתא. פסק דין לירד המלוה לתוך נכסים של לוה וליטלם בשומא בחובו [ב"ק קיב:]. שלא מצאו לו עכשיו נכסים וכתבו לו שירדוף לחזור על נכסיו ואם ימצא יגבה. אדרכתא לשון רודף ומשיג כמו פרסה בתלא ולא אדרכיה (כתובות דף ס:) ולשון המקרא כתרו את בנימין הרדיפוהו מנוחה הדריכוהו [לעיל טז:]. עדיו בחתומיו זכין לו. מיום שחתמוהו זכין לו השעבוד [לעיל יג.].

The Gemara discusses yet another issue involving the return of seized property:

אַגְבְּיֵה אִיהוּ בְּחוֹבוֹ – Where [the debtor] himself gave his creditor [the property] in repayment of his debt[1] and he later offers a cash payment in return for the property, פְּלִיגֵי בָּהּ רַב אַחָא וְרָבִינָא – Rav Acha and Ravina dispute the ruling in [such a case]: חַד אָמַר הָדְרָה – One says that [the property] must be returned to the debtor, וְחַד אָמַר לֹא הָדְרָה – and one says that it is not returned to him.

The Gemara explains the basis of their dispute:

מַאן דְּאָמַר לֹא הָדְרָה – The one who says that [the property] need not be returned סָבַר הַאי זְבִינֵי מְעַלְּיָא הִיא – holds that this transfer of the property is a proper sale, דְּהָא מִדַּעְתָּא דְּנַפְשֵׁיהּ אַגְבְּיֵהּ – for [the debtor] gave him [the property] of his own free will.[2] וּמַאן דְּאָמַר הָדְרָה – But the one who says that [the property] is returned סָבַר לֹא זְבִינֵי מְעַלְּיָא הוּא – holds that it is not a proper sale, וְהַאי דְּאַגְבְּיֵהּ מִדַּעְתֵּיהּ – and that which he voluntarily gave the creditor [the property] לֹא אָתָא לְדִינָא – and did not go to court for an adjudication of the matter מֵחֲמַת כִּיסוּפָא הוּא דְּאַגְבְּיֵהּ – is because he was embarrassed to go to court and he therefore gave the creditor [the property] on his own, but not that he actually intended to part with his property.

The Gemara discusses the point at which a creditor is entitled to benefit from property seized for him by *beis din:*

וּמֵאֵימַת אָכִיל פֵּירֵי – And from when may [the creditor] eat the produce?[3] רַבָּה אָמַר – Rabbah says: מִכִּי מָטְיָא אַדְרַכְתָּא לִידֵיהּ – From when the document of seizure reaches his hands.[4] אַבַּיֵי אָמַר – Abaye says: עֵדָיו בַּחֲתוּמָיו זָכִין לוֹ – The witnesses [of the seizure document] acquire these rights for [the creditor] by their signatures.[5] רָבָא אָמַר – Rava says: מִכִּי שְׁלִימוּ יְמֵי אַכְרַזְתָּא – From when the days of public announcement of the sale have been completed.[6]

**Mishnah** This Mishnah discusses another case in which a *shomer* may profit from the deposited item: הַשּׂוֹכֵר פָּרָה מֵחֲבֵירוֹ – If someone rents a cow from his friend, וְהִשְׁאִילָהּ לְאַחֵר – and [the renter] lent it to another person to use during the period of the rental, וּמֵתָה כְּדַרְכָּהּ – and it subsequently died a natural death, unrelated to its work, יִשָּׁבַע הַשּׂוֹכֵר שֶׁמֵּתָה כְּדַרְכָּהּ – the renter should swear to the owner that [the cow] died naturally, thereby freeing himself from having to pay for it;[7] וְהַשּׁוֹאֵל יְשַׁלֵּם לַשּׂוֹכֵר – and the borrower, who is liable for this type of loss, pays the value of the cow to the renter. אָמַר רַבִּי יוֹסֵי – R' Yose said: כֵּיצַד הַלָּה עוֹשֶׂה סְחוֹרָה – How can that one (the renter) do business בְּפָרָתוֹ שֶׁל חֲבֵירוֹ – with his friend's cow? אֶלָּא תַּחֲזוֹר פָּרָה לַבְּעָלִים – Rather, the value of the cow should be returned to its owner.[8]

**Gemara** The Gemara discusses the rationale for the Mishnah's ruling:

אָמַר לֵיהּ רַב אִידִי בַּר אָבִין לְאַבַּיֵי – Rav Idi bar Avin commented to Abaye: מִכְּדֵי שׂוֹכֵר בְּמַאי קָנֵי לְהַאי פָּרָה – Now, with what act did the renter acquire that cow, that he should be entitled to the borrower's payment? בִּשְׁבוּעָה – With the oath that he swore to the owner that he is not liable. וְנֵימָא לֵיהּ מַשְׂכִּיר לַשּׂוֹכֵר – But if so, let the owner tell the renter: דַּל אַנְתְּ וְדַל שְׁבוּעָתָךְ – "Eliminate yourself and eliminate your oath, i.e. I release you from liability, וַאֲנָא מִשְׁתָּעֵינָא דִּינָא בַּהֲדֵי שׁוֹאֵל – and I will take up the case directly with the borrower."[9] אָמַר לֵיהּ – [Abaye] told him: מִי סָבְרַתְּ שׂוֹכֵר בִּשְׁבוּעָה הוּא דְּקָא קָנֵי לָהּ – Do you think that it is with the oath that the renter acquires [the cow]? מִשְּׁעַת מִיתָה הוּא דְּקָנֵי – No! He acquires it automatically from the time of the animal's death, וּשְׁבוּעָה – and the purpose of the oath כְּדֵי לְהָפִיס דַּעְתּוֹ שֶׁל בַּעַל הַבַּיִת – is only to appease the owner, so that he will not charge the renter with negligence. Hence, it is impossible for the owner to prevent the renter from acquiring the cow — and with it the borrower's payment.

The Gemara discusses some unusual consequences of the Mishnah's ruling:

NOTES

1. I.e. since he did not have the cash to pay, he voluntarily gave his property to the creditor in payment of the debt, and did not trouble the creditor to collect through the court [as in the previous cases] (*Rashi*).

2. The court did not take the property from him and give it to the creditor; he gave it himself. This is like any other sale of property, and when a person sells his property willingly, he cannot later demand that he be allowed to take it back in return for the money.

[The commentators debate whether this reasoning applies if the debtor was forced to go to *beis din*, but once there, he willingly gave his property (see *Shach* to *Choshen Mishpat* 103:15).]

3. I.e. at what point does he acquire the property, so that he may enjoy its proceeds? (*Rashi*).

4. Ninety days after its decision, when the court is convinced that the debtor will not pay, the court gives the creditor a document of seizure, which authorizes him to collect his debt from any property of the debtor that he might discover (*Rashi*, from *Bava Kamma* 112b).

Even though all agree that a creditor does not take possession of the seized property until the days of public announcement are completed (see below and note 6), Rabbah maintains that upon that occasion, the creditor acquires the property retroactively from the time the document of seizure reaches his hands. Hence, all profits from that time on belong to him.

5. According to Abaye, the creditor is entitled to benefit from the seized property from the time witnesses sign the document of seizure in court — i.e. even before the creditor actually receives the document (*Rashi*).

6. Rava holds that although the creditor may have received the document of seizure, he has no right to the produce until he actually locates land belonging to the debtor, even if that takes some time. He must then wait until *beis din* conducts a public auction. Then, if he is the highest bidder, *beis din* awards him the property, and he acquires the right to its proceeds only at that time (*Rashi; cf. Ritva;* see *Arachin* 21b).

7. A renter does not pay for unavoidable loss [such as the natural death of the animal] (*Rashi;* see Chapter Introduction).

The Mishnah speaks of a renter because a renter has the right to use the cow; therefore, his loan of the cow to another person is not considered a misuse of it. However, if a paid or unpaid *shomer*, who does not have the right to use the cow, lent the cow to another person, he would be guilty of improperly taking the cow for personal use, and he would be liable for anything that happened afterward (see Chapter Introduction, note 2).

8. R' Yose maintains that the renter does not acquire the right to the borrower's payment until he frees himself from his obligation to the owner by swearing that the animal died naturally. R' Yose therefore says that the owner of the cow may release the renter from his obligation to swear and deal directly with the borrower, who is then liable to him. The Sages, on the other hand, maintain that the renter acquires the right to the borrower's payment immediately upon the natural death of the animal; the oath is merely to help establish the truth of his claim. Therefore, even if the owner releases the renter from the oath, he cannot claim payment from the borrower (*Tosafos* ד״ה תחזור; see *Rashba* and *Ritva* for a different explanation). [The Gemara below will present both of these arguments without attributing them to the Tannaim of the Mishnah.]

9. By forgoing the oath the owner prevents the renter from acquiring the right to collect from the borrower. The owner may therefore collect from the borrower himself.

אגביה איהו בחובו פליגי בה רב אחא ורבינא חד אמר הדרה וחד אמר [א]לא הדרה מאן דאמר לא הדרה סבר האי זביני מעליא היא דהא מדעתא דנפשיה אגביה ומאן דאמר הדרה סבר לא זביני מעליא הוא והאי דאגביה מדעתיה ולא אתא לדינא מחמת כיסופא הוא דאגביה ומאימת אכיל פירי רבה אמר מכי מטיא אדרכתא לידיה [א] אביי אמר עדיו בחתומיו זכין לו רבא אמר [ב]מכי שלימו ימי אכרזתא: **מתני'** השוכר פרה מחבירו והשאילה לאחר ומתה כדרכה ישבע השוכר שמתה כדרכה [ג]והשואל ישלם לשוכר א"ר יוסי [ג]כיצד הלה עושה סחורה בפרתו של חבירו אלא תחזור פרה לבעלים: **גמ'** א"ל רב אידי בר אבין לאביי מכדי שוכר במאי קני להאי פרה בשבועה ונימא ליה משכיר לשוכר דל אנת ודל שבועתך ואנא משתעינא דינא בהדי שואל א"ל מי סברת שוכר בשבועה הוא דקא קני לה משעת מיתה הוא דקני ושבועה כדי להפיס דעתו של בעל הבית א"ר זירא פעמים שהבעלים משלמין כמה פרות לשוכר היכי דמי אגרה מיניה מאה יומי והדר שיילה מיניה תשעין יומי הדר אגרה מיניה תמנן יומי והדר שיילה מיניה שבעין יומי ומתה בתוך ימי שאלתה דאכל שאלה ושאלה מיחייב חדא פרה א"ל רב אחא מדיפתי לרבינא מכדי חדא פרה היא עיילה ואפקה אפקה משכירות ועיילה לשאילה אפקה משאילה ועיילה לשכירות א"ל ומי איתא לפרה בעינא דנימא ליה הכי מר בר רב אשי אמר אין לו עליהן אלא שתי פרות חדא דשאלה וחדא דשכירות שום שאלה אחת היא ושום שכירות אחת היא דשאלה קני לגמרי דשכירות עבד בה ימי שכירותיה ומיהדר ליה למרה אמר ר' ירמיה פעמים ששניהם בחטאת פעמים

**רבא** אמר מכי שלמו ימי אכרזתא. וא"ת שלהי הגוזל (כתובות דף קד: ושם ד"ה ה"ג) דאמר רבא אחוי אדרכתיך והתם רבא גרסינן מדאמר והא מר הוא דאמר אחריות טעות סופר הוא והיינו רבא דפסיק כן לעיל בפ"ק (דף טו: ושם) וי"ל אחוי לי אדרכתיך דאי שפיר כתיבא הוה גבי מיומא דאכרזתא ואית דגרסי בשמעתין רבא אמר מכי מטא אדרכתא לידיה ובתר הכי רבה ולפי זה אתי טפי בפשיטות ההיא דהגוזל והקדים רבא לאביי ורבה משום דאדרכתא קודם לאכרזתא ודברי אביי דאמר עדיו בחתומיו זכין לו מיושב טפי לשנות בתר דברי רבא מקודם:

**תחזור** פרה לבעלים הראשונים. אין לפרש משום דא"ל משכיר לשוכר פרתי גבך דהשואל שילם דמיה דבפ' השואל (לקמן דף צו: ושם) בעי רמי בר חמא בעל בנכסי אשתו שוכר הוי או שואל הוי היכא דאגרה פרה מעלמא ואינסיבא אליבא דרבנן ודאי בעלה פטור משום דאשתו עמו במלאכתו והויא שאלה בבעלים [ד](ואשה חייבת כדין שוכר) כי תבעי לך אליבא דר' יוסי שואל הוי להתחייב לבעלים הראשונים במתה כדרכה או שוכר הוי ופטור והשתא התם כיון דלרבנן הבעל פטור מן האשה משום דהוי שאלה בבעלים לא יתחייב נמי לר' יוסי לבעלים הראשונים אלא טעמא דרבי יוסי הוי משום דסבר דשוכר לא קני אלא בשבועה ומשכיר יאמר לו דל אנת ודל שבועתך ומשתעינא דינא בהדי שואל ואפילו אם יש עדים שמתה כדרכה דאין השוכר צריך לישבע מ"מ לא קני לה אלא בהבאת עדים ויאמר לו אני פוטרך מהבאת עדים ורבנן סברי דשוכר קני לה במיתה ופליגי בדברי המקשה והמתרץ שבגמ' ונראה אם המשכיר עצמו היה שם בשעת שמתה ביד שואל שר' יוסי יודה לדברי רבנן דהתם ודאי קני לה במיתה גרידא דהשתא אין השוכר צריך לעשות כלום:

(א) **אגרה** ק' יום ושיילה צ' יום. השתא אם מתה חייב שתי פרות לשוכר אחת שתהא שלו ואחת שיעשה בה מלאכה י' ימים ויחזירנה למשכיר אבל אי שיילוה ק' יום לא יתחייב לו רק אחת של שאלה:

**אגרה** פ' יום. ה"מ למימר אגרה נ' יום אלא לפי שבשאלה הולכך לפחות פוחת גם בשכירות ועי"ל דאי אגרה נ' יום דהיינו כל ימי השאלה הוי כאילו נתן לו מעות לבטל השאלה כיון שאינה חוזרת לו לאחר השכירות להשלים ימי השאלה ואי הדר שיילה [ה]ע' יום לא יתחייב רק אחת דשאלה ודשכירות [ו]ק' יום וכן י"ל ברישא דאי שיילה ק' יום בימי השכירות כאילו ביקש שיתבטל השכירות ולא יתחייב כלום ומתני' דהשוכר הוי בעלים דשואל לרבנן אי מיירי שלא שאל כל ימי השכירות אתי שפיר דלאחר ימי השאלה תחזור לשוכר ואפילו אם השאילה כל ימי השכירות מ"מ כיון שהיא באחריות השוכר מגניבה ואבידה ופשיעה אם היה עם השואל במלאכתו דאז השואל פטור והשוכר חייב מקרי בעלים אבל הכא אי שיילה ק' יום השוכר פטור מכל דבר: שוכר

אגביה איהו בחובו. לעיל מיהדר גבי שומא כלומר אם לא שמוה ב"ד למלוה על כרחו של לוה וקם ליה מעצמו ולא הטריחו לדין ואמר לו טול קרקע זה בחובך: מאימתי אוכל פירות. מי ששמו לו ב"ד קרקע בחובו מאימת היא קנויה לו לאכול פירות: אדרכתא. לאחר תשעים יום שנפסק הדין דאמרינן [ג] בפ"ק (דף טו) דב"ד כותבין אדרכתא שטר פסק דין אנכסי לוה שבכל מקום שימצאם משלו יקחם ומוסרין לו השטר: עדיו בחתומיו. מיום שנחתם שטר האדרכתא בב"ד אע"פ שלא בא לידו: מכי שלמו ימי אכרזתא. אע"פ שבאה אדרכתא לידו ולא מצא נכסים ללוה עד לאחר זמן וכשמצא הוזקק לבא לב"ד ומכריזין שיש כאן קרקע למכור כדאמרינן בערכין (דף כא:) ואם בא זה וקיבלה ביותר ממה ששמוה אחרים מוסרין אותה בידו לאחר שכלו ימי הכרזה ובמסכת ערכין מפרש כמה ימים מכריזין בפ' שום היתומים (שם) ועד דשלמו הנך יומי הוי פירי דלוה: **מתני'** השוכר פרה מחבירו. ועמד שוכר והשאילה לאחר לעשות בה ימי שכירותו: ישבע השוכר. למשכיר: שמתה כדרכה. ופטור שהשוכר אינו חייב באונסין: והשואל. שהוא חייב באונסין משלם לשוכר: **גמ'** בשבועה. שהוא נשבע למשכיר: להפיס דעתו. שלא יאמר פשעת בה: פעמים שהבעלים. המשכירין הראשונים: משלמין. לשוכר זה כמה פרות על פרה זו לפי דברי משנתנו יש שיהו כולם שלו ויש שיעשה בהם ימי שכירותו ויחזירם: כיצד אגרה מיניה מאה יומי והדר שיילה מיניה תשעין יומי וכו'. ראובן ששכר פרה משמעון שיעשה בה מלאכה מאה יום וחזר שמעון ואמר לו עשה עמי טובה והשאילני אותה תשעים יום מן המאה ששכרת ולאחר תשעים אחזירנה לך לעשות אצלך י' ימים להשלים המאה וכן עשה יש כאן דין משנתנו דתנן השוכר פרה מחבירו והשאילה לאחר בתוך ימי שכירותה דמה לי בעלים ומה לי אחר אם מתה אצל שואל הרי שוכר פטור בשבועה והשואל משלם לשוכר חזר ראובן ובא אצלו ואמר לו השכירנה לי מתשעים יום שהיא שאולה בידך ממני ואשתעבד בה שמונים יום וטול שכרך וכן עשה הרי היא בחזקת שאילתו על שמעון כאילו השכירה לאחר שהרי נוטל שכרו וכל הנאה שלו ואם היתה מתה אצל ראובן היה ראובן פטור בשבועה ושמעון משלם לו פרה אחת ששאל ממנו והוא חייב באונסים ופרה אחרת לעשות אצלו עשרה ימים להשלים המאה חזר שמעון ושאלה ממנו שבעים יום מן השמונים ששכרה תחנו על מנת שיחזירנה לו ויעשה בה עשרים ימים להשלים השמונים של שכירות השני ואם היתה מתה בתוך שבעים יום הללו הרי יש כאן דין השני כדין הראשון וישבע ראובן שמתה כדרכה ושמעון השואל משלם לו ד' פרות שתים נחלטות לו בשביל שתי פרות שאולות שהשאילו ראובן ובפעם זה כאילו מתו שתיהן שהרי אין פרתו בעין שהשאילו בראשון דנימא הרי החזיר לו פרתו וזו שהוא משלם לו עכשיו בתורת תשלומין באה לידו והרי יש לו עליו שתי תביעות על שתי שאילות ושתי תביעות על שתי שכירות לעשות אצלו עשרים יום: מכדי חדא פרה הואי כו'. ולענין תשלומין נמי לשלם ליה פרה אחת ותעמוד במקום הראשונה תחת שתי השאילות ותהא שלו ואחת ימסור לו לעשות בה עשרים יום: מי איתא לפרה בעינא דנימא הכי. אילו היתה קיימת היה פטור לגמרי אלא שיעשה בה עשרים יום עכשיו שמתה בא עליו בתורת תשלומין שואל לשוכר על שתי תביעות: מר בר רב אשי ס"ל כאתקפתא דרב אחא מדפתי: שום שאלה אחת היא. דכיון דחדא פרה הואי אלא משמתת שוכר שהשאיל הוא בא עליו שני שאילות פרה אחת אין שאלה אלא אחת: פעמים ששניהם בחטאת. ממתניתין קאי השוכר והשואל נשבעו לשקר ולא כפרו ממון והרי הן בשבועות ביטוי וקרבן שלו חטאת כדכתיב בויקרא או נפש כי תשבע וגו': שניהם

עין משפט
נר מצוה

כ א מיי' פכ"ב מהל' מלוה ולוה הל' יז סמג עשין לד טוש"ע ח"מ סי' קג סעי' י:
כא ב מיי' שם הל' יב סמג שם טוש"מ סי' קג:
כב ג מיי' פ"א מהל' שכירות הל' ו סמג עשין פב טוש"ע ח"מ סי' שז סעי' ה:

רבינו חננאל

אגביה הלוה מדעתו ומכרה למלוה פליגי בה רב אחא ורבינא וקיימא לן הלכה כדברי המיקל הלכך לא מיהדר. זה ששמוה לו מאימת אכיל הפירות [א] רבא אמר מכי מטיא אדרכתא לידיה. סדר הדין מוציא מלוה שטרו בב"ד ומקיימו ומחייבין הלוה לפורעו לא פרע קורעין שטר חוב וכותבין למלוה אדרכתא על נכסי הלוה ומכריזין ואחרי ההכרזה שמין נכסי הלוה ומחליטין למלוה לא מצא נכסין בני חורין כותבין לו טירפא ואחרי שיטרוף קורעין הטירפא וכותבין לו אדרכתא על הנכסין הללו ואחר כך קורעין האדרכתא וכותבין לו שומא על שדה זו ומחליטין אותה למלוה. אביי אמר בחתימת העדים על האדרכת' מיד זכה המלוה בשדה. רבא אמר מכי שלמן (אדרכתא) [אכרזתא] וקיי"ל כרבא: **מתני' השוכר פרה והשאילה לאחר ומתה כדרכה ישבע השוכר שמתה כדרכה והשואל משלם לשוכר.** אוקמה ר' אמי [לקמן דף לו] בשנתנו לו הבעלים רשות כגון שאמרו לו לדעתו כלומ' אם רצונך להשאילה לו הרשות בידך. עכשיו אם ראה אותה השוכר שמתה ברשות השואל כדרכה ישבע ויפטר. וישלם השואל לשוכר. אמר ר' זירא פעמים שמשלמים הבעלים כמה פרות לשוכר כו' ודברים פשוטין הן. אמר ר' ירמיה פעמים שהשוכר והשואל שניהן בחטאת. פעמים ששניהן באשם. פעמים שהשוכר בחטאת והשואל באשם. פעמים שהשואל בחטאת והשוכר באשם. תפרש האי כללא בידך כפירת ממון באשם. אין שם כפירת ממון אלא ביטוי שפתים כלומר נשבע בשקר על דבר שאין לו בו הנאת ממון חייב חטאת. וקיימא לן שומר חנם נשבע על הכל. שואל משלם את הכל חוץ ממתה מחמת מלאכה. נושא שכר והשוכר נשבעין על השבורה ועל השבויה ועל המתה ומשלמין הגניבה והאבידה וכבר פירשנום. שניהן בחטאת כו' כגון שמתה מחמת מלאכה דתרוייהו פטורין מלשלם וכחשו ונשבעו שנאנסה אין אחד מהן נהנה לפיכך שניהן בחטאת.

חשק שלמה על ר"ח

א) נראה דל"ל רבה ועי' תוס' ד"ה רבא. ב) לפנינו בגמ' הגי' כגון שמתה כדרכה ואמרו נאנסה וכו' ואולי דגרסינן ר"ח לגי' אחרת בגמ' וצ"ע.

מסורת הש"ס

א) לעיל יג. [וש"נ], ב) [לקמן לו:], ג) [ל"ל בבבא קמא קיב:], ד) ע' מהרש"א, ה) ל"ל פ מהרש"ל, ו) ל"ל כ מהרש"ל.

הגהות הב"ח

(א) תוס' ד"ה אגרה כ' וד"ה אגרה פ' הד"א:

ליקוטי רש"י

אדרכתא. פסק ד' ליד המלוה לחוף נכסי של לוה ולעולם בשום בחובו [ב"ק קיב:]. של מלאו לו עכשיו נכסי וכתבו לו שירדוף וחוזר נכסיו ואם ימלא יגבה אדרכתא לשון רודף ומשי אדריכא (כתובות דף ...) ולשון המקרא כתרו את בנימין הרדיפוהו מנוחה הדריכוהו [לעיל טז:]. עדיו בחתומיו זכי לו. מיום שחתמוהו זכי לו השעבוד [לעיל יג.].

איתא לדרב הונא כיון דמשתבע מלוה שאינה ברשותו היכי מצי מפיק לה אמר (א) [א] רבא שיש עדים שנשרפה אי הכי מהיכא מייתי לה אלא אמר רב יוסף שיש עדים שנגנבה סוף סוף מהיכא מייתי לה דטרח ומייתי לה אי הכי כי משתבע מלוה נמי לטרח לוה וליתי בשלמא מלוה ידע מאן קא עייל ונפק בביתיה ואזיל וטרח ומייתי לה אלא לוה מי ידע מאן עייל ונפיק בביתיה דמלוה אביי אומר גזירה שמא יטעון ויאמר לו אחר שבועה מצאתיה [ב] רב אשי אמר [א] זה נשבע וזה נשבע זה נשבע שאינה ברשותו וזה נשבע כמה היה שוה והכי קאמר מי נשבע תחילה [ב] מלוה נשבע תחילה שמא ישבע זה ויוציא הלה את הפקדון רב הונא בר תחליפא משמיה דרבא אמר רישא דסיפא תיובתא לרב הונא סלע הלויתני עליו שתים היה שוה והלה אומר לא כי אלא סלע הלויתיך עליו סלע היה שוה פטור ואם איתא לדרב הונא מגו דמשתבע מלוה שאינה ברשותו [ג] לישתבע נמי אגילגול שבועה כמה היה שוה אמר רב אשי אמריתה לשמעתא קמיה דרב כהנא ואמר לי [ג] [ד] תהא במאמינו ונהמניה לוה למלוה נמי בהא כמה הוה שוה לא קים ליה בגויה ונהמניה מלוה ללוה דקים ליה בגויה לא מהימן ליה ומאי שנא לוה דמהימן ליה למלוה ומאי שנא מלוה דלא מהימן ליה ללוה לוה מקיים ביה במלוה [א] תומת ישרים תנחם מלוה מקיים ביה בלוה [א] וסלף בוגדים ישדם: ההוא גברא דאפקיד כיפי גביה חבריה אמר ליה הב לי (ב) כיפי אמר ליה לא ידענא היכא אותבינהו אתא לקמיה דרב נחמן אמר ליה [ד] [ה] כל לא ידענא פשיעותא היא זיל שלים לא שילם אזל רב נחמן אגביה לאפדניה מיניה לסוף אישתכח כיפי ואיקור אמר רב נחמן [ו] הדרי כיפי למרייהו והדרא אפדנא למרה אמר רבא הוה יתיבנא קמיה דרב נחמן ופרקין המפקיד הוה ואמרי ליה שילם ולא רצה לישבע ולא אהדר לי ושפיר עבד דלא אהדר לי מאי טעמא [ז] התם לא אטרחיה לבי דינא הכא אטרחיה לבי דינא למימרא דסבר רב נחמן דשומא הדר שאני התם דשומא בטעות הוה דקא הוה כיפי מעיקרא [ה] אמרי נהרדעי שומא הדר עד תריסר ירחי שתא ואמר אמימר אנא מנהרדעא אנא וסבירא לי שומא הדר לעולם [ח] והלכתא שומא הדר לעולם משום שנאמר [ב] ועשית הישר והטוב [ט] פשיטא שמו ליה לבעל חוב ואזל איהו ושמה לבעל חוב דידיה אמרינן ליה לא עדיף את מגברא דאתית מיניה [י] זבנה (ג) אורתא ויהבה במתנה ודאי הני מעיקרא אדעתא דארעא נחות ולאו אדעתא דזוזי נחות [כ] שמו לה לאשה ואינסיבא או שמו מינה דאשה ואינסיבא ומתה [ו] בעל בנכסי אשתו לוקח הוי לא מיהדר ולא מהדרינן ליה [ז] דאמר רבי יוסי בר חנינא באושא התקינו [ל] האשה שמכרה בנכסי מלוג בחיי בעלה ומתה הבעל מוציא מיד הלקוחות

אגביה

**רש"י**

**איתא לדרב הונא.** שהשומר המשלם דמים נשבע שאינה ברשותו דאמאי חיישינן לשמא יוציאה הא אשתבע: **שיש עדים שנשרפה.** דהשתא לא אשבעינהו שהרי הביא עדים: **טרח ומייתי לה.** מחזר ושואל אחר הנכנסים בביתו וימצא הגנב: **וזה נשבע.** הלוה שהשבועה עליו נשבע כמה שוה: **מלוה נשבע תחילה.** שאינה ברשותו: **רישא דסיפא.** הויא תיובתא לרב הונא רישא תביעת מלוה סיפא תביעת לוה רישא דסיפא דקתני פטור בתביעת לוה: **אגילגול שבועה.** דטענה שאין בה שבועה עם טענה שיש בה שבועה מגלגלין עליו שבועה לישבע על שתיהן וגילגול שבועה דאורייתא היא בקדושין (דף כז:): **תהא במאמינו.** הא דקתני פטור במאמינו לוה למלוה שאינה ברשותו: **לא קים ליה בגויה.** מימר אמר לוה לא קים למלוה בגויה דמשכון דלא נתן דעתו עליו לדעת דמיו: **מאי שנא כו'.** דנקט תנא למלתיה בהכי שזה נאמן על זה וזה אינו נאמן על זה: **לוה מקיים במלוה.** מקרא זה תומת ישרים תנחם אם לא שאדם נאמן וישר הוא לא היו מעשרין אותו מן השמים שנאמר תומת ישרים תנחם: **כיפי.** נזמים: **ואייקור.** יתר על הדמים שפרע לבעלים: **הוה יתיבנא.** כשדן דין זה: **ופרקין המפקיד הוה.** ובפרק זה היינו עוסקין: **ואמרי ליה שילם ולא רצה לישבע.** קתני מתני' דקני כפילא והאי נמי שילם וליקני רווחא דאייקור: **דשומא הדר.** נכסי לוה ששמו ב"ד לבעל חוב חוזרין אליו אם נותן מעות לבעל חוב כי הכא דהדר אפדנא למרה: **דשומא בטעות הוה.** דסבור היה שאבדו הנזמים והרי לא אבדו: **דהא הוו כיפי מעיקרא.** שהרי בתחילת השומא היו הנזמים בידו ולא היה יודע דאילו היה יודע שכן לא שמו לו הטרקלין אבל שומא שב"ד שמין על שאין לו מעות והוא חייב לו הרי הוא כמכר גמור ואינה חוזרת: **אמרינן.** לבעל חוב שני: **לא עדיפת.** מבעל חוב ראשון שבאת מכחו כשם שהוא מחזירה ויטול מעותיו משום ועשית הישר והטוב אף אתה קבל מעותיך מבעלים הראשונים משום ועשית הישר והטוב: **זבנה אורתה כו'.** בעל חוב ששמו לו קרקע ומכרה או שנתנה או הוריש: **הני.** אחרונים או לוקח או יורש או מקבל מתנה: **אדעתא דארעא נחות.** שיהא קרקע שלהם ולא שיקבלו מעות דאילו בעל חוב אית ביה משום ועשית הישר והטוב דאמרינן לא היה לך עליו אלא מעות והרי הן לך אבל אלו קרקע קנו: **ואנסיבא.** אפילו לא שמאתן לבעלה בכתובתה להיות נכסי צאן ברזל שהן קנויין לבעל אלא עיכבתן לעצמה להיות נכסי מלוג הקרן שלה והבעל אוכל פירות: **בעל.** בנכסי מלוג של אשתו: **לוקח הוי.** דין לוקח נתנו בו חכמים הלכך לא מיהדר היכא דשמו לה ואינסיבא ומתה וירשה בעלה כדאמרינן זבנה אדעתא דארעא נחות: **ולא מהדרינן ליה.** היכא דשמו מינה ואינסיבא ומתה וירשה בעלה ובא להחזיר החוב וליטול הקרקע לא מצי למימר יורשה אני דלוקח שוייה רבנן ולא כיורש: **האשה שמכרה בנכסי מלוג.** להיות הבעל אוכל פירות בחייה וגוף הקרקע יהיה ללוקח לכשתמות ומתה: **בעל מוציא.** גוף הקרקע מיד הלקוחות והכי מוקי לה בפרק האשה בכתובות (דף עח:) תקנת אושא בגופה של קרקע לאחר מיתה אלמא כלוקח שוויהו רבנן וא"ל אני לקחתי ראשון דאי כשאר יורש שוויהו רבנן יורש שמכר אביו נכסיו בחייו אין לו ירושה בהן: **באושא התקינו.** כשהיתה סנהדרין באושא שגלתה וישבה שם סנהדרי גדולה כדאמרינן בר"ה (דף לא.) גבי עשרה מסעות:

אגביה

**תוספות**

**מגו** דמשתבע מלוה שאינו ברשותו כו'. [ח] לרבה ולרב יוסף לא פריך אלא לאביי ורב אשי:

**תהא** במאמינו. ברישא לא מצי לאוקמי הכי משום דהתם לא ירצה להאמינו כיון שע"י כן לא יוכל לישבע אבל הכא אין כאן שבועה ואע"פ שמפסיד במה שמאמינו שבועה שהיה יכול לגלגל עליו אינו חושש:

**ואותביניה** שילם. וצ"ל דיוקרא דכיפי הוי שבחא דעלמא כמו כפילא ולא דמי לגיזות וולדות דאותו שבח ניכר בגוף הבהמה: **אטרחיה** לב"ד. דלא דמי לאטרחיה לשבועה דקני כפילא לרבא כששילם אחרי כן (ב"ק דף קח.) דהתם משלם ברצונו אבל רב נחמן הולך לגבות אפדנו:

**זבנה** כו'. וא"ת ואמאי לא מהדר (ד) מה מכר ראשון לשני כל זכות שתבא לידו וי"ל דהראשון מן הדין נמי אין מחזיר שמכורה היא לו שהרי אוכל פירות בלא נכייתא אלא משום ועשית הישר והטוב מהדר ולכך שני לא מהדר:

**לוקח** הוי. אפי' אי הוי יורש לא מהדר כדאמר זבנה אורתה כו' אלא משום לא מהדרינן ליה נקטיה דאי יורש הוי מהדרינן ליה שהבן פודה קרקע של אביו ואע"ג דבפרק יש נוחלין (ב"ב דף קלט: ושם ד"ה התם) מסיק דטבא ליה עבדו ליה או יורש או לוקח הא אמרינן התם בר היכא דאיכא פסידא לאחריני לא עבדי ליה טבא ולכך הכא לא הוי כיורש משום פסידא דמלוה ולא מהדר ממה נפשך דאפי' יורש הוי לא מהדר ודר' יוסי בר חנינא מפרש התם דלקוחות אפסדו אנפשייהו:

רבא

**מסורת הש"ס**

א) [נראה דצ"ל רבה], [שבועות מג: ע"ש], [בבא קמא לח:], [לקמן מג.], ה) לעיל ;, ו) [בבא בתרא ט:], ז) לקמן לו:, ...ובות נ., עח:, בבא ...א פח:, בבא בתרא קלט:, ח) גירסת מהרש"א לרב הונא.

**הגהות הב"ח**

(א) גמ' אמר רבא אמר ... יוסף שיש עדים ...שרפה: (ב) שם הב לי ...פאי אמר: (ג) שם ...נה אורתה: (ד) תום' ...ה זבנה וכו' לא מהדר ...נימא מה מכר:

**תורה אור השלם**

א) תֻּמַּת יְשָׁרִים תַּנְחֵם וְסֶלֶף בֹּגְדִים יְשָׁדֵּם: [משלי יא, ג]

ב) וְעָשִׂיתָ הַיָּשָׁר וְהַטּוֹב בְּעֵינֵי יְיָ לְמַעַן יִיטַב לָךְ וּבָאתָ וְיָרַשְׁתָּ אֶת הָאָרֶץ הַטֹּבָה אֲשֶׁר נִשְׁבַּע יְיָ לַאֲבֹתֶיךָ: [דברים ו, יח]

**ליקוטי רש"י**

**מלוה נשבע תחילה.** ...י שהפקדון אצלו נשבע ...חילה שאינה ברשותו ...עולם אסיפא דרישא ...אי היכא דשבועה גבי ...ה [שבועות מג:]. **תהא במאמינו.** בכל מה ...אומר [ב"ק צח:]. **...נחם.** תנהלם. **ישדם.** ...שדדם [משלי יא, ג]. **...כיפי.** מרגליות ל"א ...זמים וכן עיקר [עירובין ...ו:]. עגילים אנור"ש ...דאמרינן בעלמא ...עירובין דף נו:) כיפי ...אלא ליה עגילים תלה ...אוניהם [רשב"ם ב"ב נב.]. **...שומא הדר עד תריסר ירחי שתא.** ...אם יפרע לו מעות עד ...שנה [לעיל טז:]. **הישר והטוב.** זו פשרה לפנים משורת הדין [דברים ו, יח]. **האשה שמכרה בנכסי מלוג.** הקרן ...כתובות נ.]. **בחיי בעלה.** שאם ימות בעלה זכה בהן ואם תמות היא יירשה בעל יפסידו. ונכסי מלוג הן נכסים שנפלו לה מבית אביה או שהכניסה קרקעות שלא נשומו בכתובתה ולא קיבל בעל עליו אחריות ואוכל פירותיהן בחייה כתקנת חכמים תחת פרקונה ולהכי מיקרי מלוג שמולגן וממסרן בעל שאוכל הפירות כמליגת הראש [רשב"ם ב"ב קלט:]. **הבעל מוציא.** דאע"ג דבעלמא לאו כקנין הגוף דמי בעל בנכסי אשתו אלמוה רבנן לשעבודיה משום איבה והוי כלוקח ראשון שהבעל יורש את אשתו והוא היה לוקח ראשון [ב"ק פח:].

**עין משפט נר מצוה**

יג א ב מיי' פי"ג מהל' מלוה ולוה הל' ד סמג עשין לד טוש"ע ח"מ סי' עב סעי' י:

יד ג ד מיי' שם טוש"ע שם סעי' יב:

טו ה מיי' פ"ד מהל' שאלה ופקדון הל' ז סמג עשין פח טוש"ע ח"מ סי' רלא סעי' ז:

טז ו ז מיי' שם פ"ח הל' ג סמג שם טוש"מ סי' רלה:

יז ח מיי' פכ"ב מהל' מלוה הל' טו סמג עשין לד טוש"ע ח"מ סי' קג סעי' ט:

יח ט י כ מיי' שם הל' יח טוש"ע שם סעי' י:

יט ל מיי' פכ"ב מהל' אישות הל' ז ועיין במ"מ סמג עשין מח טוש"ע אה"ע סי' צ סעי' ט:

**רבינו חננאל**

וקשיא לן וכי תקנתא לרשיעי עבדינן אלא שמא ישבע הלוה ויוציא המלוה את הפקדון ונמצאת שבועת הלוה שיצאה לבטלה. ואמרי' אם איתא לדרב הונא כיון שנשבע המלוה שאינה ברשותו אינו יכול להוציא הפקדון שכבר נשבע שאינו ברשותו א) והלה נשבע כמה היה שוה ומתני' הכי קתני מי נשבע תחלה מי שהפקדון אצלו שאם ישבע הלוה תחלה חיישינן שמא יוציא המלוה את המשכון ונמצאת שבועה זו לבטלה. ושאר השמועה פשוטה היא. ההוא דאפקיד כיפי גביה חבריה ואמר לא ידענא היכא אנחתינהו אמר ר' נחמן כל לא ידענא פשיעותא היא חייביה לשלומי לא שילם ירד רב נחמן לנכסיו ושם לאפדני ויהביה לבעל הפקדון בדמי דהנהו כיפי דפשע בהו. פי' אפדנא חצר. לסוף אישתכח כיפי ואוקירו בדמיהן. מריה דכיפי אמר הב לי כיפאי וטול אפדנא והלה אומר לא כי אלא מעידנא דשקלית לאפדניי זבינא אנא בכיפי וברשותי אוקירו ודן ר' נחמן כיון דהא שומא דשמו ליה לאפדנא שומא בטעות הואי דהא הוו כיפי ולא אבדו וקיימא לן פקדון כל היכא דאיתיה ברשותיה דמריה קאי לאו שומא הוא והדר אפדנא למריה והדרי כיפי למרייהו. ואסיק' שומא הדרא לעולם משום שנאמר ועשית הישר והטוב והני מילי אם לא מכרה אבל אם מכרה לאחר או נתנה במתנה או הורישה לא הדרא. וכן אם שמו ב"ד שדה לאשה במלוה שהיא נושה לאחרים וניסת והכניסה שדה זו לבעלים או שמו שדה אשה לנושה שלה וניסת לא מהדרינן ליה לבעל ולא מהדרינן מיניה דבעל דכזביני דמי וקיימא לן בעל בנכסי אשתו לוקח הוי לא מהדר ולא מהדרינן ליה דאמר ר' יוסי בר' חנינא באושא התקינו האשה שמכרה נכסי מלוג בחיי בעלה סומתה הבעל מוציא מיד הלקוחות.

אגביה

חשק שלמה על ר"ח א) נראה דחסר כאן וצ"ל ופריק רב אשי דזה נשבע שאינו ברשותו והלה נשבע כמה היה שוה וכו'.

The Gemara distinguishes between this case and other types of econdary ownership:

**זַבְנָ** – If **[a creditor]** acquired seized property and later **sold t,** **אוֹרְתָא** – or died and **left it as an inheritance,** **וִיהֲבָה בְּמַתָּנָ** – **or gave it as a present,** and subsequently the debtor ffers to repay the debt with cash and reclaim his property, **וַדַּאי הָנֵי מֵעִיקָּרָא אַדַּעְתָּא דְאַרְעָא נָחוּ** – **certainly these** three second-ry owners[28] **originally entered** the property **with the intent of** cquiring **the land,** **וְלָאו אַדַּעְתָּא דְזוּזֵי נָחוּת** – **and did not enter** vith **the intent of** acquiring **money.** Therefore, the verse cited bove does not require them to return the property.[29]

The Gemara continues its discussion of the laws of seized roperty:

**שָׁמוּ לָהּ לְאִשָּׁה וְאִינְסִיבָ** – If the court **seized** property **for a wom-n and she** subsequently **got married,**[30] **אוֹ שָׁמוּ מִינָּהּ דְּאִשָּׁה וְאִינְסִיבָ** – **or if they seized** property **from a woman and she** subsequently **got married,** **וּמֵתָה** – **and** then **she died,** **בַּעַל בְּנִכְסֵי אִשְׁתּוֹ לוֹקֵחַ הָוֵי** – since **a husband is** considered **a "buyer" with regard to his wife's** *melog* **property,** which he acquires upon her death,[31] **לֹא מִיהֲדַר** – **he need not return** the property if the debtor should later offer a cash repayment,[32] **וְלֹא מְהַדְּרִינַן לֵיהּ** – **nor do we return** the property **to him** if he later offers to pay cash for his wife's debt.[33]

The Gemara cites the basis for this last ruling:

**דְּאָמַר רַבִּי יוֹסֵי בַּר חֲנִינָא** – **For R' Yose bar Chanina said:** **בְּאוּשָׁא הִתְקִינוּ** – **In Usha**[34] the Sages **enacted** **הָאִשָּׁה שֶׁמָּכְרָה בְּנִכְסֵי מְלוֹג בְּחַיֵּי בַעְלָהּ** – that **if a woman sells** ***melog*** **property in her husband's lifetime**[35] **וּמֵתָה** – **and** then she **dies,** **הַבַּעַל מוֹצִיא מִיַּד הַלָּקוֹחוֹת** – **the husband may remove** the property **from the possession of the buyers.** We see from this that the Sages gave a husband the status of a buyer vis-à-vis his wife's *melog* property.[36]

NOTES

8. The buyer, the heir, or the person receiving the gift (*Rashi*).

9. When a creditor accepts property as payment, he does so only in *lace* of money. It is therefore fair for him to return the property when e is later offered the money he originally expected to be paid, in fulfill-nent of the verse, *And you shall do that which is fair and good.* A buyer, eir, or beneficiary of a gift, on the other hand, intended to acquire the roperty, not cash. Hence, the verse does not apply to him (*Rashi*).

0. This property was subsequently brought into the marriage either s *tzon-barzel* property, of which the husband becomes the owner once hey marry, or as *melog* property, of which the wife is considered to e the owner, with the husband receiving only the profits (*Rashi;* see bove, 34b note 13).

1. That is, when his wife dies and he inherits her property, he is consid-red to have bought it from her while she was still alive. This Rabbinic nactment gives him certain legal rights he would not have if he were imply her heir, as the Gemara will explain below (*Rashi*). It goes with-ut saying that he is considered the "buyer" of her *tzon-barzel* property, s explained in the previous note.

2. I.e. if the debtor whose property was seized for this woman before he married wants to pay back the money and reclaim his property, the usband does not need to give it back to him. The husband has the sta-us of a buyer, and as we learned above, a buyer is not required to return eized property (*Rashi*).

[The commentators raise the question that even if the husband had nly the status of an heir, he would also not have to return the prop-rty, as the Gemara explained above. Why did the Gemara have to base his ruling on the fact that the husband is considered a buyer? Some xplain that, in fact, the husband's status as a buyer is needed only or the Gemara's next ruling, not this one (see the next note). Others xplain that indeed a regular inheritance (or a husband's inheritance f his wife's *melog* property, if he were considered only an heir) must e returned when the debtor wants to pay cash and get it back. This is because it cannot be said about an heir that he "originally intended to acquire the property." When the Gemara said above that an heir need not return the seized property for cash, it referred only to someone who inherited the property as a result of a specific bequest by the person who died (see *Tosafos, Ramban*).

33. Property seized from a debtor must be returned to him or his heirs, but not to someone else who later acquired rights to the property. Since the inheriting husband is regarded as a buyer of his wife's property, he has no right to redeem the property she lost when she could not repay her debt (see *Rashi, Tosafos*).

34. One of the ten seats of the exiled Great Sanhedrin (*Rashi*, from *Rosh Hashanah* 31a-b).

35. A wife cannot sell her husband's right to use and profit from the *melog* property during their marriage. She can, however, sell the own-ership of the property. This enables the buyer to take possession of it after she dies [when the husband no longer has the right to use it] (see *Rashi*).

36. The Sages' enactment strengthened the husband's rights to his wife's *melog* property. According to Torah law, he would not have inher-ited his wife's *melog* property in this case, since she sold the ownership of it before she died and there was nothing left to inherit. The Sages de-creed, however, that the husband should get the property, not the buyer.

In strengthening his *melog* rights in this manner, the Sages in effect decreed that, when a man marries, not only does he get the right to use his wife's *melog* property and keep its profits, but in case she dies first, he should be considered the *buyer* of this property retroactive to the time of the marriage. As a result, if she dies first the husband can claim that he "bought" the property *before* the wife sold it to someone else, and it therefore comes to him after her death (*Rashi*). [Accordingly, once this decree went into effect, when a woman sells the ownership of her *melog* property during her marriage, the sale is effective only if the husband dies before the wife.]

איתא לדרב הונא כיון דמשתבע מלוה שאינה ברשותו היכי מצי מפיק לה אמר (א) [א] רבא שיש עדים שנשרפה אי הכי מהיכא מייתי לה אלא אמר רב יוסף שיש עדים שנגנבה סוף סוף מהיכא מייתי לה דטרח ומייתי לה אי הכי כי משתבע מלוה נמי לטרח לוה וליתי בשלמא מלוה ידע מאן קא עייל ונפק בביתיה ואזיל וטרח ומייתי לה אלא לוה מי ידע מאן עייל ונפיק בביתיה דמלוה אביי אומר גזירה שמא יטעון ויאמר לו אחר שבועה מצאתיה [ג] רב אשי אמר [א] זה נשבע וזה נשבע זה נשבע שאינה ברשותו וזה נשבע כמה היה שוה והכי קאמר מי נשבע תחילה [ב] מלוה נשבע תחילה שמא ישבע זה ויוציא הלה את הפקדון רב הונא בר תחליפא משמיה דרבא אמר רישא דסיפא תיובתא לרב הונא סלע הלויתני עליו שתים היה שוה והלה אומר לא כי אלא סלע הלויתיך עליו סלע היה שוה פטור ואם איתא לדרב הונא מגו דמשתבע מלוה שאינה ברשותו [ג] לישתבע נמי אגילגול שבועה כמה היה שוה אמר רב אשי אמריתה לשמעתא קמיה דרב כהנא ואמר לי [ג] [ד] תהא במאמינו ונהמניה לוה למלוה נמי בהא כמה הוה שוה לא קים ליה בגויה ונהמניה מלוה ללוה דקים ליה בגויה לא מהימן ליה ומאי שנא לוה דמהימן ליה למלוה ומאי שנא מלוה דלא מהימן ליה ללוה לוה מקיים ביה במלוה [א] תומת ישרים תנחם מלוה מקיים ביה בלוה [א] וסלף בוגדים ישדם: ההוא גברא דאפקיד כיפי גביה חבריה אמר ליה הב לי (ב) כיפי אמר ליה לא ידענא היכא אותבינהו אתא לקמיה דרב נחמן אמר ליה [ד] [ה] כל לא ידענא פשיעותא היא זיל שלים לא שילם אזל רב נחמן אגביה לאפדניה מיניה לסוף אישתכח כיפי ואיקור אמר רב נחמן [ו] הדרי כיפי למרייהו והדרא אפדנא למרה אמר רבא הוה יתיבנא קמיה דרב נחמן ופרקין המפקיד הוה ואמרי ליה שילם ולא רצה לישבע ולא אהדר לי ושפיר עבד דלא אהדר לי מאי טעמא [ז] התם לא אטרחיה לבי דינא הכא אטרחיה לבי דינא למימרא דסבר רב נחמן דשומא הדר שאני התם דשומא בטעות הוה דקא הוה כיפי מעיקרא [ה] אמרי נהרדעי שומא הדר עד תריסר ירחי שתא ואמר אמימר אנא מנהרדעא אנא וסבירא לי שומא הדר לעולם [ח] והלכתא שומא הדר לעולם משום שנאמר [ב] ועשית הישר והטוב [ט] פשיטא שמו ליה לבעל חוב ואזל איהו ושמה לבעל חוב דידיה אמרינן ליה לא עדיף את מגברא דאתית מיניה [י] זבנה (ג) אורתא ויהבה במתנה ודאי הני מעיקרא אדעתא דארעא נחות ולאו אדעתא דזוזי נחות [כ] שמו לה לאשה ואינסיבא או שמו מינה דאשה ואינסיבא ומתה [י] בעל בנכסי אשתו לוקח הוי לא מיהדר ולא מהדרינן ליה [י] דאמר רבי יוסי בר חנינא באושא התקינו [ל] האשה שמכרה בנכסי מלוג בחיי בעלה ומתה הבעל מוציא מיד הלקוחות אגביה

**רש"י**

**איתא לדרב הונא.** שהשומר המשלם דמים נשבע שאינה ברשותו אמאי חיישינן לשמא יוציא הא אשתבע: **שיש עדים שנשרפה.** דהשתא לא אשבעינהו שהרי הביא עדים: **טרח ומייתי לה.** מחזר ושואל אחר הנכנסים בביתו וימצא הגנב: **וזה נשבע.** הלוה שהשבועה עליו נשבע כמה שוה: **מלוה נשבע תחילה.** שאינה ברשותו: **רישא דסיפא.** הויא תיובתא לרב הונא רישא תביעת מלוה סיפא תביעת לוה רישא דסיפא דקתני פטור בתביעת לוה: **אגילגול שבועה.** דטענה שאין בה שבועה עם טענה שיש בה שבועה מגלגלין עליו שבועה לישבע על שתיהן וגילגול שבועה דאורייתא היא בקדושין (דף כז:): **תהא במאמינו.** הא דקתני פטור במאמינו לוה למלוה שאינה ברשותו: **לא קים ליה בגויה.** מימר אמר לוה לא קים למלוה בגויה דמשכון דלא נתן דעתו עליו לדעת דמיו: **מאי שנא כו'.** דנקט תנא למלתיה בהכי שזה נאמן על זה וזה אינו נאמן על זה: **לוה מקיים במלוה.** מקרא זה תומת ישרים תנחם אם לא שאדם נאמן וישר הוא לא היו מעשרין אותו מן השמים שנאמר תומת ישרים תנחם: **כיפי.** נזמים: **ואייקור.** יתר על הדמים שפרע לבעלים: **הוה יתיבנא.** כשדן דין זה: **ופרקין המפקיד הוה.** ובפרק זה היינו עוסקין: **ואמרי ליה שילם ולא רצה לישבע.** קתני מתני' דקני כפילא והאי נמי שילם וליקני רווחא דאייקור: **דשומא הדר.** נכסי לוה ששמו ב"ד לבעל חוב חוזרין אליו אם נותן מעות לבעל חוב כי הכא דהדר אפדנא למרה: **דשומא בטעות הוה.** דסבור היה שאבדו הנזמים והרי לא אבדו: **דהא הוו כיפי מעיקרא.** שהרי בתחילת השומא היו הנזמים בידו ולא היה יודע דאילו היה יודע שכן לא שמו לו הטרקלין אבל שומא שב"ד שמין על שאין לו מעות והוא חייב לו הרי הוא כמכר גמור ואינה חוזרת: **אמרינן.** לבעל חוב שני: **לא עדיפת.** מבעל חוב ראשון שבאת מכחו כשם שהוא מחזירה ויטול מעותיו משום ועשית הישר והטוב אף אתה קבל מעותיך מבעלים הראשונים משום ועשית הישר והטוב: **זבנה אורתה כו'.** בעל חוב ששמו לו קרקע ומכרה או שנתנה או הוריש: **הני.** אחרונים או לוקח או יורש או מקבל מתנה: **אדעתא דארעא נחות.** שיהא קרקע שלהם ולא שיקבלו מעות דאילו בעל חוב אית ביה משום ועשית הישר והטוב דאמרינן לא היה לך עליו אלא מעות והרי הן לך אבל אלו קרקע קנו: **ואנסיבא.** אפילו לא שמאתן לבעלה בכתובתה להיות נכסי צאן ברזל שהן קנויין לבעל אלא עיכבתן לעצמה להיות נכסי מלוג הקרן שלה והבעל אוכל פירות: **בעל.** בנכסי מלוג של אשתו: **לוקח הוי.** דין לוקח נתנו בו חכמים הלכך לא מיהדר היכא דשמו לה ואינסיבא ומתה וירשה בעלה כדאמרינן זבנה אדעתא דארעא נחות: **ולא מהדרינן ליה.** היכא דשמו מינה ואינסיבא ומתה וירשה בעלה ובא להחזיר החוב וליטול הקרקע לא מצי למימר יורשה אני דכלוקח שוייה רבנן ולא כיורש: **האשה שמכרה בנכסי מלוג.** להיות הבעל אוכל פירות בחייה וגוף הקרקע יהיה ללוקח לכשתמות ומתה: **בעל מוציא.** גוף הקרקע מיד הלקוחות והכי מוקי לה בפרק האשה בכתובות (דף עח:) תקנת אושא בגופה של קרקע לאחר מיתה אלמא כלוקח שויוהו רבנן וא"ל אני לקחתי ראשון דאי כשאר יורש שויוהו רבנן יורש שמכר אביו נכסיו בחייו אין לו ירושה בהן: **באושא התקינו.** כשהיתה סנהדרין באושא שגלתה וישבה שם סנהדרי גדולה כדאמרינן בר"ה (דף לא.) גבי עשרה מסעות: אגביה

**תוספות**

**מגו** דמשתבע מלוה שאינו ברשותו כו'. [ח] לרבה ולרב יוסף לא פריך אלא לאביי ורב אשי:

**תהא** במאמינו. ברישא לא מצי לאוקמי הכי משום דהתם לא ירצה להאמינו כיון שע"י כן לא יוכל לישבע אבל הכא אין כאן שבועה ואע"פ שמפסיד במה שמאמינו שבועה שהיה יכול לגלגל עליו אינו חושש:

**ואותביניה** שילם. וא"ל דיוקרא דכיפי הוי שבחא דעלמא כמו כפילא ולא דמי לגיזות וולדות דאותו שבח ניכר בגוף הבהמה: **אטרחיה** לב"ד. דלא דמי לאטרחיה לשבועה דקני כפילא לרבא כששילם אחרי כן (ב"ק דף קח.) דהתם משלם ברצונו אבל רב נחמן הולך לגבות אפדנו:

**זבנה** כו'. וא"ת ואמאי לא מהדר (ד) מה מכר ראשון לשני כל זכות שתבא לידו וי"ל דהראשון מן הדין נמי אין מחזיר שמכורה היא לו שהרי אוכל פירות בלא נכייתא אלא משום ועשית הישר והטוב מהדר ולכך שני לא מהדר:

**לוקח** הוי. אפי' אי הוי יורש לא מהדר כדאמר זבנה אורתה כו' אלא משום לא מהדרינן ליה נקטיה דאי יורש הוי מהדרינן ליה שהבן פודה קרקע של אביו ואע"ג דבפרק יש נוחלין (ב"ב דף קלט: ושם ד"ה התם) מסיק דטבא ליה עבדו ליה או יורש או לוקח הא אמרינן התם בר היכא דאיכא פסידא לאחריני לא עבדי ליה טבא ולכך הכא לא הוי כיורש משום פסידא דמלוה ולא מהדר ממה נפשך דאפי' יורש הוי לא מהדר ודר' יוסי בר חנינא מפרש התם דלקוחות אפסדו אנפשייהו: רבא

**עין משפט נר מצוה**

יג א ב מיי' פי"ג מהל' מלוה ולוה הל' ד סמג עשין לד טוש"ע ח"מ סי' עב סעי' י:
יד ג ד מיי' שם טוש"ע שם סעי' יב:
טו ה מיי' פ"ד מהל' שאלה ופקדון הל' ז סמג עשין פח טוש"ע ח"מ סי' רלא סעי' ז:
טז ו ז מיי' שם פ"ח הל' ג סמג שם טוח"מ סי' רלה:
יז ח מיי' פכ"ב מהל' מלוה הל' טז סמג עשין לד טוש"ע ח"מ סי' קג סעי' ט:
יח ט י כ מיי' שם הל' יח טוש"ע שם סעי' י:
יט ל מיי' פכ"ב מהל' אישות הל' ז ועיין במ"מ סמג עשין מח טוש"ע אה"ע סי' צ סעי' ט:

**רבינו חננאל**

וקשיא לן וכי תקנתא לרשיעי עבדינן אלא שמא ישבע הלוה ויוציא המלוה את הפקדון ונמצאת שבועת הלוה שיצאה לבטלה. ואמרי' אם איתא לדרב הונא כיון שנשבע המלוה שאינה ברשותו אינו יכול להוציא הפקדון שכבר נשבע שאינו ברשותו א) והלה נשבע כמה היה שוה ומתני' הכי קתני מי נשבע תחלה מי שהפקדון אצלו שאם ישבע הלוה תחלה חיישינן שמא יוציא המלוה את המשכון ונמצאת שבועה זו לבטלה. ושאר השמועה פשוטה היא. ההוא דאפקיד כיפי גביה חבריה ואמר לא ידענא היכא אנחתינהו אמר ר' נחמן כל לא ידענא פשיעותא היא חייביה לשלומי לא שילם יהד רב נחמן לנכסיו ושם לאפדני ויהביה לבעל הפקדון בדמי דהנהו כיפי דפשע בהו. פי' אפדנא חצר. לסוף אישתכח כיפי ואוקירו בדמיהן. מריה דכיפי אמר הב לי כיפאי וטול אפדנא והלה אומר לא כי אלא מעידנא דשקלית לאפדניי זבינא אנא בכיפי וברשותי אוקירו ודן ר' נחמן כיון דהא שומא דשמו ליה לאפדנא שומא בטעות הואי דהא הוו כיפי ולא אבדו וקיימא לן פקדון כל היכא דאיתיה ברשותיה דמריה קאי לאו שומא הוא והדר אפדנא למריה והדרי כיפי למרייהו. ואסיק' שומא הדרא לעולם משום שנאמר ועשית הישר והטוב והני מילי אם לא מכרה אבל אם מכרה לאחר או נתנה במתנה או הורישה לא הדרא. וכן אם שמו ב"ד שדה לאשה במלוה שהיא נושה לאחרים וניסת והכניסה שדה זו לבעלים או שמו שדה אשה לנושה שלה וניסת לא מהדרינן ליה לבעל ולא מהדרינן מיניה דבעל דכזביני דמי וקיימא לן בעל בנכסי אשתו לוקח הוי לא מהדר ולא מהדרינן ליה דאמר ר' יוסי בר' חנינא באושא התקינו האשה שמכרה נכסי מלוג בחיי בעלה ומתה הבעל מוציא מיד הלקוחות. אגביה

**מסורת הש"ם**

א) [נראה דל"ל רבה], [שבועות מג: ע"ש], [בבא קמא לח:], [לקמן מג.], ה) לעיל ...;, ו) [בבא בתרא ...ט:], ז) לקמן לו:, ...ובות כ., עח:, בבא ...תא פח:, בבא בתרא קלט:, ח) גירסת מהרש"א לרב הונא.

**הגהות הב"ח**

(א) גמ' אמר רבא אמר ...: יוסף שיש עדים ...שרפה: (ב) שם הב לי ...פאי אמר: (ג) שם ...נה אורתה: (ד) תוס' ...ה זבנה וכו' לא מהדר ...נימא מה מכר:

**תורה אור השלם**

א) תֻּמַּת יְשָׁרִים תַּנְחֵם ...סֶלֶף בֹּגְדִים יְשָׁדֵּם: [משלי יא, ג]

ב) וְעָשִׂיתָ הַיָּשָׁר וְהַטּוֹב ...עֵינֵי יְיָ לְמַעַן יִיטַב ...ךְ וּבָאתָ וְיָרַשְׁתָּ אֶת ...אָרֶץ הַטֹּבָה אֲשֶׁר ...נִשְׁבַּע יְיָ לַאֲבֹתֶיךָ: [דברים ו, יח]

**ליקוטי רש"י**

...לוה נשבע תחילה. ...י שהפקדון אצלו נשבע ...חילה שאינה ברשותו ...לעולם אסיפא דרישא ...אי היכא דשבועה גבי ...ה [שבועות מג:]. תהא ...מאמינו. בכל מה ...אומר [ב"ק צח:]. ...תנחם. תנהלם. ישדם. ...שדדם [משלי יא, ג]. ...יפי. מרגליות ל"א ...זמים וכן עיקר [עירובין ...י:]. עגילים אור"ש ...דאמרינן בעלמא ...עירובין דף לו:) כיפי ...לא ליה עגילים תלה ...אזניהם [רשב"ם ב"ב נב.]. ...שומא הדר עד תריסר ירחי שתא. ...אם יפרע לו מעות עד ...שנה [לעיל טז:]. הישר ...הטוב. זו פשרה לפנים ...משורת הדין [דברים ו, יח]. ...האשה שמכרה ...בנכסי מלוג. הקרן ...כתובות נ.]. בחיי ...בעלה. שאם ימות בעלה ...כה בהן ואם תמות היא ...יירשה בעל יפסידו. ונכסי ...מלוג הן נכסים שנפלו לה ...בית אביה או שהכניסה ...קרקעות שלא נשומו ...בכתובתה ולא קיבל בעל ...עליו אחריות ואוכל ...פירותיהן בחייה כתקנת ...חכמים תחת פרקונה ...להכי מיקרי מלוג שמולגן ...ומחסרן בעל שאוכל ...הפירות כמליגת הראש ...[רשב"ם ב"ב קלט:]. ...הבעל מוציא. דאע"ג ...דבעלמא לאו כקנין הגוף ...דמי בעל בנכסי אשתו ...אלמוה רבנן לשעבודיה ...משום איבה והוי כלוקח ...ראשון שהבעל יורש את ...אשתו והוא היה לוקח ראשון [ב"ק פח:].

loss." לֹא שִׁילֵּם – [The *shomer*] did not pay, however. אָזַל רַב נַחְמָן אַגְבֵּיהּ לְאַפַּדְנֵיהּ מִינֵּיהּ – Thereupon, **Rav Nachman went** and **seized his mansion from him** for payment. לְסוֹף אִישְׁתַּכַּח כִּיפֵי – **Eventually, the earrings were found,** וְאַיְּקוּר – **and they had become more valuable** in the interim than what had been seized by the court to pay their owner. אָמַר רַב נַחְמָן – **Rav Nachman said:** הַדְרֵי כִּיפֵי לְמָרַיְיהוּ – **The earrings should be returned to their owner,** וְהַדְרָא אַפַּדְנָא לְמָרֵהּ – **and the mansion should be returned to its owner.**

The Gemara analyzes this ruling:

אָמַר רָבָא – **Rava said:** הֲוָה יָתִיבְנָא קַמֵּיהּ דְּרַב נַחְמָן – **I was sitting in front of Rav Nachman** when this matter was decided, וּפִרְקִין הַמַּפְקִיד הֲוָה – **and our chapter** of study at the time **was** ***Hamafkid*** (our chapter), וְאָמְרִי לֵיהּ – **and I commented to him** שִׁילֵּם וְלֹא רָצָה לִישָּׁבַע – that the Mishnah states: If THE SHOMER PAID for the lost item AND HE DID NOT WANT TO SWEAR, he acquires any future penalty payment. Here, too, the *shomer* should acquire the increased value of the earrings, since he paid for their loss.[20] וְלֹא אַהְדַּר לִי – **[Rav Nachman] did not respond to me,** וְשַׁפִּיר עֲבַד דְּלֹא אַהְדַּר לִי – **and he was right not to respond to me.** מַאי טַעְמָא – **What is the reason** that my argument was wrong? הָתָם לֹא אַטְרְחֵיהּ לְבֵי דִּינָא – **There,** in the case of the Mishnah, **[the *shomer*] did not trouble [the owner]** to go **to *beis din*** to collect from him the payment for the deposit. Since he paid it voluntarily, the owner is willing to transfer the added value to him in exchange. הָכָא אַטְרְחֵיהּ לְבֵי דִּינָא – **Here,** in Rav Nachman's case, the **[the *shomer*] troubled [the owner]** to go **to *beis din*** to collect the payment; he did not pay it willingly. Therefore, the owner has no reason to transfer anything to him in return.

The Gemara questions an implication of Rav Nachman's ruling:

לְמֵימְרָא דְּסָבַר רַב נַחְמָן – **Is this to say that Rav Nachman holds** דְּשׁוּמָא הָדַר – **that property seized** by *beis din* for payment of an obligation[21] **must be returned** to the debtor if he later offers money as payment? Is this why Rav Nachman ordered the mansion returned to the *shomer*?[22]

The Gemara rejects this conclusion:

שָׁאנֵי הָתָם – **There,** in Rav Nachman's case, **it is different,** דְּשׁוּמָא בְּטָעוּת הֲוָה – **since** taking the mansion **was an erroneous** and invalid **seizure,**[23] דְּקָא הֲוָה כִּיפֵי מֵעִיקָּרָא – **for the earrings were,** in fact, in the *shomer's* possession **from the outset,** i.e. at the time *beis din* seized his mansion.[24]

The Gemara now discusses the issue of returning property seized by the court to pay a debt:

אָמְרֵי נְהַרְדָּעֵי – **The Nehardean** scholars **say:** שׁוּמָא הָדַר – **Seized** property **is returned** when the debtor offers money עַד תְּרֵיסַר יַרְחֵי שַׁתָּא – **up to twelve months' time** following the seizure. וְאָמַר אֲמֵימָר – **And Ameimar said:** אֲנָא מִנְּהַרְדְּעָא אֲנָא – **I am from Nehardea,** וּסְבִירָא לִי שׁוּמָא הָדַר לְעוֹלָם – **yet I hold that seized** property **is returned forever** (whenever the debtor comes forward with the money to repay the debt). וְהִלְכְתָא – **And the halachah** is that שׁוּמָא הָדַר לְעוֹלָם – **seized** property **is returned forever,** מִשּׁוּם שֶׁנֶּאֱמַר – **because it is stated:** "וְעָשִׂיתָ הַיָּשָׁר וְהַטּוֹב" – ***And you shall do that which is fair and good*** *in the eyes of Hashem.*[25]

The Gemara applies this principle to the case of a secondary creditor:

פְּשִׁיטָא – **It is obvious,** שָׁמוּ לֵיהּ לְבַעַל חוֹב – if **[the court] seized** property **for a creditor** וְאָזַל אִיהוּ וְשָׁמָהּ לְבַעַל חוֹב דִּידֵיהּ – **and then [the creditor] went and awarded** the property **to** ***his*** **creditor,** that if the original debtor subsequently offers to repay his debt with cash,[26] אָמְרִינַן לֵיהּ – **we tell [the second creditor]:** לֹא עֲדִיף אַתְּ מִגַּבְרָא דְּאָתֵית מִינֵּיהּ – **You are no better than the man from whom your** claim **derives.** Just as he [i.e. the first creditor] would have had to return the property in exchange for money, you must do the same.[27]

NOTES

20. [The Mishnah's ruling applies even when the *shomer* admits that he was negligent, as Rav Pappa said on 34a. Thus, here too, although the *shomer* admits his negligence, once he paid, he should acquire any extra value that comes through the earrings.]

Rava's question is difficult to understand. Above (34a), R' Zeira ruled that an owner generally does not transfer to a *shomer* future profits that come from the item itself (such as shearings and offspring). How, then, can Rava suggest that the *shomer* acquires the increased value of the earrings, which is a profit that comes from the item itself, and not from an outside source? *Tosafos* explain that this rule applies only to those profits that can be seen emerging from the body of the deposit (such as the wool of the sheep or the offspring of an animal). An increase in the value of the object is not obvious in the object itself [rather, it is caused by a change in market conditions]. Thus, it qualifies as an external profit, similar to penalty payments (see *Ramban;* see, however, *Tos. HaRosh* and *Maharam Schif*).

21. The word שׁוּמָא actually means *appraisal.* Here and below, however, the Gemara means that *beis din* has appraised and then seized the property for the creditor.

The issue the Gemara will now discuss is whether property collected by the court to pay a debt must be returned by the lender if the borrower later comes up with the money and wishes to get his property back. Since the court gave the property to the lender as *payment,* perhaps the lender no longer has any obligation to return it.

22. The Gemara assumes that the return of the earrings to their owner is equivalent to a cash payment to a lender. Just as Rav Nachman required the owner of the earrings to take back his earrings and return the mansion to the *shomer,* so too he would require a lender to take the money the borrower now wants to give him and return the property he collected from him (see *Ritva*).

The commentators note that the two cases are not similar. In the case of a loan, the borrower *wants* his property back once he comes up with the money. In the case of the earrings, however, the *shomer* would prefer to keep the earrings and not get his mansion back, since the earrings are now worth more than the house! *Ramban* explains that since the Gemara has already concluded above that the *shomer* has no right to the increased value of the earrings, he has no advantage in keeping them; therefore, he would surely prefer to get his mansion back. See *Ritva* for another explanation.

23. It was thought that the earrings were gone when, in fact, they were not (*Rashi*).

24. Had *beis din* known this fact, they would not have seized the mansion for the owner of the earrings; they would instead have compelled him to return the earrings. [Hence, it makes sense to say that the seizure is nullified when the earrings are found.] In the case of an ordinary debt, however, *beis din* seizes the property of one who *lacks* the money with which to pay his debt. Such a seizure might be considered equivalent to a sale (*Rashi;* cf. *Ramban* and *Rambam, Hil. She'eilah U'Fikadon* 8:3).

25. *Deuteronomy* 6:18. Although according to the strict letter of the law the creditor has acquired the seized property, he is obligated to return it in exchange for money so as to do what *"is fair and good"* (see *Tosafos* ד"ה זבנה). See above, 16b note 23, for a fuller explanation of this obligation; see also *Ramban's* commentary on the verse.

26. To illustrate: Reuven borrowed money from Shimon and was not able to repay it. As a result, the court took a property from Reuven and gave it to Shimon to satisfy the debt. Shimon took that property and gave it to Levi to repay the money that he (Shimon) owed Levi. Reuven now comes back with the cash to pay his debt and wants to give this money to Levi and reclaim the property taken from him by Shimon.

27. I.e. just as the first creditor (Shimon) would have been obligated by the verse, *And you shall do that which is fair and good,* to accept a cash reimbursement and give back the property, so too the second creditor (Levi) must accept the cash reimbursement for the same reason (*Rashi*).

איתא לדרב הונא כיון דמשתבע מלוה שאינה ברשותו היכי מצי מפיק לה אמר (א) [א] רבא שיש עדים שנשרפה אי הכי מהיכא מייתי לה אלא אמר רב יוסף שיש עדים שנגנבה סוף סוף מהיכא מייתי לה דטרח ומייתי לה אי הכי כי משתבע מלוה נמי לטרח לוה וליתי בשלמא מלוה ידע מאן קא עייל ונפק בביתיה ואזיל וטרח ומייתי לה אלא לוה מי ידע מאן עייל ונפיק בביתיה דמלוה אביי אומר גזירה שמא יטעון ויאמר לו אחר שבועה מצאתיה [ג] רב אשי אמר [א] זה נשבע וזה נשבע זה נשבע שאינה ברשותו וזה נשבע כמה היה שוה והכי קאמר מי נשבע תחילה [ב] מלוה נשבע תחילה שמא ישבע זה ויוציא הלה את הפקדון רב הונא בר תחליפא משמיה דרבא אמר רישא דסיפא תיובתא לרב הונא סלע הלויתני עליו שתים היה שוה והלה אומר לא כי אלא סלע הלויתיך עליו סלע היה שוה פטור ואם איתא לדרב הונא מגו דמשתבע מלוה שאינה ברשותו [ג] לישתבע נמי אגילגול שבועה כמה היה שוה אמר רב אשי אמריתה לשמעתא קמיה דרב כהנא ואמר לי [ג] [ד] תהא במאמינו ונהמניה לוה למלוה נמי בהא כמה הוה שוה לא קים ליה בגויה ונהמניה מלוה ללוה דקים ליה בגויה לא מהימן ליה ומאי שנא לוה דמהימן ליה למלוה ומאי שנא מלוה דלא מהימן ליה ללוה לוה מקיים ביה במלוה [א] תומת ישרים תנחם מלוה מקיים ביה בלוה [א] וסלף בוגדים ישדם: ההוא גברא דאפקיד כיפי גביה חבריה אמר ליה הב לי (ב) כיפי אמר ליה לא ידענא היכא אותבינהו אתא לקמיה דרב נחמן אמר ליה [ד] [ה] כל לא ידענא פשיעותא היא זיל שלים לא שילם אזל רב נחמן אגביה לאפדניה מיניה לסוף אישתכח כיפי ואיקור אמר רב נחמן [ו] הדרי כיפי למרייהו והדרא אפדנא למרה אמר רבא הוה יתיבנא קמיה דרב נחמן ופרקין המפקיד הוה ואמרי ליה שילם ולא רצה לישבע ולא אהדר לי ושפיר עבד דלא אהדר לי מאי טעמא [ז] התם לא אטרחיה לבי דינא הכא אטרחיה לבי דינא למימרא דסבר רב נחמן דשומא הדר שאני התם דשומא בטעות הוה דקא הוה כיפי מעיקרא [ה] אמרי נהרדעי שומא הדר עד תריסר ירחי שתא ואמר אמימר אנא מנהרדעא אנא וסבירא לי שומא הדר לעולם [ח] והלכתא שומא הדר לעולם משום שנאמר [ב] ועשית הישר והטוב [ט] פשיטא שמו ליה לבעל חוב ואזל איהו ושמה לבעל חוב דידיה אמרינן ליה לא עדיף את מגברא דאתית מיניה [י] זבנה (ג) אורתא ויהבה במתנה ודאי הני מעיקרא אדעתא דארעא נחות ולאו אדעתא דזוזי נחות [כ] שמו לה לאשה ואינסיבא או שמו מינה דאשה ואינסיבא ומתה [ו] בעל בנכסי אשתו לוקח הוי לא מיהדר ולא מהדרינן ליה [ז] דאמר רבי יוסי בר חנינא באושא התקינו [ל] האשה שמכרה בנכסי מלוג בחיי בעלה ומתה הבעל מוציא מיד הלקוחות

אגביה

**רש"י**

**איתא לדרב הונא.** שהשומר המשלם דמים נשבע שאינה ברשותו אמאי חיישינן לשמא יוציא הא אשתבע: **שיש עדים שנשרפה.** דהשתא לא אשבעינהו שהרי הביא עדים: **טרח ומייתי לה.** מחזר ושואל אחר הנכנסים בביתו וימצא הגנב: **וזה נשבע.** הלוה שהשבועה עליו נשבע כמה שוה: **מלוה נשבע תחילה.** שאינה ברשותו: **רישא דסיפא.** הויא תיובתא לרב הונא רישא תביעת מלוה סיפא תביעת לוה רישא דסיפא דקתני פטור בתביעת לוה: **אגילגול שבועה.** דטענה שאין בה שבועה עם טענה שיש בה שבועה מגלגלין עליו שבועה לישבע על שתיהן וגילגול שבועה דאורייתא היא בקדושין (דף כז:): **תהא במאמינו.** הא דקתני פטור במאמינו לוה למלוה שאינה ברשותו: **לא קים ליה בגויה.** מימר אמר לוה לא קים למלוה בגויה דמשכון דלא נתן דעתו עליו לדעת דמיו: **מאי שנא כו'.** דנקט תנא למלתיה בהכי שזה נאמן על זה וזה אינו נאמן על זה: **לוה מקיים במלוה.** מקרא זה תומת ישרים תנחם אם לא שאדם נאמן וישר הוא לא היו מעשרין אותו מן השמים שנאמר תומת ישרים תנחם: **כיפי.** נזמים: **ואייקור.** יתר על הדמים שפרע לבעלים: **הוה יתיבנא.** כשדן דין זה: **ופרקין המפקיד הוה.** ובפרק זה היינו עוסקין: **ואמרי ליה שילם ולא רצה לישבע.** קתני מתני' דקני כפילא והאי נמי שילם וליקני רווחא דאייקור: **דשומא הדר.** נכסי לוה ששמו ב"ד לבעל חוב חוזרין אליו אם נותן מעות לבעל חוב כי הכא דהדר אפדנא למרה: **דשומא בטעות הוה.** דסבור היה שאבדו הנזמים והרי לא אבדו: **דהא הוו כיפי מעיקרא.** שהרי בתחילת השומא היו הנזמים בידו ולא היה יודע דאילו היה יודע שכן לא שמו לו הטרקלין אבל שומא שב"ד שמין על שאין לו מעות והוא חייב לו הרי הוא כמכר גמור ואינה חוזרת: **אמרינן.** לבעל חוב שני: **לא עדיפת.** מבעל חוב ראשון שבאת מכחו כשם שהוא מחזירה ויטול מעותיו משום ועשית הישר והטוב אף אתה קבל מעותיך מבעלים הראשונים משום ועשית הישר והטוב: **זבנה אורתה כו'.** בעל חוב ששמו לו קרקע ומכרה או שנתנה או הוריש: **הני.** אחרונים או לוקח או יורש או מקבל מתנה: **אדעתא דארעא נחות.** שיהא קרקע שלהם ולא שיקבלו מעות דאילו בעל חוב אית ביה משום ועשית הישר והטוב דאמרינן לא היה לך עליו אלא מעות והרי הן לך אבל אלו קרקע קנו: **ואנסיבא.** אפילו לא שמאתן לבעלה בכתובתה להיות נכסי צאן ברזל שהן קנויין לבעל אלא עיכבתן לעצמה להיות נכסי מלוג הקרן שלה והבעל אוכל פירות: **בעל.** בנכסי מלוג של אשתו: **לוקח הוי.** דין לוקח נתנו בו חכמים הלכך לא מיהדר היכא דשמו לה ואינסיבא ומתה וירשה בעלה כדאמרינן זבנה אדעתא דארעא נחות: **ולא מהדרינן ליה.** היכא דשמו מינה ואינסיבא ומתה וירשה בעלה ובא להחזיר החוב וליטול הקרקע לא מצי למימר יורשה אני דלוקח שויה רבנן ולא כיורש: **האשה שמכרה בנכסי מלוג.** להיות הבעל אוכל פירות בחייה וגוף הקרקע יהיה ללוקח לכשתמות ומתה: **בעל מוציא.** גוף הקרקע מיד הלקוחות והכי מוקי לה בפרק האשה בכתובות (דף עח:) תקנת אושא בגופה של קרקע לאחר מיתה אלמא כלוקח שויוהו רבנן וא"ל אני לקחתי ראשון דאי כשאר יורש שמכר אביו נכסיו בחייו אין לו ירושה בהן: **באושא התקינו.** כשהיתה סנהדרין באושא שגלתה וישבה שם סנהדרי גדולה כדאמרינן בר"ה (דף לא.) גבי עשרה מסעות:

**תוספות**

**מגו** דמשתבע מלוה שאינו ברשותו כו'. [ח] לרבה ולרב יוסף לא פריך אלא לאביי ורב אשי:

**תהא** במאמינו. ברישא לא מצי לאוקמי הכי משום דהתם לא ירצה להאמינו כיון שע"י כן לא יוכל לישבע אבל הכא אין כאן שבועה ואע"פ שמפסיד במה שמאמינו שבועה שהיה יכול לגלגל עליו אינו חושש:

**ואותביניה** שילם. וצ"ל דיוקרא דכיפי הוי שבחא דעלמא כמו כפילא ולא דמי לגיזות וולדות דאותו שבח ניכר בגוף הבהמה:

**אטרחיה** לב"ד. דלא דמי לאטרחיה לשבועה דקני כפילא לרבא כששילם אחרי כן (ב"ק דף קח.) דהתם משלם ברצונו אבל רב נחמן הולך לגבות אפדנו:

**זבנה** כו'. וא"ת ואמאי לא מהדר (ד) מה מכר ראשון לשני כל זכות שתבא לידו וי"ל דהראשון מן הדין נמי אין מחזיר שמכורה היא לו שהרי אוכל פירות בלא נכייתא אלא משום ועשית הישר והטוב מהדר ולכך שני לא מהדר:

**לוקח** הוי. אפי' אי הוי יורש לא מהדר כדאמר זבנה אורתה כו' אלא משום לא מהדרינן ליה נקטיה דאי יורש הוי מהדרינן ליה שהבן פודה קרקע של אביו ואע"ג דבפרק יש נוחלין (ב"ב דף קלט: ושם ד"ה התם) מסיק דטבא ליה עבדו ליה או יורש או לוקח הא אמרינן התם בר היכא דאיכא פסידא לאחריני לא עבדי ליה טבא ולכך הכא לא הוי כיורש משום פסידא דמלוה ולא מהדר ממה נפשך דאפי' יורש הוי לא מהדר ודר' יוסי בר חנינא מפרש התם דלקוחות אפסדו אנפשייהו:

רבא

**עין משפט נר מצוה**

יג א ב מיי' פי"ג מהל' מלוה ולוה הל' ד סמג עשין צד טוש"ע ח"מ סי' עב סעי' י:

יד ג ד מיי' שם טוש"ע שם סעי' יב:

טו ה מיי' פ"ד מהל' שאלה ופקדון הל' ז סמג עשין פח טוש"ע ח"מ סי' רלא סעי' ז:

טז ו ז מיי' שם פ"ח הל' ג סמג שם טוח"מ סי' רלה:

יז ח מיי' פכ"ב מהל' מלוה הל' טו סמג עשין צד טוש"ע ח"מ סי' קג סעי' ט:

יח ט י כ מיי' שם הל' יח טוש"ע שם סעי' י:

יט ל מיי' פכ"ב מהל' אישות הל' ז ועיין במ"מ סמג עשין מח טוש"ע אה"ע סי' צ סעי' ט:

**רבינו חננאל**

וקשיא לן וכי תקנתא לרשיעי עבדינן אלא שמא ישבע הלוה ויוציא המלוה את הפקדון ונמצאת שבועת הלוה שיצאה לבטלה. ואמרי' אם איתא לדרב הונא כיון שנשבע המלוה שאינה ברשותו אינו יכול להוציא הפקדון שכבר נשבע שאינו ברשותו א) והלה נשבע כמה היה שוה ומתני' הכי קתני מי נשבע תחלה מי שהפקדון אצלו שאם ישבע הלוה תחלה חיישינן שמא יוציא המלוה את המשכון ונמצאת שבועה זו לבטלה. ושאר השמועה פשוטה היא. ההוא דאפקיד כיפי גביה חבריה ואמר לא ידענא היכא אנחתינהו אמר ר' נחמן כל לא ידענא פשיעותא היא חייביה לשלומי לא שילם ירד רב נחמן לנכסיו ושם לאפדני ויהביה לבעל הפקדון בדמי דהנהו כיפי דפשע בהו. פי' אפדנא חצר. לסוף אישתכח כיפי ואוקירו בדמיהן. מריה דכיפי אמר הב לי כיפאי וטול אפדנא והלה אומר לא כי אלא מעידנא דשקלית לאפדניי זבינא אנא בכיפי וברשותי אוקירו ודן ר' נחמן כיון דהא שומא דשמו ליה לאפדנא שומא בטעות הואי דהא הוו כיפי ולא אבדו וקיימא לן פקדון כל היכא דאיתיה ברשותיה דמריה קאי לאו שומא הוא והדר אפדנא למריה והדרי כיפי למרייהו. ואסיק' שומא הדרא לעולם משום שנאמר ועשית הישר והטוב והני מילי אם לא מכרה אבל אם מכרה לאחר או נתנה במתנה או הורישה לא הדרא. וכן אם שמו ב"ד שדה לאשה במלוה שהיא נרשה לאחרים וניסת והכניסה שדה זו לבעלים או שמו שדה אשה לנושה שלה וניסת לא מהדרינן ליה לבעל ולא מהדרינן מיניה דבעל דכזביני דמי וקיימא לן בעל בנכסי אשתו לוקח הוי לא מהדר ולא מהדרינן ליה דאמר ר' יוסי בר' חנינא באושא התקינו האשה שמכרה נכסי מלוג בחיי בעלה ומתה הבעל מוציא מיד הלקוחות.

אגביה

**מסורת הש"ס**

א) [נראה דל"ל רבה], ב) [שבועות מג: ע"ש], ג) [בבא קמא קח:], ד) [לקמן מב.], ה) לעיל ?:, ו) [בבא בתרא לט:], ז) לקמן לו:, כתובות נ., עח., בבא מציעא פח., בבא בתרא קלט:, ח) גירסת מהרש"א לרב הונא.

**הגהות הב"ח**

(א) גמ' אמר רבא אמר רב יוסף שיש עדים שנשרפה: (ב) שם הב לי כיפאי אמר: (ג) שם זבנה אורתה: (ד) תוס' ד"ה זבנה וכו' לא מהדר נימא מה מכר:

**תורה אור השלם**

א) תֻּמַּת יְשָׁרִים תַּנְחֵם וְסֶלֶף בֹּגְדִים יְשָׁדֵּם: [משלי יא, ג]

ב) וְעָשִׂיתָ הַיָּשָׁר וְהַטּוֹב בְּעֵינֵי יְיָ לְמַעַן יִיטַב לָךְ וּבָאתָ וְיָרַשְׁתָּ אֶת הָאָרֶץ הַטֹּבָה אֲשֶׁר נִשְׁבַּע יְיָ לַאֲבֹתֶיךָ: [דברים ו, יח]

**ליקוטי רש"י**

מלוה נשבע תחילה. מי שהפקדון אצלו נשבע תחלה שאינה ברשותו לעולם קודם שיפרע דרישא קאי היכא דשבועה גבי מלוה [שבועות מג:]. תהא במאמינו. כלל מה שאומר [ב"ק צח.]. תנחם. תנהלם. ישדם. שודדם [משלי יא, ג]. כיפי. מרגליות ל"א נזמים וכן עיקר [עירובין נד:]. עגילים ... דאמרינן בעלמא [עירובין דף נד:] כיפי תלה ליה עגילים תלה [לשבת דף נב.]. שומא הדר עד תריסר ירחי שתא. אם יפרע לו מעות עד תריסר ירחי שתא. הישר והטוב. זו פשרה לפנים משורת הדין [דברים ו, יח]. האשה שמכרה בנכסי מלוג. הקרן שלה [כתובות נ.]. בחיי בעלה. שאם ימות בעלה היא יורשה בעל יפסידו. נכסי מלוג הן נכסים שמולגה לה ... בעל מוציא. ... [ב"ב קלט:]. לוקח הוי. ... [ב"ק פח.].

HE DEPOSIT (the collateral) in court and thereby disqualify the orrower if the object's value is not what the borrower said.[11]

The Gemara continues its discussion of Rav Huna's ruling that *shomer* who pays must still swear that the item deposited with im is no longer in his possession:

**רַב הוּנָא בַּר תַּחְלִיפָא מִשְּׁמֵיהּ דְּרָבָא אָמַ – Rav Huna bar Tachlifa aid in the name of Rava:** **רֵישָׁא דְּסֵיפָא תְּיוּבְתָּא לְרַב הוּנָא – The irst case of the end** of the Mishnah[12] **is a refutation of Rav Iuna's** ruling, for the Mishnah stated: סֶלַע הִלְוִיתַנִי עָלָיו – If the orrower claims, "YOU LENT ME A *SELA* ON [COLLATERAL] שְׁתַּיִם הָיָה שָׁו – but IT WAS WORTH TWO *selas*, and you therefore owe ıe one *sela*"; וְהַלָּה אוֹמֵר – AND THAT ONE (the lender) SAYS, לֹא כ – "NOT SO; אֶלָּא סֶלַע הִלְוִיתִיךָ עָלָיו – RATHER, I LENT YOU *SELA* ON [COLLATERAL] סֶלַע הָיָה שָׁוֶה – and IT WAS WORTH nly A *SELA*, and so I owe you nothing"; פָּטוּר – HE (the lender) S EXEMPT from taking an oath about the value of the collateral, ince he does not admit to owing any part of the borrower's claim.

The Gemara explains the challenge to Rav Huna from this uling:

**וְאִם אִיתָא לְדְרַב הוּנ – Now, if Rav Huna**'s ruling is correct, מִגּוֹ **דְּמִשְׁתַּבַּע מַלְוֶה שֶׁאֵינָהּ בִּרְשׁוּת – since the lender must swear that the collateral] is not in his possession,** **לִישְׁתַּבַּע נַמִּי אַגִּלְגּוּל שְׁבוּעָ – let him also** be required to **swear, based on** the rule f **"extending an oath,"**[13] **כַּמָּה הָיָה שָׁוֶה – how much it was vorth.** Why does the Mishnah say in this case that the lender is xempt from swearing this oath?

The Gemara answers:

**אָמַר רַב אַשְׁ – Rav Ashi said:** **אֲמַרִיתָהּ לִשְׁמַעְתָּא קַמֵּיהּ דְּרַב כַּהֲנ – I related this question in front of Rav Kahana,** **וְאָמַר ל – and he told me:** **תְּהֵא בְּמַאֲמִינוֹ – That** case of the Mishnah hould be explained as referring **to [a borrower] who trusts the lender]** when he claims that the collateral is not in his possession; for that reason the lender is released from Rav Huna's ath.[14]

The Gemara asks:

**וְנִהֵמְנֵיהּ לֹוֶה לַמַּלְוֶה נַמִּי בָּהּ – If** so, **then let the borrower also rust the lender regarding this** matter **כַּמָּה הָוֵה שָׁוֶה – of ow much [the collateral] was worth,** so that the lender should not have to swear even when he admits to part of the borrower's claim.[15] **– ? –**

The Gemara answers:

**לֹא קִים לֵיהּ בְּגַוֵּיהּ – The borrower assumes that [the lender] is not familiar with [the collateral],** i.e. he did not pay close enough attention to the collateral to correctly estimate its value.

The Gemara again asks:

**וְנִהֵמְנֵיהּ מַלְוֶה לַלֹּוֶה – If** so, **then let the lender trust the borrower** regarding the value of the collateral, **דְּקִים לֵיהּ בְּגַוֵּיהּ – for he** (the borrower) **is familiar with it** and knows precisely how much it is worth. Hence, the borrower should not have to swear when he acknowledges part of the lender's claim.[16] **– ? –**

The Gemara answers:

**לֹא מְהֵימַן לֵיהּ – [The lender] does not trust [the borrower].**

The Gemara questions:

**וּמַאי שְׁנָא לֹוֶה דִּמְהֵימַן לֵיהּ לַמַּלְוֶה – And why** do we assume that **the borrower trusts the lender** when he claims that the collateral is not in his possession, **וּמַאי שְׁנָא מַלְוֶה דְּלֹא מְהֵימַן לֵיהּ לַלֹּוֶה – and why** do we assume that **the lender does not trust the borrower** to assess the value of the collateral?

The Gemara explains:

**לֹוֶה מְקַיֵּים בֵּיהּ בַּמַּלְוֶה – The borrower applies to the lender** the following Scriptural maxim: "תֻּמַּת יְשָׁרִים תַּנְחֵם" – ***The perfection of the upright shall lead them*** to good fortune.[17] **מַלְוֶה מְקַיֵּים בֵּיהּ בַּלֹּוֶה – And the lender applies to the borrower** the second half of that verse: "וְסֶלֶף בּוֹגְדִים יְשָׁדֵּם" – ***and the perverseness of traitors will plunder them.***[18]

The Gemara relates a particular incident to a ruling in our Mishnah:

**הַהוּא גַּבְרָא דְּאַפְקִיד כִּיפֵי גַּבֵּיהּ חַבְרֵיהּ** – There was once **a certain man who deposited earrings with his friend** for safekeeping. **אָמַר לֵיהּ הַב לִי כִּיפֵי** – After a time **he said to [the *shomer*], "Give me my earrings."**[19] **אָמַר לֵיהּ – [The *shomer*] told him,** **לֹא יָדַעְנָא הֵיכָא אוֹתְבִינְהוּ – "I do not know where I put them."** **אָתָא לְקַמֵּיהּ דְּרַב נַחְמָן – [The *shomer*] came before Rav Nachman** for a ruling. **אָמַר לֵיהּ – [Rav Nachman] told him:** **כָּל לֹא יָדַעְנָא פְּשִׁיעוּתָא הִיא – "Any** claim of **'I do not know' is** indicative of **negligence;** **זִיל שַׁלֵּים** – therefore, **go** and **pay** for the

NOTES

1. The Mishnah never says that the borrower does *not* swear. The Iishnah only says that the lender swears. According to Rav Ashi this ıeans that the lender swears *first,* but in fact the borrower also swears. 'he lender swears that the collateral is not in his possession, as Rav Iuna ruled. Once he does this we are no longer concerned that he will roduce the collateral. Since this is no longer a concern, we have the orrower swear how much it was worth.

2. I.e. the first of the last two cases of the Mishnah (see above, 34b ote 28).

3. The Gemara (*Kiddushin* 27b) learns from a verse that when a deendant is confronted with two claims, one of which would normally equire him to swear and the other not, once he must swear about ne of them he can be required to swear about the other one as well. 'his principle is called גִּלְגּוּל שְׁבוּעָה, *the rolling* (i.e. extending) *of an ath* (*Rashi*).

In this case, according to Rav Huna, the lender is claiming two things: a) that he no longer has the collateral, and (b) that the value of the ost collateral equaled the amount of the loan. Regarding the first claim, e must swear an oath; that is the ruling of Rav Huna. The Gemara herefore asks that if this is so, then based on the principle of גִּלְגּוּל שְׁבוּעָה, *xtending an oath,* the lender should also be required to take an oath bout his claim concerning the value of the collateral (*Rashi*).

4. Since he does not have to swear the first oath, the principle of גִּלְגּוּל שְׁבוּעָ, *extending an oath,* cannot be applied.

[The second of the first set of cases of the Mishnah, regarding which Rav Ashi himself stated above that the lender must swear that the collateral is not in his possession, must be speaking of a borrower who does not trust the lender (see *Ramban, Tosafos*).]

15. If the borrower is willing to trust the lender that the item deposited with him is no longer in his possession, he should be willing to take his word about the value of the collateral as well. Why then does the Mishnah say in its fourth case that if the lender admits that the collateral was worth more than the loan, but not as much as the borrower claims, that the lender must swear that it was worth only as much as he claims? Why is he making him swear about the value of the collateral if he trusts him?

16. Why then does the Mishnah say in its second case that if the borrower admits that the collateral was worth less than the loan, he must swear that his claim is true? If the borrower and lender trust each other, the lender should accept the borrower's word for how much the collateral was worth, since the borrower was familiar with the object he gave as collateral and presumably knew how much it was worth.

17. *Proverbs* 11:3. That is, if a person were not upright and trustworthy, he would not be blessed by Heaven with wealth (*Rashi*).

18. I.e. the fact that a man is poor and must borrow money may indicate that he is not trustworthy. In other words, the Tanna discusses a case of a borrower who trusts his lender while the lender does not trust the borrower because it is common for this to happen. Poor people look at successful people as being trustworthy, while wealthy people do not generally consider poor people trustworthy.

19. *Bach* emends the text to read כִּיפַאי, *my earrings.* Our translation follows his emendation.

איתא לדרב הונא כיון דמשתבע מלוה שאינה ברשותו היכי מצי מפיק לה אמר (א) רבא שיש עדים שנשרפה אי הכי מהיכא מייתי לה אלא אמר רב יוסף שיש עדים שנגנבה סוף סוף מהיכא מייתי לה דטרח ומייתי לה אי הכי כי משתבע מלוה נמי לטרח לוה וליתי בשלמא מלוה ידע מאן קא עייל ונפק בביתיה ואזיל וטרח ומייתי לה אלא לוה מי ידע מאן עייל ונפיק בביתיה דמלוה אביי אומר גזירה שמא יטעון ויאמר לו אחר שבועה מצאתיה רב אשי אמר זה נשבע וזה נשבע זה נשבע שאינה ברשותו וזה נשבע כמה היה שוה והכי קאמר מי נשבע תחילה מלוה נשבע תחילה שמא ישבע זה ויוציא הלה את הפקדון רב הונא בר תחליפא משמיה דרבא אמר רישא דסיפא תיובתא לרב הונא סלע הלויתני עליו שתים היה שוה והלה אומר לא כי אלא סלע הלויתך עליו סלע היה שוה פטור ואם איתא לדרב הונא מגו דמשתבע מלוה שאינה ברשותו לישתבע נמי אגילגול שבועה כמה היה שוה אמר רב אשי אמריתה לשמעתא קמיה דרב כהנא ואמר לי תהא במאמינו ונהמניה לוה למלוה נמי בהא כמה הוה שוה לא קים ליה בגויה ונהמניה מלוה ללוה דקים ליה בגויה לא מהימן ליה ומאי שנא לוה דמהימן ליה למלוה ומאי שנא מלוה דלא מהימן ליה ללוה לוה מקיים ביה במלוה א) תומת ישרים תנחם מלוה מקיים ביה בלוה א) וסלף בוגדים ישדם: ההוא גברא דאפקיד כיפי גביה חבריה אמר ליה הב לי (ב) כיפי אמר ליה לא ידענא היכא אותבינהו אתא לקמיה דרב נחמן אמר ליה כל לא ידענא פשיעותא היא זיל שלים לא שילם אזל רב נחמן אגביה לאפדניה מיניה לסוף אישתכח כיפי ואיקור אמר רב נחמן הדרי כיפי למרייהו והדרא אפדנא למרה אמר רבא הוה יתיבנא קמיה דרב נחמן ופרקין המפקיד הוה ואמרי ליה שילם ולא רצה לישבע ולא אהדר לי ושפיר עבד דלא אהדר לי מאי טעמא התם לא אטרחיה לבי דינא הכא אטרחיה לבי דינא למימרא דסבר רב נחמן דשאני התם דשומא הדר בטעות הוה דקא הוה כיפי מעיקרא אמרי נהרדעי שומא הדר עד תריסר ירחי שתא ואמר אמימר אנא מנהרדעא אנא וסבירא לי שומא הדר לעולם והלכתא שומא הדר לעולם משום שנאמר ב) ועשית הישר והטוב פשיטא שמו ליה לבעל חוב ואזל איהו ושמה לבעל חוב דידיה אמרינן ליה לא עדיף את מגברא דאתית מיניה זבנה (ג) אורתא ויהבה במתנה ודאי הני מעיקרא אדעתא דארעא נחות ולאו אדעתא דזוזי נחות שמו לה לאשה ואינסיבא או שמו מינה דאשה ואינסיבא ומתה בעל בנכסי אשתו לוקח הוי לא מיהדר ולא מהדרינן ליה דאמר רבי יוסי בר חנינא באושא התקינו האשה שמכרה בנכסי מלוג בחיי בעלה ומתה הבעל מוציא מיד הלקוחות אגביה

**רש"י**

**איתא לדרב הונא.** שהשומר המשלם דמים נשבע שאינה ברשותו אמאי חיישינן לשמא יוציא הא אשתבע: **שיש עדים שנשרפה.** דהשתא לא אשבעינהו שהרי הביא עדים: **טרח ומייתי לה.** מחזר ושואל אחר הנכנסים בביתו וימצא הגנב: **וזה נשבע.** הלוה שהשבועה עליו נשבע כמה שוה: **מלוה נשבע תחילה.** שאינה ברשותו: **רישא דסיפא.** הויא תיובתא לרב הונא רישא תביעת מלוה סיפא תביעת לוה רישא דסיפא דקתני פטור בתביעת לוה: **אגילגול שבועה.** דטענה שאין בה שבועה עם טענה שיש בה שבועה מגלגלין עליו שבועה לישבע על שתיהן וגילגול שבועה דאורייתא היא בקדושין (דף כז:): **תהא במאמינו.** הא דקתני פטור במאמינו לוה למלוה שאינה ברשותו: **לא קים ליה בגויה.** מימר אמר לוה לא קים למלוה בגויה דמשכון דלא נתן דעתו עליו לדעת דמיו: **מאי שנא כו'.** דנקט תנא למלתיה בהכי שזה נאמן על זה וזה אינו נאמן על זה: **לוה מקיים במלוה.** מקרא זה תומת ישרים תנחם אם לא שאדם נאמן וישר הוא לא היו מעשרין אותו מן השמים שנאמר תומת ישרים תנחם: **כיפי.** נזמים: **ואייקור.** יתר על הדמים שפרע לבעלים: **הוה יתיבנא.** כשדן דין זה: **ופרקין המפקיד הוה.** ובפרק זה היינו עוסקין: **ואמרי ליה שילם ולא רצה לישבע.** קתני מתני' דקני כפילא והאי נמי שילם וליקני רווחא דאייקור: **דשומא הדר.** נכסי לוה ששמו ב"ד לבעל חוב חוזרין אליו אם נותן מעות לבעל חוב כי הכא דהדר אפדנא למרה: **דשומא בטעות הוה.** דסבור היה שאבדו הנזמים והרי לא אבדו: **דהא הוו כיפי מעיקרא.** שהרי בתחילת השומא היו הנזמים בידו ולא היה יודע דאילו היה יודע שכן לא שמו לו הטרקלין אבל שומא שב"ד שמין לו שאין לו מעות והוא חייב לו הרי הוא כמכר גמור ואינה חוזרת: **אמרינן.** לבעל חוב שני: **לא עדיפת.** מבעל חוב ראשון שבאת מכחו שאם הוא מחזירה ויטול מעותיו משום ועשית הישר והטוב אף אתה קבל מעותיך מבעלים הראשונים משום ועשית הישר והטוב: **זבנה אורתה כו'.** בעל חוב ששמו לו קרקע ומכרה או נתנה או הוריש: **הני.** אחרונים או לוקח או יורש או מקבל מתנה: **אדעתא דארעא נחות.** שיהא קרקע שלהם ולא שיקבלו מעות דאילו בעל חוב לא אית ביה משום ועשית הישר והטוב דאמרינן לא היה לך עליו אלא מעות והרי הן לך אבל אלו קרקע קנו: **ואנסיבא.** אפילו לא שמאתן לבעלה בכתובתה להיות נכסי צאן ברזל שהן קניין לבעל אלא עיכבתן לעצמה להיות נכסי מלוג הקרן שלה והבעל אוכל פירות: **בעל.** בנכסי מלוג של אשתו: **לוקח הוי.** דין לוקח נתנו בו חכמים הלכך לא מיהדר היכא דשמו לה ולאינסיבא ומתה וירשה בעלה דאמרינן אדעתא דארעא נחות: **ולא מהדרינן ליה.** היכא דשמו מינה ואינסיבא ומתה וירשה בעלה ובא להחזיר החוב וליטול הקרקע לא מצי למימר יורשה אני דלוקח שויה רבנן ולא כיורש: **האשה שמכרה בנכסי מלוג.** להיות הבעל אוכל פירות בחייה וגוף הקרקע יהיה ללוקח לכשתמות ומתה: **בעל מוציא.** גוף הקרקע מיד הלקוחות והכי מוקי לה בפרק האשה בכתובות (דף עח:) תקנת אושא בגופה של קרקע לאחר מיתה אלמא כלוקח שוויה רבנן וה"ל אי לקתני ראשון דאי כאשר יורש שמכר שוויהו רבנן יורש שמכר אביו נכסיו בחייו אין לו ירושה בהן: **באושא התקינו.** כשגלתה סנהדרין באושא גלתה וישבה שם סנהדרי גדולה כדאמרינן בר"ה (דף לא.) גבי עשרה מסעות: אגביה

**תוספות**

**מגו** דמשתבע מלוה שאינו ברשותו כו'. ו) לרבה ולרב יוסף לא פריך אלא לאביי ורב אשי:

**תהא** במאמינו. ברישא לא מצי לאוקמי הכי משום דהתם לא ירצה להאמינו כיון שע"י כן לא יוכל לישבע אבל הכא אין כאן שבועה ואע"פ שמפקיד במה שמאמינו שבועה שהיה יכול לגלגל עליו אינו חושש:

**ואותבינהו** שילם. וה"ל דיוקרא דכיפי הוי שבחא דעלמא כמו כפילא ולא דמי לגיזות וולדות דאותו שבח ניכר בגוף הבהמה: **אטרחיה** לב"ד. דלא דמי לאטרחיה לשבועה דקני כפילא לרבא כששילם אחרי כן (בב"ק דף קח.) דהתם משלם ברצונו אבל רב נחמן הולכן לגבות אפדנו:

**זבנה** כו'. וה"ה ולמאי לא מהדר (ד) מה מכר ראשון לשני כל זכות שתבא לידו וי"ל דהראשון מן הדין נמי אין מחזיר שמכורה היא לו שהרי אוכל פירות בלא נכייתא אלא משום ועשית הישר והטוב מהדר ולכך שני לא מהדר:

**לוקח** הוי. אפי' אי הוי יורש לא מהדר כדאמר זבנה אורתה כו' אלא משום לא מהדרין ליה נקטיה דאי יורש הוי מהדרינן ליה שכבן פודה קרקע של אביו ואע"ג דבפרק יש נוחלין (ב"ב דף קלט: ושם ד"ה התם) מסיק דטבא ליה עבדו ליה אי יורש או לוקח הא אמרינן התם בר היכא דליכא פסידא לאחריני לא עבדי ליה טבא ולכך הכא הוי כיורש משום פסידא דמלוה ולא מהדר ממה נפשך דאפי' יורש הוי לא מהדר ודר' יוסי בר חנינא מפרש התם דלקוחות אפסדו אנפשייהו: רבא

**מסורת הש"ס**

א) [גמרא לא"ל רבה], ב) [שבועות מג: ע"ש], ג) [בבא קמא לא:], ד) [לקמן מב.], ה) לעיל לט:, ו) לקמן לו:, כתובות נ, עח, ב"ב מא, בבא בתרא קלט., ח) גירסת מהרש"ל לרב הונא.

**הגהות הב"ח**

(א) גמ' אמר רבא אמר רב יוסף שיש עדים שנשרפה: (ב) שם הב לי כיפאי אמר: (ג) שם זבנה אורתה: (ד) תוס' ד"ה זבנה וכו' לא מהדר נימא מה מכר:

**תורה אור השלם**

א) תֻּמַּת יְשָׁרִים תַּנְחֵם וְסֶלֶף בֹּגְדִים יְשָׁדֵּם: [משלי יא, ג]

ב) וְעָשִׂיתָ הַיָּשָׁר וְהַטּוֹב בְּעֵינֵי יְיָ לְמַעַן יִיטַב לָךְ וּבָאתָ וְיָרַשְׁתָּ אֶת הָאָרֶץ הַטֹּבָה אֲשֶׁר נִשְׁבַּע יְיָ לַאֲבֹתֶיךָ: [דברים ו, יח]

**ליקוטי רש"י**

מלוה נשבע תחילה. מי שהפקדון אצלו נשבע תחלה שאינה ברשותו ולעולם אסיפא דרישא קאי היכא דשבועה גבי תהא במאמינו. כלל מה שאומר [ב"ק צה:]. תנחם. תנהלם. ישדם. ישדדם [משלי יא, ג]. כיפי. מרגליות וכו' נזמים וכן עיקר [ערכין ...]. עגולים. שומא הדר עד תריסר ירחי שתא. שאם יפרע לו מעות עד שנה [לעיל טז:]. הישר והטוב. זו פשרה לפנים משורת הדין [דברים ו, יח]. האשה שמכרה בנכסי מלוג. הקרן שלה ... בחיי בעלה. ... הבעל מוציא. ... [ב"ק פח.].

**עין משפט נר מצוה**

יג א ב מיי' פ"ג מהל' מלוה ולוה הל' ד סמג עשין לד טוש"ע ח"מ סי' עב סעי' ו:
יד ג ד מיי' שם טוש"ע שם סעי' יב:
טו ה מיי' פ"ד מהל' שאלה ופקדון הל' ז סמג עשין פח טוש"ע ח"מ סי' רצא סעי' ז:
טז ו ז מיי' פ"ד שם הל' ג סמג שם טוש"ע ח"מ סי' רלא סעי' ...:
יז ח מיי' פכ"ב מהל' מלוה ולוה הל' טו סמג עשין לד טוש"ע ח"מ סי' קג סעי' ט:
יח ט י מיי' שם הל' יז טוש"ע שם סעי' יא:
יט ל מיי' פכ"ב מהל' אישות הל' ז ועיין במ"מ שם טוש"ע אה"ע סי' צ סעי' ט:

**רבינו חננאל**

וקשיא לן וכי תקנתא לרשיעי עבדינן אלא שמא ישבע הלוה ויוציא המלוה את הפקדון ונמצאת שבועת הלוה שיצאה לבטלה. ואמרי' אם איתא לדרב הונא כיון שנשבע המלוה שאינה ברשותו אינו יכול להוציא הפקדון שכבר נשבע שאינו ברשותו: א) הלוה נשבע כמה היה שוה ומתני' הכי קתני מי נשבע תחלה מי שהפקדון אצלו שאם ישבע הלוה תחלה חיישינן שמא יוציא המלוה את המשכון ונמצאת שבועה זו לבטלה. ושאר השמועה פשוטה היא. ההוא דאפקיד כיפי גביה חבריה ואמר לא ידענא היכא אנחתינהו אמר ר' נחמן כל לא ידענא פשיעותא היא חייביה לשלומי לא שילם ידר רב נחמן לנכסיו ושם לאפדני ויהביה לבעל הפקדון בדמי דהנהו כיפי דפשע בהו. פי' אפדנא חצר. לסוף אישתכח כיפי ואוקירו בדמיהן. מריה דכיפי אמר הב לי כיפאי וטול אפדנך והלה אומר לא כי אלא מעידנא דשקלית לאפדנאי זבינא אנא בכיפי וברשותי אוקיר ודן ר' נחמן כיון דהא שומא דשמו ליה לאפדנא שומא בטעות הואי דהא הוו כיפי ולא אבדו וקיימא לן פקדון כל היכא דאיתיה ברשותיה דמריה קאי לאו שומא הוא הדרא אפדנא למריה והדרי כיפי למרייהו. ואסיק' שומא הדרא לעולם משום שנאמר ועשית הישר והטוב והני מילי אם מכרה לאחר או נתנה במתנה או הורישה לא הדרא. וכן אם שמו לו ב"ד שדה לאשה במלוה שהיא נושה לאחרים וניסת והכניסה שדה זו לבעלים או שמו שדה אשה לנושה שלה וניסת ולא מהדרינן ליה לבעל ולא מהדרינן מיניה דבעל דכזביני דמי וקיימא לן בעל בנכסי אשתו לוקח הוי לא מהדר ולא מהדרינן ליה דאמר ר' יוסי בר' חנינא באושא התקינו האשה שמכרה בנכסי מלוג בחיי בעלה ומתה הבעל מוציא מיד הלקוחות. אגביה

חשק שלמה על ר"ח א) נראה דחסר כאן וה"ל ופריך רב אשי זה נשבע שאינו ברשותו והלה נשבע כמה היה שוה וכו'.

**אִיתָא לְדְרַב הוּנָא — Rav Huna's** ruling **is true,** why were the Rabbis concerned that the lender might produce the collateral after the borrower swears about its value? Since the lender is a *shomer* on the collateral,[1] he will have to swear that the deposit is no longer in his possession, **כֵּיוָן דְּמִשְׁתַּבַּע מַלְוֶה שֶׁאֵינָהּ בִּרְשׁוּתוֹ — and once he swears that [the collateral] is not in his possession, הֵיכִי מָצֵי מַפִּיק לָהּ — how can he** later **produce it?** Hence, Rav Huna's oath alone would suffice to prevent the lender from discrediting the borrower.[2]

The Gemara proposes that the Mishnah's ruling (that the oath is transferred from the borrower to the lender) applies only in a specific case:

**אָמַר רָבָא — Rava**[3] **said: שֶׁיֵּשׁ עֵדִים שֶׁנִּשְׂרְפָה** — The borrower's oath is transferred to the lender only **when there are witnesses that** the collateral **was destroyed by fire.**[4] In such a case, there is no need for the lender to swear that the collateral is not in his possession, since that point is established by the testimony of the witnesses. Therefore, the lender must swear as to the value of the collateral in order to ensure that the borrower will not later become disqualified.[5]

The Gemara rejects this explanation:

**אִי הָכִי — If it is so** that witnesses testified that the collateral was destroyed, **מֵהֵיכָא מַיְיתֵי לָהּ — from where does [the lender] bring [the collateral]** to show that it is worth less than the borrower swore?[6]

The Gemara therefore proposes that the Mishnah's ruling refers to a different case:

**אֶלָּא אָמַר רַב יוֹסֵף — Rather, Rav Yosef said: שֶׁיֵּשׁ עֵדִים שֶׁנִּגְנְבָה** — The borrower's oath is transferred to the lender only **when there are witnesses that** the collateral **was stolen.** In this case as well the lender does not need to swear that the collateral is not in his possession, since witnesses establish that point. Therefore, he must swear about the value of the collateral; since the collateral is still in existence, he may eventually produce it and refute the borrower.

The Gemara challenges this explanation as well:

**סוֹף סוֹף — Be that as it may,**[7] **מֵהֵיכָא מַיְיתֵי לָהּ — from where will** the lender **bring it** to show in court? The collateral has been removed from his possession, and he does not know its whereabouts!

The Gemara answers:

**דְּטָרַח וּמַיְיתֵי לָהּ — [The lender] will trouble** himself to discover who had entered his home, and he will eventually find the thief **and bring [the collateral].**

The Gemara asks:

**אִי הָכִי — If it is so** that we allow for the possibility that stolen collateral will be recovered, **כִּי מִשְׁתַּבַּע מַלְוֶה** — even **when the lender swears, נַמִּי לִטְרַח לוֶֹה וְלַיְתֵי — the borrower may also** do the same thing: he **will trouble** himself to find the thief **and bring** the collateral and show that the *lender* was lying about its value! Although the borrower's eligibility has been preserved by shifting the burden of swearing from him to the lender, the lender's eligibility has now been jeopardized. — ? —

The Gemara explains that such a development is unlikely:

**בִּשְׁלָמָא מַלְוֶה — It is appropriate** to fear that **the lender** will find the thief, **יָדַע מַאן קָא עַיֵּיל וְנָפַק בְּבֵיתֵיהּ** — because **he knows** generally **who enters and exits his house,**[8] **וְאָזִיל וְטָרַח וּמַיְיתֵי לָהּ — and he will go and trouble** himself to find the person who stole the collateral **and** eventually **bring it** to court. **אֶלָּא לוֶֹה — However, the borrower** certainly will not find the thief, **מִי יָדַע מַאן עַיֵּיל וְנָפִיק בְּבֵיתֵיהּ דְּמַלְוֶה — for does he know who enters and exits the lender's house?**

The Gemara now proposes another answer, according to which the Mishnah's last statement (transferring the oath about the value of the collateral from the borrower to the lender) applies in all cases:[9]

**אַבַּיֵּי אוֹמֵר — Abaye says: גְּזֵירָה** — The Rabbis transferred the oath from the borrower to the lender by **decree, שֶׁמָּא יִטְעוֹן וְיֹאמַר לוֹ** — because of **the possibility that [the lender] will claim and say to [the borrower]: אַחַר שְׁבוּעָה מְצָאתִיהָ — "I found [the collateral] after** I took **the oath** that it was not in my possession."[10]

The Gemara now proposes another answer, according to which the Mishnah actually means that the *borrower* swears about the value of the collateral:

**רַב אַשִׁי אָמַר — Rav Ashi said: זֶה נִשְׁבָּע וְזֶה נִשְׁבָּע** — What the Mishnah means when it says that the lender swears is that both **this one** (the lender) **must swear and this one** (the borrower) **must swear. זֶה נִשְׁבָּע שֶׁאֵינָהּ בִּרְשׁוּתוֹ — [The lender] must swear that [the collateral] is not in his possession, וְזֶה נִשְׁבָּע כַּמָּה הָיָה שָׁוֶה — and [the borrower] must swear how much it was worth. וְהָכִי קָאָמַר — And** the Mishnah **is** actually **saying thus: מִי נִשְׁבָּע תְּחִילָּה — Who swears** ***first?*** **מַלְוֶה נִשְׁבָּע תְּחִילָּה — The lender swears first** that the collateral is not in his possession. **שֶׁמָּא יִשָּׁבַע זֶה** — For otherwise **PERHAPS THIS ONE** (the borrower) **WILL SWEAR** how much the collateral was worth, **וְיוֹצִיא הַלָּה אֶת הַפִּקָּדוֹן — AND THAT ONE** (the lender) **WILL** then **PRODUCE**

NOTES

1. As we learned above (34b note 20), the lender is considered a paid *shomer* on the collateral. Thus, even when he pays the borrower for what the lost collateral was worth, he must swear, according to Rav Huna, that it is not in his possession (*Rashi*).

2. Thus, from the fact that the Rabbis felt it necessary to transfer the oath from the borrower to the lender, we see that they did *not* accept Rav Huna's rule that a *shomer* who pays for a lost deposit must swear that it is no longer in his possession.

3. *Mesoras HaShas* emends this to read "Rabbah" [since Rava's opinion is customarily stated after Abaye's, which is cited below]. See also *Hagahos HaBach*.

4. I.e. witnesses testify that an article fitting the borrower's description of the collateral was consumed by fire (*Ritva*). [If they testify with certainty that the collateral was destroyed, then surely the lender need not swear, since he cannot possibly produce the collateral at a later date (see next note).]

5. We are concerned that the destroyed article was not actually the collateral, but something that looked like it, and that the lender may someday produce the collateral. To prevent this, the Rabbis transferred the borrower's oath (for admitting part of the claim) to the lender (*Ritva*). [Nevertheless, the fact that the witnesses testified that it looked like the collateral is enough to exempt the lender from swearing Rav Huna's oath that the deposit is no longer in his possession.]

6. The Gemara now insists that the lender should not be required to swear at all. Since we rely on the testimony of the witnesses to exempt the lender from swearing Rav Huna's oath (that the collateral is not in his possession), we should also rely on it to assure us that he will not later produce the collateral and refute the borrower. Thus, there is no reason to transfer the borrower's oath to the lender (*Ritva*).

7. I.e. despite the fact that the collateral has not been destroyed.

8. He therefore has a better idea of who may have stolen the item from him.

9. I.e. even in cases when the lender must swear that the collateral is no longer in his possession.

10. According to Abaye, the lender is not suspected of having sworn falsely; rather, we are concerned that even though he searched for the collateral before swearing that it was not in his possession, he may afterward find it and bring it to court (*Tos. HaRosh*; see *Chasam Sofer* for a more novel interpretation).

ON [COLLATERAL], שֶׁקֶל הָיָה שָׁוֶה – but IT WAS WORTH only A *SHEKEL*, and you therefore owe me one *shekel* (two *dinars*)"; וְהַלָּה אוֹמֵר – AND THAT borrower RESPONDS, לֹא כִּי – "NOT SO; אֶלָּא סֶלַע הִלְוִיתָנִי עָלָיו – RATHER, YOU LENT ME A *SELA* ON [COLLATERAL], שְׁלֹשָׁה דִּינָרִין הָיָה שָׁוֶה – and IT WAS WORTH THREE *DINARS*, and I owe you only one *dinar*"; חַיָּיב – in such a case HE (the borrower) should be OBLIGATED to swear that the collateral was worth three *dinars*, דִּשְׁבוּעָה גַּבֵּי לֹוֶה הוּא – for by rights **the oath falls on the borrower,** since he admits to part of the lender's claim. וְאָמוּר רַבָּנָן – **But the Rabbis said:** לִשְׁתַּבַּע מַלְוֶה – **Let the lender swear** that the collateral was worth only a *shekel*, and then collect the *shekel* that he claims th borrower still owes him;[30] מָא יִשָּׁבַע זֶה וְיוֹצִיא הַלָּה אֶת הַפִּקָּדוֹן – otherwise, PERHAPS THIS borrower WILL SWEAR to support h claim, AND THAT lender WILL afterward PRODUCE THE DEPOS (i.e. the collateral) and show that it was not worth what th borrower said, and thereby disqualify him from ever giving test mony or swearing.

The Gemara now explains the challenge from this Mishnah t Rav Huna's ruling that we make a *shomer* who pays for a depos swear that he does not still have it in his possession:

וְאִם – **And if**

NOTES

30. Although the borrower is the one who should swear, the Rabbis did not want him to do so since this might jeopardize his eligibility to bear witness and take other oaths. Nevertheless, since he is Biblically obligated to swear (having admitted partial liability), it is impossible to exempt him from paying the rest of the claim without an oath. Hence, the Rabbis transferred the obligation to swear from the borrower tc the lender, whose eligibility would not be jeopardized by his swearing (*Rashi*). [The lender will not become disqualified as a result of this oath since if he is lying about its value, he will never produce the collateral ir court to show that he lied.]

וחזר ואמר איני משלם מאי מי אמרינן מהדר קא הדר ביה או דלמא במלתיה קאי ודחויי הוא דקא מדחי ליה אמר הריני משלם ומת ואמרו בניו אין אנו משלמין מאי מי אמרינן מהדר קא הדרי בהו או דלמא במלתא דאבוהון קיימי ודחויי הוא דקא מדחו ליה שלמו בנים מאי מצי אמר להו כי אקנאי כפילא לאבוכון דעבד לי נייח נפשאי לדידכו לא או דלמא לא שנא שילם לבנים מאי מצו אמרי ליה כי אקני לך [א] אבונא כפילא דעבדת ליה נייח נפשיה אבל אנן לדידן לא או דלמא לא שנא שלמו בנים לבנים מאי שילם מחצה מאי שאל שתי פרות ושילם אחת מהן מאי שאל מן השותפין ושילם לאחד מהן מאי שותפין ששאלו ושילם אחד מהן מאי שאל מן האשה ושילם לבעלה מאי אשה ששאלה ושילם בעלה מאי תיקו [ב] אמר רב הונא משביעין אותו שבועה שאינה ברשותו מאי טעמא חיישינן שמא עיניו נתן בה מיתיבי [ג] המלוה את חבירו על המשכון ואבד המשכון ואמר לו סלע הלויתיך עליו שקל היה שוה והלה אומר לא כי אלא סלע הלויתני עליו סלע היה שוה פטור [ד] סלע הלויתיך עליו שקל היה שוה והלה אומר לא כי אלא סלע הלויתני עליו שלשה דינרים היה שוה חייב סלע הלויתני עליו ב' היה שוה והלה אומר לא כי אלא סלע הלויתיך עליו סלע היה שוה פטור סלע הלויתני עליו שנים היה שוה והלה אומר לא כי אלא סלע הלויתיך עליו ה' דינרים היה שוה חייב מי נשבע מי שהפקדון אצלו שמא ישבע זה ויוציא הלה את הפקדון [ד] אהייא אילימא אסיפא ותיפוק ליה דשבועה גבי מלוה היא דהא קא מודי מקצת הטענה אלא אמר שמואל ארישא מאי ארישא אסיפא דרישא סלע הלויתיך עליו שקל היה שוה והלה אומר לא כי אלא סלע הלויתני עליו שלשה דינרין היה שוה חייב דשבועה גבי לוה הוא ואמור רבנן לשתבע מלוה שמא ישבע זה ויוציא הלה את הפקדון ואם איתא

ואמרו בנים אין אנו משלמין. (א) לא הספיק לשלם עד שמת: שלמו בנים. והאב לא הספיק לומר הריני משלם עד שמת: דעבד לי נייח נפשאי. פעמים רבות עשה לי קורת רוח: שילם לבנים. מתו הבעלים ונגנבה ואמר השומר לבנים הריני משלם או שילם מהו: שלמו בנים לבנים מהו. דליכא שום נייחא נפשא באלו שהם קיימים שלא הם ולא אביהם עשו קורת רוח לאלו ולא אביהם של אלו קיבל קורת רוח מבני השומר: או דלמא. כיון שאביהם הראשונים הוה להו נייחא נפשא בהדדי קנו כפילא אף בנים מן הבנים: שילם מחצה. מתחילתו אמר הריני משלם מחצה ולא יותר: מהו. לקנות חצי הכפל: שאל שתי פרות. אם תימצי לומר לא קני מחצה שאל שתי פרות ונגנבו ואמר הריני משלם אחת ולא אמר מתה מחמת מלאכה: מהו. לקנות כפל שלה מי אמרינן כיון דפרה שלימה שילם קנה או דלמא כיון דתרוייהו חד פקדון הוו ואינו משלם את שתיהם לא אקני ליה כפילא שהרי הוא נפסד על ידו: ושילם לאחד מהם. חלקו חצי דמיה שעליו מהו לקנות חלקו המגיעו מי אמרינן כל הקרן שלו שילם או דלמא בעינן עד שישלם כל הפרה: ושילם אחד מהם. חצי דמיו שעליו: מהו. שיקנה חצי הכפל מי אמרינן הרי שילם כל המוטל עליו: שאל מן האשה. פרה של נכסי מלוג שהקרן שלה והפירות לבעל: ושילם. הפרה לבעל: מהו. לקנות הכפל מי אמרי' כיון דקרן לאו דבעל הוא לאו תשלומין מעליא נינהו ולא קני כפילא או דלמא כיון דאפוטרופוס הוא על הנכסים ואוכל הפירות בעלים הוי עלייהו ותשלומין הן: אשה ששאלה. לצורך קרקע מלוג שלה: משביעין אותו. אמתני' קאי אע"פ שהוא משלם כדקתני שילם ולא רצה לישבע משביעין אותו שבועה שאינה ברשותו: שקל. חצי סלע: פטור. הלוה מן השבועה שאין כאן הודאה במקצת: חייב. לישבע שכך היה שוה ומשלם לו דינר שהודה לו: ושתים היה שוה. והלוה תובע את המלוה את יתר דמיו וקא סבר האי תנא המלוה על המשכון שומר שכר הוא: פטור. מן השבועה שאין כאן הודאה שחייב לו כלום: ויוציא הלה כו'. ויפסלנו: אהייא. קאי מי נשבע דקתני בה: אילימא אסיפא. אחיוב דסיפא: תיפוק ליה כו'. ולמה ליה למתלי טעמא בשמא יוציא הפקדון ויפסלנו לעדות ולשבועה: מאי ארישא. הא רישא פטור קתני: אסיפא דרישא. אחיוב דקתני ברישא קאי: לשתבע מלוה. שלא היתה שוה אלא שקל ויטול שקל דכיון דאיכא שבועה על הלוה מן התורה אי אתה יכול לפוטרו בולא כלום ומשום תיקון עולם שלא יפסל ישראל שקלוה לשבועה מיניה ושדיוה אמלוה: ואם איתא

וחזר ואמר איני משלם [מאי] מי אמרינן מהדר קהדר ביה. מכאן מוכיח ר"ת דאם אמר לחבירו השבע וטול קודם שנשבע יכול לחזור בו ולומר אשבע ולא אשלם ובפרק יש נוחלין (ב"ב דף קכח. ושם) דאמר עבדי גנבת והלה אומר אתה מכרתו לי רצונך השבע וטול ונשבע אינו יכול לחזור בו לא גרס נשבע בלא וא"ו דמשמע שבע"כ ישבע וברים שבועת הדיינים (שבועות דף לט. ושם ד"ה אם) דאמר אם אמר איני נשבע פוטרין אותו מיד לא כפרש"י שפוטרין אותו לפי שאינו יכול לחזור בו אלא יש לומר מסלקין אותו מב"ד כדי שיתבייש לחזור ולומר אשבע מיהו שוב פירש ר"ת בתשובה אחת דשפיר גרסינן נשבע בלא וא"ו וישבע בע"כ והא דאמרינן בפרק זה בורר (סנהדרין דף כד. ושם: ד"ה שלא) גבי נאמן עלי אבא ואביך מחלוקת לאחר גמר דין אבל קודם גמר דין דברי הכל יכול לחזור בו הכא אפילו קודם שנשבע אינו יכול לחזור בו דכיון שקבל עליו לשלם אם ישבע זה שכנגדו הוי כמו לאחר גמר דין והכא דקאמר מהדר קהדר ביה לא שיוכל לחזור אלא רוצה הוא לחזור אף על פי שאינו יכול ולא מקני ליה כפילא משום דאטרחיה לב"ד כדאמר בסמוך גבי ההוא דאפקיד כיפי וכה"ג איכא בפ' יש נוחלין (ב"ב דף קלח.) מדאשתיק קנגהו וכשלוא לבסוף מהדר קהדר ביה פירוש רוצה לחזור ואינו יכול:

הריני משלם ומת כו'. תימה היאך ישלם לבני הנפקד כפל הא אין אדם מוריש קנס לבניו כדתנן בריש פרק נערה שנתפתתה [ה] (כתובות דף מא:):

שאל מן האשה. פי' רש"י פרה מנכסי מלוג שהקרן שלה ופירות לבעל וקשה דמאי קבעי דכי שאל פרה מן האשה כאילו שאל הפירות מן הבעל וכששילם הפרה לבעל כאילו שילם הקרן לאשה ויש ליישב ששילם לבעל חלקו כמו שהיתה שוה לפירותיה ולא שילם הקרן וגרע משילם לאחד משותפים חלקו דהתם שילם קרן ודוחק ויש לפרש שאל מן האשה כשהיתה פנויה שהיו שלה הקרן והפירות וניסת דהשתא שילם הפירות לבעל אפילו נתן הכל לאשה דכיון דניסת יש לו פירות כדין נכסי מלוג וכן אשה ששאלה כשהיא פנויה וניסת ושלמה דהשתא שילם הבעל דהוו הפירות שלו והריב"ן פי' שאל מן האשה ומתה ושילם לבעל מהו דאפילו אם תמצא לומר דשילם לבנים קנה כפילא משום ניחותא דאבוהון אבל בעל לא חיים לניחותא דאשה ולישנא דמעכשיו אשה אינה חסה על בעלה וכן אשה ששאלה ומתה ושילם בעל אפי' אם מפקיד מקני כפילא לבני נפקד משום דרחים להו משום אבוהון אבל לא מקני להו לבעל משום אשתו שמתה:

שמא יוציא הלה הפקדון. פירש רש"י ויפסלנו לעדות ולשבועה וקשה לר"ת דכל שכן שישבע הלוה שהוא ידקדק יותר לישבע באמת כדי שלא יפסלנו המלוה וכי עבדינן תקנה לרמאי וכי תימא דחיישינן שמא המשכון יתקלקל אחרי כן ויוציא עליו לעז אע"פ שנשבע באמת [ו] א"כ מאי פריך בסמוך כי משתבע מלוה נמי לטרח לוה ולייתי והשתא אי שוה יותר אם כן נשבע לשקר וכל שכן שיזהר בשבועתו ונראה לרבינו תם כפירוש רבינו חננאל דנראה כמו שבועה לבטלה וגנאי הוא לישבע היכא שהדבר מתברר אחרי כן שהמלוה יוציא את הפקדון אבל כי רמינן לה על המלוה לא ישבע עד שידע שלא יוכל למצאה וא"ת אמאי לא חשיב הא בפרק כל הנשבעין (שבועות דף מד: ושם ד"ה ואלו) עם הנשבעין ונוטלין דליכא למימר תנא ושייר דאלו קתני כלדייק בפ"ק דקידושין (דף טז: ושם) גבי אלו מעניקין להם ויש לומר דלא חשיב התם אלא אותם שאין יכולין לישבע כגון גזלן וחובל דניכרים הדברים כיון שנכנס שלם בביתו ונתקוטטו ויצא חבול שהוא חבלו וכן בחנוני אינו יכול לישבע בעה"ב שאינו יודע אם נתן חנוני לפועלים וכן שכיר שאין בעה"ב יכול לישבע לפי שהוא טרוד בפועליו ומהאי טעמא נמי במוציא הוצאות על נכסי אשתו אמרי' בפרק האשה שנפלו לה כו' (כתובות דף פ. ושם ד"ה ישבע) ישבע כמה הוציא ויטול דאין האשה יודעת כמה הוציא בעלה ולא חשיב לה פ' כל הנשבעים דהוי בכלל שכיר אבל הכא הלוה יכול לישבע דקים ליה טפי ממלוה אך שלא רצו חכמים גזירה שמא יוציא הלה כו': [וע"ע תוס' כתובות פ. ד"ה ישבע ועוד שם פז: ד"ה ואלו]



עין משפט
נר מצוה

ט א מיי' פ"ח מהל' שאלה הל' ה סמג עשין פח טוש"מ סי' רלה:
י ב מיי' פ"ו מהל' שאלה ופקדון הל' א סמג עשין פח טוש"ע ח"מ סי' רלה סעי' א וסי' שה סעי' א:
יא ג מיי' פי"ג מהל' מלוה ולוה הל' ד סמג עשין לד טוש"ע ח"מ סי' עב סעי' ע:
יב ד מיי' שם טוש"ע שם סעי' י:

רבינו חננאל

כפילא דידיה היא ודלא כר' יוסי דאמר כיצד הלה עושה סחורה וכו'. שלמו בני שואל למשאיל או א) לבני המשאיל או שילם מחצה ולא הספיק להשלים הנשאר עד שנמצא הגנב או שאל מאשה ושילם לבעלה או שאלה האשה ושילם בעלה או שאל משני שותפין ושילם לאחד מהן או שאלו שני שותפין ושילם אחד מהן אלו כולן עלו בתיקו. וקיימא לן ממון המוטל בספק חולקין. אמר רב הונא ומשביעין. פי' אע"פ שמשלם אמר רב הונא משביעין אותו שבועה שאינה ברשותו חיישינן שמא עיניו נתן בה ותלמוד ארץ ישראל מסייע דגרסינן לא סוף דבר שילם אלא כיון דאמר הריני משלם חוששין ב) שמא שלא שלח בה יד. אמר הריני נשבע וראה שמגלגלין עליו שבועות אחרות חזר ואמר הריני משלם חוששין. אמר ר' יוסי לא חייבתו התורה להחמיר עליו אלא להקל עליו שאם רצה לשלם ישלם ואם אינו רוצה לשלם ישבע. היו [לו] עדים שנגנבה באונס הדה היא דאמר ר' אלעזר המוכר קנסיו לאחר לא עשה כלום. ואותבינן אהא דרב הונא הא דתנן המלוה את חבירו על המשכון ואבד ואמר לו סלע הלויתיך ושקל היה שוה והלה אומר לא כי אלא סלע הלויתני עליו וסלע היה שוה פטור וכו' פי' הסלע הוא ד' דינרין והשקל הוא שני דינרין חצי סלע ג) כשאבד המשכון וטוען המלוה כי הלויתיך עליו ד' דינרין והיה שוה שני דינר הריני מחשב על ב' דינרין דמי המשכון שאבד מפני שאמרו חכמים כשומר שכר אני שמשלם הגניבה והאבידה עכשיו חייב אתה לתת לי ב' דינר תשלום הסלע והלה אומר לא כי אלא ד' דינרין הלויתני וד' היה שוה המשכון ולא נשאר לך כלום פטור הלוה משבועה דאורייתא שהרי לא הודה לו במקצת מן התביעה אבל אם [טען] הלוה סלע הלויתני וג' דינרין היה שוה המשכון ונשאר לך עלי דינר והמלוה אמר לא היה שוה המשכון אלא ב' דינר ונשארו לי עליך ב' דינר כיון שהודה בדינר חייב לשלם (על) הדינר וישבע על הדינר האחר שבועה דאורייתא ותנן בהדא מתני' מי נשבע מי שהפקדון אצלו שמא ישבע זה ויוציא הלה את הפקדון ואינו שוה ג' דינ' כמו שנשבע ונמצא הלה חשוד על השבועה. וקשיא

מסורת הש"ס

א) גירסת מהרש"ל כפילא אבונא, ב) לעיל ה:, ג) שבועות מג., ד) [שם ע"ב, ע"ש], ה) [ועיין תוספות בבא קמא עב. ד"ה סיפא כו'], ו) נ"ל מכל מקום, מהרש"א.

הגהות הב"ח

(א) רש"י ד"ה ואמרו וכו' משלמים והאב לא הספיק:

ליקוטי רש"י

שמא עיניו נתן בה. ורוצה לקנותה בדמים [שבועות מג: בד"ה והשתא]. מי נשבע. כמה היתה שוה. מי שהפקדון אצלו. המלוה ובגמרא מפרש אהייא קאי. ויוציא הלה את הפקדון. ושמא לא דקדק זה בשומא ויפסלנו לעדות ולשבועה [שם ע"א].

חשק שלמה על ר"ח א) או ששילם השואל לבני המשאיל או ששלמו בני השואל לבני המשאיל. ב) בירושלמי לפנינו הגי' אלא כיון דאמר הריני משלם כמי ששילם. אמר משלם אני חוששין שמא שלח בו יד וכו' וכצ"ל גם כאן. ג) וכשאבד המשכון טוען המלוה וכו'.

חֲבֵירוֹ עַל הַמַּשְׁכּוֹן – IF SOMEONE LENT HIS FELLOW money ON COLLATERAL[19] וְאָבַד הַמַּשְׁכּוֹן – AND THE COLLATERAL WAS LOST;[20] וְאָמַר לוֹ סֶלַע הִלְוִיתִיךָ עָלָיו – later, when the lender asked for the loan to be repaid, HE SAID TO [THE BORROWER], "I LENT YOU A *SELA* ON [COLLATERAL], שֶׁקֶל הָיָה שָׁוֶה – and [THE COLLATERAL] WAS WORTH only A *SHEKEL* (a coin worth half a *sela*) and you therefore owe me one *shekel*";[21] וְהַלָּה אוֹמֵר – AND THAT ONE (the borrower) RESPONDS, לֹא כִּי – "NOT SO; אֶלָּא סֶלַע הִלְוִיתַנִי עָלָיו – RATHER, YOU LENT ME A *SELA* ON [COLLATERAL], סֶלַע הָיָה שָׁוֶה – and [THE COLLATERAL] WAS WORTH A *SELA*, and so I owe you nothing"; פָּטוּר – in such a case [THE BORROWER] IS EXEMPT from swearing an oath that his claim is true, since he does not admit to owing anything.[22]

The Mishnah continues:

סֶלַע הִלְוִיתִיךָ עָלָיו – However, if the lender said to him, "I LENT YOU A *SELA* ON [COLLATERAL], שֶׁקֶל הָיָה שָׁוֶה – and IT WAS WORTH only A *SHEKEL* (half a *sela*), and you therefore owe me a *shekel*"; וְהַלָּה אוֹמֵר – AND THAT ONE (the borrower) RESPONDS, לֹא כִּי – "NOT SO; אֶלָּא סֶלַע הִלְוִיתַנִי עָלָיו – RATHER, YOU LENT ME A *SELA* ON [COLLATERAL], שְׁלֹשָׁה דִּינָרִים הָיָה שָׁוֶה – and [THE COLLATERAL] WAS WORTH THREE *DINARS*, and I owe you only one *dinar*";[23] חַיָּיב – HE IS OBLIGATED to swear that the collateral was worth three *dinars*,[24] and the borrower then pays only the one *dinar* he admits owing.

In the previous two cases the issue was whether the collateral was worth *less* than the loan. In the next two cases the issue is whether the collateral was worth *more* than the loan.

The Mishnah's third case:

סֶלַע הִלְוִיתַנִי עָלָיו – If the borrower claims, "YOU LENT ME A *SELA* ON [COLLATERAL], שְׁנַיִם הָיָה שָׁוֶה – but IT WAS WORTH TWO *SELAS*, and you (the lender) therefore owe me one *sela*";[25] וְהַלָּה אוֹמֵר – AND THAT ONE (the lender) SAYS, לֹא כִּי – "NOT SO; אֶלָּא סֶלַע הִלְוִיתִיךָ עָלָיו – RATHER, I LENT YOU A *SELA* ON [COLLATERAL], סֶלַע הָיָה שָׁוֶה – and IT WAS WORTH only A *SELA*, and I owe you nothing"; פָּטוּר – in such a case [THE LENDER] IS EXEMPT from taking an oath, for there is no admission of partial liability.

The fourth and final case:

סֶלַע הִלְוִיתַנִי עָלָיו – If the borrower claims, "YOU LENT ME A *SELA* ON [COLLATERAL], שְׁנַיִם הָיָה שָׁוֶה – but IT WAS WORTH TWO *selas*, and you therefore owe me one *sela*"; וְהַלָּה אוֹמֵר – AND THAT ONE (the lender) SAYS, לֹא כִּי – "NOT SO; אֶלָּא סֶלַע הִלְוִיתִיךָ עָלָיו – RATHER, I LENT YOU A *SELA* ON [COLLATERAL], חָמֵשׁ דִּינָרִים הָיָה שָׁוֶה – and IT WAS WORTH FIVE *DINARS*, and I owe you only one *dinar*"; חַיָּיב – in such a case [THE LENDER IS] OBLIGATED to swear that the collateral was worth only five *dinars*,[26] and he then pays only the *dinar* that he admits owing.

The Mishnah concludes:

מִי נִשְׁבָּע – WHO SWEARS as to the value of the collateral? מִי שֶׁהַפִּקָּדוֹן אֶצְלוֹ – THE ONE IN WHOSE POSSESSION THE DEPOSIT WAS IN prior to the loss, i.e. the lender. שֶׁמָּא יִשָּׁבַע זֶה – For if we were to do otherwise, PERHAPS THIS ONE (the borrower) WILL SWEAR to support his claim, וְיוֹצִיא הַלָּה אֶת הַפִּקָּדוֹן – AND THAT ONE (the lender) WILL afterward PRODUCE THE DEPOSIT (i.e. the collateral) and show that it was not as the borrower said, and thereby disqualify him from ever again swearing or testifying in court.[27]

The Gemara analyzes this last statement:

אַהֵייא – **On which** of the four cases does the Mishnah now rule? אִילֵימָא אַסֵּיפָא – **If we say** that it rules **on the end** of the Mishnah (i.e. the fourth case, where the lender admits the collateral was worth more than the loan but not as much as the borrower says),[28] וְתִיפּוֹק לֵיהּ דִּשְׁבוּעָה גַּבֵּי מַלְוֶה הִיא – **let [the Tanna] base** his ruling that the lender is the one who swears on the fact **that the oath** by rights **falls on the lender,** דְּהָא קָא מוֹדֵי מִקְצָת הַטַּעֲנָה – **for** the reason that **he admits to part of the** borrower's **claim!**[29] Why should the Tanna explain that the Sages require the lender to swear in order that he not disqualify the borrower from testifying and swearing?

The Gemara thus concludes:

אֶלָּא אָמַר שְׁמוּאֵל – **Rather, Shmuel said:** אַרֵישָׁא – The last statement of the Mishnah rules **on the beginning** of the Mishnah (where the borrower is being asked to pay the lender).

The Gemara asks:

מַאי אַרֵישָׁא – **What** did Shmuel mean when he said that the Mishnah's last statement goes **on the beginning** of the Mishnah? In the first case of the Mishnah no one is obligated to swear!

The Gemara explains:

אַסֵּיפָא דְּרֵישָׁא – He meant that it goes **on the end** (i.e. the second case) **of the "beginning"** of the Mishnah, which states: סֶלַע הִלְוִיתִיךָ עָלָיו – If the lender claims, "I LENT YOU A *SELA*

NOTES

19. Collateral is an object of value that a borrower gives a lender to hold as security, so that if he cannot repay the loan, the lender will be able to collect from the object he is holding as collateral.

20. The Tanna of this Mishnah is of the opinion that a lender holding collateral on a loan is considered a paid *shomer* for it, and he is therefore responsible for its loss (*Rashi* below ד״ה ושתים היה שוה). This is the subject of a dispute, which the Gemara cites below, 80b.

21. Since the lender is responsible for the loss of the collateral, he must subtract its value from the amount of the loan. Since a *sela* is worth two *shekels*, and the collateral was worth one *shekel*, the lender claims that he is still owed one *shekel*.

22. Someone who is sued for money and admits to part of the claim is required by the Torah to swear that he does not owe the rest of it; if he refuses, he must pay the full claim. This is known as שְׁבוּעַת מוֹדֶה בְּמִקְצָת, *the oath of one who admits to part [of a claim]* (see above, 3a with note 23). In this case, however, the borrower does not admit to owing anything and he is therefore exempt from swearing an oath.

23. There are four *dinars* in a *sela*. Thus, the borrower, by saying that the collateral was worth three *dinars*, is admitting that he still owes the lender one *dinar*, half of what the lender claims.

24. The Mishnah will explain below who must swear.

25. Since the lender is liable for loss of the collateral (see above, note 20), if it is worth more than the loan he must pay the borrower the amount that was in excess of the loan (see *Rashi*).

26. Since the borrower claims he is owed a *sela* (four *dinars*) and the lender admits he owes one *dinar*, the lender has admitted part of the borrower's claim and he must therefore swear that he does not owe the rest of the claim.

27. *Rashi*. [A person who swears falsely cannot be believed again with an oath. He is also disqualified from offering testimony (*Sanhedrin* 27a).]

Others explain the point to be that since the question of the collateral's worth can be resolved by producing the collateral, even if the borrower swears truthfully, if the collateral is eventually found his oath will look like a שְׁבוּעַת שָׁוְא, *vain oath*, which will be embarrassing to him. [A "vain oath" is an oath about something that is either obviously true or obviously false. Such an oath is forbidden (see Mishnah, *Shevuos* 29a).] To avoid this, the Mishnah requires the lender to take the oath, for he will not do so until he is certain that the collateral cannot be found (*Rabbeinu Chananel;* see also *Tosafos, Ritva*).

28. [The Gemara calls the first two cases of the Mishnah, in which the lender claims that the borrower still owes him money, the "beginning" of the Mishnah. The final two cases, in which the borrower claims that the lender owes him, are called the "end" of the Mishnah.] The Gemara here intends specifically to the second case of the "end," where the lender must swear that the collateral was worth only five *dinars* (*Rashi*).

29. Since the lender admits to part of the borrower's claim, he is Biblically obligated to swear (see above, note 22). It is unnecessary for the Mishnah to give another reason!

וחזר ואמר איני משלם מאי מי אמרינן מהדר קא הדר ביה או דלמא במלתיה קאי ודחויי הוא דקא מדחי ליה אמר הריני משלם ומת ואמרו בניו אין אנו משלמין מאי מי אמרינן מהדר קא הדרי בהו או דלמא במלתא דאבוהון קיימי ודחויי הוא דקא מדחו ליה שלמו בנים מאי מצי אמר להו כי אקנאי כפילא לאבוכון דעבד לי נייח נפשאי לדידכו לא או דלמא לא שנא שילם לבנים מאי מצו אמרי ליה כי אקני לך א) אבונא כפילא דעבדת ליה נייח נפשיה אבל אנן לדידן לא או דלמא לא שנא שלמו בנים לבנים מאי שילם מחצה מאי שאל שתי פרות ושילם אחת מהן מאי שאל מן השותפין ושילם לאחד מהן מאי שותפין ששאלו ושילם אחד מהן מאי שאל מן האשה ושילם לבעלה מאי אשה ששאלה ושילם בעלה מאי א תיקו ב) אמר רב הונא ב משביעין אותו שבועה שאינה ברשותו מאי טעמא חיישינן שמא עיניו נתן בה מיתיבי ג) ג המלוה את חבירו על המשכון ואבד המשכון ואמר לו סלע הלויתיך עליו שקל היה שוה והלה אומר לא כי אלא סלע הלויתני עליו סלע היה שוה פטור ד סלע הלויתיך עליו שקל היה שוה והלה אומר לא כי אלא סלע הלויתני עליו שלשה דינרים היה שוה חייב סלע הלויתני עליו ב' היה שוה והלה אומר לא כי אלא סלע הלויתיך עליו סלע היה שוה פטור סלע הלויתני עליו שנים היה שוה והלה אומר לא כי אלא סלע הלויתיך עליו ה' דינרים היה שוה חייב מי נשבע מי שהפקדון אצלו שמא ישבע זה ויוציא הלה את הפקדון ד) אהייא אילימא אסיפא ותיפוק ליה דשבועה גבי מלוה היא דהא קא מודי מקצת הטענה אלא אמר שמואל ארישא מאי ארישא אסיפא דרישא סלע הלויתיך עליו שקל היה שוה והלה אומר לא כי אלא סלע הלויתני עליו שלשה דינרין היה שוה חייב דשבועה גבי לוה הוא ואמור רבנן לשתבע מלוה שמא ישבע זה ויוציא הלה את הפקדון ואם
איתא

ואמרו בנים אין אנו משלמין. (א) לא הספיק לשלם עד שמת: שלמו בנים. והאב לא הספיק לומר הריני משלם עד שמת: דעבד לי נייח נפשאי. פעמים רבות עשה לי קורת רוח: שילם לבנים. מתו הבעלים ונגנבה ואמר השומר לבנים הריני משלם או שילם מהו: שלמו בנים לבנים מהו. דליכא שום לד נייחא נפשא באלו שהם קיימים שלא הם ולא אביהם עשו קורת רוח לאלו ולא אביהם של אלו קיבל קורת רוח מבני השומר: או דלמא. כיון שניהם הראשונים הוה להו נייחא נפשא בהדדי קנו כפילא אף בנים מן הבנים: שילם מחצה. מתחילתו אמר הריני משלם מחצה ולא יותר: מהו. לקנות חצי הכפל: שאל שתי פרות. אם תימצי לומר לא קני מחצה שאל שתי פרות ונגנבו ואמר הריני משלם אחת ולא אמר מתה מחמת מלאכה: מהו. לקנות כפל שלה מי אמרינן כיון דפרה שלימה שילם קנה או דלמא כיון דתרוייהו חד פקדון הוו ואינו משלם את שתיהם לא אקני ליה כפילא שהרי הוא נפסד על ידו: ושילם לאחד מהם. חלקו חצי דמיה שעליו מהו לקנות חלקו המגיעו מי אמרינן כל הקרן שלו שילם או דלמא בעינן עד שישלם כל הפרה: ושילם אחד מהם. חצי דמיו שעליו: מהו. שיקנה חצי הכפל מי אמרינן הרי שילם כל המוטל עליו: שאל מן האשה. פרה של נכסי מלוג שהקרן שלה והפירות לבעל: ושילם. הפרה לבעל: מהו. לקנות הכפל מי אמרי' כיון דקרן לאו דבעל הוא לאו תשלומין מעליא נינהו ולא קני כפילא או דלמא כיון דאפוטרופוס הוא על הנכסים ואוכל הפירות בעלים הוי עלייהו ותשלומין הן: אשה ששאלה. לצורך קרקע מלוג שלה: משביעין אותו. אמתני' קאי אע"פ שהוא משלם כדקתני שילם ולא רצה לישבע משביעין אותו שבועה שאינה ברשותו: שקל. חצי סלע: פטור. הלוה מן השבועה שאין כאן הודאה במקצת: חייב. לישבע שכך היה שוה ומשלם לו דינר שהודה לו: ושתים היה שוה. והלוה תובע את המלוה את יתר דמיו וקא סבר האי תנא המלוה על המשכון שומר שכר הוא: פטור. מן השבועה שאין כאן הודאה שחייב לו כלום: ויוציא הלה כו'. ויפסלנו: אהייא. קאי מי נשבע דקתני בה: אילימא אסיפא. אחיוב דסיפא: תיפוק ליה כו'. ולמה ליה למתלי טעמא דשמא יוציא הפקדון ויפסלנו לעדות ולשבועה: מאי ארישא. הא רישא פטור קתני: אסיפא דרישא. אחיוב דקתני ברישא קאי: לשתבע מלוה. שלא היתה שוה אלא שקל ויטול שקל דכיון דאיכא שבועה על הלוה מן התורה אי אתה יכול לפוטרו בולא כלום ומשום תיקון עולם שלא יפסל ישראל שקלוה לשבועה מיניה ושדיוה אמלוה: ואם
איתא

**וחזר** ואמר איני משלם [מאי] מי אמרינן מהדר קהדר ביה. מכאן מוכיח ר"ת דאם אמר לחברו השבע וטול קודם שנשבע יכול לחזור בו ולומר אשבע ולא אשלם ובפרק יש נוחלין (ב"ב דף קכח. ושם) דאמר עבדי גנבת והלה אומר אתה מכרתו לי רצונך השבע וטול ונשבע אינו יכול לחזור בו לא גרס נשבע בלא וא"ו דמשמע שבע"כ ישבע וכריש שבועת הדיינים (שבועות דף לט. ושם ד"ה אם) דאמר אם אמר איני נשבע פוטרין אותו מיד לא כפרש"י שפוטרין אותו לפי שאינו יכול לחזור בו אלא יש לומר מסלקין אותו מב"ד כדי שיתבייש לחזור ולומר אשבע מיהו שוב פירש ר"ת בתשובה אחת דשפיר גרסינן נשבע בלא וא"ו וישבע בע"כ והא דאמרינן בפרק זה בורר (סנהדרין דף כד. ושם: ד"ה שלא) גבי נאמן עלי אבא ואביך מחלוקת לאחר גמר דין אבל קודם גמר דין דברי הכל יכול לחזור בו הכא אפילו קודם שנשבע אינו יכול לחזור בו דכיון שקבל עליו לשלם אם ישבע זה שכנגדו הוי כמו לאחר גמר דין והכא דקאמר מהדר קהדר ביה לא שיוכל לחזור אלא רוצה הוא לחזור אף על פי שאינו יכול ולא מקני ליה כפילא משום דאטרחיה לב"ד כדאמר בסמוך גבי ההוא דאפקיד כיפי וכה"ג איכא בפ' יש נוחלין (ב"ב דף קלח.) מדאשתיק קנהו וכשצוח לבסוף מהדר קהדר ביה פירוש רוצה לחזור ואינו יכול:

**הריני** משלם ומת כו'. תימה היאך ישלם לבני הנפקד כפל הא אין אדם מוריש קנס לבניו כדתנן בריש פרק נערה שנתפתתה ה) (כתובות דף מא:):

**שאל** מן האשה. פי' רש"י פרה מנכסי מלוג שהקרן שלה ופירות לבעל וקשה דמאי קבעי דכי שאל פרה מן האשה כאילו שאל הפירות מן הבעל וכששילם הפרה לבעל כאילו שילם הקרן לאשה ויש ליישב ששילם לבעל חלקו כמו שהיתה שוה לפירותיה ולא שילם הקרן וגרע משילם לאחד משותפים חלקו דהתם שילם קרן ודוחק ויש לפרש שאל מן האשה כשהיתה פנויה שהיו שלה הקרן והפירות וניסת דהשתא שילם הפירות לבעל אפילו נתן הכל לאשה דכיון דניסת יש לו פירות כדין נכסי מלוג וכן אשה ששאלה כשהיא פנויה וניסת ושלמה דהשתא שילם הבעל דהוו הפירות שלו והריב"ן פי' שאל מן האשה ומתה ושילם לבעל מהו דאפילו אם תמצא לומר דשילם לבנים קנה כפילא משום ניחותא דאבוהון אבל בעל לא חיים לניחותא דאשה ולישנא דמעכשיו אשה אינה חסה על בעלה וכן אשה ששאלה ומתה ושילם בעל אפי' אם מפקיד מקני כפילא לבני נפקד משום דרחים להו משום אבוהון אבל לא מקני להו לבעל משום אשתו שמתה:

**שמא** יוציא הלה הפקדון. פירש רש"י ויפסלנו לעדות ולשבועה וקשה לר"ת דכל שכן שישבע הלוה שהוא ידקדק יותר לישבע באמת כדי שלא יפסלנו המלוה וכי עבדינן תקנה לרמאי וכי תימא דחיישינן שמא המשכון יתקלקל אחרי כן ויוציא עליו לעז אע"פ שנשבע באמת ו) א"כ מאי פריך בסמוך כי משתבע מלוה נמי לטרח לוה ולייתי והשתא אי שוה יותר אם כן נשבע לשקר וכל שכן שיזהר בשבועתו ונראה לרבינו תם כפירוש רבינו חננאל דנראה כמו שבועה לבטלה וגנאי הוא לישבע היכא שהדבר מתברר אחרי כן שהמלוה יוציא את הפקדון אבל כי רמינן לה על המלוה לא ישבע עד שידע שלא יוכל למצאה וא"ת אמאי לא חשיב הא בפרק כל הנשבעין (שבועות דף מד: ושם ד"ה ואלו) עם הנשבעין ונוטלין דליכא למימר תנא ושייר דאלו קתני כדדייק בפ"ק דקידושין (דף טז: ושם) גבי אלו מעניקין להם ויש לומר דלא חשיב התם אלא אותם שאין יכולין לישבע כגון גזלן וחובל דניכרים הדברים כיון שנכנס שלם בביתו ונתקוטטו ויצא חבול שהוא חבלו וכן בחנוני אינו יכול לישבע בעה"ב שאינו יודע אם נתן חנוני לפועלים וכן שכיר שאין בעה"ב יכול לישבע לפי שהוא טרוד בפועליו ומהאי טעמא נמי במוציא הוצאות על נכסי אשתו אמרי' בפרק האשה שנפלו לה כו' (כתובות דף פ. ושם ד"ה ישבע) ישבע כמה הוציא ויטול דאין האשה יודעת כמה הוציא בעלה ולא חשיב לה פ' כל הנשבעים דהוי בכלל שכיר אבל הכא הלוה יכול לישבע דקים ליה טפי ממלוה אך שלא רצו חכמים גזירה שמא יוציא הלה כו': [וע"ע תוס' כתובות פ. ד"ה ישבע ועוד שם פז: ד"ה ואלו]:
מגו

עין משפט
נר מצוה

ט א מיי' פ"ח מהל' שאלה הל' ה סמג עשין פח טוש"מ סי' רלה:
י ב מיי' פ"ו מהל' שאלה ופקדון הל' א סמג עשין פח טוש"ע ח"מ סי' רלה סעי' א וסי' שה סעי' א:
יא ג מיי' פי"ג מהל' מלוה ולוה הל' ד סמג עשין לד טוש"ע ח"מ סי' עב סעי' ע:
יב ד מיי' שם טוש"ע שם סעי' י:

רבינו חננאל

כפילא דידיה היא ודלא כר' יוסי דאמר כיצד הלה עושה סחורה וכו'. שלמו בני שואל למשאיל או א) לבני המשאיל או שילם מחצה ולא הספיק להשלים הנשאר עד שנמצא הגנב או שאל מאשה ושילם לבעלה או שאלה האשה ושילם בעלה או שאל משני שותפין ושילם לאחד מהן או שאלו שני שותפין ושילם אחד מהן אלו כולן עלו בתיקו. וקיימא לן ממון המוטל בספק חולקין. אמר רב הונא ומשביעין. פי' אע"פ שמשלם אמר רב הונא משביעין אותו שבועה שאינה ברשותו חיישינן שמא עיניו נתן בה ותלמוד ארץ ישראל מסייע דגרסינן לא סוף דבר שילם אלא כיון דאמר הריני משלם חוששין ב) שמא שלא שלח בה יד. אמר הריני נשבע וראה שמגלגלין עליו שבועות אחרות חזר ואמר הריני משלם חוששין. אמר ר' יוסי לא חייבתו התורה להחמיר עליו אלא להקל עליו שאם רצה לשלם ישלם ואם אינו רוצה לשלם ישבע. היו [לו] עדים שנגנבה באונס הדה היא דאמר ר' אלעזר המוכר קנסיו לאחר לא עשה כלום. ואותבינן אהא דרב הונא הא דתנן המלוה את חבירו על המשכון ואבד ואמר לו סלע הלויתיך ושקל היה שוה והלה אומר לא כי אלא סלע הלויתני עליו וסלע היה שוה פטור וכו' פי' הסלע הוא ד' דינרין והשקל הוא שני דינרין חצי סלע ג) כשאבד המשכון וטוען המלוה כי הלויתיך עליו ד' דינרין והיה שוה שני דינר הריני מחשב על ב' דינרין דמי המשכון שאבד מפני שאמרו חכמים כשומר שכר אני שמשלם הגניבה והאבידה עכשיו חייב אתה לתת לי ב' דינר תשלום הסלע והלה אומר לא כי אלא ד' דינרין הלויתני וד' היה שוה המשכון ולא נשאר לך כלום פטור הלוה משבועה דאורייתא שהרי לא הודה לו במקצת מן התביעה אבל אם [טען] הלוה סלע הלויתני וג' דינרין היה שוה המשכון ונשאר לך עלי דינר והמלוה אמר לא היה שוה המשכון אלא ב' דינר ונשארו לי עליך ב' דינר כיון שהודה בדינר חייב לשלם (על) הדינר וישבע על הדינר האחר שבועה דאורייתא ותנן בהדא מתני' מי נשבע מי שהפקדון אצלו שמא ישבע זה ויוציא הלה את הפקדון ואינו שוה ג' דינ' כמו שנשבע ונמצא הלה חשוד על השבועה.
וקשיא

מסורת הש"ס

א) גירסת מהרש"ל כפילא אבונא, ב) לעיל ה:, ג) שבועות מג., ד) [שם ע"ב, ע"ש], ה) [ועיין תוספות בבא קמא עב. ד"ה סיפא כו'], ו) נ"ל מכל מקום, מהרש"א.

הגהות הב"ח

(א) רש"י ד"ה ואמרו וכו' משלמים והאב לא הספיק:

ליקוטי רש"י

שמא עיניו נתן בה. ורוצה לקנותה בדמים [שבועות מג: בד"ה והשתא]. מי נשבע. כמה היתה שוה. מי שהפקדון אצלו. המלוה ובגמרא מפרש אהייא קאי. ויוציא הלה את הפקדון. ושמא לא דקדק זה בשומא ויפסלנו לעדות ולשבועה [שם ע"א].

חשק שלמה על ר"ח א) או ששילם השואל לבני המשאיל או שלמו בני השואל לבני המשאיל. ב) בירושלמי לפנינו הגי' אלא כיון דאמר הריני משלם כמי ששילם. אמר משלם אני חוששין שמא שלח בו יד וכו' וכצ"ל גם כאן. ג) וכשאבד המשכון טוען המלוה וכו'.

payment for that animal, whose loss he paid in full?[10] שָׁאַל מִן הַשּׁוּתָּפִין – If someone borrowed a cow from partners and it was stolen, וְשִׁילֵּם לְאֶחָד מֵהֶן – and [the borrower] paid one of them his share of the loss, מַאי – what is the law; does the borrower acquire that partner's share of the penalty payment?[11] שׁוּתָּפִין שֶׁשָּׁאֲלוּ – If partners borrowed a cow and it was stolen, וְשִׁילֵּם אֶחָד מֵהֶן – and one of them paid his share of the loss, מַאי – what is the law; does he acquire his share of the penalty payment?[12]

Two final questions:

שָׁאַל מִן הָאִשָּׁה – If someone borrowed an object of *melog* property from a woman[13] and it was stolen, וְשִׁילֵּם לְבַעְלָהּ – and [the borrower] paid her husband for the loss, מַאי – what is the law; does paying the husband, who does not own the property outright, entitle the borrower to the penalty payment?[14] אִשָּׁה שֶׁשָּׁאֲלָה – If a woman borrowed an object needed for her *melog* property and it was stolen, וְשִׁילֵּם בַּעְלָהּ – and her husband paid for its loss, מַאי – what is the law; does the woman acquire the penalty payment even though she did not herself pay the lender?[15]

The Gemara comments on all of these questions:

תֵּיקוּ – [The question] stands.[16] All of these issues remain undecided.[17]

The Mishnah implies that by paying the owner, a *shomer* avoids having to take the oaths of a *shomer* (see Chapter Introduction). The Gemara now teaches that he is not exempt from all the oaths even if he pays:

אָמַר רַב הוּנָא – Rav Huna said: מַשְׁבִּיעִין אוֹתוֹ שְׁבוּעָה – We make [the *shomer*] who agrees to pay swear an oath שֶׁאֵינָהּ בִּרְשׁוּתוֹ – that [the item] is not in his possession. מַאי טַעְמָא – What is the reason for this? חַיְישִׁינַן שֶׁמָּא עֵינָיו נָתַן בָּהּ – We are concerned that perhaps he set his eyes on [the object] and wishes to take it for himself and pay for it.[18]

Rav Huna's ruling is challenged from a long Mishnah in *Shevuos* (43a). The Gemara cites the entire Mishnah and explains it before returning to explain the challenge from it to Rav Huna's ruling:

מֵיתִיבֵי – They challenged this from a Mishnah: הַמַּלְוֶה אֶת

NOTES

because the Gemara concluded above (34a) that a borrower does not acquire the penalty payment unless he actually pays for the loss; agreeing to pay is not sufficient.]

10. Even if we conclude in the preceding case that the *shomer* does not acquire half of the penalty payment, this may be because the owner has not been paid completely for the one object he gave the *shomer*. However, where he gave him two animals and was paid in full for one of them, it is possible that the borrower acquires the penalty payment for that animal. Or, perhaps, since the two animals were given together as one loan, and the owner was paid for only part of it, the owner is not willing to transfer even part of the penalty payment, since he has suffered a loss on account of the borrower (*Rashi*).

11. Since he paid this one partner everything that is due him, this partner transfers his share of the penalty payment to the *shomer*. Or, perhaps the agreement to transfer the penalty payment was based on the *shomer* paying for the animal, which he has not done by paying one partner for his half of the animal (*Rashi*).

*Ritva* explains the second side of the question differently: Since they are really partners in each part of the animal, when the *shomer* pays one partner for half of the animal, half of *that* payment really belongs to the other partner. Thus, he has not really paid anyone his full share (see *Chidushei R' Akiva Eiger*).

12. Since he has completely paid his share of the obligation (*Rashi*).

[*Rashi* indicates that when two people jointly accept to be *shomrim* for an object and it is lost, each is obligated to pay for only half the loss. *Ramban* maintains, however, that each partner independently assumes responsibility for the object, so that if it is lost, each one is responsible for all of it. Alternatively, although each partner is obligated only for his share, each one also guarantees his partner's share. See *Ramban* for an explanation of the Gemara's question according to his view.]

13. When a woman marries and brings property into the marriage, her husband has control of the property during the marriage. This can be arranged in one of two ways: as נִכְסֵי מְלוֹג, *melog property,* or as נִכְסֵי צֹאן בַּרְזֶל, *tzon-barzel property*. In the *melog* arrangement, the husband has the right to use the property throughout the marriage and keep whatever it produces or earns. If they divorce or he dies, the property is returned to her in whatever condition it is in. If it has become damaged or lost, the loss is hers; if it has become more valuable during the marriage, the gain is hers.

In the *tzon-barzel* arrangement, the property is evaluated before the marriage and its value is recorded in the *kesubah* (marriage contract). If they divorce or he dies, she collects the recorded amount from the estate [in addition to the regular *kesubah* payments], regardless of what the property is actually worth at that time. Even if the property was damaged or lost completely, she collects the full amount recorded in the *kesubah*. Thus, in this arrangement, it is obvious that the husband is considered the real owner of the property. The question the Gemara will now ask is therefore relevant only to the case of *melog* property, where the wife is considered owner of the property (see *Rashi*).

[The word *melog* literally means *plucking*. *Melog* property is property whose profits a husband can *pluck* without actually owning the property itself (like plucking feathers from a bird without taking the bird itself). The term *tzon-barzel* literally means *iron sheep*. It is called this because the property's value remains preserved for the wife like *iron*. The word *sheep* was added because it was the custom at that time to assess the value of sheep entrusted to shepherds, who were then required to repay that amount in the event the sheep were lost or injured (*Rav* to *Yevamos* 7:1).]

14. I.e. do we say that since the husband does not own the cow itself, paying him for it does not earn for the borrower the right to the penalty payments? Or perhaps we say that since the husband manages the cow and keeps its profits, he is considered an owner and paying him does earn the borrower the right to the penalty payments (*Rashi*).

[*Tosafos* question *Rashi's* explanation. When someone borrows a *melog* animal, he is essentially doing two things: borrowing the body of the cow from the wife and the use of it from the husband. Similarly, when he pays for the stolen cow (for example, by giving another cow in its place), he is giving back the body of the cow to the wife and the use of it to the husband. He should therefore acquire the right to the penalty payment without question! *Tosafos* therefore explain that the cow was borrowed from the woman before she married. Thus, he borrowed both the body of the cow and its use from her. When the cow was stolen and the *shomer* paid for it, she was married. Thus, when he gave back a cow, he was returning only the body of the cow to her, but the use of it he was giving to the husband. The Gemara inquires whether this is enough to acquire the penalty payments for the *shomer*.]

Our explanation of this case as well as the next one follows *Rashi*.

15. The issue here, as in the previous case, is whether the husband is considered an owner of the *melog* property in regard to acquiring the penalty payment (see previous note). If so, then when the wife borrowed the cow for the benefit of the *melog* property, she was acting on behalf of her husband. Thus, when he pays for the stolen cow it is the same as if the wife pays for it and he acquires the right to the penalty payment.

16. The term תֵּיקוּ derives from תֵּיקוּם, *let it stand,* and indicates that the question(s) still stands and the matter remains in doubt. Others suggest that the four letters form an acronym for: תִּשְׁבִּי יְתָרֵץ קוּשְׁיוֹת וְאִבַּעְיוֹת, *Tishbi* (the prophet Elijah, a native of Toshav) *will resolve all the difficulties and questions* (*Tos. Yom Tov,* end of tractate *Eduyos; Mussaf HeAruch* ערך תק; *Shelah*).

17. *Rambam* (*Hil. She'eilah U'Fikadon* 8:5) rules that since these questions have not been resolved, and neither the owner nor the *shomer* is in prior possession of the penalty payment, the payment is divided equally between them. However, if one of them went ahead and collected the whole thing he can keep it, since the other one cannot prove that he is entitled to half of it. See, however, *Rosh* (§2), who disputes *Rambam's* ruling.

18. Although this, too, is forbidden, the *shomer* rationalizes that since he is paying for it he is not doing anything wrong.

וחזר ואמר איני משלם מאי מי אמרינן מהדר קא הדר ביה או דלמא במלתיה קאי ודחויי הוא דקא מדחי ליה אמר הריני משלם ומת ואמרו בניו אין אנו משלמין מאי מי אמרינן מהדר קא הדרי בהו או דלמא במלתא דאבוהון קיימי ודחויי הוא דקא מדחו ליה שלמו בנים מאי מצי אמר להו כי אקנאי כפילא לאבוכון דעבד לי נייח נפשאי לדידכו לא או דלמא לא שנא שילם לבנים מאי מצו אמרי ליה כי אקני לך [א] אבונא כפילא דעבדת ליה נייח נפשיה אבל אנן לדידן לא או דלמא לא שנא שלמו בנים לבנים מאי שילם מחצה מאי שאל שתי פרות ושילם אחת מהן מאי שאל מן השותפין ושילם לאחד מהן מאי שותפין ששאלו ושילם אחד מהן מאי שאל מן האשה ושילם לבעלה מאי אשה ששאלה ושילם בעלה מאי [א] תיקו [ב] אמר רב הונא [ב] משביעין אותו שבועה שאינה ברשותו מאי טעמא חיישינן שמא עיניו נתן בה מיתיבי [ג] [ג] המלוה את חבירו על המשכון ואבד המשכון ואמר לו סלע הלויתיך עליו שקל היה שוה והלה אומר לא כי אלא סלע הלויתני עליו סלע היה שוה פטור [ד] סלע הלויתיך עליו שקל היה שוה והלה אומר לא כי אלא סלע הלויתני עליו שלשה דינרים היה שוה חייב סלע הלויתני עליו ב' היה שוה והלה אומר לא כי אלא סלע הלויתיך עליו סלע היה שוה פטור סלע הלויתני עליו שנים היה שוה והלה אומר לא כי אלא סלע הלויתיך עליו ה' דינרים היה שוה חייב מי נשבע מי שהפקדון אצלו שמא ישבע זה ויוציא הלה את הפקדון [ד] אהייא אילימא אסיפא ותיפוק ליה דשבועה גבי מלוה היא דהא קא מודי מקצת הטענה אלא אמר שמואל ארישא מאי ארישא אסיפא דרישא סלע הלויתיך עליו שקל היה שוה והלה אומר לא כי אלא סלע הלויתני עליו שלשה דינרין היה שוה חייב דשבועה גבי לוה הוא ואמור רבנן לשתבע מלוה שמא ישבע זה ויוציא הלה את הפקדון ואם איתא

**רש"י**

ואמרו בנים אין אנו משלמין. (א) לא הספיק לשלם עד שמת: שלמו בנים. והא"ג לא הספיק לומר הריני משלם עד שמת: דעבד לי נייח נפשאי. פעמים רבות עשה לי קורת רוח: שילם לבנים. מתו הבעלים ונגנבה ואמר השומר לבנים הריני משלם או שילם מהו: שלמו בנים לבנים מהו. דליכא שום לד נייחא נפשא באלו שהם קיימים שלא הם ולא אביהם עשו קורת רוח לאלו ולא אביהם של אלו קיבל קורת רוח מבני השומר: או דלמא. כיון שאביהם הראשונים הוה להו נייחא נפשא בהדדי קנו כפילא אף בנים מן הבנים: שילם מחצה. מתחילתו אמר הריני משלם מחצה ולא יותר: מהו. לקנות חצי הכפל: שאל שתי פרות. אם תימצי לומר לא קני מחצה שאל שתי פרות ונגנבו ואמר הריני משלם אחת ולא אמר מתה מחמת מלאכה: מהו. לקנות כפל שלה מי אמרינן כיון דפרה שלימה שילם קנה או דלמא כיון דתרווייהו חד פקדון הוו ואינו משלם את שתיהם לא אקני ליה כפילא שהרי הוא נפסד על ידו: ושילם לאחד מהם. חלקו חצי דמיה שעליו מהו לקנות חלקו המגיעו מי אמרינן כל הקרן שלו שילם או דלמא בעינן עד שישלם כל הפרה: ושילם אחד מהם. חצי דמיו שעליו: מהו. שיקנה חצי הכפל מי אמרינן הרי שילם כל המוטל עליו: שאל מן האשה. פרה של נכסי מלוג שהקרן שלה והפירות לבעל: ושילם. הפרה לבעל: מהו. לקנות הכפל מי אמרי' כיון דקרן לאו דבעל הוא לאו תשלומין מעליא נינהו ולא קני כפילא או דלמא כיון דאפוטרופוס הוא על הנכסים ואוכל הפירות בעלים הוי עלייהו ותשלומין הן: אשה ששאלה. לצורך קרקע מלוג שלה: משביעין אותו. אמתני' קאי אע"פ שהוא משלם כדקתני שילם ולא רצה לישבע משביעין אותו שבועה שאינה ברשותו: שקל. חצי סלע: פטור. הלוה מן השבועה שאין כאן הודאה במקצת: חייב. לישבע שכך היה שוה ומשלם לו דינר שהודה לו: ושתים היה שוה. והלוה תובע את המלוה את יתר דמיו וקא סבר האי תנא המלוה על המשכון שומר שכר הוא: פטור. מן השבועה שאין כאן הודאה שחייב לו כלום: ויוציא הלה כו'. ויפסלנו: אהייא. קאי מי נשבע דקתני בה: אילימא אסיפא. אחיוב דסיפא: תיפוק ליה כו'. ולמה ליה למתלי טעמא בשמא יוציא הפקדון ויפסלנו לעדות ולשבועה: מאי ארישא. הא רישא פטור קתני: אסיפא דרישא. אחיוב דקתני ברישא קאי: לשתבע מלוה. שלא היתה שוה אלא שקל ויטול שקל דכיון דאיכא שבועה על הלוה מן התורה אי אתה יכול לפוטרו בולא כלום ומשום תיקון עולם שלא יפסל ישראל שקלוה לשבועה מיניה ושדיוה אמלוה: ואם איתא

**תוספות**

וחזר ואמר איני משלם [מאי] מי אמרינן מהדר קהדר ביה. מכאן מוכיח ר"ת דאם אמר לחברו השבע וטול קודם שנשבע יכול לחזור בו ולומר אשבע ולא אשלם ובפרק יש נוחלין (ב"ב דף קכח. ושם) דאמר עבדי גנבת והלה אומר אתה מכרתו לי רצונך השבע וטול ונשבע אינו יכול לחזור בו לא גרס נשבע בלא וא"ו דמשמע שבע"כ ישבע ובריש שבועת הדיינים (שבועות דף לח. ושם ד"ה אם) דאמר אם אמר איני נשבע פוטרין אותו מיד לא כפרש"י שפוטרין אותו לפי שאינו יכול לחזור בו אלא יש לומר מסלקין אותו מב"ד כדי שיתבייש לחזור ולומר אשבע מיהו שוב פירש ר"ת בתשובה אחת דשפיר גרסינן נשבע בלא וא"ו וישבע בע"כ והא דאמרינן בפרק זה בורר (סנהדרין דף כד. ושם: ד"ה שלא) גבי נאמן עלי אבא ואביך מחלוקת לאחר גמר דין אבל קודם גמר דין דברי הכל יכול לחזור בו הכא אפילו קודם שנשבע אינו יכול לחזור בו דכיון שקבל עליו לשלם אם ישבע זה שכנגדו הוי כמו לאחר גמר דין והכא דקאמר מהדר קהדר ביה לא שיוכל לחזור אלא רוצה הוא לחזור אף על פי שאינו יכול ולא מקני ליה כפילא משום דאטרחיה לב"ד כדאמר בסמוך גבי ההוא דאפקיד כיפי וכה"ג איכא בפ' יש נוחלין (ב"ב דף קלח.) מדאשתיק קנינהו וכשצוח לבסוף מהדר קהדר ביה פירוש רוצה לחזור ואינו יכול:

הריני משלם ומת כו'. תימה היאך ישלם לבני הנפקד כפל הא אין אדם מוריש קנס לבניו כדתנן בריש פרק נערה שנתפתתה [ה] (כתובות דף מא:):

שאל מן האשה. פי' רש"י פרה מנכסי מלוג שהקרן שלה ופירות לבעל וקשה דמאי קבעי דכי שאל פרה מן האשה כאילו שאל הפירות מן הבעל וכששילם הפרה לבעל כאילו שילם הקרן לאשה ויש ליישב ששילם לבעל חלקו כמו שהיתה שוה לפירותיה ולא שילם הקרן וגרע משילם לאחד משותפים חלקו דהתם שילם קרן ודוחק ויש לפרש שאל מן האשה כשהיתה פנויה שהיו שלה הקרן והפירות וניסת דהשתא שילם הפירות לבעל אפילו נתן הכל לאשה דכיון דניסת יש לו פירות כדין נכסי מלוג וכן אשה ששאלה כשהיא פנויה וניסת ושלמה דהשתא שילם הבעל דהוו הפירות שלו והריב"ן פי' שאל מן האשה ומתה ושילם לבעל מהו דאפילו אם תמצא לומר דשילם לבנים קנה כפילא משום ניחותא דאבוהון אבל בעל לא חייש לניחותא דאשה ולאיקרא דמינהשיו אשה אינה חסה על בעלה וכן אשה ששאלה ומתה ושילם בעל אפי' אם מפקיד מקני כפילא לבני נפקד משום דרחים להו משום אבוהון אבל לא מקני להו לבעל משום אשתו שמתה:

שמא יוציא הלה הפקדון. פירש רש"י ויפסלנו לעדות ולשבועה וקשה לר"ת דלכל שכן שישבע הלוה שהוא ידקדק יותר לישבע באמת כדי שלא יפסלנו המלוה וכי עבדינן תקנה לרמאי וכי תימא דחיישינן שמא המשכון יתקלקל אחרי כן ויוציא עליו לעז אע"פ שנשבע באמת [ו] א"כ מאי פריך בסמוך כי משתבע מלוה נמי לטרח לוה ולייתי והשתא אי שוה יותר אם כן נשבע לשקר וכל שכן שיזהר בשבועתו ונראה לרבינו תם כפירוש רבינו חננאל דנראה כמו שבועה לבטלה וגנאי הוא לישבע היכא שהדבר מתברר אחרי כן שהמלוה יוציא את הפקדון אבל כי רמינן לה על המלוה לא ישבע עד שידע שלא יוכל למצאה וא"ת אמאי לא חשיב הא בפרק כל הנשבעין (שבועות דף מד: ושם ד"ה ואלו) עם הנשבעין ונוטלין דליכא למימר תנא ושייר דאלו קתני כדדייק בפ"ק דקידושין (דף טז: ושם) גבי אלו מעניקין להם ויש לומר דלא חשיב התם אלא אותם שאין יכולין לישבע כגון גזלן וחובל דניכרים הדברים כיון שנכנס שלא ברשות בביתו ונתקוטטו ויש לומר שחבל שהוא חבלו וכן בחנוני אינו יכול לישבע בעה"ב שאינו יודע אם נתן חנוני לפועלים וכן שכיר שאין בעה"ב יכול לישבע לפי שהוא טרוד בפועליו ומהאי טעמא נמי במוציא הוצאות על נכסי אשתו אמרי' בפרק האשה שנפלו לה כו' (כתובות דף פ. ושם ד"ה ישבע) ישבע כמה הוציא ויטול דאין האשה יודעת כמה הוציא בעלה ולא חשיב לה פ' כל הנשבעים דהוי בכלל שכיר אבל הכא הלוה יכול לישבע דקים ליה טפי ממלוה אך שלא רצו חכמים גזירה שמא יוציא הלה כו': [וע"ע תוס' כתובות פ. ד"ה ישבע ועוד שם פז: ד"ה ואלו]:

מגו

**עין משפט נר מצוה**

ט א מיי' פ"ח מהל' שאלה הל' ה סמג עשין פח טוש"מ סי' רלה:

י ב מיי' פ"ו מהל' שאלה ופקדון הל' א סמג עשין פח טוש"ע ח"מ סי' רלה סעי' א וסי' שה סעי' א:

יא ג מיי' פי"ג מהל' מלוה ולוה הל' ד סמג עשין לד טוש"ע ח"מ סי' עב סעי' ט:

יב ד מיי' שם טוש"ע שם סעי' י:

**רבינו חננאל**

כפילא דידיה היא ודלא כר' יוסי דאמר כיצד הלה עושה סחורה וכו'. שלמו בני שואל למשאיל או א) לבני המשאיל או שילם מחצה ולא הספיק להשלים הנשאר עד שנמצא הגנב או שאל מאשה ושילם לבעלה או שאלה האשה ושילם בעלה או שאל משני שותפין ושילם לאחד מהן או שאלו שני שותפין ושילם אחד מהן אלו כולן עלו בתיקו. וקיימא לן ממון המוטל בספק חולקין. אמר רב הונא ומשביעין. פי' אע"פ שמשלם אמר רב הונא משביעין אותו שבועה שאינה ברשותו חיישינן שמא עיניו נתן בה ותלמוד ארץ ישראל מסייע דגרסינן לא סוף דבר שילם אלא כיון דאמר הריני משלם חוששין ב) שמא שלא שלח בה יד. אמר הריני נשבע וראה שמגלגלין עליו שבועות אחרות חזר ואמר הריני משלם חוששין. אמר ר' יוסי לא חייבתו התורה להחמיר עליו אלא להקל עליו שאם רצה לשלם ישלם ואם אינו רוצה לשלם ישבע. היו [לו] עדים שנגנבה באונס הדה היא דאמר ר' אלעזר המוכר קנסיו לאחר לא עשה כלום. ואותבינן אהא דרב הונא הא דתנן המלוה את חבירו על המשכון ואבד ואמר לו סלע הלויתיך ושקל היה שוה והלה אומר לא כי אלא סלע הלויתני עליו וסלע היה שוה פטור וכו' פי' הסלע הוא ד' דינרין והשקל הוא שני דינרין חצי סלע ג) כשאבד המשכון וטוען המלוה כי הלויתיך עליו ד' דינרין והיה שוה שני דינר הריני מחשב על ב' דינרין דמי המשכון שאבד מפני שאמרו חכמים כשומר שכר אני שמשלם הגניבה והאבידה עכשיו חייב אתה לתת לי ב' דינר תשלום הסלע והלה אומר לא כי אלא ד' דינרין הלויתני וד' היה שוה המשכון ולא נשאר לך כלום פטור הלוה משבועה דאורייתא שהרי לא הודה לו במקצת מן התביעה אבל אם [טען] הלוה סלע הלויתני וג' דינרין היה שוה המשכון ונשאר לך עלי דינר והמלוה אמר לא היה שוה המשכון אלא ב' דינר ונשארו לי עליך ב' דינר כיון שהודה בדינר חייב לשלם (על) הדינר וישבע על הדינר האחר שבועה דאורייתא ותנן בהדא מתני' מי נשבע מי שהפקדון אצלו שמא ישבע זה ויוציא הלה את הפקדון ואינו שוה ג' דינ' כמו שנשבע ונמצא הלה חשוד על השבועה. וקשיא

**מסורת הש"ס**

א) גירסת מהרש"ל כפילא אבונא, ב) לעיל ה:, ג) שבועות מג., ד) [שם ע"ב, ע"ש], ה) [ועיין תוספות בבא קמא עב. ד"ה סיפא כו'], ו) נ"ל מכל מקום, מהרש"א.

**הגהות הב"ח**

(א) רש"י ד"ה ואמרו וכו' משלמים והא"ג לא הספיק:

**ליקוטי רש"י**

שמא עיניו נתן בה. ורוצה לקנותה בדמים [שבועות מג: בד"ה והשתא]. מי נשבע. כמה היתה שוה. מי שהפקדון אצלו. המלוה ובגמרא מפרש אהייא קאי. ויוציא הלה את הפקדון. ושמא לא דקדק זה בשומא ויפסלנו לעדות ולשבועה [שם ע"א].

וְחָזַר וְאָמַר אֵינִי מְשַׁלֵּם – **and** then **he returned and said, "I will not pay,"** מַאי – **what** is the law; does he still receive the penalty payment? מִי אָמְרִינַן מְהַדַּר קָא הָדַר בֵּיהּ – **Do we say that he is taking back** his offer to pay, and therefore he forfeits his rights to the penalty payment,[1] אוֹ דִּלְמָא בְּמִלְּתֵיהּ קָאֵי – **or perhaps he stands by his word** to pay, וְדַחוּיֵי הוּא דְּקָא מַדְחֵי לֵיהּ – **and is** only **stalling [the owner]** so as to put off paying him?

The second question:

אָמַר הֲרֵינִי מְשַׁלֵּם – If [a *shomer*] **said, "I will pay,"** וּמֵת – **and he died** before paying, וְאָמְרוּ בָנָיו אֵין אָנוּ מְשַׁלְּמִין – **and his sons said, "We will not pay,"** מַאי – **what** is the law; do they nonetheless inherit the penalty payment?[2] מִי אָמְרִינַן מְהַדַּר קָא הָדְרִי בְּהוּ – **Do we say that they are taking back** their father's offer to pay, and therefore forfeit the rights to the penalty payment, אוֹ דִּלְמָא בְּמִלְּתָא דַּאֲבוּהוֹן קַיְימִי – **or perhaps they stand by their father's word,** וְדַחוּיֵי הוּא דְּקָא מַדְחוּ לֵיהּ – **and are** only **stalling [the owner]** so as to put off paying him?[3]

A third question:

שִׁלְּמוּ בָנִים – If **the sons** of the *shomer* **paid** for the lost item, even though the *shomer* died without committing himself to pay,[4] מַאי – **what** is the law; do the sons thereby acquire the penalty payment? מָצֵי אָמַר לְהוּ – **Can** the owner **tell [the sons]:** כִּי אַקְנַאי כְּפֵילָא – **"When I** committed myself to **transfer the double payment** or other penalties, לַאֲבוּכוֹן – I did so only **to your father,** דַּעֲבַד לִי נַיְיחָ נַפְשָׁאי – **who** many times **did favors for me.** Therefore, I was willing to transfer these payments to him if he would agree to pay for the lost item. לְדִידְכוּ לֹא – However, I did **not** have any intention to transfer this payment **to you,** his children, even if you would agree to pay." אוֹ דִּלְמָא לֹא שְׁנָא – **Or, perhaps, it does not make any difference** to the owner, who only wishes to be sure to get back the value of his lost item and is therefore willing to transfer the penalty payment to the *shomer's* children as well, if they pay for the deposit. – ? –

A fourth question:

שִׁילֵּם לְבָנִים – If the owner died and then the object was stolen, and **[the *shomer*] paid** or promised to pay **to the** owner's **sons,** מַאי – **what** is the law; do the owner's sons also transfer the penalty payment to the *shomer*?[5] מָצוּ אָמְרֵי לֵיהּ – **Can they tell [the *shomer*]:** כִּי אַקְנֵי לָךְ אֲבוּנָא כְּפֵילָא – **"When our father** committed himself to **transfer the double payment to you,** דַּעֲבַדְתְּ לֵיהּ נַיְיחָ נַפְשֵׁיהּ – he did so **because you did favors for him.** אֲבָל אֲנַן לְדִידָן לֹא – **But** you have **not** done any favors for **us,** and so we see no reason to transfer the penalty payment to you." אוֹ דִּלְמָא לֹא שְׁנָא – **Or perhaps it does not make a difference** to the children, and they transfer the payment to the *shomer* even though he has not done any favors for them.[6] – ? –

A fifth question:

שִׁלְּמוּ בָנִים לְבָנִים – If the *shomer* and the owner both died, and **the sons** of the *shomer* **paid the sons** of the owner, מַאי – **what** is the law; do the owner's sons transfer the penalty payment to the *shomer's* sons?[7]

A group of related questions:

שִׁילֵּם מֶחֱצָה – If **[the *shomer*] paid** or agreed to pay for only **one-half** of the value of the stolen animal,[8] מַאי – **what** is the law; does he acquire one-half of the penalty payment? שָׁאַל שְׁתֵּי פָרוֹת – If **someone borrowed two cows** and they were both stolen, וְשִׁילֵּם אַחַת מֵהֶן – **and he paid** or agreed to pay for only **one of them,**[9] מַאי – **what** is the law; does he acquire the penalty

NOTES

1. Once a *shomer* promises to pay, he is obligated to do so and cannot back out. However, by trying to take back his promise, he forfeits the penalty payment, since the owner must now take him to court to force him to pay. An owner transfers the penalty payment to a *shomer* only because he voluntarily pays him (*Tosafos, Ramban*).

2. If they had fulfilled their father's promise, they would certainly have received the penalty payment (*Tosafos*). The Gemara's question is where they refused to fulfill it.

[Although there is a principle that אֵין אָדָם מוֹרִישׁ קְנָס לְבָנָיו, *a person cannot leave penalty payments as an inheritance to his sons* (*Kesubos* 41b), our case is different. Once the father agreed to pay, he acquired the animal retroactively, as we learned above (34a). Since if the animal had still been alive when he died, ownership of it would have passed to his sons, the penalty payment that derives from that animal can also pass to the sons. The only time we say that a penalty payment cannot be inherited by the sons [even though it was incurred before the father died] is when the object from which the penalty derives could also not have been inherited by the sons (see *Rashba* for further discussion of this distinction; see also *Tosafos* here and to *Bava Kamma* 72a ד״ה סיפא; *Kesef Mishneh, Hil. She'eilah U'Fikadon* 8:5; and *Derush VeChidush* of *R' Akiva Eiger* for other approaches).]

3. This question is built on the previous one. Assuming the father does not really mean to take back his promise to pay and is just stalling for time, this may be because he gave his word. But his sons, who did not promise to pay, may really mean it when they say they will not pay (*Ritva*).

4. *Rashi.* Others explain that the Gemara's inquiry applies to a case where the theft occurred after the *shomer's* death and he never had the opportunity to volunteer to pay (*Ritva;* see *Pnei Yehoshua* and *Even HaAzel, Hil. She'eilah U'Fikadon* 8:5, no. 2).

5. As we learned above (34a), when a *shomer* agrees to pay he acquires the penalty payment because the owner transfers the animal to him retroactively to the moment just before the theft. In our case, where the owner died before the animal was stolen, he cannot be considered to have transferred the animal at that time, since he is no longer alive to make any transaction. The question therefore becomes whether the owner's sons (who inherited the animal from him) are willing to transfer the animal to the *shomer* in return for his agreeing to pay for it (see *Rashba*).

[This question is relevant only according to the second version of Rava's explanation above (34a), that the transfer takes place retroactively to just before the theft. However, according to the first version of Rava's explanation, which states that the transfer occurs retroactively to the time when the *shomer* was first given the animal to care for, the Gemara has no question, because the *shomer* can have acquired it from the father, who was still alive at that time (*Rashi*, as interpreted by *Chidushei Ritva HaChadashim;* cf. *Raavad,* cited in *Shitah Mekubetzes*).]

6. [The issue here (and in the next several questions) is not what this particular owner meant to do. He may not have thought about the transfer at all when he entrusted the animal to the *shomer.* Rather, the Sages understood that this is what most people would feel if they thought about it, and they therefore established the rules we have learned as a condition of every agreement to care for something [לֵב בֵּית דִּין מַתְנֶה]. The Gemara is exploring with these questions the limits of that innovation (*Rashba* to the Gemara's next question).]

7. Although when a *shomer* dies, his sons do not become *shomrim* in his place (see *Kesubos* 34b and *Rashi* ד״ה אין חייבים באונסה), it is possible that the owner nonetheless intended to transfer the penalty payment to the *shomer's* children if they would voluntarily pay him.

Where the owner and the *shomer* both died, the *shomer's* sons never did any favors for the original owner's sons [and so there is no motivation for the owner's sons to transfer the penalty payment for their own sakes], nor did the *shomer's* sons ever do any favors for the original owner [and so there is no motivation for the current owners to make the transfer for the sake of their father]. On the other hand, since the *shomer* probably did do favors for the original owner, perhaps the children of the original owner agree to transfer penalty payments to the *shomer* and even to his children (*Rashi*).

8. I.e. he agreed from the very beginning to pay one-half of the animal's value but no more (*Rashi*). This was done as a voluntary compromise, to save the owner from suffering a total loss (*Meiri*). Accordingly, the Gemara's question is whether the owner is so appreciative of this partial payment that he is willing to transfer half the penalty payment to the *shomer*. See *Ritva* and *Rabbeinu Chananel* for other interpretations.

9. I.e. he agreed to pay for one of them and did not try to absolve himself from responsibility by claiming that it died on account of its work (*Rashi*; see above, 34a note 15). [*Rashash* questions this interpretation,

וחזר ואמר איני משלם מאי מי אמרינן מהדר קא הדר ביה או דלמא במלתיה קאי ודחויי הוא דקא מדחי ליה אמר הריני משלם ומת ואמרו בניו אין אנו משלמין מאי מי אמרינן מהדר קא הדרי בהו או דלמא במלתא דאבוהון קיימי ודחויי הוא דקא מדחו ליה שלמו בנים מאי מצי אמר להו כי אקנאי כפילא לאבוכון דעבד לי נייח נפשאי לדידכו לא או דלמא לא שנא שילם לבנים מאי מצו אמרי ליה כי אקני לך (א) אבונא כפילא דעבדת ליה נייח נפשיה אבל אנן לדידן לא או דלמא לא שנא שלמו בנים לבנים מאי שילם מחצה מאי שאל שתי פרות ושילם אחת מהן מאי שאל מן השותפין ושילם לאחד מהן מאי שותפין ששאלו ושילם אחד מהן מאי שאל מן האשה ושילם לבעלה מאי אשה ששאלה ושילם בעלה מאי [א] תיקו (ב) אמר רב הונא [ב] משביעין אותו שבועה שאינה ברשותו מאי טעמא חיישינן שמא עיניו נתן בה מיתיבי (ג) [ג] המלוה את חבירו על המשכון ואבד המשכון ואמר לו סלע הלויתיך עליו שקל היה שוה והלה אומר לא כי אלא סלע הלויתני עליו סלע היה שוה פטור [ד] סלע הלויתיך עליו שקל היה שוה והלה אומר לא כי אלא סלע הלויתני עליו שלשה דינרים היה שוה חייב סלע הלויתני עליו ב' היה שוה והלה אומר לא כי אלא סלע הלויתיך עליו סלע היה שוה פטור סלע הלויתני עליו שנים היה שוה והלה אומר לא כי אלא סלע הלויתיך עליו ה' דינרים היה שוה חייב מי נשבע מי שהפקדון אצלו שמא ישבע זה ויוציא הלה את הפקדון (ד) אהייא אילימא אסיפא ותיפוק ליה דשבועה גבי מלוה היא דהא קא מודי מקצת הטענה אלא אמר שמואל ארישא מאי ארישא אסיפא דרישא סלע הלויתיך עליו שקל היה שוה והלה אומר לא כי אלא סלע הלויתני עליו שלשה דינרין היה שוה חייב דשבועה גבי לוה הוא ואמור רבנן לשתבע מלוה שמא ישבע זה ויוציא הלה את הפקדון ואם

איתא

---

ואמרו בנים אין אנו משלמין. (א) לא הספיק לשלם עד שמת: שלמו בנים. והאב לא הספיק לומר הריני משלם עד שמת: דעבד לי נייח נפשאי. פעמים רבות עשה לי קורת רוח: שילם לבנים. מתו הבעלים ונגנבה ואמר השומר לבנים הריני משלם או שילם מהו: שלמו בנים לבנים מהו. דליכא שום צד נייחא נפשא באלו שהם קיימים שלא הם ולא אביהם עשו קורת רוח לאלו ולא אביהם של אלו קיבל קורת רוח מבני השומר: או דלמא. כיון שאביהם הראשונים הוה להו נייחא נפשא בהדדי קנו כפילא אף בנים מן הבנים: שילם מחצה. מתחילתו אמר הריני משלם מחצה ולא יותר: מהו. לקנות חצי הכפל: שאל שתי פרות. אם תימצי לומר לא קני מחצה שאל שתי פרות ונגנבו ואמר הריני משלם אחת ולא אמר מתה מחמת מלאכה: מהו. לקנות כפל שלה מי אמרינן כיון דפרה שלימה שילם קנה או דלמא כיון דתרוייהו חד פקדון הוו ואינו משלם את שתיהם לא אקני ליה כפילא שהרי הוא נפסד על ידו: ושילם לאחד מהם. חלקו חצי דמיה שעליו מהו לקנות חלקו המגיעו מי אמרינן כל הקרן שלו שילם או דלמא בעינן עד שישלם כל הפרה: ושילם אחד מהם. חצי דמיו שעליו: מהו. שיקנה חצי הכפל מי אמרינן הרי שילם כל המוטל עליו: שאל מן האשה. פרה של נכסי מלוג שהקרן שלה והפירות לבעל: ושילם. הפרה לבעל: מהו. לקנות הכפל מי אמרי' כיון דקרן לאו דבעל הוא לאו תשלומין מעליא נינהו ולא קני כפילא או דלמא כיון דאפוטרופוס הוא על הנכסים ואוכל הפירות בעלים הוי עלייהו ותשלומין הן: אשה ששאלה. לצורך קרקע מלוג שלה: משביעין אותו. אמתני' קאי אע"פ שהוא משלם כדקתני שילם ולא רצה לישבע משביעין אותו שבועה שאינה ברשותו: שקל. חצי סלע: פטור. הלוה מן השבועה שאין כאן הודאה במקצת: חייב. לישבע שכך היה שוה ומשלם לו דינר שהודה לו: ושתים היה שוה. והלוה תובע את המלוה את יתר דמיו וקא סבר האי תנא המלוה על המשכון שומר שכר הוא: פטור. מן השבועה שאין כאן הודאה שחייב לו כלום: ויוציא הלה כו'. ויפסלנו: אהייא. קאי מי נשבע דקתני בה: אילימא אסיפא. אחיוב דסיפא: תיפוק ליה כו'. ולמה ליה למתלי טעמא בשמא יוציא הפקדון ויפסלנו לעדות ולשבועה: מאי ארישא. הא רישא פטור קתני: אסיפא דרישא. אחיוב דקתני ברישא קאי: לשתבע מלוה. שלא היתה שוה אלא שקל ויטול שקל דכיון דאיכא שבועה על הלוה מן התורה אי אתה יכול לפוטרו בולא כלום ומשום תיקון עולם שלא יפסל ישראל שקלוה לשבועה מיניה ושדיוה אמלוה: ואם איתא

---

**וחזר** ואמר איני משלם [מאי] מי אמרינן מהדר קהדר ביה. מכאן מוכיח ר"ת דאם אמר לחברו השבע וטול קודם שנשבע יכול לחזור בו ולומר אשבע ולא אשלם ובפרק יש נוחלין (ב"ב דף קכח. ושם) דאמר עבדי גנבת והלה אומר אתה מכרתו לי רצונך השבע וטול ונשבע אינו יכול לחזור בו לא גרס נשבע בלא וא"ו דמשמע שבע"כ ישבע ובריש שבועת הדיינים (שבועות דף לג. ושם ד"ה אם) דאמר אם אמר איני נשבע פוטרין אותו מיד לא כפרש"י שפוטרין אותו לפי שאינו יכול לחזור בו אלא יש לומר מסלקין אותו מב"ד כדי שיתבייש לחזור ולומר אשבע מיהו שוב פירש ר"ת בתשובה אחת דשפיר גרסינן נשבע בלא וא"ו וישבע בע"כ והא דאמרינן בפרק זה בורר (סנהדרין דף כד. ושם: ד"ה שלא) גבי נאמן עלי אבא ואביך מחלוקת לאחר גמר דין אבל קודם גמר דין דברי הכל יכול לחזור בו הכא אפילו קודם שנשבע אינו יכול לחזור בו דכיון שקבל עליו לשלם אם ישבע זה שכנגדו הוי כמו לאחר גמר דין והכא דקאמר מהדר קהדר ביה לא שיוכל לחזור אלא רוצה הוא לחזור אף על פי שאינו יכול ולא מקני ליה כפילא משום דאטרחיה לב"ד כדאמר בסמוך גבי ההוא דאפקיד כיפי וכה"ג איכא בפ' יש נוחלין (ב"ב דף קלח.) מדאשתיק קנינהו וכשלוה לבסוף מהדר קהדר ביה פירוש רוצה לחזור ואינו יכול:

**הריני** משלם ומת כו'. תימה היאך ישלם לבני הנפקד כפל הא אין אדם מוריש קנס לבניו כדתנן בריש פרק נערה שנתפתתה (ה) (כתובות דף מא:):

**שאל** מן האשה. פי' רש"י פרה מנכסי מלוג שהקרן שלה ופירות לבעל וקשה דמאי קבעי דכי שאל פרה מן האשה כאילו שאל הפירות מן הבעל וכששילם הפרה לבעל כאילו שילם הקרן לאשה ויש ליישב ששילם לבעל חלקו כמו שהיתה שוה לפירותיה ולא שילם הקרן וגרע משילם לאחד משותפים חלקו דהתם שילם קרן ודוחק ויש לפרש שאל מן האשה כשהיתה פנויה שהיו שלה הקרן והפירות וניסת דהשתא שילם הפירות לבעל אפילו נתן הכל לאשה דכיון דניסת יש לו פירות כדין נכסי מלוג וכן אשה ששאלה כשהיא פנויה וניסת ושלמה דהשתא שילם הבעל דהוו הפירות שלו והריב"ן פי' שאל מן האשה ומתה ושילם לבעל מהו דאפילו אם תמצא לומר דשילם לבנים קנה כפילא משום ניחותא דאבוהון אבל בעל לא חייש לניחותא דאשה ולישנא דמעכשיו אשה אינה חסה על בעלה וכן אשה ששאלה ומתה ושילם בעל אפי' אם מפקיד מקני כפילא לבני נפקד משום דרחים להו משום אבוהון אבל לא מקני להו לבעל משום אשתו שמתה:

**שמא** יוציא הלה הפקדון. פירש רש"י ויפסלנו לעדות ולשבועה וקשה לר"ת דכל שכן שישבע הלוה שהוא ידקדק יותר לישבע באמת כדי שלא יפסלנו המלוה וכי עבדינן תקנה לרמאי וכי תימא דחיישינן שמא המשכון יתקלקל אחרי כן ויוציא עליו לעז אע"פ שנשבע באמת (ו) א"כ מאי פריך בסמוך כי משתבע מלוה נמי לטרח לוה ולייתי והשתא אי שוה יותר אם כן נשבע לשקר וכל שכן שיזהר בשבועתו ונראה לרבינו תם כפירוש רבינו חננאל דנראה כמו שבועה לבטלה וגנאי הוא לישבע היכא שהדבר מתברר אחרי כן שהמלוה יוציא את הפקדון אבל כי רמינן לה על המלוה לא ישבע עד שידע שלא יוכל למנאה וא"ת אמאי לא חשיב הא בפרק כל הנשבעין (שבועות דף מד: ושם ד"ה ואלו) עם הנשבעין ונוטלין דליכא למימר תנא ושייר דאלו קתני כדדייק בפ"ק דקידושין (דף טז: ושם) גבי אלו מעניקין להם ויש לומר דלא חשיב התם אלא אותם שאין יכולין לישבע כגון גזלן וחובל דניכרים הדברים כיון שנכנס שלם בביתו ונתקוטטו ויצא חבול שהוא חבלו וכן בחנוני אינו יכול לישבע בעה"ב שאינו יודע אם נתן חנוני לפועלים וכן שכיר שאין בעה"ב יכול לישבע לפי שהוא טרוד בפועליו ומהאי טעמא נמי במוציא הוצאות על נכסי אשתו אמרי' בפרק האשה שנפלו לה כו' (כתובות דף פ. ושם ד"ה ישבע) ישבע כמה הוציא ויטול דאין האשה יודעת כמה הוציא בעלה ולא חשיב לה פ' כל הנשבעים דהוי בכלל שכיר אבל הכא הלוה יכול לישבע דקים ליה טפי ממלוה אך שלא רצו חכמים גזירה שמא יוציא הלה כו': [וע"ע תוס' כתובות פ. ד"ה ישבע ועוד שם פז: ד"ה ואלו]

מגו

---

עין משפט נר מצוה

ט א מיי' פ"ח מהל' שאלה הל' ה סמג עשין פח טוש"מ סי' רלה:
י ב מיי' פ"ו מהל' שאלה ופקדון הל' א סמג עשין פח טוש"ע ח"מ סי' רלה סעי' א וסי' שה סעי' א:
יא ג מיי' פי"ג מהל' מלוה ולוה הל' ד סמג עשין לד טוש"ע ח"מ סי' עב סעי' ט:
יב ד מיי' שם טוש"ע שם סעי' י:

רבינו חננאל

כפילא דידיה היא ודלא כר' יוסי דאמר כיצד הלה עושה סחורה וכו'. שלמו בני שואל למשאיל או (א) לבני המשאיל או שילם מחצה ולא הספיק להשלים הנשאר עד שנמצא הגנב או שאל מאשה ושילם לבעלה או שאלה האשה ושילם בעלה או שאל משני שותפין ושילם לאחד מהן או שאלו שני שותפין ושילם אחד מהן אלו כולן עלו בתיקו. וקיימא לן ממון המוטל בספק חולקין. אמר רב הונא ומשביעין. פי' אע"פ שמשלם אמר רב הונא משביעין אותו שבועה שאינה ברשותו חיישינן שמא עיניו נתן בה ותלמוד ארץ ישראל מסייע דגרסינן לא סוף דבר שילם אלא כיון דאמר הריני משלם חוששין ב) שמא שלא שלח בה יד. אמר הריני נשבע וראה שמגלגלין עליו שבועות אחרות חזר ואמר הריני משלם חוששין. אמר ר' יוסי לא חייבתו התורה להחמיר עליו אלא להקל עליו שאם רצה לשלם ישלם ואם אינו רוצה לשלם ישבע. היו [לו] עדים שנגנבה באונס הדה היא דאמר ר' אלעזר המוכר קנסיו לאחר לא עשה כלום. ואותבינן אהא דרב הונא הא דתנן המלוה את חבירו על המשכון ואבד ואמר לו סלע הלויתיך ושקל היה שוה והלה אומר לא כי אלא סלע הלויתני עליו וסלע היה שוה פטור וכו' פי' הסלע הוא ד' דינרין והשקל הוא שני דינרין חצי סלע ג) כשאבד המשכון וטוען המלוה כי הלויתיך עליו ד' דינרין והיה שוה שני דינר הריני מחשב על ב' דינרין דמי המשכון שאבד מפני שאמרו חכמים כשומר שכר אני שמשלם הגניבה והאבידה עכשיו חייב אתה לתת לי ב' דינר תשלום הסלע והלה אומר לא כי אלא ד' דינרין הלויתני וד' היה שוה המשכון ולא נשאר לך כלום פטור הלוה משבועה דאורייתא שהרי לא הודה לו במקצת מן התביעה אבל אם [טען] הלוה סלע הלויתני וג' דינרין היה שוה המשכון ונשאר לך עלי דינר והמלוה אמר לא היה שוה המשכון אלא ב' דינר ונשארו לי עליך ב' דינר כיון שהודה בדינר חייב לשלם (על) הדינר וישבע על הדינר האחר שבועה דאורייתא ותנן בהדא מתני' מי נשבע מי שהפקדון אצלו שמא ישבע זה ויוציא הלה את הפקדון ואינו שוה ג' דינ' כמו שנשבע ונמצא הלה חשוד על השבועה.

וקשיא

---

מסורת הש"ס

א) גירסת מהרש"ל כפילא אבונא, ב) לעיל ה:, ג) שבועות מג:, ד) [שם ע"ב, ע"ש], ה) [ועיין תוספות ב"ק קמא: ד"ה טיפל כו'], ו) נ"ל מכל מקום מהרש"ל.

הגהות הב"ח

(א) רש"י ד"ה ולמי וכו' משלמים והאב לא הספיק:

ליקוטי רש"י

שמא עיניו נתן בה ורוצה לקנותה בדמי [שבועות מג: ד"ה והשתא]. מי נשבע כמה היתה שוה. שהפקדון אצלו המלוה ונגמגם מפני שהייה קאי. ויוציא הלה את הפקדון. ושמא לא דקדק זה בשומא ויפסלנו לעדות ולשבועה [שם ע"א].

---

חשק שלמה על ר"ח א) או ששילם השואל לבני המשאיל או ששלמו בני השואל לבני המשאיל. ב) בירושלמי לפנינו הגי' אלא כיון דאמר הריני משלם כמי ששילם. אמר משלם אני חוששין שמא שלח בו יד וכו' וכצ"ל גם כאן. ג) וכשאבד המשכון טוען המלוה וכו'.

מי יימר דמגנבא ואם תימצי לומר דמגנבא מי יימר דמשתכח גנב ואי משתכח גנב מי יימר דמשלם דלמא מודי ומפטר ° אמר רבא נעשה כאומר לו לכשתגנב ותרצה ותשלמני הרי פרתי קנויה לך מעכשיו מתקיף לה ר' זירא אי הכי אפי' גיזותיה וולדותיה נמי אלמה תניא [א]חוץ מגיזותיה וולדותיה אלא אמר ר' זירא נעשה כאומר לו חוץ מגיזותיה וולדותיה ומאי פסקא סתמא דמלתא שבחא דאתא מעלמא עביד איניש דמקני שבחא דמגופה לא עביד איניש דמקני איכא דאמרי אמר רבא נעשה כאומר לו לכשתגנב ותרצה ותשלמני סמוך לגניבתה קנויה לך מאי בינייהו איכא בינייהו קושיא דרבי זירא אי נמי [ב]דקיימא באגם: שילם ולא רצה לישבע [וכו']: [א]א"ר חייא בר אבא א"ר יוחנן לא שילם שילם ממש אלא [ג]כיון שאמר הריני משלם אע"פ שלא שילם תנן שילם ולא רצה לישבע שילם אין לא שילם לא אימא סיפא נשבע ולא רצה לשלם טעמא דלא רצה הא רצה אע"פ שלא שילם ° אלא [ב]מהא ליכא למשמע מינה תניא כותיה דר' יוחנן [ג][ד]השוכר פרה מחבירו ונגנבה ואמר הלה הריני משלם ואיני נשבע ואח"כ נמצא הגנב משלם תשלומי כפל לשוכר אמר רב פפא [ה]שומר חנם כיון שאמר פשעתי מקנה ליה כפילא דאי בעי פטר נפשיה בגניבה [ו]שומר שכר כיון שאמר נגנבה מקנה ליה כפילא דאי בעי פטר נפשיה בשבורה ומתה שואל שאומר הריני משלם לא מקני ליה כפילא במאי הוה ליה למפטר נפשיה במתה מחמת מלאכה מתה מחמת מלאכה לא שכיח איכא דאמרי אמר רב פפא שואל נמי כיון שאמר הריני משלם מקני ליה כפילא דאי בעי פטר נפשיה במתה מחמת מלאכה אמר ליה רב זביד הכי אמר אביי [ז]שואל עד שישלם מאי טעמא הואיל וכל הנאה שלו בדיבורא לא מקני ליה כפילא תניא כוותיה דרב זביד [ח]השואל פרה מחבירו ונגנבה וקידם השואל ושילם ואח"כ נמצא הגנב משלם תשלומי כפל לשואל ללישנא קמא דרב פפא ודאי לא הויא תיובתא ללישנא בתרא לימא תיהוי תיובתיה אמר לך רב פפא מי אלימא ממתניתין דקתני שילם ואוקימנא באמר הכא נמי באמר מי דמי התם לא קתני קידם הכא קתני קידם מאי קידם ואמר הא מדקתני גבי שוכר ואמר וגבי שואל קידם ש"מ דוקא קתני מידי [ד]גבי הדדי תניא שיילינהו לתנאי דבי רבי חייא ודבי ר' אושעיא ואמרי גבי הדדי תניין [ט]פשיטא אמר איני משלם וחזר ואמר הריני משלם הא קאמר הריני משלם אלא אמר הריני משלם וחזר

מי יימר דמגנבא. שעתיד להיגנב דליקני ליה כפל בשעת מסירה דעל כרחך משעת מסירה בעי לאקנויה שמשכה ממנו על מנת כן: נעשה כאומר לו. בשעה שמסרה לו דקים להו לרבנן דניחא להו לבעלים שיהא בטוח בקרן על מנת שיהא ספק כפל העתיד לבא של שומר והרי היא כמסרה לו על מנת כן שאם תיגנב וישלם לו קרן שתהא פרה קנויה לו משעה שמסרה נמלא למפרע כשגנב הגנב של שומר היתה דפרה כבר היא בעולם: אי הכי. דנמלא שהיתה שלו משעה ראשונה יזכה אף בגיזות וולדות שהיו לה משבאה לביתו דכיון דנגנב ורלה ושילם נמלאת שלו למפרע: פסקא. פסקת הדבר בכל אדם שדעתו להקנות כפל אם יבא לכך ואין דעתו להקנות הולדות: נעשה כאומר לו. בשעה שמסרה לו: לכשתגנב ותרצה ותשלמני. אם תשלם לי הקרן: סמוך לגניבתה קנויה לך. שעה אחת לפני גניבתה תהא הפרה קנויה לך והיא כבר היתה בעולם: קושיא דר' זירא. ללישנא בתרא ליכא לאקשויי גיזות וולדות דהא סמוך לגניבתה הוא דאקנייה: א"נ דהוה קיימא באגם. כשגנבה גנב ללישנא בתרא לא קני כפילא דהא סמוך לגניבתה לא היתה בחלירו שתהא חלירו קונה לו ומשיכה ההוא שעתא לא הואי ובמאי נקני וא"ת תקני לו משיכה ראשונה שמשכה לו על מנת לקנותה שעה הסמוכה לגניבתה הא אמרינן בכתובות בהאשה שנפלו לה נכסים (דף פב.) האומר לחבירו משוך פרה זו ולא תיקני לך אלא לאחר שלשים לא קנה: השוכר פרה ונגנבה כו'. אע"פ שהשוכר חייב בגניבה ואבידה מ"מ אם רוצה לשקר ולישבע שנאנסה היה נפטר בשבועה הלכך כי אמר נגנבה וחייב עצמו בקרן נקנה לו הכפל: מקנה ליה כפילא. נקנה לו הכפל: כל חיובי ופטורי דד' שומרין ילפינן מקראי לקמן בפרק השואל (דף לד:) שומר חנם ישבע על הכל אם לא פשע והשואל משלם את הכל נושא שכר והשוכר פטורין מן האונסין וחייבין בגניבה ואבידה שואל פטור במתה מחמת מלאכה הראויה לה דאמר ליה להכי אושלת לי ולא לאוקמה בכילתא: וכל הנאה שלו. שהיה עושה בה מלאכתו בלא שום שכר: בדיבורא. דהריני משלם: לא מקני ליה. הבעלים כפל שאין זו שום טובה מוטל היה עליו להניח דעתו שהשאילה לו חנם: ללישנא קמא דר"פ. ודאי לא הוי תיובתא דנימא כיון דטעמא דרב פפא משום דלא הוה (א) למפטר נפשיה דהא מתה מחמת מלאכה לא שכיחא אפי' קדם ושילם נמי אית ליה לרב פפא דלא קני ליה כפילא ותיקשי ליה הא ודאי ליכא לאותובי דמלי אמר לך אנא אע"פ שאמר הריני משלם אמרי ולא אמרי אע"פ שילם: נימא תיהוי תיובתא. מי נימא דשילם דוקא קאמר תנא דברייתא: והא מדקתני. תנא דברייתא גבי שוכר ואמר כדאמרינן לעיל תניא כוותיה דר' יוחנן וגבי שואל (ב) ושילם בהך דתניא כוותיה דרב זביד: שיילינהו. בני הישיבה: לתנאי. שהיו שונין תוספתא דרבי חייא ותוספתא דרבי אושעיא שהם עיקר כדאמרינן בעלמא (חולין דף קמא.) כל מתניתא דלא מיתניא בי רבי אושעיא ורבי חייא לא תותבוה בי מדרשא: ואמרו

**דלמא** מודה ומפטר. פי' דלמא ימהר להודות קודם שיבאו עדים והיינו כרב דאמר מודה בקנס ואח"כ באו עדים פטור ואע"ג דמתני' דמרובה (ב"ק דף עה:) דייקי' דלא כרב על פי עצמו דומיא דעל פי עד אחד לפי מסקנא דהתם דאמר מסתברא מלתיה דרב בשחייב עצמו בקרן אבל היכא דפטר עצמו מכלום לא אמר לא מפקא מדרב וכן הלכה ולא כשמואל דמחייב דר' יוחנן סבר נמי התם דפטור ושמואל ור' יוחנן הלכה כר' יוחנן כדאמר פ' מי שהוציאוהו (עירובין דף מז:):

**אי** נמי דקיימא באגם. תימה דנימא נעשה כאמר לו לכשתגנב ותשלמני הרי פרתי קנויה לך מעכשיו סמוך לגניבה דהשתא קני אפילו עומדת באגם כדאמר ר' יוחנן בפ' האשה שנפלו (כתובות ד' פב. ושם) משוך פרה זו ותקנה לך מעכשיו ולאחר שלשים יום קנה אפי' עומדת באגם וגיזותיה וולדותיה לא קנה אע"פ שאומר מעכשיו שאין הקנין נגמר עד סמוך לגניבתה כדאמר ר' יוחנן בפ' האומר (קידושין דף ס.) בא אחד וקדשה מעכשיו ולאחר שלשים יום בא אחר וקדשה מעכשיו ולאחר כ' יום בא אחר וקדשה מעכשיו ולאחר עשרה ימים בא אחר וקדשה מעכשיו אפי' הן מאה כולם תופסים בה דכל חד וחד רווחא לחבריה שבק ושמא י"ל דקדושין אלימי וכיון דאשכחו רווחא תו לא פקעי אבל הכא גיזות וולדות לכל הפחות הנהו דאיתנהו בשעת מסירה אהני מעכשיו לקנותה סמוך לגניבתה למפרע:

**אלא** מהא ליכא למשמע מינה. תימה כיון דקשיא ליה רישא לסיפא נימא נעשה כדאמרינן בפרק קמא דקידושין (דף ה:) ותקשה לר' יוחנן ° וי"ל דשילם נקט לאביי דפרק הגוזל קמא (ב"ק ד' קח.) לאורויי דאם נשבע ושילם דאין הכפל שלו ולרבא לאורויי שילם אע"פ שנשבע תחלה שהכפל שלו ולא רצה לישבע היינו לא רצה לעמוד בשבועה אבל אם אמר הריני משלם אם נשבע תחלה אין הכפל שלו:

**שואל** עד שישלם. הואיל וכל הנאה שלו ולהאי טעמא אפי' אם התנה להיות כש"ח לא קנה עד שישלם ולטעמא דלעיל דמשום לא: שכיחא אם התנה להיות כש"ח קנה כפל במגו דפטר נפשיה בגניבה ואבידה דשכיחא:

**ללישנא** קמא דרב פפא ודאי לא הויא תיובתא. דאמר הריני משלם לא קנה כפל אבל שילם קנה כפל ור"ח גרס ודאי הויא תיובתא דכיון דרב פפא מפרש טעמא משום דלא שכיח האי טעמא שייך אפילו בשילם והא דנקט ואמר הריני משלם משום דנקט גבי ש"ח וש"ש נקט נמי גבי שואל:



ד א מיי' פ"ח מהל' שאלה הל' א סמג עשין פב טוש"מ סי' רלה:
ה ב טוש"מ שם:
ו ג ד מיי' שם סמג שם טוש"מ שם:
ז ה ו ז ח מיי' שם הל' ג טוש"מ שם:
ח ט מיי' שם הלכה ד טוש"מ שם:

### רבינו חננאל

ופריק רבא נעשה כאומר לו בשעה שהפקיד אצלו לכשתיגנב ותרצה ותשלם לי הרי פרתי זו קנויה לך מעכשיו. אי הכי כי מאותה שעה שהפקידה אצלו הקנה אותה לו. יהיה אפילו גיזותיה וולדותיה לו. א) ופריק איכא דאמרי אמר רבא נעשה כאומר לו לכשתגנב ותרצה ותשלם לי תהיה פרתי זו קנויה לך סמוך לגניבה שעה אחת. פי' ללישנא קמא דרבא קנה דהא אית ליה בידיה. ללישנא בתרא דרבא לא קנה דהא באגמא הות קיימא וליתה ברשותיה דליקני לה ליה. פירוש אחר מאי בינייהו איכא בינייהו קשיא דר' זירא. פירוש ללישנא בתרא דרבא דאמ' סמוך לגניבתה קנויה לך לית אורחא לאקשויי אי הכי גיזותיה וולדותיה דליכא סמוך לגניבתה לא גיזות ולא ולדות. אי נמי דקיימא באגם. פי' ללישנא קמא דרבא לא קני כפל ב) דהא ליתה ברשותיה דליקני לה במשיכה ויזכה בכפילא לפיכך ג) אמר פרתי קנויה לך מעכשיו בעידנא דעיילא ברשותיה חרץ מגיזותיה וולדותיה. וללישנא בתרא דרבא אע"ג דהות באגמא קני לה דהא ברשותיה קיימא מעידנא דאפקיד מרה לגביה דהא מיחייב בשמירתה ומיגו דאיחייב בשמירתה כל היכא דאיתה ברשותיה קיימא הלכך זכי ליה בכפילא דאמרינן סמוך לגניבתה אקנייה ליה מרה ונפקא מרשותיה ואשכחתא דממי שהפקדון אצלו נגנבה. א"ר יוחנן לא שילם ממש אלא כיון שאמר הריני משלם אע"פ שלא שילם עדיין קנה. תניא נמי הכי השוכר פרה מחבירו ונגנבה ואמר השוכר הריני משלם ואיני נשבע שנאנסה ונמצא הגנב משלם תשלומי כפל לשוכר. אוקמוה [ב"ק נז ע"ב] לר"מ שאמר שוכר כשומר חנם משלם. אמר רב פפא שומר חנם שאמר פשעתי בה מיקני ליה כפל דאי בעי הוה פטר נפשיה בגניבה ואבידה וכיון שאמר פשעתי ואני חייב לשלם כאילו שילם וקנה הכפל וכן שומר שכר שהודה לו כי נגנבה. אבל שואל אע"פ שאמר הריני משלם לא קנה הכפל דלית ליה למיפטר נפשיה אלא במתה מחמת מלאכה והא נגנבה וליתה גביה דנימא מחמת מלאכה מתה. איכא דאמרי שואל נמי כיון דאמר הריני משלם קני כפל וכו' אמר ליה רב זביד הכי אמר אביי שואל עד שישלם מאי טעמא הואיל וכל הנאה שלו היא בדיבורא לא קני ליה כפל.

והלכתא כרב פפא בשומר חנם ובשומר שכר מיגו דאי בעו הוו יכלי למיפטר נפשייהו וקא מודו בההוא הנאה מקנה להו כפילא. חדא דשמעתיה דר' יוחנן סתמא היא. ורב זביד נמי לא פליג עליה אלא בשואל בלחוד ובשואל הלכתא כרב זביד דתניא בהדיא כוותיה ודייקינן ללישנא קמא דרב פפא דאמר שואל כיון שאין לו דרך להפטר מן התשלומין אע"פ שאמר הריני משלם לא קנה כפל הוא הדין ואפי' שילם דהא חיוביה קא פרע ולא מהני מידי למשאל דליקני ליה כפילא אי הכי קשיא ליה הא דתניא השואל פרה מחבירו ונגנבה וקדם השואל ושילם ואחר כך נמצא הגנב משלם תשלומי כפל לשואל ואתינן לדחויה ד) ולא נדחית אלא מדקתני גבי שוכר ואמר הריני משלם וגבי שואל תני וקדם ושילם ושתי הברייתות הללו ביחד הם שנויות במקום אחד זו אחר זו במתניתא דבי רבי חייא דוקא קתני וקדם ושילם ש"מ דאפילו שואל אם שילם קנה כפל קשיא לרב פפא לפום דוקיא דדייקינן משמעתיה דהוא הדין אפילו שילם לא קנה. ויש מי שגורס הכי ללישנא קמא דרב פפא ודאי לא הויא הא דתניא כוותיה דרב זביד תיובתא ומאן דגרים הכי פשוטה היא אינה צריכה לפנים ולא לפני לפנים. תוב [מקשינן] ללישנא בתרא דרב פפא דאמר כיון דאמר השואל הריני משלם קנה כפל קשיא ליה הא מתניתא דקתני גבי שואל וקדם ושילם ואוקימנא דוקא שילם אבל אמר ואכתי לא שילם לא קנה ונדחו דברי רב פפא בשואל לתרתי לישני ובשילם השואל דברי הכל

### חשק שלמה על ר"ח

א) נראה דנתחלפו השורות בכאן וכן צ"ל ופריק נעשה כאומר לו חוץ מגיזותיה וולדותיה איכא דאמרי אמר רבא וכו' עד תיהוי שעה אחת. מאי בינייהו איכא בינייהו קושיא דר' זירא וכו' עד תיהוי דקיימא באגם. פי' ללישנא קמא דרבא קנה וכו' עד תיהוי דליקני לה ליה. פירוש אחר ללישנא קמא דרבא לא קני כפל וכו'. ב) ר"ל אם לא הי' אומר מעכשיו. ג) נראה דצ"ל לפיכך צריך שיאמר הרי פרתי קנויה לך מעכשיו דאז קנה לה בעידנא דעיילא ברשותיה. ד) דברי רבינו צריך ביאור בזה דלל"ק דרב פפא אין זה דיחוי כלל דשלם לאו דוקא דאדרבה דכ"ש דהוי תיובתא ואולי דגי' אחרת היה לו ול"ע.

### מסורת הש"ס

א) [לקמן לז.], ב) [ברכות כה. וש"נ, עיין נדרים עב.], ג) בבא קמא מז:, ד) [לקמן לב., שבת יח., עירובין כ:, גיטין סד.].

### הגהות הב"ח

(א) רש"י ד"ה ללישנא וכו' דלא הוה ליה למפטר: (ב) ד"ה והא מדקתני וכו' וגבי שואל וקידם ושילם:

### גליון הש"ס

גמ' אמר רבא נעשה. עיין במרדכי פ"ק דב"מ אות (רל"ח) [רמז]: שם אלא מהא ליכא למשמע מינה. נדה לג ע"ב: תוס' ד"ה אלא וכו'. וי"ל דשילם נקט לאביי. עיין נדרים דף ס ע"ב ול"ע:

### ליקוטי רש"י

משלם תשלומי כפל לשוכר. דכיון דשילם נמלאת הגניבה שלו [ב"ק נז:]. הואיל וכל הנאה שלו. שבחנם הוא עושה מלאכתו וגו היה לו להחמיר יותר [לקמן צד:]. מידי גבי הדדי תניא. הלא תניא ר' חייא והלא תניא רבי אושעיא [שבת יח.]. הני תרי תנאי ניניהו [גיטין סד.]. שיילינהו לתנאי דבי רבי חייא ודבי רבי אושעיא. סדרו את הברייתות ודקדקו בדברי כל חכם לומר כמו שאמר [חולין קמא:].

The Gemara supports Rav Zevid's ruling:
תַּנְיָא כְּוָותֵיהּ דְּרַב זְבִיד — **It was taught in a Baraisa in accordance with** the opinion of **Rav Zevid:** הַשּׁוֹאֵל פָּרָה מֵחֲבֵירוֹ — IF ONE BORROWS A COW FROM HIS FELLOW וְנִגְנְבָה — AND IT WAS STOLEN, וְקִידֵּם הַשּׁוֹאֵל וְשִׁילֵּם — AND THE BORROWER WENT AHEAD AND PAID for the animal's loss, וְאַחַר כָּךְ נִמְצָא הַגַּנָּב — AND AFTERWARD THE THIEF WAS FOUND, מְשַׁלֵּם תַּשְׁלוּמֵי כֶּפֶל לַשּׁוֹאֵל — [THE THIEF] PAYS A DOUBLE PAYMENT TO THE BORROWER. The Baraisa thus states that the borrower acquires the rights to the penalty payment by actually *paying* for the animal's loss, which implies that he does *not* receive it simply for promising to pay.

The Gemara debates whether the Baraisa refutes Rav Pappa's ruling:
לְלִישָּׁנָא קַמָּא דְּרַב פָּפָּא — **According to the first version of Rav Pappa's** opinion, in which he said that a borrower does *not* acquire the penalty payment by promising to pay, וַדַּאי לָא הָוְיָא תְּיוּבְתָּא — **[the Baraisa] is certainly not a refutation,** because Rav Pappa agrees that if the borrower *pays*, he acquires that payment from the lender.[20]

לְלִישָּׁנָא בָּתְרָא — However, **according to the last version of Rav Pappa**'s opinion, in which he rules that a borrower *does* acquire the penalty payment with a mere promise to pay, לֵימָא תֶּיהֱוֵי תְּיוּבְתֵּיהּ — **shall we say** that **[the Baraisa] is his refutation?** אָמַר לָךְ רַב פָּפָּא — Not necessarily, because **Rav Pappa could respond to you:** מִי אַלִּימָא מִמַּתְנִיתִין — **Is** the Baraisa a **stronger** refutation **than** our **Mishnah,** דְּקָתָנֵי שִׁילֵּם — **which** also **taught** that the *shomer* acquires the penalty payment if **"he paid,"** וְאוֹקִימְנָא בְּאָמַר — **and** yet **I explained**[21] it to mean that the *shomer* only **said** he would pay, and not that he actually paid? הָכָא נַמִּי בְּאָמַר — **Here, too,** although the Baraisa said "he paid," it means that the borrower **said** he would pay, and not that he actually paid.

The Gemara argues that the Baraisa cannot be explained to mean this:
מִי דָּמֵי — **Is** the Baraisa **comparable** to the Mishnah? הָתָם לָא קָתָנֵי קִידֵּם — **There** (in the Mishnah) **it does not say** that the *shomer* **"went ahead"** and paid;[22] הָכָא קָתָנֵי קִידֵּם — however, **here** (in the Baraisa) **it says** that the borrower **"went ahead"** and paid, which implies that he actually paid.[23]

Rav Pappa would respond:
מַאי קִידֵּם — **What** does **"he went ahead"** actually mean? קִידֵּם וְאָמַר — That **he went ahead** before the thief was caught **and said** he would pay.[24]

The Gemara tries to disprove this interpretation on other grounds:
הָא מִדְּקָתָנֵי גַּבֵּי שׂוֹכֵר וְאָמַר — **Since the Baraisa** quoted earlier[25] **says regarding a renter** that he acquires the penalty payment because **"he said"** he would pay, וְגַבֵּי שׁוֹאֵל קִידֵּם — **and** yet **regarding a borrower** it says [26] that he acquires this payment because **"he went ahead"** and paid, שְׁמַע מִינָּהּ — **we learn from this** difference of expression דַּוְקָא קָתָנֵי — that when the Baraisa says "he went ahead and paid" **it says** this **literally,** that a borrower acquires the penalty payment only if he actually pays.

The Gemara challenges this proof:
מִידֵי גַּבֵּי הֲדָדֵי תַּנְיָא — **Were** these two Baraisos **taught together?** It is possible that they are separate Baraisos, in which case no inference may be drawn from the difference of expression.[27]

The Gemara rejects this possibility:
שַׁיְילִינְהוּ לְתַנָּאֵי דְּבֵי רַבִּי חִיָּיא וּדְבֵי ר׳ אוֹשַׁעְיָא — **[The students of the yeshivah] inquired of the Tannaim** who taught the Baraisos **of the academies of R' Chiya and R' Oshaya**[28] whether these were separate Baraisos or not, וְאָמְרֵי גַּבֵּי הֲדָדֵי תַּנְיָין — **and they said** that these two Baraisos **were taught together;** that is, they were indeed both parts of the same Baraisa. We may therefore infer from the difference of expression that when the Baraisa says about a borrower that he acquires the penalty payment because "he went ahead and paid," it means literally that he paid (and not that he promised to pay). This refutes the last version of Rav Pappa, that promising to pay is enough even for a borrower.

The Gemara poses a series of questions about the extent to which penalty payments are transferred to a *shomer* when he accepts the responsibility to pay for the lost deposit (*pikadon*):
פְּשִׁיטָא — **It is obvious** that אָמַר אֵינִי מְשַׁלֵּם — if [a ***shomer***] **said, "I will not pay,"** וְחָזַר וְאָמַר הֲרֵינִי מְשַׁלֵּם — **and then he returned and said, "I will pay,"** he acquires the penalty payment, הָא קָאָמַר הֲרֵינִי מְשַׁלֵּם — **for he said** in the end, **"I will pay."** Since he agreed in the end to pay, his initial refusal to do so is not legally significant. אֶלָּא אָמַר הֲרֵינִי מְשַׁלֵּם — **However, if he** originally **said, "I will pay,"**

NOTES

20. Although Rav Pappa's reason for saying that the borrower does not acquire the penalty payment for promising to pay is that he is afraid to make the only claim that would free him from paying ("it died from its work"), nevertheless he agrees that the lender is willing to give him the rights to the penalty payment if he actually pays him for his loss (*Rashi,* as explained by *Ritva;* cf. *Tosafos'* quote of *Rabbeinu Chananel,* who rejects this approach and suggests a textual change).

[According to this explanation, Rav Pappa and Rav Zevid (who disputes the second version of Rav Pappa's statement) hold the same thing: A borrower does not acquire the right to the penalty payment by promising to pay but he does acquire it by actually paying. Nevertheless, they disagree about *why* a borrower does not acquire this right by promising. According to Rav Pappa it is because he has no choice but to admit the truth (since he does not want to look like a liar by claiming it died from its work), and according to Rav Zevid it is because the lender does not feel that he owes him anything for admitting his responsibility (see note 19). See *Tosafos* (ד״ה שואל), *Tos. Rabbeinu Peretz, Tos. HaRosh,* and *Ritva* for practical differences between these explanations.]

21. Literally: established.

22. It says only that "he paid," which lends itself to the interpretation that he "said he would pay."

23. [If the Baraisa meant that he merely *said* he would pay, it should have said the same thing the Mishnah said: שִׁילֵּם, *he paid.* Why does it add the word קִידֵּם, *he went ahead,* unless it is to indicate that he went ahead and *paid* (קִידֵּם וְשִׁילֵּם)?]

24. [The Baraisa adds this word to show that the borrower *went ahead and said* this before the thief was caught. This is part of the statement that the thief was found afterward (קִידֵּם...וְאַחַר כָּךְ נִמְצָא..., *he went ahead ... and afterward he was found*).] The Baraisa is thus teaching that a borrower acquires the penalty payment simply by promising to pay.

25. This is the Baraisa cited above in support of R' Yochanan (*Rashi*).

26. The Gemara assumes that the Baraisa it quoted about a borrower is the second part of that earlier Baraisa, which deals with a renter.

27. The Gemara is saying that the Baraisa about the borrower is not the second part of the Baraisa about the renter but an independent Baraisa. Since these Baraisos may have been authored by different Tannaim, no proof can be drawn from the change of expression.

28. [The word "Tannaim" here does not refer to the Rabbis quoted in a Baraisa but to Rabbis of later generations who were experts in remembering all the Baraisos and their exact language. The students of the yeshivah who discussed the opinions of Rav Pappa and Rav Zevid (who lived many generations after the Mishnah and Baraisos were composed) asked these experts in Baraisos ("Tannaim") whether the two Baraisos they were discussing were parts of the same Baraisa or separate Baraisos.]

The most authoritative Baraisos were those collected and edited by R' Chiya and R' Oshaya [who were students of Rebbi, who put together the Mishnah] (*Rashi,* from *Chullin* 141a,b). [The collections of these Baraisos were known as "the Baraisos of the academies of R' Chiya and R' Oshaya, and the specialists who remembered these Baraisos were called "the Tannaim [of the Baraisos] of the academies of R' Chiya and R' Oshaya."]

מי יימר דמגנבא ואם תימצי לומר דמגנבא מי יימר דמשתכח גנב ואי משתכח גנב מי יימר דמשלם דלמא מודי ומפטר אמר רבא נעשה כאומר לו לכשתגנב ותרצה ותשלמני הרי פרתי קנויה לך מעכשיו מתקיף לה ר' זירא אי הכי אפי' גיזותיה וולדותיה נמי אלמה תניא חוץ מגיזותיה וולדותיה אלא אמר ר' זירא נעשה כאומר לו חוץ מגיזותיה וולדותיה ומאי פסקא סתמא דמלתא שבחא דאתא מעלמא עביד איניש דמקני שבחא דמגופה לא עביד איניש דמקני איכא דאמרי אמר רבא נעשה כאומר לו לכשתגנב ותרצה ותשלמני סמוך לגניבתה קנויה לך מאי בינייהו איכא בינייהו קושיא דרבי זירא אי נמי דקיימא באגם: שילם ולא רצה לישבע [וכו']: א"ר חייא בר אבא א"ר יוחנן לא שילם שילם ממש אלא כיון שאמר הריני משלם אע"פ שלא שילם תנן שילם ולא רצה לישבע שילם אין לא שילם לא אימא סיפא נשבע ולא רצה לשלם טעמא דלא רצה הא רצה אע"פ שלא שילם מהא ליכא למשמע מינה תניא כותיה דר' יוחנן השוכר פרה מחבירו ונגנבה ואמר הלה הריני משלם ואיני נשבע ואח"כ נמצא הגנב משלם תשלומי כפל לשוכר אמר רב פפא שומר חנם כיון שאמר פשעתי מקנה ליה כפילא דאי בעי פטר נפשיה בגניבה שומר שכר כיון שאמר נגנבה מקנה ליה כפילא דאי בעי פטר נפשיה בשבורה ומתה שואל שאומר הריני משלם לא מקני ליה כפילא במאי הוה ליה למפטר נפשיה במתה מחמת מלאכה מתה מחמת מלאכה לא שכיח איכא דאמרי אמר רב פפא שואל נמי כיון שאמר הריני משלם מקני ליה כפילא דאי בעי פטר נפשיה במתה מחמת מלאכה אמר ליה רב זביד הכי אמר אביי שואל עד שישלם מאי טעמא הואיל וכל הנאה שלו בדיבורא לא מקני ליה כפילא תניא כוותיה דרב זביד השואל פרה מחבירו ונגנבה וקדם השואל ושילם ואח"כ נמצא הגנב משלם תשלומי כפל לשואל ללישנא קמא דרב פפא ודאי לא הויא תיובתא ללישנא בתרא לימא תיהוי תיובתיה אמר לך רב פפא מי אלימא ממתניתין דקתני שילם ואוקימנא באמר הכא נמי באמר מי דמי התם לא קתני קידם הכא קתני קידם מאי קידם ואמר הא מדקתני גבי שוכר ואמר וגבי שואל קידם ש"מ דוקא קתני מידי גבי הדדי תניא שיילינהו לתנאי דבי רבי חייא ודבי ר' אושעיא ואמרי גבי הדדי תניין פשיטא אמר איני משלם וחזר ואמר הריני משלם הא קאמר הריני משלם אלא אמר הריני משלם וחזר

וחזר

## רש"י

מי יימר דמגנבא. שעתיד להיגנב דליקני ליה כפל בשעת מסירה דעל כרחך משעת מסירה בעי לאקנויה שמשכה ממנו על מנת כן: נעשה כאומר לו. בשעה שמסרה לו דקים להו לרבנן דניחא להו לבעלים שיהא בטוח בקרן על מנת שיהא ספק כפל העתיד לבא של שומר והרי היא כמסרה לו על מנת כן שאם תיגנב וישלם לו קרן שתהא פרה קנויה לו משעה שמסרה נמצא למפרע כשגנב הגנב של שומר היתה דפרה כבר היא בעולם: אי הכי. דנמצא שהיתה שלו משעה ראשונה יזכה אף בגיזות וולדות שהיו לה משבאה לביתו דכיון דנגנב ורצה ושילם נמצאת שלו למפרע: פסקא. פסקת הדבר בכל אדם שדעתו להקנות כפל אם יבא לכך ואין דעתו להקנות הולדות: נעשה כאומר לו. בשעה שמסרה לו: לכשתגנב ותרצה ותשלמני. אם תשלם לי הקרן: סמוך לגניבתה קנויה לך. שעה אחת לפני גניבתה תהא הפרה קנויה לך והיא כבר היתה בעולם: קושיא דר' זירא. ללישנא בתרא ליכא לאקשויי גיזות וולדות דהא סמוך לגניבתה הוא דאקנייה: א"נ דהוה קיימא באגם. כשגנבה גנב ללישנא בתרא לא קני כפילא דהא סמוך לגניבתה לא היתה בחצירו שתהא חצירו קונה לו ומשיכה ההוא שעתא לא הואי ובמאי נקני וא"ת תקני לו משיכה ראשונה שמשכה לו על מנת לקנותה שעה הסמוכה לגניבתה הא אמרינן בכתובות בהאשה שנפלו לה נכסים (דף פב.) האומר לחבירו משוך פרה זו ולא תיקני לך אלא לאחר שלשים לא קנה: השוכר פרה ונגנבה כו'. אע"פ שהשוכר חייב בגניבה ואבידה מ"מ אם רוצה לשקר ולישבע שנאנסה היה נפטר בשבועה הלכך כי אמר נגנבה וחייב עצמו בקרן נקנה לו הכפל: מקנה ליה כפילא. נקנה לו הכפל: כל חיובי ופטורי דד' שומרין ילפינן מקראי לקמן בפרק השואל (דף צד:) שומר חנם ישבע על הכל אם לא פשע והשואל משלם את הכל נושא שכר והשוכר פטורין מן האונסין וחייבין בגניבה ואבידה שואל פטור במתה מחמת מלאכה הראויה לה דאמר ליה להכי אושלת לי ולא לאוקמה בכילתא: וכל הנאה שלו. שהיה עושה בה מלאכתו בלא שום שכר: בדיבורא. דהריני משלם: לא מקני ליה. הבעלים כפל שאין זו שום טובה מוטל היה עליו להניח דעתו שהשאילה לו חנם: ללישנא קמא דר"פ. ודאי לא הוי תיובתא דנימא כיון דטעמא דרב פפא משום דלא הוה (א) למפטר נפשיה דהא מתה מחמת מלאכה לא שכיחא אפי' קדם ושילם נמי אית ליה לרב פפא דלא קני ליה כפילא ותיקשי ליה הא ודאי ליכא לאותובי דמאי אמר לך אנא אע"פ שאמר הריני משלם אמרי ולא אמרי אע"פ ששילם: נימא תיהוי תיובתא. מי נימא דשילם דוקא קאמר תנא דברייתא: והא מדקתני. תנא דברייתא גבי שוכר ואמר כדאמרינן לעיל תניא כוותיה דר' יוחנן וגבי שואל (ג) ושילם בהך דתניא כוותיה דרב זביד: שיילינהו. בני הישיבה: לתנאי. שהיו שונין תוספתא דרבי חייא ותוספתא דרבי אושעיא שהם עיקר כדאמרינן בעלמא (חולין דף קמא.) כל מתניתא דלא מיתניא בי רבי אושעיא ורבי חייא לא תותבוה בי מדרשא:

ואמרו

## תוספות

**דלמא** מודה ומפטר. פי' דלמא ימהר להודות קודם שיבאו עדים והיינו כרב דאמר מודה בקנס ואח"כ באו עדים פטור ואע"ג דממתני' דמרובה (ב"ק דף עה:) דייקי' דלא כרב על פי עצמו דומיא דעל פי עד אחד לפי מסקנא דהתם דאמר מסתברא מלתיה דרב בשחייב עצמו בקרן אבל היכא דפטר עצמו מכלום לא אמר לא מפקא מדרב וכן הלכה ולא כשמואל דמחייב דר' יוחנן סבר נמי התם דפטור ושמואל ור' יוחנן הלכה כר' יוחנן כדאמר פ' מי שהוציאוהו (עירובין דף מז:):

**אי** נמי דקיימא באגם. תימה דנימא נעשה כאמר לו לכשתגנב ותשלמני הרי פרתי קנויה לך מעכשיו סמוך לגניבה דהשתא קני אפילו עומדת באגם כדאמר ר' יוחנן בפ' האשה שנפלו (כתובות ד' פב. ושם) משוך פרה זו ותקנה לך מעכשיו ולאחר שלשים יום קנה אפי' עומדת באגם וגיזותיה וולדותיה לא קנה אע"פ שאומר מעכשיו שאין הקנין נגמר עד סמוך לגניבתה כדאמר ר' יוחנן בפ' האומר (קידושין דף ס.) בא אחד וקדשה מעכשיו ולאחר שלשים יום בא אחר וקדשה מעכשיו ולאחר כ' יום בא אחר וקדשה מעכשיו ולאחר עשרה ימים בא אחר וקדשה מעכשיו אפי' הן מאה כולם תופסים בה דכל חד וחד רווחא לחבריה שבק ושמא י"ל דקדושין אלימי וכיון דאשכחו רווחא תו לא פקעי אבל הכא גיזות וולדות לכל הפחות הנהו דאיתנהו בשעת מסירה אהני מעכשיו לקנותה סמוך לגניבתה למפרע:

**אלא** מהא ליכא למשמע מינה. תימה כיון דקשיא ליה רישא לסיפא נימא נעשה כדאמרינן בפרק קמא דקידושין (דף ה:) ותקשה לר' יוחנן ° וי"ל דשילם נקט לאביי דפרק הגוזל קמא (ב"ק ד' קח.) לאורויי דאם נשבע ושילם דאין הכפל שלו ולרבא לאורויי שילם אע"פ שנשבע תחלה שהכפל שלו ולא רצה לישבע היינו לא רצה לעמוד בשבועה אבל אם אמר הריני משלם אם נשבע תחלה אין הכפל שלו:

**שואל** עד שישלם. הואיל וכל הנאה שלו ולהאי טעמא אפי' אם התנה להיות כש"ח לא קנה עד שישלם ולטעמא דלעיל דמשום לא: שכיחא אם התנה להיות כש"ח קנה כפל במגו דפטר נפשיה בגניבה ואבידה דשכיחא:

**ללישנא** קמא דרב פפא ודאי לא הויא תיובתא. דאמר הריני משלם לא קנה כפל אבל שילם קנה כפל ור"ח גרס ודאי הויא תיובתא דכיון דרב פפא מפרש טעמא משום דלא שכיח האי טעמא שייך אפילו בשילם והא דנקט ואמר הריני משלם משום דנקט גבי ש"ח וש"ש נקט נמי גבי שואל:

## עין משפט נר מצוה

ד א מיי' פ"ח מהל' שאלה הל' א סמג עשין פב טוש"ע ח"מ סי' רצה:
ה ב טוש"ע שם:
ו ג ד מיי' שם סמג שם טוש"ע שם:
ז ה ו ז ח מיי' שם הל' ב טוש"ע שם:
ח ט מיי' שם הלכה ד טוש"ע שם:

## רבינו חננאל

ופריק רבא נעשה כאומר לו בשעה שהפקיד אצלו לכשתיגנב ותרצה ותשלם לי הרי פרתי זו קנויה לך מעכשיו. אי הכי כי מאותה שעה שהפקידה אצלו הקנה אותה לו. יהיה אפילו גיזותיה וולדותיה לו. א) ופריק איכא דאמרי אמר רבא נעשה כאומר לו לכשתגנב ותרצה ותשלם לי תהיה פרתי זו קנויה לך סמוך לגניבה שעה אחת. פי' ללישנא קמא דרבא קנה דהא אית ליה בידיה. ללישנא בתרא דרבא לא קנה דהא באגמא הות קיימא וליתה ברשותיה דליקני לה ליה. פירוש אחר מאי בינייהו איכא בינייהו קשיא דר' זירא. פירוש ללישנא בתרא דרבא דאמ' סמוך לגניבתה קנויה לך לית אורחא לאקשויי אי הכי גיזותיה וולדותיה דליכא סמוך לגניבתה לא גיזות ולא ולדות. אי נמי דקיימא באגם. פי' ללישנא קמא דרבא לא קני כפל ב) דהא ליתה ברשותיה דליקני לה במשיכה ויזכה בכפילא לפיכך ג) אמר פרתי קנויה לך מעכשיו בעידנא דעיילא ברשותיה חוץ מגיזותיה וולדותיה. וללישנא בתרא דרבא אע"ג דהות באגמא קני לה דהא ברשותיה קיימא מעידנא דאפקיד מרה לגביה דהא מיחייב בשמירתה ומיגו דאיחייב בשמירתה כל היכא דאיתה ברשותיה קיימא הלכך זכי ליה בכפילא דאמרינן סמוך לגניבתה אקנייה ליה מרה ונפקא מרשותיה ואשכחתא דממי שהפקדון אצלו נגנבה. א"ר יוחנן לא שילם ממש אלא כיון שאמר הריני משלם אע"פ שלא שילם עדיין קנה. תניא נמי הכי השוכר פרה מחבירו ונגנבה ואמר השוכר הריני משלם ואיני נשבע שנאנסה ונמצא הגנב משלם תשלומי כפל לשוכר. אוקמוה [ב"ק נז ע"ב] לר"מ שאמר שוכר כשומר חנם משלם. אמר רב פפא שומר חנם שאמר פשעתי בה מיקני ליה כפל דאי בעי הוה פטר נפשיה בגניבה ואבידה וכיון שאמר פשעתי ואני חייב לשלם כאילו שילם וקנה הכפל וכן שומר שכר שהודה לו כי נגנבה. אבל שואל אע"פ שאמר הריני משלם לא קנה הכפל דלית ליה למיפטר נפשיה אלא במתה מחמת מלאכה והא נגנבה וליתה גביה דנימא מחמת מלאכה מתה. איכא דאמרי שואל נמי כיון דאמר הריני משלם קני כפל וכו' אמר ליה רב זביד הכי אמר אביי שואל עד שישלם מאי טעמא הואיל וכל הנאה שלו היא בדיבורא לא קני ליה כפל.

והלכתא כרב פפא בשומר חנם ובשומר שכר מיגו דאי בעו הוו יכלי למיפטר נפשייהו וקא מודו בההוא הנאה מקנה להו כפילא. חדא דשמעתיה דר' יוחנן סתמא היא. ורב זביד נמי לא פליג עליה אלא בשואל בלחוד ובשואל הלכתא כרב זביד דתניא בהדיא כוותיה ודייקינן ללישנא קמא דרב פפא דאמר שואל כיון שאין לו דרך להפטר מן התשלומין אע"פ שאמר הריני משלם לא קנה כפל הוא הדין ואפי' שילם דהא חיוביה קא פרע ולא מהני מידי למשאיל דליקני ליה כפילא אי הכי קשיא ליה הא דתניא השואל פרה מחבירו ונגנבה וקדם השואל ושילם ואחר כך נמצא הגנב משלם תשלומי כפל לשואל ואתינן לדחויה ד) ולא נדחית אלא מדקתני גבי שוכר ואמר הריני משלם וגבי שואל תני וקדם ושילם ושתי הברייתות הללו ביחד הם שנויות במקום אחד זו אחר זו במתניתא דבי רבי חייא דוקא קתני וקדם ושילם ש"מ דאפילו שואל אם שילם קנה כפל קשיא לרב פפא לפום דוקיא דדייקינן משמעתיה דהוא הדין אפילו שילם לא קנה. ויש מי שגורס הכי ללישנא קמא דרב פפא ודאי לא הויא הא דתניא כוותיה דרב זביד תיובתא ומאן דגריס הכי פשוטה היא אינה צריכה לפנים ולא לפני לפנים. תוב [מקשינן] ללישנא בתרא דרב פפא דאמר כיון דאמר השואל הריני משלם קנה כפל קשיא ליה הא מתניתא דקתני גבי שואל וקדם ושילם ואוקימנא דוקא שילם אבל אמר ואכתי לא שילם לא קנה ונדחו דברי רב פפא בשואל לתרתי לישני ובשילם השואל דברי הכל

## מסורת הש"ס

א) [לקמן לז.], ב) [ברכות כה. וש"נ, עיין נדרים עב.], ג) בבא קמא מז:, ד) [לקמן צג, שבת יח, עירובין כ:, גיטין סד.].

## הגהות הב"ח

(א) רש"י ד"ה ללישנא וכו' דלא הוה ליה למפטר: (ב) ד"ה והא מדקתני וכו' וגבי שואל וקידם ושילם:

## גליון הש"ס

גמ' אמר רבא נעשה. עיין במרדכי פ"ק דב"מ אות (רל"ח) [רמו]: שם אלא מהא ליכא למשמע מינה. נדה לג ע"ב: תוס' ד"ה אלא וכו'. וי"ל דשילם נקט לאביי. עיין נדרים דף ס ע"ב וצ"ע:

## ליקוטי רש"י

משלם תשלומי כפל לשוכר. דכיון דשילם נמצאת הגניבה שלו [ב"ק נז:]. הואיל וכל הנאה שלו. שבחנם הוא עושה מלאכתו וכו היה לו להחמיר יותר [לקמן צד:]. מידי גבי הדדי תניא. חדא תניא ר' חייא וחדא תניא רבי אושעיא [שבת יח.]. הני תרי תנאי ניינהו [גיטין סד.]. שיילינהו לתנאי דבי רבי חייא ודבי רבי אושעיא. סדרו את הברייתות ודקדקו בדברי כל חכם לומר כמו שאמר [חולין קמא:].

### חשק שלמה על ר"ח

א) נראה דנתחלפו השורות בכאן וכן צ"ל ופריק נעשה כאומר לו חוץ מגיזותיה וולדותיה איכא דאמרי אמר רבא וכו' עד תיבות שעה אחת. מאי בינייהו איכא בינייהו קושיא דר' זירא וכו' עד תיבות דקיימא באגם. פי' ללישנא קמא דרבא קנה וכו' עד תיבות דליקני לה ליה. פירוש אחר ללישנא קמא דרבא לא קני כפל וכו'. ב) ר"ל אם לא הי' אומר מעכשיו. ג) נראה דצ"ל לפיכך צריך שיאמר הרי פרתי קנויה לך מעכשיו דאז קנה לה בעידנא דעיילא ברשותיה. ד) דברי רבינו צריך ביאור כזה דלל"ק דרב פפא אין זה דיחוי כלל דשלם לאו דוקא דאדרבה דכ"ש דהוי תיובתא ואולי דגי' אחרת היה לו וצ"ע.

The Mishnah stated:

שִׁילֵּם וְלֹא רָצָה לִישָּׁבַע [וכו' — If the *shomer* **PAID, AND HE DID NOT WANT TO SWEAR etc.,** he receives any future penalty payment.

The Gemara discusses whether a mere promise to pay is enough:

אָמַר רַבִּי חִיָּיא בַּר אַבָּא אָמַר רַבִּי יוֹחָנָן — **R' Chiya bar Abba said in the name of R' Yochanan:** לֹא שִׁילֵּם שִׁילֵּם מַמָּשׁ — **The** Mishnah's statement that the *shomer* **paid** does **not** mean that he actually paid. אֶלָּא כֵּיוָן שֶׁאָמַר הֲרֵינִי מְשַׁלֵּם — **Rather, once he said, "I will pay,"** he receives any future penalty payment אַף עַל פִּי שֶׁלֹּא שִׁילֵּם — **even though he did not** yet **pay.**

The Gemara attempts to refute this ruling from the words of the Mishnah:

תְּנַן — **We learned in the Mishnah:** שִׁילֵּם וְלֹא רָצָה לִישָּׁבַע — If the *shomer* **PAID, AND HE DID NOT WANT TO SWEAR.** The Mishnah implies that שִׁילֵּם אִין — if **he paid,** he **indeed** receives the penalty payment, לֹא שִׁילֵּם לֹא — but that if **he did not pay,** even though he promised to do so, he does **not** receive the payment. — ? —

The Gemara rejects this proof:

אֵימָא סֵיפָא — **I will cite the end** of the Mishnah in support of R' Yochanan's ruling: נִשְׁבַּע וְלֹא רָצָה לְשַׁלֵּם — If the *shomer* **SWORE, AND HE DID NOT WANT TO PAY,** he does not receive the penalty payment. Here the Mishnah implies that טַעְמָא דְּלֹא רָצָה — **the reason** he does not receive the payment in this case **is because he did not want** to pay; הָא רָצָה — **but had he wanted** to pay, אַף עַל פִּי שֶׁלֹּא שִׁילֵּם — he would receive the payment **even though he did not** yet **pay!**

The Gemara thus concludes:

אֶלָּא מֵהָא לֵיכָּא לְמִשְׁמַע מִינַּהּ — **Rather, it is not possible to prove** anything **from this** Mishnah about R' Yochanan's statement, since the implications of the Mishnah's rulings are contradictory.

The Gemara supports R' Yochanan's ruling from a Baraisa:

תַּנְיָא כְּוָתֵיהּ דְּרַבִּי יוֹחָנָן — **A Baraisa was taught in accordance with** the opinion of **R' Yochanan:** הַשּׂוֹכֵר פָּרָה מֵחֲבֵירוֹ — **IF ONE RENTED A COW FROM HIS FELLOW** וְנִגְנְבָה — **AND IT WAS STOLEN,** וְאָמַר הֲלָה — **AND THAT** renter **SAID,** הֲרֵינִי מְשַׁלֵּם וְאֵינִי נִשְׁבָּע — **"I WILL PAY** for the cow **AND NOT SWEAR,"** וְאַחַר כָּךְ נִמְצָא הַגַּנָּב — **AND AFTERWARD THE THIEF WAS FOUND,** מְשַׁלֵּם תַּשְׁלוּמֵי כֶּפֶל לַשּׂוֹכֵר — **[THE THIEF] PAYS THE DOUBLE PAYMENT TO THE RENTER.**[11] The Baraisa clearly indicates that a *shomer* acquires the rights to the penalty payment merely by *saying* that he will pay.

The Baraisa just quoted makes clear that a *shomer* acquires the rights to the penalty payments not only by agreeing to pay, but also by committing himself to pay. Based on this, the Gemara now explains which admission causes each type of *shomer* to acquire the double payment:

אָמַר רַב פָּפָּא — **Rav Pappa said:** שׁוֹמֵר חִנָּם כֵּיוָן שֶׁאָמַר פָּשַׁעְתִּי — **Once an unpaid** ***shomer*** **says, "I was negligent** in the care of the animal given to me to watch and consequently it was lost or stolen," מַקְנֶה לֵיהּ כְּפֵילָא — **he acquires**[12] **the double payment,** דְּאִי בָּעֵי פָּטַר נַפְשֵׁיהּ בִּגְנֵיבָה — **because if** [**the** ***shomer***] **wanted, he could have freed himself** from responsibility **by** claiming that the deposit was **stolen** through no fault of his own.[13] שׁוֹמֵר שָׂכָר כֵּיוָן שֶׁאָמַר נִגְנְבָה — **Once a paid** ***shomer*** **says, "[The animal] was stolen,"** מַקְנֶה לֵיהּ כְּפֵילָא — **he acquires the double payment,** דְּאִי בָּעֵי פָּטַר נַפְשֵׁיהּ בִּשְׁבוּרָה וּמֵתָה — **because if** [**the** ***shomer***] **wanted, he could have freed himself** from responsibility **by** claiming that it had either **been broken or it died.**[14] שׁוֹאֵל שֶׁאוֹמֵר הֲרֵינִי מְשַׁלֵּם — However, if **a borrower says, "I will pay** for the loss of the object," לֹא מַקְנֵי לֵיהּ כְּפֵילָא — **he does not acquire the double payment,** because he must pay no matter how the animal was lost, stolen, or destroyed.[15] בְּמַאי הֲוָה לֵיהּ לְמִפְטַר נַפְשֵׁיהּ — **With what** claim **could [the borrower] have freed himself** from liability? בְּמֵתָה מֵחֲמַת מְלָאכָה — Only **with** the claim that **[the animal] died on account of** its **work.**[16] מֵתָה מֵחֲמַת מְלָאכָה לֹא שְׁכִיחַ — An animal **dying on account of** its **work is uncommon,** and the borrower could not have claimed this exemption without being suspected of lying.[17]

The Gemara presents another version of Rav Pappa's final ruling:

אִיכָּא דְּאָמְרֵי — **There are those who say** that אָמַר רַב פָּפָּא — **Rav Pappa said:** שׁוֹאֵל נַמִּי כֵּיוָן שֶׁאָמַר הֲרֵינִי מְשַׁלֵּם — **Even** in the case of **a borrower, once he says, "I will pay** for the loss of the animal," מַקְנֵי לֵיהּ כְּפֵילָא — **he acquires the double payment,** דְּאִי בָּעֵי פָּטַר נַפְשֵׁיהּ בְּמֵתָה מֵחֲמַת מְלָאכָה — **because if [the borrower] wanted, he could have freed himself** from liability **with** a claim that **[the animal] died on account of** its **work.**

The Gemara presents a dissenting opinion:

אָמַר לֵיהּ רַב זְבִיד — **Rav Zevid told [Rav Pappa]:** הָכִי אָמַר אַבַּיֵי — **This is how Abaye ruled:** שׁוֹאֵל עַד שֶׁיְּשַׁלֵּם — **A borrower** does not acquire the penalty payment **until he pays** for the loss of the object. מַאי טַעְמָא — **What is the reason?** הוֹאִיל וְכָל הֲנָאָה שֶׁלּוֹ — **Since the entire benefit** of the loan **is his,**[18] בְּדִיבּוּרָא לֹא מַקְנֵי לֵיהּ כְּפֵילָא — the lender **does not transfer the double payment to him** in exchange **for** a mere **verbal commitment** to pay.[19]

NOTES

*Kesubos* 82a). Thus, the only thing that can acquire the animal for the *shomer* just before it is stolen is his yard. [One's property can acquire for a person things that are present in it (see above, 10b note 10).] But if the animal is not in his yard when it is stolen, the yard never acquired it for him (*Rashi*).

11. Even though a renter is responsible for theft and loss (see Chapter Introduction), he can nonetheless falsely claim that the item disappeared due to circumstances beyond his control, swear to this, and thereby be exempt from paying for it. [To prevent this and be sure of getting back his principal, the owner is willing to give the future double payment even to a *shomer* who must pay for theft and loss, in return for his agreeing to pay for it.] Therefore, when the renter admits that it was stolen or lost and thereby obligates himself to pay for it, the future penalty payments become his (*Rashi*).

12. Our translation follows *Rashi*. See *Maharsha*.

13. An unpaid *shomer* does not have to pay for theft or loss — provided he was not negligent in guarding the *pikadon*. Thus, an unpaid *shomer* who admits that he was negligent must pay for what was lost or stolen. Since this admission requires him to pay, it also entitles him to the penalty payment.

For a brief statement of the extent of liability for each type of *shomer*, see Chapter Introduction.

14. A paid *shomer* must pay for theft and loss but not for damages or losses that resulted from circumstances beyond his control. See Chapter Introduction. ["Broken" means in this context that it was killed by a predator (see *Targum* to *Exodus* 22:9 and *Rashi* there).]

15. Thus, he is giving the owner nothing by admitting that he is responsible, since he would be responsible even if he did not admit it. The owner therefore has no reason to transfer to him the right to the penalty payment (see note 11).

16. Since the lender gave the object to the borrower to use, the borrower is not liable for work-related breakage or death, as long as the borrowed object was put to normal use (*Rashi;* Gemara below, 96b).

17. He is thus reluctant to make this claim. For this reason, the lender does not feel he needs to transfer future payment penalties to the borrower in order to get him to admit that he is responsible for the loss of the animal (*Ritva*).

18. The borrower can use the object for his own purposes without paying the owner (*Rashi*).

19. Since the lender gave the borrower free use of his property, when the animal is lost in circumstances for which the borrower must pay, it is only right that the borrower should reassure the lender that he will pay for it. Since this is expected, the lender feels no need to transfer the penalty payment to the borrower simply in return for being promised that he will be paid (*Rashi*).

מי יימר דמגנבא ואם תימצי לומר דמגנבא מי יימר דמשתכח גנב ואי משתכח גנב מי יימר דמשלם דלמא מודי ומפטר ° אמר רבא נעשה כאומר לו לכשתגנב ותרצה ותשלמני הרי פרתי קנויה לך מעכשיו מתקיף לה ר' זירא אי הכי אפי' גיזותיה וולדותיה נמי אלמה תניא [א] חוץ מגיזותיה וולדותיה אלא אמר ר' זירא נעשה כאומר לו חוץ מגיזותיה וולדותיה ומאי פסקא סתמא דמלתא שבחא דאתא מעלמא עביד איניש דמקני שבחא דמגופה לא עביד איניש דמקני איכא דאמרי אמר רבא נעשה כאומר לו לכשתגנב ותרצה ותשלמני סמוך לגניבתה קנויה לך מאי בינייהו איכא בינייהו קושיא דרבי זירא אי נמי [ב] דקיימא באגם: שילם ולא רצה לישבע [וכו']: (א) א"ר חייא בר אבא א"ר יוחנן לא שילם שילם ממש אלא [ג] כיון שאמר הריני משלם אע"פ שלא שילם תנן שילם ולא רצה לישבע שילם אין לא שילם לא אימא סיפא נשבע ולא רצה לשלם טעמא דלא רצה הא רצה אע"פ שלא שילם ° אלא (ג) מהא ליכא למשמע מינה תניא כותיה דר' יוחנן (ד) [ד] השוכר פרה מחבירו ונגנבה ואמר הלה הריני משלם ואיני נשבע ואח"כ נמצא הגנב משלם תשלומי כפל לשוכר אמר רב פפא [ה] שומר חנם כיון שאמר פשעתי מקנה ליה כפילא דאי בעי פטר נפשיה בגניבה [ו] שומר שכר כיון שאמר נגנבה מקנה ליה כפילא דאי בעי פטר נפשיה בשבורה ומתה שואל שאומר הריני משלם לא מקני ליה כפילא במאי הוה ליה למפטר נפשיה במתה מחמת מלאכה מתה מחמת מלאכה לא שכיח איכא דאמרי אמר רב פפא שואל נמי כיון שאמר הריני משלם מקני ליה כפילא דאי בעי פטר נפשיה במתה מחמת מלאכה אמר ליה רב זביד הכי אמר אביי [ז] שואל עד שישלם מאי טעמא הואיל וכל הנאה שלו בדיבורא לא מקני ליה כפילא תניא כוותיה דרב זביד [ח] השואל פרה מחבירו ונגנבה וקידם השואל ושילם ואח"כ נמצא הגנב משלם תשלומי כפל לשואל ללישנא קמא דרב פפא ודאי לא הויא תיובתא ללישנא בתרא לימא תיהוי תיובתיה אמר לך רב פפא מי אלימא ממתניתין דקתני שילם ואוקימנא באמר הכא נמי באמר מי דמי התם לא קתני קידם הכא קתני קידם מאי קידם קידם ואמר הא מדקתני גבי שוכר ואמר וגבי שואל קידם ש"מ דוקא קתני מידי (ה) גבי הדדי תניא שיילינהו לתנאי דבי רבי חייא ודבי ר' אושעיא ואמרי גבי הדדי תניין [ט] פשיטא אמר איני משלם וחזר ואמר הריני משלם הא קאמר הריני משלם אלא אמר הריני משלם וחזר

**רש"י**

מי יימר דמגנבא. שעתיד להיגנב דליקני ליה כפל בשעת מסירה דעל כרחך משעת מסירה בעי לאקנויה שמשכה ממנו על מנת כן: נעשה כאומר לו. בשעה שמסרה לו דקים להו לרבנן דניחא להו לבעלים שיהא בטוח בקרן על מנת שיהא ספק כפל העתיד לבא של שומר והרי היא כמסרה לו על מנת כן שאם תיגנב וישלם לו קרן שתהא פרה קנויה לו משעה שמסרה נמלא למפרע כשגנב הגנב של שומר היתה דפרה כבר היא בעולם: אי הכי. דנמלא שהיתה שלו משעה ראשונה יזכה אף בגיזות וולדות שהיו לה משבאה לביתו דכיון דנגנב ורלה ושילם נמלאת שלו למפרע: פסקא. פסקת הדבר בכל אדם שדעתו להקנות כפל אם יבא לכך ואין דעתו להקנות הולדות: נעשה כאומר לו. בשעה שמסרה לו: לכשתגנב ותרצה ותשלמני. אם תשלם לי הקרן: סמוך לגניבתה קנויה לך. שעה אחת לפני גניבתה תהא הפרה קנויה לך והיא כבר היתה בעולם: קושיא דר' זירא. ללישנא בתרא ליכא לאקשויי גיזות וולדות דהא סמוך לגניבתה הוא דאקנייה: א"נ דהוה קיימא באגם. כשגנבה גנב ללישנא בתרא לא קני כפילא דהא סמוך לגניבתה לא היתה בחצירו שתהא חצירו קונה לו ומשיכה ההוא שעתא לא הואי ובמאי נקני וא"ת תקני לו משיכה ראשונה שמשכה לו על מנת לקנותה שעה הסמוכה לגניבתה הא אמרינן בכתובות בהאשה שנפלו לה נכסים (דף פב.) האומר לחבירו משוך פרה זו ולא תיקני לך אלא לאחר שלשים לא קנה: השוכר פרה ונגנבה כו'. אע"פ שהשוכר חייב בגניבה ואבידה מ"מ אם רוצה לשקר ולישבע שנאנסה היה נפטר בשבועה הלכך כי אמר נגנבה וחייב עצמו בקרן נקנה לו הכפל: מקנה ליה כפילא. נקנה לו הכפל: כל חיובי ופטורי דד' שומרין ילפינן מקראי לקמן בפרק השואל (דף צד:) שומר חנם ישבע על הכל אם לא פשע והשואל משלם את הכל נושא שכר והשוכר פטורין מן האונסין וחייבין בגניבה ואבידה שואל פטור במתה מחמת מלאכה הראויה לה דאמר ליה להכי אושלת לי ולא לאוקמה בכילתא: וכל הנאה שלו. שהיה עושה בה מלאכתו בלא שום שכר: בדיבורא. דהריני משלם: לא מקני ליה. הבעלים כפל שאין זו שום טובה מוטל היה עליו להניח דעתו שהשאילה לו חנם: ללישנא קמא דר"פ. ודאי לא הוי תיובתא דנימא כיון דטעמא דרב פפא משום דלא הוה (א) למפטר נפשיה דהא מתה מחמת מלאכה לא שכיחא אפי' קדם ושילם נמי אית ליה לרב פפא דלא קני ליה כפילא ותיקשי ליה הא ודאי ליכא לאותובי דמלי אמר לך אנא אע"פ שאמר הריני משלם אמרי ולא אמרי אע"פ ששילם: נימא תיהוי תיובתא. מי נימא דשילם דוקא קאמר תנא דברייתא: והא מדקתני. תנא דברייתא גבי שוכר ואמר כדאמרינן לעיל תניא כוותיה דר' יוחנן וגבי שואל (ב) ושילם בהך דתניא כוותיה דרב זביד: שיילינהו. בני הישיבה: לתנאי. שהיו שונין תוספתא דרבי חייא ותוספתא דרבי אושעיא שהם עיקר כדאמרינן בעלמא (חולין דף קמא.) כל מתניתא דלא מיתניא בי רבי אושעיא ורבי חייא לא תותבוה בי מדרשא: ואמרו

**תוספות**

דלמא מודה ומפטר. פי' דלמא ימהר להודות קודם שיבאו עדים והיינו כרב דאמר מודה בקנס ואח"כ באו עדים פטור ואע"ג דממתני' דמרובה (ב"ק דף עה:) דייקי' דלא כרב על פי עצמו דומיא דעל פי עד אחד לפי מסקנא דהתם דאמר מסתברא מלתיה דרב בשחייב עצמו בקרן אבל היכא דפטר עצמו מכלום לא אמר לא מפקא מדרב וכן הלכה ולא כשמואל דמחייב דר' יוחנן סבר נמי התם דפטור ושמואל ור' יוחנן הלכה כר' יוחנן כדאמר פ' מי שהוציאוהו (עירובין דף מז:):

אי נמי דקיימא באגם. תימה דנימא נעשה כאמר לו לכשתגנב ותשלמני הרי פרתי קנויה לך מעכשיו סמוך לגניבה דהשתא קני אפילו עומדת באגם כדאמר ר' יוחנן בפ' האשה שנפלו (כתובות ד' פב. ושם) משוך פרה זו ותקנה לך מעכשיו ולאחר שלשים יום קנה אפי' עומדת באגם וגיזותיה וולדותיה לא קנה אע"פ שאומר מעכשיו שאין הקנין נגמר עד סמוך לגניבתה כדאמר ר' יוחנן בפ' האומר (קידושין דף ס.) בא אחד וקדשה מעכשיו ולאחר שלשים יום בא אחר וקדשה מעכשיו ולאחר כ' יום בא אחר וקדשה מעכשיו ולאחר עשרה ימים בא אחר וקדשה מעכשיו אפי' הן מאה כולם תופסים בה דכל חד וחד רווחא לחבריה שבק ושמא י"ל דקודשין אלימי וכיון דאשכחו רווחא תו לא פקעי אבל הכא גיזות וולדות לכל הפחות הנהו דאיתנהו בשעת מסירה אהני מעכשיו לקנותה סמוך לגניבתה למפרע:

אלא מהא ליכא למשמע מינה. תימה כיון דקשיא ליה רישא לסיפא נימא נעשה כדאמרינן בפרק קמא דקידושין (דף ה:) ותקשה לר' יוחנן ° וי"ל דשילם נקט לאביי דפרק הגוזל קמא (ב"ק ד' קח.) לאורויי דאם נשבע ושילם דאין הכפל שלו ולרבא לאורויי שילם אע"פ שנשבע תחלה שהכפל שלו ולא רצה לישבע היינו לא רצה לעמוד בשבועה אבל אם אמר הריני משלם אם נשבע תחלה אין הכפל שלו:

שואל עד שישלם. הואיל וכל הנאה שלו והאי טעמא אפי' אם התנה להיות כש"ח לא קנה עד שישלם ולטעמא דלעיל דמשום לא: שכיחא אם התנה להיות כש"ח קנה כפל במגו דפטר נפשיה בגניבה ואבידה דשכיחא:

ללישנא קמא דרב פפא ודאי לא הויא תיובתא. דאמר הריני משלם לא קנה כפל אבל שילם קנה כפל ור"ח גרס ודאי הויא תיובתא דכיון דרב פפא מפרש טעמא משום דלא שכיח האי טעמא שייך אפילו בשילם והא דנקט ואמר הריני משלם משום דנקט גבי ש"ח וש"ש נקט נמי גבי שואל:

**עין משפט נר מצוה**

ד א מיי' פ"ח מהל' שאלה הל' א סמג עשין פב טוש"מ סי' רלה:
ה ב טוש"מ שם:
ו ג ד מיי' שם סמג שם טוש"מ שם:
ז ה ו ז ח מיי' שם הל' ג טוש"מ שם:
ח ט מיי' שם הלכה ד טוש"מ שם:

**רבינו חננאל**

ופריק רבא נעשה כאומר לו בשעה שהפקיד אצלו לכשתיגנב ותרצה ותשלם לי הרי פרתי זו קנויה לך מעכשיו. אי הכי כי מאותה שעה שהפקידה אצלו הקנה אותה לו. יהיה אפילו גיזותיה וולדותיה לו. א) ופריק איכא דאמרי אמר רבא נעשה כאומר לו לכשתגנב ותרצה ותשלם לי תהיה פרתי זו קנויה לך סמוך לגניבה שעה אחת. פי' ללישנא קמא דרבא קנה דהא אית ליה בידיה. ללישנא בתרא דרבא לא קנה דהא באגמא הות קיימא וליתה ברשותיה דליקני לה ליה. פירוש אחר מאי בינייהו איכא בינייהו קשיא דר' זירא. פירוש ללישנא בתרא דרבא דאמ' סמוך לגניבתה קנויה לך לית אורחא לאקשויי אי הכי גיזותיה וולדותיה דליכא סמוך לגניבתה לא גיזות ולא ולדות. אי נמי דקיימא באגם. פי' ללישנא קמא דרבא לא קני כפל ב) דהא ליתה ברשותיה דליקני לה במשיכה ויזכה בכפילא לפיכך ג) אמר פרתי קנויה לך מעכשיו בעידנא דעיילא ברשותיה חוץ מגיזותיה וולדותיה. וללישנא בתרא דרבא אע"ג דהות באגמא קני לה דהא ברשותיה קיימא מעידנא דאפקיד מרה לגביה דהא מיחייב בשמירתה ומיגו דאיחייב בשמירתה כל היכא דאיתה ברשותיה קיימא הלכך זכי ליה בכפילא דאמרינן סמוך לגניבתה אקנייה ליה מרה ונפקא מרשותיה ואשכחתא דממי שהפקדון אצלו נגנבה. א"ר יוחנן לא שילם ממש אלא כיון שאמר הריני משלם אע"פ שלא שילם עדיין קנה. תניא נמי הכי השוכר פרה מחבירו ונגנבה ואמר השוכר הריני משלם ואיני נשבע שנאנסה ונמצא הגנב משלם תשלומי כפל לשוכר. אוקמוה [ב"ק נז ע"ב] לר"מ שאמר שוכר כשומר חנם משלם. אמר רב פפא שומר חנם שאמר פשעתי בה מיקני ליה כפל דאי בעי הוה פטר נפשיה בגניבה ואבידה וכיון שאמר פשעתי ואני חייב לשלם כאילו שילם וקנה הכפל וכן שומר שכר שהודה לו כי נגנבה. אבל שואל אע"פ שאמר הריני משלם לא קנה הכפל דלית ליה למיפטר נפשיה אלא במתה מחמת מלאכה והא נגנבה וליתה גביה דנימא מחמת מלאכה מתה. איכא דאמרי שואל נמי כיון דאמר הריני משלם קני כפל וכו' אמר ליה רב זביד הכי אמר אביי שואל עד שישלם מאי טעמא הואיל וכל הנאה שלו היא בדיבורא לא קני ליה כפל.

והלכתא כרב פפא בשומר חנם ובשומר שכר מיגו דאי בעו הוו יכלי למיפטר נפשייהו וקא מודו בההוא הנאה מקנה להו כפילא. חדא דשמעתיה דר' יוחנן סתמא היא. ורב זביד נמי לא פליג עליה אלא בשואל בלחוד ובשואל הלכתא כרב זביד דתניא בהדיא כוותיה ודייקינן ללישנא קמא דרב פפא דאמר שואל כיון שאין לו דרך להפטר מן התשלומין אע"פ שאמר הריני משלם לא קנה כפל הוא הדין ואפי' שילם דהא חיוביה קא פרע ולא מהני מידי למשאיל דליקני ליה כפילא אי הכי קשיא ליה הא דתניא השואל פרה מחבירו ונגנבה וקדם השואל ושילם ואחר כך נמצא הגנב משלם תשלומי כפל לשואל ואתינן לדחויה ד) ולא נדחית אלא מדקתני גבי שוכר ואמר הריני משלם וגבי שואל תני וקדם ושילם ושתי הברייתות הללו ביחד הם שנויות במקום אחד זו אחר זו במתניתא דבי רבי חייא דוקא קתני וקדם ושילם ש"מ דאפילו שואל אם שילם קנה כפל קשיא לרב פפא לפום דוקיא דדייקינן משמעתיה דהוא הדין אפילו שילם לא קנה. ויש מי שגורס הכי ללישנא קמא דרב פפא ודאי לא הויא הא דתניא כוותיה דרב זביד תיובתא ומאן דגריס הכי פשוטה היא אינה צריכה לפנים ולא לפני לפנים. תוב [מקשינן] ללישנא בתרא דרב פפא דאמר כיון דאמר השואל הריני משלם קנה כפל קשיא ליה הא מתניתא דקתני גבי שואל וקדם ושילם ואוקימנא דוקא שילם אבל אמר ואכתי לא שילם לא קנה ונדחו דברי רב פפא בשואל לתרתי לישני ובשילם השואל דברי הכל

**מסורת הש"ס**

א) [לקמן לז.], ב) [ברכות כה. וש"נ, עיין נדרים עב.], ג) בבא קמא מז:, ד) [לקמן לב., שבת יח., ערובין כ:, גיטין סד.].

**הגהות הב"ח**

(א) רש"י ד"ה ללישנא וכו' דלא הוה ליה למפטר: (ב) ד"ה והא מדקתני וכו' וגבי שואל וקידם ושילם:

**גליון הש"ס**

גמ' אמר רבא נעשה. עיין במרדכי פ"ק דב"מ אות (רל"ח) [רמז]: שם אלא מהא ליכא למשמע מינה. נדה לג ע"ב: תוס' ד"ה אלא וכו'. וי"ל דשילם נקט לאביי. עיין נדרים דף ס ע"ב וצ"ע:

**ליקוטי רש"י**

משלם תשלומי כפל לשוכר. דכיון דשילם נמלאת הגניבה שלו [ב"ק נז:]. הואיל וכל הנאה שלו. שבתנם הוא עושה מלאכתו וכו היה לו להחמיר יותר [לקמן צד:]. מידי גבי הדדי תניא. הדא תניא ר' חייא והדא תניא רבי אושעיא [שבת יח.]. הני תרי תנאי נינהו [גיטין סד.]. שיילינהו לתנאי דבי רבי חייא ודבי רבי אושעיא. סדרו את הברייתות ודקדקו בדברי כל חכם לומר כמו שאמר [חולין קמא:].

**חשק שלמה על ר"ח**

א) נראה דנתחלפו השורות בכאן וכן צ"ל ופריק נעשה כאומר לו חוץ מגיזותיה וולדותיה איכא דאמרי אמר רבא וכו' עד תיבות שעה אחת. מאי בינייהו איכא בינייהו קושיא דר' זירא וכו' עד תיבות דקיימא באגם. פי' ללישנא קמא דרבא קנה וכו' עד תיבות דליקני לה ליה. פירוש אחר ללישנא קמא דרבא לא קני כפל וכו'. ב) ר"ל אם לא הי' אומר מעכשיו. ג) נראה דצ"ל לפיכך צריך שיאמר הרי פרתי קניה לך מעכשיו דאז קנה לה בעידנא דעיילא ברשותיה. ד) דברי רבינו צריך ביאור בזה דלל"ק דרב פפא אין זה דיחוי כלל דשלם לאו דוקא דאדרבה דכ"ש דהוי תיובתא ואולי דגי' אחרת היה לו וצ"ע.

**מִי יֵימַר דְּמִגַּנְבָא – who says that [the deposit] will be stolen?**[1] **וְאִם תִּמְצֵי לוֹמַר דְּמִגַּנְבָא – And even if it is** eventually **stolen, מִי יֵימַר דְּמִשְׁתְּכַח גַּנָּב – who says that the thief will be caught? וְאִי מִשְׁתְּכַח גַּנָּב – And even if the thief is caught, מִי יֵימַר דְּמִשַׁלֵּם – who says that he will** have to **pay? דִּלְמָא מוֹדֵי וּמִפְּטַר – Perhaps he will confess** his crime **and** thereby **avoid** having to pay the penalty?[2] Since there are so many uncertainties about ever collecting the penalty payments, they can certainly not be considered *likely* to come, and therefore should not be transferable even according to R' Meir.

The Gemara answers:

**אָמַר רָבָא – Rava said: נַעֲשָׂה כְּאוֹמֵר לוֹ – It is as if** the owner **told [the *shomer*]** when he handed him the animal: **לִכְשֶׁתִּגָּנֵב וְתִרְצֶה וּתְשַׁלְּמֵנִי – "Should [this cow] be stolen, and you will be willing and pay me** for its loss, **הֲרֵי פָּרָתִי קְנוּיָה לְךָ מֵעַכְשָׁיו – my cow is hereby transferred to you as of now."**[3] By making such a stipulation, the cow itself can become the *shomer's* retroactively to the time he received it from the owner. He is therefore entitled to the penalty payments because it turns out that it was *his* cow that was stolen.[4]

The Gemara objects:

**מַתְקִיף לָהּ רַבִּי זֵירָא – R' Zeira challenges [this explanation]: אִי הָכִי – If it is so** that the *shomer* retroactively acquires the animal from the moment he took it to watch, **אֲפִילוּ גִּיזּוֹתֶיהָ וּוְלָדוֹתֶיהָ נַמִּי –** he should acquire **even her shearings and offspring** from the time she entered his possession.[5] **אַלְמָה תַּנְיָא – Why, then, was it taught in a Baraisa** that the *shomer* collects any additional revenue generated by the animal if he pays the owner for its loss, **חוּץ מִגִּיזּוֹתֶיהָ וּוְלָדוֹתֶיהָ – WITH THE EXCEPTION OF HER SHEARINGS AND OFFSPRING?**

R' Zeira therefore gives a slightly different explanation:

**אֶלָּא אָמַר רַבִּי זֵירָא – Rather, R' Zeira said: נַעֲשָׂה כְּאוֹמֵר לוֹ – It is as if** the owner had expressly **told [the *shomer*]** that he will retroactively acquire the animal **חוּץ מִגִּיזּוֹתֶיהָ וּוְלָדוֹתֶיהָ – with the exception of her shearings and offspring.**

The Gemara questions:

**וּמַאי פַּסְקָא – And why did you decide** that every depositor intends to keep for himself the shearings and offspring, but not the penalty payment?

The Gemara explains:

**סְתָמָא דְּמִלְּתָא – Ordinarily,**[6] **שִׁבְחָא דְּאָתְיָא מֵעָלְמָא – a profit that derives from an outside** source, **עָבִיד אִינִישׁ דְּמַקְנֵי – a person is accustomed to transfer** to others; **שִׁבְחָא דְּמִגּוּפָהּ –** however, **a profit that comes** directly **from the body of [the animal],** such as its wool or offspring, **לָא עָבִיד אִינִישׁ דְּמַקְנֵי – a person is not accustomed to transfer** to others.[7]

The Gemara cites a different version of Rava's explanation of the Mishnah:

**אִיכָּא דְּאָמְרֵי – There are those who say אָמַר רָבָא –** that **Rava said: נַעֲשָׂה כְּאוֹמֵר לוֹ – It is as if** the owner **told [the *shomer*]** when he handed him the animal: **לִכְשֶׁתִּגָּנֵב וְתִרְצֶה וּתְשַׁלְּמֵנִי – "Should [this cow] be stolen, and you will be willing and pay me** for its loss, **סָמוּךְ לִגְנֵיבָתָהּ קְנוּיָה לְךָ – it is** hereby **transferred to you** as of a moment **before its theft."**[8] Therefore, the *shomer* does not receive the shearings or offspring that grew before the animal was stolen, because the animal belonged to the owner until a moment before it was stolen.

The Gemara asks:

**מַאי בֵּינַיְיהוּ – What is** the difference **between these** two versions of Rava's explanation? **אִיכָּא בֵּינַיְיהוּ – There is** a difference **between them קוּשְׁיָא דְּרַבִּי זֵירָא –** with regard to **the objection of R' Zeira.**[9] **אִי נַמִּי – Alternatively,** there is a practical difference **דְּקַיְימָא בַּאֲגַם – when** the animal **is standing in a marsh** at the time of the theft, and not in the *shomer's* property.[10]

NOTES

1. As explained above (33b note 13), the *shomer* must acquire the right to collect the penalty payments at the time he first receives the deposit (*pikadon*) from its owner. At that time, there is no reason to assume it will eventually be stolen (*Rashi*).

2. The Torah states: אֲשֶׁר יַרְשִׁיעֻן אֱלֹהִים יְשַׁלֵּם שְׁנַיִם לְרֵעֵהוּ, *he whom the judges will condemn shall pay double to his fellow* (*Exodus* 22:8). The Gemara (*Bava Kamma* 64b) derives from this verse that a penalty is paid only by someone found guilty by the court, not by someone who confesses on his own. Thus, if the thief confesses his crime, he will have to pay only the amount he stole, but not the extra penalty payment.

[Our Gemara indicates that a thief can forever free himself from the double payment by confessing his crime before witnesses come to court to testify about it. This follows the opinion of Rav, who maintains (*Bava Kamma* 74b, 75a) that once a person confesses to a crime involving a penalty, he is exempt from paying it even if witnesses later come to court and testify to his guilt (*Tosafos*). Shmuel (ibid. 75a) disputes this.]

3. [A transaction can be made based on a condition, in such a way that if the condition is later fulfilled, the transaction is seen to have taken effect from the time it was originally made.] Here too, when the owner hands the cow to the *shomer* and he takes it from him, with the condition that if it is eventually stolen and the *shomer* pays for it the cow will become his from the time he took possession of it, once the *shomer* pays for it, the cow becomes his retroactively, from the time he took it from the owner (*Rashi*).

4. Although the owner did not actually say this when he handed the cow to the *shomer,* we presume that he meant it, because an owner is happy to give up a potential penalty payment so as to be guaranteed being paid for his lost principal (*Rashi*).

5. If the animal that had been given to him was a sheep, and he sheared its wool for the owner while he was caring for it, that wool should now belong to the *shomer,* since it turns out that the sheep had become his at the moment it was deposited with him. Similarly, if it was a female animal and it give birth while in his care, the offspring should belong to the *shomer*!

6. Literally: the ordinary way of things.

7. Therefore, when an owner deposits an animal with someone, we assume he is willing to give away the outside profits (the penalty payments) to guarantee his principal in case it is stolen or lost. But we do not assume he is willing to give away the profits that come from the body of the animal itself, such as its shearings and offspring.

8. [A person may agree to give away something to another person, and say that the transfer should take effect at a later time. When that time arrives, the transfer will take effect without any new declaration being needed.] This is what is happening here, according to the new explanation. When the owner delivers the animal to the *shomer,* he in effect says to him that if the animal is stolen and the *shomer* pays for it, the animal should become retroactively the *shomer's*. But the owner sets the *time* for the transfer to take effect in the future – at a moment before the animal is stolen. Thus, even if the animal is eventually stolen and paid for, and the animal becomes the *shomer's* retroactively, it only becomes his from just before the theft. For this reason, it is obvious that the *shomer* will have no claim on the shearings or offspring that happened before this time (see *Rashi*).

Of course, the owner did not say any of this when he handed the animal to the *shomer,* but he is assumed to have meant it. See above, note 4.

9. According to the second version, there is no basis for R' Zeira's question that the shearings and offspring should be acquired retroactively by the *shomer*, since he does not acquire the animal until just before the theft (*Rashi*).

10. According to the first version of Rava's explanation, the *shomer* receives the penalty payments, since he acquired the animal retroactively with the *kinyan* (act of transfer) he performed when he first took the animal from the owner into his care. [Taking the animal is a *kinyan* known as *meshichah,* which is effective for acquiring animals and most movable property (see above, 33b note 13).] However, according to the second version of Rava's explanation, the *shomer* does not acquire even the animal, much less any penalty payment, because at the time stipulated for him to acquire it (immediately preceding the theft), no method of *kinyan* is available to him to acquire it. The *meshichah* he made when he first took the animal cannot help because *meshichah* can acquire only at the time it is done, not at a later time

owner transfers the future penalty payments to the *shomer,* if he is willing to pay for the stolen item and not swear and free himself from payment.[10]

The Gemara questions how the owner can transfer the future penalty payments to the *shomer:*[11]

מַתְקִיף לָהּ רָמִי בַּר חָמָא – **Rami bar Chama challenges [this ruling]:** וְהָא אֵין אָדָם מַקְנֶה דָּבָר שֶׁלֹּא בָּא לָעוֹלָם – **But a person cannot transfer** to someone else **something that has not** yet **come into existence!**[12] How, then, can the owner transfer a penalty payment that no thief is yet obligated to pay?[13]

Rami bar Chama reinforces his challenge:

וַאֲפִילּוּ לְרַבִּי מֵאִיר דְּאָמַר – **And even according to R' Meir, wh** says אָדָם מַקְנֶה דָּבָר שֶׁלֹּא בָּא לָעוֹלָם – that **a person *can* transfe something that has not** yet **come into existence,** the Mishnah' ruling is still difficult. הָנֵי מִילֵּי – For **that teaching** of R' Mei applies only כְּגוֹן פֵּירוֹת דֶּקֶל – when someone transfers, **fo instance, the** future **fruits of a palm tree,**[14] דַּעֲבִידֵי דְּאָתוּ – **which are likely to come** (i.e. grow);[15] אֲבָל הָכָא – **but her** in the case of a penalty payment,

NOTES

10. [It is more important to the owner to be paid for his stolen *pikadon* right away than to take a chance and see if the thief is caught and can be forced to make the extra penalty payments.]

11. *Rashi. Ritva,* however, argues that the expression מַתְקִיף never introduces a challenge to a Mishnah, only to an Amoraic statement. He therefore explains that the Gemara does not find the Mishnah's ruling difficult in itself, for perhaps the Sages awarded the penalty payments to the *shomer* as a matter of public policy, to encourage *shomrim* to pay rather than swear. However, the previous discussion of the Gemara made it clear that it is the owner of the item who transfers the penalty payments to the *shomer*. The Gemara now challenges that interpretation by asking how this can work.

12. Literally: come into the world.

13. *Rashi.* Rami bar Chama takes for granted that the right to collect the penalty payment must be transferred to the *shomer* at the time the item is first given to him and he takes possession of it (*Rashi* 34a ד״ה מי יימר דמגנבא). [It cannot take place at the time the *shomer* pays for the stolen item because money by itself cannot acquire מְטַלְטְלִין, *movable property* (or anything else other than real estate). Thus, it must be the act of taking possession of the animal or utensil (*meshichah*) that is considered the act of *kinyan* for the penalty payments (*Tosafos* ד״ה כגון).] But at the time this item was given to the *shomer* nothing had yet been stolen and no one had yet become liable to pay anything! The eventual penalty payment was something that had not yet come into existence (*Rashi*).

14. R' Meir's opinion is recorded in *Kiddushin* (63a), where he rule that a non-Jew may perform an act of marriage with a Jewish womar to take effect when he converts. We see from this that R' Meir uphold a transaction (such as marriage) in which a vital element (in this case the man entering the marriage) has not come into existence (since non-Jew is not subject to the laws of Jewish marriage).

R' Meir never actually discusses the case of selling "the fruit of palm tree." However, in the Gemara below (66b) Rav Huna states tha a person can sell the future fruit of his tree even before the fruit start growing. The Gemara in *Yevamos* (93a) says that this ruling follows th opinion of R' Meir, who holds that one can transfer something that ha not yet come into the world. For this reason our Gemara speaks of R Meir's opinion in terms of the sale of the fruit of his tree, even thoug R' Meir actually never spoke about this case (*Rashi, Ramban, Ritva*).

15. The Gemara's statement is difficult to understand. The case tha R' Meir ruled on in *Kiddushin* (see previous note) involves a situatio where the object that must come into existence (a Jewish man) is nc necessarily likely to happen, since the non-Jew may decide in the en not to convert. Yet R' Meir considers his *kiddushin* to be effective!

Some explain that, in R' Meir's cases, the thing that must come int existence *is* likely to happen. Since the non-Jew knows that he wishe to convert, he will most likely be able to arrange for a *beis din* to ove see his conversion. See *Ramban, Tosafos* to *Kesubos* 58b ד״ה לאחר, *To HaRosh,* and *Ritva* for this and other answers.

א) בימי רבי נשנית משנה זו שבקו כולא עלמא מתניתין ואזלו בתר גמרא הדר דרש להו ולעולם הוי רץ למשנה יותר מן הגמרא מאי דרוש כדדריש רבי יהודה ברבי אלעאי מאי דכתיב א) הגד לעמי פשעם ולבית יעקב חטאתם הגד לעמי פשעם אלו תלמידי חכמים ב) ששגגות נעשות להם כזדונות ולבית יעקב חטאתם אלו עמי הארץ שזדונות נעשות להם כשגגות והיינו דתנן ג) ר' יהודה אומר הוי זהיר בתלמוד ששגגת תלמוד עולה זדון דרש ר' יהודה בר' אלעאי מאי דכתיב ב) שמעו דבר ה' החרדים אל דברו אלו תלמידי חכמים [אמרו] אחיכם אלו בעלי מקרא שנאיכם אלו בעלי משנה מנדיכם ו) אלו עמי הארץ שמא תאמר פסק סברם ובטל סיכוים ת"ל ונראה בשמחתכם שמא תאמר ישראל יבושו תלמוד לומר והם יבושו עובדי כוכבים יבושו וישראל ישמחו:

## הדרן עלך אלו מציאות

**המפקיד** ד) אצל חבירו בהמה או כלים ונגנבו או שאבדו שילם ולא רצה לישבע א שהרי אמרו שומר חנם נשבע ויוצא ב נמצא הגנב משלם תשלומי כפל טבח ומכר משלם תשלומי ארבעה וחמשה למי משלם ג למי שהפקדון אצלו ד נשבע ולא רצה לשלם נמצא הגנב משלם תשלומי כפל טבח ומכר משלם תשלומי ארבעה וחמשה למי משלם לבעל הפקדון: **גמ'** למה ליה למתני בהמה ולמה ליה למתני כלים צריכי דאי תנא בהמה הוה אמינא בהמה הוא דמקני ליה כפילא משום דנפיש טירחה לעיולה ולאפוקה אבל כלים דלא נפיש טירחייהו אימא לא מקני ליה כפילא ואי תנא כלים הוה אמינא כלים הוא דקמקני ליה כפילא משום דלא נפיש כפלייהו אבל בהמה דכי טבח ומכר משלם תשלומי ד' וה' אימא לא מקני ליה כפילא צריכא מתקיף לה רמי בר חמא והא ה אין אדם מקנה דבר שלא בא לעולם ואפילו ו) לר"מ דאמר אדם מקנה דבר שלא בא לעולם ה"מ כגון פירות דקל דעבידי דאתו אבל הכא

---

**רש"י**

**בימי רבי נשנית משנה זו.** הא דקתני גמרא אין לך מדה גדולה מזו לפי שמשרבו תלמידי שמאי והלל שהיו לפניו שלשה דורות רבו מחלוקות בתורה ונעשית כשתי תורות ז) מתוך עול שעבוד מלכיות וגזירות שהיו גוזרין עליהן ומתוך כך לא היו יכולים לתת לב לברר דברי החולקים עד ימיו של רבי שנתן הקב"ה לו חן בעיני אנטונינוס מלך רומי כדאמרינן בע"ז (דף י:) ונחו מצרה ושלח וקבץ כל תלמידי ארץ ישראל ועד ימיו לא היו מסכתות סדורות אלא כל תלמיד ששמע דבר מפי גדול הימנו גרסה ונתן סימנים הלכה פלונית ופלונית שמעתי משם פלוני וכשנתקבצו אמר כל אחד מה ששמע ונתנו לב לברר טעמי המחלוקת דברי מי ראוין לקיים וסידרו המסכתות דברי נזיקין לבדם ודברי יבמות לבדם ודברי קדשים לבדם וסתם נמי במשנה דברי יחידים שראה רבי את דבריהם ושנאן סתם כדי לקבוע הלכה כמותם לפיכך אמרו בגמרא אין לך מדה גדולה מזו שיתנו לב לטעמי המשנה: **שבקו כולי עלמא מתני'.** מלחזור על גרסת משנתם: **ואזלו בתר גמרא.** לחשוב בסברא: **הדר דרש להו הוי רץ למשנה.** לפי שירא פן ישתכחו המשניות ויחליפו שמות החכמים ובמקום חיוב יאמרו פטור ובמקום אסור יאמרו מותר: **מאי דרוש.** מתחילה כשדרש שגמרא גדול: **לעמי פשעם.** עמי דהיינו ת"ח את חטאתם אני קורא פשע שהיה להם לתת לב בטעמי משנתם שיבררו להם על העיקר ולא יורו הלכה מתוך משנה שאינה עיקר: **ולבית יעקב.** שאר העם: **חטאתם.** אפילו פשע שלהם אני קורא חטאת: **הוי זהיר בתלמוד.** בגמרא שהיא תירוץ [טעמי] המשניות או אם תשמע דבר משנה מרבך הזהר לשאול טעמיו ומי שנאה: **ששגגת תלמוד.** אם שגית בהוראה בשגגת תלמודך שלא ידעת טעם המשנה ונתת בה טעם אחר ומתוך כך דמית לה דין או הוראה שבא לידך ולמדת הימנה שלא כדת שאין הטעם כמו שהיית סבור שאילו ידעת טעם המשנה לא דמית לה מעשה הבא לידך: **עולה זדון.** ענוש אתה עליה כמזיד שזדון הוא בידך שלא שאלת טעם מרבך: **אלו ת"ח.** ששימשו חכמים הרבה ללמדם טעמי משנתם זה בזו וזה בזו שאין הכל בקיאין בשוין: **שנאיכם אלו בעלי משנה.** ששונאין בעלי גמרא לפי שבעלי גמרא אומרים על בעלי משנה שהן מבלי עולם כדאמרינן במסכת סוטה (דף כב.) התנאים מבלי עולם שמורים הלכה מתוך משנתם: **מנדיכם אלו ע"ה.** שת"ח שנואין ומתועבין להן כנדה: **שמא תאמר אבד סברם.** של אלו שהרי כתיב למען שמי יכבד ה' דמשמע שהם אומרים אבל אין הדבר כן: ת"ל ונראה בשמחתכם. ולא נאמר ונראה בשמחתכם כך אמר הנביא אני ואחיכם שונאיכם ומנדיכם כולנו נראה בשמחתכם: **והם יבושו.** אותם שהם עובדי כוכבים שאינם ממנו ואין נקראין על שם ישראל הם יבושו וישראל ישמחו:

הדרן עלך אלו מציאות

**המפקיד. ולא רצה לישבע.** שבועת שומרים שלא פשע בה ושלא שלח בה יד שהיה יכול ליפטר בשבועה זו שהרי אמרו כו': **למי שהפקדון אצלו.** דכיון דשילם קנה כל תשלומיה ובגמרא מפרש טעמא: **גמ' דמקני ליה כפילא.** הבעלים מקנין לשומר כפל העתיד להשתלם כדאמר לקמן שבשעה שמסרה לו לשמור על מנת כן מסרה שאם תגנב וירצה וישלם יהא כפל שלו: **אימר לא מקנה ליה כפילא.** לא מסרה לו מתחילה על מנת כן: **דלא נפיש כפלייהו.** שאין באין לידי ארבעה וחמשה שאינה נוהגת אלא בשור ושה בלבד: **מתקיף לה רמי כו'.** אמתניתין קא מתמה: **והא אין אדם מקנה דבר שלא בא לעולם.** והיאך הקנו לו בעלים כפל זה שעדיין לא נתחייב בו גנב: **ואפילו לר' מאיר דאמר.** בפ"ג דקדושין (דף סג.) הרי את מקודשת לי על מנת שאתגייר איכא למיגמר מינה מוכר פירות דקל לחבירו עד שלא באו לעולם דאפליגו בה רב הונא ורב נחמן לקמן באיזהו נשך (דף סו:): **דעבידי דאתו.** גרסינן:

מי

---

**תוספות**

**אחיכם** אלו בעלי מקרא. שאינם יודעים דינים והוראות כי אם על פי בעלי גמרא שונאיכם אלו בעלי משנה שסבורים לידע כמו בעלי גמרא ואינם יודעים בירור הדבר מנדיכם אלו ע"ה ששונאים ת"ח ושמא תאמר אבד סברן ת"ל ונראה בשמחתכם ישראל ישמחו ועובדי כוכבים יבושו:

הדרן עלך אלו מציאות

**המפקיד.** אית דלא גרסי או שאבדו משום דבאבידה ליכא כפל ויש לישב שכך טוען הנפקד ואחר כך נמצא הגנב אי נמי אנו יודעים שנגנבו מתוך ביתו אך אין אנו יודעים אם פשע או שאבדו שאנו יודעין שנאבד ממנו אך לא ידעינן אם על ידי גניבה או על ידי דבר אחר:

**נגנבו.** ה"ה אם אמר פשעתי שהכפל שלו כדאמר בגמרא מגו דאי בעי פטר נפשיה בגניבה אלא אורחא דמילתא נקט נגנבו שהוא רגילות לטעון דבר שהוא פטור אע"פ שהוא רוצה לשלם וריב"ן פי' דמתני' נמי ה"פ דהנפקד אומר שנגנבו בפשיעה ולא רצה לישבע היינו ולא רצה לישבע לשקר: **כגון** פירות דקל דעבידי דאתו. וא"ת והכא אפילו אי עבידי דאתו היאך יקנה הכפל במעות ששילם והלא מעות אינן קונות אלא למיקם עליה במי שפרע ועוד מאי קפריך בסמוך מי יימר דמיגנבא והלא כששילם כבר נגנבה והו"ל מי יימר דנגנבה פירוש שכבר נגנבה שמא נאבדה ויש לומר דהמקשה סבר דבשעת משיכה הקנה לו הפרה לקנות הכפל כשיבא ואע"ג דבפרק מי שמת (ב"ב דף קמז:) אמרי' דבדקל לפירות אפילו רבנן מודו דקני היינו משום דעבידי דאתו אבל הכא דלא עבידו דאתא אפילו לר' מאיר לא קני וקשה דבפ' השולח (גיטין מב: ושם) מיבעיא לן בעבד שמכרו רבו לקנס דדילמא אפילו לר' מאיר לא יועיל משום דלא עבידא דאתי דמנגח או דילמא אפילו לרבנן יועיל משום דהא קאי עבדא והוי כדקל לפירותיו והכא פשיטא ליה דלא מהני פרה לכפילא ואפילו לר"מ וי"ל דשמא התם שכיח טפי מהכא אי נמי הכא פריך אם תימצי לומר בעבד שמכרו רבו לקנס דלא מהני לר"מ ומשני נעשה כאומר לו לכשתגנב ותשלמני הרי פרתי קנויה לך מעכשיו שגוף הפרה מכר לו דהשתא הכפל שלו ממילא ז):

דילמא

---

**עין משפט נר מצוה**

א א מיי' פ"א מהלכות שכירות הל' ג סמג עשין פט טור ש"ע ח"מ סי' רלא סעיף א:

ב ב ג ד מיי' פ"ח מהל' שאלה ופקדון הלכה א סמג עשין פח טור ח"מ סי' רצה:

ג ה מיי' פכ"ב מהלכות מכירה הלכה י סמג עשין פ"ב טור ש"ע ח"מ סי' רט סעיף ד:

**רבינו חננאל**

שבבבל עומדין זה מלפני זה וקורעין זה על זה וכו'. פי' כיון שנושאין זה עם זה בהלכה לומדין זה מזה טעמי' הרבה כרבו הוא חשוב כל אחד לחבירו לפיכך עומדין זה מפני זה וקורעין זה על זה אבל לענין השבת אבידה אינו מניח של אביו ומחזיר לרבו אלא אם הוא רבו מובהק. רב חסדא הוא תלמיד רב הונא דגרסי' בעירובין בתחלת פרק הדר עם הנכרי בחצר. אמר רב יוסף ביעתא בכותחא בעאי מרב חסדא בשני רב הונא ולא פשט לי. פי' מפני שיש בכותח כמכא דחלבא הוצרך לשאול אם הוא מותר שיאכל ביצת שחוטה בכותח אי לא כלומר ביצת שחוטה כבשר היא וכיון שיש בכותח חלב נמצא כאילו אוכל בשר בחלב ואסור אי לא ואע"ג דדבר ברור הוא דתניא השוחט את התרנגולת ומצא בה ביצים גמורות מותרות לאכלן בחלב אפי' הכי זה שהוא דבר קל לא רצה להורות בפני רב הונא רבו. בעא מיניה רב חסדא מרב הונא תלמיד וצריך לו רבו מהו כלומר תלמיד חריף שרבו נהנה ממנו ומשאילות התלמיד ומחקריו מוסיף הרב חכמה כדאמר [בסנהדרין סח] הרבה למדתי מרבותי ומחברי יותר מהם ומתלמידי יותר מכולם תלמיד כגון זה אצל רבו יניח אבידת אביו ויחזיר או לא וחשב רב הונא בדעתו כי רב (הונא) [חסדא] על עצמו שאל וכי הוא כענין תלמיד שצריך לו רבו וכעס והשיבו חסדא חסדא לא צריכנא לך ולא לחידודך ולא לפלפולך אנת צריך לקבל ממני עד מלאת לך לפני מ' שנה שבמלאת מ' שנה עומד התלמיד על דעת רבו כדכתיב ואולך אתכם ארבעים שנה במדבר וגו' ולא נתן ה' לכם לב לדעת וגו': איקפדו להדדי ולא עול לגבי [הדדי]. רב הונא יתיב ארבעין תעניתא דחשדיה לרב חסדא. רב חסדא יתיב ארבעין תעניתא משום דחלש דעתיה דרב הונא. דרש ר' יהודה בר' אלעי שמעו דבר ה' החרדים אל דברו אלו תלמידי חכמים וכו':

הדרן עלך אלו מציאות

המפקיד אצל חבירו בהמה או כלים נגנבו או שאבדו שילם ולא רצה לישבע וכו' עד למי משלם למי שהפקדון אצלו וכן הלכה. ומקשי' והא אין [אדם] מקנה לחבירו דבר שלא בא לעולם כלומר היאך יכול המפקיד להקנות כפילו למי שהפקדון בידו והא אפי' ר' מאיר דסבר אדם מקנה לחבירו דבר שלא בא לעולם כי האי גוונא לא אמר.

---

**מסורת הש"ס**

א) [עיין תוספות בבא קמא לד: ד"ה בימי וכו'] ב) [דוגמתו סנהדרין קג:] ג) אבות פרק ד משנה יג ד) ב"ק קח., ה) יבמות לג. קדושין סב:, גיטין יג: מב:, ב"ב עט:, קמז:, קלא. קמא:, קמו., ו) [סוטה מז: סנהדרין פח:], ז) [ועי' תוספות ב"ב עט: ד"ה אימור].

**גליון הש"ס**

גמ' אלו עמי הארץ. עי' סוטה דף כב ע"א תוס' ד"ה רבי שמואל. רש"י ד"ה בימי וכו' שמשרבו תלמידי. ועיין חגיגה דף טז ע"ב תוספות ד"ה יוסי:

**הגהות מהר"ב רנשבורג**

א] ברש"י ד"ה מתקיף לה רמי. נ"ב עיין הליכות עולם דף (ז) [ה] ע"ב ודף (ח) [ו] ע"א ובדברי בעל יבין שמועה שם יעוש"ה ע"ב בד"ה ה"ע ומליץ מתקיף וכו':

**תורה אור השלם**

א) קְרָא בְגָרוֹן אַל תַּחְשֹׂךְ כַּשּׁוֹפָר הָרֵם קוֹלֶךָ וְהַגֵּד לְעַמִּי פִּשְׁעָם וּלְבֵית יַעֲקֹב חַטֹּאתָם: [ישעיה נח, א]

ב) שִׁמְעוּ דְּבַר יְיָ הַחֲרֵדִים אֶל דְּבָרוֹ אָמְרוּ אֲחֵיכֶם שֹׂנְאֵיכֶם מְנַדֵּיכֶם לְמַעַן שְׁמִי יִכְבַּד יְיָ וְנִרְאֶה בְשִׂמְחַתְכֶם וְהֵם יֵבֹשׁוּ: [ישעיה סו, ה]

**ליקוטי רש"י**

הגד לעמי. אלו תלמידי חכמים שכל שגגתם פשע ששגגת תלמוד עולה זדון [ישעיה נח, ב]. החרדים אל דברו. הצדיקים הממהרים במרוצה להתקרב אל דבריו. [ישעיה סו, ה]. ובטל סיכוים. תוחלתם ומבטם כדמתרגמינן הבט נא (בראשית טו) איסתכי כען לשמיא [סוכה מה:]. שהרי אמרו וכו'. וכי היה ליפטר בשבועה [ב"ק קח.]. פירות דקל. קודם שחנטו פירותיו [לקמן סו:]. שהמוכר פירות דקל לחבירו אע"פ שעדיין לא באו לעולם אין יכול לחזור בו משיבואו לעולם דהא ודאי עבידי דאתו דומיא דע"מ שאתגייר דדעתי' לאיגיורי ומיהו ר"מ לא איירי בפירות דקל אלא רב הונא דקאי כוותי' במסכת יבמות [רשב"ם ב"ב עט:].

# Chapter Three

**Mishnah** The Mishnah discusses cases involving a deposit that was lost or stolen while in the care of an unpaid *shomer*:

הַמַּפְקִיד אֵצֶל חֲבֵירוֹ בְּהֵמָה אוֹ כֵּלִים – **If someone deposits with his fellow an animal or utensils** for safekeeping וְנִגְנְבוּ אוֹ שֶׁאָבְדוּ – **and they were stolen or lost,**[1] שִׁילֵּם – and **[the *shomer*] paid** the owner for the lost or stolen items וְלֹא רָצָה לִישָּׁבַע – **and did not want to swear** the oaths of a *shomer* that would free him from paying...[2] The Mishnah interrupts its statement for a moment to state the law of the unpaid *shomer*: שֶׁהֲרֵי אָמְרוּ – **For [the Sages] said** that if a deposit is stolen or lost, שׁוֹמֵר חִנָּם נִשְׁבָּע וְיוֹצֵא – **an unpaid *shomer* may swear and** thereby **fulfill** his obligation to the owner, and he does not have to pay.[3] The Mishnah now returns to its main statement: In this case, where the *shomer* chose to pay rather than swear, נִמְצָא הַגַּנָּב – if **the thief is** later **found,** מְשַׁלֵּם תַּשְׁלוּמֵי כֶפֶל – **he pays a double payment,**[4] טָבַח וּמָכַר – and **if [the thief] slaughtered or sold** the animal he stole before he was caught, מְשַׁלֵּם תַּשְׁלוּמֵי אַרְבָּעָה וַחֲמִשָּׁה – **he pays a fourfold or fivefold payment.**[5] לְמִי מְשַׁלֵּם – **To whom does he pay?** לְמִי שֶׁהַפִּקָּדוֹן אֶצְלוֹ – **To the one with whom the deposit is** at the time it is stolen, i.e. to the *shomer*.[6] נִשְׁבַּע וְלֹא רָצָה לְשַׁלֵּם – If, however, the *shomer* **swore** the oaths he must swear in regard to a lost or stolen item **and did not want to pay** for it, נִמְצָא הַגַּנָּב – if **the thief is** later **found,** מְשַׁלֵּם תַּשְׁלוּמֵי כֶפֶל – **he pays a double payment,** טָבַח וּמָכַר – and if **he slaughtered or sold** the animal before being caught, מְשַׁלֵּם תַּשְׁלוּמֵי אַרְבָּעָה וַחֲמִשָּׁה – **he pays a fourfold or fivefold payment.** לְמִי מְשַׁלֵּם – **To whom does he pay?** לְבַעַל הַפִּקָּדוֹן – **To the owner of the deposit.**

**Gemara** The Mishnah stated that when an unpaid *shomer* pays the owner for a stolen animal or utensil left in his care, he acquires the right to receive any penalty payment later made by the thief. The Gemara questions the necessity of teaching this law with respect to both animals and utensils:

לָמָּה לֵיהּ לְמִתְנֵי בְּהֵמָה – **Why did [the Tanna] teach** this law in the case of a stolen **animal,** וְלָמָּה לֵיהּ לְמִתְנֵי כֵּלִים – **and why did he teach** it as well in the case of stolen **utensils?** Is one case not sufficient?

The Gemara answers:

צְרִיכֵי – **[Both]** teachings **are necessary.** דְּאִי תָּנָא בְּהֵמָה – **For if the [Tanna] had taught** this law only with respect to a stolen **animal,** הֲוָה אָמִינָא – **I might have said** בְּהֵמָה הוּא דְּמַקְנֵי לֵיהּ כְּפֵילָא – **that it is** specifically in the case of **an animal that [the owner] transfers to [the *shomer*]** any future **double payment,** מִשּׁוּם דְּנָפִישׁ טִירְחָה לְעֵיוּלָה וּלְאַפּוּקָה – **because a lot of effort** is involved **in bringing [the animal] in and taking it out** to graze.[7] אֲבָל כֵּלִים – **However,** in the case of **utensils,** דְּלָא נָפִישׁ טִירְחַיְיהוּ – **whose** care **does not** involve **a lot of effort,** אֵימָא לָא מַקְנֵי לֵיהּ כְּפֵילָא – **I might say that [the owner] does not transfer to [the *shomer*]** the right to a future **double payment.**[8] Therefore, it was necessary to teach that he does so in the case of utensils as well.

The Gemara now explains why the Tanna mentions the case of an animal:

וְאִי תָּנָא כֵּלִים – **And if [the Tanna] had taught** this law only with respect to stolen **utensils,** הֲוָה אָמִינָא – **I might have said** כֵּלִים הוּא דְּקַמַּקְנֵי לֵיהּ כְּפֵילָא – **that it is** specifically in the case of **utensils that [the owner]** is willing to **transfer to [the *shomer*]** a future **double payment,** מִשּׁוּם דְּלָא נָפִישׁ כְּפֵלַיְיהוּ – **because their double payment does not increase;** that is, the penalty payment is never more than double. אֲבָל בְּהֵמָה – **However** in the case of an **animal,** דְּכִי טָבַח וּמָכַר – **since when** the thief **slaughters or sells** the animal מְשַׁלֵּם תַּשְׁלוּמֵי ד׳ וה׳ – **he must pay a fourfold or fivefold payment,** אֵימָא לָא מַקְנֵי לֵיהּ כְּפֵילָא – **I might say that [the owner] does not transfer to [the *shomer*]** the right to **a** future **double payment.**[9] צְרִיכָא – Therefore **it was necessary** for the Tanna to teach in both cases that the

NOTES

1. That is, we know from witnesses that the item left with the unpaid *shomer* was stolen *from* his house, but we do not know if this was due to his negligence; or, we know from witnesses that it is missing from his house ("lost") but we do not know if this is because it was stolen (*Tosafos* ד״ה המפקיד, second explanation).

[Some delete the words אוֹ שֶׁאָבְדוּ, *or if they were lost*, from the Mishnah, because it is evident from the rulings that follow that the object was indeed stolen. *Tosafos*, however, keep these words by explaining as we said above, that we know that the object is missing ("lost") but we do not know if it was stolen. In the end it turns out that it was in fact stolen.]

2. A unpaid *shomer* who wishes to free himself from paying for a lost or stolen *pikadon* (an item left with him for safekeeping) must swear that he was not negligent in guarding it and that he did not take the item for his own use (*Rashi;* see *Exodus* 22:7). [He must also swear that it is no longer in his possession. However, this oath is required of him even if he agrees to pay for the missing item, as the Gemara will say below (34b).]

3. Thus, the unpaid *shomer* in our case *could* have freed himself from paying by swearing these oaths; he did not have to pay. But he chose to pay rather than swear.

4. This is the law for any thief: In addition to returning the stolen object, he must pay a fine equal to its value (*Exodus* 22:3, 6).

5. This is the law for anyone who steals livestock: If he steals a sheep and then sells or slaughters it, he must pay four times its value to the owner; and if he steals an ox and sells it or slaughters it, he must pay five times its value to the owner (ibid. 21:37).

6. By paying the owner for the loss of the animal, the *shomer* acquires the rights to any future penalty payment imposed upon the thief. The Gemara will explain how this works (*Rashi*).

[Although the Mishnah speaks of a case where the *shomer* claims the item was stolen or lost through no fault of his, the same would be true even if the *shomer* admitted he was negligent and paid the owner (*Tosafos,* from Gemara below, 34a). As long as the *shomer* could have denied responsibility but he chose instead to pay, he acquired the right to receive the payments from the thief (*Tosafos;* see *Ramban* and *Rashba*).

7. [Since the owner knows that the *shomer* will have to put a lot of effort into caring for the animal, the owner responds more generously] at the time he leaves the animal in the *shomer's* care, by transferring to the *shomer* the rights to any future penalty payments, in case the animal is stolen and the *shomer* pays the owner for it (*Rashi*). [As the Gemara will conclude below, the owner transfers the rights to the future penalty payments to the *shomer* at the time he deposits the item with him.]

8. That is, he does not have in mind at the time he leaves the utensil in the care of the *shomer* to transfer to him rights to future penalty payments (*Rashi*).

9. Since there is a possibility of collecting such a large sum of money, the owner is unwilling to give up the chance for that windfall and give it to the *shomer* in exchange for paying and not swearing. However, in the case of stolen utensils there is never a possibility of collecting more than a double payment, since the fourfold and fivefold penalties apply only to stolen sheep and oxen (*Rashi*).

א) בימי רבי נשנית משנה זו שבקו כולא עלמא מתניתין ואזלו בתר גמרא הדר דרש להו ולעולם הוי רץ למשנה יותר מן הגמרא מאי דרוש כדדריש רבי יהודה ברבי אלעאי מאי דכתיב א) הגד לעמי פשעם ולבית יעקב חטאתם הגד לעמי פשעם אלו תלמידי חכמים ג) ששגגות נעשות להם כזדונות ולבית יעקב חטאתם אלו עמי הארץ שזדונות נעשות להם כשגגות והיינו דתנן ג) ר' יהודה אומר הוי זהיר בתלמוד ששגגת תלמוד עולה זדון דרש ר' יהודה בר' אלעאי מאי דכתיב ב) שמעו דבר ה' החרדים אל דברו אלו תלמידי חכמים [אמרו] אחיכם אלו בעלי מקרא שנאיכם אלו בעלי משנה מנדיכם ° אלו עמי הארץ שמא תאמר פסק סברם ובטל סיכוים ת"ל ונראה בשמחתכם שמא תאמר ישראל יבושו תלמוד לומר והם יבושו עובדי כוכבים יבושו וישראל ישמחו:

## הדרן עלך אלו מציאות

**המפקיד** ד) אצל חבירו בהמה או כלים ונגנבו או שאבדו שילם ולא רצה לישבע א שהרי אמרו שומר חנם נשבע ויוצא ב נמצא הגנב משלם תשלומי כפל טבח ומכר משלם תשלומי ארבעה וחמשה למי משלם ג למי שהפקדון אצלו ד נשבע ולא רצה לשלם נמצא הגנב משלם תשלומי כפל טבח ומכר משלם תשלומי ארבעה וחמשה למי משלם לבעל הפקדון: **גמ'** למה ליה למתני בהמה ולמה ליה למתני כלים צריכי דאי תנא בהמה הוה אמינא בהמה הוא דמקני ליה כפילא משום דנפיש טירחה לעיולה ולאפוקה אבל כלים דלא נפיש טירחייהו אימא לא מקני ליה כפילא ואי תנא כלים הוה אמינא כלים הוא דקמקני ליה כפילא משום דלא נפיש כפלייהו אבל בהמה דכי טבח ומכר משלם תשלומי ד' וה' אימא לא מקני ליה כפילא צריכא מתקיף לה רמי בר חמא והא ה אין אדם מקנה דבר שלא בא לעולם ואפילו ה) לר"מ דאמר אדם מקנה דבר שלא בא לעולם ה"מ כגון פירות דקל דעבידי דאתו אבל הכא

**אחיכם** אלו בעלי מקרא. שאינם יודעים דינים והוראות כי אם על פי בעלי גמרא שונאיכם אלו בעלי משנה שסבורים לידע כמו בעלי גמרא ואינם יודעים בירור הדבר מנדיכם אלו ע"ה שסונאים ת"ח ושמא תאמר אבד סברן ת"ל ונראה בשמחתכם ישראל ישמחו ועובדי כוכבים יבושו:

הדרן עלך אלו מציאות

**המפקיד.** אית דלא גרסי או שאבדו משום דבאבידה ליכא כפל ויש ליישב שכך טוען הנפקד ואחר כך נמצא הגנב אי נמי אנו יודעים שנגנבו מתוך ביתו אך אין אנו יודעים אם פשע או שאבדו שאנו יודעין שנאבד ממנו אך לא ידעינן אם על ידי גניבה או על ידי דבר אחר:

**נגנבו.** ה"ה אם אמר פשעתי שהכפל שלו כדאמר בגמרא מגו דאי בעי פטר נפשיה בגניבה אלא אורחא דמילתא נקט נגנבו שהוא רגילות לטעון דבר שהוא פטור אע"פ שהוא רוצה לשלם וריב"ן פי' דמתני' נמי ה"פ דהנפקד אומר שנגנבו בפשיעה ולא רצה לישבע היינו ולא רצה לישבע לשקר: **כגון** פירות דקל דעבידי דאתו. וא"ת והכא אפילו אי עבידי דאתו היאך יקנה הכפל במעות ששילם והלא מעות אינן קונות אלא למיקם עליה במי שפרע ועוד מאי קפריך בסמוך מי יימר דמיגנבא והלא כששילם כבר נגנבה והול"ל מי יימר דנגנבה פירוש שכבר נגנבה שמא נאבדה ויש לומר דהמקשה סבר דבשעת משיכה הקנה לו הפרה לקנות הכפל כשיבא ואע"ג דבפרק מי שמת (ב"ב דף קמו:) אמרי' דבדקל לפירות אפילו רבנן מודו דקני היינו משום דעבידי דאתו אבל הכא דלא עבידו דאתא אפילו לר' מאיר לא קני וקשה דבפ' השולח (גיטין מב: ושם) מיבעיא לן בעבד שמכרו רבו לקנס דדילמא אפילו לר' מאיר לא יועיל משום דלא עבידא דאתי דמנגח או דילמא אפילו לרבנן יועיל משום דהא קאי עבדא והוי כדקל לפירותיו והכא פשיטא ליה דלא מהני פרה לכפילא ואפילו לר"מ וי"ל דשאני התם שכיח טפי מהכא אי נמי הכא פריך אם תימצי לומר בעבד שמכרו רבו לקנס דלא מהני לר"מ ומשני נעשה כאומר לו לכשתגנב ותשלמני הרי פרתי קנויה לך מעכשיו שגוף הפרה מכר לו דהשתא הכפל שלו ממילא ו): דילמא

**בימי רבי נשנית משנה זו.** הא דקתני גמרא אין לך מדה גדולה מזו לפי ° שמשרבו תלמידי שמאי והלל שהיו לפניו שלשה דורות רבו מחלוקות בתורה ונעשית כשתי תורות ו) מתוך עול שעבוד מלכיות וגזירות שהיו גוזרין עליהן ומתוך כך לא היו יכולים לתת לב לברר דברי החולקים עד ימיו של רבי שנתן הקב"ה לו חן בעיני אנטונינוס מלך רומי כדאמרינן בע"ז (דף י:) ונחו מצרה ושלח וקבץ כל תלמידי ארץ ישראל ועד ימיו לא היו מסכתות סדורות אלא כל תלמיד ששמע דבר מפי גדול הימנו גרסה ונתן סימנים הלכה פלונית ופלונית שמעתי משם פלוני וכשנתקבצו אמר כל אחד מה ששמע ונתנו לב לברר טעמי המחלוקת דברי מי ראוין לקיים וסידרו המסכתות דברי נזיקין לבדם ודברי יבמות לבדם ודברי קדשים לבדם וסתם נמי במשנה דברי יחידים שראה רבי את דבריהם ושנאן סתם כדי לקבוע הלכה כמותם לפיכך אמרו בגמרא אין לך מדה גדולה מזו שיתנו לב לטעמי המשנה: **שבקו כולי עלמא מתני'.** מלחזור על גרסת משנתם: **ואזלו בתר גמרא.** לחשוב בסברא: **הדר דרש להו הוי רץ למשנה.** לפי שירא פן ישתכחו המשניות ויחליפו שמות החכמים ובמקום חיוב יאמרו פטור ובמקום אסור יאמרו מותר: **מאי דרוש.** מתחילה כשדרש שגמרא גדול: **לעמי פשעם.** עמי דהיינו ת"ח את חטאתם אני קורא פשע שהיה להם לתת לב בטעמי משנתם שיבררו להם על העיקר ולא יורו הלכה מתוך משנה שאינה עיקר: **ולבית יעקב.** שאר העם: **חטאתם.** אפילו פשע שלהם אני קורא חטאת: **הוי זהיר בתלמוד.** בגמרא שהיא תירוץ [טעמי] המשניות או אם תשמע דבר משנה מרבך הזהר לשאול טעמיו ומי שנאה: **ששגגת תלמוד.** אם שגית בהוראה בשגגת תלמודך שלא ידעת טעם המשנה ונתת בה טעם אחר ומתוך כך דמית לה דין או הוראה שבא לידך ולמדת הימנה שלא כדת שאין הטעם כמו שהיית סבור שאילו ידעת טעם המשנה לא דמית לה מעשה הבא לידך: **עולה זדון.** ענוש אתה עליה כמזיד שזדון הוא בידך שלא שאלת טעם מרבך: **אלו ת"ח.** שימשו חכמים הרבה ללמדם טעמי משנתם זה בזו וזה בזו שאין הכל בקיאין בשוין: **שנאיכם אלו בעלי משנה.** ששונאין בעלי גמרא לפי שבעלי גמרא אומרים על בעלי משנה שהן מבלי עולם כדאמרינן במסכת סוטה (דף כב.) התנאים מבלי עולם שמורים הלכה מתוך משנתם: **מנדיכם אלו ע"ה.** שת"ח שנואין ומתועבין להן כנדה: **שמא תאמר אבד סברם.** של אלו שהרי כתיב למען שמי יכבד ה' דמשמע שהם אומרים אבל אין הדבר כן: **ת"ל ונראה בשמחתכם.** ולא נאמר ונראה בשמחתם כך אמר הנביא אני ואחיכם שונאיכם ומנדיכם כולנו נראה בשמחתכם: **והם יבושו.** אותם שהם עובדי כוכבים שאינם ממנו ואינן נקראין על שם ישראל הם יבושו וישראל ישמחו:

הדרן עלך אלו מציאות

**המפקיד.** **ולא רצה לישבע.** שבועת שומרים שלא פשע בה ושלא שלח בה יד שהיה יכול ליפטר בשבועה זו שהרי אמרו כו': **למי שהפקדון אצלו.** דכיון דשילם קנה כל תשלומיה ובגמרא מפרש טעמא: **גמ' דמקני ליה כפילא.** הבעלים מקנין לשומר כפל העתיד להשתלם כדאמר לקמן שבשעה שמסרה לו לשמור על מנת כן מסרה שאם תגנב וירצה וישלם יהא כפל שלו: **אימר לא מקנה ליה כפילא.** לא מסרה לו מתחילה על מנת כן: **דלא נפיש כפלייהו.** שאין בהן לידי ארבעה וחמשה שאינה נוהגת אלא בשור ושה בלבד: **מתקיף לה רמי כו'.** אמתניתין קא מתמה: **והא אין אדם מקנה דבר שלא בא לעולם.** והיאך הקנו לו בעלים כפל זה שעדיין לא נתחייב בו גנב: **ואפילו לר' מאיר דאמר.** בפ"ג דקדושין (דף סג.) הרי את מקודשת לי על מנת שאתגייר איכא למיגמר מינה מוכר פירות דקל לחבירו עד שלא באו לעולם דאפליגו בה רב הונא ורב נחמן לקמן באיזהו נשך (דף סו:): **דעבידי דאתו.** גרסינן: מי



א א מיי' פ"א מהלכות שכירות הל' ג סמג עשין פט טור ש"ע ח"מ סי' רצא סעיף א:
ב ב ג ד מיי' פ"ח מהל' שאלה ופקדון הלכה א סמג עשין פח טור ח"מ סי' רצה:
ג ה מיי' פכ"ב מהלכות מכירה הלכה י סמג עשין פ"ב טור ש"ע ח"מ סי' רט סעיף ד:

### רבינו חננאל

שבבבל עומדין זה מלפני זה וקורעין זה על זה וכו'. פי' כיון שנושאין זה עם זה בהלכה לומדין זה מזה טעמי' הרבה כרבו הוא חשוב כל אחד לחבירו לפיכך עומדין זה מפני זה וקורעין זה על זה אבל לענין השבת אבידה אינו מניח של אביו ומחזיר לרבו אלא אם הוא רבו מובהק. רב חסדא הוא תלמיד רב הונא דגרסי' בעירובין בתחלת פרק הדר עם הנכרי בחצר. אמר רב יוסף ביעתא בכותחא בעאי מרב חסדא בשני רב הונא ולא פשט לי. פי' מפני שיש בכותח כמכא דחלבא הוצרך לשאול אם הוא מותר שיאכל ביצת שחוטה בכותח אי לא כלומר ביצת שחוטה כבשר היא וכיון שיש בכותח חלב נמצא כאילו אוכל בשר בחלב ואסור אי לא ואע"ג דדבר ברור הוא דתניא השוחט את התרנגולת ומצא בה ביצים גמורות מותרות לאכלן בחלב אפי' הכי זה שהוא דבר קל לא רצה להורות בפני רב הונא רבו. בעא מיניה רב חסדא מרב הונא תלמיד וצריך לו רבו מהו כלומר תלמיד חריף שרבו נהנה ממנו ומשאילות התלמיד ומחקריו מוסיף הרב חכמה כדאמר [בסנהדרין סח] הרבה למדתי מרבותי ומחברי יותר מהם ומתלמידי יותר מכולם תלמיד כגון זה אצל רבו יניח אבידת אביו ויחזיר או לא וחשב רב הונא בדעתו כי רב (הונא) [חסדא] על עצמו שאל וכי הוא כענין תלמיד שצריך לו רבו וכעס והשיבו חסדא חסדא לא צריכנא לך ולא לחידודך ולא לפלפולך אנת צריך לקבל ממני עד מלאת לך לפני מ' שנה שבמלאת מ' שנה עומד התלמיד על דעת רבו כדכתיב ואולך אתכם ארבעים שנה במדבר וגו' ולא נתן ה' לכם לב לדעת וגו': איקפדו להדדי ולא עול לגבי [הדדי]. רב הונא יתיב ארבעין תעניתא דחשדיה לרב חסדא. רב חסדא יתיב ארבעין תעניתא משום דחלש דעתיה דרב הונא. דרש ר' יהודה בר' אלעי שמעו דבר ה' החרדים אל דברו אלו תלמידי חכמים וכו':

הדרן עלך אלו מציאות

המפקיד אצל חבירו בהמה או כלים נגנבו או שאבדו שילם ולא רצה לישבע וכו' עד למי משלם למי שהפקדון אצלו וכן הלכה. ומקשי' והא אין [אדם] מקנה לחבירו דבר שלא בא לעולם כלומר היאך יכול המפקיד להקנות כפילו למי שהפקדון בידו והא אפי' ר' מאיר דסבר אדם מקנה לחבירו דבר שלא בא לעולם כי האי גוונא לא אמר.



א) [עיין תוספות בבא קמא לד: ד"ה בימי וכו'] ב) [דוגמתו סנהדרין קג:] ג) אבות פרק ד משנה ... ד) ב"ק קח., ה) יבמות ... קדושין סב:, גיטין ... מב:, ב"ב עט:, קמ:, קלא: קמא:, קנז., ו) [סוטה ... סנהדרין פח:], ז) [ו... תוספות ב"ב עט: ד"... אימור].

### גליון הש"ס

גמ' אלו עמי הארץ. עי' סוטה דף כב ע"... תוס' ד"ה רבי שמואל... רש"י ד"ה בימי וכו' שמשרבו תלמידי... ועיין חגיגה דף טז ע"... תוספות ד"ה יוסי:

### הגהות מהר"ב רנשבורג

א] ברש"י ד"ה מתקיף לה רמי. נ"ב עיין הליכות עולם דף (... [ה] ע"ב ודף (ח) [... ע"א ובדברי בעל יד... שמועה שם יעוש"ה ע"ב בד"ה ה"ע ומש"... מתקיף וכו':

### תורה אור השלם

א) קְרָא בְגָרוֹן אַל תַּחְשֹׂךְ כַּשּׁוֹפָר הָרֵם קוֹלֶךָ וְהַגֵּד לְעַמִּי פִּשְׁעָם וּלְבֵית יַעֲקֹב חַטֹּאתָם: [ישעיה נח, א]

ב) שִׁמְעוּ דְּבַר יְיָ הַחֲרֵדִים אֶל דְּבָרוֹ אָמְרוּ אֲחֵיכֶם שֹׂנְאֵיכֶם מְנַדֵּיכֶם לְמַעַן שְׁמִי יִכְבַּד יְיָ וְנִרְאֶה בְשִׂמְחַתְכֶם וְהֵם יֵבֹשׁוּ: [ישעיה סו, ה]

### ליקוטי רש"י

הגד לעמי. אלו תלמידי חכמים שכל שגגתם פשע ששגגת תלמוד עולה זדון [ישעיה נח, ב]. החרדים אל דברו. הצדיקים הממהרים בחרדה להתקרב אל דבריו. [ישעיה סו, ה]. ובטל סיכוים. תוחלתם ומבטם כדמתרגמינן הבט נא (בראשית טו) אסתכי כען לשמיא [סוכה מה:]. שהרי אמרו וכו'. ויכול היה ליפטר בשבועה [ב"ק קח.]. פירות דקל. קודם שחנטו פירות [לקמן סו:]. שהמוכר פירות דקל לחבירו אע"פ שעדיין לא באו לעולם אין יכול לחזור בו משיבואו לעולם דהא ודאי עבידי דאתו דומיא דע"... שאתגייר דדעתיה לאיגיורי ומיהו ר"מ ... איירי בפירות דקל אלא רב הונא דקאי כוותיה במסכת יבמות [רשב"ם ב"ב עט:].

# Chapter Three

## Introduction

This chapter discusses the responsibilities, obligations, and liabilities of a שׁוֹמֵר, *shomer*. A *shomer* (pl. שׁוֹמְרִים *shomrim*) is one who assumes responsibility for the safekeeping of another person's property, which i placed in his care. This property is called a פִּקָּדוֹן, *pikadon,* deposit.

**The Four Shomrim** – The passages contained in *Exodus* 22:6-14 outline various categories of *shomrim*. Basing itself on those verses, the Mishnah below (93a) identifies four types c *shomrim,* each with its own unique responsibilities and liabilities: (1) שׁוֹמֵר חִנָּם – *an unpaid shomer.* He mus safeguard and maintain the object in his care, as must every *shomer,* and may not use it for his own purposes. H is liable for any loss or damage caused by his own negligence, but not for that caused by any other mishap. (2) שׁוֹמֵר שָׂכָר – *a paid shomer.* He, too, may not use the deposit for his own purposes. Since he is paid for watching it, he i held to a higher standard of care. Hence, he is liable even for theft or loss not due to his negligence. Nevertheless, h bears no responsibility for mishaps beyond his control, such as the death, breakage, or forced seizure of the deposi (3) שׂוֹכֵר – *a renter.* He pays for the right to use another's property. R' Meir and R' Yehudah dispute whether hi liability is identical to that of the unpaid *shomer* or of the paid *shomer*. The halachah follows the latter view (*Choshen Mishpat* 307:1). (4) שׁוֹאֵל – *a borrower.* He has the right to use another's property without paying, and thus bear the highest degree of responsibility – i.e. he is liable even for mishaps beyond his control, with the exception c work-related damages (as long as the *pikadon* was being put to normal use).

**The Shomer's Oath** – When a *shomer* claims exemption from liability [e.g. if an unpaid *shomer* asserted that the deposit was stolen], he must support his claim either by bringing witnesses or by swearing that his claim is true.[1] This oath is a Biblical obligation (*Shach* to *Choshen Mishpat* 294:2). In addition, he must swear that he has not been negligent in safeguarding the object, and, in the case of paid and unpaid *shomrim*, must also swear that he did not appropriate the deposit for his personal use.[2]

Even when a *shomer* is willing to pay for the loss of property in his care, he must swear that the object is not in his possession.[3]

**TERMS RELEVANT TO THIS CHAPTER**

פִּקָּדוֹן, *pikadon* – an object deposited with a *shomer* for safekeeping.

שׁוֹמֵר, *shomer* – one who has assumed responsibility for another's property.

שׁוֹמֵר חִנָּם, *unpaid shomer* – he is liable only for loss or damage resulting from his negligence.

שׁוֹמֵר שָׂכָר, *paid shomer* – he is liable for damage due to negligence, and for theft and loss.

שׂוֹכֵר, *renter* – his liability is identical to that of a paid *shomer*.

שׁוֹאֵל, *borrower* – he is liable for all losses except those unavoidable losses incurred during the normal course of work.

שְׁלִיחוּת יָד, *shelichus yad* – misappropriation; the theft by a *shomer* of part[4] of a deposit.

NOTES

1. See *Bava Kamma* 107a with *Rashi* and *Tosafos.*

2. If a *shomer* did take the deposit for himself, he is regarded as a thief and is subsequently liable even for mishaps beyond his control (see below, 41a and note 10). A *shomer* may not be charged with taking this oath unless he is otherwise obligated to swear (*Rosh* 20; *Choshen Mishpat* 294:2 and *Rama;* cf. *Tosafos* to 6b ד״ה שבועה).

3. The Rabbis instituted this oath in order to ensure that the *shomer* wil not falsely claim the loss of the object, pay for it, and thereby acquire ar item that he covets (Gemara below, 34b; see *Shach* to *Choshen Mishpa* ibid.).

4. *Rashi* to 41a ד״ה ור׳ נתן and to 44a ד״ה דניחא. According to *Tosafos* (41a ד״ה שנטלה), however, this term also signifies the theft of an entire deposit.

**scholars** for they exert themselves to clarify God's words.[9] "אָמְרוּ אֲחֵיכֶם" – The verse then continues, stating: ***your brothers.*** אֵלּוּ בַּעֲלֵי מִקְרָא – **These** persons, "your brothers," **are** the people **who study** only **Scripture.**[10] "שֹׂנְאֵיכֶם" – The verse then continues, stating: ***your enemies.*** אֵלּוּ בַּעֲלֵי מִשְׁנָה – **These are** the ones **who study** only **Mishnah,** for they despise those who delve into Talmud.[11] "מְנַדֵּיכֶם" – The next word in the verse is, ***those who cast you away.*** אֵלּוּ עַמֵּי הָאָרֶץ – **These are the common people of the land** who are unlettered.[12] The verse then states that all these people (those who study Scripture, those who study Mishnah, and those who are completely unlettered) have said: *"Because of me, HASHEM will be honored."*

שֶׁמָּא תֹּאמַר – Now, **perhaps you will say** that, in view of thei[r] attitude, פָּסַק סִבְרָם וּבָטֵל סִיכּוּיָם – **their hope is gone and thei[r] prospects are naught,** i.e. they will not be partners in the joy tha[t] will accompany the Messiah's coming.[13] תַּלְמוּד לוֹמַר – **Th[e] verse** therefore **teaches:** "וְנִרְאֶה בְשִׂמְחַתְכֶם" – ***we will** all **se[e] your joy***.[14] שֶׁמָּא תֹּאמַר – **Perhaps you will say** that יִשְׂרָאֵל יֵבוֹשׁוּ – those among **Israel,** i.e. Jews, **will be ashamed;** that i[s] that although these groups will experience joy, they will neverthe[-]less be ashamed when the Messiah comes. תַּלְמוּד לוֹמַר – **Th[e] verse** therefore **teaches** that "וְהֵם יֵבֹשׁוּ" – ***"they" will b[e] ashamed;*** עוֹבְדֵי כוֹכָבִים יֵבוֹשׁוּ – that is, **idolaters will b[e] ashamed,**[15] וְיִשְׂרָאֵל יִשְׂמָחוּ – **but Israel will rejoice.**

## הדרן עלך אלו מציאות

**WE SHALL RETURN TO YOU, EILU METZIOS**

NOTES

9. The true Torah scholar – one who is deeply involved in clarifying the principles underlying God's word – will study under many different scholars, for he will be able to gain insight into different Mishnahs from each of them (see *Rashi*).

10. Those who study only Scripture are aware that they do not fully know the laws, and, therefore, when they have questions in halachah, they will consult those who study Talmud (*Tosafos*). Since they have a relationship with those who study Talmud, they are referred to as their brothers.

11. Their feelings toward the students of Talmud come from the fact that the latter view those who decide law on the basis of the Mishnaic text alone as distorters of the law (*Rashi*, from Gemara *Sotah* 22a).

12. The word מְנַדֵּיכֶם, *those who cast you out,* refers to unlettered persons, for these individuals often view scholars with disdain, and seek to separate themselves from them (see *Rashi*; see also *Ben Yehoyada*).

13. The verse states that all these people have said, "because of me HASHEM will be honored," implying that, although they say this, they are not correct. Thus, one might have said that they will *not* join in the joy that will accompany the Messiah's coming (*Rashi*).

14. Since the prophet did not say "***I*** will see your joy," but, rather, ***we** will see your joy,* he means that he, along with all the above groups – your brothers, enemies, and those who cast you away (those who study Scripture, those who study Mishnah, and the unlettered people) will all rejoice in the Messiah's coming (see *Rashi*).

15. *They* connotes someone who is other than you, a complete foreigner to your ways. It is thus taken to refer to idolaters, not persons who can be counted among Israel (*Rashi*).

א) בימי רבי נשנית משנה זו שבקו כולא עלמא מתניתין ואזלו בתר גמרא הדר דרש להו ולעולם הוי רץ למשנה יותר מן הגמרא מאי דרוש כדדריש רבי יהודה ברבי אלעאי מאי דכתיב א) הגד לעמי פשעם ולבית יעקב חטאתם הגד לעמי פשעם אלו תלמידי חכמים ג) ששגגות נעשות להם כזדונות ולבית יעקב חטאתם אלו עמי הארץ שזדונות נעשות להם כשגגות והיינו דתנן ג) ר' יהודה אומר הוי זהיר בתלמוד ששגגת תלמוד עולה זדון דרש ר' יהודה בר' אלעאי מאי דכתיב ב) שמעו דבר ה' החרדים אל דברו אלו תלמידי חכמים [אמרו] אחיכם אלו בעלי מקרא שנאיכם אלו בעלי משנה מנדיכם ° אלו עמי הארץ שמא תאמר פסק סברם ובטל סיכוים ת"ל ונראה בשמחתכם שמא תאמר ישראל יבושו תלמוד לומר והם יבושו עובדי כוכבים יבושו וישראל ישמחו:

## הדרן עלך אלו מציאות

**המפקיד** ד) אצל חבירו בהמה או כלים ונגנבו או שאבדו שילם ולא רצה לישבע א שהרי אמרו שומר חנם נשבע ויוצא ב נמצא הגנב משלם תשלומי כפל טבח ומכר משלם תשלומי ארבעה וחמשה למי משלם ג למי שהפקדון אצלו ד נשבע ולא רצה לשלם נמצא הגנב משלם תשלומי כפל טבח ומכר משלם תשלומי ארבעה וחמשה למי משלם לבעל הפקדון: **גמ'** למה ליה למתני בהמה ולמה ליה למתני כלים צריכי דאי תנא בהמה הוה אמינא בהמה הוא דמקני ליה כפילא משום דנפיש טירחה לעיולה ולאפוקה אבל כלים דלא נפיש טירחייהו אימא לא מקני ליה כפילא ואי תנא כלים הוה אמינא כלים הוא דקמקני ליה כפילא משום דלא נפיש כפלייהו אבל בהמה דכי טבח ומכר משלם תשלומי ד' וה' אימא לא מקני ליה כפילא צריכא מתקיף לה רמי בר חמא והא ה אין אדם מקנה דבר שלא בא לעולם ואפילו ה) לר"מ דאמר אדם מקנה דבר שלא בא לעולם ה"מ כגון פירות דקל דעבידי דאתו אבל הכא

---

**אחיכם** אלו בעלי מקרא. שאינם יודעים דינים והוראות כי אם על פי בעלי גמרא שונאיכם אלו בעלי משנה שסבורים לידע כמו בעלי גמרא ואינם יודעים בירור הדבר מנדיכם אלו ע"ה ששונאים ת"ח ושמא תאמר אבד סברן ת"ל ונראה בשמחתכם ישראל ישמחו ועובדי כוכבים יבושו:

בימי רבי נשנית משנה זו. הא דקתני גמרא אין לך מדה גדולה מזו לפי ° שמשרבו תלמידי שמאי והלל שהיו לפניו שלשה דורות רבו מחלוקות בתורה ונעשית כשתי תורות ו) מתוך עול שעבוד מלכיות וגזירות שהיו גוזרין עליהן ומתוך כך לא היו יכולים לתת לב לברר דברי החולקים עד ימיו של רבי שנתן הקב"ה לו חן בעיני אנטונינוס מלך רומי כדאמרינן בע"ז (דף י:) ונחו מצרה ושלח וקבץ כל תלמידי ארץ ישראל ועד ימיו לא היו מסכתות סדורות אלא כל תלמיד ששמע דבר מפי גדול הימנו גרסה ונתן סימנים הלכה פלונית ופלונית שמעתי משם פלוני וכשנתקבצו אמר כל אחד מה ששמע ונתנו לב לברר טעמי המחלוקת דברי מי ראוין לקיים וסידרו המסכתות דברי נזיקין לבדם ודברי יבמות לבדם ודברי קדשים לבדם וסתם נמי במשנה דברי יחידים שראה רבי את דבריהם ושנאן סתם כדי לקבוע הלכה כמותם לפיכך אמרו בגמרא אין לך מדה גדולה מזו שיתנו לב לטעמי המשנה: שבקו כולי עלמא מתני'. מלחזור על גרסת משנתם: ואזלו בתר גמרא. לחשוב בסברא: הדר דרש להו הוי רץ למשנה. לפי שירא פן ישתכחו המשניות ויחליפו שמות החכמים ובמקום חיוב יאמרו פטור ובמקום אסור יאמרו מותר: מאי דרוש. מתחילה כשדרש שגמרא גדול: לעמי פשעם. עמי דהיינו ת"ח את חטאתם אני קורא פשע שהיה להם לתת לב בטעמי משנתם שיבררו להם על העיקר ולא יורו הלכה מתוך משנה שאינה עיקר: ולבית יעקב. שאר העם: חטאתם. אפילו פשע שלהם אני קורא חטאת: הוי זהיר בתלמוד. בגמרא שהיא תירוץ [טעמי] המשניות או אם תשמע דבר משנה מרבך הזהר לשאול טעמיו ומי שנאה: ששגגת תלמוד. אם שגית בהוראה בשגגת תלמודך שלא ידעת טעם המשנה ונתת בה טעם אחר ומתוך כך דמית לה דין או הוראה שבא לידך ולמדת הימנה שלא כדת שאין הטעם כמו שהיית סבור שאילו ידעת טעם המשנה לא דמית לה מעשה הבא לידך: עולה זדון. ענוש אתה עליה כמזיד שזדון הוא בידך שלא שאלת טעם מרבך: אלו ת"ח.: שימשו חכמים הרבה ללמדם טעמי משנתם זה בזו וזה בזו שאין הכל בקיאין בשוין: שנאיכם אלו בעלי משנה. ששונאין בעלי גמרא לפי שבעלי גמרא אומרים על בעלי משנה שהן מבלי עולם כדאמרינן במסכת סוטה (דף כב.) התנאים מבלי עולם שמורים הלכה מתוך משנתם: מנדיכם אלו ע"ה. שת"ח שונאין ומתועבין להן כנדה: שמא תאמר אבד סברם. של אלו שהרי כתיב למען שמי יכבד ה' דמשמע שהם אומרים אבל אין הדבר כן: ת"ל ונראה בשמחתכם. ולא נאמר וארא' בשמחתכם כך אמר הנביא אני ואחיכם שונאיכם ומנדיכם כולנו נראה בשמחתכם: והם יבושו. אותם שהם עובדי כוכבים שאינם ממנו ואין נקראין על שם ישראל הם יבושו וישראל ישמחו:

## הדרן עלך אלו מציאות

**המפקיד.** ולא רצה לישבע. שבועת שומרים שלא פשע בה ושלא שלח בה יד שהיה יכול ליפטר בשבועה זו שהרי אמרו כו': למי שהפקדון אצלו. דכיון דשילם קנה כל תשלומיה וגמרא מפרש טעמא: **גמ'** דמקני ליה כפילא. הבעלים מקנין לשומר כפל העתיד להשתלם כדאמר לקמן שבשעה שמסרה לו לשמור על מנת כן מסרה שאם תגנב וירצה וישלם יהא כפל שלו: אימר לא מקנה ליה כפילא. לא מסרה לו מתחילה על מנת כן: דלא נפיש כפליידו. שאין באין לידי ארבעה וחמשה שאינה נוהגת אלא בשור ושה בלבד: מתקיף לה רמי כו'. אמתניתין קא מתמה: והא אין אדם מקנה דבר שלא בא לעולם. והיאך הקנו לו בעלים כפל זה שעדיין לא נתחייב בו גנב: ואפילו לר' מאיר דאמר. בפ"ג דקדושין (דף סג.) הרי את מקודשת לי על מנת שאתגייר איכא למיגמר מינה מוכר פירות דקל לחבירו עד שלא באו לעולם דאפליגו בה רב הונא ורב נחמן לקמן באיזהו נשך (דף סו:): דעבידי דאתו. גרסינן: מי

---

**המפקיד.** אית דלא גרסי או שאבדו משום דבאבידה ליכא כפל ויש ליישב שכך טוען הנפקד ואחר כך נמצא הגנב אי נמי אנו יודעים שנגנבו מתוך ביתו אך אין אנו יודעים אם פשע או שאבדו שאנו יודעין שנאבד ממנו אך לא ידעינן אם על ידי גניבה או על ידי דבר אחר:

**נגנבו.** ה"ה אם אמר פשעתי שהכפל שלו כדאמר בגמרא מגו דאי בעי פטר נפשיה בגניבה אלא אורחא דמילתא נקט נגנבו שהוא רגילות לטעון דבר שהוא פטור אע"פ שהוא רוצה לשלם וריב"ן פי' דמתני' נמי ה"פ דהנפקד אומר שנגנבו בפשיעה ולא רצה לישבע היינו ולא רצה לישבע לשקר: **כגון** פירות דקל דעבידי דאתו. וא"ת והכא אפילו אי עבידי דאתו היאך יקנה הכפל במעות ששילם והלא מעות אינן קונות אלא למיקם עליה במי שפרע ועוד מאי קפריך בסמוך מי יימר דמיגנבא והלא כששילם כבר נגנבה והול"ל מי יימר דנגנבה פירוש שכבר נגנבה שמא נאבדה ויש לומר דהמקשה סבר דבשעת משיכה הקנה לו הפרה לקנות הכפל כשיבא ואע"ג דבפרק מי שמת (ב"ב דף קמז:) אמרי' דבדקל לפירות אפילו רבנן מודו דקני היינו משום דעבידי דאתו אבל הכא דלא עבידו דאתא אפילו לר' מאיר לא קני וקשה דבפ' השולח (גיטין מב: ושם) מיבעיא לן בעבד שמכרו רבו לקנם דדילמא אפילו לר' מאיר לא יועיל משום דלא עבידא דאתי דמנגח או דילמא אפילו לרבנן יועיל משום דהא קאי עבדא והוי כדקל לפירותיו והכא פשיטא ליה דלא מהני פרה לכפילא ואפילו לר"מ וי"ל דשמא התם שכיח טפי מהכא אי נמי הכא פריך אם תימצי לומר בעבד שמכרו רבו לקנס דלא מהני לר"מ ומשני נעשה כאומר לו לכשתגנב ותשלמני הרי פרתי קנויה לך מעכשיו שגוף הפרה מכר לו דהשתא הכפל שלו ממילא ז): דילמא

---



א א מיי' פ"א מהלכות שכירות הל' ג סמג עשין פט טור ש"ע ח"מ סי' רלא סעיף א:

ב ב ג ד מיי' פ"ח מהל' שאלה ופקדון הלכה א סמג עשין פח טור ח"מ סי' רנה:

ג ה מיי' פכ"ב מהלכות מכירה הלכה י סמג עשין פ"ב טור ש"ע ח"מ סי' רט סעיף ד:

### רבינו חננאל

שבבבל עומדין זה מלפני זה וקורעין זה על זה וכו'. פי' כיון שנושאין זה עם זה בהלכה לומדין זה מזה טעמי' הרבה כרבו הוא חשוב כל אחד לחבירו לפיכך עומדין זה מפני זה וקורעין זה על זה אבל לענין השבת אבידה אינו מניח של אביו ומחזיר לרבו אלא אם הוא רבו מובהק. רב חסדא הוא תלמיד רב הונא דגרסי' בעירובין בתחלת פרק הדר עם הנכרי בחצר. אמר רב יוסף ביעתא בכותחא בעאי מרב חסדא בשני רב הונא ולא פשט לי. פי' מפני שיש בכותח כמכא דחלבא הוצרך לשאול אם הוא מותר שיאכל ביצת שחוטה בכותח אי לא כלומר ביצת שחוטה כבשר היא וכיון שיש בכותח חלב נמצא כאילו אוכל בשר בחלב ואסור אי לא ואע"ג דדבר ברור הוא דתניא השוחט את התרנגולת ומצא בה ביצים גמורות מותרות לאכלן בחלב אפי' הכי זה שהוא דבר קל לא רצה להורות בפני רב הונא רבו. בעא מיניה רב חסדא מרב הונא תלמיד וצריך לו רבו מהו כלומר תלמיד חריף שרבו נהנה ממנו ומשאילות התלמיד ומחקריו מוסיף הרב חכמה כדאמר [בסנהדרין סח] הרבה למדתי מרבותי ומחברי יותר מהם ומתלמידי יותר מכולם תלמיד כגון זה אצל רבו יניח אבידת אביו ויחזיר או לא וחשב רב הונא בדעתו כי רב (הונא) [חסדא] על עצמו שאל וכי הוא כענין תלמיד שצריך לו רבו וכעס והשיבו חסדא חסדא לא צריכנא לך ולא לחידודך ולא לפלפולך אנת צריך לקבל ממני עד מלאת לך לפני מ' שנה שבמלאת מ' שנה עומד התלמיד על דעת רבו כדכתיב ואולך אתכם ארבעים שנה במדבר וגו' ולא נתן ה' לכם לב לדעת וגו': איקפדו להדדי ולא עול לגבי [הדדי]. רב הונא יתיב ארבעין תעניתא דחשדיה לרב חסדא. רב חסדא יתיב ארבעין תעניתא משום דחלש דעתיה דרב הונא. דרש ר' יהודה בר' אלעי שמעו דבר ה' החרדים אל דברו אלו תלמידי חכמים וכו':

הדרן עלך אלו מציאות

המפקיד אצל חבירו בהמה או כלים נגנבו או שאבדו שילם ולא רצה לישבע וכו' עד למי משלם למי שהפקדון אצלו וכן הלכה. ומקשי' והא אין [אדם] מקנה לחבירו דבר שלא בא לעולם כלומר היאך יכול המפקיד להקנות כפלו למי שהפקדון בידו והא אפי' ר' מאיר דסבר אדם מקנה לחבירו דבר שלא בא לעולם כי האי גוונא לא אמר.

---

### מסורת הש"ס

א) [עיין תוספות בבא קמ... לד: ד"ה בימי וכו' ב) [דוגמתו סנהדרין קג... ג) אבות פרק ד משנה ... ד) ב"ק קח., ה) יבמות ... קדושין סג., גיטין ... מב., ב"ב עט., קמ., קל... קמא., קמז., ו) [סוטה ... סנהדרין פח:], ז) [ו... תוספות ב"ב עט: ד"... אימור].

### גליון הש"ס

גמ' אלו עמי הארץ ... עי' סוטה דף כב ע"... תוס' ד"ה רבי שמוא... רש"י ד"ה בימי ו... שמשרבו תלמיד... ועיין חגיגה דף טז ע"... תוספות ד"ה יוסי:

### הגהות מהר"ב רנשבורג

א] ברש"י ד"... מתקיף לה רמי. ... עיין הליכות עולם דף ... [ה] ע"ב ודף (ח) ... ע"א ובדברי בעל י... שמועה שם יעוש"ה ... ע"ב בד"ה ה"ע ומ... מתקיף וכו':

### תורה אור השלם

א) קְרָא בְגָרוֹן ... תַּחְשֹׂךְ כַּשּׁוֹפָר הָ... קוֹלֶךָ וְהַגֵּד לְעַ... פִּשְׁעָם וּלְבֵית יַעֲ... חַטֹּאתָם: [ישעיה נח, ...]

ב) שִׁמְעוּ דְּבַר ... הַחֲרֵדִים אֶל דְּבָ... אָמְרוּ אֲחֵיכֶם שֹׂנְאֵי... מְנַדֵּיכֶם לְמַעַן שְׁ... יִכְבַּד יְיָ וְנִרְ... בְשִׂמְחַתְכֶם וְהֵם יֵבֹ... [ישעיה סו, ה]

### ליקוטי רש"י

הגד לעמי. אלו תלמ... חכמים שכל שגגתם פ... ששגגת תלמוד עולה ז... [ישעיה נח, ב]. החרד... אל דברו. הלדי... הממהרים ... בתר... להתקרב אל דבריו. [יש... סו, ה]. ובטל סיכוי... תוחלתם ומב... כדמתרגמינן הכט... (בראשית טו) איסתכי ... לשמיא [סוכה מ... שהרי אמרו וכו'. ו... היה ליפטר בשבועה [... קח.]. פירות ד... קודם שחנטו פירו... [לקמן סו:]. שהמ... פירות דקל לחבירו אע... שעדיין לא באו לעולם ... יכול לגזור בו נקנין ... לעולם דהא ודאי ע... דאתו דומיא דע... שאתגייר דדעו... לאיגיורי ומיהו ר"מ ... איירי בפירות דקל אלא ... הונא דקאי כוו... במסכת יבמות [רש... ב"ב עט:].

בִּימֵי רַבִּי נִשְׁנֵית מִשְׁנָה זוֹ — **This** first **Tannaic statement,** which extols the study of Talmud, **was taught during the days of Rebbi.** In his time, it was indeed more important to study Talmud than Mishnah, and the first part of the Baraisa reflects this.[1] שָׁבְקוּ כּוּלָּא עָלְמָא מַתְנִיתִין — Subsequently, however, **everyone abandoned** the study of **Mishnah** וְאָזְלוּ בָּתַר גְּמָרָא — **and pursued** the study of **Talmud.** I.e. they stopped reviewing the text of the Mishnahs and, instead, concentrated exclusively on analyzing them. Rebbi then feared that they would forget the Mishnahs,[2] הֲדַר דְּרַשׁ לְהוּ וּלְעוֹלָם הֱוֵי רָץ לַמִּשְׁנָה יוֹתֵר מִן הַגְּמָרָא — so **he lectured to them** that **ONE SHOULD ALWAYS RUN TO** study **MISHNAH MORE THAN TALMUD.** The statements of the Baraisa were thus taught at different times, and since each time had a different need, there is no contradiction between the two statements.

The Gemara seeks a source for Rebbi's original statement:

מַאי דָּרוּשׁ — When Rebbi originally stated that studying Talmud is more important than studying Mishnah, **what** verse **did he expound** to derive this?

The Gemara replies:

כִּדְדָרֵישׁ רַבִּי יְהוּדָה בְּרַבִּי אִלְעַאי — **He expounded as R' Yehudah son of R' Ilai** did: מַאי דִּכְתִיב — **What is** the meaning of this **that is written:** "הַגֵּד לְעַמִּי פִּשְׁעָם — *Tell My nation of their willful transgressions,* "וּלְבֵית יַעֲקֹב חַטֹּאתָם — *and the Hous of Jacob their unwitting transgressions?*[3] הַגֵּד לְעַמִּי פִּשְׁעָם" — As for the first phrase, ***Tell*** **My** ***nation of their willfu transgressions,*** אֵלּוּ תַּלְמִידֵי חֲכָמִים — **this refers to the Tora scholars,** שֶׁשְּׁגָגוֹת נַעֲשׂוֹת לָהֶם כִּזְדוֹנוֹת — **whose unwittin transgressions are considered** by God to be **like willfu transgressions.**[4] "וּלְבֵית יַעֲקֹב חַטֹּאתָם" — As for the secon phrase, ***and the House of Jacob their unwillful transgression*** אֵלּוּ עַמֵּי הָאָרֶץ — **this refers to the common people of the lan** שֶׁזְּדוֹנוֹת נַעֲשׂוֹת לָהֶם כִּשְׁגָגוֹת — **whose willful transgressions ar considered** by God to be **like unwitting transgressions.** וְהַיְינוּ דִּתְנַן — **And this is as we have learned in a Mishnah:** ר׳ יְהוּדָה אוֹמֵר — **R' YEHUDAH SAYS:** הֱוֵי זָהִיר בְּתַלְמוּד — **B METICULOUS IN** the study of **TALMUD,** שֶׁשִּׁגְגַת תַּלְמוּד עוֹלָה זָדוֹן — **FOR A CARELESS MISINTERPRETATION OF TALMUD IS CONSII ERED TANTAMOUNT TO WILLFUL TRANSGRESSION.**[7]

A further exposition by R' Yehudah son of R' Ilai on the sam general theme:

דָּרַשׁ ר׳ יְהוּדָה בַּר׳ אִלְעַאי — **R' Yehudah son of R' Ilai expoundec** מַאי דִּכְתִיב — **What is** the meaning of **that which is wri ten:**[8] "שִׁמְעוּ דְּבַר ה׳ הַחֲרֵדִים אֶל דְּבָרוֹ" — *Hear the word c Hashem, those who tremble at His word?* אֵלּוּ תַּלְמִידֵי חֲכָמִים - **These** persons who "tremble at His word" **are the Tora**

NOTES

1. In order to explain why the study of Talmud — the underlying reasons of the Mishnah— was especially important in the days of Rebbi, *Rashi* provides some historical background to the period. During the days of the early Tannaim there were not many disputes in Jewish law. As the years passed, however, local governments enforced decrees prohibiting the study of Torah, and the conditions under which the Tannaim lived and taught worsened. By the time the schools of Hillel and Shammai became well established (three generations before Rebbi), disputes over points of law had become much more widespread, and the danger emerged that a time would come where few principles would remain accepted by all. Little could be done about the situation, however, for the ever-present fear of persecution prevented the Torah Sages of the period from having the time or presence of mind to resolve or categorize the various disputes.

This state of affairs remained unchanged until the days of Rebbi, when an unprecedented opportunity arose. God caused Anthony Caesar to view Rebbi with favor, and the climate of persecution eased somewhat (see *Avodah Zarah* 10b). Rebbi seized upon the auspicious conditions of his day, gathering all the Torah scholars together to compile the various teachings they knew, and to analyze the principles upon which they were based. The teachings that were found to be worthy of preservation were then divided by subject and categorized into different tractates, each dealing with a certain central theme. (The laws pertinent to *yibum,* for example, were organized into their own tractate, and were set apart from laws concerning other topics such as sacrifices or monetary judgments.) Additionally, Rebbi took the teachings he viewed as most authoritative and set them down without naming the specific Tanna that originally propounded them. By doing this, he conveyed his view that these teachings were to be accepted as halachah (*Rashi*).

It is against this backdrop that we may understand the Baraisa's teaching that "there is no greater measure than the study of Talmud." As the Gemara states, this Baraisa was initially taught in the days of Rebbi, when the principal challenge facing the Torah world was the task of analyzing and categorizing the disparate Tannaic teachings. This could be truly achieved only if the scholars of the day dedicated themselves to this work wholeheartedly, concentrating their study in the area of Talmud (the analysis of Tannaic statements) above all else.

2. As noted above, the teachings of the Tannaim had not yet been written down. Thus, when the students stopped reviewing the oral Mishnahs and involved themselves only in analysis, Rebbi feared they would forget the precise oral text of these teachings (*Rashi*).

3. *Isaiah* 58:1. The verse could have combined both phrases together by writing: Tell My nation their willful and unwitting transgressions. Since the verse instead uses two distinct terms to refer to Israel ("M nation" and the "House of Jacob"), it is expounded as referring to tw different groups within the nation of Israel (*Rif* in *Ein Yaakov;* see als *Iyun Yaakov*).

4. The word עַמִּי, *My nation,* refers to Torah scholars, persons who ar capable of discerning the principles that underly the Tannaic state ments of the Mishnah. The verse speaks of such persons who did nc devote themselves to analyze properly and were, therefore, unaware c the law in certain areas. They therefore came to transgress law unwittingly, by incorrectly construing Mishnahs and assuming that certain action was permitted when, in fact, it was not. The verse state that such transgressions are considered by God to be willful, since th offender should have analyzed the Mishnahs more carefully (*Rashi;* se also *Rabbeinu Chananel*).

5. Although they transgressed the prohibition knowing that it wa forbidden, they are not held fully accountable because their lack c learning prevents them from realizing the true significance of the actions. They thus treat even prohibitions of which they are aware wit the same careless and cavalier attitude with which more learned peop treat unwitting transgressions (see *Maharsha*).

6. *Avos* 4:16. The previously cited exposition was set forth by Yehudah son of R' Ilai, who is also known as R' Yehudah (see *Rashi* t *Beitzah* 26a ד״ה ר׳ יהודה). Thus, both that exposition and the Mishna which follows — which was authored by R' Yehudah as well — wer expounded by the same person.

7. I.e. if one carelessly misinterpreted the principle behind a Mishnah ruling and, because of this, drew an incorrect analogy to a case tha came before him to judge, he is punished for this as if he willfully dre a false ruling. He is held culpable in this matter for he should hav asked his teacher for a clarification of the concept that was unclear t him (see *Rashi*).

8. *Isaiah* 66:5. The verse in its entirety reads: שִׁמְעוּ דְּבַר־ה׳ הַחֲרֵדִים אֶל־דְּבָרוֹ אָמְרוּ אֲחֵיכֶם שֹׂנְאֵיכֶם מְנַדֵּיכֶם לְמַעַן שְׁמִי יִכְבַּד ה׳ וְנִרְאֶה בְשִׂמְחַתְכֶם וְהֵם יֵבֹשׁוּ — *Hear the word of Hashem, those who tremble at His word: You brothers, your enemies, those who cast you away, have said: "Because c me, Hashem will be honored"; and we will see your joy, and they will b ashamed.* The plain meaning of the verse is as follows: The prophe addresses "those who tremble at God's word," and tells them: Althoug other groups might scorn you, claiming that God is honored by *the* deeds, not yours, their assessment is false. In fact, God will bestow H presence at the time of your joy (i.e. in the days of the Messiah) and th other groups will be downcast (*Radak* ad loc.) The Tanna now expounc each phrase in the verse individually.

[א] בימי רבי נשנית משנה זו שבקו כולא עלמא מתניתין ואזלו בתר גמרא הדר דרש להו ולעולם הוי רץ למשנה יותר מן הגמרא מאי דרוש כדדריש רבי יהודה ברבי אלעאי מאי דכתיב [א] הגד לעמי פשעם ולבית יעקב חטאתם הגד לעמי פשעם אלו תלמידי חכמים [ב] ששגגות נעשות להם כזדונות ולבית יעקב חטאתם אלו עמי הארץ שזדונות נעשות להם כשגגות והיינו דתנן [ג] ר' יהודה אומר הוי זהיר בתלמוד ששגגת תלמוד עולה זדון דרש ר' יהודה בר' אלעאי מאי דכתיב [ב] שמעו דבר ה' החרדים אל דברו אלו תלמידי חכמים [אמרו] אחיכם אלו בעלי מקרא שנאיכם אלו בעלי משנה מנדיכם ° אלו עמי הארץ שמא תאמר פסק סברם ובטל סיכוים ת"ל ונראה בשמחתכם שמא תאמר ישראל יבושו תלמוד לומר והם יבושו עובדי כוכבים יבושו וישראל ישמחו:

## הדרן עלך אלו מציאות

**המפקיד** [ד] אצל חבירו בהמה או כלים ונגנבו או שאבדו שילם ולא רצה לישבע [א] שהרי אמרו שומר חנם נשבע ויוצא [ב] נמצא הגנב משלם תשלומי כפל טבח ומכר משלם תשלומי ארבעה וחמשה למי משלם [ג] למי שהפקדון אצלו [ד] נשבע ולא רצה לשלם נמצא הגנב משלם תשלומי כפל טבח ומכר משלם תשלומי ארבעה וחמשה למי משלם לבעל הפקדון: **גמ'** למה ליה למתני בהמה ולמה ליה למתני כלים צריכי דאי תנא בהמה הוה אמינא בהמה הוא דמקני ליה כפילא משום דנפיש טירחה לעיולה ולאפוקה אבל כלים דלא נפיש טירחייהו אימא לא מקני ליה כפילא ואי תנא כלים הוה אמינא כלים הוא דקמקני ליה כפילא משום דלא נפיש כפלייהו אבל בהמה דכי טבח ומכר משלם תשלומי ד' וה' אימא לא מקני ליה כפילא צריכא מתקיף לה רמי בר חמא והא [ה] אין אדם מקנה דבר שלא בא לעולם ואפילו [ה] לר"מ דאמר אדם מקנה דבר שלא בא לעולם ה"מ כגון פירות דקל דעבידי דאתו אבל הכא

---

**רש"י**

בימי רבי נשנית משנה זו. הא דקתני גמרא אין לך מדה גדולה מזו לפי ° שמשרבו תלמידי שמאי והלל שהיו לפניו שלשה דורות רבו מחלוקות בתורה ונעשית כשתי תורות [ו] מתוך עול שעבוד מלכיות וגזירות שהיו גוזרין עליהן ומתוך כך לא היו יכולים לתת לב לברר דברי החולקים עד ימיו של רבי שנתן הקב"ה לו חן בעיני אנטונינוס מלך רומי כדאמרינן בע"ז (דף י:) ונחו מצרה ושלא וקבץ כל תלמידי ארץ ישראל ועד ימיו לא היו מסכתות סדורות אלא כל תלמיד ששמע דבר מפי גדול הימנו גרסה ונתן סימנים הלכה פלונית ופלונית שמעתי משם פלוני וכשנתקבצו אמר כל אחד מה ששמע ונתנו לב לברר טעמי המחלוקת דברי מי ראוין לקיים וסידרו המסכתות דברי נזיקין לבדם ודברי יבמות לבדם ודברי קדשים לבדם וסתם נמי במשנה דברי יחידים שראה רבי את דבריהם ושנאן סתם כדי לקבוע הלכה כמותם לפיכך אמרו בגמרא אין לך מדה גדולה מזו שיתנו לב לטעמי המשנה: **שבקו כולי עלמא מתני'**. מלחזור על גרסת משנתם: **ואזלו בתר גמרא**. לחשוב בסברא: **הדר דרש להו הוי רץ למשנה**. לפי שירא פן ישתכחו המשניות ויחליפו שמות החכמים ובמקום חיוב יאמרו פטור ובמקום אסור יאמרו מותר: **מאי דרוש**. מתחילה כשדרש שגמרא גדול: **לעמי פשעם**. עמי דהיינו ת"ח את חטאתם אני קורא פשע שהיה להם לתת לב בטעמי משנתם שיבררו להם על העיקר ולא יורו הלכה מתוך משנה שאינה עיקר: **ולבית יעקב**. שאר העם: **חטאתם**. אפילו פשע שלהם אני קורא חטאת: **הוי זהיר בתלמוד**. בגמרא שהיא תירוץ [טעמי] המשניות או אם תשמע דבר משנה מרבך הזהר לשאול טעמיו ומי שנאה: **ששגגת תלמוד**. אם שגית בהוראה בשגגת תלמודך שלא ידעת טעם המשנה ונתת בה טעם אחר ומתוך כך דמית לה דין או הוראה שבא לידך ולמדת הימנה שלא כדת שאין הטעם כמו שהיית סבור שאילו ידעת טעם המשנה לא דמית לה מעשה הבא לידך: **עולה זדון**. ענוש אתה עליה כמזיד שזדון הוא בידך שלא שאלת טעם מרבך: **אלו ת"ח.**: שטימשו חכמים הרבה ללמדם טעמי משנתם זה בזו וזה בזו שאין הכל בקיאין בשון: **שנאיכם אלו בעלי משנה**. שסונאין בעלי גמרא לפי שבעלי גמרא אומרים על בעלי משנה שהן מבלי עולם כדאמרינן במסכת סוטה (דף כב.) התנאים מבלי עולם שמורים הלכה מתוך משנתם: **מנדיכם אלו ע"ה**. שת"ח שונאין ומתועבין להן הגדה: **שמא תאמר אבד סברם**. של אלו שהרי כתיב למען שמי יכבד ה' דמשמע שהם אומרים אבל אין הדבר כן: **ת"ל ונראה בשמחתכם**. ולא נאמר ונראה בשמחתכם כך אמר הנביא אני ואחיכם שונאיכם ומנדיכם כולנו נראה בשמחתכם: **והם יבושו**. אותם שהם עובדי כוכבים שאינם ממנו ואין נקראין על שם ישראל הם יבושו וישראל ישמחו:

הדרן עלך אלו מציאות

**המפקיד.** ולא רצה לישבע. שבועת שומרים שלא פשע בה ושלא שלח בה יד שהיה יכול ליפטר בשבועה זו שהרי אמרו כו': **למי שהפקדון אצלו**. דכיון דשילם קנה כל תשלומיה ובגמרא מפרש טעמא: **גמ' דמקני ליה כפילא**. הבעלים מקנין לשומר כפל העתיד להשתלם כדאמר לקמן שבשעה שמסרה לו לשמור על מנת כן מסרה שאם תגנב וירצה וישלם יהא כפל שלו: **אימר לא מקנה ליה כפילא**. לא מסרה לו מתחילה על מנת כן: **דלא נפיש כפלייהו**. שאין באין לידי ארבעה וחמשה שאינה נוהגת אלא בשור ושה בלבד: **מתקיף לה רמי כו'**. אמתניתין קא מתמה: **והא אין אדם מקנה דבר שלא בא לעולם**. והיאך הקנו לו בעלים כפל זה שעדיין לא נתחייב בו גנב: **ואפילו לר' מאיר דאמר**. בפ"ג דקדושין (דף סג.) הרי את מקודשת לי על מנת שאתגייר איכא למיגמר מינה מוכר פירות דקל לחבירו עד שלא באו לעולם דאפליגו בה רב הונא ורב נחמן לקמן באיזהו נשך (דף סו:): **דעבידי דאתו**. גרסינן:

מי

---

**תוספות**

**אחיכם** אלו בעלי מקרא. שאינם יודעים דינים והוראות כי אם על פי בעלי גמרא שונאיכם אלו בעלי משנה שסבורים לידע כמו בעלי גמרא ואינם יודעים בירור הדבר מנדיכם אלו ע"ה ששונאים ת"ח ושמא תאמר אבד סברן ת"ל ונראה בשמחתכם ישראל ישמחו ועובדי כוכבים יבושו:

הדרן עלך אלו מציאות

**המפקיד.** אית דלא גרסי או שאבדו משום דבאבידה ליכא כפל ויש ליישב שכך טוען הנפקד ואחר כך נמצא הגנב אי נמי אנו יודעים שנגנבו מתוך ביתו אך אין אנו יודעים אם פשע או שאבדו שאנו יודעין שנאבד ממנו אך לא ידעינן אם על ידי גניבה או על ידי דבר אחר:

**נגנבו.** ה"ה אם אמר פשעתי שהכפל שלו כדאמר בגמרא מגו דאי בעי פטר נפשיה בגניבה אלא אורחא דמילתא נקט נגנבו שהוא רגילות לטעון דבר שהוא פטור אע"פ שהוא רוצה לשלם וריב"ן פי' דמתני' נמי ה"פ דהנפקד אומר שנגנבו בפשיעה ולא רצה לישבע היינו ולא רצה לישבע לשקר: **כגון** פירות דקל דעבידי דאתו. וא"ת והכא אפילו אי עבידי דאתו היאך יקנה הכפל במעות שילם והלא מעות אינן קונות אלא למיקם עליה במי שפרע ועוד מאי קפריך בסמוך מי יימר דמיגנבא והלא כשילם כבר נגנבה והול"ל מי יימר דנגנבה פירוש שכבר נגנבה שמא נאבדה ויש לומר דהמקשה סבר דבשעת משיכה הקנה לו הפרה לקנות הכפל כשיבא ואע"ג דבפרק מי שמת (ב"ב דף קמז:) אמרי' דבדקל לפירות אפילו רבנן מודו דקני היינו משום דעבידי דאתו אבל הכא דלא עבידו דאתא אפילו לר' מאיר לא קני וקשה דבפ' השולח (גיטין מב: ושם) מיבעיא לן בעבד שמכרו רבו לקנס דדילמא אפילו לר' מאיר לא יועיל משום דלא עבידא דאתי דמנגח או דילמא אפילו לרבנן יועיל משום דהא קאי עבדא והוי כדקל לפירותיו והכא פשיטא ליה דלא מהני פרה לכפילא ואפילו לר"מ וי"ל דשמא התם שכיח טפי מהכא אי נמי הכא פריך אם תימצי לומר בעבד שמכרו רבו לקנס דלא מהני לר"מ ומשני נעשה כאומר לו לכשתגנב ותשלמני הרי פרתי קניה לך מעכשיו שגוף הפרה מכר לו דהשתא הכפל שלו ממילא [ז]:

דילמא

---

**עין משפט נר מצוה**

א א מיי' פ"א מהלכות שכירות הל' ג סמג עשין פט טור ש"ע ח"מ סי' רלא סעיף א:

ב ב ג ד מיי' פ"ח מהל' שאלה ופקדון הלכה א סמג עשין פח טור ח"מ סי' רלה:

ג ה מיי' פכ"ב מהלכות מכירה הלכה י סמג עשין פ"ב טור ש"ע ח"מ סי' רט סעיף ד:

**רבינו חננאל**

שבבבל עומדין זה מלפני זה וקורעין זה על זה וכו'. פי' כיון שנושאין זה עם זה בהלכה לומדין זה מזה טעמי' הרבה כרבו הוא חשוב כל אחד לחבירו לפיכך עומדין זה מפני זה וקורעין זה על זה אבל לענין השבת אבידה אינו מניח של אביו ומחזיר לרבו אלא אם הוא רבו מובהק. רב חסדא הוא תלמיד רב הונא דגרסי' בעירובין בתחלת פרק הדר עם הנכרי בחצר. אמר רב יוסף ביעתא בכותחא בעאי מרב חסדא בשני רב הונא ולא פשט לי. פי' מפני שיש בכותח כמכא דחלבא הוצרך לשאול אם הוא מותר שיאכל ביצת שחוטה בכותח אי לא כלומר ביצת שחוטה כבשר היא וכיון שיש בכותח חלב נמצא כאילו אוכל בשר בחלב ואסור אי לא ואע"ג דדבר ברור הוא דתניא השוחט את התרנגולת ומצא בה ביצים גמורות מותרות לאכלן בחלב אפי' הכי זה שהוא דבר קל לא רצה להורות בפני רב הונא רבו. בעא מיניה רב חסדא מרב הונא תלמיד וצריך לו רבו מהו כלומר תלמיד חריף שרבו נהנה ממנו ומשאילות התלמיד ומחקריו מוסיף הרב חכמה כדאמר [בסנהדרין סח] הרבה למדתי מרבותי ומחברי יותר מהם ומתלמידי יותר מכולם תלמיד כגון זה אצל רבו יניח אבידת אביו ויחזיר או לא וחשב רב הונא בדעתו כי רב (הונא) [חסדא] על עצמו שאל וכי הוא כענין תלמיד שצריך לו רבו וכעס והשיבו חסדא חסדא לא צריכנא לך ולא לחידודך ולא לפלפולך אנת צריך לקבל ממני עד מלאת לך לפני מ' שנה שבמלאת מ' שנה עומד התלמיד על דעת רבו כדכתיב ואולך אתכם ארבעים שנה במדבר וגו' ולא נתן ה' לכם לב לדעת וגו': איקפדו להדדי ולא עול לגבי [הדדי]. רב הונא יתיב ארבעין תעניתא דחשדיה לרב חסדא. רב חסדא יתיב ארבעין תעניתא משום דחלש דעתיה דרב הונא. דרש ר' יהודה בר' אלעי שמעו דבר ה' החרדים אל דברו אלו תלמידי חכמים וכו':

הדרן עלך אלו מציאות

המפקיד אצל חבירו בהמה או כלים נגנבו או שאבדו שילם ולא רצה לישבע וכו' עד למי משלם למי שהפקדון אצלו וכן הלכה. ומקשי' והא אין [אדם] מקנה לחבירו דבר שלא בא לעולם כלומר היאך יכול המפקיד להקנות כפילו למי שהפקדון בידו והא אפי' ר' מאיר דסבר אדם מקנה לחבירו דבר שלא בא לעולם כי האי גוונא לא אמר.

**מסורת הש"ס**

א) [עיין תוספות בבא קמא לד: ד"ה בימי וכו'] ב) [דוגמתו סנהדרין קג:] ג) אבות פרק ד משנה י ד) ב"ק קח., ה) יבמות לג קדושין סב:, גיטין יג מב:, ב"ב עט:, קמ:, קלא קמא:, קנז:, ו) [סוטה מז סנהדרין פח:], ז) [וע' תוספות ב"ב עט: ד"ה אימור].

**גליון הש"ס**

גמ' אלו עמי הארץ. עי' סוטה דף כב ע"א תוס' ד"ה רבי שמואל רש"י ד"ה בימי וכו' שמשרבו תלמידי ועיין חגיגה דף טז ע"ב תוספות ד"ה יוסי:

**הגהות מהר"ב רנשבורג**

א] ברש"י ד"ה מתקיף לה רמי. כ"ב עיין הליכות עולם דף [ה] ע"ב ודף (ח) [ו] ע"א ובדברי בעל יבין שמועה שם יעוש"ה ע"ב בד"ה ה"ע ומליץ מתקיף וכו':

**תורה אור השלם**

א) קְרָא בְגָרוֹן אַל תַּחְשֹׂךְ כַּשּׁוֹפָר הָרֵם קוֹלֶךָ וְהַגֵּד לְעַמִּי פִּשְׁעָם וּלְבֵית יַעֲקֹב חַטֹּאתָם: [ישעיה נח, א]

ב) שִׁמְעוּ דְּבַר יְיָ הַחֲרֵדִים אֶל דְּבָרוֹ אָמְרוּ אֲחֵיכֶם שֹׂנְאֵיכֶם מְנַדֵּיכֶם לְמַעַן שְׁמִי יִכְבַּד יְיָ וְנִרְאֶה בְשִׂמְחַתְכֶם וְהֵם יֵבֹשׁוּ: [ישעיה סו, ה]

**ליקוטי רש"י**

הגד לעמי. אלו תלמידי חכמים שכל שגגתם פשע ששגגת תלמוד עולה זדון [ישעיה נח, ב]. החרדים אל דברו. הצדיקים הממהרים בחרדה להתקרב אל דבריו. [ישעיה סו, ה]. ובטל סיכוים תוחלתם ומבטם כדמתרגמינן הבט נא (בראשית טו) איסתכי כען לשמיא [סוכה מה:]. שהרי אמרו וכו'. ויכול היה ליפטר בשבועה [ב"ק קח.]. פירות דקל קודם שחנטו פירותיו [לקמן סו:]. שהמוכר פירות דקל לחבירו אע"פ שעדיין לא באו לעולם אינו יכול לחזור בו משיבואו לעולם דהא ודאי עבידי דאתו דומיא דע"מ שאתגייר דלדעתיה לאיגיורי ומיהו ר"מ לא איירי בפירות דקל אלא רב הונא דקאי כוותיה במסכת יבמות [רשב"ם ב"ב עט:].

א) רובץ ולא רבצן רובץ ולא עומד תחת משאו ולא מפורק תחת משאו משאוי שיכול לעמוד בו ואי אמרת צער בעלי חיים דאורייתא מה לי רובץ ומה לי רבצן ומה לי עומד הא מני ר' יוסי הגלילי היא דאמר צער בעלי חיים דרבנן ה"נ מסתברא דקתני תחת משאו משאוי שיכול לעמוד בו מאן שמעת ליה דאית ליה האי סברא רבי יוסי הגלילי ש"מ ומי מצית מוקמת לה כרבי יוסי הגלילי והא קתני סיפא תחת משאו ולא מפורק מאי לא מפורק אילימא לא מפורק כלל הא כתיב ב) הקם תקים עמו אלא פשיטא לא מפורק בחנם אלא בשכר מאן שמעת ליה דאית ליה האי סברא רבנן לעולם ר' יוסי הגלילי היא ובטעינה סבר לה כרבנן ת"ר [א]א) כי תראה יכול אפי' מרחוק ת"ל כי תפגע אי כי תפגע יכול פגיעה ממש ת"ל כי תראה ואיזו היא ראייה שיש בה פגיעה אשיערו חכמים אחד משבע ומחצה במיל וזה הוא ריס תנא בומדדה עמו עד פרסה אמר רבה בר בר חנה גונוטל שכר: **מתני'** א) דאבדתו ואבדת אביו אבדתו קודמת אבדתו ואבדת רבו שלו קודם האבדת אביו ואבדת רבו של רבו קודמת שאביו הביאו לעולם הזה ורבו שלמדו חכמה מביאו לחיי העולם הבא ואם אביו [ב]חכם של אביו קודמת זהיה אביו ורבו נושאין משאוי מניח את של רבו ואחר כך מניח את של אביו חהיה אביו ורבו בבית השבי פודה את רבו ואחר כך פודה את אביו טואם אביו חכם פודה את אביו ואח"כ פודה את רבו: **גמ'** מנא הני מילי ג) אמר רב יהודה אמר רב קרא ג) אפס כי לא יהיה בך אביון ישלך קודם לשל כל אדם ואמר רב יהודה אמר רב כבל המקיים בעצמו כך סוף בא לידי כך: היה אביו ורבו נושאין משאוי וכו': ג) תנו רבנן רבו שאמרו רבו שלמדו חכמה ולא רבו שלמדו מקרא ומשנה דברי ר"מ ד) רבי יהודה אומר לכל שרוב חכמתו הימנו רבי יוסי אומר אפילו לא האיר עיניו אלא במשנה אחת זה הוא רבו אמר רבא כגון ה) רב סחורה דאסברן ו) זוהמא ליסטרון שמואל קרע מאניה עליה ההוא מרבנן דאסבריה ז) אחד יורד לאמת השחי ואחד פותח כיון אמר עולא מתלמידי חכמים שבבבל עומדין זה מפני זה וקורעין זה על זה נולענין אבדה במקום אביו אינן חוזרין אלא לרבו מובהק קבעי מיניה רב חסדא מרב הונא תלמיד וצריך לו רבו מאי אמר ליה חסדא חסדא לא צריכנא לך את צריכת לי עד ארבעין שנין איקפדי אהדדי ולא עיילי לגבי הדדי יתיב רב חסדא ארבעין תעניתא משום דחלש דעתיה דרב הונא יתיב רב הונא ארבעין תעניתא משום דחשדיה לרב חסדא איתמר רב יצחק בר יוסף אמר ר' יוחנן הלכה כרבי יהודה רב אחא בר רב הונא אמר רב ששת הלכה כרבי יוסי ומי אמר רבי יוחנן הכי והאמר רבי יוחנן ס) הלכה כסתם משנה ותנן רבו שלמדו חכמה מאי חכמה רוב חכמתו ת"ר העוסקין במקרא מדה ואינה מדה במשנה מדה ונוטלין עליה שכר סגמרא אין לך מדה גדולה מזו ולעולם הוי רץ למשנה יותר מן גמרא הא גופא קשיא אמרת בגמרא אין לך מדה גדולה מזו והדר אמרת ולעולם הוי רץ למשנה יותר מן הגמרא אמר רבי יוחנן

**רש"י**

רובץ. מקרה הוא לו שרובץ תחת משאו בפעם הזאת: ולא רבצן. הרגיל בכך: ולא מפורק. והוא צריך טעינה ולקמן פריך הכתיב הקם תקים: יכול מרחוק. והטיל עליו שילך שם: מדדה עמו. לאחר שהטעינו שמא יחזור ויפול: גמ' מנא הני מילי. דשלו קודם: לא יהיה בך אביון. הזהר מן עניות: כל המקיים בעצמו כך. אף על פי שלא הטילו עליו הכתוב יש לאדם ליכנס לפנים משורת הדין ולא לדקדק שלי קודם אם לא בהפסד מוכיח ואם תמיד מדקדק פורק מעליו עול ג"ח ולדקה וסוף שילטרך לבריות: שלמדו חכמה. סברת טעמי המשנה ולהבין שלא יהו סותרות זו את זו וטעמי איסור והיתר והחיוב והפטור והוא נקרא גמרא: מקרא. תורה נביאים וכתובים: משנה. כמו שהן שנויות ואין טעמן מפורש בהן: כל שרוב חכמתו הימנו. אם מקרא אם משנה אם גמרא: האיר עיניו. שהודיעו טעם משנה אחת שלא יכול להבין: דאסברן זוהמא ליסטרון. בסדר טהרות (כלים פי"ג משנה ב ופכ"ה משנה ג) היא שנויה ולא הייתי יודע מה כלי הוא ולמדני שהוא כף גדולה שמסלקין בו זוהם הקדירה והקלחת לצדדין: קרע מאניה. קרע שאין מתאחה כדין תלמיד על הרב: אחד יורד לאמת השחי. משנה היא במסכת תמיד (פרק ג משנה ו) אצל הנכנסים שחרית לפתוח דלתות ההיכל מי שזכה בדישון מזבח הפנימי כו' ושני מפתחות בידו אחד יורד לאמת השחי ואחד פותח כיון אחד מן המפתחות הללו פותח פשפש הצפוני שאצל פתח ההיכל בקרן מזרחית צפונית של אולם והיכל כדתנן התם שני פשפשים היה לו לשער הגדול אחד לצפון ההיכל והאולם ואחד לדרומו ואותו שבדרום לא נכנס בו אדם מעולם כדמפרש התם ואותו פשפש שבצפון והוא לפתח שבזוית האולם שאצל חמש אמות של כותל ההיכל שבצפון פתח ההיכל ודלת סובבת בו ואותו מפתח של אותו הפתח יורד לאמת השחי. פשפשים פתחים קטנים כמין צפות קטנות ארכו כעובי רוחב הכותל ודלת סובבת בו פושטי"ר בלעז אחד יורד לאמת השחי הבא לפתוח בו שחרית ט) [פשפש שבזוית האולם] עומד מבחוץ בתוך האולם ומכניס ידו בחור שבכותל עד בית שחיו ופותח: ואחד פותח כיון. לאחר שנכנס בזה (א) ובא לו לתא אשר על פני אחת עשרה אמה של אולם וקצת מן ההיכל ופותח במפתח שני דלת אחד שמן התא להיכל מהר בלא טורח כשאר פתחים ונכנס להיכל לפתוח דלתות ההיכל: כיון. כמו (פסחים דף לו.) יעשנה בדפוס ויקבענה כיון מהר בלא טורח והאי שער הגדול הוא פתח ההיכל שבין אולם להיכל: עומדין זה מפני זה. כדין תלמיד לרב לפי שהיו יושבין תמיד בבית המדרש יחד ומקשין ומפרקין וכולם למדים זה מזה: לרבו מובהק. שרוב חכמתו ממנו כר"י: וצריך לו רבו. ששמע שמועות שיש בידו מפי אחרים: מאי. כלומר קודם לאביו לענין אבדה: ותנן רבו שלמדו חכמה. סתמא כר' מאיר: רוב חכמתו. אם מקרא מקרא אם משנה משנה: מדה. היא קצת: ואינה מדה. שהמשנה וגמרא יפים ממנה מפני שתלוין בגירסא ומשתכחים שבימיהם לא היה גמרא בכתב וגם לא היה ניתן לכתוב אלא לפי שנתמעטו הלבבות התחילו דורות [אחרונים] לכתבו: גמרא. כבר פירשתי למעלה שהוא לתת לב להבין סתימות טעמי המשנה מה הם וכששתים סותרות זו את זו יבין לתרץ שיהיו שתיהן קיימות או לדעת דברי התנאים החלוקים בדבר וימצא האי מני פלוני תנא הוא:

בימי

**תוספות**

מה לי רבצן. וא"ת וליתני רובץ בחנם רבצן בשכר דה"נ משני ולא מפורק בחנם אלא בשכר וי"ל דניחא ליה לשנויי דאתי כרבי יוסי הגלילי כדמוכח דאתיא כוותיה: ונוטל שכר. במה שמדדה ובפריקה מיירי שירא פן ירבץ דאי בטעינה פשיטא דהא טעינה גופה בשכר וכל שכן מה שמדדה: י) וזהו ריס. אית דגרסי רוס דשבע ומחצה רוס עולה כ) אלפים דהוי שיעור מיל כדמוכח בפרק שני שעירי (יומא דף סז.) גבי סוכות דשעיר המשתלח: אבדתו קודמת. וא"ת אבדתו ואבדת רבו וכבוד אביו איזהו קודם אי אבדתו הלא כבוד אביו עדיף למאן דאמר בפ"ק דקדושין (דף לב. ושם) משל בן ואם כבוד אביו הלא אבדת רבו קודמת כדאמר לעיל ל) אני ה' ויש לומר אבדתו קודמת דהיכא דאביו נהנה מגוף הבהמה חייב לכבדו כגון שאומר לי בהמתך אבל הניחה ליאבד ותביא לי לאכול שגם לאב קשה האבדה אלא שרוצה לאכול מ): ומקרעין זה על זה. אף על פי שאינו יודע יותר לפי שלומדין זה מזה ואם תאמר דאמרינן בפרק האורג (שבת דף קה: ושם) חייב לקרוע על אדם כשר אפילו לא היה בשעת יציאת נשמה [ג] ויש לומר דהכא מיירי בקרע שאינו מתאחה כדין תלמיד על רבו וכן פירש רש"י:

אחיכם

**עין משפט נר מצוה**

קפח א מיי' פי"ג מהל' רוצח ה"ו סמג עשין פא טוש"ע חו"מ סי' רעב סעיף ה:
קפט ב מיי' שם הל' ה טוש"ע שם סעיף ד:
קצ ג מיי' שם הל' ז טוש"ע שם סעיף ו:
קצא ד מיי' פי"ב מהל' אבידה הלכה א סמג עשין עד טוש"ע חו"מ סי' רסד ס"א:
קצב ה ו מיי' שם ה"ב ופ"ה מהלכות ת"ת הלכה א סמג שם טור ש"ע שם ס"ב וטור ש"ע י"ד סי' רמב סל"ד:
קצג ז מיי' פ"ה מהל' ת"ת ה"א סמג שם טוש"ע י"ד סי' רמב סל"ד:
קצד ח ט מיי' שם ופ"ח מהל' מתנות עניים הל' יח סמג שם וסי' קסב טוש"ע שם וסי' רנב ס"ט:
קצה י מיי' פי"ב מהל' אבידה הלכה א סמג עשין עד טוש"ע ח"מ סי' רסד ס"א וטוש"ע יו"ד סי' רמב סל"ה:
קצו כ טוש"ע ח"מ שם:
קצז ל מיי' פי"ב מהל' אבדה הל' ב ופ"ה מהל' ת"ת הל' ט סמג עשין שם טוש"ע ח"מ סי' רסד ס"ב וטוש"ע י"ד סי' רמב סעיף ל:
קצח מ מיי' פ"ה מהל' ת"ת ופ"ט מהל' אבל הי"א סמג עשין יב עד פב טוש"ע יו"ד סי' רמב ס"ל וסי' שמ ס"ז וסעיף ח:
קצט נ מיי' פי"ב מהל' אבידה הל' ב סמג עשין עד טוש"ע ח"מ סי' רסד סעיף ב:
ר ס מיי' פ"א מהל' ת"ת הלכה יא סמג עשין יב טוש"ע י"ד סי' רמו ס"ד:

**רבינו חננאל**

ת"ר כי תראה יכול מרחוק ת"ל כי תפגע יכול פגיעה ממש פניא בפנים ת"ל כי תראה (הם) [הא] כיצד ראיה שיש בה פגיעה שיערו חכמים אחד משבעה ומחצה במיל וזהו ריס. ומדדה עמו עד פרסה ונוטל שכרו. קיימא לן פריקה בחנם לדברי הכל וטעינה בשכר כרבנן: מתני' אבדתו ואבדת אביו וכו' אבדת רבו שלו קודמת. פי' יניח של אביו ויניח של רבו וישיב את שלו שנאמר אפס כי לא יהיה בך אביון. והמדקדק שלא יבא לידי עניות סוף בא לידי כך: ת"ר רבו שאמרו רבו שלמדו חכמה ולא רבו שלמדו מקרא ומשנה דברי ר"מ ר' יהודה אומר כל שרוב חכמתו ממנו ור' יוסי [אמר] אפי' לא האיר עיניו אלא במשנה אחת זהו רבו. אע"ג דאמר ר' יוחנן הלכה כר' יהודה רב ששת דהוא בתרא אמר הלכה כר' יוסי. ועוד הנה שמואל עשה כמותו וקרע על ההוא מרבנן דאסבריה הא דתנן במסכת תמיד פ' אמר להן הממונה ושני מפתחות אחד יורד אמת השחי ואחד פותח כיון פירש לו מפתח אחד היה מכניס ידו ופותח בו מיד והאחר לא יכול לפתוח בו עד שהיה מוריד ידו עד שחיו וכך היה פותח וכן הוא מפורש בתלמוד ארץ ישראל א) הנה שמואל לא למד ממנו אלא פירוש משנה זו בלבד וכיון ששמע שמת קרע עליו כאשר קורע התלמיד על רבו. וכן פירש רבא כי רבו כגון רב סחורה דאסברן זומליסטרון ב) פי' התרוד שמהפך בה בשר בתוך הצלחת נקראת זומליסטרון: ובתלמוד ארץ ישראל ג) רב כר"מ חד בר נש פתח פומיה דרב ושמע דמדכן ובזע עלוהי. ומתניתין נמי כר' יוסי דייקא ד) והא דאוקימנא כר' יהודה שינויא הוא: ת"ר העוסק במקרא פי' במקרא בלבד [illegible]

**מסורת הש"ס**

א) סנהדרין סד:, ב) לעיל ..., סנהדרין סד: ע"ש, ג) [מסכת כלה, תוספתא הוריות פרק ב], ד) [עיין תוספות מועד קטן כה: ד"ה ועל רבו], ה) [עיין תוספות סנהדרין מט: ד"ה אמר, ותוספות יבמות ... ד"ה רבא, ועבודה זרה ... ד"ה אמר], ו) [כלים פרק יג משנה ב, ופרק כה משנה ג], ז) [תמיד ל:], ח) שבת מו. וש"נ, ט) מהרש"ל, י) [צ"ל קודם ד"ה ונוטל], כ) הוא אלפים חסר חמשה, ועיין בערוך ערך רוס, ל) דף לב., מ) [וע"ש בתוס' ד"ה ר"י, וכן בתוס' זבחים ל: ד"ה מטלא].

**הגהות הב"ח**

(א) רש"י ד"ה ואחד פותח כיון לאחר שנכנס בזה. נ"ב אבל הר' עובדיה פי' שאותן שני מפתחות היו שניהם בפשפש הצפוני וע"ש:

**הגהות הגר"א**

[א] גמרא ת"ר לא תראה כו' ממש ת"ל לא תראה. כצ"ל (והוא בדברים כב וכן הוא בספרי שם וא"ש דב' המקראות מיירי גבי אבידה ומוכיחין זה לזה ועיין ריטב"א בשיטה מקובצת ובהגר"א ח"מ סי' רע"ב ס"ק ב'): [ב] במשנה חכם. נ"ב גירס' הרי"ף וש"פ כאן שקול נגד רבו: [ג] תוס' ד"ה ומקרעין. וי"ל כו'. נ"ב ורמב"ם חולק וכו' דוקא ברבו מובהק (ועמ"ש רבינו ביו"ד סי' רמב ס"ק סט):

**תורה אור השלם**

א) כִּי תִרְאֶה חֲמוֹר שֹׂנַאֲךָ רֹבֵץ תַּחַת מַשָּׂאוֹ וְחָדַלְתָּ מֵעֲזֹב לוֹ עָזֹב תַּעֲזֹב עִמּוֹ: [שמות כג, ה]
ב) לֹא תִרְאֶה אֶת חֲמוֹר אָחִיךָ אוֹ שׁוֹרוֹ נֹפְלִים בַּדֶּרֶךְ וְהִתְעַלַּמְתָּ מֵהֶם הָקֵם תָּקִים עִמּוֹ: [דברים כב, ד]
ג) אֶפֶס כִּי לֹא יִהְיֶה בְּךָ אֶבְיוֹן כִּי בָרֵךְ יְבָרֶכְךָ יְיָ בָּאָרֶץ אֲשֶׁר יְיָ אֱלֹהֶיךָ נֹתֵן לְךָ נַחֲלָה לְרִשְׁתָּהּ: [דברים טו, ד]

**לעזי רש"י**

פושטי"ר. פירוש פשפש, שער קטן בתוך שער גדול (ערוך ערך פשפש ג').

**ליקוטי רש"י**

אפס וכו' בך אביון. הזהר בעצמך שלא תבוא לידי עניות [סנהדרין סד:]. זוהמא ליסטרון. אותו כף שבוחשין את הקדרה קרי להו הכי על שם שמעבירין הזוהמא לצדדין על שני צדיו תרגום על מרין סטרוהי [הוריות יג:]. מאניה. בגדיו [יומא נב.].

חשק שלמה על ר"ח א) כן מבואר בירושלמי בסוף פירקין. ב) כ"ה הגירסא בערוך זומלסטרן ובכ"י זומליסטרון בתיבה אחת. ג) [illegible] ד) [illegible]

study of MISHNAH[47] alone מִדָּה – accomplish A large MEASURE, וְנוֹטְלִין עָלֶיהָ שָׂכָר – AND THEY RECEIVE REWARD FOR studying IT. גְּמָרָא – And for those who delve into the study of TALMUD, אֵין לְךָ מִדָּה גְּדוֹלָה מִזּוֹ – THERE IS NO GREATER MEASURE THAN THIS:[48] וּלְעוֹלָם הֱוֵי רָץ לַמִּשְׁנָה יוֹתֵר מִן גְּמָרָא – YET ONE SHOULD ALWAYS RUN TO study MISHNAH MORE THAN TALMUD.

The Gemara questions the Baraisa:

הָא גוּפָא קַשְׁיָא – This is self-contradictory! אָמְרַת בִּגְמָרָא – On the one hand, **you said** concerning those who engross themselves IN the study of TALMUD, אֵין לְךָ מִדָּה גְּדוֹלָה מִזּוֹ – THERE IS NO GREATER MEASURE THAN THIS. This implies that studying Talmud is of greater importance than studying Mishnah. וְהָדַר אָמְרַת – **But then you said,** וּלְעוֹלָם הֱוֵי רָץ לַמִּשְׁנָה יוֹתֵר מִן הַגְּמָרָא – ONE SHOULD ALWAYS RUN TO study MISHNAH MORE THAN TALMUD, which implies that Mishnah is the more important area of study. This is self-contradictory! – ? –

The Gemara replies:

אָמַר רַבִּי יוֹחָנָן – **R' Yochanan said:**

---

NOTES

47. The term "Mishnah," as it is used here, seems to denote the study of Mishnaic texts without resolving the apparent difficulties they present (see above, note 31).

48. I.e. Talmud represents the most preferred area of study. The term "Talmud" (or "Gemara"), as it is used here, denotes the principles that underlie the precepts of the Mishnah, as well as the knowledge of how to reconcile Mishnahs that apparently contradict each other. Such Mishnahs can be reconciled in various ways – for example, by showing that the conflicting teachings reflect the views of Tannaim that are in dispute, or address cases that are different from one another (*Rashi*).

רובץ ולא רבצן רובץ ולא עומד תחת משאו ולא מפורק תחת משאו משאוי שיכול לעמוד בו ואי אמרת צער בעלי חיים דאורייתא מה לי רובץ ומה לי רבצן ומה לי עומד הא מני ר' יוסי הגלילי היא דאמר צער בעלי חיים דרבנן ה"נ מסתברא דקתני תחת משאו משאוי שיכול לעמוד בו מאן שמעת ליה דאית ליה האי סברא רבי יוסי הגלילי ש"מ ומי מצית מוקמת לה כרבי יוסי הגלילי והא קתני סיפא תחת משאו ולא מפורק מאי לא מפורק אילימא לא מפורק כלל הא כתיב הקם תקים עמו אלא פשיטא לא מפורק בחנם אלא בשכר מאן שמעת ליה דאית ליה האי סברא רבנן לעולם ר' יוסי הגלילי היא ובטעינה סבר לה כרבנן ת"ר [א] כי תראה יכול אפי' מרחוק ת"ל כי תפגע אי כי תפגע יכול פגיעה ממש ת"ל כי תראה ואיזו היא ראייה שיש בה פגיעה שיערו חכמים אחד משבע ומחצה במיל וזה הוא ריס תנא ומדדה עמו עד פרסה אמר רבה בר בר חנה ונוטל שכר: **מתני'** אבדתו ואבדת אביו אבדתו קודמת אבדתו ואבדת רבו אבדתו קודמת אבדת אביו ואבדת רבו של רבו קודמת שאביו הביאו לעולם הזה ורבו שלמדו חכמה מביאו לחיי העולם הבא ואם אביו [ב] חכם של אביו קודמת היה אביו ורבו נושאין משאוי מניח את של רבו ואחר כך מניח את של אביו היה אביו ורבו בבית השבי פודה את רבו ואחר כך פודה את אביו ואם אביו חכם פודה את אביו ואח"כ פודה את רבו: **גמ'** מנא הני מילי אמר רב יהודה אמר רב קרא אפס כי לא יהיה בך אביון שלך קודם לשל כל אדם ואמר רב יהודה אמר רב כל המקיים בעצמו כך סוף בא לידי כך: היה אביו ורבו נושאין משאוי וכו': תנו רבנן רבו שאמרו רבו שלמדו חכמה ולא רבו שלמדו מקרא ומשנה דברי ר"מ רבי יהודה אומר כל שרוב חכמתו הימנו רבי יוסי אומר אפילו לא האיר עיניו אלא במשנה אחת זה הוא רבו אמר רבא כגון רב סחורה דאסברן זוהמא ליסטרון שמואל קרע מאניה עליה ההוא מרבנן דאסבריה אחד יורד לאמת השחי ואחד פותח כיון אמר עולא תלמידי חכמים שבבבל עומדין זה מפני זה וקורעין זה על זה ולענין אבדה במקום אביו אינן חוזרין אלא לרבו מובהק קבעי מיניה רב חסדא מרב הונא תלמיד וצריך לו רבו מאי אמר ליה חסדא חסדא לא צריכנא לך את צריכת לי עד ארבעין שנין איקפדי אהדדי ולא עיילי לגבי הדדי יתיב רב חסדא ארבעין תעניתא משום דחלש דעתיה דרב הונא יתיב רב הונא ארבעין תעניתא משום דחשדיה לרב חסדא איתמר רב יצחק בר יוסף אמר ר' יוחנן הלכה כרבי יהודה רב אחא בר רב הונא אמר רב ששת הלכה כרבי יוסי ומי אמר רבי יוחנן הכי והאמר רבי יוחנן הלכה כסתם משנה ותנן רבו שלמדו חכמה מאי חכמה רוב חכמתו ת"ר העוסקין במקרא מדה ואינה מדה במשנה מדה ונוטלין עליה שכר גמרא אין לך מדה גדולה מזו ולעולם הוי רץ למשנה יותר מן גמרא הא גופא קשיא אמרת בגמרא אין לך מדה גדולה מזו והדר אמרת ולעולם הוי רץ למשנה יותר מן הגמרא אמר רבי יוחנן

**רש"י**

רובץ. מקרה הוא לו שרובץ תחת משאו בפעם הזאת: ולא רבצן. הרגיל בכך: ולא מפורק. והוא לריך טעינה ולקמן פריך הכתיב הקם תקים: יכול מרחוק. והטיל עליו שילך שם: מדדה עמו. לאחר שהטעינו שמא יחזור ויפול: גמ' מנא הני מילי. דשלו קודם: לא יהיה בך אביון. הזהר מן עניות: כל המקיים בעצמו כך. אף על פי שלא הטילו עליו הכתוב יש לאדם ליכנס לפנים משורת הדין ולא לדקדק שלי קודם אם לא בהפסד מוכיח ואם תמיד מדקדק פורק מעליו עול ג"ח ולדקה וסוף שילטרך לבריות: שלמדו חכמה. סברת טעמי המשנה ולהבין שלא יהו סותרות זו את זו וטעמי איסור והיתר והחיוב והפטור והוא נקרא גמרא: מקרא. תורה נביאים וכתובים: משנה. כמו שהן שנויות ואין טעמן מפורש בהן: כל שרוב חכמתו הימנו. אם מקרא אם משנה אם גמרא: האיר עיניו. שהודיעו טעם משנה אחת שלא יכול להבין: דאסברן זוהמא ליסטרון. בסדר טהרות (כלים פי"ג משנה ב ופכ"ה משנה ג) היא שנויה ולא הייתי יודע מה כלי הוא ולמדני שהוא כף גדולה שמסלקין בו זוהם הקדירה והקלחת ללדדין: קרע מאניה. קרע שאין מתאחה כדין תלמיד על הרב: אחד יורד לאמת השחי. משנה היא במסכת תמיד (פרק ג משנה ו) אלל הנכנסים שחרית לפתוח דלתות ההיכל מי שזכה בדישון מזבח הפנימי כו' ושני מפתחות בידו אחד יורד לאמת השחי ואחד פותח כיון אחד מן המפתחות הללו פותח פשפש הלפוני שאלל פתח ההיכל בקרן מזרחית לפונית של אולם והיכל כדתנן התם שני פשפשים היה לו לשער הגדול אחד ללפון ההיכל והאולם ואחד לדרומו ואותו שבדרום לא נכנס בו אדם מעולם כדמפרש התם ואותו פשפש שבלפון והוא לפתח שבזוית האולם שאלל חמש אמות של כותל ההיכל שבלפון פתח ההיכל ודלת סובבת בו ואותו מפתח של אותו הפתח יורד לאמת השחי. פשפשים פתחים קטנים כמין כיפות קטנות ארכו כעובי רוחב הכותל ודלת סובבת בו פוסטי"ר בלעז אחד יורד לאמת השחי הבא לפתוח בו שחרית ט) [פשפש שבזוית האולם] עומד מבחוץ בתוך האולם ומכניס ידו בחור שבכותל עד בית שחיו ופותח: ואחד פותח כיון. לאחר שנכנס בזה (א) ובא לו לתא אשר על פני אחת עשרה אמה של אולם וקלת מן ההיכל ופותח במפתח שני דלת אחד שמן התא להיכל מהר בלא טורח כשאר פתחים ונכנס להיכל לפתוח דלתות ההיכל: כיון. כמו (פסחים דף לז.) יעשנה בדפוס ויקבענה כיון מהר בלא טורח והאי שער הגדול הוא פתח ההיכל שבין אולם להיכל: עומדין זה מפני זה. כדין תלמיד לרב לפי שהיו יושבין תמיד בבית המדרש יחד ומקשין ומפרקין וכולם למדים זה מזה: לרבו מובהק. שרוב חכמתו ממנו כר"י: וצריך לו רבו. ששמע שמועות שיש בידו מפי אחרים: מאי. כלומר קודם לאביו לענין אבדה: ותנן רבו שלמדו חכמה. סתמא כר' מאיר: רוב חכמתו. אם מקרא מקרא אם משנה משנה: מדה. היא קלת: ואינה מדה. שהמשנה וגמרא יפים ממנה מפני שתלוין בגירסא ומשתכחים שבימיהם לא היה גמרא בכתב וגם לא היה ניתן לכתוב אלא לפי שנתמעטו הלבבות התחילו דורות [אחרונים] לכתבו: גמרא. כבר פירשתי למעלה שהוא לתת לב להבין סתימות טעמי המשנה מה הם וכשהם סותרות זו את זו יבין לתרץ שיהיו שתיהן קיימות או לדעת דברי התנאים החלוקים בדבר ונימא הא מני פלוני חכם הוא: בימי

**תוספות**

מה לי רבצן. וא"ת ולישני רובץ בחנם רבצן בשכר דה"נ משני ולא מפורק בחנם אלא בשכר וי"ל דניחא ליה לשנויי דאתי כרבי יוסי הגלילי כדמוכח דאתיא כוותיה: ונוטל שכר. במה שמדדה ובפריקה איירי שירא פן ירבץ דאי בטעינה פשיטא דהא טעינה גופה בשכר וכל שכן מה שמדדה: י) וזהו ריס. אית דגרסי רוס דשבע ומחצה רוס עולה כ) אלפים דהוי שיעור מיל כדמוכח בפרק שני שעירי (יומא דף סז.) גבי סוכות דשעיר המשתלח: אבדתו קודמת. וא"ת אבדתו ואבדת רבו וכבוד אביו איזהו קודם אי אבדתו הלא כבוד אביו עדיף למאן דאמר בפ"ק דקדושין (דף לב. ושם) משל בן ואם כבוד אביו הלא אבדת רבו קודמת כדאמר לעיל ל) אני ה' ויש לומר אבדתו קודמת דהיכא דאביו נהנה מגוף הבהמה חייב לכבדו כגון שחוט לי בהמתך אבל הניחה ליאבד ותביא לי לאכול שגם לאב קשה האבדה אלא שרוצה לאכול מ): ומקרעין זה על זה. אף על פי שאינו יודע יותר לפי שלומדין זה מזה ואם תאמר דאמרינן בפרק האורג (שבת דף קה: ושם) חייב לקרוע על אדם כשר אפילו לא היה בשעת יציאת נשמה [ג] ויש לומר דהכא איירי בקרע שאינו מתאחה כדין תלמיד על רבו וכן פירש רש"י: אחיכם

**מסורת הש"ס**

א) סנהדרין סד:, ב) לעיל לב., סנהדרין סד:, ע"ש, ג) [מסכת כלה, תוספתא הוריות פרק ב], ד) [עיין תוספות מועד קטן כה: ד"ה ועל רבו], ה) [עיין תוספות סנהדרין מט: ד"ה אמר, ותוספות יבמות קו. ד"ה רבא, ועבודה זרה ט. ד"ה אמר], ו) [כלים פרק יג משנה ב, ופרק כה משנה ג], ז) [תמיד ל:], ח) שבת מו. וש"נ, ט) מהרש"ל, י) [נ"ל קודם ד"ה ונוטל], כ) הוא אלפים וסר חמשה, ועיין בערוך ערך רוס, ל) דף לב., מ) [וע"ש בתוס' ד"ה ר"י, וכן בתוס' זבחים ל: ד"ה סתמא].

**הגהות הב"ח**

(א) רש"י ד"ה ואחד פותח כיון לאחר שנכנס בזה. נ"ב אבל הר' עובדיה פי' שאותן שני מפתחות היו שניהם בפשפש הצפוני וע"ש:

**הגהות הגר"א**

[א] גמרא ת"ר לא תראה כו' ממש ת"ל לא תראה. כצ"ל (והוא בדברים כב וכן הוא בספרי שם וא"ש דב' המקראות במיירי גבי אבידה ומוכיחין זה לזה ועיין ריטב"א שיטה מקובצת ובהגר"א ח"מ סי' רע"ב ס"ק ב'): [ב] במשנה חכם. נ"ב גירס' הרי"ף וש"פ כאן שקול נגד רבו: [ג] תוס' ד"ה ומקרעין. וי"ל כו'. נ"ב ורמב"ם חולק וכ' דוקא ברבו מובהק (ועמ"ש בביאורי ביו"ד סי' רמב ס"ק סט):

**תורה אור השלם**

א) כִּי תִרְאֶה חֲמוֹר שֹׂנַאֲךָ רֹבֵץ תַּחַת מַשָּׂאוֹ וְחָדַלְתָּ מֵעֲזֹב לוֹ עָזֹב תַּעֲזֹב עִמּוֹ: [שמות כג, ה]

ב) לֹא תִרְאֶה אֶת חֲמוֹר אָחִיךָ אוֹ שׁוֹרוֹ נֹפְלִים בַּדֶּרֶךְ וְהִתְעַלַּמְתָּ מֵהֶם הָקֵם תָּקִים עִמּוֹ: [דברים כב, ד]

ג) אֶפֶס כִּי לֹא יִהְיֶה בְּךָ אֶבְיוֹן כִּי בָרֵךְ יְבָרֶכְךָ יְיָ בָּאָרֶץ אֲשֶׁר יְיָ אֱלֹהֶיךָ נֹתֵן לְךָ נַחֲלָה לְרִשְׁתָּהּ: [דברים טו, ד]

**לעזי רש"י**

פושטי"ר. פירוש פשפש, שער קטן בתוך שער גדול (ערוך ערך פשפש ג').

**ליקוטי רש"י**

אפס וכו' בך אביון. הזהר בעלמך שלא תבוא לידי עניות [סנהדרין סד:]. זוהמא ליסטרון. אותו כף שבוחשין את הקדרה קרי להו הכי על שם שמעבירין הזוהמא ללדדין על שני לדיו תרגום על תרין סטרוהי [הוריות יג:]. מאניה. בגדיו [יומא נב.].

**עין משפט נר מצוה**

קפח א מיי' פי"ג מהל' רולח ה"ו סמג עשין פא טוש"ע חו"מ סי' רעב סעיף ה:
קפט ב מיי' שם הל' ה טוש"ע שם סעיף ד:
קצ ג מיי' שם הל' ז טוש"ע שם סעיף ו:
קצא ד מיי' פי"ב מהל' אבידה הלכה ח סמג עשין עד טוש"ע חו"מ סי' רסד ס"א:
קצב ה ו מיי' שם ה"ב ופ"ה מהלכות ת"ת הלכה א סמג שם טור ש"ע שם ס"ב וטור ש"ע י"ד סי' רמב סל"ד:
קצג ז מיי' פ"ה מהל' ת"ת ה"א סמג שם טוש"ע י"ד סי' רמב סל"ד:
קצד ח ט מיי' שם ופ"ח מהל' מתנות עניים הל' יח סמג שם וסי' קסב טוש"ע שם וסי' רנב ס"ט:
קצה י מיי' פי"ב מהל' אבידה הלכה א סמג עשין עד טוש"ע ח"מ סי' רסד ס"א וטוש"ע יו"ד סי' רמב סל"ה:
קצו כ טוש"ע ח"מ שם:
קצז ל מיי' פי"ב מהל' אבדה הל' ב ופ"ה מהל' ת"ת הל' ט סמג עשין שם טוש"ע ח"מ סי' רסד ס"ב וטוש"ע י"ד סי' רמב סעיף ל:
קצח מ מיי' פ"ה מהל' ת"ת ופ"ט מהל' אבל הי"א סמג עשין יג עד פב טוש"ע יו"ד סי' רמב ס"ל וסי' שמ ס"ז וסעיף ח:
קצט נ מיי' פי"ב מהל' אבידה הל' ב סמג עשין עד טוש"ע ח"מ סי' רסד סעיף ב:
ר ס מיי' פ"א מהל' ת"ת הלכה יא סמג עשין יב טוש"ע י"ד סי' רמו ס"ד:

**רבינו חננאל**

ת"ר כי תראה יכול מרחוק ת"ל כי תפגע יכול פגיעה ממש פניא בפנים ת"ל כי תראה (הם) [הא] כיצד ראיה שיש בה פגיעה שיערו חכמים אחד משבעה ומחצה במיל וזהו ריס. ומדדה עמו עד פרסה ונוטל שכרו. קיימא לן פריקה בחנם לדברי הכל וטעינה בשכר כרבנן: מתני' אבדתו ואבדת אביו וכו' אבדת רבו שלו קודמת. פי' יניח של אביו ויניח של רבו וישיב את שלו שנאמר אפס כי לא יהיה בך אביון. והמדקדק שלא יבא לידי עניות סוף בא לידי כך: ת"ר רבו שאמרו רבו שלמדו חכמה ולא רבו שלמדו מקרא ומשנה דברי ר"מ ר' יהודה אומר כל שרוב חכמתו ממנו ור' יוסי [אמר] אפי' לא האיר עיניו אלא במשנה אחת זהו רבו. אע"ג דאמר ר' יוחנן הלכה כר' יהודה רב ששת דהוא בתרא אמר הלכה כר' יוסי. ועוד הנה שמואל עשה כמותו וקרע על ההוא מרבנן דאסבריה הא דתנן במסכת תמיד פ' אמר להן הממונה ושני מפתחות אחד יורד אמת השחי ואחד פותח כיון פירש לו מפתח אחד היה מכניס ידו ופותח בו מיד והאחר לא יכול לפתוח בו עד שהיה מוריד ידו עד שחיו וכך היה פותח וכן הוא מפורש בתלמוד ארץ ישראל א) הנה שמואל לא למד ממנו אלא פירוש משנה זו בלבד וכיון ששמע שמת קרע עליו כאשר קורע התלמיד על רבו. וכן פירש רבא כי רבו כגון רב סחורה דאסברן זומליסטרון ב) פי' התרוד שמהפך בה בשר בתוך הצלחת נקראת זומליסטרון: ובתלמוד ארץ ישראל ג) רב כר"מ חד בר נש פתח פומיה דרב ושמע דדמך ובזע עלוהי. ומתניתין נמי כר' יוסי דייקא ד) והא דאוקימנא כר' יהודה שינויא הוא: ת"ר העוסק במקרא פי' במקרא בלבד ואין מתעסק גם בתלמוד מדה שאינה מדה היא שהרי לא נתעסק גם בפתרון המצות. במשנה מדה שנוטלין עליה שכר פי' המתעסק בפתרון המשנה שיש בה הרבה מן המצות שהן קבלה והן תלויות במשניות החיצונות וכשהוא מתעסק במשנה צריך לעיין באותן הברייתות כולן ופתרוני החכמים יש לו בזה שכר מצוה. אבל המתעסק בתלמוד ומורה ומבאר המצות כתקנן ומגיד הלכה למעשה אין לך מדה גדולה מזו כי בתלמוד פתרון התורה והמשנה והמצוה שהן בקבלה הלכה למשה מסיני. ולעולם הוי רץ למשנה יותר מן התלמוד פי' הוי רץ למשנה שהיא מדה ונוטלין עליה שכר והשוגג אינו נדון בה כמזיד אבל המתעסק בתלמוד אפי' השגגות חשובות עליו כזדונות שהיה לו לדקדק על עצמו שלא יכשל אפי' בשגגה לפי שמדקדקין עליו אפי' כחוט השערה שנאמר וסביביו נשערה מאד מלמד שהקב"ה מדקדק עם סביביו אפי' כחוט השערה ומי יכול להשמר כל זה וכבר פירשנוהו הוי זהיר בתלמוד ששגגת התלמוד עולה זדון וכו' יהודה בר' אלעי דדרש הגד לעמי פשעם אלו תלמידי חכמים ששגגות נעשות להם כזדונות וכו'. אמר עולא תלמידי חכמים

**חשק שלמה על ר"ח** א) כן מבואר בירושלמי בסוף פירקין. ב) כ"ה גירסת רבינו זומליסטרון בתיבה אחת וכ"ה גי' הערוך בערך זמלסטר וע"ש עוד גירסא אחרת. ג) נראה דלפנינו שייך כאן רק מקומו לעיל אצל דברי ר"מ. ד) וכן הובא בשמ"ק ובשו"ת מהרי"ק בשורש קס"ט דרבינו פסק כר' יוסי.

'he **Torah scholars of Babylonia**[38] are accustomed to **stand** ıp **before one another,** וְקוֹרְעִין זֶה עַל זֶה – **and** to **rend** heir garments **for one another.**[39] וּלְעִנְיַן אֲבֵדָה בִּמְקוֹם אָבִיו – **Iowever, with regard to** retrieving another's **lost object in** place **of one's father's,** אֵינָן חוֹזְרִין – **they did not return** the ther person's object in place of their father's אֶלָּא לְרַבּוֹ מוּבְהָק - **unless** it belonged **to their primary teacher.**[40]

The Gemara presents an inquiry with respect to this last idea: קָבָעֵי מִינֵּיהּ רַב חִסְדָּא מֵרַב הוּנָ: – **Rav Chisda inquired of** his eacher, **Rav Huna:** תַּלְמִיד וְצָרִיךְ לוֹ רַבּוֹ – If one is **a student whom his teacher needs,**[41] מַאי – **what** is the law? If this tudent comes across his father's object and his teacher's object, hould he retrieve his father's object or his teacher's object? אָמַר לֵיה – Suspecting that Rav Chisda was referring to himself as 'the student whom his teacher needs," **[Rav Huna] answered him:** חִסְדָּא חִסְדָּא לֹא צְרִיכְנָא לָךְ – **"Chisda, Chisda, I do not need you;** אַתְּ צְרִיכַת לִי עַד אַרְבְּעִין שְׁנִין – indeed, **you need me or** even **forty years!"**[42] אִיקְפְּדֵי אַהֲדָדֵי וְלֹא עָיְילֵי לְגַבֵּי הֲדָדֵי – After this incident, **they bore resentment towards one another and would not go to visit each other.**

The Gemara continues:

יָתֵיב רַב חִסְדָּא אַרְבְּעִין תַּעֲנִיתָ: – **Rav Chisda fasted forty fasts,** מִשּׁוּם דְּחָלַשׁ דַּעְתֵּיהּ דְּרַב הוּנָ: – **because** he had caused **Rav Huna** o **feel dejected.** יָתֵיב רַב הוּנָא אַרְבְּעִין תַּעֲנִיתָא – Likewise, **Rav Iuna fasted forty fasts,** מִשּׁוּם דְּחַשְׁדֵיהּ לְרַב חִסְדָּא – **because he** ıad unjustly **suspected Rav Chisda** of acting insolently.

The Gemara now completes its discussion of the criteria that stablish a person as "one's teacher" (whose needs take precelence over one's father's):

אִיתְּמַ – **It was taught:** רַב יִצְחָק בַּר יוֹסֵף אָמַר ר׳ יוֹחָנָן – **Rav** 'itzchak bar Yosef said in the name of R' Yochanan: הֲלָכָה כְּרַבִּי יְהוּדָ – **The halachah follows** the opinion that **R' Yehudah** stated in the aforementioned Baraisa. רַב אַחָא בַּר רַב הוּנָא אָמַר רַב שֵׁשֶׁת – Opposing this, however, **Rav Acha bar Rav Huna said in the name of Rav Sheishess:** הֲלָכָה כְּרַבִּי יוֹסֵי – **The halachah follows** the opinion that **R' Yose** stated in this Baraisa.[43]

The Gemara questions Rav Yitzchak bar Yosef's record of R' Yochanan's view:

וּמִי אָמַר רַבִּי יוֹחָנָן הָכִי – **Did R' Yochanan** indeed **say [that the halachah follows R' Yehudah]?** וְהָאָמַר רַבִּי יוֹחָנָן הֲלָכָה כִּסְתָם מִשְׁנָה – **But** we know **R' Yochanan** to have **said** that **the halachah** always **follows** the view set forth in **an anonymous Mishnah.**[44] וּתְנַן – **And,** indeed, **we learned in** our anonymously taught **Mishnah** that one's teacher takes precedence over his father because רַבּוֹ שֶׁלִּמְּדוֹ חָכְמָה – HIS TEACHER THAT TAUGHT HIM WISDOM is the one who brings him to the World to Come. This Mishnah thus seems to rule in accordance with R' Meir, that the person who taught one "wisdom" (i.e. Talmud) is his teacher. How, then, can Rav Yitzchak bar Yosef assert that R' Yochanan ruled in favor of R' Yehudah?

The Gemara answers:

מַאי חָכְמָה – **What** does our Mishnah mean when it mentions the person who "taught him WISDOM"? רוֹב חָכְמָתוֹ – It means the person who taught him **the majority of his wisdom.** The anonymous Mishnah thus indeed reflects R' Yehudah's view.[45]

The Gemara cites a Baraisa that deals with the relative merit of studying Scripture, Mishnah, and Talmud:

תָּנוּ רַבָּנָן – **The Rabbis taught in a Baraisa:** הָעוֹסְקִין בַּמִּקְרָא – THOSE WHO ENGROSS THEMSELVES IN the study of SCRIPTURE מִדָּה – accomplish A MEASURE, וְאֵינָהּ מִדָּה – BUT IT IS NOT A large MEASURE; indeed, the study of Mishnah and Talmud is of greater value.[46] בַּמִּשְׁנָה – Those who engross themselves IN the

NOTES

8. The term תַּלְמִיד חָכָם denotes learned students of the Torah – eachers as well as their disciples (see *Maharsha*; *Rashi* to 33b ד״ה אלו ת״ח; *Rosh* to *Taanis* §22).

9. The law is that when one's רַב מוּבְהָק, *primary teacher,* walks by, one nust stand up as soon as he sees him approaching (see *Kiddushin* 33a). imilarly, when one hears of the death of his primary teacher, one must ear his garment in a way that is irreparable (see above, note 36). Here, Jlla records that the scholars in Babylonia showed these signs of eference towards their peers; they were accustomed to stand for each ther, and to rend their garments upon hearing of a colleague's death. n effect, they treated each other as one normally treats only his rimary teacher (*Rashi,* as explained by *Nimukei Yosef;* see *Rosh;* cf. *Ramban* cited by *Nimukei Yosef*). Their custom was based on the fact hat they all studied together in the study hall, asking questions from, nd answering, each other. Thus, they were all students of, and eachers to, one another (see *Rashi).*

0. The Babylonian Torah scholars thus ruled in accordance with R' 'ehudah that the only person for whom one retrieves a lost object *before* ne's father is one's primary teacher (*Rashi*). Although in other natters, these scholars accepted upon themselves the stringency of iewing their colleagues as primary teachers, they could not do this vith regard to retrieving lost objects for they would have thereby hirked their more fundamental responsibilities toward their fathers see *Nimukei Yosef*).

1. Rav Chisda speaks of a student who studied under other teachers as vell, and, therefore, his teacher "needs him" to relate what he has earned from them, since this teacher himself is not familiar with those eachings (*Rashi*). Alternatively, the reference is to a student who is specially bright. Such a student would help his teacher obtain a better ınderstanding of the subject matter through their discussions *Rabbeinu Chananel,* based on *Taanis* 7a).

2. Because Rav Huna interpreted Rav Chisda as making reference to heir own relationship, he felt that the query as posed was disrespectful to him. He therefore retorted that he did not "need" Rav Chisda, but that, in fact, Rav Chisda would need *him* – for even forty years. (The forty-year specification is in line with the idea (*Avodah Zarah* 5b) that a person does not fully comprehend his master's teachings for forty years.)

The above interpretation follows *R' Chananel. Maharsha,* however, breaks up the narrative as follows: "*. . . you need me.*" *For forty years they bore resentment towards one another.*

43. In the Baraisa, R' Yehudah had ruled that "one's teacher" is the person that taught one "the majority of his wisdom." R' Yose had stated that this term applies even to a person that made a relatively small contribution to one's knowledge, enlightening him to the correct understanding of a single Mishnah.

44. An "anonymous Mishnah" is one in which the law that is taught therein is not attributed to any specific Tanna.

45. R' Yochanan could therefore have ruled in accordance with R' Yehudah, as Rav Yitzchak bar Yosef in fact attested.

46. At the time this Baraisa was taught, the Mishnah and Talmud had not yet been recorded in writing. It was, in fact, forbidden to record these teachings in writing, for they were meant to be passed on through oral tradition only. There was thus a danger that the text of the Mishnah and its attendant teachings would be forgotten unless they were reviewed constantly; hence, the Baraisa ascribes greater priority to the study of Mishnah than to the study of the written Scripture (see *Rashi*).

[The text of the Mishnah and Gemara came to be written down in later generations, as the level of scholarship declined and it became increasingly difficult to accurately preserve the teachings (see *Rashi* and *Temurah* 14b).]

*Rabbeinu Chananel* suggests an alternative interpretation of the Baraisa: The study of Scripture is seen as less important than the study of Mishnah and Talmud, since it does not provide one with a full explanation of the mitzvos.

א) רובץ ולא רבצן רובץ ולא עומד תחת משאו ולא מפורק תחת משאו משאוי שיכול לעמוד בו ואי אמרת צער בעלי חיים דאורייתא מה לי רובץ ומה לי רבצן ומה לי עומד הא מני ר' יוסי הגלילי היא דאמר צער בעלי חיים דרבנן ה"נ מסתברא דקתני תחת משאו משאוי שיכול לעמוד בו מאן שמעת ליה דאית ליה האי סברא רבי יוסי הגלילי ש"מ ומי מצית מוקמת לה כרבי יוסי הגלילי והא קתני סיפא תחת משאו ולא מפורק מאי לא מפורק אילימא לא מפורק כלל הא כתיב ב) הקם תקים עמו אלא פשיטא לא מפורק בחנם אלא בשכר מאן שמעת ליה דאית ליה האי סברא רבנן לעולם ר' יוסי הגלילי היא ובטעינה סבר לה כרבנן ת"ר [א] א) כי תראה יכול אפי' מרחוק ת"ל כי תפגע אי כי תפגע יכול פגיעה ממש ת"ל כי תראה ואיזו היא ראייה שיש בה פגיעה א שיערו חכמים אחד משבע ומחצה במיל וזה הוא רים תנא ג ומדדה עמו עד פרסה אמר רבה בר בר חנה ד ונוטל שכר: **מתני'** ה) אבדתו ואבדת אביו אבדתו קודמת אבדתו ואבדת רבו שלו קודם ה אבדת אביו ואבדת רבו של רבו קודמת שאביו הביאו לעולם הזה ורבו שלמדו חכמה מביאו לחיי העולם הבא ו ואם אביו [ב] חכם של אביו קודמת ז היה אביו ורבו נושאין משאוי מניח את של רבו ואחר כך מניח את של אביו ח היה אביו ורבו בבית השבי פודה את רבו ואחר כך פודה את אביו ט ואם אביו חכם פודה את אביו ואח"כ פודה את רבו: **גמ'** מנא הני מילי ו) אמר רב יהודה אמר רב קרא ג) אפס כי לא יהיה בך אביון י שלך קודם לשל כל אדם ואמר רב יהודה אמר רב כ כל המקיים בעצמו כך סוף בא לידי כך: היה אביו ורבו נושאין משאוי וכו': ז) תנו רבנן רבו שאמרו רבו שלמדו חכמה ולא רבו שלמדו מקרא ומשנה דברי ר"מ ח) רבי יהודה אומר ל כל שרוב חכמתו הימנו רבי יוסי אומר אפילו לא האיר עיניו אלא במשנה אחת זה הוא רבו אמר רבא כגון ט) רב סחורה דאסברן י) זוהמא ליסטרון שמואל קרע מאניה עליה ההוא מרבנן דאסבריה כ) אחד יורד לאמת השחי ואחד פותח כיון אמר עולא מ תלמידי חכמים שבבבל עומדין זה מפני זה וקורעין זה על זה נ ולענין אבדה במקום אביו אינן חוזרין אלא לרבו מובהק קבעי מיניה רב חסדא מרב הונא תלמיד וצריך לו רבו מאי אמר ליה חסדא חסדא לא צריכנא לך את צריכת לי עד ארבעין שנין איקפדי אהדדי ולא עיילי לגבי הדדי יתיב רב חסדא ארבעין תעניתא משום דחלש דעתיה דרב הונא יתיב רב הונא ארבעין תעניתא משום דחשדיה לרב חסדא איתמר רב יצחק בר יוסף אמר ר' יוחנן הלכה כרבי יהודה רב אחא בר רב הונא אמר רב ששת הלכה כרבי יוסי ומי אמר רבי יוחנן הכי והאמר רבי יוחנן ס) הלכה כסתם משנה ותנן רבו שלמדו חכמה מאי חכמה רוב חכמתו ת"ר העוסקין במקרא מדה ואינה מדה במשנה מדה ונוטלין עליה שכר ס גמרא אין לך מדה גדולה מזו ולעולם הוי רץ למשנה יותר מן גמרא הא גופא קשיא אמרת בגמרא אין לך מדה גדולה מזו והדר אמרת ולעולם הוי רץ למשנה יותר מן הגמרא אמר רבי יוחנן

בימי

---

רש"י

רובץ. מקרה הוא לו שרובץ תחת משאו בפעם אחת: ולא רבצן. הרגיל בכך: ולא מפורק. והוא לריך טעינה ולקמן פריך הכתיב הקם תקים: יכול מרחוק. והטיל עליו שילך שם: מדדה עמו. לאחר שהטעינו שמא יחזור ויפול: גמ' מנא הני מילי. דשלו קודם: לא יהיה בך אביון. הזהר מן עניות: כל המקיים בעצמו כך. אף על פי שלא הטילו עליו הכתוב יש לאדם ליכנס לפנים משורת הדין ולא לדקדק שלי קודם אם לא בהפסד מוכיח ואם תמיד מדקדק פורק מעליו עול ג"ח ולדקה וסוף שילטרך לבריות: שלמדו חכמה. סברת טעמי המשנה ולהבין שלא יהו סותרות זו את זו וטעמי איסור והיתר והחיוב והפטור והוא נקרא גמרא: מקרא. תורה נביאים וכתובים: משנה. כמו שהן שנויות ואין טעמן מפורש בהן: כל שרוב חכמתו הימנו. אם מקרא אם משנה אם גמרא: האיר עיניו. שהודיעו טעם משנה אחת שלא יכול להבין: דאסברן זוהמא ליסטרון. בסדר טהרות (כלים פי"ג משנה ב ופכ"ה משנה ג) היא שנויה ולא הייתי יודע מה כלי הוא ולמדני שהוא כף גדולה שמסלקין בו זוהם הקדירה והקלחת לגדדין: קרע מאניה. קרע שאין מתאחה כדין תלמיד על הרב: אחד יורד לאמת השחי. משנה היא במסכת תמיד (פרק ג משנה ו) אבל הנכנסים שחרית לפתוח דלתות ההיכל מי שזכה בדישון מזבח הפנימי כו' ושני מפתחות בידו אחד יורד לאמת השחי ואחד פותח כיון אחד מן המפתחות הללו פותח פשפש הלפוני שאצל פתח ההיכל בקרן מזרחית לפונית של אולם והיכל כדתנן התם שני פשפשים היה לו לשער הגדול אחד לצפון ההיכל והאולם ואחד לדרומו ואותו שבדרום לא נכנס בו אדם מעולם כדמפרש התם ואותו פשפש שבצפון והוא לפתח שבזוית האולם שאצל חמש אמות של כותל ההיכל שבצפון פתח ההיכל ודלת סובבת בו ואותו מפתח של אותו הפתח יורד לאמת השחי. פשפשים פתחים קטנים כמין ליפות קטנות ארכו כעובי רוחב הכותל ודלת סובבת בו פוסטי"ר בלעז אחד יורד לאמת השחי הבא לפתוח בו שחרית ט) [פשפש שבזוית האולם] עומד מבחוץ בתוך האולם ומכניס ידו בחור שבכותל עד בית שחיו ופותח: ואחד פותח כיון. לאחר שנכנס בזה (א) ובא לו לתא אשר על פני אחת עשרה אמה של אולם וקלת מן ההיכל ופותח במפתח שני דלת אחד שמן התא להיכל מהר בלא טורח כשאר פתחים ונכנס להיכל לפתוח דלתות ההיכל: כיון. כמו (פסחים דף לז.) יעשנה בדפוס ויקבענה כיון מהר בלא טורח והאי שער הגדול הוא פתח ההיכל שבין אולם להיכל: עומדין זה מפני זה. כדין תלמיד לרב לפי שהיו יושבין תמיד בבית המדרש יחד ומקשין ומפרקין וכולם למדים זה מזה: לרבו מובהק. שרוב חכמתו ממנו כר"י: וצריך לו רבו. שמע שמועות שיש בידו מפי אחרים: מאי. כלומר קודם לאביו לענין אבדה: ותנן רבו שלמדו חכמה. סתמא כר' מאיר: רוב חכמתו. אם מקרא מקרא אם משנה משנה: מדה. היא קלת: ואינה מדה. שהמשנה וגמרא יפיס ממנה מפני שתלוין בגירסא ומשתכחים שבימיהם לא היה גמרא בכתב וגם לא היה ניתן לכתוב אלא לפי שנתמעטו הלבבות התחילו דורות [אחרונים] לכתבו: גמרא. כבר פירשתי למעלה שהוא לתת לב להבין סתימות טעמי המשנה מה הם וכששתים סותרות זו את זו יבין לתרץ שיהיו שתיהן קיימות או לדעת דברי התנאים החלוקים בדבר ונימא הא מני פלוני חכם הוא:

---

תוספות

מה לי רבצן. וא"ת ולישני רובץ בחנם רבצן בשכר דה"נ משני ולא מפורק בחנם אלא בשכר וי"ל דניחא ליה לשנויי דאתי כרבי יוסי הגלילי כדמוכח דאתיא כוותיה: ונוטל שכר. במה שמדדה ובפריקה מיירי שירא פן ירבץ דאי בטעינה פשיטא דהא טעינה גופה בשכר וכל שכן מה שמדדה: י) וזהו רים. אית דגרסי רוס דשבע ומחצה רוס עולה כ) אלפים דהוי שיעור מיל כדמוכח בפרק שני שעירי (יומא דף סז.) גבי סוכות דשעיר המשתלח: אבדתו קודמת. וא"ת אבדתו ואבדת רבו וכבוד אביו איזהו קודם אי אבדתו הלא כבוד אביו עדיף למאן דאמר בפ"ק דקדושין (דף לב. ושם) משל בן ואם כבוד אביו הלא אבדת רבו קודמת כדאמר לעיל ל) אני ה' ויש לומר אבדתו קודמת דהיכא דאביו נהנה מגוף הבהמה חייב לכבדו כגון שחוט לי בהמתך אבל הניחה ליאבד ותביא לי לאכול שגם לאב קשה האבדה אלא שרוצה לאכול מ): ומקרעין זה על זה. אף על פי שאינו יודע יותר לפי שלומדין זה מזה ואם תאמר דאמרינן בפרק האורג (שבת דף קה: ושם) חייב לקרוע על אדם כשר אפילו לא היה בשעת יציאת נשמה [ג] ויש לומר דהכא מיירי בקרע שאינו מתאחה כדין תלמיד על רבו וכן פירש רש"י:

אחיכם

---

עין משפט
נר מצוה

קפח א מיי' פי"ג מהל' רולח ה"ו סמג עשין פא טוש"ע חו"מ סי' רעב סעיף ה:
קפט ב מיי' שם הל' ה טוש"ע שם סעיף ד:
קצ ג מיי' שם הל' ז טוש"ע שם סעיף ו:
קצא ד מיי' פי"ב מהל' אבידה הלכה ח סמג עשין עד טוש"ע חו"מ סי' רסד ס"א:
קצב ה ו מיי' שם ה"ב ופ"ה מהלכות ת"ת הלכה א סמג שם טור ש"ע שם ס"ב וטור ש"ע י"ד סי' רמב סל"ד:
קצג ז מיי' פ"ה מהל' ת"ת ה"א סמג שם טוש"ע י"ד סי' רמב סל"ד:
קצד ח ט מיי' שם ופ"ח מהל' מתנות עניים הל' יח סמג שם וסי' קסב טוש"ע שם וסי' רנב ס"ט:
קצה י מיי' פי"ב מהל' אבידה הלכה א סמג עשין עד טוש"ע ח"מ סי' רסד ס"א וטוש"ע יו"ד סי' רמב סל"ה:
קצו כ טוש"ע ח"מ שם:
קצז ל מיי' פי"ב מהל' אבדה הל' ב ופ"ה מהל' ת"ת הל' ט סמג עשין שם טוש"ע ח"מ סי' רסד ס"ב וטוש"ע י"ד סי' רמב סעיף ל:
קצח מ מיי' פ"ה מהל' ת"ת ופ"ט מהל' אבל הי"א סמג עשין יב עד פב טוש"ע יו"ד סי' רמב ס"ל וסי' שמ ס"ז וסעיף ח:
קצט נ מיי' פי"ב מהל' אבידה הל' ב סמג עשין עד טוש"ע ח"מ סי' רסד סעיף ב:
ר ס מיי' פ"א מהל' ת"ת הלכה יא סמג עשין יב טוש"ע י"ד סי' רמו ס"ד:

מסורת הש"ס

א) סנהדרין סד:, ב) לעיל לב:, ג) סנהדרין סד:, ע"ש, ד) [מסכת כלה, תוספתא הוריות פרק ב], ה) [עיין תוספות מועד קטן כה: ד"ה ועל רבו], ו) [עיין תוספות סנהדרין מט: ד"ה אמר, ותוספות יבמות ... ד"ה רבא, ועבודה זרה ... ד"ה אמר], ז) [כלים פרק יג משנה ב, ופרק כה משנה ג], ח) [תמיד ל:], ט) שבת מו. וש"נ, י) מהרש"ל, כ) [צ"ל קודם ד"ה ונוטל], ל) הוא אלפים ... מסה, ועיין בערוך ערך רוס, ל) דף לב., מ) [וע"ש בתוס' ד"ה ר"י, ... בתוס' זבחים ל: ד"ה תטאת].

הגהות הב"ח

(א) רש"י ד"ה ואחד פותח כיון לאחר שנכנס בזה. נ"ב אבל הר' עובדיה פי' שאותן שני מפתחות היו שניהם בפשפש הלפוני וע"ש:

הגהות הגר"א

[א] גמרא ת"ר לא תראה כו' ממש ת"ל לא תראה. כל"ל (והוא בדברים כב וכן הוא בספרי שם וא"ש דב' המקראות מיירי גבי אבידה ומוכיחין זה לזה ועיין ריטב"א שיטה מקובצת והגר"א ח"מ סי' רע"ב ס"ק ב'): [ב] במשנה חכם. נ"ב ... הרי"ף וש"פ כאן שקול נגד רבו: [ג] תוס' ד"ה ומקרעין. וי"ל ... נ"ב ורמב"ם חולק וכו' ... ברבו מובהק (ועמ"ש ... ביו"ד סי' רמב ס"ק סט):

תורה אור השלם

א) כִּי תִרְאֶה חֲמוֹר שֹׂנַאֲךָ רֹבֵץ תַּחַת מַשָּׂאוֹ וְחָדַלְתָּ מֵעֲזֹב לוֹ עָזֹב תַּעֲזֹב עִמּוֹ: [שמות כג, ה]
ב) לֹא תִרְאֶה אֶת חֲמוֹר אָחִיךָ אוֹ שׁוֹרוֹ נֹפְלִים בַּדֶּרֶךְ וְהִתְעַלַּמְתָּ מֵהֶם הָקֵם תָּקִים עִמּוֹ: [דברים כב, ד]
ג) אֶפֶס כִּי לֹא יִהְיֶה בְּךָ אֶבְיוֹן כִּי בָרֵךְ יְבָרֶכְךָ יְיָ בָּאָרֶץ אֲשֶׁר יְיָ אֱלֹהֶיךָ נֹתֵן לְךָ נַחֲלָה לְרִשְׁתָּהּ: [דברים טו, ד]

לעזי רש"י

פושטי"ר. פירוש פשפש, שער קטן בתוך שער גדול (ערוך ערך פשפש ג').

ליקוטי רש"י

אפס וכו' בך אביון. הזהר בעלמך שלא תבוא לידי עניות [סנהדרין סד:]. זוהמא ליסטרון. אותו כף שבוחשין את הקדרה קרי להו הכי על שם שמעבירין הזוהמא לגדדין על שני לדיו תרגום על פרין סטרוסי [הוריות יג:]. מאניה. בגדיו [יומא נב.].

רבינו חננאל

ת"ר כי תראה יכול מרחוק ת"ל כי תפגע יכול פגיעה ממש פניא בפנים ת"ל כי תראה (הם) [הא] כיצד ראיה שיש בה פגיעה שיערו חכמים אחד משבעה ומחצה במיל וזהו ריס. ומדדה עמו עד פרסה ונוטל שכרו. קיימא לן פריקה בחנם לדברי הכל וטעינה בשכר כרבנן: **מתני' אבדתו ואבדת אביו וכו' אבדת רבו שלו קודמת.** פי' יניח של אביו ויניח של רבו וישיב את שלו שנאמר אפס כי לא יהיה בך אביון. והמדקדק שלא יבא לידי עניות סוף בא לידי כך: ת"ר רבו שאמרו רבו שלמדו חכמה ולא רבו שלמדו מקרא ומשנה דברי ר"מ ר' יהודה אומר כל שרוב חכמתו ממנו ור' יוסי [אמר] אפי' לא האיר עיניו אלא במשנה אחת זהו רבו. אע"ג דאמר ר' יוחנן הלכה כר' יהודה רב ששת דהוא בתרא אמר הלכה כר' יוסי. ועוד הנה שמואל עשה כמותו וקרע על ההוא מרבנן דאסבריה הא דתנן במסכת תמיד פ' אמר להן הממונה ושני מפתחות אחד יורד אמת השחי ואחד פותח כיון פירש לו מפתח אחד היה מכניס ידו ופותח בו מיד והאחר לא יכול לפתוח בו עד שהיה מוריד ידו עד שחיו וכך היה פותח וכן הוא מפורש בתלמוד ארץ ישראל א) הנה שמואל לא למד ממנו אלא פירוש משנה זו בלבד וכיון ששמע שמת קרע עליו כאשר קורע התלמיד על רבו. וכן פירש רבא כי רבו כגון רב סחורה דאסברן זומליסטרון ב) פי' התרוד שמהפך בה בשר בתוך הצלחת נקראת זומליסטרון: ובתלמוד ארץ ישראל ג) רב כר"מ חד בר נש פתח פומיה דרב ושמע דדמך ובזע עלוהו. ומתניתין נמי כר' יוסי דייקא ד) והא דאוקימנא כר' יהודה שניא הוא: ת"ר העוסק במקרא פי' במקרא בלבד ואין מתעסק גם בתלמוד מדה שאינה מדה היא שהרי לא נתעסק גם בפתרון המצות. במשנה מדה שנוטלין עליה שכר פי' המתעסק בפתרון המשנה שיש בה הרבה מן המצות שהן קבלה והן תלויות במשניות החיצונות וכשהוא מתעסק במשנה צריך לעיין באותן הברייתות כולן ופתרוני החכמים יש לו בזה שכר מצוה. אבל המתעסק בתלמוד ומורה ומבאר המצות כתקנן ומגיד הלכה למעשה אין לך מדה גדולה מזו כי בתלמוד פתרון התורה והמשנה והמצוה שהן בקבלה הלכה למשה מסיני. ולעולם הוי רץ למשנה יותר מן התלמוד פי' הוי רץ למשנה שהיא מדה ונוטלין עליה שכר והשוגג אינו נדון בה כמזיד אבל המתעסק בתלמוד אפי' השגגות חשובות עליו כזדונות שהיה לו לדקדק על עצמו שלא יכשל אפי' בשגגה לפי שמדקדקין עליו אפי' כחוט השערה שנאמר וסביביו נשערה מאד מלמד שהקב"ה מדקדק עם סביביו אפי' כחוט השערה ומי יכול להשמר כל זה וכבר פירשנוהו הוי זהיר בתלמוד ששגגת התלמוד עולה זדון הרי זהיר אתה המתעסק בתלמוד ששגגתו עולה לך זדון וכו' יהודה בר' אלעי דדרש הגד לעמי פשעם אלו תלמידי חכמים ששגגות נעשות להם כזדונות וכו'. אמר עולא תלמידי חכמים

חשק שלמה על ר"ח א) כן מבואר בירושלמי בסוף פירקין. ב) כ"ה גירסת רבינו זומליסטרון בתיבה אחת וכ"ה גי' הערוך בערך זמלסטר וע"ש עוד גירסא אחרת. ג) נראה דלאו שייך כאן רק מקומו לעיל אלא דברי ר"מ. ד) וכן הובא בשמ"ק ובשו"ת מהרי"ק בשורש קס"ט דרבינו פסק כר' יוסי.

**Gemara** The Gemara seeks a source for the Mishnah's first ruling that retrieving one's own lost object takes precedence over retrieving an object belonging to one's father or one's teacher:

מְנָא הָנֵי מִילֵּי – **From where are these words derived?** אָמַר רַב יְהוּדָה אָמַר רַב – **Rav Yehudah said in the name of Rav:** קְרָא – **The verse states:**[26] ,,אֶפֶס כִּי לֹא יִהְיֶה־בְּךָ אֶבְיוֹן" – ***But among you there will be no destitute.*** This teaches that שֶׁלְּךָ קוֹדֶם לְשֶׁל כָּל אָדָם – **your** financial concerns **take precedence to those of everyone** else.[27] וְאָמַר רַב יְהוּדָה אָמַר רַב – **But Rav Yehudah said** also **in the name of Rav:** Although one has the right to give greater weight to his own financial concerns than to others, כָּל הַמְקַיֵּים בְּעַצְמוֹ כָּךְ – **whoever establishes such** a way of life **for himself,** סוֹף בָּא לִידֵי כָּךְ – will, **in the end, come to** endure the very **[poverty]** he seeks to avoid.[28]

An abbreviated quote from the Mishnah introduces the next discussion:

הָיָה אָבִיו וְרַבּוֹ נוֹשְׂאִין מַשּׂאוֹי וכו' – If [ONE'S] FATHER AND HIS TEACHER are both CARRYING BURDENS etc. [. . . If one's father and his teacher are both being held captive, he should first ransom his teacher, and only then should he ransom his father.]

The Gemara cites a Baraisa that defines who is considered his teacher such that ransoming him takes precedence over ransoming his father:[29]

תָּנוּ רַבָּנָן – **The Rabbis taught in a Baraisa:** רַבּוֹ שֶׁאָמְרוּ – THE TEACHER THAT [THE RABBIS] SPOKE OF רַבּוֹ שֶׁלִּמְּדוֹ חָכְמָה – is THE TEACHER THAT TAUGHT HIM WISDOM, i.e. Talmud,[30] וְלֹא רַבּוֹ שֶׁלִּמְּדוֹ מִקְרָא וּמִשְׁנָה – NOT THE TEACHER THAT TAUGHT HIM SCRIPTURE OR the plain text of MISHNAH.[31] דִּבְרֵי רַבִּי מֵאִיר – These are THE WORDS OF R' MEIR. רַבִּי יְהוּדָה אוֹמֵר – R' YEHUDAH SAYS: כָּל שֶׁרוֹב חָכְמָתוֹ הֵימֶנּוּ – The person [FROM] WHOM ONE LEARNED THE MAJORITY OF HIS WISDOM is considered "his teacher."[32] רַבִּי יוֹסֵי אוֹמֵר – R' YOSE SAYS: אֲפִילּוּ לֹא הֵאִיר עֵינָיו אֶלָּא בְּמִשְׁנָה אַחַת – EVEN if ONE CLARIFIED FOR [A PERSON] the teaching OF ONLY ONE MISHNAH that this person did not previously understand,[33] זֶה הוּא רַבּוֹ – HE IS considered HIS TEACHER with respect to the law of precedence.

The Gemara records a statement made by Rava in connection with R' Yose's ruling:

אָמַר רָבָא – **Rava said:** כְּגוֹן רַב סְחוֹרָה דְּאַסְבְּרָן זוּהֲמָא לִיסְטְרוֹן – In our case, **for example,** such a teacher would be **Rav Sechorah, who explained to us** the Mishnah that deals with **a froth spoon.**[34]

The Gemara cites an incident in illustration of this concept that one who explains to a person even a single Mishnah is considered his teacher:[35]

שְׁמוּאֵל קָרַע מָאנֵיהּ – **Shmuel rent his garment** in mourning[36] עֲלֵיהּ הַהוּא מֵרַבָּנָן דְּאַסְבְּרֵיהּ – **upon** hearing of the death of **a certain Rabbi who explained to him** the Mishnah that reads: אֶחָד יוֹרֵד לְאַמַּת הַשֶּׁחִי – ONE IS THRUST TO THE ARMPIT, וְאֶחָד פּוֹתֵחַ כִּיוָּן – AND ONE OPENS QUICKLY.[37]

The Gemara puts forth a statement by Ulla relevant to the above discussion:

אָמַר עוּלָּא – **Ulla said:** תַּלְמִידֵי חֲכָמִים שֶׁבְּבָבֶל עוֹמְדִין זֶה מִפְּנֵי זֶה –

NOTES

father takes precedence (so long as he is a scholar) regardless of whether he is of equal stature as one's teacher. (For an explanation of *Rosh's* position see *Pilpula Charifta* אות ב׳)

The Mishnah has in effect taught the same ruling (that one's teacher's needs take precedence over one's father's needs unless the father is a scholar) three times: with respect to lost objects, setting down a load, and ransoming from captivity. *Ben Yehoyada* provides an explanation for the Mishnah's need to teach all three cases (cf. *Toras Chaim, Pilpula Charifta* אות ב׳).

26. *Deuteronomy* 15:4.

27. The simple meaning of the verse is to promise that there will be no destitute among you if you observe meticulously the Sabbatical law of relinquishing debts. If so, however, the word אֶפֶס, *But,* would be redundant. Rav therefore expounds the verse as an injunction, and the word אֶפֶס as *naught*: "Make naught (i.e. take measures to insure that) there shall not be *within you* (personally) a destitute person" (*Sanhedrin* 64b as explained by *Rashi* there ד״ה התם מאפס).

28. Rav cautions that although one is permitted by law to be more concerned with his own needs than those of others, one ought nevertheless endeavor to go beyond the letter of the law in this matter; that is, he should seek to prevent monetary loss from coming to others, even if he must forfeit a small financial gain in order to do this. Indeed, if one constantly analyzes his situation to see how he might incur a loss, and he will never perform kind deeds, he will in effect see himself as exempt from the obligation to act charitably. As a punishment for this, Rav states, he will in the end become impoverished, and will be forced to rely on the generosity of others for their support (*Rashi;* see also *Maharsha*).

29. See *Tosefta* to *Horayos* 2:5. The same definition would apply to the other cases in our Mishnah: those of returning his lost object and putting down his burden.

30. As it is used here, the term "wisdom" denotes the principles that underly the precepts of Mishnah and halachah, and the teachings by which apparent contradictions between Mishnahs can be resolved. In their present written form, these teachings and precepts have come to be known as "Gemara" or "Talmud" (*Rashi*).

31. The term "Scripture" refers to Pentateuch, the Prophets, and Writings. The study of the Mishnahs as they are written, without resolving the various difficulties they present, is referred to as *Mishnah* (*Rashi*).

32. Such a teacher is referred to by the Gemara below as רַבּוֹ מוּבְהָק, *his primary teacher.* R' Yehudah differs from R' Meir in that he does not require the teacher to have taught Gemara specifically; rather, he argues that the law turns on whether the teacher has taught this person *most of his* present knowledge, be it in the area of Gemara, Mishnah, or Scripture (*Rashi*).

33. Literally: "Even one who enlightened his eyes in only one Mishnah." That is, he did nothing but explain to the person the basis for a single Mishnah's ruling (*Rashi*).

34. See *Keilim* 13:2, 25:3. Rava did not know what type of utensil was denoted by the Mishnah's term זוּהֲמָא לִיסְטְרוֹן, and Rav Sechorah explained to him that the term refers to a utensil that serves as a ladle to remove the froth from a pot (*Rashi*). [Alternatively, the term refers to a utensil that has a ladle on one end and a fork on the other (see the commentaries to *Keilim* 13:2).]

35. This follows *Rabbeinu Chananel* who states that Shmuel acted in accordance with R' Yose's ruling. Cf. *Kesef Mishnah* to *Hil. Talmud Torah* 5:9; see also *Ritva.*

36. When a person hears that his teacher has died, he is required to tear his garment in a way that it can never be fully repaired. In our case, Shmuel tore his clothing in such a manner upon hearing of the death of a Rabbi who explained to him only one Mishnah (*Rashi*).

37. This Mishnah appears in tractate *Tamid* (3:6). It describes the opening of two doors in the Temple by means of keys, teaching that "one [key] is thrust to the armpit, and one [key] opens quickly." The door that the first key opened was located in the north-west corner of the *Ulam* (the hall leading to the Temple Sanctuary), five *amos* to the right of the Sanctuary's gate. Now the lock to this door was placed on the inner part of the door, and it therefore could not be opened directly from the *Ulam* (see *Rav* ad loc.). Instead, the person with the key would thrust his arm up to his armpit through a hole in the adjacent wall, allowing him to reach the lock from the inside and open it. This is what the Mishnah means by "one [key] is thrust to the armpits."

After opening this door, the bearer of the keys would walk through an arched opening into a compartment known as a *Ta,* a small enclosure flanking the Sanctuary's north side. In the wall separating the *Ta* from the Sanctuary, he would see another door – yet the lock to this door was easily accessible, and to open it, he needed simply to insert the key directly. This is what the Mishnah means by "and one [key] opens quickly" (see *Rashi*).

א) רובץ ולא רבצן רובץ ולא עומד תחת משאו ולא מפורק תחת משאו משאוי שיכול לעמוד בו ואי אמרת צער בעלי חיים דאורייתא מה לי רובץ ומה לי רבצן ומה לי עומד הא מני ר' יוסי הגלילי היא דאמר צער בעלי חיים דרבנן ה"נ מסתברא דקתני תחת משאו משאוי שיכול לעמוד בו מאן שמעת ליה דאית ליה האי סברא רבי יוסי הגלילי ש"מ ומי מצית מוקמת לה כרבי יוסי הגלילי והא קתני סיפא תחת משאו ולא מפורק מאי לא מפורק אילימא לא מפורק כלל הא כתיב ב) הקם תקים עמו אלא פשיטא לא מפורק בחנם אלא בשכר מאן שמעת ליה דאית ליה האי סברא רבנן לעולם ר' יוסי הגלילי היא ובטעינה סבר לה כרבנן ת"ר [א]א) כי תראה יכול אפי' מרחוק ת"ל כי תפגע אי כי תפגע יכול פגיעה ממש ת"ל כי תראה ואיזו היא ראייה שיש בה פגיעה א שיערו חכמים אחד משבע ומחצה במיל וזה הוא ריס תנא ב ומדדה עמו עד פרסה אמר רבה בר בר חנה ג ונוטל שכר: מתני' א) ד אבדתו ואבדת אביו אבדתו קודמת אבדתו ואבדת רבו שלו קודם ה אבדת אביו ואבדת רבו של רבו קודמת שאביו הביאו לעולם הזה ורבו שלמדו חכמה מביאו לחיי העולם הבא ו ואם אביו [ב]חכם של אביו קודמת ז היה אביו ורבו נושאין משאוי מניח את של רבו ואחר כך מניח את של אביו ח היה אביו ורבו בבית השבי פודה את רבו ואחר כך פודה את אביו ט ואם אביו חכם פודה את אביו ואח"כ פודה את רבו: גמ' מנא הני מילי ב) אמר רב יהודה אמר רב אמר קרא ג) אפס כי לא יהיה בך אביון י שלך קודם לשל כל אדם ואמר רב יהודה אמר רב כ כל המקיים בעצמו כך סוף בא לידי כך: היה אביו ורבו נושאין משאוי וכו': ג) תנו רבנן רבו שאמרו רבו שלמדו חכמה ולא רבו שלמדו מקרא ומשנה דברי ר"מ ד) רבי יהודה אומר ל כל שרוב חכמתו הימנו רבי יוסי אומר אפילו לא האיר עיניו אלא במשנה אחת זה הוא רבו אמר רבא כגון ה) רב סחורה דאסברן ו) זוהמא ליסטרון שמואל קרע מאניה עליה ההוא מרבנן דאסבריה ז) אחד יורד לאמת השחי ואחד פותח כיון אמר עולא מ תלמידי חכמים שבבבל עומדין זה מפני זה וקורעין זה על זה נ ולענין אבדה במקום אביו אינן חוזרין אלא לרבו מובהק קבעי מיניה רב חסדא מרב הונא תלמיד וצריך לו רבו מאי אמר ליה חסדא חסדא לא צריכנא לך את צריכת לי עד ארבעין שנין איקפדי אהדדי ולא עיילי לגבי הדדי יתיב רב חסדא ארבעין תעניתא משום דחלש דעתיה דרב הונא יתיב רב הונא ארבעין תעניתא משום דחשדיה לרב חסדא איתמר רב יצחק בר יוסף אמר ר' יוחנן הלכה כרבי יהודה רב אחא בר רב הונא אמר רב ששת הלכה כרבי יוסי ומי אמר רבי יוחנן הכי והאמר רבי יוחנן ח) הלכה כסתם משנה ותנן רבו שלמדו חכמה מאי חכמה רוב חכמתו ת"ר העוסקין במקרא מדה ואינה מדה במשנה מדה ונוטלין עליה שכר ס גמרא אין לך מדה גדולה מזו ולעולם הוי רץ למשנה יותר מן גמרא הא גופא קשיא אמרת בגמרא אין לך מדה גדולה מזו והדר אמרת ולעולם הוי רץ למשנה יותר מן הגמרא אמר רבי יוחנן

רובץ. מקרה הוא לו שרובץ תחת משאו בפעם הזאת: ולא רבצן. הרגיל בכך: ולא מפורק. והוא לריך טעינה ולקמן פריך הכתיב הקם תקים: יכול מרחוק. והטיל עליו שילך שם: מדדה עמו. לאחר שהטעינו שמא יחזור ויפול: גמ' מנא הני מילי. דשלו קודם: לא יהיה בך אביון. הזהר מן עניות: כל המקיים בעצמו כך. אף על פי שלא הטילו עליו הכתוב יש לאדם ליכנס לפנים משורת הדין ולא לדקדק שלי קודם אם לא בהפסד מוכיח ואם תמיד מדקדק פורק מעליו עול ג"ח ולדקה וסוף שילטרך לבריות: שלמדו חכמה. סברת טעמי המשנה ולהבין שלא יהו סותרות זו את זו וטעמי איסור והיתר והחיוב והפטור והוא נקרא גמרא: מקרא. תורה נביאים וכתובים: משנה. כמו שהן שנויות ואין טעמן מפורש בהן: כל שרוב חכמתו הימנו. אם מקרא אם משנה אם גמרא: האיר עיניו. שהודיעו טעם משנה אחת שלא יכול להבין: דאסברן זוהמא ליסטרון. בסדר טהרות (כלים פי"ג משנה ב ופכ"ה משנה ג) היא שנויה ולא הייתי יודע מה כלי הוא ולמדני שהוא כף גדולה שמסלקין בו זוהם הקדירה והקלחת לצדדין: קרע מאניה. קרע שאין מתאחה כדין תלמיד על הרב: אחד יורד לאמת השחי. משנה היא במסכת תמיד (פרק ג משנה ו) אלא הנכנסים שחרית לפתוח דלתות ההיכל מי שזכה בדישון מזבח הפנימי כו' ושני מפתחות בידו אחד יורד לאמת השחי ואחד פותח כיון אחד מן המפתחות הללו פותח פשפש הצפוני שאצל פתח ההיכל בקרן מזרחית צפונית של אולם והיכל כדתנן התם שני פשפשים היה לו לשער הגדול אחד לצפון ההיכל והאולם ואחד לדרומו ואותו שבדרום לא נכנס בו אדם מעולם כדמפרש התם ואותו פשפש שבצפון והוא לפתח שבזוית האולם שאצל חמש אמות של כותל ההיכל שבצפון פתח ההיכל ודלת סובבת בו ואותו מפתח של אותו הפתח יורד לאמת השחי. פשפשים פתחים קטנים כמין ליפות קטנות ארכו כעובי רוחב הכותל ודלת סובבת בו פושטי"ר בלעז אחד יורד לאמת השחי הבא לפתוח בו שחרית [פשפש שבזוית האולם] עומד מבחוץ בתוך האולם ומכניס ידו בחור שבכותל עד בית שחיו ופותח: ואחד פותח כיון. לאחר שנכנס בזה (א) ובא לו לתא אשר על פני אמת עשרה אמה של אולם וקלת מן ההיכל ופותח במפתח שני דלת אחד שמן התא להיכל מהר בלא טורח כשאר פתחים ונכנס להיכל לפתוח דלתות ההיכל: כיון. כמו (פסחים דף לז.) יעשנה כדפוס ויקבענה כיון מהר בלא טורח והאי שער הגדול הוא פתח ההיכל שבין אולם להיכל: עומדין זה מפני זה. כדין תלמיד לרב לפי שהיו יושבין תמיד בבית המדרש יחד ומקשין ומפרקין וכולם למדים זה מזה: לרבו מובהק. שרוב חכמתו ממנו כר"י: וצריך לו רבו. ששמע שמועות שיש בידו מפי אחרים: מאי. כלומר קודם לאביו לענין אבדה: ותנן רבו שלמדו חכמה. סתמא כר' מאיר: רוב חכמתו. אם מקרא מקרא אם משנה משנה: מדה. היא קלת: ואינה מדה. שהמשנה וגמרא יפים ממנה מפני שתלוין בגירסא ומשתכחים שבימיהם לא היה גמרא בכתב וגם לא היה ניתן לכתוב אלא לפי שנתמעטו הלבבות התחילו דורות [אחרונים] לכתבו: גמרא. כבר פירשתי למעלה שהוא לתת לב להבין סתימות טעמי המשנה מה הם וכששתים סותרות זו את זו יבין לתרץ שיהיו שתיהן קיימות או לדעת דברי התנאים החלוקים בדבר וימצא הא מני פלוני תנא הוא:

בימי

מה לי רבצן. וא"ת וליתני רובץ בחנם רבצן בשכר דה"נ משני ולא מפורק בחנם אלא בשכר וי"ל דניחא ליה לשנויי דאתי כרבי יוסי הגלילי כדמוכח דאתיא כוותיה: ונוטל שכר. במה שמדדה ובפריקה מיירי שירא פן ירבץ דאי בטעינה פשיטא דהא טעינה גופה בשכר וכל שכן מה שמדדה: י) וזהו ריס. אית דגרסי רוס דשבע ומחצה רוס עולה כ) אלפים דהוי שיעור מיל כדמוכח בפרק שני שעירי (יומא דף סז.) גבי סוכות דשעיר המשתלח: אבדתו קודמת. וא"ת אבדתו ואבדת רבו וכבוד אביו איזהו קודם אי אבדתו הלא כבוד אביו עדיף למאן דאמר בפ"ק דקדושין (דף לב. ושם) משל בן ואם כבוד אביו הלא אבדת רבו קודמת כדאמר לעיל ל) אני ה' ויש לומר אבדתו קודמת דהיכא דאביו נהנה מגוף הבהמה חייב לכבדו כגון שחוט לי בהמתך אבל הניחה ליאבד ותביא לי לאכול שגם לאב קשה האבדה אלא שרוצה לאכול מ): ומקרעין זה על זה. אף על פי שאינו יודע יותר לפי שלומדין זה מזה ואם תאמר דאמרינן בפרק האורג (שבת דף קה: ושם) חייב לקרוע על אדם כשר אפילו לא היה בשעת יציאת נשמה [ג] ויש לומר דהכא מיירי בקרע שאינו מתאחה כדין תלמיד על רבו וכן פירש רש"י:

אחיכס

## עין משפט נר מצוה

קפח א מיי' פי"ג מהל' רולח ה"ו סמג עשין פא טוש"ע חו"מ סי' רעב סעיף ה:
קפט ב מיי' שם הל' ה טוש"ע שם סעיף ד:
קצ ג מיי' שם הל' ז טוש"ע שם סעיף ו:
קצא ד מיי' פי"ב מהל' אבידה הלכה ח סמג עשין עד טוש"ע חו"מ סי' רסד ס"א:
קצב ה ו מיי' שם ה"ב ופ"ה מהלכות ת"ת הלכה א סמג שם טור ש"ע שם ס"ב וטור ש"ע י"ד סי' רמב סל"ד:
קצג ז מיי' פ"ה מהל' ת"ת ה"א סמג שם טוש"ע י"ד סי' רמב סל"ד:
קצד ח ט מיי' שם ופ"ח מהל' מתנות עניים הל' יח סמג שם וסי' קסב טוש"ע שם וסי' רנב ס"ט:
קצה י מיי' פי"ב מהל' אבידה הלכה א סמג עשין עד טוש"ע ח"מ סי' רסד ס"א וטוש"ע יו"ד סי' רמב סל"ה:
קצו כ טוש"ע ח"מ שם:
קצז ל מיי' פי"ב מהל' אבדה הל' ב ופ"ה מהל' ת"ת הל' ט סמג עשין שם טוש"ע ח"מ סי' רסד ס"ב וטוש"ע י"ד סי' רמב סעיף ל:
קצח מ מיי' פ"ה מהל' ת"ת ופ"ט מהל' אבל הי"א סמג עשין יב עד פב טוש"ע יו"ד סי' רמב ס"ל וסי' שמ ס"ז וסעיף ח:
קצט נ מיי' פי"ב מהל' אבידה הל' ג סמג עשין עד טוש"ע ח"מ סי' רסד סעיף ג:
ר ס מיי' פ"א מהל' ת"ת הלכה יא סמג עשין יב טוש"ע י"ד סי' רמו ס"ד:

## רבינו חננאל

ת"ר כי תראה יכול מרחוק ת"ל כי תפגע יכול פגיעה ממש פניא בפנים ת"ל כי תראה (הם) [הא] כיצד ראיה שיש בה פגיעה שיערו חכמים אחד משבעה ומחצה במיל וזהו ריס. ומדדה עמו עד פרסה ונוטל שכרו. קיימא לן פריקה בחנם לדברי הכל וטעינה בשכר כרבנן: מתני' אבדתו ואבדת אביו וכו' אבדת רבו שלו קודמת. פי' יניח של אביו ויניח של רבו וישיב את שלו שנאמר אפס כי לא יהיה בך אביון. והמדקדק שלא יבא לידי עניות סוף בא לידי כך: ת"ר רבו שאמרו רבו שלמדו חכמה ולא רבו שלמדו מקרא ומשנה דברי ר"מ ר' יהודה אומר כל שרוב חכמתו ממנו ור' יוסי [אמר] אפי' לא האיר עיניו אלא במשנה אחת זהו רבו. אע"ג דאמר ר' יוחנן הלכה כר' יהודה רב ששת דהוא בתרא אמר הלכה כר' יוסי. ועוד הנה שמואל עשה כמותו וקרע על ההוא מרבנן דאסבריה הא דתנן במסכת תמיד פ' אמר להן הממונה ושני מפתחות אחד יורד אמת השחי ואחד פותח כיון פירש לו מפתח אחד היה מכניס ידו ופותח בו מיד והאחר לא יכול לפתוח בו עד שהיה מוריד ידו עד שחיו וכך היה פותח וכן הוא מפורש בתלמוד ארץ ישראל א) הנה שמואל לא למד ממנו אלא פירוש משנה זו בלבד וכיון ששמע שמת קרע עליו כאשר קורע התלמיד על רבו. וכן פירש רבא כי רבו כגון רב סחורה דאסברן זומליסטרון ב) פי' התרוד שמהפך בה בשר בתוך הצלחת נקראת זומליסטרון: ובתלמוד ארץ ישראל ג) רב כר"מ חד בר נש פתח פומיה דרב ושמע דדמך ובזע עלוהו. ומתניתין נמי כר' יוסי דייקא ד) והא דאוקימנא כר' יהודה שינויא הוא: ת"ר העוסק במקרא פי' במקרא בלבד ואין מתעסק גם בתלמוד מדה שאינה מדה היא שהרי לא נתעסק גם בפתרון המצות. במשנה מדה שנוטלין עליה שכר פי' המתעסק בפתרון המשנה שיש בה הרבה מן המצות שהן קבלה והן תלויות במשניות החיצונות וכשהוא מתעסק במשנה צריך לעיין באותן הברייתות כולן ופתרוני החכמים יש לו בזה שכר מצוה. אבל המתעסק בתלמוד ומורה ומבאר המצות כתקנן ומגיד הלכה למעשה אין לך מדה גדולה מזו כי בתלמוד פתרון התורה והמשנה והמצוה שהן בקבלה הלכה למשה מסיני. ולעולם הוי רץ למשנה יותר מן התלמוד פי' הוי רץ למשנה שהיא מדה ונוטלין עליה שכר והשוגג אינו נדון בה כמזיד אבל המתעסק בתלמוד אפי' השגגות חשובות עליו כזדונות שהיה לו לדקדק על עצמו שלא יכשל אפי' בשגגה לפי שמדקדקין עליו אפי' כחוט השערה שנאמר וסביביו נשערה מאד מלמד שהקב"ה מדקדק עם סביביו אפי' כחוט השערה ומי יכול להשמר כל זה וכבר פירשנוהו הוי זהיר בתלמוד ששגגת התלמוד עולה זדון הוי זהיר אתה המתעסק בתלמוד ששגגתו עולה לך זדון וכר' יהודה בר' אלעי דדרש הגד לעמי פשעם אלו תלמידי חכמים ששגגות נעשות להם כזדונות וכו'. אמר עולא תלמידי חכמים

## מסורת הש"ס

א) סנהדרין סד:, ב) לעיל לב., סנהדרין סד., ע"ש, ג) [מסכת כלה, תוספתא הוריות פרק ב], ד) [עיין תוספות מועד קטן כה: ד"ה ועל רבו], ה) [עיין תוספות סנהדרין מט: ד"ה אמר, ותוספות יבמות ק. ד"ה רבא, ועבודה זרה ט. ד"ה אמר], ו) [כלים פרק יג משנה ב, ופרק כה משנה ג], ז) [תמיד ל:], ח) שבת מו. וש"נ, ט) מהרש"ל, י) [נ"ל קודם רי"ס וטועל], כ) הוא אלפים וכר חמשה, ועיין בערוך ערך רום, ל) דף לב., מ) [וע"ש בתוס' ד"ה ר"י, ובתוס' זבחים ל: ד"ה תטמא].

## הגהות הב"ח

(א) רש"י ד"ה ואחד פותח כיון לאחר שנכנס בזה. נ"ב אבל הר' עובדיה פי' שאותן שני מפתחות היו שניהם בפשפש הצפוני וע"ש:

## הגהות הגר"א

[א] גמרא ת"ר לא תראה כו' ממש ת"ל לא תראה. כל"ל (והוא בדברים כב וכן הוא בספרי שם וא"ש דב' המקראות כמיני גבי אבידה ומוכיחין זה לזה ועיין ריטב"א ושיטה מקובצת והבהגר"א ח"מ סי' רע"ב ס"ק ג'): [ב] במשנה חכם. נ"ב גירס' הרי"ף וש"פ כאן שקול נגד רבו: [ג] תוס' ד"ה ומקרעין. וי"ל כו'. נ"ב ורמב"ם חולק וכ' דוקא ברבו מובהק (ועמ"ש רבינו ביו"ד סי' רמב ס"ק סט):

## תורה אור השלם

א) כִּי תִרְאֶה חֲמוֹר שֹׂנַאֲךָ רֹבֵץ תַּחַת מַשָּׂאוֹ וְחָדַלְתָּ מֵעֲזֹב לוֹ עָזֹב תַּעֲזֹב עִמּוֹ: [שמות כג, ה]

ב) לֹא תִרְאֶה אֶת חֲמוֹר אָחִיךָ אוֹ שׁוֹרוֹ נֹפְלִים בַּדֶּרֶךְ וְהִתְעַלַּמְתָּ מֵהֶם הָקֵם תָּקִים עִמּוֹ: [דברים כב, ד]

ג) אֶפֶס כִּי לֹא יִהְיֶה בְּךָ אֶבְיוֹן כִּי בָרֵךְ יְבָרֶכְךָ יְיָ בָּאָרֶץ אֲשֶׁר יְיָ אֱלֹהֶיךָ נֹתֵן לְךָ נַחֲלָה לְרִשְׁתָּהּ: [דברים טו, ד]

## לעזי רש"י

פושטי"ר. פירוש פשפש, שער קטן בתוך שער גדול (ערוך ערך פשפש ג').

## ליקוטי רש"י

אפס וכו' בך אביון. הזהר בעלמך שלא תבוא לידי עניות [סנהדרין סד:]. זוהמא ליסטרון. אותו כף שגוחשין את הקדרה קרי להו הכי על שם שמעבירין הזוהמא לצדדין על שני צדיו תרגום על תרין סטרוהי [הוריות יג:]. מאניה. בגדיו [יומא נב.].

חשק שלמה על ר"ח א) כן מבואר בירושלמי בסוף פירקין. ב) כ"ה גירסת רבינו זומליסטרון בתיבה אחת וכ"ה גי' הערוך בערך זמלסטר וע"ש עוד גירסא אחרת. ג) נראה דלפנ"ש כאן רק מקומו לעיל אבל דברי ר"מ. ד) וכן הוא בסמ"ק ובשו"ת מהרי"ק בשורש קס"ט דרבינו פסק כר' יוסי.

The Gemara now cites a Baraisa that discusses the point at which the obligation to unload or load begins:

**תָּנוּ רַבָּנַן – The Rabbis taught in a Baraisa:** "כִּי־תִרְאֶה" – With regard to unloading the verse states:[12] *WHEN YOU SEE a donkey. . .lying down under its burden. . .* יָכוֹל אֲפִילוּ מֵרָחוֹק – Now, I MIGHT HAVE THOUGHT that if you sight an animal lying under its load, EVEN FROM A DISTANCE, you are obligated to walk to it and unload it. תַּלְמוּד לוֹמַר: "כִּי תִפְגַּע" – THE VERSE therefore TEACHES that the obligation applies only *WHEN YOU MEET UP* with an animal,[13] not when you see one from a distance.

The Baraisa continues:

אִי "כִּי תִפְגַּע" – IF Scripture had written only the words: *WHEN YOU MEET UP,* יָכוֹל פְּגִיעָה מַמָּשׁ – I MIGHT HAVE THOUGHT that the obligation applies only when you ACTUALLY MEET UP with an animal, and not if you simply see it nearby. תַּלְמוּד לוֹמַר – THE VERSE therefore TEACHES that the obligation applies "כִּי תִרְאֶה" – *WHEN YOU SEE* an animal lying down, even if you have not actually met up with it. In all, then, the obligation to unload applies only when one sees the animal close by; when one "sees" it in a way that is considered "meeting" it.[14] וְאֵיזוֹ הִיא רְאִיָּה שֶׁיֵּשׁ בָּהּ פְּגִיעָה – AND from WHAT distance DOES SEEING indeed INVOLVE MEETING? שִׁיעֲרוּ חֲכָמִים אֶחָד מִשֶּׁבַע וּמֶחֱצָה בְּמִיל – THE SAGES ESTABLISHED THE MEASUREMENT to be ONE IN SEVEN AND ONE-HALF PARTS OF A *MIL*;[15] וְזֶה הוּא רִיס – AND THIS distance IS called A *RIS*.[16]

The Gemara records:

**תָּנָא – A Tanna taught:** מְדַדֶּה עִמּוֹ עַד פַּרְסָה – After one helps reload a burden upon an animal, HE MUST WALK ALONG WITH [THE ANIMAL] FOR A *PARSAH*[17] to insure that the burden does not fall off it.[18]

The Gemara issues a ruling in conjunction with this Baraisa: **אָמַר רַבָּה בַּר בַּר חָנָה – Rabbah bar bar Chanah said:** וְנוֹטֵל שָׂכָר **– One may take payment** for walking along with the animal.[19]

**Mishnah** אֲבֵדָתוֹ וַאֲבֵדַת אָבִיו – If one spotted **his own lost object and his father's lost object,** אֲבֵדָתוֹ קוֹדֶמֶת – retrieving **his own lost object takes precedence** over retrieving his father's.[20] אֲבֵדָתוֹ וַאֲבֵדַת רַבּוֹ – Likewise, if he spotted both **his lost object and his teacher's lost object,** שֶׁלּוֹ קוֹדֵם – retrieving **his** own lost object **takes precedence.**[21] אֲבֵדַת אָבִיו וַאֲבֵדַת רַבּוֹ – If one spotted both **his father's lost object and his teacher's lost object,** שֶׁל רַבּוֹ קוֹדֶמֶת – retrieving **his teacher's** lost object **takes precedence,** שֶׁאָבִיו הֱבִיאוֹ לָעוֹלָם הַזֶּה – **for his father** is the one who **brought him into this world,** וְרַבּוֹ שֶׁלִּמְּדוֹ חָכְמָה מְבִיאוֹ לְחַיֵּי הָעוֹלָם הַבָּא – **whereas his teacher that taught him wisdom** is the one who **brings him into the World to Come.**[22] וְאִם אָבִיו חָכָם – **If,** however, **his father is a scholar,** שֶׁל אָבִיו קוֹדֶמֶת – then retrieving **his father's** object **takes precedence.**[23]

הָיָה אָבִיו וְרַבּוֹ נוֹשְׂאִין מַשּׂאוֹי – If **[one's] father and his teacher** are both **carrying burdens,** and both are in need of help in putting them down, מֵנִיחַ אֶת שֶׁל רַבּוֹ – **he should** first **put down his teacher's** burden וְאַחַר כָּךְ מֵנִיחַ אֶת שֶׁל אָבִיו – **and** only **then** should **he put down his father's** burden.[24]

הָיָה אָבִיו וְרַבּוֹ בְּבֵית הַשֶּׁבִי – **If [one's] father and his teacher** are both being held **captive,** פּוֹדֶה אֶת רַבּוֹ – **he should** first **ransom his teacher,** וְאַחַר כָּךְ פּוֹדֶה אֶת אָבִיו – **and** only **then** should **he ransom his father.** וְאִם אָבִיו חָכָם – **If,** however, **his father is a scholar,** פּוֹדֶה אֶת אָבִיו – **he should ransom his father** first וְאַחַר כָּךְ פּוֹדֶה אֶת רַבּוֹ – **and** only **then ransom his teacher.**[25]

NOTES

12. See note 1. [Although this verse is written with regard to unloading, the laws derived from it are applicable to loading as well.]

13. *Exodus* 23:4. The verse in its entirety reads: כִּי תִפְגַּע שׁוֹר אֹיִבְךָ אוֹ חֲמֹרוֹ תֹּעֶה הָשֵׁב תְּשִׁיבֶנּוּ לוֹ, *When you meet up with the ox of your enemy, or his donkey that is wandering, you shall surely return it to him.* Although the verse deals with the obligation of returning a lost object, the Gemara sees the law of unloading as essentially comparable, and, thus, it derives the parameters of the latter from the former (*Tos. HaRosh*; see also *Chidushei HaRitva*).

14. One verse indicates that the bystander becomes obligated as soon as he sees the animal from a distance, whereas the other verse indicates that he does not become obligated until he actually meets up with the animal. The Baraisa resolves the apparent contradiction by finding a distance at which one could see the animal and yet be considered to have also "met up" with it.

15. I.e. 2/15 of a *mil*. A *mil* is equivalent to 2,000 *amos*, a distance roughly equal to three or four thousand feet.

16. The Baraisa thus teaches that one is obligated to help unload if he sees the animal at a distance of one *ris* or closer. If, however, he sees that the animal is further than a *ris* from him, he need *not* walk to the animal to unload it.

17. One *parsah* is equivalent to four *mil*.

18. Were it to fall off, he would be obligated to help load it up again (*Nimukei Yosef*). Alternatively, the Gemara may mean that after one helps load an animal, he must walk along with it for a *parsah* in case the animal falls and he will be needed to help unload it (see *Tosafos* ד״ה ונוטל; *R' Yehonasan,* cited by *Shitah Mekubetzes* ד״ה ומדדה עמו).

It is debatable whether the obligation of walking with the animal for a *parsah* is Biblical or Rabbinic in nature (see *Minchas Chinuch* §80 ד״ה ושמדדו and *Chazon Yechezkel* to *Tosefta* 2:10).

19. That is, one may demand remuneration for walking with the animal in case he will be needed to help unload it again (see previous note). In setting forth this ruling, the Gemara maintains that only the actual *action* of unloading must be done for free; actions that are done in conjunction with unloading may be done for payment (*Nimukei Yosef*). One may certainly then accept payment for walking with an animal in case he will be needed to help *load* it, for if he may accept payment for the actual action of loading (as per the Rabbis' opinion, which is accepted as halachah), then he certainly may accept payment for actions that are done in conjunction with loading (*Tosafos* ד״ה נוטל).

20. I.e. if the finder is able to retrieve only one of them, he may retrieve his own and leave his father's, for his own needs take precedence. If, however, he has the ability to retrieve both, he of course must do so (see *Rambam, Hil. Aveidah* 12:1).

21. See previous note.

22. Consequently, he must honor his teacher more than his father, and he must therefore return his teacher's object if he can retrieve only one (see *Rambam Hil. Talmud Torah* 5:1; compare Mishnah *Kerisos* 28a; see also *Nachalas Moshe*).

23. See *Rashash*. The text of the Mishnah as we have it seems to imply that as long as one's father is a scholar, one must return his object over his teacher's object — even if the father is not as accomplished a scholar as his teacher. *Rif* and *Rosh,* however, had a different text of our Mishnah, which read: "If his father is a scholar of the same stature as his teacher . . .," and they therefore rule that one's father's object takes precedence only if the father is as accomplished a scholar as is the teacher.

24. [The Mishnah's choice of putting down a burden as an example of whom to help first fits well with the previous discussion of the obligation to help unload an animal. It thus lends support to the view of *Rashba* cited above (30b note 9) that this obligation extends to helping a human being unload his burden.]

25. Although *Rosh* stated earlier that the retrieval of one's father's item takes precedence only if the father was as great a scholar as the teacher, he nevertheless rules that with respect to ransoming from captivity, the

א) רובץ ולא רבצן רובץ ולא עומד תחת משאו ולא מפורק תחת משאו משאוי שיכול לעמוד בו ואי אמרת צער בעלי חיים דאורייתא מה לי רובץ ומה לי רבצן ומה לי עומד הא מני ר' יוסי הגלילי היא דאמר צער בעלי חיים דרבנן ה"נ מסתברא דקתני תחת משאו משאוי שיכול לעמוד בו מאן שמעת ליה דאית ליה האי סברא רבי יוסי הגלילי ש"מ ומי מצית מוקמת לה כרבי יוסי הגלילי והא קתני סיפא תחת משאו ולא מפורק מאי לא מפורק אילימא לא מפורק כלל הא כתיב ב) הקם תקים עמו אלא פשיטא לא מפורק בחנם אלא בשכר מאן שמעת ליה דאית ליה האי סברא רבנן לעולם ר' יוסי הגלילי היא ובטעינה סבר לה כרבנן ת"ר [א]א) כי תראה יכול אפי' מרחוק ת"ל כי תפגע אי כי תפגע יכול פגיעה ממש ת"ל כי תראה ואיזו היא ראייה שיש בה פגיעה א שיערו חכמים אחד משבע ומחצה במיל וזה הוא רים תנא ב ומדדה עמו עד פרסה אמר רבה בר בר חנה ג ונוטל שכר: **מתני'** א) ד אבדתו ואבדת אביו אבדתו קודמת אבדתו ואבדת רבו שלו קודם ה אבדת אביו ואבדת רבו של רבו קודמת שאביו הביאו לעולם הזה ורבו שלמדו חכמה מביאו לחיי העולם הבא ו ואם אביו [ב]חכם של אביו קודמת ז היה אביו ורבו נושאין משאוי מניח את של רבו ואחר כך מניח את של אביו ח היה אביו ורבו בבית השבי פודה את רבו ואחר כך פודה את אביו ט ואם אביו חכם פודה את אביו ואח"כ פודה את רבו: **גמ'** מנא הני מילי ב) אמר רב יהודה אמר רב קרא ג) אפס כי לא יהיה בך אביון י שלך קודם לשל כל אדם ואמר רב יהודה אמר רב כ כל המקיים בעצמו כך סוף בא לידי כך: היה אביו ורבו נושאין משאוי וכו': ג) תנו רבנן רבו שאמרו רבו שלמדו חכמה ולא רבו שלמדו מקרא ומשנה דברי ר"מ ד) רבי יהודה אומר ל כל שרוב חכמתו הימנו רבי יוסי אומר אפילו לא האיר עיניו אלא במשנה אחת זה הוא רבו אמר רבא כגון ה) רב סחורה דאסברן ו) זוהמא ליסטרון שמואל קרע מאניה עליה ההוא מרבנן דאסבריה ז) אחד יורד לאמת השחי ואחד פותח כיון אמר עולא מ תלמידי חכמים שבבבל עומדין זה מפני זה וקורעין זה על זה נ ולענין אבדה במקום אביו אינן חוזרין אלא לרבו מובהק קבעי מיניה רב חסדא מרב הונא תלמיד וצריך לו רבו מאי אמר ליה חסדא חסדא לא צריכנא לך את צריכת לי עד ארבעין שנין איקפדי אהדדי ולא עיילי לגבי הדדי יתיב רב חסדא ארבעין תעניתא משום דחלש דעתיה דרב הונא יתיב רב הונא ארבעין תעניתא משום דחשדיה לרב חסדא איתמר רב יצחק בר יוסף אמר ר' יוחנן הלכה כרבי יהודה רב אחא בר רב הונא אמר רב ששת הלכה כרבי יוסי ומי אמר רבי יוחנן הכי והאמר רבי יוחנן ס) הלכה כסתם משנה ותנן רבו שלמדו חכמה מאי חכמה רוב חכמתו ת"ר העוסקין במקרא מדה ואינה מדה במשנה מדה ונוטלין עליה שכר ס גמרא אין לך מדה גדולה מזו ולעולם הוי רץ למשנה יותר מן גמרא הא גופא קשיא אמרת בגמרא אין לך מדה גדולה מזו והדר אמרת ולעולם הוי רץ למשנה יותר מן הגמרא אמר רבי יוחנן בימי

**רש"י**

רובץ. מקרה הוא לו שרובץ תחת משאו בפעם הזאת: ולא רבצן. הרגיל בכך: ולא מפורק. והוא לריך טעינה ולקמן פריך הכתיב הקם תקים: יכול מרחוק. והטיל עליו שילך שם: מדדה עמו. לאחר שהטעינו שמא יחזור ויפול: גמ' מנא הני מילי. דשלו קודם: לא יהיה בך אביון. הזהר מן עניות: כל המקיים בעצמו כך. אף על פי שלא הטילו עליו הכתוב יש לאדם ליכנס לפנים משורת הדין ולא לדקדק שלי קודם אם לא בהפסד מוכיח ואם תמיד מדקדק פורק מעליו עול ג"ח ולדקה וסוף שילטרך לבריות: שלמדו חכמה. סברת טעמי המשנה ולהבין שלא יהו סותרות זו את זו וטעמי איסור והיתר והחיוב והפטור והוא נקרא גמרא: מקרא. תורה נביאים וכתובים: משנה. כמו שהן שנויות ואין טעמן מפורש בהן: כל שרוב חכמתו הימנו. אם מקרא אם משנה אם גמרא: האיר עיניו. שהודיעו טעם משנה אחת שלא יכול להבין: דאסברן זוהמא ליסטרון. בסדר טהרות (כלים פי"ג משנה ב ופכ"ה משנה ג) היא שנויה ולא הייתי יודע מה כלי הוא ולמדני שהוא כף גדולה שמסלקין בו זוהם הקדירה והקלחת ללדדין: קרע מאניה. קרע שאין מתאחה כדין תלמיד על הרב: אחד יורד לאמת השחי. משנה היא במסכת תמיד (פרק ג משנה ו) אבל הנכנסים שחרית לפתוח דלתות ההיכל מי שזכה בדישון מזבח הפנימי כו' ושני מפתחות בידו אחד יורד לאמת השחי ואחד פותח כיון אחד מן המפתחות הללו פותח פשפש הלפוני שאצל פתח ההיכל בקרן מזרחית לפונית של אולם והיכל כדתנן התם שני פשפשים היה לו לשער הגדול אחד ללפון ההיכל והאולם ואחד לדרומו ואותו שבדרום לא נכנס בו אדם מעולם כדמפרש התם ואותו פשפש שבלפון והוא לפתח שבזוית האולם שאצל חמש אמות של כותל ההיכל שבלפון פתח ההיכל ודלת סובבת בו ואותו מפתח של אותו הפתח יורד לאמת השחי. פשפשים פתחים קטנים כמין ליפות קטנות ארכו כעובי רוחב הכותל ודלת סובבת בו פוסטי"ר בלעז אחד יורד לאמת השחי הבא לפתוח בו שחרית ט) [פשפש שבזוית האולם] עומד מבחוץ בתוך האולם ומכניס ידו בחור שבכותל עד בית שחיו ופותח: ואחד פותח כיון. לאחר שנכנס בזה (א) ובא לו לתא אשר על פני אחת עשרה אמה של אולם וקלת מן ההיכל ופותח במפתח שני דלת אחד שמן התא להיכל מהר בלא טורח כשאר פתחים ונכנס להיכל לפתוח דלתות ההיכל: כיון. כמו (פסחים דף לז.) יעשנה בדפוס ויקבענה כיון מהר בלא טורח והאי שער הגדול הוא פתח ההיכל שבין אולם להיכל: עומדין זה מפני זה. כדין תלמיד לרב לפי שהיו יושבין תמיד בבית המדרש יחד ומקשין ומפרקין וכולם למדים זה מזה: לרבו מובהק. שרוב חכמתו ממנו כר"י: וצריך לו רבו. ששמע שמועות שיש בידו מפי אחרים: מאי. כלומר קודם לאביו לענין אבדה: ותנן רבו שלמדו חכמה. סתמא כר' מאיר: רוב חכמתו. אם מקרא מקרא אם משנה משנה: מדה. היא קלת: ואינה מדה. שהמשנה וגמרא יפים ממנה מפני שתלוין בגירסא ומשתכחים שבימיהם לא היה גמרא בכתב וגם לא היה ניתן לכתוב אלא לפי שנתמעטו הלבבות התחילו דורות [אחרונים] לכתבו: גמרא. כבר פירשתי למעלה שהוא לתת לב להבין סתימות טעמי המשנה מה הם וכששתים סותרות זו את זו יבין לתרץ שיהיו שתיהן קיימות או לדעת דברי התנאים החלוקים בדבר וימלא הא מני פלוני חכם הוא:

**תוספות**

מה לי רבצן. וא"ת וליתני רובץ בחנם רבצן בשכר דה"נ משני ולא מפורק בחנם אלא בשכר וי"ל דניחא ליה לשנויי דאתי כרבי יוסי הגלילי כדמוכח דאתיא כוותיה: ונוטל שכר. במה שמדדה ובפריקה מיירי שירא פן ירבץ דאי בטעינה פשיטא דהא טעינה גופה בשכר וכל שכן מה שמדדה:

י) וזהו רים. אית דגרסי רום דשבע ומחצה רום עולה כ) אלפים דהוי שיעור מיל כדמוכח בפרק שני שעירי (יומא דף סז.) גבי סוכות דשעיר המשתלח: אבדתו קודמת. וא"ת אבדתו ואבדת רבו וכבוד אביו איזהו קודם אי אבדתו הלא כבוד אביו עדיף למאן דאמר בפ"ק דקדושין (דף לב. ושם) משל בן ואם כבוד אביו הלא אבדת רבו קודמת כדאמר לעיל ל) אני ה' ויש לומר אבדתו קודמת דהיכא דאביו נהנה מגוף הבהמה חייב לכבדו כגון שחוט לי בהמתך אבל הניחה ליאבד ותביא לי לאכול שגם לאב קשה האבדה אלא שרוצה לאכול מ): ומקרעין זה על זה. אף על פי שאינו יודע יותר לפי שלומדין זה מזה ואם תאמר דאמרינן בפרק האורג (שבת דף קה: ושם) חייב לקרוע על אדם כשר אפילו לא היה בשעת יציאת נשמה [ג] ויש לומר דהכא מיירי בקרע שאינו מתאחה כדין תלמיד על רבו וכן פירש רש"י: אחיכם

**עין משפט נר מצוה**

קפח א מיי' פי"ג מהל' רוצח הי"ו סמג עשין פא טוש"ע חו"מ סי' רעב סעיף ה:
קפט ב מיי' שם הל' ה טוש"ע שם סעיף ד:
קצ ג מיי' שם הל' ז טוש"ע שם סעיף ו:
קצא ד מיי' פי"ב מהל' אבידה הלכה א סמג עשין עד טוש"ע חו"מ סי' רסד ס"א:
קצב ה ו מיי' שם ה"ב ופ"ה מהלכות ת"ת הלכה א סמג שם טור ש"ע שם ס"ב וטור ש"ע י"ד סי' רמב סל"ד:
קצג ז מיי' פ"ה מהל' ת"ת ה"א סמג שם טוש"ע י"ד סי' רמב סל"ד:
קצד ח ט מיי' שם ופ"ח מהל' מתנות עניים הל' יח סמג שם וסי' קסב טוש"ע שם וסי' רנב ס"ט:
קצה י מיי' פי"ב מהל' אבידה הלכה א סמג עשין עד טוש"ע ח"מ סי' רסד ס"א וטוש"ע יו"ד סי' רמב סל"ה:
קצו כ טוש"ע ח"מ שם:
קצז ל מיי' פי"ב מהל' אבדה הל' ב ופ"ה מהל' ת"ת הל' ט סמג עשין שם טוש"ע ח"מ סי' רסד ס"ב וטוש"ע י"ד סי' רמב סעיף ל:
קצח מ מיי' פ"ה מהל' ת"ת ופ"ט מהל' אבל הי"א סמג עשין יג עד פב טוש"ע יו"ד סי' רמב ס"ל וסי' שמ ס"ז וסעיף ח:
קצט נ מיי' פי"ב מהל' אבידה הל' ב סמג עשין עד טוש"ע ח"מ סי' רסד סעיף ב:
ר ס מיי' פ"א מהל' ת"ת הלכה יא סמג עשין יב טוש"ע י"ד סי' רמו ס"ד:

**רבינו חננאל**

ת"ר כי תראה יכול מרחוק ת"ל כי תפגע יכול פגיעה ממש פניא בפנים ת"ל כי תראה (הם) [הא] כיצד ראיה שיש בה פגיעה שיערו חכמים אחד משבעה ומחצה במיל וזהו ריס. ומדדה עמו עד פרסה ונוטל שכרו. קיימא לן פריקה בחנם לדברי הכל וטעינה בשכר כרבנן: מתני' אבדתו ואבדת אביו וכו' אבדת רבו שלו קודמת. פי' יניח של אביו ויניח של רבו וישיב את שלו שנאמר אפס כי לא יהיה בך אביון. והמדקדק שלא יבא לידי עניות סוף בא לידי כך: ת"ר רבו שאמרו רבו שלמדו חכמה ולא רבו שלמדו מקרא ומשנה דברי ר"מ ר' יהודה אומר כל שרוב חכמתו ממנו ור' יוסי [אמר] אפי' לא האיר עיניו אלא במשנה אחת זהו רבו. אע"ג דאמר ר' יוחנן הלכה כר' יהודה רב ששת דהוא בתרא אמר הלכה כר' יוסי. ועוד הנה שמואל עשה כמותו וקרע על ההוא מרבנן דאסבריה הא דתנן במסכת תמיד פ' אמר להן הממונה ושני מפתחות אחד יורד אמת השחי ואחד פותח כיון פירש לו מפתח אחד היה מכניס ידו ופותח בו מיד והאחר לא יכול לפתוח בו עד שהיה מוריד ידו עד שחיו וכך היה פותח וכן הוא מפורש בתלמוד ארץ ישראל א) הנה שמואל לא למד ממנו אלא פירוש משנה זו בלבד וכיון ששמע שמת קרע עליו כאשר קורע התלמיד על רבו. וכן פירש רבא כי רבו כגון רב סחורה דאסברן זומליסטרון ב) פי' התרוד שמהפך בה בשר בתוך הצלחת נקראת זומליסטרון: ובתלמוד ארץ ישראל ג) רב כר"מ חד בר נש פתח פומיה דרב ושמע דדמך ובזע עלוהו. ומתניתין נמי כר' יוסי דייקא ד) והא דאוקימנא כר' יהודה שינויא הוא: ת"ר העוסק במקרא פי' במקרא בלבד ואין מתעסק גם בתלמוד מדה שאינה מדה היא שהרי לא נתעסק גם בפתרון המצות. במשנה מדה שנוטלין עליה שכר פי' המתעסק בפתרון המשנה שיש בה הרבה מן המצות שהן קבלה והן תלויות במשניות החיצונות וכשהוא מתעסק במשנה צריך לעיין באותן הברייתות כולן ופתרוני החכמים יש לו בזה שכר מצוה. אבל המתעסק בתלמוד ומורה ומבאר המצות כתקנן ומגיד הלכה למעשה אין לך מדה גדולה מזו כי בתלמוד פתרון התורה והמשנה והמצוה שהן בקבלה הלכה למשה מסיני. ולעולם הוי רץ למשנה יותר מן התלמוד פי' הוי רץ למשנה שהיא מדה ונוטלין עליה שכר והשוגג אינו נדון בה כמזיד אבל המתעסק בתלמוד אפי' השגגות חשובות עליו כזדונות שהיה לו לדקדק על עצמו שלא יכשל אפי' בשגגה לפי שמדקדקין עליו אפי' כחוט השערה שנאמר וסביביו נשערה מאד מלמד שהקב"ה מדקדק עם סביביו אפי' כחוט השערה ומי יכול להשמר כל זה וכבר פירשנוהו הוי זהיר בתלמוד ששגגת התלמוד עולה זדון הוי זהיר אתה המתעסק בתלמוד ששגגתו עולה לך זדון וכו' יהודה בר' אלעי דדרש הגד לעמי פשעם אלו תלמידי חכמים ששגגות נעשות להם כזדונות וכו'. אמר עולא תלמידי חכמים

**מסורת הש"ס**

א) סנהדרין סד., ב) לעיל ל:, סנהדרין סד: ע"ש, ג) [מסכת כלה, תוספתא הוריות פרק ב], ד) [עיין תוספות מועד קטן כה: ד"ה ועל רבו], ה) [עיין תוספות סנהדרין מט: ד"ה אמר, ותוספות יבמות ה. ד"ה רבא, ועבודה זרה ע. ד"ה אמר], ו) [כלים פרק יג משנה ב, ופרק כה משנה ג], ז) [תמיד ל:], ח) שבת מו. וש"נ, ט) מהרש"ל, י) [צ"ל קודם ד"ה ונוטל], כ) הוא אלפים אמר משה, ועיין בערוך ערך רוס, ל) דף לג., מ) [וע"ש בתוס' ד"ה ר"י, וכן בתוס' זבחים ל: ד"ה מטלת].

**הגהות הב"ח**

(א) רש"י ד"ה ואחד פותח כיון לאחר שנכנס בזה. נ"ב אבל הר' עובדיה פי' שאותן שני מפתחות בידו שניהם בפשפש הצפוני וע"ש:

**הגהות הגר"א**

[א] גמרא ת"ר לא תראה כו' ממש ת"ל לא תראה. כצ"ל (והוא בדברים כב וכן הוא בספרי שם וא"ש דב' המקראות במיני גבי אבידה ומוכיחין זה לזה ועיין ריטב"א בשיטה מקובצת והגר"א בח"מ סי' רע"ב ס"ק ג'): [ב] במשנה חכם. נ"ב גירס' הרי"ף וש"פ כאן שקול נגד רבו: [ג] תוס' ד"ה ומקרעין. וי"ל בר'. נ"ב ורמב"ם חולק וכ' דוקא ברבו מובהק (ועמ"ש רבינו ביו"ד סי' רמב ס"ק סט):

**תורה אור השלם**

א) כִּי תִרְאֶה חֲמוֹר שֹׂנַאֲךָ רֹבֵץ תַּחַת מַשָּׂאוֹ וְחָדַלְתָּ מֵעֲזֹב לוֹ עָזֹב תַּעֲזֹב עִמּוֹ: [שמות כג, ה]
ב) לֹא תִרְאֶה אֶת חֲמוֹר אָחִיךָ אוֹ שׁוֹרוֹ נֹפְלִים בַּדֶּרֶךְ וְהִתְעַלַּמְתָּ מֵהֶם הָקֵם תָּקִים עִמּוֹ: [דברים כב, ד]
ג) אֶפֶס כִּי לֹא יִהְיֶה בְּךָ אֶבְיוֹן כִּי בָרֵךְ יְבָרֶכְךָ יְיָ בָּאָרֶץ אֲשֶׁר יְיָ אֱלֹהֶיךָ נֹתֵן לְךָ נַחֲלָה לְרִשְׁתָּהּ: [דברים טו, ד]

**לעזי רש"י**

פושטי"ר. פירוש פשפש, שער קטן בתוך שער גדול (ערוך ערך פשפש ג').

**ליקוטי רש"י**

אפס וכו' בך אביון. הזהר בעצמך שלא תבוא לידי עניות [סנהדרין סד:]. זוהמא ליסטרון. אותו כף שבוחשין את הקדרה קרי להו הכי על שם שמעבירין הזוהמא לצדדין על שני צדיו תרגום על תרין סטרוהי [הוריות יג:]. מאניה. בגדיו [יומא נב.].

חשק שלמה על ר"ח א) כן מבואר בירושלמי בסוף פירקין. ב) כ"ה גירסת רבינו זומליסטרון בתיבה אחת וכ"ה גי' הערוך בערך זמלסטר וע"ש עוד גירסא אחרת. ג) נראה דלפ"ז שייך כאן רק מקומו לעיל אצל דברי ר"מ. ד) וכן הובא בשמ"ק ובשו"ת מהרי"ק בשורש קס"ט דרבינו פסק כר' יוסי.

״רֹבֵץ״ – The verse obligates one to unload an animal that is ***lying down*** *under its burden,*[1] which implies that וְלֹא רַבְצָן – one is NOT obligated to unload an animal that HABITUALLY LIES DOWN under its burden.[2] ״רֹבֵץ״ – Another implication of Scripture's term, *LYING DOWN,* is that one must help unload only a lying animal, וְלֹא עוֹמֵד – BUT NOT one that is STANDING.[3] ״תַּחַת מַשָּׂאוֹ״ – The verse further states: ***under its burden,*** implying that one is obligated to help an animal that has its burden upon it, וְלֹא מְפוּרָק – BUT NOT one whose burden was UNLADEN and is now in need of loading.[4] ״תַּחַת מַשָּׂאוֹ״ – Another implication of the words ***under its burden*** is that מַשָּׂאוֹי שֶׁיָּכוֹל לַעֲמוֹד בּוֹ – one is obligated to unload only if the animal had been carrying A BURDEN UNDER WHICH IT CAN STAND.[5] If, however, it had been overloaded, one is not obligated to help unload it. וְאִי אָמְרַת צַעַר בַּעֲלֵי חַיִּים דְּאוֹרַיְיתָא – Now, **if you will say** the **suffering of living creatures is** a **Biblical** concern, מַה לִּי רוֹבֵץ וּמַה לִּי רַבְצָן – **what does it matter to me** if the animal happens to be **lying down** this one time, **or** if it **habitually lies down?** וּמַה לִּי עוֹמֵד – **Furthermore, what does it matter to me** if it is still **standing?** In any case, one should be required to unload the animal to relieve its suffering. Rather, since the Baraisa ruled that one is exempt from unloading in these cases, it must hold that the suffering of living creatures is not a Biblical concern.[6] – ? –

The Gemara concedes the point, but suggests that the author of the Baraisa is a Tanna that was already known to hold this view: הָא מַנִּי – **Who is** the author of **this** Baraisa? ר׳ יוֹסֵי הַגְּלִילִי הִיא – **It is R' Yose HaGlili,** דְּאָמַר צַעַר בַּעֲלֵי חַיִּים דְּרַבָּנָן – **who said** in the Mishnah that the **suffering of living creatures is** a **Rabbinic** concern, not a Biblical one.[7]

The Gemara supports this notion that the Baraisa reflects only R' Yose HaGlili's view, but not that of other Tannaim:

הָכִי נַמִּי מִסְתַּבְּרָא – **This is indeed a logical assumption,** דְּקָתָנֵי ״תַּחַת מַשָּׂאוֹ״ – **for [the Baraisa] taught** that the words *UNDER ITS BURDEN* imply מַשָּׂאוֹי שֶׁיָּכוֹל לַעֲמוֹד בּוֹ – that one is obligated to unload only if the animal had been carrying A BURDEN UNDER WHICH IT CAN STAND. מַאן שָׁמְעַת לֵיהּ דְּאִית לֵיהּ הַאי סְבָרָא – Now, **whom did you hear of that subscribes to this idea?** רַבִּי יוֹסֵי הַגְּלִילִי – **R' Yose HaGlili!** שְׁמַע מִינָּהּ – We can thus **learn from this** that the Baraisa was indeed authored by R' Yose HaGlili.[8]

The Gemara questions this resolution:

וּמִי מָצֵית מוֹקְמַת לָהּ כְּרַבִּי יוֹסֵי הַגְּלִילִי – **But, can you** really **establish** that **[the Baraisa] represents** the view of **R' Yose HaGlili?** וְהָא קָתָנֵי סֵיפָא ״תַּחַת מַשָּׂאוֹ״ – **But the end of [the Baraisa] taught** that since the verse states *UNDER ITS BURDEN,* it implies that one is obligated to help an animal that has a burden on it, וְלֹא מְפוּרָק – BUT NOT one whose burden was UNLADEN and is now in need of loading. מַאי לֹא מְפוּרָק – Now, **what** does it mean BUT NOT one whose burden is UNLADEN? אִילֵימָא לֹא מְפוּרָק כְּלָל – **If you will say** it means one is **not** obligated to help an **unladen** animal **whatsoever,** that is, he need not assist whatsoever in loading it, הָא כְּתִיב – this is impossible, for **it is** indeed **written:**[9] ״הָקֵם תָּקִים עִמּוֹ״ – ***you shall surely raise [it] up with him***, a verse which clearly obligates a bystander to help with loading. אֶלָּא פְּשִׁיטָא לֹא מְפוּרָק בְּחִנָּם – **Rather,** the Baraisa **obviously** means to say that one is **not** obligated to load an **unladen** animal **for free,** אֶלָּא בְּשָׂכָר – **but,** rather, he may help load for **payment.** מַאן שָׁמְעַת לֵיהּ דְּאִית לֵיהּ הַאי סְבָרָא – Now, **whom did you hear of that subscribes to this idea?** רַבָּנָן – **The Rabbis** of the Mishnah who argue with R' Yose HaGlili![10] How, then, can you say that the Baraisa was authored by R' Yose HaGlili?

The Gemara answers:

לְעוֹלָם ר׳ יוֹסֵי הַגְּלִילִי הִיא – **Really,** we may indeed assert that **[the Baraisa]** represents the view of **R' Yose HaGlili.** וּבִטְעִינָה – **With regard to loading, however,** סָבַר לָהּ כְּרַבָּנָן – **[R' Yose HaGlili] concurs with the Rabbis** that one may load an animal for payment.[11]

NOTES

1. *Exodus* 23:5.

2. The word רֹבֵץ, *lying down*, connotes that the animal happened to lie down this one time, but it does not do this habitually (*Rashi*). By using this word, the Torah implies that if the animal habitually lies down, one is not obligated to help unload it.

3. That is, one is obligated to unload the animal only if the animal is actually lying down underneath its load. If, however, the animal is still standing, one is not obligated to unload it even though the animal is struggling to stand up under its burden.

4. That is, one is obligated to unload an animal, but not to load it. The Gemara will later qualify this ruling, in light of the fact that a verse explicitly obligates one to help load an animal when this is necessary (*Rashi*).

5. Although the animal was not overloaded, [due to fatigue, load slippage, etc.] the animal lay down under its burden and is now unable to stand up unless the load is temporarily taken off its back (see *Sefer HaChinuch* §80).

6. If the Baraisa indeed maintains that the suffering of living creatures is not a Biblical concern, but a Rabbinic one, then its rulings are indeed understandable. As noted before (32b note 15), a Rabbinic decree to alleviate the suffering of animals would not have required a person to alleviate the pain of *someone else's* animal. Rather, the decree would merely obligate each individual to see to it that his own animal does not suffer.

7. See 32b note 35.

8. In connection with the question of whether the suffering of living creatures is a Biblical concern, many Rishonim ask a question not dealt with by the Gemara: If the suffering of living creatures is indeed a Biblical concern, why does the Gemara (30b) exempt an elderly man from unloading an animal merely if it is beneath his dignity to do so? *Ran* (cited by *Nimukei Yosef*) answers that since we find that one may actively cause suffering to animals to promote his welfare (e.g. he may kill an animal for its hide), it stands to reason that he need not debase himself to prevent an animal from experiencing pain. See also *Ramban,* and *Shitah Mekubetzes* ד״ה ולענין.

9. *Deuteronomy* 22:4.

10. In the Mishnah, the Rabbis had stated that "It is a commandment in the Torah to unload, but not to load," a statement which is taken to mean that there is no command to help load *for free;* rather, one may load for payment. Since the Mishnah places R' Yose HaGlili's statement after this portion of the Mishnah, the Gemara assumes that R' Yose HaGlili disputes the Rabbi's view on this matter.

[*Rashba* asks that the Gemara's question here seems to imply that the Baraisa *could have been* authored by the Rabbis. This seems difficult, however, for the Baraisa set forth that one is not obligated to help unload an overburdened animal, a ruling the Rabbis of the Mishnah clearly dispute. See *Rashba* (cited in *Shitah Mekubetzes*) who provides a resolution to this problem.]

11. The Gemara now asserts that although R' Yose HaGlili disagrees with the Rabbis with respect to an over-burdened animal, it need not be assumed that he disagrees also with respect to loading for payment. Indeed, R' Yose HaGlili could agree with the Rabbis on this point. We can thus argue that the Baraisa indeed reflects only R' Yose HaGlili's view when it states that one need not unload a standing animal or one that lies down habitually. Other Tannaim, however, would dispute R' Yose HaGlili on this, and would hold that one must even unload in these cases, because of the consideration of the animal's suffering.

This now concludes the Gemara's discussion of whether the suffering of living creatures is a Biblical or Rabbinic concern. The halachic decisors have followed the view of the Rabbis that discomfort of living creatures is indeed a Biblical concern (see *Kesef Mishneh* to *Hil. Rotzei'ach U'Shemiras Nefesh* 13:9; *Rif*; see also *Nimukei Yosef*).

In order to construe the Baraisa as holding that the suffering of living creatures is a Biblical concern, the Gemara had suggested that the Baraisa is dealing with a case of loading, not a case of unloading. The Gemara now questions this premise:

וְהָא „וְחָדַלְתָּ״ וְ„עָזֹב תַּעֲזֹב״ בִּפְרִיקָה הוּא דִּכְתִיבֵי – But the phrases *you may refrain* and *you shall surely help* **are written** in the Torah **with respect to unloading!** We must thus conclude that the Baraisa, which uses these phrases to teach its laws, must have also referred to unloading! – ? –

The Gemara concedes the point:[33]

(אמר ליה) [אֶלָּא] הָא מַנִּי – **Rather,** we may suggest:[34] **Who** is the author of **this** Baraisa? רַבִּי יוֹסֵי הַגְּלִילִי הִיא – It is **R' Yose HaGlili,** דְּאָמַר צַעַר בַּעֲלֵי חַיִּים לָאו דְּאוֹרַיְיתָא – **who says** that the **suffering of living creatures is not** a **Biblical** concern.[35]

The Gemara attempts again to show that the suffering of living creatures is not a Biblical concern:

תָּא שְׁמַע – **Come, learn** the proof to this from a Baraisa: אוֹהֵב לִפְרוֹק – If one's FRIEND'S animal is lying under its burden and needs TO BE UNLOADED, וְשׂוֹנֵא לִטְעוֹן – AND one's ENEMY'S animal needs TO BE LOADED,[36] מִצְוָה בְּשׂוֹנֵא – IT IS A MITZVAH for one to assist one's ENEMY'S animal, כְּדֵי לָכוֹף אֶת יִצְרוֹ – IN ORDER TO SUBDUE ONE'S EVIL INCLINATION.[37] וְאִי סָלְקָא דַּעְתָּךְ צַעַר בַּעֲלֵי חַיִּים דְּאוֹרַיְיתָא – **Now, if you would consider** that the **suffering of living creatures is** a **Biblical** concern, then the Baraisa's ruling would seem to be incorrect; הָא עָדִיף לֵיהּ – since **this** obligation to unload **would be more important** than the other obligation to load![38] – ? –

The Gemara responds:

אֲפִילּוּ הָכִי – In fact, the suffering of living creatures could be a Biblical concern. However, **even so,** כְּדֵי לָכוֹף אֶת יִצְרוֹ עָדִיף – **it would be more important to subdue [one's] Evil Inclination** by loading his enemy's animal than to alleviate an animal's pain by unloading his friend's animal.[39]

The Gemara attempts again to prove that the suffering of living creatures is not a Biblical concern:

תָּא שְׁמַע – **Come, learn** the proof to this from the following Baraisa: שׂוֹנֵא שֶׁאָמְרוּ שׂוֹנֵא יִשְׂרָאֵל – THE ENEMY THAT THEY SAID one must assist is A JEWISH ENEMY, וְלֹא שׂוֹנֵא עוֹבֵד כּוֹכָבִים – NOT AN ENEMY that is AN IDOLATER.[40] אִי אָמְרַתְּ צַעַר בַּעֲלֵי חַיִּים דְּאוֹרַיְיתָא – Now, **if you say** that the **suffering of living creatures is** a **Biblical** concern, מָה לִי שׂוֹנֵא יִשְׂרָאֵל וּמָה לִי שׂוֹנֵא עוֹבֵד כּוֹכָבִים – **what does it matter to me** if he is **a Jewish enemy or an idolatrous enemy?** In either case one should be obligated to unload the animal![41] – ? –

The Gemara counters:

מִי סָבְרַתְּ אַשּׂוֹנֵא דִּקְרָא קָאֵי – **Did you think** that **[this Baraisa] is discussing the enemy** mentioned **in the verse** that mandates unloading? אַשּׂוֹנֵא דְּמַתְנִיתִין קָאֵי – In fact, **it is discussing the enemy** mentioned **in** the aforementioned **Baraisa,** whose animal was in need of loading.[42] There is thus no proof from here that the suffering of living creatures is not a Biblical concern.

The Gemara attempts once again to prove that the suffering of living creatures is not a Biblical concern:

תָּא שְׁמַע – **Come, learn** the proof to this from the following Baraisa:

---

NOTES

*always* be obligated to help *unload* an animal, (even if the cargo and/or the animal belonged to an idolater,) since the bystander is Biblically obligated to relieve an animal's suffering.

33. Having conceded that the present Baraisa speaks about a case of unloading, the Gemara is forced to agree that the Tanna of the Baraisa does not view the suffering of animals to be a Biblical concern. (If he viewed this to be a Biblical concern, he could not have ruled that the bystander may refrain from helping when the animal in distress belongs to an idolater.)

34. This follows the emendation of *Mesoras HaShas*.

35. R' Yose HaGlili ruled in our Mishnah that if the owner overloaded the animal, the bystander is not obligated to help unload it. The Gemara subsequently explained that R' Yose HaGlili is of the opinion that the suffering of living creatures is not a Biblical concern. The Gemara now states that although the present Baraisa indeed holds the suffering of living creatures not to be a Biblical concern, its authorship can be attributed to R' Yose HaGlili, whom the halachah does not follow.

36. Since he encounters both parties at the same time, the question arises whether he should unload or load. [It is not clear from the Gemara whether the bystander was able to do both, and the question is which he should do first, or if the bystander was able to do only one, and the question is which one should he do at all. See *Chazon Yechezkel* to *Tosefta* 2:11 for a discussion of this point.]

37. By choosing to assist his enemy, the bystander "wages war" against his natural impulse to feel hateful towards him (see *Michtav MeEliyahu, Kuntres HaChesed* Chap. 4).

38. Although loading would "subdue the [bystander's] Evil Inclination," it is still the case that unloading would alleviate an animal's suffering. Hence, if the suffering of living creatures is indeed a Biblical concern, unloading should seemingly take precedence (see *Ritva*).

39. Subduing one's impulse to hate a fellow Jew is so important that it takes precedence even over the Biblically preferred obligation of unloading (see *Ritva*).

*Minchas Chinuch* suggests a possible reason for this as follows: We find that in certain cases, man is permitted to actively cause suffering to animals to promote his own welfare. He may, for example, kill an animal for its hide. It stands to reason, then, that he may at least *refrain* from alleviating an animal's suffering if by doing this he will gain the opportunity to subdue his feelings of hate and thereby improve his character (*Minchas Chinuch* §80 ד״ה והנה סברת הש״ס, cf. *Michtav MeEliyahu, Kuntres HaChesed* Chap. 4).

40. At this point, the Gemara understands the Baraisa to mean that the enemy that *the Torah spoke of* when it set forth the obligation to unload is a Jewish enemy (the verse states . . . כִּי־תִרְאֶה חֲמוֹר שֹׂנַאֲךָ רֹבֵץ תַּחַת מַשָּׂאוֹ, *when you shall see your enemy's donkey lying down under its burden* . . .). This would imply that the Torah did not obligate one to unload the animal of his idolatrous enemy.

41. See beginning of note 25.

42. The previous Baraisa ruled that if one has a choice between unloading his friend's animal or loading his enemy's animal, he must do the latter. The current Baraisa then qualifies this previous Baraisa by saying that its ruling applies only when the enemy whose animal needed loading is a Jew. If, however, the enemy is an idolater, then the bystander's obligation to unload his friend's animal takes precedence.

According to the Gemara's answer, neither Baraisa implies an exemption from unloading an idolater's animal. Hence, the Baraisos contain no indication as to whether the suffering of living creatures is a Biblical concern.

מדברי שניהם נלמד [א] צער בעלי חיים דאורייתא ואפי' ר"ש לא קאמר אלא משום דלא מסיימי קראי אבל מסיימי קראי דרשי' ק"ו משום מאי לאו משום צער בעלי חיים דרשינן דלמא משום דאיכא חסרון כיס וה"ק ומה טעינה דלית בה חסרון כיס חייב פריקה דאית בה חסרון כיס לא כ"ש וטעינה אין בה חסרון כיס מי לא עסקינן דאדהכי והכי בטיל משוקיה אי נמי אתו גנבי ושקלי כל מה דאיכא בהדיה תדע דצער בעלי חיים דאורייתא דקתני סיפא ר' יוסי הגלילי אומר אם היה עליו יתר [על] משאו אין זקוק לו שנאמר א) תחת משאו משאוי שיכול לעמוד בו לאו מכלל דת"ק סבר [א] זקוק לו מאי טעמא לאו משום דצער בעלי חיים דאורייתא דלמא בתחת משאו פליגי דרבי יוסי סבר דרשינן תחת משאו משאוי שיכול לעמוד בו ורבנן סברי לא דרשינן תחת משאו תדע דצער בעלי חיים לאו דאורייתא דקתני רישא הלך וישב לו ואמר לו הואיל ועליך מצוה לפרוק פרוק פטור שנאמר עמו ואי סלקא דעתך צער בעלי חיים דאורייתא מה לי איתיה למריה בהדיה ומה לי כי ליתיה למריה בהדיה לעולם צער בעלי חיים דאורייתא מי סברת פטור לגמרי (א) ודלמא פטור בחנם וחייב בשכר וה"ק רחמנא כי איתיה למריה בהדיה עבד גביה בחנם וכי ליתיה למריה בהדיה עבד גביה בשכר ולעולם צער בעלי חיים דאורייתא (סימ"ן בהמ"ת אוה"ב שונ"א רבצ"ן) לימא מסייע ליה [ב] בהמת עובד כוכבים מטפל בה כבהמת ישראל אי אמרת בשלמא צער בעלי חיים דאורייתא משום הכי מטפל בה כבהמת ישראל אלא אי אמרת צער בעלי חיים לאו דאורייתא אמאי מטפל בה כבהמת ישראל התם [ג] משום איבה הכי נמי מסתברא דקתני אם היתה טעונה יין אסור אין זקוק לה אי אמרת בשלמא לאו דאורייתא משום הכי אין זקוק לה אלא אי אמרת דאורייתא אמאי אין זקוק לה ה"ק ולהטעינה יין אסור אין זקוק לה תא שמע [ד] בהמת עובד כוכבים ומשאוי ישראל וחדלת ואי אמרת צער בעלי חיים דאורייתא אמאי וחדלת עזב תעזב מבעי ליה [ה] לעולם צער בעלי חיים דאורייתא התם בטעינה אי הכי אימא סיפא [ו] בהמת ישראל ומשאוי עובד כוכבים עזב תעזב ואי בטעינה אמאי עזב תעזב משום צערא דישראל אי הכי אפילו רישא נמי רישא [ז] בחמר עובד כוכבים סיפא בחמר ישראל מאי פסקת סתמא דמלתא איניש בתר חמריה אזיל והא וחדלת ועזב תעזב בפריקה הוא דכתיבי (ג) א"ל הא מני רבי יוסי הגלילי היא דאמר (ו) צער בעלי חיים לאו דאורייתא ת"ש (ז) [ח] אוהב לפרוק ושונא לטעון מצוה בשונא כדי לכוף את יצרו ואי סלקא דעתך צער בעלי חיים דאורייתא הא עדיף ליה אפ"ה כדי לכוף את יצרו עדיף ת"ש (ה) [ט] שונא שאמרו שונא ישראל ולא שונא עובד כוכבים אי אמרת צער בעלי חיים דאורייתא מה לי שונא ישראל ומה לי שונא עובד כוכבים מי סברת אשונא דקרא קאי אשונא (ו) דמתניתין קאי תא שמע

רובץ

---

מדברי שניהם. מדקאמרי תרווייהו פריקה עדיפא: ואפילו ר"ש לא קאמר. דאצטריך למכתב פריקה: אלא משום דלא מסיימי קראי. לטעינה: לאו משום צער בעלי חיים. והכי יליף מה טעינה דליכא צער בעלי חיים חייב פריקה דאיכא צער בעלי חיים לא כ"ש: מי לא עסקינן. וכי אין המקרא מדבר אף בהולך לסחורה דאדהכי בטיל משוקיה: תדע. דלרבנן דפליגי עליה דר"ש ולר"ש צער בעלי חיים דאורייתא: מכלל דת"ק. דרבי יוסי הגלילי רבנן ור"ש: זקוק לו. ואמאי זקוק לו אי משום מצות עזב תעזב הא כתיב משאו הראוי לו אלא משום צער בעלי חיים: לא דרשינן משאו. למשא הראוי לו דמשאו כל משא שעליו משמע: ותדע. דהכי הוא כדדחינא לך דצער בעלי חיים לאו דאורייתא: עביד גביה. משום צער בעלי חיים ועל כורחו יטול שכר: לימא מסייע ליה. לרבא דאמר לעיל צער בעלי חיים דאורייתא: מטפל בה. לפרוק משאה: אי אמרת (ב) לאו דאורייתא. וטעמא משום איבה הוא מש"ה אין זקוק לה שיכול להשמט ולומר דבר איסור הוא לנו: ה"ק ולהטעינה. ולעולם דאורייתא ורישא תנא מטפל בה בין בפריקה בין בטעינה פריקה משום צער בעלי חיים וטעינה משום איבה ולהטעינה יין אסור דלאו צערא איכא ולאו איבה איכא אין זקוק לה: התם בטעינה. לקמיה פריך הא בפריקה כתיב: משום צערא דישראל. שצריך להשהות שם: בחמר עובד כוכבים. ואין בעל המשא שם ועל העובד כוכבים לטעון: מאי פסקת. וכי פסקת הדבר כן דכל בהמת עובד כוכבים הוי חמר עובד כוכבים וכל בהמת ישראל הוי חמר ישראל: שונא שאמרו. קס"ד שונא שאמרו אשונא דקרא קאי דמשתעי בפריקה כי תראה חמור שונאך רובץ וגומר: אשונא דמתניתין קאי. אהך מתניתא דלעיל דשונא לטעון הוא:

רובץ

---

מדברי שניהם נלמד צער בעלי חיים דאורייתא. וא"ת א"כ אמאי עוקרים על המלכים ולא מדרכי האמורי (ע"ז דף יא.) וי"ל משום דכבוד מלך ונשיא עדיף כמו בל תשחית דנדחה מפני כבודם דאונקלוס (ג) שרף על ר"ג ע' מנה צורי פ"ק דע"ז (שם) ועוד דכיון דכתיב את סוסיהם תעקר קל לדחות מפני המלך:

מי לא עסקינן דאדהכי והכי בטיל משוקיה. וא"ת מ"מ נדרוש ק"ו מטעינה דלית בה חסרון כיס וי"ל כיון דטעינה שיש בה חסרון כיס לא הוי בשכר דמ"ש מפריקה א"כ אף טעינה דלית בה חסרון כיס נמי הוי בחנם ופריקה נכתבה לדרוש שום דרשה אחרת:

מכלל דת"ק סבר דזקוק לו. המקשה סבור דת"ק נמי ידרוש משאו שהוא יכול לעמוד בו ושאינו יכול לעמוד בו נהי דאין חייב לסייע בחנם משום דלית ביה מצות פריקה מ"מ בשכר חייב לסייעו משום צער בעלי חיים וא"ת ולרבי יוסי הגלילי דסבר צער בעלי חיים לאו דאורייתא ואית ליה לקמן (דף לג.) דטעינה בשכר מ"ש טעינה מפריקה וי"ל דדריש ק"ו מחסרון כיס דלכתוב טעינה גרידא דיש טעינה שאין בו חסרון כיס וכ"ש פריקה אלא כתב פריקה לאגמורי דטעינה בשכר וכיון דטעינה שאין בה חסרון כיס הויא בשכר היכא דאית בה חסרון כיס נמי דהיינו היכא דבטיל משוקיה הוי בשכר דילפי' מטעינה דלית בה חסרון כיס והשתא לא בא להוכיח רק דצער בעלי חיים דאורייתא ולא לקיים שמכח ק"ו יש להוכיח דצער בעלי חיים דאורייתא דאפשר שק"ו הוי מחסרון כיס כדפרישית לר' יוסי וא"ת ודלמא זקוק לו מדרבנן וי"ל דכל הסוגיא מוכחת דאי צער בעלי חיים לאו דאורייתא אינו חייב לסייעו אפי' בשכר כדאמרינן בסמוך וכי ליתיה למריה בהדיה ליעבד גביה בשכר ולעולם צער בעלי חיים דאורייתא אבל אי הוי דרבנן פטור היה אפילו בשכר וכן בתר הכי דקאמר ואי אמרת לאו דאורייתא אמאי מטפל ביה ולישני מדרבנן:

ואי לאו דאורייתא אמאי מטפל בה. וא"ת והלא בספרי דורש שונאך אפילו שונא עובד כוכבים וי"ל דאסמכתא בעלמא היא דבערבי פסחים (פסחים דף קיג: ושם) מוקי בשונא ישראל:

ולהטעינה יין אסור אין זקוק לה. אבל שאר דברים זקוק ואפילו לטעון משום איבה: אמאי וחדלת. וא"ת ולישני בחנם אבל בשכר חייב ולעולם צער בעלי חיים דאורייתא וי"ל דוחדלת משמע לגמרי:

ואי בטעינה אמאי עזוב. וליכא למימר דבטיל משוקיה דאם כן רישא נמי:

לכוף יצרו. וא"ת כיון דבערבי פסחים (שם) מוקי לה בישראל שמותר לשנאותו כגון שראה בו דבר ערוה מה שייך בו לכוף יצרו וי"ל [א] דלא מיירי בשונא דקרא: מה לי שונא עובד כוכבים. ה"מ לשנויי ישראל בחנם ולעובד כוכבים בשכר:

מה

---

עין משפט
נר מצוה

קפ א מיי' פי"ג מהל' רוצח ושמירת נפש הל' א סמג עשין פא טוש"ע ח"מ סי' רעב סעיף א:
קפא ב ג מיי' שם הל' ט ועיין בכ"מ טוש"ע שם סעיף ט:
קפב ד מיי' שם טוש"ע שם סעיף ח:
קפג ה מיי' שם הל' יג ועיין בכ"מ טוש"ע שם סעיף ט בהג"ה:
קפד ו מיי' שם הל' ט ועיין בהל"ן טוש"ע שם סעיף ט:
קפה ז מיי' שם טוש"ע שם סעיף ח:
קפו ח מיי' שם הל' יג טוש"ע שם סעיף י:
קפז ט מיי' שם הל' יד טוש"ע שם סעיף יא:

רבינו חננאל

לפרוק בחנם ולא לטעון בחנם אלא בשכר. ר' שמעון אומר אף לטעון בחנם משום דלא מסיימי קראי איזהו לפרוק ואיזהו לטעון הילכך שניהם בחנם. אמר רבא מדברי שניהם נלמד צער בעלי חיים דאוריי' מדאמרי' פריקה דברי הכל בחנם: ר' יוסי הגלילי אומר אם הטעינו יותר ממשאו ונפל אין נזקק לו שנאמר תחת משאו משאוי שיכול לעמוד בו. בהמת עובד כוכבים מטפל בה כבהמת ישראל משום איבה. בהמת עובד כוכבים ועובד כוכבים מחמר אחריה ומשאוי של ישראל וצריך לטעון אין זקוק לו שנא' וחדלת. אבל ישראל מחמר אחרי בהמתו והמשאו לעובד כוכבים עזב תעזוב עמו. ומקשי' והא תרווייהו וחדלת עזב תעזב בפריקה הוא דכתיב ביה ואוקימנא כר' יוסי הגלילי דסבר צער בעלי חיים לאו דאורייתא. אוהב צריך לסייעו בפריקה והשונא צריך לסייעו בטעינה יניח האוהב ויסייע השונא כדי לכוף את יצרו לשלום. ופשוטה היא:

---

מסורת הש"ס

א) [שבת קכח:], ב) [צ"ל אלא הא מני], ג) [שבת קנד:], ד) [תוספתא פרק ב], ה) פסחים קיג: [תוספתא שם], ו) צ"ל דמתניתא.

הגהות הב"ח

(א) גמ' פטור לגמרי דלמא כצ"ל ואות ו' נמחק: (ב) רש"י ד"ה אי אמרת בשלמא לאו: (ג) תוס' ד"ה מדברי וכו' דאונקלוס הגר שרף:

הגהות הגר"א

[א] תוס' ד"ה לכוף. וי"ל כו'. נ"ב ר"ל דא"צ להקדים אבל מ"מ חייב כמש"ש:

תורה אור השלם

א) כִּי תִרְאֶה חֲמוֹר שֹׂנַאֲךָ רֹבֵץ תַּחַת מַשָּׂאוֹ וְחָדַלְתָּ מֵעֲזֹב לוֹ עָזֹב תַּעֲזֹב עִמּוֹ: [שמות כג, ה]

ליקוטי רש"י

צער בעלי חיים דאורייתא. שנאמר עזב תעזב עמו ואיכא מאן דדריש טעמא דקרא משום צער בעלי חיים באלו מציאות [שבת קכח:]. הלך וישב לו. הבעלים [לעיל ע"א].

does not view the suffering of animals to be a Biblical concern.

The Gemara refutes the proof:

לְעוֹלָם צַעַר בַּעֲלֵי חַיִּים דְּאוֹרַיְיתָא – **Really,** the Tanna may hold that the **suffering of living creatures is** a **Biblical** concern. הָתָם בִּטְעִינָה – Yet, **there,** in the case of the Baraisa, he does not require the Jew to help the idolater because the case was one in which **loading** was required.[26]

The Gemara challenges this reply:

אִי הָכִי – **If** it is **so,** that the Baraisa is referring to a case in which loading is required, אֵימָא סֵיפָא – **turn to the latter part of the Baraisa** which states: בֶּהֱמַת יִשְׂרָאֵל – If THE ANIMAL belongs TO A JEW, וּמַשּׂאוֹי עוֹבֵד כּוֹכָבִים – AND THE BURDEN that is on it belongs TO AN IDOLATER, "עָזֹב תַּעֲזֹב" – then we must apply the verse *YOU SHALL CERTAINLY HELP;* that is, you must assist with the burden. וְאִי בִּטְעִינָה – **Now, if** the Baraisa is truly dealing **with** a case in which **loading** is called for, אַמַּאי "עָזֹב תַּעֲזֹב" – **why** did the Baraisa rule that ***you shall certainly help?***[27] There should in fact be no obligation to help the idolater load the burden! – **?** –

The Gemara defends its explanation:

מִשּׁוּם צַעֲרָא דְיִשְׂרָאֵל – The reason the Baraisa ruled that *you shall certainly help* is **because of the anguish** experienced by the animal's **Jewish** owner when he must wait helplessly until his animal is loaded.[28]

The Gemara asks:

אִי הָכִי – **If** it is **so,** that we are concerned with the anguish of a Jew, אֲפִילוּ רֵישָׁא נָמִי – then **even** with regard to **the first case of the Baraisa,** in which the animal belonged to an idolater and the cargo belonged to a Jew, the Baraisa should have ruled that *you shall certainly help* him.[29] Why did the Baraisa rule instead that *you may refrain* from helping?

The Gemara answers:

רֵישָׁא – In **the first case of the Baraisa,** where the animal belonged to an idolater and the cargo belonged to a Jew, חַמָּר עוֹבֵד כּוֹכָבִים – the **donkey driver** was **an idolater,** and the Jewish owner of the cargo was not present.[30] סֵיפָא – In **the latter case of the Baraisa,** where the animal belonged to a Jew and the cargo belonged to an idolater, חַמָּר יִשְׂרָאֵל – the **donkey driver** was **a Jew.** It is thus understandable why, in the latter case the bystander must assist, and in the former case he need not assist.[31]

The Gemara challenges this way of construing the Baraisa:

מַאי פָּסְקַת – **Why do you assume** that when the animal belongs to an idolater, the donkey driver is an idolater, and when the animal belongs to a Jew, the donkey driver is a Jew?

The Gemara answers:

סְתָמָא דְּמִלְּתָא אִינִישׁ בָּתַר חֲמָרֵיהּ אָזִיל – **The general rule** is that **a person follows his donkey.**[32]

---

NOTES

does *not* hold the suffering of living creatures to be a Biblical concern. He must hold instead that the obligation to alleviate such suffering comes from Rabbinic law only, and the Rabbinic decree does not apply here, since the Jew is not the owner of the animal in distress (see *Tos. HaRosh,* cited above in note 15).

[*Tos. HaRosh* questions why the Tanna does not require the Jew to assist the idolater on the grounds that ignoring his plight would generate enmity (see above, note 21). He replies that, in this case, enmity is not a consideration, for since the cargo carried by the animal is owned by a Jew, the idolater will not feel that he had been discriminated against if the Jewish bystander does not load the cargo upon the animal (cf. *Rashba*).]

26. Until now it had been assumed that the Baraisa was speaking of a case in which the animal was lying down under its burden, and it needed to be unloaded in order to stand up. The Gemara now considers, however, that the Baraisa is instead speaking of a case in which the burden was on the ground and the animal was in need of reloading. In this case, the animal is not in distress, and the consideration of suffering would not be a factor. The fact that the Baraisa does not require the Jew to assist would thus not prove that suffering of animals is merely a Rabbinic concern.

The Gemara below will question this answer on the grounds that the word וְחָדַלְתָּ, which is used by the Baraisa to signify the lack of an obligation to assist, is written in the Torah with respect to unloading. It therefore seems impossible to maintain that the Baraisa refers to loading (*Rashi*).

27. The Gemara questions that if the Baraisa is speaking of a case in which טְעִינָה, *loading,* is called for, it would be impossible to understand why the Tanna obligates the bystander to assist the idolater when the animal bearing the burden belonged to a Jew. For since the load belongs to the idolater, the obligation of *loading* – which is stated only in reference to אָחִיךָ, *your brother* – should no longer apply! [The Gemara evidently takes the word אָחִיךָ to imply that both the animal and its burden must belong to a Jew in order for the Biblical obligations of טְעִינָה, *loading,* or פְּרִיקָה, *unloading,* to apply (see *Kesef Mishnah* to *Hil. Rotzeach Ushmiras Nefesh* 13:9).

It should be noted that the Gemara maintains that the Baraisa may indeed be understood if it is speaking of a case in which פְּרִיקָה, *unloading,* is called for. We would then assert that the suffering of living creatures is *not* a Biblical concern, and we would understand the Baraisa's two rulings as follows: When the animal belongs to the idolater and its cargo belongs to a Jew, the bystander need not assist the idolater in unloading packages from the animal, for the reasons described in note 18: There is no Biblical obligation of פְּרִיקָה when the animal belongs to an idolater, and the animal's suffering is not a factor when the animal belongs to someone else. When, however, the animal belongs to a Jew and its cargo belongs to an idolater, the Baraisa indeed requires the bystander to help unload. The reason for this is that although there is no *Biblical* obligation to help unload here (for the reasons that apply in the Baraisa's first case), there would nevertheless be an unrelated *Rabbinic* obligation to help unload, in order to prevent damage from coming to Jewish property (the Jew's animal could be injured if its load remains upon it, causing financial loss to its owner).

The above explanation follows *Tos. HaRosh.*

28. [It is assumed that Torah law obligates one to prevent the anguish of a Jew (see *Sma* 272:13). Accordingly, even though the cargo belongs to an idolater, the bystander would be obligated to load the animal and prevent the Jew from experiencing anguish.]

29. Here too, the Jewish owner of the cargo will experience anguish when he must wait for the cargo to be loaded.

30. Since the Jewish owner of the bundles is not present (*Rashi*), he experiences no anguish. Therefore, since the animal belongs to an idolater, and the one who is responsible for loading it is an idolater, there is no obligation upon the bystander to help him load. The Baraisa thus rules that *you may refrain* from helping.

31. In the latter case, the Jewish driver is responsible for loading the animal [and the idolater is not on hand to help load, but a bystander is]. Since the Jew experiences anguish when his bundle is not loaded, the Baraisa rules that that *you shall certainly help* him.

32. The Gemara concludes that there is reason to assume that when the owner of the donkey is an idolater so is the driver, and when the owner is a Jew so is the driver. This is so because, generally, it is the owner of the animal himself who walks behind the donkey and guides it. The Gemara has thus defended the notion that the Baraisa can be speaking of a case in which טְעִינָה, *loading,* is called for, for it has demonstrated why the two clauses of the Baraisa would set forth different rulings according to this view.

**In summary:** The Gemara was able to establish that the Tanna of the Baraisa could indeed hold that the suffering of living creatures is a Biblical concern. If the Tanna indeed holds this opinion, the Gemara concluded, the Baraisa must be dealing with a case of loading, not unloading. In respect to this case, the Baraisa's guidelines would be as follows: If a Jew would experience anguish if the bystander does not help him load, the bystander is obligated to help him load even if the animal or the cargo belongs to an idolater. If a Jew would not experience anguish, there is no obligation upon the bystander to help load [since enmity is not a concern here – see note 25,] unless both the animal and the cargo belong to a Jew. In this understanding, the bystander would

מדברי שניהם נלמד (א) צער בעלי חיים דאורייתא ואפי' ר"ש לא קאמר אלא משום דלא מסיימי קראי אבל מסיימי קראי דרשי' ק"ו משום מאי לאו משום צער בעלי חיים דרשינן דלמא משום דאיכא חסרון כיס וה"ק ומה טעינה דלית בה חסרון כיס חייב פריקה דאית בה חסרון כיס לא כ"ש וטעינה אין בה חסרון כיס מי לא עסקינן דאדהכי והכי בטיל משוקיה אי נמי אתו גנבי ושקלי כל מה דאיכא בהדיה תדע דצער בעלי חיים דאורייתא דקתני סיפא ר' יוסי הגלילי אומר אם היה עליו יתר [על] משאו אין זקוק לו שנאמר א) תחת משאו משאוי שיכול לעמוד בו לאו מכלל דת"ק סבר א זקוק לו מאי טעמא לאו משום דצער בעלי חיים דאורייתא דלמא בתחת משאו פליגי דרבי יוסי סבר דרשינן תחת משאו משאוי שיכול לעמוד בו ורבנן סברי לא דרשינן תחת משאו תדע דצער בעלי חיים לאו דאורייתא דקתני רישא הלך וישב לו ואמר לו הואיל ועליך מצוה לפרוק פרוק פטור שנאמר עמו ואי סלקא דעתך צער בעלי חיים דאורייתא מה לי איתיה למריה בהדיה ומה לי כי ליתיה למריה בהדיה לעולם צער בעלי חיים דאורייתא מי סברת פטור פטור לגמרי (א) ודלמא פטור בחנם וחייב בשכר וה"ק רחמנא כי איתיה למריה בהדיה עבד גביה בחנם וכי ליתיה למריה בהדיה עבד גביה בשכר ולעולם צער בעלי חיים דאורייתא (סימן בהמ"ת בהמ"ת אוה"ב שונ"א רבצ"ן) לימא מסייע ליה ב בהמת עובד כוכבים מטפל בה כבהמת ישראל אי אמרת בשלמא צער בעלי חיים דאורייתא משום הכי מטפל בה כבהמת ישראל אלא אי אמרת צער בעלי חיים לאו דאורייתא אמאי מטפל בה כבהמת ישראל התם ג משום איבה הכי נמי מסתברא דקתני אם היתה טעונה יין אסור אין זקוק לה אי אמרת בשלמא לאו דאורייתא משום הכי אין זקוק לה אלא אי אמרת דאורייתא אמאי אין זקוק לה ה"ק ולהטעינה יין אסור אין זקוק לה תא שמע ד בהמת עובד כוכבים ומשאוי ישראל וחדלת ואי אמרת צער בעלי חיים דאורייתא אמאי וחדלת עזב תעזב מבעי ליה ה לעולם צער בעלי חיים דאורייתא התם בטעינה אי הכי אימא סיפא ו בהמת ישראל ומשאוי עובד כוכבים עזב תעזב ואי בטעינה אמאי עזב תעזב משום צערא דישראל אי הכי אפילו רישא נמי רישא ז בחמר עובד כוכבים סיפא בחמר ישראל מאי פסקת סתמא דמלתא איניש בתר חמריה אזיל והא וחדלת ועזב תעזב בפריקה הוא דכתיבי ב) א"ל הא מני רבי יוסי הגלילי היא דאמר ג) צער בעלי חיים לאו דאורייתא ת"ש ד) ח אוהב לפרוק ושונא לטעון מצוה בשונא כדי לכוף את יצרו ואי סלקא דעתך צער בעלי חיים דאורייתא הא עדיף ליה אפ"ה כדי לכוף את יצרו עדיף ת"ש ה) ט שונא שאמרו שונא ישראל ולא שונא עובד כוכבים אי אמרת צער בעלי חיים דאורייתא מה לי שונא ישראל ומה לי שונא עובד כוכבים מי סברת אשונא דקרא קאי אשונא ו) דמתניתין קאי תא שמע

רובץ

מדברי שניהם. מדקאמרי תרווייהו פריקה עדיפא: ואפילו ר"ש לא קאמר. דאצטריך למכתב פריקה: אלא משום דלא מסיימי קראי. לטעינה: לאו משום צער בעלי חיים. והכי יליף מה טעינה דליכא צער בעלי חיים חייב פריקה דאיכא צער בעלי חיים לא כ"ש: מי לא עסקינן. וכי אין המקרא מדבר אף בהולך לסחורה דאדהכי בטיל משוקיה: תדע. דלרבנן דפליגי עליה דר"ש ולר"ש צער בעלי חיים דאורייתא: מכלל דת"ק. דרבי יוסי הגלילי רבנן ור"ש: זקוק לו. ואמאי זקוק לו אי משום מלות עזב תעזב הא כתיב משאו הראוי לו אלא משום צער בעלי חיים: לא דרשינן משאו. למשא הראוי לו דמשאו כל משא שעליו משמע: ותדע. דהכי הוא כדדחינא לך דצער בעלי חיים לאו דאורייתא: עביד גביה. משום צער בעלי חיים ועל כרחו יטול שכר: לימא מסייע ליה. לרבא דאמר לעיל צער בעלי חיים דאורייתא: מטפל בה. לפרוק משאה: אי אמרת (ב) לאו דאורייתא. וטעמא משום איבה הוא מש"ה אין זקוק לה שיכול להשמט ולומר דבר איסור הוא לנו: ה"ק ולהטעינה. ולעולם דאורייתא ורישא תנא מטפל בה בין בפריקה בין בטעינה פריקה משום צער בעלי חיים וטעינה משום איבה ולהטעינה יין אסור דלאו צערא איכא ולאו איבה איכא אין זקוק לה: התם בטעינה. לקמיה פריך הא בפריקה כתיב: משום צערא דישראל. שצריך להשהות שם: בחמר עובד כוכבים. ואין בעל המשא שם ועל העובד כוכבים לטעון: מאי פסקת. וכי פסקת הדבר כן דכל בהמת עובד כוכבים הוי חמר עובד כוכבים וכל בהמת ישראל הוי חמר ישראל: שונא שאמרו. קס"ד שונא שאמרו אשונא דקרא קאי דמשתעי בפריקה כי תראה חמור שונאך רובץ וגומר: אשונא דמתניתין קאי. אהך מתניתא דלעיל דשונא לטעון הוא:

רובץ

מדברי שניהם נלמד צער בעלי חיים דאורייתא. וא"ת א"כ אמאי עוקרים על המלכים ולא מדרכי האמורי (ע"ז דף יא.) וי"ל משום דכבוד מלך ונשיא עדיף כמו בל תשחית דנדחה מפני כבודם דאונקלוס (ג) שרף על ר"ג ע' מנה צורי פ"ק דע"ז (שם) ועוד דכיון דכתיב את סוסיהם תעקר קל לדחות מפני המלך:

מי לא עסקינן דאדהכי והכי בטיל משוקיה. וא"ת מ"מ נדרוש ק"ו מטעינה דלית בה חסרון כיס וי"ל כיון דטעינה שיש בה חסרון כיס לא הוי בשכר דמ"ש מפריקה א"כ אף טעינה דלית בה חסרון כיס נמי הוי בחנם ופריקה נכתבה לדרוש שום דרשה אחרת:

מכלל דת"ק סבר דזקוק לו. המקשה סבור דת"ק נמי ידרוש משאו שהוא יכול לעמוד בו ושאינו יכול לעמוד בו נהי דאין חייב לסייע בחנם משום דלית ביה מלות פריקה מ"מ בשכר חייב לסייעו משום צער בעלי חיים וא"ת ולרבי יוסי הגלילי דסבר צער בעלי חיים לאו דאורייתא ואית ליה לקמן (דף לג.) דטעינה בשכר מ"ש טעינה מפריקה וי"ל דדריש ק"ו מחסרון כיס דלכתוב טעינה גרידא דיש טעינה שאין בו חסרון כיס וכ"ש פריקה אלא כתב פריקה לאגמורי דטעינה בשכר וכיון דטעינה שאין בה חסרון כיס הויא בשכר היכא דאית בה חסרון כיס נמי דהיינו היכא דבטיל משוקיה הוי בשכר דילפי' מטעינה דלית בה חסרון כיס והשתא לא בא להוכיח רק לצער בעלי חיים דאורייתא ולא לקיים שמכח ק"ו יש להוכיח דלצער בעלי חיים דאורייתא דאפשר שק"ו הוי מחסרון כיס כדפרישית לר' יוסי וא"ת ודלמא זקוק לו מדרבנן וי"ל דכל הסוגיא מוכחת דאי צער בעלי חיים לאו דאורייתא אינו חייב לסייעו אפי' בשכר כדאמרינן בסמוך וכי ליתיה למריה בהדיה ליעבד גביה בשכר ולעולם צער בעלי חיים דאורייתא אבל אי הוי דרבנן פטור היה אפילו בשכר וכן בתר הכי דקאמר ואי אמרת לאו דאורייתא אמאי מטפל ביה וליתני מדרבנן:

ואי לאו דאורייתא אמאי מטפל בה. וא"ת והלא בספרי דורש שונאך אפילו שונא עובד כוכבים וי"ל דאסמכתא בעלמא היא דבערבי פסחים (פסחים דף קיג: ושם) מוקי בשונא ישראל:

ולהטעינה יין אסור אין זקוק לה. אבל שאר דברים זקוק ואפילו לטעון משום איבה: אמאי וחדלת. וא"ת וליתני בחנם אבל בשכר חייב ולעולם צער בעלי חיים דאורייתא וי"ל דוחדלת משמע לגמרי:

ואי בטעינה אמאי עזוב. וליכא למימר דבטיל משוקיה דאם כן רישא נמי:

לכוף יצרו. וא"ת כיון דבערבי פסחים (שם) מוקי לה בישראל שמותר לשנאותו כגון שראה בו דבר ערוה מה שייך בו לכוף יצרו וי"ל [א] דלא איירי בשונא דקרא: מה לי שונא עובד כוכבים. ה"מ לשנוי ישראל בחנם ולעובד כוכבים בשכר:

מה

## עין משפט נר מצוה

קפ א מיי' פי"ג מהל' רולח ושמירת נפש הל' א סמג עשין פא טוש"ע ח"מ סי' רעב סעיף א:
קפא ב ג מיי' שם הל' ט ועיין בכ"מ טוש"ע שם סעיף ט:
קפב ד מיי' שם טוש"ע שם סעיף ח:
קפג ה מיי' שם הל' יג ועיין בכ"מ טוש"ע שם סעיף ט בהג"ה:
קפד ו מיי' שם הל' ט ועיין בהג"ל טוש"ע שם סעיף ט:
קפה ז מיי' שם טוש"ע שם סעיף ח:
קפו ח מיי' שם הל' יג טוש"ע שם סעיף י:
קפז ט מיי' שם הל' יד טוש"ע שם סעיף יא:

## רבינו חננאל

לפרוק בחנם ולא לטעון בחנם אלא בשכר. ר' שמעון אומר אף לטעון בחנם משום דלא מסיימי קראי איזהו לפרוק ואיזהו לטעון הילכך שניהם בחנם. אמר רבא מדברי שניהם נלמד צער בעלי חיים דאוריי' מדאמרי' פריקה דברי הכל בחנם: ר' יוסי הגלילי אומר אם הטעינו יותר ממשאו ונפל אין נזקק לו שנאמר תחת משאו משאוי שיכול לעמוד בו. בהמת עובד כוכבים מטפל בה כבהמת ישראל משום איבה. בהמת עובד כוכבים ועובד כוכבים מחמר אחריה ומשאוי של ישראל וצריך לטעון אין זקוק לו שנא' וחדלת. אבל ישראל מחמר אחרי בהמתו והמשאו לעובד כוכבים עזב תעזוב עמו. ומקשי' והא תרוויהו וחדלת עזב תעזב בפריקה הוא דכתיב ביה ואוקימנא כר' יוסי הגלילי דסבר צער בעלי חיים לאו דאורייתא. אוהב צריך לסייעו בפריקה והשונא צריך לסייעו בטעינה יניח האוהב ויסייע השונא כדי לכוף את יצרו לשלום. ופשוטה היא:

## מסורת הש"ס

א) [שבת קכח:], ב) [ל"... אלא הא מני], ג) [שבת קנד:], ד) [תוספתא פרק ב], ה) פסחים קיג [תוספתא שם], ו) ל"... דמתניתא.

## הגהות הב"ח

(א) גמ' פטור לגמרי דלמא כצ"ל ואות ו' נמחק: (ב) רש"י ד"ה אי אמרת בשלמא לאו: (ג) תוס' ד"ה מדברי וכו' דאונקלוס הגר שרף:

## הגהות הגר"א

[א] תוס' ד"ה לכוף וי"ל כו'. נ"ב ר"ל דא"... להקדים אבל מ"מ חייב... כמש"ש:

## תורה אור השלם

א) כִּי תִרְאֶה חֲמוֹר שֹׂנַאֲךָ רֹבֵץ תַּחַת מַשָּׂאוֹ וְחָדַלְתָּ מֵעֲזֹב לוֹ עָזֹב תַּעֲזֹב עִמּוֹ: [שמות כג, ה]

## ליקוטי רש"י

צער בעלי חיים דאורייתא. שנאמר עזב תעזב עמו ואיכא מאן דדריש טעמא דקרא משום צער בעלי חיים באלו מציאות [שבת קכח:]. הלך וישב לו. הבעלים [לעיל ע"א].

The Baraisa states:

בְּהֶמַת עוֹבֵד כּוֹכָבִים מְטַפֵּל בָּהּ – ONE MUST TEND TO THE ANIMAL OF AN IDOLATER and unload it, כִּבְהֶמַת יִשְׂרָאֵל – JUST AS one must tend to THE ANIMAL OF A JEW. אִי אָמְרַת בִּשְׁלָמָא צַעַר בַּעֲלֵי חַיִּים דְּאוֹרַיְיתָא – Now, **this is understandable if you say** that the **suffering of living creatures is** a **Biblical** concern, מִשּׁוּם הָכִי מְטַפֵּל בָּהּ כִּבְהֶמַת יִשְׂרָאֵל – **for it follows** then that **he must tend to it as to the animal of a Jew.**[17] אֶלָּא אִי אָמְרַת צַעַר בַּעֲלֵי חַיִּים לָאו דְּאוֹרַיְיתָא – **But if you say** that the **suffering of living creatures is not** a **Biblical** concern, אַמַּאי מְטַפֵּל בָּהּ כִּבְהֶמַת יִשְׂרָאֵל – **why** would **he** be required to **tend to it as to the animal of a Jew?** Neither the specific command of unloading nor the general command to alleviate suffering would apply here![18] – ? –

The Gemara dismisses the proof:

הָתָם מִשּׁוּם אֵיבָה – In fact, it may be argued that the suffering of living creatures is *not* a Biblical concern. Yet, **there,** the Baraisa requires one to tend to the animal of an idolater **because of** the need to prevent **enmity.**[19]

The Gemara cites proof that this interpretation of the Baraisa is in fact correct:

הָכִי נַמִּי מִסְתַּבְּרָא – **This is indeed logical.** We may indeed assume that the the Baraisa obligates one to unload the animal only to prevent enmity. דְּקָתָנֵי – **For [the Baraisa] taught:** אִם הָיְתָה טְעוּנָה יֵין אָסוּר – IF [THE ANIMAL] WAS LADEN WITH FORBIDDEN WINE[20] אֵין זָקוּק לָהּ – HE IS NOT BOUND TO IT, i.e. he is not obligated to unload it. אִי אָמְרַת בִּשְׁלָמָא לָאו דְּאוֹרַיְיתָא – **It is understandable if you say** that the suffering of living creatures is **not** a **Biblical** concern, מִשּׁוּם הָכִי – **for it follows** then that אֵין זָקוּק לָהּ – **he is not bound to it.** For he would be obligated to unload an idolater's animal only to prevent enmity, which does not apply in this case.[21] אֶלָּא אִי אָמְרַת דְּאוֹרַיְיתָא – **However, if you say** that the suffering of living creatures is a **Biblical** concern, אַמַּאי אֵין זָקוּק לָהּ – **why** should **he not** be **bound to** relieve the suffering of **[the animal]?**[22]

The Gemara counters:

הָכִי קָאָמַר – In fact, the suffering of living creatures is a Biblical concern, yet the Baraisa is not difficult. For when it ruled that if the animal was laden with forbidden wine he is not bound to it, **this is what it** meant to **say:** וּלְהַטְעִינָהּ יֵין אָסוּר – **To load it with forbidden wine,** אֵין זָקוּק לָהּ – **he is not bound to it.** However, he would indeed be obligated to unload forbidden wine to relieve the animal of its suffering.[23]

The Gemara attempts to prove that the suffering of living creatures is not a Biblical concern:

תָּא שְׁמַע – **Come, learn** the proof to this from the following Baraisa: בְּהֶמַת עוֹבֵד כּוֹכָבִים – IF THE ANIMAL belongs TO AN IDOLATER, וּמַשָּׂאוֹי יִשְׂרָאֵל – AND THE BURDEN that is upon it belongs TO A JEW, "וְחָדַלְתָּ" – then we may apply the verse: *YOU MAY REFRAIN;* that is, you need not assist the idolater with the burden.[24] וְאִי אָמְרַת צַעַר בַּעֲלֵי חַיִּים דְּאוֹרַיְיתָא – **Now, if you say** that the **suffering of living creatures is** a **Biblical** concern, אַמַּאי "וְחָדַלְתָּ" – then **why** does the Baraisa rule that *you may refrain* from unloading the animal? "עָזֹב תַּעֲזֹב" מִבְּעֵי לֵיהּ – **[The Baraisa] should have** ruled instead that *you shall certainly help* unload the animal![25] Rather, it must be that this Tanna

NOTES

17. Since the animal is experiencing pain, he would be obligated to unload it, despite the fact that the owner is an idolater.

18. Since the verse regarding loading (*Deut.* 22:4) mentions the donkey of אָחִיךָ, *your brother*, it is clear that the obligations of טְעִינָה, *loading*, and פְּרִיקָה, *unloading,* do not apply to the animals of idolaters (*Tosafos,* as cited by *Ritva*). Furthermore, if the suffering of living creatures is not a Biblical concern, but rather a Rabbinic one, then one would not be obligated to aid anyone's animals but one's own (see *Tos. HaRosh,* cited above in note 15). Accordingly, there would be no obligation whatsoever to help unload the animal of an idolater.

19. [If Jews did not help idolaters with their needs, enmity between the groups might arise, thereby creating an unfavorable atmosphere for Jews.]

20. Wine which an idolater pours to his deity, known as *nesech* (*libation*) wine, is Biblically forbidden to Jews; it may not be drunk, nor may any benefit whatsoever be derived from it (see *Avodah Zarah* 29b). In addition to this, the Rabbis decreed that one may not even help an idolater move his forbidden wine (see Mishnah ibid. 62a).

21. Since moving the wine is prohibited (see previous note), the Jewish bystander can excuse himself to the idolater, without generating enmity, for not unloading it (the Jew can tell the idolater that the Jewish faith forbids him to handle such wine) (see *Ritva* ד״ה ה״נ מסתברא; cf. *Tos. HaRosh* ד״ה אלא אי אמרת). Thus, if the suffering of animals is not a Biblical concern, no imperative at all would obligate the Jew to unload the wine. He would not generate enmity by his refusal, and since the animal is not his own, he would not be subject to any Rabbinic injunction to be concerned with its welfare (see above, note 15).

22. Although helping the idolater move forbidden wine would usually be prohibited by Rabbinic decree, the Biblical commandment to relieve the animal of its pain would supersede the Rabbinic prohibition. Accordingly, he should be required to unload the animal (*Ritva;* cf. *Tos. HaRosh*). Since the Baraisa does not require him to unload the wine, it must hold that suffering of living creatures is not a Biblical concern.

23. The Gemara now suggests that the Tanna may indeed maintain that one is *Biblically* obligated to alleviate an animal's suffering. This is so, because the Baraisa can be interpreted as follows:

In its first clause, the Baraisa teaches that one must assist an idolater with his animal just as he would assist a fellow Jew. We would understand this part of the Baraisa as referring to both *unloading* the burden from an animal and to *loading* a burden on to an animal. In the former case, the Biblical requirement to alleviate an animal's suffering obligates the Jew to assist. In the latter case, however, his obligation to assist stems only from the Rabbinic decree to prevent enmity, since the animal itself is not in distress.

The end of the Baraisa now qualifies this last ruling. It states that when the merchandise in question was forbidden wine, the Jew is not required to help the idolater load *at all.* The reason for this is that, here, neither of the above considerations applies: The animal suffers no pain if its burden remains strewn on the ground, hence, the consideration of suffering is not a factor; and furthermore, the Jew can explain to the idolater that his religion prohibits him to handle wine used for idolatry – hence, the consideration of enmity is not a factor. The Baraisa thus rules that the Jew need not load the wine onto the idolater's animal (*Rashi*). [According to this reading, the one case the Baraisa does not address is where the idolater's animal is carrying a burden of forbidden wine, and is in need of *unloading.* In such a case the law would be that the Jew must assist the idolater, for the Biblical command to relieve the animal of its suffering would supersede the Rabbinic prohibition (see above).]

24. The Gemara presently understands the Baraisa as dealing with a situation in which *unloading* would be called for (e.g. the animal is lying down under its burden).

The term וְחָדַלְתָּ, which is rendered here as *you may refrain,* has its origins in the verse that speaks of *unloading* (*Exodus* 23:5; see 32a note 12). In that verse, the word וְחָדַלְתָּ actually serves as a rhetorical question – *shall you refrain*? [*No!*] *You shall certainly help with him.* The Gemara, however, understands that the verse can also be saying that there are indeed times when *you may refrain* from helping. [This is similar to the Gemara's interpretation (30a) that the word וְהִתְעַלַּמְתָּ teaches that there are indeed times that *you may hide,* refraining from picking up and returning a lost object (see 30a note 23) (*Shitah Mekubetzes* ד״ה ואם תאמר כיון and ד״ה ואם תאמר הא).]

25. Although the specific command of פְּרִיקָה, *unloading,* does not apply with respect to an animal owned by an idolater (see above, note 18), one should nevertheless be required to take the packages off the animal to alleviate its suffering if the suffering of living creatures is a Biblical concern. Rather, from the fact that the Baraisa does not require the Jew to assist (even in return for payment), we can surmise that the Tanna

## עין משפט נר מצוה

קפ א מיי׳ פי״ג מהל׳ רולח ושמירת נפש הל׳ א סמג עשין פא טוש״ע ח״מ סי׳ רעב סעיף א:
קפא ב ג מיי׳ שם הל׳ ט ועיין בכ״מ טוש״ע שם סעיף ט:
קפב ד מיי׳ שם טוש״ע שם סעיף ח:
קפג ה מיי׳ שם הל׳ יג ועיין בכ״מ טוש״ע שם סעיף ט בהג״ה:
קפד ו מיי׳ שם הל׳ ט ועיין בהג״ל טוש״ע שם סעיף ט:
קפה ז מיי׳ שם טוש״ע שם סעיף ח:
קפו ח מיי׳ שם הל׳ יג טוש״ע שם סעיף י:
קפז ט מיי׳ שם הל׳ יד טוש״ע שם סעיף יא:

## רבינו חננאל

לפרוק בחנם ולא לטעון בחנם אלא בשכר. ר׳ שמעון אומר אף לטעון בחנם משום דלא מסיימי קראי איזהו לפרוק ואיזהו לטעון הילכך שניהם בחנם. אמר רבא מדברי שניהם נלמד צער בעלי חיים דאוריי׳ מדאמרי׳ פריקה דברי הכל בחנם: ר׳ יוסי הגלילי אומר אם הטעינו יותר ממשאו ונפל אין נזקק לו שנאמר תחת משאו משאוי שיכול לעמוד בו. בהמת עובד כוכבים מטפל בה כבהמת ישראל משום איבה. בהמת עובד כוכבים ועובד כוכבים מחמר אחריה ומשאוי של ישראל וצריך לטעון אין זקוק לו שנא׳ וחדלת. אבל ישראל מחמר אחרי בהמתו והמשאו לעובד כוכבים עזב תעזוב עמו. ומקשי׳ והא תרווייהו וחדלת עזב תעזוב בפריקה הוא דכתיב ביה ואוקימנא כר׳ יוסי הגלילי דסבר צער בעלי חיים לאו דאורייתא. אוהב צריך לסייעו בפריקה והשונא צריך לסייעו בטעינה יניח האוהב ויסייע השונא כדי לכוף את יצרו לשלום. ופשוטה היא:

## גמרא

מדברי שניהם נלמד [א] צער בעלי חיים דאורייתא ואפי׳ ר״ש לא קאמר אלא משום דלא מסיימי קראי אבל מסיימי קראי דרשי׳ ק״ו משום מאי לאו משום צער בעלי חיים דרשינן דלמא משום דאיכא חסרון כיס וה״ק ומה טעינה דלית בה חסרון כיס חייב פריקה דאית בה חסרון כיס לא כ״ש וטעינה אין בה חסרון כיס מי לא עסקינן דאדהכי והכי בטיל משוקיה אי נמי אתו גנבי ושקלי כל מה דאיכא בהדיה תדע דצער בעלי חיים דאורייתא דקתני סיפא ר׳ יוסי הגלילי אומר אם היה עליו יתר [על] משאו אין זקוק לו שנאמר [א] תחת משאו משאוי שיכול לעמוד בו לאו מכלל דת״ק סבר [א] זקוק לו מאי טעמא לאו משום דצער בעלי חיים דאורייתא דלמא בתחת משאו פליגי דרבי יוסי סבר דרשינן תחת משאו משאוי שיכול לעמוד בו ורבנן סברי לא דרשינן תחת משאו תדע דצער בעלי חיים לאו דאורייתא דקתני רישא הלך וישב לו ואמר לו הואיל ועליך מצוה לפרוק פרוק פטור שנאמר עמו ואי סלקא דעתך צער בעלי חיים דאורייתא מה לי איתיה למריה בהדיה ומה לי כי ליתיה למריה בהדיה לעולם צער בעלי חיים דאורייתא מי סברת פטור פטור לגמרי (א) ודלמא פטור בחנם וחייב בשכר וה״ק רחמנא כי איתיה למריה בהדיה עבד גביה בחנם וכי ליתיה למריה בהדיה עבד גביה בשכר ולעולם צער בעלי חיים דאורייתא (סימ״ן בהמ״ת אוה״ב שונ״א רבצ״ן) לימא מסייע ליה [ב] בהמת עובד כוכבים מטפל בה כבהמת ישראל אי אמרת בשלמא צער בעלי חיים דאורייתא משום הכי מטפל בה כבהמת ישראל אלא אי אמרת צער בעלי חיים לאו דאורייתא אמאי מטפל בה כבהמת ישראל התם [ג] משום איבה הכי נמי מסתברא דקתני אם היתה טעונה יין אסור אין זקוק לה אי אמרת בשלמא לאו דאורייתא משום הכי אין זקוק לה אלא אי אמרת דאורייתא אמאי אין זקוק לה ה״ק ולהטעינה יין אסור אין זקוק לה תא שמע [ד] בהמת עובד כוכבים ומשאוי ישראל וחדלת ואי אמרת צער בעלי חיים דאורייתא אמאי וחדלת עזב תעזוב מבעי ליה [ה] לעולם צער בעלי חיים דאורייתא התם בטעינה אי הכי אימא סיפא [ו] בהמת ישראל ומשאוי עובד כוכבים עזב תעזוב ואי בטעינה אמאי עזב תעזוב משום צערא דישראל אי הכי אפילו רישא נמי רישא [ז] בחמר עובד כוכבים סיפא בחמר ישראל מאי פסקת סתמא דמלתא איניש בתר חמריה אזיל והא וחדלת ועזב תעזוב בפריקה הוא דכתיבי (ב) א״ל הא מני רבי יוסי הגלילי היא דאמר (ג) צער בעלי חיים לאו דאורייתא ת״ש (ד) [ח] אוהב לפרוק ושונא לטעון מצוה בשונא כדי לכוף את יצרו ואי סלקא דעתך צער בעלי חיים דאורייתא הא עדיף ליה אפ״ה כדי לכוף את יצרו עדיף ת״ש (ה) [ט] שונא שאמרו שונא ישראל ולא שונא עובד כוכבים אי אמרת צער בעלי חיים דאורייתא מה לי שונא ישראל ומה לי שונא עובד כוכבים מי סברת אשונא דקרא קאי אשונא [י] דמתניתין קאי תא שמע

רובץ

## רש״י

מדברי שניהם. מדקאמרי תרווייהו פריקה עדיפא: ואפילו ר״ש לא קאמר. דאצטריך למכתב פריקה: אלא משום דלא מסיימי קראי. לטעינה: לאו משום צער בעלי חיים. והכי יליף מה טעינה דליכא צער בעלי חיים חייב פריקה דאיכא צער בעלי חיים לא כ״ש: מי לא עסקינן. וכי אין המקרא מדבר אף בהולך לסחורה דאדהכי בטיל משוקיה: תדע. דלרבנן דפליגי עליה דר״ש ולר״ש צער בעלי חיים דאורייתא: מכלל דת״ק. דרבי יוסי הגלילי רבנן ור״ש: זקוק לו. ואמאי זקוק לו אי משום מצות עזב תעזב הא כתיב משאו הראוי לו אלא משום צער בעלי חיים: לא דרשינן משאו. למשא הראוי לו דמשאו כל משא שעליו משמע: ותדע. דהכי הוא כדדחינא לך דצער בעלי חיים לאו דאורייתא: עביד גביה. משום צער בעלי חיים ועל כורחו יטול שכר: לימא מסייע ליה. לרבא דאמר לעיל צער בעלי חיים דאורייתא: מטפל בה. לפרוק משאה: אי אמרת (ב) לאו דאורייתא. וטעמא משום איבה הוא מש״ה אין זקוק לה שיכול להשמט ולומר דבר איסור הוא לנו: ה״ק ולהטעינה. ולעולם דאורייתא ורישא תנא מטפל בה בין בפריקה בין בטעינה פריקה משום צער בעלי חיים וטעינה משום איבה ולהטעינה יין אסור דלאו צערא איכא ולאו איבה איכא אין זקוק לה: התם בטעינה. לקמיה פריך הא בפריקה כתיב: משום צערא דישראל. שצריך להשהות שם: בחמר עובד כוכבים. ואין בעל המשא שם ועל העובד כוכבים לטעון: מאי פסקת. וכי פסקת הדבר כן דכל בהמת עובד כוכבים הוי חמר עובד כוכבים וכל בהמת ישראל הוי חמר ישראל: שונא שאמרו. קס״ד שונא שאמרו אשונא דקרא קאי דמשתעי בפריקה כי תראה חמור שונאך רובץ וגומר: אשונא דמתניתין קאי. אהך מתניתא דלעיל דשונא לטעון הוא:

רובץ

## תוספות

**מדברי** שניהם נלמד צער בעלי חיים דאורייתא. וא״ת א״כ אמאי עוקרים על המלכים ולא מדרכי האמורי (ע״ז דף יא.) וי״ל משום דכבוד מלך ונשיא עדיף כמו בל תשחית דנדחה מפני כבודם דאונקלוס (ג) שרף על ר״ג ע׳ מנה צורי פ״ק דע״ז (שם) ועוד דכיון דכתיב את סוסיהם תעקר קל לדחות מפני המלך:

**מי** לא עסקינן דאדהכי והכי בטיל משוקיה. וא״ת מ״מ נדרוש ק״ו מטעינה דלית בה חסרון כיס וי״ל כיון דטעינה שיש בה חסרון כיס לא הוי בשכר דמ״ש מפריקה א״כ אף טעינה דלית בה חסרון כיס נמי הוי בחנם ופריקה נכתבה לדרוש שום דרשה אחרת:

**מכלל** דת״ק סבר דזקוק לו. המקשה סבור דת״ק נמי ידרוש משאו שהוא יכול לעמוד בו ושאינו יכול לעמוד בו נהי דאין חייב לסייע בחנם משום דלית ביה מצות פריקה מ״מ בשכר חייב לסייעו משום צער בעלי חיים וא״ת ולרבי יוסי הגלילי דסבר צער בעלי חיים לאו דאורייתא ואית ליה לקמן (דף לג.) דטעינה בשכר מ״ש טעינה מפריקה וי״ל דדריש ק״ו מחסרון כיס דלכתוב טעינה גרידא דיש טעינה שאין בו חסרון כיס וכ״ש פריקה אלא כתב פריקה לאגמורי דטעינה בשכר וכיון דטעינה שאין בה חסרון כיס הויא בשכר היכא דאית בה חסרון כיס נמי דהיינו היכא דבטיל משוקיה הוי בשכר דילפי׳ מטעינה דלית בה חסרון כיס והשתא לא בא להוכיח רק דצער בעלי חיים דאורייתא ולא לקיים שמכח ק״ו יש להוכיח דצער בעלי חיים דאורייתא דאפשר שק״ו הוי מחסרון כיס כדפרישית לר׳ יוסי וא״ת ודלמא זקוק לו מדרבנן וי״ל דכל הסוגיא מוכחת דאי צער בעלי חיים לאו דאורייתא אינו חייב לסייעו אפי׳ בשכר כדאמרינן בסמוך וכי ליתיה למריה בהדיה ליעבד גביה בשכר ולעולם צער בעלי חיים דאורייתא אבל אי הוי דרבנן פטור היה אפילו בשכר וכן בתר הכי דקאמר ואי אמרת לאו דאורייתא אמאי מטפל ביה ולישני מדרבנן:

**ואי** לאו דאורייתא אמאי מטפל בה. וא״ת והלא בספרי דורש שונאך אפילו שונא עובד כוכבים וי״ל דאסמכתא בעלמא היא דבערבי פסחים (פסחים דף קיג: ושם) מוקי בשונא ישראל:

**ולהטעינה** יין אסור אין זקוק לה. אבל שאר דברים זקוק ואפילו לטעון משום איבה: **אמאי** וחדלת. וא״ת ולישני בחנם אבל בשכר חייב ולעולם צער בעלי חיים דאורייתא וי״ל דוחדלת משמע לגמרי:

**ואי** בטעינה אמאי עזוב. וליכא למימר דבטיל משוקיה דאם כן רישא נמי:

**לכוף** יצרו. וא״ת כיון דבערבי פסחים (שם) מוקי לה בישראל שמותר לשנאותו כגון שראה בו דבר ערוה מה שייך בו לכוף יצרו וי״ל [א] דלא מיירי בשונא דקרא: **מה** לי שונא עובד כוכבים. ה״מ לשנויי ישראל בחנם ולעובד כוכבים בשכר:

מה

## מסורת הש״ס

א) [שבת קכח:], ב) [ל״ל אלא הא מני], ג) [שבת קנד:], ד) [תוספתא פרק ב], ה) פסחים קיג:, [תוספתא שם], ו) ל״ל דמתניתא.

## הגהות הב״ח

(א) גמ׳ פטור לגמרי דלמא כצ״ל ואות ו׳ נמחק: (ב) רש״י ד״ה אי אמרת בשלמא לאו: (ג) תום׳ ד״ה מדברי וכו׳ דאונקלוס הגר שרף:

## הגהות הגר״א

[א] תוס׳ ד״ה לכוף. וי״ל כו׳. נ״ב ר״ל דא״צ להקדים אבל מ״מ חייב כמש״ש:

## תורה אור השלם

א) כִּי תִרְאֶה חֲמוֹר שֹׂנַאֲךָ רֹבֵץ תַּחַת מַשָּׂאוֹ וְחָדַלְתָּ מֵעֲזֹב לוֹ עָזֹב תַּעֲזֹב עִמּוֹ: [שמות כג, ה]

## ליקוטי רש״י

צער בעלי חיים דאורייתא. שנאמר עזב תעזב עמו ואיכא מאן דדריש טעמא דקרא משום צער בעלי חיים באלו מציאות [שבת קכח:]. הלך וישב לו. הבעלים [לעיל ע״א].

Rabbis and R' Shimon] dispute R' Yose HaGlili on this point; do they not **hold** that even when the owner overloaded the animal, **זָקוּק לוֹ – [the bystander] is bound to** help **him?** This is apparently so.[11] **מַאי טַעְמָא – What,** then, is their **reasoning?**[12] **לָאו מִשּׁוּם דְּצַעַר בַּעֲלֵי חַיִּים דְּאוֹרַיְיתָא – Is it not because** they hold that the **suffering of living creatures is** a **Biblical** concern?[13]

The Gemara dismisses the proof:

**דִּלְמָא – Perhaps** all agree that the suffering of living creatures is not a Biblical concern, **וּבְ"תַחַת מַשָּׂאוֹ" פְּלִיגֵי – and [the Rabbis and R' Yose] argue** only **with respect to** the correct interpretation of the words ***under its burden.*** **דְּרַבִּי יוֹסֵי סָבַר דָּרְשִׁינַן "תַּחַת מַשָּׂאוֹ" – That is, R' Yose HaGlili holds** that **we expound** ***under its burden*** as referring to **מַשָּׂאוֹי שֶׁיָּכוֹל לַעֲמוֹד בּוֹ – a burden under which [the animal] can stand;** hence, he exempts the bystander from helping when the load is oversized. **וְרַבָּנָן סָבְרֵי לָא דָּרְשִׁינַן "תַּחַת מַשָּׂאוֹ" – And the Rabbis** (and R' Shimon) **hold** that **we do not expound** ***under its burden*** as referring to a load under which it can stand; hence, the bystander is indeed obligated to unload an animal even if the owner overloaded it.[14] The position of the Rabbis and R' Shimon can thus be understood even if they do not hold the suffering of living creatures to be a Biblical concern.

The Gemara supports this interpretation of the Rabbis' and R' Shimon's position:

**תֵּדַע דְּצַעַר בַּעֲלֵי חַיִּים לָאו דְּאוֹרַיְיתָא – Know** that all agree that the **suffering of living creatures is not** a **Biblical** concern, **דְּקָתָנֵי רֵישָׁא – for the beginning of the Mishnah taught** that **הָלַךְ וְיָשַׁב לוֹ – if** [THE OWNER] impudently **WALKED AWAY AND SAT DOWN, וְאָמַר לוֹ – SAYING TO** [THE BYSTANDER]: **הוֹאִיל וְעָלֶיךָ מִצְוָה לִפְרוֹק – "SINCE THE COMMANDMENT** to unload my animal **IS** incumbent **UPON YOU, פְּרוֹק – UNLOAD** it by yourself but I shall not help," **פָּטוּר – [THE BYSTANDER] IS EXEMPT** from unloading the animal, **שֶׁנֶּאֱמַר – FOR IT STATED: "עִמּוֹ" –** ***You shall help*** **WITH HIM,** implying that you must help only if the owner is prepared to join you. **וְאִי סָלְקָא דַּעְתָּךְ צַעַר בַּעֲלֵי חַיִּים דְּאוֹרַיְיתָא – Now, if you were to consider** that the **suffering of living creatures is** a **Biblical** concern, **מָה לִי אִיתֵיהּ לְמָרֵיהּ בַּהֲדֵיהּ – what does it matter to me whether the owner is** unloading along **with him, וּמָה לִי כִּי לֵיתֵיהּ לְמָרֵיהּ בַּהֲדֵיהּ – or whether the owner is not** unloading along **with him?** In either case, the bystander should be obligated to unload, in order to relieve the animal of its suffering![15]

The Gemara rejects the proof:

**לְעוֹלָם צַעַר בַּעֲלֵי חַיִּים דְּאוֹרַיְיתָא –** One can argue that **really,** the **suffering of living creatures is** a **Biblical** concern. **מִי סָבְרַתְּ פָּטוּר פָּטוּר לְגַמְרֵי – For can you assume** that when the Mishnah rules that **[the bystander] is exempt,** it means that **he is completely exempt? וְדִלְמָא פָּטוּר בְּחִנָּם וְחַיָּיב בְּשָׂכָר – Perhaps** it means instead that **he is exempt** from unloading **for free, but he is** indeed **obligated** to help unload **for payment. וְהָכִי קָאָמַר רַחֲמָנָא –** In effect, then, **this is what the Merciful One** would be **saying** in His Torah: **כִּי אִיתֵיהּ לְמָרֵיהּ בַּהֲדֵיהּ – When the owner is** unloading along **with [the bystander], עָבֵד גַּבֵּיהּ בְּחִנָּם – [this bystander]** must **work alongside him for free; וְכִי לֵיתֵיהּ לְמָרֵיהּ בַּהֲדֵיהּ – and when the owner is not** unloading along **with him, עָבֵד גַּבֵּיהּ בְּשָׂכָר – [the bystander]** must still **work for him,** but he may demand **payment** for his efforts.[16] **לְעוֹלָם צַעַר בַּעֲלֵי חַיִּים דְּאוֹרַיְיתָא – Really,** then, it may be that all agree (with the exception of R' Yose HaGlili) that the **suffering of living creatures is** a **Biblical** concern.

The Gemara provides a mnemonic for the ensuing discussions: **(סימן) (A mnemonic:)** (בהמ"ת בהמ"ת אוה"ב שונ"א רבצ"ן) – **Animal, animal, friend, enemy, habitually lying down.)**

The Gemara continues its discussion of whether or not the suffering of living creatures is a Biblical concern:

**לֵימָא מְסַיֵּיעַ לֵיהּ – Say** that the following Baraisa **supports [Rava]** who stated above that the suffering of living creatures is a Biblical concern.

NOTES

11. [Since the Mishnah attributes R' Yose HaGlili's statement to him specifically, it is implied that the Tannaim mentioned previously dispute his point.]

12. I.e. why, indeed, would the Rabbis maintain that the bystander must assist in this case? Not because of the general command to help unload an animal, for this does not apply when the animal was overloaded (for the verse uses the word מַשָּׂאוֹ, implying that the obligation of unloading applies only when the burden was one that the beast could carry). It must be, then, that the Rabbis require the bystander to assist here on the basis of a different principle (*Rashi*).

13. See previous note. The only conceivable explanation for the Rabbis' ruling is that they hold that there exists a Biblical imperative to alleviate the suffering of animals. Therefore, although the verse does specify מַשָּׂאוֹ, *its burden,* this merely exempts the bystander from the direct command of עָזֹב תַּעֲזֹב, *help, you shall help,* specified in this verse. The bystander would still be required to unload the oversized burden, however, for a different reason – to fulfill the Biblical requirement of alleviating an animal's suffering (*Rashi*; cf. *Ritva*).

*Tosafos* adds that the Gemara now believes that the Rabbis would permit the bystander to demand payment for his help in unloading the oversized burden. Even though a bystander is generally required to help unload for free, this applies only when he is subject to the specific command of פְּרִיקָה, *unloading,* mandated by *Exodus* 23:5 (see 32a note 12). Since in this case he is exempt from this law (it is only the *general requirement* to alleviate an animal's pain that requires him to assist), he may take payment for his actions.

See below, note 15, for an explanation of R' Yose HaGlili's position.

14. According to the Rabbis, מַשָּׂאוֹ, *its burden,* is interpreted as referring to any load that is upon the animal, not necessarily under which it can stand (*Rashi*). Accordingly, the Rabbis could hold that there is no general Biblical imperative to alleviate the suffering of an animal. There is only a specific obligation to help unload an animal's burden – and this obligation applies no matter what the size of the burden.

15. Rather, since the Mishnah does *not* obligate him to unload when the owner does not help him, it must hold that the suffering of living creatures is not a Biblical concern.

Even if the suffering of living creatures is not a Biblical concern, it would indeed still be a concern, albeit of a Rabbinic nature (see 33a). The Gemara clearly assumes, however, that a mere Rabbinic injunction to alleviate suffering would not, in this case, be sufficient grounds to require a bystander to unload another's animal. The reason for this, *Tos. HaRosh* suggests, is that the Rabbinic decree would not have required a person to inconvenience himself to alleviate the pain of *someone else's* animal. Rather, the decree would merely obligate each individual to see to it that *his own* animal does not suffer. (This would also explain why R' Yose HaGlili maintains that a bystander need not help unload if the burden was too large for the beast that was carrying it. Although R' Yose HaGlili would agree that there is at least a Rabbinic obligation to alleviate an animal's pain, he would assert that the bystander is not subject to this obligation, since he is not the owner of the animal.)

16. That is, the bystander must unload the animal alone, and the owner is legally bound to pay him for his work (*Toras Chaim* ד"ה ומה לי).

As the Gemara set forth above, the verse mandating פְּרִיקָה, *unloading,* requires a bystander to help unload for free. In this case, however, the bystander is not subject to the specific Torah command obligating פְּרִיקָה, *unloading,* for the animal's owner has refused to assist him in unloading the beast. He is thus required to unload only because of the general Biblical command to alleviate the suffering – and since this command does not mandate that one must come to the assistance of another person's animal *for free,* the bystander may demand payment for his services (see *Rashi;* see also *Rosh* §30).

מדברי שניהם נלמד [א] צער בעלי חיים דאורייתא ואפי' ר"ש לא קאמר אלא משום דלא מסיימי קראי אבל מסיימי קראי דרשי' ק"ו משום מאי לאו משום צער בעלי חיים דרשינן דלמא משום דאיכא חסרון כיס וה"ק ומה טעינה דלית בה חסרון כיס חייב פריקה דאית בה חסרון כיס לא כ"ש וטעינה אין בה חסרון כיס מי לא עסקינן דאדהכי והכי בטיל משוקיה אי נמי אתו גנבי ושקלי כל מה דאיכא בהדיה תדע דצער בעלי חיים דאורייתא דקתני סיפא ר' יוסי הגלילי אומר אם היה עליו יתר [על] משאו אין זקוק לו שנאמר א) תחת משאו משאוי שיכול לעמוד בו לאו מכלל דת"ק סבר א זקוק לו מאי טעמא לאו משום דצער בעלי חיים דאורייתא דלמא בתחת משאו פליגי דרבי יוסי סבר דרשינן תחת משאו משאוי שיכול לעמוד בו ורבנן סברי לא דרשינן תחת משאו תדע דצער בעלי חיים לאו דאורייתא דקתני רישא הלך וישב לו ואמר לו הואיל ועליך מצוה לפרוק פרוק פטור שנאמר עמו ואי סלקא דעתך צער בעלי חיים דאורייתא מה לי איתיה למריה בהדיה ומה לי כי ליתיה למריה בהדיה לעולם צער בעלי חיים דאורייתא מי סברת פטור פטור לגמרי (א) ודלמא פטור בחנם וחייב בשכר וה"ק רחמנא כי איתיה למריה בהדיה עבד גביה בחנם וכי ליתיה למריה בהדיה עבד גביה בשכר ולעולם צער בעלי חיים דאורייתא (סימ"ן בהמ"ת בהמ"ת אוה"ב שונ"א רבצ"ן) לימא מסייע ליה ב בהמת עובד כוכבים מטפל בה כבהמת ישראל אי אמרת בשלמא צער בעלי חיים דאורייתא משום הכי מטפל בה כבהמת ישראל אלא אי אמרת צער בעלי חיים לאו דאורייתא אמאי מטפל בה כבהמת ישראל התם ג משום איבה הכי נמי מסתברא דקתני אם היתה טעונה יין אסור אין זקוק לה אי אמרת בשלמא לאו דאורייתא משום הכי אין זקוק לה אלא אי אמרת דאורייתא אמאי אין זקוק לה ה"ק ולהטעינה יין אסור אין זקוק לה תא שמע ד בהמת עובד כוכבים ומשאוי ישראל וחדלת ואי אמרת צער בעלי חיים דאורייתא אמאי וחדלת עזב תעזב מבעי ליה ה לעולם צער בעלי חיים דאורייתא התם בטעינה אי הכי אימא סיפא ו בהמת ישראל ומשאוי עובד כוכבים עזב תעזב ואי בטעינה אמאי עזב תעזב משום צערא דישראל אי הכי אפילו רישא נמי רישא ז בחמר עובד כוכבים סיפא בחמר ישראל מאי פסקת סתמא דמלתא איניש בתר חמריה אזיל והא וחדלת ועזב תעזב בפריקה הוא דכתיבי ב) א"ל הא מני רבי יוסי הגלילי היא דאמר ג) צער בעלי חיים לאו דאורייתא ת"ש ד) ח אוהב לפרוק ושונא לטעון מצוה בשונא כדי לכוף את יצרו ואי סלקא דעתך צער בעלי חיים דאורייתא הא עדיף ליה אפ"ה כדי לכוף את יצרו עדיף ת"ש ה) ט שונא שאמרו שונא ישראל ולא שונא עובד כוכבים אי אמרת צער בעלי חיים דאורייתא מה לי שונא ישראל ומה לי שונא עובד כוכבים מי סברת אשונא דקרא קאי אשונא ו) דמתניתין קאי תא שמע

רובץ

---

**רש"י**

מדברי שניהם. מדקאמרי תרווייהו פריקה עדיפא: ואפילו ר"ש לא קאמר. דאצטריך למכתב פריקה: אלא משום דלא מסיימי קראי. לטעינה: לאו משום צער בעלי חיים. והכי יליף מה טעינה דליכא צער בעלי חיים חייב פריקה דאיכא צער בעלי חיים לא כ"ש: מי לא עסקינן. וכי אין המקרא מדבר אף בהולך לסחורה דאדהכי בטיל משוקיה: תדע. דלרבנן דפליגי עליה דר"ש ולר"ש צער בעלי חיים דאורייתא: מכלל דת"ק. דרבי יוסי הגלילי רבנן ור"ש: זקוק לו. ואמאי זקוק לו אי משום מצות עזב תעזב הא כתיב משאו הראוי לו אלא משום צער בעלי חיים: לא דרשינן משאו. למשא הראוי לו דמשאו כל משא שעליו משמע: ותדע. דהכי הוא כדדחינא לך דצער בעלי חיים לאו דאורייתא: עביד גביה. משום צער בעלי חיים ועל כורחו יטול שכר: לימא מסייע ליה. לרבא דאמר לעיל צער בעלי חיים דאורייתא: מטפל בה. לפרוק משאה: אי אמרת (ב) לאו דאורייתא. וטעמא משום איבה הוא מש"ה אין זקוק לה שיכול להשמט ולומר דבר איסור הוא לנו: ה"ק ולהטעינה. ולעולם דאורייתא ורישא תנא מטפל בה בין בפריקה בין בטעינה פריקה משום צער בעלי חיים וטעינה משום איבה ולהטעינה יין אסור דלאו צערא איכא ולאו איבה איכא אין זקוק לה: התם בטעינה. לקמיה פריך הא בפריקה כתיב: משום צערא דישראל. שצריך להשהות שם: בחמר עובד כוכבים. ואין בעל המשא שם ועל העובד כוכבים לטעון: מאי פסקת. וכי פסקת הדבר כן דכל בהמת עובד כוכבים הוי חמר עובד כוכבים וכל בהמת ישראל הוי חמר ישראל: שונא שאמרו. קס"ד שונא שאמרו אשונא דקרא קאי דמשתעי בפריקה כי תראה חמור שונאך רובץ וגומר: אשונא דמתניתין קאי. אהך מתניתא דלעיל דשונא לטעון הוא:

רובץ

---

**תוספות**

מדברי שניהם נלמד צער בעלי חיים דאורייתא. וא"ת א"כ אמאי עוקרים על המלכים ולא מדרכי האמורי (ע"ז דף יא.) וי"ל משום דכבוד מלך ונשיא עדיף כמו בל תשחית דנדחה מפני כבודם דאונקלוס (ג) שרף על ר"ג ע' מנה צורי פ"ק דע"ז (שם) ועוד דכיון דכתיב את סוסיהם תעקר קל לדחות מפני המלך:

מי לא עסקינן דאדהכי והכי בטיל משוקיה. וא"ת מ"מ נדרוש ק"ו מטעינה דלית בה חסרון כיס וי"ל כיון דטעינה שיש בה חסרון כיס לא הוי בשכר דמ"ש מפריקה א"כ אף טעינה דלית בה חסרון כיס נמי הוי בחנם ופריקה נכתבה לדרוש שום דרשה אחרת:

מכלל דת"ק סבר דזקוק לו. המקשה סבור דת"ק נמי ידרוש משאו שהוא יכול לעמוד בו ושאינו יכול לעמוד בו נהי דאין חייב לסייע בחנם משום דלית ביה מצות פריקה מ"מ בשכר חייב לסייעו משום צער בעלי חיים וא"ת ולרבי יוסי הגלילי דסבר צער בעלי חיים לאו דאורייתא ואית ליה לקמן (דף לג.) דטעינה בשכר מ"ש טעינה מפריקה וי"ל דדריש ק"ו מחסרון כיס דלכתוב טעינה גרידא דיש טעינה שאין בו חסרון כיס וכ"ש פריקה אלא כתב פריקה לאגמורי דטעינה בשכר וכיון דטעינה שאין בה חסרון כיס הויא בשכר היכא דאית בה חסרון כיס נמי דהיינו היכא דבטיל משוקיה הוי בשכר דילפי' מטעינה דלית בה חסרון כיס והשתא לא בא להוכיח רק דצער בעלי חיים דאורייתא ולא לקיים שמכח ק"ו יש להוכיח דצער בעלי חיים דאורייתא דאפשר שק"ו הוי מחסרון כיס כדפרישית לר' יוסי וא"ת ודלמא זקוק לו מדרבנן וי"ל דכל הסוגיא מוכחת דאי צער בעלי חיים לאו דאורייתא אינו חייב לסייעו אפי' בשכר כדאמרינן בסמוך וכי ליתיה למריה בהדיה ליעבד גביה בשכר ולעולם צער בעלי חיים דאורייתא אבל אי הוי דרבנן פטור היה אפילו בשכר וכן בתר הכי דקאמר ואי אמרת לאו דאורייתא אמאי מטפל ביה ולישני מדרבנן:

ואי לאו דאורייתא אמאי מטפל בה. וא"ת והלא בספרי דורש שונאך אפילו שונא עובד כוכבים וי"ל דאסמכתא בעלמא היא דבערבי פסחים (פסחים דף קיג: ושם) מוקי בשונא ישראל:

ולהטעינה יין אסור אין זקוק לה. אבל שאר דברים זקוק ואפילו לטעון משום איבה: אמאי וחדלת. וא"ת ולישני בחנם אבל בשכר חייב ולעולם צער בעלי חיים דאורייתא וי"ל דוחדלת משמע לגמרי:

ואי בטעינה אמאי עזוב. וליכא למימר דבטיל משוקיה דאם כן רישא נמי:

לכוף יצרו. וא"ת כיון דבערבי פסחים (שם) מוקי לה בישראל שמותר לשנאותו כגון שראה בו דבר ערוה מה שייך בו לכוף יצרו וי"ל [א] דלא מיירי בשונא דקרא: מה לי שונא עובד כוכבים. ה"מ לשנויי ישראל בחנם ולעובד כוכבים בשכר:

מה

---

**עין משפט נר מצוה**

קפ א מיי' פי"ג מהל' רוצח ושמירת נפש הל' א סמג עשין פא טוש"ע ח"מ סי' רעב סעיף א:

קפא ב ג מיי' שם הל' ט ועיין בכ"מ טוש"ע שם סעיף ט:

קפב ד מיי' שם טוש"ע שם סעיף ח:

קפג ה מיי' שם הל' יג ועיין בכ"מ טוש"ע שם סעיף ט בהג"ה:

קפד ו מיי' שם הל' ט ועיין בהה"ל טוש"ע שם סעיף ט:

קפה ז מיי' שם טוש"ע שם סעיף ח:

קפו ח מיי' שם הל' יג טוש"ע שם סעיף י:

קפז ט מיי' שם הל' יד טוש"ע שם סעיף יא:

**רבינו חננאל**

לפרוק בחנם ולא לטעון בחנם אלא בשכר. ר' שמעון אומר אף לטעון בחנם משום דלא מסיימי קראי איזהו לפרוק ואיזהו לטעון הילכך שניהם בחנם. אמר רבא מדברי שניהם נלמד צער בעלי חיים דאורי' מדאמרי' פריקה דברי הכל בחנם: ר' יוסי הגלילי אומר אם הטעינו יותר ממשאו ונפל אין נזקק לו שנאמר תחת משאו משאוי שיכול לעמוד בו. בהמת עובד כוכבים מטפל בה כבהמת ישראל משום איבה. בהמת עובד כוכבים ועובד כוכבים מחמר אחריה ומשאוי של ישראל וצריך לטעון אין זקוק לו שנא' וחדלת. אבל ישראל מחמר אחרי בהמתו והמשאו לעובד כוכבים עזב תעזוב עמו. ומקשי' והא תרווייהו וחדלת עזב תעזב בפריקה הוא דכתיב ביה ואוקימנא כר' יוסי הגלילי דסבר צער בעלי חיים לאו דאורייתא. אוהב צריך לסייעו בפריקה והשונא צריך לסייעו בטעינה יניח האוהב ויסייע השונא כדי לכוף את יצרו לשלום. ופשוטה היא:

**מסורת הש"ס**

א) [שבת קכח:], ב) [ל"... אלא הא מני], ג) [שב... קנד:], ד) [תוספתא פר... ב], ה) פסחים קיג [תוספתא שם], ו) ל"... דמתניתא.

**הגהות הב"ח**

(א) גמ' פטור לגמרי דלמ... כצ"ל ואות ו' נמחק (ב) רש"י ד"ה אי אמרת בשלמא לאו: (ג) תוס' ד"ה מדברי וכו' דאונקלוס הגר שרף:

**הגהות הגר"א**

[א] תוס' ד"ה לכוף וי"ל כו'. נ"ב ר"ל דא"... להקדים אבל מ"מ חיי... כמש"ש:

**תורה אור השלם**

א) כִּי תִרְאֶה חֲמוֹר שֹׂנַאֲךָ רֹבֵץ תַּחַת מַשָּׂאוֹ וְחָדַלְתָּ מֵעֲזֹב לוֹ עָזֹב תַּעֲזֹב עִמּוֹ: [שמות כג, ה]

**ליקוטי רש"י**

צער בעלי חיים דאורייתא. שנאמר עזב תעזב עמו ואיכא מא... דדריש טעמא דקרא משום צער בעלי חיים באלו מציאות [שבת קכח:]. הלך וישב לו. הבעלים [לעיל ע"א].

מִדִּבְרֵי שְׁנֵיהֶם – **From the words of both [the Rabbis and R' Shimon],** נִלְמַד צַעַר בַּעֲלֵי חַיִּים דְּאוֹרַיְיתָא – **it can be derived** that the **suffering of living creatures is** a **Biblical** concern.[1] For the Rabbis maintained that once the obligation to load was written, the obligation to unload could be deduced through a *kal vachomer*.[2] וַאֲפִילוּ רַבִּי שִׁמְעוֹן לֹא קָאָמַר אֶלָּא מִשּׁוּם דְּלֹא מְסַיְּימֵי קְרָאֵי – **And even R' Shimon** had **said** that it was necessary to explicitly write the obligation to unload **only because** he held that **the verses** of loading and unloading **are not conclusive;** i.e. neither of the two verses can be conclusively shown to obligate loading.[3] אֲבָל מְסַיְּימֵי קְרָאֵי – **But had the verses been conclusive,** i.e. had it been evident that a given verse referred to loading, דָּרְשִׁינַן קַל וָחוֹמֶר – R' Shimon would have agreed that the Torah could have written only this verse and **we would have expounded a** ***kal vachomer*** to derive the law of unloading. מִשּׁוּם מַאי – Now, **on what** basis would such a *kal vachomer* have been predicated? לָאו מִשּׁוּם צַעַר בַּעֲלֵי חַיִּים דָּרְשִׁינַן – **Is it not because** unloading relieves the **suffering of a living creature** that **we could have expounded** the *kal vachomer*?[4] It can thus be shown that, according to the Rabbis and R' Shimon, the suffering of living creatures is indeed a Biblical concern.

The Gemara disputes the proof:

דִּלְמָא מִשּׁוּם דְּאִיכָּא חֶסְרוֹן כִּיס – **Perhaps** the reason unloading is more compelling is because **there is monetary loss** involved if the bystander does not help unload the animal. וְהָכִי קָאָמַר – **This,** then, **is how** we would **say [the** ***kal vachomer*****]:** וּמָה טְעִינָה – Now, **if** in a situation where **loading** a burden is called for, דְּלֵית בָּהּ חֶסְרוֹן כִּיס – **where there is no monetary loss** caused to the owner if the animal is not loaded, חַיָּיב – still, we find that the bystander is **obligated** to help the owner; פְּרִיקָה – then, in a situation where **unloading** a burden is called for, דְּאִית בָּהּ חֶסְרוֹן כִּיס – **where there** ***is*** the potential of **monetary loss** to the owner if the bystander does not help,[5] לֹא כָּל שֶׁכֵּן – **should** he **not certainly** be obligated to help the owner? Accordingly, there is no indication that the Rabbis and R' Shimon view the suffering of living creatures to be a Biblical concern.[6]

The Gemara counters:

וּטְעִינָה אֵין בָּהּ חֶסְרוֹן כִּיס – **But does loading not,** in fact, prevent **monetary loss?** מִי לֹא עָסְקִינַן דְּאַדְּהָכִי וְהָכִי – **Are we not dealing** also with a case in which the animal was carrying merchandise **where, in the meantime,** so long as the animal has not been loaded, בָּטֵיל מִשּׁוּקֵיהּ – **[the owner] is idle,** being prevented **from** going to **the market place** and selling his wares? אִי נַמִּי – **Or, alternatively,** אָתוּ גַּנָּבֵי – perhaps **thieves will come** while the animal's burden lays strewn on the ground וְשָׁקְלֵי כָּל מַה דְּאִיכָּא בַּהֲדֵיהּ – **and they will take all** the goods **that [the owner] has with him?**[7] Since these are indeed some of the cases in which there is a requirement to help load, it cannot be that the *kal vachomer* is based on the consideration of potential monetary loss. It must be based instead on the consideration of suffering, in which case it can be shown that an animal's suffering is indeed a Biblical concern.[8]

The Gemara fortifies this conclusion with a proof from our Mishnah:

תֵּדַע דְּצַעַר בַּעֲלֵי חַיִּים דְּאוֹרַיְיתָא – **Know that,** according to both the Rabbis and R' Shimon, **the suffering of living creatures is a Biblical** concern; דְּקָתָנֵי סֵיפָא – **for the end of the Mishnah taught:** ר׳ יוֹסֵי הַגְּלִילִי אוֹמֵר – **R' YOSE HAGLILI SAYS:** אִם הָיָה עָלָיו יָתֵר [עַל] מַשָּׂאוֹ – **IF [THE ANIMAL] WAS BEARING MORE THAN ITS** proper **BURDEN** when it lay down, אֵין זָקוּק לוֹ – **[THE BYSTANDER] IS NOT BOUND TO** help unload **IT,** שֶׁנֶּאֱמַר – **FOR IT IS STATED**[9] that one must help unload an animal: ״תַּחַת מַשָּׂאוֹ״, – *lying down* **UNDER** ***ITS BURDEN,*** which implies that the animal had been bearing מַשּׂאוֹי שֶׁיָּכוֹל לַעֲמוֹד בּוֹ – **A BURDEN UNDER WHICH IT CAN STAND.**[10] לָאו מִכְּלָל – Now, **is it not** true, **by implication,** דְּתַנָּא קַמָּא סָבַר – **that the Tanna Kamma** [i.e. the

NOTES

1. Both the Rabbis and R' Shimon make the assumption that, in logic, the obligation to help unload is more compelling than the obligation to help load (see *Rashi*). In the case of the Rabbis, this is evident from their claim that if the Torah had written only the obligation of loading, we would have deduced by *kal vachomer* that one must certainly help in unloading. As the Gemara goes on to show, R' Shimon agrees with this idea at least in principle.

The Gemara now assumes that the reason unloading is the greater of the two obligations is because it involves relieving the suffering of an animal, while loading does not. Apparently, then, there must exist within Torah law an obligation to relieve or prevent the suffering of an animal. In other words, "the suffering of living creatures is a Biblical concern." [*Rambam* suggests that the source for this is the angel's criticism of Balaam for striking his donkey (*Numbers* 22:32); see *Moreh Nevuchim* 3:17; *Midrash Lekach Tov*; cf. *Rashi, Shabbos* 128b ד״ה צער בעלי חיים דאורייתא, and *Meiri* there and here).]

2. See previous note. The *kal vachomer* argues that if one is obligated to help load, he is certainly obligated to help unload, for the latter action is more important than the former. On the basis of this *kal vachomer*, the Rabbis had concluded that the verse stating the obligation to unload is not needed to teach the obligation itself. Rather, it is intended instead to teach that one is obligated to help unload without taking compensation for his efforts (see 32a note 37).

3. According to R' Shimon, the language of neither *Deuteronomy* 22:4 nor *Exodus* 23:5 unequivocally indicates an obligation to help load. Hence, if only one of these verses were written, we would not know that an obligation to load exists. See bottom of 32a.

4. The *kal vachomer* would run as follows: Since one is obligated to load an animal (even though he does not alleviate suffering by doing so), he is certainly obligated to unload an animal (where he *would* alleviate an animal's suffering by his actions) (*Rashi*). Now, since concern for an animal's suffering lies at the root of a *kal vachomer* that would conceivably obviate the need for the Torah to write the verse of unloading, it is evident that the suffering of an animal is a legal consideration that has weight on a *Biblical level*. That is, the obligation to alleviate such suffering must originate in *Torah law*, not the Rabbinic legislation of a subsequent period.

5. The fallen animal may die or become injured if the load is not removed from upon it (see *Rashi* to 32a ד״ה פריקה).

6. Any reason that would explain why unloading is more compelling than loading will provide a basis for the *kal vachomer*. The Gemara therefore suggests that since unloading prevents potential monetary loss to the owner whereas loading does not, the *kal vachomer* can be invoked even if the animal's suffering is not taken into account. Accordingly, the fact that the Rabbis and R' Shimon both concede the validity of the *kal vachomer* does not indicate that they deem suffering of living creatures to be a Biblical concern.

According to this explanation, when the Gemara above (32a) mentioned the animal's suffering as a factor in the *kal vachomer,* it did so because this factor adds to the *kal vachomer* according to the view that it is a Biblical concern. In fact, only the monetary loss argument is necessary (*Ritva*).

7. The Torah required one to help reload an animal in *all cases*. Since in some of these cases the owner stands to lose money if his animal is not reloaded (either through lost business or theft), we must concede that loading prevents monetary loss just as unloading does (*Rashi*).

8. There are only two conceivable arguments that would establish unloading as a more compelling obligation than loading: 1) Loading does not prevent suffering of the animal, whereas unloading does; and 2) loading does not prevent monetary loss, whereas unloading does. Since the Gemara rejects the second argument, we must conclude that the *kal vachomer* is based on the first argument. Accordingly, from the fact that the Rabbis and R' Shimon accept the *kal vachomer* it is evident that they view the suffering of animals to be a Biblical concern (see above, note 1).

9. *Exodus* 23:5.

10. The term מַשָּׂאוֹ, *"its" burden,* connotes a burden that suits the animal, not an oversized one that it cannot bear. See 32a note 15.

מדברי שניהם נלמד [א] צער בעלי חיים דאורייתא ואפי' ר"ש לא קאמר אלא משום דלא מסיימי קראי אבל מסיימי קראי דרשי' ק"ו משום מאי לאו משום צער בעלי חיים דרשינן דלמא משום דאיכא חסרון כיס וה"ק ומה טעינה דלית בה חסרון כיס חייב פריקה דאית בה חסרון כיס לא כ"ש וטעינה אין בה חסרון כיס מי לא עסקינן דאדהכי והכי בטיל משוקיה אי נמי אתו גנבי ושקלי כל מה דאיכא בהדיה תדע דצער בעלי חיים דאורייתא דקתני סיפא ר' יוסי הגלילי אומר אם היה עליו יתר [על] משאו אין זקוק לו שנאמר [א] תחת משאו משאוי שיכול לעמוד בו לאו מכלל דת"ק סבר [א] זקוק לו מאי טעמא לאו משום דצער בעלי חיים דאורייתא דלמא בתחת משאו פליגי דרבי יוסי סבר דרשינן תחת משאו משאוי שיכול לעמוד בו ורבנן סברי לא דרשינן תחת משאו תדע דצער בעלי חיים לאו דאורייתא דקתני רישא הלך וישב לו ואמר לו הואיל ועליך מצוה לפרוק פרוק פטור שנאמר עמו ואי סלקא דעתך צער בעלי חיים דאורייתא מה לי איתיה למריה בהדיה ומה לי כי ליתיה למריה בהדיה לעולם צער בעלי חיים דאורייתא מי סברת פטור פטור לגמרי (א) ודלמא פטור בחנם וחייב בשכר וה"ק רחמנא כי איתיה למריה בהדיה עבד גביה בחנם וכי ליתיה למריה בהדיה עבד גביה בשכר ולעולם צער בעלי חיים דאורייתא (סימ"ן בהמ"ת אוה"ב שונ"א רבצ"ן) לימא מסייע ליה [ב] בהמת עובד כוכבים מטפל בה כבהמת ישראל אי אמרת בשלמא צער בעלי חיים דאורייתא משום הכי מטפל בה כבהמת ישראל אלא אי אמרת צער בעלי חיים לאו דאורייתא אמאי מטפל בה כבהמת ישראל התם [ג] משום איבה הכי נמי מסתברא דקתני אם היתה טעונה יין אסור אין זקוק לה אי אמרת בשלמא לאו דאורייתא משום הכי אין זקוק לה אלא אי אמרת דאורייתא אמאי אין זקוק לה ה"ק ולהטעינה יין אסור אין זקוק לה תא שמע [ד] בהמת עובד כוכבים ומשאוי ישראל וחדלת ואי אמרת צער בעלי חיים דאורייתא אמאי וחדלת עזב תעזב מבעי ליה [ה] לעולם צער בעלי חיים דאורייתא התם בטעינה אי הכי אימא סיפא [ו] בהמת ישראל ומשאוי עובד כוכבים עזב תעזב ואי בטעינה אמאי עזב תעזב משום צערא דישראל אי הכי אפילו רישא נמי רישא [ז] בחמר עובד כוכבים סיפא בחמר ישראל מאי פסקת סתמא דמלתא איניש בתר חמריה אזיל והא וחדלת ועזב תעזב בפריקה הוא דכתיבי (ב) א"ל הא מני רבי יוסי הגלילי היא דאמר (ג) צער בעלי חיים לאו דאורייתא ת"ש (ד) [ח] אוהב לפרוק ושונא לטעון מצוה בשונא כדי לכוף את יצרו ואי סלקא דעתך צער בעלי חיים דאורייתא הא עדיף ליה אפ"ה כדי לכוף את יצרו עדיף ת"ש (ה) [ט] שונא שאמרו שונא ישראל ולא שונא עובד כוכבים אי אמרת צער בעלי חיים דאורייתא מה לי שונא ישראל ומה לי שונא עובד כוכבים מי סברת אשונא דקרא קאי אשונא (ו) [י] דמתניתין קאי תא שמע

רובץ

מדברי שניהם. מדקאמרי תרווייהו פריקה עדיפא: ואפילו ר"ש לא קאמר. דאצטריך למכתב פריקה: אלא משום דלא מסיימי קראי. לטעינה: לאו משום צער בעלי חיים. והכי יליף מה טעינה דליכא צער בעלי חיים חייב פריקה דאיכא צער בעלי חיים לא כ"ש: מי לא עסקינן. וכי אין המקרא מדבר אף בהולך לסחורה דאדהכי בטיל משוקיה: תדע. דלרבנן דפליגי עליה דר"ש ולר"ש צער בעלי חיים דאורייתא: מכלל דת"ק. דרבי יוסי הגלילי רבנן ור"ש: זקוק לו. ואמאי זקוק לו אי משום מצות עזב תעזב הא כתיב משאו הראוי לו אלא משום צער בעלי חיים: לא דרשינן משאו. למשא הראוי לו דמשאו כל משא שעליו משמע: ותדע. דהכי הוא כדדחינא לך דצער בעלי חיים לאו דאורייתא: עביד גביה. משום צער בעלי חיים ועל כורחו יטול שכר: לימא מסייע ליה. לרבא דאמר לעיל צער בעלי חיים דאורייתא: מטפל בה. לפרוק משאה: אי אמרת (ב) לאו דאורייתא. וטעמא משום איבה הוא מש"ה אין זקוק לה שיכול להשמט ולומר דבר איסור הוא לנו: ה"ק ולהטעינה. ולעולם דאורייתא ורישא תנא מטפל בה בין בפריקה בין בטעינה פריקה משום צער בעלי חיים וטעינה משום איבה ולהטעינה יין אסור דלאו צערא איכא ולאו איבה איכא אין זקוק לה: התם בטעינה. לקמיה פריך הא בפריקה כתיב: משום צערא דישראל. שצריך להשהות שם: בחמר עובד כוכבים. ואין בעל המשא שם ועל העובד כוכבים לטעון: מאי פסקת. וכי פסקת הדבר כן דכל בהמת עובד כוכבים הוי חמר עובד כוכבים וכל בהמת ישראל הוי חמר ישראל: שונא שאמרו. קס"ד שונא שאמרו אשונא דקרא קאי דמשתעי בפריקה כי תראה חמור שונאך רובץ וגומר: אשונא דמתניתין קאי. אהך מתניתא דלעיל דשונא לטעון הוא:

מדברי שניהם נלמד צער בעלי חיים דאורייתא. וא"ת א"כ אמאי עוקרים על המלכים ולא מדרכי האמורי (ע"ז דף יא.) וי"ל משום דכבוד מלך ונשיא עדיף כמו בל תשחית דנדחה מפני כבודם דאונקלוס (ג) שרף על ר"ג ע' מנה צורי פ"ק דע"ז (שם) ועוד דכיון דכתיב את סוסיהם תעקר קל לדחות מפני המלך:

מי לא עסקינן דאדהכי והכי בטיל משוקיה. וא"ת מ"מ נדרוש ק"ו מטעינה דלית בה חסרון כיס וי"ל כיון דטעינה שיש בה חסרון כיס לא הוי בשכר דמ"ש מפריקה א"כ אף טעינה דלית בה חסרון כיס נמי הוי בחנם ופריקה נכתבה לדרוש שום דרשה אחרת:

מכלל דת"ק סבר דזקוק לו. המקשה סבור דת"ק נמי ידרוש משאו שהוא יכול לעמוד בו ושאינו יכול לעמוד בו נהי דאין חייב לסייע בחנם משום דלית ביה מצות פריקה מ"מ בשכר חייב לסייעו משום צער בעלי חיים וא"ת ולרבי יוסי הגלילי דסבר צער בעלי חיים לאו דאורייתא ואית ליה לקמן (דף לג.) דטעינה בשכר מ"ש טעינה מפריקה וי"ל דדריש ק"ו מחסרון כיס דלכתוב טעינה גרידא דיש טעינה שאין בו חסרון כיס וכ"ש פריקה אלא כתב פריקה לאגמורי דטעינה בשכר וכיון דטעינה שאין בה חסרון כיס הויא בשכר היכא דאית בה חסרון כיס נמי דהיינו היכא דבטיל משוקיה הוי בשכר דילפי' מטעינה דלית בה חסרון כיס והשתא לא בא להוכיח רק דצער בעלי חיים דאורייתא ולא לקיים שמכח ק"ו יש להוכיח דצער בעלי חיים דאורייתא דאפשר שק"ו הוי מחסרון כיס כדפרישית לר' יוסי וא"ת ודלמא זקוק לו מדרבנן וי"ל דכל הסוגיא מוכחת דאי צער בעלי חיים לאו דאורייתא אינו חייב לסייעו אפי' בשכר כדאמרינן בסמוך וכי ליתיה למריה בהדיה ליעבד גביה בשכר ולעולם צער בעלי חיים דאורייתא אבל אי הוי דרבנן פטור היה אפילו בשכר וכן בתר הכי דקאמר ואי אמרת לאו דאורייתא אמאי מטפל ביה ולישני מדרבנן:

ואי לאו דאורייתא אמאי מטפל בה. וא"ת והלא בספרי דורש שונאך אפילו שונא עובד כוכבים וי"ל דאסמכתא בעלמא היא דבערבי פסחים (פסחים דף קיג: ושם) מוקי בשונא ישראל:

ולהטעינה יין אסור אין זקוק לה. אבל שאר דברים זקוק ואפילו לטעון משום איבה: אמאי וחדלת. וא"ת ולישני בחנם אבל בשכר חייב ולעולם צער בעלי חיים דאורייתא וי"ל דוחדלת משמע לגמרי:

ואי בטעינה אמאי עזוב. וליכא למימר דבטיל משוקיה דא"כ ריש' נמי:

לכוף יצרו. וא"ת כיון דבערבי פסחים (שם) מוקי לה בישראל שמותר לשנאותו כגון שראה בו דבר ערוה מה שייך בו לכוף יצרו וי"ל [א] דלא איירי בשונא דקרא: מה לי שונא עובד כוכבים. ה"מ לשנויי ישראל בחנם ולעובד כוכבים בשכר:

מה

עין משפט
נר מצוה

קפ א מיי' פי"ג מהל' רוצח ושמירת נפש הל' א סמג עשין פא טוש"ע ח"מ סי' רעב סעיף א:
קפא ב ג מיי' שם הל' ט ועיין בכ"מ טוש"ע שם סעיף ט:
קפב ד מיי' שם טוש"ע שם סעיף ח:
קפג ה מיי' שם הל' יג ועיין בכ"מ טוש"ע שם סעיף ט בהג"ה:
קפד ו מיי' שם הל' ט ועיין בהכ"ל טוש"ע שם סעיף ט:
קפה ז מיי' שם טוש"ע שם סעיף ח:
קפו ח מיי' שם הל' יג טוש"ע שם סעיף י:
קפז ט מיי' שם הל' יד טוש"ע שם סעיף יא:

רבינו חננאל

לפרוק בחנם ולא לטעון בחנם אלא בשכר. ר' שמעון אומר אף לטעון בחנם משום דלא מסיימי קראי איזהו לפרוק ואיזהו לטעון הילכך שניהם בחנם. אמר רבא מדברי שניהם נלמד צער בעלי חיים דאוריי' מדאמרי' פריקה דברי הכל בחנם: ר' יוסי הגלילי אומר אם הטעינו יותר ממשאו ונפל אין נזקק לו שנאמר תחת משאו משאוי שיכול לעמוד בו. בהמת עובד כוכבים מטפל בה כבהמת ישראל משום איבה. בהמת עובד כוכבים ועובד כוכבים מחמר אחריה ומשאוי של ישראל וצריך לטעון אין זקוק לו שנא' וחדלת. אבל ישראל מחמר אחרי בהמתו והמשאו לעובד כוכבים עזב תעזוב עמו. ומקשי' והא תרווייהו וחדלת עזב תעזב בפריקה הוא דכתיב ביה ואוקימנא כר' יוסי הגלילי דסבר צער בעלי חיים לאו דאורייתא. אוהב צריך לסייעו בפריקה והשונא צריך לסייעו בטעינה יניח האוהב ויסייע השונא כדי לכוף את יצרו לשלום. ופשוטה היא:

מסורת הש"ס

א) [שבת קכח:], ב) [נ"א הא מני], ג) [שבת קנד:], ד) [תוספתא פרק ב], ה) פסחים קיג [תוספתא שם], ו) נ"א דמתניתא.

הגהות הב"ח

(א) גמ' פטור לגמרי דלמא כצ"ל ואות ו' נמחק: (ב) רש"י ד"ה אי אמרת בשלמא לאו: (ג) תוס' ד"ה מדברי וכו' דאונקלוס הגר שרף:

הגהות הגר"א

[א] תוס' ד"ה לכוף וי"ל כו'. נ"ב ר"ל דא"ל להקדים אבל מ"מ חייב כמש"ש:

תורה אור השלם

א) כִּי תִרְאֶה חֲמוֹר שֹׂנַאֲךָ רֹבֵץ תַּחַת מַשָּׂאוֹ וְחָדַלְתָּ מֵעֲזֹב לוֹ עָזֹב תַּעֲזֹב עִמּוֹ: [שמות כג, ה]

ליקוטי רש"י

צער בעלי חיים דאורייתא. שנאמר עזב תעזב עמו ואיכא מאן דדריש טעמא דקרא משום צער בעלי חיים באלו מציאות [שבת קכח:]. הלך וישב לו. הבעלים [לעיל ע"א].

תרי מגו תלתא ואי נמי תרי סהדי דפלגת באפי בי תלתא א"ל מנא לך הא א"ל דתנן אם יש שם ב"ד מתנה בפניהם אין שם ב"ד בפני מי יתנה שלו קודם א"ל מי דמי התם דמפיק ממונא מהאי ומותיב להאי בעינן ב"ד אבל הכא (א) דידיה שקלי גילוי מילתא בעלמא הוא בתרי סגי ליה תדע דתנן [א] אלמנה מוכרת שלא בפני ב"ד אמר ליה אביי ולאו מי אתמר עלה אמר רב יוסף בר מניומי אמר ר"נ אלמנה אינה צריכה ב"ד של מומחין [ב] אבל צריכה בית דין של הדיוטות: **מתני'** [ג] מצאה ברפת אין חייב בה ברה"ר חייב בה [ד] ואם היתה בבית הקברות לא יטמא לה [ה] אם אמר לו אביו היטמא או שאמר לו אל תחזיר לא ישמע לו [ו] פרק וטען פרק וטען אפילו ארבעה וחמשה פעמים חייב שנאמר [א] עזב תעזב [ז] הלך וישב לו ואמר הואיל ועליך מצוה אם רצונך לפרוק פרוק פטור שנאמר עמו [ח] אם היה זקן או חולה חייב מצוה מן התורה לפרוק אבל לא לטעון ר"ש אומר אף לטעון רבי יוסי הגלילי אומר אם היה עליו יתר על משאו אין זקוק לו שנאמר תחת משאו משאוי שיכול לעמוד בו: **גמ'** אמר רבא [ט] רפת שאמרו [ג] אינה מתעה ואינה משמרת אינה מתעה מדקתני אינו חייב בה ואינה משמרת מדאיצטריך למיתני אינו חייב בה דאי סלקא דעתך משמרת השתא משכח לה אבראי מעייל לה לגואי משכח לה מגואי מבעיא אלא שמע מינה אינה משמרת שמע מינה: מצאה ברפת אינו חייב: א"ר יצחק [ג] והוא שעומדת תוך לתחום מכלל דברשות הרבים ואפילו בתוך התחום נמי חייב איכא דמתני לה אסיפא ברה"ר חייב בה אמר רבי יצחק והוא שעומדת חוץ לתחום מכלל דברפת אפילו עומדת חוץ לתחום נמי אינו חייב בה: בבית הקברות לא יטמא לה: [ד] ת"ר מנין שאם אמר לו אביו היטמא או שאמר לו [ה] אל תחזיר שלא ישמע לו שנאמר [ב] איש אמו ואביו תיראו ואת שבתותי תשמרו אני ה' (ג) כולכם חייבין בכבודי טעמא דכתב רחמנא את שבתותי תשמרו הא לאו הכי הוה אמינא צייתא ליה ואמאי האי עשה והאי לא תעשה ועשה [ו] ולא אתי עשה ודחי את לא תעשה ועשה איצטריך ס"ד אמינא הואיל והוקש כיבוד אב ואם לכבודו [ז] של מקום שנאמר כאן [ג] כבד את אביך ואת אמך ונאמר להלן [ד] כבד את ה' מהונך הלכך לציית ליה קמ"ל דלא לשמע ליה: מצוה מן התורה לפרוק אבל לא לטעון: מאי אבל לא לטעון אילימא אבל לא לטעון כלל מאי שנא פריקה דכתיב עזב תעזב עמו טעינה נמי הכתיב [ה] הקם תקים עמו אלא [כ] מצוה מן התורה לפרוק בחנם ולא לטעון בחנם אלא בשכר ר"ש אומר [ס] אף לטעון בחנם תנינא להא דת"ר פריקה בחנם טעינה בשכר ר"ש אומר זו וזו בחנם מאי טעמייהו דרבנן דאי ס"ד כר"ש לכתוב רחמנא טעינה ולא בעי פריקה ואנא אמינא ומה טעינה דלית בה צער בעלי חיים וליכא חסרון כיס חייב פריקה דאית בה צער בעלי חיים וחסרון כיס לא כל שכן אלא למאי הלכתא כתביה רחמנא לומר לך פריקה בחנם טעינה בשכר ורבי שמעון מאי טעמא משום דלא מסיימי קראי ורבנן אמאי לא מסיימי קראי הכא כתיב רובץ תחת משאו התם כתיב נופלין בדרך דרמו אינהו וטעונייהו באורחא משמע ורבי שמעון נופלין בדרך אינהו וטעונייהו עלוייהו משמע אמר רבא

מדברי

תרי מגו תלתא. שנים מן השלשה יבואו ויעידו לומר שלשה היינו: אם יש שם ב"ד. וסתם ב"ד שלשה אלמא אין כח להפקיר ממון זה אלא זה בפחות משלשה: גילוי מילתא. שידעו שחלקתי בשוה: אלמנה. הניזונת מנכסי יתומים מוכרת למזונות: שלא בב"ד. ובלבד שירלו שנים שלא תמכור בזול: **מתני'** מצאה ברפת. בגמרא מפרש מאי אלטריך: היתה בבית הקברות. והוא כהן: או שאמר לו אל תחזיר. והוא במקום שהוא מותר לילך שם: הלך וישב לו. הבעלים: אבל לא לטעון. בגמרא מפרש: **גמ'** רפת שאמרו. ששנינו במשנתנו עסקינן כשאינה מתעה את הבהמה שבתוכה להיות בורחת ויולאת: ואינה משתמרת. שאינה נעולה ואם באת ללאת יולאה: מעייל לגואי. כדאמרינן לעיל (דף לא.) לגינתו ולחורבתו מנין: ברישא גרסינן והוא שעומדת בתוך לתחום בסיפא גרסינן והוא שעומדת חוץ לתחום: אני ה'. אע"פ שאמרתי לך ירא את אביך אני אדון לשניכם ואם אמר לך אביך עבור על דברי לחלל שבת אל תשמע לו: הוה אמינא צייתא ליה. דאתי עשה דכיבוד ודחי לא תעשה דלא תוכל להתעלם: אבידה עשה ולא תעשה היא השב תשיבם לא תוכל להתעלם: הוקש כבודם. בגזירה שוה כבד את אביך כבד את ה' מהונך: דלית ביה חסרון כיס. אם לא יטעון: פריקה אית בה חסרון כיס. שהבהמה נשברת תחת משאה: לומר לך פריקה בחנם. אבל טעינה לא נלטוית אלא בשכר ° הלכך אי לא כתב פריקה ואתיא מק"ו מטעינה הוה אמינא דיו לבא מן הדין להיות כנדון מה טעינה בשכר אף פריקה בשכר: לא מסיימי קראי. למשמעות טעינה הלכך אי כתיב חד הוה אמינא לפריקה אתא: רובץ תחת משאו. משמע שלריך לפרוק: דרמו אינהו וטעונייהו באורחא. אף המשא מוטל על הקרקע שלריך לטעון:

מדברי

אלמנה מוכרת שלא בב"ד. וא"ת התם משום חינא או משום שלא תתבזה בב"ד כדמפרש באלמנה ניזונת (כתובות דף לז: ושם) וי"ל דס"ל כיון דאלמנה מוכרת אע"ג דאינה שלה שלא בב"ד משום חינא ה"נ שותף יטול את שלו שלא בב"ד אע"ג דליכא טעם דחינא: **בית** דין הדיוטות. וא"ת והאמרינן התם (דף לח. ושם) אלמנה ששמה לעצמה לא עשתה ולא כלום דאמרינן לה מאן שם לך הלא מכרה ע"פ ב"ד הדיוטות וי"ל כיון שלוקחת לעצמה נראה לעולם שמעכבת מנכסי יתומים בידה אע"פ שיש ב"ד הדיוטות כיון דליכא מומחין אבל כשמוכרת לאחרים אין נראה שמעכבת משלהם שהרי לא עכבה כלום וא"ת ומ"ש דאלמנה מוכרת לאחרים שלא בב"ד ובב"ד יכולה לעכב אפי' לעצמה מדאמרינן התם דא"ל מאן שם לך משמע דבב"ד יכולה לשום וקאמר נמי התם ההוא גברא דאפקידו גביה כסתא דיתמי אזל שמה לנפשיה בת' זוזי לסוף אייקור כו' אתא לקמיה דרבי א"ל מאן שם לך משמע דבב"ד יכול לשום ולקמן בפרק המפקיד (דף לח.) תנן המפקיד פירות אצל חבירו והרקיבו כו' עושה להם תקנה ומוכרן בב"ד וכשהוא מוכרן מוכרן לאחרים ואין מוכרן לעצמו כיולא בו גבאי לדקה פורטין לאחרים ואין פורטין לעצמם דאפילו בב"ד מוכרין לאחרים ואין מוכרין לעצמם ושלא בב"ד אין מוכרין אפילו לאחרים וליכא למימר הא דאמר ומוכרים לאחרים בב"ד היינו ברשות ב"ד אבל אי ידעי ב"ד השומא יכול לעכב לעצמו דבירושלמי מסיק על ההוא מעשה דרבי יוחנן חקוקאה דמייתי פ"ק דפסחים (דף יג. ושם) א"ל לך ומוכרם בב"ד אלמא אע"פ שנתן לו רשות היה לריך למוכרם בב"ד וי"ל דמוכרת שלא בב"ד משום חינא [ט] וגבי כסתא דיתמי נמי דיכול לעכב לעצמו בב"ד מלינן למימר דהיינו דוקא בדיעבד דמשום חשד לא מהדרינן עובדא א"נ דגבי יתמי ב"ד עצמם הם מפקידין ולכך יכול לעכב לעצמו על פיהם אבל פקדון של אחרים אינו יכול לעכב לעצמו על פי ב"ד: **כבד** את ה' מהונך. הא דנקט קרא לדברי קבלה ולא נקט קרא דאיש אמו ואביו תיראו וכתיב את ה' אלהיך תירא משום דניחא ליה לאתויי קרא דכבוד:

מדברי

## מסורת הש"ס

כתובות לז., ג) [פי' ור בסימן רס"א כגון אין לו פתחים בכל ארבע רוחותיו], ג) וזו גירסת ר"י ויש גירסא אחרת יפך והיא גירסת רמב"ם, וע"ש ובספר ם ישועות, ד) יבמות ו., [עיין תוס' קדושין לב. ד"ה רב יהודה], ו) [עיין יל ל. תוס' ד"ה הא אין], [קדושין ל: ע"ש], [לעיל לא.], ט) עיין תוס' דכתובות דף לח. שתירצו בענין אחר.

## תורה אור השלם

כִּי תִרְאֶה חֲמוֹר שֹׂנַאֲךָ רֹבֵץ תַּחַת מַשָּׂאוֹ וְחָדַלְתָּ מֵעֲזֹב לוֹ עָזֹב תַּעֲזֹב עִמּוֹ: [שמות כג, ה]

אִישׁ אִמּוֹ וְאָבִיו תִּירָאוּ וְאֶת שַׁבְּתֹתַי תִּשְׁמֹרוּ אֲנִי יְיָ אֱלֹהֵיכֶם: [ויקרא יט, ג]

כַּבֵּד אֶת אָבִיךָ וְאֶת אִמֶּךָ לְמַעַן יַאֲרִכוּן יָמֶיךָ עַל הָאֲדָמָה אֲשֶׁר יְיָ אֱלֹהֶיךָ נֹתֵן לָךְ: [שמות כ, יב]

כַּבֵּד אֶת יְיָ מֵהוֹנֶךָ וּמֵרֵאשִׁית כָּל תְּבוּאָתֶךָ: [משלי ג, ט]

לֹא תִרְאֶה אֶת חֲמוֹר אָחִיךָ אוֹ שׁוֹרוֹ נֹפְלִים בַּדֶּרֶךְ וְהִתְעַלַּמְתָּ מֵהֶם הָקֵם תָּקִים עִמּוֹ: [דברים כב, ד]

## רבינו חננאל

מיה תלתא. אמר ליה ב ספרא מנא לך [הא] מר ליה דתנן אם יש שם "ד מתנה בפני ב"ד מר ליה מי דמי התם פוקי ממונא הוא ובעי "ד אבל הכא דידי שקלי תרי סגי ליה תדע דקתני למנה מוכרת שלא ב"ד. ואסיק' משמיה רב נחמן בההיא דאינה ריכה ב"ד מומחה אבל ריכה (אפי') ב"ד דיוטות: **מתני'** מצאה רפת וכו' עד אמר לו ביו היטמא או אל תחזיר לא ישמע לו. ת"ר נין שאם אמר לו אביו יטמא או אל תחזיר שלא ישמע לו לבטל את המצוה שנאמר איש אמו אביו תיראו ואת שבתותי תשמורו כולכם חייבים בכבודי אע"פ שהזהרתיך בכיבוד אב אם אם יאמרו לך חלל שבת אל תשמע להן אלא את שבתותי תשמרו וכן בכל המצות. ומקשינן טעמא דכתב רחמנא הכי הא לאו הכי הוה אמינא אם יאמר לו אל תשיב שמע לו ואמאי והא כיבוד אב ואם עשה הוא שנאמר כבד את אביך השבה היא עשה שנאמר השב תשיבם לאחיך ולא תעשה שנאמר לא תוכל להתעלם ולא אתי עשה דחה לא תעשה ועשה. ופרקינן מהו דתימא הואיל ואיתקש כיבוד אב ואם לכיבוד המקום שנאמר כבד את ה' מהונך אימא ניציית ליה לאבוה קמ"ל דלא: חייב לטעון ולפרוק אפי' ק' פעמים שנאמר עזב תעזב עמו. פי' פריקה אית בה חסרון כיס שאם לא תפרקה תמות הבהמה תחת משאה טעינה אין בה חסרון כיס דליכא חששא למיתת הבהמה. ישב לו בעל הבהמה ואמר לו מצוה עליך לפרוק אם תרצה לפרוק פרוק פטור שנאמר עמו. היה בעל הבהמה זקן או חולה חייב. מצוה מן התורה לפרוק

## עין משפט נר מצוה

קעא א ב מיי' פי"ז מהל' אישות הל' יג סמג עשין מח טוש"ע אה"ע סי' קג סעיף א:

קעב ג מיי' פט"ו מהל' אבידה הל' ה סמג עשין עד טוש"ע ח"מ סי' רסא סעיף ג:

קעג ד מיי' פי"א שם הלכה יח ופי"ג מהלכות רוצח הלכה ג סמג שם טוש"ע ח"מ סי' רעב סעיף ג:

קעד ה מיי' פי"א מהל' אבידה הל' יט ופ"ו מהלכות ממרים הל' יב סמג שם וסי' עה טוש"ע ח"מ סי' רסו סעיף ה וטוש"ע י"ד סי' רמ סעיף טו:

קעה ו מיי' פי"ג מהל' רוצח הל' ה סמג עשין פא טוש"ע ח"מ סי' רעב סעיף ד:

קעו ז ח מיי' שם הל' ח טוש"ע שם סעיף ז:

קעז ט מיי' פט"ו מהל' אבידה הל' ה סמג עשין עד טוש"ע ח"מ סי' רסא סעיף ג:

קעח י טוש"ע שם בהג"ה:

קעט כ מיי' פי"ג מהל' רוצח הל' ז סמג עשין פא טוש"ע ח"מ סי' רעב סעיף ו:

## הגהות הב"ח

(א) גמ' אבל הכא דידי שקלי: (ב) שם אני ה' אלהיכם כולכם:

## גליון הש"ס

רש"י ד"ה לומר וכו' הלכך אי לא כתיב. כעין זה כתב רש"י ביצה דף ז ע"ב ד"ה שיעורו:

## ליקוטי רש"י

**אמר לו אביו.** לכהן. **היטמא.** בבית הקברות להשיב אבידה. **אל תחזיר.** שהיתה עומדת בחוץ ואמר לו אל תחזיר. **שנאמר איש אמו וכו' שבתותי תשמרו.** וילפינן לאו דטומאה ולאו דהשבת אבדה מלאוי דשבת [יבמות ו.]. סמך שמירת שבת למורא אב לומר אע"פ שהזהרתיך על מורא אב אם יאמר לך חלל את השבת אל תשמע לו וכן בשאר כל המצות. **אני ה' אלהיכם.** אתה ואביך חייבים בכבודי לפיכך לא תשמע לו לבטל את דברי [ויקרא יט, ג]. **כבד את ה' מהונך.** מכל מה שחננך [משלי ג, ט]. **הקם תקים.** זו טעינה להטעין משאוי שנפל מעליו [דברים כב, ד]. **לא מסיימי קראי.** הי משמע טעינה והי משמע פריקה ואי כתב חדא הוה אמינא לפריקה אתא אבל טעינה לא כתב רחמנא אידך לטעינה [לעיל לא.].

*raise, you shall raise up with him!* Why then, would you consider unloading a commandment, while you deny this status to loading?

The Gemara answers:

אֶלָּא – **Rather,** the Mishnah is to be understood as follows: מִצְוָה מִן הַתּוֹרָה לִפְרוֹק בְּחִנָּם – **It is a commandment in the Torah to** help **unload** an animal **for free;** וְלֹא לִטְעוֹן בְּחִנָּם – **but** it is **not** a commandment **to** help **load for free;** אֶלָּא בְּשָׂכָר – **rather,** if one wishes, he may demand **payment** for helping to reload. רַבִּי שִׁמְעוֹן אוֹמֵר – **R' Shimon says:** אַף לִטְעוֹן בְּחִנָּם – It is **even** a commandment **to** help **load for free.**[34]

On the basis of this reading of the Mishnah, the Gemara corroborates the accuracy of a Baraisa:[35]

תָּנֵינָא לְהָא דְּתָנוּ רַבָּנָן – According to the above interpretation, it emerges that **we have learned in a Mishnah that which the Rabbis taught in a Baraisa.** פְּרִיקָה בְּחִנָּם – For a Baraisa taught: UNLOADING must be done FOR FREE, טְעִינָה בְּשָׂכָר – whereas LOADING may be done FOR PAYMENT. רַבִּי שִׁמְעוֹן אוֹמֵר – R' SHIMON SAYS: זוּ וָזוּ בְּחִנָּם – Both THIS AND THIS [unloading and loading] must be done FOR FREE.

The Gemara explains the reasoning of each disputant:

מַאי טַעֲמַיְיהוּ דְּרַבָּנָן – **What is the reason of the Rabbis** who hold that a person may demand payment for his help in loading? They argue as follows: דְּאִי סָלְקָא דַּעְתָּךְ כְּרַבִּי שִׁמְעוֹן – **If you were to consider** that the law is **as R' Shimon** states it, that one must both unload and load for free, לִכְתּוֹב רַחֲמָנָא טְעִינָה – then **let the Merciful One** simply **write** in his Torah the obligation of **loading,** וְלֹא בָּעֵי פְּרִיקָה – **and** the obligation of **unloading would not need** to be written at all; וַאֲנָא אֲמִינָא – **for I will say** as follows: וּמַה טְּעִינָה – **Now, if** in a situation where **loading** a burden is called for, דְּלֵית בָּהּ צַעַר בַּעֲלֵי חַיִּים – **where there is no suffering caused to a living creature** if the bystander does not assist with the burden, וְלֵיכָּא חֶסְרוֹן כִּיס – **and** likewise **there is no monetary loss** caused to the owner if he does not assist, חַיָּיב – yet still, this bystander **is obligated** by the Torah to help reload; פְּרִיקָה – then, in a situation where **unloading** a burden is called for, דְּאִית בָּהּ צַעַר בַּעֲלֵי חַיִּים – **where there** ***is*** **discomfort to a living creature** if the bystander refrains from helping, וְחֶסְרוֹן כִּיס – **and** there *is* the potential of **monetary loss** to the owner if the bystander does not assist,[36] לֹא כָּל שֶׁכֵּן – **should** this bystander **not certainly** be obligated? אֶלָּא לְמַאי הִלְכְתָא כְּתָבֵיהּ רַחֲמָנָא – **Indeed,** then, **for what purpose did the Merciful One write [the obligation to unload]** in His Torah? לוֹמַר לָךְ – **To tell you** that the obligation to unload extends even further than the obligation to load: פְּרִיקָה בְּחִנָּם – **Unloading** must be done **for free,** טְעִינָה בְּשָׂכָר – whereas **loading** may be done **for payment.**[37]

The Gemara now explains R' Shimon's reasoning:

וְרַבִּי שִׁמְעוֹן מַאי טַעְמָא – **And R' Shimon,** for **what reason** does he reject the logic of the Sages? Why does he rule that both loading and unloading must be done for free? מִשּׁוּם דְּלָא מְסַיְּימֵי קְרָאֵי – **Because,** according to R' Shimon, **the verses are not conclusive.** I.e. it is not clear from the language of the two verses which of them teaches the obligation to load and which one teaches the obligation to unload. Therefore, had the Torah written only one, it would have been understood to teach the obligation to unload, and the obligation to load would not have been known at all.[38]

How, then, would the Rabbis respond to this? The Gemara explains:

וְרַבָּנָן – **And the Rabbis** would counter: אַמַּאי לֹא מְסַיְּימֵי קְרָאֵי – **Why** do you say that **the verses are not conclusive?** הָכָא כְּתִיב: ,,רֹבֵץ תַּחַת מַשָּׂאוֹ" – **Here,**[39] **it is written** that the animal was *lying down under its burden,* which implies that unloading the burden is the action that is called for; הָתָם כְּתִיב נוֹפְלִין בַּדֶּרֶךְ – whereas **there,**[40] **it is written** that you see the animals ***falling by the road,*** דְּרָמוּ אִינְהוּ וּטְעוּנַיְיהוּ בְּאוֹרְחָא מַשְׁמַע – **which implies that** both **[the animals]** ***and*** **their burdens are** lying **cast in the road,** in which case the fallen burdens need to be reloaded onto the animals.[41] It is thus evident that the requirement of the former verse is to assist in unloading, while the requirement of the latter verse is to assist in reloading.

The Gemara concludes:

וְרַבִּי שִׁמְעוֹן נוֹפְלִין בַּדֶּרֶךְ – **R' Shimon, however,** would explain *falling by the road* differently; אִינְהוּ וּטְעוּנַיְיהוּ עֲלָוַיְיהוּ מַשְׁמַע – in his view, these words imply that **[the animals] are** lying **in the road with their burdens** ***upon*** **them.** Thus, according to R' Shimon, even this verse could be interpreted as a command to help unload.[42]

Rava draws an inference from the positions of the Sages and R' Shimon related above:

אָמַר רָבָא – **Rava said:**

NOTES

34. A dispute exists between *Rosh* (§28) and *Ran* (cited by *Nimukei Yosef*) as to the proper interpretation of the Tanna Kamma's ruling that one must help unload for free. According to *Rosh,* this means that a person must help unload an animal without demanding payment only if he had not been working at the time. If he had been working, however, he may ask to receive wages "like an idle worker," as per the system outlined in the Mishnah earlier (see Mishnah 30b and Gemara 31b). According to *Ran,* however, a person must help unload for free in *all* instances, even if his assistance caused him to interrupt his work (see also *Pnei Yehoshua*).

35. See *Rashi* to *Bava Kamma* 13b et al. See also *Ritva* to *Kiddushin* 29a.

36. The lying animal may die or become injured if the load is not removed from it (see *Rashi*).

37. Had only the precept to load been stated, we would have deduced the obligation to unload through a *kal vachomer.* (If it is required that one help load another's animal even though the animal suffers no pain and the owner suffers no loss, it is surely required that one help unload another's animal where there is consideration of pain and loss.) Since, however, the ultimate source of the obligation to unload would have been nothing other than the obligation to load, it could not have been shown that one has a *greater* obligation to unload than he has to load. It would have thus been said that just as one may demand payment for loading, so may he demand payment for unloading. The Torah therefore explicitly stated this second command, the command to unload, to teach that one must do this action without being compensated for it (*Rashi*, as understood by *Maharsha;* cf. *Maharam Shif*).

38. In R' Shimon's view, the language of each of the two verses is ambiguous: Each one could refer to either loading or unloading. Accordingly, if only one of these verses had been written, it would have been understood to teach the more obvious obligation – that one must help *unload* an animal, preventing loss to the owner and pain to the animal. That one is also obligated to help *load* an animal – where his actions would not prevent pain or loss – would not have been known (see *Tosafos* to 31a ד״ה לרבי שמעון לא מסיימי קראי).

According to R' Shimon then, there is no indication from the fact that a second verse is written that the obligation to unload extends further than the obligation to load. He thus concludes that one is obligated to undertake both duties for free.

39. In the verse in *Exodus* 23:5.

40. In the verse in *Deuteronomy* 22:4.

41. The word נוֹפְלִים, *falling,* is in the plural form, thus implying that two things fell – the animal and its burden. Apparently, then, the verse speaks of an animal that stumbled to the ground, strewing its load in the process. In such a case, it is necessary to reload the animal, after it stands itself back upon its feet.

42. R' Shimon agrees that the plural verb נוֹפְלִים, *falling,* refers to both the animals and their burdens; however, he argues that the verse could mean that the two have fallen *together,* the animal having lain down under the weight of a burden that still remains strapped to its back. In such case, the action that would be called for is פְּרִיקָה, *unloading.*

תרי מגו תלתא ואי נמי תרי סהדי דפלגת באפי בי תלתא א"ל מנא לך הא א"ל דתנן אם יש שם ב"ד מתנה בפניהם אין שם ב"ד בפני מי יתנה שלו קודם א"ל מי דמי התם דמפיק ממונא מהאי ומותיב להאי בעינן ב"ד אבל הכא (א) דידיה שקלי גילוי מילתא בעלמא הוא בתרי סגי ליה תדע דתנן (א) [א]אלמנה מוכרת שלא בפני ב"ד אמר ליה אביי ולאו מי אתמר עלה אמר רב יוסף בר מניומי אמר ר"נ אלמנה אינה צריכה ב"ד של מומחין [ב]אבל צריכה בית דין של הדיוטות: **מתני'** [ג]מצאה ברפת אין חייב בה ברה"ר חייב בה [ד]ואם היתה בבית הקברות לא יטמא לה [ה]אם אמר לו אביו היטמא או שאמר לו אל תחזיר לא ישמע לו [ו]פרק וטען פרק וטען אפילו ארבעה וחמשה פעמים חייב שנאמר א) עזב תעזב [ז]הלך וישב לו ואמר הואיל ועליך מצוה אם רצונך לפרוק פרוק פטור שנאמר עמו [ח]אם היה זקן או חולה חייב מצוה מן התורה לפרוק אבל לא לטעון ר"ש אומר אף לטעון רבי יוסי הגלילי אומר אם היה עליו יתר על משאו אין זקוק לו שנאמר תחת משאו משאוי שיכול לעמוד בו: **גמ'** אמר רבא [ט]רפת שאמרו [ג] אינה מתעה ואינה משמרת אינה מתעה מדקתני אינו חייב בה ואינה משמרת מדאיצטריך למיתני אינו חייב בה דאי סלקא דעתך משמרת השתא משכח לה אבראי מעייל לה לגואי משכח לה מגואי מבעיא אלא שמע מינה אינה משמרת שמע מינה: מצאה ברפת אינו חייב: א"ר יצחק [ג] [י]והוא שעומדת תוך לתחום מכלל דברשות הרבים ואפילו בתוך התחום נמי חייב איכא דמתני לה אסיפא ברה"ר חייב בה אמר רבי יצחק והוא שעומדת חוץ לתחום מכלל דברפת אפילו עומדת חוץ לתחום נמי אינו חייב בה: בבית הקברות לא יטמא לה: [ד]ת"ר מנין שאם אמר לו אביו היטמא או שאמר לו [ה]אל תחזיר שלא ישמע לו שנאמר ב) איש אמו ואביו תיראו ואת שבתותי תשמרו אני ה' (ב) כולכם חייבין בכבודי טעמא דכתב רחמנא את שבתותי תשמרו הא לאו הכי הוה אמינא צייתא ליה ואמאי האי עשה והאי לא תעשה ועשה [ו]ולא אתי עשה ודחי את לא תעשה ועשה איצטריך ס"ד אמינא הואיל והוקש כיבוד אב ואם לכבודו [ז]של מקום שנאמר כאן ג) כבד את אביך ואת אמך ונאמר להלן ד) כבד את ה' מהונך הלכך לציית ליה קמ"ל דלא לשמע ליה: מצוה מן התורה לפרוק אבל לא לטעון: מאי אבל לא לטעון אילימא אבל לא לטעון כלל מאי שנא פריקה דכתיב עזב תעזב עמו טעינה נמי הכתיב ה) הקם תקים עמו אלא [כ]מצוה מן התורה לפרוק בחנם ולא לטעון בחנם אלא בשכר ר"ש אומר [ח]אף לטעון בחנם תנינא להא דת"ר פריקה בחנם טעינה בשכר ר"ש אומר זו וזו בחנם מאי טעמייהו דרבנן דאי ס"ד כר"ש לכתוב רחמנא טעינה ולא בעי פריקה ואנא אמינא ומה טעינה דלית בה צער בעלי חיים וליכא חסרון כיס חייב פריקה דאית בה צער בעלי חיים וחסרון כיס לא כל שכן אלא למאי הלכתא כתביה רחמנא לומר לך פריקה בחנם טעינה בשכר ורבי שמעון מאי טעמא משום דלא מסיימי קראי ורבנן אמאי לא מסיימי קראי הכא כתיב רובץ תחת משאו התם כתיב נופלין בדרך דרמו אינהו וטעונייהו באורחא משמע ורבי שמעון נופלין בדרך אינהו וטעונייהו עלוייהו משמע אמר רבא

מדברי

רש"י

תרי מגו תלתא. שנים מן השלשה יבואו ויעידו לומר שלשה היינו: אם יש שם ב"ד. וסתם ב"ד שלשה אלמא אין כח להפקיד ממון זה אלא זה בפחות משלשה: גילוי מילתא. שידעו שחלקתי בשוה: אלמנה. הניזונת מנכסי יתומים מוכרת למזונות: שלא בב"ד. ובלבד שיראו שנים שלא תמכור בזול: **מתני'** מצאה ברפת. בגמרא מפרש מאי אצטריך: היתה בבית הקברות. והוא כהן: או שאמר לו אל תחזיר. והוא במקום שהוא מותר לילך שם: הלך וישב לו. הבעלים: אבל לא לטעון. בגמרא מפרש: **גמ'** רפת שאמרו. ששנינו במשנתנו עסקינן כשאינה מתעה את הבהמה שבתוכה להיות בורחת ויוצאת: ואינה משתמרת. שאינה נעולה ואם באת לצאת יוצאה: מעייל לגואי. כדאמרינן לעיל (דף לא.) לגינתו ולחורבתו מנין: ברישא גרסינן והוא שעומדת בתוך לתחום בסיפא גרסינן והוא שעומדת חוץ לתחום: אני ה'. אע"פ שאמרתי לך ירא את אביך אני אדון לשניכם ואם אמר לך אביך עבור על דברי לחלל שבת אל תשמע לו: הוה אמינא צייתא ליה. דאתי עשה דכיבוד ודחי לא תעשה דלא תוכל להתעלם: אבידה עשה ולא תעשה היא השב תשיבם לא תוכל להתעלם: הוקש כבודם. בגזירה שוה כבד את אביך כבד את ה' מהונך: דלית ביה חסרון כיס. אם לא יטעון: פריקה אית בה חסרון כיס. שהבהמה נשברת תחת משאה: לומר לך פריקה בחנם. אבל טעינה לא נצטוית אלא בשכר °הלכך אי לא כתב פריקה ואתיא מק"ו מטעינה הוה אמינא דיו לבא מן הדין להיות כנדון מה טעינה בשכר אף פריקה בשכר: לא מסיימי קראי. למשמעות טעינה הלכך אי כתיב חד הוה אמינא לפריקה אתא: רובץ תחת משאו. משמע שצריך לפרוק: דרמו אינהו וטעונייהו באורחא. אף המשא מוטל על הקרקע שצריך לטעון:

מדברי

תוספות

**אלמנה** מוכרת שלא בב"ד. וא"ת התם משום חינא או משום שלא תתבזה בב"ד כדמפרש באלמנה ניזונת (כתובות דף לז: ושם) וי"ל דס"ל כיון דאלמנה מוכרת אע"ג דאינה שלה שלא בב"ד משום חינא ה"נ שותף יטול את שלו שלא בב"ד אע"ג דליכא טעם דחינא: **בית** דין הדיוטות. וא"ת והאמרינן התם (דף לח. ושם) אלמנה ששמה לעצמה לא עשתה ולא כלום דאמרינן לה מאן שם לך הלא מכרה ע"פ ב"ד הדיוטות וי"ל כיון שלוקחת לעצמה נראה לעולם שמעכבת מנכסי יתומים בידה אע"פ שיש ב"ד הדיוטות כיון דליכא מומחין אבל כשמוכרת לאחרים אין נראה שמעכבת משלהם שהרי לא עכבה כלום וא"ת ומ"ש דאלמנה מוכרת לאחרים שלא בב"ד ובב"ד יכולה לעכב אפי' לעצמה מדאמרינן התם דא"ל מאן שם לך משמע דבב"ד יכולה לשום וקאמר נמי התם ההוא גברא דאפקידו גביה כשא דיתמי אזל שמה לנפשיה בת' זוזי לסוף אייקור כו' אתא לקמיה דרבי א"ל מאן שם לך משמע דבב"ד יכול לשום ולקמן בפרק המפקיד (דף לח.) תנן המפקיד פירות אצל חבירו והרקיבו כו' עושה להם תקנה ומוכרן בב"ד וכשהוא מוכרן מוכרן לאחרים ואין מוכרן לעצמו כיוצא בו גבאי צדקה פורטין לאחרים ואין פורטין לעצמם דאפילו בב"ד מוכרין לאחרים ואין מוכרין לעצמם ושלא בב"ד אין מוכרין אפילו לאחרים וליכא למימר הא דאמר ומוכרים לאחרים בב"ד היינו ברשות ב"ד אבל אי ידעי ב"ד השומא יכול לעכב לעצמו דבירושלמי מסיק על ההוא מעשה דרבי יוחנן חקוקאה דמייתי פ"ק דפסחים (דף יג. ושם) א"ל לך ומוכרם בב"ד אלמא אע"פ שנתן לו רשות היה צריך למוכרם בב"ד וי"ל דמוכרת שלא בב"ד משום חינא [ט]וגבי כשא דיתמי נמי דיכול לעכב לעצמו בב"ד מלינן למימר דהיינו דוקא בדיעבד דמשום חסד לא מהדרינן עובדא א"נ דגבי יתמי ב"ד עצמם הם מפקידין ולכך יכול לעכב לעצמו על פיהם אבל פקדון של אחרים אינו יכול לעכב לעצמו על פי ב"ד: **כבד** את ה' מהונך. הא דנקט קרא דדברי קבלה ולא נקט קרא דאיש אמו ואביו תיראו וכתיב את ה' אלהיך תירא משום דניחא ליה לאתויי קרא דכבוד:

מדברי

עין משפט נר מצוה

קעא א ב מיי' פי"ז מהל' אישות הל' יג סמג עשין מח טוש"ע אה"ע סי' קג סעיף א:

קעב ג מיי' פט"ו מהל' אבידה הל' ה סמג עשין עד טוש"ע ח"מ סי' רסא סעיף ג:

קעג ד מיי' פי"א שם הלכה יח ופי"ג מהלכות רוצח הלכה ג סמג שם טוש"ע ח"מ סי' רעב סעיף ב:

קעד ה מיי' פי"א מהל' אבידה הל' יט ופ"ו מהלכות ממרים הל' יב סמג שם וסי' עה טוש"ע ח"מ סי' רסו סעיף ה וטוש"ע י"ד סי' רמ סעיף טו:

קעה ו מיי' פי"ג מהל' רוצח הל' ה סמג עשין פא טוש"ע ח"מ סי' רעב סעיף ד:

קעו ז ח מיי' שם הל' ח טוש"ע שם סעיף ז:

קעז ט מיי' פט"ו מהל' אבידה הל' ה סמג עשין עד טוש"ע ח"מ סי' רסא סעיף ג:

קעח י טוש"ע שם בהג"ה:

קעט כ מיי' פי"ג מהל' רוצח הל' ז סמג עשין פא טוש"ע ח"מ סי' רעב סעיף ו:

הגהות הב"ח

(א) גמ' אבל הכא דידי שקלי: (ב) שם אני ה' אלהיכם כולכם:

גליון הש"ס

רש"י ד"ה לומר וכו' הלכך אי לא כתיב. כעין זה כתב רש"י ביצה דף ז ע"ב ד"ה שיעורו:

ליקוטי רש"י

**אמר לו אביו.** לכהן. **היטמא.** בבית הקברות להשיב אבידה. **אל תחזיר.** שהיתה עומדת בחוץ ואמר לו אל תחזיר. **שנאמר איש אמו וכו' שבתותי תשמרו.** וילפינן לאו דטומאה ולאו דהשבת אבדה מלאוי דשבת [יבמות ו.]. סמך שמירת שבת למורא אב לומר אע"פ שהזהרתיך על מורא אב אם יאמר לך חלל את השבת אל תשמע לו וכן בשאר כל המצות. **אני ה' אלהיכם.** אתה ואביך חייבים בכבודי לפיכך לא תשמע לו לבטל את דברי [ויקרא יט, ג]. **כבד את ה' מהונך.** מכל מה שחננך [משלי ג, ט]. **הקם תקים.** זו טעינה להטעין משאוי שנפל מעליו [דברים כב, ד]. **לא מסיימי קראי.** הי משמע טעינה והי משמע פריקה ואי כתב חדא הוה אמינא לפריקה אתא אבל טעינה לא כתב רחמנא אידך לטעינה [לעיל לא.].

מסורת הש"ס

א) כתובות לז., ב) [פי' הטור בסימן רס"א כגון שאין לו פתחים בכל ארבע רוחותיו], ג) זהו גירסת רש"י ויש גירסא אחרת להיפך והיא גירסת הרמב"ם, וע"ש ובספר כוס ישועות, ד) יבמות ו., ה) [עיין תוס' קדושין לב. ד"ה רב יהודה], ו) [עיין לעיל ל. תוס' ד"ה הא אין], ז) [קדושין ל: ע"ש], ח) [לעיל לא.], ט) עיין בתוס' דכתובות דף לח. שתירצו בענין אחר.

תורה אור השלם

א) כִּי תִרְאֶה חֲמוֹר שֹׂנַאֲךָ רֹבֵץ תַּחַת מַשָּׂאוֹ וְחָדַלְתָּ מֵעֲזֹב לוֹ עָזֹב תַּעֲזֹב עִמּוֹ: [שמות כג, ה]

ב) אִישׁ אִמּוֹ וְאָבִיו תִּירָאוּ וְאֶת שַׁבְּתֹתַי תִּשְׁמֹרוּ אֲנִי יְיָ אֱלֹהֵיכֶם: [ויקרא יט, ג]

ג) כַּבֵּד אֶת אָבִיךָ וְאֶת אִמֶּךָ לְמַעַן יַאֲרִכוּן יָמֶיךָ עַל הָאֲדָמָה אֲשֶׁר יְיָ אֱלֹהֶיךָ נֹתֵן לָךְ: [שמות כ, יב]

ד) כַּבֵּד אֶת יְיָ מֵהוֹנֶךָ וּמֵרֵאשִׁית כָּל תְּבוּאָתֶךָ: [משלי ג, ט]

ה) לֹא תִרְאֶה אֶת חֲמוֹר אָחִיךָ אוֹ שׁוֹרוֹ נֹפְלִים בַּדֶּרֶךְ וְהִתְעַלַּמְתָּ מֵהֶם הָקֵם תָּקִים עִמּוֹ: [דברים כב, ד]

רבינו חננאל

קמיה תלתא. אמר ליה רב ספרא מנא לך [הא] אמר ליה דתנן אם יש שם ב"ד מתנה בפני ב"ד אמר ליה מי דמי התם אפוקי ממונא הוא ובעי ב"ד אבל הכא דידי שקלי בתרי סגי ליה תדע דקתני אלמנה מוכרת שלא בב"ד. ואסיק' משמיה דרב נחמן בההיא דאינה צריכה ב"ד מומחה אבל צריכה (אפי') ב"ד הדיוטות: מתני' מצאה ברפת וכו' עד אמר לו אביו היטמא או אל תחזיר לא ישמע לו. ת"ר מנין שאם אמר לו אביו היטמא או אל תחזיר שלא ישמע לו לבטל את המצוה שנאמר איש אמו ואביו תיראו ואת שבתותי תשמורו כולכם חייבים בכבודי אע"פ שהזהרתיך בכיבוד אב ואם אם יאמרו לך חלל שבת אל תשמע להן אלא ואת שבתותי תשמרו וכן בכל המצות. ומקשינן טעמא דכתב רחמנא הכי הא לאו הכי הוה אמינא אם יאמר לו אל תשיב ישמע לו אמאי והא כיבוד אב ואם עשה הוא שנאמר כבד את אביך והשבה היא עשה שנאמר השב תשיבם לאחיך ולא תעשה שנאמר לא תוכל להתעלם ולא אתי עשה ודחה לא תעשה ועשה. ופרקינן מהו דתימא הואיל ואיתקיש כיבוד אב ואם לכיבוד המקום שנאמר כבד את ה' מהונך אימא ניציית ליה לאבוה קמ"ל דלא: חייב לטעון ולפרוק אפי' ק' פעמים שנאמר עזב תעזב עמו. פי' פריקה אית בה חסרון כיס שאם לא תפרקה תמות הבהמה תחת משאה טעינה אין בה חסרון כיס דליכא חששא למיתת הבהמה. ישב לו בעל הבהמה ואמר לו מצוה עליך לפרוק אם תרצה לפרוק פרוק פטור שנאמר עמו. היה בעל הבהמה זקן או חולה חייב. מצוה מן התורה לפרוק

standing on public property **beyond the *techum* boundary;** if, however, it is standing on public property *within* the *techum,* the finder need not retrieve it.

The Gemara points out how this qualification will affect the interpretation of the Mishnah's first law as well:

**מִכְּלָל דִּבְרֵפְת** – **By implication,** then, it follows **that** when the Mishnah speaks of an animal found **in a barn,** אֲפִילוּ עוֹמֶדֶת חוּץ לַתְּחוּם נַמִּי אֵינוֹ חַיָּיב בָּהּ – it means that **even if [the barn] is situated beyond the *techum,* he is still not obligated to** return **it.**[22]

The Gemara now discusses the next section of the Mishnah. This had begun:

**בְּבֵית הַקְּבָרוֹת לֹא יִטַּמָּא לָהּ** – If the finder is a Kohen and the lost object he sights was IN A CEMETERY, HE SHOULD NOT BECOME *TAMEI* by entering the cemetery TO retrieve [THE OBJECT].

The Mishnah proceeded to state that the Kohen should not enter the cemetery even if his father orders him to. The Gemara now cites a Baraisa that elaborates on this:

**תָּנוּ רַבָּנַן** – **The Rabbis taught in a Baraisa:** מִנַּיִן שֶׁאִם אָמַר לוֹ אָבִיו – FROM WHERE IS IT DERIVED THAT IF [A KOHEN'S] FATHER TOLD HIM, הִיטַּמֵּא – "Retrieve the lost object and BECOME *TAMEI,*"[23] אוֹ שֶׁאָמַר לוֹ אַל תַּחֲזִיר – OR if [HIS FATHER] TOLD HIM; "DO NOT RETURN the lost object you see before you,"[24] שֶׁלֹּא יִשְׁמַע לוֹ – THAT HE SHOULD NOT LISTEN TO [HIS FATHER]? שֶׁנֶּאֱמַר – FOR IT IS STATED:[25] ,,אִישׁ אִמּוֹ וְאָבִיו תִּירָאוּ וְאֶת־שַׁבְּתֹתַי תִּשְׁמֹרוּ – *[EVERY] MAN, YOU SHALL REVERE YOUR MOTHER AND FATHER, AND MY SABBATH YOU SHALL OBSERVE,* אֲנִי ה׳" – and the verse then concludes: *I AM GOD,* implying: כּוּלְּכֶם חַיָּיבִין בִּכְבוֹדִי – ALL OF YOU – you, as well as your father – ARE OBLIGATED to uphold MY HONOR.[26] It can thus be shown that if your father tells you to violate the Torah's commandments, you are not to heed his demand.

The Gemara analyzes this Baraisa:

**טַעְמָא דִּכְתַב רַחֲמָנָא** – Apparently, **the reason** the son must disobey his father and return the object is **that the Merciful One wrote** in His Torah: ,,אֶת־שַׁבְּתֹתַי תִּשְׁמֹרוּ" – *My Sabbath you shall observe, I am God,* teaching that God's directives take precedence over one's father's. **הָא לָאו הָכִי הֲוָה אָמִינָא** – **Had [these words] not been** written, however, **I would have** apparently **said:** **צַיְיתָא לֵיהּ** – **[The son] should** indeed **listen to [his father],** and not return the lost item. **וְאַמַּאי** – **But why** would I have thought this? **הַאי עֲשֵׂה** – **This** obligation to obey one's father **is a positive commandment,** **וְהַאי לֹא תַעֲשֶׂה וַעֲשֵׂה** – **whereas this** obligation to return a lost object is mandated by both **a negative commandment and a positive commandment.**[27] **וְלֹא אָתֵי עֲשֵׂה וְדָחֵי אֶת לֹא תַעֲשֶׂה וַעֲשֵׂה** – **And** the rule in such cases is that a **positive commandment cannot come and push aside a negative commandment and a positive commandment.**[28] Thus, even without the teaching of the verse, I would have known that the obligation to honor one's father does not supersede the obligation to retrieve a lost object! – ? –

The Gemara answers by showing why a verse is in fact needed to teach this law:

**אִיצְטְרִיךְ** – **It was** indeed **necessary** for the Torah to write this. **סָלְקָא דַּעְתָּךְ אָמִינָא** – For had it not done so, **you might have thought to say:** הוֹאִיל וְהוּקַּשׁ כִּיבּוּד אָב וְאֵם לִכְבוֹדוֹ שֶׁל מָקוֹם – **Since the** idea of **honoring** one's **father and mother is compared** by the Torah **to the** idea of **honoring the Omnipresent,** שֶׁנֶּאֱמַר כָּאן – **for** indeed, **it is stated here:** ,,כַּבֵּד אֶת־אָבִיךָ וְאֶת־אִמֶּךָ" – *Honor your father and your mother,*[29] וְנֶאֱמַר לְהַלָּן – **and it is stated further on,** in another verse: ,,כַּבֵּד אֶת־ה׳ מֵהוֹנֶךָ" – *Honor God with your property;*[30] הִלְכָּךְ לְצַיֵּית לֵיהּ – since these two concepts are compared, it could have been thought that **one should therefore listen to [his father]** even when his father asks him to transgress a commandment.[31] **קָא מַשְׁמַע לָן דְּלָא לִשְׁמַע לֵיהּ** – **[The Torah] therefore informs us that** this is not the case; **one should not listen to him.**

The Gemara analyzes another segment of our Mishnah:

**מִצְוָה מִן הַתּוֹרָה לִפְרוֹק אֲבָל לֹא לִטְעוֹן** – IT IS A COMMANDMENT IN THE TORAH TO help UNLOAD cargo from an animal that is lying under its burden, BUT it is NOT a commandment TO help LOAD a burden upon an animal after this burden fell off of it.

The Gemara questions this statement:

**מַאי אֲבָל לֹא לִטְעוֹן** – **What is** meant by the statement BUT it is NOT a commandment TO help LOAD a burden upon an animal? **אִילֵימָא אֲבָל לֹא לִטְעוֹן כְּלָל** – **If you will say** this means: "**but there is no** commandment **to** help **load whatsoever,**" this cannot be, **מַאי שְׁנָא פְּרִיקָה** – for why **is unloading unique** that you consider only this to be a commandment? **דִּכְתִיב: ,,עָזֹב תַּעֲזֹב עִמּוֹ"** – Is it **because it is written** with respect to unloading: ***help, you shall help with him?***[32] **טְעִינָה נַמִּי הַכְּתִיב** – Then with respect to **loading as well,** a verse is also **written:**[33] ,,הָקֵם תָּקִים עִמּוֹ" –

NOTES

Thus, if the barn was within the *techum,* so, too, was the public property that was spoken of.]

22. Once again, the assumption is made that the case in which the animal is found on public property is parallel to the case in which it is found in the barn. Hence, if the public property that was spoken of is property that lies outside the *techum,* it can be assumed that the barn that was spoken of is also a barn that lies outside the *techum.*

In summary, the following laws emerge from the Gemara's discussion: According to the first version of R' Yitzchak's words, if one found an animal in public property, he must *always* retrieve it. If, however, he found it in a barn, he need retrieve it only if this barn was situated beyond the *techum*. According to the second version, if one found an animal in a barn, he should categorically not retrieve it, regardless of the barn's whereabouts. If, however, he found it in public property, he should indeed retrieve it if the animal was standing beyond the *techum*.

23. See above, note 9.

24. See above, note 10.

25. *Leviticus* 19:3.

26. The Baraisa expounds the juxtaposition of the commands to revere one's father and to observe the Sabbath with the verse's mention that "*I am God.*" The verse is taken to imply: "Although I have commanded you to revere your father, I have also stated that "*I am God,*" the ultimate authority over both of you. Thus, if your father tells you to disregard My command and violate the Sabbath, you must disobey him and observe the Sabbath" (*Rashi*).

27. The obligation to honor one's father is mandated by the positive commandment: כַּבֵּד אֶת־אָבִיךָ וְאֶת־אִמֶּךָ, *Honor your father and your mother* (*Exodus* 20:12). The obligation to return a lost object, however, is mandated by both a positive commandment: הָשֵׁב תְּשִׁיבֵם, *You shall return them* (*Deut.* 22:1), and a negative commandment: לֹא תוּכַל לְהִתְעַלֵּם, *you are not able to hide* (*Deut.* 22:3) (*Rashi*; see *Rashash*).

28. See 30a note 28.

29. *Exodus* 20:12.

30. *Proverbs* 3:9. The word כַּבֵּד, *honor,* appears in both verses, and they are therefore compared by means of a *gezeirah shavah* (see *Rashi*).

31. *Ritva* cites *Tosafos* as finding difficulty with this assertion of the Gemara. Why would the fact that a comparison exists between the ideas of honoring God and honoring parents lead us to believe that the obligation to honor parents *supersedes* the obligation to honor God? If anything, this comparison might yield that the two have equal standing, but not that one supersedes the other! As a possible solution to this problem, *Ritva* suggests that perhaps this is exactly what the Gemara means to say. In other words, perhaps when the Gemara considers that the command to honor parents might "push aside" the command to return an object, it means only that the two would have equal standing, in which case the son would be permitted to choose which command he wishes to fulfill (cf. *Tos. HaRosh*).

32. *Exodus* 23:5.

33. *Deuteronomy* 22:4.

תרי מגו תלתא ואי נמי תרי סהדי דפלגת באפי בי תלתא א"ל מנא לך הא א"ל דתנן אם יש שם ב"ד מתנה בפניהם אין שם ב"ד בפני מי יתנה שלו קודם א"ל מי דמי התם דמפיק ממונא מהאי ומותיב להאי בעינן ב"ד אבל הכא (א) דידיה שקלי גילוי מילתא בעלמא הוא בתרי סגי ליה תדע דתנן (א) אאלמנה מוכרת שלא בפני ב"ד אמר ליה אביי ולאו מי אתמר עלה אמר רב יוסף בר מניומי אמר ר"נ אלמנה אינה צריכה ב"ד של מומחין באבל צריכה בית דין של הדיוטות: **מתני'** גמצאה ברפת אין חייב בה ברה"ר חייב בה דואם היתה בבית הקברות לא יטמא לה האם אמר לו אביו היטמא או שאמר לו אל תחזיר לא ישמע לו ופרק וטען פרק וטען אפילו ארבעה וחמשה פעמים חייב שנאמר (א) עזב תעזב זהלך וישב לו ואמר הואיל ועליך מצוה אם רצונך לפרוק פרוק פטור שנאמר עמו חאם היה זקן או חולה חייב מצוה מן התורה לפרוק אבל לא לטעון ר"ש אומר אף לטעון רבי יוסי הגלילי אומר אם היה עליו יתר על משאו אין זקוק לו שנאמר תחת משאו משאוי שיכול לעמוד בו: **גמ'** אמר רבא טרפת שאמרו (ב) אינה מתעה ואינה משמרת אינה מתעה מדקתני אינו חייב בה ואינה משמרת מדאיצטריך למיתני אינו חייב בה דאי סלקא דעתך משמרת השתא משכח לה אבראי מעייל לה לגואי משכח לה מגואי מבעיא אלא שמע מינה אינה משמרת שמע מינה: מצאה ברפת אינו חייב: א"ר יצחק (ג) יוהוא שעומדת תוך לתחום מכלל דברשות הרבים ואפילו בתוך התחום נמי חייב איכא דמתני לה אסיפא ברה"ר חייב בה אמר רבי יצחק והוא שעומדת חוץ לתחום מכלל דברפת אפילו עומדת חוץ לתחום נמי אינו חייב בה: בבית הקברות לא יטמא לה: (ד) ת"ר מנין שאם אמר לו אביו היטמא או שאמר לו (ה) אל תחזיר שלא ישמע לו שנאמר (ב) איש אמו ואביו תיראו ואת שבתותי תשמרו אני ה' (ג) כולכם חייבין בכבודי טעמא דכתב רחמנא את שבתותי תשמרו הא לאו הכי הוה אמינא צייתא ליה ואמאי האי עשה והאי לא תעשה ועשה (י) ולא אתי עשה ודחי את לא תעשה ועשה איצטריך ס"ד אמינא הואיל והוקש כיבוד אב ואם לכבודו (ז) של מקום שנאמר כאן (ג) כבד את אביך ואת אמך ונאמר להלן (ד) כבד את ה' מהונך הלכך לציית ליה קמ"ל דלא לשמע ליה: מצוה מן התורה לפרוק אבל לא לטעון: מאי אבל לא לטעון אילימא אבל לא לטעון כלל מאי שנא פריקה דכתיב עזב תעזב עמו טעינה נמי הכתיב (ה) הקם תקים עמו אלא כמצוה מן התורה לפרוק בחנם ולא לטעון בחנם אלא בשכר ר"ש אומר (ח) אף לטעון בחנם תנינא להא דת"ר פריקה בחנם טעינה בשכר ר"ש אומר זו וזו בחנם מאי טעמייהו דרבנן דאי ס"ד כר"ש לכתוב רחמנא טעינה ולא בעי פריקה ואנא אמינא ומה טעינה דלית בה צער בעלי חיים וליכא חסרון כיס חייב פריקה דאית בה צער בעלי חיים וחסרון כיס לא כל שכן אלא למאי הלכתא כתביה רחמנא לומר לך פריקה בחנם טעינה בשכר ורבי שמעון מאי טעמא משום דלא מסיימי קראי ורבנן אמאי לא מסיימי קראי הכא כתיב רובץ תחת משאו התם כתיב נופלין בדרך דרמו אינהו וטעונייהו באורחא ורבי שמעון נופלין בדרך אינהו וטעונייהו עלוייהו משמע אמר רבא

מדברי

### רש"י

תרי מגו תלתא. שנים מן השלשה יבואו ויעידו לומר שלשה היינו: אם יש שם ב"ד. וסתם ב"ד שלשה אלמא אין כח להפקיר ממון זה אלא זה בפחות משלשה: גילוי מילתא. שידעו שחלקתי בשוה: אלמנה. הניזונת מנכסי יתומים מוכרת למזונות: שלא בב"ד. ובלבד שיראו שנים שלא תמכור בזול: **מתני'** מצאה ברפת. בגמרא מפרש מאי אצטריך: היתה בבית הקברות. והוא כהן: או שאמר לו אל תחזיר. והוא במקום שהוא מותר לילך שם: הלך וישב לו. הבעלים: אבל לא לטעון. בגמרא מפרש: גמ' רפת שאמרו. ששנינו במשנתנו עסקינן כשאינה מתעה את הבהמה שבתוכה להיות בורחת ויוצאת: ואינה משתמרת. שאינה נעולה ואם באת לצאת יוצאה: מעייל לגואי. כדאמרינן לעיל (דף לא.) לגינתו ולחורבתו מנין: ברישא גרסינן והוא שעומדת בתוך לתחום בסיפא גרסינן והוא שעומדת חוץ לתחום: אני ה'. אע"פ שאמרתי לך ירא את אביך אני אדון לשניכם ואם אמר לך אביך עבור על דברי לחלל שבת אל תשמע לו: הוה אמינא צייתא ליה. דאתי עשה דכיבוד ודחי לא תעשה דלא תוכל להתעלם: אבידה עשה ולא תעשה היא השב תשיבם לא תוכל להתעלם: הוקש כבודם. בגזירה שוה כבד את אביך כבד את ה' מהונך: דלית ביה חסרון כיס. אם לא יטעון: פריקה אית בה חסרון כיס. שהבהמה נשברת תחת משאה: לומר לך פריקה בחנם. אבל טעינה לא נצטוית אלא בשכר ° הלכך אי לא כתב פריקה ואתיא מק"ו מטעינה הוה אמינא דיו לבא מן הדין להיות כנדון מה טעינה בשכר אף פריקה בשכר: לא מסיימי קראי. למשמעות טעינה הלכך אי כתיב חד הוה אמינא לפריקה אתא: רובץ תחת משאו. משמע שצריך לפרוק: דרמו אינהו וטעונייהו באורחא. אף המשא מוטל על הקרקע שצריך לטעון:

מדברי

### תוספות

**אלמנה** מוכרת שלא בב"ד. וא"ת התם משום חינא או משום שלא תתבזה בב"ד כדמפרש באלמנה ניזונת (כתובות דף צז: ושם) וי"ל דס"ל כיון דאלמנה מוכרת אע"ג דאינה שלה שלא בב"ד משום חינא ה"נ שותף יטול את שלו שלא בב"ד אע"ג דליכא טעם דחינא: **בית** דין הדיוטות. וא"ת והאמרינן התם (דף צח. ושם) אלמנה ששמה לעצמה לא עשתה ולא כלום דאמרינן לה מאן שם לך הלא מכרה ע"פ ב"ד הדיוטות וי"ל כיון שלוקחת לעצמה נראה לעולם שמעכבת מנכסי יתומים בידה אע"פ שיש ב"ד הדיוטות כיון דליכא מומחין אבל כשמוכרת לאחרים אין נראה שמעכבת משלהם שהרי לא עכבה כלום וא"ת ומ"ש דאלמנה מוכרת לאחרים שלא בב"ד ובב"ד יכולה לעכב אפי' לעצמה מדאמרינן התם דא"ל מאן שם לך משמע דבב"ד יכולה לשום וקאמר נמי התם ההוא גברא דאפקידו גביה כספא דיתמי אזל שמה לנפשיה בת' זוזי לסוף אייקור כו' אתא לקמיה דרבי א"ל מאן שם לך משמע דבב"ד יכול לשום ולקמן בפרק המפקיד (דף לח.) תנן המפקיד פירות אצל חבירו והרקיבו כו' עושה להם תקנה ומוכרן בב"ד וכשהוא מוכרן מוכרן לאחרים ואין מוכרן לעצמו כיוצא בו גבאי צדקה פורטין לאחרים ואין פורטין לעצמם דאפילו בב"ד מוכרין לאחרים ואין מוכרין לעצמם ושלא בב"ד אין מוכרין אפילו לאחרים וליכא למימר הא דאמר ומוכרים לאחרים בב"ד היינו ברשות ב"ד אבל אי ידעי ב"ד השומא יכול לעכב לעצמו דבירושלמי מסיק על ההוא מעשה דרבי יוחנן חקוקאה דמייתי פ"ק דפסחים (דף יג. ושם) א"ל לך ומוכרם בב"ד אלמא אע"פ שנתן לו רשות היה צריך למוכרם בב"ד וי"ל דמוכרת שלא בב"ד משום חינא (ט) וגבי כספא דיתמי נמי דיכול לעכב לעצמו בב"ד מלינן למימר דהיינו דוקא בדיעבד דמשום חסד לא מהדרינן עובדא א"נ דגבי יתמי ב"ד עצמם הם מפקידין ולכך יכול לעכב לעצמו על פיהם אבל פקדון של אחרים אינו יכול לעכב לעצמו על פי ב"ד: **כבד** את ה' מהונך. הא דנקט קרא דדברי קבלה ולא נקט קרא דאיש אמו ואביו תיראו וכתיב את ה' אלהיך תירא משום דניחא ליה לאתויי קרא דכבוד:

מדברי

### עין משפט נר מצוה

קעא א ב מיי' פי"ז מהל' אישות הל' יג סמג עשין מח טוש"ע אה"ע סי' קג סעיף א:
קעב ג מיי' פט"ו מהל' אבידה הל' ה סמג עשין עד טוש"ע ח"מ סי' רסא סעיף ג:
קעג ד מיי' פי"א שם הלכה יח ופי"ג מהלכות רוצח הלכה ג סמג שם טוש"ע ח"מ סי' רעב סעיף ב:
קעד ה מיי' פי"א מהל' אבידה הל' יט ופ"ו מהלכות ממרים הל' יב סמג שם וסי' עה טוש"ע ח"מ סי' רסו סעיף ה וטוש"ע י"ד סי' רמ סעיף טו:
קעה ו מיי' פי"ג מהל' רוצח הל' ה סמג עשין פא טוש"ע ח"מ סי' רעב סעיף ד:
קעו ז ח מיי' שם הל' ח טוש"ע שם סעיף ז:
קעז ט מיי' פט"ו מהל' אבידה הל' ה סמג עשין עד טוש"ע ח"מ סי' רסא סעיף ג:
קעח י טוש"ע שם בהג"ה:
קעט כ מיי' פי"ג מהל' רוצח הל' ז סמג עשין פא טוש"ע ח"מ סי' רעב סעיף ו:

### הגהות הב"ח

(א) גמ' אבל הכא דידי שקלי: (ב) שם אני ה' אלהיכם כולכם:

### גליון הש"ס

רש"י ד"ה לומר וכו' הלכך אי לא כתיב. כעין זה כתב רש"י בילה דף ז ע"ב ד"ה שיעורו:

### ליקוטי רש"י

אמר לו אביו. לכהן. היטמא. בבית הקברות להשיב אבידה. אל תחזיר. שהיתה עומדת בחוץ ואמר לו אל תחזיר. שנאמר איש אמו וכו' שבתותי תשמרו. וילפינן לאו דטומאה ולאו דהשבת אבדה מלאוי דשבת [יבמות ו.]. סמך שמירת שבת למורא אב לומר אע"פ שהזהרתיך על מורא אב אם יאמר לך חלל את השבת אל תשמע לו וכן בשאר כל המצות. אני ה' אלהיכם. אתה ואביך חייבים בכבודי לפיכך לא תשמע לו לבטל את דברי [ויקרא יט, ג]. כבד את ה' מהונך. מכל מה שחנך [משלי ג, ט]. הקם תקים. זו טעינה להטעין משאוי שנפל מעליו [דברים כב, ד]. לא מסיימי קראי. הי משמע טעינה והי משמע פריקה ואי כתב חדא הוה אמינא לפריקה אתא אבל טעינה לא כתב רחמנא אידך לטעינה [לעיל לא.].

### מסורת הש"ס

[א] כתובות לז., ב) [פי' טור בסימן רס"א כגון אין לו פתחים בכל ארבע רוחותיו], ג) זהו גירסת רש"י ויש גירסא אחרת איפך והיא גירסת הרמב"ם, וע"ש ובספר [יד]ים ישועות, ד) יבמות ו., [ה] [עיין תוס' קדושין לב. ד"ה רבי יהודה], ו) [עיין לעיל ל. תוס' ד"ה הא אין], [ז] [קדושין ל: ע"ש], [ח] [לעיל לא.], ט) עיין תוס' דכתובות דף לח. שתירלו בענין אחר.

### תורה אור השלם

[א] כִּי תִרְאֶה חֲמוֹר שֹׂנַאֲךָ רֹבֵץ תַּחַת מַשָּׂאוֹ וְחָדַלְתָּ מֵעֲזֹב לוֹ עָזֹב תַּעֲזֹב עִמּוֹ: [שמות כג, ה]
[ב] אִישׁ אִמּוֹ וְאָבִיו תִּירָאוּ וְאֶת שַׁבְּתֹתַי תִּשְׁמֹרוּ אֲנִי יְיָ אֱלֹהֵיכֶם: [ויקרא יט, ג]
[ג] כַּבֵּד אֶת אָבִיךָ וְאֶת אִמֶּךָ לְמַעַן יַאֲרִכוּן יָמֶיךָ עַל הָאֲדָמָה אֲשֶׁר יְיָ אֱלֹהֶיךָ נֹתֵן לָךְ: [שמות כ, יב]
[ד] כַּבֵּד אֶת יְיָ מֵהוֹנֶךָ וּמֵרֵאשִׁית כָּל תְּבוּאָתֶךָ: [משלי ג, ט]
[ה] לֹא תִרְאֶה אֶת חֲמוֹר אָחִיךָ אוֹ שׁוֹרוֹ נֹפְלִים בַּדֶּרֶךְ וְהִתְעַלַּמְתָּ מֵהֶם הָקֵם תָּקִים עִמּוֹ: [דברים כב, ד]

### רבינו חננאל

...מיה תלתא. אמר ליה ...ב ספרא מנא לך [הא] ...מר ליה דתנן אם יש שם ...ד מתנה בפני ב"ד ...מר ליה מי דמי התם ...פוקי ממונא הוא ובעי ...ד אבל הכא דידי שקלי ...תרי סגי ליה תדע דקתני ...למנה מוכרת שלא ...ב"ד. ואסיק' משמיה ...ב נחמן בההיא דאינה ...ריכה ב"ד מומחה אבל ...ריכה (אפי') ב"ד ...דיוטות: **מתני'** מצאה ...רפת וכו' עד אמר לו ...ביו היטמא או אל ...חזיר לא ישמע לו. ת"ר ...נין שאם אמר לו אביו ...יטמא או אל תחזיר ...לא ישמע לו לבטל את ...מצוה שנאמר איש אמו ...אביו תיראו ואת ...בתותי תשמרו כולכם ...ייבים בכבודי אע"פ ...הזהרתיך בכיבוד אב ...אם אם יאמרו לך חלל ...בת אל תשמע להן אלא ...את שבתותי תשמרו וכן ...כל המצות. ומקשינן ...עמא דכתב רחמנא הכי ...א לאו הכי הוה אמינא ...ם יאמר לו אל תשיב ...שמע לו אמאי והא ...יבוד אב ואם עשה הוא ...נאמר כבד את אביך ...השבה היא עשה שנאמר ...שב תשיבם לאחיך ולא ...עשה שנאמר לא תוכל ...התעלם ולא אתי עשה ...יחה לא תעשה ועשה. ...פרקינן מהו דתימא ...ואיל ואיתקיש כיבוד ...ב ואם לכיבוד המקום ...נאמר כבד את ה' מהונך אימא ניציית ליה לאבוה קמ"ל דלא: חייב לטעון ולפרוק אפי' ק' פעמים שנאמר עזב תעזב עמו. פי' פריקה אית בה חסרון כיס שאם לא תפרקה תמות הבהמה תחת משאה טעינה ...ין בה חסרון כיס דליכא חששא למיתת הבהמה. ישב לו בעל הבהמה ואמר לו מצוה עליך לפרוק אם תרצה לפרוק פרוק פטור שנאמר עמו. היה בעל הבהמה זקן או חולה חייב. מצוה מן התורה לפרוק

The Mishnah now deals with the precept of helping another Jew with his animal when he is in need:[12] פָּרַק וְטָעַן – If one saw another person's animal lying under its burden, and **he unloaded** it, allowing it to get up, **and** then **reloaded** the burden upon it, פָּרַק וְטָעַן – and shortly thereafter, the animal lay down again, and **he unloaded** it **and reloaded** it, אֲפִילוּ אַרְבָּעָה וַחֲמִשָּׁה פְּעָמִים – **even** if this process repeated itself **four or five times,** חַיָּיב – **he is** still **obligated** to unload or reload as necessary, שֶׁנֶּאֱמַר: ,,עָזֹב תַּעֲזֹב" – **for it is stated:** ***help, you shall help.***[13] הָלַךְ וְיָשַׁב לוֹ – If [**the owner**] impudently **walked away and sat down,** וְאָמַר – **saying** to the bystander: הוֹאִיל וְעָלֶיךָ מִצְוָה – **"Since the commandment** to unload my animal **is** incumbent **upon you,** אִם רְצוֹנְךָ לִפְרוֹק פְּרוֹק – **if you wish to unload,** then **unload,** but I shall not help you"; פָּטוּר – [**the bystander**] **is exempt** from unloading the animal, שֶׁנֶּאֱמַר – **for it is stated:** ,,עִמּוֹ" – *you shall help* ***with him,*** implying that you must help only if the owner is prepared to join you. אִם הָיָה זָקֵן אוֹ חוֹלֶה – **If,** however, [**the owner**] **was an elderly or a sickly man** who has no strength to help, חַיָּיב – [**the bystander**] **is** indeed **obligated** to unload the animal by himself. מִצְוָה מִן הַתּוֹרָה לִפְרוֹק – **It is a commandment in the Torah to** help **unload** cargo from an animal that is lying under its burden, אֲבָל לֹא לִטְעוֹן – **but** it is **not** a commandment **to** help **load** a burden upon an animal after this burden fell off of it.[14] רַבִּי שִׁמְעוֹן אוֹמֵר – **R' Shimon,** however, **says:** אַף לִטְעוֹן – The Torah commands one **even to** help **load.** רַבִּי יוֹסֵי הַגְּלִילִי אוֹמֵר – **R' Yose HaGlili says:** אִם הָיָה עָלָיו יָתֵר עַל מַשָּׂאוֹ – **If** [**the animal**] **was bearing more than its** proper **burden** when it lay down, אֵין זָקוּק לוֹ – [**the bystander**] **is not bound to** help unload **it,** שֶׁנֶּאֱמַר: ,,תַּחַת מַשָּׂאוֹ" – **for it is stated** that one must help unload an animal lying down ***under its burden,*** which implies that the animal had been bearing מַשְׂאוֹי שֶׁיָּכוֹל לַעֲמוֹד בּוֹ – **a burden under which it can stand.**[15]

**Gemara** The Mishnah has ruled that if one found an animal in a barn, he is not obligated to retrieve it. The Gemara now clarifies the case:

אָמַר רָבָא – **Rava said:** רֶפֶת שֶׁאָמְרוּ – **The barn that** [**the Sages**] **spoke** of in the Mishnah אֵינָהּ מַתְעָה – **is not** one that would **incite** the animal **to run astray,**[16] וְאֵינָהּ מְשַׁמֶּרֶת – **nor is it** one that **protects** the animal from leaving if it should wish.[17]

Rava now explains how he knows this:

אֵינָהּ מַתְעָה – We may infer that **it does not incite** the animal **to run astray,** מִדְּקָתָנֵי אֵינוֹ חַיָּיב בָּהּ – **since** [**the Mishnah**] **taught** that one **is not obligated to** retrieve [**the animal**] if it is in this barn.[18] וְאֵינָהּ מְשַׁמֶּרֶת – And we may infer that **it does not protect** the animal from leaving, מִדְּאִיצְטְרִיךְ לְמִיתְנֵי אֵינוֹ חַיָּיב בָּהּ – **since** [**the Mishnah**] **found it necessary to** even **mention** that **one is not obligated to** retrieve [**the animal**] in the barn.

Rava explains this last point:

דְּאִי סָלְקָא דַּעְתָּךְ מְשַׁמֶּרֶת – **If you would consider that** [**the barn**] spoken of in the Mishnah is one that **protects** the animal from leaving, the Mishnah's law would be entirely obvious. Indeed, we could argue as follows: הַשְׁתָּא מִשְׁכַּח לָהּ אַבְרַאי – **Now,** we know that if **one finds a** [**lost animal**] **outside,** in the pasture, מְעַיֵּיל לָהּ לְגַוַּאי – **he may bring it inside** the owner's protected barn to fulfill his obligation of returning it.[19] מִשְׁכַּח לָהּ מִגַּוַּאי מִבַּעְיָא – **Is it even necessary** to state, then, that **if he finds it** already **inside** such a barn he need not retrieve it from there? This is self-evident! אֶלָּא שְׁמַע מִינָּהּ אֵינָהּ מְשַׁמֶּרֶת – **Rather, learn from this** that the barn spoken of in the Mishnah would **not protect** the animal from leaving; שְׁמַע מִינָּהּ – we can indeed **learn** it **from this.**

The Mishnah had stated:

מְצָאָהּ בָּרֶפֶת אֵינוֹ חַיָּיב – If ONE FOUND [AN ANIMAL] IN A BARN, HE IS NOT OBLIGATED TO retrieve IT.

This ruling is now qualified:

אָמַר רַבִּי יִצְחָק – **R' Yitzchak said:** וְהוּא שֶׁעוֹמֶדֶת תּוֹךְ לַתְּחוּם – **This applies** only **when** [**the barn**] **is situated within the** ***techum*** **boundary** of the nearest town;[20] if, however, it is found in a barn *outside* the *techum,* it should indeed be considered lost, and it must be returned by the finder.

The Gemara notes that R' Yitzchak's qualification will affect the interpretation of the Mishnah's second law as well:

מִכְּלָל דִּבְרְשׁוּת הָרַבִּים – **By implication,** then, it follows **that** when the Mishnah speaks of an animal found **on public property,** וַאֲפִילוּ בְּתוֹךְ הַתְּחוּם נַמִּי חַיָּיב – it means that **even** if the animal is **within the** ***techum,*** **he is still obligated** to return it.[21]

The Gemara records a second version of R' Yitzchak's statement:

אִיכָּא דְּמַתְנֵי לָהּ אַסֵּיפָא – **There are those who taught** [**R' Yitzchak's statement**] **in reference to the second clause of the Mishnah:** בִּרְשׁוּת הָרַבִּים חַיָּיב בָּהּ – If one finds the animal ON PUBLIC PROPERTY, HE IS OBLIGATED TO return IT, for it can be presumed that the owner is unaware of its whereabouts. אָמַר רַבִּי יִצְחָק – In reference to this ruling, **R' Yitzchak said:** וְהוּא שֶׁעוֹמֶדֶת חוּץ לַתְּחוּם – **This applies** only **when** [**the animal**] **is**

NOTES

bject, and in the second case he *must* retrieve the lost object, despite his ather's request to leave the object where it is.

2. When one sees an animal lying under its load, and unable to rise, he is bligated to assist the owner in unloading the animal. This duty, known s פְּרִיקָה, *unloading,* is from *Exodus* 23:5, which states: כִּי־תִרְאֶה חֲמוֹר שֹׂנַאֲךָ רֹבֵץ תַּחַת מַשָּׂאוֹ וְחָדַלְתָּ מֵעֲזֹב לוֹ עָזֹב תַּעֲזֹב עִמּ, *When you see a donkey of your nemy lying under its burden, shall you refrain from helping him* [the wner] [No!]; *help, you shall help with him.* Similarly, when one sees that burden has fallen from an animal, he is required to help the owner eload it. This duty, known as טְעִינָה, *reloading,* is from *Deut.* 22:4, which tates: לֹא־תִרְאֶה אֶת חֲמוֹר אָחִיךָ אוֹ שׁוֹרוֹ נֹפְלִים בַּדֶּרֶךְ וְהִתְעַלַּמְתָּ מֵהֶם הָקֵם תָּקִים עִמּוֹ, *'ou shall not see the donkey of your brother or his ox falling on the road; nd hide from them; raise up, you shall raise [it] up with him.*

[Although the Mishnah sets forth its rulings with respect to unloading, hey apply to loading as well.]

3. *Exodus* 23:5. An infinitive — in this case, the word עָזֹב — can refer to oing the action once or many times (see 31a note 19).

4. Scripture (*Deuteronomy* 22:4) indeed seems to require one even to eload an animal, and the Gemara will therefore discuss the meaning of he Tanna's teaching that this is "not a commandment in the Torah."

15. The term מַשָּׂאוֹ, *"its" burden,* connotes a burden that suits the animal, not an oversized one. Thus, the verse speaks of an animal that lay down under a normal, rather than oppressive, load [due to fatigue or load slippage, etc.; see *Chinuch* §80], and is now unable to rise unless the load is temporarily removed.

16. As an example of a barn that would incite an animal to run away, *Ritva* gives the case of a barn that contains no fodder from which the animal could graze (cf. *Tur, Choshen Mishpat* 261).

17. I.e. the barn is not locked (*Rashi*).

18. Clearly, if there was an immediate danger that the animal would run away, the finder would be required to retrieve it.

19. It was derived earlier (31a) that one need not return a lost object directly to its owner's house: One may also return it to his garden, deserted building, or barn (so long as these places are protected), where the owner might not immediately notice its presence (see *Rashi*).

20. The word *techum* denotes a boundary that extends two-thousand *amos* beyond the limits of a town (the term is more commonly employed in reference to the laws of *eruvin*).

21. [The Gemara assumes that the case in which the animal is found in a barn and the case in which it is found on public property are parallel.

**תרי מגו תלתא.** שנים מן השלשה יבואו ויעידו לומר שלשה היינו: **אם יש שם ב"ד.** וסתם ב"ד שלשה אלמא אין כח להפקיר ממון זה אלא זה בפחות משלשה: **גילוי מילתא.** שידעו שחלקתי בשוה: **אלמנה.** הניזונת מנכסי יתומים מוכרת למזונות: **שלא בב"ד.** ובלבד שיראו שנים שלא תמכור בזול:

תרי מגו תלתא ואי נמי תרי סהדי דפלגת באפי בי תלתא א"ל מנא לך הא א"ל דתנן אם יש שם ב"ד מתנה בפניהם אין שם ב"ד בפני מי יתנה שלו קודם א"ל מי דמי התם דמפיק ממונא מהאי ומותיב להאי בעינן ב"ד אבל הכא (א) דידיה שקלי גילוי מילתא בעלמא הוא בתרי סגי ליה תדע דתנן [א] אלמנה מוכרת שלא בפני ב"ד אמר ליה אביי ולאו מי אתמר עלה אמר רב יוסף בר מניומי אמר ר"נ אלמנה אינה צריכה ב"ד של מומחין [ב] אבל צריכה בית דין של הדיוטות: **מתני'** [ג] מצאה ברפת אין חייב בה ברה"ר חייב בה [ד] ואם היתה בבית הקברות לא יטמא לה [ה] אם אמר לו אביו היטמא או שאמר לו אל תחזיר לא ישמע לו [ו] פרק וטען פרק וטען אפילו ארבעה וחמשה פעמים חייב שנאמר [א] עזב תעזב [ז] הלך וישב לו ואמר הואיל ועליך מצוה אם רצונך לפרוק פרוק פטור שנאמר עמו [ח] אם היה זקן או חולה חייב מצוה מן התורה לפרוק אבל לא לטעון ר"ש אומר אף לטעון רבי יוסי הגלילי אומר אם היה עליו יתר על משאו אין זקוק לו שנאמר תחת משאו משאוי שיכול לעמוד בו: **גמ'** אמר רבא [ט] רפת שאמרו [ג] אינה מתעה ואינה משמרת אינה מתעה מדקתני אינו חייב בה ואינה משמרת מדאיצטריך למיתני אינו חייב בה דאי סלקא דעתך משמרת השתא משכח לה אבראי מעייל לה לגואי משכח לה מגואי מבעיא אלא שמע מינה אינה משמרת שמע מינה: מצאה ברפת אינו חייב: א"ר יצחק [ג] [י] והוא שעומדת תוך לתחום מכלל דברשות הרבים ואפילו בתוך התחום נמי חייב איכא דמתני לה אסיפא ברה"ר חייב בה אמר רבי יצחק והוא שעומדת חוץ לתחום מכלל דברפת אפילו עומדת חוץ לתחום נמי אינו חייב בה: בבית הקברות לא יטמא לה: [ד] ת"ר מנין שאם אמר לו אביו היטמא או שאמר לו [ה] אל תחזיר שלא ישמע לו שנאמר [ב] איש אמו ואביו תיראו ואת שבתותי תשמרו אני ה' (ג) כולכם חייבין בכבודי טעמא דכתב רחמנא את שבתותי תשמרו הא לאו הכי הוה אמינא ציית ליה ואמאי האי עשה והאי לא תעשה ועשה [ו] ולא אתי עשה ודחי את לא תעשה ועשה איצטריך ס"ד אמינא הואיל והוקש כיבוד אב ואם לכבודו [ז] של מקום שנאמר כאן [ג] כבד את אביך ואת אמך ונאמר להלן [ד] כבד את ה' מהונך הלכך לציית ליה קמ"ל דלא לשמע ליה: מצוה מן התורה לפרוק אבל לא לטעון: מאי אבל לא לטעון אילימא אבל לא לטעון כלל מאי שנא פריקה דכתיב עזב תעזב עמו טעינה נמי הכתיב [ה] הקם תקים עמו אלא [כ] מצוה מן התורה לפרוק בחנם ולא לטעון בחנם אלא בשכר ר"ש אומר [ל] אף לטעון בחנם תנינא להא דת"ר פריקה בחנם טעינה בשכר ר"ש אומר זו וזו בחנם מאי טעמייהו דרבנן דאי ס"ד כר"ש לכתוב רחמנא טעינה ולא בעי פריקה ואנא אמינא ומה טעינה דלית בה צער בעלי חיים וליכא חסרון כיס חייב פריקה דאית בה צער בעלי חיים וחסרון כיס לא כל שכן אלא למאי הלכתא כתביה רחמנא לומר לך פריקה בחנם טעינה בשכר ורבי שמעון מאי טעמא משום דלא מסיימי קראי ורבנן אמאי לא מסיימי קראי הכא כתיב רובץ תחת משאו התם כתיב נופלין בדרך דרמו אינהו וטעונייהו באורחא משמע ורבי שמעון נופלין בדרך אינהו וטעונייהו עלוייהו משמע אמר רבא

מדברי

## רש"י

**מתני' מצאה ברפת.** בגמרא מפרש מאי אצטריך: **היתה בבית הקברות.** והוא כהן: **או שאמר לו אל תחזיר.** והוא במקום שהוא מותר לילך שם: **הלך וישב לו.** הבעלים: **אבל לא לטעון.** בגמרא מפרש: **גמ' רפת שאמרו.** ששנינו במשנתנו עסקינן כשאינה מתעה את הבהמה שבתוכה להיות בורחת ויוצאת: **ואינה משתמרת.** שאינה נעולה ואם באת לצאת יוצאה: **מעייל לגואי.** כדאמרינן לעיל (דף לא.) לגינתו ולחורבתו מנין: ברישא גרסינן והוא שעומדת בתוך לתחום בסיפא גרסינן והוא שעומדת חוץ לתחום: **אני ה'.** אע"פ שאמרתי לך ירא את אביך אני אדון לשניכם ואם אמר לך אביך עבור על דברי לחלל שבת אל תשמע לו: **הוה אמינא צייתא ליה.** דאתי עשה דכיבוד ודחי לא תעשה דלא תוכל להתעלם: אבידה עשה ולא תעשה היא השב תשיבם לא תוכל להתעלם: **הוקש כבודם.** בגזירה שוה כבד את אביך כבד את ה' מהונך: דלית ביה חסרון כיס. אם לא יטעון: **פריקה אית בה חסרון כיס.** שהבהמה נשברת תחת משאה: **לומר לך** פריקה בחנם. אבל טעינה לא נצטוית אלא בשכר [°] הלכך אי לא כתב פריקה ואתיא מק"ו מטעינה הוה אמינא דיו לבא מן הדין להיות כנדון מה טעינה בשכר אף פריקה בשכר: **לא מסיימי קראי.** למשמעות טעינה הלכך אי כתיב חד הוה אמינא לפריקה אתא: **רובץ תחת משאו.** משמע שצריך לפרוק: **דרמו אינהו וטעונייהו באורחא.** אף המשא מוטל על הקרקע שצריך לטעון:

מדברי

## תוספות

**אלמנה** מוכרת שלא בב"ד. וא"ת התם משום חינא או משום שלא תתבזה בב"ד כדמפרש באלמנה ניזונת (כתובות דף צז: ושם) וי"ל דס"ל כיון דאלמנה מוכרת אע"ג דאינה שלה שלא בב"ד משום חינא ה"נ שותף יטול את שלו שלא בב"ד אע"ג דליכא טעם דחינא: **בית** דין הדיוטות. וא"ת והאמרינן התם (דף צח. ושם) אלמנה ששמה לעצמה לא עשתה ולא כלום דאמרינן לה מאן שם לך הלא מכרה ע"פ ב"ד הדיוטות וי"ל כיון שלוקחת לעצמה נראה לעולם שמעכבת מנכסי יתומים בידה אע"פ שיש ב"ד הדיוטות כיון דליכא מומחין אבל כשמוכרת לאחרים אין נראה שמעכבת משלהם שהרי לא עכבה כלום וא"ת ומ"ש דאלמנה מוכרת לאחרים שלא בב"ד ובב"ד יכולה לעכב אפי' לעצמה מדאמרינן התם דא"ל מאן שם לך משמע דבב"ד יכולה לשום וקאמר נמי התם ההוא גברא דאפקידו גביה כסתא דיתמי אזל שמה לנפשיה בת' זוזי לסוף אייקור כו' אתא לקמיה דרבי א"ל מאן שם לך משמע דבב"ד יכול לשום ולקמן בפרק המפקיד (דף לח.) תנן המפקיד פירות אצל חבירו והרקיבו כו' עושה להם תקנה ומוכרן בב"ד וכשהוא מוכרן מוכרן לאחרים ואין מוכרן לעצמו כיוצא בו גבאי צדקה פורטין לאחרים ואין פורטין לעצמם דאפילו בב"ד מוכרין לאחרים ואין מוכרין לעצמם ושלא בב"ד אין מוכרין אפילו לאחרים וליכא למימר הא דאמר ומוכרים לאחרים בב"ד היינו ברשות ב"ד אבל אי ידעי ב"ד השומא יכול לעכב לעצמו דבירושלמי מסיק על ההוא מעשה דרבי יוחנן חקוקאה דמייתי פ"ק דפסחים (דף יג. ושם) א"ל לך ומוכרם בב"ד אלמא אע"פ שנתן לו רשות היה צריך למוכרם בב"ד וי"ל דמוכרת שלא בב"ד משום חינא [ט] וגבי כסתא דיתמי נמי דיכול לעכב לעצמו בב"ד מצינן למימר דהיינו דוקא בדיעבד דמשום חשד לא מהדרינן עובדא א"נ דגבי יתמי ב"ד עצמם הם מפקידין ולכך יכול לעכב לעצמו על פיהם אבל פקדון של אחרים אינו יכול לעכב לעצמו על פי ב"ד: **כבד** את ה' מהונך. הא דנקט קרא דדברי קבלה ולא נקט קרא דאיש אמו ואביו תיראו וכתיב את ה' אלהיך תירא משום דניחא ליה לאתויי קרא דכבוד:

מדברי



## מסורת הש"ס

א) כתובות לז., ב) [פי' טור בסימן רס"א כגון אין לו פתחים בכל ארבע רוחותיו], ג) זהו גירסת רש"י ויש גירסא אחרת איפך והיא גירסת הרמב"ם, וע"ש ובספר ... ישועות, ד) יבמות ו., ה) [עיין תוס' קדושין לג. ד"ה רב יהודה], ו) [עיין לעיל ל. תוס' ד"ה הא אין], ז) [קדושין ל: ע"ש], ח) [לעיל לא.], ט) עיין תוס' דכתובות דף לח. שפירשו בענין אחר.

## תורה אור השלם

א) כִּי תִרְאֶה חֲמוֹר שֹׂנַאֲךָ רֹבֵץ תַּחַת מַשָּׂאוֹ וְחָדַלְתָּ מֵעֲזֹב לוֹ עָזֹב תַּעֲזֹב עִמּוֹ: [שמות כג, ה]

ב) אִישׁ אִמּוֹ וְאָבִיו תִּירָאוּ וְאֶת שַׁבְּתֹתַי תִּשְׁמֹרוּ אֲנִי יְיָ אֱלֹהֵיכֶם: [ויקרא יט, ג]

ג) כַּבֵּד אֶת אָבִיךָ וְאֶת אִמֶּךָ לְמַעַן יַאֲרִכוּן יָמֶיךָ עַל הָאֲדָמָה אֲשֶׁר יְיָ אֱלֹהֶיךָ נֹתֵן לָךְ: [שמות כ, יב]

ד) כַּבֵּד אֶת יְיָ מֵהוֹנֶךָ וּמֵרֵאשִׁית כָּל תְּבוּאָתֶךָ: [משלי ג, ט]

ה) לֹא תִרְאֶה אֶת חֲמוֹר אָחִיךָ אוֹ שׁוֹרוֹ נֹפְלִים בַּדֶּרֶךְ וְהִתְעַלַּמְתָּ מֵהֶם הָקֵם תָּקִים עִמּוֹ: [דברים כב, ד]

## רבינו חננאל

מיה תלתא. אמר ליה ב ספרא מנא לך [הא] אמר ליה דתנן אם יש שם ב"ד מתנה בפני ב"ד אמר ליה מי דמי התם מפוקי ממונא הוא ובעי ב"ד אבל הכא דידי שקלי בתרי סגי ליה תדע דקתני אלמנה מוכרת שלא בב"ד. ואסיק' משמיה דרב נחמן בההיא דאינה צריכה ב"ד מומחה אבל צריכה (אפי') ב"ד הדיוטות: **מתני'** מצאה ברפת וכו' עד אמר לו אביו היטמא או אל תחזיר לא ישמע לו. ת"ר מנין שאם אמר לו אביו היטמא או אל תחזיר שלא ישמע לו לבטל את המצוה שנאמר איש אמו ואביו תיראו ואת שבתותי תשמרו כולכם חייבים בכבודי אע"פ שהזהרתיך בכיבוד אב ואם אם יאמרו לך חלל שבת אל תשמע להן אלא את שבתותי תשמרו וכן בכל המצות. ומקשינן טעמא דכתב רחמנא הכי הא לאו הכי הוה אמינא אם יאמר לו אל תשיב שמע לו אמאי והא כיבוד אב ואם עשה הוא שנאמר כבד את אביך והשבה היא עשה שנאמר השב תשיבם לאחיך ולא תעשה שנאמר לא תוכל להתעלם ולא אתי עשה דחה לא תעשה ועשה. ופרקינן מהו דתימא הואיל ואיתקיש כיבוד אב ואם לכבוד המקום

## עין משפט נר מצוה

קעא א ב מיי' פי"ז מהל' אישות הל' יג סמג עשין מח טוש"ע אה"ע סי' קג סעיף א:

קעב ג מיי' פט"ו מהל' אבידה הל' ה סמג עשין עד טוש"ע ח"מ סי' רסא סעיף ג:

קעג ד מיי' פי"א שם הלכה יח ופי"ג מהלכות רוצח הלכה ג סמג שם טוש"ע ח"מ סי' רעב סעיף ב:

קעד ה מיי' פי"א מהל' אבידה הל' יט ופ"ו מהלכות ממרים הל' יב סמג שם וסי' עה טוש"ע ח"מ סי' רסו סעיף ה וטוש"ע י"ד סי' רמ סעיף טו:

קעה ו מיי' פי"ג מהל' רוצח הל' ה סמג עשין פא טוש"ע ח"מ סי' רעב סעיף ד:

קעו ז ח מיי' שם הל' ח טוש"ע שם סעיף ז:

קעז ט מיי' פט"ו מהל' אבידה הל' ה סמג עשין עד טוש"ע ח"מ סי' רסא סעיף ג:

קעח י טוש"ע שם בהג"ה:

קעט כ מיי' פי"ג מהל' רוצח הל' ז סמג עשין פא טוש"ע ח"מ סי' רעב סעיף ו:

## הגהות הב"ח

(א) גמ' אבל הכא דידי שקלי: (ב) שם אני ה' אלהיכם כולכם:

## גליון הש"ס

רש"י ד"ה לומר וכו' הלכך אי לא כתיב. כעין זה כתב רש"י ביצה דף ז ע"ב ד"ה שיעורו:

## ליקוטי רש"י

**אמר לו אביו.** לכהן. **היטמא.** בבית הקברות להשיב אבידה. **אל תחזיר.** שהיתה עומדת בחוץ ואמר לו אל תחזיר. **שנאמר איש אמו וכו' שבתותי תשמרו.** וילפינן לאו דטומאה ולאו דהשבת אבדה מלאוי דשבת [יבמות ו.]. סמך שמירת שבת למורא אב לומר אע"פ שהזהרתיך על מורא אב אם יאמר לך חלל את השבת אל תשמע לו וכן בשאר כל המצות. **אני ה' אלהיכם.** אתה ואביך חייבים בכבודי לפיכך לא תשמע לו לבטל את דברי [ויקרא יט, ג]. **כבד את ה' מהונך.** מכל מה שחננך [משלי ג, ט]. **הקם תקים.** זו טעינה להטעין משאוי שנפל מעליו [דברים כב, ד]. **לא מסיימי קראי.** הי משמע טעינה והי משמע פריקה ואי כתב חדא הוה אמינא לפריקה אתא אבל טעינה לא כתב רחמנא אידך לטעינה [לעיל לא.].

תְּרֵי מִגּוֹ תְּלָתָא – bring **two of** the **three** men to testify that they were indeed part of a three-man court that supervised the division; וְאִי נַמִּי – **or, alternatively,** תְּרֵי סַהֲדֵי דִּפְלַגְתְּ בְּאַפֵּי בֵּי תְּלָתָא – bring **two** other **witnesses** to testify **that you divided** the business **before** a court of **three.**[1]

אָמַר לֵיהּ – **[Rav Safra] said to him:** מְנָא לָךְ הָא – **From where do you know this,** that one is required to liquidate a partnership before a court of three?

אָמַר לֵיהּ – **He answered him:** דִּתְנַן – **For we have learned in the Mishnah:** אִם יֵשׁ שָׁם בֵּית דִּין מַתְנֶה בִּפְנֵיהֶם – IF THERE IS A COURT in the vicinity, [THE FINDER OF AN OBJECT] MAY STIPULATE BEFORE THEM to receive a higher rate of compensation. אֵין שָׁם בֵּית דִּין בִּפְנֵי מִי יַתְנֶה – If, however, THERE IS NO COURT in the vicinity, BEFORE WHOM SHOULD HE STIPULATE? He cannot collect full compensation, שֶׁלּוֹ קוֹדֵם – and therefore, HIS own financial concerns COME BEFORE those of others. Now, the Mishnah has ruled that a finder may lodge a claim against the owner for a higher rate of compensation only if he stipulates before a court [of three].[2] Evidently, then, to extract money from another person requires the sanction of a court of three.

Rav Safra disputes this reasoning:

אָמַר לֵיהּ – **[Rav Safra] said to him:** מִי דָּמֵי – **Are [our case and the case of the Mishnah] comparable** to one another? הָתָם – **There,** in the Mishnah's case, דְּמַפִּיק מָמוֹנָא מֵהַאי וּמוֹתִיב לְהַאי – **where money is** to be **extracted from this** person [the owner], **and given to this** person [the finder], בְּעֵינַן בֵּית דִּין – **we require** the sanction of **a court.** אֲבָל הָכָא – **But, here,** in our case, דִּידֵיהּ שָׁקְלִי – **[the one who divides] is** merely **taking his own** share; he does not seek to claim any more money than was already his. גִּילּוּי מִילְּתָא בְּעָלְמָא הוּא – Accordingly, the purpose of outside supervision **is merely** to **ascertain facts:** It is to see that the person divided the goods fairly, בִּתְרֵי סַגֵּי לֵיהּ – and for this, **two** men would **suffice.**[3]

Rav Safra cites a Mishnah to support his contention:

תֵּדַע – **Know** that this reasoning is valid, דִּתְנַן – **for we have learned in a Mishnah:** אַלְמָנָה מוֹכֶרֶת שֶׁלֹּא בִּפְנֵי בֵּית דִּין – A WIDOW may SELL property of her late husband's estate WITHOUT the sanction of A COURT.[4] Evidently, then, when one is entitled to a share of certain properties, he may take his share without convening a court to supervise the procedure![5] – ? –

Abaye responds to Rav Safra's objection:

אָמַר לֵיהּ אַבָּיֵי – **Abaye said to him:** וְלָאו מִי אִתְמַר עֲלָהּ – **And was it not taught in reference to that** very Mishnah: אָמַר רַב יוֹסֵף בַּר מַנְיוּמֵי אָמַר רַב נַחְמָן – **Rav Yosef bar Manyumei said in the name of Rav Nachman:** When the Mishnah states that a widow need not sell possessions of the estate before a court, it means אַלְמָנָה אֵינָהּ צְרִיכָה בֵּית דִּין שֶׁל מוּמְחִין – **a widow does not need** to sell before **a court of experts,** אֲבָל צְרִיכָה בֵּית דִּין שֶׁל הֶדְיוֹטוֹת – **but she** indeed **needs** to sell before **a court of laymen.**[6] Therefore, with regard to your partnership as well, the liquidation needed to be executed before a court of three laymen.

**Mishnah** מָצְאָה בְּרֶפֶת – If **one found [an animal] in a barn,** אֵין חַיָּיב בָּהּ – **he is not obligated to** retrieve **it,** for he should not assume that the animal is lost.[7] בִּרְשׁוּת הָרַבִּים – If, however, he found the animal **on public property,** חַיָּיב בָּהּ – **he is** indeed **obligated to** retrieve **it.** וְאִם הָיְתָה בְּבֵית הַקְּבָרוֹת – **If** the finder is a Kohen, and **[the lost object]** he sights **was in a cemetery,**[8] לֹא יִטַּמֵּא לָהּ – **he should not become *tamei*** by entering the cemetery **to** retrieve **[the object].** אִם אָמַר לוֹ אָבִיו הִיטַּמֵּא – **If,** in such a case, **his father told him,** "Retrieve the object and **become *tamei*,**"[9] אוֹ שֶׁאָמַר לוֹ אַל תַּחֲזִיר – **or** if the object was in a place the finder was permitted to enter, and **[his father] told him, "Do not return** the object,"[10] לֹא יִשְׁמַע לוֹ – **he should not** in these cases **listen to [his father],** for to comply would cause him to violate a Torah law.[11]

NOTES

1. Rabbah bar Rav Huna ruled that the liquidation had to be executed before a court of three men, and he offered Rav Safra three ways of proving that this was indeed done. In fact, however, Rav Safra had divided the assets only in front of two witnesses, not in front of a three-man court. The division was thus null according to Rabbah bar Rav Huna – it would have to be executed over again, and under the new settlement, the ultimate disbursement of the property could change.

2. The Mishnah requires a בֵּית דִּין, *beis din,* a term that denotes a court of three men (*Rashi*).

3. Rav Safra maintains that a court is needed in the Mishnah's case, because, there, the finder is claiming more than he would otherwise be entitled to. His basic right is to be compensated for his lost time "as a worker standing idle," and he seeks to extract from the object's owner an amount of compensation that goes beyond this. In the case of dividing the business, however, Rav Safra did not seek to increase his claim against Issur. Rather, he wished merely to divide their property and to take what was rightfully his. Rav Safra thus maintained that he needed only witnesses – not a full court – to supervise the transaction for, here, the role of the outside party was not to authorize a new entitlement, but merely to verify the fairness of the division.

4. *Kesubos* 97a. When a man dies, his estate must pay his widow a monetary settlement, as stipulated in her *kesubah,* marriage contract. Until the time that she demands the money, however, the widow is entitled to be supported from the estate. To receive this support, she is permitted to take property from the estate and sell it. The Mishnah states that this sale need not be executed before a court.

5. Rav Safra takes this Mishnah to mean that the property must indeed be sold before two witnesses, but it need not be sold before an actual court. The reason a court is not required, Rav Safra suggests, is that the widow is merely selling property she is already entitled to by Rabbinic decree. For her sale to be valid, then, it would merely be necessary for witnesses to attest that she sold the property at a fair price, and did not cause any undue loss to the estate's heirs (see *Rashi*).

6. I.e. the widow's sale of the assets does not need to take place before a court of experts in the law, but it *does* need to take place before three laymen who are qualified to evaluate the proper market price of the goods being sold (*Ritva*).

7. Seemingly, this ruling is obvious. The Gemara will explain why it was necessary for the Mishnah to teach it (see *Rashi*).

8. In the present case, the finder who is a Kohen is presented with two conflicting obligations: On the one hand, he is Biblically forbidden to contaminate himself by coming into contact with a corpse. This is mandated by both a positive commandment (*Leviticus* 21:6: קְדֹשִׁים יִהְיוּ, *they shall be holy*) and a negative commandment (ibid. v. 1: לְנֶפֶשׁ לֹא־יִטַּמָּא בְּעַמָּיו, *no [Kohen] shall contaminate himself with a dead body among his people*). On the other hand, a positive commandment obligates him to return the lost article (*Deuteronomy* 22:1: הָשֵׁב תְּשִׁיבֵם לְאָחִיךָ, *you shall surely return them to your brother*).

9. This explanation follows *Rashi* to Yevamos 6a ד״ה היטמא; (see also *Aruch LaNer* ad loc. who interprets *Rashi* as saying that the object in question belongs to the father – his father told him to retrieve his object from a cemetery;) cf. *Ritva* ד״ה יכול.

10. I.e. his father told him not to retrieve the object, but rather to feed him or clothe him instead (*Ramban; Rashba; Tosafos* to *Kiddushin* 32a ד״ה רב יהודה). [In a case where there was no such motive behind the father's command, it goes without saying that the son should not listen to him.] In the first case, a father tells his son – a Kohen – to expose himself to the *tumah* of a corpse. In the second case, a finder sights a lost item in a place permitted for him to enter, and his father tells him not to retrieve the item. In both instances, the son is faced with conflicting obligations: on the one hand, in both cases, he is obligated to honor his father. Yet, opposing this obligation, he is, in the first case, obligated to avoid becoming *tamei,* and in the second case, he is obligated to return the lost object.

11. I.e. in the first case he *may not* enter the cemetery to return the lost

others' donations. אָמַר רַחֲמָנָא תֵּן לוֹ דֶּרֶךְ הַלְוָאָה – Of such a person, THE MERCIFUL ONE SAID in his Torah: GIVE HIM money BY WAY OF A LOAN, since he will not accept your outright gift.[21] יֵשׁ לוֹ – But IF [A PERSON] HAS money of his own, וְאֵינוֹ רוֹצֶה לְהִתְפַּרְנֵס – AND HE DOES NOT WANT TO SUPPORT himself with this money, מִנַּיִן – FROM WHERE IS IT DERIVED that you must extend money to even this type of person?[22] תַּלְמוּד לוֹמַר – FOR THE VERSE STATES its point a second time: "תַּעֲבִיטֶנּוּ" – *YOU SHALL LEND TO HIM,* implying: מִכָּל מָקוֹם – You must extend assistance IN ALL CASES.

The Gemara, however, asks:

וּלְרַבִּי שִׁמְעוֹן – **But according to R' Shimon,** דְּאָמַר – **who says** that the verse is to understood according to its plain meaning:[23] יֵשׁ לוֹ – IF HE HAS money of his own וְאֵינוֹ רוֹצֶה לְהִתְפַּרְנֵס – AND DOES NOT WANT TO SUPPORT himself with it, אֵין נִזְקָקִין לוֹ – WE ARE indeed NOT BOUND TO HIM; we need not lend him money at all, "תַּעֲבִיטֶנּוּ" לָמָּה לִי – **why do I need** the phrase ***you shall lend to him?*** What is taught by this repetitive language according to R' Shimon?

The Gemara answers:

דִּבְּרָה תּוֹרָה כִּלְשׁוֹן בְּנֵי אָדָם – According to R' Shimon, there is no special significance in this repetition, for **the Torah** simply **spoke** in the common **language used by men.**[24]

The Gemara now cites and explains the next clause of our Mishnah:

הָיָה בָּטֵל מִן הַסֶּלַע – If [THE FINDER] STOOD IDLE FROM doing work worth A *SELA* because he was busy returning the object he found, לֹא יֹאמַר לוֹ – HE SHOULD NOT SAY TO [THE OWNER], תֵּן לִי סֶלַע – "GIVE ME the full *SELA* that I lost." אֶלָּא נוֹתֵן לוֹ שְׂכָרוֹ כְּפוֹעֵל (בטל) – RATHER, [THE OWNER] GIVES HIM HIS WAGE LIKE A WORKER.[25]

The meaning of these final words is clarified by the statement of another Tanna:

(תנן) [תָּנָא] – **A Tanna taught:** נוֹתֵן לוֹ שְׂכָרוֹ כְּפוֹעֵל בָּטֵל – [THE OWNER] GIVES HIM HIS WAGE LIKE AN IDLE WORKER.

The Gemara takes this to mean that the owner should pay t[he] finder the minimum amount of money he would accept to fore[go] his regular wage and stand completely idle from work.[26]

The Gemara therefore asks:

מַאי כְּפוֹעֵל בָּטֵל – For **what** reason is he paid only LIKE AN ID[LE] WORKER? The finder is *not* merely standing idle when he works [to] return the object and, therefore, he should be entitled to mo[re] than one would pay him to simply remain idle! – ? –

The Gemara answers:

אָמַר אַבָּיֵי – **Abaye said:** [כְּפ]וֹעֵל בָּטֵל שֶׁל אוֹתָהּ מְלָאכָה דְּבָטֵל מִינָּהּ – The Tanna means he should be paid **like a worker** who cho[oses] to stand **idle from the** type of **work he stopped,** so that he cou[ld] instead carry out a different, easier type of labor.[27]

The Mishnah had stated:

אִם יֵשׁ שָׁם בֵּית דִּין מַתְנֶה בִּפְנֵיהֶם – IF THERE IS A COURT in th[e] vicinity, [THE FINDER] MAY STIPULATE BEFORE THEM that [he] is willing to retrieve the object only if he receives full co[m]pensation for his lost labor, and he may then claim this fu[ll] amount.

The Gemara recounts an incident relevant to the above law:

אִיסוּר וְרַב סַפְרָא עֲבִיד עִיסְקָא בַּהֲדֵי הֲדָדֵי – **Issur and Rav Saf[ra]** **engaged in a business** venture **together.** When the agreed-up[on] time of their partnership expired,[28] אָזַל רַב סַפְרָא פְּלַג לֵיהּ – **R[av]** **Safra went and divided up [their merchandise],**[29] [בְּ]לָ[א] דַּעְתֵּיהּ דְּאִיסוּר בְּאַפֵּי בֵּי תְרֵי – doing this **without the awar[e]ness of Issur, in front of two** people.[30] [אֲ]תָא לְקַמֵּיהּ דְּרַבָּה בַּר רַב הוּנָא – When Issur subsequently disputed the fairness of th[e] settlement, **[Rav Safra] came before Rabbah bar Rav Hun[a]** for arbitration. אָמַר לֵיהּ – **[Rabbah bar Rav Huna] said t[o]** **him:** זִיל אַיְיתִי תְּלָתָא דִּפְלַגְתְּ קַמַּיְיהוּ – "Go bring the thre[e] **people before whom you divided** the goods; אִי נַמִּי – o[r] **alternatively,**

NOTES

21. [As noted above, the verse mentions that you shall lend him *enough [to fulfill] his lack*. The inclusion of these words seems to indicate that the verse deals with a situation in which this person lacks the means to support himself.]

22. The Gemara speaks here of an extreme miser – a person who would rather suffer from hunger while waiting for alms than use his own money to buy food (*Rashi* to *Kesubos* 67b). Of such a person, the verse implies (through its double language) that you should extend to him a loan in a way that appears as if you are giving him a gift – and you may then claim your expenses from the heirs of his estate, after this man has died (*Rashi*).

23. R' Shimon's position is recorded in a Baraisa on *Kesubos* 67b.

24. See above, note 19. Here, too, there is no indication that R' Shimon would argue with *all* the above expositions of repetitive language. He would seem to assert only that in *this* case, the word תַּעֲבִיטֶנּוּ cannot be interpreted as broadening the lending requirement to apply in "all cases," for the verse specifically states: *lend, you shall lend to him enough [to fulfill] his lack*. A miser in fact lacks nothing, so it is evident that the verse does not mean that one must lend money to him also (*Tosafos*).

25. The finder cannot claim the full *sela*, for if he had in fact continued laboring to earn this money, he would have exerted himself far more than he actually did in retrieving the object. He may thus claim only the lesser compensation signified by the Mishnah's words "his wages like a worker." The Gemara now undertakes to explain the meaning of this phrase.

26. Consider, for example, that the finder earns five *dinar* an hour at his regular job. For every hour that he remains idle, he forfeits a potential gain of five *dinar*. Nevertheless, if someone were to offer hi[m] a reduced wage of, say, one *dinar* for the opportunity to rest an hou[r] from his work, he might be willing to accept the proposal. The Gema[ra] now takes the Baraisa to mean that the owner must pay the finder f[or] his time according to the minimum amount he would be willing [to] accept under such an arrangement – one *dinar,* in our example (s[ee] *Rashi*).

27. That is, the owner must give the finder the amount of money h[e] would accept to stop doing his more difficult work, and instead car[ry] out the easier job of returning a lost object. For example, if someone i[n] the finder's line of work is paid five *dinar* for his labor, he might b[e] willing to stand completely idle and rest from his work for only o[ne] *dinar*. But if he was asked to use the time off from his ordinary job, n[ot] to rest but, to perform some easier form of labor – e.g. to return a lo[st] object – he might ask for a slightly higher amount of compensation; h[e] might, for example, request two *dinar*. In such a case the owner wou[ld] be required to pay the finder two *dinar* for his lost time (see *Rosh*, §24[)].

Generally, when one finds a lost object, he is obligated to return it f[or] free. The Gemara rules, however, that this applies only when he wou[ld] have been idle from work during the time he was busy retrieving an[d] returning the object; but if he would have otherwise been workin[g] during that time, as in our case, he is entitled to receive payment t[o] compensate for his lost wages (*Rosh*).

28. *Ritva*.

29. The assets of the partnership were not in cash form; rather, th[e] partnership owned goods whose worth needed to be assessed in order t[o] be divided equally (*Rashi*).

30. Issur was out of town at the time (*Ritva*).

עין משפט
נר מצוה

קפד א מיי' פי"ד מהל' סנהדרין הל' ח:
קפה ב ג מיי' פ"ג מהל' מלוה ולוה הל' ה סמג לאוין קפז טוש"ע ח"מ סי' לז סעיף טז:
קפו ד ה מיי' פ"ז מהל' מתנות עניים הל' יג סמג עשין קסב טוש"ע י"ד סי' רמז סעיף א וסי' רמח סעיף א וסי' רנא סעיף ג:
קפז ו מיי' פ"ג מהל' עבדים הלכה יד סמג עשין פד:
קפח ז מיי' פ"ז מהל' מתנות עניים הל' ט סמג עשין קסב טוש"ע י"ד סי' רנג סעיף י:
קפט ח מיי' פי"ב מהל' גזילה ואבידה הלכה ד סמג עשין עד טוש"ע ח"מ סי' רסה:
קצ ט מיי' פ"ה מהל' שלוחים ושותפין הל' ט סמג עשין פב טוש"ע ח"מ סי' קעו סעיף יח:

רבינו חננאל

וכן דין השב תשיב את העבוט וכן דין חבל תחבול בין כסות יום בין כסות לילה וכן פתח תפתח את ידך וגומר לענייך ואפי' לעניי עיר אחרת וכן דין נתן תתן לו א) במתנה בין מרובה בין מועטת. וכן דין הענק תעניק לו ואפי' לא נתברך הבית בגללו וכן העבט תעביטנו אפי' יש לו ואינו רוצה להתפרנס: היה בטל מסלע לא יאמר לו תן לי סלע אלא נותן לו שכרו כפועל תנא כפועל בטל. ואקשי' והא לאו בטל הוא דהא מתעסק להחזיר האבידה. ופירקה אביי כפועל בטל של אותה מלאכה פי' כגון שהיה חייט והניח מלאכתו והלך להשיב את האבידה ונשתהה בהשבתה כשיעור תפירת בגד ששכרו סלע לא יאמר לו כבר בטלתי ממלאכתי שיעור סלע תנה לי אלא משערין שכרו כעת שאין לו מה יתפור אלא יושב ובטל אם יבא אדם ויאמר לו הנך יושב ובטל תקח בתפירת בגד חצי סלע או תשאר בטל היום ובעת שהמלאכה מצויה כגון קרוב לרגל וכיוצא בו שכר תפירת הבגד סלע ומה שמתברר שנוטל בשעה שאין לו תפירה לתפור הוא שנוטל מבעל האבידה וכן אם יאמר לו אדם אתה חייט ואין תפירה מצויה אצלך תבוא ללבון עמי לבנים ותיקח שכירותך כך וכך וזה מפני שלא התנה בב"ד על שכרו. אבל התנה בב"ד נוטל לפי תנאו דתנן אם יש שם ב"ד מתנה בפני ב"ד. איסור ורב ספרא הוו שותפי בעיסקא אזל רב ספרא פלג בלא דעתיה דאיסור קמי תרי וחייביה רבא לאיתויי תלתא אי נמי תרי מיגו תלתא אי נמי תרי סהדי דפלג קמיה

חשק שלמה על ר"ח

א) נ"ל תתן לו בין מתנה מרובה בין וכו'.

---

**אבל** הני תרתי דאיתנהו למרייהו בהדייהו. ואע"ג דמרבינן לעיל אין בעלים עמו היינו שהוא זקן או חולה ונהי דאין יכול לעזור יכול לשכור פועלין ואימא לא קא משמע לן:

**אין** לי אלא משכנו. פרשתי בהמקבל (לקמן דף קיג.):

**דברה** תורה כלשון בני אדם. וא"ת וכי לית להו כל הני דרשות דלעיל ואליבא דר"ש משנינן נמי לעיל דלא מסיימי קראי ובר"ה (דף ח.) דריש נמי ר"ש עשר תעשר אחד מעשר דגן ואחד מעשר בהמה וי"ל דדוקא הכא בהני תרי קראי אמרינן דברה תורה כלשון בני אדם [°] משום דמוכחי קראי דכתיב די מחסורו ובאידך כתיב אשר ברכך ובריש השואל (לקמן דף לד: ושם ד"ה אלא) דאמר אם גנב אין לי אלא גניבה אבידה מנין ת"ל יגנב ופריך למ"ד דברה תורה כלשון בני אדם מאי איכא למימר התם נמי איכא הוכחה דגניבה משמע דוקא גניבה ולא אבידה [°]:

**אם** יש שם ב"ד יתנה בפניהם. שישלם לו כל מה שישתכר במלאכה שהוא עושה ואם אין ב"ד לא ישיב כיון שאם ישיב לא יהא לו אלא כפועל בטל אבל אם אינו עושה מלאכה ישיב בחנם וא"ת לעיל דנקט או שהיתה שלו מרובה היכי דמי אי ליכא ב"ד אפילו מועטת נמי מן האבידה לא ישיב ואי בפני ב"ד כי נמי אין מרובה אלא שוה לאבידה למה יתנו ב"ד ליתן לו כל שכרו א"כ מה ירויחו הבעלים וי"ל דנ"מ לכושרא דחיותא או לטרחא יתירא וכה"ג משני בסוף השוכר את הפועלים (לקמן דף צג:) וא"ת דהכא משלם לכל הפחות השכירות כפועל בטל וכן משני לקמן בסוף השוכר את הפועלים (שם) גבי רועה שהיה יכול לקדם ברועים ובמקלות ש"מ בשכר וש"מ בחנם חייב וש"מ שקדם בשכר חוזר ונוטל מבעל הבית ומסתמא ש"מ נמי שקדם בשכר חוזר ונוטל מבעה"ב ואילו בפרק הגוזל בתרא (ב"ק דף קטו:) תנן שטף נהר את חמורו וחמור חבירו הניח את שלו והציל את של חבירו אין לו אלא שכרו ואין משלם לו דמי חמורו שטבע וי"ל דהתם מיירי כשהיה יכול להציל ע"י הדחק דאי לאו הכי מצי אמר ליה מהפקירא קזכינא כדאיתא התם ועי"ל כיון שבעל החמור שם יכול לומר הייתי שוכר פועלים להצילו וא"ת הכא אמאי נוטל שכר וכן לקמן ש"מ שאין צריך לקדם בשכר אם קידם אמאי נוטלו מבעה"ב האמרי' פר' הכונס (שם דף נח. ושם ד"ה אי) דמבריח ארי מנכסי חבירו פטור וללישנא בתרא דהכונס דמבריח ארי פטור משום דלית ליה פסידא אתי שפיר דהכא אית ליה פסידא אבל ללישנא קמא דקאמר דמבריח ארי מדעתו משמע אפילו אית ליה פסידא פטור כיון דמדעתו הוא קשה ואור"י דמבריח ארי פטור היינו דוקא שמצילו מפחד הארי שירא שיבא וקידם ברועים והבריחו דלא ברי הזיקא דבלא הצלתו יכול להיות שלא היה בא אבל מציל מפי הארי ושטף נהר חמורו ומחזיר אבידה דברי הזיקא ובא זה והציל נוטל שכרו וא"ת דפורע חובו דשרי למודר הנאה בפרק אין בין המודר (נדרים דף לג.) ופרק בתרא דכתובות (דף קח. ושם) מחשבין ליה מבריח ארי אע"ג דברי הזיקא ואית ליה פסידא וי"ל דהתם נמי אין מצילו מן ההפסד דמה שמלוה טורף ממנו אין זה הפסד שהרי נתחייב לו ולכך חשיב ליה כמבריח ארי א"נ כדמפרש טעמא בירושלמי דנדרים הוינא מפייס ליה ומחיל לי ואפי' במשכון מפייס הוינא ליה ויהיב לי משכוני ואפילו בב"ח דוחק מסיק בירושלמי והטעם נראה משום שיכול לומר הייתי מולא אוהבים הרבה שיפרעו עבורי דהיינו מעין אותם הטעמים והא דקרי ליה בפ' ח"ה (ב"ב דף נג.) מבריח ארי נתן צרור ונטל צרור דסכר מינה מיא ואפיק מינה מיא אע"פ שמצילו מן ההפסד שהיה נהר שוטפה התם לא נקט לשון מבריח לענין שיפטר משכר הברחה אלא כלומר אין זו חזקה כיון שאין מתקן השדה אלא מגין עליה בעלמא שלא תבא לידי קלקול ונראה שגם ר"ת סובר דלא חשיב מבריח ארי במקום שמצילו מן ההפסד שהיה מעמיד ההיא דפורע חובו דוקא במזונות אשתו כדמפרש בפ' בתרא דכתובות (דף קח. ושם) משום דאפשר שתהא עושה ואוכלת או תתפרנס מן הצדקה או מקרוביה שיתנו לה בחנם אבל שאר פריעת חוב אור"ת דאין זה מבריח ארי אלא מהנה גמור וירושלמי פליג אגמרא שלנו ולפ"ז אם השר גזל ביתו של ישראל ובא חבירו ישראל ופייס אותו בדמים מועטים אם ירצה בעה"ב ליקח ביתו ישלם דמים לחבירו וכן פסק רבינו גרשום אבל רש"י פסק שיחזיר לו ביתו חנם בפ' הנזקין (גיטין דף נח:) ונראה דלא מבעיא אם קנאה בדמים שמציל הבעלים מן ההפסד שישלמו הבעלים אלא אפי' קנאן בשויו ולא דמי למבריח ארי דאם היה משתקע בידו לא היה הבית חוזר לו לעולם ואפי' בשויו ודמי למקדים ברועים ובמקלות בשכר דאמרי' שנותן שכרו עד כדי דמיהם ונ"מ לכושרא דחיותא או לטרחא יתירא ועוד נר' אפי' ידוע בודאי שאפילו לא מיהר לקנותו היה חוזר לבעלים בדמים הללו כל שעה שירצו בין קנאן בדמים מרובים בין קנאן בדמים מועטים לא דמי למבריח ארי כיון שילא הבית מחזקת ישראל ובא לידי נכרי וזה מוליאו מחזקת נכרי ומחזירו ליד ישראל נוטל מה שההנהו:

**כפועל** בטל. פירשנו באיזהו נשך (לקמן דף סח. ושם ד"ה ונותן):
אלמנה

---

אבל הני תרתי דאיתא למרה בהדה אימא לא צריכא א) [א] מות יומת המכה אין לי אלא במיתה הכתובה בו מנין שאם אי אתה יכול להמיתו במיתה הכתובה בו שאתה רשאי להמיתו בכל מיתה שאתה יכול להמיתו ת"ל א מות יומת מ"מ ב) הכה תכה אין לי אלא בהכאה הכתובה בהן מנין שאם אי אתה יכול להמיתן בהכאה הכתובה בהן שאתה רשאי להכותן בכל הכאה שאתה יכול ת"ל הכה תכה מ"מ ג) השב תשיב אין לי אלא שמשכנו ברשות ב"ד משכנו שלא ברשות ב"ד מנין ת"ל ב השב תשיב מ"מ ד) חבל תחבול אין לי אלא שמשכנו ברשות משכנו שלא ברשות מנין ת"ל ג חבל תחבול מ"מ והני תרי קראי למה לי חד לכסות יום וחד לכסות לילה ה) פתח תפתח אין לי אלא לעניי עירך לעניי עיר אחרת מנין ת"ל ד פתח תפתח מכל מקום ו) נתן תתן אין לי אלא מתנה מרובה מתנה מועטת מנין ה ת"ל נתן תתן מ"מ ז) הענק תעניק ג) אין לי אלא שנתברך הבית בגללו מעניקים לא נתברך הבית בגללו מנין ו ת"ל הענק תעניק מ"מ ולר' אלעזר בן עזריה דאמר נתברך הבית בגללו מעניקין לו לא נתברך הבית בגללו אין מעניקין תעניק למה לי ג) דברה תורה כלשון בני אדם ה) העבט תעביטנו ד) אין לי אלא שאין לו ואינו רוצה להתפרנס אמר רחמנא תן לו דרך הלואה יש לו ואינו רוצה להתפרנס מנין ת"ל תעביטנו מ"מ ולר"ש ה) דאמר ז יש לו ואינו רוצה להתפרנס אין נזקקין לו תעביטנו למה לי דברה תורה כלשון בני אדם: היה בטל מן הסלע לא יאמר לו תן לי סלע אלא נותן לו שכרו כפועל (בטל): י) (תנן) ז) נותן לו שכרו כפועל בטל מאי כפועל בטל ח) אמר אביי ח כפועל בטל של אותה מלאכה דבטל מינה: אם יש שם ב"ד מתנה בפניהם: איסור ורב ספרא עביד עיסקא בהדי הדדי אזל רב ספרא פלג ליה בלא דעתיה דאיסור באפי בי תרי ° אתא לקמי' ט) דרבה בר רב הונא א"ל ט זיל אייתי תלתא דפלגת קמייהו אי נמי תרי
תרי

---

דאיתיה למרה. דכתיב עמו אימא יחזור אחר בני אדם וישכור: שאם אי אתה יכול להמיתו במיתה הכתובה בו. והיינו סייף כגון שהיה בספינה ובורח ואתה יכול לזרוק בו חץ או לטובעו: הכה תכה. בעיר הנדחת: אין לי אלא שמשכנו ברשות ב"ד. דלעק עליו בדין ושלחו שלוחם לתפוס מטלטליו דקרא דהשבת העבוט עליה כתיב דכתיב לעיל מיניה בחוץ תעמוד והאיש ואמרינן לקמן בפ' המקבל (דף קיג.) בשליח ב"ד הכתוב מדבר: שלא ברשות ב"ד מנין. דלריך השבה: שהם חבלה ע"פ ב"ד היא דלא שכיח דחליף איניש ליכנס בבית וליטול מטלטלי שלא ברשות: חד לכסות יום וחד לכסות לילה. בפ' המקבל (לקמן קיד:) מפרש לקרא הכי: מתנה מועטת מנין. אם אי אפשר לך ליתן מתנה מרובה: אין לי אלא שנתברך הבית בגללו. דהכי כתיב קרא אשר ברכך ה' אלהיך תתן לו: דרבי אלעזר בן עזריה בקדושין (דף יז:): שאין לו. ממה שיתפרנס: ואינו רוצה להתפרנס. משלך במתנה ואמר רחמנא העבט דרך הלואה: יש לו ואינו רוצה להתפרנס. משלו אלא משלך מנין שאתה חייב להעביטו וליפרע ממנו אחר מיתה ת"ל תעביטנו והכי מפרש בכתובות פרק מציאת האשה (דף סז:): מאי כפועל בטל. והלא אינו בטל שהרי טורח בהשבתה ומתניתין תני נותנין לו כשיעור שירצה פועל ליטול להתרפות ממלאכה ולישב בטל: כפועל בטל של אותה מלאכה דבטל מינה. כמה אדם רוצה ליטול ולפחות משכרו ליבטל ממלאכה זו כבדה שהוא עוסק בה ולעסוק במלאכה קלה כזו הכל לפי כובד המלאכה וריבוי שכר יש מלאכ' שטורחה קל ושכרה רב או חילוף: פלג. בסחורה ולא היו מעות אלא דבר הצריך שומא:
תרי

כשמגיע הזמן ואינו פורע [שמות כב, כה]. הענק תעניק. לשון עדי בגובה ובמראית העין דבר שיהא ניכר שהטיבות לו ויש מפרשים לשון הטענה על צוארו [דברים טו, יד]. שאין לו. משלו. ואינו רוצה להתפרנס. מן הצדקה [כתובות סז:]. אם לא רצה במתנה תן לו בהלואה [דברים טו, ח]. יש לו ואינו רוצה להתפרנס. משלו אלא משל צדקה ומסגף עלמו ברעב [כתובות שם]. נותן לו שכרו כפועל בטל. ובמתניתין לא גרסינן בטל משמע כמה אדם רוצה ליטול ולישב בטל. אם היה נגר או נפח כמה אדם רוצה ליטול ליבטל ממלאכה כבידה כזו ולעשות מלאכה קלה [לקמן סח:]. דבטל הימנה דאם היה נוקב מרגליות שעבודתה נוחה לעשות ושכרו מרובה אם אומר לו טול כך וכך ותבטל היום ממלאכה אינו פוחת משכרו אלא דבר מועט שהרי נוחה ואין בה טורח ואי מלאכה קשה היא כמו נגר אומר לו אתה נוטל עכשיו שלשה זוזי טול זוז והבטל היום מאותה מלאכה ועשה מלאכה קלה זו נוח לו להיבטל וליטול זוז והכא נמי כי ההוא אגרא אגרא לא יהיב ליה שהרי מבטלו ממלאכתו וכוליה אגרא לא יהיב ליה שהרי אינו עסוק במלאכה קשה אלא [בכורות כט:]

---

מסורת הש"ס

א) [סנהדרין מה:, מג. עב:], ב) קדושין יז:, ג) [שם וש"נ], ד) כתובות סז:, ה) [ע"ש], ו) [ל"ע תנא], ז) לקמן סח. בכורות כט:, ח) הא לא בטיל מיניה. מהרש"ל, ט) [גרל"ע איתא ר' אבא אבל בתוס' בבא בתרא מ. ד"ה קיום מוכח דהגירסא לפניהם ר"נ], י) [וע"ע תוס' כתובות סז: ד"ה וחכמים, ועמ"ש תוס' סוטה כד. ד"ה ור' יונתן ותוס' מנחות יח: ד"ה מא בארוכות].

גליון הש"ס

גמ' אתא לקמיה דרבה בר רב הונא. עיין תוס' ב"ב מ ע"ל ד"ה קיום דנראה דהיה להם הגירסא כאן אתא לקמיה דר"נ: תוס' ד"ה דברה תורה וכו' משום דמוכחי קראי. עיי' מזרחי ריש פ' לך לך

תורה אור השלם

א) אוֹ בְאֵיבָה הִכָּהוּ בְיָדוֹ וַיָּמֹת מוֹת יוּמַת הַמַּכֶּה רֹצֵחַ הוּא גֹּאֵל הַדָּם יָמִית אֶת הָרֹצֵחַ בְּפִגְעוֹ בוֹ: [במדבר לה, כא]

ב) הַכֵּה תַכֶּה אֶת יֹשְׁבֵי הָעִיר הַהִוא לְפִי חָרֶב הַחֲרֵם אֹתָהּ וְאֶת כָּל אֲשֶׁר בָּהּ וְאֶת בְּהֶמְתָּהּ לְפִי חָרֶב: [דברים יג, טז]

ג) הָשֵׁב תָּשִׁיב לוֹ אֶת הָעֲבוֹט כְּבוֹא הַשֶּׁמֶשׁ וְשָׁכַב בְּשַׂלְמָתוֹ וּבֵרֲכֶךָּ וּלְךָ תִּהְיֶה צְדָקָה לִפְנֵי יְיָ אֱלֹהֶיךָ: [דברים כד, יג]

ד) אִם חָבֹל תַּחְבֹּל שַׂלְמַת רֵעֶךָ עַד בֹּא הַשֶּׁמֶשׁ תְּשִׁיבֶנּוּ לוֹ: [שמות כב, כה]

ה) כִּי פָתֹחַ תִּפְתַּח אֶת יָדְךָ לוֹ וְהַעֲבֵט תַּעֲבִיטֶנּוּ דֵּי מַחְסֹרוֹ אֲשֶׁר יֶחְסַר לוֹ: [דברים טו, ח]

ו) נָתוֹן תִּתֵּן לוֹ וְלֹא יֵרַע לְבָבְךָ בְּתִתְּךָ לוֹ כִּי בִּגְלַל הַדָּבָר הַזֶּה יְבָרֶכְךָ יְיָ אֱלֹהֶיךָ בְּכָל מַעֲשֶׂךָ וּבְכֹל מִשְׁלַח יָדֶךָ: [דברים טו, י]

ז) הַעֲנֵיק תַּעֲנִיק לוֹ מִצֹּאנְךָ וּמִגָּרְנְךָ וּמִיִּקְבֶךָ אֲשֶׁר בֵּרַכְךָ יְיָ אֱלֹהֶיךָ תִּתֶּן לוֹ: [דברים טו, יד]

ליקוטי רש"י

אין לי. אי לא כתיב אלא יומת. אלא מיתה הכתובה בו. סייף [סנהדרין מה:]. שאם אי אתה יכול וכו' הכתובה בו. כגון שהיה מכשף או שהיה לו נהר מפסיק ואתה יכול לירות בו חץ או אבן [שם עב:] מות יומת. ריבויא הוא [שם מה:]. הכה תכה אם אינך יכול להמיתם במיתה הכתובה בהם המיתם באחרת [דברים יג, טז]. חבל תחבול. לשון חבלה אינו משכון בשעת הלואה אלא שממשכנין את הלוה

*PROCURE, YOU PROCURE... you shall return it to him.* This repetitive language implies: מִכָּל מָקוֹם – You must return the item **IN ALL CASES,** even if it was procured without permission of the court.

In the verses just cited, the Torah twice recorded a creditor's obligation to return a collateral item to the debtor when he needs it. The Gemara now asks:

וְהָנֵי תְּרֵי קְרָאֵי לָמָּה לִי – **Why do I need these two verses** to tell me the same law?

The Gemara answers:

חַד לִכְסוּת יוֹם – **One** teaches about returning **a garment** that is worn during **the day,** וְחַד לִכְסוּת לַיְלָה – **and one** teaches about returning **a garment** that is worn during **the night.**[11]

The Gemara expounds an instance of repetitive language in connection with the command to give alms to the poor:

"פָּתֹחַ תִּפְתַּח" – The verse states: *OPEN, YOU SHALL OPEN your hand to him.*[12] אֵין לִי אֶלָּא לַעֲנִיֵּי עִירְךָ – Now, if the verse had not used repetitive language, **I [WOULD HAVE] KNOWN ONLY** that you are obligated to give alms **TO THE POOR OF YOUR TOWN.**[13] לַעֲנִיֵּי עִיר אַחֶרֶת מִנַּיִן – But **FROM WHERE IS IT DERIVED** that you are also obligated to give alms **TO THE POOR OF ANOTHER TOWN?** תַּלְמוּד לוֹמַר – **FOR THE VERSE STATES:** "פָּתֹחַ תִּפְתַּח" – *OPEN, YOU SHALL OPEN YOUR HAND,* and the double language implies: מִכָּל מָקוֹם – Open your hand **IN ALL CASES,** whether the poor person is from your town or not.

The Gemara records a similar exposition:

"נָתוֹן תִּתֵּן" – The verse states: *GIVE, YOU SHALL GIVE to him.*[14] אֵין לִי אֶלָּא מַתָּנָה מְרוּבָּה – If the verse had not used repetitive language, **I [WOULD HAVE] KNOWN ONLY** that you are obligated to give **A LARGE GIFT** if you can afford this.[15] מַתָּנָה מוּעֶטֶת מִנַּיִן – But **FROM WHERE IS IT DERIVED** that even if you cannot afford a large gift you must give **A SMALL GIFT?** תַּלְמוּד לוֹמַר – **THE VERSE STATES:** "נָתוֹן תִּתֵּן" – *GIVE, YOU SHALL GIVE,* which implies: מִכָּל מָקוֹם – you must give a gift **IN ALL CASES,** even if you can afford only a small one.

The Gemara sets forth a similar exposition regarding the obligation to give severance gifts to a Jewish servant upon his emancipation:[16]

"הַעֲנֵיק תַּעֲנִיק" – The verse states: *BESTOW, YOU SHALL BESTO[W] upon him SEVERANCE GIFTS.* אֵין לִי אֶלָּא שֶׁנִּתְבָּרֵךְ הַבַּיִת בִּגְלָלוֹ – [If] the verse had stated its law without using repetitive language, **[I WOULD HAVE] KNOWN ONLY THAT** if **THE [MASTER'S] HOUSEHO[LD] WAS BLESSED ON ACCOUNT OF [THE SERVANT],** מַעֲנִיקִים – the[n] **HE IS TO BE GIVEN SEVERANCE GIFTS.**[17] לֹא נִתְבָּרֵךְ הַבַּיִת בִּגְלָלוֹ מִנַּיִן – But **FROM WHERE IS IT DERIVED THAT** if **THE HOUSEHOL[D] WAS NOT BLESSED ON HIS ACCOUNT,** he is still to be given severan[ce] gifts? תַּלְמוּד לוֹמַר – **FOR THE VERSE STATES:** "הַעֲנֵיק תַּעֲנִיק" *BESTOW, YOU SHALL BESTOW UPON HIM SEVERANCE GIFTS,* a repet[i]tive phraseology which implies: מִכָּל מָקוֹם – the servant [is] entitled to severance gifts **IN ALL CASES,** even if his presence in t[he] master's household was not a source of great blessing.

The Gemara, however, asks:

וּלְר׳ אֶלְעָזָר בֶּן עֲזַרְיָה – **But according to R' Elazar ben Azarya[h]** דְּאָמַר – **who says** that the verse is to be understood according [to] its plain meaning:[18] נִתְבָּרֵךְ הַבַּיִת בִּגְלָלוֹ – If **THE** master['s] **HOUSEHOLD WAS BLESSED ON ACCOUNT OF [THE SERVANT]** מַעֲנִיקִין לוֹ – then **HE IS TO BE GIVEN SEVERANCE GIFTS,** לֹא נִתְבָּרֵךְ הַבַּיִת בִּגְלָלוֹ – but if **THE HOUSEHOLD WAS NOT BLESSED ON H[IS] ACCOUNT,** אֵין מַעֲנִיקִין – then **HE NEED NOT BE GIVEN SEVERAN[CE] GIFTS,** "תַּעֲנִיק" לָמָּה לִי – **why do I need** the words, *you sha[ll] bestow upon him?* What is taught by this repetitive langua[ge] according to R' Elazar ben Azaryah?

The Gemara answers:

דִּבְּרָה תּוֹרָה כִּלְשׁוֹן בְּנֵי אָדָם – According to R' Elazar ben Azarya[h] there is no special significance in this repetition, for **the Tora[h]** simply **spoke in the** common **language used by men.**[19]

The Gemara presents a final exposition of repetitive Scriptur[al] language:

"הַעֲבֵט תַּעֲבִיטֶנּוּ" – In setting forth the command to lend money [to] those in need, the verse states: *LEND, YOU SHALL LEND TO HIM.*[20] אֵין לִי אֶלָּא שֶׁאֵין לוֹ וְאֵינוֹ רוֹצֶה לְהִתְפַּרְנֵס – Now, if Scripture ha[d] stated this law without using repetitive language, **I [WOULD HAV[E]] KNOWN ONLY** that one must lend to **[A PERSON] WHO DOES NO[T] HAVE** money of his own, **AND DOES NOT WANT TO BE SUPPORTED** b[y]

NOTES

11. The verse in *Deuteronomy* 24:13 refers to a garment that is worn at night, and teaches that the creditor must return it *as the sun sets* so the debtor may sleep in it. The verse in *Exodus* 22:25 refers to a day garment, and teaches that the creditor must return it to the debtor for him to use during the day *until the sun sets* (Gemara below, 114b).

12. The passage states (*Deuteronomy* 15:7-8): כִּי־יִהְיֶה בְךָ אֶבְיוֹן מֵאַחַד אַחֶיךָ בְּאַחַד שְׁעָרֶיךָ... לֹא תְאַמֵּץ אֶת־לְבָבְךָ וְלֹא תִקְפֹּץ אֶת־יָדְךָ... כִּי פָתֹחַ תִּפְתַּח אֶת־יָדְךָ לוֹ, *When there is among you a destitute person from one of your brothers in one of your gates...do not harden your heart nor close your hand ... Rather, open, you shall open your hand to him.*

13. The verse seems to speak only of the poor of one's own city, for the poor man it mentions is located בְּאַחַד שְׁעָרֶיךָ, *in one of your gates* (*Maharsha; Toras Chaim*).

14. The verse speaks of giving financial assistance to the poor (*Deuteronomy* 15:10): נָתוֹן תִּתֵּן לוֹ וְלֹא־יֵרַע לְבָבְךָ בְּתִתְּךָ לוֹ כִּי בִּגְלַל הַדָּבָר הַזֶּה יְבָרֶכְךָ ה׳ אֱלֹהֶיךָ, Give, *you shall give him, and your heart shall not be grieved when you give to him, for because of this thing* HASHEM *your God shall bless you....*

15. The verse seems to speak of giving a large gift specifically, for it states: וְלֹא־יֵרַע לְבָבְךָ, *and your heart shall not be grieved.* One might be expected to "grieve" only if he is parting with a large sum of money (*Ritva*; see also *Tos. HaRosh;* cf. *Maharsha*).

16. Scripture gives the following instruction to a master who sends a Jewish servant free after six years (*Deuteronomy* 15:13-14): וְכִי־תְשַׁלְּחֶנּוּ חָפְשִׁי מֵעִמָּךְ לֹא תְשַׁלְּחֶנּוּ רֵיקָם. הַעֲנֵיק תַּעֲנִיק לוֹ מִצֹּאנְךָ וּמִגָּרְנְךָ וּמִיִּקְבֶךָ אֲשֶׁר בֵּרַכְךָ ה׳ אֱלֹהֶיךָ תִּתֶּן־לוֹ, *And when you send him free from you, you shall not send him empty-handed. Bestow, you shall bestow upon him severance gifts, from your sheep and from your threshing floor and from your winepres[s] [of that with] which* HASHEM *your God blessed you, you shall give hi[m].*

17. I.e. if the master realized a substantial profit since the arrival of th[e] servant, then he is required to give him severance gifts.

As noted above, the verse mentions that severance gifts should b[e] given from *"that with which* HASHEM *your God has blessed you."* Th[e] inclusion of these words seems to indicate that the verse deals with [a] situation in which the master has been blessed with an abundance [of] assets, a portion of which he must select as severance gifts (*Rashi*).

18. R' Elazer ben Azaryah's position is set forth by a Baraisa [in] *Kiddushin* (17b).

19. People often repeat themselves when they wish to motivate others [to] take a certain action. Here, too, the Torah repeated itself to motivate th[e] master to give severance gifts to his servant (*Toras Chaim*).

*Tosafos* question whether R' Elazar ben Azaryah would indeed argu[e] with *all* the above expositions by employing the argument that th[e] Torah spoke in the common language of men. Would R' Elazar see n[o] significance in *any* of the instances of repetitive language expounde[d] earlier? *Tosafos* reply that R' Elazar ben Azaryah would indeed agre[e] with the above expositions. In the case of הַעֲנֵיק תַּעֲנִיק, however, h[e] maintains that the repetitive language cannot be construed to requi[re] severance gifts in *all* cases, for the Torah explicitly links the obligatio[n] of giving severance gifts to the blessing the owner received on th[e] servant's account. Hence, in this case specifically, no special significan[ce] can be attached to the Torah's use of repetitive language.

20. The verse speaks of lending money to others: הַעֲבֵט תַּעֲבִיטֶנּוּ דֵּי מַחְסֹרוֹ, *and lend, you shall lend to him enough [to fulfill] his lack* (*Deuteronom[y]* 15:8).

עין משפט
נר מצוה

קסד א מיי׳ פי״ד מהל׳ סנהדרין הל׳ ח:
קסה ב ג מיי׳ פ״ג מהל׳ מלוה ולוה הל׳ ה סמג לאוין קפז טוש״ע ח״מ סי׳ לז סעיף טז:
קסו ד ה מיי׳ פ״ז מהל׳ מתנות עניים הל׳ יג סמג עשין קסב טוש״ע י״ד סי׳ רמז סעיף א וסי׳ רמח סעיף א וסי׳ רנא סעיף ג:
קסז ו מיי׳ פ״ג מהל׳ עבדים הלכה יד סמג עשין פד:
קסח ז מיי׳ פ״ז מהל׳ מתנות עניים הל׳ ט סמג עשין קסב טוש״ע י״ד סי׳ רנג סעיף י:
קסט ח מיי׳ פי״ב מהל׳ גזילה ואבידה הלכה ד סמג עשין עד טוש״ע ח״מ סי׳ רסה:
קע ט מיי׳ פ״ה מהל׳ שלוחים ושותפין הל׳ ט סמג עשין פב טוש״ע ח״מ סי׳ קעו סעיף יח:

אבל הני תרתי דאיתא למרה בהדה אימא לא צריכא א) [א] מות יומת המכה אין לי אלא במיתה הכתובה בו מנין שאם אי אתה יכול להמיתו במיתה הכתובה בו שאתה רשאי להמיתו בכל מיתה שאתה יכול להמיתו ת״ל [א] מות יומת מ״מ ב) הכה תכה אין לי אלא בהכאה הכתובה בהן מנין שאם אי אתה יכול להמיתן בהכאה הכתובה בהן שאתה רשאי להכותן בכל הכאה שאתה יכול ת״ל הכה תכה מ״מ ג) השב תשיב אין לי אלא שמשכנו ברשות ב״ד משכנו שלא ברשות ב״ד מנין ת״ל [ג] השב תשיב מ״מ ד) חבל תחבול אין לי אלא שמשכנו ברשות משכנו שלא ברשות מנין ת״ל [ג] חבל תחבול מ״מ והני תרי קראי למה לי חד לכסות יום וחד לכסות לילה ה) פתח תפתח אין לי אלא לעניי עירך לעניי עיר אחרת מנין ת״ל [ד] פתח תפתח מכל מקום ו) נתן תתן אין לי אלא מתנה מרובה מתנה מועטת מנין [ה] ת״ל נתן תתן מ״מ ז) העניק תעניק [ב] אין לי אלא שנתברך הבית בגללו מעניקים לא נתברך הבית בגללו מנין [י] ת״ל העניק תעניק מ״מ ולר׳ אלעזר בן עזריה דאמר נתברך הבית בגללו מעניקין לו לא נתברך הבית בגללו אין מעניקין תעניק למה לי [ג] דברה תורה כלשון בני אדם ה) העבט תעביטנו [ד] אין לי אלא שאין לו ואינו רוצה להתפרנס אמר רחמנא תן לו דרך הלואה יש לו ואינו רוצה להתפרנס מנין ת״ל תעביטנו מ״מ ולר״ש [ה] דאמר [ז] יש לו ואינו רוצה להתפרנס אין נזקקין לו תעביטנו למה לי דברה תורה כלשון בני אדם: היה בטל מן הסלע לא יאמר לו תן לי סלע אלא נותן לו שכרו כפועל (בטל): [י] (תנן) [ו] נותן לו שכרו כפועל בטל מאי כפועל בטל [ח] אמר אביי [ח] כפועל בטל של אותה מלאכה דבטל מינה: אם יש שם ב״ד מתנה בפניהם: איסור ורב ספרא עביד עיסקא בהדי הדדי אזל רב ספרא פלג ליה בלא דעתיה דאיסור באפי בי תרי [ס] אתא לקמי׳ [ט] דרבה בר רב הונא א״ל [ט] זיל אייתי תלתא דפלגת קמייהו אי נמי תרי

רש״י

דאיתיה למרה. דכתיב עמו אימא יחזור אחר בני אדם וישכור: שאם אי אתה יכול להמיתו במיתה הכתובה בו. והיינו סייף כגון שהיה בספינה ובורח ואתה יכול לזרוק בו חץ או לטובעו: הכה תכה. בעיר הנדחת: אין לי אלא שמשכנו ברשות ב״ד. דלעק עליו בדין ושלחו שלוחם לתפוס מטלטליו דקרא דהשבת העבוט עליה כתיב דכתיב לעיל מיניה בחוץ תעמוד והאיש ואמרינן לקמן בפ׳ המקבל (דף קיג.) בשליח ב״ד הכתוב מדבר: שלא ברשות ב״ד מנין. דלריך השבה: סתם חבלה ע״פ ב״ד היא דלא שכיח דחליף איניש ליכנס בבית וליטול מטלטלי שלא ברשות: חד לכסות יום וחד לכסות לילה. בפ׳ המקבל (לקמן קיד:) מפרש לקרא הכי: מתנה מועטת מנין. אם אי אפשר לך ליתן מתנה מרובה: אין לי אלא שנתברך הבית בגללו. דהכי כתיב קרא אשר ברכך ה׳ אלהיך תתן לו: דרבי אלעזר בן עזריה בקדושין (דף יז:): שאין לו. ממה שיתפרנס: ואינו רוצה להתפרנס. משלך במתנה ואמר רחמנא העבט דרך הלואה: יש לו ואינו רוצה להתפרנס. משלו אלא משלך מנין שאתה חייב להעביטו וליפרע ממנו אחר מיתה ת״ל תעביטנו והכי מפרש בכתובות פרק מציאת האשה (דף סז:): מאי כפועל בטל. והלא אינו בטל שהרי טורח בהשבתה ומתניתין תני נותנין לו כשיעור שירצה פועל ליטול להתרפות ממלאכה ולישב בטל: כפועל בטל של אותה מלאכה דבטל מינה. כמה אדם רוצה ליטול ולפחות משכרו ליבטל ממלאכה זו כבדה שהוא עוסק בה ולעסוק במלאכה קלה כזו הכל לפי כובד המלאכה וריבוי שכר יש מלאכ׳ שטורחה קל ושכרה רב או חילוף: פלג. בסחורה ולא היו מעות אלא דבר הצריך שומא:

תוספות

אבל הני תרתי דאיתנהו למרייהו בהדייהו. ואע״ג דמרבינן לעיל אין בעלים עמו היינו שהוא זקן או חולה והכי דאין יכול לעזור יכול לשכור פועלין ואימא לא קא משמע לן:

אין לי אלא משכנו. פרשתי בהמקבל (לקמן דף קיג.):

דברה תורה כלשון בני אדם. וא״ת וכי לית להו כל הני דרשות דלעיל ואליבא דר״ש משנינן נמי לעיל דלא מסיימי קראי ובר״ה (דף ח.) דריש נמי ר״ש עשר תעשר אחד מעשר דגן ואחד מעשר בהמה וי״ל דדוקא הכא בהני תרי קראי אמרינן דברה תורה כלשון בני אדם [ס] משום דמוכחי קראי דכתיב די מחסורו ובאידך כתיב אשר ברכך ובריש השואל (לקמן דף לד: ושם ד״ה אלא) דאמר אם גנב אין לי אלא גניבה אבידה מנין ת״ל יגנב ופריך למ״ד דברה תורה כלשון בני אדם מאי איכא למימר התם נמי איכא הוכחה דגניבה משמע דוקא גניבה ולא אבידה [י]:

אם יש שם ב״ד יתנה בפניהם. שישלם לו כל מה שישתכר במלאכה שהוא עושה ואם אין ב״ד לא ישיב כיון שאם ישיב לא יהא לו אלא כפועל בטל אבל אם אינו עושה מלאכה ישיב בחנם וא״ת לעיל דנקט או שהיתה שלו מרובה היכי דמי אי ליכא ב״ד אפילו מועטת נמי מן האבידה לא ישיב ואי בפני ב״ד כי נמי אין מרובה אלא שוה לאבידה למה יתנו ב״ד ליתן לו כל שכרו א״כ מה ירויחו הבעלים וי״ל דנ״מ לכושרא דחיותא או לטרחא יתירא וכה״ג משני בסוף השוכר את הפועלים (לקמן דף עג:) וא״ת דהכא משלם לכל הפחות השכירות כפועל בטל וכן משני לקמן בסוף השוכר את הפועלים (שם) גבי רועה שהיה יכול לקדם ברועים ובמקלות ש״מ בשכר וש״מ בחנם חייב וש״מ שקדם בשכר חוזר ונוטל מבעל הבית ומסתמא ש״מ נמי שקדם בשכר חוזר ונוטל מבעה״ב ואילו בפרק הגוזל בתרא (ב״ק דף קטו:) תנן שטף נהר את חמורו וחמור חבירו הניח את שלו והציל את של חבירו אין לו אלא שכרו ואין משלם לו דמי חמורו שטבע וי״ל דהתם מיירי כשהיה יכול להציל ע״י הדחק דאי לאו הכי מאי אמר ליה מהפקירא קזכינא כדאיתא התם ועי״ל כיון שבעל החמור שם יכול לומר הייתי שוכר פועלים להצילו וא״ת הכא אמאי נוטל שכר וכן לקמן ש״מ שאין צריך לקדם בשכר אם קידם אמאי נוטלו מבעה״ב האמרי׳ פר׳ הכונס (שם דף נח. ושם ד״ה אי) דמבריח ארי מנכסי חבירו פטור וללישנא בתרא דהכונס דמבריח ארי פטור משום דלית ליה פסידא אתי שפיר דהכא אית ליה פסידא אבל ללישנא קמא דקאמר דמבריח ארי מדעתו משמע אפילו אית ליה פסידא פטור כיון דמדעתו הוא קשה ואור״י דמבריח ארי פטור היינו דוקא שמצילו מפחד הארי שירא שיבא וקידם ברועים והבריחו דלא ברי היזקא דבלא הצלתו יכול להיות שלא היה בא אבל מציל מפי הארי ושטף נהר חמורו ומחזיר אבידה דברי היזקא ובא זה והציל נוטל שכרו וא״ת דפורע חובו דשרי למודר הנאה בפרק אין בין המודר (נדרים דף לג.) ופרק בתרא דכתובות (דף קח. ושם) מחשבין ליה מבריח ארי אע״ג דברי היזקא ואית ליה פסידא וי״ל דהתם נמי אין מצילו מן ההפסד דמה שמלוה טורף ממנו אין זה הפסד שהרי נתחייב לו ולכך חשיב ליה כמבריח ארי א״נ כדמפרש טעמא בירושלמי דנדרים הוינא מפייס ליה ומחיל לי ואפי׳ במשכון מפייס הוינא ליה ויהיב לי משכוני ואפילו בב״ח דוחק מסיק בירושלמי והטעם נראה משום שיכול לומר הייתי מולא אוהבים הרבה שיפרעו עבורי דהיינו מעין אותם הטעמים והא דקרי ליה בפ׳ ח״ה (ב״ב דף נג.) מבריח ארי נתן צרור ונטל צרור דסכר מינה מיא ואפיק מינה מיא אע״פ שמצילו מן ההפסד שהיה נהר שוטפה התם לא נקט לשון מבריח לענין שיפטר משכר הברחה אלא כלומר אין זו חזקה כיון שאין מתקן השדה אלא מגין עליה בעלמא שלא תבא לידי קלקול ונראה שגם ר״ת סובר דלא חשיב מבריח ארי במקום שמצילו מן ההפסד שהיה מעמיד ההיא דפורע חובו דוקא במזונות אשתו כדמפרש בפ׳ בתרא דכתובות (דף קח. ושם) משום דאפשר שתהא עושה ואוכלת או תתפרנס מן הצדקה או מקרוביה שיתנו לה בחנם אבל שאר פריעת חוב אור״ת דאין זה מבריח ארי אלא מהנה גמור וירושלמי פליג אגמרא שלנו ולפ״ז אם השר גזל ביתו של ישראל ובא חבירו ישראל ופייס אותו בדמים מועטים אם ירצה בעה״ב ליקח ביתו ישלם דמים לחבירו וכן פסק רבינו גרשום אבל רש״י פסק שיחזיר לו ביתו חנם בפ׳ הנזקין (גיטין דף נח:) ונראה דלא מבעיא אם קנאה בדמים שמציל הבעלים מן ההפסד שישלמו הבעלים אלא אפי׳ קנאן בשויו ולא דמי למבריח ארי דאם היה משתקע בידו לא היה הבית חוזר לו לעולם ואפי׳ בשויו ודמי למקדים ברועים ובמקלות בשכר דאמרי׳ שנותן שכרו עד כדי דמיהם ונ״מ לכושרא דחיותא או לטרחא יתירא ועוד נר׳ אפי׳ ידוע בודאי שאפילו לא מיהר לקנותו היה חוזר לבעלים בדמים הללו כל שעה שירלו בין קנאן בדמים מרובים בין קנאן בדמים מועטים לא דמי למבריח ארי כיון שילא הבית מחזקת ישראל ובא לידי נכרי וזה מוליאו מחזקת נכרי ומחזירו ליד ישראל נוטל מה שההנהו:

כפועל בטל. פירשנו באיזהו נשך (לקמן דף סח. ושם ד״ה ונותן): אלמנה

רבינו חננאל

וכן דין השב תשיב את העבוט וכן דין חבל תחבול בין כסות יום בין כסות לילה וכן פתח תפתח את ידך וגומר לענייך ואפי׳ לעניי עיר אחרת וכן דין נתן תתן לו א) במתנה בין מרובה בין מועטת. וכן דין העניק תעניק לו ואפי׳ לא נתברך הבית בגללו וכן העבט תעביטנו אפי׳ יש לו ואינו רוצה להתפרנס: היה בטל מסלע לא יאמר לו תן לי סלע אלא נותן לו שכרו כפועל תנא כפועל בטל. ואקשי׳ והא לאו בטל הוא דהא מתעסק להחזיר האבידה. ופירקה אביי כפועל בטל של אותה מלאכה פי׳ כגון שהיה חייט והניח מלאכתו והלך להשיב את האבידה ונשתהה בהשבתה כשיעור תפירת בגד ששכרו סלע לא יאמר לו כבר בטלתי ממלאכתי שיעור סלע תנה לי אלא משערין שכרו כעת שאין לו מה יתפור אלא יושב ובטל אם יבא אדם ויאמר לו הנך יושב ובטל תקח בתפירת בגד חצי סלע או תשאר בטל היום ובעת שהמלאכה מצויה כגון קרוב לרגל וכיוצא בו שכר תפירת הבגד סלע ומה שמתברר שנוטל בשעה שאין לו תפירה לתפור הוא שכר האבידה וכן אם יאמר לו אדם אתה חייט ואין תפירה מצויה אצלך תבוא ללבכן עמי שכירותך כך וכך וזה מפני שלא התנה בבי״ד על שכרו. אבל התנה בב״ד נוטל לפי תנאו דתנן אם יש שם ב״ד מתנה בפני ב״ד. איסור ורב ספרא הוו שותפי בעיסקא אזל רב ספרא פלג בלא דעתיה דאיסור קמי תרי ואייתיביה רבא לאיתויי תלתא אי נמי תרי מיגו תלתא אי נמי תרי סהדי דפלג קמיה

חשק שלמה על ר״ח
א) נ״ל נתן תתן בין מתנה מרובה בין וכו׳.

מסורת הש״ס

א) [סנהדרין מה:, נג., עב:], ב) קדושין יז:, ג) [שם וש״נ], ד) כתובות סז:, ה) [ע״ש], ו) [נ״ל תנא], ז) לקמן סח., בכורות כט:, ח) הא לא בטיל מיניה, מהרש״ל, ט) [גרס״ש איתא ר׳ אבא אבל בתוס׳ בבא בתרא מ. ד״ה קיום מוכח דהגירסא לפניהם ר״נ], י) [וע״ע תוס׳ כתובות סז: ד״ה וחכמים, ועמ״ש תוס׳ סוטה כד. ד״ה ור׳ יונתן, ותוס׳ מנחות יז: ד״ה מאי בארוכות].

גליון הש״ס

גמ׳ אתא לקמיה דרבה בר רב הונא. עיין תוס׳ ב״ב מ ע״א ד״ה קיום דנראה דהיה להם הגירסא כאן אתא לקמיה דר״נ: תוס׳ ד״ה דברה תורה וכו׳ משום דמוכחי קראי. עיי׳ מזרחי ריש פ׳ לך לך:

תורה אור השלם

א) אוֹ בְאֵיבָה הִכָּהוּ בְיָדוֹ וַיָּמֹת מוֹת יוּמַת הַמַּכֶּה רֹצֵחַ הוּא גֹּאֵל הַדָּם יָמִית אֶת הָרֹצֵחַ בְּפִגְעוֹ בוֹ: [במדבר לה, כא]
ב) הַכֵּה תַכֶּה אֶת יֹשְׁבֵי הָעִיר הַהִוא לְפִי חָרֶב הַחֲרֵם אֹתָהּ וְאֶת כָּל אֲשֶׁר בָּהּ וְאֶת בְּהֶמְתָּהּ לְפִי חָרֶב: [דברים יג, טז]
ג) הָשֵׁב תָּשִׁיב לוֹ אֶת הָעֲבוֹט כְּבוֹא הַשֶּׁמֶשׁ וְשָׁכַב בְּשַׂלְמָתוֹ וּבֵרְכֶךָּ וּלְךָ תִּהְיֶה צְדָקָה לִפְנֵי יְיָ אֱלֹהֶיךָ: [דברים כד, יג]
ד) אִם חָבֹל תַּחְבֹּל שַׂלְמַת רֵעֶךָ עַד בֹּא הַשֶּׁמֶשׁ תְּשִׁיבֶנּוּ לוֹ: [שמות כב, כה]
ה) כִּי פָתֹחַ תִּפְתַּח אֶת יָדְךָ לוֹ וְהַעֲבֵט תַּעֲבִיטֶנּוּ דֵּי מַחְסֹרוֹ אֲשֶׁר יֶחְסַר לוֹ: [דברים טו, ח]
ו) נָתוֹן תִּתֵּן לוֹ וְלֹא יֵרַע לְבָבְךָ בְּתִתְּךָ לוֹ כִּי בִּגְלַל הַדָּבָר הַזֶּה יְבָרֶכְךָ יְיָ אֱלֹהֶיךָ בְּכָל מַעֲשֶׂךָ וּבְכֹל מִשְׁלַח יָדֶךָ: [דברים טו, י]
ז) הַעֲנֵיק תַּעֲנִיק לוֹ מִצֹּאנְךָ וּמִגָּרְנְךָ וּמִיִּקְבֶךָ אֲשֶׁר בֵּרַכְךָ יְיָ אֱלֹהֶיךָ תִּתֶּן לוֹ: [דברים טו, יד]

ליקוטי רש״י

אין לי. אי לא כתיב יומת. אלא מיתה הכתובה בו. [סנהדרין מה:]. שאם אי אתה יכול להמיתו במיתה הכתובה בו. כגון שמכסך או שהיה על הגג ואין יכול לירד בו כן אם אין לך [שם עב:]. מות יומת. ריבויא הוא [שם מה:]. הכה תכה. אם אינך יכול להמיתם במיתה הכתובה בהם המיתם באחרת [דברים יג, טז]. חבל תחבול. כל לשון חבלה אינו משכון בשעת הלואה אלא שממשכנין את הלוה כשמגיע הזמן ואינו פורע [שמות כב, כה]. העניק תעניק. לשון עדי בגובה ובמראית העין דבר שיהא ניכר שהטיבות לו ויש מפרשים לשון הטענה על צוארו [דברים טו, יד]. שאין לו. משלו. ואינו רוצה להתפרנס. משל צדקה [כתובות סז:]. אם לא רצה במתנה תן לו בהלואה [דברים טו, ח]. יש לו ואינו רוצה להתפרנס. משלו אלא משל צדקה ומסגף עצמו ברעב [כתובות שם]. נותן לו שכרו כפועל בטל. ובמתניתין לא גרסינן בטל. משמע כמה אדם רוצה ליטול ולישב בטל. אמר אביי כפועל בטל של אותה מלאכה. אם היה נגר או נפח כמה אדם רוצה ליטול ליבטל ממלאכה כבידה כזו ולעשות מלאכה קלה [לקמן סח:]. דבטל הימנה דאם היה נוקב מרגליות שעבודתה נוחה לעשות ושכרו מרובה אם אומר לו טול כך וכך ותבטל היום ממלאכה אינו פוחת משכרו אלא דבר מועט שהרי נוחה ואין בה טורח ואי מלאכה קשה היא כמו נגר אומר לו אתה נוטל עכשיו שלשה זוזים טול זוז והבטל היום מאותה מלאכה ועשה מלאכה קלה זו נוח לו להיבטל וליטול זוז והכא נמי כי ההוא אגרא לא יהיב ליה שהרי מבטלו ממלאכתו וכוליה אגרא לא יהיב ליה שהרי אינו עסוק במלאכה קשה אלא [בכורות כט:].

אֲבָל הָנֵי תַּרְתֵּי – **But** with respect to **these two** laws, loading and unloading, דְּאִיתָא לְמָרָהּ בַּהֲדָהּ – **where [the animal's] owner is** there **with [the animal],** standing next to it, אֵימָא לֹא – **I might** have **said** that there is **no** obligation for a bystander to help him, since the owner could hire others to load or unload, if he so wished.[1] צְרִיכָא – **It is** therefore **necessary** for the Torah to write both sets of laws: the duty to load and unload, as well as the duty to return a lost object.

The Gemara now resumes its exposition of duplicative Scriptural phrases by citing a number of Baraisos that expound these: "מוֹת־יוּמַת הַמַּכֶּה" – Regarding the fate of a convicted murderer, the verse states: ***HE WHO STRUCK [THE MAN] SHALL DIE, HE SHALL DIE.***[2] Now, if Scripture had not used repetitive language here, אֵין לִי אֶלָּא בְּמִיתָה הַכְּתוּבָה בּוֹ – **I [WOULD HAVE] KNOWN ONLY** that you can put the murderer to death **THROUGH THE** method of **EXECUTION THAT IS PRESCRIBED IN HIS CASE;** namely, execution by sword.[3] מִנַּיִן שֶׁאִם אִי אַתָּה יָכוֹל לַהֲמִיתוֹ בְּמִיתָה הַכְּתוּבָה בּוֹ – **FROM WHERE IS IT DERIVED THAT IF YOU CANNOT PUT HIM TO DEATH WITH THE** method of **EXECUTION PRESCRIBED FOR HIM,** שֶׁאַתָּה רַשַּׁאי לַהֲמִיתוֹ – **THAT YOU ARE PERMITTED TO PUT HIM TO DEATH** בְּכָל מִיתָה שֶׁאַתָּה יָכוֹל לַהֲמִיתוֹ – **WITH ANY** method of **EXECUTION BY WHICH YOU ARE ABLE TO PUT HIM TO DEATH?**[4] תַּלְמוּד לוֹמַר "מוֹת־יוּמַת" – **FOR THE VERSE STATES: *HE SHALL DIE, HE SHALL DIE.*** The repetitive phraseology implies: מִכָּל מָקוֹם – He may be put to death **IN ANY MANNER** that is possible.

The Gemara expounds the repetitive language employed in connection with the obligation to destroy a city whose inhabitants are idolaters:[5]

"הַכֵּה תַכֶּה" – The verse states: ***SMITE, YOU SHALL SMITE.*** Now, if the verse had not used repetitive language here, אֵין לִי אֶלָּא בְּהַכָּאָה הַכְּתוּבָה בָּהֶן – **I [WOULD HAVE] KNOWN ONLY** that you can **SMITE** them **WITH THE** type of **BLOW THAT IS PRESCRIBED IN THEIR CASE;** i.e. you must execute the city's inhabitants by the sword. מִנַּיִן שֶׁאִם אִי אַתָּה יָכוֹל לַהֲמִיתָן בְּהַכָּאָה הַכְּתוּבָה בָּהֶן – **FROM WHERE IS IT DERIVED THAT IF YOU CANNOT EXECUTE THEM WITH THE** type of **BLOW THAT IS PRESCRIBED FOR THEM,** אַתָּה רַשַּׁאי לְהַכּוֹתָן בְּכָל הַכָּאָה שֶׁאַתָּה יָכוֹל – **THAT YOU ARE PERMITTED TO SMITE THEM WITH ANY** type of **BLOW THAT YOU ARE ABLE** to administer? תַּלְמוּד לוֹמַר "הַכֵּה תַכֶּה" – **THE VERSE** therefore **TEACHES: *SMITE, YOU SHALL SMITE,*** which implies: מִכָּל מָקוֹם – You should execute the inhabitants **IN ANY MANNER** that is available to you.

The Gemara expounds repetitive language employed in connection with a creditor's obligation to return a collateral item to his debtor:[6]

"הָשֵׁב תָּשִׁיב" – The verse states: ***RETURN, YOU SHALL RETURN** the collateral item to him.* אֵין לִי אֶלָּא שֶׁמִּשְׁכְּנוֹ בִּרְשׁוּת בֵּית דִּין – Now, if the verse had not used repetitive language here, **I [WOULD HAVE] KNOWN ONLY THAT** if **[THE CREDITOR] PROCURED THE COLLATERAL** item **WITH THE PERMISSION OF THE COURT,** he is obligated to return it when the debtor needs it.[7] שֶׁמִּשְׁכְּנוֹ שֶׁלֹּא בִּרְשׁוּת בֵּית דִּין מִנַּיִן – But **FROM WHERE IS IT DERIVED THAT** if **HE PROCURED THE COLLATERAL ITEM WITHOUT THE PERMISSION OF THE COURT,**[8] he must also return it? תַּלְמוּד לוֹמַר – **FOR THE VERSE STATES:** "הָשֵׁב תָּשִׁיב" – ***RETURN, YOU SHALL RETURN** the collateral item,* implying: מִכָּל מָקוֹם – You must return the item **IN ALL CASES,** even if it was procured without permission of the court.

A similar exposition:

"חָבֹל תַּחְבֹּל" – In reference to taking a collateral item, another verse states: *If* ***PROCURE, YOU PROCURE*** *the garment of your friend . . . you shall return it to him.*[9] אֵין לִי אֶלָּא שֶׁמִּשְׁכְּנוֹ בִּרְשׁוּת – Now, if the verse had not used repetitive language, **I [WOULD HAVE] KNOWN ONLY THAT** if **[THE CREDITOR] PROCURED THE COLLATERAL ITEM WITH** the **PERMISSION** of the courts, he is obligated to return it when the debtor needs it.[10] מִשְׁכְּנוֹ שֶׁלֹּא בִּרְשׁוּת מִנַּיִן – But if **HE PROCURED THE COLLATERAL ITEM WITHOUT PERMISSION** of the courts, **FROM WHERE IS IT DERIVED** that he must also return it? תַּלְמוּד לוֹמַר – **FOR THE VERSE STATES:** "חָבֹל תַּחְבֹּל" –

NOTES

1. The verses concerning loading and unloading indicate that the owner is there with his animal (עָזֹב תַּעֲזֹב עִמּוֹ, *help, you shall help* ***with him***; הָקֵם תָּקִים עִמּוֹ, *lift up, you shall lift up* ***with him***). Accordingly, the owner is not powerless to carry out the necessary tasks, for if it is too difficult for him to load or unload by himself, he could hire workers to help him. A bystander's obligation to help load or unload could thus not be derived from his obligation to return a lost object, for in the latter case, the owner lacks any means to retrieve the object through his own efforts.

2. The text of the verse is as follows (*Numbers* 35:21): אוֹ בְאֵיבָה הִכָּהוּ בְיָדוֹ וַיָּמֹת מוֹת־יוּמַת הַמַּכֶּה רֹצֵחַ הוּא, *Or if he hit him with his hand out of hatred and he died, he who struck [the man] shall die, he shall die; he is a murderer.*

3. The Torah mandates four different methods of execution for various capital offenses. A murderer is punished with death by sword, as described in *Sanhedrin* 52b.

4. The Gemara speaks of an instance, for example, in which the convicted murderer attempted to escape by boat. Under these circumstances, it might be impossible to kill him by sword, but it still could be possible to shoot an arrow at him, or drown him (*Rashi*).

5. If an entire town, or the majority of it, was led astray to worship false gods, they are liable to execution by the sword. In this connection, the verse states (*Deuteronomy* 13:16): הַכֵּה תַכֶּה אֶת־יֹשְׁבֵי הָעִיר הַהִוא לְפִי־חָרֶב, *Smite, you shall smite the inhabitants of that city by sword.*

6. If a debtor does not repay his loan when it comes due, the creditor may approach the courts and request that they seize some of the debtor's possessions for him to hold as collateral. After receiving the collateral, the creditor may retain it until the borrowed money is repaid. If, however, the debtor is a poor person, the creditor must periodically return the collateral item to the debtor when the debtor is in need of it. Thus, for example, if the debtor's blankets were seized as collateral, the creditor must return them to the debtor at night, and he may re-collect them in the morning. This is specifically mandated by Scripture, as the verse (*Deuteronomy* 24:13) states: הָשֵׁב תָּשִׁיב לוֹ אֶת־הָעֲבוֹט כְּבוֹא הַשֶּׁמֶשׁ וְשָׁכַב בְּשַׂלְמָתוֹ וּבֵרֲכֶךָּ וּלְךָ תִּהְיֶה צְדָקָה לִפְנֵי ה׳ אֱלֹהֶיךָ, *Return, you shall return the collateral item to him as the sun sets, and he shall sleep in his garment; he shall bless you, and [this] shall be a merit for you before* H*ASHEM* *your God.*

7. The Gemara later (113a) shows that the Scriptural section, in which the words הָשֵׁב תָּשִׁיב appear, speaks specifically of a case in which the creditor approached the court about the money owed to him, and a messenger of the court was sent to take a collateral item from the debtor. Accordingly, the plain meaning of the verse is only that the creditor must periodically return the collateral item *if* the item was originally procured for him through the offices of the court.

8. In this case, the creditor did not approach the courts with his claim. Rather, he illegally entered the debtor's house and seized property as collateral (see *Ritva*).

9. The full verse states (*Exodus* 22:25): אִם־חָבֹל תַּחְבֹּל שַׂלְמַת רֵעֶךָ עַד־בֹּא הַשֶּׁמֶשׁ תְּשִׁיבֶנּוּ לוֹ, *If procure, you procure the garment of your friend [as collateral], you shall return it to him until the sun sets.* The Gemara below will explain why two verses are necessary to teach this law (חָבֹל תַּחְבֹּל and הָשֵׁב תָּשִׁיב), and why one verse mandates that the collateral item be returned *as the sun sets,* and the other that it be returned *until the sun sets.*

10. The Gemara understands the plain meaning of the verse to be that the collateral was seized for the creditor by an agent of the court acting on the court's behalf ("with the permission of the court"). The reason for this is that the verse uses the verb חבל, *procure*, which implies that the item was actually seized from inside the debtor's house (see *Rashi* to 113a). Since the average person does not have the audacity to enter another person's home and take his property, it can be assumed that it was an agent of the courts – not the creditor himself – who seized the garment in the verse's case (see *Rashi*).

**אבל** הני תרתי דאיתנהו למרייהו בהדייהו. ואע"ג דמרבינן לעיל אין בעלים עמו היינו שהוא זקן או חולה ונהי דאין יכול לעזור יכול לשכור פועלין ואימא לא קא משמע לן: **אין** לי אלא משכנו. פרשתי בהמקבל (לקמן דף קיג.): **דברה** תורה כלשון בני אדם. וא"ת וכי לית להו כל הני דרשות דלעיל ואליבא דר"ש מסיינן נמי לעיל דלא מסיימי קראי וברי"ה (דף ח.) דריש נמי ר"ש עשר תעשר אחד מעשר דגן ואחד מעשר בהמה וי"ל דדוקא הכא בהני תרי קראי אמרינן דברה תורה כלשון בני אדם משום דמוכחי קראי דכתיב די מחסורו ובאידך כתיב אשר ברכך וברים השואל (לקמן דף לד: ושם ד"ה אלא) דאמר אם גנב אין לי אלא גניבה אבידה מנין ת"ל יגנב ופריך למ"ד דברה תורה כלשון בני אדם מאי איכא למימר התם נמי איכא הוכחה דגניבה משמע דוקא גניבה ולא אבידה: **אם** יש שם ב"ד יתנה בפניהם. שישלם לו כל מה שישתכר במלאכה שהוא עושה ואם אין ב"ד לא ישיב כיון שאם ישיב לא יהא לו אלא כפועל בטל אבל אם אינו עושה מלאכה ישיב בחנם וא"ת לעיל דנקט או שהיתה שלו מרובה היכי דמי אי ליכא ב"ד אפילו מועטת נמי מן האבידה לא ישיב ואי בפני ב"ד כי נמי אין מרובה אלא שוה לאבידה למה יתנו ב"ד ליתן לו כל שכרו א"כ מה ירויחו הבעלים וי"ל דנ"מ לכושרא דחיותא או לטרחא יתירא וכה"ג משני בסוף השוכר את הפועלים (לקמן דף עג:) וא"ת דהכא משלם לכל הפחות השכירות כפועל בטל וכן משני לקמן בסוף השוכר את הפועלים (שם) גבי רועה שהיה יכול לקדם ברועים ובמקלות ש"ש בשכר וש"ח בחנם חייב וש"ש שקדם בשכר חוזר ונוטל מבעל הבית ומסתמא ש"ח נמי שקדם בשכר חוזר ונוטל מבעה"ב ואילו בפרק הגוזל בתרא (ב"ק דף קטו:) תנן שטף נהר את חמורו וחמור חבירו הניח את שלו והציל את של חבירו אין לו אלא שכרו ואין משלם לו דמי חמורו שטבע וי"ל דהתם מיירי כשהיה יכול להציל

דאיתיה למרה. דכתיב עמו אימא יחזור אחר בני אדם וישכור: שאם אי אתה יכול להמיתו במיתה הכתובה בו. והיינו סייף כגון שהיה בספינה ובורח ואתה יכול לזרוק בו חץ או לטובעו: הכה תכה. בעיר הנדחת: **אין לי אלא שמשכנו ברשות ב"ד.** לצעק עליו בדין ושלחו שלוחם לתפוס מטלטליו דקרא דהשבת העבוט עליה כתיב דכתיב לעיל מיניה בחוץ תעמוד והאיש ואמרינן לקמן בפ' המקבל (דף קיג.) בשליח ב"ד הכתוב מדבר: **שלא ברשות ב"ד מנין.** דלריך השבה: שהם חבלה ע"פ ב"ד היא דלא שכיח דחליף איניש ליכנס בבית וליטול מטלטלי שלא ברשות: **חד לכסות יום וחד לכסות לילה.** בפ' המקבל (לקמן קיד:) מפרש לקרא הכי: **מתנה מועטת מנין.** אם אי אפשר לך ליתן מתנה מרובה: **אין לי אלא שנתברך הבית בגללו.** דהכי כתיב קרא אשר ברכך ה' אלהיך תתן לו: דרבי אלעזר בן עזריה בקדושין (דף יז:): **שאין לו.** ממה שיתפרנס: **ואינו רוצה להתפרנס.** משלך במתנה ואמר רחמנא העבט דרך הלואה: **יש לו ואינו רוצה להתפרנס.** משלו אלא משלך מנין שאתה חייב להעביטו וליפרע ממנו אחר מיתה ת"ל תעביטנו והכי מפרש בכתובות פרק מציאת האשה (דף סז:): **מאי כפועל בטל.** והלא אינו בטל שהרי טורח בהשבתה ומתניתין תני נותנין לו כשיעור שירצה פועל ליטול להתרפות ממלאכה ולישב בטל: **כפועל בטל של אותה מלאכה דבטל מינה.** כמה אדם רוצה ליטול ולפחות משכרו ליבטל ממלאכה זו כבדה שהוא עוסק בה ולעסוק במלאכה קלה כזו הכל לפי כובד המלאכה וריבוי שכר יש מלאכ' שטורחה קל ושכרה רב או חילוף: **פלג.** בסחורה ולא היו מעות אלא דבר הצריך שומא:

אבל הני תרתי דאיתא למרה בהדה אימא לא צריכא [א] (א) מות יומת המכה אין לי אלא במיתה הכתובה בו מנין שאם אי אתה יכול להמיתו במיתה הכתובה בו שאתה רשאי להמיתו בכל מיתה שאתה יכול להמיתו ת"ל [א]מות יומת מ"מ (ב) הכה תכה אין לי אלא בהכאה הכתובה בהן מנין שאם אי אתה יכול להמיתן בהכאה הכתובה בהן שאתה רשאי להכותן בכל הכאה שאתה יכול ת"ל הכה תכה מ"מ (ג) השב תשיב אין לי אלא שמשכנו ברשות ב"ד משכנו שלא ברשות ב"ד מנין ת"ל [ב]השב תשיב מ"מ (ד) חבל תחבול אין לי אלא שמשכנו ברשות משכנו שלא ברשות מנין ת"ל [ג]חבל תחבול מ"מ והני תרי קראי למה לי חד לכסות יום וחד לכסות לילה (ה) פתח תפתח אין לי אלא לעניי עירך לעניי עיר אחרת מנין ת"ל [ד]פתח תפתח מכל מקום (ו) נתן תתן אין לי אלא מתנה מרובה מתנה מועטת מנין [ה]ת"ל נתן תתן מ"מ (ז) הענק תעניק (ג) אין לי אלא שנתברך הבית בגללו לא נתברך הבית בגללו מנין [ו]ת"ל הענק תעניק מ"מ ולר' אלעזר בן עזריה דאמר נתברך הבית בגללו מעניקין לו לא נתברך הבית בגללו אין מעניקין תעניק למה לי (ג) דברה תורה כלשון בני אדם (ה) העבט תעביטנו (ד) אין לי אלא שאין לו ואינו רוצה להתפרנס אמר רחמנא תן לו דרך הלואה יש לו ואינו רוצה להתפרנס מנין ת"ל תעביטנו מ"מ ולר"ש (ט) דאמר [ז]יש לו ואינו רוצה להתפרנס אין נזקקין לו תעביטנו למה לי דברה תורה כלשון בני אדם: **היה בטל מן הסלע לא יאמר לו תן לי סלע אלא נותן לו שכרו כפועל (בטל):** (י) (תנן) [ו] נותן לו שכרו כפועל בטל מאי כפועל בטל (כ) אמר אביי [ח]כפועל בטל של אותה מלאכה דבטל מינה: **אם יש שם ב"ד מתנה בפניהם:** איסור ורב ספרא עביד עיסקא בהדי הדדי אזל רב ספרא פלג ליה בלא דעתיה דאיסור באפי בי תרי ° אתא לקמי' (ט) דרבה בר רב הונא א"ל [ט]זיל אייתי תלתא דפלגת קמייהו אי נמי תרי

ע"י הדחק דאי לאו הכי מצי אמר ליה מהפקירא קזכינא כדאיתא התם ועי"ל כיון שבעל החמור שם יכול לומר הייתי שוכר פועלים להצילו וא"ת הכא אמאי נוטל שכר וכן לקמן ש"ח שאין צריך לקדם בשכר אם קידם אמאי נוטלו מבעה"ב האמרי' פר' הכונס (שם דף נח. ושם ד"ה אי) דמבריח ארי מנכסי חבירו פטור ולישנא בתרא דהכונס דמבריח ארי פטור משום דלית ליה פסידא אתי שפיר דהכא אית ליה פסידא אבל ללישנא קמא דקאמר דמבריח ארי מדעתו משמע אפילו אית ליה פסידא פטור כיון דמדעתו הוא קשה ואור"י דמבריח ארי פטור היינו דוקא שמצילו מפחד הארי שירא שיבא וקידם ברועים והבריחו דלא ברי הזיקא דבלא הצלתו יכול להיות שלא היה בא אבל מציל מפי הארי ושטף נהר חמורו ומחזיר אבידה דברי הזיקא ובא זה והציל נוטל שכרו וא"ת דפורע חובו דשרי למודר הנאה בפרק אין בין המודר (נדרים דף לג.) ופרק בתרא דכתובות (דף קח. ושם) מחשבין ליה מבריח ארי אע"ג דברי הזיקא ואית ליה פסידא וי"ל דהתם נמי אין מצילו מן ההפסד לגמרי שנותן לו מה שהיה מוכרח לתת ולכן חשיב ליה כמבריח ארי א"נ כדמפרש טעמא בירושלמי דנדרים הוינא מפייס ליה ומחיל לי ואפי' במשכון מפייס הוינא ליה ויהיב לי משכוני ואפילו בב"ח דוחק מסיק בירושלמי והטעם נראה משום שיכול לומר הייתי מולא אוהבים הרבה שיפרעו עבורי דהיינו מעין אותם הטעמים והא דקרי ליה בפ' ח"ה (ב"ב דף נג.) מבריח ארי נתן צרור ונטל צרור דסבר מינה מיא ואפיק מינה מיא אע"פ שמצילו מן ההפסד שהיה נהר שוטפה התם לא נקט לשון מבריח לענין שיפטר משכר הברחה אלא כלומר אין זו חזקה כיון שאין מתקן השדה אלא מגין עליה בעלמא שלא תבא לידי קלקול ונראה שגם ר"ת סובר דלא חשיב מבריח ארי במקום שמצילו מן ההפסד שהיה מעמיד ההיא דפורע חובו דוקא במזונות אשתו כדמפרש בפ' בתרא דכתובות (דף קח. ושם) משום דאפשר שתהא עושה ואוכלת או תתפרנס מן הצדקה או מקרוביה שיתנו לה בחנם אבל שאר פריעת חוב אור"ת דאין זה מבריח ארי אלא מהנה גמור וירושלמי פליג אגמרא שלנו ולפ"ז אם הסר גזל ביתו של ישראל ובא חבירו ישראל ופייס אותו בדמים מועטים אם ירצה בעה"ב ליקח ביתו ישלם דמים לחבירו וכן פסק רבינו גרשום אבל רש"י פסק שיחזיר לו ביתו חנם בפ' הנזקין (גיטין דף נח:) ונראה דלא מבעיא אם קנאה בדמים שמציל הבעלים מן ההפסד שישלמו הבעלים אלא אפי' קנאן בשויו ולא דמי למבריח ארי דאם היה משתקע בידו לא היה הבית חוזר לו לעולם ואפי' בשויו ודמי למקדים ברועים ובמקלות בשכר דאמרי' שנותן שכרו עד כדי דמיהם ונ"מ לכושרא דחיותא או לטרחא יתירא ועוד נר' אפי' ידוע בודאי שאפילו לא מיהר לקנותו היה חוזר לבעלים בדמים הללו כל שעה שירצו בין קנאן בדמים מרובים בין קנאן בדמים מועטים לא דמי למבריח ארי כיון שילא הבית מחזקת ישראל ובא לידי נכרי וזה מוציאו מחזקת נכרי ומחזירו ליד ישראל נוטל מה שההנהו: **כפועל** בטל. פירשנו באיזהו נשך (לקמן דף סח. ושם ד"ה ונותן):

כשמגיע הזמן ואינו פורע [שמות כב, כה]. **העבט תעניק.** לשון עדי בגובה ובמראית העין דבר שיהא ניכר שהטיבות לו ויש מפרשים לשון הטענה על צוארו [דברים טו, יד]. **שאין לו.** משלו. **ואינו רוצה להתפרנס.** משל לדקה [כתובות סז:]. אם לא רלה במתנה תן לו בהלואה [דברים טו, ח]. **יש לו ואינו רוצה להתפרנס.** משלו אלא משל לדקה ומסגף עלמו ברעב [כתובות שם]. **נותן לו שכרו כפועל בטל.** ובמתניתין לא גרסינן בטל. משמע כמה אדם רולה ליטול ולישב בטל. **אמר אביי כפועל בטל של אותה מלאכה.** אם היה נגר או נפח כמה אדם רולה ליטול ליבטל ממלאכה כבידה כזו ולעשות מלאכה קלה [לקמן סח:]. דבטל הימנה דאם היה נוקב מרגליות שעבודתה נוחה לעשות ושכרו מרובה אם אומר לו טול כך וכך ותבטל היום ממלאכה אינו פוחת משכרו אלא דבר מועט שהרי נוחה ואין בה טורח ואי מלאכה קשה היא כמו נגר אומר לו אתה נוטל עכשיו שלשה זוזים טול זוז והבטל היום מאותה מלאכה ועשה מלאכה קלה זו נוח לו להיבטל וליטול זוז והכא נמי כי ההוא אגרא יהיב ליה שהרי מבטלו ממלאכתו וכוליה אגרא לא יהיב ליה שהרי אינו עסוק במלאכה קשה אלא [בכורות כט:].

עין משפט נר מצוה

קסד א מיי' פי"ד מהל' סנהדרין הל' ח:

קסה ב ג מיי' פ"ג מהל' מלוה ולוה הל' ה סמג לאוין קפז טוש"ע ח"מ סי' לז סעיף טו:

קסו ד ה מיי' פ"ז מהל' מתנות עניים הל' יג סמג עשין קסב טוש"ע י"ד סי' רמז סעיף א וסי' רמח סעיף א וסי' רנא סעיף ג:

קסז ו מיי' פ"ג מהל' עבדים הלכה יד סמג עשין פד:

קסח ז מיי' פ"ז מהל' מתנות עניים הל' ט סמג עשין קסב טוש"ע י"ד סי' רנג סעיף י:

קסט ח מיי' פי"ב מהל' גזילה ואבידה הלכה ד סמג עשין עד טוש"ע ח"מ סי' רסה:

קע ט מיי' פ"ה מהל' שלוחים ושותפין הל' ט סמג עשין פב טוש"ע ח"מ סי' קעו סעיף יח:

רבינו חננאל

וכן דין השב תשיב את העבוט וכן דין חבל תחבול בין כסות יום בין כסות לילה וכן פתח תפתח את ידך וגומר לענייך ואפי' לעניי עיר אחרת וכן דין נתן תתן לו א) במתנה בין מרובה בין מועטת. וכן דין הענק תעניק לו ואפי' לא נתברך הבית בגללו וכן העבט תעביטנו אפי' יש לו ואינו רוצה להתפרנס: **היה בטל מסלע לא יאמר לו תן לי סלע אלא נותן לו שכרו כפועל תנא כפועל בטל.** ואקשי' והא לאו בטל הוא דהא מתעסק להחזיר האבידה. ופירקה אביי כפועל בטל של אותה מלאכה פי' כגון שהיה חייט והניח מלאכתו והלך להשיב את האבידה ונשתהה בהשבתה כשיעור תפירת בגד ששכרו סלע לא יאמר לו כבר בטלתי ממלאכתי שיעור סלע תנה לי אלא משערין שכרו כעת שאין לו מה יתפור אלא יושב ובטל אם יבא אדם ויאמר לו הנך יושב ובטל תקח בתפירת בגד חצי סלע או תשאר בטל היום ובעת שהמלאכה מצויה כגון קרוב לרגל וכיוצא בו שכר תפירת הבגד סלע ומה שמתברר שנוטל בשעה שאין לו תפירה לתפור הוא שנוטל מבעל האבידה וכן אם יאמר לו אדם אתה חייט ואין תפירה מצויה אצלך תבוא ללבון עמי לבנים ותיקח שכירותך כך וכך וזה מפני שלא התנה בב"ד על שכרו. אבל התנה בב"ד נוטל לפי תנאו דתנן אם יש שם ב"ד מתנה בפני ב"ד. איסור ורב ספרא הוו שותפי בעיסקא אזל רב ספרא פלג בלא דעתיה דאיסור קמי תרי וחייביה רבא לאיתויי תלתא אי נמי תרי מיגו תלתא אי נמי תרי סהדי דפלג קמיה

חשק שלמה על ר"ח

א) נ"ל תתן לו בין מתנה מרובה בין וכו'.

מסורת הש"ס

א) [סנהדרין מה:, עב:], ב) קדושין יז:, ג) [שם וש"נ], ד) כתובות סז:, ה) [ע"ש], ו) [נ"ל תנא], ז) לקמן סח., בכורות כט:, ח) **הא לא בטיל מיניה**, מהרש"ל, ט) [גירס' הרא"ש איתא ר' אבא אבל בתוס' בבא בתרא מ. ד"ה קיום מוכח דהגירסא לפניהם ר"ן], י) [וע"ע תוס' כתובות סז: ד"ה וחכמים, ועמ"ש תוס' סוטה כד. ד"ה ור' יונתן, ותוס' מנחות ה: ד"ה מאי באריכות].

גליון הש"ס

גמ' **אתא לקמיה דרבה בר רב הונא.** עיין תוס' ב"ב מ ע"א ד"ה קיום דנראה דהיה להם הגירסא כאן אתא לקמיה דר"נ: **תוס' ד"ה דברה תורה וכו' משום דמוכחי קראי.** עי' מזרחי ריש פ' לך לך:

תורה אור השלם

א) אוֹ בְאֵיבָה הִכָּהוּ בְיָדוֹ וַיָּמֹת מוֹת יוּמַת הַמַּכֶּה רֹצֵחַ הוּא גֹּאֵל הַדָּם יָמִית אֶת הָרֹצֵחַ בְּפִגְעוֹ בוֹ: [במדבר לה, כא]

ב) הַכֵּה תַכֶּה אֶת יֹשְׁבֵי הָעִיר הַהִוא לְפִי חָרֶב הַחֲרֵם אֹתָהּ וְאֶת כָּל אֲשֶׁר בָּהּ וְאֶת בְּהֶמְתָּהּ לְפִי חָרֶב: [דברים יג, טז]

ג) הָשֵׁב תָּשִׁיב לוֹ אֶת הָעֲבוֹט כְּבוֹא הַשֶּׁמֶשׁ וְשָׁכַב בְּשַׂלְמָתוֹ וּבֵרְכֶךָּ וּלְךָ תִּהְיֶה צְדָקָה לִפְנֵי יְיָ אֱלֹהֶיךָ: [דברים כד, יג]

ד) אִם חָבֹל תַּחְבֹּל שַׂלְמַת רֵעֶךָ עַד בֹּא הַשֶּׁמֶשׁ תְּשִׁיבֶנּוּ לוֹ: [שמות כב, כה]

ה) כִּי פָתֹחַ תִּפְתַּח אֶת יָדְךָ לוֹ וְהַעֲבֵט תַּעֲבִיטֶנּוּ דֵּי מַחְסֹרוֹ אֲשֶׁר יֶחְסַר לוֹ: [דברים טו, ח]

ו) נָתוֹן תִּתֵּן לוֹ וְלֹא יֵרַע לְבָבְךָ בְּתִתְּךָ לוֹ כִּי בִּגְלַל הַדָּבָר הַזֶּה יְבָרֶכְךָ יְיָ אֱלֹהֶיךָ בְּכָל מַעֲשֶׂךָ וּבְכֹל מִשְׁלַח יָדֶךָ: [דברים טו, י]

ז) הַעֲנֵיק תַּעֲנִיק לוֹ מִצֹּאנְךָ וּמִגָּרְנְךָ וּמִיִּקְבֶךָ אֲשֶׁר בֵּרַכְךָ יְיָ אֱלֹהֶיךָ תִּתֶּן לוֹ: [דברים טו, יד]

ליקוטי רש"י

**אין לי.** אי לא כתיב אלא יומת. **אלא מיתה הכתובה בו.** סייף [סנהדרין מה:]. **שאם אי אתה יכול וכו' הכתובה בו.** כגון שהיה מכשף או שהיה לו נהר מפסיק ואתה יכול לירות בו חץ או אבן [שם עב:]. **מות יומת.** ריבויא הוא [שם מה:]. **הכה תכה.** אם אינך יכול להמיתם במיתה הכתובה בהם המיתם באחרת [דברים יג, טז]. **חבל תחבול.** כל לשון חבלה אינו משכון בשעת הלואה אלא שממשכנין את הלוה

א באסרטיא ופרה רצה בין הכרמים הרי זו אבידה ב טלית בצד גדר קרדום בצד גדר ופרה רועה בין [א] הכרמים אין זו אבידה ג' ימים זה אחר זה הרי זו אבידה ג ראה מים ששוטפין ובאין הרי זה גודר בפניהם אמר רבא א) לכל אבידת אחיך ד לרבות אבידת קרקע א"ל רב חנניה לרבא תניא דמסייע לך ראה מים ששוטפין ובאין הרי זה גודר בפניהם א"ל אי משום הא לא תסייעי הכא במאי עסקינן בדאיכא עומרין אי דאיכא עומרין מאי למימרא לא צריכא דאית בה עומרין דצריכי לארעא מהו דתימא כיון דצריכי לארעא כי גופה דארעא דמיין קמ"ל: מצא חמור ופרה [וכו']: הא גופה קשיא אמרת מצא חמור ופרה רועין בדרך אין זו אבידה רועין בדרך הוא דלא הוו אבידה הא רצה בדרך ורועה בין הכרמים הויא אבידה אימא סיפא חמור וכליו הפוכים ופרה רצה בין הכרמים הרי זו אבידה רצה בין הכרמים הוא דהויא אבידה הא רצה בדרך ורועה בין הכרמים אין זו אבידה א) אמר אביי ב) יגיד עליו ריעו תנא רועה בדרך דלא הויא אבידה והוא הדין לרועה בין הכרמים תנא רצה בין הכרמים דהויא אבידה והוא הדין לרצה בדרך א"ל רבא אי יגיד עליו ריעו ליתני קילתא וכ"ש חמירתא ליתני רצה בדרך דהויא אבידה וכ"ש רצה בין הכרמים ולתני רועה בין הכרמים דלא הויא אבידה וכ"ש רועה בדרך אלא אמר רבא רצה ארצה לא קשיא ה הא דאפה לגבי דברא הא דאפה לגבי מתא רועה ארועה נמי לא קשיא כאן באבידת גופה כאן באבידת קרקע ו כי קתני רועה בדרך לא הויא אבידה הא רועה בין הכרמים הויא אבידה באבידת קרקע וכי קתני רצה בין הכרמים הויא אבידה הא רועה בין הכרמים לא הויא אבידה באבידת גופה דרצה בין הכרמים ג) מסקבא ורועה בין הכרמים לא מסקבא נהי דלא מסקבא תיפוק ליה משום אבידת קרקע ז בדכותי ותיפוק ליה משום אבידת גופה דדלמא קטלו לה ח באתרא דמתרו והדר קטלי ודלמא אתרו בה אי אתרו בה ג) ולא אזדהרו בה ודאי אבידה מדעת היא: החזירה וברחה החזירה וברחה [וכו']: א"ל ההוא מדרבנן לרבא אימא השב חדא זמנא תשיבם תרי זמני א"ל ד) השב אפי' ק' פעמים משמע ה) תשיבם ט אין לי אלא לביתו לגינתו ולחורבתו מנין ת"ל תשיבם מ"מ ה"ד אי דמינטרא פשיטא אי דלא מינטרא אמאי לעולם י דמינטרא והא קמ"ל דלא בעינן דעת בעלים וכדר' אלעזר ו) דאמר כ הכל צריכין דעת בעלים ל חוץ מהשבת אבידה שהתורה ריבתה השבות הרבה ג) שלח תשלח ז) אימא שלח חדא זימנא תשלח תרי זמני א"ל שלח מ אפי' מאה פעמים משמע תשלח אין לי אלא לדבר הרשות נ לדבר מצוה מנין ת"ל תשלח מ"מ א"ל ההוא מדרבנן לרבא ואימא ח) הוכח חדא זימנא תוכיח תרי זמני א"ל ס הוכח אפי' ק' פעמים משמע תוכיח אין לי אלא הרב לתלמיד תלמיד לרב מנין ת"ל הוכח תוכיח ע מ"מ ה) עזוב תעזוב עמו אין לי אלא בעליו עמו שאין בעליו עמו מנין ת"ל עזב תעזוב פ מ"מ ו) הקם תקים עמו אין לי אלא בעליו עמו שאין בעליו עמו מנין ת"ל הקם תקים צ מ"מ ולמה ליה למכתב פריקה ולמה ליה למיכתב טעינה צריכי דאי כתב רחמנא פריקה הוה אמינא משום דאיכא צער בעלי חיים ואיכא חסרון כיס אבל טעינה דלאו צער בעלי חיים איכא ולא חסרון כיס איכא אימא לא ואי אשמעינן טעינה משום דבשכר אבל פריקה דבחנם אימא לא צריכא ולר"ש ק) דאמר אף טעינה בחנם מאי איכא למימר לר"ש לא מסיימי קראי למה לי למכתב הני תרתי ולמה לי למכתב אבידה צריכי דאי כתב רחמנא הני תרתי משום דצערא דמרה איתא צערא דידה איתא אבל אבידה דצערא דמרה איתא וצערא דידה ליתא אימא לא ואי אשמעינן אבידה משום דליתא למרה בהדה אבל

אסרטיא. דרך כבושה לרבים: ששוטפין ובאין. לשדה חבירו: אמר רבא לכל אבידת כו'. מילתא באפיה נפשיה היא דאמרה רבא בבי מדרשא: מאי למימרא. ותיפוק ליה משום עומרין שישנן בכלל אבידה דדמו לפרטא דשה ושלמה ולמה לי לכל לרבוינהו: רועה בדרך. איכא תרתי למעליותא חדא דרועה ועוד דאפילו רצה לא מסתקבא רצה בין הכרמים איכא תרתי לגריעותא חדא דרצה ועוד דכרמים מסקבי לה רצה בדרך איכא חדא לגריעותא דרצה ומתקלקלת ברגלתה אי נמי תלך למרחקים רועה בין הכרמים חדא לגריעותא דזימנין דמסתקבא: והא באבידת גופה כו'. מפרש ואזיל לה: באבידת קרקע. וחייב להוציאה משום הפסד כרמים: לגינתו ולחורבתו מנין. דהויא השבה ופטור: דעת בעלים. לומר לו שמור פרתך שהחזרתיה לגינתך שמצאתיה אובדת: הכל צריך דעת בעלים. גנב גזלן וד' שומרים שהשיבו צריכין להודיעו ואם לא הודיעו ומתה או נגנבה חייבים באחריותן דכיון דידע שאבדה ולא ידע שהושבה לא נזהר בה ולא מאכילה: שלח. לגבי שלוח הקן: תרתי זמני. ואנן תנן ט) שלחה וחזרה שלחה וחזרה אפי' ארבע וה' פעמים חייב: לדבר הרשות. שאין צריך לצפור אלא לאוכלה: לדבר מצוה מנין. היה צריך לטהר בו את המצורע מנין שאסור באם על הבנים ת"ל תשלח: עזב תעזוב. פריקה: הקם תקים. טעינה: חסרון כיס. שהבהמה מתקלקלת: משום דבשכר. שנותנין לו שכר דאיכא למ"ד לקמן (דף לב.) טעינה בשכר פריקה בחנם: לא מסיימי קראי. הי משמע טעינה והי משמע פריקה ואי כתב חדא הוה אמינא לפריקה אתא אבל טעינה לא כתב רחמנא אידך לטעינה: למה לי למכתב אבידה. השבת אבידה לכתוב או הא או הא וליגמר מניה דהא כולהו אזהרות ממון ישראל הוא: צערא דמרה. הוא העומד שם ואין יכול לטעון לבדו וכן לפרוק: דליתא למרה בהדה. שיטרח בהשבתה: דליתיה

קורדום בצד גדר. פירשתי לעיל (כה: סד"ה ואם נטל): למה לי למכתב רחמנא פריקה כו'. אין לפרש למה לי דכתב כוליה קרא דפריקה או דטעינה דא"כ היכי קאמר אי אשמועינן טעינה דבשכר הא משמע לקמן (דף לב.) דטעינה לא הוי בשכר אלא משום דנכתב פריקה ועוד דלא שייכא הך צריכותא אלא לקמן אלא י"ל למה לי דכתב רחמנא יתורא דמרבינן אין בעליו עמו בפריקה ולמה לי דכתב בטעינה:

לרבי שמעון לא מסיימי קראי. תימה דלקמן (דף לב.) משמע דקרא דנופלים בדרך לא מסיים לר"ש דהוי בטעינה דטעונייהו עלייהו משמע ואי לא כתב אלא חד הוה מוקמי ליה בפריקה אבל קרא דרובץ תחת משאו לא משמע לכ"ע אלא בפריקה וכשנכתבו שניהם ע"כ גם לר"ש קרא דנופלים בדרך הוי בטעינה וא"כ לר"ש לא יכתוב אלא חד יתורא לאין בעליו עמו בקרא דנופלים בדרך וי"ל דרובץ תחת משאו נמי לא מסיים לר"ש דאפשר למשמע בטעינה דע"י שאין הרבה בני אדם לטעון מכביד המשוי על הבהמה ורובצת ולקמן לא אצטריך למימר דלא מסיימי אלא אקרא דנופלים בדרך והא דפריך לקמן (דף לב:) והא וחדלת בפריקה הוא דכתיב לא הוי אלא איבעיא דרבנן דלר"ש מצי למהוי בטעינה:

אבל

מסורת הש"ס

[יבמות לא:, וש"נ], [פירוש עושה בה ...ורה, ערוך ערך סקב], ...ג"ל ולא איהדרו בה, ...הר"ס, ד) חולין פז., ... בבא קמא נז., ו) [בבא ...מא שם], ז) חולין קמא., ... [לקמן לב.], ט) [בחולין קמא.].

ליקוטי רש"י

אסרטיא. מסילה ...הולכין בה מעיר לעיר [...שבת ו.]. יגיד עליו ...יעו. ונלמד משנה ...חבירתה [ע"ז עו.]. ...ברא. שדה [קדושין ...א:]. מתא. עיר [שבת ...מה: ועוד]. מסקבא. ...אשי"ר בלע"ז [יבמות ...:] (וראה לעיל כז:). ...שב. השבה מעלייתא ...שמע. לגינתו ...לחורבתו מנין. דסגי ...ה למולא בהשבתו לגינתן דבעלים [ב"ק נז.].

רבינו חננאל

...יסטרטא. אמר רבה אמר ...רא לכל אבידת אחיך ...רבות אבידת קרקע: ...תני רישא רועים בדרך ...ינה אבידה הא רצים ...דרך ורועים בכרמים ...בידה היא. וקתני סיפא ...צה בכרמים הרי זו ...בידה הא רועים אינה ...בידה קשיא רישא ...סיפא. ופריק רבא הכי ...צה ופניה כלפי השדה ...בידה היא וחייב להחזיר. ...צה ופניה כלפי המדינה ...ינה אבידה. רועה בדרך ...אפי' רועה בכרמים אינה ...בידה אבל יש בה אבידת ...קרקע שאוכלת הזמורות מפסדת הכרם והאי ...קתני רצה בין הכרמים ...ויא אבידה באבידת ...ופה כי בריצתה מכין ...אותה זמורות הכרם ...עושין בה חבורות וזהו ...פי' מסתקבא כי סיקוב זה ...לשון חבורה הוא. א) והא ...תניא רועה בכרמים אינה אבידה בכרמי כותי' ...אבידת קרקע ליכא דהא ...קרקע כותים הוא. אבידת ...גופה ליכא דהא רועים ...מעט מעט והילוכם ...בניחותא ואין סיקוב. ...השב אפי' ק' פעמים ...תשיבם אפי' לגינתו ...לחרבתו דיו. אמר ר"א ...הכל צריכין דעת [בעלים] ...חוץ מהשב אבידה [לבעלים) שהרי ריבתה התורה בה השבות הרבה. ...וכן שלח תשלח את האם ...חייב לשלחה אפי' ק' פעמים ואפי' צריך לה ...לדבר מצוה כגון טהרת ...מצורע וכיוצא בו אפי' ...הכי חייב לשלח האם וכן ...דין הוכח תוכיח אפי' ק' פעמים ואפי' תלמיד לרב. ...וכן דין עזוב תעזוב וכן ...הקם תקים בין בעליו עמו ...בין אין בעליו עמו וכן

חשק שלמה על ר"ח
א) עי' לעיל ד' כ"ז ע"ב בד' ...רבינו גבי הא דאמרי' שם משום דמסקב לי' לאמרא.

עין משפט
נר מצוה

קנד א ב מיי' פט"ו מהל' אבידה הלכה ב ה סמג עשין עד טוש"ע ח"מ סי' רס סעיף י:
קנה ג ד מיי' שם פי"א הלכה כ סמג שם טוש"ע ח"מ סי' רנט סעיף ט:
קנו ה ו ז ח מיי' פט"ו שם הל' ג ד סמג שם טוש"ע ח"מ סי' רסא סעיף ג:
קנז ט י מיי' שם פי"א הל' יד טו סמג שם טוש"ע ח"מ סי' רסז סעיף א:
קנח כ מיי' פ"ד מהל' גניבה הל' י ועיין בהשגות ובמ"מ ופ"א מהל' גזילה הל' ח סמג עשין עא טוש"ע ח"מ סי' שנה סעיף א:
קנט ל מיי' פי"א מהל' אבידה הל' טז סמג עשין עד טוש"ע ח"מ סי' רסז סעיף א:
קס מ מיי' פי"ג מהל' שחיטה הל' ה סמג עשין סה טוש"ע י"ד סי' רנב סעיף ה:
קסא נ מיי' שם הל' יט:
קסב ס ע מיי' פ"ו מהל' דיעות הל' ז סמג עשין יא:
קסג פ צ מיי' פי"ג מהל' רוצח הל' ח סמג עשין פא טוש"ע ח"מ סי' רעב סעיף ז:

הגהות הגר"א

[א] גמ' ופרה רועה בין הכרמים. נ"ב העשבים וכ"ה ברי"ף וש"פ (ועמ"ש רבינו בח"מ סי' רס"א ס"ק ה):

תורה אור השלם

א) וְכֵן תַּעֲשֶׂה לַחֲמֹרוֹ וְכֵן תַּעֲשֶׂה לְשִׂמְלָתוֹ וְכֵן תַּעֲשֶׂה לְכָל אֲבֵדַת אָחִיךָ אֲשֶׁר תֹּאבַד מִמֶּנּוּ וּמְצָאתָהּ לֹא תוּכַל לְהִתְעַלֵּם: [דברים כב, ג]

ב) יַגִּיד עָלָיו רֵעוֹ מִקְנֶה אַף עַל עוֹלֶה: [איוב לו, לג]

ג) שַׁלֵּחַ תְּשַׁלַּח אֶת הָאֵם וְאֶת הַבָּנִים תִּקַּח לָךְ לְמַעַן יִיטַב לָךְ וְהַאֲרַכְתָּ יָמִים: [דברים כב, ז]

ד) לֹא תִשְׂנָא אֶת אָחִיךָ בִּלְבָבֶךָ הוֹכֵחַ תּוֹכִיחַ אֶת עֲמִיתֶךָ וְלֹא תִשָּׂא עָלָיו חֵטְא: [ויקרא יט, יז]

ה) כִּי תִרְאֶה חֲמוֹר שֹׂנַאֲךָ רֹבֵץ תַּחַת מַשָּׂאוֹ וְחָדַלְתָּ מֵעֲזֹב לוֹ עָזֹב תַּעֲזֹב עִמּוֹ: [שמות כג, ה]

ו) לֹא תִרְאֶה אֶת חֲמוֹר אָחִיךָ אוֹ שׁוֹרוֹ נֹפְלִים בַּדֶּרֶךְ וְהִתְעַלַּמְתָּ מֵהֶם הָקֵם תָּקִים עִמּוֹ: [דברים כב, ד]

*with him.* אֵין לִי אֶלָּא בְּעָלָיו עִמּוֹ – From Scripture's mention that one must reload the animal "with" the owner, **I know only** that he must reload if **the owner is** working along **with him** to replace the load upon the animal. שֶׁאֵין בְּעָלָיו עִמּוֹ – But if **the owner is not** working **with him,** because, for example, he is too old or sick to do such strenuous work, מִנַּיִן – **from where can it be derived** that one must still reload the animal? תַּלְמוּד לוֹמַר: ,,הָקֵם תָּקִים״ – For **the verse states:** ***raise up, you shall raise up,*** which implies: מִכָּל מָקוֹם – One must raise the packages onto the animal **in all cases.**[31]

In the above discussion, the Gemara had referred to the Torah laws that mandate that, when necessary, a person must help unburden an animal, and, when necessary, he must help place a burden upon an animal. The Gemara now asks:

וְלָמָּה לֵיהּ לְמִכְתַּב פְּרִיקָה – **Why did [the Torah] need to write** the law of **unloading,** וְלָמָּה לֵיהּ לְמִכְתַּב טְעִינָה – **and why did [the Torah] need to** also **write** the law of **loading?** I.e. why was it necessary for the Torah to write both laws? It could have written only one of them and derived the other by analogy.[33] – ? –

The Gemara answers:

צְרִיכֵי – **They are** indeed both **necessary.** דְּאִי כָּתַב רַחֲמָנָא פְּרִיקָה – **For had the Merciful One written** in his Torah only the law of **unloading,** הֲוָה אֲמִינָא מִשּׁוּם דְּאִיכָּא צַעַר בַּעֲלֵי חַיִּים – **I might have said** this obligation exists **because,** if the bundles are not unloaded quickly, **suffering is** caused **to the animal,** וְאִיכָּא חֶסְרוֹן כִּיס – **and monetary loss is** potentially caused to the owner.[34] אֲבָל טְעִינָה – **But** with respect to **loading,** דְּלָאו צַעַר בַּעֲלֵי חַיִּים אִיכָּא – **where no suffering is** caused **to the animal** if the bystander does not help place the load,[35] וְלָא חֶסְרוֹן כִּיס אִיכָּא – **and,** likewise, **no monetary loss is** caused to the owner if this bystander does not assist him,[36] אֵימָא לֹא – **I might say** that there is **no** obligation to help load whatsoever. וְאִי אַשְׁמַעִינַן טְעִינָה – **And if the Merciful One had informed us** in his Torah only of the law of **loading,** I might have said that this obligation exists מִשּׁוּם דְּבְשָׂכָר – **because it is** done **for payment;** that is, the owner must pay the one who helps him load.[37] אֲבָל פְּרִיקָה דְּבְחִנָּם – **But unloading, which** must be done **for free,** אֵימָא לֹא – **I might say** there is **no** obligation to help unload for free.[38] צְרִיכָא – **It is** therefore **necessary** for the Torah to write both laws.

The Gemara, however, asks:

וּלְרַבִּי שִׁמְעוֹן דְּאָמַר אַף טְעִינָה בְּחִנָּם – **But according to R' Shimon, who says** that **even loading** must be done **for free,**[39] מַאי אִיכָּא לְמֵימַר – **what can be said** as the reason the Torah wrote both laws? If the extent of one's obligation to unload is the same as his obligation to load, then let the Torah simply write the law of loading, and we will derive the law of unloading by analogy! – ? –

The Gemara answers:

לְרַבִּי שִׁמְעוֹן לָא מְסַיְּימֵי קְרָאֵי – **According to R' Shimon, the verses are not conclusive.** I.e. it is not clear from the language of the two verses which of them teaches the obligation to load and which teaches the obligation to unload. Therefore, had the Torah written only one, it would have been understood to teach the obligation to unload, and the obligation to load would not have been known.[40]

Having shown that it was necessary to teach both the law of loading and the law of unloading, the Gemara inquires:

לָמָּה לִי לְמִכְתַּב הָנֵי תַּרְתֵּי – **Why must** the Torah **write these two** laws of loading and unloading, וְלָמָּה לִי לְמִכְתַּב אֲבֵידָה – **and why must** the Torah also **write** the law of returning **a lost object?** Let the Torah write either the former set of laws or the latter law and we will derive the other by analogy![41] – ? –

The Gemara replies:

צְרִיכֵי – **[Both sets of laws] are necessary.** דְּאִי כָּתַב רַחֲמָנָא הָנֵי תַּרְתֵּי – **For had the Merciful One written** in his Torah only **these two** laws, those concerning loading and unloading, I might have said that one must help with these activities, מִשּׁוּם דְּצַעֲרָא דְּמָרֵהּ אִיתָא – **because,** if he does not, **anguish will be caused to the owner,**[42] צַעֲרָא דִידֵהּ אִיתָא – **and suffering will be** caused to **[the animal].**[43] אֲבָל אֲבֵידָה – **But** with respect to **a lost object,** דְּצַעֲרָא דְּמָרֵהּ אִיתָא – although **there will be anguish to the owner** if the finder does not return it, וְצַעֲרָא דִידֵהּ לֵיתָא – **there will be no discomfort** caused to **the [object itself]** if it remains lost. אֵימָא לֹא – Hence, **I might have said** that there is no obligation to return a lost object whatsoever.

The Gemara continues:

וְאִי אַשְׁמַעִינַן אֲבֵידָה – **And if [the Torah] had informed us** only about the law of returning **a lost object,** I might have said that this obligation exists מִשּׁוּם דְּלֵיתָא לְמָרֵהּ בַּהֲדָהּ – **because the owner is not** there along **with [his object],** and, therefore, he is unable to retrieve it on his own.[44]

NOTES

וְהִתְעַלַּמְתָּ מֵהֶם הָקֵם תָּקִים עִמּוֹ, *You shall not see your brother's donkey or his ox fallen in the road and hide from them; raise up, you shall raise up with him* [the owner].

33. Our explanation follows *Rashi* ד״ה למה לי and *Ritzvash,* cited in *Shitah Mekubetzes*; see, however, *Tosafos* ד״ה למה לי, who explains the Gemara's question somewhat differently.

34. If the overburdening load remains upon the animal, it may become permanently weakened as a result, causing financial loss to its owner (*Rashi*).

35. *Ritva* understands the Gemara to mean that helping to load does not alleviate *as much* discomfort to the animal as helping to unload does. In fact, however, helping an owner load an animal will prevent *some* discomfort to the beast, for two people can more gently place loads upon it than can one.

36. *Kos Yeshuos* understands that there can, in fact, be some monetary loss suffered if the bystander does not assist in loading – however, the potential for loss is not as great in the case of loading as it is in the case of unloading (see also *Rashi* ד״ה למה לי למכתב אבידה).

37. It is the opinion of some Tannaim that loading can be done for payment, while unloading must be done for free (*Rashi,* from 32a).

38. I.e. if only the law of loading were written, the law of unloading could indeed be inferred – but it would have been thought that one's obligation to unload is exactly the same as his obligation to load. That is, we would have supposed that just as one is entitled to compensation for helping to *load* an animal, so too, he is entitled to compensation for helping to *unload* the animal. This, however, is not the case (*Shitah Mekubetzes*).

39. See Mishnah and Gemara 32a.

40. In R' Shimon's view, the language of the two verses is ambiguous: Each one could refer to either loading or unloading. As such, if only one of these verses had been written, it would have been understood to teach the more obvious obligation – that one must help *unload* an animal, preventing loss to the owner and pain to the animal. That one is also obligated to help *load* up an animal – where his actions would not prevent pain or loss – would not have been known (*Rashi*; see *Tosafos* ד״ה לרבי שמעון).

41. In essence, the command to return a lost object and the commands to help load or unload an animal are all expressions of a common obligation: the duty to safeguard the property of a fellow Jew. Since one set of laws could simply be derived from the other, it would seem that there would be no need to write them both (*Rashi* ד״ה למה לי; cf. *Toras Chaim*).

42. Without assistance from this bystander, the owner would stand helplessly by his animal, unable to reload the fallen packages. So too, in a case where unloading is required, the owner would experience distress at being unable to unburden his struggling beast (*Rashi*).

43. When a passerby does not help an owner in unloading an overburdened animal, he causes suffering to the beast since it must endure its load that much longer. Similarly, if he does not help an owner to load fallen packages, he also causes discomfort to the beast – for one person cannot place a load upon a beast as gently as two people can (*Ritva*; see above, note 35).

44. It would seem logical that the finder must return the object, for the owner is powerless to retrieve it through his own efforts.

[א] באסרטיא ופרה רצה בין הכרמים הרי זו אבידה [ב] טלית בצד גדר קרדום בצד גדר ופרה רועה בין [א] הכרמים אין זו אבידה ג' ימים זה אחר זה הרי זו אבידה [ג] ראה מים ששוטפין ובאין הרי זה גודר בפניהם אמר רבא א) לכל אבידת אחיך [ד] לרבות אבידת קרקע א"ל רב חנניה לרבא תניא דמסייע לך ראה מים ששוטפין ובאין הרי זה גודר בפניהם א"ל אי משום הא לא תסייעי הכא במאי עסקינן בדאיכא עומרין אי דאיכא עומרין מאי למימרא לא צריכא דאית בה עומרין דצריכי לארעא מהו דתימא כיון דצריכי לארעא כי גופה דארעא דמיין קמ"ל: מצא חמור ופרה [וכו']: הא גופה קשיא אמרת מצא חמור ופרה רועין בדרך אין זו אבידה הא רצה בדרך הוא דלא הוו אבידה הא רצה בדרך ורועה בין הכרמים הויא אבידה אימא סיפא חמור וכליו הפוכים ופרה רצה בין הכרמים הרי זו אבידה רצה בין הכרמים הוא דהויא אבידה הא רצה בדרך ורועה בין הכרמים אין זו אבידה (א) אמר אביי ב) יגיד עליו ריעו תנא רועה בדרך דלא הויא אבידה והוא הדין לרועה בין הכרמים תנא רצה בין הכרמים דהויא אבידה והוא הדין לרצה בדרך א"ל רבא אי יגיד עליו ריעו ליתני קילתא וכ"ש חמירתא ליתני רצה בדרך דהויא אבידה וכ"ש רצה בין הכרמים ולתני רועה בין הכרמים דלא הויא אבידה וכ"ש רועה בדרך אלא אמר רבא רצה ארצה לא קשיא [ה] הא דאפה לגבי דברא הא דאפה לגבי מתא רועה ארועה נמי לא קשיא כאן באבידת גופה כאן באבידת קרקע [ו] כי קתני רועה בדרך לא הויא אבידה הא רועה בין הכרמים הויא אבידה באבידת קרקע וכי קתני רצה בין הכרמים הויא אבידה הא רועה בין הכרמים לא הויא אבידה באבידת גופה דרצה בין הכרמים (ב) מסקבא ורועה בין הכרמים לא מסקבא ורועה בין הכרמים נהי דלא מסקבא תיפוק ליה משום אבידת קרקע [ז] בדכותי ותיפוק ליה משום אבידת גופה דדלמא קטלו לה [ח] באתרא דמתרו והדר קטלי ודלמא אתרו בה אי אתרו בה (ג) ולא אזדהרו בה ודאי אבידה מדעת היא: החזירה וברחה החזירה וברחה [וכו']: א"ל ההוא מדרבנן לרבא אימא השב חדא זמנא תשיבם תרי זמני א"ל (ד) השב אפי' ק' פעמים משמע (ה) תשיבם [ט] אין לי אלא לביתו לגינתו ולחורבתו מנין ת"ל תשיבם מ"מ ה"ד אי דמינטרא פשיטא אי דלא מינטרא אמאי לעולם [י] דמינטרא והא קמ"ל דלא בעינן דעת בעלים וכדר' אלעזר (ו) דאמר [כ] הכל צריכין דעת בעלים [ל] חוץ מהשבת אבידה שהתורה ריבתה השבות הרבה ג) שלח תשלח (ז) אימא שלח חדא זימנא תשלח תרי זמני א"ל שלח [מ] אפי' מאה פעמים משמע תשלח אין לי אלא לדבר הרשות [נ] לדבר מצוה מנין ת"ל תשלח מ"מ א"ל ההוא מדרבנן לרבא ואימא ד) הוכח חדא זימנא תוכיח תרי זמני א"ל [ס] הוכח אפי' ק' פעמים משמע תוכיח אין לי אלא הרב לתלמיד תלמיד לרב מנין ת"ל הוכח תוכיח [ע] מ"מ ה) עזב תעזוב עמו אין לי אלא בעליו עמו שאין בעליו עמו מנין ת"ל עזב תעזוב [פ] מ"מ ו) הקם תקים עמו אין לי אלא בעליו עמו שאין בעליו עמו מנין ת"ל הקם תקים [צ] מ"מ ולמה ליה למכתב פריקה ולמה ליה למיכתב טעינה צריכי דאי כתב רחמנא פריקה הוה אמינא משום דאיכא צער בעלי חיים ואיכא חסרון כיס אבל טעינה דלאו צער בעלי חיים איכא ולא חסרון כיס איכא אימא לא ואי אשמעינן טעינה משום דבשכר אבל פריקה דבחנם אימא לא צריכא ולר"ש (ט) דאמר אף טעינה בחנם מאי איכא למימר לר"ש לא מסיימי קראי למה לי למכתב הני תרתי ולמה לי למכתב אבידה צריכי דאי כתב רחמנא הני תרתי משום דצערא דמרה איתא צערא דידה איתא אבל אבידה דצערא דמרה איתא וצערא דידה ליתא אימא לא ואי אשמעינן אבידה משום דליתא למרה בהדה אבל

---

**אסרטיא.** דרך כבושה לרבים: **ששוטפין ובאין.** לשדה חבירו: **אמר רבא לכל אבידת כו'.** מילתא באפיה נפשיה היא דאמרה רבא בבי מדרשא: **מאי למימרא.** ותיפוק ליה משום עומרין שישנן בכלל אבידה דדמו לפרטא דשה ושלמה ולמה לי לכל לרבוינהו: **רועה בדרך.** איכא תרתי למעליותא חדא דרועה ועוד דאפילו רצה לא מסתקבא רצה בין הכרמים איכא תרתי לגריעותא חדא דרצה ועוד דכרמים מסקבי לה רצה בדרך איכא חדא לגריעותא דרצה ומתקלקלת ברילתה אי נמי תלך למרחקים רועה בין הכרמים חדא לגריעותא דזימנין דמסתקבא: **והא באבידת גופה כו'.** מפרש ואזיל לה: **באבידת קרקע.** וחייב להוציאה משום הפסד כרמים: **לגינתו ולחורבתו מנין.** דהויא השבה ופטור: **דעת בעלים.** לומר לו שמור פרתך שהחזרתיה לגינתך שמצאתיה אובדת: **הכל צריך דעת בעלים.** גנב גזלן וד' שומרים שהשיבו צריכין להודיעו ואם לא הודיעו ומתה או נגנבה חייבים באחריותן דכיון דידע שאבדה ולא ידע שהושבה לא נזהר בה ולא מאכילה: **שלח.** לגבי שלוח הקן: **תרתי זמני.** ואנן תנן (ט) שלחה וחזרה שלחה וחזרה אפי' ארבע וה' פעמים חייב: **לדבר הרשות.** שאין צריך לצפור אלא לאוכלה: **לדבר מצוה מנין.** היה צריך לטהר בו את המצורע מנין שאסור בואו על הבנים ת"ל תשלח: **עזב תעזוב.** פריקה: **הקם תקים.** טעינה: **חסרון כיס.** שהבהמה מתקלקלת: **משום דבשכר.** שנותנין לו שכר דאיכא למ"ד לקמן (דף לב.) טעינה בשכר פריקה בחנם: **לא מסיימי קראי.** הי משמע טעינה והי משמע פריקה ואי כתב חדא הוה אמינא לפריקה אתא אבל טעינה לא כתב רחמנא אידך לטעינה: **למה לי למכתב אבידה.** השבת אבידה לכתוב או הא או הא וליגמר מיניה דהא כולהו אזהרות ממון ישראל הוא: **צערא דמרה.** הוא העומד שם ואין יכול לטעון לבדו וכן לפרוק: **דליתא למרה בהדה.** שיטרח בהשבתה: דאיתיה

---

**קורדום** בצד גדר. פירשתי לעיל (כה: סד"ה ואם נטל): **למה** לי למכתב רחמנא פריקה כו'. אין לפרש למה לי דכתב כוליה קרא דפריקה או דטעינה דא"כ היכי קאמר אי אשמועינן טעינה דבשכר הא משמע לקמן (דף לב.) דטעינה לא הוי בשכר אלא משום דנכתב פריקה ועוד דלא שייכא הך צריכותא אלא לקמן אלא י"ל למה לי דכתב רחמנא יתורא דמרבינן אין בעליו עמו בפריקה ולמה לי דכתב בטעינה: **לרבי** שמעון לא מסיימי קראי. תימה דלקמן (דף לב.) משמע דקרא דנופלים בדרך לא מסיים לר"ש דהוי בטעינה דטעונייהו עלייהו משמע ואי לא כתב אלא חד הוה מוקמי ליה בפריקה אבל קרא דרובץ תחת משאו לא משמע לכ"ע אלא בפריקה וכשנכתבו שניהם ע"כ גם לר"ש קרא דנופלים בדרך הוי בטעינה וא"כ לר"ש לא יכתוב אלא חד יתורא לאין בעליו עמו בקרא דנופלים בדרך וי"ל דרובץ תחת משאו נמי לא מסיים לר"ש דאפשר למשמע בטעינה דע"י שאין הרבה בני אדם לטעון מכביד המשוי על הבהמה ורובצת ולקמן לא אצטריך למימר דלא מסייני אלא אקרא דנופלים בדרך והא דפריך לקמן (דף לב:) והא וחדלת בפריקה הוא דכתיב לא הוי אלא אליבא דרבנן דלר"ש מצי למהוי בטעינה: אבל

---

### עין משפט נר מצוה

קנד א ב מיי' פט"ו מהל' אבידה הלכה ג ה סמג עשין עד טוש"ע ח"מ סי' רס סעיף י:
קנה ג ד מיי' שם פי"א הלכה כ סמג שם טוש"ע ח"מ סי' רנט סעיף ט:
קנו ה ו ז ח מיי' פט"ו שם הל' ג ד סמג שם טוש"ע ח"מ סי' רסא סעיף ג:
קנז ט י מיי' שם פי"א הל' יד טו סמג שם טוש"ע ח"מ סי' רסז סעיף א:
קנח כ מיי' פ"ד מהל' גניבה הל' י ועיין בהשגות ובמ"מ ופ"א מהל' גזילה הל' ח סמג עשין עא טוש"ע ח"מ סי' שנה סעיף א:
קנט ל מיי' פי"א מהל' אבידה הל' טו סמג עשין עד טוש"ע ח"מ סי' רסז סעיף א:
קס מ מיי' פי"ג מהל' שחיטה הל' ה סמג עשין סה טוש"ע י"ד סי' רצב סעיף ה:
קסא נ מיי' שם הל' יט:
קסב ס ע מיי' פ"ו מהל' דיעות הל' ז סמג עשין יא:
קסג פ צ מיי' פי"ג מהל' רוצח הל' ח סמג עשין פא טוש"ע ח"מ סי' רעב סעיף ז:

### הגהות הגר"א

**[א]** גמ' ופרה רועה בין הכרמים. נ"ב העשבים וכ"ה ברי"ף וש"פ (ועמ"ש רבינו בח"מ סי' רס"א ס"ק ה):

### תורה אור השלם

א) וְכֵן תַּעֲשֶׂה לַחֲמֹרוֹ וְכֵן תַּעֲשֶׂה לְשִׂמְלָתוֹ וְכֵן תַּעֲשֶׂה לְכָל אֲבֵדַת אָחִיךָ אֲשֶׁר תֹּאבַד מִמֶּנּוּ וּמְצָאתָהּ לֹא תוּכַל לְהִתְעַלֵּם: [דברים כב, ג]
ב) יַגִּיד עָלָיו רֵעוֹ מִקְנֶה אַף עַל עוֹלֶה: [איוב לו, לג]
ג) שַׁלֵּחַ תְּשַׁלַּח אֶת הָאֵם וְאֶת הַבָּנִים תִּקַּח לָךְ לְמַעַן יִיטַב לָךְ וְהַאֲרַכְתָּ יָמִים: [דברים כב, ז]
ד) לֹא תִשְׂנָא אֶת אָחִיךָ בִּלְבָבֶךָ הוֹכֵחַ תּוֹכִיחַ אֶת עֲמִיתֶךָ וְלֹא תִשָּׂא עָלָיו חֵטְא: [ויקרא יט, יז]
ה) כִּי תִרְאֶה חֲמוֹר שֹׂנַאֲךָ רֹבֵץ תַּחַת מַשָּׂאוֹ וְחָדַלְתָּ מֵעֲזֹב לוֹ עָזֹב תַּעֲזֹב עִמּוֹ: [שמות כג, ה]
ו) לֹא תִרְאֶה אֶת חֲמוֹר אָחִיךָ אוֹ שׁוֹרוֹ נֹפְלִים בַּדֶּרֶךְ וְהִתְעַלַּמְתָּ מֵהֶם הָקֵם תָּקִים עִמּוֹ: [דברים כב, ד]

### מסורת הש"ס

במות לא:, וש"נ], ...פירוש עושה בה ...ה, ערוך ערך סקב], ...ל ולא איהדרו בה, ...ס, ד) חולין פו., ...בא קמא נו., ו) [בבא ...שם], ז) חולין קמא., ...לקמן לב.], ט) [בחולין קמא.].

### ליקוטי רש"י

...סרטיא. מסילה ...לכן בה מעיר לעיר ...ת ו.]. יגיד עליו ...נו. ונלמד משנה ...ילתה [ע"ז עו.]. ...רא. שדה [קדושין ...]. מתא. עיר [שבת ...: ועוד]. מסקבא. ...י"ר בלע"ז [יבמות ...] (וראה לעיל כז:). ...זב. השבה מעלייתא ...מע. לגינתו ...חורבתו מנין. דסגי ...למוצא בהשבתו לגינתן דבעלים [ב"ק נז.].

### רבינו חננאל

...סטרטא. אמר רבה אמר ...א לכל אבידת אחיך ...בות אבידת קרקע: ...ני רישא רועים בדרך ...ה אבידה הא רצים ...רך ורועים בכרמים ...ידה היא. וקתני סיפא ...ה בכרמים הרי זו ...ידה הא רועים אינה ...ידה קשיא רישא ...יפא. ופריק רבא הכי ...ה ופניה כלפי השדה ...ידה היא וחייב להחזיר. ...ה ופניה כלפי המדינה ...נה אבידה. רועה בדרך ...פי' רועה בכרמים אינה ...ידה אבל יש בה אבידת ...קע שאוכלת הזמורות ...פסדת הכרם והאי ...קתני רצה בין הכרמים ...יא אבידה באבידת ...פה כי בריצתה מכין ...יתה זמורות הכרם ...ושין בה חבורות וזהו ...' מסתקבא כי סיקוב זה ...שון חבורה הוא. א) והא ...תניא רועה בכרמים אינה ...בידה בכרמי כותי' ...בידת קרקע ליכא דהא ...רקע כותים הוא. אבידת ...פה ליכא דהא רועים ...עט מעט והילוכם ...ניחותא ואין סיקוב. ...שב אפי' ק' פעמים ...שיבם אפי' לגינתו ...לחרבתו דיו. אמר ר"א ...כל צריכין דעת [בעלים] ...ורץ מהשב אבידה ...לבעלים) שהרי ריבתה ...תורה בה השבות הרבה. ...כן שלח תשלח את האם ...זייב לשלחה אפי' ק' ...פעמים ואפי' צריך לה ...לדבר מצוה כגון טהרת ...מצורע וכיוצא בו אפי' ...הכי חייב לשלח האם וכן ...ין הוכח תוכיח אפי' ק' ...פעמים ואפי' תלמיד לרב. ...כן דין עזוב תעזוב וכן ...הקם תקים בין בעליו עמו ...בין אין בעליו עמו וכן

### חשק שלמה על ר"ח

א) עי' לעיל ד' כ"ז ע"ב בד' ...רבינו גבי הא דאמרי' שם משום דמסקב לי' לתמרא.

The Gemara continues:

וּכְדְרַ׳ אֶלְעָזָר דְּאָמַר – **And** this teaching of Rava is **in accordance with** the opinion of **R' Elazar, who said:** הַכֹּל צְרִיכִין דַּעַת בְּעָלִים – **Every** case in which something is returned **requires the awareness of the owners,**[21] חוּץ מֵהֲשָׁבַת אֲבֵידָה – **except for** the case of **returning a lost object,** שֶׁהַתּוֹרָה רִיבְּתָה הֲשָׁבוֹת הַרְבֵּה – **for,** here, **the Torah included many** types of **returning** as being valid.[22]

The same scholar posed a similar question regarding the obligation to send away a mother bird before taking the young:[23] ,,שַׁלֵּחַ תְּשַׁלַּח׳׳ – The verse states: ***Send away, you shall send away*** the mother. אֵימָא ,,שַׁלֵּחַ׳׳ חֲדָא זִימְנָא – **Say** that the former term, ***send away,*** denotes **one time,** and the latter term, ,,תְּשַׁלַּח׳׳ תְּרֵי זִמְנֵי – ***you shall send away***, denotes **two times.** The verse would thus teach an obligation to send away the mother only twice before taking the young; if she returns yet again, one need not send her away a third time. We learned in a Mishnah, however, that this is not the case.[24] – ? –

Rava replies:

אָמַר לֵיהּ – **[Rava] said to him:** The first term, ,,שַׁלֵּחַ׳׳ – ***send away,*** אֲפִילּוּ מֵאָה פְּעָמִים מַשְׁמַע – connotes that one must send away the mother **even one hundred times,** if necessary.[25] As for the additional term, ,,תְּשַׁלַּח׳׳ – ***you shall send away,*** this teaches the following idea: אֵין לִי אֶלָּא לִדְבַר הָרְשׁוּת – From Scripture's mention that one must send away the mother, **I know only** that one is obligated to send her away when he needs the young **for a mundane matter,** such as for eating. לִדְבַר מִצְוָה מִנַּיִן – **But from where is it derived** that if he needs the mother **for the purposes of a mitzvah,** he must also send her away?[26] תַּלְמוּד לוֹמַר ,,תְּשַׁלַּח׳׳ – For **this verse states:** ***you shall send away*** *the mother,* implying: מִכָּל מָקוֹם – The obligation to send away the mother applies **in all cases.**

The Gemara records a similar discussion regarding the obligation to rebuke one's fellow who commits a wrongdoing:[27]

אָמַר לֵיהּ הַהוּא מִדְּרַבָּנָן לְרָבָא – **One of the Rabbis asked Rava:** וְאֵימָא ,,הוֹכֵחַ׳׳ חֲדָא זִימְנָא – **And say** that the term, ***rebuke,*** denotes **one time,** and the latter term, ,,תּוֹכִיחַ׳׳ תְּרֵי זִמְנֵי – ***you shall rebuke,*** denotes **two times.** The verse would thus teach that there is an obligation to rebuke a transgressor only twice.[28]

Rava replies:

אָמַר לֵיהּ – **[Rava] said to him:** ,,הוֹכֵחַ׳׳ אֲפִילּוּ ק׳ פְּעָמִים מַשְׁמַע – The term, ***rebuke*****, connotes** that one must admonish his fellow **even one hundred times,** if necessary.[25] As for the additional term, ,,תּוֹכִיחַ׳׳ – ***you shall rebuke,*** this teaches the following idea: אֵין לִי אֶלָּא הָרַב לַתַּלְמִיד – From Scripture's mention that one must rebuke his fellow, **I know only** that **a teacher** must give rebuke **to his student** if the latter commits a transgression. תַּלְמִיד לָרַב מִנַּיִן – But **from where it is derived** that even **a student** must rebuke **his teacher** if it is the teacher that is transgressing? תַּלְמוּד לוֹמַר: ,,הוֹכֵחַ תּוֹכִיחַ׳׳ – For **this verse states:** ***rebuke you shall rebuke,*** which implies: מִכָּל מָקוֹם – The obligation to rebuke remains in force **in all cases.**[29]

The Gemara sets forth a similar exposition regarding the obligation to help unload packages from an animal that collapsed under their weight:[30]

,,עָזֹב תַּעֲזֹב עִמּוֹ׳׳ – The verse states: ***help*****,** ***you shall help with him*** [i.e. with the donkey's owner]. אֵין לִי אֶלָּא בְּעָלָיו עִמּוֹ – From Scripture's command that one must help "with" the donkey's owner, **I know only** that he must help if **the owner is** working along **with him** to unload the donkey. שֶׁאֵין בְּעָלָיו עִמּוֹ – But **if the owner is not** working **with him** because, for example, he is too old or sick to lift the packages, מִנַּיִן – **from where is it derived** that one must still unload the animal? תַּלְמוּד לוֹמַר: ,,עָזֹב תַּעֲזֹב׳׳ – For **the verse states:** ***help, you shall help,*** which implies: מִכָּל מָקוֹם – you must help unload the animal **in all cases.**[31]

A further exposition of this nature is set forth regarding the obligation to help in loading cargo upon an animal:[32]

,,הָקֵם תָּקִים עִמּוֹ׳׳ – The verse states: ***raise up, you shall raise up***

NOTES

these places has fulfilled his obligation (if, of course, they are adequately protected); he need not alert the owner to the fact that the object is now upon his property, and that he must now care for it himself (see *Rashi*).

21. For example, a thief who returns a stolen animal, or a watchman who returns the animal that had been under his supervision, must each inform the owner that he has placed the animal back in his possession. This is necessary so that the owner will become aware that he must now feed the animal and protect it from thieves. If these persons place the animal on the owner's property *without* informing him, and the animal subsequently dies or is stolen, they are liable to pay for the animal's full value (*Rashi*).

22. I.e. the Torah added the extra word תְּשִׁיבֵם, *you shall return them,* to imply that there is more than one way to return an item: One need not return it to the owner's home – he may also return it to his garden or deserted building, places where the owner would not become immediately aware that he had regained his lost item.

23. The Torah sets forth that when one finds a nest of birds, he may not take the eggs or chicks while the mother bird remains present. Rather, the Torah commands (*Deuteronomy* 22:7): שַׁלֵּחַ תְּשַׁלַּח אֶת־הָאֵם וְאֶת־הַבָּנִים תִּקַּח־לָךְ לְמַעַן יִיטַב לָךְ וְהַאֲרַכְתָּ יָמִים, *Send away, you shall send away the mother, and the young you may keep for yourself; [you shall do this] so that it shall be good for you and your days shall be lengthened*.

24. The Mishnah (*Chullin* 141a) states that if the mother continues to return before the young can be taken, she must be sent away repeatedly – even four or five times, if necessary (see *Rashi*).

25. Rava interprets the word שַׁלֵּחַ in the same sense as the word הָשֵׁב. See above, note 19.

26. An example of using the birds for the purposes of a mitzvah arises in the case of a *metzora* – one who is afflicted with the malady of *tzaraas.* As part of the process by which a *metzora* becomes purified, two birds must be taken, the first of which is slaughtered, the second of which is set free after being dipped in the blood of the first (see *Leviticus*, 14:4-7). Rava teaches that the requirement to send away the mother bird remains in force even if one needs the mother for the mitzvah of carrying out the above purification process (*Rashi*; see also *Ritva*).

27. When one sees a fellow Jew committing a transgression, he is required to rebuke him privately, in an attempt to steer him towards the path of proper conduct (see *Rambam, Hil. De'os* 6:7). The source for this law is *Leviticus* 19:17, where the verse states: הוֹכֵחַ תּוֹכִיחַ אֶת־עֲמִיתֶךָ, *rebuke, you shall rebuke your friend.*

28. I.e. if, after a first rebuke, the transgressor does not change his ways, one would be required to admonish him again. If, however, he ignored this second rebuke, one would not be required to reprove him a third time.

29. *Ritva* notes that although a student must rebuke his teacher, he should do so with respect, addressing himself to his master tentatively, rather than forcefully. For example, instead of confronting the teacher openly, the student could approach him with a question that bears on the matter at hand. He might begin: "My teacher, you have taught us that such and such is the law. . ." (see *Kiddushin* 32a).

30. The obligation to assist in פְּרִיקָה, *unloading,* derives from *Exodus* 23:5, where the verse states: כִּי־תִרְאֶה חֲמוֹר שֹׂנַאֲךָ רֹבֵץ תַּחַת מַשָּׂאוֹ וְחָדַלְתָּ מֵעֲזֹב לוֹ עָזֹב תַּעֲזֹב עִמּוֹ, *Should you see your enemy's donkey lying down under its burden and refrain from helping him? Help, you shall help with him* [the owner].

31. The Mishnah later (32a) states that if the owner is able bodied and he insists that someone else unload the animal without his help, that person is *not* obligated to unload the animal by himself. It is only when the owner is *unable* to assist that the passerby must unload the animal himself. (The same ruling applies with respect to loading as well; see below.)

32. The obligation to assist in טְעִינָה, *loading*, derives from *Deuteronomy* 22:4, where the verse states: לֹא־תִרְאֶה אֶת־חֲמוֹר אָחִיךָ אוֹ שׁוֹרוֹ נֹפְלִים בַּדֶּרֶךְ

באסרטיא ופרה רצה בין הכרמים הרי זו אבידה טלית בצד גדר קרדום בצד גדר ופרה רועה בין [א] הכרמים אין זו אבידה ג' ימים זה אחר זה הרי זו אבידה ראה מים ששוטפין ובאין הרי זה גודר בפניהם אמר רבא לכל אבידת אחיך לרבות אבידת קרקע א"ל רב חנניה לרבא תניא דמסייע לך ראה מים ששוטפין ובאין הרי זה גודר בפניהם א"ל אי משום הא לא תסייעי הכא במאי עסקינן בדאיכא עומרין אי דאיכא עומרין מאי למימרא לא צריכא דאית בה עומרין דצריכי לארעא מהו דתימא כיון דצריכי לארעא כי גופה דארעא דמיין קמ"ל: מצא חמור ופרה [וכו']: הא גופה קשיא אמרת מצא חמור ופרה רועין בדרך אין זו אבידה רועין בדרך הוא דלא הוו אבידה הא רצה בדרך ורועה בין הכרמים הויא אבידה אימא סיפא חמור וכליו הפוכים ופרה רצה בין הכרמים הרי זו אבידה רצה בין הכרמים הוא דהויא אבידה הא רצה בדרך ורועה בין הכרמים אין זו אבידה אמר אביי יגיד עליו ריעו תנא רועה בדרך דלא הויא אבידה והוא הדין לרועה בין הכרמים תנא רצה בין הכרמים דהויא אבידה והוא הדין לרצה בדרך א"ל רבא אי יגיד עליו ריעו ליתני קילתא וכ"ש חמירתא ליתני רצה בדרך דהויא אבידה וכ"ש רצה בין הכרמים ולתני רועה בין הכרמים דלא הויא אבידה וכ"ש רועה בדרך אלא אמר רבא רצה ארצה לא קשיא הא דאפה לגבי דברא הא דאפה לגבי מתא רועה ארועה נמי לא קשיא כאן באבידת גופה כאן באבידת קרקע כי קתני רועה בדרך לא הויא אבידה הא רועה בין הכרמים הויא אבידה באבידת קרקע וכי קתני רצה בין הכרמים הויא אבידה הא רועה בין הכרמים לא הויא אבידה באבידת גופה דרצה בין הכרמים מסקבא ורועה בין הכרמים לא מסקבא נהי דלא מסקבא תיפוק ליה משום אבידת קרקע בדכותי ותיפוק ליה משום אבידת גופה דדלמא קטלו לה באתרא דמתרו והדר קטלי ודלמא אתרו בה אי אתרו בה ולא אזדהרו בה ודאי אבידה מדעת היא: החזירה וברחה החזירה וברחה [וכו']: א"ל ההוא מדרבנן לרבא אימא השב חדא זמנא תשיבם תרי זמני א"ל השב אפי' ק' פעמים משמע תשיבם אין לי אלא לביתו לגינתו ולחורבתו מנין ת"ל תשיבם מ"מ ה"ד אי דמינטרא פשיטא אי דלא מינטרא אמאי לעולם דמינטרא והא קמ"ל דלא בעינן דעת בעלים וכדר' אלעזר דאמר הכל צריכין דעת בעלים חוץ מהשבת אבידה שהתורה ריבתה השבות הרבה שלח תשלח אימא שלח חדא זימנא תשלח תרי זמני א"ל שלח אפי' מאה פעמים משמע תשלח אין לי אלא לדבר הרשות לדבר מצוה מנין ת"ל תשלח מ"מ א"ל ההוא מדרבנן לרבא ואימא הוכח חדא זימנא תוכיח תרי זמני א"ל הוכח אפי' ק' פעמים משמע תוכיח אין לי אלא הרב לתלמיד תלמיד לרב מנין ת"ל הוכח תוכיח מ"מ עזוב תעזוב עמו אין לי אלא בעליו עמו שאין בעליו עמו מנין ת"ל עזוב תעזוב מ"מ הקם תקים עמו אין לי אלא בעליו עמו שאין בעליו עמו מנין ת"ל הקם תקים מ"מ ולמה ליה למכתב פריקה ולמה ליה למיכתב טעינה צריכי דאי כתב רחמנא פריקה הוה אמינא משום דאיכא צער בעלי חיים ואיכא חסרון כיס אבל טעינה דלאו צער בעלי חיים איכא ולא חסרון כיס איכא אימא לא ואי אשמעינן טעינה משום דבשכר אבל פריקה דבחנם אימא לא צריכא ולר"ש דאמר אף טעינה בחנם מאי איכא למימר לר"ש לא מסיימי קראי למה לי למכתב הני תרתי ולמה לי למכתב אבידה צריכי דאי כתב רחמנא הני תרתי משום דצערא דמרה איתא צערא דידה איתא אבל אבידה דצערא דמרה איתא וצערא דידה ליתא אימא לא ואי אשמעינן אבידה משום דליתא למרה בהדה אבל

**אסרטיא.** דרך כבושה לרבים: **ששוטפין ובאין.** לשדה חבירו: **אמר רבא לכל אבידת כו'.** מילתא באפיה נפשיה היא דאמרה רבא בבי מדרשא: **מאי למימרא.** ותיפוק ליה משום עומרין שישנן בכלל אבידה דדמו לפרטא דשה ושלמה ולמה לי לכל לרבוייהו: **רועה בדרך.** איכא תרתי למעליותא חדא דרועה ועוד דאפילו רצה לא מסתקבא רצה בין הכרמים איכא תרתי לגריעותא חדא דרצה ועוד דכרמים מסקבי לה רצה בדרך איכא חדא לגריעותא דרצה ומתקלקלת ברגליה אי נמי תלך למרחקים רועה בין הכרמים חדא לגריעותא דזימנין דמסתקבא: **והא באבידת גופה כו'.** מפרש ואזיל לה: **באבידת קרקע.** וחייב להוציאה משום הפסד כרמים: **לגינתו ולחורבתו מנין.** דהויא השבה ופטור: **דעת בעלים.** לומר לו שמור פרתך שהחזרתיה לגינתך שמאתיה אובדת: **הכל צריך דעת בעלים.** גנב גזלן וד' שומרים שהשיבו צריכין להודיעו ואם לא הודיעו ומתה או נגנבה חייבים באחריותן דכיון דידע שאבדה ולא ידע שהושבה לא נזהר בה ולא מאכילה: **שלח.** לגבי שלוח הקן: **תרתי זמני.** ואנן תנן שלחה וחזרה שלחה וחזרה אפי' ארבע וה' פעמים חייב: **לדבר הרשות.** שאין צריך לצפור אלא לאוכלה: **לדבר מצוה מנין.** היה צריך לטהר בו את המצורע מנין שאסור באם על הבנים ת"ל תשלח: **עזוב תעזוב.** פריקה: **הקם תקים.** טעינה: **חסרון כיס.** שהבהמה מתקלקלת: **משום דבשכר.** שנותנין לו שכר דאיכא למ"ד לקמן (דף לב.) טעינה בשכר פריקה בחנם: **לא מסיימי קראי.** הי משמע טעינה והי משמע פריקה ואי כתב חדא הוה אמינא לפריקה אתא אבל טעינה לא כתב רחמנא אידך לטעינה: **למה לי למכתב אבידה.** השבת אבידה לכתוב או הא או הא וליגמר מניה דהא כולהו אזהרות ממון ישראל הוא: **צערא דמרה.** הוא העומד שם ואין יכול לטעון לבדו וכן לפרוק: **דליתא למרה בהדה.** שיטרח בהשבתה: דאיתיה

**קורדום** בצד גדר. פירשתי לעיל (כה: סד"ה ואם נטל): **למה** לי למכתב רחמנא פריקה כו'. אין לפרש למה לי דכתב כוליה קרא דפריקה או דטעינה דא"כ היכי קאמר אי אשמועינן טעינה דבשכר הא משמע לקמן (דף לב.) דטעינה לא הוי בשכר אלא משום דנכתב פריקה ועוד דלא שייכא הך צריכותא אלא לקמן אלא י"ל למה לי דכתב רחמנא יתורא דמרבינן אין בעליו עמו בפריקה ולמה לי דכתב בטעינה: **לרבי** שמעון לא מסיימי קראי. תימה דלקמן (דף לב.) משמע דקרא דנופלים בדרך לא מסיים לר"ש דהוי בטעינה דטעונייהו עלייהו משמע ואי לא כתב אלא חד הוה מוקמי ליה בפריקה אבל קרא דרובץ תחת משאו לא משמע לכ"ע אלא בפריקה וכשנכתבו שניהם ע"כ גם לר"ש קרא דנופלים בדרך הוי בטעינה וא"כ לר"ש לא יכתוב אלא חד יתורא לאין בעליו עמו בקרא דנופלים בדרך וי"ל דרובץ תחת משאו נמי לא מסיים לר"ש דאפשר למשמע בטעינה דע"י שאין הרבה בני אדם לטעון מכביד המשוי על הבהמה ורובצת ולקמן לא אצטריך למימר דלא מסיימי אלא אקרא דנופלים בדרך והא דפריך לקמן (דף לב:) והא וחדלת בפריקה הוא דכתיב לא הוי אלא אליבא דרבנן דלר"ש מצי למהוי בטעינה: אבל

### מסורת הש"ס

א) [יבמות לא:, וש"נ], ב) [פירוש עושה בה גבורה, ערוך ערך סקב], ג) צ"ל ולא איהדרו בה, מהרש"ם, ד) חולין פז., ה) בבא קמא נז., ו) [בבא קמא שם], ז) חולין קמא., ח) [לקמן לב.], ט) [בחולין קמא.].

### ליקוטי רש"י

**באסרטיא.** מסילה שהולכין בה מעיר לעיר [שבת ו.]. **יגיד עליו ריעו.** ונלמד משנה מחבירתה [ע"ז עו.]. **דברא.** שדה [קדושין מא:]. **מתא.** עיר [שבת קמה: ועוד]. **מסקבא.** לאשי"ר בלע"ז [יבמות קכ:] (וראה לעיל כז:). **השב.** השבה מעלייתא משמע. **לגינתו ולחורבתו מנין.** דסגי ליה למולא בהשבתו לגינתן דבעלים [ב"ק נז.].

### רבינו חננאל

איסטרטא. אמר רבה אמר קרא לכל אבידת אחיך לרבות אבידת קרקע: קתני רישא רועים בדרך אינה אבידה הא רצים בדרך ורועים בכרמים אבידה היא. וקתני סיפא רצה בכרמים הרי זו אבידה הא רועים אינה אבידה קשיא רישא אסיפא. ופריק רבא הכי רצה ופניה כלפי השדה אבידה היא וחייב להחזיר. רצה ופניה כלפי המדינה אינה אבידה. רועה בדרך אפי' רועה בכרמים אינה אבידה אבל יש בה אבידת קרקע שאוכלת הזמורות מפסדת הכרם והאי דקתני רצה בין הכרמים הויא אבידה באבידת גופה כי בריצתה מכין אותה זמורות הכרם ועושין בה חבורות וזהו פי' מסתקבא כי סיקוב זה לשון חבורה הוא. א) והא דתניא רועה בכרמים אינה אבידה בכרמי כותי' אבידת קרקע ליכא דהא קרקע כותים הוא. אבידת גופה ליכא דהא רועים מעט מעט והילוכם בניחותא ואין סיקוב. השב אפי' ק' פעמים תשיבם אפי' לגינתו ולחרבתו דיו. אמר ר"א הכל צריכין דעת [בעלים] חוץ מהשב אבידה (לבעלים) שהרי ריבתה התורה בה השבות הרבה. וכן שלח תשלח את האם חייב לשלחה אפי' ק' פעמים ואפי' צריך לה לדבר מצוה כגון טהרת מצורע וכיוצא בו אפי' הכי חייב לשלח האם וכן דין הוכח תוכיח אפי' ק' פעמים ואפי' תלמיד לרב. וכן דין עזוב תעזוב וכן הקם תקים בין בעליו עמו בין אין בעליו עמו וכן

**חשק שלמה על ר"ח** א) עי' לעיל ד' כ"ז ע"ב בד' רבינו גבי הא דאמרי' שם משום דמסקב לי' למרא.

### עין משפט נר מצוה

קנד א ב מיי' פט"ו מהל' אבידה הלכה ב ה סמג עשין עד טוש"ע ח"מ סי' רס סעיף י:
קנה ג ד מיי' שם פי"א הלכה כ סמג שם טוש"ע ח"מ סי' רנט סעיף ט:
קנו ה ו ז ח מיי' פט"ו שם הל' ג ד סמג שם טוש"ע ח"מ סי' רסא סעיף ב:
קנז ט י מיי' שם פי"א הל' יד טו סמג שם טוש"ע ח"מ סי' רסז סעיף א:
קנח כ מיי' פ"ד מהל' גניבה הל' י ועיין בהשגות ובמ"מ ופ"א מהל' גזילה הל' ח סמג עשין עא טוש"ע ח"מ סי' שנה סעיף א:
קנט ל מיי' פי"א מהל' אבידה הל' טז סמג עשין עד טוש"ע ח"מ סי' רסז סעיף א:
קס מ מיי' פי"ג מהל' שחיטה הל' ה סמג עשין סה טוש"ע י"ד סי' רצב סעיף ה:
קסא נ מיי' שם הל' יט:
קסב ס ע מיי' פ"ו מהל' דיעות הל' ז סמג עשין יא:
קסג פ צ מיי' פי"ג מהל' רוצח הל' ח סמג עשין פא טוש"ע ח"מ סי' רעב סעיף ז:

### הגהות הגר"א

[א] גמ' ופרה רועה בין הכרמים. נ"ב העשבים וכ"ה ברי"ף וש"פ (ועמ"ש רבינו בח"מ סי' רס"א ס"ק ה):

### תורה אור השלם

א) וְכֵן תַּעֲשֶׂה לַחֲמֹרוֹ וְכֵן תַּעֲשֶׂה לְשִׂמְלָתוֹ וְכֵן תַּעֲשֶׂה לְכָל אֲבֵדַת אָחִיךָ אֲשֶׁר תֹּאבַד מִמֶּנּוּ וּמְצָאתָהּ לֹא תוּכַל לְהִתְעַלֵּם: [דברים כב, ג]

ב) יַגִּיד עָלָיו רֵעוֹ מִקְנֶה אַף עַל עוֹלֶה: [איוב לו, לג]

ג) שַׁלֵּחַ תְּשַׁלַּח אֶת הָאֵם וְאֶת הַבָּנִים תִּקַּח לָךְ לְמַעַן יִיטַב לָךְ וְהַאֲרַכְתָּ יָמִים: [דברים כב, ז]

ד) לֹא תִשְׂנָא אֶת אָחִיךָ בִּלְבָבֶךָ הוֹכֵחַ תּוֹכִיחַ אֶת עֲמִיתֶךָ וְלֹא תִשָּׂא עָלָיו חֵטְא: [ויקרא יט, יז]

ה) כִּי תִרְאֶה חֲמוֹר שֹׂנַאֲךָ רֹבֵץ תַּחַת מַשָּׂאוֹ וְחָדַלְתָּ מֵעֲזֹב לוֹ עָזֹב תַּעֲזֹב עִמּוֹ: [שמות כג, ה]

ו) לֹא תִרְאֶה אֶת חֲמוֹר אָחִיךָ אוֹ שׁוֹרוֹ נֹפְלִים בַּדֶּרֶךְ וְהִתְעַלַּמְתָּ מֵהֶם הָקֵם תָּקִים עִמּוֹ: [דברים כב, ד]

therefore, there is no obligation to protect the land.[16]

The Gemara, however, objects:

**וְתִיפּוֹק לֵיהּ מִשּׁוּם אֲבֵידַת גּוּפָהּ** – **But** if the field is owned by Cuthites, **you should** still **derive** that the finder must remove the animal from their vineyard **because of the** consideration of **loss to** the animal **itself, דִּדְלְמָא קָטְלוּ לָהּ** – **for perhaps [the Cuthites]** who own the vineyard **will kill [the intruding animal]** to protect their land! – ? –

The Gemara replies:

**בְּאַתְרָא דְּמַתְרוּ** – The Mishnah is dealing **with a place in which [people] warn** a man the first time his animal is found on their land, **וְהָדַר קָטְלֵי** – **and, then,** if the animal is found on it a second time, **they kill** it. Accordingly, there is no need to fear that the Cuthites will kill this animal, for they would warn the owner first.

The Gemara retorts:

**וְדִלְמָא אַתְרוּ בֵּיהּ** – **But perhaps [the Cuthites]** have already **warned [the owner]** once before, and now if the finder does not remove the animal, they will kill it. – ? –

The Gemara answers:

**אִי אַתְרוּ בֵּהּ וְלֹא אִזְדְּהַרוּ בָּהּ** – **If,** indeed, **they** already **warned the owner and,** subsequently, **[this owner] was not careful with [his animal],** allowing it to wander into the vineyards once again, **וַדַּאי אֲבֵידָה מִדַּעַת הִיא** – then **this** animal **is certainly an intentionally abandoned object,** and the finder is under no obligation to retrieve it.[17]

The Gemara quotes the next section of the Mishnah and comments upon it:

**הֶחֱזִירָהּ וּבָרְחָה הֶחֱזִירָהּ וּבָרְחָה [וכו׳]** – IF ONE RETURNED [AN ANIMAL] AND IT RAN AWAY, and HE RETURNED IT again AND IT RAN AWAY [etc.] [even if this happens four or five times, he is still obligated to return it yet again, for it is stated: *return, you shall return them*].

The Gemara relates a discussion regarding the derivation of this law:[18]

**אֲמַר לֵיהּ הַהוּא מֵרַבָּנַן לְרָבָא** – **One of the Rabbis** in the academy **said to Rava: אֵימָא** – **Say** that the Scriptural term, ,,הָשֵׁב" – ***return,*** **חֲדָא זִמְנָא** – denotes returning **one time;** and the following term, ,,תְּשִׁיבֵם" – ***you shall return them,*** **תְּרֵי זִמְנֵי** – denotes returning **two times.** There would thus be an obligation to return a lost object only twice, not four or five times, as the Mishnah taught! – ? –

Rava replies:

**אֲמַר לֵיהּ** – **[Rava] said to him:** **,,הָשֵׁב" אֲפִילוּ ק׳ פְּעָמִים מַשְׁמַע** – The term, ***return,*** **connotes** that one must return an object **even one hundred times.**[19] As for the additional phrase, ,,תְּשִׁיבֵם" – ***you shall return them,*** this teaches the following: **אֵין לִי אֶלָּא לְבֵיתוֹ** – From Scripture's mention that one must return a lost object, **I know only** that the finder can return the lost object **to [the owner's] house.** **לְגִינָּתוֹ וּלְחוּרְבָּתוֹ מִנַּיִן** – But **from where is it derived** that if he returns it **to [the owner's] garden, or to his deserted building,** he has also fulfilled his obligation? **תַּלְמוּד לוֹמַר: ,,תְּשִׁיבֵם"** – For **the verse states:** ***you shall return them;*** which implies: **מִכָּל מָקוֹם** – you may return them **in any manner,** i.e. you may return them even to the owner's garden or to his deserted building.

The Gemara inquires:

**הֵיכִי דָּמֵי** – **How is this** ruling to be understood? **אִי דְּמִינְטְרָא** – **If [the garden or deserted building] is protected** from potential intruders, then the object would be safe there, **פְּשִׁיטָא** – and **it is obvious** that the finder may return the object to this place! **אִי דְּלֹא מִינְטְרָא** – And **if [this place] is not protected,** **אַמַּאי** – **why** indeed *should* the finder be permitted to leave the object there?

The Gemara answers:

**לְעוֹלָם דְּמִינְטְרָא** – **In fact,** Rava is referring to a place **that is protected;** **וְהָא קָא מַשְׁמַע לָן** – **and** it is of **this** that **[the verse] informs us:** **דְּלֹא בָּעֵינַן דַּעַת בְּעָלִים** – **That we do not require the awareness of the owner** that his object has been returned; i.e. the finder may return an object to the owner's protected garden or deserted building, and he need not inform the owner that he has returned it.[20]

NOTES

the animal. Accordingly, the finder should be required to remove the animal from the vineyard, despite the fact that the animal itself cannot be considered lost.

16. Thus, in the case of the second clause, loss of land is not an issue; the only consideration is whether the animal itself should be assumed lost. As regards this question, the Mishnah states that when the animal is running through the vineyard it is to be considered lost, implying that when it is only grazing there, this is not the case.

As it is used here, the word Cuthite refers to an idolater. Torah law does not obligate one to return the lost items of an idolater, for the verse refers only to returning the lost items of אָחִיךָ, *your brother* (see *Deuteronomy* 22:3; see *Bava Kamma* 113b).

17. In summary, then, the Mishnah's second clause implies that an animal grazing in a vineyard is not to be assumed lost, and therefore it need not be retrieved. In issuing this ruling, the Mishnah speaks specifically of a case in which the vineyard is owned by idolaters – hence, there is no obligation to remove the animal to prevent damage to the vineyard. Likewise, the Mishnah also speaks of a case in which the proprietors of the vineyard would not kill the animal unless they had first warned its owner; hence, the consideration that harm may come to the animal does not obligate the finder to retrieve it.

The rulings of the first and second clauses of the Mishnah may now be summarized as follows:

1) If an animal is grazing by the road, it is *not* to be assumed lost, and it should not be retrieved.
2) If it is running in vineyards, it *is* to be assumed lost, and should be retrieved.
3) If it is running along the road then:
   a) If it is running towards the city, it is *not* to be assumed lost.
   b) If it is running towards the desert it *is* to be assumed lost.
4) If it is grazing among the vineyards then:
   a) If the vineyard belongs to a Jew, the endangered *vineyard* must be considered a "lost" object, and the animal must be removed.
   b) If the vineyard belongs to a Cuthite, the *vineyard* is *not* to be considered a lost object, and:
      i. In a place where people would warn the animal's owner before killing the animal, the animal is *not* to be assumed lost.
      ii. In a place where people do not warn the owner first, the animal *is* to be assumed lost (*Rosh* §22).

In connection with the above discussion, *Ritva* posits the following distinction: If the vineyard belongs to a Jew, in which case the land is considered "lost," but the animal is not, the finder's obligation is only to *remove* the animal from the vineyard (to prevent damage coming to it); he need not actually return the animal to its owner, since the animal is not considered lost. If however, the vineyard belongs to a Cuthite (in a place where people do not warn the owner first), this is not the case. Here, where the animal is considered lost, it is not sufficient for the finder to simply remove the animal from the vineyard; he must also return the animal to its owner (*Ritva;* see also *Rashi* ד״ה באבידת קרקע; cf. *Rosh*).

18. The obligation to return a lost object is stated in the Torah (*Deuteronomy* 22:1) as follows: לֹא־תִרְאֶה אֶת־שׁוֹר אָחִיךָ אוֹ אֶת־שֵׂיוֹ נִדָּחִים וְהִתְעַלַּמְתָּ מֵהֶם הָשֵׁב תְּשִׁיבֵם לְאָחִיךָ, *You shall not see the ox of your brother or his sheep straying and hide from them; return, you shall return them to your brother.*

19. According to Rava, the word הָשֵׁב, *return*, has a dual connotation: It has the sense of both *one* and *many* acts of returning (*Rambam,* commentary to Mishnah; cf. *Toras Chaim*).

20. Presumably, an owner will notice an object that has been returned to his house. He may not, however, notice an object that has been returned to his garden or deserted building. Despite this, however, Scripture teaches that a finder who simply returns a lost object (e.g. a cow) to

באסרטיא ופרה רצה בין הכרמים הרי זו אבידה טלית בצד גדר קרדום בצד גדר ופרה רועה בין [א] הכרמים אין זו אבידה ג' ימים זה אחר זה הרי זו אבידה ראה מים ששוטפין ובאין הרי זה גודר בפניהם אמר רבא א) לכל אבידת אחיך לרבות אבידת קרקע א"ל רב חנניה לרבא תניא דמסייע לך ראה מים ששוטפין ובאין הרי זה גודר בפניהם א"ל אי משום הא לא תסייעי הכא במאי עסקינן בדאיכא עומרין אי דאיכא עומרין מאי למימרא לא צריכא דאית בה עומרין דצריכי לארעא מהו דתימא כיון דצריכי לארעא כי גופה דארעא דמיין קמ"ל: מצא חמור ופרה [וכו']: הא גופה קשיא אמרת מצא חמור ופרה רועין בדרך אין זו אבידה רועין בדרך הוא דלא הוו אבידה הא רצה בדרך ורועה בין הכרמים הויא אבידה אימא סיפא חמור וכליו הפוכים ופרה רצה בין הכרמים הרי זו אבידה רצה בין הכרמים הוא דהויא אבידה הא רצה בדרך ורועה בין הכרמים אין זו אבידה אמר אביי ב) יגיד עליו ריעו תנא רועה בדרך דלא הויא אבידה והוא הדין לרועה בין הכרמים תנא רצה בין הכרמים דהויא אבידה והוא הדין לרצה בדרך א"ל רבא אי יגיד עליו ריעו ליתני קילתא וכ"ש חמירתא ליתני רצה בדרך דהויא אבידה וכ"ש רצה בין הכרמים ולתני רועה בין הכרמים דלא הויא אבידה וכ"ש רועה בדרך אלא אמר רבא רצה ארצה לא קשיא הא דאפה לגבי דברא הא דאפה לגבי מתא רועה ארועה נמי לא קשיא כאן באבידת גופה כאן באבידת קרקע כי קתני רועה בדרך לא הויא אבידה הא רועה בין הכרמים הויא אבידה באבידת קרקע וכי קתני רצה בין הכרמים הויא אבידה הא רועה בין הכרמים לא הויא אבידה באבידת גופה דרצה בין הכרמים מסקבא ורועה בין הכרמים לא מסקבא ורועה בין הכרמים נהי דלא מסקבא תיפוק ליה משום אבידת קרקע בדכותי ותיפוק ליה משום אבידת גופה דדלמא קטלו לה באתרא דמתרו והדר קטלי ודלמא אתרו בה אי אתרו בה ולא אזדהרו בה ודאי אבידה מדעת היא: החזירה וברחה החזירה וברחה [וכו']: א"ל ההוא מדרבנן לרבא אימא השב חדא זמנא תשיבם תרי זמני א"ל השב אפי' ק' פעמים משמע תשיבם אין לי אלא לביתו לגינתו ולחורבתו מנין ת"ל תשיבם מ"מ ה"ד אי דמינטרא פשיטא אי דלא מינטרא אמאי לעולם דמינטרא והא קמ"ל דלא בעינן דעת בעלים וכדר' אלעזר דאמר הכל צריכין דעת בעלים חוץ מהשבת אבידה שהתורה ריבתה השבות הרבה שלח תשלח אימא שלח חדא זימנא תשלח תרי זמני א"ל שלח אפי' מאה פעמים משמע תשלח אין לי אלא לדבר הרשות לדבר מצוה מנין ת"ל תשלח מ"מ א"ל ההוא מדרבנן לרבא ואימא הוכח חדא זימנא תוכיח תרי זמני א"ל הוכח אפי' ק' פעמים משמע תוכיח אין לי אלא הרב לתלמיד תלמיד לרב מנין ת"ל הוכח תוכיח מ"מ עזב תעזוב עמו אין לי אלא בעליו עמו שאין בעליו עמו מנין ת"ל עזב תעזוב מ"מ הקם תקים עמו אין לי אלא בעליו עמו שאין בעליו עמו מנין ת"ל הקם תקים מ"מ ולמה ליה למכתב פריקה ולמה ליה למיכתב טעינה צריכי דאי כתב רחמנא פריקה הוה אמינא משום דאיכא צער בעלי חיים ואיכא חסרון כיס אבל טעינה דלאו צער בעלי חיים איכא ולא חסרון כיס איכא אימא לא ואי אשמעינן טעינה משום דבשכר אבל פריקה דבחנם אימא לא צריכא ולר"ש דאמר אף טעינה בחנם מאי איכא למימר לר"ש לא מסיימי קראי למה לי למכתב הני תרתי ולמה לי למכתב אבידה צריכי דאי כתב רחמנא הני תרתי משום דצערא דמרה איתא צערא דידה איתא אבל אבידה דצערא דמרה איתא וצערא דידה ליתא אימא לא ואי אשמעינן אבידה משום דליתא למרה בהדה אבל

---

**רש"י**

אסרטיא. דרך כבושה לרבים: ששוטפין ובאין. לשדה חבירו: אמר רבא לכל אבידת כו'. מילתא באפיה נפשיה היא דאמרה רבא בבי מדרשא: מאי למימרא. ותיפוק ליה משום עומרין שישנן בכלל אבידה דדמו לפרטא דשה ושלמה ולמה לי לכל לרבוינהו: רועה בדרך. איכא תרתי למעליותא חדא דרועה ועוד דאפילו רצה לא מסתקבא רצה בין הכרמים איכא תרתי לגריעותא חדא דרצה ועוד דכרמים מסקבי לה רצה בדרך איכא חדא לגריעותא דרצה ומתקלקלת ברגלתה אי נמי תלך למרחקים רועה בין הכרמים חדא לגריעותא דזימנין דמסתקבא: והא באבידת גופה כו'. מפרש ואזיל לה: באבידת קרקע. וחייב להוציאה משום הפסד כרמים: לגינתו ולחורבתו מנין. דהויא השבה ופטור: דעת בעלים. לומר לו שמור פרתך שהחזרתיה לגינתך שמצאתיה אובדת: הכל צריך דעת בעלים. גנב גזלן וד' שומרים שהשיבו צריכין להודיעו ואם לא הודיעו ומתה או נגנבה חייבים באחריותן דכיון דידע שאבדה ולא ידע שהושבה לא נזהר בה ולא מאכילה: שלח. לגבי שלוח הקן: תרתי זמני. ואנן תנן ט) שלחה וחזרה שלחה וחזרה אפי' ארבע וה' פעמים חייב: לדבר הרשות. שאין צריך לצפור אלא לאוכלה: לדבר מצוה מנין. היה צריך לטהר בו את המצורע מנין שאסור בא"ם על הבנים ת"ל תשלח: עזב תעזוב. פריקה: הקם תקים. טעינה: חסרון כיס. שהבהמה מתקלקלת: משום דבשכר. שנותנין לו שכר דאיכא למ"ד לקמן (דף לב.) טעינה בשכר פריקה בחנם: לא מסיימי קראי. הי משמע טעינה והי משמע פריקה ואי כתב חדא הוה אמינא לפריקה אתא אבל טעינה לא כתב רחמנא אידך לטעינה: למה לי למכתב אבידה. השבת אבידה לכתוב או הא או הא וליגמר מניה דהא כולהו אזהרות ממון ישראל הוא: צערא דמרה. הוא העומד שם ואין יכול לטעון לבדו וכן לפרוק: דליתא למרה בהדה. שיטרח בהשבתה: דאיתיה

---

**תוספות**

קורדום בצד גדר. פירשתי לעיל (כה: סד"ה ואם נטל):

למה לי למכתב רחמנא פריקה כו'. אין לפרש למה לי דכתב כוליה קרא דפריקה או דטעינה דא"כ היכי קאמר אי אשמועינן טעינה דבשכר הא משמע לקמן (דף לב.) דטעינה לא הוי בשכר אלא משום דנכתב פריקה ועוד דלא שייכא הך צריכותא אלא לקמן אלא י"ל למה לי דכתב רחמנא יתורא דמרבינן אין בעליו עמו בפריקה ולמה לי דכתב בטעינה:

לרבי שמעון לא מסיימי קראי. תימה דלקמן (דף לב.) משמע דקרא דנופלים בדרך לא מסיים לר"ש דהוי בטעינה דטעונייהו עלייהו משמע ואי לא כתב אלא חד הוה מוקמי ליה בפריקה אבל קרא דרובץ תחת משאו לא משמע לכ"ע אלא בפריקה וכשנכתבו שניהם ע"כ גם לר"ש קרא דנופלים בדרך הוי בטעינה וא"כ לר"ש לא יכתוב אלא חד יתורא לאין בעליו עמו בקרא דנופלים בדרך וי"ל דרובץ תחת משאו נמי לא מסיים לר"ש דאפשר למשמע בטעינה דע"י שאין הרבה בני אדם לטעון מכביד המשוי על הבהמה ורובצת ולקמן לא אצטריך למימר דלא מסיימי אלא אקרא דנופלים בדרך והא דפריך לקמן (דף לב:) והא וחדלת בפריקה הוא דכתיב לא הוי אלא אליבא דרבנן דלר"ש מצי למהוי בטעינה:

אבל

---



**ליקוטי רש"י**

אסרטיא. מסילה הולכין בה מעיר לעיר [שבת ו.]. יגיד עליו ריעו. ונלמד משנה חבירתה [ע"ז עו.]. ברא. שדה [קדושין א:]. מתא. עיר [שבת מה: ועוד]. מסקבא. אשי"ר בלע"ז [יבמות כ:] (וראה לעיל כז:). השב. השבה מעלייתא משמע. לגינתו לחורבתו מנין. דסגי יה למוצא בהשבתו לגינתן דבעלים [ב"ק נז.].

**רבינו חננאל**

איסטרטא. אמר רבה אמר קרא לכל אבידת אחיך לרבות אבידת קרקע: ותני רישא רועים בדרך אינה אבידה הא רצים בדרך ורועים בכרמים אבידה היא. וקתני סיפא רצה בכרמים הרי זו אבידה הא רועים אינה אבידה קשיא רישא אסיפא. ופריק רבא הכי רצה ופניה כלפי השדה אבידה היא וחייב להחזיר. רצה ופניה כלפי המדינה אינה אבידה. רועה בדרך אפי' רועה בכרמים אינה אבידה אבל יש בה אבידת קרקע שאוכלת הזמורות ומפסדת הכרם והאי דקתני רצה בין הכרמים הויא אבידה באבידת גופה כי בריצתה מכין אותה זמורות הכרם ועושין בה חבורות וזהו פי' מסתקבא כי סיקוב זה לשון חבורה הוא. א) והא דתניא רועה בכרמים אינה אבידה בכרמי כותי' אבידת קרקע ליכא דהא קרקע כותים הוא. אבידת גופה ליכא דהא רועים מעט מעט והילוכם בניחותא ואין סיקוב. השב אפי' ק' פעמים תשיבם אפי' לגינתו ולחרבתו דיו. אמר ר"א הכל צריכין דעת [בעלים] חוץ מהשב אבידה (לבעלים) שהרי ריבתה התורה בה השבות הרבה. וכן שלח תשלח את האם חייב לשלחה אפי' ק' פעמים ואפי' צריך לה לדבר מצוה כגון טהרת מצורע וכיוצא בו אפי' הכי חייב לשלח האם וכן דין הוכח תוכיח אפי' ק' פעמים ואפי' תלמיד לרב. וכן דין עזוב תעזוב וכן הקם תקים בין בעליו עמו בין אין בעליו עמו וכן

**חשק שלמה על ר"ח**

א) עי' לעיל ד' כ"ז ע"ב כד' רבינו גבי הא דאמרי' שם משום דמסקב לי' למרא.

---

**עין משפט נר מצוה**

קנד א ב מיי' פט"ו מהל' אבידה הלכה ג ה סמג עשין עד טוש"ע ח"מ סי' רס סעיף י:
קנה ג ד מיי' שם פי"א הלכה כ סמג שם טוש"ע ח"מ סי' רנט סעיף ט:
קנו ה ו ז ח מיי' פט"ו שם הל' ג ד סמג שם טוש"ע ח"מ סי' רסא סעיף ג:
קנז ט י מיי' שם פי"א הל' יד טו סמג שם טוש"ע ח"מ סי' רסז סעיף א:
קנח כ מיי' פ"ד מהל' גניבה הל' י ועיין בהשגות ובמ"מ ופ"א מהל' גזילה הל' ח סמג עשין עא טוש"ע ח"מ סי' שנה סעיף א:
קנט ל מיי' פי"א מהל' אבידה הל' טז סמג עשין עד טוש"ע ח"מ סי' רסז סעיף א:
קס מ מיי' פי"ג מהל' שחיטה הל' ה סמג עשין סה טוש"ע י"ד סי' רלב סעיף ה:
קסא נ מיי' שם הל' יט:
קסב ס ע מיי' פ"ו מהל' דיעות הל' ז סמג עשין יא:
קסג פ צ מיי' פי"ג מהל' רוצח הל' ח סמג עשין פא טוש"ע ח"מ סי' רעב סעיף ז:

**הגהות הגר"א**

[א] גמ' ופרה רועה בין הכרמים. נ"ב העשבים וכ"ה בר"ף וש"פ (ועמ"ש רבינו בח"מ סי' רס"א ס"ק ה):

**תורה אור השלם**

א) וְכֵן תַּעֲשֶׂה לַחֲמֹרוֹ וְכֵן תַּעֲשֶׂה לְשִׂמְלָתוֹ וְכֵן תַּעֲשֶׂה לְכָל אֲבֵדַת אָחִיךָ אֲשֶׁר תֹּאבַד מִמֶּנּוּ וּמְצָאתָהּ לֹא תוּכַל לְהִתְעַלֵּם: [דברים כב, ג]
ב) יַגִּיד עָלָיו רֵעוֹ מִקְנֶה אַף עַל עוֹלֶה: [איוב לו, לג]
ג) שַׁלֵּחַ תְּשַׁלַּח אֶת הָאֵם וְאֶת הַבָּנִים תִּקַּח לָךְ לְמַעַן יִיטַב לָךְ וְהַאֲרַכְתָּ יָמִים: [דברים כב, ז]
ד) לֹא תִשְׂנָא אֶת אָחִיךָ בִּלְבָבֶךָ הוֹכֵחַ תּוֹכִיחַ אֶת עֲמִיתֶךָ וְלֹא תִשָּׂא עָלָיו חֵטְא: [ויקרא יט, יז]
ה) כִּי תִרְאֶה חֲמוֹר שֹׂנַאֲךָ רֹבֵץ תַּחַת מַשָּׂאוֹ וְחָדַלְתָּ מֵעֲזֹב לוֹ עָזֹב תַּעֲזֹב עִמּוֹ: [שמות כג, ה]
ו) לֹא תִרְאֶה אֶת חֲמוֹר אָחִיךָ אוֹ שׁוֹרוֹ נֹפְלִים בַּדֶּרֶךְ וְהִתְעַלַּמְתָּ מֵהֶם הָקֵם תָּקִים עִמּוֹ: [דברים כב, ד]

ITS GEAR OVERTURNED, וּפָרָה רָצָה בֵּין הַכְּרָמִים – OR A COW RUNNING THROUGH THE VINEYARDS, הֲרֵי זוֹ אֲבֵידָה – THIS IS indeed A LOST OBJECT. רָצָה בֵּין הַכְּרָמִים הוּא דְּהַוְיָא אֲבֵידָה – Seemingly, then, it is only when **[the animal] is running through the vineyards, that it is** viewed as a **lost object.** הָא רָצָה בַּדֶּרֶךְ וְרוֹעָה בֵּין הַכְּרָמִים – **However,** if it was **running along the road, or grazing in the vineyards,** in which cases the animal is safer, אֵין זוֹ אֲבֵידָה – **it is not** viewed as a **lost object!** How can these clauses of the Mishnah be reconciled?

The Gemara offers a resolution:

אָמַר אַבַּיֵי – **Abaye said:** "יַגִּיד עָלָיו רֵעוֹ" – ***The thunder will tell about it;***[9] i.e. one case will shed light upon the other case. תָּנָא רוֹעָה בַּדֶּרֶךְ דְּלֹא הַוְיָא אֲבֵידָה – **[The Mishnah] taught** that an animal **grazing by the road is not** considered **a lost object,** וְהוּא הַדִּין לְרוֹעָה בֵּין הַכְּרָמִים – **and the same is true if it is grazing in the vineyards.** תָּנָא רָצָה בֵּין הַכְּרָמִים דְּהַוְיָא אֲבֵידָה – **And [the Mishnah] taught** that an animal **running through the vineyards is** considered **a lost object,** וְהוּא הַדִּין לְרָצָה בַּדֶּרֶךְ – **and the same is true if it is running in the road.** In other words, if the animal is grazing it is never assumed to be lost, and if it is running it is always assumed to be lost.[10]

Rava objects to Abaye's reconciliation of the Mishnah:

אָמַר לֵיהּ רָבָא – **Rava said to [Abaye]:** "אִי "יַגִּיד עָלָיו רֵעוֹ – **If** the Mishnah is truly employing the principle of ***the thunder will tell about it*** (that one case is taught to shed light on another that was not taught), לִיתְנֵי קִילְתָא – then **let [the Mishnah] teach** the **less extreme** cases, וְכָל שֶׁכֵּן חֲמִירְתָא – **and** from there, we will **certainly** infer the law concerning **the more extreme** cases![11] That is, לִיתְנֵי רָצָה בַּדֶּרֶךְ דְּהַוְיָא אֲבֵידָה – **let [the Mishnah] teach** that an animal **running by the road is** considered **a lost object,** וְכָל שֶׁכֵּן רָצָה בֵּין הַכְּרָמִים – **and** it will be understood that, **certainly,** if it is **running in the vineyards** it is considered lost. וְלִתְנֵי רוֹעָה בֵּין הַכְּרָמִים דְּלֹא הַוְיָא אֲבֵידָה – **And,** similarly, **let [the Mishnah] teach** that an animal **grazing in the vineyards is not** considered **a lost object,** וְכָל שֶׁכֵּן רוֹעָה בַּדֶּרֶךְ – **and** it will be understood that, **certainly,** if it is **grazing by the road** it is not considered lost. Since, however, the Mishnah did not follow this pattern, it is evident that Abaye's resolution is incorrect.

Rava thus offers a different way of reconciling the Mishnah's clauses:

אֶלָּא אָמַר רָבָא – **Rather, said Rava:** רָצָה אַרָצָה לֹא קַשְׁיָא – As for the contradictory implications about an animal that is **running, there is no difficulty,**[12] for in fact, there are times that an animal running on the road is considered lost, and there are times in which it is not. הָא דְּאַפָּהּ לְגַבֵּי דַּבְרָא – When the Mishnah implies that it *is* a lost object, **this** is speaking of a case **in which [the running animal] is headed towards the wilderness,** away from its owner. הָא דְּאַפָּהּ לְגַבֵּי מָתָא – When, however, the Mishnah implies that it is *not* a lost object, **this** is speaking of a case **in which [the running animal] is headed towards the city,** the place where its owner lives.

Rava continues:

רוֹעָה אַרוֹעָה נַמִּי לֹא קַשְׁיָא – Similarly, with respect to the contradictory implications about an animal that is **grazing, there is also no difficulty.** כָּאן בַּאֲבֵידַת גּוּפָהּ – **Here,** where the Mishnah implies that an animal grazing in vineyards is not assumed lost, the Tanna is referring **to the loss of** the animal **itself;** כָּאן בַּאֲבֵידַת קַרְקַע – whereas **here,** where the Mishnah implies the opposite, the Tanna is referring **to the loss of** the **land,** i.e. the damage the animal causes to the vineyards. To explain further: כִּי קָתָנֵי רוֹעָה בַּדֶּרֶךְ לֹא הַוְיָא אֲבֵידָה – **When [the Mishnah] taught** that an animal **grazing by the road** does **not** represent a case of **a lost object,** הָא רוֹעָה בֵּין הַכְּרָמִים הַוְיָא אֲבֵידָה – **implying** that one **grazing in the vineyards does** represent **a lost object,** בַּאֲבֵידַת קַרְקַע – this is referring **to the loss of** the **land.** That is, the Mishnah implies that the *vineyard* will suffer from the animal's presence and, therefore, one must retrieve an animal he finds grazing there.[13] וְכִי קָתָנֵי רָצָה בֵּין הַכְּרָמִים הַוְיָא אֲבֵידָה – **When, however, [the Mishnah] taught** that an animal **running through the vineyards is** considered **a lost object,** הָא רוֹעָה בֵּין הַכְּרָמִים לֹא הַוְיָא אֲבֵידָה – **implying** that one **grazing in the vineyards is not a lost object,** בַּאֲבֵידַת גּוּפָהּ – this is referring **to the loss of** the animal **itself.** That is, the Mishnah implies that one should not view an animal grazing in vineyards as being there without its owner's knowledge since the *animal itself* is not in danger there; דְּרָצָה בֵּין הַכְּרָמִים מִסַּקְּבָא – **for** only if it is **running through the vineyards will [the animal] become injured,** וְרוֹעָה בֵּין הַכְּרָמִים לֹא מִסַּקְּבָא – **but** if it is simply **grazing in the vineyards it will not become injured.**[14]

The Gemara questions Rava's explanation of this last point:

וְרוֹעָה בֵּין הַכְּרָמִים – **But** when the animal is **grazing in the vineyards,** נְהִי דְּלֹא מִסַּקְּבָא – **granted** that **it will not become injured;** תֵּיפוֹק לֵיהּ מִשּׁוּם אֲבֵידַת קַרְקַע – still, **you should derive** that the finder must remove it from the vineyard, **because of the** consideration of **loss to the land!**[15] – ? –

The Gemara answers:

בִּדְכוּתִי – In this second clause, the Mishnah is referring to a case **in which** the vineyard **belongs to a Cuthite,** i.e. an idolater, and

NOTES

it is by the road, not among the vineyards. In the fourth case, the animal is safe insofar as it is grazing, not running, but it is unsafe in the sense that it may be injured by thorns in the vineyards (*Rashi*).

9. *Job* 36:33. In the context of the verse, these words mean that the sound of thunder will indicate that it is raining.

10. The question arises how Abaye knew to make this inference from the Mishnah rather than its opposite – that an animal situated by the road is never considered lost, and one situated in the vineyards is always considered lost. See *Maharam Shif*, who offers a resolution to this difficulty.

11. A Tanna would generally prefer to teach a law of greater novelty rather than one of lesser novelty. Hence, Rava asserts, if it were truly so that a grazing animal is *never* assumed lost while a running animal is *always* assumed lost, the Mishnah should have worded its rulings to convey the full extent of these teachings. That is, the Mishnah should have taught that a grazing animal should be left alone even if it is in a vineyard, and a running animal should be retrieved even if it is traveling along the road.

12. Literally: *running on running, there is no difficulty.* The first clause of the Mishnah implied that an animal running by the road is assumed to be lost, whereas the second clause implied that it is assumed to be there with its owner's knowledge (see Gemara above). Rava contends that the two clauses do not contradict each other since each of the implied laws is true under *some* conditions.

13. In this case, it is the vineyard – not the animal – that is considered the lost object. The Tanna maintains that the "finder" must save the vineyard by removing the animal from it, in accordance with Rava's ruling above that one must prevent loss of land (*Pilpula Charifta* אות נ׳).

14. Each clause of the Mishnah thus teaches a separate law about an animal grazing in the vineyard. The first clause teaches that the *vineyard* itself is deemed a "lost object," for it stands to suffer damage from the grazing animal's presence. The second clause, however, teaches that the *animal* is not presumed to be lost, since grazing in the vineyard will cause it no harm (and, thus, there is no reason to believe that the animal's owner is unaware of its presence there).

15. According to Rava, the Mishnah's second clause implied that one who finds an animal grazing in a vineyard need not retrieve it, for since the animal is not in danger, there is no reason to assume its owner is unaware of its whereabouts. The Gemara, however, points out that although the animal will not become injured by grazing in the vineyard, Rava would surely concede that the vineyard will become damaged by

**א** באסרטיא ופרה רצה בין הכרמים הרי זו אבידה **ב** טלית בצד גדר קרדום בצד גדר ופרה רועה בין **[א]** הכרמים אין זו אבידה ג' ימים זה אחר זה הרי זו אבידה **ג** ראה מים ששוטפין ובאין הרי זה גודר בפניהם אמר רבא א) לכל אבידת אחיך **ד** לרבות אבידת קרקע א"ל רב חנניה לרבא תניא דמסייע לך ראה מים ששוטפין ובאין הרי זה גודר בפניהם א"ל אי משום הא לא תסייעי הכא במאי עסקינן בדאיכא עומרין אי דאיכא עומרין מאי למימרא לא צריכא דאית בה עומרין דצריכי לארעא מהו דתימא כיון דצריכי לארעא כי גופה דארעא דמיין קמ"ל: מצא חמור ופרה [וכו']: הא גופה קשיא אמרת מצא חמור ופרה רועין בדרך אין זו אבידה רועין בדרך הוא דלא הוו אבידה הא רצה בדרך ורועה בין הכרמים הויא אבידה אימא סיפא חמור וכליו הפוכים ופרה רצה בין הכרמים הרי זו אבידה רצה בין הכרמים הוא דהויא אבידה הא רצה בדרך ורועה בין הכרמים אין זו אבידה **ה)** אמר אביי ב) יגיד עליו ריעו תנא רועה בדרך דלא הויא אבידה והוא הדין לרועה בין הכרמים תנא רצה בין הכרמים דהויא אבידה והוא הדין לרצה בדרך א"ל רבא אי יגיד עליו ריעו ליתני קילתא וכ"ש חמירתא ליתני רצה בדרך דהויא אבידה וכ"ש רצה בין הכרמים ולתני רועה בין הכרמים דלא הויא אבידה וכ"ש רועה בדרך אלא אמר רבא רצה ארצה לא קשיא **ה** הא דאפה לגבי דברא הא דאפה לגבי מתא רועה ארועה נמי לא קשיא כאן באבידת גופה כאן באבידת קרקע **ו** כי קתני רועה בדרך לא הויא אבידה הא רועה בין הכרמים הויא אבידה באבידת קרקע וכי קתני רצה בין הכרמים הויא אבידה הא רועה בין הכרמים לא הויא אבידה באבידת גופה דרצה בין הכרמים **ט)** מסקבא ורועה בין הכרמים לא מסקבא ורועה בין הכרמים נהי דלא מסקבא תיפוק ליה משום אבידת קרקע **ז** בדכותי ותיפוק ליה משום אבידת גופה דדלמא קטלו לה **ח** באתרא דמתרו והדר קטלי ודלמא אתרו בה אי אתרו בה **ג)** ולא אזדהרו בה ודאי אבידה מדעת היא: החזירה וברחה החזירה וברחה [וכו']: א"ל ההוא מדרבנן לרבא אימא השב חדא זמנא תשיבם תרי זמני א"ל **ד)** השב אפי' ק' פעמים משמע **ה)** תשיבם **ט** אין לי אלא לביתו לגינתו ולחורבתו מנין ת"ל תשיבם מ"מ ה"ד אי דמינטרא פשיטא אי דלא מינטרא אמאי לעולם **י** דמינטרא והא קמ"ל דלא בעינן דעת בעלים וכדר' אלעזר **ו)** דאמר **כ** הכל צריכין דעת בעלים **ל** חוץ מהשבת אבידה שהתורה ריבתה השבות הרבה **ג)** שלח תשלח **ז)** אימא שלח חדא זימנא תשלח תרי זמני א"ל שלח **מ** אפי' מאה פעמים משמע תשלח אין לי אלא לדבר הרשות **נ** לדבר מצוה מנין ת"ל תשלח מ"מ א"ל ההוא מדרבנן לרבא ואימא **ד)** הוכח חדא זימנא תוכיח תרי זמני א"ל **ס** הוכח אפי' ק' פעמים משמע תוכיח אין לי אלא הרב לתלמיד תלמיד לרב מנין ת"ל הוכח תוכיח **ע** מ"מ **ה)** עזוב תעזוב עמו אין לי אלא בעליו עמו שאין בעליו עמו מנין ת"ל עזב תעזוב **פ** מ"מ **ו)** הקם תקים עמו אין לי אלא בעליו עמו שאין בעליו עמו מנין ת"ל הקם תקים **צ** מ"מ ולמה ליה למכתב פריקה ולמה ליה למיכתב טעינה צריכי דאי כתב רחמנא פריקה הוה אמינא משום דאיכא צער בעלי חיים ואיכא חסרון כיס אבל טעינה דלאו צער בעלי חיים איכא ולא חסרון כיס איכא אימא לא ואי אשמעינן טעינה משום דבשכר אבל פריקה דבחנם אימא לא צריכא ולר"ש **ק)** דאמר אף טעינה בחנם מאי איכא למימר לר"ש לא מסיימי קראי למה לי למכתב הני תרתי ולמה לי למכתב אבידה צריכי דאי כתב רחמנא הני תרתי משום דצערא דמרה איתא וצערא דידה איתא אבל אבידה דצערא דמרה איתא וצערא דידה ליתא אימא לא ואי אשמעינן אבידה משום דליתא למרה בהדה אבל

---

**רש"י**

**אסרטיא.** דרך כבושה לרבים: **ששוטפין ובאין.** לשדה חבירו: **אמר רבא לכל אבידת כו'.** מילתא באפיה נפשיה היא דאמרה רבא בבי מדרשא: **מאי למימרא.** ותיפוק ליה משום עומרין שישנן בכלל אבידה דדמו לפרעת דשה ושלמה ולמה לי לכל לרבוינהו: **רועה בדרך.** איכא תרתי למעליותא חדא דרועה ועוד דאפילו רצה לא מסתקבא רצה בין הכרמים איכא תרתי לגריעותא חדא דרצה ועוד דכרמים מסקבי לה רצה בדרך איכא חדא לגריעותא דרצה ומתקלקלת בריצתה אי נמי תלך למרחקים רועה בין הכרמים חדא לגריעותא דזימנין דמסתקבא: **והא באבידת גופה כו'.** מפרש ואזיל לה: **באבידת קרקע.** וחייב להוציאה משום הפסד כרמים: **לגינתו ולחורבתו מנין.** דהויא השבה ופטור: **דעת בעלים.** לומר לו שמור פרתך שהחזרתיה לגינתך שמלאכתיה אובדת: **הכל צריך דעת בעלים.** גנב גזלן וד' שומרים שהשיבו צריכין להודיעו ואם לא הודיעו ומתה או נגנבה חייבים באחריותן דכיון דידע שאבדה ולא ידע שהושבה לא מזהר בה ולא מאכילה: **שלח.** לגבי שלוח הקן: **תרתי זמני.** ואנן תנן ט) שלחה וחזרה שלחה וחזרה אפי' ארבע וה' פעמים חייב: **לדבר הרשות.** שאין צריך לכפור אלא לאוכלה: **לדבר מצוה מנין.** היה צריך לטהר בו את המצורע מנין שאסור באם על הבנים ת"ל תשלח: **עזוב תעזוב.** פריקה: **הקם תקים.** טעינה: **חסרון כיס.** שהבהמה מתקלקלת: **משום דבשכר.** שנותנין לו שכר דאיכא למ"ד לקמן (דף לב.) טעינה בשכר פריקה בחנם: **לא מסיימי קראי.** הי משמע טעינה והי משמע פריקה ואי כתב חדא הוה אמינא לפריקה אתא אבל טעינה לא כתב רחמנא אידך לטעינה: **למה לי למכתב אבידה.** השבת אבידה לכתוב או הא או הא וליגמר מניה דהא כולהו אזהרות ממון ישראל הוא: **צערא דמרה.** הוא העומד שם ואין יכול לטעון לבדו וכן לפרוק: **דליתא למרה בהדה.** שיטרח בהשבתה:

דאיתיה

---

**תוספות**

**קורדום** בצד גדר. פירשתי לעיל (כה: סד"ה ואם נטל):

**למה** לי למכתב רחמנא פריקה כו'. אין לפרש למה לי דכתב כוליה קרא דפריקה או דטעינה דא"כ היכי קאמר אי אשמועינן טעינה דבשכר הא משמע לקמן (דף לב.) דטעינה לא הוי בשכר אלא משום דנכתב פריקה ועוד דלא שייכא הך צריכותא אלא לקמן אלא י"ל למה לי דכתב רחמנא יתורא דמרבינן אין בעליו עמו בפריקה ולמה לי דכתב בטעינה:

**לרבי** שמעון לא מסיימי קראי. תימה דלקמן (דף לב.) משמע דקרא דנופלים בדרך לא מסיים לר"ש דהוי בטעינה דטעונייהו עלייהו משמע ואי לא כתב אלא חד הוה מוקמי ליה בפריקה אבל קרא דרובץ תחת משאו לא משמע לכ"ע אלא בפריקה וכשנכתבו שניהם ע"כ גם לר"ש קרא דנופלים בדרך הוי בטעינה וא"כ לר"ש לא יכתוב אלא חד יתורא לאין בעליו עמו בקרא דנופלים בדרך וי"ל דרובץ תחת משאו נמי לא מסיים לר"ש דאפשר למשמע בטעינה דע"י שאין הרבה בני אדם לטעון מכביד המשוי על הבהמה ורובצת ולקמן לא אצטריך למימר דלא מסיימי אלא אקרא דנופלים בדרך והא דפריך לקמן (דף לב:) והא וחדלת בפריקה הוא דכתיב לא הוי אלא אליבא דרבנן דלר"ש מצי למהוי בטעינה:

אבל

---

**מסורת הש"ס**

א) [יבמות לא:, וש"נ], ב) [פירוש עושה בה בורה, ערוך ערך סקב], ג) נ"ל ולא איהדרו בה, הר"ס, ד) חולין פז., ה) [בבא קמא נז., ו) [בבא מציעא שם], ז) חולין קמא., ח) [לקמן לב.], ט) [בחולין קמא.].

**ליקוטי רש"י**

**אסרטיא.** מסילה שהולכין בה מעיר לעיר [שבת ו.]. **יגיד עליו ריעו.** ונלמד משנה מחבירתה [ע"ז עו.]. **דברא.** שדה [קדושין א:]. **מתא.** עיר [שבת מה: ועוד]. **מסקבא.** אשי"ר בלע"ז [יבמות כ:] (וראה לעיל כז:). **תשיבם.** השבה מעלייתא משמע. **לגינתו ולחורבתו מנין.** דסגי ליה למוצא בהשבתו לגינתן דבעלים [ב"ק נז.].

**רבינו חננאל**

אסטרטא. אמר רבא אמר קרא לכל אבידת אחיך לרבות אבידת קרקע: קתני רישא רועים בדרך אינה אבידה הא רצים בדרך ורועים בכרמים אבידה היא. וקתני סיפא רצה בכרמים הרי זו אבידה הא רועים אינה אבידה קשיא רישא אסיפא. ופריק רבא הכי רצה ופניה כלפי השדה אבידה היא וחייב להחזיר. רצה ופניה כלפי המדינה אינה אבידה. רועה בדרך אפי' רועה בכרמים אינה אבידה אבל יש בה אבידת קרקע שאוכלת הזמורות ומפסדת הכרם והאי דקתני רצה בין הכרמים הויא אבידה באבידת גופה כי בריצתה מכין אותה זמורות הכרם ועושין בה חבורות וזהו אפי' מסתקבא כי סיקוב זה לשון חבורה הוא. א) והא דתניא רועה בכרמים אינה אבידה בכרמי כותי' אבידת קרקע ליכא דהא קרקע כותים הוא. אבידת גופה ליכא דהא רועים מעט מעט והילוכם בניחותא ואין סיקוב. השב אפי' ק' פעמים תשיבם אפי' לגינתו ולחרבתו דיו. אמר ר"א הכל צריכין דעת [בעלים] חוץ מהשב אבידה (לבעלים) שהרי ריבתה התורה בה השבות הרבה. וכן שלח תשלח את האם חייב לשלחה אפי' ק' פעמים ואפי' צריך לה לדבר מצוה כגון טהרת מצורע וכיוצא בו אפי' הכי חייב לשלח האם וכן דין הוכח תוכיח אפי' ק' פעמים ואפי' תלמיד לרב. וכן דין עזוב תעזוב וכן הקם תקים בין בעליו עמו בין אין בעליו עמו

וכן

**חשק שלמה על ר"ח**

א) עי' לעיל ד' כ"ז ע"ב בד' רבינו גבי הא דאמרי' שם משום דמסקב לי' לחמרא.

---

**עין משפט נר מצוה**

קנד א ב מיי' פט"ו מהל' אבידה הלכה ג ה סמג עשין עד טוש"ע ח"מ סי' רס סעיף י:

קנה ג ד מיי' שם פי"א הלכה כ סמג שם טוש"ע ח"מ סי' רנט סעיף ט:

קנו ה ו ז ח מיי' פט"ו שם הל' ג ד סמג שם טוש"ע ח"מ סי' רפא סעיף ב:

קנז ט י מיי' שם פי"א הל' יד טו סמג שם טוש"ע ח"מ סי' רסז סעיף א:

קנח כ מיי' פ"ד מהל' גניבה הל' י ועיין בהשגות ובמ"מ ופ"א מהל' גזילה הל' ח סמג עשין עא טוש"ע ח"מ סי' שנה סעיף א:

קנט ל מיי' פי"א מהל' אבידה הל' טז סמג עשין עד טוש"ע ח"מ סי' רסז סעיף א:

קס מ מיי' פי"ג מהל' שחיטה הל' ה סמג עשין סה טוש"ע י"ד סי' רצב סעיף ה:

קסא נ מיי' שם הל' יט:

קסב ס ע מיי' פ"ו מהל' דיעות הל' ז סמג עשין יא:

קסג פ צ מיי' פי"ג מהל' רוצח הל' ח סמג עשין פא טוש"ע ח"מ סי' רעב סעיף ז:

**הגהות הגר"א**

[א] גמ' ופרה רועה בין הכרמים. נ"ב העשבים וכ"ה ברי"ף וש"פ (ועמ"ש רבינו בח"מ סי' רס"א ס"ק ה):

**תורה אור השלם**

א) וְכֵן תַּעֲשֶׂה לַחֲמֹרוֹ וְכֵן תַּעֲשֶׂה לְשִׂמְלָתוֹ וְכֵן תַּעֲשֶׂה לְכָל אֲבֵדַת אָחִיךָ אֲשֶׁר תֹּאבַד מִמֶּנּוּ וּמְצָאתָהּ לֹא תוּכַל לְהִתְעַלֵּם: [דברים כב, ג]

ב) יַגִּיד עָלָיו רֵעוֹ מִקְנֶה אַף עַל עוֹלֶה: [איוב לו, לג]

ג) שַׁלֵּחַ תְּשַׁלַּח אֶת הָאֵם וְאֶת הַבָּנִים תִּקַּח לָךְ לְמַעַן יִיטַב לָךְ וְהַאֲרַכְתָּ יָמִים: [דברים כב, ז]

ד) לֹא תִשְׂנָא אֶת אָחִיךָ בִּלְבָבֶךָ הוֹכֵחַ תּוֹכִיחַ אֶת עֲמִיתֶךָ וְלֹא תִשָּׂא עָלָיו חֵטְא: [ויקרא יט, יז]

ה) כִּי תִרְאֶה חֲמוֹר שֹׂנַאֲךָ רֹבֵץ תַּחַת מַשָּׂאוֹ וְחָדַלְתָּ מֵעֲזֹב לוֹ עָזֹב תַּעֲזֹב עִמּוֹ: [שמות כג, ה]

ו) לֹא תִרְאֶה אֶת חֲמוֹר אָחִיךָ אוֹ שׁוֹרוֹ נֹפְלִים בַּדֶּרֶךְ וְהִתְעַלַּמְתָּ מֵהֶם הָקֵם תָּקִים עִמּוֹ: [דברים כב, ד]

בְּאִסְרַטְיָא – IN A PUBLIC THOROUGHFARE, וּפָרָה רָצָה בֵּין הַכְּרָמִים – OR if he found A COW RUNNING THROUGH THE VINEYARDS, הֲרֵי זוֹ אֲבֵידָה – he may be sure that THIS IS A LOST OBJECT. טַלִּית בְּצַד גָּדֵר – If, however, he found A CLOAK BESIDE A FENCE, קַרְדּוֹם בְּצַד גָּדֵר – A HATCHET BESIDE A FENCE,[1] וּפָרָה רוֹעָה בֵּין הַכְּרָמִים – OR A COW GRAZING IN THE VINEYARDS,[2] אֵין זוֹ אֲבֵידָה – he may assume that THIS IS NOT A LOST OBJECT, for it is reasonably certain that the owner left the item there intentionally. Even in such cases, however, ג׳ יָמִים זֶה אַחַר זֶה – if one sighted the object in the same place for more than THREE CONSECUTIVE DAYS, הֲרֵי זוֹ אֲבֵידָה – then he should assume that THIS IS A LOST OBJECT.[3] רָאָה מַיִם שֶׁשּׁוֹטְפִין וּבָאִין – If ONE SAW FLOWING WATER THAT WAS ADVANCING towards his friend's field, threatening to flood it, הֲרֵי זֶה גּוֹדֵר בִּפְנֵיהֶם – HE SHOULD ERECT A WALL BEFORE [THE WATERS] to protect the field.

Rava sets forth a ruling:

אָמַר רָבָא – **Rava said:** לְכָל אֲבֵידַת אָחִיךָ – In reference to returning a lost item, the verse states: *And so you should do* **for any lost object of your brother.**[4] לְרַבּוֹת אֲבֵידַת קַרְקַע – This mention of "any" lost object comes **to include loss of land;** i.e. one must prevent his friend's land from becoming ruined, if it is in his power to do so.

An attempt is made to support Rava's ruling:

אָמַר לֵיהּ רַב חֲנַנְיָה לְרָבָא – **Rav Chananyah said to Rava:** תַּנְיָא דִּמְסַיֵּיעַ לָךְ – **A Baraisa that supports your** ruling **was taught** as follows: רָאָה מַיִם שֶׁשּׁוֹטְפִין וּבָאִין – If ONE SAW FLOWING WATER THAT WAS ADVANCING towards his friend's field, הֲרֵי זֶה גּוֹדֵר בִּפְנֵיהֶם – HE SHOULD ERECT A WALL BEFORE [THE WATERS] to protect the field. Evidently, then, another person's land is something one must endeavor to save.

Rava responds:

אָמַר לֵיהּ – **[Rava] said to him:** אִי מִשּׁוּם הָא – **If it is** only **because of this** that you subscribe to my position, you are mistaken; לָא תְּסַיְּיעֵי – **you cannot support [my ruling]** from this Baraisa, for one can argue that הָכָא בְּמַאי עַסְקִינַן בִּדְאִיכָּא עוֹמָרִין – **here,** in the Baraisa, **with what** case **are we dealing? With a case in which there are bundles** of wheat placed on the field. One must therefore erect a fence to protect the bundles, even if he need not do so for the field itself.

The Gemara challenges Rava's reply:

אִי דְּאִיכָּא עוֹמָרִין – **If there are bundles** of wheat on the field, מַאי לְמֵימְרָא – **what** need **would there be to** even **say** that he must protect them? Obviously, this is so, for these bundles fall into the general category of lost objects that must be returned![5] – ? –

The Gemara answers:

לֹא צְרִיכָא דְּאִית בָּהּ עוֹמָרִין דִּצְרִיכֵי לְאַרְעָא – **[The Baraisa's law] is necessary only** for a case **in which [the field] has in it bundles that** still **need the ground;** i.e. bunches of standing wheat that have been left rooted in the ground until they dry out completely.[6] מַהוּ דְּתֵימָא כֵּיוָן דִּצְרִיכֵי לְאַרְעָא – **You might have said** that **since they** still **need the ground** somewhat, כִּי גּוּפָהּ דְּאַרְעָא דָּמְיָין – **they are** considered **like the ground itself,** and there is no obligation to protect them. קָא מַשְׁמַע לָן – **[The Baraisa]** therefore **informs us** that such bundles are treated like ordinary movable objects, and one is indeed obligated to protect them.[7]

The Gemara now returns to analyze our Mishnah:

מָצָא חֲמוֹר וּפָרָה [וכו׳] – The Mishnah had stated: If ONE FOUND A DONKEY OR A COW [etc.] [grazing by the road, this is not considered a lost object. If, however, he found a donkey with its gear overturned, or a cow running through the vineyards, this is indeed a lost object].

The Gemara asks:

אָמְרַתְּ מָצָא הָא גּוּפָהּ קַשְׁיָא – **This** Mishnah **is self-contradictory!** חֲמוֹר וּפָרָה רוֹעִין בַּדֶּרֶךְ – First, **you said that if** ONE FOUND A DONKEY OR A COW GRAZING BY THE ROAD, אֵין זוֹ אֲבֵידָה – THIS IS NOT considered A LOST OBJECT, for most likely, the owner left it there intentionally to graze. רוֹעִין בַּדֶּרֶךְ הוּא דְּלָא הָווּ אֲבֵידָה – Apparently, then, it is only when **[animals] are grazing by the road that they are not** viewed as **lost objects.** הָא רָצָה בַּדֶּרֶךְ וְרוֹעָה בֵּין הַכְּרָמִים – **However,** if an animal was found **running by the road, or grazing in the vineyards,** in which cases it is less safe, הֲוְיָא אֲבֵידָה – it would seem that **it is** viewed as **a lost object.**[8] אֵימָא סֵיפָא – **But take note of the latter part** of the Mishnah: חֲמוֹר וְכֵלָיו הֲפוּכִים – If one found A DONKEY WITH

NOTES

1. The Baraisa speaks of a case in which the cloak or hatchet is lying in a safe, protected place. Alternatively, the particular fence next to which the items were found is a place workers would often leave their belongings when working in the fields. This being the case, the Baraisa rules that a finder should leave these items as he found them (*Tosafos* 25b ד״ה ואם נטל).

2. *Gra* in *Hagahos HaGra* suggests that the proper wording of our Baraisa is: . . . *a cow grazing in the grasses* (see also *Beur HaGra* to *Choshen Mishpat* 261:5). The Baraisa appears this way in earlier texts of *Rif* as well.

3. Seemingly, the three-day limit applies not only to the case of the grazing cow, but to the case of the cloak and hatchet as well. If such items remained next to the fence in the same place for more than three days, it can be assumed that their owner forgot he placed them there (*Rashba*, as cited by *Shitah Mekubetzes*; cf. *Rambam Hil. Aveidah* 15:5).

4. *Deuteronomy* 22:3. The verse in its entirety reads: וְכֵן תַּעֲשֶׂה לַחֲמֹרוֹ וְכֵן תַּעֲשֶׂה לְשִׂמְלָתוֹ וְכֵן תַּעֲשֶׂה לְכָל־אֲבֵדַת אָחִיךָ אֲשֶׁר־תֹּאבַד מִמֶּנּוּ וּמְצָאתָהּ לֹא תוּכַל לְהִתְעַלֵּם, *And so should you do for his donkey, and so should you do for his garment, and so should you do for any lost object of your brother that may be lost from him which you find; you are not able to hide.*

5. If there were bundles of wheat lying on the field, it would be obvious that one must save them from the approaching water. The verse (*Deuteronomy* 22:3) explicitly states that one must save from loss such items as a donkey or a garment belonging to another, and a bundle of wheat – also a type of movable object – should be no different (see *Rashi;* see also *Maharam Shif* who points out a difficulty with the final words of *Rashi's* explanation).

6. *Ritva*.

7. This argument concludes Rava's objection that his ruling cannot draw support from the Baraisa: The Baraisa could, in theory, be dealing with a case that involved protecting bundles of standing wheat, in which case there would be no proof that one is required to protect land alone. Rava's law, however, has not been disproven by the Baraisa, and, indeed, the more obvious reading of the Baraisa would seem to support it [the Baraisa does not actually mention bundles of wheat, and it seems to be saying that one must protect land alone] (*Ritva*).

Rava's ruling is accepted as law by the major halachic decisors (see *Rambam, Hil. Aveidah* 11:20, and *Shulchan Aruch, Choshen Mishpat* 259:9).

8. The general discussion of the Gemara deals with four possible cases:
(1) an animal that is grazing by the road;
(2) one that is running through the vineyards;
(3) one running along the road;
(4) one grazing in the vineyards.

The Mishnah specifically discusses cases (1) and (2), ruling in the first that the animal should be left alone and in the second that the animal can be presumed lost and should be returned. The Mishnah does not explicitly discuss cases (3) and (4).

In the first case, where the animal is grazing by the road, it is safe on two accounts: (a) It is walking, not running, so there is less of a possibility that it will injure itself or wander too far; and (b) it is situated in the road, not in the vineyards, where thorny vines could injure it. In the second case, by contrast, where the animal is running through the vineyards, it is unsafe on two accounts: (a) It is running; and (b) it is situated in a vineyard where it is likely to be injured. In the third and fourth cases, the animal is unsafe on one account and safe on another: In the third case, it is unsafe by virtue of the fact it is running, but it is safe in that

**Gemara** The Mishnah had stated that a donkey whose gear is overturned and a cow running through the vineyards are lost objects. Previous Mishnahs, however, had listed many types of lost objects besides these (utensils, money in a wallet, etc.). The Gemara therefore asks:

**אָטוּ כָּל הָנֵי דְּאַמְרִינַן לָאו אֲבֵידָה הֲווּ – Are then all these that we have mentioned** previously **not lost objects?** What is our Mishnah's intent in specifying the particular cases of the donkey and cow?

The Gemara clarifies the Mishnah's statement:

**אָמַר רַב יְהוּדָה – Rav Yehudah said: הָכִי קָאָמַר – This is what the Mishnah is saying: אֵי זוֹ הִיא כְּלָל אֲבֵידָה – What is the general guideline for** establishing when something is **a lost object, שֶׁהוּא חַיָּיב בָּהּ –** such that **one is obligated to** return **it** if he finds it?[28] **מָצָא חֲמוֹר וּפָרָה רוֹעִין בַּדֶּרֶךְ – If one found a donkey or cow grazing by the road, אֵין זוֹ אֲבֵידָה וְלֹא מִיחַיֵּיב בָּהּ – this is not** considered **a lost object, and [the finder] is not obligated to** return **it,** for it can be assumed that the owner left it there intentionally. **חֲמוֹר וְכֵלָיו הֲפוּכִים –** If, however, one found **a donkey with its gear overturned, פָּרָה וְרָצָה בֵּין הַכְּרָמִים –** or **a cow running through the vineyards, הֲרֵי זוֹ אֲבֵידָה וּמִיחַיֵּיב בָּהּ – this is** indeed considered **a lost object, and he is obligated to** return **it,** for it is evident that the owner did not leave it there intentionally. Likewise, any other object that falls into this general category has the same law.[29]

The Gemara now asks:

**וּלְעוֹלָם – And** is this so **forever?** If day in and day out, one sees an animal grazing by the road, should he still assume that the owner left it there intentionally?[30]

The Gemara answers:[31]

**אָמַר רַב יְהוּדָה אָמַר רַב – Rav Yehudah said in the name of Rav: עַד שְׁלֹשָׁה יָמִים – Until three days** he can assume the owner left it there; after three days he must assume the animal is lost.

The Gemara questions Rav Yehudah's answer:

**הֵיכִי דָּמֵי –** Now, **how is this? אִי בְּלֵילְוָתָא – If** one saw the animal grazing **during the night, אֲפִילוּ חֲדָא שַׁעְתָּא נַמִּי –** then if he saw it there **even for one moment,** it should **also** be considered lost. **אִי בִּימָמָא – If,** on the other hand, he saw it grazing **during the day, אֲפִילוּ טוּבָא נַמִּי לֹא –** then even if he saw it there for **more** than three days, it should **still not** be considered lost! In what case, then, did Rav Yehudah mean that three days is the time at which the animal should be viewed as lost?

The Gemara replies:

**לֹא צְרִיכָא –** The three-day standard **is only necessary** for a case in which **דַּהֲוָה חָזֵי לָהּ בְּקַדְמְתָא – [the finder]** consistently **saw it** grazing **early in the morning,** before the morning star rose, **וּבַחֲשֶׁכְתָּא – or at night,** after sunset. **תְּלָתָא יוֹמֵי אַמְרִינַן –** For **three days, we say: אִיתְרַמּוּיֵי אִתְרַמֵּי לָהּ וְנָפְקָא – It just happened** that **[the animal] went out** to graze at these unusual times. **טְפֵי –** But once the animal was seen at these times for **more** than three days, **וַדַּאי אֲבֵידָה הִיא –** we say **it is certainly a lost object,** and the finder must return it.

The Gemara cites a Baraisa that supports this idea of a three-day limit:

**תַּנְיָא נַמִּי הָכִי – It was taught similarly in a Baraisa: מָצָא טַלִּית וְקַרְדּוֹם –** If A PERSON FOUND A CLOAK OR A HATCHET

NOTES

28. That is, how can it be determined if a given item is truly lost (i.e. that the owner is unaware of its whereabouts)? (*Rashi*).

29. I.e. whenever circumstances indicate that an object's owner is unaware of its whereabouts, the object has the legal status of a lost item, and the finder is required to return it.

30. An owner does not leave his animal to graze indefinitely; at some point, he will bring it in to the stable (see *Rashi*).

31. See *Maharam Shif* ד״ה ולעולם.

לא יהיה בך אביון שלך קודם לשל כל אדם אלא לזקן ואינו לפי כבודו (א) אמר רבה א הכישה חייב בה אביי הוה יתיב קמיה דרבה חזא להנך עיזי דקיימו שקל קלא ושדא בהו א"ל איחייבת בהו קום אהדרינהו ב איבעיא להו דרכו להחזיר בשדה ואין דרכו להחזיר בעיר מהו מי אמרינן השבה מעליא בעינן וכיון דלאו דרכיה להחזיר בעיר לא לחייב או דלמא בשדה מיהת הוא דאיחייב ליה וכיון דאיחייב ליה בשדה איחייב ליה בעיר תיקו אמר רבא ג כל שבשלו מחזיר בשל חבירו נמי מחזיר ד וכל שבשלו פורק וטוען בשל חבירו נמי פורק וטוען רבי ישמעאל ברבי יוסי הוה קאזיל באורחא פגע ביה ההוא גברא הוה דרי פתכא דאופי אותבינהו וקא מיתפח א"ל דלי לי אמר ליה כמה שוין א"ל פלגא דזוזא יהיב ליה פלגא דזוזא ואפקרה הדר זכה בהו הדר יהיב ליה פלגא דזוזא ואפקרה חזייה דהוה קא בעי למיהדר למזכיה בהו א"ל לכולי עלמא אפקרנהו ולך לא אפקרנהו ומי הוי הפקר כי האי גוונא והתנן (ג) בש"א הפקר לעניים הפקר וב"ה אומרים ה אינו הפקר עד שיהא הפקר לעניים ולעשירים כשמיטה אלא רבי ישמעאל ברבי יוסי לכולי עלמא אפקרינהו ובמילתא בעלמא הוא דאוקמיה והא רבי ישמעאל ברבי יוסי זקן ואינו לפי כבודו הוה ר' ישמעאל ברבי יוסי (ג) ו לפנים משורת הדין הוא דעבד ז דתני רב יוסף (א) והודעת להם זה בית חייהם את הדרך זו גמילות חסדים [א] (ה) (אשר) ילכו זה ביקור חולים בה זו קבורה ואת המעשה זה הדין אשר יעשון זו לפנים משורת הדין: אמר מר [ב] (אשר) ילכו זה ביקור חולים היינו גמילות חסדים לא נצרכה אלא ז לבן גילו דאמר מר (י) בן גילו נוטל אחד מששים בחליו ואפי' הכי מבעי ליה למיזל לגביה בה זו קבורה היינו גמילות חסדים לא נצרכה אלא לזקן ואינו לפי כבודו אשר יעשון זו לפנים משורת הדין דאמר ר' יוחנן לא חרבה ירושלים אלא על שדנו בה דין תורה אלא דיני דמגיזתא לדיינו אלא אימא (י) שהעמידו דיניהם על דין תורה ולא עבדו לפנים משורת הדין: מתני' אי זו היא אבידה ח מצא חמור או פרה רועין בדרך אין זו אבידה חמור וכליו הפוכין פרה רצה בין הכרמים הרי זו אבידה ט החזירה וברחה החזירה וברחה אפי' ארבעה וחמשה פעמים חייב להחזירה שנאמר (ב) השב תשיבם י היה בטל מסלע לא יאמר לו תן לי סלע אלא נותן לו (א) שכרו כפועל (ה) כ אם יש שם בית דין מתנה בפני ב"ד ל אם אין שם ב"ד בפני מי יתנה שלו קודם: גמ' אטו כל הני דאמרינן לאו אבידה הוו אמר רב יהודה הכי קאמר אי זו היא כלל אבידה שהוא חייב בה מצא חמור ופרה רועין בדרך אין זו אבידה ולא מיחייב בה חמור וכליו הפוכים פרה ורצה בין הכרמים הרי זו אבידה ומיחייב בה (ט) ולעולם אמר רב יהודה עד שלשה ימים היכי דמי אי בלילותא אפי' חדא שעתא נמי אי בימממא אפי' טובא נמי לא מ לא צריכא דהוה חזי לה בקדמתא (י) ובחשכתא תלתא יומי אמרינן איתרמויי אתרמי לה ונפקא טפי ודאי אבידה היא תניא נמי הכי מצא טלית וקרדום באסרטיא

---

**רש"י**

לא יהיה בך אביון. לא תביא עצמך לידי עניות: הכישה. זה שאינו לפי כבודו אם הכישה הכאה אחת להשיבה נתחייב בה להחזירה הואיל והתחיל: קלא. מרט"א בלע"ז: דרכו להחזיר בשדה. שאין שם רואים כל כך ואינו בוש: ואין דרכו בעיר. שהוא בוש משכיניו והוא מצא בשדה: מהו. שיתחייב להשיבה: לא מיחייב. להתחיל בהשבתה בשדה: וכיון דאיחייב. שהזיזה ממקומה חייב אף בעיר: פורק וטוען. פורק משא מן החמור וטוען עליו דכתיב עזוב תעזוב הקם תקים: פתכא דאופי. משאוי של עצים: וקא מיתפח. עומד לנוח: דלי לי. הטעינני: הדר זכה בהו. חזר האיש ההוא והחזיק בהן מן ההפקר: הפקר לעניים הוי הפקר. אע"ג שלא הפקירו אלא לעניים הוי הפקר למפטר מן המעשר: זה בית חייהם. (ס) ללמוד להם אומנות להתפרנס בו חוקות (ג) ותורות כתיבי ברישיה דקרא: (ע) דיני דמגיזתא לידיינו. בתמיה. דמגיזתא גוזאי הדנין ביסורים ובחזקה ותבירו בבבא קמא (דף קיד.) דדייני בגזתיא: מתני' איזו היא אבידה. בגמרא מפרש: אין זו אבידה. ואינו חייב להחזיר שמדעת הניחוה שם: רצה בין הכרמים. דמסתקבא: לא יאמר לו תן לי סלע. שבטלתי ממלאכתי (ג) שיאמר לו אם עשית מלאכתך היית מרבה טורח עכשיו לפי מה שטרחת טול: כפועל. בגמרא מפרש: אם יש שם בית דין. אם נוח לו לטרוח יותר כדי להרבות שכר ואינו חפץ ליבטל ממלאכתו מה יעשה אם יש שם שלשה בני אדם יתנה בפניהם ויאמר ראו שאני משתכר כך וכך ואי איפשי ליבטל ליטול שכר מועט אני אשיב אם תאמרו שאטול שכר משלם: גמ' כלל. סתם אבידה שמוכחת שהיא שם שלא מדעת בעלים: ולעולם. בתמיה וכי אף אם ימצאנה שם לעולם נאמר מדעת היא וכי דרך שלא להכניס: בקדמותא. לפני עלות השחר: חשכתא. שחשכה ערבית:

אסרטיא

---

**תוספות**

ה"מ לא תעשה ועשה השוה בכל אבל הא דאינו שוה בכל דחי כדמוכח פרק שני נזירין (נזיר דף נח:) דאתי עשה דמצורע ודחי לאו ועשה דכהנים וכן ק' לקמן (לב.) יכול אמר לו אביו הטמא כו' ופריך תיפוק ליה דאין עשה דוחה לא תעשה ועשה הא גבי כהנים שאינו שוה בכל דחי וי"ל דעשה דמצורע שאני דחמיר משום דגדול השלום כדאמר בפ' שילוח הקן (חולין דף קמא.) (מ) דעשה דמצורע הוי דחי לאו ועשה דשילוח הקן אי לאו יתורא דשלח תשלח אבל עשה דעלמא לא דחי לאו ועשה אפילו אינו שוה בכל וזה התירוץ לא יתיישב למאן דשרי מצורע בימי חלוטו בתשמיש המטה פ"ק דמועד קטן (דף ז:) ולדידיה יש לומר דהכא סמיך על ותו מי דחינן איסורא מקמי ממונא ולקמן נמי עדיפא משני דהוה דחי אפילו לאו ועשה אי לאו קרא אפי' אי בעלמא לא דחי ובפ"ב דיבמות (דף כא.) דאמר גבי פלוגתא דר' יוחנן ור"א בביאת כ"ג באלמנה מן הנישואין כ"ע לא פליגי דלא פטרה דאין עשה דוחה לא תעשה ועשה וי"ל דחשיב שוה בכל כיון שהאלמנה עשתה איסור כמו הכהן דאקרי ביה לא יקח לא יקחו אע"ג דאין שוה בכל אלא בכהנים אבל ההיא דגילוח זקן שאינו שוה בנשים נדחי מקמי עשה דמצורע:

אלא לזקן ואינו לפי כבודו. וא"ת תיפוק ליה מולאחותו דכבוד הבריות דוחה מילת בנו ושחיטת פסחו וי"ל כבוד הבריות דמת מצוה חמיר טפי שמוטל בבזיון פן יסריח או יאכלוהו כלבים אע"ג דבפ' מי שמתו (ברכות דף כ. ושם ד"ה שב) מוכח דאי הוה כלאים שב ואל תעשה היה נדחה מפני כבוד הבריות היינו משום דערום הוי גנות ובזיון גדול כדאמר (יבמות דף סג:) אין לך משוקץ יותר מאותו שהוא מהלך ערום ומהכא לא ידעי' דדחי אלא ממונא אבל איסורא כמו פסח ומילה וגם כרת לא: [וע' תוס' שבועות ל: ד"ה אבל]:

אפקרה. שלא יכשלו בני אדם בלא תגזול וא"ת הא אמר בפ' אין בין המודר (נדרים דף מה.) אין הפקר אלא בפני שלשה וי"ל דהכא נמי הוו שלשה אי נמי דאורייתא בלא שלשה נמי הוי הפקר והא דאמר שלהי פ"ק דשבת (דף יח: ושם ד"ה דמפקרא) גיגית נר וקדירה אפקורי מפקר להו אע"ג דליכא שלשה התם אנן סהדי דמפקר להו בלבו שלא יעשה איסור שביתת כלים:

לא חרבה כו'. ואם תאמר דביומא (דף ט:) אמר מפני שנאת חנם וי"ל דהא והא גרמא:

איזוהי אבידה. שיכן שאין הבעלים יודעין שהיא שם:

קורדוס

---

עין משפט נר מצוה

קמד א ב מיי' פי"א מהל' גזילה ואבידה הל' יג יד סמג עשין עד טוש"ע ח"מ סי' רסג סעיף ב:

קמה ג מיי' שם הל' יג טוש"ע שם סעיף א:

קמו ד מיי' פי"ג מהל' רוצח הל' ד סמג עשין פא טוש"ע ח"מ סי' רעב סעיף ג:

קמז ה מיי' פ"ב מהל' נדרים הלכה טו טוש"ע ח"מ סי' רעג סעיף ה:

קמח ו מיי' פי"א מהל' אבידה הלכה יז ופי"ג מהל' רוצח הל' ד סמג עשין עד פא טוש"ע ח"מ סי' רסג סעיף ג וסי' רעב סעיף ג:

קמט ז מיי' פי"ד מהל' אבילות הלכה ד סמג עשין ב טוש"ע י"ד סי' שלה סעיף ב:

קנ ח מיי' פט"ו מהל' אבידה הל' ב סמג עשין עד טוש"ע ח"מ סי' רסא סעיף א:

קנא ט מיי' שם פי"א הל' יד סמג שם טוש"ע ח"מ סי' רסו סעיף ב:

קנב י כ ל מיי' שם פי"ב הל' ד סמג שם טוש"ע ח"מ סי' רסה:

קנג מ מיי' שם פט"ו הלכה ג סמג שם טוש"ע ח"מ סי' רסא סעיף א:

**רבינו חננאל**

והיא בבית הקברות לא צריכא מאי טעמא דהא כהן מוזהר בטומאה עשה ולא תעשה עשה שנאמר וקדשתו קדשים יהיו לאלהיהם לא תעשה שנאמר לנפש לא יטמא בעמיו והשבת אבידה עשה היא שנאמר השב תשיבם לאחי' ולא אתי עשה ודחי את לא תעשה ועשה ותוב לא דחינן איסורא מקמי ממונא. שלו מרובה משל חבירו שנאמר אפס כי לא יהיה בך אביון שלך קודם לשל כל אדם. אמר רבא כל שבשלו מחזיר בשל חבירו נמי מחזיר כל שבשלו פורק וטוען בשל חבירו נמי פורק וטוען. אביי שקל קלא פתק בהני עיזי דהוו קיימי. אמר ליה רבא איחייבת בהו קום אהדרינהו. וכן אמר רב הכישה נתחייב בה. דרכו להנהיג בחמור או למשוך בגמל בשדה ואין דרכו בעיר ועלתה בתיקו: מתני' איזהו אבידה מצא חמור וכו' אוקמה רב יהודה למתני' הכי קאמר איזהו היא כלל אבידה שחייב להחזירה מצא חמור וכליו הפוכין פרה ורצה בין הכרמים הרי זו אבידה וחייב להחזיר. תניא נמי הכי. דרך בלשון יון נקראת

---

מסורת הש"ס

א) בבא בתרא פח., ב) פאה פרק ו [משנה א, עדיות פרק ד משנה ג], ג) [לעיל כד: וש"נ], ד) בבא קמא לט:, ה) [תיבת אשר מיותר], ו) [נדרים לט: ע"ש], ז) [לקמן פח.], ח) [עיין תוס' לקמן לא: ד"ה אם], ט) [עי' תוס' לעיל כא. ד"ה וכמה], י) פי' או בחשכתא, מהרש"ל, כ) ובהגוזל דף ק. פירש"י תלמוד תורה, ע"ש כ"י, ל) ס"א שזה אומר כו', מהרש"ל, מ) נ"ל דעשה דמצורע דוחה עשה דשילוח הקן אי לאו כו', ועיין מהרש"א.

הגהות הב"ח

(א) גמ' במשנה שכרו כפועל. נ"ב ע"ל בדף ס"ח: (ב) רש"י ד"ה זה בית וכו' ותורות. נ"ב ובב"ק דף ק'. פרש"י דהוא ת"ת ול"ע:

הגהות הגר"א

[א][ב] גמ' אשר. רשום קו עליו למחקו:

גליון הש"ס

רש"י ד"ה דיני. בערון ערך מגיסתא הגירסא כאן דייני דמגיסתא ופי' דדני בגסות:

תורה אור השלם

א) וְהִזְהַרְתָּה אֶתְהֶם אֶת הַחֻקִּים וְאֶת הַתּוֹרֹת וְהוֹדַעְתָּ לָהֶם אֶת הַדֶּרֶךְ יֵלְכוּ בָהּ וְאֶת הַמַּעֲשֶׂה אֲשֶׁר יַעֲשׂוּן: [שמות יח, כ]

ב) לֹא תִרְאֶה אֶת שׁוֹר אָחִיךָ אוֹ אֶת שֵׂיוֹ נִדָּחִים וְהִתְעַלַּמְתָּ מֵהֶם הָשֵׁב תְּשִׁיבֵם לְאָחִיךָ: [דברים כב, א]

לעזי רש"י

מרט"א. פירוש גושה ש קרקע (רש"י תענית דף ע"א ד"ה אפי'), פיסו רגבים (רש"י ע"ז דף י ע"ב ד"ה שקל קלא).

ליקוטי רש"י

לא יהיה בך אביון. הזהר מן עניות [לקמן לג.]. הזהר בעצמך שלא תבא לידי עניות [סנהדרין סד:]. הכישה. במקל [רשב"ם ב"ב פח.]. דרי. נושא [עי' ע"ז נט:]. בית חייהם. תלמוד תורה [ב"ק ק.]. לבן גילו. כמותו או זקן לזקן [נדרים לט:]. שנולד בפרק אחד ובמזל אחד [יבמות קכ.]. דיני דמגיזתא. כפר שאין יודעין לדון במשפט לשון אחר דמגוזתא אנסין בחזקה כמו אתו גיזאי וקא מנ ליה פריסים העומדים לרדות בחזקה [ב"ק קיד.

is indeed understandable.

The Gemara now analyzes the above exposition: אָמַר מַר – In the Baraisa, **the master said:** "(אשר) "יֵלְכוּ – *(THAT)* **THEY MAY WALK;** זֶה בִּיקּוּר חוֹלִים – **THIS** refers to **VISITING THE SICK.**

The Gemara asks: הַיְינוּ גְּמִילוּת חֲסָדִים – **[Visiting the sick] is** merely a subcategory of **kind deeds.** Why, then, must the verse specifically mention "visiting the sick" when it had already mentioned "kind deeds"?

The Gemara answers: לֹא נִצְרְכָה אֶלָּא לְבֶן גִּילוֹ – **It is necessary only for** the case of **a person of his [hour],** i.e when both the sick person and his visitor were born under the same astrological constellation. דְּאָמַר מַר – **As the master said:** בֶּן גִּילוֹ נוֹטֵל אֶחָד מִשִּׁשִּׁים בְּחָלְיוֹ – When **a person of [one's]** own **[hour]** comes to visit him when he is sick, he **takes** away **one-sixtieth of one's sickness** and is afflicted with this portion himself. וַאֲפִילוּ הָכִי מִבָּעֵי לֵיהּ לְמֵיזַל לְגַבֵּיהּ – **Yet, even so,** the verse teaches that **he must go to** visit **him.**[18]

The Gemara continues its analysis of the Baraisa: "בָּהּ" – The Baraisa had stated: *IN IT;* זוֹ קְבוּרָה – **THIS** refers to **BURYING** the dead.

The Gemara asks: הַיְינוּ גְּמִילוּת חֲסָדִים – **[Burying the dead] is** a subcategory of **kind deeds.** Why, then, must it be mentioned specifically?

The Gemara answers: לֹא נִצְרְכָה אֶלָּא לְזָקֵן וְאֵינוֹ לְפִי כְּבוֹדוֹ – **It is necessary only for** the case of **an elderly man whose honor it does not befit** to bury a corpse. Had the verse taught only that one must do kind deeds, such a person would be exempt from burying the dead. The verse thus added a reference to burial, teaching that this exemption does not apply here: One must bury the dead, even if it is not befitting his honor to do so.

The Gemara comments upon the final part of the Baraisa: "אֲשֶׁר יַעֲשׂוּן" – The Baraisa stated: *THAT THEY SHOULD DO;* זוֹ לִפְנִים מִשּׁוּרַת הַדִּין – **THIS** refers to maintaining a standard of conduct that goes **BEYOND THE LETTER OF THE LAW.**

The Gemara suggests: דְּאָמַר ר׳ יוֹחָנָן – This is **as R' Yochanan said:** לֹא חָרְבָה יְרוּשָׁלַיִם אֶלָּא עַל שֶׁדָּנוּ בָּהּ דִּין תּוֹרָה – **Jerusalem was destroyed only because [its inhabitants] decided** cases **according to Torah law.**

The Gemara asks in astonishment: אֶלָּא דִּינֵי דְמַגִּיזְתָּא לְדַיְּינוּ – **Should they have instead decided** cases **according to the law of tyranny?**[19]

The Gemara responds by clarifying R' Yochanan's statement: אֶלָּא אֵימָא – **Rather, say** the following: שֶׁהֶעֱמִידוּ דִּינֵיהֶם עַל דִּין תּוֹרָה – Jerusalem was destroyed **because they limited their decisions to the letter of the law of the Torah,** וְלֹא עָבְדוּ לִפְנִים מִשּׁוּרַת הַדִּין – **and did not perform actions** that would have gone **beyond the letter of the law.**[20]

**Mishnah** אֵי זוֹ הִיא אֲבֵידָה – **What is a lost object?**[21] מָצָא חֲמוֹר אוֹ פָרָה רוֹעִין בַּדֶּרֶךְ – **If** one **found a donkey or a cow grazing by the road,** אֵין זוֹ אֲבֵידָה – **this is not** considered **a lost object** since, most likely, the owner left it there intentionally to graze.[22] חֲמוֹר וְכֵלָיו הֲפוּכִין – If, however, he found **a donkey with its gear overturned,** פָּרָה רָצָה בֵּין הַכְּרָמִים – or **a cow running through the vineyards,**[23] הֲרֵי זוֹ אֲבֵידָה – **this is** indeed **a lost object,** for it is evident that its owner is unaware of its whereabouts.

הֶחֱזִירָהּ וּבָרְחָה הֶחֱזִירָהּ וּבָרְחָה – **If** one **returned [an animal] and it ran away,** and **he returned it** again **and it ran away,** אֲפִילוּ אַרְבָּעָה וַחֲמִשָּׁה פְּעָמִים – **even** if this happens **four or five times,** חַיָּיב לְהַחֲזִירָהּ – **he is** still **obligated to return it** yet again; שֶׁנֶּאֱמַר – **for it is stated:** "הָשֵׁב תְּשִׁיבֵם" – ***return, you shall return them.***[24]

הָיָה בָּטֵל מִסֶּלַע – If **[the finder] stood idle from** doing work worth **a *sela*** because he was busy returning the object he found, לֹא יֹאמַר לוֹ – **he should not say to [the owner]:** תֵּן לִי סֶלַע – **"Give me the full *sela*** that I lost." אֶלָּא נוֹתֵן לוֹ שְׂכָרוֹ כְּפוֹעֵל – **Rather, [the owner] gives him his wage like a worker.**[25] אִם יֵשׁ שָׁם בֵּית דִּין – **If,** however, **there is a court** in the vicinity, and the finder is dissatisfied with the above arrangement, מַתְנֶה בִּפְנֵי בֵית דִּין – **he may stipulate before the court** that he is willing to retrieve the object only if he receives full compensation for his lost labor, and he may then claim this full amount.[26] אִם אֵין שָׁם בֵּית דִּין – **If,** on the other hand, **there is no court** in the vicinity,[27] בִּפְנֵי מִי יַתְנֶה – **before whom should he stipulate?** In such a situation, he is without a means to collect full compensation, שֶׁלּוֹ קוֹדֵם – and therefore **his** own financial concerns **come before** those of **others:** He may continue performing his work, and he need not retrieve the object.

NOTES

the law, and they must also maintain an even higher standard; that is, they must go beyond the letter of the law as well.

18. By setting apart "visiting the sick" from all other acts of kindness, the verse conveys that a person must visit the sick even when this might cause him harm – as in a case in which he was born under the same constellation as the person he is to visit.

19. I.e. if the courts ought not judge according to Torah law, how then ought they judge? Should they instead hand down unfair decisions and enforce them brutally? (see *Rashi* to *Bava Kamma* 114a).

20. Although the Gemara (*Yoma* 9b) states that Jerusalem was destroyed because its inhabitants acted with unwarranted hate towards others, it is possible that it was destroyed because they were guilty of *both* acting with unwarranted hate and not acting beyond the letter of the law (*Tosafos*; cf. *Ben Yehoyada*).

21. I.e. how is a finder to determine whether the object he has found is truly lost? How is he to understand whether or not the owner knows of it whereabouts? (*Tosafos;* see *Rashi*).

22. Accordingly, the finder need not return it (*Rashi*).

23. The cow would likely become bruised by this (*Rashi*).

24. *Deuteronomy* 22:1. The language connotes that a finder must return the same lost object even many times (see 31a note 19).

25. The Gemara (31b) will explain precisely what this means. The finder cannot claim the full *sela*, for if he had in fact continued laboring to earn that money, he would have had to exert himself far more than he actually did in returning the object. The owner can therefore argue that the finder deserves payment only for the easier "work" he in fact did, not for the harder work he *might* have done (*Rashi*, from *Gemara* 31b).

26. The Mishnah describes a case in which the finder does not wish to accept the lesser payment, preferring instead to continue with the more difficult work he had been doing in order to collect a greater return on his time (*Rashi*). He may therefore stipulate before a court the conditions upon which he will return the object.

As it is used here, the term "court" refers to a group of three people.

27. The Mishnah here speaks of a case in which the finder is unable to convene a group of three before whom he could stipulate (see *Rashi*).

לא יהיה בך אביון שלך קודם לשל כל אדם אלא לזקן ואינו לפי כבודו [א] אמר רבה [א] הכישה חייב בה אביי הוה יתיב קמיה דרבה חזא להנך עיזי דקיימו שקל קלא ושדא בהו א"ל איחייבת בהו קום אהדרינהו [ב] איבעיא להו דרכו להחזיר בשדה ואין דרכו להחזיר בעיר מהו מי אמרינן השבה מעליא בעינן וכיון דלאו דרכיה להחזיר בעיר לא לחייב או דלמא בשדה מיהת הוא דאיחייב ליה וכיון דאיחייב ליה בשדה איחייב ליה בעיר תיקו אמר רבא [ג] כל שבשלו מחזיר בשל חבירו נמי מחזיר [ד] וכל שבשלו פורק וטוען בשל חבירו נמי פורק וטוען רבי ישמעאל ברבי יוסי הוה קאזיל באורחא פגע ביה ההוא גברא הוה דרי פתכא דאופי אותבינהו וקא מיתפח א"ל דלי לי אמר ליה כמה שוין א"ל פלגא דזוזא יהיב ליה פלגא דזוזא ואפקרה הדר זכה בהו הדר יהיב ליה פלגא דזוזא ואפקרה חזייה דהוה קא בעי למיהדר למזכיה בהו א"ל לכולי עלמא אפקרנהו ולך לא אפקרנהו ומי הוי הפקר כי האי גוונא והתנן [ג] בש"א הפקר לעניים הפקר וב"ה אומרים [ה] אינו הפקר עד שיהא הפקר לעניים ולעשירים כשמיטה אלא רבי ישמעאל ברבי יוסי לכולי עלמא אפקרינהו ובמלתא בעלמא הוא דאוקמיה והא רבי ישמעאל ברבי יוסי זקן ואינו לפי כבודו הוה ר' ישמעאל ברבי יוסי [ו] לפנים משורת הדין הוא דעבד [ז] דתני רב יוסף [א] והודעת להם זה בית חייהם את הדרך זו גמילות חסדים [ב] (אשר) ילכו זה ביקור חולים בה זו קבורה ואת המעשה זה הדין אשר יעשון זו לפנים משורת הדין: אמר מר [ב] (אשר) ילכו זה ביקור חולים היינו גמילות חסדים לא נצרכה אלא [ט] לבן גילו דאמר מר [י] בן גילו נוטל אחד מששים בחליו ואפ"ה הכי מבעי ליה למיזל לגביה בה זו קבורה היינו גמילות חסדים לא נצרכה אלא לזקן ואינו לפי כבודו אשר יעשון זו לפנים משורת הדין דאמר ר' יוחנן לא חרבה ירושלים אלא על שדנו בה דין תורה אלא דיני דמגיזתא לדיינו אלא אימא [י] שהעמידו דיניהם על דין תורה ולא עבדו לפנים משורת הדין:

**מתני'** אי זו היא אבידה [ח] מצא חמור או פרה רועין בדרך אין זו אבידה חמור וכליו הפוכין פרה רצה בין הכרמים הרי זו אבידה [ט] החזירה וברחה החזירה וברחה אפי' ארבעה וחמשה פעמים חייב להחזירה שנאמר [ב] השב תשיבם [י] היה בטל מסלע לא יאמר לו תן לי סלע אלא נותן לו [ל] שכרו כפועל [מ] אם יש שם בית דין מתנה בפני ב"ד [נ] אם אין שם ב"ד בפני מי יתנה שלו קודם:

**גמ'** אטו כל הני דאמרינן לאו אבידה הוו אמר רב יהודה הכי קאמר אי זו היא כלל אבידה שהוא חייב בה מצא חמור ופרה רועין בדרך אין זו אבידה ולא מיחייב בה חמור וכליו הפוכים פרה ורצה בין הכרמים הרי זו אבידה ומיחייב בה [ס] ולעולם אמר רב יהודה אמר רב עד שלשה ימים היכי דמי אי בלילותא אפי' חדא שעתא נמי אי בימממא אפי' טובא נמי לא [ע] לא צריכא דהוה חזי לה בקדמתא [פ] ובחשכתא תלתא יומי אמרינן איתרמויי איתרמי לה ונפקא טפי ודאי אבידה היא תניא נמי הכי מצא טלית וקרדום באסרטיא

---

**רש"י**

**לא יהיה בך אביון.** לא תביא עצמך לידי עניות: **הכישה.** זה שאינו לפי כבודו אם הכישה הכאה אחת להשיבה נתחייב בה לההדורה הואיל והתחיל: **קלא.** מרט"א בלע"ז: **דרכו להחזיר בשדה.** שאין שם רואים כל כך ואינו בוש: **ואין דרכו בעיר.** שהוא בוש משכיניו והוא מצא בשדה: **מהו.** שיתחייב להשיבה: **לא מיחייב.** להתחיל בהשבתה בשדה: **וכיון דאיחייב.** שהזיזה ממקומה חייב אף בעיר: **פורק וטוען.** פורק משא מן החמור וטוען עליו דכתיב עזוב תעזוב הקם תקים: **פתכא דאופי.** משאוי של עצים: **וקא מיתפח.** עומד לנוח: **דלי לי.** הטעינני: **הדר זכה בהו.** חזר האיש ההוא והחזיק בהן מן ההפקר: **הפקר לעניים הוי הפקר.** אע"ג שלא הפקירו אלא לעניים הוי הפקר למפטר מן המעשר: **זה בית חייהם.** [כ] ללמוד להם אומנות להתפרנס בו חוקות (ג) ותורות כתיבי ברישיה דקרא: [ס] **דיני דמגיזתא לידיינו.** בתמיה. דמגיזתא גוזאי הדנין ביסורים ובחזקה וחבירו בבבא קמא (דף קיד.) דדייני בגזתיא: **מתני' איזו היא אבידה.** בגמרא מפרש: **אין זו אבידה.** ואינו חייב להחזיר שמדעת הניחוה שם: **רצה בין הכרמים.** דמסתקבלא: **לא יאמר לו תן לי סלע.** שבטלתי ממלאכתי [ל] שיאמר לו אם עשית מלאכתך היית מרבה טורח עכשיו לפי מה שטרחת טול: **כפועל.** בגמרא מפרש: **אם יש שם בית דין.** אם נוח לו לטרוח יותר כדי להרבות שכר ואינו חפץ ליבטל ממלאכתו מה יעשה אם יש שם שלשה בני אדם יתנה בפניהם ויאמר ראו שאני משתכר כך וכך ואי איפשי ליבטל ליטול שכר מועט אני אשיב אם תאמרו שאטול שכר משלם: **גמ' כלל.** סתם אבידה שמוכחת שהיא שם שלא מדעת בעלים: **ולעולם.** בתמיה וכי אף אם ימצאנה שם לעולם נאמר מדעת היא וכי דרך שלא להכניס: **בקדמותא.** לפני עלות השחר: **חשכתא.** שחשכה ערבית: אסרטיא

**תוספות**

ה"מ לא תעשה ועשה השוה בכל אבל האי דאינו שוה בכל דחי כדמוכח פרק שני נזירין (נזיר דף נח:) דאתי עשה דמצורע ודחי לאו ועשה דכהנים וכן ק' לקמן (לב.) יכול אמר לו אביו הטמא כו' ופריך תיפוק ליה דאין עשה דוחה לא תעשה ועשה הא גבי כהנים שאינו שוה בכל דחי וי"ל דעשה דמצורע שאני דחמיר משום דגדול השלום כדאמר בפ' שילוח הקן (חולין דף קמא.) [מ] דעשה דמצורע הוי דחי לאו ועשה דשילוח הקן אי לאו יתורא דשלח תשלח אבל עשה דעלמא לא דחי לאו ועשה אפילו אינו שוה בכל וזה התירוץ לא יתיישב למאן דשרי מצורע בימי חלוטו בתשמיש המטה פ"ק דמועד קטן (דף ז:) ולדידיה יש לומר דהכא סמיך על ותו מי דחינן איסורא מקמי ממונא ולקמן נמי עדיפא משני דהוה דחי אפילו לאו ועשה אי לאו קרא אפי' אי בעלמא לא דחי ובפ"ב דיבמות (דף כא.) דאמר גבי פלוגתא דר' יוחנן ור"א בביאת כ"ג באלמנה מן הנישואין כ"ע לא פליגי דלא פטרה דאין עשה דוחה לא תעשה ועשה וי"ל דחשיב שוה בכל כיון שהאלמנה עשתה איסור כמו הכהן דאקרי ביה לא יקח לא יקחו אע"ג דאין שוה בכל אלא בכהנים אבל ההיא דגילוח זקן שאינו שוה בנשים נדחי מקמי עשה דמצורע:

**אלא** לזקן ואינו לפי כבודו. וא"ת תיפוק ליה מולאחותו דכבוד הבריות דוחה מילת בנו ושחיטת פסחו וי"ל כבוד הבריות דמת מצוה חמיר טפי שמוטל בבזיון פן יסריח או יאכלוהו כלבים אע"ג דבפ' מי שמתו (ברכות דף כ. ושם ד"ה שב) מוכח דאי הוה כלאים שב ואל תעשה היה נדחה מפני כבוד הבריות היינו משום דערום הוי גנות ובזיון גדול כדאמר (יבמות דף סג:) אין לך משוקץ יותר מאותו שהוא מהלך ערום ומהכא לא ידעי' דדחי אלא ממונא אבל איסורא כמו פסח ומילה וגם כרת לא: [וע' תוס' שבועות ל: ד"ה אבל]:

**אפקרה.** שלא יכשלו בני אדם בלא תגזול וא"ת הא אמר בפ' אין בין המודר (נדרים דף מה.) אין הפקר אלא בפני שלשה וי"ל דהכא נמי הוו שלשה אי נמי דאורייתא בלא שלשה נמי הוי הפקר והא דאמר שלהי פ"ק דשבת (דף יח: ושם ד"ה דמפקרא) גיגית נר וקדירה אפקורי מפקר להו אע"ג דליכא שלשה התם אנן סהדי דמפקר להו בלבו שלא יעשה איסור שביתת כלים: **לא** חרבה כו'. ואם תאמר דביומא (דף ט:) אמר מפני שנאת חנם וי"ל דהא והא גרמא:

**איזוהי** אבידה. שיבין שאין הבעלים יודעין שהיא שם: קורדוס

---

**עין משפט נר מצוה**

קמד א ב מיי' פי"א מהל' גזילה ואבידה הל' יג יד סמג עשין עד טוש"ע ח"מ סי' רסג סעיף ב:
קמה ג מיי' שם הל' יג טוש"ע שם סעיף א:
קמו ד מיי' פי"ג מהל' רוצח הל' ד סמג עשין פא טוש"ע ח"מ סי' רעב סעיף ג:
קמז ה מיי' פ"ב מהל' נדרים הלכה טו טוש"ע ח"מ סי' רעג סעיף ה:
קמח ו מיי' פי"א מהל' אבידה הלכה ח ופי"ג מהל' רוצח הל' ד סמג עשין עד פא טוש"ע ח"מ סי' רסג סעיף ג וסי' רעב סעיף ג:
קמט ז מיי' פי"ד מהל' אבילות הלכה ד סמג עשין ב טוש"ע י"ד סי' שלה סעיף ב:
קנ ח מיי' פט"ו מהל' אבידה הל' ב סמג עשין עד טוש"ע ח"מ סי' רסא סעיף א:
קנא ט מיי' שם פי"א הל' יד סמג שם טוש"ע ח"מ סי' רסו סעיף ב:
קנב י כ ל מיי' שם פי"ב הל' ד סמג שם טוש"ע ח"מ סי' רסה:
קנג מ מיי' שם פט"ו הלכה ג סמג שם טוש"ע ח"מ סי' רסא סעיף א:

**רבינו חננאל**

והיא בבית הקברות לא צריכא מאי טעמא דהא כהן מוזהר בטומאה עשה ולא תעשה עשה שנאמר וקדשתו קדשים יהיו לאלהיהם לא תעשה שנאמר לנפש לא יטמא בעמיו והשבת אבידה עשה היא שנאמר השב תשיבם לאחי' ולא אתי עשה ודחי את לא תעשה ועשה ותוב לא דחינן איסורא מקמי ממונא. שלו מרובה משל חבירו שנאמר אפס כי לא יהיה בך אביון שלך קודם לשל כל אדם. אמר רבא כל שבשלו מחזיר בשל חבירו נמי מחזיר כל שבשלו פורק וטוען בשל חבירו נמי פורק וטוען. אביי שקל קלא פתק בהני עיזי דהוו קיימי. אמר ליה רבא איחייבת בהו קום אהדרינהו. וכן אמר רב הכישה נתחייב בה. דרכו להנהיג בחמור או למשוך בגמל בשדה ואין דרכו בעיר ועלתה בתיקו: מתני' איזהו אבידה מצא חמור וכו' אוקמה רב יהודה למתני' הכי קאמר איזהו היא כלל אבידה שחייב להחזירה מצא חמור וכליו הפוכין פרה ורצה בין הכרמים הרי זו אבידה וחייב להחזיר. תניא נמי הכי. דרך בלשון יון נקראת

**מסורת הש"ס**

א) בבא בתרא פח., ב) פאה פרק ו [משנה א, עדיו פרק ד משנה ג], ג) [לעי' כד: וש"נ], ד) בבא קמא לט., ה) [סיבת אש מיוחר], ו) [נדרים לט ע"ש], ז) [לקמן פח.], ח) [עיין תוס' לקמן לג ד"ה אם], ט) [עי' תוס' לעיל כא. ד"ה וכמה], י) פי' או במשכתא מהרש"ל, כ) ובהגהות דף פירש"י תלמוד תורה, ע"כ"י, ל) ס"א שזה אומ כו', מהרש"ל, מ) נ"ל דעשה דמצורע דוחה עשה דשילוח הקן אי לאו כו' ועיין מהרש"א.

**הגהות הב"ח**

(א) גמ' במשנה שכרו כפועל. נ"ב ע"ל בד' ס"ח: (ב) רש"י ד"ה זה בית וכו' ותורות. נ"ב וכב"ק דף ק'. פרש"י דהוא ת"ת וצ"ע:

**הגהות הגר"א**

[א][ב] גמ' אשר. רשו קו עליו למחקו:

**גליון הש"ס**

רש"י ד"ה דיני. בערוך ערך מגיסתא הגירסא כא דייני דמגיסתא ופי' דדני בגסות:

**תורה אור השלם**

א) וְהִזְהַרְתָּה אֶתְהֶם אֶת הַחֻקִּים וְאֶת הַתּוֹרֹת וְהוֹדַעְתָּ לָהֶם אֶת הַדֶּרֶךְ יֵלְכוּ בָהּ וְאֶת הַמַּעֲשֶׂה אֲשֶׁר יַעֲשׂוּן: [שמות יח, כ]
ב) לֹא תִרְאֶה אֶת שׁוֹר אָחִיךָ אוֹ אֶת שֵׂיוֹ נִדָּחִים וְהִתְעַלַּמְתָּ מֵהֶם הָשֵׁב תְּשִׁיבֵם לְאָחִיךָ: [דברים כב, א]

**לעזי רש"י**

מרט"א. פירוש גושה של קרקע (רש"י תענית דף ע"א ד"ה אפי'), פיסו רגבים (רש"י ע"ז דף יו ע"ב ד"ה שקל קלא).

**ליקוטי רש"י**

**לא יהיה בך אביון.** הזהר מן עניות [לקמן לג.]. הזהר בעצמך שלא תבא לידי עניות [סנהדרין סד:]. **הכישה.** במקל [רשב"ם ב"ב פח.]. **דרי.** נושא [עי' ע"ז נט:]. **בית חייהם.** תלמוד תורה [ב"ק ק.]. **לבן גילו.** במזל כמותו או זקן לזקן [נדרים לט:]. שנולד בפרק אחד ובמזל אחד [יבמות קכ.]. **דיני דמגיזתא.** בני כפר שאין יודעין לדון במשפט לשון אחר דמגוזתא אנסין בחזקה כמו אתו גיזאי וקא מחו ליה סריסים העומדים לרדות בחזקה [ב"ק קיד.].

*zuz.*" יָהִיב לֵיהּ פַּלְגָּא דְזוּזָא וְאַפְקְרָה – [R' Yishmael son of R' Yose] then **gave him a half of a *zuz*** as payment for the wood, **and pronounced [the wood] ownerless.**[9] הֲדַר זָכָה בְּהוּ – Seeing that R' Yishmael had renounced ownership over the wood, **[the man] then** grabbed it and **took possession of it** for himself. הֲדַר יָהִיב לֵיהּ פַּלְגָּא דְזוּזָא וְאַפְקְרָה – Once **again, [R' Yishmael] gave him half a *zuz* and pronounced [the wood] ownerless.** חַזְיֵיה דַּהֲוָה קָא בָּעֵי לְמֵיהֲדַר לְמִזְכְּיֵיה בְּהוּ – He immediately **saw that [the man] wished to go after** the wood **to acquire it** yet again. אֲמַר לֵיהּ – **He** therefore **said to him:** לְכוּלֵּי עָלְמָא אַפְקַרְנְהוּ – "With respect **to the whole world, I have pronounced them ownerless;** וְלָךְ לֹא אַפְקַרְנְהוּ – **but** with respect **to you, I have not pronounced them ownerless."**

The Gemara questions this last point:

וּמִי הָוֵי הֶפְקֵר כִּי הַאי גַּוְונָא – **Can** something **really become ownerless in this way** – ownerless for some people but not for others? וְהָתְנַן – **But we learned in a Mishnah:**[10] בֵּית שַׁמַּאי אוֹמְרִים – BEIS SHAMMAI SAY: הֶפְקֵר לַעֲנִיִּים – If a person declares his produce to be OWNERLESS with respect TO THE POOR only, הֶפְקֵר – IT IS indeed considered OWNERLESS.[11] וּבֵית הִלֵּל אוֹמְרִים – HOWEVER, BEIS HILLEL SAY: אֵינוֹ הֶפְקֵר – IT IS NOT considered OWNERLESS, עַד שֶׁיְּהֵא הֶפְקֵר לַעֲנִיִּים וְלַעֲשִׁירִים כִּשְׁמִיטָּה – UNLESS IT HAS BEEN pronounced OWNERLESS FOR THE POOR AND FOR THE RICH alike, AS is the produce of the THE SABBATICAL YEAR.[12] Since the law follows the view of Beis Hillel, it is evident that something cannot become ownerless for certain people and not for others. How, then, could R' Yishmael son of R' Yose declare the bundles ownerless for everyone except the man who had been carrying them?

The Gemara answers:

אֶלָּא רַבִּי יִשְׁמָעֵאל בְּרַבִּי יוֹסֵי לְכוּלֵּי עָלְמָא אַפְקְרִינְהוּ – **Rather,** in actuality, **R' Yishmael son of R' Yose pronounced [the wood] ownerless for the whole world,** including that man; בְּמִלְּתָא בְּעָלְמָא הוּא דְּאוֹקְמֵיהּ – **and he restrained [the man]** from taking the wood **with mere words.**[13]

The Gemara now questions R' Yishmael's actions on different grounds:

וְהָא רַבִּי יִשְׁמָעֵאל בְּרַבִּי יוֹסֵי זָקֵן וְאֵינוֹ לְפִי כְּבוֹדוֹ הֲוָה – **But R' Yishmael son of R' Yose was an elderly man, and** presumably **it would not befit his honor** to pile wood on a man's back. Accordingly, he would have been exempt from helping the man, and he need not have purchased the wood from him! – ? –

The Gemara replies:

ר' יִשְׁמָעֵאל בְּרַבִּי יוֹסֵי לִפְנִים מִשּׁוּרַת הַדִּין הוּא דַּעֲבַד – **R' Yishmael son of R' Yose went beyond the letter of the law** in purchasing the wood.[14] Scripture indeed sanctions this kind of action, דְּתָנֵי רַב יוֹסֵף – **as Rav Yosef taught:** "וְהוֹדַעְתָּ לָהֶם" – Concerning the areas in which Moses should instruct the Jews, the verse states:[15] *AND YOU SHALL MAKE KNOWN TO THEM;* זֶה בֵּית חַיֵּיהֶם – THIS refers to THEIR LIVELIHOOD.[16] Next, the verse states: "אֶת־הַדֶּרֶךְ" – *THE WAY;* זוּ גְּמִילוּת חֲסָדִים – THIS refers to KIND DEEDS. The verse then states: "(אשר) יֵלְכוּ" – *(THAT) THEY MAY WALK;* זֶה בִּיקּוּר חוֹלִים – THIS refers to VISITING THE SICK. The next word of the verse is: "בָהּ" – *IN IT.* זוּ קְבוּרָה – THIS refers to BURYING the dead. The verse continues, stating: "וְאֶת־הַמַּעֲשֶׂה" – *AND THE ACTIONS;* זֶה הַדִּין – THIS refers to observing the letter of THE LAW. The verse then concludes with the words "אֲשֶׁר יַעֲשׂוּן" – *THAT THEY SHOULD DO;* זוּ לִפְנִים מִשּׁוּרַת הַדִּין – THIS refers to maintaining a standard of conduct that goes BEYOND THE LETTER OF THE LAW.[17] In light of the requirement to uphold such a standard, R' Yishmael son of R' Yose's conduct

NOTES

9. R' Yishmael purchased the wood because he did not wish to go through the process of loading it onto the man's back. He did not, however, wish to take the wood for himself. He therefore pronounced it *hefker*, renouncing his ownership over it, so that others who took the wood would not be liable for theft (*Tosafos*). *Rashba* (*Teshuvos* vol. I §252,256) infers from this incident that the obligation to help load applies not only with a burden being placed upon an animal, but also with a burden being placed on a person (see also *Sefer HaChinuch* §540,541 and *Minchas Chinuch* ad loc.). Others, however, maintain that the obligation to help a person place a burden upon himself is of Rabbinic origin (*Rabbeinu Peretz,* as cited by *Shitah Mekubetzes* to *Bava Kamma* 54b).

10. *Pe'ah* 6:1.

11. Produce that is declared ownerless – that is, freely available for acquisition – need not be tithed; neither by its original owner, nor by one who acquires it at any later time (see Mishnah, *Pe'ah* 1:6). In Beis Shammai's opinion, if one declares his produce to be "ownerless for the poor," his declaration has legal standing. The produce becomes freely available for acquisition by the poor (but not by the rich), and it becomes exempt from tithes just like produce that is unconditionally *hefker* (see *Rav* to *Pe'ah* 6:1).

12. I.e. just as the produce of the Sabbatical year (*shemittah*) is ownerless and available for acquisition to all, so too, must produce declared ownerless be made available to all. According to Beis Hillel, an owner's declaration of *hefker* (ownerlessness) has no legal effect if the declaration limits the potential of acquisition to poor people alone or rich people alone. Therefore, if someone declared produce to be ownerless for the poor, it does not become ownerless at all (it is not exempted from tithes, nor is it available for acquisition *even by the poor*).

[Beis Hillel find support for their position in the verse (*Exodus* 23:11): וְהַשְּׁבִיעִת תִּשְׁמְטֶנָּה וּנְטַשְׁתָּהּ, *And on the seventh year you shall release it and abandon it.* The seemingly superfluous addition of *and abandon it* indicates that voluntary abandonment of property – i.e. making it ownerless – must resemble the state of seventh-year produce, which is freely available to anyone, rich or poor. Therefore, in order for voluntary abandonment to be legally effective, the owner must declare it available to all, rich and poor alike (*Rav* to *Pe'ah* 6:1).]

13. I.e. he fooled the man with the false assertion that he could not re-acquire the wood.

14. *Rosh* (§21) gives R' Yishmael son of R' Yose's actions as an example of how a sage should conduct himself if he wishes to forego his exemption to return a lost object: The sage is not to degrade himself by actually retrieving the lost object; rather, he may, if he wishes, choose to financially compensate the owner for his loss. *Rambam,* however (*Hil. Aveidah* 11:17), disputes *Rosh* on this, maintaining that the sage is permitted to actually retrieve the object if he so wishes.

15. *Exodus* 18:20. The verse records Jethro's advice to Moses as to how he should guide the Jewish people. In its entirety, it states: וְהִזְהַרְתָּה אֶתְהֶם אֶת־הַחֻקִּים וְאֶת־הַתּוֹרֹת וְהוֹדַעְתָּ לָהֶם אֶת־הַדֶּרֶךְ יֵלְכוּ בָהּ וְאֶת־הַמַּעֲשֶׂה אֲשֶׁר יַעֲשׂוּן, *And you shall advise them of the [Torah's] statutes and [its] laws, and you shall make known to them the way [that] they may walk in it and the actions that they should do.* The Baraisa expounds the latter section of the verse, interpreting each individual clause as a reference to a particular area of conduct in which Moses should instruct the people.

16. I.e. Moses was instructed to inform the nation of an individual's obligation to learn a craft or trade to provide a livelihood for himself.

According to *Maharsha*, the basis for this interpretation of the words וְהוֹדַעְתָּ לָהֶם comes from the implication of the word לָהֶם, as well as from the preceding section of the verse [not cited in the Baraisa] which reads: וְהִזְהַרְתָּה אֶתְהֶם אֶת־הַחֻקִּים וְאֶת־הַתּוֹרֹת, *and you shall advise them of the [Torah's] statutes and [its] laws.* Essentially, the Baraisa reads the verse as follows: After instructing the Jews about *the [Torah's] statutes and [its] laws,* Moses was to *make known* (וְהוֹדַעְתָּ) something that concerned *them* [physically] (לָהֶם). That is, he was to advise them of the obligation to learn a craft to provide for their physical welfare (*Rashi*, as interpreted by *Maharsha*; cf. *Rashi* to *Bava Kamma* 100a).

[As the Baraisa continues, it expounds each successive clause of this verse as referring to another area of conduct in which Moses should instruct the Jews. In each case, *Maharsha* endeavors to show the connection between the particular word expounded and the area of conduct it is taken to represent.]

17. In all, then, Moses was instructed to inform the people that they must involve themselves in the pursuit of a livelihood, kind deeds, visiting the sick and burying the dead. They must adhere to the letter of

לא יהיה בך אביון שלך קודם לשל כל אדם אלא לזקן ואינו לפי כבודו [א] אמר רבה [א] הכישה חייב בה אביי הוה יתיב קמיה דרבה חזא להנך עיזי דקיימו שקל קלא ושדא בהו א"ל איחייבת בהו קום אהדרינהו [ב] איבעיא להו דרכו להחזיר בשדה ואין דרכו להחזיר בעיר מהו מי אמרינן השבה מעליא בעינן וכיון דלאו דרכיה להחזיר בעיר לא לחייב או דלמא בשדה מיהת הוא דאיחייב ליה וכיון דאיחייב ליה בשדה איחייב ליה בעיר תיקו אמר רבא [ג] כל שבשלו מחזיר בשל חבירו נמי מחזיר [ד] וכל שבשלו פורק וטוען בשל חבירו נמי פורק וטוען רבי ישמעאל ברבי יוסי הוה קאזיל באורחא פגע ביה ההוא גברא הוה דרי פתכא דאופי אותבינהו וקא מיתפח א"ל דלי לי אמר ליה כמה שוין א"ל פלגא דוזא יהיב ליה פלגא דוזא ואפקרה הדר זכה בהו הדר יהיב ליה פלגא דוזא ואפקרה חזייה דהוה קא בעי למיהדר למזכיה בהו א"ל לכולי עלמא אפקרנהו ולך לא אפקרנהו ומי הוי הפקר כי האי גוונא והתנן [ג] בש"א הפקר לעניים הפקר וב"ה אומרים [ה] אינו הפקר עד שיהא הפקר לעניים ולעשירים כשמיטה אלא רבי ישמעאל ברבי יוסי לכולי עלמא אפקרינהו ובמלתא בעלמא הוא דאוקמיה והא רבי ישמעאל ברבי יוסי זקן ואינו לפי כבודו הוה ר' ישמעאל ברבי יוסי [ו] לפנים משורת הדין הוא דעבד [ז] דתני רב יוסף [א] והודעת להם זה בית חייהם את הדרך זו גמילות חסדים [א] [ט] (אשר) ילכו זה ביקור חולים בה זו קבורה ואת המעשה זה הדין אשר יעשון זו לפנים משורת הדין: אמר מר [ב] (אשר) ילכו זה ביקור חולים היינו גמילות חסדים לא נצרכה אלא [ח] לבן גילו דאמר מר [י] בן גילו נוטל אחד משששים בחליו ואפי' הכי מבעי ליה למיזל לגביה בה זו קבורה היינו גמילות חסדים לא נצרכה אלא לזקן ואינו לפי כבודו אשר יעשון זו לפנים משורת הדין דאמר ר' יוחנן לא חרבה ירושלים אלא על שדנו בה דין תורה אלא דיני דמגיזתא לדיינו אלא אימא [י] שהעמידו דיניהם על דין תורה ולא עבדו לפנים משורת הדין:

**מתני'** אי זו היא אבידה [ח] מצא חמור או פרה רועין בדרך אין זו אבידה חמור וכליו הפוכין פרה רצה בין הכרמים הרי זו אבידה [ט] החזירה וברחה החזירה וברחה אפי' ארבעה וחמשה פעמים חייב להחזירה שנאמר [ב] השב תשיבם [י] היה בטל מסלע לא יאמר לו תן לי סלע אלא נותן לו (א) שכרו כפועל [מ] [כ] אם יש שם בית דין מתנה בפני ב"ד [ל] אם אין שם ב"ד בפני מי יתנה שלו קודם:

**גמ'** אטו כל הני דאמרינן לאו אבידה הוו אמר רב יהודה הכי קאמר אי זו היא כלל אבידה שהוא חייב בה מצא חמור ופרה רועין בדרך אין זו אבידה ולא מיחייב בה חמור וכליו הפוכים פרה ורצה בין הכרמים הרי זו אבידה ומיחייב בה [ט] ולעולם אמר רב יהודה אמר רב עד שלשה ימים היכי דמי אי בלילותא אפי' חדא שעתא נמי אי בימממא אפי' טובא נמי לא [מ] לא צריכא דהוה חזי לה בקדמתא [י] ובחשכתא תלתא יומי אמרינן איתרמויי אתרמי לה ונפקא טפי ודאי אבידה היא תניא נמי הכי מצא טלית וקרדום באסרטיא

---

לא יהיה בך אביון. לא תביא עצמך לידי עניות: הכישה. זה שאינו לפי כבודו אם הכישה הכאה אחת להשיבה נתחייב בה להחזירה הואיל והתחיל: קלא. מרט"א בלע"ז: דרכו להחזיר בשדה. שאין שם רואים כל כך ואינו בוש: ואין דרכו בעיר. שהוא בוש משכניו והוא מצא בשדה: מהו. שיתחייב להשיבה: לא מיחייב. להתחיל בהשבתה בשדה: וכיון דאיחייב. שהזיזה ממקומה חייב אף בעיר: פורק וטוען. פורק משא מן החמור וטוען עליו דכתיב עזוב תעזוב הקם תקים: פתכא דאופי. משאוי של עצים: וקא מיתפח. עומד לפוש: דלי לי. הטעינני: הדר זכה בהו. חזר האיש ההוא והחזיק בהן מן ההפקר: הפקר לעניים הוי הפקר. אע"ג שלא הפקירו אלא לעניים הוי הפקר למפטר מן המעשר: זה בית חייהם. [ס] ללמוד להם אומנות להתפרנס בו חוקות (ב) ותורות כתיבי ברישיה דקרא: [ע] דיני דמגיזתא לידיינו. בתמיה. דמגיזתא גוזאי הדנין ביסורים ובחזקה וחבירו בבבא קמא (דף קיד.) דדייני דגזותא: מתני' איזו היא אבידה. בגמרא מפרש: אין זו אבידה. ואינו חייב להחזיר שמדעת הניחוה שם: רצה בין הכרמים. דמסתקבא: לא יאמר לו תן לי סלע. שבטלתי ממלאכתי [פ] שיאמר לו אם עשית מלאכתך היית מרבה טורח עכשיו לפי מה שטרחת טול: כפועל. בגמרא מפרש: אם יש שם בית דין. אם נוח לו לטרוח יותר כדי להרבות שכר ואינו חפץ ליבטל ממלאכתו מה יעשה אם יש שם שלשה בני אדם יתנה בפניהם ויאמר ראו שאני משתכר כך וכך ואי איפשי ליבטל ליטול שכר מועט אני אשיב אם תאמרו שאטול שכר משלם: גמ' כלל. סתם אבידה שמוכחת שהיא שם שלא מדעת בעלים: ולעולם. בתמיה וכי אף אם ימצאנה שם לעולם נאמר מדעת היא וכי דרך שלא להכנים: בקדמותא. לפני עלות השחר: חשכתא. מחשכה ערבית: אסרטיא

---

ה"מ לא תעשה ועשה השוה בכל אבל הכא דאינו שוה בכל דחי כדמוכח פרק שני נזירין (נזיר דף נח:) דאתי עשה דמצורע ודחי לאו ועשה דכהנים וכן ק' לקמן (לב.) יכול אמר לו אביו הטמא כו' ופריך תיפוק ליה דאין עשה דוחה לא תעשה ועשה הא גבי כהנים שאינו שוה בכל דחי וי"ל דעשה דמצורע שאני דחמיר משום דגדול השלום כדאמר בפ' שילוח הקן (חולין דף קמא.) [מ] דעשה דמצורע הוי דחי לאו ועשה דשילוח הקן אי לאו יתורא דשלח תשלח אבל עשה דעלמא לא דחי לאו ועשה אפילו אינו שוה בכל וזה התירוץ לא יתיישב למאן דשרי מצורע בימי חלוטו בתשמיש המטה פ"ק דמועד קטן (דף ז:) ולדידיה יש לומר דהכא סמיך על ותו מי דאין איסורא מקמי ממונא ולקמן נמי עדיפא משני דהוה דחי אפילו לאו ועשה אי לאו קרא אפי' אי בעלמא לא דחי ובפ"ב דיבמות (דף כא.) דאמר גבי פלוגתא דר' יוחנן ור"א בביאת כ"ג באלמנה מן הנישואין כ"ע לא פליגי דלא פטרה דאין עשה דוחה לא תעשה ועשה וי"ל דחשיב שוה בכל כיון שהאלמנה עשתה איסור כמו הכהן דאקרי ביה לא יקח לא יקחו אע"ג דאין שוה בכל אלא בכהנים אבל הכא דגילות זקן שאינו שוה בנשים נדחי מקמי עשה דמצורע:

**אלא** לזקן ואינו לפי כבודו. וא"ת תיפוק ליה מולאחותו דכבוד הבריות דוחה מילת בנו ושחיטת פסחו וי"ל כבוד הבריות דמת מצוה חמיר טפי שמוטל בבזיון פן יסריח או יאכלוהו כלבים אע"ג דבפ' מי שמתו (ברכות דף כ. ושם ד"ה שב) מוכח דלאו הוה כלאים שב ואל תעשה היה נדחה מפני כבוד הבריות היינו משום דערום הוי גנות ובזיון גדול כדאמר (יבמות דף סג:) אין לך משוקץ יותר מאותו שהוא מהלך ערום ומהכא לא ידעי' דדחי אלא ממונא אבל איסורא כמו פסח ומילה וגם כרת לא: [וע' תוס' שבועות ל: ד"ה אבל]:

**אפקרה.** שלא יכשלו בני אדם בלא תגזול וא"ת הא אמר בפ' אין בין המודר (נדרים דף מה.) אין הפקר אלא בפני שלשה וי"ל דהכא נמי הוו שלשה אי נמי דאורייתא בלא שלשה נמי הוי הפקר והא דאמר שלהי פ"ק דשבת (דף יח: ושם ד"ה דמפקרא) גיגית נר וקדירה אפקורי מפקר להו אע"ג דליכא שלשה התם אין סהדי דמפקר להו בלבו שלא יעשה איסור שביתת כלים: **לא** חרבה כו'. ואם תאמר דביומא (דף ט:) אמר מפני שנאת חנם וי"ל דהא והא גרמא:

**איזוהי** אבידה. שיבין שאין הבעלים יודעין שהיא שם:

קורדוס

---

### עין משפט נר מצוה

קמד א ב מיי' פי"א מהל' גזלה ואבידה הל' יג יד סמג עשין עד טוש"ע ח"מ סי' רסג סעיף ב:

קמה ג מיי' שם הל' יג טוש"ע שם סעיף א:

קמו ד מיי' פי"ג מהל' רוצח הל' ד סמג עשין פא טוש"ע ח"מ סי' רעב סעיף ג:

קמז ה מיי' פ"ב מהל' נדרים הלכה טו טוש"ע ח"מ סי' רעג סעיף ה:

קמח ו מיי' פי"א מהל' אבידה הלכה יח ופי"ג מהל' רוצח הל' ד סמג עשין עד פא טוש"ע ח"מ סי' רסג סעיף ג וסי' רעב סעיף ג:

קמט ז מיי' פי"ד מהל' אבילות הלכה ד סמג עשין ב טוש"ע י"ד סי' שלה סעיף ב:

קנ ח מיי' פט"ו מהל' אבידה הל' ב סמג עשין עד טוש"ע ח"מ סי' רפא סעיף א:

קנא ט מיי' שם פי"א הל' יד סמג שם טוש"ע ח"מ סי' רסז סעיף ב:

קנב י כ ל מיי' שם פי"ב הל' ד סמג שם טוש"ע ח"מ סי' רסה:

קנג מ מיי' שם פט"ו הלכה ג סמג שם טוש"ע ח"מ סי' רפא סעיף א:

### רבינו חננאל

והיא בבית הקברות לא צריכא מאי טעמא דהא כהן מוזהר בטומאה עשה ולא תעשה עשה שנאמר וקדשתו קדשים יהיו לאלהיהם לא תעשה שנאמר לנפש לא יטמא בעמיו והשבת אבידה עשה היא שנאמר השב תשיבם לאחי' ולא אתי עשה ודחי את לא תעשה ועשה ותוב לא דחינן איסורא מקמי ממונא. שלו מרובה משל חבירו שנאמר אפס כי לא יהיה בך אביון שלך קודם לשל כל אדם. אמר רבא כל שבשלו מחזיר בשל חבירו נמי מחזיר כל שבשלו פורק וטוען בשל חבירו נמי פורק וטוען. אביי שקל קלא פתק בהני עיזי דהוו קיימי. אמר ליה רבא איחייבת בהו קום אהדרינהו. וכן אמר רב הכישה נתחייב בה. דרכו להנהיג בחמור או למשוך בגמל בשדה ואין דרכו בעיר ועלתה בתיקו: מתני' איזהו אבידה מצא חמור וכו' אוקמה רב יהודה למתני' הכי קאמר איזהו היא כלל אבידה שחייב להחזירה מצא חמור וכליו הפוכין פרה ורצה בין הכרמים הרי זו אבידה וחייב להחזיר. תניא נמי הכי. דרך בלשון יון נקראת

### מסורת הש"ס

א) בבא בתרא פח., ב) פא פרק ו [משנה א, עדיו פרק ד משנה ג], ג) [לע כד: וש"נ], ד) בבא קמ לט., ה) [מיבת אש מיותר], ו) [נדרים לג ע"ש], ז) [לקמן פח. ח) [עיין תוס' לקמן לג ד"ה אם], ט) [עי' תוס לעיל כח. ד"ה וכמה י) פי' או במשכת מהרש"ל, כ) ובהגהל דף פירש"י תלמוד תורה, ע" כ"י, ל) ס"א שזה אומ כו', מהרש"ל, מ) נ' דעשה דמצורע דוחה עש דשילוח הקן אי לאו כ ועיין מהרש"א.

### הגהות הב"ח

(א) גמ' במשנה שכ כפועל. נ"ב ע"ל דף ס"א: (ב) רש"י ד"ה בית וכו' ותורות. נ" ובב"ק דף ק'. פרש"י דה ת"ת וצ"ע:

### הגהות הגר"א

[א] [ב] גמ' אשר. רש קו עליו למחקו:

### גליון הש"ס

רש"י ד"ה דיני. בער ערך מגיסתא הגירסא כ דייני דמגיסתא ופי' דדי בגסות:

### תורה אור השלם

א) וְהִזְהַרְתָּה אֶתְהֶם אֶת הַחֻקִּים וְאֶת הַתּוֹרֹת וְהוֹדַעְתָּ לָהֶם אֶת הַדֶּרֶךְ יֵלְכוּ בָהּ וְאֶת הַמַּעֲשֶׂה אֲשֶׁר יַעֲשׂוּן: [שמות יח, כ]

ב) לֹא תִרְאֶה אֶת שׁוֹר אָחִיךָ אוֹ אֶת שֵׂיוֹ נִדָּחִים וְהִתְעַלַּמְתָּ מֵהֶם הָשֵׁב תְּשִׁיבֵם לְאָחִיךָ: [דברים כב, א]

### לעזי רש"י

מרט"א. פירוש גושה ש קרקע (רש"י תענית דף ע"א ד"ה אפי'), פיס רגבים (רש"י ע"ז דף ע"ב ד"ה שקל קלא).

### ליקוטי רש"י

לא יהיה בך אביון. הזהר מן עניות [לקו לג.]. הזהר בעצמך של תבא לידי עניות [סנהדר סד:]. הכישה. במכ [רשב"ם ב"ב פח.]. דר נושא [עי' ע"ז נט:]. בי חייהם. תלמוד תור [ב"ק ק.]. לבן גילו. בן כמותו או זקן לזקן [נדר לט:]. שנולד בפרק אח ובמזל אחד [יבמות קכ. דיני דמגיזתא. כפר שאין יודעין לד במשפט לשון אר דמגוזתא אנסין בחזק כמו אתו גיזאי וקא מ ליה סריסים העומדי לרדות בחזקה [ב"ק קיד.

"לֹא־יִהְיֶה בְּךָ אֶבְיוֹן – **among you there will be no destitute.**[1] This teaches that שֶׁלְּךָ קוֹדֵם לְשֶׁל כָּל אָדָם – **your** financial concerns **take precedence to those of everyone** else. Accordingly, it is evident that the finder is exempt when retrieving the object would cause him financial loss; no special verse is necessary to teach this. – ? –

The Gemara concludes:

אֶלָּא – **Rather,** the verse is needed לְזָקֵן וְאֵינוֹ לְפִי כְבוֹדוֹ – **for the** case in which the finder is an **elderly man and it is not befitting his honor** to pick up this particular lost object. In such a case, the verse teaches that he is indeed not required to do so.

The Gemara now qualifies the Baraisa's ruling regarding the elderly finder:

אָמַר רַבָּה – **Rabbah said:** הִכִּישָׁהּ – **If [the elderly person] hit [the animal]** even once, prodding it to walk towards its owner, חַיָּיב בָּהּ – **he is obligated to** finish returning **it.**[2]

The Gemara records an incident in which Rabbah's ruling is applied:

אַבַּיֵי הֲוָה יָתִיב קַמֵּיהּ דְּרַבָּה – **Abaye was sitting**[3] **before Rabbah,** חֲזָא לְהָנָךְ עִיזֵּי דְּקָיְימוּ – **when he saw some goats that were standing** and were apparently lost. שְׁקַל קָלָא וְשָׁדָא בְּהוּ – **He took a clump of dirt and threw it at them,** hoping to chase them towards their owner.[4] אָמַר לֵיהּ – **[Rabbah] said to him:** אִיחַיַּיבְתְּ בְּהוּ – Through your action, **you have become obligated to** restore **them** to their owner; קוּם אַהְדְּרִינְהוּ – **get up and return them.**

A related query:

אִיבַּעְיָא לְהוּ – **[The Rabbis of the academy] inquired:** If a distinguished elder finds an object in a field and the owner of the object lives in the city, דַּרְכּוֹ לְהַחֲזִיר בַּשָּׂדֶה – and **it would be [the elder's] practice to return** such an object **in the field,** where few people would observe him, וְאֵין דַּרְכּוֹ לְהַחֲזִיר בָּעִיר – **but it would not be his practice to return** it **in the city,** where many people would observe him, causing him shame, מַהוּ – **what** is the law? Is he obligated to return it or not?

The Gemara clarifies the underlying issue involved in th[e] query:

מִי אַמְרִינַן הֲשָׁבָה מַעֲלְיָא בְּעֵינַן – **Do we say: We require** one t[o] undertake **a complete** act of **return** or none at all; [כֵּ]יוָן דְּלָאו דַּרְכֵּיהּ לְהַחֲזִיר בָּעִיר – **and since it is not [this person's] practic[e] to return** such an object **in the city,** לֹא לִחַיַּיב – **he should no[t] become obligated** to return it at all, even in the field? [א]וֹ דִלְמָא – **Or perhaps we say:** בְּשָׂדֶה מִיהַת הוּא דְּאִיחַיַּיב לֵיהּ – **In th[e] field, at least, he is obligated** to begin the act of returning [it] (since it does not compromise his dignity to do so there), [כֵּ]יוָן דְּאִיחַיַּיב לֵיהּ בְּשָׂדֶה – **and once he becomes obligated in th[e] field,** אִיחַיַּיב לֵיהּ בָּעִיר – **he** remains **obligated** even **in th[e] city?**[5]

The Gemara responds:

תֵּיקוּ – **The question remains unresolved.**[6]

The Baraisa had ruled that one need not return an object whe[n] it compromises his dignity to do so. The Gemara now defines th[e] criterion by which this exemption is applied:

אָמַר רָבָא – **Rava said:** כָּל שֶׁבְּשֶׁלּוֹ מַחֲזִיר – **Any** object **that on[e] would return** if it were **his own,** בְּשֶׁל חֲבֵירוֹ נַמִּי מַחֲזִיר – **h[e] must also return** if it is **his friend's.**[7] וְכָל שֶׁבְּשֶׁלּוֹ פּוֹרֵק וְטוֹעֵן – **And,** similarly, **any bundle that one would unload or load** if [i]t were **his own,** בְּשֶׁל חֲבֵירוֹ נַמִּי פּוֹרֵק וְטוֹעֵן – **he must also** hel[p] **unload or load** if it is **his friend's.**[8]

The Gemara recounts an incident in connection with Rava'[s] ruling:

רַבִּי יִשְׁמָעֵאל בְּרַבִּי יוֹסֵי הֲוָה קָאָזִיל בְּאוֹרְחָא – **R' Yishmael son of R[']** **Yose was traveling on the road** פָּגַע בֵּיהּ הַהוּא גַּבְרָא – when **a certain man** chanced to **meet him.** [הֲ]וָה דָּרֵי פִּתְכָּא דְאוּפֵי – **[The man] had been carrying a bundle of wood,** [א]וֹתְבִינְהוּ – which **he placed** on the ground **and,** now, **h[e] was resting.** When he was ready to go on, וְקָא מִיתְפַּח אָמַר לֵיהּ – **[the man] said to [R' Yishmael son of R' Yose]:** דְּלֵי לִי – **"Load** th[e] wood back upon **me."** אָמַר לֵיהּ – **[R' Yishmael son of R' Yose] replied to him:** כַּמָּה שָׁוֵין – **"How much is** your **[bundle] worth?"** אָמַר לֵיהּ פַּלְגָּא דְזוּזָא – **He answered him: "Half [a]**

NOTES

1. The simple meaning of the verse is to promise that there will be no destitute among you if you observe meticulously the Sabbatical law of relinquishing debts. If so, however, the word אֶפֶס, *But,* would be redundant. Rav therefore expounds the verse as an injunction, and the word אֶפֶס as *naught*: "Make naught (i.e. take measures to insure that) there shall not be *within you* (personally) a destitute person" (*Sanhedrin* 64b as explained by *Rashi* there ד"ה התם מאפס).

2. Such a person would normally have been exempt from returning the animal. Since, however, he began the act of returning it, he is obligated to complete this process (*Rashi*).

*Ritva* challenges *Rashi's* explanation from the Gemara in *Bava Basra* (88a). There, the Gemara qualifies Rabbah's ruling as applying only to a case in which the elderly person chased the animal *away* from its owner, thereby increasing the chance that it would remain lost. In such a case, *Ritva* asserts, the person is required to return the animal, but he need not continue returning it if he merely prodded it to walk *towards* its owner.

3. [This expression denotes a pupil sitting before his teacher, studying Torah.]

4. Our rendering here follows *Rashi's* interpretation of Rabbah's law (see above, note 2).

5. I.e. once he begins the process of returning, he must complete it, as Rabbah stated earlier (see *Rashi*; for an explanation of the query according to *Ritva,* see *R' Akiva Eiger*).

6. For a discussion of the halachic ruling here, see *Rosh* §21 and *Nimukei Yosef.*

7. Rava rules that the following test be applied to determine whether a finder is exempt from retrieving a given lost object: If the finder himself were the owner of this object, would he leave it in its present state rathe[r] than degrade himself by retrieving it? If the finder would answer "yes" to this question, then he need not return the object when it belongs t[o] his fellow either. If, however, he would answer "no" to this question then he must indeed retrieve the object for his fellow.

In connection with this ruling, *Chochmas Shlomo* asks the followin[g] question: If Rava's standard is indeed the criterion for determinin[g] whether a person is obligated to return an object, why is it that th[e] Mishnah and Baraisa mention this exemption regarding a sage o[r] elderly man specifically? Seemingly, any person would be exempt, s[o] long as he would not retrieve the object were it his own! *Chochma[s] Shlomo* answers that the Mishnah specifically mentions a sage or elderl[y] man because such a person is assumed to be exempt from returnin[g] objects unless it is known otherwise [i.e. unless it is known that h[e] *would* "return" the object in question had it been his own]. An ordinar[y] person, on the other hand, is assumed to be obligated to return objects unless it is known otherwise [i.e. unless it is known that he would *no[t]* "return" the object were it his own].

8. When one sees that a person's animal has collapsed under the weigh[t] of its load, he is obligated by the Torah to assist the owner in unloadin[g] the goods from upon the animal's back. Similarly, when one sees tha[t] bundles of goods have fallen off an animal, he is required to help th[e] owner reload the fallen items.

These duties, mandated by *Exodus* 23:5 and *Deuteronomy* 22:4 respectively, are known as פְּרִיקָה, *unloading*, and טְעִינָה, *loading*. As wit[h] returning a lost object, one becomes exempt from *unloading* or *loadin[g]* when his performance of these actions would compromise his dignity Rava here sets forth the criterion for determining when this exemptio[n] applies.

לא יהיה בך אביון שלך קודם לשל כל אדם אלא לזקן ואינו לפי כבודו [א] אמר רבה [א] הכישה חייב בה אביי הוה יתיב קמיה דרבה חזא להנך עיזי דקיימו שקל קלא ושדא בהו א"ל איחייבת בהו קום אהדרינהו [ב] איבעיא להו דרכו להחזיר בשדה ואין דרכו להחזיר בעיר מהו מי אמרינן השבה מעליא בעינן וכיון דלאו דרכיה להחזיר בעיר לא לחייב או דלמא בשדה מיהת הוא דאיחייב ליה וכיון דאיחייב ליה בשדה איחייב ליה בעיר תיקו אמר רבא [ג] כל שבשלו מחזיר בשל חבירו נמי מחזיר [ד] וכל שבשלו פורק וטוען בשל חבירו נמי פורק וטוען רבי ישמעאל ברבי יוסי הוה קאזיל באורחא פגע ביה ההוא גברא הוה דרי פתכא דאופי אותבינהו וקא מיתפח א"ל דלי לי אמר ליה כמה שוין א"ל פלגא דזוזא יהיב ליה פלגא דזוזא ואפקרה הדר זכה בהו הדר יהיב ליה פלגא דזוזא ואפקרה חזייה דהוה קא בעי למיהדר למזכיה בהו א"ל לכולי עלמא אפקרנהו ולך לא אפקרנהו ומי הוי הפקר כי האי גוונא והתנן [ב] בש"א הפקר לעניים הפקר ובה"א [ה] אינו הפקר עד שיהא הפקר לעניים ולעשירים כשמיטה אלא רבי ישמעאל ברבי יוסי לכולי עלמא אפקרינהו ובמלתא בעלמא הוא דאוקמיה והא רבי ישמעאל ברבי יוסי זקן ואינו לפי כבודו הוה ר' ישמעאל ברבי יוסי [ג] [ו] לפנים משורת הדין הוא דעבד [ד] דתני רב יוסף [א] והודעת להם זה בית חייהם את הדרך זו גמילות חסדים [א] [ה] (אשר) ילכו זה ביקור חולים בה זו קבורה ואת המעשה זה הדין אשר יעשון זו לפנים משורת הדין: אמר מר [ב] (אשר) ילכו זה ביקור חולים היינו גמילות חסדים לא נצרכה אלא [ז] לבן גילו דאמר מר [ו] בן גילו נוטל אחד מששים בחליו ואפי' הכי מבעי ליה למיזל לגביה בה זו קבורה היינו גמילות חסדים לא נצרכה אלא לזקן ואינו לפי כבודו אשר יעשון זו לפנים משורת הדין דאמר ר' יוחנן לא חרבה ירושלים אלא על שדנו בה דין תורה אלא דיני דמגיזתא לדיינו אלא אימא [ז] שהעמידו דיניהם על דין תורה ולא עבדו לפנים משורת הדין: **מתני'** אי זו היא אבידה [ח] מצא חמור או פרה רועין בדרך אין זו אבידה חמור וכליו הפוכין פרה רצה בין הכרמים הרי זו אבידה [ט] החזירה וברחה החזירה וברחה אפי' ארבעה וחמשה פעמים חייב להחזירה שנאמר [ב] השב תשיבם [י] היה בטל מסלע לא יאמר לו תן לי סלע אלא נותן לו (א) שכרו כפועל [ט] [כ] אם יש שם בית דין מתנה בפני ב"ד [ל] אם אין שם ב"ד בפני מי יתנה שלו קודם: **גמ'** אטו כל הני דאמרינן לאו אבידה הוו אמר רב יהודה הכי קאמר אי זו היא כלל אבידה שהוא חייב בה מצא חמור ופרה רועין בדרך אין זו אבידה ולא מיחייב בה חמור וכליו הפוכים פרה ורצה בין הכרמים הרי זו אבידה ומיחייב בה [ט] ולעולם אמר רב יהודה אמר רב עד שלשה ימים היכי דמי אי בלילותא אפי' חדא שעתא נמי אי ביממא אפי' טובא נמי לא [מ] לא צריכא דהוה חזי לה בקדמתא [י] ובחשכתא תלתא יומי אמרינן איתרמויי אתרמי לה ונפקא טפי ודאי אבידה היא תניא נמי הכי מצא טלית וקרדום באסרטיא

**רש"י**

לא יהיה בך אביון. לא תביא עצמך לידי עניות: **הכישה.** זה שאינו לפי כבודו אם הכישה הבהמה אחת להשיבה נתחייב בה להחזירה הואיל והתחיל: **קלא.** מרט"א בלע"ז: **דרכו להחזיר בשדה.** שאין שם רואים כל כך ואינו בוש: **ואין דרכו בעיר.** שהוא בוש משכיניו והוא מלא בשדה: **מהו.** שיתחייב להשיבה: **לא מיחייב.** להתחיל בהשבתה בשדה: **וכיון דאיחייב.** שהזיזה ממקומה חייב אף בעיר: **פורק וטוען.** פורק משא מן החמור וטוען עליו דכתיב עזוב תעזוב הקם תקים: **פתכא דאופי.** משאוי של עצים: **וקא מיתפח.** עומד לפוש: **דלי לי.** הטעינני: **הדר זכה בהו.** חזר האיש ההוא והחזיק בהן מן ההפקר: **הפקר לעניים הוי הפקר.** אע"ג שלא הפקירו אלא לעניים הוי הפקר למפטר מן המעשר: **זה בית חייהם.** [י] ללמוד להם אומנות להתפרנס בו חוקות (ג) ותורות כתיבי ברישיה דקרא: [ט] **דיני דמגיזתא לידיינו.** בתמיה. דמגיזתא גוזאי הדנין ביסורים ובחזקה וחבירו בבבא קמא (דף קיד.) דדייני בגזתיא: **מתני'** איזו היא אבידה. בגמרא מפרש: **אין זו אבידה.** ואינו חייב להחזיר שמדעת הניחוה שם: **רצה בין הכרמים.** דמסתקבלא: **לא יאמר לו תן לי סלע.** שבטלתי ממלאכתי [ל] שיאמר לו אם עשית מלאכתך היית מרבה טורח עכשיו לפי מה שטרחת טול: **כפועל.** בגמרא מפרש: **אם יש שם בית דין.** אם נוח לו לטרוח יותר כדי להרבות שכר ואינו חפץ ליבטל ממלאכתו מה יעשה אם יש שם שלשה בני אדם יתנה בפניהם ויאמר ראו שאני משתכר כך וכך ואי איפשי ליבטל ליטול שכר מועט אני אשיב אם תאמרו שאטול שכר משלם: **גמ'** כלל. סתם אבידה שמוכחת שהיא שם שלא מדעת בעלים: **ולעולם.** בתמיה וכי אף אם ימצאנה שם לעולם נאמר מדעת היא וכי דרך שלא להכניס: **בקדמותא.** לפני עלות השחר: **חשכתא.** שחשכה ערבית: **אסרטיא**

**תוספות**

ה"מ לא תעשה ועשה השוה בכל אבל האי דאינו שוה בכל דחי כדמוכח פרק שני נזירין (נזיר דף נח:) דאתי עשה דמצורע ודחי לאו ועשה דכהנים וכן ק' לקמן (לב.) יכול אמר לו אביו הטמא כו' ופריך תיפוק ליה דאין עשה דוחה לא תעשה ועשה הא גבי כהנים שאינו שוה בכל דחי וי"ל דעשה דמצורע שאני דחמיר משום דגדול השלום כדאמר בפ' שילוח הקן (חולין דף קמא.) [מ] דעשה דמצורע הוי דחי לאו ועשה דשילוח הקן אי לאו יתורא דשלח תשלח אבל עשה דעלמא לא דחי לאו ועשה אפילו אינו שוה בכל וזה התירוץ לא יתיישב למאן דשרי מצורע בימי חלוטו בתשמיש המטה פ"ק דמועד קטן (דף ז:) ולדידיה יש לומר דהכא סמיך על ותו מי דחינן איסורא מקמי ממונא ולקמן נמי עדיפא משני דהוה דחי אפילו לאו ועשה אי לאו קרא אפי' אי בעלמא לא דחי ובפ"ב דיבמות (דף כא.) דאמר גבי פלוגתא דר' יוחנן ור"א בביאת כ"ג באלמנה מן הנישואין כ"ע לא פליגי דלא פטרה דאין עשה דוחה לא תעשה ועשה וי"ל דחשיב שוה בכל כיון שהאלמנה עשתה איסור כמו הכהן דאקרי ביה לא יקחו לא יקחו אע"ג דאין שוה בכל אלא בכהנים אבל ההיא דגילוח זקן שאינו שוה בנשים נדחי מקמי עשה דמצורע:

**אלא** לזקן ואינו לפי כבודו. וא"ת תיפוק ליה מולאחותו דכבוד הבריות דוחה מילת בנו ושחיטת פסחו וי"ל כבוד הבריות דמת מצוה חמיר טפי שמוטל בבזיון פן יסריח או יאכלוהו כלבים אע"ג דבפ' מי שמתו (ברכות דף כ. ושם ד"ה שב) מוכח דלאו הוה כלאים שב ואל תעשה היה נדחה מפני כבוד הבריות היינו משום דערום הוי גנות ובזיון גדול כדאמר (יבמות דף סג:) אין לך משוקץ יותר מאותו שהוא מהלך ערום ומהכא לא ידעי' דדחי אלא ממונא אבל איסורא כמו פסח ומילה וגם כרת לא: [וע' תוס' שבועות ל: ד"ה אבל]:

**אפקרה.** שלא יכשלו בני אדם בלא תגזול וא"ת הא אמר בפ' אין בין המודר (נדרים דף מה.) אין הפקר אלא בפני שלשה וי"ל דהכא נמי הוו שלשה אי נמי לאורייתא בלא שלשה נמי הוי הפקר והא דאמר שלהי פ"ק דשבת (דף יח: ושם ד"ה דמפקרא) גיגית נר וקדירה אפקורי מפקר להו אע"ג דליכא שלשה התם אנן סהדי דמפקר להו בלבו שלא יעשה איסור שביתת כלים:

**לא** חרבה כו'. ואם תאמר דביומא (דף ט:) אמר מפני שנאת חנם וי"ל דהא והא גרמא:

**איזוהי** אבידה. סימן שאין הבעלים יודעין שהיא שם: קורדוס

ע"ש

**עין משפט נר מצוה**

קמד א ב מיי' פי"א מהל' גזלה ואבידה הל' יג יד סמג עשין עד טוש"ע ח"מ סי' רסג סעיף ב:

קמה ג מיי' שם הל' יג טוש"ע שם סעיף א:

קמו ד מיי' פי"ג מהל' רוצח הל' ד סמג עשין פא טוש"ע ח"מ סי' רעב סעיף ג:

קמז ה מיי' פ"ב מהל' נדרים הלכה טו טוש"ע ח"מ סי' רעג סעיף ה:

קמח ו מיי' פי"א מהל' אבידה הלכה יח ופי"ג מהל' רוצח הל' ד סמג עשין עד פא טוש"ע ח"מ סי' רסג סעיף ג וסי' רעב סעיף ג:

קמט ז מיי' פי"ד מהל' אבילות הלכה ד סמג עשין ב טוש"ע י"ד סי' שלה סעיף ב:

קנ ח מיי' פט"ו מהל' אבידה הל' ב סמג עשין עד טוש"ע ח"מ סי' רסא סעיף א:

קנא ט מיי' שם פי"א הל' יד סמג שם טוש"ע ח"מ סי' רסו סעיף ב:

קנב י כ ל מיי' שם פי"ב הל' ד סמג שם טוש"ע ח"מ סי' רסה:

קנג מ מיי' שם פט"ו הלכה ג סמג שם טוש"ע ח"מ סי' רסא סעיף א:

**רבינו חננאל**

והיא בבית הקברות לא צריכא מאי טעמא דהא כהן מוזהר בטומאה עשה ולא תעשה עשה שנאמר וקדשתו קדשים יהיו לאלהיהם לא תעשה שנאמר לנפש לא יטמא בעמיו והשבת אבידה עשה היא שנאמר השב תשיבם לאחי' ולא אתי עשה ודחי את לא תעשה ועשה ותוב לא דחינן איסורא מקמי ממונא. שלו מרובה משל חבירו שנאמר אפס כי לא יהיה בך אביון שלך קודם לשל כל אדם. אמר רבא כל שבשלו מחזיר בשל חבירו נמי מחזיר כל שבשלו פורק וטוען בשל חבירו נמי פורק וטוען. אביי שקל קלא פתק בהני עיזי דהוו קיימי. אמר ליה רבא איחייבת בהו קום אהדרינהו. וכן אמר רב הכישה נתחייב בה. דרכו להנהיג בחמור או למשוך בגמל בשדה ואין דרכו בעיר ועלתה בתיקו: **מתני'** איזהו אבידה מצא חמור וכו' אוקמה רב יהודה למתני' הכי קאמר איזהו היא כלל אבידה שחייב להחזירה מצא חמור וכליו הפוכין פרה ורצה בין הכרמים הרי זו אבידה וחייב להחזיר. תניא נמי הכי. דרך בלשון יון נקראת

**מסורת הש"ס**

א) בבא בתרא פח., ב) פאה פרק ו [משנה א, עדיות פרק ד משנה ג], ג) [לעיל כד: וש"נ], ד) בבא קמא לט:, ה) [מיבת אש מיותר], ו) [נדרים לט ע"ש], ז) [לקמן פח.], ח) [עיין תוס' לקמן לא ד"ה אם], ט) [עי' תוס' לעיל כא. ד"ה וכמה], י) פי' או בחשכת מהרש"ל, כ) ובהגהל דף פירש"י תלמוד תורה, ע" כ"י, ל) ס"א שזה אומ כו', מהרש"ל, מ) ל' דעשה דמצורע דוחה עש דשילוח הקן אי לאו כו ועיין מהרש"א.

**הגהות הב"ח**

(א) גמ' במשנה שכו כפועל. נ"ב ע"ל דד ס"ח: (ב) רש"י ד"ה ז בית וכו' ותורות. נ" ובב"ק דף ק'. פרש"י דהו ת"ת ול"ע:

**הגהות הגר"א**

[א][ב] גמ' אשר. רשו קו עליו למחקו:

**גליון הש"ס**

רש"י ד"ה דיני. בערו ערך מגיסתא הגירסא כל דייני דמגיסתא ופי' דדנ בגסות:

**תורה אור השלם**

א) וְהִזְהַרְתָּה אֶתְהֶם אֶת הַחֻקִּים וְאֶת הַתּוֹרֹת וְהוֹדַעְתָּ לָהֶם אֶת הַדֶּרֶךְ יֵלְכוּ בָהּ וְאֶת הַמַּעֲשֶׂה אֲשֶׁר יַעֲשׂוּן: [שמות יח, כ]

ב) לֹא תִרְאֶה אֶת שׁוֹר אָחִיךָ אוֹ אֶת שֵׂיוֹ נִדָּחִים וְהִתְעַלַּמְתָּ מֵהֶם הָשֵׁב תְּשִׁיבֵם לְאָחִיךָ: [דברים כב, א]

**לעזי רש"י**

מרט"א. פירוש גושה בקרקע (רש"י תענית דף ע"א ד"ה אפי'), פיס רגבים (רש"י ע"ז דף ע"ב ד"ה שקל קלא).

**ליקוטי רש"י**

**לא יהיה בך אביון.** הזהר מן עניות [לקו לג.]. הזהר בעצמך שלא תבא לידי עניות [סנהדרין סד:]. **הכישה.** במק [רשב"ם ב"ב פח.]. **דרך** נושא [עי' ע"ז נט:]. **בית חייהם.** תלמוד תורה [ב"ק ק.]. **לבן גילו.** כמו כמותו או זקן לזקן [נדרים לט:]. שנולד בפרק אחד ובמזל אחד [יבמות קכ.]. **דיני דמגיזתא.** כפר שאין יודעין לדון במשפט לשון אחר דמגוזתא אנסין בחזקה כמו אתו גיזאי וקא מ ליה סריסים העומדים לרדות בחזקה [ב"ק קיד.].

א) בתורי דנפיש פסידייהו: שוטחה לצורכה אבל לא לכבודו וכו': איבעיא להו לצורכו ולצורכה מאי ת"ש שוטחה לצורכה לצורכה אין א הא לצורכו ולצורכה לא אימא סיפא אבל לא לכבודו לכבודו הוא דלא הא לצורכה ולצורכו שפיר דמי ב) אלא מהא ליכא למשמע מינה ת"ש ג) לא ישטחנה לא על גבי מטה ולא על גבי ד) מגוד לצרכו אבל ישטחנה על גבי מטה ועל גבי מגוד לצרכה נזדמנו לו אורחים לא ישטחנה לא על גבי מטה ולא על גבי מגוד בין לצורכו בין לצורכה שאני התם דמקלא קלי לה אי משום עינא אי משום גנבי תא שמע ה) ב הכניסה לרבקה ודשה כשירה בשביל שתינק ותדוש פסולה והא הכא דלצורכו ולצורכה הוא וקתני פסולה שאני התם דאמר קרא א) אשר לא עובד בה מ"מ אי הכי אפילו רישא נמי הא לא דמיא אלא להא ו) דתנן ג שכן עליה עוף כשירה עלה עליה זכר פסולה מאי טעמא כדרב פפא דאמר רב פפא אי כתיב עובד וקרינן עובד הוה אמינא אפילו ממילא ואי כתיב עבד וקרינן עבד הוה אמינא עד דעבד בה איהו השתא דכתיב עבד וקרינן עובד בעינן עובד דומיא דעבד ד מה עבד דניחא ליה אף עובד דניחא ליה: כלי כסף וכלי נחושת משתמש בהן בחמין וכו': ת"ר ה המוצא כלי עץ משתמש בהן בשביל שלא ירקבו ו כלי נחושת משתמש בהן בחמין אבל לא על ידי האור מפני ששוחקן ז כלי כסף משתמש בהן בצונן אבל לא בחמין מפני שמשחירן ח מגריפות וקרדומות משתמש בהן ברך אבל לא בקשה מפני שמפחיתן כלי זהב וכלי זכוכית לא יגע בהן עד שיבא אליהו ט כדרך שאמרו באבידה כך אמרו בפקדון פקדון מאי עבידתיה גביה אמר רב אדא בר חמא אמר רב ששת י בפקדון שהלכו בעליהן למדינת הים: מצא שק או קופה [וכל דבר] שאין דרכו ליטול הרי זה לא יטול: מנהני מילי ז) דת"ר ב) והתעלמת פעמים שאתה מתעלם ופעמים שאי אתה מתעלם הא כיצד כ היה כהן והיא בבית הקברות ל או שהיה זקן ואינה לפי כבודו מ או שהיתה מלאכה שלו מרובה משל חבירו לכך נאמר והתעלמת מהם למאי איצטריך קרא אילימא לכהן והיא בבית הקברות פשיטא האי עשה והאי לא תעשה ועשה נ ולא אתי עשה ודחי את לא תעשה ועשה ותו לא דחינן איסורא מקמי ממונא אלא לשלו מרובה משל חבירו מדרב יהודה אמר רב נפקא ח) דאמר רב יהודה אמר רב ג) אפס כי

**רש"י**

דנפיש פסידייהו. שרוב עבודת קרקעות שלהן בשוורים היתה אף חרישת הכרמים ובצירתם מנהיגים כלי שורות הכרם עם הבוצרים ונותנין שם הענבים לפיכך אם אין הבעלים עליהם יש הפסד גדול שאין דרך הפועלים לחוס על הכרם ועל השוורים ומנהיגים אותן על הגפנים ועל הנטיעות והם מתקלקלין והשוורין נסחבין ונשברים: מגוד. קביל"א בלע"ז: נזדמנו לו אורחים. קס"ד טעמא משום דמתכבד בהם ואיכא לצורכה ולצרכו: שאני התם דקא קלי לה. בשטיחה זו הוא שורפה ומה הוא שריפתה: אי משום עינא. שתשלוט בה עין רע של אורחין: אי משום גנבי. פן יגנבוה האורחים: הכניסה לרבקה. בעגלה ערופה קאי. רבקה קופל"ה בלע"ז שמדבקים שלש בהמות או ארבעה בצואריהן זו אצל זו ודשים הדישה: כשירה. הואיל ולא נתכוון שתדוש: ואם בשביל שתינק ותדוש. שהיתה אמה דשה והכניס את הבת לשם שתינק ואף נתכוין שתדוש פסולה: הא לא דמיא. תירוצא היא: שכן עליה עוף. בפרה אדומה קאי: עלה עליה זכר פסולה. שנאמר אשר לא עלה עליה עול ותניא עול אין לי אלא עול כו' במסכת סוטה (דף מו.) והאי הכניסה לרבקה ודשה דלא ניחא ליה בה דמיא לשכן עליה עוף: משתמש בהן בחמין. וכ"ש בצונן: אבל לא ע"י האור. לא יתן הכלי על האור: מגריפות. ודיל"ש עשוין לגרוף הכירות או להפריש תאנים המדובקים: שמפחיתן. פוגמן: מאי עבידתיה גביה. מה לו להשתמש בו יבא בעליו וישתמש בו: והתעלמת מהם. וללמדך בא שמותר להתעלם: ופעמים שאי אתה מתעלם. דכתיב לא תוכל להתעלם: והיא בבית הקברות. האבידה בבית הקברות: ואינה לפי כבודו. שישיבנה: או שהיה בטל ממלאכה שלו. שיבטל בהשבתה מרובה על דמי האבידה: האי עשה. השב תשיבם ואע"ג דלא תעשה נמי איכא אין לא תעשה מועיל לדחות לא תעשה אלא עשה הוא דקא דחי ליה כדאמרינן ביבמות (דף כא.): לא תעשה ועשה. לנפש לא יטמא קדושים יהיו: לא

**תוספות**

בתורי דנפיש פסידייהו. ר"ח גרס בתוורי פירוש פועלים שמוליכים השוורים לחרישה ואין מעמיקין המחרישה שלשה טפחים ואין הזרע נקלט היטב ט):

לצורכו ולצורכה מאי. דוקא בשיטוח כסות מבעיא ליה וכל דדמי ליה דשמא יניחנה שטוחה יותר מכדי צורכה עד שיתקלקל אבל בספר אמרינן דקורא בהן אף ע"ג דלצורכו הוא כמו צורכה ולא גזרינן דליכא למיחש למידי כיון שקבעו לו זמן אחד לשלשים יום או אחד לי"ב חדש ולא ילמוד בו בתחלה גם לא יקרא וישנה וכלי נחשת דתניא לקמן דמשתמש אפי' בחמין וכלי כסף בצונן אפי' לצורכו מותר כיון שעל ידי אותו תשמיש אינו יכול לבא לידי קלקול ותדע דאי דוקא לצורך הכלי מאי פריך פקדון מאי עבידתיה גביה כיון שהוא שומר יש לו לעיין שלא יתקלקל אע"פ שהבעלים אינם אומרים לו להשתמש:

הכניסה לרבקה ודשה. בתוספת' (דפרה) י) תני לה גבי פרה אדומה: בשביל שתינק ותדוש פסולה. ובסיפא (דתוספתא כ) קתני לצורכו פסולה לצורכה כשירה ולכך פריך אלמא לצורכו ולצורכה חשיב כמו צורכו ואסור ומשני דהתם דאורייתא פסולה כמו בא עלי' זכר דפסולה מדרב פפא וא"ת ואמאי מייתי ההיא דשכן עליה עוף ואי משום דרב פפא אמר למלתיה עלה אמאי לא אמר אהך דהכניסה לרבק' וי"ל משום דברייתא היא אבל הך דשכן עליה עוף היא מתניתין:

אף עובד דניחא ליה. וא"ת ובפרה אדומה מנלן דבעינן דניחא ליה דבשלמא למאן דיליף (סוטה דף מו.) עבודות בפרה מג"ש דעול עול ניחא אלא למאן דלית ליה ג"ש ומשכח עבודות בפרה גופיה מנלן דבעינן דניחא ליה וי"ל דכיון דשוין בפסול עול ועבודות גם לענין דניחא ליה יש להשוותן וא"ת ועלה עליה זכר אמאי פסולה הא ודאי לא ניחא ליה להפסיל פרה שדמיה יקרים בשביל דבר מועט וי"ל דאם היתה כשירה הוה ניחא ליה ולכך אין להכשיר וא"ת הכניסה לרבקה ודשה אמאי כשירה מאי שנא מעלה עליה זכר דפסולה וי"ל דהתם לא ניחא ליה בדישה שאינו מרויח כ"כ דבלאו הכי נדושת התבואה וא"ת אי לא ידע בשעת עליית הזכר אמאי פסולה מאי שנא מהכשר דאמרינן לעיל (דף כב.) נגבו אינן בכי יותן ואם נאמר דלא מיפסלא אלא כשידע בשעת עלייתו א"ש ואתי נמי שפיר הא דתנן (פרה פ"ב מ"א) פרה מעוברת ר"א מכשיר וקשה וכי לית ליה עלה עליה זכר פסולה ולמאי דפרישית אתי שפיר אי נמי סבר כר"י דאמר דוקא העלה עליה זכר אבל עלה מאליו כשירה וה"ר יצחק מסימפון פירש דלא פליגי בפרה עצמה אלא בבתה וטעמא דרבנן דפסולה כדדרשינן בספרי ויקחו אליך פרה בעינן שתהא בשעת לקיחה פרה ור"א לית ליה ההיא דרשה וה"ה דמצו פליגי בלקחו פרה קטנה וא"ת העושה מלאכה בפרת חטאת דאמר בפ' הכונס (ב"ק דף נו. ושם) דחייב בדיני שמים אמאי מיפסלא הא ודאי לא ניחא להו לבעלים וי"ל כגון שהיה שותף אי נמי לא בעינן ניחותא דבעלים רק ניחותא דעושה מלאכה וא"ת בפרק אין מעמידין (ע"ז דף כג:) דפוסל ר"א פרה הניקחת מן הנכרים דחיישינן לרביעה ודייק ש"מ קדשי מזבח היא דאי קדשי בדק הבית היא אמאי פסולה משום רביעה לימא דפסולה משום עול וי"ל דמשמע ליה דלאו מטעם עול פוסל דקתני בסיפא וכן היה ר"א פוסל בשאר קרבנות לכך קאמר דקדשי מזבח היא דממעטינן נרבע מקרא דמן הבהמה: [וע"ע תוס' ע"ז כג: ד"ה ש"מ]:

הא אין עשה דוחה לא תעשה ועשה. וא"ת דבפ"ב דיבמות (דף כא.) ובפ' כ"ג (סנהדרין דף יט.) לא חשיב אלמנה לכהן גדול אלא לא תעשה גרידא ואמאי והא איכא עשה דקדושים יהיו וי"ל דלא קאי עשה דקדושים יהיו אלא אמאי דכתיב בההיא פרשה וא"ת והא כי אמרינן דאין עשה דוחה את לא תעשה ועשה ה"מ



**מסורת הש"ס**

א) [לקמן עג., חולין פד:], ב) [ברכות כה., וש"נ], ג) פסחים כו: [ע"ש], ד) פי' [בערוך] דבר מזומן לשטוח עליו כלי כיסה, פ"א גודא ממש ותוס' פרק כ"ש דף כו: פירשו כמו נגוד לגלימא, ה) שם ע"א, ו) שם ע"ב, פרה פרק ב משנה ד, ז) ברכות יט:, סנהדרין יח:, ח) [לקמן לג., סנהדרין סד:, ע"ש], ט) [ועיין היטב תוס' לקמן לג., ותוס' חולין פד:], י) [פרק א וע"ש היטב], כ) [ע"ש היטב].

**תורה אור השלם**

א) וְהָיָה הָעִיר הַקְּרֹבָה אֶל הֶחָלָל וְלָקְחוּ זִקְנֵי הָעִיר הַהִוא עֶגְלַת בָּקָר אֲשֶׁר לֹא עֻבַּד בָּהּ אֲשֶׁר לֹא מָשְׁכָה בְּעֹל: [דברים כא, ג]

ב) לֹא תִרְאֶה אֶת שׁוֹר אָחִיךָ אוֹ אֶת שֵׂיוֹ נִדָּחִים וְהִתְעַלַּמְתָּ מֵהֶם הָשֵׁב תְּשִׁיבֵם לְאָחִיךָ: [דברים כב, א]

ג) אֶפֶס כִּי לֹא יִהְיֶה בְּךָ אֶבְיוֹן כִּי בָרֵךְ יְבָרֶכְךָ יְיָ בָּאָרֶץ אֲשֶׁר יְיָ אֱלֹהֶיךָ נֹתֵן לְךָ נַחֲלָה לְרִשְׁתָּהּ: [דברים טו, ד]

**לעזי רש"י**

קביל"א. פירוש יתד (רש"י ערובין דף עח ע"א ד"ה יתד). דבר שמזומן לשטוח עליו כלי כביסה (ערוך ערך מגד ב'). קופל"ה. פירוש למד הבהמות (קשורות יחד). ודיל"ש. פירוש מגריפות, יעים (רש"י שמות כז ג).

**ליקוטי רש"י**

בתורי. ישכור פועלים וימסור להן שוורים שלו לחרוש והם יכחישו השוורים ויקצצו ביערות בכרמים והמלאכה לא תעלה לכלום שאין חוששין לכך [חולין פד:]. שבולרין כרמים בשוורים בעגלה מוליכין את העגלה בין שורות הכרמים ומתקלקלין רגלי השוורים בקלחי שרשים שבקרקע הפסדן רב [לקמן עג.]. לא ישטחנה. כמולא כנגד עבודה קאי. לצורכה. כדי שלא יאכלנו עש. נזדמנו לו אורחים וכו'. אע"ג דלצורכה הוא הואיל ומתכוין להתכבד בשל חבירו באורחין חשיב ליה גזל ואסור. דמקלא קלי לה. דבשטיחה זו קלי לה כלומר מאבדה בידים [פסחים כו:]. ודשה. תבואה עם חברותיה. כשירה. שלא נתכוין לכך שלאו עבודה היא. אשר לא עובד בה מ"מ. ואע"ג דבעלמא לא מיתסר הכא אסור [שם בע"א]. שכן עליה עוף. בפרה אדומה קאי שפרח ונח על גבה אע"ג דכתיב לא עלה עליה עול דמשמע עליה אפילו עליה בעלמא ואי משום דכתיב עול הא מרבינן ביה שאר עבודות במסכת סוטה (דף מו.) אפ"ה בהא עלייה כשרה דלא ניחא ליה והוא הדין להכניסה לרבקה ודשה.

**עין משפט נר מצוה**

קלו א מיי' פי"ג מהל' גזילה ואבידה הל' יא סמג עשין עד טוש"ע ח"מ סי' רסז סעיף יח:

קלז ב ג ד מיי' פ"י מהל' רוצח הל' ג ופ"א מהל' פרה אדומה הלכה ז סמג עשין עח רלב:

קלח ה ו ז ח מיי' פי"ג מהל' גזילה ואבידה הלכה יב סמג עשין עד טוש"ע ח"מ סי' רסז סעיף יט:

קלט ט י מיי' שם הל' יג ופ"ז מהלכות שאלה ופקדון הלכה ד סמג שם טוש"ע ח"מ סי' רצב סעיף כא כב:

קמ כ מיי' פי"א מהל' גזילה ואבידה הל' יח סמג עשין עד טוש"ע ח"מ סי' רעב סעיף ב:

קמא ל מיי' שם הלכה יג סמג שם טוש"ע ח"מ סי' רסג סעיף א:

קמב מ מיי' שם פי"ב הלכה א סמג שם טוש"ע ח"מ סי' רסד סעיף יא:

קמג נ מיי' פי"א שם הלכה יח ופ"ז מהלכות נזירות הל' טו:

**רבינו חננאל**

שלא הוחמו כל צרכן כי קשין הן לגוף מאד והוא שהוחמו בכלי מתכות. ויש אומרי' פושרין הן הלוחשין ושאר שמעתתא דר' יוחנן פירשנום בפ' כיסוי הדם. ושוטחה לצורכה אבל לא לכבודו מיבעיא לן לצרכה ולצרכו מאי ת"ש שוטחה לצרכו וכו' ת"ש לא ישטחנה לא על גבי מיטה ולא על גבי מגוד לצרכו ולא איפשיטה. פי' לרבקה לפטמה מלשון עגלי מרבק. ת"ש הכניס לעגלה לרבקה ובהליכתה דשה ברגליה בתבואה שבגורן כשירה בשביל שתינק משדי אמו ותדוש פסולה ופשוטה היא. ת"ש מהא דתנן במסכת פרה שכן עליה עוף כשירה עלה עליה זכר פסולה והא עליית עליה זכר לצרכו ולצרכה היא וקתני פסולה. ודחי רב פפא ואמר כל מלתא דניחא ליה אע"ג שלא עשאה בידים מעשיו הן ודייק מדכתב עבד וקרינן עובד: מצא כלי חרש וכלי נחשת משתמש בהן לצרכן אבל לא לשחקן מצא כלי עץ משתמש בהן שלא ירקבו כלי נחשת משתמש בהן בחמין אבל לא על ידי האור. כלי כסף משתמש בהן בצונן אבל לא בחמין מפני שמשחירן. מגרפות וקרדומות משתמש בהן ברך אבל לא בקשה מפני שמפחיתן כלי זהב וכלי זכוכית לא יגע בהן עד שיבא אליהו כדרך שאמרו באבידה כך אמרו בפיקדון שהלכו בעליו למדינת הים. מצא שק או קופה שאין דרכו ליטול הרי זה לא יטול אלא אם רוצה לעשות לפנים משורת הדין כר' ישמעאל. פי' פתכא דאופי חבילה של חריות של דקל. פי' וקא מיתפח יגע והניח משאו לארץ כדי ליפוש. לא חרבה ירושלם אלא מפני שהעמידו דבריהם על דין תורה ולא עשו לפנים משורת הדין. ת"ר והתעלמת פעמים שאתה מתעלם כיצד זקן ואינה לפי כבודו אבל כהן

וְהִיא בְּבֵית הַקְּבָרוֹ – **AND [THE LOST OBJECT]** he sighted **WAS IN A** CEMETERY, then the Kohen should "hide" from it; he may not pick it up.[25] אוֹ שֶׁהָיָה זָקֵן – **OR,** similarly, if **[THE FINDER] WAS A** SAGE,[26] וְאֵינָהּ לְפִי כְבוֹדוֹ – **AND IT IS NOT BEFITTING HIS HONOR** to pick up this particular object and return it, he need not do so. אוֹ שֶׁהָיְתָה מְלַאכָה שֶׁלּוֹ מְרוּבָּה מִשֶּׁל חֲבֵירוֹ – **OR** if **THE WORK** [the finder was engaged in] **IS OF GREATER** monetary **VALUE THAN HIS** FRIEND'S object, he likewise need not pick it up.[27] לְכָךְ נֶאֱמַר: "וְהִתְעַלַּמְתָּ מֵהֶם" – **BECAUSE** of these situations, **IT IS STATED** in the verse: ***AND YOU SHALL HIDE FROM THEM,*** thereby teaching that in certain situations, one may "hide" from a lost object; that is, he need not pick it up.

The Baraisa set forth three cases in which a finder is released from the obligation to pick up the lost object he sees before him. The Gemara now asks:

לְמַאי אִיצְטְרִיךְ קְרָא – **For which** of these cases **is the verse needed** to teach the finder's exemption?

The Gemara suggests and rejects a possibility:

אִילֵימָא לְכֹהֵן וְהִיא בְּבֵית הַקְּבָרוֹת – **If you will say for the** case in which the finder is a **Kohen and [the object]** he sights **is in a cemetery,** this cannot be, פְּשִׁיטָא – for here **it is obvious** that he may not retrieve the object.

The Gemara explains why this is indeed obvious:

הַאי עֲשֵׂה – **This** obligation to return a lost object constitutes **a positive commandment,** וְהַאי לֹא תַעֲשֶׂה וַעֲשֵׂה – **whereas this** requirement that a Kohen not expose himself to the tumah of a corpse constitutes both **a negative commandment and a positive commandment;** וְלֹא אָתֵי עֲשֵׂה וְדָחֵי אֶת לֹא תַעֲשֶׂה וַעֲשֵׂה – **and** the rule in such cases is that **a positive commandment cannot come and push aside** both **a negative commandment and a positive commandment!**[28] וְתוּ – **And, furthermore,** yet another principle dictates that the Kohen should not retrieve the object: לֹא דָּחִינַן אִיסּוּרָא מִקַּמֵּי מָמוֹנָא – **We do not push aside prohibitory law on account of monetary** considerations![29] We must conclude, then, that the verse is not necessary to teach the Kohen's exemption. – ? –

The Gemara suggests and rejects another possibility:

אֶלָּא – **Rather,** you might argue that the verse is needed לְשֶׁלּוֹ מְרוּבֶּה מִשֶּׁל חֲבֵירוֹ – **to** teach the finder's exemption when **his** work **is of greater value than his friend's** object. מִדְּרַב יְהוּדָה אָמַר רַב נָפְקָא – **This,** however, **can** simply **be derived from** the exposition that **Rav Yehudah stated in the name of Rav.** דְּאָמַר רַב יְהוּדָה אָמַר רַב – **For Rav Yehudah stated in the name of Rav:** "אֶפֶס כִּי – The verse states:[30] ***But***

NOTES

25. The Torah enjoins a Kohen not to contract *tumah* from a human corpse (see *Leviticus* 21:1,6). By entering the cemetery to retrieve this object, he would almost certainly violate this prohibition.

26. *Ritva; Nimukei Yosef* to 32b, citing *Ramban*; see *Rambam, Hil. Gezeilah* 11:13 who explain this to refer to an old person as well.

27. The Baraisa here speaks of a case in which the finder would forego a profit exceeding the lost object's value if he were to stop working long enough to pick it up.

The Mishnah later (30b) sets forth a system for calculating the amount of compensation a finder can claim for time he expended retrieving a lost object. The compensation is generally minimal, unless the finder declares before a court that he wishes to receive *full* compensation for his lost work. In these circumstances, the object's owner must indeed pay the full sum – unless, of course, it exceeds the entire worth of the object. In such a case, the court would not award the finder full compensation – and, our Baraisa declares, the finder is thus released from the obligation to retrieve the object. (This explanation follows the second interpretation set forth by *Ritva*.)

28. One's obligation to return a lost object is mandated by the positive commandment (*Deuteronomy* 22:1): הָשֵׁב תְּשִׁיבֵם, *you shall return them*; whereas the Kohen's duty to avoid becoming *tamei* stems from the negative commandment (*Leviticus* 21:1): לְנֶפֶשׁ לֹא־יִטַּמָּא, *he shall not become tamei to a [dead] person,* as well as from the positive commandment (ibid. v. 6): קְדֹשִׁים יִהְיוּ, *they shall be holy.* These sets of commands stand in conflict with one another in our case, where retrieving the object from the cemetery would entail contracting *tumah*.

In cases of conflict between commandments, the general Talmudic rule dictates that a positive commandment supersedes a negative one. A positive commandment does not, however, supersede a negative and positive commandment *combined*. A simple application of this principle thus yields that the Kohen's obligation to restore the object does not supersede his duty to avoid contracting *tumah*. No verse is required to teach this law, for it is evident on its own.

In connection with the above, *Rashi* addresses the following question: The requirement to return lost objects involves not just a positive command but a negative prohibition as well – the prohibition set forth in the words: *you are not able to hide* (*Deuteronomy* 22:3; see note 23). Why, then, does the Gemara refer to this requirement as a positive commandment only? *Rashi* answers that the power to "push aside" is vested only in positive commandments, not negative ones (see *Yevamos* 21a; see also *Beis Aharon*). Thus, the negative command involved in "hiding" from an object has no bearing in this context (see *Ritva*).

29. The requirement that a Kohen not contract *tumah* falls in the category of *prohibitory law,* whereas the duty to return a lost object is a *monetary* obligation. The Gemara seizes upon this distinction, arguing that a monetary obligation [the Kohen's duty to return the object] cannot outweigh a prohibition [the Kohen's duty not to contract *tumah*]. Hence, even if the Kohen's obligation to retrieve the object conflicted with a negative command *only,* no verse would be required to teach the Kohen's exemption from returning the object, for this could be determined solely through the above argument.

According to *Ritva,* the basis for the idea that monetary duties do not outweigh prohibitions lies in the fact that monetary obligations can be waived, while prohibitions cannot be. (For example, the owner of a lost object may waive his claim to the lost item – releasing a finder from the obligation to return it. No one, however can "waive" the Kohen's obligation to avoid contracting *tumah*.) A monetary obligation is thus considered less "steadfast" than a prohibition; hence, the former cannot outweigh the latter.

30. *Deuteronomy* 15:4.

# בתורי

בתורי דנפיש פסידייהו: שוטחה לצורכה אבל לא לכבודו וכו': איבעיא להו לצורכו ולצורכה מאי ת"ש שוטחה לצורכה אבל לא לכבודו ואי אמרת לצורכו ולצורכה לא אימא סיפא לכבודו הוא דלא הא לצורכה ולצורכו שפיר דמי אלא מהא ליכא למשמע מינה ת"ש לא ישטחנה לא על גבי מטה ולא על גבי מגוד לצרכו אבל ישטחנה על גבי מטה ועל גבי מגוד לצרכה נזדמנו לו אורחים לא ישטחנה לא על גבי מטה ולא על גבי מגוד בין לצורכו בין לצורכה שאני התם דמקלא קלי לה אי משום עינא אי משום גנבי תא שמע הכניסה לרבקה ודשה כשירה בשביל שתינק ותדוש פסולה והא הכא דלצורכו ולצורכה הוא וקתני פסולה שאני התם דאמר קרא אשר לא עובד בה מ"מ אי הכי אפילו רישא נמי הא לא דמיא אלא להא דתנן שכן עליה עוף כשירה עלה עליה זכר פסולה מאי טעמא כדרב פפא דאמר רב פפא אי כתיב עובד וקרינן עובד הוה אמינא אפילו ממילא ואי כתיב עבד וקרינן עבד הוה אמינא עד דעבד בה איהו השתא דכתיב עבד וקרינן עובד בעינן עובד דומיא דעבד מה עבד דניחא ליה אף עובד דניחא ליה: כלי כסף וכלי נחושת משתמש בהן וכו': ת"ר המוצא כלי עץ משתמש בהן בשביל שלא ירקבו כלי נחושת משתמש בהן בחמין אבל לא על ידי האור מפני שמשחיקן כלי כסף משתמש בהן בצונן אבל לא בחמין מפני שמשחירן מגריפות וקרדומות משתמש בהן ברך אבל לא בקשה מפני שמפחיתן כלי זהב וכלי זכוכית לא יגע בהן עד שיבא אליהו כדרך שאמרו באבידה כך אמרו בפקדון פקדון מאי עבידתיה גביה אמר רב אדא בר חמא אמר רב ששת בפקדון שהלכו בעליהן למדינת הים: מצא שק או קופה [וכל דבר] שאין דרכו ליטול הרי זה לא יטול: מנהני מילי דת"ר והתעלמת פעמים שאתה מתעלם ופעמים שאי אתה מתעלם הא כיצד היה כהן והיא בבית הקברות או שהיה זקן ואינה לפי כבודו או שהיתה מלאכה שלו מרובה משל חבירו לכך נאמר והתעלמת מהם למאי איצטריך קרא אילימא לכהן והיא בבית הקברות פשיטא האי עשה והאי לא תעשה ועשה ולא אתי עשה ודחי את לא תעשה ועשה ותו לא דחינן איסורא מקמי ממונא אלא לשלו מרובה משל חבירו מדרב יהודה אמר רב נפקא דאמר רב יהודה אמר רב אפס כי

## רש"י

דנפיש פסידייהו. שרוב עבודת קרקעות שלהן בשוורים היתה אף חרישת הכרמים ובצירתם מנהיגים כלי המחרישה בעגלה בין שורות הכרם עם הבוצרים ונותנין שם הענבים לפיכך אם אין הבעלים עליהם יש הפסד גדול שאין דרך הפועלים לחוס על הכרם ועל השוורים ומנהיגים אותן על הגפנים ועל הנטיעות והם מתקלקלין והשוורין נסתכין ונשברים: מגוד. קביל"א בלע"ז: נזדמנו לו אורחים. קס"ד טעמא משום דמתכבד בהם ואיכא לצורכה ולצרכו: שאני התם דקא קלי לה. בשטיחה זו הוא שורפה ומה הוא שריפתה: אי משום עינא. שתשלוט בה עין רע של אורחין: אי משום גנבי. פן יגנבוה האורחים: הכניסה לרבקה. בעגלה ערופה קאי. רבקה קופל"ה בלע"ז שמדבקים שלש בהמות או ארבעה בצואריהן זו אצל זו ודשים הדישה: כשירה. הואיל ולא נתכוון שתדוש: ואם בשביל שתינק ותדוש. שהיתה אמה דשה והכניס את הבת לשם שתינק ואף נתכוון שתדוש פסולה: הא לא דמיא. מירולא היא: שכן עליה עוף. בפרה אדומה קאי: עלה עליה זכר פסולה. שנאמר אשר לא עלה עליה עול ותניא עול אין לי אלא עול כו' במסכת סוטה (דף מו.) והאי הכניסה לרבקה ודשה דלא ניחא ליה בה דמיא לשכן עליה עוף: משתמש בהן בחמין. וכ"ש בצונן: אבל לא ע"י האור. לא יתן הכלי על האור: מגריפות. ווידיל"ש עשויין לגרוף הפירות או להפריש תאנים המדובקים: שמפחיתן. פוגמן: מאי עבידתיה גביה. מה לו להשתמש בו יבא בעליו וישתמש בו: והתעלמת מהם. וללמדך בא שמותר להתעלם: ופעמים שאי אתה מתעלם. דכתיב לא תוכל להתעלם: והיא בבית הקברות. האבידה בבית הקברות: ואינה לפי כבודו. שישיבנה: או שהיה בטל ממלאכה שלו. שיבטל בהשבתה מרובה על דמי האבידה: האי עשה. השב תשיבם ואע"ג דלא תעשה נמי איכא אין לא תעשה מועיל לדחות לא תעשה אלא עשה הוא דקא דחי ליה כדאמרינן ביבמות (דף כא.): לא תעשה ועשה. לנפש לא יטמא קדושים יהיו: לא

## תוספות

בתורי דנפיש פסידייהו. ר"ח גרס בתוורי פירוש פועלים שמוליכים השוורים לחרישה ואין מעמיקין המחרישה שלשה טפחים ואין הזרע נקלט היטב:

ולצורכה מאי. דוקא בשיטוח כסות מבעיא ליה וכל דדמי ליה דשמא יניחנה שטוחה יותר מכדי צורכה עד שיתקלקל אבל בספר אמרינן דקורא בהן אף ע"ג דלצורכו הוא כמו צורכה ולא גזרינן דליכא למיחש למידי כיון שקבעו לו זמן אחד לשלשים יום או אחד לי"ב חדש ולא ילמוד בו בתחלה גם לא יקרא וישנה וכלי נחשת דתניא לקמן דמשתמש אפי' בחמין וכלי כסף בצונן אפי' לצורכו מותר כיון שעל ידי אותו תשמיש אינו יכול לבא לידי קלקול ותדע דאי דוקא לצורך הכלי מאי פריך פקדון מאי עבידתיה גביה כיון שהוא שומר יש לו לעיין שלא יתקלקל אע"פ שהבעלים אינם אומרים לו להשתמש:

הכניסה לרבקה ודשה. בתוספתא' (דפרה) תני לה גבי פרה אדומה: בשביל שתינק ותדוש פסולה. ובסיפא (דתוספתא) קתני לצורכו פסולה לצורכה כשירה ולכך פריך אלמא לצורכו ולצורכה חשיב כמו צורכו ואסור ומשני דהתם דאורייתא פסולה כמו בא עלי' זכר דפסולה מדרב פפא וא"ת ואמאי מייתי ההיא דשכן עליה עוף ואי משום דרב פפא אמר למלתיה עלה אמאי לא אמר אהך דהכניסה לרבק' וי"ל משום דברייתא היא אבל הך דשכן עליה עוף היא מתניתין:

אף עובד דניחא ליה. וא"ת ובפרה אדומה מנלן דבעינן דניחא ליה דבשלמא למאן דיליף (סוטה דף מו.) עבודות בפרה מג"ש דעול עול ניחא אלא למאן דלית ליה ג"ש ומשכח עבודות בפרה גופיה מנלן דבעינן דניחא ליה וי"ל דכיון דשוין בפסול עול ועבודות גם לענין דניחא ליה יש להשוותן וא"ת ועלה עליה זכר אמאי פסולה הא ודאי לא ניחא ליה להפסיל פרה שדמיה יקרים בשביל דבר מועט וי"ל דאם היתה כשירה הוה ניחא ליה ולכך אין להכשיר וא"ת הכניסה לרבקה ודשה אמאי כשירה מאי שנא מעלה עליה זכר דפסולה וי"ל דהתם לא ניחא ליה בדישתה שאינו מרויח כ"כ דבלאו הכי נדושת התבואה וא"ת אי לא ידע בשעת עליית הזכר אמאי פסולה מאי שנא מהכשר דאמרינן לעיל (דף כב.) נגבו אינן בכי יותן ואם נאמר דלא מיפסלא אלא כשידע בשעת עלייתו א"ש ואתי נמי שפיר הא דתנן (פרה פ"ב מ"א) פרה מעוברת ר"א מכשיר וקשה וכי לית ליה עלה עליה זכר פסולה ואמאי דפריש אתי שפיר אי נמי סבר כר"י דאמר דוקא העלה עליה זכר אבל עלה מאליו כשירה וה"ר יצחק מסימפון פירש דלא פליגי בפרה עצמה אלא בבתה וטעמא דרבנן דפסולה כדדרשינן בספרי ויקחו אליך פרה בעינן שתהא בשעת לקיחה פרה ור"א לית ליה ההיא דרשה וה"ה דמצו פליגי בלקחו פרה קטנה וא"ת העושה מלאכה בפרת חטאת דאמר בפ' הכונס (ב"ק דף נו. ושם) דחייב בדיני שמים אמאי מיפסלא הא ודאי לא ניחא להו לבעלים וי"ל כגון שהיה שותף אי נמי לא בעינן ניחותא דבעלים רק ניחותא דעושה מלאכה וא"ת בפרק אין מעמידין (ע"ז דף כג:) דפוסל ר"א פרה הניקחת מן הנכרים דחייש לרביעה ודייק ש"מ קדשי מזבח היא דאי קדשי בדק הבית היא אמאי פסולה משום רביעה לימא דפסולה משום עול וי"ל דמשמע ליה דלאו מטעם עול פוסל דקתני בסיפא וכן היה ר"א פוסל בשאר קרבנות לכך קאמר דקדשי מזבח היא דממעטינן נרבע מקרא דמן הבהמה: [וע"ע תוס' ע"ז כג: ד"ה ש"מ]:

הא אין עשה דוחה לא תעשה ועשה. וא"ת דבפ"ב דיבמות (דף כא.) ובפ' כ"ג (סנהדרין דף יט.) לא חשיב אלמנה לכהן גדול אלא לא תעשה גרידא ואמאי והא איכא עשה דקדושים יהיו וי"ל דלא קאי עשה דקדושים יהיו אלא אמאי דכתיב בההיא פרשה וא"ת והא כי אמרינן דאין עשה דוחה את לא תעשה ועשה ה"מ

## עין משפט נר מצוה

קלו א מיי' פי"ג מהל' גזילה ואבידה הל' יא סמג עשין עד טוש"ע ח"מ סי' רסז סעיף יח:

קלז ב ג ד מיי' פ"י מהל' רוצח הל' ג ופ"א מהל' פרה אדומה הלכה ז סמג עשין עם רלב:

קלח ה ו ז ח מיי' פי"ג מהל' גזילה ואבידה הלכה יב סמג עשין עד טוש"ע ח"מ סי' רסז סעיף יט:

קלט ט י מיי' שם הל' יג ופ"ז מהלכות שאלה ופקדון הלכה ד סמג שם טוש"ע ח"מ סי' רצב סעיף כא כב:

קמ כ מיי' פי"א מהל' גזילה ואבידה הל' יח סמג עשין עד טוש"ע ח"מ סי' רעב סעיף ג:

קמא ל מיי' שם הלכה יג סמג שם טוש"ע ח"מ סי' רסג סעיף א:

קמב מ מיי' שם פי"ג הלכה א סמג שם טוש"ע ח"מ סי' רסד סעיף יא:

קמג נ מיי' פי"א שם הלכה יח ופ"ז מהלכות נזירות הל' טו:

## רבינו חננאל

שלא הוחמו כל צרכן כי קשין הן לגוף מאד והוא שהוחמו בכלי מתכות. ויש אומרי' פושרין הן הלוחשין ושאר שמעתתא דר' יוחנן פירשנום בפ' כיסוי הדם. **ושוטחה** לצורכה אבל לא לכבודו מיבעיא לן לצרכה ולצרכו מאי ת"ש שוטחה לצרכו וכו' ת"ש לא ישטחנה לא על גבי מיטה ולא על גבי מגוד לצרכו ולא איפשיטה. פי' לרבקה לפטמה מלשון עגלי מרבק. ת"ש הכניס לעגלה לרבקה ובהליכתה דשה ברגליה בתבואה שבגורן כשירה בשביל שתינק משדי אמו ותדוש פסולה ופשוטה היא. ת"ש מהא דתנן במסכת פרה שכן עליה עוף כשירה עלה עליה זכר פסולה והא עליית עליה זכר לצרכו ולצרכה היא וקתני פסולה. ודחי רב פפא ואמר כל מלתא דניחא ליה אע"ג שלא עשאה בידים מעשיו הן ודייק מדכתב עבד וקרינן עובד: **מצא כלי חרש וכלי נחשת** משתמש בהן לצרכן אבל לא לשחקן מצא כלי עץ משתמש בהן שלא ירקבו כלי נחשת משתמש בהן בחמין אבל לא על ידי האור. כלי כסף משתמש בהן בצונן אבל לא בחמין מפני שמשחירן. מגרפות וקרדומות משתמש בהן ברך אבל לא בקשה מפני שמפחיתן כלי זהב וכלי זכוכית לא יגע בהן עד שיבא אליהו כדרך שאמרו באבידה כך אמרו בפיקדון שהלכו בעליו למדינת הים. מצא שק או קופה שאין דרכו ליטול הרי זה לא יטול אלא אם רוצה לעשות לפנים משורת הדין כר' ישמעאל. פי' פתכא דאופי חבילה של חריות של דקל. פי' וקא מיתפח יגע והניח משאו לארץ כדי ליפוש. לא חרבה ירושלם אלא מפני שהעמידו דבריהם על דין תורה ולא עשו לפנים משורת הדין. **ת"ר** והתעלמת פעמים שאתה מתעלם כיצד זקן ואינה לפי כבודו אבל כהן

## מסורת הש"ס

א) [לקמן עג., חולין פד:], ב) [ברכות כה., וש"נ], ג) פסחים כו: [ע"ש], ד) פי' [בערוך] דבר המזומן לשטות עליו כלי כביסה, פ"א גודא ממש התום' פרק כ"ש דף כו: פירשו כמו נגוד לגלימא, ה) שם ע"א, ו) שם ע"ב, פרה פרק ב משנה ד, ז) ברכות יט:, סנהדרין מ:, ח) [לקמן לג., סנהדרין סד: ע"ש], ט) [ועיין היטב תוס' לקמן עג., ותוס' חולין פד:], י) [פרק א וע"ש היטב], כ) [ע"ש היטב].

## תורה אור השלם

א) וְהָיָה הָעִיר הַקְּרֹבָה אֶל הֶחָלָל וְלָקְחוּ זִקְנֵי הָעִיר הַהִוא עֶגְלַת בָּקָר אֲשֶׁר לֹא עֻבַּד בָּהּ אֲשֶׁר לֹא מָשְׁכָה בְּעֹל: [דברים כא, ג]

ב) לֹא תִרְאֶה אֶת שׁוֹר אָחִיךָ אוֹ אֶת שֵׂיוֹ נִדָּחִים וְהִתְעַלַּמְתָּ מֵהֶם הָשֵׁב תְּשִׁיבֵם לְאָחִיךָ: [דברים כב, א]

ג) אֶפֶס כִּי לֹא יִהְיֶה בְּךָ אֶבְיוֹן כִּי בָרֵךְ יְבָרֶכְךָ יְיָ בָּאָרֶץ אֲשֶׁר יְיָ אֱלֹהֶיךָ נֹתֵן לְךָ נַחֲלָה לְרִשְׁתָּהּ: [דברים טו, ד]

## לעזי רש"י

קביל"א. פירוש יתד (רש"י ערובין דף עח ע"א ד"ה יתד). דבר שמזומן לשטות עליו כלי כביסה (ערוך ערך מגד ג'). קופל"ה. פירוש למד בהמות (קשורות יחד). ווידיל"ש. פירוש מגריפות, יעים (רש"י שמות כז ג).

## ליקוטי רש"י

**בתורי.** ישכור פועלים וימסור להן שוורים שלו לחרוש והם יכחישו השוורים ויסקבום ביערות ובכרמים והמלאכה לא תעלה לכלום שאין חוששין לכך [חולין פד:]. שבוצרין כרמים בשוורים בעגלה ומוליכין את העגלה בין שורות הכרמים ומתקלקלין רגלי השוורים בקלחי שרשים שבקרקע והפסדן רב [לקמן עג.]. **לא ישטחנה.** במולא בגד אבודה קאי. **לצורכה.** כדי שלא יאכלנו עש. **נזדמנו לו אורחים וכו'.** אע"ג דלצורכה הוא הואיל ומתכוין להתכבד בשל חבירו באורחין חשיב ליה גזל ואסור. **דמקלא קלי לה.** דבשטיחה זו קלי לה כלומר מאבדה בידים [פסחים כו:]. **ודשה.** תבואה עם חברותיה. **כשירה.** שלא נתכוין לכך ולאו עבודה היא. **אשר לא עובד בה מ"מ.** דאע"ג דבעלמא לא מיתסר הכא אסור [שם בע"א]. **שכן עליה עוף.** בפרה אדומה קאי שפרח ונח על גבה אע"ג דכתיב לא עלה עליה עול דמשמע עליה אפילו עליה בעלמא ואי משום דכתיב עול הא מרבינן ביה שאר עבודות במסכת סוטה (דף מו.) אפ"ה בהא עלייה כשרה דלא ניחא ליה והוא הדין להכניסה לרבקה ודשה.

**עלה עליה זכר פסולה.** דניחא ליה והוא הדין לתינק ותדוש. **עובד.** משמע ממילא עבד משמע בידים ואף על גב דהאי בעגלה כתיב תרוייהו ילפינן מהדדי בגזירה שוה דעול עול במסכת סוטה [שם בע"ב]. **וקרדומות.** קרדום עשוי כמין כלי אומנות שעושין בו אוכפות וסרגות שקורין אישי"ש [ביצה לא.]. **והתעלמת.** כובש עין כאילו אינו רואהו ורבותינו אמרו פעמים שאתה מתעלם [דברים כב, א]. **ואינה לפי כבודו.** אין האבדה חשובה לפי כבודו להשיבה [ברכות יט:]. שאם היתה שלו לא היה מחזירה [סנהדרין יח:]. **או שהיתה מלאכה שלו מרובה משל חבירו.** שדמי בטול מלאכתו לרדוף אחריה יתירים על דמי האבידה ולא ירצו הבעלים להשיב לו יותר ממה שמשיב להם ונמצא הוא מפסיד [ברכות שם]. כגון עוקב מרגליות שאם ילך ויחזירנה יפסיד בבטלותו יותר מדמיה [סנהדרין שם]. **לא דחינן איסורא מקמי ממונא.** ממונא קל מאיסורא [ברכות שם].

leasing to [the owner] in order to disqualify the animal.[17]

The discussion now turns to the next clause of our Mishnah, which states:

כְּלֵי כֶסֶף וּכְלֵי נְחוֹשֶׁת מִשְׁתַּמֵּשׁ בָּהֶן וכו׳ – If he found SILVER UTENSILS OR COPPER UTENSILS, HE SHOULD MAKE USE OF THEM etc. [as necessary for their needs, but not to the extent that he wears them down].

The Gemara cites a Baraisa that describes how a finder is to care for various utensils:

תָּנוּ רַבָּנַן – The Rabbis taught in a Baraisa: הַמּוֹצֵא כְּלֵי עֵץ – ONE WHO FINDS WOODEN UTENSILS מִשְׁתַּמֵּשׁ בָּהֶן בִּשְׁבִיל שֶׁלֹּא יִרְקְבוּ – SHOULD USE THEM SO THAT THEY SHOULD NOT ROT. כְּלֵי נְחוֹשֶׁת – One who finds COPPER UTENSILS מִשְׁתַּמֵּשׁ בָּהֶן בְּחַמִּין – SHOULD USE THEM to serve or prepare HOT dishes,[18] אֲבָל לֹא עַל יְדֵי הָאוּר – BUT he should NOT place these utensils OVER FIRE, מִפְּנֵי שֶׁמְּשַׁחִיקָן – BECAUSE [FIRE] WEARS THEM OUT. כְּלֵי כֶסֶף – One who finds SILVER UTENSILS מִשְׁתַּמֵּשׁ בָּהֶן בְּצוֹנֵן – SHOULD USE THEM to serve or prepare COLD dishes, אֲבָל לֹא בְּחַמִּין – BUT he should NOT use them WITH HOT dishes, מִפְּנֵי שֶׁמַּשְׁחִירָן – BECAUSE HEAT BLACKENS [THE UTENSILS]. מַגְרֵיפוֹת וְקַרְדּוּמוֹת – One who finds SHOVELS[19] or HATCHETS מִשְׁתַּמֵּשׁ בָּהֶן בְּרַךְ – SHOULD USE THEM WITH SOFT objects, אֲבָל לֹא בְּקָשֶׁה – BUT NOT WITH HARD objects, מִפְּנֵי שֶׁמְּפַחִיתָן – BECAUSE [HARD OBJECTS] DAMAGE THEM. כְּלֵי זָהָב וּכְלֵי זְכוּכִית – One who finds GOLD UTENSILS OR GLASS UTENSILS לֹא יִגַּע בָּהֶן – SHOULD NOT TOUCH THEM whatsoever עַד שֶׁיָּבֹא אֵלִיָּהוּ – UNTIL ELIJAH the prophet COMES and reveals the identity of the owner.[20]

The Baraisa now concludes:

כְּדֶרֶךְ שֶׁאָמְרוּ בַּאֲבֵידָה – JUST AS [THE RABBIS] STATED these guidelines WITH RESPECT TO A LOST OBJECT, כָּךְ אָמְרוּ בְּפִקָּדוֹן – SO THEY also STATED them WITH RESPECT TO A DEPOSITED OBJECT; i.e. the custodian of a deposit must care for the object entrusted him in the same way that he would be required to care for a lost object that he found.

The Gemara questions this last ruling:

פִּקָּדוֹן – As for a deposited object, מַאי עֲבִידְתֵּיהּ גַּבֵּיהּ – what is his business with it? I.e. why must the custodian care for it? Let the owner come and care for it himself![21] – ? –

The Gemara answers:

אָמַר רַב אַדָּא בַּר חָמָא אָמַר רַב שֵׁשֶׁת – Rav Ada bar Chama said in the name of Rav Sheishess: בְּפִקָּדוֹן שֶׁהָלְכוּ בְּעָלֶיהָ לִמְדִינַת הַיָּם – The Baraisa speaks of deposited objects whose owners have traveled overseas and are thus unable to care for them. The burden of care therefore falls on the custodian.[22]

The Gemara now turns to analyze the next clause of our Mishnah:

מָצָא שַׂק אוֹ קוּפָּה – If ONE FOUND A SACK OR A BOX, [וְכָל דָּבָר] שֶׁאֵין דַּרְכּוֹ לִיטּוֹל – OR ANY other OBJECT THAT would NOT be HIS PRACTICE TO PICK UP if it were his own, הֲרֵי זֶה לֹא יִטּוֹל – HE NEED NOT PICK it UP.

The Gemara seeks a source for this:

מְנָהָנֵי מִילֵּי – From where is this derived? דְּתָנוּ רַבָּנַן – From that which the Rabbis taught in a Baraisa: "וְהִתְעַלַּמְתָּ" – The verse states: *AND YOU SHALL HIDE* from them.[23] This teaches that when you sight a lost object, פְּעָמִים שֶׁאַתָּה מִתְעַלֵּם – THERE ARE TIMES THAT YOU MAY HIDE, וּפְעָמִים שֶׁאִי אַתָּה מִתְעַלֵּם – AND THERE ARE TIMES THAT YOU MAY NOT HIDE.[24] הָא כֵּיצַד – HOW IS THIS manifest? הָיָה כֹּהֵן – If [THE FINDER] WAS A KOHEN,

NOTES

17. In setting forth the law that labor disqualifies an animal from consideration as an *eglah arufah,* the Torah writes the phrase אֲשֶׁר לֹא עֻבַּד בָּ. Now, the word עָבַד means *he worked* – which in this context would signify that the owner actually imposed labor upon the animal. The word עוּבַד, by contrast, means *work was done* by the animal – which in this context would mean that the animal performed work without the owner prompting it. (Examples of this second category of labor would include: the animal performing work of its own accord, or another animal mating with it, or a bird resting upon it, thereby causing it to "work.") Whereas the first category would include only work that benefits the owner, the second category would include all types of work – even those that do not benefit the owner.

In our case, the Torah writes the word עֻבַּד. In a sense, this represents a cross between the two words described above, for although the *vowelization* of the word causes it to be read *ubad,* the *spelling* of the word – that is, the way it is *written* – could point also to a pronunciation of *avad*. Rav Pappa thus understands that *both* implications of the word are to play a role in the law that is being taught here: On the one hand, even labor that the animal performs *on its own* (עוּבַד) disqualifies it from consideration as an *eglah arufah.* On the other hand, however, such labor disqualifies that animal only if its performance is beneficial to the owner (עָבַד) (*Meiri*).

[As noted earlier (note 14), the Gemara understands that the definition of disqualifying labor is the same for both *parah adumah* and *eglah arufah.* Thus, although Rav Pappa stated his teaching with reference to *eglah arufah*, the Gemara takes it as an explanation of the Mishnah's rulings regarding *parah adumah* as well. That is, the Mishnah rules that an animal remains eligible to be a *parah adumah* if it carries a resting bird – for here, the owner gains no benefit from the animal's action. When, however, the cow mates with a bull, the Mishnah rules that it becomes ineligible to be a *parah adumah* – for although the animal performed the action of its own accord, this action was beneficial to the owner.]

This concludes the Gemara's discussion of whether it is permissible for a finder to make use of the garment in his care in a way that serves its purposes as well as his own. After advancing and rejecting several proofs, the Gemara now leaves the question unresolved. *Shulchan Aruch* (*Choshen Mishpat* 267:18) and other halachic decisors set forth stringent positions on the issue, ruling that the finder may not make use of the garment in this way.

18. He may certainly use those utensils to prepare cold dishes (*Rashi*).

19. The Baraisa refers to those shovels that were used to clean out fireplaces or to separate dried figs that were clumped together (*Rashi*).

20. See 29b note 14.

21. [It is understandable that a finder is required to care for the lost object in his charge – for the object's owner is unaware of its whereabouts and is therefore unable to care for it himself. When, however, one deposits his object with a custodian, he is aware of its whereabouts – hence, it seems unreasonable that the burden of caring for the object should fall on the custodian.]

22. This explanation of the Gemara's question and answer follows *Rashi* and *Rashba*. See, however, *Tosafos* ד״ה לצורכו, and *Tos. HaRosh* ד״ה לצרכה, who seem to interpret the Gemara differently.

23. *Deuteronomy* 22:1. The verse in its entirety reads: לֹא־תִרְאֶה אֶת־שׁוֹר אָחִיךָ אוֹ אֶת־שֵׂיוֹ נִדָּחִים וְהִתְעַלַּמְתָּ מֵהֶם הָשֵׁב תְּשִׁיבֵם לְאָחִיךָ, *You shall not see the ox of your brother or his sheep wandering and hide from them; [rather,] you shall return them to your brother.* In this context, the word *hide* means to ignore the object one has seen – to refrain from picking it up and returning it.

In its simple explanation, the verse means that one must not "hide" from one's brother's animal after recognizing that it has been lost (i.e. after "seeing it wandering"). Since, however, this basic idea is explicitly taught two verses later (v. 3 states לֹא תוּכַל לְהִתְעַלֵּם, *you are not able to hide*), the first verse is read exegetically to convey an additional teaching. Under this reading, the word וְהִתְעַלַּמְתָּ is interpreted in isolation, set apart from the earlier words לֹא תִרְאֶה, *you shall not see...* It thus conveys the meaning "you *shall* hide from them," teaching that there are times in which one may indeed ignore a lost object that crosses his path (*Rabbeinu Yehonasan*, cited by *Shitah Mekubetzes*).

24. Depending on the situation, we sometimes apply the verse וְהִתְעַלַּמְתָּ [the teaching that one may ignore a lost object], and other times we apply the verse לֹא תוּכַל לְהִתְעַלֵּם [the teaching that one may not ignore a lost object] (see *Rashi,* and previous note). The Baraisa proceeds to illustrate this point.

בתורי דנפיש פסידייהו: שוטחה לצורכה אבל לא לכבודו וכו': איבעיא להו לצורכו ולצורכה מאי ת"ש שוטחה לצורכה אין א הא לצורכו ולצורכה לא אימא סיפא אבל לא לכבודו לכבודו הוא דלא הא לצורכה ולצורכו שפיר דמי ב אלא מהא ליכא למשמע מינה ת"ש ג לא ישטחנה לא על גבי מטה ולא על גבי ד מגוד לצרכו אבל ישטחנה על גבי מטה ועל גבי מגוד לצרכה נזדמנו לו אורחים לא ישטחנה לא על גבי מטה ולא על גבי מגוד בין לצורכו בין לצורכה שאני התם דמקלא קלי לה אי משום עינא אי משום גנבי תא שמע ה ב הכניסה לרבקה ודשה כשירה בשביל שתינק ותדוש פסולה והא הכא דלצורכו ולצורכה הוא וקתני פסולה שאני התם דאמר קרא א) אשר לא עובד בה מ"מ אי הכי אפילו רישא נמי הא לא דמיא אלא להא ו דתנן ג שכן עליה עוף כשירה עלה עליה זכר פסולה מאי טעמא כדרב פפא דאמר רב פפא אי כתיב עובד וקרינן עובד הוה אמינא אפילו ממילא ואי כתיב עבד וקרינן עבד הוה אמינא עד דעבד בה איהו השתא דכתיב עבד וקרינן עובד בעינן עובד דומיא דעבד ד מה עבד דניחא ליה אף עובד דניחא ליה: כלי כסף וכלי נחושת משתמש בהן וכו': ת"ר ה המוצא כלי עץ משתמש בהן בשביל שלא ירקבו ו כלי נחושת משתמש בהן בחמין אבל לא על ידי האור מפני שמשחיקן ז כלי כסף משתמש בהן בצונן אבל לא בחמין מפני שמשחירן ח מגריפות וקרדומות משתמש בהן ברך אבל לא בקשה מפני שמפחיתן כלי זהב וכלי זכוכית לא יגע בהן עד שיבא אליהו ט כדרך שאמרו באבידה כך אמרו בפקדון פקדון מאי עבידתיה גביה אמר רב אדא בר חמא אמר רב ששת י בפקדון שהלכו בעליהן למדינת הים: מצא שק או קופה [וכל דבר] שאין דרכו ליטול הרי זה לא יטול: מנהני מילי ז) דת"ר ב) והתעלמת פעמים שאתה מתעלם ופעמים שאי אתה מתעלם הא כיצד כ היה כהן והיא בבית הקברות ל או שהיה זקן ואינה לפי כבודו מ או שהיתה מלאכה שלו מרובה משל חבירו לכך נאמר והתעלמת מהם למאי איצטריך קרא אילימא לכהן והיא בבית הקברות פשיטא האי עשה והאי לא תעשה ועשה נ ולא אתי עשה ודחי את לא תעשה ועשה ותו לא דחינן איסורא מקמי ממונא אלא לשלו מרובה משל חבירו מדרב יהודה אמר רב ח) דאמר רב יהודה אמר רב ג) אפס כי

## רש"י

דנפיש פסידייהו. שרוב עבודת קרקעות שלהן בשוורים היתה אף חרישת הכרמים ובצירתם מנהיגים כלי המחרישה בעגלה בין שורות הכרם עם הבוצרים ונותנין שם הענבים לפיכך אם אין הבעלים עליהם יש הפסד גדול שאין דרך הפועלים לחוס על הכרם ועל השוורים ומנהיגים אותן על הגפנים ועל הנטיעות והם מתקלקלין והשוורין נסחבין ונשברים: מגוד. קביל"א בלע"ז: נזדמנו לו אורחים. קס"ד טעמא משום דמתכבד בהם ואיכא לצורכה ולצרכו: שאני התם דקא קלי לה. בשטיחה זו הוא שורפה ומה הוא שריפתה: אי משום עינא. שתשלוט בה עין רע של אורחין: אי משום גנבי. פן יגנבוה האורחים: הכניסה לרבקה. בעגלה ערופה קאי. רבקה קופל"ה בלע"ז שמדבקים שלש בהמות או ארבעה בצואריהן זו אצל זו ודשים הדישה: כשירה. הואיל ולא נתכוון שתדוש: ואם בשביל שתינק ותידוש. שהיתה אמה דשה והכניס את הבת לשם שתינק ואף נתכוין שתדוש פסולה: הא לא דמיא. תירוצא היא: שכן עליה עוף. בפרה אדומה קאי: עלה עליה זכר פסולה. שנאמר אשר לא עלה עליה עול ותניא עול אין לי אלא עול כו' במסכת סוטה (דף מו.) והאי הכניסה לרבקה ודשה דלא ניחא ליה בה דמיא לשכן עליה עוף: משתמש בהן בחמין. וכ"ש בצונן: אבל לא ע"י האור. לא יתן הכלי על האור: מגריפות. ווידיל"ש עשויין לגרוף הפירות או להפריש תאנים המדובקים: שמפחיתן. פוגמן: מאי עבידתיה גביה. מה לו להשתמש בו יבא בעליו וישתמש בו: והתעלמת מהם. וללמדך בא שמותר להתעלם: ופעמים שאי אתה מתעלם. דכתיב לא תוכל להתעלם: והיא בבית הקברות. האבידה בבית הקברות: ואינה לפי כבודו. שישיבנה: או שהיה בטל ממלאכה שלו. שיבטל בהשבתה מרובה על דמי האבידה: האי עשה. השב תשיבם ואע"ג דלא תעשה נמי איכא אין לא תעשה מועיל לדחות לא תעשה אלא עשה הוא דקא דחי ליה כדאמרינן ביבמות (דף כא.): לא תעשה ועשה. לנפש לא יטמא קדושים יהיו: לא

## תוספות

בתורי דנפיש פסידייהו. ר"ח גרס בתוורי פירוש פועלים שמוליכים השוורים לחרישה ואין מעמיקין המחרישה שלשה טפחים ואין הזרע נקלט היטב ט): לצורכו ולצורכה מאי. דוקא בשיטוח כסות מבעיא ליה וכל דדמי ליה דשמא יניחנה שטוחה יותר מכדי צורכה עד שיתקלקל אבל בספר אמרינן דקורא בהן אף ע"ג דלצורכו הוא כמו צורכה ולא גזרינן דליכא למיחש למידי כיון שקבעו לו זמן אחד לשלשים יום או אחד לי"ב חדש ולא ילמוד בו בתחלה גם לא יקרא וישנה וכלי נחשת דתניא לקמן דמשתמש אפי' בחמין וכלי כסף בצונן אפי' לצורכו מותר כיון שעל ידי אותו תשמיש אינו יכול לבא לידי קלקול ותדע דאי דוקא לצורך הכלי מאי פריך פקדון מאי עבידתיה גביה כיון שהוא שומר יש לו לעיין שלא יתקלקל אע"פ שהבעלים אינם אומרים לו להשתמש:

הכניסה לרבקה ודשה. בתוספת' (דפרה) י) תני לה גבי פרה אדומה: בשביל שתינק ותדוש פסולה. ובסיפא (דתוספתא כ) קתני לצורכו פסולה לצורכה כשירה ולכך פריך אלמא לצורכו ולצורכה חשיב כמו צורכו ואסור ומשני דהתם דאורייתא פסולה כמו בא עלי' זכר דפסולה מדרב פפא וא"ת ואמאי מייתי ההיא דשכן עליה עוף ואי משום דרב פפא אמר למלתיה עלה אמאי לא אמר אהך דהכניסה לרבק' וי"ל משום דברייתא היא אבל הך דשכן עליה עוף היא מתניתין:

אף עובד דניחא ליה. וא"ת ובפרה אדומה מנלן דבעינן דניחא ליה דבשלמא למאן דיליף (סוטה דף מו.) עבודות בפרה מג"ש דעול עול ניחא אלא למאן דלית ליה ג"ש ומשכח עבודות בפרה גופיה מנלן דבעינן דניחא ליה וי"ל דכיון דשוין בפסול עול ועבודות גם לענין דניחא ליה יש להשוותן וא"ת ועלה עליה זכר אמאי פסולה הא ודאי לא ניחא ליה להפסיל פרה שדמיה יקרים בשביל דבר מועט וי"ל דאם היתה כשירה הוה ניחא ליה ולכך אין להכשיר וא"ת הכניסה לרבקה ודשה אמאי כשירה מאי שנא מעלה עליה זכר דפסולה וי"ל דהתם לא ניחא ליה בדישתה שאינו מרויח כ"כ דבלאו הכי נדושת התבואה וא"ת אי לא ידע בשעת עליית הזכר אמאי פסולה מאי שנא מהכשר דאמרינן לעיל (דף כב.) נגבו אין בכי יותן ואם נאמר דלא מיפסלא אלא כשידע בשעת עלייתו א"ש ואתי נמי שפיר הא דתנן (פרה פ"ב מ"א) פרה מעוברת ר"א מכשיר וקשה וכי לית ליה עלה עליה זכר פסולה ולמאי דפרישית אתי שפיר אי נמי סבר כר"י דאמר דוקא העלה עליה זכר אבל עלה מאליו כשירה וה"ר יצחק מסימפון פירש דלא פליגי בפרה עצמה אלא בבתה וטעמא דרבנן דפסולה כדדרשינן בספרי ויקחו אליך פרה בעינן שתהא בשעת לקיחה פרה ור"א לית ליה ההיא דרשה וה"ה דמצו פליגי בלקחו פרה קטנה וא"ת העושה מלאכה בפרת חטאת דאמר בפ' הכונס (ב"ק דף נו. ושם) דחייב בדיני שמים אמאי מיפסלא הא ודאי לא ניחא להו לבעלים וי"ל כגון שהיה שותף אי נמי לא בעינן ניחותא דבעלים רק ניחותא דעושה מלאכה וא"ת בפרק אין מעמידין (ע"ז דף כג:) דפוסל ר"א פרה הניקחת מן הנכרים דחייש לרביעה ודייק ש"מ קדשי מזבח היא דאי קדשי בדק הבית היא אמאי פסולה משום רביעה לימא דפסולה משום עול וי"ל דמשמע ליה דלאו מטעם עול פוסל דקתני בסיפא וכן היה ר"א פוסל בשאר קרבנות לכך קאמר דקדשי מזבח היא דממעטינן נרבע מקרא דמן הבהמה: [וע"ע תוס' ע"ז כג: ד"ה ש"מ]:

הא אין עשה דוחה לא תעשה ועשה. וא"ת דבפ"ב דיבמות (דף כא.) ובפ' כ"ג (סנהדרין דף יט.) לא חשיב אלמנה לכהן גדול אלא לא תעשה גרידא ואמאי והא איכא עשה דקדושים יהיו וי"ל דלא קאי עשה דקדושים יהיו אלא אמאי דכתיב בההיא פרשה וא"ת והא כי אמרינן דאין עשה דוחה את לא תעשה ועשה ה"מ

## עין משפט נר מצוה

קלו א מיי' פי"ג מהל' גזילה ואבידה הל' יא סמג עשין עד טוש"ע ח"מ סי' רסז סעיף יח:

קלז ב ג ד מיי' פ"י מהל' רוצח הל' ג ופ"א מהל' פרה אדומה הלכה ז סמג עשין עח רלב:

קלח ה ו ז ח מיי' פי"ג מהל' גזילה ואבידה הלכה יג סמג עשין עד טוש"ע ח"מ סי' רסז סעיף יט:

קלט ט י מיי' שם הל' יג ופ"ז מהלכות שאלה ופקדון הלכה ד סמג שם טוש"ע ח"מ סי' רלב סעיף כא כב:

קמ כ מיי' פי"א מהל' גזילה ואבידה הל' יח סמג עשין עד טוש"ע ח"מ סי' רעב סעיף ב:

קמא ל מיי' שם הלכה יג סמג שם טוש"ע ח"מ סי' רסג סעיף א:

קמב מ מיי' שם פי"ב הלכה א סמג שם טוש"ע ח"מ סי' רסד סעיף יא:

קמג נ מיי' פי"א שם הלכה יח ופ"ז מהלכות נזירות הל' טו:

## רבינו חננאל

שלא הוחמו כל צרכן כי קשין הן לגוף מאד והוא שהוחמו בכלי מתכות. ויש אומרי' פושרין הן הלוחשין ושאר שמעתתא דר' יוחנן פירשנום בפ' כיסוי הדם. ושוטחה לצורכה אבל לא לכבודו מיבעיא לן לצרכה ולצרכו מאי ת"ש שוטחה לצרכו וכו' ת"ש לא ישטחנה לא על גבי מיטה ולא על גבי מגוד לצרכו ולא איפשיטה. פי' לרבקה לפטמה מלשון עגלי מרבק. ת"ש הכניס לעגלה לרבקה ובהליכתה דשה ברגליה בתבואה שבגורן כשירה בשביל שתינק משדי אמו ותדוש פסולה ופשוטה היא. ת"ש מהא דתנן במסכת פרה שכן עליה עוף כשירה עלה עליה זכר פסולה והא עליית עליה זכר לצרכו ולצרכה היא וקתני פסולה. ודחי רב פפא ואמר כל מלתא דניחא ליה אע"ג שלא עשאה בידים מעשיו הן ודייק מדכתב עבד וקרינן עובד: מצא כלי חרש וכלי נחשת משתמש בהן לצרכן אבל לא לשחקן מצא כלי עץ משתמש בהן שלא ירקבו כלי נחשת משתמש בהן בחמין אבל לא על ידי האור. כלי כסף משתמש בהן בצונן אבל לא בחמין מפני שמשחירן. מגרפות וקרדומות משתמש בהן ברך אבל לא בקשה מפני שמפחיתן כלי זהב וכלי זכוכית לא יגע בהן עד שיבא אליהו כדרך שאמרו באבידה כך אמרו בפיקדון שהלכו בעליו למדינת הים. מצא שק או קופה שאין דרכו ליטול הרי זה לא יטול אלא אם רוצה לעשות לפנים משורת הדין כר' ישמעאל. פי' פתכא דאופי חבילה של חריות של דקל. פי' וקא מיתפח יגע והניח משאו לארץ כדי ליפוש. לא חרבה ירושלם אלא מפני שהעמידו דבריהם על דין תורה ולא עשו לפנים משורת הדין. ת"ר והתעלמת פעמים שאתה מתעלם כיצד זקן ואינה לפי כבודו אבל כהן

## מסורת הש"ס

א) [לקמן עג. חולין פד:], ב) [ברכות כה. וש"נ], ג) פסחים כו: [ע"ש], ד) פי' [בערוך] דבר מזומן לשטוח עליו כלי כיסה, פ"א גודא ממש ותוס' פרק כ"ש דף כו: ירסו כמו נגוד לגלימא, ה) שם ע"א, ו) שם ע"ב, פרה פרק ב משנה ד, ז) ברכות יט., סנהדרין ח., ח) [לקמן לג. סנהדרין סד. ע"ש], ט) [ועיין היטב תוס' לקמן עג. ותוס' חולין פד:], י) [פרק א וע"ש היטב], כ) [ע"ש היטב].

## תורה אור השלם

א) וְהָיָה הָעִיר הַקְּרֹבָה אֶל הֶחָלָל וְלָקְחוּ זִקְנֵי הָעִיר הַהִוא עֶגְלַת בָּקָר אֲשֶׁר לֹא עֻבַּד בָּהּ אֲשֶׁר לֹא מָשְׁכָה בְּעֹל: [דברים כא, ג]

ב) לֹא תִרְאֶה אֶת שׁוֹר אָחִיךָ אוֹ אֶת שֵׂיוֹ נִדָּחִים וְהִתְעַלַּמְתָּ מֵהֶם הָשֵׁב תְּשִׁיבֵם לְאָחִיךָ: [דברים כב, א]

ג) אֶפֶס כִּי לֹא יִהְיֶה בְּךָ אֶבְיוֹן כִּי בָרֵךְ יְבָרֶכְךָ יְיָ בָּאָרֶץ אֲשֶׁר יְיָ אֱלֹהֶיךָ נֹתֵן לְךָ נַחֲלָה לְרִשְׁתָּהּ: [דברים טו, ד]

## לעזי רש"י

ביל"א. פירוש יתד (רש"י ערכין דף עח ע"א ד"ה יתד). דבר שמזומן לשטוח עליו כלי כביסה (ערוך ערך מגד ג'). קופל"ה. פירוש למד בהמות (קשורות יחד). ודיל"ש. פירוש מגריפות, יעים (רש"י שמות כז ג).

## ליקוטי רש"י

בתורי. ישכור פועלים וימסור להן שוורים שלו לחרוש והם יכחישו השוורים ויקלקלו ביערות וכרמים והמלאכה לא תעלה לכלום שאין חוששין לכך [חולין פד:]. שבוצרין כרמים בשוורים בעגלה ומוליכין את העגלה בין שורות הכרמים ומתקלקלין רגלי השוורים וקולטי שרשים שבקרקע והפסדן רב [לקמן עג.]. לא ישטחנה. כמולא בגד אבידה קאי. לצורכה. כדי שלא יאכלנו עש. נזדמנו לו אורחים וכו'. אע"ג דלצורכה הוא הואיל ומתכוין להתכבד בשל חבירו באורחין חשיב ליה גזל ואסור. דמקלא קלי לה. דבשטיחה זו קלי לה כלומר מאבדה בידים [פסחים כו:]. ודשה. תבואה עם חברותיה. כשירה. שלא נתכוון לכך דלאו עבודה היא. אשר לא עובד בה מ"מ. ואע"ג דבעלמא לא מיתסר הכא אסור [שם בע"א]. שכן עליה עוף. בפרה אדומה קאי שפרח ונח על גבה אע"ג דכתיב לא עלה עליה עול דמשמע עגליה אפילו עליה בעלמא אי משום דכתיב עול הא מרבינן ביה שאר עבודות במסכת סוטה (דף מו.) אפ"ה בהא עלייה כשרה דלא ניחא ליה והוא הדין להכניסה לרבקה ודשה.

עלה עליה זכר פסולה. דניחא ליה והוא הדין לתינק ותידוש. עובד. משמע ממילא עבד משמע בידים ואף על גב דהאי בעגלה כתיב תרווייהו ילפינן מהדדי בגזירה שוה דעול עול במסכת סוטה [שם בע"ב]. וקרדומות. קרדום עשוי כמין כלי אומנות שעושין בו אוכפות וסרגות שקורין איישי"ש [ביצה לא.]. והתעלמת. כובש עין כאלו אינו רואהו ורבותינו אמרו פעמים שאתה מתעלם [דברים כב, א]. ואינה לפי כבודו. אין האבדה חשובה לפי כבודו להשיבה [ברכות יט:]. שאם היתה שלו לא היה מחזירה [סנהדרין יח:]. או שהיתה מלאכה שלו מרובה משל חבירו. שדמי בטול מלאכתו לרדוף אחריה יתירים על דמי האבידה ולא ירצו הבעלים להשיב לו יותר ממה שמשיב להם ונמצא הוא מפסיד [ברכות שם]. כגון נוקב מרגליות שאם ילך ויחזירנה יפסיד בבטלותו יותר מדמיה [סנהדרין שם]. לא דחינן איסורא מקמי ממונא. ממונא קל מאיסורא [ברכות שם].

בִּשְׁבִיל שֶׁתִּינַק וְתָדוּשׁ – SO THAT IT SHOULD SUCKLE AND THRESH at the same time, פְּסוּלָה – then IT IS UNFIT to be an *eglah arufah.*[10] וְהָא הָכָא – Now here, in the Baraisa's second clause, דִּלְצוֹרְכּוֹ וּלְצוֹרְכָּהּ הוּא – we have a case **in which** the animal entered the harness **for** both **[the owner's] needs and its** own **needs,** וְקָתָנֵי פְּסוּלָה – **and,** nevertheless, **[the Baraisa] teaches** that it becomes **unfit** to be an *eglah arufah.* Apparently, then, using something for one's own needs and its needs is tantamount to using it solely for one's own needs.[11]

The Gemara rejects the proof:

שָׁאנֵי הָתָם – Perhaps in the case of the garment, using the item for his needs and its needs would be permitted. **There,** however, with respect to *eglah arufah,* the law **is different,** דְּאָמַר קְרָא – **for the verse states** that the calf must be „אֲשֶׁר לֹא־עֻבַּד בָּהּ" – ***[one] with which work was not done.***[12] This implies: מִכָּל מָקוֹם – No work can have been done with it **whatsoever,** even if this work served the animal's own needs.[13]

The Gemara challenges this reply:

אִי הָכִי – **If** it were **so** that any work renders a calf unfit to be an *eglah arufah,* אֲפִילּוּ רֵישָׁא נַמִּי – then **even** in **the first case of the Baraisa** [where the owner did not intend the calf to thresh, but it did so anyway], the calf should also be rendered unfit. In fact, however, the Tanna rules that the calf remains fit in that case! – ? –

The Gemara explains the Baraisa's ruling, using a principle found in another Mishnah:

הָא לֹא דָּמְיָא אֶלָּא לְהָא דִּתְנַן – **That** case of the Baraisa **is** actually **comparable only to [the case] we learned in** the following **Mishnah:**[14] שָׁכַן עָלֶיהָ עוֹף – If A BIRD RESTED UPON [A COW], כְּשֵׁירָה – [THE COW] IS still FIT to be a *parah adumah,* for even though the cow labored in carrying the bird, the cow's owner views this occurrence with indifference. עָלָה עָלֶיהָ זָכָר – If, however, A [BULL] MOUNTED [THIS COW] and mated with it, פְּסוּלָה – then IT IS UNFIT to be a *parah adumah* because, in this case, the labor it performed was pleasing to its owner.[15] The principle found in the Mishnah now explains the ruling of the Baraisa: Just as an animal remains fit to be a *parah adumah* when it performs work about which its owner is indifferent, so too, an animal remains fit to be an *eglah arufah* when it performs work about which its owner is indifferent.[16]

The Gemara explains the basis for the Mishnah's distinction:

מַאי טַעְמָא – **What,** indeed, **is the reason** that a *parah adumah* is rendered unfit when it mates, whereas it remains fit when a bird rests upon it? כִּדְרַב פַּפָּא – It is as **Rav Pappa** stated with respect to the law of an *eglah arufah.* דְּאָמַר רַב פַּפָּא – **For Rav Pappa said:** אִי כְּתִיב עוּבַד – **If [the verse] had written *"ubad":*** that the calf need be one with which "work was not done," וְקָרִינַן עוּבַד – **and we had** likewise **pronounced** the word ***"ubad,"*** הֲוָה אָמִינָא אֲפִילּוּ מִמֵּילָא – then **I would have said** that **even** when the calf labors **on its own** [without the owner's prompting it], the calf would be rendered unfit. וְאִי כְּתִיב עָבַד – **And if [the verse] had written *"avad":*** "he worked it," וְקָרִינַן עָבַד – **and we had** likewise **pronounced** the word ***"avad,"*** הֲוָה אָמִינָא עַד דְּעָבַד בָּהּ אִיהוּ – then **I would have said** that the calf remains fit **unless [the owner]** actually **worked with it himself.** הַשְׁתָּא דִּכְתִיב עָבַד – **Now,** however, **that it is written *"avad,"*** וְקָרִינַן עוּבַד – **and it is pronounced *"ubad,"*** בְּעִינַן עוּבַד דּוּמְיָא דְּעָבַד – **we** compare the two words, and **require** that ***"ubad"*** be **similar to *"avad":*** That is, מָה עָבַד דְּנִיחָא לֵיהּ – **just as** the performance of ***"avad"*** [work the owner imposes upon the animal] is by definition **pleasing to [the owner],** אַף עוּבַד דְּנִיחָא לֵיהּ – **so, too,** the performance of ***"ubad"*** [work the animal undertakes on its own] must **be**

NOTES

10. In the first case, the owner placed the calf in the harness with the sole intent that it nurse from its mother while there; he did not intend also for it to thresh grain during this time (*Meiri;* see *Rashi*; cf. *Tosafos Chitzoniyos* as cited in *Shitah Mekubetzes*). The Tanna thus rules that the fact that the calf indeed threshed while nursing does not disqualify it to be an *eglah arufah.* In the second case, however, the owner placed the calf in the harness for a dual purpose: He wished it to nurse from its mother – but he also hoped that it would assist the other cows in threshing. In this case, the Tanna rules that the calf indeed becomes disqualified (see *Rashi*).

11. According to *Rosh,* the Gemara at this point interprets the Baraisa's second ruling as being the product of a Rabbinic decree. In Torah law, the Gemara assumes, the calf would become unfit only when its owner causes it to labor *for his purposes exclusively* (e.g. when the owner wishes the calf to thresh, and he has *no other motive* in joining it to the harness). The Rabbis, however, instituted a safeguard to this law, decreeing that even when the calf joins the harness for its purposes as well as the owner's (e.g. to nurse and thresh at the same time), it likewise becomes unfit to be an *eglah arufah.* The motivation for this decree was as follows: A fear existed that if the owner utilized the cow to thresh while it was nursing, he would be tempted to let it continue threshing even after it had stopped to nurse. In such a case, the calf would be laboring in fulfillment of the owner's needs alone, and it would become disqualified as an *eglah arufah* even in the realm of Torah law (see *Tos. HaRosh*; see also *Tos. Rabbeinu Peretz* ad loc.).

The Gemara is now making an analogy from the ruling of the Baraisa, arguing that a similar decree should apply in the case of a found garment: The finder should not be permitted to use the garment for his needs and its needs [e.g. to hang the garment in a way that airs it out and also decorates his home], for in doing so, he would be tempted to leave the garment hanging longer than its own needs demand.

12. *Deuteronomy* 21:3.

13. Previously, the Gemara had assumed that the Baraisa's second ruling was based on a Rabbinic decree. That is, the Rabbis decreed that placing a calf in a harness to nurse and thresh renders it unfit as an *eglah arufah,* for they feared that the owner might allow it to continue threshing after it had stopped to nurse (see above, note 11). Now, however, the Gemara establishes that the calf's labor under these circumstances renders it unfit in *Torah law,* even if it does not continue to thresh after nursing. [The Torah declares that the *eglah arufah* shall have performed no work *whatsoever* (even if this labor served its own needs).] The Gemara thus concludes that the case of the Baraisa is irrelevant to our inquiry, for it contains no precedent for a Rabbinic decree preventing the use of an object for its needs at the same time it is being used for one's own personal needs.

14. *Parah* 2:4. This Mishnah deals with the laws of a *parah adumah,* a red cow. The Torah declares that when a person becomes *tamei* through contact with a corpse, he remains so for seven days. In order for him to become purified, the ashes of a red heifer mixed with fresh spring water must be sprinkled upon him on the third and seventh days of his *tumah.* The purification process is then completed on the evening of the seventh day, when he immerses himself in a *mikveh* (see *Numbers* 19:12,19).

In describing the heifer used as a *parah adumah,* the Torah states that this animal must be one upon which a yoke was not placed (*Numbers* 19:2). Although the verse specifies only a yoke, the Baraisa (*Sotah* 46a) derives through exegesis that the law of the heifer is similar to that of the *eglah arufah:* It cannot have undergone *any* work, whether or not this work involved a yoke per se. The Mishnah now gives further definition to the type of work that renders a heifer unfit to be a *parah adumah.*

15. The process of mating is classified as a type of labor (*Tosafos* to *Pesachim* 26b ד״ה עלה עליה זכר פסולה). [It can be assumed that the owner would be pleased for his cow to mate, for he stands to profit from any offspring of the union.]

16. I.e. in the Baraisa's first case, the calf remains fit to be an *eglah arufah* because its owner placed it in the harness to nurse only: Whether or not the suckling calf also threshed was of no consequence to the owner [his grain would be threshed anyway by the other cows already in the harness (*Tosafos*)].

**מסורת הש"ס**

א) [לקמן עג., חולין פד:], ב) [ברכות כה., וש"נ], ג) פסחים כו: [ע"ש], ד) פי' [בערוך] דבר שמזומן לשטוח עליו כלי כביסה, פ"א גודא ממש והתוס' פרק כ"ש דף כו: פירשו כמו נגוד לגלימא, ה) שם ע"א, ו) שם ע"ב, פרה פרק ב משנה ד, ז) ברכות יט:, סנהדרין יח:, ח) [לקמן לג., סנהדרין סד:, ע"ש], ט) [ועיין היטב תוס' לקמן עג., ותוס' חולין פד:], י) [פרק א וע"ש היטב], כ) [ע"ש היטב].

**תורה אור השלם**

א) וְהָיָה הָעִיר הַקְּרֹבָה אֶל הֶחָלָל וְלָקְחוּ זִקְנֵי הָעִיר הַהִוא עֶגְלַת בָּקָר אֲשֶׁר לֹא עֻבַּד בָּהּ אֲשֶׁר לֹא מָשְׁכָה בְּעֹל: [דברים כא, ג]

ב) לֹא תִרְאֶה אֶת שׁוֹר אָחִיךָ אוֹ אֶת שֵׂיוֹ נִדָּחִים וְהִתְעַלַּמְתָּ מֵהֶם הָשֵׁב תְּשִׁיבֵם לְאָחִיךָ: [דברים כב, א]

ג) אֶפֶס כִּי לֹא יִהְיֶה בְּךָ אֶבְיוֹן כִּי בָרֵךְ יְבָרֶכְךָ יְיָ בָּאָרֶץ אֲשֶׁר יְיָ אֱלֹהֶיךָ נֹתֵן לְךָ נַחֲלָה לְרִשְׁתָּהּ: [דברים טו, ד]

**לעזי רש"י**

קביל"א. פירוש יתד (רש"י ערכין דף עח ע"א ד"ה יתד). דבר שמזומן לשטוח עליו כלי כביסה (ערוך ערך מגד ג'). קופל"ה. פירוש לצמד בהמות (קשורות יחד). ודיל"ש. פירוש מגריפות, יעים (רש"י שמות כז ג).

**ליקוטי רש"י**

בתורי. ישכור פועלים למסור להן שוורים שלו לחרוש והם יכחישו השוורים ויקצצום ביערות והכרמים והמלאכה לא תעלה לכלום שאינן חוששין לכך [חולין פד:]. שבולרין כרמים בשוורים בעגלה ומוליכין את העגלה בין שורות הכרמים ומתקלקלין רגלי השוורים מקלחי שרשים שבקרקע והפסדן רב [לקמן עג.]. לא ישטחנה. במולא בגד בודה קאי. לצורכה. כדי שלא יאכלנו עש. נזדמנו לו אורחים וכו'. אע"ג דלצורכה הוא הואיל ומתכוין להתכבד של חבירו באורחין חשיב זה גזל ואסור. דמקלא קלי לה. דבשטיחה זו קלי לה כלומר מאבדה בידים [פסחים כו:]. ודשה. הולכה עם חברותיה. כשירה. שלא נתכוון לכך אלו עבודה היא. אשר לא עובד בה מ"מ. אע"ג דבעלמא לא נאסר הכא אסור [שם ע"א]. שכן עליה עוף. פרה אדומה קאי שפרח ונח על גבה אע"ג דכתיב לא עלה עליה עול דמשמע אפילו עליה בעלמא משום דכתיב עול הא דרשינן ביה שאר עבודות במסכת סוטה (דף מו.) ה"ה בהא עלייה כשרה דלא ניחא ליה והוא הדין הכניסה לרבקה ודשה. ... עליה זכר פסולה. דניחא ליה והוא הדין לתינק ותידוש. עובד. משמע ממילא עבד משמע בידים ואף על גב דהאי בעגלה כתיב תרווייהו ילפינן מהדדי בגזירה שוה דעול עול במסכת סוטה [שם בע"ב]. וקרדומות. קרדום ... עושין בו אוכפות וסרגות שקורין איישי"ש [ביצה לא.]. והתעלמת. כובש עין כאילו אינו רואהו ורבותינו אמרו פעמים שאתה מתעלם [דברים כב, א]. ואינה לפי כבודו. אין האבדה חשובה לפי כבודו להשיבה [ברכות יט:]. שאם היתה ... [סנהדרין יח:]. או שהיתה מלאכה שלו מרובה משל חבירו. שדמי בטול מלאכתו לרדוף אחריה יתירים על דמי האבידה ולא ירצו הבעלים להשיב לו יותר ממה שמשיב להם ונמצא הוא מפסיד [ברכות שם]. כגון נוקב מרגליות ש... בבטלותו יותר מדמיה [סנהדרין שם]. לא דחינן איסורא מקמי ממונא. ממונא קל מאיסורא [ברכות שם].

**עין משפט נר מצוה**

קלו א מיי' פי"ג מהל' גזילה ואבידה הל' יא סמג עשין עד טוש"ע ח"מ סי' רסז סעיף יח:

קלז ב ג ד מיי' פי"ג מהל' רוצח הל' ג ופ"א מהל' פרה אדומה הלכה ז סמג עשין עם רלב:

קלח ה ו ז ח מיי' פי"ג מהל' גזילה ואבידה הלכה יג סמג עשין עד טוש"ע ח"מ סי' רסז סעיף יט:

קלט ט י מיי' שם הל' יג ופ"ז מהלכות שאלה ופקדון הלכה ד סמג שם טוש"ע ח"מ סי' רצב סעיף כא כב:

קמ כ מיי' פי"א מהל' גזילה ואבידה הל' יח סמג עשין עד טוש"ע ח"מ סי' רעב סעיף ב:

קמא ל מיי' שם הלכה יג סמג שם טוש"ע ח"מ סי' רסג סעיף א:

קמב מ מיי' שם פי"ב הלכה א סמג שם טוש"ע ח"מ סי' רסד סעיף יא:

קמג נ מיי' פי"א שם הלכה יח ופ"ז מהלכות נזירות הל' טו:

**רבינו חננאל**

שלא הוחמו כל צרכן כי קשין הן לגוף מאד והוא שהוחמו בכלי מתכות. ויש אומרי' פורשרין הן הלוחשין ושאר שמעתתא דר' יוחנן פירשנום בפ' כיסוי הדם. **ושוטחה לצורכה אבל לא לכבודו** מיבעיא לן לצרכה ולצרכו מאי ת"ש שוטחה לצרכו וכו' ת"ש לא ישטחנה לא על גבי מיטה ולא על גבי מגוד לצרכו ולא איפשיטא. פי' לרבקה לפטמה מלשון עגלי מרבק. ת"ש הכניס לעגלה לרבקה והבליכתה דשה ברגליה בתבואה שבגורן כשירה בשביל שתינק משדי אמו ותדוש פסולה ופשוטה היא. ת"ש מהא דתנן במסכת פרה שכן עליה עוף כשירה עלה עליה זכר פסולה והא עליית עליה זכר לצרכו ולצרכה היא וקתני פסולה. ודחי רב פפא ואמר כל מלתא דניחא ליה אע"ג שלא עשאה בידים מעשיו הן ודייק מדכתב עבד וקרינן עובד: **מצא כלי חרש וכלי נחשת** משתמש בהן לצרכן אבל לא לשחקן מצא כלי עץ משתמש בהן שלא ירקבו כלי נחשת משתמש בהן בחמין אבל לא על ידי האור. כלי כסף משתמש בהן בצונן אבל לא בחמין מפני שמשחירן. מגרפות וקרדומות משתמש בהן ברך אבל לא בקשה מפני שמפחיתן כלי זהב וכלי זכוכית לא יגע בהן עד שיבא אליהו כדרך שאמרו באבידה כך אמרו בפיקדון שהלכו בעליו למדינת הים. מצא שק או קופה שאין דרכו ליטול הרי זה לא יטול אלא אם רוצה לעשות לפנים משורת הדין כר' ישמעאל. פי' פתכא דאופי חבילה של חריות של דקל. פי' וקא מיתפח יגע והניח משאו לארץ כדי ליפוש. לא חרבה ירושלם אלא מפני שהעמידו דבריהם על דין תורה ולא עשו לפנים משורת הדין. ת"ר והתעלמת פעמים שאתה מתעלם כיצד זקן ואינה לפי כבודו אבל כהן

**גמרא**

א) בתורי דנפיש פסידייהו: שוטחה לצורכה אבל לא לכבודו וכו': איבעיא להו לצורכו ולצורכה מאי ת"ש שוטחה לצורכה אין א) הא לצורכו ולצורכה לא אימא סיפא אבל לא לכבודו לכבודו הוא דלא הא לצורכה ולצורכו שפיר דמי ג) אלא מהא ליכא למשמע מינה ת"ש ג) לא ישטחנה לא על גבי מטה ולא על גבי ד) מגוד לצרכו אבל ישטחנה על גבי מטה ועל גבי מגוד לצרכה נזדמנו לו אורחים לא ישטחנה לא על גבי מטה ולא על גבי מגוד בין לצורכו בין לצורכה שאני התם דמקלא קלי לה אי משום עינא אי משום גנבי תא שמע ה) ב) הכניסה לרבקה ודשה כשירה בשביל שתינק ותדוש פסולה והא הכא דלצורכו ולצורכה הוא וקתני פסולה שאני התם דאמר קרא א) אשר לא עובד בה מ"מ אי הכי אפילו רישא נמי הא לא דמיא אלא להא ו) דתנן ג) שכן עליה עוף כשירה עלה עליה זכר פסולה מאי טעמא כדרב פפא דאמר רב פפא אי כתיב עובד וקרינן עובד הוה אמינא אפילו ממילא ואי כתיב עבד וקרינן עבד הוה אמינא עד דעבד בה איהו השתא דכתיב עבד וקרינן עובד בעינן עובד דומיא דעבד ד) מה עבד דניחא ליה אף עובד דניחא ליה: כלי כסף וכלי נחושת משתמש בהן וכו': ת"ר ה) המוצא כלי עץ משתמש בהן בשביל שלא ירקבו ו) כלי נחושת משתמש בהן בחמין אבל לא על ידי האור מפני שמשחיקן ז) כלי כסף משתמש בהן בצונן אבל לא בחמין מפני שמשחירן ח) מגריפות וקרדומות משתמש בהן ברך אבל לא בקשה מפני שמפחיתן כלי זהב וכלי זכוכית לא יגע בהן עד שיבא אליהו ט) כדרך שאמרו באבידה כך אמרו בפקדון פקדון מאי עבידתיה גביה אמר רב אדא בר חמא אמר רב ששת י) בפקדון שהלכו בעליהן למדינת הים: מצא שק או קופה [וכל דבר] שאין דרכו ליטול הרי זה לא יטול: מנהני מילי ז) דת"ר ב) והתעלמת פעמים שאתה מתעלם ופעמים שאי אתה מתעלם הא כיצד כ) היה כהן והיא בבית הקברות ל) או שהיה זקן ואינה לפי כבודו מ) או שהיתה מלאכה שלו מרובה משל חבירו לכך נאמר והתעלמת מהם למאי איצטריך קרא אילימא לכהן והיא בבית הקברות פשיטא האי עשה והאי לא תעשה ועשה נ) ולא אתי עשה ודחי את לא תעשה ועשה ותו לא דחינן איסורא מקמי ממונא אלא לשלו מרובה משל חבירו מדרב יהודה אמר רב נפקא ח) דאמר רב יהודה אמר רב ג) אפס כי

**רש"י**

דנפיש פסידייהו. שרוב עבודת קרקעות שלהן בשוורים היתה אף חרישת הכרמים ובצירתם מנהיגים כלי המחרישה בעגלה בין שורות הכרם עם הבוצרים ונותנין שם הענבים לפיכך אם אין הבעלים עליהם יש הפסד גדול שאין דרך הפועלים לחוס על הכרם ועל השוורים ומנהיגים אותן על הגפנים ועל הנטיעות והם מתקלקלין והשוורין נסחבין ונשברים: מגוד. קביל"א בלע"ז: נזדמנו לו אורחים. קס"ד טעמא משום דמתכבד בהם ואיכא לצורכה ולצרכו: שאני התם דקא קלי לה. בשטיחה זו הוא שורפה ומה הוא שריפתה: אי משום עינא. שתשלוט בה עין רע של אורחין: אי משום גנבי. פן יגנבוה האורחים: הכניסה לרבקה. בעגלה ערופה קאי. רבקה קופל"ה בלע"ז שמדבקים שלש בהמות או ארבעה בצואריהן זו אצל זו ודשים הדישה: כשירה. הואיל ולא נתכוון שתדוש: ואם בשביל שתינק ותידוש. שהיתה אמה דשה והכניס את הבת לשם שתינק ואף נתכוין שתדוש פסולה: הא לא דמיא. תירוצא היא: שכן עליה עוף. בפרה אדומה קאי: עלה עליה זכר פסולה. שנאמר אשר לא עלה עליה עול ותניא עול אין לי אלא עול כו' במסכת סוטה (דף מו.) והאי הכניסה לרבקה ודשה דלא ניחא ליה בה דמיא לשכן עליה עוף: משתמש בהן בחמין. וכ"ש בצונן: אבל לא ע"י האור. לא יתן הכלי על האור: מגריפות. ודיל"ש עשוין לגרוף הפירות או להפריש תאנים המדובקים: שמפחיתן. פוגמן: מאי עבידתיה גביה. מה לו להשתמש בו יבא בעליו וישתמש בו: והתעלמת מהם. וללמדך בא שמותר להתעלם: ופעמים שאי אתה מתעלם. דכתיב לא תוכל להתעלם: והיא בבית הקברות. האבידה בבית הקברות: ואינה לפי כבודו. שיתבזה: או שהיה בטל ממלאכה שלו. שיבטל בהשבתה מרובה על דמי האבידה: האי עשה. השב תשיבם ואע"ג דלא תעשה נמי איכא אין לא תעשה מועיל לדחות לא תעשה אלא עשה הוא דקא דחי ליה כדאמרינן ביבמות (דף כא.): לא תעשה ועשה. לנפש לא יטמא קדושים יהיו: לא

**תוספות**

בתורי דנפיש פסידייהו. ר"ח גרס בתוורי פירוש פועלים שמוליכים השוורים לחרישה ואין מעמיקין המחרישה שלשה טפחים ואין הזרע נקלט היטב ט): ולצורכה מאי. דוקא בשיטוח כסות מבעיא ליה וכל דדמי ליה דשמא יניחנה שטוחה יותר מכדי צורכה עד שיתקלקל אבל בספר אמרינן דקורא בהן אף ע"ג דלצורכו הוא כמו צורכה ולא גזרינן דליכא למיחש למידי כיון שקבעו לו זמן אחד לשלשים יום או אחד לי"ב חדש ולא ילמוד בו בתחלה גם לא יקרא וישנה וכלי נחשת דתניא לקמן דמשתמש אפי' בחמין וכלי כסף בצונן אפי' לצורכו מותר כיון שעל ידי אותו תשמיש אינו יכול לבא לידי קלקול ותדע דאי דוקא לצורך הכלי מאי פריך פקדון מאי עבידתיה גביה כיון שהוא שומר יש לו לעיין שלא יתקלקל אע"פ שהבעלים אינם אומרים לו להשתמש:

**הכניסה** לרבקה ודשה. בתוספת' (דפרה)[י] תני לה גבי פרה אדומה: **בשביל** שתינק ותדוש פסולה. ובסיפא (דתוספתא[כ]) קתני לצורכו פסולה לצורכה כשירה ולכך פריך אלמא לצורכו ולצורכה חשיב כמו צורכו ואסור ומשני דהתם דאורייתא פסולה כמו בא עלי' זכר דפסולה מדרב פפא וא"ת ואמאי מייתי ההיא דשכן עליה עוף ואי משום דרב פפא אמר למלתיה עלה אמאי לא אמר אהך דהכניסה לרבק' וי"ל משום דברייתא היא אבל הך דשכן עליה עוף היא מתניתין:

**אף** עובד דניחא ליה. וא"ת ובפרה אדומה מנלן דבעינן דניחא ליה דבשלמא למאן דיליף (סוטה דף מו.) עבודות בפרה מג"ש דעול עול ניחא אלא למאן דלית ליה ג"ש ומשכח עבודות בפרה גופיה מנלן דבעינן דניחא ליה וי"ל דכיון דשוין בפסול עול ועבודות גם לענין דניחא ליה יש להשוותן וא"ת ועלה עליה זכר אמאי פסולה הא ודאי לא ניחא ליה להפסיל פרה שדמיה יקרים בשביל דבר מועט וי"ל דאם היתה כשירה הוה ניחא ליה ולכך אין להכשיר וא"ת הכניסה לרבקה ודשה אמאי כשירה מאי שנא מעלה עליה זכר דפסולה וי"ל דהתם לא ניחא ליה בדישתה שאינו מרויח כ"כ דבלאו הכי נדושת התבואה וא"ת אי לא ידע בשעת עליית הזכר אמאי פסולה מאי שנא מהכשר דאמרינן לעיל (דף כב.) נגבו אינן בכי יותן ואם נאמר דלא מיפסלא אלא כשידע בשעת עלייתו א"ש ואתי נמי שפיר הא דתנן (פרה פ"ב מ"א) פרה מעוברת ר"א מכשיר וקשה וכי לית ליה עלה עליה זכר פסולה ולמאי דפרישית אתי שפיר אי נמי סבר כר"י דאמר דוקא העלה עליה זכר אבל עלה מאליו כשירה וה"ר יצחק מסימפון פירש דלא פליגי בפרה עצמה אלא בבתה וטעמא דרבנן דפסולה כדדרשינן בספרי ויקחו אליך פרה בעינן שתהא בשעת לקיחה פרה ור"א לית ליה ההיא דרשה וה"ה דמצו פליגי בלקחו פרה קטנה וא"ת העושה מלאכה בפרת חטאת דאמר בפ' הכונס (ב"ק דף נו. ושם) דחייב בדיני שמים אמאי מיפסלא הא ודאי לא ניחא להו לבעלים וי"ל כגון שהיה שותף אי נמי לא בעינן ניחותא דבעלים רק ניחותא דעושה מלאכה וא"ת בפרק אין מעמידין (ע"ז דף כג:) דפוסל ר"א פרה הניקחת מן הנכרים דחייש לרביעה ודייק ש"מ קדשי מזבח היא דאי קדשי בדק הבית היא אמאי פסולה משום רביעה לימא דפסולה משום עול וי"ל דמשמע ליה דלאו מטעם עול פוסל דקתני בסיפא וכן היה ר"א פוסל בשאר קרבנות לכך קאמר דקדשי מזבח היא דממעטין נרבע מקרא דמן הבהמה: [וע"ע תוס' ע"ז כג: ד"ה ש"מ]:

**הא** אין עשה דוחה לא תעשה ועשה. וא"ת דבפ"ב דיבמות (דף כא.) ובפ' כ"ג (סנהדרין דף יט.) לא חשיב אלמנה לכהן גדול אלא לא תעשה גרידא ואמאי והא איכא עשה דקדושים יהיו וי"ל דלא קאי עשה דקדושים יהיו אלא אמאי דכתיב בההיא פרשה וא"ת והא כי אמרינן דאין עשה דוחה את לא תעשה ועשה ה"מ

בְּתוֹר – as referring to the hiring of oxen drivers דַּנְפִּישׁ פְּסֵידַיְיהוּ – where the potential loss is great if they are not supervised.[1]

The Gemara now resumes its analysis of our Mishnah. The Mishnah had stated:
שׁוֹטְחָהּ לְצוֹרְכָּהּ אֲבָל לֹא לִכְבוֹדוֹ וכו׳ – If one found a garment . . . HE SHOULD SPREAD IT OUT as necessary FOR ITS NEEDS, BUT he should NOT spread it out FOR HIS own HONOR etc.[2]

The Gemara presents a question:
אִיבַּעְיָא לְהוּ – [The Rabbis of the academy] inquired: לְצוֹרְכּוֹ וּלְצוֹרְכָּהּ מַאי – If the finder wishes to spread out the garment to serve his own needs as well as [the garment's] needs, what is the law?[3] May he spread the garment out under these circumstances or not?

The Gemara attempts to resolve the question by analyzing the language of our Mishnah:
תָּא שְׁמַע – Come, learn the proof to this from our Mishnah: שׁוֹטְחָהּ לְצוֹרְכָּהּ – HE SHOULD SPREAD IT OUT FOR ITS NEEDS. לְצוֹרְכָּהּ אִין – This implies that if the finder intends to spread the garment out for its needs alone, then indeed, he may do this. הָא לְצוֹרְכּוֹ וּלְצוֹרְכָּהּ לֹא – But if he intends to spread it out for both his own needs and for its needs, then he may not do this.

The Gemara counters with an inference to the contrary:
אֵימָא סֵיפָא – But take note of the latter part of the Mishnah! This states: אֲבָל לֹא לִכְבוֹדוֹ – BUT he should NOT spread it out FOR HIS own HONOR, implying: לִכְבוֹדוֹ הוּא דְּלֹא – For his honor (a "need" of the finder himself), he may not spread it out, הָא לְצוֹרְכָּהּ וּלְצוֹרְכּוֹ – but if he wishes to spread it out for both its needs and his own needs, שַׁפִּיר דָּמֵי – this is fine. This stands at odds with the implication of the first clause.

Having shown that the two clauses of the Mishnah yield contradictory inferences, the Gemara concludes:
אֶלָּא מֵהָא לֵיכָּא לְמִשְׁמַע מִינָּהּ – Rather, from this Mishnah, it cannot be proven one way or the other.

The Gemara puts forth a second attempt to resolve the inquiry:
תָּא שְׁמַע – Come, learn the proof to this from the following Baraisa: לֹא יִשְׁטְחֶנָּה לֹא עַל גַּבֵּי מִטָּה – If a person finds a garment, HE SHOULD NOT SPREAD IT OUT OVER A BED וְלֹא עַל גַּבֵּי מָגוֹד – NOR should he do so OVER A PEG,[4] לְצָרְכּוֹ – if he is doing this FOR HIS NEEDS. אֲבָל יִשְׁטְחֶנָּה עַל גַּבֵּי מִטָּה וְעַל גַּבֵּי מָגוֹד לְצָרְכָּהּ – BUT HE SHOULD SPREAD IT OUT OVER A BED OR OVER A PEG FOR ITS NEEDS. נִזְדַּמְּנוּ לוֹ אוֹרְחִים – If, however, GUESTS HAPPENED TO visit HIM, לֹא יִשְׁטְחֶנָּה לֹא עַל גַּבֵּי מִטָּה – then HE SHOULD NOT under any circumstances SPREAD IT OUT OVER A BED, וְלֹא עַל גַּבֵּי מָגוֹד – NOR OVER A PEG, בֵּין לְצוֹרְכּוֹ בֵּין לְצוֹרְכָּהּ – regardless of WHETHER he wishes to do this FOR HIS NEEDS OR FOR ITS NEEDS.[5] Now, the final clause of the Baraisa clearly deals with a case in which spreading the garment could serve *both* needs [those of the garment as well as those of the finder], and, nevertheless, it rules that the garment may not be spread out. Apparently, then, we have resolved our question.

The Gemara rejects the proof:
שָׁאנֵי הָתָם – Perhaps using it for his needs and its needs would generally be permitted, but there, in the Baraisa's case, it is different, דְּמִקְלָא קָלֵי לָהּ – for by displaying the garment in front of guests he in effect burns it (i.e. he potentially brings about the garment's ruin). How is this so? אִי מִשּׁוּם עֵינָא – Either because he exposes the garment to the jealous eye of the guests,[6] אִי מִשּׁוּם גַּנָּבֵי – or because he exposes it to potential thieves.[7] Our question thus remains unresolved.

The Gemara makes a final attempt to resolve the inquiry:
תָּא שְׁמַע – Come, learn the proof to this from a Baraisa, which deals with the following case:[8] הִכְנִיסָהּ לְרִבְקָה – If ONE JOINED [HIS CALF] with a team of cows IN A MULTIPLE HARNESS, intending for the calf to suckle from its mother while it is there,[9] וְדָשָׁה – AND while in the harness IT THRESHED some grain beneath its feet. In this case, כְּשֵׁירָה – [THE CALF] IS still FIT to be an *eglah arufah*. If, however, he joined the calf with its mother

NOTES

*Rashi* explains that in the days of the Amoraim, most agricultural work, including the plowing and harvesting of vineyards, was done with the aid of oxen. When grapes were harvested, oxen would pull a wagon between rows of vines, while people picking the grapes would trail behind, depositing into the wagon the fruit they had gathered.

Although the oxen added efficiency to the process, their presence gave rise to certain risks as well. Specifically, there existed the possibility that if the oxen strayed off course, they would trample the vines, injuring themselves and uprooting the plants in the process. Because of these risks, R' Yochanan advised that the vineyard owner supervise the people who were hired to drive the oxen, to ensure that they carried out their task properly. [Since the hired workers had no personal stake in the well-being of either the oxen or the vines, they could not be trusted to take the necessary precautions on their own.]

E.g. he should not spread it out for the purpose of adorning his home.

I.e. if the garment requires airing out, may the finder spread it out in a way that not only exposes it to air, but also, for example, enhances the appearance of his home? Essentially, the question being asked here is this: Were the Rabbis concerned that the finder would leave the garment spread out longer than its own needs require if he stands to realize some benefit from the garment remaining spread out? (*Tosafos; Tos. HaRosh*). [The Gemara did not seek to resolve its question from the Mishnah's ruling that a finder may use scrolls and utensils in ways that benefit both him and the article, for in these cases, there is no reason to fear that the finder's use of the article will lead to its ruin. In the case of scrolls, for example, the Mishnah allows the finder to read them only once in thirty days, and it does not allow him to study in them material he is learning a first time. The Gemara's question, on the other hand, concerns a different case entirely. It questions the permissibility of using items such as clothes, where there is indeed reason to fear for the well-being of the article. The finder may be tempted to leave it spread out for longer than is advisable, as explained above] (*Tosafos*).

4. *Rashi* gives the French term קביל״א – which generally denotes a peg – as the translation of this word (cf. *Aruch,* and *Tosafos* to *Pesachim* 26b ד״ה מגוד).

5. In the final clause of the Baraisa, the garment itself is in need of exposure to air, and, presumably, the finder would take pride in displaying it while entertaining the guests in his home (see *Rashi*).

6. *Rashi* interprets עינא as meaning that the guests' עין רעה, *evil eye,* will rest on the garment. The concept of עין רעה appears with some frequency in the Talmud. Essentially, it affirms that when an item is looked upon with envy by people, the likelihood increases that it will become harmed.

7. When guests are entertained in the vicinity of the garment, the possibility exists that one of them will steal it (*Rashi*).

8. The Baraisa deals with the concept of *eglah arufah,* a calf that is to be decapitated (*Rashi*). Briefly, the law of this animal can be described as follows: If a person is found murdered between two cities and his murderer is not known, the elders of the Sanhedrin must measure the distance to the surrounding cities to determine the city closest to the corpse. The elders of that city must then bring a female calf and decapitate it in a valley, in accordance with the procedure outlined in *Deuteronomy* 21:1-9.

One of the requirements the Torah sets forth in this law is that an *eglah arufah* never had performed work while it was alive. In the words of the verse (*Deuteronomy* 21:3), the calf must be *[one] with which work was not done [and one] that did not pull on a yoke.* It is this requirement that the Baraisa now sets out to clarify.

The above follows *Rashi* and *R' Chananel.* According to *Tosafos,* however, the Baraisa refers not to an *eglah arufah,* but to a *parah adumah.*

9. *Ramban, Meiri;* cf. *Tosafos Chitzoniyos,* as cited in *Shitah Mekubetzes.* See also *Tos. HaRosh.*

וְלֹא יִקְרָא אַחֵר עִמּוֹ – **NOR SHOULD ANOTHER** person **READ** from the scroll together **WITH HIM.**

The Gemara asks that the second of these rulings appears to stand in contradiction to a Baraisa:

וּרְמִינְהוּ – **They noted a contradiction** from the following Baraisa: לֹא יִקְרָא פָּרָשָׁה וְיִשְׁנֶה – **ONE** who has found a scroll **SHOULD NOT READ A PORTION AND** then **REVIEW IT** while he is caring for it, וְלֹא יִקְרָא בּוֹ פָּרָשָׁה וִיתַרְגֵּם – **NOR SHOULD HE READ A PORTION IN IT AND** then **TRANSLATE IT.**[33] וְלֹא יִפְתַּח בּוֹ יוֹתֵר מִג׳ דַּפִּין – **HE SHOULD NOT OPEN IT MORE THAN THREE COLUMNS** at a time, וְלֹא יִקְרְאוּ בּוֹ שְׁלֹשָׁה בְּנֵי אָדָם בִּכְרֶךְ אֶחָד – **AND THREE PEOPLE SHOULD NOT READ FROM IT,** if they are reading **IN ONE VOLUME** at the same time. הָא שְׁנַיִם קוֹרִין – Now, by stating that three people should not read from it, **this** Baraisa **implies that two** people **may** indeed **read** from it at the same time. The Mishnah, however, said that even two people may not read together. – ? –

The Gemara reconciles the two rulings:

אָמַר אַבַּיֵי – **Abaye said:** לֹא קַשְׁיָא – This is **no difficulty.** כָּאן בְּעִנְיָן אֶחָד – **Here,** in the Mishnah's case, it **refers to** two people reading **one passage.** This is prohibited because each person has a tendency to pull the scroll towards himself, which might cause it to tear. כָּאן בִּשְׁנֵי עִנְיָנִים – **Here,** however, in the Baraisa's case, it **refers to** people reading **two** different **passages.** These two people are permitted to read at once,[34] since they can open the scroll wide enough for each to read from his own section without pulling on the scroll.[35]

The Gemara cites the next section of the Mishnah and analyzes it:

מָצָא כְּסוּת מְנַעֲרָהּ אֶחָד לִשְׁלֹשִׁים יוֹם – If **ONE FOUND A GARMENT, HE SHOULD SHAKE IT OUT ONCE EVERY THIRTY DAYS.**

The Gemara asks:

לְמֵימְרָא דְּנִיעוּר מַעֲלֵי לָהּ – **Is this to say that shaking out** a garment **is beneficial to it?** וְהָאָמַר רַבִּי יוֹחָנָן – **But R' Yochanan said** sarcastically: מִי שֶׁיֵּשׁ לוֹ גַּרְדִּי אוּמָּן בְּתוֹךְ בֵּיתוֹ יְנַעֵר כְּסוּתוֹ בְּכָל יוֹם – **Whoever has a professional weaver in his house** should shake **out his garment every day;** doing so will ruin the garment, and the weaver will then have the job of weaving another one! This is contrary to our Mishnah's ruling! – ? –

The Gemara responds:

אָמְרֵי – **They said:** בְּכָל יוֹם קָשֵׁי לָהּ – Shaking out a garment **every day is harmful to it,** as R' Yochanan said; אֶחָד לִשְׁלֹשִׁים יוֹם מַעֲלֵי לָהּ – doing so **once in thirty days is beneficial to it,** as the Mishnah says.

An alternative resolution:

אִיבָּעֵית אֵימָא – Or, **if you prefer, say** that לֹא קַשְׁיָא – there is **no difficulty** here for the following reason: הָא בְּחַד – **This** [the Mishnah] speaks of **one person** shaking it out, וְהָא בִּתְרֵי – **while this** [R' Yochanan] refers to **two people** shaking it out together.[36]

A third resolution:

אִיבָּעֵית אֵימָא – Or, **if you prefer, say** that לֹא קַשְׁיָא – there **no difficulty** here for yet another reason: הָא בְּיָדָא – **This** [th Mishnah] speaks of shaking **by hand,** וְהָא בְּחוּטְרָא – **wherea this** [R' Yochanan's] refers to beating the garment **with a stic** The former process is safe for the garment, but the latter proces may cause it to tear.

A fourth resolution:

אִיבָּעֵית אֵימָא – Or, **if you prefer, say** that לֹא קַשְׁיָא – there **no difficulty** here for still another reason: הָא בְּדַעַמְרָא – **Thi** [R' Yochanan's] **refers to** a garment made **of wool,** whic stretches and may tear when shaken vigorously; הָא בִּדְכִיתָּנָא – **whereas this** [the Mishnah's] **refers to** a garment made **of liner** which does not tear as easily.

In the previous discussion, the Gemara had mentioned a point practical advice offered by R' Yochanan. The Gemara no presents some other aphorisms of R' Yochanan concernin practical matters:

אָמַר רַבִּי יוֹחָנָן – **R' Yochanan said:** כָּסָא דְּחַרְשִׁין – Let a perso drink **a cup** prepared **by sorcerers,** וְלֹא כָּסָא דְּפוֹשְׁרִין – **but no a cup of lukewarm water,**[37] for the latter is even more dangerou than the former. וְלֹא אֲמָרָן אֶלָּא בִּכְלֵי מַתָּכוֹת – **Now this wa said** only in regard to water warmed **in a metal utensil;** אֲבָל בִּכְלֵי חֶרֶשׂ – **but** if it was warmed to a lukewarm state **in a earthenware utensil,** לֵית לָן בָּהּ – **there is no** objection **t** drinking **it.** וּבִכְלֵי מַתָּכוֹת נַמִּי – **Moreover, even** if the water wa warmed **in a metal utensil,** לֹא אֲמָרָן אֶלָּא דְּלֹא צְוִיץ – **it was no said** that it is harmful **unless it had not** been brought to a **boi** אֲבָל דִּצְוִיץ – **but if it had been** brought to a **boil,** לֵית לָן בָּהּ – **there is no** objection **to** drinking **it.** לֹא אֲמָרָן אֶלָּא דְּלֹא שָׁדָא בֵּיהּ צִיבְיָא – **Moreover, it was only said** that the water is harmfu when one did not put other **ingredients**[38] **into it;** אֲבָל שָׁדָא בֵּיהּ צִיבְיָא – **but** if **one put** other **ingredients into it,** לֵית לָן בָּהּ – **there is no** objection **to** drinking **[the mixture].**

The Gemara records another piece of advice imparted by R Yochanan:

וְאָמַר רַבִּי יוֹחָנָן – **And R' Yochanan said:** מִי שֶׁהִנִּיחַ לוֹ אָבִיו מָעוֹת הַרְבֵּה – If **one's father left him a great sum of money** as a inheritance, וְרוֹצֶה לְאַבְּדָן – **and he wishes to lose it,** יִלְבַּשׁ בִּגְדֵי פִשְׁתָּן – **let him wear linen clothing,** וְיִשְׁתַּמֵּשׁ בִּכְלֵי זְכוּכִית – **use glass utensils,** וְיִשְׂכּוֹר פּוֹעֲלִים וְאַל יֵשֵׁב עִמָּהֶן – **and hir workers and not sit with them** to supervise.[39]

The Gemara clarifies R' Yochanan's statement:

יִלְבַּשׁ בִּכְלֵי פִשְׁתָּן – When R' Yochanan stated: **"Let him wea linen clothing,"** בִּכְתָנָא רוּמִיתָא – he referred **to Roman linen** which is very expensive and wears out quickly. יִשְׁתַּמֵּשׁ בִּכְלֵי זְכוּכִית – When he further stated: **"Let him use glass utensils,"** בְּזוּגִיתָא חִיוַּרְתָּא – he referred specifically **to white glass,** whic breaks easily. וְיִשְׂכּוֹר פּוֹעֲלִים וְאַל יֵשֵׁב עִמָּהֶן – And when he stated **"Let him hire workers and not sit with them** to supervise," תַּרְגּוּמָא – **interpret this**

NOTES

33. In doing either of these, the finder may keep the scroll open for a long time, thereby increasing the possibility that it will become damaged in some way (*Tos. Shantz,* cited by *Shitah Mekubetzes*).

34. If the passages appear in separate columns (*Rashi*).

35. [Three people, however, may not read even separate passages simultaneously, because this places undue strain on the scroll.]

36. When two people shake out a garment together, they tend to pull it taut, and the increased strain on the garment can eventually cause it to tear. R' Yochanan therefore advises not to shake it out regularly. When only one person shakes it out, however, this is not a problem. The Mishnah therefore requires one who finds a garment to shake it out once i thirty days (*Rashi*).

37. I.e. it is less dangerous to drink a cup prepared by sorcerers than i is to drink a cup of lukewarm water.

38. The word צִיבְיָא refers to any ingredient that is added to water t create a beverage. The term would include spices, and flavorful roots o grasses (*Rashi*).

39. R' Yochanan's words are meant as a note of caution: One should no become accustomed to conducting himself in these ways, for these indul gences will quickly cost a man his fortune (*Rashi;* see *Ben Yehoyada*).

כדרבה [א] דאמר רבה נגנבו בלסטים מזויין אבדו שטבעה ספינתו בים אמר רב יהודה אמר שמואל הלכה כר' טרפון (א) ביד רחבה הוה ליה הנהו זוזי דיתמי אתא לקמיה דרב יוסף אמר ליה מהו לאשתמושי בגוייהו א"ל הכי אמר רב יהודה אמר שמואל הלכה כר' טרפון א"ל אביי ולאו אתמר עלה א"ר חלבו אמר רב הונא [א] לא שנו אלא בדמי אבידה הואיל וטרח בה אבל מעות אבידה דלא טרח בהו לא והני כמעות אבידה דמו א"ל זיל לא שבקו לי דאשרי לך: **מתני'** [ב] מצא ספרים קורא בהן אחד לשלשים יום ואם אינו יודע לקרות גוללן אבל לא ילמוד בהן בתחלה ולא יקרא אחר עמו [ג] מצא כסות מנערה אחד לשלשים יום ושוטחה לצרכה אבל לא לכבודו [ד] כלי כסף וכלי נחושת משתמש בהן לצרכן אבל לא לשחקן [ה] כלי זהב וכלי זכוכית לא יגע בהן עד שיבא אליהו (ג) [ו] מצא שק או קופה וכל דבר שאין דרכו ליטול הרי זה לא יטול: **גמ'** אמר שמואל [ז] המוצא תפילין בשוק שם דמיהן ומניחן לאלתר מתיב רבינא מצא ספרים קורא בהן אחד לשלשים יום ואם אינו יודע לקרות גוללן גוללן אין שם דמיהן ומניחן לא אמר אביי [ח] תפילין בי בר חבו משכח שכיחי ספרים לא שכיחי ת"ר (ג) [ט] השואל ספר תורה מחבירו הרי זה לא ישאילנו לאחר פותחו וקורא בו ובלבד שלא ילמוד בו בתחלה ולא יקרא אחר עמו [י] וכן המפקיד ס"ת אצל חבירו גוללו כל שנים עשר חדש פותחו וקורא בו אם בשבילו פתחו אסור סומכוס אומר בחדש שלשים יום בישן שנים עשר חדש ר"א בן יעקב אומר אחד זה ואחד זה שנים עשר חדש: אמר מר השואל ספר תורה מחבירו הרי זה לא ישאילנו לאחר מאי אריא ס"ת אפי' כל מילי נמי [ד] דאמר ר"ש בן לקיש כאן שנה רבי [כ] אין השואל רשאי להשאיל [ל] ואין השוכר רשאי להשכיר ס"ת איצטריכא ליה מהו דתימא (ה) ניחא ליה לאיניש דתיעביד מצוה בממוניה קמ"ל פותחו וקורא בו פשיטא ואלא למאי שייליה מיניה סיפא איצטריכא ליה ובלבד שלא ילמוד בו בתחלה וכן המפקיד ס"ת אצל חבירו גוללו כל שנים עשר חדש פותחו וקורא בו מאי עבידתיה גביה ותו אם בשבילו פתחו אסור הא אמרת פותחו וקורא בו הכי קאמר [מ] אם כשהוא גוללו פותחו וקורא בו מותר אם בשבילו פתחו אסור סומכוס אומר בחדש שלשים יום בישן שנים עשר חדש ר"א בן יעקב אומר אחד זה ואחד זה שנים עשר חדש ר"א בן יעקב היינו תנא קמא אלא אימא ר' אליעזר בן יעקב אומר אחד זה ואחד זה שלשים יום: אבל לא ילמוד בו בתחלה ולא יקרא אחר עמו: ורמינהו לא יקרא פרשה וישנה ולא יקרא בו פרשה ויתרגם ולא יפתח בו יותר מג' דפין ולא יקראו בו שלשה בני אדם בכרך אחד הא שנים קורין אמר אביי לא קשיא כאן בענין אחד כאן בשני ענינים: מצא כסות מנערה אחד לשלשים יום: למימרא דניעור מעלי לה והאמר רבי יוחנן מי שיש לו גרדי אומן בתוך ביתו ינער כסותו בכל יום אמרי בכל יום קשי לה אחד לשלשים יום מעלי לה איבעית אימא לא קשיא [נ] הא בחד והא בתרי איבעית אימא לא קשיא [ס] הא בידא והא בחוטרא איבעית אימא לא קשיא [ע] הא בדעמרא הא בדכיתנא [י] א"ר יוחנן כסא דחרשין ולא כסא דפושרין ולא אמרן אלא בכלי מתכות אבל בכלי חרש לית לן בה ובכלי מתכות נמי לא אמרן אלא דלא צויץ אבל דצויץ לית לן בה ולא אמרן אלא דלא שדא ביה ציביא אבל שדא ביה ציביא לית לן בה: וא"ר יוחנן [י] מי שהניח לו אביו מעות הרבה ורוצה לאבדן ילבש בגדי פשתן וישתמש בכלי זכוכית וישכור פועלים ואל ישב עמהן ילבש (פ) בכלי פשתן בכתנא רומיתא וישתמש בכלי זכוכית בזוגיתא חיורתא וישכור פועלים ואל ישב עמהן תרגומא בתורי

דנפיש

רש"י: כדרבה. בפרק הזהב (לקמן דף נח.) גבי בני העיר ששלחו את שקליהן: בדמי אבידה. שמכרה לאחר שנטפל בה כמו שאמרו חכמים: אבל מעות אבידה. כגון שמצא מעות בכיס או שלש מטבעות עשויין כמגדלין: **מתני'** אחת לשלשים יום. שמתעפשין כשעוהים מלפותחן וכל ספרים שלהן היו עשויין (ג) בגליון: גוללן. מתחילתן לסופן שיכנס בהן האויר: בתחלה. מה שלא למד מפני שצריך להשהותו לפניו: ולא יקרא אחר עמו. לפי שזה מושך אצלו וזה מושך אצלו ונקרע: שוטחה לצרכה. לשלוט בה אויר שלא תכלה ולא תאכלנה עש: לצרכן. שמתעפשים בקרקע שצריך לתתן בקרקע כדאמרינן לקמן שזו היא שמירתן ולפיכך משתמש בהם לפרקים: אבל לא לשחקן. לא ישתמש בהן זמן ארוך שישחקן אוזי"ר בלע"ז: לא יגע בהן. זהב אינו מתעפש בארץ וזכוכית שמא ישבר: שאין דרכו ליטול. דבר שגנאי הוא לו שאדם חשוב הוא ואין דרכו ליטול קופה שלו להכניסה מן החוץ לבית שמור לא יטול ופטור מהשבת אבידה דילפינן מוהתעלמת: **גמ'** בי בר חבו. בבית פלוני העושה תפילין מצויין לימכר ויחזור ויקנה מן הדמים: גוללו. בכל שנים עשר חדש פעם אחת: אם בשבילו פתחו. כולה מפרש לקמיה: מאי אריא ספר. שהוא נוח להתקלקל בטשטוש וקריעה: כאן שנה רבי. במסכת גיטין (דף כט.) תנן השולח גט בארץ ישראל הרי זה משלחו ביד אחר ואם אמר לו טול חפץ פלוני הימנה לא ישלחנו ביד אחר שאין רצונו שיהא פקדונו ביד אחר ואמר ר"ל עלה כאן שנה רבי במשנה זו למדנו רבי שסתם המשניות אין השואל כו' דבכולהו שייך למימר אין רצונו שיהא פקדונו ביד אחר: מאי עבידתיה גביה. קס"ד לצורכו קאמר ולא לצורך ספר תורה דהא לצורך ספר תורה תנא ליה גוללו כל שנים עשר חדש להכי פרכינן מאי עבידתיה דהאי גבי ספר תורה לקרות בו לצורך עצמו: אם כשהוא גוללו. להנאת ס"ת פתחו וקרא בו מותר: בחדש שלשים יום. החדש ממהר להתעפש מן הישן: אימא אחד זה ואחד זה שלשים יום. ומתני' נמי דקתני קורא בהן אחת לשלשים יום ולא מפליג בין ישן לחדש ר"א בן יעקב היא: בענין אחד. [א] בפרשה אחת אין קורין: בשני ענינים. זה בדף זה וזה בדף זה קורין דלא אתי לשמוטי מהדדי: מי שיש לו גרדי אומן בביתו. שיארוג לו טליתות חדשות תמיד: ינער כסותו בכל יום. ולמדנו דרך ארץ דניעור קשה לה: בחד. באדם אחד אין ניעורו קורעה: שנים. האוחזין בשני ראשיה ומנערין ממתחין אותה יותר מדאי וקשה לה: דעמרא. [ב] קשה לה שנמתחת ונקרעת: כסא דחרשין. נוח לשתות כוס של מכשפות מכוס של מים פושרין ואיידי דאיירי במילי דרבי יוחנן בהלכות דרך ארץ נקט הני שמעתא: צויץ. רותח: ציביא. כל דבר שנותנין לתוך המשקה או עשבים או תבלין או עקרי בשמים קרי ציביא: ורוצה לאבדן. ללמדנו בא שלא ירגיל אדם בכך שהעושה אלה מאבד מהר הון רב: כתנא רומיתא. דמיהם יקרין וממהרין לכלות: תרגמה. להן שכירות דפועלים: בתורי. בפועלים המנהיגים בשורי בעה"ב:

תוספות: **בזכוכית** לבנה. וא"ת והא אמרינן פרק עגלה ערופה (סוטה דף מח.) דמשחרב בית המקדש בטלה זכוכית לבנה וי"ל דלא בטלה לגמרי קאמר אלא דלא שכיחא דהא רב הונא תבר זכוכית חיורתא בחופת בנו פ' (ט) אין עומדין (ברכות דף לא. ע"ש):

בתורי

### עין משפט נר מצוה

קכד א מיי' פי"ג מהל' גזלה ואבידה הל' יח סמג עשין עד טוש"ע ח"מ סי' רסז סעיף כה:

קכה ב מיי' שם הל' יג טוש"ע שם סעיף כ:

קכו ג מיי' שם הל' יא טוש"ע שם סעיף יח:

קכז ד ה מיי' שם הל' יג טוש"ע שם סעיף יט:

קכח ו מיי' שם פי"א הל' יג סמג שם טוש"ע ח"מ סי' רסג סעיף א:

קכט ז ח מיי' שם פי"ג הל' יד סמג שם טוש"ע ח"מ סי' רסז סעיף כא [רב אלפס כאן ובהלכות תפילין דף עה.]:

קל ט מיי' פ"א מהל' שכירות הלכה ד טוש"ע ח"מ סי' שמב:

קלא י מיי' פ"ז מהל' שאלה ופקדון הל' ד ופי"ג מהלכות אבדה הלכה יג סמג עשין עד פח טוש"ע ח"מ סי' רצב סעיף כ:

קלב כ מיי' פ"א מהל' שכירות הלכה ד סמג עשין עד טוש"ע ח"מ סי' שמב:

קלג ל מיי' שם סמג שם טוש"ע ח"מ סי' שז סעיף ד:

קלד מ מיי' פ"ז מהל' שאלה ופקדון הלכה ד סמג עשין פח טוש"ע ח"מ סי' רצב סעיף כ:

קלה נ ס ע מיי' פי"ג מהל' גזילה ואבדה הלכה יא ופ"ז מהלכות שאלה ופקדון הל' ד סמג עשין עד טוש"ע ח"מ סי' רסז סעיף יח וסי' רצב סעיף כא:

### רבינו חננאל

אמר ר' יהודה אמר שמואל הלכה כר"ט והני מילי בדמי אבידה כגון שמצא אבידה ומטפל בה הזמן שאמרו חכמים ואחר כך מכרה בב"ד הואיל וטרח בה שרו ליה לאישתמושי בהו והשכר לעצמו אבל מצא צרור ובתוכו מעות לא שרו ליה לאישתמושי בהו וכן זוזי דיתמי דהוו מופקדין גביה לא שרו ליה רבנן לאישתמושי בהו מההוא מעשה דרחבה דפריש בשמעתא דא וכבר פירשנוהו בפ' הכונס צאן לדיר ביאור יפה וכי כרב יוסף קיימא לן בהא דאמר שומר אבידה כשומר שכר הוא: **מתני'** מצא ספרים קורא בהן אחד לל' יום וכו'. אמר שמואל המוצא תפילין שם דמיהן ומניחן מאי טעמא דהא בבי בר חבו שכיחי תפילין ואם אותו נו... ואמרי תפילין בעינא זבני ויהבי ליה אבל ספרים גוללן ומניחן אצלו עד שיבא בעליהן ויתנו סימנים ויקחום. ת"ר השואל ספר תורה מחבירו לא ישאילנו לאחרים. ומקשי' מאי אריא ספר תורה אפי' כל מילי נמי דהא אמר ר' שמעון בר לקיש פרק כל גט שנכתב הלכה ואם אמר לו טול לי ממנה חפץ פלוני לא ישלחנו ביד אחר כאן שנה דאין השואל רשאי להשאיל ולא השוכר רשאי להשכיר כיון דכל מתניתא דשנאה ר' חייא אמרי' ר' לא שנאה ר' חייא מנין ליה וזו שנויה במשנת ר' חייא ור' הושעיה הכי א) אין השואל רשאי להשאיל ולא השוכר להשכיר ולא השואל רשאי להשכיר ולא השוכר רשאי להשאיל ולא זה המופקדין אצלו רשאי להפקיד אצל אחר אלא אם נתנו בעלים רשות לפיכך הוצרך ריש לקיש לפרש שגם זה שנאה ר' ואסקוה ואפי' ספר תורה דמצוה הוא לא ישאיל. ב) פותחו וקורא בו כדי לנערו אבל לא ילמד בו. וכן המפקיד ס"ת אצל חבירו דינו כדין המוצא ג) מנערה אחד לל' יום. וסוגיא לנערה במאני דכיתנא קשי להו ובמאני דעמרא בתרי אינשי או בחוטרא או בכל יומא קשי להו. אבל חד גברא ביומא חדא לל' יום מעלי להו. אמר ר' יוחנן כסא דחרשין ולא כסא דפושרין פי' נוח לו לאדם לשתות כוס שיש בו מיני כשפניות כדמתרגמינן מכשפה חרשא מלשתות כוס מים פושרין

**חשק שלמה על ר"ח** א) והוא בתוספתא דמכילתין בפ"ג. ב) נראה דדיבור הזה שייך אחר דיבור וכן המפקיד ס"ת וקאי אמפקיד ס"ת ודו"ק. ג) נראה דל"ל [מצא כסות]:

### מסורת הש"ס

א) לקמן מג., ב) [שבועות ל:], ג) [מס' סופרים פרק ה הל' טו], ד) גיטין כ... ה) [פסחים ד:, בכור' יח:, נח.], ו) חולין פ... ז) [שם], ח) בגדי פשר כל"ל, ט) [וע"ע תוס' ... כ: ד"ה אגן].

### הגהות הב"ח

(א) גמ' בי רחבה הוה ... הנהו וכו' אתו לקמיה ד... יוסף אמרו ליה וכו' א... להו הכי אמר וכו' דלא... לכו כצ"ל וכ"ב ובאשכ... גורס ביד רחבא ה"ל ה... זוזי דיתמי אתא הכל כל... יחיד: (ב) רש"י ד"ה א... וכו' היו עשויין בגלי... הס"ד:

### הגהות הגר"א

[א] רש"י ד"ה בע... אחד כו'. נ"ב וכן ... הרא"ש אבל הרמב"ם ... להיפך: [ב] שם ד"... דעמרא קשה כו'. ... אבל רי"ף ורמב"ם וש... פי' להיפך:

### לעזי רש"י

אוזי"ר. פירוש לשחו...

### ליקוטי רש"י

נגנבו בלסטים מזוי... דאונס הוא [לקמן נ... וכל דבר שאין דר... ליטול. אם היה ... הרי זה לא יטול. ... מוחזר עליו בלא ת... להתעלם שנא... והתעלמת פעמים שא... מתעלם [שבועות ל:]. בר חבו. מוכר תפי... הוה [מגילה יח:]. כ... שנה רבי. במשנה שנה לנו רבי. א... השואל וכו'. דהא ד... לא ישלחנו ביד אחר משום בטולי שלי... דגיטא נקט לה אלא ה... דתנן לא ישל... לאשמועינן דאין הש... רשאי להשאיל [גיטין כ... עמרא. למר [גיטין סו... ולא כסא דפושר... שרעים הם לגוף. ד... צויץ. הרתיח. שהניח לו א... מעות. כלומר מי ש... טרח בממון וקל בעי... לאבדו זהו איבודו [חו... פד:]. זוגיתא. זכו... [שם:]. חיורתא. לב... [עי' ברכות כח.].

**all** other borrowed **objects as well,** even those that are not readily damaged?[25]

The Gemara demonstrates that the Baraisa's ruling is indeed not specific to a scroll:

דְּאָמַר רַבִּי שִׁמְעוֹן בֶּן לָקִישׁ – **For R' Shimon ben Lakish said** in connection with a Mishnah in tractate *Gittin:* כָּאן שָׁנָה רַבִּי – **Here,** in this ruling,[26] **Rebbi taught** that אֵין הַשּׁוֹאֵל רַשַּׁאי לְהַשְׁאִיל – **a borrower is not permitted to lend** to another person that which he borrowed, וְאֵין הַשּׂוֹכֵר רַשַּׁאי לְהַשְׂכִּיר – **nor is a renter permitted to rent** to another person that which he rented.[27] Since the rule applies to all objects, why does the Baraisa point it out specifically in the case of a Torah scroll?

The Gemara answers:

סֵפֶר תּוֹרָה אִיצְטְרִיכָא לֵיהּ – **It was necessary for [the Tanna]** to teach this ruling with respect to **a Torah scroll.** מַהוּ דְּתֵימָא – For **you might have said** that נִיחָא לֵיהּ לְאִינִישׁ דְּתִיעָבֵיד מִצְוָה בְּמָמוֹנֵיהּ – **a person is agreeable to having a mitzvah performed with his possessions,** and the owner would therefore not object to the borrower lending his Torah scroll to another person to read from it. קָא מַשְׁמַע לָן – **[The Tanna] therefore informs us** that, in fact, the borrower may not lend the Torah scroll to another person.[28]

The Gemara now examines the ruling of the Baraisa, which states:

פּוֹתְחוֹ וְקוֹרֵא בּוֹ – HE MAY OPEN IT AND READ FROM IT.

The Gemara asks:

פְּשִׁיטָא – **This is obvious!** וְאֶלָּא לְמַאי שַׁיְילֵיהּ מִינֵּיהּ – **Indeed, for what** purpose **did he borrow [the scroll] from him** if not to read it?

The Gemara answers:

סֵיפָא אִיצְטְרִיכָא לֵיהּ – **It was necessary for [the Tanna]** to teach this case only to inform us of **the latter ruling,** ובִלְבַד שֶׁלֹּא יִלְמוֹד בּוֹ בַּתְּחִלָּה – that he may read PROVIDED HE DOES NOT STUDY IN IT something FOR THE FIRST TIME.[29]

The Gemara examines the next ruling of the Baraisa, which states:

וְכֵן הַמַּפְקִיד סֵפֶר תּוֹרָה אֵצֶל חֲבֵירוֹ – SIMILARLY, if ONE DEPOSITS A TORAH SCROLL WITH HIS FRIEND, גּוֹלְלוֹ כָּל שְׁנֵים עָשָׂר חֹדֶשׁ – HE SHOULD ROLL IT from end to end once EVERY TWELVE MONTHS. פּוֹתְחוֹ וְקוֹרֵא בּוֹ – HE MAY OPEN IT AND READ FROM IT.

The Gemara asks:

מַאי עֲבִידְתֵּיהּ גַּבֵּיהּ – **What business does he have with [t Torah scroll]?** What right does he have to read from it?[30] ותו – **Furthermore,** the Baraisa states: אִם בִּשְׁבִילוֹ פְּתָחוֹ אָסוּר – IF OPENED IT FOR HIS OWN PURPOSES, IT IS FORBIDDEN. אָמְרַתְּ – **But you have** just **said** that פּוֹתְחוֹ וְקוֹרֵא בּוֹ – HE MAY OPEN AND READ FROM IT. – ? –

The Gemara answers:

הָכִי קָאָמַר – **This is what [the Baraisa] is saying:** He should r the Torah scroll for its own benefit once every twelve montl אִם כְּשֶׁהוּא גּוֹלְלוֹ – and **if, while he is rolling it** for its benef פּוֹתְחוֹ וְקוֹרֵא בּוֹ – **he opens it and reads from it,** מוּתָּר – **it permissible.** אִם בִּשְׁבִילוֹ פְּתָחוֹ – However, **if he opened it f his own purposes,** simply to read from it, אָסוּר – **it is fc bidden;** i.e. he may not do so.

The Gemara examines the final statement of the Baraisa, whi states:

סוּמְכוֹס אוֹמֵר – SUMCHOS SAYS: בְּחָדָשׁ שְׁלֹשִׁים יוֹם – WITH A NE [TORAH SCROLL], he should roll it from end to end once eve THIRTY DAYS; בְּיָשָׁן שְׁנֵים עָשָׂר חֹדֶשׁ – WITH AN OLD [SCROLL], on every TWELVE MONTHS. רַבִּי אֱלִיעֶזֶר בֶּן יַעֲקֹב אוֹמֵר – R' ELIEZI BEN YAAKOV SAYS: אֶחָד זֶה וְאֶחָד זֶה שְׁנֵים עָשָׂר חֹדֶשׁ – IN EITHI CASE, he is required to roll it only once every TWELVE MONTH

The Gemara asks:

רַבִּי אֱלִיעֶזֶר בֶּן יַעֲקֹב הַיְינוּ תַּנָּא קַמָּא – **R' Eliezer ben Yaakov's** ru ing **is the same as the Tanna Kamma's** ruling. The first Tanna the Barasa also ruled that a Torah scroll must be rolled once eve twelve months, and did not differentiate between a new one and a old one. What is R' Eliezer ben Yaakov adding to his ruling?[31]

The Gemara answers:

אֶלָּא אֵימָא – **Rather, say** that the Baraisa reads as follows: אֱלִיעֶזֶר בֶּן יַעֲקֹב אוֹמֵר – R' ELIEZER BEN YAAKOV SAYS: חַד זֶה וְאֶחָד זֶה – IN EITHER CASE שְׁלֹשִׁים יוֹם – once every THIRT DAYS.[32]

The Gemara now returns to its analysis of the Mishnah. Th Mishnah states:

אֲבָל לֹא יִלְמוֹד בּוֹ בַּתְּחִלָּה – HOWEVER, HE SHOULD NOT STUD IN [THE SCROLL] any text he is learning FOR THE FIRST TIM

NOTES

25. A scroll becomes smudged and tears as a result of frequent use (*Rashi*). [Since the prohibition to lend what one has borrowed is a general rule and not specific to a scroll, why should the Tanna of this Baraisa mention it in connection with a scroll, unless he means it to serve as an illustration of the general rule? But if so, it is a poor choice because it could be argued, based on this illustration, that the rule applies only to things easily damaged. To demonstrate that this rule applies to all borrowed objects, it would have been better for the Tanna to have stated the rule in the case of an object not easily damaged.]

26. The Mishnah in *Gittin* (29a) rules that if a man appointed an agent to deliver a *get* (bill of divorce) to his wife, the agent may appoint another agent and have the second agent deliver the *get* to the woman. But if the husband specified that, in addition to delivering the *get,* he wants his agent to retrieve an object of his that is in his wife's possession, the agent may not appoint another agent to deliver the *get* and retrieve the object from her. This is because the husband may not want his object in the hands of another person [whom he may not trust]. R' Shimon ben Lakish explained that, through this ruling, Rebbi (who redacted the Mishnah) taught that a borrower may not lend the object that he borrowed to another person, etc. (*Rashi;* see also *Rabbeinu Chananel*).

27. Without the owner's consent. Similarly, a borrower may not rent what he borrowed, nor may a renter lend what he rented without the owner's consent (see *Rabbeinu Chananel; Tosefta* 3:1).

28. [Thus, the rule is mentioned in the case of a Torah scroll not to illustrate the general rule, but to make it clear that it applies *even* in th case of a Torah scroll, where it might be thought not to apply.]

Indeed, there are instances in which it is assumed that a person content to have a mitzvah performed with his possessions, even withou his explicit permission. The Baraisa teaches that this rule does not appl here because the owner is not agreeable when his property stands to b damaged (*Ritva*).

29. That is, the Tanna stated the obvious – that the borrower may ope and read from the Torah scroll – as an introduction to his ruling tha the borrower may not study a portion of the Torah scroll that he has nc previously learned.

30. The Gemara assumes that since the Baraisa already stated that h must roll the scroll every twelve months for the benefit of the scroll, the when it states that he may open it and read from it, it must mean tha he may do so even for his own benefit. The Gemara therefore asks wha right he has to open and read from the scroll for his own benefit (*Rashi* cf. *Rashba* who advances an entirely different interpretation of th Gemara).

31. It is not the custom of a Mishnah or Baraisa to repeat a ruling in th name of a second Tanna. It is generally assumed that whatever seems t be a repetition is in fact a divergent opinion.

32. Accordingly, our Mishnah, which ruled that books (i.e. scrolls should be rolled once in thirty days, without differentiating betwee new scrolls and old ones, follows the opinion of R' Eliezer ben Yaako (*Rashi* ד״ה אימא).

בזכוכית לבנה. וא"ת והא אמרינן פרק עגלה ערופה (סוטה דף מח.) דמשחרב בית המקדש בטלה זכוכית לבנה וי"ל דלא בטלה לגמרי קאמר אלא דלא שכיחא דהא רב הונא תבר זכוכית חיורתא בחופת בנו פ' ט) אין עומדין (ברכות דף לא. ע"ש):

בתורי

כדרבה א) דאמר רבה נגנבו בלסטים מזויין אבדו שטבעה ספינתו בים אמר רב יהודה אמר שמואל הלכה כר' טרפון (א) ביד רחבה הוה ליה הנהו זוזי דיתמי אתא לקמיה דרב יוסף אמר ליה מהו לאשתמושי בגוייהו א"ל הכי אמר רב יהודה אמר שמואל הלכה כר' טרפון א"ל אביי ולאו אתמר עלה א"ר חלבו אמר רב הונא [א] לא שנו אלא בדמי אבידה הואיל וטרח בה אבל מעות אבידה דלא טרח בהו לא והני כמעות אבידה דמו א"ל זיל לא שבקו לי דאשרי לך: **מתני'** [ב] מצא ספרים קורא בהן אחד לשלשים יום ואם אינו יודע לקרות גוללן אבל לא ילמוד בהן בתחלה ולא יקרא אחר עמו [ג] מצא כסות מנערה אחד לשלשים יום ושוטחה לצרכה אבל לא לכבודו [ד] כלי כסף וכלי נחושת משתמש בהן לצרכן אבל לא לשחקן [ה] כלי זהב וכלי זכוכית לא יגע בהן עד שיבא אליהו ג) [ו] מצא שק או קופה וכל דבר שאין דרכו ליטול הרי זה לא יטול:

**גמ'** אמר שמואל [ז] המוצא תפילין בשוק שם דמיהן ומניחן לאלתר מתיב רבינא מצא ספרים קורא בהן אחד לשלשים יום ואם אינו יודע לקרות גוללן גוללן אין שם דמיהן ומניחן לא אמר אביי [ח] תפילין בי בר חבו משכח שכיחי ספרים לא שכיחי ת"ר [ט] ג) השואל ספר תורה מחבירו הרי זה לא ישאילנו לאחר פותחו וקורא בו ובלבד שלא ילמוד בו בתחלה ולא יקרא אחר עמו וכן המפקיד ס"ת אצל חבירו גוללו כל שנים עשר חדש פותחו וקורא בו אם בשבילו פתחו אסור סומכוס אומר בחדש שלשים יום בישן שנים עשר חדש ר"א בן יעקב אומר אחד זה ואחד זה שנים עשר חדש: אמר מר השואל ספר תורה מחבירו הרי זה לא ישאילנו לאחר מאי אריא ס"ת אפי' כל מילי נמי ז) דאמר ר"ש בן לקיש כאן שנה רבי [כ] אין השואל רשאי להשאיל [ל] ואין השוכר רשאי להשכיר ס"ת איצטריכא ליה מהו דתימא ה) ניחא ליה לאיניש דתיעביד מצוה בממוניה קמ"ל פותחו וקורא בו פשיטא ואלא למאי שייליה מיניה סיפא איצטריכא ליה ובלבד שלא ילמוד בו בתחלה וכן המפקיד ס"ת אצל חבירו גוללו כל שנים עשר חדש פותחו וקורא בו מאי עבידתיה גביה ותו אם בשבילו פתחו אסור הא אמרת פותחו וקורא בו הכי קאמר [מ] אם כשהוא גוללו פותחו וקורא בו מותר אם בשבילו פתחו אסור סומכוס אומר בחדש שלשים יום בישן שנים עשר חדש ר"א בן יעקב אומר אחד זה ואחד זה שנים עשר חדש ר"א בן יעקב היינו תנא קמא אלא אימא ר' אליעזר בן יעקב אומר אחד זה ואחד זה שלשים יום: אבל לא ילמוד בו בתחלה ולא יקרא אחר עמו: ורמינהו לא יקרא פרשה וישנה ולא יקרא בו פרשה ויתרגם ולא יפתח בו יותר מג' דפין ולא יקראו בו שלשה בני אדם בכרך אחד הא שנים קורין אמר אביי לא קשיא כאן בענין אחד כאן בשני ענינים: מצא כסות מנערה אחד לשלשים יום: למימרא דניעור מעלי לה והאמר רבי יוחנן מי שיש לו גרדי אומן בתוך ביתו ינער כסותו בכל יום אמרי בכל יום קשי לה אחד לשלשים יום מעלי לה איבעית אימא לא קשיא [נ] הא בחד והא בתרי איבעית אימא לא קשיא [ס] הא בידא והא בחוטרא איבעית אימא לא קשיא [ע] הא בדעמרא הא בדכיתנא י) א"ר יוחנן כסא דחרשין ולא כסא דפושרין ולא אמרן אלא בכלי מתכות אבל בכלי חרש לית לן בה ובכלי מתכות נמי לא אמרן אלא דלא צויץ אבל דצויץ לית לן בה ולא אמרן אלא דלא שדא ביה ציביא אבל שדא ביה ציביא לית לן בה: וא"ר יוחנן י) מי שהניח לו אביו מעות הרבה ורוצה לאבדן ילבש בגדי פשתן וישתמש בכלי זכוכית וישכור פועלים ואל ישב עמהן ילבש פ) בכלי פשתן בכתנא רומיתא וישתמש בכלי זכוכית בזוגיתא חיורתא וישכור פועלים ואל ישב עמהן תרגומא בתורי

**רש"י**

כדרבה. בפרק הזהב (לקמן דף נח.) גבי בני העיר ששלחו את שקליהן: בדמי אבידה. שמכרה לאחר שנטפל בה כמו שאמרו חכמים: אבל מעות אבידה. כגון שמצא מעות בכיס או שלש מטבעות עשויין כמגדלין: מתני' אחת לשלשים יום. שמתעפשין כשהוסיס מלפותחן וכל ספרים שלהן היו עשויין (ג) בגליון: גוללן. מתחילתן לסופן שיכנס בהן האויר: בתחלה. מה שלא למד מפני שצריך להשהותו לפניו: ולא יקרא אחר עמו. לפי שזה מושך אצלו וזה מושך אצלו ונקרע: שוטחה לצרכה. לשלוט בה אויר שלא תכלה ולא תאכלנה עש: לצרכן. שמתעפשים בקרקע שצריך לתתן בקרקע כדאמרינן לקמן שזו היא שמירתן ולפיכך משתמש בהם לפרקים: אבל לא לשחקן. לא ישתמש בהן זמן ארוך שישחקן אוזי"ר בלע"ז: לא יגע בהן. זהב אינו מתעפש בארץ וזכוכית שמא ישבר: שאין דרכו ליטול. דבר שגנאי הוא לו שאדם חשוב הוא ואין דרכו ליטול קופה שלו להכניסה מן החוץ לבית שמור לא יטול ופטור מהשבת אבידה דילפינן מוהתעלמת: גמ' בי בר חבו. בבית פלוני העושה תפילין מצויין לימכר ויחזור ויקנה מן הדמים: גוללו. בכל שנים עשר חדש פעם אחת: אם בשבילו פתחו. כולה מפרש לקמיה: מאי אריא ספר. שהוא נוח להתקלקל בטשטוש וקריעה: כאן שנה רבי. במסכת גיטין (דף כט.) תנן השולח גט בארץ ישראל הרי זה משלחו ביד אחר ואם אמר לו טול חפץ פלוני הימנה לא ישלחנו ביד אחר שאין רצונו שיהא פקדונו ביד אחר ואמר ר"ל עלה כאן שנה רבי במשנה זו למדנו רבי שסתם המשניות אין השואל כו' דבכולהו שייך למימר אין רצונו שיהא פקדונו ביד אחר: מאי עבידתיה גביה. קס"ד לצורכו קאמר ולא לצורך ספר תורה דהא לצורך ספר תורה תנא ליה גוללו כל שנים עשר חדש להכי פרכינן מאי עבידתיה דהאי גבי ספר תורה לקרות בו לצורך עצמו: אם כשהוא גוללו. להנאת ס"ת פתחו וקרא בו מותר: בחדש שלשים יום. החדש ממהר להתעפש מן הישן: אימא אחד זה ואחד זה שלשים יום. ומתני' נמי דקתני קורא בהן אחת לשלשים יום ולא מפליג בין ישן לחדש ר"א בן יעקב היא: בענין אחד. [א] בפרשה אחת אין קורין: בשני ענינים. זה בדף זה וזה בדף זה קורין דלא אתי לשמוטי מהדדי: מי שיש לו גרדי אומן בביתו. שיארוג לו טליתות חדשות תמיד: ינער כסותו בכל יום. ולמדנו דרך ארץ דניעור קשה לה: בחד. באדם אחד אין ניעורו קורעה: שנים. האוחזין בשני ראשיה ומנערין ממתחין אותה יותר מדאי וקשה לה: דעמרא. [ב] קשה לה שנמתחת ונקרעת: כסא דחרשין. נוח לשתות כוס של מכשפות מכוס של מים פושרין ואידי דאיירי במילי דרבי יוחנן בהלכות דרך ארץ נקט הני שמעתא: צויץ. רותח: ציביא. כל דבר שנותנין לתוך המשקה או עשבים או תבלין או עקרי בשמים קרי ציבא: ורוצה לאבדן. ללמדנו בא שלא ירגיל אדם בכך שהעושה אלה מאבד מהר הון רב: כתנא רומיתא. דמיהם יקרין וממהרין לכלות: תרגמה. להך שכירות דפועלים: בתורי. בפועלים המנהיגים בשורי בעה"ב:

**עין משפט נר מצוה**

קכד א מיי' פי"ג מהל' גזלה ואבדה הל' יח סמג עשין עד טוש"ע ח"מ סי' רסז סעיף כה:
קכה ב מיי' שם הל' יג טוש"ע שם סעיף כ:
קכו ג מיי' שם הל' יא טוש"ע שם סעיף יח:
קכז ד ה מיי' שם הל' יב טוש"ע שם סעיף יט:
קכח ו מיי' שם פי"א הל' יג סמג שם טוש"ע ח"מ סי' רסג סעיף א:
קכט ז ח מיי' שם פי"ג הל' יד סמג שם טוש"ע ח"מ סי' רסז סעיף כא [רב אלפס כאן ובהלכות תפילין דף עה.]:
קל ט מיי' פ"א מהל' שכירות הלכה ד טוש"ע ח"מ סי' שמב:
קלא י מיי' פ"ו מהל' שאלה ופקדון הל' ד ופי"ג מהלכות אבדה הלכה יג סמג עשין עד פח טוש"ע ח"מ סי' רצב סעיף כ:
קלב כ מיי' פ"א מהל' שכירות הלכה ד סמג עשין עד טוש"ע ח"מ סי' שמב:
קלג ל מיי' שם סמג שם טוש"ע ח"מ סי' שז סעיף ד:
קלד מ מיי' פ"ו מהל' שאלה ופקדון הלכה ד סמג עשין פח טוש"ע ח"מ סי' רצב סעיף כ:
קלה נ ס ע מיי' פי"ג מהל' גזילה ואבדה הלכה יא ופ"ז מהלכות שאלה ופקדון הל' ד סמג עשין עד טוש"ע ח"מ סי' רסז סעיף יח וסי' רצב סעיף כא:

**רבינו חננאל**

אמר ר' יהודה אמר שמואל הלכה כר"ט והני מילי בדמי אבידה כגון שמצא אבידה ומטפל בה הזמן שאמרו חכמים ואחר כך מכרה בב"ד הואיל וטרח בה שרו ליה לאישתמושי בהו והשכר לעצמו אבל מצא צרור ובתוכו מעות לא שרו ליה לאישתמושי בהו וכן זוזי דיתמי דהוו מופקדין גביה לא שרו ליה רבנן לאישתמושי בהו מההוא מעשה דרחבה דפריש בשמעתא דא וכבר פירשנוהו בפ' הכונס צאן לדיר ביאור יפה וכי כרב יוסף קיימא לן בהא דאמר שומר אבידה כשומר שכר הוא: **מתני'** מצא ספרים קורא בהן אחד לל' יום וכו'. אמר שמואל המוצא תפילין שם דמיהן ומניחן מאי טעמא דהא בבי בר חבו שכיחי תפילין ואם אתו מרייהו ואמרי תפילין בעינא זבני ויהבי ליה אבל ספרים גוללן ומניחן אצלו עד שיבא בעליהן ויתנו סימנים ויקחום. ת"ר השואל ספר תורה מחבירו לא ישאילנו לאחרים. ומקשי' מאי אריא ספר תורה אפי' כל מילי נמי דהא אמר ר' שמעון בר לקיש פרק כל גט שנכתב הלכה ואם אמר לו טול לי ממנה חפץ פלוני לא ישלחנו ביד אחר כאן שנה דאין השואל רשאי להשאיל ולא השוכר רשאי להשכיר כיון דכל מתניתא דשנאה ר' חייא אמרי' ר' לא שנאה ר' חייא מנין ליה וזו שנויה במשנת ר' חייא ור' הושעיה הכי א) אין השואל רשאי להשאיל ולא השוכר להשכיר ולא השואל רשאי להשכיר ולא השוכר רשאי להשאיל ולא זה המופקדין אצלו רשאי להפקיד אצל אחר אלא אם נתנו בעלים רשות לפיכך הוצרך ריש לקיש לפרש שגם זה שנאה ר' ואסקוה ואפי' ספר תורה דמצוה הוא לא ישאיל. ב) פותחו וקורא בו כדי לנערו אבל לא ילמד בו. וכן המפקיד ס"ת אצל חבירו דינו כדין המוצא ג) מנערה אחד לל' יום. וסוגיא לנערה במאני דכיתנא קשי להו ובמאני דעמרא בתרי אינשי או בחוטרא או בכל יומא קשי להו. אבל חד גברא ביומא חדא לל' יום מעלי להו. אמר ר' יוחנן כסא דחרשין ולא כסא דפושרין פי' נוח לו לאדם לשתות כוס שיש בו מיני כשפניות כדמתרגמינן מכשפה חרשא מלשתות כוס מים פושרין

**חשק שלמה על ר"ח** א) והוא בתוספתא דמכילתין בפ"ג. ב) נראה דדיבור הזה שייך אחר דיבור וכן המפקיד ס"ת וקאי אמפקיד ס"ת ודו"ק. ג) נראה דצ"ל [מלא כסות]:

**מסורת הש"ס**

א) לקמן מג., ב) [שבועות לו:], ג) [מס' סופרים פרק ה ה' טו], ד) גיטין כ... ה) [פסחים ד:, בכו' יח:, נח.], ו) חולין כ... ז) [שם], ח) בגדי פש... כל"ל, ט) [וע"ע תוס' ... כ: ד"ה אמן].

**הגהות הב"ח**

(א) גמ' בי רחבה הוה הנהו וכו' אתו לקמיה ... יוסף אמרו ליה וכו' ... להו הכי אמר וכו' דא... לכו כצ"ל וני"ב ובאש... גורם ביד רחבה ה"ל ה... זוזי דיתמי אתא הכל כל... יחיד: (ב) רש"י ד"ה ... וכו' היו עשויין בגל... הס"ד:

**הגהות הגר"א**

[א] רש"י ד"ה בע... אחד כו'. נ"ב וכן הרא"ש אבל הרמב"ם להיפך: [ב] שם ד... דעמרא קשה כו'. ... אבל רי"ף ורמב"ם וש... פי' להיפך:

**לעזי רש"י**

אוזי"ר. פירוש לשחו...

**ליקוטי רש"י**

נגנבו בלסטים מזוי... דאונס הוא [לקמן ... וכל דבר שאין דר... ליטול. אם היה ... הרי זה לא יטול. ... מוזהר עליו בלא ... להתעלם שנ... והתעלמת פעמים שא... מתעלם [שבועות ל:]. בר חבו. מוכר תפ... הוה [מגילה יח:]. ... שנה רבי. במשנה שנה לנו רבי. ... השואל וכו'. דהא ... לא ישלחנו ביד אחר משום בטולי שלי... דגיטא נקט לה אלא ... דתנן לא יש... לאשמועינן דאין הש... רשאי להשאיל [גיטין כ... עמרא. למר [גיטין ס... ולא כסא דפושר... שרעים הם לגוף. ... צויץ. הרמים. שהניח לו א... מעות. כלומר מי ... טרח בממון וקל בע... לאבדו זהו איבודו [... פד:]. זוגיתא. זכו... [שם:]. חיורתא. ... [עי' ברכות כח.].

אֲבָל לֹא לְשַׁחֲקָן – **but not to** the extent that he **wears them down.** כְּלֵי זָהָב וּכְלֵי זְכוּכִית – If he found **gold utensils or glass utensils,** לֹא יִגַּע בָּהֶן – **he should not touch them** at all while he holds them, עַד שֶׁיָּבֹא אֵלִיָּהוּ – **until Elijah** the Prophet **comes** and reveals the identity of their owner.[14] מָצָא שַׂק אוֹ קוּפָּה – **If one found a sack or a box,** וְכָל דָּבָר שֶׁאֵין דַּרְכּוֹ לִיטּוֹל – **or any** other **object that** would **not** be **his practice to pick up** if it were his own, הֲרֵי זֶה לֹא יִטּוֹל – **he** need **not pick** it **up.**[15]

**Gemara** The Gemara records:

אָמַר שְׁמוּאֵל – **Shmuel said:** הַמּוֹצֵא תְּפִילִּין בַּשּׁוּק – **One who finds tefillin in the marketplace** שָׁם דְּמֵיהֶן וּמַנִּיחָן לְאַלְתַּר – **assesses their worth,** sells them **immediately, and sets aside [the money].**[16]

The Gemara questions this:

מָתִיב רָבִינָא – **Ravina challenged** Shmuel's ruling from our Mishnah which states: מָצָא סְפָרִים – If ONE FOUND BOOKS, קוֹרֵא בָהֶן אֶחָד לִשְׁלֹשִׁים יוֹם – HE SHOULD READ FROM THEM ONCE IN THIRTY DAYS. וְאִם אֵינוֹ יוֹדֵעַ לִקְרוֹת – IF HE DOES NOT KNOW how TO READ, גּוֹלְלָן – HE SHOULD ROLL THEM from beginning to end. גּוֹלְלָן אִין – We see from the Mishnah that **indeed, he should roll them** from end to end to air them out and preserve them, שָׁם דְּמֵיהֶן וּמַנִּיחָן לֹא – **but he should not assess their worth,** sell them, and set aside the money for the owner. Why, then, does Shmuel teach that tefillin should be sold?[17]

The Gemara answers:

אָמַר אַבָּיֵי – **Abaye said:** תְּפִילִּין בֵּי בַר חָבוּ מִשְׁכָּח שְׁכִיחֵי – **Tefillin are readily available at the house of Bar Chavu** and it is easy to replace the ones that are sold, סְפָרִים לֹא שְׁכִיחֵי – whereas **books are not readily available** for purchase.[18]

The Gemara cites a Baraisa concerning the responsibilities of one who borrows a Torah scroll:

תָּנוּ רַבָּנָן – **The Rabbis taught in a Baraisa:** הַשּׁוֹאֵל סֵפֶר תּוֹרָה מֵחֲבֵירוֹ – IF ONE BORROWS A TORAH SCROLL FROM HIS FRIEND, הֲרֵי זֶה לֹא יַשְׁאִילֶנּוּ לְאַחֵר – HE MAY NOT LEND IT TO ANOTHER person. פּוֹתְחוֹ וְקוֹרֵא בּוֹ – HE MAY OPEN IT AND READ FR[OM] IT, וּבִלְבַד שֶׁלֹּא יִלְמוֹד בּוֹ בַּתְּחִלָּה – PROVIDED HE DOES N[OT] STUDY IN IT something FOR THE FIRST TIME,[19] [ולֹ]א יִקְרָא אַחֵר עִמּוֹ – NOR SHOULD ANOTHER person READ from the scroll togeth[er] WITH HIM.[20] וְכֵן – SIMILARLY, הַמַּפְקִיד סֵפֶר תּוֹרָה אֵצֶל חֲבֵירוֹ – if ONE DEPOSITS A TORAH SCROLL WITH HIS FRIEND, [גּוֹ]לְלוֹ כָּל שְׁנֵים עָשָׂר חֹדֶשׁ – HE SHOULD ROLL IT from end to end once EVE[RY] TWELVE MONTHS.[21] פּוֹתְחוֹ וְקוֹרֵא בּוֹ – HE MAY OPEN IT A[ND] READ FROM IT; אִם בִּשְׁבִילוֹ פְּתָחוֹ – but IF HE OPENED IT FOR H[IS] OWN PURPOSES, אָסוּר – IT IS FORBIDDEN.[22] סוּמְכוֹס אוֹמֵר – SUMCHOS SAYS: בְּחָדָשׁ – WITH A NEW [TORAH SCROLL], [אחד] לִשְׁלֹשִׁים יוֹם – he should roll it once every THIRTY DAYS; בְּיָשָׁן – WI[TH] AN OLD [TORAH SCROLL], שְׁנֵים עָשָׂר חֹדֶשׁ – once eve[ry] TWELVE MONTHS.[23] רַבִּי אֱלִיעֶזֶר בֶּן יַעֲקֹב אוֹמֵר – R' ELIEZ[ER] BEN YAAKOV SAYS: אֶחָד זֶה וְאֶחָד זֶה – IN EITHER CASE,[24] [שְׁנֵ]ים עָשָׂר חֹדֶשׁ – he is required to roll it only once every TWEL[VE] MONTHS.

The Gemara analyzes the Baraisa:

אָמַר מָר – **The master said** in the Baraisa: [ה]שּׁוֹאֵל סֵפֶר תּוֹרָה מֵחֲבֵירוֹ – IF ONE BORROWS A TORAH SCROLL FROM HIS FRIEN[D], הֲרֵי זֶה לֹא יַשְׁאִילֶנּוּ לְאַחֵר – HE MAY NOT LEND IT TO ANOTHE[R] person.

The Gemara asks:

מַאי אִרְיָא סֵפֶר תּוֹרָה – **Why** does the Tanna **state** the rule that o[ne] may not lend what he has borrowed in the case of **a Torah scro[ll]** which is easily damaged, אֲפִילּוּ כָּל מִילֵּי נַמִּי – when this is true [...]

NOTES

14. Since neither gold nor glass rusts in the ground, there is no need for the finder to take these types of utensils out for periodic use. Moreover, glass breaks easily (see *Rashi* and *Meiri*). Therefore, once the finder buries these utensils for safekeeping, he should not touch them again until their owner can be identified – if need be, until Elijah the Prophet returns to earth to herald the coming of the Messiah. [Tradition teaches that Elijah will resolve all monetary and halachic questions that have remained undecided. See Mishnah *Eduyos* 8:7 and *Tos. Yom Tov* there.]

15. The Mishnah here speaks of a distinguished individual, who finds it demeaning to trouble himself with such items. Were this person to find his own box lying outdoors, for example, he would not personally pick it up and remove it to a safe place. Since it is beneath his dignity to pick this up, he is exempt from the general obligation to return lost objects. The Gemara (30a) will state the Scriptural source for this law (*Rashi*).

16. I.e. he may not use the money while he is holding it for the owner *Rosh* §16, in explanation of *Rashi; Ritva*). [See above, 28b note 28 regarding the manner of the sale.]

We learned above (28b) that if one found animals and sold them, he is permitted to use the money, according to R' Tarfon (Mishnah 28b). Shmuel, himself, ruled in favor of R' Tarfon (Gemara above). Yet in the case of tefillin, Shmuel rules that the finder may not use the money from their sale! The distinction is that R' Tarfon's leniency is based on the fact that the finder went to a lot of trouble to care for the animals before selling them (as explained by the Gemara above). This is not the case with tefillin. Thus, the Sages did not permit using the money obtained from the sale of the tefillin (*Rosh* ibid. according to *Rashi*).

*Rosh* himself, however, explains Shmuel's ruling to mean that "he assesses the value of the tefillin, [sets aside the money for the owner,] and dons the tefillin immediately"; i.e. he may keep the tefillin for himself by setting aside their worth for the owner. [Shmuel makes no comment, according to this interpretation, as to whether the money may be used.]

17. Although Torah scrolls and the like might decay if left in a closet [o]r box indefinitely, we do not allow the finder to sell them and hold th[e] money. Rather, we require him to air them out periodically and preserv[e] them for the owner. Why should we not treat tefillin in the sam[e] manner?

18. The Mishnah speaks of scrolls, as explained in note 9, and these wer[e] not readily available. Thus, selling them and returning the money to th[e] owner represents a loss, or at least a major inconvenience to him, sinc[e] it will not be so easy for him to replace them. Tefillin, however, we[re] always available for purchase [as Abaye illustrates with his reference t[o] the well-known tefillin manufacturer of his time, Bar Chavu]. Th[e] Rabbis therefore did not put the finder to the trouble of caring for them. [Whether this rule is applicable to all found objects that are easi[ly] replaced or only to tefillin is a matter of some discussion. See *Sm*[*a*] 267:30 and *Shach* 267:16.]

19. This ruling applies only to a scroll of Scripture, which once a perso[n] has learned thoroughly, he generally rereads only quickly for review. [Therefore, unless otherwise specified, we assume the lender meant t[o] lend it only for reading, not studying.] With respect to a book of th[e] Mishnah and Talmud, however, where even a knowledgeable person wi[ll] delve into the subject deeper each time he reads it, it may be assume[d] that the book was lent with the understanding that it would be studie[d] thoroughly (*Ramban*).

20. See notes 10 and 11.

21. According to *Rosh* (§20, based on Gemara 30a), the one holding th[e] scroll must roll it from end to end once every twelve months only if th[e] owner went overseas. If he is in the area, and thus available to do thi[s] himself, the holder is under no obligation to roll it.

22. The Gemara will explain the entire Baraisa.

23. Because a new Torah scroll is more susceptible to decay than an ol[d] one (*Rashi* ד"ה בחדש שלשים יום).

24. Literally: whether this or whether this.

עין משפט
נר מצוה

קכד א מיי׳ פי״ג מהל׳ גזלה ואבידה הל׳ יח סמג עשין עד טוש״ע ח״מ סי׳ רסז סעיף כה:
קכה ב מיי׳ שם הל׳ יג טוש״ע שם סעיף כ:
קכו ג מיי׳ שם הל׳ יא טוש״ע שם סעיף יח:
קכז ד ה מיי׳ שם הל׳ יג טוש״ע שם סעיף יט:
קכח ו מיי׳ שם פי״א הל׳ יג סמג שם טוש״ע ח״מ סי׳ רסג סעיף א:
קכט ז ח מיי׳ שם פי״ג הל׳ יד סמג שם טוש״ע ח״מ סי׳ רסז סעיף כא [רב אלפס כאן ובהלכות תפילין דף עה.]:
קל ט מיי׳ פ״א מהל׳ שכירות הלכה ד טוש״ע ח״מ סי׳ שמב:
קלא י מיי׳ פ״ז מהל׳ שאלה ופקדון הל׳ ד ופי״ג מהלכות אבדה הלכה יג סמג עשין פח טוש״ע ח״מ סי׳ רנב סעיף כ:
קלב כ מיי׳ פ״א מהל׳ שכירות הלכה ד סמג עשין עד טוש״ע ח״מ סי׳ שמב:
קלג ל מיי׳ שם סמג שם טוש״ע ח״מ סי׳ שז סעיף ד:
קלד מ מיי׳ פ״ז מהל׳ שאלה ופקדון הלכה ד סמג עשין פח טוש״ע ח״מ סי׳ רנב סעיף כ:
קלה נ ס ע מיי׳ פי״ג מהל׳ גזילה ואבדה הלכה יא ופ״ז מהלכות שאלה ופקדון הל׳ ד סמג עשין עד טוש״ע ח״מ סי׳ רסז סעיף יח וסי׳ רנב סעיף כא:

כדרבה (א) דאמר רבה נגנבו בלסטים מזויין אבדו שטבעה ספינתו בים אמר רב יהודה אמר שמואל הלכה כר׳ טרפון (א) ביד רחבה הוה ליה הנהו זוזי דיתמי אתא לקמיה דרב יוסף אמר ליה מהו לאשתמושי בגויידהו א״ל הכי אמר רב יהודה אמר שמואל הלכה כר׳ טרפון א״ל אביי ולאו אתמר עלה א״ר חלבו אמר רב הונא א לא שנו אלא בדמי אבידה הואיל וטרח בה אבל מעות אבידה דלא טרח בהו לא והני כמעות אבידה דמו א״ל זיל לא שבקו לי דאשרי לך: **מתני׳** ב מצא ספרים קורא בהן אחד לשלשים יום ואם אינו יודע לקרות גוללן אבל לא ילמוד בהן בתחלה ולא יקרא אחר עמו ג מצא כסות מנערה אחד לשלשים יום ושוטחה לצרכה אבל לא לכבודו ד כלי כסף וכלי נחושת משתמש בהן לצרכן אבל לא לשחקן ה כלי זהב וכלי זכוכית לא יגע בהן עד שיבא אליהו (ג) ו מצא שק או קופה וכל דבר שאין דרכו ליטול הרי זה לא יטול: **גמ׳** אמר שמואל ז המוצא תפילין בשוק שם דמיהן ומניחן לאלתר מתיב רבינא מצא ספרים קורא בהן אחד לשלשים יום ואם אינו יודע לקרות גוללן גוללן אין שם דמיהן ומניחן לא אמר אביי ח תפילין בי בר חבו משכח שכיחי ספרים לא שכיחי ת״ר (ג) ט השואל ספר תורה מחבירו הרי זה לא ישאילנו לאחר פותחו וקורא בו ובלבד שלא ילמוד בו בתחלה ולא יקרא אחר עמו י וכן המפקיד ס״ת אצל חבירו גוללו כל שנים עשר חדש פותחו וקורא בו אם בשבילו פתחו אסור סומכוס אומר בחדש שלשים יום בישן שנים עשר חדש ר״א בן יעקב אומר אחד זה ואחד זה שנים עשר חדש: אמר מר השואל ספר תורה מחבירו הרי זה לא ישאילנו לאחר מאי אריא ס״ת אפי׳ כל מילי נמי (ד) דאמר ר״ש בן לקיש כאן שנה רבי כ אין השואל רשאי להשאיל ל ואין השוכר רשאי להשכיר ס״ת איצטריכא ליה מהו דתימא (ה) ניחא ליה לאיניש דתיעביד מצוה בממוניה קמ״ל פותחו וקורא בו פשיטא ואלא למאי שיילה מיניה סיפא איצטריכא ליה ובלבד שלא ילמוד בו בתחלה וכן המפקיד ס״ת אצל חבירו גוללו כל שנים עשר חדש פותחו וקורא בו מאי עבידתיה גביה ותו אם בשבילו פתחו אסור הא אמרת פותחו וקורא בו הכי קאמר מ אם כשהוא גוללו פותחו וקורא בו מותר אם בשבילו פתחו אסור סומכוס אומר בחדש שלשים יום בישן שנים עשר חדש ר״א בן יעקב אומר אחד זה ואחד זה שנים עשר חדש ר״א בן יעקב היינו תנא קמא אלא אימא ר׳ אליעזר בן יעקב אומר אחד זה ואחד זה שלשים יום: אבל לא ילמוד בו בתחלה ולא יקרא אחר עמו: ורמינהו לא יקרא פרשה וישנה ולא יקרא בו פרשה ויתרגם ולא יפתח בו יותר מג׳ דפין ולא יקראו בו שלשה בני אדם בכרך אחד הא שנים קורין אמר אביי לא קשיא כאן בענין אחד כאן בשני ענינים: מצא כסות מנערה אחד לשלשים יום: למימרא דניעור מעלי לה והאמר רבי יוחנן מי שיש לו גרדי אומן בתוך ביתו ינער כסותו בכל יום אמרי בכל יום קשי לה אחד לשלשים יום מעלי לה איבעית אימא לא קשיא נ הא בחד והא בתרי איבעית אימא לא קשיא ס הא בידא והא בחוטרא איבעית אימא לא קשיא ע הא בדעמרא הא בדכיתנא (ו) א״ר יוחנן כסא דחרשין ולא כסא דפושרין ולא אמרן אלא בכלי מתכות אבל בכלי חרש לית לן בה ובכלי מתכות נמי לא אמרן אלא דלא צויץ אבל דצויץ לית לן בה ולא אמרן אלא דלא שדא ביה ציביא אבל שדא ביה ציביא לית לן בה: וא״ר יוחנן (ז) מי שהניח לו אביו מעות הרבה ורוצה לאבדן ילבש בגדי פשתן וישתמש בכלי זכוכית וישכור פועלים ואל ישב עמהן ילבש (ח) בכלי פשתן בכתנא רומיתא וישתמש בכלי זכוכית בזוגיתא חיורתא וישכור פועלים ואל ישב עמהן תרגומא בתורי

**תוספות**

**בזכוכית** לבנה. וא״ת והא אמרינן פרק עגלה ערופה (סוטה דף מח.) דמשחרב בית המקדש בטלה זכוכית לבנה וי״ל דלא בטלה לגמרי קאמר אלא דלא שכיחא דהא רב הונא תבר זכוכית חיורתא בחופת בנו פ׳ (ט) אין עומדין (ברכות דף לא. ע״ש): בתורי

**רש״י**

כדרבה. בפרק הזהב (לקמן דף נח.) גבי בני העיר ששלחו את שקליהן: בדמי אבידה. שמכרה לאחר שנטפל בה כמו שאמרו חכמים: אבל מעות אבידה. כגון שמצא מעות בכיס או שלש מטבעות עשויין כמגדלין: מתני׳ אחת לשלשים יום. שמתעפשין כששוהים מלפותחן וכל ספרים שלהן היו עשויין (ג) בגליון: גוללן. מתחילתן לסופן שיכנס בהן האויר: בתחלה. מה שלא למד מפני שצריך להשהותו לפניו: ולא יקרא אחר עמו. לפי שזה מושך אצלו וזה מושך אצלו ונקרע: שוטחה לצרכה. לשלוט בה אויר שלא תכלה ולא תאכלנה עש: לצרכן. שמתעפשים בקרקע שצריך לתתן בקרקע כדאמרינן לקמן שזו היא שמירתן ולפיכך משתמש בהם לפרקים: אבל לא לשחקן. לא ישתמש בהן זמן ארוך שישחקן אוזי״ר בלע״ז: לא יגע בהן. זהב אינו מתעפש בארץ וזכוכית שמא ישבר: שאין דרכו ליטול. דבר שגנאי הוא לו שאדם חשוב הוא ואין דרכו ליטול קופה שלו להכניסה מן החוץ לבית שמור לא יטול ופטור מהשבת אבידה דילפינן מוהתעלמת: גמ׳ בי בר חבו. בבית פלוני העושה תפילין מצויין לימכר ויחזור ויקנה מן הדמים: גוללו. בכל שנים עשר חדש פעם אחת: אם בשבילו פתחו. כולה מפרש לקמיה: מאי אריא ספר. שהוא נוח להתקלקל בטשטוש וקריעה: כאן שנה רבי. במסכת גיטין (דף כט.) תנן השולח גט בארץ ישראל הרי זה משלחו ביד אחר ואם אמר לו טול חפץ פלוני הימנה לא ישלחנו ביד אחר שאין רצונו שיהא פקדונו ביד אחר ואמר ר״ל עלה כאן שנה רבי במשנה זו למדנו רבי שסתם המשניות אין השואל כו׳ דבכולהו שייך למימר אין רצונו שיהא פקדונו ביד אחר: מאי עבידתיה גביה. קס״ד לצורכו קאמר ולא לצורך ספר תורה דהא לצורך ספר תורה תנא ליה גוללו כל שנים עשר חדש להכי פרכינן מאי עבידתיה דהאי גבי ספר תורה לקרות בו לצורך עצמו: אם כשהוא גוללו. להנאת ס״ת פתחו וקרא בו מותר: בחדש שלשים יום. החדש ממהר להתעפש מן הישן: אימא אחד זה ואחד זה שלשים יום. ומתני׳ נמי דקתני קורא בהן אחת לשלשים יום ולא מפליג בין ישן לחדש ר״א בן יעקב היא: בענין אחד. [א] בפרשה אחת אין קורין: בשני ענינים. זה בדף זה וזה בדף זה קורין דלא אתי לשמוטי מהדדי: מי שיש לו גרדי אומן בביתו. שיארוג לו טליתות חדשות תמיד: ינער כסותו בכל יום. ולמדנו דרך ארץ דניעור קשה לה: בחד. באדם אחד אין ניעורו קורעה: שנים. האוחזין בשני ראשיה ומנערין ממתחין אותה יותר מדאי וקשה לה: דעמרא. [ב] קשה לה שנמתחת ונקרעת: כסא דחרשין. נוח לשתות כוס של מכשפות מכוס של מים פושרין ואיידי דאיירי במילי דרבי יוחנן בהלכות דרך ארץ נקט הני שמעתא: צויץ. רותח: ציביא. כל דבר שנותנין לתוך המשקה או עשבים או תבלין או עקרי בשמים קרי ציבא: ורוצה לאבדן. ללמדנו בא שלא ירגיל אדם בכך שהעושה אלה מאבד מהר הון רב: כתנא רומיתא. דמיסס יקרין וממהרין לכלות: תרגמה. להך שכירות דפועלים: בתורי. בפועלים המנהיגים בשורי בעה״ב:

**רבינו חננאל**

אמר ר׳ יהודה אמר שמואל הלכה כר״ט והני מילי בדמי אבידה כגון שמצא אבידה ומטפל בה הזמן שאמרו חכמים ואחר כך מכרה בב״ד הואיל וטרח בה שרו ליה לאישתמושי בהו והשכר לעצמו אבל מצא צרור ובתוכו מעות לא שרו ליה לאישתמושי בהו וכן זוזי דיתמי דהוו מופקדין גביה לא שרו ליה רבנן לאישתמושי בהו מההוא מעשה דרחבה דפריש בשמעתא דא וכבר פירשנוהו בפ׳ הכונס צאן לדיר ביאור יפה וכי כרב יוסף קיימא לן בהא דאמר שומר אבידה כשומר שכר הוא: **מתני׳ מצא ספרים קורא בהן אחד לל׳ יום וכו׳**. אמר שמואל המוצא תפילין שם דמיהן ומניחן מאי טעמא דהא בבי בר חבו שכיחי תפילין ואם אתו מרייהו ואמרי תפילין בעינא זבני ויהבי ליה אבל ספרים גוללן ומניחן אצלו עד שיבא בעליהן ויתנו סימנים ויקחום. ת״ר השואל ספר תורה מחבירו לא ישאילנו לאחרים. ומקשי׳ מאי אריא ספר תורה אפי׳ כל מילי נמי דהא אמר ר׳ שמעון בר לקיש פרק כל גט שנכתב הלכה ואם אמר לו טול לי ממנה חפץ פלוני לא ישלחנו ביד אחר כאן שנה דאין השואל רשאי

דנפיס
להשאיל ולא השוכר רשאי להשכיר כיון דכל מתניתא דשנאה ר׳ חייא אמרי׳ ר׳ לא שנאה ר׳ חייא מנין ליה וזו שנויה במשנת ר׳ חייא ור׳ הושעיה הכי (א) אין השואל רשאי להשאיל ולא השוכר להשכיר ולא השואל רשאי להשכיר ולא השוכר רשאי להשאיל ולא זה המופקדין אצלו רשאי להפקיד אצל אחר אלא אם נתנו בעלים רשות לפיכך הוצרך ריש לקיש לפרש שגם זה שנאה ר׳ ואסקוה ואפי׳ ספר תורה דמצוה הוא לא ישאיל. (ב) פותחו וקורא בו כדי לנערו אבל לא ילמד בו. וכן המפקיד ס״ת אצל חבירו דינו כדין המוצא (ג) מנערה אחד לל׳ יום. וסוגיא לנערה במאני דכיתנא קשי להו ובמאני דעמרא בתרי אינשי או בחוטרא או בכל יומא קשי להו. אבל חד גברא ביומא חדא לל׳ יום מעלי להו. אמר ר׳ יוחנן כסא דחרשין ולא כסא דפושרין פי׳ נוח לו לאדם לשתות כוס שיש בו מיני כשפניות כדמתרגמינן מכשפה חרשא מלשתות כוס מים פושרין

חשק שלמה על ר״ח (א) והוא בתוספתא דמכילתין ברפ״ג. (ב) נראה דדיבור הזה שייך אחר דיבור וכן המפקיד ס״ת וקאי אמפקיד ס״ת ודו״ק. (ג) נראה דל״ל [מצא כסות]:

**מסורת הש״ס**

א) לקמן מג., ב) [שבועות לז:], ג) [מס׳ סופרים פרק ה ה״ט], ד) גיטין כט., ה) [פסחים ד:, כמ יח:, נח.], ו) חולין ק..., ז) [שם], ח) בגדי פשתן כל״ל, ט) [וע״ע תוס׳ ... כ: ד״ה אין].

**הגהות הב״ח**

(א) גמ׳ בי רחבה הוה הנהו וכו׳ אתו לקמיה דרב יוסף אמרו ליה וכו׳ ... להו הכי אמר וכו׳ דלא ... להו כל״ל וג״ב ובהא ... גורס ביד רחבה ה״ל ... זוזי דיתמי אתא הכל ... יחיד: (ג) רש״י ד״ה לא ... וכו׳ היו עשויין בגל... הס״ד:

**הגהות הגר״א**

[א] רש״י ד״ה בע... אחד כו׳. נ״ב וכן הרא״ש אבל הרמב״ם להיפך: [ב] שם ד״ה דעמרא קשה כו׳. ... אבל רי״ף ורמב״ם ... פי׳ להיפך:

**לעזי רש״י**

אוזי״ר. פירוש לשחו...

**ליקוטי רש״י**

נגנבו בלסטים מזוי... דאונס הוא [לקמן ...] וכל דבר שאין דר... ליטול. אם היה ... הרי זה לא יטול. ... מוחזר עליו בלא ... להתעלם שנא... והתעלמת פעמים שא... מתעלם [שבועות ל:]. בר חבו. מוכר תפ... הוה [מגילה יח:]. כ... שנה רבי. במשנה ... שנה לנו רבי. א... השואל וכו׳. דהא ד... לא ישלחנו ביד אחר משום בטולי שליו... דגיטא נקט לה אלא ... דתנן לא ישל... לאשמועינן דאין הש... רשאי להשאיל [גיטין כ...]. עמרא. צמר [גיטין ס...]. ולא כסא דפושר... פרעים הם לגוף. ד... צויץ. הרמית. שהניח לו א... מעות. כלומר מי ש... טרח בממון וקל בעי... לאבדו זהו איבודו [חו... פד:]. זוגיתא. זכו... [שם:]. חיורתא. ל... [עי׳ ברכות כח.].

The Gemara answers:
כִּדְרַבָּה – Rav Yosef defines "it was lost" **in accordance with** the clarification **of Rabbah.** דְּאָמַר רַבָּה נִגְנְבוּ בְּלִסְטִים מְזוּיָּין – **For Rabbah said** in connection with another discussion,[1] that when the Mishnah quoted there says [THE MONEY] WAS STOLEN, it means it was stolen **by an armed robber;** אָבְדוּ שֶׁטָּבְעָה סְפִינָתוֹ בַּיָּם – and when it says IT WAS LOST, it means that is was lost **when his ship sank at sea.**[2] According to Rav Yosef, our Mishnah, too, refers to such an unavoidable loss. Therefore, whether the person caring for the money from the sale is held liable for such a loss depends on whether he is classified a borrower.

The halachah is decided:
אָמַר רַב יְהוּדָה אָמַר שְׁמוּאֵל – Rav Yehudah said in the name of Shmuel: הֲלָכָה כְּר׳ טַרְפוֹן – **The halachah follows** the view of **R' Tarfon,** that the finder may use the money.[3]

The Gemara relates an incident regarding the rights of a custodian to money left in his care:
בֵּיד רַחֲבָה הֲוָה לֵיהּ הָנְהוּ זוּזֵי דְיַתְמֵי – **Rachavah had in his possession money that belonged to orphans.**[4] אֲתָא לְקַמֵּיהּ דְּרַב יוֹסֵף – **He came before Rav Yosef,** אָמַר לֵיהּ – and **said to him:** מַהוּ לְאִשְׁתַּמּוּשֵׁי בְּגַוַּויְיהוּ – **What is [the law] regarding the use of this [money]?**[5] אָמַר לֵיהּ – **[Rav Yosef] replied:** כִּי אָמַר רַב יְהוּדָה אָמַר שְׁמוּאֵל – **This is what Rav Yehudah said in the name of Shmuel:** הֲלָכָה כְּר׳ טַרְפוֹן – **The halachah follows R' Tarfon,** who ruled that the finder is permitted to use the money he is holding. Thus, you too may use it.

This ruling is questioned:
אָמַר לֵיהּ אַבַּיֵי – **Abaye said to [Rav Yosef]:** וְלָאו אִתְּמַר עֲלָהּ – **But was** the following qualification **not stated in regard to that** ruling: אָמַר רַב חֶלְבּוֹ אָמַר רַב הוּנָא – **Rav Chelbo said in the name of Rav Huna:** לֹא שָׁנוּ אֶלָּא בִּדְמֵי אֲבֵידָה – **They taught** that the finder may use the money he is holding **only in regard to the money** received from the sale **of the lost object,** הוֹאִיל וְטָרַח בָּהּ – **because he exerted himself** to care **for it** before selling it. אֲבָל מָעוֹת אֲבֵידָה – **But** if he is holding **lost coins,**[7] דְּלֹא טָרַח בְּהוּ – **in which** case **[the finder] did not exert himself** to care **for them,** לֹא – he may **not** use them. Rather, he must hold those very coins for the owner to reclaim. וְהָנֵי כְּמָעוֹת אֲבֵידָה דָּמוּ – **Now these** monies belonging to the orphans **are like coins that were lost.**[8] – ? –

Rav Yosef accepts Abaye's refutation:
אָמַר לֵיהּ – **[Rav Yosef] said to [Rachavah]:** זִיל – **Go!** לָא שַׁבְקוּ לִי דְּאַשְׁרֵי לָךְ – **They do not allow me to permit this to you.**

## *Mishnah*

The following Mishnah deals with one's responsibility to care for the objects he finds:
מָצָא סְפָרִים – **If one found books,** קוֹרֵא בָּהֶן אֶחָד לִשְׁלֹשִׁים יוֹם – **he should read from them once in thirty days,** to air them out and prevent their decay. וְאִם אֵינוֹ יוֹדֵעַ לִקְרוֹת – **If he does not know** how **to read,** גּוֹלְלָן – **he should roll them** from beginning to end to air them out.[9] אֲבָל לֹא יִלְמוֹד בָּהֶן בַּתְּחִלָּה – **However, he should not study in them** any text he is learning **for the first time,** since he would then keep the scroll open for longer than necessary, which might lead to its damage.[10] וְלֹא יִקְרָא אַחֵר עִמּוֹ – **Nor should another** person **read** from the scroll together **with him,** so that they should not each pull the scroll in opposite directions, causing it to tear.[11]
מָצָא כְסוּת – **If one found a garment,** מְנַעֲרָהּ אֶחָד לִשְׁלֹשִׁים יוֹם – **he should shake it out once every thirty days,** וְשׁוֹטְחָהּ לְצָרְכָּהּ – **and spread it out** as necessary **for its needs,** to prevent its disintegration,[12] אֲבָל לֹא לִכְבוֹדוֹ – **but** he should **not** spread it out **for his own honor,** to decorate his home. כְּלֵי כֶסֶף וּכְלֵי נְחוֹשֶׁת – If he found **silver utensils or copper utensils,** מִשְׁתַּמֵּשׁ בָּהֶן לְצָרְכָּן – **he should make use of them as** necessary **for their needs,**[13]

NOTES

1. See Gemara below, 58a.

2. Generally, theft and loss are considered somewhat preventable and not unavoidable accidents. [Therefore, even though a paid *shomer* is not held liable for accidents, he is still held liable for theft and loss.] Rabbah, in response to a question raised by the Gemara on 57b-58a, explains that when the Mishnah quoted there says that the coins were "stolen," it means that they were stolen by an armed robber, and when it says that they were "lost," it means lost at sea. These are considered unavoidable accidents, for which a paid *shomer* is not held liable. Rav Yosef, noting Rabbah's statement that lost and stolen in Mishnaic terminology can refer to accidents as well as loss and theft, explains the term "lost" in our Mishnah in the same way, as referring to loss through an unavoidable accident. Therefore, whether the finder is responsible to make good such a loss depends on whether he is considered a borrower.

3. However, whether this confers upon him the status of a paid *shomer* or a borrower (which would seem to depend on the dispute of Rabbah and Rav Yosef) remains subject to the controversy among the Poskim as to whether the halachah follows Rabbah or Rav Yosef (see *Shulchan Aruch* and *Rama, Chosen Mishpat* 267:16, 25; *Beur HaGra* ibid. 37 and *Nesivos, Chidushim* 15; see also *Shach* 17).

4. Literally: these *zuz* of orphans. He was caring for the orphans and watching their money until they could take responsibility for it themselves (*Rosh*; cf. *Nimukei Yosef* and see *Taz, Choshen Mishpat* 267:25).

5. I.e. can I use the orphans' money since I care for them? Moreover, it is in their best interest that I be allowed to use the money, since I will then be responsible for it, as we learned in our Mishnah (*Rosh*).

6. As we learned in the Baraisa above (28b), the Sages required the finder to care for animals and other lost objects for varying amounts of time before selling them (*Rashi;* see *Rosh* §16).

7. I.e. he found coins in a purse [which may be identified], or he found coins stacked in a distinctive way (*Rashi*; see Mishnah 24b, 25a).

8. The Sages permitted the finder to use the money from the sale because it is in the public interest [to compensate people for the great effort expended in caring for animals for long periods of time and then selling them; otherwise people would be reluctant to undertake such commitment]. However, they did not find it necessary to permit the use of the money being safeguarded for orphans, even though the trustee devotes much effort to caring for the orphans [because this is a burden people undertake only of their own free will] (*Ramban* cited by *Ritva*).

9. The term גּוֹלְלָן, *roll them,* is used here since, during the times of the Mishnah, books were written in scroll form. The Mishnah requires the finder to roll through the scroll from end to end (if he cannot read from it) since this exposes the book to air to prevents its decay (see *Rashi*).

[Seemingly, when the Mishnah states that he may read it, it also means from end to end, since it is necessary to expose the entire scroll to air. Whatever he does not read, he would have to roll. See, however *Nachalas Moshe,* who conjectures that if one reads part of the scroll he need not roll through the rest of it because the length of time the open part is exposed to the air compensates for the lack of rolling.]

10. *Rashi.* When one reads from a scroll, he generally handles it and pulls on it somewhat (*Meiri*). The likelihood that the scroll will become damaged thus increases when one studies in it for extended periods of time.

11. Thus, even though they are merely reading the text and not studying it, they may not do so together. [See *Rashash*.]

12. From decay or moths (*Rashi*).

13. In order to safeguard these utensils from theft, the finder is required to store them in the ground (see Gemara 42a). However, vessels decay if buried for prolonged periods. The Mishnah therefore requires the finder to take them out and use them periodically (*Rashi*).

בזכוכית לבנה. וא"ת והא אמרינן פרק עגלה ערופה (סוטה דף מח.) דמשחרב בית המקדש בטלה זכוכית לבנה וי"ל דלא בטלה לגמרי קאמר אלא דלא שכיחא דהא רב הונא תבר זכוכית חיורתא בחופת בנו פ' [ט] אין עומדין (ברכות דף לא. ע"ש): בתורי

כדרבה [א] דאמר רבה נגנבו בלסטים מזויין אבדו שטבעה ספינתו בים אמר רב יהודה אמר שמואל הלכה כר' טרפון (א) ביד רחבה הוה ליה הנהו זוזי דיתמי אתא לקמיה דרב יוסף אמר ליה מהו לאשתמושי בגוייהו א"ל הכי אמר רב יהודה אמר שמואל הלכה כר' טרפון א"ל אביי ולאו אתמר עלה א"ר חלבו אמר רב הונא [א] לא שנו אלא בדמי אבידה הואיל וטרח בה אבל מעות אבידה דלא טרח בהו לא והני כמעות אבידה דמו א"ל זיל לא שבקו לי דאשרי לך: **מתני'** [ב] מצא ספרים קורא בהן אחד לשלשים יום ואם אינו יודע לקרות גוללן אבל לא ילמוד בהן בתחלה ולא יקרא אחר עמו [ג] מצא כסות מנערה אחד לשלשים יום ושוטחה לצרכה אבל לא לכבודו [ד] כלי כסף וכלי נחושת משתמש בהן לצרכן אבל לא לשחקן [ה] כלי זהב וכלי זכוכית לא יגע בהן עד שיבא אליהו (ג) [ו] מצא שק או קופה וכל דבר שאין דרכו ליטול הרי זה לא יטול: **גמ'** אמר שמואל [ז] המוצא תפילין בשוק שם דמיהן ומניחן לאלתר מתיב רבינא מצא ספרים קורא בהן אחד לשלשים יום ואם אינו יודע לקרות גוללן גוללן אין שם דמיהן ומניחן לא אמר אביי [ח] תפילין בי בר חבו משכח שכיחי ספרים לא שכיחי ת"ר (ג) [ט] השואל ספר תורה מחבירו הרי זה לא ישאילנו לאחר פותחו וקורא בו ובלבד שלא ילמוד בו בתחלה ולא יקרא אחר עמו [י] וכן המפקיד ס"ת אצל חבירו גוללו כל שנים עשר חדש פותחו וקורא בו אם בשבילו פתחו אסור סומכוס אומר בחדש שלשים יום בישן שנים עשר חדש ר"א בן יעקב אומר אחד זה ואחד זה שנים עשר חדש: אמר מר השואל ספר תורה מחבירו הרי זה לא ישאילנו לאחר מאי אריא ס"ת אפי' כל מילי נמי [ל] דאמר ר"ש בן לקיש כאן שנה רבי [כ] אין השואל רשאי להשאיל [ל] ואין השוכר רשאי להשכיר ס"ת איצטריכא ליה מהו דתימא (ה) ניחא ליה לאיניש דתיעביד מצוה בממוניה קמ"ל פותחו וקורא בו פשיטא ואלא למאי שייליה מיניה סיפא איצטריכא ליה ובלבד שלא ילמוד בו בתחלה וכן המפקיד ס"ת אצל חבירו גוללו כל שנים עשר חדש פותחו וקורא בו מאי עבידתיה גביה ותו אם בשבילו פתחו אסור הא אמרת פותחו וקורא בו הכי קאמר [מ] אם כשהוא גוללו פותחו וקורא בו מותר אם בשבילו פתחו אסור סומכוס אומר בחדש שלשים יום בישן שנים עשר חדש ר"א בן יעקב אומר אחד זה ואחד זה שנים עשר חדש ר"א בן יעקב היינו תנא קמא אלא אימא ר' אליעזר בן יעקב אומר אחד זה ואחד זה שלשים יום: אבל לא ילמוד בו בתחלה ולא יקרא אחר עמו: ורמינהו לא יקרא פרשה וישנה ולא יקרא בו פרשה ויתרגם ולא יפתח בו יותר מג' דפין ולא יקראו בו שלשה בני אדם בכרך אחד הא שנים קורין אמר אביי לא קשיא כאן בענין אחד כאן בשני ענינים: מצא כסות מנערה אחד לשלשים יום: למימרא דניעור מעלי לה והאמר רבי יוחנן מי שיש לו גרדי אומן בתוך ביתו ינער כסותו בכל יום אמרי בכל יום קשי לה אחד לשלשים יום מעלי לה איבעית אימא לא קשיא [נ] הא בחד והא בתרי איבעית אימא לא קשיא [ס] הא בידא והא בחוטרא איבעית אימא לא קשיא [ע] הא בדעמרא הא בדכיתנא [י] א"ר יוחנן כסא דחרשין ולא כסא דפושרין ולא אמרן אלא בכלי מתכות אבל בכלי חרש לית לן בה ובכלי מתכות נמי לא אמרן אלא דלא צויץ אבל דצויץ לית לן בה ולא אמרן אלא דלא שדא ביה ציביא אבל שדא ביה ציביא לית לן בה: וא"ר יוחנן [י] מי שהניח לו אביו מעות הרבה ורוצה לאבדן ילבש בגדי פשתן וישתמש בכלי זכוכית וישכור פועלים ואל ישב עמהן ילבש (ס) בכלי פשתן בכתנא רומיתא וישתמש בכלי זכוכית בזוגיתא חיורתא וישכור פועלים ואל ישב עמהן תרגומא בתורי

כדרבה. בפרק הזהב (לקמן דף נח.) גבי בני העיר ששלחו את שקליהן: בדמי אבידה. שמכרה לאחר שנטפל בה כמו שאמרו חכמים: אבל מעות אבידה. כגון שמצא מעות בכיס או שלש מטבעות עשויין כמגדלין: **מתני'** אחת לשלשים יום. שמתעפשין כשהוהים מלפותחן וכל ספרים שלהן היו עשויין (ב) בגליון: גוללן. מתחילתן לסופן שיכנס בהן האויר: בתחלה. מה שלא למד מפני שצריך להשהותו לפניו: ולא יקרא אחר עמו. לפי שזה מושך אצלו וזה מושך אצלו ונקרע: שוטחה לצרכה. לשלוט בה אויר שלא תכלה ולא תאכלנה עש: לצרכן. שמתעפשים בקרקע שצריך לתתן בקרקע כדאמרינן לקמן שזו היא שמירתן ולפיכך משתמש בהם לפרקים: אבל לא לשחקן. לא ישתמש בהן זמן ארוך שישחקן אוזי"ר בלע"ז: לא יגע בהן. זהב אינו מתעפש בארץ וזכוכית שמא ישבר: שאין דרכו ליטול. דבר שגנאי הוא לו שאדם חשוב הוא ואין דרכו ליטול קופה שלו להכניסה מן החוץ לבית שמור לא יטול ופטור מהשבת אבידה דילפינן מוהתעלמת: **גמ'** בי בר חבו. בבית פלוני העושה תפילין מצויין לימכר ויחזור ויקנה מן הדמים: גוללו. בכל שנים עשר חדש פעם אחת: אם בשבילו פתחו. כולה מפרש לקמיה: מאי אריא ספר. שהוא נוח להתקלקל בטשטוש וקריעה: כאן שנה רבי. במסכת גיטין (דף כט.) תנן השולח גט בארץ ישראל הרי זה משלחו ביד אחר ואם אמר לו טול חפץ פלוני הימנה לא ישלחנו ביד אחר שאין רצונו שיהא פקדונו ביד אחר ואמר ר"ל עלה כאן שנה רבי במשנה זו למדנו רבי שסתם המשניות אין השואל כו' דבכולהו שייך למימר אין רצונו שיהא פקדונו ביד אחר: מאי עבידתיה גביה. קס"ד לצורכו קאמר ולא לצורך ספר תורה דהא לצורך ספר תורה תנא ליה גוללו כל שנים עשר חדש להכי פרכינן מאי עבידתיה דהאי גבי ספר תורה לקרות בו לצורך עצמו: אם כשהוא גוללו. להנאת ס"ת פתחו וקרא בו מותר: בחדש שלשים יום. החדש ממהר להתעפש מן הישן: אימא אחד זה ואחד זה שלשים יום. ומתני' נמי דקתני קורא בהן אחת לשלשים יום ולא מפליג בין ישן לחדש ר"א בן יעקב היא: בענין אחד. [א] בפרשה אחת אין קורין: בשני ענינים. זה בדף זה וזה בדף זה קורין דלא אתי לשמוטי מהדדי: מי שיש לו גרדי אומן בביתו. שיארוג לו טליתות חדשות תמיד: ינער כסותו בכל יום. ולמדנו דרך ארץ דניעור קשה לה: בחד. באדם אחד אין ניעורו קורעה: שנים. האוחזין בשני ראשיה ומנערין ממתחין אותה יותר מדאי וקשה לה: דעמרא. [ב] קשה לה שנמתחת ונקרעת: כסא דחרשין. נוח לשתות כוס של מכשפות מכוס של מים פושרין ואיידי דאיירי במילי דרבי יוחנן בהלכות דרך ארץ נקט הני שמעתא: צויץ. רותח: ציביא. כל דבר שנותנין לתוך המשקה או עשבים או תבלין או עקרי בשמים קרי ציביא: ורוצה לאבדן. ללמדנו בא שלא ירגיל אדם בכך שהעושה אלה מאבד מהר הון רב: כתנא רומיתא. דמיהם יקרין וממהרין לכלות: תרגמא. להך שכירות דפועלים: בתורי. בפועלים המנהיגים בשורי בעה"ב:

דנפיש

## עין משפט נר מצוה

קכד א מיי' פי"ג מהל' גזלה ואבידה הל' יח סמג עשין עד טוש"ע ח"מ סי' רסז סעיף כה:

קכה ב מיי' שם הל' יג טוש"ע שם סעיף כ:

קכו ג מיי' שם הל' יא טוש"ע שם סעיף יח:

קכז ד ה מיי' שם הל' יב טוש"ע שם סעיף יט:

קכח ו מיי' שם פי"א הל' יג סמג שם טוש"ע ח"מ סי' רסג סעיף א:

קכט ז ח מיי' שם פי"ג הל' יד סמג שם טוש"ע ח"מ סי' רסז סעיף כא [רב אלפס כאן ובהלכות תפילין דף עה.]:

קל ט מיי' פ"א מהל' שכירות הלכה ד טוש"ע ח"מ סי' שמב:

קלא י מיי' פ"ז מהל' שאלה ופקדון הל' ד ופי"ג מהלכות אבדה הלכה יג סמג עשין עד פח טוש"ע ח"מ סי' רלב סעיף כ:

קלב כ מיי' פ"א מהל' שכירות הלכה ד סמג עשין עד טוש"ע ח"מ סי' שמב:

קלג ל מיי' שם סמג שם טוש"ע ח"מ סי' שז סעיף ד:

קלד מ מיי' פ"ז מהל' שאלה ופקדון הלכה ד סמג עשין פח טוש"ע ח"מ סי' רלב סעיף כ:

קלה נ ס ע מיי' פי"ג מהל' גזילה ואבדה הלכה יא ופ"ז מהלכות שאלה ופקדון הל' ד סמג עשין עד טוש"ע ח"מ סי' רסז סעיף יח וסי' רלב סעיף כא:

## רבינו חננאל

אמר ר' יהודה אמר שמואל הלכה כר"ט והני מילי בדמי אבידה כגון שמצא אבידה ומטפל בה הזמן שאמרו חכמים ואחר כך מכרה בב"ד הואיל וטרח בה שרו ליה לאישתמושי בהו והשכר לעצמו אבל מצא צרור ובתוכו מעות לא שרו ליה לאישתמושי בהו וכן זוזי דיתמי דהוו מופקדין גביה לא שרו ליה רבנן לאישתמושי בהו מההוא מעשה דרחבה דפריש בשמעתא דא וכבר פירשנוהו בפ' הכונס צאן לדיר ביאור יפה וכי כרב יוסף קיימא לן בהא דאמר שומר אבידה כשומר שכר הוא: **מתני'** מצא ספרים קורא בהן אחד לל' יום וכו'. אמר שמואל המוצא תפילין שם דמיהן ומניחן מאי טעמא דהא בבי בר חבו שכיחי תפילין ואם אינו כמו ייחוד ואמרי תפילין בעינא זבני ויהבי ליה אבל ספרים גוללן ומניחן אצלו עד שיבא בעליהן ויתנו סימנים ויקחום. ת"ר השואל ספר תורה מחבירו לא ישאילנו לאחרים. ומקשי' מאי אריא ספר תורה אפי' כל מילי נמי דהא אמר ר' שמעון בר לקיש פרק כל גט שנכתב הלכה ואם אמר לו טול לי ממנה חפץ פלוני לא ישלחנו ביד אחר כאן שנה דאין השואל רשאי להשאיל ולא השוכר רשאי להשכיר כיון דכל מתניתא דשנאה ר' חייא אמרי' ר' לא שנאה ר' חייא מנין ליה וזו שנויה במשנת ר' חייא ור' הושעיה הכי א) אין השואל רשאי להשאיל ולא השוכר רשאי להשכיר ולא השואל רשאי להשכיר ולא השוכר רשאי להשאיל ולא זה המופקדין אצלו רשאי להפקיד אצל אחר אלא אם נתנו בעלים רשות לפיכך הוצרך ריש לקיש לפרש שגם זה שנאה ר' ואסקוה ואפי' ספר תורה דמצוה הוא לא ישאיל. ב) פותחו וקורא בו כדי לנערו אבל לא ילמד בו. וכן המפקיד ס"ת אצל חבירו דינו כדין המוצא ג) מנערה אחד לל' יום. וסוגיא לנערה במאני דכיתנא קשי להו ובמאני דעמרא בתרי אינשי או בחוטרא או בכל יומא קשי להו. אבל חד גברא ביומא חדא לל' יום מעלי להו. אמר ר' יוחנן כסא דחרשין ולא כסא דפושרין פי' נוח לו לאדם לשתות כוס שיש בו מיני כשפניות כדמתרגמינן מכשפה חרשא מלשתות כוס מים פושרין

חשק שלמה על ר"ח א) והוא בתוספתא דמכילתין פרפ"ג. ב) נראה דדיבור זה שייך אחר דיבור וכן המפקיד ס"ת וקאי אמפקיד ס"ת ודו"ק. ג) נראה דל"ל [מלא כסות]:

## מסורת הש"ס

א) לקמן מג., נ... ב) [שבועות ל:], ג) [מס' סופרים פרק ה הל' טז], ד) גיטין כ... ה) [פסחים ד:, בכור' יח:, נח.], ו) חולין פ... ז) [שם], ח) בגדי פשר... כצ"ל, ט) [וע"ע תוס' ש... כ: ד"ה אין].

## הגהות הב"ח

(א) גמ' בי רחבה הוה ל... הנהו וכו' אתו לקמיה ד... יוסף אמרו ליה וכו' א... להו הכי אמר וכו' דאש... לכו כצ"ל וכ"ב ובאשר... גורס ביד רחבא ה"ל הנ... זוזי דיתמי אתא הכל בל... יחיד: (ב) רש"י ד"ה א... וכו' היו עשויין בגלי... הס"ד:

## הגהות הגר"א

[א] רש"י ד"ה בענ... אחד כו'. נ"ב וכן ... הרא"ש אבל הרמב"ם ... להיפך: [ב] שם ד"... דעמרא קשה כו'. נ... אבל רי"ף ורמב"ס וש... פי' להיפך:

## לעזי רש"י

אוזי"ר. פירוש לשחו...

## ליקוטי רש"י

נגנבו בלסטים מזוי... דאונס הוא [לקמן נד... וכל דבר שאין דר... ליטול. אם היה ש... הרי זה לא יטול. א... מוזהר עליו בלא ת... להתעלם שנא'... והתעלמת פעמים שא... מתעלם [שבועות ל:]. בר חבו. מוכר תפי... הוה [מגילה יח:]. כ... שנה רבי. במשנה שנה לנו רבי. א... השואל וכו'. דהא ד... לא ישלחנו ביד אחר משום בטולי שליח... דגיטא נקט לה אלא ה... דתנן לא ישל... לאשמועינן דאין השו... רשאי להשאיל [גיטין כ... עמרא. למר [גיטין סד... ולא כסא דפושר... שרעים הם לגוף. ד... צויץ. הרתית. שהניח לו א... מעות. כלומר מי ש... טרח בממון וקל בעי... לאבדו זהו איבודו [חו... פד:]. זוגיתא. זכו... [שם:]. חיורתא. לב... [עי' ברכות כח.].

אלא כשנשתמש בהן אבל לא נשתמש בהן אם אבדו פטור לימא תיהוי תיובתא דרב יוסף [א] דאתמר שומר אבידה רבה אמר כש"ח רב יוסף אמר [א] כש"ש אמר לך רב יוסף בגניבה ואבידה דכ"ע לא פליגי דחייב כי פליגי באונסין דשואל ר"ט סבר שרו ליה רבנן לאשתמושי בגווייהו [ב] והוה ליה שואל עלייהו ור"ע סבר לא שרו ליה רבנן לאשתמושי בגווייהו הלכך לא הוי שואל עלייהו א"ה לפיכך דאמר ר"ע למה לי א"א בשלמא בגניבה ואבידה הוא דפליגי היינו דקתני ר"ע אומר לא ישתמש בהן לפיכך אם אבדו אינו חייב באחריותן ס"ד אמינא שומר שכר הוי כדרב יוסף ובגניבה ואבידה מחייב קא משמע לן לפיכך השתא דאמרת לא ישתמש בהן שומר שכר לא הוי ולא מחייב בגניבה ואבידה אלא אי אמרת בגניבה ואבידה דכולי עלמא לא פליגי דחייב כי פליגי באונסין דשואל מאי לפיכך דרבי עקיבא הכי מבעי ליה למתנא ר"ע אומר לא ישתמש בהן ואנא ידענא דכיון דלא ישתמש בהן לאו שואל הוי ואינו חייב באחריותן ° לפיכך דרבי עקיבא למה לי משום לפיכך דרבי טרפון ולפיכך דרבי טרפון למה לי [ג] הכי קאמר כיון דשרו ליה רבנן לאשתמושי בגווייהו כמאן דאישתמש בגווייהו דמי וחייב באחריותן והא אבדו קתני כדרבה

אלא. משום שכר שימוש מעות אבל שכר שמירת מלוה דנימא מגו דלא בעי למיתב ריפתא לעניא דהעוסק במלוה פטור מן המלוה לא מחייבינן ליה: כשנשתמש. לאו דוקא אלא משום שכר שימוש קאמר מפני שמותר להשתמש בהן: כשומר חנם. ואינו חייב אלא בפשיעה: כשומר שכר. וחייב בגניבה ואבידה דשומר שכר מלוה הוא דהעוסק במלוה פטור מן המלוה: כולי עלמא לא פליגי דמחייב. כדין שומר שכר: מאי לפיכך דר"ע. כיון דאמר לא ישתמש מהיכא תיסק אדעתין לחיוביה דאיצטריך למימר אינו חייב:

והוי שואל עליהו. תימה דהוה ליה למימר והוה לוה עלייהו ואם נאמר דאם באו בעלים קודם שהוציאם חייב להחזיר אותם מעות עצמם ולא אחרים הוה א"ש דקרי ליה שואל אך אי אפשר לומר כן דבפרק המפקיד (לקמן דף מג.) פריך אי נאנסו חייב מאי אריא הוציא כי לא הוציא נמי והשתא אי חייב להחזיר הן עצמן כשיתבע הגזבר אם כן לא קנאם השולחני בשלא הוציאם ולא מעל כדאמר פרק השואל (לקמן דף לט.) לא בקע בו לא מעל כיון שהמשאיל יכול לחזור בו וא"כ מאי פריך כי לא הוציא נמי אלא ודאי אפילו אם אותן המעות עדיין בעין אין צריך להחזיר הן עצמן וי"ל דנקט שואל משום דנקט אונסין דכתיב בקרא גבי שואל וגם לפי שמזכיר שומר חנם ושומר שכר. ר"ח וה"ג פסקו דהלכה כרב יוסף מההיא דאין בין המודר (נדרים דף לג:) דקאמר ומחזיר לו אבידתו חד אמר דוקא מדיר למודר אבל מודר למדיר לא משום דקא מתהני פרוטה דרב יוסף וחד אמר פרוטה דרב יוסף לא שכיחא ש"מ דכולהו אית להו דרב יוסף ואין זו ראיה דגם רבה מודה דבשעה שמתעסק באבידה שפטור מלמיתב ריפתא לעניים אלא דס"ל דלא שכיחא שיבא עני בשעה שמתעסק בה לצורכה ואין סברא שיהא שומר שכר בעבור זה כיון דלא שכיח דבשעה שהאבידה בביתו ואינו מתעסק בה פשיטא דאף לרב יוסף אינו פטור מלמיתב ריפתא לעני שהרי אדם שלבוש ציצית או שיש לו תפילין בראשו וכי יפטר מכל המצות והא דלקמן (דף לא.) מוקי רבא קרא (א) דוהשב תשיבם לגינתו המשתמרת וקמ"ל דלא בעינן דעת בעלים כדמוקי רב יוסף בפרק הכונס (ב"ק דף נו. ושם) דרבה מוקי לה בשאינה משתמרת שמירה מעולה כמו בביתו ומייתי ראיה מינה דשומר אבידה כשומר חנם הוי אין ראיה דהלכה כרב יוסף דרבה גופיה הדר ביה כשתירך לו רב יוסף דקמ"ל דלא בעינן דעת בעלים ומוקי לה בגינתו המשתמרת דהא בקרא שור ושה כתיב ומודה רבה בבעלי חיים דהוי עלייהו שומר שכר דאנקטינהו נגרי ברייתא וכשרולה להביא ראיה לדבריו ולא ידע שינויא דרב יוסף היה צריך לדחוק ולהעמיד בכפותים ועוד דוחק אחר דהוי מוקי קרא לגינתו שאינה משתמרת ואשמועינן קרא דהוי שומר חנם ולרבה אית ליה מסברא דהוי שומר חנם דלא מטי הנאה לידו ועוד [ג] י"ל דלקמן ה"פ היכי דמי אי דלא מינטרא למר כדאית ליה מפשיעה ולמר כדאית ליה מגניבה ואבידה אמאי פטור ואי דמנטרא למר כדאית ליה ולמר כדאית ליה וכו' ושלהי האומנין (לקמן דף פא: ושם) דאמר ר"א ישבע שאבד המשכון ויטול מעותיו ר"ע אומר אבד המשכון אבדו מעותיו ומוקי מתני' דהלוהו על המשכון שומר שכר דלא כר"א ומסיק דפליגי בשומר אבידה וקאמר לימא דרב יוסף תנאי היא ופרש"י דרבה ודאי תנאי היא דלא מצי סבר כר"ע אם כן משמע דאין הלכה כרבה דהוי כר"א דשמותי הוא וגם דמתניתי' לא אתיא כוותיה וי"ל דרבה ודאי לאו תנאי היא ואפילו לר"ע משום מלוה לא הוי שומר שכר וטעמא דר"ע דאמר אבדו מעותיו כדשמואל דאפילו בדלא שוי שיעור זוזי אבדו כל מעותיו דהוי כאילו פי' שאם יאבד המשכון שיאבדו מעותיו ור"א לית ליה דשמואל ואפילו שוי שיעור זוזי לא אבדו מעותיו אלא לרב יוסף כי נמי מוקי פלוגתייהו בדשמואל לא קאי ר' אליעזר כוותיה לפי מה שמדמה עתה במסקנא מלוה על המשכון לשומר אבידה שהוא פוטר את המלוה באבידה אלמא לא הוי שומר שכר ומשני דאתי מלתיה דרב יוסף אפי' כר"א ותדע דלא מצינו למימר דרבה לא מצי סבר כר"ע דהא בשמעתין משמע דכולהו סברי דרבה ולר"ע נמי הוי שומר חנם והא דתנן פרק שבועת הדיינין (שבועות דף מד. ושם) המלוה על המשכון ואבד המשכון שחייב באבידה מה שהמשכון יתר על החוב אליבא דרבה מבעיא לן לאוקמה באבדה בפשיעה דלא הוי ביה אלא שומר חנם דמה שכנגד החוב מפסיד אפילו לא אבד בפשיעה מטעמא דשמואל ואין זה דוחק דה"נ כי בעי גמרא מעיקרא לאוקמה פלוגתא דר"א ור' עקיבא בדשמואל או בדר' יצחק ולא היה מדמה לשומר אבידה צריך נמי לאוקמה מתני' דשבועות דמיחייב לשלם באבדה מה שהמשכון יתר על החוב באבדה בפשיעה דמטעם דשמואל או דר' יצחק אין לחייב המלוה באבידת המשכון אלא במה שכנגד החוב ואדרבה מפ' האומנין (לקמן דף פב. ושם) יש להוכיח דהלכה כרבה דאי הלכה כרב יוסף אמאי מוקי גמרא אלא מחוורתא מתניתין דלא כר"א לוקמה באין מלוה צריך למשכון דהוי שומר שכר אפי' לר"א ופלוגתייהו במלוה צריך למשכון אלא ודאי משום דהלכה כרבה ואין הלכה כרב יוסף ולדידיה לא מצי לאוקמא מתניתין כר"א ועוד ראיה מפרק המפקיד (לקמן דף מג. ושם) דרב נחמן סבר נאנסו לא אלמא ס"ל דבהנאה שמותר להשתמש לא הוי אלא שומר שכר והיינו כרבה דלרב יוסף הוי שואל ואין לומר דהכא דהוי שומר אבידה דבלא היתר תשמיש הוי שומר שכר השתא דשרו ליה לאשתמושי בהו הוי שואל אבל התם דלא מיירי באבידה משום הנאת היתר תשמיש לבד לא הוי אלא שומר שכר לא היא כיון דבשביל היתר תשמיש לבד לא הוי אלא שומר שכר כרב נחמן א"כ בשביל שיש לו עוד פרוטה דרב יוסף משום שמירת אבידה אין סברא שיהא לו דין שואל דאטו אם מוסיפין שכר לשומר יהיה לו דין שואל ועוד דקי"ל כרבה בר [ג] משדה ענין ומחצה וליכא למימר דוקא במילי דבבא בתרא כדמפרש בתשובות דרב צמח דהא אמר פרק מי שאחזו (גיטין דף עד: ושם ד"ה הא) והא קי"ל כרבה ולא קאמר בהא דהוה משמע בהא ולא במילי אחרינא כדקאמר על רשב"ג ובפרק מי שהוציאוהו (עירובין דף נג:) בשמעתין דהחזיק בדרך מתיישבת ההלכה יותר במה שהלכה כרבה לגבי דרב יוסף כדפי' שם רש"י ובסדר תנאים ואמוראים פוסק דרבה ורב יוסף הלכה כרבה בר משדה ענין ומחצה וכל רבותינו שוין דבשאר דברים סתמא הלכה כרבה אי ליכא הוכחה כרב יוסף [ד]: **לפיכך** דרבי טרפון למה לי. בשלמא לרבה דלפיכך דר"ע אשמועינן לאפוקי דרב יוסף מצינו למימר דלפיכך דרבי טרפון משום לפיכך דר"ע אי נמי גם לפיכך דר"ט אתי למידק נמי דדוקא משום דמותר להשתמש חייב אבל אסור להשתמש פטור לאפוקי דרב יוסף אבל לרב יוסף מאי לפיכך וקשה דמאי בעי מאי לפיכך הלא חדוש גדול השמיעו דמעיקרא אמרינן דבמה שמותר להשתמש לא הוי אלא שומר שכר ולא כשואל דהא אבדו קתני דמשמע סתם אבידה בלא אונס והשתא מבעי לן למימר דמחמת היתר תשמיש הוי כשואל ואבדו היינו שטבע ספינתו בים ועוד דבפרק המפקיד (לקמן דף מג. ושם) איצטריך מתני' לאשמועינן דמחמת היתר תשמיש הוי שומר שכר לרב נחמן דאמר נאנסו לא גבי מפקיד מעות אצל (ב) חנווני דקתני צרורים לא ישתמש בהן לפיכך אם אבדו אינו חייב והא מלתא דפשיטא היא דאינו חייב באבידה כיון דשומר חנם הוא אלא סיפא איצטריכא ליה לאשמועינן דמותרין להשתמש בהן לפיכך אם אבדו חייב באחריותן והוי שומר שכר לרב נחמן דאמר נאנסו לא וכיון דאפילו למיהוי שומר שכר מחמת היתר תשמיש איצטריך לאשמועינן כ"ש הכא דאמר דהוי שואל דלאו מלתא דפשיטא הוא דאיצטריך שפיר לאשמועינן אלא י"ל דלאו קושיא הוא אלא פירושא בעלמא הוא:



עין משפט
נר מצוה

קכב א מיי' פי"ג מהלכות גזילה ואבידה הלכה י סמג עשין עד טוש"ע ח"מ סי' רסז סעיף טז:
קכג ב ג מיי' שם הל' יז סמג שם טוש"ע ח"מ שם סעיף כה:

רבינו חננאל

ותאכיל לנשארים דקא מיכליא אלא מכור הכל: מה יהיה בדמים ר' טרפון אומר ישתמש בהן לפיכך אם אבדו חייב באחריותן ורבי עקיבא אומר לא ישתמש בהן וכו' עד כאן לא פליגי אלא בנשתמש בהן אבל אם לא נשתמש בהן דברי הכל פטור. לימא תהוי תיובתא דרב יוסף דאיתמר בפ' הכונס צאן לדיר שומר אבידה רבה אמר כשומר חנם ונשבע על הכל. רב יוסף אמר כשומר שכר שנשבע על האונסין ומשלם הגניבה ואבידה. ודחי רב יוסף בגניבה ואבידה כולי עלמא לא פליגי דחייב כשומר שכר כי פליגי באונסין ר' טרפון סבר אע"ג דבאבידה עצמה הוה לי' שומר שכר כיון דשרי ליה לאישתמושי בדמיה נעשה עליה כשואל וחייב גם על האונסין. ור' עקיבא סבר לא שרו ליה רבנן לאישתמושי בדמי אבידה הלכך לא הוי עלייהו אלא שומר שכר. ואקשי' עליה אי הכי למה ליה לר' עקיבא למיתנא לפיכך אי אמרת בגניבה ואבידה פליגי ר' טרפון סבר כיון דשרו ליה לאישתמושי בהו הוי ליה כשומר שכר עלייהו וחייב בגניבה ואבידה. ור' עקיבא סבר לא שרו ליה רבנן לאישתמושי בהו וכשומר חנם הוא עליהו שאם אבדו פטור וכל שכן נאנסו שפטור אלא אי אמרת בגניבה ואבידה דברי הכל חייב כי פליגי באונסין לתני רבי עקיבא אומר לא ישתמש בהן וממילא ידענא דכיון דלא שרי לאישתמושי בהו לא הוי עלייהו אלא כשומר שכר אבל שואל לא הוי עלייהו לפיכך דקתני מאי אתא לאשמועינן ופרקי' ודאי ר' עקיבא לא הוי צריך למיתניה לפיכך מיהו איידי דתנא ר' טרפון לפיכך תנא איהו נמי לפיכך ומקשי' תוב לפיכך דר' טרפון נמי למה לי ופריק רב יוסף צריכא והכי קתני כיון דשרו ליה רבנן לאישתמושי בהו הוה ליה עלייהו כשואל לפיכך אע"פ שלא נשתמש בהן חייב עליהן כשואל. ומקשי' עליה אי הכי לא הוה תני לפיכך אם אבדו חייב בהן דמשמע שומר שכר הוא חשוב באבידה אלא הוה ליה למיתנא לפיכך אם נאנסו חייב בהן דמשמע דשואל הוי עליהן. ופריק רב יוסף האי אבדו דקתני נאנסו הוא. ומקשי' ומי קרו לאבדו נאנסו (היו) [אין] כדרבה דאמר בפ' הזהב הלכה שומר חנם אין נשבע וכו' נגנבו בלסטים מזוין אבדו שטבעה ספינתו בים:
אמר

מסורת הש"ס

[...]בא קמא ט:, לקמן שבועות מד., נדרים [...] ב) ר"ל כעין ז"ל והכל [...] אחד, מהרש"ל, [...]בא בתרא קיד:, [...]:], ד) [ועיין תוס' [...]ה כט: ד"ה והלכתא וכו'].

הגהות הב"ח

[...]תוס' ד"ה והוי וכו' דלקמן מוקי רבא קרא [...]ב תשיבם: (ב) ד"ה [...]ך וכו' גבי מפקיד [...]ת אצל שולחני דקתני:

גליון הש"ס

לפיכך דר"ע. כעין [...]ה דף ט ע"א ודף ס ע"ב:

ליקוטי רש"י

[...]מר אבידה. שמצא [...]דה והכניסה אל תוך [...] כדכתיב (דברים כב) [...]פתו אל תוך ביתך [לקמן פב.].

for which only **a borrower** is held liable, **מַאי לְפִיכָךְ דְּרַבִּי עֲקִיבָא** – **what** does the "THEREFORE" **of R' Akiva** teach us? It is superfluous! **הָכִי מִבָּעֵי לֵיהּ לְמִתְנָא** – Rather, **this is what [the Mishnah] should have said: רַבִּי עֲקִיבָא אוֹמֵר לֹא יִשְׁתַּמֵּשׁ בָּהֶן** – R' AKIVA SAYS: HE MAY NOT USE [THE MONEY] – and no more,[11] **וַאֲנָא יָדַעְנָא** – **and I would** have **known** on my own **דְּכֵיוָן דְּלֹא יִשְׁתַּמֵּשׁ בָּהּ** – **that since he may not use [the money], לָאו שׁוֹאֵל הֲוֵי** – **he is not a borrower, וְאֵינוֹ חַיָּיב בְּאַחֲרָיוּתָן** – **and he** is therefore **not responsible for it** if an accident occurs.[12] **לְפִיכָךְ דְּרַבִּי עֲקִיבָא לָמָּה לִי** – **Why** then is there **any need for the** "THEREFORE" clause **of R' Akiva?**

The Gemara answers that this clause is in fact unnecessary according to Rav Yosef, but:

**מִשּׁוּם לְפִיכָךְ דְּרַבִּי טַרְפוֹן** – It is added to R' Akiva's statement **because of the** "THEREFORE" **of R' Tarfon**'s statement, to maintain a symmetry with R' Tarfon's phrasing.[13]

The Gemara continues:

**וּלְפִיכָךְ דְּרַבִּי טַרְפוֹן לָמָּה לִי** – **And why** is there **any need for the** "THEREFORE" clause **of R' Tarfon?**[14]

The Gemara explains:

**הָכִי קָאָמַר** – **This is what [R' Tarfon] is saying: כֵּיוָן דְּשָׁרוּ לֵיהּ רַבָּנָן לְאִשְׁתַּמּוּשֵׁי בְּגַוַּיְיהוּ** – **Since the Rabbis permitted [the finder] to use [the money], כְּמַאן דְּאִישְׁתַּמֵּשׁ בְּגַוַּיְיהוּ דָּמֵי** – **he is** viewed **as if he used it,** i.e. he is classified as a borrower regardless of whether he actually uses it, **וְחַיָּיב בְּאַחֲרָיוּתָן** – **and he is** therefore **responsible for it** if an accident occurs.[15]

The Gemara challenges Rav Yosef's answer:

**וְהָא אָבְדוּ קָתָנֵי** – **But the Mishnah said**: IF [THE MONEY] WAS *LOST* he is responsible for it! How can Rav Yosef say that it means that he is responsible for an *accident*?[16]

NOTES

11. I.e. the Mishnah should not have added the corollary ruling that he is therefore exempt from paying for any accidents.

12. [Since the only reason to treat the finder as a borrower and hold him liable for accidents is because of his right to use the money,] once R' Akiva states that he is *not* allowed to use the money, it is quite obvious that he cannot be considered a borrower! Why should the Mishnah have to state this explicitly, when it would never occur to anyone to say otherwise? (*Rashi*).

13. Parallel phrasing is a device often employed in Mishnah [to aid in the memorization of the texts].

14. *Tosafos* explain that this is really only a rhetorical question because it is not at all obvious that one who may use the money is classified a borrower. [Earlier, the Gemara said that the right to use the money made him only a paid *shomer*, not a borrower.]

15. According to Rav Yosef, R' Tarfon considers the finder a borrower because he is permitted to use the money from the sale of the lost object. Now, it might be thought that if he does not use the money, he would not become a borrower and he would not be responsible for accidents. To preclude this interpretation, the Mishnah adds: *Therefore, if it is lost, he is responsible for it,* to indicate that he is responsible in *all* cases, whether he actually used the money or not.

16. Rav Yosef explained that R' Tarfon and R' Akiva argue whether the finder is responsible for an accident, but they agree that he is responsible for theft and loss. But the Mishnah clearly states, "Therefore, if it is *lost*..." This proves that R' Akiva and R' Tarfon dispute the liability for loss, not accident.

אלא כשנשתמש בהן אבל לא נשתמש בהן אם אבדו פטור לימא תיהוי תיובתא דרב יוסף [א] דאתמר שומר אבידה רבה אמר כש"ח רב יוסף אמר [א]כש"ש אמר לך רב יוסף בגניבה ואבידה דכ"ע לא פליגי דחייב כי פליגי באונסין דשואל ר"ט סבר שרו ליה רבנן לאשתמושי בגוייהו [ב]והוה ליה שואל עלייהו ור"ע סבר לא שרו ליה רבנן לאשתמושי בגוייהו הלכך לא הוי שואל עלייהו א"ה לפיכך דאמר ר"ע למה לי א"א בשלמא בגניבה ואבידה הוא דפליגי היינו דקתני ר"ע אומר לא ישתמש בהן לפיכך אם אבדו אינו חייב באחריותן ס"ד אמינא שומר שכר הוי כדרב יוסף ובגניבה ואבידה מחייב קא משמע לן לפיכך השתא דאמרת לא ישתמש בהן שומר שכר לא הוי ולא מחייב בגניבה ואבידה אלא אי אמרת בגניבה ואבידה דכולי עלמא לא פליגי דחייב כי פליגי באונסין דשואל מאי לפיכך דרבי עקיבא הכי מבעי ליה למתנא ר"ע אומר לא ישתמש בהן ואנא ידענא דכיון דלא ישתמש בהן לאו שואל הוי ואינו חייב באחריותן ° לפיכך דרבי עקיבא למה לי משום לפיכך דרבי טרפון ולפיכך דרבי טרפון למה לי [ג]הכי קאמר כיון דשרו ליה רבנן לאשתמושי בגוייהו כמאן דאישתמש בגוייהו דמי וחייב באחריותן והא אבדו קתני כדרבה

## רש"י

**אלא.** משום שכר שימוש מעות אבל שכר שמירת מלוה דנימא מגו דלא בעי למיתב ריפתא לעניא דהעוסק במלוה פטור מן המלוה לא מחייבינן ליה: **כשנשתמש.** לאו דוקא אלא משום שכר שימוש קאמר מפני שמותר להשתמש בהן: **כשומר חנם.** ואינו חייב אלא בפשיעה: **כשומר שכר.** וחייב בגניבה ואבידה דשומר שכר מלוה הוא דהעוסק במלוה פטור מן המלוה: **כולי עלמא לא פליגי דמחייב.** כדין שומר שכר: **מאי לפיכך דר"ע.** כיון דאמר לא ישתמש מהיכא תיסק אדעתין לחיוביה דאיצטריך למימר אינו חייב:

## תוספות

**והוי שואל עלייהו.** תימה דהוה ליה למימר והוה לוה עלייהו ואם נאמר דאם באו בעלים קודם שהוציאם חייב להחזיר אותם מעות עצמם ולא אחרים הוה א"ש דקרי ליה שואל אך אי אפשר לומר כן דבפרק המפקיד (לקמן דף מג.) פריך אי נאנסו חייב מאי אריא הוציא כי לא הוציא נמי והשתא אי חייב להחזיר הן עצמן כשיתבע הגזבר אם כן לא קנאם השולחני בשלא הוציאם ולא מעל כדאמר פרק השואל (לקמן דף צט.) לא בקע בו לא מעל כיון שהמשאיל יכול לחזור בו וא"כ מאי פריך כי לא הוציא נמי אלא ודאי אפילו אם אותן המעות עדיין בעין אין צריך להחזיר הן עצמן וי"ל דנקט שואל משום דנקט אונסין דכתיב בקרא גבי שואל וגם לפי שמזכיר שומר חנם ושומר שכר. ר"ח וה"ג פסקו דהלכה כרב יוסף מההיא דאין בין המודר (נדרים דף לג:) דקאמר ומחזיר לו אבידתו חד אמר דוקא מדיר למודר אבל מודר למדיר לא משום דקא מתהני פרוטה דרב יוסף וחד אמר פרוטה דרב יוסף לא שכיחא ש"מ דכולהו אית להו דרב יוסף ואין זו ראיה דגם רבה מודה דבשעה שמתעסק באבידה שפטור מלמיתב רפתא לעניים אלא דס"ל דלא שכיחא שיבא עני בשעה שמתעסק בה לצורכה ואין סברא שיהא שומר שכר בעבור זה כיון דלא שכיח דבשעה שהאבידה בביתו ואינו מתעסק בה פשיטא דאף לרב יוסף אינו פטור מלמיתב רפתא לעני שהרי אדם שלבוש ציצית או שיש לו תפילין בראשו וכי יפטר מכל המצות והא דלקמן (דף לא.) מוקי רבא קרא (א) דוהשב תשיבם לגינתו המשתמרת וקמ"ל דלא בעינן דעת בעלים כדמוקי רב יוסף בפרק הכונס (ב"ק דף נז. ושם) דרבה מוקי לה בשאינה משתמרת שמירה מעולה כמו בביתו ומייתי ראיה מינה דשומר אבידה כשומר חנם הוי אין ראיה דהלכה כרב יוסף דרבה גופיה הדר ביה כשתירץ לו רב יוסף דקמ"ל דלא בעינן דעת בעלים ומוקי לה בגינתו המשתמרת דהא בקרא שור ושה כתיב ומודה רבה בבעלי חיים דהוי עלייהו שומר שכר דאנקטינהו נגרי ברייתא וכשרולה להביא ראיה לדבריו ולא ידע שינויא דרב יוסף היה צריך לדחוק ולהעמיד בכפותים ועוד דוחק אחר דהוי מוקי קרא לגינתו שאינה משתמרת ואשמועינן קרא דהוי שומר חנם ולרבה אית ליה מסברא דהוי שומר חנם דלא מטי הנאה לידו ועוד [ג] י"ל דלקמן ה"פ היכי דמי אי דלא מינטרא למר כדאית ליה מפשיעה ולמר כדאית ליה מגניבה ואבידה אמאי פטור ואי דמנטרא למר כדאית ליה ולמר כדאית ליה וכו' ושלהי האומנין (לקמן דף פא: ושם) דאמר ר"א ישבע שאבד המשכון ויטול מעותיו ר"ע אומר אבד המשכון אבדו מעותיו ומוקי מתני' דהלוהו על המשכון שומר שכר דלא כר"א ומסיק דפליגי בשומר אבידה וקאמר לימא דרב יוסף תנאי היא ופרש"י דרבה ודאי תנאי היא דלא מצי סבר כר"ע אם כן משמע דאין הלכה כרבה דהוי כר"א דשמותי הוא וגם דמתניתי' לא אתיא כוותיה וי"ל דרבה ודאי לאו תנאי היא ואפילו לר"ע משום מלוה לא הוי שומר שכר וטעמא דר"ע דאמר אבדו מעותיו כדשמואל דאפילו בדלא שוי שיעור זוזי אבדו כל מעותיו דהוי כאילו פי' שאם יאבד המשכון שיאבדו מעותיו ור"א לית ליה דשמואל ואפילו שוי שיעור זוזי לא אבדו מעותיו אלא לרב יוסף כי נמי מוקי פלוגתייהו בדשמואל לא קאי ר' אליעזר כוותיה לפי מה שמדמה עתה במסקנא מלוה על המשכון לשומר אבידה שהוא פוטר את המלוה באבידה אלמא לא הוי שומר שכר ומשני דאתי מלתיה דרב יוסף אפי' כר"א ותדע דלא מצינו למימר דרבה לא מצי סבר כר"ע דהא בשמעתין משמע דכולהו סברי דרבה ולר"ע נמי הוי שומר חנם והא דתנן פרק שבועת הדיינין (שבועות דף מד. ושם) המלוה על המשכון ואבד המשכון שחייב באבידה מה שהמשכון יתר על החוב אליבא דרבה מבעיא לן לאוקמה באבדה בפשיעה דלא הוי ביה אלא שומר חנם דמה שכנגד החוב מפסיד אפילו לא אבד בפשיעה מטעמא דשמואל ואין זה דוחק דה"נ כי בעי גמרא מעיקרא לאוקמה פלוגתא דר"א ור' עקיבא בדשמואל או בדר' יצחק ולא היה מדמה לשומר אבידה צריך נמי לאוקמה מתני' דשבועות דמיחייב לשלם באבדה מה שהמשכון יתר על החוב באבדה בפשיעה דמטעם דשמואל או דר' יצחק אין לחייב המלוה באבידת המשכון אלא במה שכנגד החוב ולדרבה מפ' האומנין (לקמן דף פב. ושם) יש להוכיח דהלכה כרבה דאי הלכה כרב יוסף אמאי מוקי גמרא אלא מחוורתא מתניתין דלא כר"א לוקמה באין מלוה צריך למשכון דהוי שומר שכר אפי' לר"א ופלוגתייהו במלוה צריך למשכון אלא ודאי משום דהלכה כרבה ואין הלכה כרב יוסף ולדידיה לא מצי לאוקמא מתניתין כר"א ועוד ראיה מפרק המפקיד (לקמן דף מג. ושם) דרב נחמן סבר נאנסו לא אלמא ס"ל דבהנאה שמותר להשתמש לא הוי אלא שומר שכר והיינו כרבה דלרב יוסף הוי שואל ואין לומר דהכא דהוי שומר אבידה דבלא היתר תשמיש הוי שומר שכר השתא דשרו ליה לאשתמושי בהו הוי שואל אבל התם דלא מיירי באבידה משום הנאת היתר תשמיש לבד לא היא כיון דבשביל היתר תשמיש לבד לא הוי אלא שומר שכר כרב נחמן א"כ בשביל שיש לו עוד פרוטה דרב יוסף משום שמירת אבידה אין סברא שיהא לו דין שואל דאטו אם מוסיפין שכר לשומר יהיה לו דין שואל ועוד דקי"ל כרבה בר [ג] משדה ענין ומחצה וליכא למימר דוקא במילי דבבא בתרא כדמפרש בתשובות דרב למה דהא אמר פרק מי שאחזו (גיטין דף עד: ושם ד"ה הא) והא קי"ל כרבה ולא קאמר בהא דהוה משמע בהא ולא במילי אחרינא כדקאמר על רשב"ג ובפרק מי שהוליאוהו (עירובין דף נב:) בשמעתין דהחזיק בדרך מתיישבת ההלכה יותר במה שהלכה כרבה לגבי דרב יוסף כדפי' שם רש"י ובסדר תנאים ואמוראים פוסק דרבה ורב יוסף הלכה כרבה בר משדה ענין ומחצה וכל רבותינו שוין דבשאר דברים סתמא הלכה כרבה אי ליכא הוכחה כרב יוסף [ד]: **לפיכך** דרבי טרפון למה לי. בשלמא לרבה דלפיכך דר"ע אשמועינן לאפוקי דרב יוסף מצינו למימר דלפיכך דרבי טרפון משום לפיכך דר"ע אי נמי גם לפיכך דר"ט אתי למידק נמי דדוקא משום דמותר להשתמש חייב אבל אסור להשתמש פטור לאפוקי דרב יוסף אבל לרב יוסף מאי לפיכך וקשה דמאי בעי מאי לפיכך הלא חדוש גדול השמיענו דמעיקרא אמרינן דבמה שמותר להשתמש לא הוי אלא שומר שכר ולא כשואל דהא אבדו קתני דמשמע סתם אבידה בלא אונס והשתא מבעי לן למימר דמחמת היתר תשמיש הוי כשואל ואבדו היינו שטבע ספינתו בים ועוד דבפרק המפקיד (לקמן דף מג. ושם) אצטריך מתני' לאשמועינן דמחמת היתר תשמיש הוי שומר שכר לרב נחמן דאמר נאנסו לא גבי מפקיד מעות אצל (ג) חנוני דקתני צרורים לא ישתמש בהן לפיכך אם אבדו אינו חייב והא מלתא דפשיטא היא דאינו חייב באבידה כיון דשומר חנם הוא אלא קיפא איצטריכא ליה לאשמועינן דמותרין להשתמש בהן לפיכך אם אבדו חייב באחריותן והוי שומר שכר לרב נחמן דאמר נאנסו לא וכיון דאפילו למיהוי שומר שכר מחמת היתר תשמיש אצטריך לאשמועינן כ"ש הכא דאמר דהוי שואל דלאו מלתא דפשיטא הוא דאצטריך שפיר לאשמועינן אלא י"ל דלאו קושיא הוא אלא פירושא בעלמא הוא:

## עין משפט נר מצוה

קכב א מיי' פי"ג מהלכות גזילה ואבידה הלכה י סמג עשין עד טוש"ע ח"מ סי' רסז סעיף טז:
קכג ב ג מיי' שם הל' יז סמג שם טוש"ע ח"מ שם סעיף כה:

## רבינו חננאל

ותאכיל לנשארים דקא מיכליא אלא מכור הכל: מה יהיה בדמים ר' טרפון אומר ישתמש בהן לפיכך אם אבדו חייב באחריותן ורבי עקיבא אומר לא ישתמש בהן וכו' עד כאן לא פליגי אלא בנשתמש בהן אבל אם לא נשתמש בהן דברי הכל פטור. לימא תהוי תיובתא דרב יוסף דאיתמר בפ' הכונס צאן לדיר שומר אבידה רבה אמר כשומר חנם ונשבע על הכל. רב יוסף אמר כשומר שכר שנשבע על האונסין ומשלם הגניבה ואבידה. ודחי רב יוסף בגניבה ואבידה כולי עלמא לא פליגי דחייב כשומר שכר כי פליגי באונסין ר' טרפון סבר אע"ג דבאבידה עצמה הוה לי' שומר שכר כיון דשרי ליה לאישתמושי בדמיה נעשה עליה כשואל וחייב גם על האונסין. ור' עקיבא סבר לא שרו ליה רבנן לאישתמושי בדמי אבידה הלכך לא הוי עלייהו אלא שומר שכר. ואקשי' עליה אי הכי למה ליה לר' עקיבא למיתנא לפיכך אי אמרת בגניבה ואבידה פליגי ר' טרפון סבר כיון דשרו ליה לאישתמושי בהו הוי ליה כשומר שכר עלייהו וחייב בגניבה ואבידה. ור' עקיבא סבר לא שרו ליה רבנן לאישתמושי בהו וכשומר חנם הוא עליהו שאם אבדו פטור וכל שכן נאנסו שפטור אלא אי אמרת בגניבה ואבידה דברי הכל חייב כי פליגי באונסין לתני רבי עקיבא אומר לא ישתמש בהן וממילא ידענא דכיון דלא שרי לאישתמושי בהו לא הוי עלייהו אלא כשומר שכר אבל שואל לא הוי עלייהו לפיכך דקתני מאי אתא לאשמועינן ופרקי' ודאי ר' עקיבא לא הוי צריך למיתניה לפיכך מיהו איידי דתנא ר' טרפון לפיכך תנא איהו נמי לפיכך ומקשי' תוב לפיכך דר' טרפון נמי למה לי ופריק רב יוסף צריכא והכי קתני כיון דשרו ליה רבנן לאישתמושי בהו הוה ליה עלייהו כשואל לפיכך אע"פ שלא נשתמש בהן חייב עליהן כשואל. ומקשי' עליה אי הכי לא הוה תני לפיכך אם אבדו חייב בהן דמשמע שומר שכר הוא חשוב באבידה אלא הוה ליה למיתנא לפיכך אם נאנסו חייב בהן דמשמע דשואל הוי עליהן. ופריק רב יוסף האי אבדו דקתני נאנסו הוא. ומקשי' ומי קרו לאבדו נאנסו (היו) [אין] כדרבה דאמר בפ' הזהב הלכה שומר חנם אין נשבע וכו' נגנבו בלסטים מזוין אבדו שטבעה ספינתו בים:
אמר

## מסורת הש"ס

בבא קמא נו., לקמן ..., שבועות מד., נדרים ..., ג) ר"ל כעין צ"ל והכל ...דין אחד, מהרש"ל, [בבא בתרא קיד., ...מג:], ד) [ועיין תוס' ...ילה כט: ד"ה והלכתא וכו'].

## הגהות הב"ח

...) תוס' ד"ה והוי וכו' ...א דלקמן מוקי רבא קרא ...השב תשיבם: (ג) ד"ה ...יכך וכו' גבי מפקיד ...עות אצל שולחני דקתני:

## גליון הש"ס

...' לפיכך דר"ע. כעין נדה דף ט ע"א ודף ס ע"ב:

## ליקוטי רש"י

...ומר אבידה. שמלא ...בידה והכניסה אל תוך ...תו כדכתיב (דברים כב) ...ספתו אל תוך ביתך [לקמן פב.].

בזוכית

אֶלָּא כְּשֶׁנִּשְׁתַּמֵּשׁ בָּהּ – as he had the right to **use [the money]**,[1] אֲבָל לֹא נִשְׁתַּמֵּשׁ בָּהּ – but if **he did not** have the right to **use [the money]**, they would both agree that אִם אָבְדוּ פָּטוּר – **if it were lost, he would be exempt** from paying.[2] It follows that in a case where one holds the found object itself for the owner, the finder should be exempt from paying for its loss.[3]

The Gemara asks:

לֵימָא תֶּיהֱוֵי תְּיוּבְתָּא דְּרַב יוֹסֵף – **Shall we say that this** inference regarding R' Tarfon's and R' Akiva's position **poses a refutation to Rav Yosef's** view that one who finds and cares for any lost object is held liable for its loss?[4] דְּאִתְּמַר – For it has been stated: שׁוֹמֵר אֲבֵידָה – **The custodian of a lost object:** רַבָּה אָמַר כְּשׁוֹמֵר חִנָּם – **Rabbah says he is like an unpaid custodian,** who is not held liable for loss. רַב יוֹסֵף אָמַר כְּשׁוֹמֵר שָׂכָר – **Rav Yosef says he is like a paid custodian,** who is held liable for loss.[5] Rav Yosef's position would seem to be inconsistent with the views of both R' Tarfon and R' Akiva! – **?** –

The Gemara answers:

אָמַר לָךְ רַב יוֹסֵף – **Rav Yosef would say to you:** בִּגְנֵיבָה וַאֲבֵידָה – **With respect to theft and loss,** דְּכוּלֵּי עָלְמָא לֹא פְּלִיגֵי דְּחַיָּיב – **everyone** [both R' Tarfon and R' Akiva] **agrees that [the finder] is held liable** because he is certainly considered at least a paid custodian.[6] כִּי פְּלִיגֵי בְּאוֹנְסִין דְּשׁוֹאֵל – **Where they disagree is in regard to the accidents for** which only **a borrower** is held liable.[7] רַבִּי טַרְפוֹן סָבַר – **R' Tarfon holds** that שָׁרוּ לֵיהּ רַבָּנָן לְאִשְׁתַּמּוּשֵׁי בְּגַוַּייהוּ – **the Rabbis permitted [the finder] to use [the money]** from the sale of the object, וַהֲוָה לֵיהּ שׁוֹאֵל עֲלַייהוּ – **and he is** therefore classified **a borrower in regard to it;** thus, he pays even for accidents that befall it. וְרַבִּי עֲקִיבָא סָבַר – **But R' Akiva holds** that לֹא שָׁרוּ לֵיהּ רַבָּנָן לְאִשְׁתַּמּוּשֵׁי בְּגַוַּייהוּ – **the Rabbis did not permit [the finder] to use [the money];** הִלְכָּךְ לֹא הָוֵי שׁוֹאֵל עֲלַייהוּ – **therefore, he is not** classified as **a borrower in regard to it,** and he does not pay for accidents.[8]

The Gemara questions Rav Yosef's explanation:

אִי הָכִי – **If so,** that R' Tarfon and R' Akiva dispute only whether he is held liable for accidents, like a borrower, לְפִיכָךְ דְּאָמַר רַבִּי עֲקִיבָא לָמָּה לִי – **why** is there **any need for R' Akiva to say: "THEREFORE,** if the money is stolen or lost he is not responsible"?

The Gemara explains its question:

אִי אָמְרַת בִּשְׁלָמָא בִּגְנֵיבָה וַאֲבֵידָה הוּא דִּפְלִיגֵי – **If you say that they disagree with respect to theft and loss,** the liabilities of a paid custodian, **it is understandable** that הַיְינוּ דְּקָתָנֵי רַבִּי עֲקִיבָא אוֹמֵר לֹא יִשְׁתַּמֵּשׁ בָּהֶן – **this is why the Mishnah states: R' AKIVA SAYS HE MAY NOT USE [THE MONEY],** and adds: לְפִיכָךְ אִם אָבְדוּ אֵינוֹ חַיָּיב בְּאַחֲרָיוּתָן – **THEREFORE, IF IT IS LOST HE IS NOT RESPONSIBLE FOR IT.** סָלְקָא דַּעְתָּךְ אָמֵינָא – Because **you might** otherwise **have thought to say** that, quite apart from the question of using the money, שׁוֹמֵר שָׂכָר הָוֵי כִּדְרַב יוֹסֵף – **[the finder] is** considered **a paid custodian – in accordance with Rav Yosef's** view,[9] וּבִגְנֵיבָה וַאֲבֵידָה מִחַיֵּיב – **and** that **he is** therefore **held liable for theft and loss** even if he is not permitted to use the money. קָא מַשְׁמַע לָן לְפִיכָךְ – The sentence beginning with **"THEREFORE"** is thus added to **inform us** that הַשְׁתָּא דְּאָמְרַת לֹא יִשְׁתַּמֵּשׁ בָּהֶן – **now that you** [R' Akiva] **say he may not use [the money]** שׁוֹמֵר שָׂכָר לֹא הָוֵי – **he is *not*** considered **a paid custodian,** because we reject Rav Yosef's reasoning, וְלֹא מִחַיֵּיב בִּגְנֵיבָה וַאֲבֵידָה – **and he is** therefore **not liable for theft or loss.**[10] אֶלָּא אִי אָמְרַת – **But if you say** that בִּגְנֵיבָה וַאֲבֵידָה – **with respect to theft and loss** דְּכוּלֵּי עָלְמָא לֹא פְּלִיגֵי דְּחַיָּיב – **everyone agrees that [the finder]** is **held liable,** because both Tannaim accept Rav Yosef's reasoning, כִּי פְּלִיגֵי בְּאוֹנְסִין דְּשׁוֹאֵל – and **that they disagree** only **with respect to the accidents**

NOTES

1. Literally: except where he used [the money]. The critical factor, however, is not the use of the money but the benefit the finder derives from having the right to use it – whether or not he actually exercises this right (*Rashi*). According to R' Tarfon, the finder has the right to use the money and he is therefore considered a paid custodian [שׁוֹמֵר שָׂכָר] for it. A paid custodian (*shomer*) is held liable for the loss of an object in his care (Mishnah below, 93a; see introduction to chapter 3). According to R' Akiva, the finder is forbidden to use the money, and since he derives no benefit from having it in his care, he is considered an unpaid custodian [שׁוֹמֵר חִנָּם]. An unpaid custodian does not pay for the loss of the object in his care [unless he was negligent in caring for it] (*Rashi*).

2. I.e. if not for the possible right to use the money, all would agree that the finder is considered an unpaid *shomer* (custodian), who does not pay for the loss of the object in his care.

3. Since all agree that the finder may not use the lost object itself, they would agree that he is exempt from paying for its loss. The dispute between R' Tarfon and R' Akiva is only in regard to the money obtained from the sale of the lost object.

4. Rav Yosef's view is based on the fact that the finder of any lost object derives benefit from it in the following fashion. There is a rule that while a person fulfills one mitzvah he is exempt from performing other mitzvos. Therefore, while one is engaged in caring for a lost object, one is not obligated to give charity to a poor man who comes to the door at that moment. This represents a potential savings for the finder, and he is therefore classified as a paid *shomer* [custodian] (*Rashi*).

*Tosafos* note that one is exempt from other mitzvos only while one is actually *occupied* in performing a mitzvah. If it is possible to perform many mitzvos simultaneously, e.g. to wear tzitzis and tefillin, or give charity while there is a lost object merely lying in one's possession, one is obligated to fulfill them all. Thus, it is only at the moment that one is engaged in caring for the object that one benefits by being free from the obligation to give charity. [See Mishnah on 29b for examples of what a finder must do to care for a lost object.]

This explains why Rabbah rejects Rav Yosef's view. It is unlikely that a poor man will come knocking at precisely the moment the finder is engaged with the lost object. The slight possibility of this happening is not, in Rabbah's opinion, sufficient to recast the finder as a paid *shomer* (*Tosafos*).

5. A שׁוֹמֵר חִנָּם, *unpaid custodian,* is liable for the loss of the object in his care only if it occurred through his negligence. A שׁוֹמֵר שָׂכָר, *paid custodian*, is liable for theft or loss even if he was not at fault (*Rashi*).

6. According to Rav Yosef, even R' Akiva [who does not allow the finder to use the money] agrees with his view that a person holding a found object is classified a paid *shomer*. The disagreement between R' Tarfon and R' Akiva does not concern theft and loss – both agree that the finder is liable for them. Their disagreement concerns the finder's liability for the money in cases in which even a paid *shomer* is exempt and only a borrower is liable.

7. A borrower is held liable not only for the theft or loss of the object in his care, but even for its damage or destruction through accidents beyond his control (Mishnah 93a; see introduction to chapter 3).

8. The Mishnah would now be understood as follows: R' Tarfon says he is permitted to use the money; therefore, if an accident occurs, he is liable. R' Akiva says he is not permitted to use it; therefore, if an accident occurs, he is not liable.

9. That the custodian of any lost object is treated as a paid custodian.

10. There are two reasons why the finder might be considered a paid *shomer* and held liable for theft and loss. One is that he has the use of the money (R' Tarfon's reason), and the other is that he benefits by not having to give charity while he is caring for the money (Rav Yosef's reason). Were R' Akiva to say only that the finder may not use the money, it would still not be clear that he exempts him from paying for the theft or loss of the money. He might well consider him a paid *shomer* for Rav Yosef's reason! Thus, it was necessary for the Mishnah to add that "therefore, he is not responsible," to indicate that he rejects Rav Yosef's reason as well. This explanation of the Mishnah, however, is obviously not acceptable to Rav Yosef.

contradiction **between** the first Baraisa's ruling that **ganders and roosters** must be kept up to thirty days **and** the second Baraisa's ruling that **ganders and roosters** are kept for only three days. – ? –

The Gemara answers:

**עֲגָלִים וּסְיָיחִין אַעֲגָלִים וּסְיָיחִין לֹא קַשְׁיָא** – The first Baraisa's ruling regarding **calves and young donkeys does not contradict** the second Baraisa's ruling regarding **calves and young donkeys,** **הָא דְרַעְיָא וְהָא דְפִטּוּמָא** – because **this** Baraisa that requires one to care for them for up to three months refers to animals **that** can be left to **graze, whereas this** Baraisa that requires one to do so for only thirty days refers to animals **that** need to **be fattened** from feed, because of the lack of pasture.[31] **אַוָּוזִין וְתַרְנְגוֹלִין אַאַוָּוזִין וְתַרְנְגוֹלִין נַמִּי לֹא קַשְׁיָא** – Similarly, the first Baraisa's ruling regarding **ganders and roosters also does not contradict** the second Baraisa's ruling regarding **ganders and roosters,** **הָא בְּרַבְרְבֵי הָא בְּזוּטְרֵי** – because **this** Baraisa that requires one to care for them for only three days **refers to large ones,** which eat a lot, whereas **this** Baraisa that says for thirty days **refers to small ones,** which eat little and are inexpensive to maintain.

A quote from the Mishnah:

**וְשֶׁאֵינוֹ עוֹשֶׂה וְאוֹכֵל** – AND SOMETHING THAT DOES NOT WORK BU EATS. . .

The Gemara quotes a Baraisa that elaborates the law of th Mishnah:

**תָּנוּ רַבָּנָן** – **The Rabbis taught** in a Baraisa: "וַהֲשֵׁבֹתוֹ לוֹ" – Th verse states: AND YOU SHALL RETURN IT TO HIM, אֵה הֵיאָךְ **תְּשִׁיבֶנּוּ לוֹ** – which is interpreted homiletically to mean CONSIDE HOW YOU MAY RETURN IT TO HIM. **שֶׁלֹּא יַאֲכִיל עֵגֶל לַעֲגָלִים וּסְיָח לִסְיָיחִין** – This teaches THAT ONE SHOULD NOT FEED the value of CALF TO CALVES, OR the value of A YOUNG DONKEY TO YOUN DONKEYS,[32] **אַוְּוזָא לְאַוָּוזִין וְתַרְנְגוֹל לְתַרְנְגוֹלִין** – and not the valu of A GANDER TO GANDERS, OR the value of A ROOSTER T ROOSTERS.

The Gemara cites the final section of the Mishnah:

**מַה יְּהֵא בְּדָמִים רַבִּי טַרְפוֹן אוֹמֵר יִשְׁתַּמֵּשׁ וכו'** – WHAT IS TO BE don WITH THE MONEY after selling the lost object? R' TARFON SAYS [THE FINDER MAY] USE IT etc.

**עַד כָּאן לֹא פְּלִיגִי** – **They** [R' Tarfon and R' Akiva] **do not disagre** about the finder's liability **except insofar**

NOTES

31. Where pasture is available, little expense is incurred maintaining these animals. One must therefore keep them for up to three months before selling them. In times or places where pasture is scarce, the animals must be given feed, which is expensive. As a result, one tends them for only thirty days before selling them (*Rashi*). Although some small expense is nonetheless incurred, it does not exceed the limit set by the Baraisa below (see *Ritva*).

32. I.e. if one found a group of calves or young donkeys, he should not sell one of them and use the proceeds to pay for feeding the others (*Rabbeinu Chananel, Rashba*), because he has an obligation to return each and every one of them (*Nimukei Yosef; R' Yehonasan,* cited in *Shitah Mekubetzes*). Rather, he should sell the entire group and save the money for the owner (*Rabbeinu Chananel*).

עין משפט
נר מצוה

קח א ב מיי׳ פי״ג מהל׳ גזלה ואבדה הלכה ט סמג עשין עד טוש״ע ח״מ סי׳ רסז סעיף ג:
קט ג מיי׳ שם הל׳ א סמג שם:
קי ד מיי׳ שם הל׳ ג סמג שם טוש״ע ח״מ סי׳ רסז סעיף ה:
קיא ה ו מיי׳ שם הל׳ ג ועיין בהשגות ובמגיד משנה סמג שם טוש״ע שם סעיף ה:
קיב ז מיי׳ שם הלכה ד טוש״ע שם סעיף ו:
קיג ח טוש״ע ח״מ סי׳ כט סעיף א:
קיד ט מיי׳ פי״ג מהל׳ גזלה ואבדה הל׳ טו סמג שם טוש״ע ח״מ סי׳ רסז סעיף כג:
קטו י כ מיי׳ שם הל׳ יח טוש״ע שם סעיף כה:
קטז ל מיי׳ שם הל׳ טו טוש״ע שם סעיף כג:
קיז מ מיי׳ שם הל׳ טז טוש״ע שם סעיף כג:
קיח נ מיי׳ שם הל׳ טו ועיין בהשגות ובמגיד משנה טוש״ע שם סעיף כג:
קיט ס מיי׳ שם הל׳ טז טוש״ע שם סעיף כד:
קכ ע מיי׳ שם טוש״ע שם סעיף כג:
קכא פ מיי׳ שם טוש״ע שם סעיף כד:

אתיא לאחלופי בראשון הא קא אתי רגל שלישי ת״ר בראשונה כל מי שמצא אבידה היה מכריז עליה שלשה רגלים ואחר רגל אחרון שבעת ימים כדי שילך שלשה ויחזור שלשה ויכריז יום אחד [א]משחרב בית המקדש שיבנה במהרה בימינו התקינו שיהו מכריזים בבתי כנסיות ובבתי מדרשות ומשרבו האנסים התקינו שיהו מודיעין לשכיניו ולמיודעיו ודיו מאי משרבו האנסין [ב]דאמרי אבידתא למלכא רבי אמי אשכח אודייא דדינרי חזייה ההוא א) בר נש דקא מירתת א״ל זיל שקול לנפשך דלאו פרסאי אנן דאמרי אבידתא למלכא ת״ר [ג]אבן טוען היתה בירושלים כל מי שאבדה לו אבידה נפנה לשם וכל מי שמוצא אבידה נפנה לשם זה עומד ומכריז וזה עומד ונותן סימנין ונוטלה וזו היא ששנינו ג) צאו וראו אם נמחת אבן הטוען: **מתני׳** [ד]אמר את האבידה ולא אמר סימניה לא יתן לו [ה]והרמאי אע״פ שאמר סימניה לא יתן לו שנאמר א) עד דרוש אחיך אותו עד שתדרוש את אחיך אם רמאי הוא אם אינו רמאי: **גמ׳** אתמר רב יהודה אמר אבידתא מכריז ור״נ אמר גלימא מכריז רב יהודה אמר אבידתא מכריז דאי אמרת גלימא מכריז חיישינן לרמאי ר״נ אמר גלימא מכריז לרמאי לא חיישינן דא״כ אין לדבר סוף תנן אמר את האבידה ולא אמר את סימניה ה״ז לא יתן לו אי אמרת בשלמא אבידתא מכריז הא קמ״ל אע״ג דאמר גלימא כי לא אמר סימנין לא מהדרינן ליה אלא אי אמרת גלימא מכריז אמר איהו גלימא ואמר איהו גלימא צריכא למימר כי לא אמר סימנין לא מהדרינן ליה אמר רב ספרא לעולם גלימא מכריז אמר איהו גלימא ואמר איהו סימנין ומאי לא אמר את סימניה [ו]לא אמר סימנין מובהקין דידה: והרמאי אע״פ שאמר את סימניה ה״ז לא יתן לו: ת״ר בראשונה כל מי שאבדה לו אבידה היה נותן סימנין ונוטלה משרבו הרמאין [ז]התקינו שיהו אומרים לו צא והבא עדים דלאו רמאי את וטול כי הא דאבוה דרב פפא אירכס ליה חמרא ואשכחוה אתא לקמיה דרבה בר רב הונא אמר ליה זיל אייתי סהדי דלאו רמאי את וטול אזל אייתי סהדי אמר להו ידעיתון ביה דרמאי הוא אמרו ליה אין אמר להו אנא רמאה אנא אמרו ליה אנן לאו רמאי את קאמרינן אמר רבה בר רב הונא [ח]מסתברא לא מייתי איניש חובתא לנפשיה: **מתני׳** [ט]כל דבר שעושה ואוכל יעשה ויאכל ודבר שאין עושה ואוכל ימכר שנאמר א) והשבותו לו ראה היאך תשיבנו לו מה יהא בדמים ר״ט אומר [י]ישתמש בהן לפיכך אם אבדו [כ]חייב באחריותן ר״ע אומר לא ישתמש בהן לפיכך אם אבדו אין חייב באחריותן: **גמ׳** ולעולם אמר רב נחמן ג) אמר שמואל עד י״ב חדש תניא נמי הכי [ל]כל דבר שעושה ואוכל כגון פרה וחמור מטפל בהן עד י״ב חדש מכאן ואילך שם דמיהן ומניחן [מ]עגלים וסייחין מטפל בהן שלשה חדשים מכאן ואילך שם דמיהן ומניחן אווזין ותרנגולין מטפל בהם שלשים יום מכאן ואילך שם דמיהן ומניחן אמר רב נחמן בר יצחק תרנגולת כבהמה גסה תניא נמי הכי [נ]תרנגולת ובהמה גסה מטפל בהן שנים עשר חודש מכאן ואילך שם דמיהן ומניחן עגלים וסייחין מטפל בהן ל׳ יום מכאן ואילך שם דמיהן ומניחן [ס]אווזין ותרנגולין וכל דבר שטיפולו מרובה משכרו מטפל בהן שלשה ימים מכאן ואילך שם דמיהן ומניחן קשיא עגלים וסייחין אעגלים וסייחין אווזין ותרנגולין אאווזין ותרנגולין עגלים וסייחין אעגלים וסייחין לא קשיא [ע]הא דרעיא והא דפטומא אווזין ותרנגולין אאווזין ותרנגולין נמי לא קשיא [פ]הא ברברבי הא בזוטרי: ושאינו עושה ואוכל: תנו רבנן והשבותו לו ראה היאך תשיבנו לו שלא יאכיל עגל לעגלים וסיח לסייחין אווזא לאווזין ותרנגול לתרנגולין: מה יהא בדמים רבי טרפון אומר ישתמש וכו׳: עד כאן לא פליגי אלא

**אבן** טוען. מפרש בירושלמי כשם שהאבן אינה יכולה למחות כך אין יכולים להתפלל על רוב טובה: **שם** דמיהן. לקמן ה) גבי עסקא דרב ספרא אפרש בע״ה: **עד** כאן לא פליגי אלא בנשתמש בהן. לאו דוקא נשתמש דאם נשתמש לר״ע נמי חייב באחריותן כיון דלדידיה אסור להשתמש א״כ הוי שולח יד בפקדון ואפילו החזיר אין בכך כלום דהא ר״ע סבר בפרק המפקיד (לקמן דף מג:) דבעינן דעת בעלים אלא ולאי נשתמש לאו דוקא כדפרישית אלא בשכר שמוש שמותר להשתמש קאמר לרבי טרפון דאית ליה דמותר להשתמש חייב באחריותן דההוא הנאה דלאי מיתרמי ליה זבינא שקיל להו וחבין בהו הוי עלייהו שומר שכר ולר״ע דאסור להשתמש בהן פטור אבל אם לא היה מותר להשתמש היה פטור לכ״ע והיינו כרבה: והוי

ד) (אתי לאחלופי בשני. שמא יש שהוא סבור שאמר רגל שני:) אודיא דדינרי. כלי מלא זהובים: וזו היא ששנינו. במסכת תענית (דף יט.) בחוני המעגל: צאו וראו אם נמחת אבן טוען. אם נכסת בגשמים שגבהו הגשמים למעלה הימנו יש גשמים יותר מדאי ואתפלל עליהם שילכו: חיישינן לרמאי. שמא שמע האובד מתאונן בין שכיניו טליתי נאבדה וזה יודע את סימניה וכשישמע את מוצאה מכריז טלית מצאתי יקום ויתן סימניה הלכך אבידתא מכריז ואינו נותן לב לומר טלית זו אבדתי ואלו סימניה: אין לדבר סוף. דהשתא נמי מסיק אדעתיה ואמר אם טלית היא שמצאת אלו סימניה: אי אמרת בשלמא אבידתא מכריז. ולא מזכיר שם החפץ אצטריך תנא לאשמועינן דאע״ג דאמר האי טלית אבדתי צריך ליתן סימנין: אמרו ליה אין. כסבורין שאמר להן ידעיתון ביה דלאו רמאי הוא שכך היה לו לשואלן: מסתברא. שזה היה דעתן מתחילה ואין כאן משום מגיד וחוזר ומגיד: לא מייתי איניש חובה לנפשיה. וכשהביאן לב״ד בטוח היה שלא יעידו חובתו: **מתני׳** כל דבר שעושה ואוכל. אם אבידה זו דבר שיכולין להאכילו את שכר מעשיו כגון שור וחמור יעשה ויאכל ולא ימכור אותו המוצא אם שהו בעליו מלדרשו שכל אדם נוח לו בבהמתו שהכירה בו כבר ולימדה לרצונו: ראה היאך תשיבנו לו. שלא תאכילנו חצי דמיו שא״כ אין זו השבה: לפיכך. מפרש בגמרא: **גמ׳** ולעולם. וכי עד עולם זקוק זה לטפל בטורח שמירה: שם דמיהן. מוכרן ומניח הדמים אצלו: עגלים וסייחין. דקין שאין עושין מלאכה: תרנגולין. זכרים שאין מטילין בצים: כבהמה גסה. שעושה ואוכלת ומטפל בה י״ב חדש דיכול להאכילה דמי בצים: מטפל. אנשמיטרא בלע״ז: הא דרעיא הא דפטומא. הא דקתני שלשה [חדשים] באֶרץ מרעה ובזמן הדשאים שאין טיפולו מרובה והא דקתני ל׳ [יום] בזמן שאין מרעה וצריך לפטמה על אבוסה ממה שבבית שדמיה יקרים: רברבי. [א] אוכלין הרבה הלכך ג׳ ימים דהא אוקימנא בזכרים: שלא יאכיל עגל לעגלים. מן העגלים שנמצא לא יאכיל לו דמי עגל: עד כאן לא פליגי. לענין להתחייב באבידתו:
אלא

מסורת הש״ס

א) נ״א בר רומאד מהר״ס, ב) תענית יט [ג] [גירסת רי״ף ולעול אמר שמואל וגירס הרא״ש אמר רב יהוד אמר שמואל ד) מהרש״ל מ״ז, ה) [ד לג. ד״ה כ״ד].

הגהות הגר״א

[א] רש״י ד״ה רברב כו׳. נ״ב אבל רמב״ם פ להיפך וכן נ״י בשם ר״מ

תורה אור השלם

א) וְאִם לֹא קָרוֹב אָחִי אֵלֶיךָ וְלֹא יְדַעְ וַאֲסַפְתּוֹ אֶל תּוֹךְ בֵּית וְהָיָה עִמְּךָ עַד דְּרֹ אָחִיךָ אֹתוֹ וַהֲשֵׁבֹתוֹ ל [דברים כב, ב]

ליקוטי רש״י

עד דרוש אחיך. ו תעלה בלבבך שיתנהו קודם שידרשהו א דרשהו שלא יהא רמא והשבותו לו. שתהא השבה שלא יאכל בבית כדי דמיו ותתבעם ממ מכאן אמרו כל דב שעושה ואוכל יעשה ויאכ ושאינו עושה ואוכל ימכ [דברים כב, ב]. וסייחי בנו של חמור קרוי סי [רשב״ם ב״ב עח:].

לעזי רש״י

אנשמיטר״א. פירו לטפל, להתעסק.

רבינו חננאל

הגשמים וכו׳. והנה מהלך ט״ו ימים היא. ואסיקנא לא שנא מקדש ראשון ולא שנא מקדש שני לא הטריחו באבידה יותר מדאי ת״ר משחרב בית המקדש התקינו להיות מכריזין בכנסיות ובתי מדרשות משרבו האנסין שאומרין אבדתא למלכא התקינו שיהא מודיע המוצאה לשכניו ולמיודעיו ודיו. פי׳ מהסם מתיירא. ת״ר אבן הטוען היתה בירושלים כל מי שאבדה לו אבידה נפנה לשם וכו׳ פי׳ אבן גבוהה היתה בירושלים והיה כל מוצא אבידה עולה עליה ומכריז וזו היא ששנינו בפרק סדר תעניות השני אמר להן חוני המעגל צאו וראו אם נמחת אבן הטוען. אבקש רחמים שיפסקו הגשמים: **מתני׳** אמר את האבידה ולא אמר את סימניה. אוקמה רב ספרא אליבא דרב נחמן דאמר גלימא מכריז א) כדאמר האבידה וסימניה ומאי לא אמר סימניה דקאמר במתני׳ לא אמר סימנין מובהקין דידה. וסוגיין בעינן דיהיב סימנין מובהקין והוא דאית סהדי דליתיה רמאי. ופשטינן דלא מייתי איניש חובה לנפשיה כדאבוה דרב פפא. תלמוד ארץ ישראל שמע סימניה בהאי כנישתא ואזל לכנישתא אחריתי יהיב סימניה זהו רמאי וכן כיוצא בו: **מתני׳** כל דבר שעושה ואוכל יעשה ואוכל אוקימנא עד י״ב חדש. תניא נמי הכי כל דבר שעושה ואוכל כגון פרה וחמור מטפל בהן כל י״ב חדש מכאן ואילך שם דמיהן ומניחן עגלים וסייחים אם יכולין לרעות מטפל בהן ג׳ חדשים. אוזין ותרנגולין גדולים מטפל בהן ל׳ יום. ותניא אחריתי תרנגולת כבהמה גסה י״ב חדש וכל דבר שטיפולו מרובה משכרו ג׳ ימים. ושאינו עושה ואוכל ימכור שנאמר והשבותו לו ראה היאך תשיבנו לו. שלא יאכיל עגל לעגלים. פי׳ לא תמכור עגל היום

חשק שלמה על ר״ח א) אולי צ״ל בדאמר.

**Mishnah** כָּל דָּבָר שֶׁעוֹשֶׂה וְאוֹכֵל – **Anything that works and eats,** such as an ox or donkey, יַעֲשֶׂה וְיֹאכַל – **should,** if found, be put to **work and** given to **eat** from that which it produces;[21] וְדָבָר שֶׁאֵין עוֹשֶׂה וְאוֹכֵל – **and something that does not work but eats**[22] יִמָּכֵר – **should be sold,** and the money should be held for the owner. שֶׁנֶּאֱמַר: ,,וַהֲשֵׁבֹתוֹ לוֹ'' – **As it says in the verse:**[23] ***And return it to him*** – רְאֵה הֵיאָךְ תְּשִׁיבֶנּוּ לוֹ – **consider how you may return it to him.**[24]

מַה יְּהֵא בַּדָּמִים – **What is to be** done **with the money** that one receives for selling the lost object? רַבִּי טַרְפוֹן אוֹמֵר יִשְׁתַּמֵּשׁ בָּהֶן – **R' Tarfon says: [The finder] may use [the money];** לְפִיכָךְ אִם אָבְדוּ – **therefore, if [the money] is lost** חַיָּיב בְּאַחֲרָיוּתָן – **he is responsible for it.**[25] רַבִּי עֲקִיבָא אוֹמֵר לֹא יִשְׁתַּמֵּשׁ בָּהֶן – **R' Akiva says: He may not use the money;** לְפִיכָךְ אִם אָבְדוּ – **therefore, if [the money] is lost** אֵין חַיָּיב בְּאַחֲרָיוּתָן – **he is not responsible for it.**

**Gemara** The Mishnah taught that a finder must keep and maintain an item that works and eats. The Gemara asks:

וּלְעוֹלָם – Does he have to keep it **forever?**[26]

אָמַר רַב נַחְמָן אָמַר שְׁמוּאֵל – **Rav Nachman said in the name of Shmuel:** עַד י״ב חֹדֶשׁ – For **up to twelve months.**[27]

Rav Nachman's ruling is confirmed from a Baraisa:

תַּנְיָא נַמִּי הָכִי – **A Baraisa has taught this as well:** כָּל דָּבָר שֶׁעוֹשֶׂה וְאוֹכֵל – ANYTHING THAT WORKS AND EATS, כְּגוֹן פָּרָה וַחֲמוֹר – SUCH AS A COW OR DONKEY, מְטַפֵּל בָּהֶן עַד י״ב חֹדֶשׁ – ONE MUST CARE FOR THEM UP TO TWELVE MONTHS; מִכָּאן וְאֵילָךְ שָׁם דְּמֵיהֶן וּמַנִּיחָן – FROM HERE FORWARD, ONE MAY ASSESS THEIR VALUE, sell them, AND PLACE [THEIR MONEY] in his keep.[28] עֲגָלִים וּסְיָיחִין – CALVES AND YOUNG DONKEYS, מְטַפֵּל בָּהֶן שְׁלֹשָׁה חֳדָשִׁים – ONE MUST CARE FOR THEM up to THREE MONTHS;[29] מִכָּאן וְאֵילָךְ שָׁם דְּמֵיהֶן וּמַנִּיחָן – FROM HERE FORWARD, ONE MUST ASSESS THEIR VALUE, sell them, AND PLACE [THEIR MONEY] in his keep. אַוָּוזִין וְתַרְנְגוֹלִין – GANDERS AND ROOSTERS,[30] מְטַפֵּל בָּהֶם שְׁלֹשִׁים יוֹם – ONE MUST CARE FOR THEM up to THIRTY DAYS; מִכָּאן וְאֵילָךְ שָׁם דְּמֵיהֶן וּמַנִּיחָן – FROM HERE FORWARD, ONE MUST ASSESS THEIR VALUE, sell them, AND PLACE [THEIR MONEY] in his keep.

A related ruling:

אָמַר רַב נַחְמָן בַּר יִצְחָק – **Rav Nachman bar Yitzchak said:** תַּרְנְגוֹלֶת כִּבְהֵמָה גַּסָּה – **A hen is** treated **like a large animal** (e.g. a cow or donkey), since one can pay for its upkeep by selling its eggs. Thus, it must be kept up to twelve months.

The Gemara cites a Baraisa in support of Rav Nachman:

תַּנְיָא נַמִּי הָכִי – **A Baraisa has taught this as well:** תַּרְנְגוֹלֶת וּבְהֵמָה גַּסָּה – A HEN AND A LARGE ANIMAL, מְטַפֵּל בָּהֶן שְׁנֵים עָשָׂר חוֹדֶשׁ – ONE MUST CARE FOR THEM up to TWELVE MONTHS; מִכָּאן וְאֵילָךְ שָׁם דְּמֵיהֶן וּמַנִּיחָן – FROM HERE FORWARD, ONE MAY ASSESS THEIR VALUE, sell them, AND PLACE [THEIR MONEY] in his keep. עֲגָלִים וּסְיָיחִין – CALVES AND YOUNG DONKEYS, מְטַפֵּל בָּהֶן ל׳ יוֹם – ONE MUST CARE FOR THEM up to THIRTY DAYS; מִכָּאן וְאֵילָךְ שָׁם דְּמֵיהֶן וּמַנִּיחָן – FROM HERE FORWARD, ONE MUST ASSESS THEIR VALUE, sell them, AND PLACE [THEIR MONEY] in his keep. וְאַוָּזִין וְתַרְנְגוֹלִין וְכָל דָּבָר שֶׁטִּיפּוּלוֹ מְרוּבֶּה מִשְּׂכָרוֹ – GANDERS AND ROOSTERS, AND ANYTHING else WHOSE CARE costs MORE THAN IT EARNS, מְטַפֵּל בָּהֶן שְׁלֹשָׁה יָמִים – ONE MUST CARE FOR THEM up to THREE DAYS; מִכָּאן וְאֵילָךְ שָׁם דְּמֵיהֶן וּמַנִּיחָן – FROM HERE FORWARD, ONE MUST ASSESS THEIR VALUE, sell them, AND PLACE [THEIR MONEY] in his keep.

The Gemara points out two contradictions between this and the previous Baraisa:

קַשְׁיָא עֲגָלִים וּסְיָיחִין אַעֲגָלִים וּסְיָיחִין – **There is a contradiction between** the first Baraisa's ruling that **calves and young donkeys** must be kept for three months, **and** the second Baraisa's ruling that **calves and young donkeys** are kept for only thirty days. אַוָּוזִין וְתַרְנְגוֹלִין אַאַוָּוזִין וְתַרְנְגוֹלִין – There is also

NOTES

21. One who finds a lost object is not required to bear the expense of maintaining it until its owner reclaims it. As the Mishnah will state below, when there is expense in maintaining a found object, the finder should sell it and hold the money for the owner. However, if this object is something that can be put to work and fed from the money it earns, e.g. an ox or donkey, the finder should have it work and feed it rather than sell it. The reason is that a man is more comfortable with the animal he has gotten to know and trained to his needs (*Rashi*). [Therefore, even though it is somewhat of a burden on the finder to rent out the animal, we do not allow him to sell it, since returning the money would not be the same as returning the animal.]

22. For example, a rooster or calf (Gemara). They need to be fed but cannot do anything to earn their keep.

23. *Deuteronomy* 22:2.

24. If the feed bill should come to more than half its value, one would not in effect be returning the object to the owner (*Rashi;* see note 27 below).

The phrase וַהֲשֵׁבֹתוֹ לוֹ, *return it to him,* is seemingly superfluous since the verse says to keep it "until he seeks it out." Hence, the Mishnah explains that the verse teaches the necessity of returning the object with its value intact (*Sifsei Chachamim* to the verse). If this cannot be done with the object itself, it should be sold. Others explain that the derivation is from the word לוֹ, *to him.* By selling an animal that cannot pay for its food and holding the money, you are returning it *to him,* i.e. in the manner that best serves his interests (*Shoshanim LeDavid* to the Mishnah).

When selling a lost object, one must be careful to record its *simanim*, so that the owner can later identify it and claim the money (*Nachalas Moshe*).

25. Since the finder is permitted to use the money [and replace it], he is held liable for it if it is lost, as the Gemara will explain (29a).

26. Caring for the animal may entail considerable bother; thus, the Gemara asks how long the finder must keep it (*Rashi*).

27. If the owner does not claim it within twelve months, the finder may sell the animal and hold the money (though he is not obligated to sell it; he may continue to care for it if he does not mind doing so). In the case of animals that consume more than they earn, he *must* sell them to preserve their value for the owner, even before twelve months have elapsed, as we learned in our Mishnah (*Maharam Shif*).

28. The finder now holds for the owner the money from the sale instead of the animal. From *Rashi,* who states that the animal is *sold,* it seems that the finder cannot simply evaluate and buy the article himself because of the suspicion that he may undervalue it. The courts must assess it and sell it (*Rashba*). *Rosh* (quoting *Tosafos*), however, is of the opinion that there is no basis for distrusting the finder after he has demonstrated his honesty by announcing the find and attempting to return it to its rightful owner. Thus, he may evaluate it and purchase it for himself.

29. Unlike the cow and donkey, these are too small to work [and earn their keep] (*Rashi*). However, for up to three months, the expense of their care is not great, as the Gemara will explain below, and one must therefore care for them. [The expense is also offset to some extent by the increase in their value resulting from their growth; see *Shitah Mekubetzes.*] Beyond this point, one should sell them and preserve their value for the owner.

30. The Baraisa refers specifically to male geese and chickens, as will become evident from the Gemara below. The females compensate for the expense of their keep by laying eggs, which may be sold to buy feed (*Rashi*).

אתיא לאחלופי בראשון הא קא אתי רגל שלישי ת"ר בראשונה כל מי שמצא אבידה היה מכריז עליה שלשה רגלים ואחר רגל אחרון שבעת ימים כדי שילך שלשה ויחזור שלשה ויכריז יום אחד [א]משחרב בית המקדש שיבנה במהרה בימינו התקינו שיהו מכריזים בבתי כנסיות ובבתי מדרשות ומשרבו האנסים התקינו שיהו מודיעין לשכיניו ולמיודעיו ודיו מאי משרבו האנסין [ב]דאמרי אבידתא למלכא רבי אמי אשכח אודייא דדינרי חזייה ההוא א) בר נש דקא מירתת א"ל זיל שקול לנפשך דלאו פרסאי אנן דאמרי אבידתא למלכא ת"ר [ג]אבן טוען היתה בירושלים כל מי שאבדה לו אבידה נפנה לשם וכל מי שמוצא אבידה נפנה לשם זה עומד ומכריז וזה עומד ונותן סימנין ונוטלה וזו היא ששנינו ג) צאו וראו אם נמחת אבן הטוען: **מתני'** [ד]אמר את האבידה ולא אמר סימניה לא יתן לו [ה]והרמאי אע"פ שאמר סימניה לא יתן לו שנאמר א) עד דרוש אחיך אותו עד שתדרוש את אחיך אם רמאי הוא אם אינו רמאי: **גמ'** אתמר רב יהודה אמר אבידתא מכריז ור"נ אמר גלימא מכריז רב יהודה אמר אבידתא מכריז דאי אמרת גלימא מכריז חיישינן לרמאי ר"נ אמר גלימא מכריז לרמאי לא חיישינן דא"כ אין לדבר סוף תנן אמר את האבידה ולא אמר את סימניה ה"ז לא יתן לו אי אמרת בשלמא אבידתא מכריז הא קמ"ל אע"ג דאמר גלימא כי לא אמר סימנין לא מהדרינן ליה אלא אי אמרת גלימא מכריז אמר איהו גלימא ואמר איהו גלימא צריכא למימר כי לא אמר סימנין לא מהדרינן ליה אמר רב ספרא לעולם גלימא מכריז אמר איהו גלימא ואמר איהו סימנין ומאי לא אמר את סימניה [ו]לא אמר סימנין מובהקין דידה: והרמאי אע"פ שאמר את סימניה ה"ז לא יתן לו: ת"ר בראשונה כל מי שאבדה לו אבידה היה נותן סימנין ונוטלה משרבו הרמאין [ז]התקינו שיהו אומרים לו צא והבא עדים דלאו רמאי את וטול כי הא דאבוה דרב פפא אירכס ליה חמרא ואשכחוה אתא לקמיה דרבה בר רב הונא אמר ליה זיל אייתי סהדי דלאו רמאי את וטול אזל אייתי סהדי אמר להו ידעיתון ביה דרמאי הוא אמרו ליה אין אמר להו אנא רמאה אנא אמרו ליה אנן לאו רמאי את קאמרינן אמר רבה בר רב הונא [ח]מסתברא לא מייתי איניש חובתא לנפשיה: **מתני'** [ט]כל דבר שעושה ואוכל יעשה ויאכל ודבר שאין עושה ואוכל ימכר שנאמר א) והשבותו לו ראה היאך תשיבנו לו מה יהא בדמים ר"ט אומר [י]ישתמש בהן לפיכך אם אבדו [כ]חייב באחריותן ר"ע אומר לא ישתמש בהן לפיכך אם אבדו אין חייב באחריותן: **גמ'** ולעולם אמר רב נחמן ג) אמר שמואל עד י"ב חדש תניא נמי הכי [ל]כל דבר שעושה ואוכל כגון פרה וחמור מטפל בהן עד י"ב חדש מכאן ואילך שם דמיהן ומניחן [מ]עגלים וסייחין מטפל בהן שלשה חדשים מכאן ואילך שם דמיהן ומניחן אווזין ותרנגולין מטפל בהם שלשים יום מכאן ואילך שם דמיהן ומניחן אמר רב נחמן בר יצחק תרנגולת כבהמה גסה תניא נמי הכי [נ]תרנגולת ובהמה גסה מטפל בהן שנים עשר חודש מכאן ואילך שם דמיהן ומניחן עגלים וסייחין מטפל בהן ל' יום מכאן ואילך שם דמיהן ומניחן [ס]אווזין ותרנגולין וכל דבר שטיפולו מרובה משכרו מטפל בהן שלשה ימים מכאן ואילך שם דמיהן ומניחן קשיא עגלים וסייחין אעגלים וסייחין אווזין ותרנגולין אאווזין ותרנגולין עגלים וסייחין אעגלים וסייחין לא קשיא [ע]הא דרעיא והא דפטומא אווזין ותרנגולין אאווזין ותרנגולין נמי לא קשיא [פ]הא ברברבי הא בזוטרי: ושאינו עושה ואוכל: תנו רבנן והשבותו לו ראה היאך תשיבנו לו שלא יאכיל עגל לעגלים וסיח לסייחין אווזא לאווזין ותרנגול לתרנגולין: מה יהא בדמים רבי טרפון אומר ישתמש וכו': עד כאן לא פליגי

אלא

---

**תוספות**

**אבן** טוען. מפרש בירושלמי כשם שהאבן אינה יכולה למחות כך אין יכולים להתפלל על רוב טובה: **שם** דמיהן. לקמן ה) גבי עסקא דרב ספרא אפרש בע"ה: **עד** כאן לא פליגי אלא בנשתמש בהן. לאו דוקא נשתמש דאם נשתמש לר"ע נמי חייב באחריותן כיון דלדידיה אסור להשתמש א"כ הוי שולח יד בפקדון ואפילו החזיר אין בכך כלום דהא ר"ע סבר בפרק המפקיד (לקמן דף מג:) דבעינן דעת בעלים אלא ודאי נשתמש לאו דוקא כדפרישית אלא בשכר שמוש שמותר להשתמש קאמר דלרבי טרפון דאית ליה דמותר להשתמש חייב באחריותן דההוא הנאה דאי מיתרמי ליה זבינא שקיל להו וזבין בהו הוי עלייהו שומר שכר ולר"ע דאסור להשתמש בהן פטור אבל אם לא היה מותר להשתמש היה פטור לכ"ע והיינו כרבה:

והוי

---

**רש"י**

ד) (אתי לאחלופי בשני. שמא יש שהוא סבור שאמר רגל שני:) אודיא דדינרי. כלי מלא זהובים: וזו היא ששנינו. במסכת תענית (דף יט.) בחוני המעגל: צאו וראו אם נמחת אבן טוען. אם נכסת בגשמים שגבהו הגשמים למעלה הימנו יש גשמים יותר מדאי ואתפלל עליהם שילכו: חיישינן לרמאי. שמא שמע האובד מתאונן בין שכיניו טליתי נאבדה וזה יודע את סימניה וכשישמע את מוצאה מכריז טלית מצאתי יקום ויתן סימניה הלכך אבידתא מכריז ואינו נותן לב לומר טלית זו אבדתי ואלו סימניה: אין לדבר סוף. דהשתא נמי מסיק אדעתיה ואמר אם טלית היא שמצאת אלו סימניה: אי אמרת בשלמא אבידתא מכריז. ולא מזכיר שם החפץ אצטריך תנא לאשמועינן דאע"ג דאמר האי טלית אבדתי צריך ליתן סימנין: אמרו ליה אין. כסבורין שאמר להן ידעיתון ביה דלאו רמאי הוא שכך היה לו לשואלן: מסתברא. שזה היה דעתן מתחילה ואין כאן משום מגיד וחוזר ומגיד: לא מייתי איניש חובה לנפשיה. וכשהביאן לב"ד בטוח היה שלא יעידו חובתו: **מתני'** כל דבר שעושה ואוכל. אם אבידה זו דבר שיכולין להאכילו את שכר מעשיו כגון שור וחמור יעשה ויאכל ולא ימכור אותו המוצא אם שהו בעליו מלדרשו שכל אדם נוח לו בבהמתו שהכירה בו כבר ולימדה לרצונו: ראה היאך תשיבנו לו. שלא תאכילנו חצי דמיו שא"כ אין זו השבה: לפיכך. מפרש בגמרא: **גמ'** ולעולם. וכי עד עולם זקוק זה לטפל בטורח שמירה: שם דמיהן. מוכרן ומניח הדמים אצלו: עגלים וסייחין. דקין שאין עושין מלאכה: תרנגולין. זכרים שאין מטילין בצים: כבהמה גסה. שעושה ואוכלת ומטפל בה י"ב חדש דיכול להאכילה דמי בצים: מטפל. אנשמיטרא בלע"ז: הא דרעיא הא דפטומא. הא דקתני שלשה [חדשים] בארץ מרעה ובזמן הדשאים שאין טיפולו מרובה והא דקתני ל' [יום] בזמן שאין מרעה וצריך לפטמה על אבוסה ממה שבבית שדמיה יקרים: רברבי. [א] אוכלין הרבה הלכך ג' ימים דהא אוקימנא בזכרים: שלא יאכיל עגל לעגלים. מן העגלים שנמצא לא יאכיל לו דמי עגל: עד כאן לא פליגי. לענין להתחייב באבידתו:

אלא

---

**רבינו חננאל**

הגשמים וכו'. והנה מהלך ט"ו ימים היא. ואסיקנא לא שנא מקדש ראשון ולא שנא מקדש שני לא הטריחו באבידה יותר מדאי ת"ר משחרב בית המקדש התקינו להיות מכריזין בכנסיות ובתי מדרשות משרבו האנסין שאומרין אבדתא למלכא התקינו שיהא מודיע המוצאה לשכניו ולמיודעיו ודיו. פי' מהסם מתיירא. ת"ר אבן הטוען היתה בירושלים כל מי שאבדה לו אבידה נפנה לשם וכו' פי' אבן גבוהה היתה בירושלים והיה כל מוצא אבידה עולה עליה ומכריז וזו היא ששנינו בפרק סדר תעניות השני אמר להן חוני המעגל צאו וראו אם נמחת אבן הטוען. אבקש רחמים שיפסקו הגשמים: **מתני'** אמר את האבידה ולא אמר את סימניה. אוקמה רב ספרא אליבא דרב נחמן דאמר גלימא מכריז א) כדאמר האבידה וסימניה ומאי לא אמר סימניה דקאמר במתני' לא אמר חיווין מובהקין דידה. וסוגיין בעינן דיהיב סימנין מובהקין והוא דאית סהדי דליתיה רמאי. ופשטינן דלא מייתי איניש חובה לנפשיה כדאבוה דרב פפא. תלמוד ארץ ישראל שמע סימניה בהאי כנישתא ואזל לכנישתא אחריתי יהיב סימניה זהו רמאי וכן כיוצא בו: **מתני'** כל דבר שעושה ואוכל יעשה ואוכל אוקימנא עד י"ב חדש.

תניא נמי הכי כל דבר שעושה ואוכל כגון פרה וחמור מטפל בהן כל י"ב חדש מכאן ואילך שם דמיהן ומניחן עגלים וסייחים אם יכולין לרעות מטפל בהן ג' חדשים. אוזין ותרנגולין גדולים מטפל בהן ל' יום. ותניא אחריתי תרנגולת כבהמה גסה י"ב חדש וכל דבר שטיפולו מרובה משכרו ג' ימים. ושאינו עושה ואוכל ימכור שנאמר והשבותו לו ראה היאך תשיבנו לו. שלא יאכיל עגל לעגלים. פי' לא תמכור עגל היום

**חשק שלמה על ר"ח** א) אולי צ"ל כדאמר.

---

**עין משפט נר מצוה**

קח א ב מיי' פי"ג מהל' גזלה ואבדה הלכה ט סמג עשין עד טוש"ע ח"מ סי' רסז סעיף ג:

קט ג מיי' שם הל' א סמג שם:

קי ד מיי' שם הל' ג סמג שם טוש"ע ח"מ סי' רסז סעיף ה:

קיא ה ו מיי' שם הל' ג ועיין בהשגות ובמגיד משנה סמג שם טוש"ע שם סעיף ה:

קיב ז מיי' שם הלכה ד טוש"ע שם סעיף ו:

קיג ח טוש"ע ח"מ סי' כט סעיף א:

קיד ט מיי' פי"ג מהל' גזלה ואבדה הל' טו סמג שם טוש"ע ח"מ סי' רסז סעיף כב:

קטו י כ מיי' שם הל' יח טוש"ע שם סעיף כה:

קטז ל מיי' שם הל' טו טוש"ע שם סעיף כג:

קיז מ מיי' שם הל' טז טוש"ע שם סעיף כג:

קיח נ מיי' שם הל' טו ועיין בהשגות ובמגיד משנה טוש"ע שם סעיף כג:

קיט ס מיי' שם הל' טז טוש"ע שם סעיף כד:

קכ ע מיי' שם טוש"ע שם סעיף כג:

קכא פ מיי' שם טוש"ע שם סעיף כד:

---

**מסורת הש"ס**

א) נ"א בר רומאה מהר"ס, ב) תענית יט. ג) [גירסת רי"ף ולעולם אמר שמואל וגירסת הרא"ש אמר רב יהודה אמר שמואל] ד) מהרש"ל מ"ז, ה) [דף לג. ד"ה כ"ד].

**הגהות הגר"א**

[א] רש"י ד"ה רברבי כו'. נ"ב אבל רמב"ם פי' להיפך וכן נ"י בשם ר"ח

**תורה אור השלם**

א) וְאִם לֹא קָרוֹב אָחִיךָ אֵלֶיךָ וְלֹא יְדַעְתּוֹ וַאֲסַפְתּוֹ אֶל תּוֹךְ בֵּיתֶךָ וְהָיָה עִמְּךָ עַד דְּרֹשׁ אָחִיךָ אֹתוֹ וַהֲשֵׁבֹתוֹ לוֹ [דברים כב, ב]

**ליקוטי רש"י**

עד דרוש אחיך. וכי תעלה בלבבך שיתנהו לו קודם שידרשהו אלא דרשהו שלא יהא רמאי. והשבותו לו. שתהא בו השבה שלא יאכל בבית כדי דמיו ותתבעם ממנו מכאן אמרו כל דבר שעושה ואוכל יעשה ויאכל ושאינו עושה ואוכל ימכר [דברים כב, ב]. וסייחין בנו של חמור קרוי סייח [רשב"ם ב"ב עח:].

**לעזי רש"י**

אנשמיטר"א. פירוש לטפל, להתעסק.

**be concerned** that this will create an opening **for a dishonest person** to claim it falsely.[11] רַב נַחְמָן אָמַר גְּלִימָא מַכְרִיז – **Rav Nachman says** that **he announces a garment,** לְרַמָּאֵי לֹא חָיְישִׁינַן – and **we need not be concerned** that this will create an opening **for a dishonest person,** דְּאִם כֵּן אֵין לַדָּבָר סוֹף – **for if so, the matter would never end** and we would need to be concerned regardless of what we announced.[12]

The Gemara questions Rav Nachman's opinion:

תְּנַן – **We learned in the Mishnah:** אָמַר אֶת הָאֲבֵידָה וְלֹא אָמַר אֶת סִימָנֶיהָ – If [THE CLAIMANT] NAMED THE LOST OBJECT BUT DID NOT NAME ITS IDENTIFYING MARKS, הֲרֵי זֶה לֹא יִתֵּן לוֹ – [THE FINDER] SHOULD NOT GIVE IT TO HIM. אִי אָמְרַת בִּשְׁלָמָא אֲבֵידְתָא מַכְרִיז – Now, **if you say** that **[the finder] announces a lost object, this is understandable,** הָא קָא מַשְׁמַע לָן – because **[the Mishnah]** is then **teaching us the following:** אַף עַל גַּב דְּאָמַר גְּלִימָא – **even though [the claimant] named a garment** as the lost object,[13] כִּי לֹא אָמַר סִימָנִין – **if he does not name** its **identifying marks,** לֹא מְהַדְּרִינַן לֵיהּ – **we do not return** it **to him.**[14] אֶלָּא אִי אָמְרַת גְּלִימָא מַכְרִיז – **However, if you say** that **he announces a garment,** אָמַר אִיהוּ גְּלִימָא וְאָמַר אִיהוּ גְּלִימָא – then the case is one in which **[the finder] said** he found **a garment and [the claimant] said** he lost **a garment.**[15] צְרִיכָא לְמֵימַר כִּי לֹא אָמַר סִימָנִין – **Is it** at all **necessary** for the Tanna **to say** that **if [the claimant] does not name** its **identifying marks** לֹא מְהַדְּרִינַן לֵיהּ – **we do not return** the garment **to him?!**[16] Thus, this Mishnah seems to demonstrate that the announcement does *not* specify the type of object found. – ? –

The Gemara rejects this proof:

אָמַר רַב סַפְרָא – **Rav Safra said:** לְעוֹלָם גְּלִימָא מַכְרִיז – **Actually** we may say that **[the finder] announces a garment,** אָמַר אִיהוּ גְּלִימָא וְאָמַר אִיהוּ סִימָנִין – and the case of the Mishnah is that **he said** he found **a garment and [the claimant] named** its **identifying marks.** וּמַאי לֹא אָמַר אֶת סִימָנֶיהָ – **Now what does** the Mishnah mean when it says that HE DID NOT NAME ITS IDENTIFYING MARKS? לֹא אָמַר סִימָנִין מוּבְהָקִין דִּידָהּ – It means that **he did not name its distinctive identifying marks,** only its general features.[17]

The Gemara discusses the second ruling of the Mishnah:

וְהָרַמַּאי אַף עַל פִּי שֶׁאָמַר אֶת סִימָנֶיהָ הֲרֵי זֶה לֹא יִתֵּן לוֹ – AND if the claimant is known to be A DISHONEST PERSON, – EVEN IF HE NAMED [THE OBJECT'S] IDENTIFYING MARKS, [THE FINDER] SHOULD NOT GIVE IT TO HIM:

תָּנוּ רַבָּנַן – **The Rabbis taught in a Baraisa:** בָּרִאשׁוֹנָה כָּל מִי שֶׁאָבְדָה לוֹ אֲבֵידָה – ORIGINALLY, ANYONE WHO LOST AN OBJECT הָיָה נוֹתֵן סִימָנִין וְנוֹטְלָהּ – WOULD GIVE the evidence of its IDENTIFYING MARKS AND TAKE IT. מִשֶּׁרָבוּ הָרַמָּאִין – WHEN DISHONEST PEOPLE BECAME PREVALENT הִתְקִינוּ שֶׁיְּהוּ אוֹמְרִים לוֹ – [THE SAGES] DECREED THAT THEY SHOULD SAY TO [THE CLAIMANT]: צֵא וְהָבֵא עֵדִים דְּלָאו רַמַּאי אַתְּ – GO AND BRING WITNESSES THAT YOU ARE NOT A DISHONEST PERSON,[18] וְטוֹל – AND then TAKE it.

The Gemara relates an incident in connection with this:

כִּי הָא דַּאֲבוּהָ דְּרַב פָּפָּא – **Like that** which happened **with the father of Rav Pappa:** אִירְכַּס לֵיהּ חֲמָרָא וְאַשְׁכַּחוּהָ – **He lost a donkey and it was found.** אָתָא לְקַמֵּיהּ דְּרַבָּה בַּר רַב הוּנָא – **[Rav Pappa's father] came before Rabbah bar Rav Huna** to claim it. אָמַר לֵיהּ זִיל אַיְיתִי סַהֲדֵי דְּלָאו רַמַּאי אַתְּ וְטוֹל – **[Rabbah bar Rav Huna] said to him, "Go and bring witnesses that you are not a dishonest person and take** the donkey.'' אֲזַל אַיְיתִי סַהֲדֵי – **He went** and **brought witnesses.** אָמַר לְהוּ יָדְעִיתוּן בֵּיהּ דְּרַמַּאי הוּא – **[Rabbah bar Rav Huna] said to [the witnesses], "Do you know** whether **he** [Rav Pappa's father] **is a dishonest person?"** אָמְרוּ לֵיהּ אִין – **They said to [Rabbah bar Rav Huna], "Yes."**[19] אָמַר לְהוּ אֲנָא רַמָּאָה אֲנָא – **[Rav Pappa's father] said to them** incredulously, **"I am a dishonest person?"** אָמְרוּ לֵיהּ אֲנַן לָאו רַמַּאי אַתְּ קָאַמְרִינַן – **They said to him, "We meant to say that you are not a dishonest person."** אָמַר רַבָּה בַּר רַב הוּנָא – **Rabbah bar Rav Huna said:** מִסְתַּבְּרָא לֹא מַיְיתֵי אִינִישׁ חוֹבָתָא לְנַפְשֵׁיהּ – **It is likely** that **a person would not bring** witnesses that are **to his detriment,** and we therefore accept their revised statement.[20]

NOTES

11. [It often happens that a person is aware of the distinctive features of his neighbor's garments, having seen him wear them. Thus,] should a dishonest person hear his neighbor bemoaning the loss of his garment, and then hear that a garment was found, he might well connect the two and falsely claim the garment. It is therefore better not to specify what was lost. In this way, the dishonest person may not be sensitive to the announcement, since he himself has not lost anything [and is therefore not listening for announcements] (*Rashi;* see *Nachalas Moshe*).

12. Rav Nachman objects that even if the announcement does not specify the type of object found, there is still an opening for a dishonest person, since he may well make the connection and say, "If you found a garment, these are its *simanim*" (*Rashi*).

The benefit of announcing a garment rather than merely a lost object is that this is more likely to jog the owner's memory and remind him that he is missing something; it will at least remind him to check his garments to see if he is missing anything. Thus, announcing a garment better fulfills the obligation to return lost property (*Tos. R' Akiva Eiger* to this Mishnah; see also *Shitah Mekubetzes* to 25a ד״ה וז״ל הר״ן). Specifying the lost article also spares the owner the trouble of going to every person who found anything to inquire after his lost garment (*Nachalas Moshe*). It is thus preferable to make the announcement more specific.

Accordingly, *Ritva* suggests that the original way was to announce a garment. The dispute between Rav Yehudah and Rav Nachman concerns the period when dishonest people became numerous (see Baraisa below). According to Rav Yehudah, this necessitated a change in the method of announcing, whereas Rav Nachman is of the opinion that little would be gained by changing and the old method was therefore retained.

13. Thereby indicating that he had some knowledge of the object and might be the one who lost it.

14. If the announcement merely states that an object has been found without specifying what kind of object [it is possible for the claimant to offer some form of identification – naming the article – without naming its identifying marks]. The Tanna must therefore teach that even though the claimant knows what has been lost, we do not give it to him until he identifies its *simanim* (*Rashi*).

15. According to Rav Nachman, the one who found the object must have announced the name of the object. The Mishnah, however, speaks of a case in which the claimant named only the object but not its particular *siman.* Thus, the case is one in which he merely repeated what had been announced!

16. Quite obviously, we do not return an object to a person who does not identify it beyond repeating what was said in the announcement!

17. The claimant named general *simanim,* e.g. color. Though this narrows the field, it may still apply to many garments. The Mishnah teaches that *simanim* that are not very distinctive do not suffice to reclaim the garment (*Rashba; Rosh;* see also *Tosafos* 27b ד״ה ואנא יהיבנא).

18. I.e. character witnesses.

19. The witnesses expected to be asked whether they could testify that this man is *not* a dishonest person. They responded to the question they expected to hear and not to the question that was actually asked (*Rashi*).

20. When Rav Pappa's father brought them to court he was clearly certain that they meant to testify in his favor. Therefore, although witnesses are generally not permitted to retract their testimony, we may assume that their correction reflected what they meant to say in the first place, and did not constitute a retraction (*Rashi*).

אתיא לאחלופי בראשון הא קא אתי רגל שלישי ת"ר בראשונה כל מי שמצא אבידה היה מכריז עליה שלשה רגלים ואחר רגל אחרון שבעת ימים כדי שילך שלשה ויחזור שלשה ויכריז יום אחד [א]משחרב בית המקדש שיבנה במהרה בימינו התקינו שיהו מכריזים בבתי כנסיות ובבתי מדרשות ומשרבו האנסים התקינו שיהו מודיעין לשכיניו ולמיודעיו ודיו מאי משרבו האנסין [ב]דאמרי אבידתא למלכא רבי אמי אשכח אודייא דדינרי חזייה ההוא [א]בר נש דקא מירתת א"ל זיל שקול לנפשך דלאו פרסאי אנן דאמרי אבידתא למלכא ת"ר [ג]אבן טוען היתה בירושלים כל מי שאבדה לו אבידה נפנה לשם וכל מי שמוצא אבידה נפנה לשם זה עומד ומכריז וזה עומד ונותן סימנין ונוטלה וזו היא ששנינו [ג]צאו וראו אם נמחת אבן הטוען: **מתני'** [ד]אמר את האבידה ולא אמר סימניה לא יתן לו [ה]והרמאי אע"פ שאמר סימניה לא יתן לו שנאמר [א]עד דרוש אחיך אותו עד שתדרוש את אחיך אם רמאי הוא אם אינו רמאי: **גמ'** אתמר רב יהודה אמר אבידתא מכריז ור"נ אמר גלימא מכריז רב יהודה אמר אבידתא מכריז דאי אמרת גלימא מכריז חיישינן לרמאי ר"נ אמר גלימא מכריז לרמאי לא חיישינן דא"כ אין לדבר סוף תנן אמר את האבידה ולא אמר את סימניה ה"ז לא יתן לו אי אמרת בשלמא אבידתא מכריז הא קמ"ל אע"ג דאמר גלימא כי לא אמר סימנין לא מהדרינן ליה אלא אי אמרת גלימא מכריז אמר איהו גלימא ואמר איהו גלימא צריכא למימר כי לא אמר סימנין לא מהדרינן ליה אמר רב ספרא לעולם גלימא מכריז אמר איהו גלימא ואמר איהו סימנין ומאי לא אמר את סימניה [ו]לא אמר סימנין מובהקין דידה: והרמאי אע"פ שאמר את סימניה ה"ז לא יתן לו: ת"ר בראשונה כל מי שאבדה לו אבידה היה נותן סימנין ונוטלה משרבו הרמאין [ז]התקינו שיהו אומרים לו צא והבא עדים דלאו רמאי את וטול כי הא דאבוה דרב פפא אירכס ליה חמרא ואשכחוה אתא לקמיה דרבה בר רב הונא אמר ליה זיל אייתי סהדי דלאו רמאי את וטול אזל אייתי סהדי אמר להו ידעיתון ביה דרמאי הוא אמרו ליה אין אמר להו אנא רמאה אנא אמרו ליה אנן לאו רמאי את קאמרינן אמר רבה בר רב הונא [ח]מסתברא לא מייתי איניש חובתא לנפשיה: **מתני'** [ט]כל דבר שעושה ואוכל יעשה ויאכל ודבר שאין עושה ואוכל ימכר שנאמר [א]והשבותו לו ראה היאך תשיבנו לו מה יהא בדמים ר"ט אומר [י]ישתמש בהן לפיכך אם אבדו [כ]חייב באחריותן ר"ע אומר לא ישתמש בהן לפיכך אם אבדו אין חייב באחריותן: **גמ'** ולעולם אמר רב נחמן [ג]אמר שמואל עד י"ב חדש תניא נמי הכי [ל]כל דבר שעושה ואוכל כגון פרה וחמור מטפל בהן עד י"ב חדש מכאן ואילך שם דמיהן ומניחן [מ]עגלים וסייחין מטפל בהן שלשה חדשים מכאן ואילך שם דמיהן ומניחן אווזין ותרנגולין מטפל בהם שלשים יום מכאן ואילך שם דמיהן ומניחן אמר רב נחמן בר יצחק תרנגולת כבהמה גסה תניא נמי הכי [נ]תרנגולת ובהמה גסה מטפל בהן שנים עשר חודש מכאן ואילך שם דמיהן ומניחן עגלים וסייחין מטפל בהן ל' יום מכאן ואילך שם דמיהן ומניחן [ס]אווזין ותרנגולין וכל דבר שטיפולו מרובה משכרו מטפל בהן שלשה ימים מכאן ואילך שם דמיהן ומניחן קשיא עגלים וסייחין אעגלים וסייחין אווזין ותרנגולין אאווזין ותרנגולין עגלים וסייחין לא קשיא [ע]הא דרעיא והא דפטומא אווזין ותרנגולין אאווזין ותרנגולין נמי לא קשיא [פ]הא ברברבי הא בזוטרי: ושאינו עושה ואוכל: תנו רבנן והשבותו לו ראה היאך תשיבנו לו שלא יאכיל עגל לעגלים וסיח לסייחין אווזא לאווזין ותרנגול לתרנגולין: מה יהא בדמים רבי טרפון אומר ישתמש וכו': עד כאן לא פליגי אלא

---

**רש"י**

**אבן** טוען. מפרש בירושלמי כשם שהאבן אינה יכולה למחות כך אין יכולים להתפלל על רוב טובה: **שם** דמיהן. לקמן [ה] גבי עסקא דרב ספרא אפרש בע"ה: **עד** כאן לא פליגי אלא בנשתמש בהן. לאו דוקא נשתמש דאם נשתמש לר"ע נמי חייב באחריותן כיון דלדידיה אסור להשתמש א"כ הוי שולח יד בפקדון ואפילו החזיר אין בכך כלום דהא ר"ע סבר בפרק המפקיד (לקמן דף מג.) דבעינן דעת בעלים אלא ודאי נשתמש לאו דוקא כדפרישית אלא בשכר שמוש שמותר להשתמש קאמר דלרבי טרפון דאית ליה דמותר להשתמש חייב באחריותן דההוא הנאה דאי מיתרמי ליה זבינא שקיל להו וזבין בהו הוי עלייהו שומר שכר ולר"ע דאסור להשתמש בהן פטור אבל אם לא היה מותר להשתמש היה פטור לכ"ע והיינו כרבה: והוי

[ד] (אתי לאחלופי בשני. שמא יש שהוא סבור שאמר רגל שני:) אודיא דדינרי. כלי מלא זהובים: וזו היא ששנינו. במסכת תענית (דף יט.) בחוני המעגל: צאו וראו אם נמחת אבן טוען. אם נכסת בגשמים שגבהו הגשמים למעלה הימנו יש גשמים יותר מדאי ואתפלל עליהם שילכו: חיישינן לרמאי. שמא שמע האובד מתאונן בין שכיניו טליתי נאבדה וזה יודע את סימניה וכשישמע את מוצאה מכריז טלית מצאתי יקום ויתן סימניה הלכך אבידתא מכריז ואינו נותן לב לומר טלית זו אבדתי ואלו סימניה: אין לדבר סוף. דהשתא נמי מסיק אדעתיה ואמר אם טלית היא שמצאת אלו סימניה: אי אמרת בשלמא אבידתא מכריז. ולא מזכיר שם החפץ אצטריך תנא לאשמועינן דאע"ג דאמר האי טלית אבדתי צריך ליתן סימנין: אמרו ליה אין. כסבורין שאמר להן ידעיתון ביה דלאו רמאי הוא שכך היה לו לשואלן: מסתברא. שזה היה דעתן מתחילה ואין כאן משום מגיד וחוזר ומגיד: לא מייתי איניש חובה לנפשיה. וכשהביאן לב"ד בטוח היה שלא יעידו חובתו: **מתני'** כל דבר שעושה ואוכל. אם אבידה זו דבר שיכולין להאכילו את שכר מעשיו כגון שור וחמור יעשה ויאכל ולא ימכור אותו המוצא אם שהו בעליו מלדרשו שכל אדם נוח לו בבהמתו שהכירה בו כבר ולימדה לרצונו: ראה היאך תשיבנו לו. שלא תאכילנו חצי דמיו שא"כ אין זו השבה: לפיכך. מפרש בגמרא: **גמ'** ולעולם. וכי עד עולם זקוק זה לטפל בטורח שמירה: שם דמיהן. מוכרן ומניח הדמים אצלו: עגלים וסייחין. דקין שאין עושין מלאכה: תרנגולין. זכרים שאין מטילין בצים: כבהמה גסה. שעושה ואוכלת ומטפל בה י"ב חדש דיכול להאכילה דמי בצים: מטפל. אנשמיטרא בלע"ז: הא דרעיא הא דפטומא. הא דקתני שלשה [חדשים] בארץ מרעה ובזמן הדשאים שאין טיפולו מרובה והא דקתני ל' [יום] בזמן שאין מרעה וצריך לפטמה על אבוסה ממה שבבית שדמיה יקרים: רברבי. [א] אוכלין הרבה הלכך ג' ימים דהא אוקימנא בזכרים: שלא יאכיל עגל לעגלים. מן העגלים שנמצא לא יאכיל לו דמי עגל: עד כאן לא פליגי. לענין להתחייב באבידתו: אלא

---

**עין משפט נר מצוה**

קח א ב מיי' פי"ג מהל' גזלה ואבדה הלכה ט סמג עשין עד טוש"ע ח"מ סי' רסז סעיף ג:
קט ג מיי' שם הל' א סמג שם:
קי ד מיי' שם הל' ג סמג שם טוש"ע ח"מ סי' רסז סעיף ה:
קיא ה ו מיי' שם הל' ג ועיין בהשגות ובמגיד משנה סמג שם טוש"ע שם סעיף ה:
קיב ז מיי' שם הלכה ד טוש"ע שם סעיף ו:
קיג ח טוש"ע ח"מ סי' כט סעיף א:
קיד ט מיי' פי"ג מהל' גזלה ואבדה הל' טו סמג שם טוש"ע ח"מ סי' רסז סעיף כב:
קטו י כ מיי' שם הל' יח טוש"ע שם סעיף כה:
קטז ל מיי' שם הל' טו טוש"ע שם סעיף כב:
קיז מ מיי' שם הל' טז טוש"ע שם סעיף כג:
קיח נ מיי' שם הל' טו ועיין בהשגות ובמגיד משנה טוש"ע שם סעיף כב:
קיט ס מיי' שם הל' טז טוש"ע שם סעיף כד:
קכ ע מיי' שם טוש"ע שם סעיף כג:
קכא פ מיי' שם טוש"ע שם סעיף כד:

**רבינו חננאל**

הגשמים וכו'. והנה מהלך ט"ו ימים היא. ואסיקנא לא שנא מקדש ראשון ולא שנא מקדש שני לא הטריחו באבידה יותר מדאי ת"ר משחרב בית המקדש התקינו להיות מכריזין בכנסיות ובתי מדרשות משרבו האנסין שאומרין אבדתא למלכא התקינו שיהא מודיע המוצאה לשכניו ולמיודעיו ודיו. פי' מהסם מתיירא. ת"ר אבן הטוען היתה בירושלים כל מי שאבדה לו אבידה נפנה לשם וכו' פי' אבן גבוהה היתה בירושלים והיה כל מוצא אבידה עולה עליה ומכריז וזו היא ששנינו בפרק סדר תעניות השני אמר להן חוני המעגל צאו וראו אם נמחת אבן הטוען. אבקש רחמים שיפסקו הגשמים: **מתני'** אמר את האבידה ולא אמר את סימניה. אוקמה רב ספרא אליבא דרב נחמן דאמר גלימא מכריז [א] כדאמר האבידה וסימניה ומאי לא אמר סימניה דקאמר במתני' לא אמר חיוורין מובהקין דידה. וסוגיין בעינן דיהיב סימנין מובהקין והוא דאית סהדי דליתיה רמאי. ופשטינן דלא מייתי איניש חובה לנפשיה כדאבוה דרב פפא. תלמוד ארץ ישראל שמע סימניה בהאי כנישתא ואזל לכנישתא אחריתי יהיב סימניה זהו רמאי וכן כיוצא בו: **מתני'** כל דבר שעושה ואוכל יעשה ואוכל אוקימנא עד י"ב חדש. תניא נמי הכי כל דבר שעושה ואוכל כגון פרה וחמור מטפל בהן כל י"ב חדש מכאן ואילך שם דמיהן ומניחן עגלים וסייחים אם יכולין לרעות מטפל בהן ג' חדשים. אוזין ותרנגולין גדולים מטפל בהן ל' יום. ותניא אחריתי תרנגולת כבהמה גסה י"ב חדש וכל דבר שטיפולו מרובה משכרו ג' ימים. ושאינו עושה ואוכל ימכור שנאמר והשבותו לו ראה היאך תשיבנו לו. שלא יאכיל עגל לעגלים. פי' לא תמכור עגל היום

**חשק שלמה על ר"ח** א) אולי צ"ל כדאמר.

---

**מסורת הש"ס**

א) נ"א בר רומאה. מהרש"ס, ב) תענית יט., ג) [גירסת רי"ף ולעולם אמר שמואל וגירסת הרא"ש אמר רב יהודה אמר שמואל], ד) מהרש"ל מ"ז, ה) [דף לג. ד"ה כ"ד].

**הגהות הגר"א**

[א] רש"י ד"ה רברבי כו'. נ"ב אבל רמב"ם פי' להיפך וכן נ"י בשם ר"ח:

**תורה אור השלם**

א) וְאִם לֹא קָרוֹב אָחִיךָ אֵלֶיךָ וְלֹא יְדַעְתּוֹ וַאֲסַפְתּוֹ אֶל תּוֹךְ בֵּיתֶךָ וְהָיָה עִמְּךָ עַד דְּרשׁ אָחִיךָ אֹתוֹ וַהֲשֵׁבֹתוֹ לוֹ: [דברים כב, ב]

**ליקוטי רש"י**

עד דרוש אחיך. וכי תעלה בלבבך שיתנהו לו קודם שידרשהו אלא דרשהו שלא יהא רמאי. והשבותו לו. שתהא בו השבה שלא יאכל בביתך כדי דמיו ותתבעם ממנו מכאן אמרו כל דבר שעושה ואוכל יעשה ויאכל ושאינו עושה ואוכל ימכר [דברים כב, ב]. וסייחין. בנו של חמור קרוי סיח [רשב"ם ב"ב עח:].

**לעזי רש"י**

אנשמיטר"א. פירוש לטפל, להתעסק.

אַתְיָא לְאַחְלוּפֵי בְּרִאשׁוֹן – **might lead to confusing** it **with the first.**[1] – ? –

The Gemara answers:

הָא קָא אָתֵי רֶגֶל שְׁלִישִׁי – Even so, **the third festival is still to come,** and he will be able to reclaim his property.[2]

The Gemara cites a Baraisa:

תָּנוּ רַבָּנָן – **The Rabbis taught in a Baraisa:** בָּרִאשׁוֹנָה – AT FIRST, כָּל מִי שֶׁמָּצָא אֲבֵידָה – ANYONE WHO FOUND A LOST OBJECT הָיָה מַכְרִיז עָלֶיהָ שְׁלֹשָׁה רְגָלִים – WOULD ANNOUNCE IT for THREE FESTIVALS וְאַחַר רֶגֶל אַחֲרוֹן שִׁבְעַת יָמִים – AND AFTER THE FINAL FESTIVAL, for another SEVEN DAYS, כְּדֵי שֶׁיֵּלֵךְ שְׁלֹשָׁה וְיַחֲזוֹר שְׁלֹשָׁה וְיַכְרִיז יוֹם אֶחָד – SO THAT ONE SHOULD HAVE THREE days TO TRAVEL home and check his belongings, AND THREE days TO RETURN, AND ONE DAY TO ANNOUNCE the loss of the object and its identifying marks. מִשֶּׁחָרַב בֵּית הַמִּקְדָּשׁ שֶׁיִּבָּנֶה בִּמְהֵרָה בְיָמֵינוּ – WHEN THE TEMPLE WAS DESTROYED, MAY IT BE SPEEDILY REBUILT IN OUR TIME, הִתְקִינוּ – [THE SAGES] INSTITUTED שֶׁיְּהוּ מַכְרִיזִים בְּבָתֵּי כְּנֵסִיּוֹת וּבְבָתֵּי מִדְרָשׁוֹת – THAT THEY SHOULD ANNOUNCE [LOST OBJECTS] IN THE SYNAGOGUES AND STUDY HALLS.[3] וּמִשֶּׁרַבּוּ הָאַנָּסִים – WHEN THE CONFISCATORS BECAME PREVALENT,[4] הִתְקִינוּ שֶׁיְּהוּ מוֹדִיעִין לִשְׁכֵנָיו וְלִמְיוּדָּעָיו וְדַיּוֹ – THEY INSTITUTED THAT [FINDERS] SHOULD INFORM THEIR NEIGHBORS AND THEIR ACQUAINTANCES – AND THAT IS SUFFICIENT.

The Gemara clarifies a term:

מַאי מִשֶּׁרַבּוּ הָאַנָּסִין – **What is** the meaning of: WHEN THE CONFISCATORS BECAME PREVALENT? To whom does the term "confiscators" refer? דְּאָמְרֵי אֲבֵידְתָא לְמַלְכָּא – It refers to **those who say** that all **lost objects belong to the king.**

The Gemara relates an incident:

רַבִּי אַמִּי אַשְׁכַּח אוּדְיָא דְּדִינָרֵי – **R' Ami found a vessel of gold coins.** חַזְיֵיהּ הַהוּא בַּר נַשׁ דְּקָא מִירְתַּת – **A certain person,** a Roman who observed the discovery, **saw that [R' Ami] was frightened** that he would take it from him. אָמַר לֵיהּ זִיל שְׁקוֹל לְנַפְשָׁךְ – **He said to [R' Ami]: Go and take it for yourself** דְּלָאו פַּרְסָאֵי אֲנַן – **because we are not Persians,** דְּאָמְרֵי אֲבֵידְתָא לְמַלְכָּא – **who say** that all **lost objects belong to the king.**

The Gemara cites another Baraisa:

תָּנוּ רַבָּנָן – **The Rabbis taught in a Baraisa:** אֶבֶן טוֹעַן הָיְתָה בִּירוּשָׁלַיִם – THERE WAS A "CLAIMANTS' STONE" IN JERUSALEM. כָּל מִי שֶׁאָבְדָה לוֹ אֲבֵידָה נִפְנֶה לְשָׁם – ANYONE WHO LOST SOMETHING WOULD TURN THERE, וְכָל מִי שֶׁמּוֹצֵא אֲבֵידָה נִפְנֶה לְשָׁם – AND ANYONE WHO FOUND A LOST OBJECT WOULD TURN THERE. זֶה עוֹמֵד וּמַכְרִיז – [THE FINDER] WOULD STAND by the stone AND ANNOUNCE his find וְזֶה עוֹמֵד וְנוֹתֵן סִימָנִין וְנוֹטְלָהּ – AND [THE OWNER] WOULD STAND by the stone AND GIVE THE evidence of IDENTIFYING MARKS, AND TAKE IT. וְזוּ הִיא שֶׁשָּׁנִינוּ – AND IT WAS [ABOUT] THIS [STONE] THAT WE LEARNED צְאוּ וּרְאוּ אִם נִמְחֵת אֶבֶן הַטּוֹעַן – that Choni the Circle-maker said to the people, "GO OUT AND SEE IF THE STONE OF THE CLAIMANTS HAS BEEN EFFACED."[5]

**Mishnah** אָמַר אֶת הָאֲבֵידָה – If **[the claimant] named the lost object** וְלֹא אָמַר סִימָנֶיהָ – **but did not name its identifying marks,**[6] לֹא יִתֵּן לוֹ – **[the finder] should not give it to him.** וְהָרַמַּאי – **And** if the claimant is known to be **a dishonest person,** אַף עַל פִּי שֶׁאָמַר סִימָנֶיהָ – **even if he named its identifying marks,** לֹא יִתֵּן לוֹ – **[the finder] should not give it to him;**[7] שֶׁנֶּאֱמַר: ,,עַד דְּרֹשׁ אָחִיךָ אֹתוֹ" – **as it says:** ***until your brother seeks it out,***[8] עַד שֶׁתִּדְרוֹשׁ אֶת אָחִיךָ – which is interpreted homiletically to mean: **until you seek out** [i.e. investigate] the nature of **your brother** and determine אִם רַמַּאי הוּא אִם אֵינוֹ רַמַּאי – **whether he is a dishonest person or not.**[9]

**Gemara** The Gemara cites an Amoraic dispute regarding the way a lost object is announced:

אִתְּמַר – **It has been stated:** רַב יְהוּדָה אָמַר אֲבֵידְתָא מַכְרִיז – **Rav Yehudah says:** If someone finds a garment, for example, **he announces** that he found **a lost object,** without specifying its nature. וְרַב נַחְמָן אָמַר גְּלִימָא מַכְרִיז – **Rav Nachman says: He announces** that he found **a garment.**[10] רַב יְהוּדָה אָמַר אֲבֵידְתָא מַכְרִיז – **Rav Yehudah says** that **he announces** only that he found **a lost object,** דְּאִי אָמְרַתְּ גְּלִימָא מַכְרִיז – **because if you say** that **he announces a garment,** חַיְישִׁינַן לְרַמַּאי – **we must**

NOTES

1. If people are going to confuse the third with the second, then they are just as likely to confuse the second with the first [and think they still have two more festivals to reclaim their lost object].

2. Even if the person confuses the second festival with the first, he will still come to Jerusalem to claim his article at the next festival, the third, which he mistakenly assumes to be the second. Thus, no loss will result from the mistake. But, if he confuses the third with the second, he will mistakenly assume that he need not return to Jerusalem immediately because he can still claim the article on the following festival.

3. Since there was no longer any pilgrimage to Jerusalem the announcement was made in other public places.

4. אַנָּסִים – literally: those who take by force.

5. In *Taanis* 19a, where the Mishnah tells the story of Choni the Circle-maker.

Once when there was a drought the people asked Choni to pray for rain. He drew a circle in the dust and swore not to leave it until God sent the rain. So much rain came that the people feared it would endanger them and they asked Choni to pray that it should stop. Choni responded that since it is improper to pray that blessings should cease, he could only do so if the Stone of the Claimants was effaced by the long-lasting rain. This was a rhetorical reply. He was saying in effect that just as it is impossible for a rock to dissolve, it is also impossible to pray for a blessing to end (*Tosafos* from *Yerushalmi*). [The text of the Mishnah in *Taanis* reads אֶבֶן הַטּוֹעִין, the Stone of the Strayers. Even according to that reading, the meaning is the same. It was the stone where all those whose property had "strayed" from them would come to reclaim it.]

6. I.e. he stated what type of object he had lost, but he did not describe the *siman* that would identify this particular article as his. This will be explained further in the Gemara.

7. Since he has not positively identified the article and it may belong to someone else.

8. *Deuteronomy* 22:2. The full text of the verse is: וְאִם־לֹא קָרוֹב אָחִיךָ אֵלֶיךָ וְלֹא יְדַעְתּוֹ וַאֲסַפְתּוֹ אֶל־תּוֹךְ בֵּיתֶךָ וְהָיָה עִמְּךָ עַד דְּרֹשׁ אָחִיךָ אֹתוֹ וַהֲשֵׁבֹתוֹ לוֹ, *And if your brother is not close to you, and you do not know him, you shall gather it into your house, and it shall be with you until your brother seeks it out, and you shall return it to him.*

9. The root דרש means to *seek out* or *investigate.* The basis for this homiletical interpretation, as the Gemara explained above (27b), is that the Torah had no need to say that we wait until the unknown owner seeks out his object before returning it to him. This is perfectly obvious. The verse is thus expounded to mean that it is *we* who must investigate the character of the claimant before returning it to him solely on the basis of his identification.

A person known to be dishonest can reclaim an article only by bringing witnesses that it is his, as the Gemara stated above (27b). As to whether we return an article to him based on the identification of a truly distinctive *siman,* see *Rosh* with *Pilpula Charifta; Maggid Mishneh* to *Hil. Gezeilah* 13:3; *Sma* 267:9, and *Shach* 267:3.

10. The Gemara uses a garment by way of example.

עין משפט
נר מצוה

קח א ב מיי' פי"ג מהל' גזלה ואבדה הלכה ט סמג עשין עד טוש"ע ח"מ סי' רסז סעיף ג:
קט ג מיי' שם הל' א סמג שם:
קי ד מיי' שם הל' ג סמג שם טוש"ע ח"מ סי' רסז סעיף ה:
קיא ה ו מיי' שם הל' ג ועיין בהשגות ובמגיד משנה סמג שם טוש"ע שם סעיף ה:
קיב ז מיי' שם הלכה ד טוש"ע שם סעיף ו:
קיג ח טוש"ע ח"מ סי' כט סעיף א:
קיד ט מיי' פי"ג מהל' גזלה ואבדה הל' טו סמג שם טוש"ע ח"מ סי' רסז סעיף כג:
קטו י כ מיי' שם הל' יז טוש"ע שם סעיף כה:
קטז ל מיי' שם הל' טו טוש"ע שם סעיף כב:
קיז מ מיי' שם הל' טז טוש"ע שם סעיף כג:
קיח נ מיי' שם הל' טו ועיין בהשגות ובמגיד משנה טוש"ע שם סעיף כב:
קיט ס מיי' שם הל' טז טוש"ע שם סעיף כד:
קכ ע מיי' שם טוש"ע שם סעיף כג:
קכא פ מיי' שם טוש"ע שם סעיף כד:

אבן טוען. מפרש בירושלמי כסא שהאבן אינה יכולה למחות כך אין יכולים להתפלל על רוב טובה: שם דמיהן. לקמן ה) גבי עסקא דרב ספרא אפרש בע"ה: עד כאן לא פליגי אלא בנשתמש בהן. לאו דוקא נשתמש דאם נשתמש לר"ע נמי חייב באחריותן כיון דלדידיה אסור להשתמש א"כ הוי שולח יד בפקדון ואפילו החזיר אין בכך כלום דהא ר"ע סבר בפרק המפקיד (לקמן דף מג:) דבעינן דעת בעלים אלא ודאי נשתמש לאו דוקא כדפרישית אלא בשכר שמוש שמותר להשתמש קאמר לרבי טרפון דאית ליה דמותר להשתמש חייב באחריותן דבההוא הנאה דאי מיתרמי ליה זבינא שקיל להו וקנין בהו הוי עלייהו שומר שכר ולר"ע דאסור להשתמש בהן פטור אבל אם לא היה מותר להשתמש היה פטור לכ"ע והיינו כרבה:

והוי

ד) (אתי לאחלופי בשני. שמא יש שהוא סבור שאמר רגל שני:) אודיא דדינרי. כלי מלא זהובים: וזו היא ששנינו. במסכת תענית (דף יט.) בחוני המעגל: צאו וראו אם נמחת אבן טוען. אם נכסת בגשמים שגבהו הגשמים למעלה הימנו יש גשמים יותר מדאי ואתפלל עליהם שילכו: חיישינן לרמאי. שמא שמע האובד מתאונן בין שכיניו טליתי נאבדה וזה יודע את סימניה וכשישמע את מוצאה מכריז טלית מצאתי יקום ויתן סימניה הלכך אבידתא מכריז ואינו נותן לב לומר טלית זו אבדתי ואלו סימניה: אין לדבר סוף. דהשתא נמי מסיק אדעתיה ואמר אם טלית היא שמצאת אלו סימניה: אי אמרת בשלמא אבידתא מכריז. ולא מזכיר שם החפץ אצטריך תנא לאשמועינן דאע"ג דאמר האי טלית אבדתי צריך ליתן סימנין: אמרו ליה אין. כסבורין שאמר להן ידעיתון ביה דלאו רמאי הוא שכך היה לו לשואלן: מסתברא. שזה היה דעתן מתחילה ואין כאן משום מגיד וחוזר ומגיד: לא מייתי איניש חובה לנפשיה. וכשהביאן לב"ד בטוח היה שלא יעידו חובתו: מתני' כל דבר שעושה ואוכל. אם אבידה זו דבר שיכולין להאכילו את שכר מעשיו כגון שור וחמור יעשה ויאכל ולא ימכור אותו המוצא אם שהו בעליו מלדרשו שכל אדם נוח לו בבהמתו שהכירה בו כבר ולימדה לרצונו: ראה היאך תשיבנו לו. שלא תאכילנו חצי דמיו שא"כ אין זו השבה: לפיכך. מפרש בגמרא: גמ' ולעולם. וכי עד עולם זקוק זה לטפל בטורח שמירה: שם דמיהן. מוכרן ומניח הדמים אצלו: עגלים וסייחין. דקין שאין עושין מלאכה: תרנגולין. זכרים שאין מטילין בצים: כבהמה גסה. שעושה ואוכלת ומטפל בה י"ב חדש דיכול להאכילה דמי בצים: מטפל. אנשמיטרא בלע"ז: הא דרעיא הא דפטומא. הא דקתני שלשה [חדשים] בארץ מרעה ובזמן הדשאים שאין טיפולו מרובה והא דקתני ל' [יום] בזמן שאין מרעה וצריך לפטמה על אבוסה ממה שבבית שדמיה יקרים: רברבי. [א] אוכלין הרבה הלכך ג' ימים דהא אוקימנא בזכרים: שלא יאכיל עגל לעגלים. מן העגלים שנמצא לא יאכיל לו דמי עגל: עד כאן לא פליגי. לעניין להתחייב באבידתו:
אלא

אתיא לאחלופי בראשון הא קא אתי רגל שלישי ת"ר בראשונה כל מי שמצא אבידה היה מכריז עליה שלשה רגלים ואחר רגל אחרון שבעת ימים כדי שילך שלשה ויחזור שלשה ויכריז יום אחד א משחרב בית המקדש שיבנה במהרה בימינו התקינו שיהו מכריזים בבתי כנסיות ובבתי מדרשות ומשרבו האנסים התקינו שיהו מודיעין לשכיניו ולמיודעיו ודיו מאי משרבו האנסין ב דאמרי אבידתא למלכא רבי אמי אשכח אודייא דדינרי חזייה ההוא א) בר נש דקא מירתת א"ל זיל שקול לנפשך דלאו פרסאי אנן דאמרי אבידתא למלכא ת"ר ג אבן טוען היתה בירושלים כל מי שאבדה לו אבידה נפנה לשם וכל מי שמוצא אבידה נפנה לשם זה עומד ומכריז וזה עומד ונותן סימנין ונוטלה וזו היא ששנינו ב) צאו וראו אם נמחת אבן הטוען: **מתני'** ד אמר את האבידה ולא אמר סימניה לא יתן לו ה והרמאי אע"פ שאמר סימניה לא יתן לו שנאמר א) עד דרוש אחיך אותו עד שתדרוש את אחיך אם רמאי הוא אם אינו רמאי: **גמ'** אתמר רב יהודה אמר אבידתא מכריז ור"נ אמר גלימא מכריז רב יהודה אמר אבידתא מכריז דאי אמרת גלימא מכריז חיישינן לרמאי ר"נ אמר גלימא מכריז לרמאי לא חיישינן דא"כ אין לדבר סוף תנן אמר את האבידה ולא אמר את סימניה ה"ז לא יתן לו אי אמרת בשלמא אבידתא מכריז הא קמ"ל אע"ג דאמר גלימא כי לא אמר סימנין לא מהדרינן ליה אלא אי אמרת גלימא מכריז אמר איהו גלימא ואמר איהו גלימא צריכא למימר כי לא אמר סימנין לא מהדרינן ליה אמר רב ספרא לעולם גלימא מכריז אמר איהו גלימא ואמר איהו סימנין ומאי לא אמר את סימניה ו לא אמר סימנין מובהקין דידה: והרמאי אע"פ שאמר את סימניה ה"ז לא יתן לו: ת"ר בראשונה כל מי שאבדה לו אבידה היה נותן סימנין ונוטלה משרבו הרמאין ז התקינו שיהו אומרים לו צא והבא עדים דלאו רמאי את וטול כי הא דאבוה דרב פפא אירכס ליה חמרא ואשכחוה אתא לקמיה דרבה בר רב הונא אמר ליה זיל אייתי סהדי דלאו רמאי את וטול אזל אייתי סהדי אמר להו ידעיתון ביה דרמאי הוא אמרו ליה אין אמר להו אנא רמאה אנא אמרו ליה אנן לאו רמאי את קאמרינן אמר רבה בר רב הונא ח מסתברא לא מייתי איניש חובתא לנפשיה: **מתני'** ט כל דבר שעושה ואוכל יעשה ויאכל ודבר שאין עושה ואוכל ימכר שנאמר א) והשבותו לו ראה היאך תשיבנו לו מה יהא בדמים ר"ט אומר י ישתמש בהן לפיכך אם אבדו כ חייב באחריותן ר"ע אומר לא ישתמש בהן לפיכך אם אבדו אין חייב באחריותן: **גמ'** ולעולם אמר רב נחמן ג) אמר שמואל עד י"ב חדש תניא נמי הכי ל כל דבר שעושה ואוכל כגון פרה וחמור מטפל בהן עד י"ב חדש מכאן ואילך שם דמיהן ומניחן מ עגלים וסייחין מטפל בהן שלשה חדשים מכאן ואילך שם דמיהן ומניחן אווזין ותרנגולין מטפל בהם שלשים יום מכאן ואילך שם דמיהן ומניחן אמר רב נחמן בר יצחק תרנגולת כבהמה גסה תניא נמי הכי נ תרנגולת ובהמה גסה מטפל בהן שנים עשר חודש מכאן ואילך שם דמיהן ומניחן עגלים וסייחין מטפל בהן ל' יום מכאן ואילך שם דמיהן ומניחן ס אווזין ותרנגולין וכל דבר שטיפולו מרובה משכרו מטפל בהן שלשה ימים מכאן ואילך שם דמיהן ומניחן קשיא עגלים וסייחין אעגלים וסייחין קשיא אווזין ותרנגולין אאווזין ותרנגולין עגלים וסייחין אעגלים וסייחין לא קשיא ע הא דרעיא והא דפטומא אווזין ותרנגולין אאווזין ותרנגולין נמי לא קשיא פ הא ברברבי הא בזוטרי: ושאינו עושה ואוכל: תנו רבנן והשבותו לו ראה היאך תשיבנו לו שלא יאכיל עגל לעגלים וסיח לסייחין אווזא לאווזין ותרנגול לתרנגולין: מה יהא בדמים רבי טרפון אומר ישתמש וכו': עד כאן לא פליגי
אלא

מסורת הש"ס

א) נ"א בר רומאי מהרש"ם, ב) תענית יט. ג) [גירסת רי"ף ולעול אמר שמואל וגירס הרא"ש אמר רב יהודה אמר שמואל] ד) מהרש"ל מ"ז, ה) [ד לב. ד"ה ב"ד].

הגהות הגר"א

[א] רש"י ד"ה רברבי כו'. נ"ב אבל רמב"ם פ להיפך וכן נ"י בשם ר"ר

תורה אור השלם

א) וְאִם לֹא קָרוֹב אָחִיךָ אֵלֶיךָ וְלֹא יְדַעְתּוֹ וַאֲסַפְתּוֹ אֶל תּוֹךְ בֵּיתֶךָ וְהָיָה עִמְּךָ עַד דְּרֹשׁ אָחִיךָ אֹתוֹ וַהֲשֵׁבֹתוֹ לוֹ [דברים כב, ב]

ליקוטי רש"י

עד דרוש אחיך. וכי תעלה בלבבך שיתנהו לו קודם שידרשהו אלא דרשהו שלא יהא רמאי. והשבותו לו. שתהא השבה שלא יאכל בביתו כדי דמיו ותתבעם ממנו מכאן אמרו כל דבר שעושה ואוכל יעשה ויאכל ושאינו עושה ואוכל ימכר [דברים כב, ב]. וסייחין. בנו של חמור קרוי סייח [רשב"ם ב"ב עח:].

לעזי רש"י

אנשמיטר"א. פירו לטפל, להתעסק.

רבינו חננאל

הגשמים וכו'. והנה מהלך ט"ו ימים היא. ואסיקנא לא שנא מקדש ראשון ולא שנא מקדש שני לא הטריחו באבידה יותר מדאי. ת"ר משחרב בית המקדש התקינו להיות מכריזין בכנסיות ובתי מדרשות משרבו האנסין שאומרין אבדתא למלכא התקינו שיהא מודיע המרצאה לשכניו ולמיודעיו ודיו. פי' מהסם מתיירא. ת"ר אבן הטוען היתה בירושלים כל מי שאבדה לו אבידה נפנה לשם וכו' פי' אבן גבוהה היתה בירושלים והיה כל מוצא אבידה עולה עליה ומכריז וזו היא ששנינו בפרק סדר תעניות השני אמר להן חוני המעגל צאו וראו אם נמחת אבן הטוען. אבקש רחמים שיפסקו הגשמים: **מתני'** אמר את האבידה ולא אמר את סימניה. אוקמה רב ספרא אליבא דרב נחמן דאמר גלימא מכריז א) כדאמר האבידה וסימניה ומאי לא אמר סימניה דקאמר במתני' לא אמר סימנין מובהקין דידה. וסוגיין בעינן דיהיב סימנין מובהקין והוא דאית סהדי דליתיה רמאי. ופשטינן דלא מייתי איניש חובה לנפשיה כדאבוה דרב פפא. תלמוד ארץ ישראל שמע סימניה בהאי כנישתא ואזל לכנישתא אחריתי יהיב סימניה זהו רמאי וכן כיוצא בו: **מתני'** כל דבר שעושה ואוכל יעשה ואוכל אוקימנא עד י"ב חדש. תניא נמי הכי כל דבר שעושה ואוכל כגון פרה וחמור מטפל בהן כל י"ב חדש מכאן ואילך שם דמיהן ומניחן עגלים וסייחים אם יכולין לרעות מטפל בהן ג' חדשים. אוזין ותרנגולין גדולים מטפל בהן ל' יום. ותניא אחריתי תרגולת כבהמה גסה י"ב חדש וכל דבר שטיפולו מרובה משכרו ג' ימים. ושאינו עושה ואוכל ימכור שנאמר והשבותו לו ראה היאך תשיבנו לו. שלא יאכיל עגל לעגלים. פי' לא תמכור עגל היום

חשק שלמה על ר"ח א) אולי צ"ל כדאמר.

אלא הא דתנן [א] מצא תכריך של שטרות או אגודה של שטרות ה"ז יחזיר הכי נמי דניחא ליה ללוה לאהדורי ליה למלוה אלא אמר רבא [א]סימנין דאורייתא דכתיב [א] והיה עמך עד דרוש אחיך אותו [ב] וכי תעלה על דעתך שיתננו קודם שידרשנו אלא דרשהו אם רמאי הוא או אינו רמאי לאו בסימנין שמע מינה אמר רבא אם תמצי לומר סימנין דאורייתא אם תמצי לומר הא פשיט ליה סימנין דאורייתא משום דאיכא למימר כדשנינן סימנין וסימנין [ב]יניח סימנין ועדים [ג]ינתן לבעל העדים סימנין וסימנין ועד אחד [ד]עד אחד כמאן דליתיה דמי ויניח עדי אריגה ועדי נפילה [ה]תנתן לעדי נפילה דאמרינן זבוני זבנה ומאיניש אחרינא נפל מדת ארכו ומדת רחבו [ו]תנתן למדת ארכו דמדת רחבו שעורי קא משער לה כד מכסי לה מרה וקאי ומדת ארכו לא משתער לה מדת ארכו ומדת רחבו ומדת גמיו [ז]ינתן למדת ארכו ורחבו מדת ארכו ומדת רחבו ומדת משקלותיו [ח]ינתן למדת משקלותיו הוא אומר סימני הגט והיא אומרת סימני הגט [ט]ינתן לה במאי אילימא במדת ארכו ורחבו דלמא בהדי דנקיט ליה חזיתיה [י]אלא נקב יש בו בצד אות פלוני הוא אומר סימני החוט והיא אומרת סימני החוט [כ]ינתן לה במאי אילימא בחיורא ובסומקא ודלמא בהדי דנקיט ליה חזיתיה אלא במדת ארכו הוא אומר בחפיסה והיא אומרת בחפיסה ינתן לו מ"ט מידע ידעה דכל מה דאית ליה בחפיסה הוא דמנח ליה:

**מתני'** ועד מתי חייב להכריז עד כדי שידעו בו שכניו דברי ר"מ ר' יהודה אומר [ל]שלש רגלים ואחר הרגל האחרון שבעה ימים כדי שילך לביתו שלשה ויחזור שלשה ויכריז יום אחד:

**גמ'** תנא שכני אבידה מאי שכני אבידה אילימא שכנים דבעל אבידה אי ידע ליה ליזיל ולהדריה נהליה אלא שכני מקום שנמצאת בו אבידה: רבי יהודה אומר כו': ורמינהו [ג] בשלשה במרחשון שואלין את הגשמים ר"ג אומר [ד]בז' בו (שהוא) ט"ו יום אחר החג כדי שיגיע אחרון שבא"י לנהר פרת אמר רב יוסף לא קשיא כאן במקדש ראשון כאן במקדש שני במקדש ראשון דנפישי ישראל טובא דכתיב בהו [ב] יהודה וישראל רבים כחול אשר על הים לרוב בעינן כולי האי במקדש שני דלא נפישי ישראל טובא דכתיב בהו [ג] כל הקהל כאחד ארבע רבוא אלפים שלש מאות וששים לא בעינן כולי האי אמר ליה אביי והא כתיב [ד] וישבו הכהנים והלוים וגו' [ה] והמשוררים והשוערים וכל ישראל בעריהם וכיון דהכי הוא אפכא מסתברא מקדש ראשון דנפישי ישראל טובא דמשתכחי שיירתא דאזלי בין ביממא ובין בליליא לא בעינן כולי האי וסגי בתלתא יומא מקדש שני דלא נפישי ישראל טובא ולא משתכחי שיירתא [ס]דאזלי בין ביממא ובין בליליא בעינן כולי האי רבא אמר לא שנא במקדש ראשון ולא שנא במקדש שני לא הטריחו רבנן באבדה יותר מדאי [ע]אמר רבינא שמע מינה [י]כי מכריז גלימא מכריז דאי סלקא דעתך אבידתא מכריז בעינן למטפי ליה חד יומא לעיוני במאניה אלא שמע מינה גלימא מכריז שמע מינה רבא אמר אפילו תימא אבידתא מכריז לא הטריחו רבנן באבידה יותר מדאי ת"ר [פ]רגל ראשון אומר רגל שני אומר רגל שלישי אומר סתם ואמאי לימא רגל שלישי דלא אתי לאחלופי בשני שני נמי אתיא

**רש"י**

**אלא הא דתנן מצא תכריך.** דמשום סימנא מהדרינן ואם נתן מלוה סימן מחזירין לו ואי נפול מיניה דלוה מי ניחא ליה דתהוי הך תקנתא דניהדריה בסימן והא ניחא ליה דנהוו ביד המלוה לעולם: **כדשנינן. בעדים: אם תימצי לומר סימנים דאורייתא.** רבותא נקט דאפי' אמרינן דאורייתא אפ"ה עדים עדיפי כדמפרש ואזיל סימנין ועדים ינתן לבעל עדים: **סימנין וסימנין.** באו שנים ונתנו סימניה: **יניח.** עד שיבא אליהו: **מדת ארכו כו'.** זה אומר מדת ארכו וזה נותן מדת רחבו: **שעורי משער לה.** אם ראה אותה ביד הבעלים שיערה כשהיה בעלה מכוסה בה אם טלית היא: **מדת ארכו ורחבו ומדת גמיו.** זה אומר כך ארכה וכך רחבה וזה אומר ארכה ורחבה כך וכך אמות בין הכל אבל אינו יודע כמה באורך וכמה ברוחב: **גמיו.** גאם יוונית עשויה כמין ך' שלנו להכי קרי אורך ורוחב יחד גמיו: **הוא אומר סימני הגט.** ואומר ממני נפל שנמלכתי שלא ליתן: **והיא אומרת סימני הגט.** וממני נפל שנתנו לי וגרסתני: **ינתן לה.** שהוא נתנו ויודע סימנין אבל היא אם לא נתנו לה מהיכן ידעה: **סימני החוט.** שהגט קשור בו: **בחפיסה.** מלאת אותו: **מתני' שכיניו.** מפרש בגמרא: **כדי שילך.** כל אחד לביתו: **שלשה.** משישמע ההכרזה וידע אם אבד לו כלום ואם יבין שאבד יחזור שלשה: **ויכריז יום אחד.** אני אבדתי ואלו סימניה ובגמרא פריך דבג' ימים אין שהות לחזור לסוף א"י: **גמ' שכני מקום שנמצא בו אבידה.** שמא שלהן היא: **כדי שיגיע כו'.** ולא ידביקוהו הגשמים אלמא כולי האי בעינן ומתני' תני שלשה: **והכתיב וישבו כל ישראל בעריהם.** ואע"ג דפורתא הוו בכל עריהן היו מפוזרים ויש רחוקים מירושלים כבתחילה: **ה"ג.** וכיון דהכי הוא איפכא מסתברא: **דמצות עלמא.** לוות יש לו טובים השנים: **שמע מינה.** מדלא יהבי ליה לרבנן שהות אלא הליכה וחזרה: **גלימא מכריז.** זה שמלאה מכריז שם חפץ טלית מלאתי ולכך לא הוצרכו ליתן שהות יום אחד לעיין בכליו מה אבד שהאדם יודע כמה טליתות יש לו וכשהוא בביתו בודק אם ימלאנה ואין לריך שהות: **דאי ס"ד אבידתא מכריז.** ואינו מזכיר שם החפץ ליתבו ליה לכל חד וחד אכתי טפי יומא לעיוני במאניה אם כל כליו בידו ופלוגתא היא בהא לקמן: **לא הטריחו.** זה שיהא שוהא יותר משבעה ימים: **רגל ראשון.** שהוא מכריז: **אומר.** בהכרזתו זהו רגל ראשון שלא להטריח את האובד לחזור וכשיבא רגל שני יעלה לרגל ויתן סימניה: **שלישי אומר סתם.** אבידה מלאתי ואינו אומר איזה רגל הוא למלאתה כדי שלא יסמוך האובד על רגל הבא ויבין שזהו רגל האחרון: אתי

**תוספות**

**מצא** תכריך של שטרות מי ניחא ליה ללוה כו'. וא"ת אין ניחא ליה דכי ילוה לאחר דליהדרו ליה לדידיה וי"ל דאינו רוצה להפסיד עתה כדי להיות בספק ריוח פעם אחרת:

**חמשה** עשר יום. וא"ת והלא [ח] א"י היא ארבע מאות פרסה על ארבע מאות פרסה [ט] ומהלך אדם (א) עשרה פרסאות ביום הוי ארבעים יום באורך וירושלים מן הירדן שהוא תחום א"י מהלך יום אחד כדאיתא בבילה (דף ה.) נשאר מלד אחד ל"ט ימים וי"ל דעם כרמים ויערים היה ארבע מאות פרסה אבל מישוב לא היה כל כך [י]:

**לא** בעינן כולי האי. וסגי בתלתא יומי וא"ת דז' ימים ומתלה לריך דהיינו חלי של ט"ו יום וי"ל דכי לא שכיחי שיירתא ואין הולך בלילה גם כל היום אינו הולך לפי שלא ימלא מלון בערב:

**עין משפט נר מצוה**

צה א מיי' פי"ג מהל' אבידה הלכה ה:
צו ב מיי' שם הלכה ו סמג עשין עד טוש"ע ח"מ סי' רסז סעיף ח:
צז ג מיי' שם טוש"ע שם סעיף ט:
צח ד מיי' שם טוש"ע שם סעיף י:
צט ה מיי' שם הל' ז טוש"ע שם סעיף יא:
ק ו מיי' שם טוש"ע שם סעיף יב:
קא ז מיי' שם טוש"ע שם סעיף יד:
קב ח מיי' שם טוש"ע שם סעיף יג:
קג ט י כ מיי' שם פי"ח הלכה ו ז סמג שם טוש"ע אה"ע סי' קנג:
קד ל מיי' שם פי"ג הלכה ח סמג שם:
קה מ מיי' פ"ב מהל' תפלה הלכה טז סמג עשין יט טוש"ע א"ח סי' קיז סעיף א:
קו נ מיי' פי"ג מהל' גזלה ואבדה הל' א סמג עשין עד טוש"ע ח"מ סי' רסז סעיף ד:
קז ס מיי' שם הל' ח:

**ליקוטי רש"י**

**מצא תכריך של שטרות.** בכרך או באגודה. **ה"ז יחזיר.** לדבר שיש בו סימן הוא כדמפרש בגמרא שהכלי סימן כשיאמרו הבעלים בכלי כך וכך מלאת אותם וכן תכריך ואגודה הרי זה יחזיר לדבר שיש בו סימן הוא [לעיל כ.]. **אלא דרשהו אם רמאי הוא.** והכי משמע עד דרוש אחיך אותו עד לרשך את אחיך [לעיל כז:]. **ט"ו יום אחר החג.** כלומר בשבעה במרחשון הוא ט"ו אחר החג. **כדי שיגיע אחרון.** כלומר קודם ביאת מים לנהר פרת שהוא רחוק יותר [תענית י.]. **כל הקהל כאחד וכו'.** כשהיו כולם ביחד עם הכהנים והלוים והנתינים היו בהם חשבון זה [עזרא ב, סד].

**רבינו חננאל**

לאבידה ואסיקנא אלא אמר רבא [סימנין] דאוריית' מהכא עד דרוש אחיך אותו והשבות לו וכי תעלה על דעתך שיתנו לו קודם שיתבענו אלא עד שתדרשהו אם רמאי הוא אם לאו ובמאי תהיה דרישתו בסימנין אמור לו תן סימניה ואם יביא סימניה תנה לו ש"מ סימנין דאורייתא אמר רבא אם תמצא לומר סימנין דאורייתא אקשינן עליה אכתי אמרת אם תמצא לומר והא כבר פשטינן לה סימנין דאורייתא ודחינן משום דאיכא למימר הא דפשטינן דרשהו לאו כדקאמרת אלא דרשהו לתובע הכי אם הוא צורבא מרבנן דלא משני בדיבוריה אלא במסכתא ובפוריא ובאושפיזא בלחוד מהדרינן ליה אבידה בטביעות עינא. סימנין וסימנין יניח פי' אם באו שניהם ונתנו זה וזה סימניה וכל אחד אמר שלי הוא לא יתננה לא לזה ולא לזה אלא יניחנה מוצאה אצלו. אבל אם אחד נתן סימניה וטען נפלה ממני ובא אחר והביא עדים כי ממנו נפל תנתן לבעל עדים. א) עד אחד כמאן דליתיה דמי. מדת ארכו ומדת רחבו [תנתן למדת ארכו] זה נתן מדת ארכה ורחבה של טלית וזה נתן מדת גמיה תינתן לבעל מדת ארכה ורחבה. אשתו אומרת זה הגט נתנו לי בעלי ונפל ממני ואמרה [סימניו] והבעל אמר סימניו וטוען כי לא נתתיו לה עדיין ינתן לה והוא שנותנת סימנין מובהקין כגון נקב ישנו בצד אות פלוני ש"מ דבסימן מובהק שרינן אשת איש דהיא איסורא וכל שכן ממונא: **מתני' עד מתי חייב להכריז** וכו' תנא עד שידעו בו שכני המקום שנמצאת בה זו האבידה ורמינן על הא דתנן ואחר הרגל האחרון ז' ימים כדי שילך לביתו ג' ויחזור בג' ויכריז יום אחד פי' כדי שילך שומע המכריז למקומו ויגיד לבעל האבידה ויבא מיד וישמע ביום השביעי המכריז ויתן סימניה ויקחנה למימרא דארץ ישראל מהלך ג' ימים היא. והתנן בג' מרחשון שואלים את הגשמים

**מסורת הש"ס**

לעיל כ., ב) [לעיל כז:], תענית י., ד) מהרש"ס ז, ה) נ"א ולא אזלי, ו) נ"א וגרסני, עיין בתוספות דלעיל כב: ה אי דליכא, ח) [מגילה], ט) [פסחים לג:], [עיין תוס' ראש השנה כג: ד"ה כמה].

**הגהות הב"ח**

(א) תוס' ד"ה חמשה וכו' ומהלך אדם בינוני הוא עשרה פרסאות:

**גליון הש"ס**

גמ' ינתן למדת משקלותיו. עיין לעיל כג ע"ב תוס' ד"ה במשקל: שם אמר רבינא ש"מ. עיין ברא"ש פ"ג דחולין ס"ס כ"ג:

**תורה אור השלם**

א) וְאִם לֹא קָרוֹב אָחִיךָ אֵלֶיךָ וְלֹא יְדַעְתּוֹ וַאֲסַפְתּוֹ אֶל תּוֹךְ בֵּיתֶךָ וְהָיָה עִמְּךָ עַד דְּרֹשׁ אָחִיךָ אֹתוֹ וַהֲשֵׁבֹתוֹ לוֹ: [דברים כב, ב]

ב) יְהוּדָה וְיִשְׂרָאֵל רַבִּים כַּחוֹל אֲשֶׁר עַל הַיָּם לָרֹב אֹכְלִים וְשֹׁתִים וּשְׂמֵחִים: [מלכים א' ד, כ]

ג) כָּל הַקָּהָל כְּאֶחָד אַרְבַּע רִבּוֹא אַלְפַּיִם שְׁלֹשׁ מֵאוֹת שִׁשִּׁים: [עזרא ב, סד]

ד) וַיֵּשְׁבוּ הַכֹּהֲנִים וְהַלְוִיִּם וְהַשּׁוֹעֲרִים וְהַמְשֹׁרְרִים וּמִן הָעָם וְהַנְּתִינִים וְכָל יִשְׂרָאֵל בְּעָרֵיהֶם וַיִּגַּע הַחֹדֶשׁ הַשְּׁבִיעִי וּבְנֵי יִשְׂרָאֵל בְּעָרֵיהֶם: [נחמיה ז, עב]

ה) וַיֵּשְׁבוּ הַכֹּהֲנִים וְהַלְוִיִּם וּמִן הָעָם וְהַמְשֹׁרְרִים וְהַשּׁוֹעֲרִים וְהַנְּתִינִים בְּעָרֵיהֶם וְכָל יִשְׂרָאֵל בְּעָרֵיהֶם: [עזרא ב, ע]

**לעזי רש"י**

טודי"ש. פירוש (לשבת) לוותא (עם...) (עיין רש"י ב"ב דף כא ע"א ד"ה ליהוי לוותא לחבריה).

חשק שלמה על ר"ח א) נראה דחסר וצ"ל סימנין וסימנין ועד אחד עד אחד וכו'.

**תָּנוּ רַבָּנ – The Rabbis taught in a Baraisa:** רֶגֶל רִאשׁוֹן אוֹמֵר רֶגֶל רִאשׁוֹ – On THE FIRST FESTIVAL that one announces a find, NE SAYS, "This is THE FIRST FESTIVAL of the announcement."[38] רֶגֶל שֵׁנִי אוֹמֵר רֶגֶל שֵׁנ – On THE SECOND FESTIVAL, ONE SAYS, 'This is THE SECOND FESTIVAL of the announcement." רֶגֶל שְׁלִישִׁי אוֹמֵר סְתָ – On THE THIRD and final FESTIVAL HE SAYS nerely that he has found an article, WITHOUT SPECIFYING the estival.[39]

The Gemara asks:

**וְאַמַּאי לֵימָא רֶגֶל שְׁלִישִׁי – And why** should he not give a number? **Let him say** that it is **the third festival.** What harm would result from announcing this?

The Gemara answers:

**דְּלֹא אָתֵי לְאַחְלוּפֵי בְּשֵׁנִי** – So **that it should not lead to confusing** the "third" **with the "second."**[40]

The Gemara asks:

**שֵׁנִי נַמִּי** – If so, announcing **the second** festival **too**

NOTES

38. In this way, when one returns home and realizes he is missing something, he does not need to rush back to Jerusalem to claim it. Instead, he can wait until the next festival to claim it (*Rashi*).

39. The omission of the festival is meant to alert the listeners to the fact that this is the last announcement for the object, and that they have only seven more days to return and claim it (*Rashi*).

40. A person hearing a number might confuse one number with another, and think that he heard the announcer say the "second" festival. It is thus better to omit any reference to the festival and have that stand as the sign of the final announcement.

אלא הא דתנן [א] מצא תכריך של שטרות או אגודה של שטרות ה"ז יחזיר הכי נמי דניחא ליה ללוה לאהדורי ליה למלוה אלא אמר רבא [א] סימנין דאורייתא דכתיב [א] והיה עמך עד דרוש אחיך אותו [ג] וכי תעלה על דעתך שיתננו קודם שידרשנו אלא דרשהו אם רמאי הוא או אינו רמאי לאו בסימנין שמע מינה אמר רבא אם תמצי לומר סימנין דאורייתא אם תמצי לומר הא פשיט ליה סימנין דאורייתא משום דאיכא למימר כדשנינן סימנין וסימנין [ב] יניח סימנין ועדים [ג] ינתן לבעל העדים סימנין וסימנין ועד אחד [ד] עד אחד כמאן דליתיה דמי ויניח עדי אריגה ועדי נפילה [ה] תנתן לעדי נפילה דאמרינן זבוני זבנה ומאיניש אחרינא נפל מדת ארכו ומדת רחבו [ו] תנתן למדת ארכו דמדת רחבו שעורי קא משער לה כד מכסי לה מרה וקאי ומדת ארכו לא משתער לה מדת ארכו ומדת רחבו ומדת גמיו [ז] ינתן למדת ארכו ורחבו מדת ארכו ומדת רחבו ומדת משקלותיו [ח] ינתן למדת משקלותיו הוא אומר סימני הגט והיא אומרת סימני הגט [ט] ינתן לה במאי אילימא במדת ארכו ורחבו דלמא בהדי דנקיט ליה חזיתיה [י] אלא נקב יש בו בצד אות פלוני הוא אומר סימני החוט והיא אומרת סימני החוט [כ] ינתן לה במאי אילימא בחיורא ובסומקא ודלמא בהדי דנקיט ליה חזיתיה אלא במדת ארכו הוא אומר בחפיסה והיא אומרת בחפיסה ינתן לו מ"ט מידע ידעה דכל מה דאית ליה בחפיסה הוא דמנח ליה: **מתני'** ועד מתי חייב להכריז עד כדי שידעו בו שכניו דברי ר"מ ר' יהודה אומר [ל] שלש רגלים ואחר הרגל האחרון שבעה ימים כדי שילך לביתו שלשה ויחזור שלשה ויכריז יום אחד: **גמ'** תנא שכני אבידה מאי שכני אבידה אילימא שכינים דבעל אבידה אי ידע ליה ליזול ולהדריה נהליה אלא שכני מקום שנמצאת בו אבידה: רבי יהודה אומר כו': ורמינהו [ג] בשלשה במרחשון שואלין את הגשמים ר"ג אומר [מ] בז' בו [ד] (שהוא) ט"ו יום אחר החג כדי שיגיע אחרון שבא"י לנהר פרת אמר רב יוסף לא קשיא כאן במקדש ראשון כאן במקדש שני במקדש ראשון דנפישי ישראל טובא דכתיב בהו [ב] יהודה וישראל רבים כחול אשר על הים לרוב בעינן כולי האי במקדש שני דלא נפישי ישראל טובא דכתיב בהו [ג] כל הקהל כאחד ארבע רבוא אלפים שלש מאות וששים לא בעינן כולי האי אמר ליה אביי והא כתיב [ד] וישבו הכהנים והלוים וגו' [ה] והמשוררים והשוערים וכל ישראל בעריהם וכיון דהכי הוא אפכא מסתברא מקדש ראשון דנפישי ישראל טובא דמצוות עלמא ומשתכחי שיירתא דאזלי בין בימּמא ובין בליליא לא בעינן כולי האי וסגי בתלתא יומא מקדש שני דלא נפישי ישראל טובא ולא מצוות עלמא ולא משתכחי שיירתא [ה] דאזלי בין ביממא ובין בליליא בעינן כולי האי רבא אמר לא שנא במקדש ראשון ולא שנא במקדש שני לא הטריחו רבנן באבדה יותר מדאי [ס] אמר רבינא שמע מינה [נ] כי מכריז גלימא מכריז דאי סלקא דעתך אבידתא מכריז בעינן למטפי ליה חד יומא לעיוני במאניה אלא שמע מינה גלימא מכריז שמע מינה רבא אמר אפילו תימא אבידתא מכריז לא הטריחו רבנן באבידה יותר מדאי ת"ר [ס] רגל ראשון אומר רגל ראשון רגל שני אומר רגל שני רגל שלישי אומר סתם ואמאי לימא רגל שלישי דלא אתי לאחלופי בשני נמי

אתיא

**רש"י**

**אלא הא דתנן מצא תכריך.** דמשום סימנא מהדרינן ואם נתן מלוה סימן מחזירין לו ואי נפול מיניה דלוה מי ניחא ליה דתהוי הך תקנתא דניהדרה בסימן והא ניחא ליה דנהוו ביד המוצא לעולם: **כדשנינן.** בעדים: **אם תימצי לומר סימנים דאורייתא.** רבותא נקט דאפי' אמרינן דאורייתא אפ"ה עדים עדיפי כדמפרש ואזיל סימנין ועדים ינתן לבעל עדים: **סימנין וסימנין.** באו שנים ונתנו סימניה: **יניח.** עד שיבא אליהו: **מדת ארכו כו'.** זה אומר מדת ארכו וזה נותן מדת רחבו: **שעורי משער לה.** אם ראה אותה ביד הבעלים שיערה כשהיה בעלה מכוסה בה אם טלית היא: **מדת ארכו ורחבו ומדת גמיו.** זה אומר כך ארכה וכך רחבה וזה אומר ארכה ורחבה כך וכך אמות בין הכל אבל אינו יודע כמה באורך וכמה ברוחב: **גמיו.** גאם יוונית עשויה כמין ך' שלנו להכי קרי אורך ורוחב יחד גמיו: **הוא אומר סימני הגט.** ואומר ממני נפל שנמלכתי שלא ליתן: **והיא אומרת סימני הגט.** וממני נפל שנתנו לי [ו] וגרסתי: **ינתן לה.** שהוא נתנו ויודע סימנין אבל היא אם לא נתנו לה מהיכן ידעה: **סימני החוט.** שהגט קשור בו: **בחפיסה.** מלאת אותו: **מתני' שכיניו.** מפרש בגמרא: **כדי שילך.** כל אחד לביתו: **שלשה.** משישמע ההכרזה וידע אם אבד לו כלום ואם יבין שאבד יחזור שלשה: [ז] **ויכריז יום אחד.** אני אבדתי ואלו סימניה ובגמרא פריך דבג' ימים אין שהות לחזור לסוף א"י: **גמ' שכני מקום שנמצא בו אבידה.** שמא שלהן היא: **כדי שיגיע כו'.** ולא ידביקוהו הגשמים אלמא כולי האי בעינן ומתני' תני שלשה: **והכתיב וישבו כל ישראל בעריהם.** ואע"ג דפורתא הוו בכל עריהן היו מפוזרים ויש רחוקים מירושלים כבתחילה: **ה"ג. וכיון דהכי הוא איפכא מסתברא:** **דמצות עלמא.** לוות יש לו טובים הסנים: **שמע מינה.** מדלא יהבי ליה לרבנן שהות אלא הליכה וחזרה: **גלימא מכריז.** זה שמלאה מכריז שם חפץ טלית מלאתי ולכך לא הוצרכו ליתן שהות יום אחד לעיין בכליו מה אבד שהאדם יודע כמה טליתות יש לו כשהוא בביתו בודק אם ימלאנה ואין צריך שהות: **דאי ס"ד אבידתא מכריז.** ואינו מזכיר שם החפץ ליתבו ליה לכל חד וחד אכתי טפי יומא לעיוני במאניה אם כל כליו בידו ופלוגתא היא בהא לקמן: **לא הטריחו.** זה שיהא שוהא יותר משבעה ימים: **רגל ראשון.** שהוא מכריז: **אומר.** בהכרזתו זהו רגל ראשון שלא להטריח את האובד לחזור וכשיבא רגל שני יעלה לרגל ויתן סימניה: **שלישי אומר סתם.** אבידה מלאתי ואינו אומר איזה רגל הוא למליאתה כדי שלא יסמוך האובד על רגל הבא ויבין שזהו רגל האחרון:

אתי

**תוספות**

**מצא** תכריך של שטרות מי ניחא ליה ללוה כו'. וא"ת אין ניחא ליה דכי ילוה לאחר דליהדרו ליה לדידיה וי"ל דאינו רוצה להפסיד עתה כדי להיות בספק ריוח פעם אחרת:

**חמשה** עשר יום. וא"ת והלא [ט] א"י היא ארבע מאות פרסה על ארבע מאות פרסה [ט] ומהלך אדם (א) עשרה פרסאות ביום הוי ארבעים יום באורך וירושלים מן הירדן שהוא תחום א"י מהלך יום אחד כדאיתא בבילה (דף ה.) נשאר מלד אחד ל"ט ימים וי"ל דעם כרמים ויערים היה ארבע מאות פרסה אבל מישוב לא היה כל כך [י]:

**לא** בעינן כולי האי. וסגי בתלתא יומי וא"ת לד' ימים ומתלה צריך דהיינו אלי של ט"ו יום וי"ל דכי לא שכיחי שיירתא ואין הולך בלילה גם כל היום אינו הולך לפי שלא ימצא מלון בערב:

אבן

**עין משפט נר מצוה**

צה א מיי' פי"ג מהל' אבידה הלכה ה:
צו ב מיי' שם הלכה ו סמג עשין עד טוש"ע ח"מ סי' רסז סעיף ח:
צז ג מיי' שם טוש"ע שם סעיף ט:
צח ד מיי' שם טוש"ע שם סעיף י:
צט ה מיי' שם הל' ז טוש"ע שם סעיף יא:
ק ו מיי' שם טוש"ע שם סעיף יב:
קא ז מיי' שם טוש"ע שם סעיף יד:
קב ח מיי' שם טוש"ע שם סעיף יג:
קג ט י כ מיי' שם פי"ח הלכה ו ז סמג שם טוש"ע אה"ע סי' קנג:
קד ל מיי' שם פי"ג הלכה ח סמג שם:
קה מ מיי' פ"ב מהל' תפלה הלכה טז סמג עשין יט טוש"ע א"ח סי' קיז סעיף א:
קו נ מיי' פי"ג מהל' גזלה ואבדה הל' א סמג עשין עד טוש"ע ח"מ סי' רסז סעיף ד:
קז ס מיי' שם הל' ח:

**ליקוטי רש"י**

**מצא תכריך של שטרות.** בכרך או באגודה. **ה"ז יחזיר.** דדבר שיש בו סימן הוא כדמפרש בגמרא שהכלי סימן כשיאמרו הבעלים בכלי כך וכך מצאת אותם וכן תכריך ואגודה הרי זה יחזיר דדבר שיש בו סימן הוא [לעיל כ.]. **אלא דרשהו אם רמאי הוא.** והכי משמע עד דרוש אחיך אותו עד דרשך את אחיך [לעיל כז:]. **ט"ו יום אחר החג.** כלומר בשבעה במרחשון הוא ט"ו אחר החג. **כדי שיגיע אחרון.** כלומר קודם ביאת מים לנהר פרת שהוא רחוק יותר [תענית י.]. **כל הקהל כאחד וכו'.** כשהיו כולם ביחד עם הכהנים והלוים והנתינים היו בהם חשבון זה [עזרא ב, סד].

**רבינו חננאל**

לאבידה ואסיקנא אלא אמר רבא [סימנין] דאוריית' מהכא עד דרוש אחיך אותו והשבות לו וכי תעלה על דעתך שיתנו לו קודם שיתבענו אלא עד שתדרשהו אם רמאי הוא אם לאו ובמאי תהיה דרישתו בסימנין אמור לו תן סימניה ואם יביא סימניה תנה לו ש"מ סימנין דאורייתא אמר רבא אם תמצא לומר סימנין דאורייתא אקשינן עליה אכתי אמרת אם תמצא לומר והא כבר פשטינן לה סימנין דאורייתא ודחינן משום דאיכא למימר הא דפשטינן דרשהו לאו כדקאמרת אלא דרשהו לתובע הכי אם הוא צורבא מרבנן דלא משני בדיבוריה אלא במסכתא ובפוריא ובאושפיזא

בלחוד מהדרינן ליה אבידה בטביעות עינא. סימנין וסימנין יניח פי' אם באו שניהם ונתנו זה וזה סימניה וכל אחד אמר שלי הוא לא יתננה לא לזה ולא לזה אלא יניחנה מוצאה אצלו. אבל אם אחד נתן סימניה וטען נפלה ממני ובא אחר והביא עדים כי ממנו נפל תנתן לבעל עדים. א) עד אחד כמאן דליתיה דמי. מדת ארכו ומדת רחבו [תנתן למדת ארכו] זה נתן מדת ארכה ורחבה של טלית וזה נתן מדת גמיה תינתן לבעל מדת ארכה ורחבה. אשתו אומרת זה הגט נתנו לי בעלי ונפל ממני ואמרה [סימניו] והבעל אמר סימניו וטוען כי לא נתתיו לה עדיין ינתן לה והוא שנותנת סימנין מובהקין כגון נקב ישנו בצד אות פלוני ש"מ דבסימן מובהק שרינן אשת איש דהיא איסורא וכל שכן ממונא: **מתני' עד מתי חייב להכריז וכו'** תנא עד שידעו בו שכני המקום שנמצאת בה זו האבידה ורמינן על הא דתנן ואחר הרגל האחרון ז' ימים כדי שילך לביתו ג' ויחזור בג' ויכריז יום אחד פי' כדי שילך שומע המכריז למקומו ויגיד וישמע בעל האבידה ויבא מיד ביום השביעי המכריז ויתן סימניה ויקחנה למימרא דארץ ישראל מהלך ג' ימים היא. והתנן בג' מרחשון שואלים את הגשמים

חשק שלמה על ר"ח א) נראה דחסר וצ"ל סימנין וסימנין ועד אחד עד אחד וכו'.

**מסורת הש"ס**

א) [לעיל כ.], ב) [לעיל כז:], ג) תענית י., ד) מהר"ם ז, ה) נ"א ולא אזלי, ו) נ"א וגרסני, ז) עיין בתוספות דלעיל כב: ד"ה אי דליכא, ח) [מגילה, ט) [פסחים לג:], [עיין תוס' ראש השנה כג: ד"ה כמה].

**הגהות הב"ח**

(א) תוס' ד"ה חמשה וכו' ומהלך אדם בינוני הוה עשרה פרסאות:

**גליון הש"ס**

גמ' ינתן למדת משקלותיו. עיין לעיל דף כג ע"ב תוס' ד"ה במשקל: שם אמר רבינא ש"מ. עיין בר"ש פ"ג דחולין ס"ס כ"ג:

**תורה אור השלם**

א) וְאִם לֹא קָרוֹב אָחִיךָ אֵלֶיךָ וְלֹא יְדַעְתּוֹ וַאֲסַפְתּוֹ אֶל תּוֹךְ בֵּיתֶךָ וְהָיָה עִמְּךָ עַד דְּרֹשׁ אָחִיךָ אֹתוֹ וַהֲשֵׁבֹתוֹ לוֹ: [דברים כב, ב]

ב) יְהוּדָה וְיִשְׂרָאֵל רַבִּים כַּחוֹל אֲשֶׁר עַל הַיָּם לָרֹב אֹכְלִים וְשֹׁתִים וּשְׂמֵחִים: [מלכים א' ד, כ]

ג) כָּל הַקָּהָל כְּאֶחָד אַרְבַּע רִבּוֹא אַלְפַּיִם שְׁלֹשׁ מֵאוֹת שִׁשִּׁים: [עזרא ב, סד]

ד) וַיֵּשְׁבוּ הַכֹּהֲנִים וְהַלְוִיִּם וְהַשּׁוֹעֲרִים וְהַמְשֹׁרְרִים וּמִן הָעָם וְהַנְּתִינִים וְכָל יִשְׂרָאֵל בְּעָרֵיהֶם וַיִּגַּע הַחֹדֶשׁ הַשְּׁבִיעִי וּבְנֵי יִשְׂרָאֵל בְּעָרֵיהֶם: [נחמיה ז, עב]

ה) וַיֵּשְׁבוּ הַכֹּהֲנִים וְהַלְוִיִּם וּמִן הָעָם וְהַמְשֹׁרְרִים וְהַשּׁוֹעֲרִים וְהַנְּתִינִים בְּעָרֵיהֶם וְכָל יִשְׂרָאֵל בְּעָרֵיהֶם: [עזרא ב, ע]

**לעזי רש"י**

שול"יץ. פירוש (לשבת) לגומא (עס...) (עיין רש"י ב"ב דף כא ע"א ד"ה ליסור גומא למבריה).

from this Mishnah that from Jerusalem to the farthest border of the Land of Israel was a fifteen-day journey. Why, then, does R' Yehudah allow people only three days to travel home from Jerusalem and examine their belongings?

The Gemara answers:

אָמַר רַב יוֹסֵף – **Rav Yosef said:** לֹא קַשְׁיָא – **There is no difficulty.** כָּאן בְּמִקְדָּשׁ רִאשׁוֹן כָּאן בְּמִקְדָּשׁ שֵׁנִי – **Here,** in the Mishnah regarding the rains, **it refers to the First Temple** era; **here,** in our Mishnah, **it refers to the Second Temple** era. בְּמִקְדָּשׁ רִאשׁוֹן דִּנְפִישֵׁי יִשְׂרָאֵל טוּבָא – **In** the time of **the First Temple, when the Jews were very numerous,** דִּכְתִיב בְּהוּ: ,,יְהוּדָה וְיִשְׂרָאֵל רַבִּים כַּחוֹל אֲשֶׁר־עַל־הַיָּם לָרֹב׳ – **as it is written** in Scripture **about them:**[30] ***Judah and Israel were as many as the sand which is by the sea in multitude,*** בְּעֵינַן כּוּלֵּי הַאי – **[travelers] required this much** time (i.e. fifteen days) to traverse the distance from Jerusalem to the border. בְּמִקְדָּשׁ שֵׁנִי דְּלָא נְפִישֵׁי יִשְׂרָאֵל טוּבָא – But **in** the time of **the Second Temple, when the Jews were not so numerous,** דִּכְתִיב בְּהוּ: ,,כָּל־הַקָּהָל כְּאֶחָד אַרְבַּע רִבּוֹא אַלְפַּיִם שְׁלֹשׁ־מֵאוֹת וְשִׁשִּׁים׳ – **as is written** in Scripture **about them:**[31] ***The entire congregation together*** *numbered* ***forty-two thousand three hundred and sixty,*** לָא בְּעֵינַן כּוּלֵּי הַאי – **[travelers] did not require this much** time to traverse the distance from Jerusalem to the border, and three days was sufficient.[32]

The Gemara challenges Rav Yosef:

אָמַר לֵיהּ אַבַּיֵי – **Abaye said to Rav Yosef:** וְהָא כְּתִיב: ,,וַיֵּשְׁבוּ הַכֹּהֲנִים וְהַלְוִיִּם וגו – **But it is written in Scripture** regarding Israel's return from exile to rebuild the Second Temple:[33] ***and the Kohanim and Levites returned etc.*** וְהַמְשֹׁרְרִים וְהַשּׁוֹעֲרִים . . . וְכָל־יִשְׂרָאֵל בְּעָרֵיהֶם׳ – ***and the singers and the gatekeepers . . and all of Israel*** *settled* ***in their cities***, i.e. they resettled the cities their families had occupied during the First Temple period, just in fewer numbers than before. Thus, the distance from Jerusalem to the border must have been about the same in the Second Temple era as in the First. – ? –

Based on the previous challenge, the Gemara gives a different answer:

וְכֵיוָן דְּהָכִי הוּא אִפְּכָא מִסְתַּבְּרָא – **And since it is so,** that the same cities were resettled only in smaller numbers than before, **the opposite is** more **logical.** מִקְדָּשׁ רִאשׁוֹן דִּנְפִישֵׁי יִשְׂרָאֵל טוּבָא – In the time of **the First Temple, when Jews were very numerous,** דִּמְצַוְּתֵי עָלְמָא – **so that people would join together** in large numbers, וּמִשְׁתַּכְּחֵי שַׁיַּירְתָּא דְּאָזְלֵי בֵּין בִּימָמָא וּבֵין בְּלֵילְיָא – **and** thus **caravans were to be found that traveled by day and by night,** לָא בְּעֵינַן כּוּלֵּי הַאי – **[travelers] did not require so much time** to reach the border, וְסַגֵּי בִּתְלָתָא יוֹמָא – **and three days was sufficient.**[34] מִקְדָּשׁ שֵׁנִי – In the time of **the Second Temple,** however, דְּלָא נְפִישֵׁי יִשְׂרָאֵל טוּבָא – **when the Jews were not so numerous,** וְלָא מְצַוְּתֵי עָלְמָא – **so that people could not join together** as frequently, וְלָא מִשְׁתַּכְּחֵי שַׁיַּירְתָּא דְּאָזְלֵי בֵּין בִּימָמָא וּבֵין בְּלֵילְיָא – **and caravans were not to be found that traveled by day and by night,** בְּעֵינַן כּוּלֵּי הַאי – **[travelers] required this much** time – fifteen days – to reach the farthest borders.

The Gemara offers another solution:

רָבָא אָמַר – **Rava said:** לָא שְׁנָא בְּמִקְדָּשׁ רִאשׁוֹן וְלָא שְׁנָא בְּמִקְדָּשׁ שֵׁנִי – **There is no difference between the First and Second Temple** times with respect to R' Yehudah's law. In both periods the Rabbis allowed only three days for travel each way, לָא הַטְרִיחוּ רַבָּנַן בַּאֲבֵדָה יוֹתֵר מִדַּאי – because **the Rabbis did not** wish to **burden** a person **unduly over a lost object.** Thus, R' Yehudah only required the finder to wait seven days after the last festival.

The Gemara attempts to resolve a dispute from R' Yehudah's law:[35]

אָמַר רָבִינָא – **Ravina said:** שְׁמַע מִינָּהּ – **Learn from this** – that R' Yehudah allotted only six-days' travel time – כִּי מַכְרִיז גְּלִימָא מַכְרִיז – that **when one announces** the discovery of a garment, for example, **he announces that he found a garment.** דְּאִי סָלְקָא דַּעְתָּךְ אֲבֵידְתָּא מַכְרִיז – **For if you should think** that **he** merely **announces that he found a "lost object,"** without specifying the type of object, בְּעֵינַן לְמִיטְפֵי לֵיהּ חַד יוֹמָא – **we would have to give [the owner] one more day** at home לְעַיּוּנֵי בְּמָאנֵיהּ – **to examine his possessions** and see if he is missing anything.[36] אֶלָּא שְׁמַע מִינָּהּ גְּלִימָא מַכְרִיז – **Learn, therefore, from [Rav Yehudah's ruling]** that **[the finder] announces** that he found **a garment.** שְׁמַע מִינָּהּ – Indeed, **learn from this.**

Rava disagrees:

רָבָא אָמַר – **Rava said:** אֲפִילּוּ תֵּימָא אֲבֵידְתָּא מַכְרִיז – **You may even say** that **he announces** only **a "lost object."** The reason R' Yehudah does not allot an extra day for a person to search his belongings is because לָא הַטְרִיחוּ רַבָּנַן בַּאֲבֵידָה יוֹתֵר מִדַּאי – **the Rabbis did not** wish to **burden** a person **unduly over a lost object.**[37]

The Gemara cites a Baraisa that elaborates on R' Yehudah's law:

NOTES

would be hampered by the difficult weather and road conditions.] Since Shemini Atzeres ended on the twenty-second of Tishrei, R' Gamliel rules that the prayers for rain should not begin until the seventh of Marcheshvan – fifteen days later (see *Rashi* here; cf. *Rashi, Taanis* 4b).

30. *I Kings* 4:20.

31. *Nehemiah* 7:66.

32. The Gemara assumes at this point that because the population was smaller, so too were the borders of the Land.

33. *Ezra* 2:70.

34. The increased demand from such a large population resulted in increased caravan service, with caravans traveling constantly, even at night. Thus, it was possible for a traveler to make much better time and to reach the borders of Eretz Yisrael in three days of continuous travel (see *Tosafos*).

35. The Gemara (28b) records a dispute between Rav Yehudah (the Amora) and Rav Nachman regarding the procedure for announcing lost objects. Rav Yehudah states that one announces merely that he has found something that was lost. Rav Nachman is of the opinion that one must specify the type of object found, for example, a garment. The owner then reclaims it by providing some further identification of it.

36. Since the type of article found was not mentioned, one who suspects he may have lost something must look through *all* his possessions to determine if he is missing anything. This would require at least a day. Since R' Yehudah does not allot an extra day for this, we see that he is of the opinion that one must announce the type of object found, e.g. a garment. As a result, a person would need only to count his garments on his return home to see if one was missing, and this would take almost no time. He could then set out immediately to Jerusalem to reclaim his property, without spending a day going through his possessions (*Rashi*).

37. Just as they did not require the finder to hold the object in Jerusalem long enough for every last person in Eretz Yisrael to return home and then come back to Jerusalem, so too they did not allot a day for those living within a three-day journey of Jerusalem to go home and examine all their possessions. They did not wish to impose too great a burden on one who finds a lost object, by requiring him to remain in Jerusalem [or to find someone to care for the lost object] more than seven days after the third festival on which he announced it. [Although the mitzvah of returning lost property is a Biblical obligation, the possibility of someone from far away having lost an object, and then not hearing about it until the third festival, and then not being sure if he lost it, is somewhat remote! Thus, it was a Rabbinical stringency to allow three days back and forth in the first place, and the Sages did not wish to add any more to the stringency (*Nachalas Moshe*).]

אלא הא דתנן [א] מצא תכריך של שטרות או אגודה של שטרות ה"ז יחזיר הכי נמי דניחא ליה ללוה לאהדורי ליה למלוה אלא אמר רבא [א] סימנין דאורייתא דכתיב [א] והיה עמך עד דרוש אחיך אותו [ג] וכי תעלה על דעתך שיתננו קודם שידרשנו אלא דרשהו אם רמאי הוא או אינו רמאי לאו בסימנין שמע מינה אמר רבא אם תמצי לומר סימנין דאורייתא אם תמצי לומר הא פשיט ליה סימנין דאורייתא משום דאיכא למימר כדשנינן סימנין וסימנין [ב] יניח סימנין ועדים [ג] ינתן לבעל העדים סימנין וסימנין ועד אחד [ד] עד אחד כמאן דליתיה דמי ויניח עדי אריגה ועדי נפילה [ה] תנתן לעדי נפילה דאמרינן זבוני זבנה ומאיניש אחרינא נפל מדת ארכו ומדת רחבו [ו] תנתן למדת ארכו דמדת רחבו שעורי קא משער לה כד מכסי לה מרה וקאי ומדת ארכו לא משתער לה מדת ארכו ומדת רחבו ומדת גמיו [ז] ינתן למדת ארכו ורחבו מדת ארכו ומדת רחבו ומדת משקלותיו [ח] ינתן למדת משקלותיו הוא אומר סימני הגט והיא אומרת סימני הגט [ט] ינתן לה במאי אילימא במדת ארכו ורחבו דלמא בהדי דנקיט ליה חזיתיה [י] אלא נקב יש בו בצד אות פלוני הוא אומר סימני החוט והיא אומרת סימני החוט [כ] ינתן לה במאי אילימא בחיורא ובסומקא ודלמא בהדי דנקיט ליה חזיתיה אלא במדת ארכו הוא אומר בחפיסה והיא אומרת בחפיסה ינתן לו מ"ט מידע ידעה דכל מה דאית ליה בחפיסה הוא דמנח ליה: **מתני'** ועד מתי חייב להכריז עד כדי שידעו בו שכניו דברי ר"מ ר' יהודה אומר [ל] שלש רגלים ואחר הרגל האחרון שבעה ימים כדי שילך לביתו שלשה ויחזור שלשה ויכריז יום אחד: **גמ'** תנא שכני אבידה מאי שכני אבידה אילימא שכינים דבעל אבידה אי ידע ליה ליזול ולהדריה נהליה אלא שכני מקום שנמצאת בו אבידה: רבי יהודה אומר כו': ורמינהו [ג] בשלשה במרחשון שואלין את הגשמים ר"ג אומר [מ] בז' בו [ד] (שהוא) ט"ו יום אחר החג כדי שיגיע אחרון שבא"י לנהר פרת אמר רב יוסף לא קשיא כאן במקדש ראשון כאן במקדש שני במקדש ראשון דנפישי ישראל טובא דכתיב בהו [ב] יהודה וישראל רבים כחול אשר על הים לרוב בעינן כולי האי במקדש שני דלא נפישי ישראל טובא דכתיב בהו [ג] כל הקהל כאחד ארבע רבוא אלפים שלש מאות וששים לא בעינן כולי האי אמר ליה אביי והא כתיב [ד] וישבו הכהנים והלוים וגו' [ה] והמשוררים והשוערים וכל ישראל בעריהם וכיון דהכי הוא אפכא מסתברא מקדש ראשון דנפישי ישראל טובא דמצוות עלמא ומשתכחי שיירתא דאזלי בין בימי' ובין בליליא לא בעינן כולי האי וסגי בתלתא יומא מקדש שני דלא נפישי ישראל טובא ולא מצוות עלמא ולא משתכחי שיירתא [ס] דאזלי בין בימ' ובין בליליא בעינן כולי האי רבא אמר לא שנא במקדש ראשון ולא שנא במקדש שני לא הטריחו רבנן באבדה יותר מדאי [ס] אמר רבינא שמע מינה [נ] כי מכריז גלימא מכריז דאי סלקא דעתך אבידתא מכריז בעינן למטפי ליה חד יומא לעיוני במאניה אלא שמע מינה גלימא מכריז שמע מינה רבא אמר אפילו תימא אבידתא מכריז לא הטריחו רבנן באבידה יותר מדאי ת"ר [ס] רגל ראשון אומר רגל ראשון רגל שני אומר רגל שני רגל שלישי אומר סתם ואמאי לימא רגל שלישי דלא אתי לאחלופי בשני שני נמי אתיא

**רש"י**

אלא הא דתנן מצא תכריך. דמשום סימנא מהדרינן ואם נתן מלוה סימן מחזירין לו ואי נפול מיניה דלוה מי ניחא ליה דתהוי הך תקנתא דניהדרה בסימן והא ניחא ליה דנהוו ביד המולא לעולם: כדשנינן. בעדים: אם תימצי לומר סימנים דאורייתא. רבותא נקט דאפי' אמרינן דאורייתא אפ"ה עדים עדיפי כדמפרש ואזיל סימנין ועדים ינתן לבעל עדים: סימנין וסימנין. באו שנים ונתנו סימניה: יניח. עד שיבא אליהו: מדת ארכו כו'. זה אומר מדת ארכו וזה נותן מדת רחבו: שעורי משער לה. אם ראה אותה ביד הבעלים שיערה כשהיה בעלה מכוסה בה אם טלית היא: מדת ארכו ורחבו ומדת גמיו. זה אומר כך ארכה וכך רחבה וזה אומר ארכה ורחבה כך וכך אמות בין הכל אבל אינו יודע כמה באורך וכמה ברוחב: גמיו. גאם יוונית עשויה כמין ך' שלנו להכי קרי אורך ורוחב יחד גמיו: הוא אומר סימני הגט. ואומר ממני נפל שנמלכתי שלא ליתן: והיא אומרת סימני הגט. וממני נפל שנתנו לי [י] וגרסתני: ינתן לה. שהוא נתנו ויודע סימנין אבל היא אם לא נתנו לה מהיכן ידעה: סימני החוט. שהגט קשור בו: בחפיסה. מלאת אותו: **מתני'** שכיניו. מפרש בגמרא: כדי שילך. כל אחד לביתו: שלשה. משישמע ההכרזה וידע אם אבד לו כלום ואם יבין שאבד יחזור שלשה: [י] ויכריז יום אחד. אני אבדתי ואלו סימניה ובגמרא פריך דבג' ימים אין שהות לחזור לסוף א"י: **גמ'** שכני מקום שנמצא בו אבידה. שמא שלהן היא: כדי שיגיע כו'. ולא ידביקוהו הגשמים אלמא כולי האי בעינן ומתני' תני שלשה: והכתיב וישבו כל ישראל בעריהם. ואע"ג דפורתא הוו בכל עריהן היו מפוזרים ויש רחוקים מירושלים כבתחילה: ה"ג. וכיון דהכי הוא איפכא מסתברא: דמצות עלמא. לוות יש לו טובים השנים: שמע מינה. מדלא יהבי ליה לרבנן שהות אלא הליכה וחזרה: גלימא מכריז. זה שמלאה מכריז שם חפץ טלית מלאתי ולכך לא הוצרכו ליתן שהות יום אחד לעיין בכליו מה אבד שהאדם יודע כמה טליתות יש לו וכשהוא בביתו בודק אם ימלאנה ואין צריך שהות: דאי ס"ד אבידתא מכריז. ואינו מזכיר שם החפץ ליתבו ליה לכל חד וחד אכתי טפי יומא לעיוני במאניה אם כל כליו בידו ופלוגתא היא בהא לקמן: לא הטריחו. זה שיהא שוהא יותר משבעה ימים: רגל ראשון. שהוא מכריז: אומר. בהכרזתו זהו רגל ראשון שלא להטריח את האובד לחזור וכשיבא רגל שני יעלה לרגל ויתן סימניה: שלישי אומר סתם. אבידה מצאתי ואינו אומר איזה רגל הוא למציאתה כדי שלא יסמוך האובד על רגל הבא ויבין שזהו רגל האחרון: אתי

**תוספות**

**מצא** תכריך של שטרות מי ניחא ליה ללוה כו'. וא"ת אין ניחא ליה דכי ילוה לאחר דליהדרו ליה לדידיה וי"ל דאינו רוצה להפסיד עתה כדי להיות בספק ריוח פעם אחרת:

**חמשה** עשר יום. וא"ת והלא [ח] א"י היא ארבע מאות פרסה על ארבע מאות פרסה [ט] ומהלך אדם (א) עשרה פרסאות ביום הוי ארבעים יום באורך וירושלים מן הירדן שהוא תחום א"י מהלך יום אחד כדאיתא בבילה (דף ה.) נשאר מצד אחד ל"ט ימים וי"ל דעם כרמים ויערים היה ארבע מאות פרסה אבל מישוב לא היה כל כך [י]:

**לא** בעינן כולי האי. וסגי בתלתא יומי וא"ת דז' ימים ומחצה צריך דהיינו חצי של ט"ו יום וי"ל דכי לא שכיחי שיירתא ואין הולך בלילה גם כל היום אינו הולך לפי שלא ימצא מלון בערב:

אבן

**עין משפט נר מצוה**

צה א מיי' פי"ג מהל' אבידה הלכה ה:
צו ב מיי' שם הלכה ו סמג עשין עד טוש"ע ח"מ סי' רסז סעיף ח:
צז ג מיי' שם טוש"ע שם סעיף ט:
צח ד מיי' שם טוש"ע שם סעיף י:
צט ה מיי' שם הל' ז טוש"ע שם סעיף יא:
ק ו מיי' שם טוש"ע שם סעיף יב:
קא ז מיי' שם טוש"ע שם סעיף יד:
קב ח מיי' שם טוש"ע שם סעיף יג:
קג ט י כ מיי' שם פי"ח הלכה ו ז סמג שם טוש"ע אה"ע סי' קנג:
קד ל מיי' שם פי"ג הלכה ח סמג שם:
קה מ מיי' פ"ב מהל' תפלה הלכה טז סמג עשין יט טוש"ע א"ח סי' קיז סעיף א:
קו נ מיי' פי"ג מהל' גזלה ואבדה הל' א סמג עשין עד טוש"ע ח"מ סי' רסז סעיף ד:
קז ס מיי' שם הל' ח:

**ליקוטי רש"י**

מצא תכריך של שטרות. בכרך או באגודה. ה"ז יחזיר. לדבר שיש בו סימן הוא כדמפרש בגמרא שהכלי סימן כשיאמרו הבעלים בכלי כך וכך מצאת אותם וכן תכריך ואגודה הרי זה יחזיר לדבר שיש בו סימן הוא [לעיל כ.]. **אלא דרשהו אם רמאי הוא.** והכי משמע עד דרוש אחיך אותו עד דרשך את אחיך [לעיל כז:]. **ט"ו יום אחר החג.** כלומר בשבעה במרחשון הוא ט"ו אחר החג. **כדי שיגיע אחרון.** כלומר קודם ביאת מים לנהר פרת שהוא רחוק יותר [תענית י.]. **כל הקהל כאחד וכו'.** כשהיו כולם ביחד עם הכהנים והלוים והנתינים היו כהם חשבון זה [עזרא ב, סד].

**רבינו חננאל**

לאבידה ואסיקנא אלא אמר רבא [סימנין] דאוריית' מהכא עד דרוש אחיך אותו והשבות לו וכי תעלה על דעתך שיתנו לו קודם שיתבענו אלא עד שתדרשהו אם רמאי הוא אם לאו ובמאי תהיה דרישתו בסימנין אמור לו תן סימניה ואם יביא סימניה תנה לו ש"מ סימנין דאורייתא אמר רבא אם תמצא לומר סימנין דאורייתא אקשינן עליה אכתי אמרת אם תמצא לומר והא כבר פשטינן לה סימנין דאורייתא ודחינן משום דאיכא למימר הא דפשטינן דרשהו לאו כדקאמרת אלא דרשהו לתובע הכי אם הוא צורבא מרבנן דלא משני בדיבוריה אלא במסכתא ובפוריא ובאושפיזא בלחוד מהדרינן ליה אבידה בטביעות עינא. סימנין וסימנין יניח פי' אם באו שניהם ונתנו זה וזה סימניה וכל אחד אמר שלי הוא לא יתננה לא לזה ולא לזה אלא יניחנה מוצאה אצלו. אבל אם אחד נתן סימניה וטען נפלה ממני ובא אחר והביא עדים כי ממנו נפל תנתן לבעל עדים. א) עד אחד כמאן דליתיה דמי. מדת ארכו ומדת רחבו [תנתן למדת ארכו] זה נתן מדת ארכה ורחבה של טלית וזה נתן מדת גמיה תינתן לבעל מדת ארכה ורחבה. אשתו אומרת זה הגט נתנו לי בעלי ונפל ממני ואמרה [סימניו] והבעל אמר סימניו וטוען כי לא נתתיו לה עדיין ינתן לה והוא שנותנת סימנין מובהקין כגון נקב ישנו בצד אות פלוני ש"מ דבסימן מובהק שרינן אשת איש דהיא איסורא וכל שכן ממונא: **מתני'** **עד מתי חייב להכריז וכו'** תנא עד שידעו בו שכני המקום שנמצאת בה זו האבידה ורמינן על הא דתנן ואחר הרגל האחרון ז' ימים כדי שילך לביתו ג' ויחזור בג' ויכריז יום אחד פי' כדי שילך שומע המכריז למקומו ויגיד וישמע בעל האבידה ויבא מיד וישמע ביום השביעי המכריז ויתן סימניה ויקחנה למימרא דארץ ישראל מהלך ג' ימים היא. והתנן בג' מרחשון שואלים את הגשמים

**חשק שלמה על ר"ח** א) נראה דחסר וצ"ל סימנין וסימנין ועד אחד עד אחד וכו'.

**מסורת הש"ס**

א) לעיל כ., ב) [לעיל כז:], ג) תענית י., ד) מהר"ס י"ז, ה) כ"א ולא אזלי ו', ו) כ"א וגרסני, עיין בתוספות דלעיל כב: י"ה אי דליכא, ח) [מגילה ], ט) [פסחים לג:], [עיין תוס' ראש השנה כג: ד"ה כמה].

**הגהות הב"ח**

(א) תוס' ד"ה חמשה כו' ומהלך אדם בינוני הוה עשרה פרסאות:

**גליון הש"ס**

גמ' ינתן למדת משקלותיו. עיין לעיל דף כג ע"ב תוס' ד"ה למשקל: שם אמר רבינא ש"מ. עיין הרא"ש פ"ג דחולין ס"ם כ"ג:

**תורה אור השלם**

א) וְאִם לֹא קָרוֹב אָחִיךָ אֵלֶיךָ וְלֹא יְדַעְתּוֹ וַאֲסַפְתּוֹ אֶל תּוֹךְ בֵּיתֶךָ וְהָיָה עִמְּךָ עַד דְּרֹשׁ אָחִיךָ אֹתוֹ וַהֲשֵׁבֹתוֹ לוֹ: [דברים כב, ב]

ב) יְהוּדָה וְיִשְׂרָאֵל רַבִּים כַּחוֹל אֲשֶׁר עַל הַיָּם לָרֹב אֹכְלִים וְשֹׁתִים וּשְׂמֵחִים: [מלכים א' ד, כ]

ג) כָּל הַקָּהָל כְּאֶחָד אַרְבַּע רִבּוֹא אַלְפַּיִם שְׁלֹשׁ מֵאוֹת שִׁשִּׁים: [עזרא ב, סד]

ד) וַיֵּשְׁבוּ הַכֹּהֲנִים וְהַלְוִיִּם וְהַשּׁוֹעֲרִים וְהַמְשֹׁרְרִים וּמִן הָעָם וְהַנְּתִינִים וְכָל יִשְׂרָאֵל בְּעָרֵיהֶם וַיִּגַּע הַחֹדֶשׁ הַשְּׁבִיעִי וּבְנֵי יִשְׂרָאֵל בְּעָרֵיהֶם: [נחמיה ז, עב]

ה) וַיֵּשְׁבוּ הַכֹּהֲנִים וְהַלְוִיִּם וּמִן הָעָם וְהַמְשֹׁרְרִים וְהַשּׁוֹעֲרִים וְהַנְּתִינִים בְּעָרֵיהֶם וְכָל יִשְׂרָאֵל בְּעָרֵיהֶם: [עזרא ב, ע]

**לעזי רש"י**

שול"ין. פירוש (לשבת בלוותא (עם...) (עיין רש"י ב"ב דף כא ע"א ד"ה ליהוי לוותא לחבריה).

הוּא אוֹמֵר סִימָנֵי הַגֵּט וְהִיא אוֹמֶרֶת סִימָנֵי הַגֵּט – A bill of divorce was found, and both husband and wife claim it. If **he states the bill of divorce's identifying marks**[17] **and she states the bill of divorce's identifying marks,**[18] יִנָּתֵן לָהּ – **[the bill of divorce] should be given to her.**[19]

The Gemara asks:

בְּמַאי – **By what** marks did she identify the bill of divorce? אִילֵימָא בְּמִדַּת אָרְכּוֹ וְרָחְבּוֹ – **If you say** it was **by** providing **the measure of its length and breadth,** what proof is that? דִּלְמָא בַּהֲדֵי דְּנָקִיט לֵיהּ חֲזִיתֵיהּ – **Perhaps she saw [the bill of divorce] while he was holding it,** enabling her to gauge its dimensions without ever having received it! – ? –

The Gemara answers:

אֶלָּא נֶקֶב יֵשׁ בּוֹ בְּצַד אוֹת פְּלוֹנִית – **Rather,** she identified the bill of divorce by stating: **"It has a** small **hole on the side of a certain letter."** Since she cannot know this from a casual glance, it indeed proves that the document is hers.

הוּא אוֹמֵר סִמָּנֵי הַחוּט וְהִיא אוֹמֶרֶת סִמָּנֵי הַחוּט – If **he states the identifying marks of the cord** binding the bill of divorce **and she states the identifying marks of the cord,** יִנָּתֵן לָהּ – the bill of divorce should be given to her.[20]

The Gemara asks:

בְּמַאי – **By what** marks did she identify the cord? אִילֵימָא בְּחִיוָּרָא וּבְסוּמָּקָא – **If you say by** correctly stating that it was **white or red,** what proof is that? וְדִלְמָא בַּהֲדֵי דְּנָקִיט לֵיהּ חֲזִיתֵיהּ – **Perhaps she saw it while he was holding it,** and therefore she knows its color! – ? –

The Gemara answers:

אֶלָּא בְּמִדַּת אָרְכּוֹ – **Rather,** she identified it **by** stating **the measure of its length.**

הוּא אוֹמֵר בַּחֲפִיסָה – If **he states** it was found **in a skin** [i.e. hide] **bag** וְהִיא אוֹמֶרֶת בַּחֲפִיסָה – **and she states** it was found **in a skin bag,** יִנָּתֵן לוֹ – **[the bill of divorce] should be given to him.** מַאי טַעְמָא – **What is the reason** for this ruling? מֵידַע יָדְעָה – **She knows** דְּכָל מַה דְּאִית לֵיהּ – **that everything he owns**[21] בַּחֲפִיסָה הוּא דְּמַנַּח לֵיהּ – **he places in a skin bag.** Therefore, her knowledge that it was found in a skin bag does not prove her claim.[22]

## Mishnah

וְעַד מָתַי חַיָּב לְהַכְרִיז – **Until when is one obligated to announce** the lost article he has found? עַד כְּדֵי שֶׁיֵּדְעוּ בוֹ שְׁכֵנָיו – **Until the neighbors know about it.**[23] דִּבְרֵי ר׳ מֵאִיר – These are **the words of R' Meir.** ר׳ יְהוּדָה אוֹמֵר – **R' Yehudah says:** שָׁלֹשׁ רְגָלִים – He must announce it for **three festivals,**[24] i.e. Pesach, Shavuos, and Succos, וְאַחַר הָרֶגֶל הָאַחֲרוֹן – **and after the final festival** שִׁבְעָה יָמִים – another **seven days;** כְּדֵי שֶׁיֵּלֵךְ לְבֵיתוֹ שְׁלֹשָׁה – **so that [the owner]** of the lost object **should have three days to travel home,** check his belongings, וְיַחֲזוֹר שְׁלֹשָׁה – **and** if anything is missing, **three days to return,** וְיַכְרִיז יוֹם אֶחָד – **and one day to announce** the loss of the object and its identifying marks.[25]

## Gemara

R' Meir stated in the Mishnah that one must announce a find until the neighbors know of it. The Gemara defines this further:

תָּנָא שְׁכֵנֵי אֲבֵידָה – **A Baraisa has taught:** One must announce his find until the **NEIGHBORS OF THE LOST OBJECT** know about it. מַאי שְׁכֵנֵי אֲבֵידָה – **What is meant by the "neighbors of the lost object"?** אִילֵימָא שְׁכֵינִים דְּבַעַל אֲבֵידָה – **If you say** that it means **the neighbors of the owner of the lost object,** how can one be sure his neighbors have heard of it unless he knows the identity of the owner? אִי יָדַע לֵיהּ – And **if he knows him,** לֵיזוּל וּלְהַדְרֵיהּ נִיהְלֵיהּ – **let him go and return** it **to him!** Clearly, this phrase must refer to something or someone else. – ? –

The Gemara explains:

אֶלָּא שְׁכֵנֵי מָקוֹם שֶׁנִּמְצֵאת בּוֹ אֲבֵידָה – **Rather,** it means that he must inform **the neighbors of the place where the lost object was found,** since it might belong to one of them.[26]

The Gemara raises a difficulty with the next clause of the Mishnah:

רַבִּי יְהוּדָה אוֹמֵר כו׳ – **R' YEHUDAH SAYS:** He must announce it for three festivals, and another seven days, so that the owner has three days to travel home, and three days to return **ETC.**

וּרְמִינְהוּ – They posed a contradiction to this from the following Mishnah: בִּשְׁלֹשָׁה בְּמַרְחֶשְׁוָן שׁוֹאֲלִין אֶת הַגְּשָׁמִים – **On the third of Marcheshvan we** begin to **request the rains** in our prayers.[27] רַבָּן גַּמְלִיאֵל אוֹמֵר – **Rabban Gamliel said:** בְּז׳ בּוֹ (שֶׁהוּא) ט״ו יוֹם אַחַר הֶחָג – We commence **on the seventh [of Marcheshvan], fifteen days after the festival** of Succos-Shemini Atzeres, כְּדֵי שֶׁיַּגִּיעַ אַחֲרוֹן שֶׁבְּאֶרֶץ יִשְׂרָאֵל לִנְהַר פְּרָת – **so that the last** returning pilgrim[28] **in Eretz Yisrael can reach the Euphrates River,** the most distant border of the country, before the rains fall.[29] We see

NOTES

17. The husband claims that he never actually divorced her; after writing the *get* he changed his mind and did not deliver it to her, and subsequently he lost it (*Rashi*).

18. She claims that her husband did divorce her; hence, she lost the document (*Rashi*).

19. Her knowledge of its identifying marks is better proof of her claim, for had the husband not delivered the *get,* she would have no way of knowing its identifying marks. The husband, however, knows the identifying marks since he wrote it. Therefore, his knowledge does not support his claim (*Rashi*).

20. See previous note.

21. I.e. his important papers.

22. However, the husband's knowledge that it was in a skin bag does prove his claim. Since the woman needs her *get* as proof of her divorce (to enable her to remarry), it would be unusual for her to store the *get* in as unsafe a place as a skin bag. Therefore, although he may know that she stores her other papers in a skin bag, he would not have guessed that she stored her *get* there too (*Ritva*).

23. Literally: his or its neighbors. The Gemara will discuss the identity of these neighbors.

24. Three times a year, at Pesach, Shavuos and Succos, all Jewish males are obligated to make a pilgrimage to the Temple in Jerusalem (*Deuteronomy* 16:16). Since the entire nation would gather there, this was the ideal time for public announcements. However, sickness and other unavoidable circumstances often caused someone to miss one, or even two, festivals, but generally not three. Thus, one had to announce a find over three festivals to ensure that its owner would hear of it (*Rabbeinu Yehonasan*; see *Maharshal*). The Gemara (28b) discusses the procedure to be followed for these announcements.

25. I.e. one day upon his return to announce his lost object and its *simanim,* and thereby to locate the person who found the object (see *Rashi;* see *Tosafos* 22b ד״ה אי דליכא, and *Maharsha* ad loc.).

26. *Rashi.* R' Meir, however, does not require the finder to announce it to people outside the area in which it was found.

27. The Tanna Kamma of this Mishnah in *Taanis* 10a is of the opinion that the rainy season in Eretz Yisrael begins on the third day in Marcheshvan; thus, he considers it the appropriate time to begin to request rain in the daily prayers [by saying וְתֵן טַל וּמָטָר, *and give dew and rain*] (*Rashi, Taanis* 4b ד״ה בשלשה).

28. See note 24.

29. The Euphrates River was a fifteen-day journey from Jerusalem. [If the rains should fall before the pilgrims returned home, their return

מצא תכריך של שטרות מי ניחא ליה ללוה כו'. וא"ת אין ניחא ליה דכי ילוה לאחר דליהדרו ליה לדידיה וי"ל דאינו רוצה להפסיד עתה כדי להיות בספק ריוח פעם אחרת:

חמשה עשר יום. וא"ת והלא (ח) א"י היא ארבע מאות פרסה על ארבע מאות פרסה (ט) ומהלך אדם (א) עשרה פרסאות ביום הוי ארבעים יום באורך וירושלים מן הירדן שהוא תחום א"י מהלך יום אחד כדאיתא בגילה (דף ה.) נשאר מהלך אחד ל"ט ימים וי"ל דעם כרמים ויערים היה ארבע מאות פרסה אבל מישור לא היה כל כך (י):

לא בעינן כולי האי. וסגי בתלתא יומי וא"ת הז' ימים ומהלה לריך דהיינו חצי של ט"ו יום וי"ל דכי לא שכיחי שיירתא ואין הולך בלילה גם כל היום אינו הולך לפי שלא ימצא מלון בערב:

אבן

אלא הא דתנן מצא תכריך. דמשום סימנא מהדרינן ואם נתן מלוה סימן מחזירין לו ואי נפול מיניה דלוה מי ניחא ליה דתהוי הך תקנתא דניהדרה בסימן והא ניחא ליה דנהוו ביד המלוה לעולם: כדשנינן. בעדים: אם תימצי לומר סימנים דאורייתא. רבותא נקט דלפי' אמרינן דאורייתא אפ"ה עדים עדיפי כדמפרש ואזיל סימנין ועדים יתן לבעל עדים: סימנין וסימנין. באו שניהם ונתנו סימניה: יניח. עד שיבא אליהו: מדת ארכו כו'. זה אומר מדת ארכו וזה נותן מדת רחבו: שעורי משער לה. אם ראה אותה ביד הבעלים שיערה כשהיה בעלה מכוסה בה אם טלית היא: מדת ארכו ורחבו ומדת גמיו. זה אומר כך ארכה וכך רחבה וזה אומר ארכה ורחבה כך וכך אמות בין הכל אבל אינו יודע כמה באורך וכמה ברוחב: גמיו. גאם יוונית עשויה כמין ך' שלנו להכי קרי אורך ורוחב יחד גמיו: הוא אומר סימני הגט. ואומר ממני נפל שנמלכתי שלא ליתן: והיא אומרת סימני הגט. וממני נפל שנתנו לי ונגרשתי: ינתן לה. שהוא נתנו ויודע סימנין אבל היא אם לא נתנו לה מהיכן ידעה: סימני החוט. שהגט קשור בו: בחפיסה. מלאת אותו: מתני' שכיניו. מפרש בגמרא: כדי שילך. כל אחד לביתו: שלשה. משישמע ההכרזה וידע אם אבד לו כלום ואם יבין שאבד יחזור שלשה: ויכריז יום אחד. אני אבדתי ואלו סימניה ובגמרא פריך דבג' ימים אין שהות לחזור לסוף א"י: גמ' שכני מקום שנמצא בו אבידה. שמא שלהן היא: כדי שיגיע כו'. ולא ידביקוהו הגשמים אלמא כולי האי בעינן ומתני' תני שלשה: והכתיב וישבו כל ישראל בעריהם. ואע"ג דפורתא הוו בכל עריהן היו מפוזרים ויש רחוקים מירושלים כבתחילה: ה"ג. וכיון דהכי הוא איפכא מסתברא: דמצות עלמא. לוות יש לו טובים השנים: שמע מינה. מדלא יהבי ליה לרבנן שהות אלא הליכה וחזרה: גלימא מכריז. זה שמלאה מכריז שם חפץ טלית מצאתי ולכך לא הוצרכו ליתן שהות יום אחד לעיין בכליו מה אבד שהאדם יודע כמה טליתות יש לו וכשהוא בביתו בודק אם ימצאנה ואין צריך שהות: דאי ס"ד אבידתא מכריז. ואינו מזכיר שם החפץ ליתבו ליה לכל חד וחד אכתי טפי יומא לעיוני במאניה אם כל כליו בידו ופלוגתא היא בהא לקמן: לא הטריחו. זה שיהא שוהא יותר משבעה ימים: רגל ראשון. שהוא מכריז: אומר. בהכרזתו זהו רגל ראשון שלא להטריח את האובד לחזור וכשיבא רגל שני יעלה לרגל ויתן סימניה: שלישי אומר סתם. אבידה מצאתי ואינו אומר איזה רגל הוא למציאתה כדי שלא יסמוך האובד על רגל הבא ויבין שזהו רגל האחרון:

אתי

אלא הא דתנן (א) מצא תכריך של שטרות או אגודה של שטרות ה"ז יחזיר הכי נמי דניחא ליה ללוה לאהדורי ליה למלוה אלא אמר רבא [א] סימנין דאורייתא דכתיב (א) והיה עמך עד דרוש אחיך אותו [ג] וכי תעלה על דעתך שיתננו קודם שידרשנו אלא דרשהו אם רמאי הוא או אינו רמאי לאו בסימנין שמע מינה אמר רבא אם תמצי לומר סימנין דאורייתא אם תמצי לומר הא פשיט ליה סימנין דאורייתא משום דאיכא למימר כדשנינן סימנין וסימנין [ב] יניח סימנין ועדים [ג] ינתן לבעל העדים סימנין וסימנין ועד אחד [ד] עד אחד כמאן דליתיה דמי ויניח עדי אריגה ועדי נפילה [ה] תנתן לעדי נפילה דאמרינן זבוני זבנה ומאיניש אחרינא נפל מדת ארכו ומדת רחבו [ו] תנתן למדת ארכו דמדת רחבו שעורי קא משער לה כד מכסי לה מרה וקאי ומדת ארכו לא משתער לה מדת ארכו ומדת רחבו ומדת גמיו [ז] ינתן למדת ארכו ורחבו מדת ארכו ומדת רחבו ומדת משקלותיו [ח] ינתן למדת משקלותיו הוא אומר סימני הגט והיא אומרת סימני הגט [ט] ינתן לה במאי אילימא במדת ארכו ורחבו דלמא בהדי דנקיט ליה חזיתיה [י] אלא נקב יש בו בצד אות פלוני הוא אומר סימני החוט והיא אומרת סימני החוט [כ] ינתן לה במאי אילימא בחיורא ובסומקא ודלמא בהדי דנקיט ליה חזיתיה אלא במדת ארכו הוא אומר בחפיסה והיא אומרת בחפיסה ינתן לו מ"ט מידע ידעה דכל מה דאית ליה בחפיסה הוא דמנח ליה: מתני' ועד מתי חייב להכריז עד כדי שידעו בו שכניו דברי ר"מ ר' יהודה אומר [ל] שלש רגלים ואחר הרגל האחרון שבעה ימים כדי שילך לביתו שלשה ויחזור שלשה ויכריז יום אחד: גמ' תנא שכני אבידה מאי שכני אבידה אילימא שכינים דבעל אבידה אי ידע ליה ליזול ולהדריה נהליה אלא שכני מקום שנמצאת בו אבידה: רבי יהודה אומר כו': ורמינהו [ג] בשלשה במרחשון שואלין את הגשמים ר"ג אומר [מ] בז' בו [ד] (שהוא) ט"ו יום אחר החג כדי שיגיע אחרון שבא"י לנהר פרת אמר רב יוסף לא קשיא כאן במקדש ראשון כאן במקדש שני במקדש ראשון דנפישי ישראל טובא דכתיב בהו [ב] יהודה וישראל רבים כחול אשר על הים לרוב בעינן כולי האי במקדש שני דלא נפישי ישראל טובא דכתיב בהו [ג] כל הקהל כאחד ארבע רבוא אלפים שלש מאות וששים לא בעינן כולי האי אמר ליה אביי והא כתיב [ד] וישבו הכהנים והלוים וגו' [ה] והמשוררים והשוערים וכל ישראל בעריהם וכיון דהכי הוא אפכא מסתברא מקדש ראשון דנפישי ישראל טובא דמצוות עלמא ומשתכחי שיירתא דאזלי בין ביממא ובין בליליא לא בעינן כולי האי וסגי בתלתא יומא מקדש שני דלא נפישי ישראל טובא ולא מצוות עלמא ולא משתכחי שיירתא [ה] דאזלי בין ביממא ובין בליליא בעינן כולי האי רבא אמר לא שנא במקדש ראשון ולא שנא במקדש שני לא הטריחו רבנן באבדה יותר מדאי [ס] אמר רבינא שמע מינה [נ] כי מכריז גלימא מכריז דאי סלקא דעתך אבידתא מכריז בעינן למטפי ליה חד יומא לעיוני במאניה אלא שמע מינה גלימא מכריז שמע מינה רבא אמר אפילו תימא אבידתא מכריז לא הטריחו רבנן באבידה יותר מדאי ת"ר [ס] רגל ראשון אומר רגל ראשון רגל שני אומר רגל שני רגל שלישי אומר סתם ואמאי לימא רגל שלישי דלא אתי לאחלופי בשני שני נמי

אתיא

## עין משפט נר מצוה

צה א מיי' פי"ג מהל' אבידה הלכה ה:
צו ב מיי' שם הלכה ו סמג עשין עד טוש"ע ח"מ סי' רסז סעיף ח:
צז ג מיי' שם טוש"ע שם סעיף ט:
צח ד מיי' שם טוש"ע שם סעיף י:
צט ה מיי' שם הל' ז טוש"ע שם סעיף יא:
ק ו מיי' שם טוש"ע שם סעיף יב:
קא ז מיי' שם טוש"ע שם סעיף יד:
קב ח מיי' שם טוש"ע שם סעיף יג:
קג ט י כ מיי' שם פי"ח הלכה ו ז סמג שם טוש"ע אה"ע סי' קנג:
קד ל מיי' שם פי"ג הלכה ח סמג שם:
קה מ מיי' פ"ב מהל' תפלה הלכה טז סמג עשין יט טוש"ע א"ח סי' קיז סעיף א:
קו נ מיי' פי"ג מהל' גזלה ואבדה הל' א סמג עשין עד טוש"ע ח"מ סי' רסז סעיף ד:
קז ס מיי' שם הל' ח:

## ליקוטי רש"י

מצא תכריך של שטרות. בכרך או באגודה. ה"ז יחזיר. לדבר שיש בו סימן הוא כדמפרש בגמרא שהכלי סימן כשיאמרו הבעלים בכלי כך וכך מצאת אותם וכן תכריך ואגודה הרי זה יחזיר לדבר שיש בו סימן הוא [לעיל כ.]. אלא דרשהו אם רמאי הוא. והכי משמע עד דרוש אחיך אותו עד לדרשך את אחיך [לעיל כז:]. ט"ו יום אחר החג. כלומר בשבעה במרחשון הוא ט"ו אחר החג. כדי שיגיע אחרון. כלומר קודם ביאת מים לנהר פרת שהוא רחוק יותר [תענית י.]. כל הקהל כאחד וכו'. כשהיו כולם ביחד עם הכהנים והלוים והנתינים היו בהם חשבון זה [עזרא ב, סד].

## רבינו חננאל

לאבידה ואסיקנא אלא אמר רבא [סימנין] דאוריית' מהכא עד דרוש אחיך אותו והשבות לו וכי תעלה על דעתך שיתנו לו קודם שיתבענו אלא עד שתדרשהו אם רמאי הוא אם לאו ובמאי תהיה דרישתו בסימנין אמור לו תן סימניה ואם יביא סימניה תנה לו ש"מ סימנין דאורייתא אמר רבא אם תמצא לומר סימנין דאורייתא אקשינן עליה אכתי אמרת אם תמצא לומר והא כבר פשטינן לה סימנין דאורייתא ודחינן משום דאיכא למימר הא דפשטינן דרשהו לאו כדקאמרת אלא דרשהו לתובע הכי אם הוא צורבא מרבנן דלא משני בדיבוריה אלא במסכתא ובפוריא ובאושפיזא

## מסורת הש"ס

א) לעיל כ., ב) [לעיל כז:], ג) תענית י., ד) מהרש"ל, ה) נ"א ולא אזלי', ו) נ"א וגרסני, ז) עיין בתוספות לעיל כב: ד"ה אי לדליכא, ח) [מגילה ה.], ט) [פסחים לג:], י) [עיין תוס' ר"ה השנה כג: ד"ה כמה].

## הגהות הב"ח

(א) תוס' ד"ה חמשה וכו' ומהלך אדם ביוני הוה עשרה פרסאות:

## גליון הש"ס

ז' ינתן למדת משקלותיו. עיין לעיל כב ע"ב תוס' ד"ה משקל: שם אמר רבינא ש"מ. עיין ברא"ש פ"ג דחולין ס"ס כ"ג:

## תורה אור השלם

א) וְאִם לֹא קָרוֹב אָחִיךָ אֵלֶיךָ וְלֹא יְדַעְתּוֹ וַאֲסַפְתּוֹ אֶל תּוֹךְ בֵּיתֶךָ וְהָיָה עִמְּךָ עַד דְּרֹשׁ אָחִיךָ אֹתוֹ וַהֲשֵׁבֹתוֹ לוֹ: [דברים כב, ב]

ב) יְהוּדָה וְיִשְׂרָאֵל רַבִּים כַּחוֹל אֲשֶׁר עַל הַיָּם לָרֹב אֹכְלִים וְשֹׁתִים וּשְׂמֵחִים: [מלכים א' ד, כ]

ג) כָּל הַקָּהָל כְּאֶחָד אַרְבַּע רִבּוֹא אַלְפַּיִם שְׁלֹשׁ מֵאוֹת שִׁשִּׁים: [עזרא ב, סד]

ד) וַיֵּשְׁבוּ הַכֹּהֲנִים וְהַלְוִיִּם וְהַשּׁוֹעֲרִים וְהַמְשֹׁרְרִים וּמִן הָעָם וְהַנְּתִינִים וְכָל יִשְׂרָאֵל בְּעָרֵיהֶם וַיִּגַּע הַחֹדֶשׁ הַשְּׁבִיעִי וּבְנֵי יִשְׂרָאֵל בְּעָרֵיהֶם: [נחמיה ז, עב]

ה) וַיֵּשְׁבוּ הַכֹּהֲנִים וְהַלְוִיִּם וּמִן הָעָם וְהַמְשֹׁרְרִים וְהַשּׁוֹעֲרִים וְהַנְּתִינִים בְּעָרֵיהֶם וְכָל יִשְׂרָאֵל בְּעָרֵיהֶם: [עזרא ב, ע]

## לעזי רש"י

ול"ע. פירוש (לשבת) ווזת (עס...) (עיין רש"י ב דף כא ע"א ד"ה ליהוי לווזא לחבריה).

בלחוד מהדרינן ליה אבידה בטביעות עינא. סימנין וסימנין יניח פי' אם באו שניהם ונתנו זה וזה סימניה וכל אחד אמר שלי הוא לא יתננה לא לזה ולא לזה אלא יניחנה מוצאה אצלו. אבל אם אחד נתן סימניה וטען נפלה ממני ובא אחר והביא עדים כי ממנו נפל תנתן לבעל עדים. א) עד אחד כמאן דליתיה דמי. מדת ארכו ומדת רחבו [תנתן למדת ארכו] זה נתן מדת ארכה ורחבה של טלית וזה נתן מדת גמיה תינתן לבעל מדת ארכה ורחבה. אשתו אומרת זה הגט נתנו לי בעלי ונפל ממני ואמרה [סימניו] והבעל אמר סימניו וטוען כי לא נתתיו לה עדיין ינתן לה והוא שנותנת סימנין מובהקין כגון נקב ישנו בצד אות פלוני ש"מ דבסימן מובהק שרינן אשת איש דהיא איסורא וכל שכן ממונא: מתני' עד מתי חייב להכריז וכו' תנא עד שידעו בו שכני המקום שנמצאת בה זו האבידה ורמינן על הא דתנן ואחר הרגל האחרון ז' ימים כדי שילך לביתו ג' ויחזור בג' ויכריז יום אחד פי' כדי שילך שומע המכריז למקומו ויגיד וישמע בעל האבידה ויבא מיד וישמע ביום השביעי המכריז ויתן סימניה ויקחנה למימרא דארץ ישראל מהלך ג' ימים היא. והתנן בג' מרחשון שואלים את הגשמים

חשק שלמה על ר"ח א) נראה דחסר וצ"ל סימנין וסימנין ועד אחד עד אחד וכו'.

The Gemara again challenges Rava's explanation of the Rabbinic enactment:

אֶלָּא הָא דִּתְנַן – But, regarding that which we learned in a Mishnah:[1] מָצָא תַּכְרִיךְ שֶׁל שְׁטָרוֹת – If ONE FOUND A ROLL OF DOCUMENTS אוֹ אֲגוּדָּה שֶׁל שְׁטָרוֹת – OR A BUNDLE OF DOCUMENTS,[2] הֲרֵי זֶה יַחֲזִיר – HE SHOULD RETURN IT – הָכִי נַמֵּי דְּנִיחָא לֵיהּ לַלֹּוֶה לְאַהֲדוּרֵי לֵיהּ לַמַּלְוֶה – can you then say that here, too, the borrower is content that the Rabbis enact to return the documents to the lender?[3]

Rava accepts this argument as conclusive, and offers a Biblical source for identifying marks:

אֶלָּא אָמַר רָבָא – Rava said: Rather, סִימָנִין דְּאוֹרַיְיתָא – the law that ownership is determined based on identifying marks is Biblical, דִּכְתִיב – for it is written:[4] "וְהָיָה עִמְּךָ עַד דְּרֹשׁ אָחִיךָ אֹתוֹ" – *And it* (the lost object) *shall remain with you until your brother seeks it out.* וְכִי תַּעֲלֶה עַל דַּעְתְּךָ שֶׁיִּתְּנֶנּוּ קוֹדֶם שֶׁיִּדְרְשֶׁנּוּ – Now, could you have supposed that [the finder] should give it to its owner before he seeks it out? Certainly not, since the finder does not know who lost it! אֶלָּא דָּרְשֵׁהוּ אִם רַמַּאי הוּא אוֹ אֵינוֹ רַמַּאי – Rather, interpret the verse as follows: Investigate [the claimant] to determine whether he is a deceiver or he is not a deceiver. לָאו בְּסִימָנִין – Now, how is this investigation done? Is it not on the basis of identifying marks? שְׁמַע מִינָּהּ – We learn from this that identifying marks are Biblically reliable.[5]

Rava now considers the relative strengths of various proofs which may be employed for establishing ownership of a lost object:

אָמַר רָבָא – Rava said: אִם תִּמְצֵי לוֹמַר סִימָנִין דְּאוֹרַיְיתָא – Even if you assume that the law of identifying marks is Biblical . . .

The Gemara immediately interjects:[6]

אִם תִּמְצֵי לוֹמַר – "If you assume"?! This must be wrong, הָא פְּשִׁיט לֵיהּ סִימָנִין דְּאוֹרַיְיתָא – for [Rava] himself resolved conclusively that the law of identifying marks is Biblical! – ? –

The Gemara answers:

מִשּׁוּם דְּאִיכָּא לְמֵימַר כִּדְשַׁנִּינַן – The Scriptural source given by Rava is not conclusive, for it is possible to say, as we answered previously,[7] that the investigation is accomplished through witnesses, not on the basis of identifying marks.

Rava continues his interrupted statement:

סִימָנִין וְסִימָנִין יַנִּיחַ – If two claimants come before the court, one providing identifying marks as proof of ownership, and the other also providing identifying marks as proof of ownership, the law is that [the finder] should leave the object in his own possession.[8] סִימָנִין וְעֵדִים יִנָּתֵן לְבַעַל הָעֵדִים – If one provides identifying marks as proof, and the other provides witnesses who testify on his behalf,[9] it should be given to the one with witnesses.[10] סִימָנִין וְסִימָנִין וְעֵד אֶחָד – If one provides identifying marks as proof of ownership, and the other provides identifying marks and additionally is supported by a single witness, עֵד אֶחָד כְּמַאן דְּלֵיתֵיהּ דָּמֵי – it is as if the single witness does not exist. וְיַנִּיחַ – Hence, [the finder] should leave it in his own possession.[11] עֵדֵי אֲרִיגָה וְעֵדֵי נְפִילָה – If one is supported by witnesses to his weaving of the garment and the other is supported by witnesses to the garment's falling from him, תִּנָּתֵן לְעֵדֵי נְפִילָה – [the garment] should be given to the one supported by witnesses to the falling. דְּאָמְרִינַן זַבּוֹנֵי זַבְנָהּ – For we say [the weaver] sold [the garment], וּמֵאִינִישׁ אַחֲרִינָא נָפַל – and it fell from some other person.[12]

מִדַּת אָרְכּוֹ וּמִדַּת רָחְבּוֹ – If one provides the measure of its length as an identifying mark, and the other provides the measure of its breadth as an identifying mark, תִּנָּתֵן לְמִדַּת אָרְכּוֹ – it should be given to the one who provides the measure of its length. דְּמִדַּת רָחְבּוֹ שִׁיעוּרֵי קָא מְשַׁעֵר לָהּ כַּד מְכַסֵּי לָהּ מָרָהּ וְקָאֵי – For one can gauge the measure of its breadth when the owner is standing and wearing it, וּמִדַּת אָרְכּוֹ לֹא מִשְׁתַּעֵר לָהּ – but he cannot similarly gauge the measure of its length. Hence, knowledge of the cloak's length is better proof of ownership.[13]

מִדַּת אָרְכּוֹ וּמִדַּת רָחְבּוֹ וּמִדַּת גַּמָּיו – If one provides both the measure of its length and its breadth, and the other provides the combined measure of its length and breadth,[14] יִנָּתֵן לְמִדַּת אָרְכּוֹ וְרָחְבּוֹ – it should be given to the one who provides both the measure of its length and its breadth.[15]

מִדַּת אָרְכּוֹ וּמִדַּת רָחְבּוֹ וּמִדַּת מִשְׁקְלוֹתָיו – If one provides the measure of its length and the measure of its breadth, and the other provides the measure of its weight, יִנָּתֵן לְמִדַּת מִשְׁקְלוֹתָיו – it should be given to the one who provides the measure of its weight.[16]

Along the same lines, Rava issues additional rulings regarding a lost bill of divorce:

NOTES

1. Above, 20a.

2. In these cases, the identifying marks are the number of documents or the manner in which they are folded (above, 20b).

3. See above, 27b note 36.

4. *Deuteronomy* 22:2.

5. Although the Gemara above (27b) rejected this argument as *conclusive* proof that identifying marks are Biblically reliable, the Gemara now holds that in absence of a convincing rationale for a Rabbinic enactment, we must assume that this verse refers to identifying marks, and that they are therefore Biblically reliable (*Ritva*, see also *Rosh* §13).

6. The Gemara is disturbed by the uncertain tone of Rava's statement. The words "if you assume" imply that it is only an assumption, and that it is possible to argue otherwise.

7. Above, 27b. See above, note 5.

8. Until Elijah the prophet arrives (*Rashi*), who will identify the true owner. *Rambam*, however, explains this to mean that the finder holds it until one claimant admits that he is lying or until the two claimants compromise (*Hilchos Gezeilah V'Aveidah* 13:6).

9. The witnesses testify either that that they observed the object being lost, or that they know it is the claimant's (*Rosh* §13, *Shulchan Aruch Choshen Mishpat* 267:9).

10. Because witnesses' testimony is stronger than proof through *simanim*.

It was in reference to this law that Rava began with the words, "Even if you assume that the law of identifying marks is Biblical . . ." He means to say: Even if *simanim* are a Biblically reliable proof, witnesses' testimony nevertheless constitutes a stronger proof (*Rashi*).

11. A basic principle in monetary law is that testimony of a single witness is insufficient (*Deuteronomy* 19:15). The single witness is therefore not a factor in this case. [*Rosh* holds, however, that the claimant opposed by the witness would be required to swear (cf. *Nimukei Yosef*).]

12. The fact that one claimant wove the garment does not prove that it still belongs to him, since he may have later sold it. Therefore, the garment is awarded to the claimant who was observed losing the garment.

13. The Gemara refers to a garment that was worn in the manner that we wear a *talis* today; the breadth of the garment hung down the wearer's back, while the length was wrapped around the body. Thus, it was easier for an observer to gauge the garment's breadth than its length (*Sma, Choshen Mishpat* 267:13). Accordingly, *Shach* (ibid. 267:10) writes that a judge must base his ruling on the type of garment and the manner in which it is generally worn.

14. The Gemara's term is גַּמָּיו, its *gamma*. This refers to the upper case Greek letter *gamma,* whose shape resembles the Hebrew *chaf sofis*, or an inverted "L." Thus, it is used to express two perpendicular dimensions.

15. Since this is evidence of a more detailed acquaintance with the object.

16. Since it is unusual to weigh a cloak, knowledge of its weight constitutes greater proof of ownership than knowledge of its other measurements (see *Tosafos* above, 23b ד"ה מדמשקל).

**death.** Hence, a wart is a valid identifying mark, and as such can be relied upon even regarding Biblical laws of a prohibitory nature.[26]

A third explanation:

**אִיבָּעִית אֵימָא – If you prefer, say:** דְּכוּלֵּי עָלְמָא שׁוּמָא אֵינָהּ עֲשׂוּיָה לְהִשְׁתַּנּוֹת לְאַחַר מִיתָה – **All** concur that **a wart does not tend to change** its appearance **after death,** וְסִימָנִין דְּרַבָּנָן – **and** all concur that **identifying marks are** merely **Rabbinic** in nature. וְהָכָא בְּשׁוּמָא סִימָן מוּבְהָק הוּא קָמִיפַּלְגֵי – **But here their dispute** centers on **whether a wart is** considered to be **a unique identifying mark.** מַר סָבַר – One **master holds** שׁוּמָא סִימָן מוּבְהָק הוּא – **a wart is a unique identifying mark** and is therefore sufficient proof to permit the wife to remarry. וּמַר סָבַר – **And** the other **master holds** שׁוּמָא לַאו סִימָן מוּבְהָק הוּא – **a wart is not a unique identifying mark.** Hence, testimony identifying the corpse on the basis of a wart is insufficient to permit the wife to remarry.[27]

The Gemara continues its discussion of identifying marks by raising a basic question:

אָמַר רָבָא – **Rava said:** אִם תִּמְצֵי לוֹמַר – **If you assume** סִימָנִין לַאו דְּאוֹרַיְיתָא – that determination of ownership based on **identifying marks** is **not Biblical,** הֵיכִי מְהַדְּרִינַן אֲבֵידְתָא בְּסִימָנִין – **how,** then, **do we return a lost object on the basis of identifying marks?** Why did the Rabbis enact to rely on identifying marks for the return of lost objects if this is not Biblically ordained?[28]

The Gemara answers:

דְּנִיחָא לֵיהּ לְמוֹצֵא אֲבֵידָה – **Because the finder of the lost object is content** דְּנֶהְדַר בְּסִימָנִין – **to return** the object **on the basis of identifying marks,** כִּי הֵיכִי דְּכִי אָבְדָה לֵיהּ לְדִידֵיהּ – **in order that when an object is lost by him** נַמִּי נֶהְדְּרוּ לֵיהּ בְּסִימָנִין – **they will likewise return** it **to him on the basis of identifying marks.**

The Gemara raises an objection to this reasoning:

אָמַר לֵיהּ רַב סַפְרָא לְרָבָא – **Rav Safra said to Rava:** וְכִי אָדָם עוֹשֶׂה טוֹבָה לְעַצְמוֹ בְּמָמוֹן שֶׁאֵינוֹ שֶׁלּוֹ – **But may one do a favor to himself with property that does not belong to him?!**[29]

Rava presents another explanation:

אֶלָּא – **Rather** say: נִיחָא לֵיהּ לְבַעַל אֲבֵידָה – **The rightful owner is content** לְמֵיהַב סִימָנִין וּלְמִשְׁקְלֵיהּ – that the Rabbis enact a law allowing one **to provide** identifying **marks** as evidence of ownership **and to** thereby **take [the object].** מֵידַע יָדַע דְּעֵדִים לֵית לֵיהּ – Since **he knows that he has no identifying witnesses** to testi[fy] that the lost object is his, וּמֵימַר אָמַר – **he** therefore **says** to hi[m]self: כּוּלֵּי עָלְמָא לֹא יָדְעֵי סִימָנִין מוּבְהָקִים דִּידָהּ – It is probable th[at] **no one** but me **knows [the object's] unique**[30] **identifyi[ng] marks.** וַאֲנָא יָהֵיבְנָא סִימָנִין מוּבְהָקִים דִּידָהּ וְשָׁקְלְנָא לָהּ – Therefor[e] **I will provide its unique**[30] **identifying marks** as evidence [of] ownership, **and** thereby **retrieve [the object].**[31]

The Gemara disputes the contention that the loser of an obje[ct] always benefits from an enactment authorizing its return on th[e] basis of identifying marks:

אֶלָּא הָא דִּתְנַן – **But that which we learned in a Mishnah:**[...] רַבָּן שִׁמְעוֹן בֶּן גַּמְלִיאֵל אוֹמֵר – RABBAN SHIMON BEN GAMLIEL SAY[S]: אֶחָד הַלֹּוֶה מִשְּׁלֹשָׁה [...]זִיר לַלֹּוֶה – If one found three documents concerning ON[E] person WHO BORROWED FROM THREE different people, – HE SHOULD RETURN them TO THE BORROWER for they certain[ly] belong to him.[33] שְׁלֹשָׁה שֶׁלָּוּוּ מִן הָאֶחָד – If the three documen[ts] concern THREE people WHO BORROWED FROM ONE person, [...]זִיר לַמַּלְוֶה – [THE FINDER] SHOULD RETURN them TO THE LENDER.[...] נִיחָא לֵיהּ לַלֹּוֶה לְאַהֲדוּרֵי לֵיהּ לַמַּלְוֶה – Now, **is the borrower co[n]tent,** in the latter case, that the Rabbis enact a law **to return** th[e] documents **to the lender** based on identifying marks?[35] Obvious[ly] not, since if the finder would not return the document, the lend[er] would be unable to collect the loan![36] – ? –

Rava answers:

אָמַר לֵיהּ – **[Rava] said to [Rav Safra]:** הָתָם סְבָרָא הוּא – **Ther[e]** in the case of Rabban Shimon ben Gamliel, **it is logical** to rule th[at] the finder should return the documents.[37] [...]חַד הַלֹּוֶה מִשְּׁלֹשָׁה יַחֲזִיר לַלֹּוֶה – In the case where **one borrowed from three, h[e] should return** the documents **to the borrower,** [...]גַּבֵּי לֹוֶה שְׁכִיחֵי – **since [three documents]** bearing the name of the same bo[r]rower **are most likely** to have been **in the borrower's possessio[n]** גַּבֵּי מַלְוֶה לֹא שְׁכִיחֵי – but are **not likely** to have been **in the lender'[s] possession.** שְׁמַע מִינָּהּ מִלֹּוֶה נְפוּל – **This proves** that **[the docu]ments] fell from the borrower.** Conversely, in the case of [...]לֹשָׁה שֶׁלָּווּ מֵאֶחָד יַחֲזִיר לַמַּלְוֶה – **three** people **who borrowed from on[e]** person, **he should return** the documents **to the lender,** [...]גַּבֵּי מַלְוֶה שְׁכִיחֵי – **since** it is **most likely** that **they** were **in the lender'[s] possession,** גַּבֵּי לֹוֶה לֹא שְׁכִיחֵי – but it is **unlikely** that **they** wer[e] **in the borrower's possession.**[38]

NOTES

26. As explained by *Rashi,* a wart can change color after death, e.g. a black wart might turn white. Hence, the Tanna Kamma holds that identifying a corpse on the basis of the wart's color, even with testimony regarding the existence of a wart on a specific limb, is insufficient. Conversely, according to Elazar ben Mehavai, when testifying to a wart on a specific limb, the witnesses must *also* identify the wart's color. Even Elazar ben Mehavai would not consider the mere existence of a wart to be a valid identifying mark (see *Noda B'Yehudah, Even HaEzer* I:51).

27. The Gemara has now introduced a new concept; that there are certain identifying marks which are so unique that they are in a category by themselves. Therefore, even if generally identifying marks are not Biblically valid, these unique marks, since they prove identity beyond any reasonable doubt, are valid even on a Biblical level. [See *Rashi* to *Gittin* 27b ד״ה ודווקא, who writes that "there is no clearer testimony" than a unique identifying mark.] The Tanna Kamma and Elazar ben Mehavai argue whether a wart meets the criteria for "unique."

28. Since there exists the possibility that the object is being given not to the rightful owner, but to an impostor (*Rashi*).

29. Since our concern is that the rightful owner might be deprived of his lost object, of what significance is the fact that the *finder* is happy to return it? (*Rashi*).

30. The term מוּבְהָק, *unique,* is not used here in the same sense as it was used above. The intent here is only to distinguish this identifying mark from one that an impostor could offer (such as color), which does not prove ownership due to its prevalence (*Tosafos*).

31. If the Biblical law were left standing, the only way an owner could retrieve his lost object would be to provide witnesses who attest to his ownership. Since such witnesses are difficult to come by, owners would often be forced to forfeit their possessions. Consequently, it is their com[mon] consensus to allow people to retrieve their objects by providing ider[n]tifying marks, although there is a slight risk that an imposter might suc[c]essfully do likewise (*Rashi*).

32. Above, 20a.

33. Since the three documents indicate the same borrower, the logica[l] assumption is that he already repaid those loans and hence was in pos[]session of the documents. It is most improbable that three different cred[]itors lost the documents at the same spot (*Rashi* above, 20a ד״ה ללוה).

34. In this case, since the three documents all indicate the same lende[r] the logical assumption is that these represent unpaid loans, and wer[e] therefore in the possession of the lender who lost them all at one tim[e].

35. In this case, the identifying mark offered by the lender is that ther[e] were *three* documents from *three* separate borrowers (*Rashi*).

36. Ordinarily, the benefit of being able to retrieve a lost object by provid[]ing its identifying marks outweighs the slight risk that an imposto[r] might obtain it by likewise successfully offering its marks. However, th[e] case of the lost documents is different. A debtor is not at all intereste[d] in retrieving the note of indebtedness from the finder. Rather, his con[]cern is solely that it not be given to the creditor, so that he cannot collec[t] the debt. Therefore, in this case he prefers that there not be a Rabbini[c] enactment allowing someone to retrieve an object by providing its iden[]tifying marks (*Rashi*).

37. That is, besides the identifying marks, there is a specific logic to Rab[]ban Shimon Ben Gamliel's ruling. We are therefore unconcerned wit[h] whether the borrower is amenable to their return.

38. As explained above, notes 33 and 34.

לאהדורי גט אשה בסימנים אי אמרת דאורייתא מהדרינן ואי אמרת דרבנן כי עבוד רבנן תקנתא בממונא אבל באיסורא לא עבוד רבנן תקנתא ת"ש אף השמלה היתה בכלל כל (א) אלו ולמה יצאת להקיש אליה ולומר לך מה שמלה מיוחדת שיש לה סימנין ויש לה תובעין חייב להכריז אף כל דבר שיש לו סימנין ויש לו תובעין חייב להכריז תנא תובעין אצטריכא ליה סימנין כדי נסבא ת"ש חמור בסימני אוכף אימא בעדי אוכף ת"ש והיה עמך עד דרוש אחיך אותו וכי תעלה על דעתך שיתננו לו קודם שידרשנו אלא דרשהו אם רמאי הוא או אינו רמאי מאי לאו בסימנין לא בעדים ת"ש אין מעידין אלא על פרצוף הפנים עם החוטם אע"פ שיש סימנין בגופו ובכליו שמע מינה סימנין לאו דאורייתא אמרי גופו דארוך וגוץ כליו דחיישינן לשאלה אי חיישינן לשאלה חמור בסימני אוכף היכי מהדרינן (ג) אוכף לא שאולי אינשי אוכפא משום דמסקב ליה לחמרא איבעית אימא כליו בחיורי ובסומקי אלא הא דתניא מצאו קשור בכיס או בארנקי ובטבעת או שמצאו בין כליו אפילו לזמן מרובה כשר ואי ס"ד חיישינן לשאלה כי מצאו קשור בכיס אמאי כשר ניחוש לשאלה אמרי כיס וארנקי וטבעת לא משאלי אינשי כיס וארנקי משום דמסמני וטבעת משום דמזייף לימא כתנאי אין מעידין על השומא ואלעזר בן מהבאי אומר מעידין על השומא מאי לאו בהא קמיפלגי דת"ק סבר סימנין דרבנן ואלעזר בן מהבאי סבר סימנין דאורייתא אמר רבא דכ"ע סימנין דאורייתא והכא בשומא מצויה בבן גילו קמיפלגי מר סבר שומא מצויה בבן גילו ומ"ס שומא אינה מצויה בבן גילו איבעית אימא דכ"ע שומא אינה מצויה בבן גילו והכא בסימנין העשוין להשתנות לאחר מיתה קמיפלגי מר סבר סימנין אין עשוים להשתנות לאחר מיתה ומר סבר סימנין עשוים להשתנות לאחר מיתה אב"א דכ"ע שומא אינה עשויה להשתנות לאחר מיתה וסימנין דרבנן והכא בשומא סימן מובהק הוא קמיפלגי מ"ס שומא סימן מובהק הוא ומ"ס שומא לאו סימן מובהק הוא אמר רבא את"ל סימנין לאו דאורייתא היכי מהדרינן אבידתא בסימנין דניחא ליה למוצא אבידה דנהדר בסימנין כי היכי דכי אבדה ליה לדידיה נמי נהדרו ליה בסימנין אמר ליה רב ספרא לרבא וכי אדם עושה טובה לעצמו בממון שאינו שלו אלא ניחא ליה לבעל אבידה למיהב סימנין ולמשקליה מידע ידע דעדים לית ליה ומימר אמר כולי עלמא לא ידעי סימנין מובהקים דידה ואנא יהיבנא סימנין מובהקים דידה ושקלנא לה אלא הא דתנן רבן שמעון בן גמליאל אומר אחד הלוה משלשה יחזיר ללוה שלשה שלוו מן האחד יחזיר למלוה ניחא ליה ללוה לאהדורי ליה למלוה אמר ליה התם סברא הוא אחד הלוה משלשה יחזיר ללוה דגבי לוה שכיחי גבי מלוה לא שכיחי ש"מ מלוה נפול שלשה שלוו מאחד יחזור למלוה דגבי מלוה שכיחי גבי לוה לא שכיחי אלא

**רש"י**

לאהדורי גט. שאבד מן השליח המביאו קודם שנתן לה: תקנתא. לקמן בשמעתין מפרש מאי היא: בממונא. דהפקר ב"ד הפקר: תובעין אצטריכא ליה. קרא לתובעין אתא ולמעוטי מידי דאיאוש ואפקריה: כדי נסבה. בלא מקרא אלא אסמכינהו אקרא בעלמא: ת"ש. דאוקמינן לעיל חמור לסימני אוכף אתא: אימא בעדי אוכף. אם יש עדים המכירין בטביעות עין לאוכף שהוא שלו מחזירין לו את החמור: דרשהו. והכי משמע עד דרוש אחיך אותו עד דרשך את אחיך: בעדים. שיבא עדים שהוא שלו: אין מעידין. על אדם שמת להשיא את אשתו אלא א"כ ראו פרצוף פניו שהוא עם החוטם: דארוך או גוץ. שאין זה סימן שהרבה ארוכין וגוצים יש: כליו. בגדיו: חיישינן. שמא השאילם לאחר ואותו אחר ראו שמת: מסקב. דורויי"ר בלעז: חיורי או סומקי. אין זה סימן שהרבה כאלה יש: מצאו קשור בכיס שלו או בארנקי כו'. שליח המביא גט ואבד הימנו לאחר זמן מצאו קשור בכיס שלו או בארנקי כו': בין כליו. כלי תשמישו שבביתו: אפילו לזמן מרובה. אע"ג דתנן (גיטין דף כ.) המביא גט ואבד הימנו מצאו לזמן מרובה פסול הכא כשר: ניחוש לשאלה. שמא השאיל כיסו לאחר והוא קשרו בו: דמסמני. מנחשי ואומר סימן לאדם שמשאיל כיסו שמוכר לו מזלו: דמזייף. שהיה לכל איש חותם ניכר בטבעתו וכששולח שום דבר סתום מכסהו וחותמו בטבעתו לפיכך אינו משאיל טבעתו שמא יעשה זה חותם כנגד חותמו ויזייף בו את שליחותיו: אין מעידין על השומא. המעידין על האשה להשיאה ואמרו סימן היה בו שומא באבר פלוני: שומא. וורוא"ה בלעז: סימנין דרבנן. וגבי אשת איש דאיסור דאורייתא הוא לא סמכינן עלייהו: בבן גילו. הנולד בשעתו שנולדו במזל אחד: בסימנין העשויין כו'. אם עשויין להשתנות או אינן עשויין להשתנות אם בחייו היתה שומא שחורה במותו נעשית לבנה או איפוך: מובהק. ואפילו סימנין דרבנן יש לסמוך על זה: היכי מהדרינן. כלומר מה תקנה ראו חכמים בדבר ליכנס בספק להחזיר ממון למי שאינו שלו: אלא ל"ג: וכי אדם עושה. וניחותא דמוצא מאי איכפת לן אם מי שאבדה ממנו לא ניחא ליה: אלא. אמר רבא כל אובדי אבידה ניחא להו שתהא דת זו בישראל למיתב סימנין וכל הבא ונותנו יטלנה מאי טעמא מידע ידע דעדים לית ליה פעמים שאין לו עדים עליה ואם יזקיקוהו לעדים לא תבא לעולם לידו ומימר אמר טוב לי שיחזירוה לכל האומר סימניה דלא שכיחא דנימא סימנין דידה אלא אנא דכ"ע לא ידעי כו': אלא הא דתנן כו'. ואמרו להחזיר לו למלוה בלא עדים בסימן זה שאומר שלשה היו ומשלשה לוים ואם מן הלוה נפלו שכבר פרעם מי ניחא ליה בתקנה זו שיתנם המוצאם לכל הבא ונותן סימניהם והלא טוב לו שיהו מונחים ביד המוצאם עולמית דכל זמן שהם בידו ולא יחזירם למלוה הרי הם כשרופים ולא ניחא ליהדר להו בסימנין דלמא מיתרמי דידע מלוה בסימניהן: התם. בסימנין כי האי לא איכפת לן בניחותא דלוה דודאי לאו מיניה נפיל דהנך שטרי אחריני מאי בעו גביה: אלא

**תוספות**

ת"ש חמור בסימני אוכף. ברייתא היא: **דרשהו** אם הוא רמאי מאי לאו בסימנין. וא"ת דבמתני' (לקמן כח:) דריש מהאי קרא דלא יחזיר אף בסימנין וי"ל דאסמכתא היא כדקתני עלה בברייתא משרבו הרמאים התקינו אבל הכא משמע ליה שהיא דרשה גמורה מדקאמר וכי תעלה על דעתך לומר כו' (ג) ועי"ל דבמתני' מיירי בידוע שהוא רמאי לכך צריך עדים אבל הכא מיירי בסתם בני אדם: (ד) **מצאו.** גט קשור בכיס יחזיר המוצא לשליח או לבעל השואלו בסימני הכיס:

י) (**וניחוש** לשאלה). וא"ת ולוכח מהכא דסימנין דאורייתא ובפרק בתרא דיבמות (ה) (דף קכ. ושם ד"ה מצאו) פריך מהכא דסימנין דאורייתא וי"ל דאלי לאוקמה כגון שאותו שאבדו מצאו ומכיר הכיס בטביעות עין דכיון שבעצמו מצאו נאמן וה"נ הוה מצי למדחי התם: **כיס** וארנקי משום דמסמני. וא"ת והכתיב לא תנחשו וי"ל בשלהי במה אשה (שבת דף סז.) אמרינן כל דבר שיש בו משום רפואה אין בו משום דרכי האמורי:

**ואנא** יהיבנא סימנים מובהקין דידה. לא מובהקין ממש קאמר אלא מובהקים מסימני חבירו כמו זה אומר מדת ארכו וזה אומר מדת רחבו ולקמן (דף כח:) נמי דקאמר לעולם גלימא מכריז ולא אמר סימנין מובהקין התם נמי לאו מובהקים ממש קאמר אלא שלא אמר סימנים טובים שיש בו כי אם כסימנין דסומקי וחיורי:

מגלא



**עין משפט נר מצוה**

צא א מיי' פ"ג מהל' גירושין הלכה יא ועיין בהשגות ובמגיד משנה סמג עשין מח טוש"ע אה"ע סי' קלב סעיף ד:
צב ב ג מיי' פי"ג שם הל' כא סמג עשין נ טוש"ע אה"ע סי' יז סעיף כד:
צג ד ה מיי' פ"ג שם [דין זה לא מכר ברמב"ם ועיין בב"י סי' קלב שתמה עליו] סמג שם טוש"ע אה"ע סי' קלב סעיף ד:
צד ו מיי' פי"ג שם הלכה כא טוש"ע אה"ע סי' יז סעיף כד:

**רבינו חננאל**

איבעיא להו סימנין דאורייתא או דרבנן וכו' וסימנין כדי נסבה פי' אגב גררה הזכירה משנתנו הסימנין ולאו דוקא הן. ת"ש חמור בסימני אוכף. פי' אוכף הוא שלפעמים נתון על המרדעת של חמור כדי למנוע א) חבור המשוי על גבי חמור. ת"ש דתנן בהאשה פרק בתרא דיבמות אין מעידים אלא על פרצוף פנים עם החוטם אע"פ שיש סימנין בגופו כלומר אם נותנין העדים סימני פרצופו ואמר מי שפרצופו כך וכך ראינוהו שמת משיאין את אשתו. ופרקי' גופו דארוך וגוץ דלאו סימן מובהק הוא כליו חיישינן שמא שאולין היו לו ומקשי' אי הכי חמור בסימני אוכף נמי דלמא שאול הוא ואע"ג דאיכא סהדי ב) האי דאיכוף להאי גברא הוא נימא דלמא השאילו לאחרים דהא אמרת גבי כלים חיישינן לשאלה. ופרקי' איכוף לא מושלי אינשי למה כי פעמי' שתהיה בהמת בעל האיכוף רזה ובהמת השואל שמנה וכשנותנין עליה זה האיכוף מתפתח וכשמחזיר על בהמתו של המשאיל מסקבה פי' עושה בה חבורה כדגרסי' ג) במשקין סקבא דשתא ריגלא. אלא הא דתניא מצא לגט קשור בכיס בארנקי בטבעת או שמצאו בכליו אפי' לזמן מרובה כשר ואי חיישינן לשאלה אמאי כשר ניחוש דלמ' השאיל כיסו או טבעתו או ארנקי שלו לאדם אחר והוא שקשר זה הגט עמהם וגט זה של אדם אחר הוא ואינו זה הגט שהיה בידו של משאיל. ופרקי' כיס וטבעת וארנקי לא מושלי אינשי ופשוטה היא. והא דאמרי' אין מעידין על השומא. ושומא מצויה בבן גילו וסימנין עשוין להשתנות אחר המיתה כולן פשוטות הן. וסוגיין דשמעתין מאן דאמר סימנין דאורייתא היינו דמהדרינן אבידתא בסימניה ואפי' למאן דאמר סימנין לאו דאורייתא הן אם הן ד) סימנין מהדרינן לה

**חשק שלמה על ר"ח**

א) נ"ל חכוך וכ"ה בערוך ערך אכפא. ב) נראה דצ"ל דהאי אוכף להאי גברא וכו'. ג) במשקין ליתא אך הוא בקידושין דף פ' וכ"ה בערוך ערך סקב. ד) נראה דצ"ל אם הן סימנים מובהקין מהדרינן וכו'.

**מסורת הש"ס**

א) [ראש השנה ה. וש"נ] ב) לקמן כח., ג) יבמות קכ., [בכורות מו:] ד) יבמות קכ., [גיטין כ:] ה) יבמות קכ., ו) שם ביבמות איתא בשומא העשויה כו' וע"ש ז) לעיל כ., ח) שם ע"ב ט) [ובעל המאור הקשה לפירושו דת"ל משמלה וכו' ופי' הוא שיביא עדים שאינו רמאי כו' וע"ש] י) מהרש"ל מ"ז ועשה הכל דבור אחד.

**הגהות הב"ח**

(א) גמ' בכלל כל אלו ולמה: (ב) שם היכי מהדרינן אמרי לא משאלי כצ"ל ותיבת אוכף נמחק: (ג) תום' ד"ה דרשהו וכו' ועי"ל דבמתני' נ"ב עי' בשו"ת ב"ח סי' רמ"ו ביאור דבור זה: (ד) ד"ה מצאו וד"ה וניחוש הד"א: (ה) בא"ד ובפ' בתרא דיבמות. נ"ב דף קכ ע"א וע"ש בתוספות בד"ה אמר רבא:

**תורה אור השלם**

א) וְאִם לֹא קָרוֹב אָחִיךָ אֵלֶיךָ וְלֹא יְדַעְתּוֹ וַאֲסַפְתּוֹ אֶל תּוֹךְ בֵּיתֶךָ וְהָיָה עִמְּךָ עַד דְּרֹשׁ אָחִיךָ אֹתוֹ וַהֲשֵׁבֹתוֹ לוֹ [דברים כב, ב]

**לעזי רש"י**

דורויי"ר. פירוש לשפשף, לעשות פצע (פצע) גבן של בהמות משא, לעשות חַבּוּרָה (עיין ערך סקב). וורוא"ד פירוש יבלת (רש"י ויקרא כב, כה), (ווארצעל).

**ליקוטי רש"י**

אין מעידין. על האשה שמת אא"כ ראוהו בפרצוף פניו עם חוטמו שיכולין להכירו שזהו הוא לא ראוהו בפרצוף שניטל חוטמו אין מעידין עליו להשיא את אשתו שמא אין הוא [יבמות קכ.]. כליו. בגדיו שמא לאחר השאילן ואותו אחר מת וראוהו אלו וסבורים שזהו בעל הבגדים. אוכף לא שאולי אינשי. כי החמור לא היה שוה אוכפו של זה לחבירו. איבעית אימא כליו דמתני' דקתני בגופו ובכליו דלא סמכי' אסימנייהו. בחיורי ובסומקי. דלא אמרי הוי סימן במלבושיו שחורין היו או לבנים דאין זה סימן שהרבה שחורין ולבנים ואדומים [יבמות קכ:]. או שמצאו בין כליו. בין כלי ביתו ומכיר את הכיס ואת הטבעת שהן שלו כשר ולא חיישינן דלמא האי כיס והאי טבעת דאינש אחרינא הוה והאי גט אחר הוא [שם בע"א]. אמאי כשר וכו'. מאי איכא למימר ליחוש אע"פ שהוא מכיר את הכיס יש לא...

שמא השאילו לאחר וקשר בו גט זה והחזירו לזה ושכח בו את הגט. כיס וארנקי משום דמסמני. שלא יטול זה מזלו ... ... ויטול הימנה כל אשר ישאל [שם בע"א]. וטבעת משום דמזייף. שמא יעשה חותם וצורה כנגד טבעתו וילך וראהו לאשתו ויטול הימנה כל ...

סימנין דאורייתא. אף השמלה בכלל היתה כו' בפ' ואלו מציאות. בשומא מצויה בבן גילו. שנולד בפרק אחד ובמזל אחד ור"א בן מהבאי סבר אין שומא מצויה בבן גילו. להשתנות. ממראה. סימנין דרבנן. ולא דריש אף השמלה לסימן אלא לתובעין כו' [שם בע"א]. שומא סימן מובהק הוא. ואע"ג דסימנין דרבנן אסימן כי האי סמכינן אפילו לאיסור דאורייתא [שם בע"ב].

**concerned about** the possibility of **borrowing.**[16] Other identifying marks, however, may be relied on even Biblically.

The Gemara questions the assumption that we are concerned about the possibility that an object might be on loan:

**אִי חַיְישִׁינַן לִשְׁאֵלָה** – But, **if we are concerned for** the possibility that an object might be **borrowed,** **חֲמוֹר בְּסִימָנֵי אוּכָּף הֵיכִי מְהַדְרִינַן** – **how,** then, **do we return a donkey based on the identifying marks of the saddle?**[17]

The Gemara answers:

**אָמְרֵי** – You can **say:** **אוּכָּף לֹא שְׁאוּלֵי אִינָשֵׁי אוּכָּפָא** – As far as **a saddle** is concerned, **people do not** usually **borrow a saddle,** **מִשּׁוּם דְּמַסְקַב לֵיהּ לַחֲמָרָא** – **since it would abrade the donkey's** skin[18] due to its incorrect size. Hence, it is possible to maintain that other objects, including garments, do tend to be borrowed with sufficient frequency so as to create a concern in the case of a corpse whose identity is determined only by the identifying marks on its garments.

**אִיבָּעֵית אֵימָא** – **If you prefer, say:** **כֵּלָיו** – Perhaps the identifying marks of **[the corpse's] garments** that the Mishnah disqualifies **בְּחִיוּרֵי וּבְסוּמָקֵי** – refer only to their **being white or** their **being red.**[19]

In its first answer, the Gemara maintained that a saddle is the exception in that it is unusual for it to be borrowed. Generally, however, the concern would exist that an object was borrowed. The Gemara now disputes this contention:

**אֶלָּא הָא דְּתַנְיָא** – **But,** this seems to be contradicted by **that which was taught in a Baraisa:** **מְצָאוֹ קָשׁוּר בְּכִיס אוֹ בְּאַרְנָקִי וּבְטַבַּעַת** – If [AN AGENT] who was charged with delivering a bill of divorce lost it, and later FOUND IT TIED TO A MONEYBAG OR TO A PURSE OR TO A SIGNET RING, **אוֹ שֶׁמְּצָאוֹ בֵּין כֵּלָיו** – OR if HE FOUND IT at home AMONG HIS UTENSILS **אֲפִילּוּ לִזְמַן מְרוּבֶּה** – EVEN if he found it only AFTER A LONG TIME has passed,[20] **כָּשֵׁר** – the bill of divorce is VALID. The fact that it is tied to an object of his, or that it was found among his belongings, proves that the bill of divorce is the one he originally lost. **וְאִי סָלְקָא דַּעְתָּךְ חַיְישִׁינַן לִשְׁאֵלָה** – **Now, if you suppose** that **we are concerned with** the possibility of **a loan** **כִּי מְצָאוֹ קָשׁוּר בְּכִיס אַמַּאי כָּשֵׁר** – **when he finds [the bill of divorce] tied to a moneybag, why is it valid?** **נֵיחוּשׁ לִשְׁאֵלָה** – **Let us consider** that the agent's moneybag was **borrowed** and the *borrower* may have attached the bill of divorce to the moneybag.[21] – ? –

The Gemara answers:

**אָמְרֵי** – You can **say:** **כִּיס וְאַרְנָקִי וְטַבַּעַת לֹא מַשְׁאֲלֵי אִינָשֵׁי** – **People do not** generally **lend a moneybag, a purse or a signet ring.** **כִּיס וְאַרְנָקִי מִשּׁוּם דִּמְסַמְּנֵי** – They do not lend **a moneybag or purse because [people] superstitiously believe** that by doing so, they transfer their good fortune to the borrower. **וְטַבַּעַת מִשּׁוּם דִּמְזַיֵּיף** – **And** they do not lend **a signet ring since [the borrower] coul[d] counterfeit** its impression and use it to falsely authorize message[s] in the name of the lender. Hence, moneybags, purses and signe[t] rings are in a category by themselves. Regarding other objects, how[ever], the possibility that they were loaned must be considered.[22]

The Gemara now returns to its main topic of whether reliance o[n] identifying marks is Biblical. The Gemara suggests that this is th[e] subject of a Tannaic dispute:

**לֵימָא כְּתַנָּאֵי** – **Shall we say** the matter is the subject of a **disput[e] among Tannaim?** For it was taught in a Baraisa: **[א]ין מְעִידִין עַל הַשּׁוּמָא** – WITNESSES MAY NOT TESTIFY regarding the identity of [a] corpse, in order to permit the wife to remarry, based ON recogn[i]tion of A WART.[23] **וְאֶלְעָזָר בֶּן מְהַבַאי אוֹמֵר** – BUT ELAZAR BE[N] MEHAVAI SAYS: **מְעִידִין עַל הַשּׁוּמָא** – THEY CAN TESTIFY ON the ba[]sis of A WART.

The Gemara analyzes the Baraisa:

**מַאי לָאו בְּהָא קָמִיפַּלְגֵי** – **Do they not dispute** precisely **this** point? **דְּתַנָּא קַמָּא סָבַר סִימָנִין דְּרַבָּנָן** – For apparently, **the Tanna Kamm[a] holds** that determination by **identifying marks** is **a Rabbinic** en[]actment[24] **וְאֶלְעָזָר בֶּן מְהַבַאי סָבַר סִימָנִין דְּאוֹרַיְיתָא** – **and Elaza[r] ben Mehavai holds** that determination by **identifying marks** i[s] **Biblical** law.

Rava rejects this reasoning:

**אָמַר רָבָא** – **Rava said:** **דְּכוּלֵּי עָלְמָא** – Perhaps **all** agree **[ס]ימָנִין דְּאוֹרַיְיתָא** – that determination by **identifying marks** is **Biblica[l]**. **וְהָכָא בְּשׁוּמָא מְצוּיָה בְּבֶן גִּילוֹ קָמִיפַּלְגֵי** – Rather, **here, they disput[e]** whether **an** identical **wart is commonly found on** the body o[f] **one's contemporary.**[25] **מַר סָבַר שׁוּמָא מְצוּיָה בְּבֶן גִּילוֹ** – **One mas[ter] holds** that **an** identical **wart is commonly found on** the bod[y] of **one's contemporary.** Hence, a wart is not considered an identi[]fying mark. **וּמַר סָבַר שׁוּמָא אֵינָהּ מְצוּיָה בְּבֶן גִּילוֹ** – **And** the othe[r] **master holds** that **an** identical **wart is not commonly found o[n]** the body of **one's contemporary.** Hence, a wart is considered a[n] identifying mark, and can be relied upon even for Biblical laws o[f] a prohibitory nature.

A second explanation of the dispute:

**אִיבָּעֵית אֵימָא** – **If you prefer, say:** **[דְּ]כוּלֵּי עָלְמָא שׁוּמָא אֵינָהּ מְצוּיָה בְּבֶן גִּילוֹ** – **All agree** that **an** identical **wart is not commonl[y] found on** the body of **one's contemporary.** **[ו]הָכָא בְּסִימָנִין הָעֲשׂוּיִן לְהִשְׁתַּנּוֹת לְאַחַר מִיתָה קָמִיפַּלְגֵי** – **But here, they argue whethe[r] identifying marks tend to change** their appearance **after death**. **מַר סָבַר סִימָנִין עֲשׂוּיִם לְהִשְׁתַּנּוֹת לְאַחַר מִיתָה** – **One master holds** tha[t] **identifying marks tend to change** their appearance **after death**. Thus, a wart cannot serve as an identifying mark. **[וּ]מַר סָבַר סִימָנִין אֵין עֲשׂוּיִם לְהִשְׁתַּנּוֹת לְאַחַר מִיתָה** – **And** the other **master holds** tha[t] **identifying marks do not tend to change** their appearance **afte[r]**

NOTES

16. We are concerned that perhaps the garments were loaned to the dead man. Thus, although the garment's *simanim* determine their owner, they do not conclusively prove the dead man's identity. Hence, their owner might still be alive.

17. The Gemara above suggested that, Biblically, a donkey would be returned based not on the saddle's *simanim,* but on witnesses who attest to its ownership. However, this point is irrelevant to our discussion, for if we need to consider the possibility that the saddle is borrowed, it would make no difference how ownership of the saddle has been proven (*Ramban;* see also *R' Chananel,* and *Noda B'Yehudah Even HaEzer* I:51).

18. *Rabbeinu Chananel* explains that the *owner* of a saddle would not *lend* it to another, out of concern that it might become stretched out of shape. It would then wound his own beast after it was returned.

19. Since there are many garments of these colors, the color is not an identifying mark at all (*Rashi*).

20. The Mishnah (*Gittin* 27a) rules that if an agent lost a *get*, it is not valid unless he finds it shortly after losing it. If he finds a *get* only after a long time has passed, it is invalid, because we are concerned that it is not the same *get* that he lost. Although a *get* includes the names of husband and wife, the recovered *get* may have been written for another cou[]ple with identical names. Hence, the agent could not legally deliver it because a *get* is valid only for the couple for whom it was composed (se[e] Mishnah *Gittin* 24a).

Our Baraisa qualifies the Mishnah's ruling by giving instances wher[e] the *get* is valid even if it was retrieved only after a long time (*Rashi*).

21. We should consider the possibility that he lent his moneybag to some[]one else and later forgot that he lent it (*Ritva,* in explanation of *Rashi*).

22. The Baraisa additionally validated a *get* found among the agent' utensils. *Rashi* to *Yevamos* (120b ד״ה מנחשי) explains that these are uten[]sils not commonly lent. They are therefore in the same category as a moneybag, purse and signet ring.

23. They say that the body had a wart on a specific limb (*Rashi*).

24. As such, they cannot be relied upon for Biblical laws of a prohibitor[y] nature, such as for releasing a woman from her married status (*Rashi* see above, note 3).

25. Contemporary, in the context of our Gemara, means one who wa[s] born at the same hour and is therefore subject to identical astrologica[l] influences (*Rashi*).

## עין משפט נר מצוה

צא א מיי' פ"ג מהל' גירושין הלכה יא ועיין בהשגות ובמגיד משנה סמג עשין מח טוש"ע אה"ע סי' קלג סעיף ד:
צב ב ג מיי' פי"ג שם הל' כא סמג עשין נ טוש"ע אה"ע סי' יז סעיף כד:
צג ד ה מיי' פ"ג שם [דין זה לא מצא ברמב"ם ועיין בב"י סי' קלג שתמה עליו] סמג שם טוש"ע אה"ע סי' קלג סעיף ד:
צד ו מיי' פי"ג שם הלכה כא טוש"ע אה"ע סי' יז סעיף כד:

## רבינו חננאל

איבעיא להו סימנין דאורייתא או דרבנן וכו' וסימנין כדי נסבה פי' אגב גררה הזכירה משנתנו הסימנין ולאו דוקא הן. ת"ש חמור בסימני אוכף. פי' אוכף הוא שלפעמים נתון על המרדעת של חמור כדי למנוע א) חבור המשוי על גבי חמור. ת"ש דתנן בהאשה פרק בתרא דיבמות אין מעידים אלא על פרצוף פנים עם החוטם אע"פ שיש סימנין בגופו כלומר אם נותנין העדים סימני פרצופו ואמר מי שפרצופו כך וכך ראינוהו שמת משיאין את אשתו. ופרקי' גופו דארוך וגוץ דלאו סימן מובהק הוא כליו חיישינן שמא שאולין היו לו ומקשי' אי הכי חמור בסימני אוכף נמי דלמא שאול הוא ואע"ג דאיכא סהדי ב) האי דאיכוף להאי גברא הוא נימא דלמא השאילו לאחרים דהא אמרת גבי כלים חיישינן לשאלה. ופרקי' איכוף לא מושלי אינשי למה כי פעמי' שתהיה בהמת בעל האיכוף רזה ובהמת השואל שמנה וכשנותנין עליה זה האיכוף מתפתח וכשמחזיר על בהמתו של המשאיל מסקבה פי' עושה בה חבורה כדגרסי' ג) במשקין סקבא דשתא ריגלא. אלא הא דתניא מצא לגט קשור בכיס בארנקי בטבעת או שמצאו בכליו אפי' לזמן מרובה כשר ואי חיישינן לשאלה אמאי כשר ניחוש דלמ' השאיל כיסו או טבעתו או ארנקי שלו לאדם אחר והוא שקשר זה הגט עמהם וגט זה של אדם אחר הוא ואינו זה הגט שהיה בידו של משאיל. ופרקי' כיס וטבעת וארנקי לא מושלי אינשי ופשוטה היא. והא דאמרי' אין מעידין על השומא. ושומא מצויה בבן גילו וסימנין עשוין להשתנות אחר המיתה כולן פשוטות הן. וסוגיין דשמעתין מאן דאמר סימנין דאורייתא היינו דמהדרינן אבידתא בסימניה ואפי' למאן דאמר סימנין לאו דאורייתא הן אם הן ד) סימנין מהדרינן לה

## חשק שלמה על ר"ח

א) נ"ל חכוך וכ"ה בערוך ערך אכפא. ב) נראה דצ"ל דהאי אוכף להאי גברא וכו'. ג) במשקין ליתא אך הוא בקדושין דף פ' וכ"ה בערוך ערך סקב. ד) נראה דצ"ל אם הן סימנים מובהקין מהדרינן וכו'.

## גמרא

לאהדורי גט אשה בסימנים אי אמרת דאורייתא [א]מהדרינן ואי אמרת דרבנן כי עבוד רבנן תקנתא בממונא אבל באיסורא לא עבוד רבנן תקנתא ת"ש אף השמלה היתה בכלל כל (א) אלו ולמה יצאת להקיש אליה ולומר לך מה שמלה מיוחדת שיש לה סימנין ויש לה תובעין חייב להכריז אף כל דבר שיש לו סימנין ויש לו תובעין חייב להכריז תנא תובעין אצטריכא ליה סימנין [א]כדי נסבא ת"ש חמור בסימני אוכף אימא בעדי אוכף ת"ש [ז] א) והיה עמך עד דרוש אחיך אותו וכי תעלה על דעתך שיתננו לו קודם שידרשנו אלא דרשהו אם רמאי הוא או אינו רמאי מאי לאו בסימנין לא בעדים ת"ש [ג] [ב]אין מעידין אלא על פרצוף הפנים עם החוטם אע"פ שיש סימנין בגופו ובכליו שמע מינה סימנין לאו דאורייתא אמרי גופו דארוך וגוץ כליו [ג]דחיישינן לשאלה אי חיישינן לשאלה חמור בסימני אוכף היכי מהדרינן אמרי (ב) אוכף לא שאולי אינשי אוכפא משום דמסקב ליה לחמרא איבעית אימא כליו בחיורי ובסומקי אלא הא דתניא [ד]מצאו קשור בכיס או בארנקי ובטבעת או שמצאו בין כליו אפילו לזמן מרובה כשר ואי ס"ד חיישינן לשאלה כי מצאו קשור בכיס אמאי כשר ניחוש לשאלה אמרי כיס וארנקי וטבעת [ה]לא משאלי אינשי כיס וארנקי משום דמסמני וטבעת משום דמזייף לימא כתנאי [ט] [ו]אין מעידין על השומא ואלעזר בן מהבאי אומר מעידין על השומא מאי לאו בהא קמיפלגי דת"ק סבר סימנין דרבנן ואלעזר בן מהבאי סבר סימנין דאורייתא אמר רבא דכ"ע סימנין דאורייתא והכא בשומא מצויה בבן גילו קמיפלגי מר סבר שומא מצויה בבן גילו ומ"ס שומא אינה מצויה בבן גילו איבעית אימא דכ"ע שומא אינה מצויה בבן גילו והכא [י]בסימנין העשוין להשתנות לאחר מיתה קמיפלגי מר סבר סימנין עשוים להשתנות לאחר מיתה ומר סבר סימנין אין עשוים להשתנות לאחר מיתה אב"א דכ"ע שומא אינה עשויה להשתנות לאחר מיתה וסימנין דרבנן והכא בשומא סימן מובהק הוא קמיפלגי מ"ס שומא סימן מובהק הוא ומ"ס שומא לאו סימן מובהק הוא אמר רבא את"ל סימנין לאו דאורייתא היכי מהדרינן אבידתא בסימנין דניחא ליה למוצא אבידה דנהדר בסימנין כי היכי דכי אבדה ליה לדידיה נמי נהדרו ליה בסימנין אמר ליה רב ספרא לרבא וכי אדם עושה טובה לעצמו בממון שאינו שלו אלא ניחא ליה לבעל אבידה למיהב סימנין ולמשקליה מידע ידע דעדים לית ליה ומימר אמר כולי עלמא לא ידעי סימנין מובהקים דידה ואנא יהיבנא סימנין מובהקים דידה ושקלנא לה אלא הא דתנן [ז]רבן שמעון בן גמליאל אומר אחד הלוה משלשה יחזיר ללוה שלשה שלוו מן האחד יחזיר למלוה ניחא ליה ללוה לאהדורי ליה התם סברא הוא [ח]אחד הלוה משלשה יחזיר ללוה דגבי לוה שכיחי גבי מלוה לא שכיחי ש"מ מלוה נפול שלשה שלוו מאחד יחזור למלוה דגבי מלוה שכיחי גבי לוה לא שכיחי אלא

## תוספות

ת"ש חמור בסימני אוכף. ברייתא היא: דרשהו אם הוא רמאי מאי לאו בסימנין. וא"ת דבמתני' (לקמן כח:) דריש מהאי קרא דלא יחזיר אף בסימנין וי"ל דאסמכתא היא כדקתני עלה בברייתא משרבו הרמאים התקינו אבל הכא משמע ליה שהיא דרשה גמורה מדקאמר וכי תעלה על דעתך לומר כו' (ג) ועי"ל דבמתני' איירי בידוע שהוא רמאי לכך צריך עדים אבל הכא איירי בסתם בני אדם:

(ד) מצאו. גט קשור בכיס יחזיר המוצא לשליח או לבעל השואלו בסימני הכיס:

[י](וניחוש לשאלה). וא"ת ולוכח מהכא דסימנין דאורייתא ובפרק בתרא דיבמות (ה) (דף קכ. ושם ד"ה מצאו) פריך מהכא דסימנין דאורייתא וי"ל דמצי לאוקמה כגון שאותו שאבדו מצאו ומכיר הכיס בטביעות עין דכיון שבעצמו מצאו נאמן וה"נ הוה מצי למדחי התם: כיס וארנקי משום דמסמני. וא"ת והכתיב לא תנחשו וי"ל בשלהי במה אשה (שבת דף סז.) אמרינן כל דבר שיש בו משום רפואה אין בו משום דרכי האמורי:

ואנא יהיבנא סימנים מובהקין דידה. לא מובהקין ממש קאמר אלא מובהקים מסימני חבירו כמו זה אומר מדת ארכו וזה אומר מדת רחבו ולקמן (דף כח:) נמי דקאמר לעולם גלימא מכריז ולא אמר סימנין מובהקין התם נמי לאו מובהקים ממש קאמר אלא שלא אמר סימנים טובים שיש בו כי אם כסימנין דסומקי וחיורי:

אלא

## רש"י

לאהדורי גט. שאבד מן השליח המביאו קודם שנתן לה: תקנתא. לקמן בשמעתין מפרש מאי היא: בממונא. דהפקר ב"ד הפקר: תובעין אצטריכא ליה. קרא לתובעין אתא ולמעוטי מידי דאיאוש ואפקריה: כדי נסבה. בלא מקרא אלא אסמכינהו אקרא בעלמא:

ת"ש. דאוקמינן לעיל חמור לסימני אוכף אתא: אימא בעדי אוכף. אם יש עדים המכירין בטביעות עין לאוכף שהוא שלו מחזירין לו את החמור: דרשהו. והכי משמע עד דרוש אחיך אותו עד דרשך את אחיך: [ט] בעדים. שיבא עדים שהוא שלו: אין מעידין. על אדם שמת להשיא את אשתו אלא א"כ ראו פרצוף פניו שהוא עם החוטם: דארוך או גוץ. שאין זה סימן שהרבה ארוכין וגוצים יש: כליו. בגדיו: חיישינן. שמא השאילם לאחר ואותו אחר ראו שמת: מסקב. דורויי"ר בלעז: חיורי או סומקי. אין זה סימן שהרבה כאלה יש: מצאו קשור בכיס שלו או בארנקי כו'. שליח המביא גט ואבד הימנו לאחר זמן מצאו קשור בכיס שלו או בארנקי כו': בין כליו. כלי תשמישו שבביתו: אפילו לזמן מרובה. אע"ג דתנן (גיטין דף כז.) המביא גט ואבד הימנו מצאו לזמן מרובה פסול הכא כשר: ניחוש לשאלה. שמא השאיל כיסו לאחר והוא קשרו בו: דמסמני. מנחשי ואומר סימן לאדם שמשאיל כיסו שמוכר לו מזלו: דמזייף. שהיה לכל איש חותם ניכר בטבעתו וכששולח שום דבר סתום מכסהו וחותמו בטבעתו לפיכך אינו משאיל טבעתו שמא יעשה זה חותם כנגד חותמו ויזייף בו את שליחותיו: אין מעידין על השומא. המעידין על האשה להשיאה ואמרו סימן היה בו שומא באבר פלוני: שומא. וורוא"ה בלעז: סימנין דרבנן. וגבי אשת איש דאיסור דאורייתא הוא לא סמכינן עלייהו: בבן גילו. הנולד בשעתו שנולדו במזל אחד: בסימנין העשויין כו'. אם עשויין להשתנות או אינן עשויין להשתנות אם בחייו היתה שומא שחורה במותו נעשית לבנה או איפוך: מובהק. ואפילו סימנין דרבנן יש לסמוך על זה: היכי מהדרינן. כלומר מה תקנה ראו חכמים בדבר ליכנס בספק להחזיר ממון למי שאינו שלו: אלא ל"ג: וכי אדם עושה. ובניחותא דמוצא מאי איכפת לן אם מי שאבדה ממנו לא ניחא ליה: אלא. אמר רבא כל אובדי אבידה ניחא להו שתהא דת זו בישראל למיתב סימנין וכל הבא ונותנו יטלנה מאי טעמא מידע ידע דעדים לית ליה פעמים שאין לו עדים עליה ואם יזקיקוהו לעדים לא תבא לעולם לידו ומימר אמר טוב לי שיחזירוה לכל האומר סימניה דלא שכיחא דנימא סימנין דידה אלא אנא דכ"ע לא ידעי כו'. ואמרו להחזיר לו למלוה בלא עדים בסימן זה שאומר שלשה היו ומשלשה לוים ואם מן הלוה נפלו שכבר פרעם מי ניחא ליה בתקנה זו שיתנם המוצאם לכל הבא ונותן סימניהם והלא טוב לו שיהו מונחים ביד המוצאם עולמית דכל זמן שהם בידו ולא יחזירם למלוה הרי הם כשרופים ולא ניחא דליהדר להו בסימנין דלמא מיתרמי דידע מלוה בסימניהן: התם. בסימנין כי האי לא איכפת לן בניחותא דלוה דודאי לאו מיניה נפיל דהנך שטרי אחריני מאי בעו גביה:

אלא

## מסורת הש"ס

א) [ראש השנה ה. וש"נ] ב) לקמן כח. ג) יבמות קכ. [בכורות מו] ד) יבמות קכ. [גיטין כז] ה) יבמות קכ. ו) ביבמות איתא בשומא העשויה כו' וע"ש ז) לעיל כ. ח) שם ע"ב ט) [ובעל המאור הקשה לפירושו דת"ל משמלה ופי' הוא שיביא עד שאינו רמאי כו' וע"ש] י) מהרש"ל מ"ז ועשה הכל דבור אחד.

## הגהות הב"ח

(א) גמ' בכלל כל אלו ולמה: (ב) שם אמרי מהדרינן אמרי לא משום כל"ל ותיבת אוכף נמחק: (ג) תוס' ד"ה דרשהו וכו' ועי"ל דבמתני' נ"ב עיין בשו"ת ב"ח סי' רמ"ו ביאור דבור זה: (ד) ד"ה מצאו וד"ה וניחוש הד"א: (ה) בא"ד ובפ' בתרא דיבמות. נ"ב דף קכ ע"א וע"ש בתוספות בד"ה אי רבא:

## תורה אור השלם

א) וְאִם לֹא קָרוֹב אָחִיךָ אֵלֶיךָ וְלֹא יְדַעְתּוֹ וַאֲסַפְתּוֹ אֶל תּוֹךְ בֵּיתֶךָ וְהָיָה עִמְּךָ עַד דְּרֹשׁ אָחִיךָ אֹתוֹ וַהֲשֵׁבֹתוֹ לוֹ: [דברים כב, ב]

## לעזי רש"י

דורוייש"ר. פירוש לשפשף, לעשות פצע (גבן של בהמות משא לעשות חבורה (עיין ערוך ערך סקב). וורוא"ה פירוש יבלת (רש"י ויקרא כב, כב), (ווארצעל).

## ליקוטי רש"י

אין מעידין. על האיש שמת אא"כ ראוהו בפרצוף פניו עם חוטם שיכולין להכירו שזהו לא ראוהו בפרצוף שניטל חוטמו אין מעידין עליו להשיא את אשתו שאין הוא [יבמות קכ.]. כליו. בגדיו שמא לא השאילן ואותו אחר וראוהו אלו וסבורים שזהו בעל הבגדים. אוכף לא שאולי אינשי. החמור לא היה של אוכפו של זה לחבר. איבעית אימא כליו. דמתני' דקתני בגופו ובכליו דלא סמכינן אסימנייהו. בחיורי ובסומקי. דלא אמר הוי סימן במלבושיו שחורין היו או לבנים דאין זה סימן שהרבה שחורין ולבנים ואדום [יבמות קכ:]. או שמצאו בין כליו. בין כלי ביתו ומכיר את הכיס ואת הטבעת שהן שלו כשר חיישינן דלמא האי כיס והאי טבעת דאי אחרינא הוה והאי גט לאו הוא [שם בע"א]. אמאי כשר וכו'. מאי איכא למימר ליחוש אע"פ שהוא מכיר את הכיס יש לומר

## הערות בתחתית הדף

ג) במשקין ליתא אך הוא בקדושין דף פ' וכ"ה בערוך ערך סקב. ד) נראה דצ"ל אם הן סימנים מובהקין מהדרינן וכו'.

סימנין דאורייתא. אף השמלה בכלל היתה כו' בפ' ואלו מציאות. בשומא מצויה בבן גילו. שנולד בפרק אחד ובמזל אחד ור"א בן מהבאי סבר אין שומא מצויה בבן גילו. להשתנות. ממראה. סימנין דרבנן. ולא דריש אף השמלה לסימן אלא לתובעין כו' [שם בע"א]. שומא סימן מובהק הוא. ואע"ג דסימנין דרבנן אסימן כי האי סמכינן אפילו לאיסור דאורייתא [שם בע"ב].

שמא השאילו לאחר וקשר בו גט זה והחזירו לזה ושכח בו את הגט. כיס וארנקי משום דמסמני. שלא יטול זה מזלו וטבעת משום דמזייף. שמא יעשה חותם וצורה כנגד טבעתו וילך וירא[ה]הו לאשתו ויטול הימנה כל אשר ישאל [שם בע"א].

לְאַהֲדוּרֵי גֵט אִשָּׁה בְּסִימָנִים – The difference that emerges is whether **to return a woman's bill of divorce based on** a claimant's knowledge of its **identifying marks.**[1] אִי אָמְרַת דְּאוֹרַיְיתָא מְהַדְרִינַן – **If you say** that reliance on identifying marks is **Biblical,** then **we** would **return** a lost bill of divorce on this basis. וְאִי אָמְרַת דְּרַבָּנָן – **But if you say** that reliance on identifying marks is a **Rabbinic** enactment, we would not return a lost bill of divorce on this basis. כִּי עָבוּד רַבָּנַן תַּקַּנְתָּא – For **regarding which** matters would **the Rabbis** have **legislated an enactment** to rely on identifying marks? בְּמָמוֹנָא – They would have relied on these marks only **insofar as monetary law** is concerned.[2] אֲבָל בְּאִיסוּרָא לֹא עָבוּד רַבָּנַן תַּקַּנְתָּא – **However, insofar as prohibitory law** is concerned, **the Rabbis would not** have **legislated** such **an enactment.**[3]

The Gemara seeks a proof from the Mishnah:

תָּא שְׁמַע – **Come, learn** a proof from our Mishnah:[4] אַף הַשִּׂמְלָה הָיְתָה בִּכְלַל כָּל אֵלּוּ – THE GARMENT, TOO, WAS INCLUDED IN ALL OF THESE וְלָמָּה יָצְאת – AND WHY WAS IT SINGLED OUT? לְהַקִּישׁ אֵלֶיהָ – TO COMPARE all types of lost property TO IT וְלוֹמַר לְךָ – AND TO TELL YOU: מַה שִּׂמְלָה מְיוּחֶדֶת – JUST AS A GARMENT IS DISTINGUISHED שֶׁיֵּשׁ לָהּ סִימָנִין וְיֵשׁ לָהּ תּוֹבְעִין – IN THAT IT HAS IDENTIFYING MARKS AND HAS CLAIMANTS, חַיָּיב לְהַכְרִיז – and MUST BE ANNOUNCED, אַף כָּל דָּבָר שֶׁיֵּשׁ לוֹ סִימָנִין וְיֵשׁ לוֹ תּוֹבְעִין – SO, TOO, ANYTHING THAT HAS IDENTIFYING MARKS AND HAS CLAIMANTS חַיָּיב לְהַכְרִיז – MUST BE ANNOUNCED. Since a verse from Scripture is interpreted as limiting the obligation to return lost objects to those that have identifying marks, it is clear that identifying marks are Scripturally significant.

The Gemara rejects this proof:

תַּנָּא תּוֹבְעִין אִצְטְרִיכָא לֵיהּ – Perhaps **the Tanna** who taught this Mishnah **needed** the Scriptural interpretation only with regard to the requirement of **claimants.** סִימָנִין כְּדִי נָסְבָא – **He mentioned identifying marks,** however, only **incidentally,** but not because they are derived from Scripture.[5] Hence, this Mishnah does not prove that such identification is Biblically ordained.

The Gemara attempts another proof:

תָּא שְׁמַע – **Come, learn** a proof. חֲמוֹר בְּסִימָנֵי אוּכָּף – It was explained above (27a) that the word **chamor** in the verse teaches that a **donkey** should be returned to a claimant who provides the **identifying marks of the saddle.** Apparently, then, the law for relying on such marks is Biblically ordained.

The Gemara counters:

אֵימָא – You can **say:** בְּעֵדֵי אוּכָּף – Perhaps the verse teaches that a donkey should be returned **on the basis of witnesses** who recognize the **saddle.**[6] Proof of ownership by identifying marks however, may be merely a Rabbinic concept.

A third proof:

תָּא שְׁמַע – **Come, learn** a proof from a Baraisa. The verse states:[7] ,,וְהָיָה עִמְּךָ עַד דְּרֹשׁ אָחִיךָ אֹתוֹ" – *AND IT* (the lost object) *SHALL REMAIN WITH YOU UNTIL YOUR BROTHER SEEKS IT OUT.*[8]

The Baraisa explains this verse:

וְכִי תַּעֲלֶה עַל דַּעְתְּךָ – NOW, COULD YOU HAVE SUPPOSED[9] שֶׁיִּתְּנֶנּוּ לוֹ קוֹדֶם שֶׁיִּדְרְשֶׁנּוּ – THAT [THE FINDER] SHOULD GIVE [THE RECOVERED OBJECT] TO [ITS OWNER] BEFORE HE SEEKS IT OUT? Certainly, since the verse discusses a case in which the owner is not known to the finder, he cannot return it before it is sought out! אֶלָּא – RATHER, interpret the verse as follows: דָּרְשֵׁהוּ אִם רַמַּאי הוּא אוֹ אֵינוֹ רַמַּאי – INVESTIGATE [THE CLAIMANT] to determine WHETHER HE IS A DECEIVER OR HE IS NOT A DECEIVER.[10]

The Gemara concludes its proof by showing how this determination is made:

מַאי לָאו בְּסִימָנִין – **Is it not through identifying marks?** Since the Torah says that the claimant's knowledge of the object's identifying marks is sufficient to establish the veracity of his claim, it is clear that such identification is Biblically valid.

The Gemara rejects this proof:

לֹא בְּעֵדִים – **No!** Perhaps the status of the claimant is to be determined **through witnesses.**[11] Hence, there is no proof that Scripture accepts identifying marks as proof of ownership.

The Gemara now attempts to prove that identifying marks are not Biblically recognized:

תָּא שְׁמַע – **Come, learn** a proof from a Mishnah:[12] אֵין מְעִידִין – Witnesses MAY NOT TESTIFY regarding the identity of a corpse אֶלָּא עַל פַּרְצוּף הַפָּנִים – UNLESS their testimony is BASED ON observation of THE FACE עִם הַחוֹטֶם – INCLUDING THE NOSE.[13] אַף עַל פִּי שֶׁיֵּשׁ סִימָנִין בְּגוּפוֹ וּבְכֵלָיו – Lacking such observation, they may not testify ALTHOUGH THERE ARE IDENTIFYING MARKS ON HIS BODY AND ON HIS GARMENTS. שְׁמַע מִינָּהּ סִימָנִין לָאו דְּאוֹרַיְיתָא – We **learn from [this Mishnah]** that reliance on **identifying marks is not Biblical.**[14]

The Gemara rejects this proof:

אָמְרֵי – You can **say:** גּוּפוֹ דְּאָרוֹךְ וְגוּץ – Perhaps the identifying marks which were disqualified regarding **his body** refer to witnesses' testimony that **he was** either **tall or short,** which is not in fact an identifying feature at all, since there are many tall and short people.[15] כֵּלָיו – And identifying marks on **[the corpse's] garments** are disqualified דְּחָיְישִׁינָן לִשְׁאֵלָה – **because we are**

NOTES

1. A husband may divorce his wife by appointing an agent to deliver a *get* to her. The Gemara discusses a case of an agent who lost the *get* while en route (*Rashi*). The question is whether the finder should return it to the agent based on his identification of its *simanim*.

2. The Rabbis are authorized to declare property ownerless at their discretion (*Gittin* 36b). Likewise, although by Torah law certain property may belong to one person, the Rabbis are empowered to enact a law that, in effect, transfers ownership to another (see *Rashi*).

3. The Rabbis are not authorized to legislate where this would render permissible something forbidden by Torah law. Thus, if identification by *simanim* is merely Rabbinic, it would not extend to the case of the *get,* for it would result in granting the status of divorcee to a woman who by Torah law is still considered married.

4. Above, 27a; see Gemara there and notes.

5. The Mishnah's second law, that an object need be returned only if its owner has not yet despaired of finding it, is derived from Scripture. However, the Mishnah's first law, that an object is returned only if it has marks by which it can be identified, is not derived from Scripture. The Mishnah cited the verse for this first law merely to link a Rabbinic law to a Scriptural text (*Rashi*).

6. The witnesses must identify the owner through visual recognition of the saddle itself, not merely on the basis of its identifying marks (*Rashi*).

7. *Deuteronomy* 22:2.

8. The verse discusses a case in which the object's owner is not known to the finder.

9. Literally: could it go up unto your mind.

10. That is, the word דְּרֹשׁ can also be translated "investigate," referring not to the lost object, but to "your brother." Hence, it is interpreted to read "it shall remain with you until you investigate your brother" to determine if his claim of ownership is honest (see *Rashi*).

11. As explained by *Rashi,* the witnesses testify that the object actually belongs to the claimant. However, *Rabbeinu Chananel* (quoted by *Ramban*) maintains that the Gemara refers to character witnesses; they testify that the claimant is an honest man.

12. *Yevamos* 120a. This Mishnah establishes the minimum requirement for positive identification of a corpse to permit the wife to remarry.

13. This actually refers only to the cheeks and the nose (see *Chelkas Mechokek, Even HaEzer,* 17:41).

14. Since they do not suffice to establish positive identification of the corpse, they likewise do not suffice to establish ownership of a lost object.

15. However, if the witnesses were to base their identification of the corpse on more specific identifying marks, their testimony would be valid even if they do not recognize the face.

עין משפט
נר מצוה

צא א מיי׳ פ״ג מהל׳ גירושין הלכה יא ועיין בהשגות ובמגיד משנה סמג עשין מח טוש״ע אה״ע סי׳ קלג סעיף ד:
צב ב ג מיי׳ פי״ג שם הל׳ כא סמג עשין ג טוש״ע אה״ע סי׳ יז סעיף כד:
צג ד ה מיי׳ פ״ג שם [דין זה לא נזכר ברמב״ם ועיין בב״י סי׳ קלב שתמה עליו] סמג שם טוש״ע אה״ע סי׳ קלב סעיף ד:
צד ו מיי׳ פי״ג שם הלכה כא טוש״ע אה״ע סי׳ יז סעיף כד:

לאהדורי גט אשה בסימנים אי אמרת דאורייתא [א]מהדרינן ואי אמרת דרבנן כי עבוד רבנן תקנתא בממונא אבל באיסורא לא עבוד רבנן תקנתא ת״ש אף השמלה היתה בכלל כל (א) אלו ולמה יצאת להקיש אליה ולומר לך מה שמלה מיוחדת שיש לה סימנין ויש לה תובעין חייב להכריז אף כל דבר שיש לו סימנין ויש לו תובעין חייב להכריז תנא תובעין אצטריכא ליה סימנין (א) כדי נסבא ת״ש חמור בסימני אוכף אימא בעדי אוכף ת״ש (ב) א) והיה עמך עד דרוש אחיך אותו וכי תעלה על דעתך שיתננו לו קודם שידרשנו אלא דרשהו אם רמאי הוא או אינו רמאי מאי לאו בסימנין לא בעדים ת״ש (ג) [ב]אין מעידין אלא על פרצוף הפנים עם החוטם אע״פ שיש סימנין בגופו ובכליו שמע מינה סימנין לאו דאורייתא אמרי גופו דארוך וגוץ כליו [ג]דחיישינן לשאלה אי חיישינן לשאלה חמור בסימני אוכף היכי מהדרינן אמרי (ב) אוכף לא שאולי אינשי אוכפא משום דמסקב ליה לחמרא איבעית אימא כליו בחיורי ובסומקי אלא הא דתניא (ד) [ד]מצאו קשור בכים או בארנקי ובטבעת או שמצאו בין כליו אפילו לזמן מרובה כשר ואי ס״ד חיישינן לשאלה כי מצאו קשור בכים אמאי כשר ניחוש לשאלה אמרי כים וארנקי וטבעת [ה]לא משאלי אינשי כים וארנקי משום דמסמני וטבעת משום דמזייף לימא כתנאי (ה) [ו]אין מעידין על השומא ואלעזר בן מהבאי אומר מעידין על השומא מאי לאו בהא קמיפלגי דת״ק סבר סימנין דרבנן ואלעזר בן מהבאי סבר סימנין דאורייתא אמר רבא דכ״ע סימנין דאורייתא והכא בשומא מצויה בבן גילו קמיפלגי מר סבר שומא מצויה בבן גילו ומ״ס שומא אינה מצויה בבן גילו איבעית אימא דכ״ע שומא אינה מצויה בבן גילו והכא [ו]בסימנין העשוין להשתנות לאחר מיתה קמיפלגי מר סבר סימנין עשוים להשתנות לאחר מיתה ומר סבר סימנין אין עשוים להשתנות לאחר מיתה אב״א דכ״ע שומא אינה עשויה להשתנות לאחר מיתה וסימנין דרבנן והכא בשומא סימן מובהק הוא קמיפלגי מ״ס שומא סימן מובהק הוא ומ״ס שומא לאו סימן מובהק הוא אמר רבא את״ל סימנין לאו דאורייתא היכי מהדרינן אבידתא בסימנין דניחא ליה למוצא אבידה דנהדר בסימנין כי היכי דכי אבדה ליה לדידיה נמי נהדרו ליה בסימנין אמר ליה רב ספרא לרבא וכי אדם עושה טובה לעצמו בממון שאינו שלו אלא ניחא ליה לבעל אבידה למיהב סימנין ולמשקליה מידע ידע דעדים לית ליה ומימר אמר כולי עלמא לא ידעי סימנין מובהקים דידה ואנא יהיבנא סימנין מובהקים דידה ושקלנא לה אלא הא דתנן [ז]רבן שמעון בן גמליאל אומר אחד הלוה משלשה יחזיר ללוה שלשה שלוו מן האחד יחזיר למלוה ניחא ליה ללוה לאהדורי ליה למלוה אמר ליה התם סברא הוא (ח) אחד הלוה משלשה יחזיר ללוה דגבי לוה שכיחי גבי מלוה לא שכיחי ש״מ מלוה נפול שלשה שלוו מאחד יחזור למלוה דגבי מלוה שכיחי גבי לוה לא שכיחי
אלא

**רש״י**

לאהדורי גט. שאבד מן השליח המביאו קודם שנתן לה: **תקנתא.** לקמן בשמעתין מפרש מאי היא: **בממונא.** דהפקר ב״ד הפקר: **תובעין אצטריכא ליה.** קרא לתובעין אתא ולמעוטי מידי דאיאוש ואפקריה: **כדי נסבה.** בלא מקרא אלא אסמכינהו אקרא בעלמא: **ת״ש.** דאוקמינן לעיל חמור לסימני אוכף אתא: **אימא בעדי אוכף.** אם יש עדים המכירין בטביעות עין לאוכף שהוא שלו מחזירין לו את החמור: **דרשהו.** והכי משמע עד דרוש אחיך אותו עד דרשך את אחיך: [ט]**בעדים.** שיבא עדים שהוא שלו: **אין מעידין.** על אדם שמת להשיא את אשתו אלא א״כ ראו פרצוף פניו שהוא עם החוטם: **דארוך או גוץ.** שאין זה סימן שהרבה ארוכין וגוצים יש: **כליו.** בגדיו: **חיישינן.** שמא השאילם לאחר ואותו אחר ראו שמת: **מסקב.** דורוי״ש בלעז: **חיורי או סומקי.** אין זה סימן שהרבה כאלה יש: **מצאו קשור בכיס שלו או בארנקי כו׳.** שליח המביא גט ואבד הימנו לאחר זמן מצאו קשור בכיס שלו או בארנקי כו׳: **בין כליו.** כלי תשמישו שבביתו: **אפילו לזמן מרובה.** אע״ג דתנן (גיטין דף כז.) המביא גט ואבד הימנו מצאו לזמן מרובה פסול הכא כשר: **ניחוש לשאלה.** שמא השאיל כיסו לאחר והוא קשרו בו: **דמסמני.** מנחשי ואומר סימן לאדם שמשאיל כיסו שמוכר לו מזלו: **דמזייף.** שהיה לכל איש חותם ניכר בטבעתו וכששולח שום דבר סתום מכסהו וחותמו בטבעתו לפיכך אינו משאיל טבעתו שמא יעשה זה חותם כנגד חותמו ויזייף בו את שליחותיו: **אין מעידין על השומא.** המעידין על האשה להשיאה ואמרו סימן היה בו שומא באבר פלוני: **שומא.** וורוא״ה בלעז: **סימנין דרבנן.** וגבי אשת איש דאיסור דאורייתא הוא לא סמכינן עלייהו: **בבן גילו.** הנולד בשעתו שנולדו במזל אחד: **בסימנין העשוין כו׳.** אם עשוין להשתנות או אינן עשוין להשתנות אם בחייו היתה שומא שחורה במותו נעשית לבנה או איפוך: **מובהק.** ואפילו סימנין דרבנן יש לסמוך על זה: **היכי מהדרינן.** כלומר מה תקנה ראו חכמים בדבר ליכנס בספק להחזיר ממון למי שאינו שלו: **אלא ל״ג: וכי אדם עושה.** ובניחותא דמוצא מאי איכפת לן אם מי שאבדה ממנו לא ניחא ליה: **אלא.** אמר רבא כל אובדי אבידה ניחא להו שתהא דת זו בישראל למיתב סימנין וכל הבא ונותנו יטלנה מאי טעמא מידע ידע דעדים לית ליה שעמים שאין לו עדים עליה ואם יזקיקוהו לעדים לא תבא לעולם לידו ומימר אמר טוב לי שיחזירוה לכל האומר סימניה דלא שכיחא דנימא סימנין דידה אלא אנא דכ״ע לא ידעי כו׳: **אלא הא דתנן כו׳.** ואמרו להחזיר לו למלוה בלא עדים בסימן זה שאומר שלשה היו ומשלשה לויס ואם מן הלוה נפלו שכבר פרעם מי ניחא ליה בתקנה זו שיתנם המוצא לכל הבא ונותן סימניהם והלא טוב לו שיהו מונחים ביד המוצא עולמית דכל זמן שהם בידו ולא יחזירם למלוה הרי הם כשרופים ולא ניחא דליהדר להו בסימנין דלמא מיתרמי דידע מלוה בסימניהן: **התם.** בסימנין כי האי לא איכפת לן בניחותא דלוה דודאי לאו מיניה נפיל דהנך שטרי אחריני מאי בעו גביה:
אלא

**תוספות**

**ת״ש** חמור בסימני אוכף. ברייתא היא: **דרשהו** אם הוא רמאי מאי לאו בסימנין. וא״ת דבמתני׳ (לקמן כח:) דריש מהאי קרא דלא יחזיר אף בסימנין וי״ל דאסמכתא היא כדקתני עלה בברייתא משרבו הרמאים התקינו אבל הכא משמע ליה שהיא דרשה גמורה מדקאמר וכי תעלה על דעתך לומר כו׳ (ג) ועי״ל דבמתני׳ מיירי בידוע שהוא רמאי לכך צריך עדים אבל הכא מיירי בסתם בני אדם: (ד) **מצאו.** גט קשור בכים יחזיר המוצא לשליח או לבעל השואלו בסימני הכים:

[י](**וניחוש** לשאלה). וא״ת ולוכח מהכא דסימנין דאורייתא ובפרק בתרא דיבמות (ה) (דף קכ. ושם ד״ה מצאו) פריך מהכא דסימנין דאורייתא וי״ל דמצי לאוקמה כגון שאותו שאבדו מצאו ומכיר הכים בטביעות עין דכיון שבעצמו מצאו נאמן וה״נ הוה מצי למדחי התם: **כים** וארנקי משום דמסמני. וא״ת והכתיב לא תנחשו וי״ל בשלהי במה אשה (שבת דף סז.) אמרינן כל דבר שיש בו משום רפואה אין בו משום דרכי האמורי:

**ואנא** יהיבנא סימנים מובהקין דידה. לא מובהקין ממש קאמר אלא מובהקים מסימני חבירו כמו זה אומר מדת ארכו וזה אומר מדת רחבו ולקמן (דף כח:) נמי דקאמר לעולם גלימא מכריז ולא אמר סימנין מובהקין התם נמי לאו מובהקים ממש קאמר אלא שלא אמר סימנים טובים שיש בו כי אם כסימנין דסומקי וחיורי:
מלא

**רבינו חננאל**

איבעיא להו סימנין דאורייתא או דרבנן וכו׳ וסימנין כדי נסבה פי׳ אגב גררה הזכירה משנתנו הסימנין ולאו דוקא הן. ת״ש חמור בסימני אוכף. פי׳ אוכף הוא שלפעמים נתון על המרדעת של חמור כדי למנוע א) חבור המשוי על גבי חמור. ת״ש דתנן בהאשה פרק בתרא דיבמות אין מעידים אלא על פרצוף פנים עם החוטם אע״פ שיש סימנין בגופו כלומר אם נותנין העדים סימני פרצופו ואמר מי שפרצופו כך וכך ראינוהו שמת משיאין את אשתו. ופרקי׳ גופו דארוך וגוץ דלאו סימן מובהק הוא כליו חיישינן שמא שאולין היו לו ומקשי׳ אי הכי חמור בסימני אוכף נמי דלמא שאול הוא ואע״ג דאיכא סהדי ב) האי דאיכוף להאי גברא הוא נימא דלמא השאילו לאחרים דהא אמרת גבי כלים חיישינן לשאלה. ופרקי׳ איכוף לא מושלי אינשי למה כי פעמי׳ שתהיה בהמת בעל האיכוף רזה ובהמת השואל שמנה וכשנותנין עליה זה האיכוף מתפתח וכשמחזיר על בהמתו של המשאיל מסקבה פי׳ עושה בה חבורה כדגרסי׳ ג) במשקין סקבא דשתא ריגלא. אלא הא דתניא מצא לגט קשור בכיס בארנקי בטבעת או שמצאו בכליו אפי׳ לזמן מרובה כשר ואי חיישינן לשאלה אמאי כשר ניחוש דלמ׳ השאיל כיסו או טבעתו או ארנקי שלו לאדם אחר והוא שקשר זה הגט עמהם וגט זה של אדם אחר הוא ואינו זה הגט שהיה בידו של משאיל. ופרקי׳ כיס וטבעת וארנקי לא מושלי אינשי ופשוטה היא. והא דאהרי׳ אין מעידין על השומא. ושומא מצויה בבן גילו וסימנין עשוין להשתנות אחר המיתה כולן פשוטות הן. וסוגיין דשמעתין מאן דאמר סימנין דאורייתא היינו דמהדרינן אבידתא בסימניה ואפי׳ למאן דאמר סימנין לאו דאורייתא הן אם הן ד) סימנין מהדרינן לה

**חשק שלמה על ר״ח**

א) נ״ל חכוך וכ״ה בערוך ערך אכפא. ב) נראה דצ״ל דהאי אוכף להאי גברא וכו׳. ג) במשקין ליתא אך הוא בקדושין דף פ׳ וכ״ה בערוך ערך סקב. ד) נראה דצ״ל אם הן סימנים מובהקין מהדרינן וכו׳.

**מסורת הש״ס**

א) [ראש השנה ה. וש״נ], ב) לקמן כח., ג) יבמות קכ., [בכורות מו:], ד) יבמות קכ., [גיטין כז:], ה) יבמות קכ., ו) בבא בתרא כב. ותוספ׳ דיבמות, ז) לעיל כ., ח) שם ט״ע, ט) [ועיין המאור הקצר לפירושו דת״ל משמלה ופי׳ הוא שיבא עד שאינו רמאי כו׳ וע״ע], י) מהרש״ל מ״ז ועשה כו דבור אחד.

**הגהות הב״ח**

(א) גמ׳ בכלל כל אלו ולמה: (ב) שם הי מהדרינן אמרי לא הוה כל״ל ותיבת אוכף נמחק: (ג) תוס׳ ד״ה דרשהו ועי״ל דבמתני׳ נ״ב ע בשו״ת ב״ש סי׳ רמ״ד ביאור דבור זה: (ד) ד״ה מצאו וד״ה ונימא וכו׳ הד״א: (ה) בא״ד ונפ׳ בתרא דיבמות. נ״ב דף קכ ע״ב ועי״ש בתוספות בד״ה אי רבה:

**תורה אור השלם**

א) וְאִם לֹא קָרוֹב אָחִיךָ אֵלֶיךָ וְלֹא יְדַעְתּוֹ וַאֲסַפְתּוֹ אֶל תּוֹךְ בֵּיתֶךָ וְהָיָה עִמְּךָ עַד דְּרֹשׁ אָחִיךָ אֹתוֹ וַהֲשֵׁבֹתוֹ לוֹ: [דברים כב, ב]

**לעזי רש״י**

דורויי״ר. פי׳ לשפשף, לעשות פצע (גבן של בהמות משא) לעשות חבורה (עיין ערך סקב). וורוא״ה פירוש יבלת (רש״י ויק כב, כב), (וואדצע).

**ליקוטי רש״י**

אין מעידין. על האשה שמת אא״כ ראוהו בפרצוף פניו עם החוטם שיכולין להכירו שזהו לא שניטל חוטמו או שניכר עליו אין הוא [יבמות קכ.]. בגדיו. שמא השאילם ואותו אחר ורואהו אלו ובגדים בגבעל הבגדים. אוכף. שאולי אינשי. כ הסמור לא היה אוכפו של זה לא אביבעית אימא כלי דקמני בגופו ובכליו דלא סמכי אסימניהו. בחיורי ובסומקי. דלא אמר הוי סימן מובהק שמרין היו לו לבגדיו לאין זה סימן שהרבה לפי הנדים ילבשים [יבמות קכ:]. או שמצא בין כליו. בין כלי ומכ הטבעת או טבעת כשר ולא חיישינן דלמא הוא ולא והאי גט הוא והאי גט אחר הוא מתהו הוא [שם בע״א]. אבו כשר וכו׳. מאי איכא למימר ליחוש אע״פ שמכיר את הכיס יש לו

א) בלוקח מן התגר אבל בלוקח מבעל הבית חייב להחזיר וכן תני תנא קמיה דרב נחמן ל"ש אלא בלוקח מן התגר אבל בלוקח מבעל הבית חייב להחזיר א"ל רב נחמן וכי בעל הבית בעצמו דשן א"ל (א) איסמיה א"ל לא תתרגם מתני' ב) כגון שדשן ע"י עבדו ושפחתו הכנענים: **מתני'** ג) אף השמלה היתה בכלל כל אלו ולמה יצאת להקיש אליה לומר לך מה שמלה מיוחדת שיש בה סימנין ויש לה תובעין אף ד) כל דבר שיש בו סימנין ויש לו תובעים חייב להכריז: **גמ'** מאי בכלל כל אלו אמר רבא בכלל (א) כל אבדת אחיך אמר רבא למה לי דכתב רחמנא שור חמור שה ושמלה צריכי דאי כתב רחמנא שמלה הוה אמינא ה"מ בעדים דגופה וסימנין דגופה אבל חמור בעדים דאוכף וסימנין דאוכף אימא לא מהדרינן ליה כתב רחמנא חמור ה) דאפילו חמור בסימני האוכף שור ושה דכתב רחמנא ל"ל שור ו) דאפילו לגיזת זנבו ושה לגיזותיו ולכתוב רחמנא שור דאפילו לגיזת זנבו וכ"ש שה לגיזותיו אלא (ב) אמר רבא חמור דבור לרבי יהודה ושה דאבידה לדברי הכל קשיא ואימא לגללים הוא דאתא (ג) גללים אפקורי מפקר להו ודילמא לסימנין הוא דאתא דאיבעיא לן סימנין דאורייתא או דרבנן כתב רחמנא שה דאפילו בסימנין מהדרינן (ד) ז) וסימנין דאורייתא אמרי מדקתני להו תנא לסימנין גבי שמלה דקתני מה שמלה מיוחדת שיש בה סימנין ויש לה תובעין חייב להכריז אף כל דבר שיש בו סימנין ויש לו תובעין חייב להכריז ש"מ דשה לאו לסימנין הוא דאתא: תנו רבנן (א) אשר תאבד ח) פרט לאבידה שאין בה שוה פרוטה רבי יהודה אומר ומצאתה פרט לאבידה שאין בה שוה פרוטה מאי בינייהו אמר אביי ° משמעות דורשין איכא בינייהו מר נפקא ליה מאשר תאבד ומר נפקא ליה מומצאתה ולמאן דנפקא ליה מאשר תאבד האי ומצאתה מאי עביד ליה ההוא מיבעי ליה (א) לכדרבנאי ט) דאמר רבנאי ומצאתה דאתאי לידיה משמע ולמאן דנפקא ליה מומצאתה האי אשר תאבד מאי עביד ליה מבעי ליה לכדרבי יוחנן דאמר רבי יוחנן משום י) ר"ש בן יוחי מניין לאבידה ששטפה נהר שהיא מותרת שנאמר כן תעשה לכל אבדת אחיך אשר תאבד ממנו ומצאתה מי שאבודה הימנו ומצויה אצל כל אדם יצתה זו שאבודה הימנו ואינה מצויה אצל כל אדם ואידך הא דרבנאי מנא ליה נפקא ליה י) מומצאתה ואידך הא דרבי יוחנן מנא ליה נפקא ליה ממנו ואידך ממנו לא משמע ליה רבא אמר פרוטה שהוזלה איכא בינייהו מ"ד מאשר תאבד איכא ומ"ד מומצאתה ליכא ולמ"ד אשר תאבד הא בעינן ומצאתה וליכא אלא פרוטה שהוקרה איכא בינייהו מאן דאמר ומצאתה איכא ומאן דאמר אשר תאבד ליכא ולמאן דאמר ומצאתה הא בעינן אשר תאבד וליכא ט) אלא פרוטה (ב) שהוקרה והוזלה וחזרה והוקרה איכא בינייהו מאן דאמר אשר תאבד איכא ומאן דאמר ומצאתה בעינן דאית בה שיעור מציאה משעת אבידה ועד שעת מציאה: איבעיא להו סימנין דאורייתא (ה) או דרבנן מאי נפקא מינה

---

**רש"י**

בלוקח מן התגר. שאף הוא לקח תבואה זו מאנשים הרבה ולא ידיע דמאן ניהו וכיון דלית בהו סימן נתייאשו הבעלים: דשן. וכי הוא עצמו דש את התבואה הזאת הלא פועלים הרבה דשו אותה: איסמיה. אסיר ברייתא זו מגרסתי: אמר ליה לא תסמי תתרגם מתנית' כו': **מתני'** בכלל כל אלו. בגמרא מפרש לה: למה יצאתה. וכן תעשה לשמלתו: סתם שמלה יש בה סימן וכל שמלה יש לה בעלים תובעין אותה שלא נעשית אלא בידי אדם ולא באת מן ההפקר: אף כל שיש לו תובעין. למעוטי מידי דלדעינן ביה דמיאש: **גמ'** שור וחמור שה ושמלה. לא תראה את שור אחיך או שיו וכן תעשה לחמורו וכן תעשה לשמלתו: בסימני אוכף. אם אין לו סימן בחמור ויש לו סימן באוכף שעליו: כתב רחמנא חמור. קרא יתירא לדרשה: לגיזת זנבו. שאפי' שער שבסוף הזנב יחזיר: חמור דבור לרבי יהודה. דמחייב על נזקי כלים בבור קשיא לן למאי אתא דאילו לרבנן מבעי להו שור ולא אדם חמור ולא כלים: לגללים. להחזיר את גלליו דאי כתב שור הוה אמינא כי אתא לגיזת זנבו אתא אבל גללים לא חשיבי ולא ליהדר כתב רחמנא קרא יתירא לאתויי גללים: אפקורי מפקר להו. למי שטרח בו ולא אתא קרא לרבוייהו דאין לו תובעין הוא: לסימנין אתא. לאשמועינן דליהדריה בסימנין בלא עדים דקמיבעי' לן לקמן סימנין דאורייתא או דרבנן ובעינן למפשט ממתניתין דיליף להו משמלה ודחינן ואמר תנא תובעין אצטריכא ליה סימנין כדי נסבה נפשוט מקרא יתירא דשה לסימנין אתא וסימנין דאורייתא: אמרי מדנקט תנא. במתני' למילף סימנין משמלה בהדי תובעין פשיטא ליה דשה למלתא אחריתי אתא ואנן הוא דלא ידעינן משום הכי לא פשיטא ליה לקמן סימנין משה הלכך קשיא לן למאי אתא: אשר תאבד. שתהא קרויה אבידה: ומצאתה. שתהא קרויה מציאה: דאתא לידיה משמע. ואפילו הכי אחיך ולא עובד כוכבים ולמדך שאבידת כנעני מותרת ולא תימא כי אמעוט אבידת כנעני מלטרוח אחריה אמעוט אבל אי נקטה חייב לאהדורה: מי שאבודה ממנו. ואיידי דכתב ממנו כתב אשר תאבד: ומצאתה. הוי"ו יתירה משמע ומלאתה כבר: שהוזלה. דבשעת אבידה שוה פרוט' ובשע' מציאה הוזלה: לאהדורי

**תוספות**

**בלוקח** מן התגר. פרש"י שלקח מאנשים הרבה ועירב פירות יחד ואינו יודע של מי הן ובאין בו סימן איירי וא"ת אמאי לא מוקי בלוקח שהוא תגר וי"ל דלא פסיקא ליה דאם מלא קודם ששהא כדי לערבו בפירות אחרים חייב להחזיר אבל בלוקח מן התגר כבר עירב התגר ועי"ל בלא טעם דמערב עם שאר הפירות לא שנו אלא בלוקח מן התגר שאינו יודע למי להחזיר או לתגר או לבעה"ב אפי' אם אינו (ג) הוה ליפול בתבואה כ"א בשעת דישה ואין להסתפק בתגר מ"מ אינו יודע מאיזה בעל הבית קנה התגר ולזה הפי' הו"מ למימר בלוקח שהוא תגר ומתייאש בעל הבית שסבר שכבר מכר התגר ואין הקונה יודע למי יחזיר אלא כמו כן משום דלא פסיקא ליה דאם התגר מלאה קודם ששהה כדי למכור לאחר לא נתייאש בעה"ב וחייב להחזיר:

**מה** שמלה מיוחדת שיש לה סימני' ויש לה תובעין. במרובה (ב"ק דף סו. ושם ד"ה מולא) אמרינן בגניבה ילפינן יאוש מאבידה וא"ת ואבידה גופה מנלן וי"ל דמהכא נפקא לן דמה שמלה מיוחדת שיש בה סימן ואין הבעלים מתייאשין אלא תובעין שיחזירוה להם בסימנין אפי' אי סימנין לאו דאורייתא ואין מחזירין אלא בעדים מ"מ ילפינן משמלה דדווקא דבר שיש בו סימן חייב ט) להחזיר דע"י שיש בו סימן ימלא עדים שיאמר להם מכירים אתם שמלה שלי שהיו בה סימנין כך וכך וגם המוצא לא יוציא השמלה להראותה לכל אדם אלא למי שיתן בה סימנים אע"פ שאינו מחזירה לו בכך מ"מ דומה שהיא שלו ומראה אותה לעדים אבל דברים שאין בהן סימן הוי שלו לפי שהבעלים נתייאשו והא דקאמר בגמרא סימנין כדי נסבה אע"ג דלריך הסימנין דע"י זה יש לה תובעין מ"מ כדי נסבה דאפילו אי לא תני אלא שיש לה תובעין מ"מ ידעינן דע"י סימנין יש לה תובעין ואין הבעלים מתייאשים כדפרישית ומיהו בירושלמי יליף מניין ליאוש מן התורה אמר רבי יוחנן אשר תאבד ממנו מי שאבודה ממנו ומצויה אצל כל אדם יצאה זו כו':

**בעדי** אוכף. פי' אי סימנין לאו דאורייתא: **לגיזת** זנבו. וא"ת אם יש בה שוה פרוטה פשיטא ואם אין בה שוה פרוטה הא ממעטינן לקמן מהשבה וי"ל דאצטריך שחייב לגוזה בעתה אע"פ שאין בה שוה פרוטה בשעה שגוזה:

**חמור** דבור לרבי יהודה. הא דלא קאמר גם לב"ע י) קשה דלא חשיב אלא בהמות: **ושה** דאבידה לדברי הכל קשיא. מקשינן ונימא מלתא דאתיא בק"ו טרח וכתב לה קרא ותירץ הר"י כהן דכיון דנכתב שור לגיזת זנבו הוי גיזת שה בכלל כל אבידת אחיך: **פרט** לשאין בו שוה פרוטה. דס"ד דמחייב מכלל כל אבידת אחיך:

ת"ש

---

**מסורת הש"ס**

[בבא קמא נא:], ב) שם, ג) [לקמן סח:, בבא מח.], ד) [חולין], ה) בבא קמא קיג:, לעיל ב., ו) [לעיל כב: ושם איתא ר"ש בן וצדק], ז) [עיין תוס' סנהדרין יד. ד"ה ור"ש], ח) [לעיל יח:, חולין], ט) אולי צ"ל להכריז, [כדאיתא בבבא קמא לד.].

**הגהות הב"ח**

(א) גמ' לכדרבינא דאמר רבינא ומצאתה: (ב) שם אלא פרוטה שהוזלה וחזרה והוקרה איכא בינייהו כצ"ל ותיבת שהוקרה נמחק: (ג) תוס' ד"ה בלוקח וכו' אם אינו הווה ליפול:

**גליון הש"ס**

גמ' משמעות דורשין איכא בינייהו. שבועות דף יט ע"א:

**ליקוטי רש"י**

ושה דאבידה. כיון דחייב לכל אבידת אחיך למה לי דכתב רחמנא חמור שור ושה ושלמה ובפרק אלו מציאות דרשינן להו כולהו בר משה [ב"ק נד.]. סימנין דאורייתא. סמיך אסימנין ושרי איסורא עלייהו ש"מ הא סמכינן אסימנין בחזרת אבידה כדאמרינן באלו מציאות (ב"מ דף כז.) דאורייתא היא דאי דרבנן היכי דעבוד רבנן תקנתא למיגנא באיסורא מי מלו מתקני אלא ש"מ דאורייתא היא [חולין עט:]. אשר תאבד ממנו וכו' מי שאבודה. קרא יתירא הוא לאשמועינן שאינו אבוד אלא הימנו [לעיל כב:].

**עין משפט נר מצוה**

פג א ב מיי' פי"ו מהל' אבידה הלכה ו סמג עשין עד טוש"ע ח"מ סי' רסב סעיף יז:
פד ג מיי' שם פי"ד הלכה א:
פה ד מיי' שם וסמג שם טוש"ע ח"מ סי' רנט סעיף ג וסי' רסב סעיף ג:
פו ה מיי' שם וסמג שם טוש"ע ח"מ סי' רסב סעיף יח:
פז ו מיי' שם סמג שם טוש"ע ח"מ סי' רסז סעיף יז:
פח ז מיי' פי"ג שם הלכה ה:
פט ח מיי' שם פי"א הלכה יב סמג שם טוש"ע ח"מ סי' רנט סעיף ג וסי' רסב סעיף א:
צ ט י מיי' שם פי"ג הל' א סמג שם טוש"ע ח"מ סי' רסב סעיף א:

**רבינו חננאל**

אם מתגר לקח או מבעל הבית שדשים לו פועלים הרי הן שלו ואם מצאן צרורין או אפי' מפוזרין ולקח מבעל הבית שדשם על ידי עבדיו הכנענים וכיוצא בהן נוטל ומכריז: מתני' אף השמלה היתה בכלל כל אלו ולמה יצאת להקיש אליה לומר לך מה שמלה מיוחדת שיש לה סימנין ויש לה תובעין אף כל שיש לה סימנין ויש לה תובעין. אמר רבא [חמור] דבור לר"י ושה דאבידה לדברי הכל קשיא. חמור דבור פי' חמור שכתב בבור אליבא דרבנן דאמרי שור ולא אדם חמור ולא כלים שפיר כתיב בקרא ונפל שמה שור או חמור אלא לר' יהודה דמחייב על נזקי כלים בבור חמור מה בא למעט קשיא. שה דאבידה שנאמר כי תראה את שור אחיך או את שיו נדחים וגו' אם השור שיש לומר הוא הניחו שרוב השוורים שעושים מלאכה בהן אין נמסרין לרועה הזהירה תורה להשיבן שה לא כל שכן שה דכתב רחמנא למה לי קשיא. פי' גללין צפיעי בקר. מלשון והיא בגללי צואת האדם: ת"ר אשר תאבד ממנו פרט לאבידה שאין בה שוה פרוטה וכו' אמר ר' יוחנן משום ר' שמעון בן יוחאי מנין לאבידה ששטפה נהר שמותרת וכו' הא דאמר רבנאי ומצאתה דאתאי לידיה משמע הוא בפ' הגוזל בתרא הלכה אין פורטין מתיבת המוכסין.

**תורה אור השלם**

א) וְכֵן תַּעֲשֶׂה לַחֲמֹרוֹ וְכֵן תַּעֲשֶׂה לְשִׂמְלָתוֹ וְכֵן תַּעֲשֶׂה לְכָל אֲבֵדַת אָחִיךָ אֲשֶׁר תֹּאבַד מִמֶּנּוּ וּמְצָאתָהּ לֹא תוּכַל לְהִתְעַלֵּם: [דברים כב, ג]

The Gemara now presents a second explanation of the differ-nce between the Tanna Kamma and R' Yehudah:

רָבָא אָמַ – **Rava said:** פְּרוּטָה שֶׁהוּזְלָה אִיכָּא בֵּינַיְיהוּ – The ifference **between them is** the case of a lost object worth **a** *erutah* **that depreciated.**[33] מַאן דְּאָמַר מֵ,,אֲשֶׁר־תֹּאבַד" – **he one who said** (the Tanna Kamma) that we derive the xclusion of objects worth less than a *perutah* **from** ***which is lost*** אִיכָּ – would say that **there is** an obligation to return the lost oject.[34] וּמַאן דְּאָמַר מִ,,וּמְצָאתָהּ" – **And the one who said** (R' ehudah) that we derive the exclusion **from** ***and you have found*** לֵיכָּא – would say that **there is no** obligation to return the bject.[35]

The Gemara rejects this line of reasoning:

וּלְמַאן דְּאָמַר,,אֲשֶׁר־תֹּאבַד – **But** even **according to the one who** aid that the exclusion is derived from ***which is lost,*** הָא בְּעִינַן וּמְצָאתָהּ,, – **we surely need** to meet the requirements of ***and ou have found it,*** i.e. that the found object be worth a *perutah*,[36] וְלֵיכָּ – **and** in this case of depreciation **there is no** found object orth **a** *perutah*. Thus, according to both the Tanna Kamma and ' Yehudah there is no obligation to return a lost object that, hen found, is no longer worth a *perutah*.

Another attempt to find a difference between the Tanna amma and R' Yehudah:

אֶלָּא פְּרוּטָה שֶׁהוּקְרָה אִיכָּא בֵּינַיְי – **Rather,** the difference etween them is the case of an object worth less than **a** ***perutah*** hat appreciated.**[37] מַאן דְּאָמַר – **The one who said** (R' ehudah) that we derive the exclusion of objects worth less than a *erutah* וּמְצָאתָהּ",, – from ***and you have found it*** אִיכָּא – ould say that **there is** an obligation to return the object.[38] וּמַאן דְּאָמַ – **And the one who said** (Tanna Kamma) that we erive it אֲשֶׁר־תֹּאבַד",, – from ***which is lost*** לֵיכָּא – would ay that **there is no** obligation to return the object.[39]

The Gemara rejects this reasoning:

וּלְמַאן דְּאָמַר,,וּמְצָאתָהּ – **But** even **according to the one who said** that the exclusion is derived from ***and you have found it,*** הָא בְּעִינַן,,אֲשֶׁר־תֹּאבַד" – **surely we need** to meet the requirements of ***which is lost,***[40] וְלֵיכָּא – **and** in this case **there is no** loss of an object worth a *perutah*. Thus, according to both the Tanna Kamma and R' Yehudah there is no obligation to return an object that was not worth a *perutah* when it was lost.

The Gemara now offers a third and this time viable explanation of the difference between the Tanna Kamma and R' Yehudah:

אֶלָּא פְּרוּטָה שֶׁהוּקְרָה וְהוּזְלָה וְחָזְרָה וְהוּקְרָה אִיכָּא בֵּינַיְיהוּ – **Rather,** the difference **between them is** the case of an object worth **a** ***perutah*** **that depreciated and then appreciated once again.**[41] מַאן דְּאָמַר,,אֲשֶׁר־תֹּאבַד" – According to **the one who said** (Tanna Kamma) that the exclusion is derived from ***which is lost,*** אִיכָּא – **there is** an obligation to return the object, since the requirements of *which is lost* (that the object be worth a *perutah* when it is lost) and *and you have found it* (that the object be worth a *perutah* when it is found) are met.

וּמַאן דְּאָמַר,,וּמְצָאתָהּ" – **And** according to **the one who said** (R' Yehudah) that the exclusion is derived from ***and you have found it,*** בְּעִינַן דְּאִית בָּהּ שִׁיעוּר מְצִיאָה – **we require that [the object] have the value of a found object** (a *perutah*) מִשְּׁעַת אֲבֵידָה וְעַד שְׁעַת מְצִיאָה – **from the time of the loss until the time of the finding.**[42]

The Gemara analyzes the nature of the Mishnah's law that requires a recovered object to be returned to one who provides its identifying marks:

אִיבַּעְיָא לְהוּ – **They inquired:** סִימָנִין דְּאוֹרַיְיתָא אוֹ דְּרַבָּנָן – Is the law that we return a lost object to one who provides its **identifying marks Biblical or Rabbinic** in origin?

The Gemara explains the import of this query:

מַאי נָפְקָא מִינָּהּ – **What** practical difference **emerges from [this query]?**

NOTES

rom the extra word *and* in that verse. [It seems that the Tanna Kamma ttaches no significance to the additional word *and*] (*Shitah 1ekubetzes,* citing *Ritzbash*).

3. At the time it was lost the object was worth a *perutah*, but when it as found it was worth less (*Rashi*).

4. Since, according to the Tanna Kamma, the determination of which ost objects must be returned occurs in the verse that speaks of *losing* he object, any object that qualifies at that time falls within the purview f the mitzvah, even if later it becomes deficient.

5. According to R' Yehudah, the determination occurs in the verse that peaks of *finding* the object. Thus, since in this case the devalued object as worth less than a *perutah* at that time, the finder need not return .

6. Since the two phrases (*which is lost* and *and you have found it*) are ıxtaposed in the same verse (*Deuteronomy* 22:3), they are exegetically onnected, so that the requirements dictated by one phrase must be ound in the situation described by the other phrase. Thus, *which is lost* eaches that the object must be worth a *perutah* even at the time it is ound.

7. The object was worth less than a *perutah* when it was lost, but later appreciated and was worth a *perutah* when it was found.

38. Since, according to R' Yehudah, the determination of which lost objects must be returned occurs in the verse that speaks of *finding* the object, any object that qualifies at that time falls within the purview of the mitzvah, even if earlier it was deficient.

39. According to the Tanna Kamma, the determination occurs in the verse that speaks of *losing* the object. Thus, since at that time the object was not worth a *perutah*, the finder need not return it.

40. I.e. *and you have found it* teaches that the object must be worth a *perutah* even at the time it is lost (see above, note 36).

41. Our translation follows *Bach*, who deletes the first הוּקְרָה, *it appreciated.* The case concerns an object that was worth a *perutah* when it was lost, then depreciated, and then appreciated (to at least the value of a *perutah*) before it was found.

42. R' Yehudah, who derives the exclusion primarily from *and you have found it,* focuses on the word *and.* In addition to linking the two sections of the verse grammatically, *and* implies a sense of continuity, thus teaching that the object must be worth a *perutah* from the time of its loss until it is found (*Ritva*).

א בלוקח מן התגר אבל בלוקח מבעל הבית חייב להחזיר וכן תני תנא קמיה דרב נחמן ל"ש אלא בלוקח מן התגר אבל בלוקח מבעל הבית חייב להחזיר א"ל רב נחמן וכי בעל הבית בעצמו דשן א"ל (א) איסמיה א"ל לא תתרגם מתני' ב כגון שדשן ע"י עבדו ושפחתו הכנענים: **מתני'** ג אף השמלה היתה בכלל כל אלו ולמה יצאת להקיש אליה לומר לך מה שמלה מיוחדת שיש בה סימנין ויש לה תובעין אף ד כל דבר שיש בו סימנין ויש לו תובעים חייב להכריז: **גמ'** מאי בכלל כל אלו אמר רבא בכלל א) כל אבדת אחיך אמר רבא למה לי דכתב רחמנא שור חמור שה ושמלה צריכי דאי כתב רחמנא שמלה הוה אמינא ה"מ בעדים דגופה וסימנין דגופה אבל חמור בעדים דאוכף וסימנין דאוכף אימא לא מהדרינן ליה כתב רחמנא חמור ה דאפילו חמור בסימני האוכף שור ושה דכתב רחמנא ל"ל שור ו דאפילו לגיזת זנבו ושה לגיזותיו ולכתוב רחמנא שור דאפילו לגיזת זנבו וכ"ש שה לגיזותיו אלא ג) אמר רבא חמור דבור לרבי יהודה ושה דאבידה לדברי הכל קשיא ואימא לגללים הוא דאתא ג) גללים אפקורי מפקר להו ודילמא לסימנין הוא דאתא דאיבעיא לן סימנין דאורייתא או דרבנן כתב רחמנא שה דאפילו בסימנין מהדרינן ד) ז וסימנין דאורייתא אמרי מדקתני להו תנא לסימנין גבי שמלה דקתני מה שמלה מיוחדת שיש בה סימנין ויש לה תובעין חייב להכריז אף כל דבר שיש בו סימנין ויש לו תובעין חייב להכריז ש"מ דשה לאו לסימנין הוא דאתא: תנו רבנן א) אשר תאבד ח פרט לאבידה שאין בה שוה פרוטה רבי יהודה אומר ומצאתה פרט לאבידה שאין בה שוה פרוטה מאי בינייהו אמר אביי ° משמעות דורשין איכא בינייהו מר נפקא ליה מאשר תאבד ומר נפקא ליה מומצאתה ולמאן דנפקא ליה מאשר תאבד האי ומצאתה מאי עביד ליה ההוא מיבעי ליה (א) לכדרבנאי ט דאמר רבנאי ומצאתה דאתאי לידיה משמע ולמאן דנפקא ליה מומצאתה האי אשר תאבד מאי עביד ליה מבעי ליה לכדרבי יוחנן דאמר רבי יוחנן משום י ר"ש בן יוחי מניין לאבידה ששטפה נהר שהיא מותרת שנאמר כן תעשה לכל אבדת אחיך אשר תאבד ממנו ומצאתה מי שאבודה הימנו ומצויה אצל כל אדם יצתה זו שאבודה הימנו ואינה מצויה אצל כל אדם ואידך הא דרבנאי מנא ליה נפקא ליה י מומצאתה ואידך הא דרבי יוחנן מנא ליה נפקא ליה ממנו ואידך ממנו לא משמע ליה רבא אמר פרוטה שהוזלה איכא בינייהו מ"ד מאשר תאבד איכא ומ"ד מומצאתה ליכא ולמ"ד אשר תאבד הא בעינן ומצאתה וליכא אלא פרוטה שהוקרה איכא בינייהו מאן דאמר ומצאתה איכא ומאן דאמר אשר תאבד ליכא ולמאן דאמר ומצאתה הא בעינן אשר תאבד וליכא ° אלא פרוטה (ג) שהוקרה והוזלה וחזרה והוקרה איכא בינייהו מאן דאמר אשר תאבד איכא ומאן דאמר ומצאתה בעינן דאית בה שיעור מציאה משעת אבידה ועד שעת מציאה: איבעיא להו סימנין דאורייתא ° או דרבנן מאי נפקא מינה

---

**רש"י**

**בלוקח** מן התגר. שאף הוא לקח תבואה זו מאנשים הרבה ולא ידיע דמאן נינהו וכיון דלית בהו סימן נתייאשו הבעלים: **דשן.** וכי הוא עלמו דש את התבואה הזאת הלא פועלים הרבה דשו אותה: **איסמייה.** אסיר ברייתא זו מגרסתי: **אמר ליה לא תסמי** תתרגם מתנית' כו': **מתני' בכלל** כל אלו. בגמרא מפרש לה: **למה** יצאתה. וכן תעשה לשמלתו: סתם שמלה יש בה סימן וכל שמלה יש לה בעלים תובעין אותה שלא נעשית אלא בידי אדם ולא באת מן ההפקר: **אף כל שיש לו תובעין.** למעוטי מידי דידעינן ביה דמיאש: **גמ' שור** וחמור שה ושמלה. לא תראה את שור אחיך או שיו וכן תעשה לחמורו וכן תעשה לשמלתו: **בסימני אוכף.** אם אין לו סימן בחמור ויש לו סימן באוכף שעליו: **כתב רחמנא חמור.** קרא יתירא לדרשה: **לגיזת זנבו.** שאפי' שער שבסוף הזנב יחזיר: **חמור דבור לרבי יהודה.** דמחייב על נזקי כלים בבור קשיא לן למאי אתא דאילו לרבנן מבעי להו שור ולא אדם חמור ולא כלים: **לגללים.** להחזיר את גלליו דאי כתב שור הוה אמינא כי אתא לגיזת זנבו אתא אבל גללים לא חשיבי ולא ליהדר כתב רחמנא קרא יתירא לאתויי גללים: **אפקורי מפקר להו.** למי שטרח בו ולא אתא קרא לרבויינהו דאין לו תובעין הוא: **לסימנין אתא.** לאשמועינן דליהדריה בסימנין בלא עדים דקמיבעי' לן לקמן סימנין דאורייתא או דרבנן ובעינן למפשט ממתניתין דיליף להו משמלה ודחינן ואמר תנא תובעין אצטריכא ליה סימנין כדי נסבה נפשוט מקרא יתירא דשה לסימנין אתא וסימנין דאורייתא: **אמרי מדנקט תנא.** במתני' למילף סימנין משמלה בהדי תובעין פשיטא ליה דשה למלתא אחריתי אתא ואנן הוא דלא ידעינן משום הכי לא פשיטא ליה לקמן סימנין משה הלכך קשיא לן למאי אתא: **אשר תאבד.** שתהא קרויה אבידה: **ומצאתה.** שתהא קרויה מציאה: **דאתא לידיה משמע.** ואפילו הכי אחיך ולא עובד כוכבים ולמדך שאבידת כנעני מותרת ולא תימא כי אמעוט אבידת כנעני מלטרוח אחריה אמעוט אבל אי נקטה חייב לאהדורה: **מי שאבודה ממנו.** ואיידי דכתב ממנו כתב אשר תאבד: **ומצאתה.** הוי"ו יתירה משמע ומלאתה כבר: **שהוזלה.** דבשעת אבידה שוה פרוט' ובשע' מציאה הוזלה: לאהדורי

---

**תוספות**

**בלוקח** מן התגר. פרש"י שלקח מאנשים הרבה ועירב פירות יחד ואינו יודע של מי הן ובאין בו סימן מיירי וא"ת אמאי לא מוקי בלוקח שהוא תגר וי"ל דלא פסיקא ליה דאם מצא קודם ששהא כדי לערבו בפירות אחרים חייב להחזיר אבל בלוקח מן התגר כבר עירב התגר ועי"ל בלא טעם דמערב עם שאר הפירות לא שנו אלא בלוקח מן התגר שאינו יודע למי להחזיר או לתגר או לבעה"ב אפי' אם אינו (ג) הוה ליפול בתבואה כ"א בשעת דישה ואין להסתפק בתגר מ"מ אינו יודע מאיזה בעל הבית קנה התגר ולזה הפי' הו"מ למימר בלוקח שהוא תגר ומתייאש בעל הבית שסבר שכבר מכר התגר ואין הקונה יודע למי יחזיר אלא כמו כן משום דלא פסיקא ליה דאם התגר מצאה קודם ששהה כדי למכור לאחר לא נתייאש בעה"ב וחייב להחזיר:

**מה** שמלה מיוחדת שיש לה סימני' ויש לה תובעין. במרובה (ב"ק דף סו. ושם ד"ה מולא) אמרינן בגניבה ילפינן יאוש מאבידה וא"ת ואבידה גופה מנלן וי"ל דמהכא נפקא לן דמה שמלה מיוחדת שיש בה סימן ואין הבעלים מתייאשין אלא תובעין שיחזירוה להם בסימנין אפי' אי סימנין לאו דאורייתא ואין מחזירין אלא בעדים מ"מ ילפינן משמלה דלווקא דבר שיש בו סימן חייב ט) להחזיר דע"י שיש בו סימן ימלא עדים שיאמר להם מכירים אתם שמלה שלי שהיו בה סימנין כך וכך וגם המולא לא יוליא השמלה להראותה לכל אדם אלא למי שיתן בה סימנים אע"פ שאינו מחזירה לו בכך מ"מ דומה שהיא שלו ומראה אותה לעדים אבל דברים שאין בהן סימן הוי שלו לפי שהבעלים נתייאשו והא דקאמר בגמרא סימנין כדי נסבה אע"ג דלריך הסימנין דע"י זה יש לה תובעין מ"מ כדי נסבה דאפילו אי לא תני אלא שיש לה תובעין מ"מ ידעינן דע"י סימנין יש לה תובעין ואין הבעלים מתייאשים כדפרישית ומיהו בירושלמי יליף מניין ליאוש מן התורה אמר רבי יוחנן אשר תאבד ממנו מי שאבודה ממנו ומלויה אלל כל אדם יאלא זו כו':

**בעדי** אוכף. פי' אי סימנין לאו דאורייתא:

**לגיזת** זנבו. וא"ת אם יש בה שוה פרוטה פשיטא ואם אין בה שוה פרוטה הא ממעטינן לקמן מהשבה וי"ל דאלטריך שחייב לגוזה בעתה אע"פ שאין בה שוה פרוטה בשעה שגוזה:

**חמור** דבור לרבי יהודה. הא דלא קאמר גם לנ"ה י) קשה דלא חשיב אלא בהמות:

**ושה** דאבידה לדברי הכל קשיא. מקשין וניחא מלתא דלתיא בק"ו טרח וכתב לה קרא ותירץ הר"י כהן דכיון דנכתב שור לגיזת זנבו הוי גיזת שה בכלל כל אבידת אחיך:

**פרט** לשאין בו שוה פרוטה. דס"ד דחייב מכלל כל אבידת אחיך:

ת"ש

---

**עין משפט נר מצוה**

פג א ב מיי' פי"ו מהל' אבידה הלכה ו סמג עשין עד טוש"ע ח"מ סי' רסב סעיף יז:

פד ג מיי' שם פי"ד הלכה א:

פה ד מיי' שם וסמג שם טוש"ע ח"מ סי' רנט סעיף ג וסי' רסב סעיף ג:

פו ה מיי' שם וסמג שם טוש"ע ח"מ סי' רסב סעיף יח:

פז ו מיי' שם סמג שם טוש"ע ח"מ סי' רסז סעיף יז:

פח ז מיי' פי"ג שם הלכה ה:

פט ח מיי' שם פי"א הלכה יב סמג שם טוש"ע ח"מ סי' רנט סעיף ב וסי' רסב סעיף א:

צ ט י מיי' שם פי"ג הל' א סמג שם טוש"ע ח"מ סי' רסב סעיף א:

**רבינו חננאל**

אם מתגר לקח או מבעל הבית שדשים לו פועלים הרי הן שלו ואם מצאן צרורין או אפי' מפוזרין ולקח מבעל הבית שדשם על ידי עבדיו הכנענים וכיוצא בהן נוטל ומכריז: מתני' אף השמלה היתה בכלל כל אלו ולמה יצאת להקיש אליה לומר לך מה שמלה מיוחדת שיש לה סימנין ויש לה תובעין אף כל שיש לה סימנין ויש לה תובעין. אמר רבא [חמור] דבור לר"י ושה דאבידה לדברי הכל קשיא. חמור דבור פי' חמור שכתב בבור אליבא דרבנן דאמרי' שור ולא אדם חמור ולא כלים שפיר כתיב בקרא ונפל שמה שור או חמור אלא לר' יהודה דמחייב על נזקי כלים בבור חמור מה בא למעט קשיא. שה דאבידה שנאמר כי תראה את שור אחיך או את שיו נדחים וגו' אם השור שיש לומר הוא הניחו שרוב השוורים שעושים מלאכה בהן אין נמסרין לרועה הזהירה תורה להשיבן שה לא כל שכן שה דכתב רחמנא למה לי קשיא. פי' גללין צפיעי בקר. מלשון והיא בגללי צואת האדם: ת"ר אשר תאבד ממנו פרט לאבידה שאין בה שוה פרוטה וכו' אמר ר' יוחנן משום ר' שמעון בן יוחאי מנין לאבידה ששטפה נהר שמותרת וכו' הא דאמר רבנאי ומצאתה דאתאי לידיה משמע הוא בפ' הגוזל בתרא הלכה אין פורטין מתיבת המוכסין.

**תורה אור השלם**

א) וְכֵן תַּעֲשֶׂה לַחֲמֹרוֹ וְכֵן תַּעֲשֶׂה לְשִׂמְלָתוֹ וְכֵן תַּעֲשֶׂה לְכָל אֲבֵדַת אָחִיךָ אֲשֶׁר תֹּאבַד מִמֶּנּוּ וּמְצָאתָהּ לֹא תוּכַל לְהִתְעַלֵּם: [דברים כב, ג]

**מסורת הש"ס**

[בבא קמא לא:], ב) שם, ג) [לקמן סח:, בבא מח.], ד) [חולין :], ה) בבא קמא קיג:, לעיל ב., ו) [לעיל כב: ושם איתא ר"ש בן יוצדק], ז) [עיין תוס' סנהדרין יד. ד"ה ור"ש], ח) [לעיל יח:, חולין :], ט) אולי צ"ל להכריז, כדאיתא בבבא קמא לד.].

**הגהות הב"ח**

גמ' לכדרבינא דאמר נא ומלאתה: (ב) שם פרוטה שהוזלה רה והוקרה איכא ייהו כצ"ל ותיבת וקרה נמחק: (ג) תוס' ה בלוקח וכו' אם אינו הווה ליפול:

**גליון הש"ס**

' משמעות דורשין ב. שבועות דף יט ע"א:

**ליקוטי רש"י**

זה דאבידה. כיון חיב לכל אבידת אחיך ה לי דכתב רחמנא חמור ר ושה ושלמה ובפרק ו מליאות דרשינן להו ולהו בר משה [ב"ק נד.]. סימנין דאורייתא. יסמיך אסימנין ושרי סורא עלייהו ש"מ הא מכינן אסימנין בחזרת דה כדאמרינן באלו יאות (ב"מ דף כ.) ורייתא היא דאי דרבנן י דעבוד רבנן תקנתא מונא באיסורא מי מלו תקני אלא ש"מ אורייתא היא [חולין עט:]. שר תאבד ממנו וכו' שאבודה. קרא ירא הוא לאשמועינן אינו אבוד אלא הימנו [לעיל כב:].

omes TO EXCLUDE A LOST OBJECT THAT IS NOT WORTH A *PERUTAH*.[23]

The Gemara inquires:

מַאי בֵּינַיְיה – **What is** the difference **between [the Tanna** **Kamma and R' Yehudah]?**

The Gemara answers:

אָמַר אַבַּ – **Abaye said:** מַשְׁמָעוּת דּוֹרְשִׁין אִיכָּא בֵּינַיְיהוּ – The ifference **between them is** how **they understand** the verses xegetically. מַר נָפְקָא לֵיהּ מֵ,,אֲשֶׁר־תֹּאבַד" – One **master** (the 'anna Kamma) **derives [the exclusion of objects worth less** han a *perutah*] **from** *which is lost*, וּמַר נָפְקָא לֵיהּ מִ,,וּמְצָאתָהּ" - and the other **master** (R' Yehudah) **derives it from** *and you* *ave found it*.[24]

The Gemara asks:

וּלְמַאן דְּנָפְקָא לֵיהּ מֵ,,אֲשֶׁר־תֹּאבַד – **And according to the one** he Tanna Kamma) **who derives it from** *which is lost*, הַאי ,,וּמְצָאתָהּ" מַאי עָבֵיד לֵי – **what does he do with this** other verse, *nd you have found it?* I.e. what interpretation does he derive erefrom?

The Gemara answers:

הַהוּא מִיבָּעֵי לֵיהּ לְכִדְרַבְּנַא – The Tanna Kamma maintains that hat verse **is required** to teach **that which Rabbenai,** in fact, erived from it, דְּאָמַר רַבְּנַאי – **for Rabbenai said:** ,,וּמְצָאתָהּ – *And you have found it* דַּאֲתַאי לְיָדֵיהּ מַשְׁמַע – nplies that it has come into his hand.[25]

The Gemara asks:

וּלְמַאן דְּנָפְקָא לֵיהּ מִ,,וּמְצָאתָהּ – **And according to the one** (R' ehudah) **who derives [the exclusion of objects worth less** han a *perutah*] **from** *and you have found it*, הַאי ,,אֲשֶׁר־ תֹּאבַד" מַאי עָבֵיד לֵי – **what does he do with this** other verse, *hich is lost?* What interpretation does he derive therefrom?

The Gemara answers:

מִבָּעֵי לֵיהּ לְכִדְרַבִּי יוֹחָ – R' Yehudah maintains that that verse **is** equired to teach **that which R' Yochanan**, in fact, derived from . דְּאָמַר רַבִּי יוֹחָנָן מִשּׁוּם רַבִּי שִׁמְעוֹן בֶּן יוֹחַאי – **For R' Yochanan** aid in the name of R' Shimon ben Yochai:[26] מִנַּיִין לַאֲבֵידָה שֶׁשְּׁטָפָהּ נָהָ – **From where** do we derive **that a lost object swept** **away by a** flooding **river** שֶׁהִיא מוּתֶּרֶת – **is permitted** to whoever finds it? שֶׁנֶּאֱמַר – **As it says** concerning the commandment to return lost property: ,,כֵּן תַּעֲשֶׂה לְכָל־אֲבֵדַת אָחִיךָ" – ***So shall you do with regard to any lost object belonging to your brother***, ,,אֲשֶׁר־תֹּאבַד מִמֶּנּוּ וּמְצָאתָהּ" – ***which is lost from him and you have found it.*** מִי שֶׁאֲבוּדָה הֵימֶנּוּ וּמְצוּיָה אֵצֶל כָּל אָדָם – This teaches that only **that which is lost to him**[27] **but is accessible to any** other **man** must be returned. יָצְתָה זוֹ – **Excluded** by the verse **is this** object swept away by a flood, שֶׁאֲבוּדָה הֵימֶנּוּ – **for it is lost to him** וְאֵינָהּ מְצוּיָה אֵצֶל כָּל אָדָם – **and is inaccessible to all** other **men.**

The Gemara asks:

וְאִידָךְ – **And the other** master (R' Yehudah), who derives the exclusion of objects worth less than a *perutah* from *and you have found it*, הָא דְּרַבְּנַאי מְנָא לֵיהּ – **from where does he know that** teaching **of Rabbenai,**[28] which was derived from that very expression?

The Gemara replies:

נָפְקָא לֵיהּ מִ,,וּמְצָאתָהּ" – **He derives it from** ***and you have found it.***[29]

The Gemara asks:

וְאִידָךְ – **And the other** master (the Tanna Kamma), who derives the exclusion of objects worth less than a *perutah* from *which is lost*, הָא דְּרַבִּי יוֹחָנָן מְנָא לֵיהּ – **from where does he know that** teaching **of R' Yochanan,**[30] which was derived from that very expression?

The Gemara answers:

נָפְקָא לֵיהּ ,,מִמֶּנּוּ" – **He derives it** from the expression ***from him.***[31]

Accordingly, the Gemara inquires:

וְאִידָךְ – **And the other** master (R' Yehudah), why does he need the entire phrase, *which is lost from him,* to derive R' Yochanan's ruling? Let him derive it from just the second half, *from him.* – ? –

The Gemara answers:

מִמֶּנּוּ לֹא מַשְׁמַע לֵיהּ – **He does not regard** ***from him*** **to be significant** in its own right.[32]

NOTES

3. R' Yehudah maintains that the words *and you have found it* connote: something that is called a *found* object" (*Rashi*), which implies that me objects do not legally qualify as "found objects" that must be eturned.

4. That is, there is no practical difference between them. They differ erely in their interpretation of the Biblical verses.

5. Rabbenai refers to *Deuteronomy* 22:3, which commands that lost bjects be returned to their owners: וְכֵן תַּעֲשֶׂה לְכָל־אֲבֵדַת אָחִיךָ אֲשֶׁר־תֹּאבַד מִמֶּנּוּ וּמְצָאתָ, *and so shall you do with regard to any lost object belonging your brother, which is lost from him and you have found it.* The emara (*Bava Kamma* 113b) explains that the expression *your brother* arrows the purview of the mitzvah to those objects lost by your *Jewish* rethren; there is, however, no obligation to return the lost object of a on-Jew. The Gemara there considers the possibility that the limitation pplies only to *retrieving* and returning a lost object; that is, one is not bligated to exert himself to retrieve another's lost object unless the wner is a Jew. But once the finder has already taken the trouble to etrieve the lost object, perhaps he must return it even to a gentile wner. To this conjecture Rabbenai responds (ibid.) that since the mitation is written with regard to a lost object that "you find," i.e. one ready retrieved, we see that one need not return the lost object of a entile even if it is already in hand (see *Rashi*).

6. Above (22b), R' Yochanan attributed this ruling to R' Yishmael ben ehotzedek (see *Mesoras HaShas* there).

7. [The word מִמֶּנּוּ, *from him*, appears superfluous. If the object is lost, is obviously lost from him, its owner. It thus teaches the obligation to eturn lost objects applies only to objects that are lost specifically to him, e owner [because he does not know where he lost them], but they are still accessible to whoever sees them.] The Torah, therefore, stated *that is lost* only as a prelude to the phrase *from him*, in order to teach this law (*Rashi*).

28. Rabbenai derived from *and you have found it* that even one who has already retrieved a gentile's lost object need not return it.

29. [To teach the exclusion of objects worth less than a *perutah*, the Torah could have written only מְצָאתָהּ, *you have found it.* The addition of the *vav* to render וּמְצָאתָהּ, *and you have found it*, implies that the object has already been found and retrieved. [Accordingly, Rabbenai exempted from the mitzvah one who has found and even retrieved an object lost by a non-Jew (see note 25 above)] (*Rashi*).

30. R' Yochanan derived from *which is lost from him* that the mitzvah of returning a lost object applies only when the object is lost to the owner, but is accessible to other men.

31. Thus, the Tanna Kamma derives the exclusion of objects worth less than a *perutah* from the first half of the phrase, *which is lost*. He derives R' Yochanan's teaching from the second half, *from him.*

32. **In summary:** The Tanna Kamma perceives the phrase, *which is lost from him*, as comprised of two distinct parts: 1) *Which is lost* implies that the lost object must have the value of a *perutah;* 2) *from him* allows the finder to retain any object that is inaccessible to everyone (R' Yochanan's ruling).

R' Yehudah views *which is lost from him* as one unit, deriving from it R' Yochanan's ruling. Consequently, he derives the exclusion of objects worth less than a *perutah* from another verse – *and you have found it.*

The Tanna Kamma, however, interprets *and you have found it* as the source for Rabbenai's ruling, that one is not obligated to return even a retrieved lost object to a non-Jew. R' Yehudah derives Rabbenai's ruling

**מסורת הש"ס**

בבא קמא לא:], ג) שם ג) [לקמן סח., בבא מח.], ד) [חולין ], ה) בבא קמא קיג:, לעיל ב., ו) [לעיל כב: ושם איתא ר"ש בן צדק], ז) [עיין תוס' דרין יד. ד"ה ור"ש ], ח) [לעיל יח:, חולין :], ט) אולי צ"ל להכריז, כדאיתא בבבא קמא לד.].

**הגהות הב"ח**

גמ' לכדרבינא דאמר א ומלאתה: (ב) שם פרוטה שהוזלה ים והוקרה איכא יהו כצ"ל ותיבת יקרה נמחק: (ג) תוס' בלוקח וכו' אם אינו הווה ליפול:

**גליון הש"ס**

משמעות דורשין ב. שבועות דף יט ע"א:

**ליקוטי רש"י**

ה דאבידה. כיון זיב לכל אבידת אחיך ה לי דכתב רחמנא חמור ר ושה ושלמה ובפרק מציאות דרשינן להו להו בר משה [ב"ק נד.]. מנין דאורייתא. סמיך אסימנין ושרי ורא עלייהו ש"מ הא מכין אסימנין בחזרת דה כדאמרינן באלו אות (ב"מ דף כ.) רייתא היא דאי דרבנן דעבוד רבנן תקנתא מונא באיסורא מי מלו קי אלא ש"מ וריתא היא [חולין עט:]. שר תאבד ממנו וכו' שאבודה. קרא רא הוא לאשמועינן ינו דאבודה הימנו [לעיל כב:].

---

**רש"י**

בלוקח מן התגר. שאף הוא לקח תבואה זו מאנשים הרבה ולא ידיע דמאן ניהו וכיון דלית בהו סימן נתייאשו הבעלים: דשן. וכי הוא עצמו דש את התבואה הזאת הלא פועלים הרבה דשו אותה: איסמייה. אסיר ברייתא זו מגרסתי: אמר ליה לא תסמי תתרגם מתנית' כו': מתני' בכלל כל אלו. בגמרא מפרש לה: למה יצאתה. וכן תעשה לשמלתו: סתם שמלה יש בה סימן וכל שמלה יש לה בעלים תובעין אותה שלא נעשית אלא בידי אדם ולא באת מן ההפקר: אף כל שיש לו תובעין. למעוטי מידי דידעינן ביה דמיאש: גמ' שור וחמור שה ושמלה. לא תראה את שור אחיך או שיו וכן תעשה לחמורו וכן תעשה לשמלתו: בסימני אוכף. אם אין לו סימן בחמור ויש לו סימן באוכף שעליו: כתב רחמנא חמור. קרא יתירא לדרשה: לגיזת זנבו. שאפי' שער שבסוף הזנב יחזיר: חמור דבור לרבי יהודה. דמחייב על נזקי כלים בבור קשיא לן למאי אתא דאילו לרבנן מבעי להו שור ולא אדם חמור ולא כלים: לגללים. להחזיר את גלליו דאי כתב שור הוה אמינא כי אתא לגיזת זנבו אתא אבל גללים לא חשיבי ולא ליהדר כתב רחמנא קרא יתירא לאתויי גללים: אפקורי מפקר להו. למי שטרח בו ולא אתא קרא לרבויינהו דאין לו תובעין הוא: לסימנין אתא. לאשמועינן דליהדריה בסימנין בלא עדים דקמיבעי' לן לקמן סימנין דאורייתא או דרבנן ובעינן למפשט ממתניתין דיליף להו משמלה ודחינן ואמר תנא תובעין אצטריכא ליה סימנין כדי נסבה נפשוט מקרא יתירא דשה לסימנין אתא וסימנין דאורייתא: אמרי מדנקט תנא. במתני' למילף סימנין משמלה בהדי תובעין פשיטא ליה דשה למלתא אחריתי אתא ואנן הוא דלא ידעינן משום הכי לא פשיטא ליה לקמן סימנין מהא הלכך קשיא לן למאי אתא: אשר תאבד. שתהא קרויה אבידה: ומצאתה. שתהא קרויה מציאה: דאתא לידיה משמע. ואפילו הכי אחיך ולא עובד כוכבים ולמדך שאבידת כנעני מותרת ולא תימא כי אמעוט אבידת כנעני מלטרוח אחריה אמעוט אבל אי נקטה חייב לאהדורה: מי שאבודה ממנו. ואיידי דכתב ממנו כתב אשר תאבד: ומצאתה. הוי"ו יתירה משמע ומלאתה כבר: שהוזלה. דבשעת אבידה שוה פרוט' ובשע' מציאה הוזלה: לאהדורי

---

**גמרא**

בלוקח[א] מן התגר אבל בלוקח מבעל הבית חייב להחזיר וכן תני תנא קמיה דרב נחמן ל"ש אלא בלוקח מן התגר אבל בלוקח מבעל הבית חייב להחזיר א"ל רב נחמן וכי בעל הבית בעצמו דשן א"ל [א] איסמיה א"ל לא תתרגם מתני' [ב]כגון שדשן ע"י עבדו ושפחתו הכנענים: **מתני'** [ג]אף השמלה היתה בכלל כל אלו ולמה יצאת להקיש אליה לומר לך מה שמלה מיוחדת שיש בה סימנין ויש לה תובעין אף [ד]כל דבר שיש בו סימנין ויש לו תובעים חייב להכריז: **גמ'** מאי בכלל כל אלו אמר רבא בכלל [א] כל אבדת אחיך אמר רבא למה לי דכתב רחמנא שור חמור שה ושמלה צריכי דאי כתב רחמנא שמלה הוה אמינא ה"מ בעדים דגופה וסימנין דגופה אבל חמור בעדים דאוכף וסימנין דאוכף אימא לא מהדרינן ליה כתב רחמנא חמור [ה]דאפילו חמור בסימני האוכף שור ושה דכתב רחמנא ל"ל שור [ו]דאפילו לגיזת זנבו ושה לגיזותיו ולכתוב רחמנא שור דאפילו לגיזת זנבו וכ"ש שה לגיזותיו אלא [ב] אמר רבא חמור דבור לרבי יהודה ושה דאבידה לדברי הכל קשיא ואימא לגללים הוא דאתא [ג] גללים אפקורי מפקר להו ודילמא לסימנין הוא דאתא דאיבעיא לן סימנין דאורייתא או דרבנן כתב רחמנא שה דאפילו בסימנין מהדרינן [ד] [ז]וסימנין דאורייתא אמרי מדקתני להו תנא לסימנין גבי שמלה דקתני מה שמלה מיוחדת שיש בה סימנין ויש לה תובעין חייב להכריז אף כל דבר שיש בו סימנין ויש לו תובעין חייב להכריז ש"מ דשה לאו לסימנין הוא דאתא: תנו רבנן [א] אשר תאבד [ח]פרט לאבידה שאין בה שוה פרוטה רבי יהודה אומר ומצאתה פרט לאבידה שאין בה שוה פרוטה מאי בינייהו אמר אביי [ט] משמעות דורשין איכא בינייהו מר נפקא ליה מאשר תאבד ומר נפקא ליה מומצאתה ולמאן דנפקא ליה מאשר תאבד האי ומצאתה מאי עביד ליה ההוא מיבעי ליה (א) לכדרבנאי [ט] דאמר רבנאי ומצאתה דאתאי לידיה משמע ולמאן דנפקא ליה מומצאתה האי אשר תאבד מאי עביד ליה מבעי ליה לכדרבי יוחנן דאמר רבי יוחנן משום [י]ר"ש בן יוחי מניין לאבידה ששטפה נהר שהיא מותרת שנאמר כן תעשה לכל אבדת אחיך אשר תאבד ממנו ומצאתה מי שאבודה הימנו ומצויה אצל כל אדם יצתה זו שאבודה הימנו ואינה מצויה אצל כל אדם ואידך הא דרבנאי מנא ליה נפקא ליה [י] מומצאתה ואידך הא דרבי יוחנן מנא ליה נפקא ליה ממנו ואידך ממנו לא משמע ליה רבא אמר פרוטה שהוזלה איכא בינייהו מ"ד מאשר תאבד איכא ומ"ד מומצאתה ליכא ולמ"ד אשר תאבד הא בעינן ומצאתה וליכא אלא פרוטה שהוקרה איכא בינייהו מאן דאמר ומצאתה איכא ומאן דאמר אשר תאבד ליכא ולמאן דאמר ומצאתה הא בעינן אשר תאבד וליכא [ט]אלא פרוטה (ב) שהוקרה והוזלה וחזרה והוקרה איכא בינייהו מאן דאמר אשר תאבד איכא ומאן דאמר ומצאתה בעינן דאית בה שיעור מציאה משעת אבידה ועד שעת מציאה: איבעיא להו סימנין דאורייתא [פ] או דרבנן מאי נפקא מינה

---

**תוספות**

**בלוקח** מן התגר. פרש"י שלקח מאנשים הרבה ועירב פירות יחד ואינו יודע של מי הן ובאין בו סימן איירי וא"ת אמאי לא מוקי בלוקח שהוא תגר וי"ל דלא פסיקא ליה דאם מלא קודם ששהא כדי לערבו בפירות אחרים חייב להחזיר אבל בלוקח מן התגר כבר עירב התגר ועי"ל בלא טעם דמערב עם שאר הפירות לא שנו אלא בלוקח מן התגר שאינו יודע למי להחזיר או לתגר או לבעה"ב אפי' אם אינו (ג) הוה ליפול בתבואה כ"א בשעת דישה ואין להסתפק בתגר מ"מ אינו יודע מאיזה בעל הבית קנה התגר ולזה הפי' הו"מ למימר בלוקח שהוא תגר ומתייאש בעל הבית שסבר שכבר מכר התגר ואין הקונה יודע למי יחזיר אלא כמו כן משום דלא פסיקא ליה דאם התגר מצאה קודם ששהה כדי למכור לאחר לא נתייאש בעה"ב וחייב להחזיר:

**מה** שמלה מיוחדת שיש לה סימני' ויש לה תובעין. במרובה (ב"ק דף סו. ושם ד"ה מונא) אמרינן בגניבה ילפינן יאוש מאבידה וא"ת ואבידה גופה מנלן וי"ל דמהכא נפקא לן דמה שמלה מיוחדת שיש בה סימן ואין הבעלים מתייאשין אלא תובעין שיחזירוה להם בסימנין אפי' אי סימנין לאו דאורייתא ואין מחזירין אלא בעדים מ"מ ילפינן משמלה דדוקא דבר שיש בו סימן חייב [ט]להחזיר דע"י שיש בו סימן ימצא עדים שיאמר להם מכירים אתם שמלה שלי שהיו בה סימנין כך וכך וגם המוצא לא יוציא השמלה להראותה לכל אדם אלא למי שיתן בה סימנים אע"פ שאינו מחזירה לו בכך מ"מ דומה שהיא שלו ומראה אותה לעדים אבל דברים שאין בהן סימן הוי שלו לפי שהבעלים נתייאשו והא דקאמר בגמרא סימנין כדי נסבה אע"ג דלריך הסימנין דע"י זה יש לה תובעין מ"מ כדי נסבה דאפילו אי לא תני אלא שיש לה תובעין מ"מ ידעינן דע"י סימנין יש לה תובעין ואין הבעלים מתייאשים כדפרישית ומיהו בירושלמי יליף מניין ליאוש מן התורה אמר רבי יוחנן אשר תאבד ממנו מי שאבודה ממנו ומצויה אצל כל אדם יצאה זו כו':

**בעדי** אוכף. פי' אי סימנין לאו דאורייתא: **לגיזת** זנבו. וא"ת אם יש בה שוה פרוטה פשיטא ואם אין בה שוה פרוטה הא ממעטינן לקמן מהשבה וי"ל דאצטריך שחייב לגוזזה בעתה אע"פ שאין בה שוה פרוטה בשעה שגוזזה:

**חמור** דבור לרבי יהודה. הא דלא קאמר גם לב"ה [י] קשה דלא חשיב אלא בהמות: **ושה** דאבידה לדברי הכל קשיא. מקשינן ונימא מלתא דאתיא בק"ו טרח וכתב לה קרא ותירץ הר"י כהן דכיון דנכתב שור לגיזת זנבו הוי גיזת שה בכלל כל אבידת אחיך: **פרט** לשאין בו שוה פרוטה. דס"ד דחייב מכלל כל אבידת אחיך:

ת"ש

---

**עין משפט נר מצוה**

פג א ב מיי' פי"ו מהל' אבידה הלכה ו סמג עשין עד טוש"ע ח"מ סי' רסב סעיף יז:

פד ג מיי' שם פי"ד הלכה א:

פה ד מיי' שם וסמג שם טוש"ע ח"מ סי' רנט סעיף ג וסי' רסב סעיף ג:

פו ה מיי' שם וסמג שם טוש"ע ח"מ סי' רסב סעיף יח:

פז ו מיי' שם סמג שם טוש"ע ח"מ סי' רסז סעיף יז:

פח ז מיי' פי"ג שם הלכה ה:

פט ח מיי' שם פי"א הלכה יב סמג שם טוש"ע ח"מ סי' רנט סעיף ב וסי' רסב סעיף א:

צ ט י מיי' שם פי"ג הל' א סמג שם טוש"ע ח"מ סי' רסב סעיף א:

**רבינו חננאל**

אם מתגר לקח או מבעל הבית שדשים לו פועלים הרי הן שלו ואם מצאן צרורין או אפי' מפוזרין ולקח מבעל הבית שדשם על ידי עבדיו הכנענים וכיוצא בהן נוטל ומכריז: מתני' אף השמלה היתה בכלל כל אלו ולמה יצאת להקיש אליה לומר לך מה שמלה מיוחדת שיש לה סימנין ויש לה תובעין אף כל שיש לה סימנין ויש לה תובעין. אמר רבא [חמור] דבור לר"י ושה דאבידה לדברי הכל קשיא. חמור דבור פי' חמור שכתב בבור אליבא דרבנן דאמרי שור ולא אדם חמור ולא כלים שפיר כתיב בקרא ונפל שמה שור או חמור אלא לר' יהודה דמחייב על נזקי כלים בבור חמור מה בא למעט קשיא. שה דאבידה שנאמר כי תראה את שור אחיך או את שיו נדחים וגו' אם השור שיש לומר הוא הניחו שרוב השוורים שעושים מלאכה בהן אין נמסרין לרועה הזהירה תורה להשיבן שה לא כל שכן שה דכתב רחמנא למה לי קשיא. פי' גללין צפיעי בקר. מלשון והיא בגללי צואת האדם: ת"ר אשר תאבד ממנו פרט לאבידה שאין בה שוה פרוטה וכו' אמר ר' יוחנן משום ר' שמעון בן יוחאי מנין לאבידה ששטפה נהר שמותרת וכו' הא דאמר רבנאי ומצאתה דאתאי לידיה משמע הוא בפ' הגוזל בתרא הלכה אין פורטין מתיבת המוכסין.

**תורה אור השלם**

א) וְכֵן תַּעֲשֶׂה לַחֲמֹרוֹ וְכֵן תַּעֲשֶׂה לְשִׂמְלָתוֹ וְכֵן תַּעֲשֶׂה לְכָל אֲבֵדַת אָחִיךָ אֲשֶׁר תֹּאבַד מִמֶּנּוּ וּמְצָאתָהּ לֹא תוּכַל לְהִתְעַלֵּם: [דברים כב, ג]

inder **with the identifying marks of the saddle.**[13]

The Gemara returns to those parts of Rava's question that emained unanswered:

,,שׁוֹר״,,וָשֶׂה״ דִּכְתַב רַחֲמָנָא לָמָּה ל – **Why did the Merciful One write** in the Torah ***ox*** **and** ***lamb,*** which appear superfluous?

The Gemara answers:

,,שׁוֹר״ – דַּאֲפִילּוּ לִגְיזַּת זְנָב – ***Ox*** teaches **that even the shearing of the ox's] tail** must be returned.[14] ,,וְשֶׂה״ לִגְיזּוֹתָיו – **And** ***lamb*** eaches that even **[the lamb's] shearings** must be returned.

The Gemara asks:

וְלִכְתּוֹב רַחֲמָנָא ,,שׁוֹר – **And** if so, **let the Merciful One write** nly ***ox,*** דַּאֲפִילּוּ לִגְיזַּת זְנָבוֹ – which would teach **that even the** ainute **shearing of [the ox's] tail** must be returned, וְכָל שֶׁכֵּן שֶׂה לִגְיזּוֹתָיו – **and** we would infer **all the more so** that **the** ubstantial **shearing of a lamb** must be returned. – ? –

The Gemara concedes this point:

אֶלָּא אָמַר רָבָא – **Rather, Rava said:** ,,חֲמוֹר״ דְּבוֹר – The word ***onkey,*** which the Torah uses as an example **of** something that is amaged from falling into **a pit**[15] לְרַבִּי יְהוּדָה – **according to** **R' Yehudah,**[16] וְ,,שֶׂה״ דַּאֲבֵידָה – **and** the word ***lamb***, which he Torah uses as an example **of lost property** לְדִבְרֵי הַכֹּל – **according to all opinions,** קַשְׁיָא – **are difficult** to explain. I.e. oth of these words appear superfluous, and we cannot explain why the Torah wrote them.

The Gemara suggests an interpretation of the superfluous word *amb:*

וְאֵימָא – **But say** לִגְלָלִים הוּא דְּאָתָא – that [***lamb***] **comes** to each that even **the dung** of a lost animal must be returned to the wner.[17] – ? –

The Gemara rejects this interpretation:

גְּלָלִים אַפְקוּרֵי מַפְקַר לְהּ – **[The owner] renounces ownership of the dung.**[18] Thus, there is no obligation upon the finder to return t.

The Gemara suggests another interpretation:

וְדִילְמָא – **But perhaps** לְסִימָנִין הוּא דְּאָתָא – the superfluous ***lamb]*** **comes** to teach that, according to Torah law, **identifying marks** are a valid means of proving ownership, as effective as witnesses. דְּאִיבַּעְיָא לָן – **For it has been asked of us:**[19] סִימָנִין דְּאוֹרַיְיתָא אוֹ דְּרַבָּנָן – Is the law that we return a lost object to one who provides its **identifying marks Biblical or Rabbinic** in origin?[20] כְּתַב רַחֲמָנָא ,,שֶׂה״ – Derive instead that **the Merciful One wrote** ***lamb*** דַּאֲפִילּוּ בְּסִימָנִין מַהַדְרִינַן – to teach us **that we return** a lost article **even** to one that only provides **the identifying marks,** even though he has no witnesses, וְסִימָנִין דְּאוֹרַיְיתָא – **and** thus that the law of **identifying marks is Biblical** in origin. – ? –

The Gemara rejects this interpretation as well:

אָמְרֵי – **We say** in response, מִדְּקָתָנֵי לְהוּ תַּנָּא לְסִימָנִין גַּבֵּי שִׂמְלָה – **since the Tanna** of our Mishnah **taught** the law of **identifying marks in conjunction with** the word ***garment*** – דְּקָתָנֵי – **for the Tanna taught:** מַה שִּׂמְלָה מְיוּחֶדֶת – JUST AS A GARMENT IS DISTINGUISHED שֶׁיֵּשׁ בָּהּ סִימָנִין וְיֵשׁ לָהּ תּוֹבְעִין חַיָּיב לְהַכְרִיז – IN THAT IT HAS IDENTIFYING MARKS AND IT HAS CLAIMANTS and [its finder] **is obligated to announce** it, אַף כָּל דָּבָר שֶׁיֵּשׁ בּוֹ סִימָנִין וְיֵשׁ לוֹ תּוֹבְעִין – SO, TOO, ANYTHING THAT HAS IDENTIFYING MARKS AND HAS CLAIMANTS חַיָּיב לְהַכְרִיז – MUST BE ANNOUNCED – שְׁמַע מִינָּהּ – **conclude from [the Mishnah]** דְּ,,שֶׂה״ לָאו לְסִימָנִין הוּא דְּאָתָא – **that** the word ***lamb*** **does not come** to teach the law of **identifying marks.**[21] Since all suggested interpretations of *lamb* have been rejected, the Gemara reaches the same conclusion as did Rava – that no adequate explanation can be found for the apparently superfluous *lamb.*

The Gemara discusses the minimum value a lost object must have before it must be returned:

תָּנוּ רַבָּנַן – **Our Rabbis taught:** Scripture states: ,,אֲשֶׁר־תֹּאבַד״ – *And so shall you do with any lost article. . .* ***WHICH IS LOST.***[22] פְּרָט לַאֲבֵידָה שֶׁאֵין בָּהּ שָׁוֶה פְּרוּטָה – The verse comes TO EXCLUDE A LOST OBJECT THAT IS NOT WORTH A *PERUTAH*. Such an object is so insignificant that the Torah does not classify it as lost property. רַבִּי יְהוּדָה אוֹמֵר – R' YEHUDAH SAYS, however, that it is the passage ,,וּמְצָאתָהּ״ – ***AND YOU HAVE FOUND IT,*** which is also written in that verse, פְּרָט לַאֲבֵידָה שֶׁאֵין בָּהּ שָׁוֶה פְּרוּטָה – that

NOTES

3. Identification of the saddle is considered valid proof of the ownership f the donkey because it is improbable that someone borrowed the addle for use on his own donkey (see Gemara below and *Chidushei Chasam Sofer, Sugyos* no. 16).

4. *Rashi.* This interpretation seems to follows the opinion of *Ran* and ther Rishonim, who explain that we derive from the word *ox* that one s obligated to return the oxtail shearing even if it is worth less than a *erutah.* Although the Gemara below exempts a finder from returning n object worth less than a *perutah,* these Rishonim distinguish between self-contained object (worth less than a *perutah*) and a subordinate bject, which can be classified as part of a larger object that is worth a *erutah.* The oxtail shearings are viewed as part of the ox, and so must e returned together with the ox.

*Tosafos* (ד״ה לגיזת) understand the thrust of the Gemara differently. They explain that the lesson derived from *ox* is that the finder is bligated to shear the ox's tail periodically (see *Rashba, Maharam Shif*). The shearing of the ox's tail will promote the continual growth of its air, which will result, in turn, in more shearings. In this way the value f the lost object (the ox and its shearings) will be enhanced. This verse eaches us, then, that a finder is obligated (when possible) to improve he state and value of the lost object (*Tosefos Rabbeinu Peretz*).

5. In *Exodus* 21:33, which states: וְכִי־יִפְתַּח אִישׁ בּוֹר אוֹ כִּי־יִכְרֶה אִישׁ בֹּר וְלֹא יְכַסֶּנּוּ וְנָפַל־שָׁמָּה שׁוֹר אוֹ חֲמוֹר, *If a person digs a pit in the ground or uncovers pit and does not cover it, and an ox or donkey falls into it.*

6. The Rabbis derive (*Bava Kamma* 53b) from the word *donkey* that a it owner is liable only for damage to animals, but not for damage to essels and other inanimate objects. However, R' Yehudah obligates a it owner to pay even for damage to inanimate objects. According to R' Yehudah, then, the word *donkey* teaches no limitation or other new law; hence, its mention is difficult to explain.

The word *ox* is not problematic, because it is used to exempt the pit owner from paying compensation for the death of a person who fell into the pit (*Rashi*).

17. Without the word *lamb* we would know (from *ox*) that the finder is obligated to return the oxtail shearings [although they are of minimal value]. We would not know, however, that the dung, which is virtually insignificant, must be returned. The Gemara therefore suggests that the Torah wrote *lamb* to teach us that even the dung must be returned (*Rashi*).

18. In favor of the one who found his animal and cared for it. Thus, the dung is an "object without claimants," and the finder may keep it [as the Mishnah has already established] (*Rashi*).

19. Below 27a-b.

20. The Gemara there attempts to prove from our Mishnah that the law is Biblical, but the proof is nullified. Our Gemara thus suggests that the apparently superfluous word *lamb* actually comes to teach that the law of identifying marks is Biblical (*Rashi*).

21. Since the Tanna of our Mishnah derived the law of identifying marks as an adjunct to the requirement of claimants (see Gemara below, 27b) from the word *garment*, we may conclude that it was obvious to him that the word *lamb* came for a different teaching, of which we are ignorant. For that reason the Gemara below does not attempt to derive from *lamb* that the law of identifying marks is of Biblical origin (*Rashi*).

22. *Deuteronomy* 22:3 (see above, note 9 for a quotation of the entire verse). The words *which is lost* connote: "which shall be called a *lost* object" (*Rashi*), implying that some lost articles are not considered "lost objects" by the Halachah and need not be returned.

א בלוקח מן התגר אבל בלוקח מבעל הבית חייב להחזיר וכן תני תנא קמיה דרב נחמן ל"ש אלא בלוקח מן התגר אבל בלוקח מבעל הבית חייב להחזיר א"ל רב נחמן וכי בעל הבית בעצמו דשן א"ל (א) איסמיה א"ל לא תתרגם מתני' ב כגון שדשן ע"י עבדו ושפחתו הכנענים: **מתני'** ג אף השמלה היתה בכלל כל אלו ולמה יצאת להקיש אליה לומר לך מה שמלה מיוחדת שיש בה סימנין ויש לה תובעין אף ד כל דבר שיש בו סימנין ויש לו תובעים חייב להכריז: **גמ'** מאי בכלל כל אלו אמר רבא בכלל (א) כל אבדת אחיך אמר רבא למה לי דכתב רחמנא שור חמור שה ושמלה צריכי דאי כתב רחמנא שמלה הוה אמינא ה"מ בעדים דגופה וסימנין דגופה אבל חמור בעדים דאוכף וסימנין דאוכף אימא לא מהדרינן ליה כתב רחמנא חמור ה דאפילו חמור בסימני האוכף שור ושה דכתב רחמנא ל"ל שור ו דאפילו לגיזת זנבו ושה לגיזותיו ולכתוב רחמנא שור דאפילו לגיזת זנבו וכ"ש שה לגיזותיו אלא (ב) אמר רבא חמור דבור לרבי יהודה ושה דאבידה לדברי הכל קשיא ואימא לגללים הוא דאתא (ג) גללים אפקורי מפקר להו ודילמא לסימנין הוא דאתא דאיבעיא לן סימנין דאורייתא או דרבנן כתב רחמנא שה דאפילו בסימנין מהדרינן (ד) ז וסימנין דאורייתא אמרי מדקתני להו תנא לסימנין גבי שמלה דקתני מה שמלה מיוחדת שיש בה סימנין ויש לה תובעין חייב להכריז אף כל דבר שיש בו סימנין ויש לו תובעין חייב להכריז ש"מ דשה לאו לסימנין הוא דאתא: תנו רבנן (א) אשר תאבד ח פרט לאבידה שאין בה שוה פרוטה רבי יהודה אומר ומצאתה פרט לאבידה שאין בה שוה פרוטה מאי בינייהו אמר אביי (ה) משמעות דורשין איכא בינייהו מר נפקא ליה מאשר תאבד ומר נפקא ליה מומצאתה ולמאן דנפקא ליה מאשר תאבד האי ומצאתה מאי עביד ליה ההוא מיבעי ליה (א) לכדרבנאי (ו) דאמר רבנאי ומצאתה דאתאי לידיה משמע ולמאן דנפקא ליה מומצאתה האי אשר תאבד מאי עביד ליה מבעי ליה לכדרבי יוחנן דאמר רבי יוחנן משום (ז) ר"ש בן יוחי מניין לאבידה ששטפה נהר שהיא מותרת שנאמר כן תעשה לכל אבדת אחיך אשר תאבד ממנו ומצאתה מי שאבודה הימנו ומצויה אצל כל אדם יצתה זו שאבודה הימנו ואינה מצויה אצל כל אדם ואידך הא דרבנאי מנא ליה נפקא ליה (י) מומצאתה ואידך הא דרבי יוחנן מנא ליה נפקא ליה ממנו ואידך ממנו לא משמע ליה רבא אמר פרוטה שהוזלה איכא בינייהו מ"ד מאשר תאבד איכא ומ"ד מומצאתה ליכא ולמ"ד אשר תאבד הא בעינן ומצאתה וליכא אלא פרוטה שהוקרה איכא בינייהו מאן דאמר ומצאתה איכא ומאן דאמר אשר תאבד ליכא ולמאן דאמר ומצאתה הא בעינן אשר תאבד וליכא ט אלא פרוטה (ג) שהוקרה והוזלה וחזרה והוקרה איכא בינייהו מאן דאמר אשר תאבד איכא ומאן דאמר ומצאתה בעינן דאית בה שיעור מציאה משעת אבידה ועד שעת מציאה: איבעיא להו סימנין דאורייתא (כ) או דרבנן מאי נפקא מינה

---

**רש"י**

בלוקח מן התגר. שאף הוא לקח תבואה זו מאנשים הרבה ולא ידיע דמאן נינהו וכיון דלית בהו סימן נתייאשו הבעלים: דשן. וכי הוא עצמו דש את התבואה הזאת הלא פועלים הרבה דשו אותה: איסמייה. אסיר ברייתא זו מגרסתי: אמר ליה לא תסמי תתרגם מתנית' כו': **מתני'** בכלל כל אלו. בגמרא מפרש לה: למה יצאתה. וכן תעשה לשמלתו: סתם שמלה יש בה סימן וכל שמלה יש לה בעלים תובעין אותה שלא נעשית אלא בידי אדם ולא באת מן ההפקר: אף כל שיש לו תובעין. למעוטי מידי דידעינן ביה דמיאש: **גמ'** שור וחמור שה ושמלה. לא תראה את שור אחיך או שיו וכן תעשה לחמורו וכן תעשה לשמלתו: בסימני אוכף. אם אין לו סימן בחמור ויש לו סימן באוכף שעליו: כתב רחמנא חמור. קרא יתירא לדרשה: לגיזת זנבו. שאפי' שער שבסוף הזנב יחזיר: חמור דבור לרבי יהודה. דמחייב על נזקי כלים בבור קשיא לן למאי אתא דאילו לרבנן מבעי להו שור ולא אדם חמור ולא כלים: לגללים. להחזיר את גלליו דאי כתב שור הוה אמינא כי אתא לגיזת זנבו אתא אבל גללים לא חשיבי ולא ליהדר כתב רחמנא קרא יתירא לאתויי גללים: אפקורי מפקר להו. למי שטרח בו ולא אתא קרא לרבויינהו דאין לו תובעין הוא: לסימנין אתא. לאשמועינן דליהדריה בסימנין בלא עדים דקמיבעי' לן לקמן סימנין דאורייתא או דרבנן ובעינן למפשט ממתניתין דיליף להו משמלה ודחינן ואמר תנא תובעין אצטריכא ליה סימנין כדי נסבה נפשוט מקרא יתירא דשה לסימנין אתא וסימנין דאורייתא: אמרי מדנקט תנא. במתני' למילף סימנין משמלה בהדי תובעין פשיטא ליה דשה למלתא אחריתי אתא ואנן הוא דלא ידעינן משום הכי לא פשיטא ליה לקמן סימנין משה הלכך קשיא לן למאי אתא: אשר תאבד. שתהא קרויה אבידה: ומצאתה. שתהא קרויה מציאה: דאתא לידיה משמע. ואפילו הכי אחיך ולא עובד כוכבים ולמדך שאבידת כנעני מותרת ולא תימא כי אמעוט אבידת כנעני מלטרוח אחריה אמעוט אבל אי נקטה חייב לאהדורה: מי שאבודה ממנו. ואיידי דכתב ממנו כתב אשר תאבד: ומצאתה. הוי"ו יתירה משמע ומלאתה כבר: שהוזלה. דבשעת אבידה שוה פרוט' ובשע' מציאה הוזלה: לאהדורי

---

**תוספות**

**בלוקח** מן התגר. פרש"י שלקח מאנשים הרבה ועירב פירות יחד ואינו יודע של מי הן ובאין בו סימן מיירי וא"ת אמאי לא מוקי בלוקח שהוא תגר וי"ל דלא פסיקא ליה דאם מלא קודם ששהא כדי לערבו בפירות אחרים חייב להחזיר אבל בלוקח מן התגר כבר עירב התגר ועי"ל בלא טעם דמערב עם שאר הפירות לא שנו אלא בלוקח מן התגר שאינו יודע למי להחזיר או לתגר או לבעה"ב אפי' אם אינו (ג) הוה ליפול בתבואה כ"א בשעת דישה ואין להסתפק בתגר מ"מ אינו יודע מאיזה בעל הבית קנה התגר ולזה הפי' הו"מ למימר בלוקח שהוא תגר ומתייאש בעל הבית שסבר שכבר מכר התגר ואין הקונה יודע למי יחזיר אלא כמו כן משום דלא פסיקא ליה דאם התגר מצאה קודם ששהה כדי למכור לאחר לא נתייאש בעה"ב וחייב להחזיר:

**מה** שמלה מיוחדת שיש לה סימני' ויש לה תובעין. במרובה (ב"ק דף סו. ושם ד"ה מולא) אמרינן בגניבה ילפינן יאוש מאבידה וא"ת ואבידה גופה מנלן וי"ל דמהכא נפקא לן דמה שמלה מיוחדת שיש בה סימן ואין הבעלים מתייאשין אלא תובעין שיחזירוה להם בסימנין אפי' אי סימנין לאו דאורייתא ואין מחזירין אלא בעדים מ"מ ילפינן משמלה דוודאי דבר שיש בו סימן חייב (ט) להחזיר דע"י שיש בו סימן ימצא עדים שיאמר להם מכירים אתם שמלה שלי שהיו בה סימנין כך וכך וגם המוצא לא יוציא השמלה להראותה לכל אדם אלא למי שיתן בה סימנים אע"פ שאינו מחזירה לו בכך מ"מ דומה שהיא שלו ומראה אותה לעדים אבל דברים שאין בהן סימן הוי שלו לפי שהבעלים נתייאשו והא דקאמר בגמרא סימנין כדי נסבה אע"ג דצריך הסימנין דע"י זה יש לה תובעין מ"מ כדי נסבה דאפילו אי לא תני אלא שיש לה תובעין מ"מ ידעינן דע"י סימנין יש לה תובעין ואין הבעלים מתייאשים כדפרישית ומיהו בירושלמי יליף מניין ליאוש מן התורה אמר רבי יוחנן אשר תאבד ממנו מי שאבודה ממנו ומצויה אצל כל אדם יצאה זו כו':

**בעדי** אוכף. פי' אי סימנין לאו דאורייתא: **לגיזת** זנבו. וא"ת אם יש בה שוה פרוטה פשיטא ואם אין בה שוה פרוטה הא ממעטינן לקמן מהשבה וי"ל דאצטריך שחייב לגוזזה בעתה אע"פ שאין בה שוה פרוטה בשעה שגוזזה:

**חמור** דבור לרבי יהודה. הא דלא קאמר גם לב"ה (י) קשה דלא חשיב אלא בהמות:

**ושה** דאבידה לדברי הכל קשיא. מקשינן ונימא מלתא דאתיא בק"ו טרח וכתב לה קרא ותירץ הר"י כהן דכיון דנכתב שור לגיזת זנבו הוי גיזת שה בכלל כל אבידת אחיך: **פרט** לשאין בו שוה פרוטה. דס"ד דחייב מכלל כל אבידת אחיך:

ת"ש

---

**עין משפט נר מצוה**

פג א ב מיי' פי"ו מהל' אבידה הלכה ו סמג עשין עד טוש"ע ח"מ סי' רסב סעיף יז:
פד ג מיי' שם פי"ד הלכה א:
פה ד מיי' שם וסמג שם טוש"ע ח"מ סי' רנט סעיף ג וסי' רסב סעיף ג:
פו ה מיי' שם וסמג שם טוש"ע ח"מ סי' רסב סעיף יח:
פז ו מיי' שם סמג שם טוש"ע ח"מ סי' רסז סעיף יז:
פח ז מיי' פי"ג שם הלכה ה:
פט ח מיי' שם פי"א הלכה יג סמג שם טוש"ע ח"מ סי' רנט סעיף ג וסי' רסב סעיף א:
צ ט י מיי' שם פי"ג הל' א סמג שם טוש"ע ח"מ סי' רסב סעיף א:

**רבינו חננאל**

אם מתגר לקח או מבעל הבית שדשים לו פועלים הרי הן שלו ואם מצאן צרורין או אפי' מפוזרין ולקח מבעל הבית שדשם על ידי עבדיו הכנענים וכיוצא בהן נוטל ומכריז: מתני' אף השמלה היתה בכלל כל אלו ולמה יצאת להקיש אליה לומר לך מה שמלה מיוחדת שיש לה סימנין ויש לה תובעין אף כל שיש לה סימנין ויש לה תובעין. אמר רבא [חמור] דבור לר"י ושה דאבידה לדברי הכל קשיא. חמור דבור פי' חמור שכתב בבור אליבא דרבנן דאמרי שור ולא אדם חמור ולא כלים שפיר כתיב בקרא ונפל שמה שור או חמור אלא לר' יהודה דמחייב על נזקי כלים בבור חמור מה בא למעט קשיא. שה דאבידה שנאמר כי תראה את שור אחיך או את שיו נדחים וגו' אם השור שיש לומר הוא הניחו שרוב השוורים שעושים מלאכה בהן אין נמסרין לרועה הזהירה תורה להשיבן שה לא כל שכן שה דכתב רחמנא למה לי קשיא. פי' גללין צפיעי בקר. מלשון והיא בגללי צואת האדם: ת"ר אשר תאבד ממנו פרט לאבידה שאין בה שוה פרוטה וכו' אמר ר' יוחנן משום ר' שמעון בן יוחאי מנין לאבידה ששטפה נהר שמותרת וכו' הא דאמר רבנאי ומצאתה דאתאי לידיה משמע הוא בפ' הגוזל בתרא הלכה אין פורטין מתיבת המוכסין.

**תורה אור השלם**

א) וְכֵן תַּעֲשֶׂה לַחֲמֹרוֹ וְכֵן תַּעֲשֶׂה לְשִׂמְלָתוֹ וְכֵן תַּעֲשֶׂה לְכָל אֲבֵדַת אָחִיךָ אֲשֶׁר תֹּאבַד מִמֶּנּוּ וּמְצָאתָהּ לֹא תוּכַל לְהִתְעַלֵּם: [דברים כב, ג]

**מסורת הש"ס**

[בבא קמא לא:], ב) שם ..., ג) [לקמן סח:, בבא ... מח.], ד) [חולין ...:], ה) בבא קמא קיג: ...ס, לעיל ב., ו) [לעיל כב: ...ם ושם איתא ר"ש בן ...וצדק], ז) [עיין תוס' ...הדרין יד. ד"ה ור"ש ...ר'], ח) [לעיל יח:, חולין ...:], ט) אולי צ"ל להכריז, [כדאיתא בבבא קמא לד.].

**הגהות הב"ח**

(א) גמ' לכדרבינא דאמר ...ינא ומלאתה: (ב) שם ...לא פרוטה שהוזלה ...זרה והוקרה איכא ...נייהו כצ"ל ותיבת ...הוקרה נמחק: (ג) תוס' ...ה בלוקח וכו' אם אינו הווה ליפול:

**גליון הש"ס**

...' משמעות דורשין ...ב. שבועות דף יט ע"א:

**ליקוטי רש"י**

שה דאבידה. כיון ...כתיב לכל אבידת אחיך ...ה לי דכתב רחמנא חמור ...ור ושה ושלמה ובפרק ...ו מציאות דרשינן להו ...כולהו בר משה [ב"ק נד.]. ...סימנין דאורייתא. ...דסמיך אסימנין ושרי ...יסורא עליהו ש"מ הא ...סמכין אסימנין בחזרת ...בדה כדאמרינן באלו ...מציאות (ב"מ דף כז.) ...אורייתא היא דאי דרבנן ...י דעבוד רבנן תקנתא ...ממונא באיסורא מי מצו ...תקני אלא ש"מ ...אורייתא היא [חולין צו:]. ...אשר תאבד ממנו וכו' ...י שאבודה. קרא ...יתירא הוא לאשמועינן ...אינו אבוד אלא הימנו [לעיל כב:].

בְּלוֹקֵחַ מִן הַתַּגָּר – in a case **where one purchases the produce from a merchant,** who himself purchased his produce from many suppliers;[1] אֲבָל בְּלוֹקֵחַ מִבַּעַל הַבַּיִת – **but** in a case **where one purchases** produce **from a** private **householder** and finds something in it, חַיָּיב לְהַחֲזִיר – **he is obligated to return** it to that person.[2]

The Gemara presents another source for this view:

וְכֵן תָּנֵי תַּנָּא קַמֵּיהּ דְּרַב נַחְמָן – **And likewise a teacher of Baraisos taught** the following Baraisa **in the presence of Rav Nachman:** לֹא שָׁנוּ – [THE SAGES OF THE MISHNAH,] who permitted the finder to keep what he finds amongst the produce, **DID NOT TEACH** this leniency אֶלָּא בְּלוֹקֵחַ מִן הַתַּגָּר – **EXCEPT** in a case **WHERE HE PURCHASES** the produce **FROM A MERCHANT,** who himself purchased his produce from many suppliers; אֲבָל בְּלוֹקֵחַ מִבַּעַל הַבַּיִת – **BUT WHERE HE PURCHASES** produce **FROM A** private **HOUSEHOLDER** and finds something in it, חַיָּיב לְהַחֲזִיר – **HE IS OBLIGATED TO RETURN** it to that individual.

The Gemara asks:

אָמַר לֵיהּ רַב נַחְמָן – **Rav Nachman told him:** וְכִי בַּעַל הַבַּיִת בְּעַצְמוֹ דָּשָׁן – **But did the householder thresh them himself?** Surely not! It was his hired workers who threshed the produce. Why, if so, should the objects be returned? Since we cannot determine from which of the many threshers it fell, the finder should be allowed to keep it. – ? –

אָמַר לֵיהּ – **[The teacher of the Baraisos] told [Rav Nachman]:** אִיסְמְיֵיהּ – Should I **delete it?**[3] אָמַר לֵיהּ – **[Rav Nachman] told him:** לֹא – **No,** you need not delete it. תְּתַרְגֵּם מַתְנִיתָא – Rather, **interpret the Baraisa** as referring כְּגוֹן שֶׁדְּשָׁן עַל יְדֵי עַבְדּוֹ וְשִׁפְחָתוֹ הַכְּנַעֲנִים – to **a case in which he threshed them by means of his Canaanite slave and maidservant.**[4]

**Mishnah** The following Mishnah deduces laws pertaining to the return of lost property from a seemingly extraneous word in the Torah:

אַף הַשִּׂמְלָה הָיְתָה בִּכְלָל כָּל אֵלּוּ – **The "garment," too, was included in all of these.**[5] וְלָמָּה יָצָאת – **And why was it singled out?**[6] לְהַקִּישׁ אֵלֶיהָ – **To compare** all types of lost property **to it,** לוֹמַר לָךְ – **to tell you:** מַה שִּׂמְלָה מְיוּחֶדֶת – **Just as a garment is distinguished** שֶׁיֵּשׁ בָּהּ סִימָנִין וְיֵשׁ לָהּ תּוֹבְעִין – **in that it has identifying marks and it has claimants,**[7] אַף כָּל דָּבָר שֶׁיֵּשׁ בּוֹ סִימָנִין וְיֵשׁ לוֹ תּוֹבְעִים – **so, too, anything that has identifying marks and has claimants** חַיָּיב לְהַכְרִיז – **must be announced.**[8]

**Gemara** The Gemara inquires as to the meaning of a phrase in the Mishnah:

מַאי בִּכְלָל כָּל אֵלּוּ – **What** does **INCLUDED IN ALL OF THESE** mean?

The Gemara answers:

אָמַר רָבָא – **Rava said:** בִּכְלָל "כָּל־אֲבֵדַת אָחִיךָ" – The Mishnah means that a garment is already **included in** the phrase ***any lost article.***[9]

The Gemara questions why the Torah enumerates several examples of a lost item that requires returning:

אָמַר רָבָא – **Rava said:** לָמָּה לִי דִּכְתַב רַחֲמָנָא "שׁוֹר" "חֲמוֹר" "שֶׂה" "וְשִׂמְלָה" – **Why did the Merciful One write** in the Torah – ***(an) ox, (a) donkey, (a) lamb,*** and ***(a) garment?***[10]

The Gemara answers:

צְרִיכֵי – **They are all necessary.** דְּאִי כְּתַב רַחֲמָנָא שִׂמְלָה – **For if the Merciful One had written** only ***garment,*** הֲוָה אֲמִינָא – **I would have said** that הָנֵי מִילֵּי בְּעֵדִים דְּגוּפָהּ – **this ruling** (which obligates a finder to return lost property to the one who identifies it) applies only **where** there are **witnesses as to the object itself,** וְסִימָנִין דְּגוּפָהּ – **or** where there are **identifying marks on the object itself.** I.e. I would have said that one is obligated to return an item only when the owner can prove that the item itself belongs to him. אֲבָל חֲמוֹר בְּעֵדִים דְּאוּכָּף – **However,** in the case of **a donkey, where** there are **witnesses as to the saddle**[11] but not to the ownership of the donkey itself, וְסִימָנִין דְּאוּכָּף – **or** where there are **identifying marks on the** donkey's **saddle** but not on the donkey itself, אֵימָא לֹא מְהַדְּרִינַן לֵיהּ – **I would say** that **we would not return** the donkey **to [the one who proved only the ownership of the saddle].**[12] כְּתַב רַחֲמָנָא "חֲמוֹר" – **The Merciful One** therefore **wrote** the additional word ***donkey*** in the Torah to teach us that דַּאֲפִילּוּ חֲמוֹר בְּסִימָנֵי הָאוּכָּף – **even the donkey** itself should be returned to the claimant that provides the

NOTES

1. The finder is unable to know from which of the merchant's suppliers the object fell. The supplier who actually lost the unidentifiable object therefore despairs of recovering it, because he is aware that, in the absence of a *siman,* it cannot be traced back to him (*Rashi*).

2. Since the produce was purchased from a private person, it is clear that what was found in it belongs to him. By the same token, the owner, knowing that he sold it to a private person, does not despair of recovering it — even though it has no *siman.*

3. The teacher of Baraisos would delete from his repertoire any Baraisa found to be untenable.

4. The Canaanite slave and maidservant lack the right of ownership. Whatever they acquire belongs to their owner (see above, 12a). Consequently, regardless of who lost the object found amongst the produce, it belongs to the owner (and not the threshers). The finder is therefore obligated to return it to him.

5. I.e. in the general category of lost items that must be returned, as the Gemara explains below.

6. Why did the Torah state specifically: וְכֵן תַּעֲשֶׂה לְשִׂמְלָתוֹ, *and so shall you do with his garment* (*Deuteronomy* 22:3)?

7. Garments ordinarily have identifying marks. In addition, since they are man made and do not come into being as ownerless property, garments have owners who will claim them (*Rashi*).

8. However, one is not obligated to return a lost object that the owner has despaired of recovering (*Rashi*).

The word "garment" is the source for the right of a finder to acquire a lost article when its owner has given up hope of recovering it. The *Talmud Yerushalmi* (*Bava Metzia* 2:1) derives this law from another source (*Tosafos* ד״ה מה שמלה).

9. *Deuteronomy* 22:3. The verse in its entirety reads: וְכֵן תַּעֲשֶׂה לַחֲמֹרוֹ וְכֵן תַּעֲשֶׂה לְשִׂמְלָתוֹ וְכֵן תַּעֲשֶׂה לְכָל־אֲבֵדַת אָחִיךָ אֲשֶׁר־תֹּאבַד מִמֶּנּוּ וּמְצָאתָהּ לֹא תוּכַל לְהִתְעַלֵּם, *And so shall you do with his donkey, and so shall you do with his garment, and so shall you do with any lost article belonging to your brother, which is lost from him and you have found it; you may not hide yourself.* The Mishnah therefore questioned the Torah's specific mention of "garment," inasmuch as a garment is included in the general phrase, *any lost article.*

10. *Donkey* and *garment* are written in the verse quoted in the previous note. *Ox* and *lamb* are written in *Deuteronomy* 22:1, which states: לֹא־תִרְאֶה אֶת־שׁוֹר אָחִיךָ אוֹ אֶת־שֵׂיוֹ נִדָּחִים וְהִתְעַלַּמְתָּ מֵהֶם הָשֵׁב תְּשִׁיבֵם לְאָחִיךָ, *You shall not see your brother's ox or his lamb straying, and hide yourself from them; you shall surely return them to your brother.*

Rava continues the Mishnah's line of questioning. Although the Mishnah has explained the specific mention of "garment," Rava inquires why the Torah singles out these other objects, and does not rely on the inclusionary phrase, *any lost article.*

11. That is, where witnesses testify that the saddle belongs to the claimant, but cannot say as much for the donkey itself.

12. That is, the finder would return only the saddle, which has been identified, but not the donkey.

finder.[19]

The Gemara analyzes the Mishnah's ruling to determine whether R' Elazar's ruling is consistent with it:

**תְּנַן – We have learned** in our Mishnah: **לִפְנֵי שׁוּלְחָנִי** – If someone found coins IN FRONT OF A MONEYCHANGER, **הֲרֵי אֵלּוּ שֶׁלּוֹ** – THEY BELONG TO [THE FINDER]. The expression "in front of" connotes that they were found on the ground. **הָא עַל גַּבֵּי שׁוּלְחָן דְּשׁוּלְחָנִי** – **But,** we may infer, if they were found **on the counter,** then they belong **to the moneychanger.** This refutes R' Elazar's ruling.

The Gemara continues its analysis of the Mishnah:

**אֵימָא סֵיפָא** – Now, **consider the concluding clause** of that case in the Mishnah: **בֵּין הַכִּסֵּא וְלַשּׁוּלְחָנִי שֶׁל שׁוּלְחָנִי** – If they were found BETWEEN THE STOOL AND THE MONEYCHANGER, THEY BELONG TO THE MONEYCHANGER. **הָא עַל גַּבֵּי שׁוּלְחָן שֶׁלּוֹ** – **But,** we infer if they were found **on the counter** itself, then they belong **to [the finder].** Thus, the implications of these two clauses are contradictory!

The Gemara concludes:

**אֶלָּא מֵהָא לֵיכָּא לְמִשְׁמַע מִינָּהּ** – **Rather, from this** wording of the Mishnah **it is impossible to derive** to whom the money belongs in R' Elazar's case.[20]

Having proven that the Mishnah does not rule on R' Elazar's case, the Gemara searches for the source of his ruling:

**וְרַבִּי אֶלְעָזָר הָא מְנָא לֵיהּ** – **And R' Elazar, from where** did he derive **[his ruling]?**

The Gemara suggests two sources:

**אָמַר רָבָא – Rava said: מַתְנִיתִין קְשִׁיתֵיהּ** – The wording of **our Mishnah was difficult for him** to understand. **אי אִרְיָא דְּתָנֵי** – **Why did [the Mishnah] specifically teach: ין הַכִּסֵּא לַשּׁוּלְחָנִי** – If they were found BETWEEN THE STOOL AND TH MONEYCHANGER, **שֶׁל שׁוּלְחָנִי** – they belong TO THE MONE CHANGER? **לִיתְנֵי – Let [the Mishnah] teach** that **עַל שׁוּלְחָן** – even coins found **on the counter** belong to the mone changer.[21] Since it did not, this implies that such coins belong t the finder. **אִי נַמִּי – Or possibly,** R' Elazar noted anothe difficulty: **מָצָא בְּשׁוּלְחָנוּת** – Let the Mishnah state that **[someone] found** coins **in the moneychanger's shop,** the belong to him,[22] **כִּדְקָתָנֵי רֵישָׁא** – just **as the** Mishnah's **firs case teaches** that **מָצָא בְּחָנוּת שֶׁלּוֹ** – if **[someone] found** a article **in a store, it belongs to him.** The Mishnah would the have ruled on parallel cases. Why did the Mishnah state insteac "if he found coins *in front of* a moneychanger"? This teaches tha even coins found on the counter belong to the finder.[23] **לָא שְׁמַע מִינָּהּ – Rather, conclude from [either inference],** as R Elazar does, that **אֲפִילּוּ מוּנָּחִין עַל גַּבֵּי שׁוּלְחָן** – **even** if the coin were **lying upon the counter** **הֲרֵי אֵלּוּ שֶׁלּוֹ** – **they belong t [the finder].**

Our Mishnah stated:

**הַלּוֹקֵחַ פֵּירוֹת מֵחֲבֵירוֹ וכו'** – ONE WHO PURCHASES PRODUCE FRO ANOTHER **etc.**

The Gemara qualifies the Mishnah's ruling:

**אָמַר רֵישׁ לָקִישׁ מִשּׁוּם רַבִּי יַנַּאי – Reish Lakish said in the name o R' Yannai: לֹא שָׁנוּ אֶלָּא – [The Sages of the Mishnah,]** wh permitted the finder to keep coins found among purchase produce **taught this only**

NOTES

19. The customers as well as the moneychanger place their money on the table. Thus, when a customer loses money, he surely despairs of recovering it, for he realizes that the finder will never know to return it to him.

20. Because the contradiction can be resolved in one of two ways. Perhaps the beginning clause's wording is imprecise: Its ruling that coins found in front of a moneychanger belong to the finder actually includes those found on the counter. This would concur with the concluding clause's implication and thus support R' Elazar's ruling. On the other hand, the beginning clause's wording might indeed be precise, implying that coins found on the counter belong to the moneychanger. This would refute R' Elazar's ruling. (For a reconciliation between this and the implication of the Mishnah's concluding clause, see *Rosh* cited in *Shitah Mekubetzes*.) Since the Mishnah's meaning is in doubt, it neither supports nor refutes R' Elazar's ruling (*Rosh* cited in *Shitah Mekubetzes*).

21. We would then surely have inferred that coins found between the stool and the moneychanger belong to the moneychanger (*Rashi*). Previously, the Gemara maintained that this inference is contradicted by that from the first clause of this case. See *Toras Chaim*, who explain why Rava favors this inference over that from the first clause.

22. *Rashi;* cf. *Hagahos HaGra*.

23. According to this answer, the expression "in front of" a money changer includes the counter, whereas "in the store" does not. Hence since the Mishnah allows a finder to keep coins found "in front of" th moneychanger, he may keep even coins found on the counter.

This, however, differs from the Mishnah's first ruling, in which th Mishnah states only that a finder can keep an article found in the store This implies that if it is found on the counter it belongs to th storekeeper. *Tur (Choshen Mishpat* 260) explains the differenc between a moneychanger's shop and a store. At a moneychanger's shop both the customers and the moneychanger place their monies upon th counter. Therefore, coins found on the counter belongs to the finder (se note 16). At a store, however, only the storekeeper places his object upon the counter. Hence, if coins are found there, they belong to hir (see *Rambam*, *Hilchos Gezeilah V'Aveidah* 16:4, who rules differentl and *Kesef Mishneh* ad loc.).

שנפל משנים חייב להחזיר מאי טעמא ההוא דנפל מיניה לא מיאש מימר אמר מכדי איניש אחרינא לא הוה בהדאי אלא האי נקיטנא ליה ואמינא ליה אנת הוא דשקלתיה בשלשה אינו חייב להחזיר מאי טעמא ההוא דנפל מיניה ודאי מיאש מימר אמר מכדי תרי הוו בהדאי אי נקיטנא להאי אמר לא שקלתיה ואי נקיטנא להאי אמר לא שקלתיה אמר רבא האי דאמרת בשלשה אינו חייב להחזיר לא אמרן אלא דלית ביה שוה פרוטה לכל חד וחד אבל אית ביה שוה פרוטה לכל חד וחד חייב להחזיר מאי טעמא אימור שותפי נינהו ולא מיאשו איכא דאמרי אמר רבא [א]אע"ג דלית ביה אלא שוה שתי פרוטות חייב להחזיר מאי טעמא אימור שותפי נינהו וחד מנייהו אחולי אחליה למנתיה גבי חבריה ואמר רבא [ב]ראה סלע שנפלה נטלה לפני יאוש על מנת לגוזלה עובר בכולן משום א) לא תגזול ומשום ב) השב תשיבם ומשום ג) לא תוכל להתעלם ואע"ג דהדרה לאחר יאוש [א]מתנה הוא דיהיב ליה ואיסורא דעבד עבד [ג]נטלה לפני יאוש על מנת להחזירה ולאחר יאוש נתכוין לגוזלה עובר משום השב תשיבם [ד]המתין לה עד שנתיאשו הבעלים ונטלה [ב]אינו עובר אלא משום לא תוכל להתעלם בלבד [ג]אמר רבא [ה]האי מאן דחזי דנפל זוזי מחבריה בי חלתא ואשכחיה ושקליה לא מיחייב לאהדורי ליה מאי טעמא ההוא דנפל מיניה מיאש הוא אע"ג דחזייה דאייתי ארבלא וקא מרבל מימר אמר כי היכי דנפול מינאי דידי הכי (א) [ד]נפול מאיניש אחרינא [א] ומשכחנא מידי:

מתני' [ו]מצא בחנות הרי אלו שלו בין התיבה ולחנוני של חנוני לפני שולחני הרי אלו שלו בין הכסא ולשולחני הרי אלו של שולחני [ז]הלוקח פירות מחבירו או ששילח לו חבירו פירות ומצא בהן מעות הרי אלו שלו אם היו צרורין נוטל ומכריז: גמ' אמר רבי אלעזר [ח]אפילו מונחין על גבי שולחן תנן לפני שולחני הרי אלו שלו הא על גבי שולחן דשולחני אימא סיפא בין הכסא ולשולחני של שולחני הא על גבי שולחן שלו אלא [ד]מהא ליכא למשמע מינה ורבי אלעזר הא מנא ליה אמר רבא מתניתין קשיתיה מאי אריא דתני בין הכסא לשולחני של שולחני ליתני על (ב) שולחן אי נמי מצא בשולחנות כדקתני רישא מצא בחנות שלו [ה]אלא ש"מ אפי' מונחין על גבי שולחן הרי אלו שלו: הלוקח פירות מחבירו וכו': אמר ריש לקיש משום רבי ינאי לא שנו אלא

בלוקח

**רש"י**

נקיטנא ליה כו'. משבענא ליה שבועת היסת ולא נתייאש מיד כשמשמש ולא מצא ונמצא שבא ליד זה לפני יאוש והלכה כאביי: אי נקיטנא וכו'. ואינו יכול להשביעו בטענת שמא שאין נשבעין בטענת שמא אלא אותן השנויין במשנה ואלו נשבעים שלא בטענה כו' (שבועות דף מה.) וא"ת הא מקמי יאוש אתי לידיה ואוקימנא הלכתא כאביי ביע"ל קג"ס הא אמרן דמעות מידע ידיע מיד כרבי יצחק דאמר אדם עשוי למשמש בכיסו כו' (לעיל דף כא:): אימור שותפי נינהו. בסלע זו ונאמנים זה על זה ואין האחד חושד את חבירו בחלקו ולכי מישמש בכיסו ולא מצאה לא אייאש מימר אמר אחד מן השותפים מצאה ולצערני הוא שותק ונמצא כשבאת ליד זה לפני יאוש באת לידו והא אוקמיה כאביי הלכך אף ע"ג דסלע דבר שאין בו סימן הוא חייב להחזיר אבל כי אין בו שלש פרוטות מה נפשך אי שותפין הן בו אין כאן משום השבת אבידה ואם של אחד מהם הוא או של השנים נואשו ואמרו חברנו זה גנב הוא והרי משמש ואמר לא לקחתיו אחד מכם לקחו וגנבו מחבירו: אימור שותפי נינהו. ומהימני אהדדי ואין חושדין זה את זה ונמצאת שבאת ליד זה לפני יאוש: ראה סלע שנפלה. ולא גרסינן משנים: נטלה לפני יאוש. שלא שהה כדי למשמש זה בכיסו: עובר משום השב תשיבם. לא תגזול לא שייך אלא בשעת נטילה כמו ויגזול את החנית מיד המצרי (שמואל ב כג) כדאמר בבבא קמא (עט:) לא תוכל להתעלם אינה אזהרה אלא לכובש את עיניו ונמנע מלהציל הלכך הנוטלה על מנת להחזיר ולאחר יאוש נתכוין לגוזלה אין כאן מתעלם אבל השב תשיבם איכא משנטל עד שישיבנה: המתין לה כו'. בשעה שראה אותה ולא נטלה להחזירה: עובר בלא תוכל להתעלם. שהרי העלים עיניו: בי חלתא. בין החולות: ארבלא. כברה: מתני' מצא בחנות הרי אלו שלו. בדבר שאין בו סימן קאי דההוא דנפל מיניה מיאש שהכל נכנסים לשם: בין התיבה. שהחנוני יושב לפניה ותמיד נוטל ממנה ונותן לפניו ומוכר ומעות שנותנין לו נותן [ו]לתיבה ולא נפל שום דבר אלא מיד חנוני: שולחני. מחליף מעות ונותן מטבעותיו בשולחן שלפניו והבאין להחליף אף הן נותנין שם מעותיהן: הרי אלו שלו. דאמרינן מן הבאין נפלו שהרי השולחן מפסיק בין שולחני למעות שנמצאו ואם מן השולחני נפלו היה להם להמצא בינו לכסא שהשולחן מונח עליו: הלוקח פירות מחבירו. מפרש בגמרא: ואם היו צרורין. הוי סימן או קשר או מנין שבהם: גמ' אמר רבי אלעזר אפילו מונחין על גבי שולחן. נראה בעיני דלא גרסינן צרורין: לפני. משמע על גבי קרקע: לתני על גבי שולחן. של שולחני וכ"ש בין הכסא ולשולחני: אי נמי. [ב] ניתני ברישא מצא בשולחנות כדקתני רישא מצא בחנות מדנקט לפני השולחני אף על השולחן במשמע:

בלוקח

**תוספות**

שנפל משנים חייב להחזיר. אפילו אין בו סימן דאינו מתיאש לעולם ומיירי שניהם בקשוה יחד קודם שבא זה ומצאה ולכך סבור ודאי שחבירו לקחה כשבקשה עמו ואינו מתיאש לעולם שמחשב יחזירנה לי כשאביישנו ברבים ואוכיח לו שמצאו ולכך נמי אמרינן בסמוך אימור שותפי נינהו כיון שראינום מחפשין יחד ומה שפרש"י מטעם יאוש שלא מדעת אין נראה דהא רבא סבר דהוי יאוש ומפרש בסמוך מילתיה דרב נחמן ואין סברא לומר דהדר ביה בתר דאיתותב ומה שפירש נמי שישביענו שבועת היסת קשה וכי ישביענו בטענת ספק ומיהו י"ל דטוען ברי לפי שלא היה שם אחר כי אם הוא אך קשה דבימי בר קפרא עדיין לא נתקנה שבועת היסת ונראה לפרש שבלא שבועה אינו מתיאש לעולם כדפרישית: לא אמרן אלא כי לית ביה שוה פרוטה לכל חד וחד. דהיינו כי ליכא שלש פרוטות אלא ב' דמה נפשך אין צריך להחזיר אם שלשתן שותפין אין כאן כדי השבה לכל אחד ואם אינן שותפין האובד יתיאש כי השנים ידחוהו כל אחד על חבירו וא"ת וניחוש שמא שנים הם שותפין דאין חושדים זה את זה ולא מתיאשי שניהם יטענו בטענת ברי לשלישי וכן באיכא דאמרי אמאי קאמר הני שותפי נינהו וחד מינייהו אחיל מנתיה גבי חבריה נימא אימור שנים מהם הם שותפין ואין חושדין זה את זה ויאמרו ודאי שהשלישי לקחה וי"ל דודאי כי ליכא אלא שנים האחד יטען ברי לחבירו אבל כשיש שלשה לא יטענו טענת ברי לשלישי אפי' יהיו שנים מהן שותפין דנהי דאין חושדים זה את זה מ"מ סבור שהשותף לקחה לצערו עד זמן מרובה כדאמר בסמוך דאי איכא שלש פרוטות דאינם מתיאשים שסבורים שחבריהם מצאם ומעלים מהם להקניט ולצער עד זמן מרובה ולבסוף יחזירנה ועי"ל דכיון שבלשה הולכין יחד אין לומר שותפין שנים מהם אלא או כולם שותפין או כל אחד ואחד לבדו: מתנה בעלמא הוא דיהיב ליה. וא"ת והלא לאו דלא תגזול מקרי ניתק לעשה בפ' שילוח הקן (חולין דף קמא.) א"כ כיון דלענין גזילה לא מקרי מתנה גם השב תשיבם למה לא תיקן וי"ל דלא קאי אלא על לאו דלא תוכל להתעלם שעבר שלא החזיר קודם יאוש: אינו עובר אלא משום השב תשיבם. ובפ"ק דקדושין (דף לד. ושם ד"ה מעקה) דחשיב השבת אבידה עשה שאין הזמן גרמא היינו בענין שבכאן וא"ת ואמאי ליכא לאו דלא תגזול אי משום דבהתירא אתא לידיה הלא בכובש שכר שכיר איכא לאו כדאמר בפרק איזהו נשך (לקמן דף סא. ושם) וי"ל דהתם כשמתכוין לגזול לא נתיאשו הבעלים והכא כבר נתיאשו: אפילו צרורין. רש"י ל"ג צרורין דאם היה בו סימן מכריז וי"ל דגרים ליה ומיירי דאיכא רוב עכו"ם מצויים שם והם שלו ואע"ג דאיכא סימן דהלכה כר' שמעון בן אלעזר בהא:

בלוקח

**עין משפט נר מצוה**

עז א מיי' פי"ד מהל' אבידה הל' ח סמג עשין עד טוש"ע ח"מ סי' רסב סעיף ג וסעיף ד:

עח ב ג ד מיי' שם הל' ו ז סמג שם טוש"ע ח"מ סי' רנט סעיף א:

עט ה מיי' שם הל' ט סמג שם טוש"ע ח"מ סי' רסב סעיף יד:

פ ו מיי' פט"ז שם הלכה ד ה ועיין בהשגות ובמ"מ סמג שם טוש"ע ח"מ סי' רס סעיף ה:

פא ז מיי' שם הל' ו סמג שם טוש"ע ח"מ סי' רסב סעיף יח:

פב ח מיי' שם הלכה ה סמג שם טוש"ע ח"מ סי' רס סעיף ה:

**רבינו חננאל**

חייב להכריז דלא נתיאש. נפל מתוך שלשה אין חייב להכריז דודאי מיאש וכו' ורבא פליג עליה בהא. אמר רבא סלע שנפלה מחבירו נטלה לפני יאוש עובר משום בל תגזול ומשום השב תשיבם ומשום לא תוכל להתעלם אע"ג דאהדרה למרה לבתר יאוש איסורא כבר עבדא והשתא מתנה הוא דיהיב ליה. נטלה לפני יאוש על מנת להחזירה ולאחר יאוש נמלך לנוטלה עובר משום השב תשיבם. המתין עד שנתיאשו הבעלים ונטלה אינו עובר אלא משום לא תוכל להתעלם. אמר רבא מאן דחזא דנפל זוזא מחבריה בי חלתא ושקליה אינו חייב להחזירו אע"ג דחזיה דמייתי ארבולי ומארבל וכו': מתני' מצא בחנות הרי אלו שלו. בין תיבה לחנווני הרי אלו לחנווני. לפני שולחני למוצאן בין כסא לשולחני הרי הן לשולחני. ודייק ר' אלעזר מדקתני בין כסא לשולחני הרי הן לשולחני הא על השולחן אפי' צרורין ומונחין הרי הן של מוצאן ותוב מדלא קתני סיפא מצא בחנות של שולחני הרי אלו שלו כדקתני רישא ש"מ אפי' על השולחן עצמו הרי הן למוצאן. לקח פירות מחבירו ומצא בתוכן מעות או שילח לו חבירו פירות

**תורה אור השלם**

א) לֹא תַעֲשֹׁק אֶת רֵעֲךָ וְלֹא תִגְזֹל לֹא תָלִין פְּעֻלַּת שָׂכִיר אִתְּךָ עַד בֹּקֶר: [ויקרא יט, יג]

ב) לֹא תִרְאֶה אֶת שׁוֹר אָחִיךָ אוֹ אֶת שֵׂיוֹ נִדָּחִים וְהִתְעַלַּמְתָּ מֵהֶם הָשֵׁב תְּשִׁיבֵם לְאָחִיךָ: [דברים כב, א]

ג) וְכֵן תַּעֲשֶׂה לַחֲמֹרוֹ וְכֵן תַּעֲשֶׂה לְשִׂמְלָתוֹ וְכֵן תַּעֲשֶׂה לְכָל אֲבֵדַת אָחִיךָ אֲשֶׁר תֹּאבַד מִמֶּנּוּ וּמְצָאתָהּ לֹא תוּכַל לְהִתְעַלֵּם: [דברים כב, ג]

**מסורת הש"ס**

א) [עיין תוס' בבא קמ סו: ד"ה רבא], ב) [גירס הנמוקי יוסף ונטל עובר משום וכו' ו משמע ברש"י ד"ה עובר ג) [נ"ל ואמר וכן אי ברי"ף ורא"ש], ד) [עי' נדרים עב.], ברכות כ וש"נ, ה) [עי' רי"ף ורא"ש גירסאות אחרות, ועי' מהרש"א], ו) נ"ל לתוך מהרש"ל.

**הגהות הב"ח**

(א) גמ' הכי נמי נפ מאיניש אחרינא: (ב) ש לתני על גבי שלחן אי נמי

**הגהות הגר"א**

[א] גמ' ומשכח(נא) אותיות נא ממל ומשכחנא מוקפים [ב] רש"י ד"ה א ניתני ברישא. נ והרמב"ם מפרש דקאי ט סיפא בין הכסא כו' לית בשולחנות כו' ועהג" (ועמ"ש רבינו בח"מ ס רס ס"ק טו יז):

**ליקוטי רש"י**

וקא מרבל. מירו לשון כברה שמנענעי אותה כמו אייתי ארבו וקא מרבל באלו מציאו [חולין מט.].

מִשּׁוּם ,,לֹא תִגְזֹל" – He is guilty of: *you shall not rob;*[6] וּמִשּׁוּם ,,הָשֵׁב תְּשִׁיבֵם" – and of: *you shall surely return them;*[7] וּמִשּׁוּם ,,לֹא תוּכַל לְהִתְעַלֵּם" – and of: *you shall not hide from it.*[8] וְאַף עַל גַּב דְּהַדְרָהּ לְאַחַר יֵאוּשׁ – **And even though he returned it after the** owner **despaired** of it, מַתָּנָה הוּא דְּיָהֵיב לֵיהּ – it is considered merely **a present that [the finder] gave to [the owner],** וְאִיסּוּרָא דַּעֲבַד עֲבַד – **but the transgression that he has committed stands.**[9]

Rava states a second ruling regarding one who sees a *sela* fall from its owner:

נְטָלָהּ לִפְנֵי יֵאוּשׁ עַל מְנָת לְהַחֲזִירָהּ – If **he took it before** the owner **despaired** of it, **with the intention to return it,** וּלְאַחַר יֵאוּשׁ נִתְכַּוֵּין לְגוֹזְלָהּ – **but after the** owner **despaired** of it, **[the finder] decided to steal it,** עוֹבֵר מִשּׁוּם ,,הָשֵׁב תְּשִׁיבֵם" – **he has transgressed** the commandment: ***you shall surely return them.***[10]

Rava states a third ruling for such a case:

הִמְתִּין לָהּ עַד שֶׁנִּתְיָאֲשׁוּ הַבְּעָלִים וּנְטָלָהּ – If **[the bystander] waited until the owner despaired, and** then **took [the** ***sela*** **]** for himself, אֵינוֹ עוֹבֵר אֶלָּא מִשּׁוּם ,,לֹא תוּכַל לְהִתְעַלֵּם" בִּלְבָד – **he has transgressed only** the commandment: ***you shall not hide*** *from it.*[11]

The Gemara presents another ruling concerning a lost coin:

אָמַר רָבָא – **Rava said:** הַאי מַאן דְּחָזֵי דְּנָפַל זוּזֵי מֵחַבְרֵיהּ בֵּי חַלְתָּא – **If one saw a** ***zuz*** **fall from his fellow into the sand,** אַשְׁכְּחֵיהּ וּשְׁקָלֵיהּ – **and he found it and took it,** לֹא מִיחַיֵּיב לְאַהְדּוּרֵי לֵיהּ – **he is not obligated to return it to [his fellow].** מַאי טַעְמָא – **What is the reason?** הַהוּא דְּנָפַל מִינֵּיהּ מְיָאֵשׁ הוּא – For it can be assumed that **the one from whom it fell despairs** of ever recovering it. אַף עַל גַּב דְּחָזְיֵיהּ דְּאַיְיתִי אַרְבְּלָא וְקָא מְרַבֵּל – This is so **even though [the finder] sees that [the owner] brings a sieve and is sifting** the sand. For it can be assumed that he is sifting only because מֵימַר אָמַר – **he says** to himself, כִּי הֵיכִי דִּנְפוּל מִינַּאי דִּידִי – **"Just as my [coin] fell from me,** נְפוּל מֵאִינִישׁ אַחֲרִינָא – **so too [a coin] has fallen from another person;** וּמַשְׁכַּחְנָא מִידֵּי – perhaps **I will find something** by sifting."[12]

## Mishnah

The Mishnah discusses the laws of articles found within a business establishment or amongst merchandise:

מָצָא בַּחֲנוּת – If [one] **found** articles **in a store,** הֲרֵי אֵלּוּ שֶׁלּוֹ – **they belong to [the finder].**[13] בֵּין הַתֵּיבָה וְלַחֶנְוָנִי – If, however, he found them **between the counter and the storekeeper,** שֶׁל חֶנְוָנִי – they belong **to the storekeeper.**[14] לִפְנֵי שׁוּלְחָנִי – If someone found coins **in front of a moneychanger,**[15] הֲרֵי אֵלּוּ שֶׁלּוֹ – **they belong to [the finder].**[16] בֵּין הַכִּסֵּא וְלַשּׁוּלְחָנִי – If, however, he found them **between the stool**[17] **and the moneychanger,** הֲרֵי אֵלּוּ שֶׁל שׁוּלְחָנִי – **they belong to the moneychanger.** הַלּוֹקֵחַ פֵּירוֹת מֵחֲבֵירוֹ – If **one purchases produce from his fellow,** אוֹ שֶׁשִּׁילַּח לוֹ חֲבֵירוֹ פֵּירוֹת – **or his fellow sends him produce,** וּמָצָא בָּהֶן מָעוֹת – **and he finds coins among it,** הֲרֵי אֵלּוּ שֶׁלּוֹ – **they belong to him.** אִם הָיוּ צְרוּרִין – However, **if [the coins] were tied** and **bundled** so that they are identifiable,[18] נוֹטֵל וּמַכְרִיז – **he must take** them **and announce** his find.

## Gemara

The Gemara presents another ruling concerning coins found at a moneychanger:

אָמַר רַבִּי אֶלְעָזָר – **R' Elazar said:** אֲפִילּוּ מוּנָּחִין עַל גַּבֵּי שׁוּלְחָן – **Even** coins **lying on top of the counter** belong to the

NOTES

6. *Leviticus* 19:13. Since the owner had not yet despaired of recovering his object when the finder picked it up, it was still considered in the owner's possession at that time. By taking the article with intent to steal, it is as if the finder took the article from the owner's courtyard – in violation of the Biblical prohibition against stealing (*Ritva*).

7. *Deuteronomy* 22:1.

8. *Deuteronomy* 22:3. By stealing the coin instead of retrieving it to return it, the finder has failed to fulfill the positive mitzvah to return a lost article. In addition, he has violated the prohibition against hiding one's eyes from retrieving a lost article.

9. *Tosafos* write that this applies only to the prohibition of לֹא תוּכַל לְהִתְעַלֵּם; by not returning the coin before *ye'ush,* the finder can no longer fulfill this obligation. But when he eventually returns the coin, he will no longer be in violation of the prohibition against stealing, because he no longer holds stolen property. Similarly, when he returns the coin, he will have fulfilled his obligation to return a lost article, and will no longer be in violation of הָשֵׁב תְּשִׁיבֵם. This issue, however, is the subject of much dispute among the Rishonim (see *Shitah Mekubetzes*).

10. In this case, the finder will be in violation of the mitzvah of הָשֵׁב תְּשִׁיבֵם, which is applicable from the moment an object is taken until it is actually returned. He did not, however, violate the prohibition against stealing, because theft is defined as the physical expropriation of an object from the owner's possession [see *Bava Kamma* 79b]. Here, though, when the finder picked up the coin, he intended to return it; his "theft" occurred when it was already in his physical control (*Rashi*; see also *Ritva*).

Similarly, this finder did not violate the prohibition of לֹא תוּכַל לְהִתְעַלֵּם, for that prohibition applies to one who encounters a lost object and refrains from taking it to return it to its owner. Here, though, the finder initially took the object to return it, and only later changed his mind. Rava therefore rules that the finder has violated only the mitzvah of הָשֵׁב תְּשִׁיבֵם (*Rashi*).

11. The commandment לֹא תוּכַל לְהִתְעַלֵּם prohibits someone from failing to pick up an article and return it to its owner before *ye'ush* [hiding one's eyes from it]. In this case the finder did just that – he failed to pick up the object [before the owner despaired of it] (see *Rashi*).

However, he was not guilty of stealing, because he picked up the object only after the owner had despaired of recovering it; hence, it was no longer in the owner's possession. He also is not obligated in the positive mitzvah of הָשֵׁב תְּשִׁיבֵם because he picked up the object after *ye'ush*; the requirement to return lost property applies only to articles picked up before *ye'ush.*

12. Since it is so unlikely that the owner would ever find his coin, we assume that he has despaired of recovering it. The fact that he is sifting the sand can be attributed to his looking to find other coins in the sand (see *Meiri*).

13. The Mishnah refers to articles bearing no identifying marks that were found in a store. Since a store is open to the public, any customer who lost such an article there certainly despaired of ever recovering it (*Rashi;* cf. *Rosh*). Hence, any finder may acquire it.

14. In the Mishnah's time, the storekeeper would sit in front of the counter and reach behind him to take merchandise from it to sell. He would then take the money he received and deposit it into the counter. Therefore, anything found between the counter and the storekeeper was surely lost by the storekeeper.

15. Literally: "a table keeper." One of the trades during Mishnaic times was moneychanging, i.e. exchanging coins of different denominations for a nominal fee. The moneychanger would set up a table between himself and his customers on which both placed their money. [Apparently, the "table" consisted of a flat surface that was placed upon a stool] (*Rashi*).

16. It is presumed that the money had been lost by the customers, because had the moneychanger lost it, it would have been found between him and the table (*Rashi*). Since the moneychanger is open to the public, any customer that dropped money, which has no *simanim*, surely despairs of ever recovering it.

17. Upon which the "table" rested (see note 15).

18. I.e. the owner can identify either the type of knot or number of coins (*Rashi*).

שנפל משנים חייב להחזיר מאי טעמא ההוא דנפל מיניה לא מיאש מימר אמר מכדי איניש אחרינא לא הוה בהדאי אלא האי נקיטנא ליה ואמינא ליה אנת הוא דשקלתיה בשלשה אינו חייב להחזיר מאי טעמא ההוא דנפל מיניה ודאי מיאש מימר אמר מכדי תרי הוו בהדאי אי נקיטנא להאי אמר לא שקלתיה ואי נקיטנא להאי אמר לא שקלתיה אמר רבא האי דאמרת בשלשה אינו חייב להחזיר לא אמרן אלא דלית ביה שוה פרוטה לכל חד וחד אבל אית ביה שוה פרוטה לכל חד וחד חייב להחזיר מאי טעמא אימור שותפי נינהו ולא מיאשו איכא דאמרי אמר רבא [א]אע"ג דלית ביה אלא שוה שתי פרוטות חייב להחזיר מאי טעמא אימור שותפי נינהו וחד מניהו אחולי אחליה למנתיה גבי חבריה ואמר רבא [ב]ראה סלע שנפלה נטלה לפני יאוש על מנת לגוזלה עובר בכולן משום א) לא תגזול ומשום ב) השב תשיבם ומשום ג) לא תוכל להתעלם ואע"ג דהדרה לאחר יאוש (א)מתנה הוא דיהיב ליה ואיסורא דעבד עבד [ג]נטלה לפני יאוש על מנת להחזירה ולאחר יאוש נתכוין לגוזלה עובר משום השב תשיבם [ד]המתין לה עד שנתיאשו הבעלים ונטלה (ב)אינו עובר אלא משום לא תוכל להתעלם בלבד (ג)אמר רבא [ה]האי מאן דחזי דנפל זוזי מחבריה בי חלתא ואשכחיה ושקליה לא מיחייב לאהדורי ליה מאי טעמא ההוא דנפל מיניה מיאש הוא אע"ג דחזייה דאייתי ארבלא וקא מרבל מימר אמר כי היכי דנפול מינאי דידי הכי (א) (ה)נפול מאיניש אחרינא [א] ומשכחנא מידי:

מתני' [ו]מצא בחנות הרי אלו שלו בין התיבה ולחנוני של חנוני לפני שולחני הרי אלו שלו בין הכסא ולשולחני הרי אלו של שולחני [ז]הלוקח פירות מחבירו או ששילח לו חבירו פירות ומצא בהן מעות הרי אלו שלו אם היו צרורין נוטל ומכריז: גמ' אמר רבי אלעזר [ח]אפילו מונחין על גבי שולחן תנן לפני שולחני הרי אלו שלו הא על גבי שולחן דשולחני איפא סיפא בין הכסא ולשולחני של שולחני הא על גבי שולחן שלו אלא (ז)מהא ליכא למשמע מינה ורבי אלעזר הא מנא ליה אמר רבא מתניתין קשיתיה מאי אריא דתני בין הכסא לשולחני של שולחני ליתני על (ב) שולחן אי נמי מצא בשולחנות כדקתני רישא מצא בחנות שלו (ח)אלא ש"מ אפי' מונחין על גבי שולחן הרי אלו שלו: הלוקח פירות מחבירו וכו': אמר ריש לקיש משום רבי ינאי לא שנו אלא

בלוקח

---

**רש"י**

נקיטנא ליה כו'. משבענא ליה שבועת היסת ולא נתייאש מיד כשמשמש ולא מצא ונמצא שבא ליד זה לפני יאוש והלכה כאביי: אי נקיטנא וכו'. ואינו יכול להשביעו בטענת שמא שאין נשבעין בטענת שמא אלא אותן השנויין במשנה ואלו נשבעים שלא בטענה כו' (שבועות דף מה.) וא"ת הא מקמי יאוש אתי לידיה ואוקימנא הלכתא כאביי ביע"ל קג"ם הא אמרן דמעות מידע ידיע מיד כרבי יצחק דאמר אדם עשוי למשמש בכיסו כו' (לעיל דף כא:): אימור שותפי נינהו. בסלע זו ונאמנים זה על זה ואין האחד חושד את חבירו בחלקו ולכי מישמש בכיסו ולא מצאה לא אייאש מימר אמר אחד מן השותפים מצאה ולצערני הוא שותק ונמצא כשבאת ליד זה לפני יאוש באת לידו והא אוקמיה כאביי הלכך אף ע"ג דסלע דבר שאין בו סימן הוא חייב להחזיר אבל כי אין בו שלש פרוטות מה נפשך אי שותפין הן בו אין כאן משום השבת אבידה ואם של אחד מהם הוא או של השנים נואשו ואמרו חברנו זה גנב הוא והרי משמש ואמר לא לקחתיו אחד מכם לקחו וגנבו מחבירו: אימור שותפי נינהו. ומהימני אהדדי ואין חושדין זה את זה ונמצאת שבאת ליד זה לפני יאוש: ראה סלע שנפלה. ולא גרסינן משנים: נטלה לפני יאוש. שלא שהה כדי למשמש זה בכיסו: עובר משום השב תשיבם. לא תגזול לא שייך אלא בשעת נטילה כמו ויגזול את החנית מיד המצרי (שמואל ב כג) כדאמר בבבא קמא (עט:) לא תוכל להתעלם אינה אזהרה אלא לכובש את עיניו ונמנע מלהציל הלכך הנוטלה על מנת להחזיר ולאחר יאוש נתכוין לגוזלה אין כאן מתעלם אבל השב תשיבם איכא משנטל עד שישיבנה: המתין לה כו'. בשעה שראה אותה ולא נטלה להחזירה: עובר בלא תוכל להתעלם. שהרי העלים עיניו: בי חלתא. בין החולות: ארבלא. כברה: מתני' מצא בחנות הרי אלו שלו. בדבר שאין בו סימן קאי דההוא דנפל מיניה מיאש שהכל נכנסים לשם: בין התיבה. שהחנוני יושב לפניה ותמיד נוטל ממנה ונותן לפניו ומוכר ומעות שנותנין לו נותן [ו]לתיבה ולא נפל שום דבר אלא מיד חנוני: שולחני. מחליף מעות ונותן מטבעותיו בשולחן שלפניו והבאין להחליף אף הן נותנין שם מעותיהן: הרי אלו שלו. דאמרינן מן הבאין נפלו שהרי השולחן מפסיק בין שולחני למעות שנמצאו ואם מן השולחני נפלו היה להם להמצא בינו לכסא שהשולחן מונח עליו: הלוקח פירות מחבירו. מפרש בגמרא: ואם היו צרורין. הוי סימן או קשר או מנין שבהם: גמ' אמר רבי אלעזר אפילו מונחין על גבי שולחן. נראה בעיני דלא גרסינן צרורין: לפני. משמע על גבי קרקע: לתני על גבי שולחן. של שולחני וכ"ש בין הכסא ולשולחני: אי נמי. [ב] ניתני ברישא מצא בשולחנות כדקתני רישא מצא בחנות מדנקט לפני השולחני אף על השולחן במשמע:

בלוקח

---

**תוספות**

שנפל משנים חייב להחזיר. אפילו אין בו סימן דאינו מתיאש לעולם ומיירי שהניחם בקשוה יחד קודם שבא זה ומצאה ולכך סבור ודאי שחבירו לקחה כשבקשה עמו ואינו מתיאש לעולם שמחשב יחזירנה לי כשאביישנו ברבים ואוכיח לו שמצאו ולכך נמי אמרינן בסמוך אימור שותפי נינהו כיון שראינום מחפשין יחד ומה שפרש"י מטעם יאוש שלא מדעת אין נראה דהא רבא סבר דהוי יאוש ומפרש בסמוך מילתיה דרב נחמן ואין סברא לומר דהדר ביה בתר דאיתותב ומה שפירש נמי שישביענו שבועת היסת קשה וכי ישביענו בטענת ספק ומיהו י"ל דטוען ברי לפי שלא היה שם אחר כי אם הוא אך קשה דבימי בר קפרא עדיין לא נתקנה שבועת היסת ונראה לפרש שבלא שבועה אינו מתיאש לעולם כדפרישית: לא אמרן אלא כי לית ביה שוה פרוטה לכל חד וחד. דהיינו כי ליכא שלש פרוטות אלא ב' דמה נפשך אין צריך להחזיר אם שלשתן שותפין אין כאן כדי השבה לכל אחד ואם אינן שותפין האובד יתיאש כי השנים ידחוהו כל אחד על חבירו וא"ת וניחוש שמא שנים הם שותפין דאין חושדים זה את זה ולא מתיאשי שניהם יטענו בטענת ברי לשלישי וכן באיכא דאמרי אמאי קאמר הני שותפי נינהו וחד מינייהו אחיל מנתיה גבי חבריה נימא אימור שנים מהם הם שותפין ואין חושדין זה את זה ויאמרו ודאי שהשלישי לקחה וי"ל דודאי כי ליכא אלא שנים האחד יטען ברי לחבירו אבל כשיש שלשה לא יטענו טענת ברי לשלישי אפי' יהיו שנים מהן שותפין דנהי דאין חושדים זה את זה מ"מ סבור שהשותף לקחה לצערו עד זמן מרובה כדאמר בסמוך דאי איכא שלש פרוטות דאינם מתיאשים שסבורים שחבריהם מצאם ומעלים מהם להקניט ולצער עד זמן מרובה ולבסוף יחזירנה ועי"ל דכיון שלשה הולכין יחד אין לומר שותפין שנים מהם אלא או כולם שותפין או כל אחד ואחד לבדו: מתנה בעלמא הוא דיהיב ליה. וא"ת והלא לאו דלא תגזול מקרי ניתק לעשה בפ' שילוח הקן (חולין דף קמא.) א"כ כיון דלענין גזילה לא מקרי מתנה גם השב תשיבם למה לא תיקן וי"ל דלא קאי אלא על לאו דלא תוכל להתעלם שעבר שלא החזיר קודם יאוש: אינו עובר אלא משום השב תשיבם. ובפ"ק דקדושין (דף לד. ושם ד"ה מעקה) דחשיב השבת אבידה עשה שאין הזמן גרמא היינו בענין שבכאן וא"ת ואמאי ליכא לאו דלא תגזול אי משום דבהתירא אתא לידיה הלא בכובש שכר שכיר איכא לאו כדאמר בפרק איזהו נשך (לקמן דף סא. ושם) וי"ל דהתם כשמתכוין לגזול לא נתיאשו הבעלים והכא כבר נתיאשו: אפילו צרורין. רש"י ל"ג צרורין דאם היה בו סימן מכריז וי"ל דגרים ליה ומיירי דאיכא רוב עכו"ם מצויים שם והם שלו ואע"ג דאיכא סימן דהלכה כר' שמעון בן אלעזר בהא:

בלוקח

---

**עין משפט נר מצוה**

עז א מיי' פי"ד מהל' אבידה הל' ח סמג עשין עד טוש"ע ח"מ סי' רסב סעיף ג וסעיף ד:
עח ב ג ד מיי' שם הל' ו ז סמג שם טוש"ע ח"מ סי' רנט סעיף א:
עט ה מיי' שם הל' ט סמג שם טוש"ע ח"מ סי' רסב סעיף יד:
פ ו מיי' פט"ז שם הלכה ד ה ועיין בהשגות ובמ"מ סמג שם טוש"ע ח"מ סי' רס סעיף ה:
פא ז מיי' שם הל' ו סמג שם טוש"ע ח"מ סי' רסב סעיף יח:
פב ח מיי' שם הלכה ה סמג שם טוש"ע ח"מ סי' רס סעיף ה:

**רבינו חננאל**

חייב להכריז דלא נתיאש. נפל מתוך שלשה אין חייב להכריז דודאי מיאש וכו' ורבא פליג עליה בהא. אמר רבא סלע שנפלה מחבירו נטלה לפני יאוש עובר משום בל תגזול ומשום השב תשיבם ומשום לא תוכל להתעלם אע"ג דאהדרה למרה לבתר יאוש איסורא כבר עבדא והשתא מתנה הוא דיהיב ליה. נטלה לפני יאוש על מנת להחזירה ולאחר יאוש נמלך לנוטלה עובר משום השב תשיבם. המתין עד שנתיאשו הבעלים ונטלה אינו עובר אלא משום לא תוכל להתעלם. אמר רבא מאן דחזא דנפל זוזא מחבריה בי חלתא ושקליה אינו חייב להחזירו אע"ג דחזיה דמייתי ארבולי ומארבל וכו': מתני' מצא בחנות הרי אלו שלו. בין תיבה לחנווני הרי אלו לחנווני. לפני שולחני למוצאן בין כסא לשולחני הרי הן לשולחני. ודייק ר' אלעזר מדקתני בין כסא לשולחני הרי הן לשולחני הא על השולחן אפי' צרורין ומונחין הרי הן של מוצאן ותוב מדלא קתני סיפא מצא בחנות של שולחני הרי אלו שלו כדקתני רישא ש"מ אפי' על השולחן עצמו הרי הן למוצאן. לקח פירות מחבירו ומצא בתוכן מעות או שילח לו חבירו פירות

**תורה אור השלם**

א) לֹא תַעֲשֹׁק אֶת רֵעֲךָ וְלֹא תִגְזֹל לֹא תָלִין פְּעֻלַּת שָׂכִיר אִתְּךָ עַד בֹּקֶר: [ויקרא יט, יג]

ב) לֹא תִרְאֶה אֶת שׁוֹר אָחִיךָ אוֹ אֶת שֵׂיוֹ נִדָּחִים וְהִתְעַלַּמְתָּ מֵהֶם הָשֵׁב תְּשִׁיבֵם לְאָחִיךָ: [דברים כב, א]

ג) וְכֵן תַּעֲשֶׂה לַחֲמֹרוֹ וְכֵן תַּעֲשֶׂה לְשִׂמְלָתוֹ וְכֵן תַּעֲשֶׂה לְכָל אֲבֵדַת אָחִיךָ אֲשֶׁר תֹּאבַד מִמֶּנּוּ וּמְצָאתָהּ לֹא תוּכַל לְהִתְעַלֵּם: [דברים כב, ג]

**מסורת הש"ס**

א) [עיין תוס' בבא קמא סו: ד"ה רבא], ב) [גירסת הנמוקי יוסף ונטלה עובר משום וכו' ו... משמע ברש"י ד"ה עובר], ג) [נ"ל ואמר וכן איתא ברי"ף ורא"ש], ד) [עי' נדרים עב.], ברכות כה. וש"נ, ה) [עי' רי"ף ורא"ש גירסאות אחרות, ועי' מהרש"א], ו) נ"ל לתוכה מהרש"ל.

**הגהות הב"ח**

(א) גמ' הכי נמי נפיל מאיניש אחרינא: (ב) שם לתני על גבי שלחן אי נמי

**הגהות הגר"א**

[א] גמ' ומשכחנא. (נא) אותיות נא ממלא ומשכחנא מוקפים [ב] רש"י ד"ה א"נ ניתני ברישא. נ"... והרמב"ם מפרש דקאי ע... סיפא בין הכסא כו' ליתני בשולחנות כו' ועהג"... (ועמ"ש רבינו בח"מ סי' רס ס"ק טו יז):

**ליקוטי רש"י**

וקא מרבל. מירב לשון כברה שמנענעין אותה כמו אייתי ארבלא וקא מרבל באלו מציאות [חולין מט.].

שֶׁנָּפַל מִשְּׁנַיִם – **that fell from** one of **two** people, חַיָּיב לְהַחֲזִיר – **he is obligated to return** it. מַאי טַעְמָא – **What is the reason?** הַהוּא דְּנָפַל מִינֵּיהּ לֹא מְיָאֵשׁ – For **the one from whom it fell does not despair** of it, מֵימַר אָמַר – because **he surely says** to himself: מִכְּדִי אִינִישׁ אַחֲרִינָא לֹא הֲוָה בַּהֲדַאי אֶלָּא הַאי – **Let us see, no other person besides this** companion of mine **was with me** when I dropped the coin. נְקִיטְנָא לֵיהּ וְאָמֵינָא לֵיהּ – **I will** therefore **confront him and say to him,** אַנְתְּ הוּא דְּשַׁקַלְתֵּיהּ – **"You are [the one] who took it!"**[1] בִּשְׁלֹשָׁה – **In** a case where the coin fell from one of **three** people, אֵינוֹ חַיָּיב לְהַחֲזִיר – **[the finder] is not obligated to return** it. מַאי טַעְמָא – **What is the reason?** הַהוּא דְּנָפַל מִינֵּיהּ וַדַּאי מְיָאֵשׁ – For **the one from whom it fell certainly despairs** of it, מֵימַר אָמַר – because **he surely says** to himself: מִכְּדִי תְּרֵי הֲווּ בַּהֲדַאי – **Let us see, two** other people **were with me** when I lost the coin. אִי נְקִיטְנָא לְהַאי – Now, **if I confront this** one, אָמַר לֹא שְׁקַלְתֵּיהּ – **he will say, "I did not take it."** וְאִי נְקִיטְנָא לְהַאי – **And if I confront this** other one, אָמַר לֹא שְׁקַלְתֵּיהּ – **he** too **will say, "I did not take it."**[2]

The Gemara qualifies the previous ruling of Rav Nachman:

אָמַר רָבָא – **Rava said:** הַאי דְּאָמְרַת – **That which you** [Rav Nachman] **said,** בִּשְׁלֹשָׁה אֵינוֹ חַיָּיב לְהַחֲזִיר – **"In** a case where a coin fell from one of **three** people, **[the finder] is not obligated to return it,"** is not always true. לֹא אֲמָרָן אֶלָּא דְּלֵית בֵּיהּ שָׁוֶה פְּרוּטָה לְכָל חַד וְחַד – **It can be said only when [the coin] does not contain a** ***perutah's*** **worth for each and every one** of the three [i.e. it is worth less than three *perutos*]. אֲבָל אִית בֵּיהּ שָׁוֶה פְּרוּטָה לְכָל חַד וְחַד – **But if [the coin] does contain a** ***perutah's*** **worth for each and every one,** חַיָּיב לְהַחֲזִיר – **[the finder] is indeed obligated to return** it. מַאי טַעְמָא – **What is the reason?** אֵימוֹר שׁוּתָּפֵי נִינְהוּ – For it is possible to **say that** [the three **people] are partners** in the coin, וְלֹא מְיָאֲשׁוּ – **and,** hence **they do not despair** of it.[3]

The Gemara presents an alternative version of Rava's statement:

אִיכָּא דְּאָמְרֵי אָמַר רָבָא – **There are those who say** that **Rava stated** the following ruling: אַף עַל גַּב דְּלֵית בֵּיהּ אֶלָּא שָׁוֶה שְׁתֵּי פְּרוּטוֹת – **Even** in a case **where [the coin] has a value of only two** ***perutos***, חַיָּיב לְהַחֲזִיר – **[the finder] is obligated to return** it. מַאי טַעְמָא – **What is the reason?** אֵימוֹר שׁוּתָּפֵי נִינְהוּ – For it is possible to **say that they were** all **partners** in the coin, וְחַד מִנַּיְיהוּ אַחוּלֵי אַחֲלֵיהּ לְמְנָתֵיהּ גַּבֵּי חַבְרֵיהּ – **and one of them relinquished his share in favor of his partners.**[4]

The Gemara presents the first of several rulings that Rava issued to define the various Biblical obligations that pertain to the return of lost property:

וְאָמַר רָבָא – **Rava said:** רָאָה סֶלַע שֶׁנָּפְלָה – If **one saw a** ***sela*** **that fell** from its owner, נְטָלָהּ לִפְנֵי יֵאוּשׁ עַל מְנָת לְגוֹזְלָהּ – **and he took it before the** owner **despaired** of it, **with the intention to steal it,**[5] עוֹבֵר בְּכוּלָּן – **he has transgressed all** [of the **Biblical commandments**] that are conceivably relevant here

NOTES

1. That is, the owner can bring the other person to court and force him to take a *hesess* oath ("oath of incitement"), that he did not find the coin [see above, 5a note 26]. Since the owner has this recourse, he does not immediately despair of recovering his coin; hence, the finder must return it (*Rashi*; cf. *Tosafos*, other Rishonim).

[It is important to note that the owner will eventually despair of recovering the coin, for, in reality, the bystander found it, not the owner's companion. Therefore, when forced to take the oath, the companion will swear truthfully to defend his claim that he did not take the coin. At that time, the owner, realizing he no longer has any legal recourse, will despair of ever recovering his coin.] Nevertheless, since the bystander picked up the coin before the owner's *ye'ush,* he is obligated to return it in accordance with the Gemara's decision above (22b) in favor of Abaye's view (*Rashi*; cf. *Tosafos,* other Rishonim cited by *Shitah Mekubetzes*). [This ruling, then, applies even to a coin that has no *siman* – see note 3 below.]

2. In this situation, the owner is not certain which of his two companions found the coin. Therefore, since generally a defendant is not required to take an oath when the plaintiff is not certain of his claim against him, the owner will have no recourse against his companions and will despair of recovering his coin. Hence, the bystander who found the coin may keep it (*Rashi*). This second ruling of Rav Nachman, then, accords with the statement he made above (26a) in explanation of the Mishnah.

In this case there is no concern that the bystander found the coin before the owner's *ye'ush*, because a person becomes aware of a loss of money immediately, as we learned above (21b). Therefore, we can assume that having no recourse with which to regain his coin, the owner will have despaired before the bystander picked it up (*Rashi*).

3. The finder must be concerned that the three people in the group own the coin in partnership. If that were the case, the one who dropped the coin would not despair upon discovering that he lost the coin; rather, he would assume that one of his partners found it. Even if the others deny finding the coin, he will think that one of them actually did find it but was teasing him. Hence, even if the one who dropped the coin eventually despairs of recovering the coin, the finder may not keep it because he picked it up before the owner had reached that state of mind. The finder must therefore return the coin, even though it has no *siman* (*Rashi*).

Rav Nachman's ruling – allowing the finder to keep the coin – thus applies only in a case where the coin was worth less that three *perutos,* for then the relationship of the three people to each other is irrelevant. If they all owned the coin in partnership, then it would not have sufficient value for it to be obligated to be returned. [The Gemara states below (27a) that the Torah does not require an object worth less than a *perutah* to be returned. In this case as well, since the individual share of each partner is worth less than a *perutah,* the finder is not obligated to return it – see *Ritva*.] If, on the other hand, the coin was owned by only one of them, there would be no obligation to return it – even if the owner had a *perutah's* interest in the coin – because the owner despairs of recovering a coin when there are two people that must be confronted as Rav Nachman explained above. Even if two of the three are partners – in which case each would hold a *perutah* interest in the coin – they would despair immediately of recovering the coin. That is so because they would suspect the third person of being a thief, but could nevertheless not confront him with certainty since he could accuse one of the partners of stealing it from the other (*Rashi*).

4. Even though the coin is worth only two *perutos,* we must still be concerned that the three people were partners and consequently trusted each other. In such a case, the one who dropped the coin would likely not despair of recovering it from the others, and the finder must thus return it. In this scenario the fact that each share would be worth less than a *perutah* – and, hence, not subject to the obligation of return – does not help the finder, because it is possible that one of the partners relinquished his share in the coin, raising the remaining partners' shares to one *perutah* each (*Rashi*).

According to this version of Rava, Rav Nachman – who awards the coin to the finder – must have stated his ruling where the coin was worth even less than two *perutos.* In that case, even if one of the partners relinquished his rights, the remaining two would each hold less than a *perutah* interest in the coin. To suspect that two of the partners relinquished their rights – giving the third a *perutah's* worth – is too far fetched a possibility to consider (*Shitah Mekubetzes*).

5. In this case, an unaccompanied owner dropped a coin. A bystander [who intended to steal it] picked it up immediately – before the owner had a chance to feel his purse and become aware of the loss (*Rashi*).

*R' Peretz* (cited in *Shitah Mekubetzes*) objects to *Rashi's* implication that it is possible to pick up a lost coin before the owner has discovered his loss, because throughout this chapter the Gemara holds it to be axiomatic that a person despairs of recovering his money immediately after its loss (see, for example, note 2 above). *R' Peretz* therefore understands this case to be referring to a coin that could be identified by the way in which it was wrapped. In that case, we do not assume that the owner has despaired unless we heard him say so. [See also *Rashba* for an alternative reading of our Gemara.]

שנפל משנים חייב להחזיר מאי טעמא ההוא דנפל מיניה לא מיאש מימר אמר מכדי איניש אחרינא לא הוה בהדאי אלא האי נקיטנא ליה ואמינא ליה אנת הוא דשקלתיה בשלשה אינו חייב להחזיר מאי טעמא ההוא דנפל מיניה ודאי מיאש מימר אמר מכדי תרי הוו בהדאי אי נקיטנא להאי אמר לא שקלתיה ואי נקיטנא להאי אמר לא שקלתיה אמר רבא האי דאמרת בשלשה אינו חייב להחזיר לא אמרן אלא דלית ביה שוה פרוטה לכל חד וחד אבל אית ביה שוה פרוטה לכל חד וחד חייב להחזיר מאי טעמא אימור שותפי נינהו ולא מיאשו איכא דאמרי אמר רבא [א] אע"ג דלית ביה אלא שוה שתי פרוטות חייב להחזיר מאי טעמא אימור שותפי נינהו וחד מנייהו אחולי אחליה למנתיה גבי חבריה ואמר רבא [ב] ראה סלע שנפלה נטלה לפני יאוש על מנת לגוזלה עובר בכולן משום (א) לא תגזול ומשום (ב) השב תשיבם ומשום (ג) לא תוכל להתעלם ואע"ג דהדרה לאחר יאוש (א) מתנה הוא דיהיב ליה ואיסורא דעבד עבד [ג] נטלה לפני יאוש על מנת להחזירה ולאחר יאוש נתכוין לגוזלה עובר משום השב תשיבם [ד] המתין לה עד שנתיאשו הבעלים ונטלה (ב) אינו עובר אלא משום לא תוכל להתעלם בלבד (ג) אמר רבא [ה] האי מאן דחזי דנפל זוזי מחבריה בי חלתא ואשכחיה ושקליה לא מיחייב לאהדורי ליה מאי טעמא ההוא דנפל מיניה מיאש הוא אע"ג דחזייה דאייתי ארבלא וקא מרבל מימר אמר כי היכי דנפול מינאי דידי הכי (א) [ו] נפול מאיניש אחרינא [א] ומשכחנא מידי:

**מתני'** [ו] מצא בחנות הרי אלו שלו בין התיבה ולחנוני של חנוני לפני שולחני הרי אלו שלו בין הכסא ולשולחני הרי אלו של שולחני [ז] הלוקח פירות מחבירו או ששילח לו חבירו פירות ומצא בהן מעות הרי אלו שלו אם היו צרורין נוטל ומכריז: **גמ'** אמר רבי אלעזר [ח] אפילו מונחין על גבי שולחן תנן לפני שולחני הרי אלו שלו הא על גבי שולחן דשולחני אימא סיפא בין הכסא ולשולחני של שולחני הא על גבי שולחן שלו אלא [ד] מהא ליכא למשמע מינה ורבי אלעזר הא מנא ליה אמר רבא מתניתין קשיתיה מאי אריא דתני בין הכסא לשולחני של שולחני ליתני על (ב) שולחן אי נמי מצא בשולחנות כדקתני רישא מצא בחנות שלו [ה] אלא ש"מ אפי' מונחין על גבי שולחן הרי אלו שלו: הלוקח פירות מחבירו וכו': אמר ריש לקיש משום רבי ינאי לא שנו אלא בלוקח

---

**רש"י**

נקיטנא ליה כו'. משבענא ליה שבועת היסת ולא נתייאש מיד כשמשמש ולא מצא ונמצא שבא ליד זה לפני יאוש והלכה כאביי: אי נקיטנא וכו'. ואינו יכול להשביעו בטענת שמא שאין נשבעין בטענת שמא אלא אותן השנויין במשנה ואלו נשבעים שלא בטענה כו' (שבועות דף מה.) וא"ת הא מקמי יאוש אתי לידיה ואוקימנא הלכתא כאביי ביע"ל קג"ם הא אמרן דמעות מידע ידיע מיד כרבי יצחק דאמר אדם עשוי למשמש בכיסו כו' (לעיל דף כא:): **אימור שותפי נינהו.** בסלע זו ונאמנים זה על זה ואין האחד חושד את חבירו בחלקו ולכי מישמש בכיסו ולא מצאה לא אייאש מימר אמר אחד מן השותפים מצאה ולצערני הוא שותק ונמצא כשבאת ליד זה לפני יאוש באת לידו והא אוקמיה כאביי הלכך אף ע"ג דסלע דבר שאין בו סימן הוא חייב להחזיר אבל כי אין בו שלש פרוטות מה נפשך אי שותפין הן בו אין כאן משום השבת אבידה ואם של אחד מהם הוא או של השנים נואשו ואמרו חברנו זה גנב הוא והרי משמט ואמר לא לקחתיו אחד מכם לקחו וגנבו מחבירו: **אימור שותפי נינהו.** ומהימני אהדדי ואין חושדין זה את זה ונמצאת שבאת ליד זה לפני יאוש: ראה סלע שנפלה. ולא גרסינן משנים: נטלה לפני יאוש. שלא שהה כדי למשמש זה בכיסו: **עובר משום השב תשיבם.** לא תגזול לא שייך אלא בשעת נטילה כמו ויגזול את החנית מיד המצרי (שמואל ב כג) כדאמר בבבא קמא (עט:) לא תוכל להתעלם אינה אזהרה אלא לכובש את עיניו ונמנע מלהציל הלכך הנוטלה על מנת להחזיר ולאחר יאוש נתכוין לגוזלה אין כאן מתעלם אבל השב תשיבם איכא משנטל עד שישיבנה: המתין לה כו'. בשעה שראה אותה ולא נטלה להחזירה: **עובר בלא תוכל להתעלם.** שהרי העלים עיניו: **בי חלתא.** בין החולות: **ארבלא.** כברה: **מתני' מצא בחנות הרי אלו שלו.** בדבר שאין בו סימן קאי דההוא דנפל מיניה מיאש שהכל נכנסים לשם: **בין התיבה.** שהחנוני יושב לפניה ותמיד נוטל ממנה ונותן לפניו ומוכר ומעות שנותנין לו נותן [ו] לתיבה ולא נפל שום דבר אלא מיד חנוני: **שולחני.** מחליף מעות ונותן מטבעותיו בשולחן שלפניו והבאין להחליף אף הן נותנין שם מעותיהן: **הרי אלו שלו.** דאמרינן מן הבאין נפלו שהרי השולחן מפסיק בין שולחני למעות שנמצאו ואם מן השולחני נפלו היה להם להמצא בינו לכסא שהשולחן מונח עליו: **הלוקח פירות מחבירו.** מפרש בגמרא: **ואם היו צרורין.** הוי סימן או קשר או מנין שבהם: **גמ' אמר רבי אלעזר אפילו מונחין על גבי שולחן.** נראה בעיני דלא גרסינן צרורין: **לפני.** משמע על גבי קרקע: **לתני על גבי שולחן.** של שולחני וכ"ש בין הכסא ולשולחני: **אי נמי.** [ב] ניתני ברישא מצא בשולחנות כדקתני רישא מצא בחנות מדנקט לפני השולחני אף על השולחן במשמע:



---

**תוספות**

**שנפל** משנים חייב להחזיר. אפילו אין בו סימן דאינו מתיאש לעולם ומיירי ששניהם בקשוה יחד קודם שבא זה ומצאה ולכך סבור ודאי שחבירו לקחה כשבקשה עמו ואינו מתיאש לעולם שמחשב יחזירנה לי כשאביישנו ברבים ואוכיח לו שמצאו ולכך נמי אמרינן בסמוך אימור שותפי נינהו כיון שראינום מחפשין יחד ומה שפרש"י מטעם יאוש שלא מדעת אין נראה דהא רבא סבר דהוי יאוש ומפרש בסמוך מילתיה דרב נחמן ואין סברא לומר דהדר ביה בתר דאיתותב ומה שפירש נמי שישביענו שבועת היסת קשה וכי ישביענו בטענת ספק ומיהו י"ל דטוען ברי לפי שלא היה שם אחר כי אם הוא אך קשה דימי בר קפרא עדיין לא נתקנה שבועת היסת ונראה לפרש שבלא שבועה אינו מתיאש לעולם כדפרישית: **לא** אמרן אלא כי לית ביה שוה פרוטה לכל חד וחד. דהיינו כי ליכא שלש פרוטות אלא ב' דמה נפשך אין צריך להחזיר אם שלשתן שותפין אין כאן כדי השבה לכל אחד ואם אין שותפין האובד יתיאש כי השנים ידחוהו כל אחד על חבירו וא"ת וניחוש שמא שנים הם שותפין דאין חושדים זה את זה ולא מתיאשי ששניהם יטענו בטענת ברי לשלישי וכן באיכא דאמרי אמאי קאמר הני שותפי נינהו וחד מינייהו אחיל מנתיה גבי חבריה נימא אימור שנים מהם הם שותפין ואין חושדין זה את זה ויאמרו ודאי שהשלישי לקחה וי"ל דודאי כי ליכא אלא שנים האחד יטען ברי לחבירו אבל כשיש שלשה לא יטענו טענת ברי לשלישי אפי' יהיו שנים מהן שותפין דנהי דאין חושדים זה את זה מ"מ סבור שהשותף לקחה לצערו עד זמן מרובה כדאמר בסמוך דאי איכא שלש פרוטות דאינם מתיאשים שסבורים שחבריהם מצאם ומעלים מהם להקניט ולצער עד זמן מרובה ולבסוף יחזירנה וע"ל דכיון שלשה הולכין יחד אין לומר שותפין שנים מהם אלא או כולם שותפין או כל אחד ואחד לבדו:

**מתנה** בעלמא הוא דיהיב ליה. וא"ת והלא לאו דלא תגזול מקרי ניתק לעשה בפ' שילוח הקן (חולין דף קמא.) א"כ כיון דלענין גזילה לא מקרי מתנה גם השב תשיבם למה לא תיקן וי"ל דלא קאי אלא על לאו דלא תוכל להתעלם שעבר שלא החזיר קודם יאוש: **אינו** עובר אלא משום השב תשיבם. ובפ"ק דקדושין (דף לד. ושם ד"ה מעקה) לחשיב השבת אבידה עשה שאין הזמן גרמא היינו בענין שבכאן וא"ת ואמאי ליכא לאו דלא תגזול אי משום דבהתירא אתא לידיה הלא בכובש שכר שכיר איכא לאו כדאמר בפרק איזהו נשך (לקמן דף סא. ושם) וי"ל דהתם כשמתכוין לגזול לא נתיאשו הבעלים והכא כבר נתיאשו: **אפילו** צרורין. רש"י ל"ג צרורין דאם היה בו סימן מכריז וי"ל דגרים ליה ומיירי דאיכא רוב עכו"ם מצויים שם והם שלו ואע"ג דאיכא סימן דהלכה כר' שמעון בן אלעזר בהא:



---

**עין משפט נר מצוה**

עז א מיי' פי"ד מהל' אבידה הל' ח סמג עשין עד טוש"ע ח"מ סי' רסב סעיף ב וסעיף ד:

עח ב ג ד מיי' שם הל' ו ז סמג שם טוש"ע ח"מ סי' רנט סעיף א:

עט ה מיי' שם הל' ט סמג שם טוש"ע ח"מ סי' רסב סעיף יד:

פ ו מיי' פט"ו שם הלכה ד ה ועיין בהשגות ובמ"מ סמג שם טוש"ע ח"מ סי' רס סעיף ה:

פא ז מיי' שם הל' ו סמג שם טוש"ע ח"מ סי' רסב סעיף יז:

פב ח מיי' שם הלכה ה סמג שם טוש"ע ח"מ סי' רס סעיף ה:

**רבינו חננאל**

חייב להכריז דלא נתיאש. נפל מתוך שלשה אין חייב להכריז דודאי מיאש וכו' ורבא פליג עליה בהא. אמר רבא סלע שנפלה מחבירו נטלה לפני יאוש עובר משום בל תגזול ומשום השב תשיבם ומשום לא תוכל להתעלם אע"ג דאהדרה למרה לבתר יאוש איסורא כבר עבדא והשתא מתנה הוא דיהיב ליה. נטלה לפני יאוש על מנת להחזירה ולאחר יאוש נמלך לנוטלה עובר משום השב תשיבם. המתין עד שנתיאשו הבעלים ונטלה אינו עובר אלא משום לא תוכל להתעלם. אמר רבא מאן דחזא דנפל זוזא מחבריה בי חלתא ושקליה אינו חייב להחזירו אע"ג דחזיה דמייתי ארבולי ומארבל וכו': מתני' מצא בחנות הרי אלו שלו. בין תיבה לחנווני הרי אלו לחנווני. לפני שולחני למוצאן בין כסא לשולחני הרי הן לשולחני. ודייק ר' אלעזר מדקתני בין כסא לשולחני הרי הן לשולחני הא על השולחן אפי' צרורין ומונחין הרי הן של מוצאן ותוב מדלא קתני סיפא מצא בחנות של שולחני הרי אלו שלו כדקתני רישא ש"מ אפי' על השולחן עצמו הרי הן למוצאן. לקח פירות מחבירו ומצא בתוכן מעות או שילח לו חבירו פירות

**תורה אור השלם**

א) לֹא תַעֲשֹׁק אֶת רֵעֲךָ וְלֹא תִגְזֹל לֹא תָלִין פְּעֻלַּת שָׂכִיר אִתְּךָ עַד בֹּקֶר: [ויקרא יט, יג]

ב) לֹא תִרְאֶה אֶת שׁוֹר אָחִיךָ אוֹ אֶת שֵׂיוֹ נִדָּחִים וְהִתְעַלַּמְתָּ מֵהֶם הָשֵׁב תְּשִׁיבֵם לְאָחִיךָ: [דברים כב, א]

ג) וְכֵן תַּעֲשֶׂה לַחֲמֹרוֹ וְכֵן תַּעֲשֶׂה לְשִׂמְלָתוֹ וְכֵן תַּעֲשֶׂה לְכָל אֲבֵדַת אָחִיךָ אֲשֶׁר תֹּאבַד מִמֶּנּוּ וּמְצָאתָהּ לֹא תוּכַל לְהִתְעַלֵּם: [דברים כב, ג]

**מסורת הש"ס**

א) [עיין תוס' בבא קמא סו: ד"ה רבא], ב) [גירסת הנמוקי יוסף ונטלה עובר משום וכו' וכן משמע ברש"י ד"ה עובר], ג) [צ"ל ואמר וכן איתא ברי"ף ורא"ש], ד) [עי' נדרים עב.], ברכות כה וש"נ, ה) [עי' רי"ף ורא"ש גירסאות אחרות, ועיי' מהרש"א], ו) צ"ל לתוכה מהרש"ל.

**הגהות הב"ח**

(א) גמ' הכי נמי נפיל מאיניש אחרינא: (ב) שם לתני על גבי שלחן אי נמי

**הגהות הגר"א**

[א] גמ' ומשכח(נא) אותיות נא ממלה ומשכחנא מוקפים [ב] רש"י ד"ה א"נ ניתני ברישא. נ"ב והרמב"ם מפרש דקאי ע' סיפא בין הכסא כו' ליתני בשולחנות כו' ועהג"ה (ועמ"ש רביגו בח"מ סי' רס ס"ק טו יז):

**ליקוטי רש"י**

וקא מרבל. מירב לשון כברה שמנענעין אותה כמו אייתי ארבלא וקא מרבל באלו מציאות [חולין מט.].

[א] אדשתיך טפי: בכותל חדש מחציו ולחוץ שלו מחציו ולפנים של בעל הבית: אמר רב אשי בסכינא בתר קתא וכיסא בתר שנציה ואלא מתני' דקתני מחציו ולחוץ שלו מחציו ולפנים של בעל הבית ולחזי אי קתא לגאו אי קתא לבר אי שנציה לגאו אי שנציה לבר מתני' גבאודרא ונסכא תנא דאם היה כותל ממולא מהן חולקין פשיטא לא צריכא דמשפע בחד גיסא מהו דתימא אשתפוכי אישתפוך קמ"ל: אם היה משכירו לאחרים אפילו (מצא) בתוך הבית הרי אלו שלו: ואמאי ליזיל בתר בתרא מי לא א)תנן המעות שנמצאו לפני סוחרי בהמה לעולם מעשר בהר הבית חולין ובירושלים בשאר ימות השנה חולין בשעת הרגל הכל מעשר ואמר ר' שמעיה בר זעירא מאי טעמא הואיל ושוקי ירושלים עשוין להתכבד בכל יום אלמא אמרינן קמאי קמאי אזלו והני אחריני נינהו והכא נמי קמא קמא אזל והני דבתרא הוא אמר ריש לקיש משום בר קפרא כגון שעשאו פונדק לשלשה ב) ישראל שמע מינה הלכה כר"ש בן אלעזר ג) אפי' ברוב ישראל אלא אמר רב מנשיא בר יעקב זכגון שעשאו פונדק לשלשה עובדי כוכבים רב נחמן אמר רבה בר אבוה אפי' תימא לשלשה ישראל מאי טעמא ההוא דנפל מיניה מיאש מימר אמר מכדי איניש אחרינא לא הוה בהדי אלא הני אמרי קמייהו כמה זמני ליהדרו לי ולא הדרו לי והשתא ליהדרו אי דעתייהו לאהדורה אהדרוה ניהלי והאי דלא אהדרוה לי בדעתייהו למיגזלה ד) ואזדא רב נחמן לטעמיה דאמר רב נחמן ראה סלע שנפל

## רש"י

דשתיך טפי. העלו חלודה רבה דכולי האי לא שביק להו: סכינא. הנמצא באחד מחורי הכותל: בתר קתא. אזיל אי קתיה לגיו בני הבית נתנוהו שם אי קתא לבר בני רשות הרבים נתנוהו שם שכן דרך אחיזתו וכן כיסא בתר שנציה אשטדל"א בלע"ז: באודרא. מוכין: נסכא. פלטא של כסף: ממולא. מן החפץ שמחזיק כל רוחב הכותל: לא צריכא דמשפע. הכותל לחד גיסא: מהו דתימא. באלי הגובה היה תחילה ואשתפוכי אשתפוך לצד הנמוך קמ"ל: לפני סוחרי בהמה. בירושלים: לעולם. בין בשעת הרגל בין שלא בשעת הרגל: מעשר. שרוב בשר הנאכל בירושלים מעשר לפי שאין אדם שוהה בירושלים עד שיאכל כל מעשרותיו ונותן מעות מעשר לעניי העיר או לאוהביו יושבי העיר ורוב הולאות מעשר לוקחין בהן בהמות לשלמים כדגמר שם שם מעשר משלמים במסכת מנחות (דף פב.): ובהר הבית חולין. ואפילו בשעת הרגל ואע"פ שרוב מעות שבעיר מעשר שעולי רגלים מביאין מעות מעשרותיהן לאכלם לא שבקינן רובא דשתא ואזלינן בתר רגל אלא אמרי' מלפני הרגל נפלו כאן וחולין הן: ובירושלים. בשאר שווקים שבה: בשאר ימות השנה חולין. דרוב מעות שבעיר חולין: ובשעת הרגל מעשר. שרוב מעות העיר מעשר: ואמר רב שמעיה בר זעירא מאי טעם. בירושלים בשעת הרגל מעשר ולא אמרי' מלפני הרגל נפלו כדאמרן בהר הבית: ושוקי ירושלים עשויין להתכבד בכל יום. ואם נפלו שם לפני הרגל כבר מצאום מכבדי השוק אבל הר הבית אין צריך להתכבד בכל יום שאין טיט ועפר קולט שם מתוך שהוא משופע ועוד שאין אדם נכנס שם במנעל ובאבק שעל רגליו: אלמא. בדבר שעשוי להתכבד אמרי' קמאי קמאי אזלו והני אחריני נינהו: הכא נמי. סתם שוכר בית כשהוא יוצא מחפש כל זויותיו ונוטל את שלו ויוצא ונימא האחרונים שכחוהו שאילו הראשונים שכחוהו ה) כבר מצאו האחרונים: לשלשה ישראל. בבת אחת וכל שכן אם היו עובדי כוכבים ומי שנפל ממנו מיאש דלא ידע ממאן נבעי: פונדק. מקום שעוברים ושבים לנים לילה אחד ושנים: ואפילו ברוב ישראל. דעביד דמייאש ולא סמיך דליהדרו ניהליה דלא מפלגי בין דבר שיש בו סימן לאין בו סימן: שלשה עובדי כוכבים. איידי דנקט שלשה גבי ישראל נקט נמי גבי עובדי כוכבים וה"ה חד ובלבד שיהא אחרון: אפילו תימא לשלשה ישראל. ולא תפשוט דהלכה כרשב"א דכי פליגי רבנן עליה היכא דנפלה במקום שהרבים מצויין דלא ידע להו לכולהו דסבר האובד ומימר אמר ההוא דאשכח לא ידע ממי נפלה ולכשיגיע הרגל יכריז עליה ואתן סימן ואטול אבל הכא דידע להו לכולהו ותבעינהו ולא אודו איאושי מיאוש מימר אמר כו': אמרי קמיידהו. אמרתי לפניהם: והשתא ליהדרו. בתמיה:

נקיטנא

## תוספות

דשתיך. וא"ת וליקני ליה חצירו לבעל הגג או לבעל הכותל [ב] וי"ל דאין חצר קונה בדבר שיכול להיות שלא ימצאנו לעולם כמו הכא שהוא מוצנע בעובי הכותל וכן מוכח לקמן (עמוד ב) דתנן מצא בחנות ובשולחנות הרי אלו שלו ואין חצירו קונה לחנוני או לשולחני לפי שהמעות הם דבר קטן ואין סופו הוה לימצא וכן לקמן (דף מ.) דקאמר לא שנו אלא בלוקח מן התגר דאז הוי שלו ולא אמרי' דקנה אותם תגר כשהיה ברשותו: בכותל חדש מחציו ולחוץ שלו. וא"ת והא אמרינן ספק הינוח לא יטול ועוד דהכא כי נמי נטל להוי מקום סימן ויכריז ועוד דמשמע דמתני' איירי אפילו ביש בו סימן דבגמרא הוה בעי לאוקמי מתני' בסכין וכיס אלא מחמת פירכא אחריתי מוקי לה באודרא ונסכא וי"ל דאיירי בשתיך דומיא דכותל ישן ומסתמא כבר בקשו בעלים ולא מצאו ונתייאשו אבל מחציו ולפנים של בעל הבית דאינו שוכח חפציו ימים רבים:

בתוך הבית הרי אלו שלו. מיירי שמצא בזה הענין שנראה שהוא אבידה: וניזיל בתר בתרא. דהיינו בעל הבית דמסתמא לעולם הוא דר בביתו עם השוכרים וטרם שהלכו חפשו חפציהם וכבדו הבית ולא שכחו דבר ואין לתלות המציאה שהיא שלהם אלא בבעל הבית שעדיין נשאר בביתו באחרונה כגון מעות דתלינן בתר בתרא לפי שמכבדין השווקים בכל יום ואפילו אין בו סימן דאין בעל הבית מתיאש מה שמפסיד בביתו כסבור שימצאנו היום או למחר כיון שאין נכרים עמו דרים בביתו וכי משני שעשה פונדק לשלשה בני אדם אפילו כי יש סימן מתיאש: לעולם מעשר. ואין לתלות דמן המוכרין נפלו וכבר מעות חולין הן שנתחללו על הבהמה דאזלינן בתר לוקחין דהוו רובא דמוכר אחד מוכר לכמה בני אדם ועוד דמוקמינן להו אחזקה דהוי מעשר: בהר הבית לעולם חולין. וא"ת והא אמרינן פרק הרואה (ברכות דף סב:) לא יכנס אדם בהר הבית במעות הצרורים לו בסדינו א"כ מסתמא של הקדש הם ונפלו מן המביאין ללשכה בניסן וי"ל דאין אסור ליכנס אלא במעות הצרורים לו בסדינו בפרהסיא דנראה שנושא אותם לסחורה וגנאי הוא וכענין זה אפילו של הקדש אסור אבל ו) בידו אפילו הם של חולין מותר ליכנס [ועיין תוס' פסחים ז.]:

עשויין להתכבד בכל יום. וא"ת והלא אין מתכבדות אלא בשביל שרצים שלא יטמאו הטהרות ולא בשביל המעות ובנדה (דף נו: ושם ד"ה ש"מ) מוכח דמבוי דאינה בחזקת בדוקה משרצים אע"פ שכבדוהו אינו מועיל כיון שלא בדקו משרצים בשעת כיבוד וי"ל כיון שבודקין משרצים שלא יהא אפילו עכבר נקיטנא בכעדשה אי אפשר שלא ימצא מעות אם היו שם:

הכא נמי קמא קמא אזיל ליה. וא"ת ולוקי מתני' כגון שנמצא בגומא שלא נמצא ע"י כיבוד כדמוכח פ"ק דפסחים (דף ז. ושם) גבי תיבה שנשתמשו בה מעות מעשר וחולין דאע"ג שכיבד התיבה אזלינן בתר רוב מעות שנשתמשו שם ולא בתר בתרא כשנמצאו בגומא ויש לומר שיש גומא שנבדקת על ידי כיבוד כדאמר פרק דם נדה (נדה נו: ושם ד"ה בגומא) ויש גומא שהיא עמוקה או סדק שהוא עמוק שאינו נבדק ע"י כיבוד כי ההיא דפסחים ומתני' דקתני מצא בתוך הבית לא משמע שמצא בסדק עמוק או בגומא עמוקה כל כך שלא יוכל לו למצוא בשעת כיבוד:

לשלשה עובדי כוכבים. בפחות משלשה לא מקרי רוב ומיירי שעדיין ישנם בבית דאי לאו הכי הוי דבעל הבית שהוא בתרא: אפילו תימא לשלשה ישראל. מלתיה דבר קפרא מפרש דאמר לשלשה בני אדם מיירי אפי' בשלשה ישראל ואפילו רבנן דאמרי ברוב ישראל חייב להכריז הכא הוי שלו כדמפ' דמתיאש וא"ת ולמה לי שלשה בתרי ובעל הבית סגי דכל אחד יאמר חבירו לקחה כדאמר בסמוך גבי ראה סלע שנפלה משלשה וי"ל דלא סגי בפחות משלשה דאימר דמאחד מן השוכרים אבד והם אינם חושדים את בעל הבית ולכך אין האובד מתיאש דסבור ודאי חבירו לקחה ויחזירנו לו ז) (ועי"ל דבעי לאוקמי אפילו אין בעל הבית עמהם):

שנפל

## עין משפט נר מצוה

עב א מיי' פט"ז מהל' גזלה ואבדה הל' ז סמג עשין עד טוש"ע ח"מ סי' רס סעיף א:
עג ב ג מיי' שם הל' ט י טוש"ע שם סעיף ב:
עד ד מיי' שם הל' ט טוש"ע שם סעיף א:
עה ה מיי' פ"ו מהל' מעשר שני הלכה י:
עו ו ז מיי' פט"ז מהל' גזלה ואבדה הל' יא ועיין בהשגות ובמ"מ ובכ"מ סמג עשין עד טוש"ע ח"מ סי' רס סעיף ג:

## רבינו חננאל

הזוהמה. דשתיך טפי עלה בהן סיג הרבה. כלומר משנים רבות הם נתונים בזה המקום לפיכך עלה [בהן סיג] פי' קתא יד הסכין נקרא קתא שנצי רצועות שהכיס קשור בהן. שהרצועות נקראות שנצי: מתניתין דקתני מצא בכותל חדש מחציו לחוץ למוצאו מחציו ולפנים לבעל הבית אוקימנא באודרא ונסכא דלית להו לא קתא ולא שנצי וכן כל כיוצא בהן. אם משכירו לבית זה לאחרים אפי' מצא בתוך הבית הרי אלו שלו אוקמה רב נחמן בשעשאו פונדק ואפי' לא עשאו אלא לשלשה ישראל הרי אלו שלו מאי טעמא ההוא דנפל מניה נתיאש. ואזדא רב נחמן לטעמיה דאמר ראה סלע שנפל משנים

## מסורת הש"ס

א) פסחים ז., שקלים ה:, ב) בני אדם, מהרש"ל, ג) [לעיל כד.], ד) [עיין ברא"ש גירסא אחרת], ה) עיין מהרש"א, ו) ס"א בצנעא בכיסו, ז) ס"א.

## הגהות הגר"א

[א] גמ' דשתיך. נ"ב גירסת הרמב"ם דשחית ועמ"ש רבינו בח"מ סי' רס ס"ק ג): [ב] תום' ד"ה דשתיך כו' וי"ל כו'. נ"ב עי' הג"א בשם ראבי"ה:

## לעזי רש"י

אשטדל"א. פירוש רצועות (רש"י שבת דף לב ע"א ד"ה ופרכינן), רצועות (שהכיס קשור בהן) (רבינו חננאל ועיין ערוך ערך שנץ). פלט"א. פירוש חתיכה (רש"י מנחות דף קז ע"א ד"ה נסכא).

## ליקוטי רש"י

שנציה. רצועותיו [עי' שבת צב.]. לעולם מעשר. רוב אוכלי בשר בירושלים כל ימות השנה ממעות מעשר שני הן לפי שלא היו מספיקין לאכול כל מעות מעשר שני שלהן ברגל ונותנין אותם לבני העיר בטובת הנאה והן אוכלים אותם בקדושתן ועיקר אכילת מעות מעשר שלמים היו מביאין מהן כדקיימא לן במנחות הלכך לוקחין מהן בהמות בכל זמן שיש לו מעות מעשר אינו מוציא מעות חולין ואע"ג דאיכא למימר שמא מיד המוכר נפלו ומעות חולין הן ספק איסורא לחומרא [פסחים ז.].

Mishnah refers to **a case where [the owner] made [the house] into an inn for three idolaters.**[17]

The Gemara now goes back and defends Bar Kappara's interpretation of our Mishnah:

**רַב נַחְמָן אָמַר רַבָּה בַּר אֲבוּהָ – Rav Nachman said in the name of Rabbah bar Avuha: אֲפִילּוּ תֵּימָא לִשְׁלֹשָׁה יִשְׂרָאֵל – You may even say,** as Bar Kappara did, that the Mishnah refers to a case where the inn was rented **to three Jews.** Nonetheless, the Mishnah's ruling is unrelated to R' Shimon ben Elazar's position for the following reason: **מַאי טַעְמָא – What is the reason** the finder may keep the object in this case? **הַהוּא דְּנָפַל מִינֵּיהּ מְיָאֵשׁ –** Because **the one from whom it fell despairs** of it, **מֵימַר אָמַר – for he says** to himself, **מִכְּדִי אִינִישׁ אַחֲרִינָא לֹא הֲוָה בַּהֲדִי אֶלָּא הָנֵי – "Let me see; no other person was with me** in this inn **except for these** two. Thus, one of them must have found my lost object. **אָמְרִי קַמַּיְיהוּ כַּמָּה זִמְנֵי לְהַדְרוּ לִי –** Yet, **I have said many times in their presence that they should return it to me, וְלֹא הַדְרוּ לִי – but they have not returned it to me. וְהַשְׁתָּא לִיהַדְּרוּ – Will they now** suddenly change their minds and **return it?** Certainly not! **אִי דַּעְתַּיְיהוּ לַאֲהַדוּרָה – If their intention had been to return it, אַהַדְרוּהָ נִיהֲלִי – they would have returned it to me** by now. **וְהַאי דְּלֹא אַהַדְרוּהָ לִי –** I must therefore conclude that **[the reason] they did not return it to me** is because **בְּדַעְתַּיְיהוּ לְמִיגְזְלָהּ – it is their intention to steal it."** He therefore despairs of recovering his object. However, where someone loses something in an area where many people are to be found, and the majority of them, are Jews, it is possible that he does not despair of recovering it.[18] Thus, this explanation of the Mishnah is unrelated to R' Shimon ben Elazar's position.

The Gemara cites another ruling of Rav Nachman based on the logic he uses to explain Bar Kappara's answer:

**וְאָזְדָא רַב נַחְמָן לְטַעְמֵיהּ – Now Rav Nachman** here **follows his own reasoning** in a ruling he made elsewhere. **דְּאָמַר רַב נַחְמָן – For Rav Nachman said: רָאָה סֶלַע – If one saw a** ***sela*** coin

NOTES

17. That is, three idolaters were the last tenants in the house. Accordingly, any object found there now can be assumed to have been lost by one of them, and there is no obligation to return it.

*Rashi* points out that the same would be true if only a single idolater had been the last tenant. The Gemara speaks of three idolaters to parallel Bar Kappara's case of three Jewish tenants, in which case the ruling applies only when three Jews stayed in the house at the same time, as explained above.

18. The Gemara's answer is that the likelihood of *ye'ush* (despair) may actually be greater for an object lost among a small group of people, because once the owner challenges them to return it and they deny knowing anything about it, the owner assumes that whoever has it means to steal it. Since he cannot prove who has it, he despairs of recovering it. In R' Shimon ben Elazar's case, however, the owner does not know all the people that could possibly have found his object. Hence, he can hope that the finder – whoever he may be – is honest and will announce the find during the festival (see Mishnah 28a). Since he can then reclaim it by identifying its *siman*, he does not despair of recovering it (*Rashi*).

[א] ^א^דשתיך טפי: בכותל חדש מחציו ולחוץ שלו מחציו ולפנים של בעל הבית: אמר רב אשי ^ב^סכינא בתר קתא וכיסא בתר שנציה ואלא מתני' דקתני מחציו ולחוץ שלו מחציו ולפנים של בעל הבית ולחזי אי קתא לגאו אי קתא לבר אי שנציה לגאו אי שנציה לבר מתני' ^ג^באודרא ונסכא תנא ^ד^אם היה כותל ממולא מהן חולקין פשיטא לא צריכא דמשפע בחד גיסא מהו דתימא אשתפוכי אישתפוך קמ"ל: אם היה משכירו לאחרים אפילו (מצא) בתוך הבית הרי אלו שלו: ואמאי ליזיל בתר בתרא מי לא ^(א)^תנן ^ה^מעות שנמצאו לפני סוחרי בהמה לעולם מעשר בהר הבית חולין ובירושלים בשאר ימות השנה חולין בשעת הרגל הכל מעשר ואמר ר' שמעיה בר זעירא מאי טעמא הואיל ושוקי ירושלים עשוין להתכבד בכל יום אלמא אמרינן קמאי קמאי אזלו והני אחריני נינהו ^ו^הכא נמי קמא קמא אזל והני דבתרא הוא אמר ריש לקיש משום בר קפרא כגון שעשאו פונדק לשלשה ^(ב)^ישראל שמע מינה הלכה כר"ש בן אלעזר ^(ג)^אפי' ברוב ישראל אלא אמר רב מנשיא בר יעקב ^ז^כגון שעשאו פונדק לשלשה עובדי כוכבים רב נחמן אמר רבה בר אבוה אפי' תימא לשלשה ישראל מאי טעמא ההוא דנפל מיניה מיאש מימר אמר מכדי איניש אחרינא לא הוה בהדי אלא הני אמרי קמייהו כמה זמני לידהדרו לי ולא הדרו לי והשתא לידהדרו אי דעתייהו לאהדורה אהדורה ניהלי והאי דלא אהדרוה לי בדעתייהו למיגזלה ^(ד)^ואזדא רב נחמן לטעמיה דאמר רב נחמן ראה סלע שנפל

**רש"י**

דשתיך טפי. העלו חלודה רבה דכולי האי לא שביק להו: סכינא. הנמצא באחד מחורי הכותל: בתר קתא. אזיל אי קתיה לגיו בני הבית נתנוהו שם אי קתא לבר בני רשות הרבים נתנוהו שם שכן דרך אחיזתו וכן כיסא בתר שנציה אשטדל"א בלע"ז: באודרא. מוכין: נסכא. פלטא של כסף: ממולא. מן החפץ שמחזיק כל רוחב הכותל: לא צריכא דמשפע. הכותל לחד גיסא: מהו דתימא. בחאי הגובה היה תחילה ואשתפוכי אשתפוך לצד הנמוך קמ"ל: לפני סוחרי בהמה. בירושלים: לעולם. בין בשעת הרגל בין שלא בשעת הרגל: מעשר. שרוב בשר הנאכל בירושלים מעשר לפי שאין אדם שוהה בירושלים עד שיאכל כל מעשרותיו ונותן מעות מעשר לעניי העיר או לאוהביו יושבי העיר ורוב הוצאות מעשר לוקחין בהן בהמות לשלמים כדגמר שם שם מעשר משלמים במסכת מנחות (דף פב.): ובהר הבית חולין. ואפילו בשעת הרגל ואע"פ שרוב מעות שבעיר מעשר שעולי רגלים מביאין מעות מעשרותיהן לאכלם לא שבקינן רובא דשתא ואזלינן בתר רגל אלא אמרי' מלפני הרגל נפלו כאן וחולין הן: ובירושלים. בשאר שווקים שבה: בשאר ימות השנה חולין. דרוב מעות שבעיר חולין: ובשעת הרגל מעשר. שרוב מעות העיר מעשר: ואמר רב שמעיה בר זעירא מאי טעם. בירושלים בשעת הרגל מעשר ולא אמרי' מלפני הרגל נפלו כדאמרן בהר הבית: ושוקי ירושלים עשוין להתכבד בכל יום. ואם נפלו שם לפני הרגל כבר מצאום מכבדי השוק אבל הר הבית אין צריך להתכבד בכל יום שאין טיט ועפר קולט שם מתוך שהוא משופע ועוד שאין אדם נכנס שם במנעל ובאבק שעל רגליו: אלמא. בדבר שעשוי להתכבד אמרי' קמאי קמאי אזלו והני אחריני נינהו: הכא נמי. סתם שוכר בית כשהוא יוצא מחפש כל זוויותיו ונוטל את שלו ויוצא וניצא האחרונים שכחוהו שאילו הראשונים שכחוהו ^(ה)^כבר מצאו האחרונים: לשלשה ישראל. בבת אחת וכל שכן אם היו עובדי כוכבים ומי שנפל ממנו מיאש דלא ידע ממאן נבעי: פונדק. מקום שעוברים ושבים לנים לילה אחד ושנים: ואפילו ברוב ישראל. דעביד דמייאש ולא סמיך דליהדרו נהליה דלא מפלגי בין דבר שיש בו סימן לאין בו סימן: שלשה עובדי כוכבים. איידי דנקט שלשה גבי ישראל נקט נמי גבי עובדי כוכבים וה"ה חד ובלבד שיהא אחרון: אפילו תימא לשלשה ישראל. ולא תפשוט דהלכה כרשב"א דכי פליגי רבנן עליה היכא דנפלה במקום שהרבים מצויין דלא ידע להו לכולהו דסבר האובד ומימר אמר ההוא דאשכח לא ידע ממי נפלה ולכשיגיע הרגל יכריז עליה ואתן סימן ואטול אבל הכא דידע להו לכולהו ותבענהו ולא אודו איאושי מיאוש מימר אמר כו': אמרי קמייהו. אמרתי לפניהם: והשתא לידהדרו. בתמיה:

**תוספות**

דשתיך. וא"ת וליקני ליה חצירו לבעל הגל או לבעל הכותל [ב] וי"ל דאין חצר קונה בדבר שיכול להיות שלא ימצאנו לעולם כמו הכא שהוא מוצנע בעובי הכותל וכן מוכח לקמן (עמוד ב) דתנן מצא בחנות ובשולחנות הרי אלו שלו ואין חצירו קונה לחנוני או לשולחני לפי שהמעות הם דבר קטן ואין סופו הוה לימצא וכן לקמן (דף מ.) דקאמר לא שנו אלא בלוקח מן התגר דאז הוי שלו ולא אמרי' דקנה אותם תגר כשהיה ברשותו:

**בכותל** חדש מחציו ולחוץ שלו. וא"ת והא אמרינן ספק הינוח לא יטול ועוד דהכא כי נמי נטל להוי מקום סימן ויכריז ועוד דמשמע דמתני' מיירי אפילו ביש בו סימן דבגמרא הוה בעי לאוקמי מתני' בסכין וכיס אלא מחמת פירכא אחריתי מוקי לה באודרא ונסכא וי"ל דאיירי בשתיך דומיא דכותל ישן ומסתמא כבר בקשו בעלים ולא מצאו ונתייאשו אבל מחציו ולפנים של בעל הבית דאינו שוכח חפציו ימים רבים:

**בתוך** הבית הרי אלו שלו. מיירי שמצא בזה הענין שנראה שהוא אבידה: **וניזל** בתר בתרא. דהיינו בעל הבית דמסתמא לעולם הוא דר בביתו עם השוכרים וטרם שהלכו חפשו חפציהם וכבדו הבית ולא שכחו דבר ואין לתלות המציאה שהיא שלהם אלא בבעל הבית שעדיין נשאר בביתו באחרונה כגון מעות דתלינן בתר בתרא לפי שמכבדין השווקים בכל יום ואפילו אין בו סימן דאין בעל הבית מתיאש מה שמפסיד בביתו כסבור שימצאנו היום או למחר כיון שאין נכרים עמו דרים בביתו וכי משני שעשה פונדק לשלשה בני אדם אפילו כי יש סימן מתיאש: **לעולם** מעשר. ואין לתלות דמן המוכרין נפלו וכבר מעות חולין הן שנתחללו על הבהמה דאזלינן בתר לוקחין דהוו רובא דמוכר אחד מוכר לכמה בני אדם ועוד דמוקמינן להו אחזקה דהוי מעשר: **בהר** הבית לעולם חולין. וא"ת והא אמרינן פרק הרואה (ברכות דף סב:) לא יכנס אדם בהר הבית במעות הצרורים לו בסדינו א"כ מסתמא של הקדש הם ונפלו מן המביאין ללשכה בניסן וי"ל דאין אסור ליכנס אלא במעות הצרורים לו בסדינו בפרהסיא דנראה שנושא אותם לסחורה וגנאי הוא וכענין זה אפילו של הקדש אסור אבל ^(ו)^בידו אפילו הם של חולין מותר ליכנס [ועיין תוס' פסחים ז.]:

**עשויין** להתכבד בכל יום. וא"ת והלא אין מתכבדות אלא בשביל שרצים שלא יטמאו הטהרות ולא בשביל המעות ובנדה (דף נו: ושם ד"ה ש"מ) מוכח דמבוי דאינה בחזקת בדוקה משרצים אע"פ שכבדוהו אינו מועיל כיון שלא בדקו משרצים בשעת כיבוד וי"ל כיון שבודקין משרצים שלא יהא אפילו עלם בכעדשה אי אפשר שלא ימצא מעות אם היו שם:

**הכא** נמי קמא קמא אזיל ליה. וא"ת ולוקי מתני' כגון שנמצא נקיטנא בגומא שלא נמצא ע"י כיבוד כדמוכח פ"ק דפסחים (דף ז. ושם) גבי תיבה שנשתמשו בה מעות מעשר וחולין דאע"ג שכיבד התיבה אזלינן בתר רוב מעות שנשתמשו שם ולא בתר בתרא כשנמצאו בגומא ויש לומר שיש גומא שנבדקת על ידי כיבוד כדאמר פרק דם נדה (נדה נו: ושם ד"ה בגומא) ויש גומא שהיא עמוקה או סדק שהוא עמוק שאינו נבדק ע"י כיבוד כי ההיא דפסחים ומתני' דקתני מצא בתוך הבית לא משמע שמצא בסדק עמוק או בגומא עמוקה כל כך שלא יוכל לו למצוא בשעת כיבוד:

**לשלשה** עובדי כוכבים. בפחות משלשה לא מקרי רוב ומיירי שעדיין ישנם בבית דאי לאו הכי הוי דבעל הבית שהוא בתרא: **אפילו** תימא לשלשה ישראל. מלתיה דבר קפרא מפרש דאמר לשלשה בני אדם מיירי אפי' בשלשה ישראל ואפילו רבנן דאמרי ברוב ישראל חייב להכריז הכא הוי שלו כדמפ' דמתיאש וא"ת ולמה לי שלשה בתרי ובעל הבית סגי דכל אחד יאמר חבירו לקחה כדאמר בסמוך גבי ראה סלע שנפלה משלשה וי"ל דלא סגי בפחות משלשה דאימר דמאחד מן השוכרים אבד והם אינם חושדים את בעל הבית ולכך אין האובד מתיאש דסבור ודאי חבירו לקחה ויחזירנו לו ^(ז)^(ועי"ל דבעי לאוקמי אפילו אין בעל הבית עמהם):

שנפל

**מסורת הש"ס**

א) פסחים ז., שקלים א:, ב) בני אדם, מהרש"ל, ג) [לעיל כד.], ד) [עיין ברא"ש גירסא אחרת], ה) עיין מהרש"א, ו) ס"א בצנעא בכיסו, ז) ס"א.

**הגהות הגר"א**

[א] גמ' דשתיך. נ"ב גירסת הרמב"ם דשתית (ועמ"ש רבינו בח"מ סי' רס ס"ק ב): [ב] תוס' ד"ה דשתיך כו' וי"ל כו'. נ"ב עי' הג"א בשם ראבי"ה:

**לעזי רש"י**

אשטדל"א. פירוש רצועות (רש"י שבת דף נב ע"א ד"ה ופרכינן), רצועות (שהכיס קשור בהן) (רבינו חננאל ועיין ערוך ערך שנץ). פלט"א. פירוש חתיכה (רש"י מנחות דף קז ע"א ד"ה נסכא).

**ליקוטי רש"י**

שנציה. רצועותיו [עי' שבת צב.]. לעולם מעשר. רוב אוכלי בשר בירושלים כל ימות השנה ממעות מעשר שני הן לפי שלא היו מספיקין לאכול כל מעות מעשר שני שלהן ברגל ונותנין אותם לבני העיר בטובת הנאה והן אוכלים אותם בקדושתן ויעיקר אכילת מעות מעשר שלמים היו מביאין מהן כדקיימא לן במנחות הלכך לוקחין מהן בהמות דכל זמן שיש לו מעות מעשר אינו מוציא מעות חולין ואע"ג דאיכא למימר שמא מיד המוכר נפלו ומעות חולין הן ספק איסורא לחומרא [פסחים ז.].

**עין משפט נר מצוה**

עב א מיי' פט"ז מהל' גזלה ואבדה הל' ז סמג עשין עד טוש"ע ח"מ סי' רס סעיף א:
עג ב ג מיי' שם הל' ט י טוש"ע שם סעיף ג:
עד ד מיי' שם הל' ט טוש"ע שם סעיף א:
עה ה מיי' פ"ו מהל' מעשר שני הלכה י:
עו ו ז מיי' פט"ז מהל' גזלה ואבדה הל' יא ועיין בהשגות ובמ"מ וככ"מ סמג עשין עד טוש"ע ח"מ סי' רס סעיף ג:

**רבינו חננאל**

הזוהמה. דשתיך טפי עלה בהן סיג הרבה. כלומר משנים רבות הם נתונים בזה המקום לפיכך עלה [בהן סיג] פי' קתא יד הסכין נקרא קתא שנצי רצועות שהכיס קשור בהן. שהרצועות נקראות שנצי: מתניתין דקתני מצא בכותל חדש מחציו לחוץ למוצאו מחציו ולפנים לבעל הבית אוקימנא באודרא ונסכא דלית להו לא קתא ולא שנצי וכן כל כיוצא בהן. אם משכירו לבית זה לאחרים אפי' מצא בתוך הבית הרי אלו שלו אוקמה רב נחמן בשעשאו פונדק ואפי' לא עשאו אלא לשלשה ישראל הרי אלו שלו מאי טעמא ההוא דנפל מניה נתיאש. ואודא רב נחמן לטעמיה דאמר ראה סלע שנפל משנים

לִפְנֵי סוֹחֲרֵי בְהֵמָ – COINS WHICH ARE FOUND IN FRONT OF the remises of ANIMAL DEALERS in Jerusalem לְעוֹלָם מַעֲשֵׂר – ARE LWAYS assumed to be money of *MAASER [SHENI].*[8] בְּהַר הַבַּיִת – 'oins found ON THE TEMPLE MOUNT חוּלִּין – are assumed to be ON-SACRED.[9] וּבִירוּשָׁלַיִם – BUT the status of coins found lsewhere IN JERUSALEM depends on when they were found: בִּשְׁאָר יְמוֹת הַשָּׁנָה חוּלִ – DURING THE REST OF THE YEAR, i.e. uring periods other than the festival season, they are assumed to e NON-SACRED; בִּשְׁעַת הָרֶגֶל הַכֹּל מַעֲשֵׂר – DURING THE PILGRIM-.GE FESTIVALS, ALL coins that ARE found are assumed to be *IAASER.*[10]

The Gemara explains the Mishnah's distinction between the 'emple Mount and other parts of Jerusalem and thereby bolsters :s earlier question:

וְאָמַר ר׳ שְׁמַעְיָה בַּר זְעִירָ – And, in explanation of this Mishnah, **' Shemayah bar Ze'ira said:** מַאי טַעְמָא – **What is the reason** hat coins found elsewhere in Jerusalem during the pilgrimage estivals are assumed to be *maaser sheni* funds?[11] הוֹאִיל וְשׁוּקֵי יְרוּשָׁלַיִם עֲשׂוּיִן לְהִתְכַּבֵּד בְּכָל יוֹ – **Because the market places of 'erusalem are usually swept each day.**[12] אַלְמָא אָמְרִינַן קַמָּאֵי קַמָּאֵי אָזְ – **We see** from this that where an area is cleaned egularly **we say: The earlier [coins]**[13] **have gone,** וְהָנֵי אַחֲרִינֵי נִינְהוּ – **and these** that are found now **are others.** הָכָא נַמִּי – Therefore, **here also,** in the case of our Mishnah, we should assume that קַמָּא קַמָּא אָזַל – **the earlier [objects]** left by the earlier tenant **have gone,** וְהָנֵי דְבַתְרָא הוּא – **and these** objects found now **belong to the last [tenant].**[14] Why, then, does the Mishnah rule that the finder may keep the object that he found?

The Gemara answers:

אָמַר רֵישׁ לָקִישׁ מִשּׁוּם בַּר קַפָּרָא – **Reish Lakish said in the name of Bar Kappara:** כְּגוֹן שֶׁעֲשָׂאוֹ פּוּנְדָּק לִשְׁלֹשָׁה יִשְׂרָאֵל – The Mishnah refers to **a case where [the owner] made [the house]** into **an inn for three Jews** at once, so that he does not know who lost it.[15]

The Gemara objects to this interpretation of our Mishnah:

שְׁמַע מִינָּה – If so, **learn from this** explanation הֲלָכָה כְּרַבִּי שִׁמְעוֹן בֶּן אֶלְעָזָר – that **the halachah is in accordance with R' Shimon ben Elazar** אֲפִילוּ בְּרוֹב יִשְׂרָאֵל – **even** in a case **with a majority of Jews.**[16]

The Gemara therefore revises the interpretation of the Mishnah:

אֶלָּא אָמַר רַב מְנַשְׁיָא בַּר יַעֲקֹב – **Rather, Rav Menashya bar Yaakov said:** כְּגוֹן שֶׁעֲשָׂאוֹ פּוּנְדָּק לִשְׁלֹשָׁה עוֹבְדֵי כוֹכָבִים – The

NOTES

. The first ruling of the Mishnah presupposes that the people who isited Jerusalem for only a limited period of time were not there long nough to consume all the food they could purchase with their *maaser heni* funds. Therefore, they would leave their remaining funds with heir acquaintances or poor people in Jerusalem. Although one could urchase any type of food with the consecrated *maaser sheni* money, nost people used the money to purchase sacrificial peace offerings *shelamim*) [see *Menachos* 82a]. Consequently, throughout the year, nost animals sold in the stockyards of Jerusalem were purchased with *naaser sheni* money. The Mishnah therefore rules [in accordance with he rule of following the majority (הָלֵךְ אַחַר הָרוֹב),] that coins found year ound in the animal markets are assumed to be *maaser sheni* funds *Rashi*).

. During the three pilgrimage festivals of Pesach, Shavuos, and Succos, vhen there is an obligation to travel to Jerusalem, visitors would bring heir *maaser sheni* funds to spend there. Consequently, during the estival season most of the money circulating in Jerusalem was of *naaser sheni* status. The Mishnah nevertheless rules that coins found n the Temple Mount during that period – and certainly during the est of the year – are assumed to be non-sacred. This is so because we ave no reason to believe that the money was lost during the festival eriod; it might have been lost before. The principle of following the najority therefore dictates that because there is a preponderance of on-sacred money most of the year, any money found on the Temple Mount must be considered non-sacred – even during the festival period *Rashi*).

0. As stated in the previous note, the majority of money circulating in 'erusalem during most of the year was not consecrated for *maaser heni.* [Only in the animal market was there a preponderance of *maaser heni* money year round, because the most common use of *maaser heni* funds was the purchase of animals for *shelamim* offerings.] )uring the festival season, however, the majority of money circulating n Jerusalem's marketplaces was money of *maaser sheni.* Therefore, nly coins found during the festival season are assumed to be *maaser heni;* during the rest of the year, they are assumed to be nonconse-rated (*Rashi*).

1. Why do we not assume these coins had been lying on the ground efore the start of the festival – when most money was non-sacred – ust as we assume the money found on the Temple Mount was ion-sacred for that reason? (*Rashi*).

2. Therefore, any coins lost in Jerusalem before the festival would resumably have been found by the sweepers, and coins found during he festival period should be assumed to have been lost that day. The Temple Mount, however, did not have to be regularly swept for two easons: First, the incline of the Temple Mount naturally prevented the ccumulation of dirt and mud; second, no one was permitted to enter the Temple Mount with shoes or dusty feet. Since the Temple Mount was not swept every day, coins lost before the festival season would not necessarily have been found before the start of the festival; hence, coins found on the Temple Mount during the festival could have been lost any time of the year and are assumed to be non-sacred (*Rashi*).

13. Literally: the first ones, the first ones.

14. Here too, we should assume that the objects were lost by the last tenant, for people who rent a house search it thoroughly before leaving and take all their belongings with them. It is therefore very unlikely that the first tenants forgot anything; and even if they did, it would have certainly been found by the next tenant. Hence, by default, any article found in a rented house should be assumed to be the property of the last tenant (*Rashi,* as explained by *Ritva;* cf. *Tosafos*). Why, then, does the Mishnah rule that one may keep an object found in a rented house?

15. I.e. he rented lodging to three Jews at the same time. In this case, even if we must assume the object to have belonged to one of the last three tenants, the finder can keep it. Since the person who lost the object had rented lodging space with two others in the inn, he does not know from which one to claim his object; he therefore despairs of recovering it (*Rashi*; see Gemara below, 26b).

Although Reish Lakish mentions three "Jews," his answer would certainly hold true for a situation in which three Canaanites last occupied the house [for there is no obligation to return an article lost by a Canaanite, as we learned on 24a] (*Rashi;* see note 18 below).

16. Above (24a), R' Shimon ben Elazar ruled that one may keep what he finds in a place frequented by many people – even though it has a *siman* – because the owner despairs of recovering it. The Gemara there considered whether R' Shimon ben Elazar's ruling applies only where the majority of people are Canaanites [who would generally not return what they find], or whether his rule applies even in a place where the majority of people are Jews. The Gemara also inquired whether the halachah follows his opinion.

Now according to Bar Kappara's explanation of our Mishnah, a Jew who lost his object in an inn whose other occupants were Jews nonetheless despairs of recovering it – even though it has a *siman.* This ruling would seem to accord with the view of R' Shimon ben Elazar, but only if we assume that R' Shimon ben Elazar stated it even for a place where the majority of people are Jews (*Rashi*). We should therefore infer from our Mishnah that the halachah follows R' Shimon ben Elazar's view even in a place where the majority are Jews. The Gemara above, however, did not reach this resolution.

[See *Ritva,* who explains why the Gemara considers Bar Kappara's interpretation of our Mishnah analogous to R' Shimon ben Elazar's ruling regarding an area frequented by large numbers of people. See also *Shitah Mekubetzes.*]

[א] אדשתיך טפי: בכותל חדש מחציו ולחוץ שלו מחציו ולפנים של בעל הבית: אמר רב אשי בסכינא בתר קתא וכיסא בתר שנציה ואלא מתני' דקתני מחציו ולחוץ שלו מחציו ולפנים של בעל הבית ולחזי אי קתא לגאו אי קתא לבר אי שנציה לגאו אי שנציה לבר מתני' גבאודרא ונסכא תנא דאם היה כותל ממולא מהן חולקין פשיטא לא צריכא דמשפע בחד גיסא מהו דתימא אשתפוכי אישתפוך קמ"ל: אם היה משכירו לאחרים אפילו (מצא) בתוך הבית הרי אלו שלו: ואמאי ליזיל בתר בתרא מי לא א)תנן המעות שנמצאו לפני סוחרי בהמה לעולם מעשר בהר הבית חולין ובירושלים בשאר ימות השנה חולין בשעת הרגל הכל מעשר ואמר ר' שמעיה בר זעירא מאי טעמא הואיל ושוקי ירושלים עשוין להתכבד בכל יום אלמא אמרינן קמאי קמאי אזלו והני אחריני נינהו והכא נמי קמא קמא אזל והני דבתרא הוא אמר ריש לקיש משום בר קפרא כגון שעשאו פונדק לשלשה ב)ישראל שמע מינה הלכה כר"ש בן אלעזר ג)אפי' ברוב ישראל אלא אמר רב מנשיא בר יעקב זכגון שעשאו פונדק לשלשה עובדי כוכבים רב נחמן אמר רבה בר אבוה אפי' תימא לשלשה ישראל מאי טעמא ההוא דנפל מיניה מיאש מימר אמר מכדי איניש אחרינא לא הוה בהדי אלא הני אמרי קמייהו כמה זמני ליהדרו לי ולא הדרו לי והשתא ליהדרו אי דעתייהו לאהדורה אהדורה ניהלי והאי דלא אהדרוה לי בדעתייהו למיגזלה ד)ואזדא רב נחמן לטעמיה דאמר רב נחמן ראה סלע שנפל

דשתיך טפי. העלו חלודה רבה דכולי האי לא שביק להו: סכינא. הנמצא באחד מחורי הכותל: בתר קתא. אזיל אי קתיה לגיו בני הבית נתנוהו שם אי קתא לבר בני רשות הרבים נתנוהו שם שכן דרך אחיזתו וכן כיסא בתר שנציה אשטדל"א בלע"ז: באודרא. מוכין: נסכא. פלטא של כסף: ממולא. מן החפץ שמחזיק כל רוחב הכותל: לא צריכא דמשפע. הכותל לחד גיסא: מהו דתימא. באותו הגובה היה תחילה ואשתפוכי אשתפוך לצד הנמוך קמ"ל: לפני סוחרי בהמה. בירושלים: לעולם. בין בשעת הרגל בין שלא בשעת הרגל: מעשר. שרוב בשר הנאכל בירושלים מעשר לפי שאין אדם שוהה בירושלים עד שיאכל כל מעשרותיו ונותן מעות מעשר לעניי העיר או לאוהביו יושבי העיר ורוב הוצאות מעשר לוקחין בהן בהמות לשלמים כדגמר שם שם מעשר משלמים במסכת מנחות (דף פב.): ובהר הבית חולין. ואפילו בשעת הרגל ואע"פ שרוב מעות שבעיר מעשר שעולי רגלים מביאין מעות מעשרותיהן לאכלם לא שבקינן רובא דשתא ואזלינן בתר רגל אלא אמרי' מלפני הרגל נפלו כאן וחולין הן: ובירושלים. בשאר שווקים שבה: בשאר ימות השנה חולין. דרוב מעות שבעיר חולין: ובשעת הרגל מעשר. שרוב מעות העיר מעשר: ואמר רב שמעיה בר זעירא מאי טעם. בירושלים בשעת הרגל מעשר ולא אמרי' מלפני הרגל נפלו כדאמרן בהר הבית: ושוקי ירושלים עשויין להתכבד בכל יום. ואם נפלו שם לפני הרגל כבר מצאום מכבדי השוק אבל הר הבית אין צריך להתכבד בכל יום שאין טיט ועפר קולט שם מתוך שהוא משופע ועוד שאין אדם נכנס שם במנעל ובאבק שעל רגליו: אלמא. בדבר שעשוי להתכבד אמרי' קמאי קמאי אזלו והני אחריני נינהו: הכא נמי. סתם שוכר בית כשהוא יוצא מחפש כל זויותיו ונוטל את שלו ויוצא ונימא האחרונים שכחוהו שאילו הראשונים שכחוהו ה)כבר מצאו האחרונים: לשלשה ישראל. בבת אחת וכל שכן אם היו עובדי כוכבים ומי שנפל ממנו מיאש דלא ידע ממאן נבעי: פונדק. מקום שעוברים ושבים לנים לילה אחד ושנים: ואפילו ברוב ישראל. דעביד דמייאש ולא סמיך דליהדרו נהליה דלא מפלגי בין דבר שיש בו סימן לאין בו סימן: שלשה עובדי כוכבים. איידי דנקט שלשה גבי ישראל נקט נמי גבי עובדי כוכבים וה"ה חד ובלבד שיהא אחרון: אפילו תימא לשלשה ישראל. ולא תפשוט דהלכה כרשב"א דכי פליגי רבנן עליה היכא דנפלה במקום שהרבים מצויין דלא ידע להו לכולהו דסבר האובד ומימר אמר ההוא דאשכח לא ידע ממי נפלה ולכשיגיע הרגל יכריז עליה ואתן סימן ואטול אבל הכא דידע להו לכולהו ותבעינהו ולא אודו איאושי מיאוש מימר אמר כו': אמרי קמייהו. אמרתי לפניהם: והשתא ליהדרו. בתמיה:

דשתיך. וא"ת וליקני ליה חצירו לבעל הגג או לבעל הכותל [ב] וי"ל דאין חצר קונה בדבר שיכול להיות שלא ימצאנו לעולם כמו הכא שהוא מוצנע בעובי הכותל וכן מוכח לקמן (עמוד ב) דתנן מצא בחנות ובשולחנות הרי אלו שלו ואין חצירו קונה לחנוני או לשולחני לפי שהמעות הם דבר קטן ואין סופו הוה לימצא וכן לקמן (דף מ.) דקאמר לא שנו אלא בלוקח מן התגר דאז הוי שלו ולא אמרי' דקנה אותם תגר כשהיה ברשותו: **בכותל** חדש מחציו ולחוץ שלו. וא"ת והא אמרינן ספק הינוח לא יטול ועוד דהכא כי נמי נטל להוי מקום סימן ויכריז ועוד דמשמע דמתני' מיירי אפילו ביש בו סימן דבגמרא הוה בעי לאוקמי מתני' בסכין וכיס אלא מחמת פירכא אחריתי מוקי לה באודרא ונסכא וי"ל דאיירי בשתיך דומיא דכותל ישן ומסתמא כבר בקשו בעלים ולא מצאו ונתייאשו אבל מחציו ולפנים של בעל הבית דאינו שוכח חפציו ימים רבים:

**בתוך** הבית הרי אלו שלו. מיירי שמצא בזה הענין שנראה שהוא אבידה: **וניזיל** בתר בתרא. דהיינו בעל הבית דמסתמא לעולם הוא דר בביתו עם השוכרים וטרם שהלכו חפשו חפציהם וכבדו הבית ולא שכחו דבר ואין לתלות המציאה שהיא שלהם אלא בבעל הבית שעדיין נשאר בביתו באחרונה כגון מעות דתלינן בתר בתרא לפי שמכבדין השווקים בכל יום ואפילו אין בו סימן דאין בעל הבית מתיאש מה שמפסיד בביתו כסבור שימצאנו היום או למחר כיון שאין נכרים עמו דרים בביתו וכי משני שעשה פונדק לשלשה בני אדם אפילו כי יש סימן מתיאש: **לעולם** מעשר. ואין לתלות דמן המוכרין נפלו וכבר מעות חולין הן שנתחללו על הבהמה דאזלינן בתר לוקחין דהוו רובא דמוכר אחד מוכר לכמה בני אדם ועוד דמוקמינן להו אחזקה דהוי מעשר: **בהר** הבית לעולם חולין. וא"ת והא אמרינן פרק הרואה (ברכות דף סב:) לא יכנס אדם בהר הבית במעות הצרורים לו בסדינו א"כ מסתמא של הקדש הם ונפלו מן המביאין ללשכה בניסן וי"ל דאין אסור ליכנס אלא במעות הצרורים לו בסדינו בפרהסיא דנראה שנושא אותם לסחורה וגנאי הוא וכענין זה אפילו של הקדש אסור אבל ו)בידו אפילו הם של חולין מותר ליכנס [ועיין תוס' פסחים ז.]:

**עשויין** להתכבד בכל יום. וא"ת והלא אין מתכבדות אלא בשביל שרצים שלא יטמאו הטהרות ולא בשביל המעות ובנדה (דף נו: ושם ד"ה ש"מ) מוכח דמבוי דאינה בחזקת בדוקה משרצים אע"פ שכבדוהו אינו מועיל כיון שלא בדקו משרצים בשעת כיבוד וי"ל כיון שבודקין משרצים שלא יהא אפילו עלם בכעדשה אי אפשר שלא ימצא מעות אם היו שם:

**הכא** נמי קמא קמא אזיל ליה. וא"ת ולוקי מתני' כגון שנמצא בגומא שלא נמצא ע"י כיבוד כדמוכח פ"ק דפסחים (דף ז. ושם) גבי תיבה שנשתמשו בה מעות מעשר וחולין דאע"ג שכיבד התיבה אזלינן בתר רוב מעות שנשתמשו שם ולא בתר בתרא כשנמצאו בגומא ויש לומר שיש גומא שנבדקת על ידי כיבוד כדאמר פרק דם נדה (נדה נו: ושם ד"ה בגומא) ויש גומא שהיא עמוקה או סדק שהוא עמוק שאינו נבדק ע"י כיבוד כי ההיא דפסחים ומתני' דקתני מצא בתוך הבית לא משמע שמצא בסדק עמוק או בגומא עמוקה כל כך שלא יוכל לו למצוא בשעת כיבוד:

**לשלשה** עובדי כוכבים. בפחות משלשה לא מקרי רוב ומיירי שעדיין ישנם בבית דאי לאו הכי הוי דבעל הבית שהוא בתרא: **אפילו** תימא לשלשה ישראל. מלתיה דבר קפרא מפרש דאמר לשלשה בני אדם מיירי אפי' בשלשה ישראל ואפילו רבנן דאמרי ברוב ישראל חייב להכריז הכא הוי שלו כדמפ' דמתיאש וא"ת ולמה לי שלשה בתרי ובעל הבית סגי דכל אחד יאמר חבירו לקחה כדאמר בסמוך גבי ראה סלע שנפלה משלשה וי"ל דלא סגי בפחות משלשה דאימר דמאחד מן השוכרים אבד והם אינם חושדים את בעל הבית ולכך אין האובד מתיאש דסבור ודאי חבירו לקחה ויחזירנו לו ז)(ועי"ל דבעי לאוקמי אפילו אין בעל הבית עמהם):

שנפל



עב א מיי' פט"ז מהל' גזלה ואבדה הל' ז סמג עשין עד טוש"ע ח"מ סי' רס סעיף א:
עג ב ג מיי' שם הל' ט י טוש"ע שם סעיף ב:
עד ד מיי' שם הל' ט טוש"ע שם סעיף א:
עה ה מיי' פ"ו מהל' מעשר שני הלכה י:
עו ו ז מיי' פט"ז מהל' גזלה ואבדה הל' יא ועיין בהשגות ובמ"מ ובכ"מ סמג עשין עד טוש"ע ח"מ סי' רס סעיף ג:

רבינו חננאל

הזוהמה. דשתיך טפי עלה בהן סיג הרבה. כלומר משנים רבות הם נתונים בזה המקום לפיכך עלה [בהן סיג] פי' קתא יד הסכין נקרא קתא שנצי רצועות שהכיס קשור בהן. שהרצועות נקראות שנצי: מתניתין דקתני מצא בכותל חדש מחציו לחוץ למוצאו מחציו ולפנים לבעל הבית אוקימנא באודרא ונסכא דלית להו לא קתא ולא שנצי וכן כל כיוצא בהן. אם משכירו לבית זה לאחרים אפי' מצא בתוך הבית הרי אלו שלו אוקמה רב נחמן בשעשאו פונדק ואפי' לא עשאו אלא לשלשה ישראל הרי אלו של' מאי טעמא ההוא דנפל מניה נתיאש. ואזדא רב נחמן לטעמיה דאמר ראה סלע שנפל משנים



א) פסחים ז., שקלים ... ב) בני אדם, ... מהרש"ל, ג) [לעיל כד.], ד) [עיין ברא"ש גירסא ... אחרת], ה) עיין מהרש"א, ו) ... ס"א בצנעה בכיסו, ז) ס"א.

הגהות הגר"א

[א] גמ' דשתיך. נ"ב ... גירסת הרמב"ם דשתיך ... עמ"ש רבינו בח"מ סי' ... ס"ק ב): [ב] תוס' ד"ה דשתיך כו' וי"ל ... נ"ב עי' הג"א בשם ראבי"ה:

לעזי רש"י

אשטדל"א. פירוש רצועות (רש"י שבת דף נב ... ד"ה ופרכינן), רצועות (שהכיס קשור בהן) (רבינו חננאל ועיין ערוך ערך שנץ). פלט"א. פירוש חתיכה (רש"י מנחות דף קז ע"א ד"ה נסכא).

ליקוטי רש"י

שנציה. רצועותיו [עי' שבת צב.]. לעולם מעשר. רוב אוכלי בשר ירושלים כל ימות השנה ממעות מעשר שני הן לפי שלא היו מספיקין לאכול כל מעות מעשר שני שלהן ברגל ונותנין אותם לבני העיר בטובת הנאה והן אוכלים אותם בקדושתן ועיקר אכילת מעות מעשר שלמים היו מביאין כדקיימא לן במנחות לכך לוקחין מהן בהמות וכל זמן שיש לו מעות מעשר אינו מוציא מעות חולין ואע"ג דאיכא למימר שמא מיד המוכר נפלו ומעות חולין הן ספק ... [פסחים ז.].

דְשַׁתִּיךְ טו – **where [the object] is extremely rusty.**[1]

The next section of the Mishnah stated: בְּכוֹתֶל חָדָשׁ – If one found objects IN a hole of A NEW WALL: מֶחֱצִיו וְלַחוּץ שֶׁלּוֹ – If it was FROM THE MIDDLE [OF THE WALL] AND OUTWARD, THEY BELONG TO [THE FINDER]; מֶחֱצִיו וְלִפְנִים שֶׁל בַּעַל הַבַּיִת – if it was FROM THE MIDDLE [OF THE WALL] AND INWARD, THEY BELONG TO THE OWNER OF THE HOUSE.

The Gemara records a related ruling:

אָמַר רַב אַשִׁי – **Rav Ashi said:** סַכִּינָא – Ownership of **a knife** found in a wall בָּתַר קַתָּא – **follows its handle,** וְכִיסָא בָּתַר שְׁנָצֵי – **and** ownership of **a purse follows its straps.**[2]

The Gemara asks:

וְאֶלָּא מַתְנִיתִין דְּקָתָנֵי – **But** then in **our Mishnah, which states** that: מֶחֱצִיו וְלַחוּץ שֶׁלּוֹ – If the object was found FROM THE MIDDLE [OF THE WALL] AND OUTWARD, IT BELONGS TO [THE FINDER]; מֶחֱצִיו וְלִפְנִים שֶׁל בַּעַל הַבַּיִת – and if it was found FROM THE MIDDLE [OF THE WALL] AND INWARD, IT BELONGS TO THE OWNER OF THE HOUSE, let us disregard the object's position in the wall and apply Rav Ashi's rule: וְלֶחֱזֵי – **Let us see,** in the case of a knife, אִי קַתָּא לְגָאו אִי קַתָּא לְבַר – **whether the handle is towards the inside or whether the handle is towards the outside;** and for a purse, let us see אִי שְׁנָצֵיהּ לְגָאו אִי שְׁנָצֵיהּ לְבַר – **whether its drawstrings** are **towards the inside** or **if its drawstrings are towards the outside!** – ? –

The Gemara answers:

מַתְנִיתִין בְּאוּדְרָא וְנִסְכָּא – **Our Mishnah** is dealing **with** finds such as **flock,**[3] **and a bar** of silver. These objects give no indication as to the direction from which they were inserted into the wall; therefore, the sole criterion of ownership is the part of the wall in which they are found.

The Gemara cites a Baraisa that elaborates upon the laws of objects found in walls:

תָּנָא – **A Baraisa has taught:** אִם הָיָה כּוֹתֶל מְמוּלָּא מֵהֶן – IF THE width of the WALL WAS FILLED WITH [THE LOST OBJECTS], חוֹלְקִין – THEY [the finder and the owner of the house] DIVIDE it equally.

The Gemara asks:

פְּשִׁיטָא – This is **obvious!**

The Gemara answers:

לֹא צְרִיכָא דְּמִשְׁפַּע בְּחַד גִּיסָא – **[The Tanna's ruling] is necessary only where [the wall] is leaning towards one side,** thereby causing the hole to slant downward in that direction.[4] מַהוּ דְּתֵימָא – **You might have said** that all the objects were originally placed in the upper half of the hole, אִשְׁתַּפּוּכֵי אִישְׁתַּפּוּךְ – and later **spilled down** to extend across the entire length of the hole.[5] Hence, it would be possible to assign ownership of the entire find to the person on the higher side of the hole. קָא מַשְׁמַע לָן – **[The Tanna]** therefore **informs us** that the find is nevertheless divided equally.[6]

The Gemara cites the next part of the Mishnah:

אִם הָיָה מַשְׂכִּירוֹ לַאֲחֵרִים – IF [THE HOUSE OWNER] WAS in the habit of RENTING [HIS HOUSE] TO OTHERS, אֲפִילּוּ (מצא) בְּתוֹךְ הַבַּיִת – EVEN if one found objects INSIDE THE HOUSE, הֲרֵי אֵלּוּ שֶׁלּוֹ – THESE BELONG TO [THE FINDER].

The apparent reason for this ruling is that there is no way of knowing who the owner is. The Gemara therefore asks:

וְאַמַּאי – **Why** may the finder keep the object? לֵיזִיל בָּתַר בָּתְרָא – **Let [presumptive ownership] follow the last** person who lived in the house!

The Gemara supports its question from a Mishnah:

מִי לֹא תְּנַן – **Did we not learn in a Mishnah:**[7] מָעוֹת שֶׁנִּמְצְאוּ

NOTES

1. [The extreme degree of rust indicates that the object has been in the wall a great many years,] and it would be unusual for the owner to leave it there for that length of time (*Rashi*). It is therefore reasonable to assume that it is there since ancient times.

[The mere antiquity of this object, however, is no proof that it is from Emorite times. It may well have been left by the house owner's ancestors, who forgot to inform their heirs of its existence before they died. Why should we assume that it comes from the Emorites? *Rosh* answers that once it is possible to attribute the origin of the object to the Emorites, there is no longer any legal presumption of previous Jewish ownership. Therefore, whoever finds it may keep it.]

According to the Gemara's answer, the definition of an "old wall' is one that may date back to pre-conquest days. It follows from this that when the Mishnah speaks of a "new" wall, it refers to any wall built after the Jewish conquest of the Land (*Ritva* in explanation of *Rashi*). Any object hidden in it, no matter how rusty, must have been placed there by Jews; thus, if they are found in the inner half of the wall they belong to the owner of the house [since they are presumed to have belonged to his ancestors]. According to this reasoning, this case of the Mishnah must refer to the wall of a property that, since it was built, has always been in the hands of the family of the current owner (*Rosh*).

The Rishonim also question why the present owner of the house does not acquire the object through *kinyan chatzeir*. As we learned above (11a), one can acquire objects by virtue of their presence in his courtyard (*chatzeir*) or house, even if he is unaware of their presence. Hence, even if the object was, in fact, abandoned by the Emorites, it should not belong to the finder; rather, it should become the property of the house owner. In answer to this question, *Tosafos* write that a concealed object that may never be found (such as an object hidden in a wall) cannot be acquired through *kinyan chatzeir*. See also *Rambam*, *Hil. Gezeilah* 16:8 with *Raavad*; *Rosh, Ritva,* and *Mordechai* for alternative explanations.]

2. Since a knife is held by its handle, its position indicates who placed it there, and consequently to whom it belongs. If the handle points towards the house, the knife belongs to the owner of the house because we can assume that either he or someone from his household placed it there. If, however, the handle points towards the street, the knife belongs to the finder, because we can assume that a passerby placed it there and forgot it. The same holds true for the purse and its drawstrings (*Rashi*).

3. *Rashi* translates this word as מוֹכִין. This usually denotes material used as stuffing for mattresses – tufts of soft fabric, unprocessed wool or worn-out clothing (see *Rashi* to *Shabbos* 47b).

4. For example, if the wall leans towards the house, the hole will be higher on the outside than on the inside. We therefore could have suspected that if the objects were found throughout the hole, all of them were left by a passerby in the outer half of the hole, but in the course of time, some slid down from that higher section to the lower section on the other side of the wall. We should, in that case, treat all the objects as if they had been located in the outer half of the wall and assign them to the finder.

5. [The find did not fill the entire cavity of the hole; it merely extended across it from end to end. Thus, it is possible that it was all originally bunched in one half of the hole and then gradually spilled down to spread across the entire length of the hole.]

6. This applies even if a single object fills the hole from end to end. [Since there is no one currently holding it] and there is no knowledge of who its original owner may have been, the property in question is divided between its two claimants (*Sma* 260:5; see *R' Akiva Eiger*).

7. *Shekalim* 7:2. This Mishnah discusses the circumstances under which money found on the ground in various sections of Jerusalem is assumed to have *maaser sheni* (second tithe) status. The rules of *maaser sheni* are as follows: Produce grown in Eretz Yisrael must be tithed. The first tithe is given to a Levi. One must also separate a second tithe. During the first, second, fourth, and fifth years of each seven-year *Shemittah* cycle, this tithe is referred to as *maaser sheni* (literally: second tithe). The produce separated must be eaten in Jerusalem or must be redeemed with money that is then taken to Jerusalem and used to purchase food. The money used to redeem *maaser sheni* produce acquires the sanctity of *maaser sheni.* It can only be spent on food to be eaten in Jerusalem. Purchase of the food transfers the sanctity from the money to the food.

announce it?[22]

The Gemara modifies its answer:

אֶלָּא – **Rather,** בְּאַשְׁפָּה שֶׁאֵינָהּ עֲשׂוּיָה לְפַנּוֹת – the Baraisa refers to **a garbage heap which is not ordinarily cleared,** וְנִמְלַךְ עָלֶיהָ לְפַנּוֹתָהּ – **but [its owner]** suddenly **changed his mind** and decided **to clear it.** Therefore, the find must be taken and announced.[23]

The Gemara challenges Rav Zevid's answer:

בִּשְׁלָמָא לְרַב פָּפָּא – **According to Rav Pappa it is understandable** הַיְינוּ דְּקָתָנֵי – that **this is why the Baraisa stated** as its reason: שֶׁכֵּן דֶּרֶךְ אַשְׁפָּה לְפַנּוֹת – BECAUSE IT IS THE NATURE OF A GARBAGE HEAP TO BE CLEARED.[24] אֶלָּא לְרַב זְבִיד – **But according to Rav Zevid,** מַאי שֶׁכֵּן דֶּרֶךְ אַשְׁפָּה לְפַנּוֹת – **why do** the Baraisa state as its reason: BECAUSE IT IS THE NATURE OF GARBAGE HEAP TO BE CLEARED? According to Rav Zevid, th Baraisa refers to small utensils that were inadvertently throw out with the garbage; hence, they should have to be returned eve if the heap is never cleared! – ? –

The Gemara reinterprets the Baraisa to deflect this challeng

שֶׁכֵּן דֶּרֶךְ אַשְׁפָּה לְפַנּוֹת לָהּ כֵּלִים קְטַנִּים – The Baraisa means that or must announce what he finds **because it is in the nature of garbage heap that [people] clear away small utensils into** inadvertently.[25]

**Mishnah** מָצָא בְּגַל – If **one found** objects **in a heap** of stones,[26] וּבְכוֹתֶל יָשָׁן – **or in an old wall,** הֲרֵי אֵלּוּ שֶׁלּוֹ – **these belong to him.** מָצָא בְּכוֹתֶל חָדָשׁ – If **he found them in** a hole in **a new wall:** מֵחֶצְיוֹ וּלְחוּץ – If they were found **from the middle [of the wall] and outward,** שֶׁלּוֹ – **they belong to [the finder];**[27] מֵחֶצְיוֹ וְלִפְנִים – if they were **from the middle [of the wall] inwards,** שֶׁל בַּעַל הַבַּיִת – they **belong to the owner of the house.**[28] אִם הָיָה מַשְׂכִּירוֹ לַאֲחֵרִים – **If he was** in the habit of **renting [the house] to others,** אֲפִילוּ בְּתוֹךְ הַבַּיִת – **even** if the objects were found **inside the house,** הֲרֵי אֵלּוּ שֶׁלּוֹ – **these belong to [the finder].**[29]

**Gemara** The Gemara cites a Baraisa which explains the first ruling of the Mishnah:

תָּנָא – **A Baraisa has taught** that this is the reason one may keep what he finds in a heap of stones or an old wall: מִפְּנֵי שֶׁיָּכוֹל לוֹמַר לוֹ – BECAUSE [THE FINDER] MAY SAY TO [THE OWNER] of the heap or wall: שֶׁל אֱמוֹרִיִּים הֵן – THESE objects once BELONGED TO THE EMORITES, the ancient inhabitants of the Land of Israel.[30]

The Gemara asks:

אָטוּ אֱמוֹרִים מַצְנְעֵי – **Is it** only **Emorites who put away** things i walls, יִשְׂרָאֵל לָא מַצְנְעֵי – while **Jews do not conceal** ther there? Surely it is reasonable to assume that the object found i the wall is of more recent origin. – ? –

The Gemara answers:

לָא צְרִיכָא – **The** Mishnah's **[ruling] is necessary,** i.e. it applie only in the case

NOTES

22. One who deliberately leaves his possessions in a place where they may well be lost or destroyed cannot be said to have "lost" them; he is himself responsible for their loss! Thus, there is no obligation to return them to him (*Rambam*, *Hil. Gezeilah V'Aveidah* 11:11). Similarly, one who knowingly places his object in a garbage heap that is ordinarily cleared has not "lost" it, since it should have occurred to him that the heap would be cleared (*Rashi*). The finder therefore has no obligation to take it and announce it. According to some authorities, he may take it and keep it [on the assumption that its owner has actually abandoned it] (*Rama, Choshen Mishpat* 260:11). There is, however, considerable discussion of this matter (see *Sma* §54, *Shach* §33, *Ketzos HaChoshen,* and *Nesivos HaMishpat* ad loc.).

23. Since the garbage heap is usually kept intact, the person who concealed his object in it did not abandon it. Rather, he intended to return for it. But since he is not aware of the sudden decision to clear the heap, his object will be lost unless the finder takes the object and announces it (*Shitah Mekubetzes*).

24. That is, it often happens that the owner of a garbage heap will change his mind and decide to clear it (*Rashi*). [Thus, the finder should take the object and not assume that, since this heap is one that is not ordinarily cleared, the owner of the heap will postpone clearing it long enough for the object's owner to return for it.]

*Ritva* explains that the point the Baraisa means to make is that since it often happens that the owner of a heap suddenly decides to clear it, the person who placed his object there must bear the consequence. If, however, garbage-heap owners were not in the habit of changing their minds about them, then it would be prohibited for any particular garbage-heap owner to do so because of the potential loss it would cause for those who concealed objects there.

25. Thus, the Baraisa does not refer to the nature of the garbage heap, but to the type of object found in a garbage heap that must be announced. In fact, however, this Baraisa deals with a heap that is not ordinarily cleared. Thus, an object placed there deliberately must be left in place, and only those objects assumed to have been cast there inadvertently should be taken and announced.

26. From a wall that collapsed (*Rashi*). This case, like the next one, refers to an old wall. Even though in both cases the object was originally placed there by its owner, and it has a *siman*, the finder may keep it. Th Gemara will explain why (*Ritva*).

27. The object was found in a hole that goes completely through the wal but it was found in the outer half of the hole, on the side facing th street. In that case we assume that the object was left by a passerby, wh subsequently forgot it; hence, the finder can keep it (*Rashi*).

Seemingly, the Mishnah speaks here even of an object that has *siman.* But if so, why may the finder take it? We have learned in th previous section of the Gemara that if there is even a doubt tha an object was left in a certain place deliberately, it should not b removed. Certainly, then, where it is obvious that the object wa deliberately placed in the hole in the wall, one should have to leave i there!

The answer to this is that, as the Gemara will soon explain, ou Mishnah is discussing an object that is very rusty, which has clearly bee in the wall for a very long time. We may therefore assume that the owne despaired of recovering it; hence, the finder can keep it (*Rashi;* see als *Tosafos* below, 26a ד"ה בכותל).

28. In this case we assume that it was placed there by the owner of th house; hence, no one may take it.

Although the object's corrosion indicates that it has been there for very long time (see previous note), this is not significant where it was pu there by the owners of the house, as will be explained on 26a note 1 Therefore, an object found in the inner half of the wall belongs to th owner of the house regardless of how long it has been there (*Rosh;* se *Rashba*).

29. Since there is no way to know which of the renters lost the object, th owner despairs of recovering it (*Rashi*). This will be explained further in the Gemara.

30. The Emorites (and their related tribes, such as the Canaanites) inhabitated Eretz Yisrael prior to its conquest by the people of Israe under the leadership of Joshua. Objects left behind by these ancient inhabitants belong to whoever finds them. [See below, 26a note 1.] *Tos. Yom Tov* notes that the Tanna of this Baraisa obviously lived in Eretz Yisrael, and therefore spoke of Emorites. The same would hold true for a wall in any other land; the finder would be able to attribute the find to the ancient gentile inhabitants.

כאבני בית קולים מהו ת"ש דתניא מצא מעות מפוזרות הרי אלו שלו כאבני בית קולים [א]חייב להכריז [ב]ואלו הן (א)אבני בית קולים אחת מכאן ואחת מכאן ואחת על גביהן תנו רבנן המוצא סלע בשוק ומצאו חבירו ואמר לו שלי היא חדשה היא נירונית היא של מלך פלוני היא [ג]לא אמר כלום ולא עוד אלא [ד]אפילו שמו כתוב עליה לא אמר כלום לפי שאין סימן למטבע דאמר דלמא אפוקי אפקה ומאיניש אחרינא נפל: **מתני'** מצא [ה]אחר הגפה או אחר הגדר גוזלות מקושרים או בשבילין שבשדות הרי זה לא יגע בהן (ב)[ו]מצא כלי באשפה אם מכוסה לא יגע בו אם מגולה נוטל ומכריז: **גמ'** מאי טעמא דאמרינן הני איניש אצנעינהו (א) ואי שקיל להו לית להו למרייהו סימנא בגווייהו הלכך לשבקינהו עד דאתי מרייהו ושקיל להו ואמאי ליהוי (ג)קשר סימנא אמר רבי אבא בר זבדא אמר רב [ז]במקושרין בכנפיהן דכולי עלמא הכי מקטרי להו ולהוי מקום סימן אמר רב עוקבא בר חמא [ח]במדדין אי במדדין מעלמא אתו ומותרין איכא למימר מעלמא אתו ואיכא למימר איניש אצנעינהו והוה ליה ספק הינוח (ד)ואמר רבי אבא בר זבדא אמר רב [ט]כל ספק הינוח לכתחילה לא יטול ואם נטל לא יחזיר: מצא כלי באשפה מכוסה לא יגע בו מגולה נוטל ומכריז: ורמינהו מצא כלי טמון באשפה נוטל ומכריז שכן דרך אשפה לפנות אמר רב זביד לא קשיא [י]הא בכובי וכסי הא בסכיני והמניק בכובי וכסי לא יגע בסכיני והמניק נוטל ומכריז רב פפא אמר הא והא בכובי וכסי ולא קשיא כאן באשפה העשויה לפנות כאן באשפה שאינה עשויה לפנות אשפה העשויה לפנות [כ]אבידה מדעת היא [ל]אלא (ה)באשפה שאינה עשויה לפנות ונמלך עליה לפנותה בשלמא לרב פפא היינו דקתני שכן דרך אשפה לפנות אלא לרב זביד מאי שכן דרך אשפה לפנות שכן דרך אשפה לפנות לה כלים קטנים: **מתני'** [מ]מצא בגל ובכותל ישן (ו)הרי אלו שלו [נ]מצא בכותל חדש מחציו ולחוץ שלו מחציו ולפנים של בעל הבית [ס]אם היה משכירו לאחרים אפילו (ב) (ז)בתוך הבית הרי אלו שלו: **גמ'** תנא מפני שיכול לומר לו של אמוריים הן אטו אמורים מצנעי ישראל לא מצנעי לא צריכא

דשתיך

---

**רש"י**

כאבני בית קולים. מרקולים והיא שם ע"ז ולקמיה מפ' היכי עבדי: אחת מכאן ואחת מכאן. והשלישית אליה על זה ואליה על זה: נירונית היא. נירון קיסר כתוב עליה: **מתני'** מצא אחר הגפה [או אחר הגדר] גוזלות מקושרין. גפה סתימת כותל של עץ או של קנים: גדר. של אבנים: לא יגע בהן. טעמא מפ' בגמרא: מכוסה לא יגע בו. דאין זו אבידה שיהא מוזהר עליה בלא תוכל להתעלם דמשתמר הוא: **גמ'** במדדין. ממקום למקום: מעלמא אתו. ואין זה הינוח וכיון דאין בהן סימן נימא הרי אלו שלו: ואיכא למימר איניש אצנעינהו. הואיל ומקושרין: ספק הינוח. בדבר שאין בו סימן וכ"ש ודאי הינוח: לכתחילה לא יטול. דאי שקלת לה ליכא למרייהו סימנין למיתב בהו ויפסיד הלכך לא יטול והבעלים יזכרו ויבאו ויטלום: ואם נטל לא יחזיר. דהא ליכא דיהיב סימנא: שכן דרך אשפה ליפנות. ואי לא שקיל ליה האי השתא לכשיפנה יטלנה נכרי או ישראל חשוד הלכך אבידה היא ומוזהר עליה: כובי וכסי. טמונים מדעת הואי ולא יגע בהן: סכיני והמניק. שהן כלים קטנים אבדה הן שהשליכם שם עם האשפה שהוציאם מן הבית ולקמן פריך מאי שכן דרך אשפה לפנות: אבידה מדעת היא. דהוה ליה לאסוקי אדעתיה שיפנוה: היינו דקתני שכן דרך אשפה לפנות. שהבעלים נמלכים לפנות: לפנות לה כלים קטנים. מן הבית שלא מדעת: **מתני'** מצא בגל. גל אבנים מחומה שנפלה: הרי אלו שלו. בגמרא מפרש: מחציו ולחוץ. באחד מחורי כותל הסמוכים לרשות הרבים מלאה מחצי עוביו של כותל ולחוץ שלו דאמרינן אחד מבני רשות הרבים נתנו שם ושכח דאע"ג דאמרן לעיל ספק הינוח לא יטול והאי ודאי הינוח הוא הא מוקמי' למתני' בגמרא דשתיך טפי דאיכא יאוש בעלים: ואפילו מצא בתוך הבית כו'. דלא ידוע דמאן נינהו ובעליו נואשו: **גמ'** תנא. גבי גל וכותל ישן: שיכול לומר לו. לבעל הגל או לבעל הכותל: של אמוריים. שהורישו אבותינו היו: ישראל לא מצנעי. ומחציו ולפנים אמאי שלו הרי בעל הבית זה משתמש בה זה כמה שנים:

דשתיך

---

**תוספות**

**כאבני** בית קולים. מכאן אר"ת דאין שם ע"ז מרקולים אלא קולים כדאמרינן הכא והא דקרי ליה בעלמא מרקולים היינו אילוף קילוס דהם קורים קילוס לשון שבח וחכמים החליפו לגנאי לשון לעג וקלס (תהלים מד) ומר הוא אילוף כמו מר דשחוטה דפרק גיד הנשה (חולין דף לד.) ומר דפרזלא דהגוזל בתרא (ב"ק קיג:)(ח):

**אחר** הגפה. מקום שמשתמרות קצת אבל מצא במקום שאין משתמר כלל ודאי אבידה היא ונתייאשו הבעלים כיון שאין בה סימן ולא איירי הכא במשתמר לגמרי מדפריך בגמרא ולהוי קשר סימן כלומר ויטול ויכריז ובמקום המשתמר אפי' יש בו סימן לא יגע בו דהא תנן מצא כלי טמון באשפה לא יגע בו וביש בו סימן איירי מדקאמר ואם מגולה נוטל ומכריז וכן לעיל (דף כד.) אמר מצא אבידה אם רוב ישראל חייב להכריז א"כ ביש בה סימן איירי ומוקי לה בטמון באשפה ונמלך עליה לפנותה אבל אם לא נמלך לא יגע בה ולרבא דאמר מקום הוי סימן נקט דוקא גוזלות דמדדין אבל דבר אחר לא דהוי מקום סימן ויטול ויכריז כיון דאינו משתמר לגמרי ולרבה דאמר מקום לא הוי סימן נקט גוזלות לאשמועינן דאע"ג דהוי ספק הינוח דאיכא למימר דמעלמא אתו לא יגע בהן:

(ט) **ואמר** ר' אבא בר זבדא אמר רב ספק הינוח לכתחילה לא יטול. כדמפרש לעיל דלמא איניש אצנעינהו: **ואם** נטל לא יחזיר. יש מפרש דהיינו דוקא כשנטלהו והוליכו לביתו דיש לחוש שמא באו בעלים בתוך כך ולא מצאו מה שהניחו שם ושוב לא יחזרו לבקשה לכך לא יחזיר למקום שנטל אבל אם נטלו ולא זז משם ורואה שלא באו בעלים בתוך כך יחזיר וכן יש בירושלמי עובדא ברבי אבא בר זבדא גופיה דקאמר רבי אבא בר זבדא אשכח חמרא מכוסה בחפיסה ונסביה אתא ושאיל בבי רב אמרו ליה לאו יאות עבדת אמר להו אהדריה א"ל לא דלמא אתא מריה ולא אשכחיה ומיאש מיניה ומיהו אם נטל לא יחזיר משמע רק שנטלה ואע"ג דלא הוליכה לשום מקום לא יחזיר ויש לפרש דמיירי הכא בספק אבידה דאפי' הניחה בעלים שם מדעת דומה ששכחוהו דבלא משתמר כ"א קצת מיירי דומיא דמתני' דעל מתני' קאי רבי אבא ולכך אם נטל לא יחזיר דהשתא אבידה היא ושכחוה הבעלים וכיון שאם היה יודע שהיא אבידה היה מחויב בהשבתה בלא שום הגבהה אם הוא יודע של מי הוא דכיון שהוא משתמר קצת לא יתייאשו הבעלים היכא דהגביה הוי מחויב בשמירתה מספק לרבה הוי שומר חנם ולרב יוסף שומר שכר עד שתבא ליד הבעלים ולא דמי לזקן ואינה לפי כבודו דאמר רבה בפרקין (י) הכישה נתחייב בה ואמרינן בהמוכר את הספינה (ב"ב דף פח.) אימור דאמר רבה בבעלי חיים דאנקטינהו נגרי ברייתא אבל בשאר דברים לא היינו משום דזקן לא מיחייב בהשבה כלל ולכך כי יחזיר למקומה אינו חייב בשמירתה וכן לגלוסקין דפרק הספינה (שם דף פז:) לא מיחייב כלל בנטילה דאבידה מדעת היא ואינו חייב כלל בהשבתה אבל הכא אם היה יודע שהיא אבידה היה חייב ליקחנה ולהשיבה לבעלים אם היה יודע של מי (ג) הם עתה שהוא ספק אם הגביה חייב בשמירתה כדין אבידה ממש וכן משמע בפרק הספינה (שם) דקאמר לגלוסקין אבידה מדעת היא משמע דאם לא היתה אבידה מדעת א"ש דמחייב בנטילתה ועובדא דירושלמי דקאמר דאימור אתא מריה ולא אשכחיה מיירי שמצאו במקום שמשתמר לגמרי שלא היתה אבידה ואינה בת השבה ולכך אי לא הוה לן למיחש לאתא מריה יחזיר שפיר וכן משמע דסתם חפיסה יש בו סימן ואי לא הוה משתמר לגמרי א"כ שפיר עשה שנטלה ואמאי אמר דלאו יאות עבד וכן הא דתניא לקמן (דף לא.) מצא טלית או קורדום בצד גדר אין זו אבידה ולא יגע בו אפילו יש בו סימן מיירי במקום המשתמר אי נמי התם לדעת הונח שם ולא יגע בו אפילו יש בו סימן דדרך פועלים שמניחים טליתן או קורדומם בצד גדר של אותה שדה ולפירוש רש"י דפירש דלא יחזיר דליכא איניש דיהיב סימנא קשה דפשיטא דלא יחזירנו לשום אדם שאינו יודע מי הם הבעלים כיון שאין בו סימן:

דשתיך

---

**עין משפט נר מצוה**

סא א ב מיי' פט"ז מהל' אבדה הלכה ג סמג עשין עד טוש"ע ח"מ סי' רסב סעיף יג:
סב ג ד מיי' שם פי"ד הלכה י סמג שם טוש"ע שם סעיף יג:
סג ה מיי' שם פט"ו הל' ו ועיין בהשגות ובמ"מ סמג שם טוש"ע ח"מ סי' רס סעיף י:
סד ו מיי' שם הלכה ז טוש"ע שם סעי' יא:
סה ז ח מיי' שם הל' ו טוש"ע שם סעיף י:
סו ט מיי' שם הל"א ועי' בהשגות טוש"ע שם סעיף ט:
סז י מיי' שם הלכה ז טוש"ע שם סעיף יא:
סח כ מיי' שם פי"א הל' יא סמג שם טוש"ע ח"מ סי' רסא סעיף ד:
סט ל מיי' שם פט"ו הלכה ז טוש"ע ח"מ סי' רס סעיף יא:
ע מ נ מיי' שם פט"ז הלכה ט ועיין בהשגות ובמגיד משנה סמג שם טוש"ע שם סעיף א:
עא ס מיי' שם הל' יא ועיין בהשגות ובמ"מ טוש"ע שם סעיף ג:

**הגהות הב"ח**

(א) גמ' הני איניש אצנעינהו הכא ואי: (ב) שם במשנה אפילו מצא בתוך הבית: (ג) תום' ד"ה ואם וכו' אם היה יודע של מי הוא עתה:

**ליקוטי רש"י**

קשר סימנא. שיש קשרים שאין דומין זה לזה ויאמר כך וכך הוא עשוי [לעיל כ:]. ספק הינוח. אלא דבר שאין בו סימן בצד מקום שמשתמר קצת דלא שכיחי אינשי דאזלי ויש לספוקי שמא מדעת הונח שם לגניזה. לכתחילה לא יטול. המוצאו שכשיבא בעליו לא ימצאנו וסימן אין בו שיכריז לפיכך יניחנו זה ובעליו יבא ויטלנו. ואם נטל לא יחזיר. ואם בא אחר ואמר שלי הוא וסימן אינו נותן בו לא יחזירנו שמא אינו שלו וסוף הבעלים לבוא ויביא עדים שהניחו שם לפיכך יהא מונח ביד זה עד שיבא אליהו דהאי לא יחזיר לא שיהא שלו קאמר דהא מעיקרא באיסורא אתא לידיה אם הינוח הוא [לקמן לז:]. הא בכובי. קנקן [שבת מח.]. כסי. כוסות [ביצה יג:]. והמניק. ימוספו"ר של ברזל של סופרים שיש לו שני ראשים ולאחד אחד מפולל [סוכה לב.]. אבידה מדעת היא. שהיה לו לחוש שמא יפנה. שאינה עשויה לפנות. רגילים היו בעלים להניחה ימים רבים ולא לפנותה מיד. ונמלך עליה לפנותה. מיד ועל כרחו או יטלנו או יהא הפקר [לעיל כד.].

**מסורת הש"ס**

א) [עבודה זרה נ. ב) [לעיל כד.], ג) [לעיל כ... כג:], ד) לקמן לז... ה) [לעיל כד.], ו) [עי' תוס' בבא בתרא נד. ד"ה אדעתא], ז) [גירסת הרי"ף והרא"ש כגירסת רש"י אפילו מצא וכו' בפיסקא לקמן כו. ח) [ועיין תוס' סנהדרין סד. ד"ה מרקולים ועבודה זרה נ. ד"ה אבני], ט) ... דברי מהרש"ל דיבור זה ע... ד"ה ואם הד"א, י) [לקמן ל:].

**רבינו חננאל**

כחצובה זה למעלה מז... במקום א) מרודד. כסול... נתונים כסדר באו... והפרש ביניהן. הי... מכריז אם היו עשויי... כמגדלים. אמר רבי... טיבעא מכריז ויב... בעליהם ויתן סימנ... ויטלם. אבני בית קולי... בית ע"ז שמה מרקולי... עבודתו גרימת אבני... ועיקרו ג' אבנים שתים... כנגד זו ואחד על גביה... ואם מצא מטבעות... האי גוונא חייב להכרי... ת"ר המוצא סלע בש... ואמר לו חבירו שלי הי... נירונית היא פי' כמטב... נירון קיסר היא כו' ו... ולא עוד אפי' שמו כת... עליה לא אמר כלו... שאין סימן למטב... דאמרי' אפוקי אפק... ומאחרינא נפל: מתנ... מצא אחר הגפה. ... הגפה סגירה מלש... יגיפו הדלתות וכדתנן ... האגף ולפנים. גוזל... מקושרות או בשביל... שבשדות הרי זה לא י... בהן ואוקימנא בדלי... בהו סימן ובמדד... דאיכא למימר מעלמ... אתו ואיכא למימר איני... אצנעינהו הוי ליה ספ... הינוח וכל ספק הינ... לכתחלה לא יטול וא... נטל לא יחזיר. תלמ... ארץ ישראל ר' אבא ב... זבדא אשכח חמר מכוס... בחפיסה ונסביה או... שאיל לרב אמר ליה ... עבדת יאות אמר ל... אהדריה אמר ליה ... דנימר אתא מריה ו... אשכחיה ונתיאש מיני... פי' מדדין מהלכין מ... מעט כדכתיב אדדם ... בית אלהים. ותנן ... האשה מדדה את בנ... מצא כלי טמון באשפ... לא יגע בו. איני והתנ... נוטל ומכריז. ופריק ... זביד לא קשיא מת... בכובי וכסי דמצנעי ל... אינשי. בהמנק וסכ... דאיכא למימר בטאנ... שקלינהו בהדי עפ... דביתא וזרקינהו לאשפ... ולא ידע שכן דרך ב... אדם לכבד הב... ולהשליך העפר לאשפ... פי' המנק כלי שיש... שני ראשים כגון המז... שיש לו ג' שינים וד... בני יון להחזיק חתי... הבשר ולחתוך עם הסכ... ולאכול ונוטל זה שחו... ונותנו לתוך פיו ואין יז... נוגעות בבשר כלל מ...

**חשק שלמה על ר"ח**

א) עי' בערוך ערך אגב שכתב זה למעלה מזה במק... מורד עכ"ל ונראה שכן ... גס כאן בדברי רבינו וע... עוד פי' אחר.

**וְלֶהֱוֵי מָקוֹם סִימָן** – **But let the place** where they were found **serve as an identifying mark!**[13] – ? –

The Gemara answers:

**אָמַר רַב עוּקְבָא בַּר חָמָא** – **Rav Ukva bar Chama said:** **בִּמְדַדִּין** – The Mishnah is dealing **with [birds] that** can **hop** from place to place.[14]

The Gemara asks:

**אִי בִּמְדַדִּין** – If the Mishnah is dealing **with [birds] that** can **hop,** **מֵעָלְמָא אָתוּ** – then **they** might have **come from elsewhere,** **וּמוּתָּרִין** – **and they** should be **permitted** for the finder to keep. Why does the Mishnah forbid the finder to take the birds?[15]

The Gemara answers:

**אִיכָּא לְמֵימַר מֵעָלְמָא אָתוּ** – Indeed, **it is possible to say that they came from elsewhere,** **וְאִיכָּא לְמֵימַר אִינָשׁ אַצְנְעִינְהוּ** – **but it is** also possible **to say that a person concealed them** behind this fence.[16] **וַהֲוָה לֵיהּ סָפֵק הִינּוּחַ** – Thus, **it is** a find regarding which **a doubt** exists whether it was deliberately **placed** there for safekeeping; **וְאָמַר רַבִּי אַבָּא בַּר זַבְדָּא אָמַר רַב** – **and R' Abba bar Zavda said in the name of Rav:** **כָּל סָפֵק הִינּוּחַ** – **Any** found object regarding which a **doubt** exists whether it was deliberately **placed** there, **לְכַתְּחִילָּה לֹא יִטּוֹל** – **one should not pick** it **up as a first resort;**[17] **וְאִם נָטַל** – **but if he picked** it **up,** **לֹא יַחֲזִיר** – **he should not return** it to any claimant.[18]

The Gemara cites the next section of our Mishnah:

**מָצָא כְּלִי בְּאַשְׁפָּה** – IF ONE FOUND A UTENSIL IN A GARBAGE HEAP: **מְכוּסֶּה** – if [THE UTENSIL] IS COVERED, **לֹא יִגַּע** – HE SHOULD NOT TOUCH IT; **מְגוּלֶּה** – if IT IS UNCOVERED, **נוֹטֵל וּמַכְרִיז** – HE MUST TAKE it AND ANNOUNCE it.

The Gemara asks:

**וּרְמִינְהוּ** – **They noted a contradiction** between our Mishnah and the following Baraisa: **מָצָא כְּלִי טָמוּן בְּאַשְׁפָּה** – IF ONE FOUND A UTENSIL BURIED IN A GARBAGE HEAP, **נוֹטֵל וּמַכְרִיז** – HE MUST TAKE it AND ANNOUNCE it, **שֶׁכֵּן דֶּרֶךְ אַשְׁפָּה לְפַנּוֹת** – BECAUSE IT IS THE NATURE OF A GARBAGE HEAP to BE CLEARED.[19] This Baraisa apparently contradicts our Mishnah, which instructed the finder not to touch an object found concealed in a garbage heap. – ? –

The Gemara reconciles the rulings of the Mishnah and the Baraisa:

**אָמַר רַב זְבִיד** – **Rav Zevid said:** **לֹא קַשְׁיָא** – **There is no difficulty.** **הָא בְּכוּבֵי וְכַסֵּי** – **This** [the Mishnah] is dealing **with** finds such as **barrels and cups;** **הָא בְּסַכִּינֵי וְהַמְנִיק** – whereas **that** [the Baraisa] is dealing **with** finds such as **knives and a *hamnik.***[20] **בְּכוּבֵי וְכַסֵּי** – **With** regard to large vessels, such as **barrels and cups,** **לֹא יִגַּע** – the Mishnah rules that **[the finder] should not touch** them, because they are assumed to have been placed there deliberately. Thus, they are not lost. **בְּסַכִּינֵי וְהַמְנִיק** – But **with** small utensils, such as **knives and a *hamnik,*** **נוֹטֵל וּמַכְרִיז** – the Baraisa rules that **he must take** them **and announce** them, because they might have been taken out inadvertently from the house with the garbage.[21]

An alternative solution:

**רַב פָּפָּא אָמַר** – **Rav Pappa said:** **הָא וְהָא בְּכוּבֵי וְכַסֵּי** – **This** Mishnah **and this** Baraisa can both be dealing **with** large objects such as **barrels and cups;** **וְלֹא קַשְׁיָא** – **yet, there is no difficulty.** **כָּאן בְּאַשְׁפָּה הָעֲשׂוּיָה לְפַנּוֹת** – For **here,** the Baraisa is dealing **with a garbage heap that is ordinarily cleared;** thus, even an object concealed in it must be considered lost. **כָּאן בְּאַשְׁפָּה שֶׁאֵינָהּ עֲשׂוּיָה לְפַנּוֹת** – **Here,** the Mishnah is dealing **with a garbage heap that is not ordinarily cleared;** thus, an object concealed in it is not lost.

The Gemara objects to this reconciliation:

**אַשְׁפָּה הָעֲשׂוּיָה לְפַנּוֹת** – If the object was found in **a garbage heap that is ordinarily cleared,** **אֲבֵידָה מִדַּעַת הִיא** – **it is an intentional loss,** since the owner realizes that it may well be cleared at any time! Why should one who finds it have to

NOTES

13. The Gemara above (22b) cited a dispute between Rabbah and Rava whether the location of a lost article is acceptable as a *siman.* This question is based on Rava's opinion that it is acceptable.

14. Although their wings are immobilized, the birds may still be able to hop. Thus, they may have moved since they were lost, and the owner will be unable to use their location as a *siman* to reclaim them (see *Rashi*).

15. The only situation in which the Mishnah rules that one should leave an unidentifiable object in place is where it seems likely that the owner deliberately placed his property there. [Leaving them then offers a chance for the owner to return and retrieve them.] However, in the case of mobile birds, it seems somewhat unlikely that the owner would place them down deliberately, knowing that they could hop away. We should therefore assume that they fell from their owner without his knowledge. Since they have no *siman,* the finder should be permitted to keep them for himself (*Rashi,* as explained by *Pnei Yehoshua*).

16. People do not ordinarily tie the wings of their birds unless they are planning to put them down somewhere. Therefore, although their mobility gives us reason to suspect that they fell from their owner, their tied wings give support to the notion that they were deliberately left in this place (*Rashi*).

17. R' Abba bar Zavda refers to an unidentifiable object found in a partially protected place. If it had been deliberately placed there by its owner, it would not be in the owner's best interest for the finder to take it and announce it, since the owner will have no way of reclaiming it. It is therefore preferable for the finder to leave the object in its place, so that the owner can return and retrieve it (*Rashi* here and below, 37b). Hence, in the case of our Mishnah, since there is a possibility that the owner deliberately placed his birds behind the fence, the finder should not take them.

18. Since this object has no *siman,* no one will be able to identify it. Hence, the finder cannot return it to any claimant (*Rashi*; cf. *Tosafos*). Nor should he return it to its place, since the owner might have returned in the interim to look for it and found it missing. Thus, he will not think to look for it there again, and the object will eventually be lost (see *Tosafos* and *Nimukei Yosef*). Rather, having taken it wrongfully, he becomes responsible for it, and he must hold it until the identity of its owner is determined by witnesses, or until Elijah comes and clarifies its ownership (*Rashi* on 37b, see note 6 there; cf. *Rambam, Hil. Gezeilah* 15:31).

**In summary:** There are three conditions in which an object may be found, and the law for returning them varies accordingly:

(1) *Totally protected* – The finder should not take and announce the object even if it has a *siman,* because there is no reason to assume that it was lost by its owner. We rather assume that the object is being kept there for safekeeping.

(2) *Partially protected* – If the find has a *siman,* the finder should take it and announce it, for it may well be a lost object. Even if the owner deliberately placed it there for a short time intending to come back for it, we must be concerned that a dishonest person will find it in the interim and keep it for himself. Thus, it is preferable to take it and announce it. However, if the object has no *siman,* the finder should leave it, because the owner cannot identify it, and taking it therefore diminishes the chance of his recovering it.

(3) *Not protected at all* – It is certainly a lost object. Therefore, if the find has a *siman,* then the finder should take it and announce it. If it has no *siman,* the finder may keep the object for his own use, because the owner has surely despaired of recovering it (*Rosh*).

19. Consequently, if the finder does not take the object now, it may be taken later by a dishonest person when the heap is cleared. It is thus in effect a lost object (*Rashi*).

20. A *hamnik* is a metal instrument, pointed at both ends, used by scribes. One end was split in the shape of a "Y" (*Rashi, Succah* 32a ד"ה אלא דעביד כי המניק).

21. The Gemara below will ask why, according to this explanation, the Baraisa states as its reason for announcing the object that the garbage heap is usually cleared; that fact is irrelevant according to Rav Zevid's reconciliation.

עין משפט
נר מצוה

סא א ב מיי' פט"ו מהל' אבדה הלכה ג סמג עשין עד טוש"ע ח"מ סי' רסב סעיף יג:
סב ג ד מיי' שם פי"ד הלכה י סמג שם טוש"ע שם סעיף יג:
סג ה מיי' שם פט"ו הל' ו ועיין בהשגות ובמ"מ סמג שם טוש"ע ח"מ סי' רס סעיף י:
סד ו מיי' שם הלכה ז טוש"ע שם סעי' יא:
סה ז ח מיי' שם הל' ו טוש"ע שם סעיף י:
סו ט מיי' שם הל"א ועי' בהשגות טוש"ע שם סעיף ט:
סז י מיי' שם הלכה ז טוש"ע שם סעיף יא:
סח כ מיי' שם פי"א הל' יא סמג שם טוש"ע ח"מ סי' רסא סעיף ד:
סט ל מיי' שם פט"ו הלכה ז טוש"ע ח"מ סי' רס סעיף יא:
ע מ נ מיי' שם פט"ו הלכה ט ועיין בהשגות ובמגיד משנה סמג שם טוש"ע שם סעיף א:
עא ס מיי' שם הל' יא ועיין בהשגות ובמ"מ טוש"ע שם סעיף ג:

כאבני בית קולים מהו ת"ש דתניא מצא מעות מפוזרות הרי אלו שלו כאבני בית קולים [א]חייב להכריז [ב]ואלו הן [א)]אבני בית קולים אחת מכאן ואחת מכאן ואחת על גביהן תנו רבנן המוצא סלע בשוק ומצאו חבירו ואמר לו שלי היא חדשה היא נירונית היא של מלך פלוני היא [ג]לא אמר כלום ולא עוד אלא [ד]אפילו שמו כתוב עליה לא אמר כלום לפי שאין סימן למטבע דאמר דלמא אפוקי אפקה ומאיניש אחרינא נפל: **מתני'** מצא [ה]אחר הגפה או אחר הגדר גוזלות מקושרים או בשבילין שבשדות הרי זה לא יגע בהן [ג)][ו]מצא כלי באשפה אם מכוסה לא יגע בו אם מגולה נוטל ומכריז: **גמ'** מאי טעמא דאמרינן הני איניש אצנעינהו (א) ואי שקיל להו לית להו למרייהו סימנא בגווייהו הלכך לשבקינהו עד דאתי מרייהו ושקיל להו ואמאי לידהוי [ג)]קשר סימנא אמר רבי אבא בר זבדא אמר רב [ז]במקושרין בכנפיהן דכולי עלמא הכי מקטרי להו ולהוי מקום סימן אמר רב עוקבא בר חמא [ח]במדדין אי במדדין מעלמא אתו ומותרין איכא למימר מעלמא אתו ואיכא למימר איניש אצנעינהו והוה ליה ספק הינוח [ד)]ואמר רבי אבא בר זבדא אמר רב [ט]כל ספק הינוח לכתחילה לא יטול ואם נטל לא יחזיר: מצא כלי באשפה מכוסה לא יגע בו מגולה נוטל ומכריז: ורמינהו מצא כלי טמון באשפה נוטל ומכריז שכן דרך אשפה לפנות אמר רב זביד לא קשיא [י]הא בכובי וכסי הא בסכיני והמניק בכובי וכסי לא יגע בסכיני והמניק נוטל ומכריז רב פפא אמר הא והא בכובי וכסי ולא קשיא כאן באשפה העשויה לפנות כאן באשפה שאינה עשויה לפנות אשפה העשויה לפנות [כ]אבידה מדעת היא [ל]אלא [ה)]באשפה שאינה עשויה לפנות ונמלך עליה לפנותה בשלמא לרב פפא היינו דקתני שכן דרך אשפה לפנות אלא לרב זביד מאי שכן דרך אשפה לפנות שכן דרך אשפה לפנות לה כלים קטנים: **מתני'** [מ]מצא בגל ובכותל ישן [ו)]הרי אלו שלו [נ]מצא בכותל חדש מחציו ולחוץ שלו מחציו ולפנים של בעל הבית [ס]אם היה משכירו לאחרים אפילו (ב) [ז)]בתוך הבית הרי אלו שלו: **גמ'** תנא מפני שיכול לומר לו של אמוריים הן אטו אמורים מצנעי ישראל לא מצנעי לא צריכא

דשתיך

רש"י

כאבני בית קולים. מרקולים והיא שם ע"ז ולקמיה מפ' היכי עבדי: אחת מכאן ואחת מכאן. והשלישית חליה על זה וחליה על זה: נירונית היא. נירון קיסר כתוב עליה: **מתני'** מצא אחר הגפה [או אחר הגדר] גוזלות מקושרין. גפה סתימת כותל של עץ או של קנים: גדר. של אבנים: לא יגע בהן. טעמא מפ' בגמרא: מכוסה לא יגע בו. דאין זו אבידה שיהא מוזהר עליה דלא תוכל להתעלם דמשתמר הוא: **גמ'** במדדין. ממקום למקום: מעלמא אתו. ואין זה הינוח וכיון דאין בהן סימן נימא הרי אלו שלו: ואיכא למימר איניש אצנעינהו. הואיל ומקושרין: ספק הינוח. בדבר שאין בו סימן וכ"ש ודאי הינוח: לכתחילה לא יטול. דאי שקלת לה ליכא למרייהו סימנין למיתב בהו ויפסיד הלכך לא יטול והבעלים יזכרו ויבאו ויטלום: ואם נטל לא יחזיר. דהא ליכא דיהיב סימנא: שכן דרך אשפה ליפנות. ואי לא שקיל ליה האי השתא לכשיפנה יטלנה נכרי או ישראל חשוד הלכך אבידה היא ומוזהר עליה: כובי וכסי. טמונים מדעת הואי ולא יגע בהן: סכיני והמניק. שהן כלים קטנים אבדה הן שהשליכם שם עם האשפה שהוציאם מן הבית ולקמן פריך מאי שכן דרך אשפה לפנות: אבידה מדעת היא. דהוה ליה לאסוקי אדעתיה שיפנוה: היינו דקתני שכן דרך אשפה לפנות. שהבעלים נמלכים לפנות: לפנות לה כלים קטנים. מן הבית שלא מדעת: **מתני'** מצא בגל. גל אבנים מחומה שנפלה: הרי אלו שלו. בגמרא מפרש: מחציו ולחוץ. באחד מחורי כותל הסמוכים לרשות הרבים מאלה מחצי עוביו של כותל ולחוץ שלו דאמרינן אחד מבני רשות הרבים נתנו שם ושכח דאע"ג דאמרן לעיל ספק הינוח לא יטול והאי ודאי הינוח הוא הא מוקמי' למתני' בגמרא דשתיך טפי דאיכא יאוש בעלים: ואפילו מצא בתוך הבית כו'. דלא ידוע דמאן נינהו ובעליו נואשו: **גמ'** תנא. גבי גל וכותל ישן: שיכול לומר לו. לבעל הגל או לבעל הכותל: של אמוריים. שהורישו אבותינו היו: ישראל לא מצנעי. ומחציו ולפנים אמאי שלו הרי בעל הבית זה משתמש בה זה כמה שנים:

דשתיך

תוספות

**כאבני** בית קולים. מכאן אר"ת דאין שם ע"ז מרקולים אלא קולים כדאמרינן הכא והא דקרי ליה בעלמא מרקולים היינו חילוף קילוס דהם קוריס קילוס לשון שבח וחכמים החליפו לגנאי לשון לעג וקלס (תהלים מד) ומר הוא חילוף כמו מר דשחוטה דפרק גיד הנשה (חולין דף צג.) ומר דפרזלא דהגוזל בתרא (ב"ק קיג:)[ט]:

**אחר** הגפה. מקום שמשתמרות קצת אבל מצא במקום שאין משתמר כלל ודאי אבידה היא ונתייאשו הבעלים כיון שאין בה סימן ולא איירי הכא במשתמר לגמרי מדפריך בגמרא ולהוי קשר סימן כלומר ויטול ויכריז ובמקום המשתמר אפי' יש בו סימן לא יגע בו דהא תנן מצא כלי טמון באשפה לא יגע בו וביש בו סימן איירי מדקאמר ואם מגולה נוטל ומכריז וכן לעיל (דף כד.) אמר מצא אבידה אם רוב ישראל חייב להכריז א"כ ביש בה סימן איירי ומוקי לה בטמון באשפה ונמלך עליה לפנותה אבל אם לא נמלך לא יגע בה ולרבה דאמר מקום הוי סימן נקט דוקא גוזלות דמדדין אבל דבר אחר לא דהוי מקום סימן ויטול ויכריז כיון דאינו משתמר לגמרי ולרבה דאמר מקום לא הוי סימן נקט גוזלות לאשמועינן דאע"ג דהוי ספק הינוח דאיכא למימר דמעלמא אתו לא יגע בהן:

[ט)] **ואמר** ר' אבא בר זבדא אמר רב ספק הינוח לכתחילה לא יטול. כדמפרש לעיל דלמא איניש אצנעינהו: **ואם** נטל לא יחזיר. יש מפרש דהיינו דוקא כשנטלהו והוליכו לביתו דיש לחוש שמא באו בעלים בתוך כך ולא מצאו מה שהניחו שם ושוב לא יחזרו לבקשה לכך לא יחזיר למקום שנטל אבל אם נטלו ולא זז משם ורואה שלא באו בעלים בתוך כך יחזיר וכן יש בירושלמי עובדא ברבי אבא בר זבדא גופיה דקאמר רבי אבא בר זבדא אשכח חמרא מכוסה בחפיסה ונסביה אתא ושאיל בבי רב אמרו ליה לאו יאות עבדת אמר להו אהדריה א"ל לא דלמא אתא מריה ולא אשכחיה ומיאש מיניה ומיהו אם נטל לא יחזיר משמע רק שנטלה ואע"ג דלא הוליכה לשום מקום לא יחזיר ויש לפרש דמיירי הכא בספק אבידה דאפי' הניחה בעלים שם מדעת דומה ששכחוהו דבלא משתמר כ"א קצת מיירי דומיא דמתני' דעל מתני' קאי רבי אבא ולכך אם נטל לא יחזיר דהשתא אבידה היא ושכחוה הבעלים וכיון שאם היה יודע שהיא אבידה היה מחויב בהשבתה בלא שום הגבהה אם הוא יודע של מי הוא דכיון שהוא משתמר קצת לא יתייאשו הבעלים היכא דהגביה הוי מחויב בשמירתה מספק לרבה הוי שומר חנם ולרב יוסף שומר שכר עד שתבא ליד הבעלים ולא דמי לזקן ואינה לפי כבודו דאמר רבה בפרקין [י)] הכישה נתחייב בה ואמרינן בהמוכר את הספינה (ב"ב דף פז.) איסור דאמר רבה בבעלי חיים דאנקטינהו נגרי ברייתא אבל בשאר דברים לא היינו משום דזקן לא מיחייב בהשבה כלל ולכך כי יחזיר למקומה אינו חייב בשמירתה וכן גלוסית דפרק הספינה (שם דף פז:) לא מיחייב כלל בנטילה דאבידה מדעת היא ואינו חייב כלל בהשבתה אבל הכא אם היה יודע שהיא אבידה היה חייב ליקחנה ולהשיבה לבעלים אם היה יודע של מי (ג) הם עתה שהוא ספק אם הגביה חייב בשמירתה כדין אבידה ממש וכן משמע בפרק הספינה (שם) דקאמר גלוסית אבידה מדעת היא משמע דאם לא היתה אבידה מדעת א"ש דמחייב בנטילתה ועובדא דירושלמי דקאמר דאימור דאתא מריה ולא אשכחיה איירי שמצאו במקום שמשתמר לגמרי שלא היתה אבידה ואינה בת השבה ולכך אי לא הוה לן למיחש לאתא מריה יחזיר שפיר וכן משמע דבתם חפיסה יש בו סימן ואי לא הוה משתמר לגמרי א"כ שפיר עשה שנטלה ואמאי אמר דלאו יאות עבד וכן הא דתניא לקמן (דף לא.) מצא טלית או קורדום בצד גדר אין זו אבידה ולא יגע בו אפילו יש בו סימן איירי במקום המשתמר אי נמי התם לדעת הונח שם ולא יגע בו אפילו יש בו סימן דדרך פועלים שמניחים טליתן או קורדומם בצד גדר של אותה שדה ולפירוש רש"י דפירש דלא יחזיר דליכא איניש דיהיב סימנא קשה דפשיטא דלא יחזירנו לשום אדם שאינו יודע מי הם הבעלים כיון שאין בו סימן:

דשתיך

הגהות הב"ח

(א) גמ' הני איניש אצנעינהו הכא ואי: (ב) שם במשנה אפילו מצא בתוך הבית: (ג) תוס' ד"ה ואם וכו' אם היה יודע של מי הוא עתה:

ליקוטי רש"י

קשר סימנא. שיש קשרים שאין דומין זה לזה ויאמר כך וכך הוא עשוי [לעיל כ:]. ספק הינוח. מצא דבר שאין בו סימן בצד מקום שמשתמר קצת דלא שכיחי אינשי דאזלי ויש לספוקי שמא מדעת הונח שם לגניזה. לכתחילה לא יטול. המוצאו שכשיבא בעליו לא ימצאנו וסימן אין בו שיכריז לפיכך יניחנו זה ובעליו יבא ויטלנו. ואם נטל לא יחזיר. ואם בא אחר ואמר שלי הוא וסימן אינו נותן בו לא יחזירנו שמא אינו שלו וסוף הבעלים לבוא ויביא עדים שהניחו שם לפיכך יהא מונח ביד זה עד שיבא אליהו דהאי לא יחזיר לא שיהא שלו קאמר דהא מעיקרא באיסורא אתא לידיה אם הינוח הוא [לקמן לז:]. הא בכובי. קנקן [שבת מח.]. כסי. נוטוע [ביצה יג:]. והמניק. יפוילפו"ר של ברזל של סופרים שיש לו שני ראשים וראשו אחד מפולל [סוכה לב.]. אבידה מדעת היא. שהיה לו לחוש שמא יפנה. שאינה עשויה לפנות. רגילים היו בעלים להניחה ימים רבים ולא לפנותה מיד. ונמלך עליה לפנותה. מיד ועל כרחו או יטלנו או יהא הפקר [לעיל כד.].

מסורת הש"ס

א) [עבודה זרה ב) [לעיל כד.], ג) [לעיל כג:], ד) לקמן ה) [לעיל כד.], ו) [תוס' בבא בתרא נד. לדעתא], ז) [גירסת הר והרא"ש כגירסת ר אפילו מצא ו בפיסקא לקמן כ ח) [ועיין תוס' סנהד סד. ד"ה מרקולים ועב זרה נ. ד"ה אבנין], ט) דברי מהר"ס דיבור זה ד"ה ואם הד"א, י) [לע ל:].

רבינו חננאל

כחצובה זה למעלה במקום א) מרודד. כסו נתונים כסדר בא והפרש ביניהן. מכריז אם היו עשו כמגדלים. אמר רב טיבעא מכריז ו בעליהם ויתן סי ויטלם. אבני בית קו בית ע"ז שמה מרקו עבודתו גרימת אב ועיקרו ג' אבנים שתים כנגד זו ואחד על גביו ואם מצא מטבעות האי גוונא חייב להכר ת"ר המוצא סלע בש ואמר לו חבירו שלי ז נירונית היא פי' כמט נירון קיסר היא כו' ולא עוד אפי' שמו כו עליה לא אמר כ שאין סימן למט דאמרי' אפוקי אפ ומאחרינא נפל: מת מצא אחר הגפה. הגפה סגירה מלי יגיפו הדלתות וכדתנן האגף ולפנים. גוז מקושרות או בשבי שבשדות הרי זה לא בהן ואוקימנא בד בהו סימן ובמד דאיכא למימר מעל אתו ואיכא למימר אי אצנעינהו הוי ליה ס הינוח וכל ספק הינ לכתחלה לא יטול ו נטל לא יחזיר. תלכ ארץ ישראל ר' אבא זבדא אשכח חמר מכו בחפיסה ונסביה א שאיל לרב אמר ליה עבדת יאות אמר ל אהדריה אמר ליה דנימר אתא מריה ו אשכחיה ונתיאש מינ פי' מדדין מהלכין מ מעט כדכתיב אדדם בית אלהים. ותנן נ האשה מדדה את בו מצא כלי טמון באש לא יגע בו. איני והתנ נוטל ומכריז. ופריק זביד לא קשיא מת בכובי וכסי דמצנעי ל אינשי. בהמנק וס דאיכא למימר בטא שקלינהו בהדי עפ דביתא וזרקינהו לאשפ ולא ידע שכן דרך ג אדם לכבד הב ולהשליך העפר לאשפ פי' המנק כלי שיש שני ראשים כגון המז שיש לו ג' שינים וד בני יון להחזיק חתי הבשר ולחתוך פה ולאכול ונוטל זה שח ונותנו לתוך פיו ואין נוגעות בבשר כלל כו

חשק שלמה על ר'

א) עי' בערוך ערך הלב שכתב זה למעלה מזה במר מורד עכ"ל ונראה שגם כאן בדברי רבינו וצ עוד פי' אחר.

If ONE FOUND A *SELA* coin IN THE MARKET, וּמְצָאוֹ חֲבֵירוֹ וְאָמַר לוֹ – AND HIS FRIEND ENCOUNTERED HIM AND SAID TO HIM: לִי הִיא – "[THE COIN] IS MINE," and the claimant went on to state one of the following features of the coin: חֲדָשָׁה הִיא – "IT IS NEW," – or "שֶׁל מֶלֶךְ פְּלוֹנִי הִיא – נֵירוֹנִית הִיא – or "IT IS A NERONIAN";[3] IS OF KING SO-AND-SO" – לֹא אָמַר כְּלוּם – HE HAS SAID NOTHING of significance, and the finder may keep the coin. וְלֹא עוֹד – NOT ONLY THAT, אֶלָּא אֲפִילּוּ שְׁמוֹ כָּתוּב עָלֶיהָ – BUT EVEN IF [THE CLAIMANT'S] NAME IS WRITTEN ON [THE COIN], לֹא אָמַר כְּלוּם – HE HAS SAID NOTHING of significance, לְפִי שֶׁאֵין סִימָן לְמַטְבֵּעַ – BECAUSE THERE IS NO valid IDENTIFYING MARK FOR A COIN.

The Gemara explains the last case of the Baraisa:

דְּאָמַר – For [the finder] can say: דִּלְמָא אַפּוּקֵי אַפְּקָהּ – Perhaps [the claimant] spent [the coin], וְאִינִישׁ אַחֲרִינָא נָפַל – and it fell from another person.[4]

כְּאַבְנֵי בֵּית קוּלִיס מַהוּ – What is [the law] if the coins are arranged like the stones of the House of Kulis?[1]

The Gemara answers:

תָּא שְׁמַע – Come, learn the resolution to this inquiry; דְּתַנְיָא – for it was taught in a Baraisa: מָצָא מָעוֹת מְפוּזָּרוֹת – If ONE FOUND SCATTERED COINS, הֲרֵי אֵלּוּ שֶׁלּוֹ – THESE BELONG TO HIM. כְּאַבְנֵי בֵּית קוּלִיס – But if they were arranged LIKE THE STONES OF THE HOUSE OF KULIS, חַיָּיב לְהַכְרִיז – HE IS OBLIGATED TO ANNOUNCE them. וְאֵלּוּ הֵן אַבְנֵי בֵּית קוּלִיס – AND THIS IS how THE STONES OF THE HOUSE OF KULIS were arranged: אַחַת מִכָּאן – ONE ON THIS SIDE, וְאַחַת מִכָּאן – AND ONE ON THAT SIDE, וְאַחַת עַל גַּבֵּיהֶן – AND ONE ON TOP OF THEM.[2]

The Gemara elaborates upon another aspect of finding money:

תָּנוּ רַבָּנַן – The Rabbis taught in a Baraisa: הַמּוֹצֵא סֶלַע בַּשּׁוּק – 

## Mishnah

מָצָא אַחַר הַגַּפָּה אוֹ אַחַר הַגָּדֵר – If one found behind a fence or behind a wall[5] גּוֹזָלוֹת מְקוּשָּׁרִים – young pigeons that were tied; אוֹ בִּשְׁבִילִין שֶׁבִּשְׂדוֹת – or if he found such birds in the paths of the fields, הֲרֵי זֶה לֹא יִגַּע בָּהֶן – he should not touch them.[6] מָצָא כְּלִי בְּאַשְׁפָּה – If he found a utensil in a garbage heap: אִם מְכוּסֶּה – If [the utensil] is covered, לֹא יִגַּע בּוֹ – he should not touch it;[7] אִם מְגוּלֶּה – if it is uncovered, נוֹטֵל וּמַכְרִיז – he must take it and announce it.[8]

## Gemara

The Gemara elaborates upon the first ruling of the Mishnah:

מַאי טַעְמָא – What is the reason that the finder must not touch the birds? דְּאָמְרִינַן – For we say הָנֵי אִינָשׁ אַצְנְעִינְהוּ – that a person perhaps concealed these birds behind the fence,[9] וְאִי שָׁקֵיל לְהוּ – and, if [the finder] takes them in order to return them, לֵית לְהוּ לְמָרַיְיהוּ סִימָנָא בְּגַוַּויְיהוּ – their owner does not have available any identifying mark on [these birds] by which to reclaim them. הִלְכָּךְ לִשְׁבְקִינְהוּ – Therefore, let [the finder] leave them עַד דְּאָתֵי מָרַיְיהוּ וְשָׁקֵיל לְהוּ – until their owner comes and takes them.[10]

The Gemara objects:

וְאַמַּאי – But why does the owner not have any identifying mark? לֶיהֱוֵי קֶשֶׁר סִימָנָא – Let the type of knot serve as the identifying mark![11] – ? –

The Gemara answers:

אָמַר רַבִּי אַבָּא בַּר זַבְדָּא אָמַר רַב – R' Abba bar Zavda said in the name of Rav: בִּמְקוּשָּׁרִין בִּכְנַפֵיהֶן – The Mishnah is dealing with [birds] tied by their wings, which cannot serve as an identifying mark, דְּכוּלֵּי עָלְמָא הָכִי מְקַטְרֵי לְהוּ – because everyone ties [birds] in this particular manner.[12]

The Gemara objects again:

NOTES

1. Kulis is a Roman deity referred to in Mishnah as Markulis (see, for example, *Sanhedrin* 60b). This deity was often represented as a heap of stones in the configuration described later in this Baraisa. *Tosafos* write that the prefix *Mar* connotes a reversal; thus, Markulis is a derogatory appellation for the pagan diety meaning "the opposite of praise."

2. Two stones standing next to each other, with a third stone resting across the other two (*Rashi*).

3. That is, it was inscribed with the name of the Roman emperor Nero (*Rashi*).

4. Since coins are commonly spent, we must consider the possibility that the claimant previously bought something with one of his inscribed coins, and it was the seller who subsequently lost it. Moreover, it is probable that the claimant wrote his name on more than one coin. Therefore, even if the claimant really lost a coin with his name on it, the coin that was found may not be his. Thus, a signature on a coin is never considered a *siman* (*Ramban*). However, if someone found a coin with a unique identifying mark, it would be treated as any other lost object, which must be announced and returned (*Ramban; cf. Ritva*).

5. A גַּפָּה is a fence made of wood or reeds; a גָּדֵר is one made of stone (*Rashi*). Both provide partial protection to objects placed behind them (*Tosafos*).

6. Rather, he should leave them where they are. The Gemara will explain this ruling.

7. Something buried in a garbage heap is considered concealed and therefore secure (*Tosafos*; see *Rashi*). Thus, there is no reason to assume that an object found there was lost by its owner; rather, it should be assumed that the owner concealed his object in the heap and will return for it. Hence, the obligation of returning lost articles does not apply, and it should be left where its owner placed it (*Rashi*). This is true whether or not the vessel has a *siman*. Since it is not assumed to have been lost, it must be left in its place (*Tosafos, Rosh*).

8. Since no one would deliberately leave his possessions in an open, unprotected place, we must assume that the owner lost this article in the garbage heap. The finder should therefore take it and announce it, if it has a *siman* (*Ritva*).

9. A fence or wall offers partial protection to the object behind it. It is therefore reasonable to assume that someone deliberately left his birds there for a short time, but forgot to return for them (*Nimukei Yosef*, see also *Rashi* below ד״ה לכתחלה and *Beis Aharon*; cf. *Rosh*).

10. The purpose of taking a find and announcing it is to return the lost object to its owner. In this case, taking the birds and announcing them would lessen the owner's chance of recovering them, for he has no *siman* by which to identify the birds. It is therefore in the owner's best interest for the finder to leave the object in place, so that the owner should have a chance to return for them when he remembers that he left them there.

11. Since people often tie their knots differently, the type of knot – if it is somewhat unusual – can serve to identify the birds (*Ritva* cited by *Shitah Mekubetzes*). Now, a fence offers only partial protection to the birds. It is therefore in the owner's best interest for the finder to take them and announce them, for if he does not, a dishonest person might then find them and keep them (*Nimukei Yosef*; see also *Rashi* below ד״ה שכן).

[Had the fence supplied complete protection to the birds, we would not assume that the owner temporarily placed them there and then forgot them; rather, we would assume that the owner was keeping them there. In that case, there would obviously be no obligation for the finder to take them, even if they had a *siman*. This would be like the case of the garbage heap in the second half of the Mishnah, in which we assume that the vessel was placed there by its owner for safekeeping (see *Tosafos, Rosh, Nimukei Yosef*).]

12. Trappers immobilize the wings of a captured bird by intertwining the feathers of one wing with those of the other. This method was employed even by ordinary people, so that it cannot be considered a *siman* (*Ritzvash* cited by *Shitah Mekubetzes*).

כאבני בית קולים מהו ת"ש דתניא מצא מעות מפוזרות הרי אלו שלו כאבני בית קולים [א] חייב להכריז [ב] ואלו הן (א) אבני בית קולים אחת מכאן ואחת מכאן ואחת על גביהן תנו רבנן המוצא סלע בשוק ומצאו חבירו ואמר לו שלי היא חדשה היא נירונית היא של מלך פלוני היא [ג] לא אמר כלום ולא עוד אלא [ד] אפילו שמו כתוב עליה לא אמר כלום לפי שאין סימן למטבע דאמר דלמא אפוקי אפקה ומאיניש אחרינא נפל: **מתני'** מצא [ה] אחר הגפה או אחר הגדר גוזלות מקושרים או בשבילין שבשדות הרי זה לא יגע בהן (ג) [ו] מצא כלי באשפה אם מכוסה לא יגע בו אם מגולה נוטל ומכריז: **גמ'** מאי טעמא דאמרינן הני איניש אצנעינהו (א) ואי שקיל להו לית להו למרייהו סימנא בגווייהו הלכך לשבקינהו עד דאתי מרייהו ושקיל להו ואמאי ליהוי (ג) קשר סימנא אמר רבי אבא בר זבדא אמר רב [ז] במקושרין בכנפיהן דכולי עלמא הכי מקטרי להו ולהוי מקום סימן אמר רב עוקבא בר חמא [ח] במדדין אי במדדין מעלמא אתו ומותרין איכא למימר מעלמא אתו ואיכא למימר איניש אצנעינהו והוה ליה ספק הינוח (ד) ואמר רבי אבא בר זבדא אמר רב [ט] כל ספק הינוח לכתחילה לא יטול ואם נטל לא יחזיר: מצא כלי באשפה מכוסה לא יגע בו מגולה נוטל ומכריז: ורמינהו מצא כלי טמון באשפה נוטל ומכריז שכן דרך אשפה לפנות אמר רב זביד לא קשיא [י] הא בכובי וכסי הא בסכיני והמניק בכובי וכסי לא יגע בסכיני והמניק נוטל ומכריז רב פפא אמר הא והא בכובי וכסי ולא קשיא כאן באשפה העשויה לפנות כאן באשפה שאינה עשויה לפנות אשפה העשויה לפנות [כ] אבידה מדעת היא [ל] אלא (ה) באשפה שאינה עשויה לפנות ונמלך עליה לפנותה בשלמא לרב פפא היינו דקתני שכן דרך אשפה לפנות אלא לרב זביד מאי שכן דרך אשפה לפנות שכן דרך אשפה לפנות לה כלים קטנים: **מתני'** [מ] מצא בגל ובכותל ישן (ו) הרי אלו שלו [נ] מצא בכותל חדש מחציו ולחוץ שלו מחציו ולפנים של בעל הבית [ס] אם היה משכירו לאחרים אפילו (ב) (ז) בתוך הבית הרי אלו שלו: **גמ'** תנא מפני שיכול לומר לו של אמוריים הן אטו אמורים מצנעי ישראל לא מצנעי לא צריכא

דשתיך

### רש"י

כאבני בית קולים. מרקולים והיא שם ע"ז ולקמיה מפ' היכי עבדי: אחת מכאן ואחת מכאן. והשלישית חליה על זה וחליה על זה: נירונית היא. נירון קיסר כתוב עליה: **מתני'** מצא אחר הגפה [או אחר הגדר] גוזלות מקושרין. גפה סתימת כותל של עץ או של קנים: גדר. של אבנים: לא יגע בהן. טעמא מפ' בגמרא: מכוסה לא יגע בו. דאין זו אבידה שיהא מוזהר עליה בלא תוכל להתעלם דמשתמר הוא: **גמ'** במדדין. ממקום למקום: מעלמא אתו. ואין זה הינוח וכיון דאין בהן סימן נימא הרי אלו שלו: ואיכא למימר איניש אצנעינהו. הואיל ומקושרין: ספק הינוח. בדבר שאין בו סימן וכ"ש ודאי הינוח: לכתחילה לא יטול. דאי שקלא לה ליכא למרייהו סימנין למיתב בהו ויפסיד הלכך לא יטול והבעלים יזכרו ויבאו ויטלום: ואם נטל לא יחזיר. דהא ליכא דיהיב סימנא: שכן דרך אשפה ליפנות. ואי לא שקיל ליה האי השתא לכשיפנה יטלנה נכרי או ישראל חשוד הלכך אבידה היא ומוזהר עליה: כובי וכסי. טמונים מדעת הואי ולא יגע בהן: סכיני והמניק. שהן כלים קטנים אבדה הן שהשליכם שם עם האשפה שהוציאם מן הבית ולקמן פריך מאי שכן דרך אשפה לפנות: אבידה מדעת היא. דהוה ליה לאסוקי אדעתיה שיפנוה: היינו דקתני שכן דרך אשפה לפנות. שהבעלים נמלכים לפנות: לפנות לה כלים קטנים. מן הבית שלא מדעת: **מתני'** מצא בגל. גל אבנים מחומה שנפלה: הרי אלו שלו. בגמרא מפרש: מחציו ולחוץ. באחד מחורי כותל הסמוכים לרשות הרבים מגאה מחצי עוביו של כותל ולחוץ שלו דאמרינן אחד מבני רשות הרבים נתנו שם ושכח דאע"ג דאמרן לעיל ספק הינוח לא יטול והאי ודאי הינוח הוא הא מוקמי' למתני' בגמרא דשתיך טפי דליכא יאוש בעלים: ואפילו מצא בתוך הבית כו'. דלא ידוע דמאן ניהו ובעליו נואשו: **גמ'** תנא. גבי גל וכותל ישן: שיכול לומר לו. לבעל הגל או לבעל הכותל: של אמוריים. שהורישו אבותיהו היו: ישראל לא מצנעי. ומחציו ולפנים אמאי שלו הרי בעל הבית זה משתמש בה זה כמה שנים:

דשתיך

### תוספות

**כאבני** בית קולים. מכאן אר"ת דאין שם ע"ז מרקולים אלא קולים כדאמרינן הכא והא דקרי ליה בעלמא מרקולים היינו חילוף קילוס דהם קורים קילוס לשון שבח וחכמים החליפו לגנאי לשון לעג וקלס (תהלים מד) ומר הוא חילוף כמו מר דשחוטה דפרק גיד הנשה (חולין דף צג.) ומר דפרזלא דהגוזל בתרא (ב"ק קיג:)[ס]:

**אחר** הגפה. מקום שמשתמרות קצת אבל מצא במקום שאין משתמר כלל ודאי אבידה היא ונתייאשו הבעלים כיון שאין בה סימן ולא איירי הכא במשתמר לגמרי מדפריך בגמרא ולהוי קשר סימן כלומר ויטול ויכריז ובמקום המשתמר אפי' יש בו סימן לא יגע בו דהא תנן מצא כלי טמון באשפה לא יגע בו וביש בו סימן איירי מדקאמר ואם מגולה נוטל ומכריז וכן לעיל (דף כד.) אמר מצא אבידה אם רוב ישראל חייב להכריז א"כ ביש בה סימן איירי ומוקי לה בטמון באשפה ונמלך עליה לפנותה אבל אם לא נמלך לא יגע בה ולרבה דאמר מקום הוי סימן נקט דוקא גוזלות דמדדין אבל דבר אחר לא דהוי מקום סימן ויטול ויכריז כיון דאינו משתמר לגמרי ולרבה דאמר מקום לא הוי סימן נקט גוזלות לאשמועינן דאע"ג דהוי ספק הינוח דאיכא למימר דמעלמא אתו לא יגע בהן:

(ט) **ואמר** ר' אבא בר זבדא אמר רב ספק הינוח לכתחילה לא יטול. כדמפרש לעיל דלמא איניש אצנעינהו: **ואם** נטל לא יחזיר. יש מפרש דהיינו דוקא כשנטלהו והוליכו לביתו דיש לחוש שמא באו בעלים בתוך כך ולא מצאו מה שהניחו שם ושוב לא יחזרו לבקשה לכך לא יחזיר למקום שנטל אבל אם נטלו ולא זז משם וראה שלא באו בעלים בתוך כך יחזיר וכן יש בירושלמי עובדא ברבי אבא בר זבדא גופיה דקאמר רבי אבא בר זבדא אשכח חמרא מכוסה בחפיסה ונסביה אתא ושאיל בבי רב אמרו ליה לאו יאות עבדת אמר להו אהדריה א"ל לא דלמא אתא מריה ולא אשכחיה ומיאש מיניה ומיהו אם נטל לא יחזיר משמע רק שנטלה ואע"ג דלא הוליכה לשום מקום לא יחזיר ויש לפרש דמיירי הכא בספק אבידה דאפי' הניחה בעלים שם מדעת דומה ששכחוהו דבלא משתמר כ"א קצת מיירי דומיא דמתני' דעל מתני' קאי רבי אבא ולכך אם נטל לא יחזיר דהשתא אבידה היא ושכחוה הבעלים וכיון שאם היה יודע שהיא אבידה היה מחויב בהשבתה בלא שום הגבהה אם הוא יודע של מי הוא דכיון שהוא משתמר קצת לא יתייאשו הבעלים היכא דהגביה הוי מחויב בשמירתה מספק לרבה הוי שומר חנם ולרב יוסף שומר שכר עד שתבא ליד הבעלים ולא דמי לזקן ואינה לפי כבודו דאמר רבה בפרקין [י] הכישה נתחייב בה ואמרינן בהמוכר את הספינה (ב"ב דף פח.) אימור דאמר רבה בבעלי חיים דאנקטינהו נגרי ברייתא אבל בשאר דברים לא היינו משום דזקן לא מחייב בהשבה כלל ולכך כי יחזיר למקומה אינו חייב בשמירתה וכן גלוסית דפרק הספינה (שם דף פז:) לא מחייב כלל בנטילה דאבידה מדעת היא ואינו חייב כלל בהשבתה אבל הכא אם היה יודע שהיא אבידה היה חייב ליקחנה ולהשיבה לבעלים אם היה יודע של מי (ג) הם עתה שהוא ספק אם הגביה חייב בשמירתה כדין אבידה ממש וכן משמע בפרק הספינה (שם) דקאמר גלוסית אבידה מדעת היא משמע דאם לא היתה אבידה מדעת א"ש דמחייב בנטילתה ועובדא דירושלמי דקאמר דאימור אתא מריה ולא אשכחיה מיירי שמצאו במקום שמשתמר לגמרי שלא היתה אבידה ואינה בת השבה ולכך אי לא הוה לן למיחש לאתא מריה יחזיר שפיר וכן משמע דשם חפיסה יש בו סימן ואי לא הוה משתמר לגמרי א"כ שפיר עשה שנטלה ואמאי אמר דלאו יאות עבד וכן הא דתניא לקמן (דף לא.) מצא טלית או קורדום בצד גדר אין זו אבידה ולא יגע בו אפילו יש בו סימן מיירי במקום המשתמר אי נמי התם לדעת הונח שם ולא יגע בו אפילו יש בו סימן דדרך פועלים שמניחים טליתן או קורדומם בצד גדר של אותה שדה ולפירוש רש"י דפירש דלא יחזיר דליכא איניש דיהיב סימנא קשה דפשיטא דלא יחזירנו לשום אדם שאינו יודע מי הם הבעלים כיון שאין בו סימן:

דשתיך

### עין משפט נר מצוה

סא א ב מיי' פט"ו מהל' אבדה הלכה ג סמג עשין עד טוש"ע ח"מ סי' רסב סעיף יג:
סב ג ד מיי' שם פי"ד הלכה י סמג שם טוש"ע שם סעיף יג:
סג ה מיי' שם פט"ו הל' ו ועיין בהשגות וכמ"מ סמג שם טוש"ע ח"מ סי' רס סעיף י:
סד ו מיי' שם הלכה ז טוש"ע שם סעי' יא:
סה ז ח מיי' שם הל' ו טוש"ע שם סעיף י:
סו ט מיי' שם הל"א ועי' בהשגות טוש"ע שם סעיף ט:
סז י מיי' שם הלכה ז טוש"ע שם סעיף יא:
סח כ מיי' שם פי"א הל' יא סמג שם טוש"ע ח"מ סי' רסא סעיף ד:
סט ל מיי' שם פט"ו הלכה ז טוש"ע ח"מ סי' רס סעיף יא:
ע מ נ מיי' שם פט"ז הלכה ט ועיין בהשגות ובמגיד משנה סמג שם טוש"ע שם סעיף א:
עא ס מיי' שם הל' יא ועיין בהשגות וכמ"מ טוש"ע שם סעיף ג:

### הגהות הב"ח

(א) גמ' הני איניש אצנעינהו הכא ואי: (ב) שם במשנה אפילו מצא בתוך הבית: (ג) תום' ד"ה ואם וכו' אם היה יודע של מי הוא עתה:

### ליקוטי רש"י

קשר סימנא. שיש קשרים שאין דומין זה לזה ויאמר כך וכך הוא עשוי [לעיל כ:]. ספק הינוח. מצא דבר שאין בו סימן בצד מקום שמשתמר קצת דלא שכיחי אינשי דאזלי ויש לספוקי שמא מדעת הונח שם לגניזה. לכתחילה לא יטול. המוצאו שכשיבא בעליו לא ימצאנו וסימן אין בו שיכריז לפיכך יניחנו זה ובעליו יבא ויטלנו. ואם נטל לא יחזיר. ואם בא אחר ואמר שלי הוא וסימן אינו נותן בו לא יחזירנו שמא אינו שלו וסוף הבעלים לבוא ויביא עדים שהניחו שם לפיכך יהא מונח ביד זה עד שיבא אליהו דהאי לא יחזיר לא שיהא שלו קאמר דהא מעיקרא באיסורא אתא לידיה אם הינוח הוא [לקמן לז:]. הא בכובי. קנקן [שבת מח.]. כסי. כוסות [ביצה יג:]. והמניק. יפוילפו"ר של ברזל של סופרים שיש לו שני ראשים וראשו אחד מפולל [סוכה לב.]. אבידה מדעת היא. שהיה לו לחוש שמא יפנה. שאינה עשויה לפנות. רגילים היו בעלים להניחה ימים רבים ולא לפנותה מיד. ונמלך עליה לפנותה. מיד ועל כרחו או יטלנו או יהא הפקר [לעיל כד.].

### מסורת הש"ס

א) [עבודה זרה ... ב) [לעיל כד.], ג) [לעיל כג:], ד) לקמן ... ה) [לעיל כד.], ו) [... תוס' בבא בתרא נד. ד... אדעתא], ז) [גירסת הרי... והרא"ש כגירסת ר... אפילו מצא וכ... בפיסקא לקמן ... ח) [ועיין תוס' סנהד... סד. ד"ה מרקולים ועבו... זרה נ. ד"ה אבני], ט) ... דברי מהר"ם דיבור זה ... ד"ה ואם הד"א, י) [לק... ל:].

### רבינו חננאל

כחצובה זה למעלה מ... במקום א) מרודד. כסו... נתונים כסדר בא... והפרש ביניהן. ה... מכריז אם היו עשוי... כמגדלים. אמר רבי... טיבעא מכריז וי... בעליהם ויתן סימ... ויטלם. אבני בית קו... בית ע"ז שמה מרקו... עבודתו גרימת אבנ... ועיקרו ג' אבנים שתים... כנגד זו ואחד על גביה... ואם מצא מטבעות... האי גוונא חייב להכר... ת"ר המוצא סלע בש... ואמר לו חבירו שלי ד... נירונית היא פי' כמט... נירון קיסר היא כו'... ולא עוד אפי' שמו כת... עליה לא אמר כל... שאין סימן למט... דאמרי' אפוקי אפ... ומאחרינא נפל: מת... מצא אחר הגפה. הגפה סגירה מלו... יגיפו הדלתות וכדתנן... האגף ולפנים. גוזל... מקושרות או בשבי... שבשדות הרי זה לא י... בהן ואוקימנא בדל... בהו סימן ובמד... דאיכא למימר מעל... אתו ואיכא למימר אינ... אצנעינהו הוי ליה ס... הינוח וכל ספק הינ... לכתחלה לא יטול ו... נטל לא יחזיר. תלמ... ארץ ישראל ר' אבא... זבדא אשכח חמר מכו... בחפיסה ונסביה א... שאיל לרב אמר ליה... עבדת יאות אמר ... אהדריה אמר ליה... דנימר אתא מריה ו... אשכחיה ונתיאש מינ... פי' מדדין מהלכין מ... מעט כדכתיב אדדם... בית אלהים. ותנן... האשה מדדה את ב... מצא כלי טמון באש... לא יגע בו. איני והתנ... נוטל ומכריז. ופריק... זביד לא קשיא מר... בכובי וכסי דמצנעי ... אינשי. בהמנק וס... דאיכא למימר בטא... שקלינהו בהדי עפ... דביתא וזרקינהו לאש... ולא ידע שכן דרך... אדם לכבד הב... ולהשליך העפר לאשפ... פי' המנק כלי שיש... שני ראשים כגון המ... שיש לו ג' שינים וד... בני יון להחזיק חתי... הבשר ולחתוך עם הס... ולאכול ונוטל זה שח... ונותנו לתוך פיו ואין י... נוגעות בבשר כלל מ...

### חשק שלמה על ר"ח

א) עי' בערוך ערך אלב שכתב זה למעלה מזה כמו... מורד עכ"ל ונראה שכן... גם כאן בדברי רבינו וש... עוד פי' אחר.

**עין משפט נר מצוה**

נ א מיי' פט"ו מהלכות אבידה הל' ג סמג עשין עד טוש"ע ח"מ סי' רסב סעיף יג:
נא ב מיי' שם פט"ו הלכה י סמג שם טוש"ע שם סעיף ט:
נב ג מיי' שם הלכה ט טוש"ע שם סעיף ח:
נג ד מיי' שם הלכה יג סמג שם טוש"ע ח"מ סי' רסב סעיף יט:
נד ה מיי' שם פט"ו הל' ג סמג שם טוש"ע שם סעיף כ:
נה ו מיי' שם פט"ו הל' טו סמג שם טוש"ע שם סעיף יט:
נו ז מיי' שם פי"ד הל' יא סמג שם:
נז ח ט מיי' שם פט"ו הלכה יד סמג שם טוש"ע ח"מ סי' רסב סעיף יט:
נח י מיי' שם פט"ו הל' ג סמג שם טוש"ע ח"מ שם סעיף יג:
נט כ מיי' שם טוש"ע שם סעיף יא:
ס ל מ מיי' שם טוש"ע שם סעיף יב:

**רבינו חננאל**

מצא פירות בכלי או כלי כמות שהוא וכו' אמרי' תנינא להא דתנו רבנן מצא כלי ולפניו פירות כיס ולפניו מעות הרי אלו שלו. מקצתן בכלי ומקצתן בקרקע חייב להכריז ואם בא ישראל ונתן סימני הכלי נוטל גם הפירות וכן כל כיוצא בהן. ורמינן עלה הא דתניא מצא דבר שאין בו סימן בצד דבר שיש בו סימן א) נוטל הדבר שיש בו סימן וזכה הלה בדבר שאין בו סימן. ופרקינן הא והא בצנא ופרי וכגון שנותרו מן הפירות בצנא ולא קשיא הא דתני חייב להכריז דמשמע שמחזיר גם הפירות בצנא דאית ליה אוגנים והן כפופות לתוכה דאמרי' האי צנא איתהפכא והני פירי אישתפוך מן הצנא והני פירי (דאישתפוך) [דאשתייר] בגוה אוגנים מנעום מלהשפך בחוץ הלכך הפירות בתר צנא גרירי בא מי שנתן סימני צנא נוטל גם הפירות. והא דתני דזכה הלה במה שבידו בצנא דלית ליה אוגנים ונמצאו הפירות בחוץ ופירות בצנא דאמרי' הני פירי דבחוץ לאו מן הצנא אישתפוך דאילו מינה אישתפוך הוו להו לאישתפוכי כולהו דהא לית לה לצנא אוגנים אלא הני פירי דבחוץ לאחרינא אינון לפיכך זכה בהם המוצאן דהא דבר שאין בו סימן נינהו. ציבורי פירות. ש"מ מנין הוי סימן. ג' מטבעות זו על גבי זו חייב להכריז. פי' כמגדלים מכוונות אבנים זו על גבי זו אין אחת עודפת על חבירתה. מפוזרין שלו הא אי הוו שלחופי משלחפי שאין מיושבות זו על גב זו אלא מקצתן עליה ומקצתן יוצאה מעליה כגון כנפי הכרובים כדגרסי' בסוף המוכר את הבית ודלמא שלחופי הוו משלחפי אהדדי ועיקרו כדמתרגמי' בתרגום ארץ ישראל שכל את ידיו שלחופינן לידוהי. אסקינן כל שאינן עשויים כמגדלים מפוזרין נינהו והרי הן שלו רויחא לתתא ומיצעא עילויה וזוטא עילוי מצעי זהו כמגדלים. בעי ר' ירמיה כשיר או כשורה או כחצובה או כסולם מהו ועלו בתיקו. פי' כשיר עגול כצמידין דמתרגמ' לה שירין. כשורה זה בצד זה. כחצובה

**[גמרא]**

אשלשה מטבעות זה על גב זה בכריכות ברה"י גוככרות של בעה"ב וגיזי צמר הלקוחין מבית האומן א) כדי יין וכדי שמן הרי אלו חייב להכריז: **גמ'** טעמא דמצא פירות בכלי ומעות בכיס הא כלי ולפניו פירות כים ולפניו מעות הרי אלו שלו תנינא להא דתנו רבנן דמצא כלי ולפניו פירות הכים ולפניו מעות הרי אלו שלו ומקצתן בכלי ומקצתן על גבי קרקע מקצתן בכים ומקצתן על גבי קרקע חייב להכריז ורמינהו זמצא דבר שאין בו סימן בצד דבר שיש בו סימן חייב להכריז בא בעל סימן ונטל את שלו זכה הלה בדבר שאין בו סימן אמר רב זביד לא קשיא הא בכובא וכיתנא הא בצנא ופירי [א] רב פפא אמר הא והא בצנא ופירי ולא קשיא הא דאשתייר בה מידי הא דלא אשתייר בה מידי [ב] ואיבעית אימא הא והא דלא אשתייר בה מידי ולא קשיא חהא דמהדרי אפיה לגבי פירי הא דלא מהדרי אפיה לגבי פירי ואיבעית אימא הא והא דמהדרי אפיה לגבי פירי ולא קשיא טהא דאית לה אוגנין לצנא הא דלית לה אוגנין לצנא: צבורי פירות וצבורי מעות: שמעת מינה מנין הוי סימן תני צבור פירות שמעת מינה מקום הוי סימן תני צבורי פירות: שלשה מטבעות זה על גב זה: אמר רבי יצחק מגדלאה יוהוא שעשויין כמגדלין תניא נמי הכי מצא מעות מפוזרות הרי אלו שלו עשויין כמגדלים חייב להכריז ואלו הן עשויין כמגדלים שלשה מטבעין זה על גב זה הא גופא קשיא אמרת מצא מעות מפוזרות הרי אלו שלו הא משלחפי שלחופי חייב להכריז אימא סיפא עשויין כמגדלין חייב להכריז הא משלחפי שלחופי הרי אלו שלו תנא כל שאין עשויין כמגדלין כמפוזרות קרי להו [ג] א"ר חנינא לא שנו אלא של שלשה מלכים אבל של מלך אחד אינו חייב להכריז היכי דמי אי דעשויין כמגדלין אפילו של מלך אחד נמי ואי דאין עשויין כמגדלין אפילו של שלשה מלכים נמי לא אלא אי אתמר הכי אתמר לא שנו אלא של מלך אחד כעין שלשה מלכים ג) (אבל של מלך אחד אינו חייב להכריז) והיכי דמי דעשויין כמגדלים רויחא תתאה ומציעא עילויה וזוטא עילויה מציעא דאמרינן אנוחי אנחינהו אבל של מלך אחד דכולהו כי הדדי נינהו אע"ג דמנחי אהדדי הרי אלו שלו אימר אתרמויי אתרמי ובהדי הדדי נפול ורבי יוחנן אמר אפילו של מלך אחד נמי מכריז גמאי מכריז מנין מאי איריא תלתא אפי' תרין נמי אמר רבינא (א) דטבעא מכריז ה) לבעי ר' ירמיה כשיר מהו כשורה מהו כחצובה מהו כסולם מהו [ד] פשוט מהא חדא דאמר רב נחמן אמר רבה בר אבוה מכל שאילו מכנים לה קיסם ביניהן ונוטלם בבת אחת חייב להכריז בעי רב אשי

**[רש"י]**

שלשה מטבעות זו ע"ג זו. בגמרא מפרש סימנייהו: גמ' טעמא דמצא כו'. התם הוא דאמר שהפירות לבעל הכלי: הא כלי ולפניו פירות. הרי אלו הפירות של מוצאן ואע"פ שהכלי לבעל הסימן את הכלי יחזיר ואת הפירות יעכב לו ולא אמרינן מהאי מנא נפל: מקצתן בכלי כו'. הדבר מוכיח דהנך דעל גבי קרקע דהנך הוא וחייב להחזירם למי שיתן סימן בכלי וכן מעות לבעל הכיס: ה"ג מצא דבר שאין בו סימן בצד דבר שיש בו סימן. כגון מעות לפני כיס: חייב להכריז. על הכל וינתנו המעות לבעל הכיס: בא בעל סימן ונטל את שלו. את הכיס ואמר אין המעות שלי זכה הלה במעות: הא. דקתני הרי אלו שלו: בכובא וכיתנא. גיגית מוטלת ופשתן לפניה דודאי האי פשתן לאו מכובא נפל דאי מינה נפל הוה משתייר בה והוא הדין לכיס ולפניו מעות מהאי טעמא והא דקתני חייב בצנא ופירי דעבידי דשרקי ונפלי מיניה כולהו: הא דקתני חייב בדאשתייר. ואיכא למימר הנך דאבראי מיניה נפל: והא דלא אשתייר. כיון דסתם צנא יש לו אוגנין כפולים לתוכו אי מתוכו נפל הוה משתייר ביה דאוגנין מעכבי ליה: ה"ג הא והא דלא אשתייר ביה מידי: הא דאית ליה אוגנין. לאו מיניה נפל דאי מיניה נפל הוה משתייר ביה מידי: ש"מ מנין הוי סימן. דאי לאו הכי מאי סימן איכא: תני צבור פירות. דאין כאן מנין (ג) מאי סימניה מקום דכיון דצבורין הינוח הוה ויהיב סימנא במקום פלוני הנחתים: תני צבורי פירות. סימני מנין (ג) דהוי מדחי ליה לא הא תפשוט ולא הא תפשוט: והוא שעשוין כמגדלין. לקמיה מפרש שנלשתן רחבין זה מזה ומניח מלמטה את הרחב ועליו את הבינוני ועליון הוא הקצר שבכולן כמגדל זה העשוי היסוד רחב ומקצר ועולה וכי מנחי הכי לאו דרך נפילה הוא אלא דרך הינוח והיה דעתו לחזור וליטלן ושכח הלכך נוטל ומכריז וזה בא ונותן סימן ואומר מגדלין היו עשוין: ג' מטבעות. שאין דומות זו לזו ברחבן: משלחפי שלחופי. מקצת זו על חבירתה ומקצת על גבי קרקע: חייב להכריז. אלמא כי האי גוונא לאו דרך נפילה הוא: של שלשה מלכים. קס"ד שלא היו צורותיהם שוות שכל מלך כותב שמו וצורתו על מטבע שלו: אי דעשויין כמגדלין. שאין שוין ברחבן ומונחים כמו שפרישית: אפילו של מלך אחד. שצורת שלשתן שוות: של מלך אחד כעין שלשה מלכים. כלומר אפי' הן של מלך אחד שצורת שלשתן שוה והן כעין שלשה מלכים שחלוקין ברחבן ודומין לג' מטבעות: ה"ג והיכי דמי כגון שעשויין כמגדלין חייב להכריז: דכולהו כי הדדי נינהו. שוין ברחבן: אע"ג דכי הדדי מנחי. זה על זה ולאו משלחפי: אימור [אתרמויי] אתרמי. דהכי נפל ואין זה הינוח וסימן אין לו בהם ואפי' מקום דלא ידע היכן נפל: אפי' של מלך אחד מכריז. הואיל ומטבעות הוו זו ע"ג זו יש כאן סימן דלא אתרמי דנפול הכי: ופרכינן מאי מכריז מנין. כך וכך מטבעות מצאתי וזה בא ונתן סימן זו ע"ג זו מצאתם: טבעא מכריז. מטבעות מצאתי הלכך תרי לאו סימנא הוא דמיעוט מטבעות ג': כשיר. מוטלין בעגול כאלעדה: כשורה. זו אצל זו: כחצובה. כג' רגלי קנקן כל אחד כנגד אויר של שני כזה ∴: כסולם. רוב אמצעי על התחתון ורוב העליון על האמצעי כמו מעלות שקורין אשקולינו"ש: פשוט מהא. דר"נ הלא: כל שאילו מכנים כו'. וכי הוו כסולם ניטלים בבת אחת:

כאבני

**[תוספות]**

הא בכובא וכיתנא. פי' רש"י דמתני' בכובא וכיתנא וקשה דקתני מלא פירות וי"א דכיתנא אקרי פירי כדאמרינן (בבראשית רבה) ויבא קין מפרי האדמה זרע פשתן הביא ודוחק ונראה דמתני' בצנא ופירי דכיון דאין הפירות מחוברים יחד אילו מן הכלי נפלו היה קצת נשאר מהם בכלי אבל פשתן שקשור ביחד יכול להיות שבכלי היה ונפל ור"ח פי' דפריך אמאי דקאמר מקצתן על גבי קרקע חייב להכריז ורמינהו מצא דבר כו' בא בעל סימן ונטל את שלו זכה המוצא במה שבידו היינו מה שבחוץ אע"פ שיש בפנים קצת פירות ואפילו בעל כלי אומר שכולן שלו ולפי זה גרס בסמוך הא והא דאשתיירי ביה:

שמעת מינה מנין הוי סימן. אע"ג דפשיטא ליה לעיל י) מדמשקל הוי סימן מדה ומנין נמי הוי סימן בעי לאוכוחי הכא ממתני' ולעיל (דף כד.) נמי דקתני אבל מצא שנים חייב לא קאמר ש"מ מנין הוי סימן (י) דלא אלימא ליה ברייתא למפשט מינה) אי נמי דמצי למדחי דמנין וקשירה הוי סימן:

והוא שעשויין כמגדלין. אי מנין הוי סימן במה שעשויין כמגדלין ידעינן דדרך הינוח הוה ובתרי לא סגי דטבעא מכריז אבל אם מקום הוי סימן אפילו בתרי ועשויין כמגדלין ידעינן דדרך הינוח הוה דאי בתרי אפי' עשוין כמגדלין לא ידעינן דדרך הינוח הוה דאימור דרך נפילה הוה דאתרמי הכי א"כ לקמן מאי פריך ס) (אר' יוחנן) מאי אריא תלתא אפי' בתרי סגי וי"ל דשפיר משני טבעא מכריז:

הא גופא קשיא. אמתני' לא פריך דמלינן למימר דג' מטבעות היינו פירוש לצבורי מעות:

כאבני

**מסורת הש"ס**

[לעיל כג:], ב) מהרש"ל ... ר"ס מ"ז, ג) לפירוש ... "ף והרא"ש קאי על ... שנה וע"ש, ד) [לעיל ... ה) בבא בתרא קג., ... ף כג:], ו) ס"א ... ימא היא ומאי אולמא ... דמשקל, ח) ס"א ל"ג.

**הגהות הב"ח**

גמ' טבעי מכריז: רש"י ד"ה תני צבור ומאי סימניה: ד"ה תני צבורי וכו' מנין הוא דהוי:

**הגהות הגר"א**

גמ' רב פפא וכו'. הרמב"ם פסק ככולהו ... ימתא דר"פ אבל דר"ז ... מיטה. והרא"ש וטור ... קו גם לדר"ז: [ב] שם ... ב"א הא והא דלא ... תייר בה מידי ... ק הא דא"ל אוגנין ... נא הא דל"ל אוגנין ... נא ואב"א הא והא ... "ל אוגנין ול"ק הא ... הדרי אפיה לגבי ... י הא דלא מהדרי ... יה לגבי פירי כצ"ל ... "נ מרש"י ד"ה והא כו' ... תס לנא כו' אבל הרא"ש ... ם כגירסא שלנו וע"ש ... ברי רבינו בח"מ סי' ... ס"ק כ"ה): [ג] שם ... ר חנינא כו'. נ"ב ... "פ הרא"ש וש"פ אבל ... מב"ס השמיטה דס"ל ... "ח ור' יוחנן פליגי ... בא דר"י מגדלאה ופסק ... יוחנן וע' רי"ף ... מפרש כהרמב"ם וע' ... ): [ד] שם (פשוט ... הא חדא ד)אמר. אות ... ממלת דאמר עם ג' ... ת שלפניו מוקפים ... גולים ונ"ב הרמב"ם ל"ג ... אלא גרים אמר ר"נ כו' ... לם לא איפשיטא וחסר ... "ע כאן וע' ברמב"ם:

**לעזי רש"י**

שקולינו"ש. פירוש ... לות (רש"י שמות כ, ... מדרגות (רש"י ... קאל לח, כ. שה"ש ב, יד).

**ליקוטי רש"י**

... גנין. שפה לפיהם [עי' ... לין כה.]. צנא. סל ... ילה כח:]. כשיר ... ר. שעשוי כאלעדה ... צורה מהו. שתי וערב [רשב"ם ב"ב קג:].

חשק שלמה על ר"ח א) נראה דלא גרס בברייתא השניה נוטל ומכריז רק נוטל הדבר וכו' וע' בתוס' כאן ד"ה הא גירסת רבינו ופירושו.

hat if they are arranged **like** the three legs of **a tripod?**[37] בְּסוּלָם מַ – **What** if they are arranged **like a ladder?**[38]

The Gemara responds:

פְּשׁוֹט מֵהָא חֲדָ – **Resolve one** of the questions **from this** llowing statement: דְּאָמַר רַב נַחְמָן אָמַר רַבָּה בַּר אֲבוּהָ – **For** av **Nachman said in the name of Rabbah bar Avuha:** כָּל שֶׁאִילוּ מַכְנִיס לָהּ קִיסָם בֵּינֵי – **Any** coins arranged in a way **that if one would insert a sliver** of wood **between them,** וְנוֹטְלָם בְּבַת אַחַת – **he could lift** all of **them together,** חַיָּיב לְהַכְרִיז – **one is obligated to announce.** Since coins arranged like a ladder fulfill this condition, it is clear that they must be announced.

The Gemara inquires about another formation:

בָּעֵי רַב אַשִׁי – **Rav Ashi asked:**

NOTES

vare of the arrangement and can identify his coins by it, or whether ey could have fallen accidentally and landed in that formation.

. That is, they were arranged in triangular formation (*Rashi*).

38. The coins were arranged like steps, with most of the middle coin resting on the bottom coin, and most of the top coin resting on the middle coin (*Rashi*).

א שלשה מטבעות זה על גב זה ב כריכות ברה"י ג וככרות של בעה"ב וגיזי צמר הלקוחין מבית האומן [א] כדי יין וכדי שמן הרי אלו חייב להכריז: **גמ'** טעמא דמצא פירות בכלי ומעות בכים הא כלי ולפניו פירות כים ולפניו מעות הרי אלו שלו תנינא להא דתנו רבנן ד מצא כלי ולפניו פירות ה כים ולפניו מעות הרי אלו שלו ו מקצתן בכלי ומקצתן על גבי קרקע מקצתן בכים ומקצתן על גבי קרקע חייב להכריז ורמינהו ז מצא דבר שאין בו סימן בצד דבר שיש בו סימן חייב להכריז בא בעל סימן ונטל את שלו זכה הלה בדבר שאין בו סימן אמר רב זביד לא קשיא הא בכובא וכיתנא הא בצנא ופירי [א] רב פפא אמר הא והא בצנא ופירי ולא קשיא הא דאשתייר בה מידי הא דלא אשתייר בה מידי [ב] ואיבעית אימא הא והא דלא אשתייר בה מידי ולא קשיא ח הא דמהדרי אפיה לגבי פירי הא דלא מהדרי אפיה לגבי פירי ואיבעית אימא הא והא דמהדרי אפיה לגבי פירי ולא קשיא ט הא דאית לה אוגנין לצנא הא דלית לה אוגנין לצנא: צבורי פירות וצבורי מעות: שמעת מינה מנין הוי סימן תני צבור פירות שמעת מינה מקום הוי סימן תני צבורי פירות: שלשה מטבעות זה על גב זה: אמר רבי יצחק מגדלאה י והוא שעשויין כמגדלין תניא נמי הכי מצא מעות מפוזרות הרי אלו שלו עשויין כמגדלים חייב להכריז ואלו הן עשויין כמגדלים שלשה מטבעין זה על גב זה הא גופא קשיא אמרת מצא מעות מפוזרות הרי אלו שלו הא משלחפי שלחופי חייב להכריז אימא סיפא עשויין כמגדלין חייב להכריז הא משלחפי שלחופי הרי אלו שלו תנא כל שאין עשויין כמגדלין כ מפוזרות קרי להו [ג] א"ר חנינא לא שנו אלא של שלשה מלכים אבל של מלך אחד אינו חייב להכריז היכי דמי אי דעשויין כמגדלין אפילו של מלך אחד נמי ואי דאין עשויין כמגדלין אפילו של שלשה מלכים נמי לא אלא אי אתמר הכי אתמר לא שנו אלא של מלך אחד כעין שלשה מלכים (ב) (אבל של מלך אחד אינו חייב להכריז) והיכי דמי דעשויין כמגדלים רויחא תתאה ומציעא עילויה וזוטא עילויה מציעא דאמרינן אנוחי אנחינהו אבל של מלך אחד דכולהו כי הדדי נינהו אע"ג דמנחי אהדדי הרי אלו שלו אימר אתרמויי אתרמי ובהדי הדדי נפול ורבי יוחנן אמר אפילו של מלך אחד נמי מכריז (ג) מאי מכריז מנין מאי איריא תלתא אפי' תרין נמי אמר רבינא (א) ל טבעא מכריז (ה) מ בעי ר' ירמיה כשיר מהו כשורה מהו כחצובה מהו כסולם מהו [ד] פשוט מהא חדא דאמר רבה בר אבוה נ כל שאילו מכנים לה קיסם ביניהן ונוטלם בבת אחת חייב להכריז בעי רב אשי

**רש"י**

שלשה מטבעות זו ע"ג זו. בגמרא מפרש סימנייהו: **גמ'** טעמא דמצא כו'. התם הוא דאמר שהפירות לבעל הכלי: הא כלי ולפניו פירות. הרי אלו הפירות של מוצאן ואע"פ שהכלי לבעל הסימן את הכלי יחזיר ואת הפירות יעכב לו ולא אמרינן מהאי מנא נפל: מקצתן בכלי כו'. הדבר מוכיח דהנך דעל גבי קרקע דהנך הוא וחייב להחזירם למי שיתן סימן בכלי וכן מעות לבעל הכים: ה"ג מצא דבר שאין בו סימן בצד דבר שיש בו סימן. כגון מעות לפני כים: חייב להכריז. על הכל ויתנו המעות לבעל הכים: בא בעל סימן ונטל את שלו. את הכים ואמר אין המעות שלי זכה הלה במעות: הא. דקתני הרי אלו שלו: בכובא וכיתנא. גיגית מוטלת ופשתן לפניה דודאי האי פשתן לאו מכובא נפל דאי מינה נפל הוה משתייר בה והוא הדין לכים ולפניו מעות מהאי טעמא והא דקתני חייב בצנא ופירי דעבידי דשרקי ונפלי מיניה כולהו: הא דקתני חייב בדאשתייר. ואיכא למימר הנך דאבראי מיניה נפל: והא דלא אשתייר. כיון דסתם צנא יש לו אוגנין כפולים לתוכו אי מתוכו נפל הוה משתייר ביה דאוגנין מעכבי ליה: ה"ג הא והא דלא אשתייר ביה מידי: הא דאית ליה אוגנין. לאו מיניה נפל דאי מיניה נפל הוה משתייר ביה מידי: ש"מ מנין הוי סימן. דאי לאו הכי מאי סימן איכא: תני צבור פירות. דאין כאן מנין (ב) מאי סימניה מקום דכיון דצבורין הינוח הוה ויהיב סימנא במקום פלוני הנחתים: תני צבורי פירות. סימני מנין (ג) דהוי מדחי ליה לא הא תפשוט ולא הא תפשוט: והוא שעשוין כמגדלין. לקמיה מפרש שנלשתן רחבין זה מזה ומניח מלמטה את הרחב ועליו את הבינוני ועליון הוא הקצר שכולן כמגדל זה העשוי היסוד רחב ומקצר ועולה וכי מנחי הכי לאו דרך נפילה הוה אלא דרך הינוח והיה דעתו לחזור ולטלן ושכח הלכך נוטל ומכריז וזה בא ונותן סימן ואומר מגדלין היו עשוין: ג' מטבעות. שאין דומות זו לזו ברחבן: משלחפי שלחופי. מקצת זו על חבירתה ומקצת על גבי קרקע: חייב להכריז. אלמא כי האי גוונא לאו דרך נפילה הוא: של שלשה מלכים. קס"ד שלא היו צורותיהם שוות שכל מלך כותב שמו וצורתו על מטבע שלו: אי דעשויין כמגדלין. שאין שוין ברחבן ומונחים כמו שפרישית: אפילו של מלך אחד. שצורת שלשתן שוות: של מלך אחד כעין שלשה מלכים. כלומר אפי' הן של מלך אחד שצורת שלשתן שוה והן כעין שלשה מלכים שחלוקין ברחבן ודומין לג' מטבעות: ה"ג והיכי דמי כגון שעשויין כמגדלין חייב להכריז: דכולהו כי הדדי נינהו. שוין ברחבן: אע"ג דכי הדדי מנחי. זה על זה ולאו משלחפי: אימור [אתרמויי] אתרמי. דהכי נפל ואין זה הינוח וסימן אין לו בהם ואפי' מקום דלא ידע היכן נפל: אפי' של מלך אחד מכריז. הואיל ומטבעות הוו זו ע"ג זו יש כאן סימן דלא אתרמי דנפול הכי: ופרכינן מאי מכריז מנין. כך וכך מטבעות מצאתי וזה בא ונתן סימן זו ע"ג זו מצאתם: טבעא מכריז. מטבעות מצאתי הלכך תרי לאו סימנא הוא דמיעוט מטבעות ב': כשיר. מוטלין בעגול כאצעדה: כשורה. זו אצל זו: כחצובה. כג' רגלי קנקן כל אחד כנגד אויר של שני כזה ∴: כסולם. רוב אמצעי על התחתון ורוב העליון על האמצעי כמו מעלות שקורין אשקלונ"ש: פשוט מהא. דר"נ חדא: כל שאילו מכנים כו'. וכי הוו כסולם ניטלים בבת אחת:

**תוספות**

**הא** בכובא וכיתנא. פי' רש"י דמתני' בכובא וכיתנא וקשה דקתני מלא פירות וי"א דכיתנא אקרי פירי כדאמרינן (בבראשית רבה) ויבא קין מפרי האדמה זרע פשתן היא ודוחק ונראה דמתני' בצנא ופירי דכיון דאין הפירות מחוברים יחד אילו מן הכלי נפלו היה קצת נשאר מהם בכלי אבל פשתן שקשור ביחד יכול להיות שבכלי היה ונפל ור"ח פי' דפריך אמאי דקאמר מקצתן על גבי קרקע חייב להכריז ורמינהו מצא דבר כו' בא בעל סימן ונטל את שלו זכה המוצא במה שבידו היינו מה שבחוץ אע"פ שיש בפנים קצת פירות ואפילו בעל כלי אומר שכולן שלו ולפי זה גרס בסמוך הא והא דאשתיירי ביה:

**שמעת** מינה מנין הוי סימן. אע"ג דפשיטא ליה לעיל (י) מדמסקל הוי סימן מדה ומנין נמי הוי סימן בעי לאוכוחי הכא ממתני' ולעיל (דף כד.) נמי דקתני אבל מצא שנים חייב לא קאמר ש"מ מנין הוי סימן (ז) דלא אלימא ליה ברייתא למפשט מינה) אי נמי דמצי למדחי דמנין וקרוזא הוי סימן:

**והוא** שעשויין כמגדלין. אי מנין הוי סימן במה שעשוין כמגדלין ידעינן דדרך הינוח הוה ובתרי לא סגי דטבעא מכריז אבל אם מקום הוי סימן אפילו בתרי ועשויין כמגדלין ידעינן דדרך הינוח הוה דאי בתרי אפי' עשוין כמגדלין לא ידעינן דדרך הינוח הוה דאימור דרך נפילה הוה דאתרמי הכי א"כ לקמן מאי פריך (ס) (אר' יוחנן) מאי אריא תלתא אפי' בתרי סגי וי"ל דשפיר משני טבעא מכריז:

**הא** גופא קשיא. אמתני' לא פריך דמצינן למימר דג' מטבעות היינו פירוש לצבורי מעות:

**עין משפט נר מצוה**

נ א מיי' פט"ז מהלכות אבידה הל' ג סמג עשין עד טוש"ע ח"מ סי' רסב סעיף יב:
נא ב מיי' שם פט"ו הלכה י סמג שם טוש"ע שם סעיף ט:
נב ג מיי' שם הלכה ט טוש"ע שם סעיף ח:
נג ד מיי' שם הלכה יג סמג שם טוש"ע ח"מ סי' רסב סעיף יט:
נד ה מיי' שם פט"ז הל' ג סמג שם טוש"ע שם סעיף כ:
נה ו מיי' שם פט"ו הל' טו סמג שם טוש"ע שם סעיף יט:
נו ז מיי' שם פי"ד הל' יא סמג שם:
נז ח ט מיי' שם פט"ו הלכה יד סמג שם טוש"ע ח"מ סי' רסב סעיף יט:
נח י מיי' שם פט"ז הל' ב סמג שם טוש"ע ח"מ שם סעיף יב:
נט כ מיי' שם טוש"ע שם סעיף יא:
ס ל מ מיי' שם טוש"ע שם סעיף יב:

**רבינו חננאל**

מצא פירות בכלי או כלי כמות שהוא וכו' אמרי' תנינא להא דתנו רבנן מצא כלי ולפניו פירות כיס ולפניו מעות הרי אלו שלו. מקצתן בכלי ומקצתן בקרקע חייב להכריז ואם בא ישראל ונתן סימני הכלי נוטל גם הפירות וכן כל כיוצא בהן. ורמינן עלה הא דתניא מצא דבר שאין בו סימן בצד דבר שיש בו סימן א) נוטל הדבר שיש בו סימן וזכה הלה בדבר שאין בו סימן. ופרקינן הא והא בצנא ופרי וכגון שנותרו מן הפירות בצנא ולא קשיא הא דתני חייב להכריז דמשמע שמחזיר גם הפירות בצנא דאית ליה אוגנים והן כפופות לתוכה דאמרי' האי צנא איתהפכא והני פירי אישתפוך מן הצנא והני פירי (דאישתפוך) [דאשתייר] בגוה אוגנים מנעום מלהשפך בחוץ הלכך הפירות בתר צנא גרירי בא מי שנתן סימני צנא נוטל גם הפירות. והא דתני דזכה הלה במה שבידו בצנא דלית ליה אוגנים ונמצאו הפירות בחוץ ופירות בצנא דאמרי' הני פירי דבחוץ לאו מן הצנא אישתפוך דאילו מינה אישתפוך הוו להו לאישתפוכי כולהו דהא לית לה לצנא אוגנים אלא הני פירי דבחוץ לאחרינא אינון לפיכך זכה בהם המוצאן דהא דבר שאין בו סימן נינהו. ציבורי פירות. ש"מ מנין הוי סימן. ג' מטבעות זו על גבי זו חייב להכריז. פי' כמגדלים מכוונות אבנים זו על גבי זו אין אחת עודפת על חבירתה. מפוזרין שלו הא אי הוו שלחופי משלחפי שאין מיושבות זו על גב זו אלא מקצתן עליה ומקצתן יוצאה מעליה כגון כנפי הכרובים כדגרסי' בסוף המוכר את הבית ודלמא שלחופי הוו משלחפי אהדדי ועיקרו כדמתרגמי' בתרגום ארץ ישראל שכל

**מסורת הש"ס**

[לעיל כג:], ב) מהרש"ל גר"ס מ"ז, ג) לפירוש ר"ף והרא"ש קאי על שנה וע"ש, ד) [לעיל ...], ה) בבא בתרא קג., דף כג:], ז) ס"א ... היא ומאי אולמא ... דמשקל, ח) ס"א ל"ג.

**הגהות הב"ח**

(א) גמ' טבעי מכריז: (ב) רש"י ד"ה תני לצבור ... ומאי סימניה: (ג) ד"ה תני לצבורי וכו' מנין הוא דהוי:

**הגהות הגר"א**

[א] גמ' רב פפא וכו'. ... הרמב"ם פסק כרב זביד ... דמתא דר"פ אבל דר"ז ... מיטה. והרא"ש וטור ... קו גם לדר"ז: [ב] שם ... ב"א הא והא דלא ... אשתייר בה מידי ... ק הא דא"ל אוגנין ... נא הא דל"ל אוגנין ... נא ואב"א הא והא ... ל אוגנין ול"ק הא ... דהדרי אפיה לגבי ... פירי הא דלא מהדרי ... אפיה לגבי פירי כצ"ל ... נ מרש"י ד"ה והא כו' ... תם לנא כו' אבל הרא"ש ... ים כגירסא שלנו וע"ש ... דברי רבינו בח"מ סי' ... ב ס"ק כ"ה): [ג] שם ... ר חנינא כו'. נ"ב ... פ הרא"ש וש"פ אבל ... מב"ם השמיטה דס"ל ... "ח ור' יוחנן פליגי ... בא דר"י מגדלאה ופסק ... יוחנן וע' רי"ף ... מפרש כהרמב"ם וע' ... ): [ד] שם (פשוט ... מהא חדא ד)אמר. אות ... ממלת דאמר עם ג' ... ות שלפניו מוקפים ... גוליס וני"ב הרמב"ם ל"ג ... אלא גרים אמר ר"נ כו' ... לם לא איפשיטא וחסר ... "ע כאן וע' ברמב"ם:

**לעזי רש"י**

אשקולינו"ש. פירוש ... מעלות (רש"י שמות כ, כג), מדרגות (רש"י יחזקאל מ, כ. שה"ש ב, יד).

**ליקוטי רש"י**

[עי' ...] לין כה.]. צנא. סל ... גילה כח:]. כשיר ... ורה. שעשוין כאצעדה. ... שורה מהו. שתי וערב ... [רשב"ם ב"ב קג:].

את ידיו שלחופינן לידודי. אסקינן כל שאינן עשויים כמגדלים מפוזרין נינהו והרי הן שלו רויחא לתתא ומיצעא עילויה וזוטא עילוי מצעי זהו כמגדלים. בעי ר' ירמיה כשיר או כשורה או כחצובה או כסולם מהו ועלו בתיקו. פי' כשיר עגול כצמידין דמתרגמי' לה שירין. כשורה זה בצד זה. כחצובה

חשק שלמה על ר"ח א) נראה דלא גרס בברייתא השניה נוטל הדבר וכו' ומכריז רק נוטל הדבר וכו' ועי' בתוס' כאן ד"ה הא גירסת רבינו ופירושו.

The Gemara elaborates further on the Mishnah's requirement o announce a find of three coins:

**אָמַר רַבִּי חֲנִינָ** – **R' Chanina said:** **לֹא שָׁנוּ אֶלָּא שֶׁל שְׁלֹשָׁה מְלָכִים** - **The Mishnah taught** its ruling **only** for the coins **of three** ifferent **kings;** **אֲבָל שֶׁל מֶלֶךְ אֶחָד** – **but** if one finds the coins **of** ne **king,** **אֵינוֹ חַיָּיב לְהַכְרִיז** – **he is not obligated to announce** hem.[27]

The Gemara questions this distinction:

**הֵיכִי דָּמֵ** – **Under what circumstances** is this true? **אִי דַּעֲשׂוּיִין כְּמִגְדָּלִי** – **If [the coins] were arranged like towers,** **אֲפִילוּ שֶׁל מֶלֶךְ אֶחָד נַמ** – **even** if they were minted **by one king** they should lso be announced, since they are identifiable by their unusual ormation. **וְאִי דְּאֵין עֲשׂוּיִין כְּמִגְדָּלִין** – **And if they were not** rranged **like towers,** **אֲפִילוּ שֶׁל שְׁלֹשָׁה מְלָכִים נַמִּי לֹא** – then ven if they were minted **by three kings** they should **also not** ave to be announced.[28] – ? –

The Gemara revises R' Chanina's statement:

**אֶלָּא אִי אִתְּמַ** – **Rather, if [R' Chanina's ruling] was stated,** **הָכִי אִתְּמַ** – **it was stated thus:** **לֹא שָׁנוּ אֶלָּא שֶׁל מֶלֶךְ אֶחָד** – **The** Mishnah **taught** its ruling that one must announce a find of coins nly for coins **of one king** **בְּעֵין שְׁלֹשָׁה מְלָכִים** – that are **similar** o the coins **of three kings.**[29] (אבל של מלך אחד אינו חייב להכריז)[30]

**וְהֵיכִי דָּמֵ** – **And how is this?** **דַּעֲשׂוּיִין כְּמִגְדָּלִים** – **Where [the** oins**] are arranged like towers:** **רְוִיחָא תַּתָּאָה** – **a wide** oin **on the bottom,** **וּמְצִיעָא עִילָוֵיהּ** – **with a medium-sized** oin **on top of it,** **וְזוּטָא עִילָוֵיהּ מְצִיעָא** – **and a small** coin n **top of the medium-sized** coin. **דְּאָמְרִינַן אֱנוֹחֵי אַנְחִינְהוּ** – or we may **say** in such a case that **[the owner] surely placed** hem in this arrangement, and he can therefore identify them y the arrangement. **אֲבָל שֶׁל מֶלֶךְ אֶחָד** – **But** in the case of oins **of one king** **דְּכוּלְּהוּ כִּי הֲדָדֵי נִינְהוּ** – **where all [the coins] are of equal** size, **אַף עַל גַּב דְּמַנְחֵי אַהֲדָדֵי** – then **even though they are lying upon one another,** **הֲרֵי אֵלּוּ שֶׁלּוֹ** – **these belong to [the finder],** **אֵימַר אִתְרַמּוּיֵי אִתְרְמִי** – for we may **say it just so happened** **וּבַהֲדָדֵי נָפוּל** – **that the coins fell together.**[31]

The Gemara cites a dissenting opinion:

**וְרַבִּי יוֹחָנָן אָמַר** – **R' Yochanan says:** **אֲפִילוּ שֶׁל מֶלֶךְ אֶחָד** – **Even** identically sized coins **of one king,** which are stacked one directly upon the other, **נַמִּי מַכְרִיז** – **[the finder] must also announce.**[32]

The Gemara raises an objection:

**מַאי מַכְרִיז** – **What does [the finder] announce?** **מִנְיָן** – Seemingly, **the number** of coins he found.[33] The owner can then identify them by describing their arrangement. **מַאי אִירְיָא תְּלָתָא** – But if that is so, **why** does the Mishnah **discuss** a case of **three** coins? **אֲפִילוּ תְּרֵין נַמִּי** – **Even two** should **also** have to be announced, for in that case, too, the owner can identify them by describing their arrangement![34] – ? –

The Gemara answers:

**אָמַר רָבִינָא** – **Ravina said:** **טִבְעָא מַכְרִיז** – **[The finder] announces** merely that he found **coins,** without mentioning the number. The owner must then state how many coins he lost – in addition to their arrangement – in order to reclaim them. Since two coins cannot be identified by their number, the finder may keep them.[35]

The Gemara inquires if one must announce coins found in other arrangements:

**בָּעֵי ר׳ יִרְמְיָה** – **R' Yirmiyah inquired:** **כְּשִׁיר מַהוּ** – **What is [the law]** if the coins are arranged in a circle **like a bracelet?**[36] **כְּשׁוּרָה מַהוּ** – **What** if they are arranged **in a line?** **בַּחֲצוּבָה מַהוּ** –

NOTES

7. Every king would mint coins which bore his name and image. The iemara now assumes R' Chanina to be making the following tatement: Only a find of coins with images of three different kings ıust be announced; but coins with the same image may be kept by the nder (*Rashi*).

8. As explained earlier, coins that are not arranged like a tower are ssumed to have fallen from the owner. Hence, they have no *siman*.

9. That is, even though they were actually minted by the same king – nd all contain his image – they differ in diameter. In this respect, hen, they are similar to coins of different kings (*Rashi*).

0. *Maharshal* deletes this clause.

1. Thus, according to R' Chanina, if the coins are all of the same size, here is no reason to suspect that they were placed there deliberately by heir owner, even when they are stacked one upon the other. Since we ssume they fell without the owner's knowledge, we assume that he will ot know in what arrangement they landed on the ground, nor where e lost them. The finder may therefore keep the coins, because the wner knows no *siman* by which to reclaim them (*Rashi*; see *Pnei* 'ehoshua).

2. R' Yochanan maintains that coins do not fall directly upon one nother by chance. Hence, coins found in this arrangement [as well as ı a tower arrangement] should be assumed to have been placed there eliberately by their owner, who will be able to provide the *siman* [of heir arrangement] to reclaim them (*Rashi*).

R' Yochanan disputes the ruling of R' Chanina, and of the Baraisa bove that supports him, because he feels that our Mishnah's failure to pecify a tower-like arrangement indicates that it accepts any type f stack as evidence of deliberate placement and a *siman* (*Rashi;* cf. 'ra).

3. [When one finds an object, it is best that he describe it with as much etail as possible (without mentioning its outstanding *siman*), so that he owner will realize that his object has been found (see below, 28b ote 12).] The Gemara now assumes that the finder therefore includes ı his announcement the number of coins found, and the owner comes nd identifies them by their arrangement (*Rashi*).

34. By specifying that a find of *three* coins must be announced, the Mishnah implies that a find of two coins may be kept by the finder. If, however, coins may be identified even if they are not stacked in a tower-like formation, and if even coins of equal size stacked one upon the other are assumed to have been left deliberately by their owner and to be identifiable by their arrangement (as R' Yochanan ruled), two coins should be no different than three.

This objection does not hold for R' Chanina's view. According to him, a mere neat arrangement of coins of identical size is not considered sufficient evidence that the coins were left deliberately. Only if coins of different sizes are stacked like a tower does R' Chanina assume that they were left there deliberately. A tower, however, [by definition] can be created only from three coins of different sizes, not two. It is therefore understandable why, according to R' Chanina, the Mishnah ruled that only a find of three [or more] coins must be announced (*Shitah Mekubetzes;* see *Ran* and other Rishonim cited there for alternative explanations of the Gemara's objection).

35. Ravina answers that according to R' Yochanan (who does not require a tower-like arrangment), an ordinary arrangement of coins is not significant enough to be considered a *siman* (see *Shitah Mekubetzes* p. 152 ד״ה וז״ל גלוין התוס׳). Rather, the primary *siman* is the number of coins lost. Accordingly, the finder cannot include this information in his announcement. Nevertheless, since he *does* announce that he found "coins" – not a single coin – he has intimated that he has found at least two. Naming two coins as the number lost would not suffice to identify them, since the claimant would merely be repeating the information contained in the announcement. Therefore, if one found only two coins, even if they are stacked one upon the other, he may keep them, since their owner will have no opportunity to identify them. Thus, only if there are three or more coins can the number serve to identify them (*Ritva;* see Gemara 20b and note 14 there). However, even in this case, the claimant must mention the way they were stacked, since his lack of knowledge of this would tend to indicate that he was not the one who lost them (ibid.).

36. At issue is whether coins found in such a formation should be assumed to have been put there deliberately, in which case the owner is

שלשה מטבעות זה על גב זה כריכות ברה"י וככרות של בעה"ב וגיזי צמר הלקוחין מבית האומן כדי יין וכדי שמן הרי אלו חייב להכריז: **גמ'** טעמא דמצא פירות בכלי ומעות בכיס הא כלי ולפניו פירות כיס ולפניו מעות הרי אלו שלו תנינא להא דתנו רבנן מצא כלי ולפניו פירות כיס ולפניו מעות הרי אלו שלו מקצתן בכלי ומקצתן על גבי קרקע מקצתן בכיס ומקצתן על גבי קרקע חייב להכריז ורמינהו מצא דבר שאין בו סימן בצד דבר שיש בו סימן חייב להכריז בא בעל סימן ונטל את שלו זכה הלה בדבר שאין בו סימן אמר רב זביד לא קשיא הא בכובא וכיתנא הא בצנא ופירי [א] רב פפא אמר הא והא בצנא ופירי ולא קשיא הא דאשתייר בה מידי הא דלא אשתייר בה מידי [ב] ואיבעית אימא הא והא דלא אשתייר בה מידי ולא קשיא הא דמהדרי אפיה לגבי פירי הא דלא מהדרי אפיה לגבי פירי ואיבעית אימא הא והא דמהדרי אפיה לגבי פירי ולא קשיא הא דאית לה אוגנין לצנא הא דלית לה אוגנין לצנא: צבורי פירות וצבורי מעות: שמעת מינה מנין הוי סימן תני צבור פירות שמעת מינה מקום הוי סימן תני צבורי פירות: שלשה מטבעות זה על גב זה: אמר רבי יצחק מגדלאה והוא שעשויין כמגדלין תניא נמי הכי מצא מעות מפוזרות הרי אלו שלו עשויין כמגדלים חייב להכריז ואלו הן עשויין כמגדלים שלשה מטבעין זה על גב זה הא גופא קשיא אמרת מצא מעות מפוזרות הרי אלו שלו הא משלחפי שלחופי חייב להכריז אימא סיפא עשויין כמגדלין חייב להכריז הא משלחפי שלחופי הרי אלו שלו תנא כל שאין עשויין כמגדלין מפוזרות קרי להו [ג] א"ר חנינא לא שנו אלא של שלשה מלכים אבל של מלך אחד אינו חייב להכריז היכי דמי אי דעשויין כמגדלין אפילו של מלך אחד נמי ואי דאין עשויין כמגדלין אפילו של שלשה מלכים נמי לא אלא אי אתמר הכי אתמר לא שנו אלא של מלך אחד כעין שלשה מלכים (אבל של מלך אחד אינו חייב להכריז) והיכי דמי דעשויין כמגדלים רויחא תתאה ומציעא עילויה וזוטא עילויה מציעא דאמרינן אנוחי אנחינהו אבל של מלך אחד דכולהו כי הדדי נינהו אע"ג דמנחי אהדדי הרי אלו שלו אימר אתרמויי אתרמי ובהדי הדדי נפול ורבי יוחנן אמר אפילו של מלך אחד נמי מכריז מאי מכריז מנין מאי איריא תלתא אפי' תרין נמי אמר רבינא (א) טבעא מכריז בעי ר' ירמיה כשיר מהו כשורה מהו כחצובה מהו כסולם מהו [ד] פשוט מהא חדא דאמר רב נחמן אמר רבה בר אבוה כל שאילו מכנים לה קיסם ביניהן ונוטלם בבת אחת חייב להכריז בעי רב אשי

---

**רש"י**

שלשה מטבעות זו ע"ג זו. בגמרא מפרש סימנייהו: **גמ'** טעמא דמצא כו'. התם הוא דאמר שהפירות לבעל הכלי: הא כלי ולפניו פירות. הרי אלו הפירות של מוצאן ואע"פ שהכלי לבעל הסימן את הכלי יחזיר ואת הפירות יעכב לו ולא אמרינן מהאי מנא נפל: מקצתן בכלי כו'. הדבר מוכיח דהנך דעל גבי קרקע דהנך הוא וחייב להחזירם למי שיתן סימן בכלי וכן מעות לבעל הכיס: ה"ג מצא דבר שאין בו סימן בצד דבר שיש בו סימן. כגון מעות לפני כיס: חייב להכריז. על הכל ויתנו המעות לבעל הכיס: **בא בעל סימן ונטל את שלו.** את הכיס ואמר אין המעות שלי זכה הלה במעות: הא. דקתני הרי אלו שלו: בכובא וכיתנא. גיגית מוטלת ופשתן לפניה דודאי האי פשתן לאו מכובא נפל דאי מינה נפל הוה משתייר בה והוא הדין לכיס ולפניו מעות מהאי טעמא והא דקתני חייב בצנא ופירי דעבידי דשרקי ונפלי מיניה כולהו: הא דקתני חייב בדאשתייר. ואיכא למימר הנך דאברא מיניה נפל: והא דלא אשתייר. כיון דסתם צנא יש לו אוגנין כפולים לתוכו אי מתוכו נפל הוה משתייר ביה דאוגנין מעכבי ליה: ה"ג הא והא דלא אשתייר ביה מידי: הא דאית ליה אוגנין. לאו מיניה נפל דאי מיניה נפל הוה משתייר ביה מידי: ש"מ מנין הוי סימן. דאי לאו הכי מאי סימן איכא: תני צבור פירות. דאין כאן מנין (ב) מאי סימניה מקום דכיון דצבורין הינוח הוה ויהיב סימנא במקום פלוני הנחתים: תני צבורי פירות. סימני מנין (ג) דהוי מדחי ליה לא הא תפשוט ולא הא תפשוט: והוא שעשוין כמגדלין. לקמיה מפרש שאלשתן רחבין זה מזה ומניח מלמטה את הרחב ועליו את הבינוני ועליון הוא הקצר שבכולן כמגדל זה העשוי היסוד רחב ומקצר ועולה וכי מנחי הכי לאו דרך נפילה הוה אלא דרך הינוח והיה דעתו לחזור ולטלן ושכח הלכך נוטל ומכריז וזה בא ונותן סימן ואומר מגדלין היו עשוין: ג' מטבעות. שאין דומות זו לזו ברחבן: משלחפי שלחופי. מקצת זו על חבירתה ומקצת על גבי קרקע: חייב להכריז. אלמא כי האי גוונא לאו דרך נפילה הוא: של שלשה מלכים. קס"ד שלא היו צורותיהם שוות שכל מלך כותב שמו וצורתו על מטבע שלו: אי דעשויין כמגדלין. שאין שוין ברחבן ומונחים כמו שפרישית: אפילו של מלך אחד. שצורת שלשתן שוות: של מלך אחד כעין שלשה מלכים. כלומר אפי' הן של מלך אחד שצורת שלשתן שוה והן כעין שלשה מלכים שחלוקין ברחבן ודומין לג' מטבעות: ה"ג והיכי דמי כגון שעשויין כמגדלין חייב להכריז: דכולהו כי הדדי נינהו. שוין ברחבן: אע"ג דכי הדדי מנחי. זה על זה ולאו משלחפי: אימור [אתרמויי] אתרמי. דהכי נפל ואין זה הינוח וסימן אין לו בהם ואפי' מקום דלא ידע היכן נפל: אפי' של מלך אחד מכריז. הואיל ומטבעות הוו זו ע"ג זו יש כאן סימן דלא אתרמי דנפול הכי: ופרכינן מאי מכריז מנין. כך וכך מטבעות מצאתי וזה בא ונתן סימן זו ע"ג זו מצאתם: טבעא מכריז. מטבעות מצאתי הלכך תרי לאו סימנא הוא דמיעוט מטבעות ב': כשיר. מוטלין בעגול כצלעדה: כשורה. זו אצל זו: כחצובה. כג' רגלי קנקן כל אחד כנגד אויר של שני כזה ∴: כסולם. רוב אמצעי על התחתון ורוב העליון על האמצעי כמו מעלות שקורין אשקולינו"ש: פשוט מהא. דר"נ חדא: כל שאילו מכנים כו'. וכי הוו כסולם ניטלים בבת אחת:

---

**תוספות**

**הא** בכובא וכיתנא. פי' רש"י דמתני' בכובא וכיתנא וקשה דקתני מלא פירות וי"א דכיתנא אקרי פירי כדאמרינן (בבראשית רבה) ויבא קין מפרי האדמה זרע פשתן הביא ודוחק ונראה דמתני' בצנא ופירי דכיון דאין הפירות מחוברים יחד אילו מן הכלי נפלו היה קצת נשאר מהם בכלי אבל פשתן שקשור ביחד יכול להיות שבכלי היה ונפל ור"ח פי' דפריך אמאי דקאמר מקצתן על גבי קרקע חייב להכריז ורמינהו מצא דבר כו' בא בעל סימן ונטל את שלו זכה המוצא במה שבידו היינו מה שבחוץ אע"פ שיש בפנים קצת פירות ואפילו בעל כלי אומר שכולן שלו ולפי זה גרס בסמוך הא והא דאשתיירי ביה:

**שמעת** מינה מנין הוי סימן. אע"ג דפשיטא ליה לעיל מדמשקל הוי סימן מדה ומנין נמי הוי סימן בעי לאוכוחי הכא ממתני' ולעיל (דף כד.) נמי דקתני אבל מלא שנים חייב לא קאמר ש"מ מנין הוי סימן (דלא אלימא ליה ברייתא למפשט מינה) אי נמי דמצי למדחי דמנין וחרוזא הוי סימן:

**והוא** שעשויין כמגדלין. אי מנין הוי סימן במה שעשוין כמגדלין ידעינן דדרך הינוח הוה ובתרי לא סגי דטבעא מכריז אבל אם מקום הוי סימן אפילו בתרי ועשוין כמגדלין ידעינן דדרך הינוח הוה דאי בתרי אפי' עשוין כמגדלין לא ידעינן דדרך הינוח הוה דאימור דרך נפילה הוה דאתרמי הכי א"כ לקמן מאי פריך (אר' יוחנן) מאי אריא תלתא אפי' בתרי סגי וי"ל דשפיר משני טבעא מכריז:

**הא** גופא קשיא. אמתני' לא פריך דמלינן למימר דג' מטבעות היינו פירוש לצבורי מעות:

כאבני

---

**עין משפט נר מצוה**

נ א מיי' פט"ו מהלכות אבידה הל' ב סמג עשין עד טוש"ע ח"מ סי' רסב סעיף יב:
נא ב מיי' שם פט"ו הלכה י סמג שם טוש"ע שם סעיף ט:
נב ג מיי' שם הלכה ט טוש"ע שם סעיף ח:
נג ד מיי' שם הלכה יג סמג שם טוש"ע ח"מ סי' רסב סעיף יט:
נד ה מיי' שם פט"ו הל' ג סמג שם טוש"ע שם סעיף כ:
נה ו מיי' שם פט"ו הל' טו סמג שם טוש"ע שם סעיף יט:
נו ז מיי' שם פי"ד הל' יא סמג שם:
נז ח ט מיי' שם פט"ו הלכה יד סמג שם טוש"ע ח"מ סי' רסב סעיף יט:
נח י מיי' שם פט"ו הל' ב סמג שם טוש"ע ח"מ שם סעיף יב:
נט כ מיי' שם טוש"ע שם סעיף יא:
ס ל מ מיי' שם טוש"ע שם סעיף יב:

**רבינו חננאל**

מצא פירות בכלי או כלי כמות שהוא וכו' אמרי' תנינא להא דתנו רבנן מצא כלי ולפניו פירות כיס ולפניו מעות הרי אלו שלו. מקצתן בכלי ומקצתן בקרקע חייב להכריז ואם בא ישראל ונתן סימני הכלי נוטל גם הפירות וכן כל כיוצא בהן. ורמינן עלה הא דתניא מצא דבר שאין בו סימן בצד דבר שיש בו סימן א) נוטל הדבר שיש בו סימן וזכה הלה בדבר שאין בו סימן. ופרקינן הא והא בצנא ופרי וכגון שנותרו מן הפירות בצנא ולא קשיא הא דתני חייב להכריז דמשמע שמחזיר גם הפירות בצנא דאית ליה אוגנים והן כפופות לתוכה דאמרי' האי צנא איתהפכא והני פירי אישתפוך מן הצנא והני פירי (דאישתפוך) [דאשתייר] בגוה אוגנים מנעום מלהשפך בחוץ הלכך הפירות בתר צנא גרירי בא מי שנתן סימני צנא נוטל גם הפירות. והא דתני דזכה הלה במה שבידו בצנא דלית ליה אוגנים ונמצאו הפירות בחוץ ופירות בצנא דאמרי' הני פירי דבחוץ לאו מן הצנא אישתפוך דאילו מינה אישתפוך הוו להו לאישתפוכי כולהו דהא לית לה לצנא אוגנים אלא הני פירי דבחוץ לאחרינא אינון לפיכך זכה בהם המוצאן דהא דבר שאין בו סימן נינהו. ציבורי פירות. ש"מ מנין הוי סימן. ג' מטבעות זו על גבי זו חייב להכריז. פי' כמגדלים מכוונות אבנים זו על גבי זו אין אחת עודפת על חבירתה. מפוזרין שלו הא אי הוו שלחופי משלחפי שאין מיושבות זו על גב זו אלא מקצתן עליה ומקצתן יוצאה מעליה כגון כנפי הכרובים כדגרסי' בסוף המוכר את הבית ודלמא שלחופי הוו משלחפי אהדדי ועיקרו כדמתרגמי' בתרגום ארץ ישראל שכל את ידיו שלחופינון לידוהי. אסקינן כל שאינן עשויים כמגדלים מפוזרין נינהו והרי הן שלו רויחא לתתא ומיצעא עילויה וזוטא עילוי מצעי זהו כמגדלים. בעי ר' ירמיה כשיר או כשורה או כחצובה או כסולם מהו ועלו בתיקו. פי' כשיר עגול כצמידין דמתרגמ' לה שירין. כשורה זה בצד זה.

כחצובה

---

**מסורת הש"ס**

א) [לעיל כג:], ב) מהרש"ל גורס מ"ז, ג) לפירוש רש"י והרא"ש קאי על משנה וע"ש, ד) [לעיל ...], ה) בבא בתרא קג., ו) [לעיל דף כג:], ז) ס"א מייתא היא ומאי אולמא דמשקל, ח) ס"א ל"ג.

**הגהות הב"ח**

(א) גמ' טבעי מכריז: (ב) רש"י ד"ה תני צבור ומאי סימניה: (ג) ד"ה תני צבורי וכו' מנין הוא דהוי:

**הגהות הגר"א**

[א] גמ' רב פפא וכו'. הרמב"ם פסק ככולהו [illegible] דר"פ אבל דר"ז [illegible] מיטה. והרא"ש וטור [illegible] גם לדר"ז: [ב] שם [illegible] הא והא דלא אשתייר בה מידי [illegible] הא דא"ל אוגנין [illegible] הא דל"ל אוגנין [illegible] ואב"א הא והא [illegible] אוגנין ול"ק הא [illegible] מהדרי אפיה לגבי [illegible] הא דלא מהדרי [illegible] לגבי פירי כצ"ל [illegible] ד"ה והא כו' [illegible] [ג] שם [illegible] חנינא כו' [illegible] [ד] שם פשוט [illegible] חדא דאמר [illegible]

**לעזי רש"י**

[illegible] שקולינ"ש. פירוש [illegible]

**ליקוטי רש"י**

[illegible] אגנין. שפה [illegible] כשיר [illegible] כשורה. [illegible] שתי וערב [רשב"ם ב"ב קג:].

---

**חשק שלמה על ר"ח** א) נראה דלא גרס בברייתא השניה נוטל ומכריז רק נוטל הדבר וכו' ועי' בתוס' כאן ד"ה הא גירסת רבינו ופירושו.

The Gemara suggests yet another answer:

וְאִיבָּעֵית אֵימָא — Or, if you prefer, say: הָא וְהָא דִּמְהַדְּרֵי אַפֵּיהּ לְגַבֵּי פֵּי — Both this Baraisa and that Baraisa refer to cases where the opening of [the basket] is facing the produce, וְלָא קַשְׁיָא — and still there is no difficulty. הָא דְּאִית לָהּ אוֹגְנִין לְצַנָּא — For this first Baraisa, which permits the finder to keep the produce, refers to a case where [the basket] has a rim; הָא דְּלֵית לָהּ אוֹגְנִין לְצַנָּא — whereas this second Baraisa, which requires the finder to return the produce, refers to a case where [the basket] does not have a rim.[16]

The Gemara considers the next items that our Mishnah requires the finder to announce and return:

צִבּוּרֵי פֵּירוֹת וְצִבּוּרֵי מָעוֹ — PILES OF PRODUCE OR PILES OF MONEY.

The Gemara infers:

שְׁמַעַת מִינָּ — Learn from this Mishnah מִנְיָן הָוֵי סִימָן — that the number of items found together is treated as a valid identifying mark![17]

The Gemara rejects this inference:

תְּנִי צִבּוּר פֵּירוֹ — Perhaps the Mishnah means to teach: A single pile of produce must be returned.[18] Thus, the number of piles cannot serve as the identifying mark.[19]

Based on this new understanding of the Mishnah, the Gemara attempts to derive another ruling:

שְׁמַעַת מִינָּ — Learn from this מָקוֹם הָוֵי סִימָן — that the location of a lost object is treated as an identifying mark.[20]

The Gemara rejects this deduction, as well:

תְּ — Perhaps the Mishnah means to teach: צִבּוּרֵי פֵּירוֹת — Piles of produce.[21] In that case, the number of piles would serve as the identifying feature rather than the location.

The next item that the Mishnah required one to announce was:

שְׁלֹשָׁה מַטְבְּעוֹת זֶה עַל גַּב זֶה — THREE COINS ONE UPON THE OTHER.

The Gemara explains:

אָמַר רַבִּי יִצְחָק מִגְדְּלָאָה — R' Yitzchak Migdelaah said: וְהוּא שֶׁעֲשׂוּיִין כְּמִגְדָּלִין — This ruling is true only when the coins were arranged like towers.[22]

The Gemara supports this explanation:

תַּנְיָא נַמִּי הָכִי — This was also taught in a Baraisa: מָצָא מָעוֹת מְפוּזָּרוֹת — IF ONE FOUND SCATTERED COINS, הֲרֵי אֵלּוּ שֶׁלּוֹ — THESE BELONG TO HIM. עֲשׂוּיִין כְּמִגְדָּלִים — IF THEY WERE ARRANGED LIKE TOWERS, חַיָּיב לְהַכְרִיז — HE IS OBLIGATED TO ANNOUNCE his find.[23] וְאֵלּוּ הֵן עֲשׂוּיִין כְּמִגְדָּלִים — AND THESE ARE THE ONES THAT ARE ARRANGED LIKE TOWERS: שְׁלֹשָׁה מַטְבְּעִין — THREE COINS of unequal size זֶה עַל גַּב זֶה — ONE UPON THE OTHER.

The Gemara notes a difficulty in the Baraisa:

הָא גּוּפָא קַשְׁיָא — This Barasisa is self-contradictory! אָמְרַת — First you say: מָצָא מָעוֹת מְפוּזָּרוֹת הֲרֵי אֵלּוּ שֶׁלּוֹ — IF ONE FOUND SCATTERED COINS, THESE BELONG TO HIM. This implies: הָא מְשַׁלְּחֲפֵי שַׁלְחוּפֵי — But if [the coins] were leaning on each other, one resting partially atop the next and partially on the ground, חַיָּיב לְהַכְרִיז — he is obligated to announce his find.[24] אֵימָא סֵיפָא — Consider, however, the end of the Baraisa: עֲשׂוּיִין כְּמִגְדָּלִין חַיָּיב לְהַכְרִיז — IF [THE COINS] WERE ARRANGED LIKE TOWERS, HE IS OBLIGATED TO ANNOUNCE his find. This implies: הָא מְשַׁלְּחֲפֵי שַׁלְחוּפֵי — But if [the coins] were leaning on each other, הֲרֵי אֵלּוּ שֶׁלּוֹ — these belong to [the finder].[25] Thus, the implications of two sections of the Baraisa contradict each other! — ? —

The Gemara resolves the contradiction:

תַּנָּא כָּל שֶׁאֵין עֲשׂוּיִין כְּמִגְדָּלִין מְפוּזָּרוֹת קָרֵי לְהוּ — The Tanna of the Baraisa refers to whatever is not arranged like a tower as "scattered."[26]

NOTES

16. As Rav Pappa stated in his first answer, we assume that the produce did not fall from the basket, for had it done so, some produce would certainly have been trapped by the rim and remained inside. Where the basket does not have a rim, however, there is no reason to assume that the produce did not originate in the basket; hence, the one who identifies the *siman* on the basket takes the produce as well.

17. The Gemara assumes that this produce can be identified only by stating the number of piles in which it was kept. Since the Mishnah requires them to be announced, it can be inferred that the number of items found together constitutes a valid *siman* (*Rashi*).

Although the Gemara previously proved from a Baraisa that the number of items found is considered a valid *siman* [see 23b], it now wishes to prove this point from a Mishnah (*Tosafos*; see there for an alternative explanation).

18. The Gemara suggests that the Mishnah means to include a single pile of produce in its listing of items that must be announced by the finder. Although the Mishnah lists the find as צִבּוּרֵי פֵּירוֹת, *piles of produce* (in the plural), it uses the plural to connote a general condition, as if to say one who found one of the many piles of produce in the world that are lost (*Ritva*).

19. It is common for produce to be heaped in a pile. Thus, if the owner attempts to reclaim his produce by stating that he lost a single pile, he has not identified anything distinctive about the produce, and his identification is thus not meaningful. Only where he states that he left two or more piles is the number significant, since it is not common for people to heap their produce in more than one pile (*Nachalas Moshe*). The number of fruits in the pile cannot serve as the *siman* because the Mishnah may be referring to a pile of wheat grains, which are impossible to count (*Shitah Mekubetzes*).

20. Accordingly, when the Mishnah states that a pile of produce must be announced, it is because it can be identified by its location. The fact that the produce was piled rather than scattered indicates that it had been placed there intentionally; hence, the owner will be able to identify the location of this pile and reclaim it by virtue of that *siman* (*Rashi*).

21. If the Mishnah should be understood to be teaching that one must announce a find of a single pile of produce, what *siman* other than its location can the owner provide in order to reclaim his property?

I.e. it is not clear whether the Mishnah is speaking of a single pile of produce or several piles. If it speaks of a single pile, then indeed location must be the *siman;* if it speaks of several piles, then number is the *siman*. However, since it is unclear which of these the Mishnah is discussing, it cannot be *proven* from our Mishnah which kind of *siman* is valid (*Rashi*).

22. [One need only announce an object if it can be identified by its owner. R' Yitzchak states that the three coins listed in our Mishnah need be announced only when they are stacked like a tower.] The Gemara will soon explain this to apply to three coins of different diameters, with the largest coin on the bottom and the smallest coin on top. Since the coins were found stacked in such a stable arrangement, it is evident that they were deliberately placed there by the owner. Although he subsequently forgot them there, the owner could remember their arrangement and reclaim them by virtue of that *siman*. Therefore, the finder must announce his find (*Rashi*; see *Maharam Shif*).

*Maharatz Chayos* suggests that since R' Yitzchak Migdelaah is mentioned rarely in the Talmud, he was surnamed "Migdelaah" (from the root *migdal,* tower) because his most famous ruling refers to coins stacked like towers.

23. As R' Yitzchak Migdelaah stated.

24. [The term "scattered" ordinarily means that they are lying on the ground completely apart from each other.] Thus, the Baraisa's first ruling implies that if the coins were even partially on top of each other, the finder may not keep them, because we assume that even a formation that is not like a tower is the result of deliberate placement rather than the haphazard pattern of a fall (*Rashi*).

25. This statement implies that coins found in any arrangement other than a "tower" are assumed to have fallen from their owner and therefore to lack a *siman*.

26. The Tanna indeed holds that coins found in any arrangement other than that of a tower can be assumed to have fallen from the owner. He refers to *all* such haphazard arrangements when he rules in the first part of the Baraisa that "scattered" coins may be kept.

שלשה מטבעות זה על גב זה [ב]כריכות ברה"י [ג]וככרות של בעה"ב וגיזי צמר הלקוחין מבית האומן (א) כדי יין וכדי שמן הרי אלו חייב להכריז: **גמ'** טעמא דמצא פירות בכלי ומעות בכים הא כלי ולפניו פירות כים ולפניו מעות הרי אלו שלו תנינא להא דתנו רבנן [ד]מצא כלי ולפניו פירות [ה]כים ולפניו מעות הרי אלו שלו [ו]מקצתן בכלי ומקצתן על גבי קרקע מקצתן בכים ומקצתן על גבי קרקע חייב להכריז ורמינהו [ז]מצא דבר שאין בו סימן בצד דבר שיש בו סימן חייב להכריז בא בעל סימן ונטל את שלו זכה הלה בדבר שאין בו סימן אמר רב זביד לא קשיא הא בכובא וכיתנא הא בצנא ופירי [א] רב פפא אמר הא והא בצנא ופירי ולא קשיא הא דאשתייר בה מידי הא דלא אשתייר בה מידי [ב] ואיבעית אימא הא והא דלא אשתייר בה מידי ולא קשיא [ח]הא דמהדרי אפיה לגבי פירי הא דלא מהדרי אפיה לגבי פירי ואיבעית אימא הא והא דמהדרי אפיה לגבי פירי ולא קשיא [ט]הא דאית לה אוגנין לצנא הא דלית לה אוגנין לצנא: צבורי פירות וצבורי מעות: שמעת מינה מנין הוי סימן תני צבור פירות שמעת מינה מקום הוי סימן תני צבורי פירות: שלשה מטבעות זה על גב זה: אמר רבי יצחק מגדלאה [י]והוא שעשויין כמגדלין תניא נמי הכי מצא מעות מפוזרות הרי אלו שלו עשויין כמגדלים חייב להכריז ואלו הן עשויין כמגדלים שלשה מטבעין זה על גב זה הא גופא קשיא אמרת מצא מעות מפוזרות הרי אלו שלו הא משלחפי שלחופי חייב להכריז אימא סיפא עשויין כמגדלין חייב להכריז הא משלחפי שלחופי הרי אלו שלו תנא כל שאין עשויין כמגדלין [כ]מפוזרות קרי להו [ג] א"ר חנינא לא שנו אלא של שלשה מלכים אבל של מלך אחד אינו חייב להכריז היכי דמי אי דעשויין כמגדלין אפילו של מלך אחד נמי ואי דאין עשויין כמגדלין אפילו של שלשה מלכים נמי לא אלא אי אתמר הכי אתמר לא שנו אלא של מלך אחד כעין שלשה מלכים [ג](אבל של מלך אחד אינו חייב להכריז) והיכי דמי דעשויין כמגדלים רויחא תתאה ומציעא עילויה וזוטא עילויה מציעא דאמרינן אנוחי אנחינהו אבל של מלך אחד דכולהו כי הדדי נינהו אע"ג דמנחי אהדדי הרי אלו שלו אימר אתרמויי אתרמי ובהדי הדדי נפול ורבי יוחנן אמר אפילו של מלך אחד נמי מכריז [ג]מאי מכריז מנין מאי איריא תלתא אפי' תרין נמי אמר רבינא (א) [ד]טבעא מכריז [ה][ל]בעי ר' ירמיה כשיר מהו כשורה מהו כחצובה מהו כסולם מהו [ד] פשוט מהא חדא דאמר רבה בר אבוה [מ]כל שאילו מכנים לה קיסם ביניהן ונוטלם בבת אחת חייב להכריז בעי רב אשי

**רש"י**

שלשה מטבעות זו ע"ג זו. בגמרא מפרש סימנייהו: **גמ'** טעמא דמצא כו'. התם הוא דאמר שהפירות לבעל הכלי: הא כלי ולפניו פירות. הרי אלו הפירות של מוצאן ואע"פ שהכלי לבעל הסימן את הכלי יחזיר ואת הפירות יעכב לו ולא אמרינן מהאי מנא נפל: מקצתן בכלי כו'. הדבר מוכיח דהנך דעל גבי קרקע דהנך הוא וחייב להחזירם למי שיתן סימן בכלי וכן מעות לבעל הכים: ה"ג מצא דבר שאין בו סימן בצד דבר שיש בו סימן. כגון מעות לפני כים: חייב להכריז. על הכל ויתנו המעות לבעל הכים: בא בעל סימן ונטל את שלו. את הכים ואמר אין המעות שלי זכה הלה במעות: הא. דקתני הרי אלו שלו: בכובא וכיתנא. גיגית מוטלת ופשתן לפניה דודאי האי פשתן לאו מכובא נפל דאי מינה נפל הוה משתייר בה והוא הדין לכים ולפניו מעות מהאי טעמא והא דקתני חייב בצנא ופירי דעבידי דשרקי ונפלי מיניה כולהו: הא דקתני חייב בדאשתייר. ואיכא למימר הנך דאברא מיניה נפל: והא דלא אשתייר. כיון דפתח לצנא יש לו אוגנין כפולים לתוכו אי מתוכו נפל הוה משתייר ביה דאוגנין מעכבי ליה: ה"ג הא והא דלא אשתייר ביה מידי: הא דאית ליה אוגנין. לאו מיניה נפל דאי מיניה נפל הוה משתייר ביה מידי: ש"מ מנין הוי סימן. דאי לאו הכי מאי סימן איכא: תני צבור פירות. דאין כאן מנין (ב) מאי סימניה מקום דכיון דצבורין הינוח הוה ויהיב סימנא במקום פלוני הנחתים: תני צבורי פירות. סימני מנין (ג) דהוי מדחי ליה לא הא תפשוט ולא הא תפשוט: והוא שעשויין כמגדלין. לקמיה מפרש שלשתן רחבין זה מזה ומניח מלמטה את הרחב ועליו את הבינוני ועליון הוא הקצר שכולן כמגדל זה העשוי היסוד רחב ומקצר ועולה וכי מנחי הכי לאו דרך נפילה הוה אלא דרך הינוח והיה דעתו לחזור וליטלן ושכח הלכך נוטל ומכריז וזה בא ונותן סימן ואומר מגדלין היו עשויין: ג' מטבעות. שאין דומות זו לזו ברחבן: משלחפי שלחופי. מקצת זו על חבירתה ומקצת על גבי קרקע: חייב להכריז. אלמא כי האי גוונא לאו דרך נפילה הוא: של שלשה מלכים. קס"ד שלא היו צורותיהם שוות שכל מלך כותב שמו וצורתו על מטבע שלו: אי דעשויין כמגדלין. שאין שוין ברחבן ומונחים כמו שפרישית: אפילו של מלך אחד. שצורת שלשתן שוות: של מלך אחד כעין שלשה מלכים. כלומר אפי' הן של מלך אחד שצורת שלשתן שוה והן כעין שלשה מלכים שחלוקין ברחבן ודומין לג' מטבעות: ה"ג והיכי דמי כגון שעשויין כמגדלין חייב להכריז: דכולהו כי הדדי נינהו. שוין ברחבן: אע"ג דכי הדדי מנחי. זה על זה ולאו משלחפי: אימור [אתרמויי] אתרמי. דהכי נפל ואין זה הינוח וסימן אין לו בהם ואפי' מקום דלא ידע היכן נפל: אפי' של מלך אחד מכריז. הואיל ומטבעות הוו זו ע"ג זו יש כאן סימן דלא אתרמי דנפול הכי: ופרכינן מאי מכריז מנין. כך וכך מטבעות מצאתי וזה בא ונתן סימן זו ע"ג זו מצאתם: טבעא מכריז. מטבעות מצאתי הלכך תרי לאו סימנא הוא דמיעוט מטבעות ב': כשיר. מוטלין בעגול כאלעדה: כשורה. זו אצל זו: כחצובה. כג' רגלי קנקן כל אחד כנגד אויר של שני כזה ∴: כסולם. רוב אמצעי על התחתון ורוב העליון על האמצעי כמו מעלות שקורין אשקולינו"ש: פשוט מהא. דר"נ הלא: כל שאילו מכנים כו'. וכי הוו כסולם ניטלים בבת אחת: כאבני

**תוספות**

**הא** בכובא וכיתנא. פי' רש"י דמתני' בכובא וכיתנא וקשה דקתני מלא פירות וי"א דכיתנא אקרי פירי כדאמרינן (בבראשית רבה) ויבא קין מפרי האדמה זרע פשתן היא ודוחק ונראה דמתני' בצנא ופירי דכיון דאין הפירות מחוברים יחד אילו מן הכלי נפלו היה קצת נשאר מהם בכלי אבל פשתן שקשור ביחד יכול להיות שבכלי היה ונפל ור"ח פי' דפריך אמאי דקאמר מקצתן על גבי קרקע חייב להכריז ורמינהו מצא דבר כו' בא בעל סימן ונטל את שלו זכה המוצא במה שבידו היינו מה שבחוץ אע"פ שיש בפנים קצת פירות ואפילו בעל כלי אומר שכולן שלו ולפי זה גרס בסמוך הא והא דאשתיירי ביה:

**שמעת** מינה מנין הוי סימן. אע"ג דפשיטא ליה לעיל [י] מדמשקל הוי סימן מדה ומנין נמי הוי סימן בעי לאוכוחי הכא ממתני' ולעיל (דף כד.) נמי דקתני אבל מלא שנים חייב לא קאמר ש"מ מנין הוי סימן ([י] דלא אלימא ליה ברייתא למפשט מינה) אי נמי דמלי למדחי דמנין וחרוזא הוי סימן:

**והוא** שעשויין כמגדלין. אי מנין הוי סימן במה שעשויין כמגדלין ידעינן דדרך הינוח הוה ובתרי לא סגי דטבעא מכריז אבל אם מקום הוי סימן אפילו בתרי ועשויין כמגדלין ידעינן דדרך הינוח הוה דאי בתרי אפי' עשויין כמגדלין לא ידעינן דדרך הינוח הוה דאימור דרך נפילה הוה דאתרמי הכי א"כ לקמן מאי פריך [ח](אר' יוחנן) מאי איריא תלתא אפי' בתרי סגי וי"ל דשפיר משני טבעא מכריז:

**הא** גופא קשיא. אמתני' לא פריך דמצינן למימר דג' מטבעות היינו פירוש לצבורי מעות:
כאבני

**עין משפט נר מצוה**

נ א מיי' פט"ז מהלכות אבידה הל' ג סמג עשין עד טוש"ע ח"מ סי' רסב סעיף יב:
נא ב מיי' שם פט"ו הלכה י סמג שם טוש"ע שם סעיף ט:
נב ג מיי' שם הלכה ט טוש"ע שם סעיף ח:
נג ד מיי' שם הלכה יג סמג שם טוש"ע ח"מ סי' רסב סעיף יט:
נד ה מיי' שם פט"ז הל' ג סמג שם טוש"ע שם סעיף כ:
נה ו מיי' שם פט"ו הל' טו סמג שם טוש"ע שם סעיף יט:
נו ז מיי' שם פי"ד הל' יא סמג שם:
נז ח ט מיי' שם פט"ו הלכה יד סמג שם טוש"ע ח"מ סי' רסב סעיף יט:
נח י מיי' שם פט"ז הל' ג סמג שם טוש"ע ח"מ שם סעיף יב:
נט כ מיי' שם טוש"ע שם סעיף יא:
ס ל מ מיי' שם טוש"ע שם סעיף יב:

**רבינו חננאל**

מצא פירות בכלי או כלי כמות שהוא וכו' אמרי' תנינא להא דתנו רבנן מצא כלי ולפניו פירות כיס ולפניו מעות הרי אלו שלו. מקצתן בכלי ומקצתן בקרקע חייב להכריז ואם בא ישראל ונתן סימני הכלי נוטל גם הפירות וכן כל כיוצא בהן. ורמינן עלה הא דתניא מצא דבר שאין בו סימן בצד דבר שיש בו סימן א) נוטל הדבר שיש בו סימן וזכה הלה בדבר שאין בו סימן. ופרקינן הא והא בצנא ופרי וכגון שנותרו מן הפירות בצנא ולא קשיא הא דתני חייב להכריז דמשמע שמחזיר גם הפירות בצנא דאית ליה אוגנים והן כפופות לתוכה דאמרי' האי צנא איתהפכא והני פירי אישתפוך מן הצנא והני פירי (דאישתפוך) [דאשתייר] בגוה אוגנים מנעום מלהשפך בחרץ הלכך הפירות בתר צנא גרירי בא מי שנתן סימני צנא נוטל גם הפירות. והא דתני דזכה הלה במה שבידו בצנא דלית ליה אוגנים ונמצאו הפירות בחרץ ופירות בצנא דאמרי' הני פירי דבחרץ לאו מן הצנא אישתפוך דאילו מינה אישתפוך הוו להו לאישתפוכי כולהו דהא לית לה לצנא אוגנים אלא הני פירי דבחרץ לאחרינא אינון לפיכך זכה בהם המוצאן דהא דבר שאין בו סימן נינהו. ציבורי פירות. ש"מ מנין הוי סימן. **ג' מטבעות זו על גבי זו חייב להכריז.** פי' כמגדלים מכוונות אבנים זו על גבי זו אין אחת עודפת על חבירתה. מפוזרין שלו הא אי הוו שלחופי משלחפי שאין מיושבות זו על גב זו אלא מקצתן עליה ומקצתן יוצאה מעליה כגון כנפי הכרובים כדגרסי' בסוף המוכר את הבית ודלמא שלחופי הוו משלחפי אהדדי ועיקרו כדמתרגמי' בתרגום ארץ ישראל שכל את ידיו שלחופינון לידוהי. אסקינן כל שאינן עשויים כמגדלים מפוזרין נינהו והרי הן שלו רויחא לתתא ומיצעא עילויה וזוטא עילוי מצעי זהו כמגדלים. בעי ר' ירמיה כשיר או כשורה או כחצובה או כסולם מהו ועלו בתיקו. פי' כשיר עגול כצמידין דמתרגמ' לה שירין. כשורה זה בצד זה.
כחצובה

**מסורת הש"ס**

[א] לעיל כג:], ב) מהרש"ל ...ר"ס מ"ז, ג) לפירוש ...ף והרא"ש קאי על ...נה וע"ש, ד) [לעיל ...], ה) בבא בתרא קג., ...ף כג:], ז) ס"א ...ייתא היא ומאי אולמא ... דמשקל, ח) ס"א ל"ג.

**הגהות הב"ח**

(א) גמ' טבעי מכריז: (ב) רש"י ד"ה תני צבור ומאי סימניה: (ג) ד"ה תני צבורי וכו' מנין הוא דהוי:

**הגהות הגר"א**

[א] גמ' רב פפא וכו'. הרמב"ם פסק ככולהו ...ימתא דר"פ אבל דר"ז ...ניטה. והרא"ש וטור ...ק גם לדר"ז: [ב] שם ...א הא והא דלא ...תייר בה מידי ...ק הא דא"ל אוגנין ...א הא דל"ל אוגנין ...א ואב"א הא והא ...ל אוגנין ול"ק הא ...הדרי אפיה לגבי ...י הא דלא מהדרי ...יה לגבי פירי כצ"ל ...נ מרש"י ד"ה והא כו' ...ס לנא כו' אבל הרא"ש ...ם כגירסא שלנו וע"ש ...כרי רבינו בח"מ סי' ... ס"ק כ"ה): [ג] שם ... חנינא כו'. נ"ב ...פ הרא"ש וש"פ אבל ...נב"ס השמיטה דס"ל ...ח ור' יוחנן פליגי ...נא דר"י מגדלאה ופסק ... יוחנן וע' רי"ף ...פרש כהרמב"ם וע' ...: [ד] שם (פשוט ...א חדא ד)אמר. אות ... ממלת דאמר עם ג' ...ת שלפניו מוקפים ...ולים וכ"ב הרמב"ם ל"ג ...אלא גרים אמר ר"נ כו' ...לם לא איפשיטא ותסר ...ע כאן וע' ברמב"ם:

**לעזי רש"י**

אשקולינו"ש. פירוש מעלות (רש"י שמות כ, ...), מדרגות (רש"י ...).

**ליקוטי רש"י**

מנין. ... [עי' לק כה.]. צנא. ... כשיר ... עשוין כאלעדה ... [רשב"ם ב"ב קג:].

חשק שלמה על ר"ח א) נראה דלא גרס בברייתא השניה נוטל ומכריז רק נוטל הדבר וכו' ועי' בתוס' כאן ד"ה הא גירסת רבינו ופירושו.

**שְׁלֹשָׁה מַטְבְּעוֹת זֶה עַל גַּב זֶה – three coins one upon the other,**[1] **כְּרִיכוֹת בִּרְשׁוּת הַיָּחִיד – small sheaves in a private domain,**[2] **וְכִכָּרוֹת שֶׁל בַּעַל הַבַּיִת** – or homemade **loaves of a householder,**[3] **וְגִיזֵּי צֶמֶר הַלְּקוּחִין מִבֵּית הָאוּמָּן – or fleeces of wool taken from the craftsman's workshop,**[4] **כַּדֵּי יַיִן – jugs of wine וְכַדֵּי שֶׁמֶן – or jugs of oil**[5] – **הֲרֵי אֵלּוּ חַיָּיב לְהַכְרִיז – these** finds **one is obligated to announce.**

**Gemara** The first two examples given by the Mishnah of finds that need to be announced are produce in a ssel and coins in a purse. The Gemara draws an inference from ese:

**טַעְ – The reason** that one must announce the entire find is **דְּמָצָא פֵּירוֹת בִּכְלִי וּמָעוֹת בְּכ – because he found** the **produce in vessel and** the **coins in a purse; הָא כְּלִי וּלְפָנָיו פֵּירוֹת – but** if found **a vessel with produce in front of it, כִּיס וּלְפָנָיו מָעוֹת – a purse with coins in front of it, הֲרֵי אֵלּוּ שֶׁלּוֹ – these** [the oduce and money] **belong to [the finder].**[6]

On the basis of this inference, the Gemara corroborates the ling of a Baraisa:

**תְּנֵינָא לְהָא דְּתָנוּ רַבָּ – We have learned in** our **Mishnah that hich the Rabbis taught in** the following **Baraisa: מָצָא כְּלִי – ONE FOUND A VESSEL וּלְפָנָיו פֵּירוֹת – WITH PRODUCE IN FRONT IT, כִּיס וּלְפָנָיו מָעוֹת –** or **A PURSE WITH COINS IN FRONT OF IT, הֲרֵי אֵלּוּ שֶׁ – THESE** [the produce and money] **BELONG TO [THE NDER].**[7] **מִקְצָתָן בִּכְלִי –** If **SOME OF [THE PRODUCE] WAS IN THE SSEL וּמִקְצָתָן עַל גַּבֵּי קַרְקַע – AND SOME OF IT WAS** lying nearby **THE GROUND, מִקְצָתָן בְּכִיס –** or, if **SOME OF [THE COINS] WERE THE PURSE וּמִקְצָתָן עַל גַּבֵּי קַרְקַע – AND SOME OF THEM WERE** ing nearby **ON THE GROUND, חַיָּיב לְהַכְרִיז – [THE FINDER] IS BLIGATED TO ANNOUNCE** the entire find.[8]

The Gemara asks:

**וּרְמִינְ – They pointed out a contradiction** between this araisa and another Baraisa, which states: **מָצָא דָּבָר שֶׁאֵין בּוֹ סִימָן –** If **ONE FOUND AN OBJECT THAT DOES NOT HAVE AN IDENTIFYING ARK בְּצַד דָּבָר שֶׁיֵּשׁ בּוֹ סִימָן – NEXT TO AN OBJECT THAT HAS AN ENTIFYING MARK, חַיָּיב לְהַכְרִיז – HE IS OBLIGATED TO ANOUNCE** the entire find.[9] **בָּא בַּעַל סִימָן –** If **THE ONE WHO PRODED THE IDENTIFYING MARK CAME וְנָטַל אֶת שֶׁלּוֹ – AND TOOK HAT WHICH WAS HIS,** but admitted that the unidentifiable object did not belong to him, **זָכָה הַלָּה בְּדָבָר שֶׁאֵין בּוֹ סִימָן – THE OTHER ONE** [i.e. the finder] **IS ENTITLED TO THE OBJECT THAT DOES NOT HAVE AN IDENTIFYING MARK.**[10] At any rate, the first ruling of the Baraisa, which requires the finder to announce the unidentifiable object, contradicts the previous Baraisa, which ruled that the finder may keep the unidentifiable produce or coins. – ? –

The Gemara reconciles the Baraisos:

**אָמַר רַב זְבִיד – Rav Zevid said: לֹא קַשְׁיָא – There is no difficulty. הָא בְּכוּבָא וְכִיתְנָא – This** first Baraisa, which permits the finder to keep the unidentifiable object, deals **with** a find such as **a barrel and flax;**[11] **הָא בְּצַנָּא וּפֵירֵי –** whereas **this** second Baraisa, which obligates the finder to return even the unidentifiable object, deals **with** a find such as **a basket and produce.**[12]

The Gemara offers an alternative answer:

**רַב פָּפָּא אָמַר – Rav Pappa said: הָא וְהָא בְּצַנָּא וּפֵירֵי –** Both **this** Baraisa **and that** Baraisa can be dealing **with a a basket and produce, וְלֹא קַשְׁיָא – and** still **there is no difficulty. הָא דְּאִשְׁתַּיֵּיר בָּהּ מִידֵּי –** For **this** second **Baraisa,** which requires the finder to return the produce, refers to a case **where some** produce **remains in [the basket];**[13] **הָא דְּלֹא אִשְׁתַּיֵּיר בָּהּ מִידֵּי – whereas this** first Baraisa, which permits the finder to keep the produce, refers to a case **where no** produce **remains in [the basket].**[14]

The Gemara suggests yet another answer:

**וְאִיבָּעֵית אֵימָא – Or, if you prefer, say: הָא וְהָא דְּלֹא אִשְׁתַּיֵּיר בָּהּ מִידֵּי –** Both **this** Baraisa **and that** Baraisa refer to cases **where nothing remains in [the basket], וְלֹא קַשְׁיָא –** and still **there is no difficulty. הָא דִּמְהַדְּרֵי אַפֵּיהּ לְגַבֵּי פֵּירֵי –** For **this** second Baraisa, which requires the finder to return the produce, refers to a case **where the opening of [the basket] faces the produce; הָא דְּלֹא מְהַדְּרֵי אַפֵּיהּ לְגַבֵּי פֵּירֵי –** whereas **this** first Baraisa, which permits the finder to keep the produce, refers to a case **where the opening of [the basket] is not facing the produce.**[15]

NOTES

The Gemara will discuss what their *siman* is.

For example, a sown field which, while being open to the public, is tually used by only a few people (*Rashi* to 22b; see note 21 there).

Each householder bakes his bread somewhat differently, and their aves are therefore identifiable, as we learned on 23a (cf. *R' Yehonasan* ed by *Shitah Mekubetzes*).

When a craftsman is given wool for dyeing, he knots it in order to cognize each customer's fleece. Thus, it has an identifying mark *Ieiri*).

The Gemara above (23b) explained that the *siman* is the container's al.

The finder must return the vessel and purse to the one who identifies eir *siman;* nevertheless, he may keep the produce or coins for himself nce they have no *siman* of their own]. We do not assume that they fell om that vessel or purse (*Rashi*).

Thus, our Mishnah supports the first ruling of the Baraisa.

Since some produce or coins remain in the vessel or purse, it is ear that any of these items lying on the ground nearby originated from e same container (*Rashi*). The finder must thus return all of the oduce or coins to the person who identifies the *siman* in the vessel or irse.

For example, if a person found money in front of a purse, he must nounce the entire find. If someone comes and identifies the *siman* in e purse, he receives the money, as well as the purse (*Rashi*).

. For example, someone came and identified his purse, but admitted at he had not lost any money. In that case, the finder may keep the oney (*Rashi;* see *Pnei Yehoshua* and *Nesivos HaMishpat* 262:6).

11. If someone finds an overturned barrel with flax in front of it, he may conclude that the flax did not originate from the barrel. For if it had, it is certain that not all of the flax would have fallen out when the barrel turned over. This deduction also applies to coins found outside of a purse: Had they originated in the purse, some of them would have remained inside it.

12. Even if no produce remains in the basket, there is no reason to suspect that the produce on the ground nearby did not fall from the basket, because produce commonly slides completely out of its container (*Rashi*).

13. Since some produce remains in the basket, it is logical to assume that the produce in front of the basket fell out of it (*Rashi*).

14. The outer rims of most baskets were folded into the basket. Therefore, if the produce had originated from the basket, some would certainly have been trapped inside by the rim when the basket overturned (*Rashi*; cf. *Tosafos*). [According to *Rashi,* Rav Zevid, who previously answered that ordinary produce found in front of a basket must *always* be returned (even if none remains in the basket), disagrees with Rav Pappa (*Ritva, Shitah Mekubetzes*).

15. Where the mouth of the basket faces the produce, we must suspect that the produce originated from the basket even though nothing remains in the basket. Therefore, the person who identifies the *siman* of the basket takes the produce as well. Only where the mouth of the basket faces away from the produce do we assume that the produce did not originate in it.

Hence, two conditions must be fulfilled in order to conclude that the produce did not originate in the basket: (1) No produce remains in the basket; (2) the basket's opening does not face the produce.

רַבִּי אַמִּי אַשְׁכַּח פַּרְגִיּוֹת שְׁחוּטוֹת בֵּין טְבֶרְיָא לְצִיפּוֹרִי – **R' Ami found slaughtered pigeons between** the cities of **Tiberias and Tzippori.** אָתָא לְקַמֵּיהּ דְּר׳ אַסִּי – **He came before R' Assi** to ask about them, וְאָמְרֵי לָהּ לְקַמֵּיהּ דְּר׳ יוֹחָנָן – **and others say he came before R' Yochanan** to inquire, וְאָמְרֵי לָהּ בֵּי מִדְרְשָׁא – **and** still **others say** that he came before the sages in **the study hall** to pose his query. וְאָמְרוּ לֵיהּ – **They said to him:** זִיל שְׁקוֹל לְנַפְשָׁךְ – **Go, take** it **for yourself.**[29]

Another incident:
רַבִּי יִצְחָק נַפְחָא אַשְׁכַּח קִיבּוּרָא – **R' Yitzchak Nafcha** fou **coils of spun string** דְּאָזְלֵי בֵּיהּ אַזְלוּיֵי – **that the trappers u for making nets.** אָתָא לְקַמֵּיהּ דְּר׳ יוֹחָנָן – **He came before Yochanan** to ask about them, וְאָמְרֵי לָהּ בְּבֵי מִדְרָשָׁא – **a others say** he came before the sages **in the study hall** to pose question. וְאָמְרוּ לֵיהּ – **They said to him:** זִיל שְׁקוֹל לְנַפְשָׁךְ **Go, take** them **for yourself.**[30]

**Mishnah** This Mishnah enumerates the articles that the finder must announce and return to the owner. וְאֵלּוּ חַיָּיב לְהַכְרִיז – **And these** finds **one is obligated to announce:**[31] מָצָא פֵּירוֹת בִּכְלִי – If **he found produce in a vessel,**[32] אוֹ כְּלִי כְּמוֹת שֶׁהוּא – **or a vessel just as it is,**[33] מָעוֹת בְּכִיס – **coins in a purse,**[34] אוֹ כִּיס כְּמוֹת שֶׁהוּא – **or a purse just as it is,**[35] צִיבּוּרֵי פֵּירוֹת – **piles of produce,** צִיבּוּרֵי מָעוֹת – **piles of coins,**[36]

NOTES

29. Since R' Ami was told that he could keep the pigeons (and presumably eat them), it is clear that they were found in an area with a Jewish majority.

*Raavad* (cited in *Shitah Mekubetzes*) proves from this incident that the halachah follows the view of R' Shimon ben Elazar even in an area with a majority of Jews. The Gemara's previous answer, that most of the slaughterers were Jews, is inappropriate here because birds (as opposed to animals) were slaughtered privately, by Jew and Canaanite alike, and not by professional slaughterers.

*Rashba* and *Ran* reject this proof. They propose that it was the trappers who slaughtered the pigeons immediately after they were caught. Thus, we may still apply the framework of the Gemara's previous answer to this case as well. We are dealing with a general Canaanite majority, with a majority of the trappers being Jewish.

30. It may be assumed that in this case as well most of the inhabitants of the area were Canaanites. R' Yochanan permitted the finder to kee them in accordance with R' Shimon ben Elazar's opinion (see note above).

31. If one finds any of the following items, he must announce them sinc they all have a *siman* (identifying mark); hence, the owner ha presumably not despaired of recovering them.

32. An ordinary vessel has an identifying mark (*Rashi*).

33. That is, an empty vessel (*Rashi*).

34. A purse, too, usually has a *siman* and can therefore be identified b its owner (*Rashi*).

35. That is, an empty purse.

36. The Gemara below (25a) will discuss two features that could possibl serve as a *siman* – either the number of piles or the place where the were found.

ואיבעית אימא לעולם רבנן מי קתני הן שלו אינו חייב להכריז קתני ויניח וייתי ישראל ויהיב ביה סימנא ושקיל ת"ש דאמר רב אסי [א]מצא חבית יין בעיר שרובה כנענים מותרת משום מציאה ואסורה בהנאה בא ישראל ונתן בה סימן מותרת בשתיה למוצאה כמאן כר"ש בן אלעזר שמע מינה כי קאמר ר"ש בן אלעזר ברוב כנענים אבל ברוב ישראל לא לעולם אימא לך ר"ש בן אלעזר אפי' ברוב ישראל נמי קאמר ורב אסי סבר לה כוותיה בחדא ופליג עליה בחדא וכי מאחר דאסירא בהנאה מותרת משום מציאה למאי הלכתא אמר רב אשי [ב]לקנקנה: ההוא גברא דאשכח ארבעה זוזי דצייריי בסדינא ושדו בנהר בירן אתא לקמיה דרב יהודה א"ל זיל אכריז והא זוטו של ים הוא שאני נהר בירן [ג]כיון דמתקיל לא מיאש והא רובא כנענים נינהו ש"מ אין הלכה כר"ש בן אלעזר אפי' ברוב כנענים שאני נהר בירן דישראל סכרו ליה וישראל כרו ליה כיון דישראל סכרו ליה אימור מישראל נפל וכיון דישראל כרו ליה לא מיאש רב יהודה הוה שקיל ואזיל בתריה דמר שמואל בשוקא דבי דיסא א"ל מצא כאן ארנקי מהו אמר ליה הרי אלו שלו בא ישראל ונתן בה סימן מהו א"ל חייב להחזיר תרתי אמר ליה [ד][א]לפנים משורת הדין כי הא דאבוה דשמואל אשכח הנך חמרי במדברא ואהדרינהו למרייהו לבתר תריסר ירחי שתא לפנים משורת הדין רבא הוה שקיל ואזיל בתריה דר"נ [ה]בשוקא דגלדאי ואמרי לה בשוקא דרבנן א"ל מצא כאן ארנקי מהו א"ל הרי אלו שלו בא ישראל ונתן בה סימן מהו אמר ליה [ה]הרי אלו שלו והלא עומד וצווח נעשה כצווח על ביתו שנפל ועל ספינתו שטבעה בים ההוא דיו דשקיל בשרא בשוקא ושדיה בצנייתא דבי בר מריון אתא לקמיה דאביי א"ל [ו]זיל שקול לנפשך והא רובא דישראל נינהו שמעת מינה הלכה כרבי שמעון בן אלעזר אפי' ברוב ישראל שאני דיו דכזוטו של ים דמי והא [ג]אמר רב [ז]בשר שנתעלם מן העין אסור בעומד ורואהו: ר' חנינא מצא גדי שחוט בין טבריא לציפורי והתירוהו לו אמר רבי אמי התירוהו לו [ח]משום מציאה כר"ש בן אלעזר משום שחיטה כרבי חנניא בנו של רבי יוסי הגלילי דתניא [ד]הרי שאבדו לו גדייו ותרנגוליו והלך ומצאן שחוטין ר' יהודה אוסר ורבי חנניא בנו של רבי יוסי הגלילי מתיר אמר רבי נראין דברי רבי יהודה כשמצאן באשפה [ט]ודברי רבי חנניא בנו של רבי יוסי הגלילי כשמצאן בבית מדהתירוהו לו משום שחיטה רובא ישראל נינהו שמעת מינה הלכה כר"ש בן אלעזר אפי' ברוב ישראל אמר רבא [י]רוב כנענים ורוב טבחי ישראל רבי אמי אשכח פרגיות שחוטות בין טבריא לציפורי אתא לקמיה דר' אסי ואמרי לה לקמיה דר' יוחנן ואמרי לה בי מדרשא ואמרו ליה זיל שקול לנפשך רבי יצחק נפחא אשכח קיבורא דאזלי ביה אזלויי אתא לקמיה דר' יוחנן ואמרי לה בבי מדרשא ואמרו ליה זיל שקול לנפשך: **מתני'** [כ]ואלו חייב להכריז מצא פירות בכלי או כלי כמות שהוא [ל]מעות בכיס או כיס כמות שהוא [מ]צבורי פירות [נ]צבורי מעות שלשה

---

**רש"י**

ואיבעית אימא לעולם רבנן. ובשאינה טמון ולא תפשוט מינה דמודו ליה ברוב כנענים: מי קתני כו' אינו חייב להכריז קתני. דכיון דרובא כנענים דלמא דכנענים הוא ושלו נמי לא הויא דלא אזלי רבנן בתר רובא בממונא: מותרת משום מציאה. דאינו חייב להכריז: ואסורה בהנאה. ולקמיה פריך א"כ מה היתר יש במציאתה: בא ישראל ונתן סימן. יצאת מספק יין כנענים ומותרת בשתיה למוצאה דכיון דרובא כנענים נתייאשו הבעלים: ושדו בנהר בירן. ומושלכין בנהר בירן: דמתקיל. יש בו מכשולים אבנים וסתימת גדר שעושין לדגים ולא מיאש סבר לא יוכל הנהר להוליכם חוץ למכשולים ורגילים היו לסוכרו ולנקותו ולכרותו שישטפו מימיו וסומך שימצאם כשיסכרו אותו וינקום: סכרו ליה. שקורין נשנ"ש בלע"ז כמו עושי שכר [ה]אגמי נפש (ישעיה יט): אימא מישראל נפיל. לפיכך חייב להכריז ולא אמרי' יניח כדאמרינן לעיל ברוב כנענים לרבנן: לא מיאש. שהכורה ימצאם: דבי דיסא. שמוכרים שם חטים כתושין לדייסא ורבים מצויין שם: בתר תריסר ירחי שתא. מצאם: דגלדאי. רצענים: דיו. עוף שקורין אוזלטו"ר והוא לשון דיה: ושדיה בצנייתא דבי בר מריון. השליכתו בין דקלים של בר מריון: אסור. שמא נתחלף בנבילה: ורואהו. משנטלו עד שהשליכו: כשמצאו באשפה. שדרך נבילה להשליכה באשפה: פרגיות. גוזלות: אשכח קיבורי דאזלי ביה אזלויי. מלא פקעיות של טווי למכמורות ורשתות במקום שהציידין מצויין: אזלוי. ציידים העושים מכמורות: **מתני'** מצא פירות בכלי. וסתם כלי יש בו סימן: כמות שהוא. ריקן: כיס. יש בו סימן לבעלים: צבורי פירות. בגמ' מפרש סימנייהו או מנין או מקום: שלשה

---

**תוספות**

**סבר** כוותיה בחדא. ולא בעי למימר דסבר כרבנן דא"כ תפשוט דמודו רבנן ברוב כנענים ומכל מקום יש לפשוט דהלכה כמותו ברוב כנענים: **לבתר** תריסר ירחי שתא כו'. פי' הן עצמן החזיר אע"ג דלא היה צריך ליתן רק דמיהם כדתנן בפרקין (דף כח:) כל דבר שעושה ואוכל מטפל בו י"ב חדש מכאן ואילך שם דמיהן ומניחן אבל רש"י פירש שמצאן אחר י"ב חדש שנאבדו קשה דמנלן [י]שיהא בשביל כך למוצא דהאובד אינו מתיאש שסבור שהמוצא יסבור שמקרוב נאבדו ויכריז:

**לפנים** משורת הדין. מאשר יעשון נפקא לן לקמן בפרקין (דף ל:) תימה דלא מייתי קרא הכא כדמייתי לקמן בעובדא דר' ישמעאל ובהגוזל קמא (ב"ק דף ק. ושם ד"ה לפנים) בעובדא דרבי חייא במראה דינר לשולחני ונמצא רע ולקמן בסוף פרק האומנין (דף פג.) מייתי קרא אחרינא למען תלך בדרך טובים שהוא מדברי קבלה ושביק קרא דאשר יעשון שהוא מדברי תורה וי"ל דלא מייתי קרא דאשר יעשון אלא במקום שאחרים חייבין והוא פטור כמו במראה דינר דאחרים דבעו למילף חייבים ור' חייא דלא בעי למילף פטור ולפנים משורת הדין שילם כמו אחרים וכן בעובדא דרבי ישמעאל דזקן ואינו לפי כבודו הוה ועשה לפנים משורת הדין כמו אחרים והכא בשמעתין דהדרינהו בתר תריסר ירחי שתא כ"ע פטורים לכך לא מייתי קרא הכא ומ"מ משום לפנים משורת הדין בעי ליה לאהדורי כיון שאינו מתחסר ממונא אבל בסוף האומנין (שם) בהנהו שקולאי שסברו לו החבית ועשו לו הפסד גדול משום לפנים משורת הדין אין לו להפסיד לכך מייתי קרא למען תלך בדרך טובים: **אתא** לקמיה דרב גרסי' כדמשמע בירושלמי פרק אין מעמידין ואפילו לספרים דגרסי אביי פריך שפיר מבשר שנתעלם מן העין דאף ע"ג דלא קיימא לן כרב כדפרישית לעיל (דף כג: ד"ה מחרוזות) מדפריך בפרק גיד הנשה (חולין דף צה: ושם) ורב היכי אכיל בשרא מ"מ פריך שפיר דכיון דחזי המוצא שהעוף השליכם שם אפילו מאן דפליג ארב מודה הכא דאסור דאימור נטלה מעיר שרובה כנענים ומשני בעומד ורואהו שנטלה מעיר שרובה טבחי ישראל ולרב מיירי בעומד ורואה שנטלה לפני טבחי ישראל:

**הרי** שאבדו כו'. ה"ה נגנבו ואע"ג דעבר על לא תגנוב לא עבר על לאו דנבילה ובתוספתא (פ"ב דחולין) תניא בהדיא הרי שאבדו או נגנבו והכא נקט אבדו אורחא דמילתא: **שמצאן** באשפה. בפ"ק דחולין (ד' יג:) מפרש נראין דברי רבי יהודה לרבי חנניא כשמצאן באשפה שבשוק שאף רבי חנניא לא פליג עליה אלא באשפה שבבית ובעובדא דהכא שמצאן בדרך בלא אשפה הוי כאשפה שבבית: **אתא** לקמיה דרבי אסי גרסי' אע"ג דבכל דוכתי חשיב רבי אמי ברישא כדאמר (גיטין דף נט:) רבי אמי ורבי אסי כהני חשיבי דארעא דישראל אף על גב שגדול ממנו אין תימה שבא לפניו לישאל לפי שחבירו היה אבל אי גרסינן רבי אבא קשה דרבי אבא היה תלמידו של רבי אמי כדמוכח גבי נסכא דרבי אבא (שבועות דף מז.) ואיך היה בא לפניו ([י]לעולם):

---

**עין משפט נר מצוה**

לח א ב מיי' פי"א מהל' גזלה ואבדה הל' ח ופי"ב מהלכות מאכלות אסורות הל' כח סמג עשין עד טוש"ע ח"מ סי' רנט סעיף ד וטוש"ע י"ד סי' קכט סעיף יז:

לט ג טוש"ע ח"מ סי' רנט סעיף ז וטוש"ע י"ד סי' קכט סעיף יז:

מ ד ה מיי' פי"א מהל' גזלה ואבדה הלכה ז סמג עשין עד טוש"ע ח"מ סי' רנט סעיף ה:

מא ו מיי' שם הל' ט טוש"ע שם סעיף ו:

מב ז מיי' פ"ח מהל' מאכלות אסורות הל' יב סמג לאוין קמג טוש"ע י"ד סי' סג סעיף א:

מג ח טוש"ע ח"מ סי' רנט סעיף ו:

מד ט מיי' פ"ד מהל' שחיטה הל' ח ועיין שם בכ"מ סמג לאוין קמג טוש"ע י"ד סי' א סעיף ד:

מה י טוש"ע ח"מ סי' רנט סעיף ו:

מו כ מיי' פט"ו מהל' גזלה ואבדה הל' יג סמג עשין עד טוש"ע ח"מ סי' רסב סעיף י:

מז ל מיי' שם פט"ו הל"ג סמג שם טוש"ע שם סעיף כ:

מח מ מיי' שם פט"ו הלכה יג סמג שם טוש"ע שם סעיף י:

מט נ מיי' שם פט"ז הלכה ב סמג שם טוש"ע ח"מ שם סעיף יא:

---

**רבינו חננאל**

היא וכן הא דא"ר אסי מצא חבית של יין בעיר שרובה כנענים קנקנה מותר [משום] מציאה ויינה אסור אפי' בהנאה בא ישראל ונתן סימניה מותרת אפי' בשתיה למוצאה. ש"מ דברוב כנענים הרי הן שלו. ההוא דאשכח ד' זוזי דציירי בסדינא בנהר בירן כו' ואסיקנא כיון דישראל כרו ליה וישראל סכרו ליה אימור מישראל נפול ולא מיאש. רב יהודה הוה אזיל בתריה דמר שמואל בשוקא דבי דיסא אמר ליה מצא כאן ארנקי מהו אמר ליה הרי הן שלו. בא ישראל ונתן סימניה מהו אמר לו אם רוצה לעשות לפנים משורת הדין מחזיר כדאבוה דשמואל אשכח חמרא במדברא ואהדרינהו בתר י"ב ירחי שתא והא דרבה דאמר ליה רב נחמן מצא ארנקי בשוקא דרבנן הרי הן שלו ואפי' הלה עומד וצווח נעשה כצווח על ביתו שנפל ועל ספינתו שטבעה בים כלומר כשם מי שטבעה ספינתו המציל ממנה הרי הן שלו ואע"פ שבעלה עומד וצווח כדאמרינן המציל מזוטו של ים התורה התירתו לו כן גם זה מותר למוצאו ש"מ אפי' ברוב ישראל. עוף הנקרא דיו שקיל בישרא ושדא בצינייתא דבי בר מריון. אסיקנא אם הוא עומד וראה את המקום שחוטף זה הבשר ממנה והוא מישראל מותר לו דכזוטו של ים [דמי] ואם לאו אסור באכילה כרב דאמר בשר כיון שנתעלם מן העין אסור באכילה. והא דרב חנינא דאשכח גדי שחוט בין טבריא לצפורי והתירוהו לו משום מציאה כר"ש בן אלעזר ומשום שחיטה כר' יוסי בר חנינא וכו' ופשוטה היא. פי' פרגיות צפרים טהורים. רב אמי אשכח פרגיות בין טבריא לצפורי וא"ל ר' יוחנן שקול לנפשך. וכן רב יצחק אשכח (פגעיות) [פקעיות] של מטוה דאמר ר' יצחק אשכח קיבורי דאיזלו בי אזלויי וא"ל ר' יוחנן זיל שקול לנפשך: **מתני'** ואלו חייב להכריז מצא

---

**מסורת הש"ס**

א) [לקמן ל:, ברכות מה:, כתובות לז., בבא ק... לט:], ב) [חולין מה... ג) חולין לה., ד) חולין [תוספתא דחולין פרק... ה) פירוש האגמים של... בהם הדגים, שרשי רד"... ו) [עיין רש"י ברכות... ד"ה ככלי אובד], ז) ... לישאל, מהר"מ.

**לעזי רש"י**

נשנ"ש. פירוש ע... סכר (עיין רש"י ישע... יט, י). אוזלטו"ר. פיר... עוף הנקרא דיה (רש... ישעיה לד, טו).

**ליקוטי רש"י**

בשר שנתעלם ... העין. שהיה שעה א... שלא ראהו ואפילו ה... מונח על שולחנו [חו... צה.].

The Gemara relates an incident, in an attempt to resolve one of the questions raised on 24a:

הַהוּא דַּיּוֹ – There was **this vulture** דְּשָׁקִיל בִּשְׂרָא בְּשׁוּקָא – **that took meat in the market** וְשַׁדְיֵהּ בִּצְנִיָּיתָא דְּבֵי בַּר מָרְיוֹן – **and threw it between the palm trees of Bar Marion.** אֲתָא לְקַמֵּיהּ דְּאַבָּיֵי – **[Bar Marion] came before Abaye** to inquire as to his responsibilities, if any. אָמַר לֵיהּ – **[Abaye] said to him:** זִיל שְׁקוֹל לְנַפְשָׁךְ – **Go, take** the meat **for yourself.**

The Gemara proceeds with its resolution:

וְהָא רוּבָּא דְיִשְׂרָאֵל נִינְהוּ – **But** surely **the majority** of the residents in that area **were Jews.** שְׁמַעְתְּ מִינָּהּ – **Learn from this** ruling of Abaye הֲלָכָה כְּרַבִּי שִׁמְעוֹן בֶּן אֶלְעָזָר – that **the halachah is in accordance** with the opinion of **R' Shimon ben Elazar,** אֲפִילּוּ בְּרוֹב יִשְׂרָאֵל – **even** in an area **with a majority of Jews.**

The Gemara rejects this proof:

שָׁאנֵי דַּיּוֹ – This situation with regard to **the vulture is different** from the conventional case of an object lost in an area with a majority of Jews, דִּכְזוּטוֹ שֶׁל יָם דָּמֵי – **because it resembles** the case of an object swept away by **the tides of the sea,** which belongs to whoever finds it.[22]

The Gemara raises another question in regard to Abaye's ruling:

וְהָא אָמַר רַב – **But** surely **Rav said:** בָּשָׂר שֶׁנִּתְעַלֵּם מִן הָעַיִן אָסוּר – **Meat that has disappeared from sight is forbidden.**[23]

The Gemara answers:

בְּעוֹמֵד וְרוֹאֵהוּ – The case was one **in which he** [Bar Marion] **was standing and observing [the meat]** from the moment the vulture took it until it threw it among his palm trees.[24]

The Gemara cites yet another incident in a final attempt to resolve one of the questions raised earlier:

ר׳ חֲנִינָא מָצָא גְּדִי שָׁחוּט – **R' Chanina found a slaughtered kid** בֵּין טְבֶרְיָא לְצִיפּוֹרִי – **between** the cities of **Tiberias and Tzippori,** וְהִתִּירוּהוּ לוֹ – **and [the Sages] permitted it to him.** אָמַר רַבִּי אַמִי – **R' Ami said,** in elaboration of the Sages' ruling: הִתִּירוּהוּ לוֹ מִשּׁוּם מְצִיאָה – **They permitted it to him as regards a found object,** and did not obligate him to announce and return it, כְּרַבִּי שִׁמְעוֹן בֶּן אֶלְעָזָר – **in accordance with** th[e] opinion of **R' Shimon ben Elazar,** as the Gemara will explai[n] below. מִשּׁוּם שְׁחִיטָה – They also permitted the meat to hi[m] **as regards** the law of ritual **slaughter,**[25] [ר]בִּי חֲנַנְיָא בְּנוֹ שֶׁל רַבִּי יוֹסֵי הַגְּלִילִי – **in accordance with** the opinion of **R' Chana[n]ya the son of R' Yose HaGlili.** דְּתַנְיָא – **For it has bee[n] taught** in a Baraisa: הֲרֵי שֶׁאָבְדוּ לוֹ גְּדָיָיו וְתַרְנְגוֹלָיו – IF ON[E] LOST HIS KIDS OR CHICKENS, וְהָלַךְ וּמְצָאָן שְׁחוּטִין – AND H[E] WENT AND FOUND THEM SLAUGHTERED: ר׳ יְהוּדָה אוֹסֵר – R' YEHUDAH PROHIBITS them to be eaten, since they may n[ot] have been slaughtered properly, [ר]בִּי חֲנַנְיָא בְּנוֹ שֶׁל רַבִּי יוֹסֵי הַגְּלִילִי מַתִּיר – AND R' CHANANYA THE SON OF R' YOSE HAGLILI PE[R]MITS them to be eaten. אָמַר רַבִּי – REBBI SAID: [ר]אִין דִּבְרֵי רַבִּי יְהוּדָה – THE WORDS OF R' YEHUDAH SEEM more CORREC[T] כְּשֶׁמְּצָאָן בָּאַשְׁפָּה – WHEN HE FOUND THEM IN A GARBAGE HEA[P] where it was customary to discard the carcasses of improper[ly] slaughtered animals,[26] וְדִבְרֵי רַבִּי חֲנַנְיָא בְּנוֹ שֶׁל רַבִּי יוֹסֵי הַגְּלִילִי – AND THE WORDS OF R' CHANANYA THE SON OF R' YOSE HAGLI[LI] seem more correct, כְּשֶׁמְּצָאָן בַּבַּיִת – WHEN HE FOUND THEM IN [THE] HOUSE.[27]

The Gemara now attempts to resolve one of its questions fro[m] this ruling:

מִדְּהִתִּירוּהוּ לוֹ מִשּׁוּם שְׁחִיטָה – **From** the fact **that [the Sage]s permitted it to him as regards** the law of proper **slaughter,** it [is] evident that the incident occurred רוּבָּא יִשְׂרָאֵל נִינְהוּ – in a[n] area with **a majority of Jews.** Otherwise, we would certainly n[ot] presume that the meat is kosher. שְׁמַעְתְּ מִינָּהּ – Therefor[e] **learn from here** הֲלָכָה כְּרַבִּי שִׁמְעוֹן בֶּן אֶלְעָזָר – that **th[e] halachah is in accordance with** the opinion of **R' Shimon be[n] Elazar** אֲפִילּוּ בְּרוֹב יִשְׂרָאֵל – **even** if the object was found in a[n] area **with a majority of Jews!**

The Gemara rejects the proof:

אָמַר רָבָא – **Rava said:** Nothing can be proven from this inc[i]dent רוֹב כְּנַעֲנִים – because the area in which the slaughtere[d] kid was found had **a majority of Canaanites,** [ר]וֹב טַבָּחֵי יִשְׂרָאֵל – **but a majority of** the **slaughterers** in that area **wer[e] Jews.** Thus, R' Chanina was permitted to keep the kid and eat [it] because of the probability that it had been slaughtered by [a] Jew.[28]

The Gemara cites a similar incident:

NOTES

22. The meat seized by the vulture and the object washed away by the sea are similar inasmuch as they are both presumed to be lost to everyone. As we have learned earlier (22b), any object that appears to be beyond anyone's reach and lost forever may be kept if it should become accessible.

23. [Literally: meat that has disappeared from the eye.] Rav rules that meat that has not been under constant supervision is prohibited. While it was unattended, it may have been exchanged for non-kosher meat. Is it not possible in this case as well that the meat the vulture dropped was not the same piece of kosher meat it took from the market?

24. The meat was taken from the stand of a Jewish butcher. If, however, the vulture had taken meat lying unattended on the ground, even in an area with a majority of Jewish butchers, the meat would be prohibited according to Rav (*Tosafos* ד״ה אתא).

25. I.e. they permitted him to eat the meat of the animal on the assumption that it was properly slaughtered.

26. Thus, the presence of the carcasses on the garbage heap makes it likely that something happened with their slaughter to render them invalid.

27. The assumption is that the majority of those who undertake to slaughter an animal are knowledgeable of the law and proficient at the task (see *Chullin* 12a).

The Gemara there explains that R' Chananya the son of R' Yo[se] HaGlili permits the meat even if it was found in a household dump, [a]s long as it was not found in the public dump. Our Gemara states tha[t] based on this ruling, the Sages permitted R' Chanina to eat the meat h[e] found on the road between Tiberias and Tzippori. Since it was not dis[-]carded on a public dump, it is assumed to have been properly slaugh[-]tered (*Tosafos*).

28. Since the majority of inhabitants were Canaanites, R' Chanina wa[s] allowed to keep the meat, in accordance with the view of R' Shimon be[n] Elazar [who holds that even if the owner was a Jew, he certainly de[-]spaired of recovering the meat in an area with a Canaanite majority. However, in regard to the permissibility of eating the meat, the are[a] was considered to have a Jewish majority, because the majority of thos[e] who slaughtered animals in that area were Jews, and even Canaanite[s] would buy from them.

The Rishonim question this ruling, in light of Rav's statement abov[e] prohibiting meat not kept under constant supervision. Although a ma[-]jority of the slaughterers were Jews, nonetheless this meat was foun[d] unattended on the road, and it should therefore be prohibited out o[f] concern that it was exchanged for non-kosher meat. *Rosh* proves fro[m] this case that the accepted halachah does not follow Rav's view. Conse[-]quently, even unattended meat found in an area with a majority of Jew[-]ish slaughterers is permitted. [See further, *Meiri; Rashba* to *Chulli[n]* 93b סד״ה במאי; *Sma, Choshen Mishpat* 259:13, for alternative explana[-]tions.]

ואיבעית אימא לעולם רבנן מי קתני הן שלו אינו חייב להכריז קתני ויניח וייתי ישראל ויהיב ביה סימנא ושקיל ת"ש דאמר רב אסי [א] מצא חבית יין בעיר שרובה כנענים מותרת משום מציאה ואסורה בהנאה בא ישראל ונתן בה סימן מותרת בשתיה למוצאה כמאן כר"ש בן אלעזר שמע מינה כי קאמר ר"ש בן אלעזר ברוב כנענים אבל ברוב ישראל לא לעולם אימא לך ר"ש בן אלעזר אפי' ברוב ישראל נמי קאמר ורב אסי סבר לה כוותיה בחדא ופליג עליה בחדא וכי מאחר דאסירא בהנאה מותרת משום מציאה למאי הלכתא אמר רב אשי [ב] לקנקנה: ההוא גברא דאשכח ארבעה זוזי דצייררי בסדינא ושדו בנהר בירן אתא לקמיה דרב יהודה א"ל זיל אכריז והא זוטו של ים הוא שאני נהר בירן [ג] כיון דמתקיל לא מיאש והא רובא כנענים נינהו ש"מ אין הלכה כר"ש בן אלעזר אפי' ברוב כנענים שאני נהר בירן דישראל סכרו ליה וישראל כרו ליה כיון דישראל סכרו ליה אימור מישראל נפל וכיון דישראל כרו ליה לא מיאש רב יהודה הוה שקיל ואזיל בתריה דמר שמואל בשוקא דבי דיסא א"ל מצא כאן ארנקי מהו אמר ליה הרי אלו שלו בא ישראל ונתן בה סימן מהו א"ל חייב להחזיר תרתי אמר ליה [ד] [א] לפנים משורת הדין כי הא דאבוה דשמואל אשכח הנך חמרי במדברא ואהדרינהו למרייהו לבתר תריסר ירחי שתא לפנים משורת הדין רבא הוה שקיל ואזיל בתריה דר"נ [ב] בשוקא דגלדאי ואמרי לה בשוקא דרבנן א"ל מצא כאן ארנקי מהו א"ל הרי אלו שלו בא ישראל ונתן בה סימן מהו אמר ליה [ה] הרי אלו שלו והלא עומד וצווח נעשה כצווח על ביתו שנפל ועל ספינתו שטבעה בים ההוא דיו דשקיל בשרא בשוקא ושדיה בצנייתא דבי בר מריון אתא לקמיה דאביי א"ל [ו] זיל שקול לנפשך והא רובא דישראל נינהו שמעת מינה הלכה כרבי שמעון בן אלעזר אפי' ברוב ישראל שאני דיו דכזוטו של ים דמי והא [ג] אמר רב [ז] בשר שנתעלם מן העין אסור בעומד ורואהו: ר' חנינא מצא גדי שחוט בין טבריא לציפורי והתירוהו לו אמר רבי אמי התירוהו לו [ח] משום מציאה כר"ש בן אלעזר משום שחיטה כרבי חנניא בנו של רבי יוסי הגלילי דתניא [ד] הרי שאבדו לו גדייו ותרנגוליו והלך ומצאן שחוטין ר' יהודה אוסר ורבי חנניא בנו של רבי יוסי הגלילי מתיר אמר רבי נראין דברי רבי יהודה כשמצאן באשפה [ט] ודברי רבי חנניא בנו של רבי יוסי הגלילי כשמצאן בבית מדהתירוהו לו משום שחיטה רובא ישראל נינהו שמעת מינה הלכה כר"ש בן אלעזר אפי' ברוב ישראל אמר רבא [י] רוב כנענים ורוב טבחי ישראל רבי אמי אשכח פרגיות שחוטות בין טבריא לציפורי אתא לקמיה דר' אסי ואמרי לה לקמיה דר' יוחנן ואמרי לה בי מדרשא ואמרו ליה זיל שקול לנפשך רבי יצחק נפחא אשכח קיבורא דאזלי ביה אזלויי אתא לקמיה דר' יוחנן ואמרי לה בבי מדרשא ואמרו ליה זיל שקול לנפשך: **מתני'** [כ] ואלו חייב להכריז מצא פירות בכלי או כלי כמות שהוא [ל] מעות בכיס או כיס כמות שהוא [מ] צבורי פירות [נ] צבורי מעות שלשה

## רש"י

ואיבעית אימא לעולם רבנן. ובשאינה טמון ולא תפשוט מינה דמודו ליה ברוב כנענים: מי קתני כו' אינו חייב להכריז קתני. דכיון דרובא כנענים דלמא דכנענים הוא ושלו נמי לא הויא דלא אזלי רבנן בתר רובא בממונא: מותרת משום מציאה. דאינו חייב להכריז: ואסורה בהנאה. ולקמיה פריך א"כ מה היתר יש במציאתה: בא ישראל ונתן סימן. יצאת מספק יין כנענים ומותרת בשתיה למוצאה דכיון דרובא כנענים נתייאשו הבעלים: ושדו בנהר בירן. ומושלכין בנהר בירן: דמתקיל. יש בו מכשולים אבנים וסתימת גדר שעושין לדגים ולא מיאש סבר לא יוכל הנהר להוליכם חוץ למכשולים ורגילים היו לסוכרו ולנקותו ולכרותו שישטפו מימיו וסומך שימצאם כשיסכרו אותו וינקום: סכרו ליה. שקורין נשנ"ש בלע"ז כמו עושי שכר [ה] אגמי נפש (ישעיה יט): אימא מישראל נפיל. לפיכך חייב להכריז ולא אמרי' יניח כדאמרינן לעיל ברוב כנענים לרבנן: לא מיאש. שהכורה ימצאם: דבי דיסא. שמוכרים שם חטים כתושין לדייסא ורבים מצויין שם: בתר תריסר ירחי שתא. מצאם: דגלדאי. רצענים: דיו. עוף שקורין אוזלטו"ר והוא לשון דיה: ושדיה בצנייתא דבי בר מריון. השליכתו בין דקלים של בר מריון: אסור. שמא נתחלף בנבילה: ורואהו. משנטלו עד שהשליכו: כשמצאו באשפה. שדרך נבילה להשליכה באשפה: פרגיות. גוזלות: אשכח קיבורי דאזלי ביה אזלויי. מלא פקעיות של טווי למכמורות ורשתות במקום שהציידין מצויין: אזלויי. ציידים העושים מכמורות: **מתני'** מצא פירות בכלי. ושם כלי יש בו סימן: כמות שהוא. ריקן: כיס. יש בו סימן לבעלים: צבורי פירות. בגמ' מפרש סימנייהו או מנין או מקום: שלשה

## תוספות

**סבר** כוותיה בחדא. ולא בעי למימר דסבר כרבנן דא"כ תפשוט דמודו רבנן ברוב כנענים ומכל מקום יש לפשוט דהלכה כמותו ברוב כנענים: **לבתר** תריסר ירחי שתא כו'. פי' הן עצמן החזיר אע"ג דלא היה צריך ליתן רק דמיהם כדתנן בפרקין (דף כח:) כל דבר שעושה ואוכל מטפל בו י"ב חדש מכאן ואילך שם דמיהן ומניחן אבל רש"י פירש שמאחר י"ב חדש שנאבדו קשה דמנלן [י] שיהא בשביל כך למוצא דהאובד אינו מתיאש שסבור שהמוצא יסבור שמקרוב נאבדו ויכריז: **לפנים** משורת הדין. מאשר יעשון נפקא לן לקמן בפרקין (דף ל:) תימה דלא מייתי קרא הכא כדמייתי לקמן בעובדא דר' ישמעאל ובהגוזל קמא (ב"ק דף ק. ושם ד"ה לפנים) בעובדא דרבי חייא במראה דינר לשולחני ונמצא רע ולקמן בסוף פרק האומנין (דף פג.) מייתי קרא אחרינא למען תלך בדרך טובים שהוא מדברי קבלה ושביק קרא דאשר יעשון שהוא מדברי תורה וי"ל דלא מייתי קרא דאשר יעשון אלא במקום שאחרים חייבין והוא פטור כמו במראה דינר דאחרים דבעו למילף חייבים ור' חייא דלא בעי למילף פטור ולפנים משורת הדין שילם כמו אחרים וכן בעובדא דרבי ישמעאל דזקן ואינו לפי כבודו הוה ועשה לפנים משורת הדין כמו אחרים והכא בשמעתין דהדרינהו בתר תריסר ירחי שתא כ"ע פטורים לכך לא מייתי קרא הכא ומ"מ משום לפנים משורת הדין בעי ליה לאהדורי כיון שאינו מתחסר ממונא אבל בסוף האומנין (שם) בהנהו שקולאי שסברו לו החבית ועשו לו הפסד גדול משום לפנים משורת הדין אין לו להפסיד לכך מייתי קרא למען תלך בדרך טובים: **אתא** לקמיה דרב גרסי' כדמשמע בירושלמי פרק אין מעמידין ואפילו לספרים דגרסי אביי פריך שפיר מבשר שנתעלם מן העין דאף ע"ג דלא קיימא לן כרב כדפרישית לעיל (דף כג: ד"ה מחרוזות) מדפריך בפרק גיד הנשה (חולין דף צה: ושם) ורב היכי אכיל בשרא מ"מ פריך שפיר דכיון דחזי המוצא שהעוף השליכם שם אפילו מאן דפליג ארב מודה הכא דאסור דאימור נטלה מעיר שרובה כנענים ומשני בעומד ורואהו שנטלה מעיר שרובה טבחי ישראל ולרב מיירי בעומד ורואה שנטלה לפני טבחי ישראל: **הרי** שאבדו כו'. ה"ה נגנבו ואע"ג דעבר על לא תגנוב לא עבר על לאו דנבילה ובתוספתא (פ"ב דחולין) תניא בהדיא הרי שאבדו או נגנבו והכא נקט אבדו אורחא דמילתא: **שמצאן** באשפה. בפ"ק דחולין (ד' יב:) מפרש נראין דברי רבי יהודה לרבי חנניא כשמצאן באשפה שבשוק שאף רבי חנניא לא פליג עליה אלא באשפה שבבית ובעובדא דהכא שמצאן בדרך בלא אשפה הוי כאשפה שבבית: **אתא** לקמיה דרבי אסי גרסי' אע"ג דבכל דוכתי חשיב רבי אמי ברישא כדאמר (גיטין דף נט:) רבי אמי ורבי אסי כהני חשיבי דארעא דישראל אף על גב שגדול ממנו אין תימה שבא לפניו לישאל לפי שחבירו היה אבל אי גרסינן רבי אבא קשה דרבי אבא היה תלמידו של רבי אמי כדמוכח גבי נסכא דרבי אבא (שבועות דף מז.) ואיך היה בא לפניו ([י] לעולם):

## עין משפט נר מצוה

לח א ב מיי' פי"א מהל' גזלה ואבדה הל' ח ופי"ב מהלכות מאכלות אסורות הל' כח סמג עשין עד טוש"ע ח"מ סי' רנט סעיף ד וטוש"ע י"ד סי' קכט סעיף יז:
לט ג טוש"ע ח"מ סי' רנט סעיף ז וטוש"ע י"ד סי' קכט סעיף יז:
מ ד ה מיי' פי"א מהל' גזלה ואבדה הלכה ז סמג עשין עד טוש"ע ח"מ סי' רנט סעיף ה:
מא ו מיי' שם הל' ט טוש"ע שם סעיף ו:
מב ז מיי' פ"ח מהל' מאכלות אסורות הל' יג סמג לאוין קמג טוש"ע י"ד סי' סג סעיף א:
מג ח טוש"ע ח"מ סי' רנט סעיף ו:
מד ט מיי' פ"ד מהל' שחיטה הל' ח ועיין שם בכ"מ סמג לאוין קמג טוש"ע י"ד סי' א סעיף ד:
מה י טוש"ע ח"מ סי' רנט סעיף ו:
מו כ מיי' פט"ו מהל' גזלה ואבדה הל' יג סמג עשין עד טוש"ע ח"מ סי' רסב סעיף י:
מז ל מיי' שם פט"ז הל"ג סמג שם טוש"ע שם סעיף כ:
מח מ מיי' שם פט"ו הלכה יג סמג שם טוש"ע שם סעיף י:
מט נ מיי' שם פט"ז הלכה ג סמג שם טוש"ע ח"מ שם סעיף יא:

## רבינו חננאל

היא וכן הא דא"ר אסי מצא חבית של יין בעיר שרובה כנענים קנקנה מותר [משום] מציאה ויינה אסור אפי' בהנאה בא ישראל ונתן סימניה מותרת אפי' בשתיה למוצאה. ש"מ דברוב כנענים הרי הן שלו. ההוא דאשכח ד' זוזי דציירי בסדינא בנהר בירן כו' ואסיקנא כיון דישראל כרו ליה וישראל סכרו ליה אימור מישראל נפול ולא מיאש. רב יהודה הוה אזיל בתריה דמר שמואל בשוקא דבי דיסא אמר ליה מצא כאן ארנקי מהו אמר ליה הרי הן שלו. בא ישראל ונתן סימניה מהו אמר לו אם רוצה לעשות לפנים משורת הדין מחזיר כדאבוה דשמואל אשכח חמרא במדברא ואהדרינהו בתר י"ב ירחי שתא והא דרבה דאמר ליה רב נחמן מצא ארנקי בשוקא דרבנן הרי הן שלו ואפי' חלח עומד וצווח נעשה כצווח על ביתו שנפל ועל ספינתו שטבעה בים כלומר כשם מי שטבעה ספינתו המציל ממנה הרי הן שלו ואע"פ שבעלה עומד וצווח כדאמרינן המציל מזוטו של ים התורה התירתו לו כן גם זה מותר למוצאו ש"מ אפי' ברוב ישראל. עוף הנקרא דיו שקיל בישרא ושדא בצינייתא דבי בר מריון. אסיקנא אם הוא עומד וראה את המקום שחוטף זה הבשר ממנה והוא מישראל מותר לו דכזוטו של ים [דמי] ואם לאו אסור באכילה כרב דאמר בשר כיון שנתעלם מן העין אסור באכילה. והא דרב חנינא דאשכח גדי שחוט בין טבריא לצפורי והתירוהו לו משום מציאה כר"ש בן אלעזר ומשום שחיטה כר' יוסי בר חנינא וכו' ופשוטה היא. פי' פרגיות צפרים טהורים. רב אמי אשכח פרגיות בין טבריא לצפורי וא"ל ר' יוחנן שקול לנפשך. וכן רב יצחק אשכח (פגעיות) [פקעיות] של מטוה דאמר ר' יצחק אשכח קיבורי דאיזלו בי אזלויי וא"ל ר' יוחנן זיל שקול לנפשך: מתני' ואלו חייב להכריז

מצא

## מסורת הש"ס

א) [לקמן ל:, ברכות מה:, כתובות לו., בבא ק... לט:], ב) [חולין מ...], ג) חולין לה., ד) חולין [תוספתא דחולין פרק ...] ה) פירוש האגמים שי... בהם הדגים, פרש"י רד"... ו) [עיין רש"י ברכות ... ד"ה ככלי אובד], ז) ... לישאל, מהר"מ.

## לעזי רש"י

נשנ"ש. פירוש ... סכר (עיין רש"י ישע... יט, י). אוזלטו"ר. פיר... עוף הנקרא דיה (רש... ישעיה לד, טו).

## ליקוטי רש"י

בשר שנתעלם ... העין. שהיה שעה א... שלא ראהו ואפילו ה... מונח על שולחנו [חו... צה.].

The Gemara asks:

**וְהָא רוּבָּא כְּנַעֲנִים נִינְהוּ** – **But surely a majority** of the residents along the Biran River **are Canaanites!** **שְׁמַע מִינָּהּ** – **Learn from this** ruling, that one is obligated to announce his find even in an area with a Canaanite majority, **אֵין הֲלָכָה כְּרַבִּי שִׁמְעוֹן בֶּן אֶלְעָזָר** – that **the halachah is not in accordance with** the opinion of **R' Shimon ben Elazar,** **אֲפִילּוּ בְּרוֹב כְּנַעֲנִים** – **even** in an area **with a majority of Canaanites.**

The Gemara rejects this proof:

**שָׁאנֵי נְהַר בִּירָן** – The situation with regard to **the Biran River is different,** **דְּיִשְׂרָאֵל סָכְרוּ לֵיהּ** – **because** it is **Jews** who **dam it** **וְיִשְׂרָאֵל כָּרוּ לֵיהּ** – **and Jews** who **dredge it.** **כֵּיוָן דְּיִשְׂרָאֵל סָכְרוּ לֵיהּ** – **Since** it is **Jews** who **dam it,** **אֵימוּר מִיִּשְׂרָאֵל נָפַל** – **one may say that it fell from a Jew;**[11] **וְכֵיוָן דְּיִשְׂרָאֵל כָּרוּ לֵיהּ** – **and since** it is **Jews** who **dredge it,** **לֹא מְיָאֵשׁ** – **[the owner] does not despair** of recovering it.[12]

The Gemara relates an incident pertaining to the obligation to return lost objects:

**רַב יְהוּדָה הֲוָה שָׁקִיל וְאָזִיל בָּתְרֵיהּ דְּמַר שְׁמוּאֵל** – **Rav Yehudah was following behind the master, Shmuel,**[13] **בְּשׁוּקָא דְבֵי דַיְסָא** – **in the market of cereal stores.**[14] **אָמַר לֵיהּ** – **[Rav Yehudah] said to [Shmuel]:** **מָצָא כָּאן אַרְנָקִי** – **If one found a purse here,** **מַהוּ** – **what is [the law]?** **אָמַר לֵיהּ** – **[Shmuel] said to him:** **הֲרֵי אֵלּוּ שֶׁלּוֹ** – **These belong to [the finder].**

Rav Yehudah continued:

**בָּא יִשְׂרָאֵל וְנָתַן בָּהּ סִימָן** – **If a Jew comes and gives an identifying mark for it,** **מַהוּ** – what is [the law]?

Shmuel replied:

**אָמַר לֵיהּ** – **He said to him:** **חַיָּיב לְהַחֲזִיר** – **He is obligated to return** it.

Rav Yehudah asked:

**תַּרְתֵּי** – Can **both** these rulings be true?[15]

Shmuel replied:

**אָמַר לֵיהּ** – **He said to [Rav Yehudah]:** **לִפְנִים מִשּׁוּרַת הַדִּין** – My second statement reflects the moral obligation of going **beyor the letter of the law.**[16]

The Gemara illustrates this with a story:

**כִּי הָא דַּאֲבוּהָ דִּשְׁמוּאֵל** – It is **like this** incident **involving Shmue father,** **אַשְׁכַּח הָנָךְ חֲמָרֵי בְּמַדְבְּרָא** – who **found these donkeys i the desert,** **וְאַהַדְרִינְהוּ לְמָרַיְיהוּ** – **and he returned them t their owners** **לְבָתַר תְּרֵיסַר יַרְחֵי שַׁתָּא** – **after** a full **twelv months of the year** had elapsed, **לִפְנִים מִשּׁוּרַת הַדִּין** – **goir beyond the letter of the law.**[17]

The Gemara relates another incident pertaining to the laws lost objects:

**רָבָא הֲוָה שָׁקִיל וְאָזִיל בָּתְרֵיהּ דְּרַב נַחְמָן** – **Rava was follov ing behind Rav Nachman** **בְּשׁוּקָא דְגִלְדָּאֵי** – **in the mark of the leather workers,** **וְאָמְרֵי לָהּ** – **and some say** **שׁוּקָא דְּרַבָּנָן** – it was **in the market of the rabbis.** **אָמַר לֵיהּ** – **[Rav said to [Rav Nachman]:** **מָצָא כָּאן אַרְנָקִי** – **If one found purse here,** **מַהוּ** – **what is [the law]?** **אָמַר לֵיהּ** – **[Ra Nachman] said to him:** **הֲרֵי אֵלּוּ שֶׁלּוֹ** – **These belong to [th finder].**[18]

Rava continued:

**בָּא יִשְׂרָאֵל וְנָתַן בָּהּ סִימָן** – **If a Jew comes and gives a identifying mark for it,** **מַהוּ** – **what is [the law]?**

Rav Nachman replied:

**אָמַר לֵיהּ** – He **said to him:** **הֲרֵי אֵלּוּ שֶׁלּוֹ** – **These** still **belong t [the finder].**[19]

Rava questioned this ruling:

**וַהֲלֹא עוֹמֵד וְצוֹוֵחַ** – **But is [the original owner] not standing an shouting** that it is his?[20]

Rav Nachman responded:

**נַעֲשָׂה כְּצוֹוֵחַ עַל בֵּיתוֹ שֶׁנָּפַל** – **This is like someone who shou about his house that fell,** **וְעַל סְפִינָתוֹ שֶׁטָּבְעָה בַּיָּם** – **or abou his ship that sank at sea.** Clearly, the owner has despaired finding it and has already relinquished his ownership. H subsequent protest is of no avail.[21]

NOTES

object will be found in these places during the periodic dredging and cleaning of the river (*Rashi*).

11. In a conventional situation of a Canaanite majority, R' Shimon ben Elazar rules that we may assume that it was lost by a Canaanite, and the finder may keep it. In this case, however, due to the preponderance of Jewish river-workers, the assumption is that the object was lost by a Jew (*Rashi* ד״ה אימא, according to *Maharsha*).

12. He is confident that they will announce what they recover from the river and he will be able to identify his bundle of coins.

13. This expression is employed to describe the accompaniment of a rabbinical teacher by his disciple. As a sign of deference, the student would walk slightly behind his teacher (see *Yoma* 37a; *Tur, Yoreh De'ah* 242).

14. An area frequented by many people (*Rashi;* see *Rosh* and *Tos. HaRosh*).

15. Since the owner has already despaired of finding it, as evidenced by Shmuel's first ruling, what right does he have to reclaim it upon his identification?

16. Literally: inside the line of judgment. There are three opinions as to the nature of going beyond the requirement of the law in this case:

*Rambam* (*Hil. Gezeilah V'Aveidah* 11:7) states that, "One who wishes to walk upon a good and righteous way, and do beyond the requirement of the law" will return an article to an owner who identifies it, even after the owner's *ye'ush*. Accordingly, Shmuel's intent was only to obligate someone who wishes do more than the law's basic requirements (see also *Rabbeinu Chananel*).

*Rabbeinu Yehonasan* (cited in *Shitah Mekubetzes* ד״ה נעשה) seems to rule that a person of distinction, by virtue of his stature, is legally obligated to go beyond the letter of the law. Shmuel's second ruling was intended for such a person (see below, Gemara 83a). *Mordechai* (257) rules that although the law for lost objects permits one to keep an object after the owner's *ye'ush,* one is legally obligated to go beyond th law, and return the object to its owner. If, however, the finder is po and the owner is a person of means, then the finder is permitted to follo the strict letter of the law and *not* return an object after the owner *ye'ush*.

17. *Rashi* ד״ה בתר explains that Shmuel's father found them after the had been lost for twelve months. According to the letter of the law, h was permitted to keep them, because of the assumed *ye'ush* of the owne

*Tosafos* ד״ה לבתר question this position. Why should we assume th the owner despairs of finding it after one year? We should assume, on th contrary, that the owner anticipates that any prospective finde unaware of the duration of the loss, will attempt to return it. (Se *Tosafos* for an alternative explanation.) However, *Rashi* (*Berachos* 58 ד״ה ככלי) explains, based on a Scriptural analogy between a lost obje and a deceased person, that a person forgets about an object after a yea and despairs of ever recovering it.

18. According to the view accepted as halachah (see note 6), we must sa that although rabbis frequented this market, it was nonetheless an are with a majority of Canaanites (*Rosh; Ritzbash* cited in *Shita Mekubetzes*).

19. Rav Nachman states the letter of the law. Above we learned that i is proper for a person to go beyond the letter of the law. See note 1

20. I.e. what if the original owner declares loudly that he neve abandoned hope of recovering his lost object?

21. We see from this that in a situation in which it is assumed that reasonable person abandons hope of recovering his object, we do no believe him to say otherwise. His protest is like one who says that he ha not abandoned hope of recovering his house that collapsed or his shi that sank (*Maharik, Shoresh* 3). [This is disputed by *Rosh;* see *Pilpul Charifta,* and *Derishah* to *Choshen Mishpat* 259, para. 13, who explai the Gemara's statement here according to *Rosh.*]

ואיבעית אימא לעולם רבנן מי קתני הן שלו אינו חייב להכריז קתני ויניח וייתי ישראל ויהיב ביה סימנא ושקיל ת"ש דאמר רב אסי [א] מצא חבית יין בעיר שרובה כנעניםמותרת משום מציאה ואסורה בהנאה בא ישראל ונתן בה סימן מותרת בשתיה למוצאה כמאן כר"ש בן אלעזר שמע מינה כי קאמר ר"ש בן אלעזר ברוב כנענים אבל ברוב ישראל לא לעולם אימא לך ר"ש בן אלעזר אפי' ברוב ישראל נמי קאמר ורב אסי סבר לה כוותיה בחדא ופליג עליה בחדא וכי מאחר דאסירא בהנאה מותרת משום מציאה למאי הלכתא אמר רב אשי [ב] לקנקנה: ההוא גברא דאשכח ארבעה זוזי דציירי בסדינא ושדו בנהר בירן אתא לקמיה דרב יהודה א"ל זיל אכריז והא זוטו של ים הוא שאני נהר בירן [ג] כיון דמתקיל לא מיאש והא רובא כנענים נינהו ש"מ אין הלכה כר"ש בן אלעזר אפי' ברוב כנענים שאני נהר בירן דישראל סכרו ליה וישראל כרו ליה כיון דישראל סכרו ליה אימור מישראל נפל וכיון דישראל כרו ליה לא מיאש רב יהודה הוה שקיל ואזיל בתריה דמר שמואל בשוקא דבי דיסא א"ל מצא כאן ארנקי מהו אמר ליה הרי אלו שלו בא ישראל ונתן בה סימן מהו א"ל חייב להחזיר תרתי אמר ליה [ד][א] לפנים משורת הדין כי הא דאבוה דשמואל אשכח הנך חמרי במדברא ואהדרינהו למרייהו לבתר תריסר ירחי שתא לפנים משורת הדין רבא הוה שקיל ואזיל בתריה דר"נ [ב] בשוקא דגלדאי ואמרי לה בשוקא דרבנן א"ל מצא כאן ארנקי מהו א"ל הרי אלו שלו בא ישראל ונתן בה סימן מהו אמר ליה [ה] הרי אלו שלו והלא עומד וצווח נעשה כצווח על ביתו שנפל ועל ספינתו שטבעה בים ההוא דיו דשקיל בשרא בשוקא ושדיה בצנייתא דבי בר מריון אתא לקמיה דאביי א"ל [ו] זיל שקול לנפשך והא רובא דישראל נינהו שמעת מינה הלכה כרבי שמעון בן אלעזר אפי' ברוב ישראל שאני דיו דכזוטו של ים דמי והא [ג] אמר רב [ז] בשר שנתעלם מן העין אסור בעומד ורואהו: ר' חנינא מצא גדי שחוט בין טבריא לציפורי והתירוהו לו אמר רבי אמי התירוהו לו [ח] משום מציאה כר"ש בן אלעזר משום שחיטה כרבי חנניא בנו של רבי יוסי הגלילי דתניא [ד] הרי שאבדו לו גדייו ותרנגוליו והלך ומצאן שחוטין ר' יהודה אוסר ורבי חנניא בנו של רבי יוסי הגלילי מתיר אמר רבי נראין דברי רבי יהודה כשמצאן באשפה [ט] ודברי רבי חנניא בנו של רבי יוסי הגלילי כשמצאן בבית מדהתירוהו לו משום שחיטה רובא ישראל נינהו שמעת מינה הלכה כר"ש בן אלעזר אפי' ברוב ישראל אמר רבא [י] רוב כנענים ורוב טבחי ישראל רבי אמי אשכח פרגיות שחוטות בין טבריא לציפורי אתא לקמיה דר' אסי ואמרי לה לקמיה דר' יוחנן ואמרי לה בי מדרשא ואמרו ליה זיל שקול לנפשך רבי יצחק נפחא אשכח קיבורא דאזלי ביה אזלויי אתא לקמיה דר' יוחנן ואמרי לה בבי מדרשא ואמרו ליה זיל שקול לנפשך: **מתני'** [כ] ואלו חייב להכריז מצא פירות בכלי או כלי כמות שהוא [ל] מעות בכיס או כיס כמות שהוא [מ] צבורי פירות [נ] צבורי מעות שלשה

**רש"י**

ואיבעית אימא לעולם רבנן. ובשאינה טמון ולא תפשוט מינה דמודו ליה ברוב כנענים: מי קתני כו' אינו חייב להכריז קתני. דכיון דרובא כנענים דלמא דכנענים הוא ושלו נמי לא הויא דלא אזלי רבנן בתר רובא בממונא: מותרת משום מציאה. דאינו חייב להכריז: ואסורה בהנאה. ולקמיה פריך א"כ מה היתר יש במציאתה: בא ישראל ונתן סימן. יצאת מספק יין כנענים ומותרת בשתיה למוצאה דכיון דרובא כנענים נתייאשו הבעלים: ושדו בנהר בירן. ומושלכין בנהר בירן: דמתקיל. יש בו מכשולים אבנים וסתימת גדר שעושין לדגים ולא מיאש סבר לא יוכל הנהר להוליכם חוץ למכשולים ורגילים היו לסוכרו ולנקותו ולכרותו שישטפו מימיו וסומך שימצאם כשיסכרו אותו וינקוס: סכרו ליה. שקורין נשנ"ש בלע"ז כמו עושי שכר [ה] אגמי נפש (ישעיה יט): אימא מישראל נפיל. לפיכך חייב להכריז ולא אמרי' יניח כדאמרינן לעיל ברוב כנענים לרבנן: לא מיאש. שהכורה ימצאם: דבי דיסא. שמוכרים שם חטים כתושין לדייסא ורבים מצויין שם: בתר תריסר ירחי שתא. מצאם: דגלדאי. רצענים: דיו. עוף שקורין אוזלטו"ר והוא לשון דיה: ושדיה בצנייתא דבי בר מריון. השליכתו בין דקלים של בר מריון: אסור. שמא נתחלף בנבילה: ורואהו. משנטלו עד שהשליכו: כשמצאו באשפה. שדרך נבילה להשליכה באשפה: פרגיות. גוזלות: אשכח קיבורי דאזלי ביה אזלויי. מלא פקעיות של טווי למכמורות ורשתות במקום שהציידין מצויין: אזלוי. ציידים העושים מכמורות: **מתני'** מצא פירות בכלי. וסתם כלי יש בו סימן: כמות שהוא. ריקן: כיס. יש בו סימן לבעלים: צבורי פירות. בגמ' מפרש סימנייהו או מנין או מקום: שלשה

**תוספות**

**סבר** כוותיה בחדא. ולא בעי למימר דסבר כרבנן דא"כ תפשוט דמודו רבנן ברוב כנענים ומכל מקום יש לפשוט דהלכה כמותו ברוב כנענים: **לבתר** תריסר ירחי שתא כו'. פי' הן עצמן החזיר אע"ג דלא היה צריך ליתן רק דמיהם כדתנן בפרקין (דף כח:) כל דבר שעושה ואוכל מטפל בו י"ב חדש מכאן ואילך שם דמיהן ומניחן אבל רש"י פירש שמצאן אחר י"ב חדש שנאבדו קשה דמנלן [י] שיהא בשביל כך למוצא דהאובד אינו מתיאש שסבור שהמוצא יסבור שמקרוב נאבדו ויכריז:

**לפנים** משורת הדין. מאשר יעשון נפקא לן לקמן בפרקין (דף ל:) תימה דלא מייתי קרא הכא כדמייתי לקמן בעובדא דר' ישמעאל ובהגוזל קמא (ב"ק דף ק. ושם ד"ה לפנים) בעובדא דרבי חייא במראה דינר לשולחני ונמצא רע ולקמן בסוף פרק האומנין (דף פג.) מייתי קרא אחרינא למען תלך בדרך טובים שהוא מדברי קבלה ושביק קרא דאשר יעשון שהוא מדברי תורה וי"ל דלא מייתי קרא דאשר יעשון אלא במקום שאחרים חייבין והוא פטור כמו במראה דינר דאחרים דבעו למילף חייבים ור' חייא דלא בעי למילף פטור ולפנים משורת הדין שילם כמו אחרים וכן בעובדא דרבי ישמעאל דזקן ואינו לפי כבודו הוה ועשה לפנים משורת הדין כמו אחרים והכא בשמעתין דהדרינהו בתר תריסר ירחי שתא כ"ע פטורים לכך לא מייתי קרא הכא ומ"מ משום לפנים משורת הדין בעי ליה לאהדורי כיון שאינו מתחסר ממונא אבל בסוף האומנין (שם) בהנהו שקולאי שסברו לו החבית ועשו לו הפסד גדול משום לפנים משורת הדין אין לו להפסיד לכך מייתי קרא למען תלך בדרך טובים: **אתא** לקמיה דרב גרסי' כדמשמע בירושלמי פרק אין מעמידין ואפילו לספרים דגרסי אביי פריך שפיר מבשר שנתעלם מן העין דאף ע"ג דלא קיימא לן כרב כדפרישית לעיל (דף כג: ד"ה מתרחות) מדפריך בפרק גיד הנשה (חולין דף צה: ושם) ורב היכי אכיל בשרא מ"מ פריך שפיר דכיון דחזי המוצא שהעוף השליכם שם אפילו מאן דפליג ארב מודה הכא דאסור דאימור נטלה מעיר שרובה כנענים ומשני בעומד ורואהו שנטלה מעיר שרובה טבחי ישראל ולרב מיירי בעומד ורואה שנטלה לפני טבחי ישראל: **הרי** שאבדו כו'. ה"ה נגנבו ואע"ג דעבר על לא תגנוב לא עבר על לאו דנבילה ובתוספתא (פ"ב דחולין) תניא בהדיא הרי שאבדו או נגנבו והכא נקט אבדו אורחא דמילתא: **שמצאן** באשפה. בפ"ק דחולין (ד' יב:) מפרש נראין דברי רבי יהודה לרבי חנניא כשמצאן באשפה שבשוק שאף רבי חנניא לא פליג עליה אלא באשפה שבבית ובעובדא דהכא שמצאן בדרך בלא אשפה הוי כאשפה שבבית: **אתא** לקמיה דרבי אסי גרסי' אע"ג דבכל דוכתי חשיב רבי אמי ברישא כדאמר (גיטין דף נט:) רבי אמי ורבי אסי כהני חשיבי דארעא דישראל אף על גב שגדול ממנו אין תימה שבא לפניו לישאל לפי שחבירו היה אבל אי גרסינן רבי אבא קשה דרבי אבא היה תלמידו של רבי אמי כדמוכח גבי נסכא דרבי אבא (שבועות דף מז.) ואיך היה בא לפניו ([י] לעולם):

**רבינו חננאל**

היא וכן הא דא"ר אסי מצא חבית של יין בעיר שרובה כנענים קנקנה מותר [משום] מציאה ויינה אסור אפי' בהנאה בא ישראל ונתן סימניה מותרת אפי' בשתיה למוצאה. ש"מ דברוב כנענים הרי הן שלו. ההוא דאשכח ד' זוזי דציירי בסדינא בנהר בירין כו' ואסיקנא כיון דישראל כרו ליה וישראל סכרו ליה אימור מישראל נפול ולא מיאש. רב יהודה הוה אזיל בתריה דמר שמואל בשוקא דבי דיסא אמר ליה מצא כאן ארנקי מהו אמר ליה הרי הן שלו. בא ישראל ונתן סימניה מהו אמר לו אם רוצה לעשות לפנים משורת הדין מחזיר כדאבוה דשמואל אשכח חמרא במדברא ואהדרינהו בתר י"ב ירחי שתא והא דרבה דאמר ליה רב נחמן מצא ארנקי בשוקא דרבנן הרי הן שלו ואוק' חלה עומד וצווח נעשה כצווח על ביתו שנפל ועל ספינתו שטבעה בים כלומר כשם מי שטבעה ספינתו המציל ממנה הרי הן שלו ואע"פ שבעלה עומד וצווח כדאמרינן המציל מזוטו של ים התורה התירתו לו כן גם זה מותר למוצאו ש"מ אפי' ברוב ישראל. עוף הנקרא דיו שקיל בישרא ושדא בציניתא דבי בר מריון. אסיקנא אם הוא עומד וראה את המקום שחוטף זה הבשר ממנה והוא מישראל מותר לו דכזוטו של ים [דמי] ואם לאו אסור באכילה כרב דאמר בשר כיון שנתעלם מן העין אסור באכילה. והא דרב חנינא דאשכח גדי שחוט בין טבריא לצפורי והתירוהו לו משום מציאה כר"ש בן אלעזר ומשום שחיטה כר' יוסי בר חנינא וכו' ופשוטה היא. פי' פרגיות צפרים טהורים. רב אמי אשכח פרגיות בין טבריא לצפורי וא"ל ר' יוחנן שקול לנפשך. וכן רב יצחק אשכח (פגעיות) [פקעיות] של מטוה דאמר ר' יצחק אשכח קיבורי דאיזלו בי אזלויי וא"ל ר' יוחנן זיל שקול לנפשך: מתני' ואלו חייב להכריז מצא

**עין משפט נר מצוה**

לח א ב מיי' פי"א מהל' גזלה ואבדה הל' ח ופי"ב מהלכות מאכלות אסורות הל' כח סמג עשין עד טוש"ע ח"מ סי' רנט סעיף ד וטוש"ע י"ד סי' קכט סעיף יז:
לט ג טוש"ע ח"מ סי' רנט סעיף ז וטוש"ע י"ד סי' קכט סעיף יז:
מ ד ה מיי' פי"א מהל' גזלה ואבדה הלכה ז סמג עשין עד טוש"ע ח"מ סי' רנט סעיף ה:
מא ו מיי' שם הל' ט טוש"ע שם סעיף ו:
מב ז מיי' פ"ח מהל' מאכלות אסורות הל' יב סמג לאוין קמג טוש"ע י"ד סי' סג סעיף א:
מג ח טוש"ע ח"מ סי' רנט סעיף ו:
מד ט מיי' פ"ד מהל' שחיטה הל' ח ועיין שם בכ"מ סמג לאוין קמג טוש"ע י"ד סי' א סעיף ד:
מה י טוש"ע ח"מ סי' רנט סעיף ו:
מו כ מיי' פט"ו מהל' גזלה ואבדה הל' יג סמג עשין עד טוש"ע ח"מ סי' רסב סעיף י:
מז ל מיי' שם פט"ז הל"ג סמג שם טוש"ע שם סעיף כ:
מח מ מיי' שם פט"ו הלכה יג סמג שם טוש"ע שם סעיף י:
מט נ מיי' שם פט"ז הלכה ב סמג שם טוש"ע ח"מ שם סעיף יא:

**מסורת הש"ס**

א) [לקמן ל:, ברכות ז מה:, כתובות לז., בבא קמ לט:], ב) [חולין מח. ג) חולין לה., ד) חולין י [תוספתא דחולין פרק ב ה) פירוש האגמים שילו בהם הדגים, שרשי רד"ק ו) [עיין רש"י ברכות נה ד"ה ככלי אובד], ז) צ"ל לישאל, מהר"מ.

**לעזי רש"י**

נשנ"ש. פירוש עו סכר (עיין רש"י ישעי יט, י). אוזלטו"ר. פירו עוף הנקרא דיה (רש" ישעיה לד, טו).

**ליקוטי רש"י**

בשר שנתעלם מ העין. שהיה שעה אח שלא ראהו ואפילו הי מונח על שולחנו [חול צה.].

The Gemara presents an alternative explanation:

וְאִיבָּעִית אֵימָא לְעוֹלָם רַבָּנָן – **And if you prefer, say in fact** that the Mishnah follows the view of **the Rabbis.**[1] Nonetheless, it cannot be proven from here that the Rabbis agree with R' Shimon ben Elazar that one may keep what he finds in an area with a Canaanite majority. מִי קָתָנֵי הֵן שֶׁלּוֹ – **Does [the Mishnah]** actually **state** that **they** [the lost objects] **are [the finder's]?** אֵינוֹ חַיָּיב לְהַכְרִיז קָתָנֵי – **The Mishnah says** only: [THE FINDER] IS NOT OBLIGATED TO ANNOUNCE his find. וְנֵינֵיהּ – Rather, **he should set** it **aside** in his possession, וְיֵיתֵי יִשְׂרָאֵל – and **let a Jew come** וְיָהִיב בֵּיהּ סִימָנָא וְשָׁקִיל – **and give** the evidence of its **identifying mark and take** it.[2]

The Gemara attempts to demonstrate the scope of R' Shimon ben Elazar's ruling from an Amoraic statement:

תָּא שְׁמַע – **Come, learn** a resolution to our first question from the following: דְּאָמַר רַב אַסִּי – For Rav Assi said: מָצָא חָבִית יַיִן – If **one found a keg of wine** בְּעִיר שֶׁרוּבָּהּ כְּנַעֲנִים – **in a city whose majority is Canaanite,** מוּתֶּרֶת מִשּׁוּם מְצִיאָה – **it is permitted as regards** the law of **a found object,** i.e. there is no obligation to announce it, וַאֲסוּרָה בַּהֲנָאָה – but it is forbidden to derive any benefit from it, because we must assume that it is the wine of a Canaanite.[3] בָּא יִשְׂרָאֵל וְנָתַן בָּהּ סִימָן – If **a Jew came and gave an identifying mark for it,** מוּתֶּרֶת בִּשְׁתִיָּה לְמוֹצְאָהּ – **it is permitted to its finder for drinking.**[4]

The Gemara now demonstrates how Rav Assi's ruling resolves one of the questions:

כְּמַאן – **In accordance with whom** did Rav Assi formulate his ruling? כְּרַבִּי שִׁמְעוֹן בֶּן אֶלְעָזָר – It would seem to be **in accordance with** the opinion of **R' Shimon ben Elazar,** who considers the multitudes of people who frequent an area a significant factor determining the obligation to return lost objects.[5] שְׁמַע מִינָּהּ – Therefore, **learn from this** ruling of Rav Assi, that one may keep the wine in an area with a Canaanite majority, כִּי קָאָמַר רַבִּי שִׁמְעוֹן בֶּן אֶלְעָזָר – that **in what** case **does R' Shimon ben Elazar state** that one may keep what he finds in a place frequented by many people? בְּרוֹב כְּנַעֲנִים – Only in an area **with a majority of Canaanites;** אֲבָל בְּרוֹב יִשְׂרָאֵל לֹא – **but** in an area **with a majority of Jews,** he does **not** permit one to keep it.

The Gemara rejects the proof:

לְעוֹלָם אֵימָא לָךְ – **Actually, I could say to you** כִּי שִׁמְעוֹן בֶּן אֶלְעָזָר אֲפִילּוּ בְּרוֹב יִשְׂרָאֵל נַמִּי קָאָמַר – that **R' Shimon ben Elazar says** one may keep what he finds **even** in an area **with a majority of Jews.** וְרַב אַסִּי – **But Rav Assi,** who distinguishes between areas with Jewish and Canaanite majorities, סָבַר לָהּ כְּוָותֵיהּ בְּחֲדָא – **agrees with [R' Shimon ben Elazar] in one** case (where there is a Canaanite majority), וּפְלִיג עֲלֵיהּ בְּחֲדָא – **and disagrees with him in one** case (where there is a Jewish majority). Thus, Rav Assi's statement can give us no real indication of R' Shimon ben Elazar's position.[6]

The Gemara questions the actual ruling of Rav Assi:

וְכִי מֵאַחַר דַּאֲסִירָא בַּהֲנָאָה – **Now, since [the wine]** that was found **is forbidden for benefit,** מוּתֶּרֶת מִשּׁוּם מְצִיאָה לְמַאי הִלְכְתָא – to **what** practical matter of **law** is it relevant that **it is permitted as regards a found object?**[7]

The Gemara answers:

אָמַר רַב אַשִׁי – **Rav Ashi said:** לְקַנְקַנָּהּ – **In regard to its container.** Although the wine is prohibited, the container may be kept and used, because it is assumed to have belonged to a Canaanite.

The Gemara relates an incident and ruling that may resolve one of the questions raised above:

הַהוּא גַּבְרָא – There was **a certain man** דְּאַשְׁכַּח אַרְבָּעָה זוּזֵי – **who found four** ***zuzim***[8] דִּצְיִירֵי בְּסְדִינָא – **tied up in a cloth** וְשָׁדוּ בִּנְהַר בִּירָן – **and cast in the Biran River.** אָתָא לְקַמֵּיהּ דְּרַב יְהוּדָה – **He came before Rav Yehudah,** and asked him what to do with the money. אָמַר לֵיהּ – **[Rav Yehudah] told him:** זִיל אַכְרִיז – **Go** and **announce** your find.

The Gemara questions this ruling:

וְהָא זוּטוֹ שֶׁל יָם הוּא – **But surely that is** like an object swept away by **the tides of the sea,**[9] which one is permitted to keep. – ? –

The Gemara answers:

שָׁאנֵי נְהַר בִּירָן – The situation with regard to **the Biran River is different,** and not to be compared to an object swept out to sea, for the following reason: כֵּיוָן דְּמִתְקִיל – **Since there are obstacles** in the Biran River, which might catch an object, לֹא מְיָאֵשׁ – **[the owner] does not despair** of recovering it.[10]

NOTES

1. [I.e. the Mishnah in *Machshirin,* concerning the object found in a city with a mixed population, follows the view of the Rabbis, rather than R' Shimon ben Elazar.] Thus, there is no necessity to say, as the first explanation did, that this Mishnah deals with a buried object (*Rashi*).

2. The Rabbis make the following distinction: The law of majority (which permits us to assume that the object was lost by a Canaanite) absolves the finder from making any effort toward returning the lost object. Thus, he need not announce his find in a city whose majority is Canaanite. The law of majority, however, is insufficient to establish ownership conclusively. This follows the well-established rule (*Bava Kamma* 27b) that monetary matters cannot be established on the basis of majority (*Rashi*; cf. *Ran*). Thus, though the finder need not announce the find, at the same time, he is not permitted to use the object, since it may in fact belong to a Jew. [Rather, he must hold the object against the possibility that a Jew will step forward and identify it.]

According to this view, the Rabbis maintain that an owner does not despair of recovering an object with a *siman* even if he lost it in a place in which the multitudes are to be found and the majority of them are Canaanites. This does not accord with R' Shimon ben Elazar's opinion.

3. It is forbidden to derive any kind of benefit from the wine of a Canaanite because of the possibility that he poured some of it off as a libation to his pagan deity (Mishnah, *Avodah Zarah* 29b; see *Rashi* and *Tosafos* ad loc.).

The Gemara will soon raise the obvious question: If it is forbidden to derive benefit from it, of what significance is the permissibility of taking it? (*Rashi*).

4. The Jew's ability to identify the container of wine dispels our doubts that it may have belonged to a Canaanite. Nonetheless, it is presumed that the original owner has already despaired of finding the container because it was lost in an area with a Canaanite majority. Therefore the finder may keep it and drink it.

5. See 24a note 16.

6. R' Shimon ben Elazar certainly permits one to keep what he finds in a place where the majority of people are Canaanites. It is uncertain whether he permits this where the majority are Jews. If he does, Rav Assi rules against him in this case.

Nevertheless, we can at least demonstrate from this that the halachah follows R' Shimon ben Elazar where there is a Canaanite majority (*Tosafos*). *Rif* and *Rosh* go further and conclude that the halachah follows the view of Rav Assi, that though one may keep what he finds in a place where the majority are Canaanites, he cannot do so where the majority are Jews. See also *Shulchan Aruch, Choshen Mishpat* 259:3.

7. Since there is nothing he can do with the wine, what is the point of saying that he is permitted to keep it?

8. *Zuz* [pl. *zuzim*] – an ancient coin.

9. Although the phrase 'the surge of a river' seems more appropriate here than 'tides of the sea,' it is common to refer to a legal principle by the first of its several phrases [see Baraisa on 24a] (*Teshuvos HaRashba* 3:337).

10. There were stone obstacles and dams in the Biran River for the purpose of catching fish. The owner, therefore, is confident that the lost

ואיבעית אימא לעולם רבנן מי קתני הן שלו אינו חייב להכריז קתני ויניח וייתי ישראל ויהיב ביה סימנא ושקיל ת"ש דאמר רב אסי מצא חבית יין בעיר שרובה כנענים מותרת משום מציאה ואסורה בהנאה בא ישראל ונתן בה סימן מותרת בשתיה למוצאה כמאן כר"ש בן אלעזר שמע מינה כי קאמר ר"ש בן אלעזר ברוב כנענים אבל ברוב ישראל לא לעולם אימא לך ר"ש בן אלעזר אפי' ברוב ישראל נמי קאמר ורב אסי סבר לה כוותיה בחדא ופליג עליה בחדא וכי מאחר דאסירא בהנאה מותרת משום מציאה למאי הלכתא אמר רב אשי לקנקנה: ההוא גברא דאשכח ארבעה זוזי דציירי בסדינא ושדו בנהר בירן אתא לקמיה דרב יהודה א"ל זיל אכריז והא זוטו של ים הוא שאני נהר בירן כיון דמתקיל לא מיאש והא רובא כנענים נינהו ש"מ אין הלכה כר"ש בן אלעזר אפי' ברוב כנענים שאני נהר בירן דישראל סכרו ליה וישראל כרו ליה כיון דישראל סכרו ליה אימור מישראל נפל וכיון דישראל כרו ליה לא מיאש רב יהודה הוה שקיל ואזיל בתריה דמר שמואל בשוקא דבי דיסא א"ל מצא כאן ארנקי מהו אמר ליה הרי אלו שלו בא ישראל ונתן בה סימן מהו א"ל חייב להחזיר תרתי אמר ליה לפנים משורת הדין כי הא דאבוה דשמואל אשכח הנך חמרי במדברא ואהדרינהו למרייהו לבתר תריסר ירחי שתא לפנים משורת הדין רבא הוה שקיל ואזיל בתריה דר"נ בשוקא דגלדאי ואמרי לה בשוקא דרבנן א"ל מצא כאן ארנקי מהו א"ל הרי אלו שלו בא ישראל ונתן בה סימן מהו אמר ליה הרי אלו שלו והלא עומד וצווח נעשה כצווח על ביתו שנפל ועל ספינתו שטבעה בים ההוא דיו דשקיל בשרא בשוקא ושדיה בצנייתא דבי בר מריון אתא לקמיה דאביי א"ל זיל שקול לנפשך והא רובא דישראל נינהו שמעת מינה הלכה כרבי שמעון בן אלעזר אפי' ברוב ישראל שאני דיו דכזוטו של ים דמי והא אמר רב בשר שנתעלם מן העין אסור בעומד ורואהו: ר' חנינא מצא גדי שחוט בין טבריא לציפורי והתירוהו לו אמר רבי אמי התירוהו לו משום מציאה כר"ש בן אלעזר משום שחיטה כרבי חנניא בנו של רבי יוסי הגלילי דתניא הרי שאבדו לו גדייו ותרנגוליו והלך ומצאן שחוטין ר' יהודה אוסר ורבי חנניא בנו של רבי יוסי הגלילי מתיר אמר רבי נראין דברי רבי יהודה כשמצאן באשפה ודברי רבי חנניא בנו של רבי יוסי הגלילי כשמצאן בבית מדהתירוהו לו משום שחיטה רובא ישראל נינהו שמעת מינה הלכה כר"ש בן אלעזר אפי' ברוב ישראל אמר רבא רוב כנענים ורוב טבחי ישראל רבי אמי אשכח פרגיות שחוטות בין טבריא לציפורי אתא לקמיה דר' אסי ואמרי לה לקמיה דר' יוחנן ואמרי לה בי מדרשא ואמרו ליה זיל שקול לנפשך רבי יצחק נפחא אשכח קיבורא דאזלי ביה אזלויי אתא לקמיה דר' יוחנן ואמרי לה בבי מדרשא ואמרו ליה זיל שקול לנפשך: **מתני'** ואלו חייב להכריז מצא פירות בכלי או כלי כמות שהוא מעות בכים או כים כמות שהוא צבורי פירות צבורי מעות שלשה

---

**רש"י**

ואיבעית אימא לעולם רבנן. ובשאינה טמון ולא תפשוט מינה דמודו ליה ברוב כנענים: מי קתני כו' אינו חייב להכריז קתני. דכיון דרובא כנענים דלמא דכנענים הוא ושלו נמי לא הויא דלא אזלי רבנן בתר רובא בממונא: מותרת משום מציאה. דאינו חייב להכריז: ואסורה בהנאה. ולקמיה פריך א"כ מה היתר יש במציאה: בא ישראל ונתן סימן. יצאת מספק יין כנענים ומותרת בשתיה למוצאה דכיון דרובא כנענים נתיאשו הבעלים: ושדו בנהר בירן. ומושלכין בנהר בירן: דמתקיל. יש בו מכשולים אבנים וסתימת גדר שעושין לדגים ולא מיאש סבר לא יוכל הנהר להוליכם חוץ למכשולים ורגילים היו לסוכרו ולנקותו ולכרותו שישטפו מימיו וסומך שימצאם כשיסכרו אותו וינקום: סכרו ליה. סוקרין נשנ"ש בלע"ז כמו עושי שכר (ישעיה יט) אגמי נפש (ישעיה יט): אימור מישראל נפל. לפיכך חייב להכריז ולא אמרי' יניח כדאמרינן לעיל ברוב כנענים לרבנן: לא מיאש. שהסכורה ימצאם: דבי דיסא. שמוכרים שם חטים כתושין לדייסא ודגים מלוחין שם: בתר תריסר ירחי שתא. מלאם: דגלדאי. רצענים: דיו. עוף שקורין אולטו"ר והוא לשון דיה: ושדיה בצנייתא דבי בר מריון. השליכתו בין דקלים של בר מריון: אסור. שמא נתחלף בנבילה: ורואהו. משנטלו עד שהשליכו: כשמצאן באשפה. שדרך נבילה להשליכה באשפה: פרגיות. גוזלות: אשכח קיבורי דאזלי ביה אזלויי. מלא פקעיות של טווי למכמורות ולרשתות במקום שהצידין מצוין: אזלוי. ציידים העושים מכמורות: **מתני'** מצא פירות בכלי. וסתם כלי יש בו סימן: כמות שהוא. ריקן: כים. יש בו סימן לבעלים: צבורי פירות. בגמ' מפרש סימנייהו או מנין או מקום: שלשה

---

**תוספות**

**סבר** כוותיה בחדא. ולא בעי למימר דסבר כרבנן דא"כ תפשוט דמודו רבנן ברוב כנענים ומכל מקום יש לפשוט דהלכה כמותו ברוב כנענים: **לבתר** תריסר ירחי שתא כו'. פי' הן עצמן החזיר אע"ג דלא היה צריך ליתן רק דמיהם כדתנן בפרקין (דף כח:) כל דבר שעושה ואוכל מטפל בו י"ב חדש מכאן ואילך שם דמיהן ומניחן אבל רש"י פירש שמצאן אחר י"ב חדש שנאבדו קשה דמנלן שיהא בשביל כך לפנים משורת הדין אינו מתיאש שסבור שהמוצא יסבור שמקרוב נאבדו ויכריז: **לפנים** משורת הדין. מאשר יעשון נפקא לן לקמן בפרקין (דף ל:) תימה דלא מייתי קרא הכא כדמייתי לקמן בעובדא דר' ישמעאל ובהגוזל קמא (ב"ק דף ק. ושם ד"ה לפנים) בעובדא דרבי חייא במראה דינר לשולחני ונמצא רע ולקמן בסוף פרק האומנין (דף פג.) מייתי קרא אחרינא למען תלך בדרך טובים שהוא מדברי קבלה ושביק קרא דאשר יעשון שהוא מדברי תורה וי"ל דלא מייתי קרא דאשר יעשון אלא במקום שאחרים חייבין והוא פטור כמו במראה דינר דאחרים דבעו למיקם חייבים ור' חייא דלא בעי למיקם פטור ולפנים משורת הדין שילם כמו אחרים וכן בעובדא דרבי ישמעאל דזקן ואינו לפי כבודו הוה ועשה לפנים משורת הדין כמו אחרים והכא בשמעתין דהדרינהו בתר תריסר ירחי שתא כ"ע פטורים לכך לא מייתי קרא הכא ומ"מ משום לפנים משורת הדין בעי ליה לאהדורי כיון שאינו מתחסר ממונא אבל בסוף האומנין (שם) בההוא שקולאי שסברו לו החבית ועשו לו הפסד גדול משום לפנים משורת הדין אין לו להפסיד לכך מייתי קרא למען תלך בדרך טובים: **אתא** לקמיה דרב גרסי' כדמשמע בירושלמי פרק אין מעמידין ולפיכך לספרים דגרסי אביי פריך שפיר מבשר שנתעלם מן העין דאף ע"ג דלא קיימא לן כרב כדפרישית לעיל (דף כג: ד"ה מתרוצת) מדפריך בפרק גיד הנשה (חולין דף צה: ושם) ורב היכי אכיל בשרא מ"מ פריך שפיר דכיון דחזי המוצא שהעוף השליכם שם אפילו מאן דפליג ארב מודה הכא דאסור דאימור נטלה מעיר שרובה כנענים ומשני בעומד ורואהו שנטלה מעיר שרובה טבחי ישראל ולרב מיירי בעומד ורואהו שנטלה לפני טבחי ישראל: **הרי** שאבדו כו'. ה"ה נגנבו ואע"ג דעבר על לא תגנוב לא עבר על לאו דנבילה ובתוספתא (פ"ב דחולין) תניא בהדיא הרי שאבדו או נגנבו והכא נקט אבדו אורחא דמילתא: **שמצאן** באשפה. בפ"ק דחולין (ד' יב:) מפרש נראין דברי רבי יהודה לרבי חנניא כשמצאן באשפה שבשוק שאף רבי חנניא לא פליג עליה אלא באשפה שבבית ובעובדא דהכא שמצאן בדרך בלא אשפה הוי כאשפה שבבית: **אתא** לקמיה דרבי אסי גרסי' דאע"ג דבכל דוכתי חשיב רבי אמי ברישא כדאמר (גיטין דף נט:) רבי אמי ורבי אסי כהני חשיבי דארעא דישראל אף על גב שגדול ממנו אין תימה שבא לפניו לישאל לפי שחבירו היה אבל אי גרסינן רבי אבא קשה דרבי אבא היה תלמידו של רבי אמי כדמוכח גבי נסכא דרבי אבא (שבועות דף מז.) ואיך היה בא לפניו (ז) לעולם:

---

**עין משפט נר מצוה**

לח א ב מיי' פי"א מהל' גזלה ואבדה הל' ח ופי"ב מהלכות מאכלות אסורות הל' כח סמג עשין עד טוש"ע ח"מ סי' רנט סעיף ד וטוש"ע י"ד סי' קכט סעיף יז:
לט ג טוש"ע ח"מ סי' רנט סעיף ז וטוש"ע י"ד סי' קכט סעיף יז:
מ ד ה מיי' פי"א מהל' גזלה ואבדה הלכה ז סמג עשין עד טוש"ע ח"מ סי' רנט סעיף ה:
מא ו מיי' שם הל' ט טוש"ע שם סעיף ו:
מב ז מיי' פ"ח מהל' מאכלות אסורות הל' יב סמג לאוין קמג טוש"ע י"ד סי' סג סעיף א:
מג ח טוש"ע ח"מ סי' רנט סעיף ו:
מד ט מיי' פ"ד מהל' שחיטה הל' ח ועיין שם בכ"מ סמג לאוין קמג טוש"ע י"ד סי' א סעיף ד:
מה י טוש"ע ח"מ סי' רנט סעיף ו:
מו כ מיי' פט"ו מהל' גזלה ואבדה הל' יג סמג עשין עד טוש"ע ח"מ סי' רסב סעיף י:
מז ל מיי' שם פט"ז הל"ג סמג שם טוש"ע שם סעיף כ:
מח מ מיי' שם פט"ו הלכה יג סמג שם טוש"ע שם סעיף י:
מט נ מיי' שם פט"ז הלכה ב סמג שם טוש"ע ח"מ שם סעיף יא:

---

**רבינו חננאל**

היא וכן הא דא"ר אסי מצא חבית של יין בעיר שרובה כנענים קנקנה מותר [משום] מציאה ויינה אסור אפי' בהנאה בא ישראל ונתן סימניה מותרת אפי' בשתיה למוצאה. ש"מ דברוב כנענים הרי הן שלו. ההוא דאשכח ד' זוזי דצייר בסדינא בנהר בירן כו' ואסיקנא כיון דישראל כרו ליה וישראל סכרו ליה אימור מישראל נפול ולא מיאש. רב יהודה הוה אזיל בתריה דמר שמואל בשוקא דבי דיסא אמר ליה מצא כאן ארנקי מהו אמר ליה הרי הן שלו. בא ישראל ונתן סימניה מהו אמר לו אם הוא רוצה לעשות לפנים משורת הדין מחזיר כדאבוה דשמואל אשכח חמרא במדברא ואהדרינהו בתר י"ב ירחי שתא והא דרבה דאמר ליה רב נחמן מצא ארנקי בשוקא דרבנן הרי הן שלו ואפי' הלה עומד וצווח נעשה כצווח על ביתו שנפל ועל ספינתו שטבעה בים כלומר כשם מי שטבעה ספינתו המציל ממנה הרי הן שלו ואע"פ שבעלה עומד וצווח כדאמרינן המציל מזוטו של ים התורה התירתו לו כן גם זה מותר למוצאו ש"מ אפי' ברוב ישראל. עוף הנקרא דיו דשקיל בישרא ושדא בצנייתא דבי בר מריון. אסיקנא אם הוא עומד וראה את המקום שחוטף זה הבשר ממנו והוא מישראל מותר לו דכזוטו של ים [דמי] ואם לאו אסור באכילה כרב דאמר בשר כיון שנתעלם מן העין הא אסור באכילה. והא דרב חנינא דאשכח גדי שחוט בין טבריא לצפורי והתירוהו לו משום מציאה כר"ש בן אלעזר ומשום שחיטה כר' יוסי בר חנינא וכו' ופשוטה היא. פי' פרגיות צפרים טהורים. רב אמי אשכח פרגיות בין טבריא לצפורי וא"ל ר' יוחנן שקול לנפשך. וכן רב יצחק אשכח [פקעיות] של מטוה דאמר ר' יצחק אשכח קיבורי דאיזלו בי אזלויי וא"ל ר' יוחנן זיל שקול לנפשך: מתני' ואלו חייב להכריז מצא

---

**מסורת הש"ס**

א) [לקמן ל:, ברכות מה:, כתובות לז., בבא קמא לט:], ב) [חולין מח.], ג) חולין לה., ד) חולין י [תוספתא דחולין פרק ב], ה) פירוש האגמים שעושים בהם הדגים, שרשי רד"ק, ו) [עיין רש"י ברכות נ ד"ה ככלי אובד], ז) ל' לישאל, מהר"מ.

**לעזי רש"י**

נשנ"ש. פירוש עושי סכר (עיין רש"י ישעיה יט, י). אוזלטו"ר. פירוש עוף הנקרא דיה (רש"י ישעיה לד, טו).

**ליקוטי רש"י**

בשר שנתעלם מן העין. שהיה שעה אחת שלא ראהו ואפילו היה מונח על שולחנו [חולין צה.].

ובאושפיזא מאי נפקא מינה אמר מר זוטרא לאהדורי ליה אבידתא בטביעות עינא אי [א]ידעינן ביה דלא משני אלא בהני תלת מהדרינן ליה ואי משני במילי אחריני לא מהדרינן ליה מר זוטרא חסידא אגניב ליה כסא דכספא מאושפיזא חזיא להוא בר בי רב דמשי ידיה ונגיב בגלימא דחבריה אמר היינו האי דלא איכפת ליה אממונא דחבריה [א]כפתיה ואודי תניא (א) מודה ר"ש בן אלעזר בכלים חדשים ששבעתן העין שחייב להכריז ואלו הן כלים חדשים שלא שבעתן העין שאינו חייב להכריז כגון [א] בדי מחטין וצינוריות ומחרוזות של קרדומות כל אלו שאמרו [ב]אימתי מותרים בזמן שמצאן אחד אחד אבל מצאן שנים שנים חייב להכריז מאי בדי שוכי ואמאי קרו ליה בדי דבר דתלו ביה מידי בד קרו ליה כי ההוא [ב] דתנן התם [ג]עלה אחד בבד אחד וכן היה ר"ש בן אלעזר אומר [ג]המציל מן הארי ומן הדוב ומן הנמר ומן הברדלס ומן זוטו של ים ומשלוליתו של נהר המוצא בסרטיא ופלטיא גדולה ובכל מקום שהרבים מצויין שם הרי אלו שלו מפני שהבעלים מתיאשין מהן איבעיא להו כי קאמר ר"ש בן אלעזר [ד]ברוב כנענים אבל ברוב ישראל לא או דלמא [ד]אפי' ברוב ישראל נמי אמר אם תמצא לומר אפילו ברוב ישראל נמי אמר [ה]פליגי רבנן עליה או לא פליגי ואם תמצא לומר פליגי ברוב ישראל ודאי פליגי ברוב כנענים פליגי או לא פליגי ואם תמצא לומר פליגי אפי' [ה]ברוב כנענים הלכה כמותו או אין הלכה כמותו אם תמצא לומר הלכה כמותו דוקא ברוב כנענים או אפילו ברוב ישראל ת"ש [ו]המוצא מעות בבתי כנסיות ובבתי מדרשות ובכל מקום שהרבים מצויין שם הרי אלו שלו מפני שהבעלים מתיאשין מהן מאן שמעת ליה דאזיל בתר רובא ר"ש בן אלעזר שמעת מינה אפילו ברוב ישראל נמי הב"ע במפוזרין אי במפוזרין מאי אריא מקום שהרבים מצויין שם אפילו אין הרבים מצויין שם אלא לעולם [ז]בצרורין והכא במאי עסקינן [ה]בבתי כנסיות של כנענים בתי מדרשות מאי איכא למימר בתי מדרשות דידן דיתבי בהו כנענים השתא דאתית להכי בתי כנסיות נמי דידן דיתבי בהו כנענים ת"ש [ח]מצא בה אבידה [ו]אם רוב ישראל חייב להכריז אם רוב כנענים אינו חייב להכריז מאן שמעת ליה דאמר אזלינן בתר רובא רשב"א שמעת מינה כי קאמר רשב"א ברוב כנענים אבל ברוב ישראל לא הא מני רבנן היא תפשוט מינה דמודו ליה רבנן לרשב"א ברוב כנענים אלא לעולם רשב"א היא ואפי' ברוב ישראל נמי והכא במאי עסקי' בטמון אי בטמון מאי עבידתיה גביה והתנן [ט]מצא כלי באשפה מכוסה לא יגע בו מגולה נוטל ומכריז [י]כדאמר רב פפא באשפה שאינה עשויה לפנות ונמלך עליה לפנותה הכא נמי באשפה שאינה עשויה לפנות ונמלך עליה לפנותה

ואיבעית

**באושפיזא.** שאלוהו על אושפיזו אם קבלו בסבר פנים יפות ואמר לאו מדה טובה היא כדי שלא יקפצו בו בני אדם שאינן מהוגנין לבא תמיד עליו ויכלו את ממונו: **אגניב ליה כסא דכספא.** כלי של אושפיזו היה: **בדי מחטין וצינוריות.** לקמיה מפרש בדי מחטין שתולין בו מחטין: **וצינוריות.** מזלגות קטנים שטוות בו זהב: **אחת אחת.** בד אחת ומחרוז אחד: **חייב להכריז.** דמנין הוי סימן: **שוכי.** ענפים של אילן: **עלה אחד בבד אחד.** [ג] במס' סוכה (דף מד:) גבי ערבה שנשרו מקצת עליה ונשתיירו בה שלשה עלין לחין ואיכא דאמרי אפילו עלה אחד בבד אחד כשירה: **ברדלס.** צבוע וי"א פוטיא"ש [כ] ודרך להרוג אווזים ותרנגולים: **ובכל מקום שהרבים כו'.** ואפילו דבר שיש בו סימן: **פליגי רבנן עליה.** בתרוייהו: **המוצא מעות.** קא ס"ד צבורי מעות דקתני מתני' חייב להכריז והכא הואיל ורבים מצויין שם הרי אלו שלו שנתייאשו הבעלים: **דאזיל בתר רובא.** כלומר שהולך בדין מציאה אחר טעם רבים מצויים שם: **ברוב ישראל.** דסתם בתי כנסיות ישראל נהן: **במפוזרים.** ורבנן היא דמודו במפוזרין דתנן מעות מפוזרין הרי אלו שלו: **כנסיות.** אסיפת מקום שמתכנסים שם להתיעץ ולהוועד: **דיתבי בהו כנענים.** שהן חוץ לעיר ומושיבין בה כנענים לשמור: **מצא בה אבידה.** משנה היא בסדר טהרות בעיר שישראל וכנענים דרים בה במסכת מכשירין: **ותפשוט מיהא.** מקצת משאלותיך דמודו רבנן ברוב כנענים ופליגי ברוב ישראל: **בטמון.** דכיון דטמנו לאו אבידה היא הלכך ברוב ישראל יכריז: **שאינה עשויה לפנות.** רגילים היו בעלים להניחה ימים רבים ולא לפנותה מיד: **ונמלך עליה לפנותה.** מיד ועל כרחו או יטלנו או יהא הפקר להכי נקט (ב) שאינה עשויה לפנות דאי עשויה לפנות אבידה מדעת היא שהיה לו לחוש שמא יפנה:

**ומודה** ר"ש בכלים ששבעתן העין כו'. מדקאמר ומודה משמע דלרבנן אפילו לא שבעתן העין חייב להכריז וכן מצינו ברבה בר בר חנה דאמר בפ"ק (לעיל דף יט.) אי טביעות עינא אית לי בגויה וגט לא שבעתו העין דלא משהה איניש גיטא בידיה וקשה דלא מצינו דאמרו רבנן זה בפירוש וי"ל דמדנקט במתני' כריכות ועיגולי דבילה ומחרוזות וככרות הרי אלו שלו ואלו דברים אין דרכן להיות בהן טביעות העין משמע דדברים שדרכן להיות בהן טביעות עין בכל ענין חייב להכריז אפילו לא שבעתן העין אי מצא במקום דשכיחי רבנן: **אבל** שנים חייב להכריז. דמנין הוי סימן ומתניתין דקתני מחרוזות וככרות הרי אלו שלו אי איירי דרך נפילה אתי שפיר דאז לא היה מנין סימן שאינו יודע שנפלו בבת אחת א"נ איירי דרך הינוח וליכא אלא מחרוזה אחת וכן עיגול וככר והא דקאמר מחרוזות היינו מחרוזות דעלמא ולקמן (דף כה.) גבי צבורי פירות וגבי צבורי מעות דפריך ש"מ מנין הוי סימן ולא משני צבורי דעלמא דומיא דרישא מחרוזות ועיגול וככרות וכריכות היינו משום דלא הוה ליה למתני אלא מעות צבורות ופירות צבורות כדקתני מעות מפוזרות ופירות מפוזרות: **כי** קאמר ר"ש ברוב כנענים. וא"ת א"כ מה צריך טעם מפני שהבעלים מתיאשים ת"ל דיש לתלות דמכנענים נפל דהוו רובא וי"ל דאיצטריך דאפילו יודע ודאי שמישראל נפל קאמר הרי אלו שלו [ל] דהמפסיד מתיאש ואומר דכנענים שקלי ליה ואפילו אם ישראל ימצאם לא יכריז דתולה דמן הכנענים נפל דהן רובא: **אפילו** ברוב ישראל נמי. הוי שלו וטעמא משום דאיכא אינשי דלא מעלי ושקלי לה: **אם** תמצי לומר פליגי פליגי ברוב כנענים או לא. להך גירסא מספקא אי פליגי אפילו ברוב ישראל ואית ספרים דלא גרסי הכי אלא גרסי את"ל אפילו ברוב ישראל פליגי רבנן עליה ברוב כנענים או לא ולהך גירסא פשיטא ליה דרבנן פליגי עליה ברוב ישראל וחייב להכריז ולא חיישינן לאינשי דלא מעלי וכן נראה דהא תנן אלו שחייב להכריז מצא פירות בכלי וכן כולהו דאית בהו סימן ומשמע דאפילו ברה"ר דרבים מצויים שם חייב להכריז דלא מדכר רה"י אלא גבי כריכות ודוחק הוא להעמיד בסמטא וכן לקמן אמר לעולם רבנן כו' ומי קתני הרי אלו שלו אינו חייב להכריז קתני ויניח והשתא מ"מ תפשוט דפליגי רבנן ברוב ישראל דקתני אם רוב ישראל חייב להכריז אלא ודאי הא לא מספקא ליה אם פליגי ברוב ישראל ופשיטא ליה דפליגי מכח מתני' כדפרישית: **מאן** שמעת ליה דאזיל בתר רובא. פירוש גבי מציאה ולא שייך הא לפלוגתא דחיישינן למיעוט: **ותפשוט** מינה דמודו רבנן לר"ש כו'. וא"ת אי בעי למפשט דמודו רבנן נימא ר"ש היא וי"ל דמ"מ תפשוט דלא מצינו למימר דלר"ש אפילו ברוב ישראל הרי אלו שלו ולרבנן אפילו ברוב כנענים חייב להכריז דאי כר"ש אתיא אם כן ברוב ישראל חייב [להכריז] לר"ש ואי כרבנן אתיא א"כ ברוב כנענים הרי אלו שלו: **בטמון.** ולא בעי לאוקמה שאין רבים מצויין שם מדמפליג בין רוב העיר כנענים לרוב העיר ישראל משמע שמצא במקום שרוב בני העיר מצויים שם דאי מצא במקום שאין רבים מצויין לא הוה ליה למנקט רוב העיר אלא אם רוב כנענים או ישראל שכיחי במקום שמצא וא"ת ובטמון למה יגע בו אי משום שיפנה אותה המפנה יקחנה ויכריז וי"ל דשמא המפנה יהיה כנעני או שמא לא ימצאנה המפנה וישליכנה לחוץ עם הזבל וא"ת ואמאי יכריז יקחנה לעצמו דכשלא ימצאנה בעליה יתייאש ויאמר שאדם שאינו הגון לקחה ואע"ג דאיכא רובא ישראל דהיינו טעמא דר"ש דשרי ברוב ישראל וי"ל דהוי יאוש שלא מדעת דבשעה שלוקחה עדיין לא ידע האובד שנלקחה וברוב כנענים הוי שלו דתלינן דכנענים הטמינוה דהוו רובא:

סבר

### מסורת הש"ס

א) [בבא בתרא קסז.], ב) סוכה מד: [ע"ש מימרא הוא], ג) עבודה זרה מג., ד) [לקמן כו.], ה) [עיין תוס' בבא בתרא ... ד"ה חוץ], ו) [לעיל ...], ז) ס"א צבורין, ח) מכשירין פ"ב משנה ח ע"ש, ט) לקמן כה:, י) שם, כ) [צ"ל ודרכו. יעב"ץ], ל) נ"א דהאובד.

### הגהות הב"ח

(א) גמ' תניא ומודה ר"ש: (ב) רש"י ד"ה ונמלך וכו' להכי נקט. נ"ב ע"ל דף כה ע"ב:

### הגהות הגר"א

[א] גמ' בדי מחטין. נ"ב הרמב"ם וש"ע לא כתבו בדי אלא מחטין כו' לא בדין וע' רא"ש ומש"ש בסי' רס"ב ס"ק כ"ג): [ב] שם דתנן. רשום קו עליו ונ"ב דאמרינן וכ"ה ברי"ף ורא"ש: [ג] רש"י ד"ה עלה. במס' סוכה כו'. נ"ב תמוה מאד וע' בדברי רבינו בא"ח סי' תרמ"ו ס"ק י"ד):

### גליון הש"ס

גמ' פליגי רבנן עליה. עיין זה נדרים כ"ג ע"ב:

### לעזי רש"י

פוטיא"ש. פירוש חיה קטנה כעין חולדה (תוספות סנהדרין דף טו ע"ב סוד"ה והברדלס).

### ליקוטי רש"י

**כפתיה.** הכריחו [קדושין ה:]. **ברדלס.** הוא צבוע ... לישנא אחרינא ועיקר צבוע נקבה [ב"ק טז.]. **ומן זוטו של ים.** לשון ים שחוזר לאחוריו עשר וחמש עשרה פרסאות ושוטף כל מה שמוצא בדרך חזרתו וכן עושה בכל יום. **ומשלוליתו של נהר.** שהנהר גדל ויוצא על גדותיו ופושט [ע"ז מג.]. **המוצא בסרטיא.** מסילה שהולכין בה מעיר לעיר. **ופלטיא.** רחבה של עיר ששם מתקבלין לסחורה [שבת ו.]. **מכוסה לא יגע בו.** שאין זו אבידה שיהא מוזהר עליה בלא תוכל להתעלם דמשמר הוא [לקמן כה:].

### עין משפט נר מצוה

לד א מיי' פי"ד מהל' גזילה ואבידה הלכה יג סמג עשין עד טוש"ע ח"מ סי' רסב סעיף כא:

לה ב מיי' פט"ו שם הל' א סמג עשין עד טוש"ע ח"מ סי' רסב סעיף טו:

לו ג מיי' שם פ"ו הל' ג ועיין בהשגות ובמגיד משנה סמג שם טוש"ע ח"מ סי' רנט סעיף ז:

לז ד ה ו מיי' שם פי"א הל' ז סמג שם טוש"ע שם סעיף ג וע"ש:

### רבינו חננאל

הלילה שפיר עבד שאין דרך ארץ לגלות בני אדם שיחתם עם נשיהם לבני אדם וכן באושפיזא אם כיבדו ועשה לו מטעמים הרבה ותיקן הבית בכלים מכובדים ושינה האורח מפני כי פחד שלא ירגישו בני אדם וירדו אחריו בביתו כדכתיב מברך רעהו בקול גדול וגו' ושינה כל שינוי בענין זה אין מחזיקין אותו בשקרי אלא הרי הוא באמונתו ואם יאמר ברי לי שאלו כליי הן מחזירין אותו בטביעות עין בלבד בלא נתינת סימנין לפיכך מודה ר' שמעון בן אלעזר בכלים חדשים ששבעתן העין שחייב להכריז מאי טעמא דלמא אתי צורבא מרבנן דלא משנה בדיבוריה דאמר טביעות עינא אית לי בהו ושקיל להו. ואלו הן (הן) כלים חדשים שאין חייב להכריז בדי מחטין וצינורות ומחרוזות [של] קרדומות שמצאן אחד אחד וכן היה ר"ש אומר המציל מן הארי ומן הדוב ומזוטו של ים ומשלוליתו של נהר והמוצא באיסרטיא ופלטיא ומעות בבתי כנסיות ובתי מדרשות ואפי' צרורין ובכל מקום שהרבים מצוין שם הרי אלו שלו מפני שהבעלים מתיאשים מהן. ואיבעיא לן ברוב כנענים או אפי' ברוב ישראל נמי הרי אלו שלו ולא איפשיטא וקיימא לן תיקו דממונא לקולא. מעשה דמר זוטרא חסידא פשוטה

אֶלָּא – Rather, לְעוֹלָם רַבִּי שִׁמְעוֹן בֶּן אֶלְעָזָר הִיא – [the Mishnah] may actually be in accordance with R' Shimon ben Elazar, וַאֲפִילוּ בְּרוֹב יִשְׂרָאֵל נַמ – and it is conceivable that R' Shimon ben Elazar ordinarily allows one to keep even what he finds in an area with a majority of Jews. Why then does this Mishnah state that one must announce what he finds in an area with a majority of Jews? Because this Mishnah is not dealing with an ordinary find. וְהָכָא בְּמַאי עַסְקִינָ – Rather, with what case are we dealing here? בְּטָמוּן – With the case of a buried [object]. Since the owner concealed it, and is presumably aware of its whereabouts, the object is not considered lost. Therefore, the finder is not permitted to keep it.

The Gemara questions this answer:

אִי בְּטָמוּ – If the Mishnah refers to a buried [object], מַאי עֲבִידְתֵּיהּ גַּבֵּי – what is it doing in his possession, i.e. why does the finder take it at all? וְהָתְנַן – Surely we have learned in a Mishnah:[32] מָצָא כְּלִי בְּאַשְׁפָּה – If [ONE] FOUND A VESSEL IN A GARBAGE HEAP, the following determination should be made: מְכוּסֶּ – If the vessel IS COVERED, indicating that it had been concealed there intentionally, לֹא יִגַּע בּוֹ – HE SHOULD NOT TOUCH IT, because it is not lost.[33] מְגוּלֶּה – If the vessel IS UNCOVERED, indicating that the owner is unaware of its whereabouts, נוֹטֵל וּמַכְרִיז – HE MUST TAKE it AND ANNOUNCE his find. Thus, if the object is concealed, why is the finder taking it into his possession at all?

The Gemara answers:

כִּדְאָמַר רַב פָּפָּא – The earlier Mishnah may be explained as Rav Pappa said in reference to a Baraisa quoted later.[34] בְּאַשְׁפָּה שֶׁאֵינָהּ עֲשׂוּיָה לְפַנּוֹת – It deals with a garbage heap that is ordinarily not cleared away, וְנִמְלַךְ עָלֶיהָ לְפַנּוֹתָהּ – but [whose owner] changed his mind and decided to clear it away immediately.[35] הָכָא נַמִי – Here too, we may say that the Mishnah that speaks of an object found in a city with a mixed population בְּאַשְׁפָּה שֶׁאֵינָהּ עֲשׂוּיָה לְפַנּוֹת – refers to an object found buried in a garbage heap that is ordinarily not cleared away, וְנִמְלַךְ עָלֶיהָ לְפַנּוֹתָהּ – but [whose owner] changed his mind and decided to clear it away immediately.[36]

NOTES

32. Below, 25b.

33. We assume that the owner knows where it is and is planning to return for it.

34. Gemara 25b, regarding an object found in a garbage heap.

35. Private garbage heaps were left in place for long periods of time without being cleared (*Rashi*). Thus, a passerby who buried an object in a garbage heap for safekeeping could expect to retrieve it weeks or even months later. In this case, however, the owner unexpectedly decided to clear the garbage heap.

36. [Since the garbage heap is about to be cleared, there is no point in leaving the object in place. It is thus considered a lost object,] and it must either be announced and returned to its owner, or be deemed ownerless [and therefore permitted to the finder] (*Rashi*). In this case, R' Shimon ben Elazar rules that in an area with a Jewish majority the finder must announce the object, since the owner buried it and obviously did not despair of recovering it. [However, where there is a Canaanite majority he may keep it, because we then assume that it belonged to a Canaanite (*Tosafos* ד״ה בטמון).] In ordinary circumstances, it is possible that R' Shimon ben Elazar would allow one to keep what he finds even in an area with a majority of Jews, because the owner despairs of recovering it.

The reason the Gemara explains this as referring to a garbage heap that is ordinarily not cleared away is because one who places his object in a heap which is expected to be cleared has willfully abandoned it [and there would be no obligation to return it to him] (*Rashi*).

ובאושפיזא מאי נפקא מינה אמר מר זוטרא לאהדורי ליה אבידתא בטביעות עינא אי ידעינן ביה דלא משני אלא בהני תלת מהדרינן ליה ואי משני במילי אחריני לא מהדרינן ליה מר זוטרא חסידא אגניב ליה כסא דכספא מאושפיזא חזיא להההוא בר בי רב דמשי ידיה ונגיב בגלימא דחבריה אמר היינו האי דלא איכפת ליה אממונא דחבריה כפתיה ואודי תניא (א) מודה ר"ש בן אלעזר בכלים חדשים ששבעתן העין שחייב להכריז ואלו הן כלים חדשים שלא שבעתן העין שאינו חייב להכריז כגון [א] בדי מחטין וצינוריות ומחרוזות של קרדומות כל אלו שאמרו אימתי מותרים בזמן שמצאן אחד אחד אבל מצאן שנים שנים חייב להכריז מאי בדי שוכי ואמאי קרו ליה בדי דבר דתלו ביה מידי בד קרו ליה כי ההוא [ב] דתנן התם עלה אחד בבד אחד וכן היה ר"ש בן אלעזר אומר המציל מן הארי ומן הדוב ומן הנמר ומן הברדלס ומן זוטו של ים ומשלוליתו של נהר המוצא בסרטיא ופלטיא גדולה ובכל מקום שהרבים מצויין שם הרי אלו שלו מפני שהבעלים מתיאשין מהן איבעיא להו כי קאמר ר"ש בן אלעזר ברוב כנענים אבל ברוב ישראל לא או דלמא אפי' ברוב ישראל נמי אמר אם תמצא לומר אפילו ברוב ישראל נמי אמר פליגי רבנן עליה או לא פליגי ואם תמצא לומר פליגי ברוב ישראל ודאי פליגי ברוב כנענים פליגי או לא פליגי ואם תמצא לומר פליגי אפי' ברוב כנענים הלכה כמותו או אין הלכה כמותו אם תמצא לומר הלכה כמותו דוקא ברוב כנענים או אפילו ברוב ישראל ת"ש המוצא מעות בבתי כנסיות ובבתי מדרשות ובכל מקום שהרבים מצויין שם הרי אלו שלו מפני שהבעלים מתיאשין מהן מאן שמעת ליה דאזיל בתר רובא ר"ש בן אלעזר שמעת מינה אפילו ברוב ישראל נמי הב"ע במפוזרין אי במפוזרין מאי אריא מקום שהרבים מצויין שם אפילו אין הרבים מצויין שם אלא לעולם בצרורין והכא במאי עסקינן בבתי כנסיות של כנענים בתי מדרשות מאי איכא למימר בתי מדרשות דידן דיתבי בהו כנענים השתא דאתית להכי בתי כנסיות נמי דידן דיתבי בהו כנענים ת"ש מצא בה אבידה אם רוב ישראל חייב להכריז אם רוב כנענים אינו חייב להכריז מאן שמעת ליה דאמר אזלינן בתר רובא רשב"א שמעת מינה כי קאמר רשב"א ברוב כנענים אבל ברוב ישראל לא הא מני רבנן היא תפשוט מינה דמודו ליה רבנן לרשב"א ברוב כנענים אלא לעולם רשב"א היא ואפי' ברוב ישראל נמי והכא במאי עסקי' בטמון אי בטמון מאי עבידתיה גביה והתנן מצא כלי באשפה מכוסה לא יגע בו מגולה נוטל ומכריז כדאמר רב פפא באשפה שאינה עשויה לפנות ונמלך עליה לפנותה הכא נמי באשפה שאינה עשויה לפנות ונמלך עליה לפנותה

ואיבעית

## רש"י

באושפיזא. שאלוהו על אושפיזו אם קבלו בסבר פנים יפות ואמר לאו מדה טובה היא כדי שלא יקפלו בו בני אדם שאינן מהוגנין לבא תמיד עליו ויכלו את ממונו: אגניב ליה כסא דכספא. כלי של אושפיזו היה: בדי מחטין וצינוריות. לקמיה מפרש בדי מחטין שתולין בו מחטין: וצינוריות. מזלגות קטנים שטווית בו זהב: אחת אחת. בד אחת ומחרוזת אחד: חייב להכריז. דמנין הוי סימן: שוכי. ענפים של אילן: עלה אחד בבד אחד. [ג] במס' סוכה (דף מד:) גבי ערבה שנשרו מקצת עליה ונשתיירו בה שלשה עלין לחין ואיכא דאמרי אפילו עלה אחד בבד אחד כשירה: ברדלס. צבוע וי"א פוטיא"ש ודרך להרוג אווזים ותרנגולים: ובכל מקום שהרבים כו'. ואפילו דבר שיש בו סימן: פליגי רבנן עליה. בתרוייהו: המוצא מעות. קא ס"ד צבורי מעות דקתני מתני' חייב להכריז והכא הואיל ורבים מצויין שם הרי אלו שלו שנתייאשו הבעלים: דאזיל בתר רובא. כלומר שהולך בדין מציאה אחר טעם רבים מצויים שם: ברוב ישראל. דסתם בתי כנסיות ישראל בהן: במפוזרים. ורבנן היא דמודו במפוזרין דתנן מעות מפוזרין הרי אלו שלו: כנסיות. אסיפת מקום שמתכנסים שם להתיעץ ולהוועד: דיתבי בהו כנענים. שהן חוץ לעיר ומושיבין בה כנענים לשמור: מצא בה אבידה. משנה היא בסדר טהרות בעיר שישראל וכנענים דרים בה במסכת מכשירין: ותפשוט מיהא. מקצת מאבעיא דמודו רבנן ברוב כנענים ופליגי ברוב ישראל: בטמון. דכיון דטמנו לאו אבידה היא הלכך ברוב ישראל יכריז: שאינה עשויה לפנות. רגילים היו בעלים להניחה ימים רבים ולא לפנותה מיד: ונמלך עליה לפנותה. מיד ועל כרחו או יטלנו או יהא הפקר להכי נקט (ג) שאינה עשויה לפנות דאי עשויה לפנות אבידה מדעת היא שהיה לו לחוש שמא יפנה:

## תוספות

ומודה ר"ש בכלים ששבעתן העין כו'. מדקאמר ומודה משמע דלרבנן אפילו לא שבעתן העין חייב להכריז וכן מלינו ברבה בר בר חנה דאמר בפ"ק (לעיל דף יט.) אי טביעות עינא אית לי בגויה וגט לא שבעתו העין דלא משהה איניש גיטא בידיה וקשה דלא מלינו דאמרו רבנן זה בפירוש וי"ל דמדנקט במתני' כריכות ועיגולי דבילה ומחרוזות וככרות הרי אלו שלו ואלו דברים אין דרכן להיות בהן טביעות העין משמע דדברים שדרכן להיות בהן טביעות עין בכל ענין חייב להכריז אפילו לא שבעתן העין אי מלא במקום דשכיחי רבנן:

אבל שנים חייב להכריז. דמנין הוי סימן ומתניתין דקתני מחרוזות וככרות הרי אלו שלו אי מיירי דרך נפילה אתי שפיר דאז לא היה מנין סימן שאינו יודע שנפלו בבת אחת א"נ מיירי דרך הינוח וליכא אלא מחרוזה אחת וכן עיגול וככר והא דקאמר מחרוזות היינו מחרוזות דעלמא ולקמן (דף כה.) גבי צבורי פירות וגבי צבורי מעות דפריך ש"מ מנין הוי סימן ולא משני צבורי דעלמא דומיא דרישא מחרוזות ועיגול וככרות וכריכות היינו משום דלא הוה ליה למתני אלא מעות צבורות ופירות צבורות כדקתני מעות מפוזרות ופירות מפוזרות:

כי קאמר ר"ש ברוב כנענים. וא"ת א"כ מה צריך טעם מפני שהבעלים מתיאשים ת"ל דיש לתלות דמכנענים נפל דהוו רובא וי"ל דאיצטריך דאפילו יודע ודאי שמישראל נפל קאמר הרי אלו שלו דהמפסיד מתיאש ואומר דכנענים שקלי ליה ואפילו אם ישראל ימצאנו לא יכריז דתולה דמן הכנענים נפל דהן רובא:

אפילו ברוב ישראל נמי. הוי שלו וטעמא משום דאיכא אינשי דלא מעלי ושקלי לה:

אם תמצי לומר פליגי ברוב כנענים או לא. להך גירסא מספקא אי פליגי אפילו ברוב ישראל ואית ספרים דלא גרסי הכי אלא גרסי את"ל אפילו ברוב ישראל פליגי רבנן עליה ברוב כנענים או לא ולהך גירסא פשיטא ליה דרבנן פליגי עליה ברוב ישראל וחייב להכריז ולא חיישינן לאינשי דלא מעלי וכן נראה דהא תנן אלו שחייב להכריז מצא פירות בכלי וכן כולהו דאית בהו סימן ומשמע דאפילו ברה"ר דרבים מצויים שם חייב להכריז דלא מדכר רה"י אלא גבי כריכות ודוחק הוא להעמיד בסמטא וכן לקמן אמר לעולם רבנן כו' ומי קתני הרי אלו שלו אינו חייב להכריז קתני ויניח והשתא מ"מ תפשוט דפליגי רבנן ברוב ישראל דקתני אם רוב ישראל חייב להכריז אלא ודאי הא לא מספקא ליה אם פליגי ברוב ישראל ופשיטא ליה דפליגי מכח מתני' כדפרישית:

מאן שמעת ליה דאזיל בתר רובא. פירוש גבי מציאה ולא שייך הא לפלוגתא דחיישינן למיעוט:

ותפשוט מינה דמודו רבנן לר"ש כו'. וא"ת אי בעי למפשט דמודו רבנן נימא ר"ש היא וי"ל דמ"מ תפשוט דלא מלינו למימר דלר"ש אפילו ברוב ישראל הרי אלו שלו ולרבנן אפילו ברוב כנענים חייב להכריז דאי כר"ש אתיא אם כן ברוב ישראל חייב [להכריז] לר"ש ואי כרבנן אתיא א"כ ברוב כנענים הרי אלו שלו:

בטמון. ולא בעי לאוקמה שאין רבים מצויין שם מדמפליג בין רוב העיר כנענים לרוב העיר ישראל משמע שמצא במקום שרוב בני העיר מצויים שם דאי מצא במקום שאין רבים מצויין לא הוה ליה למנקט רוב העיר אלא אם רוב כנענים או ישראל שכיחי במקום שמצא וא"ת ובטמון למה יגע בו אי משום שיפנה אותה המפנה יקחנה ויכריז וי"ל דשמא המפנה יהיה כנעני או שמא לא ימצאנה המפנה וישליכנה לחוץ עם הזבל וא"ת ואמאי יכריז יקחנה לעצמו דכשלא ימצאנה בעליה יתייאש ויאמר שאדם שאינו הגון לקחה ואע"ג דאיכא רובא ישראל דהיינו טעמא דר"ש דשרי ברוב ישראל וי"ל דהוי יאוש שלא מדעת דבשעה שלוקחה עדיין לא ידע האובד שנלקחה וברוב כנענים הוי שלו דתלינן דכנענים הטמינוה דהוו רובא:

סבר

## עין משפט נר מצוה

לד א מיי' פי"ד מהל' גזלה ואבידה הלכה יג סמג עשין עד טוש"ע ח"מ סי' רסב סעיף כא:

לה ב מיי' פט"ז שם הל' א סמג עשין עד טוש"ע ח"מ סי' רסב סעיף טז:

לו ג מיי' שם פ"ו הל' ג ועיין בהשגות ובמגיד משנה סמג שם טוש"ע ח"מ סי' רנט סעיף ז:

לז ד ה ו מיי' שם פי"א הל' ז סמג שם טוש"ע שם סעיף ג וע"ש:

## רבינו חננאל

הלילה שפיר עבד שאין דרך ארץ לגלות בני אדם שיחתם עם נשיהם לבני אדם וכן באושפיזא אם כיבדו ועשה לו מטעמים הרבה ותיקן הבית בכלים מכובדים ושינה האורח מפני כי פחד שלא ירגישו בני אדם וירדו אחריו בביתו כדכתיב מברך רעהו בקול גדול וגו' ושינה כל שינוי בענין זה אין מחזיקין אותו בשקרי אלא הרי הוא באמונתו ואם יאמר ברי לי שאלו כליי הן מחזירין אותו בטביעות עין בלבד בלא נתינת סימנין לפיכך מודה ר' שמעון בן אלעזר בכלים חדשים ששבעתן העין שחייב להכריז מאי טעמא דלמא אתי צורבא מרבנן דלא משנה בדיבוריה דאמר טביעות עינא אית לי בהו ושקיל להו. ואלו הן (הן) כלים חדשים שאין חייב להכריז בדי מחטין וצינורות ומחרוזות [של] קרדומות שמצאן אחד אחד וכן היה ר"ש אומר המציל מן הארי ומן הדוב ומזוטו של ים ומשלוליתו של נהר והמוצא באיסרטיא ופלטיא ומעות בבתי כנסיות ובתי מדרשות ואפי' צרורין ובכל מקום שהרבים מצוין שם הרי אלו שלו מפני שהבעלים מתיאשים מהן. ואיבעיא לן ברוב כנענים או אפי' ברוב ישראל נמי הרי אלו שלו ולא איפשיטא וקיימא לן תיקו דממונא לקולא. מעשה דמר זוטרא חסידא פשוטה

## מסורת הש"ס

[בבא בתרא קסז.], סוכה מד: [ע"ש זימרא הוא], ג) עבודה זרה מג., ד) [לקמן כו.], [עיין תוס' בבא בתרא ד"ה חוץ], ו) [לעיל ...:], ז) פ"א צבורין, עיין מהרש"ל, ח) מכשירין פ"ב משנה ח ע"ש, לקמן כה., י) שם, [צ"ל ודרכו. יעב"ץ], ל) נ"א דהאובד.

## הגהות הב"ח

(א) גמ' תניא ומודה ר"ש: (ג) רש"י ד"ה ונמלך וכו' להכי נקט. נ"ב ע"ל דף כה ע"ב:

## הגהות הגר"א

[א] גמ' בדי מחטין. נ"ב הרמב"ם וש"ע לא גרסו בדי אלא מחטין כו' ... בדין וע' רא"ש ומש"ש סי' רס"ב ס"ק כ"ג): [ב] שם דתנן. רשום קו ... ונ"ב דאמרינן וכ"ה ... י"ף ורא"ש: [ג] רש"י ד"ה עלה. במס' סוכה ... כו'. נ"ב תמוה מאד ... בדברי רבינו בא"ח סי' תרמ"ו ס"ק י"ד):

## גליון הש"ס

... פליגי רבנן עליה. ... עין זה נדרים כ"ג ע"ב:

## לעזי רש"י

... פוטיא"ש. פירוש חיה ... כעין חולדה ... וספות סנהדרין דף טו ... ב סוד"ה והברדלס).

## ליקוטי רש"י

... כפתיה. הכריחו [קדושין ...:]. ברדלס. הוא צבוע ..., לישנא אחרינא ועיקר ... נקבה [ב"ק טז.]. ומן זוטו של ים. לשון ים ... חוזר לאחוריו עשר וחמש ... פרסאות ושוטף כל ... שמוצא בדרך חזרתו ... עושה בכל יום. ומשלוליתו של נהר. ... הנהר גדל ויוצא על ... ותיו ופושט [ע"ז מג.]. המוצא בסרטיא. ... שהולכין בה מעיר ... לעיר. ופלטיא. רחבה של ... שם מתקבצין ... סחורה [שבת ו.]. ... מכוסה לא יגע בו. ... אין זו אבידה שהיא ... זהר עליה אלא תוכל ... מעלם דמשתמר הוא [לקמן כה:].

e agrees that the finder may keep them, as we learned in our ishnah.[22]

The Gemara questions this explanation of the Baraisa:

אִי בִּמְפוּזָּר – **If** the Baraisa is dealing **with** a case of **scattered oins],** מַאי אִרְיָא – **why** does it **speak of** מָקוֹם שֶׁהָרַבִּים מְצוּיִין שָׁ – **a place where large numbers of people are commonly und?** אֲפִילוּ אֵין הָרַבִּים מְצוּיִין שָׁם – **Even** in a place **where rge numbers of people are not commonly found,** it is rmissible to keep scattered coins which cannot be identified![23]

The Gemara accepts this argument, but rejects the proof in nother manner:

אֶ – **Rather,** we must say that לְעוֹלָם בִּצְרוּרִין – the Baraisa tually refers **to bundled [coins],** which are identifiable. וְהָכָא בְּמַאי עָסְקִי – **But with what** case **are we dealing here?** בְּבָתֵּי כְּנֵסִיּוֹת שֶׁל כְּנַעֲ – We are dealing with **the houses of assembly Canaanites.**[24] Thus, it is impossible to prove from the Baraisa at R' Shimon ben Elazar's ruling refers to areas with a majority Jews.

The Gemara questions the applicability of this answer to the her example of the Baraisa:

בָּתֵּי מִדְרָשׁוֹת מַאי אִיכָּא לְמֵימַ – **What is there to say** in regard to e **study halls** mentioned by the Baraisa? These obviously refer places for the public study of Torah.[25] If so, it may still be ferred that R' Shimon ben Elazar's ruling applies even where ere is a Jewish majority.

The Gemara rejects this as well:

בָּתֵּי מִדְרָשׁוֹת דִּי – The Baraisa is indeed referring to **our** (i.e. wish) **study halls,** דְּיָתְבֵי בְהוּ כְּנַעֲנִים – **in which Canaanites ay** as guards. Thus, as regards the law of lost objects, the study alls are not considered a place primarily of Jews.[26] הַשְׁתָּא דְּאָתֵית לְהָ – **Now that you have arrived at this** understanding the Baraisa, בָּתֵּי כְּנֵסִיּוֹת נַמִּי דִּידַן – it is possible that the araisa's term **"houses of assembly" also** refers to **our** houses of ssembly, i.e. synagogues, דְּיָתְבֵי בְהוּ כְּנַעֲנִים – **in which anaanites stay** as guards.[27]

The Gemara once again attempts to clarify the scope of R' Shimon ben Elazar's ruling:

תָּא שְׁמַע – **Come, learn** the resolution to our question from a Mishnah[28] which states: מָצָא בָהּ אֲבֵידָה – If **ONE FOUND A LOST OBJECT THERE,** in a city with Jewish and Canaanite residents, the following determination should be made: אִם רוֹב יִשְׂרָאֵל – **IF THE MAJORITY** of residents are **JEWS,** חַיָּיב לְהַכְרִיז – **[THE FINDER] IS OBLIGATED TO ANNOUNCE** his find. אִם רוֹב כְּנַעֲנִים – **IF THE MAJORITY** of residents are **CANAANITES,** אֵינוֹ חַיָּיב לְהַכְרִיז – **[THE FINDER] IS NOT OBLIGATED TO ANNOUNCE** his find. מַאן שָׁמְעַת לֵיהּ דְּאָמַר אָזְלִינַן בָּתַר רוּבָּא – **Whom have you heard saying** that **we take into consideration the multitudes** who frequent an area in deciding what should be done with a lost object?[29] רַבִּי שִׁמְעוֹן בֶּן אֶלְעָזָר – It is **R' Shimon ben Elazar** who, in the Baraisa cited above, permits one to keep what he finds in an area frequented by many people. Thus, it would seem that this anonymous Mishnah also reflects the view of R' Shimon ben Elazar. שְׁמַעַת מִינָּהּ – Therefore, **learn from this** Mishnah's differentiation between Jewish and Canaanite majorities, כִּי קָאָמַר רַבִּי שִׁמְעוֹן בֶּן אֶלְעָזָר – that **in which** case **does R' Shimon ben Elazar state** his rule? בְּרוֹב כְּנַעֲנִים – Only **in** areas with **a majority of Canaanites;** אֲבָל בְּרוֹב יִשְׂרָאֵל – **but in** areas with **a majority of Jews,** לֹא – R' Shimon ben Elazar does **not** rule that one may keep whatever he finds.

The Gemara rejects the proof as well:

הָא מַנִּי – **Who is** the Tanna of **this** Mishnah? רַבָּנַן הִיא – **It is the Rabbis** who disagree with R' Shimon ben Elazar.[30]

But if so, asks the Gemara:

תִּפְשׁוֹט מִינָּהּ – **Resolve from this** interpretation of the Mishnah דְּמוֹדוּ לֵיהּ רַבָּנַן לְרַבִּי שִׁמְעוֹן בֶּן אֶלְעָזָר – **that the Sages agree with R' Shimon ben Elazar** בְּרוֹב כְּנַעֲנִים – **in** an area with **a majority of Canaanites.**[31]

The Gemara accepts this argument and therefore offers another interpretation, in which none of the previous questions is resolved:

NOTES

2. Above, 21a. Thus, the Baraisa can follow even the opinion of the abbis, who may disagree with R' Shimon ben Elazar. Their dispute ncerns an object identifiable through a *siman*, which a person dinarily expects to recover. Nevertheless, R' Shimon ben Elazar ntends that if he loses it in a place frequented by many people, he spairs of recovering it despite the *siman* because he fears it will be und by someone who will not return it to him (see note 16). This novel ling is possibly the subject of a dispute with the Rabbis, as the Gemara ated above. However, where the object has no *siman* and is nidentifiable, everyone agrees that the owner despairs. Thus, if this araisa speaks of coins without a *siman,* it tells us nothing about R' himon ben Elazar's personal view.

3. By stating a rule for places in which large numbers of people are und, the Baraisa implies that what causes the owner to despair is the esence of crowds, not the lack of a *siman.* Thus, the Baraisa must be eaking of coins that are in fact identifiable. [This question is so vious that it is difficult to understand what the Gemara could have eant when it originally proposed this answer. See *Ritva* and *Shitah ekubetzes* for possible explanations.]

4. Although the Baraisa's term בָּתֵּי כְּנֵסִיּוֹת is commonly used to mean *nagogues,* it can be understood in its literal sense as well – *houses of ssembly.* [The word synagogue itself comes from the Greek word eaning *to bring together,* or *assemble*.] Such buildings were common in her cultures as well, as places for councils to meet and for the public assemble (*Rashi*).

5. [The term מִדְרָשׁ, *midrash,* refers specifically to the exposition of orah, and is not a general term for learning. Thus, the phrase בָּתֵּי מִדְרָשׁ, literally: *houses of midrash,* can only refer to halls for the study f Torah, not any other studies.]

6. The study halls were located outside the cities [where they were xposed to marauders]. Canaanite guards would be hired and placed there to protect the students (*Rashi*).

This explanation seems difficult. Although there are Canaanite watchmen guarding in the study halls, they are certainly a minority as compared to the Jews who study there. Thus, the Baraisa is still dealing with a situation in which there is a Jewish majority. How then has the Gemara refuted the proof?

*Rashba* answers that though there is a numerical majority of Jews, nonetheless, the Canaanites who live there constantly are more apt to search for and find lost objects than the Jews who come there for the purpose of studying. For this reason, the owner despairs of recovering his loss, because he considers it likely that it will be found by the Canaanites. Therefore, this situation is analogous to the case of a Canaanite majority, not a Jewish majority.

27. Thus, the term "houses of assembly" [בָּתֵּי כְּנֵסִיּוֹת] may be understood in its usual sense of synagogues.

28. *Machshirin* 2:8.

29. Since the Mishnah bases its distinction on the population of the city as a whole, rather than on the residents of the particular street in which the object was found, it seems clear that the Mishnah is discussing an object found in a part of the city frequented by most of its inhabitants. Thus, we see that even in areas frequented by the multitudes, the Mishnah requires one to announce the find if there are a majority of Jews (*Tosafos* ד״ה בטמון).

30. Although the ruling of the Mishnah seems to follow R' Shimon ben Elazar's line of reasoning, it may well be that the Rabbis agree with him in an area with a majority of Canaanites. Thus, the Mishnah may reflect their view, whereas R' Shimon ben Elazar may hold that a lost object may be kept even where there is a majority of Jews.

31. By the same token, we see that the Rabbis disagree with R' Shimon ben Elazar in an area with a Jewish majority (see *Rashi* ד״ה ותפשוט, and *Tosafos*). Thus the second and third questions may be resolved.

ובאושפיזא מאי נפקא מינה אמר מר זוטרא לאהדורי ליה אבידתא בטביעות עינא אי [א]ידעינן ביה דלא משני אלא בהני תלת מהדרינן ליה ואי משני במילי אחריני לא מהדרינן ליה מר זוטרא חסידא אגניב ליה כסא דכספא מאושפיזא חזיא להההוא בר בי רב דמשי ידיה ונגיב בגלימא דחבריה אמר היינו האי דלא איכפת ליה אממונא דחבריה [א]כפתיה ואודי תניא (א) מודה ר"ש בן אלעזר בכלים חדשים ששבעתן העין שחייב להכריז ואלו הן כלים חדשים שלא שבעתן העין שאינו חייב להכריז כגון [א] בדי מחטין וצינוריות ומחרוזות של קרדומות כל אלו שאמרו [ב]אימתי מותרים בזמן שמצאן אחד אחד אבל מצאן שנים שנים חייב להכריז מאי בדי שוכי ואמאי קרו ליה בדי דבר דתלו ביה מידי בד קרו ליה כי ההוא [ב]דתנן התם [ג]עלה אחד בבד אחד וכן היה ר"ש בן אלעזר אומר [ג]המציל מן הארי ומן הדוב ומן הנמר ומן הברדלס ומן זוטו של ים ומשלוליתו של נהר המוצא בסרטיא ופלטיא גדולה ובכל מקום שהרבים מצויין שם הרי אלו שלו מפני שהבעלים מתיאשין מהן איבעיא להו כי קאמר ר"ש בן אלעזר [ד]ברוב כנענים אבל ברוב ישראל לא או דלמא [ד]אפי' ברוב ישראל נמי אמר אם תמצא לומר אפילו ברוב ישראל נמי אמר [ה]פליגי רבנן עליה או לא פליגי ואם תמצא לומר פליגי ברוב ישראל ודאי פליגי ברוב כנענים פליגי או לא פליגי ואם תמצא לומר פליגי אפי' [ה]ברוב כנענים הלכה כמותו או אין הלכה כמותו אם תמצא לומר הלכה כמותו דוקא ברוב כנענים או אפילו ברוב ישראל ת"ש [ו]המוצא מעות בבתי כנסיות ובבתי מדרשות ובכל מקום שהרבים מצויין שם הרי אלו שלו מפני שהבעלים מתיאשין מהן מאן שמעת ליה דאזיל בתר רובא ר"ש בן אלעזר שמעת מינה אפילו ברוב ישראל נמי הב"ע במפוזרין אי במפוזרין מאי אריא מקום שהרבים מצויין שם אפילו אין הרבים מצויין שם אלא לעולם [ז]בצרורין והכא במאי עסקינן [ח]בבתי כנסיות של כנענים בתי מדרשות מאי איכא למימר בתי מדרשות דידן דיתבי בהו כנענים השתא דאתית להכי בתי כנסיות נמי דידן דיתבי בהו כנענים ת"ש [ט]מצא בה אבידה [י]אם רוב ישראל חייב להכריז אם רוב כנענים אינו חייב להכריז מאן שמעת ליה דאמר אזלינן בתר רובא רשב"א שמעת מינה כי קאמר רשב"א ברוב כנענים אבל ברוב ישראל לא הא מני רבנן היא תפשוט מינה דמודו ליה רבנן לרשב"א ברוב כנענים אלא לעולם רשב"א היא ואפי' ברוב ישראל נמי והכא במאי עסקי' בטמון אי בטמון מאי עבידתיה גביה והתנן [ט]מצא כלי באשפה מכוסה לא יגע בו מגולה נוטל ומכריז [י]כדאמר רב פפא באשפה שאינה עשויה לפנות ונמלך עליה לפנותה הכא נמי באשפה שאינה עשויה לפנות ונמלך עליה לפנותה ואיבעית

**רש"י**

**באושפיזא.** שאלוהו על אושפיזו אם קבלו בסבר פנים יפות ואמר לאו מדה טובה היא כדי שלא יקפצו בו בני אדם שאינן מהוגנין לבא תמיד עליו ויכלו את ממונו: **אגניב ליה כסא דכספא.** כלי של אושפיזו היה: **בדי מחטין וצינוריות.** לקמיה מפרש בדי מחטין שתולין בו מחטין: **וצינוריות.** מזלגות קטנים שטוות בו זהב: **אחת אחת.** בד אחת ומחרוז אחד: **חייב להכריז.** דמנין הוי סימן: **שוכי.** ענפים של אילן: **עלה אחד בבד אחד.** [ג] במס' סוכה (דף מד:) גבי ערבה שנשרו מקצת עליה ונשתיירו בה שלשה עלין לחין ואיכא דאמרי אפילו עלה אחד בבד אחד כשירה: **ברדלס.** לבוע וי"א פוטיא"ש [כ] ודרך להרוג אווזים ותרנגולים: **וכל מקום שהרבים כו'.** ואפילו דבר שיש בו סימן: **פליגי רבנן עליה.** בתרוייהו: **המוצא מעות.** קא ס"ד לצורי מעות דקתני מתני' חייב להכריז והכא הואיל ורבים מצויין שם הרי אלו שלו שנתייאשו הבעלים: **דאזיל בתר רובא.** כלומר שהולך בדין מציאה אחר טעם רבים מצויים שם: **ברוב ישראל.** דסתם בתי כנסיות ישראל בהן: **במפוזרים.** ורבנן היא דמודו במפוזרין דתנן מעות מפוזרין הרי אלו שלו: **כנסיות.** אסיפת מקום שמתכנסים שם להתיעץ ולהוועד: **דיתבי בהו כנענים.** שהן חוץ לעיר ומושיבין בה כנענים לשמור: **מצא בה אבידה.** משנה היא בסדר טהרות בעיר שישראל וכנענים דרים בה במסכת מכשירין: **ותפשוט מידא.** מקצת משאלותיך דמודו רבנן ברוב כנענים ופליגי ברוב ישראל: **בטמון.** דכיון דטמנו לאו אבידה היא הלכך ברוב ישראל יכריז: **שאינה עשויה לפנות.** רגילים היו בעלים להניחה ימים רבים ולא לפנותה מיד: **ונמלך עליה לפנותה.** מיד ועל כרחו או יטלנו או יהא הפקר להכי נקט (ג) שאינה עשויה לפנות דאי עשויה לפנות אבידה מדעת היא שהיה לו לחוש שמא יפנה:

**תוספות**

**ומודה** ר"ש בכלים ששבעתן העין כו'. מדקאמר ומודה משמע דלרבנן אפילו לא שבעתן העין חייב להכריז וכן מלינו ברבה בר בר חנה דאמר בפ"ק (לעיל דף יט.) אי טביעות עינא אית לי בגויה וגט לא שבעתו העין דלא משהה איניש גיטא בידיה וקשה דלא מלינו דאמרו רבנן זה בפירוש וי"ל דמדנקט במתני' כריכות ועיגולי דבילה ומחרוזות וככרות הרי אלו שלו ואלו דברים אין דרכן להיות בהן טביעות העין משמע דדברים שדרכן להיות בהן טביעות עין בכל ענין חייב להכריז אפילו לא שבעתן העין אי מלא במקום דשכיחי רבנן: **אבל** שנים חייב להכריז. דמנין הוי סימן ומתניתין דקתני מחרוזות וככרות הרי אלו שלו אי מיירי דרך נפילה אתי שפיר דאז לא היה מנין סימן שאינו יודע שנפלו בבת אחת א"נ מיירי דרך הינוח וליכא אלא מחרוזה אחת וכן עיגול וככר והא דקאמר מחרוזות היינו מחרוזות דעלמא ולקמן (דף כה.) גבי לבורי פירות וגבי לבורי מעות דפריך ש"מ מנין הוי סימן ולא משני לבורי דעלמא דומיא דרישא מחרוזות ועיגול וככרות וכריכות היינו משום דלא הוה ליה למתני אלא מעות לבורות ופירות לבורות כדקתני מעות מפוזרות ופירות מפוזרות: **כי** קאמר ר"ש ברוב כנענים. וא"ת א"כ מה לריך טעם מפני שהבעלים מתיאשים ת"ל דיש לתלות דמכנענים נפל דהוו רובא וי"ל דאיצטריך דאפילו יודע ודאי שמישראל נפל קאמר הרי אלו שלו [ל]דהמפסיד מתיאש ואומר דכנענים שקלי ליה ואפילו אם ישראל ימצאם לא יכריז דתולה דמן הכנענים נפל דהן רובא: **אפילו** ברוב ישראל נמי. הוי שלו וטעמא משום דליכא איניש דלא מעלי ושקלי לה: **אם** תמצי לומר פליגי פליגי ברוב כנענים או לא. להך גירסא מספקא אי פליגי אפילו ברוב ישראל ואית ספרים דלא גרסי הכי אלא גרסי את"ל אפילו ברוב ישראל פליגי רבנן עליה ברוב כנענים או לא ולהך גירסא פשיטא ליה דרבנן פליגי עליה ברוב ישראל וחייב להכריז ולא חיישינן לאינשי דלא מעלי וכן נראה דהא תנן אלו שחייב להכריז מלא פירות בכלי וכן כולהו דאית בהו סימן ומשמע דאפילו ברה"ר דרבים מצויים שם חייב להכריז דלא מדכר רה"י אלא גבי כריכות ודוקא הוא להעמיד בסמטא וכן לקמן אמר לעולם רבנן כו' ומי קתני הרי אלו שלו אינו חייב להכריז קתני ויניח והשתא מ"מ תפשוט דפליגי רבנן ברוב ישראל דקתני אם רוב ישראל חייב להכריז אלא ודאי הא לא מספקא ליה אם פליגי ברוב ישראל ופשיטא ליה דפליגי מכח מתני' כדפרישית: **מאן** שמעת ליה דאזיל בתר רובא. פירוש גבי מציאה ולא שייך הא לפלוגתא דחיישינן למיעוט:

**ותפשוט** מינה דמודו רבנן לר"ש כו'. וא"ת אי בעי למפשט דמודו רבנן נימא ר"ש היא וי"ל דמ"מ תפשוט דלא מלינו למימר דלר"ש אפילו ברוב ישראל הרי אלו שלו ולרבנן אפילו ברוב כנענים חייב להכריז דאי כר"ש אתיא אם כן ברוב ישראל חייב [להכריז] לר"ש ואי כרבנן אתיא א"כ ברוב כנענים הרי אלו שלו: **בטמון.** ולא בעי לאוקמה שאין רבים מצויין שם מדמפליג בין רוב העיר כנענים לרוב העיר ישראל משמע שמלא במקום שרוב בני העיר מצויים שם דאי מלא במקום שאין רבים מצויין לא הוה ליה למנקט רוב העיר אלא אם רוב כנענים או ישראל שכיחי במקום שמלא וא"ת ובטמון למה יגע בו אי משום שיפנה אותה המפנה יקחנה ויכריז וי"ל דשמא המפנה יהיה כנעני או שמא לא ימלאנה המפנה וישליכנה לחוץ עם הזבל וא"ת ואמאי יכריז יקחנה לעצמו דכשלא ימלאנה בעליה יתייאש ויאמר שאדם שאינו הגון לקחה ועוד דאיכא רובא ישראל דהיינו טעמא דר"ש דשרי ברוב ישראל וי"ל דהוי יאוש שלא מדעת דבשעה שלוקחה עדיין לא ידע האובד שנלקחה וברוב כנענים הוי שלו דתלינן דכנענים הטמינוה דהוו רובא:

סבר

**מסורת הש"ס**

[...]בבא בתרא קמז.], [...]סוכה מד: [ע"ש [...]מרא הוא], ג) עבודה [...] מג., ד) [לקמן כו.], [...] [עיין תוס' בבא בתרא [...]ד"ה מון], ו) [לעיל [...]], ז) פ"א צבורין, [...] מהרש"ל, ח) מכשירין [...] ב משנה ח ע"ש, [...] לקמן כה:, י) שם, [...]צ"ל ודרכו. יעב"ן], [...]ל) נ"א להאובד.

**הגהות הב"ח**

[...] גמ' תניא ומודה [...]: (ב) רש"י ד"ה [...]לך וכו' להכי נקט. נ"ב [...] ע"ל דף כה ע"ב:

**הגהות הגר"א**

[...] גמ' בדי מחטין. [...]: הרמב"ם וש"ע לא [...]כו בדי אלא מחטין כו' [...] בדין וע' רא"ש ומש"ש [...]סי' רמ"ב ס"ק כ"ג): [...] שם דתנן. רשום קו [...] ונ"ב דאמרינן וכ"ה [...]י"ף ורא"ש: [ג] רש"י [...]ה עלה. במס' סוכה [...] כו'. נ"ב תמוה מאד [...] בדברי רבינו בא"ח סי' [...] תרמ"ו ס"ק י"ד):

**גליון הש"ס**

[...] פליגי רבנן עליה. [...]ין זה נדרים כ"ג ע"ב:

**לעזי רש"י**

[...]טיא"ש. פירוש חיה [...]ונה כעין חולדה [...] וספות סנהדרין דף טו [...]"ב סוד"ה והברדלס).

**ליקוטי רש"י**

[...]תיה. הכריחו [קדושין [...]:]. **ברדלס.** הוא לבוע [...], לישנא אחרינא ועיקר [...]וע נקבה [ב"ק טז.]. **ומן** [...]טו של ים. לשון ים [...]חזר לאחוריו עשר וחמש [...]רה פרסאות ושוטף כל [...] שמולא בדרך חזרתו [...] עושה בכל יום. [...]**משלוליתו של נהר.** [...]שהנהר גדל ויולא על [...]ותיו ופושט [ע"ז מג.]. **מוצא בסרטיא.** [...]סילה שהולכין בה מעיר [...]ניר. **ופלטיא.** רחבה של [...]יר ששם מתקבלין [...]סחורה [שבת ו.]. [...]כוסה לא יגע בו. [...]אין זו אבידה שהיא [...]חזר עליה בלא תוכל [...]תעלם דמשתמר הוא [לקמן כה:].

**עין משפט נר מצוה**

לד א מיי' פי"ד מהל' גזילה ואבידה הלכה יג סמג עשין עד טוש"ע ח"מ סי' רסב סעיף כא:
לה ב מיי' פט"ז שם הל' א סמג עשין עד טוש"ע ח"מ סי' רסב סעיף טז:
לו ג מיי' שם פ"ו הל' ג ועיין בהשגות ובמגיד משנה סמג שם טוש"ע ח"מ סי' רנט סעיף ז:
לז ד ה ו מיי' שם פי"א הל' ז סמג שם טוש"ע שם סעיף ג וע"ש:

**רבינו חננאל**

הלילה שפיר עבד שאין דרך ארץ לגלות בני אדם שיחתם עם נשיהם לבני אדם וכן באושפיזא אם כיבדו ועשה לו מטעמים הרבה ותיקן הבית בכלים מכובדים ושינה האורח מפני כי פחד שלא ירגישו בני אדם וירדו אחריו בביתו כדכתיב מברך רעהו בקול גדול וגו' ושינה כל שינוי בענין זה אין מחזיקין אותו בשקרי אלא הרי הוא באמונתו ואם יאמר ברי לי שאלו כליי הן מחזירין אותו בטביעות עין בלבד בלא נתינת סימנין לפיכך מודה ר' שמעון בן אלעזר בכלים חדשים ששבעתן העין שחייב להכריז מאי טעמא דלמא אתי צורבא מרבנן דלא משנה בדיבוריה דאמר טביעות עינא אית לי בהו ושקיל להו. ואלו הן (הן) כלים חדשים שאין חייב להכריז בדי מחטין וצינורות ומחרוזות [של] קרדומות שמצאן אחד אחד וכן היה ר"ש אומר המציל מן הארי ומן הדוב ומזוטו של ים ומשלוליתו של נהר והמוצא באיסרטיא ופלטיא ומעות בבתי כנסיות ובתי מדרשות ואפי' צרורין ובכל מקום שהרבים מצוין שם הרי אלו שלו מפני שהבעלים מתיאשים מהן. ואיבעיא לן ברוב כנענים או אפי' ברוב ישראל נמי הרי אלו שלו ולא איפשיטא וקיימא לן תיקו דממונא לקולא. מעשה דמר זוטרא חסידא פשוטה

thing FROM A LION, וּמִן הַנָּמֵר – OR FROM A BEAR, וּמִן הַדּוֹב – OR FROM A LEOPARD, וּמִן הַבַּרְדְּלָס – OR FROM A HYENA,[13] וּמִן זוּטוֹ שֶׁל יָם – OR FROM THE TIDES OF THE SEA, וּמִשְּׁלוּלִיתוֹ שֶׁל נָהָר – OR FROM THE SURGE OF A flooding RIVER may retain it for himself.[14] הַמּוֹצֵא בְּסְרַטְיָא וּפְלַטְיָא גְּדוֹלָה – Similarly, ONE WHO FINDS something IN A MAJOR THOROUGHFARE[15] OR IN A LARGE PUBLIC SQUARE, וּבְכָל מָקוֹם – OR IN ANY PLACE שֶׁהָרַבִּים מְצוּיִין שָׁם – IN WHICH LARGE NUMBERS OF PEOPLE ARE COMMONLY FOUND, הֲרֵי אֵלּוּ שֶׁלּוֹ – THESE BELONG TO [THE FINDER], even if the objects are identifiable; מִפְּנֵי שֶׁהַבְּעָלִים מִתְיָאֲשִׁין מֵהֶן – BECAUSE THE OWNER DESPAIRS OF recovering THEM.

The Gemara now poses a series of five questions regarding the scope of R' Shimon ben Elazar's last statement and the final halachah:

אִיבַּעְיָא לְהוּ – **They inquired:** כִּי קָאָמַר רַבִּי שִׁמְעוֹן בֶּן אֶלְעָזָר – **When R' Shimon ben Elazar said** that one who finds an object in a place frequented by many people is permitted to keep it, was he referring to בְּרוֹב כְּנַעֲנִים – an area **where the majority** of people **are Canaanites,**[16] אֲבָל בְּרוֹב יִשְׂרָאֵל – **but** in an area **where the majority** of people **are Jews,** לֹא – R' Shimon ben Elazar would **not** permit the finder to keep it? אוֹ דִלְמָא – **Or perhaps,** אֲפִילּוּ בְּרוֹב יִשְׂרָאֵל נַמִּי אָמַר – **even** in an area **where the majority** of people **are Jews,** R' Shimon ben Elazar **also said** that the finder is permitted to keep the object.[17] – ? –

The Gemara further questions whether R' Shimon ben Elazar's contemporaries agree with him:

אִם תִּמְצָא לוֹמַר – **If you will say** אֲפִילּוּ בְּרוֹב יִשְׂרָאֵל נַמִּי אָמַר – that he **said** his ruling **even** in an area **where the majority** of people **are Jews,** פְּלִיגֵי רַבָּנָן עֲלֵיהּ – **do the Rabbis** (i.e. his colleagues) **disagree with him** and obligate the finder to announce his find regardless of the makeup of the population, אוֹ לֹא פְּלִיגֵי – **or do** they **not disagree** with R' Shimon ben Elazar at all? Rather, they too agree that one may keep what he finds in a place frequented by many people, even where the majority is Jewish. – ? –

A further question:

וְאִם תִּמְצָא לוֹמַר פְּלִיגֵי – **And if you will say** that **[the Rabbis] do disagree** with R' Shimon ben Elazar, what is the extent of their disagreement? בְּרוֹב יִשְׂרָאֵל וַדַּאי פְּלִיגֵי – If they disagree at all, **they certainly disagree where the majority** of people **are Jews,** and obligate the finder to announce the lost object. בְּרוֹב כְּנַעֲנִים – However, **where the majority are Canaanites,** פְּלִיגֵי – **do [the Rabbis] disagree** and obligate the finder to announce the lost object,[18] אוֹ לֹא פְּלִיגֵי – **or do they** perhaps **not disagree** in this case, but accept R' Shimon ben Elazar's ruling that one is permitted to keep what he finds in an area with a Canaanite majority?

The Gemara now questions what the authoritative ruling should be:

וְאִם תִּמְצָא לוֹמַר פְּלִיגֵי – **And if you will say** that **[the Rabbis] disagree** with R' Shimon ben Elazar אֲפִילּוּ בְּרוֹב כְּנַעֲנִים – **even** in an area **where the majority** of people **are Canaanites,** and they obligate the finder to announce his find, הֲלָכָה כְּמוֹתוֹ – **does the halachah follow his** [R' Shimon ben Elazar's] **view,** אוֹ אֵין הֲלָכָה כְּמוֹתוֹ – **or does the halachah not follow his view?**

A final question:

אִם תִּמְצָא לוֹמַר – **If you will say** הֲלָכָה כְּמוֹתוֹ – that **the halachah follows his** [R' Shimon ben Elazar's] **view,** דַּוְקָא בְּרוֹב כְּנַעֲנִים – does it follow his view **only** in regard to an area **where the majority** of people **are Canaanites,** אוֹ אֲפִילּוּ בְּרוֹב יִשְׂרָאֵל – **or even where the majority are Jews?**

The Gemara attempts to resolve the first question:

תָּא שְׁמַע – **Come, learn** a resolution to our question from the Baraisa which states: הַמּוֹצֵא מָעוֹת – ONE WHO FINDS COINS בְּבָתֵּי כְנֵסִיּוֹת – IN SYNAGOGUES, וּבְבָתֵּי מִדְרָשׁוֹת – OR IN STUDY HALLS, וּבְכָל מָקוֹם שֶׁהָרַבִּים מְצוּיִין שָׁם – OR IN ANY PLACE IN WHICH LARGE NUMBERS OF PEOPLE ARE COMMONLY FOUND, הֲרֵי אֵלּוּ שֶׁלּוֹ – THESE BELONG TO [THE FINDER], מִפְּנֵי שֶׁהַבְּעָלִים מִתְיָאֲשִׁין מֵהֶן – BECAUSE THE OWNER DESPAIRS OF recovering THEM. מַאן שָׁמְעַתְּ לֵיהּ – **Whom have you heard** דְּאָזִיל בָּתַר רוּבָּא – **taking into consideration** the **multitudes**[19] in determining what should be done with a lost object? רַבִּי שִׁמְעוֹן בֶּן אֶלְעָזָר – It is **R' Shimon ben Elazar** who, in the earlier Baraisa, permits the finder to keep objects found in areas frequented by multitudes of people. Thus, this anonymous Baraisa too must be the ruling of R' Shimon ben Elazar.[20] שְׁמַעַתְּ מִינַּהּ – Therefore, **learn from this** anonymous Baraisa, which permits the finder to keep coins found in a synagogue, אֲפִילּוּ בְּרוֹב יִשְׂרָאֵל נַמִּי – that R' Shimon ben Elazar permits him to keep it **even where a majority** of the people **are Jews.**[21]

The Gemara rejects this proof:

הָכָא בְּמַאי עַסְקִינַן – **With what** case **are we dealing here,** in the ruling regarding the synagogues? בִּמְפוּזָּרִין – **With** a case of **scattered [coins].** Since these have no identifying mark, every-

NOTES

13. *Rashi* cites another opinion that this is a polecat, which preys upon geese and chickens.

14. The Scriptural basis for the license to keep objects washed away by a flood was stated on 22b. R' Shimon ben Elazar elaborates upon this rule and adds other objects at imminent risk of being lost to mankind (e.g. something about to be devoured by a lion). All of these are considered ownerless; thus, in case of an unexpected rescue, the finder is permitted to keep them.

15. A highway going from city to city (*Rashi*, *Shabbos* 6a). These highways, as well as the large public plazas, are used constantly by *many* people, in contrast to the ordinary public domain (*Rashba, Ritva*).

16. There are two reasons why one is permitted to keep a found object in such an area — because it was likely lost by a Canaanite and there is no obligation to return a lost object to a Canaanite (see Gemara 27a), and because even if it was lost by a Jew, he despairs of recovering it. The reason he despairs is because he thinks it likely that a Canaanite will find it and not return it, or that even if a Jew finds it, he will not announce it because will assume that it was lost by a Canaanite. Although both reasons are valid, the second (the owner's despair of recovery) is more inclusive, since it permits to keep what he finds even if he knows that it was lost by a Jew. R' Shimon ben Elazar therefore gives this second reason as the basis for the finder's right to keep the object (*Tosafos*).

17. In areas frequented by many people there is a greater chance of the lost object being found by a dishonest person. For this reason, it is possible that even though the object is identifiable, the owner despairs of recovering it (*Tosafos*).

18. As a special Rabbinic decree, in case a Jew lost it (*Rosh,* cited by *Shitah Mekubetzes).*

19. *Rashi.* Literally: going after the many.

20. The Baraisa cited above in the name of R' Shimon ben Elazar records his ruling that one who finds something in any place in which the public is commonly found may keep it. The anonymous Baraisa just quoted, whose authorship the Gemara is attempting to establish, states that one who finds money in a synagogue, study hall, or any other place in which the public is commonly found may keep it. The final ruling [and even phrasing] of this latter Baraisa is virtually identical to R' Shimon ben Elazar's ruling in the earlier Baraisa. The Gemara establishes from this that the author of the anonymous Baraisa is also R' Shimon ben Elazar.

21. The Gemara assumes now that we are dealing with piles of coins, which are identifiable (see Mishnah 24b). The only possible justification for the finder to keep them is that the owner despairs of recovering the lost coins due to the steady flow of people through the synagogue (*Rashi*). This Baraisa, therefore, makes it clear that R' Shimon ben Elazar permits one to keep what he finds even in an area with a Jewish majority.

ובאושפיזא מאי נפקא מינה אמר מר זוטרא לאהדורי ליה אבידתא בטביעות עינא אי ידעינן ביה דלא משני אלא בהני תלת מהדרינן ליה ואי משני במילי אחריני לא מהדרינן ליה מר זוטרא חסידא אגניב ליה כסא דכספא מאושפיזא חזיא להההוא בר בי רב דמשי ידיה ונגיב בגלימא דחבריה אמר היינו האי דלא איכפת ליה אממונא דחבריה כפתיה ואודי תניא (א) מודה ר"ש בן אלעזר בכלים חדשים ששבעתן העין שחייב להכריז ואלו הן כלים חדשים שלא שבעתן העין שאינו חייב להכריז כגון [א] בדי מחטין וצינוריות ומחרוזות של קרדומות כל אלו שאמרו אימתי מותרים בזמן שמצאן אחד אחד אבל מצאן שנים שנים חייב להכריז מאי בדי שוכי ואמאי קרו ליה בדי דבר דתלו ביה מידי בד קרו ליה כי ההוא [ב] דתנן התם עלה אחד בבד אחד וכן היה ר"ש בן אלעזר אומר המציל מן הארי ומן הדוב ומן הנמר ומן הברדלס ומן זוטו של ים ומשלוליתו של נהר המוצא בסרטיא ופלטיא גדולה ובכל מקום שהרבים מצויין שם הרי אלו שלו מפני שהבעלים מתיאשין מהן איבעיא להו כי קאמר ר"ש בן אלעזר ברוב כנענים אבל ברוב ישראל לא או דלמא אפי' ברוב ישראל נמי אמר אם תמצא לומר אפילו ברוב ישראל נמי אמר פליגי רבנן עליה או לא פליגי ואם תמצא לומר פליגי ברוב ישראל ודאי פליגי ברוב כנענים פליגי או לא פליגי ואם תמצא לומר פליגי אפי' ברוב כנענים הלכה כמותו או אין הלכה כמותו אם תמצא לומר הלכה כמותו דוקא ברוב כנענים או אפילו ברוב ישראל ת"ש המוצא מעות בבתי כנסיות ובבתי מדרשות ובכל מקום שהרבים מצויין שם הרי אלו שלו מפני שהבעלים מתיאשין מהן מאן שמעת ליה דאזיל בתר רובא ר"ש בן אלעזר שמעת מינה אפילו ברוב ישראל נמי הב"ע במפוזרין אי במפוזרין מאי אריא מקום שהרבים מצויין שם אפילו אין הרבים מצויין שם אלא לעולם בצרורין והכא במאי עסקינן בבתי כנסיות של כנענים בתי מדרשות מאי איכא למימר בתי מדרשות דידן דיתבי בהו כנענים השתא דאתית להכי בתי כנסיות נמי דידן דיתבי בהו כנענים ת"ש מצא בה אבידה אם רוב ישראל חייב להכריז אם רוב כנענים אינו חייב להכריז מאן שמעת ליה דאמר אזלינן בתר רובא רשב"א שמעת מינה כי קאמר רשב"א ברוב כנענים אבל ברוב ישראל לא הא מני רבנן היא תפשוט מינה דמודו ליה רבנן לרשב"א ברוב כנענים אלא לעולם רשב"א היא ואפי' ברוב ישראל נמי והכא במאי עסקי' בטמון אי בטמון מאי עבידתיה גביה והתנן מצא כלי באשפה מכוסה לא יגע בו מגולה נוטל ומכריז כדאמר רב פפא באשפה שאינה עשויה לפנות ונמלך עליה לפנותה הכא נמי באשפה שאינה עשויה לפנות ונמלך עליה לפנותה ואיבעית

## רש"י

באושפיזא. שאלוהו על אושפיזו אם קבלו בסבר פנים יפות ואמר לאו מדה טובה היא כדי שלא יקפלו בו בני אדם שאינן מהוגנין לבא תמיד עליו ויכלו את ממונו: אגניב ליה כסא דכספא. כלי של אושפיזו היה: בדי מחטין וצינוריות. לקמיה מפרש בדי מחטין שתולין בו מחטין: וצינוריות. מזלגות קטנים שטווין בו זהב: אחת אחת. בד אחת ומחרוז אחד: חייב להכריז. דמנין הוי סימן: שוכי. ענפים של אילן: עלה אחד בבד אחד. [ג] במס' סוכה (דף מד:) גבי ערבה שנשרו מקצת עליה ונשתיירו בה שלשה עלין לחין ואיכא דאמרי אפילו עלה אחד בבד אחד כשירה: ברדלס. לבוע וי"א פוטיא"ש ודרך להרוג אווזים ותרנגולים: ובכל מקום שהרבים כו'. ואפילו דבר שיש בו סימן: פליגי רבנן עליה. בתרוייהו: המוצא מעות. קא ס"ד לבורי מעות דקתני מתני' חייב להכריז והכא הואיל ורבים מצויין שם הרי אלו שלו שנתייאשו הבעלים: דאזיל בתר רובא. כלומר שהולך בדין מציאה אחר טעם רבים מצויים שם: ברוב ישראל. דסתם בתי כנסיות ישראל בהן: במפוזרים. ורבנן היא דמודו במפוזרין דתנן מעות מפוזרין הרי אלו שלו: כנסיות. אסיפת מקום שמתכנסים שם להתיעץ ולהוועד: דיתבי בהו כנענים. שהן חוץ לעיר ומושיבין בה כנענים לשמור: מצא בה אבידה. משנה היא בסדר טהרות בעיר שישראל וכנענים דרים בה במסכת מכשירין: ותפשוט מידא. מקצת משאלותיך דמודו רבנן ברוב כנענים ופליגי ברוב ישראל: בטמון. דכיון דטמנו לאו אבידה היא הלכך ברוב ישראל יכריז: שאינה עשויה לפנות. רגילים היו בעלים להניחה ימים רבים ולא לפנותה מיד: ונמלך עליה לפנותה. מיד ועל כרחו או יטלנו או יהא הפקר להכי נקט (ג) שאינה עשויה לפנות דאי עשויה לפנות אבידה מדעת היא שהיה לו לחוש שמא יפנה: ואיבעית

## תוספות

ומודה ר"ש בכלים ששבעתן העין כו'. מדקאמר ומודה משמע דלרבנן אפילו לא שבעתן העין חייב להכריז וכן מלינו ברבה בר בר חנה דאמר בפ"ק (לעיל דף יט.) אי טביעות עינא אית לי בגויה וגט לא שבעתו העין דלא משהה איניש גיטא בידיה וקשה דלא מלינו דאמרו רבנן זה בפירוש וי"ל דמדנקט במתני' כריכות ועיגולי דבילה ומחרוזות וככרות הרי אלו שלו ואלו דברים אין דרכן להיות בהן טביעות העין משמע דדברים שדרכן להיות בהן טביעות עין בכל ענין חייב להכריז אפילו לא שבעתן העין אי מלא במקום דשכיחי רבנן: אבל שנים חייב להכריז. דמנין הוי סימן ומתניתין דקתני מחרוזות וככרות הרי אלו שלו אי מיירי דרך נפילה אתי שפיר דאז לא היה מנין סימן שאינו יודע שנפלו בבת אחת א"נ מיירי דרך הינוח וליכא אלא מחרוזה אחת וכן עיגול וככר והא דקאמר מחרוזות היינו מחרוזות דעלמא ולקמן (דף כה.) גבי צבורי פירות וגבי צבורי מעות דפריך ש"מ מנין הוי סימן ולא משני צבורי דעלמא דומיא דרישא מחרוזות ועיגול וככרות וכריכות היינו משום דלא הוה ליה למתני אלא מעות צבורות ופירות צבורות כדקתני מעות מפוזרות ופירות מפוזרות: כי קאמר ר"ש ברוב כנענים. וא"ת א"כ מה צריך טעם מפני שהבעלים מתיאשים ת"ל דיש לתלות דמכנענים נפל דהוו רובא וי"ל דאיצטריך דאפילו יודע ודאי שמישראל נפל קאמר הרי אלו שלו דהמפסיד מתיאש ואומר דכנענים שקלי ליה ואפילו אם ישראל ימצאם לא יכריז דתולה דמן הכנענים נפל דהן רובא: אפילו ברוב ישראל נמי. הוי שלו וטעמא משום דאיכא אינשי דלא מעלי ושקלי לה: אם תמצי לומר פליגי ברוב כנענים או לא. להך גירסא מספקא אי פליגי אפילו ברוב ישראל ואית ספרים דלא גרסי הכי אלא גרסי את"ל אפילו ברוב ישראל פליגי רבנן עליה ברוב כנענים או לא ולהך גירסא פשיטא ליה דרבנן פליגי עליה ברוב ישראל וחייב להכריז ולא חיישינן לאינשי דלא מעלי וכן נראה דהא תנן אלו שחייב להכריז מצא פירות בכלי וכן כולהו דאית בהו סימן ומשמע דאפילו ברה"ר דרבים מצויים שם חייב להכריז דלא מדכר רה"י אלא גבי כריכות ודוחק הוא להעמיד בסמטא וכן לקמן אמר לעולם רבנן כו' ומי קתני הרי אלו שלו אינו חייב להכריז קתני ויניח והשתא מ"מ תפשוט דפליגי רבנן ברוב ישראל דקתני אם רוב ישראל חייב להכריז אלא ודאי הא לא מספקא ליה אם פליגי ברוב ישראל ופשיטא ליה דפליגי מכח מתני' כדפרישית: מאן שמעת ליה דאזיל בתר רובא. פירוש גבי מציאה ולא שייך הא לפלוגתא דחיישינן למיעוט: ותפשוט מינה דמודו רבנן לר"ש כו'. וא"ת אי בעי למפשט דמודו רבנן נימא ר"ש היא וי"ל דמ"מ תפשוט דלא מלינו למימר דלר"ש אפילו ברוב ישראל הרי אלו שלו ולרבנן אפילו ברוב כנענים חייב להכריז דאי כר"ש אתיא אם כן ברוב ישראל חייב [להכריז] לר"ש ואי כרבנן אתיא א"כ ברוב כנענים הרי אלו שלו: בטמון. ולא בעי לאוקמה שאין רבים מצויין שם מדמפליג בין רוב העיר כנענים לרוב העיר ישראל משמע שמצא במקום שרוב בני העיר מצויים שם דאי מצא במקום שאין רבים מצויין לא הוה ליה למנקט רוב העיר אלא אם רוב כנענים או ישראל שכיחי במקום שמצא וא"ת ובטמון למה יגע בו אי משום שיפנה אותה המפנה יקחנה ויכריז וי"ל דשמא המפנה יהיה כנעני או שמא לא ימצאנה המפנה וישליכנה לחוץ עם הזבל וא"ת ולמאי יכריז יקחנה לעצמו דכשלא ימצאנה בעליה יתייאש ויאמר שאדם שאינו הגון לקחה ועי"ג דאיכא רובא ישראל דהיינו טעמא דר"ש דשרי ברוב ישראל וי"ל דהוי יאוש שלא מדעת דבשעה שלוקחה עדיין לא ידע האובד שנלקחה וברוב כנענים הוי שלו דתלינן דכנענים הטמינוה דהוו רובא:

סבר

## עין משפט נר מצוה

לד א מיי' פי"ד מהל' גזילה ואבידה הלכה יג סמג עשין עד טוש"ע ח"מ סי' רסב סעיף כא:
לה ב מיי' פט"ז שם הל' א סמג עשין עד טוש"ע ח"מ סי' רסב סעיף טז:
לו ג מיי' שם פ"ו הל' ב ועיין בהשגות ובמגיד משנה סמג שם טוש"ע ח"מ סי' רנט סעיף ז:
לז ד ה ו מיי' שם פי"א הל' ז סמג שם טוש"ע שם סעיף ג וע"ש:

## רבינו חננאל

הלילה שפיר עבד שאין דרך ארץ לגלות בני אדם שיחתם עם נשיהם לבני אדם וכן באושפיזא אם כיבדו ועשה לו מטעמים הרבה ותיקן הבית בכלים מכובדים ושינה האורח מפני כי פחד שלא ירגישו בני אדם וירדו אחריו בביתו כדכתיב מברך רעהו בקול גדול וגו' ושינה כל שינוי בענין זה אין מחזיקין אותו בשקרי אלא הרי הוא באמונתו ואם יאמר ברי לי שאלו כליי הן מחזירין אותו בטביעות עין בלבד בלא נתינת סימנין לפיכך מודה ר' שמעון בן אלעזר בכלים חדשים ששבעתן העין שחייב להכריז מאי טעמא דלמא אתי צורבא מרבנן דלא משנה בדיבוריה דאמר טביעות עינא אית לי בהו ושקיל להו. ואלו הן (הן) כלים חדשים שאין חייב להכריז בדי מחטין וצינורות ומחרוזות [של] קרדומות שמצאן אחד אחד וכן היה ר"ש אומר המציל מן הארי ומן הדוב ומזוטו של ים ומשלוליתו של נהר והמוצא באיסרטיא ופלטיא ומעות בבתי כנסיות ובתי מדרשות ואפי' צרורין ובכל מקום שהרבים מצוין שם הרי אלו שלו מפני שהבעלים מתיאשים מהן. ואיבעיא לן ברוב כנענים או אפי' ברוב ישראל נמי הרי אלו שלו ולא איפשיטא וקיימא לן תיקו דממונא לקולא. מעשה דמר זוטרא חסידא פשוטה

## מסורת הש"ס

[בבא בתרא קמז.], סוכה מד: [ע"ש דימרא הוא], ג) עבודה זרה מג., ד) [לקמן כו.], ה) [עיין תוס' בבא בתרא ... ד"ה תוך], ו) [לעיל ...], ז) ס"א צבורין, [עיין מהרש"ל], ח) מכשירין פרק ב משנה ח ע"ש, ט) לקמן כה:, י) שם, [צ"ל ודרכו. יעב"ץ], ל) נ"א דהאובד.

## הגהות הב"ח

(א) גמ' תניא ומודה ר"ש: (ג) רש"י ד"ה ונמלך וכו' להכי נקט. נ"ב ע"ל דף כה ע"ב:

## הגהות הגר"א

[א] גמ' בדי מחטין. נ"ב הרמב"ם וש"ע לא כתבו בדי אלא מחטין כו' ... [ב] שם דתנן. רשום קו ... [ג] רש"י ד"ה עלה. במס' סוכה כו'. נ"ב תמוה מאד ... תרמ"ו ס"ק י"ז):

## גליון הש"ס

גמ' פליגי רבנן עליה. עין זה נדרים כ"ג ע"ב:

## לעזי רש"י

פוטיא"ש. פירוש חיה קטנה כעין חולדה (תוספות סנהדרין דף טו ע"ב סוד"ה והברדלס).

## ליקוטי רש"י

כפתיה. הכריחו [קדושין ...]. ברדלס. הוא לבוע ... בבא קמא טז.]. ומן זוטו של ים. לשון ים ... משלוליתו של נהר. כשהנהר גדל ויוצא על ... [ע"ז מג.] ... בסרטיא. ... ופלטיא. ... מכוסה לא יגע בו. ...

וּבְאוּשְׁפִּיזָ – and in regard to hospitality.[1]

The Gemara explains the point of Shmuel's statement:

מַאי נָפְקָא מִינָּ – What is the practical consequence of Shmuel's bservation? אָמַר מַר זוּטְרָא – Mar Zutra said: It is relevant to now in which matters a rabbinical scholar is permitted to lie, לְאַהֲדוּרֵי לֵיהּ אֲבֵידְתָא בִּטְבִיעוּת עֵינָ – to determine whether to eturn a lost object to him based on his visual recognition of . אִי יָדְעִינַן בֵּיהּ דְּלָא מְשַׁנֵּי – If we know about him that he does ot deviate from the truth אֶלָּא בְּהָנֵי תְּלָת – except in regard to hese three matters, מְהַדְּרִינַן לֵיהּ – we return the lost object to im on the basis of his visual recognition of it.[2] וְאִי מְשַׁנֵּי בְּמִילֵּי אַחֲרִינָ – But if he deviates from the truth in regard to other natters as well, לָא מְהַדְּרִינַן לֵיהּ – we do not return a lost bject to him on the basis of his visual recognition.

The Gemara records an incident:

מַר זוּטְרָא חֲסִידָ – Mar Zutra the Pious was involved in an ncident אִגְּנִיב לֵיהּ כַּסָּא דְּכַסְפָּא מֵאוּשְׁפִּיזָא – in which a silver cup vas stolen from his host. חַזְיָא לְהַהוּא בַּר בֵּי רַב – Later, [Mar utra] saw a certain young student[3] דְּמָשֵׁי יָדֵיהּ – wash his ands וְנָגִיב בִּגְלִימָא דְּחַבְרֵיהּ – and dry them on his friend's arment. אָמַר – [Mar Zutra] said: הַיְינוּ הַאי – This is the ne who stole the cup, דְּלָא אִיכְפַּת לֵיהּ אַמָּמוֹנָא דְּחַבְרֵיהּ – for he as no consideration for his friend's property. כַּפְתֵּיהּ – Mar Zutra] bound him to a post and coerced him,[4] וְאוֹדֵי – nd he confessed to the crime.[5]

The Gemara cites a Baraisa which further defines R' Shimon en Elazar's position:

תַּנְיָ – It was taught in a Baraisa: מוֹדֶה רַבִּי שִׁמְעוֹן בֶּן אֶלְעָזָר – ' SHIMON BEN ELAZAR AGREES בְּכֵלִים חֲדָשִׁים שֶׁשְּׁבָעָתַן הָעַיִן – N the case of NEW VESSELS TO WHICH THE EYE of the owner AS GROWN ACCUSTOMED, i.e. which the owner will recognize, שֶׁחַיָּיב לְהַכְרִיז – THAT [THE FINDER] IS OBLIGATED TO ANNOUNCE his find.[6] וְאֵלּוּ הֵן כֵּלִים חֲדָשִׁים שֶׁלֹּא שְׁבָעָתַן הָעַיִן – AND THESE ARE THE NEW VESSELS TO WHICH THE EYE HAS NOT GROWN ACCUSTOMED, שֶׁאֵינוֹ חַיָּיב לְהַכְרִיז – WHICH [THE FINDER] IS therefore NOT OBLIGATED TO ANNOUNCE. כְּגוֹן – FOR EXAMPLE, בַּדֵּי מְחָטִין וְצִינּוֹרִיּוֹת – *BADEI* OF NEEDLES, AND OF SPINNING FORKS,[7] a term the Gemara will soon define, וּמַחֲרוֹזוֹת שֶׁל קַרְדּוּמּוֹת – AND STRINGS OF AXES, are all considered new vessels to which the eye has not yet grown accustomed.[8]

The Baraisa adds a qualification:

כָּל אֵלּוּ שֶׁאָמְרוּ – ALL THESE objects WHICH THEY HAVE SAID are unidentifiable, אֵימָתַי מוּתָּרִים – WHEN ARE THEY PERMITTED to the finder to keep? בִּזְמַן שֶׁמְּצָאָן אֶחָד אֶחָד – WHEN HE FOUND THEM ONE by ONE; אֲבָל מְצָאָן שְׁנַיִם שְׁנַיִם – BUT IF HE FOUND THEM TWO by TWO, חַיָּיב לְהַכְרִיז – HE IS OBLIGATED TO ANNOUNCE them. As stated earlier, the number of lost objects is considered an identifying mark.[9]

Before continuing the Baraisa, the Gemara pauses to clarify the meaning of the word *badei*:

מַאי בַּדֵּי – What are *badei*? שׁוֹכֵי – Literally, the branches of a tree. Thus, "*badei* of needles and spinning forks" are rods holding a collection of needles or forks.[10] וְאַמַּאי קָרוּ לֵיהּ בַּדֵּי – And why are they called *badei*? דָּבָר דְּתָלוּ בֵּיהּ מִידֵּי – An object on which [people] hang anything בַּד קָרוּ לֵיהּ – is called a *bad*.

The Gemara supports this definition:

כִּי הַהוּא (דתנן) [דְּאָמְרִינַן] הָתָם[11] – The word *badei* is like that which we said there: עָלֶה אֶחָד בְּבַד אֶחָד – The willow branch used on Hoshanah Rabbah need have only one leaf upon one *bad* (branch).[12]

The Gemara now resumes the citation of the Baraisa:

וְכֵן הָיָה רַבִּי שִׁמְעוֹן בֶּן אֶלְעָזָר אוֹמֵר – SIMILARLY, R' SHIMON BEN ELAZAR WOULD SAY: הַמַּצִּיל מִן הָאֲרִי – ONE WHO SAVES some-

NOTES

. When questioned about one's experiences as a guest, it is preferable to ownplay the owner's hospitality and avoid giving a favorable report. his is so that a gracious host should not be deluged with undesirable uests, who would return repeatedly and ultimately exhaust his esources (*Rashi*).

. The *Ohr Zarua* writes that it is not necessary for a rabbinical scholar o prove his integrity. Rather, he is presumed honest unless it is proven hat he has lied impermissibly. Should that happen, he is no longer rusted on the basis of visual recognition alone (see also *Rama, Choshen Aishpat* 262:21).

. Literally: a child of the teacher's house.

. He lashed him until he confessed [and returned the silver cup] (*Rosh, hitah Mekubetzes*). Others maintain that he coerced him verbally by hreatening to excommunicate him (see *Shitah Mekubetzes*).

. What is the connection between this incident and the previous assage concerning the integrity of rabbinical scholars? *Meiri* explains hat one who is inconsiderate of other people's property is not entitled o reclaim a lost object by visual recognition alone, even if he is a abbinical scholar (with a record of integrity). See *Toras Chaim* for nother approach.

. As stated earlier (23b, note 27) this holds true either where the owner s known to be a rabbinical scholar, or else in a place where rabbinical cholars are commonly found (see also *Tosafos* ד״ה ומודה).

There is a question whether R' Shimon ben Elazar's ruling regarding ew vessels is universally accepted. *Tosafos* conclude from the Gemara's vording, "R' Shimon ben Elazar *agrees* in the case of new vessels to vhich the eye has grown accustomed," that his ruling in the case in vhich the eye has *not* grown accustomed is the subject of a dispute. According to *Tosafos,* the Tanna Kamma of our Mishnah (who does not ifferentiate between new and old vessels) holds that one must nnounce even objects to which the eye has not grown accustomed *Tosafos*), because of the possibility that a rabbinical scholar might ecognize them (*Rosh*). *Ritva* disagrees on the grounds that the rgument to exempt one from announcing new vessels with which the owner is unfamiliar is so convincing that it is inconceivable that anyone challenges it. He notes other instances in which the expression "R' . . . agrees" is used even when no one disputes the issue.

7. These were small forked [needles] used for spinning gold thread (*Rashi*).

8. Why are the items which the Baraisa lists presumed to be unidentifiable by means of visual recognition? *Raavad* explains that we assume that the owner's eye has not grown accustomed to the peculiarities of his new needles and the like on account of their smallness. Larger vessels and utensils, even if they are new, are presumed to be identifiable by visual recognition (cf. *Shitah Mekubetzes*).

*Tos. Rid* draws another distinction. He reasons that the objects which the Baraisa lists are all items of merchandise. As such, the owner does not recognize them.However, personal household items, even if they are new, are presumed to be recognizable to their owners.

9. Provided it is not a standard number (Gemara, beginning of 23b). Thus, the number of needles hanging from a *bad* (rod; see next note) cannot serve as a *siman,* since it is standard. But the number of *badin* (rods) can serve as a *siman* (*Gra, Choshen Mishpat* 262:23). In this case, he announces that he has found needles or spinning forks, and the owner identifies them by saying that he lost so many rods of them (*Rosh*).

10. *Gra, Choshen Mishpat* 262:23, based on *Rosh* here. Needles of various types were commonly suspended from a rod [to prevent their getting lost]. A rod generally contained a standard number of needles, so that the number of needles on the stick would not constitute a *siman* (ibid.).

11. As emended by *Hagahos HaGra*. See *Succah* 44b.

12. On the seventh day of Succos (Hoshanah Rabbah), it is the custom to take a willow branch in hand and beat it. The Gemara here quotes the opinion of Rav Sheishess on *Succah* 44b, that one leaf on one stem suffices for this. The Gemara there also records the opinion of Rav Nachman, who mandates a minimum of three stems, each with fresh leaves (see *Rashash's* emendation to *Rashi* ד״ה עלה, and *Hagahos HaGra*).

follows: אָמַר רַב מָרִי – **Rav Mari said:** מַאי טַעֲמָא אָמְרוּ רַבָּנַן – **What is the reason the Rabbis said** מָקוֹם – that **location** along a riverbank לֹא הָוֵי סִימָן – **is not** acceptable as **an identifying mark?** כִּי הֵיכִי – דְּאָמְרִינַן לֵיהּ – **Because we say to [the claimant]:** דְּאִתְרְמִי לְדִידָךְ הַאי מָקוֹם – **Just as this** particular **location happened to** be convenient to **you,** אִתְרְמִי נַמִּי לְחַבְרָךְ הַאי מָקוֹם – **so too this** particular location may have **happened to** be convenient to **another person.** Thus, even if the claimant identifies the precise location along the riverbank where these containers were placed, it is not considered a valid identification, according to this second version.[20]

The Gemara reports an incident relating to identification by means of location:

הַהוּא גַּבְרָא – There was **a certain man** דְּאַשְׁכַּח כּוּפְרָא – **who found pitch** בֵּי מַעֲצַרְתָּא – **in a winepress.** אֲתָא לְקַמֵּיהּ דְּרַב – **He came before Rav,** and inquired as to the proper course of action. אָמַר לֵיהּ – **[Rav] said to him:** זִיל שְׁקוֹל לְנַפְשָׁךְ – **Go, take it for yourself,** since it is unidentifiable. חַזְיֵיהּ דַּהֲוָה קָא מְחַסֵּם – **[Rav] saw that the man was hesitating,** because of his concern as to the correctness of Rav's ruling. אָמַר לֵיהּ – **[Rav] said to him,** in order to demonstrate his conviction that the ruling was correct: זִיל פְּלוֹג לֵיהּ לְחִיָּיא בְּרִי מִינֵּיהּ – **Go, give a portion of it to Chiya, my son.**

The Gemara analyzes Rav's ruling:

לֵימָא קָא סָבַר רַב – **Are we to say that Rav,** who ruled that the pitch is unidentifiable, **holds** that מָקוֹם לֹא הָוֵי סִימָן – **the place** where an object was lost **is not** considered **an identifying mark?**

The Gemara answers:

אָמַר רַבִּי אַבָּא – **R' Abba said:** מִשּׁוּם יֵאוּשׁ בְּעָלִים נָגְעוּ בָהּ – **It was the abandonment of the owner** that **they touched upon** to permit it,[21] דַּחֲזָא דְּקָדְחֵי בֵיהּ חַלְפֵי – **for [Rav] saw that weeds had grown upon it.** This was evidence that the pitch had been there so long that the owner must certainly have abandoned it.[22]

The Gemara explains the last clause of the Mishnah:

רַבִּי שִׁמְעוֹן בֶּן אֶלְעָזָר אוֹמֵר וכו׳ – **R' SHIMON BEN ELAZAR SAYS etc.** that one who finds *anporya* vessels is not obligated to announce them.

The Gemara defines the term *anporya:*

מַאי אַנְפּוּרְיָא – **What are *anporya*** vessels? אָמַר רַב יְהוּדָה אָמַר שְׁמוּאֵל – **Rav Yehudah said in the name of Shmuel:** לים חֲדָשִׁים שֶׁלֹּא שְׁבָעָתָן הָעַיִן – **New vessels to which the eye has not** yet **grow accustomed.**[23] The owner has not used them long enough to b able to recognize them.

The Gemara questions this ruling:

הֵיכִי דָמֵי – **What are the circumstances** in which we speak? י אִית בְּהוּ סִימָן – **If [the new vessels] have an identifying mark o them,** כִּי לֹא שְׁבָעָתָן הָעַיִן מַאי הָוֵי – of **what** concern **is it that th** owner's **eye has not** yet **grown accustomed to them?** The owne is likely aware of their identifying mark, and the finder should b obligated to announce them in any event. אִי דְּלֵית בְּהוּ סִימָן – **they do not have an identifying mark on them,** י שְׁבָעָתָן הָעַיִן מַאי הָוֵי – of **what** benefit **is** it **that the** owner's **eye has grow accustomed to them?** Since they have no identifying mark, th owner has no way of reclaiming them. Why must the finde announce them?

The Gemara answers:

לְעוֹלָם – **Actually,** R' Shimon ben Elazar's rule holds true in a cas דְּלֵית בְּהוּ סִימָן – **in which they do not have an identifying mark** נַפְקָא מִינָּהּ – **The** practical **consequence of [this ruling] is**[2 לַאֲהַדוּרֵי לְצוּרְבָא מֵרַבָּנַן – whether **to return them to a rabbinica scholar** בִּטְבִיעוּת עֵינָא – **on the basis of visual recognition.**[2 שְׁבָעָתָן הָעַיִן – If **the** owner's **eye has grown accustomed to them** קִים לֵיהּ בְּגַוַּיְיהוּ – **he is certain about them,** וּמַהַדְרִינַן לֵיהּ – **an we return** them **to him** on the basis of his visual recognitio alone.[26] Therefore, the finder must announce them, in case the were lost by a rabbinical scholar. כִּי לֹא שְׁבָעָתָן הָעַיִן – **But if th eye has not yet grown accustomed to them,** א קִים לֵיהּ בְּגַוַּיְיהוּ – **he is not certain about them,** וְלֹא מַהַדְרִינַן לֵיהּ – **and we d not return** them **to him.**[27] Therefore, there is no reason t announce them and the finder may keep them, as R' Shimon be Elazar ruled.

The Gemara cites an Amoraic statement in support of thi principle:

דְּאָמַר רַב יְהוּדָה אָמַר שְׁמוּאֵל – **For Rav Yehudah said in the nam of Shmuel:** בְּהָנֵי תְּלָת מִילֵּי – **In** only **these three matter** עָבְידֵי רַבָּנַן דִּמְשַׁנּוּ בְּמִלַּיְיהוּ – **is it the practice of rabbis to deviat in their speech** from the truth: בְּמַסֶּכֶת – **in regard** to knowledg **of a tractate,**[28] וּבְפוּרְיָא – **in regard to** matters **of the bed,**[2

NOTES

20. However, according to the first version, if he specified the exact location along the riverbank where he left his goods, the claimant could take the kegs (*Rashi* ד״ה איכא דאמרי). Other Rishonim understand that, according to this version, Rav Mari is not dealing with the issue of a riverbank but is explaining why the location of *any* lost object can never be used as its *siman*. Thus, he is supporting Rav Nachman's conclusion (see *Shitah Mekubetzes*). [As we learned above (22b), this is in fact a dispute between Rabbah and Rava.]

21. Literally: It was because of the abandonment of the owner that they touched upon it.

22. Thus, even if it could be identified, it would belong to the finder (*Ritva*).

This still leaves the question of why it should not belong to the owner of the winepress rather than the finder, by virtue of the fact that it lies in his property (see Gemara above, 11a). *Ritva* answers that this winepress did not constitute a protected area. As stated earlier (ibid.), acquisition by one's property is effected without the owner's knowledge only when the property is protected for its owner. [Otherwise, the owner must be present and declare his intent to acquire the object by means of his property.] Since the winepress was not protected, the pitch remained available to anyone who took possession of it after *ye'ush*.

23. Literally: which with the eye has not become satisfied. *Anporya* may be understood as an acronym for the Hebrew words: אֵין פֹּה רְאִיָּה (*ain po r'iyah*), which means, "there is no visual [recognition] here" (*Rashi*; see *Mossaf HeAruch*).

24. Literally: that which emerges from this.

25. Literally: imprinting of the eye, as explained by *R' Yaakov Emder* (cited in *Moriah* vol. 5:9-10). *Tos. Yom Tov* translates it literally as "th sinking or immersion of the eye" into the characteristics of the vessel

26. Although there are no identifying marks by which to verify the rab binical scholar's claim, we rely upon his integrity, and return an objec to him on his word alone. Others, who cannot lay claim to such scrupu lousness, must verify their claim by naming the identifying marks.

27. Although the integrity of the rabbinical scholar is not in question, i is possible that he is making a mistake (see *R' Akiva Eiger*).

*Ritva* asks, based on this, why it should not be necessary to announce every lost object, even one without a *siman,* since it might belong to a rabbinical scholar who could identify it by visual recognition. He answers that we are only required to announce an object without a *siman* wher it was *seen* to have fallen from a rabbinical scholar, or in a place where such scholars are common. Otherwise, it is not necessary to be concernec that the object might have been lost by such a person (see *Rama, Chosher Mishpat* 262:21). *Ritva* also cites the view of *Raavad*, that if it is though that a found object might belong to a rabbinical scholar, the finder neec only announce it in places frequented by them, such as the study halls

28. A rabbi, for the sake of modesty, is permitted to understate the true extent of his knowledge (*Rashi*). If however, someone is in need of instruction or tutelage, he should be forthcoming with his knowledge anc not pretend ignorance (*Tosafos*).

29. One who was asked whether he engaged in conjugal relations is permitted to reply untruthfully. As a matter of decency, intimate matters should not be publicized (*Rashi*).

ומחרוזות של דגים: אמאי להוי א) אקשר סימן בקטרא דציידא דכולי עלמא הכי מקטרי ולהוי מנין סימן במנינא דשוין בעו מיניה מרב ששת ב) [מנין] הוי סימן או לא הוי סימן אמר להו רב ששת תניתוה מצא [א] בכלי כסף וכלי נחושת גסטרון של אבר וכל כלי מתכות הרי זה לא יחזיר עד שיתן אות או עד שיכוין משקלותיו בומדמשקל הוי סימן ג) גמדה דומנין נמי הוי סימן: וחתיכות של בשר וכו': אמאי להוי משקלא סימן במשקלא דשוין ותהוי חתיכה גופה סימן או דדפקא או דאטמא מי לא תניא המצא חתיכות דגים ודג נשוך חייב להכריז וחביות של יין ושל שמן ושל תבואה ושל גרוגרות ושל זיתים הרי אלו שלו זהכא במאי עסקינן בדאיכא סימנא בפסקא כי הא ד) דרבה בר רב הונא מחתיך ליה אתלתא קרנתא דיקא נמי דקתני דומיא דדג נשוך שמע מינה אמר מר חביות של יין ושל שמן ושל תבואה ושל גרוגרות ושל זיתים הרי אלו שלו והא תנן ה) כדי יין וכדי שמן חייב להכריז א"ר זירא אמר רב מתניתין ברשום מכלל דברייתא בפתוח אי בפתוח אבידה מדעת היא אמר רב הושעיא במציף אביי אמר אפילו תימא אידי ואידי ברשום חולא קשיא כאן קודם שנפתחו האוצרות כאן לאחר שנפתחו האוצרות כי הא דרב יעקב בר אבא אשכח חביתא דחמרא לאחר שנפתחו האוצרות אתא לקמיה דאביי א"ל זיל שקול לנפשך בעא מיניה רב ביבי מרב נחמן מקום הוי סימן או לא הוי סימן אמר ליה תניתוה מצא חביות של יין ושל שמן ושל תבואה ושל גרוגרות ושל זיתים הרי אלו שלו ואי ס"ד דמקום הוי סימן לכרוז מקום אמר רב זביד הכא במאי עסקינן ברקתא דנהרא אמר רב מרי מאי טעמא אמרו רבנן רקתא דנהרא לא הוי סימן דאמרינן ליה כי היכי דאתרמי לדידך אתרמי נמי לחברך איכא דאמרי אמר רב מרי מאי טעמא אמרו רבנן מקום לא הוי סימן דאמרינן ליה כי היכי דאתרמי לדידך האי מקום אתרמי נמי לחברך האי מקום ההוא גברא דאשכח כופרא בי מעצרתא אתא לקמיה דרב א"ל זיל שקול לנפשך חזייה דהוה קא מחסם א"ל זיל פלוג ליה לחייא ברי מיניה לימא קא סבר רב מקום לא הוי סימן א"ר אבא משום יאוש בעלים נגעו בה דחזא דקדחי ביה חלפי: ר"ש בן אלעזר אומר וכו': מאי אנפוריא א"ר יהודה אמר שמואל כלים חדשים שלא שבעתן העין היכי דמי אי אית בהו סימן כי לא שבעתן העין מאי הוי אי דלית בהו סימן כי שבעתן העין מאי הוי לעולם דלית בהו סימן נפקא מינה טלאהדורי לצורבא מרבנן בטביעות עינא שבעתן העין קים ליה בגוייהו ומהדרינן ליה כי לא שבעתן העין לא קים ליה בגוייהו ולא מהדרינן ליה דאמר רב יהודה אמר שמואל יבהני תלת מילי עבידי רבנן דמשנו במלייהו י) במסכת ובפוריא ובאושפיזא

## רש"י

במנינא דשוין. כבר נהגו הציידין לחרוז כמנין הזה בחרוז אחד: וגסטרון של אבר. שברי חתיכות של אבר: שיכוין משקלותיו. שיאמר משקלו ויכוין האמת: במתקלא דשוין. שנהגו הטבחים לעשות החתיכות במשקל הזה: חתיכה גופה סימן. יאמר מאבר פלוני היה: או דדפקא. לועז שמעתי ומשום רבי יצחק בר' מנחם שמעתי דדפקא פלנק"ן מקום שדופק כשהוא יגע: חתיכות דג חייב להכריז. קא ס"ד כשאין בהן סימן והחתיכה גופה סימן או מאצל הראש או מן הזנב: ודג נשוך. זהו סימן שלו: הכא במאי עסקינן. דקתני חתיכות דג חייב להכריז: בדאיכא סימנא בפסקא. שלא נחתכה כדרך החותכין: כי הא דרבה. כשהיה שולח בשר לאשתו ביד נכרי: מחתך לה אתלת קרנתא. עושה החתיכה בת ג' קרנות כזה:

דומיא דדג נשוך. דיש בו סימן: מתני'. דחייב להכריז: ברשום. חביותיהם של חרס היו וגפין אותם במגופת חרס וטורקין טיט סביב לדבק המגופה שלא יצא ריח היין ובימי שבט או ניסן שמוכרין בעלי בתים חביות לחנווני כעשר או כט"ו יחד נוטלין מגופותיהם וטועמין את היין וחוזר וסותמו וטח בו טיט סביב המגופה והוא קרוי רושם ונושאן החנווני לביתו ומתניתין בחבית רשומה והיינו סימן שיש רושמין ויש שנושאין אותה פתוחה למוכרה מיד: ופרכינן מכלל דברייתא. דקתני הרי אלו שלו בפתוחה קתני בתמיה פשיטא דהא אבידה מדעת היא שהניחה פתוחה וכל שקצים ורמשים ונחשים שותים הימנה: במציף. שהניח מגופה עליה ולא שרקה בטיט סימן ליכא ואבידה מדעת נמי ליכא: קודם שנפתחו האוצרות. שעדיין לא הגיע זמן מוכרי החביות ויחיד בעלמא הוא דעביד הוי רושם סימן: ברקתא דנהרא. והיין בא לעיר בספינה והלוקחין מפנין הספינה ומניחו על שפת הנהר ונושאין אחת אחת ופעמים ששוכח: איכא דאמרי כו'. נפקא מינה דאפי' כוון ואמר מקום מושבה מסוים לא הוי סימן: כופרא. זפת דבר שאין בו סימן הוא: מחסם. לשון לא תחסום (דברים כה) מגמגם בדבר ולבו נוקפו: דקדחו ביה חלפי. אורטי"א בלעז גדלו עליה ש"מ מימים רבים היה שם וכבר נואשו הבעלים: שלא שבעתן. עדיין לא הורגל בראייתן ותשמישן שיהא מכירן יפה ולשון אנפוריא נוטריקון אין פה ראיה: נפקא מינה כו'. וכגון דזה התובען צורבא מרבנן הוא: במסכת. יש בידך מסכת פלוני סדורה בגירסא או לאו ואע"ג שסדורה היא לו יאמר לו לאו ומדת ענוה היא: בפוריא. שימשת מטתך יאמר לאו מדת צניעות הוא:

באושפיזא

## תוספות

מחרוזות של דגים הרי אלו שלו. וה"ה מחרוזות של בשר כדאמר בתוספתא (פ"ב) וא"ת והא אמר בפ' גיד הנשה (חולין דף צה: ושם ד"ה במרוזים) אל תהא שוטה בשר במרוזים הוי סימן וי"ל גבי בשר שנתעלם מן העין הקילו טפי ו) דאין הלכה כרב מדפריך (שם) ורב היכי אכל בשרא משמע דאנן שפיר אכלינן:

מדמשקל הוי סימן מדה ומנין נמי הוי סימן. משמע דמדה עדיפא וא"ת והא אמרי' (לקמן דף כח.) יתנן לאומר משקלותיו ולא לאומר מדת ארכו ורחבו משמע דמשקל הוי סימן טפי וי"ל דה"מ בבגד דאין דרך לשקול התם ודאי משקל עדיף:

חביות של יין ושל גרוגרות הרי אלו שלו. אע"ג דתנן (לקמן דף כד:) מצא פירות בכלי חייב להכריז משום סימן של הכלי הכא רגילות הוא דכל החביות שוין וא"ת מדת היין להוי סימן וי"ל שהחבית מלאה וכל החביות שוין אבל אם אין החבית מלאה יהא סימן לומר כמה יין יש בו:

אתלתא קרנתא. וא"ת דרב אמר בפ' אין מעמידין (ע"ז דף לט: ושם) חבי"ת אסור בחותם אחד ושמואל נמי לא פליג עליה אלא בחלב אבל בשר יין ותכלת מודה ומפרש ר"ת דהתם איירי בישראל חשוד וכן משמע דמיירי התם לעיל בחבר ועם הארץ וישראל חשוד לא מרתת כמו נכרי ח):

ברשום. שכל בעל הבית עושה רשימתו משונה משל חבירו והוי סימן ברייתא בלא רשימה:

ט) אביי אמר. אפילו רשום לא הוי סימן אחר שנפתחו האוצרות שבעל הבית אחד מוכר להרבה חנוונים וכולם רשומים בענין אחד ופרש"י אינו נראה:

במסכת. וא"ת והאמר (קדושין דף ל.) ושננתם שיהו דברי תורה מחודדין בפיך שאם ישאלך אדם אל תגמגם ותאמר לו אלא אמור לו מיד וי"ל דהיינו דוקא באדם הבא לשאול דין או הוראה או להתלמד אבל הכא שבא לנסותו אם יודע מותר לשנות ולומר לא למדתי זה:

בפוריא. אין רגילות שישאלוהו כפירוש רש"י אם שימש מטתו אלא אם בעל קרי היה ולא בא לבית המדרש ושאלוהו למה לא בא ישנה ויאמר שחולה היה או שאר אונס אירע לו אי נמי שאלוהו שכבת על מטה זו לא יאמר לו כן פן יראה בה קרי ויתגנה:

באושפיזא. אם שאלוהו אם קבלוהו בסבר פנים יפות יאמר לא כדפירש רש"י דאמרינן בערכין (דף טז.) מברך רעהו בקול גדול י) בבקר השכם בערב קללה תחשב לו וא"ת והא אמרינן בברכות (דף נח.) אורח טוב אומר כל מה שטרח בעל הבית לא טרח אלא בשבילי וי"ל דהתם מיירי בין בני אדם מהוגנים והכא בין בני אדם שאינם מהוגנים והא דלא חשיב הכא מותר לשנות מפני דרכי שלום כדאמרינן פרק הבא על יבמתו (יבמות דף סה:) משום דהני נמי משום דרכי שלום הן ורגילין יותר מאחרים להכי נקט הני:

ומודה

## עין משפט נר מצוה

כז א מיי' פט"ו מהל' גזלה ואבידה הל' ו טוש"ע ח"מ סי' רסב סעיף ג וסעיף ו:

כח ב ג ד מיי' שם פי"ג הל' ה סמג עשין עד טוש"ע ח"מ סי' רסב סעיף ג וסי' רסז סעיף ז:

כט ה מיי' שם פט"ו הלכה יא סמג שם טוש"ע שם סי' רסב סעיף ח וסעיף טו:

ל ו מיי' שם הלכה ט ועיין בהשגות ובמגיד משנה טוש"ע שם סעיף ט בהג"ה:

לא ז מיי' שם הל' יא טוש"ע שם סעי' טו:

לב ח מיי' שם הלכה ט ועיין בהשגות ובמגיד משנה טוש"ע שם סעיף ט בהג"ה:

לג ט י מיי' שם פי"ד הלכה יג סמג שם טוש"ע שם סעיף כא:

## רבינו חננאל

מחרוזות של דגים דלית בהו סימן לא במדה ולא במשקל ולא בקשירה אלא מצאן בקשירת הציידין ובמניינא דשוין כלומר כל מחרוזות עשרה עשרה דגים הרי אלו שלו. וכן בשר שאין בו סימן. אבל יש בו סימן בחתיכות כדרבה דהוה מחתך בה בתלת קרנתא חייב להכריז דתניא מצא כלי כסף או כלי נחושת וגסטרון וכל מיני מתכות לא יחזיר עד שיתן אות או עד שיתן משקלותיו ש"מ דמשקל הוי סימן. ומדמשקל הוי סימן מדה ומנין נמי הוי סימן וכן הלכה. (מסובריא דנשייתא) א). כסוי הקנקנים כשהוא מהודק וטחוי בטיט נקרא רשום. כשהוא מרופרף נקרא מצוף מלשון ציפוי. ואסקינן בה אידי ואידי ברשום ומתניתא דקתני הרי אלו שלו לאחר פתיחת האוצרות שהכל כשהן באוצרות כשהן רשומין כן מוציאין אותו והכל ענין אחד הן כי הא דר' יעקב בר אבא אשכח חביתא דחמרא אחר פתיחת האוצרות ואמר ליה אביי זיל שקול לנפשך. סוגיין דשמעתא מקום לא הוי סימן. פי' כופרא אצטלע פי' מהסם מדקדק על עצמו מליגע בו כיוצא בו בהאשה שנתאלמנה (דף כ ע"ב) חזייה רב אשי לרב כהנא דהוה קא מהסם א"ל מי סברת עלך סמיכנא ומתיירא מן העבירה. ואמר רב לההוא גברא אין בו איסור אם רצונו חלקיהו עם חייא ברי כלומר אין בו איסור. פי' קדח בהו חילפי צמחו בו עשבים הנקראים חילפי והן קמשונים שצומחין בכרמים כלומר מזמן רב הוא (מוטב הוא) [מונח] הנה בזה המקום וכבר נתיאשו הבעלים: מתני' ר' יהודה אומר כל דבר שיש בו שינוי חייב להכריז כיצד עיגול ובתוכו חרש וכו' פי' עיגול של דבילה מאי כלי אנפוריא כלים חדשים שלא שבעתן העין כלומר לא עיין בהן הרבה ולא שבעה עינו בראייתם לפיכך אינו מכירן ושמועה זו בכלים שאין בהם סימן אם שבעתן עינו ומכירן ידיעה ברורה מהדרינן להו לצורבא מרבנן בטביעות עינא והני מילי בצורבא מרבנן דלא משני בדיבוריה אבל בהני תלת מילי במסכתא שקראה ואמר איני יודע אותה כי לא קריתיה כגון זה לא מחזקינן ליה בשקרי דעבד כרבנן דאמרי לעולם למד לשונך לומר איני יודע וכן בפוריא אם יאמר לך לא שימשתי וכי לא ישנה אשתי אצלי הלילה

חשק שלמה על ר"ח א) נראה דל"ל מסוברא דמייתא ועי' בערוך ערך סבר ה'.

## מסורת הש"ס

א) [לעיל כ:, לקמן כה:], ב) מהרש"ל, ג) [עיין תוס' יבמות קטו: ד"ה אתרמויי], ד) [ביצה כח.], חולין לה:, ה) [לקמן כה.], ו) [עיין תוס' קדושין ל. ד"ה אלא], ז) [עיין מהרש"ם ופר"ח סימן סג ס"ק ג ביו"ד], ח) [ועיין תוס' עבודה זרה דף לט. ד"ה אמר רב], ט) הס דיבור אחד, מהרש"ם ועיין שם, י) פירוש שמשכים בבוקר לברכו או בערב קללה תחשב לו לבעה"ב, מהרש"ל.

## הגהות הגר"א

[א] גמ' מצא כסף ונחשת גסטרון של אבר וכל מיני מתכות. כצ"ל (ועי' רא"ש ועי' רש"י לקמן כד ב' במתני' ד"ה מצא כו'):

## לעזי רש"י

פלנק"ן. פירוש הכסלים (דיא פלאנקען) (רש"י ויקרא ג, ד ועיין רש"י יהושע יט יב). אורטי"א. פירוש מיני קוצים (רש"י ישעיה לד, יג).

## ליקוטי רש"י

קשר סימן. שיש קשרים שאין דומין זה לזה ויאמר כך וכך הוא עשוי [לעיל כ:]. קטרא. קשר [שבת קיא:]. דאטמא. ירך [חולין נד.]. מחתיך ליה אתלתא קרנתא. כשהיה משלח הבשר לביתו היה רגיל לעשות כל חתיכה בעלת שלש קרנות וכבר היו מכירין אנשי ביתו שזה היה סימן שלו [ביצה כח.]. לכל חתיכה ג' קרנות ומשום סימן שלא יגנבו ממנה אנשי ביתו [חולין צה:]. רקתא דנהרא. שפת הנהר גבוה מן הנהר [מגילה ו.]. על שפת הנהר מקום שהספינות עולות לנמל [לקמן קח.]. מעצרתא. גת [עי' ע"ז ס.]. לאהדורי וכו' בטביעות עינא. כיון שאמר אני מכירה אע"פ שאינו נותן בה סימן כדאמר באלו מציאות [שבת קיד.]. פוריא. מטה [מו"ק כה.].

means of identification.[13]

The Gemara questions this answer:

מִכְּלָל – **This** explanation **implies** דִּבְרַיְיתָא בְּפָתוּחַ – **that the Baraisa,** which permits the finder to keep the jug, is dealing **with an open [container],** which is considered an object without an identifying mark.[14]

אִי בְּפָתוּחַ – However, **if** the Baraisa is dealing **with an open [container],** אֲבֵידָה מִדַּעַת הִיא – **it is** surely **an** instance of **intentional loss.** Someone who leaves his wine keg open and unguarded is surely aware that insects and rodents may well render the wine unfit for consumption. Thus, his leaving it exposed demonstrates his conscious abandonment of the wine, and it is unnecessary for the Baraisa to teach that the finder may keep it. – ? –

The Gemara clarifies its earlier explanation:

אָמַר רַב הוֹשַׁעְיָא – **Rav Hoshaya said:** בְּמֵצִיף – The Baraisa refers to a container **which he covered** but did not reseal. The covered contents cannot be considered abandoned, because they are protected from vermin. Nonetheless, the unsealed container is considered unidentifiable and may be kept by the finder.

The Gemara presents another answer:

אַבַּיֵי אָמַר – **Abaye said:** אֲפִילּוּ תֵּימָא – **You may even say** אִידִי וְאִידִי בְּרָשׁוּם – that **this** Mishnah **and this** Baraisa both deal **with a resealed [container],** וְלֹא קַשְׁיָא – **and** still **there is no contradiction.** כָּאן – **Here,** in the Mishnah, קוֹדֶם שֶׁנִּפְתְּחוּ הָאוֹצָרוֹת – it deals with a resealed container found **before the storehouses opened,** i.e. before the season in which the winemakers sell to the storekeepers, when resealed containers are uncommon.[15] Therefore, one must announce a container with such a seal. כָּאן – **Here,** in the Baraisa, לְאַחַר שֶׁנִּפְתְּחוּ הָאוֹצָרוֹת – it deals with a sealed container found **after the storehouses opened** to sell wine to the storekeepers, when thick seals are more common and therefore not an effective means of identification. Accordingly, one who finds a container with such a seal may keep it.

The Gemara cites an incident in which Abaye actually ruled according to his distinction:

כִּי הָא דְּרַב יַעֲקֹב בַּר אַבָּא – This is **like that** ruling which was issued in the case **of Rav Yaakov bar Abba,** אַשְׁכַּח חָבִיתָא דְּחַמְרָא – who **found a container of wine** לְאַחַר שֶׁנִּפְתְּחוּ הָאוֹצָרוֹת – **after the** winemakers' **storehouses had opened** and their wine was sold to the stores. אֲתָא לְקַמֵּיהּ דְּאַבַּיֵי – **He came before Abaye** to ask what he should do with the wine. אָמַר לֵיהּ – **[Abaye] said to him:** זִיל שְׁקוֹל לְנַפְשָׁךְ – **"Go, take it for yourself."**[16]

The Gemara quotes a discussion related to the previously quoted Baraisa:

בְּעָא מִינֵּיהּ רַב בִּיבִי מֵרַב נַחְמָן – **Rav Bivi inquired of Rav Nachman:** מָקוֹם הָוֵי סִימָן – **Is the place** where an object was lost considered **an** acceptable **identifying mark,** אוֹ לֹא הָוֵי סִימָן – **or is it not an** acceptable **identifying mark?**

Rav Nachman replies:

אָמַר לֵיהּ – **He answered him:** תְּנֵיתוּהָ – **You have learned the** answer to **this in the Baraisa** which states: מָצָא חָבִיּוֹת שֶׁל יַיִן – IF ONE FOUND KEGS OF WINE, וְשֶׁל שֶׁמֶן – OR OF OIL, שֶׁל תְּבוּאָה – OR OF GRAIN, וְשֶׁל גְּרוֹגְרוֹת – OR OF DRIED FIGS, וְשֶׁל זֵיתִים – OR OF OLIVES, הֲרֵי אֵלּוּ שֶׁלּוֹ – THESE BELONG TO [THE FINDER]. וְאִי סָלְקָא דַּעְתָּךְ – **Now, if you should think** דְּמָקוֹם הָוֵי סִימָן – **that the place** where an object was lost **is** considered **an** acceptable **identifying mark,** לִכְרוֹז מָקוֹם – **let [the finder] announce the place** of the find so that the owner may reclaim his containers by naming the objects left there.[17]

The Gemara rejects this proof:

אָמַר רַב זְבִיד – **Rav Zevid said:** הָכָא בְּמַאי עַסְקִינַן – **What case are we dealing with here?** בְּרַקְתָּא דְּנַהֲרָא – **With** containers found on **the riverbank,**[18] where they have been unloaded from boats. Since containers are common here, naming wine containers as the objects lost in this place does not suffice to identify them as the claimant's.

The Gemara elaborates on the status of a riverbank:

אָמַר רַב מָרִי – **Rav Mari said:** מַאי טַעְמָא אָמְרוּ רַבָּנָן – **What is the reason the Rabbis said** רַקְתָּא דְּנַהֲרָא לֹא הָוֵי סִימָן – that **a riverbank is not** acceptable as **an identifying mark?**[19] דְּאָמְרִינַן לֵיהּ – **Because we say to [the claimant]:** כִּי הֵיכִי דְּאִתְרְמֵי לְדִידָךְ – **Just as it happened to you,** that you left your goods on the riverbank, אִתְרְמֵי נַמֵּי לְחַבְרָךְ – **so too it** may have **happened to another person,** that he left the same type of goods there. Since so many goods pass through the riverbank, the mere identification of the riverbank is too vague to prove ownership.

The Gemara presents an alternative version of the above statement:

אִיכָּא דְּאָמְרֵי – **There are those who say** that the reason is as

NOTES

13. Wine was [produced in late summer and autumn and] stored by winemakers in earthenware kegs covered with earthenware lids. To seal the containers (and preserve the wine's bouquet), clay was smeared around the lid. In winter and early spring, storekeepers would come to buy the wine, and they would remove the lids to sample it. Those wine containers which were purchased for immediate resale were carried away unsealed. Those purchased for sale at a later date were resealed with a heavy layer of clay. Thus, specifying a lost wine container as resealed served to identify it (*Rashi*, as explained by *R' Betzalel Ashkenazi* in *Shitah Mekubetzes*; cf. *Ritva*).

Other Rishonim question this interpretation, and explain instead that each person's seal was distinctive. By describing the distinctive seal one could identify the wine container (*Tosafos* ד"ה ברשום).

14. Since R' Zeira considers a seal an identifying mark, the implication is that being unsealed is not an identifying mark. [The reason for this is that once the containers were opened, most were not resealed (*Nachalas Moshe*; cf. *Rashash* and *Maharam Shif*).]

The Gemara considers only two possibilities – that the found containers were open or resealed – but not that the containers still had their original seal. The reason for this is that it would be very unusual to find a container with its original seal in the street, since containers were not commonly transported through the streets with their original seals intact (*R' Betzalel Ashkenazi* in explanation of *Rashi*).

15. During this period, it is extremely uncommon for a wine container to be sealed with the thick layer of clay which is the hallmark of resealing. (The first containers to have such a seal do not ordinarily appear until several months later.) This heavier seal therefore serves as a valid identifying mark for the container.

16. Abaye issued his ruling without even inquiring whether the container was resealed, based on his view stated above, that even resealed containers are classified as unidentifiable once the winemakers' storehouses have opened for business.

17. If place serves as a marker to identify an object, it can be used in one of two ways – either by announcing the specific object found and having the owner identify the place where it was left, or by announcing that an unspecified object was found in a particular place and having the owner name the object left there. However, if place is not considered a *siman*, then naming the object found in a specified place is also not an acceptable means of identification. These two issues are interdependent as explained above (22b note 24). Thus, Rav Nachman argues, if place is an acceptable *siman*, then one should have to announce kegs and jugs of wine, by announcing the place of his find and having the owner identify what he left there (see *Rashi* 22b ד"ה מכריז מקום and note 22 there).

18. Specifically, an elevated portion of a riverbank (*Aruch*). [This served as a wharf,] where riverboats would dock to sell their wares. When someone purchased several containers of wine or other produce, he would carry them off the boat and onto the bank, and then carry them away one at a time. Occasionally, some would be forgotten (*Rashi*).

19. I.e. that one cannot identify a lost object by naming the riverbank as the place where it was lost (see note 17).

ומחרוזות של דגים: אמאי להוי [א] אקשר סימן בקטרא דצײדא דכולי עלמא הכי מקטרי ולהוי מנין סימן במנינא דשוין בעו מיניה מרב ששת ג)[מנין] הוי סימן או לא הוי סימן אמר להו רב ששת תניתוה מצא [א] כלי כסף וכלי נחושת גסטרון של אבר וכל כלי מתכות הרי זה לא יחזיר עד שיתן אות או עד שיכוין משקלותיו בומדמשקל הוי סימן ג) גמדה דומנין נמי הוי סימן: וחתיכות של בשר וכו': אמאי להוי משקלא סימן במשקלא דשוין ותהוי חתיכה גופה סימן או דדפקא או דאטמא מי לא תניא המצא חתיכות דגים ודג נשוך חייב להכריז וחביות של יין ושל שמן ושל תבואה ושל גרוגרות ושל זיתים הרי אלו שלו זהכא במאי עסקינן בדאיכא סימנא בפסקא כי הא ד) דרבה בר רב הונא מחתיך ליה אתלתא קרנתא דיקא נמי דקתני דומיא דדג נשוך שמע מינה אמר מר חביות של יין ושל שמן ושל תבואה ושל גרוגרות ושל זיתים הרי אלו שלו והא תנן ה) כדי יין וכדי שמן חייב להכריז א"ר זירא אמר רב מתניתין ברשום מכלל דברייתא בפתוח אי בפתוח אבידה מדעת היא אמר רב הושעיא במציף אביי אמר אפילו תימא אידי ואידי ברשום חולא קשיא כאן קודם שנפתחו האוצרות כאן לאחר שנפתחו האוצרות כי הא דרב יעקב בר אבא אשכח חביתא דחמרא לאחר שנפתחו האוצרות אתא לקמיה דאביי א"ל זיל שקול לנפשך בעא מיניה רב ביבי מרב נחמן מקום הוי סימן או לא הוי סימן אמר ליה תניתוה מצא חביות של יין ושל שמן ושל תבואה ושל גרוגרות ושל זיתים הרי אלו שלו ואי ס"ד דמקום הוי סימן לכרוז מקום אמר רב זביד הכא במאי עסקינן ברקתא דנהרא אמר רב מרי מאי טעמא אמרו רבנן רקתא דנהרא לא הוי סימן דאמרינן ליה כי היכי דאתרמי לדידך אתרמי נמי לחברך איכא דאמרי אמר רב מרי מאי טעמא אמרו רבנן מקום לא הוי סימן דאמרינן ליה כי היכי דאתרמי לדידך האי מקום אתרמי נמי לחברך האי מקום ההוא גברא דאשכח כופרא בי מעצרתא אתא לקמיה דרב א"ל זיל שקול לנפשך חזייה דהוה קא מחסם א"ל זיל פלוג ליה לחייא ברי מיניה לימא קא סבר רב מקום לא הוי סימן א"ר אבא משום יאוש בעלים נגעו בה דחזא דקדחי ביה חלפי: ר"ש בן אלעזר אומר וכו': מאי אנפוריא א"ר יהודה אמר שמואל כלים חדשים שלא שבעתן העין היכי דמי אי אית בהו סימן כי לא שבעתן העין מאי הוי אי דלית בהו סימן כי שבעתן העין מאי הוי לעולם דלית בהו סימן נפקא מינה טלאהדורי לצורבא מרבנן בטביעות עינא שבעתן העין קים ליה בגוייהו ומהדרינן ליה כי לא שבעתן העין לא קים ליה בגוייהו ולא מהדרינן ליה דאמר רב יהודה אמר שמואל יבהני תלת מילי עבידי רבנן דמשנו במלייהו י) במסכת ובפוריא ובאושפיזא

**רש"י**

קשר סימן. במנינא דשוין. כבר נהגו הצײדין לחרוז כמנין הזה בחרוז אחד: וגסטרון של אבר. שברי חתיכות של אבר: שיכוין משקלותיו. שיאמר משקלו ויכוין האמת: במתקלא דשוין. שנהגו הטבחים לעשות החתיכות במשקל הזה: חתיכה גופה סימן. יאמר מאבר פלוני היה: או דדפקא. לואר שמעתי ומשום רבי יצחק בר' מנחם שמעתי דדפקא פלנק"ן מקום שדופק כשהוא יגע: חתיכות דג חייב להכריז. קא ס"ד כשאין בהן סימן והחתיכה גופה סימן או מאצל הראש או מן הזנב: ודג נשוך. זהו סימן שלו: הכא במאי עסקינן. דקתני חתיכות דג חייב להכריז: בדאיכא סימנא בפסקא. שלא נחתכה כדרך החותכין: כי הא דרבה. כשהיה שולח בשר לאשתו ביד נכרי: מחתך לה אתלת קרנתא. עושה החתיכה בת ג' קרנות כזה:

דומיא דדג נשוך. דיש בו סימן: מתני'. דחייב להכריז: ברשום. חביותיהם של חרס היו וגפין אותם במגופת חרס וטורקין טיט סביב לדבק המגופה שלא יצא ריח היין ובימי שבט או ניסן שמוכרין בעלי בתים חביות לחנווני כעשר או כט"ו יחד נוטלין מגופותיהם וטועמין את היין וחוזר וסותמו וטח בו טיט סביב המגופה והוא קרוי רושם ונושאו החנווני לביתו ומתניתין בחבית רשומה והיינו סימן שיש רושמין ויש שנושאין אותה פתוחה למוכרה מיד: ופרכינן מכלל דברייתא. דקתני הרי אלו שלו בפתוחה קתני בתמיה פשיטא דהא אבידה מדעת היא שהניחה פתוחה וכל שקלים ורמשים ונחשים שותים הימנה: במציף. שהניח מגופה עליה ולא שרקה בטיט סימן ליכא ואבידה מדעת נמי ליכא: קודם שנפתחו האוצרות. שעדיין לא הגיע זמן מוכרי החביות ויחיד בעלמא הוא דעביד הוי רושם סימן: ברקתא דנהרא. והיין בא לעיר בספינה והלוקחין מפנין הספינה ומניחו על שפת הנהר ונושאין אחת אחת ופעמים ששוכח: איכא דאמרי כו'. נפקא מינה דאפי' כוון ואמר מקום מושבה מסוים לא הוי סימן: כופרא. זפת דבר שאין בו סימן הוא: מחסם. לשון לא תחסום (דברים כה) מגמגם בדבר ולבו נוקפו: דקדחו ביה חלפי. אורטיי"א בלעז גדלו עליה ש"מ מימים רבים היה שם וכבר נואשו הבעלים: שלא שבעתן. עדיין לא הורגל בראייתן ותשמישן שיהא מכירן יפה ולשון אנפוריא נוטריקון אין פה ראיה: נפקא מינה כו'. וכגון דזה התובען צורבא מרבנן הוא: במסכת. יש בידך מסכת פלוני סדורה בגירסא או לאו ואע"ג שסדורה היא לו יאמר לו לאו ומדת ענוה היא: בפוריא. שימשת מטתך יאמר לאו מדת צניעות הוא: באושפיזא

**תוספות**

**מחרוזות** של דגים הרי אלו שלו. וה"ה מחרוזות של בשר כדאמר בתוספתא (פ"ב) וא"ת והא אמר בפ' גיד הנשה (חולין דף צה: ושם ד"ה בחרוזים) אל תהא שוטה בשר בחרוזים הוי סימן וי"ל גבי בשר שנתעלם מן העין הקילו טפי ו) דאין הלכה כרב מדפריך (שם) ורב היכי אכל בשרא משמע דאכן שפיר אכלינן:

**מדמשקל** הוי סימן מדה ומנין נמי הוי סימן. משמע דמדה עדיפא וא"ת והא אמרי' (לקמן דף כח.) יתנן לאומר משקלותיו ולא לאומר מדת ארכו ורחבו משמע דמשקל הוי סימן טפי וי"ל דה"מ בבגד דאין דרך לשקול התם ודאי משקל עדיף:

**חביות** של יין ושל גרוגרות הרי אלו שלו. אע"ג דתנן (לקמן דף כד:) מלא פירות בכלי חייב להכריז משום סימן של הכלי הכא רגילות הוא דכל החביות שוין וא"ת מדת היין להוי סימן וי"ל שהחבית מלאה וכל החביות שוין אבל אם אין החבית מלאה יהא סימן לומר כמה יין יש בו:

**אתלתא** קרנתא. וא"ת דרב אמר בפ' אין מעמידין (ע"ז דף לט: ושם) חבי"ת אסור בחותם אחד ושמואל נמי לא פליג עליה אלא בחלב אבל בשר יין ותכלת מודה ומפרש ר"ת דהתם איירי בישראל חשוד וכן משמע דמיירי התם לעיל בחבר ועם הארץ וישראל חשוד לא מרתת כמו נכרי ח):

**ברשום.** שכל בעל הבית עושה רשימתו משונה משל חבירו והוי סימן ברייתא בלא רשימה:

ט) **אביי** אמר. אפילו רשום לא הוי סימן אחר שנפתחו האוצרות שבעל הבית אחד מוכר להרבה חנונים וכולם רשומים בענין אחד ופרש"י אינו נראה:

**במסכת.** וא"ת והאמר (קדושין דף ל.) ושננתם שיהו דברי תורה מחודדין בפיך שאם ישאלך אדם אל תגמגם ותאמר לו אלא אמור לו מיד וי"ל דהיינו דוקא באדם הבא לשאול דין או הוראה או להתלמד אבל הכא שבא לנסותו אם יודע מותר לשנות ולומר לא למדתי זה:

**בפוריא.** אין רגילות שישאלוהו כפירוש רש"י אם שימש מטתו אלא אם בעל קרי היה ולא בא לבית המדרש ושאלוהו למה לא בא ישנה ויאמר שחולה היה או שאר אונס אירע לו אי נמי שאלוהו שכבת על מטה זו לא יאמר לו כן פן ירצה בה קרי ויתגנה:

**באושפיזא.** אם שאלוהו אם קבלוהו בסבר פנים יפות יאמר לא כדפירש רש"י דאמרינן בערכין (דף טז.) מברך רעהו בקול גדול י) בבקר השכם בערב קללה תחשב לו וא"ת והא אמרינן בברכות (דף נח.) אורח טוב אומר כל מה שטרח בעל הבית לא טרח אלא בשבילי וי"ל דהתם איירי בין בני אדם מהוגנים והכא בין בני אדם שאינם מהוגנים והא דלא חשיב הכא מותר לשנות מפני דרכי שלום כדאמרינן פרק הבא על יבמתו (יבמות דף סה:) משום דהני נמי משום דרכי שלום הן ורגילין יותר מאחרים להכי נקט הני: ומודה

**עין משפט נר מצוה**

כז א מיי' פט"ו מהל' גזילה ואבידה הל' ו טוש"ע ח"מ סי' רסב סעיף ג וסעיף ו:

כח ב ג ד מיי' שם פי"ג הל' ה סמג עשין עד טוש"ע ח"מ סי' רסב סעיף ג וסי' רסז סעיף ז:

כט ה מיי' שם פט"ו הלכה יא סמג שם טוש"ע שם סי' רסב סעיף ח וסעיף טו:

ל ו מיי' שם הלכה ט ועיין בהשגות ובמגיד משנה טוש"ע שם סעיף ט בהג"ה:

לא ז מיי' שם הל' יא טוש"ע שם סעי' טו:

לב ח מיי' שם הלכה ט ועיין בהשגות ובמגיד משנה טוש"ע שם סעיף ט בהג"ה:

לג ט י מיי' שם פי"ד הלכה יג סמג שם טוש"ע שם סעיף כא:

**רבינו חננאל**

מחרוזות של דגים דלית בהו סימן לא במדה ולא במשקל ולא בקשירה אלא מצאן בקשירת הצײדין ובמניינא דשוין כלומר כל מחרוזות עשרה עשרה דגים הרי אלו שלו. וכן בשר שאין בו סימן. אבל יש בו סימן בחתיכות כדרבה דהוה מחתך בה בתלת קרנתא חייב להכריז דתניא מצא כלי כסף או כלי נחושת וגסטרון וכל מיני מתכות לא יחזיר עד שיתן אות או עד שיתן משקלותיו ש"מ דמשקל הוי סימן. ומדמשקל הוי סימן מדה ומנין נמי הוי סימן וכן הלכה. (מסובריא דנשייתא) א). כסוי הקנקנים כשהוא מהודק וטחוי בטיט נקרא רשום. כשהוא מרופרף נקרא מצוף מלשון ציפוי. ואסקינן בה אידי ואידי ברשום ומתניתא דקתני הרי אלו שלו לאחר פתיחת האוצרות שהכל כשהן באוצרות כשהן רשומין כן מוציאין אותו והכל ענין אחד הן כי הא דר' יעקב בר אבא אשכח חביתא דחמרא אחר פתיחת האוצרות ואמר ליה אביי זיל שקול לנפשך. סוגיין דשמעתא מקום לא הוי סימן. פי' כופרא אצטלע פי' מהסם מדקדק על עצמו מליגע בו כיוצא בו בהאשה שנתאלמנה (דף כ ע"ב) חזייה רב אשי לרב כהנא דהוה קא מהסם א"ל מי סברת עלך סמיכנא ומתיירא מן העבירה. ואמר רב לההוא גברא אין בו איסור אם רצונו חלקיהו עם חייא ברי כלומר אין בו איטור. עי' קדח בהו חילפי צמחו בו עשבים הנקראים חילפי והן קמשונים שצומחין בכרמים כלומר מזמן רב הוא (מוטב הוא) [מונח] הנה בזה המקום וכבר נתיאשו הבעלים: **מתני'** ר' יהודה אומר כל דבר שיש בו שינוי חייב להכריז כיצד עיגול ובתוכו חרש וכו' פי' עיגול של דבילה מאי כלי אנפוריא כלים חדשים שלא שבעתן העין כלומר לא עיין בהן הרבה ולא שבעה עינו בראייתם לפיכך אינו מכירן ושמועה זו בכלים שאין בהם סימן אם שבעתן עינו ומכירן ידיעה ברורה מהדרינן להו לצורבא מרבנן בטביעות עינא והני מילי בצורבא מרבנן דלא משני בדיבוריה אבל בהני תלת מילי במסכתא שקראה ואמר איני יודע אותה כי לא קריתיה כגון זה לא מחזקינן ליה בשקרי דעבד כרבנן דאמרי לעולם למד לשונך לומר איני יודע וכן בפוריא אם יאמר לך לא שימשתי וכי לא ישנה אשתי אצלי הלילה

**חשק שלמה על ר"ח** א) נראה דצ"ל מסוברא דמייתא ועי' בערוך ערך סבר ה'.

**מסורת הש"ס**

א) [לעיל כ:, לקמן כה:] ב) מהרש"ל, ג) [עיין תוס' יבמות קטו: ד"ה אתרמויי], ד) [ביצה כח.] חולין צה:, ה) [לקמן כה.] ו) [עיין תוס' קדושין ל: ד"ה אלו], ז) [עיין מהרש"ל ופר"ח סימן סג ס"ק ביו"ד], ח) [ועיין תוס' עבודה זרה דף לט. ד"ה אמר רב], ט) הם דיבור אחד, מהרש"ל ועיין שם י) פירוש שמשבח בקול רם לברכו או בערב קללה תחשב לו לבעה"ב, מהרש"ל.

**הגהות הגר"א**

[א] גמ' מצא כסף ונחשת גסטרון של אבר וכל מיני מתכות. כצ"ל (ועי' רא"ש ועי' רש"י לקמן כד ב' במתני' ד"ה מצא כו'):

**לעזי רש"י**

פלנק"ן. פירוש הכסלים (דיא פלאנקען) (רש"י ויקרא ג, ד ועיין רש"י יהושע יט יב). אורטי"א. פירוש מיני קוצים (רש"י ישעיה לד, יג).

**ליקוטי רש"י**

קשר סימן. שיש קשרים שאין דומין זה לזה ויאמר כך וכך הוא עשוי [לעיל כ:]. קטרא. קשר [שבת קיא:]. דאטמא. ירך [חולין נד.]. מחתיך ליה אתלתא קרנתא. כשהיה משלח הבשר לביתו היה רגיל לעשות כל חתיכה בעלת שלש קרנות וכבר היו מכירין אנשי ביתו שזה היה סימן שלו [ביצה כח.]. לכל חתיכה ג' קרנות ומשום סימן שלא יגנבו ממנה אנשי ביתו [חולין צה:]. רקתא דנהרא. שפת הנהר גבוה מן הנהר [מגילה ו.]. על שפת הנהר מקום שהספינות עולות לנמל [לקמן קח.]. מעצרתא. גת [עי' ע"ז ס.]. לאהדורי וכו' בטביעות עינא. כיון שאמר אני מכירה אע"פ שאינו נותן בה סימן כדאמר באלו מציאות [שבת קיד.]. פוריא. מטה [מו"ק כה.].

The Gemara analyzes the next clause of our Mishnah:

וּמַחֲרוֹזוֹת שֶׁל דָּגִים – AND STRINGS OF FISH that were found belong to the finder, because they lack any identifying mark.

The Gemara asks:

אַמַּאי – **Why** is this **so?** לֶהֱוֵי קֶשֶׁר סִימָן – **Let the** distinctive pattern of the **knot serve as the identifying mark.**[1] – ? –

The Gemara answers:

בְּקִטְרָא דְּצַיָּידָא – The Mishnah is dealing with a case where the strings of fish were tied **with a fisherman's knot,** דְּכוּלֵּי עָלְמָא הָכִי מְקַטְּרֵי – **which everyone knots in this** particular **manner.**[2] A widely used knot cannot serve as an identifying mark.

The Gemara raises another objection:

וְלֶהֱוֵי מִנְיָן סִימָן – **Let the number** of fish on the string **serve as an identifying mark.** – ? –

The Gemara answers:

בְּמִנְיָנָא דְּשָׁוִין – The Mishnah is dealing with a case **where the number** of fish sold on the string **is the standard** number.[3] Thus, the number of fish cannot serve as an identifying mark.

The previous discussion assumed that the number of fish can serve as an identifying mark. The Gemara now cites a question regarding this:

בָּעוּ מִינֵּיהּ מֵרַב שֵׁשֶׁת – **[The rabbis] inquired of Rav Sheishess:** מִנְיָן הָוֵי סִימָן – Is the **number** of items found together considered **an identifying mark,** אוֹ לֹא הָוֵי סִימָן – **or is it not** considered **an identifying mark?**

Rav Sheishess responds:

אָמַר לְהוּ רַב שֵׁשֶׁת – **Rav Sheishess said to them:** תְּנֵיתוּהָ – **You have learned** the answer to **this in a Baraisa,** which states: מָצָא כְּלֵי כֶסֶף – If ONE FOUND SILVER VESSELS, וּכְלֵי נְחוֹשֶׁת – OR COPPER VESSELS, גַּסְטְרוֹן שֶׁל אֲבָר – OR BROKEN PIECES OF LEAD, וְכָל כְּלֵי מַתָּכוֹת – OR ANY METAL VESSELS, הֲרֵי זֶה לֹא יַחֲזִיר – HE SHOULD NOT RETURN THESE to any claimant, עַד שֶׁיִּתֵּן אוֹת – UNTIL [THE CLAIMANT] PROVIDES A SIGN, אוֹ עַד שֶׁיְּכַוֵּין מִשְׁקְלוֹתָיו – OR UNTIL HE STATES THEIR WEIGHT ACCURATELY.

Rav Sheishess concludes:

וּמִדְּמִשְׁקָל הָוֵי סִימָן – **Now, since** the **weight** of a lost object **is** considered **an identifying mark,** מִדָּה וּמִנְיָן נַמִּי הָוֵי סִימָן – its **dimensions or** its **number are also** considered **an identifying mark.**[4]

The Gemara analyzes the next case of our Mishnah:

וַחֲתִיכוֹת שֶׁל בָּשָׂר וכו׳ – PIECES OF MEAT **etc.** belong to the finder.

The Gemara asks:

אַמַּאי – **Why** is this **so?** לֶהֱוֵי מִשְׁקְלָא סִימָן – **Let the weight** of the pieces **serve as an identifying mark.**[5]

The Gemara answers:

בְּמִשְׁקְלָא דְּשָׁוִין – The Mishnah is dealing with a case **where the weight** of the pieces **was uniform.**[6]

The Gemara raises another objection:

וְתֶהֱוֵי חֲתִיכָה גּוּפָהּ סִימָן – **Let the piece itself serve as the identifying feature,** אוֹ דְּדַפְקָא אוֹ דְּאַטְמָא – that is, **whether** it **comes from the neck**[7] **or from the thigh.** Why are pieces of meat considered unidentifiable objects when the owner can identify them by the part of the animal from which they come?

The Gemara cites a Baraisa to bolster its question:

מִי לֹא תַּנְיָא – **Has it not been taught** in a Baraisa: מָצָא חֲתִיכוֹת דָּגִים – If ONE FOUND PIECES OF FISH, וְדָג נָשׁוּךְ – OR A FISH THAT WAS BITTEN,[8] חַיָּיב לְהַכְרִיז – HE IS OBLIGATED TO ANNOUNCE his find. חָבִיּוֹת שֶׁל יַיִן – If one found KEGS OF WINE, וְשֶׁל שֶׁמֶן – OR OF OIL, וְשֶׁל תְּבוּאָה – OR OF GRAIN, וְשֶׁל גְּרוֹגְרוֹת – OR OF DRIED FIGS, וְשֶׁל זֵיתִים – OR OF OLIVES, הֲרֵי אֵלּוּ שֶׁלּוֹ – THESE BELONG TO [THE FINDER] because they cannot be identified. But what is the identifying feature of a piece of fish? Seemingly, the part of the fish from which the piece comes.[9] If so, pieces of meat should be considered identifiable in the same way!

The Gemara rejects the proof from the Baraisa:

הָכָא בְּמַאי עַסְקִינַן – **Here,** in this Baraisa, **with what** situation **are we dealing?** בִּדְאִיכָּא סִימָנָא בְּפַסְקָא – **Where there is an identifying mark in** the unusual shape of **the cut,** כִּי הָא דְּרַבָּה בַּר רַב הוּנָא – for example, **like that** practice **of Rabbah bar Rav Huna** מְחַתֵּיךְ לֵיהּ אַתְּלָתָא קַרְנָתָא – who **would cut** his **[meat] into triangles.**[10]

The Gemara bolsters this interpretation of the Baraisa:

דַּיְקָא נַמִּי – One can **infer** this **as well** from a **precise** reading of the Baraisa, דְּקָתָנֵי – **for the Baraisa teaches** the law for pieces of fish דּוּמְיָא דְּדָג נָשׁוּךְ – **as** being **comparable to** the law for a **bitten fish,** indicating that both share the characteristic of a distinctive cut.[11] שְׁמַע מִינָּהּ – **Learn from this** that the Baraisa indeed refers to pieces of fish cut in an unusual manner.

The Gemara questions the second clause of the Baraisa quoted above:

אָמַר מַר – **The master said:** חָבִיּוֹת שֶׁל יַיִן – If one found KEGS OF WINE, וְשֶׁל שֶׁמֶן – OR OF OIL, וְשֶׁל תְּבוּאָה – OR OF GRAIN, וְשֶׁל גְּרוֹגְרוֹת – OR OF DRIED FIGS, וְשֶׁל זֵיתִים – OR OF OLIVES, הֲרֵי אֵלּוּ שֶׁלּוֹ – THESE BELONG TO [THE FINDER]. וְהָא תְּנַן – **But we have learned in a Mishnah:**[12] כַּדֵּי יַיִן – If one found JUGS OF WINE וְכַדֵּי שֶׁמֶן – OR JUGS OF OIL, חַיָּיב לְהַכְרִיז – HE IS OBLIGATED TO ANNOUNCE his find.

The Gemara reconciles the Baraisa with the Mishnah:

אָמַר רַבִּי זֵירָא אָמַר רַב – **R' Zeira said in the name of Rav:** מַתְנִיתִין בְּרְשׁוּם – **Our Mishnah** deals **with resealed [containers].** The fact that the keg was resealed rather than open serves as a

NOTES

1. People tend to knot their strings in different ways. Thus, one who finds a string of fish should have to announce his find, since the owner can identify it by its knot.

2. I.e. it is common for fishermen to knot strings of fish in this manner and sell them. However, a string of fish that was knotted distinctively is regarded as an object with a *siman* and must be announced.

3. Fishermen would generally sell a standard number of fish on a string (*Rashi*). However, a string holding an unusual number of fish would be considered an object with a *siman* and would have to be announced.

4. [The Baraisa mentions weight explicitly, because it is the least convincing *siman* of these number-related signs.] The ability to state the number or dimensions of lost objects is even a more convincing proof of ownership than the ability to state their weight (see *Tosafos* ד״ה מדמשקל).

5. Thus, one who finds a piece of meat should have to announce it.

6. It was the practice of butchers to cut and sell pieces of a uniform weight (*Rashi*). However, a piece of meat with an unusual weight would be regarded as an object with a *siman* and would have to be announced.

7. This follows *Rashi's* first interpretation. His second interpretation, which he quotes in the name of *R' Yitzchak ben R' Menachem,* is *flank.* The word דפק means to knock or pound. The flank can be seen to heave back and forth when the animal is exhausted.

8. The bite mark serves as a *siman* (*Rashi*).

9. For example, from near the head or near the tail (*Rashi*).

10. Rabbah bar Rav Huna would cut his meat into triangular pieces and have them delivered to his house by a gentile (*Rashi*). [He did this to protect himself against the substitution of non-kosher meat. His wife would use only meat that came in this form.]

11. A fish with a piece bitten out of it has a clearly distinctive and identifiable cut. Since the Baraisa includes in the same ruling pieces of fish and a bitten fish, it is evident that the Baraisa speaks of pieces with characteristics similar to the bitten fish – i.e. an unusual cut.

However, the identification of the particular section of fish or meat is a less precise identification, and it is not considered a valid identifying mark. It is for this reason that our Mishnah rules that a finder may keep uniformly cut pieces of meat.

12. Below, 25a.

ומחרוזות של דגים: אמאי להוי [א] [א]קשר סימן בקטרא דציידא דכולי עלמא הכי מקטרי ולהוי מנין סימן במנינא דשוין בעו מיניה מרב ששת [ג][מנין] הוי סימן או לא הוי סימן אמר להו רב ששת תניתוה מצא [א]כלי כסף וכלי נחושת גסטרון של אבר וכל כלי מתכות הרי זה לא יחזיר עד שיתן אות או עד שיכוין משקלותיו [ב]ומדמשקל הוי סימן [ג][ג]מדה [ד]ומנין נמי הוי סימן: וחתיכות של בשר וכו': אמאי להוי משקלא סימן במשקלא דשוין ותהוי חתיכה גופה סימן או דדפקא או דאטמא מי לא תניא [ה]מצא חתיכות דגים ודג נשוך חייב להכריז [ו]חביות של יין ושל שמן ושל תבואה ושל גרוגרות ושל זיתים הרי אלו שלו [ז]הכא במאי עסקינן בדאיכא סימנא בפסקא כי הא [ד]דרבה בר רב הונא מחתיך ליה אתלתא קרנתא דיקא נמי דקתני דומיא דדג נשוך שמע מינה אמר מר חביות של יין ושל שמן ושל תבואה ושל גרוגרות ושל זיתים הרי אלו שלו והא תנן [ה]כדי יין וכדי שמן חייב להכריז א"ר זירא אמר רב מתניתין ברשום מכלל דברייתא בפתוח אי בפתוח אבידה מדעת היא אמר רב הושעיא במציף אביי אמר אפילו תימא אידי ואידי ברשום [ח]ולא קשיא כאן קודם שנפתחו האוצרות כאן לאחר שנפתחו האוצרות כי הא דרב יעקב בר אבא אשכח חביתא דחמרא לאחר שנפתחו האוצרות אתא לקמיה דאביי א"ל זיל שקול לנפשך בעא מיניה רב ביבי מרב נחמן מקום הוי סימן או לא הוי סימן אמר ליה תניתוה מצא חביות של יין ושל שמן ושל תבואה ושל גרוגרות ושל זיתים הרי אלו שלו ואי ס"ד דמקום הוי סימן לכרוז מקום אמר רב זביד הכא במאי עסקינן ברקתא דנהרא אמר רב מרי מאי טעמא אמרו רבנן רקתא דנהרא לא הוי סימן דאמרינן ליה כי היכי דאתרמי לדידך אתרמי נמי לחברך איכא דאמרי אמר רב מרי מאי טעמא אמרו רבנן מקום לא הוי סימן דאמרינן ליה כי היכי דאתרמי לדידך האי מקום אתרמי נמי לחברך האי מקום ההוא גברא דאשכח כופרא בי מעצרתא אתא לקמיה דרב א"ל זיל שקול לנפשך חזייה דהוה קא מחסם א"ל זיל פלוג ליה לחייא ברי מיניה לימא קא סבר רב מקום לא הוי סימן א"ר אבא משום יאוש בעלים נגעו בה דחזא דקדחי ביה חלפי: ר"ש בן אלעזר אומר וכו': מאי אנפוריא א"ר יהודה אמר שמואל כלים חדשים שלא שבעתן העין היכי דמי אי איכא בהו סימן כי לא שבעתן העין מאי הוי אי דלית בהו סימן כי שבעתן העין מאי הוי לעולם דלית בהו סימן נפקא מינה [ט]לאהדורי לצורבא מרבנן בטביעות עינא שבעתן העין קים ליה בגוייהו ומהדרינן ליה כי לא שבעתן העין לא קים ליה בגוייהו ולא מהדרינן ליה דאמר רב יהודה אמר שמואל [י]בהני תלת מילי עבידי רבנן דמשנו במלייהו [י]במסכת ובפוריא ובאושפיזא

**רש"י**

במנינא דשוין. כבר נהגו הציידין לחרוז כמנין הזה בחרוז אחד: וגסטרון של אבר. סברי חתיכות של אבר: שיכוין משקלותיו. שיאמר משקלו ויכוין האמת: במתקלא דשוין. שנהגו הטבחים לעשות החתיכות במשקל הזה: חתיכה גופה סימן. יאמר מאבר פלוני היה: או דדפקא. לוא"ר שמעתי ומשום רבי יצחק בר' מנחם שמעתי דדפקא פלנק"ן מקום שדופק כשהוא יגע: חתיכות דג חייב להכריז. קא ס"ד כשאין בהן סימן והחתיכה גופה סימן או מאצל הראש או מן הזנב: ודג נשוך. זהו סימן שלו: הכא במאי עסקינן. דקתני חתיכות דג חייב להכריז: בדאיכא סימנא בפסקא. שלא נחתכה כדרך החותכין: כי הא דרבה. כשהיה שולח בשר לאשתו ביד נכרי: מחתך לה אתלת קרנתא. עושה החתיכה בת ג' קרנות כזה:

דומיא דדג נשוך. דיש בו סימן: מתני'. דחייב להכריז: ברשום. חביותיהם של חרס היו וגפין אותם במגופת חרס וטורקין טיט סביב לדבק המגופה שלא יצא ריח היין ובימי שבט או ניסן שמוכרין בעלי בתים חביות לחנווני כעשר או כט"ו יחד נוטלין מגופותיהם וטועמין את היין וחוזר וסותמו וטח בו טיט סביב המגופה והוא קרוי רושם ונושאן החנווני לביתו ומתניתין בחבית רשומה והיינו סימן שיש רושמין ויש שנושאין אותה פתוחה למוכרה מיד: ופרכינן מכלל דברייתא. דקתני הרי אלו שלו בפתוחה קתני בתמיה פשיטא דהא אבידה מדעת היא שהניחה פתוחה וכל שקצים ורמשים ונחשים שותים הימנה: במציף. שהניח מגופה עליה ולא שרקה בטיט סימן ליכא ואבידה מדעת נמי ליכא: קודם שנפתחו האוצרות. שעדיין לא הגיע זמן מוכרי החביות ויחיד בעלמא הוא דעביד הוי רושם סימן: ברקתא דנהרא. והיין בא לעיר בספינה והלוקחין מפנין הספינה ומניחו על שפת הנהר ונושאין אחת אחת ופעמים ששוכח: איכא דאמרי כו'. נפקא מינה דלפי' כוון ואמר מקום מושבה מסוים לא הוי סימן: כופרא. זפת דבר שאין בו סימן הוה: מחסם. לשון לא תחסום (דברים כה) מגמגם בדבר ולבו נוקפו: דקדחו ביה חלפי. אורטי"א בלעז גדלו עליה ש"מ מימים רבים היה שם וכבר נואשו הבעלים: שלא שבעתן. עדיין לא הורגל בראייתן ותשמישן שיהא מכירן יפה ולשון אנפוריא נוטריקון אין פה רואה: נפקא מינה כו'. וכגון דזה התובען צורבא מרבנן הוא: במסכת. יש בידך מסכת פלוני סדורה בגירסא או לאו ואע"ג שסדורה היא לו יאמר לו לאו ומדת ענוה היא: בפוריא. שימשת מטתך יאמר לאו מדת צניעות הוא:

באושפיזא

**תוספות**

מחרוזות של דגים הרי אלו שלו. וה"ה מחרוזות של בשר כדאמר בתוספתא (פ"ב) וא"ת והא אמר בפ' גיד הנשה (חולין דף צה: ושם ד"ה במחרוזים) אל תהא שוטה בשר במחרוזים הוי סימן וי"ל גבי בשר שנתעלם מן העין הקילו טפי [י] דאין הלכה כרב מדפריך (שם) ורב היכי אכל בשרא משמע דאנן שפיר אכלינן:

מדמשקל הוי סימן מדה ומנין נמי הוי סימן. משמע דמדה עדיפא וא"ת והא אמרי' (לקמן דף כח.) יכול לאומר משקלותיו ולא לאומר מדת ארכו ורחבו משמע דמשקל הוי סימן טפי וי"ל דה"מ בבגד דאין דרך לשקול התם ודאי משקל עדיף:

חביות של יין ושל גרוגרות הרי אלו שלו. אע"ג דתנן (לקמן דף כד:) מלא פירות בכלי חייב להכריז משום סימן של הכלי הכא רגילות הוא דכל החביות שוין וא"ת מדת היין להוי סימן וי"ל שהחבית מלאה וכל החביות שוין אבל אם אין החבית מלאה יהא סימן לומר כמה יין יש בו:

אתלתא קרנתא. וא"ת דרב אמר בפ' אין מעמידין (ע"ז דף לט: ושם) חבי"ת אסור בחותם אחד ושמואל נמי לא פליג עליה אלא בחלב אבל בשר יין ותכלת מודה ומפרש ר"ת דהתם מיירי בישראל חשוד וכן משמע דמיירי התם לעיל בחבר ועם הארץ וישראל חשוד לא מרתת כמו נכרי [ח]:

ברשום. שכל בעל הבית עושה רשימתו משונה משל חבירו והוי סימן ברייתא בלא רשימה:

[ט] אביי אמר. אפילו רשום לא הוי סימן אחר שנפתחו האוצרות שבעל הבית אחד מוכר להרבה חנונים וכולם רשומים בענין אחד ופרש"י אינו נראה:

במסכת. וא"ת והאמר (קדושין דף ל.) ושננתם שיהו דברי תורה מחודדין בפיך שאם ישאלך אדם אל תגמגם ותאמר לו אלא אמור לו מיד וי"ל דהיינו דוקא באדם הבא לשאול דין או הוראה או להתלמד אבל הכא שבא לנסותו אם יודע מותר לשנות ולומר לא למדתי זה:

בפוריא. אין רגילות שישאלוהו כפירוש רש"י אם שימש מטתו אלא אם בעל קרי היה ולא בא לבית המדרש ושאלוהו למה לא בא ישנה ויאמר שחולה היה או שאר אונס אירע לו אי נמי שאלוהו שכבת על מטה זו לא יאמר לו כן פן ירא בה קרי ויתגנה:

באושפיזא. אם שאלוהו אם קבלוהו בסבר פנים יפות יאמר לא כדפירש רש"י דאמרינן בערכין (דף טז.) מברך רעהו בקול גדול [י] בבקר השכם בערב קללה תחשב לו וא"ת והא אמרינן בברכות (דף נח.) אורח טוב אומר כל מה שטרח בעל הבית לא טרח אלא בשבילי וי"ל דהתם מיירי בין בני אדם מהוגנים והכא בין בני אדם שאינם מהוגנים והא דלא חשיב הכא מותר לשנות מפני דרכי שלום כדאמרינן פרק הבא על יבמתו (יבמות דף סה:) משום דהני נמי משום דרכי שלום הן ורגילין יותר מאחרים להכי נקט הני:

ומודה

**עין משפט נר מצוה**

כז א מיי' פט"ו מהל' גזילה ואבידה הל' ו טוש"ע ח"מ סי' רסב סעיף ג וסעיף ו:

כח ב ג ד מיי' שם פי"ג הל' ה סמג עשין עד טוש"ע ח"מ סי' רסב סעיף ג וסי' רסז סעיף ז:

כט ה מיי' שם פט"ו הלכה יא סמג שם טוש"ע שם סי' רסב סעיף ח וסעיף טו:

ל ו מיי' שם הלכה ט ועיין בהשגות ובמגיד משנה טוש"ע שם סעיף ט בהג"ה:

לא ז מיי' שם הל' יא טוש"ע שם סעי' טו:

לב ח מיי' שם הלכה ט ועיין בהשגות ובמגיד משנה טוש"ע שם סעיף ט בהג"ה:

לג ט י מיי' שם פי"ד הלכה יג סמג שם טוש"ע שם סעיף כא:

**רבינו חננאל**

מחרוזות של דגים דלית בהו סימן לא במדה ולא במשקל ולא בקשירה אלא מצאן בקשירת הציידין ובמניינא דשוין כלומר כל מחרוזות עשרה עשרה דגים הרי אלו שלו. וכן בשר שאין בו סימן. אבל יש בו סימן בחתיכות כדרבה דהוה מחתך בה בתלת קרנתא חייב להכריז דתניא מצא כלי כסף או כלי נחושת וגסטרון וכל מיני מתכות לא יחזיר עד שיתן אות או עד שיתן משקלותיו ש"מ דמשקל הוי סימן. ומדמשקל הוי סימן מדה ומנין נמי הוי סימן וכן הלכה. (מסובריא דנשייתא) א). כסוי הקנקנים כשהוא מהודק וטחוי בטיט נקרא רשום. כשהוא מרופרף נקרא מצוף מלשון ציפוי. ואסקינן בה אידי ואידי ברשום ומתניתא דקתני הרי אלו שלו לאחר פתיחת האוצרות שהכל כשהן באוצרות כשהן רשומין כן מוציאין אותו והכל ענין אחד הן כי הא דר' יעקב בר אבא אשכח חביתא דחמרא אחר פתיחת האוצרות ואמר ליה אביי זיל שקול לנפשך. סוגיין דשמעתא מקום לא הוי סימן. פי' כופרא אצטלע פי' מהסם מדקדק על עצמו מליגע בו כיוצא בו בהאשה שנתאלמנה (דף כ ע"ב) חזייה רב אשי לרב כהנא דהוה קא מהסם א"ל מי סברת עלך סמיכנא ומתיירא מן העבירה. ואמר רב לההוא גברא אין בו איסור אם רצונו חלקיהו עם חייא ברי כלומר אין בו איסור. פי' קדח בהו חילפי צמחו בו עשבים הנקראים חילפי והן קמשונים שצומחין בכרמים כלומר מזמן רב הוא (מוטב הוא) [מונח] הנה בזה המקום וכבר נתיאשו הבעלים: מתני' ר' יהודה אומר כל דבר שיש בו שינוי חייב להכריז כיצד עיגול ובתוכו חרש וכו' פי' עיגול של דבילה מאי כלי אנפוריא כלים חדשים שלא שבעתן העין כלומר לא עיין בהן הרבה ולא שבעה עינו בראייתם לפיכך אינו מכירן ושמועה זו בכלים שאין בהם סימן אם שבעתן עינו ומכירן ידיעה ברורה מהדרינן להו לצורבא מרבנן בטביעות עינא והני מילי בצורבא מרבנן דלא משני בדיבוריה אבל בהני תלת מילי במסכתא שקראה ואמר איני יודע אותה כי לא קריתיה כגון זה לא מחזקינן ליה בשקרי דעבד כרבנן דאמרי לעולם למד לשונך לומר איני יודע וכן בפוריא אם יאמר לך לא שימשתי וכי לא ישנה אשתי אצלי הלילה

חשק שלמה על ר"ח א) נראה דצ"ל מסוברא דמייתא ועי' בערוך ערך סבר ה'.

**מסורת הש"ס**

א) [לעיל כ:, לקמן כה: ב) מהרש"ל, ג) [עיין תוס' יבמות קטו: ד"ה אתרמוי], ד) [ביצה כח. חולין לה:, ה) [לקמן כה. ו) [עיין תוס' קדושין ד"ה אלא], ז) [עיין מהר"ם ופר"ח סימן סג ס"ק ביו"ד], ח) [ועיין תוס' עבודה זרה דף לא. ד"ה אמר רב], ט) הס דיבור אחד, מהר"ם ועיין שם י) פירוש שמשכים בבוקר לברכו אז בערב קללה תחשב לו לבעה"ב, מהרש"ל.

**הגהות הגר"א**

[א] גמ' מצא כס ונחשת גסטרון ש אבר וכל מיני מתכות כצ"ל (ועי' רא"ש ועי' רש"י לקמן כד ב' במתני' ד"ה מלא כו'):

**לעזי רש"י**

פלנק"ן. פירוש הכסלי (דיא פלאנקען) (רש"י ויקרא ג, ד ועיין רש"י יהושע יט יב). אורטי"א. פירוש מי קוצים (רש"י ישעיה לד יג).

**ליקוטי רש"י**

קשר סימן. שיש קשרי שאינן דומין זה לזה ויאמ כך וכך הוא עשוי [לעיל כ:]. קטרא. קשר [שבת קיא:]. דאטמא. יר [חולין נד.]. מחתיך ליה אתלתא קרנתא כשהיה משלח הבשר לבית היה רגיל לעשות כ חתיכה בעלת שלש קרנות וכבר היו מכירין אנשי ביתו שזה היה סימן של [ביצה כח.]. לכל חתיכה ג קרנות ומשום סימן שלא יגנבו ממנה אנשי ביתו [חולין צה:]. רקתא דנהרא. שפת הנהר גבוה מן הנהר [מגילה ו.]. על שפת הנהר מקום שהספינות עולות לנמל [לקמן קח.]. מעצרתא גת [עי' ע"ז ס.]. לאהדורי וכו' בטביעות עינא. כי שאמר אני מכירה אע"פ שאינו נותן בה סימן כדאמר באלו מציאות [שבת קיד.]. פוריא. מטה [מו"ק כה.].

דמדרסא ברשות היחיד נוטל ומכריז דלא מדרסא והאלומות בין ברשות הרבים ובין ברה"י נוטל ומכריז כיון דגביהן לא מדרסא ורבא מתרץ לטעמיה במקום כריכות ברה"ר הרי אלו שלו דמינשתפא ברה"י חייב להכריז דלא מינשתפא והאלומות בין ברה"ר ובין ברה"י נוטל ומכריז כיון דיקירי לא מינשתפא ת"ש ככרות של נחתום הרי אלו שלו הא של בעל הבית חייב להכריז של בעל הבית מאי טעמא כיון דאית בהו סימן דמידע ידיע רפתא דאיניש איניש הוא ולא שנא רשות הרבים ולא שנא רשות היחיד נוטל ומכריז אלמא סימן העשוי לידרס הוי סימן תיובתא דרבה אמר לך רבה התם היינו טעמא משום [א] דאין מעבירין על האוכלין והא איכא נכרים נכרים חיישי לכשפים והאיכא בהמה וכלבים באתרא דלא שכיחי בהמה וכלבים לימא כתנאי ר"י אומר [ג] כל דבר שיש בו שינוי חייב להכריז כיצד מצא עיגול ובתוכו חרס ככר ובתוכו מעות מכלל דתנא קמא סבר הרי אלו שלו סברוה דכולי עלמא סימן הבא מאיליו הוי סימן ומעבירין על האוכלין מאי לאו בסימן העשוי לידרס קא מיפלגי מר סבר לא הוי סימן ומר סבר הוי סימן אמר רב זביד משמיה דרבא אי ס"ד דקא סבר תנא קמא סימן העשוי לידרס לא הוי סימן ומעבירין על האוכלין ככרות של בעל הבית ברה"ר אמאי מכריז אלא אמר רב זביד משמיה דרבא דכולי עלמא סברי סימן העשוי לידרס הוי סימן ומעבירין על האוכלין והכא בסימן הבא מאיליו קא מיפלגי דתנא קמא סבר סימן הבא מאיליו לא הוי סימן ור"י סבר הוי סימן ורבה אמר לך דכ"ע סימן העשוי לידרס לא הוי סימן ואין מעבירין על האוכלין והכא בסימן הבא מאיליו קמיפלגי ת"ק סבר לא הוי סימן ור"י סבר הוי סימן איכא דאמרי סברוה דכ"ע סימן הבא מאיליו הוי סימן וסימן העשוי לידרס לא הוי סימן מאי לאו במעבירין על האוכלין קא מיפלגי דמר סבר מעבירין ומר סבר אין מעבירין אמר רב זביד משמיה דרבא אי ס"ד סבר ת"ק סימן העשוי לידרס לא הוי סימן ומעבירין על האוכלין ככרות של בעל הבית ברה"ר אמאי מכריז אלא אמר רב זביד משמיה דרבא דכולי עלמא סברי סימן העשוי לידרס הוי סימן ומעבירין על האוכלין והכא בסימן הבא מאיליו קא מיפלגי דתנא קמא סבר סימן הבא מאיליו לא הוי סימן ור"י סבר הוי סימן ורבה אמר לך דכולי עלמא סימן העשוי לידרס לא הוי סימן ואין מעבירין על האוכלין והכא בסימן הבא מאיליו קא מיפלגי תנא קמא סבר סימן הבא מאיליו לא הוי סימן ור"י סבר הוי סימן אמר רב זביד משמיה דרבא [א] כללא דאבידתא כיון דאמר ווי לה לחסרון כיס מיאש ליה מינה ואמר רב זביד משמיה דרבא [ב] הלכתא כריכות ברשות הרבים הרי אלו שלו ברשות היחיד אי דרך נפילה הרי אלו שלו אי דרך הנחה נוטל ומכריז וזה וזה בדבר שאין בו סימן אבל בדבר שיש בו סימן לא שנא ברה"ר ולא שנא ברשות היחיד בין דרך נפילה ובין דרך הנחה חייב להכריז:

ומחרוזות

## רש"י

דמדרסא. וסימן העשוי לידרס הוא: דמינשתפא. מתגלגל ברגלי אדם ובהמה ואינה נמצאת במקום שנפלה תחילה: דיקירי. כבידות: הא של בעל הבית חייב להכריז. ואע"ג דבהדיא תני לה במתניתין [ג] איידי דנקט לאותביה מרישא כריכות ברשות הרבים דאותיב מינה לרבא נקט נמי לאותוביה לרבה מדוקי' דרישא: אין מעבירין על האוכלין. המוצא אוכלין בדרך אין רשאי לעבור עליהם ולהניחם שם הלכך לא נדרסו שמי שמצאן ראשון הגביהן: אין מעבירין על האוכלין. לאו לשון דריסה הוא אלא כמו אין מעבירין על המצות (יומא דף לג.): חיישי לכשפים. סבורים שמחמת כשפים הונחו לשם כדי להכשיל הדורסים עליהן והוי נמי דאין מגביהין אותם מיהו לא דרסי עליהן משום כשפים: לימא כתנאי. פלוגתא דרבה ורבא: הבא מאיליו. הראוי לבא מאיליו כגון חרס פעמים שנופל בעיגול: הוי סימן. דאמרינן לשם סימן נתנו שם ולא נפל מאליו ודבר שיש בו סימן הוא ואפילו הכי פליגי רבנן ואמרי הרי אלו שלו משום דקסברי מעבירין על האוכלין והוה ליה סימן העשוי לידרס: ור"י סבר הוי סימן. ואע"פ שזה עשוי לידרס נמי הוי סימן: ומעבירין על האוכלין. ואפילו הכי ככרות של בעל הבית חייב להכריז דסימן העשוי לידרס הוי סימן ועיגול היינו טעמא דסימן הבא מאיליו לאו סימן הוא ור"י סבר הוי סימן: ורבה אמר לך כו'. והכא היינו טעמא דר"י משום דאין מעבירין על האוכלין ות"ק הכי נמי אית ליה אין מעבירין ומשום הכי ככרות של בעל הבית חייב להכריז וטעמייהו בעיגול משום דסימן הבא מאיליו הוא ור"י סבר הוי סימן: איכא דאמרי סברוה כו'. וכי אתמר לימא כתנאי אאין מעבירין על האוכלין אתמר: הלכתא כריכות ברה"ר כו'. כדמוקי לה בשאין בו סימן: ברשות היחיד אי דרך נפילה הרי אלו שלו. דליכא למימר מקום הוי סימן דהא לא ידע היכא נפיל מיניה: אי דרך הינוח נוטל ומכריז. מקום ולא יניחם שם שמא ימצאם עכו"ם ויטלם ושמא שכחום הבעלים: אבל בדבר שיש בו סימן כו'. רבא לטעמיה דאמר סימן העשוי לידרס הוי סימן:

במנינא

## תוספות

**אין** מעבירין על האוכלין. פי' אינו רשאי לעבור מעליהן כדפירש רש"י אלא צריך להגביהן אבל אין לפרש דאין מעבירין היינו אין דורסין עליהם כדאמר בפרק הדר (עירובין דף סד:) דא"ל ר"ג לרבי אלעאי טול גלוסקא משום דאין מעבירין הרי משמע שצריך להגביהם ועוד דקאמר התם אבל בדורות אחרונים שפרוצות בכשפים מעבירין ואי אין מעבירין היינו אין דורסין א"כ האי דקאמר נמי שפרוצות בכשפים היינו דורסים והכא משמע [ד] דבאתרא דחיישי לכשפים אין דורסין אלא ודאי צריך לומר כדפרישית: **והא** איכא נכרים דלא איכפת להו. פירוש שידרסו הנכרים קודם שיבא שם שום ישראל ויגביה וא"ת ולפרוך והלא נכרים שקלי ליה וי"ל דדריסה שכיח אי לאו משום כשפים לפי שדורסין דרך הילוכן אבל נטילה לא שכיח שיראים שבעל הככר רואה שסבורים שלדעת הניחו שם אבל קשה דהיכי פריך שניחוש שידרסוהו נכרים קודם שיבא שם שום ישראל ויפטר מהכרזה אדרבה ניחוש לרוב ישראל שרואין הככר ויגביהוהו וניחוש לחומרא לחייבו הכרזה דהא בליבורי מעות מכריז אע"פ שאם יראו אותם הנכרים קודם ודאי שקלי להו ועוד דבעי למימר דאפילו ברוב נכרים פליגי רבנן ומחייבי להכריז ואע"ג דאיכא למיחש דלמא שקלי להו ומסתמא נתייאש ועוד דהוה ליה למימר דמנכרים נפול וניזיל בתר רובא אפילו לשמואל דאמר בממון אין הולכין אחר הרוב היכא דליכא חזקה מודה כדמוכח בפרק לא יחפור (ב"ב דף כג: ושם ד"ה חוץ) גבי ניפול הנמצא (א) [ה] אבל כל היכא דאפשר לתקן להשיב ממון לבעלים ע"י הכרזה מתקנינן וא"כ מאי פריך הכא: **והא** איכא בהמה וכלבים. וא"ת לרבא נמי יקשה והא איכא בהמה וכלבים דאכלי להו כדאמר לעיל דאיכא שקצים ורמשים דאכלי וי"ל דהכא מיירי בככרות גדולות שאי אפשר שיאכלום: **סימן** הבא מאיליו הוי סימן. פרש"י דלשם סימן נתנו שם ולא נפל מאיליו וקשה דאין דרך לתת מעות בככר לסימן אלא י"ל דאימור ידע שנפלו לו שם ומ"ד לא הוי סימן כיון דרגילות לבא מאיליו מסתמא לא ידע כיון שאין ניכר בחוץ אבל סימני בהמה שהן מאליהן הוי סימן כיון שניכר (ב) וכן דבר שאין ניכר בחוץ אם אין רגילות לבא מאיליו הוי סימן:

מחרוזות

## עין משפט נר מצוה

כה א מיי' פי"ד מהל' גזילה ואבידה הל' ג סמג עשין עד טוש"ע ח"מ סי' רסב סעיף ה:
כו ב מיי' שם פט"ו הל' ח סמג שם טוש"ע שם סעיף ט:

## רבינו חננאל

ת"ש ככרות של נחתום שלו של בעל הבית נוטל ומכריז והנה ככרות של בעל הבית אע"פ שידועין הן ריפתא דכל חד וחד כיון שאם ידרסו מתפתחין ואין ניכרין למי הן למה מכריזין תיובתא לרבה דאמר לא הוי סימן. ופריק רבה שאני ככרות דלא מדרסי כלל דאין מעבירין על האוכלין ומתני' באתרא דלית ביה לא בהמה ולא אפי' כלבים. פי' סימן הבא מאליו כגון מעות שנפלו בעיסה ונאפו בתוך הככר וכיוצא בהן. אמר רב זביד כללא דאבידתא כיון דאמר ווי ליה לחסרון כיס מיאש מינה. אמר רב זביד משמיה דרבא הלכתא כריכות ברשות הרבים הרי אלו שלו ברשות היחיד אי דרך נפילה מצאן הרי אלו שלו אי דרך הנחה נוטל ומכריז וזה וזה בדבר שאין בו סימן [אבל ביש בו סימן] לא שנא רשות הרבים ולא שנא רשות היחיד לא שנא דרך הינוח ולא שנא דרך נפילה נוטל ומכריז

## מסורת הש"ס

עירובין סד:, ב) [לעיל ], ג) [לקמן כה.], נכרים, מהר"מ, ה) אלא, מהרש"ל.

## הגהות הב"ח

תום' ד"ה והא איכא גבי ניפול הנמצא אלמא היכא: (ב) ד"ה סימן כיון שניכר בחוץ וכן דבר:

## ליקוטי רש"י

רות של נחתום י אלו שלו וכו'. כל ות הנחתומין שוין אבל ות של בעל הבית יש סימן [לעיל כא.]. תא. פת [עי' סנהדרין ]. עיגול. של דבילה [לעיל כא.].

Another ruling:
וְאָמַר רַב זְבִיד מִשְּׁמֵיהּ דְּרָבָ – **Rav Zevid also said in the name** of **Rava:** הִלְכְתָא – The **halachah** is that כְּרִיכוֹת בִּרְשׁוּת הָרַבִּ – **small sheaves** found **in the public domain,** הֲרֵי אֵלּוּ שֶׁ – **these belong to [the finder],** as the Mishnah stated.[27] בִּרְשׁוּת הַיָּחִ – If they are found **in the private domain,** the rule is as follows: אִי דֶּרֶךְ נְפִילָה – **If** they lie **in a way indicating that they had fallen,** הֲרֵי אֵלּוּ שֶׁלּוֹ – **these belong to [the finder].**[28] אִי דֶּרֶךְ הַנָּחָה – However, **if** they lie **in a way indicating that they had been placed** there deliberately by their owner, נוֹטֵל וּמַכְרִיז – **[the finder] must take** them **and announce** his find.[29]

Rava qualifies his ruling:
וְזֶה וָזֶה בְּדָבָר שֶׁאֵין בּוֹ סִימָן – **Both** these rulings **apply** only **to an object without an identifying mark,** אֲבָל בְּדָבָר שֶׁיֵּשׁ בּוֹ סִימָן – **but for an object with an identifying mark,** לֹא שְׁנָא בִּרְשׁוּת הָרַבִּים וְלֹא שְׁנָא בִּרְשׁוּת הַיָּחִיד – **there is no difference** whether it is found in **a public domain or in a private domain,** בֵּין דֶּרֶךְ נְפִילָה וּבֵין דֶּרֶךְ הַנָּחָה – or **whether** it lies **in a way indicating that it had fallen or in a way indicating that it had been placed** there deliberately by its owner; חַיָּיב לְהַכְרִיז – in all of these cases **[the finder] is obligated to announce** his find.[30]

NOTES

27. Rava, following his interpretation of the Mishnah (22b), is referring to small, unmarked sheaves [i.e. sheaves without any *siman* of their own] (*Rashi*). In the private domain these can be identified by referring to their place, as Rava explained above. In the public domain the location cannot be used as a reference for identification because of the likelihood that the object has been moved about by the traffic. However, identifiable sheaves (i.e. sheaves with a *siman*) must be returned, as Rava will soon say.

28. The location cannot be used as a marker for identification because the owner is unaware of the place where they fell (*Rashi*). Since these sheaves lack any *siman* of their own, the owner can never identify them and they therefore belong to the finder.

29. He announces that he found (unspecified) objects in a certain place, and the owner reclaims them by naming the objects, as explained above (22b).

The reason one should take them and announce them (rather than leave them in place) is because it is possible that the one who placed them there has forgotten them, and that by the time he remembers and returns for them, they will have been taken by a gentile [who does not observe the Torah's laws] (*Rashi*).

30. Rava's ruling is in accordance with his own opinion that an identifying mark that tends to be trampled and obliterated is nonetheless treated as an identifying mark, if found intact (*Rashi*).

דמדרסא ברשות היחיד נוטל ומכריז דלא מדרסא והאלומות בין ברשות הרבים ובין ברה"י נוטל ומכריז כיון דגביהן לא מדרסא ורבא מתרץ לטעמיה במקום כריכות ברה"ר הרי אלו שלו דמינשתפא ברה"י חייב להכריז דלא מינשתפא והאלומות בין ברה"ר ובין ברה"י נוטל ומכריז כיון דיקירי לא מינשתפא ת"ש ככרות של נחתום הרי אלו שלו הא של בעל הבית חייב להכריז של בעל הבית מאי טעמא כיון דאית בהו סימן דמידע ידיע רפתא דאיניש איניש הוא ולא שנא רשות הרבים ולא שנא רשות היחיד נוטל ומכריז אלמא סימן העשוי לידרס הוי סימן תיובתא דרבה אמר לך רבה התם היינו טעמא משום [א] דאין מעבירין על האוכלין והא איכא נכרים נכרים חיישי לכשפים והאיכא בהמה וכלבים באתרא דלא שכיחי בהמה וכלבים לימא כתנאי ר"י אומר [ג] כל דבר שיש בו שינוי חייב להכריז כיצד מצא עיגול ובתוכו חרס ככר ובתוכו מעות מכלל דתנא קמא סבר הרי אלו שלו סברוה דכולי עלמא סימן הבא מאיליו הוי סימן ומעבירין על האוכלין מאי לאו בסימן העשוי לידרס קא מיפלגי מר סבר לא הוי סימן ומר סבר הוי סימן אמר רב זביד משמיה דרבא אי ס"ד דקא סבר תנא קמא סימן העשוי לידרס לא הוי סימן ומעבירין על האוכלין ככרות של בעל הבית ברה"ר אמאי מכריז אלא אמר רב זביד משמיה דרבא דכולי עלמא סברי סימן העשוי לידרס הוי סימן ומעבירין על האוכלין והכא בסימן הבא מאיליו קא מיפלגי דתנא קמא סבר סימן הבא מאיליו לא הוי סימן ור"י סבר הוי סימן ורבה אמר לך דכ"ע סימן העשוי לידרס לא הוי סימן ואין מעבירין על האוכלין והכא בסימן הבא מאיליו קמיפלגי ת"ק סבר לא הוי סימן ור"י סבר הוי סימן איכא דאמרי סברוה דכ"ע סימן הבא מאיליו הוי סימן וסימן העשוי לידרס לא הוי סימן מאי לאו במעבירין על האוכלין קא מיפלגי דמר סבר מעבירין ומר סבר אין מעבירין אמר רב זביד משמיה דרבא אי ס"ד סבר ת"ק סימן העשוי לידרס לא הוי סימן ומעבירין על האוכלין ככרות של בעל הבית ברה"ר אמאי מכריז אלא אמר רב זביד משמיה דרבא דכולי עלמא סברי סימן העשוי לידרס הוי סימן ומעבירין על האוכלין והכא בסימן הבא מאיליו קא מיפלגי דתנא קמא סבר סימן הבא מאיליו לא הוי סימן ור"י סבר הוי סימן ורבה אמר לך דכולי עלמא סימן העשוי לידרס לא הוי סימן ואין מעבירין על האוכלין והכא בסימן הבא מאיליו קא מיפלגי תנא קמא סבר סימן הבא מאיליו לא הוי סימן ור"י סבר הוי סימן אמר רב זביד משמיה דרבא [א] כללא דאבידתא כיון דאמר ווי לה לחסרון כים מיאש ליה מינה ואמר רב זביד משמיה דרבא [ב] הלכתא כריכות ברשות הרבים הרי אלו שלו ברשות היחיד אי דרך נפילה הרי אלו שלו אי דרך הנחה נוטל ומכריז וזה וזה בדבר שאין בו סימן אבל בדבר שיש בו סימן לא שנא ברה"ר ולא שנא ברשות היחיד בין דרך נפילה ובין דרך הנחה חייב להכריז:

ומחרוזות

---

דמדרסא. וסימן העשוי לידרס הוא: דמינשתפא. מתגלגל ברגלי אדם ובהמה ואינה נמצאת במקום שנפלה תחילה: דיקירי. כבידות: הא של בעל הבית חייב להכריז. ואע"ג דבהדיא תני לה במתניתין [ג] איידי דנקט לאותביה מרישא כריכות ברשות הרבים דאותיב מינה לרבא נקט נמי לאותוביה לרבה מדוקי' דרישא: אין מעבירין על האוכלין. המוצא אוכלין בדרך אין רשאי לעבור עליהם ולהניחם שם הלכך לא נדרסו שמי שמצאן ראשון הגביהן: אין מעבירין על האוכלין. לאו לשון דריסה הוא אלא כמו אין מעבירין על המצות (יומא דף לג.): חיישי לכשפים. סבורים שמחמת כשפים הונחו לשם כדי להכשיל הדורסים עליהן והני נמי דאין מגביהין אותם מיהו לא דרסי עליהן משום כשפים: לימא כתנאי. פלוגתא דרבה ורבא: הבא מאיליו. הראוי לבא מאליו כגון חרס פעמים שנופל בעיגול: הוי סימן. דאמרינן לשם סימן נתנו שם ולא נפל מאליו ודבר שיש בו סימן הוא ואפילו הכי פליגי רבנן ואמרי הרי אלו שלו משום דקסברי מעבירין על האוכלין והוה ליה סימן העשוי לידרס: ור"י סבר הוי סימן. ואע"פ שזה עשוי לידרס נמי הוי סימן: ומעבירין על האוכלין. ואפילו הכי ככרות של בעל הבית חייב להכריז דסימן העשוי לידרס הוי סימן ועיגול היינו טעמא דסימן הבא מאיליו לאו סימן הוא ור"י סבר הוי סימן: ורבה אמר לך כו'. והכא היינו טעמא דר"י משום דאין מעבירין על האוכלין ות"ק הכי נמי אית ליה אין מעבירין ומשום הכי ככרות של בעל הבית חייב להכריז וטעמייהו בעיגול משום דסימן הבא מאיליו הוא ור"י סבר הוי סימן: איכא דאמרי סברוה כו'. וכי תימא לימא כתנאי אין מעבירין על האוכלין איתמר: הלכתא כריכות ברה"ר כו'. כדמוקי לה בשאין בו סימן: ברשות היחיד אי דרך נפילה הרי אלו שלו. דליכא למימר מקום הוי סימן דהא לא ידע היכא נפיל מיניה: אי דרך הינוח נוטל ומכריז. מקום ולא יניחם שם שמא ימצאם עכו"ם ויטלם ושמא שכחום הבעלים: אבל בדבר שיש בו סימן כו'. רבא לטעמיה דאמר סימן העשוי לידרס הוי סימן:

במנינא

---

**אין** מעבירין על האוכלין. פי' אינו רשאי לעבור מעליהן כדפירש רש"י אלא צריך להגביהן אבל אין לפרש דאין מעבירין היינו אין דורסין עליהם כדאמר בפרק הדר (עירובין דף סד:) דא"ל ר"ג לרבי אלעאי טול גלוסקא משום דאין מעבירין הרי משמע שצריך להגביהם ועוד דקאמר התם אבל בדורות אחרונים שפרוצות בכשפים מעבירין ואי אין מעבירין היינו אין דורסין א"כ האי דקאמר נמי שפרוצות בכשפים היינו דורסים והכא משמע [ד] דבאתרא דחיישי לכשפים אין דורסין אלא ודאי צריך לומר כדפרישית: **והא** איכא נכרים דלא איכפת להו. פירוש שידרסו הנכרים קודם שיבא שם שום ישראל ויגביה וא"ת ולפרוך והלא נכרים שקלי ליה וי"ל דדריסה שכיח אי לאו משום כשפים לפי שדורסין דרך הילוכן אבל נטילה לא שכיח שיראים שבעל הככר רואה שסבורים שלדעת הניחו שם אבל קשה דהיכי פריך שניחוש שידרסוהו נכרים קודם שיבא שם שום ישראל ויפטר מהכרזה אדרבה ניחוש לרוב ישראל שרואין הככר ויגביהוהו וניחוש לחומרא לחייבו הכרזה דהא בליבורי מעות מכריז אע"פ שאם יראו אותם הנכרים קודם ודאי שקלי להו ועוד דבעי למימר דאפילו ברוב נכרים פליגי רבנן ומחייבי להכריז ואע"ג דאיכא למיחש דלמא שקלי להו ומסתמא נתייאש ועוד דהוה ליה למימר דמנכרים נפול וניזיל בתר רובא אפילו לשמואל דאמר בממון אין הולכין אחר הרוב היכא דליכא חזקה מודה כדמוכח בפרק לא יחפור (ב"ב דף כג: ושם ד"ה חוץ) גבי ניפול הנמצא (א) [ה] אבל כל היכא דאפשר לתקן להשיב ממון לבעלים ע"י הכרזה מתקנינן וא"כ מאי פריך הכא: **והא** איכא בהמה וכלבים. וא"ת לרבא נמי יקשה והא איכא בהמה וכלבים דאכלי להו כדאמר לעיל דאיכא שקצים ורמשים דאכלי וי"ל דהכא מיירי בככרות גדולות שאי אפשר שיאכלום:

**סימן** הבא מאיליו הוי סימן. פרש"י דלשם סימן נתנו שם ולא נפל מאיליו וקשה דאין דרך לתת מעות בככר לסימן אלא י"ל דאימור ידע שנפלו לו שם ומ"ד לא הוי סימן כיון דרגילות לבא מאיליו מסתמא לא ידע כיון שאין ניכר בחוץ אבל סימני בהמה שהן מאיליהן הוי סימן כיון שניכר (ב) וכן דבר שאין ניכר בחוץ אם אין רגילות לבא מאיליו הוי סימן:

מחרוזות

---

עין משפט
נר מצוה

כה א מיי' פי"ד מהל' גזילה ואבידה הל' ג סמג עשין עד טוש"ע ח"מ סי' רסב סעיף ה:
כו ב מיי' שם פט"ו הל' ח סמג שם טוש"ע שם סעיף ט:

## רבינו חננאל

ת"ש ככרות של נחתום שלו של בעל הבית נוטל ומכריז והנה ככרות של בעל הבית אע"פ שידועין הן ריפתא דכל חד וחד כיון שאם ידרסו מתפתחין ואין ניכרין למי הן למה מכריזין תיובתא לרבה דאמר לא הוי סימן. ופריק רבה שאני ככרות דלא מדרסי כלל דאין מעבירין על האוכלין ומתני' באתרא דלית ביה לא בהמה ולא אפי' כלבים. פי' סימן הבא מאליו כגון מעות שנפלו בעיסה ונאפו בתוך הככר וכיוצא בהן. אמר רב זביד כללא דאבידתא כיון דאמר ווי ליה לחסרון כיס מיאש מינה. אמר רב זביד משמיה דרבא הלכתא כריכות ברשות הרבים הרי אלו שלו ברשות היחיד אי דרך נפילה מצאן הרי אלו שלו אי דרך הנחה נוטל ומכריז וזה וזה בדבר שאין בו סימן [אבל ביש בו סימן] לא שנא רשות הרבים ולא שנא רשות היחיד לא שנא דרך הינוח ולא שנא דרך נפילה נוטל ומכריז

---

מסורת הש"ם

...ירובין סד:], ב) [לעיל ...
ג) [לקמן כה.],
...כרים, מהר"מ,
ה) אלא, מהרש"ל.

## הגהות הב"ח

...תוס' ד"ה והא איכא ...גבי ניפול הנמצא אלמא ...איכא: (ב) ד"ה סימן כיון שניכר בחוץ וכן דבר:

## ליקוטי רש"י

...ות של נחתום אלו שלו וכו'. כל ...ת הנחתומין שוין אבל ...ת של בעל הבית יש סימן [לעיל כא.]. ...תא. פת [עי' סנהדרין ...]. עיגול. של דבילה [לעיל כא.].

anna Kamma holds that לֹא הָוֵי סִימָן – it is not treated as an lentifying mark. Thus, one who finds a fig cake with a pottery hard in it is *not* required to announce it. וְרַבִּי יְהוּדָה סָבַר – lowever, R' Yehudah holds that הָוֵי סִימָן – it is treated as an lentifying mark. Thus, one who finds a fig cake with a pottery hard in it must announce it.[21]

The Gemara presents a different version of the previous disussion. According to this version, the discussion began with an ttempt to demonstrate that there is a dispute of Tannaim egarding the question of passing by food in the street without icking it up:[22]

אִיכָּא דְּאָמְרֵ – There are those who say that the discussion went s follows: סְבָרוּהָ – They assumed דְּכוּלֵּי עָלְמָא – that everyne (both the Tanna Kamma and R' Yehudah) agrees that סִימָן הַבָּא מֵאֵילָיו הָוֵי סִי – an identifying mark that may have come bout on its own is nonetheless treated as an identifying nark. וְסִימָן הֶעָשׂוּי לִידָּרֵס לֹא הָוֵי סִימָן – Moreover, everyone agrees nat an identifying mark that tends to be trampled is *not* eated as an identifying mark, even if it is found intact. מַאי לָ – Is it not בְּמַעֲבִירִין עַל הָאוֹכָלִין קָא מִיפַּלְגֵי – that they isagree about whether one is permitted to pass by food on the round and leave it there? דְּמַר סָבַר – This master, the Tanna amma, holds that מַעֲבִירִין – one is permitted to pass by food n the ground and leave it there. Thus, the identifying mark of the aves or fig cakes may very well be trampled underfoot. וּמַר סָבַר – However, the other master, R' Yehudah, holds that אֵין מַעֲבִיר – one is not permitted to pass by food on the ground and ave it there. It is likely, therefore, that the identifying mark will emain intact.[23]

The Gemara rejects this interpretation of the dispute because ne position it attributes to the Tanna Kamma contradicts an arlier ruling of the Mishnah:

אָמַר רַב זְבִיד מִשְּׁמֵיהּ דְּרָבָ – Rav Zevid said in the name of Rava: אִי סָלְקָא דַּעְתָּ – If you should think סָבַר תַּנָּא קַמָּא – that the anna Kamma holds סִימָן הֶעָשׂוּי לִידָּרֵס לֹא הָוֵי סִימָן – that an lentifying mark that tends to be trampled and obliterated is ot treated as an identifying mark, even if it is found intact, וּמַעֲבִירִין עַל הָאוֹכָל – and that he also holds that one is ermitted to pass by food on the ground and leave it there, as iggested above, כִּכָּרוֹת שֶׁל בַּעַל הַבַּיִת בִּרְשׁוּת הָרַבִּים אַמַּאי מַכְרִיז – then why does the Mishnah rule earlier that one who finds a ouseholder's homemade loaves must announce his find? The istinctiveness of the homemade breads is apt to be obliterated as ne bread is trampled underfoot.[24] – ? –

Having refuted the previous interpretation of the dispute, Rava offers another interpretation, one consistent with his view:

אֶלָּא אָמַר רַב זְבִיד מִשְּׁמֵיהּ דְּרָבָא – Rather, Rav Zevid said in the name of Rava that the dispute should be explained as follows:[25] דְּכוּלֵּי עָלְמָא סָבְרֵי – Everyone (both the Tanna Kamma and R' Yehudah) agrees סִימָן הֶעָשׂוּי לִידָּרֵס הָוֵי סִימָן – that an identifying mark that tends to be trampled and obliterated is nonetheless treated as an identifying mark, if found intact. וּמַעֲבִירִין עַל הָאוֹכָלִין – Moreover, everyone agrees that one may pass by food on the ground and leave it there. וְהָכָא – And here, in the case of the fig cake with a pottery shard in it, בְּסִימָן הַבָּא מֵאֵילָיו קָא מִיפַּלְגֵי – they disagree regarding the significance of an identifying mark that may have come about on its own. דְּתַנָּא קַמָּא סָבַר סִימָן הַבָּא מֵאֵילָיו לֹא הָוֵי סִימָן – The Tanna Kamma holds that an identifying mark that may have come about on its own is not treated as an identifying mark. Thus, one who finds a fig cake with only a pottery shard to identify it is not required to announce it. וְרַבִּי יְהוּדָה סָבַר – However, R' Yehudah holds that הָוֵי סִימָן – it is indeed treated as an identifying mark. Therefore, one who finds a fig cake with a pottery shard in it must announce his find.

The Gemara now offers a second explanation of the dispute, this one consistent with Rabbah's view:

וְרַבָּה אָמַר לָךְ – Now Rabbah would say to you דְּכוּלֵּי עָלְמָא – that everyone agrees that סִימָן הֶעָשׂוּי לִידָּרֵס לֹא הָוֵי סִימָן – an identifying mark that tends to be trampled and obliterated is not treated as an identifying mark, even if it is found intact. וְאֵין מַעֲבִירִין עַל הָאוֹכָלִין – Moreover, everyone agrees that we may not pass by food on the ground and leave it there. וְהָכָא – And here, in the case of the fig cake with the pottery shard in it, בְּסִימָן הַבָּא מֵאֵילָיו קָא מִיפַּלְגֵי – they disagree regarding the significance of an identifying mark that may have come about on its own. תַּנָּא קַמָּא סָבַר סִימָן הַבָּא מֵאֵילָיו לֹא הָוֵי סִימָן – The Tanna Kamma holds that it is not treated as an identifying mark. Thus, one who finds a fig cake with a shard in it is not required to announce it. וְרַבִּי יְהוּדָה סָבַר הָוֵי סִימָן – However, R' Yehudah holds that it is treated as an identifying mark. Thus, one who finds a fig cake with a shard in it must announce it.

The Gemara cites a general rule in regard to lost objects:

אָמַר רַב זְבִיד מִשְּׁמֵיהּ דְּרָבָא – Rav Zevid said in the name of Rava: כְּלָלָא דַּאֲבֵידְתָא – The rule for lost objects is: כֵּיוָן דְּאָמַר – Once [the owner] has said, וַוי לֵהּ לְחֶסְרוֹן כִּיס – "Woe to me for the monetary loss I have sustained," מִיָּאֵשׁ לֵיהּ מִינָּהּ – he has given up hope of ever recovering it, and whoever finds it now may keep it.[26]

NOTES

arks will remain intact. Consequently, one who finds a fig cake with a nard in it or a homemade loaf should have to announce his find. The eason there is a dispute in regard to the fig cake is because the shard is mething that might have fallen into the cake without the owner's nowledge (*Rashi*).

1. **In summary:** According to both explanations, the dispute is hether a *siman* that might have come about on its own is treated as a *man*. In all other respects, however, the shard would qualify as a *man*. According to Rava, this is because a *siman* that tends to be ampled is nonetheless treated as a *siman*. Therefore, even though the ard will often be dislodged by the passing traffic (since it is permissible r people to pass by food without picking it up), should it remain in the ke, it serves as a *siman* and the finder must announce the find. ccording to Rabbah, the shard serves as a *siman* because it is not likely have been dislodged, inasmuch as it is forbidden to pass by food lying the street and not pick it up. See chart below.

2. This is in contrast to the first version, which began with an attempt prove that the validity of an identifying mark that tends to be ampled is the subject of the Tannaic dispute. In this version, the permissibility of leaving food on the ground is proposed as the subject of that Tannaic dispute (*Rashi*).

23. The owner therefore counts on the *siman* remaining intact and does not despair of recovering his lost article.

24. See note 17 above.

25. From here on, the second version of the discussion is identical to the first version. See notes above and accompanying chart.

| | PASSING BY FOOD | *SIMAN* THAT MAY COME ABOUT ON ITS OWN | *SIMAN* THAT TENDS TO BE TRAMPLED |
|---|---|---|---|
| FIRST EXPLANATION | PERMISSIBLE | *SIMAN* | DISPUTED |
| RAVA | PERMISSIBLE | DISPUTED | *SIMAN* |
| RABBAH | FORBIDDEN | DISPUTED | NOT A *SIMAN* |
| OTHERS SAY | DISPUTED | *SIMAN* | NOT A *SIMAN* |

26. There is no need for the owner to renounce his rights formally. Rather, the termination of his rights occurs when the owner expresses, in any manner, his belief in the hopelessness of recovering the lost object (see *Chazon Ish, Bava Kamma* 18:1; see also note 2 to the Mishnah on 21a).

דמדרסא ברשות היחיד נוטל ומכריז דלא מדרסא והאלומות בין ברשות הרבים ובין ברה"י נוטל ומכריז כיון דגביהן לא מדרסא ורבא מתרץ לטעמיה במקום כריכות ברה"ר הרי אלו שלו דמינשתפא ברה"י חייב להכריז דלא מינשתפא והאלומות בין ברה"ר ובין ברה"י נוטל ומכריז כיון דיקירי לא מינשתפא ת"ש ככרות של נחתום הרי אלו שלו הא של בעל הבית חייב להכריז של בעל הבית מאי טעמא כיון דאית בהו סימן דמידע ידיע רפתא דאיניש איניש הוא ולא שנא רשות הרבים ולא שנא רשות היחיד נוטל ומכריז אלמא סימן העשוי לידרס הוי סימן תיובתא דרבה אמר לך רבה התם היינו טעמא משום [א] דאין מעבירין על האוכלין והא איכא נכרים נכרים חיישי לכשפים והאיכא בהמה וכלבים באתרא דלא שכיחי בהמה וכלבים לימא כתנאי ר"י אומר [ג] כל דבר שיש בו שינוי חייב להכריז כיצד מצא עיגול ובתוכו חרס ככר ובתוכו מעות מכלל דתנא קמא סבר הרי אלו שלו סברוה דכולי עלמא סימן הבא מאליו הוי סימן ומעבירין על האוכלין מאי לאו בסימן העשוי לידרס קא מיפלגי מר סבר לא הוי סימן ומר סבר הוי סימן אמר רב זביד משמיה דרבא אי ס"ד דקא סבר תנא קמא סימן העשוי לידרס לא הוי סימן ומעבירין על האוכלין ככרות של בעל הבית ברה"ר אמאי מכריז אלא אמר רב זביד משמיה דרבא דכולי עלמא סברי סימן העשוי לידרס הוי סימן ומעבירין על האוכלין והכא בסימן הבא מאליו קא מיפלגי דתנא קמא סבר סימן הבא מאליו לא הוי סימן ור"י סבר הוי סימן ורבה אמר לך דכ"ע סימן העשוי לידרס לא הוי סימן ואין מעבירין על האוכלין והכא בסימן הבא מאליו קמיפלגי ת"ק סבר לא הוי סימן ור"י סבר הוי סימן איכא דאמרי סברוה דכ"ע סימן הבא מאליו הוי סימן וסימן העשוי לידרס לא הוי סימן מאי לאו במעבירין על האוכלין קא מיפלגי דמר סבר מעבירין ומר סבר אין מעבירין אמר רב זביד משמיה דרבא אי ס"ד סבר ת"ק סימן העשוי לידרס לא הוי סימן ומעבירין על האוכלין ככרות של בעל הבית ברה"ר אמאי מכריז אלא אמר רב זביד משמיה דרבא דכולי עלמא סברי סימן העשוי לידרס הוי סימן ומעבירין על האוכלין והכא בסימן הבא מאליו קא מיפלגי דתנא קמא סבר סימן הבא מאליו לא הוי סימן ור"י סבר הוי סימן ורבה אמר לך דכולי עלמא סימן העשוי לידרס לא הוי סימן ואין מעבירין על האוכלין והכא בסימן הבא מאליו קא מיפלגי תנא קמא סבר סימן הבא מאליו לא הוי סימן ור"י סבר הוי סימן אמר רב זביד משמיה דרבא [א]כללא דאבידתא כיון דאמר ווי לה לחסרון כיס מיאש ליה מינה ואמר רב זביד משמיה דרבא [ב]הלכתא כריכות ברשות הרבים הרי אלו שלו ברשות היחיד אי דרך נפילה הרי אלו שלו אי דרך הנחה נוטל ומכריז וזה וזה בדבר שאין בו סימן אבל בדבר שיש בו סימן לא שנא ברה"ר ולא שנא ברשות היחיד בין דרך נפילה ובין דרך הנחה חייב להכריז:

ומחרוזות

**רש"י**

**דמדרסא.** וסימן העשוי לידרס הוא: **דמינשתפא.** מתגלגל ברגלי אדם ובהמה ואינה נמצאת במקום שנפלה תחילה: **דיקירי.** כבידות: **הא של בעל הבית חייב להכריז.** ואע"ג דבהדיא תני לה במתניתין [ג] איידי דנקט לאותביה מרישא כריכות ברשות הרבים דאותיב מינה לרבא נקט נמי לאותוביה לרבה מדוקי' דרישא: **אין מעבירין על האוכלין.** המוצא אוכלין בדרך אין רשאי לעבור עליהם ולהניחם שם הלכך לא נדרסו שמי שמצאן ראשון הגביהן: **אין מעבירין על האוכלין.** לאו לשון דריסה הוא אלא כמו אין מעבירין על המצות (יומא דף לג.): **חיישי לכשפים.** סבורים שמחמת כשפים הונחו לשם כדי להכשיל הדורסים עליהן ונהי נמי דאין מגביהין אותם מיהו לא דרסי עליהן משום כשפים: **לימא כתנאי.** פלוגתא דרבה ורבא: **הבא מאליו.** הראוי לבא מאליו כגון חרס פעמים שנופל בעיגול: **הוי סימן.** דאמרינן לשם סימן נתנו שם ולא נפל מאליו ודבר שיש בו סימן הוא ואפילו הכי פליגי רבנן ואמרי הרי אלו שלו משום דקסברי מעבירין על האוכלין והוה ליה סימן העשוי לידרס: **ור"י סבר** הוי סימן. ואע"פ שזה עשוי לידרס נמי הוי סימן: **ומעבירין על האוכלין.** ואפילו הכי ככרות של בעל הבית חייב להכריז דסימן העשוי לידרס הוי סימן ועיגול היינו טעמא דסימן הבא מאליו לאו סימן הוא ור"י סבר הוי סימן: **ורבה אמר לך כו'.** והכא היינו טעמא דר"י משום דאין מעבירין על האוכלין ות"ק הכי נמי אית ליה אין מעבירין ומשום הכי ככרות של בעל הבית חייב להכריז וטעמייהו בעיגול משום דסימן הבא מאליו הוא ור"י סבר הוי סימן: **איכא דאמרי סברוה כו'.** וכי אתמר לימא כתנאי אאין מעבירין על האוכלין אתמר: **הלכתא כריכות ברה"ר כו'.** כדמוקי לה בשאין בו סימן: **ברשות היחיד אי דרך נפילה הרי אלו שלו.** דליכא למימר מקום הוי סימן דהא לא ידע היכא נפיל מיניה: **אי דרך הינוח נוטל ומכריז.** מקום ולא יניחם שם שמא ימצאם עכו"ם ויטלם ושמא שכחום הבעלים: **אבל בדבר שיש בו סימן כו'.** רבא לטעמיה דאמר סימן העשוי לידרס הוי סימן:

במנינא

**תוספות**

**אין** מעבירין על האוכלין. פי' אינו רשאי לעבור מעליהן כדפירש רש"י אלא צריך להגביהן אבל אין לפרש דאין מעבירין היינו אין דורסין עליהם כדאמר בפרק הדר (עירובין דף סד:) דא"ל ר"ג לרבי אלעאי טול גלוסקא משום דאין מעבירין הרי משמע שצריך להגביהם ועוד דקאמר התם אבל בדורות אחרונים שפרוצות בכשפים מעבירין ואי אין מעבירין היינו אין דורסין א"כ האי דקאמר נמי שפרוצות בכשפים היינו דורסים והכא משמע [ד]דבאתרא דחיישי לכשפים אין דורסין אלא ודאי צריך לומר כדפרישית: **והא** איכא נכרים דלא איכפת להו. פירוש שידרסו הנכרים קודם שיבא שם שום ישראל ויגביה וא"ת ולפרוך והלא נכרים שקלי ליה וי"ל דדריסה שכיח אי לאו משום כשפים לפי שדורסין דרך הילוכן אבל נטילה לא שכיח שיראים שבעל הככר רואה שסבורים שלדעת הניחו שם אבל קשה דהיכי פריך שניחוש שידרסוהו נכרים קודם שיבא שם שום ישראל ויפטר מהכרזה אדרבה ניחוש לרוב ישראל שרואין הככר ויגביהוהו וניחוש לחומרא לחייבו הכרזה דהא בליבורי מעות מכריז אע"פ שאם יראו אותם הנכרים קודם ודאי שקלי להו ועוד דבעי למימר דאפילו ברוב נכרים פליגי רבנן ומחייבי להכריז ואע"ג דאיכא למיחש דלמא שקלי להו ומסתמא נתייאש ועוד דהוה ליה למימר דמנכרים נפול וניזיל בתר רובא אפילו לשמואל דאמר בממון אין הולכין אחר הרוב היכא דליכא חזקה מודה כדמוכח בפרק לא יחפור (ב"ב דף כג: ושם ד"ה חוץ) גבי ניפול הנמצא (א) [ה] אבל כל היכא דאפשר לתקן להשיב ממון לבעלים ע"י הכרזה מתקנינן וא"כ מאי פריך הכא: **והא** איכא בהמה וכלבים. וא"ת לרבא נמי יקשה והא איכא בהמה וכלבים דאכלי להו כדאמר לעיל דאיכא שקצים ורמשים דאכלי וי"ל דהכא מיירי בככרות גדולות שאי אפשר שיאכלום: **סימן** הבא מאליו הוי סימן. פרש"י דלשם סימן נתנו שם ולא נפל מאליו וקשה דאין דרך לתת מעות בככר לסימן אלא י"ל דאימור ידע שנפלו לו שם ומ"ד לא הוי סימן כיון דרגילות לבא מאליו מסתמא לא ידע כיון שאין ניכר בחוץ אבל סימני בהמה שהן מאליהן הוי סימן כיון שניכר (ב) וכן דבר שאין ניכר בחוץ אם אין רגילות לבא מאליו הוי סימן:

מחרוזות

**עין משפט נר מצוה**

כה א מיי' פי"ד מהל' גזילה ואבידה הל' ג סמג עשין עד טוש"ע ח"מ סי' רסב סעיף ה:

כו ב מיי' שם פט"ו הל' ח סמג שם טוש"ע שם סעיף ט:

**רבינו חננאל**

ת"ש ככרות של נחתום שלו של בעל הבית נוטל ומכריז והנה ככרות של בעל הבית אע"פ שידועין הן ריפתא דכל חד וחד כיון שאם ידרסו מתפתחין ואין ניכרין למי הן למה מכריזין תיובתא לרבה דאמר לא הוי סימן. ופריק רבה שאני ככרות דלא מדרסי כלל דאין מעבירין על האוכלין ומתני' באתרא דלית ביה לא בהמה ולא אפי' כלבים. פי' סימן הבא מאליו כגון מעות שנפלו בעיסה ונאפו בתוך הככר וכיוצא בהן. אמר רב זביד כללא דאבידתא כיון דאמר ווי ליה לחסרון כיס מיאש מינה. אמר רב זביד משמיה דרבא הלכתא כריכות ברשות הרבים הרי אלו שלו ברשות היחיד אי דרך נפילה מצאן הרי אלו שלו אי דרך הנחה נוטל ומכריז וזה וזה בדבר שאין בו סימן [אבל ביש בו סימן] לא שנא רשות הרבים ולא שנא רשות היחיד לא שנא דרך הינוח ולא שנא דרך נפילה נוטל ומכריז

**מסורת הש"ס**

עירובין סד:, ב) [לעיל ..., ג) [לקמן כה.], ...נכרים, מהר"מ, ה) אלא, מהרש"ל.

**הגהות הב"ח**

תוס' ד"ה והא איכא גבי ניפול הנמצא אלמא היכא: (ב) ד"ה סימן כיון שניכר בחוץ וכן דבר:

**ליקוטי רש"י**

...רות של נחתום ...י אלו שלו וכו'. כל ...ות הנחתומין שוין אבל ...ות של בעל הבית יש סימן [לעיל כא.]. ...תא. פת [עי' סנהדרין ...]. עיגול. של דבילה [לעיל כא.].

ampled is in effect **the same as** the following dispute between **nnaim** recorded in our Mishnah?[13] רַבִּי יְהוּדָה אוֹמֵר — R' HUDAH SAYS: כָּל דָּבָר שֶׁיֵּשׁ בּוֹ שִׁינּוּי — ANYTHING THAT HAS METHING UNUSUAL IN IT, חַיָּיב לְהַכְרִיז — ONE IS OBLIGATED TO NOUNCE. כֵּיצַד — HOW SO? What is an example of this? מָצָא עִיגּוּל וּבְתוֹכוֹ חֶ — If ONE FOUND A ROUND CAKE of pressed figs TH A POTTERY SHARD INSIDE IT, כִּכָּר וּבְתוֹכוֹ מָעוֹת — or A LOAF TH COINS INSIDE IT. מִכְּלָל — **This implies** דְּתַנָּא קַמָּא סָבַר — **at the Tanna Kamma,** who does not offer this rule, **holds** הֲרֵי אֵלּוּ שֶׁ — that **these** cakes of pressed figs **belong to [the finder]** en if they contain a shard!

Before explaining its argument, the Gemara clarifies the sumptions underlying it:

דְּכוּלֵּי עָלְמָא סָבַר — **They** [those posing this question] **assumed that everyone** (i.e. both the Tanna Kamma and R' Yehudah) lds סִימָן הַבָּא מֵאֵילָיו הָוֵי סִימָן — that **an identifying mark that ay have come about on its own,** i.e. accidentally, **is** treated as **identifying mark.**[14] וּמַעֲבִירִין עַל הָאוֹכָלִין — **Moreover,** both e Tanna Kamma and R' Yehudah are of the opinion that **one ay pass by food** on the ground and leave it there. Thus, the cake pressed figs and the loaf are apt to be trampled underfoot and ve their unusual features obliterated.

Having explained its two assumptions regarding the points of reement between the Tanna Kamma and R' Yehudah, the emara states its understanding of their disagreement:

מַאי לָ — **Is it not** בְּסִימָן הֶעָשׂוּי לִידָּרֵס קָא מִיפַּלְגֵי — **that ey disagree about an identifying mark that tends to be ampled** and obliterated by passersby? מַר סָבַר — **This aster,** the Tanna Kamma, **holds** לֹא הָוֵי סִימָן — that **it is not** eated as **an identifying mark.** Thus, whoever finds the object, en with its identifying mark intact, is not obligated to announce [15] וּמַר סָבַר — **However,** the other **master,** R' Yehudah, holds at הָוֵי סִימָן — **it is** treated as **an identifying mark,** despite its ndency to be obliterated. Thus, one who finds it with the shard coin still in place is obligated to announce it. This interpreta-on of the dispute makes it identical to the dispute of Rabbah and ava.[16] — ? —

The Gemara rejects this interpretation of the dispute because e position it attributes to the Tanna Kamma contradicts an rlier ruling of the Mishnah:

אָמַר רַב זְבִיד מִשְּׁמֵיהּ דְּרָבָ — **Rav Zevid said in the name of Rava:** אִי סָלְקָא דַּעְתָּ — **If you should think** דְּקָא סָבַר תַּנָּא קַמָּא — **that e Tanna Kamma holds** סִימָן הֶעָשׂוּי לִידָּרֵס לֹא הָוֵי סִימָן — **that n identifying mark that tends to be trampled** and obliterated **is not** treated as **an identifying mark,** even if it is found intact, וּמַעֲבִירִין עַל הָאוֹכָלִין — **and** that he also holds that **one may pass by food** on the ground and leave it there, as suggested above, כִּכָּרוֹת שֶׁל בַּעַל הַבַּיִת בִּרְשׁוּת הָרַבִּים אַמַּאי מַכְרִיז — then **why** does the Mishnah imply earlier that **one who finds a householder's** homemade **loaves in a public domain must announce** his find? The distinctiveness of the homemade loaves is likely to be obliterated as the bread is trampled underfoot.[17] — ? —

It is clear from this that the previous interpretation of the dispute is untenable. The Gemara now records two other explanations of the disagreement. The first follows Rava's opinion:

אֶלָּא אָמַר רַב זְבִיד מִשְּׁמֵיהּ דְּרָבָא — **Rather, Rav Zevid said in the name of Rava** that the dispute should be explained as follows: דְּכוּלֵּי עָלְמָא סָבְרֵי — **Everyone** (i.e. both the Tanna Kamma and R' Yehudah) **agrees** סִימָן הֶעָשׂוּי לִידָּרֵס הָוֵי סִימָן — that **an identifying mark that tends to be trampled** and obliterated **is** nonetheless treated as **an identifying mark,** if found intact. וּמַעֲבִירִין עַל הָאוֹכָלִין — **Moreover,** everyone agrees that **one may pass by food** on the ground and leave it there. What then is the dispute? וְהָכָא בְּסִימָן הַבָּא מֵאֵילָיו קָא מִיפַּלְגֵי — **And here,** in the case of the fig cake with the pottery shard, or the loaf with the coin in it, they **disagree regarding** the significance of **an identifying mark that may have come about on its own.** דְּתַנָּא קַמָּא סָבַר — **The Tanna Kamma holds** that סִימָן הַבָּא מֵאֵילָיו לֹא הָוֵי סִימָן — **an identifying mark that may have come about on its own is not** treated as **an identifying mark.** Thus, one who finds a fig cake with no identifying mark other than a pottery shard in it is not required to announce it.[18] וְרַבִּי יְהוּדָה סָבַר — **However, R' Yehudah holds** that הָוֵי סִימָן — **it is** indeed treated as **an identifying mark.** Thus, one who finds a fig cake with a pottery shard in it must announce it.[19]

The Gemara presents a second explanation of the dispute in our Mishnah. This one follows Rabbah's opinion:

וְרַבָּה אָמַר לָךְ — **Now Rabbah could say to you** דְּכוּלֵּי עָלְמָא — **that everyone** agrees that סִימָן הֶעָשׂוּי לִידָּרֵס לֹא הָוֵי סִימָן — **an identifying mark that tends to be trampled** and obliterated **is not** treated as **an identifying mark,** even if it is found intact. וְאֵין מַעֲבִירִין עַל הָאוֹכָלִין — **Moreover,** everyone agrees that **one may not pass by food** on the ground and leave it there. What then is the dispute? וְהָכָא — **And here,** in the case of the fig cake with the pottery shard in it, בְּסִימָן הַבָּא מֵאֵילָיו קָמִיפַּלְגֵי — **they disagree regarding** the significance of **an identifying mark that may have come about on its own.**[20] תַּנָּא קַמָּא סָבַר — **The**

NOTES

3. Above, 21a.

4. The presence of the shard in the round fig cake or the coins in the loaf ay well be accidental and unknown to the owner. [There would erefore be no point in announcing these objects, because the owner ould not know of the existence of the shard or coins and could never entify the object by them.] However, the assumption of those posing is question was that both the Tanna Kamma and R' Yehudah agree at we accept the possibility that these objects were intentionally aced as identifying marks. Thus, the unusual fig cake or loaf is to be eated as something with a *siman.*

5. It may be assumed that the owner already gave up hope of recovering , because of the tendency of the shard or coin to be separated from the ke or loaf by being trampled.

6. Why then do Rabbah and Rava dispute this matter without noting at it is a dispute of Tannaim?

7. I.e. if the Tanna Kamma holds that one may pass by food and leave in the street, these loaves will tend to be trampled and their *siman* will obliterated. If he further holds that a *siman* that tends to be trampled es not count, the loaves should not be considered to have a *siman* even by chance their distinctive shape remains intact.

18. Because its owner may not be aware of its presence in the cake; see note 14.

19. Rava offers an explanation in which both the Tanna Kamma and R' Yehudah agree with his opinion that a *siman* that tends to be trampled is considered a *siman.* According to Rava, both Tannaim also hold that it is *permissible* to pass by food and leave it in the street. Thus, the fig cakes will tend to be trampled and lose their identifying shard. The dispute, however, concerns a case in which the shard was not lost. According to Rava, the shard would therefore rank as a *siman.*

The same is true for homemade breads. These, too, are apt to be trampled. Nonetheless, if one finds them with their *siman* intact, he must announce them. The reason there is a dispute in regard to a fig cake marked by a shard is because the shard might have come to be there without the owner's knowledge (*Rashi*).

20. Rabbah would formulate an explanation in which both the Tanna Kamma and R' Yehudah agree with his opinion that a *siman* that tends to be trampled is *not* considered a *siman.* According to Rabbah's explanation, however, both Tannaim hold that it is *forbidden* to pass by food in the street and leave it there. For this reason, we presume that the first person to pass these loaves will pick them up, and their distinctive

דמדרסא ברשות היחיד נוטל ומכריז דלא מדרסא והאלומות בין ברשות הרבים ובין ברה"י נוטל ומכריז כיון דגביהן לא מדרסא ורבא מתרץ לטעמיה במקום כריכות ברה"ר הרי אלו שלו דמינשתפא ברה"י חייב להכריז דלא מינשתפא והאלומות בין ברה"ר ובין ברה"י נוטל ומכריז כיון דיקירי לא מינשתפא ת"ש ככרות של נחתום הרי אלו שלו הא של בעל הבית חייב להכריז של בעל הבית מאי טעמא כיון דאית בהו סימן דמידע ידיע רפתא דאיניש איניש הוא ולא שנא רשות הרבים ולא שנא רשות היחיד נוטל ומכריז אלמא סימן העשוי לידרס הוי סימן תיובתא דרבה אמר לך רבה התם היינו טעמא משום [א] דאין מעבירין על האוכלין והא איכא נכרים נכרים חיישי לכשפים והאיכא בהמה וכלבים באתרא דלא שכיחי בהמה וכלבים לימא כתנאי ר"י אומר [ג] כל דבר שיש בו שינוי חייב להכריז כיצד מצא עיגול ובתוכו חרס ככר ובתוכו מעות מכלל דתנא קמא סבר הרי אלו שלו סברוה דכולי עלמא סימן הבא מאליו הוי סימן ומעבירין על האוכלין מאי לאו בסימן העשוי לידרס קא מיפלגי מר סבר לא הוי סימן ומר סבר הוי סימן אמר רב זביד משמיה דרבא אי ס"ד דקא סבר תנא קמא סימן העשוי לידרס לא הוי סימן ומעבירין על האוכלין ככרות של בעל הבית ברה"ר אמאי מכריז אלא אמר רב זביד משמיה דרבא דכולי עלמא סברי סימן העשוי לידרס הוי סימן ומעבירין על האוכלין והכא בסימן הבא מאליו קא מיפלגי דתנא קמא סבר סימן הבא מאליו לא הוי סימן ור"י סבר הוי סימן ורבה אמר לך דכ"ע סימן העשוי לידרס לא הוי סימן ואין מעבירין על האוכלין והכא בסימן הבא מאליו קמיפלגי ת"ק סבר לא הוי סימן ור"י סבר הוי סימן איכא דאמרי סברוה דכ"ע סימן הבא מאליו הוי סימן וסימן העשוי לידרס לא הוי סימן מאי לאו במעבירין על האוכלין קא מיפלגי דמר סבר מעבירין ומר סבר אין מעבירין אמר רב זביד משמיה דרבא אי ס"ד סבר ת"ק סימן העשוי לידרס לא הוי סימן ומעבירין על האוכלין ככרות של בעל הבית ברה"ר אמאי מכריז אלא אמר רב זביד משמיה דרבא דכולי עלמא סברי סימן העשוי לידרס הוי סימן ומעבירין על האוכלין והכא בסימן הבא מאליו קא מיפלגי דתנא קמא סבר סימן הבא מאליו לא הוי סימן ור"י סבר הוי סימן ורבה אמר לך דכולי עלמא סימן העשוי לידרס לא הוי סימן ואין מעבירין על האוכלין והכא בסימן הבא מאליו קא מיפלגי תנא קמא סבר סימן הבא מאליו לא הוי סימן ור"י סבר הוי סימן אמר רב זביד משמיה דרבא [א] כללא דאבידתא כיון דאמר ווי לה לחסרון כיס מיאש ליה מינה ואמר רב זביד משמיה דרבא [ב] הלכתא כריכות ברשות הרבים הרי אלו שלו ברשות היחיד אי דרך נפילה הרי אלו שלו אי דרך הנחה נוטל ומכריז וזה וזה בדבר שאין בו סימן אבל בדבר שיש בו סימן לא שנא ברה"ר ולא שנא ברשות היחיד בין דרך נפילה ובין דרך הנחה חייב להכריז:

ומחרוזות

**רש"י**

דמדרסא. וסימן העשוי לידרס הוא: דמינשתפא. מתגלגל ברגלי אדם ובהמה ואינה נמצאת במקום שנפלה תחילה: דיקירי. כבידות: הא של בעל הבית חייב להכריז. ואע"ג דבהדיא תני לה במתניתין [ג] איידי דנקט לאותביה מרישא כריכות ברשות הרבים דאותיב מינה לרבא נקט נמי לאותוביה לרבה מדוקי' דרישא: אין מעבירין על האוכלין. המוצא אוכלין בדרך אין רשאי לעבור עליהם ולהניחם שם הלכך לא נדרסו שמי שמצאן ראשון הגביהן: אין מעבירין על האוכלין. לאו לשון דריסה הוא אלא כמו אין מעבירין על המצות (יומא דף לג.): חיישי לכשפים. סבורים שמחמת כשפים הונחו לשם כדי להכשיל הדורסים עליהן והכי נמי דאין מגביהין אותם מיהו לא דרסי עליהן משום כשפים: לימא כתנאי. פלוגתא דרבה ורבא: הבא מאליו. הראוי לבא מאליו כגון חרס פעמים שנופל בעיגול: הוי סימן. דאמרינן לשם סימן נתנו שם ולא נפל מאליו ודבר שיש בו סימן הוא ואפילו הכי פליגי רבנן ואמרי הרי אלו שלו משום דקסברי מעבירין על האוכלין והוה ליה סימן העשוי לידרס: ור"י סבר הוי סימן. ואע"פ שזה עשוי לידרס נמי הוי סימן: ומעבירין על האוכלין. ואפילו הכי ככרות של בעל הבית חייב להכריז דסימן העשוי לידרס הוי סימן ועיגול היינו טעמא דסימן הבא מאליו לאו סימן הוא ור"י סבר הוי סימן: ורבה אמר לך כו'. והכא היינו טעמא דר"י משום דאין מעבירין על האוכלין ות"ק הכי נמי אית ליה אין מעבירין ומשום הכי ככרות של בעל הבית חייב להכריז וטעמייהו בעיגול משום דסימן הבא מאליו הוא ור"י סבר הוי סימן: איכא דאמרי סברוה כו'. וכי אתמר לימא כתנאי אאין מעבירין על האוכלין אתמר: הלכתא כריכות ברה"ר כו'. כדמוקי לה בשאין בו סימן: ברשות היחיד אי דרך נפילה הרי אלו שלו. דליכא למימר מקום הוי סימן דהא לא ידע היכא נפיל מיניה: אי דרך הינוח נוטל ומכריז. מקום ולא יניחם שם שמא ימצאם עכו"ם ויטלם ושמא שכחום הבעלים: אבל בדבר שיש בו סימן כו'. רבא לטעמיה דאמר סימן העשוי לידרס הוי סימן:

במנינא

**תוספות**

**אין** מעבירין על האוכלין. פי' אינו רשאי לעבור מעליהן כדפירש רש"י אלא צריך להגביהן אבל אין לפרש דאין מעבירין היינו אין דורסין עליהם כדאמר בפרק הדר (עירובין דף סד:) דא"ל ר"ג לרבי אלעאי טול גלוסקא משום דאין מעבירין הרי משמע שצריך להגביהם ועוד דקאמר התם אבל בדורות אחרונים שפרוצות בכשפים מעבירין ואי אין מעבירין היינו אין דורסין א"כ האי דקאמר נמי שפרוצות בכשפים היינו דורסים והכא משמע [ד] דבאתרא דחיישי לכשפים אין דורסין אלא ודאי צריך לומר כדפרישית: **והא** איכא נכרים דלא איכפת להו. פירוש שידרסו הנכרים קודם שיבא שם שום ישראל ויגביה וא"ת ולפרוך והלא נכרים שקלי ליה וי"ל דדריסה שכיח אי לאו משום כשפים לפי שדורסין דרך הילוכן אבל נטילה לא שכיח שיראים שבעל הככר רואה שסבורים שלדעת הניחו שם אבל קשה דהיכי פריך שניחוש שידרסוהו נכרים קודם שיבא שם שום ישראל ויפטר מהכרזה אדרבה ניחוש לרוב ישראל שרואין הככר ויגביהוהו וניחוש לחומרא לחייבו הכרזה דהא בליבורי מעות מכריז אע"פ שאם יראו אותם הנכרים קודם ודאי שקלי להו ועוד דבעי למימר דאפילו ברוב נכרים פליגי רבנן ומחייבי להכריז ואע"ג דאיכא למיחש דלמא שקלי להו ומסתמא נתייאש ועוד דהוה ליה למימר דמנכרים נפול וניזיל בתר רובא אפילו לשמואל דאמר בממון אין הולכין אחר הרוב היכא דליכא חזקה מודה כדמוכח בפרק לא יחפור (ב"ב דף כג: ושם ד"ה חוץ) גבי ניפול הנמצא (א) [ה] אבל כל היכא דאפשר לתקן להשיב ממון לבעלים ע"י הכרזה מתקנינן וא"כ מאי פריך הכא: **והא** איכא בהמה וכלבים. וא"ת לרבא נמי יקשה והא איכא בהמה וכלבים דאכלי להו כדאמר לעיל דאיכא שקלים ורמשים דאכלי וי"ל דהכא מיירי בככרות גדולות שאי אפשר שיאכלום:

**סימן** הבא מאליו הוי סימן. פרש"י דלשם סימן נתנו שם ולא נפל מאליו וקשה דאין דרך לתת מעות בככר לסימן אלא י"ל דאימור ידע שנפלו לו שם ומ"ד לא הוי סימן כיון דרגילות לבא מאליו מסתמא לא ידע כיון שאין ניכר בחוץ אבל סימני בהמה שהן מאליהן הוי סימן כיון שניכר (ג) וכן דבר שאין ניכר בחוץ אם אין רגילות לבא מאליו הוי סימן:

מחרוזות

**עין משפט נר מצוה**

כה א מיי' פי"ד מהל' גזילה ואבידה הל' ג סמג עשין עד טוש"ע ח"מ סי' רסב סעיף ה:
כו ב מיי' שם פט"ו הל' ח סמג שם טוש"ע שם סעיף ט:

**רבינו חננאל**

ת"ש ככרות של נחתום שלו של בעל הבית נוטל ומכריז והנה ככרות של בעל הבית אע"פ שידועין הן ריפתא דכל חד וחד כיון שאם ידרסו מתפתחין ואין ניכרין למי הן למה מכריזין תיובתא לרבה דאמר לא הוי סימן. ופריק רבה שאני ככרות דלא מדרסי כלל דאין מעבירין על האוכלין ומתני' באתרא דלית ביה לא בהמה ולא אפי' כלבים. פי' סימן הבא מאליו כגון מעות שנפלו בעיסה ונאפו בתוך הככר וכיוצא בהן. אמר רב זביד כללא דאבידתא כיון דאמר ווי ליה לחסרון כיס מיאש מינה. אמר רב זביד משמיה דרבא הלכתא כריכות ברשות הרבים הרי אלו שלו ברשות היחיד אי דרך נפילה מצאן הרי אלו שלו אי דרך הנחה נוטל ומכריז וזה וזה בדבר שאין בו סימן [אבל ביש בו סימן] לא שנא רשות הרבים ולא שנא רשות היחיד לא שנא דרך הינוח ולא שנא דרך נפילה נוטל ומכריז

**מסורת הש"ס**

עירובין סד:], ג) [לעיל ... , ג) [לקמן כה.], ... נכרים, מהר"מ, ה) אלא, מהרש"ל.

**הגהות הב"ח**

... תום' ד"ה והא איכא ... גבי ניפול הנמצא אלמא ... איכא: (ג) ד"ה סימן ... כיון שניכר בחוץ וכן דבר:

**ליקוטי רש"י**

... ות של נחתום ... אלו שלו וכו'. כל ... ות הנחתומין שוין אבל ... ות של בעל הבית יש ... סימן [לעיל כא.]. ... תא. פת [עי' סנהדרין ...]. עיגול. של דבילה [לעיל כא.].

דְּמִדְּרָס – [a small sheaf] **gets trampled** by the passing traffic, ıd its identifying mark tends to be obliterated, as explained ɔove.[1] בִּרְשׁוּת הַיָּחִיד נוֹטֵל וּמַכְרִיז – If they were found IN THE RIVATE DOMAIN, [THE FINDER] MUST TAKE them AND ANNOUNCE is find, דְּלָא מִדְּרְסָא – **because [a small sheaf] is not ampled** in the private domain, and its identifying mark ıerefore remains intact.[2] וְהָאֲלוּמוֹת – BUT if LARGE SHEAVES ere found, בֵּין בִּרְשׁוּת הָרַבִּים – WHETHER they were found IN HE PUBLIC DOMAIN, וּבֵין בִּרְשׁוּת הַיָּחִיד – OR WHETHER they ere found IN THE PRIVATE DOMAIN, נוֹטֵל וּמַכְרִיז – [THE NDER] MUST TAKE them AND ANNOUNCE his find. Why? כֵּיוָן דְּגְבִי – **Since they are tall,** לָא מִדְּרְסָא – **[the sheaf] does ot get trampled** even in the public domain.[3]

The Gemara now explains the Baraisa according to Rava:

וְרָבָא מְתָרֵץ לְטַעְמֵיהּ בִּמְקוֹ – **And Rava explains** the Baraisa **ccording to his view** that the sheaves are identifiable **by** their **lace.** Therefore:[4] כְּרִיכוֹת בִּרְשׁוּת הָרַבִּים הֲרֵי אֵלוּ שֶׁלּוֹ – SMALL HEAVES found IN THE PUBLIC DOMAIN BELONG TO [THE FINDER], דְּמִינַּשְׁתְּפָ – **because [a small sheaf] is moved about** by people ıd animals who kick it. The place where it is found is therefore ten not the place where it was lost. Thus, its place cannot serve identify it.[5] בִּרְשׁוּת הַיָּחִיד חַיָּיב לְהַכְרִיז – If they were found **in e private domain, [the finder] is obligated to announce** his nd, דְּלָא מִינַּשְׁתְּפָא – **because [the sheaf] is not moved about** y the limited traffic of the private domain. Thus, the owner does ɔt despair of being able to identify them by their place and reɔvering them. וְהָאֲלוּמוֹת – BUT if LARGE SHEAVES were found, בֵּין בִּרְשׁוּת הָרַבִּי – WHETHER they were found IN THE PUBLIC OMAIN, וּבֵין בִּרְשׁוּת הַיָּחִיד נוֹטֵל וּמַכְרִיז – OR WHETHER they were und IN THE PRIVATE DOMAIN, [THE FINDER] MUST TAKE them ND ANNOUNCE his find. Why? כֵּיוָן דְּיַקִּירֵי – **Since they are eavy,** לָא מִינַּשְׁתְּפָא – **they are not moved about.**[6]

The Gemara cites support for Rava's view that an identifying ark likely to be trampled is nonetheless treated as an identifying ark:

תָּא שְׁמַ – **Come, learn** a proof to Rava's view from our Mishnah, hich states: כִּכָּרוֹת שֶׁל נַחְתּוֹם – If A BAKER'S LOAVES were und . . . הֲרֵי אֵלוּ שֶׁלּוֹ – THEY BELONG TO [THE FINDER], because ey are uniform and have no identifying marks. הָא שֶׁל בַּעַל הַבַּ – We may infer from this **that** the homemade loaves **of a ouseholder,** חַיָּיב לְהַכְרִיז – **[the finder] is obligated to nnounce.**[7]

The Gemara analyzes this inference:

שֶׁל בַּעַל הַבַּיִת מַאי טַעְמָ – **What is the reason** that the finder ust announce the homemade loaves **of a householder?** כֵּיוָן דְּאִית בְּהוּ סִימָן – **Because they** [the homemade loaves] **have an identifying mark in them,** דְּמֵידַע יְדִיעַ – **inasmuch as they are recognizable,** רִפְתָּא דְּאִינִישׁ אִינִישׁ הוּא – for **the bread of a person is that person.**[8]

The Gemara now concludes its proof:

וְלָא שְׁנָא רְשׁוּת הָרַבִּים – **Now,** since the Mishnah does not specify otherwise, **there is no difference** between homemade loaves found in **the public domain,** where they are likely to be trampled, וְלָא שְׁנָא רְשׁוּת הַיָּחִיד – **and** those found in **the private domain,** where they are likely to remain intact;[9] נוֹטֵל וּמַכְרִיז – in either case, **[the finder] takes** them **and announces** his find. אַלְמָא – **We see** from this סִימָן הֶעָשׂוּי לִידָּרֵס הָוֵי סִימָן – that **an identifying mark that tends to be trampled** and obliterated **is** nonetheless treated as **an identifying mark,** if it is found intact. תְּיוּבְתָּא דְּרַבָּה – This would seem to be **a refutation of Rabbah's** position. – ? –

The Gemara rejects the proof:

אָמַר לָךְ רַבָּה – **Rabbah would say to you:** הָתָם – **There,** in the case of the homemade loaves, הַיְינוּ טַעְמָא – **this is the reason** one assumes their identifying mark will remain intact: מִשּׁוּם דְּאֵין מַעֲבִירִין עַל הָאוֹכָלִין – **because** of the rule **that one may not pass by food** on the ground and leave it there.[10] Therefore, the identifying marks of bread loaves are not likely to be obliterated by passersby. Rather, it is assumed that the first one who encounters the loaves will pick them up.

The Gemara objects to this answer:

וְהָא אִיכָּא נָכְרִים – **But there are gentiles** who are not enjoined to pick up food lying on the ground. Thus, the distinctive aspect of the loaves is still apt to be obliterated by gentiles stepping on them. – ? –

The Gemara answers:

נָכְרִים חָיְישֵׁי לִכְשָׁפִים – **Gentiles are concerned about witchcraft** and are therefore careful not to step on loaves of bread.[11]

The Gemara raises another objection:

וְהָאִיכָּא בְּהֵמָה וּכְלָבִים – **But there are livestock and dogs** that trample the loaves and obliterate their identifying marks. – ? –

The Gemara answers:

בְּאַתְרָא דְּלָא שְׁכִיחֵי בְּהֵמָה וּכְלָבִים – The Mishnah's ruling speaks of loaves found **in a place in which livestock and dogs are not common.** Therefore, one who finds homemade loaves there must announce them.[12]

The Gemara attempts to draw a parallel between this dispute and an earlier Tannaic dispute:

לֵימָא כְּתַנָּאֵי – **Are we to say** that the dispute between Rabbah and Rava regarding the status of an identifying mark that tends to be

NOTES

Gemara 22b; see note 19 there.

The owner therefore expects to be able to identify and reclaim his lost ject, and does not abandon it.

Because of their height, large sheaves are not stepped on by people ssing through the public domain, and their identifying marks do not come obliterated.

I.e. by announcing the place where they were found and having the aimant identify the object, as explained above (22b note 22).

Since according to Rava the Baraisa speaks of sheaves that do *not* ssess any identifying mark of their own, the owner has no way of entifying them and he therefore despairs of recovering them.

I.e. they retain their places even in the public domain. Therefore, cation can serve as a marker.

Actually, the next Mishnah (25a) states this explicitly. The reason the emara does not quote the next Mishnah, rather than infer this from r Mishnah, is because the Gemara prefers to maintain a symmetry th the previous proof, which drew support for Rabbah's position from the ruling in our Mishnah [regarding small sheaves] *(Rashi).*

8. I.e. each person bakes his bread somewhat differently, and the breads are therefore identifiable as his. [Thus, the folk expression: The bread of a person is the person.]

9. Since the Mishnah does not distinguish in the case of homemade loaves between a public domain and a private domain, as it did in the case of small sheaves, it is evident that the Mishnah considers the rule the same regardless of the domain in which it was found.

10. Food, which is essential to life, must be treated with respect. Thus, one may not leave it in the road to be trampled by passersby.

11. Gentiles were constantly mindful of the possibility of witchcraft and would not touch food left in the public domain out of a concern that it had been cast under a spell and placed in the public domain to ensnare passersby. Thus, though gentiles would not pick up the loaves, they would not step on them either *(Rashi).*

12. The owner does not abandon them because he assumes that their identifying marks will remain intact and he will be able to identify and reclaim them once they are found.

**location** where an object was found **is not** treated as **an identifying mark.**[24] דְּאִיתְּמַר – **For it was stated:** מָקוֹם – **Location** – רַבָּה אָמַר – **Rabbah said:** לֹא הָוֵי סִימָן – **It is not** treated as **an identifying mark,** and one cannot reclaim a lost object merely by identifying the place in which it was found; וְרָבָא אָמַר – **but Rava said:** הָוֵי סִימָן – **It is** treated as **an identifying mark,** and one can reclaim an object by identifying the place in which it was found.

The Gemara now presents a Baraisa which raises difficulties for both Rabbah and Rava:

תָּא שְׁמַע – **Come, learn** from the following Baraisa: כְּרִיכוֹת בִּרְשׁוּת הָרַבִּים הֲרֵי אֵלּוּ שֶׁלּוֹ – If SMALL SHEAVES were found IN THE PUBLIC DOMAIN, THESE BELONG TO [THE FINDER]. בִּרְשׁוּת הַיָּחִיד – If they were found IN THE PRIVATE DOMAIN, נוֹטֵל וּמַכְרִיז – [THE FINDER] MUST TAKE them AND ANNOUNCE his find. וְהָאֲלוּמוֹת – BUT if LARGE SHEAVES were found, בֵּין בִּרְשׁוּת הָרַבִּים – WHETHER they were found IN THE PUBLIC DOMAIN, בֵּין בִּרְשׁוּת הַיָּחִיד – or WHETHER they were found IN THE PRIVATE DOMAIN, נוֹטֵל וּמַכְרִיז – [THE FINDER] MUST TAKE them AN[D] ANNOUNCE his find. רַבָּה הֵיכִי מְתָרֵץ לָהּ – **How does Rabba[h] explain this** Baraisa,[25] וְרָבָא הֵיכִי מְתָרֵץ לָהּ – **and how do[es] Rava explain it?**[26] Why should large sheaves found in the publ[ic] domain need to be announced?

The Gemara explains how each resolves the difficulties rais[ed] against his view:

רַבָּה מְתָרֵץ לְטַעְמֵיהּ בְּסִימָן – **Rabbah explains** the Barai[sa] **according to his view** that the sheaves of which we speak posse[ss] **an identifying mark,** וְרָבָא מְתָרֵץ לְטַעְמֵיהּ בְּמָקוֹם – **and Rav[a] explains** the Baraisa **according to his view** that the sheaves [of] which we speak are identifiable **by** their **location.**

The Gemara first explains the Baraisa according to Rabbah:

רַבָּה מְתָרֵץ לְטַעְמֵיהּ בְּסִימָן – **Rabbah explains** the Barai[sa] **according to his view** that the sheaves possess **an identifyin[g] mark**. Therefore, כְּרִיכוֹת בִּרְשׁוּת הָרַבִּים הֲרֵי אֵלּוּ שֶׁלּוֹ – SMAL[L] SHEAVES found IN THE PUBLIC DOMAIN BELONG TO [THE FINDER] מִשּׁוּם – **because**

NOTES

24. I.e. one cannot claim a lost object merely by identifying the place in which it was found.

It is because Rabbah holds this view that he cannot accept Rava's answer to the previous question (see *Tosafos* ד"ה ורבה). As we explained above (note 22), naming the lost object is ordinarily not enough to identify and reclaim it. Only in a case in which the finder announces the location of the object does naming it serve as a *siman,* because we assume that it is unlikely that two people lost the same type of object in the same location. This view is tenable, however, only if we accept that the location in which an object is found is a significant factor in determining its ownership. Since Rabbah does not accept that location can identify an object, he obviously assumes that it is not beyond reason that two people lost the same type of thing in the same location (see below, 23b, and note 17 there). Accordingly, he cannot hold that announcing the location an[d] having someone name the object found there serves to identify [it] (*Lechem Abirim* in explanation of *Rashi;* cited in *Otzar Mefarsh[ei] HaTalmud*).

25. Seemingly, the identifying marks of large sheaves are as apt to b[e] obliterated as those on small sheaves. Consequently, why must larg[e] sheaves found in the public domain be announced, if, as Rabbah hold[s,] a *siman* that tends to be trampled and obliterated is not treated as [a] *siman* (*Rashi*)?

26. As Rava explained above, the Mishnah and Baraisa speak of sma[ll] sheaves that have no identifying mark upon them. But if so, the larg[e] sheaves are similarly not identifiable. Why must they be announce[d] when they are found in the public domain (*Rashi*)?

אינן בכי יותן טעמא מאי לאו משום דלא אמרינן כיון דאיגלאי מילתא דהשתא ניחא ליה מעיקרא נמי ניחא ליה שאני התם דכתיב כי יתן עד שיתן אי הכי רישא נמי התם [א] כדרב פפא דרב פפא רמי כתיב כי יתן וקרינן כי יותן הא כיצד בעינן כי יותן דומיא דכי יתן [א] מה יתן לדעת אף כי יותן נמי לדעת ת"ש [ב] דא"ר יוחנן משום [ג] רבי ישמעאל בן יהוצדק [ב] מנין לאבידה ששטפה נהר שהיא מותרת דכתיב [א] וכן תעשה לחמורו וכן תעשה לשמלתו וכן תעשה לכל אבידת אחיך אשר תאבד ממנו ומצאתה מי שאבודה הימנו ומצויה אצל כל אדם יצאתה זו שאבודה ממנו ואינה מצויה אצל כל אדם ואיסורא דומיא דהיתירא מה היתירא בין דאית בה סימן ובין דלית בה סימן שרא אף איסורא בין דאית בה סימן ובין דלית בה סימן אסורה תיובתא דרבא תיובתא [ד] והלכתא כוותיה דאביי [ס] ביע"ל קג"ם א"ל רב אחא בריה דרבא לרב אשי וכי מאחר דאיתותב רבא הני תמרי דזיקא היכי אכלינן להו אמר ליה [ג] כיון [א] דאיכא שקצים ורמשים דקא אכלי להו מעיקרא יאושי מיאש מנייהו [ס] [ה] יתמי דלאו בני מחילה נינהו מאי אמר ליה באגא בארעא דיתמי לא מחזקינן מוחזק ועומד מאי ברכתא מאי אמר ליה [ד] אסירן: כריכות ברה"ר הרי אלו שלו: אמר רבה ואפילו בדבר שיש בו סימן אלמא קסבר רבה סימן העשוי לידרס לא הוי סימן רבא אמר [ה] לא שנו אלא בדבר שאין בו סימן אבל בדבר שיש בו סימן חייב להכריז אלמא קסבר רבא סימן העשוי לידרס הוי סימן ואיכא דמתני להא שמעתא באנפי נפשה סימן העשוי לידרס רבה אמר לא הוי סימן ורבא אמר [ו] הוי סימן תנן כריכות ברה"ר הרי אלו שלו ברה"י נוטל ומכריז ה"ד אי דלית בהו סימן ברה"י מאי מכריז אלא לאו דאית בהו סימן וקתני ברה"ר הרי אלו שלו אלמא סימן העשוי לידרס לא הוי סימן תיובתא דרבא אמר לך רבא לעולם דלית בהו סימן ודקא אמרת ברה"י מאי מכריז מכריז מקום ורבה אמר מקום לא הוי סימן דאיתמר מקום רבה אמר לא הוי סימן ורבא אמר [ז] הוי סימן ת"ש כריכות ברה"ר הרי אלו שלו ברה"י נוטל ומכריז [ח] והאלומות בין ברה"ר ובין ברה"י נוטל ומכריז רבה היכי מתרץ לה ורבא היכי מתרץ לה רבה מתרץ לטעמיה בסימן ורבא מתרץ לטעמיה במקום רבה מתרץ לטעמיה בסימן כריכות ברשות הרבים הרי אלו שלו משום דמדרסא

---

**איסורא** דומיא דהתירא. מה שמתיר אבודה ממנו ומכל אדם ע"כ לא איצטריך קרא בידע ומתיאש דהא אפילו במצויין אצל כל אדם מותרת ביאוש אלא לא אצטריך אלא כי לא ידע ואע"ג דלכי ידע לא מתיאש אפי' אם יש בו סימן כיון שהיא אבודה מכל אדם ה"נ איסורא דהיינו מצוייה אצל כל אדם דאסור כה"ג דלא [ב] ידעינן דמיאש בין יש בו סימן בין שאין בו סימן ואין להתיר אלא דמיאש קודם דאתא לידיה דשריא רחמנא: **מאחר** דאיתותב רבא כו'. בשלמא לרבא אע"ג דאותם שתחת האילן או בסמוך לאילן אסירי דחזותו מוכיח עליו אבל תמרי שהרוח מוליכן ברחוק דלא שייך חזותו מוכיח עליו אע"פ שבעלים סבורין שיפלו תחת האילן מ"מ אם היו יודעין שהרוח מוליכן מרחוק היו מתיאשין אלא לאביי הא הוי יאוש שלא מדעת שהבעלים סבורים שיפלו תחת האילן ולא יקחום עוברי דרכים משום דחזותו מוכיח עליו ומשני דאפילו אותן שתחת האילן שרו אפילו לאביי [ח] באתרא דשכיחי שקצים ורמשים דמיאש וצ"ל דעבידי דנתרי כמו תאנים דאל"כ היו אסורים לאביי דהוי יאוש שלא מדעת דאינו סובר שיפלו כיון דלא עבידי דנתרי כמו זתים וחרובים דאסור כיון דלא עבידי דנתרי: **דלאו** בני מחילה נינהו מאי. בשלמא לרבא כיון דלכי גדלי מיאשי השתא נמי מיקרי יאוש: [ט] **תיובתא** דרבא. רבא ידע שפיר הך ברייתא כדמשמע קצת לעיל (דף כא:) דקאמר בזוטו של ים כ"ע לא פליגי דשרי כדבעינן למימר לקמן אלא דלא דייק איסורא דומיא דהתירא:

[ב] **ברכתא** מאי. אם יש גדר סביב האילן מי שרו אותם שהרוח מוליך אותן חוץ לגדר דכך עליו הלא הבעלים סבורין שכולן יפלו תחת האילן ושם ישתמרו משקצים ורמשים:

**אי** דליכא סימן מאי מכריז. פירוש למה צריך להכריז המוצא מאחר שהאבוד אין בו סימן ליתן ומשני דזה מכריז שאותו שאבד יתן סימן מקום וכן לקמן (דף כח.) דקאמר כדי שילך שלשה ויחזור שלשה ויכריז יום אחד היינו נמי שהמוצא מכריז והאובד יתן סימן [ס] אך קשה דבפרק אלו עוברין (דף מט: ושם ד"ה וים) אמרינן ע"ה אין מכריזין על אבידתו והיאך אנו יודעין זה אם הוא של ע"ה ויש לומר דמיירי במוצא במקום דשכיח ע"ה ורש"י שפירש דהמוצא מכריז מקום שיאמר מצאתי חפץ במקום פלוני והוא יאמר חפץ פלוני ויקחנה ק"ק דהא תנן בפירקין (דף כח:) אמר אבידה ולא אמר סימנין לא אמר כלום אלמא במה שמכוין החפץ אינו סימן וי"ל דהתם נמי לאו משום שהוא חשוד לשקר שהפסיד חפץ אלא משום דא"ל כי היכי דאת אבדת חפץ ה"נ אימר אדם אחר הפסיד אבל הכא מהדרינן דאין רגילות ששני בני אדם אבדו חפץ זה כזה ובמקום אחד ולפרש"י הוה מכריז מקום דהכא פירושו ממש דומיא דמכריז מנין דשלהי פרק קמא (דף כ:): **ורבה** אמר מקום לא הוי סימן. ולפי דסבירא ליה לרבה מקום לא הוי סימן הוצרך לומר דסי' העשוי לידרס לא הוי סימן:

---

אינן בכי יותן. ולא אמרינן כיון דהשתא ניחא מהני האי דעתא למעיקרא ותיהוי הכשר וקשיא לרבא: כתיב כי יתן. ולא כתיב כי יותן: לדעת. שידע בנתינה והוכשר בעיניו ועודהו הטל עליהן עדיין הן בנתינתו: ממנו. קרא יתירא הוא לאשמועינן שאינו אבוד אלא הימנו: ואיסורא דומיא דהיתירא. כיון דמחד קרא ילפינן מצויה אצל כל אדם שיחזור ושאינה מצויה יזכה בה איתקושי אתקוש להדדי זו לאיסורא וזו להיתירא: מה היתירא. שאינה מצויה לא חילק בין שיש בה סימן לשאין בה סימן: אף איסורא. דמצויה אצל כל אדם לא חילק בין אין סימן דכי ידע מיאש ליש סימן דלכי ידע לא מיאש וכי היכי דיש סימן אסירא כי אין סימן נמי אסירא היכא דאיכא למימר לא ידע דנפלה קודם שבאת ליד זה: יע"ל קג"ם. סימני הלכות הן יאוש שלא מדעת דהכא עד זומם למפרע הוא נפסל בסנהדרין (דף כז.) לחי העומד מאיליו בעירובין (דף טו.) קדושין שלא נמסרו לביאה בקדושין (דף נא.) גלוי דעתא בגיטא בגיטין (דף לד.) מומר אוכל נבילות להכעיס פסול לענין עדות בסנהדרין (דף כז.): הני תמרי דזיקא. שהרוח משיר: היכי אכלינן להו. הא לא מיאש והא דנקט למיבעי בעיא מאחר דאיתותב רבא קשיא לי דבלא איתותב רבא איכא למיבעי דהא מודה רבא בכל דבר שחזותו מוכיח עליו חוץ מן התאנה מפני שנמאסת עם נפילתה ונראה בעיני דלא נקט לה אלא להרבות בחומר איסור כלומר מאחר דאיתותב אפילו בדבר שאין בו סימן כ"ש שאלו אסורין שיש בהן סימן: מעיקרא. מקודם נפילתו: יאושי מיאש. דיודע הוא שהרוח משיר מהן והשקצים מזומנים לאוכלן: יתמי. קטנים שאין הפקירן הפקר: באגא בארעא דיתמי לא מחזקינן. אין עלינו להחזיק כל הבקעה בחזקת הקרקע של יתומין ולאסור כל התמרים משום ספק קרקע של יתומים אלא הולכין אחר הרוב: מוחזק ועומד מאי. קרקע עצמה של יתומין מאי: ברכתא מאי. דקלים הכרוכין ומוקפין בגדר של אבנים סביב שאין שקצים ורמשים נכנסין שם: העשוי לידרס. שהמקום שהוא שם רגיל בדריסת בני אדם והחפץ נמוך ונוח לידרס: לא הוי סימן. שאין בעליו סומך לתת בו סימן מימר אמר נשחת הסימן בדריסת הרגלים: ברה"י. כגון בשדה זרועה שאין רוב בני אדם דורכין בה ויש מיעוט שהולכין בה: ה"ג אי דלית בהו סימן ברה"י מאי מכריז. כלומר כי מכריז זה מצא אבידה מאי מכריז שיוכל ליתן האובד סימן בה: מכריז מקום. ואינו מכריז שם האבידה אלא שם המקום מי שאבדה ממנו אבידה במקום פלוני יבא ויאמר מה איבד וזה בא ואומר אבדתי שם חפץ פלוני: והאלומות. עומרים גדולים: רבה היכי מתרץ לה. רבה דאמר טעמא דרה"ר משום דנדרס מאי שנא אלומות: ורבא. דמוקים לכריכות כשאין בו סימן מאי שנא כריכות ומאי שנא אלומות: רבה מתרץ לטעמיה. דטעמא [י] דרשות הרבים דכריכות משום סימן ובדבר שיש (א) בה סימן: במקום. טעמא דכריכות [י] ברשות הרבים משום מקום ובדבר שאין בו סימן:

---

עין משפט
נר מצוה

יט א מיי' פ"א מהלכות טומאת אוכלין הל' ב ופי"ב הלכה א:
כ ב מיי' פי"א מהלכות גזילה ואבידה הלכה י סמג עשין עד טוש"ע ח"מ סי' רנט סעיף ז:
כא ג ד מיי' פט"ו מהל' גזילה ואבידה הל' יו סמג שם טוש"ע ח"מ סי' רס סעיף ו:
כב ה מיי' שם הל' ח סמג שם טוש"ע ח"מ סי' רסב סעיף ח:
כג ו מיי' שם:
כד ז ח מיי' שם הל' י ופי"ג הל' ה סמג שם טוש"ע שם סעיף ט וסי' רסז סעיף ז:

רבינו חננאל

יותן: פי' סימן העשוי לידרס כגון קשירת כריכות וכיוצא בהן שאם ידרסו יותרו הקשרים ובטל הסימן. וקתני סימן העשוי לידרס רבה אמר לא הוי סימן ודינו כדין דבר שאין בו סימן ורבא אמר הוי סימן. ואקשי' עליה דרבא ממתני' דקתני כריכות ברשות הרבים הרי אלו שלו ברשות היחיד נוטל ומכריז מאי לאו דאית בהו סימן העשוי לידרס וברשות הרבים דשכיחי רבים דדרסי עליה ובטיל מיאש לפיכך הרי אלו שלו אבל ברשות היחיד דלא מידרסי חייב להכריז אלמא סימן העשוי לידרס לא הוי סימן ודחי רבא לא מתני' בדליכא בהו סימן כלל וברשות היחיד אמאי מכריז מכריז מקום שהמקום הוא הסימן. ורבה אמר מקום לא הוי סימן. פי' מינשתפי מתגלגלין ברגלי בני אדם. פי' כיון דיקירי לא מינשתפי כיון שהן כבדים אינן מתגלגלין ברגלי בני אדם

---

מסורת הש"ס

א) קודשין נט:, ב) ל... כז., ג) [צ"ל ר' שמ... וכ"ה בילקוט], ד) [קיד... נג., בבא קמא ... סנהדרין כז.], ה) [פס... כ:], ו) ס"א דרשות הי..., ז) ס"א ברשות הי..., ח) ס"א כיון דאיכא את..., ט) [צ"ל קודס ... מאחר].

הגהות הב"ח

(א) רש"י ד"ה רבה מ... וכו' שיש בו סי...
(ב) תוס' ד"ה איסורא דלא ידע דמיאש בין...

הגהות הגר"א

[א] גמ' דאיכא ... נ"ב מחמת מתיקו... רמב"ס. משא"כ ... פירות. מ"מ: [ב] ת... ד"ה ברכתא כו'. ... אבל הרמב"ם כתב ... הקפיד והקיף כו' ש... גילה דעתו שלא מח...

גליון הש"ס

גמ' ביע"ל קג"ם. ... שבת דף קנה ע"א ... ד"ה והלכתא: שם ית... דלאו בני מחילה. ... ב"ב דף קמג ע"ב ... ד"ה ואם: תוס' ד"ה דליכא כו' אך קש... עיין תשובת רשד"ם ח... סימן ר"נ:

תורה אור השלם

א) וְכֵן תַּעֲשֶׂה לַחֲמֹ... וְכֵן תַּעֲשֶׂה לְשִׂמְ... וְכֵן תַּעֲשֶׂה לְכָל אֲבֵ... אָחִיךָ אֲשֶׁר תֹּא... מִמֶּנּוּ וּמְצָאתָהּ... תוּכַל לְהִתְעַלֵּם: [דברים כב, ג]

ליקוטי רש"י

התם כדרב פפא ו... דרחמנא קרייה מט... דכתיב כי יתן והיינו כי... ואע"ג דמחשבה בעו... הוא דאפילו נפלו מ... וניחא ליה הוי ה... ומיקרי כי יותן [קיד... נט:]. באגא. בקעה ... נט.].

The Gemara explains the next passage of the Mishnah, which states:

כְּרִיכוֹת בִּרְשׁוּת הָרַבִּים הֲרֵי אֵלּוּ שֶׁלּוֹ – SMALL SHEAVES found IN THE PUBLIC DOMAIN. . .THESE BELONG TO [THE FINDER].

The Gemara records a disagreement in regard to the explanation of this ruling of the Mishnah:

אָמַר רַבָּה – **Rabbah said:** וַאֲפִילּוּ בְּדָבָר שֶׁיֵּשׁ בּוֹ סִימָן – This ruling holds true **even for something that has an identifying mark on it.**[18]

The Gemara comments:

אַלְמָא קָסָבַר רַבָּה – **We see** from this **that Rabbah is of the opinion** that סִימָן הֶעָשׂוּי לִידָּרֵס – **an identifying mark that tends to be trampled** underfoot by passersby לֹא הָוֵי סִימָן – **is not** treated as **an identifying mark,** i.e. one who finds something with such a mark need not announce it, because the owner does not believe the mark will survive intact and he therefore despairs of recovering the object.[19]

The Gemara records a conflicting view:

רָבָא אָמַר – **Rava said:** לֹא שָׁנוּ אֶלָּא בְּדָבָר שֶׁאֵין בּוֹ סִימָן – **[The Sages]** of the Mishnah **taught** the permissibility of small sheaves **only for something that has no identifying mark on it,** אֲבָל בְּדָבָר שֶׁיֵּשׁ בּוֹ סִימָן – **but for something that does have an identifying mark on it,** חַיָּיב לְהַכְרִיז – **[the finder] is obligated to announce [it].** Thus, small sheaves with no identifying mark may be kept; identifiable sheaves must be returned.

The Gemara comments:

אַלְמָא קָסָבַר רָבָא – **We see** from this **that Rava is of the opinion** that סִימָן הֶעָשׂוּי לִידָּרֵס – **an identifying mark that tends to be trampled** underfoot by passing people הָוֵי סִימָן – **is** treated as **an identifying mark,** and one who finds something with such a mark must therefore announce it.[20]

The Gemara presents a different version of this disagreement:

וְאִיכָּא דְּמַתְנֵי לְהָא שְׁמַעְתָּא – **There are others who teach this discussion** regarding identifying marks that tend to be obliterated בְּאַנְפֵּי נַפְשָׁהּ – as a discussion **in its own right,** and not in connection with the explanation of the Mishnah. As follows:

סִימָן הֶעָשׂוּי לִידָּרֵס – **An identifying mark that tends to be trampled** and obliterated – רַבָּה אָמַר – **Rabbah said:** לֹא הָוֵי סִימָן – **It is not** treated as **an identifying mark;** therefore, one who finds an object with such a mark may keep it. וְרָבָא אָמַר – **Rava said:** הָוֵי סִימָן – **It is** treated as **an identifying mark;** therefore, one who finds an object with such a mark must announce it.

The Gemara attempts to prove Rabbah's position:

תְּנַן – **We have learned in** our **Mishnah:** [כְּר]יכוֹת בִּרְשׁוּת הָרַבִּים הֲרֵי אֵלּוּ שֶׁלּוֹ – SMALL SHEAVES found IN THE PUBLIC DOMAIN . . . THESE BELONG TO [THE FINDER]. We have also learned in t[he] next Mishnah: בִּרְשׁוּת הַיָּחִיד – If they are found IN THE PRIVA[TE] DOMAIN,[21] נוֹטֵל וּמַכְרִיז – [THE FINDER] MUST TAKE them A[ND] ANNOUNCE his find.

The Gemara analyzes these rulings:

הֵיכִי דָּמֵי – **What are the circumstances** surrounding the[se] rulings? אִי דְּלֵית בְּהוּ סִימָן – **If [the small sheaves]** of whi[ch] these Mishnahs speak **have no identifying mark on the[m]** בִּרְשׁוּת הַיָּחִיד מַאי מַכְרִיז – then when they are found **in the priva[te] domain, what can one announce** that the owner might be ab[le] to identify? It would be pointless to announce an object which t[he] owner cannot identify. אֶלָּא לָאו דְּאִית בְּהוּ סִימָן – **Rather,** mu[st] you **not** say that these Mishnahs are dealing with small sheav[es] **that have an identifying mark on them?** וְקָתָנֵי – **And** still o[ur] Mishnah **teaches** that בִּרְשׁוּת הָרַבִּים הֲרֵי אֵלּוּ שֶׁלּוֹ – if they a[re] found IN THE PUBLIC DOMAIN where they are likely to [be] trampled, THESE BELONG TO [THE FINDER], indicating that th[ey] are treated as if they have no identifying mark. אַלְמָא – **We se[e]** from this סִימָן הֶעָשׂוּי לִידָּרֵס – that **an identifying mark th[at] tends to be trampled** and obliterated לֹא הָוֵי סִימָן – **is n[ot]** treated as **an identifying mark.** תְּיוּבְתָּא דְּרָבָא – This wou[ld] seem to be **a refutation of Rava's** view. – ? –

The Gemara rejects the proof:

אָמַר לָךְ רָבָא – **Rava would say to you:** לְעוֹלָם דְּלֵית בְּהוּ סִימָן – **Actually,** we are dealing with small sheaves **that do not hav[e] identifying marks on them.** It is for this reason that they do n[ot] have to be announced if they are found in the public domai[n]. וּדְקָא אָמְרַתְּ – **Now,** in regard to **that which you said** that if s[o,] בִּרְשׁוּת הַיָּחִיד מַאי מַכְרִיז – when the sheaves are found **in th[e] private domain, what does [the finder] announce** that th[e] owner might be able to identify, since they lack any identifyin[g] marks? מַכְרִיז מָקוֹם – **He announces** that he found "som[e]thing" in **a** certain **location;** the owner may then reclaim them b[y] identifying the small sheaves as the objects he lost.[22]

The Gemara presents the opinion of Rabbah regarding th[is] issue – reclaiming an object by identifying the place where it wa[s] lost:[23]

וְרַבָּה אָמַר – **Now Rabbah said:** מָקוֹם לֹא הָוֵי סִימָן – Th[e]

NOTES

in advance. Accordingly, even those dates blown beyond the walls should be prohibited.

18. I.e. the small sheaves may be kept by the finder even if they possess a *siman* (identifying mark) by which they may be recognized.

19. The owner, knowing that the identifying mark is apt to be obliterated by people stepping on the object, does not think he will be able to identify and reclaim what he has lost and he therefore despairs of recovering it. Thus, the one who finds it, even with its *siman* intact, is permitted to keep it.

Small sheaves of grain, because of their softness and small size, are easily trampled. Thus, if they are in a public area, whatever *siman* they possess is deemed a *siman* that tends to be trampled and obliterated. For this reason, Rabbah permits one who finds small sheaves to keep them even if they possess a *siman* (*Rashi*).

20. [According to Rava, a person does not necessarily despair of recovering what he lost, because he hopes the *siman* will survive intact. Thus, the find must be announced.]

21. For example, in a planted field, which, while being open to the public, is actually used by only a few people (*Rashi*). Thus, the term *private domain* does not, in this context, refer to an area which outsiders may not enter, but to an open area which only few people pass through. Similarly, the term *public domain* may, in this context, refe[r] even to a privately owned area (such as an unplanted field) whic[h] people nevertheless pass through in number (see *Sma* 262:17).

22. The finder does not name the object he found in his announcemen[t] but merely states that he found something in a certain location. Th[e] owner can then identify it by saying that he lost sheaves in that plac[e] (*Rashi*).

[In the public domain, however, where the sheaves are kicked abou[t] one cannot announce the location, because the place where they we[re] found may not be the place where they were lost, as the Gemara wi[ll] explain below (23a).] Although the Mishnah will state below (28b) tha[t] naming the lost article does not suffice to reclaim it, this is because it i[s] possible that someone else also lost the same type of article. It is highl[y] unlikely, however, that another person lost the very same thing in th[e] very same place. Therefore, naming the object found in a specific plac[e] suffices to reclaim it, according to Rava (*Tosafos* in explanation o[f] *Rashi*).

*Tosafos* and other Rishonim explain the Gemara's answer in th[e] reverse manner: *He announces* the lost object in order that the owne[r] be able to name *the location* and thereby reclaim it.

23. Rabbah's position in this matter explains why he cannot accep[t] Rava's answer to the previous question (*Tosafos*). See next note.

אינן בכי יותן טעמא מאי לאו משום דלא אמרינן כיון דאיגלאי מילתא דהשתא ניחא ליה מעיקרא נמי ניחא ליה שאני התם דכתיב כי יתן עד שיתן אי הכי רישא נמי התם [א] כדרב פפא דרב פפא רמי כתיב כי יתן וקרינן כי יותן הא כיצד בעינן כי יותן דומיא דכי יתן [א] מה יתן לדעת אף כי יותן נמי לדעת ת"ש [ב] דא"ר יוחנן משום [ג] רבי ישמעאל בן יהוצדק [ב] מנין לאבידה ששטפה נהר שהיא מותרת דכתיב [א] וכן תעשה לחמורו וכן תעשה לשמלתו וכן תעשה לכל אבידת אחיך אשר תאבד ממנו ומצאתה מי שאבודה הימנו ומצויה אצל כל אדם יצאתה זו שאבודה ממנו ואינה מצויה אצל כל אדם ואיסורא דומיא דהיתירא מה היתירא בין דאית בה סימן ובין דלית בה סימן שרא אף איסורא בין דאית בה סימן ובין דלית בה סימן אסורה תיובתא דרבא תיובתא [ד] והלכתא כוותיה דאביי [ה] ביע"ל קג"ם א"ל רב אחא בריה דרבא לרב אשי וכי מאחר דאיתותב רבא הני תמרי דזיקא היכי אכלינן להו אמר ליה [ג] כיון [א] דאיכא שקצים ורמשים דקא אכלי להו מעיקרא יאושי מיאש מנייהו [ה] [ו] יתמי דלאו בני מחילה נינהו מאי אמר ליה באגא בארעא דיתמי לא מחזקינן מוחזק ועומד מאי כרכתא מאי אמר ליה [ד] אסירן: כריכות ברה"ר הרי אלו שלו: אמר רבה ואפילו בדבר שיש בו סימן אלמא קסבר רבה סימן העשוי לידרס לא הוי סימן רבא אמר [ה] לא שנו אלא בדבר שאין בו סימן אבל בדבר שיש בו סימן חייב להכריז אלמא קסבר רבא סימן העשוי לידרס הוי סימן ואיכא דמתני להא שמעתא באנפי נפשה סימן העשוי לידרס רבה אמר לא הוי סימן ורבא אמר [ו] הוי סימן תנן כריכות ברה"ר הרי אלו שלו ברה"י נוטל ומכריז ה"ד אי דלית בהו סימן ברה"י מאי מכריז אלא לאו דאית בהו סימן וקתני ברה"ר הרי אלו שלו אלמא סימן העשוי לידרס לא הוי סימן תיובתא דרבא אמר לך רבא לעולם דלית בהו סימן ודקא אמרת ברה"י מאי מכריז מכריז מקום ורבה אמר מקום לא הוי סימן דאיתמר מקום רבה אמר לא הוי סימן ורבא אמר [ז] הוי סימן ת"ש כריכות ברה"ר הרי אלו שלו ברה"י נוטל ומכריז [ח] והאלומות בין ברה"ר ובין ברה"י נוטל ומכריז רבה היכי מתרץ לה ורבא היכי מתרץ לה רבה מתרץ לטעמיה בסימן ורבא מתרץ לטעמיה במקום רבה מתרץ לטעמיה בסימן כריכות ברשות הרבים הרי אלו שלו משום

דמדרסא

**רש"י**

אינן בכי יותן. ולא אמרינן כיון דהשתא ניחא מהני האי דעתא למעיקרא ותיהוי הכשר וקשיא לרבא: כתיב כי יתן. ולא כתיב כי יותן: לדעת. שידע בנתינה והוכשר בעיניו ועודהו הטל עליהן עדיין הן בנתינתו: ממנו. קרא יתירא הוא לאשמועינן שאינו אבוד אלא הימנו: ואיסורא דומיא דהיתירא. כיון דמחד קרא ילפינן מצויה אצל כל אדם שיחזור ושאינה מצויה יזכה בה איתקושי אתקוש להדדי זו לאיסורא וזו להיתירא: מה היתירא. שאינה מצויה לא חילק בין שיש בה סימן לשאין בה סימן: אף איסורא. דמצויה אצל כל אדם לא חילק בין אין סימן דכי ידע מיאש ליש סימן דלכי ידע לא מיאש וכי היכי דיש סימן אסירא כי אין סימן נמי אסירא היכא דאיכא למימר לא ידע דנפלה קודם שבאת ליד זה: יע"ל קג"ם. סימני הלכות הן יאוש שלא מדעת דהכא עד זומם למפרע הוא נפסל בסנהדרין (דף כז.) לחי העומד מאליו בעירובין (דף טו.) קדושין שלא נמסרו לביאה בקדושין (דף נא.) גלוי דעתא בגיטא בגיטין (דף לד.) מומר אוכל נבילות להכעיס פסול לענין עדות בסנהדרין (דף כז.): הני תמרי דזיקא. שהרוח משיר: היכי אכלינן להו. הא לא מיאש והא דנקט למיבעי בעיא מאחר דאיתותב רבא קשיא לי דבלא איתותב רבא איכא למיבעי דהא מודה רבא בכל דבר שחזותו מוכיח עליו חוץ מן התאנה מפני שנמאסת עם נפילתה ונראה בעיני דלא נקט לה אלא להרבות בחומר איסור כלומר מאחר דאיתותב אפילו בדבר שאין בו סימן כ"ש שאלו אסורין שיש בהן סימן: מעיקרא. מקודם נפילתו: יאושי מיאש. דיודע הוא שהרוח משיר מהן והשקצים מזומנים לאוכלן: יתמי. קטנים שאין הפקירן הפקר: באגא בארעא דיתמי לא מחזקינן. אין עלינו להחזיק כל הבקעה בחזקת הקרקע של יתומין ולאסור כל התמרים משום ספק קרקע של יתומים אלא הולכין אחר הרוב: מוחזק ועומד מאי. קרקע עצמה של יתומין מאי: כרכתא מאי. דקלים הכרוכין ומוקפין בגדר של אבנים סביב שאין שקצים ורמשים נכנסין שם: העשוי לידרס. שהמקום שהוא שם רגיל בדריסת בני אדם והחפץ נמוך ונוח לידרס: לא הוי סימן. שאין בעליו סומך לתת בו סימן מימר אמר נשחת הסימן בדריסת הרגלים: ברה"י. כגון בשדה זרועה שאין רוב בני אדם דורכין בה ויש מיעוט שהולכין בה: ה"ג אי דלית בהו סימן ברה"י מאי מכריז. כלומר כי מכריז זה מצא אבידה מאי מכריז שיוכל ליתן האובד סימן בה: מכריז מקום. ואינו מכריז שם האבידה אלא שם המקום מי שאבדה ממנו אבידה במקום פלוני יבא ויאמר מה איבד וזה בא ואומר אבדתי שם חפץ פלוני: והאלומות. עומרים גדולים: רבה היכי מתרץ לה. רבה דאמר טעמא דרה"ר משום דנדרס מאי שנא אלומות: ורבא. דמוקים לכריכות כשאין בו סימן מאי שנא כריכות ומאי שנא אלומות: רבה מתרץ לטעמיה. דטעמא [י] דרשות הרבים דכריכות משום סימן ובדבר שיש (א) בה סימן: במקום. טעמא דכריכות [י] ברשות הרבים משום מקום ובדבר שאין בו סימן:

**תוספות**

**איסורא** דומיא דהתירא. מה שמתיר אבודה ממנו ומכל אדם ע"כ לא איצטריך קרא בידע ומתיאש דהא אפילו במלווין אצל כל אדם מותרת ביאוש אלא לא אצטריך אלא כי לא ידע ואע"ג דלכי ידע לא מתיאש אפי' אם יש בו סימן כיון שהיא אבודה מכל אדם ה"נ איסורא דהיינו מלוייה אצל כל אדם דאסור כה"ג דלא (ב) ידעינן דמיאש בין יש בו סימן בין שאין בו סימן ואין להתיר אלא דמיאש קודם דאתא לידיה דשריא רחמנא: **מאחר** דאיתותב רבא כו'. בשלמא לרבא אע"ג דאותם שתחת האילן או בסמוך לאילן אסירי דחזותו מוכיח עליו אבל תמרי שהרוח מוליכן ברחוק דלא שייך חזותו מוכיח עליו אע"פ שבעלים סבורין שיפלו תחת האילן מ"מ אם היו יודעין שהרוח מוליכן מרחוק היו מתיאשין אלא לאביי הא הוי יאוש שלא מדעת שהבעלים סבורים שיפלו תחת האילן ולא יקחום עוברי דרכים משום דחזותו מוכיח עליו ומשני דאפילו אותן שתחת האילן שרו אפילו לאביי [ס] באתרא דשכיחי שקלים ורמשים דמיאש וצ"ל דעבידי דנתרי כמו תאנים דאל"כ היו אסורים לאביי דהוי יאוש שלא מדעת דאינו סובר שיפלו כיון דלא עבידי דנתרי כמו זתים ותרובים דאסור כיון דלא עבידי דנתרי: **דלאו** בני מחילה נינהו מאי. בשלמא לרבא כיון דלכי גדלי מיאשי השתא נמי מיקרי יאוש: [ט] **תיובתא** דרבא. רבא ידע שפיר הך ברייתא כדמשמע קצת לעיל (דף כא:) דקאמר בזוטו של ים כ"ע לא פליגי דשרי כדבעינן למימר לקמן אלא דלא דייק איסורא דומיא דהתירא:

[ב] **כרכתא** מאי. אם יש גדר סביב האילן מי שרו אותם שהרוח מוליך אותן חוץ לגדר דרך עליו הלא הבעלים סבורין שכולן יפלו תחת האילן ושם ישתמרו משקלים ורמשים:

**אי** דליכא סימן מאי מכריז. פירוש למה צריך להכריז המוצא מאחר שהאבוד אין בו סימן ליתן ומשני דזה מכריז שאותו שאבד יתן סימן מקום וכן לקמן (דף כח.) דקאמר כדי שילך שלשה ויחזור שלשה ויכריז יום אחד היינו נמי שהמוצא מכריז והאובד יתן סימן [ס] אך קשה דבפרק אלו עוברין (דף מט: ושם ד"ה ויש) אמרינן ע"ה אין מכריזין על אבידתו והיאך אנו יודעין זה אם הוא של ע"ה ויש לומר דמיירי במוצא במקום דשכיח ע"ה ורש"י שפירש דהמוצא מכריז מקום שיאמר מצאתי חפץ במקום פלוני והוא יאמר חפץ פלוני ויקחנה ק"ק דהא תנן בפירקין (דף כח:) אמר אבידה ולא אמר סימנין לא אמר כלום אלמא במה שמכוין החפץ אינו סימן וי"ל דהתם נמי לאו משום שהוא חשוד לשקר שהפסיד חפץ אלא משום דא"ל כי היכי דאת אבדת חפץ ה"נ אימר אדם אחר הפסיד אבל הכא מהדרינן דאין רגילות ששני בני אדם אבדו חפץ זה כזה ובמקום אחד ולפרש"י הוה מכריז מקום דהכא פירושו ממש דומיא דמכריז מנין דשלהי פרק קמא (דף כ:): **ורבה** אמר מקום לא הוי סימן. ולפי דסבירא ליה לרבה מקום לא הוי סימן הוצרך לומר דסי' העשוי לידרס לא הוי סימן:

**עין משפט נר מצוה**

יט א מיי' פ"א מהלכות טומאת אוכלין הל' ג ופי"ב הלכה א:
כ ב מיי' פי"א מהלכות גזילה ואבידה הלכה י סמג עשין עד טוש"ע ח"מ סי' רנט סעיף ז:
כא ג ד מיי' פט"ו מהל' גזילה ואבידה הל' יו סמג שם טוש"ע ח"מ סי' רס סעיף ו:
כב ה מיי' שם הל' ח סמג שם טוש"ע ח"מ סי' רסב סעיף ח:
כג ו מיי' שם:
כד ז ח מיי' שם הל' י ופי"ג הל' ה סמג שם טוש"ע שם סעיף ט וסי' רסז סעיף ז:

**רבינו חננאל**

יותן: פי' סימן העשוי לידרס כגון קשירת כריכות וכיוצא בהן שאם ידרסו יותרו הקשרים ובטל הסימן. וקתני סימן העשוי לידרס רבה אמר לא הוי סימן ודינו כדין דבר שאין בו סימן ורבא אמר הוי סימן. ואקשי' עליה דרבא ממתני' דקתני כריכות ברשות הרבים הרי אלו שלו ברשות היחיד נוטל ומכריז מאי לאו דאית בהו סימן העשוי לידרס וברשות הרבים דשכיחי רבים דדרסי עליה ובטיל מיאש לפיכך הרי אלו שלו אבל ברשות היחיד דלא מידרסי חייב להכריז אלמא סימן העשוי לידרס לא הוי סימן ודחי רבא לא מתני' בדליכא בהו סימן כלל וברשות היחיד אמאי מכריז מכריז מקום שהמקום הוא הסימן. ורבה אמר מקום לא הוי סימן. פי' מינשתפי מתגלגלין ברגלי בני אדם. פי' כיון דיקירי לא מינשתפי כיון שהן כבדים אינן מתגלגלין ברגלי בני אדם

**מסורת הש"ס**

א) קדושין נט:, ב) [...] ס., ג) [צ"ל ר' שמ... וכ"ה בילקוט], ד) [קיד... נב., בבא קמא... סנהדרין כז.], ה) [פס... ג:], ו) ס"א דרשות הר... ז) ס"א ברשות הר... ח) ס"א כיון דליכא א... ט) [צ"ל קודם... מאחר].

**הגהות הב"ח**

(א) רש"י ד"ה רבה מ... וכו' שיש בו סי... (ב) תוס' ד"ה איסורא... דלא ידע דמיאש בין...

**הגהות הגר"א**

[א] גמ' דאיכא ... נ"ב מחמת ממיקו... רמב"ם. משא"כ ... פירות. מ"מ: [ב] ת... ד"ה כרכתא כו'. אבל הרמב"ם כתב ... הקפיד והקיף כו' ש... גילה דעתו שלא מח...

**גליון הש"ס**

גמ' ביע"ל קג"ם. ... שבת דף קנה ע"א ... ד"ה והלכתא: שם ית... דלאו בני מחילה. ... ב"ב דף קמג ע"ב ... ד"ה ושם: תוס' ד"ה דליכא כו' אך קש... עיין תשובת רשד"ם ... סימן ר"נ:

**תורה אור השלם**

א) וְכֵן תַּעֲשֶׂה לַחֲ... וְכֵן תַּעֲשֶׂה לְשִׂמְלָ... וְכֵן תַּעֲשֶׂה לְכָל אֲבֵ... אָחִיךָ אֲשֶׁר תֹּא... מִמֶּנּוּ וּמְצָאתָהּ ... תוּכַל לְהִתְעַלֵּם: [דברים כב, ג]

**ליקוטי רש"י**

התם כדרב פפא וכ... דרחמנא קרייה מע... דכתיב כי יתן וסיינו ב... ואע"ג דמחשבה בעל... הוא דאפילו נפלו ממ... וניחא ליה הוי הכ... ומיקרי כי יותן [קידו... נט:]. באגא. בקעה [... נט.].

return the lost object, **is likened to** the case of **the** object **permitted** to the finder, i.e. the case of an object beyond anyone's reach.[9] **מַה הֶיתֵּרָא** – Therefore, **just as the** object **permitted** to the finder (the one carried away by the flood) **בֵּין דְאִית בָּהּ סִימָן וּבֵין דְלֵית בָּהּ סִימָן שָׁרָא** – **is permitted** to him **whether it has an identifying mark in it, or whether it does not have an identifying mark in it,**[10] **אַף אִיסוּרָא** – **so too the** object **forbidden** to the finder, (the ordinary lost object, which must be returned) **בֵּין דְאִית בָּהּ סִימָן וּבֵין דְלֵית בָּהּ סִימָן אֲסוּרָה** – **is forbidden** (i.e. must be returned) **whether it has an identifying mark in it, or whether it does not have an identifying mark in it.**[11] According to Abaye, this ruling holds true where the owner has not discovered his loss and has therefore not consciously abandoned his object. However, according to Rava this is never true, since he rules that an object that cannot be identified may *always* be kept by the finder, because the owner is sure to eventually despair of it. **תְּיוּבְתָּא דְרָבָא תְּיוּבְתָּא** – This is therefore **a refutation of Rava;** it is indeed **a** conclusive **refutation.**

The Gemara now concludes with a ruling on the dispute:

**וְהִלְכְתָא כְּוָותֵיהּ דְאַבַּיֵי** – **The halachah is according to Abaye** in his disputes with Rava **בְּיַעַ״ל קְגַ״ם** – **in** the six disputes indicated by the mnemonic ***yal kgm.*** The situation of *ye'ush* (abandonment) without the owner's awareness of it is the first of these disputes.[12]

An objection is raised in light of the previous ruling:

**אֲמַר לֵיהּ רַב אַחָא בְּרֵיהּ דְרָבָא לְרַב אַשִׁי** – **Rav Acha the son of Rava said to Rav Ashi:** **וְכִי מֵאַחַר דְאִיתּוֹתַב רָבָא** – **Now that Rava h**[as] **been refuted** in regard to his acceptance of a state of abando[n]ment even without the owner's awareness of it, **[ה]ָ[נ]ֵי תַּמְרֵי דְזִיקָא** – **these wind-blown dates, הֵיכִי אַכְלִינַן לְהוּ** – **how are** [we] permitted **to eat them?**[13]

Rav Ashi replies:

**אֲמַר לֵיהּ** – **[Rav Ashi] said to [Rav Acha the son of Rava]:** **דְאִיכָּא שְׁקָצִים וּרְמָשִׂים** – **Since there are vermin and crawli**[ng] **creatures דְקָא אָכְלֵי לְהוּ** – **that eat [the fallen date**[s]**],** **מֵיעִקָּרָא יֵאוּשֵׁי מְיָאֵשׁ מִנַּיְיהוּ** – **[the owner] certainly despairs** [of] **recovering them from the** very **beginning,** even before they a[re] blown from the tree.[14]

Rav Acha continues his line of questioning:

**יַתְמֵי דְלַאו בְּנֵי מְחִילָה נִינְהוּ** – **Orphans who** are minors, and **are n**[ot] yet legally **capable of relinquishing** their rights, **מַאי** – **wh**[at] will you say in regard to their dates?[15]

Rav Ashi responds:

**אֲמַר לֵיהּ** – **[Rav Ashi] said to him:** **[בְּ]אַרְעָא דְיַתְמֵי לָא מַחְזְקִינַן** – **We do not presume an entire valley** to be compris[ed] **of the land of orphans.**[16]

Rav Acha pursues this further:

**מוּחְזָק וְעוֹמֵד מַאי** – **What** is the law in regard to dates from trees [on] land **well established** to belong to orphans? **כַּרְבְּתָא מַאי** – **What** is the law in regard to dates that have fallen off trees th[at] are **surrounded by** stone **walls?**[17]

Rav Ashi responds:

**אֲמַר לֵיהּ** – **[Rav Ashi] told him:** **אֲסִירָן** – **They are inde**[ed] **forbidden** to the finder.

NOTES

9. The law requiring one who finds a lost object to return it is stated explicitly in this verse; the law permitting one to keep an object lost to all mankind is stated by implication. Since both are derived from the same verse, their laws, though different, must be parallel (*Rashi*).

10. An object swept away by a flood is permitted to the finder even if it has a *siman* (identifying mark), as we learned in the Gemara on 21b.

11. Thus, it may be derived from this verse that even an object without a *siman* may not be kept by the finder. However, we learn from another verse that if the owner despairs of finding his object, the finder may keep it (see Mishnah on 27a). Thus, the verse quoted here, which *prohibits* the finder to keep even an object without any *siman,* must be dealing with a case in which the owner was unaware of the loss and had therefore not *consciously* abandoned it. This proves Abaye's position (see *Ritva*).

12. *Rashi* explains the mnemonic as follows (cf *Tosafos* to *Kiddushin* 52a ד״ה ביע״ל קג״ם):

י = יֵאוּשׁ שֶׁלֹּא מִדַּעַת, *abandonment without the owner's awareness.*

ע=עֵדִים זוֹמְמִין, *zomemin witnesses.* The dispute is whether their personal disqualification takes effect only henceforward or is retroactive to the time of their testimony (see *Sanhedrin* 27a).

ל= לֶחִי הָעוֹמֵד מֵאֵלָיו, *a lechi that stands by itself.* The dispute is whether a sidepost that *happens* to be standing at the entrance of a *mavoi* can permit carrying in it on the Sabbath (see *Eruvin* 15a).

ק= קִידּוּשִׁין שֶׁלֹּא נִמְסְרוּ לְבִיאָה, *kiddushin that are not given to cohabitation.* The dispute involves the validity of a marriage which cannot by law be consummated (see *Kiddushin* 51a).

ג = גִּלּוּי דַּעְתָּא בְּגִיטָּא, *clarification of intention regarding a get.* The issue is whether certain statements or actions of a husband can be interpreted as nullifications of the bill of divorce he sent to his wife (see *Gittin* 34a).

מ= מוּמָר אוֹכֵל נְבֵילוֹת לְהַכְעִיס, *a renegade who eats unkosher meat in defiance [of the Torah].* The dispute is whether somebody who eats non-kosher food not for personal gain or pleasure, but simply in defiance of the Torah's law, may serve as a witness (see *Sanhedrin* 27a).

13. It was the common practice for passersby to eat dates that had been blown from privately owned date trees. Rav Acha the son of Rava questions this practice in light of the ruling favoring Abaye. It may often be the case that the owner is unaware that his dates have been blown away by the wind. Since according to Abaye, the owner's eventual *ye'ush* is not sufficient to render the fruit ownerless now, it should be prohibited for passersby to eat them.

*Rashi* suggests that Rav Acha's objection to the practice holds tr[ue] even according to Rava. As stated earlier (21b), even Rava agrees th[at] fruit that has fallen from a tree may not be kept by the finder becau[se] they are identifiable by their similarity to the fruit on the nearby tr[ee] [with the exception of figs, which are damaged by the fall]. Therefor[e] even according to Rava, wind-blown dates should not be permitted to t[he] finder until the owner actually abandons them. Rav Acha, howeve[r] cited the Talmudical ruling in favor of Abaye to strengthen his questio[n]. If a state of *ye'ush* cannot take effect without the owner's awareness i[n] the case of unidentifiable objects, it certainly does not take effect i[n] regard to identifiable fruit. What basis exists, therefore, to legitimize t[he] common practice of eating fallen fruit?

*Tosafos,* however, resolves *Rashi's* problem by suggesting that t[he] wind blows the dates far enough away from the tree that it is no longe[r] identifiable by it. Thus, one would be allowed to eat such fruit accordin[g] to Rava. It is only according to Abaye that there is a problem, inasmuc[h] as the owner may not yet be aware of his loss.

14. The owner, who is aware of the possibility of the wind blowing aw[ay] his dates and the fate they will encounter, abandons in advance a[ny] dates that are blown from his tree.

According to this, the Baraisa (21b) that rules that fallen fruit may n[ot] be kept by the finder is referring to a locale which is relative[ly] vermin-free. In such places the owner does not automatically give u[p] hope of recovering fallen fruit (*Tosafos,* ד״ה מאחר according t[o] *Maharsha;* cf. *Hagahos HaGra*).

15. The actions of minors (boys less than thirteen years old and girls les[s] than twelve) are not legally recognized. They can neither sell nor giv[e] away property, nor relinquish their rights to property. Accordingly, th[e] wind-blown dates of minors should be prohibited. This in turn shoul[d] lead to a prohibition of all wind-blown dates because of the possibilit[y] that they belong to a minor. [Minors are referred to here as orphans t[o] account for their owning property although they are not yet of age.]

16. At worst, only a small fraction of plots in any given area belongs t[o] orphans. The great majority of land is owned by adults capable of *ye'us[h]* and relinquishment. This allows us to apply the rule of majority and t[o] presume that any given date is from the majority of owners who ar[e] capable of *ye'ush (Rashi).*

17. The owner anticipates that the dates will fall within the walls, wher[e] they are protected from vermin. He therefore does not despair of the[m]

אינן בכי יותן טעמא מאי לאו משום דלא אמרינן כיון דאיגלאי מילתא דהשתא ניחא ליה מעיקרא נמי ניחא ליה שאני התם דכתיב כי יתן עד שיתן אי הכי רישא נמי התם [א]כדרב פפא דרב פפא רמי כתיב כי יתן וקרינן כי יותן הא כיצד בעינן כי יותן דומיא דכי יתן [א]מה יתן לדעת אף כי יותן נמי לדעת ת"ש [ג]דא"ר יוחנן משום [ג]רבי ישמעאל בן יהוצדק [ב]מנין לאבידה ששטפה נהר שהיא מותרת דכתיב [א]וכן תעשה לחמורו וכן תעשה לשמלתו וכן תעשה לכל אבידת אחיך אשר תאבד ממנו ומצאתה מי שאבודה הימנו ומצויה אצל כל אדם יצאתה זו שאבודה ממנו ואינה מצויה אצל כל אדם ואיסורא דומיא דהיתירא מה היתירא בין דאית בה סימן ובין דלית בה סימן שרא אף איסורא בין דאית בה סימן ובין דלית בה סימן אסורה תיובתא דרבא תיובתא [ד]והלכתא כוותיה דאביי ביע"ל קג"ם א"ל רב אחא בריה דרבא לרב אשי וכי מאחר דאיתותב רבא הני תמרי דזיקא היכי אכלינן להו אמר ליה [ג]כיון [א] דאיכא שקצים ורמשים דקא אכלי להו מעיקרא יאושי מיאש מנייהו [ה]יתמי דלאו בני מחילה נינהו מאי אמר ליה באגא בארעא דיתמי לא מחזקינן מוחזק ועומד מאי ברכתא מאי אמר ליה [ד]אסירן: כריכות ברה"ר הרי אלו שלו: אמר רבה ואפילו בדבר שיש בו סימן אלמא קסבר רבה סימן העשוי לידרס לא הוי סימן רבא אמר [ה]לא שנו אלא בדבר שאין בו סימן אבל בדבר שיש בו סימן חייב להכריז אלמא קסבר רבא סימן העשוי לידרס הוי סימן ואיכא דמתני להא שמעתא באנפי נפשה סימן העשוי לידרס רבה אמר לא הוי סימן ורבא אמר [ו]הוי סימן תנן כריכות ברה"ר הרי אלו שלו ברה"י נוטל ומכריז ה"ד אי דלית בהו סימן ברה"י מאי מכריז אלא לאו דאית בהו סימן וקתני ברה"ר הרי אלו שלו אלמא סימן העשוי לידרס לא הוי סימן תיובתא דרבא אמר לך רבא לעולם דלית בהו סימן ודקא אמרת ברה"י מאי מכריז מכריז מקום ורבה אמר מקום לא הוי סימן דאיתמר מקום רבה אמר לא הוי סימן ורבא אמר [ז]הוי סימן ת"ש כריכות ברה"ר הרי אלו שלו ברה"י נוטל ומכריז [ח]והאלומות בין ברה"ר ובין ברה"י נוטל ומכריז רבה היכי מתרץ לה ורבא היכי מתרץ לה רבה מתרץ לטעמיה בסימן ורבא מתרץ לטעמיה במקום רבה מתרץ לטעמיה בסימן כריכות ברשות הרבים הרי אלו שלו משום
דמדרסא

**רש"י**

אינן בכי יותן. ולא אמרינן כיון דהשתא ניחא מהני האי דעתא למעיקרא ותיהוי הכשר וקשיא לרבא: כתיב כי יתן. ולא כתיב כי יותן: לדעת. שידע בנתינה והוכשר בעיניו ועודהו הטל עליהן עדיין הן בנתינתו: ממנו. קרא יתירא הוא לאשמועינן שאינו אבוד אלא הימנו: **ואיסורא דומיא דהיתירא.** כיון דמחד קרא ילפינן מצויה אצל כל אדם שיחזור ושאינה מצויה יזכה בה איתקושי אתקוש להדדי זו לאיסורא וזו להיתירא: **מה היתירא.** שאינה מצויה לא חילק בין שיש בה סימן לשאין בה סימן: **אף איסורא.** דמצויה אצל כל אדם לא חילק בין אין סימן דכי ידע מיאש ליש סימן דלכי ידע לא מיאש וכי היכי דיש סימן אסירא כי אין סימן נמי אסירא היכא דאיכא למימר לא ידע דנפלה קודם שבאת ליד זה: יע"ל קג"ם. סימני הלכות הן יאוש שלא מדעת דהכא עד זומם למפרע הוא נפסל בסנהדרין (דף כז.) לחי העומד מאליו בעירובין (דף טו.) קדושין שלא נמסרו לביאה בקדושין (דף נא.) גלוי דעתא בגיטא בגיטין (דף לד.) מומר אוכל נבילות להכעיס פסול לענין עדות בסנהדרין (דף כז.): **הני תמרי דזיקא.** שהרוח משיר: **היכי אכלינן להו.** הא לא מיאש והא דנקט למיבעי בעיא מאחר דאיתותב רבא קשיא לי דבלא איתותב רבא איכא למיבעי דהא מודה רבא בכל דבר שחזותו מוכיח עליו חוץ מן התאנה מפני שנמאסת עם נפילתה ונראה בעיני דלא נקט לה אלא להרבות בחומר איסור כלומר מאחר דאיתותב אפילו בדבר שאין בו סימן כ"ש שאלו אסורין שיש בהן סימן: מעיקרא. מקודם נפילתו: **יאושי מיאש.** דיודע הוא שהרוח משיר מהן והשקצים מזומנים לאוכלן: **יתמי.** קטנים שאין הפקירן הפקר: **באגא בארעא דיתמי לא מחזקינן.** אין עלינו להחזיק כל הבקעה בחזקת הקרקע של יתומין ולאסור כל התמרים משום ספק קרקע של יתומים אלא הולכין אחר הרוב: מוחזק ועומד מאי. קרקע עצמה של יתומין מאי: ברכתא מאי. דקלים הכרוכין ומוקפין בגדר של אבנים סביב שאין שקצים ורמשים נכנסין שם: העשוי לידרס. שהמקום שהוא שם רגיל בדריסת בני אדם והחפץ נמוך ונוח לידרס: **לא הוי סימן.** שאין בעליו סומך לתת בו סימן מימר אמר נשחת הסימן בדריסת הרגלים: **ברה"י.** כגון בשדה זרועה שאין רוב בני אדם דורכין בה ויש מיעוט שהולכין בה: **ה"ג אי דלית בהו סימן ברה"י מאי מכריז.** כלומר כי מכריז זה מצא אבידה מאי מכריז שיוכל ליתן האובד סימן בה: **מכריז מקום.** ואינו מכריז שם האבידה אלא שם המקום מי שאבדה ממנו אבידה במקום פלוני יבא ויאמר מה איבד וזה בא ואומר אבדתי שם חפץ פלוני: **והאלומות.** עומרים גדולים: **רבה היכי מתרץ לה.** רבה דאמר טעמא דרה"ר משום דנדרס מאי שנא אלומות: **ורבא.** דמוקים לכריכות כשאין בו סימן מאי שנא כריכות ומאי שנא אלומות: **רבה מתרץ לטעמיה.** דטעמא [י]דרשות הרבים דכריכות משום סימן ובדבר שיש (א) בה סימן: **במקום.** טעמא דכריכות [י]ברשות הרבים משום מקום ובדבר שאין בו סימן:

**תוספות**

**איסורא** דומיא דהתירא. מה שמתיר אבודה ממנו ומכל אדם ע"כ לא איצטריך קרא בידע ומתיאש דהא אפילו במצויין אצל כל אדם מותרת ביאוש אלא לא אצטריך אלא כי לא ידע ואע"ג דלכי ידע לא מתיאש אפי' אם יש בו סימן כיון שהיא אבודה מכל אדם ה"נ איסורא דהיינו מצוייה אצל כל אדם דאסור כה"ג דלא (ב) ידעינן דמיאש בין יש בו סימן בין שאין בו סימן ואין להתיר אלא דמיאש קודם דאתא לידיה דשריא רחמנא: **מאחר** דאיתותב רבא כו'. בשלמא לרבה אע"ג דאותם שתחת האילן או בסמוך לאילן אסירי דחזותו מוכיח עליו אבל תמרי שהרוח מוליכן ברחוק דלא שייך חזותו מוכיח עליו אע"פ שבעלים סבורין שיפלו תחת האילן מ"מ אם היו יודעין שהרוח מוליכן מרחוק היו מתיאשין אלא לאביי הא הוי יאוש שלא מדעת שהבעלים סבורים שיפלו תחת האילן ולא יקחום עוברי דרכים משום דחזותו מוכיח עליו ומשני דאפילו אותן שתחת האילן שרו אפילו לאביי [ח]באתרא דשכיחי שקצים ורמשים דמיאש וצ"ל דעבידי דנתרי כמו תאנים דאל"כ היו אסורים לאביי דהוי יאוש שלא מדעת דאינו סובר שיפלו כיון דלא עבידי דנתרי כמו זתים וחרובים דאסור כיון דלא עבידי דנתרי: **דלאו** בני מחילה נינהו מאי. בשלמא לרבה כיון דלכי גדלי מיאשי השתא נמי מיקרי יאוש: [ט]**תיובתא** דרבא. רבא ידע שפיר הך ברייתא כדמשמע קצת לעיל (דף כא:) דקאמר בזוטו של ים כ"ע לא פליגי דשרי כדבעינן למימר לקמן אלא דלא דייק איסורא דומיא דהתירא: [ב] **ברכתא** מאי. אם יש גדר סביב האילן מי שרו אותם שהרוח מוליך אותן חוץ לגדר דרך עליו הלא הבעלים סבורין שכולן יפלו תחת האילן ושם ישתמרו משקצים ורמשים: **אי** דליכא סימן מאי מכריז. פירוש למה צריך להכריז המוצא מאחר שהאבוד אין בו סימן ליתן ומשני דזה מכריז שאותו שאבד יתן סימן מקום וכן לקמן (דף כח.) דקאמר כדי שילך שלשה ויחזור שלשה ויכריז יום אחד היינו נמי שהמוצא מכריז והאובד יתן סימן אך קשה דבפרק אלו עוברין (דף מט: ושם ד"ה ויש) אמרינן ע"ה אין מכריזין על אבידתו והיאך אנו יודעין זה אם הוא של ע"ה ויש לומר דמיירי במוצא במקום דשכיח ע"ה ורש"י שפירש דהמוצא מכריז מקום שיאמר מצאתי חפץ במקום פלוני והוא יאמר חפץ פלוני ויקחנה ק"ק דהא תנן בפירקין (דף כח:) אמר אבידה ולא אמר סימנין לא אמר כלום אלמא במה שמכוין החפץ אינו סימן וי"ל דהתם נמי לאו משום שהוא חשוד לשקר שהפסיד חפץ אלא משום דא"ל כי היכי דאת אבדת חפץ ה"נ אימר אדם אחר הפסיד אבל הכא מהדרינן דאין רגילות ששני בני אדם אבדו חפץ זה כזה ובמקום אחד ולפרש"י הוה מכריז מקום דהכא פירושו ממש דומיא דמכריז מנין דשלהי פרק קמא (דף כ:): **ורבה** אמר מקום לא הוי סימן. ולפי דסבירא ליה לרבה מקום לא הוי סימן הוצרך לומר דסי' העשוי לידרס לא הוי סימן:

**עין משפט נר מצוה**

יט א מיי' פ"א מהלכות טומאת אוכלין הל' ב ופי"ב הלכה א:
כ ב מיי' פי"א מהלכות גזילה ואבידה הלכה י סמג עשין עד טוש"ע ח"מ סי' רנט סעיף ז:
כא ג ד מיי' פט"ו מהל' גזילה ואבידה הל' יו סמג שם טוש"ע ח"מ סי' רס סעיף ו:
כב ה מיי' שם הל' ח סמג שם טוש"ע ח"מ סי' רסב סעיף ח:
כג ו מיי' שם:
כד ז ח מיי' שם הל' י ופי"ג הל' ה סמג שם טוש"ע שם סעיף ט וסי' רסז סעיף ז:

**רבינו חננאל**

יותן: פי' סימן העשוי לידרס כגון קשירת כריכות וכיוצא בהן שאם ידרסו יותרו הקשרים ובטל הסימן. וקתני סימן העשוי לידרס רבה אמר לא הוי סימן ודינו כדין דבר שאין בו סימן ורבא אמר הוי סימן. ואקשי' עליה דרבא ממתני' דקתני כריכות ברשות הרבים הרי אלו שלו ברשות היחיד נוטל ומכריז מאי לאו דאית בהו סימן העשוי לידרס וברשות הרבים דשכיחי רבים דדרסי עליה ובטיל מיאש לפיכך הרי אלו שלו אבל ברשות היחיד דלא מידרסי חייב להכריז אלמא סימן העשוי לידרס לא הוי סימן ודחי רבא לא מתני' בדליכא בהו סימן כלל וברשות היחיד אמאי מכריז מכריז מקום שהמקום הוא הסימן. ורבה אמר מקום לא הוי סימן. פי' מינשתפי מתגלגלין ברגלי בני אדם. פי' כיון דיקירי לא מינשתפי כיון שהן כבדים אינן מתגלגלין ברגלי בני אדם

**מסורת הש"ס**

א) קדושין נט:, ב) לק... כ., ג) [ל"ל ר' שמע... וכ"ה בילקוט], ד) [קידו... נג., בבא קמא ע... סנהדרין כז.], ה) [פסח... כ:], ו) ס"א דרשות הים... ז) ס"א ברשות היח... ח) ס"א כיון דליכא אמ... ט) [צ"ל קודס ד... מאחר].

**הגהות הב"ח**

(א) רש"י ד"ה רבה מת... וכו' שיש בו סימ... (ב) תוס' ד"ה איסורא ו... דלא ידע דמיאש בין...

**הגהות הגר"א**

[א] גמ' דאיכא כ... נ"ב מחמת מתיקות... רמב"ס. משא"כ ש... פירות. מ"מ: [ב] תו... ד"ה ברכתא כו'. נ... אבל הרמב"ם כתב... הקפיד והקיף כו' שה... גילה דעתו שלא מחל...

**גליון הש"ס**

גמ' ביע"ל קג"ם. ע... שבת דף קנה ע"א תו... ד"ה והלכתא: שם ית... דלאו בני מחילה. ע... ב"ב דף קמג ע"ב תו... ד"ה ושם: תוס' ד"ה... דליכא כו' אך קש... עיין תשובת רשד"ס חי... סימן ר"נ:

**תורה אור השלם**

א) וְכֵן תַּעֲשֶׂה לַחֲמֹ... וְכֵן תַּעֲשֶׂה לְשִׂמְלָ... וְכֵן תַּעֲשֶׂה לְכָל אֲבֵ... אָחִיךָ אֲשֶׁר תֹּא... מִמֶּנּוּ וּמְצָאתָהּ ... תוּכַל לְהִתְעַלֵּם: [דברים כב, ג]

**ליקוטי רש"י**

התם כדרב פפא וכ... דרחמנא קרייה מע... דכתיב כי יתן והיינו בי... ואע"ג דמחשבה בעל... הוא דאפילו נפלו ממי... וניחא ליה הוי הכ... ומיקרי כי יותן [קידו... נט:]. באגא. בקעה [... נט.].

אֵינָן בְּ„כִּי יִתֵּן" – the Scriptural term of *'IF WATER IS PLACED'* DOES NOT APPLY TO [THIS PRODUCE]. טַעְמָא מַאי – **What is the reason** for the Baraisa's ruling that once the produce has dried, the owner's satisfaction is irrelevant? לָאו מִשּׁוּם דְּלָא אָמְרִינַן – **Is it not because we do** ***not*** **say** that כֵּיוָן דְּאִיגַּלַּאי מִילְּתָא דְּהַשְׁתָּא נִיחָא לֵיהּ – **since it has become clear**[1] **that he is satisfied** with the liquid contact **now,** מֵעִיקָּרָא נַמִּי נִיחָא לֵיהּ – **he was also satisfied originally,** while the produce was still wet?[2] We see from this Baraisa that the owner's eventual satisfaction is *not* viewed as having been in place while the produce was still wet. Similarly, the owner's eventual despair of recovering his lost object should not be viewed as having been in place at the time of the loss. This Baraisa, therefore, seems to support Abaye's position. – ? –

The Gemara rejects the proof:

שָׁאנֵי הָתָם – **It is different there** in the case of the produce, דִּכְתִיב: „כִּי יִתֵּן" – **for it is written** in regard to this law:[3] ***If he places,*** עַד שֶׁיִּתֵּן – which implies that food does not become susceptible to *tumah* **unless [the owner]** himself **places** the liquid upon the food.

The Gemara challenges this interpretation:

אִי הָכִי – **If so,**[4] רֵישָׁא נַמִּי – then in **the first case as well,** where the owner was pleased while the produce was still wet, it should also not become susceptible to *tumah*, since he did not personally wet it! – ? –

The Gemara clarifies its previous explanation in answer to this challenge:

הָתָם – **There,** in the first ruling of the Baraisa, כִּדְרַב פָּפָּא – **it is as Rav Pappa** said. דְּרַב פָּפָּא רָמֵי – **For Rav Pappa posed a contradiction:** כְּתִיב: „כִּי יִתֵּן" – **It is written** in the Torah *ki yiten*, which means *if he shall place.* This implies that food becomes susceptible to *tumah* only if the owner wets it himself. וְקָרֵינַן: „כִּי יוּתַּן" – **However, we read** this word, according to the pronunciation handed down by tradition, **as** ***ki yutan,*** which means *if it should be placed.* This implies that food becomes susceptible in any manner in which it becomes wet, even witho[ut] the owner's action. הָא כֵּיצַד – **How** may **this** contradiction [be] reconciled? בְּעִינַן „כִּי יוּתַּן" – We must say that for food [to] become susceptible to *tumah* by natural means, **we require** t[he] situation implied by the pronounced form: *ki yutan* (natur[al] contact), דּוּמְיָא דְּ„כִּי יִתֵּן" – to be **comparable to** the situati[on] implied by the written form: *ki yiten* (man-made contact). ה[מה] „יִתֵּן" לְדַעַת – **Just as** the man-made contact implied by *yiten* (*I*[*f he*] *shall place*) occurs **with** the owner's **knowledge**, since the own[er] is certainly aware that he himself wet the produce, „כִּי יוּתַּן" [אַף] נַמִּי לְדַעַת – **so too** the natural contact implied by the reading: *[ki] yutan* (*if it should be placed*), must occur **with** the owner['s] **knowledge.**[5]

The Gemara cites support for Abaye:

תָּא שְׁמַע – **Come, learn** a proof to Abaye's view from the followin[g]: דְּאָמַר רַבִּי יוֹחָנָן מִשּׁוּם רַבִּי יִשְׁמָעֵאל בֶּן יְהוֹצָדָק – **For R' Yochana[n] said in the name of R' Yishmael ben Yehotzadak:** [מ]ִנַּיִן לַאֲבֵידָה שֶׁשְּׁטָפָהּ נָהָר – **From where** do we derive **that a lost object swep[t] away by a** flooding **river** שֶׁהִיא מוּתֶּרֶת – **is permitted** [t]o whoever finds it? דִּכְתִיב – **For it is written** in the Torah concerning the commandment to return lost property: [וְ]כֵן תַּעֲשֶׂה לַחֲמֹרוֹ – ***And so shall you do for his donkey,*** [וְכֵ]ן תַּעֲשֶׂה לְשִׂמְלָתוֹ – ***and so shall you do for his garment,*** [וְכֵ]ן תַּעֲשֶׂה לְכָל־אֲבֵדַת אָחִיךָ – ***and so shall you do for any lost object of you[r] brother*** אֲשֶׁר־תֹּאבַד מִמֶּנּוּ וּמְצָאתָהּ – ***that is lost from him an[d] you have found."*** מִי שֶׁאֲבוּדָה הֵימֶנּוּ וּמְצוּיָה אֵצֶל כָּל אָדָם – Th[is] teaches that only **that which is lost to him but is accessible to a[ll] mankind** must be returned.[7] יָצְאָתָה זוֹ – **This** case of the obje[ct] swept away by a flood **is** therefore **excluded** from the law of retur[n] שֶׁאֲבוּדָה מִמֶּנּוּ – **inasmuch as [the object] is lost** not only t[o] **him,** וְאֵינָהּ מְצוּיָה אֵצֶל כָּל אָדָם – **but is inaccessible to a[ll] mankind.**[8] וְאִיסּוּרָא דּוּמְיָא דְּהֶיתֵּירָא – **Now** the case of th[e] object **forbidden** to the finder, i.e. the case in which a finder mus[t]

NOTES

1. Literally: the matter has been revealed.

2. Were we to say this, his satisfaction would be viewed as having been present while the produce was still wet and it would therefore be susceptible to *tumah.* Since the Baraisa rules that the produce is *not* susceptible in this case, we see that his current satisfaction *cannot* be viewed as having been in place at the earlier time, and cannot affect any legal classification that was to take effect at that time (*Rashi*).

3. *Leviticus* 11:38. See 22a note 26. In the Torah, the word for *placed* in this verse is spelled with only three letters – יתן. The accepted pronunciation is יֻתַּן, *yutan.* However, this spelling could also be read as יִתֵּן, *yiten.* To make the pronunciation *yutan* unmistakable would require adding a *vav* to the word, to spell יוּתַּן. Since the Torah does not use this more explicit form, the Gemara now assumes that the exposition of the halachah assigns primacy to the written form, and expounds the word as if it were pronounced יִתֵּן, *yiten* – he *places*. This would mean that produce does not become susceptible to *tumah* unless the owner wets it himself. For this reason, his subsequent satisfaction at a natural wetting cannot render the produce susceptible.

4. I.e. if we indeed learn from this verse that the owner must personally make the produce wet in order for it to become susceptible to *tumah.*

5. Rav Pappa reconciles the contradiction by stating that both elements of the Scriptural source – the spelling and the pronunciation – must be considered in formulating the rule concerning *hechsher tumah* (rendering food susceptible to *tumah*). [The synthesis of the spelling and the pronunciation teaches that natural contact (i.e. contact without the owner's intervention) can also render food susceptible to *tumah*, but only in circumstances in which it shares the basic elements of owner-induced contact.] This means that the owner must have knowledge of the contact and be satisfied with it while the produce is still wet (*Rashi*). Therefore, where the owner felt satisfaction while the produce was still wet, as in the Baraisa's first case, the produce becomes susceptible to *tumah.* But where this happens only after the produce is dry, as in the Baraisa's second case, the produce does n[ot] become susceptible. Without the owner's *conscious* knowledge, natur[al] wetting does not sufficiently resemble the case of owner-induce[d] wetting to qualify for this rule. It is for this reason that the owner['s] subsequent satisfaction is ineffective, even according to Rava. N[o] inference can be drawn from here to the law of *ye'ush,* because the law of *hechsher tumah* may be uncharacteristic, based as they are on [a] specific verse requiring *conscious* knowledge for *hechsher tuma[h]* (*Ritva*).

6. *Deuteronomy* 22:3.

7. The word מִמֶּנּוּ, *from him,* is seemingly superfluous. If the object is los[t] it is obviously lost from him, its owner. This is therefore understood a[s] emphasizing that the obligation to return lost objects applies only t[o] objects that are lost specifically to him, the owner [because he does n[ot] know where he lost them], but they are still accessible to whoever see[s] them (*Rashi*).

8. Under ordinary circumstances, an object swept away by a flood is los[t] to all mankind. Therefore, even if one finds it by sheer chance, one is no[t] obligated to return it.

There seems to be a dispute among the Rishonim as to how t[o] understand this Biblical decree. *Rashba* (21b ד״ה זוטו של ים) understand[s] this to mean that the Torah declared ownerless (*hefker*) any object los[t] to all mankind. Therefore, even if the owner protests loudly that he doe[s] not despair of recovering his object, it nonetheless belongs to whoeve[r] finds it. This seems to be the view of *Tosafos* as well (here ד״ה איסורא; se[e] also *Tosafos* cited by *Ritva* 24a ד״ה מפני שהבעלים מתיאשים). *Ritva* (ibid.) however, as well as *Rabbeinu Chananel* (to Gemara 21b) and *Ramban* (*Hil. Gezeilah V'Aveidah* 11:10), explain this to mean that the Torah i[s] telling us that the owner has certainly abandoned hope of recoverin[g] this object, since it is lost to all mankind. Thus, even if he protests tha[t] he has not abandoned it, we do not accept his protest (see *Ritva;* cf. hi[s] statements on 21b).

אינן בכי יותן טעמא מאי לאו משום דלא אמרינן כיון דאיגלאי מילתא דהשתא ניחא ליה מעיקרא נמי ניחא ליה שאני התם דכתיב כי יתן עד שיתן אי הכי רישא נמי התם [א] כדרב פפא דרב פפא רמי כתיב כי יתן וקרינן כי יותן הא כיצד בעינן כי יותן דומיא דכי יתן [א] מה יתן לדעת אף כי יותן נמי לדעת ת"ש [ב] דא"ר יוחנן משום [ג] רבי ישמעאל בן יהוצדק [ב] מנין לאבידה ששטפה נהר שהיא מותרת דכתיב [א] וכן תעשה לחמורו וכן תעשה לשמלתו וכן תעשה לכל אבידת אחיך אשר תאבד ממנו ומצאתה מי שאבודה הימנו ומצויה אצל כל אדם יצאתה זו שאבודה ממנו ואינה מצויה אצל כל אדם ואיסורא דומיא דהיתירא מה היתירא בין דאית בה סימן ובין דלית בה סימן שרא אף איסורא בין דאית בה סימן ובין דלית בה סימן אסורה תיובתא דרבא תיובתא [ד] והלכתא כוותיה דאביי ביע"ל קג"ם א"ל רב אחא בריה דרבא לרב אשי וכי מאחר דאיתותב רבא הני תמרי דזיקא היכי אכלינן להו אמר ליה [ג] כיון [א] דאיכא שקצים ורמשים דקא אכלי להו מעיקרא יאושי מיאש מנייהו [ה] יתמי דלאו בני מחילה נינהו מאי אמר ליה באגא בארעא דיתמי לא מחזקינן מוחזק ועומד מאי כרכתא מאי אמר ליה [ד] אסירן: כריכות ברה"ר הרי אלו שלו: אמר רבה ואפילו בדבר שיש בו סימן אלמא קסבר רבה סימן העשוי לידרס לא הוי סימן רבא אמר [ה] לא שנו אלא בדבר שאין בו סימן אבל בדבר שיש בו סימן חייב להכריז אלמא קסבר רבא סימן העשוי לידרס הוי סימן ואיכא דמתני להא שמעתא באנפי נפשה סימן העשוי לידרס רבה אמר לא הוי סימן ורבא אמר [ו] הוי סימן תנן כריכות ברה"ר הרי אלו שלו ברה"י נוטל ומכריז ה"ד אי דלית בהו סימן ברה"י מאי מכריז אלא לאו דאית בהו סימן וקתני ברה"ר הרי אלו שלו אלמא סימן העשוי לידרס לא הוי סימן תיובתא דרבא אמר לך רבא לעולם דלית בהו סימן ודקא אמרת ברה"י מאי מכריז מכריז מקום ורבה אמר מקום לא הוי סימן דאיתמר מקום רבה אמר לא הוי סימן ורבא אמר [ז] הוי סימן ת"ש כריכות ברה"ר הרי אלו שלו ברה"י נוטל ומכריז [ח] והאלומות בין ברה"ר ובין ברה"י נוטל ומכריז רבה היכי מתרץ לה ורבא היכי מתרץ לה רבה מתרץ לטעמיה בסימן ורבא מתרץ לטעמיה במקום רבה מתרץ לטעמיה בסימן כריכות ברשות הרבים הרי אלו שלו משום

דמדרסא

**רש"י**

אינן בכי יותן. ולא אמרינן כיון דהשתא ניחא מהני האי דעתא למעיקרא ותיהוי הכשר וקשיא לרבא: כתיב כי יתן. ולא כתיב כי יותן: לדעת. שידע בנתינה והוכשר בעיניו ועודהו הטל עליהן עדיין הן בנתינתו: ממנו. קרא יתירא הוא לאשמועינן שאינו אבוד אלא הימנו: ואיסורא דומיא דהיתירא. כיון דמחד קרא ילפינן מצויה אצל כל אדם שיחזור ושאינה מצויה יזכה בה איתקושי אתקוש להדדי זו לאיסורא וזו להיתירא: מה היתירא. שאינה מצויה לא חילק בין שיש בה סימן לשאין בה סימן: אף איסורא. דמצויה אצל כל אדם לא חילק בין אין סימן דכי ידע מיאש ליש סימן דלכי ידע לא מיאש וכי היכי דיש סימן אסירא כי אין סימן נמי אסירא היכא דאיכא למימר לא ידע דנפלה קודם שבאת ליד זה: יע"ל קג"ם. סימני הלכות הן יאוש שלא מדעת דהכא עד זומם למפרע הוא נפסל בסנהדרין (דף כז.) לחי העומד מאיליו בעירובין (דף טו.) קדושין שלא נמסרו לביאה בקדושין (דף נא.) גלוי דעתא בגיטא בגיטין (דף לד.) מומר אוכל נבילות להכעים פסול לענין עדות בסנהדרין (דף כז.): הני תמרי דזיקא. שהרוח משיר: היכי אכלינן להו. הא לא מיאש והא דנקט למיבעי בעיא מאחר דאיתותב רבא קשיא לי דבלא איתותב רבא איכא למיבעי דהא מודה רבא בכל דבר שחזותו מוכיח עליו חוץ מן התאנה מפני שנמאסת עם נפילתה ונראה בעיני דלא נקט לה אלא להרבות בחומר איסור כלומר מאחר דאיתותב אפילו בדבר שאין בו סימן כ"ש שאלו אסורין שיש בהן סימן: מעיקרא. מקודם נפילתו: יאושי מיאש. דיודע הוא שהרוח משיר מהן והשקצים מזומנים לאוכלן: יתמי. קטנים שאין הפקירן הפקר: באגא בארעא דיתמי לא מחזקינן. אין עלינו להחזיק כל הבקעה בחזקת הקרקע של יתומין ולאסור כל התמרים משום ספק קרקע של יתומים אלא הולכין אחר הרוב: מוחזק ועומד מאי. קרקע עצמה של יתומין מאי: כרכתא מאי. דקלים הכרוכין ומוקפין בגדר של אבנים סביב שאין שקצים ורמשים נכנסין שם: העשוי לידרס. שהמקום שהוא שם רגיל בדריסת בני אדם והחפץ נמוך ונוח לידרס: לא הוי סימן. שאין בעליו סומך לתת בו סימן מימר אמר נשחת הסימן בדריסת הרגלים: ברה"י. כגון בשדה זרועה שאין רוב בני אדם דורכין בה ויש מיעוט שהולכין בה: ה"ג אי דלית בהו סימן ברה"י מאי מכריז. כלומר כי מכריז זה מלא אבידה מאי מכריז שיוכל ליתן האובד סימן בה: מכריז מקום. ואינו מכריז שם האבידה אלא שם המקום מי שאבדה ממנו אבידה במקום פלוני יבא ויאמר מה איבד וזה בא ואומר אבדתי שם חפץ פלוני: והאלומות. עומרים גדולים: רבה היכי מתרץ לה. רבה דאמר טעמא דרה"ר משום דנדרס מאי שנא אלומות: ורבא. דמוקים לכריכות כשאין בו סימן מאי שנא כריכות ומאי שנא אלומות: רבה מתרץ לטעמיה. דטעמא [ו] דרשות הרבים דכריכות משום סימן ובדבר שיש (א) בה סימן: במקום. טעמא דכריכות [ז] ברשות הרבים משום מקום ובדבר שאין בו סימן:

**תוספות**

**איסורא** דומיא דהתירא. מה שמתיר אבודה ממנו ומכל אדם ע"כ לא איצטריך קרא בידע ומתיאש דהא אפילו במצויין אצל כל אדם מותרת ביאוש אלא לא אצטריך אלא כי לא ידע ואע"ג דלכי ידע לא מתיאש אפי' אם יש בו סימן כיון שהיא אבודה מכל אדם ה"נ איסורא דהיינו מצוייה אצל כל אדם דאסור כה"ג דלא (ב) ידעינן דמיאש בין יש בו סימן בין שאין בו סימן ואין להתיר אלא דמיאש קודם דאתא לידיה דשריא רחמנא: **מאחר** דאיתותב רבא כו'. בשלמא לרבא אע"ג דאותם שתחת האילן או בסמוך לאילן אסירי דחזותו מוכיח עליו אבל תמרי שהרוח מוליכן ברחוק דלא שייך חזותו מוכיח עליו אע"פ שבעלים סבורין שיפלו תחת האילן מ"מ אם היו יודעין שהרוח מוליכן מרחוק היו מתיאשין אלא לאביי הא הוי יאוש שלא מדעת שהבעלים סבורים שיפלו תחת האילן ולא יקחום עוברי דרכים משום דחזותו מוכיח עליו ומשני דאפילו אותן שתחת האילן שרו אפילו לאביי [ח] באתרא דשכיחי שקצים ורמשים דמיאש וצ"ל דעבידי דנתרי כמו תאנים דאל"כ היו אסורים לאביי דהוי יאוש שלא מדעת דאינו סובר שיפלו כיון דלא עבידי דנתרי כמו זתים ותרובים דאסור כיון דלא עבידי דנתרי: **דלאו** בני מחילה נינהו מאי. בשלמא לרבא כיון דלכי גדלי מיאשי השתא נמי מיקרי יאוש: [ט] **תיובתא** דרבא. רבא ידע שפיר הך ברייתא כדמשמע קצת לעיל (דף כא:) דקאמר בזוטו של ים כ"ע לא פליגי דשרי כדבעינן למימר לקמן אלא דלא דייק איסורא דומיא דהתירא: [ב] **כרכתא** מאי. אם יש גדר סביב האילן מי שרו אותם שהרוח מוליך אותן חוץ לגדר דכך עליו הלא הבעלים סבורין שכולן יפלו תחת האילן ושם ישתמרו משקצים ורמשים: **אי** דליכא סימן מאי מכריז. פירוש למה צריך להכריז המוצא מאחר שהאבוד אין בו סימן ליתן ומשני דזה מכריז שאותו שאבד יתן סימן מקום וכן לקמן (דף כח.) דקאמר כדי שילך שלשה ויחזור שלשה ויכריז יום אחד היינו נמי שהמוצא מכריז והאובד יתן סימן ° אך קשה דבפרק אלו עוברין (דף מט: ושם ד"ה ויש) אמרינן ע"ה אין מכריזין על אבידתו והיאך אנו יודעין זה אם הוא של ע"ה ויש לומר דמיירי במוצא במקום דשכיח ע"ה ורש"י שפירש דהמוצא מכריז מקום שיאמר מצאתי חפץ במקום פלוני והוא יאמר חפץ פלוני ויקחנה ק"ק דהא תנן בפירקין (דף כח:) אמר אבידה ולא אמר סימנין לא אמר כלום אלמא במה שמכוין החפץ אינו סימן וי"ל דהתם נמי לאו משום שהוא חשוד לשקר שהפסיד חפץ אלא משום דא"ל כי היכי דאת אבדת חפץ ה"נ איכא אדם אחר הפסיד אבל הכא מהדרינן דאין רגילות ששני בני אדם אבדו חפץ זה כזה ובמקום אחד ולפרש"י הוה מכריז מקום דהכא פירושו ממש דומיא דמכריז מנין דשלהי פרק קמא (דף כ:): **ורבה** אמר מקום לא הוי סימן. ולפי דסבירא ליה לרבה מקום לא הוי סימן הוצרך לומר דסי' העשוי לידרס לא הוי סימן:

**עין משפט נר מצוה**

יט א מיי' פ"א מהלכות טומאת אוכלין הל' ג ופי"ב הלכה א:
כ ב מיי' פי"א מהלכות גזילה ואבידה הלכה י סמג עשין עד טוש"ע ח"מ סי' רנט סעיף ז:
כא ג ד מיי' פט"ו מהל' גזילה ואבידה הל' יו סמג שם טוש"ע ח"מ סי' רס סעיף ו:
כב ה מיי' שם הל' ח סמג שם טוש"ע ח"מ סי' רסב סעיף ח:
כג ו מיי' שם:
כד ז ח מיי' שם הל' י ופי"ג הל' ה סמג שם טוש"ע שם סעיף ט וסי' רסז סעיף ז:

**רבינו חננאל**

יותן: פי' סימן העשוי לידרס כגון קשירת כריכות וכיוצא בהן שאם ידרסו יותרו הקשרים ובטל הסימן. וקתני סימן העשוי לידרס רבה אמר לא הוי סימן ודינו כדין דבר שאין בו סימן ורבא אמר הוי סימן. ואקשי' עליה דרבא ממתני' דקתני כריכות ברשות הרבים הרי אלו שלו ברשות היחיד נוטל ומכריז מאי לאו דאית בהו סימן העשוי לידרס וברשות הרבים דשכיחי רבים דדרסי עליה ובטיל מיאש לפיכך הרי אלו שלו אבל ברשות היחיד דלא מידרסי חייב להכריז אלמא סימן העשוי לידרס לא הוי סימן ודחי רבא לא מתני' בדליכא בהו סימן כלל וברשות היחיד אמאי מכריז מכריז מקום שהמקום הוא הסימן. ורבה אמר מקום לא הוי סימן. פי' מינשתפי מתגלגלין ברגלי בני אדם. פי' כיון דיקירי לא מינשתפי כיון שהן כבדים אינן מתגלגלין ברגלי בני אדם

**מסורת הש"ס**

א) קדושין נט:, ב) ל... ס., ג) [צ"ל ר' שמ... וכ"ה בילקוט], ד) [קיד... נב., בבא קמא... סנהדרין כז.], ה) [פס... ג:], ו) ס"א דרשות הר..., ז) ס"א ברשות הר..., ח) ס"א כיון דאיכא את..., ט) [צ"ל קודם... מאחר].

**הגהות הב"ח**

(א) רש"י ד"ה רבה מ... וכו' שיש בו סי..., (ב) תוס' ד"ה איסורא... דלא ידע דמיאש בי...

**הגהות הגר"א**

[א] גמ' דאיכא... נ"ב מחמת מתיקו... רמב"ם. משא"כ... פירות. מ"מ: [ב] ת... ד"ה כרכתא כו'... אבל הרמב"ם כתב... הקפיד והקיף כו' ש... גילה דעתו שלא מח...

**גליון הש"ס**

גמ' ביע"ל קג"ם... שבת דף קנה ע"א ... ד"ה והלכתא: שם יו... דלאו בני מחילה... ב"ב דף קמג ע"ב ... ד"ה ואם: תוס' ד"ה דליכא כו' אך קש... עיין תשובת רשד"ם ... סימן ר"נ:

**תורה אור השלם**

א) וְכֵן תַּעֲשֶׂה לַחֲמֹ... וְכֵן תַּעֲשֶׂה לְשִׂמְלָ... וְכֵן תַּעֲשֶׂה לְכָל אֲבֵ... אָחִיךָ אֲשֶׁר תֹּא... מִמֶּנּוּ וּמְצָאתָהּ תוּכַל לְהִתְעַלֵּם: [דברים כב, ג]

**ליקוטי רש"י**

התם כדרב פפא וכ... דרחמנא קרייה מ... דכתיב כי יתן והיינו בי... ואע"ג דמחשבה בעל... הוא דאפילו נפלו מ... וניחא ליה הוי הכ... ומיקרי כי יותן [קידו... נט:]. באגא. בקעה... נט.].

וכן ירדן שנטל מזה ונתן לזה מה שנטל נטל ומה שנתן נתן בשלמא גזלן וירדן דקא חזי להו ומיאש אלא גנב מי קא חזי ליה דמיאש תרגמה רב פפא בלסטים מזוין אי הכי היינו גזלן תרי גווני גזלן ת"ש שטף נהר קוריו עציו ואבניו ונתנו בתוך שדה חבירו הרי אלו שלו מפני שנתיאשו הבעלים טעמא דנתיאשו הבעלים הא סתמא לא הכא במאי עסקינן כשיכול להציל אי הכי אימא סיפא אם היו הבעלים מרדפין אחריהם חייב להחזיר אי ביכולין להציל מאי אריא מרדפין אפילו אין מרדפין נמי הכא במאי עסקינן ביכולין להציל על ידי הדחק מרדפין לא אייאוש אין מרדפין אייאושי מיאש ת"ש כיצד אמרו התורם שלא מדעת תרומתו תרומה הרי שירד לתוך שדה חבירו וליקט ותרם שלא ברשות אם חושש משום גזל אין תרומתו תרומה ואם לאו תרומתו תרומה ומנין הוא יודע אם חושש משום גזל ואם לאו הרי שבא בעל הבית ומצאו ואמר לו כלך אצל יפות אם נמצאו יפות מהן תרומתו תרומה ואם לאו אין תרומתו תרומה ליקטו הבעלים והוסיפו עליהן בין כך ובין כך תרומתו תרומה וכי נמצאו יפות מהן תרומתו תרומה אמאי בעידנא דתרם הא לא הוה ידע תרגמה רבא אליבא דאביי דשויה שליח [א]ה"נ מסתברא דאי ס"ד דלא שוויה שליח מי הויא תרומתו תרומה והא אתם גם אתם אמר רחמנא לרבות שלוחכם מה אתם לדעתכם אף שלוחכם לדעתכם אלא הכא במאי עסקינן כגון דשויה שליח וא"ל זיל תרום ולא א"ל תרום מהני וסתמיה דבעל הבית כי תרום מבינונית הוא תרום ואזל איהו ותרם מיפות ובא בעל הבית ומצאו וא"ל כלך אצל יפות אם נמצאו יפות מהן תרומתו תרומה ואם לאו אין תרומתו תרומה אמימר ומר זוטרא ורב אשי אקלעו לבוסתנא דמרי בר איסק אייתי אריסיה תמרי ורימוני ושדא קמייהו אמימר ורב אשי אכלי מר זוטרא לא אכיל אדהכי אתא מרי בר איסק אשכחינהו וא"ל לאריסיה אמאי לא אייתית להו לרבנן מהנך שפירתא אמרו ליה אמימר ורב אשי למר זוטרא השתא אמאי לא אכיל מר והתניא אם נמצאו יפות מהן תרומתו תרומה אמר להו הכי אמר רבא לא אמרו כלך אצל יפות אלא לענין תרומה בלבד משום דמצוה הוא וניחא ליה אבל הכא משום כסיפותא הוא דאמר הכי תא שמע עודהו הטל עליהן ושמח הרי זה בכי יותן נגבו אף על פי ששמח אינן

**רש"י**

ירדן. וכן שאר נהרות ותנא זה על יד הירדן היה יושב: בלסטים מזוין. ובחזקה נטלה הימנו ומעיקרא ידע ומייאש: שטף נהר קוריו. של זה ומלאן אחר: הרי אלו כו'. ה"ג הרי אלו שלו מפני שנתיאשו הבעלים דכל שטיפת נהר כקורות עצים ואבנים הבעלים ידעו בה מיד דיש לה קול: הא סתמא. הא אם היתה אבידה אחרת שאין לנו לומר שידעו הבעלים לא הויא של מוצאה קשיא לרבא: כשיכול להציל. ודכוותה במציאה אחרת דבר שיש בו סימן דיכול ליתן סימן וליטול מודינא בה דחייב להחזיר: אפילו אין מרדפין נמי. דסמכי אהצלה דלמחר וליומא אוחרא ולא מייאשי: ע"י הדחק. ואם לא ימהר להציל לא יצילו הלכך אין מרדפין אפקורי אפקרינהו דהא ידעו ולא הצילו: שלא מדעת. בעלים: וליקט. לצורך בעל הבית: ואם חושש. בעל הבית ומקפיד על מה שעשה זה: משום גזל. שתרם תרומתו בלא רשותו: כלך אצל יפות. היה לך לילך אצל יפות לתת מהן לכהן: לא הוה ידע. אלמא כיון דלכי ידע דניחא ליה אמרינן מעיקרא נמי ניחא ליה ולענין יאוש נמי כיון דלכי ידע מייאש מעיקרא נמי הוי יאוש: אתם גם אתם. כן תרימו גם אתם מהכא נפקא לן שלוחו של אדם כמותו לתרומה שהשליח שתרם תרומתו תרומה וכיון דשליחות מהכא נפקא לן על כרחך שלוחכם דומיא דאתם בעינן: אף שלוחכם לדעתכם. שהבעלים מינוהו שליח: לבוסתנא. פרדס: לא אכל. דגזל נינהו שהבעלים לא ידעו: אם נמצאו יפות כו'. אלמא גלי דעתיה דניחא ליה ה"נ גלי דעתיה דניחא ליה במה שנתן לנו: לא אמרו כלך אצל יפות. דהוי גלוי דעת אלא לענין תרומה: עודהו הטל עליהן. המעלה פירותיו לגג וירד עליהן הטל: ושמח. בטל שירד עליהן: הרי זה בכי יותן. והוכשרו לטומאה מעתה ועד עולם: נגבו. עד שלא מלאן: אע"פ ששמח. עכשיו בטל שירד עליהן:
אינן

**תוספות**

מה שנתן נתן. אתיא כר' דאמר בפרק הגוזל [בתרא] (ב"ק דף קיד.) סתם גנב וגזלן הוי יאוש בעלים:

שטף נהר קוריו עציו ואבניו. ה"ג אם נתיאשו הבעלים הרי אלו שלו וצ"ל דמיירי ביכול להציל בקל אם רודף בשעת שטיפה דאי לאו הכי הוה כזוטו של ים שאבוד ממנו ומכל אדם ועל זה לא היה אומר הא סתם לא אלא איירי ביכול להציל בקל בשעת שטיפה ואפילו אין בהן סימן ולפי שיעכבן עקולי ופשורי ויקחם שם ואפי' יקדמו אחרים ויקחו יחזירום לו לפי שניכר שהוא בעליו לפי שרדף מיד וס"ד דמיירי דאם לא רדף מיד בשעת שטיפה שלא יכול עוד כלל להציל דמוכח בסיפא לפי שיקחום אחרים כשיעכבום עקולי ופשורי ולא יחזירו לפי שאין בהן סימן וה"פ אם נתיאשו הבעלים דהיינו שהיו שם בשעת שטיפה ולא רדפו ואפילו אומרים שאין מתיאשים אין בכך כלום דודאי הן מתיאשים בלבן הא סתמא שלא היו בעלים בשעת שטיפה ולא נתיאשו עד שידעו הבעלים ששטפה נהר ואז כבר אינו יכול להציל לפי שאין בו סימן לא דכשמצאן באיסורא אתא לידיה שהבעלים לא ידעו עדיין אלמא יאוש שלא מדעת לא הוי יאוש ומשני דיכול להציל אפי' אחר שטיפה כגון שיש באבידה סימן שהבעלים אינן מתיאשין כשידעו ופריך אי הכי אימא סיפא ואם היו הבעלים מרדפין כו' מאי אריא מרדפין אפילו היו בעלים שם בשעת שטיפה ולא רדפו נמי יחזיר ומשני דיכול להציל אחר שטיפה ע"י הדחק דאע"פ שיש בו סימן בטורח יכול להציל לפי שיתרחקו הרבה שהנהר מוליכן ברחוק ולכך אם היה בשעת שטיפה ואינו מרדף ודאי מתיאש כיון שעתה יכול להציל בלא דוחק ואינו מציל אבל אין הבעלים בשעת שטיפה יחזיר דכשידעו הבעלים לא יתיאשו ויצילו על ידי הדחק וא"ת מנלן הא סתמא חייב להחזיר דלמא נתיאשו אתא לאפוקי שהיו שם ורדפו דחייב להחזיר וי"ל דא"כ לא ליתני אם נתיאשו אלא לתני סתמא שטף נהר קוריו עציו ואבניו הרי אלו שלו דפשיטא דלא מיירי ברדפו בשעת שטיפה דהא קתני סיפא דאם היו הבעלים מרדפים חייב ואין להקשות דמאי דייק מסיפא טעמא דמרדפין הא סתמא הרי אלו שלו דלעולם נימא דהוא הדין סתמא דיחזיר ולא נקט מרדפין אלא לאפוקי שהיו הבעלים בשעת שטיפה ולא רדפו וע"י סיפא ידעינן דמיירי באין יכול להציל אבל רש"י דגרס מפני שנתיאשו הבעלים משמע לישנא דפשיט ליה דנתיאשו א"כ מרישא גופיה מצי לאוכוחי דמיירי באין יכול להציל ולא היה צריך להביא סיפא ותו מנלן דהא סתמא לא דאפילו סתמא נמי מצי מיירי:

הכי גרסינן ה"נ מסתברא דאי לא שויה שליח ולא גרסינן ותסברא:

אם יש יפות מהן תרומתו תרומה. דמסתמא גם מתחילה היה דעתו כן וא"ת ונימא דהשתא ודאי ניחא ליה ביפות אבל מתחילה בשעה שתרם אי הוה ידע לא הוה ניחא ליה דאין דרך לתרום מן היפות כדאמרינן לעיל (דף כא:) גבי דבר שיש בו סימן דאפילו לרבא חייב להכריז דאע"ג דהשתא מתיאש אין בכך כלום וי"ל דשאני הכא דכיון דחזינן ביה דניחא ליה השתא אמרינן נמי ניחא ליה מעיקרא משום מצוה:

ואם לאו אין תרומתו תרומה. וא"ת דבפרק אלמנה ניזונית (כתובות דף נד: ושם ד"ה פיחת) אמרינן דסתמיה דבעל הבית הוי אחד מחמשים ואם השליח פיחת י' או הוסיף י' תרומתו תרומה דמאי א"ל בהכי אמדתיך ה"נ נימא הכי וי"ל דהתם הוי כולה שיעור תרומה ויש שתורם כך ויש שתורם כך לכך מצי א"ל כיון שלא פירשת לי בהכי אמדתיך אבל מיפות אין רגילות לתרום ולכך לא היה לו לתרום בשום ענין מהם בלא רשותו:

מר זוטרא לא אכל. וא"ת ואמאי לא אכל והאמר רבא פרק הגוזל בתרא (ב"ק דף קיט.) אריסא מדנפשיה קא זבן ויש לומר דהתם שהביא האריס מבית דמסתמא ממה שהגיע לחלקו מביא אבל הכא שהביא מן הפרדס היה חושש מר זוטרא שמא בשעת חלוקה לא יאמר לבעל הפרדס תטול כנגד מה שנתתי להם ורב אשי לא היה חושש לזה ולכך אכל קודם שבא מרי בר איסק משום דאריס מדנפשיה קא יהיב דאין לומר שהיה סומך שיתרצה מרי בר איסק כשידע דהלכה כאביי ואע"ג דהשתא ניחא ליה מעיקרא לא הוה ניחא ליה:
איסורא

**עין משפט נר מצוה**

טו א מיי' פ"ו מהלכות גזילה ואבידה הל' א טוש"מ סי' רנט:
טז ב ג ד מיי' פ"ד מהל' תרומות הל' ג:
יז ה מיי' שם הלכה א:
יח ו (מיי' פי"ג מהל' טומאת אוכלין הלכה ג):

**רבינו חננאל**

הן ממשמש בהן כל שעה והללו אע"פ שהן בצד שדה קצוצות דמוכחא מילתא דמשדה זו הן כבר נתיאש מהן כמו המעות. וכן תאנה הנוטה לדרך התאנים שהן נופלות ממנה מיד נמאסות לפיכך מתיאש מהן ומותרין משום גזל ופטורין מן המעשר דאינו נשמר ותנן כלל אמרו במעשרות כל שהוא אוכל ונשמר וגידוליו מן הארץ חייב במעשרות. גנב שנטל מזה ונתן לזה לא גנב הוא שגונב בסתר. אבל האי גנב דקתני גזלן הוא שנוטל בגלוי ותרי גווני גזלן קתני חד גזלן וחד ליסטים מזויין. ת"ש שטף נהר קורותיו ונתנן לתוך שדה חבירו אם נתיאשו הבעלים הרי אלו שלו מכלל דבסתמא חייב להחזיר ואוקימנא כשבעלין מרדפין אחריהן ויכולין להציל על ידי הדחק. ת"ש כיצד אמרו התורם שלא מדעת תרומתו תרומה וכו' אוקימנא כגון שתרם ובא בעל הפירות ומצאו שתרם ואמר לו למה [לא] היתה תורם מאלו היפות מוכחא מילתא שנתרצה ואסיקנא לא אמרי' כלך אצל יפות רצון בעלים הן במה שנעשה אלא לענין תרומה בלבד משום דמצוה היא וניחא ליה ביפה. אבל בזולתי תרומה לא ואע"פ שאמר לו כלך אצל יפות משום כסיפותא הוא דאמר ליה הכי ואסורין משום גזל. ת"ש עודהו הטל עליהם ושמח הרי הן בכי

**מסורת הש"ס**

א) בבא קמא נז. וש"נ, ב) [תוספתא דכתובות פ"ח], ג) [בתוספתא ... אם נתיאשו הבעלים הרי אלו ...], ועיין תוס' ד"ה ..., ד) [תוספתא שם ...], ה) קדושין נב:, [תוספתא דתרומות פרק ...], ו) [עירובין עא.], ז) שבת נג: וש"נ, ח) לקמן עא., קדושין ..., ט) [תוספתא ...], י) ... פרק ג ע"ש], ... למאי דסבירא לן ... דאיירי בגנב ממש אתיא כו'.

**הגהות הגר"א**

[א] גמ' ה"נ מסתברא. נ"ב גירסת ... ותסברא והא ... כו' ור"ל ואמאי ... לכלך אצל יפות הא ... כמותו אלא הב"ע ... וכל זה לתירוץ דרבא ... אבל א"צ לכ"ז דמצוה ... כמ"ש בקדושין נב ... ועי' תוס' שם ד"ה אם ... וא"כ צ"ל כו' ואולי ... שכתבו כאן ... ה"ג כו' ול"ג כו' ... מ"ש רבינו ביו"ד סי' של"א ס"ק ע"ו):

**גליון הש"ס**

גמ' דשויה שליח. עיין עירובין דף עא ע"א תוס' ד"ה כלך: שם לבוסתנא דמרי בר איסק. עיין יבמות דף כא ע"ב תוס' ד"ה ר"א:

**תורה אור השלם**

א) כֵּן תָּרִימוּ גַם אַתֶּם תְּרוּמַת יְיָ מִכֹּל מַעְשְׂרֹתֵיכֶם אֲשֶׁר תִּקְחוּ מֵאֵת בְּנֵי יִשְׂרָאֵל וּנְתַתֶּם מִמֶּנּוּ אֶת תְּרוּמַת יְיָ לְאַהֲרֹן הַכֹּהֵן: [במדבר יח, כח]
ב) וְכִי יֻתַּן מַיִם עַל זֶרַע וְנָפַל מִנִּבְלָתָם עָלָיו טָמֵא הוּא לָכֶם: [ויקרא יא, לח]

**ליקוטי רש"י**

ואם חושש משום גזל. שמקפיד בעל הבית על מה שעשה ודומה לו כגזלה. אין תרומתו תרומה. דהשתא ודאי כי קאמר ליה אם מצאת מיד יפות מאלו היית גוזלן. בין כך ובין כך. בין שיש יפות בין שאין יפות מהן [קדושין נב:]. כלך אצל יפות. גבי תורם את של חבירו שלא מדעת תניא [ב"מ דף כב.] בא בעל הבית ומצאו שהוא תורם ואמר לו כלך אצל יפות אם יש לו יפות מהן תרומתו תרומה דגלי אדעתיה דניחא ליה ואמרינן כמאן דשויה שליח מעיקרא דמי [עירובין עא.]. אתם גם אתם. והאי גם יתירא הוא [קדושין מא:]. לבוסתנא. גינה של אילנות [לקמן לט:].

UPON THEM [the produce a person had placed on his roof],[25] וְשָׂמַח – AND HE WAS PLEASED that they had become wet, הֲרֵי זֶה בְּ,,כִי יֻתַּן״ – THIS case IS SUBJECT TO the Scriptural rule of *'IF WATER IS PLACED.'*[26] The produce is now susceptible to *tumah*-contamination, even after it becomes dry.[27] נָגְבוּ – If [THE PRODUCE] HAD already DRIED before the owner became aware of the contact with dew, אַף עַל פִּי שֶׁשָּׂמַח – then EVEN THOUGH HE WAS PLEASED that they had become wet,

NOTES

25. Fresh produce was sometimes placed on the roof to prevent it from becoming infested (see *Machshirin* 6:1).

26. *Leviticus* 11:38. The full verse reads: וְכִי יֻתַּן־מַיִם עַל־זֶרַע וְנָפַל מִנִּבְלָתָם עָלָיו טָמֵא הוּא לָכֶם, *And if water is placed upon seed, and any part of their carcasses* [i.e. of the eight species of *sheretz* enumerated earlier] *should fall upon it, it is tamei to you.* Although the owner did not place the dew upon the produce [nor even place the produce on the roof for the sake of having it become wet], his satisfaction at its having become wet is equivalent to having "placed water upon them." The source for this will be explained on 22b (see note 3).

27. Once food has become susceptible to *tumah,* it remains susceptible even after it dries.

וכן ירדן שנטל מזה ונתן לזה מה שנטל נטל ומה שנתן נתן בשלמא גזלן וירדן דקא חזי להו ומיאש אלא גנב מי קא חזי ליה דמיאש תרגמה רב פפא בלסטים מזוין אי הכי היינו (א) גזלן תרי גווני גזלן ת"ש (ב) א שטף נהר קוריו עציו ואבניו ונתנו בתוך שדה חבירו (ג) הרי אלו שלו מפני שנתיאשו הבעלים טעמא דנתיאשו הבעלים הא סתמא לא הכא במאי עסקינן כשיכול להציל אי הכי אימא סיפא (ד) אם היו הבעלים מרדפין אחריהם חייב להחזיר אי ביכולין להציל מאי אריא מרדפין אפילו אין מרדפין נמי הכא במאי עסקינן ביכולין להציל על ידי הדחק מרדפין לא אייאוש אין מרדפין אייאושי מיאש ת"ש (ה) כיצד אמרו התורם שלא מדעת תרומתו תרומה ב הרי שירד לתוך שדה חבירו וליקט ותרם שלא ברשות אם חושש משום גזל אין תרומתו תרומה ואם לאו תרומתו תרומה ומנין הוא יודע אם חושש משום גזל ואם לאו ג הרי שבא בעל הבית ומצאו ואמר לו (ו) כלך אצל יפות אם נמצאו יפות מהן תרומתו תרומה ואם לאו אין תרומתו תרומה ד ליקטו הבעלים והוסיפו עליהן בין כך ובין כך תרומתו תרומה וכי נמצאו יפות מהן תרומתו תרומה אמאי בעידנא דתרם הא לא הוה ידע (ז) תרגמה רבא אליבא דאביי ◦ דשויה שליח [א]ה"נ מסתברא דאי ס"ד דלא שוויה שליח מי הויא תרומתו תרומה והא אתם (א) גם אתם אמר רחמנא (ח) ה לרבות שלוחכם מה אתם לדעתכם אף שלוחכם לדעתכם אלא הכא במאי עסקינן כגון דשויה שליח וא"ל זיל תרום ולא א"ל תרום מהני וסתמיה דבעל הבית כי תרום מבינונית הוא תרום ואזל איהו ותרם מיפות ובא בעל הבית ומצאו וא"ל כלך אצל יפות אם נמצאו יפות מהן תרומתו תרומה ואם לאו אין תרומתו תרומה אמימר ומר זוטרא ורב אשי אקלעו ◦ לבוסתנא דמרי בר איסק אייתי אריסיה תמרי ורימוני ושדא קמייהו אמימר ורב אשי אכלי מר זוטרא לא אכיל אדהכי אתא מרי בר איסק אשכחינהו וא"ל לאריסיה אמאי לא אייתית להו לרבנן מהנך שפירתא אמרו ליה אמימר ורב אשי למר זוטרא השתא אמאי לא אכיל מר והתניא אם נמצאו יפות מהן תרומתו תרומה אמר להו הכי אמר רבא לא אמרו כלך אצל יפות אלא לענין תרומה בלבד משום דמצוה הוא וניחא ליה אבל הכא משום כסיפותא הוא דאמר הכי תא שמע (ט) ו עודהו הטל עליהן ושמח הרי זה (ב) בכי יותן נגבו אף על פי ששמח אינן

ירדן. וכן שאר נהרות ותנא זה על יד הירדן היה יושב: בלסטים מזוין. ובחזקה נטלה הימנו ומעיקרא ידע ומייאש: שטף נהר קוריו. של זה ונתנן אחר: הרי אלו כו'. ה"ג הרי אלו שלו מפני שנתיאשו הבעלים דכל שטיפת נהר כקורות עצים ואבנים הבעלים ידעו בה מיד דיש לה קול: הא סתמא. הא אם היתה אבידה אחרת שאין לנו לומר שידעו הבעלים לא הויא של מוצאה קשיא לרבא: כשיכול להציל. ודכוותה במציאה אחרת דבר שיש בו סימן דיכול ליתן סימן וליטול מודינא בה דחייב להחזיר: אפילו אין מרדפין נמי. דסמכי אהצלה דלמחר וליומא אוחרא ולא מייאשי: ע"י הדחק. ואם לא ימהר להציל לא יצילו הלכך אין מרדפין אפקורי אפקרינהו דהא ידעו ולא הצילו: שלא מדעת. בעלים: וליקט. לצורך בעל הבית: ואם חושש. בעל הבית ומקפיד על מה שעשה זה: משום גזל. שתרם תרומתו בלא רשותו: כלך אצל יפות. היה לך לילך אצל יפות לתת מהן לכהן: לא הוה ידע. אלמא כיון דלכי ידע דניחא ליה אמרינן מעיקרא נמי ניחא ליה ולענין יאוש נמי כיון דלכי ידע מייאש מעיקרא נמי הוי יאוש: אתם גם אתם. כן תרימו גם אתם מהכא נפקא לן שלוחו של אדם כמותו לתרומה שהשליח שתרם תרומתו תרומה וכיון דשליחות מהכא נפקא לן על כרחך שלוחכם דומיא דאתם בעינן: אף שלוחכם לדעתכם. שהבעלים מינוהו שליח: לבוסתנא. פרדס: לא אכל. דגזל נינהו שהבעלים לא ידעו: אם נמצאו יפות כו'. אלמא גלי דעתיה דניחא ליה ה"נ גלי דעתיה דניחא ליה במה שנתן לנו: לא אמרו כלך אצל יפות. דהוי גלוי דעת אלא לענין תרומה: עודהו הטל עליהן. המעלה פירותיו לגג וירד עליהן הטל: ושמח. בטל שירד עליהן: הרי זה בכי יותן. והוכשרו לטומאה מעתה ועד עולם: נגבו. עד שלא מצאן: אע"פ ששמח. עכשיו בטל שירד עליהן: אינן

מה שנתן נתן. (י) אתיא כר' דאמר בפרק הגוזל [בתרא] (ב"ק דף קיד.) סתם גנב וגזלן הוי יאוש בעלים:

שטף נהר קוריו עציו ואבניו. ה"ג אם נתיאשו הבעלים הרי אלו שלו וצ"ל דמיירי ביכול להציל בקל אם רודף בשעת שטיפה דאי לאו הכי הוה כזוטו של ים שאבוד ממנו ומכל אדם ועל זה לא היה אומר הא סתם לא אלא איירי דיכול להציל בקל בשעת שטיפה ואפילו אין בהן סימן ולפי שיעכבן עקולי ופשורי ויקחם שם ואפי' יקדמו אחרים ויקחו יחזירום לו לפי שניכר שהוא בעליו לפי שרדף מיד וס"ד דמיירי דאם לא רדף מיד בשעת שטיפה שלא יכול עוד כלל להציל כדמוכח בסיפא לפי שיקחום אחרים כשיעכבום עקולי ופשורי ולא יחזירו לפי שאין בהן סימן וה"פ אם נתיאשו הבעלים דהיינו שהיו שם בשעת שטיפה ולא רדפו ואפילו אומרים שאין מתיאשים אין בכך כלום דודאי הן מתיאשים בלבן הא סתמא שלא היו בעלים בשעת שטיפה ולא נתיאשו עד שידעו הבעלים ששטפה נהר ואז כבר אינו יכול להציל לפי שאין בו סימן לא דכשמלאן באיסורא אתא לידיה שהבעלים לא ידעו עדיין אלמא יאוש שלא מדעת לא הוי יאוש ומשני ביכול להציל אפי' אחר שטיפה כגון שיש באבידה סימן שהבעלים אינן מתיאשין כשידעו ופריך אי הכי אימא סיפא ואם היו הבעלים מרדפין כו' מאי אריא מרדפין אפילו היו בעלים שם בשעת שטיפה ולא רדפו נמי יחזיר ומשני ביכול להציל אחר שטיפה ע"י הדחק דאע"פ שיש בו סימן בטורח יכול להציל לפי שיתרחקו הרבה שהנהר מוליכן ברחוק ולכך אם היה בשעת שטיפה ואינו מרדף ודאי מתיאש כיון שעתה יכול להציל בלא דוחק ואינו מציל אבל אין הבעלים בשעת שטיפה יחזיר דכשידעו הבעלים לא יתיאשו ויצילו על ידי הדחק וא"ת מנלן הא סתמא חייב להחזיר דלמא נתיאשו אתא לאפוקי שהיו שם ורדפו דחייב להחזיר וי"ל דא"כ לא ליתני אם נתיאשו אלא לתני סתמא שטף נהר קוריו עציו ואבניו הרי אלו שלו דפשיטא דלא מיירי ברדפו בשעת שטיפה דהא קתני סיפא דאם היו הבעלים מרדפים חייב ואין להקשות דמאי דייק מסיפא טעמא דמרדפין הא סתמא הרי אלו שלו דלעולם נימא דהוא הדין סתמא דיחזיר ולא נקט מרדפין אלא לאפוקי שהיו הבעלים בשעת שטיפה ולא רדפו וע"י סיפא ידעינן דמיירי באין יכול להציל אבל רש"י דגרס מפני שנתיאשו הבעלים משמע ליישנא דפשיט ליה דנתיאשו א"כ מרישא גופיה מצי לאוכוחי דמיירי באין יכול להציל ולא היה צריך להביא סיפא ותו מנלן דהא סתמא לא דאפילו סתמא נמי מצי מיירי:

**הכי** גרסינן ה"נ מסתברא דאי לא שויה שליח ולא גרסינן ותסברא:

**אם** יש יפות מהן תרומתו תרומה. דמסתמא גם מתחילה היה דעתו כן וא"ת ונימא דהשתא ודאי ניחא ליה ביפות אבל מתחילה בשעה שתרם אי הוה ידע לא הוה ניחא ליה דאין דרך לתרום מן היפות כדאמרינן לעיל (דף כא:) גבי דבר שיש בו סימן דאפילו לרבא חייב להכריז דאע"ג דהשתא מתיאש אין בכך כלום וי"ל דשאני הכא דכיון דחזינן ביה דניחא ליה השתא אמרינן נמי ניחא ליה מעיקרא משום מצוה:

**ואם** לאו אין תרומתו תרומה. וא"ת דבפרק אלמנה ניזונית (כתובות דף צט: ושם ד"ה פיחת) אמרינן דסתמיה דבעל הבית הוי אחד מחמשים ואם השליח פיחת י' או הוסיף י' תרומתו תרומה דמאי א"ל בהכי אמדתיך ה"נ נימא הכי וי"ל דהתם הוי כולה שיעור תרומה ויש שתורם כך ויש שתורם כך לכך מצי א"ל כיון שלא פירשת לי בהכי אמדתיך אבל מיפות אין רגילות לתרום ולכך לא היה לו לתרום בשום ענין מהם בלא רשותו:

**מר** זוטרא לא אכל. וא"ת ואמאי לא אכל האמר רבא פרק הגוזל בתרא (ב"ק דף קיט.) אריסא מדנפשיה קא זבן ויש לומר דהתם שהביא האריס מבית דמסתמא ממה שהגיע לחלקו מביא אבל הכא שהביא מן הפרדס היה חושש מר זוטרא שמא בשעת חלוקה לא יאמר לבעל הפרדס תטול כנגד מה שנתתי להם ורב אשי לא היה חושש לזה ולכך אכל קודם שבא מרי בר איסק משום דאריס מדנפשיה קא יהיב דאין לומר שהיה סומך שיתרצה מרי בר איסק כשידע דהלכה כאביי ואע"ג דהשתא ניחא ליה מעיקרא לא הוה ניחא ליה:

איסורא

## עין משפט נר מצוה

טו א מיי' פ"ו מהלכות גזלה ואבידה הל' א טוש"מ סי' רנט:

טז ב ג ד מיי' פ"ד מהל' תרומות הל' ג:

יז ה מיי' שם הלכה א:

יח ו (מיי' פי"ב מהל' טומאת אוכלין הלכה ב):

## רבינו חננאל

הן ממשמש בהן כל שעה והללו אע"פ שהן בצד שדה קצוצות דמוכחא מילתא דמשדה זו הן כבר נתיאש מהן כמו המעות. וכן תאנה הנוטה לדרך התאנים שהן נופלות ממנה מיד נמאסות לפיכך מתיאש מהן ומותרין משום גזל ופטורין מן המעשר דאינו נשמר ותנן כלל אמרו במעשרות כל שהוא אוכל ונשמר וגידוליו מן הארץ חייב במעשרות. גנב שנטל מזה ונתן לזה לא גנב הוא שגונב בסתר. אבל האי גנב דקתני גזלן הוא שנוטל בגלוי ותרי גווני גזלן קתני חד גזלן וחד ליסטים מזויין. ת"ש שטף נהר קורותיו ונתנן לתוך שדה חבירו אם נתיאשו הבעלים הרי אלו שלו מכלל דבסתמא חייב להחזיר ואוקימנא כשבעלין מרדפין אחריהן ויכולין להציל על ידי הדחק. ת"ש כיצד אמרו התורם שלא מדעת תרומתו תרומה וכו' אוקימנא כגון שתרם ובא בעל הפירות ומצאו שתרם ואמר לו למה [לא] היתה תורם מאלו היפות מוכחא מילתא שנתרצה ואסיקנא לא אמרי' כלך אצל יפות רצון בעלים הן במה שנעשה אלא לענין תרומה בלבד משום דמצוה היא וניחא ליה ביפות. אבל בזולתי תרומה לא ואע"פ שאמר לו כלך אצל יפות משום כסיפותא הוא דאמר ליה הכי ואסורין משום גזל. ת"ש עודהו הטל עליהם ושמח הרי הן בכי

## מסורת הש"ס

[בבא קמא נז, וש"נ], [תוספתא דכתובות פ"ק ח], ג) [בתוספתא אם נתיאשו בעלים הרי אלו שלו, ועיין תוס' ד"ה ...], ד) [תוספתא שם ...], ה) קדושין נב:, [תוספתא דתרומות פרק ...], ו) [עירובין עא.], [שבת נג: וש"נ], [לקמן עא:, קדושין ...], ט) [תוספתא ...שירין פרק ג ע"ש], ...ס"א למאי דסבירא לן ...תא דאיירי בגנב ממש אתיא כו'.

## הגהות הגר"א

[א] גמ' ה"נ מסתברא. נ"ב גירסת ...רמב"ם ותסברא והא ...תם כו' ור"ל ואמאי ...יכן לכלך אצל יפות הא ...ומו כמותו אלא הב"ע ...' וכל זה לתירוץ דרבא ...ן אבל א"צ לכ"ז דמצוה ...אני כמ"ש בקדושין נב ...ועי' תוס' שם ד"ה אם ...' וא"כ צ"ל כו' ואולי ...יטתייהו שכתבו כאן ...'ה ה"ג כו' ול"ג כו' ...צמ"ש רבינו ביו"ד סי' של"א ס"ק ע"ו):

## גליון הש"ס

...מ' דשויה שליח. עיין ...ירובין דף עא ע"א ...ים' ד"ה כלך: שם ...בוסתנא דמרי בר ...יסק. עיין יבמות דף כא ע"ב תוס' ד"ה ר"א:

## תורה אור השלם

א) כֵּן תָּרִימוּ גַם אַתֶּם תְּרוּמַת יְיָ מִכֹּל מַעְשְׂרֹתֵיכֶם אֲשֶׁר תִּקְחוּ מֵאֵת בְּנֵי יִשְׂרָאֵל וּנְתַתֶּם מִמֶּנּוּ אֶת תְּרוּמַת יְיָ לְאַהֲרֹן הַכֹּהֵן: [במדבר יח, כח]

ב) וְכִי יֻתַּן מַיִם עַל זֶרַע וְנָפַל מִנִּבְלָתָם עָלָיו טָמֵא הוּא לָכֶם: [ויקרא יא, לח]

## ליקוטי רש"י

...אם חושש משום גזל. ...ם מקפיד בעל הבית על ...ה שעשה ודומה לו ...גזלה. אין תרומתו תרומה. דהשתא ודאי ...כי קאמר ליה אם מצאת ...וד יפות מאלו היית גוזלן. ...בין כך ובין כך. בין שיש ...פות בין שאין יפות מהן ...[קדושין נב:]. כלך אצל ...יפות. גבי תורם את של ...חבירו שלא מדעת תניא ...[ב"מ דף כב.] בא בעל ...הבית ומצאו שהוא תורם ...אמר לו כלך אצל יפות אם ...יש לו יפות מהן תרומתו ...תרומה דגלי אדעתיה ...דניחא ליה ואמרינן כמאן ...דשויה שליח מעיקרא דמי ...[עירובין עא.]. אתם גם ...אתם. והאי גם יתירא ...הוא [קדושין מא:]. ...לבוסתנא. גינה של אילנות [לקמן לט:].

אַתֶּם" אָמַר רַחֲמָנָא – But the Merciful One has said in His Torah not only: *you shall separate terumah,* but rather: *you also shall separate terumah,*[18] לְרַבּוֹת שְׁלוּחֲכֶם – to include your agent as one who may legitimately separate *terumah* on your behalf. This establishes the following parallel between the owner's act and his agent's:[19] מָה "אַתֶּם" לְדַעְתְּכֶם – Just as *you,* the owner, separate *terumah* only with your knowledge, אַף שְׁלוּחֲכֶם לְדַעְתְּכֶם – so too your agent must separate *terumah* only with your knowledge, having been appointed by you to act on your behalf.[20] Thus, the Baraisa cannot be speaking of *terumah* separated by an unauthorized person, since his separation would not be valid even if the owner later consented.

The Gemara now concludes its interpretation of the Baraisa: אֶלָּא – Rather, הָכָא בְּמַאי עַסְקִינַן – with what case are we dealing here in the Baraisa? כְּגוֹן דְּשַׁוְּיֵהּ שָׁלִיחַ – With a case in which he appointed him as his agent, וְאָמַר לֵיהּ זִיל תְּרוֹם – and told him: "Go, separate *terumah,*" וְלֹא אָמַר לֵיהּ תְּרוֹם מֵהֶן – but he did not specifically tell him to separate *terumah* from these better fruits. וּסְתָמֵיהּ דְּבַעַל הַבַּיִת – Now ordinarily, a householder, כִּי תְּרוּם – when he separates *terumah,* מִבֵּינוֹנִית הוּא תְּרוּם – separates *terumah* from an intermediate grade of [produce]; וְאָזַל אִיהוּ וְתָרַם מִיָּפוֹת – however, this [agent] went and separated *terumah* from a better grade of [produce].[21] וּבָא בַּעַל הַבַּיִת וּמְצָאוֹ – [The owner] then came and found [the agent], וְאָמַר לֵיהּ – and said to him: כְּלָךְ אֵצֶל יָפוֹת – "You really should go to the better [produce] and designate it as *terumah.*" אִם נִמְצְאוּ יָפוֹת מֵהֶן – Therefore, if better [produce] was found in the owner's stock, תְּרוּמָתוֹ תְּרוּמָה – what [the agent] separated is considered *terumah*; וְאִם לַאו – and if better produce was not found in the owner's stock, אֵין תְּרוּמָתוֹ תְּרוּמָה – what he separated is not considered *terumah*.[22]

The Gemara now relates an incident that pertains to the Baraisa just cited:

אֲמֵימָר וּמָר זוּטְרָא וְרַב אַשִׁי אִקְלְעוּ לְבוּסְתָּנָא דְּמָרִי בַּר אִיסַק – Ameimar, Mar Zutra, and Rav Ashi came to the orchard of Mari bar Isak. אַיְיתִי אֲרִיסֵיהּ תַּמְרֵי וְרִימּוֹנֵי – His sharecropper brought out dates and pomegranates, וְשָׁדָא קַמַּיְיהוּ – and placed the fruits before them. אֲמֵימָר וְרַב אַשִׁי אָכְלֵי – Ameimar and Rav Ashi ate the fruit, מָר זוּטְרָא לֹא אָכֵיל – but Mar Zutra did not eat, out of concern that the sharecropper was offering the owner's fruit without his consent.[23] אַדְּהָכִי אָתָא מָרִי בַּר אִיסַק אַשְׁכַּחִינְהוּ – Meanwhile, Mari bar Isak came and found them, וְאָמַר לֵיהּ לַאֲרִיסֵיהּ – and told his sharecropper: אַמַּאי לֹא אַיְיתִית לְהוּ לְרַבָּנָן מֵהֶנָךְ שַׁפִּירָתָא – "Why did you not bring for the Rabbis from those fine [fruits]?" Mar Zutra, however, still refused to eat. אָמְרוּ לֵיהּ אֲמֵימָר וְרַב אַשִׁי לְמָר זוּטְרָא – Ameimar and Rav Ashi then said to Mar Zutra: הַשְׁתָּא אַמַּאי לֹא אָכֵיל מָר – "Why do you, master, not eat now? וְהָתַנְיָא – Has a Baraisa not taught: אִם נִמְצְאוּ יָפוֹת מֵהֶן – IF BETTER [PRODUCE] WAS FOUND in the owner's stock, תְּרוּמָתוֹ תְּרוּמָה – WHAT HE HAS SEPARATED IS considered *TERUMAH?*" By the same token, Mari bar Isak's generous comment should be taken as a genuine expression of approval for the action of the sharecropper!

Mar Zutra explains his continued decision not to partake of the fruit:

אָמַר לְהוּ – He said to them: הָכִי אָמַר רָבָא – So said Rava: כְּלָךְ אֵצֶל יָפוֹת לֹא אָמְרוּ – [The Sages] of the Baraisa did not say – that the statement, "You really should go to the better [produce]," is a validation of the agent's act אֶלָּא לְעִנְיַן תְּרוּמָה בִּלְבַד – except in regard to *terumah* separation, מִשּׁוּם דְּמִצְוָה הוּא – because [*terumah*] is a mitzvah, וְנִיחָא לֵיהּ – and it is therefore likely that [the owner] is genuinely satisfied to fulfill the mitzvah in a generous fashion. אֲבָל הָכָא – But here, in regard to the fruit served to the rabbis, מִשּׁוּם כְּסִיפוּתָא הוּא דְּאָמַר הָכִי – it may be because of the embarrassment of appearing miserly to the rabbis that [Mari bar Isak] said this, and not because he was genuinely happy that the sharecropper had offered them fruit. Mar Zutra therefore refused to eat.

The Gemara now cites support for Abaye's view from a Baraisa dealing with the laws of *hechsher l'tumah,* rendering a food susceptible to *tumah*-contamination. This requires a brief introduction.

**Susceptibility to *tumah*:**

Food cannot contract *tumah* unless it has first come into contact with one of seven liquids – water, dew, milk, bee's honey, olive oil, wine, or blood.[24] However, contact with these liquids renders a food capable of contracting *tumah* only when the owner is satisfied with that contact. The following Baraisa further defines the element of owner satisfaction with the contact:

תָּא שְׁמַע – Come, learn a proof to Abaye's position from the following Baraisa: עוֹדֵהוּ הַטַּל עֲלֵיהֶן – If THE DEW WAS STILL

NOTES

18. The verse (*Numbers* 18:28) reads: כֵּן תָּרִימוּ גַם־אַתֶּם תְּרוּמַת ה׳, *So too, you* [the Leviim] *also shall separate the terumah of HASHEM,* etc.

19. This verse is one of the sources of the law empowering an agent to act on behalf of the person who appoints him (see *Kiddushin* 41b). By alluding to the law of שְׁלִיחוּת, *agency,* with the phrase גַם־אַתֶּם, *you also,* the Torah indicates that the agent's power to act is limited to situations in which he is an extension of "you," the principal (*Rashi*). The Gemara now elaborates.

20. When a person separates *terumah,* his act is valid only if he is aware of what he is doing. Thus, it may be derived from the Scriptural source cited above that, similarly, the agent's acts are valid only if the principal is aware of what he is doing, having appointed him beforehand (*Rashi*).

21. Thus, there is no question that the owner authorized this person to separate *terumah* on his behalf. The only question is whether he meant for him to give this higher-grade produce.

[Had the agent separated intermediate-grade produce, however, the owner's subsequent remarks would have been irrelevant. Since he did not specify what grade to take, it is assumed that he meant at least to give intermediate-grade fruits.]

22. See notes 13 and 14. The *Toras Chaim* questions the Gemara's reconciliation of this Baraisa with the view of Abaye. Although the agent was appointed in advance, the consent to separate *terumah* from the high-grade produce was granted only after the fact. According to Abaye, this consent should not be viewed as having been in effect at the time of the separation, and the separation should therefore not be valid. He answers that Abaye agrees that once the actual agency has been established, we may assume that whatever the principal agrees to in the end was his actual intent from the very beginning, and implicit in his original instruction.

23. Ameimar and Rav Ashi, though, ate because they assumed the sharecropper would not be giving them from the owner's share of the fruit, but from his own. They could not, however, have relied on Mari bar Isak's eventual consent, because the halachah follows the view of Abaye, that *ye'ush* without knowledge is not considered an abandonment (Gemara 22b). This demonstrates that eventual knowledge and consent is not sufficient to permit taking a thing in advance (*Tosafos*).

From *Tosafos'* explanation it follows that one is not permitted to eat food belonging to another person without his knowledge, even if it is certain that the owner will consent wholeheartedly when he hears of it. Others take issue with *Tosafos'* view; see *Shach, Choshen Mishpat* 358:1.

24. This requirement is based upon *Leviticus* 11:34, which reads: מִכָּל־הָאֹכֶל אֲשֶׁר יֵאָכֵל אֲשֶׁר יָבוֹא עָלָיו מַיִם יִטְמָא, *Of any food that is edible – upon which water comes – it shall become [susceptible to becoming] contaminated.* The Mishnah (*Machshirin* 6:4) states that six other liquids have the same status as water.

וכן ירדן שנטל מזה ונתן לזה מה שנטל נטל ומה שנתן נתן בשלמא גזלן וירדן דקא חזי להו ומיאש אלא גנב מי קא חזי ליה דמיאש תרגמה רב פפא בלסטים מזוין אי הכי היינו א) גזלן תרי גווני גזלן ת"ש ב) א שטף נהר קוריו עציו ואבניו ונתנו בתוך שדה חבירו ג) הרי אלו שלו מפני שנתיאשו הבעלים טעמא דנתיאשו הבעלים הא סתמא לא הכא במאי עסקינן כשיכול להציל אי הכי אימא סיפא ד) אם היו הבעלים מרדפין אחריהם חייב להחזיר אי ביכולין להציל מאי אריא מרדפין אפילו אין מרדפין נמי הכא במאי עסקינן ביכולין להציל על ידי הדחק מרדפין לא אייאוש אין מרדפין אייאושי מיאש ת"ש ה) כיצד אמרו התורם שלא מדעת תרומתו תרומה ב הרי שירד לתוך שדה חבירו וליקט ותרם שלא ברשות אם חושש משום גזל אין תרומתו תרומה ואם לאו תרומתו תרומה ומנין הוא יודע אם חושש משום גזל ואם לאו ג הרי שבא בעל הבית ומצאו ואמר לו ו) כלך אצל יפות אם נמצאו יפות מהן תרומתו תרומה ואם לאו אין תרומתו תרומה ד ליקטו הבעלים והוסיפו עליהן בין כך ובין כך תרומתו תרומה וכי נמצאו יפות מהן תרומתו תרומה אמאי בעידנא דתרם הא לא הוה ידע ז) תרגמה רבא אליבא דאביי ° דשויה שליח [א] ה"נ מסתברא דאי ס"ד דלא שוויה שליח מי הויא תרומתו תרומה והא אתם א) גם אתם אמר רחמנא ח) ה לרבות שלוחכם מה אתם לדעתכם אף שלוחכם לדעתכם אלא הכא במאי עסקינן כגון דשויה שליח וא"ל זיל תרום ולא א"ל תרום מהני וסתמיה דבעל הבית כי תרום מבינונית הוא תרום ואזל איהו ותרם מיפות ובא בעל הבית ומצאו וא"ל כלך אצל יפות אם נמצאו יפות מהן תרומתו תרומה ואם לאו אין תרומתו תרומה אמימר ומר זוטרא ורב אשי אקלעו ° לבוסתנא דמרי בר איסק אייתי אריסיה תמרי ורימוני ושדא קמייהו אמימר ורב אשי אכלי מר זוטרא לא אכיל אדהכי אתא מרי בר איסק אשכחינהו וא"ל לאריסיה אמאי לא אייתית להו לרבנן מהנך שפירתא אמרו ליה אמימר ורב אשי למר זוטרא השתא אמאי לא אכיל מר והתניא אם נמצאו יפות מהן תרומתו תרומה אמר להו הכי אמר רבא לא אמרו כלך אצל יפות אלא לענין תרומה בלבד משום דמצוה הוא וניחא ליה אבל הכא משום כסיפותא הוא דאמר הכי תא שמע ט) י עודהו הטל עליהן ושמח הרי זה ב) בכי יותן נגבו אף על פי ששמח אינן

## רש"י

ירדן. וכן שאר נהרות ותנא זה על יד הירדן היה יושב: בלסטים מזוין. ובחזקה נטלה הימנו ומעיקרא ידע ומייאש: שטף נהר קוריו. של זה ומלאן אחר: הרי אלו כו'. ה"ג הרי אלו שלו מפני שנתיאשו הבעלים דכל שטיפת נהר כקורות עלים ואבנים הבעלים ידעו בה מיד דיש לה קול: הא סתמא. הא אם היתה אבידה אחרת שאין לנו לומר שידעו הבעלים לא הויא של מוצאה קשיא לרבא: כשיכול להציל. ודכוותה במציאה אחרת דבר שיש בו סימן דיכול ליתן סימן וליטול מודינא בה דחייב להחזיר: אפילו אין מרדפין נמי. דסמכי אהצלה דלמחר וליומא אוחרא ולא מייאשי: ע"י הדחק. ואם לא ימהר להציל לא יצילו הלכך אין מרדפין אפקורי אפקרינהו דהא ידעו ולא הצילו: שלא מדעת. בעלים: וליקט. לצורך בעל הבית: ואם חושש. בעל הבית ומקפיד על מה שעשה זה: משום גזל. שתרם תרומתו בלא רשותו: כלך אצל יפות. היה לך לילך אצל יפות לתת מהן לכהן: לא הוה ידע. אלמא כיון דלכי ידע דניחא ליה אמרינן מעיקרא נמי ניחא ליה ולענין יאוש נמי כיון דלכי ידע מייאש מעיקרא נמי הוי יאוש: אתם גם אתם. כן תרימו גם אתם מהכא נפקא לן שלוחו של אדם כמותו לתרומה שהשליח שתרם תרומתו תרומה וכיון דשליחות מהכא נפקא לן על כרחך שלוחכם דומיא דאתם בעינן: אף שלוחכם לדעתכם. שהבעלים מינוהו שליח: לבוסתנא. פרדס: לא אכל. דגזל ניהו שהבעלים לא ידעו: אם נמצאו יפות כו'. אלמא גלי דעתיה דניחא ליה ה"נ גלי דעתיה דניחא ליה במה שנתן לנו: לא אמרו כלך אצל יפות. דהוי גלוי דעת אלא לענין תרומה: עודהו הטל עליהן. המעלה פירותיו לגג וירד עליהן הטל: ושמח. בטל שירד עליהן: הרי זה בכי יותן. והוכשרו לטומאה מעתה ועד עולם: נגבו. עד שלא מלאן: אע"פ ששמח. עכשיו בטל שירד עליהן:

אינן

## תוספות

מה שנתן נתן. י) אתיא כר' דאמר בפרק הגזול [בתרא] (ב"ק דף קיד.) סתם גנב וגזלן הוי יאוש בעלים:

שטף נהר קוריו עציו ואבניו. ה"ג אם נתיאשו הבעלים הרי אלו שלו וצ"ל דמיירי ביכול להציל בקל אם רודף בשעת שטיפה דאי לאו הכי הוה כזוטו של ים שאבוד ממנו ומכל אדם ועל זה לא היה אומר הא סתם לא אלא איירי ביכול להציל בקל בשעת שטיפה ואפילו אין בהן סימן ולפי שיעכבן עקולי ופשורי ויקחם שם ואפי' יקדמו אחרים ויקחו יחזירום לו לפי שניכר שהוא בעליו לפי שרדף מיד וס"ד דמיירי דאם לא רדף מיד בשעת שטיפה שלא יכול עוד כלל להציל כדמוכח בסיפא לפי שיקחום אחרים כשיעכבום עקולי ופשורי ולא יחזירו לפי שאין בהן סימן וה"פ אם נתיאשו הבעלים דהיינו שהיו שם בשעת שטיפה ולא רדפו ואפילו אומרים שאין מתיאשים אין בכך כלום דודאי הן מתיאשים בלבן הא סתמא שלא היו בעלים בשעת שטיפה ולא נתיאשו עד שידעו הבעלים ששטפה נהר ואז כבר אינו יכול להציל לפי שאין בו סימן לא דכשמלאן באיסורא אתא לידיה שהבעלים לא ידעו עדיין אלמא יאוש שלא מדעת לא הוי יאוש ומשני ביכול להציל אפי' אחר שטיפה כגון שיש באבידה סימן שהבעלים אינן מתיאשין כשידעו ופריך אי הכי אימא סיפא ואם היו הבעלים מרדפין כו' מאי אריא מרדפין אפילו היו בעלים שם בשעת שטיפה ולא רדפו נמי יחזיר ומשני ביכול להציל אחר שטיפה ע"י הדחק דאע"פ שיש בו סימן בטורח יכול להציל לפי שיתרחקו הרבה שהנהר מוליכן ברחוק ולכך אם היה בשעת שטיפה ואינו מרדף ודאי מתיאש כיון שעתה יכול להציל בלא דוחק ואינו מציל אבל אין הבעלים בשעת שטיפה יחזיר דכשידעו הבעלים לא יתיאשו ויצילו על ידי הדחק וא"ת מנלן הא סתמא חייב להחזיר דלמא נתיאשו אתא לאפוקי שהיו שם ורדפו דחייב להחזיר וי"ל דא"כ לא ליתני אם נתיאשו אלא לתני סתמא שטף נהר קוריו עציו ואבניו הרי אלו שלו דפשיטא דלא מיירי ברדפו בשעת שטיפה דהא קתני סיפא דאם היו הבעלים מרדפים חייב ואין להקשות דמאי דייק מסיפא טעמא דמרדפין הא סתמא הרי אלו שלו דלעולם נימא דהוא הדין סתמא דיחזיר ולא נקט מרדפין אלא לאפוקי שהיו הבעלים בשעת שטיפה ולא רדפו וע"י סיפא ידעינן דמיירי באין יכול להציל אבל רש"י דגרס מפני שנתיאשו הבעלים משמע לישנא דפשיט ליה דנתיאשו א"כ מרישא גופיה מצי לאוכוחי דמיירי באין יכול להציל ולא היה צריך להביא סיפא ותו מנלן דהא סתמא לא דאפילו סתמא נמי מצי מיירי:

הכי גרסינן ה"נ מסתברא דאי לא שוייה שליח ולא גרסינן ותסברא:

אם יש יפות מהן תרומתו תרומה. דמסתמא גם מתחילה היה דעתו כן וא"ת ונימא דהשתא ודאי ניחא ליה ביפות אבל מתחילה בשעה שתרם אי הוה ידע לא הוה ניחא ליה דאין דרך לתרום מן היפות כדאמרינן לעיל (דף כא:) גבי דבר שיש בו סימן דאפילו לרבא חייב להכריז דאע"ג דהשתא מתיאש אין בכך כלום וי"ל דשאני הכא דכיון דחזינן ביה דניחא ליה השתא אמרינן נמי ניחא ליה מעיקרא משום מצוה:

ואם לאו אין תרומתו תרומה. וא"ת דבפרק אלמנה ניזונית (כתובות דף נט: ושם ד"ה פיחת) אמרינן דסתמיה דבעל הבית הוי אחד מחמשים ואם השליח פיחת י' או הוסיף י' תרומתו תרומה דמאי א"ל בהכי אמדתיך ה"נ נימא הכי וי"ל דהתם הוי כולה שיעור תרומה ויש שתורם כך ויש שתורם כך לכך מצי א"ל כיון שלא פירשת לי בהכי אמדתיך אבל מיפות אין רגילות לתרום ולכך לא היה לו לתרום בשום ענין מהם בלא רשותו:

מר זוטרא לא אכל. וא"ת ואמאי לא אכל האמר רבא פרק הגוזל בתרא (ב"ק דף קיט.) אריסא מדנפשיה קא זבן ויש לומר דהתם שהביא האריס מבית דמסתמא ממה שהגיע לחלקו מביא אבל הכא שהביא מן הפרדס היה חושש מר זוטרא שמא בשעת חלוקה לא יאמר לבעל הפרדס תטול כנגד מה שנתתי להם ורב אשי לא היה חושש לזה ולכך אכל קודם שבא מרי בר איסק משום דאריס מדנפשיה קא יהיב דאין לומר שהיה סומך שיתרצה מרי בר איסק כשידע דהלכה כאביי ואע"ג דהשתא ניחא ליה מעיקרא לא הוה ניחא ליה:

איסורא

## עין משפט נר מצוה

טו א מיי' פ"ו מהלכות גזילה ואבידה הל' א טוש"מ סי' רנט:

טז ב ג ד מיי' פ"ד מהל' תרומות הל' ג:

יז ה מיי' שם הלכה א:

יח ו (מיי' פי"ב מהל' טומאת אוכלין הלכה ג):

## רבינו חננאל

הן ממשמש בהן כל שעה והללו אע"פ שהן בצד שדה קצוצות דמוכחא מילתא דמשדה זו הן כבר נתיאש מהן כמו המעות. וכן תאנה הנוטה לדרך התאנים שהן נופלות ממנה מיד נמאסות לפיכך מתיאש מהן ומותרין משום גזל ופטורין מן המעשר דאינו נשמר ותנן כלל אמרו במעשרות כל שהוא אוכל ונשמר וגידוליו מן הארץ חייב במעשרות. גנב שנטל מזה ונתן לזה לא גנב הוא שגונב בסתר. אבל האי גנב דקתני גזלן הוא שנוטל בגלוי ותרי גווני גזלן קתני חד גזלן וחד ליסטים מזויין. ת"ש שטף נהר קורותיו ונתנן לתוך שדה חבירו אם נתיאשו הבעלים הרי אלו שלו מכלל דבסתמא חייב להחזיר ואוקימנא כשבעלין מרדפין אחריהן ויכולין להציל על ידי הדחק. ת"ש כיצד אמרו התורם שלא מדעת תרומתו תרומה וכו' אוקימנא כגון שתרם ובא בעל הפירות ומצאו שתרם ואמר לו למה [לא] היתה תורם מאלו היפות מוכחא מילתא שנתרצה ואסיקנא לא אמרי' כלך אצל יפות רצון בעלים הן במה שנעשה אלא לענין תרומה בלבד משום דמצוה היא וניחא ליה ביפה. אבל בזולתי תרומה לא ואע"פ שאמר לו כלך אצל יפות משום כסיפותא הוא דאמר ליה הכי ואסורין משום גזל. ת"ש עודהו הטל עליהם ושמח הרי הן בכי

## מסורת הש"ס

[בבא קמא נז., וש"נ], [תוספתא דכתובות פ"ק ה], ג) [בתוספתא ליתא אם נתיאשו הבעלים הרי אלו שלו, ועיין תוס' ד"ה שטף], ד) [תוספתא שם וש"נ], ה) קדושין נב:, [תוספתא דתרומות פרק א], ו) [עירובין עא.], [שבת נג: וש"נ], [לקמן עא:, קדושין מא:], ט) [תוספתא דמכשירין פרק ג ע"ש], י) ס"א למאי דסבירא לן סתמא דאיירי בגנב ממש אתיא כו'.

## הגהות הגר"א

א] גמ' ה"נ מסתברא. נ"ב גירסת רמב"ם ותסברא והא אתם כו' ור"ל ואמאי יכון לכלך אצל יפות הא שלוחו כמותו אלא הכ"ע ... וכל זה לתירוץ דרבא אבל א"נ לכ"ז דמצוה ... כמ"ש בקדושין נב ... ועי' תוס' שם ד"ה אם ... וא"כ צ"ל כו' ואולי ... גירסתייהו שכתבו כאן ... ה"ג כו' ול"ג כו' ... עמ"ש רבינו ביו"ד סי' של"א ס"ק ע"ו):

## גליון הש"ס

גמ' דשויה שליח. עיין עירובין דף עא ע"א ותוס' ד"ה כלך: שם לבוסתנא דמרי בר איסק. עיין יבמות דף כא ע"ב תוס' ד"ה ר"א:

## תורה אור השלם

א) כֵּן תָּרִימוּ גַם אַתֶּם תְּרוּמַת יְיָ מִכֹּל מַעְשְׂרֹתֵיכֶם אֲשֶׁר תִּקְחוּ מֵאֵת בְּנֵי יִשְׂרָאֵל וּנְתַתֶּם מִמֶּנּוּ אֶת תְּרוּמַת יְיָ לְאַהֲרֹן הַכֹּהֵן: [במדבר יח, כח]

ב) וְכִי יֻתַּן מַיִם עַל זֶרַע וְנָפַל מִנִּבְלָתָם עָלָיו טָמֵא הוּא לָכֶם: [ויקרא יא, לח]

## ליקוטי רש"י

אם חושש משום גזל. אם מקפיד בעל הבית על זה שעשה ודומה לו כגזלה. אין תרומתו תרומה. דהשתא ודאי הכי קאמר ליה אם מלאת עוד יפות מאלו היית גוזלן. בין כך ובין כך. בין שיש יפות בין שאין יפות מהן [קדושין נב:]. כלך אצל יפות. גבי תורם את של חבירו שלא מדעת תניא [ב"מ דף כב.] בא בעל הבית ומצאו שהוא תורם ואמר לו כלך אצל יפות אם יש לו יפות מהן תרומתו תרומה דגלי אדעתיה דניחא ליה ואמרינן כמאן דשוויה שליח מעיקרא דמי [עירובין עא.]. אתם גם אתם. והאי גם יתירא הוא [קדושין מא:]. לבוסתנא. גינת אילנות [לקמן לט:].

To resolve this problem, the Gemara modifies the previous explanation:

הָכָא בְּמַאי עָסְקִינַן – **With what** case **are we dealing here?** בִּיכוֹלִין לְהַצִּיל עַל יְדֵי הַדְּחָק – With a case **in which he is able to save** the lost items only **with difficulty.**[10] מְרַדְּפִין לֹא אַיְיאוּשׁ – Therefore, if **he** immediately **chases** after them, he indicates that **he does not despair** of them. אֵין מְרַדְּפִין – If, however, **he does not chase** after them, אַיְיאוּשֵׁי מְיָאֵשׁ – he indicates that **he despairs** of them.[11]

The Gemara again attempts to support Rava's position:

תָּא שְׁמַע – **Come, learn** a proof to Rava's opinion from the following Baraisa: כֵּיצַד אָמְרוּ – IN WHAT CIRCUMSTANCES HAVE [THE SAGES] SAID: הַתּוֹרֵם שֶׁלֹּא מִדַּעַת – ONE WHO SEPARATES *TERUMAH*[12] WITHOUT THE KNOWLEDGE of the owner of the produce, תְּרוּמָתוֹ תְּרוּמָה – WHAT HE HAS SEPARATED IS nonetheless considered *TERUMAH?* הֲרֵי שֶׁיָּרַד לְתוֹךְ שְׂדֵה חֲבֵירוֹ וְלִיקֵּט וְתָרַם שֶׁלֹּא בִּרְשׁוּת – IF SOMEONE WENT DOWN INTO HIS NEIGHBOR'S FIELD, – AND GATHERED some produce on behalf of the owner AND SEPARATED *TERUMAH* from it WITHOUT the owner's PERMISSION, אִם חוֹשֵׁשׁ מִשּׁוּם גֶּזֶל – IF [THE OWNER] OBJECTS to the unauthorized separation of *terumah* ON THE GROUNDS OF ROBBERY, אֵין תְּרוּמָתוֹ תְּרוּמָה – WHAT HE HAS SEPARATED IS NOT considered *TERUMAH.* The unauthorized designation is meaningless, and what was separated therefore acquires none of the sanctity or characteristics of genuine *terumah.* וְאִם לָאו – AND IF the owner does NOT object to the unauthorized separation, תְּרוּמָתוֹ תְּרוּמָה – WHAT HE HAS SEPARATED IS considered *TERUMAH.*

The Baraisa elaborates:

וּמִנַּיִן הוּא יוֹדֵעַ אִם חוֹשֵׁשׁ מִשּׁוּם גֶּזֶל וְאִם לָאו – NOW HOW DOES HE KNOW WHETHER [THE OWNER] OBJECTS to the unauthorized separation ON THE GROUNDS OF ROBBERY OR NOT? הֲרֵי שֶׁבָּא בַּעַל הַבַּיִת וּמְצָאוֹ – IF THE OWNER CAME AND FOUND HIM [the one who separated the *terumah*] וְאָמַר לוֹ – AND SAID TO HIM: כְּלָךְ אֵצֶל יָפוֹת – "YOU SHOULD HAVE GONE TO THE BETTER grade of PRODUCE] to take the fruits to give to a Kohen as *terumah,*" אִם נִמְצְאוּ יָפוֹת מֵהֶן – THEN IF BETTER [PRODUCE] WAS FOUND in the owner's stock, תְּרוּמָתוֹ תְּרוּמָה – WHAT HE [the unauthorized person] HAS SEPARATED IS considered TERUMAH.[13] וְאִם לָאו – AND IF better produce was NOT found in the owner's stock, אֵין תְּרוּמָתוֹ תְּרוּמָה – WHAT HE HAS SEPARATED IS NOT considered *TERUMAH.*[14] לִיקְּטוּ הַבְּעָלִים וְהוֹסִיפוּ עֲלֵיהֶן – If THE OWNER GATHERED additional produce, separated *terumah* from it, – AND ADDED IT [the new *terumah*] TO [THE PREVIOUSLY DESIGNATED] *TERUMAH,* בֵּין כָּךְ וּבֵין כָּךְ – then IN EITHER CASE, i.e. whether better produce was actually found or not, תְּרוּמָתוֹ תְּרוּמָה – WHAT HE [the unauthorized person] HAD SEPARATED IS considered *TERUMAH.* The owner's act of adding to the previously separated *terumah* indicates his approval of the unsolicited separation.[15]

The Gemara now demonstrates how this Baraisa seems to support Rava's view:

וְכִי נִמְצְאוּ יָפוֹת מֵהֶן תְּרוּמָתוֹ תְּרוּמָה – **Now if better [produce] was** actually **found,** the Baraisa stated that **what he separated is** considered ***terumah.*** אַמַּאי – **Why** so? בְּעִידְּנָא דְּתָרַם הָא לֹא הֲוָה יָדַע – **At the time [the unauthorized person] separated** it, **[the owner] did not know** that this person was separating *terumah* on his behalf! Obviously, the Baraisa must consider his eventual consent as demonstrating his consent at the time of the separation. By the same token, we should say that the eventual abandonment of a lost object is viewed as demonstrating abandonment at the time of the loss![16] This supports Rava's view.[17] – ? –

The Gemara rejects this proof:

תַּרְגְּמָהּ רָבָא אַלִּיבָּא דְּאַבָּיֵי – **Rava explained [the Baraisa] according to Abaye** to refer to a case דְּשַׁוְּיֵהּ שָׁלִיחַ – **in which [the owner] appointed [this person]** his **agent** to separate *terumah* for him. Thus, the owner consented in advance and indeed authorized the action of the person who separated the *terumah.*

Before elaborating upon the particulars of the case, the Gemara proceeds to bolster this explanation of the Baraisa:

הָכִי נַמִּי מִסְתַּבְּרָא – **Indeed, this** explanation of the Baraisa **seems more logical.** דְּאִי סָלְקָא דַּעְתָּךְ דְּלֹא שַׁוְּיֵהּ שָׁלִיחַ – **For if you should think that [the owner] did not appoint him** his **agent,** to separate the *terumah,* מִי הַוְיָא תְּרוּמָתוֹ תְּרוּמָה – **would that which he separated be** considered ***terumah?*** וְהָא ,,אַתֶּם" ,,גַּם

NOTES

10. By racing after the objects immediately, the owner has a chance to recover them. Otherwise, it is highly improbable that the objects will be retrieved (*Rashi*).

11. The failure of the owner to take immediate action is the indication that he has given up hope of retrieving his objects. Thus, although this case of the Baraisa deals with a situation in which the objects are somewhat retrievable, this factor is significant only if the owner chases after them immediately.

12. *Terumah* is the portion of the crop that must be given to a Kohen, generally between 1/40 and 1/60 of the crop. [This obligation applies only to the crops of Eretz Yisrael and, by Rabbinic decree, to certain nearby lands outside Eretz Yisrael.] The *terumah,* once it has been designated, acquires a sanctity, which, among other things, prohibits its consumption by a non-Kohen.

13. The owner's willingness to be even more generous in his choice of produce for *terumah* than the unauthorized person indicates that he approves of the unsolicited act of *terumah* separation.

14. If there was no better produce, the owner's response is interpreted as a sarcastic expression of displeasure toward the person who separated the produce, as if to say, "If only I had better produce, you would have taken that as well" (*Rashi, Kiddushin* 52b).

15. When the owner objects to the separation, the *terumah* classification does not take effect. The produce previously separated remains *tevel* and in need of *terumah* separation. Thus, he would not add the *terumah* he just separated to that other pile of produce, since one does not mix *terumah* and *tevel.* By mixing it, he indicates that he accepts what was previously separated as *terumah.*

16. In the case of *terumah,* it is not the owner's active will that renders the separated portion *terumah;* this is accomplished by the one who performs the separation. Rather, it is only the owner's consent that is required (*R' Akiva Eiger*) Thus, we see from this Baraisa that a subsequent consent is assumed to reflect the owner's consent at the time of the action (the separation of *terumah*) as well.

By the same token, the loss of ownership that occurs through *ye'ush* is not the result of the owner's *intent* to abandon the object; rather, it is the result of the fact that the object is lost to him. His subsequent *ye'ush* (acceptance of the loss) is needed only to formalize the condition of loss (see *Chazon Ish, Bava Kamma* 18:1). Accordingly, his subsequent acceptance of this loss should be seen as formalizing the state of loss from the very moment it occurred (see *Avi Ezri, Tinyana, Hil. Terumos* 4:3; *Nachalas Moshe*). See *Rashi* 21b ד״ה מהשתא הוי יאוש; and note 9 there.

17. In truth, this question could be raised even against Rava. His view in regard to *ye'ush* is predicated on the assumption that the owner of the lost object will *undoubtedly* despair of it once he discovers the loss. In the case of *terumah,* however, the owner may decide that he wishes to separate lower-grade produce as his *terumah* portion. Since the Gemara considers this a problem only according to Abaye's view (as is evident from the Gemara's answer), we must conclude that people do not generally object to the separation of good produce for *terumah* because *terumah* is a *mitzvah* [and it is a gift to a Kohen (see *Rashi* ד״ה כלך אצל יפות)]. Therefore, since this produce needed to have its *terumah* separated, there is reason to assume that the owner would consent to the separation if he knew of it (*Rashba; Tosafos,* see *Maharam Shif*).

## מסורת הש"ס

[בבא קמא נז. וש"נ], [תוספתא דכתובות פ"ק ה], ג) [בתוספתא איתא אם נתיאשו הבעלים הרי אלו שלו, ועיין תוס' ד"ה שטף], ד) [תוספתא שם ע"ש], ה) קדושין מא:, [תוספתא דתרומות פרק ד], ו) [עירובין עא.], [שבת נג: וש"נ], [לקמן עא:, קדושין נב:], ט) [תוספתא מכשירין פרק ג ע"ש], ס"א למאי דסבירא לן השתא דאיירי בגנב ממש אתיא כו'.

## הגהות הגר"א

[א] גמ' ה"נ מסתברא. נ"ב גירסת הרמב"ם ותסברא והא אתם כו' ור"ל ואמאי ליכין לכלך אצל יפות הא שלוחו כמותו אלא הב"ע כו' וכל זה לתירוץ דרבא אבל א"ג לכ"ז דמלוה ... כמ"ש בקדושין נב ועי' תוס' שם ד"ה אם ... וא"כ נ"ל כו' ואולי ...יטתייהו שכתבו כאן ...ה ה"ג כו' ול"ג כו' עמ"ש רבינו ביו"ד סי' של"א ס"ק ע"ו):

## גליון הש"ס

גמ' דשויה שליח. עיין עירובין דף עא ע"א ותוס' ד"ה כלך: שם לבוסתנא דמרי בר איסק. עיין יבמות דף כא ע"ב תוס' ד"ה ר"א:

## תורה אור השלם

א) כֵּן תָּרִימוּ גַם אַתֶּם תְּרוּמַת יְיָ מִכֹּל מַעְשְׂרֹתֵיכֶם אֲשֶׁר תִּקְחוּ מֵאֵת בְּנֵי יִשְׂרָאֵל וּנְתַתֶּם מִמֶּנּוּ אֶת תְּרוּמַת יְיָ לְאַהֲרֹן הַכֹּהֵן: [במדבר יח, כח]

ב) וְכִי יֻתַּן מַיִם עַל זֶרַע וְנָפַל מִנִּבְלָתָם עָלָיו טָמֵא הוּא לָכֶם: [ויקרא יא, לח]

## ליקוטי רש"י

אם חושש משום גזל. אם מקפיד בעל הבית על מה שעשה ודומה לו כגזלה. אין תרומתו תרומה. דהשתא ודאי הכי קאמר ליה אם מצאת עוד יפות מאלו היית גוזלן. בין כך ובין כך. בין שיש יפות בין שאין יפות מהן [קדושין נב:]. כלך אצל יפות. גבי תורם את של חבירו שלא מדעת תניא (ב"מ דף כב.) בא בעל הבית ומצאו שהוא תורס ואמר לו כלך אצל יפות אם יש לו יפות מהן תרומתו תרומה דגלי אדעתיה דניחא ליה ואמרינן כמאן דשויה שליח מעיקרא דמי [עירובין עא.]. אתם גם אתם. ואלו גם יתירא הוא [קדושין מא:]. לבוסתנא. גינה של אילנות [לקמן לט:].

## גמרא

וכן ירדן שנטל מזה ונתן לזה מה שנטל נטל ומה שנתן נתן בשלמא גזלן וירדן דקא חזי להו ומיאש אלא גנב מי קא חזי ליה דמיאש תרגמה רב פפא בלסטים מזוין אי הכי היינו [א] גזלן תרי גווני גזלן ת"ש [ג] א שטף נהר קוריו עציו ואבניו ונתנו בתוך שדה חבירו [ג] הרי אלו שלו מפני שנתיאשו הבעלים טעמא דנתיאשו הבעלים הא סתמא לא הכא במאי עסקינן כשיכול להציל אי הכי אימא סיפא [ד] אם היו הבעלים מרדפין אחריהם חייב להחזיר אי ביכולין להציל מאי אריא מרדפין אפילו אין מרדפין נמי הכא במאי עסקינן ביכולין להציל על ידי הדחק מרדפין לא אייאוש אין מרדפין אייאושי מיאש ת"ש [ה] כיצד אמרו התורם שלא מדעת תרומתו תרומה ב הרי שירד לתוך שדה חבירו וליקט ותרם שלא ברשות אם חושש משום גזל אין תרומתו תרומה ואם לאו תרומתו תרומה ומנין הוא יודע אם חושש משום גזל ואם לאו ג הרי שבא בעל הבית ומצאו ואמר לו [ו] כלך אצל יפות אם נמצאו יפות מהן תרומתו תרומה ואם לאו אין תרומתו תרומה ד ליקטו הבעלים והוסיפו עליהן בין כך ובין כך תרומתו תרומה וכי נמצאו יפות מהן תרומתו תרומה אמאי בעידנא דתרם הא לא הוה ידע [ז] תרגמה רבא אליבא דאביי [ם] דשויה שליח [א]ה"נ מסתברא דאי ס"ד דלא שוויה שליח מי הויא תרומתו תרומה והא אתם [א] גם אתם אמר רחמנא [ם] ה לרבות שלוחכם מה אתם לדעתכם אף שלוחכם לדעתכם אלא הכא במאי עסקינן כגון דשויה שליח וא"ל זיל תרום ולא א"ל תרום מהני וסתמיה דבעל הבית כי תרום מבינונית הוא תרום ואזל איהו ותרם מיפות ובא בעל הבית ומצאו וא"ל כלך אצל יפות אם נמצאו יפות מהן תרומתו תרומה ואם לאו אין תרומתו תרומה אמימר ומר זוטרא ורב אשי אקלעו [ם] לבוסתנא דמרי בר איסק אייתי אריסיה תמרי ורימוני ושדא קמייהו אמימר ורב אשי אכלי מר זוטרא לא אכיל אדהכי אתא מרי בר איסק אשכחינהו וא"ל לאריסיה אמאי לא אייתית להו לרבנן מהנך שפירתא אמרו ליה אמימר ורב אשי למר זוטרא השתא אמאי לא אכיל מר והתניא אם נמצאו יפות מהן תרומתו תרומה אמר להו הכי אמר רבא לא אמרו כלך אצל יפות אלא לענין תרומה בלבד משום דמצוה הוא וניחא ליה אבל הכא משום כסיפותא הוא דאמר הכי תא שמע [ט] ו עודהו הטל עליהן ושמח הרי זה [ב] בכי יותן נגבו אף על פי ששמח אינן

## רש"י

ירדן. וכן שאר נהרות ותנא זה על יד הירדן היה יושב: בלסטים מזוין. ובחזקה נטלה הימנו ומעיקרא ידע ומייאש: שטף נהר קוריו. של זה ומצאן אחר: הרי אלו כו'. ה"ג הרי אלו שלו מפני שנתיאשו הבעלים דכל שטיפת נהר כקורות עצים ואבנים הבעלים ידעו בה מיד דיש לה קול: הא סתמא. הא אם היתה אבידה אחרת שאין לנו לומר שידעו הבעלים לא הויא של מוצאה קשיא לרבא: כשיכול להציל. ודכוותה במציאה אחרת דבר שיש בו סימן דיכול ליתן סימן וליטול מודינא בה דחייב להחזיר: אפילו אין מרדפין נמי. דסמכי אהצלה דלמחר וליומא אוחרא ולא מייאשי: ע"י הדחק. ואם לא ימהר להציל לא יצילו הלכך אין מרדפין אפקורי אפקרינהו דהא ידעו ולא הצילו: שלא מדעת. בעלים: וליקט. לצורך בעל הבית: ואם חושש. בעל הבית ומקפיד על מה שעשה זה: משום גזל. שתרם תרומתו בלא רשותו: כלך אצל יפות. היה לך לילך אצל יפות לתת מהן לכהן: לא הוה ידע. אלמא כיון דלכי ידע דניחא ליה אמרינן מעיקרא נמי ניחא ליה ולענין יאוש נמי כיון דלכי ידע מייאש מעיקרא נמי הוי יאוש: אתם גם אתם. כן תרימו גם אתם מהכא נפקא לן שלוחו של אדם כמותו לתרומה שהשליח שתרם תרומתו תרומה וכיון דשליחות מהכא נפקא לן על כרחך שלוחכם דומיא דאתם בעינן: אף שלוחכם לדעתכם. שהבעלים מינוהו שליח: לבוסתנא. פרדס: לא אכל. דגזל נינהו שהבעלים לא ידעו: אם נמצאו יפות כו'. אלמא גלי דעתיה דניחא ליה ה"נ גלי דעתיה דניחא ליה במה שנתן לנו: לא אמרו כלך אצל יפות. דהוי גלוי דעת אלא לענין תרומה: עודהו הטל עליהן. המעלה פירותיו לגג וירד עליהן הטל: ושמח. בטל שירד עליהן: הרי זה בכי יותן. והוכשרו לטומאה מעתה ועד עולם: נגבו. עד שלא מצאן: אע"פ ששמח. עכשיו בטל שירד עליהן: אינן

## תוספות

מה שנתן נתן. [י] אתיא כר' דאמר בפרק הגוזל [בתרא] (ב"ק דף קיד.) סתם גנב וגזלן הוי יאוש בעלים:

שטף נהר קוריו עציו ואבניו. ה"ג אם נתיאשו הבעלים הרי אלו שלו וי"ל דמיירי ביכול להציל בקל אם רודף בשעת שטיפה דאי לאו הכי הוה כזוטו של ים שאבוד ממנו ומכל אדם ועל זה לא היה אומר הא סתם לא אלא איירי ביכול להציל בקל בשעת שטיפה ואפילו אין בהן סימן ולפי שיעכבן עקולי ופשורי ויקחם שם ואפי' יקדמו אחרים ויקחו יחזירום לו לפי שניכר שהוא בעליו לפי שרדף מיד וס"ד דמיירי דאם לא רדף מיד בשעת שטיפה שלא יכול עוד כלל להציל כדמוכח בסיפא לפי שיקחום אחרים כשיעכבום עקולי ופשורי ולא יחזירו לפי שאין בהן סימן וה"פ אם נתיאשו הבעלים דהיינו שהיו שם בשעת שטיפה ולא רדפו ואפילו אומרים שאין מתיאשים אין בכך כלום דודאי הן מתיאשים בלבן הא סתמא שלא היו בעלים בשעת שטיפה ולא נתיאשו עד שידעו הבעלים ששטפה נהר ואז כבר אינו יכול להציל לפי שאין בו סימן לא דכשמצאן באיסורא אתא לידיה שהבעלים לא ידעו עדיין אלמא יאוש שלא מדעת לא הוי יאוש ומשני ביכול להציל אפי' אחר שטיפה כגון שיש באבידה סימן שהבעלים אינן מתיאשין כשידעו ופריך אי הכי אימא סיפא ואם היו הבעלים מרדפין כו' מאי אריא מרדפין אפילו היו בעלים שם בשעת שטיפה ולא רדפו נמי יחזיר ומשני ביכול להציל אחר שטיפה ע"י הדחק דאע"פ שיש בו סימן בטורח יכול להציל לפי שיתרחקו הרבה שהנהר מוליכן ברחוק ולכך אם היה בשעת שטיפה ואינו מרדף ודאי מתיאש כיון שעתה יכול להציל בלא דוחק ואינו מציל אבל אין הבעלים בשעת שטיפה יחזיר דכשידעו הבעלים לא יתיאשו ויצילו על ידי הדחק וא"ת מנלן הא סתמא חייב להחזיר דלמא נתיאשו אתא לאפוקי שהיו שם ורדפו דחייב להחזיר וי"ל דא"כ לא ליתני אם נתיאשו אלא לתני סתמא שטף נהר קוריו עציו ואבניו הרי אלו שלו דפשיטא דלא מיירי ברדפו בשעת שטיפה דהא קתני סיפא דאם היו הבעלים מרדפים חייב ואין להקשות דמאי דייק מסיפא טעמא דמרדפין הא סתמא הרי אלו שלו דלעולם נימא דהוא הדין סתמא דיחזיר ולא נקט מרדפין אלא לאפוקי שהיו הבעלים בשעת שטיפה ולא רדפו וע"י סיפא ידעינן דמיירי באין יכול להציל אבל רש"י דגרס מפני שנתיאשו הבעלים משמע לישנא דפשיט ליה דנתיאשו א"כ מרישא גופיה מצי לאוכוחי דמיירי באין יכול להציל ולא היה צריך להביא סיפא ותו מנלן דהא סתמא לא דאפילו סתמא נמי מצי מיירי:

הכי גרסינן ה"נ מסתברא דאי לא שוויה שליח ולא גרסינן ותסברא:

אם יש יפות מהן תרומתו תרומה. דמסתמא גם מתחילה היה דעתו כן וא"ת ונימא דהשתא ודאי ניחא ליה ביפות אבל מתחילה בשעה שתרם אי הוה ידע לא הוה ניחא ליה דאין דרך לתרום מן היפות כדאמרינן לעיל (דף כא:) גבי דבר שיש בו סימן דאפילו לרבא חייב להכריז דאע"ג דהשתא מתיאש אין בכך כלום וי"ל דשאני הכא דכיון דחזינן ביה דניחא ליה השתא אמרינן נמי ניחא ליה מעיקרא משום מצוה:

ואם לאו אין תרומתו תרומה. וא"ת דבפרק אלמנה ניזונית (כתובות דף קא: ושם ד"ה פיתת) אמרינן דסתמיה דבעל הבית הוי אחד מחמשים ואם השליח פיחת י' או הוסיף י' תרומתו תרומה דמאי א"ל בהכי אמדתיך ה"נ נימא הכי וי"ל דהתם הוי כולה שיעור תרומה ויש שתורם כך ויש שתורם כך לכך מצי א"ל כיון שלא פירשת לי בהכי אמדתיך אבל מיפות אין רגילות לתרום ולכך לא היה לו לתרום בשום ענין מהם בלא רשותו:

מר זוטרא לא אכל. וא"ת ואמאי לא אכל האמר רבא פרק הגוזל בתרא (ב"ק דף קיט.) אריסא מדנפשיה קא זבן ויש לומר דהתם שהביא האריס מבית דמסתמא ממה שהגיע לחלקו מביא אבל הכא שהביא מן הפרדס היה חושש מר זוטרא שמא בשעת חלוקה לא יאמר לבעל הפרדס תטול כנגד מה שנתתי להם ורב אשי לא היה חושש לזה ולכך אכל קודם שבא מרי בר איסק משום דאריס מדנפשיה קא יהיב דאין לומר שהיה סומך שיתרצה מרי בר איסק כשידע דהלכה כאביי ואע"ג דהשתא ניחא ליה מעיקרא לא הוה ניחא ליה:

איסורא

## עין משפט נר מצוה

טו א מיי' פ"ו מהלכות גזילה ואבידה הל' א טוש"ע ח"מ סי' רנט:

טז ב ג ד מיי' פ"ד מהל' תרומות הל' ג:

יז ה מיי' שם הלכה א:

יח ו (מיי' פי"ג מהל' טומאת אוכלין הלכה ג):

## רבינו חננאל

הן ממשמש בהן כל שעה והללו אע"פ שהן בצד שדה קצוצות דמוכחא מילתא דמשדה זו הן כבר נתיאש מהן כמו המעות. וכן תאנה הנוטה לדרך התאנים שהן נופלות ממנה מיד נמאסות לפיכך מתיאש מהן ומותרין משום גזל ופטורין מן המעשר דאינו נשמר ותנן כלל אמרו במעשרות כל שהוא אוכל ונשמר וגידוליו מן הארץ חייב במעשרות. גנב שנטל מזה ונתן לזה לא גנב הוא שגונב בסתר. אבל האי גנב דקתני גזלן הוא שנוטל בגלוי ותרי גווני גזלן קתני חד גזלן וחד ליסטים מזויין. ת"ש שטף נהר קורותיו ונתנן לתוך שדה חבירו אם נתיאשו הבעלים הרי אלו שלו מכלל דבסתמא חייב להחזיר ואוקימנא כשבעלין מרדפין אחריהן ויכולין להציל על ידי הדחק. ת"ש כיצד אמרו התורם שלא מדעת תרומתו תרומה וכו' אוקימנא כגון שתרם ובא בעל הפירות ומצאו שתרם ואמר לו למה [לא] היתה תורם מאלו היפות מוכחא מילתא שנתרצה ואסיקנא לא אמרי' כלך אצל יפות רצון בעלים הן במה שנעשה אלא לענין תרומה בלבד משום דמצוה היא וניחא ליה ביפה. אבל בזולתי תרומה לא ואע"פ שאמר לו כלך אצל יפות משום כסיפותא הוא דאמר ליה הכי ואסורין משום גזל. ת"ש עודהו הטל עליהם ושמח הרי הן בכי

**וְכֵן יַרְדֵּן** – AND SIMILARLY, THE JORDAN River[1] **שֶׁנָּטַל מִזֶּה וְנָתַן לָזֶה** – WHICH flooded and TOOK AN OBJECT FROM THIS ONE AND GAVE IT TO THAT ONE, **מַה שֶּׁנָּטַל נָטַל וּמַה שֶּׁנָּתַן נָתַן** – WHAT IT [the thief, robber, or river] TOOK IT TOOK, AND WHAT IT GAVE IT GAVE. The recipient may keep the object.[2] **בִּשְׁלָמָא גַּזְלָן וְיַרְדֵּן** – **Now it is understandable** that objects taken by **the robber and the Jordan** River belong to the recipient, **דְּקָא חָזֵי לְהוּ וּמְיָאֵשׁ** – **because [the owner] sees them** being taken away **and despairs** of recovering them.[3] Thus, the recipient is permitted to keep them. **אֶלָּא גַּנָּב** – **But** in the case of **a thief, מִי קָא חָזֵי לֵיהּ דְּמְיָאֵשׁ** – **does the owner see the thief** so that we may be certain **that he** actually **despaired** of finding it before it came into the recipient's possession? Since the Baraisa nevertheless permits the recipient to keep it, we see that it accepts Rava's position that actual knowledge and despair are not necessary.[4] – ? –

The Gemara answers:

**תַּרְגְּמָה רַב פָּפָּא** – **Rav Pappa interpreted [the Baraisa]** according to Abaye as follows: **בְּלִסְטִים מְזוּיָּן** – The Baraisa's reference to "thief" deals **with an armed robber.** Thus, the owner is aware immediately of the theft, and consciously despairs of recovering the stolen object.

But, the Gemara asks:

**אִי הָכִי** – **If so, הַיְינוּ גַּזְלָן** – **this** case of the armed robber **is** identical to **the case of the robber.** Why state this case twice?

The Gemara answers:

**תְּרֵי גַּוְונֵי גַּזְלָן** – The Baraisa lists **two kinds of robbers.** The Baraisa's term "robber" refers to one who robs openly and fearlessly, without the threat of weapons. The term "thief" refers to one who robs less confidently, who must therefore rely upon weapons.[5] In both cases, however, the owner is immediately aware of his loss and consciously despairs of recovering the stolen object. This ruling therefore does not contradict Abaye's position.

The Gemara attempts to support Abaye's position:

**תָּא שְׁמַע** – **Come, learn** a proof to Abaye's opinion from the following Baraisa: **שָׁטַף נָהָר** – If A RIVER flooded and WASHED AWAY **קוֹרָיו עֵצָיו וַאֲבָנָיו** – [SOMEONE'S] BEAMS, WOOD, OR STONES, **וּנְתָנוֹ בְּתוֹךְ שְׂדֵה חֲבֵירוֹ** – AND DEPOSITED THEM IN SOMEONE ELSE'S FIELD, **הֲרֵי אֵלּוּ שֶׁלּוֹ** – THESE BELONG TO [THE FINDER], **מִפְּנֵי שֶׁנִּתְיָאֲשׁוּ הַבְּעָלִים** – BECAUSE THE OWNER HAS DESPAIRED of recovering them.

The Gemara deduces from this Baraisa:

**טַעְמָא דְּנִתְיָאֲשׁוּ הַבְּעָלִים** – **The reason** the finder may keep these **is because** we can be sure, in this case, that **the owner has despaired** of finding them.[6] **הָא סְתָמָא** – **But ordinarily,** in cases in which it is possible that the owner is not yet aware of his loss and has therefore not consciously despaired, **לֹא** – the lost item would **not** belong to the finder. This supports Abaye's view. – ? –

The Gemara rejects this proof by explaining that the Baraisa's reason does not mean to imply anything in regard to an ordinary case of loss but rather something else entirely:

**הָכָא בְּמַאי עַסְקִינָן** – **With what** case **are we dealing here** when the Baraisa implies that one may not keep what he finds if it is not certain the owner has despaired of it? **כְּשֶׁיָּכוֹל לְהַצִּיל** – With a case **in which he is able to save** the lost objects. Since they are salvageable, there is no reason to suppose that the owner despairs of them. The finder may therefore not keep them, as even Rava would agree.[7]

The Gemara questions this explanation:

**אִי הָכִי** – **If so, אֵימָא סֵיפָא** – **consider the last part** of the Baraisa, which states: **אִם הָיוּ הַבְּעָלִים מְרַדְּפִין אַחֲרֵיהֶם** – IF THE OWNER WAS CHASING AFTER THEM [the beams, wood, and stones], **חַיָּיב לְהַחֲזִיר** – [THE FINDER] IS OBLIGATED TO RETURN them to their owner, because his pursuit is clear proof that he has not despaired of them. **אִי בִּיכוֹלִין לְהַצִּיל** – Now **if** this latter case of the Baraisa refers to a situation **in which he is able to save** them,[8] **מַאי אִרְיָא מְרַדְּפִין** – **why speak of** a case in which **[the owner] was chasing** after them? **אֲפִילּוּ אֵין מְרַדְּפִין נָמֵי** – **Even if he was not chasing** after them, the same ruling should **also** apply. The owner's lack of pursuit does not indicate his abandonment of them since he may very well intend to reclaim them later.[9] – ? –

NOTES

1. The same holds true for any river. The author of this Baraisa, however, lived in the vicinity of the Jordan River and chose it as an example (*Rashi*).

2. This Baraisa is of the opinion that, under ordinary circumstances, an owner despairs of recovering objects stolen or robbed from him (see *Tosafos* ד״ה מה). Thus, the eventual recipient of the object may keep it.

3. An owner is immediately aware of a robbery because the event occurs openly and by force. A theft, however, occurs secretly, and the owner may not discover it until sometime later.

The Rishonim question the need for *ye'ush* in regard to objects swept away by the Jordan River. We learned earlier (21b) that objects washed away by flood are Scripturally permitted – even without the owner's knowledge and despair! For this and other reasons, many Rishonim delete the phrase "and the Jordan River" from the text of the Gemara's question (see *Shitah Mekubetzes* for alternative explanations).

4. Rather, since the owner would certainly despair of recovering it if he were to become aware of the theft, the law of *ye'ush* (abandonment) takes effect.

5. The armed robber resembles the thief inasmuch as they both are afraid to rob openly and brazenly. The thief attempts to steal without being seen; the armed robber ambushes his victim where others will not see him. [The Gemara in *Bava Kamma* (57a) cites an opinion that an armed robber is subject to the laws of the גַּנָּב, *thief,* not the laws of the גַּזְלָן, *robber.* Thus, if he is caught, the armed robber pays the double-payment penalty (כֶּפֶל), for example. Nevertheless, Rav Pappa's explanation of the word "thief" in this Baraisa to mean an armed robber is consistent even with the view that he is classified a robber. Since the armed robber hides to rob, his behavior resembles that of the thief (see *Tosafos* ד״ה ת״ש, *Bava Kamma* 114a).

6. It may be assumed that the news of a flood with sufficient force to wash away heavy objects becomes known to the owner almost immediately (*Rashi*).

7. The Baraisa itself speaks of a case in which the objects are *not* salvageable, which is why it is certain that he despairs of them. It means to *imply,* however, that where they are salvageable, the finder may not keep them (*Rashi,* as explained by *Ritva*).

According to this interpretation (which follows Rava's view), the reason the Baraisa states that one may keep the beams, wood and stones "because the owner has despaired of them," is to imply that one may *not* keep them in flood situations in which the owner is not certain to despair, for example, where the objects are still salvageable, and similarly, where lost objects of any kind can be identified and recovered through a *siman.* This is entirely consistent with Rava's view (*Ritva* in explanation of *Rashi;* cf. *Tosafos* and *Rashba,* who challenge *Rashi's* explanation based on their understanding that the Gemara means at this point to reinterpret the *case* of the Baraisa, not its *implied* ruling).

8. According to this last explanation, the final ruling of the Baraisa must be speaking of a case in which the owner can save his objects. This is because the Baraisa requires the finder to return flood-swept objects only where the owner can save them. Since the final ruling of the Baraisa requires the finder to return the objects in some cases, it must be speaking of such a case (*Ritva* in explanation of *Rashi*).

9. The Gemara understands the term "salvageable" to mean that the objects cannot get too far away and they may be retrieved at the owner's leisure.

ted to keep them.[33] תְּאֵנָה נַמִּי – In the case of the **fig tree, too,** we may say that מֵידַע יְדִיעַ דְּנַתְרָא – **[the owner] is aware that the figs** tend to **drop** from the tree, and he therefore despairs in advance of recovering any figs.[34] These are therefore cases of conscious abandonment. אֶלָּא סֵיפָא לְרָבָא קַשְׁיָא – **But the concluding section of the Mishnah contradicts Rava's** opinion, דְּקָתָנֵי – **for it states** that, בְּזֵיתִים וּבַחֲרוּבִים אָסוּר – IN REGARD TO OLIVES AND CAROBS found under the same conditions, IT IS PROHIBITED for the finder to keep them. According to Rava, however, since the owner would despair of them if he became aware of their loss, they should be considered abandoned as of now, and the finder should be *permitted* to keep them. – ? –

The Gemara answers:

אָמַר רַבִּי אַבָּהוּ – **R' Abahu said** in defense of Rava: שָׁאנֵי זַיִת – **An olive is different** הוֹאִיל וַחֲזוּתוֹ מוֹכִיחַ עָלָיו – **because its appearance attests to its** owner's identity, וְאַף עַל גַּב דְּנָתְרִין זֵיתֵי – so that **even though the olives drop** to the ground, מֵידַע יְדִיעַ – **it is recognizable,** דּוּכְתָּא דְּאִינִישׁ אִינִישׁ הוּא – for **the place of a person is that person,** i.e. the olives found in a person's place are recognized as belonging to the person of th place.[35] Therefore, the owner expects to be able to recover th olives that drop from his tree, and even Rava agrees that they ar not deemed abandoned.

The Gemara asks:

אִי הָכִי – **If so,** i.e. if the fruit's appearance can indicate to whor it belongs, אֲפִילוּ רֵישָׁא נַמִּי – then **even** in **the opening case o the Mishnah,** in the case of the figs, say the same **as well.** Wh does the Mishnah permit the finder to keep figs found in the road

The Gemara answers:

אָמַר רַב פָּפָּא – Rav Pappa said: תְּאֵנָה עִם נְפִילָתָהּ נִמְאֶסֶת – **A fi becomes unappealing upon falling to the ground.** Thus, th owner abandons figs even though they are identifiable.[36]

The Gemara offers another proof:

תָּא שְׁמַע – **Come, learn** a proof to Rava's opinion from th following Baraisa: הַגַּנָּב שֶׁנָּטַל מִזֶּה וְנָתַן לָזֶה – A THIEF WHO TOO an object FROM THIS ONE AND GAVE TO THAT ONE, כֵּן גַּזְלָן שֶׁנָּטַל מִזֶּה וְנָתַן לָזֶה – AND SIMILARLY, A ROBBER[37] WHO TOOK some thing FROM THIS ONE AND GAVE TO THAT ONE,

NOTES

33. Because the owner has already discovered the loss and has given up hope of recovering them.

34. By contrast, the Gemara assumes at this point that olives and carobs do not commonly fall off the tree [before the owner is ready to pick them]. Thus, the owner does not consciously despair of fallen olives and carobs, which is why the Mishnah rules that the finder is *not* permitted to keep them (*Rashi*). This fits well with Abaye's view.

35. It is possible to tell that olives in the road have fallen from the nearby tree [and not from a passerby] by comparing them with the olives still hanging on the tree [and seeing the similarity of shading] (*Tosafos*). [This common wisdom is captured in the folk saying: The place of a person is the person.] Thus, the owner is confident that any passerby will identify the fallen olives as coming from his tree and not take them (*Rashi*). The same reasoning applies to carobs (see *Shitah Mekubetzes*).

Accordingly, there is no longer any need to assume that olives and carobs are less prone to falling off than figs. Even if the owner expects them to fall, he does not abandon them (*Rashba;* see also *Rashi*).

36. *Rashi* (see *Maharam Shif* and *Nachalas David*). However, olives and carobs are hardier and retain their value even after falling to the ground. The owner therefore does not abandon them but expects to recover them, as explained in the previous note.

37. The difference between the thief (גַּנָּב) and robber (גַּזְלָן) is that the thief steals surreptitiously, while the robber steals openly. This distinction is the basis for the question that follows.

יאוש שלא מדעת אביי אמר לא הוי יאוש ורבא אמר הוי יאוש בדבר שיש בו סימן כולי עלמא לא פליגי דלא הוי יאוש ואף על גב דשמעיניה דמיאש (א) לסוף לא הוי יאוש דכי אתא לידיה באיסורא הוא דאתא לידיה דלכי ידע דנפל מיניה לא מיאש מימר אמר סימנא אית לי בגויה יהבנא סימנא ושקילנא ליה בזוטו של ים ובשלוליתו של נהר אע"ג דאית ביה סימן רחמנא שרייה כדבעינן למימר לקמן כי פליגי בדבר שאין בו סימן אביי אמר [א]לא הוי יאוש דהא לא ידע דנפל מיניה רבא אמר הוי יאוש דלכי ידע דנפל מיניה מיאש מימר אמר סימנא לית לי בגויה מהשתא הוא דמיאש (סימן פמג"ש ממקגט"י ככסע"ז) תא שמע פירות מפוזרין הא לא ידע דנפל מיניה הא אמר רב עוקבא בר חמא הכא במכנשתא (ב) דביזרי עסקינן דאבידה מדעת היא ת"ש מעות מפוזרות הרי אלו שלו אמאי הא לא ידע דנפל מיניה התם נמי כדרבי [א] יצחק דאמר [ב]אדם עשוי למשמש בכיסו בכל שעה ושעה [ג]הכא נמי אדם עשוי למשמש בכיסו בכל שעה ושעה ת"ש עיגולי דבילה וככרות של נחתום הרי אלו שלו אמאי והא לא ידע דנפל מיניה התם נמי [א] [ד]אגב דיקירי מידע ידע בהו ת"ש ולשונות של ארגמן הרי אלו שלו ואמאי הא לא ידע דנפל מיניה התם נמי [ה]אגב דחשיבי משמושי ממשמש בהו וכדרבי יצחק ת"ש [ו]המוצא מעות בבתי כנסיות ובבתי מדרשות ובכל מקום שהרבים מצויין שם הרי אלו שלו מפני שהבעלים מתיאשין מהן והא לא ידע דנפל מיניה אמר רבי יצחק אדם עשוי למשמש בכיסו בכל שעה ת"ש (ב) [ז]מאימתי כל אדם מותרים בלקט משילכו בה הנמושות ואמרינן מאי נמושות וא"ר יוחנן סבי דאזלי (ג) אתיגרא ריש לקיש אמר לקוטי בתר לקוטי ואמאי נהי דעניים דהכא מיאשי איכא עניים בדוכתא אחריתא דלא מיאשי אמרי כיון דאיכא עניים הכא הנך ° מעיקרא איאושי מיאש ואמרי עניים דהתם מלקטי ליה ת"ש (ד) [ח] קציעות (ה) בדרך ואפילו בצד שדה קציעות [ט]וכן תאנה הנוטה לדרך ומצא תאנים תחתיה מותרות משום גזל ופטורות מן המעשר בזיתים ובחרובים אסור בשלמא רישא לאביי לא קשיא אגב דחשיבי ממשמש בהו תאנה נמי מידע ידיע דנתרא אלא סיפא לרבא קשיא דקתני בזיתים ובחרובים אסור אמר רבי אבהו שאני זית הואיל וחזותו מוכיח עליו ואע"ג דנתרין זיתי מידע ידיע (ו)דוכתא דאיניש איניש הוא אי הכי אפילו רישא נמי אמר רב פפא תאנה עם נפילתה נמאסת תא שמע (י)הגנב שנטל מזה ונתן לזה וכן גזלן שנטל מזה ונתן לזה וכן

## רש"י

יאוש שלא מדעת. דבר שסתמו יאוש לכשידע שנפל ממנו וכשמצאו עדיין לא ידעו הבעלים שנפל מהן: לא הוי יאוש. לקמיה מפרש פלוגתייהו: דמיאש לבסוף. לאחר שמצאו זה וכללא דיאוש כגון דאמר ווי ליה לחסרון כיס דגלי דעתיה שנואש מהן: באיסורא אתא לידיה. דדבר שאינו עשוי להתיאש הוא: זוטו של ים. מקומות בשפת הים שדרך הים לחזור לאחוריו י' פרסאות או חמשה עשר פרסאות פעמיים ביום ושוטף מה שמוצא שם והולך. זוטו לשון גודל ושירוע בלשון יווני כמו שכתבו הזקנים לתלמי המלך ואל אצילי ואל זאטוטי (מגילה דף ט.): ושלוליתו של נהר. כשהוא גדל ויוצא חוץ לגדותיו ושולל שלל ושוטף הנמצא: רחמנא שרייה. ואפי' באת ליד המוצא לפני יאוש: לקמן [ח]. בשמעתין מנין לאבידה ששטפה נהר כו': מהשתא הוי יאוש. שהרי נפל וכשיודע שוב אין דעתו עליו: דאבידה מדעת היא. שלא נפלו ממנו ומדעת הניחם הפקר: עשוי למשמש. וקודם שמצאו זה נודע לבעלים שנפלו ונואשו: דיקירי. כבד משא: סבי דאזלי אתיגרא. זקנים עניים הולכים על משענתם בנחת ורואין כל שבולת ושבולת ולשון נמושות כמו [ט] לא ימושו (ישעיה נט) שממשמשין והולכים: לקוטי בתר לקוטי. לשון נמושות כמו לא ימיש (שמות יג) שנוטלין ומשין הכל מלפניהם: ואמאי. אי יאוש שלא מדעת לאו יאוש הוא: נהי. דלגבי עניים דהכא הוי יאוש מדעת שראו שהלכו בה הנמושות ונתיאשו אלא עניים דעיר אחרת עדיין לא ידעי והיאך מותרין בו אלא משום כיון דלכי ידעי מיאשי הוי יאוש משעה שהלכו בו והיתר באו ליד זה: קציעות. תאנים שקוצצין אותם באיזמל ומוהל שלהן זב ושוטחן בשדה ליבש: ואפי' בצד שדה קציעות. שדה ששוטחים בה קציעות דידע דמהנהו אתו: מותרות משום גזל. אע"ג דכי נפל לא ידע כיון דלכי ידע מיאש מהשתא הוי יאוש כרבא: ופטורות מן המעשר. כדין הפקר דהפקר פטור מן המעשר: בזיתים ובחרובים אסור. כאביי: בשלמא רישא לאביי. מלי לתרולי דמעיקרא ידע ואיאש כדמפרש ואזיל: דקתני בזיתים ובחרובין אסור. וסלקא דעתך משום דלא עבידי דנתרי וליכא למימר ידע דאיאש ואע"ג דלכי ידע מיאש לא הוי יאוש מהשתא: חזותו מוכיח עליו. מראיתו ניכר של מי הוא הלכך מריה לכי ידע דנפיל לא מיאש דמימר אמר כולי עלמא ידעי דדידי נינהו ולא הפקר הן ולא שקלי להו: עם נפילתה נמאסת. הלכך כיון דידיע דנתרא מעיקרא מיאש משום מאיסותא דמכי נפלה לא חשיבא עליה ומפקר לה: לא ידיע. לא גרסינן ופירוש היה משובש בספרים:

ירדן

## תוספות

דלכי נפל מיניה לא מיאש. ואע"ג דהשתא מיאש אקראי בעלמא הוא ומתחילה לא היה עומד ליאש: ת"ש המוצא מעות כו'. תימה כיון דכבר הקשה ממתני' דמעות מפוזרות אמאי פריך תו מהך ברייתא ורבי יצחק נמי אמאי לא אמר למלתיה אמתני' וי"ל דברייתא אלימא ליה לאקשויי דמשמע דבכל ענין הרי אלו שלו אע"ג דאיכא סימן מדמוקי טעמא (ג) שהרבים מצויין שם ומשמע נמי אע"ג דכשזה הגביה עדיין היה בעל אבידה בבית המדרש ולא ידע שנפל מיניה:

ופטורות ממעשר. במס' פאה (פ"א מ"ו) מוכח דוקא בהפקיר קודם גמר מלאכה פטור מן המעשר אבל אם הפקיר לאחר גמר מלאכה שנתחייב כבר במעשר אין בכך כלום וה"נ מיירי קודם גמר מלאכה שלא נתחייבו עדיין כדמוכח בגילה פרק המביא (דף לד:) דתאנים העומדין לשוטחן בשדה ולעשות מהן קציעות לא נגמר מלאכתן למעשר עד שיתייבשו ואפילו זכה בהן המוצא קודם שיתייבשו פטורות מן המעשר כדאמרינן בב"ק (דף כח.) המפקיר כרמו והשכים בבקר ובצרו פטור מן המעשר וגבי הקדש אינו כן שאם הקדיש קודם גמר מלאכה ונפדה קודם גמר מלאכה חייב במעשר כדמוכח קצת בפרק האומר (סב:)[י]:

תאנה נמי מידע ידיע דנתרא. פירוש בשלמא לאביי תאנה מותרת כיון דרגילות היא דנתרא מעיקרא מתיאש לפי שסבור שהמוצא יקחנה כי הוא לא ידע שנפלה מן האילן אלא סבור הוא מעוברי דרכים נפלה ובזיתים ובחרובין אסור דלא עבידי דנתרי אע"ג דאם היה יודע דנפלו היה מתיאש לפי שעוברי דרכים יקחו כי יתלו דנפל מעוברי דרכים השתא דלא ידע סבור שלא נפלו אסורה דהוה ליה יאוש שלא מדעת אבל לרבא דהוי יאוש אמאי אסור וא"ת אם דין הוא לתלות בעוברי דרכים ולא באילן שאלו אמאי אסור בזיתים ובחרובין וי"ל דבדין ודאי אין לתלות בעוברי דרכים אלא באילן אלא שהבעלים מתיאשים לפי שסבורין שעוברי דרכים דלא מעלי יורו היתירא בפירות שמוצאים ויתלו בעוברי דרכים וא"ת אם כן מאי פריך לרבא נימא דזיתים וחרובין אסירי משום דאף לאחר שידעו הבעלים שנפלו לא נתיאשו לפי שיודעין שהמוצא לא יקחם שיתלה שנפלו מן האילן כאשר הוא האמת שאין לתלות בעוברי דרכים וי"ל דאם אינן מתיאשים בתאנה אמאי מותרים מיהו אית ספרים דגרסינן שאני זית הואיל וזיתו מוכיח עליו דבזה מתורץ מה שהקשינו כלומר לפי שהם תחת הזית יחשבו הבעלים שהמוצא לא יקחם לתלות בעוברי דרכים אבל תאנה עם נפילתה נמאסת פירוש מתלכלכת ונמאסת בעיניו ומפקירה אבל ברוב ספרים גרסינן הואיל וחזותו מוכיח עליו ואע"ג דמנתרא מידע ידעי דוכתא דאיניש איניש פירוש זיתים שנפלו דומין לזיתים שעומדין באילן ולפיכך אף כשידעו הבעלים שנפלו לא יתיאשו דיודעין שהמוצא לא יקחם אבל תאנה עם נפילתה נמאסת כן גרסינן בערוך נמסת בלא אל"ף ואין דומין לאותן שבאילן אי נמי גרסינן נמאסת ומחמת שמתלכלכת אינה דומה לתאנה שבאילן:

מה

## עין משפט נר מצוה

ח א מיי' פי"ד מהלכות גזלה ואבדה הל' ה סמג עשין סי' עד טוש"ע ח"מ סי' רסב סעיף ג:

ט ב ג מיי' פ"א מהלכות גזלה ואבדה הל' ח ופ"ד מהל' גניבה הל' י סמג עשין עא טוש"ע ח"מ סי' שנה סעיף א:

י ד ה מיי' פט"ו מהל' גזלה ואבדה הל' ח ועיין בכסף משנה סמג עשין עד טוש"ע ח"מ סי' רסב סעיף ג:

יא ו מיי' שם פי"א הל' ז טוש"ע ח"מ סי' רנט סעיף ג:

יב ז מיי' פ"א מהלכות מתנות עניים הל' יא:

יג ח מיי' פ"ג מהלכות מעשר הלכה כא:

יד ט מיי' שם הל' כד ופט"ו מהלכות גזלה ואבדה הל' טו טוש"ע ח"מ סי' רס סעיף ו:

## ליקוטי רש"י

בזוטו של ים. לשון ים החוזר לאחוריו עשר וחמש עשרה פרסאות ושוטף כל מה שמוצא בדרך חזרתו וכן עושה בכל יום [ע"ז מג.]. במכנשתא דבי דרי. בשעת אסיפת גרנות וכאן דשו בעליהן ונשאו את העיקר ומותרו אלו [לעיל ע"א.]. המוצא מעות בבתי כנסיות. אסיפת מקום שמתכנסים שם להתיעץ ולהוועד [לקמן כד.]. אדם עשוי למשמש בכיסו. ולמנות כמה בכיסו [ב"ק קיח:]. כל אדם. אפילו העשירים. משילכו הנמושות. בשדה דמכאן ואילך נתיאשו שאר העניים לפי שיודעין אם נשאר לקט שכחה ופאה נמושות נטלום. נמושות. לשון ממשש. דאזלי אתיגרא. הולכין בנחת ומעייני טפי מחזיק בפלך (שמואל ב, ג) מתרגמא אתיגרא. לקוטי בתר לקוטי. עני מוליך בנו אחריו שמכאן ואילך פוסקין שאר עניים מללקט [תענית ו:].

## רבינו חננאל

איפשיט אי הוי סימן אי לא בעיות דר' ירמיה הם ופשוטות הן ועלו כולן בתיקו. איתמר יאוש שלא מדעת אביי אמר לא הוי יאוש ורבא אמר הוי יאוש בדבר שיש בו סימן כולי עלמא לא פליגי דלא הוי יאוש ואע"ג דשמעיניה לבסוף דמיאש (לבסוף) לא הוי יאוש דכי אתא לידיה באיסורא אתא לידיה דהא לפני יאוש הוה כי פליגי בדבר שאין בו סימן אביי אמר לא הוה יאוש דלא ידע דנפל מיניה דחזיאש ארל המוצא בזוטו של ים. פי' בקרקעית הים ובשלוליתו של נהר פי' בתוך הנהר מקום שמי גשמים שוללים והוא מקום שטיפתו אע"ג דאית ביה סימן רחמנא שרייה למוצאה דאמר ר' יוחנן משום ר' שמעון בן יהוצדק מנין לאבדה ששטפה נהר שהיא מותרת שנאמר כן תעשה לכל אבדת אחיך אשר תאבד ממנו ומצאתה מי שאבודה ממנו בלבד ומצויה אצל כל אדם. פרה ורועה בשדה וכיוצא בה שכל הרואה אותה יכול ליטלה יצאת זו ששטפה נהר שאבודה ממנו ומכל אדם הלכך הרי היא למוצאה בין אית ליה בה סימן בין לית ליה בה סימן שרי דהא ודאי נתייאש הימנה. וזה שהתיר בים ובנהר כנגדו אסור ביבשה ודייקינן מינה מה היתירה בין אית ביה סימן בין לית ביה סימן ואפי' לפני יאוש שרי כך מה שאסר ביבשה ואפי' לית ביה סימן לפני יאוש אסורה ועלתה תיובתא דרבא תיובתא. והלכתא כוותיה דאביי ביע"ל קג"ם י' יאוש שלא מדעת והלכתא כאביי דיאוש שלא מדעת לא הוי יאוש. ואמרי' ומאחר דאיתותב רבא הני תמרי דזיקאי כלומר התמרים שהפילם הרוח מן הדקל והם מושלכים בדרך מפני מה אוכלין אותן העוברין ושבים והנה בעליהן לא נתייאשו שלא ידעו שהפילם הרוח ואמר ר' אשי כיון דאיכא שקצים דשכיחי דאזלי התם ואכלי להו יאושי מיאש להו מרייהו מעיקרא דכי האי גוונא אפי' אביי שרי ואם היו דקלים מוחזקין ליתמי דלאו בני יאוש נינהו או דקלים בכרכים דלא שכיחי בהו שקצים למיכלינהו אסירא. יש מי שאומרים פי' כרכתא דקלים הרבה שמוקפות גדר ומקשי רבא לאביי מצא מעות מפוזרות. ופריק אביי מתני' כר' יצחק דאמר אדם עשוי למשמש בכיסו בכל שעה ושעה וכן המוצא מעות בבתי כנסיות ובתי מדרשות הרי אלו שלו. ואקשי' והא דלמא לא ידע דנפלי מיניה. ופריק הכי נמי כר' יצחק. וכן כל דבר חשוב ממשמש בכל שעה כמו מעות. פי' נמושות סבי דאזלי אתיגרא. זקנים תשושי כח שמהלכין במשענת בידם שאין בהן כח לילך הרבה והשדה שיכנסו בה ללקט לא יניחו אחריהן כלום. האי דאמר מצא קציצות ואפי' בצד שדה קציצות מותרות משום גזל כיון שאלו הקציצות דבר חשוב

הז

## מסורת הש"ס

א) בבא קמא קיח:, ב) תענית ו:, פאה פרק ח משנה א, ג) גירסת רש"ל אתיגדא, וכן הוא בערוך ערך נמש, ד) מעשרות פרק ג [משנה ד], ה) ס"א קציצות, ו) ס"א דזיתא, ז) [תוספתא דכתובות פרק ח], ח) [דף כג:], ט) גירסת מהרש"ל ולא ימישון (תהלים קטו), י) [חפשנו בפ' האומר דקדושין ובפרק האומר דגיטין ולא מצאנו אך בפ' ר' ישמעאל דמנחות סו: משמע כן ואולי צ"ל בפ' העומר בעי"ן והיינו פ' ר' ישמעאל הנ"ל דכל הפרק מיירי בדיני עומר כמו שרגילים הפוסקים לכנות פרק איזהו נשך בשם פרק הרבית ולכאורה צ"ע על התוס' שהוצרכו לדקדק מן הגמ' והלא משנה שלימה היא פ"ד ממס' פאה מ"ח ואפשר לומר שהתוספות רצו לאשמועי' רבותא טפי שאפי' היה תחלת גידולו ביד הקדש אפ"ה חייב אם פדאו קודם מירוח והא לא שמעינן ממתני' דמאי מיירי שגדל ביד הדיוט ואח"כ הקדיש אבל מפרק ר"י הנ"ל משמע דאפי' גדל ביד הקדש נמי חייב אם פדאו קודם מירוח וחילוק זה בין בגדל ביד הדיוט או ביד הקדש כעין זה מצינו גבי מירוח הנכרי ודוק. העתק מחלופי גרסאות].

## הגהות הב"ח

(א) גמ' דמיאש לבסוף לא: (ב) שם במכנשתא דבי דרי עסקינן: (ג) תוס' ד"ה ת"ש וכו' שהרבים מצויין שם. נ"ב ע"ל דף כד ע"א:

## הגהות הגר"א

[א] גמ' אגב דיקירי. נ"ב גירסת הרא"ש דחשיבי כיון דמידי דמיכל נינהו וכן מחרוזות וחתיכות וכן בלשונות אבל גיזי ואניצי כתב משום דיקירי ולא פריך גמ' מכריכות משום דהתם דרך הינוח וטעמא אחרינא להו ועי' תוס' (ע"א) ד"ה אלו כו' (ועמ"ש רבינו בח"מ סי' רס"ב ס"ק ז):

## גליון הש"ס

גמ' מעיקרא איאושי. קשה לי הא גם לעניים קטנים יש להם חלק ומקרי יאוש שלא מדעת כדלקמן דף כב ע"ב ועיין בתוס' ב"ב דף קמג ע"ב ד"ה ואם ועדיין צ"ע:

owner was already aware of their loss, and had despaired of finding them.

The Gemara again attempts to prove Rava's view: תָּא שְׁמַע – **Come, learn** a proof to Rava's opinion from the following Mishnah, which deals with the law of *leket*.[19] The Mishnah begins by posing the following question: מֵאֵימָתַי כָּל אָדָם מוּתָּרִים בְּלֶקֶט – FROM WHEN ARE ALL PEOPLE PERMITTED TO keep any *LEKET* they find? I.e. at what point do the poor give up hope of finding any more *leket,* thereby rendering whatever remains ownerless and freely available to all? מִשֶּׁיֵּלְכוּ בָהּ הַנְּמוּשׁוֹת – FROM WHEN THE RUMMAGERS GO THROUGH [THE FIELD].[20]

Before proceeding to the actual proof, the Gemara parenthetically records a dispute regarding the meaning of the term "rummagers":

וְאָמְרִינַן מַאי נְמוּשׁוֹת – **And we have said** in reference to this Mishnah:[21] **What is** meant by the term RUMMAGERS? וְאָמַר רַבִּי יוֹחָנָן – **R' Yochanan said:** סָבֵי דְּאָזְלֵי אַתִּיגְרָא – **The elderly** poor **who walk with a cane.**[22] רֵישׁ לָקִישׁ אָמַר – **Reish Lakish said:** לְקוֹטֵי בָּתַר לְקוֹטֵי – **Those who glean after the gleaners.**[23]

The Gemara now returns to its original point:

וְאַמַּאי – **But, why** does the remaining *leket* become free for anyone to take once the "rummagers" have passed through the field? נְהִי דַּעֲנִיִּים דְּהָכָא מִיָּאֲשֵׁי – **Granted that the local poor**[24] **have given up hope** of finding additional *leket* once they have seen the "rummagers" go through the field, אִיכָּא עֲנִיִּים בְּדוּכְתָּא אַחֲרִיתָא – but **there are** also the **poor in other places,** דְּלָא מִיָּאֲשֵׁי – **who have not** consciously **given up hope,** since they are not aware that the "rummagers" have passed through. How have those poor surrendered their right to the *leket?* This Mishnah seems to indicate that there is no need for their actual, conscious abandonment, as Rava contends.[25] – ? –

The Gemara rejects this proof as well:

אָמְרֵי – **They said** in defense of Abaye: כֵּיוָן דְּאִיכָּא עֲנִיִּים הָכָא – **Since there are poor in this locale,** הָנָךְ – **those** more distant poor מֵעִיקָּרָא אִיאוּשֵׁי מְיָאֵשׁ – **despair from the very beginning** of acquiring any of the local *leket,* וְאָמְרֵי – **and say** to themselves: עֲנִיִּים דְּהָתָם מְלַקְּטֵי לֵיהּ – **The poor people of that place will** certainly **collect it** all.[26] Thus, once the local poor despair of finding any more *leket*, *all* the poor have knowingly despaired. This Mishnah therefore does not contradict Abaye's opinion.

The Gemara now cites a Mishnah with conflicting indications but which is more readily explained according to Abaye:

תָּא שְׁמַע – **Come, learn** a proof from the following Mishnah:[27] קְצִיעוֹת בַּדֶּרֶךְ – CUT FIGS found IN THE ROAD, אֲפִילּוּ בְּצַד שָׂדֶה קְצִיעוֹת – AND EVEN those found BESIDE A FIELD OF CUT FIGS spread out to dry;[28] וְכֵן – AND SIMILARLY, תְּאֵנָה הַנּוֹטָה לַדֶּרֶךְ – in the case of A FIG TREE THAT HANGS OVER THE ROAD,[29] וּמָצָא תְּאֵנִים תַּחְתֶּיהָ – AND ONE FOUND FIGS BENEATH IT; מֻתָּרוֹת מִשּׁוּם גָּזֵל – THEY ARE PERMISSIBLE WITH RESPECT TO the prohibition of THEFT, i.e. they are deemed ownerless and taking them does not constitute theft, וּפְטוּרוֹת מִן הַמַּעֲשֵׂר – AND THEY ARE EXEMPT FROM THE requirement of MAASER, as is the law with all ownerless produce.[30] בְּזֵיתִים וּבֶחָרוּבִים – However, IN REGARD TO OLIVES AND CAROBS found under the same conditions, אָסוּר – IT IS PROHIBITED for the finder to keep them.

The two rulings of this Mishnah seem to contradict each other. The first ruling seems to reflect Rava's view and the second Abaye's.[31] The Gemara offers a resolution of this contradiction in accordance with Abaye's position, but sees a difficulty according to Rava's:

בִּשְׁלָמָא רֵישָׁא לְאַבַּיֵי לֹא קַשְׁיָא – **Now, it is understandable that the opening section** of the Mishnah **does not contradict Abaye's** view for the following reason: אַגַּב דַּחֲשִׁיבֵי – **Since [the cut figs] are valuable,** מְמַשְׁמֵשׁ בְּהוּ – **the owner constantly checks on them**[32] and is aware of their loss almost as soon as it occurs. Therefore, one who encounters them is permi

NOTES

19. *Leket* (gleanings) refers to the one or two stalks that fall from the reaper's hand while he cuts the grain. The Torah (*Leviticus* 19:9,10) prohibits him to retrieve these and decrees that they be left for the poor (Mishnah, *Pe'ah* 6:5). The Mishnah quoted here is from *Pe'ah* 8:1.

20. Whatever *leket* is found in the field after the "rummagers" have passed through in search of it may be taken by any person, because the poor have abandoned hope of finding anything further in that field.

21. The discussion that follows is from *Taanis* 6b.

22. They go through the field more slowly than their younger counterparts and are therefore more apt to notice each and every *leket*-stalk. Once these poor pass through a field, the others abandon hope of discovering any further *leket* in it.

According to this explanation, the word נְמוּשׁוֹת is from the root משש, to *touch* or *feel* [since those who walk with a cane probe the area before them] (*Rashi*).

23. Once the second wave of collectors has searched through the field, it is assumed that nothing remains to be found; therefore, any remaining *leket* may be taken by anybody (*Rav* to *Pe'ah* 8:1; *Rambam, Matnos Aniyim* 1:10; see *Rashi* to *Taanis* 6b for a different explanation of this expression).

According to this explanation the word נְמוּשׁוֹת is from the root מוש, meaning to *remove* or *depart*. Once the second wave has passed through, the area has been swept clean of everything likely to be found (*Rashi*).

24. Literally: the poor of here.

25. The right to *leket* belongs to all the world's poor. Therefore, though it is true that the local poor abandoned hope of finding any remaining *leket* in the field after seeing the rummagers pass through it, this does not constitute a *ye'ush* (abandonment) on the part of the poor who live elsewhere, who are not aware of the passage of the local rummagers. What, if so, divests them of their right to the *leket*? Seemingly, we must accept Rava's view that *ye'ush* without the owner's awareness is effective. We may then say that since the distant poor would despair of finding any further *leket* if only they knew that the rummagers have passed through, their abandonment can be taken as a legal fact even now.

26. The out-of-town poor *never* expect to obtain *leket* from this place since they assume it will all be collected before they can come to look for it. This constitutes a conscious abandonment on their part.

27. *Maasros* 3:4.

28. [Figs were commonly dried and pressed into large cakes, as we learned in the Mishnah (21a). The stems of] figs intended for this purpose were cut off by knife, so that the juice of the figs could ooze out through the cut at the top of the fruit. The cut figs were then spread out in a field to dry in the sun (*Rashi*). [Because of this, the term קְצִיעוֹת, which literally means *cut* (figs), is often used to refer to dried figs.]

29. I.e. a tree growing in private property whose branches overhang the road.

30. The produce of Eretz Yisrael must be tithed prior to its consumption. The owner must separate the share of the Kohen (known as *terumah*) and the share of the Levi (known as *maaser*), as well as a second *maaser* (tithe) whose distribution varies. Ownerless produce, however, is exempt from this requirement and may be eaten without tithing.

31. The Gemara sees the two rulings of the Mishnah as reflecting the conflicting views of Abaye and Rava. The reason the finder may not keep the olives and carobs (the second ruling) would seem to be because the owner may not be aware of their loss, and may therefore not actually have despaired of them. This agrees with Abaye's view, that the owner must actually give up hope of recovering a lost object before the law of abandonment takes effect. However, the Mishnah's first ruling (regarding figs) seems to contradict this, since it deems the figs ownerless regardless of whether the owner is yet aware of their loss. This agrees with Rava's view.

32. Literally: feels through them.

יאוש שלא מדעת אביי אמר לא הוי יאוש ורבא אמר הוי יאוש בדבר שיש בו סימן כולי עלמא לא פליגי דלא הוי יאוש ואף על גב דשמעיניה דמיאש (א) לסוף לא הוי יאוש דכי אתא לידיה באיסורא הוא דאתא לידיה דלכי ידע דנפל מיניה לא מיאש מימר אמר סימנא אית לי בגויה יהבנא סימנא ושקילנא ליה בזוטו של ים ובשלוליתו של נהר אע"ג דאית ביה סימן רחמנא שרייה כדבעינן למימר לקמן כי פליגי בדבר שאין בו סימן אביי אמר א לא הוי יאוש דהא לא ידע דנפל מיניה רבא אמר הוי יאוש דלכי ידע דנפל מיניה מיאש מימר אמר סימנא לית לי בגויה מהשתא הוא דמיאש (סימן פמג"ש ממקגט"י ככסע"ז) תא שמע פירות מפוזרין הא לא ידע דנפל מיניה הא אמר רב עוקבא בר חמא הכא במכנשתא (ג) דביזרי עסקינן דאבידה מדעת היא ת"ש מעות מפוזרות הרי אלו שלו אמאי הא לא ידע דנפל מיניה התם נמי כדרבי א) יצחק דאמר ב אדם עשוי למשמש בכיסו בכל שעה ושעה ג הכא נמי אדם עשוי למשמש בכיסו בכל שעה ושעה ת"ש עיגולי דבילה וככרות של נחתום הרי אלו שלו אמאי והא לא ידע דנפל מיניה התם נמי [א] ד אגב דיקירי מידע ידע בהו ת"ש ולשונות של ארגמן הרי אלו שלו ואמאי הא לא ידע דנפל מיניה התם נמי ה אגב דחשיבי משמושי ממשמש בהו וכדרבי יצחק ת"ש ו המוצא מעות בבתי כנסיות ובבתי מדרשות ובכל מקום שהרבים מצויין שם הרי אלו שלו מפני שהבעלים מתיאשין מהן והא לא ידע דנפל מיניה אמר רבי יצחק אדם עשוי למשמש בכיסו בכל שעה ת"ש ג) ז מאימתי כל אדם מותרים בלקט משילכו בה הנמושות ואמרינן מאי נמושות וא"ר יוחנן סבי דאזלי ג) אתיגרא ריש לקיש אמר לקוטי בתר לקוטי ואמאי נהי דעניים דהכא מיאשי איכא עניים בדוכתא אחריתא דלא מיאשי אמרי כיון דאיכא עניים הכא הנך ט מעיקרא איאושי מיאש ואמרי עניים דהתם מלקטי ליה ת"ש ד) ח קציעות ה) בדרך ואפילו בצד שדה קציעות ט וכן תאנה הנוטה לדרך ומצא תאנים תחתיה מותרות משום גזל ופטורות מן המעשר בזיתים ובחרובים אסור בשלמא רישא לאביי לא קשיא אגב דחשיבי ממשמש בהו תאנה נמי מידע ידיע דנתרא אלא סיפא לרבא קשיא דקתני בזיתים ובחרובים אסור אמר רבי אבהו שאני זית הואיל וחזותו מוכיח עליו ואע"ג דנתרין זיתי מידע ידיע ו) דוכתא דאיניש הוא אי הכי אפילו רישא נמי אמר רב פפא תאנה עם נפילתה נמאסת תא שמע י הגנב שנטל מזה ונתן לזה וכן גזלן שנטל מזה ונתן לזה וכן

## רש"י

יאוש שלא מדעת. דבר שסתמו יאוש לכשידע שנפל ממנו וכשמצאו עדיין לא ידעו הבעלים שנפל מהן: לא הוי יאוש. לקמיה מפרש פלוגתייהו: דמיאש לבסוף. לאחר שמצאו זה וכללא דיאוש כגון דאמר ווי ליה לחסרון כיס דגלי דעתיה שנואש מהן: באיסורא אתא לידיה. דדבר שאינו עשוי להתיאש הוא: זוטו של ים. מקומות בשפת הים שדרך הים לחזור לאחוריו י' פרסאות או חמשה עשר פרסאות פעמיים ביום ושוטף מה שמולא שם והולך. זוטו לשון גודל ושירוע בלשון יווני כמו שכתבו הזקנים לתלמי המלך ואל אצילי ואל זאטוטי (מגילה דף ט.): ושלוליתו של נהר. כשהוא גדל ויולא חוץ לגדותיו ושולל שלל ושוטף הנמלא: רחמנא שרייה. ואפי' באת ליד המולא לפני יאוש: לקמן ס). בשמעתין מנין לאבידה ששטפה נהר כו': מהשתא הוי יאוש. שהרי נפל וכשיודע שוב אין דעתו עליו: דאבידה מדעת היא. שלא נפלו ממנו ומדעת הניחם הפקר: עשוי למשמש. וקודם שמלאו זה נודע לבעלים שנפלו ונואשו: דיקירי. כבד משא: סבי דאזלי אתיגרא. זקנים עניים הולכים על משענתם בנחת ורואין כל שבולת ושבולת ולשון נמושות כמו ט) לא ימושו (ישעיה נט) שממשמשין והולכים: לקוטי בתר לקוטי. לשון נמושות כמו לא ימיש (שמות יג) שנוטלין ומשין הכל מלפניהם: ואמאי. אי יאוש שלא מדעת לאו יאוש הוא: נהי. דלגבי עניים דהכא הוי יאוש מדעת שראו שהלכו בה הנמושות ונתיאשו אלא עניים דעיר אחרת עדיין לא ידעי והיאך מותרין בו אלא משום כיון דלכי ידעי מיאשי הוי יאוש משעה שהלכו בו ובהיתר באו ליד זה: קציעות. תאנים שקוללין אותם באיזמל ומוהל שלהן זב ושוטחן בשדה ליבש: ואפי' בצד שדה קציעות. שדה ששוטחים בה קליעות דידע דמהנהו אתו: מותרות משום גזל. אע"ג דכי נפל לא ידע כיון דלכי ידע מיאש מהשתא הוי יאוש כרבא: ופטורות מן המעשר. כדין הפקר דהפקר פטור מן המעשר: בזיתים ובחרובים אסור. כאביי: בשלמא רישא לאביי. מלי לתרולי דמעיקרא ידע ואיאש כדמפרש ואזיל: דקתני בזיתים ובחרובין אסור. וסלקא דעתך משום דלא עבידי דנתרי וליכא למימר ידע דאיאש ואע"ג דלכי ידע מיאש לא הוי יאוש מהשתא: חזותו מוכיח עליו. מראיתו ניכר של מי הוא הלכך מריה לכי ידע דנפיל לא מיאש דמימר אמר כולי עלמא ידעי דדידי נינהו ולא הפקר הן ולא שקלי להו: עם נפילתה נמאסת. הלכך כיון דידיע דנתרא מעיקרא מיאש משום מאיסותא דמכי נפלה לא חשיבא עליה ומפקר לה: לא ידיע. לא גרסינן ופירוש היה משובש בספרים:

ירדן

## תוספות

דלכי נפל מיניה לא מיאש. ואע"ג דהשתא מיאש אקראי בעלמא הוא ומתחילה לא היה עומד ליאש: ת"ש המוצא מעות כו'. תימה כיון דכבר הקשה ממתני' דמעות מפוזרות אמאי פריך תו מהך ברייתא ורבי יצחק נמי אמאי לא אמר למלתיה אמתני' וי"ל דברייתא אלימא ליה לאקשויי דמשמע דבכל ענין הרי אלו שלו אע"ג דאיכא סימן מדמוקי טעמא (ג) שהרבים מלויין שם ומשמע נמי אע"ג דכשזה הגביה עדיין היה בעל אבידה בבית המדרש ולא ידע שנפל מיניה:

ופטורות ממעשר. במס' פאה (פ"א מ"ו) מוכח דוקא בהפקיר קודם גמר מלאכה פטור מן המעשר אבל אם הפקיר לאחר גמר מלאכה שנתחייב כבר במעשר אין בכך כלום וה"נ מיירי קודם גמר מלאכה שלא נתייבשו עדיין כדמוכח בבילה פרק המביא (דף לד:) דתאנים העומדין לשוטחן בשדה ולעשות מהן קליעות לא נגמר מלאכתן למעשר עד שיתייבשו ואפילו זכה בהן המולא קודם שיתייבשו פטורות מן המעשר כדאמרינן בב"ק (דף כח.) המפקיר כרמו והשכים בבקר ובלרו פטור מן המעשר וגבי הקדש אינו כן שאם הקדיש קודם גמר מלאכה ונפדה קודם גמר מלאכה חייב במעשר כדמוכח קלת בפרק האומר (סג:):

תאנה נמי מידע ידיע דנתרא. פירוש בשלמא לאביי תאנה מותרת כיון דרגילות היא דנתרא מעיקרא מתיאש לפי שסבור שהמולא יקחנה כי הוא לא ידע שנפלה מן האילן אלא סבור הוא מעוברי דרכים נפלה ובזיתים ובחרובין אסור דלא עבידי דנתרי אע"ג דאם היה יודע דנפלו היה מתיאש לפי שעוברי דרכים יקחו כי יתלו דנפל מעוברי דרכים השתא דלא ידע סבור שלא נפלו אסורה דהוה ליה יאוש שלא מדעת אבל לרבא דהוי יאוש אמאי אסור וא"ת אם דין הוא לתלות בעוברי דרכים ולא באילן שאלו אמאי אסור בזיתים ובחרובין וי"ל דבדין ודאי אין לתלות בעוברי דרכים אלא באילן אלא שהבעלים מתיאשים לפי שסבורין שעוברי דרכים דלא מעלי יורו היתירא בפירות שמולאים ויתלוס בעוברי דרכים וא"ת אם כן מאי פריך לרבא נימא דזיתים וחרובין אסירי משום דאף לאחר שידעו הבעלים שנפלו לא נתיאשו לפי שיודעין שהמולא לא יקחם שיתלה שנפלו מן האילן כאשר הוא האמת שאין לתלות בעוברי דרכים וי"ל דאם אינן מתיאשים בתאנה אמאי מותרים מיהו אית ספרים דגרסינן שאני זית הואיל וזיתו מוכיח עליו דבזה מתורץ מה שהקשינו כלומר לפי שהם תחת הזית יחשבו הבעלים שהמולא לא יקחם לתלות בעוברי דרכים אבל תאנה עם נפילתה נמאסת פירוש מתלכלכת ונמאסת בעיניו ומפקירה אבל ברוב ספרים גרסינן הואיל וחזותו מוכיח עליו ואע"ג דמנתרא מידע ידעי דוכתא דאיניש איניש פירוש זיתים שנפלו דומין לזיתים שעומדין באילן ולפיכך אף כשידעו הבעלים שנפלו לא יתיאשו דידעין שהמולא לא יקחם אבל תאנה עם נפילתה נמסת כן גרסינן בערוך נמסת בלא אל"ף ואין דומין לאותן שבאילן אי נמי גרסינן נמאסת ומחמת שמתלכלכת אינה דומה לתאנה שבאילן:

מה

## עין משפט נר מצוה

ח א מיי' פי"ד מהלכות גזלה ואבידה הל' ה סמג עשין סי' עד טוש"ע ח"מ סי' רסב סעיף ג:

ט ב ג מיי' פי"א מהלכות גזלה ואבידה הל' ח ופ"ד מהל' גניבה הל' י סמג עשין עא טוש"ע ח"מ סי' שנה סעיף א:

י ד ה מיי' פט"ו מהל' גזלה ואבידה הל' ח ועיין בכסף משנה סמג עשין עד טוש"ע ח"מ סי' רסב סעיף ג:

יא ו מיי' שם פי"א הל' ז טוש"ע ח"מ סי' רנט סעיף ג:

יב ז מיי' פ"א מהלכות מתנות עניים הל' יא:

יג ח מיי' פ"ג מהלכות מעשר הלכה כא:

יד ט מיי' שם הל' כד ופט"ו מהלכות גזלה ואבידה הל' טו טוש"ע ח"מ סי' רס סעיף ו:

## ליקוטי רש"י

בזוטו של ים. לשון ים החוזר לאחוריו עשר וחמש עשרה פרסאות ושוטף כל מה שמולא בדרך חזרתו וכן עושה בכל יום [ע"ז מג.]. במכנשתא דבי דרי. בשעת אסיפת גרנות וכאן דשן בעליהן ונשאו את העיקר ונותרו אלו [לעיל ע"א.]. המוצא מעות בבתי כנסיות. אסיפת מקום שמתכנסים שם להתיעץ ולהוועד [לקמן כד.]. אדם עשוי למשמש בכיסו. ולמנות כמה בכיסו [ב"ק קיח:]. כל אדם. אפילו העשירים. משילכו הנמושות. בשדה למכאן ואילך נמייאשו שאר העניים לפי שיודעין אם נשאר לקט שכחה ופאה נמושות נטלום. נמושות. לשון ממשש. דאזלי אתיגרא. הולכין בנחת ומעייני טפי מחזיק בפלך (שמואל ב, ג) מתרגמא אתיגרא. לקוטי בתר לקוטי. עני מוליך בנו אחריו שמכאן ואילך פוסקין שאר עניים מללקוט [תענית ו:].

## רבינו חננאל

איפשיט אי הוי סימן אי לא בעיות דר' ירמיה הם ופשוטות הן ועלו כולן בתיקו. איתמר יאוש שלא מדעת אביי אמר לא הוי יאוש ורבא אמר הוי יאוש בדבר שיש בו סימן כולי עלמא לא פליגי דלא הוי יאוש ואע"ג דשמעיניה לבסוף דמיאש (לבסוף) לא הוי יאוש דכי אתא לידיה באיסורא אתא לידיה דהא לפני יאוש הוה כי פליגי בדבר שאין בו סימן אביי אמר לא הוה יאוש דלא ידע דנפל מיניה דמיאש. אבל המוצא בזוטו של ים. פי' בקרקעית הים ובשלוליתו של נהר פי' בתוך הנהר מקום שמי גשמים שוללים והוא מקום שטיפתו אע"ג דאית ביה סימן רחמנא שרייה למוצאה דאמר ר' יוחנן משום ר' שמעון בן יהוצדק מנין לאבדה ששטפה נהר שהיא מותרת שנאמר כן תעשה לכל אבדת אחיך אשר תאבד ממנו ומצאתה מי שאבודה ממנו בלבד ומצויה אצל כל אדם. פרה ורועה בשדה וכיוצא בה שכל הרואה אותה יכול ליטלה יצאת זו ששטפה נהר שאבודה ממנו ומכל אדם הלכך הרי היא למוצאה בין אית ליה בה סימן בין לית ליה בה סימן שרי דהא ודאי נתייאש הימנה. וזה שהיתיר בים ובנהר כנגדו אסור ביבשה ודייקינן מינה מה היתירה בין אית ביה סימן בין לית ביה סימן ואפי' לפני יאוש שרי כך מה שאסר ביבשה ואפי' לית ביה סימן לפני יאוש אסורה ועלתה רבא תיובתא דרבא תיובתא. והלכתא כוותיה דאביי ביע"ל קג"ם י' יאוש שלא מדעת והלכתא כאביי דיאוש שלא מדעת לא הוי יאוש. ואמרי' ומאחר דאיתותב רבא הני תמרי דזיקאי כלומר התמרים שהפילם הרוח מן הדקל והם מושלכים בדרך מפני מה אוכלין אותן העוברין ושבים והנה בעליהן לא נתיאשו שלא ידעו שהפילם הרוח ואמר ר' אשי כיון דאיכא שקצים דשכיחי דאזלי התם ואכלי להו יאושי מיאש להו מרייהו מעיקרא דכי האי גוונא אפי' אביי שרי ואם היו דקלים מוחזקין ליתמי דלאו בני יאוש נינהו או דקלים בכרכים דלא שכיחי בהו שקצים למיכלינהו אסירא. יש מי שאומרים פי' כרכתא דקלים הרבה שמוקפות גדר ומקשי רבא לאביי מצא מעות מפוזרות. ופריק אביי מתני' כר' יצחק דאמר אדם עשוי למשמש בכיסו בכל שעה ושעה וכן המוצא מעות בבתי כנסיות ובתי מדרשות הרי אלו שלו. ואקשי' והא דלמא לא ידע דנפלי מיניה. ופריק הכי נמי כר' יצחק. וכן כל דבר חשוב ממשמש בכל שעה כמו מעות. פי' נמושות סבי דאזלי אתיגרא. זקנים תשושי כח שמהלכין במשענת בידם שאין בהן כח לילך הרבה והשדה שיכנסו בה ללקט לא יניחו אחריהן כלום. האי דאמר מצא קציצות ואפי' בצד שדה קציצות מותרות משום גזל כיון שאלו הקציצות דבר חשוב

הז

## מסורת הש"ס

א) בבא קמא קיח:, ב) תענית ו:, פאה פרק ח משנה א, ג) גירסת רש"ל אתיגדא, וכן הוא בערוך ערך נמש, ד) מעשרות פרק ג [משנה ד], ה) ס"א קציצות, ו) ס"א דזיתא, ז) [תוספתא דכתובות פרק ס], ח) [דף כב:], ט) גירסת מהרש"ל ולא ימישון (תהלים קטו), י) [חפשתי בפ' האומר דקדושין ובפרק האומר דגיטין ולא מצאתי אך בפ' ר' ישמעאל דמנחות סו: משמע כן ואולי צ"ל בפ' העומר בע"ן והיינו פ' ר' ישמעאל הנ"ל דכל הפרק מיירי בדיני עומר כמו שרגילים הפוסקים לכנות פרק אחד בשם פרק הרכים ולכאורה צ"ע על התוס' שהוצרכו לדקדק מן הגמ' והלא משנה שלימה היא פ"ד ממס' פאה מ"ח ואפשר לומר שהתוספות רצו לאשמועי' רבותא טפי שאפי' היה תחלת גידולו ביד הקדש אפ"ה חייב אם פדאו קודם מירוח והא לא שמעינן ממתני' דמלי מיירי שגדל ביד הדיוט ואח"כ הקדיש אבל מפרק ר"י הנ"ל משמע דאפי' גדל ביד הקדש נמי חייב אם פדאו קודם מירוח וחילוק זה בין גדל ביד הדיוט או ביד הקדש כעין זה מלינו גבי מירוח הנכרי ודוק. העתק מחלופי גרסאות].

## הגהות הב"ח

(א) גמ' דמיאש לבסוף לא: (ב) שם במכנשתא דבי דרי עסקינן: (ג) תוס' ד"ה ת"ש וכו' שהרבים מלוין שם. נ"ב ע"ל דף כד ע"א:

## הגהות הגר"א

[א] גמ' אגב דיקירי. נ"ב גירסת הרא"ש דחשיבי כיון דמידי דמיכל נינהו וכן מחרוזות וחתיכות וכן בלשונות אבל גחי ואולי כתב משום דיקירי ולא פריך גמ' מכריכות משום דהתם דרך היגוח וטעמא אחרינא להו ועי' תוס' (ע"א) ד"ה אלו כו' (ועמ"ש רבינו בח"מ סי' רס"ב ס"ק ז):

## גליון הש"ס

גמ' מעיקרא איאושי. קשה לי הא גם לעניים קטנים יש להם חלק ומקרי יאוש שלא מדעת כדלקמן דף כב ע"ב ועיין בתוס' ב"ב דף קמג ע"ב ד"ה ואם ועדיין צ"ע:

the Mishnah nonetheless allows the finder to keep the scattered produce, it would seem that it follows Rava's view that the law of abandonment goes into effect even if the owner is *not* aware of his loss.[10] – ? –

The Gemara rejects this proof:

**הָא אָמַר רַב עוּקְבָא בַּר חָמָא – But Rav Ukva bar Chama has** already **said:**[11] **הָכָא בְּמַכְנַשְׁתָּא דְבִיזְרֵי עָסְקִינַן – Here,** in our Mishnah's case of scattered produce, **we are dealing with** the produce left behind at **the clearing of the threshing floor, דַּאֲבֵידָה מִדַּעַת הִיא – which is a loss with** the owner's **awareness.**[12] Since our Mishnah deals with conscious abandonment, it is not a proof to Rava's opinion regarding a state of abandonment of which the owner is unaware.

The Gemara again attempts to prove Rava's position:

**תָּא שְׁמַע – Come, learn** a proof to Rava's opinion from the second case of our Mishnah, which stated: **מָעוֹת מְפוּזָּרוֹת הֲרֵי אֵלּוּ שֶׁלּוֹ – SCATTERED COINS ... THESE BELONG TO [THE FINDER]. אַמַּאי – Why** is this so, **הָא לֹא יָדַע דְּנָפַל מִינֵּיהּ – when [the owner] does not** necessarily **know that [the money] has fallen from him?** It would seem from this that the Mishnah allows a finder to keep scattered coins regardless of whether the owner is aware of their loss.[13] This supports Rava's view. – ? –

The Gemara rejects this proof:

**הָתָם נַמִּי – There, too,** the Mishnah can be explained **כִּדְרַבִּי יִצְחָק דְּאָמַר – in accordance with R' Yitzchak, who said** in connection with a Baraisa quoted below: **אָדָם עָשׂוּי לְמַשְׁמֵשׁ בְּכִיסוֹ בְּכָל שָׁעָה וְשָׁעָה – A person is in the habit of touching his purse all the time**[14] to make sure that his money is secure. **הָכָא נַמִּי – Here too,** in the case of our Mishnah, we may explain that **אָדָם עָשׂוּי לְמַשְׁמֵשׁ בְּכִיסוֹ בְּכָל שָׁעָה וְשָׁעָה – a person is in the habit of touching his purse all the time** to make sure that his money is secure. Therefore, it may safely be assumed that the owner was *aware* of the loss shortly after it occurred, and had already despaired by the time the coins were found. Thus, this case is not relevant to the issue of an object whose owner is not aware of his loss.

The Gemara once again attempts to support Rava's position:

**תָּא שְׁמַע – Come, learn** a proof to Rava's opinion from another case of our Mishnah, which stated: **עִיגּוּלֵי דְבֵילָה – ROUND CAKES OF PRESSED FIGS וְכִכְּרוֹת שֶׁל נַחְתּוֹם – AND A BAKER'S LOAVES ... הֲרֵי אֵלּוּ שֶׁלּוֹ – THESE BELONG TO [THE FINDER]. אַמַּאי – Why** may he keep them, **וְהָא לֹא יָדַע דְּנָפַל מִינֵּיהּ – when [the owner] does not** necessarily **know that they have fallen from him?** It would seem that the Mishnah allows a finder to keep the figs and loaves even if the owner is not aware of their loss, a Rava contends. – ? –

The Gemara rejects this proof as well:

**הָתָם נַמִּי – There too,** in that case of the Mishnah, we may sa that **אַגַּב דְּיַקִּירֵי – since they** [the cakes of pressed figs an baker's loaves] **are heavy, מֵידַע יָדַע בְּהוּ – [the owner] i certainly aware** of their loss not long afterwards, even befo they are found.[15] Thus, it may be assumed that he abandone hope of recovering them before they were found.

The Gemara once again attempts to support Rava's view:

**תָּא שְׁמַע – Come, learn** a proof to Rava's opinion from ye another clause of our Mishnah, which stated: **לְשׁוֹנוֹת שֶׁל אַרְגָּמָן הֲרֵי אֵלּוּ שֶׁלּוֹ – TONGUES OF PURPLE WOOL ... THESE BELONG T [THE FINDER]. וְאַמַּאי – But why, הָא לֹא יָדַע דְּנָפַל מִינֵּיהּ – when [the owner] does not** necessarily **know that they** [th tongues of purple wool] **have fallen from him?** It would see that the Mishnah allows the finder to keep them even if the owne is not aware of their loss, as Rava maintains. – ? –

The Gemara rejects this proof as well:

**הָתָם נַמִּי – There too,** we may say that **אַגַּב דַּחֲשִׁיבֵי – since the are valuable, מַשְׁמוּשֵׁי מְמַשְׁמֵשׁ בְּהוּ – [the owner] constant touches them** to check that he has not lost them, **וְכִדְרַבִּי יִצְחָק – as R' Yitzchak** said concerning money.[16] Thus, it may b assumed that by the time the tongues were found, the owner ha already discovered their loss and despaired of recovering them

The Gemara now cites a Baraisa in support of Rava's view:

**תָּא שְׁמַע – Come, learn** a proof to Rava's opinion from th Baraisa which states: **הַמּוֹצֵא מָעוֹת – ONE WHO FINDS COIN בְּבָתֵּי כְנֵסִיּוֹת – IN SYNAGOGUES, וּבְבָתֵּי מִדְרָשׁוֹת – OR IN STUD HALLS, וּבְכָל מָקוֹם שֶׁהָרַבִּים מְצוּיִין שָׁם – OR IN ANY PLACE I WHICH LARGE NUMBERS OF PEOPLE ARE COMMONLY FOUND, הֲרֵי אֵלּוּ שֶׁלּוֹ – THESE BELONG TO [THE FINDER], מִפְּנֵי שֶׁהַבְּעָלִים מִתְיָאֲשִׁין מֵהֶן – BECAUSE THE OWNER DESPAIRS OF** recoverin **THEM.**[17] **וְהָא לֹא יָדַע דְּנָפַל מִינֵּיהּ – But** why is the finder permitted to keep the money, when **[the owner] is not** necessaril **aware that [the money] has fallen from him?** The Barais seems to imply that one who finds coins in a public area ma keep them even if the owner is not aware of their loss, as Rav says! – ? –

The Gemara rejects this proof:

**אָדָם עָשׂוּי אָמַר רַבִּי יִצְחָק – R' Yitzchak said** regarding this case: **אָדָם עָשׂוּי לְמַשְׁמֵשׁ בְּכִיסוֹ בְּכָל שָׁעָה – A person is in the habit of touchin his purse all the time** to check that his money is secure.[18] It ma be assumed, therefore, that by the time the coins were found, th

NOTES

*ye'ush* is considered to take effect from the time of the loss (*Rashi*; see 22a note 16 for further explanation).

10. Since there is generally no way to know whether the person who lost the produce has already discovered its loss, we must assume that the Mishnah permits the finder to keep the produce regardless of whether the owner is aware.

11. Above on 21a, in explanation of R' Yitzchak's rule. *Bach* emends the quotation here to conform to the reading on 21a, changing the word דְּבִיזְרֵי to דְּבֵי דָרֵי.

12. [The owner was aware that he had left behind a small amount of grain on the threshing floor, and he chose to leave it there, rather than bother to return for it.] Thus, he knowingly abandoned the grain (*Rashi*).

13. Since the finder cannot be sure that the owner of the coins has discovered their loss.

14. Literally: every moment and moment.

15. Due to the weight of these items, their absence is readily noticeable. Therefore, as in the previous case, it may be assumed that by the time they were found, the owner has already discovered their loss and despaired of recovering them. Consequently, this ruling has no bearin on the issue of an object whose owner is not aware of his loss.

16. The Gemara above cited the statement of R' Yitzchak that a perso is in the habit of touching his purse all the time to check on his money In the same way we may say that a person also constantly checks o his other valuables, such as tongues of purple wool. He therefor becomes aware of their loss almost immediately. This ruling is therefor also not relevant to Rava's ruling concerning an owner who is unawar of his loss.

17. Even if they have a *siman* [identifying mark] (*Tosafos* ד"ה ת"ש). Th reason for this is because he is afraid that it will be picked up by someon who does not observe the law of returning lost objects. The Gemara (24a will discuss whether this ruling applies even where the majority of peopl are Jews. Even among Jews the owner may have reason to despair because among the many people who frequent the place, there are a certain number who do not observe the law as they should (*Tosafos* 24a ד"ה אפילו ברוב ישראל).

18. R' Yitzchak's original statement was made in regard to the ruling of this Baraisa. The Gemara above used it to explain the Mishnah as well

יאוש שלא מדעת אביי אמר לא הוי יאוש ורבא אמר הוי יאוש בדבר שיש בו סימן כולי עלמא לא פליגי דלא הוי יאוש ואף על גב דשמעיניה דמיאש (א) לסוף לא הוי יאוש דכי אתא לידיה באיסורא הוא דאתא לידיה דלכי ידע דנפל מיניה לא מיאש מימר אמר סימנא אית לי בגויה יהבנא סימנא ושקילנא ליה בזוטו של ים ובשלוליתו של נהר אע"ג דאית ביה סימן רחמנא שרייה כדבעינן למימר לקמן כי פליגי בדבר שאין בו סימן אביי אמר [א] לא הוי יאוש דהא לא ידע דנפל מיניה רבא אמר הוי יאוש דלכי ידע דנפל מיניה מיאש מימר אמר סימנא לית לי בגויה מהשתא הוא דמיאש (סימן פמג"ש ממקגט"י ככסע"ז) תא שמע פירות מפוזרין הא לא ידע דנפל מיניה הא אמר רב עוקבא בר חמא הכא במכנשתא (ב) דביזרי עסקינן דאבידה מדעת היא ת"ש מעות מפוזרות הרי אלו שלו אמאי הא לא ידע דנפל מיניה התם נמי כדרבי (א) יצחק דאמר [ב] אדם עשוי למשמש בכיסו בכל שעה ושעה [ג] הכא נמי אדם עשוי למשמש בכיסו בכל שעה ושעה ת"ש עיגולי דבילה וככרות של נחתום הרי אלו שלו אמאי והא לא ידע דנפל מיניה התם נמי [א] [ד] אגב דיקירי מידע ידע בהו ת"ש ולשונות של ארגמן הרי אלו שלו ואמאי הא לא ידע דנפל מיניה התם נמי [ה] אגב דחשיבי משמושי ממשמש בהו וכדרבי יצחק ת"ש [ו] המוצא מעות בבתי כנסיות ובבתי מדרשות ובכל מקום שהרבים מצויין שם הרי אלו שלו מפני שהבעלים מתיאשין מהן והא לא ידע דנפל מיניה אמר רבי יצחק אדם עשוי למשמש בכיסו בכל שעה ת"ש (ב) [ז] מאימתי כל אדם מותרים בלקט משילכו בה הנמושות ואמרינן מאי נמושות וא"ר יוחנן סבי דאזלי (ג) אתיגרא ריש לקיש אמר לקוטי בתר לקוטי ואמאי נהי דעניים דהכא מיאשי איכא עניים בדוכתא אחריתא דלא מיאשי אמרי כיון דאיכא עניים הכא הנך (ה) מעיקרא איאושי מיאש ואמרי עניים דהתם מלקטי ליה ת"ש (ד) [ח] קציעות (ה) בדרך ואפילו בצד שדה קציעות [ט] וכן תאנה הנוטה לדרך ומצא תאנים תחתיה מותרות משום גזל ופטורות מן המעשר בזיתים ובחרובים אסור בשלמא רישא לאביי לא קשיא אגב דחשיבי ממשמש בהו תאנה נמי מידע ידיע דנתרא אלא סיפא לרבא קשיא דקתני בזיתים ובחרובים אסור אמר רבי אבהו שאני זית הואיל וחזותו מוכיח עליו ואע"ג דנתרין זיתי מידע ידיע (י) דוכתא דאיניש איניש הוא אי הכי אפילו רישא נמי אמר רב פפא תאנה עם נפילתה נמאסת תא שמע (ז) הגנב שנטל מזה ונתן לזה וכן גזלן שנטל מזה ונתן לזה וכן

**רש"י**

יאוש שלא מדעת. דבר שסתמו יאוש לכשידע שנפל ממנו וכשמלאו עדיין לא ידעו הבעלים שנפל מהן: לא הוי יאוש. לקמיה מפרש פלוגתייהו: דמיאש לבסוף. לאחר שמלאו זה וכללא דיאוש כגון דאמר ווי ליה לחסרון כיס דגלי דעתיה שנואש מהן: באיסורא אתא לידיה. דדבר שאינו עשוי להתיאש הוא: זוטו של ים. מקומות בשפת הים שדרך הים לחזור לאחוריו י' פרסאות או חמשה עשר פרסאות פעמיים ביום ושוטף מה שמוצא שם והולך. זוטו לשון גודל ושירוע בלשון יווני כמו שכתבו הזקנים לתלמי המלך ואל אצילי ואל זאטוטי (מגילה דף ט.): ושלוליתו של נהר. כשהוא גדל ויוצא חוץ לגדותיו ושולל שלל ושוטף הנמצא: רחמנא שרייה. ואפי' באת ליד המוצא לפני יאוש: לקמן (ח). בשמעתין מנין לאבידה ששטפה נהר כו': מהשתא הוי יאוש. שהרי נפל וכשיודע שוב אין דעתו עליו: דאבידה מדעת היא. שלא נפלו ממנו ומדעת הניחם הפקר: עשוי למשמש. וקודם שמצאו זה נודע לבעלים שנפלו ונואשו: דיקירי. כבד משא: סבי דאזלי אתיגרא. זקנים עניים הולכים על משענתם בנחת ורואין כל שבולת ושבולת ולשון נמושות כמו (ט) לא ימושו (ישעיה נט) שממשמשין והולכים: לקוטי בתר לקוטי. לשון נמושות כמו לא ימיש (שמות יג) שנוטלין ומשין הכל מלפניהם: ואמאי. אי יאוש שלא מדעת לאו יאוש הוא: נהי. דלגבי עניים דהכא הוי יאוש מדעת שראו שהלכו בה הנמושות ונתיאשו אלא עניים דעיר אחרת עדיין לא ידעי והיאך מותרין בו אלא משום כיון דלכי ידעי מיאשי הוי יאוש משעה שהלכו בו והיתר באו ליד זה: קציעות. תאנים שקוצצין אותם באיזמל ומוהל שלהן זב ושוטחן בשדה ליבש: ואפי' בצד שדה קציעות. שדה ששוטחים בה קליעות דידע דמהנהו אתו: מותרות משום גזל. אע"ג דכי נפל לא ידע כיון דלכי ידע מיאש מהשתא הוי יאוש כרבא: ופטורות מן המעשר. כדין הפקר דהפקר פטור מן המעשר: בזיתים ובחרובים אסור. קתני: בשלמא רישא לאביי. מצי לתרולי דמעיקרא ידע ואיאש כדמפרש ואזיל: דקתני בזיתים ובחרובין אסור. וסלקא דעתך משום דלא עבידי דנתרי וליכא למימר ידע דאיאש ואע"ג דלכי ידע מיאש לא הוי יאוש מהשתא: חזותו מוכיח עליו. מראיתו ניכר של מי הוא הלכך מריה לכי ידע דנפיל לא מיאש דמימר אמר כולי עלמא ידעי דדידי נינהו ולא הפקר הן ולא שקלי להו: עם נפילתה נמאסת. הלכך כיון דידיע דנתרא מעיקרא מיאש משום מאיסותא דמכי נפלה לא חשיבא עליה ומפקר לה: לא ידיע. לא גרסינן ופירוש היה משובש בספרים:

ידן

**תוספות**

דלכי נפל מיניה לא מיאש. ואע"ג דהשתא מיאש אקראי בעלמא הוא ומתחילה לא היה עומד ליאש: ת"ש המוצא מעות כו'. תימה כיון דכבר הקשה ממתני' דמעות מפוזרות אמאי פריך תו מהך ברייתא ורבי יצחק נמי אמאי לא אמר למלתיה אמתני' וי"ל דברייתא אלימא ליה לאקשויי דמשמע דבכל ענין הרי אלו שלו אע"ג דאיכא סימן מדמוקי טעמא (ג) שהרבים מצויין שם ומשמע נמי אע"ג דכשזה הגביה עדיין היה בעל אבידה בבית המדרש ולא ידע שנפל מיניה:

ופטורות ממעשר. במס' פאה (פ"א מ"ו) מוכח דוקא בהפקיר קודם גמר מלאכה פטור מן המעשר אבל אם הפקיר לאחר גמר מלאכה שנתחייב כבר במעשר אין בכך כלום וה"נ מיירי קודם גמר מלאכה שלא נתחייבו עדיין כדמוכח בגילה פרק המביא (דף לד:) דתאנים העומדין לשוטחן בשדה ולעשות מהן קליעות לא נגמר מלאכתן למעשר עד שיתייבשו ואפילו זכה בהן המוצא קודם שיתייבשו פטורות מן המעשר כדאמרינן בב"ק (דף כח.) המפקיר כרמו והשכים בבקר ובצרו פטור מן המעשר וגבי הקדש אינו כן שאם הקדיש קודם גמר מלאכה ונפדה קודם גמר מלאכה חייב במעשר כדמוכח קצת בפרק האומר (סג:)(ל):

תאנה נמי מידע ידיע דנתרא. פירוש בשלמא לאביי תאנה מותרת כיון דרגילות היא דנתרא מעיקרא מתיאש לפי שסבור שהמוצא יקחנה כי הוא לא ידע שנפלה מן האילן אלא סבור הוא מעוברי דרכים נפלה וזיתים וחרובין אסור דלא עבידי דנתרי אע"ג דאם היה יודע דנפלו היה מתיאש לפי שעוברי דרכים יקחו כי יתלו דנפל מעוברי דרכים השתא דלא ידע סבור שלא נפלו אסורה דהוה ליה יאוש שלא מדעת אבל לרבא דהוי יאוש אמאי אסור וא"ת אם דין הוא לתלות בעוברי דרכים ולא באילן שאכלו אמאי אסור בזיתים ובחרובין וי"ל דבדין ודאי אין לתלות בעוברי דרכים אלא באילן אלא שהבעלים מתיאשים לפי שסבורין שעוברי דרכים דלא מעלי יורו היתירא בפירות שמוצאים ויתלום בעוברי דרכים וא"ת אם כן מאי פריך לרבא נימא דזיתים וחרובין אסירי משום דאף לאחר שידעו הבעלים שנפלו לא נתיאשו לפי שיודעין שהמוצא לא יקחם שיתלה שנפלו מן האילן כאשר הוא האמת שאין לתלות בעוברי דרכים וי"ל דאם אין מתיאשים בתאנה אמאי מותרים מיהו אית ספרים דגרסינן שאני זית הואיל וחזותו מוכיח עליו דבזה מתורץ מה שהקשינו כלומר לפי שהם תחת הזית יחשבו הבעלים שהמוצא לא יקחם לתלות בעוברי דרכים אבל תאנה עם נפילתה נמאסת פירוש מתלכלכת ונמאסת בעיניו ומפקירה אבל ברוב ספרים גרסינן הואיל וחזותו מוכיח עליו ואע"ג דמנתרא מידע ידעי דוכתא דאיניש איניש פירוש זיתים שנפלו דומין לזיתים שעומדין באילן ולפיכך אף כשידעו הבעלים שנפלו לא יתיאשו דיודעין שהמוצא לא יקחם אבל תאנה עם נפילתה נמסת כן גרסינן בערוך נמסת בלא אל"ף ואין דומין לאותן שבאילן אי נמי גרסינן נמאסת ומחמת שמתלכלכת אינה דומה לתאנה שבאילן:

מה

**עין משפט נר מצוה**

ח א מיי' פי"ד מהלכות גזלה ואבידה הל' ה סמג עשין סי' עד טוש"ע ח"מ סי' רסב סעיף ג:
ט ב ג מיי' פי"א מהלכות גזלה ואבידה הל' ח ופ"ד מהל' גניבה הל' י סמג עשין עא טוש"ע ח"מ סי' שנה סעיף א:
י ד ה מיי' פט"ו מהל' גזלה ואבידה הל' ח ועיין בכסף משנה סמג עשין עד טוש"ע ח"מ סי' רסב סעיף ג:
יא ו מיי' שם פי"א הל' ז טוש"ע ח"מ סי' רנט סעיף ג:
יב ז מיי' פ"א מהלכות מתנות עניים הל' יא:
יג ח מיי' פ"ג מהלכות מעשר הלכה כא:
יד ט מיי' שם הל' כד ופט"ו מהלכות גזלה ואבידה הל' טו טוש"ע ח"מ סי' רס סעיף ו:

**ליקוטי רש"י**

בזוטו של ים. לשון ים החוזר לאחוריו עשר וחמש עשרה פרסאות ושוטף כל מה שמוצא בדרך חזרתו וכן עושה בכל יום [ע"ז מג.]. במכנשתא דבי דרי. בשעת אסיפת גרנות וכאן דשן בעליהן ונשאו את העיקר ונותרו אלו [לעיל ע"א.]. המוצא מעות בבתי כנסיות. אסיפת מקום שמתכנסים שם להתיעץ ולהוועד [לקמן כד.]. אדם עשוי למשמש בכיסו. ולמנות כמה בכיסו [ב"ק קיח:]. כל אדם. אפילו העשירים. משילכו הנמושות. בשדה דמכאן ואילך נתייאשו שאר העניים לפי שיודעין אם נשאר לקט שכחה ופאה נמושות נטלום. נמושות. לשון ממשש. דאזלי אתיגרא. הולכין בנחת ומעייני טפי מחזיק בפלך (שמואל ב, ג) מתרגמא אתיגרא. לקוטי בתר לקוטי. עני מוליך בנו אחריו שמכאן ואילך פוסקין שאר עניים מללקוט [תענית ו:].

**רבינו חננאל**

איפשיט אי הוי סימן אי לא בעיות דר' ירמיה הם ופשוטות הן ועלו כולן בתיקו. איתמר יאוש שלא מדעת אביי אמר לא הוי יאוש ורבא אמר הוי יאוש בדבר שיש בו סימן כולי עלמא לא פליגי דלא הוי יאוש ואע"ג דשמעיניה לבסוף דמיאש (לבסוף) לא הוי יאוש דכי אתא לידיה באיסורא אתא לידיה דהא לפני יאוש הוה כי פליגי בדבר שאין בו סימן אביי אמר לא הוה יאוש דלא ידע דנפל מיניה דמיאש. אבל המוצא בזוטו של ים. פי' בקרקעית הים ובשלוליתו של נהר פי' בתוך הנהר מקום שמי גשמים שוללים והוא מקום שטיפתו אע"ג דאית ביה סימן רחמנא שרייה למוצאה דאמר ר' יוחנן משום ר' שמעון בן יהוצדק מנין לאבדה ששטפה נהר שהיא מותרת שנאמר כן תעשה לכל אבדת אחיך אשר תאבד ממנו ומצאתה מי שאבודה ממנו בלבד ומצויה אצל כל אדם. פרה ורועה בשדה וכיוצא בה שכל הרואה אותה יכול ליטלה יצאת זו ששטפה נהר שאבודה ממנו ומכל אדם הלכך הרי היא למוצאה בין אית ליה בה סימן בין לית ליה בה סימן שרי דהא ודאי נתייאש הימנה. וזה שהיתיר בים ובנהר כנגדו אסור ביבשה ודייקינן מינה מה היתירה בין אית ביה סימן בין לית ביה סימן ואפי' לפני יאוש שרי כך מה שאסר ביבשה ואפי' לית ביה סימן לפני יאוש אסורה ועלתה תיובתא דרבא תיובתא. והלכתא כוותיה דאביי ביע"ל קג"ם י' יאוש שלא מדעת והלכתא כאביי דיאוש שלא מדעת לא הוי יאוש. ואמרי' ומאחר דאיתותב רבא הני תמרי דזיקאי כלומר התמרים שהפילם הרוח מן הדקל והם מושלכים בדרך מפני מה אוכלין אותן העוברין ושבים והנה בעליהן לא נתייאשו שלא ידעו שהפילם הרוח ואמר ר' אשי כיון דאיכא שקצים דשכיחי דאזלי התם ואכלי להו יאושי מיאש להו מרייהו מעיקרא דכי האי גוונא אפי' אביי שרי ואם היו דקלים מוחזקין ליתמי דלאו בני יאוש נינהו או דקלים בכרכים דלא שכיחי בהו שקצים למיכלינהו אסירא. יש מי שאומרים פי' כרכתא דקלים הרבה שמוקפות גדר ומקשי רבא לאביי מצא מעות מפוזרות. ופריק אביי מתני' כר' יצחק דאמר אדם עשוי למשמש בכיסו בכל שעה ושעה וכן המוצא מעות בבתי כנסיות ובתי מדרשות הרי אלו שלו. ואקשי' והא דלמא לא ידע דנפלי מיניה. ופריק הכי נמי כר' יצחק. וכן כל דבר חשוב ממשמש בכל שעה כמו מעות. פי' נמושות סבי דאזלי אתיגרא. זקנים תשושי כח שמהלכין במשענת בידם שאין בהן כח לילך הרבה והשדה שיכנסו בה ללקט לא יניחו אחריהן כלום. האי דאמר מצא קציצות ואפי' בצד שדה קציצות מותרות משום גזל כיון שאלו הקציצות דבר חשוב

הז

**מסורת הש"ס**

א) בבא קמא קיח., ב) תענית ו:, פאה פרק ח משנה א, ג) גירסת רש"ל אתיגדא, וכן הוא בערוך ערך נמש, ד) מעשרות פרק ג [משנה ד], ה) ס"א קציצות, ו) ס"א דזיתא, ז) [תוספתא דכתובות פרק ח], ח) [דף כב:], ט) גירסת מהרש"ל ולא ימישון (תהלים קטו), י) [חפשנו בפ' האומר דקדושין ובפרק האומר דגיטין ולא מצאנו אך בפ' ר' ישמעאל דמנחות סו: משמע כן ואולי צ"ל בפ' העומר בעי"ן והיינו פ' ר' ישמעאל הנ"ל דכל הפרק מיירי בדיני עומר כמו שרגילים הפוסקים לכנות פרק אחהו נשך בשם פרק הרבית ולכאורה צ"ע על התוס' שהוצרכו לדקדק מן הגמ' והלא משנה שלימה היא פ"ד ממס' פאה מ"ח ואפשר לומר שהתוספות רצו לאשמועי' רבותא טפי שאפי' היה תחלת גידולו ביד הקדש אפ"ה חייב אם פדאו קודם מירוח והא לא שמעינן ממתני' דמלי מיירי שגדל ביד הדיוט ואח"כ הקדיש אבל מפרק ר"י הנ"ל משמע דאפי' גדל ביד הקדש נמי חייב אם פדאו קודם מירוח ואילוק זה בין בגדל ביד הדיוט או ביד הקדש כעין זה מלינו גבי מירוח הנכרי ודוק. העתק מחלופי גרסאות].

**הגהות הב"ח**

(א) גמ' דמיאש לבסוף לא: (ב) שם במכנשתא דבי דרי עסקינן: (ג) תוס' ד"ה ת"ש וכו' שהרבים מצויין שם. נ"ב ע"ל דף כד ע"א:

**הגהות הגר"א**

[א] גמ' אגב דיקירי. נ"ב גירסת הרא"ש דחשיבי כיון דמידי דמיכל נינהו וכן מפרחות ותתיכות וכן בלשונות אבל גיזי ואניצי כתב משום דיקירי ולא פריך גמ' מכריכות משום דהתם דרך הינוח וטעמא אחרינא להו ועי' תוס' (ע"א) ד"ה אלו כו' (ועמ"ש רבינו בח"מ סי' רס"ב ס"ק ז):

**גליון הש"ס**

גמ' מעיקרא איאושי. קשה לי הא גם לעניים קטנים יש להם חלק ומקרי יאוש שלא מדעת כדלקמן דף כב ע"ב ועיין בתוס' ב"ב דף קמג ע"ב ד"ה ואם ועדיין צ"ע:

יֵאוּשׁ שֶׁלֹּא מִדַּעַת – **Abandonment without** the owner's **awareness**, i.e. a situation in which an object which the owner would ordinarily abandon hope of recovering was lost, but he did not do so because he was not yet aware that it was lost.[1] Such a situation is the subject of the following dispute: אַבַּיֵי אָמַר – **Abaye says:** לֹא הָוֵי יֵאוּשׁ – **It is not** considered **an abandonment,** since the owner has not yet actually despaired of finding his object. Therefore, the finder is not permitted to keep it.[2] וְרָבָא אָמַר – **However, Rava said:** הָוֵי יֵאוּשׁ – **It is** considered **an abandonment.** Although the owner is not yet aware of the loss, it is considered as if he has already abandoned hope of recovering the object. Thus, the finder is permitted to keep it.

The Gemara will now explain the specific area of disagreement between Abaye and Rava. It begins by noting a case in which both agree that abandonment without awareness is *not* effective:

בְּדָבָר שֶׁיֵּשׁ בּוֹ סִימָן – **In regard to an object that has an identifying mark on it,** כּוּלֵּי עָלְמָא לֹא פְּלִיגִי – **there is no argument,** for all agree (even Rava) דְּלֹא הָוֵי יֵאוּשׁ – **that** unless he knowingly abandons it, **it is not** considered **an abandonment.**[3] וְאַף עַל גַּב דְּשָׁמְעִינֵיהּ דְּמִיָּאֵשׁ לְסוֹף – **And even though we** later **hear that in the end,** *after* the object was found, **[the owner]** discovered his loss and **abandoned hope** of recovering his object, לֹא הָוֵי יֵאוּשׁ – **it is** nevertheless **not** considered **an abandonment,**[4] דְּכִי אָתָא לִידֵיהּ – **because when it came into [the finder's] hand,** בְּאִיסּוּרָא הוּא דְּאָתָא לִידֵיהּ – **it was** in a **prohibited** state **that it came into his hand,** i.e. it came to him at a time when he was not permitted to keep it, for the following reason: דִּלְכִי יָדַע דְּנָפַל מִינֵּיהּ – **For when [the owner] becomes aware that it has fallen from him,** לֹא מִיָּאֵשׁ – **he does not** ordinarily **abandon hope** of recovering it, מֵימַר אָמַר – because **he says** to himself: סִימָנָא אִית לִי בְּגַוֵּיהּ – **I have a mark** by which **to identify it;** יָהֲבְנָא סִימָנָא – **I will give** the evidence of **the identifying mark,** וְשָׁקֵילְנָא לֵיהּ – **and take it** back from the finder.[5] Therefore, even if the owner should later abandon hope of recovering it, the finder is not permitted to keep it.[6]

The Gemara now states a case in which both Abaye and Ra[va] agree that a lost object belongs to the finder even if its origin[al] owner did not actually abandon it yet:

בְּזוּטוֹ שֶׁל יָם – If the object was swept away **by the tides of the se[a]** וּבִשְׁלוּלִיתוֹ שֶׁל נָהָר – **or by the surge of** the flooding of **a river** and it later washed up on shore and was found, [א]ַעַל גַּב דְּאִית בֵּיהּ סִימָן – then **even though it has an identifying mar[k]** רַחֲמָנָא שַׁרְיֵיהּ – **the Merciful One permitted** the finder to ke[ep] **it,** כִּדְבְעֵינָן לְמֵימַר לְקַמָּן – **as we intend to explain below.** Therefore, even Abaye agrees that the finder may keep it.

After listing the areas of agreement between Abaye and Rav[a], the Gemara explains the case in which they disagree:

כִּי פְּלִיגִי – **Where they disagree is** בְּדָבָר שֶׁאֵין בּוֹ סִימָן – **regard to an object without any identifying mark** which w[as] found before the owner became aware of its loss. אַבַּיֵי אָמַר – **Abaye says:** לֹא הָוֵי יֵאוּשׁ – **It is not** considered a case [of] **abandonment,** דְּהָא לֹא יָדַע דְּנָפַל מִינֵּיהּ – **because [the owne[r]] does not know that it has fallen from him,** i.e. he does not kn[ow] that he has lost it, and he has therefore not actually abandoned [it]. רָבָא אָמַר – **Rava says:** הָוֵי יֵאוּשׁ – **It is a** case of **abandonme[nt]** דִּלְכִי יָדַע דְּנָפַל מִינֵּיהּ – **because when he becomes aware that [it] has fallen from him,** מִיָּאֵשׁ – **he will abandon hope** [of] recovering it. מֵימַר אָמַר – **He will say** to himself: [סִימָ]נָא לֵית לִי בְּגַוֵּיהּ – **I have no mark** by which **to identify it;** [מֵהָ]שְׁתָּא הוּא דְּמִיָּאֵשׁ – it is, therefore, deemed as if **he has abandoned ho[pe] from now,** the moment of loss.[9]

The Gemara presents a mnemonic for the long list of proo[fs] about to be cited to resolve the debate between Abaye and Rav[a]:

(סִימָן פמג״ש ממקגט״י כבסע״ז)

The Gemara attempts to prove Rava's view:

תָּא שְׁמַע – **Come, learn** a proof to Rava's view from our Mishna[h] which stated: פֵּירוֹת מְפוּזָּרִין – SCATTERED PRODUCE belongs [to] the finder. הָא לֹא יָדַע דְּנָפַל מִינֵּיהּ – **But** why, when **[the owne[r]] does not** necessarily **know that it has fallen from him?** Sin[ce]

NOTES

1. The object was found before the owner realized he had lost it, and he had therefore not actually despaired of it (*Rashi*). The question is whether the finder may keep it.

[The term "abandonment" (*ye'ush*) is used in reference to both the owner's state of mind (despairing of recovering the lost article) and the legal condition that results from that state of mind (the loss of ownership and the right of the finder to keep the object).]

*Ye'ush* occurs when the owner, realizing his loss [and accepting its finality], declares, "Woe [to me] because of the monetary loss I have incurred" [or words to that effect] (*Rashi*). For this reason the Gemara will speak below of "hearing" of his abandoning hope, i.e. of his declaration of *ye'ush*.

2. Even if the owner should later discover his loss and despair, the finder must still return the object to him, as the Gemara will soon explain.

3. Therefore, even Rava agrees that the finder is *not* permitted to keep his find.

4. I.e. the *ye'ush* (abandonment) is not effective and the finder must therefore return the object to its original owner even though he has despaired of it.

5. I.e. I will identify the object by describing its distinctive mark and reclaim it. As we have learned previously, an object found with a *siman* (identifying mark) must be announced by the finder, and can be reclaimed by the owner if he identifies the mark. As a result, someone who loses such an object does not ordinarily abandon hope of recovering it (*Rashi*). Such an object can therefore not be said to be in a state of "abandonment" until the owner actually despairs of it.

6. The commentators offer two reasons for this. *Ritva* explains that when one finds an object before *ye'ush*, he not only becomes obligated to return it, he also becomes a *shomer* (custodian) over the object until he returns it (see Gemara 29a). Thus, he is in effect holding the object on behalf of the owner, and the object is therefore considered in the owner's possession no less so than if he would have appointed someone to care f[or] it. Now the law is that *ye'ush* is ineffective for something that is still [in] the owner's possession [יֵאוּשׁ בִּרְשׁוּת]. Therefore, once the finder becom[es] obligated to return the object, the legal state of *ye'ush* can no longer ta[ke] effect. [This explanation is also quoted by *Shitah Mekubetzes* in the nam[e] of *Ri*, and is also stated in brief by *Ramban* in his *Milchamos* to 26[b].]

From *Tosafos* (*Bava Kamma* 66a ד״ה הכא נמי) it seems that the reas[on] is that once the Torah's obligation to return a lost object has taken effe[ct], *ye'ush* cannot absolve the person of that obligation. It is only when o[ne] finds the object after *ye'ush*, when the owner is no longer seeking his lo[st] object, that the Torah does not impose an obligation to try and return [it] to him. But once the obligation has taken effect, it remains in effect, t[he] owner's subsequent abandonment notwithstanding (see *Kehilos Yaak[ov]* ch. 22).

7. [The word זוטו means increase or extension, as in the verse [וְאֶל]־אֲצִילֵי בְּנֵי יִשְׂרָאֵל (*Exodus* 24:11), which the Sages translated as וְאָטוּטֵי בְּנֵי יִשְׂרָאֵל, *t[he] great ones of the Children of Israel* (see *Megillah* 9a and *Rashi* to t[he] verse). Thus, the phrase זוטו שֶׁל יָם refers to the twice daily extension [of] the sea inland, i.e. high tide. When the high tide retreats out to sea, [it] carries with it any objects it has encountered (*Rashi*).

The word שְׁלוּלִית refers to the capture and removal of property, fr[om] the word שָׁלָל, *spoils of war*. In this context it refers to the action of a riv[er] when it overflows and washes away objects along its banks (*Rashi*; s[ee] *Aruch* for a different explanation).

8. Gemara 22b. The Gemara will provide a Scriptural basis for t[his] ruling. The Torah deems such an object ownerless; therefore, ev[en] Abaye agrees that the finder may keep it (*Rashba*; see below, 22b not[e] for a discussion of this point).

9. Since the object has fallen [and is already lost to him], and when [he] subsequently discovers the loss he will realize that he will never ag[ain] have it [i.e. he will abandon hope of recovering it], the legal state

יאוש שלא מדעת אביי אמר לא הוי יאוש ורבא אמר הוי יאוש בדבר שיש בו סימן כולי עלמא לא פליגי דלא הוי יאוש ואף על גב דשמעיניה דמיאש (א) לסוף לא הוי יאוש דכי אתא לידיה באיסורא הוא דאתא לידיה דלכי ידע דנפל מיניה לא מיאש מימר אמר סימנא אית לי בגויה יהבנא סימנא ושקילנא ליה בזוטו של ים ובשלוליתו של נהר אע"ג דאית ביה סימן רחמנא שרייה כדבעינן למימר לקמן כי פליגי בדבר שאין בו סימן אביי אמר [א]לא הוי יאוש דהא לא ידע דנפל מיניה רבא אמר הוי יאוש דלכי ידע דנפל מיניה מיאש מימר אמר סימנא לית לי בגויה מהשתא הוא דמיאש (סימן פמג"ש ממקגט"י ככסע"ז) תא שמע פירות מפוזרין הא לא ידע דנפל מיניה הא אמר רב עוקבא בר חמא הכא במכנשתא (ב) דביזרי עסקינן דאבידה מדעת היא ת"ש מעות מפוזרות הרי אלו שלו אמאי הא לא ידע דנפל מיניה התם נמי כדרבי [א] יצחק דאמר [ב]אדם עשוי למשמש בכיסו בכל שעה ושעה [ג]הכא נמי אדם עשוי למשמש בכיסו בכל שעה ושעה ת"ש עיגולי דבילה וככרות של נחתום הרי אלו שלו אמאי והא לא ידע דנפל מיניה התם נמי [א] [ד]אגב דיקירי מידע ידע בהו ת"ש ולשונות של ארגמן הרי אלו שלו ואמאי הא לא ידע דנפל מיניה התם נמי [ה]אגב דחשיבי משמושי ממשמש בהו וכדרבי יצחק ת"ש [ו]המוצא מעות בבתי כנסיות ובבתי מדרשות ובכל מקום שהרבים מצויין שם הרי אלו שלו מפני שהבעלים מתיאשין מהן והא לא ידע דנפל מיניה אמר רבי יצחק אדם עשוי למשמש בכיסו בכל שעה ת"ש (ב) [ז]מאימתי כל אדם מותרים בלקט משילכו בה הנמושות ואמרינן מאי נמושות וא"ר יוחנן סבי דאזלי (ג) אתיגרא ריש לקיש אמר לקוטי בתר לקוטי ואמאי נהי דעניים דהכא מיאשי איכא עניים בדוכתא אחריתא דלא מיאשי אמרי כיון דאיכא עניים הכא הנך (ה) מעיקרא איאושי מיאש ואמרי עניים דהתם מלקטי ליה ת"ש (ד) [ח] קציעות (ה) בדרך ואפילו בצד שדה קציעות [ט]וכן תאנה הנוטה לדרך ומצא תאנים תחתיה מותרות משום גזל ופטורות מן המעשר בזיתים ובחרובים אסור בשלמא רישא לאביי לא קשיא אגב דחשיבי ממשמש בהו תאנה נמי מידע ידיע דנתרא אלא סיפא לרבא קשיא דקתני בזיתים ובחרובים אסור אמר רבי אבהו שאני זית הואיל וחזותו מוכיח עליו ואע"ג דנתרין זיתי מידע ידיע [י]דוכתא דאיניש איניש הוא אי הכי אפילו רישא נמי אמר רב פפא תאנה עם נפילתה נמאסת תא שמע [י]הגנב שנטל מזה ונתן לזה וכן גזלן שנטל מזה ונתן לזה וכן

יאוש שלא מדעת. דבר שסתמו יאוש לכשידע שנפל ממנו וכשמצאו עדיין לא ידעו הבעלים שנפל מהן: לא הוי יאוש. לקמיה מפרש פלוגתייהו: דמיאש לבסוף. לאחר שמצאו זה וכללא דיאוש כגון דאמר ווי ליה לחסרון כיס דגלי דעתיה שנואש מהן: באיסורא אתא לידיה. דדבר שאינו עשוי להתיאש הוא: זוטו של ים. מקומות בשפת הים שדרך הים לחזור לאחוריו י' פרסאות או חמשה עשר פרסאות פעמיים ביום ושוטף מה שמוצא שם והולך. זוטו לשון גודל ושירוע בלשון יווני כמו שכתבו הזקנים לתלמי המלך ואת אילי ואת זאטוטי (מגילה דף ט.): ושלוליתו של נהר. כשהוא גדל ויוצא חוץ לגדותיו ושולל שלל ושוטף הנמצא: רחמנא שרייה. ואפי' באת ליד המוצא לפני יאוש: לקמן [ח]. בשמעתין מנין לאבידה ששטפה נהר כו': מהשתא הוי יאוש. שהרי נפל וכשיודע שוב אין דעתו עליו: דאבידה מדעת היא. שלא נפלו ממנו ומדעת הניחם הפקר: עשוי למשמש. וקודם שמצאו זה נודע לבעלים שנפלו ונואשו: דיקירי. כבד משא: סבי דאזלי אתיגרא. זקנים עניים הולכים על משענתם בנחת ורואין כל שבולת ושבולת ולשון נמושות כמו [ט] לא ימושו (ישעיה נט) שממשמשין והולכים: לקוטי בתר לקוטי. לשון נמושות כמו לא ימיש (שמות יג) שנוטלין ומשין הכל מלפניהם: ואמאי. אי יאוש שלא מדעת לאו יאוש הוא: נהי. דלגבי עניים דהכא הוי יאוש מדעת שראו שהלכו בה הנמושות ונתיאשו אלא עניים דעיר אחרת עדיין לא ידעי והיאך מותרין בו אלא משום כיון דלכי ידעי מיאשי הוי יאוש משעה שהלכו בו ובהיתר באו ליד זה: קציעות. תאנים שקוצצין אותם באיזמל ומוהל שלהן זב ושוטחן בשדה ליבש: ואפי' בצד שדה קציעות. שדה ששוטחים בה קציעות דידע דמהנהו אתו: מותרות משום גזל. אע"ג דכי נפל לא ידע כיון דלכי ידע מיאש מהשתא הוי יאוש כרבא: ופטורות מן המעשר. כדין הפקר דהפקר פטור מן המעשר: בזיתים ובחרובים אסור. כאביי: בשלמא רישא לאביי. מצי לתרוצי דמעיקרא ידע ואיאש כדמפרש ואזיל: דקתני בזיתים ובחרובין אסור. וסלקא דעתך משום דלא עבידי דנתרי וליכא למימר ידע דאיאש ואע"ג דלכי ידע מיאש לא הוי יאוש מהשתא: חזותו מוכיח עליו. מראיתו ניכר של מי הוא הלכך מריה לכי ידע דנפיל לא מיאש דמימר אמר כולי עלמא ידעי דדידי נינהו ולא הפקר הן ולא שקלי להו: עם נפילתה נמאסת. הלכך כיון דידיע דנתרא מעיקרא מיאש משום מאיסותא דמכי נפלה לא חשיבא עליה ומפקר לה: לא ידיע. לא גרסינן ופירוש היה משובש בספרים:

ירדן

**דלכי** נפל מיניה לא מיאש. ואע"ג דהשתא מיאש אקראי בעלמא הוא ומתחילה לא היה עומד ליאש: **ת"ש** המוצא מעות כו'. תימה כיון דכבר הקשה ממתני' דמעות מפוזרות אמאי פריך תו מהך ברייתא ורבי יצחק נמי אמאי לא אמר למלתיה אמתני' וי"ל דברייתא אלימא ליה לאקשויי דמשמע דבכל ענין הרי אלו שלו אע"ג דאיכא סימן מדמוקי טעמא (ג) שהרבים מצויין שם ומשמע נמי אע"ג דכשזה הגביה עדיין היה בעל אבידה בבית המדרש ולא ידע שנפל מיניה:

**ופטורות** ממעשר. במס' פאה (פ"א מ"ו) מוכח דוקא בהפקיר קודם גמר מלאכה פטור מן המעשר אבל אם הפקיר לאחר גמר מלאכה שנתחייב כבר במעשר אין בכך כלום וה"נ מיירי קודם גמר מלאכה שלא נתייבשו עדיין כדמוכח בביצה פרק המביא (דף לד:) דתאנים העומדין לשוטחן בשדה ולעשות מהן קציעות לא נגמר מלאכתן למעשר עד שיתייבשו ואפילו זכה בהן המוצא קודם שיתייבשו פטורות מן המעשר כדאמרינן בב"ק (דף כח.) המפקיר כרמו והשכים בבקר ובצרו פטור מן המעשר וגבי הקדש אינו כן שאם הקדיש קודם גמר מלאכה ונפדה קודם גמר מלאכה חייב במעשר כדמוכח קצת בפרק האומר (סב:[י]):

**תאנה** נמי מידע ידיע דנתרא. פירוש בשלמא לאביי תאנה מותרת כיון דרגילות היא דנתרא מעיקרא מתיאש לפי שסבור שהמוצא יקחנה כי הוא לא ידע שנפלה מן האילן אלא סבור הוא מעוברי דרכים נפלה ובזיתים ובחרובין אסור דלא עבידי דנתרי אע"ג דאם היה יודע דנפלו היה מתיאש לפי שעוברי דרכים יקחו כי יתלו דנפל מעוברי דרכים השתא דלא ידע סבור שלא נפלו אסורה דהוה ליה יאוש שלא מדעת אבל לרבא דהוי יאוש אמאי אסור וא"ת אם דין הוא לתלות בעוברי דרכים ולא באילן שאלו אמאי אסור בזיתים ובחרובין וי"ל דבדין ודאי אין לתלות בעוברי דרכים אלא באילן אלא שהבעלים מתיאשים לפי שסבורין שעוברי דרכים דלא מעלי יורו היתירא בפירות שמוצאים ויתלו בעוברי דרכים וא"ת אם כן מאי פריך לרבא נימא דזיתים וחרובין אסירי משום דאף לאחר שידעו הבעלים שנפלו לא נתיאשו לפי שיודעין שהמוצא לא יקחם שיתלה שנפלו מן האילן כאשר הוא האמת שאין לתלות בעוברי דרכים וי"ל דאם אין מתיאשים בתאנה אמאי מותרים מיהו אית ספרים דגרסינן שאני זית הואיל וזיתו מוכיח עליו דבזה מתורץ מה שהקשינו כלומר לפי שהם תחת הזית יחשבו הבעלים שהמוצא לא יקחם לתלות בעוברי דרכים אבל תאנה עם נפילתה נמאסת פירוש מתלכלכת ונמאסת בעיניו ומפקירה אבל ברוב ספרים גרסינן הואיל וחזותו מוכיח עליו ואע"ג דמנתרא מידע ידעי דוכתא דאיניש איניש פירוש זיתים שנפלו דומין לזיתים שעומדין באילן ולפיכך אף כשידעו הבעלים שנפלו לא יתיאשו דיודעין שהמוצאים לא יקחם אבל תאנה עם נפילתה נמסת כן גרסינן בערוך נמסת בלא אל"ף ואין דומין לאותן שבאילן אי נמי גרסינן נמאסת ומחמת שמתלכלכת אינה דומה לתאנה שבאילן:

מה

## עין משפט נר מצוה

ח א מיי' פי"ד מהלכות גזלה ואבידה הל' ה סמג עשין סי' עד טוש"ע ח"מ סי' רסב סעיף ג:
ט ב ג מיי' פ"א מהלכות גזלה ואבידה הל' ח ופ"ד מהל' גניבה הל' י סמג עשין עא טוש"ע ח"מ סי' שנח סעיף א:
י ד ה מיי' פט"ו מהל' גזלה ואבידה הל' ח ועיין בכסף משנה סמג עשין עד טוש"ע ח"מ סי' רסב סעיף ג:
יא ו מיי' שם פי"א הל' ז טוש"ע ח"מ סי' רנט סעיף ג:
יב ז מיי' פ"א מהלכות מתנות עניים הל' יא:
יג ח מיי' פ"ג מהלכות מעשר הלכה כא:
יד ט מיי' שם הל' כד ופט"ו מהלכות גזלה ואבידה הל' טו טוש"ע ח"מ סי' רס סעיף ו:

## ליקוטי רש"י

**בזוטו של ים.** לשון ים החוזר לאחוריו עשר וחמש עשרה פרסאות ושוטף כל מה שמוצא בדרך חזרתו וכן עושה בכל יום [ע"ז מג.]. **במכנשתא דבי דרי.** בשעת אסיפת גרנות וכאן דשן בעליהן ונשאו את העיקר ונותרו אלו [לעיל ע"א.]. **המוצא מעות בבתי כנסיות.** אסיפת מקום שמתכנסים שם להתיעץ ולהוועד [לקמן כד.]. **אדם עשוי למשמש בכיסו.** ולמנות כמה בכיסו [ב"ק קיח:]. **כל אדם.** אפילו העשירים. **משילכו הנמושות.** בשדה דמכאן ואילך נתייאשו שאר העניים לפי שיודעין אם נשאר לקט שכחה ופאה נמושות נטלום. **נמושות.** לשון ממשש. **דאזלי אתיגרא.** הולכין בנחת ומעייני טפי מחזיק בפלך (שמואל ב, ג) מתרגמא אתיגרא. **לקוטי בתר לקוטי.** עני מוליך בנו אחריו שמכאן ואילך פוסקין שאר עניים מללקוט [תענית ו:].

## רבינו חננאל

איפשיט אי הוי סימן אי לא בעיות דר' ירמיה הם ופשוטות הן ועלו כולן בתיקו. איתמר יאוש שלא מדעת אביי אמר לא הוי יאוש ורבא אמר הוי יאוש בדבר שיש בו סימן כולי עלמא לא פליגי דלא הוי יאוש ואע"ג דשמעיניה לבסוף דמיאש (לבסוף) לא הוי יאוש דכי אתא לידיה באיסורא אתא לידיה דהא לפני יאוש הוה כי פליגי בדבר שאין בו סימן אביי אמר לא הוה יאוש דלא ידע דנפל מיניה דחיאש ארל המוצא בזוטו של ים. פי' בקרקעית הים ובשלוליתו של נהר פי' בתוך הנהר מקום שמי גשמים שוללים והוא מקום שטיפתו אע"ג דאית ביה סימן רחמנא שרייה למוצאה דאמר ר' יוחנן משום ר' שמעון בן יהוצדק מנין לאבדה ששטפה נהר שהיא מותרת שנאמר כן תעשה לכל אבדת אחיך אשר תאבד ממנו ומצאתה מי שאבודה ממנו בלבד ומצויה אצל כל אדם. פרה ורועה בשדה וכיוצא בה שכל הרואה אותה יכול ליטלה יצאת זו ששטפה נהר שאבודה ממנו ומכל אדם הלכך הרי היא למוצאה בין אית ליה בה סימן בין לית ליה בה סימן שרי דהא ודאי נתייאש הימנה. וזה שהיתיר בים ובנהר כנגדו אסור ביבשה ודייקינן מינה מה היתירה בין אית ביה סימן בין לית ביה סימן ואפי' לפני יאוש שרי כך מה שאסר ביבשה ואפי' לית ביה סימן לפני יאוש אסורה ועלתה תיובתא דרבא תיובתא. והלכתא כוותיה דאביי ביע"ל קג"ם י' יאוש שלא מדעת והלכתא כאביי דיאוש שלא מדעת לא הוי יאוש. ואמרי' ומאחר דאיתותב רבא הני תמרי דזיקאי כלומר התמרים שהפילם הרוח מן הדקל והם מושלכים בדרך מפני מה אוכלין אותן העוברין ושבים והנה בעליהן לא נתייאשו שלא ידעו שהפילם הרוח ואמר ר' אשי כיון דאיכא שקצים דשכיחי דאזלי התם ואכלי להו יאושי מיאש להו מרייהו מעיקרא דכי האי גוונא אפי' אביי שרי ואם היו דקלים מוחזקין ליתמי דלאו בני יאוש נינהו או דקלים בכרכים דלא שכיחי בהו שקצים למיכלינהו אסירא. יש מי שאומרים פי' כרכתא דקלים הרבה שמוקפות גדר ומקשי רבא לאביי מצא מעות מפוזרות. ופריק אביי מתני' כר' יצחק דאמר אדם עשוי למשמש בכיסו בכל שעה ושעה וכן המוצא מעות בבתי כנסיות ובתי מדרשות הרי אלו שלו. ואקשי' והא דלמא לא ידע דנפלי מיניה. ופריק הכי נמי כר' יצחק. וכן כל דבר חשוב ממשמש בכל שעה כמו מעות. פי' נמושות סבי דאזלי אתיגרא. זקנים תשושי כח שמהלכין במשענת בידם שאין בהן כח לילך הרבה והשדה שיכנסו בה ללקט לא יניחו אחריהן כלום. האי דאמר מצא קציצות ואפי' בצד שדה קציצות מותרות משום גזל כיון שאלו הקציצות דבר חשוב

הז

## מסורת הש"ס

א) בבא קמא קיח:, ב) תענית ו:, פאה פרק ח משנה א, ג) גירסת רש"ל אתיגדא, וכן הוא בערוך ערך נמש, ד) מעשרות פרק ג [משנה ד], ה) ס"א קציצות, ו) ס"א דזיתא, ז) [תוספתא דכתובות פרק ח], ח) [דף כב:], ט) גירסת מהרש"ל ולא ימישון (תהלים קטו), י) [חפשתי בפ' האומר דקדושין ובפרק האומר דגיטין ולא מצאתי אך בפ' ר' ישמעאל דמנחות סו: משמע כן ואולי צ"ל בפ' העומר בעי"ן והיינו פ' ר' ישמעאל הנ"ל דכל הפרק מיירי בדיני עומר כמו שרגילים הפוסקים לכנות פרק איזהו נשך בשם פרק הרבית ולכאורה צ"ע על התוס' שהוצרכו לדקדק מן הגמ' והלא משנה שלימה היא פ"ד ממס' פאה מ"ח ואפשר לומר שהתוספות רצו לאשמועי' רבותא טפי שאפי' היה תחלת גידולו ביד הקדש אפ"ה חייב אם פדאו קודם מירוח והא לא שמעינן ממתני' דמאי מיירי שגדל ביד הדיוט ואח"כ הקדיש אבל מפרק ר"י הנ"ל משמע דאפי' גדל ביד הקדש נמי חייב אם פדאו קודם מירוח וחילוק זה בין גדל ביד הדיוט או ביד הקדש כעין זה מצינו גבי מירוח הנכרי ודוק. העתק מחלופי גרסאות].

## הגהות הב"ח

(א) גמ' דמיאש לבסוף לא: (ב) שם במכנשתא דבי דרי עסקינן: (ג) תוס' ד"ה ת"ש וכו' שהרבים מצויין שם. נ"ב ע"ל דף כד ע"א:

## הגהות הגר"א

[א] גמ' אגב דיקירי. נ"ב גירסת הרא"ש דחשיבי כיון דמידי דמיכל נינהו וכן מתרחות ותחיכות וכן בלשונות אבל גיזי ואולי כתב משום דיקירי ולא פריך גמ' מכריכות משום דהתם דרך היטות וטעמא אחרינא להו ועי' תוס' (ע"א) ד"ה אלו כו' (ועמ"ש רבינו בח"מ סי' רס"ב ס"ק ז):

## גליון הש"ס

גמ' מעיקרא איאושי. קשה לי הא גם לעניים קטנים יש להם חלק ומקרי יאוש שלא מדעת כדלקמן דף כב ע"ב ועיין בתוס' ב"ב דף קמג ע"ב ד"ה ואם ועדיין צ"ע:

דשיילינן להו לסהדי אי לא פרוע ת"ש סמפון שיש עליו עדים כשר מאי עדים עדי קיום הכי נמי מסתברא מדקתני סיפא ושאין עליו עדים פסול מאי אין עליו עדים אילימא דליכא עלויה עדים כלל צריכא למימר דפסול אלא לאו עדי קיום גופא סמפון שיש עליו עדי' יתקיים בחותמיו אין עליו עדים ויוצא מתחת ידי שליש או שיוצא לאחר חיתום שטרות כשר יוצא מתחת ידי שליש דהא הימניה מלוה לשליש יוצא לאחר חיתום שטרות נמי דאי לאו דפריע לא הוה מרע ליה לשטריה:

## הדרן עלך שנים אוחזין

**אלו** מציאות שלו ואלו חייב להכריז אלו מציאות שלו מצא פירות מפוזרין מעות מפוזרות כריכות ברשות הרבים ועגולי דבילה ככרות של נחתום מחרוזות של דגים וחתיכות של בשר וגיזי צמר הלקוחין ממדינתן ואניצי פשתן ולשונות של ארגמן הרי אלו שלו דברי רבי מאיר ר' יהודה אומר כל שיש בו שינוי חייב להכריז כיצד מצא עגול ובתוכו חרס ככר ובתוכו מעות רבי שמעון בן אלעזר אומר כל כלי אנפוריא אין חייב להכריז:

**גמ'** מצא פירות מפוזרין וכמה א"ר יצחק קב בארבע אמות היכי דמי אי דרך נפילה אפילו טובא נמי ואי דרך הינוח אפילו בציר מהכי נמי לא א"ר עוקבא בר חמא במכנשתא דבי דרי עסקינן קב בארבע אמות דנפיש טרחייהו לא טרח איניש ולא הדר אתי ושקיל להו אפקורי מפקר להו בציר מהכי טרח והדר אתי ושקיל להו ולא מפקר להו בעי רבי ירמיה חצי קב בשתי אמות מהו קב בארבע אמות טעמא מאי משום דנפיש טרחייהו חצי קב בשתי אמות כיון דלא נפיש טרחייהו לא מפקר להו או דלמא משום דלא חשיבי וחצי קב בשתי אמות כיון דלא חשיבי מפקר להו קביים בשמונה אמות מהו קב בארבע אמות טעמא מאי משום דנפיש טרחייהו וכ"ש קביים בשמונה אמות כיון דנפישא טרחייהו טפי מפקר להו או דלמא משום דלא חשיבי וקביים בשמונה אמות כיון דחשיבי לא מפקר להו [א] קב שומשמין בארבע אמות מהו קב בארבע אמות טעמא מאי משום דלא חשיבי ושומשמין כיון דחשיבי לא מפקר להו או דלמא משום דנפיש טרחייהו וכ"ש שומשמין כיון דנפיש טרחייהו טפי מפקר להו קב תמרי בארבע אמות קב רמוני בארבע אמות מהו קב בארבע אמות טעמא מאי משום דלא חשיבי קב תמרי בארבע אמות קב רמוני בארבע אמות נמי כיון דלא חשיבי מפקר להו או דלמא משום דנפישא טרחייהו וקב תמרי בארבע אמות וקב רמוני בארבע אמות כיון דלא נפיש טרחייהו לא מפקר להו מאי תיקו: איתמר

יאוש

### רש"י

דשיילינן להו. אם ראו הפרעון ואם לאו נאמן המלוה לומר שלא נכתב אלא להיות מוכן לכשיפרע: עדי קיום. שכתבו הנפק דדי דינא לא מקיימי ליה אלא א"כ פרע: סמפון שיש עליו עדים. בעדי קיום מוקמינן לה: יתקיים בחותמיו. ואפי' יוצא מתחת יד מלוה כשר: אין עליו עדי קיום. אבל עדים חתומין עליו: ויוצא מתחת ידי שליש. שאין הלוה מוציאו ולא המלוה אלא שליש שביניהם נאמן: או שיצא אחר חיתום שטרות. שילא לפנינו כשהוא כתוב בשטר חוב אחר החתימה כשר: דהא הימניה מלוה לשליש. דעל כרחך אין כותב שובר אלא מלוה והוא מסרו ליד השליש:

הדרן עלך שנים אוחזין

**אלו** מציאות: מצא פירות מפוזרין. נתייאשו הבעלים מהן כדאמר בגמרא והפקר הן: מעות מפוזרות. הואיל ואין להם סימן ניכר איאושי מיאש והוו להו הפקר וזהו טעם כולם: כריכות. עומרים קטנים כמו מאלמים אלומים ומתרגמינן בירושל' מכרכן כריכן (בראשית לז): ברה"ר. שהכל דשין עלייהו ואם היה סימן נקשר עליהן הרי הוא נשחת: של נחתום. כל ככרות הנחתומין שוין אבל ככרות של בעל הבית יש בהן סימן: ממדינתן. כמות שהן גזוזות כשאר כל גיזת המדינה לאפוקי הבאות מבית האומן כדקתני סיפא: אניצי פשתן. ריסט"א בל' אשכנז ובמקומינו פופי"ר: ולשון של ארגמן. למר סרוק ומשוך כמין לשון וצבוע ארגמן ומלויין הן: מצא עיגול. של דבילה: אנפוריא. בגמ' מפרש: גמ' וכמה. חשוב פיזור: קב. מפוזר בארבע אמות אבל בג' אמות לא הוי פיזור וטעמא מפרש ואזיל: אי דרך נפילה. אם מצאם דרך נפילה שיש לדעת שלא הונחו שם מדעת אלא נפלו: אפילו טובא. מקב נמי דכיון דאין בהן סימן איאושי מיאש: ואי דרך הינוח וכו'. עתיד לחזור וליטלן: במכנשתא דבי דרי. בשעת אסיפת גרנות וכאן דשו בעליהן ונשאו את העיקר ונותרו אלו: נפיש טרחייהו. לקבלן: בציר מהכי. אם היה פזורן בפחות מכן: משום דלא חשיבי. עליה קב פירות לטרוח עליהן טורח קיבוץ של ארבע אמות: שומשמין. דקין מאד ויש טורח בקיבוצן יותר מחטין אבל דמיהן יקרין: תמרים ורמונין. גסים הן ואין טורח בקבוצן:

יאוש

### תוספות

**אלו** מציאות שלו: כריכות ברה"ר. בכריכות דוקא מפליג בין רה"ר לרה"י משום דלמ"ד (לקמן כב:) סימן העשוי לידרס הוי סימן ומקום הוי סימן מיירי הכא דליכא סימן ומקום נמי לא הוי סימן ברה"ר משום דמנשתפי וברה"י הוי מקום סימן וחייב להכריז ומיירי דאשכח דרך הינוח וככרות של נחתום ועיגולי דבילה אין בהם סימן והוי שלו אף ברה"י ומיירי דמלא דרך נפילה ולכך לא הוי מקום סימן וא"ת אמאי נקט כריכות דאשכח דרך הינוח טפי משאר דאיירי דרך נפילה וי"ל דכריכות איידי דיקירי אינון לא הוה שיפלו שלא מדעת אלא כשעומד לפוש מניח לארץ ושכחם שם וככרות של בעה"ב יש להן סימן דבעלי בתים רגילים לעשות סימן בככרותיהן ולכך אפילו ברשות הרבים חייב להכריז דסימן העשוי לידרס הוי סימן וליבורי מעות ופירות דהוי מקום סימן אף ברה"ר כדאמר לקמן משום דלא שייך בהו מנשתפי ואם תאמר כריכות ברה"ר דמיירי דרך הינוח היאך לוקחם הא אמרינן לקמן ספק הינוח לא יטול וכל שכן ודאי הינוח וי"ל דה"מ כשמלא במקום מוצנע ומשתמר דלא יטול (א) אם אין בו סימן ואם יש בו סימן נוטל ומכריז ולמ"ד (לקמן כב:) סימן העשוי לידרס לא הוי סימן ומקום נמי לא הוי סימן מיירי בכריכות שיש בהם סימן ולכך ברה"י מכריז וככרות של נחתום ושאר דמתניתין לית בהו סימן ולכך אף ברה"י הם שלו וככרות של בעה"ב שיש בהם סימן חייב להכריז אף ברה"ר דאין עשוי לידרס משום דאין מעבירין על האוכלין וכולה מתני' מיירי בין דרך נפילה בין דרך הינוח וא"ת כריכות אי דרך נפילה היא אם כן אינו יודע היכן נפלו וברשות היחיד אמאי צריך להכריז הא מתייאש שסבור ברה"ר נפיל וי"ל דאע"פ שאינו יודע לכוין המקום יודע הוא אם נפל ברשות הרבים או ברשות היחיד:

**וכמה** א"ר יצחק קב בארבע אמות. צריך לומר דרבי יצחק גופיה בעי וכמה דאי גמרא בעי מאי בעי וכמה לוקי דרך נפילה ואפילו טובא כדפריך גמ' בתר הכי אלא מדברי רבי יצחק הוא ורבי יצחק לא בעי לאוקמי דרך נפילה ואפילו טובא משום דסבר כאביי דיאוש שלא מדעת לא הוי יאוש אלא מוקי לה במכנשתא דבי דרי שהניחם שם מדעת וכה"ג איכא בפירקין (דף ל:) דבעי ולעולם אמר רב יהודה כו' דצריך לומר דרב יהודה אמר ולעולם וכן בפרק לא יחפור (ב"ב דף כג: ושם ד"ה וכמה) גבי מרחיקין מן החלונות דקאמר וכמה אמר רב ייבא כמלוא רוחב חלון: **חצי** קב בשתי אמות מהו. תימה הלא קב בארבע אמות הוי נמי חצי קב בשתי אמות ומאי קמבעיא ליה וי"ל כיון דליכא אלא חצי קב ילקוט: כיון שאין לו טורח לגמור אבל קב בארבע אמות יש לו טורח ללקוט הכל ואין מלקט כלל אי נמי קב בארבע אמות מרובעין הוי חצי קב בשתי אמות רוחב וארבע אמות אורך והכא בעי חצי קב בב' אמות על ב' אמות:

דלכי

### מסורת הש"ס

סנהדרין לא:], ב) [עי' לקמן כג: ד"ה חוזם], ג) [בגמרא למי ורא"ש ליתא להך יבום], ד) [לקמן כג.], כל שכן חצי, ש"ל, ו) [דף כה:], עיין עוד תוס' פסחים לג. ד"ה תמן].

### הגהות הב"ח

תוס' ד"ה אלו וכו' אין בו סימן. נ"ב ע"ל דף כג סוף ע"א:

### לעזי רש"י

ט"א, פופי"ר. אניצי פשתן, של פשתן מנופץ שבת דף יז ע"ב אונין ועיין רש"י דף יב ע"ב ד"ה באניצי פשתן פסולה).

### ליקוטי רש"י

מתחת ידי שליש. ולא מתחת יד הלוה ושניהם שזה מינהו להיות ביניהם כשר. או יצא אחר חיתום שטרות. בתוך שטר שהוא נכתב השובר תחת החתימה כשר. דאי לאו דפרעיה לשטריה. שהרי הלוה עצמו מוחזק ואי לאו דפרעיה הוה שביק למיכתב בגוויה [סנהדרין]. ועגולי דבילה. שנתייבשו בשדה מקצועין במקלוע והוא שם העשוי לכך ומוחכין בו התאנים ואחר כך אותם בכלי עגול נדבקין יחד ונעשין והוא נקרא עגולי דבילה [ביצה ג:].

### עין משפט נר מצוה

קעו א ב מיי' פט"ז מהלכות מלוה ולוה הלכה ט סמג עשין לד טוש"ע ח"מ סי' סה סעיף יח:

קעז ג מיי' שם הל' ח טוש"ע שם סעיף יט:

קעח ד מיי' שם הל' י טוש"ע שם סעיף כ:

א ה מיי' פט"ו מהלכות גזילה ואבידה הל' ח סמג עשין עד טוש"ע ח"מ סי' רסב סעיף ז:

ב ו מיי' שם פט"ז הל' ב טוש"ע שם סעיף ו:

ג ז מיי' שם פט"ו הל' ח טוש"ע שם סעיף ט:

ד ח מיי' שם טוש"ע שם סעיף ו:

ה ט מיי' שם הלכה יא טוש"ע שם סעיף טו:

ו י כ מיי' שם הלכה ח טוש"ע שם סעיף ז:

ז ל מ נ מיי' שם הל' יב סמג שם טוש"ע ח"מ סי' רמ סעיף ז:

### רבינו חננאל

שיש עליו עדים כשר. ופריק מאי עדים דקתני עדי קיום הכי נמי מסתברא וכו'. גופא סמפון שיש עליו עדים יתקיים בחותמיו. אוקימנא יתקיים מחותמיו אם מעידין שפרעו בפניהם. אין עליו עדים כלומר אינם יודעין העדים לא סמכינן עליה ואם יוצא מתחת ידי שליש ואמר השליש שודאי פרע הלוה למלוה מיגו דאי בעי השליש למיתביה ללוה כי אמר פרעיה מהימן. וכן אם נמצא זה הסמפון כתוב בשטר חוב עצמו אחר חתימת עדי השטר כשר דאי לאו דפרעיה לא הוה מרע ליה לשטריה:

הדרן עלך שנים אוחזין

אלו מציאות שלו ואלו חייב להכריז מצא פירות מפוזרין וכו'. אמר רבי יצחק קב מפוזר בד' אמות ומקשי' עלה אי דרך נפילה אשכחינהו אפי' יותר מקב שלו הן. אי דרך הנחה אשכחינהו אפי' פחות מקב לא יגע בהן ופריק מר עוקבא מתני' במכנשתא דבי דרי עסקינן. א) הגרנות כשמכבדין הגורן בשעה שמניפין התבואה מן הגורן אם מצא כשיעור קב פירות מפוזרין בגורן ברחוק ד' אמות לא טרח איניש למכנשינהו ומפקר להו לפיכך הן שלו. אבל קב בפחות מד' אמות לא מפקר להו הלכך לא שקיל. הא דתנן וציבורי פירות ומקשי ופרקי תני וציבור פירות אינון ואיפשיט דמנין הוי סימן. אבל מקום לא

### חשק שלמה על ר"ח

א) אולי צ"ל פי' בשעת אסיפת הגרנות כשמכבדין.

### הגהות הגר"א

[א] גמ' קב שומשמין כו'. נ"ב גירסת הרמב"ם שומשמי ותמרי ורמוני מאי תיקו ור"ל מב' וג' מינים:

ᵊsame seeds, which are tiny, כֵּיוָן דְּנָפִישׁ טִרְחַיְיהוּ טְפֵי — nce the effort needed to collect them is even greater, מַפְקַר לְ — [the owner] certainly renounces his ownership of ıem.

R' Yirmiyah's fourth question:
קַב תַּמְרֵי בְּאַרְבַּע אַמּוֹ — One who finds a ***kav*** **of dates** spread **over** **ur *amos*** square, קַב רִמּוֹנֵי בְּאַרְבַּע אַמּוֹת מַהוּ — or **a *kav* of** **omegranates** spread **over four *amos* — what is [the law]?** hould it be presumed that the owner will return for them or has e abandoned them? The Gemara explains. קַב בְּאַרְבַּע אַמּוֹת טַעְמָא מַ — **What is the** principal **reason** that a person abandons ***kav*** of grain kernels spread **over four *amos*?** מִשּׁוּם דְּלֹא חֲשִׁיבֵי - Is it **because they are not significant** enough to warrant ᵊturning for them? קַב תַּמְרֵי בְּאַרְבַּע אַמּוֹת — If so, it follows that the case of **a *kav* of dates** spread **over four *amos*,** קַב רִמּוֹנֵי בְּאַרְבַּע אַמּוֹת נַ — or **a *kav* of pomegranates** spread **over four** ***mos,*** **also,** כֵּיוָן דְּלֹא חֲשִׁיבֵי — **since they are not significant** nough to warrant returning for them, מַפְקַר לְהוּ — **[the** **wner] renounces** his **ownership of them.**
אוֹ דִּלְמָ — **Or perhaps,** the principal reason one abandons a *kav* of grain kernels spread over four *amos* is מִשּׁוּם דִּנְפִישָׁא טִרְחַיְיהוּ — **because the effort** needed **to** collect **them is** too **great.** וְקַב תַּמְרֵי בְּאַרְבַּע אַמּוֹת — **However,** in the case of **a *kav* of dates** spread **over four *amos*,** וְקַב רִמּוֹנֵי בְּאַרְבַּע אַמּוֹת — **or a *kav* of pomegranates** spread **over four *amos*,** כֵּיוָן דְּלֹא נְפִישׁ טִרְחַיְיהוּ — **since the effort** needed **to** collect **them is not** too **great,** because of their larger size, לֹא מַפְקַר לְהוּ — **[the owner] does not renounce** his **ownership of them.** מַאי — **What** is the law in the four questions posed above?[23]

The Gemara concludes:
תֵּיקוּ — **Let it stand.** The questions remain unresolved.[24]

We learned above that the right to keep a lost object one finds is based on the fact that its owner has despaired of recovering it — a legal condition known as *ye'ush.* In circumstances in which he does not despair, one has an obligation to announce the lost object and return it to its owner. The following Gemara considers the law in a case in which the object was one that the owner would despair of recovering, but it was found before its loss was discovered by the owner:
אִיתְמַר — **It has been stated:**[25]

NOTES

3. All of R' Yirmiyah's questions seem to hinge on the same issue. ᵊamely, is it the meagerness of the return or the amount of trouble ᵊhich is the crucial factor in the owner's decision to abandon produce on ıe threshing floor? Why, if so, did R' Yirmiyah raise the identical ᵊuestion in four different forms? *Rashba* suggests that R' Yirmiyah aised each question in a separate study hall. Rav Ashi, the redactor of ıe Gemara, gathered all of R' Yirmiyah's questions and arranged them ı this format. In addition, *Rashba* suggests various distinctions etween the four cases, which might account for the need to pose them ᵊparately.

24. [See below, 34b note 16, for an explanation of the word תֵּיקוּ.] The Gemara does not resolve these questions. *Rosh* therefore rules that, since the obligation to return a lost article is of Biblical origin, the finder must follow the stringent approach in each of these cases and make an effort to return the produce. Other codifiers (*Rambam, Hil. Gezeilah V'Aveidah* 15:12; and *Ohr Zarua,* cited in *Hagahos Ashrei*) have different opinions as to the course of action to be followed in actual practice. See *Choshen Mishpat* 260:7; *Beur HaGra* 24.

25. This phrase introduces an Amoraic statement; in this case, a dispute among Amoraim.

<sup></sup>

א דשיילינן להו לסהדי אי פרוע אי לא פרוע ת"ש סמפון שיש עליו עדים כשר ב מאי עדים עדי קיום הכי נמי מסתברא מדקתני סיפא ושאין עליו עדים פסול מאי אין עליו עדים אילימא דליכא עלויה עדים כלל צריכא למימר דפסול אלא לאו עדי קיום גופא א) סמפון שיש עליו עדי' יתקיים בחותמיו אין עליו עדים ג ויוצא מתחת ידי שליש או ד שיוצא לאחר חיתום שטרות כשר יוצא מתחת ידי שליש דהא הימניה מלוה לשליש יוצא לאחר חיתום שטרות נמי דאי לאו דפריע לא הוה מרע ליה לשטריה:

## הדרן עלך שנים אוחזין

**אלו** מציאות שלו ואלו חייב להכריז אלו מציאות שלו ה מצא פירות מפוזרין ו מעות מפוזרות ז כריכות ברשות הרבים ח ועגולי דבילה ככרות של נחתום ט מחרוזות של דגים וחתיכות של בשר וגיזי צמר הלקוחין ממדינתן ואניצי פשתן ולשונות של ארגמן הרי אלו שלו י דברי רבי מאיר ר' יהודה אומר כ כל שיש בו שינוי חייב להכריז כיצד ל מצא עגול ובתוכו חרס ככר ובתוכו מעות רבי שמעון בן אלעזר אומר כל כלי אנפוריא אין חייב להכריז: **גמ'** מצא פירות מפוזרין וכמה א"ר יצחק קב בארבע אמות היכי דמי אי דרך נפילה אפילו טובא נמי ואי דרך הינוח נ אפילו בציר מהכי נמי לא א"ר עוקבא בר חמא ס במכנשתא דבי דרי עסקינן ע קב בארבע אמות דנפיש טרחייהו לא טרח איניש ולא הדר אתי ושקיל להו אפקורי מפקר להו בציר מהכי טרח והדר אתי ושקיל להו ולא מפקר להו בעי רבי ירמיה חצי קב בשתי אמות מהו קב בארבע אמות טעמא מאי משום דנפיש טרחייהו חצי קב בשתי אמות כיון דלא נפיש טרחייהו לא מפקר להו או דלמא משום דלא חשיבי פ וחצי קב בשתי אמות כיון דלא חשיבי מפקר להו קביים בשמונה אמות מהו קב בארבע אמות טעמא מאי משום דנפיש טרחייהו וכ"ש קביים בשמונה אמות כיון דנפישא טרחייהו טפי מפקר להו או דלמא משום דלא חשיבי וקביים בשמונה אמות כיון דחשיבי לא מפקר להו [א] קב שומשמין בארבע אמות מהו קב בארבע אמות טעמא מאי משום דלא חשיבי ושומשמין כיון דחשיבי לא מפקר להו או דלמא משום דנפיש טרחייהו וכ"ש שומשמין כיון דנפיש טרחייהו טפי מפקר להו קב תמרי בארבע אמות קב רמוני בארבע אמות מהו קב בארבע אמות טעמא מאי משום דלא חשיבי קב תמרי וקב רמוני בארבע אמות נמי כיון דלא חשיבי מפקר להו או דלמא משום דנפישא טרחייהו וקב תמרי בארבע אמות וקב רמוני בארבע אמות כיון דלא נפיש טרחייהו לא מפקר להו מאי צ תיקו: איתמר יאוש

---

**רש"י**

דשיילינן להו. אם ראו הפרעון ואם לאו נאמן המלוה לומר שלא נכתב אלא להיות מוכן לכשיפרע: עדי קיום. שכתבו הנפקק דבי דינא לא מקיימי ליה אלא א"כ פרע: סמפון שיש עליו עדים. בעדי קיום מוקמינן לה: יתקיים בחותמיו. ואפי' יוצא מתחת יד מלוה כשר: אין עליו עדי קיום. אבל עדים חתומין עליו: ויוצא מתחת ידי שליש. שאין הלוה מוליאו ולא המלוה אלא שליש שביניהם נאמן: או שיצא אחר חיתום שטרות. שילא לפנינו כשהוא כתוב בשטר חוב אחר החתימה כשר: דהא הימניה מלוה לשליש. דעל כרחך אין כותב שובר אלא מלוה והוא מסרו ליד השליש:

הדרן עלך שנים אוחזין

**אלו** מציאות: מצא פירות מפוזרין. נתייאשו הבעלים מהן כדאמר בגמרא והפקר הן: מעות מפוזרות. הואיל ואין להם סימן ניכר איאושי מיאש והוו להו הפקר וזהו טעם כולם: כריכות. עומרים קטנים כמו מאלמים אלומים ומתרגמינן בירושל' מכרכן כריכן (בראשית לז): ברה"ר. שהכל דשין עלייהו ואם היה סימן נקשר עליהן הרי הוא נשחת: של נחתום. כל ככרות הנחתומין שוין אבל ככרות של בעל הבית יש בהן סימן: ממדינתן. כמות שהן גזוזות כשאר כל גיזת המדינה לאפוקי הבאות מבית האומן כדקתני סיפא: אניצי פשתן. ריסט"א בל' אשכנז ובמקומינו פופי"ר: ולשון של ארגמן. צמר סרוק ומשוך כמין לשון וצבוע ארגמן ומלויין הן: מצא עיגול. של דבילה: אנפוריא. בגמ' מפרש: גמ' וכמה. חשוב פיזור: קב. מפוזר בארבע אמות אבל בג' אמות לא הוי פיזור וטעמא מפרש ואזיל: אי דרך נפילה. אם מאליהם דרך נפילה שיש לדעת שלא הונחו שם מדעת אלא נפלו: אפילו טובא. מקב נמי דכיון דאין בהן סימן איאושי מיאש: ואי דרך הינוח וכו'. עתיד לחזור וליטלן: במכנשתא דבי דרי. בשעת אסיפת גרנות וכאן דשו בעליהן ונשאו את העיקר ועותרו אלו: נפיש טרחייהו. לקבצן: בציר מהכי. אם היה פוזר בפחות מכן: משום דלא חשיבי. עליה קב פירות לטרוח עליהן טורח קיבוץ של ארבע אמות: שומשמין. דקין מאד ויש טורח בקיבוצן יותר מחטין אבל דמיהן יקרין: תמרים ורמונים. גסים הן ואין טורח בקיבוצן:

---

**תוספות**

**אלו** מציאות שלו: כריכות ברה"ר. בכריכות דוקא מפליג בין רה"ר לרה"י משום דלמ"ד (לקמן כב:) סימן העשוי לידרס הוי סימן ומקום הוי סימן מיירי הכא דליכא סימן ומקום נמי לא הוי סימן ברה"ר משום דמנשתפי וברה"י הוי מקום סימן וחייב להכריז ומיירי דאשכחא דרך הינוח וככרות של נחתום ועיגולי דבילה אין בהם סימן והוי שלו אף ברה"י ומיירי דמלא דרך נפילה ולכך לא הוי מקום סימן וא"ת אמאי נקט כריכות דאשכחא דרך הינוח טפי משאר דאיירי דרך נפילה וי"ל דכריכות אידי דיקירי אינון לא הוה שיפלו שלא מדעת אלא כשעומד לפוש מניח לארץ ושכחם שם וככרות של בעה"ב יש להן סימן דבעלי בתים רגילים לעשות סימן בככרותיהן ולכך אפילו ברשות הרבים חייב להכריז דסימן העשוי לידרס הוי סימן וליבורי מעות ופירות דהוי מקום סימן אף ברה"ר כדאמר לקמן משום דלא שייך בהו מנשתפי ואם תאמר כריכות ברה"ר דמיירי דרך היגוח היאך לוקחם הא אמרינן לקמן ו) ספק היגוח לא יטול וכל שכן ודאי היגוח וי"ל דה"מ כשמלא במקום מוצנע ומשתמר דלא יטול (א) אם אין בו סימן ואם יש בו סימן נוטל ומכריז ולמ"ד (לקמן כב:) סימן העשוי לידרס לא הוי סימן ומקום נמי לא הוי סימן מיירי בכריכות שיש בהם סימן ולכך ברה"י מכריז וככרות של נחתום ושאר דמתניתין לית בהו סימן ולכך אף ברה"י הם שלו וככרות של בעה"ב שיש בהם סימן חייב להכריז אף ברה"ר דאין עשוי לידרס משום דאין מעבירין על האוכלין ולהלן מתני' מיירי בין דרך נפילה בין דרך היגוח וא"ת כריכות אי דרך נפילה היא אם כן אינו יודע היכן נפלו וברשות היחיד אמאי צריך להכריז הא מתייאש שסבור ברה"ר נפיל וי"ל דלע"פ שאינו יודע לכוין המקום יודע הוא אם נפל ברשות הרבים או ברשות היחיד:

**וכמה** א"ר יצחק קב בארבע אמות. נריך לומר דרבי יצחק גופיה בעי וכמה דאי גמרא בעי מאי בעי וכמה לוקי דרך נפילה ואפילו טובא דפריך גמ' בתר הכי אלא מדברי רבי יצחק הוא ורבי יצחק לא בעי לאוקמי דרך נפילה ואפילו טובא משום דסבר כאביי דיאוש שלא מדעת לא הוי יאוש אלא מוקי לה במכנשתא דבי דרי שהניחם שם מדעת וכה"ג איכא בפירקין (דף כ:) דבעי ולעולם אמר רב יהודה כו' דלריך לומר לרב יהודה אמר ולעולם וכן בפרק לא יחפור (ב"ב דף כג: ושם ד"ה וכמה) גבי מרחיקין מן החלונות דקאמר וכמה אמר רב יצחק כמלוא רוחב חלון ו): **חצי** קב בשתי אמות מהו. תימה הלא קב בארבע אמות הוי נמי חלי קב בשתי אמות ומאי קמבעיא ליה וי"ל כיון דליכא אלא חלי קב ילקוט: כיון שאין לו טורח לגמור אבל קב בארבע אמות יש לו טורח ללקוט הכל ואין מלקט כלל אי נמי קב בארבע אמות מרובעין הוי חלי קב בשתי אמות רוחב וארבע אמות אורך והכא בעי חלי קב בב' אמות על ב' אמות:

דלכי

---

**מסורת הש"ס**

א) [סנהדרין לא:], ב) [עי' לקמן כג: ד"ה רחוק], ג) [בגמרא שלמי ורא"ש ליתא להך מיבות], ד) [לקמן כג.], ה) ופי' שבכן חצי, רש"ל, ו) [דף כה:], [ועיין עוד תוס' פסחים גג. ד"ה תתן].

**הגהות הב"ח**

(א) תוס' ד"ה אלו וכו' אין בו סימן. נ"ב ע"ל דף כג סוף ע"א.

**לעזי רש"י**

שמ"א, פופי"ר. רוש אגילי פשתן, דוס של פשתן מנופץ (ר"ש שבת דף יז ע"ב ד"ה אונין ועיין רש"י כה דף יג ע"ב ד"ה כה באגילי פשתן פסולה).

**ליקוטי רש"י**

יוצא מתחת ידי שליש. ולא מתחת יד הלוה הואיל ושניהם יש בידם אלא כך מוציאו ושלא נכתב שום ליה. שהלוה זו ביניהם כשר. או יוצא אחר חיתום השטרות. בתוך שטר המלוה נכתב השובר תחת העדים כשר. דאי לאו דפריע לא מרע ליה לשטריה. שהרי המלוה עלמו מוחזק בשטר ואי לאו דפרעיה לא הוה שביק למיכתב שובר בגווייהו [סנהדרין לא:]. ועגולי דבילה. תאנים שנתייבשו בשדה ודנין במקלעת והוא שם העשוי לכך ותותכין בו כלי החלאים ואחר כך דורסין אותם בכלי עגול כדי שידבקו יחד ונעשין גוש והוא נקרא עגולי דבילה [ביצה ג:].

---

**עין משפט נר מצוה**

קטו א ב מיי' פט"ו מהלכות מלוה ולוה הלכה ט סמג עשין נד טוש"ע ח"מ סי' סה סעיף יח:

קטז ג מיי' שם הל' ח טוש"ע שם סעיף יט:

קיז ד מיי' שם הל' י טוש"ע שם סעיף כ:

א ה מיי' פט"ו מהלכות גזלה ואבדה הל' ח סמג עשין עד טוש"ע ח"מ סי' רסב סעיף ז:

ב ו מיי' שם פט"ו הל' ג טוש"ע שם סעיף ו:

ג ז מיי' שם פט"ז הל' ח טוש"ע שם סעיף ט:

ד ח מיי' שם טוש"ע שם סעיף ו:

ה ט מיי' שם הלכה יא טוש"ע שם סעיף טו:

ו י כ מיי' שם הלכה ח טוש"ע שם סעיף ח:

ז ל מ נ מיי' שם הל' יב סמג שם טוש"ע ח"מ סי' רס סעיף ז:

**רבינו חננאל**

שיש עליו עדים כשר. ופריק מאי עדים דקתני עדי קיום הכי נמי מסתברא וכו'. גופא סמפון שיש עליו עדים יתקיים בחותמיו. אוקימנא יתקיים מחותמיו אם מעידין שפרעו בפניהם. אין עליו עדים כלומר אינם יודעין העדים לא סמכינן עליה ואם יוצא מתחת ידי שליש ואמר השליש שודאי פרע הלוה למלוה מיגו דאי בעי השליש לא מיתהבה ללוה כי אמר פרעיה מהימן. וכן אם נמצא זה הסמפון כתוב בשטר חוב עצמו אחר חתימת עדי השטר כשר דאי לאו דפרעיה לא הוה מרע ליה לשטריה:

הדרן עלך שנים אוחזין

אלו מציאות שלו ואלו חייב להכריז מצא פירות מפוזרין וכו'. אמר רבי יצחק קב מפוזר בד' אמות ומקשי' עלה אי דרך נפילה אשכחינהו אפי' יותר מקב שלו הן. אי דרך הנחה אשכחינהו אפי' פחות מקב לא יגע בהן ופריק מר עוקבא מתני' במכנשתא דבי דרי עסקינן. א) הגרנות שמכנשין הגורן בשעה שמניפין התבואה מן הגורן אם מצא כשיעור קב פירות מפוזרין בגורן ברחוק ד' אמות לא יקחם איניש למכנשינהו ומפקר להו לפיכך הן שלו. אבל קב בפחות מד' אמות לא מפקר הלכך לא שקיל. והא דתנן וציבורי פירות ומקשי ופריק תני וציבור פירות אינון ואיפשט דמנין הוי סימן. אבל מקום לא

**חשק שלמה על ר"ח**

א) אולי צ"ל פי' בשעת אסיפת הגרנות שמכנסין.

**הגהות הגר"א**

[א] גמ' קב שומשמין כו'. נ"ב גירסת הרמב"ם שומשמי ותמרי ורמוני מאי מיקו ור"ל מב' וג' מינים:

here a **kav** of grain kernels remains spread **over** an area **four** ***nos*** square, דְּנְפִישׁ טִרְחַיְיהוּ – **in which** case **the effort** needed collect **them is great,** לֹא טָרַח אִינִישׁ – **a person does not ake the effort,** וְלֹא הָדַר אָתֵי וְשָׁקִיל לְהוּ – **and does not turn to take them** [the remaining kernels];[15] אַפְקוּרֵי מַפְקַר לְ – rather, **he renounces** his **ownership of them.**[16] בָּצִיר מִיָּ – However, where a *kav* of grain is spread over an area naller than this, טָרַח וְהָדַר אָתֵי וְשָׁקִיל לְהוּ – [a person] does **ake the effort, and does return to take them,**[17] וְלֹא מַפְקַר לְ – **and he does not renounce** his **ownership of them.**

The Gemara records four questions raised by R' Yirmiyah ncerning the applicability of R' Yitzchak's formula (a *kav* read over an area four *amos* square) to other situations:

חֲצִי קַב בִּשְׁתֵּי אַמּוֹת מַהוּ – בָּעֵי רַבִּי יִרְמְ – **R' Yirmiyah inquired:** One who finds on the threshing floor **half a *kav*** spread **over** an ea of **two *amos*** – **what is [the law]?**[18] The Gemara explains e question. קַב בְּאַרְבַּע אַמּוֹת טַעְמָא מַאי – **What is the** principal ason that **a *kav*** of kernels spread **over four *amos*** belongs to e finder? מִשּׁוּם דְּנָפִישׁ טִרְחַיְיהוּ – Is it **because the effort** eded **to** collect **them is** too **great,** and the owner therefore andons them? If so, it follows that in the case of חֲצִי קַב בִּשְׁתֵּי אַמ – **half a *kav*** spread **over** an area of **two *amos*,** כֵּיוָן דְּלֹא נָפִישׁ טִרְחַי – **since the effort to** collect **them is not** that **great,** לֹא מַפְקַר לְ – **[the owner] does not renounce** his **ownership of em.**[19]

אוֹ דִּלְמָא מִשּׁוּם דְּלֹא חֲשִׁי – **Or perhaps** the principal reason a rson abandons a *kav* of kernels spread over four *amos* is **ecause they are not significant** enough for him to make the fort to return and collect them. וַחֲצִי קַב בִּשְׁתֵּי אַמּוֹת – **ccordingly,** in the case of **half a *kav*** of kernels spread **over two *nos*,** כֵּיוָן דְּלֹא חֲשִׁיבֵי – **since they are** certainly **not signifi- nt** enough, מַפְקַר לְהוּ – **[the owner] renounces** his **owner- ip of them.**[20]

R' Yirmiyah's second question:

קַבַּיִים בִּשְׁמוֹנָה אַמּוֹת מַהוּ – One who finds **two *kavs*** spread **over** an area of **eight *amos***[21] – **what is [the law]?** The Gemara explains the question. קַב בְּאַרְבַּע אַמּוֹת טַעְמָא מַאי – **What is the** principal **reason** that a person abandons **a *kav*** of kernels spread **over four *amos*?** מִשּׁוּם דְּנָפִישׁ טִרְחַיְיהוּ – Is it **because the effort** needed **to** collect **them is** too **great?** If so, it follows וְכָל שֶׁכֵּן קַבַּיִים בִּשְׁמוֹנָה אַמּוֹת – **that all the more so,** in the case of **two *kavs*** spread **over** eight ***amos*,** כֵּיוָן דִּנְפִישָׁא טִרְחַיְיהוּ טְפֵי – **since the effort** needed **to** collect **them is even greater,** מַפְקַר לְהוּ – **[the owner]** certainly **renounces** his **ownership of them,** despite the greater return available.

אוֹ דִּלְמָא – **Or perhaps** the principal reason one abandons a *kav* spread over four *amos* is מִשּׁוּם דְּלֹא חֲשִׁיבֵי – **because they are not significant** enough for him to make the effort to return to collect them. וְקַבַּיִים בִּשְׁמוֹנָה אַמּוֹת – **However,** in the case of **two *kavs*** spread **over eight *amos*,** כֵּיוָן דַּחֲשִׁיבֵי – **since they are significant,** לֹא מַפְקַר לְהוּ – **[the owner] does not renounce** his **ownership of them.**[22]

R' Yirmiyah's third question:

קַב שׁוּמְשְׁמִין בְּאַרְבַּע אַמּוֹת מַהוּ – One who finds **a *kav* of sesame** seeds spread **over** an area of **four *amos*** square – **what is [the law]?** Should it be presumed that the owner will return for them or has he abandoned them? The Gemara explains. קַב בְּאַרְבַּע אַמּוֹת טַעְמָא מַאי – **What is the** principal **reason** that a person abandons **a *kav*** of grain kernels spread **over four *amos*?** מִשּׁוּם דְּלֹא חֲשִׁיבֵי – Is it **because they are not significant** enough to warrant the owner's return for them? וְשׁוּמְשְׁמִין כֵּיוָן דַּחֲשִׁיבֵי – If so, **then** in the case of **sesame seeds, since they are** more **valuable** than grain, לֹא מַפְקַר לְהוּ – **[the owner] does not renounce** his **ownership of them.**

אוֹ דִּלְמָא – **Or, perhaps,** the principal reason one abandons a *kav* of grain kernels spread over four *amos* is מִשּׁוּם דְּנָפִישׁ טִרְחַיְיהוּ – **because the effort** needed **to** collect **them is** too **great.** וְכָל שֶׁכֵּן שׁוּמְשְׁמִין – If so, it follows **that all the more so** in the case of

NOTES

earing of the winnowed grain from the threshing floor to the silo *ashi; Aruch*).

R' Yitzchak explains this case of the Mishnah to refer to grain that was t behind, rather than grain that dropped. He therefore offers a rule for w much grain can be assumed to have been abandoned. The reason he d not explain the Mishnah to refer simply to a case of spilled grain [in hich case any amount would belong to the finder] will emerge from the emara's discussion on 21b (see *Tosafos*).

. [Because the effort of gathering kernels spread so sparsely over this rge an area is in any case great, a person would not trouble to go back the threshing floor and retrieve them.]

. His abandonment of the small quantity of grain too bothersome to llect is, in effect, a renouncement of his ownership of it.

. Since less effort is required to collect produce concentrated in a naller area.

. That is, does R' Yitzchak's ruling hold ue for half the amount of grain in half e area. Accordingly, R' Yirmiyah's estion refers to an area 2x4 *amos* *osafos* in their first explanation; see ere for another view as well). See agram.

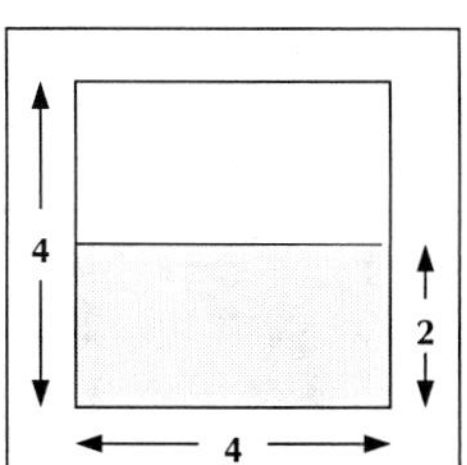


. If the degree of effort is the critical ctor in the owner's decision to abandon e grain, then it is quite possible that he ould not abandon half a *kav* in half the area, since collecting it involves uch less effort. Hence, the finder would *not* be permitted to keep half *kav* found spread over an area of two *amos*.

This raises an interesting problem. A full *kav* spread over four *amos* in effect two half-*kavs* each spread over two *amos*. If it is indeed true at a person is willing to return for half a *kav* spread over two *amos*, we should assume that the owner of a full *kav* spread over four *amos* will return for at least half of what he left behind! Why then does a full *kav* belong to the finder? *Tosafos* answer that a person has a psychological barrier against returning for just half of what he left behind. Thus, if the effort to collect the entire *kav* is too great, he will not return for any of it; but if only half a *kav* remains, he will return. [See *Tosafos* for an alternative explanation.]

20. If the critical factor in the owner's abandonment of a *kav* of kernels in four *amos* square is the meagerness of the return relative to the effort involved (*Rashi*), then it stands to reason that half a *kav*, which offers even less of a return, will certainly be abandoned, even though only half the effort is needed to collect it.

21. That is, an area of eight *amos* by four, double the amount and area of R' Yitzchak's formula. See diagram.

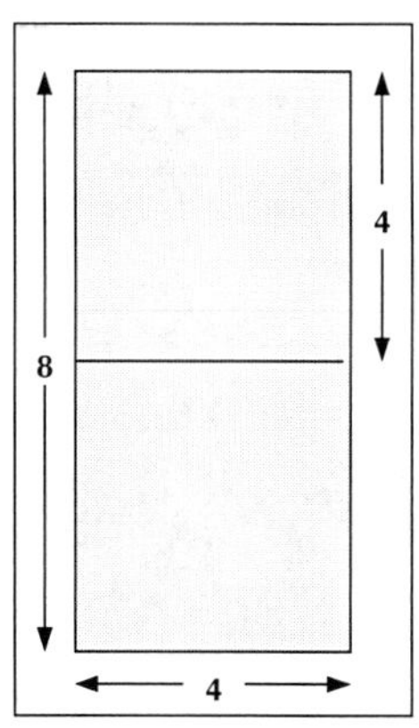


22. If the critical factor in the owner's decision to abandon a *kav* in four *amos* is the insignificance of the return rather than the effort involved, then it cannot be assumed that a larger amount in a proportionately larger area would also be abandoned.

This second question of R' Yirmiyah is in essence the reverse of his first question. In short, if the key factor in a person's abandonment of a *kav* spread over four *amos* is the difficulty of collecting it, then we must assume that a person would return for half a *kav* in two *amos* but not for two *kavs* in eight *amos*. If the principal consideration is the meagerness of the return, then the reverse is true.

דשיילינן להו לסהדי אי לא פרוע ת"ש סמפון שיש עליו עדים כשר מאי עדים עדי קיום הכי נמי מסתברא מדקתני סיפא ושאין עליו עדים פסול מאי אין עליו עדים אילימא דליכא עלויה עדים כלל צריכא למימר דפסול אלא לאו עדי קיום גופא (א) סמפון שיש עליו עדי' יתקיים בחותמיו אין עליו עדים ויוצא מתחת ידי שליש או שיוצא לאחר חיתום שטרות כשר יוצא מתחת ידי שליש דהא הימניה מלוה לשליש יוצא לאחר חיתום שטרות נמי דאי לאו דפריע לא הוה מרע ליה לשטריה:

## הדרן עלך שנים אוחזין

**אלו** מציאות שלו ואלו חייב להכריז אלו מציאות שלו מצא פירות מפוזרין מעות מפוזרות כריכות ברשות הרבים ועגולי דבילה ככרות של נחתום מחרוזות של דגים וחתיכות של בשר וגיזי צמר הלקוחין ממדינתן ואניצי פשתן ולשונות של ארגמן הרי אלו שלו דברי רבי מאיר ר' יהודה אומר כל שיש בו שינוי חייב להכריז כיצד מצא עגול ובתוכו חרס ככר ובתוכו מעות רבי שמעון בן אלעזר אומר כל כלי אנפוריא אין חייב להכריז: **גמ'** מצא פירות מפוזרין וכמה א"ר יצחק קב בארבע אמות היכי דמי אי דרך נפילה אפילו טובא נמי ואי דרך הינוח אפילו בציר מהכי נמי לא א"ר עוקבא בר חמא במכנשתא דבי דרי עסקינן קב בארבע אמות דנפיש טרחייהו לא טרח איניש ולא הדר אתי ושקיל להו אפקורי מפקר להו בציר מהכי טרח והדר אתי ושקיל להו ולא מפקר להו בעי רבי ירמיה חצי קב בשתי אמות מהו קב בארבע אמות טעמא מאי משום דנפיש טרחייהו חצי קב בשתי אמות כיון דלא נפיש טרחייהו לא מפקר להו או דלמא משום דלא חשיבי וחצי קב בשתי אמות כיון דלא חשיבי מפקר להו קביים בשמונה אמות מהו קב בארבע אמות טעמא מאי משום דנפיש טרחייהו וכ"ש קביים בשמונה אמות כיון דנפישא טרחייהו טפי מפקר להו או דלמא משום דלא חשיבי וקביים בשמונה אמות כיון דחשיבי לא מפקר להו [א] קב שומשמין בארבע אמות מהו קב בארבע אמות טעמא מאי משום דלא חשיבי ושומשמין כיון דחשיבי לא מפקר להו או דלמא משום דנפיש טרחייהו וכ"ש שומשמין כיון דנפיש טרחייהו טפי מפקר להו קב תמרי בארבע אמות קב רמוני בארבע אמות מהו קב בארבע אמות טעמא מאי משום דלא חשיבי קב תמרי בארבע אמות קב רמוני בארבע אמות נמי כיון דלא חשיבי מפקר להו או דלמא משום דנפישא טרחייהו וקב תמרי בארבע אמות וקב רמוני בארבע אמות כיון דלא נפיש טרחייהו לא מפקר להו מאי תיקו: איתמר

יאוש

---

### רש"י

דשיילינן להו. אם ראו הפרעון ואם לאו נאמן המלוה לומר שלא נכתב אלא להיות מוכן לכשיפרע: עדי קיום. שכתבו הנפק דדי דינא לא מקיימי ליה אלא א"כ פרע: סמפון שיש עליו עדים. בעדי קיום מוקמינן לה: יתקיים בחותמיו. ואפי' יוצא מתחת יד מלוה כשר: אין עליו עדי קיום. אבל עדים חתומין עליו: ויוצא מתחת ידי שליש. שאין הלוה מוליאו ולא המלוה אלא שליש שביניהם נאמן: או שיצא אחר חיתום שטרות. שילא לפנינו כשהוא כתוב בשטר תוך אחר החתימה כשר: דהא הימניה מלוה לשליש. דעל כרחך אין כותב שובר אלא מלוה והוא מסרו ליד השליש:

הדרן עלך שנים אוחזין

**אלו** מציאות: מצא פירות מפוזרין. נתייאשו הבעלים מהן כדאמר בגמרא והפקר הן: מעות מפוזרות. הואיל ואין להם סימן ניכר איאושי מיאש והוו להו הפקר וזהו טעם כולם: כריכות. עומרים קטנים כמו מאלמים אלומים ומתרגמינן בירושל' מכרכן כריכן (בראשית לז): ברה"ר. שהכל דשין עלייהו ואם היה סימן נקשר עליהן הרי הוא נשחת: של נחתום. כל ככרות הנחתומין שוין אבל ככרות של בעל הבית יש בהן סימן: ממדינתן. כמות שהן גזוזות כשאר כל גיזת המדינה לאפוקי הבאות מבית האומן כדקתני סיפא: אניצי פשתן. ריסט"א בל' אשכנז ובמקומינו פופי"ר: ולשון של ארגמן. צמר סרוק ומשוך כמין לשון וצבוע ארגמן ומלויין הן: מצא עיגול. של דבילה: אנפוריא. בגמ' מפרש: **גמ'** וכמה. חשוב פיזור: קב. מפוזר בארבע אמות אבל בג' אמות לא הוי פיזור וטעמא מפרש ואזיל: אי דרך נפילה. אם מלאם דרך נפילה שיש לדעת שלא הונחו שם מדעת אלא נפלו: אפילו טובא. מקב נמי דכיון דאין בהן סימן איאושי מיאש: ואי דרך הינוח וכו'. עתיד לחזור וליטלן: במכנשתא דבי דרי. בשעת אסיפת גרנות וכאן דשן בעליהן ונשאו את העיקר ונותרו אלו: נפיש טרחייהו. לקבלן: בציר מהכי. אם היה פזורן בפחות מכן: משום דלא חשיבי. עליה קב פירות לטרוח עליהן טורח קיבוץ של ארבע אמות: שומשמין. דקין מאד ויש טורח בקיבוצן יותר מחטין אבל דמיהן יקרין: תמרים ורמונין. גסים הן ואין טורח בקבוצן:

יאוש

---

### תוספות

**אלו** מציאות שלו: כריכות ברה"ר. בכריכות דוקא מפליג בין רה"ר לרה"י משום דלמ"ד (לקמן כב:) סימן העשוי לידרס הוי סימן ומקום הוי סימן מיירי הכא דליכא סימן ומקום נמי לא הוי סימן ברה"ר משום דמנשתפי וברה"י הוי מקום סימן וחייב להכריז ומיירי דאשכח דרך הינוח וככרות של נחתום ועיגולי דבילה אין בהם סימן והוי שלו אף ברה"י ומיירי דמלא דרך נפילה ולכך לא הוי מקום סימן וא"ת אמאי נקט כריכות דאשכח דרך הינוח טפי משאר דאיירי דרך נפילה וי"ל דכריכות איידי דיקירי אינון לא הוה שיפלו שלא מדעת אלא כשעומד לפוש מניח לארץ ושכחם שם וככרות של בעה"ב יש להן סימן דבעלי בתים רגילים לעשות סימן בככרותיהן ולכך אפילו ברשות הרבים חייב להכריז דסימן העשוי לידרס הוי סימן וליבורי מעות ופירות דהוי מקום סימן אף ברה"ר כדאמר לקמן משום דלא שייך בהו מנשתפי ואם תאמר כריכות ברה"ר דמיירי דרך הינוח היאך לוקחם הא אמרינן לקמן (ו) ספק הינוח לא יטול וכל שכן ודאי הינוח וי"ל דה"מ כשמלא במקום מוצנע ומשתמר דלא יטול (א) אם אין בו סימן ואם יש בו סימן נוטל ומכריז ולמ"ד (לקמן כב:) סימן העשוי לידרס לא הוי סימן ומקום נמי לא הוי סימן מיירי בכריכות שיש בהם סימן ולכך ברה"י מכריז וככרות של נחתום ושאר דמתניתין לית בהו סימן ולכך אף ברה"י הם שלו וככרות של בעה"ב שיש בהם סימן חייב להכריז אף ברה"ר דאין עשוי לידרס משום דאין מעבירין על האוכלין וכולה מתני' מיירי בין דרך נפילה בין דרך הינוח וא"ת כריכות אי דרך נפילה היא אם כן אינו יודע היכן נפלו וברשות היחיד אמאי צריך להכריז הא מתייאש שסבור ברה"ר נפיל וי"ל דאע"פ שאינו יודע לכוין המקום יודע הוא אם נפל ברשות הרבים או ברשות היחיד:

**וכמה** א"ר יצחק קב בארבע אמות. צריך לומר דרבי יצחק גופיה בעי וכמה דאי גמרא בעי מאי בעי וכמה לוקי דרך נפילה ואפילו טובא כדפריך גמ' בתר הכי אלא מדברי רבי יצחק הוא ורבי יצחק לא בעי לאוקמי דרך נפילה ואפילו טובא משום דסבר כאביי דיאוש שלא מדעת לא הוי יאוש אלא מוקי לה במכנשתא דבי דרי שהניחם שם מדעת וכה"ג איכא בפירקין (דף ל:) דבעי ולעולם אמר רב יהודה כו' דצריך לומר דרב יהודה אמר ולעולם וכן בפרק לא יחפור (ב"ב דף כב: ושם ד"ה וכמה) גבי מרחיקין מן החלונות דקאמר וכמה אמר רב ייבא כמלוא רוחב חלון (ז): **חצי** קב בשתי אמות מהו. תימה הלא קב בארבע אמות הוי נמי חצי קב בשתי אמות ומאי קמבעיא ליה וי"ל כיון דליכא אלא חצי קב ילקוט: כיון שאין לו טורח לגמור אבל קב בארבע אמות יש לו טורח ללקוט הכל ואין מלקט כלל אי נמי קב בארבע אמות מרובעין הוי חצי קב בשתי אמות רוחב וארבע אמות אורך והכא בעי חצי קב בב' אמות על ב' אמות:

דלכי

---

### עין משפט נר מצוה

קעו א ב מיי' פט"ז מהלכות מלוה ולוה הלכה ט סמג עשין לד טוש"ע ח"מ סי' סה סעיף יח:

קעז ג מיי' שם הל' ח טוש"ע שם סעיף יט:

קעח ד מיי' שם הל' י טוש"ע שם סעיף כ:

א ה מיי' פט"ו מהלכות גזילה ואבידה הל' ח סמג עשין עד טוש"ע ח"מ סי' רסב סעיף ז:

ב ו מיי' שם פט"ז הל' ג טוש"ע שם סעיף ו:

ג ז מיי' שם פט"ו הל' ח טוש"ע שם סעיף ט:

ד ח מיי' שם טוש"ע שם סעיף ו:

ה ט מיי' שם הלכה יא טוש"ע שם סעיף טו:

ו י כ מיי' שם הלכה ח טוש"ע שם סעיף ז:

ז ל מ נ מיי' שם הל' יב סמג שם טוש"ע ח"מ סי' רס סעיף ז:

### רבינו חננאל

שיש עליו עדים כשר. ופריק מאי עדים דקתני עדי קיום הכי נמי מסתברא וכו'. גופא סמפון שיש עליו עדים יתקיים בחותמיו. אוקימנא יתקיים מחותמיו אם מעידין שפרעו בפניהם. אין עליו עדים כלומר אינם יודעין העדים לא סמכינן עליה ואם יוצא מתחת ידי שליש ואמר השליש שודאי פרע הלוה למלוה מיגו דאי בעי השליש למיתביה ללוה כי אמר פרעיה מהימן. וכן אם נמצא זה הסמפון כתוב בשטר חוב עצמו אחר חתימת עדי השטר כשר דאי לאו דפרעיה לא הוה מרע ליה לשטריה:

הדרן עלך שנים אוחזין

אלו מציאות שלו ואלו חייב להכריז מצא פירות מפוזרין וכו'. אמר רבי יצחק קב מפוזר בד' אמות ומקשי' עלה אי דרך נפילה אשכחינהו אפי' יותר מקב שלו הן. אי דרך הנחה אשכחינהו אפי' פחות מקב לא יגע בהן ופריק מר עוקבא מתני' במכנשתא דבי דרי עסקינן. א) הגרנות כשמכבדין הגורן בשעה שמניפין התבואה מן הגורן אם מצא כשיעור קב פירות מפוזרין בגורן ברחוק ד' אמות לא טרח איניש למכנשינהו ומפקר להו לפיכך הן שלו. אבל קב בפחות מד' אמות לא מפקר להו הלכך לא שקיל. הא דתנן וציבורי פירות ומקשי ופרקי תני וציבור פירות אינון ואיפשיט דמנין הוי סימן. אבל מקום לא

### חשק שלמה על ר"ח

א) אולי צ"ל פי' בשעת אסיפת הגרנות כשמכבדין.

### הגהות הגר"א

[א] גמ' קב שומשמין כו'. נ"ב גירסת הרמב"ם שומשמי ותמרי ורמוני מאי תיקו ור"ל מב' וג' מינים:

### מסורת הש"ס

א) [סנהדרין לא:], ב) [עי' לקמן כג: ד"ה [illegible]], ג) [בגמרא [illegible] מי ורא"ש ליתא להנך [illegible]], ד) [לקמן כג.], [illegible] כל שכן חצי, [illegible] ו) [דף כה:], [illegible] עיין עוד תוס' פסחים לג. ד"ה תתן].

### הגהות הב"ח

(א) תוס' ד"ה אלו וכו' אין בו סימן. נ"ב ע"ל [illegible] דף כג סוף ע"א:

### לעזי רש"י

[illegible] ט"א, פופי"ר. [illegible] אנילי פשתן, [illegible] של פשתן מנופץ [illegible] שבת דף יז ע"ב [illegible] אונין ועיין רש"י [illegible] דף יב ע"ב ד"ה [illegible] באנילי פשתן פסולה).

### ליקוטי רש"י

[illegible]

# Chapter Two

**Mishnah** אֵלּוּ מְצִיאוֹת שֶׁלּוֹ – **These finds belong to him,** וְאֵלּוּ חַיָּיב לְהַכְרִיז – **and these he is obligated to announce.**[1] אֵלּוּ מְצִיאוֹת שֶׁלּוֹ – **These finds belong to him:**[2] מָצָא פֵּירוֹת מְפוּזָּרִין – **If one found scattered produce,** מָעוֹת מְפוּזָּרוֹת – **scattered coins,** כְּרִיכוֹת בִּרְשׁוּת הָרַבִּים – **small sheaves in a public domain,**[3] וְעִגּוּלֵי דְבֵילָה – **round cakes of pressed figs,** כִּכָּרוֹת שֶׁל נַחְתּוֹם – **a baker's loaves,**[4] מַחֲרוֹזוֹת שֶׁל דָּגִים – **strings of fish,** וַחֲתִיכוֹת שֶׁל בָּשָׂר – **pieces of meat,** וְגִיזֵּי צֶמֶר הַלְּקוּחִין מִמְּדִינָתָן – **fleeces of wool brought from their province,**[5] i.e. unprocessed wool, וַאֲנִיצֵי פִשְׁתָּן – **bundles of flax,**[6] וּלְשׁוֹנוֹת שֶׁל אַרְגָּמָן – **tongues of purple wool,**[7] הֲרֵי אֵלּוּ שֶׁלּוֹ – all **these belong to** [**the finder**]; דִּבְרֵי רַבִּי מֵאִיר – these are **the words of R' Meir.** ר׳ יְהוּדָה אוֹמֵר – **R' Yehudah says:** כָּל שֶׁיֵּשׁ בּוֹ שִׁינּוּי – **Anything that has something unusual in it,** חַיָּיב לְהַכְרִיז – **one is obligated to announce.** כֵּיצַד – **How so?** What is an example of an item with something unusual in it? מָצָא עִגּוּל – **If one found a round cake** of pressed figs וּבְתוֹכוֹ חֶרֶס – **with a pottery shard inside it,** כִּכָּר וּבְתוֹכוֹ מָעוֹת – or **a loaf with coins inside it.** רַבִּי שִׁמְעוֹן בֶּן אֶלְעָזָר אוֹמֵר – **R' Shimon ben Elazar says:** כָּל כְּלֵי אַנְפּוֹרְיָא – **Any** ***anporya*** **vessels**[8] אֵין חַיָּיב לְהַכְרִיז – **one is not obligated to announce.**

**Gemara** The Gemara analyzes the first case of the Mishnah. The Mishnah began:

מָצָא פֵּירוֹת מְפוּזָּר – If ONE FOUND SCATTERED PRODUCE, he may keep it.

The Gemara inquires:

וְכַמָּה – **How much** produce scattered over what size area is considered "scattered"?

The Gemara answers:

אָמַר רַבִּי יִצְחָק – **R' Yitzchak said:** קַב בְּאַרְבַּע אַמּוֹת – **A** ***kav*** of produce spread **over** an area **four** ***amos*** by four *amos*[9] is considered "scattered produce." However, a higher concentration of produce[10] must be announced.

The Gemara questions R' Yitzchak's statement:

הֵיכִי דָּמֵי – **What are the circumstances** in which R' Yitzchak's rule holds true? אִי דֶּרֶךְ נְפִילָה – **If** the produce lies **in a way indicating that it has fallen** from the owner unintentionally,[11] אֲפִילּוּ טוּבָא נַמִּי – then **even more** than a *kav* in four *amos* should **also** belong to the finder. Since the produce has no identifying marks, the one who lost it has certainly despaired of recovering it.[12] Therefore, whoever finds it should be allowed to keep it. וְאִי דֶּרֶךְ הִינּוּחַ – **And if** the produce was found **in a way indicating that it had been placed** there deliberately, אֲפִילּוּ בָּצִיר מֵהָכִי נַמִּי לֹא – then **even less than this** should **also not** belong to the finder, since its owner plans to return for it.[13] In what situation is R' Yitzchak's formulation (a *kav* in four *amos* square) valid?

The Gemara answers:

אָמַר רַב עוּקְבָא בַּר חָמָא – **Rav Ukva bar Chama said** in explanation of R' Yitzchak's rule: בְּמַכְנִשְׁתָּא דְבֵי דָרֵי עָסְקִינַן – **We are dealing** in this Mishnah not with grain that was lost, but **with** the produce left behind at the time of **the clearing of the threshing floor,**[14] i.e. what remains on the floor after the owner has threshed his grain and carried it away. קַב בְּאַרְבַּע אַמּוֹת –

NOTES

1. I.e. some finds belong to the finder, and some finds he is obligated to announce so that the owner may hear of the recovery of his object and come and reclaim it. This Mishnah will illustrate the types of finds one may keep. Those that must be announced will be illustrated in the next Mishnah (24b).

2. The objects the Mishnah will enumerate as belonging to the finder lack any *siman* (identifying mark) by which to recognize and distinguish them. It is assumed that someone who loses an object without any *siman* despairs of recovering it, because he knows that even if it is found, he will be unable to prove that it is his (*Rashi*). This state of mind is known as *ye'ush* (abandoning hope).

The legal consequence of *ye'ush* is that the object abandoned becomes ownerless and may therefore be kept by the finder (*Rashi*). According to *Nesivos HaMishpat* (262:3; see also *Ketzos HaChoshen* 406:2), a lost object does not become ownerless upon the owner's despair. Instead, the legal state of *ye'ush* which results from the owner's despair permits the finder to acquire the lost object for himself. However, until someone actually acquires the object, it remains technically under the ownership of the one who lost it. [See *Nesivos HaMishpat* for the practical differences between *ye'ush* and true ownerlessness (*hefker*).] This approach is disputed by others, who consider *ye'ush* to render an object immediately ownerless (see *Chazon Ish, Bava Kamma* 18:1).

3. Any *siman* (identifying mark) which might be attached to the sheaves (e.g. a tag) is likely to be obliterated by the many passersby in the public domain who step on it. Knowing this, the owner despairs of recovering them (*Rashi*). This explanation follows the opinion of Rabbah (Gemara 22b). The Gemara there will also cite the opinion of Rava, who explains the Mishnah differently.

4. All bakers' loaves are uniform. Homemade loaves, however, are different from each other and therefore identifiable (see Mishnah 25a).

5. That is, wool that has been sheared but has not been processed any further: raw wool. It therefore is identical to all the wool brought from that province. However, wool processed by a craftsman is identifiable and must be announced (see Mishnah 25a).

6. This refers to flax that has been beaten and carded, and is ready for spinning (*Aruch* from *Succah* 12b; *Tiferes Yisrael*).

7. Wool that was combed, drawn out into tongue-shaped strips, and dyed purple. Since purple wool commonly came in this shape, anyone losing a tongue of purple wool would despair of recovering it.

8. The Gemara (23b) will explain that this means vessels so new that the owner is not yet familiar with them.

9. A *kav* is a measure of volume. There are differing opinions regarding the conversion of Talmudic measures into contemporary ones. Opinions regarding a *kav* range from approximately 1.5 quarts (*R' Avraham Chaim Noeh*) to 2.65 quarts (*Chazon Ish*). Opinions regarding an *amah* (cubit; a linear measure) range from 18-24 inches.

10. I.e. a *kav* concentrated in an area of less than four *amos* by four *amos*. The basis for this distinction will emerge from the Gemara below (*Rashi*).

11. That is, it was found in a way that makes it clear that it had not been put there deliberately but had fallen from the owner's possession without his knowledge [e.g. it was found scattered about without any pattern, as though it had spilled from a container] (*Rashi*).

12. Since he has no way of identifying it as his even if it is eventually found, he gives up hope of being able to reclaim his lost produce. The produce is therefore considered ownerless (as explained in note 2), and it belongs to the finder regardless of how concentrated it may be.

13. If the produce was piled in a manner indicating that it had been left deliberately, it must be assumed that the owner intends to come back for it (*Rashi*); it is therefore not lost. Consequently, even when there is less than a *kav* in four *amos*, so that the produce is more widely scattered, the finder should still not be allowed to keep it.

14. Literally: the gathering of the winnowing place. The word דָּרֵי means to winnow (*Aruch*) [related to the Hebrew root זרה (see *Targum* to *Ruth* 3:2); the letters ד and ז are often interchanged from Hebrew to Aramaic]. Grain is winnowed at the threshing floor. The "gathering" refers to the

# Chapter Two

# Introduction

The second chapter of *Bava Metzia* deals with the obligation to return a lost object to its owner. This obligation stated in *Deuteronomy* 22:1-3: *You shall not see your brother's ox or his lamb straying, and hide yourself from them you shall surely return them to your brother. And if your brother is not close to you, and you do not know him; you sha gather it into your house, and it shall be with you, until your brother seeks it out, and you shall return it to him. An so shall you do with his donkey, and so shall you do with his garment, and so shall you do with any lost object of you brother, which is lost from him and you have found it; you may not hide yourself* [*from it*].

The obligation to return a lost object includes an obligation to announce the find, so that its owner knows from whom to reclaim it (see Mishnah 28a). It also requires the finder to make sure that he returns it to its rightful owner. Thu he may not return it to any claimant unless the claimant proves that it is his, either through witnesses or, mo commonly, by describing it sufficiently to show that it is his. The marking or feature that serves to identify a lost obje is known as a סִימָן, *siman* [pl. *simanim*], or *identifying mark*. What constitutes an identifying mark [other than unique marking] is the subject of much discussion in this chapter.

There is one major qualification to the obligation to return a lost object. The obligation exists only so long as th owner has not given up hope of recovering his lost property. Should he give up hope, the object becomes, in effec ownerless and whoever finds it at that point may keep it. Abandonment of hope is known as יֵאוּשׁ, *ye'ush*.

A corollary of this is that one may keep a lost object that lacks a *siman* (identifying mark). Since the owner ha no way of identifying this object, he can not retrieve it from the person who finds it. Accordingly, as soon as person realizes that he has lost an object without a *siman*, he abandons hope of recovering it, and whoever finds it ma keep it.

Abandonment is effective even for an object with a *siman;* however, it is not usual for a person to abandon an obje with a *siman,* since he may reasonably expect to recover it from those who find it.

**TERMS RELEVANT TO THIS CHAPTER**

יֵאוּשׁ, *abandonment* — the state of mind of an owner who has despaired of recovering his lost object; once th owner despairs, the object may be kept by whoever finds it.

הַכְרָזָה, *announcing* — publicizing the discovery of a lost object.

מְצִיאָה, *find; found object* — a lost object that has been found.

מוֹצֵא, *finder* — a person who has found a lost object.

סִימָן, *identifying mark* — the special marks, features, or characteristics of a lost object whose description allow one to reclaim a lost object.

^א^דשיילינן להו לסהדי אי לא פרוע ת"ש סמפון שיש עליו עדים כשר ^ב^מאי עדים עדי קיום הכי נמי מסתברא מדקתני סיפא ושאין עליו עדים פסול מאי אין עליו עדים אילימא דליכא עלויה עדים כלל צריכא למימר דפסול אלא לאו עדי קיום גופא (א) סמפון שיש עליו עדי' יתקיים בחותמיו אין עליו עדים ^ג^ויוצא מתחת ידי שליש או ^ד^שיוצא לאחר חיתום שטרות כשר יוצא מתחת ידי שליש דהא הימניה מלוה לשליש יוצא לאחר חיתום שטרות נמי דאי לאו דפריע לא הוה מרע ליה לשטריה:

## הדרן עלך שנים אוחזין

**אלו** מציאות שלו ואלו חייב להכריז אלו מציאות שלו ^ה^מצא פירות מפוזרין ^ו^מעות מפוזרות ^ז^כריכות ברשות הרבים ^ח^ועגולי דבילה ככרות של נחתום (ג) מחרוזות של דגים וחתיכות של בשר וגיזי צמר הלקוחין ממדינתן ואניצי פשתן ולשונות של ארגמן הרי אלו שלו (ג) דברי רבי מאיר ר' יהודה אומר (ד) כל שיש בו שינוי חייב להכריז כיצד ^ט^מצא עגול ובתוכו חרס ככר ובתוכו מעות רבי שמעון בן אלעזר אומר כל כלי אנפוריא אין חייב להכריז: **גמ'** מצא פירות מפוזרין וכמה א"ר יצחק קב בארבע אמות היכי דמי אי דרך נפילה ^י^אפילו טובא נמי ואי דרך הינוח ^כ^אפילו בציר מהכי נמי לא א"ר עוקבא בר חמא ^ל^במכנשתא דבי דרי עסקינן ^מ^קב בארבע אמות דנפיש טרחייהו לא טרח איניש ולא הדר אתי ושקיל להו אפקורי מפקר להו בציר מהכי טרח והדר אתי ושקיל להו ולא מפקר להו בעי רבי ירמיה חצי קב בשתי אמות מהו קב בארבע אמות טעמא מאי משום דנפיש טרחייהו חצי קב בשתי אמות כיון דלא נפיש טרחייהו לא מפקר להו או דלמא משום דלא חשיבי (ה) וחצי קב בשתי אמות כיון דלא חשיבי מפקר להו קביים בשמונה אמות מהו קב בארבע אמות טעמא מאי משום דנפיש טרחייהו וכ"ש קביים בשמונה אמות כיון דנפישא טרחייהו טפי מפקר להו או דלמא משום דלא חשיבי וקביים בשמונה אמות כיון דחשיבי לא מפקר להו [א] קב שומשמין בארבע אמות מהו קב בארבע אמות טעמא מאי משום דלא חשיבי ושומשמין כיון דחשיבי לא מפקר להו או דלמא משום דנפיש טרחייהו וכ"ש שומשמין כיון דנפיש טרחייהו טפי מפקר להו קב תמרי בארבע אמות קב רמוני בארבע אמות מהו קב בארבע אמות טעמא מאי משום דלא חשיבי קב תמרי בארבע אמות קב רמוני בארבע אמות נמי כיון דלא חשיבי מפקר להו או דלמא משום דנפישא טרחייהו וקב תמרי בארבע אמות וקב רמוני בארבע אמות כיון דלא נפיש טרחייהו לא מפקר להו מאי ^נ^תיקו: איתמר

יאוש

### רש"י

דשיילינן להו. אם ראו הפרעון ואם לאו נאמן המלוה לומר שלא נכתב אלא להיות מוכן לכשיפרע: עדי קיום. שכתבו הנפק דבי דינא לא מקיימי ליה אלא א"כ פרע: סמפון שיש עליו עדים. בעדי קיום מוקמינן לה: יתקיים בחותמיו. ואפי' יוצא מתחת יד מלוה כשר: אין עליו עדי קיום. אבל עדים חתומין עליו: ויוצא מתחת ידי שליש. שאין הלוה מוציאו ולא המלוה אלא שליש שביניהם נאמן: או שיצא אחר חיתום שטרות. שיצא לפנינו כשהוא כתוב בשטר חוב אחר החתימה כשר: דהא הימניה מלוה לשליש. דעל כרחך אין כותב שובר אלא מלוה והוא מסרו ליד השליש:

הדרן עלך שנים אוחזין

**אלו** מציאות: מצא פירות מפוזרין. נתייאשו הבעלים מהן כדאמר בגמרא והפקר הן: מעות מפוזרות. הואיל ואין להם סימן ניכר אייאושי מייאש והוו להו הפקר וזהו טעם כולם: כריכות. עומרים קטנים כמו מאלמים אלומים ומתרגמינן בירושל' מכרכן כריכן (בראשית לז): ברה"ר. שהכל דשין עלייהו ואם היה סימן נקשר עליהן הרי הוא נשחת: של נחתום. כל ככרות הנחתומין שוין אבל ככרות של בעל הבית יש בהן סימן: ממדינתן. כמות שהן גזוזות כשאר כל גיזת המדינה לאפוקי הבאות מבית האומן כדקתני סיפא: אניצי פשתן. ריסט"א בל' אשכנז ובמקומינו פופי"ר: ולשון של ארגמן. צמר סרוק ומשוך כמין לשון וצבוע ארגמן ומצויין הן: מצא עיגול. של דבילה: אנפוריא. בגמ' מפרש: גמ' וכמה. חשוב פיזור: קב. מפוזר בארבע אמות אבל בג' אמות לא הוי פיזור וטעמא מפרש ואזיל: אי דרך נפילה. אם מצאם דרך נפילה שיש לדעת שלא הונחו שם מדעת אלא נפלו: אפילו טובא. מקב נמי דכיון דאין בהן סימן אייאושי מייאש: ואי דרך הינוח וכו'. עתיד לחזור וליטלן: במכנשתא דבי דרי. בשעת אסיפת גרנות וכאן דשן בעליהן ונשאו את העיקר ועותרו אלו: נפיש טרחייהו. לקבצן: בציר מהכי. אם היה פוזרן בפחות מכן: משום דלא חשיבי. עליה קב פירות לטרוח עליהן טורח קיבוץ של ארבע אמות: שומשמין. דקין מאד ויש טורח בקיבוצן יותר מחטין אבל דמיהן יקרין: תמרים ורמונין. גסים הן ואין טורח בקבוצן:

יאוש

### תוספות

**אלו** מציאות שלו: כריכות ברה"ר. בכריכות דוקא מפליג בין רה"ר לרה"י משום דלמ"ד (לקמן כב:) סימן העשוי לידרס הוי סימן ומקום הוי סימן מיירי הכא דליכא סימן ומקום נמי לא הוי סימן ברה"ר משום דמנשתפי וברה"י הוי מקום סימן וחייב להכריז ומיירי דאשכח דרך הינוח וככרות של נחתום ועיגולי דבילה אין בהם סימן והוי שלו אף ברה"י ומיירי דמצא דרך נפילה ולכך לא הוי מקום סימן וא"ת אמאי נקט כריכות דאשכח דרך הינוח טפי משאר דאיירי דרך נפילה וי"ל דכריכות איידי דיקירי אינון לא הוה שיפלו שלא מדעת אלא כשעומד לפוש מניח לארץ ושכחם שם וככרות של בעה"ב יש להן סימן דבעלי בתים רגילים לעשות סימן בככרותיהן ולכך אפילו ברשות הרבים חייב להכריז דסימן העשוי לידרס הוי סימן וציבורי מעות ופירות דהוי מקום סימן אף ברה"ר כדאמר לקמן משום דלא שייך בהו מנשתפי ואם תאמר כריכות ברה"ר דמיירי דרך הינוח היאך לוקחם הא אמרינן לקמן (י) ספק הינוח לא יטול וכל שכן ודאי הינוח וי"ל דה"מ כשמצא במקום מוצנע ומשתמר דלא יטול (א) אם אין בו סימן ואם יש בו סימן נוטל ומכריז ולמ"ד (לקמן כב:) סימן העשוי לידרס לא הוי סימן ומקום נמי לא הוי סימן מיירי בכריכות שיש בהם סימן ולכך ברה"י מכריז וככרות של נחתום ושאר דמתניתין לית בהו סימן ולכך אף ברה"י הם שלו וככרות של בעה"ב שיש בהם סימן חייב להכריז אף ברה"ר דאין עשוי לידרס משום דאין מעבירין על האוכלין וכולה מתני' מיירי בין דרך נפילה בין דרך הינוח וא"ת כריכות אי דרך נפילה היא אם כן אינו יודע היכן נפלו וברשות היחיד אמאי צריך להכריז הא מתייאש שסבור ברה"ר נפיל וי"ל דאע"פ שאינו יודע לכוין המקום יודע הוא אם נפל ברשות הרבים או ברשות היחיד:

**וכמה** א"ר יצחק קב בארבע אמות. צריך לומר דרבי יצחק גופיה בעי וכמה דאי גמרא בעי מאי בעי וכמה לוקי דרך נפילה ואפילו טובא כדפריך גמ' בתר הכי אלא מדברי רבי יצחק הוא ורבי יצחק לא בעי לאוקמי דרך נפילה ואפילו טובא משום דסבר כאביי דיאוש שלא מדעת לא הוי יאוש אלא מוקי לה במכנשתא דבי דרי שהניחם שם מדעת וכה"ג איכא בפירקין (דף ל:) דבעי ולעולם אמר רב יהודה כו' דצריך לומר דרב יהודה אמר ולעולם וכן בפרק לא יחפור (ב"ב דף כב: ושם ד"ה וכמה) גבי מרחיקין מן החלונות דקאמר וכמה אמר רב ייבא כמלוא רוחב חלון (י"): **חצי** קב בשתי אמות מהו. תימה הלא קב בארבע אמות הוי נמי חצי קב בשתי אמות ומאי קמבעיא ליה וי"ל כיון דליכא אלא חצי קב ילקוט: כיון שאין לו טורח לגמור אבל קב בארבע אמות יש לו טורח ללקוט הכל ואין מלקט כלל אי נמי קב בארבע אמות מרובעין הוי חצי קב בשתי אמות רוחב וארבע אמות אורך והכא בעי חצי קב בב' אמות על ב' אמות:

דלכי

### עין משפט נר מצוה

קעו א ב מיי' פט"ז מהלכות מלוה ולוה הלכה ט סמג עשין צד טוש"ע ח"מ סי' סה סעיף יח:
קעז ג מיי' שם הל' ח טוש"ע שם סעיף יט:
קעח ד מיי' שם הל' י טוש"ע שם סעיף כ:
א ה מיי' פט"ו מהלכות גזילה ואבידה הל' ח סמג עשין עד טוש"ע ח"מ סי' רסב סעיף ז:
ב ו מיי' שם פט"ז הל' ב טוש"ע שם סעיף ו:
ג ז מיי' שם פט"ו הל' ח טוש"ע שם סעיף ט:
ד ח מיי' שם טוש"ע שם סעיף ו:
ה ט מיי' שם הלכה יא טוש"ע שם סעיף טו:
ו י כ מיי' שם הלכה ח טוש"ע שם סעיף ז:
ז ל מ נ מיי' שם הל' יב סמג שם טוש"ע ח"מ סי' רס סעיף ז:

### רבינו חננאל

שיש עליו עדים כשר. ופריק מאי עדים דקתני עדי קיום הכי נמי מסתברא וכו'. גופא סמפון שיש עליו עדים יתקיים בחותמיו. אוקימנא יתקיים מחותמיו אם מעידין שפרעו בפניהם. אין עליו עדים כלומר אינם יודעין העדים לא סמכינן עליה ואם יוצא מתחת ידי שליש ואמר השליש שודאי פרע הלוה למלוה מיגו דאי בעי השליש למיתביה ללוה כי אמר פרעיה מהימן. וכן אם נמצא זה הסמפון כתוב בשטר חוב עצמו אחר חתימת עדי השטר כשר דאי לאו דפרעיה לא הוה מרע ליה לשטריה:

הדרן עלך שנים אוחזין

אלו מציאות שלו ואלו חייב להכריז מצא פירות מפוזרין וכו'. אמר רבי יצחק קב מפוזר בד' אמות ומקשי' עלה אי דרך נפילה אשכחינהו אפי' יותר מקב שלו הן. אי דרך הנחה אשכחינהו אפי' פחות מקב לא יגע בהן ופריק מר עוקבא מתני' במכנשתא דבי דרי עסקינן. (א) הגרנות כשמכבדין הגורן בשעה שמניפין התבואה מן הגורן אם מצא כשיעור קב פירות מפוזרין בגורן ברחוק ד' אמות לא טרח איניש למכנשינהו ומפקר להו לפיכך הן שלו. אבל קב בפחות מד' אמות לא מפקר להו הלכך לא שקיל. הא דתנן וציבורי פירות ומקשי ופרקי תני וציבור פירות אינון ואיפשיט דמנין הוי סימן. אבל מקום לא

### חשק שלמה על ר"ח

א) אולי צ"ל פי' בשעת אסיפת הגרנות כשמכבדין.

### הגהות הגר"א

[א] גמ' קב שומשמין כו'. נ"ב גירסת הרמב"ם שומשמי ותמרי ורמוני מאי תיקו ור"ל מב' וג' מינים:

### מסורת הש"ס

...סנהדרין לא:], ב) [עי' לקמן כג: ד"ה ...זות], ג) [בגמרא ...מי ורא"ש ליתא להך ...יבות], ד) [לקמן כג.], ...כל שכן חצי, ...ש"ל, ו) [דף כה:], עיין עוד תוס' פסחים לג. ד"ה תתן].

### הגהות הב"ח

...תוס' ד"ה אלו וכו' ...אין בו סימן. נ"ב ע"ל ...דף כג סוף ע"א:

### לעזי רש"י

...ט"א, פופי"ר. ...ם אניצי פשתן, ...יות של פשתן מנופץ ...י שבת דף יז ע"ב ...אונין ועיין רש"י ...דף יב ע"ב ד"ה ...ה באניצי פשתן פסולה).

### ליקוטי רש"י

...א מתחת ידי ...יש. ולא מתחת יד ...הואיל ושניהם ...ים שזה מינהו להיות ...ביניהם כשר. או ...צא אחר חיתום ...רות. בתוך שטר ...וה נכתב השובר תחת ...יים כשר. דאי לאו ...לשטריה. שהרי ...וה עצמו מוחזק ...רו ואי לאו דפרעיה ...הוה שביק למיכתב ...יא בגוויה [סנהדרין ...]. ועגולי דבילה. ...ים שנתייבשו בשדה ...ען במקלוע והוא שם ...העשוי לכך וחותכין בו ...לי התאנים ואחר כך ...סין אותם בכלי עגול ...נדבקין יחד ונעשין ...נה והוא נקרא עגולי דבילה [ביצה ג:].

דְּשַׁיְילִינַן לְהוּ לְסָהֲ – **We ask the witnesses** אִי פְּרוּעַ – **whether** [the obligation] for which the receipt was written **was repaid,** אִי לֹא פְּר – **or not repaid.** If they say they saw it repaid, the lender must obviously relinquish his claim. If not, he need not abide by the receipt, in accordance with the ruling of Rav Yirmiyah bar Abba.[1]

The Gemara challenges Rav Yirmiyah bar Abba's ruling yet one more time:

תָּא שְׁמַ – **Come, learn** from the following Baraisa: סִמְפּוֹן שֶׁיֵּשׁ עָלָיו עֵד – A RECEIPT in the possession of a lender, THAT HAS ON it the signatures of WITNESSES, כָּשֵׁר – IS VALID. This contradicts Rav Yirmiyah bar Abba's ruling. – ? –

The Gemara answers:

מַאי עֵדִ – **What are the witnesses** referred to by the Baraisa? עֵדֵי קִיּ – **Witnesses of certification,** i.e. the signatures of the judges who certify that the signatures of the witnesses on the receipt are authentic. Even Rav Yirmiyah bar Abba agrees that a lender must abide by a certified receipt.[2]

The Gemara corroborates this explanation:

הָכִי נַמִּי מִסְתַּבְּרָ – **This is also** the **more reasonable** explanation. מִדְּקָתָנֵי סֵיפָ – **For the conclusion of the Baraisa has taught:** וְשֶׁאֵין עָלָיו עֵדִ – AND [A RECEIPT] THAT DOES NOT HAVE the signatures of WITNESSES ON IT פָּסוּל – IS INVALID. מַאי אֵין עָלָיו עֵדִ – **What** does the Baraisa mean when it states that [THE RECEIPT] DOES NOT HAVE WITNESSES ON IT? אִילֵימָא דְּלֵיכָּא עִלָּוֵיהּ עֵדִים כְּלָ – **If you say** it means that **there are no** signatures of **witnesses on it at all,** צְרִיכָא לְמֵימַר דְּפָסוּל – **is it** even **necessary to mention that it is invalid?** It is quite obvious that the lender need not abide by such a receipt![3] אֶלָּא לָאו עֵדֵי קִיּוּם – **Rather,** must you **not** say that the "witnesses" mentioned in this Baraisa refer to the **witnesses who certify** the signatures on the receipt?[4] Thus, the Baraisa teaches that if the receipt found in the lender's possession is not certified, even if it is signed by witnesses, it is not valid, as Rav Yirmiyah bar Abba taught.

The Gemara now quotes the full text of the Baraisa cited above (20b) and analyzes it:

גּוּפָא – **[The Baraisa] itself** taught: סִמְפּוֹן שֶׁיֵּשׁ עָלָיו עֵדִים – A RECEIPT in the possession of a lender, THAT HAS the signatures of WITNESSES ON IT, יִתְקַיֵּים בְּחוֹתְמָיו – SHOULD BE CERTIFIED THROUGH ITS SIGNERS.[5] אֵין עָלָיו עֵדִים – IF [THE RECEIPT] DOES NOT HAVE the signatures of WITNESSES ON IT, וְיוֹצֵא מִתַּחַת יְדֵי שָׁלִישׁ – BUT IT EMERGES FROM THE HANDS OF A THIRD PARTY who was trusted to hold it and give it to the borrower when he paid the debt, אוֹ שֶׁיּוֹצֵא לְאַחַר חִיתּוּם שְׁטָרוֹת – OR IT EMERGES in court BELOW THE SIGNATURES ON THE loan DOCUMENT, כָּשֵׁר – IT IS VALID.

The Gemara explains:

יוֹצֵא מִתַּחַת יְדֵי שָׁלִישׁ – When **[the receipt] emerges from the hands of a third party** we accept his statement that the loan was paid, דְּהָא הֵימְנֵיהּ מַלְוֶה לְשָׁלִישׁ – **because the lender** himself agreed to **believe the third party** when he deposited the receipt with him.[6] יוֹצֵא לְאַחַר חִיתּוּם שְׁטָרוֹת נַמִּי – When **[the receipt] emerges in court below the signatures on the** loan **document,** it is **also** valid, דְּאִי לָאו דִּפְרִיעַ – **for if [the loan] were not paid,** לֹא הֲוָה מֵרַע לֵיהּ לִשְׁטָרֵי – **[the lender] would not have compromised his** loan **document** by writing a receipt on it.[7]

## הדרן עלך שנים אוחזין

## WE SHALL RETURN TO YOU, SHENAYIM OCHAZIN

NOTES

[Accordingly, the receipt in itself has no validity; it serves only to identify possible witnesses to the repayment.] If the witnesses who signed the receipt cannot testify to having seen the repayment, the lender may ignore the receipt and claim that he prepared the receipt in advance, to have it ready for the expected repayment (*Rashi*).

Since the receipt contains a *henpeik* (certification of signatures), we may be sure that it would not have been certified by the court unless they had determined that the debt had been paid (*Rashi*; see 16b note 16).

If there are no witnesses signed on it, who is to say it is valid?

Accordingly, it is clear that the first case of the Baraisa must also be referring to the certifying witnesses – i.e. the judges – and not to the witnesses to the text itself.

[I.e. it is valid by virtue of its certification.] As the Gemara explained above, the witnesses referred to by the Baraisa are those who certify the document [not those who signed it in the first place]. A court would not certify the receipt unless it knew that the note was paid (*Rashi;* see note 2).

Actually, the Gemara did not give this explanation regarding the Baraisa now being discussed (cited on 20b), but in regard to a second Baraisa (cited at the beginning of this *amud*). However, once the Gemara demonstrated in connection with the second Baraisa that the expression, "a receipt that does not have witnesses on it," means that it lacks signatures attesting to its certification, but it does contain the signatures of the witnesses to the receipt itself, it follows that the earlier Baraisa must also be referring to such a case, since it, too, refers to a document without signatures [as the Gemara now quotes] (*Maharsha* in explanation of *Rashi*).

6. The lender trusted the third party to give the borrower the receipt once the debt was paid. Thus, he in effect trusted him to say that the debt was paid and that the receipt is valid. Therefore, the court believes him to nullify the lender's claim.

[Clearly, the Baraisa is discussing a case in which the receipt is signed by witnesses.] Thus, it could only have been written by the lender, who then entrusted it to the the third party (*Rashi*). [If there were no witnesses at all, the lender could contest the validity of the receipt by claiming that he had never written it (see *Choshen Mishpat* 65:19, *Sma* 65:66).] As we explained above, when the Baraisa says that there were no witnesses on this document, it means that the document was not certified by judges. The receipt itself, however, was signed (see note 5).

7. Although a lender does occasionally prepare a receipt in advance, he would not write it below the debt note and cast doubts on its validity.

Another challenge:

תָּא שְׁמַע – **Come, learn** a disproof of Rav Yirmiyah bar Abba's ruling from the following Mishnah:[33] The Mishnah states that when orphans come to collect money from other orphans for a debt involving their fathers, they must swear שְׁבוּעָה שֶׁלֹּא פְּקָדָנוּ אַבָּא – **AN OATH: "THAT OUR FATHER DID NOT INSTRUCT US** on his deathbed that he had been paid, וְשֶׁלֹּא אָמַר לָנוּ אַבָּא – **NOR DID OUR FATHER TELL US** at anytime that he had been paid, וְשֶׁלֹּא מָצָאנוּ בֵּין שְׁטָרוֹתָיו שֶׁל אַבָּא – **NOR HAVE WE FOUND** a receipt **AMONG OUR FATHER'S DOCUMENTS,** שֶׁשְּׁטָר זֶה פָּרוּעַ – stating **THAT THIS** loan **DOCUMENT** of your father **IS PAID."** This implies that had they found such a receipt, they would have been obliged to abide by it. – ? –

The Gemara answers:

אָמַר רַב סַפְרָא – **Rav Safra said:** שֶׁנִּמְצָא בֵּין שְׁטָרוֹת קְרוּעִין – That Mishnah's concern is **for [a receipt] discovered among t[he]** father's **ripped documents.** The orphans must swear that th[ey] found no receipt among his discards.[34]

Another challenge:

תָּא שְׁמַע – **Come, learn** from the following Baraisa: [ש]וֹבֵר שֶׁיֵּשׁ עָלָיו עֵדִים – **A RECEIPT** in the possession of a lender, **WHICH H[AS]** the signatures of **WITNESSES ON IT,** יִתְקַיֵּים בְּחוֹתְמָיו – **SHOU[LD] BE CERTIFIED BY ITS SIGNERS.**[35] If the witnesses verify that th[ey] signed the receipt, the lender must abide by it. This contradic[ts] Rav Yirmiyah bar Abba's ruling. – ? –

The Gemara answers:

אֵימָא – **Say** in the text of the Baraisa: יִתְקַיֵּים מֵחוֹתְמָיו – T[he] essence of **[the receipt] should be certified from its signers,** [in] the following manner:[36]

NOTES

33. *Shevuos* 45a.

34. They are not, however, obliged to swear that they found no receipt among his current documents, because such a receipt would be disregarded in any case.

35. The debtor claims that the note held by the lender has been paid, and cites as evidence the receipt found in the lender's possession. The lender counters by claiming that the receipt was written in anticipation of a payment that was never received. As evidence, the lender cites the fact that he still holds the receipt. As the Gemara now understands this, the Baraisa rules that if the debtor can have the witnesses confirm their signatures on the receipt, he need not pay (*Rashi*).

However, as long as the debtor does not have the signatures certifie[d] the lender would be believed to say that he wrote the receipt i[n] anticipation of a payment that never arrived. Since he, himself, produce[d] the receipt, he is believed to say it is invalid as long as the signature[s] have not been authenticated (see *Rashi*).

36. I.e. the courts should try to locate the witnesses who signed th[e] receipt, and ascertain from them whether the debt had actually bee[n] paid. The receipt itself, however, is not accepted as evidence, as Ra[v] Yirmiyah bar Abba ruled.

חיישינן לשני שוירי א"ל רב חסדא לרבה פוק עיין דלאורתא בעי לה רב הונא מינך נפק דק ואשכח דתנן כל מעשה ב"ד הרי זה יחזיר א"ל רב עמרם לרבה היכי פשיט מר (א) איסורא מממונא א"ל ° (ג) תרדא שטרי חליצה ומיאונין תנן פקע ארזא דבי רב מר אמר משום לתאי דידי פקע ומר אמר משום לתאי דידי פקע: מצא בחפיסה או בדלוסקמא: (ג) מאי חפיסה אמר רבה בר בר חנה חמת קטנה מאי דלוסקמא אמר רבה בר שמואל טליקא דסבי: תכריך של שטרות או אגודה של שטרות וכו': ת"ר [א] כמה הוא תכריך של שטרות שלשה כרוכין זה בזה וכמה היא אגודה של שטרות שלשה קשורין זה בזה שמעת מינה (ד) קשר סימן הא תני רבי חייא [ב] שלשה כרוכין זה בזה אי הכי היינו תכריך [ג] תכריך כל חד וחד בראשה דחבריה אגודה דרמו אהדדי וכרוכות מאי מכריז מנין מאי אריא תלתא אפילו תרין נמי אלא כדאמר רבינא (ה) טבעא מכריז הכא נמי [ד] שטרי מכריז: רשב"ג אומר אחד הלוה משלשה יחזיר ללוה וכו': דאי ס"ד דמלוין נינהו מאי בעו גבי הדדי דלמא לקיומינהו אזלי דמקיימי דלמא מידא דספרא נפיל לא משהי איניש קיומיה בידא דספרא: שלשה שלוו מאחד יחזיר למלוה וכו': דאי ס"ד דלוין נינהו מאי בעו גבי הדדי דלמא למכתבנהו אזלי [ה] דכתיבי בתלת ידי ספרי ודלמא לקיומינהו אזלי מלוה מקיים שטריה לוה לא מקיים שטריה: אם יש עמהן סמפונות יעשה מה שבסמפונות: אמר רב ירמיה בר אבא אמר רב (ו) סמפון היוצא מתחת ידי מלוה אע"פ שכתוב בכתב ידו אינו אלא כמשחק ופסול לא מבעיא כתוב בכתב יד סופר דאיכא למימר ספרא אתרמי ליה וכתב אלא אפילו כתוב בכתב ידו פסול סבר דלמא מתרמי ואתי בין השמשות וקא פרע לי דאי לא יהיבנא ליה לא יהיב לי זוזי אכתוב אנא דכי אייתי לי זוזי אתן ליה תנן (ז) אם יש עמהן סמפונות יעשה מה שבסמפונות כדאמר רב ספרא שנמצא בין שטרות (י) קרועין הכא נמי [ח] שמצאו בין שטרות קרועין ת"ש (ז) [ט] נמצא לאחד בין שטרותיו שטרו של יוסף בן שמעון פרוע שטרות שניהם פרועין כדאמר רב ספרא שנמצא בין שטרות (כ) קרועין הכא נמי שנמצא בין שטרות קרועין ת"ש (ט) שבועה שלא פקדנו אבא ושלא אמר לנו אבא ושלא מצאנו בין שטרותיו של אבא ששטר זה פרוע אמר רב ספרא שנמצא בין שטרות קרועין ת"ש (י) סמפון שיש עליו עדים יתקיים בחותמיו אימא יתקיים מחותמיו דשיילינן

### רש"י

חיישינן לשני שוירי. אע"פ שבשוירי הידוע לנו אין בה שני יוסף בן שמעון שמא יש שוירי אחרת שיש שם יוסף בן שמעון ושם נכתב ומשליח אחר נפל: הרי זה יחזיר. דכיון דלא הוחזקו שני יוסף בן שמעון בעיר אחת לעיר אחרת שאינה ידועה לנו לא חיישינן: (א) תרדא. (ב) משועמם: פקע ארזא דבי רב. נשבר העמוד שבית המדרש נשען עליו: מר אמר משום לתאי דידי פקע. בשביל מזלי שקינא על שגדפתני: ומר אמר משום לתאי דידי פקע. שהשבת על דברי לביישני בבית המדרש: חמת. של עור שנותנין בו יין: טליקא דסבי. טסקא שהזקנים מצניעים בה כלי תשמישן שלא יצטרכו לחפש אחריהם: כרוכין זה בזה. וזהו סימן שהבעלים נותנים בהם זה יכריז מציאה שטרות מצאתי וזה יאמר שלי הם ושלשה הן כרוכין הן זה בזה: ש"מ קשר סימן. שיש קשרים שאינן דומין זה לזה ויאמר כך וכך הוא עשוי דאי לא תימא הכי מאי סימנא איכא הכא ותפשוט מינה בעלמא דקשר סימן ובעיא בעלמא היא ומשני מהכא לא תפשוט דתני רבי חייא ג' כרוכין זה בזה הוא אגודה דכרך הוי סימן דכולי עלמא כרכי שטרא שטרא לעצמו וקושרין אותן יחד וזה כרך שלשתן יחד: דרמו אהדדי. השכיבן זה על זה אורכו על אורכו של חבירו: מאי מכריז. המוצא מאי מכריז: מנין. ג' שטרות וזה בא ונותן סימן שכרוכין היו יחד: אפי' תרי נמי. הואיל ואין צריך לבעלים לתת סימן אלא כריכתן: כדאמר רבינא. באלו מציאות (דף כה.): שטרי מכריז. שטרות מצאתי וזה צריך שיאמר כך וכך היו וכרוכין היו הלכך דוקא תלתא אבל תרי מידע ידיע דמיעוט שטרות שתים ואין מנין סימן: ודלמא לקיומינהו אזלי. אצל סופר הדיינין הכותב הנפק לכל השטרות: דלווין היו. שפרעום והוחזרו להם: למכתבנהו אזלי. ומן הסופר נפל ומעולם לא לוו: סמפון. שובר המבטל שטר וכל דבר המבטל דבר קרי סמפון כדאמר (מ) גבי קדושי אשה ומכירת עבד שהמום קרוי סמפון מפני שמבטל את המקח: היוצא מתחת ידי מלוה. שהוא מונח בידו ולא ביד הלוה: ספרא אתרמי ליה. וסבר אם יבא בעל חובי לפרעני ואני אין שטרי עכשיו בידי ואם לא יהא שובר מוכן לי לא יפרע כלום: אפי' כתוב בכתב ידו. שיש לומר אם לא שנפרע למה ליה למהר ולכתוב לפני פרעון הואיל ויודע לכתוב: ואם יש עמהן סמפון. והכא במלוה עסקינן דקתני מצא שטר בין שטרותיו כו': כדאמר רב ספרא. לקמן בשמעתין: שנמצא לו. השטר שהשובר יוצא עליו: בין שטרותיו קרועים. והוא אינו קרוע לפיכך סומכין על השובר שמקום השטר מוכיח על השובר שהוא אמת שאם לא נפרע לא היה נותן השטר אצל השטרות קרועין כך שמעתי ולי נראה שנמצא השובר בין השטרות קרועין הלכך איכא למימר שנתקבל החוב והשובר הזה אין צריך למלוה הזה אלא ללוה והלוה שכח ביד זה לפיכך נתנו זה עם השטרות שאין צריכין לו דאי ס"ד מלוה כתבו להיות מוכן לו כשירצה לוה לפרעו לא נתנו עם שטרות שאין צריכין לו: נמצא בין שטרותיו. מתני' היא בגט פשוט (ב"ב דף קעב.) שני יוסף בן שמעון בעיר אחת ונמצא שובר לאדם אחד בין שטרותיו וכתוב בו שטרו של יוסף בן שמעון שבידי פרוע הוא והיה לו שני שטרות על שניהם: שטרות שניהם פרועין. שכל אחד יכול לומר על שלי נכתב שובר ובבבא בתרא פרכינן בלא שובר נמי הא תנן אין אחד יכול להוציא שטר חוב עליהם ומוקמינן ליה במשולשין בשטר ואין משולשין בשובר והא הכא דיוצא מתחת יד מלוה הוא: שנמצא. השטר בין השטרות פרועין וכל אחד אמר זהו שטר שלי: שבועה שלא פקדנו אבא. משנה היא בשבועות (דף מה.) יתומין מן היתומין לא יפרעו אלא בשבועה ומהו שבועתן שבועה שלא פקדנו אבא בגוססת מיתה ושלא אמר לנו קודם לכן ושלא מצינו שובר בין שטרותיו של אבא על שטר זה שיהא פרוע הא אם מצאו סמכינן עליה: יתקיים בחותמיו. קא ס"ד אם אמר מלוה לא נפרעתי ותדע שהרי לא מסרתי לידך יתקיים בחותמיו ע"פ חותמיו יתקיים אם החותמיו מעידין שחתמוהו אין המלוה נאמן אבל כל כמה דלא מקיים מהימן דמאן מפיק ליה מלוה ומלוה הא אמר פסול הוא:
דשיילינן

### תוספות

**איסורא** ממונא. וא"ת טפי אנן מחמירין בממונא (י) דהא אין אנו הולכים בממון אחר הרוב ובאיסורא אזלינן בתר רובא אפי' היכא דאיכא חזקה דאיסורא כנגד הרוב ולא חיישינן שמא במקום נקב קא שחיט וי"ל דמ"מ באשת איש החמירו דמים שאין להם סוף לא תנשא לכתחילה אע"פ שרובם מתים ועוד יש לומר דמדאורייתא לא חיישינן לשני יוסף בן שמעון אבל מדרבנן חיישינן משום לעז ובממונא לא שייך לעז לכך פריך שפיר היכי פשיט מר איסורא ממונא:

**מצא** בחפיסה או בדלוסקמא. תימה בשלמא חפיסה הוי סימן כדאמר בפרק שני (דף כח.) הוא אומר בחפיסה והיא אומרת בחפיסה ינתן לו דמידע ידעה דכל מאי דאית ליה בחפיסה מנח ליה משמע דלאיניש מעלמא הוי סימן אלא דלוסקמא היכי הוי סימן הלא דרך להניח שטרות בדלוסקמא כדתניא בתוספתא דשבועות עשרה דלוסקמאות מלאים שטרות מסרתי לך וי"ל דמיירי הכא שנותן בדלוסקמא עצמה סימן שאינו מובהק ולא חיישינן לשאלה לשמא השאיל לאחר והוא הניח בו שטרות דהכי תקון רבנן דלא חיישינן כמו שתקנו (ס) להחזיר אבידה בסימן שאינו מובהק אפילו סימנין לאו דאורייתא:

**סמפון** שיש עליו עדים יתקיים בחותמיו. נראה דמשמע ליה שהוא ביד המלוה מדקרי ליה סמפון דביד הלוה קרי ליה שובר ולשון סמפון לשון ביטול ועוד דביד הלוה פשיטא דכשר ע"י קיום:

הדרן עלך שנים אוחזין

### עין משפט נר מצוה

קעב א ב ג ד מיי' פי"ח מהלכות גזילה ואבידה הלכה ג סמג עשין עד טוש"ע ח"מ סי' סה סעיף י ע"ש:
קעג ה מיי' שם הלכה ד טוש"ע שם סעיף יא:
קעד ו ז ח מיי' פי"ו מהל' מלוה ולוה הלכה ח י סמג עשין צד טוש"ע ח"מ סי' סה סעיף יח:
קעה ט מיי' שם פכ"ד הל' ח סמג שם טוש"ע ח"מ סי' מט סעיף ט:

### רבינו חננאל

אמר רב הונא חיישינן לשני שורי נפק רבא דק ואשכח כל מעשה ב"ד הרי זה יחזיר. אמר ליה רב עמרם לרבא מתני' דקתני כל מעשה ב"ד ממונא הוא וגט אשה איסורא היכי פשיט מר איסורא מממונא. אמר ליה תרדי (א) שטרי חליצה ומיאונין תנן דאינון איסורא ואיסורא מאיסורא פשטינן. פקע ארזא דבי רב פי' נשברה קורת בית המדרש. רבא אמר בשביל שבא לדחות דבריי נשברה הקורה. ורב עמרם אמר בשביל שביזוני וקראני מוריד ריר מפי נשברה: **מצא בחפיסה** פי' חפיסה חמת קטנה. דלוסקומא תיבה בלשון יון. תכריך של שטרות ג' שטרות. כגון מגילה ראש זה בזנב זה. אגודה ג' שטרות נתונים זה על גבי זה (ב) וכתובים כולן כרך אחד. מה מכריז המוצאם מכריז הכי מי אבדו לו שטרות. **רשב"ג אומר אחד לוה** מג' כגון ראובן לוה משמעון ועוד לוה מלוי ועוד מיהודה וכתב השטר לכל אחד בפני עצמו ונמצאו עכשיו שלשתן קשורין ודאי פרעם הלוה ולקח השטר שעליו ומן הלוה נפלו. וכן ג' שלוו מאחד ונמצאו שלשתן קשורין ודאי מן המלוה נפלו והוא שנמצאו מקוימים ובכתב שלשה סופרין שאם שלשתן בכתב סופר אחד חיישינן דלמא מן הסופר נפלו: **מצא שטר בין** שטרותיו ואינו יודע מה טיבו יהא מונח עד שיבוא אליהו. אם יש עמהן סמפון פי' סמפון שובר או תנאים. אמר רבי ירמיה בר אבא אמר רבי יוחנן סמפון היוצא מתחת ידי מלוה אע"פ שכתוב בכתב ידו אינו אלא כמשחק ופסול וכל מה דאקשי' עליה פריק כגון שנמצא בין שטרותיו קרועין. ת"ש שבועה שלא פקדנו אבא ושלא אמר לנו אבא ושלא מצינו בשטרותיו ששטר זה פרוע. אמר רב ספרא כגון שנמצא זה השטר חוב בין שטרותיו קרועין דמוכחא מילתא דאי לאו דפריען לא הוה יהיב ליה בהדי שטרותיו קרועין אבל בסמפון לבדו לא. ת"ש סמפון שיש עליו עדים יתקיים בחותמיו. ופריק אימא יתקיים מחותמיו דשאלינן לסהדי דחתימין חזיתון דפרעיה קמייכו אי לא. ת"ש סמפון שיש

### מסורת הש"ס

א) [ברכות יט:, כת... מ:, מו:, קדושין ...] ב) [זבחים כה: ...] ג) גיטין כח., ד) [... כג:, כה:], ה) [לקמן ...] ו) פרועין, מהר... ז) בבא בתרא ... ח) פרועין, ט) שב... מה., י) פרו... כ) סנהדרין לא:, ל) ... בבא קמא קה: רש"י ... תדורא, מ) [כתובות ...] נ) [וע"ע תוס' בבא ...] ס: ד"ה קמ"ל, ס) [... ס:].

### הגהות הב"ח

(א) רש"י ד"ה ... משועמם. נ"ב ובכרי... דף יח ע"ב פי' רש"י ... שוטה או עצל:

### גליון הש"ס

גמ' תרדא. עיין ב"ק קה ע"ב וזבחים דף ... ע"ב:

### ליקוטי רש"י

חיישינן לשני שוירי. אע"פ שבא אחד ... ואמר ממני נפל ... היה משלחו לאשתו ... אנו שאין שם בשוירי ... אנשים ששמותיהן ... חיישינן שמא שוירי ... יש ויש בה יוסף בן ... אחר [לעיל ...] דלאורתא. בלילה [ברכות ג:]. כל מעשה ב"ד ה"ז יחזיר. מילתא דאתא לב"ד ... דליכא למיחש ... עליהן שלא ליתן ... יחזיר וזה מקויים ... היה ולכך הוצא שם [... יח:]. היכי פשיט איסורא ממונא ... ממונא קל מאיס... [ברכות יט:]. תרד... שוטה לשון אחר ... [כריתות יח:]. שוטה ... [זבחים כה:]. חמת בוטי"ל בלע"ז ... עור [גיטין כח.]. נוד עור [חולין ...] דלוסקמא. כמו ... וסק לשום בו [... מגילה כו:]. טליק... טסק"א בלע"ז [גיטין ...] טבעא מכריז. מטב... מצאתי הלכך תרי... סימנא הוא דמי... מטבעות ג' [לקמן ...] שבועה שלא פקד... אבא. בשעת מי... ששטר זה פרוע. ... אמר לנו קודם ... ושלא מצאנו. שובר ... שטר זה [שבועות ...] סמפון שיש ע... עדים. שובר ולא מת... ידי לוה כמשפ... יתקיים בחותמ... יתקיים [השובר] בחות... ויעידו עדים על חתי... ידיהן וכשר [סנהדרין לא...]

### לעזי רש"י

טסק"א. פירוש ... ולמחמת (רש"י מגילה כו ע"ב ד"ה דלוסק... ועיין רש"י מעילה דף ... ע"א ד"ה דלוסקמא).

lender's benefit. Thus, they would not have been found together unless they had fallen from the possession of the lender.

The Mishnah states:

אִם יֵשׁ עִמָּהֶן סִמְפּוֹנוֹת – IF THERE ARE unissued RECEIPTS AMONG [HIS DOCUMENTS], יַעֲשֶׂה מַה שֶּׁבַּסִּמְפּוֹנוֹת – HE SHOULD ABIDE BY THAT WHICH IS recorded IN THE RECEIPTS.

The Gemara cites a related ruling:

אָמַר רַב יִרְמְיָה בַּר אַבָּא אָמַר רַב – **Rav Yirmiyah bar Abba said in the name of Rav:** סִמְפּוֹן הַיּוֹצֵא מִתַּחַת יְדֵי מַלְוֶה – **A receipt that emerges from the hands of the lender,**[24] i.e. it is found in his possession rather than the borrower's, אַף עַל פִּי שֶׁכָּתוּב בִּכְתַב יָדוֹ – **even if it is written in [the lender's] own handwriting,** אֵינוֹ אֶלָּא כִּמְשַׂחֵק – **does nothing more than mock** the borrower, וּפָסוּל – **and it is invalid.**[25] Thus, the note against which the receipt was written may still be collected.

The Gemara explains:

לֹא מִבַּעְיָא – **It is not** even **necessary** to say that the receipt is invalid כָּתוּב בִּכְתַב יַד סוֹפֵר – when it is **written in the handwriting of a scribe,** דְּאִיכָּא לְמֵימַר – **for we may** then **say** that סָפְרָא אִתְרַמֵּי לֵיהּ וְכָתַב – **[the lender] chanced upon a scribe and** had **him write** the receipt in anticipation of the note's payment.[26] Thus, the existence of the receipt in the lender's possession proves nothing. אֶלָּא אֲפִילּוּ כָּתוּב בִּכְתַב יָדוֹ פָּסוּל – **However, even if [the receipt] is written in [the lender's] own handwriting it is invalid,** for it is still possible that he wrote it in advance of payment for the following reason:[27] סָבַר – **He thought** to himself: דִּלְמָא מִתְרַמֵּי וְאָתֵי בֵּין הַשְּׁמָשׁוֹת – **It might happen that [the borrower] will appear** near **sunset** on Friday afternoon, when there is no time to write a receipt before the onset of the Sabbath, וְקָא פָּרַע לִי – **and he will** offer **to pay me.** דְּאִי לֹא יְהִיבְנָא לֵיהּ – **Now, if I do not give him** a receipt, לֹא יָהֵיב לִי זוּזֵי – **he will not give me** my **money.** אֶכְתּוֹב אֲנָא – Therefore, **let me write** a receipt in advance, דְּכִי אַיְיתֵי לִי זוּזֵי – **so that when he brings me the money,** אֶתֵּן לֵיהּ – **I will** have it ready to **give to him.** Thus, the presence of the receipt in the lender's hands does not prove that the debt has been paid.[28]

The Gemara questions this ruling:

תְּנַן – **We learned in** our **Mishnah:** אִם יֵשׁ עִמָּהֶן סִמְפּוֹנוֹת – THERE ARE unissued RECEIPTS AMONG [HIS DOCUMENTS], יַעֲשֶׂה מַה שֶּׁבַּסִּמְפּוֹנוֹת – HE [the lender][29] SHOULD ABIDE BY THAT WHI[CH] IS recorded IN THE RECEIPTS. This contradicts Rav Yirmiyah b[ar] Abba's ruling that a lender need not abide by a receipt [he] discovers in his possession. – ? –

The Gemara answers:

כִּדְאָמַר רַב סָפְרָא – Our Mishnah's ruling may be explained **as R[av] Safra said** in explanation of another Mishnah cited belo[w]: שֶׁנִּמְצָא בֵּין שְׁטָרוֹת קְרוּעִין – That Mishnah speaks of a case [in] which **[the receipt] was discovered** by the lender's fam[ily] **among** his **ripped documents.** Therefore, we presume that t[he] loan for which it was written was paid. הָכָא נַמִּי – **Here too** [we] may say that our Mishnah's ruling to abide by the receipt refers [to] a case שֶׁמְּצָאוֹ בֵּין שְׁטָרוֹת קְרוּעִין – **in which [the lende[r]] discovered [the receipt] among** his **ripped documents,** indica[t]ing that it had been discarded and the debt had been paid.[30]

The Gemara again challenges Rav Yirmiyah bar Abba's rulin[g]: תָּא שְׁמַע – **Come, learn** from the following Mishnah:[31] [נִמְ]צָא לְאֶחָד בֵּין שְׁטָרוֹתָיו – If **there** WAS DISCOVERED AMONG SOMEONE['S] DOCUMENTS a receipt stating: שְׁטָרוֹ שֶׁל יוֹסֵף בֶּן שִׁמְעוֹן פָּרוּעַ – "THE loan DOCUMENT OF YOSEF BEN SHIMON IS PAID," and the[re] are two people by this name living in this town who owe money [to] this lender, שְׁטָרוֹת שְׁנֵיהֶם פְּרוּעִין – THE loan DOCUMENTS [OF] BOTH ARE treated as PAID,[32] i.e. the lender cannot successful[ly] sue either Yosef ben Shimon for payment based on the[se] documents. This Mishnah states that a lender is obliged to abi[de] by a receipt he discovers in his possession, contrary to R[av] Yirmiyah bar Abba's ruling. – ? –

The Gemara answers:

כִּדְאָמַר רַב סָפְרָא – That Mishnah's ruling may be explained [as] **Rav Safra said** in explanation of another Mishnah: [שֶׁ]נִּמְצָא בֵּין שְׁטָרוֹת קְרוּעִין – The Mishnah speaks of a case in which **[th[e] receipt] was discovered** by the lender's family **among** h[is] **ripped documents,** indicating that the debt was paid. [הָכָ]א נַמִּי – **Here too,** we may say that the Mishnah's ruling requiring th[e] lender to abide by the receipt made out to Yosef ben Shimon refe[rs] to a case שֶׁנִּמְצָא בֵּין שְׁטָרוֹת קְרוּעִין – **in which [the receipt] wa[s] discovered among** his **ripped documents.**

NOTES

24. Literally: from under the hands of the lender. Rav Yirmiyah [and the Mishnahs which the Gemara will soon cite] refers to a case in which the lender does not remember whether the debt was paid (see 20a note 30; see next note).

25. A receipt is effective only when it is held by the borrower, since it is then evident that it was given to him by the lender. In the hands of the lender, however, it proves nothing, because it is possible that the lender wrote it in anticipation of being paid, but never actually received payment. Its presence in the hands of the lender therefore does nothing more than mock the borrower, by seeming to demonstrate his release from the debt when in fact he must still pay it.

26. The lender is concerned that he may not have the original loan document on hand to return to the borrower when he comes to repay the loan [and that he will also not be able to get a scribe to write a receipt at that moment]. Since this will result in the borrower refusing to pay, the lender arranges to have a receipt written in advance (*Rashi*).

27. Since the lender knows how to write a receipt himself, there would seem to be no reason to write it in advance. Thus, the Gemara must explain why a literate lender would do so (*Rashi*).

28. As long as the borrower cannot prove that he paid the debt, the presence of the loan document in the hands of the lender is considered sufficient evidence that he did not pay.

29. Clearly, the Mishnah is saying that the lender found the receipt, since it begins its discussion of documents found in one's possession by stating that the unknown document was found among his othe[r] documents (*Rashi*). That first sentence clearly refers to documents [of] debts owed to the lender. Thus, the case of the receipt that follows mus[t] also refer to a receipt found among the lender's [loan] documents (*Pn[ei] Yehoshua*).

30. Had the debt remained unpaid, the lender would not have placed th[e] receipt together with his discarded documents, but would have kept [it] ready for the borrower among his current documents. Its presenc[e] among the discarded documents indicates that the note was paid, an[d] the borrower forgot to take the receipt. The lender, having no furthe[r] need for the receipt, discarded it among his other useless document[s] (*Rashi,* second explanation).

31. *Bava Basra* 172a.

32. Although only one Yosef ben Shimon paid his debt, each Yosef be[n] Shimon can claim that he is the one who paid, and the burden of proo[f] of non-payment falls on the lender.

The Gemara in *Bava Basra* (173a) asks that if the loan documents d[o] not specify which Yosef ben Shimon borrowed money, then even if w[e] were to disregard the receipt, the lender could still not press fo[r] payment, since he would not be able to prove which Yosef ben Shimo[n] is the one mentioned in the loan documents! The Gemara explains tha[t] the Mishnah refers to a case in which the names of the borrower'[s] grandfathers were included in the loan documents, but not in th[e] receipt. Therefore, the lender can identify the borrower in each loa[n] document, but not in the receipt (*Rashi*).

חיישינן לשני שוירי א"ל רב חסדא לרבה פוק עיין דלאורתא בעי לה רב הונא מינך נפק דק ואשכח דתנן כל מעשה ב"ד הרי זה יחזיר א"ל רב עמרם לרבה היכי פשיט מר איסורא מממונא א"ל תרדא שטרי חליצה ומיאונין תנן פקע ארזא דבי רב מר אמר משום לתאי דידי פקע ומר אמר משום לתאי דידי פקע: מצא בחפיסה או בדלוסקמא: מאי חפיסה אמר רבה בר בר חנה חמת קטנה מאי דלוסקמא אמר רבה בר שמואל טליקא דסבי: תכריך של שטרות או אגודה של שטרות וכו': ת"ר כמה הוא תכריך של שטרות שלשה כרוכין זה בזה וכמה היא אגודה של שטרות שלשה קשורין זה בזה שמעת מינה קשר סימן הא תני רבי חייא שלשה כרוכין זה בזה אי הכי היינו תכריך תכריך כל חד וחד בראשה דחבריה אגודה דרמו אהדדי וכרוכות מאי מכריז מנין מאי אריא תלתא אפילו תרין נמי אלא כדאמר רבינא טבעא מכריז הכא נמי שטרי מכריז: רשב"ג אומר אחד הלוה משלשה יחזיר ללוה וכו': דאי ס"ד דמלוין נינהו מאי בעו גבי הדדי דלמא לקוימינהו אזלי דמקיימי דלמא מידא דספרא נפיל לא משהי איניש קיומיה בידא דספרא: שלשה שלוו מאחד יחזיר למלוה וכו': דאי ס"ד דלוין נינהו מאי בעו גבי הדדי דלמא למכתבנהו אזלי דכתיבי בתלת ידי ספרי ודלמא לקוימינהו אזלי מלוה מקיים שטריה לוה לא מקיים שטריה: אם יש עמהן סמפונות יעשה מה שבסמפונות: אמר רב ירמיה בר אבא אמר רב סמפון היוצא מתחת ידי מלוה אע"פ שכתוב בכתב ידו אינו אלא כמשחק ופסול לא מבעיא כתוב בכתב יד סופר דאיכא למימר ספרא אתרמי ליה וכתב אלא אפילו כתוב בכתב ידו פסול סבר דלמא מתרמי ואתי בין השמשות וקא פרע לי דאי לא יהיבנא ליה לא יהיב לי זוזי אכתוב אנא דכי אייתי לי זוזי אתן ליה תנן אם יש עמהן סמפונות יעשה מה שבסמפונות כדאמר רב ספרא שנמצא בין שטרות קרועין הכא נמי שמצאו בין שטרות קרועין ת"ש נמצא לאחד בין שטרותיו שטרו של יוסף בן שמעון פרוע שטרות שניהם פרועין כדאמר רב ספרא שנמצא בין שטרות קרועין הכא נמי שנמצא בין שטרות קרועין ת"ש שבועה שלא פקדנו אבא ושלא אמר לנו אבא ושלא מצאנו בין שטרותיו של אבא ששטר זה פרוע אמר רב ספרא שנמצא בין שטרות קרועין ת"ש סמפון שיש עליו עדים יתקיים בחותמיו אימא יתקיים מחותמיו
דשיילינן

**רש"י**

חיישינן לשני שוירי. אע"פ שבשוירי הידוע לנו אין בה שני יוסף בן שמעון שמא יש שוירי אחרת שיש שם יוסף בן שמעון ושם נכתב ומשליח אחר נפל: הרי זה יחזיר. דכיון דלא הוחזקו שני יוסף בן שמעון בעיר אחת לעיר אחרת שאינה ידועה לנו לא חיישינן: (א) תרדא. משועמם: פקע ארזא דבי רב. נשבר העמוד שבית המדרש נשען עליו: מר אמר משום לתאי דידי פקע. בשביל מזלי שקינא על שגדפתני: ומר אמר משום לתאי דידי פקע. שהשבת על דברי לביישני בבית המדרש: חמת. של עור שנותנין בו יין: טליקא דסבי. טסקא שהזקנים מצניעים בה כלי תשמישן שלא יצטרכו לחפש אחריהם: כרוכין זה בזה. וזהו סימן שהבעלים נותנים בהם זה יכריז מציאה שטרות מצאתי וזה יאמר שלי הם ושלשה הן כרוכין הן זה בזה: ש"מ קשר סימן. שיש קשרים שאין דומין זה לזה ויאמר כך וכך הוא עשוי דאי לא תימא הכי מאי סימנא איכא הכא ותפשוט מינה בעלמא דקשר סימן ובעיא בעלמא היא ומשני מהכא לא תפשוט דתני רבי חייא ג' כרוכין זה בזה הוא אגודה דבכך הוי סימן דכולי עלמא כרכי שטרא שטרא לעצמו וקושרין אותן יחד וזה כרך שלשתן יחד: דרמו אהדדי. השכיבן זה על זה אורכו על אורכו של חבירו: מאי מכריז. המוצא מאי מכריז: מנין. ג' שטרות וזה בא ונותן סימן שכרוכין היו יחד: אפי' תרי נמי. הואיל ואין צריך לבעלים לתת סימן אלא כריכתן: כדאמר רבינא. באלו מציאות (דף כה.): שטרי מכריז. שטרות מצאתי וזה צריך שיאמר כך וכך היו וכרוכין היו הלכך דוקא תלתא אבל תרי מידע ידיע דמיעוט שטרות שתים ואין מנין סימן: ודלמא לקוימינהו אזלי. אצל סופר הדיינין הכותב הנפק לכל השטרות: דלווין היו. שפרעום והוחזרו להם: למכתבנהו אזלי. ומן הסופר נפל ומעולם לא לוו: סמפון. שובר המבטל שטר וכל דבר המבטל דבר קרי סמפון כדאמר גבי קדושי אשה ומכירת עבד שהמום קרוי סמפון מפני שמבטל את המקח: היוצא מתחת ידי מלוה. שהוא מונח בידו ולא ביד הלוה: ספרא אתרמי ליה. וסבר אם יבא בעל חובי לפרעני ואני אין שטרי עכשיו בידי ואם לא יהא שובר מוכן לי לא יפרע כלום: אפי' כתוב בכתב ידו. שיש לומר אם לא שנפרע למה ליה למהר ולכתוב לפני פרעון הואיל ויודע לכתוב: ואם יש עמהן סמפון. והכא במלוה עסקינן דקתני מצא שטר בין שטרותיו כו': כדאמר רב ספרא. לקמן בשמעתין: שנמצא לו. השטר שהשובר יוצא עליו: בין שטרותיו קרועים. והוא אינו קרוע לפיכך סומכין על השובר שמקום השטר מוכיח על השובר שהוא אמת שאם לא נפרע לא היה נותן השטר אצל השטרות קרועין כך שמעתי ולי נראה שנמצא השובר בין השטרות קרועין הלכך איכא למימר שנתקבל החוב והשובר הזה אין צריך למלוה הזה אלא ללוה והלוה שכח ביד זה לפיכך נתנו זה עם השטרות שאין צריכין לו דאי ס"ד מלוה כתבו להיות מוכן לו כשילוה לוה לפרעו לא נתנו עם שטרות שאין צריכין לו: נמצא בין שטרותיו. מתני' היא בגט פשוט (ב"ב דף קעב.) שני יוסף בן שמעון בעיר אחת ונמצא שובר לאדם אחד בין שטרותיו וכתוב בו שטרו של יוסף בן שמעון שבידי פרוע הוא והיה לו שני שטרות על שניהם: שטרות שניהם פרועין. שכל אחד יכול לומר על שלי נכתב שובר ובבבא בתרא פרכינן בלא שובר נמי הא תנן אין אחד יכול להוציא שטר חוב עליהם ומוקמינן ליה במשולשין בשטר ואין משולשין בשובר והא הכא דיוצא מתחת יד מלוה הוא: שנמצא. השטר בין השטרות פרועין וכל אחד אמר זהו שטר שלי: שבועה שלא פקדנו אבא. משנה היא בשבועות (דף מה.) יתומין מן היתומין לא יפרעו אלא בשבועה ומהו שבועתן שבועה שלא פקדנו אבא בצוואת מיתה ושלא אמר לנו קודם לכן ושלא מצינו שובר בין שטרותיו של אבא על שטר זה שיהא פרוע הא אם מצאו סמכינן עליה: יתקיים בחותמיו. קא ס"ד אם אמר מלוה לא נפרעתי ותדע שהרי לא מסרתי לידך יתקיים בחותמיו ע"פ חותמיו יתקיים אם החותמיו מעידין שחתמוהו אין המלוה נאמן אבל כל כמה דלא מקיים מהימן דמאן מפיק ליה מלוה ומלוה הא אמר פסול הוא:
דשיילינן

**תוספות**

איסורא מממונא. וא"ת טפי אנן מחמירין בממונא דהא אין אנו הולכים בממון אחר הרוב ובאיסורא אזלינן בתר רובא אפי' היכא דאיכא חזקה דאיסורא כנגד הרוב ולא חיישינן שמא במקום נקב קא שחיט וי"ל דמ"מ באשת איש החמירו דמים שאין להם סוף לא תנשא לכתחילה אע"פ שרובם מתים ועוד יש לומר דמדאורייתא לא חיישינן לשני יוסף בן שמעון אבל מדרבנן חיישינן משום לעז ובממונא לא שייך לעז לכך פריך שפיר היכי פשיט מר איסורא מממונא: מצא בחפיסה או בדלוסקמא. תימה בשלמא חפיסה הוי סימן כדאמר בפרק שני (דף כח.) הוא אומר בחפיסה והיא אומרת בחפיסה ינתן לו דמידע ידעה דכל מאי דאית ליה בחפיסה מנח ליה משמע דלאינש מעלמא הוי סימן אלא דלוסקמא היכי הוי סימן הלא דרך להניח שטרות בדלוסקמא כדתניא בתוספתא דשבועות עשרה דלוסקמאות מלאים שטרות מסרתי לך וי"ל דמיירי הכא שנותן בדלוסקמא עצמה סימן שאינו מובהק ולא חיישינן לשאלה לשמא השאיל לאחר ואותו הניח בו שטרות דהכי תקון רבנן דלא חיישינן כמו שתקנו להחזיר אבידה בסימן שאינו מובהק אפילו סימנין לאו דאורייתא: סמפון שיש עליו עדים יתקיים בחותמיו. נראה דמשמע ליה שהוא ביד המלוה מדקרי ליה סמפון דביד הלוה קרי ליה שובר ולשון סמפון לשון ביטול ועוד דביד הלוה פשיטא דכשר ע"י קיום:

הדרן עלך שנים אוחזין

**עין משפט נר מצוה**

קעב א ב ג ד מיי' פי"ח מהלכות גזילה ואבידה הלכה ג סמג עשין עד טוש"ע ח"מ סי' סה סעיף י ע"ש:
קעג ה מיי' שם הלכה ד טוש"ע שם סעיף יא:
קעד ו ז ח מיי' פי"ו מהל' מלוה ולוה הלכה ח י סמג עשין לד טוש"ע ח"מ סי' סה סעיף יח:
קעה ט מיי' שם פכ"ד הל' ח סמג שם טוש"ע ח"מ סי' מט סעיף ט:

**רבינו חננאל**

אמר רב הונא חיישינן לשני שוירי נפק רבא דק ואשכח כל מעשה ב"ד הרי זה יחזיר. אמר ליה רב עמרם לרבא מתני' דקתני כל מעשה ב"ד ממונא הוא וגט אשה איסורא היכי פשיט מר איסורא מממונא. אמר ליה תרדי א) שטרי חליצה ומיאונין תנן דאינון איסורא ואיסורא מאיסורא פשטינן. פקע ארזא דבי רב פי' נשברה קורת בית המדרש. רבא אמר בשביל שבא לדחות דבריי נשברה הקורה. ורב עמרם אמר בשביל שביזני וקראני מוריד ריר מפי נשברה: מצא בחפיסה פי' חפיסה חמת קטנה. דלוסקומא תיבה בלשון יון. תכריך של שטרות ג' שטרות. כגון מגילה ראש זה בזנב זה. אגודה ג' שטרות נתונים זה על גבי זה ב) וכתובים כולן כרך אחד. מה מכריז המוצאם מכריז הכי מי אבדו לו שטרות. רשב"ג אומר אחד לוה מג' כגון ראובן לוה משמעון ועוד לוה מלוי ועוד מיהודה וכתב השטר לכל אחד בפני עצמו ונמצאו עכשיו שלשתן קשורין ודאי פרעם הלוה ולקח השטר שעליו ומן הלוה נפלו. וכן ג' שלוו מאחד ונמצאו שלשתן קשורין ודאי מן המלוה נפלו והוא שנמצאו מקוימים ובכתב שלשה סופרין שאם שלשתן בכתב סופר אחד חיישינן דלמא מן הסופר נפלו: מצא שטר בין שטרותיו ואינו יודע מה טיבו יהא מונח עד שיבוא אליהו. אם יש עמהן סמפון פי' סמפון שובר או תנאים. אמר רבי ירמיה בר אבא אמר רבי יוחנן סמפון היוצא מתחת ידי מלוה אע"פ שכתוב בכתב ידו אינו אלא כמשחק ופסול וכל מה דאקשי' עליה פריק כגון שנמצא בין שטרותיו קרועין. ת"ש שבועה שלא פקדנו אבא ושלא אמר לנו אבא ושלא מצינו בשטרותיו ששטר זה פרוע. אמר רב ספרא כגון שנמצא זה השטר חוב בין שטרותיו קרועין דמוכחא מילתא דאי לאו דפריען לא הוה יהיב ליה בהדי שטרותיו קרועין אבל בסמפון לבדו לא. ת"ש סמפון שיש עליו עדים יתקיים בחותמיו. ופריק אימא יתקיים מחותמיו דשאלינן לסהדי דחתימין חזיתון דפרעיה קמייכו אי לא. ת"ש סמפון
שיש

**מסורת הש"ס**

א) [ברכות יט:, כתו... מ:, מו:, קדושין ...] ב) [זבחים כה: וש...] ג) גיטין כח., ד) [ל... כג:, כה:], ה) [לקמן כ...] ו) פרועין, מהרש... ז) בבא בתרא קע... ח) פרועין, ט) שבו... מה., י) פרו... כ) סנהדרין לא., ל) בבא קמא קה: רש"י ... מ) [כתובות ...] נ) [וע"ע תוס' בבא ק... ס: ד"ה קמ"ל], ס) [ל... ס:].

**הגהות הב"ח**

(א) רש"י ד"ה ת... משועמם. נ"ב ובכרי... דף יח ע"ב פי' רש"י ת... שוטה או עלג:

**גליון הש"ס**

גמ' תרדא. עיין ב"ק קה ע"ב וזבחים דף ... ע"ב:

**ליקוטי רש"י**

חיישינן לשני שוי... אע"פ שבא אחד לפ... ואמר ממני נפל ופ... היה משלחו לאשתו ויוד... אנו שאין שם בשוירי... אנשים ששמותיהן ... חיישינן שמא שוירי אח... יש ויש בה יוסף בן שמ... אחר [לעיל יח... דלאורתא. ללילה ... ברכות ג:]. כל מעש... ב"ד ה"ז יחזיר. מילתא דאתא לב"ד לק... דליכא למיחש לגנ... עליהן שלא ליתנן ... יחזיר וזה מקויים ב... היה ולכך הוצא שם [ל... יח:]. היכי פשיט ... איסורא ממונ... ממונא קל מאיס... [ברכות יט:]. תרד... שוטה לשון אחר ... [כריתות יח:]. שוטה ... [זבחים כה:]. חמ... בולזול"א בלע"ז והיא ... עור [גיטין כח.]. נוד ... עור [חולין ק... דלוסקמא. כמו אמת... ושק לשום בו [ס... [מגילה כו:]. טליק... טשק"א בלע"ז [גיטין ש... טבעא מכריז. מטבע... מצאתי הלכך תרי ... סימנא הוא דמיע... מטבעות ב' [לקמן כ... שבועה שלא פקד... אבא. בשעת מי... ששטר זה פרוע. ... אמר לנו קודם ... ושלא מצאנו. שובר ... שטר זה [שבועות מ... סמפון שיש ע... עדים. שובר ויצא מת... ידי לוה כמשפ... יתקיים בחותמ... יתקיים [השובר] בחות... יעידו עדים על חתי... ידיהן וכשר [סנהדרין לא...

**לעזי רש"י**

טסק"א. פירוש ... ואמתחת (רש"י מגילה כו ע"ב ד"ה דלוסק... ועיין רש"י מעילה דף ... ע"א ד"ה דלוסקמא)

The case of **a bundle** is דְּרָמוּ אַהֲדָדֵי – **where they are placed one atop the other,** וּכְרוּכוֹת – **and** then **rolled together.**

The Gemara details the procedure for announcing the documents so that they can be claimed:[12]

מַאי מַכְרִיז – **What does [the finder] announce** to let the owner know that he found them? מִנְיָן – **The number** of documents; in the case of the Mishnah, for example, he announces that he found three documents.[13]

The Gemara asks:

מַאי אִרְיָא תְּלָתָא – If so, **why** does the Mishnah **discuss** a case of **three** documents? אֲפִילוּ תְּרֵין נַמִּי – **Even** if only **two** documents are found, they may **also** be announced and identified by the Mishnah's method![14] –? –

The Gemara concludes:

אֶלָּא – **Rather,** כִּדְאָמַר רָבִינָא – the procedure here must be **as Ravina said** concerning the return of lost coins: טִבְעָא מַכְרִיז – **[The finder] announces** that he found **coins,** without specifying the number. The number of coins must be provided by the owner. הָכָא נַמִּי – **Here too,** שְׁטָרֵי מַכְרִיז – **[the finder] announces** that he found **documents,** without specifying the number. The number of documents mentioned by the owner then serves to identify the bundle. Therefore, the Mishnah must discuss a case of at least three documents, for if only two documents were lost, mentioning the number would not suffice to identify them.[15]

The Mishnah states:

רַבָּן שִׁמְעוֹן בֶּן גַּמְלִיאֵל אוֹמֵר – **RABBAN SHIMON BEN GAMLIEL SAYS:** אֶחָד הַלֹּוֶה מִשְּׁלֹשָׁה – If one found three documents concerning **ONE** person **WHO BORROWED FROM THREE** different people, יַחֲזִיר לַלֹּוֶה וכו׳ – **HE SHOULD RETURN** them **TO THE BORROWER etc.** for they certainly belong to him.

The Gemara explains the reason for this:

דְּאִי סָלְקָא דַּעְתָּךְ דְּמַלְוִין נִינְהוּ – **For if you should think that [the documents]** perhaps **belong to the** three **lenders,** מַאי בָּעוּ גַּבֵּי הֲדָדֵי – **what are they doing together!?**[16]

The Gemara counters:

דִּלְמָא לְקִיּוּמִינְהוּ אָזְלֵי – **Perhaps they were going to have** the documents **certified,** and they were lost in the process.[17] Thus, the documents found might in fact belong to the lenders and n the borrower. – ? –

The Gemara answers:

דִּמְקַיְּימֵי – The Mishnah refers to a case **in which [the doc ments]** found **were** already **certified.**[18]

The Gemara persists:

דִּלְמָא מִיָּדָא דְסָפְרָא נָפִיל – Even so, **perhaps they fell from t hands of the scribe** after he certified them, but in fact they belo to the lenders?

The Gemara answers:

לֹא מַשְׁהֵי אִינִישׁ קִיּוּמֵיהּ בִּיָדָא דְסָפְרָא – **A person does not leave h certified [document] in the hands of a scribe.** Thus, they a not likely to have been lost from the scribe's possession.[19]

The Mishnah states:

שְׁלֹשָׁה שֶׁלָּווּ מֵאֶחָד – If the three documents concern **THREE** peop **WHO BORROWED FROM ONE** person, יַחֲזִיר לַמַּלְוֶה וכו׳ – [TH **FINDER] SHOULD RETURN** them **TO THE LENDER etc.**

The Gemara explains the reason for this:

דְּאִי סָלְקָא דַּעְתָּךְ דְּלֹוִין נִינְהוּ – **For if you should think that [t documents] belong to the borrowers,**[20] מַאי בָּעוּ גַּבֵּי הֲדָדֵי **what are they doing together?!**

The Gemara questions this:

דִּלְמָא לְמִכְתְּבִנְהוּ אָזְלֵי – **Perhaps [the borrowers] were going a scribe to have [the documents] written** for the loans they we planning to take out, and the scribe lost them?[21] Thus, t documents found may belong to the borrowers! – ? –

The Gemara answers:

דִּכְתִיבֵי בִּתְלָת יְדֵי סָפְרֵי – The Mishnah refers to a case **in whic [the three documents] were written in the handwritings three** different **scribes.**[22]

The Gemara counters:

וְדִלְמָא לְקִיּוּמִינְהוּ אָזְלֵי – **Perhaps they were going to have** t documents **certified,** and they were lost in the process.[23] Thu the documents might still belong to the borrowers. – ? –

The Gemara answers:

מַלְוֶה מְקַיֵּים שְׁטָרֵיהּ – **A lender** goes to court to **certify h document,** to make it easier to collect his debt; לֹא מְקַיֵּים שְׁטָרֵיהּ – **a borrower does not** go to **certify his document** for th

NOTES

ingly, when one rolls a second document over it, one is rolling it over the top part ["head"] of the first document.]

12. The obligation to return lost objects requires the finder to announce his find, so that the owner will know from whom to claim them. See next chapter.

13. The owner can then identify them by stating that they were rolled together (*Rashi*).

14. However, if the Mishnah requires the number to be part of the identification, it is understandable why it chooses a case of three rather than two documents. This is because even if the finder does not announce the number of documents, he must at least announce that he found documents. Now the word "documents," being plural, implies at least two. Thus, the claimant would not be able to reclaim his documents by specifying that he lost two, because he would not be saying anything more than was implicit in the announcement (*Rashi* ד״ה שטרי מכריז).

*Rashi* states that even when identifying the number of documents in the bundle, the owner must also specify that they are rolled together. *Maharshal* (*Chochmas Shlomo*) explains that ordinarily, either of these two identifications would suffice. [See Gemara 23b, which states that number constitutes a *siman* (identifying mark).] However, since in this case there are two means of identification, if the claimant is aware of only one of them, it indicates that the documents are not his (see also *Ritva* for a slightly different version of this answer; cf. *Rosh;* see also *Ketzos HaChoshen* 65:11, *Nesivos HaMishpat* 65:19).

15. See previous note.

16. Clearly, we must assume that they fell from the borrower, who had repaid these three loans and thereby regained the documents.

17. Perhaps all three lenders had taken their documents to court to hav the signatures of the witnesses certified. Once the court certifies t signatures as valid, the documents are sent to a court scribe to have th text of the certification written on them. It was the practice for sever people to send their documents together to the scribe. Were the perso carrying the documents to lose them, it would account for all th documents being lost together even though they still belong to th lenders (*Shitah Mekubetzes*; see *Rashi* and *Ritva*).

18. Thus, they were not lost on their way to certification.

19. We should also not be concerned that one person was sent to pick u all the documents from the scribe, because although documents ar often sent in a group to have their certification inscribed, they ar retrieved from the scribe by the lenders themselves. Thus, they woul not have all been lost in one place had they still belonged to the lender (*Ritva, Tos. HaRosh*). It is therefore clear that the notes were paid, an they fell from the possession of the debtor.

20. Who had paid the obligations and had the notes returned to ther (*Rashi*).

21. Thus it is possible that [despite the existence of these documents] th loans were in fact never taken out (*Rashi*).

22. Thus, if the scribes lost them they would not all have been found i one place.

23. This would account for the documents being together even thoug the loans had not yet been taken out. See note 17.

חיישינן לשני שורי א"ל רב חסדא לרבה פוק עיין דלאורתא בעי לה רב הונא מינך נפק דק ואשכח דתנן כל מעשה ב"ד הרי זה יחזיר א"ל רב עמרם לרבה היכי פשיט מר (א) איסורא ממונא א"ל ◦ ג) תרדא שטרי חליצה ומיאונין תנן פקע ארזא דבי רב מר אמר משום לתאי דידי פקע ומר אמר משום לתאי דידי פקע: מצא בחפיסה או בדלוסקמא: ג) מאי חפיסה אמר רבה בר בר חנה חמת קטנה מאי דלוסקמא אמר רבה בר שמואל טליקא דסבי: תכריך של שטרות או אגודה של שטרות וכו': ת"ר א כמה הוא תכריך של שטרות שלשה כרוכין זה בזה וכמה היא אגודה של שטרות שלשה קשורין זה בזה שמעת מינה ד) קשר סימן הא תני רבי חייא ב שלשה כרוכין זה בזה אי הכי היינו תכריך ג תכריך כל חד וחד בראשה דחבריה אגודה דרמו אהדדי וכרוכות מאי מכריז מנין מאי אריא תלתא אפילו תרין נמי אלא כדאמר רבינא ה) טבעא מכריז הכא נמי ד שטרי מכריז: רשב"ג אומר אחד הלוה משלשה יחזיר ללוה וכו': דאי ס"ד דמלוין נינהו מאי בעו גבי הדדי דלמא לקיומינהו אזלי דמקיימי דלמא מידא דספרא נפיל לא משהי איניש קיומיה בידא דספרא: שלשה שלוו מאחד יחזיר למלוה וכו': דאי ס"ד דלוין נינהו מאי בעו גבי הדדי דלמא למכתבנהו אזלי ה דכתיבי בתלת ידי ספרי ודלמא לקיומינהו אזלי מלוה מקיים שטריה לוה לא מקיים שטריה: אם יש עמהן סמפונות יעשה מה שבסמפונות: אמר רב ירמיה בר אבא אמר רב ו סמפון היוצא מתחת ידי מלוה אע"פ שכתוב בכתב ידו אינו אלא כמשחק ופסול לא מבעיא כתוב בכתב יד סופר דאיכא למימר ספרא אתרמי ליה וכתב אלא אפילו כתוב בכתב ידו פסול סבר דלמא מתרמי ואתי בין השמשות וקא פרע לי דאי לא יהיבנא ליה לא יהיב לי זוזי אכתוב אנא דכי אייתי לי זוזי אתן ליה תנן ז אם יש עמהן סמפונות יעשה מה שבסמפונות כדאמר רב ספרא שנמצא בין שטרות ו) קרועין הכא נמי ח שמצאו בין שטרות קרועין ת"ש ז) ט נמצא לאחד בין שטרותיו שטרו של יוסף בן שמעון פרוע שטרות שניהם פרועין כדאמר רב ספרא שנמצא בין שטרות ח) קרועין הכא נמי שנמצא בין שטרות קרועין ת"ש ט) שבועה שלא פקדנו אבא ושלא אמר לנו אבא ושלא מצאנו בין שטרותיו של אבא ששטר זה פרוע אמר רב ספרא שנמצא בין שטרות י) קרועין ת"ש כ) סמפון שיש עליו עדים יתקיים בחותמיו אימא יתקיים מחותמיו דשיילינן

חיישינן לשני שורי. אע"פ שבשורי הידוע לנו אין בה שני יוסף בן שמעון שמא יש שורי אחרת שיש שם יוסף בן שמעון ושם נכתב ומשליח אחר נפל: הרי זה יחזיר. דכיון דלא הוחזקו שני יוסף בן שמעון בעיר אחת לעיר אחרת שאינה ידועה לנו לא חיישינן: (א) תרדא. ל) משועמם: פקע ארזא דבי רב. נשבר העמוד שבית המדרש נשען עליו: מר אמר משום לתאי דידי פקע. בשביל מזלי שקינא על שגדפתני: ומר אמר משום לתאי דידי פקע. שהשבת על דברי לביישני בבית המדרש: חמת. של עור שנותנין בו יין: טליקא דסבי. טסקא שהזקנים מצניעים בה כלי תשמישן שלא יצטרכו לחפש אחריהם: כרוכין זה בזה. וזהו סימן שהבעלים נותנים בהם זה יכריז מציאה שטרות מצאתי וזה יאמר שלי הם ושלשה הן כרוכין הן זה בזה: ש"מ קשר סימן. שיש קשרים שאין דומין זה לזה ויאמר כך וכך הוא עשוי דאי לא תימא הכי מאי סימנא איכא הכא ותפשוט מינה בעלמא דקשר סימן ובעיא בעלמא היא ומשני מהכא לא תפשוט דתני רבי חייא ג' כרוכין זה בזה הוא אגודה דכרך הוי סימן דכולי עלמא כרכי שטרא שטרא לעצמו וקושרין אותן יחד וזה כרך שלשתן יחד: דרמו אהדדי. השכיבן זה על זה אורכו על אורכו של חבירו: מאי מכריז. המוצא מאי מכריז: מנין. ג' שטרות וזה בא ונותן סימן שכרוכין היו יחד: אפי' תרי נמי. הואיל ואין צריך לבעלים לתת סימן אלא כריכתן: כדאמר רבינא. באלו מציאות (דף כה.): שטרי מכריז. שטרות מצאתי וזה צריך שיאמר כך וכך היו וכרוכין היו הלכך דוקא תלתא אבל תרי מידע ידיע דמיעוט שטרות שתים ואין מנין סימן: ודלמא לקיומינהו אזלי. אצל סופר הדיינין הכותב הנפק לכל השטרות: דלווין היו. שפרעום והוחזרו להם: למכתבנהו אזלי. ומן הסופר נפל ומעולם לא לוו: סמפון. שובר המבטל שטר וכל דבר המבטל דבר קרי סמפון כדאמר מ) גבי קדושי אשה ומכירת עבד שהמום קרוי סמפון מפני שמבטל את המקח: היוצא מתחת ידי מלוה. שהוא מונח בידו ולא ביד הלוה: ספרא אתרמי ליה. וסבר אם יבא בעל חובי לפרעני ואני אין שטרי עכשיו בידי ואם לא יהא שובר מוכן לי לא יפרע כלום: אפי' כתוב בכתב ידו. שיש לומר אם לא שנפרע למה ליה למהר ולכתוב לפני פרעון הואיל ויודע לכתוב: ואם יש עמהן סמפון. והכא במלוה עסקינן דקתני מצא שטר בין שטרותיו כו': כדאמר רב ספרא. לקמן בשמעתין: שנמצא לו. השטר שהשובר יוצא עליו: בין שטרותיו קרועים. והוא אינו קרוע לפיכך סומכין על השובר שמקום השטר מוכיח על השובר שהוא אמת שאם לא נפרע לא היה נותן השטר אצל השטרות קרועין כך שמעתי ולי נראה שנמצא השובר בין השטרות קרועין הלכך איכא למימר שנתקבל החוב והשובר הזה אין צריך למלוה הזה אלא ללוה והלוה שכח ביד זה לפיכך נתנו זה עם השטרות שאין צריכין לו דאי ס"ד מלוה כתבו להיות מוכן לו כשילוה לוה לפרעו לא נתנו עם שטרות שאין צריכין לו: נמצא בין שטרותיו. מתני' היא בגט פשוט (ב"ב דף קעב.) שני יוסף בן שמעון בעיר אחת ונמצא שובר לאדם אחד בין שטרותיו וכתוב בו שטרו של יוסף בן שמעון שבידי פרוע הוא והיה לו שני שטרות על שניהם: שטרות שניהם פרועין. שכל אחד יכול לומר על שלי נכתב שובר ובבבא בתרא פרכינן בלא שובר נמי הא תנן אין אחד יכול להוציא שטר חוב עליהם ומוקמינן ליה במשולשין בשטר ואין משולשין בשובר והא הכא דיוצא מתחת יד מלוה הוא: שנמצא. השטר בין השטרות פרועין וכל אחד אמר זהו שטר שלי: שבועה שלא פקדנו אבא. משנה היא בשבועות (דף מה.) יתומין מן היתומין לא יפרעו אלא בשבועה ומהו שבועתן שבועה שלא פקדנו אבא בשעת מיתה ושלא אמר לנו קודם לכן ושלא מצינו שובר בין שטרותיו של אבא על שטר זה שיהא פרוע הא אם מצאו סמכינן עליה: יתקיים בחותמיו. קא ס"ד אם אמר מלוה לא נפרעתי ותדע שהרי לא מסרתי לידך יתקיים בחותמיו ע"פ חותמיו יתקיים אם החותמיו מעידין שחתמוהו אין המלוה נאמן אבל כל כמה דלא מקיים מהימן דמאן מפיק ליה מלוה ומלוה הא אמר פסול הוא: דשיילינן

**איסורא** ממונא. וא"ת טפי אנן מחמירין בממונא י) דהא אין אנו הולכים בממון אחר הרוב ובאיסורא אזלינן בתר רובא אפי' היכא דאיכא חזקה דאיסורא כנגד הרוב ולא חיישינן שמא במקום נקב קא שחיט וי"ל דמ"מ באשת איש החמירו דמים שאין להם סוף לא תנשא לכתחילה אע"פ שרובם מתים ועוד יש לומר דמדאורייתא לא חיישינן לשני יוסף בן שמעון אבל מדרבנן חיישינן משום לעז ובממונא לא שייך לעז לכך פריך שפיר היכי פשיט מר איסורא ממונא:

**מצא** בחפיסה או בדלוסקמא. תימה בשלמא חפיסה הוי סימן כדאמר בפרק שני (דף כח.) הוא אומר בחפיסה והיא אומרת בחפיסה ינתן לו דמידע ידעה דכל מאי דאית ליה בחפיסה מנח ליה משמע דלאיניש מעלמא הוי סימן אלא דלוסקמא היכי הוי סימן הלא דרך להניח שטרות בדלוסקמא כדתניא בתוספתא דשבועות עשרה דלוסקמאות מלאים שטרות מסרתי לך וי"ל דמיירי הכא שנותן בדלוסקמא עצמה סימן שאינו מובהק ולא חיישינן לשאלה לשמא השאיל לאחר ואותו הניח בו שטרות דהכי תקון רבנן דלא חיישינן כמו שתקנו ס) להחזיר אבידה בסימן שאינו מובהק אפילו סימנין לאו דאורייתא: **סמפון** שיש עליו עדים יתקיים בחותמיו. נראה דמשמע ליה שהוא ביד המלוה מדקרי ליה סמפון דביד הלוה קרי ליה שובר ולשון סמפון לשון ביטול ועוד דביד הלוה פשיטא דכשר ע"י קיום:

הדרן עלך שנים אוחזין



רבינו חננאל

אמר רב הונא חיישינן לשני שורי נפק רבא דק ואשכח כל מעשה ב"ד הרי זה יחזיר. אמר ליה רב עמרם לרבא מתני' דקתני כל מעשה ב"ד ממונא הוא וגט אשה איסורא היכי פשיט מר איסורא מממונא. אמר ליה תרדי א) שטרי חליצה ומיאונין תנן דאינון איסורא ואיסורא מאיסורא פשטינן. פקע ארזא דבי רב פי' נשברה קורת בית המדרש. רבא אמר בשביל שבא לדחות דבריי נשברה הקורה. ורב עמרם אמר בשביל שביזני וקראני מוריד ריר מפי נשברה: **מצא בחפיסה** פי' חפיסה חמת קטנה. דלוסקומא תיבה בלשון יון. תכריך של שטרות ג' שטרות. כגון מגילה ראש זה בזנב זה. אגודה ג' שטרות נתונים זה על גבי זה ב) וכתובים כולן כרך אחד. מה מכריז המוצאם מכריז הכי מי אבדו לו שטרות. **רשב"ג אומר** אחד לוה מג' כגון ראובן לוה משמעון ועוד לוה מלוי ועוד מיהודה וכתב השטר לכל אחד בפני עצמו ונמצאו עכשיו שלשתן קשורין ודאי פרעם הלוה ולקח השטר שעליו ומן הלוה נפלו. וכן ג' שלוו מאחד ונמצאו שלשתן קשורין ודאי מן המלוה נפלו והוא שנמצאו מקוימים ובכתב שלשה סופרין שאם שלשתן בכתב סופר אחד חיישינן דלמא מן הסופר נפלו: **מצא שטר בין** שטרותיו ואינו יודע מה טיבו יהא מונח עד שיבוא אליהו. אם יש עמהן סמפון פי' סמפון שובר או תנאים. אמר רבי ירמיה בר אבא אמר רבי יוחנן סמפון היוצא מתחת ידי מלוה אע"פ שכתוב בכתב ידו אינו אלא כמשחק ופסול וכל מה דאקשי' עליה פריק כגון שנמצא בין שטרותיו קרועין. ת"ש שבועה שלא פקדנו אבא ושלא אמר לנו אבא ושלא מצינו בשטרותיו ששטר זה פרוע. אמר רב ספרא כגון שנמצא זה השטר חוב בין שטרותיו קרועין דמוכחא מילתא דאי לאו דפריען לא הוה יהיב ליה בהדי שטרותיו קרועין אבל בסמפון לבדו לא. ת"ש סמפון שיש עליו עדים יתקיים בחותמיו. ופריק אימא יתקיים מחותמיו דשאלינן לסהדי דחתימין חזיתון דפרעיה קמייכו אי לא. ת"ש סמפון שיש

עין משפט
נר מצוה

קעב א ב ג ד מיי' פי"ח מהלכות גזילה ואבידה הלכה ג סמג עשין עד טוש"ע ח"מ סי' סה סעיף י ע"ש:
קעג ה מיי' שם הלכה ד טוש"ע שם סעיף יא:
קעד ו ז ח מיי' פי"ו מהל' מלוה ולוה הלכה ח י סמג עשין צד טוש"ע ח"מ סי' סה סעיף יח:
קעה ט מיי' שם פכ"ד הל' ח סמג שם טוש"ע ח"מ סי' מט סעיף ט:

מסורת הש"ס

א) [ברכות יט:, כתוב... מ:, מו:, קדושין ג... ב) [זבחים כה: וש"... ג) גיטין כח., ד) [לק... כג:, כה:], ה) [לקמן כה... ו) פרועין, מהרש"... ז) בבא בתרא קע... ח) פרועין, ט) שבוע... מה., י) פרועי... כ) סנהדרין לא:, ל) ... בבא קמא קה: רש"י ד"... תדורא, מ) [כתובות ... נ) [וע"ע תוס' בבא ק... ס: ד"ה קמ"ל], ס) [לק... ס:].

הגהות הב"ח

(א) רש"י ד"ה תרד... משועמם. נ"ב ובכריתו... דף יח ע"ב פי' רש"י תר... שוטה או עצל:

גליון הש"ס

גמ' תרדא. עיין ב"ק ... קה ע"ב וזבחים דף ... ע"ב:

ליקוטי רש"י

חיישינן לשני שורי... אע"פ שבא אחד לפני... ואמר ממני נפל ופל... היה משלחו לאשתו ויודע... אנו שאין שם בשורי ש... אנשים ששמותיהן ש... חיישינן שמא שורי אחר... ים ויש בה יוסף בן שמע... אחר [לעיל יח... דלאורתא. ללילה [ע... ברכות ג:]. כל מעש... ב"ד ה"ז יחזיר. ... מילתא דאתא לב"ד לקי... דליכא למיחש לגמ... עליהן שלא ליתנן ה... יחזיר וזה מקויים בב"... היה ולכך הוצא שם [לע... יח:]. היכי פשיט מ... איסורא ממונא... ממונא קל מאיסור... [ברכות יט:]. תרדא... שוטה לשון אחר ע... [כריתות יח:]. שוטה בה... [זבחים כה:]. חמר... בולזו"א בלע"ז והיא ... עור [גיטין כח.]. נוד ... עור [חולין קז.]. דלוסקמא. כמו אמתח... ושק לשום בו [ספ... [מגילה כו:]. טליקא... טסק"א בלע"ז [גיטין שם... טבעא מכריז. מטבעו... מצאתי הלכך תרי לו... סימנא הוא דמיעו... מטבעות ב' [לקמן כה... שבועה שלא פקד... אבא. בשעת מית... ששטר זה פרוע. של... אמר לנו קודם לכ... ושלא מצאנו. שובר ... שטר זה [שבועות מה... סמפון שיש על... עדים. שובר ויצא מתח... ידי לוה כמשפט... יתקיים בחותמי... יתקיים [השובר] בחותמ... יעידו עדים על חתימו... ידיהן וכשר [סנהדרין לא:

לעזי רש"י

טסק"א. פירוש ש... ואמתחת (רש"י מגילה ד... כו ע"ב ד"ה דלוסק... ועיין רש"י מעילה דף ... ע"א ד"ה דלוסקמא).

חַיְישִׁינָן לִשְׁנֵי שְׁוִירֵי – **We are concerned** that **there are** perhaps **two** towns named **Shviri,** and that the *get* found here was written for a couple with identical names who live in that second Shviri.[1] The *get,* therefore, may not be returned to the agent who claims it. אֲמַר לֵיהּ רַב חִסְדָּא לְרַבָּה – **Rav Chisda told Rabbah:** פּוּק עַיֵּין – **Go out** and **look into** this matter, דִּלְאוּרְתָּא בָּעֵי לָהּ רַב הוּנָא מִינָּךְ – **for in the evening Rav Huna will inquire of you concerning it.** נְפַק דָּק וְאַשְׁכַּח – **[Rabbah] went out, investigated, and found** a relevant source. דִּתְנַן – **For we have learned in** our **Mishnah:** כָּל מַעֲשֵׂה בֵית דִּין – If one finds ANY ACT OF THE COURT, such as a document certified by a court, הֲרֵי זֶה יַחֲזִיר – HE SHOULD RETURN it.[2] Since this *get* was certified, it should be returned to the agent.

An objection is raised:

אֲמַר לֵיהּ רַב עַמְרָם לְרַבָּה – **Rav Amram told Rabbah:** הֵיכִי פָּשִׁיט מַר אִיסּוּרָא מִמָּמוֹנָא – **How can** you, **master, resolve** a question of **prohibition from** a ruling dealing with **monetary** law?[3]

The Gemara responds:

אֲמַר לֵיהּ – **[Rabbah] told [Rav Amram]:** תְּרָדָא – **Lunatic!** שְׁטָרֵי חֲלִיצָה וּמֵיאוּנִין תְּנַן – **We** also **learned in the Mishnah** that **certificates of *chalitzah* and *mi'un*** should be returned, although they are relevant to matters of prohibition rather than money. My proof is therefore valid!

The Gemara relates:

פְּקַע אַרְזָא דְּבֵי רַב – **The cedar** column which supported the **study hall**[4] **split.** מַר אָמַר – **One master** [Rav Amram] **said:** מִשּׁוּם לְתַאי דִּידִי פְּקַע – **It was due to my fortune that it split,** because Rabbah insulted me. וּמַר אָמַר – **And the** other **master** [Rabbah] **said:** מִשּׁוּם לְתַאי דִּידִי פְּקַע – **It was due to my fortune that it split,** because Rav Amram criticized my dissertation publicly and embarrassed me.[5]

The Mishnah states:

מָצָא בַּחֲפִיסָה אוֹ בִּדְלוּסְקְמָא – If ONE FINDS a document IN A *CHAFISAH* OR IN A *DELUSKEMA* ... he should return it.

The Gemara explains:

מַאי חֲפִיסָה – **What is a *chafisah?*** אָמַר רַבָּה בַּר בַּר חָנָה – **Rabbah bar bar Chanah said:** חֵמֶת קְטַנָּה – **A small skin** (i.e. hide) bottle ordinarily used to contain wine. מַאי דְּלוּסְקְמָא – **What is a *deluskema?*** אָמַר רַבָּה בַּר שְׁמוּאֵל – **Rabbah bar Shmuel said:** תִּיקָא דְּסָבֵי – **A box of** the type used by **elderly people** to keep their household utensils, so that they do not have to go looking for them.

The Mishnah states:

תַּכְרִיךְ שֶׁל שְׁטָרוֹת – If one finds A ROLL OF DOCUMENTS אֲגוּדָּה שֶׁל שְׁטָרוֹת וכו׳ – OR A BUNDLE OF DOCUMENTS, **etc.** he should return them.

The Gemara elaborates:

תָּנוּ רַבָּנַן – **The Rabbis taught in a Baraisa:** כַּמָּה הוּא תַּכְרִיךְ שֶׁל שְׁטָרוֹת – HOW MANY documents CONSTITUTE A ROLL OF DOCUMENTS? שְׁלֹשָׁה כְּרוּכִין זֶה בָּזֶה – THREE, ROLLED TOGETHER. וְכַמָּה הִיא אֲגוּדָּה שֶׁל שְׁטָרוֹת – AND HOW MANY documents CONSTITUTE A BUNDLE OF DOCUMENTS? שְׁלֹשָׁה קְשׁוּרִין זֶה בָּזֶה – THREE, TIED TOGETHER.

The Gemara comments:

שְׁמַעַת מִינָּהּ – **Should one learn from this** Baraisa's explanation of the Mishnah קֶשֶׁר סִימָן – that the type of **knot** used in tying together a bundle **is** considered **an identifying mark?**[8]

The Gemara counters:

הָא תָּנֵי רַבִּי חִיָּיא – **But R' Chiya taught** in his text of the Baraisa that the *bundle* of documents discussed by the Mishnah refers to שְׁלֹשָׁה כְּרוּכִין זֶה בָּזֶה – THREE, ROLLED TOGETHER.[9] Therefore there is no indication that our Mishnah considers the knot to be the identifying characteristic.[10]

The Gemara asks:

אִי הָכִי – **If so,** that the Mishnah's case of a bundle of documents also refers to documents rolled together, הַיְינוּ תַּכְרִיךְ – **it is identical to** the case of **a roll** of documents! What difference is there between the two cases?

The Gemara answers:

תַּכְרִיךְ – The case of **a roll** is כָּל חַד וְחַד בְּרֵאשָׁה דְּחַבְרֵיהּ – where they are rolled **each one over the top of the other.**[11] אֲגוּדָּה –

NOTES

1. Thus, although we are aware of only one couple in the known town of Shviri whose names correspond to those on the *get,* we are concerned that perhaps there is another town named Shviri in which lives a couple with identical names, and that a *get* written for them was lost here. See 18b note 1.

2. Once a document has been certified, there is no longer any concern that it has been retracted. The Mishnah therefore tells us to return it. We see from this that the Mishnah does not require us to consider the possibility that there might be another person with the same name. See 18b notes 2,3.

3. Returning the *get* to the agent and allowing him to use it to divorce the woman named in it is a matter of prohibitory law, since the effect will be to release the woman from her marriage and allow her to marry someone else. Returning an "act of the court" to someone, however, is relevant only to monetary law, allowing the recipient to pursue some monetary claim. The fact that the Mishnah allows a lost document concerning a monetary matter to be returned cannot serve as a precedent for returning a document relating to a matter of prohibition, since the latter branch of law is generally subject to more stringent regulations, especially in matters dealing with marriage and divorce (see *Tosafos*).

4. Literally: house of the teacher.

5. *Maharsha* explains that they were not each claiming that they had been vindicated by the calamity. Rather, each one was accepting responsibility for the calamity that befell the building. Each felt that his fortune (*mazal*) was to blame for the fact that the insult or embarrassment was avenged in such a damaging manner.

See *Teshuvos Chavos Yair* 152 for a discussion of the occasional use of sharp language in Talmudic discourse. See also Gemara, *Taanis* 4a.

6. In the case of a *deluskema* box, merely naming it as the document's container does not suffice to identify it, since it is common for documents to be stored in a *deluskema* box. One must offer a *siman* that identifies the particular box (*Tosafos*).

7. When the finder announces that he has found documents, the owner may claim them by providing their number and mentioning that they were rolled up together (*Rashi*). [Documents were rolled up like scrolls. In this case, all three were rolled together in a single roll. The Gemara will explain this further.]

8. If not, what other identification does the owner provide? [Since documents are customarily tied together in a bundle, it is not sufficient to mention that they are tied together (see *Rashi*).] Accordingly, we have proof that since there are different types of knots used by people, identifying the type of knot suffices to identify the lost object (*Rashi*). This is a question considered by the Gemara below (23b, 25b), and the Gemara here seeks to resolve it from our Mishnah.

9. Since it is customary to roll up each document separately and then tie them together, to note that they were rolled up together suffices to identify them (*Rashi*).

10. Although the version of the Baraisa cited above does speak of the documents being tied together, rather than rolled, we see from R' Chiya that "tied" is being used here not in its literal sense, but in the broader sense of joined together [by whatever means]. Thus, it cannot be demonstrated that a knot alone can serve as a *siman* (see *Tos. HaRosh* who cites other instances in which קשר is used in a broad sense).

11. I.e. after rolling up one document, another one was rolled over it. [The literal translation of the Gemara's statement is: each one on the head of the other. Ordinary documents, being longer than they are wide, are rolled from bottom to top (rather than from side to side ). One begins rolling from the bottom so that the beginning [or top] of the document should remain the outermost layer of the scroll. In this manner, one has only to unroll a bit of the scroll to be able to read its beginning. Accord-

חיישינן לשני שוירי א"ל רב חסדא לרבה פוק עיין דלאורתא בעי לה רב הונא מינך נפק דק ואשכח דתנן כל מעשה ב"ד הרי זה יחזיר א"ל רב עמרם לרבה היכי פשיט מר איסורא מממונא א"ל תרדא שטרי חליצה ומיאונין תנן פקע ארזא דבי רב מר אמר משום לתאי דידי פקע ומר אמר משום לתאי דידי פקע: מצא בחפיסה או בדלוסקמא: מאי חפיסה אמר רבה בר בר חנה חמת קטנה מאי דלוסקמא אמר רבה בר שמואל טליקא דסבי: תכריך של שטרות או אגודה של שטרות וכו': ת"ר כמה הוא תכריך של שטרות שלשה כרוכין זה בזה וכמה היא אגודה של שטרות שלשה קשורין זה בזה שמעת מינה קשר סימן הא תני רבי חייא שלשה כרוכין זה בזה אי הכי היינו תכריך תכריך כל חד וחד בראשה דחבריה אגודה דרמו אהדדי וכרוכות מאי מכריז מנין מאי אריא תלתא אפילו תרין נמי אלא כדאמר רבינא טבעא מכריז הכא נמי שטרי מכריז: רשב"ג אומר אחד הלוה משלשה יחזיר ללוה וכו': דאי ס"ד דמלוין נינהו מאי בעו גבי הדדי דלמא לקוימינהו אזלי דמקיימי דלמא מידא דספרא נפיל לא משהי איניש קיומיה בידא דספרא: שלשה שלוו מאחד יחזיר למלוה וכו': דאי ס"ד דלוין נינהו מאי בעו גבי הדדי דלמא למכתבנהו אזלי דכתיבי בתלת ידי ספרי ודלמא לקוימינהו אזלי מלוה מקיים שטריה לוה לא מקיים שטריה: אם יש עמהן סמפונות יעשה מה שבסמפונות: אמר רב ירמיה בר אבא אמר רב סמפון היוצא מתחת ידי מלוה אע"פ שכתוב בכתב ידו אינו אלא כמשחק ופסול לא מבעיא כתוב בכתב יד סופר דאיכא למימר ספרא אתרמי ליה וכתב אלא אפילו כתוב בכתב ידו פסול סבר דלמא מתרמי ואתי בין השמשות וקא פרע לי דאי לא יהיבנא ליה לא יהיב לי זוזי אכתוב אנא דכי אייתי לי זוזי אתן ליה תנן אם יש עמהן סמפונות יעשה מה שבסמפונות כדאמר רב ספרא שנמצא בין שטרות קרועין הכא נמי שמצאו בין שטרות קרועין ת"ש נמצא לאחד בין שטרותיו שטרו של יוסף בן שמעון פרוע שטרות שניהם פרועין כדאמר רב ספרא שנמצא בין שטרות קרועין הכא נמי שנמצא בין שטרות קרועין ת"ש שבועה שלא פקדנו אבא ושלא אמר לנו אבא ושלא מצאנו בין שטרותיו של אבא ששטר זה פרוע אמר רב ספרא שנמצא בין שטרות קרועין ת"ש סמפון שיש עליו עדים יתקיים בחותמיו אימא יתקיים מחותמיו דשיילינן

---

**תוספות**

**איסורא** ממונא. וא"ת טפי אנן מחמרינן בממונא דהא אין אנו הולכים בממון אחר הרוב ובאיסורא אזלינן בתר רובא אפי' היכא דאיכא חזקה דאיסורא כנגד הרוב ולא חיישינן שמא במקום נקב קא שחיט וי"ל דמ"מ באשת איש החמירו דמים שאין להם סוף לא תנשא לכתחילה אע"פ שרובם מתים ועוד יש לומר דמדאורייתא לא חיישינן לשני יוסף בן שמעון אבל מדרבנן חיישינן משום לעז ובממונא לא שייך לעז לכך פריך שפיר היכי פשיט מר איסורא מממונא:

**מצא** בחפיסה או בדלוסקמא. תימה בשלמא חפיסה הוי סימן כדאמר בפרק שני (דף כח.) הוא אומר בחפיסה והיא אומרת בחפיסה ינתן לו דמידע ידעה דכל מאי דלית ליה בחפיסה מנח ליה משמע דלאיניש מעלמא הוי סימן אלא דלוסקמא היכי הוי סימן הלא דרך להניח שטרות בדלוסקמא כדתניא בתוספתא דשבועות עשרה דלוסקמאות מלאים שטרות מסרתי לך וי"ל דמיירי הכא שנותן בדלוסקמא עלמה סימן שאינו מובהק ולא חיישינן לשאלה לשמא השאיל לאחר ואותו הניח בו שטרות דהכי תקון רבנן דלא חיישינן כמו שתקנו להחזיר אבידה בסימן שאינו מובהק אפילו סימנין לאו דאורייתא:

**סמפון** שיש עליו עדים יתקיים בחותמיו. נראה דמשמע ליה שהוא ביד המלוה מדקרי ליה סמפון דביד הלוה קרי ליה שובר ולשון סמפון לשון ביטול ועוד דביד הלוה פשיטא דכשר ע"י קיום:

הדרן עלך שנים אוחזין

---

**רש"י**

חיישינן לשני שוירי. אע"פ שבשוירי הידוע לנו אין בה שני יוסף בן שמעון שמא יש שוירי אחרת שיש שם יוסף בן שמעון ושם נכתב ומשליח אחר נפל: הרי זה יחזיר. דכיון דלא הוחזקו שני יוסף בן שמעון בעיר אחת לעיר אחרת שאינה ידועה לנו לא חיישינן: (א) תרדא. משועמם: פקע ארזא דבי רב. נשבר העמוד שבית המדרש נשען עליו: מר אמר משום לתאי דידי פקע. בשביל מזלי שקינא על שגדפתני: ומר אמר משום לתאי דידי פקע. שהשבת על דברי לביישני בבית המדרש: חמת. של עור שנותנין בו יין: טליקא דסבי. טסקא שהזקנים מצניעים בה כלי תשמישן שלא יצטרכו לחפש אחריהם: כרוכין זה בזה. וזהו סימן שהבעלים נותנים בהם זה יכריז מציאה שטרות מצאתי וזה יאמר שלי הם ושלשה הן כרוכין הן זה בזה: ש"מ קשר סימן. שיש קשרים שאינן דומין זה לזה ויאמר כך וכך הוא עשוי דאי לא תימא הכי מאי סימנא איכא הכא ותפשוט מינה בעלמא דקשר סימן ובעיא בעלמא היא ומשני מהכא לא תפשוט דתני רבי חייא ג' כרוכין זה בזה הוא אגודה דכרך הוי סימן דכולי עלמא כרכי שטרא שטרא לעצמו וקושרין אותן יחד וזה כרך שלשתן יחד: דרמו אהדדי. השכיבן זה על זה ארכו על ארכו של חבירו: מאי מכריז. המוצא מאי מכריז: מנין. ג' שטרות וזה בא ונותן סימן שכרוכין היו יחד: אפי' תרי נמי. הואיל ואין צריך לבעלים לתת סימן אלא כריכתן: כדאמר רבינא. באלו מציאות (דף כה.): שטרי מכריז. שטרות מצאתי וזה צריך שיאמר כך וכך היו וכרוכין היו הלכך דוקא תלתא אבל תרי מידע ידיע דמיעוט שטרות שתים ואין מנין סימן: ודלמא לקוימינהו אזלי. אבל סופר הדיינין הכותב הנפק לכל השטרות: דלווין היו. שפרעום והוחזרו להם: למכתבנהו אזלי. ומן הסופר נפל ומעולם לא לוו: סמפון. שובר המבטל שטר וכל דבר המבטל דבר קרי סמפון כדאמר גבי קדושי אשה ומכירת עבד שהמום קרוי סמפון מפני שמבטל את המקח: היוצא מתחת ידי מלוה. שהוא מונח בידו ולא ביד הלוה: ספרא אתרמי ליה. וסבר אם יבא בעל חובי לפרעני ואני אין שטרי עכשיו בידי ואם לא יהא שובר מוכן לי לא יפרע כלום: אפי' כתוב בכתב ידו. שיש לומר אם לא שנפרע למה ליה למהר ולכתוב לפני פרעון הואיל וידע לכתוב: ואם יש עמהן סמפון. והכא במלוה עסקינן דקתני מצא שטר בין שטרותיו כו': כדאמר רב ספרא. לקמן בשמעתין: שנמצא לו. השטר שהשובר יוצא עליו: בין שטרותיו קרועים. והוא אינו קרוע לפיכך סומכין על השובר שמקום השטר מוכיח על השובר שהוא אמת שאם לא נפרע לא היה נותן השטר אצל השטרות קרועין כך שמעתי ולי נראה שנמצא השובר בין השטרות קרועין הלכך איכא למימר שנתקבל החוב והשובר הזה אין צריך למלוה הזה אלא ללוה והלוה שכח ביד זה לפיכך נתנו זה עם השטרות שאין צריכין לו דאי ס"ד מלוה כתבו להיות מוכן לו כשילוה לוה לפרעו לא נתנו עם שטרות שאין צריכין לו: נמצא בין שטרותיו. מתני' היא בגט פשוט (ב"ב דף קעג.) שני יוסף בן שמעון בעיר אחת ונמצא שובר לאדם אחד בין שטרותיו וכתוב בו שטרו של יוסף בן שמעון שבידי פרוע הוא והיה לו שני שטרות על שניהם: שטרות שניהם פרועין. שכל אחד יכול לומר על שלי נכתב שובר ובבבא בתרא פרכינן בלא שובר נמי הא תנן אין אחד יכול להוציא שטר חוב עליהם ומוקמינן ליה במשולשין בשטר ואין משולשין בשובר והא הכא דיוצא מתחת יד מלוה הוא: שנמצא. השטר בין השטרות פרועין וכל אחד אמר זהו שטר שלי: שבועה שלא פקדנו אבא. משנה היא בשבועות (דף מה.) יתומין מן היתומין לא יפרעו אלא בשבועה ומהו שבועתן שבועה שלא פקדנו אבא בצואת מיתה ושלא אמר לנו קודם לכן ושלא מצינו שובר בין שטרותיו של אבא על שטר זה שיהא פרוע הא אם מצאו סמכינן עליה: יתקיים בחותמיו. קא ס"ד אם אמר מלוה לא נפרעתי ותדע שהרי לא מסרתי לידך יתקיים בחותמיו ע"פ חותמיו יתקיים אם החותמיו מעידין שחתמוהו אין המלוה נאמן אבל כל כמה דלא מקיים מהימן דמאן דמפיק ליה מלוה ומלוה הא אמר פסול הוא: דשיילינן

---

**עין משפט נר מצוה**

קעב א ב ג ד מיי' פי"ח מהלכות גזילה ואבידה הלכה ג סמג עשין עד טוש"ע ח"מ סי' סה סעיף י ע"ש:

קעג ה מיי' שם הלכה ד טוש"ע שם סעיף יא:

קעד ו ז ח מיי' פי"ו מהל' מלוה ולוה הלכה ח י סמג עשין צד טוש"ע ח"מ סי' סה סעיף יח:

קעה ט מיי' שם פכ"ד הל' ח סמג שם טוש"ע ח"מ סי' מט סעיף ט:

**רבינו חננאל**

אמר רב הונא חיישינן לשני שורי נפק רבא דק ואשכח כל מעשה ב"ד הרי זה יחזיר. אמר ליה רב עמרם לרבא מתני' דקתני כל מעשה ב"ד ממונא הוא וגט אשה איסורא היכי פשיט מר איסורא מממונא. אמר ליה תרדי (א) שטרי חליצה ומיאונין תנן דאינון איסורא ואיסורא מאיסורא פשטינן. פקע ארזא דבי רב פי' נשברה קורת בית המדרש. רבא אמר בשביל שבא לדחות דבריי נשברה הקורה. ורב עמרם אמר בשביל שביזוני וקראני מוריד ריר מפי נשברה: מצא בחפיסה פי' חפיסה חמת קטנה. דלוסקומא תיבה בלשון יון. תכריך של שטרות ג' שטרות. כגון מגילה ראש זה בזנב זה. אגודה ג' שטרות נתונים זה על גבי זה ב) וכתובים כולן כרך אחד. מה מכריז המוצאם מכריז הכי מי אבדו לו שטרות. **רשב"ג אומר אחד לוה** מג' כגון ראובן לוה משמעון ועוד לוה מלוי ועוד מיהודה וכתב השטר לכל אחד בפני עצמו ונמצאו עכשיו שלשתן קשורין ודאי פרעם הלוה ולקח השטר שעליו ומן הלוה נפלו. וכן ג' שלוו מאחד ונמצאו שלשתן קשורין ודאי מן המלוה נפלו והוא שנמצאו מקוימים ובכתב שלשה סופרין שאם שלשתן בכתב סופר אחד חיישינן דלמא מן הסופר נפלו: **מצא שטר בין שטרותיו ואינו יודע מה טיבו יהא מונח עד שיבוא אליהו**. אם יש עמהן סמפון פי' סמפון שובר או תנאים. אמר רבי ירמיה בר אבא אמר רבי יוחנן סמפון היוצא מתחת ידי מלוה אע"פ שכתוב בכתב ידו אינו אלא כמשחק ופסול וכל מה דאקשי' עליה פריק כגון שנמצא בין שטרותיו קרועין. ת"ש שבועה שלא פקדנו אבא ושלא אמר לנו אבא ושלא מצינו בשטרותיו ששטר זה פרוע. אמר רב ספרא כגון שנמצא זה השטר חוב בין שטרותיו קרועין דמוכחא מילתא דאי לאו דפריען לא הוה יהיב ליה בהדי שטרותיו קרועין אבל בסמפון לבדו לא. ת"ש סמפון שיש עליו עדים יתקיים בחותמיו. ופריק אימא יתקיים מחותמיו דשאלינן לסהדי דחתימין חזיתון דפרעיה קמייכו אי לא. ת"ש סמפון שיש

---

**מסורת הש"ס**

א) [ברכות יט:, כתוב מ:, מו:, קדושין ג ב) [זבחים כה: וש" ג) גיטין כח., ד) [לק כג:, כה:], ה) [לקמן כה ו) פרועין, מהרש" ז) בבא בתרא קע ח) פרועין, ט) שבוע מה., י) פרוע כ) סנהדרין לא:, ל) בבא קמא קה: רש"י ד" תדורא, מ) [כתובות מ נ) [וע"ע תוס' בבא קי ס: ד"ה קמ"ל], ס) [לק ס:].

**הגהות הב"ח**

(א) רש"י ד"ה תר משועמם. נ"ב ובכרית דף יח ע"ב פי' רש"י תר שוטה או עגל:

**גליון הש"ס**

גמ' תרדא. עיין ב"ק קה ע"ב וזבחים דף ע"ב:

**ליקוטי רש"י**

חיישינן לשני שויר אע"פ שבא אחד לפנ ואמר ממני נפל ופל היה משלחו לאשתו ויוד אנו שאין שם בשורי אנשים ששמותיהן ש חיישינן שמא שורי אח יש ויש בה יוסף בן שמ אחר [לעיל יח דלאורתא. ללילה ברכות ג:]. כל מעש ב"ד ה"ז יחזיר. מילתא דאתא לב"ד לק דליכא למיחש לגנ עליהן שלא ליתנן יחזיר וזה מקויים בב היה ולכך הובא שם [ל יח:]. היכי פשיט איסורא ממונ ממונא קל מאיסו [ברכות יט:]. תרד שוטה לשון אחר [כריתות יח:]. שוטה ב [זבחים כה:]. חמ בולזול"א בלע"ז והיא עור [גיטין כח.]. נוד עור [חולין ק דלוסקמא. כמו אמת ושק לשום בו [ס [מגילה כו:]. טליק טסק"א בלע"ז [גיטין ש טבעא מכריז. מטב מצאתי הלכך תרי סימנא הוא דמיו מטבעות ג' [לקמן כ שבועה שלא פקד אבא. בשעת מי ששטר זה פרוע. אמר לנו קודם ושלא מצאנו. שובר שטר זה [שבועות מ סמפון שיש ע עדים. שובר ויצא מת ידי לוה כמשכ יתקיים בחותמ יתקיים [השובר] בחות יעידו עדים על חתי ידיהן וכשר [סנהדרין לא

**לעזי רש"י**

טסק"א. פירוש ולמתחת (רש"י מגילה כו ע"ב ד"ה דלוסק ועיין רש"י מעילה דף ע"א ד"ה דלוסקמא

---

חשק שלמה על ר"ח א) גי' הערוך תרדא ופירש שוטה ומוריד ריר [ותרדא הוא מלשון רר בשרו] ע"ש ואולי דכן היה ג"כ גי' רבינו. ב) אולי צ"ל וכרוכים כולם בכרך אחד.

שמע מינה איתא לדשמואל [א] דאמר שמואל [א] המוכר שטר חוב לחבירו וחזר ומחלו מחול [ב] ואפי' יורש מוחל אביי אמר אפילו תימא ליתיה לדשמואל הכא במאי עסקינן בששטר כתובה יוצא מתחת ידה ורבא אמר אי משום שטר כתובה חיישינן לשתי כתובות ואביי אמר חדא לשתי כתובות לא חיישינן ועוד שובר בזמנו טריף אביי לטעמיה דאמר [ב] עדיו בחתומיו זכין לו:

מתני' [ג] [ג] מצא איגרות שום ואיגרות מזון שטרי חליצה ומיאונין ושטרי בירורין [ד] וכל מעשה ב"ד הרי זה יחזיר [ה] [ד] מצא בחפיסה או בדלוסקמא [ו] [ה] תכריך של שטרות או אגודה של שטרות הרי זה יחזיר וכמה אגודה של שטרות שלשה קשורין זה בזה רשב"ג אומר [ז] [ו] אחד הלוה משלשה יחזיר ללוה שלשה הלוין מן האחד יחזיר למלוה [ז] מצא שטר בין שטרותיו ואינו יודע מה טיבו יהא מונח עד שיבא אליהו אם יש עמהן [ח] סמפונות יעשה מה שבסמפונות:

גמ' [ט] מאי שטרי ברורין הכא תרגמו שטרי טענתא רבי ירמיה אמר זה בורר לו אחד וזה בורר לו אחד: וכל מעשה ב"ד הרי זה יחזיר: [י] ההוא גיטא דאשתכח בי דינא דרב הונא דהוה כתיב ביה בשוירי מתא דעל רכים נהרא אמר רב הונא חיישינן

## רש"י

ש"מ. מדלא חיישינן להכי דאי נמי הוה הכי שפיר זכי בעל בשובר שנכתב לשמה: איתא לדשמואל. דאמר המוכר שטר חוב לחבירו וחזר המוכר הזה ומחלו מחול הוא אצל הלוה הלכך אם מכרה זו כתובתה באייר דהיינו שטר חוב וחזרה ומחלתה לבעל בתשרי מחול ושפיר טריף בעל: בששטר כתובה יוצא מתחת ידה. שמביאה לפנינו דליכא למיחש לשמא מכרה בטובת הנאה שאילו מכרתה היתה מוסרת הכתובה ביד הלוקח: לשתי כתובות. שמא שני שטרי כתובה היו לה [ויש] לחוש שמא מסרה אחד ללוקח ובאה לחזור בה ולמחול אצל בעלה ומוסרת לו שובר המוקדם לשטרו של לוקח אלא ודאי איתא לדשמואל ומתוך שבידה למחול שטר כתובה לבעלה עכשיו לא חיישינן לשמא כתבה ליתן בניסן כו': ואביי אמר. מהכא לא תסייע לשמואל: חדא דלשתי כתובות לא חיישינן. הלכך ליכא למיחש לדלמא זבנתה בטובת הנאה: ועוד. אי נמי זבנתה בטובת הנאה לית לן למיחש לשמא כתבה לשובר בניסן ולא קבלה עד תשרי דאי נמי הכי הוה כי מטא שובר לידיה בתשרי זוכה למפרע בו מזמן חתימתו ולא היה ממכרה שבנתיים כלום ושובר מזמן הכתוב בו טורף ואביי לטעמיה כו': מתני' איגרות שום. ששמו ב"ד נכסי לוה למלוה בחובו: ואיגרות מזון. שקיבל עליו לזון את בת אשתו: מיאונין. קטנה יתומה שהשיאוה אמה ואחיה לדעתה יוצאה ממנו במיאון ואינה צריכה גט אלא אומרת בפני שלשה אי אפשי בפלוני בעלי וכותבין לה ב"ד שטר שמיאנה בפניהם להיות לה עדות שמותרת לינשא: שטרי ברורין. בגמרא מפרש: הרי זה יחזיר. דליכא למיחש לשמא נמלך דהא ב"ד לא כתבום אלא בדבר מקויים ולפרעון נמי ליכא למיחש דבהני שטרות לא שייך בהו פרעון כדאמרינן לעיל (דף טז:) ואפילו למ"ד שומא הדר איהו דאפסיד אנפשיה: מצא בחפיסה או בדלוסקמא. שום שטר: או שמצא תכריך של שטרות. בכרך או באגודה ובגמרא מפרש מאי חפיסה ודלוסקמא ותכריך ואגודה: הרי זה יחזיר. דדבר שיש בו סימן הוא כדמפרש בגמרא שהכלי סימן כשיאמרו הבעלים בכלי כך וכך מצאת אותם וכן תכריך ואגודה הרי זה יחזיר לדבר שיש בו סימן הוא כדמפרש בגמרא: אחד הלוה משלשה. אם שלשה שטרות של לוה אחד הן שלוה משלשה בני אדם: יחזירם. מוצאם: ללוה. דודאי פרעם והחזירם לו ומידו נפלו שאם מידם נפלו מי קבצם למקום אחד: ואם שלשה לוים הם. שלוו מאדם אחד: יחזירם. המוצאם: למלוה. שהדבר ידוע שממנו נפלו: מצא שטר בין שטרותיו ואין יודע מה טיבו. אצלו אם הלוה הפקידו אצלו או המלוה או שמא מקצתו פרוע ומסרוהו לו להיות שליש ביניהם ושכח: יהא מונח. בידו ולא יחזיר לא לזה ולא לזה: ואם יש עמהן סמפון. מילי מילי קתני המוצא בין שטרותיו שובר שנכתב על אחד משטרותיו: יעשה מה שבסמפון. והשטר בחזקת פרוע ואע"פ שהיה לשובר הזה להיות מונח ביד הלוה אמרינן האמינו הלוה ואומר מחר תנה לי ושכח: גמ' זה בורר לו אחד. כשבוררין להן דיינין כותבין להן זה בירר לו את פלוני וזה בירר לו את פלוני שלא יוכלו לחזור בהן: דאשתכח בי דינא. מקויים בהנפק והשליח המביאו אומר ממנו נפל:

## תוספות

ש"מ איתא לדשמואל. וא"ת וניחוש שמא מכרה במעמד שלשתן שאינה יכולה למחול כדמוכח פרק האיש מקדש (קדושין ד' מח. ושם ד"ה כי) גבי התקדשי לי בשטר חוב או במלוה שיש לי ביד אחרים דקאמר במלוה בשטר במאי פליגי בדשמואל דאמר שמואל המוכר שטר חוב לחבירו וחזר ומחלו מחול ואיבעית אימא כ"ע אית להו דשמואל ובאשה סמכה דעתה פליגי כו' ובמלוה על פה פליגי בדרב הונא דאמר במעמד שלשתן קנה ולא מסיק כ"ע אית להו דרב הונא ובאשה סמכה דעתה פליגי כדאמר לעיל ש"מ דאינו יכול למחול וי"ל דליכא למיחש שמא מכרה במעמד שלשתן דאי ליכא עדים שמכרה הבעל והאשה יכפרו המכירה ואי איכא עדים נשיילינהו היכי הוה אם אומרים שנתרצה הבעל או שתק א"כ מודה שהשובר שקר ואם מוחה שאמר כבר פרעתי לה א"כ השובר נעשה קודם המכירה ואינהו דאפסידו אנפשייהו ועוד י"ל דלא תקנו מעמד שלשתן אלא בדבר שראוי לגבות מיד אבל בכתובה דאינו חייב עתה עד אחר גרושין וגם שמא לא תתגרש לא תקנו מעמד שלשתן וכן צריך לומר בפרק החובל (ב"ק דף פט. ושם) גבי האשה שחבלה [מ] (בבעלה) לא הפסידה כתובתה ואמאי תזבין במעמד שלשתן אלא משום דלא תקנו בכתובה כדפרישית וזה אין לחוש שמא מכרה אחר גרושין במעמד שלשתן כי אחר גרושין מסתמא מכרה בדמים יקרים וכשיוציא הבעל שוברו שקדם היא צריכה לשלם ולא תרויח כלום בקנוניא ולא חיישינן אלא שמא מכרה בעודה תחתיו בטובת הנאה שהיא דבר מועט ואינה צריכה לשלם אלא מעט ומרווחת הרבה ומשני איתא לדשמואל ואם היתה מוחלת לבעלה לא תפרע ללקוחות אלא דבר שנתנו ותרויח הרבה ואע"ג דגבי ערב לאשה בכתובה ורוצה לגרשה תנן בפרק גט פשוט (ב"ב ד' קעג:) דידור הנאה אלמא חיישינן לקנוניא אע"פ שיתחייב לפרוע הכל לערב ולכך חיישינן לקנוניא לפי שאין לו במה לשלם לא דמי דהתם מפסיד הערב מיד וחיישינן לקנוניא אבל הכא דאינו אלא חששא בעלמא שמא לא מכרה ואפי' מכרה שמא לא יפסידו הלקוחות כי אינו מוציא מהם אלא חוב שהיה להם על הבעל יהיה להם על האשה וגבי חייב מודה דחיישינן לעיל לקנוניא לפי שיוציא מיד מן הלקוחות ועוד יש לחוש משום לקוחות שלא באחריות שיפסידו לגמרי: שובר בזמנו טורף. אע"פ שטר מכירה נמסר ללקוחות תחילה אינו מועיל וטורף הבעל כדין וכן אמר לעיל גבי שחרורי עבדים ונראה שתקנת חכמים היא שזוכה משעת חתימה אע"פ שלא נמסר לו עד ימים רבים אחרי כן שאם לא כן לעולם לא יוכלו העדים לחתום אלא אם יראו המסירה משום חששא דכתב בניסן ולא נתן עד תשרי ומזבין ביני וביני ולענין איסור נראה דאם עבד בא על בת ישראל קודם שבא לידו גט שחרור שפסלה ושמא גם גבי איסור זכין לו משעת חתימה אע"פ דלא שייך טעמא דפרישית מ"מ לא פלוג רבנן ויש כח ביד חכמים לעקור דבר מן התורה וא"ת והא אביי סבר כר"א דאמר עידי מסירה כרתי גבי מתנתא [ל] דחתימי עלה תרי גיסי ור"א סבר בפרק מי שהיה נשוי (כתובות דף לד:) כתב לזה ולא מסר לו לזה ומסר לו לזה שמסר לו תחילה קנה וי"ל דהיינו בשני שטרות שזמנן כתוב בשוה ביום אחד שאין ניכר מתוכו איזהו מהם קודם לכך אזלינן בתר מסירה אבל אין זמנן שוה החתום קודם זכה אע"פ שהמאוחר נמסר תחילה ובעובדא דהתם דכתבינהו לרמי בר חמא בצפרא ולרב עוקבא בפניא ואוקמיה רב ששת בידיה דרמי בר חמא משום דקדים ורב נחמן אוקמיה לרב עוקבא בנכסיה משום שודא התם איירי דלא ידעינן למי נמסר תחילה ורב ששת סבר כמו שנכתב תחילה לרמי מסתמא גם לו נמסר קודם ורב נחמן סבר כיון דאינו מוכיח מכח השטר שקדם אין לומר שנמסר לו תחילה אע"ג שנכתב קודם ולכך הוי דינא שודא אבל אם הוה ידעינן למי נמסר קודם היה זוכה כיון ששניהם כתובים ביום אחד וא"ת וניחוש דלמא זבנה כתובה ביום שנכתב השובר דהשתא ליכא למימר עדיו בחתומיו זכין לו וכשיוציאו הבעל והלקוחות שטרם יהא זמנם שוה ואין ידוע דמי קדם ויאמר הבעל ללקוחות תביאו ראיה שקדמתם לפי שהוא מוחזק שהנכסים שלו והלקוחות רוצין לטרוף בשביל האשה וי"ל דהא ליכא למיחש שתמכור ביום כתיבת השובר:

איסורא

## מסורת הש"ס

כתובות פה:, פו., ... קדושין מח., בבא קמא ..., בבא בתרא קמז., ... לעיל יג., יט., לקמן ..., ג) [עי' תוס' כתובות ... ד"ה אגרת], ד) [לעיל ... יח:], ה) [עי' תוס' ... ד"ה מלא, ועי' תוס' ... כח. ד"ה מלאו], ... לקמן כח., ז) לקמן ...:, [פירושו תמצא ברש"י ... ע"ב ד"ה סמפון], ... בבא בתרא קסח. ..., י) [לעיל יח.], ... כ) מהר"מ מ"ז, ל) [סנהדרין כח:].

## ליקוטי רש"י

... ומכר שט"ח. שחייב לוה למלוה ממון ומסר המלוה את השטר ליד ... ומכרו לו וכתב לו ... לך וכל שעבודיה אי ... דמספקינן התם ... נמא אותיות נקנות ... סירה בפרק המוכר את ... פינה (לעיל עז:). ... זר. המוכר ומחל ללוה. ... זול. דלא מכר לו ... מון לשני אלא כל זכות ... בא לידו ולא עדיף האי ... ממלוה דאתי ... מחיה דמלוה ומיהו ... ותיו יחזיר לו מוכר ... קח דהא הלכתא היא ... יינין דינא דגרמי וזה ... סיד מעותיו כשורף ... רותיו של חבירו ... יימא לן דחייב מהטוח ... בלא דכפייה רפרס לרב ... י ואגבי מיניה כי ... ורא ללמי. ואפילו ... יש. של מלוה מוחל ... רא הוא דלא אלים כח ... לוקח במה שנמסר לו ... ר המלוה אלא לזכות ... וב הכתוב במקום ... לוה או היורש אך לא ... קר שעבודו מן המלוה ... יינא ביה עבד לוה לאיש ... וה ויכול למחול שעבודו ... שב"ם ב"ב קמז:]. שהלוה ... נתחייב ללוקח כלום ... א מחמת המוכר והרי ... לו אצלו [קדושין מח.]. ... מעשה ב"ד. כל ... לתא דאתא לב"ד לקיים ... יכא למיחש לנמלך ... יהן שלא ליתנן הרי זה ... יר [לעיל יח:]. ... מפונות. ולשון סימפון ... א ביטול כגון שובר ... מבטל שטר קרוי סימפון ... ום באשה או בבהמה ... מבטל המקח קרוי ... מפון [כתובות נז:]. ... שטרי טענתא. שני ... פרי הדיינין היו כותבין ... טענות אנשי הריב כדי ... א יהו טוענין וחוזרין ... ועונין ועל פי אותן ... טענות פוסקין הדיינין את ... הדין. זה בורר לו ... אחד. דיין אחד כו' והיו ... כותבין בשטר פלוני בירר ... דיין פלוני ופלוני בירר ... את פלוני [רשב"ם ב"ב ... קסח.]. בי דינא דרב ... הונא. במקום שהוא יושב ... ן ומתוך שהכל רגילין ... לו לדון הוי ליה מקום ... שיירות מצויות שם ... [לעיל יח.].

## עין משפט נר מצוה

קסו א ב מיי' פ"ו מהל' מכירה הלכה יב ועיין בהשגות ובמ"מ ובכ"מ סמג עשין פב טוש"ע ח"מ סי' סו סעיף כג:

קסז ג מיי' פי"ח מהל' גזלה ואבידה הל' יג סמג עשין עד טוש"ע ח"מ סי' סה סעיף יב:

קסח ד מיי' שם הל' ג טוש"ע שם סעיף ט:

קסט ה מיי' שם טוש"ע שם סעיף י:

קע ו מיי' שם הל' ד טוש"ע שם סעיף יא:

קעא ז מיי' פי"ו מהל' מלוה ולוה הלכה יא סמג עשין לד טוש"ע שם סעיף א:

## רבינו חננאל

אמר רבא ש"מ איתא לדשמואל דאמר המוכר שטר חוב לחבירו וחזר ומחלו מחול ואפי' יורש מוחל ומגו דאיבעי מחלה לה לכתובתה לבעלה כי אמרה שובר האי דידיה הוא תנהו לו נאמנת ואין תקנה שלא יהא המוכר רשאי למחול כלל וכבר ביארנוהו באר היטב בפרק החובל:

[מתני'] מצא איגרות שום פי' שטר שומת ב"ד ואיגרות מזון כמשמעו כגון מזון האשה והבנות. שטרי בירורין שטרי טענתא וזהו א) שימוש ב"ד. שטרי חליצה ומיאונין. ההוא גיטא דאישתכח בבי דינא דרב הונא דהוה כתיב ביה בשוירי מתא דעל רכיס נהרא מותבא

## חשק שלמה על ר"ח

א) אולי צ"ל וזהו מעשה ב"ד.

**Gemara** The Gemara defines one of the documents mentioned in the Mishnah's first ruling:

מַאי שְׁטָרֵי בֵּירוּרִי – **What are documents of clarification?** הָכָא תַּרְגְּמוּ – **Here,** in Babylonia, **they explained** that these are שְׁטָרֵי טַעֲנָתָא – **documents recording the arguments** of the litigants.[31] רַבִּי יִרְמְיָה אָמַר – **R' Yirmiyah,** who lived in Eretz Yisrael, **said** these are documents recording the judges chosen by the litigants, based on the Mishnaic dictum: זֶה בּוֹרֵר לוֹ אֶחָד – THIS litigant CHOOSES FOR HIMSELF ONE judge, וְזֶה בּוֹרֵר לוֹ אֶחָד – AND THIS other litigant CHOOSES FOR HIMSELF ONE judge.[32]

The Mishnah states:

הֲרֵי זֶה וְכָל מַעֲשֵׂה בֵּית דִּין – If one finds ANY ACT OF THE COURT, יַחֲזִיר – HE SHOULD RETURN it to the party named to receive it.

The Gemara cites an incident:

הַהוּא גִּיטָּא דְּאִשְׁתַּכַּח בֵּי דִינָא דְּרַב הוּנָא – There was **this bill of divorce that was found in Rav Huna's courthouse,** דַּהֲוָה כְּתִיב בֵּיהּ – **in which was written:** בְּשְׁוִירֵי מָתָא דְּעַל רָכִיס נַהֲרָא – **In Shviri, a town on the River Rachis.**[33] A man appeared claiming that he was the agent sent to deliver this bill of divorce to the woman named in it, and that he had dropped and lost the bill of divorce. אָמַר רַב הוּנָא – **Rav Huna said:**

NOTES

refers to a receipt, which nullifies the loan document. In other instances, it refers to a blemish that invalidates a marriage or the sale of a slave (*Rashi* to 20b ד״ה סמפון).

31. The documents contain the clarification of their claims. Court scribes would record this information to prevent the litigants from later reversing their arguments (*Shitah Mekubetzes*).

32. Litigants in a monetary case may each choose one of the three judges needed to try such a case, with the third judge being chosen by either both litigants together, or by the two judges already empaneled (see Mishnah, *Sanhedrin* 23a). The purpose of having a document recording each litigant's choice of a judge is to prevent them from retracting their choices (*Rashi*). The commentators debate whether, if this document was not written, the litigants may retract their choice of judge once the proceedings have begun (see *Ramban, Shitah Mekubetzes*).

33. I.e. the *get* recorded that the man and woman being divorced were from the town of Shviri. [See *Even HaEzer* 128:2 regarding the current practice. See also *Pischei Teshuvah, Even HaEzer* 128:9 regarding the translation of this phrase.]

## גמרא

שמע מינה איתא לדשמואל [א] דאמר שמואל א המוכר שטר חוב לחבירו וחזר ומחלו מחול ב ואפי' יורש מוחל אביי אמר אפילו תימא ליתיה לדשמואל הכא במאי עסקינן בששטר כתובה יוצא מתחת ידה ורבא אמר אי משום שטר כתובה חיישינן לשתי כתובות ואביי אמר חדא לשתי כתובות לא חיישינן ועוד שובר בזמנו טריף אביי לטעמיה דאמר [ב] עדיו בחתומיו זכין לו:

**מתני'** [ג] ג מצא איגרות שום ואיגרות מזון שטרי חליצה ומיאונין ושטרי בירורין [ד] וכל מעשה ב"ד הרי זה יחזיר [ה] ד מצא בחפיסה או בדלוסקמא [ו] ה תכריך של שטרות או אגודה של שטרות הרי זה יחזיר וכמה אגודה של שטרות שלשה קשורין זה בזה רשב"ג אומר [ז] ו אחד הלוה משלשה יחזיר ללוה שלשה הלוין מן האחד יחזיר למלוה ז מצא שטר בין שטרותיו ואינו יודע מה טיבו יהא מונח עד שיבא אליהו אם יש עמהן [ח] סמפונות יעשה מה שבסמפונות:

**גמ'** [ט] מאי שטרי ברורין הכא תרגמו שטרי טענתא רבי ירמיה אמר זה בורר לו אחד וזה בורר לו אחד: וכל מעשה ב"ד הרי זה יחזיר: [י] ההוא גיטא דאשתכח בי דינא דרב הונא דהוה כתיב ביה בשוירי מתא דעל רכים נהרא אמר רב הונא חיישינן

## רש"י

ש"מ. מדלא חיישינן להכי דאי נמי הוה הכי שפיר זכי בעל בשובר שנכתב לשמה: **איתא לדשמואל.** דאמר המוכר שטר חוב לחבירו וחזר המוכר הזה ומחלו מחול הוא אצל הלוה הלכך אם מכרה זו כתובתה באייר דהיינו שטר חוב וחזרה ומחלתה לבעל בתשרי מחול ושפיר טריף בעל: **בששטר כתובה יוצא מתחת ידה.** שמביאה לפנינו דליכא למיחש לשמא מכרה בטובת הנאה שאילו מכרתה היתה מוסרת הכתובה ביד הלוקח: **לשתי כתובות.** שמא שני שטרי כתובה היו לה [ויש] לחוש שמא מסרה אחד ללוקח ובאה לחזור בה ולמחול אצל בעלה ומוסרת לו שובר המוקדם לשטרו של לוקח אלא ודאי איתא לדשמואל ומתוך שבידה למחול שטר כתובה לבעלה עכשיו לא חיישינן לשמא כתבה ליתן בניסן כו': **ואביי אמר.** מהכא לא תסייע לשמואל: **חדא דלשתי כתובות לא חיישינן.** הלכך ליכא למיחש לדלמא זבנתה בטובת הנאה: **ועוד.** אי נמי זבנתה בטובת הנאה לית לן למיחש לשמא כתבה לשובר בניסן ולא קבלה עד תשרי דאי נמי הכי הוה כי מטא שובר לידיה בתשרי זוכה למפרע בו מזמן חתימתו ולא היה ממכרה שבנתיים כלום ושובר מזמן הכתוב בו טורף ואביי לטעמיה כו': **מתני' איגרות שום.** ששמו ב"ד נכסי לוה למלוה בחובו: **ואיגרות מזון.** שקיבל עליו לזון את בת אשתו: **מיאונין.** קטנה יתומה שהשיאוה אמה ואחיה לדעתה יוצאה ממנו במיאון ואינה צריכה גט אלא אומרת בפני שלשה אי אפשי בפלוני בעלי וכותבין לה ב"ד שטר שמיאנה בפניהם להיות לה עדות שמותרת לינשא: **שטרי ברורין.** בגמרא מפרש: **הרי זה יחזיר.** דליכא למיחש לשמא נמלך דהא ב"ד לא כתבום אלא בדבר מקויים ולפרעון נמי ליכא למיחש דבהני שטרות לא שייך בהו פרעון כדאמרינן לעיל (דף טז:) ואפילו למ"ד שומא הדר איהו דאפסיד אנפשיה: **מצא בחפיסה או בדלוסקמא.** שום שטר: **או שמצא תכריך של שטרות.** בככך או באגודה ובגמרא מפרש מאי חפיסה ודלוסקמא ותכריך ואגודה: **הרי זה יחזיר.** לדבר שיש בו סימן הוא כדמפרש בגמרא שהכלי סימן כשיאמרו הבעלים בכלי כך וכך מצאת אותם וכן תכריך ואגודה הרי זה יחזיר לדבר שיש בו סימן הוא כדמפרש בגמרא: **אחד הלוה משלשה.** אם שלשה שטרות של לוה אחד הן שלוה משלשה בני אדם: **יחזירם.** מוצאם: **ללוה.** דודאי פרעם והחזירם לו ומידו נפלו שאם מידם נפלו מי קבצם למקום אחד: **ואם שלשה לוים הם.** שלוו מאדם אחד: **יחזירם.** המוצאם: **למלוה.** שהדבר ידוע שממנו נפלו: **מצא שטר בין שטרותיו ואין יודע מה טיבו.** אצלו אם הלוה הפקידו אצלו או המלוה או שמא מתחלתו פרוע ומסרוהו לו להיות שליש ביניהם ושכח: **יהא מונח.** בידו ולא יחזיר לא לזה ולא לזה: **ואם יש עמהן סמפון.** מילי מילי קתני המוצא בין שטרותיו שובר שנכתב על אחד משטרותיו: **יעשה מה שבסמפון.** והשטר בחזקת פרוע ואע"פ שהיה לשובר הזה להיות מונח ביד הלוה אמרינן האמינו הלוה ואומר מחר תנה לי ושכח: **גמ' זה בורר לו אחד.** כשבוררין להן דיינין כותבין להן זה בירר לו את פלוני וזה בירר לו את פלוני שלא יוכלו לחזור בהן: **דאשתכח בי דינא.** מקויים בהנפק והשליח המביאו אומר ממנו נפל:

## תוספות

**ש"מ איתא לדשמואל.** וא"ת וניחוש שמא מכרה במעמד שלשתן שאינה יכולה למחול כדמוכח פרק האיש מקדש (קדושין ד' מח. ושם ד"ה כי) גבי התקדשי לי בשטר חוב או במלוה שיש לי ביד אחרים דקאמר במלוה בשטר במאי פליגי בדשמואל דאמר שמואל המוכר שטר חוב לחבירו וחזר ומחלו מחול ואיבעית אימא כ"ע אית להו דשמואל ובאשה סמכה דעתה פליגי כו' ובמלוה על פה פליגי בדרב הונא דאמר במעמד שלשתן קנה ולא מסיק כ"ע אית להו דרב הונא ובאשה סמכה דעתה פליגי כדאמר לעיל ש"מ דאינו יכול למחול וי"ל דליכא למיחש שמא מכרה במעמד שלשתן דאי ליכא עדים שמכרה הבעל והאשה יכפרו המכירה ואי איכא עדים נשיילינהו היכי הוה אם אומרים שנתרצה הבעל או שתק א"כ מודה שהשובר שקר ואם מוחה שאמר כבר פרעתי לה א"כ השובר נעשה קודם המכירה ואינהו דאפסידו אנפשייהו ועוד י"ל דלא תקנו מעמד שלשתן אלא בדבר שראוי לגבות מיד אבל בכתובה דאינו חייב עתה עד אחר גרושין וגם שמא לא תתגרש לא תקנו מעמד שלשתן וכן צריך לומר בפרק החובל (ב"ק דף פט. ושם) גבי האשה שחבלה [כ] (בבעלה) לא הפסידה כתובתה ואמאי תזבין במעמד שלשתן אלא משום דלא תקנו בכתובה כדפרישית וזה אין לחוש שמא מכרה אחר גרושין במעמד שלשתן כי אחר גרושין מסתמא מכרה בדמים יקרים וכשיוציא הבעל שוברו שקדם היא צריכה לשלם ולא תרויח כלום בקנוניא ולא חיישינן אלא שמא מכרה בעודה תחתיו בטובת הנאה שהיא דבר מועט ואינה צריכה לשלם אלא מעט ומרווחת הרבה ומשני איתא לדשמואל ואם היתה מוחלת לבעלה לא תפרע ללקוחות אלא דבר שנתנו ותרויח הרבה ואע"ג דגבי ערב לאשה בכתובה ורוצה לגרשה תנן בפרק גט פשוט (ב"ב ד' קעג:) דידור הנאה אלמא חיישינן לקנוניא אע"פ שיתחייב לפרוע הכל לערב ולכך חיישינן לקנוניא לפי שאין לו במה לשלם לא דמי דהתם מפסיד הערב מיד וחיישינן לקנוניא אבל הכא דאינו אלא חששא בעלמא שמא לא מכרה ואפי' מכרה שמא לא יפסידו הלקוחות כי אינו מוציא מהם אלא חוב שהיה להם על הבעל יהיה להם על האשה וגבי חייב מודה דחיישינן לעיל לקנוניא לפי שיוציא מיד מן הלקוחות ועוד יש לחוש משום לקוחות שלא באחריות שיפסידו לגמרי: **שובר בזמנו טורף.** אע"פ ששטר מכירה נמסר ללקוחות תחילה אינו מועיל וטורף הבעל כדין וכן אמר לעיל גבי שחרורי עבדים ונראה שתקנת חכמים היא שזוכה משעת חתימה אע"פ שלא נמסר לו עד ימים רבים אחרי כן שאם לא כן לעולם לא יוכלו העדים לחתום אלא אם יראו המסירה משום חששא דכתב בניסן ולא נתן עד תשרי ומזבין ביני ביני ולענין איסור נראה דאם עבד בא על בת ישראל קודם שבא לידו גט שחרור שפסלה ושמא גם גבי איסור זכין לו משעת חתימה אע"פ דלא שייך טעמא דפרישית מ"מ לא פלוג רבנן ויש כח ביד חכמים לעקור דבר מן התורה וא"ת והא אביי סבר כר"א דאמר עידי מסירה כרתי גבי מתנתא [ל] דחתימי עלה תרי גיסי ור"א סבר בפרק מי שהיה נשוי (כתובות דף לד:) כתב לזה ולא מסר לו לזה ומסר לו לזה שמסר לו תחילה קנה וי"ל דהיינו בשני שטרות שזמנן כתוב בשוה ביום אחד שאין ניכר מתוכו איזהו מהם קודם לכך אזלינן בתר מסירה אבל אין זמנן שוה החתום קודם זכה אע"פ שהמאוחר נמסר תחילה ובעובדא דהתם דכתבתינהו לרמי בר חמא בפרהא ולרב עוקבא בפניא ואוקמיה רב ששת בידיה דרמי בר חמא משום דקדים ורב נחמן אוקמיה לרב עוקבא בנכסיה משום שודא התם מיירי דלא ידעינן למי נמסר תחילה ורב ששת סבר כמו שנכתב תחילה לרמי מסתמא גם לו נמסר קודם ורב נחמן סבר כיון דאינו מוכיח מכח השטר שקדם אין לומר שנמסר לו תחילה אע"ג שנכתב קודם ולכך הוי דינא שודא אבל אם הוה ידעינן למי נמסר קודם היה זוכה כיון ששניהם כתובים ביום אחד וא"ת וניחוש דלמא זבנה כתובה ביום שנכתב השובר דהשתא ליכא למימר עדיו בחתומיו זכין לו וכשיוציאו הבעל והלקוחות שטרם יהא זמנם שוה ואין ידוע דמי קדם ויאמר הבעל ללקוחות תביאו ראיה שקדמתם לפי שהוא מוחזק שהנכסים שלו והלקוחות רוצין לטרוף בשביל האשה וי"ל דהא ליכא למיחש שתמכור ביום כתיבת השובר:

איסורא

## עין משפט נר מצוה

קסו א ב מיי' פ"ו מהל' מכירה הלכה יב ועיין בהשגות ובמ"מ ובכ"מ סמג עשין פב טוש"ע ח"מ סי' סו סעיף כג:

קסז ג מיי' פי"ח מהל' גזילה ואבידה הל' יג סמג עשין עד טוש"ע ח"מ סי' סה סעיף יב:

קסח ד מיי' שם הל' ג טוש"ע שם סעיף ט:

קסט ה מיי' שם טוש"ע שם סעיף י:

קע ו מיי' שם הל' ד טוש"ע שם סעיף יא:

קעא ז מיי' פי"ו מהל' מלוה ולוה הלכה יא סמג עשין לד טוש"ע שם סעיף א:

## רבינו חננאל

אמר רבא ש"מ איתא לדשמואל דאמר המוכר שטר חוב לחבירו וחזר ומחלו מחול ואפי' יורש מוחל ומגו דאיבעי מחלה לה לכתובתה לבעלה כי אמרה שובר האי דידיה הוא תנהו לו נאמנת ואין תקנה שלא יהא המוכר רשאי למחול כלל וכבר ביארנוהו באר היטב בפרק החובל:

[מתני'] מצא איגרות שום פי' שטר שומת ב"ד ואיגרות מזון כמשמעו כגון מזון האשה והבנות. שטרי בירורין שטרי טענתא וזהו א) שימוש ב"ד. שטרי חליצה ומיאונין. ההוא גיטא דאשתכח בבי דינא דרב הונא דהוה כתיב ביה בשוירי מתא דעל רכים נהרא

חשק שלמה על ר"ח

א) אולי צ"ל וזהו מעשה ב"ד.

## מסורת הש"ס

א) כתובות פה:, פו., [קידו]שין מח., בבא קמא [קיב]., בבא בתרא קמז:, ב) [לעיל יג., יט., לקמן ...:], ג) [עי' תוס' כתובות ... ד"ה אגרת], ד) [לעיל ...:, יח:], ה) [עי' תוס' ... ע"ב ד"ה מלא, ועי' תוס' גיטין כח. ד"ה מצאו], ו) לקמן כח., ז) לקמן ס:, ח) [פירושו תמצא ברש"י לקמן ע"ב ד"ה סמפון], ט) בבא בתרא קסח., י) [לעיל יח.], כ) מהר"מ מ"ז, ל) [סנהדרין כח:].

## ליקוטי רש"י

מוכר שט"ח. שחייב לו למלוה ממון ומסר המלוה את השטר ליד [לו]קח ומכרו לו וכתב לו [קני] לך וכל שעבודיה אי... כדפסקינן התם [בה]לכתא אותיות נקנות [ב]מסירה בפרק המוכר את [ה]ספינה (לעיל עז:). [ו]חזר. המוכר ומחל ללוה. [מ]חול. דלא מכר לו [ל]שון לשני אלא כל זכות [ש]בא לידו ולא עדיף האי [לו]קח ממלוה דאתי [מ]חמתיה דמלוה ומיהו [מ]עותיו יחזיר לו מוכר [ל]לוקח דהא הלכתא היא [ד]דיינינן דינא דגרמי וזה [מ]פסיד מעותיו כשורף [ש]טרותיו של חבירו [ו]קיימא לן דחייב מההוא [ע]ובדא דכפייה רפרם לרב [א]שי ואגבי מיניה כי [ס]ורא לצלמי. **ואפילו [יו]רש.** של מלוה מוחל [ד]סברא הוא דלא אלים כח [ש]ל לוקח במה שנמסר לו [ש]טר המלוה אלא לזכות [ח]וב הכתוב במקום [ה]מלוה או היורש אך לא [ל]עקר שעבודו מן המלוה [ד]קרינא ביה עבד לוה לאיש [מ]לוה ויכול למחול שעבודו [ר]שב"ם ב"ב קמז:]. שהלוה [ל]א נתחייב ללוקח כלום [א]לא מחמת המוכר והרי [מ]חלו אצלו [קדושין מח.]. **[כ]ל מעשה ב"ד.** כל [מ]ילתא דאתא לב"ד לקיים [ל]יכא למיחש לנמלך [ו]אינן שלא ליתנן הרי זה [י]חזיר [לעיל יח:]. **[ס]מפונות.** ולשון סימפון [ה]וא ביטול כגון שובר [ה]מבטל שטר קרוי סימפון [מ]ום באשה או בבהמה [ה]מבטל המקח קרוי [ס]ימפון [כתובות נז:]. **שטרי טענתא.** שני [ס]ופרי הדיינין היו כותבין [ט]ענות אנשי הריב כדי [ש]לא יהו טוענין ותוזרין [ו]טוענין ועל פי אותן [ט]ענות פוסקין הדיינין [ה]דין. **זה בורר לו** [illegible] ...

**certificates of *chalitzah***[17] **or of *mi'un,***[18] וּשְׁטָרֵי בֵּירוּרִין – **documents of clarification,**[19] וְכָל מַעֲשֵׂה בֵּית דִּין – **or any act of the court,**[20] הֲרֵי זֶה יַחֲזִיר – **he should return** these to the party named in them to receive the document.[21]

The Mishnah now considers whether an ordinary document can be returned on the basis of external evidence:[22] מָצָא בַּחֲפִיסָה אוֹ בִּדְלוּסְקְמָא – If **one found** a document **in a *chafisah* or in a *deluskema*** (two types of containers),[23] תַּכְרִיךְ שֶׁל שְׁטָרוֹת – or if he found **a roll of documents,** אוֹ אֲגוּדָּה שֶׁל שְׁטָרוֹת – **or a bundle of documents,** הֲרֵי זֶה יַחֲזִיר – **he should return it.**[24] וְכַמָּה אֲגוּדָּה שֶׁל שְׁטָרוֹת – **How many** documents constitute **a bundle of documents?** שְׁלֹשָׁה קְשׁוּרִין זֶה בָּזֶה – **Three, tied together.**

רַבָּן שִׁמְעוֹן בֶּן גַּמְלִיאֵל אוֹמֵר – **Rabban Shimon ben Gamliel says:** אֶחָד הַלֹּוֶה מִשְּׁלֹשָׁה – If one found three documents regarding **one** person **who borrowed from three** different people,[25] יַחֲזִיר לַלֹּוֶה – **he should return** them **to the borrower,** for they certainly belong to him.[26] שְׁלֹשָׁה הַלּוִֹין מִן הָאֶחָד – But if the three documents concern **three** people **who borrowed from one** person, יַחֲזִיר לַמַּלְוֶה – **[the finder] should return** them **to the lender,** for they certainly belong to him.[27]

The Mishnah now discusses what to do with unknown documents that turn up in one's possession: מָצָא שְׁטָר בֵּין שְׁטָרוֹתָיו – If **one found a document** belonging to others **among his own documents,** וְאֵינוֹ יוֹדֵעַ מַה טִּיבוֹ – **and he does not know its status,**[28] יְהֵא מוּנָּח עַד שֶׁיָּבֹא אֵלִיָּהוּ – **it should be set aside until Elijah** the Prophet **comes** and resolves its ownership. He should not return it to either the borrower or to the lender. אִם יֵשׁ עִמָּהֶן סִמְפּוֹנוֹת – **If there are** unissued **receipts**[29] **among [his documents],** and he does not remember whether or not he received payment, יַעֲשֶׂה מַה שֶּׁבַּסִּמְפּוֹנוֹת – **he should abide by that which is** recorded **in the receipts.**[30]

NOTES

t is drawn merely to give the stepdaughter proof of the obligation. [The obligation itself is effected by means of a *kinyan chalifin*] (*Rashash*). Thus, if it is lost it is returned to the stepdaughter; see note 21.

7. When a childless man dies, his widow is not free to remarry anyone but his (paternal) brothers. Should they all refuse to marry her, one of them must perform with her the procedure known as *chalitzah* (literally: *the removal* of the shoe) to release her from her bond to them and allow her to marry anyone she wishes (*Deut.* 25:5-10). The court then draws a document certifying that she has undergone *chalitzah* and is eligible to remarry. Should such a document be found, it is returned to the widow.

8. Under Biblical law, a father may contract a marriage for his underage daughter. In the case of an orphan, the Rabbis gave this right to her mother or brothers. Since the marriage contracted by them is valid only by Rabbinic law, should she wish to dissolve the marriage, the Rabbis did not require her to obtain a regular divorce from her husband. Rather, she may herself annul the marriage at any time before reaching her majority by declaring before a *beis din* of three judges her unwillingness to continue in the marriage. This process is called *mi'un* (refusal). The court then gives her a document certifying that she has annulled her marriage and is now permitted to remarry (see *Rashi*).

9. The Gemara below will explain the function of these documents.

0. For example, the certification of a document or note by a court (see Gemara below). Also included in this are an אַדְרַכְתָּא, *seizure warrant,* and חֲלָטָאתָא, *certificate of seizure* (Gemara 16b).

This presents a problem, inasmuch as a certificate of seizure would seem to be identical to the letter of assignment mentioned earlier in the Mishnah. *Rabbeinu Tam* (quoted by *Tosafos* in *Kesubos* 100b ד״ה אגרת) is of the opinion that the use of the term *letters* (אִגְּרוֹת) rather than certificates (שְׁטָרוֹת) suggests that it is a letter sent by a court in one city to a court in another city to seize property on behalf of a creditor (see *Tos. Yom Tov*). This would serve to distinguish the letter of assignment from the certificate of seizure.

*Tos. Yom Tov* quotes an explanation given by *Sma* (65:36) in the name of *Sefer HaTerumos,* that אִגֶּרֶת שׁוּם, *letter of assignment,* refers to a certificate issued to the creditor in the presence of the debtor. A חֲלָטָאתָא, *certificate of seizure,* refers to a seizure made by the court in the absence of the debtor. This latter document is included here under the heading of "an act of the court."

1. Since these documents are issued by the courts, there is no concern that the document was written in advance of the fact or obligation, because the courts do not draw documents in advance. In addition, there is no concern that the obligations of some of these documents were paid [so that the document should not be returned to the creditor], because it is the debtor's responsibility to make sure that his documents are returned to him and destroyed when he pays the obligation. If he failed to do so, he is responsible for his own loss (*Rashi;* see Gemara above, 16b).

Although a letter of sustenance is a personal obligation, not an act of the court, since it is written to attest to an obligation transacted by other means (see note 16), it would not be signed until the *kinyan* establishing the obligation had been made. Thus, if it is signed, there is no concern that the obligation was never effected (*Rashash*).

22. I.e. a document which is not an "act of the court," but a private document (*Rashi*), such as a loan document or a will. [Ordinarily, these cannot be returned to either party without proof, as we learned in the Mishnahs on 12b and 18a.] This Mishnah teaches that if the document can be identified by its special container or by the way it is bundled [something the other party to the document is not likely to know], it may be returned to the party that identifies it (*Rashi*).

23. The Gemara (20b) will explain these terms.

24. The container in which a document is found, and the method by which a number of documents are bundled together, are considered identifying marks (*simanim*). Thus, one must return them to the one who identifies them (*Rashi*). [The next chapter will discuss at length the law for returning a lost object based on identification.] The Gemara below (20b) will delineate what constitutes a roll and a bundle of documents.

25. I.e. each document records a separate loan taken out by this borrower from a different lender.

26. If the three lenders each lost their document, how are we to account for the fact that all three are together? Undoubtedly, what happened is that the borrower paid these notes and they were returned to him, and *he* lost them. Thus, we return them to him (*Rashi*).

27. Here the logic is reversed. Had the three borrowers each lost the loan document returned to them, all three documents would not have been found together. Undoubtedly, it was the lender, who kept all his uncollected bills together, who lost the three documents. They are therefore returned to him.

28. For example, he found among his papers a document recording a loan between two other parties, and he does not remember whether it was entrusted to him by the creditor or the debtor, or whether the note was partially paid and was therefore entrusted to him by both parties to hold until the remainder was paid (*Rashi*).

29. This case refers to a person who holds a note stating that he is owed a certain debt, who then finds among his papers a receipt stating that the debt has been paid.

30. That is, he should treat the debt as paid. Although this receipt, if it is valid, ought to be in the hands of the debtor, we presume in this case that the debtor paid the note, but trusted the creditor to provide him with a receipt at a later date. The creditor wrote the receipt but failed to deliver it, and eventually forgot why the receipt was in his possession (*Rashi*). The Gemara (20b) will discuss the reason for such a presumption.

The word סִמְפּוֹן refers to something that invalidates. In this context, it

שמע מינה איתא לדשמואל [א] דאמר שמואל [א] המוכר שטר חוב לחבירו וחזר ומחלו מחול [ב] ואפי' יורש מוחל אביי אמר אפילו תימא ליתיה לדשמואל הכא במאי עסקינן בששטר כתובה יוצא מתחת ידה ורבא אמר אי משום שטר כתובה חיישינן לשתי כתובות ואביי אמר חדא לשתי כתובות לא חיישינן ועוד שובר בזמנו טריף אביי לטעמיה דאמר [ב] עדיו בחתומיו זכין לו:

מתני' [ג] [ג] מצא איגרות שום ואיגרות מזון שטרי חליצה ומיאונין ושטרי בירורין [ד] וכל מעשה ב"ד הרי זה יחזיר [ה] [ד] מצא בחפיסה או בדלוסקמא [ו] [ה] תכריך של שטרות או אגודה של שטרות הרי זה יחזיר וכמה אגודה של שטרות שלשה קשורין זה בזה רשב"ג אומר [ז] [ו] אחד הלוה משלשה יחזיר ללוה שלשה הלוין מן האחד יחזיר למלוה [ז] מצא שטר בין שטרותיו ואינו יודע מה טיבו יהא מונח עד שיבא אליהו אם יש עמהן [ח] סמפונות יעשה מה שבסמפונות:

גמ' [ט] מאי שטרי ברורין הכא תרגמו שטרי טענתא רבי ירמיה אמר זה בורר לו אחד וזה בורר לו אחד: וכל מעשה ב"ד הרי זה יחזיר: [י] ההוא גיטא דאשתכח בי דינא דרב הונא דהוה כתיב ביה בשוירי מתא דעל רכים נהרא אמר רב הונא חיישינן

## רש"י

ש"מ. מדלא חיישינן להכי דאי נמי הוה הכי שפיר זכי בעל בשובר שנכתב לשמה: איתא לדשמואל. דאמר המוכר שטר חוב לחבירו וחזר המוכר הזה ומחלו מחול הוא אבל הלוה הלכך אם מכרה זו כתובתה בא"י דהיינו שטר חוב וחזרה ומחלתה לבעל בתשרי מחול ושפיר טריף בעל: בששטר כתובה יוצא מתחת ידה. שמביאה לפנינו דליכא למיחש לשמא מכרה בטובת הנאה שאילו מכרתה היתה מוסרת הכתובה ביד הלוקח: לשתי כתובות. שמא שני שטרי כתובה היו לה [ויש] לחוש שמא מסרה אחד ללוקח ובאה לחזור בה ולמחול אצל בעלה ומוסרת לו שובר המוקדם לשטרו של לוקח אלא ודאי איתא לדשמואל ומתוך שבידה למחול שטר כתובה לבעלה עכשיו לא חיישינן לשמא כתבה ליתן בניסן כו': ואביי אמר. מהכא לא תסייע לשמואל: חדא דלשתי כתובות לא חיישינן. הלכך ליכא למיחש לדלמא זבנתה בטובת הנאה: ועוד. אי נמי זבנתה בטובת הנאה לית לן למיחש לשמא כתבה לשובר בניסן ולא קבלה עד תשרי דאי נמי הכי הוה כי מטא שובר לידיה בתשרי זוכה למפרע בו מזמן חתימתו ולא היה ממכרה שבנתיים כלום ושובר מזמן הכתוב בו טורף ואביי לטעמיה כו': מתני' איגרות שום. ששמו ב"ד נכסי לוה למלוה בחובו: ואיגרות מזון. שקיבל עליו לזון את בת אשתו: מיאונין. קטנה יתומה שהשיאוה אמה ואחיה לדעתה יוצאה ממנו במיאון ואינה צריכה גט אלא אומרת בפני שלשה אי אפשי בפלוני בעלי וכותבין לה ב"ד שטר שמיאנה בפניהם להיות לה עדות שמותרת לינשא: שטרי ברורין. בגמרא מפרש: הרי זה יחזיר. דליכא למיחש לשמא נמלך דהא ב"ד לא כתבוס אלא בדבר מקויים ולפרעון נמי ליכא למיחש דבהני שטרות לא שייך בהו פרעון כדאמרינן לעיל (דף יח:) ואפילו למ"ד שומא הדר איהו דאפסיד אנפשיה: מצא בחפיסה או בדלוסקמא. שום שטר: או שמצא תכריך של שטרות. בכרך או באגודה ובגמרא מפרש מאי חפיסה ודלוסקמא ותכריך ואגודה: הרי זה יחזיר. דדבר שיש בו סימן הוא כדמפרש בגמרא שהכלי סימן כשיאמרו הבעלים בכלי כך וכך מצאת אותם וכן תכריך ואגודה הרי זה יחזיר דדבר שיש בו סימן הוא כדמפרש בגמרא: אחד הלוה משלשה. אם שלשה שטרות של לוה אחד הן שלוה משלשה בני אדם: יחזירם. מוצאם: ללוה. דודאי פרעם והחזירם לו ומידו נפלו שאם מידם נפלו מי קבצם למקום אחד: ואם שלשה לוים הם. שלוו מאדם אחד: יחזירם. המוצאם: למלוה. שהדבר ידוע שממנו נפלו: מצא שטר בין שטרותיו ואין יודע מה טיבו. אצלו אם הלוה הפקידו אצלו או המלוה או שמא מקלתו פרוע ומסרוהו לו להיות שליש ביניהם ושכח: יהא מונח. בידו ולא יחזיר לא לזה ולא לזה: ואם יש עמהן סמפון. מילי מילי קתני המוצא בין שטרותיו שובר שנכתב על אחד משטרותיו: יעשה מה שבסמפון. והשטר בחזקת פרוע ואע"פ שהיה לשובר הזה להיות מונח ביד הלוה אמרינן האמינו הלוה ואומר מחר תנה לי ושכח: גמ' זה בורר לו אחד. כשבוררין להן דיינין כותבין להן זה בירר לו את פלוני וזה בירר לו את פלוני שלא יוכלו לחזור בהן: דאשתכח בי דינא. מקויים בהנפק והשליח המביאו אומר ממנו נפל:

## תוספות

ש"מ איתא לדשמואל. וא"ת וניחוש שמא מכרה במעמד שלשתן שאינה יכולה למחול כדמוכח פרק האיש מקדש (קדושין ד' מח. ושם ד"ה מי) גבי התקדשי לי בשטר חוב או במלוה שיש לי ביד אחרים דקאמר במלוה בשטר במאי פליגי בדשמואל דאמר שמואל המוכר שטר חוב לחבירו וחזר ומחלו מחול ואיבעית אימא כ"ע אית להו דשמואל ובאשה סמכה דעתה פליגי כו' ובמלוה על פה פליגי בדרב הונא דאמר במעמד שלשתן קנה ולא מסיק כ"ע אית להו דרב הונא ובאשה סמכה דעתה פליגי כדאמר לעיל ש"מ דאינו יכול למחול וי"ל דליכא למיחש שמא מכרה במעמד שלשתן דאי ליכא עדים שמכרה הבעל והאשה יכפרו המכירה ואי איכא עדים נשיילינהו היכי הוה אם אומרים שנתרצה הבעל או שתק א"כ מודה שהשובר שקר ואם מוחה שאמר כבר פרעתי לה א"כ השובר נעשה קודם המכירה ואינהו דאפסידו אנפשייהו ועוד י"ל דלא תקנו מעמד שלשתן אלא בדבר שראוי לגבות מיד אבל בכתובה דאינו חייב עתה עד אחר גרושין וגם שמא לא תתגרש לא תקנו מעמד שלשתן וכן צריך לומר בפרק החובל (ב"ק דף פט. ושם) גבי האשה שחבלה [כ] (בבעלה) לא הפסידה כתובתה ואמאי תזבין במעמד שלשתן אלא משום דלא תקנו בכתובה כדפרישית וזה אין לחוש שמא מכרה אחר גרושין במעמד שלשתן כי אחר גרושין מסתמא מכרה בדמים יקרים וכשיוציא הבעל שוברו שקדם היא צריכה לשלם ולא תרויח כלום בקנוניא ולא חיישינן אלא שמא מכרה בעודה תחתיו בטובת הנאה שהיא דבר מועט ואינה צריכה לשלם אלא מעט ומרווחת הרבה ומשני איתא לדשמואל ואם היתה מוחלת לבעלה לא תפרע ללקוחות אלא דבר שנתנו ותרויח הרבה ואע"ג דגבי ערב לאשה בכתובה ורוצה לגרשה תנן בפרק גט פשוט (ב"ב ד' קעג:) דידור הנאה אלמא חיישינן לקנוניא אע"פ שיתחייב לפרוע הכל לערב ולכך חיישינן לקנוניא לפי שאין לו במה לשלם לא דמי דהתם מפסיד הערב מיד וחיישינן לקנוניא אבל הכא דאינו אלא חששא בעלמא שמא לא מכרה ואפי' מכרה שמא לא יפסידו הלקוחות כי אינו מוציא מהם אלא חוב שהיה להם על הבעל יהיה להם על האשה וגבי חייב מודה דחיישינן לעיל לקנוניא לפי שיוציא מיד מן הלקוחות ועוד יש לחוש משום לקוחות שלא באחריות שיפסידו לגמרי: שובר בזמנו טורף. אע"פ ששטר מכירה נמסר ללקוחות תחילה אינו מועיל וטורף הבעל כדין וכן אמר לעיל גבי שחרורי עבדים ונראה שתקנת חכמים היא שזוכה משעת חתימה אע"פ שלא נמסר לו עד ימים רבים אחרי כן שאם לא כן לעולם לא יוכלו העדים לחתום אלא אם יראו המסירה משום חששא דכתב בניסן ולא נתן עד תשרי ומזבין ביני וביני ולענין איסור נראה דאם עבד בא על בת ישראל קודם שבא לידו גט שחרור שפסלה ושמא גם גבי איסור זכין לו משעת חתימה אע"פ דלא שייך טעמא דפרישית מ"מ לא פלוג רבנן ויש כח ביד חכמים לעקור דבר מן התורה וא"ת והא אביי סבר כר"א דאמר עידי מסירה כרתי גבי מתנתא [ל] דחתימי עלה תרי גיסי ור"א סבר בפרק מי שהיה נשוי (כתובות דף צד:) כתב לזה ולא מסר לו לזה ומסר לו לזה שמסר לו תחילה קנה וי"ל דהיינו בשני שטרות שזמנן כתוב בשוה ביום אחד שאין ניכר מתוכו איזהו מהם קודם לכך אזלינן בתר מסירה אבל אין זמנן שוה החתום קודם זכה אע"פ שהמאוחר נמסר תחילה ובעובדא דהתם דכתבתינהו לרמי בר חמא בגפרא ולרב עוקבא בפניא ואוקמיה רב ששת בידיה דרמי בר חמא משום דקדים ורב נחמן אוקמיה לרב עוקבא בנכסיה משום שודא התם מיירי דלא ידעינן למי נמסר תחילה ורב ששת סבר כמו שנכתב תחילה לרמי מסתמא גם לו נמסר קודם ורב נחמן סבר כיון דאינו מוכיח מכח השטר שקדם אין לומר שנמסר לו תחילה אע"ג שנכתב קודם ולכך הוה דינא שודא אבל אם הוה ידעינן למי נמסר קודם היה זוכה כיון ששניהם כתובים ביום אחד וא"ת וניחוש דלמא זבנה כתובה ביום שנכתב השובר דהשתא ליכא למימר עדיו בחתומיו זכין לו וכשיוציאו הבעל והלקוחות שטרם יהא זמנם שוה ואין ידוע דמי קדם ויאמר הבעל ללקוחות תביאו ראיה שקדמתם לפי שהוא מוחזק שהנכסים שלו והלקוחות רוצין לטרוף בשביל האשה וי"ל דהא ליכא למיחש שתמכור ביום כתיבת השובר:

איסורא

## עין משפט נר מצוה

קנו א ב מיי' פ"ו מהל' מכירה הלכה יב ועיין בהשגות ובמ"מ ובכ"מ סמג עשין פב טוש"ע ח"מ סי' סו סעיף כג:

קנז ג מיי' פי"ח מהל' גזילה ואבידה הל' יג סמג עשין עד טוש"ע ח"מ סי' סה סעיף יב:

קנח ד מיי' שם הל' ג טוש"ע שם סעיף ט:

קנט ה מיי' שם טוש"ע שם סעיף י:

קס ו מיי' שם הל' ד טוש"ע שם סעיף יא:

קסא ז מיי' פי"ו מהל' מלוה ולוה הלכה יא סמג עשין צד טוש"ע שם סעיף א:

## רבינו חננאל

אמר רבא ש"מ איתא לדשמואל דאמר המוכר שטר חוב לחבירו וחזר ומחלו מחול ואפי' יורש מוחל ומגו דאיבעי מחלה לה לכתובתה לבעלה כי אמרה שובר האי דידיה הוא תנהו לו נאמנת ואין תקנה שלא יהא המוכר רשאי למחול כלל וכבר ביארנוהו באר היטב בפרק החובל:

[מתני'] מצא איגרות שום פי' שטר שומת ב"ד ואיגרות מזון כמשמעו כגון מזון האשה והבנות. שטרי בירורין שטרי טענתא וזהו א) שימוש ב"ד. שטרי חליצה ומיאונין. ההוא גיטא דאישתכח בבי דינא דרב הונא דהוה כתיב ביה בשוירי מתא דעל רכיס נהרא מותבא

### חשק שלמה על ר"ח

א) אולי צ"ל וזהו מעשה ב"ד.

## מסורת הש"ס

א) כתובות פה:, פו., קידושין מח., בבא קמא ט., בבא בתרא קמז:, ב) [לעיל יג., יט., לקמן ...:], ג) [עי' תוס' כתובות ...: ד"ה אגרת], ד) [לעיל ...:, יח:], ה) [עי' תוס' ...ב ד"ה מצא, ועי' תוס' גיטין כח. ד"ה מצאו], ו) לקמן כח., ז) לקמן כ:, ח) [פירושו תמצא ברש"י לקמן ע"ב ד"ה סמפון], ט) בבא בתרא קסח., י) [...צ"ש], י) [לעיל יח.], כ) גיטין כ., כ) מהר"מ מ"ז, ל) [סנהדרין כח:].

## ליקוטי רש"י

המוכר שט"ח. שחייב לוה למלוה ממון ומסר המלוה את השטר ליד לוקח ומכרו לו וכתב לו קני לך וכל שעבודיה אי נמי כדפסקינן התם הלכתא אותיות נקנות במסירה בפרק המוכר את הספינה (לעיל עז:). וחזר. המוכר ומחל ללוה. מחול. דלא מכר לו ראשון לשני אלא כל זכות שבא לידו ולא עדיף האי לוקח ממלוה דאתי מחמתיה דמלוה ומיהו מעותיו יחזיר לו מוכר ללוקח דהא הלכתא היא ודיינין דינא דגרמי וזה הפסיד מעותיו כשורף שטרותיו של חבירו וקיימא לן דחייב מההוא עובדא דכפייה רפרם לרב אשי ואגבי מיניה כי שורא ללמי. ואפילו יורש. של מלוה מוחל סברא הוא דלא אלים כח של לוקח במה שנמסר לו שטר המלוה אלא לזכות חוב הכתוב במקום מלוה או היורש אך לא עקר שעבודו מן המלוה וקרינא ביה עבד לוה לאיש מלוה ויכול למחול שעבודו [רשב"ם ב"ב קמז:]. שהלוה לא נתחייב ללוקח כלום אלא מחמת המוכר והרי מחלו אצלו [קדושין מח.]. וכל מעשה ב"ד. כל מילתא דאתא לב"ד לקיים וליכא למיחש לנמלך ועליהן שלא ליתנן הרי זה יחזיר [לעיל יח:]. סמפונות. ולשון סימפון הוא ביטול כגון שובר שמבטל שטר קרוי סימפון ומום באשה או בבהמה שמבטל המקח קרוי סימפון [כתובות נז:]. שטרי טענתא. שני סופרי הדיינין היו כותבין טענות אנשי הריב כדי שלא יהו טוענין וחוזרין וטוענין ועל פי אותן טענות פוסקין הדיינין את הדין. זה בורר לו אחד. דיין אחד כו' והיו כותבין בשטר פלוני בירר לו דיין פלוני ופלוני בירר לו את פלוני [רשב"ם ב"ב קסח.]. בי דינא דרב הונא. במקום שהיה יושב לדון ומתוך שהכל רגילין אצלו לדון הוי ליה מקום שהשיירות מצויות [לעיל יח.].

**שְׁמַע מִינָּהּ** – Let us **learn from [the Baraisa],** which is unconcerned for fraud, **אִיתָא לִדְשְׁמוּאֵל** – that **Shmuel's** following opinion **is** correct. **דְּאָמַר שְׁמוּאֵל** – **For Shmuel said: הַמּוֹכֵר שְׁטַר חוֹב לַחֲבֵירוֹ** – **If one sells a note of indebtedness to his fellow, וְחָזַר וּמְחָלוֹ** – **and afterward forgives [the debt], מָחוּל** – **[the debt] is forgiven.**[1] **וַאֲפִילּוּ יוֹרֵשׁ מוֹחֵל** – **Even the** seller's **heir can forgive** the debt after the seller's death.[2] According to Shmuel's ruling, here we can accept the woman's word that her husband lost the receipt, because if she wanted to relieve her husband of his *kesubah* obligation she would not resort to fraud, for she may lawfully forgive him.[3] Thus, the Baraisa which rules that her word is accepted supports Shmuel's opinion.

The Gemara challenges Rava's assertion that the Baraisa supports Shmuel's opinion, explaining instead that the Baraisa's ruling is limited to a specific case:

**אַבָּיֵי אָמַר** – **Abaye said: אֲפִילּוּ תֵּימָא לֵיתֵיהּ לִדְשְׁמוּאֵל** – **Even if you say** that **Shmuel's** opinion **is not** correct, the Baraisa can be explained in the following manner: **הָכָא בְּמַאי עַסְקִינָן** – **What do we refer to here,** in the Baraisa that permits the return of a receipt? **בְּשֶׁשְּׁטַר כְּתוּבָּה יוֹצֵא מִתַּחַת יָדָהּ** – To a case **where** we see that **the *kesubah* document is** still **in her possession.**[4] In such a case we know that she has not sold the *kesubah,*[5] and we therefore return the receipt to her husband. Ordinarily, however, the Baraisa may agree that we should not return the receipt because we must be concerned that a purchaser of her *kesubah* might be defrauded.[6]

The Gemara explains why Rava did not interpret the Baraisa as referring to this case, but rather asserted that the Baraisa agrees with Shmuel's opinion:

**וְרָבָא אָמַר** – **But Rava says: אִי מִשּׁוּם שְׁטַר כְּתוּבָּה** – **If the basis** for returning the receipt was **that the *kesubah* document** is in her possession, we would nevertheless have to consider the possibility of fraud; **חָיְישִׁינַן לִשְׁתֵּי כְּתוּבּוֹת** – **we must be concerned** that perhaps her husband gave her **two *kesubah* documents.** Thus, she may have sold her *kesubah* entitlement, and given one of the documents to a purchaser, while retaining the other, which we now see in her possession.[7] Therefore, the only possible explanation of the Baraisa's lack of concern for the defraudment of a purchaser is that it concurs with Shmuel's opinion.

The Gemara presents Abaye's rebuttal to this argument:

**וְאַבָּיֵי אָמַר** – **But Abaye says** that the Baraisa does not necessarily support Shmuel's opinion, for two reasons: **חֲדָא** – **Firstly, לִשְׁתֵּי כְּתוּבּוֹת לֹא חָיְישִׁינַן** – **we need not be concerned for** the unlikely possibility that the woman was given **two *kesubah* documents** by her husband. Therefore, seeing a *kesubah* document in her possession *does* eliminate the concern that she sold the *kesubah*.

Abaye's rebuttal continues, offering a new reason that we need not be concerned for fraud:

**וְעוֹד** – **And furthermore,** even in a case where she sold her *kesubah,* we may nevertheless return the receipt to her husband, for the following reason: **שׁוֹבֵר בִּזְמַנּוֹ טָרִיף** – **A receipt deprives**[8] the creditor of the right to collect payment of a debt **from the date [recorded in the receipt]** onward, even if it is handed over to the debtor at a later date.[9] Accordingly, the receipt that she wrote in Nissan is valid even if her husband did not pay her then,[10] and if anyone purchased the *kesubah* after the receipt was signed, he is not entitled to payment.[11]

The Gemara explains why Abaye holds that a receipt takes effect at the time it is written:

**אַבָּיֵי לְטַעְמֵיהּ** – **Abaye,** in this ruling, **follows his own reasoning, דְּאָמַר** – **for [Abaye] said**[12] **עֵדָיו בַּחֲתוּמָיו זָכִין לוֹ** – that when a document confers a benefit upon its recipient, **its witnesses, by** their **signatures, acquire for him** the benefit recorded in the document.[13] Thus, a receipt, which is beneficial to the debtor, takes effect at the time it is signed.[14]

## Mishnah

The Mishnah continues its discussion of returning lost documents: **מָצָא אִיגְּרוֹת שׁוּם** – **If one found letters of assignment,**[15] **וְאִיגְּרוֹת מָזוֹן** – **letters of sustenance,**[16] **שְׁטָרֵי חֲלִיצָה וּמֵיאוּנִין** –

NOTES

1. By selling a note of indebtedness to another person, the creditor transfers to that person the right to collect the debt. Nevertheless, according to Shmuel, the original creditor retains the right to forgive the debt. This is because a debt, being intangible, cannot be sold under Biblical law. Therefore, although the Rabbis decreed that one can transfer the right to collect a debt to another person, such a transaction does not divest the seller of his status as the true creditor. He therefore retains the right to forgive the debt (see *Tosafos* to *Kesubos* 85b ד״ה המוכר; cf. *Rosh* ad loc. §10).

2. This last clause emphasizes the extent of Shmuel's ruling, but is not essential for the Gemara's argument.

3. [See *Rashi* ד״ה לישתי.] Since she is the original creditor for the *kesubah* obligation, she retains the right to forgive this obligation even though she sold it (see above, note 1). In this respect, a *kesubah* is no different than a note of indebtedness.

4. Literally: the *kesubah* document comes out from underneath her hand.

5. If she had in fact sold the *kesubah* to another, he would have taken the *kesubah* document from her (*Rashi*).

6. Thus, the Baraisa does not necessarily support Shmuel's opinion, according to which the return of a receipt never presents a danger of fraud.

7. We must now be concerned that the husband may use the receipt to free himself from his obligation to pay her *kesubah* which was sold.

8. Literally: collects.

9. A receipt takes effect at the time it was signed. The Gemara will shortly explain why this is so.

10. Since, now in the end, he receives the receipt (see below, note 13; see *Shach* to *Choshen Mishpat* 39:39).

11. Indeed, she had no right to sell the *kesubah* after drafting the receipt, and the sale is null and void (*Rashi*).

12. Above, 13a; 19a.

13. I.e. the witnesses act on behalf of the beneficiary to acquire for him the benefit conferred in the document. When the beneficiary receives the document, his acquisition is retroactive to the time of the document's signing.

14. To summarize: According to Abaye, a receipt takes effect at the time it is signed. Therefore, the Baraisa correctly rules that a receipt may be returned to the husband, for if anyone purchased the *kesubah* after the receipt was signed, they are not entitled to payment. One could also interpret the Baraisa as referring to a case where we see the *kesubah* document in her possession and thus we know that she did not sell it.

Rava argues that a receipt does not take effect until it is handed over to the debtor. Thus, one who purchased the *kesubah* before the husband was given the receipt is entitled to payment. We cannot interpret the Baraisa as referring to a case where we see the *kesubah* document in her possession, for even then we would have to be concerned that perhaps her husband gave her two *kesubah* documents, and one of them was given to a purchaser. Therefore, the only possible explanation of the Baraisa is that it concurs with Shmuel's opinion that she can forgive the *kesubah* obligation even after selling it, and she therefore has no need to resort to fraud.

15. Literally: of assessment; i.e. an official letter stating that a property has been assessed and confiscated to satisfy a debt. Letters of assignment are given to a creditor by a court to certify that a property belonging to the debtor has been seized by the court and assigned to his creditor (*Rashi*). If such a letter is found, it is to be returned to the creditor named in it, as will be explained in note 21.

16. These certify that a husband has agreed to provide for his stepdaughter's support (*Rashi*). This document is not used to effect the obligation;

I am unable to retract my gift legally, אֵימַר לְהוּ – I will tell [the court] דְּאַבָּא יְהָבָהּ לֵיהּ לְהַאי – that my father gave [the will] to this person, וְנֶהְדְּרוּ לֵיהּ כְּתָבֵיהּ – and they will therefore return the document to him. וְנֵיזִיל וְנַפֵּיק מִינֵּיהּ – Then we will be able to go and take away the property from [the beneficiary of my gift], דְּהוּא זָכֵי – because if my father's beneficiary presents the will in court he will win ownership of the property, since the will indicates that I did not inherit the property and my gift was unauthorized. וְנִפְלוֹג בַּהֲדֵיהּ – I will then divide with him the proceeds of this illicit seizure."[14] Thus, by returning the will we may be assisting the son in the perpetration of a fraud. Therefore, the Baraisa rules that in such a case we do not return the will.

The Gemara now records the court's response to the son who instructs it to return the will:

אֲנַן הִלְכָּךְ אָמְרִינַן לֵיהּ – Due to this concern, we tell [the son]: הַאי כְּתָבָא לֹא יָהֲבִינַן לֵיהּ לְהַאי – We will not give this document to [your father's beneficiary] דִּדְלְמָא מִכְתַּב כְּתָבֵיהּ אֲבוּהָ – because we are concerned that perhaps your father wrote it וִיהַבְתֵּיהּ אַתְּ מֵיהַב לֹא יְהָבָהּ לֵיהּ – but did not give it to him, לְאִינִישׁ אַחֲרִינָא – and after you inherited your father's estate, you gave [the property] to another person as a gift, וְקָא הָדְרַתְּ בֵּיהּ – which you now wish to retract. אֶלָּא – Rather, we tell the son, אִי קוּשְׁטָא קָא אָמְרַתְּ דִּיהַב לֵיהּ אֲבוּךְ – if you are telling the truth – that your father gave him the will, and you did not give the property to somebody else – you have the following option: זִיל אַתְּ הַשְׁתָּא – Go now, yourself, כְּתִיב לֵיהּ שְׁטָרָא אַחֲרִינָא – and write him another document, dated today, in which you grant him the property. You can thus provide him with evidence that he owns the property. דְּאִי נַמִּי לֹא יְהָבָהּ לֵיהּ אֲבוּהָ – However, we will still be assured that even if you are lying and your father did not give him [the will], וּכְתַבְתֵּיהּ אַתְּ לְאִינִישׁ אַחֲרִינָא – and you wrote a gift document in which you granted [the property] to another person, לֵית בָּהּ פְּסֵידָא – no loss will result from this new document, for the following reason: דְּקַמָּא וּבַתְרָא – Between the earlier gift document and this later one that you will now write, קַמָּא זָכֵי – the earlier prevails, and its beneficiary receives the property.[15]

The Gemara proceeds to the last item mentioned in the Mishnah – receipts – and cites a Baraisa which discusses this subject at length:

תָּנוּ רַבָּנַן – The Rabbis taught in a Baraisa: מָצָא שׁוֹבֵר – IF ONE FOUND A RECEIPT that a woman wrote her husband for pre-payment of her *kesubah*,[16] he should do as follows: זְמַן שֶׁהָאִשָּׁה מוֹדָה – WHEN THE WOMAN ADMITS that her husband paid off the *kesubah*, יַחֲזִיר לַבַּעַל – [THE FINDER] SHOULD RETURN the receipt TO THE HUSBAND. אֵין הָאִשָּׁה מוֹדָה – But if THE WOMAN DOES NOT ADMIT that her husband paid the *kesubah*, לֹא יַחֲזִיר לֹא לָזֶה וְלֹא לָזֶה – [THE FINDER] SHOULD NOT RETURN the receipt TO either [THE HUSBAND] OR [THE WOMAN]. זְמַן שֶׁהָאִשָּׁה מוֹדָה מִיהַת יַחֲזִיר לַבַּעַל – In any event, the Baraisa teaches that when the woman admits that her husband paid the *kesubah*, [the finder] should return the receipt to the husband.

The Gemara raises a question:

וְלֵיחוּשׁ דִּלְמָא כָּתְבָה לִיתֵּן בְּנִיסָן – But how can we permit this? Let us be concerned that perhaps she wrote the receipt in Nissan anticipating payment, and expected to give it to her husband then, וְלֹא נָתְנָה עַד תִּשְׁרֵי – but actually did not receive payment and did not give him the receipt until a later date, in Tishrei. וְאָזְלָה וְזַבְנְתָּה לִכְתוּבָּה בְּטוֹבַת הֲנָאָה מִנִּיסָן עַד תִּשְׁרֵי – Meanwhile, between Nissan and Tishrei, she went and sold her *kesubah* to another person for a small amount,[17] thereby transferring to the buyer the right to collect the *kesubah* payment. Thus, she had no right to accept payment in Tishrei and the receipt she wrote her husband is void. Now, our concern is the following: וּמַפֵּיק לֵיהּ לְשׁוֹבֵר דִּכְתִיב בְּנִיסָן – If he divorces her [the husband] may produce this receipt that was written in Nissan, and claim that he had already paid off her *kesubah* before she sold it, וְאָתָא לְמִטְרַף לְקוֹחוֹת שֶׁלֹּא כַּדִּין – and he will thus come to take the property from the purchasers unlawfully or the property that had been set aside for payment of the *kesubah* to which they are entitled.[18] – ? –

The Gemara answers that the Baraisa follows a halachic opinion according to which this concern does not apply:

אָמַר רָבָא – Rava said:

NOTES

14. The Gemara assumes that the son would not retract his own gift on behalf of his father's beneficiary unless he could achieve personal gain by doing so. Accordingly, our concern is that the son is conspiring with his father's beneficiary to defraud his own beneficiary; afterward, they will divide the profit (see *Ritva*).

15. [Since both documents were written by the son, the beneficiary of the one that is dated earlier is awarded the property.]

16. At the time of marriage, a woman becomes entitled, under the *kesubah* agreement, to collect two hundred *zuz* (or, in the case of a second marriage, one hundred *zuz*) from her husband if he divorces her or if he predeceases her. [In the event that he predeceases her, payment is made from his estate.] The husband may choose to pre-pay the *kesubah* while they are still married, in which case his wife writes him a receipt.

17. [Literally: for satisfaction.] If a woman sells her *kesubah*, the buyer assumes her right to payment in the event that the husband divorces her or predeceases her. The price for such a sale is usually minimal since there is some risk to the buyer, for if the husband does not divorce her and she predeceases him there is no payment at all (*Rashi*).

18. The husband may use the predated receipt to prove that he had paid her *kesubah* entitlement before she sold it. He will thus defraud the purchasers of the payment to which they are entitled.

הא בבריא והא בשכיב מרע [א]מתניתין דקתני הא אמר תנו נותנין בשכיב מרע דבר מהדר הוא דאמרינן מאי איכא למימר דלמא כתבה מעיקרא להאי ואמליך ולא יהבה ניהליה והדר כתבה לאיניש אחרינא ויהביה ניהליה השתא קא הדר ביה מההוא דיהבה ניהליה אי במתנת בריא יהבה ליה לית ליה פסידא דכי נפקא תרתי בתרייתא זכי דהא הדר ביה מקמייתא אי במתנת שכיב מרע נמי יהבה ניהליה לית בה פסידא דבתרייתא זכי דקא הדר ביה מקמייתא [ב]כי קתני בברייתא אע"פ ששניהם מודים לא יחזיר לא לזה ולא לזה בבריא דלאו בר מהדר הוא דאמרינן דלמא כתבה להאי מעיקרא ואמליך ולא יהבה ליה והדר כתבה לאיניש אחרינא ויהבה ליה השתא קא הדר ביה מההוא דיהבה ליה וסבר מהדר לא מצינא הדרנא בי אימר להו דאנא להאי יהבתא ונידהדרו ניהליה כתבא כי היכי דכי מפיק האי כתבא דקדים זכה ביה הוא אלא אמרינן ליה אנן האי כתבא לא יהבינן ליה להאי דלמא מכתב כתבת מיהב לא יהבת ניהליה ויהבתה לאיניש אחרינא וקא הדרת ביה אי לא יהבתה לאיניש אחרינא וקא בעית דתתבה להאי כתיב ליה השתא כתבא אחרינא ויהביה ניהליה דאי יהבת לאיניש אחרינא לית בה פסידא דקדים זכי מתקיף לה רב זביד והא אידי ואידי דייתקאות קא תני אלא אמר רב זביד הא והא בשכיב מרע ולא קשיא הא ביה והא בבריה מתניתין דקא אמר תנו נותנין בדידיה דבר מהדר הוא דאמרינן א"נ יהבה לאיניש אחרינא לית בה פסידא דקמא ובתרא בתרא זכי דהא הדר ביה מקמא כי קא תני בברייתא אע"פ ששניהם מודים לא יחזיר לא לזה ולא לזה [ג]בבריה דאמרינן דלמא כתב אבוה להאי ואמלך ולא יהביה ניהליה ובתר אבוה כתב איהו לאיניש אחרינא ויהבה ליה והשתא קא הדר ביה מההוא סבר מהדר לא מצינא הדרנא בי אימר להו דאבא יהבה ליה להאי ונתבו ליה כתביה (א) וניזיל ונפיק מיניה דהוא זכי ונפלוג בהדיה הלכך אמרינן ליה אנן האי כתבא לא יהבינן ליה להאי דדלמא מכתב כתביה אבוה מיהב לא יהבה ליה ויהבתיה את לאיניש אחרינא וקא הדרת ביה אלא אי קושטא קא אמרת דיהב ליה אבוך זיל את השתא כתיב ליה שטרא אחרינא דאי נמי לא יהבה ליה אבוה וכתבתיה את לאיניש אחרינא לית בה פסידא דקמא ובתרא קמא זכי: ת"ר [ד]מצא שובר בזמן שהאשה מודה יחזיר לבעל אין האשה מודה לא יחזיר לא לזה ולא לזה בזמן שהאשה מודה מיהת יחזיר לבעל וליחוש דלמא כתבה ליתן בניסן ולא נתנה עד תשרי ואזלה זבנתה לכתובה בטובת הנאה מניסן עד תשרי ומפיק ליה לשובר דכתיב בניסן ואתא למטרף לקוחות שלא כדין אמר רבא

## תוספות

**ברייתא** בבריא דלמא כתבה להאי ולא יהביה ליה. היינו דלא כאביי דלדידיה אמאי לא נהדר כיון שהוא רוצה דעדיו בחתומיו זכין לו היכא דמטא שטרא לידיה ואביי יתרץ כדרב זביד דבסמוך: **והא** אידי ואידי דייתיקאות קתני. וא"ת ולפרוך נמי והא מתנות קתני ואור"ת דמיירי מתני' שפירש שנותן לו גוף ופירי מהיום אם לא יחזור עד לאחר מיתה דמצי הדר ביה ורש"י דחק לפרש דגבי מתנות אפי' אם אמר תנו אין נותנין וה"פ דמתניתין שאני אומר כתובין היו ונמלך עליהם שלא ליתנן ויהיב לאיניש אחרינא ועתה רוצה לחזור בו מן השני וליתנה לראשון לפיכך אפילו אם אמר תנו אין נותנין אבל דייתיקי אם אמר תנו נותנין דאפילו נמלך ונתן לאחר יכול לחזור וקשה לפירושו דא"כ פירוש דנמלך דמתני' יהיה בשני ענינים ותו לעיל גבי גט דדייק הא אמר תנו נותנין אפילו לזמן מרובה לפרש"י ז"ל מנ"ל לפרושי הכי דלמא ה"פ משום דנמלך איכא למיחש שמא לא ניתן הגט עדיין ולכך אפילו אם אמר תנו אין נותנין אלא לשון ונמלך משמע שעתה אינו רוצה כדפרישית לעיל (י"ח. ד"ה הא): **ובתר** אבוה כתבה איהו לאיניש אחרינא. תימה אמאי לא אמרינן נמי שנתנה האב תחלה במתנת שכיב מרע ואח"כ האב עצמו כתבה להאי ולא יהבה ליה ומת האב ונתקיימה המתנה לראשון והבן רוצה שתהיה לשני: **מצא** שובר כו' וליחוש דלמא כתב ליתן בניסן כו'. וא"ת לפרוך על מתני' דגט פשוט (ב"ב דף קסז.) דכותבין שובר לאשה וכ"ת לא חיישינן אלא היכא שנפל ואתרע הא פריך לעיל (יז:) גבי כותבין שטר ללוה אע"ג דליכא ריעותא וי"ל דמצי לדחויי בשטרי הקנאה אבל הכא אי בשטרי הקנאה מיירי כי אין האשה מודה נמי יחזיר לבעל דאין אשה מודה משמע אפילו אינה אומרת שהוא מזויף אלא אומרת שכתבה ליתן ולא נתנה ואומרת עתה אל תתנו לפי שנמלכה דומיא דמלא שוברין דמתניתין דלא יחזיר שאני אומר כתובים היו ונמלך כו':

ש"מ

## רש"י

הא בבריא. שהיה שטר מתנת בריא דלא כתיב ביה כדקליר ורמי בערסיה (א) כדין שכותבין בשטרי מתנות שכיב מרע: דבר מהדר הוא. שיכול לחזור במתנתו אם כתב שני שטרות השני זוכה שהרי חזר בו מראשון: אי במתנת בריא יהבה ניהליה. להוא בתרא: לית ליה פסידא. בהאי שטרא דמהדרא ליה להאי: בבריא. כגון שהיה השטר זה הנמצא מתנת בריא שהוא זוכה לשטר המאוחר לו שאינו יכול לחזור במתנתו: דאי יהבתיה לאיניש אחרינא לית ליה פסידא. בשטרא דכתבת השתא דמאן דקדים שטריה זכה: ביה. שעדיין הוא קיים ואמר תנו לזה: הא בבריה. שמת מחליו וזה בנו אומר החזירהו: דבר מהדר הוא. ממתנה זו אם חזר בו לאחר שיצאו שני שטרות בב"ד יזכה האחרון: א"נ יהבה. שוב לאיניש אחרינא במתנת בריא: לית ליה פסידא. להוא בתרא בהאי שטרא דמהדרינא ליה להאי: כתבה איהו. הבן: דהוא קדים. שיהא שטרו קודם דכיון דמת אביו מחליו זכה משנתנה לו: ונפלוג בהדיה. אחלוק עמו בקנויא זו: קמא זכה. מאחר ששני השטרות יצאו משמך הקודם זכה שמתנת בריא הם והשתא דאוקימנא טעמא דלא יחזיר משום דלמא כתבה להאי ואמליך ולא יהבה ליה והדר כתבה לאיניש אחרינא ליכא למרמי אמתנות ולא תידוק מתני' גבי מתנות הא אמר תנו נותנין דכי נמי אמר תנו שייך למימר טעמא דלא יחזיר משום שאני אומר כתובין היו ונמלך עליהן שלא לתנן והדר כתבה לאיניש אחרינא וגבי דייתקאות ע"כ אם אמר תנו נותנין אם הוא קיים דהא תלה תנא דידן טעמא משום שאני אומר נמלך עליהן שלא לתנן ואי נמי הכי הוה דנמלך השתא אם אמר תנו נותנין דליכא למיחש למידי וה"ק מלא דייתיקי או מתנה לא יחזיר שאני אומר כו' והיכא דאמר תנו [אי] שייך למימר לא יחזיר משום טעמא דשאני אומר כגון מתנת בריא או בשכיב מרע ומת ובריה קאמר תנו שמעי' ממתני' דלא יחזיר ולא דייקינן האמר תנו נותנין והיכא דלא שייך למימר שאני אומר כגון בשכיב מרע שלא מת מחליו דייקינן האמר תנו דבטל שאני אומר הלכך נותנין: מצא שובר. שכתבה אשה לבעלה התקבלתי כתובתי ועודה תחתיו: ולא נתנה עד תשרי. והוא לא פרע עד תשרי: ואזלה. איהי בעודה תחתיו בין ניסן לתשרי: וזבנתה לכתובה. לאחר: בטובת הנאה. כלומר בזול לפי שנותן מעותיו בספק שאם תמות היא יירשנה בעלה ויפסיד מי שלקחה ואם ימות בעלה או יגרשנה יהיה לוקח במקומה ויגבה כתובתה ושוב לא היה לבעלה לפרוע לה הכתובה אלא ללוקח ושובר שנכתב בשמה אינו כלום: ומפיק לשובר. שכתוב בניסן ויקדום לשטרו של לוקח ויחזיק הבעל בקרקע המיוחדת לכתובתה שלא כדין:

ש"מ

## עין משפט נר מצוה

קסד א ב ג מיי' פי"ח מהלכות גזילה ואבידה הלכה ט י ועיין במ"מ סמג עשין עד טוש"ע ח"מ סי' סה סעיף יד:

קסה ד מיי' שם הלכה יא סמג שם וטוש"ע שם סעיף יח וטוש"ע אה"ע סי' קי סעיף ג:

## רבינו חננאל

ופרקינן מתני' דדייקת מינה הא אמר תנו נותנין במתנת שכיב מרע שאפי' נתנם לאחר אי הדר ביה בר מיהדר הוא וליכא פסידא כלל. ברייתא בבריא דלאו בר מיהדר הוא דחיישינן דלמא כתביה להאי מעיקרא ולא יהב ליה שטרא והדר כתביה לאיניש אחרינא ויהב ליה שטרא והשתא בעי למיהדר במה דיהב לבתרא ועבד קנוניא בהדי קמא ומשום הכי מודה ליה לפיכך תני לא יחזיר ואתקיף עלה רב זביד והא מתניתא נמי דיתיקאות קתני אלא הא והא בשכיב מרע ולא קשיא מתני' בדידיה דבר מיהדר הוא ברייתא (באבוה) [בבריה] וכו' ופשוטה היא. ת"ר מצא שובר בזמן שהאשה מודה יחזיר לבעל וניחוש דלמא כתבה בניסן ולא נתנה לו השטר עד תשרי וזבנתה לכתובה ביני וביני ומפיק לשובר דכתב בניסן ומבטיל לה לכתובה.

## מסורת הש"ס

א) ס"א וליזול וליפ... מיניה דהאי וכן ... ברא"ש, מהרש"ל.

## הגהות הב"ח

(א) רש"י ד"ה הא בב... וכו' בערסיה כ... שכותבין:

## ליקוטי רש"י

קושטא. אמת ... סנהדרין צז.]. בטו... הנאה. דבר מועט ש... אלא כמיזוק טובה שק... גרי"ד מפיק רלון [כתו... פה:].

attempting to do so fraudulently.

The Gemara describes how the benefactor intends to accomplish this:

וְסָבַר – **He reasons:** מֵהֲדַר לֹא מָצֵינָא הַדַּרְנָא בִּי – "Since **I am unable to retract** my gift legally, אֵימַר לְהוּ – **I will tell [the court]** דְּאֵנָא לְהַאי יְהַבְתָּא – **that I gave** this first document **to [its beneficiary]** at the time that I wrote it, וְנִיהַדְרוּ נִיהֲלֵיהּ כְּתָבָא – **and they will** therefore **return the document to him.** כִּי הֵיכִי דְּכִי מַפֵּיק הַאי כְּתָבָא דְּקָדֵים – **This way, when he produces this document, which is** dated **earlier** than the gift document that I wrote for the second person, זָכָה בֵּיהּ הוּא – **he will prevail,** and retain ownership of **[the property].**"[10] Thus, by returning the gift document we may be assisting in the perpetration of a fraud. The Baraisa therefore rules that we do not return the document.

The Gemara records the court's response to the benefactor:

אֶלָּא אֲמְרִינַן לֵיהּ – **Rather, we tell [the benefactor]:** אֲנַן הַאי כְּתָבָא לֹא יָהֲבִינַן לֵיהּ לְהַאי – **We will not give this document to this** person from whom you claim it was lost, דִּלְמָא מִכְתַּב כְּתַבְתְּ – because we are concerned that **perhaps you wrote** the document מֵיהַב לֹא יְהַבְתְּ נִיהֲלֵיהּ – **but did not give it to him,** וִיהַבְתָּהּ לְאִינִישׁ אַחֲרִינָא – **and** instead, **you gave [the property] to another person** as a gift, וְקָא הָדַרְתְּ בֵּיהּ – **which you** now wish to **retract** illegally. אִי לֹא יְהַבְתָּהּ לְאִינִישׁ אַחֲרִינָא – However, **if,** as you claim, **you have not given [the property] to another person,** וְקָא בָּעֵית דְּתִתְּבָהּ לְהַאי – **and you** still **wish to give it to this** person,[11] you have the following option: כְּתִיב לֵיהּ הַשְׁתָּא כְּתָבָא אַחֲרִינָא – **Write him another** gift **document now,** וִיהָבֵיהּ נִיהֲלֵיהּ – **and give it to him.** This new document will provide him evidence that he owns the property. דְּאִי יְהַבְתְּ לְאִינִישׁ אַחֲרִינָא – However, we will still be assured **that if** you are lying and **you gave** the property **to another person,** לֵית בָּהּ פְּסֵידָא – **there is no** chance that he will suffer any **loss** as a result **of this** new document, דְּקַדְּמִים זָכֵי – **because** between two gift documents, **the** one dated **earlier prevails,** and its beneficiary is awarded ownership of the property.

The Gemara objects to the previous resolution to the contradiction between the Mishnah and Baraisa – that the Mishnah refers to a seriously ill benefactor while the Baraisa refers to a healthy benefactor:

מַתְקִיף לָהּ רַב זְבִיד – **Rav Zevid objected:** וְהָא אִידִי וְאִידִי – **But both [the Mishnah] and [the Baraisa]** דְּיַיתִּקְאוֹת קָא תָּנֵי – **state** explicitly that their rulings apply to sickbed **wills,** and nevertheless, the Mishnah implies that if the benefactor tells us to return the will we do so, while the Baraisa rules that we do not.[12] – ? –

The Gemara proposes an alternative resolution to the contradiction between the Mishnah and the Baraisa:

אֶלָּא אָמַר רַב זְבִיד – **Rather, Rav Zevid said:** הָא וְהָא בִּשְׁכִיב מְרַע – Both **this** ruling of the Mishnah **and that** ruling of the Baraisa **refer to** the will of **a seriously ill person,** וְלֹא קַשְׁיָא – **and** nevertheless, the contradiction poses **no difficulty,** for the following reason: הָא בֵּיהּ – **This** implied ruling of the Mishnah, that we return the will as instructed, **refers to** a case where t[he] benefactor **himself** tells us to return it, וְהָא בִּבְרֵיהּ – **while [t]he other]** ruling of the Baraisa, that we do not return the will as instructed, **refers to** a case where the benefactor died and **his s[on]** tells us to return it.

The Gemara explains why we need not be concerned f[or] possible fraud when the benefactor himself tells us to return t[he] will, while we need be concerned for fraud when his son tells us [to] return it:

מַתְנִיתִין – **Our Mishnah** – which teaches by implication [דְּ]אָ[מַר] אָמַר תְּנוּ נוֹתְנִין – **that if [the benefactor] said** to **give** the w[ill] to the beneficiary, **we give** it – בְּדִידֵיהּ – **refers to** a ca[se] where the benefactor **himself** tells us to return it. [מָצֵי]ר מֵהֲדַר הוּא – We need not be concerned for fraud because **he can retra[ct]** his will.

The Gemara now explains why this is so:

דְּאָמְרִינַן – **For we say:** אִי נַמִּי יְהָבָהּ לְאִינִישׁ אַחֲרִינָא – **Even if [he] gave [the property] to another person** by writing him a gi[ft] document after he wrote this will, לֵית בָּהּ פְּסֵידָא – **no loss** to t[he] other person can result **from** returning **this** will, for the followi[ng] reason: דְּקַמָּא וּבַתְרָא – Between **an earlier** dated will **and** [a] **later** gift document for the same property, בַּתְרָא זָכֵי – t[he] **later** gift document **prevails,** and its beneficiary receives the pr[o]perty, דְּהָא הָדַר בֵּיהּ מִקַּמָּא – **since** his document's later da[te] proves that **[the benefactor] retracted the earlier** will.[13] Thu[s] we need not be concerned that any fraud will result if we retur[n] the will. The Mishnah therefore rules that in such a case it may b[e] returned.

כִּי קָא תָּנֵי בִּבְרַיְיתָא – But **when the Baraisa teaches:** [אַ]ף עַל פִּי שֶׁשְּׁנֵיהֶם מוֹדִים – EVEN THOUGH BOTH [PARTIES] AGREE that th[e] will belongs to the beneficiary, לֹא יַחֲזִיר לֹא לָזֶה וְלֹא לָזֶה – [TH]E FINDER] SHOULD NOT RETURN the will TO EITHER [PART]Y – בִּבְרֵיהּ – **it refers to** a case where the benefactor died of his illne[ss] and **his son** instructs us to return the will. In this case, we do n[ot] return it.

The Gemara now explains why we must be concerned f[or] fraud in a case where the benefactor's son tells us to return th[e] will:

דְּאָמְרִינַן – **For we say** that one must be concerned for th[e] following: דִּלְמָא כָּתַב אֲבוּהָ לְהַאי – **Perhaps the fathe[r] wrote** the will, bequeathing his property **to this** person, [וְאִ]מְּלִיךְ וְלֹא יְהָבֵיהּ נִיהֲלֵיהּ – **but reconsidered and did not give it t[o] him.** וּבָתַר אֲבוּהָ – **After the father** died, [כְּ]תַב אִיהוּ לְאִינִישׁ אַחֲרִינָא – **[the son,]** having inherited the property, **wrote** a gi[ft] document in which he granted the property **to another per[]son,** וִיהָבָהּ לֵיהּ – **and gave [the document] to him.** Thus, th[e] beneficiary of the son's gift acquired the property. [וְ]הַשְׁתָּא קָא הָדַר בֵּיהּ מֵהַהוּא – Our concern is that **[the son]** now **wishes t[o] retract [the gift]** that he gave to the second person. Since h[e] cannot retract it legally, he is perhaps attempting to do s[o] fraudulently.

The Gemara now describes how the son intends to accomplis[h] this:

סָבַר – **[The son] reasons:** מֵהֲדַר לֹא מָצֵינָא הַדַּרְנָא בִּי – "Sinc[e]

NOTES

10. If this earlier document is one day produced in court, the court will assume that it was handed over to its beneficiary at the time it was written, and will therefore award him the property.

11. I.e. you want the beneficiary of the recovered document to retain ownership of the property, to which he is entitled, according to your claim.

12. It would seem that the Gemara could have further objected to the previous resolution by pointing out that both the Mishnah and the Baraisa explicitly refer to *gift documents* of healthy people as well. Se[e] *Rashi* and *Tosafos* (ד״ה והא) who explain why the Gemara ignored thi[s] possible objection.

13. [See note 6.] The Gemara curtails its explanation of the Mishnah a[t] this point and does not consider the possibility that the secon[d] document was a will. This possibility was dealt with at length earlie[r] where the Gemara explained why we need not be concerned for fraud i[n] that case (see note 8).

הא בבריא והא בשכיב מרע [א]מתניתין דקתני הא אמר תנו נותנין בשכיב מרע דבר מהדר הוא דאמרינן מאי איכא למימר דלמא כתבה מעיקרא להאי ואמליך ולא יהבה ניהליה והדר כתבה לאיניש אחרינא ויהביה ניהליה השתא קא הדר ביה מההוא דיהבה ניהליה אי במתנת בריא יהבה ליה לית ליה פסידא דכי נפקא תרתי בתרייתא זכי דהא הדר ביה מקמייתא אי במתנת שכיב מרע נמי יהבה ניהליה לית בה פסידא דבתרייתא זכי דקא הדר ביה מקמייתא [ב]כי קתני בברייתא אע"פ ששניהם מודים לא יחזיר לא לזה ולא לזה בבריא דלאו בר מהדר הוא דאמרינן דלמא כתבה להאי מעיקרא ואמליך ולא יהבה ליה והדר כתבה לאיניש אחרינא ויהבה ליה השתא קא הדר ביה מההוא דיהבה ליה וסבר מהדר לא מצינא הדרנא בי אימר להו דאנא להאי יהבתא ונהדרו ניהליה כתבא כי היכי דכי מפיק האי כתבא דקדים זכה ביה הוא אלא אמרינן ליה אנן האי כתבא לא יהבינן ליה להאי דלמא מכתב כתבת מיהב לא יהבת ניהליה ויהבתה לאיניש אחרינא וקא הדרת ביה אי לא יהבתה לאיניש אחרינא וקא בעית דתתבה להאי כתיב ליה השתא כתבא אחרינא ויהביה ניהליה דאי יהבת לאיניש אחרינא לית בה פסידא דקדים זכי מתקיף לה רב זביד והא אידי ואידי דייתקאות קא תני אלא אמר רב זביד הא והא בשכיב מרע ולא קשיא הא ביה והא בבריה מתניתין דקא אמר תנו נותנין בדידיה דבר מהדר הוא דאמרינן א"נ יהבה לאיניש אחרינא לית בה פסידא דקמא ובתרא בתרא זכי דהא הדר ביה מקמא כי קא תני בברייתא אע"פ ששניהם מודים לא יחזיר לא לזה ולא לזה [ג]בבריה דאמרינן דלמא כתב אבוה להאי ואמלך ולא יהביה ניהליה ובתר אבוה כתב איהו לאיניש אחרינא ויהבה ליה והשתא קא הדר ביה מההוא סבר מהדר לא מצינא הדרנא בי אימר להו דאבא יהבה ליה להאי ונתבו ליה כתביה [ד]וניזיל ונפיק מיניה דהוא זכי ונפלוג בהדיה הלכך אמרינן ליה אנן האי כתבא לא יהבינן ליה להאי דדלמא מכתב כתביה אבוה מיהב לא יהבה ליה ויהבתיה את לאיניש אחרינא וקא הדרת ביה אלא אי קושטא קא אמרת דיהב ליה אבוך זיל את השתא כתיב ליה שטרא אחרינא דאי נמי לא יהבה ליה אבוה וכתבתיה את לאיניש אחרינא לית בה פסידא דקמא ובתרא קמא זכי: ת"ר [ד]מצא שובר בזמן שהאשה מודה יחזיר לבעל אין האשה מודה לא יחזיר לא לזה ולא לזה בזמן שהאשה מודה מיהת יחזיר לבעל וליחוש דלמא כתבה ליתן בניסן ולא נתנה עד תשרי ואזלה זבנתה לכתובה בטובת הנאה מניסן עד תשרי ומפיק ליה לשובר דכתיב בניסן ואתא למטרף לקוחות שלא כדין אמר רבא

ש"מ

**רש"י**

**הא בבריא.** שהיה שטר מתנת בריא דלא כתיב ביה כדקליר ורמי בערסיה (א) כדין שכותבין בשטרי מתנות שכיב מרע: **דבר מהדר הוא.** שיכול לחזור במתנתו אם כתב שני שטרות השני זוכה שהרי חזר בו מראשון: **אי במתנת בריא יהבה ניהליה.** להוא בתרא: **לית ליה פסידא.** בהאי שטרא דמהדרא ליה להאי: **בבריא.** כגון שהיה השטר זה הנמצא מתנת בריא שהוא זוכה לשטר המאוחר לו שאינו יכול לחזור במתנתו: **דאי יהבתיה לאיניש אחרינא לית ליה פסידא.** בשטרא דכתבת השתא דמאן דקדים שטריה זכה: **ביה.** שעדיין הוא קיים ואמר תנו לזה: **הא בבריה.** שמת מחליו וזה בנו אומר החזירהו: **דבר מהדר הוא.** ממתנה זו אם חזר בו לאחר שיצאו שני שטרות בב"ד יזכה האחרון: **א"נ יהבה.** שוב לאיניש אחרינא במתנת בריא: **לית ליה פסידא.** להוא בתרא בהאי שטרא דמהדרינא ליה להאי: **כתבה איהו.** הבן: **דהוא קדים.** שיהא שטרו קודם דכיון דמת אביו מחליו זכה משנתנה לו: **ונפלוג בהדיה.** אחלוק עמו בקרקע זו: **קמא זכה.** מאחר ששני השטרות יצאו משמך הקודם זכה שמתנת בריא הם והשתא דאוקימנא טעמא דלא יחזיר משום דלמא כתבה להאי ואמליך ולא יהבה ליה והדר כתבה לאיניש אחרינא ליכא למרמי אמתנות ולא תידוק מתני' גבי מתנות הא אמר תנו נותנין דכי נמי אמר תנו שייך למימר טעמא דלא יחזיר משום שאני אומר כתובין היו ונמלך עליהן שלא לתתן והדר כתבה לאיניש אחרינא וגבי דייתקאות ע"כ אם אמר תנו נותנין אם הוא קיים דהא תלה תנא דידן טעמא משום שאני אומר נמלך עליהן שלא לתתן ואי נמי הכי הוה דנמלך השתא אם אמר תנו נותנין דליכא למיחש למידי וה"ק מלא דייתיקי או מתנה לא יחזיר שאני אומר כו' והיכא דאמר תנו [אי] שייך למימר לא יחזיר משום טעמא דשאני אומר כגון מתנת בריא או בשכיב מרע ומת ובריה קאמר תנו שמעי' ממתני' דלא יחזיר ולא דייקינן האמר תנו נותנין והיכא דלא שייך למימר שאני אומר כגון בשכיב מרע שלא מת מחליו דייקינן האמר תנו דבטל שאני אומר הלכך נותנין: **מצא שובר.** שכתבה אשה לבעלה התקבלתי כתובתי ועודה תחתיו: **ולא נתנה עד תשרי.** והוא לא פרעו עד תשרי: **ואזלה.** איהי בעודה תחתיו בין ניסן לתשרי: **וזבנתה לכתובה.** לאחר: **בטובת הנאה.** כלומר בזול לפי שנותן מעותיו בספק שאם תמות היא יירשנה בעלה ויפסיד מי שלקחה ואם ימות בעלה או יגרשנה יהיה לוקח במקומה ויגבה כתובתה ושוב לא היה לבעלה לפרוע לה הכתובה אלא ללוקח ושובר שנכתב בשמה אינו כלום: **ומפיק לשובר.** שכתוב בניסן ויקדום לשטרו של לוקח ויחזיק הבעל בקרקע המיוחדת לכתובתה שלא כדין:

ש"מ

**תוספות**

**בברייתא** בבריא דלמא כתבה להאי ולא יהביה ליה. היינו דלא כאביי דלדידיה אמאי לא נהדר כיון שהוא רוצה דעדיו בחתומיו זכין לו היכא דמטא שטרא לידיה ואביי יתרץ כדרב זביד דבסמוך: **והא** אידי ואידי דייתיקאות קתני. וא"ת ולפרוך נמי והא מתנות קתני ואור"ת דמיירי מתני' שפירש שנותן לו גוף ופירי מהיום אם לא יחזור עד לאחר מיתה דמצי הדר ביה ורש"י דחק לפרש דגבי מתנות אפי' אם אמר תנו אין נותנין וה"פ דמתניתין שאני אומר כתובין היו ונמלך עליהם שלא ליתנן ויהיב לאיניש אחרינא ועתה רוצה לחזור בו מן השני וליתנה לראשון לפיכך אפילו אם אמר תנו אין נותנין אבל דייתיקי אם אמר תנו נותנין דאפילו נמלך ונתן לאחר יכול לחזור וקשה לפירושו דא"כ פירוש דנמלך דמתני' יהיה בשני עניינים ותו לעיל גבי גט דדייק הא אמר תנו נותנין אפילו לזמן מרובה לפרש"י ז"ל מנ"ל לפרושי הכי דלמא ה"פ משום דנמלך איכא למיחש שמא לא ניתן הגט עדיין ולכך אפילו אם אמר תנו אין נותנין אלא לשון ונמלך משמע שעתה אינו רוצה כדפרישית לעיל (י"ח. ד"ה הא): **ובתר** אבוה כתבה איהו לאיניש אחרינא. תימה אמאי לא אמרינן נמי שנתנה האב תחלה במתנת שכיב מרע ואח"כ האב עצמו כתבה להאי ולא יהבה ליה ומת האב ונתקיימה המתנה לראשון והבן רוצה שתהיה לשני: **מצא** שובר כו' וליחוש דלמא כתב ליתן בניסן כו'. וא"ת לפרוך על מתני' דגט פשוט (ב"ב דף קסו.) דכותבין שובר לאשה וכ"ת לא חיישינן אלא היכא שנפל ואתרע הא פריך לעיל (יג:) גבי כותבין שטר ללוה אע"ג דליכא ריעותא וי"ל דמצי לדחויי בשטרי הקנאה אבל הכא אי בשטרי הקנאה מיירי כי אין האשה מודה נמי יחזיר לבעל דאין אשה מודה משמע אפילו אינה אומרת שהוא מזויף אלא אומרת שכתבה ליתן ולא נתנה ואומרת עתה אל תתנו לפי שנמלכה דומיא דמלא שוברין דמתניתין דלא יחזיר שאני אומר כתובים היו ונמלך כו':

ש"מ

**עין משפט נר מצוה**

קסד א ב ג מיי' פי"ח מהלכות גזלה ואבידה הלכה ט י ועיין במ"מ סמג עשין עד טוש"ע ח"מ סי' סה סעיף יד:

קסה ד מיי' שם הלכה יא סמג שם וטוש"ע שם סעיף יח וטוש"ע אה"ע סי' קי סעיף ג:

**רבינו חננאל**

ופרקינן מתני' דדייקת מינה הא אמר תנו נותנין במתנת שכיב מרע שאפי' נתנם לאחר אי הדר ביה בר מיהדר הוא וליכא פסידא כלל. ברייתא בבריא דלאו בר מיהדר הוא דחיישינן דלמא כתביה להאי מעיקרא ולא יהב ליה שטרא והדר כתביה לאיניש אחרינא ויהב ליה שטרא והשתא בעי למיהדר במה דיהב לבתרא ועבד קנוניא בהדי קמא ומשום הכי מודה ליה לפיכך תני לא יחזיר ואתקיף עלה רב זביד והא מתניתא נמי דיתיקאות קתני אלא הא והא בשכיב מרע ולא קשיא מתני' בדידיה דבר מיהדר הוא ברייתא (באבוה) [בבריה] וכו' ופשוטה היא. **ת"ר** מצא שובר בזמן שהאשה מודה יחזיר לבעל וניחוש דלמא כתבה בניסן ולא נתנה לו השטר עד תשרי וזבנתה לכתובה ביני וביני ומפיק לשובר דכתב בניסן ומבטיל לה לכתובה.

**מסורת הש"ס**

א) ס"א וליזול ולי[...] מיניה דהאי וכן ברא"ש, מהרש"ל.

**הגהות הב"ח**

(א) רש"י ד"ה הא בב[...] וכו' בערסיה כ[...] שכותבין:

**ליקוטי רש"י**

קושטא. אמת [סנהדרין צז.]. בטו[בת] הנאה. דבר מועט ש[...] אלא כמיזוק טובה שק[...] גרי"ד מפיק רצון [כתו' פה:].

הָא בְּבָרִיא – **This** ruling, that we do not return the document as the benefactor instructs, **refers to** the gift document of **a healthy person,**[1] וְהָא בִּשְׁכִיב מְרַע – **while [the other]** ruling, that we do return the document as the benefactor instructs, **refers to** the will of **a seriously ill person.**

The Gemara explains why we must be concerned for the possibility of fraud with regard to a gift document but not with regard to a will:

מַתְנִיתִין דְּקָתָנֵי – **Our Mishnah – which teaches** by implication הָא אָמַר תְּנוּ – that **if [the benefactor] said** to **give** the document to its designated beneficiary, נוֹתְנִין – **we give** it – בִּשְׁכִיב מְרַע – **refers to** a will of **a seriously ill person.** A will may be returned to its beneficiary, דְּבַר מִהְדַר הוּא – because **[the benefactor] can** legally **retract** it,[2] and consequently, returning the will does not enable the beneficiary to perpetrate a fraud.

The Gemara explains how the fact that a will can be retracted eliminates our concern for possible fraud. First, the Gemara describes what our concern might be:

דְּאָמְרִינַן – **For we say:** מַאי אִיכָּא לְמֵימַר – **What** possible defraudment **could one speak of?** Only the following: דִּלְמָא כְּתָבָהּ מֵעִיקָּרָא לְהַאי – **Perhaps [the benefactor] first wrote this** will, bequeathing his property **to this** person, וְאִמְלִיךְ וְלֹא יְהָבָהּ נִיהֲלֵיהּ – then **reconsidered and did not give it to him,** וְהָדַר כְּתָבָהּ לְאִינִישׁ אַחֲרִינָא – **and afterward wrote** another document[3] in which he granted **[the property] to another person,** וִיהָבֵיהּ נִיהֲלֵיהּ – **and he gave him [the document].** The second person therefore receives the property. הַשְׁתָּא קָא הָדַר בֵּיהּ מֵהַהוּא דִּיהָבָהּ נִיהֲלֵיהּ – Our concern is that perhaps **[the benefactor] now wishes to retract [the gift] that he gave to [the second person],** and he therefore tells us to return the will to the first person.[4]

The Gemara will now explain why this concern does not deter us from returning the will. This must be considered in the light of two possibilities: that the second document was an ordinary gift document or that it was another will.[5] First the Gemara explores the possibility that it was a gift document:

אִי בְּמַתְּנַת בָּרִיא יְהָבָהּ לֵיהּ – **If he gave [the property] to [the second person] by means of a healthy person's gift** document, לֵית לֵיהּ פְּסֵידָא – **[the second person] will not lose** anything as a result of our returning the will to the first, for the following reason: דְּכִי נָפְקָא תַּרְתֵּי – **When both** documents **are produced** in court, בַּתְרַיְיתָא זָכֵי – **the** gift document, which is dated **last, will prevail,** and its beneficiary will receive the property, דְּהָא הָדַר בֵּיהּ מִקַּמַּיְיתָא – **since** its later date proves that [t… benefactor] **retracted the earlier** will.[6] Thus, the recipient … the property as a gift cannot be defrauded by the return of t… will.

Now the Gemara explores the possibility that the seco… document was a will:

אִי בְּמַתְּנַת שְׁכִיב מְרַע נַמִּי יְהָבָהּ נִיהֲלֵיהּ – **Even if he gave [t… property] to [the second person] by means of a seriously … person's gift,**[7] לֵית בָּהּ פְּסֵידָא – **no** undue **loss** to the seco… person can result from the return **of this** will, for the followi… reason: דְּבַתְרַיְיתָא זָכֵי – Between two wills **the last prevai…** and its beneficiary receives ownership of the property, …א הָדַר בֵּיהּ מִקַּמַּיְיתָא – **since** by implementing a later will **[the benefa…tor] retracted the earlier** one.[8] Thus, the second person w… not be unjustly deprived of the property as a result of o… returning this will. Accordingly, the Mishnah rules that we m… return a lost will to its designated beneficiary if the benefact… tells us to do so.

The Gemara now goes on to explain why the Baraisa does n… concur with the Mishnah's ruling:

כִּי קָתָנֵי בְּבָרַיְיתָא – But **when the Baraisa teaches:** …עַל פִּי שֶׁשְּׁנֵיהֶם מוֹדִים – EVEN THOUGH BOTH [PARTIES] AGREE that t… document belongs to its beneficiary, לֹא יַחֲזִיר לֹא לָזֶה וְלֹא לָזֶה – [THE FINDER] SHOULD NOT RETURN the document TO EITH… [PARTY], בְּבָרִיא – **it refers to** the gift document of **a health… person.** A gift document may not be returned, …לָאו בַּר מִהְדַר הוּא – because under the law, **[the benefactor] cannot retra…** his gift, and consequently, returning the document enables hi… to perpetrate a fraud.

The Gemara now explains how the fact that a gift cannot … retracted creates the possibility that this document may be us… fraudulently:

דְּאָמְרִינַן **For we say** that one must be concerned for t… following: דִּלְמָא כְּתָבָהּ לְהַאי מֵעִיקָּרָא – **Perhaps [the benefa…tor] first wrote this** recovered gift document, granting t… property **to this** person, וְאִמְלִיךְ וְלֹא יְהָבָהּ לֵיהּ – then **reconsi…ered and did not give it to him,** …וְהָדַר כְּתָבָהּ לְאִינִישׁ אַחֲרִינָא – **and afterward wrote** another gift **document,** in which … granted **[the property] to another person,** וִיהָבָהּ לֵיהּ – **an… gave him [the document].** Thus, the beneficiary of t… second document acquired the property.[9] …שְׁתָּא קָא הָדַר בֵּיהּ מֵהַהוּא דִּיהָבָהּ לֵיהּ – Our concern is that **[the benefactor] no… wishes to retract [the gift] that he gave to the [secon… person].** Since he cannot retract it legally, he is perha…

NOTES

1. I.e. an ordinary gift document.

2. Although a sickbed will is effective without any formal *kinyan*, it does not take effect until the benefactor's death. He may retract it at any time before his death.

3. I.e. another will or a gift document. [The Gemara will shortly consider each of these possibilities individually.]

4. By telling the finder to return the will, the writer affords the first person the opportunity to prove that it was he who acquired the property, since the will of which he is the beneficiary is dated earlier than the document of which the other person is the beneficiary. This is the writer's way of illegally retracting the gift or bequest to the second person.

5. Of course, we do not know for certain that the benefactor wrote any other document at all. Nevertheless, we must consider the possibility that he wrote either a gift document or another will.

6. Gifting property to another subsequent to a will constitutes a retraction of the will (*Rashi* ד"ה דבר מהדר הוא). Therefore, the later date on the gift document provides sufficient evidence that the will was retracted and the beneficiary of the gift document is awarded ownership of the property.

7. I.e. a will.

8. The meaning of the term *the last* shifts in this segment of th… Gemara. Whereas previously the Gemara used this term to refer to th… second will, which bears a *later date* than that of the first, here the ter… has the opposite meaning. It refers to the first will, which is now bein… given to its beneficiary upon the instruction of the benefactor. [Thus, … is the document *received* at a *later* date.]

In this case, the beneficiary of the second will loses the property t… the beneficiary of the first will, for the following reason: When th… benefactor tells us to return this will to the first person, he is i… effect retracting the will that he gave the second person. Thus, th… first will, which was previously retracted in favor of the second one, … now reinstated, and its beneficiary acquires the property upon th… benefactor's death. Since this retraction is legal, we may follow th… benefactor's instructions and return the will to the first beneficiar… (*Ritva*).

9. Since the first document was not handed over to its beneficiary, th… transaction recorded in it did not take effect. Therefore, th… second beneficiary, whose document *was* handed over, acquired th… property.

הא בבריא והא בשכיב מרע א מתניתין דקתני הא אמר תנו נותנין בשכיב מרע דבר מהדר הוא דאמרינן מאי איכא למימר דלמא כתבה מעיקרא להאי ואמליך ולא יהבה ניהליה והדר כתבה לאיניש אחרינא ויהביה ניהליה השתא קא הדר ביה מההוא דיהבה ניהליה אי במתנת בריא יהבה ליה לית ליה פסידא דכי נפקא תרתי בתרייתא זכי דהא הדר ביה מקמייתא אי במתנת שכיב מרע נמי יהבה ניהליה לית בה פסידא דבתרייתא זכי דקא הדר ביה מקמייתא ב כי קתני בברייתא אע"פ ששניהם מודים לא יחזיר לא לזה ולא לזה בבריא דלאו בר מהדר הוא דאמרינן דלמא כתבה להאי מעיקרא ואמליך ולא יהבה ליה והדר כתבה לאיניש אחרינא ויהבה ליה השתא קא הדר ביה מההוא דיהבה ליה וסבר מהדר לא מצינא הדרנא בי אימר להו דאנא להאי יהבתא ונהדרו ניהליה כתבא כי היכי דכי מפיק האי כתבא דקדים זכה ביה הוא אלא אמרינן ליה אנן האי כתבא לא יהבינן ליה להאי דלמא מכתב כתבת מיהב לא יהבת ניהליה ויהבתה לאיניש אחרינא וקא הדרת ביה אי לא יהבתה לאיניש אחרינא וקא בעית דתתבה להאי כתיב ליה השתא כתבא אחרינא ויהביה ניהליה דאי יהבת לאיניש אחרינא לית בה פסידא דקדים זכי מתקיף לה רב זביד והא אידי ואידי דייתקאות קא תני אלא אמר רב זביד הא והא בשכיב מרע ולא קשיא הא ביה והא בבריה מתניתין דקא אמר תנו נותנין בדידיה דבר מהדר הוא דאמרינן א"נ יהבה לאיניש אחרינא לית בה פסידא דקמא ובתרא בתרא זכי דהא הדר ביה מקמא כי קא תני בברייתא אע"פ ששניהם מודים לא יחזיר לא לזה ולא לזה ג בבריה דאמרינן דלמא כתב אבוה להאי ואמלך ולא יהביה ניהליה ובתר אבוה כתב איהו לאיניש אחרינא ויהבה ליה והשתא קא הדר ביה מההוא סבר מהדר לא מצינא הדרנא בי אימר להו דאבא יהבה ליה להאי ונתבו ליה כתביה (א) וניזיל ונפיק מיניה דהוא זכי ונפלוג בהדיה הלכך אמרינן ליה אנן האי כתבא לא יהבינן ליה להאי דדלמא מכתב כתביה אבוה מיהב לא יהבה ליה ויהבתיה את לאיניש אחרינא וקא הדרת ביה אלא אי קושטא קא אמרת דיהב ליה אבוך זיל את השתא כתיב ליה שטרא אחרינא דאי נמי לא יהבה ליה אבוה וכתבתיה את לאיניש אחרינא לית בה פסידא דקמא ובתרא קמא זכי: ת"ר ד מצא שובר בזמן שהאשה מודה יחזיר לבעל אין האשה מודה לא יחזיר לא לזה ולא לזה בזמן שהאשה מודה מיהת יחזיר לבעל וליחוש דלמא כתבה ליתן בניסן ולא נתנה עד תשרי ואזלה זבנתה לכתובה בטובת הנאה מניסן עד תשרי ומפיק ליה לשובר דכתיב בניסן ואתא למטרף לקוחות שלא כדין אמר רבא

ש"מ

### רש"י

הא בבריא. שהיה שטר מתנת בריא דלא כתיב ביה כדקא' ורמי בערסיה (א) כדין שכותבין בשטרי מתנות שכיב מרע: דבר מהדר הוא. שיכול לחזור במתנתו אם כתב שני שטרות השני זוכה שהרי חזר בו מראשון: אי במתנת בריא יהבה ניהליה. לההוא בתרא: לית ליה פסידא. בהאי שטרא דמהדרא ליה להאי: בבריא. כגון שהיה השטר זה הנמצא מתנת בריא שהוא זוכה לשטר המאוחר לו שאינו יכול לחזור במתנתו: דאי יהבתיה לאיניש אחרינא לית ליה פסידא. בשטרא דכתבת השתא דמאן דקדים שטריה זכה: ביה. שעדיין הוא קיים ואמר תנו לזה: הא בבריה. שמת מחליו וזה בנו אומר החזירהו: דבר מהדר הוא. ממתנה זו אם חזר בו לאחר שיצאו שני שטרות בב"ד יזכה האחרון: א"נ יהבה. שוב לאיניש אחרינא במתנת בריא: לית ליה פסידא. לההוא בתרא בהאי שטרא דמהדרינא ליה להאי: כתבה איהו. הבן: דהוא קדים. שיהא שטרו קודם דכיון דמת אביו מחליו זכה משנתנה לו: ונפלוג בהדיה. אחלוק עמו בקנוניא זו: קמא זכה. מאחר ששני השטרות יצאו משמך הקודם זכה שמתנת בריא הם והשתא דאוקימנא טעמא דלא יחזיר משום דלמא כתבה להאי ואמליך ולא יהבה ליה והדר כתבה לאיניש אחרינא ליכא למרמי אמתנות ולא תידוק מתני' גבי מתנות הא אמר תנו נותנין דכי נמי אמר תנו שייך למימר טעמא דלא יחזיר משום שאני אומר כתובין היו ונמלך עליהן שלא לתנן והדר כתבה לאיניש אחרינא וגבי דייתקאות ע"כ אם אמר תנו נותנין אם הוא קיים דהא תלה תנא דידן טעמא משום שאני אומר נמלך עליהן שלא לתנן ואי נמי הכי הוה דנמלך השתא אם אמר תנו נותנין דליכא למיחש למידי וה"ק מצא דייתיקי או מתנה לא יחזיר שאני אומר כו' והיכא דאמר תנו [אי] שייך למימר לא יחזיר משום טעמא דשאני אומר כגון מתנת בריא או בשכיב מרע ומת ובריה קאמר תנו שמעי' ממתני' דלא יחזיר ולא דייקינן האמר תנו נותנין והיכא דלא שייך למימר שאני אומר כגון בשכיב מרע שלא מת מחליו דייקינן האמר תנו דבטל שאני אומר הלכך נותנין: מצא שובר. שכתבה אשה לבעלה התקבלתי כתובתי ועודה תחתיו: ולא נתנה עד תשרי. והוא לא פרע עד תשרי: ואזלה. איהי בעודה תחתיו בין ניסן לתשרי: וזבנתה לכתובה. לאחר: בטובת הנאה. כלומר בזול לפי שנותן מעותיו בספק שאם תמות היא יירשנה בעלה ויפסיד מי שלקחה ואם ימות בעלה או יגרשנה יהיה לוקח במקומה ויגבה כתובתה ושוב לא היה לבעלה לפרוע לה הכתובה אלא ללוקח ושובר שנכתב בשמה אינו כלום: ומפיק לשובר. שכתוב בניסן ויקדום לשטרו של לוקח ויחזיק הבעל בקרקע המיוחדת לכתובתה שלא כדין:

ש"מ

### תוספות

בברייתא בבריא דלמא כתבה להאי ולא יהביה ליה. היינו דלא כאביי דלדידיה אמאי לא נהדר כיון שהוא רוצה דעדיו בחתומיו זכין לו היכא דמטא שטרא לידיה ואביי יתרץ כדרב זביד דבסמוך: והא אידי ואידי דייתיקאות קתני. וא"ת ולפרוך נמי והא מתנות קתני ואור"ת דמיירי מתני' שפירש שנותן לו גוף ופירי מהיום אם לא יחזור עד לאחר מיתה דמצי הדר ביה ורש"י דחק לפרש דגבי מתנות אפי' אם אמר תנו אין נותנין וה"פ דמתניתין שאני אומר כתובין היו ונמלך עליהם שלא ליתן ויהיב לאיניש אחרינא ועתה רוצה לחזור בו מן השני וליתנה לראשון לפיכך אפילו אם אמר תנו אין נותנין אבל דייתיקי אם אמר תנו נותנין דאפילו נמלך ונתן לאחר יכול לחזור וקשה לפירושו דא"כ פירוש דנמלך דמתני' יהיה בשני עניינים ותו לעיל גבי גט דדייק הא אמר תנו נותנין אפילו לזמן מרובה לפרש"י ז"ל מנ"ל לפרושי הכי דלמא ה"פ משום דנמלך איכא למיחש שמא לא ניתן הגט עדיין ולכך אפילו אם אמר תנו אין נותנין אלא לשון ונמלך משמע שעתה אינו רוצה כדפרישית לעיל (י"ח. ד"ה הא): ובתר אבוה כתבה איהו לאיניש אחרינא. תימה אמאי לא אמרינן נמי שנתנה האב תחלה במתנת שכיב מרע ואח"כ האב עצמו כתבה להאי ולא יהבה ליה ומת האב ונתקיימה המתנה לראשון והבן רוצה שתהיה לשני: מצא שובר כו' וליחוש דלמא כתב ליתן בניסן כו'. וא"ת לפרוך על מתני' דגט פשוט (ב"ב דף קסז.) דכותבין שובר לאשה וכ"ת לא חיישינן אלא היכא שנפל ואתרע הא פריך לעיל (יג:) גבי כותבין שטר ללוה אע"ג דליכא ריעותא וי"ל דמצי לדחויי בשטרי הקנאה אבל הכא אי בשטרי הקנאה מיירי כי אין האשה מודה נמי יחזיר לבעל דאין אשה מודה משמע אפילו אינה אומרת שהוא מזויף אלא אומרת שכתבה ליתן ולא נתנה ואומרת עתה אל תתנו לפי שנמלכה דומיא דמלא שוברין דמתניתין דלא יחזיר שאני אומר כתובים היו ונמלך כו':

ש"מ

### עין משפט נר מצוה

קסד א ב ג מיי' פי"ח מהלכות גזלה ואבידה הלכה ט י ועיין במ"מ סמג עשין עד טוש"ע ח"מ סי' סה סעיף יד:

קסה ד מיי' שם הלכה יא סמג שם וטוש"ע שם סעיף יח וטוש"ע אה"ע סי' קי סעיף ג:

### רבינו חננאל

ופרקינן מתני' דדייקת מינה הא אמר תנו נותנין במתנת שכיב מרע שאפי' נתנם לאחר אי הדר ביה בר מיהדר הוא וליכא פסידא כלל. ברייתא בבריא דלאו בר מיהדר הוא דחיישינן דלמא כתביה להאי מעיקרא ולא יהב ליה שטרא והדר כתביה לאיניש אחרינא ויהב ליה שטרא והשתא בעי למיהדר במה דיהב לבתרא ועבד קנוניא בהדי קמא ומשום הכי מודה ליה לפיכך תני לא יחזיר ואתקיף עלה רב זביד והא מתניתא נמי דיתיקאות קתני אלא הא והא בשכיב מרע ולא קשיא מתני' בדידיה דבר מיהדר הוא ברייתא (באבוה) [בבריה] וכו' ופשוטה היא. ת"ר מצא שובר בזמן שהאשה מודה יחזיר לבעל וניחוש דלמא כתבה בניסן ולא נתנה לו השטר עד תשרי וזבנתה לכתובה ביני וביני ומפיק לשובר דכתב בניסן ומבטיל לה לכתובה.

### מסורת הש"ס

א) ס"א וליזול וליפ... מיניה דהאי וכן ... ברא"ש, מהרש"ל.

### הגהות הב"ח

(א) רש"י ד"ה הא בב... וכו' בערסיה כ... שכותבין:

### ליקוטי רש"י

קושטא. אמת [סנהדרין צז.]. בטו... הנאה. דבר מועט ש... אלא כחיזוק טובה שק... גרי"ד מפיק רלון [כתו... פה:].

אירכס ליה גיטא בי מדרשא אמר אי סימנא אית לי בגויה אי טביעות עינא אית לי בגויה אהדרוה ניהליה אמר לא ידענא אי משום סימנא אהדרוה ניהלי וקא סברי סימנין דאורייתא אי משום טביעות עינא אהדרוה ניהלי ודוקא צורבא מדרבנן אבל אינש דעלמא לא גופא מצא גט אשה בשוק בזמן שהבעל מודה יחזיר לאשה אין הבעל מודה לא יחזיר לא לזה ולא לזה בזמן שהבעל מודה מיהא יחזיר לאשה וליחוש שמא כתב ליתן בניסן ולא נתן לה עד תשרי ואזל בעל זבין פירי מניסן ועד תשרי ומפקא לגיטא דכתב בניסן ואתיא למטרף לקוחות שלא כדין הניחא למ"ד [א] כיון שנתן עיניו לגרשה שוב אין לבעל פירות שפיר אלא למ"ד יש לבעל פירות עד שעת נתינה מאי איכא למימר כי אתיא למטרף אמרינן לה אייתי ראיה אימת מטא גיטא לידך ומאי שנא משטרי חוב דתנן [ב] מצא שטרי חוב אם יש בהן אחריות נכסים לא יחזיר ואוקימנא כשחייב מודה ומשום שמא כתב ללוות בניסן ולא לוה עד תשרי וקא טריף לקוחות שלא כדין התם נמי ליהדר וכי אתי למטרף נימא ליה אייתי ראיה אימת מטא שטר חוב לידך אמרי הכא גבי גט אשה אתי לוקח ותבעה אמר האי דהדרוה ניהלה רבנן לגיטא משום דלא תעגין ותיתיב השתא דקא אתיא למטרף תיזל ותיתי ראיה אימת מטא גיטא לידה הכא גבי שטר חוב לא אתי לוקח ותבע [א] מדאהדרוה ניהליה רבנן לשטר חוב פשיטא למאי הלכתא אהדרוה ניהליה למטרף הוא שמע מינה קמו רבנן במילתא ומקמי דידי מטא שטרא לידיה: שחרורי עבדים וכו': ת"ר [א] מצא שטר שחרור בשוק בזמן שהרב מודה יחזיר לעבד אין הרב מודה לא יחזיר לא לזה ולא לזה בזמן שהרב מודה מיהא יחזיר לעבד ואמאי ניחוש שמא כתב ליתן לו בניסן ולא נתן לו עד תשרי ואזיל עבדא וקנה נכסין מניסן ועד תשרי ואזיל הרב וזבנינהו ומפיק ליה לשחרור דכתב בניסן וקא טריף לקוחות שלא כדין [ג] הניחא למ"ד זכות הוא לעבד שיוצא מתחת רבו לחירות וכאביי דאמר [ד] עדיו בחתומיו זכין ליה שפיר אלא למ"ד חוב הוא לעבד שיוצא מתחת יד רבו לחירות מאי איכא למימר דכי אתי למטרף אמרינן ליה [ב] אייתי ראיה אימת מטא שטר שחרור לידך: [ג] דייתיקי מתנה וכו': [ה] ת"ר איזו היא דייתיקי דא תהא למיקם ולהיות שאם מת נכסיו לפלוני מתנה כל שכתוב בו מהיום ולאחר מיתה אלמא אי כתיבא מהיום ולאחר מיתה הוא דקני ואי לא לא קני אמר אביי הכי קאמר [ו] איזו היא מתנת בריא שהיא כמתנת שכיב מרע דלא קני אלא לאחר מיתה כל שכתוב בה מהיום ולאחר מיתה טעמא דלא אמר תנו הא אמר תנו נותנין ורמינהו מצא דייתקאות אפותיקאות ומתנות אע"פ ששניהם מודין לא יחזיר לא לזה ולא לזה אמר רבי אבא בר ממל לא קשיא
הא

**רש"י**

אירכס ליה גיטא. שהיה שליח להביא ולירכס ליה ולשכחוהו: אמר אי סימנא. חשיבא לכו אית לי בגויה סימנא: ואי טביעות עין. חשיבא לכו אית לי בגויה טביעות עינא מכירו אני בכתב ידי הסופר והעדים מדת ארכו ורחבו כאדם המכיר את חבירו בטביעות עין שטבע בו ואין בו סימן: וקסברי. רבנן סימנין דאורייתא שלא אמרתי סימן מובהק והחזירוהו לי: ודוקא לצורבא מדרבנן. דמוחזק לן ביה דלא משני בדיבוריה: ולא נתן עד תשרי. וכל זמן שלא נתן היה לו לאכול ולמכור פירי נכסי מלוג שלה שתקנו חכמים לבעל לאכול פירות של נכסי מלוג אשתו שנפלו לה לירושה: וזבין פירי. כמשפטו: שפיר. יש לה לטרוף כל מה שמכר משעת כתיבה והא פלוגתא במס' גיטין בפ' שני (דף יח:): אימת מטא גיטא לידך. מיד בעליך: אימת מטא שטרא לידך. מיד הלוה מתחלה: אתי לוקח ותבע. אי אתיא למיטרף מסיק אדעתיה לתבוע אייתי ראיה אימת מטא גיטא לידך בזמנא קמא: מקמי דידי. מקודם שמכר לי הלוה נכסיו מטא שטר מיד לוה למלוה בראשונה: הניחא למ"ד כו'. פלוגתא בפ"ק דגיטין (דף יג:): זכות הוא לעבד. טובה היא אצלו שמתירו בקהל וכיון דזכות הוא איכא לתרוצי דמשעה שנכתב זוכה בשחרור דלכי מטא (ב) שטר גט לידיה נעשה בן חורין למפרע משעת חתימה: חוב הוא לעבד. חובתו הוא שיוצא מתחת רבו כלומר הפסד הוא לו שאם עבד (ג) כהן הוא פוסלו מן התרומה ואם של ישראל אוסרו בשפחה כנענית דזילא ליה ושכיחא ליה ופריצא ליה: מאי איכא למימר. דהשתא ליכא למימר עדיו בחתומיו [ז] חבין לו דאין חבין לאדם שלא בפניו: דא תהא למיקם. שטר זה יהיה לקום ולהיות בכל הכתוב בו דדברי שכיב מרע ככתובין וכמסורין דמי: מתנה. מתנת בריא איזו היא כל שכתוב בו כו': מהיום ולאחר מיתה. גוף הקרקע קנוי לו מן היום ואין לו עוד רשות למוכרה וליתנה ולהורישה והפירות אינו אוכל כל ימי חייו אלא לאחר מיתה: ואי לא לא קני. בתמיה כל שכן דאם יהיב ליה גוף ופירות במעכשיו דקני טפי: סתם מתנת שכיב מרע לא קניא לו אלא לאחר מיתה דמחמת מיתה הוא מצוה: הא אמר תנו נותנין. אמתני' פריך דתלי טעמא בשאני אומר נמלך עליהם שלא לתתן: אפותיקאות. שעשה לו שדה אפותיקי למלוה על פה שהיתה לו עליו מלוה ישנה: לא יחזיר. שמא כתבה לזה ולא מסר לו ולא זכה בקרקע וחזר וכתב לאחר ומסר לו השטר וזכה בו ובא לחזור בו מן השני ורוצה לתת לראשון וחפץ שימסרו לו שטר זה שיוציאנה בבית דין ונמצא זמן שטר של זה קודם לשטרו של שני ויוציאנה מידו בדין:
הא

**תוספות**

אי סימנין דאורייתא. בגט נמי מהדרינן ואי סימנין דרבנן מה שמחזירין אבידה בסימן שאינו מובהק מדרבנן משום דהפקר בית דין הפקר אבל מדאורייתא צריך או עדים או סימן מובהק וגט נמי דאיסור הוא לא מהדרינן אלא בסימן מובהק:

אבל אינש דעלמא לא. מפרש ר"ת דעם הארץ נמי אית ליה טביעות עינא כדאמר בפ' גט פשוט (ב"ב דף קסח.) האי מאן דבעי לקדושי איתתא לידבר עם הארץ בהדיה והאי דלא מהדרינן ליה משום דלא מהימן: **וליחוש** דלמא כתב ליתן בניסן כו'. ואפילו לאביי דאמר עדיו בחתומיו זכין לו הכא גבי אשה חוב הוא לה ואמתני' דדייקינן הא אמר תנו נותנין וכן אמתני' דהמביא גט ממדינת הים לא פריך ניחוש שמא כתב ליתן בניסן כו' כיון דעתה שבא לגרשה רואין שהזמן מוקדם ויש קול שלא נמסר ביום שנכתב ויזכרו לקוחות לומר אייתי ראיה אימת מטא גיטא לידך אבל הכא שהבעל מודה שממנה נפל וגירשה ביום הכתיבה פריך וניחוש שמא יסברו לקוחות שאמרה אמת ולא יאמרו בשעת טריפה אייתי ראייה אימת מטא גיטא לידך וא"ת ואמאי לא פריך אמתני' (ד) דכותבין גט לאיש אע"פ שאין אשתו עמו ליחוש שמא לא יתן עד שנה וכי תימא כיון דליכא ריעותא דנפילה י"ל יום שנכתב נמסר ואפי' נמסר נמי אחר זמן יש קול שלא נמסר ביום שנכתב כי רואים בשעת קבלת הגט שהוא מוקדם ויזכרו לקוחות לומר כשתטרף אייתי ראיה דהא לעיל (דף יג:) פריך גבי כותבין שטר ללוה ויש לומר דגבי כותבין שטר ללוה פריך שפיר משום דמאן דזיף בצנעא יזיף (ב"ב מג.) ויש לחוש שמא לאחר זמן ימסור לו בצנעא ויסברו לקוחות שנמסר לו משעת כתיבה אבל גט דיהבי בפרהסיא דצריך עדי מסירה אפילו לר"מ דאין דבר שבערוה פחות משנים כדפירש ר"ת ורשב"ם בגיטין (ד. ד"ה דקי"ל) ועוד דרגילות לגרש בפרהסיא לגלות שהיא פנויה יש קול שנתגרשה אחר זמן כתיבה ולא יטעו הלקוחות אבל אכתי קשה אמאי כותבין גט לאיש כו' ניחוש שמא תזנה אחר הכתיבה ויתן לה בצנעא כדי לחפות עליה וי"ל דמיד שנכתב הגט נותן לה דלא מקדים איניש פורענות לנפשיה: **אימת** מטא גיטא לידך. בשאר גיטין לא אמרינן כן דמסתמא ביום שנכתב נמסר אבל זה דנפל אתרע:
בריית

**עין משפט נר מצוה**

קסא א ב מיי' פי"ח מהל' גזילה ואבידה הל' ח ועיין בכ"מ סמג עשין עד טוש"ע ח"מ סי' סה סעיף יג:
קסב ג מיי' שם הל' ט טוש"ע שם סעיף יד:
קסג ד מיי' פי"ב מהל' זכייה ומתנה הל' יד סמג עשין פב טוש"ע ח"מ סי' רנז סעיף ו:

**רבינו חננאל**

לחומרא עבדינן הא דאירכס ליה גיטא בבי מדרשא לרבה בר [בר] חנא ואהדרוה ליה ולא ידע אי בסימנא דאית ליה בגויה אי בטביעות עינא מסייעא להא דאמרנא. גופא מצא גט אשה בזמן שהבעל מודה יחזיר לאשה וכו' פשוטה היא וסוגייא דשמעתתא כל כי הא גוונא מצריכינן ליה לברורי בעדים אימת מטא גט לידה וכן כל שטר הנמצא חיישינן דלמא אתי למיטרף לקוחות שלא כדין. וכן גט שחרור דינו נמי הכי. פי' דיאתיקי צואת שכיב מרע בלשון יון נקראת דייתיקי. דייתיקי מתנה ושוברים לא יחזיר שאני אומר כתובין היו ונמלך עליהם שלא ליתנם. הא אמר תנו נותנים ורמינהי דיתיקאות אפותיקאות ומתנות אע"פ ששניהן מודין לא יחזיר לא לזה ולא לזה

**מסורת הש"ס**

[א] גיטין יח:], ב) לעיל ... ג) [גיטין יג:], ... לעיל יג. וש"נ], ... בתרא קלה:, ו) זכין, מהרש"ל.

**הגהות הב"ח**

... גמ' ותבע אמר ... הדרוה ניהליה רבנן ... חוב: (ב) רש"י ... זכות הוא וכו' דלכי ... גט שחרור לידיה: ... ד"ה חוב וכו' שאם ... של כהן: (ד) תוס' ... וליחוש וכו' לא פריך ... גיטין דגט פשוט דכותבין:

**ליקוטי רש"י**

טביעות עינא ... לי בגויה. בעיתו ... ניהלי אית לי ... עינא בגויה ... עיני בו עד שאני ... יפה בלא שום ... סימנים דאורייתא. שלא נתן בו ... מובהק אלא סימנא ... מה ומדאסמכו ... בלאיסורא קסברי ... לאהדורי אבידתא ... מוכן תעשה ... וכו'. צורבא מדרבנן. דידע בטביעות ... ולא משני בדיבוריה ... כז:]. אין לו ... פירות. וכי טרפה מזמן ... בדין טרפה [גיטין ...]. עדיו בחתומיו ... לו. מיום שחתמוהו ... לו השעבוד [לעיל ...]. איזו היא דייתיקי. איזו היא מתנת שכיב מרע שגובה ... מיתה אע"ג דלא ... בה מהיום. דא תהא למיקם ולהיות. ... מיתתי והיינו לשון ... דייתיקי. כל שכתוב בו מהיום ולאחר מיתה. ... משמע הכי גופה קנוי ... מהיום ופירי לאחר ... אבל אי לא הוה ... בה מהיום אינו קונה ... מתנה לאחר מיתה ... דאין כח לאדם ליתן ... לכן דבר שלא יוכל ... קנות באותו הזמן ... רוצה שתתקיים ... מתנה ולאחר מיתה היאך ... אדם ליתן אחרי ... ונקבר. לא קני. ... אלא לאחר מיתה ... דמתנת שכיב מרע ... קונה אלא לאחר ... ומיהו בהכי עדיפא ... שכיב מרע דמתנת שכיב ... יכול לחזור בו וליתן ... כדלקמן דייתיקי ... דייתיקי אבל ... בריא דמהיום ... לאחר מיתה אינו יכול ... עוד הגוף כל ימי ... אלא פירות [רשב"ם ב"ב קלה:].

Its effect is **that if [the benefactor] dies** of his illness, **his property** passes **to so-and-so.**[27]

The Baraisa continues:

מַתָּנָה – Which is a GIFT document? כָּל שֶׁכָּתוּב בּוֹ מֵהַיּוֹם וּלְאַחַר מִיתָה – ANY document IN WHICH a clause IS WRITTEN stipulating that the gift is to take effect FROM TODAY, AND AFTER the benefactor's DEATH.[28]

The Gemara questions the Baraisa's definition of gift documents:

אַלְמָא – **Evidently** the Baraisa means to teach אִי כְּתִיבָא מֵהַיּוֹם וּלְאַחַר מִיתָה הוּא דְּקָנֵי – that **only when** the text of **a document** includes a clause which **states** that the gift is to take effect **from today and after death does [the beneficiary]** indeed **acquire ownership** of the gift. וְאִי לֹא – **But if** the text of the document does **not** include this clause, and the gift is intended to take effect immediately, לֹא קָנֵי – **[the beneficiary] does not acquire** ownership of the gift!?[29] Can it be true that a gift document that is to take effect immediately is not valid?

The Gemara explains that the Baraisa, which requires a gift document to include this clause, does not refer to an ordinary gift but rather to a specific type of gift:

אָמַר אַבַּיֵי – **Abaye said:** הָכִי קָאָמַר – **This is what [the Baraisa]** means to **say:** אֵיזוֹ הִיא מַתְּנַת בָּרִיא – **Which is the gift** document **of a healthy person** שֶׁהִיא כְּמַתְּנַת שְׁכִיב מְרַע – **[whose effectiveness] is similar to** that of **the gift of a seriously ill person,**[30] דְּלֹא קָנֵי אֶלָּא לְאַחַר מִיתָה – **in that [the beneficiary] does not acquire** full ownership of the gift **until after** the benefactor's **death?**[31] כָּל שֶׁכָּתוּב בָּהּ מֵהַיּוֹם וּלְאַחַר מִיתָה – **Any** document **in which** a clause **is written** stipulating that the gift is to take effect **from today and after death.**[32] An ordinary gift document, which does not contain this clause, takes effect immediately and is not similar to the will of a seriously ill person; however, it is certainly valid.

The Gemara notes the Mishnah's reason for not returning these documents and draws a conclusion:

טַעְמָא – **The reason** the Mishnah gives not to return a will or a gift document דְּלֹא אָמַר תְּנוּ – is **that [the benefactor] did not say to give** it to the beneficiary.[33] הָא אָמַר תְּנוּ – This implies that **if he** did **say to give** it to the beneficiary, נוֹתְנִין – **we** would **give** it.[34]

The Gemara points out a contradiction to this ruling:

וּרְמִינְהוּ – **But they contrasted** this with the ruling of a Baraisa: מָצָא דְּיַיְתִּקָאוֹת – If ONE FOUND sickbed WILLS, אַפּוֹתִיקָאוֹת – or APOTIKI documents,[35] וּמַתָּנוֹת – OR GIFT documents, אַף עַל פִּי שֶׁשְּׁנֵיהֶם מוֹדִין – EVEN THOUGH BOTH [PARTIES] AGREE that these documents belong to the beneficiary, לֹא יַחֲזִיר לֹא לָזֶה וְלֹא לָזֶה – [THE FINDER] SHOULD NOT RETURN them TO EITHER party, because we must be concerned for the possibility that the document may be used fraudulently.[36] This contradicts our Mishnah's implication that if the writer of the document instructs us to give it to the recipient, we may do so. Why is the Baraisa concerned for fraud and our Mishnah not concerned?

The Gemara answers:

אָמַר רַבִּי אַבָּא בַּר מָמָל – **R' Abba bar Memal said:** לֹא קַשְׁיָא – **This is not a difficulty.**

NOTES

death, even if no formal *kinyan* was performed (see above, 18a note 10). Accordingly, the will need not be handed over to its beneficiary for it to take effect — it is "valid and enduring" even though no formal *kinyan* has been performed (*Rashi*).

27. I.e. the beneficiary named in the will. Since the reason the benefactor wrote this will was because of his concern that he might die of his illness, it does not take effect unless he in fact dies. Should he recover from the illness, he is presumed to have retracted his will (see *Tosafos* to *Bava Basra* 153a ד״ה ולא).

28. Under this clause, the gift is granted to its beneficiary in two stages: The property itself is granted immediately, the benefactor thereby relinquishing his right to transfer it to anyone else. However, the right to the property's yield (i.e. including such things as produce and rental income) is not granted to the beneficiary until the benefactor's death. Thus, the benefactor, although no longer the property's owner, continues to enjoy the use of the property for the remainder of his life. The beneficiary, on the other hand, although the property's legal owner, derives no practical benefit from it until the benefactor dies (*Rashi;* cf. *Tosafos* 19b ד״ה והא; *Tosafos* to *Bava Basra* 135b ד״ה כל.)

29. Certainly if one deeded ownership of both the property itself and its yield to take effect immediately, the gift should surely be valid (*Rashi*).

30. In general, a deathly ill person's bequest is effective only after his death, for it is presumed that he is giving instructions how to distribute his belongings after his death (*Rashi*).

31. Wills are not valid under Torah law; upon a person's death, all property passes to his natural heirs. However, the Rabbis instituted a law allowing a seriously ill person to bequeath his property orally, out of concern that an ill person's condition might deteriorate if he were frustrated by his inability to arrange his affairs before his death as he desired. Thus, it is only a seriously ill person who is empowered to make a will. A healthy person has no recourse other than to give his property away as a bona fide gift, effective during the donor's lifetime.

The Baraisa therefore asks: In what way can a healthy person write a gift document so that it will not take effect until he dies, in the manner of a will? Is there a clause that he can insert which will accomplish this?

32. A gift granted "from today and after death," and a gift bestowed by a seriously ill person in his will, are alike in that the beneficiary acquires no practical benefit from the property as long as the benefactor lives. It is only upon his death that the beneficiary acquires the right to the property's yield. [However, unlike a will which does not take effect at all unless the benefactor dies of his illness, this gift takes effect immediately with regard to the fact that the recipient becomes the legal owner of the property.] (*Ritva*, in explanation of *Rashi*; see also *Rashbam* to *Bava Basra* 135b ד״ה דלא).

33. I.e. our only concern is that the writer lost the document before implementing it and he no longer wants it to be implemented (see Mishnah 18a).

34. Should the document's author instruct the finder to give it to the recipient named in it, the finder would hand the document over to its beneficiary. [Thus, even if it is the writer who lost the document, it will now be implemented legally.]

35. I.e. a document designating a lien on a specific property of the debtor, for an outstanding, previously unrecorded loan (*Rashi*). See above, 15b note 7.

36. We must be concerned that perhaps the writer neglected to implement this document and in the interim gave the property away to someone else. If we now return this document to the recipient named in it, he may use it to prove that he acquired the property first, since the date on his document precedes the date on the document of the later recipient, who is really the rightful owner. Therefore, although the writer agrees that he had implemented this document and it was the recipient who lost it, we do not return it because we must be concerned that perhaps the writer wishes to retract his legitimate gift to the second person and restore it to the first (*Rashi*).

This concern applies in the same way to an *apotiki* document, for a lien may subsequently be placed against the property, and the holder of the *apotiki* will fraudulently establish a precedence. The Gemara below (19b) will discuss how this concern operates with regard to a sickbed will.

אירכס ליה גיטא בי מדרשא אמר אי סימנא אית לי בגויה אי טביעות עינא אית לי בגויה אהדרוה ניהליה אמר לא ידענא אי משום סימנא אהדרוה ניהלי וקא סברי סימנין דאורייתא אי משום טביעות עינא אהדרוה ניהלי ודוקא צורבא מדרבנן אבל איניש דעלמא לא גופא מצא גט אשה בשוק בזמן שהבעל מודה יחזיר לאשה אין הבעל מודה לא יחזיר לא לזה ולא לזה בזמן שהבעל מודה מיהא יחזיר לאשה וליחוש שמא כתב ליתן בניסן ולא נתן לה עד תשרי ואזל בעל זבין פירי מניסן ועד תשרי ומפקא לגיטא דכתב בניסן ואתיא למטרף לקוחות שלא כדין הניחא למ"ד [א] כיון שנתן עיניו לגרשה שוב אין לבעל פירות שפיר אלא למ"ד יש לבעל פירות עד שעת נתינה מאי איכא למימר כי אתיא למטרף אמרינן לה אייתי ראיה אימת מטא גיטא לידך ומאי שנא משטרי חוב דתנן [ג] מצא שטרי חוב אם יש בהן אחריות נכסים לא יחזיר ואוקימנא כשחייב מודה ומשום שמא כתב ללוות בניסן ולא לוה עד תשרי וקא טריף לקוחות שלא כדין התם נמי ליהדר וכי אתי למטרף נימא ליה אייתי ראיה אימת מטא שטר חוב לידך אמרי הכא גבי גט אשה אתי לוקח ותבעה אמר האי דהדרוה רבנן לגיטא משום דלא תעגין ותיתיב השתא דקא אתיא למטרף תיזל ותיתי ראיה אימת מטא גיטא לידה הכא גבי שטר חוב לא אתי לוקח ותבע (א) מדאהדרוה ניהליה רבנן לשטר חוב פשיטא למאי הלכתא אהדרוה ניהליה למטרף הוא שמע מינה קמו רבנן במילתא ומקמי דידי מטא שטרא לידיה: שחרורי עבדים וכו': ת"ר [א] מצא שטר שחרור בשוק בזמן שהרב מודה יחזיר לעבד אין הרב מודה לא יחזיר לא לזה ולא לזה בזמן שהרב מודה מיהא יחזיר לעבד ואמאי ניחוש שמא כתב ליתן לו בניסן ולא נתן לו עד תשרי ואזל עבדא וקנה נכסין מניסן ועד תשרי ואזיל הרב וזבנינהו ומפיק ליה לשחרור דכתב בניסן וקא טריף לקוחות שלא כדין [ג] הניחא למ"ד זכות הוא לעבד שיוצא מתחת רבו לחירות וכאביי דאמר [ד] עדיו בחתומיו זכין ליה שפיר אלא למ"ד חוב הוא לעבד שיוצא מתחת יד רבו לחירות מאי איכא למימר דכי אתי למטרף אמרינן ליה [ב] אייתי ראיה אימת מטא שטר שחרור לידך: [ג] דייתיקי מתנה וכו': [ו] ת"ר איזו היא דייתיקי דא תהא למיקם ולהיות שאם מת נכסיו לפלוני מתנה כל שכתוב בו מהיום ולאחר מיתה אלמא אי כתיבא מהיום ולאחר מיתה הוא דקני ואי לא לא קני אמר אביי הכי קאמר [ד] איזו היא מתנת בריא שהיא כמתנת שכיב מרע דלא קני אלא לאחר מיתה כל שכתוב בה מהיום ולאחר מיתה טעמא דלא אמר תנו הא אמר תנו נותנין ורמינהו מצא דייתיקאות אפותיקאות ומתנות אע"פ ששניהם מודין לא יחזיר לא לזה ולא לזה אמר רבי אבא בר ממל לא קשיא
הא

**רש"י**

**אירכס ליה גיטא.** שהיה שליח להביא ואירכס ליה ואשכחוהו: **אמר אי סימנא.** חשיבא לכו אית לי בגויה סימנא: **ואי טביעות עין.** חשיבא לכו אית לי בגויה טביעות עינא מכירו אני בכתב ידי הסופר והעדים מדת ארכו ורחבו כאדם המכיר את חבירו בטביעת עין שטבע בו ואין בו סימן: **וקסברי.** רבנן סימנין דאורייתא שלא אמרתי סימן מובהק והחזירוהו לי: **ודוקא לצורבא מדרבנן.** דמוחזק לן ביה דלא משני בדיבוריה: **ולא נתן עד תשרי.** וכל זמן שלא נתן היה לו לאכול ולמכור פירי נכסי מלוג שלה שתקנו חכמים לבעל לאכול פירות של נכסי מלוג אשתו שנפלו לה לירושה: **וזבין פירי.** כמשפטו: **שפיר.** יש לה לטרוף כל מה שמכר משעת כתיבה והא פלוגתא במס' גיטין בפ' שני (דף יז:): **אימת מטא גיטא לידך.** מיד בעליך: **אימת מטא שטרא לידך.** מיד הלוה מתחלה: **אתי לוקח ותבע.** אי אתיא למיטרף מסיק אדעתיה לתבוע אייתי ראיה אימת מטא גיטא לידך בזמנא קמא: **מקמי דידי.** מקודם שמכר לי הלוה נכסיו מטא שטר מיד לוה למלוה בראשונה: **הניחא למ"ד כו'.** פלוגתא בפ"ק דגיטין (דף יב:): **זכות הוא לעבד.** טובה היא אצלו שמתירו בקהל וכיון דזכות הוא איכא לתרולי דמשעה שנכתב זוכה בשחרור דלכי מטא (ב) שטר גט לידיה נעשה בן חורין למפרע משעת חתימה: **חוב הוא לעבד.** חובתו הוא שיוצא מתחת רבו כלומר הפסד הוא לו שאם עבד (ג) כהן הוא פוסלו מן התרומה ואם של ישראל אוסרו בשפחה כנענית דזילא ליה ושכיחא ליה ופריצא ליה: **מאי איכא למימר.** דהשתא ליכא למימר עדיו בחתומיו [ו] זכין לו דאין זכין לאדם שלא בפניו: **דא תהא למיקם.** שטר זה יהיה לקום ולהיות בכל הכתוב בו דדברי שכיב מרע ככתובין וכמסורין דמי: **מתנה.** מתנת בריא איזו היא כל שכתוב בו כו': **מהיום ולאחר מיתה.** גוף הקרקע קנוי לו מן היום ואין לו עוד רשות למוכרה וליתנה ולהורישה והפירות אינו אוכל כל ימי חייו אלא לאחר מיתה: **ואי לא לא קני.** בתמיה כל שכן דאם יהיב ליה גוף ופירות במעכשיו דקני טפי: סתם מתנת שכיב מרע לא קניא לו אלא לאחר מיתה דמחמת מיתה הוא מצווה: **הא אמר תנו נותנין.** אמתני' פריך דתלי טעמא בשאני אומר נמלך עליהם שלא לתנן: **אפותיקאות.** שעשה לו שדה אפותיקי למלוה על פה שהיתה לו עליו מלוה ישנה: **לא יחזיר.** שמא כתבה לזה ולא מסר לו ולא זכה בקרקע וחזר וכתב לאחר ומסר לו השטר וזכה בו ובא לחזור בו מן השני ורוצה לתת לראשון וחפץ שימסרו לו שטר זה שיוציאנה בבית דין ונמצא זמן שטר של זה קודם לשטרו של שני ויוציאנה מידו בדין:
הא

**תוספות**

**אי סימנין דאורייתא.** בגט נמי מהדרינן ואי סימנין דרבנן מה שמחזירין אבידה בסימן שאינו מובהק מדרבנן משום דהפקר בית דין הפקר אבל מדאורייתא צריך או עדים או סימן מובהק וגט נמי דאיסור הוא לא מהדרינן אלא בסימן מובהק:

**אבל איניש דעלמא לא.** מפרש ר"ת דעם הארץ נמי אית ליה טביעות עינא כדאמר בפ' גט פשוט (ב"ב דף קסח.) האי מאן דבעי לקדושי איתתא לידבר עם הארץ בהדיה והאי דלא מהדרינן ליה משום דלא מהימן:

**וליחוש** דלמא כתב ליתן בניסן כו'. ואפילו לאביי דאמר עדיו בחתומיו זכין לו הכא גבי אשה חוב הוא לה ואמתני' דדייקינן הא אמר תנו נותנין וכן אמתני' דהמביא גט ממדינת הים לא פריך ניחוש שמא כתב ליתן בניסן כו' כיון דעתה שבא לגרשה רואין שהזמן מוקדם ויש קול שלא נמסר ביום שנכתב ויזכרו לקוחות לומר אייתי ראיה אימת מטא גיטא לידך אבל הכא שהבעל מודה שממנה נפל וגירשה ביום הכתיבה פריך וניחוש שמא יסברו לקוחות שאמרה אמת ולא יאמרו בשעת טריפה אייתי ראייה אימת מטא גיטא לידך וא"ת ואמאי לא פריך אמתני' (ד) דכותבין גט לאיש אע"פ שאין אשתו עמו ליחוש שמא לא יתן עד שנה וכי תימא כיון דליכא ריעותא דנפילה י"ל יום שנכתב נמסר ואפי' נמסר נמי אחר זמן יש קול שלא נמסר ביום שנכתב כי רואים בשעת קבלת הגט שהוא מוקדם ויזכרו לקוחות לומר כשתטרף אייתי ראיה דהא לעיל (דף יג:) פריך גבי כותבין שטר ללוה ויש לומר דגבי כותבין שטר ללוה פריך שפיר משום דמאן דיזיף בצנעא יזיף (ב"ב מג.) ויש לחוש שמא לאחר זמן ימסור לו בצנעא ויסברו לקוחות שנמסר לו משעת כתיבה אבל גט דיהבי בפרהסיא דצריך עדי מסירה אפילו לר"מ דאין דבר שבערוה פחות משנים כדפירש ר"ת ורשב"ס בגיטין (ד. ד"ה דקי"ל) ועוד דרגילות לגרש בפרהסיא לגלות שהיא פנויה יש קול שנתגרשה אחר זמן כתיבה ולא יטעו הלקוחות אבל אכתי קשה אמאי כותבין גט לאיש כו' ניחוש שמא תזנה אחר הכתיבה ויתן לה בצנעא כדי לחפות עליה וי"ל דמיד שנכתב הגט נותן לה דלא מקדים איניש פורענות לנפשיה: **אימת** מטא גיטא לידך. בשאר גיטין לא אמרינן כן דמסתמא ביום שנכתב נמסר אבל זה דנפל אתרע:
ברייתא

**עין משפט נר מצוה**

קסא א ב מיי' פי"ח מהל' גזילה ואבידה הל' ח ועיין בכ"מ סמג עשין עד טוש"ע ח"מ סי' סה סעיף יג:
קסב ג מיי' שם הל' ט טוש"ע שם סעיף יד:
קסג ד מיי' פי"ב מהל' זכייה ומתנה הל' יד סמג עשין פב טוש"ע ח"מ סי' רנז סעיף ו:

**רבינו חננאל**

לחומרא עבדינן הא דאירכס ליה גיטא בבי מדרשא לרבה בר [בר] חנא ואהדרוה ליה ולא ידע אי בסימנא דאית ליה בגויה אי בטביעות עינא מסייעא להא דאמרנא. גופא מצא גט אשה בזמן שהבעל מודה יחזיר לאשה וכו' פשוטה היא וסוגייא דשמעתתא כל כי הא גוונא מצריכינן ליה לברורי בעדים אימת מטא גט לידה וכן כל שטר הנמצא חיישינן דלמא אתי למיטרף לקוחות שלא כדין. וכן גט שחרור דינו נמי הכי. פי' דיאתיקי צואת שכיב מרע בלשון יון נקראת דייתיקי. דייתיקי מתנה ושוברים לא יחזיר שאני אומר כתובין היו ונמלך עליהם שלא ליתנם. הא אמר תנו נותנים ורמינהי דיתיקאות אפותיקאות ומתנות אע"פ ששניהן מודין לא יחזיר לא לזה ולא לזה

**מסורת הש"ס**

גיטין יח:, ג) לעיל ג) [גיטין יב:], לעיל יג. וש"נ], בא בתרא קלה:, ו) זכין, מהרש"ל.

**הגהות הב"ח**

גמ' ותבע אמר הדרוה ניהליה רבנן ר חוב: (ב) רש"י זכות הוא וכו' דלכי גט שחרור לידיה: ד"ה חוב וכו' שאם של כהן: (ד) תוס' וליחוש וכו' לא פריך תניתין דגט פשוט דכותבין:

**ליקוטי רש"י**

טביעות עינא ת לי בגויה. בעינו ורי ניהלי אית לי עות עינא בגויה תי עיני בו עד שאני רו יפה בלא שום ן. סימנים ורייתא. שלא נתן בו ן מובהק אלא סימנא מא ומדאסמכו ימנא באיסורא קסברי נין לאהדורי אבידתא ייתא מוכן מעשה לחו וכו'. צורבא רבנן. דידע בטביעות א ולא משני בדיבוריה ין כז:]. אין לו רות. וכי טרפה מזמן יבה בדין טרפה [גיטין . עדיו בחתומיו ין לו. מיום שחתמוהו לו השעבוד [לעיל . איזו היא יתיקי. איזו היא נת שכיב מרע שגובה חר מיתה אע"ג דלא ב בה מהיום. דא א למיקם ולהיות. ר מיתתי והיינו לשון תיקי. כל שכתוב בו היום ולאחר מיתה. שמע הכי גופה קנוי מהיום ופירי לאחר תה אבל אי לא הוה ב בה מהיום אינו קונה ין מתנה לאחר מיתה רי אין כח לאדם ליתן קודם לכן דבר שלא יוכל קנות באותו הזמן וא רוצה שתתקיים מתנה ואחר מיתה היאך ל אדם ליתן אחרי ת ונקבר. לא קני. רות אלא לאחר מיתה מיא דמתנת שכיב מרע אינו קונה אלא לאחר תה ומיהו בהכי עדיפא שכיב מרע דמתנת שכיב רע יכול לחזור בו וליתן חר כדלקמן דייתיקי בטלת דייתיקי אבל תנת בריא דמהיום אחר מיתה אינו יכול מכור עוד הגוף כל ימי יו אלא פירות [רשב"ם ב"ב קלה:].

e slave, לֹא יַחֲזִיר לֹא לָזֶה וְלֹא לָזֶה – [THE FINDER] SHOULD NOT ETURN the bill of emancipation TO either [THE MASTER] OR [THE AVE].

The Gemara raises a question:

בִּזְמַן שֶׁהָרַב מוֹדֶה מִיהָא יַחֲזִיר לָעֶ – **In any event,** the Baraisa aches that in a case **when the master admits** that he freed the ave, **[the finder] should return** the bill of emancipation **to the ave.** וְאַמַּאי – **But why** do we allow this? נֵיחוּשׁ שֶׁמָּא כָּתַב לִיתֵּן לוֹ בְּנִי – **Let us be concerned that perhaps [the master] wrote** e bill of emancipation **in Nissan,** intending **to give** it **to** [the ave] then, וְלֹא נָתַן לוֹ עַד תִּשְׁרֵי – **but he did not** actually **give to him until** a later date, in **Tishrei.** וְאָזַל עַבְדָּא – In the eanwhile, **the slave,** who had not yet been freed, **went** וְקָנָה נְכָסִין מִנִּיסָן וְעַד תִּשׁ – **and purchased properties** between issan and Tishrei. Since the slave was not yet free, these operties belonged to his master. וְאָזִיל הָרַב וְזַבְּנִינְהוּ – Accordgly, **the master went and sold those** properties, as he was ntitled to do.[18] וּמַפֵּיק לֵיהּ לִשְׁחָרוּר דִּכְתַב בְּנִיסָן – Now, if we turn the bill of emancipation to the slave, **he may** one day roduce this bill of emancipation written **in Nissan,** claim that e was freed then and that the master had no right to sell the operty that he purchased between Nissan and Tishrei, וְקָא טָרֵיף לְקוּחוֹת שֶׁלֹּא כַּדִּ – **and he will** be able to **take away** the operty **unlawfully from those who purchased** it from his aster.[19] Given this possibility, how can we return the bill of nancipation to the slave?

The Gemara qualifies its question:

הָנִיחָא לְמַאן דְּאָמַ – **This** ruling, that the bill of emancipation ould be returned, **fits well** according **to the one who says** שֶׁיּוֹצֵא מִתַּחַת זְכוּת הוּא לָעֶ – that **it is advantageous to a slave** רַבּוֹ לְחֵירוּ – **that he should leave his master's authority to go ee,**[20] וּכְאַבַּיֵי דְּאָמַר – if we **also** concur **with Abaye who id**[21] עֵדָיו בַּחֲתוּמָיו זָכִין לֵיהּ – that when a document is to confer benefit upon its recipient, **its witnesses, by their signatures, quire** the benefit **for him.**[22] שַׁפִּיר – **It** then **fits well** that we turn the bill of emancipation to the slave. Since emancipation is vantageous to a slave, the witnesses who signed the bill of emancipation back in Nissan acquired the slave's freedom for him with their signatures. Thus, the emancipation did in fact take effect in Nissan when the bill was signed, and the slave is indeed entitled to any property he purchased between Nissan and Tishrei.[23] אֶלָּא לְמַאן דְּאָמַר – **However, according to the one who says** חוֹב הוּא לָעֶבֶד – that **it is disadvantageous to a slave** שֶׁיּוֹצֵא מִתַּחַת יַד רַבּוֹ לְחֵירוּת – **that he should leave his master's authority to go free,** מַאי אִיכָּא לְמֵימַר – **what is there to say?** If freedom is deemed disadvantageous to the slave, the witnesses to the bill of emancipation could not acquire his freedom for him when they signed it, and the emancipation did not take effect until the bill was handed to the slave in Tishrei.[24] Thus, by returning it, we are placing in his hands a document by which he can defraud the one who purchased property that he acquired between Nissan and Tishrei. – ? –

The Gemara answers that we need not be concerned for such a possibility:

דְּכִי אָתֵי לְמִטְרַף – The bill of emancipation may be returned **because when [the slave] will come to take** the property from the purchaser on the basis of this bill of emancipation, אָמְרִינַן לֵיהּ – **we will tell him:** אַיְיתֵי רְאָיָה אֵימַת מְטָא שְׁחָרוּר לִידָךְ – **"Prove** to us **when the bill of emancipation** actually **came into your hand,** and only then will we let you take the property from the purchaser."[25] Thus, we need not be concerned that one who purchased property from the master between Nissan and Tishrei might be defrauded.

The Gemara proceeds to the next items in the Mishnah. The Mishnah states:

דַּיְיתִיקֵי מַתָּנָה וכו׳ – If one found ... sickbed WILLS, GIFT DOCUMENTS, etc.

The Gemara cites a Baraisa that examines these two types of documents – *daitiki* wills and gift documents:

תָּנוּ רַבָּנָן – **The Rabbis taught in a Baraisa:** אֵיזוֹ הִיא דַּיְיתִיקֵי – WHICH document IS A *DAITIKI?* דָּא תְהֵא לְמֵיקַם וְלִהְיוֹת – It is a sickbed will, whose name, *daitiki,* is a contraction of the phrase – THIS will SHALL BE VALID AND ENDURING.[26] שֶׁאִם מֵת נְכָסָיו לִפְלוֹנִי

NOTES

. The Gemara speaks here of a Canaanite slave. A Canaanite slave is nsidered the absolute property of his master. Thus, the master of a naanite slave automatically assumes ownership of any property the ave acquires (see *Pesachim* 88b). If the slave was not freed until shrei, the master was entitled to sell any property the slave acquired fore that date.

. Since the emancipation did not actually take place until Tishrei, the aster had every right to sell the property purchased by his slave before en. The earlier date of Nissan on the bill of emancipation, however, ll seem to prove otherwise.

. Literally: to go out to freedom from under his master. The Mishnah *Gittin* (11b) cites a dispute whether emancipation is viewed as vantageous to a Canaanite slave or not. The Sages hold that emancition is advantageous, since it permits the slave to marry a Jewess, who as previously prohibited to him. The Gemara explains, however, from e slave's point of view emancipation may be viewed as disadvantaous, since it forbids him to live with a lewd Canaanite slavewoman, nich he may prefer over marriage to a virtuous Jewish woman. lditionally, if he was the slave of a Kohen, emancipation deprives him the permission to eat *terumah* which he previously enjoyed (see *ıshi*).

. Above, 13a.

. Under Torah law, one can act as an intermediary to acquire property behalf of another person even without that person's knowledge, if the quisition is clearly to his benefit. On the basis of this principle [known *zechiyah*], Abaye ruled that any document which confers a benefit on its recipient takes effect from the time the witnesses sign it, even ough it is not handed to the beneficiary until later, for the witnesses act on behalf of the beneficiary to acquire for him the benefit conferred in the document (see 13a).

23. Thus, the former slave is not perpetrating any fraud when he takes away the property from the purchasers, since the property is indeed his, and his former master had no right to sell it.

24. Abaye's premise, that witnesses cause a document to take effect from its signing, applies only to documents that are beneficial to their recipients, since one can act on behalf of another person without his knowledge only when it is to his benefit. Therefore according to the opinion that freedom is disadvantageous to a slave, the witnesses cannot cause a bill of emancipation to take effect by signing it (*Rashi*). Thus, the slave's emancipation is not effected until the bill is actually handed to him.

25. A bill of emancipation is similar to a *get* in that we may rely on one who purchased property from the master to demand verification of the actual date of emancipation before he returns any property to the slave. We may assume that he will think that the reason the rabbis allowed the bill of emancipation to be returned is merely to provide the slave with evidence of his emancipation and not to enable him to reclaim property from one who may have purchased it. Thus, he will not assume that the court verified the date of emancipation when they authorized the bill's return, since they had no reason to do so.

26. The word *daitiki* (d,t,k,y) is a contraction of דא תהא למיקם ולהיות. ***Da*** *(this)* ***Tehai*** *(shall be)* ***Lemeikam*** *(valid)* ***Velihyos*** *(and enduring).* [See above, 15b note 8.]

Transactions are normally not valid unless a *kinyan* is performed. However, a sickbed will is an exception to this rule, for the Rabbis decreed that the instructions of a seriously ill person take effect upon his

אירכס ליה גיטא בי מדרשא אמר אי סימנא אית לי בגויה אי טביעות עינא אית לי בגויה אהדרוה ניהליה אמר לא ידענא אי משום סימנא אהדרוה ניהלי וקא סברי סימנין דאורייתא אי משום טביעות עינא אהדרוה ניהלי ודוקא צורבא מדרבנן אבל איניש דעלמא לא גופא מצא גט אשה בשוק בזמן שהבעל מודה יחזיר לאשה אין הבעל מודה לא יחזיר לא לזה ולא לזה בזמן שהבעל מודה מיהא יחזיר לאשה וליחוש שמא כתב ליתן בניסן ולא נתן לה עד תשרי ואזל בעל זבין פירי מניסן ועד תשרי ומפקא לגיטא דכתב בניסן ואתיא למטרף לקוחות שלא כדין הניחא למ"ד [א] כיון שנתן עיניו לגרשה שוב אין לבעל פירות שפיר אלא למ"ד יש לבעל פירות עד שעת נתינה מאי איכא למימר כי אתיא למטרף אמרינן לה אייתי ראיה אימת מטא גיטא לידך ומאי שנא משטרי חוב דתנן [ב] מצא שטרי חוב אם יש בהן אחריות נכסים לא יחזיר ואוקימנא כשחייב מודה ומשום שמא כתב ללוות בניסן ולא לוה עד תשרי וקא טריף לקוחות שלא כדין התם נמי ליהדר וכי אתי למטרף נימא ליה אייתי ראיה אימת מטא שטר חוב לידך אמרי הכא גבי גט אשה אתי לוקח ותבעה אמר האי דהדרוה ניהלה רבנן לגיטא משום דלא תעגין ותיתיב השתא דקא אתיא למטרף תיזל ותיתי ראיה אימת מטא גיטא לידה הכא גבי שטר חוב לא אתי לוקח ותבע (א) מדאהדרוה ניהליה רבנן לשטר חוב פשיטא למאי הלכתא אהדרוה ניהליה למטרף הוא שמע מינה קמו רבנן במילתא ומקמי דידי מטא שטרא לידיה: שחרורי עבדים וכו': ת"ר [א] מצא שטר שחרור בשוק בזמן שהרב מודה יחזיר לעבד אין הרב מודה לא יחזיר לא לזה ולא לזה בזמן שהרב מודה מיהא יחזיר לעבד ואמאי ניחוש שמא כתב ליתן לו בניסן ולא נתן לו עד תשרי ואזל עבדא וקנה נכסין מניסן ועד תשרי ואזיל הרב וזבנינהו ומפיק ליה לשחרור דכתב בניסן וקא טריף לקוחות שלא כדין [ג] הניחא למ"ד זכות הוא לעבד שיוצא מתחת רבו לחירות וכאביי דאמר [ד] עדיו בחתומיו זכין ליה שפיר אלא למ"ד חוב הוא לעבד שיוצא מתחת יד רבו לחירות מאי איכא למימר דכי אתי למטרף אמרינן ליה [ב] אייתי ראיה אימת מטא שחרור לידך: [ג] דייתיקי מתנה וכו': [ה] ת"ר איזו היא דייתיקי דא תהא למיקם ולהיות שאם מת נכסיו לפלוני מתנה כל שכתוב בו מהיום ולאחר מיתה אלמא אי כתיבא מהיום ולאחר מיתה הוא דקני ואי לא לא קני אמר אביי הכי קאמר [ד] איזו היא מתנת בריא שהיא כמתנת שכיב מרע דלא קני אלא לאחר מיתה כל שכתוב בה מהיום ולאחר מיתה טעמא דלא אמר תנו הא אמר תנו נותנין ורמינהו מצא דייתקאות אפותיקאות ומתנות אע"פ ששניהם מודין לא יחזיר לא לזה ולא לזה אמר רבי אבא בר ממל לא קשיא

הא

---

אירכס ליה גיטא. שהיה שליח להביא ואירכס ליה ואשכחוהו: אמר אי סימנא. חשיבא לכו אית לי בגויה סימנא: ואי טביעות עין. חשיבא לכו אית לי בגויה טביעות עינא מכירו אני בכתב ידי הסופר והעדים מדת ארכו ורחבו כאדם המכיר את חבירו בטביעת עין שטבע בו ואין בו סימן: וקסברי. רבנן סימנין דאורייתא שלא אמרתי סימן מובהק והחזירוהו לי: ודוקא לצורבא מדרבנן. דמוחזק לן ביה דלא משני בדיבוריה: ולא נתן עד תשרי. וכל זמן שלא נתן היה לו לאכול ולמכור פירי נכסי מלוג שלה שתקנו חכמים לבעל לאכול פירות של נכסי מלוג אשתו שנפלו לה לירושה: וזבין פירי. כמשפטו: שפיר. יש לה לטרוף כל מה שמכר משעת כתיבה והא פלוגתא במס' גיטין בפ' שני (דף יז:): אימת מטא גיטא לידך. מיד בעליך: אימת מטא שטרא לידך. מיד הלוה מתחלה: אתי לוקח ותבע. אי אתיא למיטרף מסיק אדעתיה לתבוע אייתי ראיה אימת מטא גיטא לידך בזמנא קמא: מקמי דידי. מקודם שמכר לי הלוה נכסיו מטא שטר מיד לוה למלוה בראשונה: הניחא למ"ד כו'. פלוגתא בפ"ק דגיטין (דף יב:): זכות הוא לעבד. טובה היא אצלו שמתירו בקהל וכיון דזכות הוא איכא לתרולי דמשעה שנכתב זוכה בשחרור דלכי מטא (ב) שטר גט לידיה נעשה בן חורין למפרע משעת חתימה: חוב הוא לעבד. חובתו הוא שיוצא מתחת רבו כלומר הפסד הוא לו שאם עבד (ג) כהן הוא פוסלו מן התרומה ואם של ישראל אוסרו בשפחה כנענית דזילא ליה ושכיחא ליה ופריצא ליה: מאי איכא למימר. דהשתא ליכא למימר עדיו בחתומיו [ו] חבין לו דאין חבין לאדם שלא בפניו: דא תהא למיקם. שטר זה יהיה לקום ולהיות בכל הכתוב בו דדברי שכיב מרע ככתובין וכמסורין דמי: מתנה. מתנת בריא איזו היא כל שכתוב בו כו': מהיום ולאחר מיתה. גוף הקרקע קנוי לו מן היום ואין לו עוד רשות למוכרה וליתנה ולהורישה והפירות אינו אוכל כל ימי חייו אלא לאחר מיתה: ואי לא לא קני. בתמיה כל שכן דאם יהיב ליה גוף ופירות במעכשיו דקני טפי: סתם מתנת שכיב מרע לא קניא לו אלא לאחר מיתה דמחמת מיתה הוא מלווה: הא אמר תנו נותנין. אמתני' פריך דתלי טעמא בשאני אומר נמלך עליהם שלא לתתן: אפותיקאות. שעשה לו שדה אפותיקי למלוה על פה שהיתה לו עליו מלוה ישנה: לא יחזיר. שמא כתבה לזה ולא מסר לו ולא זכה בקרקע וחזר וכתב לאחר ומסר לו השטר וזכה בו ובא לחזור בו מן השני ורוצה לתת לראשון וחפץ שימסרו לו שטר זה שיוציאנה בבית דין ונמצא זמן שטר של זה קודם לשטרו של שני ויוציאנה מידו בדין:

הא

---

אי סימנין דאורייתא. בגט נמי מהדרינן ואי סימנין דרבנן מה שמחזירין אבידה בסימן שאינו מובהק מדרבנן משום דהפקר בית דין הפקר אבל מדאורייתא צריך או עדים או סימן מובהק וגט נמי דאיסור הוא לא מהדרינן אלא בסימן מובהק:

אבל איניש דעלמא לא. מפרש ר"ת דעם הארץ נמי אית ליה טביעות עינא כדאמר בפ' גט פשוט (ב"ב דף קסח.) האי מאן דבעי לקדושי איתתא לידבר עם הארץ בהדיה והאי דלא מהדרינן ליה משום דלא מהימן: וליחוש דלמא כתב ליתן בניסן כו'. ואפילו לאביי דאמר עדיו בחתומיו זכין לו הכא גבי אשה חוב הוא לה ואמתני' דדייקינן הא אמר תנו נותנין וכן אמתני' דהמביא גט ממדינת הים לא פריך ניחוש שמא כתב ליתן בניסן כו' כיון דעתה שבא לגרשה רואין שהזמן מוקדם ויש קול שלא נמסר ביום שנכתב ויזכרו לקוחות לומר אייתי ראיה אימת מטא גיטא לידך אבל הכא שהבעל מודה שממנה נפל וגירשה ביום הכתיבה פריך וניחוש שמא יסברו לקוחות שאמרה אמת ולא יאמרו בשעת טריפה אייתי ראייה אימת מטא גיטא לידך וא"ת ואמאי לא פריך אמתני' (ד) דכותבין גט לאיש אע"פ שאין אשתו עמו ליחוש שמא לא יתן עד שנה וכי תימא כיון דליכא ריעותא דנפילה י"ל יום שנכתב נמסר ואפי' נמסר נמי אחר זמן יש קול שלא נמסר ביום שנכתב כי רואים בשעת קבלת הגט שהוא מוקדם ויזכרו לקוחות לומר כשתטרף אייתי ראיה דהא לעיל (דף יג:) פריך גבי כותבין שטר ללוה ויש לומר דגבי כותבין שטר ללוה פריך שפיר משום דמאן דיזיף בצנעא יזיף (ב"ב מג.) ויש לחוש שמא לאחר זמן ימסור לו בצנעא ויסברו לקוחות שנמסר לו משעת כתיבה אבל גט דיהבי בפרהסיא דצריך עדי מסירה אפילו לר"מ דאין דבר שבערוה פחות משנים כדפירש ר"ת ורשב"ם בגיטין (ד. ד"ה דקי"ל) ועוד דרגילות לגרש בפרהסיא לגלות שהיא פנויה יש קול שנתגרשה אחר זמן כתיבה ולא יטעו הלקוחות אבל אכתי קשה אמאי כותבין גט לאיש כו' ניחוש שמא תזנה אחר הכתיבה ויתן לה בצנעא כדי לחפות עליה וי"ל דמיד שנכתב הגט נותן לה דלא מקדים איניש פורענות לנפשיה: אימת מטא גיטא לידך. בשאר גיטין לא אמרינן כן דמסתמא ביום שנכתב נמסר אבל זה דנפל אתרע:

בריית'

---

עין משפט נר מצוה

קפא א ב מיי' פי"ח מהל' גזילה ואבידה הל' ח ועיין בכ"מ סמג עשין עד טוש"ע ח"מ סי' סה סעיף יג:

קפב ג מיי' שם הל' ט טוש"ע שם סעיף יד:

קפג ד מיי' פי"ב מהל' זכייה ומתנה הל' יד סמג עשין פב טוש"ע ח"מ סי' רנז סעיף ו:

## רבינו חננאל

לחומרא עבדינן הא דאירכס ליה גיטא בבי מדרשא לרבה בר [בר] חנא ואהדרוה ליה ולא ידע אי בסימנא דאית ליה בגויה אי בטביעות עינא מסייעא להא דאמרנא. גופא מצא גט אשה בזמן שהבעל מודה יחזיר לאשה וכו' פשוטה היא וסוגייא דשמעתתא כל כי הא גוונא מצריכינן ליה לברורי בעדים אימת מטא גט לידה וכן כל שטר הנמצא חיישינן דלמא אתי למיטרף לקוחות שלא כדין. וכן גט שחרור דינו נמי הכי. פי' דיאתיקי צואת שכיב מרע בלשון יון נקראת דייתיקי. דייתיקי מתנה ושוברים לא יחזיר שאני אומר כתובין היו ונמלך עליהם שלא ליתנם. הא אמר תנו נותנים ורמינהי דיתיקאות אפותיקאות ומתנות אע"פ ששניהן מודין לא יחזיר לא לזה ולא לזה

---

## מסורת הש"ס

[ג]יטין יז:, ב) לעיל [...] ג) [גיטין יב:], [ל]עיל יג. וש"נ], [...]א בתרא קלה:, [...]ו) זכין, מהרש"ל.

## הגהות הב"ח

[...]מ' ותבע אמר [...]הדרוה ניהליה רבנן [...]ר חוב: (ב) רש"י [...] זכות הוא וכו' דלכי [...] גט שחרור לידיה: [...]"ה חוב וכו' שאם [...]של כהן: (ד) תוס' [...] וליחוש וכו' לא פריך [...]ניתין דגט פשוט דכותבין:

## ליקוטי רש"י

[...] טביעות עינא [...] לי בגויה. בעיתו [...]רי ניהלי אית לי [...]ות עינא בגויה [...]תי עיני בו עד שאני [...]ו יפה בלא שום [...] סימנים [...]רייתא. שלא נתן בו [...] מובהק אלא סימנא [...]א ומדאסמכו [...]מנא באיסורא קסברי [...]ין לאהדורי אבידתא [...]ייתא מוכן מעשה [...]לתו וכו'. צורבא [...]רבנן. דידע בטביעות [...] ולא משני בדיבוריה [...]ן כז:]. אין לו [...]ות. וכי טרפה מזמן [...]ה בדין טרפה [גיטין [...] עדיו בחתומיו [...] לו. מיום שחתמוהו [...] לו השעבוד [לעיל [...] איזו היא [...]תיקי. איזו היא [...]ת שכיב מרע שגובה [...]ר מיתה אע"ג דלא [...] בה מהיום. דא [...]א למיקם ולהיות. [...] מיתתי והיינו לשון [...]יקי. כל שכתוב בו [...]יום ולאחר מיתה. [...]מע הכי גופה קנוי [...] מהיום ופירי לאחר [...]ה אבל אי לא הוה [...] בה מהיום אינו קונה [...] מתנה לאחר מיתה [...]י אין כח לאדם ליתן [...]דם לכן דבר שלא יוכל [...]נות באותו הזמן [...]א רוצה שתתקיים [...]תנה ואחר מיתה היאך [...] אדם ליתן אחרי [...]ת ונקבר. לא קני. [...]ות אלא לאחר מיתה [...]יא דמתנת שכיב מרע [...]נו קונה אלא לאחר [...]ה ומיהו בהכי עדיפא [...]כיב מרע דמתנת שכיב [...] יכול לחזור בו וליתן [...]ר כדלקמן דייתיקי [...]לת דייתיקי אבל [...]ת בריא דמהיום [...]חר מיתה אינו יכול [...]ור עוד הגוף כל ימי [...] אלא פירות [רשב"ם ב"ב קלה:].

יש אֶלָּא לְמַאן דְּאָמַ – However, according to the one who says לְבַעַל פֵּירוֹת עַד שְׁעַת נְתִי – that a husband retains the yield until the time he actually gives the bill of divorce, מַאי אִיכָּא לְמֵימַ – what is there to say? How can we return the bill of divorce to the woman when she might use it to prove that she was divorced in Nissan and defraud those who purchased the rights to the yield of her property from her husband?

The Gemara answers:

כִּי אָתְיָא לְמִטְרַ – According to this view, when [the woman] comes to take the yield from the buyer, אָמְרִינַן לָהּ – we tell her: אַיְיתִי רְאָיָה אֵימַת מָטָא גִּיטָּא לְיָדָךְ – "Prove to us when the bill of divorce actually came into your hand, and only then may you collect compensation from the buyers for the subsequent yield of your field."[12]

The Gemara challenges this by adducing proof that this safeguard is inadequate:

וּמַאי שְׁנָא מִשְּׁטָרֵי ח – But what is the difference between a recovered bill of divorce, which may be returned pending proof of the accuracy of its date, and recovered notes of indebtedness which may not be returned? דִּתְנַן – For we learned in a Mishnah:[13] מָצָא שְׁטָרֵי חוֹב – If ONE FOUND NOTES OF INDEBTEDNESS; אִם יֵשׁ בָּהֶן אַחֲרָיוּת נְכָסִים – IF THEY INCLUDE a provision for A LIEN ON the debtor's real PROPERTY, לֹא יַחֲזִיר – HE SHOULD NOT RETURN them to the creditor. וְאוֹקִימְנָא בְּשֶׁחַיָּיב מוֹדֶ – And we established[14] that this Mishnah refers to a case in which the debtor admits that the debt is unpaid, וּמִשּׁוּם שֶׁמָּא כָּתַב לִלְווֹת בְּנִי – and nevertheless, we do not return the note because we are concerned that perhaps [the debtor] wrote it in Nissan, intending to borrow then, וְלֹא לָוָה עַד תִּשְׁרֵי – but he did not actually borrow until later, in Tishrei. וְקָא טָרִיף לָקוֹחוֹת שֶׁלֹּא כְּדִ – Now if we return this note to the creditor, he might use it to take away property unlawfully from those who purchased properties from the debtor between Nissan and Tishrei.[15]

The Gemara now explains the question that emerges from this Mishnah:

הָתָם נַמִּי לִיהַדַ – If the safeguard suggested above is acceptable, here also, in the case of a note of indebtedness, let us return the note, וְכִי אָתֵי לְמִטְרַף – and when [the creditor] will come to take the property from the buyer on the basis of this note, נֵימָא לֵי – let us tell him: אַיְיתִי רְאָיָה אֵימַת מָטָא שְׁטַר חוֹב לְיָדָךְ – "Prove to us when the note of indebtedness actually came into your hand,[16] and only then will we allow you to take the property from the purchaser." Why does the Mishnah state that we do *not* return a note of indebtedness because of the possibility of fraud, when we do return a bill of divorce under similar circumstances and rely on this safeguard to protect against fraud?

The Gemara deflects the challenge:

אָמְ – They said: הָכָא גַּבֵּי גֵּט אִשָּׁה – Here, in the case of a bill of divorce, אָתֵי לוֹקֵחַ וּתְבָעָהּ – if she requests compensation for the dividends that accrued from her property between Nissan and Tishrei, the purchaser of the property's yield will come to court and demand of her to prove when she was actually divorced; אָמַר – for he will say to himself: הַאי דְּהַדְרוּהָ נִיהֲלָהּ רַבָּנַן לְגִיטָּא – The reason the rabbis returned the bill of divorce to her מִשּׁוּם דְּלָא תַּעֲגִין וְתֵיתִיב – is so that she should not have to remain unwed. Thus, they authorized the return of the bill of divorce to provide her with evidence of her divorce, without determining the accuracy of its date. הַשְׁתָּא דְּקָא אָתְיָא לְמִטְרַף – However, now that she is coming to take the yield of the property from me on the basis of this bill of divorce, תֵּיזִיל וְתֵיתֵי רְאָיָה – let her go and prove אֵימַת מָטָא גִּיטָּא לְיָדָהּ – when the bill of divorce actually came into her hand, and only then will I pay her. Thus, in the case of a bill of divorce we can rely on the purchaser to demand verification of the date of divorce, and we may therefore allow the bill of divorce to be returned.

הָכָא גַּבֵּי שְׁטַר חוֹב – But here, in the case of a note of indebtedness that was found, לָא אָתֵי לוֹקֵחַ וְתָבַע – when the creditor attempts to collect from him, the purchaser of the debtor's property will not come to court and demand that the creditor prove when the loan actually took place, מִדְּאַהַדְרוּהָ נִיהֲלֵיהּ רַבָּנַן לִשְׁטַר חוֹב – because he will reason: Since the rabbis allowed the finder to return the note of indebtedness to [the creditor], פְּשִׁיטָא – it is obvious that the date recorded in the note is reliable; לְמַאי הִלְכְתָא אַהַדְרוּהָ נִיהֲלֵיהּ – otherwise, for what purpose did they return [the note] to him? לְמִטְרַף הוּא – It is only in order to enable him to take the property that is subject to the lien! שְׁמַע מִינָּהּ – I must conclude from [the fact] that they authorized the return of the note, קָמוּ רַבָּנַן בְּמִילְּתָא – that the rabbis must have resolved the matter of when the loan actually took place, וּמִקַּמֵּי דִּידִי מָטָא שְׁטָרָא לִידֵיהּ – and it is true that the note of indebtedness came into [the creditor's] hand on its recorded date before I purchased the debtor's property.[17] Thus, in the case of a note of indebtedness, we cannot assume that when it is presented for collection the purchaser will demand verification of the date of the loan. Consequently, we cannot allow it to be returned.

Having concluded its discussion regarding the return of a lost bill of divorce, the Gemara proceeds to the next item in the Mishnah. The Mishnah states:

שִׁחְרוּרֵי עֲבָדִים וכו׳ – If one found . . . BILLS OF EMANCIPATION, etc.

The Gemara cites a Baraisa that elaborates on this topic:

תָּנוּ רַבָּנַן – The Rabbis taught in a Baraisa: מָצָא שְׁטַר שִׁחְרוּר בַּשּׁוּק – If ONE FOUND A BILL OF EMANCIPATION IN THE MARKETPLACE, he should do the following: בִּזְמַן שֶׁהָרַב מוֹדֶה – WHEN THE MASTER ADMITS that he freed the slave, יַחֲזִיר לָעֶבֶד – [THE FINDER] SHOULD RETURN the bill of emancipation TO THE SLAVE; אֵין הָרַב מוֹדֶה – when THE MASTER DOES NOT ADMIT that he freed

NOTES

nsumed by the buyers during this period, why should we not return the *get* to her once her husband admits that he divorced her?

12. Thus, no loss will result from our return of the *get* to her, because her need to prove when she actually received it before collecting anything will prevent her from defrauding the buyers.

13. Above, 12b.

14. Ibid.

15. When the loan goes into effect, it creates a lien on all property held by the debtor at that time. Should he subsequently sell the property and later have no money to pay the debt, the creditor would have the right to collect his debt by foreclosing on the property held by the purchaser. In the case of this debt, however, he would only have the right to collect property sold after Tishrei. Property sold between Nissan and Tishrei would not be subject to the lien because the loan was not actually implemented until Tishrei. Returning the note to the creditor, however, would enable him to "prove" that the loan was made at the earlier date in Nissan, and he would then be able to foreclose unlawfully on property that had been sold between Nissan and Tishrei.

16. I.e. when the debtor handed it to you (*Rashi*), and the loan actually took place.

17. The buyer will assume that since the rabbis returned the note of indebtedness for the sole purpose of enabling the creditor to collect his debt in court, they must have determined that the note was not pre-dated, and that anyone who purchased property from the debtor after the date recorded in the document is legally liable. Thus, they will not think to demand verification of the date.

אירכס ליה גיטא בי מדרשא אמר אי סימנא אית לי בגויה אי טביעות עינא אית לי בגויה אהדרוה ניהליה אמר לא ידענא אי משום סימנא אהדרוה ניהלי וקא סברי סימנין דאורייתא אי משום טביעות עינא אהדרוה ניהלי ודוקא צורבא מדרבנן אבל איניש דעלמא לא גופא מצא גט אשה בשוק בזמן שהבעל מודה יחזיר לאשה אין הבעל מודה לא יחזיר לא לזה ולא לזה בזמן שהבעל מודה מיהא יחזיר לאשה וליחוש שמא כתב ליתן בניסן ולא נתן לה עד תשרי ואזל בעל זבין פירי מניסן ועד תשרי ומפקא לגיטא דכתב בניסן ואתיא למטרף לקוחות שלא כדין הניחא למ"ד [א] כיון שנתן עיניו לגרשה שוב אין לבעל פירות שפיר אלא למ"ד יש לבעל פירות עד שעת נתינה מאי איכא למימר כי אתיא למטרף אמרינן לה אייתי ראיה אימת מטא גיטא לידך ומאי שנא משטרי חוב דתנן [ב] מצא שטרי חוב אם יש בהן אחריות נכסים לא יחזיר ואוקימנא כשחייב מודה ומשום שמא כתב ללוות בניסן ולא לוה עד תשרי וקא טריף לקוחות שלא כדין התם נמי ליהדר וכי אתי למטרף נימא ליה אייתי ראיה אימת מטא שטר חוב לידך אמרי הכא גבי גט אשה אתי לוקח ותבעה אמר האי דהדרוה ניהלה רבנן לגיטא משום דלא תעגין ותיתיב השתא דקא אתיא למטרף תיזל ותיתי ראיה אימת מטא גיטא לידה הכא גבי שטר חוב לא אתי לוקח ותבע (א) מדאהדרוה ניהליה רבנן לשטר חוב פשיטא למאי הלכתא אהדרוה ניהליה למטרף הוא שמע מינה קמו רבנן במילתא ומקמי דידי מטא שטרא לידיה: שחרורי עבדים וכו': ת"ר [א] מצא שטר שחרור בשוק בזמן שהרב מודה יחזיר לעבד אין הרב מודה לא יחזיר לא לזה ולא לזה בזמן שהרב מודה מיהא יחזיר לעבד ואמאי ניחוש שמא כתב ליתן לו בניסן ולא נתן לו עד תשרי ואזל עבדא וקנה נכסין מניסן ועד תשרי ואזיל הרב וזבנינהו ומפיק ליה לשחרור דכתב בניסן וקא טריף לקוחות שלא כדין [ג] הניחא למ"ד זכות הוא לעבד שיוצא מתחת רבו לחירות וכאביי דאמר [ד] עדיו בחתומיו זכין ליה שפיר אלא למ"ד חוב הוא לעבד שיוצא מתחת יד רבו לחירות מאי איכא למימר דכי אתי למטרף אמרינן ליה [ב] אייתי ראיה אימת מטא שחרור לידך: [ג] דייתיקי מתנה וכו': [ה] ת"ר איזו היא דייתיקי דא תהא למיקם ולהיות שאם מת נכסיו לפלוני מתנה כל שכתוב בו מהיום ולאחר מיתה אלמא אי כתיבא מהיום ולאחר מיתה הוא דקני ואי לא לא קני אמר אביי הכי קאמר [ד] איזו היא מתנת בריא שהיא כמתנת שכיב מרע דלא קני אלא לאחר מיתה כל שכתוב בה מהיום ולאחר מיתה טעמא דלא אמר תנו הא אמר תנו נותנין ורמינהו מצא דייתקאות אפותיקאות ומתנות אע"פ ששניהם מודין לא יחזיר לא לזה ולא לזה אמר רבי אבא בר ממל לא קשיא הא

---

**רש"י**

אירכס ליה גיטא. שהיה שליח להביא ואירכס ליה ואשכחוהו: אמר אי סימנא. חשיבא לכו אית לי בגויה סימנא: ואי טביעות עין. חשיבא לכו אית לי בגויה טביעות עינא מכירו אני בכתב ידי הסופר והעדים מדת ארכו ורחבו כאדם המכיר את חבירו בטביעת עין שטבע בו ואין בו סימן: וקסברי. רבנן סימנין דאורייתא שלא אמרתי סימן מובהק והחזירוהו לי: ודוקא לצורבא מדרבנן. דמוחזק לן ביה דלא משני בדיבוריה: ולא נתן עד תשרי. וכל זמן שלא נתן היה לו לאכול ולמכור פירי נכסי מלוג שלה שתקנו חכמים לבעל לאכול פירות של נכסי מלוג אשתו שנפלו לה לירושה: וזבין פירי. כמשפטו: שפיר. יש לה לטרוף כל מה שמכר משעת כתיבה והא פלוגתא במס' גיטין בפ' שני (דף יח:): אימת מטא גיטא לידך. מיד בעליך: אימת מטא שטרא לידך. מיד הלוה מתחלה: אתי לוקח ותבע. אי אתיא למיטרף מסיק אדעתיה לתבוע אייתי ראיה אימת מטא גיטא לידך בזמנא קמא: מקמי דידי. מקודם שמכר לי הלוה נכסיו מטא שטר מיד לוה למלוה בראשונה: הניחא למ"ד כו'. פלוגתא בפ"ק דגיטין (דף יג:): זכות הוא לעבד. טובה היא אללו שמתירו בקהל וכיון דזכות הוא איכא לתרולי דמשעה שנכתב זוכה בשחרור דלכי מטא (ב) שטר גט לידיה נעשה בן חורין למפרע משעת חתימה: חוב הוא לעבד. חובתו הוא שיוצא מתחת רבו כלומר הפסד הוא לו שאם עבד (ג) כהן הוא פוסלו מן התרומה ואם של ישראל אוסרו בשפחה כנענית דזילא ליה ושכיחא ליה ופריצא ליה: מאי איכא למימר. דהשתא ליכא למימר עדיו בחתומיו [ו] חבין לו דאין חבין לאדם שלא בפניו: דא תהא למיקם. שטר זה יהיה לקום ולהיות בכל הכתוב בו דדברי שכיב מרע ככתובין וכמסורין דמי: מתנה. מתנת בריא איזו היא כל שכתוב בו כו': מהיום ולאחר מיתה. גוף הקרקע קנוי לו מן היום ואין לו עוד רשות למוכרה וליתנה ולהורישה והפירות אינו אוכל כל ימי חייו אלא לאחר מיתה: ואי לא לא קני. בתמיה כל שכן דאם יהיב ליה גוף ופירות במעכשיו דקני טפי: סתם מתנת שכיב מרע לא קניא לו אלא לאחר מיתה דמחמת מיתה הוא מצוה: הא אמר תנו נותנין. אמתני' פריך דתלי טעמא בשאני אומר נמלך עליהם שלא לתתן: אפותיקאות. שעשה לו שדה אפותיקי למלוה על פה שהיתה לו עליו מלוה ישנה: לא יחזיר. שמא כתבה לזה ולא מסר לו ולא זכה בקרקע וחזר וכתב לאחר ומסר לו השטר וזכה בו ובא לחזור בו מן השני ורוצה לתת לראשון וחפץ שימסרו לו שטר זה שיוציאנה בבית דין ונמצא זמן שטר של זה קודם לשטרו של שני ויוציאנה מידו בדין: הא

---

**תוספות**

אי סימנין דאורייתא. בגט נמי מהדרינן ואי סימנין דרבנן מה שמחזירין אבידה בסימן שאינו מובהק מדרבנן משום דהפקר בית דין הפקר אבל מדאורייתא צריך או עדים או סימן מובהק וגט נמי דאיסור הוא לא מהדרינן אלא בסימן מובהק:

אבל איניש דעלמא לא. מפרש ר"ת דעם הארץ נמי אית ליה טביעות עינא כדאמר בפ' גט פשוט (ב"ב דף קסח.) האי מאן דבעי לקדושי איתתא לידבר עם הארץ בהדיה והאי דלא מהדרינן ליה משום דלא מהימן: וליחוש דלמא כתב ליתן בניסן כו'. ואפילו לאביי דאמר עדיו בחתומיו זכין לו הכא גבי אשה חוב הוא לה ואמתני' דדייקין הא אמר תנו נותנין וכן אמתני' דהמביא גט ממדינת הים לא פריך ניחוש שמא כתב ליתן בניסן כו' כיון דעתה שבא לגרשה רואין שהזמן מוקדם ויש קול שלא נמסר ביום שנכתב ויזכרו לקוחות לומר אייתי ראיה אימת מטא גיטא לידך אבל הכא שהבעל מודה שממנה נפל וגירשה ביום הכתיבה פריך וניחוש שמא יסברו לקוחות שאמרה אמת ולא יאמרו בשעת טריפה אייתי ראייה אימת מטא גיטא לידך וא"ת ואמאי לא פריך אמתני' (ד) דכותבין גט לאיש אע"פ שאין אשתו עמו ליחוש שמא לא יתן עד שנה וכי תימא כיון דליכא ריעותא דנפילה י"ל יום שנכתב נמסר ואפי' נמסר נמי אחר זמן יש קול שלא נמסר ביום שנכתב כי רואים בשעת קבלת הגט שהוא מוקדם ויזכרו לקוחות לומר כשתטרף אייתי ראיה דהא לעיל (דף יג:) פריך גבי כותבין שטר ללוה ויש לומר דגבי כותבין שטר ללוה פריך שפיר משום דמאן דזיף בצנעא יזיף (ב"ב מג.) ויש לחוש שמא לאחר זמן ימסור לו בצנעא ויסברו לקוחות שנמסר לו משעת כתיבה אבל גט דיהבי בפרהסיא דצריך עדי מסירה אפילו לר"מ דאין דבר שבערוה פחות משנים כדפירש ר"ת ורשב"ם בגיטין (ד. ד"ה דקי"ל) ועוד דרגילות לגרש בפרהסיא לגלות שהיא פנויה יש קול שנתגרשה אחר זמן כתיבה ולא יטעו הלקוחות אבל אכתי קשה אמאי כותבין גט לאיש כו' ניחוש שמא תזנה אחר הכתיבה ויתן לה בצנעא כדי לחפות עליה וי"ל דמיד שנכתב הגט נותן לה דלא מקדים איניש פורענות לנפשיה: אימת מטא גיטא לידך. בשאר גיטין לא אמרינן כן דמסתמא ביום שנכתב נמסר אבל זה דנפל אתרע:

בר״יתא

---



גיטין יז:], ב) לעיל ... ג) [גיטין יג:], [לעיל יג. וש"נ], ...בא בתרא קלה:, ו) וכזין, מהרש"ל.

**הגהות הב"ח**

(א) גמ' ותבע אמר ...דהדרוה ניהליה רבנן ...ר חוב: (ב) רש"י ...זכות הוא וכו' דלכי ...א גט שחרור לידיה: ...ד"ה חוב וכו' שאם ... של כהן: (ד) תום' ... וליחוש וכו' לא פריך ...תניתין דגט פשוט דכותבין:

**ליקוטי רש"י**

...טביעות עינא ...ת לי בגויה. בעיתו ...ורי ניהלי אית לי ...עות עינא בגויה ...תי עיני בו עד שאני ...רו יפה בלא שום ...ן. סימנים ...ורייתא. שלא נתן בו ...ן מובהק אלא סימנא ...מא ומדאסמכו ...מנא באיסורא קסברי ...נין לאהדורי אבידתא ...רייתא מוכן תעשה ...נלתו וכו'. צורבא ...רבנן. דידע בטביעות ...א ולא משני בדיבוריה ...ין כז:]. אין לו ...רות. וכי טרפה מזמן ...בה בדין טרפה [גיטין ...]. עדיו בחתומיו ...ין לו. מיום שחתמוהו ... לו השעבוד [לעיל ...]. איזו היא ...יתיקי. איזו היא ...נת שכיב מרע שגובה ...חר מיתה אע"ג דלא ... בה מהיום. דא ...הא למיקם ולהיות. ...ר מיתתי והיינו לשון ...תיקי. כל שכתוב בו ...היום ולאחר מיתה. ...שמע הכי גופה קנוי ... מהיום ופירי לאחר ...תה אבל אי לא הוה ... בה מהיום אינו קונה ...ין מתנה לאחר מיתה ...רי אין כח לאדם ליתן ...ודם לכן דבר שלא יוכל ...קנות באותו הזמן ...וא רוצה שתתקיים ...מתנה ואחר מיתה היאך ...ל אדם ליתן אחרי ...ת ונקבר. לא קני. ...רות אלא לאחר מיתה ...מיא דמתנת שכיב מרע ...ינו קונה אלא לאחר ...תה ומיהו בהכי עדיפא ...כיב מרע דמתנת שכיב ...ע יכול לחזור בו וליתן ...חר כדלקמן דייתיקי ...טלת דייתיקי אבל ...נת בריא דמהיום ...אחר מיתה אינו יכול ...כור עוד הגוף כל ימי ...יו אלא פירות [רשב"ם ב"ב קלה:].

---



קסא א ב מיי' פי"ח מהל' גזילה ואבידה הל' ח ועיין במ"מ סמג עשין עד טוש"ע ח"מ סי' סה סעיף יג:

קסב ג מיי' שם הל' ט טוש"ע שם סעיף יד:

קסג ד מיי' פי"ב מהל' זכייה ומתנה הל' יד סמג עשין פב טוש"ע ח"מ סי' רנז סעיף ו:

**רבינו חננאל**

לחומרא עבדינן הא דאירכס ליה גיטא בבי מדרשא לרבה בר [בר] חנא ואהדרוה ליה ולא ידע אי בסימנא דאית ליה בגויה אי בטביעות עינא מסייעא להא דאמרנא. גופא מצא גט אשה בזמן שהבעל מודה יחזיר לאשה וכו' פשוטה היא וסוגייא דשמעתתא כל כי הא גוונא מצריכינן ליה לברורי בעדים אימת מטא גט לידה וכן כל שטר הנמצא חיישינן דלמא אתי למיטרף לקוחות שלא כדין. וכן גט שחרור דינו נמי הכי. פי' דיאתיקי צוואת שכיב מרע בלשון יון נקראת דייתיקי. דייתיקי מתנה ושוברים לא יחזיר שאני אומר כתובין היו ונמלך עליהם שלא ליתנם. הא אמר תנו נותנים ורמינהי דיתיקאות אפותיקאות ומתנות אע"פ ששניהן מודין לא יחזיר לא לזה ולא לזה

אִירְכַּס לֵיהּ גִּיטָּא בֵּי מִדְרְשָׁ – lost the bill of divorce in a study all, and the scholars who studied there found it.[1] אָמַר – [Rabbah bar bar Chanah] said to them: אִי סִימָנָא – If you will accept an identifying mark to return the bill of divorce to me, אִית לִי בְּגַוֵּ – I have an identifying mark for it; אִי טְבִיעוּת עֵינָא – and if you will accept visual recognition, אִית לִי בְּגַוֵּיהּ – I have the ability to recognize it visually.[2] אַהַדְרוּהָ נִיהֲלֵיהּ – They returned it to him. אָמַר – Afterward, [Rabbah bar bar Chanah] said: לֹא יָדַעְנָא – I do not know אִי מִשּׁוּם סִימָנָא אַהַדְרוּהָ נִיהֲ – whether they returned it to me because of the identifying mark that I described to them, וְקָא סָבְרֵי סִימָנִין דְּאוֹרַיְיתָא – and they hold that ordinary identifying marks are considered reliable identification under Biblical law,[3] אִי מִשּׁוּם טְבִיעוּת עֵינָא אַהַדְרוּהָ נִיהֲ – or whether they returned it to me because of my visual recognition of it. וְדַוְקָא צוּרְבָא מִדְּרַבָּנָן – so, they would return the bill of divorce only to a completely scrupulous rabbinical scholar, אֲבָל אִינִישׁ דְּעָלְמָא לֹא – but not to an ordinary person.[4]

The Gemara quotes the text of the Baraisa cited above and analyzes it:

גּוּפָ – We return to the text of the Baraisa cited above:[5] מָצָא גֵּט אִשָּׁה בַּשּׁ – If ONE FOUND A BILL OF DIVORCE IN THE MARKET PLACE, he should do the following: בִּזְמַן שֶׁהַבַּעַל מוֹדֶה – WHEN THE HUSBAND ADMITS that he divorced his wife, יַחֲזִיר לָאִשָּׁה – [THE FINDER] SHOULD RETURN it TO THE WIFE; אֵין הַבַּעַל מוֹדֶה – but when THE HUSBAND DOES NOT ADMIT that he divorced his wife, לֹא יַחֲזִיר לֹא לָזֶה וְלֹא לָזֶה – [THE FINDER] SHOULD NOT RETURN the bill of divorce TO either [THE HUSBAND] OR [THE WIFE].

The Gemara raises a question:

בִּזְמַן שֶׁהַבַּעַל מוֹדֶה מִיהָא יַחֲזִיר לָאִשָּׁה – In any event, the Baraisa teaches that when the husband admits that he divorced her, [the finder] should return the bill of divorce to the wife. וְלֵיחוּשׁ שֶׁמָּא כָּתַב לִיתֵּן בְּנִיסָן – But how can we permit this? Let us be concerned that perhaps [the husband] wrote the bill of divorce in Nissan, intending to give it to his wife then, וְלֹא נָתַן לָהּ עַד תִּשְׁרֵי – but he did not actually give it to her until a later date, in Tishrei,[6] וְאָזַל בַּעַל זַבִּין פֵּירֵי מִנִּיסָן וְעַד תִּשְׁרֵי – and in the interim the husband went and sold the yield of her *melog* property[7] for the period between Nissan and Tishrei, which he was entitled to do since they were still married during that period. וּמַפְקָא לְגִיטָּא דִּכְתַב בְּנִיסָן – However, if we return the bill of divorce to the woman, she may then produce this bill of divorce that was written in Nissan, claiming that she was divorced then, and that the yield of her property for that period rightfully belonged to her, וְאָתְיָא לְמִטְרַף לְקוֹחוֹת שֶׁלֹּא כְּדִין – and she will thereby be able to take away the value of that yield unlawfully from those who purchased it for the period between Nissan and Tishrei.[8] Given this possibility, how can we allow the bill of divorce to be returned to her?

The Gemara qualifies its question:

הָנִיחָא לְמַאן דְּאָמַר – This ruling, that the bill of divorce should be returned, fits well according to the one who says בֵּיוָן שֶׁנָּתַן עֵינָיו לְגָרְשָׁהּ – that once [the husband] sets his mind[9] to divorce [his wife] and writes a bill of divorce, שׁוּב אֵין לַבַּעַל פֵּירוֹת – the husband forfeits his right to the yield of her property;[10] שַׁפִּיר – according to this view, it fits well that we return the bill of divorce, because the woman truly owns the yield that accrued from the property between Nissan and Tishrei.[11]

NOTES

1. The *get* was found a considerable amount of time after its loss by Rabbah bar bar Chanah. A study hall (*beis hamidrash*) is comparable to an area where travelers are common, due to the large number of students it attracts. Therefore, it was necessary for Rabbah bar bar Chanah to identify the document in order that it be returned to him.

2. The Gemara in the following chapter (23b) rules that if a scrupulously honest rabbinical scholar claims a lost object that lacks any *siman*, it should be shown to him. If he claims to recognize it as his own, his word is accepted and the object is returned to him.

3. Rabbah bar bar Chanah was unable to describe a distinctive *siman* for the *get*, only an ordinary one. He was therefore uncertain whether the scholars would return the *get* on the basis of his *siman*, for perhaps they accepted the position that ordinary *simanim* may not be relied upon in cases that fall under Biblical law. He therefore offered to identify the *get* visually. Rabbah was familiar enough with the *get* to recognize it by its general appearance, i.e. its script, signatures, and dimensions. Identification by means of visual recognition is not based on a claimant's familiarity with any particular identifying mark, but rather on his general familiarity with the entire object. This is comparable to the way one can recognize a person with whom he is familiar even though he is unable to describe any particular feature of that person (*Rashi*). [Indeed, visual recognition is considered a more reliable method of identification than a *siman*, since it is based on familiarity with the entire object rather than with a single outstanding feature (see *Chullin* 96a).]

If they returned the *get* to Rabbah bar bar Chanah on the basis of an ordinary *siman* and did not require that he give a truly distinctive *siman*, it must be because they held that even an ordinary *siman* is acceptable on the Biblical level (*Rashi*).

4. Although anybody is capable of definite visual recognition of an object, we do not accept a claim of recognition except from a rabbinical scholar whose scrupulous honesty is known to us (*Rashi*; see Gemara 23b, 24a). Interestingly, if an agent who lost a *get* found it himself, he would be permitted to rely on his own visual recognition and give it to the wife, even if he is not a rabbinical scholar, since he knows that he recognizes the *get* (*Ritva*; see also *Ramban, Gittin* 27a ד״ה הא דתנן; *Toras Gittin* 2:4, ד״ה שמצאו).

5. Gemara 18b; see notes there.

6. A husband may have a *get* written for him even if his wife is not present at the writing (see Mishnah, *Bava Basra* 167a). It is thus possible that he did not divorce his wife on the day the *get* was written. However, the date on the *get* reflects the date of its writing.

7. A married woman's personal property (e.g. an inheritance) is known as *melog* property. As one of a husband's marital privileges, he enjoys the right to the production of this property, e.g. any crops or dividends (i.e. rent) the property may yield. Nevertheless, the wife retains ownership of the property itself. [In Talmudic parlance this is known as אֲכִילַת פֵּירוֹת, literally: *eating fruit*. This corresponds exactly to the modern legal term *usufruct*.] The husband may either use the property himself (e.g. farm it) and keep the production, or he may sell the right to use the property to another person and keep the money.

These properties are known as *melog* [lit. plucking or scalding] property because the husband's treatment of them can be compared to one who plucks the feathers of a bird without taking the bird itself (*Aruch* ד״ה מלג; *Rav* to *Yevamos* 7:1).

8. At this point the Gemara assumes that even if the *get* was drafted in Nissan, the husband retains his right to the yield of his wife's properties until he actually divorces her (*Rashi*). [Thus, the woman may take unlawful advantage of the pre-dated *get* to support her claim that she was divorced in Nissan which would mean that the right of usufruct had reverted to her as of that date. One who purchased the right to the yield for the period between Nissan and Tishrei would then be forced to compensate her for his use of the field during that period, when in fact the yield from the property rightfully belongs to him, since she was in fact not divorced until Tishrei.]

9. Literally: set his eyes.

10. The Gemara in *Gittin* (17b) cites a dispute regarding the point at which a divorcing husband loses this right to the yield of his wife's property. One opinion is that he forfeits this right as soon as he *sets his mind* to divorce her, even though they are still married. The second opinion is that he does not lose this right until he actually divorces her.

11. Thus, nothing unjust would result from her extracting the profit from the buyers, since it was no longer within her husband's right to sell it to them. Since she is legally entitled to compensation for the yield

**the Mishnah teach:** כָּל מַעֲשֶׂה בֵּית דִּין שֶׁנִּמְצְאוּ בְּבֵית דִּין – **"Any act of the court that was found in the courthouse?"** No! כָּל מַעֲשֶׂה בֵּית דִּין יַחֲזִיר קָתָנֵי – **It teaches** merely that if one found ANY ACT OF THE COURT, HE SHOULD RETURN it, וּלְעוֹלָם דְּאִשְׁתַּכַּח אַבְרָאֵי – **and in reality** it is referring only to cases **where [the document] was found outside** the courthouse, in a place where caravans are not common.[22]

The Gemara presents other interpretations of the Baraisa's ruling to permit returning a bill of divorce long after its disappearance.[23]

רַבִּי יִרְמְיָה אָמַר – **R' Yirmiyah said:** כְּגוֹן דְּקָא אָמְרֵי עֵדִים – The Baraisa refers to **a case where the witnesses** who signed the bill of divorce **say** to us: מֵעוֹלָם לֹא חָתַמְנוּ – **"We never signed** אֶלָּא עַל גֵּט אֶחָד שֶׁל יוֹסֵף בֶּן שִׁמְעוֹן – **on more than one bill of divorce for** a man named **Yosef ben Shimon."** In such a case the bill of divorce may be returned, since there is no concern for another, identical document.[24]

The Gemara questions this interpretation:

אִי הָכִי – **If so,** מַאי לְמֵימְרָא – **what** need is there for the Baraisa **to state** such an obvious ruling?

The Gemara answers:

מַהוּ דְּתֵימָא – If not for this ruling, **you might have said** לֵיחוּשׁ דִּלְמָא אִתְרַמִּי שְׁמָא כִּשְׁמָא – that **we should be concerned** that **it chanced that the name** on one bill of divorce **is identical to the name** on another bill of divorce, וְעֵדִים כְּעֵדִים – **and** that the names of **the witnesses are identical to** the names of **the witnesses** on that other bill of divorce. Thus, it would still not be certain that the bill of divorce found here was the same bill of divorce that was lost, and we should not return the bill of divorce due to tl concern. קָא מַשְׁמַע לָן – **[The Baraisa]** therefore **informs** that we need not be concerned about such an unlikely occurrenc

Rav Ashi offers yet another explanation:

רַב אַשִׁי אָמַר – **Rav Ashi said:** כְּגוֹן דְּקָא אָמַר – The Barai refers to **a case where [the agent]** who claims the bill of divor **says:** נֶקֶב יֵשׁ בּוֹ בְּצַד אוֹת פְּלוֹנִית – **There is a** small **hole besi a certain letter** in the text of the document. Since he accurate describes an identifying mark found in the bill of divorce that w recovered, we may be certain that it his.[25]

Rav Ashi qualifies this ruling:

וְדַוְקָא בְּצַד אוֹת פְּלוֹנִית – This is so, however, **only** if he specifies hole **alongside a certain letter,** because that is considered very distinctive identifying mark, which certainly suffices reclaim a lost bill of divorce. אֲבָל נֶקֶב בְּעָלְמָא – **However,** if merely says that the bill of divorce has **a hole someplace,** witho identifying the specific spot, לֹא – it may **not** be returned, ev if it indeed has a hole.[26]

The Gemara explains the basis for this limitation:

רַב אַשִׁי מְסַפְּקָא לֵיהּ – **Rav Ashi is uncertain** סִימָנִים – wheth an **identifying mark** אִי דְּאוֹרַיְיתָא אִי דְּרַבָּנָן – **is** accepted evidence under **Biblical** law **or** only by **Rabbinic** decree. Ther fore, the bill of divorce may not be returned unless a tru distinctive identifying mark is provided.[27]

The Gemara discusses a related incident:

רַבָּה בַּר בַּר חָנָה – **Rabbah bar bar Chanah** while acting as agent to deliver a bill of divorce,

NOTES

22. However, where caravans are common, we would not return the document even if the existence of a second party by that name had not been established. Thus, there is no proof from this Mishnah to Rabbah's position. R' Zeira's understanding of the Mishnah formed the basis for Rav Huna's ruling above, which Rabbah disputed (*Tosafos* to *Gittin* 27a ד״ה כל).

23. The following interpretations agree with R' Zeira that a document found in a place where caravans are common should not be returned even if we are unaware of a second party with the same name. They differ with R' Zeira in that they interpret the Baraisa to refer to a *get* that was indeed found in a place where caravans are common. They explain that the reason the Baraisa permits returning a lost *get* despite the prevalence of caravans is because it deals with special circumstances in which there is no concern that an identical *get* may have been lost (see *Ritva* here, and *Rashi* to *Gittin* 27b ד״ה ר׳ ירמיה).

24. I.e. they testify that they signed a *get* for the Yosef ben Shimon who claims it, and that they never signed more than one *get* for a person of that name. Thus, there is no question that this is the *get* lost by the person claiming it (*Ritva* in explanation of *Rashi*).

25. Lost objects are returned to a claimant who can accurately describe their identifying marks (*simanim*), because his familiarity with the identifying mark proves that he is indeed the one who lost the object (see introduction to Chapter 2).

26. Although most lost objects may be returned to a claimant who describes even an ordinary identifying mark, a *get* may not be return in the absence of a truly distinctive mark, as the Gemara will nc explain.

27. We will learn in the next chapter that lost objects are returned the person who claims them if he can name their *siman* (identifyi mark). However, the Gemara below (27a) raises the question wheth ordinary *simanim* are considered a reliable means of identificati under Biblical law and should therefore be accepted in all areas of la including marital affairs (e.g. returning a *get* or identifying a dead m so that his wife may remarry), or whether they are considered reliat only under Rabbinic law, as a special leniency applied to moneta matters. [The basis of such a leniency would be the power of t Rabbinic courts to declare property ownerless (הֶפְקֵר בֵּית דִּין הֶפְקֵר); sin they could declare any lost object ownerless, they can just as w decree that it be returned to a claimant on the basis of an identificati that falls short of the normal requirements of evidence.] If t latter view is correct, the leniency is obviously limited to moneta matters and cannot be extended to matters of prohibition. Thu naming the *siman* would not be sufficient for the return of a *get,* sin returning it would enable a woman to remarry. Since Rav Ashi does n permit returning a *get* with anything less than a truly distincti *siman,* the Gemara concludes that Rav Ashi is undecided in this matt which indeed remains unresolved in the discussion in the next chapt [27b, 28a] (*Rashi*).

חיישינן לשני שוירי וא"ל [א] רב חסדא לרבה פוק עיין בה דלאורתא בעי מינך רב הונא נפק דק ואשכח דתנן [ב] כל מעשה ב"ד הרי זה יחזיר והא בי דינא דרב הונא דכי מקום שהשיירות מצויות דמי וקא פשיט רבה דיחזיר אלמא אי הוחזקו שני יוסף בן שמעון אין אי לא לא עבד רבה עובדא [ג] (בההוא גיטא דאשתכח) בי כיתנא דפומבדיתא כשמעתיה איכא דאמרי היכא דמזבני כיתנא והוא שלא הוחזקו אע"ג דשכיחין שיירתא ואיכא דאמרי היכא דתרו כיתנא ואע"ג דהוחזקו דלא שכיחא שיירות רבי זירא רמי מתניתין אברייתא ומשני תנן המביא גט ואבד הימנו מצאו לאלתר כשר ואם לאו פסול ורמינהי [ד] [א] מצא גט אשה בשוק בזמן שהבעל מודה יחזיר לאשה אין הבעל מודה לא יחזיר לא לזה ולא לזה קתני מיהת בזמן שהבעל מודה יחזיר לאשה ואפילו לזמן מרובה ומשני כאן במקום שהשיירות מצויות וכאן במקום שאין השיירות מצויות איכא דאמרי והוא שהוחזקו דלא נהדר והיינו דרבה איכא דאמרי [ב] אע"ג דלא הוחזקו לא נהדר ופליגא דרבה בשלמא רבה לא אמר כר' זירא מתניתין אלימא ליה לאקשויי אלא רבי זירא מ"ט לא אמר כרבה אמר לך מי קא תני הא אמר תנו נותנין ואפי' לזמן מרובה דלמא הא אמר תנו נותנין ולעולם כדקיימא לן לאלתר למ"ד לר' זירא במקום שהשיירות מצויות ואע"ג שלא הוחזקו שני יוסף בן שמעון ופליגא דרבה במאי קא מיפלגי רבה סבר דקתני כל מעשה ב"ד הרי זה יחזיר דאשתכח בב"ד עסקינן וב"ד כמקום שהשיירות מצויות והוא שהוחזקו לא יחזיר לא הוחזקו יחזיר ורבי זירא אמר לך מי קתני כל מעשה ב"ד שנמצאו בב"ד כל מעשה ב"ד יחזיר קתני ולעולם דאשתכח אבראי ר' ירמיה אמר [ג] כגון דקא אמרי עדים מעולם לא חתמנו אלא על גט אחד של יוסף בן שמעון אי הכי מאי למימרא מהו דתימא ליחוש דלמא אתרמי שמא כשמא ועדים כעדים קא משמע לן רב אשי אמר [ה] [ד] כגון דקא אמר נקב יש בו בצד אות פלונית ודוקא בצד אות פלונית אבל נקב בעלמא לא רב אשי מספקא ליה [ו] סימנים אי דאורייתא אי דרבנן רבה בר בר חנה

אירכס

**רש"י**

חיישינן לשני שוירי. אע"פ שבא אחד לפניו ואמר ממני נפל ופלוני היה משלחו לאשתו ויודעין אנו שאין שם בשוירי שני אנשים ששמותיהן שוין חיישינן שמא שוירי אחרת יש ויש בה יוסף בן שמעון אחר: ואמר ליה רב חסדא לרבה גרסינן: כל מעשה ב"ד הרי זה יחזיר. כל מילתא דאתא לב"ד לקיים דליכא למיחש לנמלך עליהן שלא ליתנן הרי זה יחזיר וזה מקוים בב"ד היה ולכך הובא שם: כשמעתיה. דבעינן תרתי והכא חדא הוא דהואי ואכשריה: היכא דמזבני כיתנא. דשיירות מצויות שם לבא ולקנות ואהדריה משום דלא הוחזקו שני יוסף בן שמעון בעיר שנכתב בה ולא חיישינן לומר יש עיר אחרת ששמה כמו: ואיכא דאמרי היכא דתרו כיתנא. במי המשרה שם נמצא הגט ומאי כשמעתיה שהוחזקו שני יוסף בן שמעון באותה עיר שנכתב בה ואכשריה דבמקום שנמצא בו לא היו שיירות מצויות: בשלמא רבה. דאמר שינויא ארומיא דמתניתין דגיטין אמתני' דנזיקין: לא אמר כר' זירא. דרמא מתני' אברייתא: דמתניתין אלימא ליה לאקשויי. משום דהיא עיקר ויש תימה כשסותרות זו את זו וצריך לחזר שיתיישבו דאילו ברייתא יש לומר אינה עיקר רבי לא שנאה רבי חייא מניין לו: ולעולם כדקיימא לן כשנמצא לאלתר. ואם לאו פסול שמא אינו של זה אבל ברייתא ליכא לשנויי הכי דכיון דתנא בהדיא יחזיר לאשה הוה ליה לפלוגי בין לאלתר בין לזמן מרובה דלא דמיא למתניתין דהתם לא יחזיר תנא ומדוקיא הוה דייק יחזיר היכא דאמר תנו וכיון דלא תנא יחזיר לא הוה ליה לפלוגי: דאשתכח אבראי. שאין השיירות מצויות: ר' ירמיה אמר. הא דקתני יחזיר כגון דאמרי עדים החתומין בו מעולם לא חתמנו כו': ודוקא בצד אות פלונית. דהוה ליה סימן מובהק ואפילו אם תימצי לומר גבי חזרת אבידה בסימנין דאיבעיא לן לקמן (דף כז.) דאורייתא או דרבנן אפילו פשטת סימנין דרבנן יש לסמוך על סימן מובהק כזה למשרי אשת איש דאורייתא: מספקא ליה לרב אשי סימנין. שמחזירין בהן אבידה אי דאורייתא היא ואפילו באיסור דאורייתא סמכינן אסימן כל דהו: אי דרבנן. ודוקא באבידה שהפקר ב"ד הפקר אבל במידי דאיסורא לא סמכינן ואי קשיא נימא הכי קסבר סימנין דרבנן ונפשוט בעיין דלקמן לאו מילתא היא דנהי דפשיטא ליה אי נמי מספקא ליה אית עליה למיסר מספיקא:

**תוספות**

חיישינן לשני שוירי. וא"ת א"כ לרב הונא היאך יגרש כל אדם את אשתו לר"מ דאינו מוכיח מתוכו כיון דחיישינן לשני שוירי וי"ל כיון דלא הוחזקו הוי שפיר מוכיח מתוכו ומ"מ כשנפל חיישינן: נפק דק ואשכח כל מעשה ב"ד הרי זה יחזיר. פרש"י דההוא גיטא הוה כתיב ביה הנפק ופשיט שפיר ממתני' דמעשה ב"ד יחזיר אך מה שפירש כשנפל מן השליח קשה דא"כ מה מועיל ההנפק כיון שלא בא ליד האשה עדיין דאם יש לחוש לנמלך בלא הנפק הכי נמי יש לחוש להנפק ותו דבעל לא מקיים גיטא וי"ל דאי כתיב ביה הנפק מיירי שנפל מן האשה ושואלת אותו האשה ואומרת שהוא שלה וקא פשיט דיחזיר ולא חיישינן שמא משקרת ומאשה אחרת נפל אע"ג דהשיירות מצויות כיון דלא הוחזקו כמו במעשה ב"ד דיחזיר ואע"ג דאשתכח בב"ד שהשיירות מצויות ולא חיישינן שמא מאחר נפל כיון דלא הוחזקו ואי מיירי שהשליח שואלו לגרש את האשה י"ל דלא כתיב בו הנפק ומוכיח נמי שפיר כיון דבמעשה ב"ד יחזיר דלא חיישינן לנמלך דכיון שכתוב בו הנפק ודאי נעשה הלואה דלוה לא מקיים שטרא כדאמרינן לקמן בפרקין (דף כ:) ולא חיישינן נמי שמא מאחר נפל אע"ג דהשיירות מצויות כיון דלא הוחזקו בההיא גיטא נמי דאשתכח שהשליח שואל הגט ולא שייך למימר נמלך כיון שהגט ביד השליח דאין יכול לבטל הגט שלא בפני השליח ולא ניחוש כמו כן שמא מאחר נפל אף על גב דהשיירות מצויות כיון דלא הוחזקו וא"ת אביי דאמר פ' האשה שהלכה (יבמות דף קטו: ושם) דחיישינן לתרי יצחק אפי' לא הוחזקו תקשי ליה ממתניתין דכל מעשה ב"ד הרי זה יחזיר וי"ל דמוקי לה דאשתכח חוץ לב"ד שאין השיירות מצויות כר' זירא אבל לגבי תרי יצחק לא שייך לפלוגי בין מצויות לשאין מצויות דלעולם יש להסתפק ביצחק מעיר אחרת כמו מעיר זאת אי נמי מוקי מתני' דאשתכח בב"ד ואפי' הכי לא חיישינן לאחר כיון שזה האיש שואל גט וידעינן שאבד גט ואין אנו מכירין אחר אין לחוש שמאחר נפל ונפל ממנו כמו כן כאן אבל התם אין אנו יודעים איזה יצחק מת אם מעיר זאת או מעיר אחרת [ז]:

אין הבעל מודה לא יחזיר. אע"ג דנאמנת לומר גרשתני (גיטין דף סד:) הכא אינה נאמנת דמעיזה פניה כיון דהגט מסייעה.

ואפילו לזמן מרובה. תימה כיון שמודה שממנה נפל וכבר גירשה אמאי הוה לן למימר דלא יחזיר כיון דנאמן לומר גרשתיה כדאמר פרק יש נוחלין (ב"ב דף קלד:) אפילו נפל מאחר נחזיר לה לראיה בעלמא וי"ל דנאמן לומר גרשתיה ותהא מגורשת מכאן ולהבא הואיל ובידו לגרשה אבל הכא שאומר שכבר גרשה מזמן הכתוב בגט כמו שאינו נאמן למפרע כך אינו נאמן להבא ויחזיר לאשה דקתני היינו בעדים ותתגרש בו בחזרה זו ולא חיישינן שמא מאחר נפל ואפילו לזמן מרובה:

מעולם לא חתמנו אלא על גט אחד כו'. ואומר הבעל שהוא אותו יוסף וא"ת והלא כשאין העדים אומרים כן אינו נאמן לומר שהוא שלו אלא אנו חוששין שמא מאחר נפל ועתה שעדים אומרים שלא חתמו אלא על גט אחד של יוסף בן שמעון למה יהא נאמן ליחוש שמא לאחר חתמו ולא לזה וי"ל דאף כי אין עדים מה שאינו נאמן אע"ג שאומר מכיר אני שהוא שלי לפי שמספק אומר שהוא שלו לפי שסבור שלא איבד אחר גט רק הוא לכך אומר שהוא שלו אע"פ שאינו מכיר אבל כשעדים אומרים שלא חתמו רק על גט אחד של יוסף בן שמעון במזיד לא ישקר אם חתמו לאחר לומר [ח] שלא חתמו דאינו חשוד לקלקלה כמו שנאמן לומר גרשתיה ואית ספרים דגרסי אלא על גט אחד של יוסף בן שמעון זה אתי שפיר טפי וצריך לומר שלא ראו עדים החתימה דאי ראו החתימה שהיא שלהם א"כ הוה ליה למימר מהו דתימא דלמא אתרמאי עדים כעדים וחתימה כחתימה:

אי

**עין משפט נר מצוה**

קנט א מיי' פי"ח מהל' גזלה ואבידה הל' ו ועיין בהשגות ובמ"מ סמג עשין עד טוש"ע אה"ע סי' קנג סעיף א וע"ש:

קס ב ג ד מיי' פ"ג מהלכות גירושין הל' ט י יא ועיין בהשגות ובמגיד משנה סמג עשין מח טוש"ע אה"ע שם סי' קלב סעיף ד וע"ש:

**רבינו חננאל**

בעיר אחת עבד רבא עובדא כשמעתיה איכא דאמרי היכא דמזבני כיתנא והוא שלא הוחזקו ואע"ג שהשיירות מצויות שם. איכא דאמרי היכא דתרו כיתנא ואע"ג דהוחזקו דהא לא שכיחן שיירתא התם. ר' זירא רמי מתני' אברייתא ומשני תנן המביא גט ואבד ממנו וכו' דברים פשוטים הם מיהו איצטרכינן לברורי דכר' זירא מסתברא וכלישנא בתרא דתני איכא דאמרי אע"ג דלא הוחזקו שני יוסף בן שמעון בעיר אחת לא נהדר ופליגא דרבא מדחזינן מתני' דפשיט מינה רבא כל מקום שלא הוחזקו שני יוסף בן שמעון בעיר אחת יחזיר ועבד עובדא וסמך אהא דתני כל מעשה ב"ד הרי זה יחזיר ולא סלקא שמעתא כטעמא דרבא אלא אוקמא ר' ירמיה כגון דאמרי עדים מעולם לא חתמנו אלא על גט אחד של יוסף בן שמעון וכו' ורב אשי דהוא בתרא אוקמא כגון דאמר (עדים) נקב יש בו בצד אות פלוני שהוא סימן מובהק אבל נקב בעלמא לא מכלל דשינויא דרבא לא שינויא דסמכא הוא ואע"ג דעבד עובדא כשמעתיה איהו הוא דעבד ואחריני לא עבדו כוותיה וכי האי גוונא

**מסורת הש"ס**

א) [לקמן כ:, גיטין ... בבא בתרא קעג ...], ב) [לעיל טז:, לקמן ...], ג) מהרש"ל ..., ד) גיטין ס., ה) [גי... ס:], ו) [לקמן כז:, ... עט:], ז) [ועי' תוס' יב... קטו: ד"ה יצחק], ח) ... שלו, מהרש"ל.

**ליקוטי רש"י**

חיישינן לשני שוירי ... ושמא לא זה הוא ש... מזה [גיטין כז.]. אע... שבשוירי הידוע לנו ... בה שני יוסף בן שמ... שמא יש שוירי אח... שיש שם יוסף בן שמ... ושם נכתב ומשליח ... נפל [לקמן כ:]. ... מעשה ב"ד. המ... שטר מקויים בב... דליכא למיחש לכתו... היו ונמלך עליהם ... ליתנם דלא ע... לקיומיה שטרא ... מלוה לאחר שנמסר ... דחיישי שמא ימותו עד ... הרי זה יחזיר. ... חיישינן לשמא אינו ... [גיטין שם]. דכיון ד... הוחזקו שני יוסף ... שמעון בעיר אחת ל... אחרת שאינה ידועה ... לא חיישינן [לקמן ש... בי דינא דרב הונ... היו צריכין לו ... ולהוראה ובאים ... וקפשיט רבה דיח... ש"מ משום דלא הוח... שני יוסף הוא דל... שוירי לא חיי... כשמעתיה. דלא ... תרתי בעינן והכא ... הוה אלא חדא והח... לתובע. איכא דאמ... היכא דמזב... כיתנא. בשוק שש... מצויות והחזירו לפי ... הוחזקו. ואיכא דאמ... היכא דתרו כיתנא. האי בי כי... היכא דתרו כיתנא ב... מי המשרה ששורין פשתן ואין שיי... מצויות שם והח... ואע"פ שהוחזקו ש... באותה העיר בא... השם. מודה. שאו... ליתנו לה. לא לזה ו... לזה. לבעל לא יח... שמא כבר נתנו וממנה נפל וכשיבא ... יחזור אחר עדי מס... ויעידו שגירשה וכשתת... כתובתה יאמר פרע... שהואלת הגט בבית ותנן הוליאה גט ו... עמו כתובה ג... כתובתה וחייבוני לפ... ונתנו לי את הגט שלא תחזור ותג... ולאשה לא יחזיר ש... מינסא בו [גיטין ש... איכא דאמרי. דשני ר' זירא במ... שהשיירות מצויות פ... והוא דהוחזקו דבנ... תרתי כרבה. אלא זירא. דרמי מתני... אברייתא מאי טעמא ... אמר שינויא ד... אתרתי מתני' כר... אמר לך. ר' ז... מתניתין לא ק... אהדדי. דלמא ... אמר תנו נות... ולעולם כדקי... כלומר ודאי על כר... הא אמר תנו טו... דייק' מינה מד... טעמא בנמלך עליהן ... לזמן מרובה מה ... דייקת דילמא לע... כדקי"ל בהכשירא דגי... מצאו לאלתר כשר ... ברייתא ודאי ק... דקתני יחזיר לאשה

לאלתר והבעל מודה פשיטא למאי ניחוש לה אי לאו דאשמועינן אפילו לזמן מרובה לא איצטריך למיתנייה דבשלמא מתני' לא תנא בה בהדיא האמר תנו נותנין ואצטריך למתנייה משום היא גופא לאשמועינן דלא יחזיר שאני אומר ... ר' ירמיה אמר. לא מתניתין קשיא ולא ברייתא קשיא דכל הני דאמרינן יחזיר לזמן מרובה. כגון דקאמרי עדים. החתומים בו. אלא על גט אחד. ואותו חתמנו לאיש זה המודעו. כגון דקאמר. האי שליח שאבדו. ודוק... נקט רב אשי בצד אות פלונית דהוי סימן מובהק דאין עדות ברורה מזו [גיטין כז:]. סימנים אי דאורייתא אי דרבנן. הא דאמרי' באלו מציאות (ב"מ דף כז.) שמחזירין אבדה בסימנין ואיבעיא לן התם דאורייתא או דרבנן ... אשי נמי מספקא ליה הילכך באיסור אשת איש לא סמכינן אסימנין בעלמא דלמא סימנין דרבנן וכממונא הוא דמלו רבנן להפקיע דהפקר ב"ד היה הפקר וטעמא דתקנתא התם מפרש אבל למישרי איסורא לא מצו רבנן לעקור ... מן התורה והאי דלא אמר קסבר סימנין דרבנן משום דהתם מיבעיא לן ומהכא לא מצינן למיפשט דהא אי נמי מספקא ליה קאסר מספיקא [גיטין כז:].

Baraisa contradicts the Mishnah cited above, which disqualifies such a *get* unless it is discovered immediately. – ? –

The Gemara stated above that R' Zeira posed this contradiction and offered a resolution. The following is his resolution:

וּמְשַׁנֵּי – **And [R' Zeira] answered:** כַּאן בְּמָקוֹם שֶׁהַשַּׁיָּירוֹת מְצוּיוֹת – **Here,** in the Mishnah, it refers to a bill of divorce found **in a place where caravans are common.** Therefore, the bill of divorce may be returned only if it was discovered immediately. וְכַאן בְּמָקוֹם שֶׁאֵין הַשַּׁיָּירוֹת מְצוּיוֹת – **Whereas here,** in the Baraisa, it refers to a bill of divorce found **in a place where caravans are not common.** Therefore, it is returned even if it was discovered long after its disappearance.[14]

The Gemara offers two interpretations of R' Zeira's position: אִיכָּא דְּאָמְרֵי – **There are those who say** R' Zeira holds וְהוּא שֶׁהוּחְזְקוּ דְּלֹא נַהְדַר – that it is **only where** the existence of **[a second couple with the same names] has been established that we do not return** the bill of divorce:[15] וְהַיְינוּ דְּרַבָּה – **and this is** identical to **Rabbah's** view, as we learned above. אִיכָּא דְּאָמְרֵי – **And there are those who say** R' Zeira holds אַף עַל גַּב דְּלֹא הוּחְזְקוּ לֹא נַהְדַר – that **even if** the existence of **[another couple with the same names] has not been established, we do not return** a bill of divorce found in an area where caravans are common;[16] וּפְלִיגָא דְּרַבָּה – **and this conflicts with Rabbah's** opinion.

Rabbah and R' Zeira both noted a contradiction between the Mishnah in *Gittin* cited above and another Tannaic ruling. Rabbah (on 18a) cited our Mishnah as the contradiction to that Mishnah,[17] whereas R' Zeira cited the Baraisa quoted above. The Gemara analyzes why they chose different rulings to contrast with the Mishnah in *Gittin:*

בִּשְׁלָמָא רַבָּה לֹא אָמַר כְּר׳ זֵירָא – **It is understandable that Rabbah did not say as R' Zeira** did, i.e. pose the contradiction between the Mishnah and the Baraisa, מַתְנִיתִין אַלִּימָא לֵיהּ לְאַקְשׁוּיֵי – because **a contradiction between two Mishnahs is more compelling to him** than a contradiction between a Mishnah and a Baraisa.[18] אֶלָּא רַבִּי זֵירָא מַאי טַעְמָא לֹא אָמַר כְּרַבָּה – **But why did R' Zeira not say as Rabbah** did? Why did he pose the contradiction from a Baraisa when he could have noted a contradiction between two Mishnahs?

The Gemara explains R' Zeira's reasoning:

אָמַר לָךְ – **[R' Zeira] would tell you:** מִי קָא תָּנֵי הָא אָמַר תְּנוּ נוֹתְנִין – **Does [our Mishnah] state** explicitly that **if [the husbar said: "Give** the bill of divorce," **they may give** it to her אֲפִילוּ לִזְמַן מְרוּבֶּה – **even** if it was discovered **a long time** after disappearance? No! That was merely an inference. דִּלְמָא הָא אָמַר תְּנוּ נוֹתְנִין – **Perhaps** all the Mishnah means to imply is that **if [t husband] said: "Give** the bill of divorce," **they may give** it to h under *certain* circumstances, וּלְעוֹלָם כִּדְקַיְימָא לָן לְאַלְתַּר – b **only** if it was found **immediately, as we established** in the oth Mishnah. Since our Mishnah does not clearly contradict the oth Mishnah, R' Zeira presented the contradiction as between t Mishnah and the Baraisa.[19]

The Gemara above noted two versions of R' Zeira's rulir According to the first, R' Zeira agrees with Rabbah, but accordi to the second he disagrees. The Gemara now examines the ba for the dispute according to the second version:

לְמַאן דְּאָמַר לר׳ זֵירָא – **According to the one who said that Zeira holds** בְּמָקוֹם שֶׁהַשַּׁיָּירוֹת מְצוּיוֹת – that a bill of divor recovered **in a place where caravans are common** should not returned, וְאַף עַל גַּב שֶׁלֹּא הוּחְזְקוּ שְׁנֵי יוֹסֵף בֶּן שִׁמְעוֹן – **even thou it has not been established** that there are **two** men named **Yos ben Shimon** in the town mentioned in the bill of divorce, וּפְלִיגָא דְּרַבָּה – **and** that **[R' Zeira's opinion] is in conflict with Ra bah's,** בְּמַאי קָא מִיפַּלְגִי – **what is** at the root of **the dispute?**

The Gemara explains:

רַבָּה סָבַר – **Rabbah holds** דְּקָתָנֵי כָּל מַעֲשֵׂה בֵּית דִּין – **that** wh **the Mishnah taught** that if one finds ANY ACT OF THE COURT יַחֲזִיר – HE SHOULD RETURN it, דְּאִשְׁתַּכַּח בְּבֵית דִּין עַסְקִינַן – **refers to** a case **where [the document] was discovered in t courthouse.**[21] וּבֵית דִּין כְּמָקוֹם שֶׁהַשַּׁיָּירוֹת מְצוּיוֹת – **Now t courthouse is like a place where caravans are common,** due the constant arrival of litigants. Nevertheless, the Mishnah rul that the document should be returned, without concern that may belong to another person of the same name. We must ther fore conclude that וְהוּא שֶׁהוּחְזְקוּ לֹא יַחֲזִיר – **only when** t existence of **[others with the same name] has been establish is [the finder] not** allowed **to return** the document, לֹא הוּחְזְקוּ יַחֲזִיר – but if **[their existence] has not been established,** l **should return** it.

The reason why R' Zeira does not accept this proof:

וְרַבִּי זֵירָא אָמַר לָךְ – **But R' Zeira would tell you:** מִי קָתָנֵי – **Do**

NOTES

14. Where caravans are common, we are concerned that a traveler passing through this place might also have lost a *get* with identical names. Where caravans are not common, this is not a concern.

15. I.e. even where caravans are common, we only refrain from returning the lost *get* where it is *known* that there is another couple with the same names in the town mentioned in the *get.*

16. According to this interpretation, R' Zeira is concerned that perhaps unbeknownst to us, there is another couple with identical names in the city mentioned in the *get,* and that it was a *get* written for them that was found here.

17. The Gemara above (18a) did not quote Rabbah as having explicitly posed the contradiction between the two Mishnahs, but rather asked the question anonymously and quoted Rabbah's solution. Nevertheless, since Rabbah is the one who resolved that contradiction, the Gemara assumes that he asked the question as well.

18. The Mishnah, as codified by R' Yehudah HaNasi, comprises the main body of Tannaic law, and it is therefore imperative to resolve contradictions between Mishnahs. In contrast, most Baraisos were recorded by R' Chiya, the student of R' Yehudah HaNasi, and they are considered secondary in relation to the Mishnah. Consequently, a contradiction between a Mishnah and a Baraisa is not as problematic, since if it cannot be resolved, we may disregard the Baraisa as a teaching that R' Yehudah HaNasi dismissed (*Rashi;* see *Eruvin* 92a, *Rashi* ad loc.).

19. Our Mishnah states that if one finds a bill of divorce he should n return it to the woman because perhaps the husband lost it before ] ever gave it to her and he no longer wants to give it to her.] Now, ε though we may infer from the Mishnah that if the husband says to gi her the *get* we give it, we cannot definitely extend this inference to a ca in which the *get* was found long after its disappearance. Perhaps o Mishnah would agree that it should not be returned unless it was fou immediately. Since our Mishnah never *explicitly* states that we retu the *get* to her, its failure to specify a limitation on this permission is n conclusive.

The Baraisa, however, does explicitly state that we return the *get* the husband admits to the divorce). Accordingly, its failure to limit th ruling to a case where it was discovered immediately is more significan R' Zeira therefore found the Baraisa a more compelling contradiction the Mishnah (*Rashi*).

20. The actual disagreement between R' Zeira and Rabbah is obvious: Zeira maintains that one must be concerned for the *possible* existence another couple with the same names, while Rabbah maintains th unless we know of such a couple, we need not be. The Gemara's concer is for the Tannaic source from which the disagreement springs.

21. Since the Mishnah does not qualify its ruling, we may assume th it refers even to an act of the court that was found at the courthous where such documents are common (see *Chidushei HaRan* to *Gittin* 27 ד״ה נפק).

עין משפט
נר מצוה

קנט א מיי' פי"ח מהל' גזילה ואבידה הל' ו ועיין בהשגות ובמ"מ סמג עשין עד טוש"ע אה"ע סי' קנג סעיף א וע"ש:
קס ב ג ד מיי' פ"ג מהלכות גירושין הל' ט י יא ועיין בהשגות ובמגיד משנה סמג עשין מח טוש"ע אה"ע שם סי' קלב סעיף ד וע"ש:

חיישינן לשני שוורי וא"ל [א] רב חסדא לרבה פוק עיין בה דלאורתא בעי מינך רב הונא נפק דק ואשכח דתנן [ב] כל מעשה ב"ד הרי זה יחזיר והא בי דינא דרב הונא דכי מקום שהשיירות מצויות דמי וקא פשיט רבה דיחזיר אלמא אי הוחזקו שני יוסף בן שמעון אין אי לא לא עבד רבה עובדא [ג] (בההוא גיטא דאשתכח) בי כיתנא דפומבדיתא כשמעתיה איכא דאמרי היכא דמזבני כיתנא והוא שלא הוחזקו אע"ג דשכיחין שיירתא ואיכא דאמרי היכא דתרו כיתנא ואע"ג דהוחזקו דלא שכיחא שיירות רבי זירא רמי מתניתין אברייתא ומשני תנן המביא גט ואבד הימנו מצאו לאלתר כשר ואם לאו פסול ורמינהי [ד] [א] מצא גט אשה בשוק בזמן שהבעל מודה יחזיר לאשה אין הבעל מודה לא יחזיר לא לזה ולא לזה קתני מיהת בזמן שהבעל מודה יחזיר לאשה ואפילו לזמן מרובה ומשני כאן במקום שהשיירות מצויות וכאן במקום שאין השיירות מצויות איכא דאמרי והוא שהוחזקו דלא נהדר והיינו דרבה איכא דאמרי [ב] אע"ג דלא הוחזקו לא נהדר ופליגא דרבה בשלמא רבה לא אמר כר' זירא מתניתין אלימא ליה לאקשויי אלא רבי זירא מ"ט לא אמר כרבה אמר לך מי קא תני הא אמר תנו נותנין ואפי' לזמן מרובה דלמא הא אמר תנו נותנין ולעולם כדקיימא לן לאלתר למ"ד לר' זירא במקום שהשיירות מצויות ואע"ג שלא הוחזקו שני יוסף בן שמעון ופליגא דרבה במאי קא מיפלגי רבה סבר דקתני כל מעשה ב"ד הרי זה יחזיר דאשתכח בב"ד עסקינן וב"ד כמקום שהשיירות מצויות והוא שהוחזקו לא יחזיר לא הוחזקו יחזיר ורבי זירא אמר לך מי קתני כל מעשה ב"ד שנמצאו בב"ד כל מעשה ב"ד יחזיר קתני ולעולם דאשתכח אבראי ר' ירמיה אמר [ג] כגון דקא אמרי עדים מעולם לא חתמנו אלא על גט אחד של יוסף בן שמעון אי הכי מאי למימרא מהו דתימא ליחוש דלמא אתרמי שמא כשמא ועדים כעדים קא משמע לן רב אשי אמר [ה] [ד] כגון דקא אמר נקב יש בו בצד אות פלונית ודוקא בצד אות פלונית אבל נקב בעלמא לא רב אשי מספקא ליה [ו] סימנים אי דאורייתא אי דרבנן רבה בר בר חנה

רש"י

חיישינן לשני שוורי. אע"פ שבא אחד לפניו ואמר ממני נפל ופלוני היה משלחו לאשתו ויודעין אנו שאין שם בשוורי שני אנשים ששמותיהן שוין חיישינן שמא שוורי אחרת יש ויש בה יוסף בן שמעון אחר: ואמר ליה רב חסדא לרבה גרסינן: כל מעשה ב"ד הרי זה יחזיר. כל מילתא דאתא לב"ד לקיים דליכא למיחש לנמלך עליהן שלא ליתנן הרי זה יחזיר וזה מקוים בב"ד היה ולכך הובא שם: כשמעתיה. דבעינן תרתי והכא חדא הוא דהואי ואכשריה: היכא דמזבני כיתנא. דשיירות מצויות שם לבא ולקנות ואהדריה משום דלא הוחזקו שני יוסף בן שמעון בעיר שנכתב בה ולא חיישינן לומר יש עיר אחרת ששמה כזו: ואיכא דאמרי היכא דתרו כיתנא. במי המשרה שם נמצא הגט ומאי כשמעתיה שהוחזקו שני יוסף בן שמעון באותה עיר שנכתב בה ואכשריה דבמקום שנמצא בו לא היו שיירות מצויות: בשלמא רבה. דאמר שינויא ארומיא דמתניתין דגיטין אמתני' דנזיקין: לא אמר כר' זירא. דרמא מתני' אברייתא: דמתניתין אלימא ליה לאקשויי. משום דהיא עיקר ויש תימה כשסותרות זו את זו וצריך לחזר שיתיישבו דאילו ברייתא יש לומר אינה עיקר רבי לא שנאה רבי חייא מניין לו: ולעולם כדקיימא לן כשנמצא לאלתר. ואם לאו פסול שמא אינו של זה אבל ברייתא ליכא לשנויי הכי דכיון דתנא בהדיא יחזיר לאשה הוה ליה לפלוגי בין לאלתר בין לזמן מרובה דלא דמיא למתניתין דהתם לא יחזיר תנא ומדוקיא הוה דייק יחזיר היכא דאמר תנו וכיון דלא תנא יחזיר לא הוה ליה לפלוגי: דאשתכח אבראי. שאין השיירות מצויות: ר' ירמיה אמר. הא דקתני יחזיר כגון דאמרי עדים החתומין בו מעולם לא חתמנו כו': ודוקא בצד אות פלונית. דהוה ליה סימן מובהק ואפילו אם תימצי לומר גבי חזרת אבידה בסימנין דאיבעיא לן לקמן (דף כז.) דאורייתא או דרבנן אפילו פשטת סימנין דרבנן יש לסמוך על סימן מובהק כזה למשרי אשת איש דאורייתא: מספקא ליה לרב אשי סימנין. שמחזירין בהן אבידה אי דאורייתא היא ואפילו באיסור דאורייתא סמכינן אסימן כל דהו: אי דרבנן. ודוקא באבידה שהפקר ב"ד הפקר אבל במידי דאיסורא לא סמכינן ואי קשיא נימא הכי קסבר סימנין דרבנן ונפשוט בעיין דלקמן לאו פירכא היא דמנלן דפשיטא ליה אי נמי מספקא ליה אית עליה למיסר מספיקא:

אירכס

תוספות

חיישינן לשני שוורי. וא"ת א"כ לרב הונא היאך יגרש כל אדם את אשתו לר"מ דאינו מוכיח מתוכו כיון דחיישינן לשני שוורי וי"ל כיון דלא הוחזקו הוי שפיר מוכיח מתוכו ומ"מ כשנפל חיישינן: נפק דק ואשכח כל מעשה ב"ד הרי זה יחזיר. פרש"י דההוא גיטא הוה כתיב ביה הנפק ופשיט שפיר ממתני' דמעשה ב"ד יחזיר אך מה שפירש כשנפל מן השליח קשה דא"כ מה מועיל ההנפק כיון שלא בא ליד האשה עדיין דאם יש לחוש לנמלך בלא הנפק הכי נמי יש לחוש להנפק ותו דבעל לא מקיים גיטא וי"ל דאי כתיב ביה הנפק מיירי שנפל מן האשה ושואלת אותו האשה ואומרת שהוא שלה וקא פשיט דיחזיר ולא חיישינן שמא משקרת ומאשה אחרת נפל אע"ג דהשיירות מצויות כיון דלא הוחזקו כמו במעשה ב"ד דיחזיר ואע"ג דאשתכח בב"ד שהשיירות מצויות ולא חיישינן שמא מאחר נפל כיון דלא הוחזקו ואי מיירי שהשליח שואלו לגרש את האשה י"ל דלא כתיב בו הנפק ומוכיח נמי שפיר כיון דבמעשה ב"ד יחזיר דלא חיישינן לנמלך דכיון שכתוב בו הנפק ודאי נעשה הלואה דלוה לא מקיים שטרא כדאמרינן לקמן בפרקין (דף כ:) ולא חיישינן נמי שמא מאחר נפל אע"ג דהשיירות מצויות כיון דלא הוחזקו בההיא גיטא נמי דאשתכח שהשליח שואל הגט ולא שייך למימר נמלך כיון שהגט ביד השליח דאין יכול לבטל הגט שלא בפני השליח ולא ניחוש כמו כן שמא מאחר נפל אף על גב דהשיירות מצויות כיון דלא הוחזקו וא"ת אביי דאמר פ' האשה שהלכה (יבמות דף קטו: ושם) דחיישינן לתרי יצחק אפי' לא הוחזקו תקשי ליה ממתניתין דכל מעשה ב"ד הרי זה יחזיר וי"ל דמוקי לה דאשתכח חוץ לב"ד שאין השיירות מצויות כר' זירא אבל לגבי תרי יצחק לא שייך לפלוגי בין מצויות לשאין מצויות דלעולם יש להסתפק בילחק מעיר אחרת כמו מעיר זאת אי נמי מוקי מתני' דאשתכח בב"ד ואפי' הכי לא חיישינן לאחר כיון שזה האיש שואל גט וידעינן שאבד גט ואין אנו מכירין אחר אין לחוש שמאחר נפל ונפל ממנו כמו כן כאן אבל התם אין אנו יודעים איזה יצחק מת אם מעיר זאת או מעיר אחרת [ז]:

אין הבעל מודה לא יחזיר. אע"ג דנאמנת לומר גרשתני (גיטין דף סד:) הכא אינה נאמנת דמעיזה פניה כיון דהגט מסייעה:

ואפילו לזמן מרובה. תימה כיון שמודה שממנה נפל וכבר גירשה אמאי הוה לן למימר דלא יחזיר כיון דנאמן לומר גרשתיה כדאמר פרק יש נוחלין (ב"ב דף קלד:) אפילו נפל מאחר נחזיר לה לראיה בעלמא וי"ל דנאמן לומר גרשתיה ותהא מגורשת מכאן ולהבא הואיל ובידו לגרשה אבל הכא שאומר שכבר גרשה מזמן הכתוב בגט כמו שאינו נאמן למפרע כך אינו נאמן להבא ויחזיר לאשה דקתני היינו בעדים ותתגרש בו בחזרה זו ולא חיישינן שמא מאחר נפל ואפילו לזמן מרובה:

מעולם לא חתמנו אלא על גט אחד כו'. ואומר הבעל שהוא אותו יוסף וא"ת והלא כשאין העדים אומרים כן אינו נאמן לומר שהוא שלו אלא אנו חוששין שמא מאחר נפל ועתה שעדים אומרים שלא חתמו אלא על גט אחד של יוסף בן שמעון למה יהא נאמן ליחוש שמא לאחר חתמו ולא לזה וי"ל דאף כי אין עדים מה שאינו נאמן אע"ג שאומר מכיר אני שהוא שלי לפי שמספק אומר שהוא שלו לפי שסבור שלא איבד אחר גט רק הוא לכך אומר שהוא שלו אע"פ שאינו מכיר אבל כשעדים אומרים שלא חתמו רק על גט אחד של יוסף בן שמעון במזיד לא ישקר אם חתמו לאחר לומר [ח] שלא חתמו דאינו חשוד לקלקלה כמו שנאמן לומר גרשתיה ואית ספרים דגרסי אלא על גט אחד של יוסף בן שמעון זה אתי שפיר טפי וצריך לומר שלא ראו עדים החתימה דאי ראו החתימה שהיא שלהם א"כ הוה ליה למימר מהו דתימא דלמא אתרמאי עדים כעדים וחתימה כחתימה:

אי

רבינו חננאל

בעיר אחת עבד רבא עובדא כשמעתיה איכא דאמרי היכא דמזבני כיתנא והוא שלא הוחזקו ואע"ג שהשיירות מצויות שם. איכא דאמרי היכא דתרו כיתנא ואע"ג דהוחזקו דהא לא שכיחן שיירתא התם. ר' זירא רמי מתני' אברייתא ומשני תנן המביא גט ואבד ממנו וכו' דברים פשוטים הם מיהו איצטרכינן לברורי דכר' זירא מסתברא וכלישנא בתרא דתני איכא דאמרי אע"ג דלא הוחזקו שני יוסף בן שמעון בעיר אחת לא נהדר ופליגא דרבא מדחזינן מתני' דפשיט מינה רבא כל מקום שלא הוחזקו שני יוסף בן שמעון בעיר אחת יחזיר ועבד עובדא וסמך אהא דתני כל מעשה ב"ד הרי זה יחזיר ולא סלקא שמעתא כטעמא דרבא אלא אוקמא ר' ירמיה כגון דאמרי עדים מעולם לא חתמנו אלא על גט אחד של יוסף בן שמעון וכו' ורב אשי דהוא בתרא אוקמא כגון דאמר (עדים) נקב יש בו בצד אות פלוני שהוא סימן מובהק אבל נקב בעלמא לא מכלל דשינויא דרבא לא שינויא דסמכא הוא ואע"ג דעבד עובדא כשמעתיה איהו הוא דעבד ואחריני לא עבדו כוותיה וכי האי גוונא

מסורת הש"ס

א) [לקמן כ:, גיטין כ... בבא בתרא קעב
ב) [לעיל טז:, לקמן כ...
ג) מהרש"ל מ...
ד) גיטין מ., ה) [גיט... מ:], ו) [לקמן כז:, חו... עט:], ז) [ועי' תוס' יבמ... קטו: ד"ה יצחק], ח) ... שלו, מהרש"ל.

ליקוטי רש"י

חיישינן לשני שוור... ושמא לא זה הוא שנ... מזה [גיטין כז.]. אע"... שבשוורי הידוע לנו ל... בה שני יוסף בן שמע... שמא יש שוורי אחר... שיש שם יוסף בן שמע... ושם נכתב ומשליח א... נפל [לקמן כ:]. כ... מעשה ב"ד. המו... שטר מקויים בב'... דליכא למיחש לכתו... היו ונמלך עליהם ש... ליתנם דלא עב... לקיומיה שטרא א... מלוה לאחר שנמסר לי... דחיים שמא ימותו עדי... הרי זה יחזיר. ו... חיישינן לשמא אינו... [גיטין שם]. דכיון ד... הוחזקו שני יוסף... שמעון בעיר אחת לש... אחרת שאינה ידועה... לא חיישינן [לקמן שנ... בי דינא דרב הונ... היו צריכין לו ל... ולהוראה ובאים... וקפשיט רבה דיח... ש"מ משום דלא הוח... שני יוסף הוא דל... שוורי לא חיישי... כשמעתיה. דא... תרתי בעינן והכא... הוה אלא חדא והחז... לתובע. איכא דאמ... היכא דמזב... כיתנא. בשוק שייר... מצויות והחזירו לפי ש... הוחזקו. ואיכא דאמ... היכא דתרו... כיתנא. האי בי כית... היכא דתרו כיתנא בנ... מי המשרה ששורין... פשתן ואין שייר... מצויות שם והחז... ואע"פ שהוחזקו ש... באותה העיר באו... השם. מודה. שאו... ליתנו לה. לא לזה ו... לזה. לבעל לא יח... שמא כבר נתנו... וממנה נפל וכשיבא ל... יחזור אחר עדי מסי... ויעידו שגירשה וכשתת... כתובתה יאמר פרער... שהוצאת הגט בבית... ותנן הוציאה גט ו... עמו כתובה גו... כתובתה וחיובי לפר... ונתנו לי את הגט... שלא תחזור ותג... ולאשה לא יחזיר ש... שינשא בו [גיטין ש... איכא דאמרי. ... דשני ר' זירא במק... שהשיירות מצויות שם... והוא דהוחזקו דבע... תרתי כרבה. אלא... זירא. דרמי מתני... אברייתא מאי טעמא... אמר שינויא דיד... אתרתי מתני' כרב... אמר לך. ר' ז... מתניתין לא ק... אהדדי. דלמא א... אמר תנו נות... ולעולם כדקי"... כלומר ודאי על כר... הא אמר תנו נו... דייקי' מינה מדא... טעמא בנמלך עליהן א... לזמן מרובה מהי... דייקת דילמא לעו... כדקי"ל בהכשירא דגי... מצאו לאלתר כשר ל... ברייתא ודאי קי... דקתני יחזיר לאשה

...לאלתר והבעל מודה פשיטא למאי ניחוש לה אי לאו דלאשמועינן אפילו לזמן מרובה לא איצטריך למיתנייה דבשלמא מתני' לא תנא בה בהדיא האמר תנו נותנין ואצטריך למתנייה משום היא גופא לאשמועינן דלא יחזיר שאני אומר כ... ר' ירמיה אמר. לא מתניתין קשיא ולא ברייתא קשיא דכל הני דאמרינן יחזיר לזמן מרובה. כגון דקאמרי עדים. החתומים בו. אלא על גט אחד. ואותו חתמנו לאיש זה התובעו. כגון דקאמר. האי שליח שאבדו. ודוק... נקט רב אשי בצד אות פלונית דהוי סימן מובהק דאין עדות ברורה מזו [גיטין כז:]. סימנים אי דאורייתא אי דרבנן. הא דאמרי' באלו מציאות (ב"מ דף כז.) שמחזירין אבדה בסימנין ואיבעיא לן התם דאורייתא או דרבנן ל... אשי נמי מספקא ליה הילכך באיסור אשת איש לא סמכינן אסימנין בעלמא דלמא סימנין דרבנן וממונא הוא דמלו רבנן להפקיע דהפקר ב"ד היה הפקר וטעמא דתקנתא התם מפרש אבל למישרי איסורא לא מלו רבנן לעקור ד... מן התורה והאי דלא אמר קסבר סימנין דרבנן משום דהתם מיבעיא לן ומהכא לא מצינן למיפשט דהא אי נמי מספקא ליה קאסר מספיקא [גיטין כז:].

חָיְישִׁינַן לִשְׁנֵי שְׁוִירִי – We are concerned that there are perhaps two towns named Shviri, and that the bill of divorce found here was written for another couple with identical names who live in that second town of Shviri.[1]

וְאָמַר לֵיהּ רַב חִסְדָּא לְרַבָּה – And Rav Chisda told Rabbah: פּוּק עַיֵּין בָּהּ – Go out and look into this matter, דְּלְאוּרְתָּא בָּעֵי מִינָּךְ רַב הוּנָא – for in the evening Rav Huna will inquire of you concerning it. נְפַק דָּק וְאַשְׁכַּח – [Rabbah] went out, investigated, and found a relevant source. דִּתְנַן – For we learned in a Mishnah:[2] כָּל מַעֲשֵׂה בֵּית דִּין – If one finds ANY ACT OF THE COURT, such as a document certified by a court,[3] הֲרֵי זֶה יַחֲזִיר – HE SHOULD RETURN it to the party named in it. We see from this Mishnah that we need not be concerned about the possible existence of an unknown party with the same name.[4] This contradicts Rav Huna's ruling.

The Gemara now explains how Rabbah's ruling here relates to his earlier statement (on 18a):

וְהָא בֵּי דִינָא דְּרַב הוּנָא – Now, Rav Huna's courthouse דְּכִי מָקוֹם שֶׁהַשַּׁיָּירוֹת מְצוּוֹת דָּמֵי – is comparable to a place where caravans are common, due to the constant arrival of litigants, וְקָא פָּשִׁיט רַבָּה דְּיַחֲזִיר – and yet Rabbah concluded that one should return the bill of divorce to the agent who claimed it. This would seem to contradict his earlier ruling that where caravans are common, we do not return a lost bill of divorce because it might have been lost by others with the same names. אַלְמָא – Evidently, we must say that Rabbah holds that אִי הוּחְזְקוּ שְׁנֵי יוֹסֵף בֶּן שִׁמְעוֹן אִין – only if it has indeed been established that two men named Yosef ben Shimon[5] reside in the city named in the bill of divorce are we concerned for the possibility of a second bill of divorce; אִי לָא לָא – but if this has not been established, we are not concerned.[6]

The Gemara cites a related incident:

עֲבַד רַבָּה עוּבְדָּא (בְּהַהוּא גִּיטָא) – Rabbah ruled in an actual case (דְּאִשְׁתַּכַּח) בֵּי כִּיתְנָא דְּפוּמְבְּדִיתָא – (concerning a bill of divorce that was discovered) in a flax-house in Pumbedisa, that it should be returned, כִּשְׁמַעְתֵּיהּ – in accordance with his aforementioned conclusion. The details of this incident are the subject of debate: אִיכָּא דְּאָמְרֵי הֵיכָא דְּמְזַבְּנֵי כִּיתְנָא – There are tho[se] who say the bill of divorce was found in the place where flax w[as] sold, וְהוּא שֶׁלֹּא הוּחְזְקוּ – and it was returned because the ex[is]tence of [a second couple with identical names] had not be[en] established; אַף עַל גַּב דִּשְׁכִיחִין שַׁיָּירָתָא – therefore, ev[en] though caravans of buyers and sellers were common in the fl[ax] market, the bill of divorce was nonetheless returned.[7] [אִיכָּ]א דְּאָמְרֵי הֵיכָא דְּתָרוּ כִּיתְנָא – And there are those who say the b[ill] of divorce was discovered in the place where flax was soaked[8] וְאַף עַל גַּב דְּהוּחְזְקוּ – so that even though the existence of [a se[c]ond couple with identical names] had been established, it w[as] nevertheless returned, דְּלָא שְׁכִיחָא שַׁיָּירוֹת – because carava[ns] were not common in the place where flax was soaked.[9]

The Gemara continues its discussion of the validity of a reco[v]ered bill of divorce:

רַבִּי זֵירָא רָמֵי מַתְנִיתִין אַבָּרַיְיתָא – R' Zeira contrasted the Mis[h]nah cited above with a seemingly conflicting Barais[a] וּמְשַׁנֵּי – and he resolved the contradiction between them:

– We learned in that Mishnah quoted above:[10] [הֵ]בִיא גֵט וְאָבַד הֵימֶנּוּ – If [A MAN'S AGENT] BROUGHT A BILL OF DIVORCE AND LO[ST] it, מְצָאוֹ לְאַלְתַּר כָּשֵׁר – if HE FOUND IT IMMEDIATELY, IT IS VAL[ID]; וְאִם לָאו פָּסוּל – BUT IF he did NOT find it immediately, it is N[OT] VALID. וּרְמִינְהִי – But he contrasted [this Mishnah] with t[he] following Baraisa: מָצָא גֵט אִשָּׁה בַּשּׁוּק – If ONE FOUND A BILL [OF] DIVORCE IN THE MARKETPLACE he should do the following: [בִּזְ]מַן שֶׁהַבַּעַל מוֹדֶה – WHEN THE HUSBAND ADMITS that he gave it to h[is] wife and divorced her, יַחֲזִיר לְאִשָּׁה – [THE FINDER] SHOULD R[E]TURN it TO THE WOMAN;[11] אֵין הַבַּעַל מוֹדֶה – but if THE HUSBA[ND] DOES NOT ADMIT that he divorced his wife, [לֹ]א יַחֲזִיר לֹא לָזֶה וְלֹא לָזֶה – [THE FINDER] SHOULD NOT RETURN the bill of divorce TO [EI]THER [THE HUSBAND] OR [THE WIFE].[12]

R' Zeira articulates the contradiction:

מִיהַת קָתָנֵי [בִּזְ]מַן שֶׁהַבַּעַל מוֹדֶה – In any event, the Baraisa teaches that WHEN THE HUSBAND ADMITS he divorced his wi[fe] יַחֲזִיר לְאִשָּׁה – [THE FINDER] SHOULD RETURN it TO THE WOMA[N] וַאֲפִילּוּ לִזְמַן מְרוּבֶּה – This would seem to mean even if the bill [of] divorce was discovered a long time after its disappearance.[13] Th[e]

NOTES

1. Although there is only one couple in Shviri whose names correspond to those on the *get,* Rav Huna still rules that it should not be returned to their agent because there may be another town somewhere by the name of Shviri in which another couple with identical names resides. Such a possibility seems remote; nevertheless, Rav Huna holds that since documents are usually guarded carefully, the very fact that this document was lost raises doubts as to its validity (see above, 12b). It should therefore not be returned unless its validity is proven beyond the shadow of a doubt (*Pnei Yehoshua*; see also *Tosafos* ד״ה חיישינן, and *Tosafos* 13b ד״ה הא קאמר).

2. Below, 20a.

3. See Gemara 16b.

4. Once a document has been certified by the court, we are no longer concerned that it may never have been implemented. We may therefore return it to the indicated party if it is found. We see from this ruling of the Mishnah that once the concern for a change of heart has been removed, there is no further reason to withhold a found document. The court does *not* withhold the document out of concern that there is perhaps another person with the same name to whom it might belong. Now, the *get* found in Rav Huna's courthouse had been certified by the court (which is why it had been brought there in the first place). Thus, Rabbah contends, there was no reason for Rav Huna not to return the *get* to the agent (*Rashi* as explained by *Toras Gittin* to *Gittin* 27a ד״ה בי דינא; cf. *Tosafos* and *Rosh;* see also *Pnei Yehoshua*).

5. Whose wives also share the same name.

6. This corroborates the Gemara's assessment of Rabbah's position, that even where caravans are common, concern for identical documents applies only where other parties by the same name are known to exist.

7. Rabbah was not concerned for the possibility that a couple with ide[n]tical names lived in an unknown city of the same name as the o[ne] recorded in the *get* (*Rashi*). Therefore, he had the *get* returned ev[en] though it had been found in a place where caravans were common.

8. Flax is soaked to loosen its fibers, so that it can be made into lin[en] thread.

9. We see again that Rabbah's concern for the possibility of a seco[nd] couple with the same names in the case of a lost *get* is only where bo[th] critical factors are present: There is *known* to be another couple wi[th] these names in the town named in the *get,* and the place where the *g[et]* was found is one which travelers commonly traverse (see *Rashi*).

10. This Mishnah was cited on 18a.

11. I.e. he should return it to her in the presence of witnesses, so th[at] even if it was lost by the husband before he gave it to her, she would no[t] be divorced with it (see *Tosafos*).

12. The *get* should not be returned to the husband because of the poss[i]bility that he did in fact divorce her and she lost it. Were she now [to] demand payment of her *kesubah*, he could claim that he had alrea[dy] paid her and received the *get* back from her in lieu of a receipt. Thu[s,] returning the *get* to him would enable him to defraud her of the *kesuba[h]* payment. On the other hand, it should not be returned to the woma[n] because of the possibility that she was not in fact divorced. In that cas[e,] possession of the *get* would enable her to falsely demonstrate her rig[ht] to remarry (*Rashi* to *Gittin* 27a ד״ה לא לזה).

13. Had the Baraisa's ruling been limited to a case in which the *get* w[as] discovered immediately, the Baraisa would have specified the limitatio[n] (*Rashi*).

חיישינן לשני שוירי וא"ל [א] רב חסדא לרבה פוק עיין בה דלאורתא בעי מינך רב הונא נפק דק ואשכח דתנן [ב] כל מעשה ב"ד הרי זה יחזיר והא בי דינא דרב הונא דכי מקום שהשיירות מצויות דמי וקא פשיט רבה דיחזיר אלמא אי הוחזקו שני יוסף בן שמעון אין אי לא לא עבד רבה עובדא [ג] (בההוא גיטא דאשתכח) בי כיתנא דפומבדיתא כשמעתיה איכא דאמרי היכא דמזבני כיתנא והוא שלא הוחזקו אע"ג דשכיחין שיירתא ואיכא דאמרי היכא דתרו כיתנא ואע"ג דהוחזקו דלא שכיחא שיירות רבי זירא רמי מתניתין אברייתא ומשני תנן המביא גט ואבד הימנו מצאו לאלתר כשר ואם לאו פסול ורמינהי [ד] [א]מצא גט אשה בשוק בזמן שהבעל מודה יחזיר לאשה אין הבעל מודה לא יחזיר לא לזה ולא לזה קתני מיהת בזמן שהבעל מודה יחזיר לאשה ואפילו לזמן מרובה ומשני כאן במקום שהשיירות מצויות וכאן במקום שאין השיירות מצויות איכא דאמרי והוא שהוחזקו דלא נהדר והיינו דרבה איכא דאמרי [ב]אע"ג דלא הוחזקו לא נהדר ופליגא דרבה בשלמא רבה לא אמר כר' זירא מתניתין אלימא ליה לאקשויי אלא רבי זירא מ"ט לא אמר כרבה אמר לך מי קא תני הא אמר תנו נותנין ואפי' לזמן מרובה דלמא הא אמר תנו נותנין ולעולם כדקיימא לן לאלתר למ"ד לר' זירא במקום שהשיירות מצויות ואע"ג שלא הוחזקו שני יוסף בן שמעון ופליגא דרבה במאי קא מיפלגי רבה סבר דקתני כל מעשה ב"ד הרי זה יחזיר דאשתכח בב"ד עסקינן וב"ד כמקום שהשיירות מצויות והוא שהוחזקו לא יחזיר לא הוחזקו יחזיר ורבי זירא אמר לך מי קתני כל מעשה ב"ד שנמצאו בב"ד כל מעשה ב"ד יחזיר קתני ולעולם דאשתכח אבראי ר' ירמיה אמר [ג]כגון דקא אמרי עדים מעולם לא חתמנו אלא על גט אחד של יוסף בן שמעון אי הכי מאי למימרא מהו דתימא ליחוש דלמא אתרמי שמא כשמא ועדים כעדים קא משמע לן רב אשי אמר [ה] [ד]כגון דקא אמר נקב יש בו בצד אות פלונית ודוקא בצד אות פלונית אבל נקב בעלמא לא רב אשי מספקא ליה [ו] סימנים אי דאורייתא אי דרבנן רבה בר בר חנה

---

**רש"י**

חיישינן לשני שוירי. אע"פ שבא אחד לפנינו ואמר ממני נפל ופלוני היה משלחו לאשתו ויודעין אנו שאין שם בשוירי שני אנשים ששמותיהן שוין חיישינן שמא שוירי אחרת יש ויש בה יוסף בן שמעון אחר: ואמר ליה רב חסדא לרבה גרסינן: כל מעשה ב"ד הרי זה יחזיר. כל מילתא דאתא לב"ד לקיים דליכא למיחש לנמלך עליהן שלא ליתנן הרי זה יחזיר וזה מקוים בב"ד היה ולכך הובא שם: כשמעתיה. דבעינן תרתי והכא חדא הוא דהואי ואכשריה: היכא דמזבני כיתנא. דשיירות מצויות שם לבא ולקנות ואהדריה משום דלא הוחזקו שני יוסף בן שמעון בעיר שנכתב בה ולא חיישינן לומר יש עיר אחרת ששמה כזו: ואיכא דאמרי היכא דתרו כיתנא. במי המשרה שם נמצא הגט ומאי כשמעתיה שהוחזקו שני יוסף בן שמעון באותה עיר שנכתב בה ואכשריה דבמקום שנמצא בו לא היו שיירות מצויות: בשלמא רבה. דאמר שינויא ארומיא דמתניתין דגיטין אמתני' דנזיקין: לא אמר כר' זירא. דרמא מתני' אברייתא: דמתניתין אלימא ליה לאקשויי. משום דהיא עיקר ויש תימה כשסותרות זו את זו וצריך לחזר שיתיישבו דאילו ברייתא יש לומר אינה עיקר רבי לא שנאה רבי חייא מניין לו: ולעולם כדקיימא לן כשנמצא לאלתר. ואם לאו פסול שמא אינו של זה אבל ברייתא ליכא לשנויי הכי דכיון דתנא בהדיא יחזיר לאשה הוה ליה לפלוגי בין לאלתר בין לזמן מרובה דלא דמיא למתניתין דהתם לא יחזיר תנא ומדוקיא הוה דייק יחזיר היכא דאמר תנו וכיון דלא תנא יחזיר לא הוה ליה לפלוגי: דאשתכח אבראי. שאין השיירות מצויות: ר' ירמיה אמר. הא דקתני יחזיר כגון דאמרי עדים החתומין בו מעולם לא חתמנו כו': ודוקא בצד אות פלונית. דהוה ליה סימן מובהק ואפילו אם תימצי לומר גבי חזרת אבידה בסימנין דאיבעיא לן לקמן (דף כ.) דאורייתא או דרבנן אפילו פשטת סימנין דרבנן יש לסמוך על סימן מובהק כזה למשרי אשת איש דאורייתא: מספקא ליה לרב אשי סימנין. שמחזירין בהן אבידה אי דאורייתא היא ואפילו באיסור דאורייתא סמכינן אסימן כל דהו: אי דרבנן. ודוקא באבידה שהפקר ב"ד הפקר אבל במידי דאיסורא לא סמכינן ואי קשיא נימא הכי קסבר סימנין דרבנן ונפשוט בעיין דלקמן לאו פירכא היא דמגלן דפשיטא ליה אי נמי מספקא ליה אית עליה למיסר מספיקא:

אירכס

---

**תוספות**

חיישינן לשני שוירי. וא"ת א"כ לרב הונא היאך יגרש כל אדם את אשתו לר"מ דאינו מוכיח מתוכו כיון דחיישינן לשני שוירי וי"ל כיון דלא הוחזקו הוי שפיר מוכיח מתוכו ומ"מ כשנפל חיישינן: נפק דק ואשכח כל מעשה ב"ד הרי זה יחזיר. פרש"י דההוא גיטא הוה כתיב ביה הנפק ופשיט שפיר ממתני' דמעשה ב"ד יחזיר אך מה שפירש כשנפל מן השליח קשה דא"כ מה מועיל ההנפק כיון שלא בא ליד האשה עדיין דאם יש לחוש לנמלך בלא הנפק הכי נמי יש לחוש להנפק ותו דבעל לא מקיים גיטא וי"ל דאי כתיב ביה הנפק מיירי שנפל מן האשה ושואלת אותו האשה ואומרת שהוא שלה וקא פשיט דיחזיר ולא חיישינן שמא משקרת ומאשה אחרת נפל אע"ג דהשיירות מצויות כיון דלא הוחזקו כמו במעשה ב"ד דיחזיר ואע"ג דאשתכח בב"ד שהשיירות מצויות ולא חיישינן שמא מאחר נפל כיון דלא הוחזקו ואי מיירי שהשליח שואלו לגרש את האשה י"ל דלא כתיב בו הנפק ומוכיח נמי שפיר כיון דבמעשה ב"ד יחזיר דלא חיישינן לנמלך דכיון שכתוב בו הנפק ודאי נעשה הלואה דלוה לא מקיים שטרא כדאמרינן לקמן בפרקין (דף כ:) ולא חיישינן נמי שמא מאחר נפל אע"ג דהשיירות מצויות כיון דלא הוחזקו בההיא גיטא נמי דאשתכח שהשליח שואל הגט ולא שייך למימר נמלך כיון שהגט ביד השליח דאין יכול לבטל הגט שלא בפני השליח ולא ניחוש כמו כן שמא מאחר נפל אף על גב דהשיירות מצויות כיון דלא הוחזקו וא"ת אביי דאמר פ' האשה שהלכה (יבמות דף קטו: ושם) דחיישינן לתרי יצחק אפי' לא הוחזקו תקשי ליה ממתניתין דכל מעשה ב"ד הרי זה יחזיר וי"ל דמוקי לה דאשתכח חוץ לב"ד שאין השיירות מצויות כר' זירא אבל לגבי תרי יצחק לא שייך לפלוגי בין מצויות לשאין מצויות דלעולם יש להסתפק ביצחק מעיר אחרת כמו מעיר זאת אי נמי מוקי מתני' דאשתכח בב"ד ואפי' הכי לא חיישינן לאחר כיון שזה האיש שואל גט וידעינן שאבד גט ואין אנו מכירין אחר אין לחוש שמאחר נפל ונפל ממנו כמו כן כאן אבל התם אין אנו יודעים איזה יצחק מת אם מעיר זאת או מעיר אחרת [ז]:

אין הבעל מודה לא יחזיר. אע"ג דנאמנת לומר גרשתני (גיטין דף סד:) הכא אינה נאמנת דמעיזה פניה כיון דהגט מקיימה:

ואפילו לזמן מרובה. תימה כיון שמודה שממנה נפל וכבר גירשה אמאי הוה לן למימר דלא יחזיר כיון דנאמן לומר גרשתיה כדאמר פרק יש נוחלין (ב"ב דף קלד:) אפילו נפל מאחר נחזיר לה לראיה בעלמא וי"ל דנאמן לומר גרשתיה ותהא מגורשת מכאן ולהבא הואיל ובידו לגרשה אבל הכא שאומר שכבר גרשה מזמן הכתוב בגט כמו שאינו נאמן למפרע כך אינו נאמן להבא ויחזיר לאשה דקתני היינו בעדים ותתגרש בו בחזרה זו ולא חיישינן שמא מאחר נפל ואפילו לזמן מרובה:

מעולם לא חתמנו אלא על גט אחד כו'. ואומר הבעל שהוא אותו יוסף וא"ת והלא כשאין העדים אומרים כן אינו נאמן לומר שהוא שלו אלא אנו חוששין שמא מאחר נפל ועתה שעדים אומרים שלא חתמו אלא על גט אחד של יוסף בן שמעון למה יהא נאמן ליחוש שמא לאחר חתמו ולא לזה וי"ל דאף כי אין עדים מה שאינו נאמן אע"ג שאומר מכיר אני שהוא שלי לפי שמספק אומר שהוא שלו לפי שסבור שלא איבד אחר גט רק הוא לכך אומר שהוא שלו אע"פ שאינו מכיר אבל כשעדים אומרים שלא חתמו רק על גט אחד של יוסף בן שמעון במזיד לא ישקר אם חתמו לאחר לומר [ח] שלא חתמו דאינו חשוד לקלקלה כמו שנאמן לומר גרשתיה ואית ספרים דגרסי אלא על גט אחד של יוסף בן שמעון זה אתי שפיר טפי וצריך לומר שלא ראו עדים החתימה דאי ראו החתימה שהיא שלהם א"כ הוה ליה למימר מהו דתימא דלמא אתרמאי עדים כעדים וחתימה כחתימה:

אי

---

**עין משפט נר מצוה**

קנט א מיי' פי"ח מהל' גזילה ואבידה הל' ו עיין בהשגות ובמ"מ סמג עשין עד טוש"ע אה"ע סי' קנג סעיף א וע"ש:

קס ב ג ד מיי' פ"ג מהלכות גירושין הל' ט י יא ועיין בהשגות ובמגיד משנה סמג עשין מח טוש"ע אה"ע שם סי' קלב סעיף ד וע"ש:

**רבינו חננאל**

בעיר אחת עבד רבא עובדא כשמעתיה איכא דאמרי היכא דמזבני כיתנא והוא שלא הוחזקו ואע"ג שהשיירות מצויות שם. איכא דאמרי היכא דתרו כיתנא ואע"ג דהוחזקו דהא לא שכיחן שיירתא התם. ר' זירא רמי מתני' אברייתא ומשני תנן המביא גט ואבד ממנו וכו' דברים פשוטים הם מיהו איצטרכינן לברורי דכר' זירא מסתברא וכלישנא בתרא דתני איכא דאמרי אע"ג דלא הוחזקו שני יוסף בן שמעון בעיר אחת לא נהדר ופליגא דרבא מדחזינן מתני' דפשיט מינה רבא כל מקום שלא הוחזקו שני יוסף בן שמעון בעיר אחת יחזיר ועבד עובדא וסמך אהא דתני כל מעשה ב"ד הרי זה יחזיר ולא סלקא שמעתא כטעמא דרבא אלא אוקמא ר' ירמיה כגון דאמרי עדים מעולם לא חתמנו אלא על גט אחד של יוסף בן שמעון וכו' ורב אשי דהוא בתרא אוקמא כגון דאמר (עדים) נקב יש בו בצד אות פלוני שהוא סימן מובהק אבל נקב בעלמא לא מכלל דשינויא דרבא לא שינויא דסמכא הוא ואע"ג דעבד עובדא כשמעתיה איהו הוא דעבד ואחריני לא עבדו כוותיה וכי האי גוונא

**מסורת הש"ס**

א) [לקמן כ:, גיטין כ... בבא בתרא קעב... ב) [לעיל טז:, לקמן כ... ג) מהרש"ל... ד) גיטין כו., ה) [גיטין כו:], ו) [לקמן כז:, חו... עט:], ז) [ועי' תוס' יבמ... קטו: ד"ה יצחק], ח) ... שלו, מהרש"ל.

**ליקוטי רש"י**

חיישינן לשני שוירי ושמא לא זה הוא של... מזה [גיטין כז.]. אע"... שבשוירי הידוע לנו ... בה שני יוסף בן שמע... שמא יש שוירי אחר... שיש שם יוסף בן שמע... ושם נכתב ומשליח א... נפל [לקמן כ:]. כ... מעשה ב"ד. המו... שטר מקויים בב"... דליכא למיחש לכתו... היו ונמלך עליהם ש... ליתנם דלא ע... לקיומיה שטרא א... מלוה לאחר שנמסר ל... דחיים שמא ימותו עד... הרי זה יחזיר. ו... חיישינן לשמא אינו ... [גיטין שם]. דכיון ד... הוחזקו שני יוסף שמעון בעיר אחת לע... אחרת שאינה ידועה ל... לא חיישינן [לקמן שב... בי דינא דרב הונא היו צריכין לו ל... ולהוראה ובאים ... וקפשיט רבה דיחז... ש"מ משום דלא הוחז... שני יוסף הוא דלא... שוירי לא חיישי... כשמעתיה. דלא... תרתי בעינן והכא ... הוה אלא חדא והחזי... לתובע. איכא דאמרי היכא דמזב... כיתנא. בשוק שיירו... מצויות והחזירו לפי ש... הוחזקו. ואיכא דאמרי היכא דתרו ... כיתנא. האי בי כית... היכא דתרו כיתנא בבי... מי המשרה ששורין ש... פשתן ואין שייר... מצויות שם והחזי... ואע"פ שהוחזקו שני... באותה העיר באו... השם. מודה. שאו... ליתנו לה. לא לזה ול... לזה. לבעל לא יחז... שמא כבר נתנו ל... וממנה נפל וכשיבא ל... יחזור אחר עדי מסיר... ויעידו שגירשה וכשתתב... כתובתה יאמר פרעתי... שהוצאת הגט בבית ד... ותנן הוציאה גט ול... עמו כתובה גוב... כתובתה וחייבוני לפרו... ונתנו לי את הגט כ... שלא תחזור ותגב... ולאשה לא יחזיר שמ... תינשא בו [גיטין שם... איכא דאמרי. ה... דשני ר' זירא במקו... שהשיירות מצויות הח... והוא דהוחזקו דבעי... תרתי כרבה. אלא ר' זירא. דרמי מתניתי... אברייתא מאי טעמא ל... אמר שינויא דידי... אתרתי מתני' כרבה... אמר לך. ר' זיר... מתניתין לא קשי... אהדדי. דלמא א... אמר תנו נותני... ולעולם בדקי"ל... כלומר ודאי על כרח... הא אמר תנו נותנ... דייקי' מינה מדתל... טעמא בנמלך עליהן א... לזמן מרובה מסיק... דייקת דילמא לעול... כדקי"ל בהכשירא דגיט... מצאו לאלתר כשר א... ברייתא ודאי קשי... דקתני יחזיר לאשה ול...

לאלתר והבעל מודה פשיטא למאי ניחוש לה אי לאו דאשמועינן אפילו לזמן מרובה לא איצטריך למיתנייה דבשלמא מתני' לא תנא בה בהדיא האמר תנו נותנין ואצטריך למתנייה משום היא גופא לאשמועינן דלא יחזיר שאני אומר כו' ר' ירמיה אמר. לא מתניתין קשיא ולא ברייתא קשיא דכל הני דאמרינן יחזיר לזמן מרובה. כגון דקאמרי עדים. החתומים בו. אלא על גט אחד. ואותו חתמנו לאיש זה התובעו. כגון דקאמר. האי שליח שאבדו. ודוקא נקב רב אשי בצד אות פלונית דהוי סימן מובהק דאין עדות ברורה מזו [גיטין כז:]. סימנים אי דאורייתא אי דרבנן. הא דאמרי' באלו מציאות (ב"מ דף כז.) שמחזירין אבדה בסימנין ואיבעיא לן התם דאורייתא או דרבנן לר' אשי נמי מספקא ליה הילכך באיסור אשת איש לא סמכינן אסימנין בעלמא דלמא סימנין דרבנן וכממונא הוא דמלו רבנן להפקיע דהפקר ב"ד היה הפקר וטעמא דתקנתא התם מפרש אבל למישרי איסורא לא מצו רבנן לעקור דבר מן התורה והאי דלא אמר קסבר סימנין דרבנן משום דהתם מיבעיא לן ומהכא לא מצינן למיפשט דהא אי נמי מספקא ליה קאסר מספיקא [גיטין כז:].

מאי גובה את הכל מנה ומאתים הוא דאית לה ואלא (א) מדתני רב חייא בר אמי א אשתו ארוסה לא אונן ולא מטמא לה וכן היא לא אוננת ולא מטמאה לו ב מתה אינו יורשה ג מת הוא גובה כתובתה דלמא דכתב לה וכי תימא (א) דכתב לה מאי למימרא מתה אינו יורשה איצטריכא ליה אלא אביי מגופה דמתני' קא הדר ביה דאי ס"ד במקום שאין כותבין כתובה עסקינן דגט היינו כתובתה אטו גט מנה מאתים כתיב ביה וכי תימא כיון דתקינו רבנן למגבא לה כמאן דכתיב ביה דמי לטעון ולימא פרעתי וכי תימא דאמרינן ליה אי פרעתה איבעי לך למיקרעיה אמר לן לא שבקתן אמרה בעינא לאנסובי ביה וכי תימא אמרינן ליה איבעי לך למיקרעיה ומכתב אגביה גיטא דנן דקרענוהו לא משום דגיטא פסולה הוא אלא כי היכי דלא תגבי ביה זמנא אחריתי אטו כל דמגבי בבי דינא מגבי:

מתני' ג מצא גיטי נשים ושחרורי עבדים דייתיקי מתנה ושוברין הרי זה לא יחזיר שאני אומר כתובין היו ונמלך עליהן שלא לתנן: גמ' טעמא דנמלך שלא לתנן הא אמר תנו נותנין ואפילו לזמן מרובה ורמינהו ג ד המביא גט ואבד הימנו מצאו לאלתר כשר אם לאו פסול אמר רבה לא קשיא ה כאן במקום שהשיירות מצויות כאן במקום שאין השיירות מצויות ואפי' במקום שהשיירות מצויות והוא שהוחזקו שני יוסף בן שמעון בעיר אחת דאי לא תימא הכי קשיא דרבה אדרבה ו דההוא גיטא דאשתכח בי דינא דרב הונא דהוה כתוב ביה בשוירי מתא דעל רכים נהרא אמר רב הונא חיישינן

## רש"י

מאי גובה את הכל. מאחר שלא התנה עמה כלום מהו התוספת: לא אונן. אין אנינות חל עליו לאיסור אכילת קדשים: ולא מטמא לה. אם כהן הוא דכתיב (ויקרא כא) כי אם לשארו והיינו אשתו והאי לאו שארו הוא דלא באו עדיין לידי קירוב בשר: ולא מטמאה לו. לאו משום כהונה קאמר דאין כהנות מוזהרות על הטומאה דכתיב (שם) בני אהרן אלא אינה זקוקה (ב) לטמא לו לא כהנת ולא ישראלית שמצוה להתעסק בשבעה מתי מצוה האמורים בפרשה דכתיב לה יטמא ותניא לה יטמא מצוה ואם לא רצה מטמאין אותו על כרחו ומעשה ביוסף הכהן כו' בתורת כהנים ה): מתה אינו יורשה. דירושת הבעל נפקא לן משארו הקרוב אליו ממשפחתו וירש אותה וגו' בב"ב (דף קיא:) והא לאו שארו הוא: אלא אביי. דאמר לעיל לאו מילתא היא דאמרי מגופא דמתני' דהוליאה גט משום דהיא גופא קשיא ליה הדר ביה: דאי ס"ד. דטעמא לאו משום דאין טוענין אחר מעשה ב"ד הוא אלא משום דגט היינו כתובה: אטו גט מנה מאתים כתיב ביה. דנימא הוא מוכיח על החוב: כמו דכתיב ביה דמי. דהא פסיקא לן מילתא דכתובה מנה מאתים: אטו כל דמגבי בבי דינא מגבי לה. וכי כל הפורע חוב בא לב"ד במקום שפרע לה לא היו ב"ד שיכתבו לו כן: הא אמר תנו. עכשיו: נותנין. ואפילו נמצא לזמן מרובה משנפל ולא חיישינן שמא גט אחר הוא ששמותיהן שוין ומאדם אחר נפל: מצאו לאלתר. התם (גיטין כז:) מפרש כדי שתעבור שיירא ותשרה ובתוך כך ליכא למימר משיירא שעברה שם נפל שהרי לא שהה שיעור שתחנה: ואפילו במקום כו'. לאו רבה קא מסיק אלא גמרא הוא דקאמר לן דכי אמר רבה במקום שהשיירות מלויות לא אמר אלא כשהוחזקו בעיר אחת שנכתב בה הגט שנים ששמותיהן שוין ושמות נשותיהן שוות: דאי לא תימא הכי. דרבה תרתי בעי קשיא דרבה אדרבה: בי דינא דרב הונא. במקום שהוא יושב ודן ומתוך שהכל רגילין אצלו לדון הוי ליה (ג) מקום שהשיירות מלויות שם: חיישינן

## תוספות

אטו גט מנה ומאתים כתיב ביה. תימה היכי מוכח דאפילו במקום שכותבין כתובה דגביא אפי' כי לא נקיטא כתובה דלמא הכא במקום שאין כותבין וגביא בשטר גט וכותבין בגט שטרא דנן כו' כדסבר (ז) רבא [רב] בפ' הכותב (כתובות דף פט:) ואביי נמי לוקמא הכי אי נמי נוקי במקום שאין כותבין כתובה וגביא בעדי הגט אבל גט לא קרעינן משום דבעיא לאנסובי ביה והוי כמו היכא דלא אפשר דכותבין שובר אבל במקום שכותבין כתובה לא יפרע עד שתוליא שטר כתובה מידה או משום שיהא נאמן לומר פרעתי דלא כרבי יוחנן או משום דאין כותבין שובר ועוד כיון דמן אלמנה מן הנשואין במקום שאין כותבין לא בעי לאוכוחי כמו שפי' לעיל (דף יז: ד"ה אלמנה) איך מוכח מגרושה מן הנישואין במקום שאין כותבין כיון דגט לאו היינו כתובה ומשום דבעינא לאנסובי ביה פשיטא דאין נאמן לומר פרעתי כיון דלא ניתקנה כתובה באותו מקום וי"ל דלאביי מתניתין קשיתיה דתנן כתובה ואין עמה גט אלמא במקום שכותבין כתובה עסקינן דאין סברא להעמיד שכן אירע שכתב לה בעבור אהבתה לכך פריך כיון שיש לה כתובה ואין מוליאה רק גט לימא פרעתי אלא ודאי לא אמר כלום וכותבין שובר:

הא אמר תנו נותנין. וא"ת מנלן דלמא אפילו אמר תנו אין נותנין והא דקתני נמלך ה"ק ונמלך שלא ליתנן ומחמת כן לא חשש לשמור ונאבד ועכשיו רוצה לחזור ולגרשה דסבר שזהו הגט שאבד ממנו ואמר תנו ואפילו הכי אין נותנין דשמא אין זה גיטו אלא נפל מאחר ששמו כשמו אבל לא נמלך לכתחילה מלגרשה וגרשה מחזירין לה הגט לראיה אפי' אינו שלה וי"ל דדייק מדלא קתני כתובים היו ולא נתנן ומדקתני ונמלך משמע שחושש שמא אינו רוצה עתה לגרשה אבל אם אמר תנו לה נותנים ואין לחוש שמא מאחר נפל וא"ת ומנלן ואפי' לזמן מרובה דלמא לאלתר דוקא כדפריך ר' זירא לקמן ור' זירא גופיה מנלן דיחזיר לאשה אפילו לזמן מרובה וממה פשוט לו דברייתא קאמר לזמן מרובה יותר ממתני' וי"ל דמברייתא משמע דבזמן שהבעל מודה יחזיר לאשה אפי' לזמן מרובה דאי לאלתר דוקא פשיטא אבל במתני' מאי למימר לאלתר דוקא דאם אמר תנו נותנין אינו מפורש במתני' והיא גופה אתא לאשמועינן דלא יחזיר דחיישינן לשמא נמלך אבל רבה דייק מדקתני ונמלך ולא קתני כתובין היו ולא נתן א"כ אתא לאשמועינן אם אמר תנו נותנין והיינו אפי' לזמן מרובה דאי לאלתר פשיטא וא"ת והלא אפילו אי הוי לאלתר הוי חידוש דלא חיישינן דלמא כתב בניסן ולא נתן עד תשרי כדפריך לקמן (דף יט.) וכן לקמן (עמוד ב) דפריך על רבי ירמיה דמוקי כגון דקאמרי עדים כו' מאי למימרא לימא דקא משמע לן דלא חיישינן דלמא כתב בניסן כו' וי"ל דס"ל כמאן דאמר אין לבעל פירות משעת חתימה ואז ליכא חידוש דכתב בניסן ולא נתן עד תשרי דאפילו הכי שפיר טרפה ועוד י"ל דרבי זירא דייק אפי' לזמן מרובה מדקתני בזמן שהבעל מודה יחזיר לאשה משמע שמודה שממנה נפל וכבר גירשה בו ואי לאלתר דוקא א"כ נ"ל שראינו הגט בידה דאי לא ראינו א"כ במה אנו יודעין שהוא לאלתר ואחרי שראינו הגט בידה הרי כבר מגורשת פשיטא דיחזיר ומאי קא משמע לן * והלא אפילו לא גיטה הוא זה ניתן לה לראייה ואין הבעל מודה נמי אמאי לא יחזיר אלא ודאי מיירי שלא ראינו הגט בידה וקמשמע לן דאע"פ דחיישינן שמא מבעל נפל ועדיין לא גירשה תתגרש עתה בהחזרת הגט ולא חיישינן שמא מאחר נפל א"כ הוי אפי' לזמן מרובה כיון דלא ידעינן ממי נפל מן הבעל או מן האשה ורבה דייק דמתני' נמי אפי' לזמן מרובה דומיא דשטרי הלואה ומיאונין דיחזיר אפי' לזמן מרובה דלאלתר היינו שראינו בידה פשיטא כיון דחלוה נחזיר לה לראיה אפילו אינו שלה אלא מיירי שלא ראינו בידה ואף לא ידעינן שחלוה והיינו לזמן מרובה ודומיא דהכי משמע ליה דמיירי ברישא ורבי זירא לא מוקי לה דומיא דסיפא: לאלתר כשר. אפילו אביי דחייש לתרי יצחק אפילו היכא דלא הוחזק (יבמות דף קטו:) בגט שמלאו לאלתר לא חייש דהתם הוי כמו לזמן מרובה דלא שייך התם לאלתר:

גליון תימה דלמא קמ"ל דלא חיישינן דשמא זה הגט זמנו קודם לגט זה שנתגרשה בו ותטרף בגט זה שימכן לראייה פירות שלא כדין אפי' למ"ד אין לבעל פירות משעת חתימה וי"ל דכיון שהבעל מודה וסובר שהוא שלו א"כ בודאי זמנו שוה לאותו שנאבד. ע"כ גליון:

והוא שהוחזקו. תימה אמאי לא מוקי אידי ואידי שהשיירות מלויות ומתני' בלא הוחזקו דהשתא הוי דומיא דסיפא דכל מעשה ב"ד דמיירי בהכי וי"ל דעובדא דבסמוך דהוי בבי דינא דרב הונא הוי ברישא ואשמועינן דבלא הוחזקו יחזיר אפי' שיירות מלויות והכא אשמועינן דאם הוחזקו נמי יחזיר אם אין שיירות מלויות וא"ת ומאי טעמא יחזיר לאשה כיון שיש שני יוסף בן שמעון בעיר וי"ל כיון שאנו יודעים שזה אבד גט כאן אין לחוש שגם האחר איבד כיון שאין שיירות מלויות ושמעתין אתיא כר"א דלרבי מאיר כיון שהוחזקו שני יוסף בן שמעון אין הגט כשר עד שיהא מוכיח מתוכו שהוא של זה כדמוכח פרק כל הגט (גיטין דף כד:) דתנן כתב לגרש את הגדולה לא יגרש בו את הקטנה ודייק הא גדולה מצי לגרש מני ר"א היא ובעדי מסירה משמע דלר"מ אפילו גדולה לא מצי מגרש וההוא דהמגרש (שם דף פו:) דשני גיטין שוין שנתערבו ומוקי כר"מ מיירי במשולשים דמוכיח מתוכו: [וע"ע תוס' גיטין כד: ד"ה בעדי]:

חיישינן

## עין משפט נר מצוה

קנה א מיי' פ"ב מהל' אבל הלכה ג סמג לאוין רלה טור ש"ע י"ד סי' שעג סעיף ד וסי' שעד סעיף ד וטוש"ע אה"ע סי' נה סעיף ה:

קנו ב מיי' פכ"ב מהל' אישות הל' ג סמג עשין מח טוש"ע אה"ע שם וסי' מ:

קנז ג מיי' פ"י שם הל' יא ועיין שם סמג שם טוש"ע אה"ע סי' נה סעיף ו:

קנח ד ה מיי' פ"ג מהלכות גירושין הל' ט ועיין במ"מ סמג עשין מח טוש"ע אה"ע סי' קלב סעיף ד:

## רבינו חננאל

והדר ביה אביי מגופה דמתניתין ואסיקנא דאם איתא דפרעה איבעי ליה למיקרעיה לגיטה ולמכתב על גביה גיטה דנן דקרעינוהי לאו משום דפסול הוא אלא משום דלא תיהדר ותיגביה ביה זימנא אחריתי. ואי טעין לא הוינא ידע האי דינא ואף לא גירשתיה א) שיודיעני לא אמר כלום אלא הוציאה גט גובה כתובתה. סוגיא דשמעתא אלמנה מן האירוסין אם כתב לה אית לה מנה מאתים אבל תוספת לית לה אע"ג דכתב לה: מתני' מצא גיטי נשים ושחרורי עבדים וכו' עד שאני אמר כתובין היו ונמלך עליהם שלא ליתנם מדמותבינן מינה לאביי דאמר עדיו בחתומיו זכין לו ופריק הני מילי היכא דמטא שטרא בידיה דמקבל ש"מ דהא מתני' הלכתא היא וכל שטרא מתנה דלא מטא לידיה דמקבל לא זכה ביה וצריך לברורי דמטא לידיה אי לא נפיק מתותי ידיה. ודייקינן מינה הא אמר תנו נותנין ואפי' לזמן מרובה. ורמינן עלה הא דתנן המביא גט ממדינת הים ואבד לו מצאו לאלתר כשר ואם לאו פסול ופריק רבא הכי מתני' אפי' במקום שהשיירות מצויות והוא שלא הוחזקו שני יוסף בן שמעון בעיר אחת. כלומר דלא הוחזק באותה העיר אדם אחר ששמו כשם זה שגט זה כתוב כשמו הלכך אם הבעל מודה ואמר תנהו לאשה נותנין זה הגט לזו האשה ואפי' לזמן [מרובה]. ואוקים להא דתנן המביא גט מצאו לאלתר כשר ואם לאו פסול במקום שהשיירות מצויות והוא שהוחזקו שני יוסף בן שמעון

## חשק שלמה על ר"ח

א) אולי צ"ל לא גרשתיה בב"ד שיודיעו אותי לא אמר כלום וכו'.

## מסורת הש"ס

א) כמות כט:, עיין שם ... ב) כתובות נג, פט:, ג) סנהדרין כח: ע"ש, ... יבמות ... ד) [לעיל יג.], גיטין כז:, ה) [לקמן כ.], ו) [וק בזבחים ק.], ז) מהרש"ל.

## הגהות הב"ח

(א) גמ' וכי תימא אי ... (ב) רש"י ד"ה ולא מטמאה לו וכו' אלא אינה זקוקה. נ"ב ועיין ספרים בסנהדרין כח ע"ב וביבמות דף ע"ב ובתוס' שם: (ג) ד"ה בי דינא וכו' הוי ליה כמקום:

## ליקוטי רש"י

אונן. אם מתה אינו ... בקדשים ... [סנהדרין כח:]. אוננת. ... בקדשים. ולא מטמאה. ... [יבמות כט:] ... אינו יורשה. ... דייתיקי. ... [גיטין ...] ... [לעיל יג.] ... מתנת בריא. ... שוברין. פרעון שטר. ... יחזיר. ... הא אמר ... אם לאו פסול. ... שהשיירות מצויות. ... והוא שהוחזקו ... בי דינא דרב הונא. ... [לקמן כ.].

perhaps **they were written** with the intent to give them, וְנִמְלַךְ עֲלֵיהֶן שֶׁלֹּא לִתְּנָן – **but [the author] reconsidered** and decided **not to give them** and it is he who lost them.[12]

**Gemara** The Gemara notes the Mishnah's reason for not returning the documents and draws a conclusion from it:

טַעְמָא דְנִמְלַךְ שֶׁלֹּא לִתְּ[נָן] – **The reason** the Mishnah gives for not returning these documents **is that** perhaps, after preparing them, **[the author] reconsidered** and decided **not to give them** to the person named in them. הָא אָמַר תְּנוּ – This implies that **if he would** now **say to give** them to the persons named in them, נוֹתְנִ[ין] – **we would give** them,[13] וַאֲפִילּוּ לִזְמַן מְרוּבֶּה – **even** if they were found **a long time after** their disappearance.[14]

The Gemara points out a contradiction to this ruling:

וּרְמִינְהוּ – **They contrasted** this ruling with that of another Mishnah:[15] הַמֵּבִיא גֵּט וְאָבַד הֵימֶנּוּ – If [A MAN'S AGENT] BROUGHT A *GET* to deliver to the man's wife AND HE LOST IT, מְצָאוֹ לְאַלְתַּר כָּשֵׁר – if [THE AGENT] FOUND IT IMMEDIATELY, IT IS VALID;[16] אִם לָאו פָּסוּל – and IF NOT, IT IS NOT VALID, because the *get* found now may not be the one he lost, but an identical *get* written by another man.[17] This contradicts the inference from our Mishnah that a lost *get* may be used even if it is discovered long after its disappearance. – ? –

The Gemara answers:

אָמַר רַבָּה – **Rabbah said:** לֹא קַשְׁיָא – **It is not a difficulty.** כָּאן – **Here,** in that Mishnah that rules that a lost *get* may not be used unless it is recovered immediately, בְּמָקוֹם שֶׁהַשְּׁיָירוֹת מְצוּוֹת – we refer to a *get* found **in a place where caravans are common.**[18] Therefore, we are concerned that the *get* that was found may have been lost by one of the travelers and not the agent who is claiming it. כָּאן – **Here,** in our Mishnah, which implies that the *get* may be used even if found much later, בְּמָקוֹם שֶׁאֵין הַשְּׁיָירוֹת מְצוּוֹת – we refer to a *get* found **in a place where caravans are not common.** Therefore, we are not concerned for the possibility that an identical *get* fell from a traveler.[19]

The Gemara elaborates on Rabbah's ruling:

וַאֲפִילּוּ בְּמָקוֹם שֶׁהַשְּׁיָירוֹת מְצוּוֹת – **Now even** if the *get* was found **in a place where caravans are common,** וְהוּא שֶׁהוּחְזְקוּ שְׁנֵי יוֹסֵף בֶּן שִׁמְעוֹן בְּעִיר אַחַת – **[Rabbah's concern]** that the *get* that was found might not be the *get* that was lost is **only if it has** also **been established that two** men named **Yosef ben Shimon,** for example,[20] reside **in the same city,** i.e. in the city named in the *get,*[21] and they are married to women with identical names. דְּאִי לֹא תֵּימָא הָכִי – **For if you do not say so,** קַשְׁיָא דְּרַבָּה אַדְּרַבָּה – then this ruling **of Rabbah contradicts** another ruling **of Rabbah.**[22]

The Gemara relates the incident from which Rabbah's other ruling emerged:

דְּהַהוּא גִּיטָּא דְּאִשְׁתַּכַּח בֵּי דִינָא דְּרַב הוּנָא – **For** there was **this *get* that was found in Rav Huna's courthouse,** דַּהֲוָה כָּתוּב בֵּיהּ – **in which** the place of the *get's* origin **was written** as follows: בְּשְׁוִירִי מָתָא דְּעַל רָכִיס נַהֲרָא – **In Shviri, a town on the river Rachis.**[23] An agent appointed by the Shviri resident to deliver the *get* appeared, claiming that he had lost this *get.* אָמַר רַב הוּנָא – **Rav Huna said:**

NOTES

12. I.e. we are concerned that the author lost the documents before the transactions described in them were concluded and that he does not now wish to complete these transactions. Returning the documents to the persons named in them would enable those persons to claim something that never took effect (divorce, emancipation, gift, etc.). This is because the transactions referred to in the Mishnah do not take effect until the documents are handed over to the recipient. Thus, if the writer lost them, the transactions never took effect. Even sickbed wills, which take effect without a formal transfer of the document, can nevertheless be retracted by the writer until his death (see below, 19b). We must therefore be concerned that perhaps he retracted this will.

13. I.e. upon the author's instruction, we may act as his agents and implement these documents on his behalf.

14. We are not concerned that perhaps in the course of time another, identical document was lost, whose principals have the same names as those in the first document (*Rashi*).

15. *Gittin* 27a.

16. *Rashi* defines the term "immediately," based on *Gittin* 27b: If the agent found the *get* before another caravan could have arrived in this place and pitched camp, there is no concern that he found an identical *get* that fell from a traveler. *R' Akiva Eiger* questions this definition, noting that the Gemara in *Gittin* concludes differently: The *get* may be returned only if we are certain that *not a single traveler* passed by from the time it was lost until it was found! (See *Chidushei R' Akiva Eiger;* cf. *Rambam, Hil. Gerushin* 3:9,10; *Raavad* and *Maggid Mishneh* ad loc.)

17. A *get* written for another man and woman is not valid for this couple, because a *get* must be written specifically for the man and woman who will be divorced with it (see Mishnah, *Gittin* 24a).

18. I.e. in a place that is commonly traversed, so that there is room for concern that an identical *get* was dropped by a passerby. [The concern for *caravans* is only in the case of a *get* that comes from out of town. If the *get* originated in the city in which it was found, the concern is for a local passerby.]

19. Thus, there are two concerns with a *get* that was lost and then found:
1) The husband may have lost it and he no longer wishes to grant the divorce. (This is the concern of our Mishnah.)
2) The *get* that was found may not be the *get* that was lost, so that even if the husband still wishes to divorce his wife, he cannot do so with the found *get.* (This is the concern of the Mishnah in *Gittin.*)

20. A hypothetical name for the husband whose name appears in the *get.*

21. The text of a *get* would generally include the place of the husband and wife. (See *Even HaEzer* 128:2, with regard to current practice.) Thus, identical *gittin* are a possibility only if two identically named couples reside in the same city. The Gemara states, in effect, that Rabbah's concern that an identical *get* was lost by a passerby applies only in a case where it is an *established fact* that there are two couples bearing the names that appear in the *get* who reside in the city named in the *get.*

Thus, the Gemara explains that according to Rabbah, the concern for another *get* applies only if two factors are present: 1) Caravans are common here, and 2) it has been established that two couples with the same names reside in the town from which the lost *get* originates. If either factor is absent, we assume (according to Rabbah) that only one *get* was lost here and it is the original *get* that was recovered (*Rashi* ד״ה דאי; see also *Tosafos* ד״ה והוא). The Gemara will now demonstrate that this is Rabbah's view.

22. I.e. if you will say that Rabbah is concerned for the possibility of a second *get* even when it has *not* been established that two couples with the same names reside in the city named in the *get,* and that his concern is based solely on the prevalence of caravans, you will be faced with the following contradiction in Rabbah's rulings.

23. [See *Pischei Teshuvah, Even HaEzer* 128:9.]

מאי גובה את הכל מנה ומאתים הוא דאית לה ואלא (א) מדתני רב חייא בר אמי א אשתו ארוסה לא אונן ולא מטמא לה וכן היא לא אוננת ולא מטמאה לו ב מתה אינו יורשה ג מת הוא גובה כתובתה דלמא דכתב לה וכי תימא (א) דכתב לה מאי למימרא מתה אינו יורשה איצטריכא ליה אלא אביי מגופה דמתני' קא הדר ביה דאי ס"ד במקום שאין כותבין כתובה עסקינן דגט היינו כתובתה אטו גט מנה מאתים כתיב ביה וכי תימא כיון דתקינו רבנן למגבא לה כמאן דכתיב ביה דמי לטעון ולימא פרעתי וכי תימא דאמרינן ליה אי פרעתה איבעי לך למיקרעיה אמר לן לא שבקתן אמרה בעינא לאנסובי ביה וכי תימא אמרינן ליה איבעי לך למיקרעיה ומכתב אגביה גיטא דנן דקרענוהו לא משום דגיטא פסולה הוא אלא כי היכי דלא תגבי ביה זמנא אחריתי אטו כל דמגבי בבי דינא מגבי:

מתני' ג מצא גיטי נשים ושחרורי עבדים דייתיקי מתנה ושוברין הרי זה לא יחזיר שאני אומר כתובין היו ונמלך עליהן שלא לתתן: גמ' טעמא דנמלך שלא לתתן הא אמר תנו נותנין ואפילו לזמן מרובה ורמינהו (ג) ד המביא גט ואבד הימנו מצאו לאלתר כשר אם לאו פסול אמר רבה לא קשיא ה כאן במקום שהשיירות מצויות כאן במקום שאין השיירות מצויות ואפי' במקום שהשיירות מצויות והוא שהוחזקו שני יוסף בן שמעון בעיר אחת דאי לא תימא הכי קשיא דרבה אדרבה ו דההוא גיטא דאשתכח בי דינא דרב הונא דהוה כתוב ביה בשוירי מתא דעל רכים נהרא אמר רב הונא חיישינן

**רש"י**

מאי גובה את הכל. מאחר שלא התנה עמה כלום מהו התוספת: לא אונן. אין אנינות חל עליו לאיסור אכילת קדשים: ולא מטמא לה. אם כהן הוא דכתיב (ויקרא כא) כי אם לשארו והיינו אשתו והאי לאו שארו הוא דלא באו עדיין לידי קירוב בשר: ולא מטמאה לו. לאו משום כהונה קאמר דאין כהנות מוזהרות על הטומאה דכתיב (שם) בני אהרן אלא אינה זקוקה (ב) לטמא לו לא כהנת ולא ישראלית שמצוה להתעסק בשבעה מתי מצוה האמורים בפרשה דכתיב לה יטמא ותניא לה יטמא מצוה ואם לא רצה מטמאין אותו על כרחו ומעשה ביוסף הכהן כו' בתורת כהנים: מתה אינו יורשה. דירושת הבעל נפקא לן משארו הקרוב אליו ממשפחתו וירש אותה וגו' בב"ב (דף קיא:) והא לאו שארו הוא: אלא אביי. דאמר לעיל לאו מילתא היא דאמרי מגופה דמתני' דהוציאה גט משום דהיא גופה קשיא ליה הדר ביה: דאי ס"ד. דטעמא לאו משום דאין טוענין אחר מעשה ב"ד הוא אלא משום דגט היינו כתובה: אטו גט מנה מאתים כתיב ביה. דנימא הוא מוכיח על החוב: כמו דכתיב ביה דמי. דהא פסיקא לן מילתא דכתובה מנה מאתים: אטו כל דמגבי בבי דינא מגבי לה. וכי כל הפורע חוב בלא ב"ד במקום שפרע לה לא היו ב"ד שיכתבו לו כן: הא אמר תנו. עכשיו: נותנין. ואפילו נמצא לזמן מרובה משנפל ולא חיישינן שמא גט אחר הוא ששמותיהן שוין ומאדם אחר נפל: מצאו לאלתר. התם (גיטין כ:) מפרש כדי שתעבור שיירא ותשרה ובתוך כך ליכא למימר משיירא שעברה שם נפל שהרי לא שהה שיעור שתחנה: ואפילו במקום כו'. לאו רבה קא מסיק אלא גמרא הוא דקאמר לן דכי אמר רבה במקום שהשיירות מצויות לא אמר אלא כשהוחזקו בעיר אחת שנכתב בה הגט שנים ששמותיהן שוין ושמות נשותיהן שוות: דאי לא תימא הכי. דרבה תרתי בעי קשיא דרבה אדרבה: בי דינא דרב הונא. במקום שהוא יושב ודן ומתוך שהכל רגילין אצלו לדון הוי ליה (ג) מקום שהשיירות מצויות שם: חיישינן

**תוספות**

אטו גט מנה ומאתים כתיב ביה. תימה היכי מוכח דאפילו במקום שכותבין כתובה דגביא אפי' כי לא נקיטא כתובה דלמא הכא במקום שאין כותבין וגביא בשטר גט וכותבין בגט שטרא דנן כו' כדסבר (י) רבא) [רב] בפ' הכותב (כתובות דף פט:) ואביי נמי לוקמא הכי אי נמי נוקי במקום שאין כותבין כתובה וגביא בעדי הגט אבל גט לא קרעינן משום דבעיא לאנסובי ביה והוי כמו היכא דלא אפשר דכותבין שובר אבל במקום שכותבין כתובה לא יפרע עד שתוציא שטר כתובה מידה או משום שיהא נאמן לומר פרעתי דלא כרבי יוחנן או משום דאין כותבין שובר ועוד כיון דמן אלמנה מן הנשואין במקום שאין כותבין לא בעי לאוכוחי כמו שפי' לעיל (דף יז: ד"ה אלמנה) איך מוכח מגרושה מן הנישואין במקום שאין כותבין כיון דגט לאו היינו כתובה ומשום דבעינא לאנסובי ביה פשיטא דאין נאמן לומר פרעתי כיון דלא ניתקנה כתובה באותו מקום וי"ל דלאביי מתניתין קשיתיה דתנן כתובה ואין עמה גט אלמא במקום שכותבין כתובה עסקינן דאין סברא להעמיד שכן אירע שכתב לה בעבור אהבתה לכך פריך כיון שיש לה כתובה ואין מוציאה רק גט לימא פרעתי אלא ודאי לא אמר כלום וכותבין שובר:

הא אמר תנו נותנין. וא"ת מנלן דלמא אפילו אמר תנו אין נותנין והא דקתני נמלך ה"ק ונמלך שלא ליתנן ומחמת כן לא חשש לשמור ונאבד ועכשיו רוצה לחזור ולגרשה דסבר שזהו הגט שאבד ממנו ואמר תנו ואפילו הכי אין נותנין דשמא אין זה גיטו אלא נפל מאחר ששמו כשמו אבל לא נמלך לכתחילה מלגרשה וגרשה מחזירין לה הגט לראיה אפי' אינו שלה וי"ל דדייק מדלא קתני כתובים היו ולא נתנן ומדקתני ונמלך משמע שחושש שמא אינו רוצה עתה לגרשה אבל אם אמר תנו לה נותנים ואין לחוש שמא מאחר נפל וא"ת ומנלן ואפי' לזמן מרובה דלמא לאלתר דוקא כדפריך ר' זירא לקמן ור' זירא גופיה מנלן דיחזיר לאשה אפילו לזמן מרובה וממה פשוט לו דברייתא קאמר לזמן מרובה יותר ממתני' וי"ל דמברייתא משמע דבזמן שהבעל מודה יחזיר לאשה אפי' לזמן מרובה דאי לאלתר דוקא פשיטא אבל במתני' מצי למימר לאלתר דוקא דאם אמר תנו נותנין אינו מפורש במתני' והיא גופה אתא לאשמועינן דלא יחזיר דחיישינן לשמא נמלך אבל רבה דייק מדקתני ונמלך ולא קתני כתובין היו ולא נתן א"כ אתא לאשמועינן אם אמר תנו נותנין והיינו אפי' לזמן מרובה דאי לאלתר פשיטא וא"ת והלא אפילו אי הוי לאלתר הוי חידוש דלא חיישינן דלמא כתב בניסן ולא נתן עד תשרי כדפריך לקמן (דף יט.) וכן לקמן (עמוד ב) דפריך על רבי ירמיה דמוקי כגון דקאמרי עדים כו' מאי למימרא לימא דקא משמע לן דלא חיישינן דלמא כתב בניסן כו' וי"ל דס"ל כמאן דאמר אין לבעל פירות משעת חתימה ואז ליכא חידוש דכתב בניסן ולא נתן עד תשרי דאפילו הכי שפיר טרפה ועוד י"ל דרבי זירא דייק אפי' לזמן מרובה מדקתני בזמן שהבעל מודה יחזיר לאשה משמע שמודה שממנה נפל וכבר גירשה בו ואי לאלתר דוקא א"כ צ"ל שראינו הגט בידה דאי לא ראינו א"כ במה אנו יודעין שהוא לאלתר ואחרי שראינו הגט בידה הרי כבר מגורשת פשיטא דיחזיר ומאי קא משמע לן * והלא אפילו לא גיטה הוא זה ניתן לה לראייה ואין הבעל מודה נמי אמאי לא יחזיר אלא ודאי מיירי שלא ראינו הגט בידה וקמשמע לן דאע"פ דחיישינן שמא מבעל נפל ועדיין לא גירשה תתגרש עתה בהחזרת הגט ולא חיישינן שמא מאחר נפל א"כ הוי אפי' לזמן מרובה כיון דלא ידעינן ממי נפל מן הבעל או מן האשה ורבה דייק דמתני' נמי אפי' לזמן מרובה דומיא דשטרי חליצה ומיאונין דיחזיר אפי' לזמן מרובה דלאלתר היינו שראינו בידה פשיטא כיון דחלצה נחזיר לה לראיה אפילו אינו שלה אלא מיירי שלא ראינו בידה ואף לא ידעינן שחלצה והיינו לזמן מרובה ודומיא דהכי משמע ליה דמיירי ברישא ורבי זירא לא מוקי לה דומיא דסיפא:

לאלתר כשר. אפילו אביי דחייש לתרי יוסף בן שמעון היכא דלא הוחזק (יבמות דף קטו:) בגט שמצאו לאלתר לא חייש דהתם הוי כמו לזמן מרובה דלא שייך התם לאלתר:

והוא שהוחזקו. תימה אמאי לא מוקי אידי ואידי שהשיירות מצויות ומתני' בלא הוחזקו דהשתא הוי דומיא דסיפא דכל מעשה ב"ד דמיירי בהכי וי"ל דעובדא דבסמוך דהוי בבי דינא דרב הונא הוי ברישא ואשמועינן דבלא הוחזקו יחזיר אפי' שיירות מצויות והכא אשמועינן דאם הוחזקו נמי יחזיר אם אין שיירות מצויות וא"ת ומאי טעמא יחזיר לאשה כיון שיש שני יוסף בן שמעון בעיר וי"ל כיון שאנו יודעים שזה אבד גט כאן אין לחוש שגם האחר איבד כיון שאין שיירות מצויות ושמעתין אתיא כר"א דלרבי מאיר כיון שהוחזקו שני יוסף בן שמעון אין הגט כשר עד שיהא מוכיח מתוכו שהוא של זה כדמוכח פרק כל הגט (גיטין דף כד:) דתנן כתב לגרש את הגדולה לא יגרש בו את הקטנה ודייק הא גדולה מצי לגרש מני ר"א היא ובעדי מסירה משמע דלר"מ אפילו גדולה לא מצי מגרש והיינו דהמגרש (שם דף פו:) דשני גיטין שוין שנתערבו ומוקי כר"מ מיירי במשולשים דמוכיח מתוכו: [וע"ע תוס' גיטין כד: ד"ה בעדי]:

גליון תימה דלמא קמ"ל דלא חיישינן דשמא זה הגט זמנו קודם לגט זה שנתגרשה בו ומטרף בגט זה שניתן לראייה פירות שלא כדין אפי' למ"ד אין לבעל פירות משעת חתימה וי"ל דכיון שהבעל מודה וסובר שהוא שלו א"כ בודאי זמנו שוה לאותו שנאבד. ע"כ גליון:

**מסורת הש"ס**

[...]במות כט:, עיין שם [...], כתובות נג., פט:, [...] סנהדרין כח:, ע"ש, [...]יטין כ., [לעיל יג.], [...]יטין שם, ד) [לקמן כ., [...]ן מ.], ה) [וכן בזבחים [...]ק.], ו) מהרש"ל.

**הגהות הב"ח**

(א) גמ' וכי תימא אי דכתב: (ב) רש"י ד"ה ולא מטמאה לו וכו' אלא אינה זקוקה. נ"ב ועיין שפרש"י בסנהדרין כח ע"ב וביבמות דף [...] ע"ב ובתוס' שם: (ג) ד"ה בי דינא וכו' הוי ליה כמקום:

**ליקוטי רש"י**

[...] אונן. אם מתה אינו [...]ר בקדשים מחמת [...]ות [סנהדרין כח:]. [...] אוננת. להיות [...]רה בקדשים. ולא [...]טמאת. אינה צריכה [...]עסק בו ולאו דוקא [...] ולא מיטמאת דהא [...]ת אהרן לא הוזהרו [...] הטומאה אלא איידי [...]קט לא אוננת [...]צטריך ליה נקט ולא [...]מאת דבעי למתני [...]תי בדידה ובדידיה קך [...]עתי ולי נראה ולא [...]מאה כגון ברגל [...]ראלים מוזהרים על [...]ומאה מוגבלתם לא [...]עו [יבמות כט:]. ואית [...]"ג אינה מטמאה [...] הדרין שם]. אינו [...]ישה. נדוניית בית [...]יה דלא תקון ירושת [...]על עד שתכנס לחופה [...] שתמסר לשלוחים. [...]ת הוא. במייה. גובה [...]תובתה. מנה מאתים [...]וספת אם כתב לה [...]תובות נג.]. ודכתב לה [...] האירוסין מיתוקמא [...]תובות פרק הכותב [...]מות שם]. דייתיקי. [...]את שכ"מ דא תהא [...]יקס ולהיות [גיטין [...]]. ולשון דייתיקי דא [...]קו זאת תיקום דדברי [...]יב מרע ככתובין [...]מסורין דמי [לעיל יג.]. [...]תנה. מתנת בריא. [...]זוברין. פרעון שטר. [...] יחזיר. לא לבעל [...] לאשה וכן שחרור [...] כולם. הא אמר [...]נו וכו'. ומדלא [...]נמא בשאני אומר [...]עינן מינה דאם אמר [...]על תנו לה שאני [...]בתיו לה נותנין ולא [...]ישינן לשמא אינו זה. [...]ם לאו פסול. שמא [...]אחר נפל ואין זה שלו. [...]מקום שהשיירות [...]צויות. פסול שמא [...]עוברים ושבים אחרים [...]ל. והוא שהוחזקו [...]גר'. והוא שהוחזקו שני [...]שים בשם זה באותה [...]עיר אבל אם לא [...]וחזקו מספיקא לא [...]מרינן דילמא איתנהו [...]א ידעינן או דילמא יש [...]יר אחרת ששמה כו [...]ם בה אדם אחר ששמו [...]ם אשתו כזה שמוצעו. [...] דינא דרב הונא. [...]וגא שם לקיימו בב"ד [...]מוב בו הנפק ונפל [...]ה והוא תובעו ולא [...]וחזקו שני יוסף בן [...]מעון באותה העיר [...]יטין כז.]. מקויים [...]הנפק והשליח המביאו [...]ימר ממנו נפל [לקמן כ.].

**עין משפט נר מצוה**

קנה א מיי' פ"ב מהל' אבל הלכה ג סמג לאוין רלה טור ש"ע י"ד סי' שעג סעיף ד וסי' שעד סעיף ד וטוש"ע אה"ע סי' נה סעיף ה:

קנו ב מיי' פכ"ב מהל' אישות הל' ג סמג עשין מח טוש"ע אה"ע שם וסי' מ:

קנז ג מיי' פ"י שם הל' יא ועיין שם סמג שם טוש"ע אה"ע סי' נה סעיף ו:

קנח ד ה מיי' פ"ג מהלכות גירושין הל' ט ועיין במ"מ סמג עשין מח טוש"ע אה"ע סי' קלב סעיף ד:

**רבינו חננאל**

והדר ביה אביי מגופה דמתניתין ואסיקנא דאם איתא דפרעה איבעי ליה למיקרעיה לגיטה ולמכתב על גביה גיטה דנן דקרעינוהי לאו משום דפסול הוא אלא משום דלא תיהדר ותיגביה ביה זימנא אחריתי. ואי טעין לא הוינא ידע האי דינא ואף לא גירשתיה א) שידיעני לא אמר כלום אלא הוציאה גט גובה כתובתה. סוגיא דשמעתא אלמנה מן האירוסין אם כתב לה אית לה מנה מאתים אבל תוספת לית לה אע"ג דכתב לה: מתני' מצא גיטי נשים ושחרורי עבדים וכו' עד שאני אמר כתובין היו ונמלך עליהם שלא ליתנם מדמותבינן מינה לאביי דאמר עדיו בחתומיו זכין לו ופריק הני מילי היכא דמטא שטרא בידיה דמקבל ש"מ דהא מתני' הלכתא היא וכל שטרא מתנה דלא מטא לידיה דמקבל לא זכה ביה וצריך לברורי דמטא לידיה אי לא נפיק מתותי ידיה. ודייקינן מינה הא אמר תנו נותנין ואפי' לזמן מרובה. ורמינן עלה הא דתנן המביא גט ממדינת הים ואבד לו מצאו לאלתר כשר ואם לאו פסול ופריק רבא הכי מתני' אפי' במקום שהשיירות מצויות והוא שלא הוחזקו שני יוסף בן שמעון בעיר אחת. כלומר דלא הוחזק באותה העיר אדם אחר ששמו כשם זה שגט זה כתוב כשמו הלכך אם הבעל מודה ואמר תנוהו לאשה נותנין זה הגט לזו האשה ואפי' לזמן [מרובה]. ואוקים להא דתנן המביא גט מצאו לאלתר כשר ואם לאו פסול במקום שהשיירות מצויות והוא שהוחזקו שני יוסף בן שמעון

**חשק שלמה על ר"ח**

א) אולי צ"ל לא גרשתיה בב"ד שידעו אותי לא אמר כלום וכו'.

מַאי גּוֹבָה אֶת הַכּ – what does **SHE COLLECTS** ***EVERYTHING*** mean? f the husband did not write a *kesubah* to his wife, what additional bligations are there? מָנֶה וּמָאתַיִם הוּא דְּאִית לָהּ – **She has** claim only to the basic obligation of either **one hundred or two** **undred** *zuz*![1]

The Gemara proposes an alternative proof that an *arusah* ollects the basic *kesubah* obligation, even if her husband did not rite her a *kesubah*:

וְאֶלָּא מִדְּתָנֵי רַב חִיָּיא בַּר אַמ – **Rather,** it may be deduced **from a** **araisa taught by Rav Chiya bar Ami:** אִשְׁתּוֹ אֲרוּסָה – If [A AN'S] *ARUSAH* dies, the law is that לֹא אוֹנֵן – HE DOES NOT OURN AS AN *ONEIN*,[2] וְלֹא מִטַּמֵּא לָהּ – AND if he is a Kohen HE AY NOT CONTAMINATE HIMSELF with *tumah* FOR HER.[3] וְכֵן - LIKEWISE, if her husband dies, הִיא לֹא אוֹנֶנֶת – SHE DOES NOT OURN AS AN *ONENES*, וְלֹא מִטַּמְּאָה לוֹ – AND SHE NEED NOT ONTAMINATE HERSELF with *tumah* FOR HIM.[4] מֵתָה אֵינוֹ יוֹרְשָׁהּ - If SHE DIES, [HER HUSBAND] DOES NOT INHERIT HER.[5] מֵת הוּא גּוֹבָה כְּתוּבָּתָ – If HE DIES, SHE COLLECTS HER *KESUBAH*. It seems lear from the Baraisa that a widow from *erusin* collects the esubah obligation.

The Gemara rejects this proof:

דִּלְמָא דְּכָתַב לָ – **Perhaps** the Baraisa discusses a case **where [the** **usband]** voluntarily **wrote [his** ***arusah*** **]** a *kesubah*. Ordinarily, owever, she does not collect the *kesubah* obligation. וְכִי תֵּימָא דְּכָתַב לָהּ מַאי לְמֵימְרָ – **And if you will say: If he wrote** a *kesubah* or her, **why** is it necessary for the Baraisa **to state** that she ollects it? It is obvious! מֵתָה אֵינוֹ יוֹרְשָׁהּ אִיצְטְרִיכָא לֵיהּ – **It is** **ecessary** to teach the law that if **SHE DIES, HE DOES NOT INHERIT** **ER.** The law for the collection of her *kesubah* upon his death was ncluded only incidentally. Thus, we have no definitive source that widow from *erusin* collects a *kesubah,* and we cannot say that baye reversed himself based on this unfounded obligation.

The Gemara proposes an alternative explanation for Abaye's eversal:

אֶלָּ – **Rather,** אַבַּיֵי מִגּוּפָהּ דְּמַתְנִיתִין קָא הָדַר בֵּיהּ – **Abaye** **eversed himself based on** analysis of **the Mishnah itself.** דְּאִי סָלְקָא דַּעְתָּךְ בְּמָקוֹם שֶׁאֵין כּוֹתְבִין כְּתוּבָּה עָסְקִינַן – **For if you suppose we discuss,** in the Mishnah, **a locale where they do not write a** ***kesubah,*** and she may collect the *kesubah* obligation דְּגֵט הַיְינוּ כְּתוּבָּתָהּ – **because the** ***get*** **is** in place of **her** ***kesubah,*** and not because in general one may not claim he paid an obligation of the court, אַטּוּ גֵּט מָנֶה מָאתַיִם כְּתִיב בֵּיהּ – you may ask: **Is** the basic *kesubah* obligation of **one hundred or two hundred** *zuz* **written in a** ***get?*** How does the *get* demonstrate that the *kesubah* obligation has not been paid?

וְכִי תֵּימָא – **And if you will say** that כֵּיוָן דְּתַקִּינוּ רַבָּנָן לְמִגְבָּא לָהּ – **since the Rabbis instituted that [a divorcee] collects** her *kesubah* obligation, כְּמַאן דִּכְתִיב בֵּיהּ דָּמֵי – then in a place where they do not write a *kesubah* **it is as if [the amount of the obligation] is written in [the** ***get*** **],**[6] לִטְעוֹן וְלֵימָא פְּרַעְתִּי – **let [the husband]** nevertheless **claim: "I paid** this obligation!" וְכִי תֵּימָא דְּאָמְרִינַן לֵיהּ – **And if you will say that we tell [the husband]:** אִי פְּרַעְתָּהּ – **"If you** indeed **paid her,** אִיבָּעֵי לָךְ לְמִיקְרְעֵיהּ – **you should have ripped [the** ***get*** **],"** אָמַר לָן לֹא שְׁבַקְתַּן – **he may respond to us: "She did not allow me** to rip the *get*, אָמְרָה – for **she said:** בְּעֵינָא לְאִנְסוֹבֵי בֵּיהּ – **'I need to use it** as proof of my divorced status in order **to remarry.' "** וְכִי תֵּימָא אָמְרִינַן לֵיהּ – **And if you will say that we tell [the husband]:** אִיבָּעֵי לָךְ לְמִיקְרְעֵיהּ – **"You should have ripped [the** ***get*** **],** וּמִכְתַּב אַגַּבֵּיהּ – **and written on its reverse** side: גִּיטָּא דְּנַן דִּקְרַעֲנוּהוּ – **'This** ***get*** **we have ripped,** לֹא מִשּׁוּם דְּגִיטָּא פְּסוּלָה הוּא – **not because it is an invalid** ***get,*** אֶלָּא כִּי הֵיכִי דְּלֹא תִּגְבֵּי בֵּיהּ זִמְנָא אַחֲרִיתִי – **but so that [the woman] should not reuse it again to collect** her *kesubah*,' " one may respond: אַטּוּ כָּל דְּמַגְבֵּי בְּבֵי דִינָא מַגְבֵּי – **Does everyone who pays** an obligation **– pay in** court? The husband was unaware that he could rip the *get* and still let his divorcee retain it as proof of divorce.[7] If so, the unripped *get* produced by the woman does not demonstrate that the *kesubah* obligation was not paid. Abaye therefore reversed his position, concluding from the Mishnah that one is never believed to claim payment of a court-imposed obligation without proof.

## Mishnah

מָצָא גִּיטֵּי נָשִׁים – If **one found bills of divorce,**[8] וְשִׁחְרוּרֵי עֲבָדִים – **or bills of emancipation,**[9] דְּיָיתֵיקֵי – or sickbed **wills,**[10] מַתָּנָה – or **gift** documents,[11] וְשׁוֹבָרִין – **or receipts,** הֲרֵי זֶה לֹא יַחֲזִיר – **he should not return** them to the recipients named in them. שֶׁאֲנִי אוֹמֵר – **For I say** כְּתוּבִין הָיוּ – that

NOTES

1. Depending on her status prior to her marriage (see 17b note 11).

2. *Onein* – first-day mourning. On the day that one's close relative dies, ne is classified an *onein* (*onenes* for female), and he may not eat ortions of offerings or *maasar sheni* (see *Rashi; Yevamos* 73,74). A an's *arusah*, however, is not a sufficiently close relative to bring about *nein* status (see next note).

3. A Kohen may not come in contact with a dead body, unless the eceased is one of seven close relatives. That a wife is one of these xceptions is derived from the words *except for his flesh* (*Leviticus* 21:2) which the Sages take to refer to a wife [who is considered "one flesh" with her husband (*Genesis* 2:24); see *Rashbam* to *Bava Basra* 111b ד"ה שאר]. An *arusah,* with whom relations are forbidden (see 17b note 8), is ot included in this (*Rashi;* see *Yevamos* 22b).

4. The Baraisa cannot possibly refer to the previously mentioned rohibition of defilement (see previous note), for the Torah limits this to ale Kohanim. Rather, the Baraisa refers to one's obligation (Kohen nd non-Kohen alike) to contaminate himself for his seven close elatives, as derived from the verse: לָהּ יִטַּמָּא, *he* ***shall*** *contaminate imself for her* (ibid. v. 3). [In fact, if a *Kohen* refuses to contaminate imself when a close relative dies, we forcibly contaminate him (see *evachim* 100a).] An *arusah* need not contaminate herself for her eceased husband, who is not considered a sufficiently close relative (see *ashi;* cf. *Rambam* and *Raavad, Hil. Aveilus* 2:6, with commentaries).

5. The husband's right to inherit his wife's estate is derived from the verse: לִשְׁאֵרוֹ הַקָּרֹב אֵלָיו מִמִּשְׁפַּחְתּוֹ וְיָרַשׁ אֹתָהּ, which is interpreted homiletically, *his flesh, who is close to him, from his family; he will inherit her* (*Numbers* 27:11; see *Bava Basra* 111b). Since relations with an *arusah* are forbidden, she is not considered "his flesh" (*Rashi*).

6. Since the basic obligation of one hundred or two hundred *zuz* is fixed (*Rashi*).

7. In the place where he paid the *kesubah* to his ex-wife, there was no *beis din* to instruct him about the proper procedure (*Rashi*).

8. Literally: women's documents. The term *get* means a document. Though it is used primarily in reference to divorce documents, it is occasionally applied generically to other documents as well. To make itself clear, the Mishnah explicitly states that here it refers to a woman's *get,* i.e. a bill of divorce (see *Tosafos* to *Gittin* 2a ד"ה המביא).

9. Literally: emancipations of slaves.

10. Wills are generally not effective in Torah law; unless a formal gift has been made before death, property passes automatically to the rightful heirs defined by the Torah. The Rabbis, however, decreed that a seriously ill person [שְׁכִיב מְרַע] be able to transfer his property to others by verbal declaration, without a formal act of *kinyan.* They instituted this decree out of concern that a seriously ill person, fearing that his end was near, might deteriorate mentally if he were unable to arrange his affairs according to his wishes (*Bava Basra* 147b). A דְּיָיתֵיקֵי is a document recording such a sickbed testament.

11. I.e. a document for transferring property to another as a gift.

***erusin*** **has** a right to collect the ***kesubah*** obligation? אִילֵימָא מֵהָא דִּתְנַן – **If you say** it is **from that which we learned in a Mishnah:**[10] נִתְאַרְמְלָה אוֹ נִתְגָּרְשָׁה – If [A WOMAN] IS WIDOWED OR DIVORCED, בֵּין מִן הָאֵירוּסִין וּבֵין מִן הַנִּישׂוּאִין – WHETHER FROM *ERUSIN* OR *NISUIN,* גּוֹבָה אֶת הַכֹּל – SHE COLLECTS EVERYTHING [i.e. both the basic *kesubah* obligation[11] and any additional obligations voluntarily accepted by the husband], this is not a valid source. דִּלְמָא הֵיכָא דִּכְתַב לָהּ – **Perhaps** the Mishnah states that an *arusah* collects the *kesubah* obligation only **where [her husband]** voluntarily **wrote her** a *kesubah.* However, if a husband chooses not to obligate himself, an *arusah* does not collect the *kesubah* obligation. – ? –

The Gemara dismisses a possible rejoinder:

וְכִי תֵּימָא מַאי לְמֵימְרָא – **And if you will say: Why,** then, was it necessary **to say** such an obvious ruling in the Mishnah? If a husband writes a *kesubah* for his wife, of course she may collect! לְאַפּוּקֵי מִדְּרַבִּי אֶלְעָזָר בֶּן עֲזַרְיָה – It is necessary to teach this ruling in order **to exclude** from halachah the opinion of **R' Elazar ben Azaryah,** דְּאָמַר שֶׁלֹּא כָּתַב לָהּ אֶלָּא עַל מְנָת לְכוֹנְסָהּ – **who said** that although a husband accepted and wrote additional oblig tions to his *arusah,* **he wrote them to her only with th intention of bringing her** into *nisuin.* If the marriage is neve consummated, she cannot collect these additional obligation אִצְטְרִיכָא לֵיהּ – **It was** therefore **necessary** to teach the Mishnah ruling that even an *arusah* collects these additional obligation

The Gemara supports its contention that the Mishnah discusse a case in which the husband voluntarily wrote a *kesubah* for h wife:

דַּיְקָא נַמִּי – **Also,** the Mishnah itself **implies** this explanatio דְּקָתָנֵי – **for it taught:** גּוֹבָה אֶת הַכֹּל – SHE COLLECT EVERYTHING. אִי אָמְרַת בִּשְׁלָמָא – **It is understandable if yo say** דִּכְתַב לָהּ – that the Mishnah refers to a case in which **[th husband] wrote** a *kesubah* **for [his wife].** יְינוּ דְּקָא תָנֵי גּוֹבָה אֶת הַכֹּל – **That,** then, **is why the Mishnah taught:** SHE COLLECT *EVERYTHING,* to include the additional obligations that her hu band accepted and wrote in her *kesubah.* לָא אִי אָמְרַת דְּלֹא כָּתַב לָהּ – **However, if you say that** the Mishnah refers to a case i which **he did not write** a *kesubah* **for [his wife],**

NOTES

10. *Kesubos* 54b.

11. I.e. one hundred *zuz* for a non-virgin and two hundred *zuz* for a virgin

לא אמר כלום מאי טעמא כל מעשה בית דין כמאן דנקיט שטרא בידיה דמי א"ל רבי חייא בר אבא לרבי יוחנן ולא משנתינו היא זו א) אהוציאה גט ואין עמו כתובה גובה כתובתה א"ל ג) אי לאו דדלאי לך חספא לא משכחת מרגניתא תותה אמר אביי מאי מרגניתא דלמא בבמקום שאין כותבין כתובה עסקינן דגט היינו כתובתה גאבל במקום שכותבין כתובה אי נקיטא כתובה גביא אי לא לא גביא הדר אמר אביי לאו מלתא היא דאמרי דאי סלקא דעתך במקום שאין כותבין כתובה עסקינן אבל במקום שכותבין כתובה אי נקיטא כתובה גביא אי לא לא גביא אלמנה מן האירוסין במאי גביא בעדי מיתת בעל לטעון ולימא פרעתיה וכי תימא הכי נמי אם כן מה הועילו חכמים בתקנתן א"ל מר קשישא בריה דרב חסדא לרב אשי ג) ואלמנה מן האירוסין דאית לה כתובה מנא לן אילימא מהא דתנן ד) נתארמלה או נתגרשה בין מן האירוסין ובין מן הנישואין גובה את הכל דלמא היכא דכתב לה וכי תימא מאי למימרא לאפוקי מדרבי אלעזר בן עזריה דאמר דשלא כתב לה אלא על מנת לכונסה אצטריכא ליה דיקא נמי דקתני גובה את הכל אי אמרת בשלמא דכתב לה היינו דקא תני גובה את הכל אלא אי אמרת דלא כתב לה מאי

נאמן לומר פרעתי הכל במגו דאי בעי אמר אין את אשתי וא"ת דבפרק אלמנה ניזונית (כתובות דף לו. ושם ד"ה יתומים) בעי רבי יוחנן היא אמרה לא נתנו מזונות ויתומים אמרו נתננו על מי להביא ראיה והא אית ליה הכא דלא אמר כלום וי"ל דהתם מיירי במזונות דלשעבר ולא בלהבא:

לא אמר כלום. ולא מבעי' במקום שאין כותבין כתובה או במקום שכותבין ויש עדים שנשרפה כתובתה דאינו נאמן לומר פרעתי אם יש לה עדי גירושין אלא אפי' במקום שכותבין כתובה ואינה מוציאה הכתובה אינו נאמן לומר פרעתי אפי' אם היא מודה שהכתובה היא בידה וגם הגט בידה נפרעת בעדי הגט גרידא ואע"ג דבמה שנשאר שטר כתובה בידה הוא מפסיד שאם תחזור ותתבע הכתובה הוא יכתוב שובר שלא תגבה פעם שניה ואפילו אם יפסיד שוברו יכול לומר פרעתי מנה מגו דאלמנה נשאתיך אם אין לה עדי הינומא או פרעתי הכל במגו דאין את אשתי אם אין לה עידי קדושין אבל עכשיו שהכתובה היא בידה תגבה שנית מאתים אם יפסיד שוברו שכתוב בכתובה בתולתא דא מ"מ נפרעת בעדי גירושין לבד בלא חזרת כתובתה וגט דר' יוחנן אית ליה פרק גט פשוט (ב"ב דף קעא: ושם) כותבין שובר:

הוציאה גט [ואין עמו כתובה] גובה כתובתה. והכי פירושא דמתני' לר' יוחנן הוציאה גט אפי' עדי הגט ואע"פ שמודה שכתובה וגט בידה נפרעת בעדי הגט דכותבין שובר הוציאה כתובתה ואין עמה גט פי' עדי הגט היא אומרת אבד גיטי שהלכו להם עדי הגט והוא אומר פרעתי ואבד שוברי שעשו לי שלא תגבה שנית נאמן במגו דאי בעי אמר לא גרשתיך וא"ת אם אמר לא גרשתיך יתחייב לה שאר כסות ועונה וי"ל דטענו חטין והודה לו בשעורין פטור אף מן השעורין כדאיתא בהמניח (ב"ק דף לה:) והא דתניא ברים שני דייני גזירות (כתובות דף קז:) האשה שאמרה גרשני בעלי מתפרנסת עד כדי כתובתה התם שמא אם היה הבעל בפנינו היה מודה לדבריה אבל אם היה אומר לא גרשתיך פטור אף מן המזונות וא"ת והיכי מצי אמר לא גרשתיך הא איהי מהימנא דאמר רב המנונא ה) אשה שאמרה לבעלה גירשתני נאמנת יש לומר אם תובעת כתובתה או אם יש קטטה בינו לבינה אינה נאמנת כמו במת בעלה דנאמנת ובזה הענין אינה נאמנת בפ' האשה שהלכה (יבמות דף קטז. קיז.) ומן הסכנה ואילך שירצה להביא עדי הגט נפרעת אע"פ שיש לו מגו ואע"ג דבשילהי הכותב (כתובות דף פט: ושם) פריך אי ליכא עדי גירושין במאי גביא ליהמניה במגו היינו דוקא לרב דלית ליה דר' יוחנן דאמר הכא דלא אמר כלום אבל לר' יוחנן שיפה כחה קודם הסכנה שאינו נאמן לומר פרעתי לאחר הסכנה נמי יש ליפות כחה דלא יועיל מגו שלו ואיירי כולה מתני' אף במקום שכותבין כתובה ואביי נמי מסיק כר' יוחנן ומוקי מתני' אף במקום שכותבין כתובה וקשה דבפרק גט פשוט (ב"ב דף קעא:) אמר אביי אבד שוברו של זה יאכל הלה וחדי משמע דסבר דאין כותבין שובר וא"כ הוציאה גט ואין עמו כתובה אמאי נפרעת הא כיון דמפסיד במה שנשאר שטר כתובה בידה כדפירש' לא יפרע עד שתוציא כתובה ויקרעוה ויש לומר דאביי קבל דברי רבא דאמר עבד לוה לאיש מלוה ובפרק המקנא (סוטה דף ז: ושם ד"ה אמר) דתנן אמרה נטמאתי שוברת כתובתה ופריך בגמ' ש"מ דכותבין שובר אמר אביי תני מקרעת דהויא בעלמא הוא כלומר מהכא לא תדוק שגם רבא דאית ליה כותבין שובר דחי התם במקום שאין כותבין כתובה ושמואל דאית ליה אין כותבין שובר ומוקי הך מתני' פרק הכותב במקום שאין כותבין כתובה מצי סבר כר' יוחנן דלא אמר כלום והוציאה הגט היינו עדי הגט ואע"פ שמפסיד בגט שנשאר בידה שאם לא היה בידה יכול לומר פעם אחרת אם יפסיד שוברו לא גרשתיך אם אין לה עדי הגט מ"מ היא תאמר בעינא לאנסובי ביה דלית ליה דכתבינן ביה גיטא דנן קרענוהו כאביי דבסמוך והוי כמו היכא דלא אפשר דכתבינן שובר כדאיתא בשילהי הכותב (כתובות דף פט: ושם) כתובה ואין עמה גט שכך אירע שכתב לה ואין עמה גט היינו עדי הגט לא יפרע דנאמן לומר פרעתי מגו דלא גרשתיך ומן הסכנה ואילך גובה אפילו בלא עדי הגט כדפרישית לר"י ורב מוקי התם מתני' בין במקום שאין כותבין כתובה בין במקום שכותבין כתובה וגביא מנה מאתים ע"י שטר גט וקרעינן ליה דלא תיהדר ותגבי ביה וכתבינן ע"ג גיטא דנן כו' ופליג אאביי דבסמוך ותוספת ע"י כתובה לבדה עם עדי הגט שלא יהא לו מגו דלא גרשתיך ופליג נמי אדרבי יוחנן דאמר לא אמר כלום וגביא בעדי הגט גרידא:

אי לאו דדלאי לך חספא כו'. וא"ת וכי דרך למצא מרגליות תחת חרסי' ומפרש ר"ת דבקרקעית הים אבנים רחבות ונראות כחרסים ותחתיהן נמצאים המרגליות ובהחובל (ב"ק דף צא.) נמי אמרינן ללת במים אדירים והעלית ביד' חרס:

אלמנה מן האירוסין במאי גביא. וא"ת אלמנה מן הנישואין ובמקום שאין כותבין כתובה לפרוך במאי גביא אי לא אמרינן דלא אמר כלום דמן האירוסין אין יכול להוכיח דאית לה כתובה ולפרוך מן הנישואין במקום שאין כותבין וי"ל דבמקום שאין כותבין אתי שפיר דאינו נאמן לומר פרעתי כיון דלא נתקנה כתובה באותו מקום אלא במקום שכותבין בשלמא אי לא נתקנה כתובה אלא בשביל תוספת אבל מנה ומאתים אינו נאמן לומר פרעתי להכי מן האירוסין דאין לה תוספת לא תקינו כתובה אבל אי אף משום מנה ומאתים תקנו לכתוב כתובה דנאמן לומר פרעתי מן האירוסין נמי יהא נאמן לומר פרעתי ויתקנו לכתוב כתובה:

מן האירוסין מנא ליה דאית לה כתובה. ולא מצי למיפשט מהא דתניא פ' מי שמת (ב"ב ד' קמה.) המארס את האשה בתולה גובה מאתים כו' דאיכא לאוקמי נמי בדכתב לה וסיפא איצטריך ליה דקתני מקום שנהגו להחזיר קדושין כו' ומ"מ אמת הוא דארוסה יש לה כתובה אפי' לא כתב לה כדמוכח פרק האומר (קדושין ד' סה. ושם) דקאמר היא אומרת קדשתני והוא אומר לא קדשתיך הוא מותר בקרובותיה ואם נתן גט מעצמו כופין אותו ונותן לה כתובה והתם ע"כ לא כתב לה דאי כתב לה היכי מצי למימר לא קדשתיך דאין דרך לכתוב כתובה קודם קדושין וכן מוכח פרק נערה (כתובות ד' מד.) וכאן אינו רוצה להוכיח אלא מן ברייתא או מן משנה ולא מן מימרות האמוראים אי נמי הכי קבעי באלמנה מן האירוסין דלא תגבי בעדי מיתה דליטעון ולימא פרעתיה אבל בגרושה אף מן האירוסין פשיטא ליה דאית לה כתובה דגובה בשטר גט כמו גרושה מן הנישואין במקום שאין כותבין וקורעין הגט וכתוב אגביה גיטא דנן כו' ובמסקנא דסבר אביי כרבי יוחנן הטוען כו' דלא אמר כלום אפי' אלמנה מן האירוסין אית לה כתובה ו):

אטו

---

עין משפט
נר מצוה

קנג א ב ג מיי' פט"ז מהל' אישות הל' כח סמג עשין מח טוש"ע אה"ע סי' ק סעי' יב:

קנד ד מיי' פ"י שם הל' יא ועיין שם במ"מ סמג שם טוש"ע אה"ע סי' נה סעי' ו:

רבינו חננאל

נמחל שעבודו ומפסדו לי. הלכך לא חיישינן דהכא לית ליה [רווחא] אבל היכא דאית ליה רווחא חיישינן. אמר ר' חייא בר אבא א"ר יוחנן הטוען אחר מעשה ב"ד לא אמר כלום. ואמר ליה ר' חייא ר' לא משנתינו היא זו הוציאה גט ואין עמו כתובה גובה כתובתה כלומר לא גרש עד שבא בב"ד וקרע כתובתה ואחרי כן נתן לה גיטה שתקנת חכמים היא לגבות כתובת מנה מאתים בגט והנה הוא כמו מעשה ב"ד לפיכך אין לו לטעון שפרעתי. ודחה אביי ואמר דילמא מתני' במקום שאין כותבין כתובה קתני אבל מקום שכותבין כתובה אינו גובה בגיטה אלא בכתובתה.

---

מסורת הש"ס

א) כתובות פח:, ב) [יב... לב:, מכות כא:], ג) [כת... פט:], ד) כתובות מז:, ... פט:, ה) [יבמות קט... ו) [וע"ע תוס' יומא ... ד"ה מי איכא].

ליקוטי רש"י

גובה כתובתה. ו... יכול לטעון פרע... והחזרת לי שטר כתוב... וקרעתיו משום דל... כתובה מעשה ב"ד [כתובות פט.]. דדל... הגבהתי [מכות כא:]. משכחת מרגניתא לאו דאמרי לך לא ... מיסק אדעתיך [יב... צב:]. אלמנה האירוסין. דאית כתובה בתנאי ב"ד אם כתב לה. גובה ... הכל. עיקר ותוס... שלא כתב ... התוספת אלא ... לכונסה ואם מת באיר... אין לה אלא עיקר כתו... אלא אי אמרת ד... כתב לה. ובתנאי ... הוא דגביא לאלמנה ... ומאתיים לבתולה דאית לה שהרי אין תוספת [כתובות פט...

מַאי לֹא אָמַר כְּלוּם – **he has said nothing,** i.e. he is not believed. טַעְמָא – **What is the reason?** כָּל מַעֲשֵׂה בֵּית דִּין – **Any** claimant of an obligation resulting from an **act of the court** כְּמַאן דְּנָקִיט שְׁטָרָא בִּידֵיהּ דָּמֵי – **is like one who holds in his hand a document** recording that obligation.[1]

The Gemara questions the need for R' Yochanan's teaching:

אָמַר לֵיהּ רַבִּי חִיָּיא בַּר אַבָּא לְרַבִּי יוֹחָנָן – **R' Chiya bar Abba told R' Yochanan:** וְלֹא מִשְׁנָתֵינוּ הִיא זוֹ – **Is this not** already learned in **our Mishnah?**[2] הוֹצִיאָה גֵּט – IF [A WOMAN] PRODUCES A *GET,* וְאֵין עִמּוֹ כְּתוּבָּה – BUT IT IS NOT ACCOMPANIED BY A *KESUBAH,* גּוֹבָה כְּתוּבָּתָהּ – SHE MAY nevertheless COLLECT HER *KESUBAH* money, even if the husband claims he has paid her.[3] Thus, R' Yochanan's ruling that one may not claim he paid an obligation of the court was already taught explicitly in a Mishnah. What, then, was the need for R' Yochanan's teaching?

The Gemara answers:

אָמַר לֵיהּ – **[R' Yochanan] told [R' Chiya]:** אִי לָאו דִּדְלַאי לָךְ חַסְפָּא – **"If I did not lift up for you a shard,** לֹא מַשְׁכַּחַת מַרְגָּנִיתָא תּוּתָהּ – **you would not have discovered the pearl underneath it!"**[4] If I had not taught my ruling, you would not have induced a generality from that Mishnah.[5]

The Gemara challenges:

אָמַר אַבַּיֵי – **Abaye said:** מַאי מַרְגָּנִיתָא – **What** type of **pearl** can be learned from that Mishnah; i.e. can such a generality indeed be induced? דִּלְמָא בְּמָקוֹם שֶׁאֵין כּוֹתְבִין כְּתוּבָּה עָסְקִינָן – **Perhaps** in the Mishnah **we discuss a locale where** the custom is that **they do not write a** ***kesubah,*** but rely instead on the obligation of the court, דְּגֵט הַיְינוּ כְּתוּבָּתָהּ – **for** there **a** ***get*** **is** in place of **her** ***kesubah.***[6] אֲבָל בְּמָקוֹם שֶׁכּוֹתְבִין כְּתוּבָּה – **However, in a locale where they write a** ***kesubah,*** אִי נְקִיטָא כְּתוּבָּה גָּבְיָא – **if she is holding a** ***kesubah*** **she may collect** the obligation, אִי לֹא לֹא גָּבְיָא – but **if** she is **not** holding her *kesubah,* **she may not collect** the obligation.[7] Hence, the Mishnah does not indicate that eve[n] where the creditor does not produce a document, the debtor is n[ot] believed to claim that he paid an obligation of the court. – ?

The Gemara retracts its challenge:

הֲדַר אָמַר אַבַּיֵי – **Abaye later said:** לָאו מִלְּתָא הִיא דְּאָמְרִי – **What I have said is nothing;** R' Yochanan's ruling, in fact, ma[y] be induced from the Mishnah. דְּאִי סָלְקָא דַּעְתָּךְ – **For if yo[u] suppose** בְּמָקוֹם שֶׁאֵין כּוֹתְבִין כְּתוּבָּה עָסְקִינָן – **that we discuss,** [in] the Mishnah, **a locale where they do not write a** ***kesuba[h]*** אֲבָל בְּמָקוֹם שֶׁכּוֹתְבִין כְּתוּבָּה – **but in a locale where they write** [a] ***kesubah,*** אִי נְקִיטָא כְּתוּבָּה גָּבְיָא – **if she is holding he[r]** ***kesubah,*** **she may collect** the obligation; אִי לֹא לֹא גָּבְיָא – an[d] **if** she is **not** holding her *kesubah,* **she may not collect** th[e] obligation, a difficulty arises: אַלְמָנָה מִן הָאֵירוּסִין בְּמַאי גָּבְיָא – **With what does a widow from** ***erusin*** **collect?**[8] בְּעֵדֵי מִיתַת בַּעַל – **With witnesses to her husband's death.** וְלֵימָא טָעוּן פְּרַעְתִּיהָ – But **let [the husband's heir] claim: "I have paid [th]e obligation]!"**[9] וְכִי תֵּימָא הָכִי נַמִּי – **And if you say** that, **indee[d]** an heir is believed to claim that the widow was paid, אִם כֵּן מַה הוֹעִילוּ חֲכָמִים בְּתַקָּנָתָן – **if so, what have the Sages accomplishe[d] with their enactment** of the *kesubah* obligation for an *arusa[h]*? The husband's heir can always successfully claim payme[nt] without proof! Rather, he is not believed to claim payment, and w[e] may induce from the Mishnah that one cannot successfully clai[m] without proof, that he paid any obligation of the court, even if th[e] creditor does not produce a document.

The Gemara questions Abaye's assumption that an *arusah* [is] entitled to the *kesubah* obligation:

אָמַר לֵיהּ מָר קְשִׁישָׁא בְּרֵיהּ דְּרַב חִסְדָּא לְרַב אַשִׁי – **Mar Keshisha, so[n] of Rav Chisda, told Rav Ashi:** אַלְמָנָה מִן הָאֵירוּסִין דְּאִית לָהּ כְּתוּבָּה מְנָא לָן – **And from where do we know that a widow fro[m]**

NOTES

1. Generally, there are two ways in which a plaintiff may press a claim: He can bring witnesses that attest to the creation of the obligation, e.g. they attest that a loan was given, or he can produce a document that records it. Where the claim is based on witnesses, the defendant is believed to claim that he already paid. The plaintiff's possession of a document, however, proves that the obligation is still outstanding, because we presume that the defendant would not have paid without demanding the document in return (see *Shevuos* 41a).

R' Yochanan states that the Rabbis regarded a plaintiff's demand for payment of a court-imposed obligation as if it were supported by possession of a document (see *Tosafos* to *Kesubos* 88b ד״ה הוציאה). Consequently, the defendant is not believed to claim he paid without producing a receipt (or testimony) to that effect. This is true even if a particular court-imposed obligation is known to have been recorded in a document, which the plaintiff claims he lost. The fact that he does not produce the document is not taken as proof that the debt was paid, because the document was written merely to augment the obligation of the court, not to replace it. Therefore, the plaintiff may claim that he was not careful to guard the document because he relied for collection on the obligation's status as an act of the court (*Pnei Yehoshua;* cf. *Ramban* in *Milchamos Hashem*).

2. *Kesubos* 88b. "Our Mishnah" refers to the body of Tannaic teaching codified by R' Yehudah HaNasi as the six orders of the Mishnah.

3. According to R' Yochanan, although she need not produce a *kesubah,* a *get* is needed to prove her divorce. In lieu of a *get*, she could likewise produce witnesses that she was divorced (*Tosafos;* cf. *Ramban*).

4. *Tosafos* comment that on the sea floor there are wide rocks, resembling shards, underneath which pearls are found.

R' Yochanan likens a superficial understanding of the Mishnah to a shard, and his induced ruling to a pearl.

5. You would have assumed the law to be restricted to the *kesubah* obligation rather than have induced a general rule for all court-imposed obligations (*Chochmas Manoach,* cf. *Rashba*).

6. Abaye maintains (at this point) that a court-imposed obligation is no different than an ordinary obligation; in either case the defendant [is] believed to claim he paid unless the plaintiff produces a documen[t]. Accordingly, a woman must produce her *kesubah* in order to collec[t]. However, in a locale where a *kesubah* is customarily not written, th[e] Rabbis accepted her *get* in lieu of the *kesubah*, presuming that th[e] husband would not have paid without ripping the *get* (*Ritva*).

7. The husband is believed to claim that he paid his wife. Alternativel[y], although he admits that he owes the money, he has the right to withho[ld] payment until the *kesubah* is produced, for fear that she might produ[ce] it on another occasion and collect again. [He cannot be forced to pay an[d] accept a receipt to prevent a second collection] (*Rashi*).

8. There are two stages to marriage in Jewish law. *Erusin* is effected b[y] one of several acts – most commonly by the man giving the woman a[n] object of a certain minimum value – after which the bride (known as a[n] *arusah*) is considered a married woman for most matters. However, th[e] couple do not yet live together; the woman returns to her father's hous[e] until the second stage is performed. *Nisuin* is effected when the husban[d] formally brings the woman into his home, after which the couple is full[y] married and may live together as man and wife.

Abaye presumes that an *arusah* collects the basic *kesubah* obligatio[n] (see below, note 11) when she is divorced or widowed (see Gemar[a] below). However, even in a locale where a *kesubah* is written, it wa[s] customary not to write it until *nisuin* (*Rashi*).

9. A divorcee from *erusin* can collect with her *get,* but a wido[w] from *erusin* has neither a *get* nor a *kesubah* with which to colle[ct] (*Tosafos* ד״ה מן).

[Abaye does not ask how a widow from *nisuin* can collect in a local[e] where a *kesubah* is not written. Since she has no *kesubah*, the Rabb[is] perforce allowed her to collect by presenting witnesses who testify t[o] her husband's death. However, it is not logical to assume that in [a] locale where a *kesubah* is written, a widow from *erusin* can collect b[y] merely presenting testimony of her husband's death, while a wido[w] from *nisuin* is required to produce a *kesubah* (see *Tosafos* and *To[s.] HaRosh*).]

לא אמר כלום מאי טעמא כל מעשה בית דין כמאן דנקיט שטרא בידיה דמי א"ל רבי חייא בר אבא לרבי יוחנן ולא משנתינו היא זו [א] א הוציאה גט ואין עמו כתובה גובה כתובתה א"ל [ג] אי לאו דדלאי לך חספא לא משכחת מרגניתא תותה אמר אביי מאי מרגניתא דלמא ב במקום שאין כותבין כתובה עסקינן דגט היינו כתובתה ג אבל במקום שכותבין כתובה אי נקיטא כתובה גביא אי לא לא גביא הדר אמר אביי לאו מלתא היא דאמרי דאי סלקא דעתך במקום שאין כותבין כתובה עסקינן אבל במקום שכותבין כתובה אי נקיטא כתובה גביא אי לא לא גביא אלמנה מן האירוסין במאי גביא בעדי מיתת בעל לטעון ולימא פרעתיה וכי תימא הכי נמי אם כן מה הועילו חכמים בתקנתן א"ל מר קשישא בריה דרב חסדא לרב אשי [ג] ואלמנה מן האירוסין דאית לה כתובה מנא לן אילימא מהא דתנן [ד] נתארמלה או נתגרשה בין מן האירוסין ובין מן הנישואין גובה את הכל דלמא היכא דכתב לה וכי תימא מאי למימרא לאפוקי מדרבי אלעזר בן עזריה דאמר ד שלא כתב לה אלא על מנת לכונסה אצטריכא ליה דיקא נמי דקתני גובה את הכל אי אמרת בשלמא דכתב לה היינו דקא תני גובה את הכל אלא אי אמרת דלא כתב לה מאי

נאמן לומר פרעתי הכל במגו דאי בעי אמר אין את אשתי וא"ת דבפרק אלמנה ניזונית (כתובות דף נו. ושם ד"ה יתומים) בעי רבי יוחנן היא אמרה לא נתנו מזונות ויתומים אמרו נתננו על מי להביא ראיה והא אית ליה הכא דלא אמר כלום וי"ל דהתם מיירי במזונות דלשעבר ולא בלהבא:

**לא** אמר כלום. ולא מבעי' במקום שאין כותבין כתובה או במקום שכותבין ויש עדים שנשרפה כתובתה דאינו נאמן לומר פרעתי אם יש לה עדי גירושין אלא אפי' במקום שכותבין כתובה ואינה מוציאה הכתובה אינו נאמן לומר פרעתי אפי' אם היא מודה שהכתובה היא בידה וגם הגט בידה נפרעת בעדי הגט גרידא ואע"ג דבמה שנשאר שטר כתובה בידה הוא מפסיד שאם תחזור ותתבע הכתובה הוא יכתוב שובר שלא תגבה פעם שניה ואפילו אם יפסיד שוברו יכול לומר פרעתי מנה מגו דאלמנה נשאתיך אם אין לה עדי היינומא או פרעתי הכל במגו דאין את אשתי אם אין לה עידי קדושין אבל עכשיו שהכתובה היא בידה תגבה שנית מאתים אם יפסיד שוברו שכתוב בכתובה בתולתא דא מ"מ נפרעת בעדי גירושין לבד בלא חזרת כתובתה וגט דר' יוחנן אית ליה פרק גט פשוט (ב"ב דף קעא: ושם) כותבין שובר:

**הוציאה** גט [ואין עמו כתובה] גובה כתובתה. והכי פירושא דמתני' לר' יוחנן הוציאה גט אפי' עדי הגט ואע"פ שמודה שכתובה וגט בידה נפרעת בעדי הגט דכותבין שובר הוציאה כתובתה ואין עמה גט פי' עדי הגט היא אומרת אבד גיטי שהלכו להם עדי הגט והוא אומר פרעתי ואבד שוברי שעשו לי שלא תגבה שנית נאמן במגו דאי בעי אמר לא גרשתיך וא"ת אם אמר לא גרשתיך יתחייב לה שאר כסות ועונה וי"ל דטענו חטין והודה לו בשעורין פטור אף מן השעורין כדאיתא בהמניח (ב"ק דף לה:) והא דתניא בריש שני דייני גזירות (כתובות דף קז:) האשה שאמרה גרשני בעלי מתפרנסת עד כדי כתובתה התם שמא אם היה הבעל בפנינו היה מודה לדבריה אבל אם היה אומר לא גרשתיך פטור אף מן המזונות וא"ת והיכי מצי אמר לא גרשתיך הא איהי מהימנא דאמר רב המנונא [ה] אשה שאמרה לבעלה גירשתני נאמנת יש לומר אם תובעת כתובתה או אם יש קטטה בינו לבינה אינה נאמנת כמו במת בעלה דנאמנת ובזה הענין אינה נאמנת בפ' האשה שהלכה (יבמות דף קטז. קיז.) ומן הסכנה ואילך שיראה להביא עדי הגט נפרעת אע"פ שיש לו מגו ואע"ג דבשילהי הכותב (כתובות דף פט: ושם) פריך אי ליכא עדי גירושין במאי גביא ליהמניה במגו היינו דוקא לרב דלית ליה דר' יוחנן דאמר הכא דלא אמר כלום אבל לר' יוחנן שיפה כחה קודם הסכנה שאינו נאמן לומר פרעתי לאחר הסכנה נמי יש ליפות כחה דלא יועיל מגו שלו ואיירי כולה מתני' אף במקום שכותבין כתובה ואביי נמי מסיק כר' יוחנן ומוקי מתני' אף במקום שכותבין כתובה וקשה דבפרק גט פשוט (ב"ב דף קעא:) אמר אביי אבד שוברו של זה יאכל הלה וחדי משמע דסבר דאין כותבין שובר וא"כ הוציאה גט ואין עמו כתובה אמאי נפרעת הא כיון דמפסיד במה שנשאר שטר כתובה בידה כדפירש' לא יפרע עד שתוציא כתובה ויקרעוה ויש לומר דאביי קבל דברי רבא דאמר עבד לוה לאיש מלוה ובפרק המקנא (סוטה דף ז: ושם ד"ה אמר) דתנן אמרה נטמאתי שוברת כתובתה ופריך בגמ' ש"מ דכותבין שובר אמר אביי תני מקרעת דהויא בעלמא הוא כלומר מהכא לא תדוק שגם רבא דאית ליה כותבין שובר דחי התם במקום שאין כותבין כתובה ושמואל דאית ליה אין כותבין שובר ומוקי הך מתני' פרק הכותב במקום שאין כותבין כתובה מצי סבר כר' יוחנן דלא אמר כלום והוציאה הגט היינו עדי הגט ואע"פ שמפסיד בגט שנשאר בידה שאם לא היה בידה יכול לומר פעם אחרת אם יפסיד שוברו לא גרשתיך אם אין לה עדי הגט מ"מ היא תאמר בעינא לאנסובי ביה דלית ליה דכתבין ביה גיטא דנן קרענוהו כאביי דבסמוך והוי כמו היכא דלא אפשר דכתבין שובר כדאיתא בשילהי הכותב (כתובות דף פט: ושם) כתובה ואין עמה גט שכך אירע שכתב לה ואין עמה גט היינו עדי הגט לא יפרע דנאמן לומר פרעתי מגו דלא גרשתיך ומן הסכנה ואילך גובה אפילו בלא עדי הגט כדפרישית לר"י ורב מוקי התם מתני' בין במקום שאין כותבין כתובה בין במקום שכותבין כתובה וגביא מנה מאתים ע"י שטר גט וקרעינן ליה דלא תיהדר ותגבי ביה וכתבינן ע"ג גיטא דנן כו' ופליג אאביי דבסמוך ותוספת ע"י כתובה לבדה עם עדי הגט שלא יהא לו מגו דלא גרשתיך ופליג נמי ארבי יוחנן דאמר לא אמר כלום וגביא בעדי הגט גרידא:

**אי** לאו דדלאי לך חספא כו'. וא"ת וכי דרך למצא מרגליות תחת חרסי' ומפרש ר"ת דבקרקעית הים אבנים רחבות ונראות כחרסים ותחתיהן נמצאים המרגליות ובהחובל (ב"ק דף צא.) נמי אמרי"נן צללת במים אדירים והעלית בידך חרס:

**אלמנה** מן האירוסין במאי גביא. וא"ת אלמנה מן הנישואין ובמקום שאין כותבין כתובה לפרוך במאי גביא אי לא אמרינן דלא אמר כלום דמן האירוסין אין יכול להוכיח דאית לה כתובה ולפרוך מן הנישואין במקום שאין כותבין וי"ל דבמקום שאין כותבין אתי שפיר דאינו נאמן לומר פרעתי כיון דלא נתקנה כתובה באותו מקום אלא במקום שכותבין בשלמא אי לא נתקנה כתובה אלא בשביל תוספת אבל מנה ומאתים אינו נאמן לומר פרעתי להכי מן האירוסין דאין לה תוספת לא תקינו כתובה אבל אי אף משום מנה ומאתים תקנו לכתוב כתובה דנאמן לומר פרעתי מן האירוסין נמי יהא נאמן לומר פרעתי ויתקנו לכתוב כתובה:

**מן** האירוסין מנא ליה דאית לה כתובה. ולא מצי למיפשט מהא דתניא פ' מי שמת (ב"ב ד' קמה.) המארס את האשה בתולה גובה מאתים כו' דאיכא לאוקמי נמי בדכתב לה וסיפא איצטריך ליה דקתני מקום שנהגו להחזיר קדושין כו' ומ"מ אמת הוא דארוסה יש לה כתובה אפי' לא כתב לה כדמוכח פרק האומר (קדושין ד' סה. ושם) דקאמר היא אומרת קדשתני והוא אומר לא קדשתיך הוא מותר בקרובותיה ואם נתן גט מעצמו כופין אותו ונותן לה כתובה והתם ע"כ לא כתב לה דאי כתב לה היכי מצי למימר לא קדשתיך דאין דרך לכתוב כתובה קודם קדושין וכן מוכח פרק נערה (כתובות ד' מד.) וכאן אינו רוצה להוכיח אלא מן ברייתא או מן משנה ולא מן מימרות האמוראים אי נמי הכי קבעי באלמנה מן האירוסין דלא תגבי בעדי מיתה דליטעון ולימא פרעתיה אבל בגרושה אף מן האירוסין פשיטא ליה דאית לה כתובה דגובה בשטר גט כמו גרושה מן הנישואין במקום שאין כותבין וקורעין הגט וכתוב אגביה גיטא דנן כו' ובמסקנא דסבר אביי כרבי יוחנן הטוען כו' דלא אמר כלום אפי' אלמנה מן האירוסין אית לה כתובה [ו]:
אטו

במקום שאין כותבין כתובה. אלא סומכין על תנאי ב"ד ותגבה לעולם עד שיוציא הבעל שובר דגט שמעיד שגירשה הוא מוכיח שחייב הוא לה כתובה: אי לא. נקיט לה: לא גביא. אי משום דחיישינן דלמא הדרא ומפקא כתובה וגביא זימנא אחריתי א"נ משום דאי בעי אמר פרעתיה: לאו מלתא היא דאמרי. דבמקום שכותבין שטר כתובה יכול לטעון פרעתי דאם כן אלמנה מן האירוסין דאף במקום שכותבין אין כותבין מן האירוסין: במאי גביא. כתובה על כרחך בעדי מיתת בעל: לטעון. יורש ולומר פרעתי': בתקנתן. שתקנו כתובה לארוסה והלא הכל יטענו פרעתי: גובה את הכל. בין כתובה של תנאי ב"ד דהיינו מנה לאלמנה ומאתים לבתולה בין תוספת: שלא כתב לה. את התוספת: דיקא נמי. דבכתב לה מיירי:
מאי



קנג א ב ג מיי' פט"ז מהל' אישות הל' כח סמג עשין מח טוש"ע אה"ע סי' ק סעי' יב:
קנד ד מיי' פ"י שם הל' יא ועיין שם במ"מ סמג שם טוש"ע אה"ע סי' נה סעי' ו:

רבינו חננאל

נמחל שעבודו ומפסדו לי. הלכך לא חיישינן דהכא לית ליה [רווחא] אבל היכא דאית ליה רווחא חיישינן. אמר ר' חייא בר אבא א"ר יוחנן הטוען אחר מעשה ב"ד לא אמר כלום. ואמר ליה ר' חייא ר' לא משנתינו היא זו הוציאה גט ואין עמו כתובה גובה כתובתה כלומר לא גרש עד שבא בב"ד וקרע כתובתה ואחרי כן נתן לה גיטה שתקנת חכמים היא לגבות כתובת מנה מאתים בגט והנה הוא כמו מעשה ב"ד לפיכך אין לו לטעון שפרעתי. ודחה אביי ואמר דילמא מתני' במקום שאין כותבין כתובה קתני אבל מקום שכותבין כתובה אינו גובה בגיטה אלא בכתובתה.

מסורת הש"ס

א) כתובות פח:, ב) [יבמות לב:, מכות כא:], ג) [כתובות פט:], ד) כתובות מז., נד: פט:, ה) [יבמות קטז.] ו) [וע"ע תוס' יומא יט ד"ה מי איכא].

ליקוטי רש"י

גובה כתובתה. ואינו יכול לטעון פרעתי והחזרת לי שטר כתובתי וקרעתיו משום דתנאי כתובה מעשה ב"ד הוא [כתובות פט.]. דדלאי הגבהתי [מכות כא:]. לא משכחת מרגניתא. אי לאו דאמרי לך לא הוי מיסק אדעתיך [יבמות צב:]. אלמנה מן האירוסין. דאית לה כתובה בתנאי ב"ד אם לא כתב לה. גובה את הכל. עיקר ותוספת. שלא כתב לה התוספת אלא ע"מ לכונסה ואם מת באירוסין אין לה אלא עיקר כתובה. אלא אי אמרת דלא כתב לה. ובתנאי ב"ד הוא דגביא לאלמנה מנה ומאתיים לבתולה הוא דאית לה שהרי אין כאן תוספת [כתובות פט:].

ואמר פרעתי נאמן בא מלוה לכתוב אין כותבין ונותנין לו חייב אתה ליתן לו ואמר פרעתי אינו נאמן בא מלוה לכתוב כותבין ונותנין לו רב זביד משמיה דר"נ אמר [א]בין צא תן לו בין חייב אתה ליתן לו ואמר פרעתי נאמן [ב]בא מלוה לכתוב אין כותבין ונותנין לו אלא אי איכא לפלוגי הכי הוא דאיכא לפלוגי [ג]אמרו לו צא תן לו ואמר פרעתי והעדים מעידין אותו שלא פרעו (א) וחזר ואמר פרעתי) הוחזק כפרן לאותו ממון [ד]חייב אתה ליתן לו ואמר פרעתי והעדים מעידין אותו שלא פרע וחזר ואמר פרעתי לא הוחזק כפרן לאותו ממון מ"ט אשתמוטי הוא קא משתמיט מיניה סבר עד דמעיינו בי רבנן בדיני אמר רבה בר בר חנה א"ר יוחנן [ה]מנה לי בידך והלה אומר אין לך בידי כלום והעדים מעידים אותו שיש לו וחזר ואמר פרעתי הוחזק כפרן לאותו ממון כי הא דשבתאי בריה דרבי מרינוס כתב לה לכלתיה איצטלא דמילתא בכתובתה וקבלה עליה אירכס כתובתה אמר (ג) להו) לא היו דברים מעולם [ג]אתו סהדי ואמרי אין כתב לה לסוף אמר להו פרעתיה אתא לקמיה דרבי חייא א"ל הוחזקת כפרן לאותה איצטלא: א"ר אבין א"ר אלעא א"ר יוחנן [ו]היה חייב לחבירו שבועה ואמר נשבעתי והעדים מעידין אותו שלא נשבע [ד](וחזר ואמר נשבעתי) הוחזק כפרן לאותה שבועה אמרוה קמיה דר' אבהו אמר להו מסתברא מלתא דרבי אבין [ז]שנתחייב שבועה בב"ד אבל חייב עצמו שבועה [ה][נאמן] עביד איניש דמקרי ואמר אהדרוה קמיה דר' אבין אמר להו אנא נמי בב"ד אמרי איתמר נמי א"ר אבין א"ר אלעא א"ר יוחנן היה חייב לחבירו שבועה בב"ד ואמר נשבעתי והעדים מעידין אותו שלא נשבע [ו](וחזר ואמר נשבעתי) הוחזק כפרן לאותה שבועה א"ר אסי א"ר יוחנן [ח]המוצא שטר חוב בשוק וכתוב בו הנפק וכתוב בו זמנו בו ביום יחזירו לבעלים אי משום כתב ללות ולא לוה הא כתוב בו הנפק אי משום פרעון לפריעה בת יומא לא חיישנן א"ל ר' זירא לר' אסי מי א"ר יוחנן הכי הא את הוא דאמרת משמיה דר' יוחנן [ז][ט]שטר שלוה בו ופרעו אינו חוזר ולוה בו שכבר נמחל שיעבודו אימת אילימא למחר וליומא חרא מאי אריא שכבר נמחל שעבודו תיפוק ליה דהוה ליה מוקדם ותנן [ח][י]שטרי חוב המוקדמין פסולין אלא לאו ביומיה אלמא פרעי אינשי ביומיה א"ל מי קא אמינא דלא פרעי כלל דלא שכיחי אינשי דפרעי ביומיה קא אמינא רב כהנא אמר [כ]כשחייב מודה אי הכי מאי למימרא מהו דתימא האי מפרע פרעיה והאי דקא אמר לא פרעתיה משום דקבעי מהדר למזפא ביה זמנא אחריתי ולפשיטי דספרא חייש קמ"ל דאם כן מלוה גופיה לא שבק סבר שמעי בי רבנן ומפסדי לי מאי שנא מהא דתנן [ט]מצא שטרי חוב אם יש בהן אחריות נכסים לא יחזיר ואוקימנא כשחייב מודה ומשום שמא כתב ללות בניסן ולא לוה עד תשרי ואתי למטרף לקוחות מניסן ועד תשרי שלא כדין ולא אמרינן דא"כ מלוה גופיה לא שביק דא"ל כתוב שטרא אחרינא בתשרי דדלמא שמעי רבנן ומפסדי לי אמרי התם משום דאית ליה רווחא דקא טריף לקוחות מניסן ועד תשרי מינח ניחא ליה ולא אמר ולא מידי הכא כיון דלית ליה רווחא דסוף סוף שטרא האידנא כתיב (א) מאי איכא דקטריף לקוחות בשטר שנמחל שיעבודו לא שביק: אמר רבי חייא בר אבא א"ר יוחנן הטוען אחר מעשה ב"ד לא

## רש"י

ואמר. לאחר זמן: פרעתי. ע"פ ב"ד: נאמן. ובשבועת היסת: בא מלוה. לפנינו לכתוב לו אדרכתא עליו אין כותבין ונותנין לו: אינו נאמן. לישבע אלא שכנגדו נשבע ונוטל דכיון דתחילתו הוצרך לתובעו לדין אין דרכו למהר לפרוע עד שיפסקו דינו פסק גמור: ואמר פרעתי. לאחר זמן ע"פ ב"ד: והעדים מעידים אותו שלא פרע. בפנינו תבעו לפרוע לו ע"פ ב"ד ולא פרעו הואיל ובפניהם העיז לעבור ע"פ ב"ד אינו נאמן שוב לומר פרעתיו שלא בעדים: הוחזק כפרן לאותו ממון. שאין נאמן עוד עליו לומר החזרתי ופרעתי עד שיפרע בעדים: לא הוחזק כפרן. ונשבע שפרעו ואע"פ שלא פרעו מיד כשתבעו בפני עדים ואין זה מעיז בב"ד דכיון דלא פסקו לו פסק גמור נשמט ממנו סבר כו': אצטלא. לבוש: הוחזק כפרן לאותה אצטלא. עד שיפרע: הוחזק כפרן לאותה שבועה. לומר נשבעתי עד שישבע בפנינו: כשנתחייב שבועה בב"ד. דכיון דתבעו בעדים לקיים דברי ב"ד ולא אבה אינו נאמן לומר עוד קיימתי אחרי כן: אבל חייב עצמו שבועה. שאמר לו אשבע לך ותבעו בעדים ולא אבה ואחר כך אמר נשבעתי נאמן ואע"ג דקמי עדים דחייה: עביד איניש דמקרי ואמר. לא אעשה מה שלא חייבוני ב"ד אלא אני בעצמי ואין זו סרבנות ותרטה אלא דחייה בעלמא: וכתוב בו זמנו בו ביום. שביום שנמצא נכתב: שכבר נמחל שעבודו. משפרע מלוה ראשונה ועל האחרונה לא נכתב והויא לה מלוה על פה וטורף לקוחות שלא כדין דאין מלוה על פה גובה מן הלקוחות: אימת. דפרעיה אימתי וחזר ולוה אימתי: אי נימא למחר. ולא ביום שנכתב: וליומא חרא. שתי תיבות הן וליום אחריו וקילור סופרים הוא: תיפוק ליה. דאפילו נכתב על מלוה זו אחרונה וכתוב בו יום מוקדם כזה הוה ליה השטר מוקדם: דלא שכיחי [אינשי] דפרעי [ביומיה] קאמינא. הלכך לא חיישינן למידי דלא שכיח ואי אתרמי הוצרכו לומר דאין חוזר ולוה בו: רב כהנא אמר. הא דא"ר יוחנן יחזיר לבעלים: כשחייב מודה. שלא פרע: שמעי בי רבנן. שנמחל שעבודו: ומפסדי לי. למטרף לקוחות משום דשטרי חוב המוקדמין פסולין דכיון דהאי דאוקמא הכי לית ליה עדיו בחתומיו זכין לו אף זה מן המוקדמין: מינח ניחא ליה. ברמאות ותלי נפשיה בספיקא ואמר דלמא לא שמעי ואיכא רווחא: מאי איכא דטריף לקוחות. מה טרפא יש בזה שלא יהא בשטר שיחזור ויכתוב לו והלא שניהם ביום אחד הלכך בשטר שנמחל שעבודו לא שביק: הטוען אחר מעשה ב"ד. דבר שהוא תנאי ב"ד כגון כתובה ומזון האשה והבנות הטוען ואמר פרעתי שלא בעדים לא אמר כלום: במקום

## תוספות

חייב אתה ליתן לו. הכא משמע דחייב אתה ליתן לו לא הוי פסק דין גמור כי אם לא ותן לו וכן משמע במרובה (ב"ק דף סט. ושם) וקשה דבפ"ק דסנהדרין (דף ו: ושם) אמרינן ה"ד גמר דין פלוני אתה חייב פלוני אתה זכאי וי"ל דהתם מקרי גמר דין לענין שאסור לבלוע לפי שיודע להיכן הדין נוטה:

רב כהנא אמר כשחייב מודה. תימה א"כ למה נקט הנפק במילתא דר' יוחנן וי"ל דנקטיה משום דיוקא דאי אין כתוב בו ביום אפילו כתוב בו הנפק דודאי לוה לא יחזיר דחיישינן לקנוניא או לפשיטי דספרא:

הטוען אחר מעשה ב"ד לא אמר כלום. אינו נאמן לומר פרעתי מעשה ב"ד קרי כל דבר שחייב לה אפי' לא כתב כגון מנה ומאתים ומזון האשה והבנות לאחר מותו וא"ת למה כותבין כתובה כיון דבלאו כתובה נמי אין נאמן לומר פרעתי וי"ל משום תוספת אבל מנה ומאתים גבייה בלא כתובה ותוספת נראה דאפי' אית לה סהדי דהתנה לה נאמן לומר פרעתי [י]ואין ראיה מכלתי' [כ]דר' שבתאי דהוה מהימן לומר פרעתי אי לאו דהוחזק כפרן דר' שבתאי ערב היה אבל בעל שמא לא היה נאמן ואין ראיה נמי מדתני לעיל (דף ז:) מלא כתובה לא יחזיר ומשמע דלא יחזיר משום תוספת שהיה נאמן לומר פרעתי דלגבי מנה ומאתים נמי מפסיד דהא נאמן לומר פרעתי מנה מגו דאי בעי אמר אלמנה נשאתיך אם אין לה עדי הינומא או אם אין לה עדי קדושין נאמן

## עין משפט נר מצוה

קמה א ב מיי' פ"ז מהל' טוען ונטען הל' ה סמג עשין לה טוש"ע ח"מ סי' לט סעי' ט וסי' עט סעי' יב:

קמו ג ד מיי' שם הל' ו סמג שם טוש"ע ח"מ סי' עט סעי' יג:

קמז ה מיי' שם פ"ו הל' א סמג שם טוש"ע ח"מ שם סעי' ה:

קמח ו ז מיי' פ"ז שם הל' ה סמג שם טוש"ע ח"מ סי' פז סעי' ט:

קמט ח מיי' פי"ח מהל' גזילה ואבידה הל' ב סמג עשין עד טוש"ע ח"מ סי' סה סעי' ז:

קנ ט מיי' פי"ד מהל' מלוה ולוה הל' ז סמג עשין לד טוש"ע ח"מ סי' מח סעי' א וסי' נז סעי' ב:

קנא י מיי' פכ"ג מהל' מלוה ולוה הל' א סמג עשין שם טוש"ע ח"מ סי' מג סעי' ז:

קנב כ מיי' פי"ח מהל' גזילה ואבידה הל' ב סמג עשין עד טוש"ע ח"מ סי' סה סעי' ז:

## רבינו חננאל

אמר רב יהודה אמר רב נחמן אמר לו ב"ד צא תן לו או חייב אתה ליתן לו ואמר פרעתי נאמן בא מלוה לכתוב אין כותבין ונותנין לו. אבל אמר לו צא תן לו ואמר נתתי ועדים מעידים אותו שלא נתן הוחזק כפרן לאותו ממון ואם אמר לו חייב אתה ליתן ואמר נתתי והעדים מעידים אותו שלא נתן לא הוחזק כפרן לאותו ממון מאי טעמא אמרינן אישתמוטי הוא דקא משתמיט סבר עד דמעייני רבנן בדיני. א) זה כגון הכופר במלוה כשר לעדות. אמר רבה בר בר חנא אמר ר' יוחנן מנה לי בידך והלה אומר אין לך עלי כלום ועדים מעידים שיש לו וחזר ואמר פרעתי הוחזק כפרן לאותו ממון. והוא שכפר בב"ד כי הא ב) בגמ' שבתאי דשבתי' כתב לכלתיה איצטלא דמילתא וקיבלה עילויה וכפר ובאו עדים והעידו שכתב לה איצטלא דמילתא חזר ואמר פרעתי. אמר ליה רב חייא כבר הוחזקת כפרן לאותה איצטלא וכן הלכה. וכן מי שנתחייב שבועה בב"ד ואמר נשבעתי ועדים מעידים אותו שלא נשבע הוחזק כפרן לאותה שבועה וחייב לישבע עכשיו. א"ר יוחנן המוצא שטר חוב וזמנו בו ביום וכתוב בו הנפק יחזירו לבעלים דאי משום [כתב] ללות ולא לוה הא כתוב בו הנפק. אי משום פרעון כיון דרובא דעלמא לא פרעי ביומיה אלא מיעוטא הוא דפרעי ביומיה למיעוטא לא חיישינן. ותוב מלוה גופיה לא שביק אמר דילמא שמעי רבנן דהאי שטרא שלוה בו ופרעו הוא וכבר

## חשק שלמה על ר"ח

א) אולי צ"ל ומטעם זה אמרי' דהכופר במלוה כשר לעדות ור"ל דהתם נמי הטעם משום דאמרי' דמישתמיטו וכדאיתא לעיל דף ו. ב) אולי צ"ל כי הא מעשה דשבתאי.

## מסורת הש"ס

מהר"מ מ"ז, ב) [צ"ל ...], ג) [אתא לקמיה ... ' חייא אתו סהדי ... מרי אין כתב לה ... ר' חייא ז"ל הב ... לסוף אמר לה ... יעתיק אמר לו ... חזקת כפרן וכו' כ"ה ... רי"ף ורא"ש והוא ...], ד) מהר"מ מ"ז, ... מהרש"ל, ו) מהר"מ ... ז) כתובות פה., גיטין ... ח) לקמן עב., סנהדרין ... ר"ה ב, ח., שביעית ... י משנה ה, בבא בתרא ... קעא., ט) לעיל יב:, [ועיין תוס' יבמות סה: ... כי הא], כ) צ"ל דשבתאי, מהרש"ל.

## הגהות הב"ח

(א) גמ' האידנא כתיב (אי) תז"מ ונ"ב גי' רש"י מי:

## ליקוטי רש"י

שכבר נמחל שעבודו. כשפרעו ובטל השטר ואין הקרקעות משועבדות שוב למלוה שניה שלא עליה נחתם השטר זה והויא לה מלוה על פה [גיטין כו:]. משפרעו בטל השטר מלאת מלוה השני' מלוה על פה ואינו גובה מן הלקוחות [כתובות פה.]. שטרי חוב המוקדמין. ליכתב קודם מלוה [סנהדרין לב.]. שהקדים זמן הכתוב בשטר ליום כמיכתו ... שנכתב השטר באחד בניסן וכן כתוב בו באחד בניסן לוה פלוני מפלוני והוא לא לוה ממנו כלום ... ט"ו בניסן גם זה קודם [רשב"ם ב"ב קנז:]. פסולין. דבעי למיטרף לקוחות מזמן הכתוב בו ועדיין לא הלוה ושטר לקוחות קודם למלוה וזה ... שטרו והוא קודם והוא שקר ואינו טורף מן המשועבדין ואפי' מן המאוחר למלוה [לקמן עב.]. לפי שרצה לטרוף לקוחות שלקחו שדה מן הלוה מזמן שבשטר ושלא כדין הוא שהרי קדמה מכירה להלואה ובשטר עדיו שהלואה קדמה ... קנסוהו מלגבות בו לא יטרוף אפילו מזמן מלוה ואינו אלא כמלוה על פה שאינו גובה מן משועבדים [ר"ה ב.]. פסול שאין לו לטרוף אלא מזמן ההלואה ואילך ודלא אביי דאמר עדיו בחתומיו זכין לו בשנים ומזין [רשב"ם ב"ב קנז:]. קנסינן היתרא אטו איסורא ופסול אפי' מזמן ... [סנהדרין שם]. אלא לאו ביומיה. אינו חוזר לוה בו ואפי' ביום מלוה ראשונה לאחר פרעון ליכא למיחש למוקדם הכי מפרשינן לה בשנים ומזין [גיטין כו:]. אחריות נכסים וכו'. שעבוד קרקעות שיגבה ... כשחייב מודה. שהלוה מודה שהשטר אינו פרוע [לעיל יב:].

הָכָ – **Here,** in the case of R' Yochanan's ruling, we are not ɔncerned the lender will accept a paid note, **כֵּיוָן דְּלֵית לֵיהּ רַוְוחָא** · **since he has no benefit** from accepting such a note. **דְּסוֹף סוֹף שְׁטָרָא הָאִידְנָא כְּתִי** – **For after all, the note was written today,** n the same day as the second loan, **מַאי אִיכָּא דְּקָטָרִיף לְקוֹחוֹת** – nd **what could he collect from purchasers** of the debtor's land ith a paid note that he could not collect with a new note written ıat day? **בִּשְׁטָר שֶׁנִּמְחַל שִׁיעְבּוּדוֹ לֹא שָׁבִיק** – Therefore, **[the** nder**] will not permit** the debtor to re-use **a note whose lien has lapsed,** for he fears discovery and loss. For this reason, R' Yochanan ruled that a note dated the day of its discovery may be returned if the debtor acknowledges it has not been paid.

The Gemara discusses another case in which a defendant is not believed to claim he paid:

**אָמַר רַבִּי חִיָּיא בַּר אַבָּא אָמַר רַבִּי יוֹחָנָן** – **R' Chiya bar Abba said in the name of R' Yochanan:** **הַטּוֹעֵן אַחַר מַעֲשֵׂה בֵּית דִּין** – **If one claims** he paid, in absence of witnesses, an obligation imposed by **an act of the court,**[38]

NOTES

38. Included in this category are the basic *kesubah* obligation of a man o his wife, the obligation of a man to pay for the food of his wife and laughters, and all other mandatory *kesubah* obligations enumerated in Tractate *Kesubos*. Even if these obligations were not recorded in a woman's *kesubah,* her husband is still obligated, and he may not claim he has paid them in absence of witnesses (*Rashi*; see 17b note 1).

ואמר פרעתי נאמן בא מלוה לכתוב אין כותבין ונותנין לו חייב אתה ליתן לו ואמר פרעתי אינו נאמן בא מלוה לכתוב כותבין ונותנין לו רב זביד משמיה דר"נ אמר [א]בין צא תן לו בין חייב אתה ליתן לו ואמר פרעתי נאמן [ב]בא מלוה לכתוב אין כותבין ונותנין לו אלא אי איכא לפלוגי הכי הוא דאיכא לפלוגי [ג]אמרו לו צא תן לו ואמר פרעתי והעדים מעידין אותו שלא פרעו (א) וחזר ואמר פרעתי) הוחזק כפרן לאותו ממון [ד]חייב אתה ליתן לו ואמר פרעתי והעדים מעידין אותו שלא פרע וחזר ואמר פרעתי לא הוחזק כפרן לאותו ממון מ"ט אשתמוטי הוא קא משתמיט מיניה סבר עד דמעיינו בי רבנן בדיני אמר רבה בר בר חנה א"ר יוחנן [ה]מנה לי בידך והלה אומר אין לך בידי כלום והעדים מעידים אותו שיש לו וחזר ואמר פרעתי הוחזק כפרן לאותו ממון כי הא דשבתאי בריה דרבי מרינוס כתב לה לכלתיה איצטלא דמילתא בכתובתה וקבלה עליה אירכס כתובתה אמר (ג) להו) לא היו דברים מעולם [ו]אתו סהדי ואמרי אין כתב לה לסוף אמר להו פרעתיה אתא לקמיה דרבי חייא א"ל הוחזקת כפרן לאותה איצטלא: א"ר אבין א"ר אלעא א"ר יוחנן [ו]היה חייב לחבירו שבועה ואמר נשבעתי והעדים מעידין אותו שלא נשבע [ז](וחזר ואמר נשבעתי) הוחזק כפרן לאותה שבועה אמרוה קמיה דר' אבהו אמר להו מסתברא מלתא דרבי אבין [ז]שנתחייב שבועה בב"ד אבל חייב עצמו שבועה [ח][נאמן] עביד איניש דמקרי ואמר אהדרוה קמיה דר' אבין אמר להו אנא נמי בב"ד אמרי איתמר נמי א"ר אבין א"ר אלעא א"ר יוחנן היה חייב לחבירו שבועה בב"ד ואמר נשבעתי והעדים מעידין אותו שלא נשבע [ט](וחזר ואמר נשבעתי) הוחזק כפרן לאותה שבועה א"ר אסי א"ר יוחנן [ח]המוצא שטר חוב בשוק וכתוב בו הנפק וכתוב בו זמנו בו ביום יחזירו לבעלים אי משום כתב ללות ולא לוה הא כתוב בו הנפק אי משום פרעון לפריעה בת יומא לא חיישינן א"ל ר' זירא לר' אסי מי א"ר יוחנן הכי הא את הוא דאמרת משמיה דר' יוחנן [י][ט]שטר שלוה בו ופרעו אינו חוזר ולוה בו שכבר נמחל שיעבודו אימת אילימא למחר וליומא חרא מאי אריא שכבר נמחל שעבודו תיפוק ליה דהוה ליה מוקדם ותנן [כ][י]שטרי חוב המוקדמין פסולין אלא לאו ביומיה אלמא פרעי אינשי ביומיה א"ל מי קא אמינא דלא פרעי כלל דלא שכיחי אינשי דפרעי ביומיה קא אמינא רב כהנא אמר [כ]כשחייב מודה אי הכי מאי למימרא מהו דתימא האי מפרע פרעיה והאי דקא אמר לא פרעתיה משום דקבעי מהדר למזפא ביה זמנא אחריתי ולפשיטי דספרא חייש קמ"ל דאם כן מלוה גופיה לא שבק סבר שמעי בי רבנן ומפסדי לי מאי שנא מהא דתנן [ל]מצא שטרי חוב אם יש בהן אחריות נכסים לא יחזיר ואוקימנא כשחייב מודה ומשום שמא כתב ללות בניסן ולא לוה עד תשרי ואתי למטרף לקוחות מניסן ועד תשרי שלא כדין ולא אמרינן דא"כ מלוה גופיה לא שביק דא"ל כתוב שטרא אחרינא בתשרי דדלמא שמעי רבנן ומפסדי לי אמרי התם משום דאית ליה רווחא דקא טריף לקוחות מניסן ועד תשרי מינח ניחא ליה ולא אמר ולא מידי הכא כיון דלית ליה רווחא דסוף סוף שטרא האידנא כתיב (א) מאי איכא דקטריף לקוחות בשטר שנמחל שיעבודו לא שביק: אמר רבי חייא בר אבא א"ר יוחנן הטוען אחר מעשה ב"ד

לא

**רש"י**

ואמר. לאחר זמן: פרעתי. ע"פ ב"ד: נאמן. ובשבועת היסת: בא מלוה. לפניו לכתוב לו אדרכתא עליו אין כותבין ונותנין לו: אינו נאמן. לישבע אלא שכנגדו נשבע ונוטל דכיון דתחילתו הולרך לתובעו לדין אין דרכו למהר לפרוע עד שיפסקו דינו פסק גמור: ואמר פרעתי. לאחר זמן ע"פ ב"ד: והעדים מעידים אותו שלא פרע. בפנינו תבעו לפרוע לו ע"פ ב"ד ולא פרעו הואיל ובפניהם העיז לעבור ע"פ ב"ד אינו נאמן שוב לומר פרעתיו שלא בעדים: הוחזק כפרן לאותו ממון. שאין נאמן עוד עליו לומר החזרתי ופרעתי עד שיפרע בעדים: לא הוחזק כפרן. ונשבע שפרעו ואע"פ שלא פרעו מיד כשתבעו בפני עדים ואין זה מעיז בב"ד דכיון דלא פסקו לו פסק גמור נשמט ממנו סבר כו': אצטלא. לבוש: הוחזק כפרן לאותה אצטלא. עד שיפרע: הוחזק כפרן לאותה שבועה. לומר נשבעתי עד שישבע בפנינו: כשנתחייב שבועה בב"ד. דכיון דתבעו בעדים לקיים דברי ב"ד ולא אבה אינו נאמן לומר עוד קיימתי אחרי כן: אבל חייב עצמו שבועה. שאמר לו אשבע לך ותבעו בעדים ולא אבה ואחר כך אמר נשבעתי נאמן ואע"ג דקמי עדים דחייה: עביד איניש דמקרי ואמר. לא אעשה מה שלא חייבוני ב"ד אלא אני בעצמי ואין זו סרבנות ותרטה אלא דחייה בעלמא: וכתוב בו זמנו בו ביום. שביום שנמצא נכתב: שכבר נמחל שעבודו. משפרע מלוה ראשונה ועל האחרונה לא נכתב והויא לה מלוה על פה וטורף לקוחות שלא כדין דאין מלוה על פה גובה מן הלקוחות: אימת. דפרעיה אימתי וחזר ולוה אימתי: אי נימא למחר. ולא ביום שנכתב: וליומא חרא. שתי תיבות הן וליום אחריו וקיצור סופרים הוא: תיפוק ליה. דאפילו נכתב על מלוה זו אחרונה וכתוב בו יום מוקדם כזה הוה ליה השטר מוקדם: דלא שכיחי [אינשי] דפרעי [ביומיה] קאמינא. הלכך לא חיישינן למידי דלא שכיח ואי אתרמי הולרכו לומר דאין חוזר ולוה בו: רב כהנא אמר. הא דא"ר יוחנן יחזיר לבעלים: כשחייב מודה. שלא פרע: שמעי בי רבנן. שנמחל שעבודו: ומפסדי לי. למטרף לקוחות משום דשטרי חוב המוקדמין פסולין דכיון דהאי דאוקמא הכי לית ליה עדיו בחתומיו זכין לו אף זה מן המוקדמין: מינח ניחא ליה. ברמאות ותלי נפשיה בספיקא ואמר דלמא לא שמעי ואיכא רווחא: מאי איכא דטריף לקוחות. מה טרפא יש בזה שלא יהא בשטר שיחזור ויכתוב לו והלא שניהם ביום אחד הלכך בשטר שנמחל שעבודו לא שביק: הטוען אחר מעשה ב"ד. דבר שהוא תנאי ב"ד כגון כתובה ומזון האשה והבנות הטוען ואמר פרעתי שלא בעדים לא אמר כלום:

במקום

**תוספות**

**חייב** אתה ליתן לו. הכא משמע דחייב אתה ליתן לו לא הוי פסק דין גמור כי אם צא ותן לו וכן משמע במרובה (ב"ק דף סט. ושם) וקשה דבפ"ק דסנהדרין (דף ו: ושם) אמרינן ה"ד גמר דין פלוני אתה חייב פלוני אתה זכאי וי"ל דהתם מקרי גמר דין לענין שאסור לבצוע לפי שיודע להיכן הדין נוטה:

**רב** כהנא אמר כשחייב מודה. תימה א"כ למה נקט הנפק במילתא דר' יוחנן וי"ל דנקטיה משום דיוקא דאי אין כתוב בו ביום אפילו כתוב בו הנפק דודאי לוה לא יחזיר דחיישינן לקנוניא או לפשיטי דספרא:

**הטוען** אחר מעשה ב"ד לא אמר כלום. אינו נאמן לומר פרעתי מעשה ב"ד קרי כל דבר שחייב לה אפי' לא כתב כגון מנה ומאתים ומזון האשה והבנות לאחר מותו וא"ת למה כותבין כתובה כיון דבלאו כתובה נמי אין נאמן לומר פרעתי וי"ל משום תוספת אבל מנה ומאתים גבייה בלא כתובה ותוספת נראה דאפי' אית לה סהדי דהתנה לה נאמן לומר פרעתי [י] ואין ראיה מכלתי' [כ] דר' שבתאי דהוה מהימן לומר פרעתי אי לאו דהוחזק כפרן דר' שבתאי ערב היה אבל בעל שמא לא היה נאמן ואין ראיה נמי מדתני לעיל (דף ז:) מגלה כתובה לא יחזיר ומשמע דלא יחזיר משום תוספת שהיה נאמן לומר פרעתי דלגבי מנה ומאתים נמי מפסיד דהא נאמן לומר פרעתי מנה מגו דאי בעי אמר אלמנה נשאתיך אם אין לה עדי הינומא או אם אין לה עדי קדושין נאמן

**עין משפט נר מצוה**

קמה א ב מיי' פ"ז מהל' טוען ונטען הל' ה סמג עשין לה טוש"ע ח"מ סי' לט סעי' ט וסי' עט סעי' יב:

קמו ג ד מיי' שם הל' ו סמג שם טוש"ע ח"מ סי' עט סעי' יג:

קמז ה מיי' שם פ"ו הל' א סמג שם טוש"ע ח"מ שם סעי' ה:

קמח ו ז מיי' פ"ז שם הל' ה סמג שם טוש"ע ח"מ סי' פז סעי' כ:

קמט ח מיי' פי"ח מהל' גזילה ואבידה הל' ב סמג עשין עד טוש"ע ח"מ סי' סה סעי' ז:

קנ ט מיי' פי"ד מהל' מלוה ולוה הל' ז סמג עשין לד טוש"ע ח"מ סי' מח סעי' א וסי' נז סעי' ב:

קנא י מיי' פכ"ג מהל' מלוה ולוה הל' א סמג עשין שם טוש"ע ח"מ סי' מג סעי' ז:

קנב כ מיי' פי"ח מהל' גזילה ואבידה הל' ב סמג עשין עד טוש"ע ח"מ סי' סה סעי' ז:

**רבינו חננאל**

אמר רב יהודה אמר רב נחמן אמר לו ב"ד צא תן לו או חייב אתה ליתן לו ואמר פרעתי נאמן בא מלוה לכתוב אין כותבין ונותנין לו. אבל אמר לו צא תן לו ואמר נתתי ועדים מעידים אותו שלא נתן הוחזק כפרן לאותו ממון ואם אמר לו חייב אתה ליתן ואמר נתתי והעדים מעידים אותו שלא נתן לא הוחזק כפרן לאותו ממון מאי טעמא אמרינן אישתמוטי הוא דקא משתמיט סבר עד דמעייני רבנן בדיני. א) זה כגון הכופר במלוה כשר לעדות. אמר רבה בר בר חנא אמר ר' יוחנן מנה לי בידך והלה אומר אין לך עלי כלום ועדים מעידים שיש לו וחזר ואמר פרעתי הוחזק כפרן לאותו ממון. והוא שכפר בב"ד כי הא ב) בגמ' שבתאי דשבתי' כתב לכלתיה איצטלא דמילתא וקיבלה עילויה וכפר ובאו עדים והעידו שכתב לה איצטלא דמילתא חזר ואמר פרעתי. אמר ליה רב חייא כבר הוחזקת כפרן לאותה איצטלא וכן הלכה. וכן מי שנתחייב שבועה בב"ד ואמר נשבעתי ועדים מעידים אותו שלא נשבע הוחזק כפרן לאותה שבועה וחייב לישבע עכשיו. א"ר יוחנן המוצא שטר חוב חמנו בו ביום וכתוב בו הנפק יחזירו לבעלים דאי משום [כתב] ללות ולא לוה הא כתוב בו הנפק. אי משום פרעון כיון דרובא דעלמא לא פרעי ביומיה אלא מיעוטא הוא דפרעי ביומיה למיעוטא לא חיישינן. ותוב מלוה גופיה לא שביק אמר דילמא שמעי רבנן דהאי שטרא שלוה בו ופרעו הוא וכבר

**חשק שלמה על ר"ח**

א) אולי צ"ל ומטעם זה אמרי' דהכופר במלוה כשר לעדות ור"ל דהתם נמי הטעם משום דאמרי' דמישתמיט וכדאיתא לעיל דף ו. ב) אולי צ"ל כי הא מעשה דשבתאי.

**מסורת הש"ס**

...הר"מ מ"ז, ב) [צ"ל ..., ג) [אתא לקמיה ... חייא אתו סהדי ...רי אין כתב לה ... ר' חייא ז"ל הב ... לסוף אמר לה ...תיך אמר לו ...זקת כפרן וכו' כ"ה ... רי"ף ורא"ש והוא ..., ד) מהר"מ מ"ז, ...הרש"ל, ו) מהר"מ ..., ז) כתובות פה., גיטין ... ח) לקמן עב., סנהדרין ... ר"ה ב., ח., שביעית ... י משנה ה, בבא בתרא ..., קעא., ט) לעיל יב:, ...עיין תוס' יבמות סה: ... כי הא], כ) צ"ל ... דשבתאי, מהרש"ל.

**הגהות הב"ח**

(א) גמ' האידנא כתיב (א) תז"מ ונ"ב גי' רש"י מי:

**ליקוטי רש"י**

...בר נמחל ...עבודו. כשפרעו ובטל ...טר ואין הקרקעות ...ועבדות שוב למלוה ...ניה שלא עליה נחתם ...ר זה והויא לה מלוה ... פה [גיטין כו:]. ...ופרעו בטל השטר ...גלאת מלוה השני' מלוה ... פה ואינו גובה מן ...קוחות [כתובות פה.]. ...טרי חוב ...מוקדמין. ליכתב קודם ...לוה [סנהדרין לב.]. ...פרישית שהקדים זמן ...חוב בשטר ליום כתיבתו ...' שנכתב השטר באחד ...יסן וכן כתוב בו באחד ...יסן לוה פלוני מפלוני ...וא לא לוה ממנו כלום ...' ט"ו בניסן גם זה ...קדם [רשב"ם ב"ב קנז:]. ...סולין. דבעי למיטרף ...קוחות מזמן הכתוב בו ...דין לא הלוה ושטר ...לקוחות קודם למלוה זה ...ולא שטרו והוא קודם ...וא שקר ואינו טורף מן ...משועבדין ואפי' מן ...מאוחר למלוה [לקמן ...ב.]. לפי שרלה לטרוף ...קוחות שלקחו שדה מן ...לוה מזמן שבשטר ושלא ...דין הוא שהרי קדמה ...כירה להלואה ובשטר ...עיד שהלואה קדמה ...ליכך קנסוהו מלגבות בו ...לא יטרוף אפילו מזמן ...מלוה ואינו אלא כמלוה ...ל פה שאינו גובה מן ...משועבדים [ר"ה ב.]. ...פסול שאין לו לטרוף אלא ...זמן ההלואה ואילך ודלא ...אביי דאמר עדיו ...חתומיו זכין לו בשנים ...ומזין [רשב"ם ב"ב קנז:]. ...קנסינן היתרא אטו ...יסורא ופסול אפי' מזמן ...ני [סנהדרין שם]. אלא ...לאו ביומיה. אינו חוזר ...לוה בו ואפי' ביום מלוה ...ראשונה לאחר פרעון ...ליכא למיחש למוקדם ...הכי מפרשינן לה בשנים ...אוחזין [גיטין כו:]. ...אחריות נכסים וכו'. ...שעבוד קרקעות שיגבה ...מהן. כשחייב מודה. ...שהלוה מודה שהשטר אינו ...פרוע [לעיל יב:].

**predated,** וּתְנַן – **for we learned in a Mishnah:** שְׁטָרֵי חוֹב הַמּוּקְדָּמִין פְּסוּלִין – NOTES OF INDEBTEDNESS THAT ARE PREDATED ARE INVALID.[28] – ! – אֶלָּא לָאו בְּיוֹמֵיהּ – **Rather, is it not** referring to a case in which the second loan is contracted **on the same day** as the first loan which is written in the note?[29] אַלְמָא – **Thus,** we see פָּרְעֵי אִינָשֵׁי בְּיוֹמֵיהּ – **people do** sometimes **pay** a loan **on the very day** it was contracted.[30] If so, why did R' Yochanan permit the return of a note dated the day of its discovery, if possibly it was paid?

The Gemara deflects the challenge:

אָמַר לֵיהּ – **[R' Assi] told [R' Zeira]:** מִי קָא אָמִינָא דְּלָא פָּרְעֵי כְּלָל – **Did I say** that R' Yochanan holds **people never repay** a loan on the same day it was contracted? דְּלָא שְׁכִיחֵי אִינָשֵׁי דְּפָרְעֵי בְּיוֹמֵיהּ קָא אָמִינָא – **I said** merely that he holds **it is uncommon for people to repay** a loan **on the same day** it was contracted. Therefore, a note dated the day of its discovery should be returned to the creditor, because we need not be concerned about the remote possibility of repayment. However, it was necessary for R' Yochanan to invalidate a paid note in the rare case it was paid on the same day it was written.

The Gemara presents an alternative explanation of R' Yochanan's ruling permitting the return of a note dated the day of its discovery:

רַב כָּהֲנָא אָמַר – **Rav Kahana said:** כְּשֶׁחַיָּיב מוֹדֶה – The note may be returned to the creditor **where the debtor acknowledges** that the debt has not been paid.

The Gemara questions the novelty of R' Yochanan's ruling according to this explanation:

אִי הָכִי – **If so,** מַאי לְמֵימְרָא – **why** was it necessary **to teach** this ruling? If the debtor acknowledges his liability, how might I reason that the note should not be returned to the creditor?

The Gemara answers:

מַהוּ דְּתֵימָא – Without this ruling **you might have said** הַאי מִפְרַע פַּרְעֵיהּ – perhaps **this [debtor] paid [the note].** וְהַאי דְּקָא אָמַר לֹא פְּרַעְתִּיו – **And [the reason]** that **he said: "I did not pay it"** is מִשּׁוּם דְּקָבָעֵי מֶהְדַּר לְמִזְפָּא בֵּיהּ זִמְנָא אַחֲרִיתִי – **because he desires to borrow with it again** from this creditor **another time,** וְלִפְשִׁיטֵי דְסָפְרָא חָיֵיס – **and he is concerned about** the additional expenditure of **the coins charged by the scribe** to write a new note.[31] If so, the note may not be returned to either the creditor or the debtor, because it is possibly invalid.[32] קָא מַשְׁמַע לָן – Therefore, **[R' Yochanan] teaches us** that we are not concerned about this possibility. דְּאִם כֵּן – **For if, in fact,** the note was already paid, מַלְוֶה גּוּפֵיהּ לֹא שָׁבֵק – **the lender himself would not permit** the debtor to re-use the note for the second loan. סָבַר – For **[the lender] thinks:** שָׁמְעֵי בֵּי רַבָּנָן – **The rabbis will hear about me** that I have re-used a note whose lien has lapsed, וּמַפְסְדֵי לִי – **and they will cause me a loss.**[33]

The Gemara questions this explanation:

מַאי שְׁנָא מֵהָא דִּתְנַן – **How does this differ from that which we learned in the Mishnah:**[34] מָצָא שְׁטָרֵי חוֹב – IF ONE FINDS NOTES OF INDEBTEDNESS, אִם יֵשׁ בָּהֶן אַחֲרָיוּת נְכָסִים – IF THEY CONTAIN A clause creating a LIEN ON the debtor's PROPERTY, לֹא יַחֲזִיר – HE MAY NOT RETURN them to either the creditor or the debtor? וְאוֹקִימְנָא – **And we interpreted**[34] that Mishnah to refer to a case כְּשֶׁחַיָּיב מוֹדֶה – **wherein [the debtor] acknowledges** that the note is unpaid, וּמִשּׁוּם שֶׁמָּא כָּתַב לִלְווֹת בְּנִיסָן וְלֹא לָוָה עַד תִּשְׁרֵי – **and** it may not be returned **because perhaps [the debtor] wrote** the note intending **to borrow in Nissan, but did not borrow until Tishrei.** וְאָתֵי לְמִטְרַף לְקוֹחוֹת מִנִּיסָן וְעַד תִּשְׁרֵי שֶׁלֹּא כְּדִין – **Thus, [the lender] may come to collect illegally from purchasers** who bought the debtor's land during the interval **from** the note's date in **Nissan until** the actual loan date in **Tishrei.**[35]

The Gemara concludes its question:

וְלָא אָמְרִינַן – **And we do not say** no harm will result from returning the note דְּאִם כֵּן – by arguing **that if, in fact,** the debtor did not borrow on the date of the note as he claims, מַלְוֶה גּוּפֵיהּ לֹא שָׁבֵיק – **the lender himself would not permit** the use of this predated note. דְּאָמַר לֵיהּ – **For he would tell [the debtor]:** כְּתוֹב שְׁטָרָא אַחֲרִינָא בְּתִשְׁרֵי – **"Write another note** now **in Tishrei,** דִּדִלְמָא שָׁמְעֵי רַבָּנַן – **because** otherwise **perhaps the rabbis will hear** that this original note is predated, וּמַפְסְדֵי לִי – **and they will cause me a loss."** Why does R' Yochanan say that a lender will prevent the debtor from re-using a paid note, whereas we do not say that he will prevent him from using a predated note?

The Gemara answers:

אָמְרֵי – **[The scholars] say:** The cases are not comparable. הָתָם – **There,** in the Mishnah, we are concerned that the lender will agree to accept a predated note. מִשּׁוּם דְּאִית לֵיהּ רַוְוחָא – **Since he has benefit** from this, דְּקָא טָרֵיף לְקוֹחוֹת מִנִּיסָן וְעַד תִּשְׁרֵי – **for he can** use the invalid note illegally **to collect from purchasers** who bought the debtor's land during the interval **from Nissan until Tishrei,** מֵינָח נִיחָא לֵיהּ – **this** deceit **is desirable to him,** וְלָא אָמַר וְלָא מִידֵּי – **and he will not tell** the debtor **anything,** hoping to avoid detection.[36] Therefore, a note whose date precedes the date of discovery may not be returned.[37]

NOTES

8. *Sheviis* 10:5. [A note whose date is earlier than the actual date that the note was drawn up is invalid, because the creditor could use it unlawfully to collect the debt from those who purchased the debtor's land prior to the obligation but after the date recorded in the note. According to R' Yochanan, a predated note is invalid even in regard to collection from those who purchased the debtor's land after the obligation was created (see below, 72a).]

9. If R' Yochanan's ruling that a paid note is invalid is limited to cases in which the second obligation was created at a later date than the original obligation, why did he limit his ruling to a paid note? Even a new note, written specifically for this second loan, is invalid if it is predated (*Rashi*). It is thus clear that R' Yochanan cannot be referring to a predated note.

9. Since he refers to such a case, R' Yochanan invalidates the note only because its lien has lapsed.

0. Since R' Yochanan discusses a case in which the second loan was contracted on the same day as the note was written, it follows that the first loan was paid on that day as well.

1. As noted above (16b note 25), this expense is the obligation of the borrower.

32. If the note is returned, it might be illegally used to collect payment for the second loan from purchasers of the debtor's property (see above, note 26).

33. The lender is concerned that the note will be invalidated, and he will be unable to collect the debt from purchasers of the debtor's property (*Rashi*; see above, note 26).

34. Above, 12b.

35. Earlier (12b-13a), the Gemara cited an Amoraic dispute as to whether the lien carried by a documented loan takes effect when the witnesses sign the note or when the loan is actually granted. The interpretation cited here – that the Mishnah's concern is for a note written in Nissan when the loan it records was not granted until Tishrei – follows the latter opinion. Hence, returning the note to the creditor sets up a danger of unlawful collection from the debtor's purchasers (*Rashi*).

36. Since use of the predated note is beneficial to him, he takes the chance that the rabbis will not hear about his trickery (*Rashi*).

37. Although the debtor admits that he has not paid, the note may not be returned, for perhaps its date precedes the obligation.

ואמר פרעתי נאמן בא מלוה לכתוב אין כותבין ונותנין לו חייב אתה ליתן לו ואמר פרעתי אינו נאמן בא מלוה לכתוב כותבין ונותנין לו רב זביד משמיה דר"נ אמר [א] בין צא תן לו בין חייב אתה ליתן לו ואמר פרעתי נאמן [ב] בא מלוה לכתוב אין כותבין ונותנין לו אלא אי איכא לפלוגי הכי הוא דאיכא לפלוגי [ג] אמרו לו צא תן לו ואמר פרעתי והעדים מעידין אותו שלא פרעו (א) (וחזר ואמר פרעתי) הוחזק כפרן לאותו ממון [ד] חייב אתה ליתן לו ואמר פרעתי והעדים מעידין אותו שלא פרע וחזר ואמר פרעתי לא הוחזק כפרן לאותו ממון מ"ט אשתמוטי הוא קא משתמיט מיניה סבר עד דמעיינו בי רבנן בדיני אמר רבה בר בר חנה א"ר יוחנן [ה] מנה לי בידך והלה אומר אין לך בידי כלום והעדים מעידים אותו שיש לו וחזר ואמר פרעתי הוחזק כפרן לאותו ממון כי הא דשבתאי בריה דרבי מרינוס כתב לה לכלתיה איצטלא דמילתא בכתובתה וקבלה עליה אירכס כתובתה אמר ([ג] להו) לא היו דברים מעולם [ג] אתו סהדי ואמרי אין כתב לה לסוף אמר להו פרעתיה אתא לקמיה דרבי חייא א"ל הוחזקת כפרן לאותה איצטלא: א"ר אבין א"ר אלעא א"ר יוחנן [ו] היה חייב לחבירו שבועה ואמר נשבעתי והעדים מעידין אותו שלא נשבע [ד] (וחזר ואמר נשבעתי) הוחזק כפרן לאותה שבועה אמרוה קמיה דר' אבהו אמר להו מסתברא מלתא דרבי אבין [ז] שנתחייב שבועה בב"ד אבל חייב עצמו שבועה [ה] [נאמן] עביד איניש דמקרי ואמר אהדרוה קמיה דר' אבין אמר להו אנא נמי בב"ד אמרי איתמר נמי א"ר אבין א"ר אלעא א"ר יוחנן היה חייב לחבירו שבועה בב"ד ואמר נשבעתי והעדים מעידין אותו שלא נשבע [ו] (וחזר ואמר נשבעתי) הוחזק כפרן לאותה שבועה א"ר אסי א"ר יוחנן [ח] המוצא שטר חוב בשוק וכתוב בו הנפק וכתוב בו זמנו בו ביום יחזירו לבעלים אי משום כתב ללות ולא לוה הא כתוב בו הנפק אי משום פרעון לפריעה בת יומא לא חיישינן א"ל ר' זירא לר' אסי מי א"ר יוחנן הכי הא את הוא דאמרת משמיה דר' יוחנן [ז] [ט] שטר שלוה בו ופרעו אינו חוזר ולוה בו שכבר נמחל שיעבודו אימת אילימא למחר וליומא חרא מאי אריא שכבר נמחל שעבודו תיפוק ליה דהוה ליה מוקדם ותנן [ח] [י] שטרי חוב המוקדמין פסולין אלא לאו ביומיה אלמא פרעי אינשי ביומיה א"ל מי קא אמינא דלא פרעי כלל דלא שכיחי אינשי דפרעי ביומיה קא אמינא רב כהנא אמר [כ] כשחייב מודה אי הכי מאי למימרא מהו דתימא האי מפרע פרעיה והאי דקא אמר לא פרעתיה משום דקבעי מהדר למזפא ביה זמנא אחריתי ולפשיטי דספרא חייש קמ"ל דאם כן מלוה גופיה לא שבק סבר שמעי בי רבנן ומפסדי לי מאי שנא מהא דתנן [ט] מצא שטרי חוב אם יש בהן אחריות נכסים לא יחזיר ואוקימנא כשחייב מודה ומשום שמא כתב ללות בניסן ולא לוה עד תשרי ואתי למטרף לקוחות מניסן ועד תשרי שלא כדין ולא אמרינן דא"כ מלוה גופיה לא שביק דא"ל כתוב שטרא אחרינא בתשרי דדלמא שמעי רבנן ומפסדי לי אמרי התם משום דאית ליה רווחא דקא טריף לקוחות מניסן ועד תשרי מינח ניחא ליה ולא אמר ולא מידי הכא כיון דלית ליה רווחא דסוף סוף שטרא האידנא כתיב (א) מאי איכא דקטריף לקוחות בשטר שנמחל שיעבודו לא שביק: אמר רבי חייא בר אבא א"ר יוחנן הטוען אחר מעשה ב"ד לא

## רש"י

**ואמר.** לאחר זמן: **פרעתי.** ע"פ ב"ד: **נאמן.** ובשבועת היסת: **בא מלוה.** לפנינו לכתוב לו אדרכתא עליו אין כותבין ונותנין לו: **אינו נאמן.** לישבע אלא שכנגדו נשבע ונוטל דכיון דתחילתו הולך לתובעו לדין אין דרכו למהר לפרוע עד שיפסקו דינו פסק גמור: **ואמר פרעתי.** לאחר זמן ע"פ ב"ד: **והעדים מעידים אותו שלא פרע.** בפנינו תבעו לפרוע לו ע"פ ב"ד ולא פרעו הואיל ובפניהם העיז לעבור ע"פ ב"ד אינו נאמן שוב לומר פרעתיו שלא בעדים: **הוחזק כפרן לאותו ממון.** שאין נאמן עוד עליו לומר החזרתי ופרעתי עד שיפרע בעדים: **לא הוחזק כפרן.** ונשבע שפרעו ואע"פ שלא פרעו מיד כשתבעו בפני עדים ואין זה מעיז בב"ד דכיון דלא פסקו לו פסק גמור נשמט ממנו סבר כו': **אצטלא.** לבוש: **הוחזק כפרן לאותה אצטלא.** עד שיפרע: **הוחזק כפרן לאותה שבועה.** לומר נשבעתי עד שישבע בפנינו: **כשנתחייב שבועה בב"ד.** דכיון דתבעו בעדים לקיים דברי ב"ד ולא אבה אינו נאמן לומר עוד קיימתי אחרי כן: **אבל חייב עצמו שבועה.** שאמר לו אשבע לך ותבעו בעדים ולא אבה ואחר כך אמר נשבעתי נאמן ואע"ג דקמי עדים דחייה: **עביד איניש דמקרי ואמר.** לא אעשה מה שלא חייבוני ב"ד אלא אני בעצמי ואין זו סרבנות ותרעה אלא דחייה בעלמא: **וכתוב בו זמנו בו ביום.** שביום שנמלא נכתב: **שכבר נמחל שעבודו.** משפרע מלוה ראשונה ועל האחרונה לא נכתב והויא לה מלוה על פה וטורף לקוחות שלא כדין דאין מלוה על פה גובה מן הלקוחות: **אימת.** דפרעיה אימתי וחזר ולוה אימתי: **אי נימא למחר.** ולא ביום שנכתב: **וליומא חרא.** שתי תיבות הן וליום אחריו וקיצור סופרים הוא: **תיפוק ליה.** דאפילו נכתב על מלוה זו אחרונה וכתוב בו יום מוקדם כזה הוה ליה השטר מוקדם: **דלא שכיחי [אינשי] דפרעי [ביומיה] קאמינא.** הלכך לא חיישינן למידי דלא שכיח ואי אתרמי הוצרכו לומר דאין חוזר ולוה בו: **רב כהנא אמר.** הא דא"ר יוחנן יחזיר לבעלים: **כשחייב מודה.** שלא פרע: **שמעי בי רבנן.** שנמחל שעבודו: **ומפסדי לי.** למטרף לקוחות משום דשטרי חוב המוקדמין פסולין דכיון דהאי דאוקמא הכי לית ליה עדיו בחתומיו זכין לו אף זה מן המוקדמין: **מינח ניחא ליה.** ברמאות ותלי נפשיה בספיקא ואמר דלמא לא שמעי ואיכא רווחא: **מאי איכא דטריף לקוחות.** מה טרפא יש בזה שלא יהא בשטר שיחזור ויכתוב לו והלא שניהם ביום אחד הלכך בשטר שנמחל שעבודו לא שביק: **הטוען אחר מעשה ב"ד.** דבר שהוא תנאי ב"ד כגון כתובה ומזון האשה והבנות הטוען ואמר פרעתי שלא בעדים לא אמר כלום:

במקום

## תוספות

**חייב** אתה ליתן לו. הכא משמע דחייב אתה ליתן לו לא הוי פסק דין גמור כי אם לא ותן לו וכן משמע במרובה (ב"ק דף סט. ושם) וקשה דבפ"ק דסנהדרין (דף ו: ושם) אמרינן ה"ד גמר דין פלוני אתה חייב פלוני אתה זכאי וי"ל דהתם מקרי גמר דין לענין שאסור לבצוע לפי שיודע להיכן הדין נוטה:

**רב** כהנא אמר כשחייב מודה. תימה א"כ למה נקט הנפק במילתא דר' יוחנן וי"ל דנקטיה משום דיוקא דאי אין כתוב בו ביום אפילו כתוב בו הנפק דודאי לוה לא יחזיר דחיישינן לקנוניא או לפשיטי דספרא:

**הטוען** אחר מעשה ב"ד לא אמר כלום. אינו נאמן לומר פרעתי מעשה ב"ד קרי כל דבר שחייב לה אפי' לא כתב כגון מנה ומאתים ומזון האשה והבנות לאחר מותו וא"ת למה כותבין כתובה כיון דבלאו כתובה נמי אין נאמן לומר פרעתי וי"ל משום תוספת אבל מנה ומאתים גבייה בלא כתובה ותוספת נראה דאפי' אית לה סהדי דהתנה לה נאמן לומר פרעתי [י] ואין ראיה מכלתי' [כ] דר' שבתאי דהוה מהימן לומר פרעתי אי לאו דהוחזק כפרן דר' שבתאי ערב היה אבל בעל עצמו לא היה נאמן ואין ראיה נמי מדתני לעיל (דף ז:) מלא כתובה לא יחזיר ומשמע דלא יחזיר משום תוספת שהיה נאמן לומר פרעתי דלגבי מנה ומאתים נמי מפסיד דהא נאמן לומר פרעתי מנה מגו דאי בעי אמר אלמנה נשאתיך אם אין לה עדי הינומא או אם אין לה עדי קדושין נאמן

## מסורת הש"ס

א) מהר"מ מ"ז, ב) [ל"ל ...ה], ג) [אתא לקמיה ...ר' חייא אתו סהדי ...אמרי אין כתב לה ...א"ל ר' חייא זיל הב ...ה לסוף אמר לה ...פרעתיך אמר לו ...הוחזקת כפרן וכו' כ"ה ... רי"ף ורא"ש והוא ...ון], ד) מהר"מ מ"ז, ...) מהרש"ל, ו) מהר"מ ...מ"ז, ז) כתובות פה., גיטין ...:, ח) לקמן עב., סנהדרין ...:, ר"ה ב, ח, שביעית ...פרק י משנה ה, בבא בתרא ...ז:, קעא., ט) לעיל יב:, [ועיין תוס' יבמות סה: ...ד"ה כי הא], כ) צ"ל דשבתאי, מהרש"ל.

## הגהות הב"ח

(א) גמ' האידנא כתיב (מאי) תז"מ ונ"ב גי' רש"י מי:

## ליקוטי רש"י

...שכבר נמחל ...שיעבודו. כשפרעו ובטל שטר ואין הקרקעות ...שועבדות שוב למלוה ...שניה שלא עליה נחתם ...שטר זה והויא לה מלוה ...על פה [גיטין כו:]. ...שפרעו בטל השטר ...מלאת מלוה השני' מלוה ...על פה ואינו גובה מן ...הלקוחות [כתובות פה.]. ...שטרי חוב ...המוקדמין. ליכתב קודם מלוה [סנהדרין לב.]. ...דפריסית שהקדים זמן ...כתוב בשטר ליום כתיבתו ...שנכתב השטר באחד ...ניסן וכן כתוב בו באחד ...ניסן לוה פלוני מפלוני ...הוא לא לוה ממנו כלום ...ט"ו בניסן גם זה ...וקדם [רשב"ם ב"ב קנז:]. ...פסולין. דבעי למיטרף ...לקוחות מזמן הכתוב בו ...דיין לא הלוה ושטר ...לקוחות קודם למלוה ...ואיא שטרו והוא קודם ...הוא שקר ואינו טורף מן ...משועבדין ואפי' מן ...המאוחר למלוה [לקמן ...ב.]. לפי שרצה לטרוף ...לקוחות שלקחו שדה מן ...הלוה מזמן שבשטר ושלא ...דין הוא שהרי קדמה ...כירה להלואה ובשטר ...עיד שהלואה קדמה ...פיכך קנסוהו מלגבות בו ...לא יטרוף אפילו מזמן ...מלוה ואינו אלא כמלוה ...על פה שאינו גובה מן ...משועבדים [ר"ה ב.]. ...פסול שאין לו לטרוף אלא ...זמן ההלואה ואילך ודלא ...אביי דאמר עדיו ...בחתומיו זכין לו בשניים ...וחזין [רשב"ם ב"ב קנז:]. ...קנסינן היתרא אטו ...יסורא ופסול אפי' מזמן ...י [סנהדרין שם]. **אלא ...או ביומיה.** אינו חוזר ...לוה בו ואפי' ביום מלוה ...אשונה לאחר פרעון ...ליכא למיחש למוקדם ...הכי מפרשינן לה בשניים ...וחזין [גיטין כו:]. ...**אחריות נכסים וכו'.** ...שעבוד קרקעות שיגבה ...הן. **כשחייב מודה.** ...הלוה מודה שהשטר אינו ...פרוע [לעיל יב:].

## עין משפט נר מצוה

קמה א ב מיי' פ"ז מהל' טוען ונטען הל' ה סמג עשין לה טוש"ע ח"מ סי' לט סעי' ט וסי' עט סעי' יב:
קמו ג ד מיי' שם הל' ו סמג שם טוש"ע ח"מ סי' עט סעי' יג:
קמז ה מיי' שם פ"ו הל' א סמג שם טוש"ע ח"מ שם סעי' ה:
קמח ו ז מיי' פ"ז שם הל' ה סמג שם טוש"ע ח"מ סי' פז סעי' ס:
קמט ח מיי' פי"ח מהל' גזילה ואבידה הל' ב סמג עשין עד טוש"ע ח"מ סי' סה סעי' ז:
קנ ט מיי' פי"ד מהל' מלוה ולוה הל' ז סמג עשין לד טוש"ע ח"מ סי' מח סעי' א וסי' נז סעי' ב:
קנא י מיי' פכ"ג מהל' מלוה ולוה הל' א סמג עשין שם טוש"ע ח"מ סי' מג סעי' ז:
קנב כ מיי' פי"ח מהל' גזילה ואבידה הל' ב סמג עשין עד טוש"ע ח"מ סי' סה סעי' ז:

## רבינו חננאל

אמר רב יהודה אמר רב נחמן אמר לו ב"ד צא תן לו או חייב אתה ליתן לו ואמר פרעתי נאמן בא מלוה לכתוב אין כותבין ונותנין לו. אבל אמר לו צא תן לו ואמר נתתי ועדים מעידים אותו שלא נתן הוחזק כפרן לאותו ממון ואם אמר לו חייב אתה ליתן לו ואמר נתתי והעדים מעידים אותו שלא נתן לא הוחזק כפרן לאותו ממון מאי טעמא אמרינן אישתמוטי הוא דקא משתמיט סבר עד דמעייני רבנן בדיני. א) זה כגון הכופר במלוה כשר לעדות. אמר רבה בר בר חנא אמר ר' יוחנן מנה לי בידך והלה אומר אין לך עלי כלום ועדים מעידים שיש לו וחזר ואמר פרעתי הוחזק כפרן לאותו ממון. והוא שכפר בב"ד כי הא ב) בגמ' שבתאי דשבתי' כתב לכלתיה איצטלא דמילתא וקיבלה עילויה וכפר ובאו עדים והעידו שכתב לה איצטלא דמילתא חזר ואמר פרעתי. אמר ליה רב חייא כבר הוחזקת כפרן לאותה איצטלא וכן הלכה. וכן מי שנתחייב שבועה בב"ד ואמר נשבעתי ועדים מעידים אותו שלא נשבע הוחזק כפרן לאותה שבועה וחייב לישבע עכשיו. א"ר יוחנן המוצא שטר חוב וזמנו בו ביום וכתוב בו הנפק יחזירו לבעלים דאי משום [כתב] ללות ולא לוה הא כתוב בו הנפק. אי משום פרעון כיון דרובא דעלמא לא פרעי ביומיה אלא מיעוטא הוא דפרעי ביומיה למיעוטא לא חיישינן. ותוב מלוה גופיה לא שביק אמר דילמא שמעי רבנן דהאי שטרא שלוה בו ופרעו הוא וכבר

## חשק שלמה על ר"ח

א) אולי צ"ל ומטעם זה אמרי' הכופר במלוה כשר לעדות וי"ל דהכא נמי הטעם משום דאמרי' דמישתמיט וכדאיתא לעיל דף ו. ב) אולי צ"ל כי הא מעשה דשבתאי.

אירכס כתובתה – **Her *kesubah* was** then **lost.** She demanded the garment,[17] אָמַר לְהוּ לֹא הָיוּ דְבָרִים מֵעוֹלָם – and [Shabsai] told [the court]: **"These things never occurred"** [i.e. I never agreed to give her a garment]. אָתוּ סַהֲדֵי וְאָמְרֵי – **Witnesses came and said:** אֵין כָּתַב לָהּ – **"Yes, he did write** the garment **to her** in her *kesubah!"* לְסוֹף אָמַר לְהוּ פְּרַעְתִּיהָ – **In the end, he told [the court]: "I already gave her** the garment." אָתָא לְקַמֵּיהּ דְּרַבִּי חִיָּיא – [Shabsai] **came before R' Chiya,** אָמַר לֵיהּ – **and [R' Chiya] told [Shabsai]:** הוּחְזַקְתָּ כַּפְרָן לְאוֹתָהּ אִיצְטְלָא – **"You have been presumed a liar in reference to that garment,** and you are not believed that you paid without providing witnesses to that effect."

Another related ruling:

אָמַר רַבִּי אָבִין אָמַר רַבִּי אִלְעָא אָמַר רַבִּי יוֹחָנָן – **R' Avin said in the name of R' Ila'a who said in the name of R' Yochanan:** הָיָה חַיָּיב לַחֲבֵירוֹ שְׁבוּעָה – **If a person was obligated** to swear **an oath to his fellow,** וְאָמַר נִשְׁבַּעְתִּי – **and he said: "I** already **swore,"** וְהָעֵדִים מְעִידִין אוֹתוֹ שֶׁלֹּא נִשְׁבַּע – **but witnesses testify against him that he did not swear** upon demand,[18] (וחזור ואמר נשבעתי)[8] הוּחְזַק כַּפְרָן לְאוֹתָהּ שְׁבוּעָה – **he is presumed a liar in reference to that oath.**[19]

This ruling is qualified:

אָמְרוּהָ קַמֵּיהּ דְּר׳ אַבָּהוּ – **[The students] related this** ruling **to R' Abahu.** אָמַר לְהוּ – **He told them:** מִסְתַּבְּרָא מִלְּתָא דְּרַבִּי אָבִין – **R' Avin's ruling is logical** שֶׁנִּתְחַיֵּיב שְׁבוּעָה בְּבֵית דִּין – **where [the defendant] was obligated by the court** to swear **an oath.**[20] אֲבָל חִיֵּיב עַצְמוֹ שְׁבוּעָה – **However, if he** voluntarily **obligated himself** to swear **an oath,**[21] [נֶאֱמָן] – **he is believed** to claim that he swore, even if witnesses testify that he did not swear upon demand,[22] עָבִיד אִינִישׁ דְּמִקְרֵי וְאָמַר – for **a person is wont to say** he will not perform that which the court has not obligated him to do. Therefore, his prior refusal to swear in the presence of the witnesses does not demonstrate a brazen unwillingness to swear.[23]

אַהַדְרוּהָ קַמֵּיהּ דְּר׳ אָבִין – **[The students] returned [the matter] to R' Avin** to inquire if he concurred with R' Abahu's qualification of his ruling. אָמַר לְהוּ – **He told them:** אֲנָא נַמִּי בְּבֵית דִּין אָמַר – **I also said** this ruling only **where the court** obligated the defendant to swear.

אִיתְּמַר נַמִּי – This ruling **was also related** with R' Abahu's qualification: אָמַר רַבִּי אָבִין אָמַר רַבִּי אִלְעָא אָמַר רַבִּי יוֹחָנָן – **R' Avin said in the name of R' Ila'a who said in the name of R' Yochanan,** הָיָה חַיָּיב לַחֲבֵירוֹ שְׁבוּעָה בְּבֵית דִּין – If one was **obligated by the court** to swear **an oath to his fellow,** וְאָמַר נִשְׁבַּעְתִּי – **and he said I** already **swore,** וְהָעֵדִים מְעִידִין אוֹתוֹ שֶׁלֹּא נִשְׁבַּע – **but witnesses testify against him that he did not swear** upon demand, (וחזור ואמר נשבעתי)[8] הוּחְזַק כַּפְרָן לְאוֹתָהּ שְׁבוּעָה – **he is presumed a liar in reference to that oath.**

The Gemara returns to its discussion of the laws for the return of recovered documents:

אָמַר רַבִּי אַסִּי אָמַר רַבִּי יוֹחָנָן – **R' Assi said in the name of R' Yochanan:** הַמּוֹצֵא שְׁטַר חוֹב בַּשּׁוּק – If **one finds a note of indebtedness in the street,** וְכָתוּב בּוֹ הֶנְפֵּק – **and a certification is written in it,** וְכָתוּב בּוֹ זְמַנּוֹ בּוֹ בַּיּוֹם – **and its date of** that **very day is written in it,**[24] יַחֲזִירוֹ לַבְּעָלִים – **he should return it to its owner** [i.e. to the creditor].

R' Yochanan justifies his ruling by dismissing all reasons there could be to withhold this note from the creditor:

אִי מִשּׁוּם כָּתַב לִלְוֹת וְלֹא לָוָה – **If** you argue that the note should be withheld **because** perhaps **[the debtor] wrote** it intending **to borrow, but** ultimately **did not borrow,** this is not a concern here, הָא כָּתוּב בּוֹ הֶנְפֵּק – **for a certification is written in [the note].**[25] אִי מִשּׁוּם פֵּרָעוֹן – **And if** you argue that the note should be withheld **because of repayment** – i.e. that perhaps the debtor already paid the loan – this too is not a consideration, לִפְרִיעָה בַּת יוֹמָא לֹא חָיְישִׁינַן – for **we are not concerned about** the unlikely possibility of **repayment** of a loan **on the very day** it was granted.

The Gemara challenges this ruling:

אָמַר לֵיהּ ר׳ זֵירָא לְר׳ אַסִּי – **R' Zeira told R' Assi:** מִי אָמַר רַבִּי יוֹחָנָן הָכִי – **Did R' Yochanan** really **say this?** הָא אַתְּ הוּא דְּאָמְרַתְּ מִשְּׁמֵיהּ דְּר׳ יוֹחָנָן – **But you are the one who said in the name of R' Yochanan:** שְׁטָר שֶׁלָּוָה בּוֹ וּפְרָעוֹ – If a debtor has **a note that he** once **used** in order **to borrow, and he** subsequently **repaid [the loan]** recorded therein, אֵינוֹ חוֹזֵר וְלֹוֶה בּוֹ – **he may not borrow again with [the note]** a second time, שֶׁכְּבָר נִמְחַל שִׁיעְבּוּדוֹ – **for the lien** recorded therein **has already lapsed.**[26]

The Gemara explains its challenge by analyzing this other ruling of R' Yochanan:

אֵימַת – **When** did the second loan occur?[27] אִילֵימָא לְמָחָר וּלְיוֹמָא אַחֲרָא – **If you say** on **the day after** the first loan **or** on **a subsequent day,** but not on the date written in the note, מַאי אִרְיָא שֶׁכְּבָר נִמְחַל שִׁעְבּוּדוֹ – **why teach** that the note's invalidity for the second loan is **because its lien already lapsed?** תֵּיפּוֹק לֵיהּ דַּהֲוָה לֵיהּ מוּקְדָּם – **Derive [its invalidity] because it is**

NOTES

7. The Gemara refers to a case in which when she was widowed or divorced and demanded payment of her *kesubah*.

8. They testify that in their presence his opponent demanded that he swear the required oath, and he refused to comply (see *Rashi* ד״ה רשוחחיי).

[According to *Rosh* (cited above in note 9), the Gemara means that the witnesses testify that they were present at the time he now claims to have sworn, and he did not in fact swear (*Shach, Choshen Mishpat* 87:62).]

9. He is not believed to say that he already swore; he must swear in the presence of witnesses (see *Rashi*).

10. Since, in the presence of witnesses, he refused to honor the court's instruction when summoned by the creditor to swear, he is not believed to claim that he subsequently swore (*Rashi*).

[The Gemara implies that one is believed to claim he swore an oath required by the court, as long as he is not refuted by witnesses (*Rif*). *Ramban* limits this rule to one who was obligated to swear in his own defense. One who must swear in order to collect, however, is not believed that he already swore; if the defendant disputes his claim, the plaintiff must prove that he has sworn. This follows the universal law that the burden of proof always rests with the claimant. Since the plaintiff has not substantiated his claim to have sworn, he cannot collect.]

21. Even a person who is not required to swear can, with certain limitations, voluntarily obligate himself to do so (see *Choshen Mishpat* 22:3 and *Shach* 87:62).

22. *Rashi*. [According to *Rosh*, however, he is believed with a subsequent claim that he swore even if witnesses testify that he did not swear at the time he claims he swore (*Shach* ibid.).]

23. This refusal is viewed as a delaying tactic, and not as a retraction of his offer to swear (*Rashi*).

24. I.e. it was found on the day it was written (*Rashi*).

25. See 16b note 16.

26. As explained above (15a note 7), only a debt recorded in a document may be collected from subsequent purchasers of the debtor's land if he defaults. Since the note was written for the first loan, only that debt may be collected from sold properties. However, a second loan in the same amount may not be collected from sold properties, because it was never recorded in a document. Using this note for the second loan could result in illegal collection of the debt from purchasers of the debtor's land (*Rashi*).

27. The Gemara attempts to prove, by this line of analysis, when the first loan was repaid (see *Rashi*).

**ואמר.** לאחר זמן: **פרעתי.** ע"פ ב"ד: **נאמן.** ובשבועת היסת: **בא מלוה.** לפנינו לכתוב לו אדרכתא עליו אין כותבין ונותנין לו: **אינו נאמן.** לישבע אלא שכנגדו נשבע ונוטל דכיון דתחילתו הולכך לתובעו לדין אין דרכו למהר לפרוע עד שיפסקו דינו פסק גמור: **ואמר פרעתי.** לאחר זמן ע"פ ב"ד: **והעדים מעידים אותו שלא פרע.** בפנינו תבעו לפרוע לו ע"פ ב"ד ולא פרעו הואיל ובפניהם העיז לעבור ע"פ ב"ד אינו נאמן שוב לומר פרעתיו שלא בעדים: **הוחזק כפרן לאותו ממון.** שאין נאמן עוד עליו לומר החזרתי ופרעתי עד שיפרע בעדים: **לא הוחזק כפרן.** ונשבע שפרעו ואע"פ שלא פרעו מיד כשתבעו בפני עדים ואין זה מעיז בב"ד דכיון דלא פסקו לו פסק גמור נשמט ממנו סבר כו': **אצטלא.** לבוש: **הוחזק כפרן לאותה אצטלא.** עד שיפרע: **הוחזק כפרן לאותה שבועה.** לומר נשבעתי עד שישבע בפנינו: **כשנתחייב שבועה בב"ד.** דכיון דתבעו בעדים לקיים דברי ב"ד ולא אבה אינו נאמן לומר עוד קיימתי אחרי כן: **אבל חייב עצמו שבועה.** שאמר לו אשבע לך ותבעו בעדים ולא אבה ואחר כך אמר נשבעתי נאמן ואע"ג דקמי עדים דחייה: **עביד איניש דמקרי ואמר.** לא אעשה מה שלא חייבוני ב"ד אלא אני בעלמי ואין זו סרבנות וחרטה אלא דחייה בעלמא: **וכתוב בו זמנו בו ביום.** שביום שנמלא נכתב: **שכבר נמחל שעבודו.** משפרע מלוה ראשונה ועל האחרונה לא נכתב והויא לה מלוה על פה וטורף לקוחות שלא כדין דאין מלוה על פה גובה מן הלקוחות: **אימת.** דפרעיה אימתי וחזר ולוה אימתי: **אי נימא למחר.** ולא ביום שנכתב: **וליומא חרא.** שתי תיבות הן וליום אחריו וקיצור סופרים הוא: **תיפוק ליה.** דאפילו נכתב על מלוה זו אחרונה וכתוב בו יום מוקדם כזה הוה ליה השטר מוקדם: **דלא שכיחי [אינשי] דפרעי [ביומיה] קאמינא.** הלכך לא חיישינן למידי דלא שכיח ואי אתרמי הולרכו לומר דאין חוזר ולוה בו: **רב כהנא אמר.** הא דא"ר יוחנן יחזיר לבעלים: **כשחייב מודה.** שלא פרע: **שמעי בי רבנן.** שנמחל שעבודו: **ומפסדי לי.** למטרף לקוחות משום דשטרי חוב המוקדמין פסולין דכיון דהאי דאוקמא הכי לית ליה עדיו בחתומיו זכין לו אף זה מן המוקדמין: **מינח ניחא ליה.** ברמאות ותלי נפשיה בספיקא ואמר דלמא לא שמעי ואיכא רווחא: **מאי איכא דטריף לקוחות.** מה טרפא יש בזה שלא יהא בשטר שיחזור ויכתוב לו והלא שניהם ביום אחד הלכך בשטר שנמחל שעבודו לא שביק: **הטוען אחר מעשה ב"ד.** דבר שהוא תנאי ב"ד כגון כתובה ומזון האשה והבנות הטוען ואמר פרעתי שלא בעדים לא אמר כלום:
במקום

**חייב** אתה ליתן לו. הכא משמע דחייב אתה ליתן לו לא הוי פסק דין גמור כי אם צא ותן לו וכן משמע במרובה (ב"ק דף סט. ושם) וקשה דבפ"ק דסנהדרין (דף ו: ושם) אמרינן ה"ד גמר דין פלוני אתה חייב פלוני אתה זכאי וי"ל דהתם מקרי גמר דין לענין שאסור לבלוע לפי שיודע להיכן הדין נוטה:

**רב** כהנא אמר כשחייב מודה. תימה א"כ למה נקט הנפק במילתא דר' יוחנן וי"ל דנקטיה משום דיוקא דאי אין כתוב בו ביום אפילו כתוב בו הנפק דודאי לוה לא יחזיר דחיישינן לקנוניא או לפשיטי דספרא:

**הטוען** אחר מעשה ב"ד לא אמר כלום. אינו נאמן לומר פרעתי מעשה ב"ד קרי כל דבר שחייב לה אפי' לא כתב כגון מנה ומאתים ומזון האשה והבנות לאחר מותו וא"ת למה כותבין כתובה כיון דבלאו כתובה נמי אין נאמן לומר פרעתי וי"ל משום תוספת אבל מנה ומאתים גבייה בלא כתובה ותוספת נראה דאפי' אית לה סהדי דהתנה לה נאמן לומר פרעתי [ו] ואין ראיה מכלתי' [ז] דר' שבתאי דהוה מהימן לומר פרעתי אי לאו דהוחזק כפרן דר' שבתאי ערב היה אבל בעל עצמו לא היה נאמן ואין ראיה נמי מדתני לעיל (דף ז:) מלא כתובה לא יחזיר ומשמע דלא יחזיר משום תוספת שהיה נאמן לומר פרעתי דלגבי מנה ומאתים נמי מפסיד דהא נאמן לומר פרעתי מנה מגו דאי בעי אמר אלמנה נשאתיך אם אין לה עדי הינומא או אם אין לה עדי קדושין נאמן

ואמר פרעתי נאמן בא מלוה לכתוב אין כותבין ונותנין לו חייב אתה ליתן לו ואמר פרעתי אינו נאמן בא מלוה לכתוב כותבין ונותנין לו רב זביד משמיה דר"נ אמר [א] בין צא תן לו בין חייב אתה ליתן לו ואמר פרעתי נאמן [ב] בא מלוה לכתוב אין כותבין ונותנין לו אלא אי איכא לפלוגי הכי הוא דאיכא לפלוגי [ג] אמרו לו צא תן לו ואמר פרעתי והעדים מעידין אותו שלא פרעו (א) וחזר ואמר פרעתי) הוחזק כפרן לאותו ממון [ד] חייב אתה ליתן לו ואמר פרעתי והעדים מעידין אותו שלא פרע וחזר ואמר פרעתי לא הוחזק כפרן לאותו ממון מ"ט אשתמוטי הוא קא משתמיט מיניה סבר עד דמעיינו בי רבנן בדיני אמר רבה בר בר חנה א"ר יוחנן [ה] מנה לי בידך והלה אומר אין לך בידי כלום והעדים מעידים אותו שיש לו וחזר ואמר פרעתי הוחזק כפרן לאותו ממון כי הא דשבתאי בריה דרבי מרינוס כתב לה לכלתיה איצטלא דמילתא בכתובתה וקבלה עליה אירכס כתובתה אמר (ב) להו) לא היו דברים מעולם [ג] אתו סהדי ואמרי אין כתב לה לסוף אמר להו פרעתיה אתא לקמיה דרבי חייא א"ל הוחזקת כפרן לאותה איצטלא: א"ר אבין א"ר אלעא א"ר יוחנן [ו] היה חייב לחבירו שבועה ואמר נשבעתי והעדים מעידין אותו שלא נשבע [ד] (וחזר ואמר נשבעתי) הוחזק כפרן לאותה שבועה אמרוה קמיה דר' אבהו אמר להו מסתברא מלתא דרבי אבין [ז] שנתחייב שבועה בב"ד אבל חייב עצמו שבועה [ה] [נאמן] עביד איניש דמקרי ואמר אהדרוה קמיה דר' אבין אמר להו אנא נמי בב"ד אמרי איתמר נמי א"ר אבין א"ר אלעא א"ר יוחנן היה חייב לחבירו שבועה בב"ד ואמר נשבעתי והעדים מעידין אותו שלא נשבע [ו] (וחזר ואמר נשבעתי) הוחזק כפרן לאותה שבועה א"ר אסי א"ר יוחנן [ח] המוצא שטר חוב בשוק וכתוב בו הנפק וכתוב בו זמנו בו ביום יחזירו לבעלים אי משום כתב ללות ולא לוה הא כתוב בו הנפק אי משום פרעון לפריעה בת יומא לא חיישינן א"ל ר' זירא לר' אסי מי א"ר יוחנן הכי הא את הוא דאמרת משמיה דר' יוחנן [ז] [ט] שטר שלוה בו ופרעו אינו חוזר ולוה בו שכבר נמחל שיעבודו אימת אילימא למחר וליומא חרא מאי אריא שכבר נמחל שעבודו תיפוק ליה דהוה ליה מוקדם ותנן [ח] [י] שטרי חוב המוקדמין פסולין אלא לאו ביומיה אלמא פרעי אינשי ביומיה א"ל מי קא אמינא דלא פרעי כלל דלא שכיחי אינשי דפרעי ביומיה קא אמינא רב כהנא אמר [כ] כשחייב מודה אי הכי מאי למימרא מהו דתימא האי מפרע פרעיה והאי דקא אמר לא פרעתיה משום דקבעי מהדר למזפא ביה זמנא אחריתי ולפשיטי דספרא חייש קמ"ל דאם כן מלוה גופיה לא שבק סבר שמעי בי רבנן ומפסדי לי מאי שנא מהא דתנן [ט] מצא שטרי חוב אם יש בהן אחריות נכסים לא יחזיר ואוקימנא כשחייב מודה ומשום שמא כתב ללות בניסן ולא לוה עד תשרי ואתי למטרף לקוחות מניסן ועד תשרי שלא כדין ולא אמרינן דא"כ מלוה גופיה לא שביק דא"ל כתוב שטרא אחרינא בתשרי דדלמא שמעי רבנן ומפסדי לי אמרי התם משום דאית ליה רווחא דקא טריף לקוחות מניסן ועד תשרי מינח ניחא ליה ולא אמר ולא מידי הכא כיון דלית ליה רווחא דסוף סוף שטרא האידנא כתיב (א) מאי איכא דקטריף לקוחות בשטר שנמחל שיעבודו לא שביק: אמר רבי חייא בר אבא א"ר יוחנן הטוען אחר מעשה ב"ד לא

---

**עין משפט נר מצוה**

קמה א ב מיי' פ"ז מהל' טוען ונטען הל' ה סמג עשין לה טוש"ע ח"מ סי' לט סעי' ט וסי' עט סעי' יב:
קמו ג ד מיי' שם הל' ו סמג שם טוש"ע ח"מ סי' עט סעי' יג:
קמז ה מיי' שם פ"ו הל' א סמג שם טוש"ע ח"מ שם סעי' ה:
קמח ו ז מיי' פ"ז שם הל' ה סמג שם טוש"ע ח"מ סי' פז סעי' ס:
קמט ח מיי' פי"ח מהל' גזילה ואבידה הל' ב סמג עשין עד טוש"ע ח"מ סי' סה סעי' ז:
קנ ט מיי' פי"ד מהל' מלוה ולוה הל' ז סמג עשין לד טוש"ע ח"מ סי' מח סעי' א וסי' נז סעי' ב:
קנא י מיי' פכ"ג מהל' מלוה ולוה הל' א סמג עשין שם טוש"ע ח"מ סי' מג סעי' ז:
קנב כ מיי' פי"ח מהל' גזילה ואבידה הל' ב סמג עשין עד טוש"ע ח"מ סי' סה סעי' ז:

**רבינו חננאל**

אמר רב יהודה אמר רב נחמן אמר לו ב"ד צא תן לו או חייב אתה ליתן לו ואמר פרעתי נאמן בא מלוה לכתוב אין כותבין ונותנין לו. אבל אמר לו צא תן לו ואמר נתתי ועדים מעידים אותו שלא נתן הוחזק כפרן לאותו ממון ואם אמר לו חייב אתה ליתן ואמר נתתי והעדים מעידים אותו שלא נתן לא הוחזק כפרן לאותו ממון מאי טעמא אמרינן אישתמוטי הוא דקא משתמיט סבר עד דמעייני רבנן בדיני. א) זה כגון הכופר במלוה כשר לעדות. אמר רבה בר בר חנא אמר ר' יוחנן מנה לי בידך והלה אומר אין לך עלי כלום ועדים מעידים שיש לו וחזר ואמר פרעתי הוחזק כפרן לאותו ממון. והוא שכפר בב"ד כי הא ב) בגמ' שבתאי דשבתי' כתב לכלתיה איצטלא דמילתא וקיבלה עילויה וכפר ובאו עדים והעידו שכתב לה איצטלא דמילתא חזר ואמר פרעתי. אמר ליה רב חייא כבר הוחזקת כפרן לאותה איצטלא וכן הלכה. וכן מי שנתחייב שבועה בב"ד ואמר נשבעתי ועדים מעידים אותו שלא נשבע הוחזק כפרן לאותה שבועה וחייב לישבע עכשיו. א"ר יוחנן המוצא שטר חוב וזמנו בו ביום וכתוב בו הנפק יחזירו לבעלים דאי משום [כתב] ללות ולא לוה הא כתוב בו הנפק. אי משום פרעון כיון דרובא דעלמא לא פרעי ביומיה אלא מיעוטא הוא דפרעי ביומיה למיעוטא לא חיישינן. ותוב מלוה גופיה לא שביק אמר דילמא שמעי רבנן דהאי שטרא שלוה בו ופרעו הוא וכבר

**חשק שלמה על ר"ח**

א) אולי צ"ל ומטעם זה אמרי' דהכופר במלוה כשר לעדות וכ"ל דהתם נמי הטעם משום דאמרי' דמישתמיט וכדאיתא לעיל דף ו. ב) אולי צ"ל כי הא מעשה דשבתאי.

---

**מסורת הש"ס**

...הר"מ מ"ז, ב) [צ"ל ...ג) [אתא לקמיה ...חייא אתו סהדי ...רי אין כתב לה ...ר' חייא ז"ל הב ...לסוף אמר לה ...נתיך אמר לו ...זקת כפרן וכו' כ"ה ...רי"ף ורא"ש והוא ...ד) מהר"מ מ"ז, ...מהרש"ל, ו) מהר"מ ...ז) כתובות פה., גיטין ...ח) לקמן עב., סנהדרין ...ר"ה ב, ח., שביעית ...י משנה ה, בבא בתרא ...קעא., ט) לעיל יב., ...עיין תוס' יבמות סה: ...כי הא], כ) צ"ל ...לשבתאי, מהרש"ל.

**הגהות הב"ח**

(א) גמ' האידנא כתיב ...(ו) תו"מ ונ"ב ג' רש"י מי:

**ליקוטי רש"י**

...בר נמחל ...עבודו. כשפרעו ובטל ...ער ואין הקרקעות ...ועבדות שוב למלוה ...יה שלא עליה נחתם ...ר זה והויא לה מלוה ...פה [גיטין כו:]. ...פרעו בטל השטר ...לאת מלוה השני' מלוה ...פה ואינו גובה מן ...קוחות [כתובות פה.]. ...טרי חוב ...מוקדמין. ליכתב קודם ...לוה [סנהדרין לב.]. ...פרישית שהקדים זמן ...חוב בשטר ליום כתיבתו ...ג שנכתב השטר באחד ...סן וכן כתוב בו באחד ...סן לוה פלוני מפלוני ...יא לא לוה ממנו כלום ...ט"ו בניסן גם זה ...קדם [רשב"ם ב"ב קנז:]. ...סולין. דבעי למיטרף ...ומות מזמן הכתוב בו ...דיין לא הלוה ושטר ...קוחות קודם למלוה וזה ...ליא שטרו והוא קודם ...וא שקר ואינו טורף מן ...שועבדין ואפי' מן ...אוחר למלוה [לקמן ...]. לפי שרלה לטרוף ...ומות שלקחו שדה מן ...ה מזמן שבשטר ושלא ...ין הוא שהרי קדמה ...ירה להלואה ובשטר ...עיד שהלואה קדמה ...יכך קנסוהו מלגבות בו ...א יטרוף אפילו מזמן ...מלוה ואינו אלא כמלוה ...ל פה שאינו גובה מן ...משועבדים [ר"ה ב.]. ...פסול שאין לו לטרוף אלא ...זמן ההלואה ואילך ודלא ...אביי דאמר עדיו ...חתומיו זכין לו בשנים ...וחזין [רשב"ם ב"ב קנז:]. ...קנסינן היתרא אטו ...יסורא ופסול אפי' מזמן ...ני [סנהדרין שם]. **אלא** ...או ביומיה. אינו חוזר ...לוה בו ואפי' ביום מלוה ...אשונה לאחר פרעון ...ליכא למיחש למוקדם ...הכי מפרשינן לה בשנים ...וחזין [גיטין כו:]. ...**אחריות נכסים וכו'.** ...עבוד קרקעות שיגבה ...הן. **כשחייב מודה.** ...הלוה מודה שהשטר אינו פרוע [לעיל יב:].

**וְאָמַר פָּרַעְתִּי** – and [the debtor] later **said: "I paid** the lender as nstructed by the court," **נֶאֱמָן – he is believed.**[1] **בָּא מַלְוֶה לִכְתּוֹב** – If after the debtor was instructed to pay, **the lender approaches** the court and asks them **to write** for him a record of he verdict,[2] **אֵין כּוֹתְבִין וְנוֹתְנִין לוֹ – they do not write and give t to him.**[3]

**חַיָּיב אַתָּה לִיתֵּן ל** – If the court told the debtor: **"You are oblig- ated to give [the lender]** the money you owe him," **וְאָמַר פָּרַעְתִּי – and [the debtor]** later **said: "I paid** the lender," **אֵינוֹ נֶאֱמָן – e is not believed.**[4] **בָּא מַלְוֶה לִכְתּוֹב** – If after the decision, **the ender approaches** the court **to write** for him a record of the erdict, **כּוֹתְבִין וְנוֹתְנִין לוֹ – they write and give** it **to him.**[5]

The Gemara presents a different version of Rav Nachman's uling:

**רַב זְבִיד מִשְּׁמֵיהּ דְּרַב נַחְמָן אָמַר – Rav Zevid said in the name of Rav Nachman: בֵּין צֵא תֵּן לוֹ – Whether** the court told the ebtor: **"Go out and give [the lender]** the money you owe him," **בֵּין חַיָּיב אַתָּה לִיתֵּן ל – or** they told him: **"You are obligated to ive [the lender]** the money you owe him," **וְאָמַר פָּרַעְתִּי – and the debtor]** later **said: "I paid** as instructed by the court," **נֶאֱמָן – he is believed.**[6] **בָּא מַלְוֶה לִכְתּוֹב** – If in either case **the ender approaches** the court **to write** a record of the verdict for im, **אֵין כּוֹתְבִין וְנוֹתְנִין לוֹ – they do not write and give him** the ecord.

Rav Zevid suggests a different distinction between the two ases:

**אֶלָּא – Rather, אִי אִיכָּא לְפַלּוּגֵי – if it is** possible **to distinguish** etween the two cases, **הָכִי הוּא דְּאִיכָּא לְפַלּוּגֵי – this is the istinction which may be drawn: אָמְרוּ לוֹ צֵא תֵּן לוֹ** – If [the ourt] told [the debtor]: **"Go out** and **give [the lender]** the noney you owe him," **וְאָמַר פָּרַעְתִּי – and [the debtor]** later aid: **"I paid** as instructed by the court," **וְהָעֵדִים מְעִידִין אוֹתוֹ שֶׁלֹּא פָּרַע – and witnesses testify against him that he did not ay [the lender]** upon demand,[7] **(וחזר ואמר פרעתי)**[8] **הוּחְזַק כַּפְרָן לְאוֹתוֹ מָמ – he is presumed a liar in reference to that money,** and he is not believed to claim subsequently that the debt has been paid, without producing witnesses to that effect.[9] **חַיָּיב אַתָּה לִיתֵּן לוֹ** – However, if the court told him: **"You are obligated to give [the lender]** the money you owe him," **וְאָמַר פָּרַעְתִּי – and [the debtor]** later **said: "I paid** as instructed by the court," **וְהָעֵדִים מְעִידִין אוֹתוֹ שֶׁלֹּא פָּרַע – and witnesses testify against him that he did not pay** upon demand, **(וחזר ואמר פרעתי)**[8] **לֹא הוּחְזַק כַּפְרָן לְאוֹתוֹ מָמוֹן** – he is believed,[10] for **he is not presumed a liar in reference to that money. מַאי טַעְמָא – What is the reason? אִשְׁתַּמּוּטֵי הוּא קָא מִשְׁתַּמֵּיט מִינֵּיהּ** – By refusing to pay, **[the debtor]** may have been merely temporarily **evading [the lender],** and his response does not necessarily indicate an unwillingness to pay. **סָבַר עַד דִּמְעַיְּינוּ בֵּי רַבָּנָן בְּדִינַי – He** may have **thought:** "I will not pay **until the rabbis** [i.e. the judges] further **examine my case.** Since they did not *order* me to pay, it is still possible that they will reverse themselves and decide in my favor."[11]

The Gemara presents a related ruling:

**אָמַר רַבָּה בַּר בַּר חָנָה אָמַר רַבִּי יוֹחָנָן – Rabbah bar bar Chanah said in the name of R' Yochanan: מָנֶה לִי בְּיָדְךָ** – If a creditor tells his debtor: **"You owe me a *maneh*,"**[12] **וְהַלָּה אוֹמֵר – and [the debtor] says: אֵין לְךָ בְּיָדִי כְּלוּם – "I owe you nothing**[13] because I never borrowed," **וְהָעֵדִים מְעִידִים אוֹתוֹ שֶׁיֵּשׁ לוֹ – and witnesses testify against [the debtor] that** indeed **he** did borrow and **owes** money to **[the creditor], וְחָזַר וְאָמַר פָּרַעְתִּי – and subsequently [the debtor] said: "I paid** this debt,"[14] **הוּחְזַק כַּפְרָן לְאוֹתוֹ מָמוֹן – he is presumed a liar in reference to that money,** and he is not believed that it was repaid without providing witnesses to that effect.[15]

An incident wherein this ruling was applied:

**כִּי הָא דְּשַׁבְּתַאי בְּרֵיהּ דְּרַבִּי מָרִינוּס** – This is **as** occurred in **[the case] of Shabsai, the son of R' Marinos. כְּתַב לָהּ לְכַלְּתֵיהּ אִיצְטְלָא דְּמֵילְתָא בִּכְתוּבְּתָהּ – He wrote to his daughter-in-law in her *kesubah* a fine wool garment** as part of her dowry, **וְקִבְּלָהּ עֲלֵיהּ – and he accepted it** as an obligation **upon himself.**[16]

NOTES

. However, [as is the law for any defendant who entirely denies the laintiff's claim] he must swear a *heses* oath supporting his claim *Rashi;* see above, 5a note 26, for a detailed explanation of a *heses* oath).

. [*Tur* (*Choshen Mishpat* 39) explains that he requests a written record f the verdict (see also *Shach* 39:29 who maintains that Rashi concurs; . *Beis Yosef* ad loc.).]

. Since it is possible that the debtor already paid, the court may not rite a record of the verdict for the lender, because he can use it to lsely prove that the debt is still outstanding (*Rif;* cf. *Ritva*).

It is presumed that the debtor would not have paid unless the court *rdered* him to do so (by saying, "go and pay the lender"). The court's atement that the debtor *is obligated* to pay falls short of an order *lashi*); rather, it indicates that the court still needs to consider the atter before it issues a final verdict (*Nimukei Yosef;* cf. *Ritva*). herefore, the debtor is not believed to swear that he paid. Instead, the nder swears that he has not been paid and collects the debt.

Ordinarily, even where a plaintiff has proof of the creation of an bligation (but not of repayment), the debtor is believed to assert that he ready paid. In this case, however, the fact that the debtor contested the bligation in court leads us to presume that he would not have paid nless the court ordered him to do so (see *Rashi*).

Since it is presumed that the debtor has not yet paid, no harm will be used by writing a record of the verdict for the lender (see note 3).

The average person does not distinguish between the two statements the court, and regards even the words "you are obligated to pay" as court order. Therefore, the debtor's claim that he paid is believed *losh*).

They testify that in their presence the lender demanded of the btor that he pay as instructed by the court, and he refused to pay *lashi*).

8. *Maharam* deletes the words enclosed in parentheses (see also *Rashash*).

9. Since, in the presence of witnesses, the debtor was brazen enough to refuse to honor the court's instruction, he is no longer trusted concerning that money (*Rashi*).

*Rosh,* however, argues that such testimony should not establish the debtor as a liar, since it is possible that he was only stalling due to a temporary lack of funds. This does not prove that he would be so brazen as to claim that he repaid when in fact he did not (see above, 4a). Rather, he explains that the Gemara discusses a case in which the debtor names the date on which he claims to have paid. The witnesses contradict him, testifying that they were with him at the time and he did not repay. The debtor is therefore presumed a liar, and is henceforth not believed to claim the debt was paid at a later date.

10. I.e. he may swear that he paid (*Rashi;* see note 1).

11. Since he did not disobey a court order, he is not presumed to be lying if he subsequently claims repayment (*Rashi*).

12. Literally: I have a *maneh* in your hand.

A *maneh* is a denomination equivalent in value to one hundred silver *dinars.*

13. Literally: you have nothing in my hand.

14. He claims to have paid after the witnesses testified that he borrowed the money.

15. [This applies only when the debtor denies his obligation in court (*Rif*). However, if the denial was merely in the presence of witnesses, the debtor is not presumed a liar because it is common that a litigant presents a fictitious claim out of court in order to conceal from his opponent the claim he really intends to use in court (*Sma, Choshen Mishpat* 79:24, based on *Bava Basra* 31a).]

16. He signed as a guarantor to his son's *kesubah* (*Ritva*).

הִלְכָּךְ מֵרֵישָׁא הוּא דְּקָא זָבֵין – **Therefore, [the debtor] now purchases** the land **anew,** אִיבָּעֵי לֵיהּ לְמִכְתַּב שְׁטַר זְבִינֵי – **and he should have** insisted that **a bill of sale** be **written** to prove his ownership.[24]

The Gemara now concludes its explanation of the contrast between a certificate of foreclosure, which is returned to the creditor, and a note of indebtedness, which is not returned, because we are concerned that it might have been paid:

גַּבֵּי שְׁטַר חוֹב – **Regarding a** recovered **note of indebtedness,** מַאי אִיכָּא לְמֵימַר – **what is there to say;** i.e. how could you argue that it is certainly not paid? אִם אִיתָא דְּפַרְעֵיהּ – Can we presume that **if it is** true **that he paid [the creditor],** אִיבָּעֵי לֵיהּ לְמִיקְרְעֵיהּ לִשְׁטָרֵיהּ – **he should have ripped his note?** This is not necessarily so, אֵימוֹר אִשְׁתַּמּוּטֵי קָא מִשְׁתַּמֵּיט לֵיהּ – for **I can say that** perhaps **[the creditor] avoided** having to return the note to **him,** דְּאָמַר לֵיהּ לְמָחָר יְהַבְנָא לָךְ – **by telling [the debtor]: "I will give it to you tomorrow,** דְּהַשְׁתָּא לֵיתֵיהּ גַּבַּאי – **for it is not with me right now."** אִי נַמִּי – **Or else** אַפְּשִׁיטֵי דְסָפְרָא זָיֵיר לֵיהּ – perhaps **he withheld [the note]** until the debtor repays him **for the coins** he gave **the scribe** for writing the note.[25] Therefore, the recovered note may not be returned to the creditor, because it was possibly paid although we see that it was not ripped.[26] Thus, Shmuel's ruling is not supported by the Mishnah.

The Gemara presents a conflicting ruling to Shmuel's opinion:

אָמַר רַבִּי אַבָּהוּ אָמַר רַבִּי יוֹחָנָן – **R' Abahu said in the name of R' Yochanan:** הַמּוֹצֵא שְׁטַר חוֹב בַּשּׁוּק – **If one finds a note of indebtedness in the street,** אַף עַל פִּי שֶׁכָּתוּב בּוֹ הֶנְפֵּק – **even though a certification**[27] **is written in it,** לֹא יַחֲזִירוֹ לַבְּעָלִים – **he may not return it to its owner** [i.e. the creditor]. לֹא מִיבַּעְיָא – **It is not necessary** to teach that the note should not be returned הֵיכָא דְּלֹא כָּתוּב בּוֹ הֶנְפֵּק – **where a certification is not written in it,** דְּאִיכָּא לְמֵימַר כָּתַב לִלְוֹת וְלֹא לָוָה – **because it is possible that [the debtor] wrote** the note intending **to borrow, but** in the end **did not** actually **borrow.** Therefore, returning the note to the creditor might allow him to collect a debt which is not due him. אֶלָּא אֲפִילּוּ כָּתוּב בּוֹ הֶנְפֵּק – It is, **however,** necessary to teach that **even if a certification is written in [the note]** – וּמַאי נִיהוּ דִּמְקוּיָּם – **and what does this mean? That [the note] has been certified** by verifying the witnesses' signatures – לֹא יַחֲזִיר – **he may not return it,** דְּחַיְישִׁינַן לְפֵרָעוֹן – **because we are concerned about** the possibility of **payment** of the note.[28]

The Gemara challenges this ruling:

אֵיתִיבֵיהּ רַבִּי יִרְמְיָה לְר׳ אַבָּהוּ – **R' Yirmiyah refuted R' Abah** from a Mishnah:[29] כָּל מַעֲשֵׂה בֵּית דִּין – If one finds AN document recording an ACT OF THE COURT, הֲרֵי זֶה יַחֲזִיר – H SHOULD RETURN it to the creditor named therein. This refutes I Abahu's ruling that a note of indebtedness which contains certification, which is also an act of the court, may not b returned. – ? –

The Gemara answers:

אָמַר לֵיהּ – **[R' Abahu] told him:** יִרְמְיָה בְּרִי – **My so Yirmiyah,**[30] לֹא כָּל מַעֲשֵׂה בֵּית דִּין שָׁוִים – **not all acts of th court are alike** in this regard. אֶלָּא כְּגוֹן שֶׁהוּחְזַק כַּפְרָן – **Rathe** the Mishnah refers specifically to **an instance in which [th debtor] has been presumed a liar.** Only then does the Mishna teach that a document recording an act of the court should b returned, because the debtor is not trusted to claim that he pai the note. Ordinarily, however, when the debtor is not presumed liar, he is trusted to claim the note was paid, and it may not b returned.

The Gemara objects to this explanation of the Mishnah:

אָמַר רָבָא – **Rava said:** וּמִשּׁוּם דְּהוּחְזַק כַּפְרָן חֲדָא זִמְנָא – **And d** we say that **because [this debtor] was once presumed a lia** תּוּ לֹא פָּרַע כְּלָל – **he will never pay** his debt? The possibility o repayment exists here as well![31] – ? –

The Gemara proposes an alternative explanation:

אֶלָּא אָמַר רָבָא – **Rather, Rava said** מַתְנִיתִין בִּשְׁטַר חַלְטָאתָא וְאַדְרַכְתָּא – **that the Mishnah** that rules that document recording acts of the court should be returned **refers to certificate of foreclosure and a seizure warrant,** וּכְדְרַבִּי זֵירָא – **and follows R' Zeira** who explained above that we are nc concerned that these documents were paid. Recovered notes o indebtedness, however, even if they contain a certification, ma not be returned to the creditor if the debtor claims they were pai

Rava digresses to discuss the laws of a debtor who is presume a liar:

וְכַפְרָן – **And** the topic of **a liar,** הוֹאִיל וְאָתָא לְיָדָן – **since i came up** in discussion,[32] נֵימָא בֵּיהּ מִלְּתָא – **let us sa something about it.** דְּאָמַר רַב יוֹסֵף בַּר מִנְיוֹמִי אָמַר רַב נַחְמָן – **Fo Rav Yosef bar Minyomi said in the name of Rav Nachman** אָמְרוּ לוֹ – **If [the court] told [the debtor]:** צֵא תֵּן לוֹ – **Go ou and give [the lender]** the money you owe him,

NOTES

24. If the creditor refuses to return the certificate of foreclosure by claiming it was lost, the debtor is within his rights to demand another document, since this is not a redemption of his land, but a purchase of the creditor's land (*Rashi*).

25. It is the obligation of the debtor to pay the scribe for his services (*Bava Basra* 167b). Sometimes, however, when the debtor does not have the money to pay for his services at the time, the creditor volunteers to pay the scribe, intending that the debtor will later reimburse him. If the creditor has not yet been reimbursed by the time the debt is paid, he might withhold the note from the debtor until he is reimbursed (see *Rashi*).

26. The commentators ask why the debtor is not expected to demand a receipt for payment if the creditor withholds the note, just as the debtor is expected to ask for a new bill of sale if the creditor withholds the certificate of seizure (see Gemara above). *Tos. HaRosh* explains that because the debtor feels beholden to the creditor for extending the loan to him, he is embarrassed to ask for written proof of payment as a condition for his payment of the outstanding debt. However, in a case in which his land has already been collected as payment, he is not embarrassed to ask for written proof of his repossessment of the land, since this is a document recording a separate transaction, and is nc essentially connected with the loan (cf. *Nimukei Yosef*).

27. See note 16.

28. [R' Abahu indicates that R' Yochanan forbids the finder to return th note only in a case in which the debtor denies owing the money. Thi contrasts with other Amoraim (above, 13b, and below, 17a) who quote F Yochanan as forbidding the note's return even where the debtor admit to owing the money. See *Tosafos* for a fuller discussion of this.]

29. Below, 20a.

30. "My son" is an endearment; R' Abahu was not R' Yirmiyahu's fathe (*Nimukei Yosef*).

31. Although the Gemara will soon teach that where a man was found t have lied about a certain obligation, he is no longer trusted to say he pai that obligation, the fact that this document was found in the stree raises the suspicion that it has already been repaid. Therefore, w should consider the possibility of repayment even regarding a presume liar (*Tosafos*).

32. Literally: since it came to our hands.

משום כדי חייו [א] אמר רב הונא אמר רב [א] האומר לחברו שדה שאני לוקח לכשאקחנה קנויה לך מעכשיו קנה ° אמר רבא מסתברא מלתא דרב בשדה סתם אבל בשדה זו לא מי יימר דמזבין לה ניהליה והאלהים אמר רב אפי' בשדה זו מכדי רב כמאן אמרה לשמעתי' כר"מ דאמר אדם מקנה דבר שלא בא לעולם דתניא [ב] א האומר לאשה התקדשי לי לאחר שאתגייר לאחר שתתגיירי לאחר שאשתחרר לאחר שתשתחררי לאחר שימות בעליך לאחר שיחלוץ לך יבמיך לאחר שתמות אחותיך אינה מקודשת ר"מ אומר מקודשת והא אשה כשדה זו דמיא וא"ר מאיר מקודשת: אמר שמואל [ג] המוצא שטר הקנאה בשוק יחזירו לבעלים דאי משום דכתב ללות ולא לוה ° הא שעבד נפשיה ואי משום פרעון [ד] לא חיישינן לפרעון דאם איתא דפרעיה מקרע הוה קרע ליה אמר רב נחמן אבא מן ספרי דייני דמר שמואל הוה והוינא כבר שיתא כבר שבע ודכרנא דהוו מכרזי ואמרי הני שטרי אקנייתא דמשתכחי בשוקא נהדרינהו למרייהו אמר רב עמרם אף אנן (א) תנינא [ה] כל מעשה בית דין הרי זה יחזיר אלמא לא חיישינן לפירעון א"ל רבי זירא מתניתין בשטרי חלטאתא ואדרכתא דלאו בני פרעון נינהו אמר רבא והני לאו בני פרעון נינהו והא [ו] אמרי נהרדעי שומא הדר עד תריסר ירחי שתא ואמר אמימר אנא מנהרדעא אנא וסבירא לי ב דשומא הדר לעולם אלא אמר רבא התם היינו טעמא דאמרי איהו הוא דאפסיד אנפשיה דבעידנא דפרעיה אבעי ליה למקרעיה לשטריה א"נ למכתב שטרא אחרינא עילויה דמדינא ארעא לא בעיא למיהדר ג ומשום א) ועשית הישר והטוב בעיני ה' הוא דאמור רבנן תהדר הלכך מרישא הוא דקא זבין איבעי ליה למכתב שטר זביני גבי שטר חוב מאי איכא למימר אם איתא דפרעיה איבעי ליה למיקרעיה לשטריה אימור אשתמוטי קא משתמיט ליה דא"ל למחר יהבנא לך דהשתא ליתיה גבאי אי נמי אפשיטי דספרא זייר ליה: א"ר אבהו א"ר יוחנן המוצא שטר חוב בשוק אע"פ שכתוב בו הנפק לא יחזירו לבעלים לא מיבעיא היכא דלא כתוב בו הנפק דאיכא למימר כתב ללות ולא לוה אלא אפי' כתוב בו הנפק ומאי ניהו דמקוים לא יחזיר דחיישינן לפרעון איתיביה רבי ירמיה לר' אבהו כל מעשה ב"ד הרי זה יחזיר א"ל ירמיה ברי לא כל מעשה ב"ד שוים אלא כגון שהוחזק כפרן אמר רבא ומשום דהוחזק כפרן חדא זמנא תו לא פרע כלל אלא אמר רבא מתניתין בשטר חלטאתא ואדרכתא וכדרבי זירא וכפרן הואיל ואתא לידן נימא ביה מלתא דאמר רב יוסף בר מניומי אמר רב נחמן אמרו לו [ז] צא תן לו ואמר

**רש"י**

משום כדי חייו. מה שתעלה מצודתי היום תקנו חכמים שיהיו דבריו קיימין שמא צריך הוא למזונות דבר מועט אבל מה שתעלה מצודתי כל חדש או כל שנה אין שם משום כדי חייו: קנויה לך מעכשיו. שכשאקחנה לא אוכל לחזור בו קנה. אם יקחנה ואין יכול לחזור כשלקחה: בשדה סתם. שדה שאני לוקח ולא אמר זו דסמכא דעתיה דמקבל מתנה לסמוך עליו שיקח שדה ויתננה לו שהרבה שדות מצויות ליקח אבל אמר לו שדה זו לא סמכא דעתיה דמקבל מתנה ולא האמינו דנימא ניחא ליה דליקו בהימנותיה ולא מסתבר כוותיה דרב בהא: והאלהים. בשבועה רב אמרה אפילו בשדה זו דמכדי רב כמאן אמר לשמעתיה כר"מ כו': והא אשה כשדה זו דמיא. דיש באלו שאין בידו להביא עצמו לכלל קדושין כאשר אין ביד זה לכוף את בעל השדה למוכרה לו דעבד ושפחה אין בידם לשחרר עצמם ואין ביד אשה להמית את בעלה או אחותה ואמר רבי מאיר דלכשיבאו לכלל קדושין מקודשת היא למפרע: שטר הקנאה. שקנו ממנו שאפילו לא ילוה המעות שיעבד עצמו לשלם: כל מעשה ב"ד. קס"ד שטר שכתב בו הנפק שנתקיים בב"ד אלמא כיון דליכא למיחש לשמא לא לוה שהרי אין מקיימין את השטר אלא בפני בעל דין כדאמרי' בהגוזל (ב"ק דף קיב:) לפרעון לא חיישינן: בשטרי חלטאתא. שטר שכתבו ב"ד למוציא שטר על חבירו וחייבוהו לשלם ולא שילם וירדו לנכסיו ושמו לבעל חוב אחד מהם ונתנו לו שטר שעל פי ב"ד באה לו: אדרכתא. שלא מצאו לו עכשיו נכסים וכתבו לו שירדוף לחזור על נכסיו ואם ימצא יגבה. אדרכתא לשון רודף ומשיג כמו פרסה בחלא ולא אדרכיה (כתובות דף ס:) ולשון המקרא כתרו את בנימין הרדיפוהו מנוחה הדריכוהו (שופטים כ): שומא. ששמו ב"ד לבעל חוב קרקע הלוה: הדר. אם יפרע לו מעות עד שנה: אפסיד אנפשיה. אם פרע ולא קרע השטר ואם דחהו לומר אבד היה לו לומר כתוב לי שטר מיד שאתה חוזר ומוכרה לי: דמדינא ארעא לא בעי למיהדר. טעם נותן לדבריו שראוי לכתוב שטר מכירה עליה שקנויה לו לחלוטין ומדינא לא בעי למיהדר בפדיון אם לא מדעתו: מרישא דקא זבין. כלומר אין זה פדיון אלא תחילת קניין כאילו שלו היתה לפיכך הכותב שטר מכירה עליה אינו טועה והיה לו לזה לתבוע שטר מכירה הואיל ודחהו מלהחזיר לו שטר של ב"ד: אי נמי אפשיטי דספרא זייר ליה. שעל הלוה ליתן שכר הסופר ופעמים שאין לו מעות ללוה בשעת הלואה והמלוה נותן שכר לכתיבת השטר וכשפרעו מעכב השטר בידו עד שיפרע השכר: זייר. לשון עוצר כמו מעצרת' זיירא (ע"ז דף ס.) ובלשון המקרא ויזר את הגזה (שופטים ו): כל מעשה ב"ד. והאי נמי מעשה ב"ד הוא: ירמיה ברי גרסינן: שהוחזק. לוה זה כפרן פעם אחרת לפיכך אין נאמן לומר פרעתי ובההיא תנן יחזיר: ותו לא פרע כלל. בתמיה ואי חיישינן לפרעון זה שלא נזהר לשמור שטרו יפסיד: צא תן לו. שפסקו לו דינו בב"ד שציוו עליו לתת לו: ואמר

**תוספות**

שדה שאני לוקח. ל"ג זו מדקאמר והאלהים אפילו בשדה זו הלא בפירוש אמר זו:

בשטרי חלטאתא ואדרכתא דלאו בני פרעון נינהו. תימה שטרי אדרכתא אמאי לאו בני פרעון נינהו כיון דעדיין לא זכה בקרקע עד שכתבו לו שטרי חלטאתא וכן בסמוך דקאמר איהו דאפסיד אנפשיה דבעי ליה למקרעיה או אבעי ליה למכתב שטר מכירה בשטרי אדרכתא שעדיין הקרקע היא בידו במה אפסיד אנפשיה והלא יכול לטעון פרעתי וי"ל דשטרי אדרכתא נקט אליבא דרבה דאית ליה בפרק המפקיד (לקמן דף לה: ושם) דאכיל פירי מכי מטא אדרכתא לידיה א"כ לא יוכל לומר עוד פרעתי כיון שכבר זכה בקרקע ולרבא דאית ליה מכי שלמו יומי דאכרזתא לדבריו יעמיד מתני' בחלטאתא גרידא ויש ספרים דל"ג אדרכתא:

אע"פ שכתוב בו הנפק לא יחזיר. תימה דמשמע דאיירי באין חייב מודה כדאמר שמא כתב ללות ולא לוה לכך לא יחזיר דחיישינן לפרעון אבל אם לוה מודה יחזיר דלא חיישינן לקנוניא ולא לשמא פרעו ורוצה לחזור וללות בו כדי להרויח פשיטי דספרא וקשה דלקמן (דף יז.) א"ר יוחנן שטר שכתוב זמנו בו ביום וכתוב בו הנפק יחזיר ומוקי לה רב כהנא כשחייב מודה ודוקא שכתוב בו ביום אבל אין כתוב בו ביום לא יחזיר או משום פשיטי דספרא או משום קנוניא וכן לעיל (דף יג:) אוקי ר"י מתני' דמלא שטרי חוב לא יחזיר בחייב מודה ומשום קנוניא דסברי רבנן דאין בו אחריות גבי (לוה) נמי ממשעבדי ([ח] ותניא כוותיה דרבי יוחנן) וי"ל דאמוראי נינהו ואליבא דרבי יוחנן דרב כהנא יעמיד הכא מלתא דרבי יוחנן אף כשחייב מודה ומשום קנוניא ורבי אבהו דמפרש דוקא כשאין חייב מודה אבל כשחייב מודה יחזיר דלא חיש לקנוניא יעמיד נמי מתני' דלעיל כשחייב מודה ומשום שמא כתב ללות ולא לוה כרב אסי אבל היכא דליכא למיחש לכתב ללות ולא לוה כמו בשטרי הקנאה או כתוב בו הנפק כי הכא יחזיר דלא חיישינן לקנוניא וגמרא דנקט לעיל טעמא דקנוניא סבר כאביי דאמר עדיו בחתומיו זכין לו או אקרי וכתיב לא אמרינן:

ומשום דהוחזק כפרן תו לא פרע כלל. ואף על גב דאמרינן לקמן (דף יז.) הוחזק כפרן לאותו ממון הכא דנפל שאני דמוכחא מלתא דמשום הכי לא היה נזהר לשומרו לפי שפרעו הלוה:

חייב

**עין משפט נר מצוה**

[א] [מיי' פכ"ב מהל' מכירה הל' ה ש"ע ח"מ סי' ריא סעי' א דלא כרב]:
קמג א מיי' פ"ז מהל' אישות הלכה יד סמג עשין מח טוש"ע אה"ע סי' מ סעי' ה:
קמד ב ג מיי' פכ"ב מהל' מלוה ולוה הלכה טז סמג עשין צד טוש"ע ח"מ סי' קג סעי' ט:

**גליון הש"ס**

גמ' אמר רבא מסתברא. כעין זה גיטין יג ע"ב וש"נ: שם הא שעבד נפשיה. עיין בר"ן פ"ק דקדושין דף ריד ע"ב:

**תורה אור השלם**

א) וְעָשִׂיתָ הַיָּשָׁר וְהַטּוֹב בְּעֵינֵי יְיָ לְמַעַן יִיטַב לָךְ וּבָאתָ וְיָרַשְׁתָּ אֶת הָאָרֶץ הַטֹּבָה אֲשֶׁר נִשְׁבַּע יְיָ לַאֲבֹתֶיךָ: [דברים ו, יח]

**רבינו חננאל**

מצודתי היום מכור לך דבריו קיימים. אבל הא דאמר רב האומר לחבירו שדה זו שאני לוקח לכשאקחנה קנויה לך מעכשיו קני לית הלכתא כרב דאשכחן ביבמות פ' האשה רבה הלכתא האשה שהלך בעלה ובנה למדינת הים וכו'. אמר רב נחמן בר יצחק רב הונא כרב ורב כר' ינאי ור' ינאי כר' חייא ור' חייא כר' ור' כר' מאיר ור' מאיר כר' אליעזר בן יעקב ורבי אליעזר בן יעקב כר' עקיבא כולהו סבירא להו אדם מקנה לחבירו דבר שלא בא לעולם. וקיימא לן דהני כולהו שיטה אינון ולית הלכתא אפילו כחד מינייהו. אמר שמואל המוצא שטר הקנאה בשוק יחזיר לבעלים ולית הילכתא כוותיה דהא איתותב וקיימא לן חוששין לפרעון. והא דאמר רב נחמן דכירנא דהוו מכריזי הני שטרי אקנייתא דמשתכחי בשוקא ניהדרינהו למרייהו לטעמיה דשמואל היא ולית הלכתא כוותיה. אמר ר' יוחנן המוצא שטר חוב בשוק אע"ג דכתיב ביה הנפק. פי' הנפק אשרתא דדייני לא יחזיר מאי טעמא חיישינן לפרעון. איני והתנן כל מעשה ב"ד הרי זה יחזיר. ופרקי' מתני' בשטרי חלטאתא ואדרכתא דלאו בני פרעון נינהו. ר' אבהו אמר בשהוחזק הלוה כפרן. אמר רבא ומשום דהוחזק כפרן תוב לא פרע ודילמא הדר ופרע וכו'. כפרן הואיל ואתא לידן נימא בה מילתא.

**מסורת הש"ס**

א) יבמות נג., ב) שם ...
קדושין סג., כתובות ...
ג) [לעיל יד.], ד) [לעיל ...
יד.], ה) [לקמן יח:, ...
ו) לקמן לה., ז) [דומה ...
בבא קמא סח:, ק...
ח) ס"א ל"ג.

**הגהות הב"ח**

(א) גמ' אף אנן תנינא:

**ליקוטי רש"י**

האומר לחברו. ק... שקנה את השדה. ק... והוא מתנה [יבמות צ... והאלקים. שבו... [סנהדרין עב.]. ש... הקנאה. שמקנה לו נכ... מהיום בין ילוה בין לא י... יגבה מהן לאותו ... מהיום. לא חייש... לפרעון. בשטר הנ... ואפי' אין חייב מודה. ד... איתא דפרעיה מקרע ה... קרע ליה וכו' וכ"ש כשח... מודה מהאי טעמא גו... דמיום פריעתו הוא קו... [לעיל יג.]. כל מעש... ב"ד הרי זה יחזיר. מילתא דאתא לב"ד לק... דליכא למיחש לנמלך על... שלא ליתנן הרי זה יח... [לקמן יח:]. אדרכת... שכתבו פסק דין ונ... ללוקח על נכסיו של ... שבכ"מ שימצאם יחזיק ... והיינו תשעים יום לא... שעמד בדין כדאמ... בהגוזל בתרא [לעיל בע"... שומא הדר. נכסי ... ששמו ב"ד לבעל ... חוזרין אליו אם נותן מ... לבעל חוב [לקמן ל... ועשית הישר והט... זו פשרה לפנים משו... הדין [דברים ו, י... אפשיטי. זוזי מד... שמונה מהן זוז ... [כתובות סז.].

the document is intact, the debt was clearly not paid.

The Gemara verifies that this is Shmuel's opinion:

אָמַר רַב נַחְמָן – **Rav Nachman said:** אַבָּא מִן סָפְרֵי דַיָּינֵי דְּמָר שְׁמוּאֵל הֲוָה – **My father was** one **of Shmuel's court scribes** וַהֲוֵינָא כְּבַר שִׁיתָּא כְּבַר שֶׁבַע – **and I was six or seven years old** at the time, וּדְכַרְנָא דַּהֲווּ מַכְרְזֵי וְאָמְרֵי – **and I recall that they would announce and say:** הָנֵי שְׁטָרֵי אַקְנָייתָא דְּמִשְׁתַּכְּחֵי בְּשׁוּקָא – **These documents of acquisition that are found in the street** נַהַדְרִינְהוּ לְמָרַיְיהוּ – **should be returned to their owners** [i.e. to the creditors].

The Gemara supports Shmuel's ruling:

אָמַר רַב עַמְרָם – **Rav Amram said:** אַף אֲנַן תְּנֵינָא – **We also learned** a similar ruling **in a Mishnah:**[15] כָּל מַעֲשֵׂה בֵּית דִּין – If one finds ANY document recording an ACT OF THE COURT, הֲרֵי זֶה יַחְזִיר – HE SHOULD RETURN it to the creditor named therein. Rav Amram presumes that this refers to a note of indebtedness which has been certified by the court.[16] אַלְמָא לֹא חָיְישִׁינַן לְפֵירָעוֹן – **It follows, then, that** the Mishnah holds that when we are certain of the authenticity of the debt recorded in a recovered document, **we are not concerned about** the possibility of the debt's **payment.** This supports Shmuel's ruling.

The Gemara refutes this proof:

אָמַר לֵיהּ רַבִּי זֵירָא – **R' Zeira told [Rav Amram]:** מַתְנִיתִין בִּשְׁטָרֵי חַלְטָאתָא וְאַדְרַכְתָּא – **The Mishnah's** phrase "act of the court" **refers** not to a certified note of indebtedness but **to certificates of foreclosure**[17] **and seizure warrants,**[18] דְּלָאו בְּנֵי פֵּרָעוֹן נִינְהוּ – **which are not payable.**[19] Therefore, they must be returned to the creditor. An ordinary payable note, however, cannot be returned to the creditor even if it has been certified, because the debt might have already been paid.

The refutation is challenged:

אָמַר רָבָא – **Rava said:** וְהָנֵי לָאו בְּנֵי פֵּרָעוֹן נִינְהוּ – **And are these** documents indeed **not payable?** וְהָא אָמְרֵי נְהַרְדְּעֵי – **But the Nehardean** scholars **say:** שׁוּמָא הָדַר עַד תְּרֵיסַר יַרְחֵי שַׁתָּא – **Seized property must be returned** to the debtor if he offers money instead **up to twelve months** after its collection.[20] וַאֲמֵימָר – **And Ameimar said:** אֲנָא מִנְּהַרְדְּעָא אֲנָא – **I am fr**[om] **Nehardea,** וּסְבִירָא לִי דְּשׁוּמָא הָדַר לְעוֹלָם – **yet I hold that seiz**[ed] **property must be returned** to the debtor **forever,** no matter h[ow] long after the seizure he offers money in payment of the obligati[on]. Apparently, the debt may be paid even after the creditor recei[ves] a certificate of foreclosure. If we were concerned about the possi[bi]lity of repayment, we would not return these documents to the c[re]ditor. Since the Mishnah rules that we return them, the Mishn[ah] obviously does not consider the possibility that the loan was paid. Thus, the Mishnah does indeed corroborate Shmuel's rulin[g].

The Gemara explains that the Mishnah nevertheless does n[ot] support Shmuel's ruling:

אֶלָּא אָמַר רָבָא – **Rather, Rava said:** הָתָם הַיְינוּ טַעֲמָא – **The**[re] in the Mishnah, **the reason** we return the documents to t[he] creditor is דְּאָמְרֵי אִיהוּ הוּא דְּאַפְסִיד אַנַּפְשֵׁיהּ – **because we s**[ay] that if the debtor paid the obligation **he brought** an undue l[oss] **upon himself;** דְּבְעִידְּנָא דְּפַרְעֵיהּ – **for at the time that he pa**[id] **[the creditor],** אִבָּעֵי לֵיהּ לְמִקְרְעֵיהּ לִשְׁטָרֵיהּ – **he should ha**[ve] **ripped the document,** אִי נַמִּי לְמִכְתַּב שְׁטָרָא אַחֲרִינָא עִילָּוֵיהּ – [or] asked the creditor **to write** him **another document concerni**[ng] **[the land],** stating that he repossessed it.[21] Since the debtor d[id] not rip the document, and he is not in possession of a differe[nt] document stating that the land was returned to him, we presu[me] that the obligation remained unpaid. Therefore, the document [is] returned to the creditor.

In a somewhat tangential way, the Gemara explains how it [is] that the debtor can demand that a document be drawn up stati[ng] that the land was again acquired by him:

דְּמִדִּינָא אַרְעָא לֹא בָּעְיָא לְמִיהֲדַר – **According to the** letter of t[he] **law, the land need not be returned** to the debtor, unless t[he] creditor desires to do so. [אֶלָּ]א וּמִשּׁוּם: ,,וְעָשִׂיתָ הַיָּשָׁר וְהַטּוֹב בְּעֵינֵי ה׳ ״ – **And** it is only **because** of the verse: ***You shall do that whi***[ch] ***is fair and good in the eyes of Hashem,***[22] דְּאָמוּר רַבָּנָן תִּהֲדַר – **that the Sages said [the land]** must **be returned.**

NOTES

15. Below, 20a.

16. When a note is presented by a creditor for payment, the debtor may deny having borrowed, arguing that the witnesses' signatures are forged. The creditor then cannot collect unless he can prove to the court that the signatures are genuine. If he succeeds, the court appends to the document a paragraph attesting to the authenticity of the signatures, and the judges sign their names below. This certification is called a הֶנְפֵּק.

Because a creditor may be concerned that he will have difficulty verifying the witnesses' signatures when the note becomes due, he often asks the court to verify the signatures even before he presents the note for collection. A debtor, however, generally does not bother to certify a note before giving it to his creditor. Consequently, since our Mishnah discusses recovery of a certified note, it is obvious that the note was lost by the creditor and that the loan actually occurred (*Ritva*). Additionally, the certification negates any suspicion of forgery that the note's loss may raise, because the court certifies a note for the creditor only in the presence of the debtor. Clearly, the debtor either had agreed to the note's authenticity, or was unable to prove to the court that it was forged (see *Rashi* and commentary of *Maharsha*).

17. When the court collects property of the debtor in payment of his obligation and assigns it to the creditor, the court writes a certificate of foreclosure for the creditor to serve as his proof that he legally possessed the land (*Rashi*).

18. See 16a note 12.

19. A certificate of foreclosure and a seizure warrant record a creditor's rights of collection, and not the obligation; therefore, they cannot be paid.

[*Tosafos* question why a seizure warrant is not payable. Since the creditor receives the warrant before he collects the land, the debtor could have repaid the loan and received the warrant in return. Indeed, *Tosafos* note that some texts of the Gemara do not have the word "אַדְרַכְתָּא." See תוס׳ ד״ה בשטרי and *Ritva* for possible explanations of o[ur] text.]

20. That is, although the creditor has already received payment in t[he] form of the debtor's land, the debtor may force the creditor to return [the] land in exchange for a cash payment of the original debt. The schola[rs] of Nehardea and Amaimar argue about when this can be done.

21. If the creditor claimed that he lost the certificate and therefore cou[ld] not return it, the debtor should have insisted that the creditor write h[im] a new document to serve as proof that he repossessed the land (*Rash*[*i*]; see Gemara below).

22. *Deuteronomy* 6:18.

23. Because it could not possibly list the specific proper conduct for ea[ch] situation of human relations, the Torah sums up man's obligation to [his] fellow with the general directive "you shall do that which is fair a[nd] good in the eyes of Hashem" (*Ramban* to *Deuteronomy* 6:18). The spe[ci]fic applications of this general command were left up to the Sages' jud[g]ment. They listed a number of these applications, some of which th[ey] described as preferred conduct, and some of which they required of eve[ry] Jew and are enforceable in court, but all of which have only the force [of] Rabbinic law (*Maggid Mishneh* to *Rambam Hilchos Shecheinim* 14:[5]).

Allowing a debtor to buy back property that the court awarded t[he] creditor in payment of the debtor's obligation falls under this headin[g]. Since a man generally feels an attachment to his own field, it is distres[s]ful to be forced to part with it when it is awarded to his creditor (*Aru*[*ch*] *HaShulchan Choshen Mishpat* 103:12). The creditor, on the oth[er] hand, has no special attachment to the field, since he originally count[ed] on receiving money as payment for the loan (see *Rashi* below 35a, ד״ה ארעתא). Therefore, although by Torah law he should be able to retain t[he] field once he collected it, the Sages considered it "fair and good" that [he] allow the debtor to buy it back, and they obligated the creditor to reli[n]quish the field in exchange for payment of the erstwhile debt.

משום כדי חייו [א] אמר רב הונא אמר רב [א] האומר לחברו שדה שאני לוקח לכשאקחנה קנויה לך מעכשיו קנה ° אמר רבא מסתברא מלתא דרב בשדה סתם אבל בשדה זו לא מי יימר דמזבין לה ניהליה והאלהים אמר רב אפי' בשדה זו מכדי רב כמאן אמרה לשמעתי' כר"מ דאמר אדם מקנה דבר שלא בא לעולם דתניא [ג] [א] האומר לאשה התקדשי לי לאחר שאתגייר לאחר שתתגיירי לאחר שאשתחרר לאחר שתשתחררי לאחר שימות בעליך לאחר שיחלוץ לך יבמיך לאחר שתמות אחותיך אינה מקודשת ר"מ אומר מקודשת והא אשה כשדה זו דמיא וא"ר מאיר מקודשת: אמר שמואל [ג] המוצא שטר הקנאה בשוק יחזירו לבעלים דאי משום דכתב ללות ולא לוה ° הא שעבד נפשיה ואי משום פרעון [ד] לא חיישינן לפרעון דאם איתא דפרעיה מקרע הוה קרע ליה אמר רב נחמן אבא מן ספרי דייני דמר שמואל הוה והוינא כבר שיתא כבר שבע ודכרנא דהוו מכרזי ואמרי הני שטרי אקנייתא דמשתכחי בשוקא נהדרינהו למרייהו אמר רב עמרם אף אנן (א) תנינא [ה] כל מעשה בית דין הרי זה יחזיר אלמא לא חיישינן לפירעון א"ל רבי זירא מתניתין בשטרי חלטאתא ואדרכתא דלאו בני פרעון נינהו אמר רבא והני לאו בני פרעון נינהו והא [ו] אמרי נהרדעי שומא הדר עד תריסר ירחי שתא ואמר אמימר אנא מנהרדעא אנא וסבירא לי [ב] דשומא הדר לעולם אלא אמר רבא התם היינו טעמא דאמרי איהו הוא דאפסיד אנפשיה דבעידנא דפרעיה אבעי ליה למקרעיה לשטריה א"נ למכתב שטרא אחרינא עילויה דמדינא ארעא לא בעיא למיהדר [ג] ומשום [א] ועשית הישר והטוב בעיני ה' הוא דאמור רבנן תהדר הלכך מרישא הוא דקא זבין איבעי ליה למכתב שטר זביני גבי שטר חוב מאי איכא למימר אם איתא דפרעיה איבעי ליה למיקרעיה לשטריה אימור אשתמוטי קא משתמיט ליה דא"ל למחר יהבנא לך דהשתא ליתיה גבאי אי נמי אפשיטי דספרא זייר ליה: א"ר אבהו א"ר יוחנן המוצא שטר חוב בשוק אע"פ שכתוב בו הנפק לא יחזירו לבעלים לא מיבעיא היכא דלא כתוב בו הנפק דאיכא למימר כתב ללות ולא לוה אלא אפי' כתוב בו הנפק ומאי ניהו דמקוים לא יחזיר דחיישינן לפרעון איתיביה רבי ירמיה לר' אבהו כל מעשה ב"ד הרי זה יחזיר א"ל ירמיה ברי לא כל מעשה ב"ד שוים אלא כגון שהוחזק כפרן אמר רבא ומשום דהוחזק כפרן חדא זמנא תו לא פרע כלל אלא אמר רבא מתניתין בשטר חלטאתא ואדרכתא וכדרבי זירא וכפרן הואיל ואתא לידן נימא ביה מלתא דאמר רב יוסף בר מניומי אמר רב נחמן אמרו לו [ז] צא תן לו ואמר

משום כדי חייו. מה שתלה מלודתי היום תקנו חכמים שיהיו דבריו קיימין שמא צריך הוא למזונות דבר מועט אבל מה שתלה מלודתי כל חדש או כל שנה אין שם משום כדי חייו: קנויה לך מעכשיו. שכשאקחנה לא אוכל לחזור בו קנה. אם יקחנה ואין יכול לחזור כשלקחה: בשדה סתם. שדה שאני לוקח ולא אמר זו דסמכא דעתיה דמקבל מתנה לסמוך עליו שיקח שדה ויתננה לו שהרבה שדות מצויות ליקח אבל אמר לו שדה זו לא סמכא דעתיה דמקבל מתנה ולא האמינו דנימא ניחא ליה דליקו בהימנותיה ולא מסתבר כוותיה דרב בהא: והאלהים. בשבועה רב אמרה אפילו בשדה זו דמכדי רב כמאן אמר לשמעתיה כר"מ כו': והא אשה כשדה זו דמיא. דיש באלו שאין בידו להביא עצמו לכלל קדושין כאשר אין ביד זה לכוף את בעל השדה למוכרה לו דעבד ושפחה אין בידם לשחרר עצמם ואין ביד אשה להמית את בעלה או אחותה ואמר רבי מאיר דלכשיבאו לכלל קדושין מקודשת היא למפרע: שטר הקנאה. שקנו ממנו שאפילו לא ילוה המעות שיעבד עצמו לשלם: כל מעשה ב"ד. קס"ד שטר שכתב בו הנפק שנתקיים בב"ד אלמא כיון דליכא למיחש לשמא לא לוה שהרי אין מקיימין את השטר אלא בפני בעל דין כדאמרי' בהגוזל (ב"ק דף קיב:) לפרעון לא חיישינן: בשטרי חלטאתא. שטר שכתבו ב"ד למוציא שטר על חבירו וחייבוהו לשלם ולא שילם וירדו לנכסיו ושמו לבעל חוב אחד מהם ונתנו לו שטר שעל פי ב"ד באה לו: אדרכתא. שלא מצאו לו עכשיו נכסים וכתבו לו שירדוף לחזור על נכסיו ואם ימצא יגבה. אדרכתא לשון רודף ומשיג כמו פרסה בחלא ולא אדרכיה (כתובות דף ס:) ולשון המקרא כתרו את בנימין הרדיפוהו מנוחה הדריכוהו (שופטים כ): שומא. ששמו ב"ד לבעל חוב קרקע הלוה: הדר. אם יפרע לו מעות עד שנה: אפסיד אנפשיה. אם פרע ולא קרע השטר ואם דחהו לומר אבד היה לו לומר כתוב לי שטר מיד שאתה חוזר ומוכרה לי: דמדינא ארעא לא בעי למיהדר. טעם נותן לדבריו שראוי לכתוב שטר מכירה עליה שקנויה לו לחלוטין ומדינא לא בעי למיהדר בפדיון אם לא מדעתו: מרישא דקא זבין. כלומר אין זה פדיון אלא תחילת קניין כאילו שלו היתה לפיכך הכותב שטר מכירה עליה אינו טועה והיה לו לזה לתבוע שטר מכירה הואיל ודחהו מלהחזיר לו שטר של ב"ד: אי נמי אפשיטי דספרא זייר ליה. שעל הלוה ליתן שכר הסופר ופעמים שאין לו מעות ללוה בשעת הלואה והמלוה נותן שכר לכתיבת השטר וכשפרעו מעכב השטר בידו עד שיפרע השכר: זייר. לשון עוצר כמו מעצרת' זיירא (ע"ז דף ס.) וכלשון המקרא ויזר את הגזה (שופטים ו): כל מעשה ב"ד. והאי נמי מעשה ב"ד הוא: ירמיה ברי גרסינן: שהוחזק. לוה זה כפרן פעם אחרת לפיכך אין נאמן לומר פרעתי וההיא תנן יחזיר: ותו לא פרע כלל. בתמיה ואי חיישינן לפרעון זה שלא נזהר לשמור שטרו יפסיד: צא תן לו. שפסקו לו דינו בב"ד שאיו עליו לתת לו:
ואמר

שדה שאני לוקח. ל"ג זו מדקאמר והאלהים אפילו בשדה זו הלא בפירוש אמר זו:

בשטרי חלטאתא ואדרכתא דלאו בני פרעון נינהו. תימה שטרי אדרכתא אמאי לאו בני פרעון נינהו כיון דעדיין לא זכה בקרקע עד שכתבו לו שטרי חלטאתא וכן בסמוך דקאמר איהו דאפסיד אנפשיה דבעי ליה למקרעיה או אבעי ליה למכתב שטר מכירה בשטרי אדרכתא שעדיין הקרקע היא בידו במה אפסיד אנפשיה והלא יכול לטעון פרעתי וי"ל דשטרי אדרכתא נקט אליבא דרבה דאית ליה בפרק המפקיד (לקמן דף לה: ושם) דאכיל פירי מכי מטא אדרכתא לידיה א"כ לא יוכל לומר עוד פרעתי כיון שכבר זכה בקרקע ולרבא דאית ליה מכי שלמו יומי דאכרזתא לדבריו יעמיד מתני' בחלטאתא גרידא ויש ספרים דל"ג אדרכתא:

אע"פ שכתוב בו הנפק לא יחזיר. תימה דמשמע דאיירי באין חייב מודה כדאמר שמא כתב ללות ולא לוה לכך לא יחזיר דחיישינן לפרעון אבל אם לוה מודה יחזיר דלא חיישינן לקנוניא ולא לשמא פרעו ורוצה לחזור וללות בו כדי להרויח פשיטי דספרא וקשה דלקמן (דף יז.) א"ר יוחנן שטר שכתוב זמנו בו ביום וכתוב בו הנפק יחזיר ומוקי לה רב כהנא כשחייב מודה ודוקא שכתוב בו ביום אבל אין כתוב בו ביום לא יחזיר או משום פשיטי דספרא או משום קנוניא וכן לעיל (דף יג:) אוקי ר"י מתני' דמצא שטרי חוב לא יחזיר בחייב מודה ומשום קנוניא דסברי רבנן דאין בו אחריות גבי (לוה) נמי ממשעבדי ([ח] ותניא כוותיה דרבי יוחנן) וי"ל דאמוראי נינהו ואליבא דרבי יוחנן דרב כהנא יעמיד הכא מלתא דרבי יוחנן אף כשחייב מודה ומשום קנוניא ורבי אבהו דמפרש דוקא כשאין חייב מודה אבל כשחייב מודה יחזיר דלא חיים לקנוניא יעמיד נמי מתני' דלעיל כשחייב מודה ומשום שמא כתב ללות ולא לוה כרב אסי אבל היכא דליכא למיחש לכתב ללות ולא לוה כמו בשטרי הקנאה או כתוב בו הנפק כי הכא יחזיר דלא חיישינן לקנוניא וגמרא דנקט לעיל טעמא דקנוניא סבר כאביי דאמר עדיו בחתומיו זכין לו או אקרי וכתיב לא אמרינן:

ומשום דהוחזק כפרן תו לא פרע כלל. ואף על גב דאמרינן לקמן (דף יז.) הוחזק כפרן לאותו ממון הכא דנפל שאני דמוכחא מלתא דמשום הכי לא היה נזהר לשומרו לפי שפרעו הלוה:
חייב



[א] [מיי' פכ"ב מהל' מכירה הל' ה ש"ע ח"מ סי' ריא סעי' א דלא כרב]:
קמג א מיי' פ"ז מהל' אישות הלכה יד סמג עשין מח טוש"ע אה"ע סי' מ סעי' ה:
קמד ב ג מיי' פכ"ב מהל' מלוה ולוה הלכה טז סמג עשין לד טוש"ע ח"מ סי' קג סעי' ט:

גליון הש"ס

גמ' אמר רבא מסתברא. כעין זה גיטין יג ע"ב וש"נ: שם הא שעבד נפשיה. עיין בר"ן פ"ק דקדושין דף ריד ע"ב:

תורה אור השלם

א) וְעָשִׂיתָ הַיָּשָׁר וְהַטּוֹב בְּעֵינֵי יְיָ לְמַעַן יִיטַב לָךְ וּבָאתָ וְיָרַשְׁתָּ אֶת הָאָרֶץ הַטֹּבָה אֲשֶׁר נִשְׁבַּע יְיָ לַאֲבֹתֶיךָ: [דברים ו, יח]

רבינו חננאל

מצודתי היום מכור לך דבריו קיימים. אבל הא דאמר רב האומר לחבירו שדה זו שאני לוקח לכשאקחנה קנויה לך מעכשיו קני לית הלכתא כרב דאשכחן ביבמות פ' האשה רבה הלכתא האשה שהלך בעלה ובנה למדינת הים וכו'. אמר רב נחמן בר יצחק רב הונא כרב ורב כר' ינאי ור' ינאי כר' חייא ור' חייא כר' ור' כר' מאיר ור' מאיר כר' אליעזר בן יעקב ורבי אליעזר בן יעקב כר' עקיבא כולהו סבירא להו אדם מקנה לחבירו דבר שלא בא לעולם. וקיימא לן דהני כולהו שיטה אינון ולית הלכתא אפילו כחד מינייהו. אמר שמואל המוצא שטר הקנאה בשוק יחזיר לבעלים ולית הילכתא כוותיה דהא איתותב וקיימא לן חוששין לפרעון. והא דאמר רב נחמן דכירנא דהוו מכריזי הני שטרי אקנייתא דמשתכחי בשוקא ניהדרינהו למרייהו לטעמיה דשמואל היא ולית הלכתא כוותיה. אמר ר' יוחנן המוצא שטר חוב בשוק אע"ג דכתיב ביה הנפק. פי' הנפק אשרתא דדייני לא יחזיר מאי טעמא חיישינן לפרעון. איני והתנן כל מעשה ב"ד הרי זה יחזיר. ופרקי' מתני' בשטרי חלטאתא ואדרכתא דלאו בני פרעון נינהו. ר' אבהו אמר בשהוחזק הלוה כפרן. אמר רבא ומשום דהוחזק כפרן תוב לא פרע ודילמא הדר ופרע וכו'. כפרן הואיל ואתא לידן נימא בה מילתא.



א) יבמות לג., ב) שם ... קדושין סג., כתובות ... ג) [לעיל יד.], ד) [לעיל יד.], ה) [לקמן יח:], ו) לקמן לה., ז) [דומה בבא קמא סח:, ... ח) ס"א ל"ג.

הגהות הב"ח

(א) גמ' אף אנן תנינא:

ליקוטי רש"י

האומר לחברו. ... שקנה את השדה. ... והוא מתנה [יבמות ...] והאלקים. ... [סנהדרין עב.]. ... הקנאה. שמקנה לו ... מהיום בין ילוה בין לא ... יגבה מהן לאותו ... מהיום. לא חייש... לפרעון. בשטר הקנ... ואפי' אין חייב מודה. ... איתא דפרעיה מקרע ... קרע ליה וכו' וכ"ש כש... מודה מהאי טעמא גו... דמיום פריעתו הוא קו... [לעיל יג.]. כל מע... ב"ד הרי זה יחזיר. מילתא דאתא לב"ד לק... דליכא למיחש לנמלך על... שלא ליתנן הרי זה יח... [לקמן יח:]. אדרכת... שכתבו פסק דין ו... ללוקח על נכסיו של ... שבכ"מ שימצאם יחזיק ... והיינו תשעים יום ל... שעמד בדין כדאמ... בהגוזל בתרא [לעיל בע... שומא הדר. נכסי... ששמו ב"ד לבעל ... חוזרין אליו אם נותן מ... לבעל חוב [לקמן ל... ועשית הישר והט... זו פשרה לפנים מש... הדין [דברים ו, ... אפשיטי. זוזי מד... שמונה מהן זוז ... [כתובות סז.].

מִשּׁוּם כְּדֵי חַיָּיו – **because of his livelihood.**[1]

The Gemara discusses another case of the sale of property in advance of its acquisition:

אָמַר רַב הוּנָא אָמַר רַב – **Rav Huna said in the name of Rav:** הָאוֹמֵר לַחֲבֵרוֹ – If **one tells his fellow:** שָׂדֶה שֶׁאֲנִי לוֹקֵחַ – **The field that I** am about to **purchase** לִכְשֶׁאֶקָּחֶנָּה קְנוּיָה לָךְ מֵעַכְשָׁיו – **is conveyed to you when I acquire it, retroactively to now,** קָנָה – **[the recipient] acquires** the field when the giver purchases it, and the giver may then not rescind the conveyance.[2]

The Gemara cites a dissenting opinion:

אָמַר רָבָא – **Rava said:** מִסְתַּבְּרָא מִלְּתָא דְּרַב – **Rav's ruling is** indeed **logical** בְּשָׂדֶה סְתָם – **where** the giver conveyed **an unspecified field** that he plans to purchase, for the recipient is confident that the giver will purchase a field.[3] אֲבָל בְּשָׂדֶה זוֹ לֹא – **However,** if he gave him **"this" field** that he plans to purchase, Rav's ruling is **not** logical. The gift should not be valid, because the recipient thinks: מִי יֵימַר דְּמִזַּבֵּין לָהּ נִיהֲלֵיהּ – **"Who can say** whether **[the owner]** of 'this' field **will sell it to him?"**[4]

Rava asserts, however, that Rav himself rejects this distinction: וְהָאֱלֹהִים – **But by God,** אָמַר רַב אֲפִילּוּ בְּשָׂדֶה זוֹ – **Rav stated** his ruling **even concerning** the advance sale of **"this" field.** מִכְּדִי רַב כְּמַאן אֲמָרָהּ לִשְׁמַעְתֵּיהּ – **For let us see** now, **according to whom did Rav state his ruling?** כְּרַבִּי מֵאִיר – **According to R' Meir,** דְּאָמַר אָדָם מַקְנֶה דָּבָר שֶׁלֹּא בָּא לָעוֹלָם – **who said a person can convey** ownership to another **of an item that has not yet come into existence.**[5] דְּתַנְיָא – **For it was taught in a Baraisa:** הָאוֹמֵר לְאִשָּׁה – If, while performing an act of betrothal, [A MAN] TELLS A WOMAN: הִתְקַדְּשִׁי לִי – "BECOME BETROTHED TO ME לְאַחַר שֶׁאֶתְגַּיֵּיר – AFTER I CONVERT to Judaism"; לְאַחַר שֶׁתִּתְגַּיְּירִי – or, "AFTER YOU CONVERT to Judaism";[6] לְאַחַר שֶׁאֶשְׁתַּחְרֵר – or, "AFTER I AM EMANCIPATED from slavery"; לְאַחַר שֶׁתִּשְׁתַּחְרְרִי – or, "AFTER YOU ARE EMANCIPATED from slavery";[7] לְאַחַר שֶׁיָּמוּת בַּעְלֵיךְ – or, "AFTE[R] YOUR HUSBAND DIES"; לְאַחַר שֶׁיַּחֲלוֹץ לָךְ יְבָמֵיךְ – or, "AFTE[R] YOUR *YAVAM* PERFORMS *CHALITZAH* FOR YOU";[8] [לְ]אַחַר שֶׁתָּמוּת אֲחוֹתֵיךְ – or, "AFTER YOUR SISTER DIES";[9] אֵינָהּ מְקוּדֶּשֶׁת – SH[E] IS NOT BETROTHED, even after the specified event take plac[e]. רַבִּי מֵאִיר אוֹמֵר מְקוּדֶּשֶׁת – R' MEIR SAYS: SHE IS BETROTHED.

Rava analyzes the Baraisa and proves his assertion regardir[ng] Rav's opinion:

וְהָא אִשָּׁה כְּשָׂדֶה זוֹ דָּמְיָא – **Now** this case of the advance betrothal [of] **a woman is like** the advance gift of **"this" field,** for there is n[o] guarantee that these events will take place.[10] [אָ]מַר רַבִּי מֵאִיר מְקוּדֶּשֶׁת – **Yet R' Meir said she is betrothed** when the even[t] takes place. Rav likewise rules that even the advance conveyanc[e] of "this" field is effective when it is subsequently purchased b[y] the giver.[11]

The Gemara returns to its primary discussion of the laws fo[r] the return of recovered documents:

אָמַר שְׁמוּאֵל – **Shmuel said:** הַמּוֹצֵא שְׁטַר הַקְנָאָה בַּשּׁוּק – If **on[e] finds a document of acquisition**[12] **in the street,** [יַחֲ]זִירוֹ לִבְעָלִים – **he should return it to its owner** [i.e. the creditor]. Wha[t] reason could there be for withholding it from the creditor? אִי מִשּׁוּם דִּכְתַב לִלְווֹת וְלֹא לָוָה – If you argue **that** perhaps **[th]e debtor] wrote** the document intending **to borrow, but** in the en[d] **did not** actually **borrow,**[13] this is not a concern here, [הָ]א שַׁעְבֵּד נַפְשֵׁיהּ – **for he obligated himself** to pay the creditor regardles[s] of whether he borrowed. וְאִי מִשּׁוּם פֵּרָעוֹן – **And if** you argu[e] that the note should be withheld **because of repayment,**[14] thi[s] too is not a consideration, לֹא חַיְישִׁינַן לְפֵרָעוֹן – for **we are no[t] concerned about** the possibility of **payment** of a debt recorded i[n] a recovered document. דְּאִם אִיתָא דִּפְרָעֵיהּ – **For if it were tru[e] that [the debtor]** already **repaid [the creditor],** [מִ]קְרַע הֲוָה קָרַע לֵיהּ – **[the debtor] would have ripped [the document].** Sinc[e]

NOTES

1. Since a person might sometimes be in dire need of food, the Sages validated the hunter's advance sale of a day's catch. However, he may not sell more than a day's catch in advance, because it is not necessary for his sustenance on that day (*Rashi*).

*Rav Hai Gaon* and *R' Chananel* limit the validity of this sale to one who does not have food and to the amount that he must sell in order to purchase his day's food. *Ramban* disagrees, arguing that since a hunter generally sells so small an amount as one day's catch only when in dire need and only for a low price, the Sages allowed such a sale no matter what the motive or the price charged.

2. The giver may, however, nullify the gift before he purchases the field (see *Rashi*). The giver's stipulation that the conveyance should be effective retroactively is necessary only to ensure that the gift will not be nullified if the document that effects the transaction is lost or destroyed before the giver purchases the field. It does not, however, prevent the giver from nullifying the gift before he purchases the field from its owner (see *Tosafos* to 16a ד״ה קנויה, cf. *Ketzos HaChoshen* 209:8).

3. The giver told the recipient: "I am giving you a field that I will purchase," without specifying the field. Since there are always many fields available for sale, the recipient is confident that the giver will honor his commitment (*Rashi*).

4. The recipient is not confident that the owner will sell the giver the specified field. Thus, it is impossible to say that the giver desires to requite the recipient's trust (see above, 15b), because the recipient has not invested any trust in him (*Rashi*).

5. I.e. from statements made elsewhere by Rav, it is known that he subscribes to this view of R' Meir (*Shitah Mekubetzes* in the name of *Ritzbash*).

6. A gentile's betrothal of a Jewess, or a Jew's betrothal of a gentile woman, is ineffective (*Kiddushin* 68b).

7. A Canaanite slave's betrothal of a Jewess, or a Jew's betrothal of a Canaanite slavewoman, is ineffective (*Kiddushin* 68a).

8. When a man who dies childless is survived by at least one brother, his widow may not remarry someone from the general population. Instead, a brother of the deceased (known as the *yavam*) must take her as a wif[e]. If he refuses, however, the Torah provides a mechanism known a[s] *chalitzah* (taking off the shoe), by which the widow can be released fro[m] her restricted status (*Deuteronomy* 25:9). This Baraisa assumes tha[t] until the *chalitzah* is performed, her marriage to another is ineffectiv[e] (see *Ritva*).

9. This refers to a case in which the man is married (or has bee[n] previously married) to the woman's sister. His betrothal of this woma[n] is ineffective during her sister's lifetime (see *Leviticus* 18:18, *Rashi* a[d] loc.; *Kiddushin* 67b).

10. Some of these events are beyond the control of the man and th[e] woman, just as the sale of "this" field is beyond the control of the giver who cannot force the owner to sell the field; specifically, if the man o[r] woman are slaves they cannot force their master to free them, nor ma[y] the woman kill her husband or her sister (*Rashi*).

11. Rava, however, follows the Sages, who maintain that since the ma[n] or woman is presently ineligible for marriage, the betrothal i[s] ineffective. Similarly, the Sages would hold that one cannot gift away [a] specified field that he does not yet own. Nevertheless, one can gift a[n] unspecified field even according to the Sages, for since there are alway[s] fields available for purchase, it is as if the giver already owns the fiel[d] (*Shitah Mekubetzes* in the name of *Ritzbash*).

12. Unlike an ordinary document of indebtedness which records a[n] obligation that takes effect only if the debtor actually borrows, [a] document of acquisition states that the witnesses, acting on behalf of th[e] creditor, secured an agreement from the debtor to pay the stated amoun[t] regardless of whether he subsequently borrows. This is accomplished b[y] the performance of an act of acquisition (see above, 15a note 19); hence the document's name (*Rashi*).

13. If this were true, the document would belong to the debtor, an[d] wrongly returning it to the creditor would allow him to collect a debt tha[t] is not due him.

14. If the debtor had indeed repaid, returning the note to the credito[r] would allow him to illegally collect a second time.

משום כדי חייו [א] אמר רב הונא אמר רב [א] האומר לחבירו שדה שאני לוקח לכשאקחנה קנויה לך מעכשיו קנה • אמר רבא מסתברא מלתא דרב בשדה סתם אבל בשדה זו לא מי יימר דמזבין לה ניהליה והאלהים אמר רב אפי' בשדה זו מכדי רב כמאן אמרה לשמעתי' כר"מ דאמר אדם מקנה דבר שלא בא לעולם דתניא [ב] א האומר לאשה התקדשי לי לאחר שאתגייר לאחר שתתגיירי לאחר שאשתחרר לאחר שתשתחררי לאחר שימות בעליך לאחר שיחלוץ לך יבמיך לאחר שתמות אחותיך אינה מקודשת ר"מ אומר מקודשת והא אשה כשדה זו דמיא וא"ר מאיר מקודשת: אמר שמואל [ג] המוצא שטר הקנאה בשוק יחזירו לבעלים דאי משום דכתב ללות ולא לוה • הא שעבד נפשיה ואי משום פרעון [ד] לא חיישינן לפרעון דאם איתא דפרעיה מקרע הוה קרע ליה אמר רב נחמן אבא מן ספרי דייני דמר שמואל הוה והוינא כבר שיתא כבר שבע ודכרנא דהוו מכרזי ואמרי הני שטרי אקנייתא דמשתכחי בשוקא נהדרינהו למרייהו אמר רב עמרם אף אנן (א) תנינא [ה] כל מעשה בית דין הרי זה יחזיר אלמא לא חיישינן לפירעון א"ל רבי זירא מתניתין בשטרי חלטאתא ואדרכתא דלאו בני פרעון נינהו אמר רבא והני לאו בני פרעון נינהו והא [ו] אמרי נהרדעי שומא הדר עד תריסר ירחי שתא ואמר אמימר אנא מנהרדעא אנא וסבירא לי [ב] דשומא הדר לעולם אלא אמר רבא התם היינו טעמא דאמרי איהו הוא דאפסיד אנפשיה דבעידנא דפרעיה אבעי ליה למקרעיה לשטריה א"נ למכתב שטרא אחרינא עילויה דמדינא ארעא לא בעיא למיהדר [ג] ומשום (א) ועשית הישר והטוב בעיני ה' הוא דאמור רבנן תהדר הלכך מרישא הוא דקא זבין איבעי ליה למכתב שטר זביני גבי שטר חוב מאי איכא למימר אם איתא דפרעיה איבעי ליה למיקרעיה לשטריה אימור אשתמוטי קא משתמיט ליה דא"ל למחר יהבנא לך דהשתא ליתיה גבאי אי נמי אפשיטי דספרא זייר ליה: א"ר אבהו א"ר יוחנן המוצא שטר חוב בשוק אע"פ שכתוב בו הנפק לא יחזירו לבעלים לא מיבעיא היכא דלא כתוב בו הנפק דאיכא למימר כתב ללות ולא לוה אלא אפי' כתוב בו הנפק ומאי ניהו דמקוים לא יחזיר דחיישינן לפרעון איתיביה רבי ירמיה לר' אבהו כל מעשה ב"ד הרי זה יחזיר א"ל ירמיה ברי לא כל מעשה ב"ד שוים אלא כגון שהוחזק כפרן אמר רבא ומשום דהוחזק כפרן חדא זמנא תו לא פרע כלל אלא אמר רבא מתניתין בשטר חלטאתא ואדרכתא וכדרבי זירא וכפרן הואיל ואתא לידן נימא ביה מלתא דאמר רב יוסף בר מניומי אמר רב נחמן אמרו לו [ז] צא תן לו ואמר

## תוספות

**שדה** שאני לוקח. ל"ג זו מדקאמר והאלהים אפילו בשדה זו הלא בפירוש אמר זו:

**בשטרי** חלטאתא ואדרכתא דלאו בני פרעון נינהו. תימה שטרי אדרכתא אמאי לאו בני פרעון נינהו כיון דעדיין לא זכה בקרקע עד שכתבו לו שטרי חלטאתא וכן בסמוך דקאמר איהו דאפסיד אנפשיה דבעי ליה למקרעיה או אבעי ליה למכתב שטר מכירה בשטרי אדרכתא שעדיין הקרקע היא בידו במה אפסיד אנפשיה והלא יכול לטעון פרעתי וי"ל דשטרי אדרכתא נקט אליבא דרבה דאית ליה בפרק המפקיד (לקמן דף לה: ושם) דאכיל פירי מכי מטא אדרכתא לידיה א"כ לא יוכל לומר עוד פרעתי כיון שכבר זכה בקרקע ולרבא דאית ליה מכי שלמו יומי דאכרזתא לדבריו יעמיד מתני' בחלטאתא גרידא ויש ספרים דל"ג אדרכתא:

**אע"פ** שכתוב בו הנפק לא יחזיר. תימה דמשמע דאיירי באין חייב מודה כדאמר שמא כתב ללות ולא לוה לכך לא יחזיר דחיישינן לפרעון אבל אם לוה מודה יחזיר דלא חיישינן לקנוניא ולא לשמא פרעו ורוצה לחזור וללות בו כדי להרויח פשיטי דספרא וקשה דלקמן (דף יז.) א"ר יוחנן שטר שכתוב זמנו בו ביום וכתוב בו הנפק יחזיר ומוקי לה רב כהנא כשחייב מודה ודוקא שכתוב בו ביום אבל אין כתוב בו ביום לא יחזיר או משום פשיטי דספרא או משום קנוניא וכן לעיל (דף יג:) אוקי ר"י מתני' דמלא שטרי חוב לא יחזיר בחייב מודה ומשום קנוניא דסברי רבנן דאין בו אחריות גבי (לוה) נמי ממשעבדי (ס) ותניא כוותיה דרבי יוחנן) וי"ל דאמוראי נינהו ואליבא דרבי יוחנן דרב כהנא יעמיד הכא מלתא דרבי יוחנן אף כשחייב מודה ומשום קנוניא ורבי אבהו דמפרש דוקא כשאין חייב מודה אבל כשחייב מודה יחזיר דלא חייש לקנוניא יעמיד נמי מתני' דלעיל כשחייב מודה ומשום שמא כתב ללות ולא לוה כרב אסי אבל היכא דליכא למיחש לכתב ללות ולא לוה כמו בשטרי הקנאה או כתוב בו הנפק כי הכא יחזיר דלא חיישינן לקנוניא וגמרא דנקט לעיל טעמא דקנוניא סבר כאביי דאמר עדיו בחתומיו זכין לו או אקרי וכתיב לא אמרינן:

**ומשום** דהוחזק כפרן תו לא פרע כלל. ואף על גב דאמרינן לקמן (דף יז.) הוחזק כפרן לאותו ממון הכא דנפל שאני דמוכחא מלתא דמשום הכי לא היה נזהר לשומרו לפי שפרעו הלוה:

## רש"י

משום כדי חייו. מה שתעלה מצודתי היום תקנו חכמים שיהיו דבריו קיימין שמא צריך הוא למזונות דבר מועט אבל מה שתעלה מצודתי כל חדש או כל שנה אין שם משום כדי חייו: קנויה לך מעכשיו. שכשאקחנה לא אוכל לחזור בו קנה. אם יקחנה ואין יכול לחזור כשלקחה: בשדה סתם. שדה שאני לוקח ולא אמר זו דסמכא דעתיה דמקבל מתנה לסמוך עליו שיקח שדה ויתננה לו שהרבה שדות מצויות ליקח אבל אמר לו שדה זו לא סמכא דעתיה דמקבל מתנה ולא האמינו דנימא ניחא ליה דליקו בהימנותיה ולא מסתבר כוותיה דרב בהא: והאלהים. בשבועה רב אמרה אפילו בשדה זו דמכדי רב כמאן אמר לשמעתיה כר"מ כו': והא אשה כשדה זו דמיא. דיש באלו שאין בידו להביא עצמו לכלל קדושין כאשר אין ביד זה לכוף את בעל השדה למוכרה לו דעבד ושפחה אין בידם לשחרר עצמם ואין ביד אשה להמית את בעלה או אחותה ואמר רבי מאיר דלכשיבאו לכלל קדושין מקודשת היא למפרע: שטר הקנאה. שקנו ממנו שאפילו לא ילוה המעות שיעבד עצמו לשלם: כל מעשה ב"ד. קס"ד שטר שכתב בו הנפק שנתקיים בב"ד אלמא כיון דליכא למיחש לשמא לא לוה שהרי אין מקיימין את השטר אלא בפני בעל דין כדאמרי' בהגוזל (ב"ק דף קיב:) לפרעון לא חיישינן: בשטרי חלטאתא. שטר שכתבו ב"ד למוציא שטר על חבירו וחייבוהו לשלם ולא שילם וירדו לנכסיו ושמו לבעל חוב אחד מהם ונתנו לו שטר שעל פי ב"ד באה לו: אדרכתא. שלא מצאו לו עכשיו נכסים וכתבו לו שירדוף לחזור על נכסיו ואם ימצא יגבה. אדרכתא לשון רודף ומשיג כמו פרסה בחלא ולא אדרכיה (כתובות דף ס:) ולשון המקרא כתרו את בנימין הרדיפוהו מנוחה הדריכוהו (שופטים כ): שומא. ששמו ב"ד לבעל חוב קרקע הלוה: הדר. אם יפרע לו מעות עד שנה: אפסיד אנפשיה. אם פרע ולא קרע השטר ואם דחהו לומר אבד היה לו לומר כתוב לי שטר מיד שאתה חוזר ומוכרה לי: דמדינא ארעא לא בעי למיהדר. טעם נותן לדבריו שראוי לכתוב שטר מכירה עליה שקנויה לו לחלוטין ומדינא לא בעי למיהדר בפדיון אם לא מדעתו: מרישא דקא זבין. כלומר אין זה פדיון אלא תחילת קניין ה"אילו שלו היתה לפיכך הכותב שטר מכירה עליה אינו טועה והיה לו לזה לתבוע שטר מכירה הואיל ודחהו מלהחזיר לו שטר של ב"ד: אי נמי אפשיטי דספרא זייר ליה. שעל הלוה ליתן שכר הסופר ופעמים שאין לו מעות ללוה בשעת הלואה והמלוה נותן שכר לכתיבת השטר וכשפרעו מעכב השטר בידו עד שיפרע השכר: זייר. לשון עולר כמו מעצרת' זיירא (ע"ז דף ס.) ובלשון המקרא ויזר את הגזה (שופטים ו): כל מעשה ב"ד. והאי נמי מעשה ב"ד הוא: ירמיה ברי גרסינן: שהוחזק. לוה זה כפרן פעם אחרת לפיכך אין נאמן לומר פרעתי ובההיא תנן יחזיר: ותו לא פרע כלל. בתמיה ואי חיישינן לפרעון זה שלא נזהר לשמור שטרו יפסיד: צא תן לו. שפסקו לו דינו בב"ד שציוו עליו לתת לו: ואמר

## עין משפט נר מצוה

[א] [מיי' פכ"ב מהל' מכירה הל' ה ש"ע ח"מ סי' ריא סעי' א דלא כרב]:

קמג א מיי' פ"ז מהל' אישות הלכה יד סמג עשין מח טוש"ע אה"ע סי' מ סעי' ה:

קמד ב ג מיי' פכ"ב מהל' מלוה ולוה הלכה טז סמג עשין לד טוש"ע ח"מ סי' קג סעי' ט:

## גליון הש"ס

גמ' אמר רבא מסתברא. כעין זה גיטין יג ע"ב וש"נ: שם הא שעבד נפשיה. עיין בר"ן פ"ק דקדושין דף ריד ע"ב:

## תורה אור השלם

א) וְעָשִׂיתָ הַיָּשָׁר וְהַטּוֹב בְּעֵינֵי יְיָ לְמַעַן יִיטַב לָךְ וּבָאתָ וְיָרַשְׁתָּ אֶת הָאָרֶץ הַטֹּבָה אֲשֶׁר נִשְׁבַּע יְיָ לַאֲבֹתֶיךָ: [דברים ו, יח]

## רבינו חננאל

מצודתי היום מכור לך דבריו קיימים. אבל הא דאמר רב האומר לחבירו שדה זו שאני לוקח לכשאקחנה קנויה לך מעכשיו קני לית הלכתא כרב דאשכחן ביבמות פ' האשה רבה הלכתא האשה שהלך בעלה ובנה למדינת הים וכו'. אמר רב נחמן בר יצחק רב הונא כרב ורב כר' ינאי ור' ינאי כר' חייא ור' חייא כר' ור' כר' מאיר ור' מאיר כר' אליעזר בן יעקב ורבי אליעזר בן יעקב כר' עקיבא כולהו סבירא להו אדם מקנה לחבירו דבר שלא בא לעולם. וקיימא לן דהני כולהו שיטה אינון ולית הלכתא אפילו כחד מינייהו. **אמר שמואל המוצא שטר הקנאה בשוק יחזיר לבעלים** ולית הילכתא כוותיה דהא איתותב וקיימא לן חוששין לפרעון. והא דאמר רב נחמן דכירנא דהוו מכריזי הני שטרי אקנייתא דמשתכחי בשוקא ניהדרינהו למרייהו לטעמיה דשמואל היא ולית הלכתא כוותיה. **אמר ר' יוחנן המוצא שטר חוב בשוק אע"ג דכתיב ביה הנפק.** פי' הנפק אשרתא דדייני לא יחזיר מאי טעמא חיישינן לפרעון. איני והתנן כל מעשה ב"ד הרי זה יחזיר. ופרקי' מתני' בשטרי חלטאתא ואדרכתא דלאו בני פרעון נינהו. ר' אבהו אמר בשהוחזק הלוה כפרן. אמר רבא ומשום דהוחזק כפרן תוב לא פרע ודילמא הדר ופרע וכו'. כפרן הואיל ואתא לידן נימא בה מילתא.

## מסורת הש"ס

א) יבמות לג., ב) שם קדושין סג., כתובות ... ג) [לעיל יד.], ד) [לעיל יד.], ה) [לקמן יח:], ו) לקמן לה., ז) [דומה בבא קמא סח:, ... ח) ס"א ל"ג.

## הגהות הב"ח

(א) גמ' אף אנן תנינא:

## ליקוטי רש"י

האומר לחברו. ... שקנה את השדה. ... והוא מתנה [יבמות ...] והאלקים. ... [סנהדרין עב.]. ... הקנאה. שמקנה לו ... מהיום בין ילוה בין לא ... יגבה מהן לאותו ... מהיום. לא חייש... לפרעון. בשטר הנ... ואפי' אין חייב מודה. ... איתא דפרעיה מקרע ... קרע ליה וכו' וכ"ש כש... מודה מהאי טעמא ג... דמיום פריעתו הוא ק... [לעיל יג.]. כל מע... ב"ד הרי זה יחזיר ... מילתא דאתא לב"ד ל... דליכא למיחש לנמלך ... שלא ליתנן הרי זה י... [לקמן יח:]. אדרכת... שכתבו פסק דין ... ללוקח על נכסיו של ... שבכ"מ שימצאם יחזיק ... והיינו תשעים יום ... שעמד בדין כדא... בהגוזל בתרא [לעיל בע... שומא הדר. נכסי... ששמו ב"ד לבעל ... חוזרין אליו אם נותן מ... לבעל חוב [לקמן ... ועשית הישר והט... זו פשרה לפנים מ... הדין [דברים ו, ... אפשיטי. זוזי מ... שמונה מהן זוז ... [כתובות סז.].

הא מית ליה ומאן דאמר ניחא ליה דליקום בהמנותיה בהדי בני נמי ניחא ליה דליקום בהמנותיה סוף סוף קרו ליה בני לוקח גזלנא אלא איכא בינייהו דמית גזלן מאן דאמר ניחא ליה לאיניש דלא לקריוהו גזלן הא מית ליה למ"ד ניחא ליה דליקום בהמנותיה ה"נ אע"ג דמית ניחא ליה דליקום בהמנותיה סוף סוף קרו לבניה בני גזלנא אלא איכא בינייהו דיהבה במתנה מאן דאמר ניחא ליה דליקום בהמנותיה [א]מתנה נמי ניחא ליה דליקום בהמנותיה מאן דאמר ניחא ליה דלא נקריוהו גזלנא א"ל מאי גזלינא מינך: [ב]פשיטא זבנה אורתה ויהבה במתנה לאו לאוקמה קמי לוקח קא בעי [ג]נפלה ליה בירושה ירושה ממילא היא ולאו איהו קא טרח אבתרה גבי איהו בחובו [ד]חזינא אי אית ליה ארעא אחריתי ואמר האי בעינא לאוקמה קמיה לוקח קא בעי ואי לא זוזי הוא דבעי אפרועי יהבה נהליה [א]במתנה פליגי בה רב אחא ורבינא חד אמר מתנה כירושה דהא ממילא וחד אמר [ה]מתנה כמכר דאי לאו דטרח וארצי קמיה לא הוי יהיב ליה מתנה להכי טרח וארצי קמיה כי היכי דליקום בהמנותיה ועד אימת ניחא ליה דליקום בהמנותיה אמר רב הונא עד שעת העמדה בדין חייא בר רב אמר עד דמטא אדרכתא לידיה רב פפא אמר [ו]עד דמתחלן יומי אכרזתא מתקיף לה רמי בר חמא מכדי האי לוקח במאי קני להאי ארעא בהאי שטרא האי שטרא חספא בעלמא הוא א"ל רבא תהא במאמינו בההוא הנאה דלא קאמר ליה מידי וקא סמיך עליה טרח ומייתי ליה גמר ומקני ליה מתיב רב ששת [ז]מה שאירש מאבא מכור לך מה שתעלה מצודתי מכור לך לא אמר כלום מה שאירש מן אבא היום מכור לך מה שתעלה מצודתי היום מכור לך דבריו קיימין אמר רמי בר חמא הא גברא והא תיובתא אמר רבא גברא קא חזינא ותיובתא לא קא חזינא הכא סמכא דעתיה והכא לא סמכא דעתיה הכא סמכא דעתיה דאזיל טרח ומייתי ליה כי היכי דלא נקרייה גזלנא הכא לא סמכא דעתיה שלחוה לקמיה דרבי אבא בר זבדא אמר להו זו אינה צריכה לפנים אמר רבא זו צריכה לפנים ולפני לפנים הכא סמכא דעתיה והכא לא סמכא דעתיה הוה עובדא בפומבדיתא ואותביה אמר להו רב יוסף זו אינה צריכה לפנים ואמר ליה אביי צריכה לפנים ולפני לפנים הכא סמכא דעתיה הכא לא סמכא דעתיה ומאי שנא רישא ומאי שנא סיפא אמר רבי יוחנן סיפא מה שאירש מאבא היום משום כבוד אביו מה שתעלה מצודתי היום משום

**רש"י**

הא מית. לוקח ומי יחרפנו עוד הלכך לא נתכוון לזה אלא להעמידה בידו בחייו ולא לאחר מותו מ"ד כו': דמית גזלן. לאחר שלקחה והכניס באיס להוציא מיד הלוקח: הא מית ליה. ולא נתכוון להעמיד ממכרו אלא בימי חייו שלא יחרפוהו: אע"ג דמית ניחא ליה. מעיקרא: דליקו בהימנותיה. אפילו לאחר מיתה: סוף סוף קרו לבניה בני גזלנא. נמלא שאף לאחר מיתה מחרפין אותו: זבנה אורתה. אם [א] קודם שלקח מן הבעלים חזר ומכרה לאיש אחר לבד מן הראשון או הורישה לאחד מבניו או יהבה במתנה ואחר כך לקחה האי ודאי איגלי דעתיה דלאו לאוקמי קמיה לוקח ראשון בעי ולא ניחא ליה דליקום בהימנותיה שהרי מכרה לשני: נפלה ליה. לגזלן בירושה שמתחילה גזלה לאחד ממורישיו ומת הנגזל: ירושה ממילא הויא. והא ליכא למימר ניחא ליה דליקו בהימנותיה דהא לא טרח אבתרה דנימא גלי דעתיה דניחא ליה דליקו הלכך הוי כיורש דעלמא וחוזר ותובעה ונותן מעות ללוקח: גבייה בחובו. לאחר שגזלה ומכר לו ובא לו אצל נגזל ואמר לו הגבה לי בחובי קרקע שגזלתיך: אי אית ליה ארעא אחריתי. לנגזל שיכול לגבות חובו ממנה ואמר ליה בזו שגזלתי אני חפץ הא טרח אבתרה ואמרינן לאוקמה קמיה לוקח בעי: יהביה ניהליה במתנה. נגזל לגזלן: ועד אימת. יקחנה מבעלים הראשונים דאמרינן דמשום דניחא ליה דליקו בהימנותיה לקחה: עד שעת העמדה בדין. עד שיטרפוה מן הלוקח ויעמידהו בדין אבל משעמד ברשעו עד שעת העמדה בדין גלי אדעתיה דלא מהימן הוא ואם לקחה אחרי כן לאו לאוקמיה קמיה לוקח בעי: עד דמטא אדרכתא לידיה. עד שיחייבוהו ב"ד לפרוע ללוקח מעותיו ועמד במרדו עד שכתבו פסק דין ונתנו ללוקח על נכסיו של גזלן שבכ"מ שימצאם יחזיק בהן והיינו תשעים יום לאחר שעמד בדין כדאמרי' בהגוזל [בתרא] (ב"ק דף קיב:): עד דמתחלן יומא דאכרזתא. לאחר שמצא זה קרקע משל גזלן ובא לב"ד והן מכריזין שכל מי שרוצה לקנות קרקע יבא ויקחנה כדאמרי' בערכין (דף כא:) שום היתומין שלשים יום [ג]: מתקיף לה רמי בר חמא. אהא מה מכר ראשון לשני כו': תהא. הא דרב: במאמינו. שאמר לו אני סומך עליך שתתננה בידי: גמר ומקני. כשלקחה מבעלים הראשונים: מצודתי. של חיות ועופות ושל דגים: דבריו קיימין. לקמן פריך מאי שנא רישא כו': הא גברא והא תיובתא. הרי אדם גדול וכמוהו תשובתו דקתני לא אמר כלום ולכשיירש לא קנה לוקח כיון דההיא שעתא לאו דידיה הוו נכסי אביו ולא אמרינן מה מכר לו ראשון לשני כל זכות שתבא לידו: לא סמכא דעתיה. דלוקח דקאמר מי יימר שירש מאביו כלום שמא ימכור אביו נכסיו בחייו: שלחוה. להא תיובתא דרב ששת דאותיב אדרב: אינה צריכה לפנים. אינה צריכה כדי לתרצה להכניסה לפני בני הישיבה שאין בהן יודע לפרקה ותשובת הגאונים פורשין לגגאי דליכא קושיא מעליא אל תעלוה לגיו: הוה עובדא בפומבדיתא. שדנו דין כרב ואותבינן מהא מתניתין ואמר רב יוסף כו': משום כבוד אביו. כשהיה אביו גוסס וצריך מעות לקבורתו ולתכריכין מוהר לכבוד אביו שלא לשהותו בבזיון:

**תוספות**

מאי גזלינא מינך. וא"ת וכי מכרה נמי מה גזלו והלא צריך להחזיר לו מעותיו וי"ל דמ"מ יקראנו גזלנא כל זמן שלא יפרע לו:

ארצי קמיה כי היכי דליקום בהימנותיה. משמע דהכי הלכתא מדלא נקט לישנא דלא נקרייה גזלן ועוד דהלכה כרב אשי דהוא בתרא וגדול בחכמה ובמנין:

האי שטרא חספא בעלמא הוא. וא"ת ולימא דקני לה במה שהחזיק בה אחר שקנאה גזלן וי"ל דמשמע ליה משעה שקנאה הגזלן היא של לוקח אע"פ שלא עשה בו שום מעשה וא"ת מעותיו שהיו תחלה מלוה נעשו עתה מכר וי"ל באתרא דלא קנו בכספא א"נ במלוה אינו יכול לקנות כדאמרינן פ"ק דקדושין (דף ו:) המקדש במלוה אינה מקודשת ובמכר לא קנה והא דאמר בהאיש מקדש (שם דף מז.) ושוין שבמכר קנה היינו במלוה שיש לו על אחרים דאז באשה בענין זה מקודשת לכ"ע אי לאו דאשה לא סמכא דעתה ויראה שיחזור וימחול אבל מלוה שאשה חייבת לו אם מוחל לה ומקדשה בה אינה מקודשת דלא נתן לה כלום דמקמי הכי היה ברשותה וכן במכר לא קנה אע"ג דכשמקדשה בהנאת מחילת מלוה היא מקודשת דלא גרע מארווח לה זמנא ואדבר עליך לשלטון דמקודשת וכן במכר אם מכר בהנאת מחילה קונה כמו בהחליף דמי שור בפרה מ"מ לא משמע ליה שהיה מקנה לו בהנאת מחילת מלוה משום דמשמע מיד שלקחה הגזלן קנה לוקח ראשון:

בההיא הנאה דקא סמיך כו'. והויא כאילו א"ל שדה זו תהא קנויה לך לכשאקחנה:

מה שאירש מאבא מכור לך לא אמר כלום. וא"ת לימא דרב דאמר כר"מ וברייתא כרבנן וי"ל דלדידן קפריך דאית לן כרב כדאיתא פרק איזהו נשך (לקמן דף עב:) דמייתי גמרא טעמא דלא ליקריה גזלנא וניחא ליה דליקו בהימנותיה וסבירא לן כרבנן דאין אדם מקנה דבר שלא בא לעולם דשמואל פסיק כרבי יוחנן הסנדלר פרק אע"פ (כתובות דף נט.) ורב נחמן סבר בפירות דקל אף משבאו לעולם יכול לחזור בו ורב האי פסק דאין הלכה כרב בהא משום דס"ל דאין אדם מקנה דבר שלא בא לעולם וכו' ולא נהירא מכח דאיזהו נשך (לקמן דף עב:):

[ד]קנויה לך מעכשיו. תימה מה צריך מעכשיו כיון דאדם מקנה דבר שלא בא לעולם דאי לענין חזרה הא כל זמן שלא בא לעולם יכול לחזור אע"ג דאמר מעכשיו וי"ל דנ"מ אם נקרע השטר או שאבד קודם שלקחה זה דקני כיון דאמר מעכשיו [ה]:

**עין משפט נר מצוה**

קלז א מיי' פ"ט מהל' גזילה הל' ט סמג עשין עג טוש"ע ח"מ סי' שעד סעי' א:
קלח ב ג מיי' שם הל' יא טוש"ע שם סעי' ב:
קלט ד מיי' שם הל' יב טוש"ע שם סעי' ג:
קמ ה מיי' שם הל' יג טוש"ע שם סעי' ד:
קמא ו מיי' שם הל' י טוש"ע שם סעי' א:
קמב ז מיי' פכ"ב מהל' מכירה הלכה ה סמג עשין פב טוש"ע ח"מ סי' ריא סעי' א:

**רבינו חננאל**

מיהו איצטריכינן לפרושה דחזינן מר זוטרא ורב אשי דאינון בתראי שקלו וטרו לפרושי טעמיה דרב הני מילי בעידנא דקנאה הגזלן מן הנגזל אבל אם נפלה לו לגזלן בירושה מן הניגזל לא אמרי' קנאה לוקח או מי שניתנה לו במתנה. וחזינן נמי בפרק איזהו נשך הלכה מלוה ישראל מעותיו של נכרי. תוב התם שקלי וטרו מרימר ורבינא בהא דאמר רבא התם ניתן ליכתב הכא לא ניתן ליכתב אלא הא דתניא לשבח קרקעות כיצד הרי שגזל [שדה] מחבירו ומכרה לאחר והשביחה והרי היא יוצאה מתחת ידו כשהוא גובה גובה את הקרן מנכסים משועבדים ושבח גובה מבני חורין ואמרינן אמאי נימא לא ניתן ליכתב. ופרקי' הכי השתא התם אי למאן דאמר ניחא ליה דלא ליקריוה גזלן אי למאן דאמר ניחא ליה דליקום בהימנותיה מפייס למריה ומוקים ליה לשטריה הכא אברוחי אברח ליה מוקים ליה לשטריה ש"מ דהלכתא כוותיה דרב בהאי וסוגיא דשמעתא כרב אשי דאמר ניחא ליה דליקום בהימנותיה. הלא תראה כדאתקיף ליה רמי בר חמא פריק ליה רבא תהא במאמינו פירוש בההוא הנאה דלא אמר ליה ולא מידי [א] דסמיך ליה ואזיל ומפייס לנגזל וקני ליה מיניה גמר ומקנה ליה והוא דמחזיק בה. והא דאותיב רב ששת הכא הא דתני מה שאירש מאבא מכור לך מה שתעלה מצודתי מכור לך לא אמר כלום דקיימא לן אין אדם מקנה לחבירו דבר שלא בא לעולם. היא בתוספתא במסכת נדרים ומפורש בתלמוד ארץ ישראל בכתובות פרק אע"פ מה שאירש מאבא היום מכור לך בלוה לתכריכי אביו מפני שהיה גוסס וזה פי' משום כבוד אביו. מה שתעלה מצודתי היום מכור לך דבריו קיימים משום כדי חייו. קשיא ליה לרב דאמר מה מכר ראשון לשני (לשני) כל זכות שתבוא לידו. ופרקי אביי ורבא הכי הא מתניתא דתנא [בתוספתא] בסוף מסכת נדרים ליכא למימר דסמכא דעתיה דהא כי הדר ביה לא מצי קרי ליה גזלנא לפיכך לא אמר כלום אבל הא דרב דאי לא טרח ומייתי ומוקים לה בידיה מצו קרו ליה גזלנא סמך דעתיה דאזיל וטרח ומוקים לה בידיה כי היכי דלא ליקריוה גזלנא. ואמרי' מה שנא רישא ומאי שנא סיפא אמר ר' יוחנן סיפא דקתני מה שאירש מאבא היום מכור לך דבריו קיימים משום כבוד אביו אמרו חכמים מכירתו קיימת. וכבר פירשנוהו בתלמוד ארץ ישראל בלוה בתכריכי אביו פי' כגון שהיה אביו גוסס ומוכר לעשות לו תכריכין וכן מי שאין לו [מה] יאכל משום כדי חייו אמרו חכמים אם אמר מה שתעלה

**מסורת הש"ס**

...יומה לדהכא פליגי ...ר' אחא ורבינא ...לה כו: וע"ש], ...תוספתא דנדרים סוף ...ו, ועי' תוס' כתובות ...ד"ה לזבנה], ג) [ע"ש ...ד"ה שום], ד) (שייך ...:), ה) [וע"ע תוס' ...ות לג. ד"ה קנויה].

**הגהות הגר"א**

...רש"י ד"ה זבנה ...תה אם קודם כו'. ...ורמב"ם פי' אפילו ...שלקחה (ועמ"ש רבינו ...מ סי' שע"ג ס"ק ג):

**גליון הש"ס**

...לאוקמה קמי ...ח קבעי. עיין בר"ש ...ו משנה ג ...ומות: שם מתנה ...בר. עיין מגילה כו: ...ש רפ"ב דמעשרות:

**ליקוטי רש"י**

...רכתא. פסק דין ...המלוה לתוך ...ים של לוה וליטלם ...מא בחובו [ב"ק ...]. שלא מצאו לו ...יו נכסים וכתבו לו ...רוף לחזור על נכסיו ...ימצא יגבה אדרכתא ...רודף ומשיג כמו ...ה בחלא ולא ...כיה ולשון המקרא ...ו את בנימין ...יפוהו מנוחה ...יכוהו (שופטים כ) ...מן ע"ב]. אכרזתא. ...פ שבאה אדרכתא ...ולא מצא נכסים ...עד לאחר זמן ...מצא הוקק לבא ...ד ומכריזין שיש כאן ...קע למכור כדאמרינן ...יכין (כא:) ואם בא ...וקילה ביותר ממה ...מוה אחרים מוסרין ...בידו לאחר שכלו ...הכרוז ובמסכת ...ין מפרש כמה ימים ...ירין בפ' שום ...ומים (שם) [לקמן לה:].

חשק שלמה על ר"ח א) נראה דל"ל וסמיך עליה דאזיל ומפיס כו'.

The Gemara questions this explanation:
מָתִיב רַב שֵׁשֶׁת – **Rav Sheishess challenged** this reasoning from Baraisa: מַה שֶּׁאִירַשׁ מֵאַבָּא מָכוּר לָךְ – If one transacts a deal ith his fellow, telling him: **"THAT WHICH I WILL INHERIT FROM MY ATHER IS SOLD TO YOU,"** מַה שֶּׁתַּעֲלֶה מְצוּדָתִי מָכוּר לָךְ – or he lls him: **"THAT WHICH MY NET**[19] **WILL CATCH IS SOLD TO YOU,"** לֹא אָמַר כְּלוּם – **HE HAS NOT SAID ANYTHING** [i.e. the sale is inef- ctive]. מַה שֶּׁאִירַשׁ מִן אַבָּא הַיּוֹם מָכוּר לָךְ – However, if he tells s fellow: **"THAT WHICH I WILL INHERIT FROM MY FATHER TODAY SOLD TO YOU,"** מַה שֶּׁתַּעֲלֶה מְצוּדָתִי הַיּוֹם מָכוּר לָךְ – or he tells m: **"THAT WHICH MY NET WILL CATCH TODAY IS SOLD TO YOU,"** דְּבָרָיו קַיָּימִ – **HIS WORDS STAND** [i.e. the sale is binding].[20]

אָמַר רָמִי בַּר חָמָ – **Rami bar Chama said:** הָא גַּבְרָא וְהָא תְּיוּבְתָּא – **Here** you have **a great man** (Rav Sheishess) **and here is the** futation he raised, befitting his greatness.[21] Just as the araisa, in the first two cases, teaches that a purchaser does not quire future acquisitions of the seller, so too, in this case, the irchaser should not acquire the stolen land which is only a iture acquisition of the robber.[22]

The Gemara contests this refutation:
אָמַר רָבָ – **Rava said:** גַּבְרָא קָא חֲזֵינָא – **I see a great man,** וּתְיוּבְתָּא לֹא קָא חָזֵינָ – **yet I do not see a refutation** that befits s greatness, הָכָא סָמְכָא דַּעְתֵּיהּ – for **here,** in Rav's ruling, **[the urchaser] is confident,** וְהָכָא לֹא סָמְכָא דַּעְתֵּיהּ – **but here,** in e Baraisa's case, **[the purchaser] is not confident.**

The Gemara elaborates:
הָכָא סָמְכָא דַּעְתֵּ – **Here,** in Rav's ruling, **[the purchaser] is** nfident דְּאָזִיל טָרַח וּמַיְיתֵי לֵיהּ – **that [the robber] will go** nd trouble himself **to acquire** the land **for him,** כִּי הֵיכִי דְּלֹא נִקְרְיֵיהּ גַּזְלָנָ – **in order that he not be called a robber.** herefore, the sale is binding. הָכָא לֹא סָמְכָא דַּעְתֵּיהּ – But **here,** the Baraisa's case, **[the purchaser] is not confident** that the ller will inherit his father.[23] Therefore, the sale is not binding. o contradiction exists![24]

The Gemara presents other assessments of Rav Sheishess' futation:

שְׁלַחוּהָ לְקַמֵּיהּ דְּרַבִּי אַבָּא בַּר זַבְדָּא – **They sent this** refutation of Rav Sheishess **to R' Abba bar Zavda,** אָמַר לְהוּ – and **he told them:** זוּ אֵינָהּ צְרִיכָה לִפְנִים – **This** question **is not necessary** to bring **inside** to the yeshivah.[25] אָמַר רָבָא – **Rava said:** זוּ צְרִיכָה לִפְנִים וְלִפְנֵי לִפְנִים – **This** question **is necessary** to bring **far inside** the yeshivah to the most distinguished scholars, who will resolve the difficulty as follows: הָכָא סָמְכָא דַּעְתֵּיהּ – **Here,** in Rav's ruling, **[the purchaser] is confident,** וְהָכָא לֹא סָמְכָא דַּעְתֵּיהּ – **but here,** in the Baraisa's case, **[the purchaser] is not confident.**

הֲוָה עוּבְדָא בְּפוּמְבְּדִיתָא – **There was an incident in Pumbedisa** where they ruled according to Rav, וְאוֹתְבֵיהּ – and **they challenged [Rav Yosef]** from the Baraisa. אָמַר לְהוּ רַב יוֹסֵף – **Rav Yosef told them:** זוּ אֵינָהּ צְרִיכָה לִפְנִים – **This question is not necessary** to bring **inside** to the yeshivah. וְאָמַר לֵיהּ אַבַּיֵי – **But Abaye told him:** צְרִיכָה לִפְנִים וְלִפְנֵי לִפְנִים – **This** question **is necessary** to bring **far inside** the yeshivah to the most distinguished scholars, who will resolve the difficulty as follows: הָכָא סָמְכָא דַּעְתֵּיהּ – **Here,** in Rav's ruling, **[the purchaser] is confident,** הָכָא לֹא סָמְכָא דַּעְתֵּיהּ – **but here,** in the Baraisa's case, **[the purchaser] is not confident.**

The Gemara analyzes the Baraisa:
וּמַאי שְׁנָא רֵישָׁא – **And what is the difference between the first case** of the Baraisa in which the sale is invalid וּמַאי שְׁנָא סֵיפָא – **and the last case** of the Baraisa in which the sale is valid?[26] In both cases, the purchaser is not confident. – ? –

The Gemara answers:
אָמַר רַבִּי יוֹחָנָן – **R' Yochanan said:** סֵיפָא – **The last case** of the Baraisa is explained as follows: מַה שֶּׁאִירַשׁ מֵאַבָּא הַיּוֹם – When a person tells his fellow: **"That which I will inherit from my father today** is sold to you," the sale is valid מִשּׁוּם כְּבוֹד אָבִיו – **because of the honor of [the seller's] father.**[27] מַה שֶּׁתַּעֲלֶה מְצוּדָתִי הַיּוֹם – When a person tells his fellow: **"That which my net will catch today** is sold to you," the sale is valid

NOTES

:change for this "money" (*Ran, Nimukei Yosef;* cf. *Rashba*).

. I.e. he is planning to hunt or fish and he now sells the animals, birds, id fish that he will later succeed in trapping.

. The Gemara below explains why the sale is effective only in the last o cases (*Rashi*).

. I.e. only a man as great as Rav Sheishess would have asked so strong question.

. We do not say, as Rav said above, that a seller transfers to a purchaser y right that may later come into his possession (*Rashi*). Although is issue is disputed by Tannaim, and R' Meir rules that future acquisi- ons may be sold (see below, 16b), the accepted halachah is that such a le is invalid. Since the ruling of Rav is also adopted as halachah (see low, 72b), the ruling of Rav must be reconciled with the opinion of the araisa that future acquisitions may not be sold (*Tosafos*).

. His father might sell his property before he dies, leaving nothing to s son (*Rashi*). [It is also impossible to predict whether his net will catch y fish, birds, or animals.]

. Where the purchaser is not confident that the seller will obtain the ject sold, the sale of a future acquisition is invalid. However, where the purchaser is confident that the seller will obtain the object that he sold, the acquisition is valid even though the seller did not yet own the object at the time of the sale (see *Maharsha* to תוס׳ ד״ה בההיא and *Kovetz Shiurim* to *Bava Basra* §276).

25. Some explain that R' Abba remarked that it would be futile to bring the question to the scholars since it was so strong that none of them would be able to resolve the difficulty. Others explain that R' Abba derided the question, commenting that it was not a strong question and it was not befitting to present it to the scholars (*Rashi*).

26. Why is it that if the seller specifies that he sells what he will inherit or trap "today" the sale is valid, while if he does not specify "today" the sale is invalid?

27. The Baraisa discusses a case in which the father is near death, and his son needs money for burial expenses. Since it is dishonorable to his father to delay his burial, the Sages instituted that the son may sell his future inheritance in advance in order to fulfill his duty to honor his father (see *Rashi*). *Ramban* comments that the sale is valid only for property close in value to the burial expenses, and only if the son does not have sufficient means to pay these expenses without this advance sale.

הא מית ליה ומאן דאמר ניחא ליה דליקום בהמנותיה בהדי בני נמי ניחא ליה דליקום בהמנותיה סוף סוף קרו ליה בני לוקח גזלנא אלא איכא בינייהו דמית גזלן מאן דאמר ניחא ליה לאיניש דלא לקריוהו גזלן הא מית ליה למ"ד ניחא ליה דליקום בהמנותיה ה"נ אע"ג דמית ניחא ליה דליקום בהמנותיה סוף סוף קרו לבניה בני גזלנא אלא איכא בינייהו דיהבה במתנה מאן דאמר ניחא ליה דליקום בהמנותיה [א]מתנה נמי ניחא ליה דליקום בהמנותיה מאן דאמר ניחא ליה דלא נקריוהו גזלנא א"ל מאי גזלינא מינך: [ב]פשיטא זבנה אורתה ויהבה במתנה לאו לאוקמה קמי לוקח קא בעי [ג]נפלה ליה בירושה ירושה ממילא היא ולאו איהו קא טרח אבתרה גבי איהו בחובו [ד]חזינא אי אית ליה ארעא אחריתי ואמר האי בעינא לאוקמה קמיה לוקח קא בעי ואי לא זוזי הוא דבעי אפרועי יהבה נהליה [א]במתנה פליגי בה רב אחא ורבינא חד אמר מתנה כירושה דהא ממילא וחד אמר [ה]מתנה כמכר דאי לאו דטרח וארצי קמיה לא הוי יהיב ליה מתנה להכי טרח וארצי קמיה כי היכי דליקום בהמנותיה ועד אימת ניחא ליה דליקום בהמנותיה אמר רב הונא עד שעת העמדה בדין חייא בר רב אמר עד דמטא אדרכתא לידיה רב פפא אמר [ו]עד דמתחלן יומי אכרזתא מתקיף לה רמי בר חמא מכדי האי לוקח במאי קני להאי ארעא בהאי שטרא האי שטרא חספא בעלמא הוא א"ל רבא תהא במאמינו בההוא הנאה דלא קאמר ליה מידי וקא סמיך עליה טרח ומייתי ליה גמר ומקני ליה מתיב רב ששת [ג][ז]מה שאירש מאבא מכור לך מה שתעלה מצודתי מכור לך לא אמר כלום מה שאירש מן אבא היום מכור לך מה שתעלה מצודתי היום מכור לך דבריו קיימין אמר רמי בר חמא הא גברא והא תיובתא אמר רבא גברא קא חזינא ותיובתא לא קא חזינא הכא סמכא דעתיה והכא לא סמכא דעתיה הכא סמכא דעתיה דאזיל טרח ומייתי ליה כי היכי דלא נקרייה גזלנא הכא לא סמכא דעתיה שלחוה לקמיה דרבי אבא בר זבדא אמר להו זו אינה צריכה לפנים אמר רבא זו צריכה לפנים ולפני לפנים הכא סמכא דעתיה והכא לא סמכא דעתיה הוה עובדא בפומבדיתא ואותביה אמר להו רב יוסף זו אינה צריכה לפנים ואמר ליה אביי צריכה לפנים ולפני לפנים הכא סמכא דעתיה הכא לא סמכא דעתיה ומאי שנא רישא ומאי שנא סיפא אמר רבי יוחנן סיפא מה שאירש מאבא היום משום כבוד אביו מה שתעלה מצודתי היום משום

**רש"י**

הא מית. לוקח ומי יחרפנו עוד הלכך לא נתכוון לזה אלא להעמידה בידו בחייו ולא לאחר מותו מ"ד כו': דמית גזלן. לאחר שלקחה והבנים באים להוציא מיד הלוקח: הא מית ליה. ולא נתכוון להעמיד ממכרו אלא בימי חייו שלא יחרפוהו: אע"ג דמית ניחא ליה. מעיקרא: דליקו בהימנותיה. אפילו לאחר מיתה: סוף סוף קרו לבניה בני גזלנא. נמלא שאף לאחר מיתה מחרפין אותו: זבנה אורתה. אם [א] קודם שלקח מן הבעלים חזר ומכרה לאיש אחר לבד מן הראשון או הורישה לאחד מבניו או יהבה במתנה ואחר כך לקחה האי ודאי איגלי דעתיה דלאו לאוקמי קמיה לוקח ראשון בעי ולא ניחא ליה דליקום בהימנותיה שהרי מכרה לשני: נפלה ליה. לגזלן בירושה שמתחילה גזלה לאחד ממורישיו ומת הנגזל: ירושה ממילא הויא. והא ליכא למימר ניחא ליה דליקו בהימנותיה דהא לא טרח אבתרה דנימא גלי דעתיה דניחא ליה דליקו הלכך הוי כיורש דעלמא וחוזר ותובעה ונותן מעות ללוקח: גבייה בחובו. לאחר שגזלה ומכר לו ובא לו אצל נגזל ואמר לו הגבה לי בחובי קרקע שגזלתיך: אי אית ליה ארעא אחריתי. לנגזל שיכול לגבות חובו ממנה ואמר ליה בזו שגזלתי אני חפץ הא טרח אבתרה ואמרינן לאוקמה קמיה לוקח בעי: יהביה ניהליה במתנה. נגזל לגזלן: ועד אימת. יקחנה מבעלים הראשונים דאמרינן דמשום דניחא ליה דליקו בהימנותיה לקחה: עד שעת העמדה בדין. עד שיטרפוה מן הלוקח ויעמידוהו בדין אבל משעמד ברשעו עד שעת העמדה בדין גלי אדעתיה דלא מהימן הוא ואם לקחה אחרי כן לאו לאוקמיה קמיה לוקח בעי: עד דמטא אדרכתא לידיה. עד שיחייבוהו ב"ד לפרוע ללוקח מעותיו ועמד במרדו עד שכתבו פסק דין ונתנו ללוקח על נכסיו של גזלן שבכ"מ שימצאם יחזיק בהן והיינו תשעים יום לאחר שעמד בדין כדאמרי' בהגוזל [בתרא] (ב"ק דף קיב:): עד דמתחלן יומא דאכרזתא. לאחר שמצא זה קרקע משל גזלן ובא לב"ד והן מכריזין שכל מי שרוצה לקנות קרקע יבא ויקחנה כדאמרי' בערכין (דף כא:) שום היתומין שלשים יום [ג]: מתקיף לה רמי בר חמא. אהא מה מכר ראשון לשני כו': תהא. הא דרב: במאמינו. שאמר לו אני סומך עליך שתתננה בידי: גמר ומקני. כשלקחה מבעלים הראשונים: מצודתי. של חיות ועופות ושל דגים: דבריו קיימין. לקמן פריך מאי שנא רישא כו': הא גברא והא תיובתא. הרי אדם גדול וכמוהו תשובתו דקתני לא אמר כלום ולכשיירש לא קנה לוקח כיון דההיא שעתא לאו דידיה הוו נכסי אביו ולא אמרינן מה מכר לו ראשון לשני כל זכות שתבא לידו: לא סמכא דעתיה. דלוקח דקאמר מי יימר שירש מאביו כלום שמא ימכור אביו נכסיו בחייו: שלחוה. להא תיובתא דרב ששת דאותיב אדרב: אינה צריכה לפנים. אינה צריכה כדי לתרלה להכניסה לפני בני הישיבה שאין בהן יודע לפרקה ותשובת הגאונים פורשין לגנאי דליכא קושיא מעליא אל תעלוה לגיו: הוה עובדא בפומבדיתא. שדנו דין כרב ואותבינן מהא מתניתין ואמר רב יוסף כו': משום כבוד אביו. כשהיה אביו גוסס וצריך מעות לקבורתו ולתכריכין מוהר לכבוד אביו שלא לשהותו בבזיון:

**תוספות**

מאי גזלינא מינך. וא"ת וכי מכרה נמי מה גזלו והלא צריך להחזיר לו מעותיו וי"ל דמ"מ יקראנו גזלנא כל זמן שלא יפרע לו:

ארצי קמיה כי היכי דליקום בהימנותיה. משמע דהכי הלכתא מדלא נקט לישנא דלא נקרייה גזלן ועוד דהלכה כרב אשי דהוא בתרא וגדול בחכמה ובמנין:

האי שטרא חספא בעלמא הוא. וא"ת ולימא דקני לה במה שהחזיק בה אחר שקנאה גזלן וי"ל דמשמע ליה משעה שקנאה הגזלן היא של לוקח אע"פ שלא עשה בו שום מעשה וא"ת מעותיו שהיו תחלה מלוה נעשו עתה מכר וי"ל באתרא דלא קנו בכספא א"נ במלוה אינו יכול לקנות כדאמרינן פ"ק דקדושין (דף ו:) המקדש במלוה אינה מקודשת ובמכר לא קנה והא דאמר בהאיש מקדש (שם דף מז.) ושוין שבמכר קנה היינו במלוה שיש לו על אחרים דאז באשה בענין זה מקודשת לכ"ע אי נמי דאשה לא סמכא דעתה וירא שיחזור וימחול אבל מלוה שאשה חייבת לו אם מוחל לה ומקדשה בה אינה מקודשת דלא נתן לה כלום דמקמי הכי היה ברשותה וכן במכר לא קנה אע"ג דכשמקדשה בהנאת מחילת מלוה היא מקודשת דלא גרע מארווח לה זמנא ואדבר עליך לשלטון דמקודשת וכן במכר אם מכר בהנאת מחילה קונה כמו בהחליף דמי שור בפרה מ"מ לא משמע ליה שהיה מקנה לו בהנאת מחילת מלוה משום דמשמע מיד שלקחה הגזלן קנה לוקח ראשון:

בההיא הנאה דקא סמיך כו'. והויא כאילו א"ל שדה זו תהא קנויה לך לכשאקחנה:

מה שאירש מאבא מכור לך לא אמר כלום. וא"ת לימא דרב דאמר כר"מ ובברייתא כרבנן וי"ל דלדידן קפריך דאית לן כרב כדאיתא פרק איזהו נשך (לקמן דף עב:) דמייתי גמרא טעמא דלא ליקריה גזלנא וניחא ליה דליקו בהימנותיה וסבירא לן כרבנן דאין אדם מקנה דבר שלא בא לעולם דשמואל פסיק כרבי יוחנן הסנדלר פרק אע"פ (כתובות דף נט.) ורב נחמן סבר בפירות דקל אף משבאו לעולם יכול לחזור בו ורב האי פסק דאין הלכה כרב בהא משום דס"ל דאין אדם מקנה דבר שלא בא לעולם וכו' ולא נהירא מכח דאיזהו נשך (לקמן דף עב:):

[ז]קנויה לך מעכשיו. תימה מה צריך מעכשיו כיון דאדם מקנה דבר שלא בא לעולם דאי לעניין חזרה הא כל זמן שלא בא לעולם יכול לחזור אע"ג דאמר מעכשיו וי"ל דנ"מ אם נקרע השטר או שאבד קודם שלקחה זה דקני כיון דאמר מעכשיו [ה]: שדה

**עין משפט נר מצוה**

קלז א מיי' פ"ט מהל' גזילה הל' ט סמג עשין עג טוש"ע ח"מ סי' שעד סעי' א:
קלח ב ג מיי' שם הל' יא טוש"ע שם סעי' ב:
קלט ד מיי' שם הל' יב טוש"ע שם סעי' ג:
קמ ה מיי' שם הל' יג טוש"ע שם סעי' ד:
קמא ו מיי' שם הל' י טוש"ע שם סעי' א:
קמב ז מיי' פכ"ב מהל' מכירה הלכה ה סמג עשין פב טוש"ע ח"מ סי' ריא סעי' א:

**רבינו חננאל**

מיהו איצטריכינן לפרושה דחזינן מר זוטרא ורב אשי דאינון בתראי שקלו וטרו לפרושי טעמיה דרב הני מילי בעידנא דקנאה הגזלן מן הנגזל אבל אם נפלה לו לגזלן בירושה מן הניגזל לא אמרי' קנאה לוקח או מי שניתנה לו במתנה. וחזינן נמי בפרק איזהו נשך הלכה מלוה ישראל מעותיו של נכרי. תוב התם שקלי וטרו מרימר ורבינא בהא דאמר רבא התם ניתן ליכתב הכא לא ניתן ליכתב אלא הא דתניא לשבח קרקעות כיצד הרי שגזל [שדה] מחבירו ומכרה לאחר והשביחה והרי היא יוצאה מתחת ידו כשהוא גובה גובה את הקרן מנכסים משועבדים ושבח גובה מבני חורין ואמרינן אמאי נימא לא ניתן ליכתב. ופרקי' הכי השתא התם אי למאן דאמר ניחא ליה דלא ליקריוה גזלן אי למאן דאמר ניחא ליה דליקום בהימנותיה מפייס למריה ומוקים ליה לשטריה הכא אברוחי אברח ליה מוקים ליה לשטריה ש"מ דהלכתא כוותיה דרב בהאי וסוגיא דשמעתא כרב אשי דאמר ניחא ליה דליקום בהימנותיה. הלא תראה כדאתקיף ליה רמי בר חמא פריק ליה רבא תהא במאמינו פירוש בההוא הנאה דלא אמר ליה ולא מידי א) דסמיך ליה ואזיל ומפייס לנגזל וקני ליה מיניה גמר ומקנה ליה והוא דמחזיק בה. והא דאותיב רב ששת הכא הא דתני מה שאירש מאבא מכור לך מה שתעלה מצודתי מכור לך לא אמר כלום דקיימא לן אין אדם מקנה לחבירו דבר שלא בא לעולם. היא בתוספתא במסכת נדרים ומפורש בתלמוד ארץ ישראל בכתובות פרק אע"פ מה שאירש מאבא היום מכור לך בלוה לתכריכי אביו מפני שהיה גוסס וזה פי' משום כבוד אביו. מה שתעלה מצודתי היום מכור לך דבריו קיימים משום כדי חייו. קשיא ליה לרב דאמר מה מכר ראשון לשני (לשני) כל זכות שתבוא לידו. ופרקי אביי ורבא הכי הא מתניתא דתנא [בתוספתא] בסוף מסכת נדרים ליכא למימר דסמכא דעתיה דהא כי הדר ביה לא מצי קרי ליה גזלנא לפיכך לא אמר כלום אבל הא דרב דאי לא טרח ומייתי ומוקים לה בידיה מצו קרו ליה גזלנא סמך דעתיה דאזיל וטרח ומוקים לה בידיה כי היכי דלא ליקריוה גזלנא. ואמרי' מה שנא רישא ומאי שנא סיפא אמר ר' יוחנן סיפא דקתני מה שאירש מאבא היום מכור לך דבריו קיימים משום כבוד אביו אמרו חכמים מכירתו קיימת. וכבר פירשנוהו בתלמוד ארץ ישראל בלוה בתכריכי אביו פי' כגון שהיה אביו גוסס ומוכר לעשות לו תכריכין וכן מי שאין לו [מה] יאכל משום כדי חייו אמרו חכמים אם אמר מה שתעלה

**חשק שלמה על ר"ח** א) נראה דל"ל וסמיך עליה דאזיל ומפייס כו'.

**מסורת הש"ס**

...רומה לדהכא פליגי ...ר' אחא ורבינא ...לה כו: וע"ש], ...תוספתא לנדרים סוף ...ו, ועי' תוס' כתובות ...ד"ה דזבנה], ג) [ע"ש ...ד"ה שום], ד) (שייך ...), ה) [וע"ע תוס' ...מות לג. ד"ה קנויה].

**הגהות הגר"א**

...רש"י ד"ה זבנה ...יתה אם קודם כו'. ...ורמב"ם פי' אפילו שלקחה (ועמ"ש רבינו ...מ סי' שע"ג ס"ק ג):

**גליון הש"ס**

...לאוקמה קמי ...ח קבעי. עיין בר"ש ...ו משנה ג ...ומות: שם מתנה ...בר. עיין מגילה כו: ...ש רפ"ב דמעשרות:

**ליקוטי רש"י**

...רכתא. פסק דין ...המלוה לתוך ...יס של לוה וליטלס ...מה בחובו [ב"ק ...:]. שלא מצאו לו ...סיו נכסים וכתבו לו ...רוף לחזור על נכסיו ...ימצא יגבה אדרכתא ...ן רודף ומשיג כמו ...ה בהלא ולא ...יכיה ולשון המקרא ...ו את בנימין ...יפוהו מנוחה ...יכוהו (שופטים כ ...מן ע"ב]. אכרזתא. ...פ שבאה אדרכתא ...ולא מצא נכסים ...ה עד לאחר זמן ...מצא הוזקק לבא ...ד ומכריזין שיש כאן ...קע למכור כדאמרינן ...רכין (כא:) ואם בא ...וקיבלה ביותר ממה ...מוה אחרים מוסרין ...זה בידו לאחר שלכו ...הכרזה ובמסכת ...כין מפרש כמה ימים ...ריזין בפ' שום ...תומים (שם) [לקמן ...לה:].

ere is no indication that he wants to preserve the rights of the ırchaser.[6] גַּבֵי אִיהוּ בְּחוֹבוֹ – If after he sold the land, **[the** **›bber,]** who was a creditor of the owner, **collected [the field]** in ıyment of **his debt,**[7] חָזֵינָא – **we must investigate** the case. אִי אִית לֵיהּ אַרְעָא אַחֲרִי – **If [the owner] had other land** with ıich to pay his debt, וְאָמַר הַאי בְּעֵינָא – **and [the robber] said** him: **"I desire** as payment **this** land that I stole," לְאוֹקְמָהּ קַמֵּיהּ לוֹקֵחַ קָא בָּ – we presume that **[the robber] intended to cure [the land] for the purchaser,**[8] and he may not seize the ınd from the purchaser. וְאִי לֹא – **If** the owner did **not** have her land, זוּזֵי הוּא דְּבָעֵי אִפָּרוּעֵי – we presume that **[the robber]** erely **intended to be paid** his **money,** but did not intend to otect the rights of the purchaser.[9]

יְהָבָהּ נִהֲלֵיהּ בְּמַתָּ – If after the robber sold the stolen land, **[the** **›wner] gave it to [the robber] as a gift,** פְּלִיגֵי בָהּ רַב אַחָא וְרָבִינָא **Rav Acha and Ravina dispute** the ruling in **this** case. חַד אָמַר מַתָּנָה כִּירוּשָּׁ – **One says a gift is like an inheritance,** דְּהָא מִמֵּילָ – **for,** like an inheritance, **it is** also a **passive** quisition and there is no indication that the robber wants to eserve the rights of the purchaser. The robber may therefore ize the land from the purchaser. וְחַד אָמַר מַתָּנָה כְּמֶכֶר – **And** **›e says a gift is like a purchase,** and he may not seize the land ›m the purchaser, just as he may not do if he purchased the land ›m its owner. דְּאִי לָאו דְּטָרַח וְאַרְצֵי קַמֵּיהּ – **For had [the** **bber] not exerted** himself **to find favor with [the owner],** לֹא הֲוֵי יָהֵיב לֵיהּ מַתָּ – **[the owner] would not have given him a** **ft.** לְהָכִי טָרַח וְאַרְצֵי קַמֵּיהּ – **Therefore,** we conclude that **[the** **bber] exerted himself to find favor with [the owner]** כִּי הֵיכִי דְּלֵיקוּם בְּהֵמְנוּתֵ – **in order that** the owner would give him the ıd as a gift and **he** could thus **stand by his word.**

The Gemara defines the parameters of Rav's ruling that a ›bber may not seize the land from its purchaser if he subse- ıently purchased it from its owner:

וְעַד אֵימַת נִיחָא לֵיהּ דְּלֵיקוּם בְּהֵמְנוּתֵיהּ – **And until how long** after he sells the stolen land do we presume that **[the robber] wants to stand by his word?**[10]

Three opinions are presented:

אָמַר רַב הוּנָא – **Rav Huna says:** עַד שְׁעַת הַעֲמָדָה בְּדִין – **Until the time when** the case is **brought** to court **for judgment.**[11] חִיָּיא בַּר רַב אָמַר – **Chiya bar Rav says:** עַד דְּמָטָא אַדְרַכְתָּא לִידֵיהּ – **Until the seizure warrant reaches [the purchaser's] hand.**[12] רַב פַּפָּא אָמַר – **Rav Pappa says:** עַד דְּמַתְחֲלָן יוֹמֵי אַכְרָזְתָּא – **Until the days of** public **announcement** of the sale of the robber's property **begin.**[13]

The Gemara challenges Rav's ruling that the robber may not seize the land from the purchaser if the robber subsequently purchases it from the owner:

מַתְקִיף לָהּ רָמִי בַּר חָמָא – **Rami bar Chama objects:** מִכְּדִי – **Now,** let us see הַאי לוֹקֵחַ בְּמַאי קָנֵי לְהַאי אַרְעָא – **with what does this purchaser acquire this land** – בְּהַאי שְׁטָרָא – **with this document** [i.e. his original bill of sale]? הַאי שְׁטָרָא חַסְפָּא בְּעָלְמָא הוּא – **This document is merely** like **a** useless **shard!** Since the land did not yet belong to the seller at the time that he sold it, the sale was a meaningless act and the bill of sale was a useless instrument. How, then, does the purchaser acquire the land?[14]

The Gemara answers:

אָמַר לֵיהּ רָבָא – **Rava told [Rami]:** תְּהָא – **Let this** ruling of Rav be explained in a case בְּמַאֲמִינוֹ – **where [the purchaser] relied on [the robber].**[15] בְּהַהוּא הֲנָאָה דְּלָא קָאָמַר לֵיהּ מִידֵי – In exchange **for the satisfaction that** the robber receives from **[the purchaser]** that he has faith in his integrity and **does not tell him anything** regarding the fact that the land was stolen, וְקָא סָמִיךְ עֲלֵיהּ – **and he relies upon [the robber]** טָרַח וּמַיְיתֵי לֵיהּ – that[16] **he will exert** himself **to acquire**[17] it **for [the purchaser],** גָּמַר וּמַקְנֵי לֵיהּ – **[the robber] makes up** his mind **and conveys** its **ownership to him** when he purchases it from its legitimate owner.[18]

NOTES

Therefore, he is like any other person who inherits property that has ›en stolen and sold, and he may seize it from the purchaser. However, must refund the purchaser's money (*Rashi*).

The robber approached the owner subsequent to the sale, asking him pay off his debt with the stolen land (*Rashi*).

We presume this to be his intention since he bothered to specifically ›quest as payment the field which he sold (*Rashi*).

Since the owner had no other land, there is no indication that the ›ber desired to preserve the rights of the purchaser rather than just ›lect payment of his loan.

I.e. until how long after the sale will we interpret the robber's ›rchase of the stolen land from its owner as intended to protect the ›hts of the original purchaser (*Rashi*)?

I.e. until the owner repossesses the land, and the purchaser begins ›oceedings for the refund of his money from the robber. If the robber ›rchased the land from the owner after this time, we do not presume ›at the robber intended to protect the rights of the purchaser. Since he ›l not correct his wrongdoing until now, he has already demonstrated ›at he is not trustworthy (*Rashi*). [This is the logic of all three ›inions presented here. They disagree merely concerning *when* the ›ber has demonstrated his lack of trustworthiness.]

Ninety days after a court's decision, when the court is convinced a ›btor will not pay, the court gives the creditor a seizure warrant that ›titles him to collect from any of the debtor's property that he might ›cover (from *Bava Kamma* 112b). [*Rashi* (16b ד"ה אדרכתא) explains ›at a seizure warrant is called an *adrachta* because the word means to ›rsue and overtake. The document is so named because the creditor is ›structed to pursue property which may be available for collection.] In this case, if the court was forced to issue a seizure document to the ›rchaser because the robber refused to reimburse him, we no longer ›sume that the robber desires to protect the interests of the ›rchaser (see *Rashi*).

13. After a creditor locates property of the debtor, the court begins a thirty-day public-auction process (see *Arachin* 21b). If the robber did not purchase the land from its owner until the court began to auction off one of the robber's properties in order to repay the purchaser, it is clear that he is not interested in remaining trustworthy to the purchaser (see *Rashi*).

14. [Although it is possible that the purchaser performed a proprietary act on the field subsequent to the robber's purchase from the seller, Rav indicates that the purchaser acquires the field as soon as the robber purchases it, without performing a proprietary act. If so, it must be that the purchaser acquires the land with the original bill of sale. The Gemara's question is thus valid (*Tosafos*).]

15. He told the robber: "I trust that you will give me the land" (*Rashi*). He has faith in the seller (i.e. the robber) that he will transfer ownership of the property to him and that its ownership will not be legally contested (see *Rashba.*)

16. This translation reflects the emendation of the *Rashash*.

17. Literally: bring.

18. *Tosafos* explain that it is as if the robber originally told the purchaser that the ownership of the land will be conveyed to him when he purchases it from its owner. Since the purchaser was confident that the seller would convey the property to him, the transaction is valid even though the seller did not yet own the property at the time of the sale (see *Maharsha* and *Maharam* to תוס' ד"ה בההיא). According to this explanation, the act of acquisition on the property takes place at the time the robber sells the property to the purchaser.

Others explain that the sale is transacted at the time the robber purchases the land from the owner. The faith that the purchaser has in the seller (i.e. the robber) has monetary value to the seller; it is thus as if the seller received money from the purchaser. Since payment of money is a method by which land may be acquired, the robber sells the land to the purchaser at the time he acquires it from the owner, in

הא מית ליה ומאן דאמר ניחא ליה דליקום בהמנותיה בהדי בני נמי ניחא ליה דליקום בהמנותיה סוף סוף קרו ליה בני לוקח גזלנא אלא איכא בינייהו דמית גזלן מאן דאמר ניחא ליה לאיניש דלא לקריוהו גזלן הא מית ליה למ"ד ניחא ליה דליקום בהמנותיה ה"נ אע"ג דמית ניחא ליה דליקום בהמנותיה סוף סוף קרו לבניה בני גזלנא אלא איכא בינייהו דיהבה במתנה מאן דאמר ניחא ליה דליקום בהמנותיה [א]מתנה נמי ניחא ליה דליקום בהמנותיה מאן דאמר ניחא ליה דלא נקריוהו גזלנא א"ל מאי גזלינא מינך: [ב]פשיטא זבנה אורתה ויהבה במתנה לאו לאוקמה קמי לוקח קא בעי [ג]נפלה ליה בירושה ירושה ממילא היא ולאו איהו קא טרח אבתרה גבי איהו בחובו [ד]חזינא אי אית ליה ארעא אחריתי ואמר האי בעינא [ה]לאוקמה קמיה לוקח קא בעי ואי לא זוזי הוא דבעי אפרועי יהבה נהליה [א]במתנה פליגי בה רב אחא ורבינא חד אמר מתנה כירושה דהא ממילא וחד אמר [ה]מתנה כמכר דאי לאו דטרח וארצי קמיה לא הוי יהיב ליה מתנה להכי טרח וארצי קמיה כי היכי דליקום בהמנותיה ועד אימת ניחא ליה דליקום בהמנותיה אמר רב הונא עד שעת העמדה בדין חייא בר רב אמר עד דמטא אדרכתא לידיה רב פפא אמר [ו]עד דמתחלן יומי אכרזתא מתקיף לה רמי בר חמא מכדי האי לוקח במאי קני להאי ארעא בהאי שטרא האי שטרא חספא בעלמא הוא א"ל רבא תהא במאמינו בההוא הנאה דלא קאמר ליה מידי וקא סמיך עליה טרח ומייתי ליה גמר ומקני ליה מתיב רב ששת [ג][ז]מה שאירש מאבא מכור לך מה שתעלה מצודתי מכור לך לא אמר כלום מה שאירש מן אבא היום מכור לך מה שתעלה מצודתי היום מכור לך דבריו קיימין אמר רמי בר חמא הא גברא והא תיובתא אמר רבא גברא קא חזינא ותיובתא לא קא חזינא הכא סמכא דעתיה והכא לא סמכא דעתיה הכא סמכא דעתיה דאזיל טרח ומייתי ליה כי היכי דלא נקרייה גזלנא הכא לא סמכא דעתיה שלחוה לקמיה דרבי אבא בר זבדא אמר להו זו אינה צריכה לפנים אמר רבא זו צריכה לפנים ולפני לפנים הכא סמכא דעתיה והכא לא סמכא דעתיה הוה עובדא בפומבדיתא ואותביה אמר להו רב יוסף זו אינה צריכה לפנים ואמר ליה אביי צריכה לפנים ולפני לפנים הכא סמכא דעתיה הכא לא סמכא דעתיה ומאי שנא רישא ומאי שנא סיפא אמר רבי יוחנן סיפא מה שאירש מאבא היום משום כבוד אביו מה שתעלה מצודתי היום משום

---

**רש"י**

הא מית. לוקח ומי יחרפנו עוד הלכך לא נתכוון לזה אלא להעמידה בידו בחייו ולא לאחר מותו מ"ד כו': דמית גזלן. לאחר שלקחה והבנים באים להוציא מיד הלוקח: הא מית ליה. ולא נתכוון להעמיד ממכרו אלא בימי חייו שלא יחרפוהו: אע"ג דמית ניחא ליה. מעיקרא: דליקו בהימנותיה. אפילו לאחר מיתה: סוף סוף קרו לבניה בני גזלנא. נמצא שאף לאחר מיתה מחרפין אותו: זבנה אורתה. אם [א] קודם שלקח מן הבעלים חזר ומכרה לאיש אחר לבד מן הראשון או הורישה לאחד מבניו או יהבה במתנה ואחר כך לקחה האי ודאי איגלי דעתיה דלאו לאוקמי קמיה לוקח ראשון בעי ולא ניחא ליה דליקום בהימנותיה שהרי מכרה לשני: נפלה ליה. לגזלן בירושה שמתחילה גזלה לאחד ממורישיו ומת הנגזל: ירושה ממילא הויא. והא ליכא למימר ניחא ליה דליקו בהימנותיה דהא לא טרח אבתרה דנימא גלי דעתיה דניחא ליה דליקו הלכך הוי כיורש דעלמא וחוזר ותובעה ונותן מעות ללוקח: גבייה בחובו. לאחר שגזלה ומכר לו ובא לו אצל נגזל ואמר לו הגבה לי בחובי קרקע שגזלתיך: אי אית ליה ארעא אחריתי. לנגזל שיכול לגבות חובו ממנה ואמר ליה בזו שגזלתי אני חפץ הא טרח אבתרה ואמרינן לאוקמה קמיה לוקח בעי: יהביה ניהליה במתנה. נגזל לגזלן: ועד אימת. יקחנה מבעלים הראשונים דאמרינן דמשום דניחא ליה דליקו בהימנותיה לקחה: עד שעת העמדה בדין. עד שיטרפוה מן הלוקח ויעמידהו בדין אבל משעמד ברשעו עד שעת העמדה בדין גלי אדעתיה דלא מהימן הוא ואם לקחה אחרי כן לאו לאוקמיה קמיה לוקח בעי: עד דמטא אדרכתא לידיה. עד שיחייבוהו ב"ד לפרוע ללוקח מעותיו ועמד במרדו עד שכתבו פסק דין ונתנו ללוקח על נכסיו של גזלן שבכ"מ שימצאם יחזיק בהן והיינו תשעים יום לאחר שעמד בדין כדאמרי' בהגוזל [בתרא] (ב"ק דף קיב:): עד דמתחלן יומא דאכרזתא. לאחר שמצא זה קרקע משל גזלן ובא לב"ד והן מכריזין שכל מי שרוצה לקנות קרקע יבא ויקחנה כדאמרי' בערכין (דף כא:) שום היתומין שלשים יום [ג]: מתקיף לה רמי בר חמא. אהא מה מכר ראשון לשני כו': תהא. הא דרב: במאמינו. שאמר לו אני סומך עליך שתתננה בידי: גמר ומקני. כשלקחה מבעלים הראשונים: מצודתי. של חיות ועופות ושל דגים: דבריו קיימין. לקמן פריך מאי שנא רישא כו': הא גברא והא תיובתא. הרי אדם גדול וכמוהו תשובתו דקתני לא אמר כלום ולכשיירש לא קנה לוקח כיון דהיא שעתא לאו דידיה הוו נכסי אביו ולא אמרינן מה מכר לו ראשון לשני כל זכות שתבא לידו: לא סמכא דעתיה. דלוקח דקאמר מי יימר שירש מאביו כלום שמא ימכור אביו נכסיו בחייו: שלחוה. להא תיובתא דרב ששת דאותיב אדרב: אינה צריכה לפנים. אינה צריכה כדי לתרלה להכניסה לפני בני הישיבה שאין בהן יודע לפרקה ותשובת הגאונים פורשין לגנאי דליכא קושיא מעליא אל תעלוה לגיו: הוה עובדא בפומבדיתא. שדנו דין כרב ואותבינן מהא מתניתין ואמר רב יוסף כו': משום כבוד אביו. כשהיה אביו גוסס וצריך מעות לקבורתו ולתכריכין מוזהר לכבוד אביו שלא לשהותו בבזיון:

---

**תוספות**

מאי גזלינא מינך. וא"ת וכי מכרה נמי מה גזלו והלא צריך להחזיר לו מעותיו וי"ל דמ"מ יקראנו גזלנא כל זמן שלא יפרע לו: ארצי קמיה כי היכי דליקום בהימנותיה. משמע דהכי הלכתא מדלא נקט לישנא דלא נקרייה גזלן ועוד דהלכה כרב אשי דהוא בתרא וגדול בחכמה ובמנין:

האי שטרא חספא בעלמא הוא. וא"ת ולימא דקני לה במה שהחזיק בה אחר שקנאה גזלן וי"ל דמשמע ליה משעה שקנאה הגזלן היא של לוקח אע"פ שלא עשה בו שום מעשה וא"ת מעותיו שהיו תחלה מלוה נעשו עתה מכר וי"ל באתרא דלא קנו בכספא א"נ במלוה אינו יכול לקנות כדאמרינן פ"ק דקדושין (דף ו:) המקדש במלוה אינה מקודשת ובמכר לא קנה והא דאמר בהאיש מקדש (שם דף מז.) ושוין שבמכר קנה היינו במלוה שיש לו על אחרים דאז באשה בענין זה מקודשת לכ"ע אי לאו דאשה לא סמכא דעתה וירא' שיחזור וימחול אבל מלוה שאשה חייבת לו אם מוחל לה ומקדשה בה אינה מקודשת דלא נתן לה כלום דמקמי הכי היה ברשותה וכן במכר לא קנה אע"ג דכשמקדשה בהנאת מחילת מלוה היא מקודשת דלא גרע מארווח לה זמנא ואדבר עליך לשלטון דמקודשת וכן במכר אם מכר בהנאת מחילה קונה כמו בהחליף דמי שור בפרה מ"מ לא משמע ליה שהיה מקנה לו בהנאת מחילת מלוה משום דמשמע מיד שלקחה הגזלן קנה לוקח ראשון:

בההיא הנאה דקא סמיך כו'. והוא כאילו א"ל שדה זו תהא קנויה לך לכשאקחנה:

מה שאירש מאבא מכור לך לא אמר כלום. וא"ת לימא דרב דאמר כר"מ ובריית' כרבנן וי"ל דלדידן קפריך דאית לן כרב כדאית' פרק איזהו נשך (לקמן דף עב:) דמייתי גמרא טעמא דלא ליקריה גזלנא וניחא ליה דליקו בהימנותיה וסבירא לן כרבנן דאין אדם מקנה דבר שלא בא לעולם דשמואל פסיק כרבי יוחנן הסנדלר פרק אע"פ (כתובות דף נט.) ורב נחמן סבר בפירות דקל אף משבאו לעולם יכול לחזור בו ורב האי פסק דאין הלכה כרב בהא משום דס"ל דאין אדם מקנה דבר שלא בא לעולם וכו' ולא נהירא מכח דאיזהו נשך (לקמן דף עב:):

[ד]קנויה לך מעכשיו. תימה מה צריך מעכשיו כיון דאדם מקנה דבר שלא בא לעולם דאי לעניין חזרה הא כל זמן שלא בא לעולם יכול לחזור אע"ג דאמר מעכשיו וי"ל דנ"מ אם נקרע השטר או שאבד קודם שלקחה זה דקני כיון דאמר מעכשיו [ה]: שדה

---



קלז א מיי' פ"ט מהל' גזילה הל' ט סמג עשין עג טוש"ע ח"מ סי' שעד סעי' א:
קלח ב ג מיי' שם הל' יא טוש"ע שם סעי' ב:
קלט ד מיי' שם הל' יב טוש"ע שם סעי' ג:
קמ ה מיי' שם הל' יג טוש"ע שם סעי' ד:
קמא ו מיי' שם הל' י טוש"ע שם סעי' א:
קמב ז מיי' פכ"ב מהל' מכירה הלכה ה סמג עשין פב טוש"ע ח"מ סי' ריא סעי' א:

**רבינו חננאל**

מיהו איצטריכינן לפרושה דחזינן מר זוטרא ורב אשי דאינון בתראי שקלו וטרו לפרושי טעמיה דרב הני מילי בעידנא דקנאה הגזלן מן הנגזל אבל אם נפלה לו לגזלן בירושה מן הניגזל לא אמרי' קנאה לוקח או מי שניתנה לו במתנה. וחזינן נמי בפרק איזהו נשך הלכה מלוה ישראל מעותיו של נכרי. תוב התם שקלי וטרו מרימר ורבינא בהא דאמר רבא התם ניתן ליכתב הכא לא ניתן ליכתב אלא הא דתניא לשבח קרקעות כיצד הרי שגזל [שדה] מחבירו ומכרה לאחר והשביחה והרי היא יוצאה מתחת ידו כשהוא גובה גובה את הקרן מנכסים משועבדים ושבח גובה מבני חורין ואמרינן אמאי נימא לא ניתן ליכתב. ופרקי' הכי השתא התם אי למאן דאמר ניחא ליה דלא ליקריוה גזלן אי למאן דאמר ניחא ליה דליקום בהימנותיה מפייס למריה ומוקים ליה לשטריה הכא אברוחי אברח ליה מוקים ליה לשטריה ש"מ דהלכתא כוותיה דרב בהאי וסוגיא דשמעתא כרב אשי דאמר ניחא ליה דליקום בהימנותיה. הלא תראה כדאתקיף ליה רמי בר חמא פריק ליה רבא תהא במאמינו פירוש בההוא הנאה דלא אמר ליה ולא מידי א) דסמיך ליה ואזיל ומפייס לנגזל וקני ליה מיניה גמר ומקנה ליה והוא דמחזיק בה. והא דאותיב רב ששת הכא הא דתני מה שאירש מאבא מכור לך מה שתעלה מצודתי מכור לך לא אמר כלום דקיימא לן אין אדם מקנה לחבירו דבר שלא בא לעולם. היא בתוספתא במסכת נדרים ומפורש בתלמוד ארץ ישראל בכתובות פרק אע"פ מה שאירש מאבא היום מכור לך בלוה לתכריכי אביו מפני שהיה גוסס וזה פי' משום כבוד אביו. מה שתעלה מצודתי היום מכור לך דבריו קיימים משום כדי חייו. קשיא ליה לרב דאמר מה מכר ראשון לשני (לשני) כל זכות שתבוא לידו. ופרקי אביי ורבא הכי הא מתניתא דתנא [בתוספתא] בסוף מסכת נדרים ליכא למימר דסמכא דעתיה דהא כי הדר ביה לא מצי קרי ליה גזלנא לפיכך לא אמר כלום אבל הא דרב דאי לא טרח ומייתי ומוקים לה בידיה מצו קרו ליה גזלנא סמך דעתיה דאזיל וטרח ומוקים לה בידיה כי היכי דלא ליקריוה גזלנא. ואמרי' מה שנא רישא ומאי שנא סיפא אמר ר' יוחנן סיפא דקתני מה שאירש מאבא היום מכור לך דבריו קיימים משום כבוד אביו אמרו חכמים מכירתו קיימת. וכבר פירשנוהו בתלמוד ארץ ישראל בלוה בתכריכי אביו פי' כגון שהיה אביו גוסס ומוכר לעשות לו תכריכין וכן מי שאין לו [מה] יאכל משום כדי חייו אמרו חכמים אם אמר מה שתעלה

חשק שלמה על ר"ח א) נראה דצ"ל וסמיך עליה דאזיל ומפייס כו'.

---

**מסורת הש"ס**

דומה להכא פליגי ר' אחא ורבינא ... לה כו: וע"ש], תוספתא דנדרים סוף ו, ועי' תוס' כתובות ... ד"ה דזבנה], ג) [ע"ש ... ד"ה שום], ד) [שייך ... ג], ה) [וע"ע תוס' ... עות נג. ד"ה קנויה].

**הגהות הגר"א**

[א] רש"י ד"ה זבנה אורתה אם קודם כו'. ... ורמב"ם פי' אפילו ... שלקחה (ועמ"ש רבינו ... מ סי' שע"ג ס"ק ג):

**גליון הש"ס**

לאוקמה קמי לוקח קבעי. עיין בר"ש ... ו משנה ג ... יבמות: שם מתנה כמכר. עיין מגילה כו: ... ר"ש רפ"ב דמעשרות:

**ליקוטי רש"י**

אדרכתא. פסק דין ... המלוה לתוך ... נכסים של לוה וליטלם ... מה בחובו [ב"ק ...]. שלא מצאו לו ... לו נכסים וכתבו לו ... רודף לחזור על נכסיו ... ימצא יגבה אדרכתא ... רודף ומשיג כמו ... בתלא ולא ... ולשון המקרא ... את בנימין ... מנוחה ... (שופטים כ) ... [ע"ב]. אכרזתא. ... פ שבאה אדרכתא ... ולא מצא נכסים ... עד לאחר זמן ... מצא החוקק לבא ... ד ומכריזין שיש כאן ... (כא:) ואם לא ... וקילנה ביותר ממה ... אחרים מוכרין ... בידו לאחר שכלו ... הכריזה והמכבת ... מפרש כמה ימים ... בפ' שום ... ימים (שם) [לקמן לה:].

הָא מִית לֵ – Since **[the purchaser] has died,** no one will call the ller a robber. According to Mar Zutra's reason, with his rchase, the robber intends to protect only the rights of the rchaser himself, but not the rights of the purchaser's heirs. וּמַאן דְּאָ – **And** according to **the one** [Rav Ashi] **who says** that e reason why the robber purchases the land to protect the rights the purchaser is because נִיחָא לֵיהּ דְּלֵיקוּם בְּהֵמָנוּתֵיהּ – **he ants to stand by his word,** the robber may not seize the land om the children, בַּהֲדֵי בְּנֵי נַמִּי נִיחָא לֵיהּ דְּלֵיקוּם בְּהֵמָנוּתֵיהּ – for **wants to stand by his word with the children as well.** erefore, with his purchase, the robber intends to protect the ghts of the purchaser's heirs as well.[1]

The Gemara challenges this distinction between the two inions:

סוֹף ס – **After all,** קָרוּ לֵיהּ בְּנֵי לוֹקֵחַ גַּזְלָנָא – **the children of e purchaser will call [the seller] a robber.** Therefore, even ar Zutra should agree that with his purchase, the robber tends to protect the rights of the heirs, and he may not seize the nd from them.

The Gemara accepts this objection and presents an alternative stinction between the two opinions:

אֶלָּא אִיכָּא בֵּינַיְי – **Rather, the** practical **difference between em** emerges דְּמִית גַּזְלָן – in a case **where the robber died** ter he purchased the land from its owner. They disagree hether the robber's children may seize the land from its original rchaser, although the robber himself could not.

מַאן דְּאָ – According to **the one who says** that the reason why e robber purchases the land to protect the rights of the puraser is because נִיחָא לֵיהּ לְאִינִישׁ דְּלֹא לִקְרִיוּהוּ גַּזְלָן – **a man sires that [people] not call him a robber,** the robber's ildren may seize the land from the purchaser. הָא מִית לֵיהּ – nce **[the robber] has died,** he will no longer be disparaged. erefore, with his purchase, the robber intends to protect the ghts of the purchaser only during his own lifetime, but not after s death.

לְמַאן דְּאָ – And **according to the one who says** that the ason why the robber purchases the land to protect the rights of e purchaser is because נִיחָא לֵיהּ דְּלֵיקוּם בְּהֵמָנוּתֵיהּ – **he wants stand by his word,** the robber's children may not seize the nd from the purchaser, הָכִי נַמִּי אַף עַל גַּב דְּמִית – because **here so, although [the robber] has died,** נִיחָא לֵיהּ דְּלֵיקוּם בְּהֵמָנוּתֵ – **he wants to stand by his word** even posthumously. Therefore, with his purchase, the robber intends to protect the rights of the purchaser even after his own death.

The Gemara contests this distinction as well:

סוֹף סוֹף – **After all,** קָרוּ לִבְנֵיהּ בְּנֵי גַּזְלָנָא – **[people] will call his children the children of a robber.**[2] Therefore, even Mar Zutra should agree that with his purchase, the robber intends to protect the rights of the purchaser even after his own death, and his children may not seize the land from the purchaser.

The Gemara accepts this objection and suggests yet another distinction between the two opinions:

אֶלָּא אִיכָּא בֵּינַיְיהוּ – **Rather, the** practical **difference between them** emerges דִּיהֲבָהּ בְּמַתָּנָה – in a case **where [the robber] gave [the land]** to another **as a gift,** not as a sale. If the robber then purchases the land from its owner, they disagree whether he may seize it from the recipient, although he could not seize it from a purchaser.

מַאן דְּאָמַר – According to **the one who says** that the reason why the robber purchases the land to protect the rights of a purchaser is because נִיחָא לֵיהּ דְּלֵיקוּם בְּהֵמָנוּתֵיהּ – **he wants to stand by his word,** מַתָּנָה נַמִּי – regarding **a gift as well** נִיחָא לֵיהּ דְּלֵיקוּם בְּהֵמָנוּתֵיהּ – **he wants to stand by his word.** Therefore, he may not seize the land from the recipient, because, with his purchase, he intends to protect the rights of the recipient.

מַאן דְּאָמַר – According to **the one who says** that the reason why the robber purchases the land to protect the rights of a purchaser is because נִיחָא לֵיהּ דְּלֹא נִקְרִיוּהוּ גַּזְלָנָא – **he wants that we should not call him a robber,** he may seize the land from the recipient, אָמַר לֵיהּ – for **[the robber] may tell him:** מַאי גְּזַלִינָא מִינָךְ – **What have I stolen from you?**[3]

The Gemara continues its discussion of the laws of the sale of stolen property which was later acquired by the robber:

פְּשִׁיטָא – It is **clear** זַבְּנָהּ – that if **[the robber] sold [the stolen land]** to a second purchaser, אוֹרְתָהּ – **or bequeathed it** to one of his sons, וִיהָבָהּ בְּמַתָּנָה – **or gave it as a gift** to another, and then purchased it from the legitimate owner, לָאו לְאוֹקְמָהּ קַמֵּי לוֹקֵחַ קָא בָּעֵי – **he does not intend to secure [the land] for the** first **purchaser.**[4] נָפְלָה לֵיהּ בִּירוּשָּׁה – It is likewise clear that if **[the robber] inherited [the land]**[5] after he sold it, he may seize it from the purchaser. יְרוּשָּׁה מִמֵּילָא הִיא – Since **an inheritance is a passive** acquisition, וְלָאו אִיהוּ קָא טָרַח אַבָּתְרָהּ – **and [the robber] did not exert himself** to acquire **[the land],**

NOTES

We have followed *Rashi* who explains that the purchaser died *after* the bber purchased the land from its owner. According to Mar Zutra, since e robber's goal in obtaining the land for the purchaser is to avoid being anded a robber by the purchaser, we presume that the robber wants o purchaser to own the land only as long as the purchaser lives. The bber does not intend that the land be passed on to the purchaser's irs, since upon the purchaser's death the robber's fear of disparageent ceases to be a concern.

[This is difficult to understand. Since the purchaser was alive at e time the robber purchased the land from its owner, the puraser acquired the land at that time. How, then, does the land tomatically revert to the robber's possession upon the purchaser's ath?]

[*Tosafos* and other Rishonim therefore explain that the Gemara scusses a case in which the purchaser died *before* the robber bought the nd from its owner. In this case, according to Mar Zutra, the land never comes the property of the purchaser's children, since the robber does t fear disparagement by them.]

This is a disgrace to the memory of the robber, which he will attempt prevent (see *Rashi*).

Since the recipient did not pay for the land, he does not lose anything it is seized; therefore, he will not disparage the robber. This is unlike e case of a sale, in which the purchaser paid for the land, and he might thus disparage the seller if it is seized. Indeed, even in the case of a sale the purchaser does not incur a loss, since the seller will have to refund the purchaser's money. However, since probably there will be an interval of time between the owner's seizure of the property and the robber's refund to the purchaser, the purchaser could disparage the robber during that time. Therefore, the robber endeavors to preserve the rights of the purchaser (*Tosafos*).

4. It is clear from the robber's actions that he is unconcerned with requiting the first purchaser's trust, since he conveyed the land to someone else before buying it from the owner (*Rashi*). It is also clear that he is indifferent to his possible disparagement as a robber (*Ramban*). Thus, we do not assume that he purchased the land from its owner for the purpose of obtaining it for the first purchaser.

*Rashi* indicates that if the robber conveyed the land to another *after* he purchased it from its owner, the conveyance does not retroactively invalidate our presumption that the robber desires to protect the rights of the first purchaser. *Rambam* (*Gezeilah V'Aveidah* 9:11), however, rules that even a post-purchase conveyance indicates that the robber was not interested in the rights of the first purchaser at the time he acquired the land from its owner.

5. This refers to a case in which the robber stole from someone to whom he is an heir-apparent (*Rashi*). Thus, when the owner died, the robber inherited the land.

between Rav and Shmuel concerning the purchase of stolen land: בֵּין לְרַב דְּאָמַר פִּקָּדוֹן – **Both according to Rav who says** the money is **a deposit** בֵּין לִשְׁמוּאֵל דְּאָמַר מַתָּנָה – **and according to Shmuel who says** the money is **a gift,** הַאי לְאַרְעָא בְּמַאי קָא נָחִית – **how does [the purchaser] go down to** work **the land,** וּפֵירוֹת הֵיכִי אָכִיל – **and how does he consume** its **produce?** If, as we have explained according to Rav and Shmuel, he does not intend to purchase the land, how can he justifiably possess it?[13]

The Gemara explains that although the purchaser realizes the sale is invalid, he nevertheless justifies his possession of the stolen property:

סָבַר – **He thinks:** אֵנָא אֵיחוֹת לְאַרְעָא – **I will go down to the land** וְאִיעֲבִיד וְאֵיכוֹל בְּגַוַּיהּ – **and I will work** it **and consume** its produce **in it** כִּי הֵיכִי דַּהֲוָה קָא עָבִיד אִיהוּ – **just as [the seller] did** until now. לְכִי אָתֵי מָרֵיהּ דְּאַרְעָא – **When the** legitimate **owner of the land arrives** to claim his property, זוּזַאי נֶהֱווּ – **my money will be** לְרַב דְּאָמַר פִּקָּדוֹן פִּקָּדוֹן – either **a deposit according to Rav who says** it is **a deposit** לִשְׁמוּאֵל דְּאָמַר מַתָּנָה מַתָּנָה – or **a gift, according to Shmuel who says** it is **a gift.**[14]

The Gemara issues a ruling regarding the disagreement between Rav and Shmuel (above, 14b) concerning the purchase of land which was later discovered to be stolen:

אָמַר רָבָא – **Rava said:** הִלְכְתָא – **The halachah is** that if the purchaser improves the land and it is subsequently seized by its legitimate owner, יֵשׁ לוֹ מָעוֹת – **[the purchaser] has** the right to compensation from the seller for the **money** which he paid for the property, וְיֵשׁ לוֹ שֶׁבַח – **and he has** the right to compensation from the seller for his **improvements** to the field וְאַף עַל פִּי שֶׁלֹּא פֵּירַשׁ לוֹ אֶת הַשֶּׁבַח – **even though [the seller] did not explicitly state to him** that he would compensate him for his **improvements.**[15]

Another ruling:

הִכִּיר בָּהּ שֶׁאֵינָהּ שֶׁלּוֹ – **If [the purchaser] recognized that [the property] was not [the seller's],** וְלָקְחָהּ – **but** nevertheless he **purchased it** and improved it, and then it was seized by its owner, מָעוֹת יֵשׁ לוֹ – **he has** the right to compensation from the seller for the **money** which he paid for the property,[16] שֶׁבַח אֵין לוֹ – **but he does not have the** right to compensation for his **improvements.**

Another ruling:

[...]ת סוֹפֵר אַחֲרָיוּת – The absence of **a guarantee** in a document הוּא – **is** presumed to be **an oversight of the scribe,** and not intentional omission.[17] בֵּין בִּשְׁטָרֵי הַלְוָאָה – This ruling appl[...] **both** to **a note of indebtedness,** בֵּין בִּשְׁטָרֵי מִקָּח וּמִמְכָּר – **and bills of purchase and sale.**[18]

The Gemara returns to its discussion of the sale of sto[...] property:

בְּעָא מִינֵּיהּ שְׁמוּאֵל מֵרַב – **Shmuel inquired of Rav:** [...] וְלָקְחָהּ מִבְּעָלִים הָרִאשׁוֹנִים – If after [the robber] sold the stolen land **returned and purchased it from its original** [i.e. legitima[...] **owner,** מַהוּ – **what** is the law? May the robber now seize t[...] land from the purchaser, just as the original owner could ha[...] done?[19] אָמַר לֵיהּ – **[Rav] told [Shmuel]:** מֶכֶר לוֹ רִאשׁוֹן לַשֵּׁנִי – **What did the first** [i.e. the robber ] **sell to the second** [i.[...] his purchaser]? כָּל זְכוּת שֶׁתָּבֹא לְיָדוֹ – **Any right that m[...] subsequently **come into his possession** concerning the land. [...] may therefore now not seize the land from the purchaser.[20]

The Gemara analyzes Rav's ruling:

מַאי טַעְמָא – **What is the reason** that the robber purchases t[...] land to protect his purchaser? מַר זוּטְרָא אָמַר – **Mar Zutra sa[ys]** נִיחָא לֵיהּ דְּלָא נִקְרְיֵיהּ גַּזְלָנָא – **[The robber] desires that [t[...] purchaser] not call him a robber** when the legitimate own[...] repossesses his land. The robber's preemptive purchase saves [...] reputation. רַב אַשִׁי אָמַר – **Rav Ashi says:** [...]א לֵיהּ דְּלֵיקוּ בְּהֵימָנוּתֵיהּ – **[The robber] wants to stand by his word.** Since t[...] purchaser trusted that he would retain his purchase, it is [...] violation of this trust to allow the owner to seize the land. By t[...] robber's preemptive purchase, he requites this trust.

The Gemara elaborates:

מַאי בֵּינַיְיהוּ – **What is** the practical difference **between these** t[...] explanations? אִיכָּא בֵּינַיְיהוּ – **The** practical **difference betwe[en] them** emerges דְּמִית לוֹקֵחַ – in a case in which **the origin[al] purchaser died** after the robber purchased the land from [...] legitimate owner. They disagree whether the robber may seize t[...] land from the heirs of the purchaser, although he could not sei[...] the land from the purchaser himself. מַאן דְּאָמַר – According **the one** [Mar Zutra] **who says** that the reason why the robb[...] purchases the land to protect the rights of the purchaser is becau[...] נִיחָא לֵיהּ דְּלָא לִקְרְיֵיהּ גַּזְלָנָא – **he desires that [the purchaser] n[ot] call him a robber,** the robber may seize the land from the childre[...]

NOTES

13. The Gemara argues that the purchaser must have been an unknowledgeable person who thought that he was entitled to purchase stolen property. Thus, the disagreement between Rav and Shmuel must hinge on some other point (*Rashi*).

14. The purchaser rationalizes as follows: It is possible that the rightful owner will never attempt to repossess his land and the robber will retain it and consume all its produce. If so, I will cause no additional harm to the owner by "purchasing" the field and consuming the produce myself. [In that case, the seller will keep the money as "payment" for the field.] In the event that the owner reclaims his field, I will take back my money from the seller (according to Rav), or (according to Shmuel) I will allow the seller to retain the money as a gift (see *Ritva*).

15. This ruling opposes Shmuel's opinion (15a) that the seller does not compensate the buyer for seized improvements unless the seller explicitly agreed to do so at the time of the sale [and the seller either owns other land or legally pre-committed himself to this compensation] (*Rashi*).

16. As Rav ruled above.

17. Thus, unless the document explicitly states that the loan or sale is not guaranteed, it is presumed that the scribe inadvertently omitted the guarantee clause, and we treat the document as one that contains a guarantee.

18. [In the case of a note of indebtedness, this means that the note carries a mortgage on the debtor's real property. Thus, in the event that the debtor defaults, the creditor may collect that property even from someone who subsequently purchased it.]

[In the case of a bill of sale, this means that the seller agrees to co[m]pensate the purchaser if the property is subsequently discovered to [be] stolen and is seized by its rightful owner, or if the seller's creditor collec[ts] it in payment of the seller's debt.]

[The reason for the presumption that the guarantee clause was n[ot] intentionally omitted is that a lender or purchaser generally does n[ot] risk loss of his money. Therefore, he would not lend money or make [a] purchase without insisting on a guarantee.]

Rava's ruling regarding a bill of sale is in opposition to Shmuel's rulir[ng] above (14a) that a purchaser holding a bill of sale without a guarant[ee] clause cannot demand compensation from the seller if the property [is] collected by the seller's creditor (see *Rashi*).

19. Since the robber's original sale to the purchaser was a meaningle[ss] act, the rightful owner retains title to the field and may sell it to anoth[er] party. That party could then seize the field from the original "pu[r]chaser." Shmuel now poses the following query: What is the law whe[n] the robber himself subsequently purchased the field from its legitima[te] owner; may he then seize it from the first "purchaser"? (*Rashi*).

20. Although the robber did not originally own the land, and its sale [at] the time was therefore meaningless, we presume (for reasons which th[e] Gemara will explain) that the robber intended to subsequently obtai[n] the land for his buyer so that the buyer could legally retain his purchas[e]. Since the robber did indeed later purchase the land, it now belongs to th[e] purchaser and the robber may not seize it from him (see *Rashi*).

המגיע לכתפים כאן בשבח שאינו מגיע לכתפים [א] והא מעשים בכל יום וקא מגבי שמואל אפי' בשבח המגיע לכתפים לא קשיא הא דמסיק ביה כשיעור ארעא ושבחא הא דלא מסיק ביה אלא כשיעור ארעא דיהיב ליה שבחיה ומסליק ליה [ג] הניחא למ"ד אי אית ליה זוזי ללוקח לא מצי מסליק ליה לבעל חוב שפיר אלא למאן דאמר כי [א] אית ליה זוזי ללוקח מצי מסליק ליה לבעל חוב נימא ליה אילו הוה לי זוזי הוה מסלקינך מכולה ארעא השתא דלית לי זוזי הב לי [ג] גרבא דארעא בארעא שיעור שבחאי הכא במאי עסקינן [ב] כגון שעשאו אפותיקי דאמר ליה לא יהא לך פרעון אלא מזו: הכיר בה שאינה שלו ולקחה אמר רב מעות יש לו שבח אין לו ושמואל אמר אפי' מעות אין לו במאי קמיפלגי רב סבר אדם יודע שקרקע אין לו וגמר ונתן לשום פקדון ונימא ליה לשום פקדון סבר לא מקבל ושמואל סבר אדם יודע שקרקע אין לו וגמר ונתן לשום מתנה ונימא ליה לשום מתנה כסיפא ליה מילתא והא פליגי ביה חדא זימנא [ד] דאיתמר המקדש את אחותו רב אמר [ה] מעות חוזרין ושמואל אמר [ג] מעות מתנה רב אמר מעות חוזרין אדם יודע שאין קידושין תופסין באחותו וגמר ונתן לשום פקדון ונימא לה לשום פקדון סבר לא מקבלה מיניה ושמואל אמר מעות מתנה אדם יודע שאין קידושין תופסין באחותו וגמר ונתן לשום מתנה ונימא לה לשום מתנה כסיפא לה מילתא צריכא דאי איתמר בהא בהא קאמר רב דלא עבדי אינשי דיהבי מתנות לנוכראה אבל גבי אחותו אימא מודה ליה לשמואל ואי איתמר בהך בהך קאמר שמואל אבל בהא אימא מודה ליה לרב צריכא בין לרב דאמר פקדון בין לשמואל דאמר מתנה האי לארעא במאי קא נחית ופירות היכי אכיל סבר אנא איחות לארעא ואיעביד ואיכול בגויה כי היכי דהוה קא עביד איהו (א) לכי אתי מריה דארעא זוזאי נהוו לרב דאמר פקדון פקדון לשמואל דאמר מתנה מתנה אמר רבא [ד] הלכתא יש לו מעות ויש לו שבח ואע"פ שלא פירש לו את השבח [ה] הכיר בה שאינה שלו ולקחה מעות יש לו שבח אין לו [ח] [ו] אחריות טעות סופר הוא בין בשטרי הלואה [ז] בין בשטרי מקח וממכר בעא מיניה שמואל מרב [ט] חזר ולקחה מבעלים הראשונים מהו אמר ליה [ח] מה מכר לו ראשון לשני כל זכות שתבא לידו מאי טעמא מר זוטרא אמר ניחא ליה [י] דלא נקרייה גזלנא רב אשי אמר [ט] ניחא ליה דליקו בהמנותיה מאי בינייהו איכא בינייהו דמית לוקח מאן דאמר ניחא ליה דלא לקרייה גזלנא

הא

**רש"י**

**המגיע לכתפים.** קרוב ליקצר אלא שעדיין צריכין לקרקע הוי להו כפירות גמורין ואין בעל חוב גובה אותו בלא יציאה: **והא מעשים בכל יום.** דיני טורפי מקח באין לפני שמואל ומגבי לבעל חוב כל השבח עם הקרקע ואפילו מגיע לכתפים כל זמן שצריכין לקרקע: **הא.** דקתני נוטל יציאה מבעל חוב דלא מסיק ביה בעל חוב במוכר שיעור ארעא ושבחא הלכך יהיב בעל חוב ללוקח שבחיה ומסליק ליה והאי דנקט למלתיה בלשון יציאה ולא תנא נוטל כנגד החוב מבעל הקרקע והמותר מבע"ח לאשמועינן היא גופא אתא דהיכא דיציאה יתירה על השבח אין לו אלא יציאה שיעור שבח: **הניחא למאן דאמר כו'.** פלוגתא היא בכתובות (דף נא:): **אי אית ליה זוזי ללוקח.** לפרוע החוב: **לא מצי מסלק ליה לבע"ח.** מן ארעא דבע"ח קדים: **שפיר.** דמצי למימר דהיכא דיש קרקע מותר על החוב עם השבח מסלק ליה ללוקח בזוזי על כרחו דלוקח ולא מצי אמר לוקח הב לי מן ארעא שיעור שבחי דאמר כוליה דידי ואת ירדת בה שלא ברשות: **דשוייא נהליה.** לוה לבעל חוב אפותיקי להא ארעא והכל מודים בזו דאי הוה ליה זוזי ללוקח לא הוה מצי מסלק ליה: [י] **הכא במאי עסקינן.** האי ברייתא דלעיל: **הכיר בה.** לוקח בקרקע זו: **שאינה שלו.** של מוכר שגזולה היתה אצלו ולקחה: **מעות יש לו.** מן המוכר לכשיוציאנה נגזל מידו: **שבח אין לו.** שקרקע זה אינו קנוי לו: **לא מקבל.** לשמור: **מעות חוזרין.** הקדושין חוזרין לו: **בין לרב דאמר כו'.** כלומר היכי מצינן לומר טעמא דרב משום דגמר ונתן לשום פקדון וטעמא דשמואל משום דגמר ונתן לשום מתנה ואי הוה דעתיה לחד מהנך היכי הוה נחית להאי ארעא לעובדה ולאכול פירותיה על כרחיה סבור היה שיהא המכר קיים ולא היה בקי בדין וטעמא דפלוגתא דרב ושמואל טעם אחרינא הוא: **דהוה עביד.** הגזלן: **לרב דאמר פקדון פקדון.** כלומר אליבא דרב מפרשינן דהאי מימר אמר זוזי נהוו פקדון ולשמואל מפרשינן דהאי אמר זוזי נהוו מתנה: **הלכתא.** בפלוגתא קמייתא יש לו מעות ויש לו שבח: **ואע"פ דלא פירש.** ולית לן דשמואל דאמר שבח צריך לימלך: **ואחריות טעות סופר הוא.** ולית לן דשמואל דאמר שיעבוד צריך לימלך: **חזר.** גזלן ולקחה מבעלים הראשונים לאחר שמכר ללוקח: **מהו.** להיות במקום בעלים כאילו לקחה אחר ויוציאה מיד הלוקח: **אמר ליה.** לא מצי לאפוקה שכשמכר מכר לו כל זכות שתבא לידו וכשלקחה לא לקחה אלא כדי שתהא מקוים ביד הלוקח: **דלא ליקרייה גזלנא.** שלא יחרפנו לוקח זה כשיוציאנה נגזל מידו ויקראנו גזלן לכך חוזר להעמיד ממכרו: **דמית לוקח.** לאחר שלקחה גזלן מן הבעלים והגזלן בא להוציאה מבניו: **למ"ד.** לא חזר להעמיד ממכרו אלא דלא ליקרייה לוקח גזלן:

הא

**תוספות**

**הא דלא מסיק אלא שיעור ארעא.** תימה כיון דלא מסיק אלא שיעור ארעא אמאי נוטל שבח היתר על היציאה [א] וי"ל דבלאו הכי פריך שפיר הניחא כו' ולפי המסקנא דמוקי באפותיקי א"ש דאע"פ דלא מסיק ביה אלא שיעור ארעא נותן לו היציאה ללוקח והשבח היתר על היציאה לוקח הנס כדין יורד לתוך שדה חבירו שלא ברשות: **הניחא למ"ד כו'.** מפורש בהמקבל (לקמן דף קי:)[ח] (ועיין בכתובות דף נא: ד"ה מאי): **כגון דשוייא אפותיקי.** השתא מלי איירי דמסיק ביה אפי' שיעור ארעא ושבחא ואפ"ה כיון דשוייא אפותיקי צריך ליתן היציאה כדין יורד כו' כדאמרי' בפרק המקבל (שם) גבי יתומים אומרים אנו השבחנו ורוצים היציא' דמיירי באפותיקי ואע"ג דמסיק בהו שיעור ארעא ושבחא דהא אם אביהם השביח גובה הכל ומיהו אין ראיה דשאני יתומים שאין להם על מי לחזור ליקח היציאה דכיון שעשה אביהם אפותיקי הרי הוא כיורד לתוך שדה חבירו שלא ברשות שאינו מפסיד היציאה אבל בלוקח שאינו מפסיד כלום שהמוכר משלם לו היציאה והשבח שזה פוטרו מחובו מצינו למימר דאפילו באפותיקי כיון דמסיק ביה שיעור ארעא ושבחא שקיל הכל שבשביל שעשאה אפותיקי לא יגרע כחו וא"ת כיון דאמר ליה לא יהא לך פרעון אלא מזו כשמוכר לאחר הוה ליה כלוקח מגזלן שהרי אינו של מוכר א"כ למה נוטל מן המוכר השבח היתר על היציאה והא לוקח מגזלן לשמואל לית ליה שבחא וי"ל כגון שמכרה קודם שבא זמנו של בעל חוב דחל המקח עד הזמן ולא דמי לגזלן שלא חל המקח כלל דזוזי הוו הלואה ואם ישלם שבח הוה ליה רבית ואפילו מכרה אחר הזמן היה סבור לפייס בע"ח בזוזי וחל המקח עד שטרפה ממנו: **מעות יש לו שבח אין לו.** תימה דהגוזל קמא (ב"ק דף צה. ושם: ד"ה דלמא) תנא ה' גובין מן המשועבדין שבח ומוקי לה בת"ח דידע דקרקע אינה נגזלת אלמא אפילו בהכיר בה יש לו שבח וי"ל דהתם מיירי כשקיבל עליו אחריות: **ונתן לו לשם מתנה.** אבל בערכין פרק המוכר שדה (דף כט: ושם) גבי המוכר שדהו בשנת היובל עצמה דאמר שמואל מעות חוזרין ליכא למימר אדם יודע שאין מכר ביובל דאין זה פשוט דהא אמר רב מכורה ויוצאה: **חזר ולקחה כו'.** בלא הכיר בה איירי וקמיבעיא ליה אם הגזלן יכול לבטל המקח ולהחזיר לו מעותיו או לאו: **דמית לוקח.** פרש"י אחר שלקחה ואין נראה דמיד שקנה הגזלן זכה בו לוקח ולאו משום דמית ליה בתר הכי פקע כחו אלא יש לומר דמית קודם שלקחה הגזלן מנגזל [ט] (ומית גזלן) נ"ל שהיה חולה או גוסס בשעה שלקחה מנגזל:

מאי

**עין משפט נר מצוה**

קלא א ב מיי' פכ"א מהל' מלוה ולוה הל' ה ו ועיין בהשגות ובמ"מ סמג עשין צד טוש"ע ח"מ סי' קטו סעיף ב:

קלב ג מיי' פ"ו מהל' זכייה ומתנה הל' כ סמג עשין פח טוש"ע אה"ע סי' נ סעיף ב:

קלג ד מיי' פ"ט מהל' גזילה ואבידה הל' ח ופכ"א מהל' מלוה ולוה הל' א סמג עשין עג לה טוש"ע ח"מ סי' קטו סעיף א וסי' שעג סעיף א:

קלד ה מיי' פ"ט מהל' גזילה הל' ז סמג עשין עג טוש"ע ח"מ סי' שע"ג סעיף א:

קלה ו ז מיי' פי"ח מהל' גזילה ואבידה הל' א ופי"ט מהל' מכירה הל' ג ופי"ח מהל' מלוה ולוה הל' ג סמג עשין לה טוש"ע ח"מ סי' לט סעיף א וסי' קיא סעיף א וסי' רכה סעיף א:

קלו ח ט מיי' פ"ט מהל' גזילה ואבידה הל' ט סמג עשין עג טוש"ע ח"מ סי' שעד סעיף א:

**רבינו חננאל**

והני מילי בדלא מסיק ביה בעל חוב אלא ק' בלבד אבל אם נושה בו כשיעור ארעא ושבחא נוטל הכל ואינו נותן ללוקח אפי' ההוצאה חו שינויא דשמואל היא ולא סמכינן עלה א) אלא לעולם נותן הבעל חוב ההוצאה ללוקח כפשוטה דהא מתניתא וכי יהיב ליה דמים ולא מן הקרקע עצמו בשעשאה לו אפותיקי דאמר ליה לא יהא לך פרעון אלא מזו השדה ואליבא דמ"ד אי אית ליה זוזי ללוקח מצי מסלק ליה לבע"ח בזוזי מוקים להא מתניתא בשעשאה לו הלוה אפותיקי וחזר ומכרה. ואסקי' אפי' שבח המגיע בכתפים כגון ענבים שהגיעו להבצר וקמה להקצר שהגיעו ליטלם בכתפו ולצאת כיון שעדיין כקרקע הן הכל נוטלם הבעל חוב בחובו. וכבר פירש' היטב בפרק המקבל שדה מחבירו בענין שלשה שמין להן השבח ומעלין אותן בדמים ואלו הן בכור לפשוט ובע"ח ליתומין ובעל חוב ללקוחות דלעולם נוטל הלוקח ההוצאה מן הבעל חוב כפשוטה דהא מתניתא דלא גרע מן היורד לשדה חבירו ונטעה שלא מרשותו דקי"ל שמין לו וידו על התחתונה ופירשנוה בפ' מי שמת. **הכיר בה שאינה שלו ולקחה רב אמר מעות יש לו שבח אין לו. ושמואל** אמר אפי' מעות אין לו. ואסיקנא רב אמר מעות פקדון ושמואל אמר מעות מתנה וכן לענין מקדש אחותו רב אמר מעות פקדון וחוזרין ושמואל [אמר] מעות מתנה ואינן חוזרין וצריכא. אמר רבא הלכתא המוכר שדה לחבירו ונמצאת שאינו שלו יש לו מעות ויש לו שבח דאושבחא ארעא ממילא כגון שקנאה במנה ועתה הוקרה ושוה מאתים יש לו כגון זה השבח ואע"פ שלא פירש לו את השבח. הכיר בה שאינה שלו ולקחה מעות יש לו שבח אין לו ואחריות טעות סופר הוא בין בשטרי הלואה בין בשטרי מקח וממכר ב) אבל אם נטע אילנות והשביח בין הלוקח בין הגזלן לוקחין שיעור שבחם מן הנגזל. הא דבעא שמואל מרב חזר ולקחה מן הבעלים הראשונים מהו. ופשט ... מה מכר ראשון לשני כל זכות שתבוא לידו מאי טעמא מר זוטרא אמר ניחא ליה דלא ניקרייה גזלנא. רב אשי אמר ניחא ליה דליקום בהימנותיה. דברים פשוטים הן דודאי קנאה הקונה אותה מן הגזלן כיון שקנאה הגזלן מן הנג...

**מסורת הש"ס**

א) בבא קמא לה: ... לקמן קי:, ב) [לקמן בבא קמא לו.], ג) [... קמא לו. ולקמן קי: ... גריווא], ד) גיטין ... [קדושין מו:], ערכין ... ה) [לעיל יד., כתובות ... בבא בתרא קס...], ו) [לקמן עב:], ז) ... קודם ד"ה דשוי... ח) [וכן עוד בתוס' ... קמא לו. ד"ה הניחא, ו... תוס' לקמן לה. ... הניחא], ט) ס"א וכתר מית גזלן שהיה כו'.

**הגהות הב"ח**

(א) גמ' ולכי אתי מר...

**הגהות הגר"א**

**[א] תוס' ד"ה הא** אמאי נוטל ש"ה היציאה. נ"ב ול"נ ... קושית גמ' באמת הכ... כו' כדין יורד שלא בר... וכמו באפותיקי (ו... הרמב"ן במלחמות ... כש"ך סי' קט"ו ס"ק ...

**גליון הש"ס**

גמ' מעות חוזרין. ב"ב עם ע"א תוס' ד... אבל: שם חזר ולק... מבעלים. עי' בהר... פ"ו מ"ג דתרומות

**ליקוטי רש"י**

**המגיע לכתפים.** ... תבואה שגדלה כל צ... נותנה ללוקח או ד... [ב"ק צה:]. **צריכין לקר...** דבר מועט דאילו צריכין לקרקע הוו פירות ולא מיקרו ... ובע"ח גובה השבח ק... ולא פירות גמורין. **אית ליה זוזי ללו...** שיעור דמי החוב. **שפי...** איכא למימר דאר מעיקרא דידיה הואי ו... דנחת לה שלא ברשות ... שבחא בזוזי ולא באר... הואיל והוה מסיק ... שיעור ארעא כולה [לי... קי:]. **אפותיקי.** ... תהא קאי כלומר מזה ... לך פרעון [ב"ק יא:]. **אמר מעות.** של קדו... חוזרין דאדם יודע ש... קדושין תופסין באח... וגמר ונתן לשם פק... [גיטין מה.]. ולשמואל ג... ונתן לשם מתנה [ערכין ...]. **אחריות טעות סופ...** כשאינו כתוב בשטר ס... הוא שטעה אבל זה לא ... לו מעותיו בלא אחר... נכסים דלא שדי איניש בכדי [לעיל יד. ועי"ש ע... שאינו כתוב בשטר ... נכתב השטר סתם ע... ושגגת הסופר הוא ו... שכתב בו אחריות ... ופלוגתא הוא בשנים או... (ב"מ דף יד.) והכי מסר... התם (טו:) דטעות סו... הוא בין בשטרי מקח בשטרי הלואה [רשב"ם ב... קסט:]. **דלא ניקרי... גזלנא.** אדם שמכר ש... גזולה לחבירו מחזר הבעלים הראשונים ולוק... מהם להעמיד ביד הלו... כי היכי דלא ליקרייה גז... [לקמן עב:].

 א) דברי רבינו אלו הובא ברי"ף כאן בשם ואיכא מאן דאמר ויעוין שם מש"כ שם ע"ז. ב) וכ"כ הרי"ף כאן והביא ראיה לזה מפ' הגוזל עצים ע"ש.

Consequently, the creditor may possess the improvements even if the debt is only equivalent in value to the field without the improvements.

The Gemara continues its discussion of the laws concerning the purchase of stolen property:

הִכִּיר בָּהּ שֶׁאֵינָהּ שֶׁלּוֹ – If **[the purchaser] recognized that [the property] was not [the seller's],**[9] וּלְקָחָהּ – **but** nevertheless **he purchased it** and improved it, and then it was seized by its legitimate owner, אָמַר רַב – **Rav says:** מָעוֹת יֵשׁ לוֹ – **[The purchaser] has** the right to compensation from the seller for **the money** which he paid for the property, שְׁבָח אֵין לוֹ – but **he does not have the** right to compensation for his **improvements.**[10] וּשְׁמוּאֵל אָמַר – **But Shmuel says:** אֲפִילּוּ מָעוֹת אֵין לוֹ – **He does not even have** the right to receive compensation for **the money** which he paid for the property.[11]

The Gemara explains the disagreement:

בְּמַאי קָמִיפַּלְגֵי – **On what** basic point **do they disagree?** רַב סָבַר – **Rav holds** אָדָם יוֹדֵעַ שֶׁקַּרְקַע אֵין לוֹ – that since **[the purchaser] realizes that the land is not [the seller's], he** clearly **did not intend to give the money as payment.** וְגָמַר וְנָתַן לְשׁוּם פִּקָּדוֹן – **Rather,** we presume that **he made up** his mind **and gave** the money to the seller **as a deposit.** The money therefore must be returned to the purchaser.

The Gemara questions:

וְנֵימָא לֵיהּ לְשׁוּם פִּקָּדוֹן – If so, **let [the purchaser]** explicitly **tell [the seller]** that the money is being given **as a deposit!** Why does he pretend to give the money as payment?

The Gemara answers:

סָבַר לֹא מְקַבֵּל – **He thinks [the seller] will not accept** the money for safekeeping. Therefore, he offers it in the guise of the purchase price of the stolen land.

וּשְׁמוּאֵל סָבַר – **But Shmuel holds** אָדָם יוֹדֵעַ שֶׁקַּרְקַע אֵין לוֹ – that since **[the purchaser] realizes the land is not [the seller's],** he clearly did not intend to give the money as payment. וְגָמַר וְנָתַן לְשׁוּם מַתָּנָה – Rather, we presume that **he made up** his mind **and gave** the money to the seller **as a gift.** The money therefore need not be returned to the purchaser.

The Gemara asks:

וְנֵימָא לֵיהּ לְשׁוּם מַתָּנָה – If so, **let [the purchaser]** explicitly **tell [the seller]** that the money is being given **as a gift!** Why does he pretend to give the money as payment?

The Gemara answers:

כְּסִיפָא לֵיהּ מִילְּתָא – The purchaser did not tell him because the purchaser reasoned that it would be **an embarrassment for [the seller]** to accept a gift.

The Gemara questions the necessity for stating this disagreement:

וְהָא פְּלִיגֵי בֵּיהּ חֲדָא זִימְנָא – **But [Rav and Shmuel]** already **disagreed one time** in a similar case! דְּאִיתְּמַר – **As it was said:** הַמְקַדֵּשׁ אֶת אֲחוֹתוֹ – **If one betroths his sister** by giving her money to effect the betrothal,[12] רַב אָמַר – **Rav says:** מָעוֹת חוֹזְרִין – **The money** must be **returned.** וּשְׁמוּאֵל אָמַר – **B[ut] Shmuel says:** מָעוֹת מַתָּנָה – **The money is a gift,** and need n[ot] be returned.

The Gemara explains the disagreement:

רַב אָמַר מָעוֹת חוֹזְרִין – **Rav says the money is returned,** [אָדָ]ם יוֹדֵעַ שֶׁאֵין קִידּוּשִׁין תּוֹפְסִין בַּאֲחוֹתוֹ – because since **a man knows that** [an] act of **marriage is ineffective with his sister,** he clearly did n[ot] intend to give her the money for betrothal. [וְגָמַ]ר וְנָתַן לְשׁוּם פִּקָּדוֹן – Rather, we presume that **he made up** his mind **and gave** her t[he] money **as a deposit.**

The Gemara questions:

וְנֵימָא לָהּ לְשׁוּם פִּקָּדוֹן – If so, **let him tell her** explicitly that t[he] money is being given **as a deposit!** Why does he pretend to give h[er] the money for betrothal?

The Gemara answers:

סָבַר לֹא מְקַבְּלָה מִינֵּיהּ – **He thinks she will not accept it from h[im]** as a deposit. Therefore, he offers it in the guise of an act [of] betrothal. וּשְׁמוּאֵל אָמַר מָעוֹת מַתָּנָה – **But Shmuel says t[he] money is a gift,** אָדָם יוֹדֵעַ שֶׁאֵין קִידּוּשִׁין תּוֹפְסִין בַּאֲחוֹתוֹ – becau[se] since **a man knows** that an act of **betrothal is ineffective with h[is] sister,** he clearly did not intend to give her the money for betroth[al.] וְגָמַר וְנָתַן לְשׁוּם מַתָּנָה – Rather, we presume that **he made up** h[is] mind **and gave** the money to his sister **as a gift.**

The Gemara asks:

וְנֵימָא לָהּ לְשׁוּם מַתָּנָה – If so, **let him tell her** explicitly that t[he] money is being given **as a gift!** Why does he pretend to give her t[he] money for betrothal?

The Gemara answers:

כְּסִיפָא לָהּ מִילְּתָא – He did not tell her because he reasoned that [it] would **be an embarrassment for her** to accept a gift. In this cas[e,] just as in the case of the purchase of stolen property, Rav a[nd] Shmuel disagree whether the money offered under false pretens[es] is a deposit or a gift. Why, then, was it necessary for them to sta[te] their disagreement in both cases?

The Gemara explains:

צְרִיכָא – Both cases are **necessary.** דְּאִי אִיתְּמַר בְּהָא – **Had [the disagreement] been stated** only **in this** case of the purchase [of] stolen property, בְּהָא קָאָמַר רַב – I might have thought that on[ly] **in this** case **Rav says** that the money is a deposit, [דְּלָ]א עָבְדֵי אִינָשֵׁי דְּיָהֲבֵי מַתָּנוֹת לְנוּכְרָאָה – **for it is not customary for people to gi[ve] gifts to a non-relative.** אֲבָל גַּבֵּי אֲחוֹתוֹ – **However, concernin[g]** the man who betrothed **his sister,** אֵימָא מוֹדֶה לֵיהּ לִשְׁמוּאֵל – **[I] might say [Rav] agrees with Shmuel** that the money is a gi[ft.] וְאִי אִיתְּמַר בְּהָךְ – **And had [the disagreement] been stated** on[ly] **in that** case of the man who betrothed his sister, [בְּהָ]ךְ קָאָמַר שְׁמוּאֵל – I might have thought that only **in that case Shmuel sa[ys]** that the money is a gift, since it is customary to give gifts [to] relatives. אֲבָל בְּהָא – **However, in this** case of the purchase [of] stolen property, אֵימָא מוֹדֶה לֵיהּ לְרַב – **I might say [Shmue]l agrees with Rav** that the money is a deposit. צְרִיכָא – There[fore,] both cases are **necessary.**

The Gemara questions its explanation of the disagreeme[nt]

NOTES

9. I.e. the purchaser realized that it was stolen property (*Rashi*).

10. This contrasts with Rav's ruling above (14b) concerning the purchase of property that was only later discovered to be stolen. In that case, the purchaser receives compensation from the seller even for his improvements.

11. This contrasts with Shmuel's ruling above (14b) concerning the purchase of property that was only later discovered to be stolen. In that case, the purchaser receives a refund of his purchase price.

The Gemara will now explain the reasons for the disagreement regarding the purchase price. Both agree, however, that the purchaser is not compensated for his improvements, since he was aware that the land he improved was not his (see *Rashi*, cf. *Rosh*). Rather, he may clai[m] compensation from the legitimate owner for the lesser of his expenses [or] the value of the improvements (*Shitah Mekubetzes;* see 14b note 10[)].

12. One of the methods by which betrothal (*kiddushin*) is effected is th[e] giving of money by a man to a woman for this purpose (*Kiddushin* 2a[).] However, the Gemara in *Kiddushin* (67b) teaches that an act [of] betrothal is ineffective between a man and a woman whose cohabitatio[n] carries either the death penalty or *kares* (excision). Since one's sister [is] forbidden to him on pain of *kares*, the betrothal of a sister is [a] meaningless act. Therefore, the question arises as to what must be do[ne] with the betrothal money.

המגיע לכתפים כאן בשבח שאינו מגיע לכתפים [א] והא מעשים בכל יום וקא מגבי שמואל אפי' בשבח המגיע לכתפים לא קשיא הא דמסיק ביה כשיעור ארעא ושבחא הא דלא מסיק ביה אלא כשיעור ארעא דיהיב ליה שבחיה ומסליק ליה [ג] הניחא למ"ד אי אית ליה זוזי ללוקח לא מצי מסליק ליה לבעל חוב שפיר אלא למאן דאמר כי [א] אית ליה זוזי ללוקח מצי מסליק ליה לבעל חוב נימא ליה אילו הוה לי זוזי הוה מסלקינך מכולה ארעא השתא דלית לי זוזי הב לי [ג] גרבא דארעא בארעא שיעור שבחאי הכא במאי עסקינן [ב] כגון שעשאו אפותיקי דאמר ליה לא יהא לך פרעון אלא מזו: הכיר בה שאינה שלו ולקחה אמר רב מעות יש לו שבח אין לו ושמואל אמר אפי' מעות אין לו במאי קמיפלגי רב סבר אדם יודע שקרקע אין לו וגמר ונתן לשום פקדון ונימא ליה לשום פקדון סבר לא מקבל ושמואל סבר אדם יודע שקרקע אין לו וגמר ונתן לשום מתנה ונימא ליה לשום מתנה כסיפא ליה מילתא והא פליגי ביה חדא זימנא [ד] דאיתמר המקדש את אחותו רב אמר [ה] מעות חוזרין ושמואל אמר [ג] מעות מתנה רב אמר מעות חוזרין אדם יודע שאין קידושין תופסין באחותו וגמר ונתן לשום פקדון ונימא לה לשום פקדון סבר לא מקבלה מיניה ושמואל אמר מעות מתנה אדם יודע שאין קידושין תופסין באחותו וגמר ונתן לשום מתנה ונימא לה לשום מתנה כסיפא לה מילתא צריכא דאי איתמר בהא בהא קאמר רב דלא עבדי אינשי דיהבי מתנות לנוכראה אבל גבי אחותו אימא מודה ליה לשמואל ואי איתמר בהך בהך קאמר שמואל אבל בהא אימא מודה ליה לרב צריכא בין לרב דאמר פקדון בין לשמואל דאמר מתנה האי לארעא במאי קא נחית ופירות היכי אכיל סבר אנא איחות לארעא ואיעביד ואיכול בגויה כי היכי דהוה קא עביד איהו (א) לכי אתי מריה דארעא זוזאי נהוו לרב דאמר פקדון פקדון לשמואל דאמר מתנה מתנה אמר רבא [ד] הלכתא יש לו מעות ויש לו שבח ואע"פ שלא פירש לו את השבח [ה] הכיר בה שאינה שלו ולקחה מעות יש לו שבח אין לו [ה] [ו] אחריות טעות סופר הוא בין בשטרי הלואה [ז] בין בשטרי מקח וממכר בעא מיניה שמואל מרב [ט] חזר ולקחה מבעלים הראשונים מהו אמר ליה [ח] מה מכר לו ראשון לשני כל זכות שתבא לידו מאי טעמא מר זוטרא אמר ניחא ליה [י] דלא נקרייה גזלנא רב אשי אמר [ט] ניחא ליה דליקו בהמנותיה מאי בינייהו איכא בינייהו דמית לוקח מאן דאמר ניחא ליה דלא לקרייה גזלנא

הא

**רש"י**

המגיע לכתפים. קרוב ליקצר אלא שעדיין צריכין לקרקע הוי להו כפירות גמורין ואין בעל חוב גובה אותו בלא יציאה: והא מעשים בכל יום. דיני טורפי מקח באין לפני שמואל ומגבי לבעל חוב כל השבח עם הקרקע ואפילו מגיע לכתפים כל זמן שצריכין לקרקע: הא. דקתני נוטל יציאה מבעל חוב דלא מסיק ביה בעל חוב במוכר שיעור ארעא ושבחא הלכך יהיב בעל חוב ללוקח שבחיה ומסליק ליה והאי דנקט למלתיה בלשון יציאה ולא תנא נוטל כנגד החוב מבעל הקרקע והמותר מבע"ח לאשמועינן היא גופא אתא דהיכא דיציאה יתירה על השבח אין לו אלא יציאה שיעור שבח: הניחא למאן דאמר כו'. פלוגתא היא בכתובות (דף נא:): אי אית ליה זוזי ללוקח. לפרוע החוב: לא מצי מסלק ליה לבע"ח. מן ארעא דבע"ח קדים: שפיר. דמצי למימר דהיכא דיש קרקע מותר על החוב עם השבח מסלק ליה ללוקח בזוזי על כרחו דלוקח ולא מצי אמר לוקח הב לי מן ארעא שיעור שבחי דאמר כוליה דידי ואת ירדת בה שלא ברשות: דשוייא נהליה. לוה לבעל חוב אפותיקי להא ארעא והכל מודים בזו דאי הוה ליה זוזי ללוקח לא הוה מצי מסלק ליה: [י] הכא במאי עסקינן. האי ברייתא דלעיל: הכיר בה. לוקח בקרקע זו: שאינה שלו. של מוכר שגזולה היתה אצלו ולקחה: מעות יש לו. מן המוכר לכשיוציאנה נגזל מידו: שבח אין לו. שקרקע זה אינו קנוי לו: לא מקבל. לשמור: מעות חוזרין. הקדושין חוזרין לו: בין לרב דאמר כו'. כלומר היכי מצינן לומר טעמא דרב משום דגמר ונתן לשום פקדון וטעמא דשמואל משום דגמר ונתן לשום מתנה ואי הוה דעתיה לחד מהנך היכי הוה נחית להאי ארעא לעובדה ולאכול פירותיה על כרחיה סבור היה שיהא המכר קיים ולא היה בקי בדין וטעמא דפלוגתא דרב ושמואל טעם אחרינא הוא: דהוה עביד. הגזלן: לרב דאמר פקדון פקדון. כלומר אליבא דרב מפרשינן דהאי מימר אמר זוזי נהוו פקדון ולשמואל מפרשינן דהאי אמר זוזי נהוו מתנה: הלכתא. בפלוגתא קמייתא יש לו מעות ויש לו שבח: ואע"פ דלא פירש. ולית לן דשמואל דאמר שבח צריך לימלך: ואחריות טעות סופר הוא. ולית לן דשמואל דאמר שעבוד צריך לימלך: חזר. גזלן ולקחה מבעלים הראשונים לאחר שמכר ללוקח: מהו. להיות במקום בעלים כאילו לקחה אחר ויוציאה מיד הלוקח: אמר ליה. לא מצי לאפוקה שכשמכר מכר לו כל זכות שתבא לידו וכשלקחה לא לקחה אלא כדי שתהא מקוים ביד הלוקח: דלא ליקרייה גזלנא. שלא יחרפנו לוקח זה כשיוציאנה נגזל מידו ויקראנו גזלן לכך חוזר להעמיד ממכרו: דמית לוקח. לאחר שלקחה גזלן מן הבעלים והגזלן בא להוציאה מבניו: למ"ד. לא חזר להעמיד ממכרו אלא דלא ליקרייה לוקח גזלן:

הא

**תוספות**

הא דלא מסיק אלא שיעור ארעא. תימה כיון דלא מסיק אלא שיעור ארעא אמאי נוטל שבח היתר על היציאה [א] וי"ל דבלאו הכי פריך שפיר הניחא כו' ולפי המסקנא דמוקי באפותיקי א"ש דאע"פ דלא מסיק ביה אלא שיעור ארעא נותן לו היציאה ללוקח והשבח היתר על היציאה לוקח חנם כדין יורד לתוך שדה חבירו שלא ברשות: הניחא למ"ד כו'. מפורש בהמקבל (לקמן דף קי:)[ח] (ועיין בכתובות דף נא: ד"ה מאי): כגון דשוייא אפותיקי. השתא מלי איירי דמסיק ביה אפי' שיעור ארעא ושבחא ואפ"ה כיון דשוייא אפותיקי צריך ליתן היציאה כדין יורד כו' כדאמרי' בפרק המקבל (שם) גבי יתומים אומרים אנו השבחנו ורוצים היציא' דמיירי באפותיקי ואע"ג דמסיק בהו שיעור ארעא ושבחא דהא אם אביהם השביח גובה הכל ומיהו אין ראיה דשאני יתומים שאין להם על מי לחזור ליקח היציאה דכיון שעשה אביהם אפותיקי הרי הוא כיורד לתוך שדה חבירו שלא ברשות שאינו מפסיד היציאה אבל בלוקח שאינו מפסיד כלום שהמוכר משלם לו היציאה והשבח שזה פוטרו מחובו מצינו למימר דאפילו באפותיקי כיון דמסיק ביה שיעור ארעא ושבחא שקיל הכל שבשביל שעשאה אפותיקי לא יגרע כחו וא"ת כיון דאמר ליה לא יהא לך פרעון אלא מזו כשמוכר לאחר הוה ליה כלוקח מגזלן שהרי אינו של מוכר א"כ למה נוטל מן המוכר השבח היתר על היציאה והא לוקח מגזלן לשמואל לית ליה שבחא וי"ל כגון שמכרה קודם שבא זמנו של בעל חוב דאל המקח עד הזמן ולא דמי לגזלן שלא חל המקח כלל דזוזי הוו הלואה ואם ישלם שבח הוה ליה רבית ואפילו מכרה אחר הזמן היה סבור לפיים בע"ח בזוזי וחל המקח עד שטרפה ממנו: מעות יש לו שבח אין לו. תימה דהגוזל קמא (ב"ק דף לה. ושם: ד"ה דלמא) תנא ה' גוזין מן המחוררין שבח ומוקי לה בת"ח דידע דקרקע אינה נגזלת אלמא אפילו בהכיר בה יש לו שבח וי"ל דהתם מיירי כשקיבל עליו אחריות: ונתן לו לשם מתנה. אבל בערכין פרק המוכר שדה (דף כט: ושם) גבי המוכר שדהו בשנת היובל עצמה דאמר שמואל מעות חוזרין ליכא למימר אדם יודע שאין מכר ביובל דאין זה פשוט דהא אמר רב מכורה ויוצאה: חזר ולקחה כו'. בלא הכיר בה מיירי וקמיבעיא ליה אם הגזלן יכול לבטל המקח ולהחזיר לו מעותיו או לאו: דמית לוקח. פרש"י אחר שלקחה ואין נראה דמיד שקנה הגזלן זכה בו לוקח ואטו משום דמית ליה בתר הכי פקע כחו אלא יש לומר דמית קודם שלקחה. הגזלן מנגזל [ט] (ומית גזלן) צ"ל שהיה חולה או גוסס בשעה שלקחה מנגזל:

מאי

**עין משפט נר מצוה**

קלא א ב מיי' פכ"א מהל' מלוה ולוה הל' ה ו ועיין בהשגות ובמ"מ סמג עשין לד טוש"ע ח"מ סי' קטו סעיף ב:

קלב ג מיי' פ"ו מהל' זכייה ומתנה הל' כ סמג עשין מח טוש"ע אה"ע סי' נ סעיף ג:

קלג ד מיי' פ"ט מהל' גזילה ואבידה הל' ח ופכ"א מהל' מלוה ולוה הל' א סמג עשין עג לה טוש"ע ח"מ סי' קטו סעיף א וסי' שעג סעיף א:

קלד ה מיי' פ"ט מהל' גזילה הל' ז סמג עשין עג טוש"ע ח"מ סי' שע"ג סעיף א:

קלה ו ז מיי' פי"ח מהל' גזילה ואבידה הל' א ופי"ט מהל' מכירה הל' ג ופי"ח מהל' מלוה ולוה הל' ג סמג עשין לה טוש"ע ח"מ סי' לט סעיף א וסי' קיא סעיף א וסי' רכה סעיף א:

קלו ח ט מיי' פ"ט מהל' גזילה ואבידה הל' ט סמג עשין עג טוש"ע ח"מ סי' שעד סעיף א:

**רבינו חננאל**

והני מילי בדלא מסיק ביה בעל חוב אלא ק' בלבד אבל אם נושה בו כשיעור ארעא ושבחא נוטל הכל ואינו נותן ללוקח אפי' ההוצאה וחו שינויא דשמואל היא ולא סמכינן עלה א) אלא לעולם נותן הבעל חוב ההוצאה ללוקח כפשוטה דהא מתניתא וכי יהיב ליה דמים ולא מן הקרקע עצמו בשעשאה לו אפותיקי דאמר ליה לא יהא לך פרעון אלא מזו השדה ואליבא דמ"ד אי אית ליה זוזי ללוקח מצי מסלק ליה לבע"ח בזוזי מוקים להא מתניתא בשעשאה לו הלוה אפותיקי וחזר ומכרה. ואסקי' אפי' שבח המגיע בכתפים כגון ענבים שהגיעו להבצר וקמה להקצר שהגיעו ליטלם בכתפו ולצאת כיון שעדיין בקרקע הן הכל נוטלם הבעל חוב בחובו. וכבר פירש' היטב בפרק המקבל שדה מחבירו בענין שלשה שמין להן השבח ומעלין אותן בדמים ואלו הן בכור לפשוט ובע"ח ליתומין ובעל חוב ללקוחות דלעולם נוטל הלוקח ההוצאה מן הבעל חוב כפשוטה דהא מתניתא דלא גרע מן היורד לשדה חבירו ונטעה שלא מרשותו דקי"ל שמין לו וידו על התחתונה ופירשנוה בפ' מי שמת. **הכיר בה שאינה שלו ולקחה רב אמר מעות יש לו שבח אין לו. ושמואל אמר אפי' מעות אין לו.** ואסיקנא רב אמר מעות פקדון ושמואל אמר מעות מתנה וכן לענין מקדש אחותו רב אמר מעות פקדון וחוזרין ושמואל [אמר] מעות מתנה ואינן חוזרין וצריכא. אמר רבא הלכתא המוכר שדה לחבירו ונמצאת שאינו שלו יש לו מעות ויש לו שבח דאושבחא ארעא ממילא כגון שקנאה במנה ועתה הוקרה ושוה מאתים יש לו כגון זה השבח ואע"פ שלא פירש לו את השבח. הכיר בה שאינה שלו ולקחה מעות יש לו שבח אין לו ואחריות טעות סופר הוא בין בשטרי הלואה בין בשטרי מקח וממכר ב) אבל אם נטע אילנות והשביח בין הלוקח בין הגזלן לוקחין שיעור שבחם מן הנגזל. הא דבעא שמואל מרב חזר ולקחה מן הבעלים הראשונים מהו. ופשט מה מכר ראשון לשני כל זכות שתבוא לידו מאי טעמא מר זוטרא אמר ניחא ליה דלא ניקרייה גזלנא. רב אשי אמר ניחא ליה דליקום בהימנותיה. דברים פשוטים הן דודאי קנאה הקונה אותה מן הגזלן כיון שקנאה הגזלן מן ה

**מסורת הש"ס**

א) בבא קמא לה: לקמן קי:, ב) [לקמן בבא קמא נו.], ג) [ קמא נו. ולקמן קי: גריווא], ד) גיטין [קדושין מו:], ערכ ה) [לעיל יד., כתובות בבא בתרא ק ו) [לקמן עב:], ז) קודם ד"ה ד ח) [וכן עוד בתוס' קמא נו. ד"ה הניחא, תוס' לקמן לה. הניחא], ט) ס"א ובת מית גזלן שהיה כ

**הגהות הב"ח**

(א) גמ' ולכי אתי מ

**הגהות הגר"א**

[א] תוס' ד"ה הא אמאי נוטל ש"ה היציאה. נ"ב ול"נ קושית גמ' באמת כו' כדין יורד שלא ב וכמו באפותיקי הרמב"ן במלחמות כס"ך סי' קט"ו ס"ק

**גליון הש"ס**

גמ' מעות חוזרין ב"ב עם ע"א תוס' אבל: שם חזר ול מבעלים. עי' ב פ"ו מ"ג דתרומו

**ליקוטי רש"י**

המגיע לכתפים. תבואה שגדלה כל נותנה ללוקח או [ב"ק צה:]. צריכין לר דבר מועט דאילו צריכין לקרקע הוו פירות ולא מיקרו ובע"ח גובה השבח ולא פירות גמורין. אית ליה זוזי לל שיעור דמי החוב. ש איכא למימר דל מעיקרא דידיה הואי דנחת לה שלא ברשות שבחא בזוזי ולא בל הואיל והוה מסיק שיעור ארעא כולה [ קי:]. אפותיקי. תהא קאי כלומר מזה לך פרעון [ב"ק יא:]. אמר מעות. של ק חוזרין לאדם יודע קדושין תופסין בא וגמר ונתן לשם פ [גיטין מה.]. ולשמואל ונתן לשם מתנה [ערכי אחריות טעות סו כשאינו כתוב בשטר הוא שטעה אבל זה לא לו מעותיו בלא אח נכסים דלא שדי איני בכדי [לעיל יד. ועי"ש שאינו כתוב בשטר והחז הזוזר תחת ב ושגגת הסופר הוא שכתב בו אחריות ופלוגתא הוא בשנים א (ב"מ דף יד.) והכי מכ התם (טו:) דטעות הוא בין בשטרי מקח בשטרי הלואה [רשב"ם קסט:]. דלא ניקר גזלנא. אדם שמכר גזולה לחבירו מחזר הבעלים הראשונים ולו מהם להעמיד ביד ה כי היכי דלא ליקרייה ג [לקמן עב:].

**חשק שלמה על ר"ח**

א) דברי רבינו אלו הובא ברי"ף כאן בשם ואיכא מאן דאמר ויעוין שם מש"כ שם ע"ז. ב) וכ"כ הרי"ף כאן והביא ראיה לזה מפ' הגוזל עצים ע"ש.

הַמַּגִּיעַ לְכְתֵפַיִם – almost **ready for the harvesters.**[1] Therefore, the creditor must compensate the purchaser for his expenses. כָּאן – **Here,** in Shmuel's ruling, בְּשֶׁבַח שֶׁאֵינוֹ מַגִּיעַ לִכְתֵפַיִם – **it refers to** the seizure of **improved** produce which is **not ready for the harvesters.**[2] Therefore, the creditor need not compensate the purchaser for his expenses.

The Gemara rejects the second answer:

וְהָא מַעֲשִׂים בְּכָל יוֹם – **But there are instances daily** when creditors approach Shmuel וְקָא מַגְבֵּי שְׁמוּאֵל – **and Shmuel allows them to collect** from purchasers of their debtor's land, אֲפִילוּ בְּשֶׁבַח הַמַּגִּיעַ לִכְתֵפַיִם – **even improved** produce almost **ready for the harvesters,** without compensating the purchaser for his expenses! – ? –

The Gemara suggests another answer:

לָא קַשְׁיָא – **This is not a difficulty.** הָא – **This** report of Shmuel's customary procedure דְּמַסֵּיק בֵּיהּ כְּשִׁיעוּר אַרְעָא וְשִׁבְחָא – refers to cases in which **[the creditor] demands from [the seller]** an amount **equivalent to the value of the land and** its **improvements.** Therefore, he collects his entire debt without compensating the purchaser for his expenses. הָא – **This** Baraisa דְּלָא מַסֵּיק בֵּיהּ אֶלָּא כְּשִׁיעוּר אַרְעָא – refers to a case in which **[the creditor] demands from [the seller] only** an amount **equivalent to the value of the land** without the improvements. דְּיָהֵיב לֵיהּ שִׁבְחֵיהּ – Therefore, **[the creditor]** must **give [the purchaser]** compensation for **his improvements,**[3] וּמְסַלֵּיק לֵיהּ – **and** then **removes him** from the property.

The Gemara questions this explanation:

הָנִיחָא לְמַאן דְּאָמַר – Now, **it is acceptable according to the o**[ne] **who says** that אִי אִית לֵיהּ זוּזֵי לְלוֹקֵחַ – even **if a purchaser** of t[he] debtor's land **has money,** לָא מָצֵי מְסַלֵּיק לֵיהּ לְבַעַל חוֹב – **he m**[ay] **not prevent**[4] **a creditor** who holds a lien on the debto[r's] property from possessing the land by offering him mon[ey] instead,[5] שַׁפִּיר – **for the Baraisa's ruling is then approp**[ri]**ate** that the creditor may collect even the improvements whi[ch] are valued in excess of the loan, by compensating the purchas[er] for those improvements.[6] אֶלָּא לְמַאן דְּאָמַר – **Howeve**[r,] **according to the one who says** that כִּי אִית לֵיהּ זוּזֵי לְלוֹקֵחַ – **when the purchaser has money,** מָצֵי מְסַלֵּיק לֵיהּ לְבַעַל חוֹב – **[he] may prevent the creditor** from possessing the land by offeri[ng] him money instead, נֵימָא לֵיהּ – **let [the purchaser] tell [t**[he]**] creditor]:** אִילּוּ הֲוָה לִי זוּזֵי – **"If I would have** the **money,** [ה]מְסַלְּקִינָךְ מִכּוּלָּה אַרְעָא – **I could remove you from all the lan**[d.] הַשְׁתָּא דְּלֵית לִי זוּזֵי – **Now that I do not have money** to preve[nt] you from possessing the land whose value is equivalent to yo[ur] debt, הַב לִי גַּרְבָּא דְּאַרְעָא בְּאַרְעָא שִׁיעוּר שִׁבְחַאי – **give me a sma**[ll] **piece of land in this property,** equivalent to **the value of m**[y] **improvements."**[7] – ? –

The Gemara answers:

הָכָא בְּמַאי עָסְקִינָן – **With what** case **are we dealing here** in t[he] Baraisa? כְּגוֹן שֶׁעֲשָׂאוֹ אַפּוֹתִיקֵי – **In an instance where [t**[he]**] seller] made [this field] an *apotiki*** [8] to the creditor, אָמַר לֵיהּ – **by telling him:** לָא יְהֵא לָךְ פֵּרָעוֹן אֶלָּא מִזּוֹ – **You will have n**[o] right to **collect** the debt **except from this** field. In such a case, t[he] creditor need not accept money from the purchaser if offere[d]

NOTES

1. Literally: that reaches the shoulders. The produce is almost ready to be harvested and carried on the shoulders (see *Ramban* to 15a ד״ה שבח). Since the produce will be harvested in the near future, it is somewhat comparable to ripe produce and is not considered as much a part of the land as are other land improvements. Therefore, the creditor may not collect it without first compensating the purchaser for his expenses.

The Gemara refers to a case in which the produce still derives some nourishment from the ground (*Rashi*). However, if the produce is fully ready for harvest, it is no longer regarded as a land improvement at all. Rather, it is regarded as an already-harvested crop which is not subject to collection by creditors as Shmuel stated above, 14b (*Ramban* to 15a ד״ה שבח; *Rashi* above, 14b ד״ה לאכילת פירות and to 110b ד״ה מגיע).

2. Since the produce is totally unripe and must remain attached to the ground for yet a long time, it is regarded as part of the land itself, like land improvements. Therefore, a creditor may seize it from the purchaser without compensating him for his expenses (see *Ritva* to 14b ד״ה אימא).

To summarize, there are three levels: Crops that are totally unripe are considered as part of the land and may be seized by a creditor without compensating the purchaser. Conversely, crops that are totally ripe, although still attached to the ground, are considered like unattached produce and may not be seized. Finally, crops that are almost ripe are subject to a law in between the previous two – they may be seized, but the purchaser must be compensated for his expenses.

3. *Rashi* explains that the creditor cannot collect an amount greater than the debt owed to him. Consequently, he must compensate the purchaser for the improvements he seizes which in this case exceed the value of the loan.

[Although the Baraisa states that the creditor must compensate the purchaser only for his expenses, *Rashi* explains that he must in fact pay even for the value of the improvements above the expenses. *Rashi* goes on to reconcile his explanation with the Baraisa (see *Milchamos Hashem* and *Maharam Shif* to *Rashi* ד״ה הא, who explain *Rashi*; cf. *Tosafos* ד״ה הא and *Ramban*).]

4. Literally: remove.

5. It is an Amoraic dispute in *Kesubos* (91b) whether a purchaser of mortgaged land may prevent the seller's creditor from seizing that land in payment of the seller's debt, by paying up the debt with money (*Rashi;* see *Tosafos* there ד״ה מאי).

6. The purchaser may not demand that he retain land equal in value [to] his improvements, for the creditor may claim that the land belongs [to] him [as evidenced by his right to refuse the purchaser's offer [of] monetary payment (see previous note)], and it was improved without h[is] consent. It is therefore sufficient to compensate the purchaser for h[is] improvements (*Rashi*).

7. Since the purchaser may prevent the creditor from seizing th[e] mortgaged property by offering money instead, it is clear that the lan[d] is not considered to belong to the creditor from the moment the debt [is] contracted, and he is entitled to collect only as much of the property a[s] is necessary to satisfy his debt. Why, then, does the Baraisa imply th[at] the creditor may seize all the land and improvements, compensating th[e] purchaser with money for his improvements? Let the purchaser argue a[s] follows: "You must pay me for the improvements which are in excess [of] the seller's debt to you. Instead, keep that money and leave me with [a] piece of land of equal value."

8. *Rashi* (to *Bava Kamma* 11b ד״ה אפותקי) explains that אפותיקי is a[n] acronym for אַפֹּה תְּהֵא קָאֵי, *you* [the creditor] *will stand here.* Thus, [it] refers to property specifically designated by the debtor as set aside f[or] payment of the obligation in case he defaults. [It should be noted th[at] the Greek word *hypotheke* means "a pledge" or "a property placed unde[r] obligation" and the word hypothec is used even today in that legal sens[e.] *Tosefos Anshei Shem* (*Sheviis* 10:3) writes that the Talmudic sages ofte[n] provided Hebrew or Aramaic interpretations for words they knew to b[e] of foreign origin. They did not mean these interpretations to be etymo[-] logical, but explanatory.] When property is so designated, everyon[e] agrees that its purchaser may not prevent the creditor from possessin[g] it by offering money instead (*Rashi*).

[*Tosafos* contend that the *apotiki* field is considered as belonging t[o] the creditor from the time the obligation is due. Therefore, he mus[t] compensate the purchaser for his expenses even if the obligation is equa[l] in value to the land and improvements, just as he compensates one wh[o] improves his field without prior consent (see above, 14b note 10). Thi[s] contrasts to non-*apotiki* property seized by the creditor, for which th[e] Gemara said above he need not compensate the purchaser for hi[s] expenses if the obligation is equal in value to the land and improve[-] ments. In that case, the land is not considered as belonging to th[e] creditor until its seizure. Therefore, the purchaser improved his ow[n] property, and lost his investment when it was seized by the creditor[.] Here, however, he improves the creditor's *apotiki* field, and is entitled t[o] compensation for his expenses.]

המגיע לכתפים כאן בשבח שאינו מגיע לכתפים (א) והא מעשים בכל יום וקא מגבי שמואל אפי' בשבח המגיע לכתפים לא קשיא הא דמסיק ביה כשיעור ארעא ושבחא הא דלא מסיק ביה אלא כשיעור ארעא דיהיב ליה שבחיה ומסליק ליה ג) הניחא למ"ד אי אית ליה זוזי ללוקח לא מצי מסליק ליה לבעל חוב שפיר אלא למאן דאמר כי א איח ליה זוזי ללוקח מצי מסליק ליה לבעל חוב נימא ליה אילו הוה לי זוזי הוה מסלקינך מכולה ארעא השתא דלית לי זוזי הב לי ג) גרבא דארעא בארעא שיעור שבחאי הכא במאי עסקינן ב כגון שעשאו אפותיקי דאמר ליה לא יהא לך פרעון אלא מזו: הכיר בה שאינה שלו ולקחה אמר רב מעות יש לו שבח אין לו ושמואל אמר אפי' מעות אין לו במאי קמיפלגי רב סבר אדם יודע שקרקע אין לו וגמר ונתן לשום פקדון ונימא ליה לשום פקדון סבר לא מקבל ושמואל סבר אדם יודע שקרקע אין לו וגמר ונתן לשום מתנה ונימא ליה לשום מתנה כסיפא ליה מילתא והא פליגי ביה חדא זימנא ד) דאיתמר המקדש את אחותו רב אמר ה) מעות חוזרין ושמואל אמר ג מעות מתנה רב אמר מעות חוזרין אדם יודע שאין קידושין תופסין באחותו וגמר ונתן לשום פקדון ונימא לה לשום פקדון סבר לא מקבלה מיניה ושמואל אמר מעות מתנה אדם יודע שאין קידושין תופסין באחותו וגמר ונתן לשום מתנה ונימא לה לשום מתנה כסיפא לה מילתא צריכא דאי איתמר בהא בהא קאמר רב דלא עבדי אינשי דיהבי מתנות לנוכראה אבל גבי אחותו אימא מודה ליה לשמואל ואי איתמר בהך בהך קאמר שמואל אבל בהא אימא מודה ליה לרב צריכא בין לרב דאמר פקדון בין לשמואל דאמר מתנה האי לארעא במאי קא נחית ופירות היכי אכיל סבר אנא איחות לארעא ואיעביד ואיכול בגויה כי היכי דהוה קא עביד איהו (א) לכי אתי מריה דארעא זוזאי נהוו לרב דאמר פקדון פקדון לשמואל דאמר מתנה מתנה אמר רבא ד הלכתא יש לו מעות ויש לו שבח ואע"פ שלא פירש לו את השבח ה הכיר בה שאינה שלו ולקחה מעות יש לו שבח אין לו ה) ו אחריות טעות סופר הוא בין בשטרי הלואה ז בין בשטרי מקח וממכר בעא מיניה שמואל מרב ט) חזר ולקחה מבעלים הראשונים מהו אמר ליה ח מה מכר לו ראשון לשני כל זכות שתבא לידו מאי טעמא מר זוטרא אמר ניחא ליה י) דלא נקרייה גזלנא רב אשי אמר ט ניחא ליה דליקו בהמנותיה מאי בינייהו איכא בינייהו דמית לוקח מאן דאמר ניחא ליה דלא לקרייה גזלנא הא

## רש"י

המגיע לכתפים. קרוב ליקצר אלא שעדיין צריכין לקרקע הוי להו כפירות גמורין ואין בעל חוב גובה אותו בלא יציאה: והא מעשים בכל יום. דיני טורפי מקח באין לפני שמואל ומגבי לבעל חוב כל השבח עם הקרקע ואפילו מגיע לכתפים כל זמן שצריכין לקרקע: הא. דקתני נוטל יציאה מבעל חוב דלא מסיק ביה בעל חוב במוכר שיעור ארעא ושבחא הלכך יהיב בעל חוב ללוקח שבחיה ומסליק ליה והאי דנקט למלתיה בלשון יציאה ולא תנא נוטל כנגד החוב מבעל הקרקע והמותר מבע"ח לאשמועינן היא גופא אתא דהיכא דיציאה יתירה על השבח אין לו אלא יציאה שיעור שבח: הניחא למאן דאמר כו'. פלוגתא היא בכתובות (דף צא:): אי אית ליה זוזי ללוקח. לפרוע החוב: לא מצי מסלק ליה לבע"ח. מן ארעא דבע"ח קדים: שפיר. דמצי למימר דהיכא דיש קרקע מותר על החוב עם השבח מסלק ליה ללוקח בזוזי על כרחו דלוקח ולא מצי אמר לוקח הב לי מן ארעא שיעור שבחי דאמר כוליה דידי ואת ירדת בה שלא ברשות: דשוייא נהליה. לוה לבעל חוב אפותיקי להא ארעא והכל מודים בזו דאי הוה ליה זוזי ללוקח לא הוה מצי מסלק ליה: ז) הכא במאי עסקינן. האי ברייתא דלעיל: הכיר בה. לוקח בקרקע זו: שאינה שלו. של מוכר שגזולה היתה אצלו ולקחה: מעות יש לו. מן המוכר לכשיוציאנה נגזל מידו: שבח אין לו. שקרקע זה אינו קנוי לו: לא מקבל. לשמור: מעות חוזרין. הקדושין חוזרין לו: בין לרב דאמר כו'. כלומר היכי מצינן לומר טעמא דרב משום דגמר ונתן לשום פקדון וטעמא דשמואל משום דגמר ונתן לשום מתנה ואי הוה דעתיה לחד מהנך היכי הוה נחית להאי ארעא לעובדה ולאכול פירותיה על כרחיה סבור היה שיהא המכר קיים ולא היה בקי בדין וטעמא דפלוגתא דרב ושמואל טעם אחרינא הוא: דהוה עביד. הגזלן: לרב דאמר פקדון פקדון. כלומר אליבא דרב מפרשינן דהאי מימר אמר זוזי נהוו פקדון ולשמואל מפרשינן דהאי אמר זוזי נהוו מתנה: הלכתא. בפלוגתא קמייתא יש לו מעות ויש לו שבח: ואע"פ דלא פירש. ולית לן דשמואל דאמר שבח צריך לימלך: ואחריות טעות סופר הוא. ולית לן דשמואל דאמר שעבוד צריך לימלך: חזר. גזלן ולקחה מבעלים הראשונים לאחר שמכר ללוקח: מהו. להיות במקום בעלים כאילו לקחה אחר ויוציאה מיד הלוקח: אמר ליה. לא מצי לאפוקה שכשמכר מכר לו כל זכות שתבא לידו וכשלקחה לא לקחה אלא כדי שתהא מקוים ביד הלוקח: דלא ליקרייה גזלנא. שלא יחרפנו לוקח זה כשיוציאנה נגזל מידו ויקראנו גזלן לכך חוזר להעמיד ממכרו: דמית לוקח. לאחר שלקחה גזלן מן הבעלים והגזלן בא להוציאה מבניו: למ"ד. לא חזר להעמיד ממכרו אלא דלא ליקרייה לוקח גזלן: הא

## תוספות

הא דלא מסיק אלא שיעור ארעא. תימה כיון דלא מסיק אלא שיעור ארעא אמאי נוטל שבח היתר על היציאה [א] וי"ל דבלאו הכי פריך שפיר הניחא כו' ולפי המסקנא דמוקי באפותיקי א"ש דאע"פ דלא מסיק ביה אלא שיעור ארעא נותן לו היציאה ללוקח והשבח היתר על היציאה לוקח חנם כדין יורד לתוך שדה חבירו שלא ברשות: הניחא למ"ד כו'. מפורש בהמקבל (לקמן דף קי:) ח) (ועיין בכתובות דף צא: ד"ה מאי): כגון דשוייא אפותיקי. השתא מצי איירי דמסיק ביה אפי' שיעור ארעא ושבחא ואפ"ה כיון דשוייא אפותיקי צריך ליתן יציאה כדין יורד כו' כדאמרי' בפרק המקבל (שם) גבי יתומים אומרים אנו השבחנו ורוצים היציא' דמיירי באפותיקי ואע"ג דמסיק בהו שיעור ארעא ושבחא דהא אם אביהם השביח גובה הכל ומיהו אין ראיה דשאני יתומים שאין להם על מי לחזור ליקח היציאה דכיון שעשה אביהם אפותיקי הרי הוא כיורד לתוך שדה חבירו שלא ברשות שאינו מפסיד היציאה אבל בלוקח שאינו מפסיד כלום שהמוכר משלם לו היציאה והשבח שזה פוטרו מחובו מצינו למימר דאפילו באפותיקי כיון דמסיק ביה שיעור ארעא ושבחא שקיל הכל שבשביל שעשאה אפותיקי לא יגרע כחו וא"ת כיון דאמר ליה לא יהא לך פרעון אלא מזו כשמוכר לאחר הוה ליה כלוקח מגזלן שהרי אינו של מוכר א"כ למה נוטל מן המוכר השבח היתר על היציאה והא לוקח מגזלן לשמואל לית ליה שבחא וי"ל כגון שמכרה קודם שבא זמנו של בעל חוב דחל המקח עד הזמן ולא דמי לגזלן שלא חל המקח כלל דזוזי הוו הלואה ואם ישלם שבח הוה ליה רבית ואפילו מכרה אחר הזמן היה סבור לפייס בע"ח בזוזי וחל המקח עד שטרפה ממנו: מעות יש לו שבח אין לו. תימה דהגוזל קמא (ב"ק דף צה. ושם: ד"ה דלמא) תנא ה' גוזין מן המחוררין שבח ומוקי לה בת"ח דידע דקרקע אינה נגזלת אלמא אפילו בהכיר בה יש לו שבח וי"ל דהתם מיירי כשקיבל עליו אחריות: ונתן לו לשם מתנה. אבל בערכין פרק המוכר שדה (דף כט: ושם) גבי המוכר שדהו בשנת היובל עצמה דאמר שמואל מעות חוזרין ליכא למימר אדם יודע שאין מכר ביובל דאין זה פשוט דהא אמר רב מכורה ויוצאה: חזר ולקחה כו'. בלא הכיר בה נ"ל וקמיבעיא ליה אם הגזלן יכול לבטל המקח ולהחזיר לו מעותיו או לאו: דמית לוקח. פרש"י אחר שלקחה ואין נראה דמיד שקנה הגזלן זכה בו לוקח ואטו משום דמית ליה בתר הכי פקע כחו אלא יש לומר דמית קודם שלקחה הגזלן מנגזל ט) (ומית גזלן) נ"ל שהיה חולה או גוסס בשעה שלקחה מנגזל: מאי

## עין משפט נר מצוה

קלא א ב מיי' פכ"א מהל' מלוה ולוה הל' ה ו ועיין בהשגות ובמ"מ סמג עשין צד טוש"ע ח"מ סי' קטו סעיף ב:

קלב ג מיי' פ"ו מהל' זכייה ומתנה הל' כ סמג עשין מח טוש"ע אה"ע סי' נ סעיף ב:

קלג ד מיי' פ"ט מהל' גזילה ואבידה הל' ח ופכ"א מהל' מלוה ולוה הל' א סמג עשין עג צה טוש"ע ח"מ סי' קטו סעיף א וסי' שעג סעיף א:

קלד ה מיי' פ"ט מהל' גזילה הל' ז סמג עשין עג טוש"ע ח"מ סי' שע"ג סעיף א:

קלה ו ז מיי' פי"ח מהל' גזילה ואבידה הל' א ופי"ט מהל' מכירה הל' ג ופי"ח מהל' מלוה ולוה הל' ג סמג עשין צה טוש"ע ח"מ סי' לט סעיף א וסי' קיא סעיף א וסי' רכה סעיף א:

קלו ח ט מיי' פ"ט מהל' גזילה ואבידה הל' ט סמג עשין עג טוש"ע ח"מ סי' שעד סעיף א:

## רבינו חננאל

והני מילי בדלא מסיק ביה בעל חוב אלא ק' בלבד אבל אם נושה בו כשיעור ארעא ושבחא נוטל הכל ואינו נותן ללוקח אפי' ההוצאה חוץ שינויא דשמואל היא ולא סמכינן עלה א) אלא לעולם נותן הבעל חוב ההוצאה ללוקח כפשוטה דהא מתניתא וכי יהיב ליה דמים ולא מן הקרקע עצמו בשעשאה לו אפותיקי דאמר ליה לא יהא לך פרעון אלא מזו השדה ואליבא דמ"ד אי אית ליה זוזי ללוקח מצי מסלק ליה לבע"ח בזוזי מוקים להא מתניתא בשעשאה לו הלוה אפותיקי וחזר ומכרה. ואסקי' אפי' שבח המגיע בכתפים כגון ענבים שהגיעו להבצר וקמה להקצר שהגיעו ליטלם בכתפו ולצאת כיון שעדיין כקרקע הן הכל נוטלם הבעל חוב בחובו. וכבר פירש' היטב בפרק המקבל שדה מחבירו בענין שלשה שמין להן השבח ומעלין אותן בדמים ואלו הן בכור לפשוט ובע"ח ליתומין ובעל חוב ללקוחות דלעולם נוטל הלוקח ההוצאה מן הבעל חוב כפשוטה דהא מתניתא דלא גרע מן היורד לשדה חבירו ונטעה שלא מרשותו דקי"ל שמין לו וידו על התחתונה ופירשנוה בפ' מי שמת. הכיר בה שאינה שלו ולקחה רב אמר מעות יש לו שבח אין לו. ושמואל אמר אפי' מעות אין לו. ואסיקנא רב אמר מעות פקדון ושמואל אמר מעות מתנה וכן לענין מקדש אחותו רב אמר מעות פקדון וחוזרין ושמואל [אמר] מעות מתנה ואינן חוזרין וצריכא. אמר רבא הלכתא המוכר שדה לחבירו ונמצאת שאינו שלו יש לו מעות ויש לו שבח דאושבחא ארעא ממילא כגון שקנאה במנה ועתה הוקרה ושוה מאתים יש לו כגון זה השבח ואע"פ שלא פירש לו את השבח. הכיר בה שאינה שלו ולקחה מעות יש לו שבח אין לו ואחריות טעות סופר הוא בין בשטרי הלואה בין בשטרי מקח וממכר ג) אבל אם נטע אילנות והשביח בין הלוקח בין הגזלן לוקחין שיעור שבחם מן הנגזל. הא דבעא שמואל מרב חזר ולקחה מן הבעלים הראשונים מהו. ופשט ל[ה] מה מכר ראשון לשני כל זכות שתבוא לידו מאי טעמא מר זוטרא אמר ניחא ליה דלא ניקרייה גזלנא. רב אשי אמר ניחא ליה דליקום בהימנותיה. דברים פשוטים הן דודאי קנאה הקונה אותה מן הגזלן כיון שקנאה הגזלן מן הנג[זל]

## מסורת הש"ס

א) בבא קמא צה: ו[...] לקמן קי:, ב) [לקמן בבא קמא נו.], ג) [ב]בא קמא נו. ולקמן קי: א[...] גריווא], ד) גיטין [...] [קדושין מו:], ערכין [...] ה) [לעיל יד., כתובות [...] בבא בתרא קס[...] ו) [לקמן עב:], ז) [...] קודס ד"ה דשו[...] ח) [וכן עוד בתוס' [...] קמא נו. ד"ה הניחא, ו[...] תוס' לקמן לה. [...] הניחא], ט) ס"א ובתר מית גזלן שהיה כו'.

## הגהות הב"ח

(א) גמ' ולכי אתי מר[יה]

## הגהות הגר"א

[א] תוס' ד"ה הא אמאי נוטל ש"ה היציאה. נ"ב ול"נ ד[...] קושית גמ' באמת הנ[...] כו' כדין יורד שלא בר[שות] וכמו באפותיקי (ו[...] הרמב"ן במלחמות [...] כש"ך סי' קט"ו ס"ק [...]

## גליון הש"ס

גמ' מעות חוזרין. ע"ב עם ע"א תוס' ד[...] אבל: שם חזר ולק[חה] מבעלים. עי' בהר[...] פ"ו מ"ג דתרומות.

## ליקוטי רש"י

המגיע לכתפים. [...] תבואה שגדלה כל צ[...] נותנה ללוקח או ד[...] [ב"ק צה:]. צריכין לקר[קע] דבר מועט דאילו צריכין לקרקע הוו [...] פירות ולא מיקרו [...] ובע"ח גובה השבח ק[...] ולא פירות גמורין. אית ליה זוזי ללוק[ח] שיעור דמי החוב. שפי[ר] איכא למימר דאר[...] מעיקרא דידיה הואי ו[...] דנחת לה שלא ברשות [...] שבחא בזוזי ולא באר[...] הואיל והוה מסיק [...] שיעור ארעא כולה [לק' קי:]. אפותיקי. [...] שהא קאי כלומר מזה [...] לך פרעון [ב"ק יא:]. [...] אמר מעות. של קדו[שין] חוזרין דאדם יודע [...] קדושין תופסין באח[ותו] וגמר ונתן לשם פק[דון] [גיטין מה.]. ולשמואל [...] ונתן לשם מתנה [ערכין...] אחריות טעות סופ[ר] כשאינו כתוב בשטר [...] הוא שטעה אבל זה לא [...] לו מעותיו בלא אחרי[ות] נכסים דלא שדי איניש [...] בכדי [לעיל יד. ועי"ש עו[ד] שאינו כתוב בשטר [...] נכתב השטר סתם טע[ות] [...] שכתב בו אחריות [...] ופלוגתא הוא בשנים או[...] (ב"מ דף יד.) והכי מסק[...] התם (טו:) דטעות סו[פר] הוא בין בשטרי מקח [...] בשטרי הלואה [רשב"ם ב"ב קסט:]. דלא ניקריי[ה] גזלנא. אדם שמכר ש[דה] גזולה לחבירו מחזר [...] הבעלים הראשונים ולוקח מהם להעמיד ביד הלו[קח] כי היכי דלא ליקרייה גזל[ן] [לקמן עב:].

חשק שלמה על ר"ח א) דברי רבינו אלו הובא בר"ף כאן בשם ויש מאן דאמר ויעין שם מש"כ שם ע"ז. ב) וכ"כ הרי"ף כאן והביא ראיה לזה מפ' הגוזל עצים ע"ש.

שנטלוה מסיקין [א] בא נגזל לגבות קרן גובה מנכסים משועבדים בא נגזל לגבות פירות גובה מנכסים בני חורין רבא לא אמר כרבה בר רב הונא הרי היא יוצאה מתחת ידו בדינא משמע ורבה בר רב הונא לא אמר כרבא הרי היא יוצאה מתחת ידו בעינא משמע רב אשי אמר לצדדין קתני כגון שגזל שדה מחבירו מלאה פירות ואכל את הפירות ומכר את השדה בא לוקח לגבות קרן גובה מנכסים משועבדים בא נגזל לגבות פירות גובה מנכסים בני חורין בין לרבא בין לרבה בר רב הונא מלוה על פה הוא [ב] ומלוה על פה אינו גובה מנכסים משועבדים הכא במאי עסקינן [ג] כשעמד בדין והדר זבין אי הכי פירות נמי כשעמד בדין על הקרן ולא עמד בדין על הפירות ומאי פסקא סתמא דמילתא כי תבע איניש קרנא תבע ברישא וסבר שמואל לוקח מגזלן לית ליה שבחא והא א"ל שמואל לרב חיננא בר שילת אמליך וכתוב שופרא שבחא ופירי במאי אי בבעל חוב מי אית ליה פירי [א] והאמר שמואל בעל חוב גובה את השבח שבח אין אבל פירות לא אלא לאו בלוקח מגזלן אמר רב יוסף הכא במאי עסקינן כגון שיש לו קרקע א"ל אביי וכי מותר ללות סאה בסאה במקום שיש לו קרקע א"ל התם הלואה הכא זביני איכא דאמרי אמר רב יוסף הכא במאי עסקינן כגון [ג] שקנו מידו א"ל אביי וכי מותר ללות סאה בסאה במקום שקנו מידו א"ל התם הלואה והכא זביני: גופא אמר שמואל בעל חוב גובה את השבח אמר רבא תדע שכך כותב לו מוכר ללוקח אנא איקום ואשפי ואדכי ואמריק זביני אילין אינון ועמלידון ושבחיהון ואיקום קדמך וצבי זבינא דנן וקביל עלוהי א"ל רב חייא בר אבין לרבא אלא מעתה מתנה דלא כתיב ליה הכי ה"נ [ד] דלא טריף שבחא א"ל אין וכי יפה כח מתנה ממכר א"ל אין [ה] יפה ויפה אמר רב נחמן הא מתניתא מסייע ליה למר שמואל [ו] והונא חברין מוקים לה במילי אחריני דתניא המוכר שדה לחבירו והרי היא יוצאה מתחת ידו [ה] כשהוא גובה גובה את הקרן מנכסים משועבדים ושבח גובה מנכסים בני חורין והונא חברין מוקים לה במילי אחריני בלוקח מגזלן תניא אידך המוכר שדה לחבירו והשביחה ובא בעל חוב וטרפה [ו] כשהוא גובה אם השבח יותר על היציאה נוטל את השבח מבעל הקרקע והיציאה מבעל חוב ואם היציאה יתירה על השבח אין לו אלא הוצאה שיעור שבח מבעל חוב והא שמואל במאי מוקים לה אי [ז] בלוקח מגזלן קשיא רישא דאמר שמואל לוקח מגזלן לית ליה שבחא אי בבעל חוב קשיא רישא וסיפא דאמר שמואל בעל חוב גובה את השבח איבעית אימא בלוקח מגזלן כגון שיש לו קרקע אי נמי בשקנו מידו איבעית אימא בבעל חוב ולא קשיא כאן בשבח

המגיע

## רש"י

שנטלוה מסיקין. אנסים עכו"ס נטלוה מן הגזלן ומחמתו ותנן בבבא קמא (דף קטז:) הגוזל שדה מחבירו ונטלוה מסיקין אם מחמת הגזלן חייב להעמיד לו שדה אחר והרי היא יוצאה מתחת ידו דקתני בנטילת מסיקין הוא: בדינא משמע. הלכך בהוצאת נגזל קאמר וגובה את הקרן דקאמר כשחפר בו בורות: בעינא משמע. כמו שהיתה ולא שחפר בה בורות: ומכר את השדה. והרי היא יוצאה מתחת ידו של לוקח בדינא ובעינא: בין לרבה בין לרבא. דמוקמי גביית קרן מן הגזלן בנגזל הא מלוה על פה הוא ולא טרפא ממשעבדי: כשעמד בדין. קודם שמכר נכסיו וכיון דחייבוהו ב"ד אית ליה קלא והוה ליה כמלוה בשטר: מאי פסקא. בתמיה פסקא תנא למלתיה דהעומד בדין אינו עומד על הפירות: רב חיננא בר שילת. סופר היה: אמליך. כשאתה כותב שטר המלך במוכר אם יקבל עליו להגבות ללוקח משפר נכסיו קרנא ושבחא ופרי אם יטרפוה ממנו: כגון שיש לו קרקע. לגזלן זה שמגבהו ללוקח קרקע ולא מעות דהשתא לא מחזי כרבית: אסור ללות סאה בסאה. שמא יוקרו חטין: בהלואה. שייך רבית טפי ממכר: שקנו מידו. על השבח דהוה ליה מחויב משעת המכר קודם שיש שכר המתנת מעות: תדע. דגובה ולא מלי לוקח למימר אנא אשבחי: שכך כותב לו מוכר ללוקח. באחריות שטר המכר: ואשפי. אשקיט ודומה לו על הר נשפה דמתרגם על טורא שליוא (ישעיה יג): ואדכי. אטהר מכל ערעור: אינון ועמלידון ושבחיהון. וכיון דעל מוכר הדר גבי שבחא בעל חוב מלוקח וחוזר הלוקח על המוכר: מתנה דלא כתיב ביה הכי. שאין אדם מקבל עליו אחריות מה שהוא נותן: ה"נ. דאם נותן נכסיו במתנה לא גבי בעל חוב שבחא הואיל ולא הדר על הנותן: וכי יפה כח מתנה כו'. בתמיה: יפה ויפה. בדבר זה דכיון דלא הדר גבי ליה לא מפסיד ליה במידי דלא אפסדיה לבעל חוב דבשלמא גופה של קרקע א"ל אמאי [ג] (זבנתיה) מאין אגבה חובי אבל שבחא א"ל מאי אפסדתיך: מסייע ליה למר שמואל. דבעל חוב גובה את השבח: כשהוא גובה. כשלוקח חוזר וגובה מן המוכר: במילי אחריני. בדבר אחר: בלוקח מגזלן. דנגזל ודאי טריף שבחא דאמר ליה ארעאי אשבח אבל בעל חוב כל כמה דלא טרפה לה לאו דידיה הוא וברשותא דלוקח אשבח: על הוצאה. שהוציא הלוקח בשבחה: נוטל. הלוקח: את השבח מבעל הקרקע. מה שעודף על היציאה דאמר ליה פרעתי את חובך: אין לו. ללוקח אלא מן היציאה שהוציא בה פורע לו שיעור שבח והשאר מפסיד: אי בלוקח מגזלן. האי בע"ח היינו נגזל: קשיא רישא. דקתני נוטל את השבח מבעל הקרקע: קשיא רישא וסיפא. דקתני בע"ח נותן את היציאה ולשמואל בעל חוב גובה השבח ואינו נותן כלום:

המגיע

## תוספות

**כשעמד** בדין על הקרן ולא על הפירות. תימה אם כן מאי מפני תיקון העולם הלא בדין לא גבי דמלוה על פה לא גבי ממשעבדי ויש לומר דאי לאו מפני תיקון העולם הוה אמינא הואיל ועמד בדין על הקרן יש קול גם לפירות:

**כגון** שקנו מידו. וא"ת א"כ אמאי קאמר אמליך הלא סתם קנין לכתיבה עומד וי"ל ה"מ כגון שהקנה לו דבר שהוא בעין דכיון דיפה כחו לעשות קנין רוצה שיכתבו לו:

**בעל** חוב גובה את השבח. נראה דגבי אפי' מן השבח שהשביחו יתומים אע"פ שאין להם על מי לחזור והוה ליה כמתנה דאמרינן לקמן דלא גבי שבחא מ"מ גובה מהן משום דכרעיה דאבוהון נינהו כדמוכח בפרק יש בכור (בכורות דף נב. ושם) דתנן אין הבכור נוטל פי שנים בראוי כבמוחזק ולא בשבח ולא האשה בכתובתה ולא הבנות במזונותיהן ופריך בגמרא והאמר שמואל בעל חוב גובה את השבח ומשני מקולי כתובה שנו כאן ומזון בנות נמי תנאי כתובה ככתובה דמי והתם משבח יתומים איירי דאי משבח לקוחות אם כן מאי איריא דלא טרפי בנות משבח והלא מגוף הקרקע נמי לא טרפי דאין מוציאין למזון האשה והבנות מנכסים משועבדים אלא ודאי בשבח יתומים איירי ודוקא כתובת אשה ומזונות דקילי לא גבו משבח אבל שאר בע"ח גבי ורש"י פירש התם מזון הבנות כגון נשא אשה ופסק לזון בתה ה' שנים ולפירושו אין ראיה דמאי איירי בשבח לקוחות אך לא נהירא דלא שייך בהו תנאי כתובה והא דאמר בהמקבל (לקמן דף קי.) יתומים אומרים אנו השבחנו ואין השבח שלך משמע דלא גבי משבח יתומים התם איירי כשעשה אפותיקי ואומרים אנו השבחנו ותן לנו היציאה כדין יורד לתוך שדה חבירו שלא ברשות וכן מוקי התם במסקנא כשעשאה אפותיקי:

**תדע** שכך כתב כו'. אין לפרש דהכי מוכח דבע"ח גובה את השבח דבשביל דבע"ח גובה את השבח כותב מוכר ללוקח שישלם לו את השבח דא"כ מאי פריך מתנה דלא כתיב בה (א) הכי נמי דלא טריף שבח והלא אין תלוי גביית הבע"ח בכתיבת המוכר אלא יש לומר מדמשלם מוכר ללוקח את השבח אין לחוש אם יגבהו בעל חוב ממנו דאין הלוקח מפסיד כל כך וא"ת ומאי ראיה היא (ב) דלמא מיירי בלוקח מגזלן דנגזל ודאי אית ליה שבחא וי"ל דאי בלוקח מן הגזלן איירי הוה ליה למכתב נמי [ד] ופירייהו אלא מיירי בבעל חוב דלית ליה פירי אי נמי מדקאמר ועמליהון היינו הוצאה ושבחיהון היינו השבח היתר על היציאה ואי בנגזל הא נגזל גופיה יהיב ליה יציאה כדין יורד לתוך שדה חבירו שלא ברשות:

הא

## עין משפט נר מצוה

קכה א מיי' פ"ט מהל' גזילה ואבידה הל' ב ג סמג עשין עג טוש"ע ח"מ סי' שעב סעיף א:

קכו ב מיי' פי"א מהל' מלוה ולוה הל' ד סמג עשין לד טוש"ע ח"מ סי' לט סעיף א וסי' קיא סעיף א:

קכז ג מיי' פ"ט מהל' גזילה ואבידה הל' ד סמג עשין עג טוש"ע ח"מ סי' שעב סעיף א וסעיף ב:

קכח ד מיי' פכ"א מהל' מלוה ולוה הל' ג סמג עשין לה טוש"ע ח"מ סי' קטו סעיף ג:

קכט ה מיי' שם הל' א טוש"ע שם סעיף א:

קל ו ז מיי' פ"ט מהל' גזילה הל' ו סמג עשין עג טוש"ע ח"מ סי' שעג סעיף א וע"ש ובר"ף:

## רבינו חננאל

רבה בר רב הונא אמר כגון שגזל שדה ונטלוה מסיקין מחמתו בא נגזל לגבות דמי השדה גובה אפי' ממשעבדי בא לגבות דמי פירות אינו גובה אלא מבני חרי. ומקשי' בין לרבא דאמר דמי היזק חפירות בורות שיחין ומערות ובין לרבה בר רב הונא דאמר דמי השדה שנטלוה מסיקין אמאי טריף ממשעבדי מלוה על פה היא ומלוה על פה אינו גובה (אלא) ממשעבדי. ופרקי' הכא במאי עסקינן כגון שתבע הנגזל לגזלן בב"ד וחייבוהו ב"ד לשלם ואחר שנתחייב הלך ומכר נכסיו בזה הדין לטרוף הנגזל כל הנכסין שמכר הגזלן מאחר שנתחייב בב"ד א) מיהא שמעינן חיוב ב"ד לאדם לשלם כמלוה בשטר דמי וגבי אפי' ממשעבדי. הא דאמר שמואל אימליך ובתר הכי כתוב שופרא שבחא ופירי כלומר לא תכתוב אלו עד שתימלך במקנה ויאמר לו כתוב שהללו מעין תורפי השטר [הן] חשובין ולא מטופסא דשטרא שאין בהן ממש. ומקשי' ואי בבעל חוב שמואל מי אמר דאית ליה פירי והא איהו דאמר בעל חוב גובה את השבח שבח אין פירי לא. ופריק רב יוסף בשיש ללוה קרקע. איכא דאמרי בשקנו מידו. ומקשי עלה אביי וכי מותר ללות סאה בסאה למי שיש לו קרקע או למי שקנו מידו. ופריק רב יוסף האי בהלואה אסור אבל בזביני שרי. ואע"ג דאמר רב נחמן קרקע אין לו כלומר כיון שנטרפה שדה זו מידיו נמצא כאילו לא היתה מכירתו מכירה וכי זה השבח או הפירות שכר מעותיו הוא נוטלה הא אמר רב יוסף כי האי גוונא בזביני שרי. ומסקנא דשמעתא הנותן שדהו מתנה ובא בעל חוב לטורפה אינו גובה השבח דלא גבי בעל חוב השבח אלא מן הקונה שדה משועבדת לבעל חוב ודייק רבא מדפריש בשטר זביני אנא אשפי ואמרק ואדכי זביני אילין אינון ועמליהון ושבחיהון ואוקים קדמך וצבי זבינא דנן וקביל עילויה משום הכי גבי בעל חוב שבחא דהא קביל עליה המוכר ונתרצה הקונה בזה אבל המתנה שאין כתוב בה זה

## מסורת הש"ס

...יל יד: וש"נ, ...קמן נח., לד., בבא ...ג.], ג) קבלתיה, ...ס"ל, ועיין מהרש"א, ...עי' היטב תוס' גיטין ...ד"ה לפי שאין וכו' וקל"ע].

## הגהות הב"ח

(א) תוס' ד"ה תדע וכו' כתיב בה הכי הכי (ב) בא"ד וא"ת ראיה דלמא הכא מיירי:

## גליון הש"ס

...יפה ויפה. עיין כ"כ נג ע"א תוס' ד"ה ...: שם והונא ...ין. קדושין מז ע"א:

## ליקוטי רש"י

...בע"ח וטרפה. ...יא משוכנת בזיבול ...שה חריעה [רשב"ם ב"ב קנז:].

---

ג) כולו לא גבי הבעל חוב מן המקבל מתנה שבח ובזה אמר יפה כח המתנה מכח המכר. תניא המוכר שדהו לחבירו ובא בעל חוב וטרפה אם השבח יותר על ההוצאה כו' פי' כגון שקנאה בק' והוציא י' כספים ושוה עתה ק"כ נוטל בע"ח השדה כולה והשבח כמות שהוא ונותן לקונה י' כספים שהוציא על השדה וחוזר הקונה ונוטל מן המוכר ק"י כספים ואם ההוצאה יתירה על השבח כגון שהוציא עליה כ' ושוה עכשיו ק"י אין לו מבע"ח אלא י' כספים מן ההוצאה כשיעור השבח שהשביח בקרקע ונוטל ק' מן המוכר ומפסיד י' הלוקח. וזו שנוטל הקונה חלק בקרקע הוא נוטל.

חשק שלמה על ר"ח א) עי' בר"ף לקמן דף ח גבי מימרא דר"נ באמרו לו ב"ד לא מן לו כו' עי"ש היטיב. ב) אולי צ"ל שאין כתוב בה זה כלל.

pensated.

וְהָא שְׁמוּאֵל בְּמַאי מוּקִים – **To what** case **can Shmuel explain** [this **Baraisa] as referring?** אִי בְּלוֹקֵחַ מִגַּזְלָן – **If it refers to** one **who purchases** stolen land **from a robber,**[30] קַשְׁיָא רֵישָׁא – **the first case is difficult,** דְּאָמַר שְׁמוּאֵל לוֹקֵחַ מִגַּזְלָן לֵית לֵיהּ שֶׁבַח – **for Shmuel said one who purchases** land **from a** robber **does not receive** compensation from the seller for his improvements when they are repossessed together with the land. The Baraisa, however, states in its first case that the purchaser does receive compensation from the seller for lost improvements in excess of his expenses. אִי בְּבַעַל חוֹב – **If [the Baraisa] refers** to land seized by **a creditor** of the seller, קַשְׁיָא רֵישָׁא וְסֵיפָא – both **the first and last case are difficult,** דְּאָמַר שְׁמוּאֵל בַּעַל חוֹב גּוֹבֶה אֶת הַשֶּׁבַח – **for Shmuel said a creditor collects** even **the** improvements to the debtor's sold land, without compensating the purchaser at all. The Baraisa, however, says in both cases that the creditor does compensate the purchaser for his expenses.

The Gemara explains:

אִיבָּעִית אֵימָא – **If you prefer, I can say** בְּלוֹקֵחַ מִגַּזְלָן – **[the Baraisa] refers to one who purchases** a stolen field **from a robber.** Nevertheless, he receives compensation from the robber for the value of the improvements in excess of his expenses, כְּגוֹן שֶׁיֵּשׁ לוֹ קַרְקַע – in a case in which, **for instance, [the robber] has land,** אִי נַמִּי בְּשֶׁקָּנוּ מִיָּדוֹ – **or else when [the witnesses] acquired** a commitment **from [the robber]** at the time of the sale to compensate the purchaser for lost improvements.[31]

אִיבָּעִית אֵימָא – Or **if you prefer, I can say** בְּבַעַל חוֹב – **[the Baraisa] refers to** land seized by the seller's **creditor.** וְלֹא קַשְׁיָא – Nevertheless, the Baraisa's ruling requiring the creditor to compensate the purchaser for his expenses is **not difficult:** כָּאן – **Here,** in the Baraisa, בְּשֶׁבַח – **it refers to** the seizure of **improved** produce

NOTES

reimbursed by the seller (*Rashi*).

30. According to this explanation, the "creditor" referred to by the Baraisa is in fact the rightful owner of the field (*Rashi*).

31. The Gemara above said that Shmuel agrees that the purchaser may receive compensation for improvements from the robber in these cases (see notes 15, 20).

שנטלוה מסיקין ‎א‎בא נגזל לגבות קרן גובה מנכסים משועבדים בא נגזל לגבות פירות גובה מנכסים בני חורין רבא לא אמר כרבה בר רב הונא הרי היא יוצאה מתחת ידו בדינא משמע ורבה בר רב הונא לא אמר כרבא הרי היא יוצאה מתחת ידו בעינא משמע רב אשי אמר לצדדין קתני כגון שגזל שדה מחבירו מלאה פירות ואכל את הפירות ומכר את השדה בא לוקח לגבות קרן גובה מנכסים משועבדים בא נגזל לגבות פירות גובה מנכסים בני חורין בין לרבא בין לרבה בר רב הונא מלוה על פה הוא ‎ב‎ומלוה על פה אינו גובה מנכסים משועבדים הכא במאי עסקינן ‎ג‎כשעמד בדין והדר זבין אי הכי פירות נמי כשעמד בדין על הקרן ולא עמד בדין על הפירות ומאי פסקא סתמא דמילתא כי תבע איניש קרנא תבע ברישא וסבר שמואל לוקח מגזלן לית ליה שבחא והא א"ל שמואל לרב חיננא בר שילת אמליך וכתוב שופרא שבחא ופירי במאי אי בבעל חוב מי אית ליה פירי ‎(א)‎ והאמר שמואל בעל חוב גובה את השבח שבח אין אבל פירות לא אלא לאו בלוקח מגזלן אמר רב יוסף הכא במאי עסקינן כגון שיש לו קרקע א"ל אביי וכי מותר ללות סאה בסאה במקום שיש לו קרקע א"ל התם הלואה הכא זביני איכא דאמרי אמר רב יוסף הכא במאי עסקינן כגון ‎ד‎שקנו מידו א"ל אביי וכי מותר ללות סאה בסאה במקום שקנו מידו א"ל התם הלואה והכא זביני: גופא אמר שמואל בעל חוב גובה את השבח אמר רבא תדע שכך כותב לו מוכר ללוקח אנא איקום ואשפי ואדכי ואמריק זביני אילין אינון ועמליהון ושבחיהון ואיקום קדמך וצבי זבינא דנן וקביל עלוהי א"ל רב חייא בר אבין לרבא אלא מעתה מתנה דלא כתיב ליה הכי ה"נ ‎ה‎דלא טריף שבחא א"ל אין וכי יפה כח מתנה ממכר א"ל אין ‎ו‎ יפה ויפה אמר רב נחמן הא מתניתא מסייע ליה למר שמואל ‎ז‎ והונא חברין מוקים לה במילי אחריני דתניא המוכר שדה לחבירו והרי היא יוצאה מתחת ידו ‎ח‎כשהוא גובה גובה את הקרן מנכסים משועבדים ושבח גובה מנכסים בני חורין והונא חברין מוקים לה במילי אחריני בלוקח מגזלן תניא אידך המוכר שדה לחבירו והשביחה ובא בעל חוב וטרפה ‎ט‎כשהוא גובה אם השבח יותר על היציאה נוטל את השבח מבעל הקרקע והיציאה מבעל חוב ואם היציאה יתירה על השבח אין לו אלא הוצאה שיעור שבח מבעל חוב והא שמואל במאי מוקים לה אי ‎י‎בלוקח מגזלן קשיא רישא דאמר שמואל לוקח מגזלן לית ליה שבחא אי בבעל חוב קשיא רישא וסיפא דאמר שמואל בעל חוב גובה את השבח איבעית אימא בלוקח מגזלן כגון שיש לו קרקע אי נמי בשקנו מידו איבעית אימא בבעל חוב ולא קשיא כאן בשבח המגיע

**רש"י**

שנטלוה מסיקין. אנסים עכו"ם נטלוה מן הגזלן ומחמתו ותנן בבבא קמא (דף קטז:) הגוזל שדה מחבירו ונטלוה מסיקין אם מחמת הגזלן חייב להעמיד לו שדה אחר והרי היא יוצאה מתחת ידו דקתני בנטילת מסיקין הוא: בדינא משמע. הלכך בהוצאת נגזל קאמר וגובה את הקרן דקאמר כשחפר בו בורות: בעינא משמע. כמו שהיתה ולא שחפר בה בורות: ומכר את השדה. והרי היא יוצאה מתחת ידו של לוקח בדינא ובעינא: בין לרבה בין לרבא. דמוקמי גביית קרן מן הגזלן בנגזל הא מלוה על פה הוא ולא טרפא ממשעבדי: כשעמד בדין. קודם שמכר נכסיו וכיון דחייבוהו ב"ד אית ליה קלא והוה ליה כמלוה בשטר: מאי פסקא. בתמיה פסקא תנא למלתיה דהעומד בדין אינו עומד על הפירות: רב חיננא בר שילת. סופר היה: אמליך. כשאתה כותב שטר המלך במוכר אם יקבל עליו להגבות ללוקח משפר נכסיו קרנא ושבחא ופרי אם יטרפוה ממנו: כגון שיש לו קרקע. לגזלן זה שמגבהו ללוקח קרקע ולא מעות דהשתא לא מחזי כרבית: אסור ללות סאה בסאה. שמא יוקרו חטין: בהלואה. שייך רבית טפי ממכר: שקנו מידו. על השבח דהוה ליה מחויב משעת המכר קודם שיש שכר המתנת מעות: תדע. דגובה ולא מצי לוקח למימר אנא אשבחי: שכך כותב לו מוכר ללוקח. באחריות שטר המכר: ואשפי. אשקיט ודומה לו על הר נשפה דמתרגם על טורא שליוא (ישעיה יג): ואדכי. אטהר מכל ערעור: אינון ועמלידהון ושבחיהון. וכיון דבעל מוכר הדר גבי שבחא בעל חוב מלוקח וחוזר הלוקח על המוכר: מתנה דלא כתיב ביה הכי. שאין אדם מקבל עליו אחריות מה שהוא נותן: ה"נ. דאם נותן נכסיו במתנה לא גבי בעל חוב שבחא הואיל ולא הדר על הנותן: וכי יפה כח מתנה כו'. בתמיה: יפה ויפה. בדבר זה דכיון דלא הדר גבי ליה לא מפסיד ליה במידי דלא אפסדיה לבעל חוב דבשלמא גופה של קרקע א"ל אמאי ‎ג)‎ (זבנתיה) מאין אגבה חובי אבל שבחא א"ל מאי אפסדתיך: מסייע ליה למר שמואל. דבעל חוב גובה את השבח: כשהוא גובה. כשלוקח חוזר וגובה מן המוכר: במילי אחריני. בדבר אחר: בלוקח מגזלן. דנגזל ודאי טריף שבחא דאמר ליה ארעאי אשבח אבל בעל חוב כל כמה דלא טרפה לה לאו דידיה הוא וברשותא דלוקח אשבח: על הוצאה. שהוציא הלוקח בשבחה: נוטל. הלוקח: את השבח מבעל הקרקע. מה שעודף על היציאה דאמר ליה פרעתי את חובך: אין לו. ללוקח אלא מן היציאה שהוציא בה פורע לו שיעור שבח והשאר מפסיד: אי בלוקח מגזלן. הא בע"ח היינו נגזל: קשיא רישא. דקתני נוטל את השבח מבעל הקרקע: קשיא רישא וסיפא. דקתני בע"ח נותן את היציאה ולשמואל בעל חוב גובה השבח ואינו נותן כלום:

המגיע

**תוספות**

כשעמד בדין על הקרן ולא על הפירות. תימה אם כן מאי מפני תיקון העולם הלא בדין לא גבי דמלוה על פה לא גבי ממשעבדי ויש לומר דאי לאו מפני תיקון העולם הוה אמינא הואיל ועמד בדין על הקרן יש קול גם לפירות:

כגון שקנו מידו. וא"ת א"כ אמאי קאמר אמליך הלא סתם קנין לכתיבה עומד וי"ל ה"מ כגון שהקנה לו דבר שהוא בעין דכיון דיפה כחו לעשות קנין רוצה שיכתבו לו:

בעל חוב גובה את השבח. נראה דגבי אפי' מן השבח שהשביחו יתומים אע"פ שאין להם על מי לחזור והוה ליה כמתנה דאמרינן לקמן דלא גבי שבחא מ"מ גובה מהן משום דכרעיה דאבוהון נינהו כדמוכח בפרק יש בכור (בכורות דף נב. ושם) דתנן אין הבכור נוטל פי שנים בראוי כבמוחזק ולא בשבח ולא האשה בכתובתה ולא הבנות במזונותיהן ופריך בגמרא והאמר שמואל בעל חוב גובה את השבח ומשני מקולי כתובה שנו כאן ומזון בנות נמי תנאי כתובה ככתובה דמי והתם משבח יתומים מיירי דאי משבח לקוחות אם כן מאי איריא דלא טרפי בנות משבח והלא מגוף הקרקע נמי לא טרפי דאין מוציאין למזון האשה והבנות מנכסים משועבדים אלא ודאי בשבח יתומים מיירי ודוקא כתובת אשה ומזונות דקילי לא גבו משבח אבל שאר בע"ח גבי ורש"י פירש התם מזון הבנות כגון נשא אשה ופסק לזון בתה ה' שנים ולפירושו אין ראיה דמאי מיירי בשבח לקוחות אך לא נהירא דלא שייך בהו תנאי כתובה והא דאמר בהמקבל (לקמן דף קי.) יתומים אומרים אנו השבחנו ואין השבח שלך משמע דלא גבי משבח יתומים התם מיירי כשעשה אפותיקי ואומרים אנו השבחנו ותן לנו היציאה כדין יורד לתוך שדה חבירו שלא ברשות וכן מוקי התם במסקנא כשעשאה אפותיקי: תדע שכך כתב כו'. אין לפרש דהכי מוכח דבע"ח גובה את השבח דבשביל דבע"ח גובה את השבח כותב מוכר ללוקח שישלם לו את השבח דא"כ מאי פריך מתנה דלא כתיב בה ‎(א)‎ הכי נמי דלא טריף שבח והלא אין תלוי גביית הבע"ח בכתיבת המוכר אלא יש לומר מדמשלם מוכר ללוקח את השבח אין לחוש אם יגבהו בעל חוב ממנו דאין הלוקח מפסיד כל כך וא"ת ומאי ראיה ‎(ב)‎ היא דלמא מיירי בלוקח מגזלן דנגזל ודאי אית ליה שבחא וי"ל דאי בלוקח מן הגזלן איירי הוה ליה למכתב נמי ‎ד)‎ ופיריהון אלא מיירי בבעל חוב דלית ליה פירי אי נמי מדקאמר ועמליהון היינו הוצאה ושבחיהון היינו השבח היתר על היציאה ואי בנגזל הא נגזל גופיה יהיב ליה יציאה כדין יורד לתוך שדה חבירו שלא ברשות:

הא

**עין משפט נר מצוה**

קכה א מיי' פ"ט מהל' גזילה ואבידה הל' ג ג סמג עשין עג טוש"ע ח"מ סי' שעב סעיף א:

קכו ב מיי' פי"א מהל' מלוה ולוה הל' ד סמג עשין לד טוש"ע ח"מ סי' לט סעיף א וסי' קיא סעיף א:

קכז ג מיי' פ"ט מהל' גזילה ואבידה הל' ד סמג עשין עג טוש"ע ח"מ סי' שעב סעיף א וסעיף ג:

קכח ד מיי' פכ"א מהל' מלוה ולוה הל' ג סמג עשין לה טוש"ע ח"מ סי' קטו סעיף ג:

קכט ה מיי' שם הל' א טוש"ע שם סעיף א:

קל ו ז מיי' פ"ט מהל' גזילה הל' ו סמג עשין עג טוש"ע ח"מ סי' שעג סעיף א וע"ש ובר"ף:

**רבינו חננאל**

רבה בר רב הונא אמר כגון שגזל שדה ונטלוה מסיקין מחמתו בא נגזל לגבות דמי השדה גובה אפי' ממשעבדי בא לגבות דמי פירות אינו גובה אלא מבני חרי. ומקשי' בין לרבא דאמר דמי היזק חפירות בורות שיחין ומערות ובין לרבה בר רב הונא דאמר דמי השדה שנטלוה מסיקין אמאי טריף ממשעבדי מלוה על פה היא ומלוה על פה אינו גובה (אלא) ממשעבדי. ופרקי' הכא במאי עסקינן כגון שתבע הנגזל לגזלן בב"ד וחייבוהו ב"ד לשלם ואחר שנתחייב הלך ומכר נכסיו בזה הדין לטרוף הנגזל כל הנכסין שמכר הגזלן מאחר שנתחייב בב"ד ‎א)‎ מיהא שמעינן חיוב ב"ד לאדם לשלם כמלוה בשטר דמי וגבי אפי' ממשעבדי. הא דאמר שמואל אימליך ובתר הכי כתוב שופרא שבחא ופירי כלומר לא תכתוב אלו עד שתימלך במקנה ויאמר לו כתוב שהללו מעין תורפי השטר [הן] חשובין ולא מטופסא דשטרא שאין בהן ממש. ומקשי' ואי בבעל חוב שמואל מי אמר דאית ליה פירי והא איהו דאמר בעל חוב גובה את השבח שבח אין פירי לא. ופריק רב יוסף בשיש ללוה קרקע. איכא דאמרי בשקנו מידו. ומקשי עלה אביי וכי מותר ללות סאה בסאה למי שיש לו קרקע או למי שקנו מידו. ופריק רב יוסף האי בהלואה אסור אבל בזביני שרי. ואע"ג דאמר רב נחמן קרקע אין לו כלומר כיון שנטרפה שדה זו מידיו נמצא כאילו לא היתה מכירתו מכירה וכי זה השבח או הפירות שכר מעותיו הוא נוטלה הא אמר רב יוסף כי האי גוונא בזביני שרי. ומסקנא דשמעתא הנותן שדהו מתנה ובא בעל חוב לטורפה אינו גובה השבח דלא גבי בעל חוב השבח אלא מן הקונה שדה משועבדת לבעל חוב ודייק רבא מדפריש בשטר זביני אנא אשפי ואמרק ואדכי זביני אילין אינון ועמליהון ושבחיהון ואוקים קדמך וצבי זבינא דנן וקביל עילויה משום הכי גבי בעל חוב שבחא דהא קביל עליה המוכר ונתרצה הקונה בזה אבל המתנה שאין כתוב בה זה

**תורת הש"ס**

יד: וש"נ, ...ן נח., לד., בבא ...ג.], ג) קבלתיה, ...ל, ועיין מהרש"א, ... היטב תוס' גיטין ...ה לפי שאין וכו' וקל"ע].

**הגהות הב"ח**

...ים' ד"ה תדע וכו' ...תיב בה הכי הכי (ב) בא"ד וא"ת ...ראיה דלמא ההיא מיירי:

**גליון הש"ס**

...פה ויפה. עיין ב"ב ...: ע"א תוס' ד"ה ... שם והונא ...ין. קדושין מז ע"א:

**ליקוטי רש"י**

... בע"ח וטרפה. ...ז משובחת בזיבול ...ה וחריעה [רשב"ם ב"ב קנז:].

ג) כולו לא גבי הבעל חוב מן המקבל מתנה שבח ובזה אמר יפה כח המתנה מכח המכר. תניא המוכר שדהו לחבירו ובא בעל חוב וטרפה אם השבח יותר על ההוצאה כו' פי' כגון שקנאה בק' והוציא י' כספים ושוה עתה ק"כ נוטל בע"ח השדה כולה והשבח כמות שהוא ונותן לקונה י' כספים שהוציא על השדה וחוזר הקונה ונוטל מן המוכר ק"י כספים ואם ההוצאה יתירה על השבח כגון שהוציא עליה כ' ושוה עכשיו ק"י אין לו מבע"ח אלא י' כספים מן ההוצאה כשיעור השבח שהשביח בקרקע ונוטל ק' מן המוכר ומפסיד י' הלוקח. וזו שנוטל הקונה חלק בקרקע הוא נוטל.

חשק שלמה על ר"ח א) עי' בר"ף לקמן דף יח גבי מימרא דר"נ באמרו לו ב"ד לא מן לו סי' ע"ש היטב. ב) אולי צ"ל שאין כתוב בה זה כלל.

ɔmmitment to pay the *se'ah* of grain? This is prohibited! ikewise, the interest-appearing compensation for improve-ıents should not be permitted because of the seller's pre-ɔmmitment. – ? –

The Gemara answers:

לֵי אָמַר – **[Rav Yosef] told [Abaye]:** הָתָם הַלְוָאָה – **There** it is case of **a loan,** for which the laws of interest are more stringent. וְהָכָא זְבִי – **Here** it is a case of **a purchase,** for which the laws of ıterest are less stringent.[21]

The Gemara discusses a creditor's rights to seize the improve-ıents to the debtor's sold land:

גּוּפָ – Let us return to Shmuel's statement **itself:** אָמַר שְׁמוּאֵל – **Shmuel said:** בַּעַל חוֹב גּוֹבֶה אֶת הַשְּׁבָח – **The** seller's **creditor ollects the improvements** of the land from the purchaser. אָמַר רָבָ – **Rava said:** תֵּדַע – **You should know** this is true, nd the purchaser may not prevent him by claiming the improve-ıents are his,[22] שֶׁכַּךְ כּוֹתֵב לוֹ מוֹכֵר לַלּוֹקֵחַ – **for this** is the text f the bill of sale that **the seller writes to the purchaser:** אֲנָא אֵיקוּ – **I will stand** וַאֲשַׁפֵּי – **and silence** וַאֲדַכֵּי – **and urify** וַאֲמָרֵיק זְבִינֵי אִילֵּין – **and cleanse this sale** from all rotest. אִינּוּן – This concerns **[the properties purchased],** וְעַמְלֵיהּ – **and their expenses** [i.e. the money you spend to nprove them], וְשִׁבְחֵיהוֹן – **and their improvements** [i.e. the alue of the improvements in excess of the expenses].[23] וְאֵיקוּם קֳדָמָ – **And I will stand before you** in this agreement. וּצְבִי וּבִינָא דְּ – The witnesses add: **And our** [i.e. this] **purchaser has greed** to these conditions, וְקַבִּיל עֲלוֹהִי – **and he accepted** hese terms **upon himself.**[24] Since the seller will compensate the urchaser for his improvements, the creditor may collect them rom the purchaser.[25]

אָמַר לֵיהּ רַב חִיָּיא בַּר אָבִין לְרָבָ – **Rav Chiya bar Avin said to ava:** אֶלָּא מֵעַתָּה – **But now,** if this logic is true, מַתָּנָה דְּלָא כָּתִיב לֵיהּ הָ – from the recipient of **a gift, to whom [the enefactor] does not write [this guarantee],**[26] הָכִי נַמִּי דְּלָא טָרִיף שְׁבָח – **would [the benefactor's creditor] not** be entitled ɔ **seize the improvements,** since the beneficiary would not be ompensated by the benefactor? אָמַר לֵיהּ – **[Rava] told [Rav Chiya]:** אִין – **Yes,** it is true. The improvements may not be eized from the beneficiary.

Rav Chiya asks:

וְכִי יָפֶה כֹּחַ מַתָּנָה מִמֶּכֶ – **Is the strength of a gift greater than hat of a sale?** אָמַר לֵיהּ – **[Rava] told [Rav Chiya]:** אִין יָפֶה וְיָפֶ – **Yes,** it is **definitely stronger** than a sale in this respect! ince the beneficiary cannot receive compensation from the benefactor, the creditor may not seize the improvements of the land.[27]

The Gemara adduces proof for Shmuel's ruling that a creditor may collect the improvements of the debtor's sold land:

אָמַר רַב נַחְמָן – **Rav Nachman said:** הָא מַתְנִיתָא מְסַיַּיע לֵיהּ לְמַר שְׁמוּאֵל – **The** following **Baraisa supports** the ruling of **the Master, Shmuel,** וְהוּנָא חַבְרִין מוֹקִים לָהּ בְּמִילֵּי אַחֲרִינֵי – **but our colleague Huna interprets [the Baraisa]** as **referring to a different case.** דְּתַנְיָא – **As it was taught in a Baraisa:** הַמּוֹכֵר שָׂדֶה לַחֲבֵירוֹ – IF ONE SELLS A FIELD TO HIS FELLOW, וַהֲרֵי הִיא יוֹצְאָה מִתַּחַת יָדוֹ – AND IT later LEAVES [THE PURCHASER'S] POSSESSION. כְּשֶׁהוּא גּוֹבֶה – WHEN [THE PURCHASER] COLLECTS compensation from the seller for his loss, גּוֹבֶה אֶת הַקֶּרֶן מִנְּכָסִים מְשׁוּעְבָּדִים – HE COLLECTS for THE PRINCIPAL FROM ENCUMBERED PROPERTIES, וּשְׁבָח גּוֹבֶה מִנְּכָסִים בְּנֵי חוֹרִין – AND HE COLLECTS for THE IMPROVEMENTS FROM PROPERTIES FREE OF ENCUMBER-ANCE. Rav Nachman argues that the Baraisa refers to land seized by a creditor. Since the seller must compensate the purchaser for his lost improvements from his unsold property, it is clear that his creditor may seize these improvements from the purchaser. וְהוּנָא חַבְרִין מוֹקִים לָהּ בְּמִילֵּי אַחֲרִינֵי – **However, our colleague Huna interprets [the Baraisa]** as **referring to a different case:** בְּלוֹקֵחַ מִגַּזְלָן – **when one purchases from a robber.** Although the Baraisa indicates that the rightful owner may seize the improvements from the purchaser of his stolen land, a creditor may not likewise seize the improvements from the purchaser of his debtor's land.[28]

The Gemara analyzes a Baraisa in light of Shmuel's rulings:

תַּנְיָא אִידָךְ – **It was taught in another Baraisa:** הַמּוֹכֵר שָׂדֶה לַחֲבֵירוֹ – IF ONE SELLS A FIELD TO HIS FELLOW, וְהִשְׁבִּיחָהּ – AND [THE PURCHASER] IMPROVES IT, וּבָא בַּעַל חוֹב וּטְרָפָהּ – AND the seller's CREDITOR COMES AND SEIZES IT, כְּשֶׁהוּא גּוֹבֶה – WHEN [THE PURCHASER] COLLECTS compensation from the seller for his loss, אִם הַשֶּׁבַח יוֹתֵר עַל הַיְצִיאָה – IF THE value of the IMPROVE-MENTS EXCEEDS THE EXPENSES of the purchaser in generating the improvements, נוֹטֵל אֶת הַשֶּׁבַח מִבַּעַל הַקַּרְקַע – HE COLLECTS THE excess IMPROVEMENTS FROM THE OWNER OF THE LAND [i.e. from the seller],[29] וְהַיְצִיאָה מִבַּעַל חוֹב – AND THE EXPENSES FROM THE CREDITOR. וְאִם הַיְצִיאָה יְתֵירָה עַל הַשֶּׁבַח – IF THE EXPENSES EXCEED THE value of the IMPROVEMENTS, אֵין לוֹ אֶלָּא הוֹצָאָה שִׁיעוּר שֶׁבַח מִבַּעַל חוֹב – [THE PURCHASER] COLLECTS compensa-tion FROM THE CREDITOR ONLY for THE EXPENSES UP TO THE VALUE OF THE IMPROVEMENTS. His additional expenses are not

NOTES

nprovements therefore do not resemble interest (see *Rashi*).

1. See note 18.

2. Since the property was improved due to the purchaser's efforts and while in his possession, one would logically assume that the creditor ɔuld not seize the improvements without compensating the purchaser. Nevertheless, Shmuel states that the creditor may seize them without aying the purchaser. Rava explains why this is so (*Rashba*).

3. The Rishonim ask how Rava knows that the seller intends to uarantee compensation in the event of seizure by a creditor; perhaps it s in case the field is discovered to be stolen and is seized by its rightful wner. *Tosafos* answer that the omission of a guarantee for seizure of ipe produce indicates that the seller's intention is for a creditor's ollection, since a creditor does not collect ripe produce. An owner who epossesses his field, however, collects even ripe produce.

4. The purchaser accepted that a creditor may collect the improve-ıents from him (*Tosefos Shantz* in *Shitah Mekubetzes*).

5. Although the purchaser should logically be allowed to retain his nprovements, the Sages allowed the creditor to collect them since the urchaser will not sustain a loss (see *Rashi*).

26. A benefactor generally does not guarantee his gift as a seller does his sale.

27. Since the creditor does not hold a mortgage on the improvements (only on the land), he can seize them only where the one from whom they are seized does not sustain a loss. In the case of a sale, the purchaser will be able to recover his loss from the seller, pursuant to the seller's guarantee. A recipient of a gift, however, has no guarantee from his benefactor and would therefore sustain a loss if his improvements were seized. Therefore, the creditor may not seize them.

The mortgaged land itself, however, may be seized even from one who received it as a gift, because the creditor may rightfully argue that the recipient should not have accepted a gift that was mortgaged to him without leaving him property from which to collect the debt (see *Rashi*).

28. The owner may claim the improvements, to his stolen land, because they accrued to his field. A creditor, however, may not claim the improvements, since the field is not his until he collects it. The improvements, therefore, rightfully belong to the purchaser, since the field is his until it is seized (*Rashi*).

29. The purchaser argues that the excess improvements were seized by the creditor in payment of the seller's debt; he should therefore be

כשעמד בדין על הקרן ולא על הפירות. תימה אם כן מאי מפני תיקון העולם הלא בדין לא גבי דמלוה על פה לא גבי ממשעבדי ויש לומר דאי לאו מפני תיקון העולם הוה אמינא הואיל ועמד בדין על הקרן יש קול גם לפירות:

שנטלוה מסיקין [א]בא נגזל לגבות קרן גובה מנכסים משועבדים בא נגזל לגבות פירות גובה מנכסים בני חורין רבא לא אמר כרבה בר רב הונא הרי היא יוצאה מתחת ידו בדינא משמע ורבה בר רב הונא לא אמר כרבא הרי היא יוצאה מתחת ידו בעינא משמע רב אשי אמר לצדדין קתני כגון שגזל שדה מחבירו מלאה פירות ואכל את הפירות ומכר את השדה בא לוקח לגבות קרן גובה מנכסים משועבדים בא נגזל לגבות פירות גובה מנכסים בני חורין בין לרבא בין לרבה בר רב הונא מלוה על פה הוא [ב]ומלוה על פה אינו גובה מנכסים משועבדים הכא במאי עסקינן [ג]כשעמד בדין והדר זבין אי הכי פירות נמי כשעמד בדין על הקרן ולא עמד בדין על הפירות ומאי פסקא סתמא דמילתא כי תבע איניש קרנא תבע ברישא וסבר שמואל לוקח מגזלן לית ליה שבחא והא א"ל שמואל לרב חיננא בר שילת אמליך וכתוב שופרא שבחא ופירי במאי אי בבעל חוב מי אית ליה פירי [א)]והאמר שמואל בעל חוב גובה את השבח שבח אין אבל פירות לא אלא לאו בלוקח מגזלן אמר רב יוסף הכא במאי עסקינן כגון שיש לו קרקע א"ל אביי וכי מותר ללות סאה בסאה במקום שיש לו קרקע א"ל התם הלואה הכא זביני איכא דאמרי אמר רב יוסף הכא במאי עסקינן כגון [ג)]שקנו מידו א"ל אביי וכי מותר ללות סאה בסאה במקום שקנו מידו א"ל התם הלואה והכא זביני: גופא אמר שמואל בעל חוב גובה את השבח אמר רבא תדע שכך כותב לו מוכר ללוקח אנא איקום ואשפי ואדכי ואמריק זביני אילין אינון ועמליהון ושבחיהון ואיקום קדמך וצבי זבינא דנן וקביל עלוהי א"ל רב חייא בר אבין לרבא אלא מעתה מתנה דלא כתיב ליה הכי ה"נ [ד]דלא טריף שבחא א"ל אין וכי יפה כח מתנה ממכר א"ל אין [°]יפה ויפה אמר רב נחמן הא מתניתא מסייע ליה למר שמואל [°]והונא חברין מוקים לה במילי אחריני דתניא המוכר שדה לחבירו והרי היא יוצאה מתחת ידו [ה]כשהוא גובה גובה את הקרן מנכסים משועבדים ושבח גובה מנכסים בני חורין והונא חברין מוקים לה במילי אחריני בלוקח מגזלן תניא אידך המוכר שדה לחבירו והשביחה ובא בעל חוב וטרפה [ו]כשהוא גובה אם השבח יותר על היציאה נוטל את השבח מבעל הקרקע והיציאה מבעל חוב ואם היציאה יתירה על השבח אין לו אלא הוצאה שיעור שבח מבעל חוב והא שמואל במאי מוקים לה אי [ז]בלוקח מגזלן קשיא רישא דאמר שמואל לוקח מגזלן לית ליה שבחא אי בבעל חוב קשיא רישא וסיפא דאמר שמואל בעל חוב גובה את השבח איבעית אימא בלוקח מגזלן כגון שיש לו קרקע אי נמי בשקנו מידו איבעית אימא בבעל חוב ולא קשיא כאן בשבח המגיע

**רש"י**

שנטלוה מסיקין. אנסים עכו"ם נטלוה מן הגזלן ומחמתו ותנן בבבא קמא (דף קטז:) הגוזל שדה מחבירו ונטלוה מסיקין אם מחמת הגזלן חייב להעמיד לו שדה אחר והרי היא יוצאה מתחת ידו דקתני בנטילת מסיקין הוא: בדינא משמע. הלכך בהוצאת גזל קאמר וגובה את הקרן דקאמר כשחפר בו בורות: בעינא משמע. כמו שהיתה ולא שחפר בה בורות: ומכר את השדה. והרי היא יוצאה מתחת ידו של לוקח בדינא ובעינא: בין לרבה בין לרבא. דמוקמי גביית קרן מן הגזלן בנגזל הא מלוה על פה הוא ולא טרפא ממשעבדי: כשעמד בדין. קודם שמכר נכסיו וכיון דחייבוהו ב"ד אית ליה קלא והוה ליה כמלוה בשטר: מאי פסקא. בתמיה פסקא תנא למלתיה דהעומד בדין אינו עומד על הפירות: רב חיננא בר שילת. סופר היה: אמליך. כשאתה כותב שטר המלך במוכר אם יקבל עליו להגבות ללוקח משפר נכסיו קרנא ושבחא ופרי אם יטרפוה ממנו: כגון שיש לו קרקע. לגזלן זה שמגבהו ללוקח קרקע ולא מעות דהשתא לא מחזי כרבית: אסור ללות סאה בסאה. שמא יוקרו חטין: בהלואה. שייך רבית טפי ממכר: שקנו מידו. על השבח דהוה ליה מחויב מעת המכר קודם שיש שכר המתנת מעות: תדע. דגובה ולא מצי לוקח למימר אנא אשבחי: שכך כותב לו מוכר ללוקח. באחריות שטר המכר: ואשפי. אסקיט ודומה לו על הר נשפה דמתרגם על טורא שליוא (ישעיה יג): ואדכי. אטהר מכל ערעור: אינון ועמליהון ושבחיהון. וכיון דעל מוכר הדר גבי שבחא בעל חוב מלוקח וחוזר הלוקח על המוכר: מתנה דלא כתיב ביה הכי. שאין אדם מקבל עליו אחריות מה שהוא נותן: ה"נ. דאם נותן נכסיו במתנה לא גבי בעל חוב שבחא הואיל ולא הדר על הנותן: וכי יפה כח מתנה כו'. בתמיה: יפה ויפה. בדבר זה דכיון דלא הדר גבי ליה לא מפסיד ליה במידי דלא אפסדיה לבעל חוב דבשלמא גופה של קרקע א"ל אמאי [ג)](זבנתיה) מאין אגבה חובי אבל שבחא א"ל מאי אפסדתיך: מסייע ליה למר שמואל. דבעל חוב גובה את השבח: כשהוא גובה. כשלוקח חוזר וגובה מן המוכר: במילי אחריני. בדבר אחר: בלוקח מגזלן. דנגזל ודאי טריף שבחא דאמר ליה ארעאי אשבח אבל בעל חוב כל כמה דלא טרפה לה לאו דידיה הוא וברשותא דלוקח אשבח: על הוצאה. שהוציא הלוקח בשבחה: נוטל. הלוקח: את השבח מבעל הקרקע. מה שעודף על היציאה דאמר ליה פרעתי את חובך: אין לו. ללוקח אלא מן היציאה שהוציא בה פורע לו שיעור שבח והשאר מפסיד: אי בלוקח מגזלן. האי בע"ח היינו נגזל: קשיא רישא. דקתני נוטל את השבח מבעל הקרקע: קשיא רישא וסיפא. דקתני בע"ח נותן את היציאה ולשמואל בעל חוב גובה השבח ואינו נותן כלום:

המגיע

**תוספות**

כגון שקנו מידו. וא"ת א"כ אמאי קאמר אמליך הלא סתם קנין לכתיבה עומד וי"ל ה"מ כגון שהקנה לו דבר שהוא בעין דכיון דיפה כחו לעשות קנין רוצה שיכתבו לו:

בעל חוב גובה את השבח. נראה דגבי אפי' מן השבח שהשביחו יתומים אע"פ שאין להם על מי לחזור והוה ליה כמתנה דאמרינן לקמן דלא גבי שבחא מ"מ גובה מהן משום דכרעיה דאבוהון נינהו כדמוכח בפרק יש בכור (בכורות דף נב. ושם) דתנן אין הבכור נוטל פי שנים בראוי כבמוחזק ולא בשבח ולא האשה בכתובתה ולא הבנות במזונותיהן ופריך בגמרא והאמר שמואל בעל חוב גובה את השבח ומשני מקולי כתובה שנו כאן ומזון בנות נמי תנאי כתובה ככתובה דמי והתם משבח יתומים איירי דאי משבח לקוחות אם כן מאי איריא דלא טרפי בנות משבח והלא מגוף הקרקע נמי לא טרפי דאין מוציאין למזון האשה והבנות מנכסים משועבדים אלא ודאי בשבח יתומים איירי ודוקא כתובת אשה ומזונות דקילי לא גבו משבח אבל שאר בע"ח גבי ורש"י פירש התם מזון הבנות כגון נשא אשה ופסק לזון בתה ה' שנים ולפירושו אין ראיה דמאי איירי בשבח לקוחות אך לא נהירא דלא שייך בהו תנאי כתובה והא דאמר בהמקבל (לקמן דף קי.) יתומים אומרים אנו השבחנו ואין השבח שלך משמע דלא גבי משבח יתומים התם איירי כשעשה אפותיקי ואומרים אנו השבחנו ותן לנו היציאה כדין יורד לתוך שדה חבירו שלא ברשות וכן מוקי התם במסקנא כשעשאה אפותיקי:

תדע שכך כתב כו'. אין לפרש דהכי מוכח דבע"ח גובה את השבח דבשביל דבע"ח גובה את השבח כותב מוכר ללוקח שישלם לו את השבח דא"כ מאי פריך מתנה דלא כתיב בה (א) הכי נמי דלא טריף שבח והלא אין תלוי גביית הבע"ח בכתיבת המוכר אלא יש לומר מדמשלם מוכר ללוקח את השבח אין לחוש אם יגבהו בעל חוב ממנו דאין הלוקח מפסיד כל כך וא"ת ומאי ראיה (ג) היא דלמא מיירי בלוקח מגזלן דנגזל ודאי אית ליה שבחא וי"ל דאי בלוקח מן הגזלן איירי הוה ליה למכתב נמי [ד)]ופיריהון אלא מיירי בבעל חוב דלית ליה פירי אי נמי מדקאמר ועמליהון היינו הוצאה ושבחיהון היינו השבח היתר על היציאה ואי בנגזל הא נגזל גופיה יהיב ליה יציאה כדין יורד לתוך שדה חבירו שלא ברשות:

הא

**עין משפט נר מצוה**

קכה א מיי' פ"ט מהל' גזילה ואבידה הל' ב ג סמג עשין עג טוש"ע ח"מ סי' שעב סעיף א:
קכו ב מיי' פי"א מהל' מלוה ולוה הל' ד סמג עשין לד טוש"ע ח"מ סי' לט סעיף א וסי' קיא סעיף א:
קכז ג מיי' פ"ט מהל' גזילה ואבידה הל' ד סמג עשין עג טוש"ע ח"מ סי' שעב סעיף א וסעיף ב:
קכח ד מיי' פכ"א מהל' מלוה ולוה הל' ג סמג עשין לה טוש"ע ח"מ סי' קטו סעיף ג:
קכט ה מיי' שם הל' א טוש"ע שם סעיף א:
קל ו ז מיי' פ"ט מהל' גזילה הל' ו סמג עשין פג טוש"ע ח"מ סי' שעג סעיף א וע"ש ובר"ף:

**רבינו חננאל**

רבה בר רב הונא אמר כגון שגזל שדה ונטלוה מסיקין מחמתו בא נגזל לגבות דמי השדה גובה אפי' ממשעבדי בא לגבות דמי פירות אינו גובה אלא מבני חרי. ומקשי' בין לרבא דאמר דמי היזק חפירות בורות שיחין ומערות ובין לרבה בר רב הונא דאמר דמי השדה שנטלוה מסיקין אמאי טריף ממשעבדי מלוה על פה היא ומלוה על פה אינו גובה (אלא) ממשעבדי. ופרקי' הכא במאי עסקינן כגון שתבע הנגזל לגזלן בב"ד וחייבוהו ב"ד לשלם ואחר שנתחייב הלך ומכר נכסיו בזה הדין לטרוף הנגזל כל הנכסין שמכר הגזלן מאחר שנתחייב בב"ד א) מיהא שמעינן חיוב ב"ד לאדם לשלם כמלוה בשטר דמי וגבי אפי' ממשעבדי. הא דאמר שמואל אימליך ובתר הכי כתוב שופרא שבחא ופירי כלומר לא תכתוב אלו עד שתימלך במקנה ויאמר לו כתוב שהללו מעין תורפי השטר [הן] חשובין ולא מטופסא דשטרא שאין בהן ממש. ומקשי' ואי בבעל חוב שמואל מי אמר דאית ליה פירי והא איהו דאמר בעל חוב גובה את השבח שבח אין פירי לא. ופריק רב יוסף בשיש ללוה קרקע. איכא דאמרי בשקנו מידו. ומקשי עלה אביי וכי מותר ללות סאה בסאה למי שיש לו קרקע או למי שקנו מידו. ופריק רב יוסף האי בהלואה אסור אבל בזביני שרי. ואע"ג דאמר רב נחמן קרקע אין לו כלומר כיון שנטרפה שדה זו מידיו נמצא כאילו לא היתה מכירתו מכירה וכי זה השבח או הפירות שכר מעותיו הוא נוטלה הא אמר רב יוסף כי האי גוונא בזביני שרי. ומסקנא דשמעתא הנותן שדהו מתנה ובא בעל חוב לטורפה אינו גובה השבח דלא גבי בעל חוב השבח אלא מן הקונה שדה משועבדת לבעל חוב ודייק רבא מדפריש בשטר זביני אנא אשפי ואמרק ואדכי זביני אילין אינון ועמליהון ושבחיהון ואוקים קדמך וצבי זבינא דנן וקביל עילויה משום הכי גבי בעל חוב שבחא דהא קביל עליה המוכר ונתרצה הקונה בזה אבל המתנה שאין כתוב בה זה

**מסורת הש"ס**

[fragmentary, right edge cut off in scan] ...יל יד: וש"נ, לקמן נח., לד., בבא ...ג.], ג) קבלתיה, ...ם"ל, ועיין מהרש"א, עי' היטב תוס' גיטין ...ד"ה לפי שאין וכו' וקל"ע].

**הגהות הב"ח**

(א) תוס' ד"ה תדע וכו' כתיב בה הכי הכי: (ג) בא"ד וא"ת ראיה דלמא ההיא מיירי:

**גליון הש"ס**

...יפה ויפה. עיין כ"ב ...נג ע"א תוס' ד"ה ...: שם והונא ...יין. קדושין מז ע"א:

**ליקוטי רש"י**

...בע"ח וטרפה. ...יא משובחת בזיבול ...שה חריעה [רשב"ם ב"ב קנז:].

ג) כולו לא גבי הבעל חוב מן המקבל מתנה שבח ובזה אמר יפה כח המתנה מכח המכר. תניא המוכר שדהו לחבירו ובא בעל חוב וטרפה אם השבח יותר על ההוצאה כו' פי' כגון שקנאה בק' והוציא י' כספים ושוה עתה ק"כ נוטל בע"ח השדה כולה והשבח כמות שהוא ונותן לקונה י' כספים שהוציא על השדה וחוזר הקונה ונוטל מן המוכר ק"י כספים ואם ההוצאה יתירה על השבח כגון שהוציא עליה כ' ושוה עכשיו ק"י אין לו מבע"ח אלא י' כספים מן ההוצאה כשיעור השבח שהשביח בקרקע ונוטל ק' מן המוכר ומפסיד י' הלוקח. וזו שנוטל הקונה חלק בקרקע הוא נוטל.

חשק שלמה על ר"ח א) עי' בר"ף לקמן דף ח גבי מימרא דר"נ באמרו לו ב"ד לא תן לו כו' ע"ש היטיב. ב) אולי צ"ל שאין כתוב בה זה כלל.

The Gemara responds:
סְתָמָא דְּמִילְּתָא כִּי תָּבַע אִינִישׁ – **This is the regular procedure,** for **when a person demands** compensation, קַרְנָא תָּבַע בְּרֵישָׁא – **he first demands** compensation for the **principal.** It is therefore logical for the Tanna to discuss a case in which the robber's encumbered property was sold after he was obligated by the court to compensate the owner for the lost principal, but before he was obligated to compensate the owner for the produce.

The Gemara now returns to analyze Shmuel's ruling, as related by Rav Nachman:[12]
וְסָבַר שְׁמוּאֵל לוֹקֵחַ מִגַּזְלָן לֵית לֵיהּ שְׁבָחָא – **And does Shmuel** actually **hold that one who purchases** stolen land **from a robber does not receive compensation** for the improvements he added to the land before it was repossessed, even if the seller specified that he would be compensated for these improvements? וְהָא אָמַר לֵיהּ שְׁמוּאֵל לְרַב חִינָּנָא בַּר שֵׁילַת – **But Shmuel instructed Rav Chinana bar Shilas,** the scribe: אַמְלִיךְ – When you write a bill of sale for land, **inquire** of the seller whether he agrees to obligate himself to the purchaser for collection of lost principal, improvements and produce, from his best property, וּכְתוֹב – **and** then **record** in the document that if the land is seized he agrees to compensate the purchaser שׁוּפְרָא – from his **best** property, שְׁבָחָא – for the purchaser's **improvements,** וּפֵירֵי – **and** for the ripe **produce.**

The Gemara explains Shmuel's instructions:
בְּמַאי – **Regarding what** case of seizure did Shmuel issue his instructions? אִי בְּבַעַל חוֹב – **If** he referred to seizure **by a creditor,** his instructions are incorrect, מִי אִית לֵיהּ פֵּירֵי – for **is [the creditor] entitled to** seize the ripe **produce** together with the land? וְהָאָמַר שְׁמוּאֵל – **But Shmuel said:** בַּעַל חוֹב גּוֹבֶה אֶת הַשְּׁבָח – **The** seller's **creditor collects the improvements** of the land from the purchaser. שְׁבָח אִין – We deduce that he **indeed** collects the **improvements,** אֲבָל פֵּירוֹת לֹא – **but not** ripe **produce.**[13] Therefore, Shmuel could not have been referring to seizure by a creditor.
אֶלָּא לָאו בְּלוֹקֵחַ מִגַּזְלָן – **Rather, is** Shmuel **not referring to** compensation for **a purchaser** of stolen land **from a robber,** from whom the owner may seize the produce?[14] Apparently, Shmuel holds that the purchaser of stolen land is compensated by the seller for his lost improvements, in contradiction to Rav Nachman's ruling in his name. – ? –

The Gemara answers:
אָמַר רַב יוֹסֵף – **Rav Yosef said:** הָכָא בְּמַאי עַסְקִינַן – **What are we discussing here?** כְּגוֹן שֶׁיֵּשׁ לוֹ קַרְקַע – **For instance, when [the robber] has land** which he gives the purchaser as compensation for his lost principal and improvements. The additional payment for the improvements, therefore, does not appear as interest for the "loaned" money.[15]

The Gemara objects:
אָמַר לֵיהּ אַבָּיֵי – **Abaye told [Rav Yosef]:** וְכִי מוּתָּר לִלְווֹת סְאָה בִּסְאָה – **And is it permitted to loan a *se'ah*** of grain **for** payment of **a *se'ah*** of grain at a later date, בְּמָקוֹם שֶׁיֵּשׁ לוֹ קַרְקַע – **in a situation where [the borrower] has land** and will pay land equivalent to the value of a *se'ah* of grain? Even this is forbidden as interest![16] Likewise, the interest-appearing compensation for improvements should not be permitted even if the seller offers land, and not money, as compensation.[17] – ? –

The Gemara answers:
אָמַר לֵיהּ – **[Rav Yosef] told [Abaye]:** הָתָם הַלְוָאָה – **There** it is a case of **a loan,** for which the laws of interest are more stringent. הָכָא זְבִינֵי – **Here** it is a case of **a purchase,** for which the laws of interest are less stringent.[18]

The Gemara presents a different version of Rav Yosef's explanation of Shmuel's instructions to the scribe, which also upholds Rav Nachman's ruling:
אִיכָּא דְּאָמְרֵי – **There are those who say** that אָמַר רַב יוֹסֵף – **Rav Yosef said:** הָכָא בְּמַאי עַסְקִינַן – **What are we discussing here?** כְּגוֹן שֶׁקָּנוּ מִיָּדוֹ – **For instance, when [the witnesses] acquired from [the robber]** a commitment to pay for the purchaser's lost improvements if the land is seized from the purchaser by its owner.[19] Since the robber pre-commits himself to the additional payment, it is not considered as interest.[20]

The Gemara objects:
אָמַר לֵיהּ אַבָּיֵי – **Abaye said to [Rav Yosef]:** וְכִי מוּתָּר לִלְווֹת סְאָה בִּסְאָה – **And is it permitted to loan a *se'ah*** of grain **for** payment of **a *se'ah*** of grain at a later date, בְּמָקוֹם שֶׁקָּנוּ מִיָּדוֹ – **in a situation where they initially acquired from [the borrower]** a

NOTES

12. Above, 14b.

13. See 14b note 26.

14. See 14b note 27.

15. The Gemara above (14b) commented that Shmuel holds that the money forwarded to the seller by the purchaser is viewed as a loan, and compensation for the improvements resembles interest (see 14b notes 11 and 12). Our Gemara comments that when the robber compensates the purchaser with land, but not money, the additional payment for the improvements does not resemble interest (*Rashi*). Instead, we view the seller's conveyance of land as a discounted sale to the purchaser in exchange for the money the seller originally paid (see *Ra'avad,* cited in *Shitah Mekubetzes*).

16. The Mishnah below (75a) prohibits the loan of commodities for the payment of equivalent commodities at a later date. *Rashi* and *Tosafos* ad loc. (ד״ה הלוהי) explain that this practice is prohibited because if the price of the loaned commodity rises, the additional value of the repayment is considered as interest. The Gemara there does not stipulate that if the borrower owns land, it is permitted.

17. Although the interest-prohibition of "loaning a *se'ah* for a *se'ah*" is only Rabbinic, there is no leniency where the borrower owns land. Similarly, Abaye argues, there should be no such leniency for the Rabbinic interest-prohibition of compensation for improvements.

18. Although we regard the transfer of money from the purchaser as a loan (see 14b note 11), the purchaser certainly did not *intend* it to be a loan. Rather, the money was initially given as a payment for land, and it is only in retrospect that it is viewed as a loan (see R' Chananel). Therefore, the Sages are more lenient with regard to the interest-prohibition in this case.

*Ritva* brings the Gemara's answer into sharper focus. There are two cases of Rabbinically prohibited interest: one that the Rabbis labeled as a form of interest, and one that is really not interest at all, but merely *resembles* interest. The case of "a *se'ah* for a *se'ah,*" since it involves a loan, is Rabbinically forbidden because it is a form of interest. Therefore, there are no special leniencies for it. Compensation for improvements, on the other hand, is not interest at all, since it does not involve a loan. Rather, it is forbidden merely because it resembles interest; consequently, it has leniencies not applied to the former category of Rabbinically prohibited interest.

19. One can obligate himself to another through a procedure known as קִנְיַן סוּדָר, *acquisition by the cloth.* The obligor lifts up a cloth belonging to the obligee and thereby commits himself to make a payment to the obligee. Commonly, the obligor lifts a cloth belonging to the witnesses, who act as agents of the obligee. Hence, in our case, the witnesses used their cloth to obligate the seller to compensate the purchaser in the event that the land is later discovered to be stolen and his improvements are seized.

20. The Gemara below (63b) notes that the general rule concerning interest is that any compensation offered by the borrower to the lender for the time he was without his money is prohibited. In this case, however, the seller agrees to pay for the improvements even before he has retained the purchaser's money for any amount of time. The payments for

שנטלוה מסיקין ^א^בא נגזל לגבות קרן גובה מנכסים משועבדים בא נגזל לגבות פירות גובה מנכסים בני חורין רבא לא אמר כרבה בר רב הונא הרי היא יוצאה מתחת ידו בדינא משמע ורבה בר רב הונא לא אמר כרבא הרי היא יוצאה מתחת ידו בעינא משמע רב אשי אמר לצדדין קתני כגון שגזל שדה מחבירו מלאה פירות ואכל את הפירות ומכר את השדה בא לוקח לגבות קרן גובה מנכסים משועבדים בא נגזל לגבות פירות גובה מנכסים בני חורין בין לרבא בין לרבה בר רב הונא מלוה על פה הוא ^ב^ומלוה על פה אינו גובה מנכסים משועבדים הכא במאי עסקינן ^ג^כשעמד בדין והדר זבין אי הכי פירות נמי כשעמד בדין על הקרן ולא עמד בדין על הפירות ומאי פסקא סתמא דמילתא כי תבע איניש קרנא תבע ברישא וסבר שמואל לוקח מגזלן לית ליה שבחא והא א"ל שמואל לרב חיננא בר שילת אמליך וכתוב שופרא שבחא ופירי במאי אי בבעל חוב מי אית ליה פירי [א] והאמר שמואל בעל חוב גובה את השבח שבח אין אבל פירות לא אלא לאו בלוקח מגזלן אמר רב יוסף הכא במאי עסקינן כגון שיש לו קרקע א"ל אביי וכי מותר ללות סאה בסאה במקום שיש לו קרקע א"ל התם הלואה הכא זביני איכא דאמרי אמר רב יוסף הכא במאי עסקינן כגון [ג] שקנו מידו א"ל אביי וכי מותר ללות סאה בסאה במקום שקנו מידו א"ל התם הלואה והכא זביני: גופא אמר שמואל בעל חוב גובה את השבח אמר רבא תדע שכך כותב לו מוכר ללוקח אנא איקום ואשפי ואדכי ואמריק זביני אילין אינון ועמליהון ושבחיהון ואיקום קדמך וצבי זבינא דנן וקביל עלוהי א"ל רב חייא בר אבין לרבא אלא מעתה מתנה דלא כתיב ליה הכי ה"נ ^ד^דלא טריף שבחא א"ל אין וכי יפה כח מתנה ממכר א"ל אין [ה] יפה ויפה אמר רב נחמן הא מתניתא מסייע ליה למר שמואל [ו] והונא חברין מוקים לה במילי אחריני דתניא המוכר שדה לחבירו והרי היא יוצאה מתחת ידו ^ה^כשהוא גובה גובה את הקרן מנכסים משועבדים ושבח גובה מנכסים בני חורין והונא חברין מוקים לה במילי אחריני בלוקח מגזלן תניא אידך המוכר שדה לחבירו והשביחה ובא בעל חוב וטרפה ^ו^כשהוא גובה אם השבח יותר על היציאה נוטל את השבח מבעל הקרקע והיציאה מבעל חוב ואם היציאה יתירה על השבח אין לו אלא הוצאה שיעור שבח מבעל חוב והא שמואל במאי מוקים לה אי ^ז^בלוקח מגזלן קשיא רישא דאמר שמואל לוקח מגזלן לית ליה שבחא אי בבעל חוב קשיא רישא וסיפא דאמר שמואל בעל חוב גובה את השבח איבעית אימא בלוקח מגזלן כגון שיש לו קרקע אי נמי בשקנו מידו איבעית אימא בבעל חוב ולא קשיא כאן בשבח המגיע

**רש"י**

שנטלוה מסיקין. אנסים עכו"ם נטלוה מן הגזלן ומחמתו ותנן בבבא קמא (דף קטז:) הגוזל שדה מחבירו ונטלוה מסיקין אם מחמת הגזלן חייב להעמיד לו שדה אחר והרי היא יוצאה מתחת ידו דקתני בנטילת מסיקין הוא: בדינא משמע. הלכך בהוצאת נגזל קאמר וגובה את הקרן דקאמר כשחפר בו בורות: בעינא משמע. כמו שהיתה ולא שחפר בה בורות: ומכר את השדה. והרי היא יוצאה מתחת ידו של לוקח בדינא ובעינא: בין לרבה בין לרבא. דמוקמי גביית קרן מן הגזלן בנגזל הא מלוה על פה הוא ולא טרפא ממשעבדי: כשעמד בדין. קודם שמכר נכסיו וכיון דחייבוהו ב"ד אית ליה קלא והוה ליה כמלוה בשטר: מאי פסקא. בתמיה פסקא תנא למלתיה דהעומד בדין אינו עומד על הפירות: רב חיננא בר שילת. סופר היה: אמליך. כשאתה כותב שטר המלך במוכר אם יקבל עליו להגבות ללוקח משפר נכסיו קרנא ושבחא ופרי אם יטרפוה ממנו: כגון שיש לו קרקע. לגזלן זה שמגבהו ללוקח קרקע ולא מעות דהשתא לא מחזי כרבית: אסור ללות סאה בסאה. שמא יוקרו חטין: בהלואה. שייך רבית טפי ממכר: שקנו מידו. על השבח דהוה ליה מחויב משעת המכר קודם שיש שכר המתנת מעות: תדע. דגובה ולא מצי לוקח למימר אנא אשבחי: שכך כותב לו מוכר ללוקח. באחריות שטר המכר: ואשפי. אשקיט ודומה לו על הר נשפה דמתרגם על טורא שליוא (ישעיה יג): ואדכי. אטהר מכל ערעור: אינון ועמליהון ושבחיהון. וכיון דעל מוכר הדר גבי שבחא בעל חוב מלוקח וחוזר הלוקח על המוכר: מתנה דלא כתיב ביה הכי. שאין אדם מקבל עליו אחריות מה שהוא נותן: ה"נ. דאם נותן נכסיו במתנה לא גבי בעל חוב שבחא הואיל ולא הדר על הנותן: וכי יפה כח מתנה כו'. בתמיה: יפה ויפה. בדבר זה דכיון דלא הדר גבי ליה לא מפסיד ליה במידי דלא אפסדיה לבעל חוב דבשלמא גופה של קרקע א"ל אמאי [ג] (זבנתיה) מאין אגבה חובי אבל שבחא א"ל מאי אפסדתיך: מסייע ליה למר שמואל. דבעל חוב גובה את השבח: כשהוא גובה. כשלוקח חוזר וגובה מן המוכר: במילי אחריני. בדבר אחר: בלוקח מגזלן. דנגזל ודאי טריף שבחא דאמר ליה ארעאי אשבח אבל בעל חוב כל כמה דלא טרפה לה לאו דידיה הוא וברשותא דלוקח אשבח: על היציאה. שהוציא הלוקח בשבחה: נוטל. הלוקח: את השבח מבעל הקרקע. מה שעודף על היציאה דאמר ליה פרעתי את חובך: אין לו. ללוקח אלא מן היציאה שהוציא בה פורע לו שיעור שבח והשאר מפסיד: אי בלוקח מגזלן. הא בע"ח היינו נגזל: קשיא רישא. דקתני נוטל את השבח מבעל הקרקע: קשיא רישא וסיפא. דקתני בע"ח נותן את היציאה ולשמואל בעל חוב גובה השבח ואינו נותן כלום:

המגיע

**תוספות**

כשעמד בדין על הקרן ולא על הפירות. תימה אם כן מאי מפני תיקון העולם הלא בדין לא גבי דמלוה על פה לא גבי ממשעבדי ויש לומר דאי לאו מפני תיקון העולם הוה אמינא הואיל ועמד בדין על הקרן יש קול גם לפירות:

כגון שקנו מידו. וא"ת א"כ אמאי קאמר אמליך הלא סתם קנין לכתיבה עומד וי"ל ה"מ כגון שהקנה לו דבר שהוא בעין דכיון דיפה כחו לעשות קנין רוצה שיכתבו לו:

בעל חוב גובה את השבח. נראה דגבי אפי' מן השבח שהשביחו יתומים אע"פ שאין להם על מי לחזור והוה ליה כמתנה דאמרינן לקמן דלא גבי שבחא מ"מ גובה מהן משום דכרעיה דאבוהון נינהו כדמוכח בפרק יש בכור (בכורות דף נב. ושם) דתנן אין הבכור נוטל פי שנים בראוי כבמוחזק ולא בשבח ולא האשה בכתובתה ולא הבנות במזונותיהן ופריך בגמרא והאמר שמואל בעל חוב גובה את השבח ומשני מקולי כתובה שנו כאן ומזון בנות נמי תנאי כתובה ככתובה דמי והתם משבח יתומים מיירי דאי משבח לקוחות אם כן מאי אריא דלא טרפי בנות משבח והלא מגוף הקרקע נמי לא טרפי דאין מוציאין למזון האשה והבנות מנכסים משועבדים אלא ודאי בשבח יתומים מיירי ודוקא כתובת אשה ומזונות דקילי לא גבו משבח אבל שאר בע"ח גבי ורש"י פירש התם מזון הבנות כגון נשא אשה ופסק לזון בתה ה' שנים ולפירושו אין ראיה דמאי מיירי בשבח לקוחות אך לא נהירא דלא שייך בהו תנאי כתובה והא דאמר בהמקבל (לקמן דף קי.) יתומים אומרים אנו השבחנו ואין השבח שלך משמע דלא גבי משבח יתומים התם מיירי כשעשה אפותיקי ואומרים אנו השבחנו ותן לנו היציאה כדין יורד לתוך שדה חבירו שלא ברשות וכן מוקי התם במסקנא כשעשאה אפותיקי:

תדע שכך כתב כו'. אין לפרש דהכי מוכח דבע"ח גובה את השבח דבשביל דבע"ח גובה את השבח כותב מוכר ללוקח שישלם לו את השבח דא"כ מאי פריך מתנה דלא כתיב בה (א) הכי נמי דלא טריף שבח והלא אין תלוי גביית הבע"ח בכתיבת המוכר אלא יש לומר מדמשלם מוכר ללוקח את השבח אין לחוש אם יגבהו בעל חוב ממנו דאין הלוקח מפסיד כל כך וא"ת ומאי ראיה (ב) היא דלמא מיירי בלוקח מגזלן דנגזל ודאי אית ליה שבחא וי"ל דאי בלוקח מן הגזלן איירי הוה ליה למכתב נמי [ד] ופיריהון אלא מיירי בבעל חוב דלית ליה פירי אי נמי מדקאמר ועמליהון היינו הוצאה ושבחיהון היינו השבח היתר על היציאה ואי בנגזל הא נגזל גופיה יהיב ליה יציאה כדין יורד לתוך שדה חבירו שלא ברשות:

הא

**עין משפט נר מצוה**

קכה א מיי' פ"ט מהל' גזילה ואבידה הל' ב ג סמג עשין עג טוש"ע ח"מ סי' שעב סעיף א:

קכו ב מיי' פי"א מהל' מלוה ולוה הל' ד סמג עשין לד טוש"ע ח"מ סי' לט סעיף א וסי' קיא סעיף א:

קכז ג מיי' פ"ט מהל' גזילה ואבידה הל' ד סמג עשין עג טוש"ע ח"מ סי' שעב סעיף א וסעיף ב:

קכח ד מיי' פכ"א מהל' מלוה ולוה הל' ג סמג עשין לה טוש"ע ח"מ סי' קטו סעיף ג:

קכט ה מיי' שם הל' א טוש"ע שם סעיף א:

קל ו ז מיי' פ"ט מהל' גזילה הל' ו סמג עשין פג טוש"ע ח"מ סי' שעג סעיף א וע"ש וברי"ף:

**רבינו חננאל**

רבה בר רב הונא אמר כגון שגזל שדה ונטלוה מסיקין מחמתו בא נגזל לגבות דמי השדה גובה אפי' ממשעבדי בא לגבות דמי פירות אינו גובה אלא מבני חרי. ומקשי' בין לרבא דאמר דמי היזק חפירות בורות שיחין ומערות ובין לרבה בר רב הונא דאמר דמי השדה שנטלוה מסיקין אמאי טריף ממשעבדי מלוה על פה היא ומלוה על פה אינו גובה (אלא) ממשעבדי. ופרקי' הכא במאי עסקינן כגון שתבע הנגזל לגזלן בב"ד וחייבוהו ב"ד לשלם ואחר שנתחייב הלך ומכר נכסיו בזה הדין לטרוף הנגזל כל הנכסין שמכר הגזלן מאחר שנתחייב בב"ד א) מיהא שמעינן חיוב ב"ד לאדם לשלם כמלוה בשטר דמי וגבי אפי' ממשעבדי. הא דאמר שמואל אימליך ובתר הכי כתוב שופרא שבחא ופירי כלומר לא תכתוב אלו עד שתימלך במקנה ויאמר לו כתוב שהללו מעין תורפי השטר [הן] חשובין ולא מטופסא דשטרא שאין בהן ממש. ומקשי' ואי בבעל חוב שמואל מי אמר דאית ליה פירי והא איהו דאמר בעל חוב גובה את השבח שבח אין פירי לא. ופריק רב יוסף בשיש ללוה קרקע. איכא דאמרי' בשקנו מידו. ומקשי עלה אביי וכי מותר ללות סאה בסאה למי שיש לו קרקע או למי שקנו מידו. ופריק רב יוסף האי בהלואה אסור אבל בזביני שרי. ואע"ג דאמר רב נחמן קרקע אין לו כלומר כיון שנטרפה שדה זו מידו נמצא כאילו לא היתה מכירתו מכירה וכי זה השבח או הפירות שכר מעותיו הוא נוטלה הא אמר רב יוסף כי האי גוונא בזביני שרי. ומסקנא דשמעתא הנותן שדהו מתנה ובא בעל חוב לטורפה אינו גובה השבח דלא גבי בעל חוב השבח אלא מן הקונה שדה משועבדת לבעל חוב ודייק רבא מדפריש בשטר זביני אנא אשפי ואמרק ואדכי זביני אילין אינון ועמליהון ושבחיהון ואוקים קדמך וצבי זבינא דנן וקביל עילויה משום הכי גבי בעל חוב שבחא דהא קביל עליה המוכר ונתרצה הקונה בזה אבל המתנה שאין כתוב בה זה ב) כולו לא גבי הבעל חוב מן המקבל מתנה שבח ובזה אמר יפה כח המתנה מכח המכר. תניא המוכר שדהו לחבירו ובא בעל חוב וטרפה אם השבח יותר על ההוצאה כו' פי' כגון שקנאה בק' והוציא י' כספים ושוה עתה ק"כ נוטל בע"ח השדה כולה והשבח כמות שהוא ונותן לקונה י' כספים שהוציא על השדה וחוזר הקונה ונוטל מן המוכר ק"י כספים ואם ההוצאה יתירה על השבח כגון שהוציא עליה כ' ושוה עכשיו ק"י אין לו מבע"ח אלא י' כספים מן ההוצאה כשיעור השבח שהשביח בקרקע ונוטל ק' מן המוכר ומפסיד י' הלוקח. וזו שנוטל הקונה חלק בקרקע הוא נוטל.

**חשק שלמה על ר"ח**

א) עי' ברי"ף לקמן דף ח גבי מימרא דר"נ באמרו לו ב"ד צא תן לו כו' עי"ש היטיב. ב) אולי צ"ל שאין כתוב בה זה כלל.

**מסורת הש"ס**

א) לעיל יד: וש"נ, [לקמן נח, לד, בבא בתרא ג.], ג) קבלתיה, רש"ל, ועיין מהרש"א, [ועי' היטב תוס' גיטין ... ד"ה לפי שאין וכו' וקל"ע].

**הגהות הב"ח**

(א) תוס' ד"ה תדע וכו' לא כתיב בה הכי הכי נמי: (ב) בא"ד וא"ת ומאי ראיה דלמא הסיא מיירי:

**גליון הש"ס**

רש"י ד"ה יפה ויפה. עיין ב"ב נג ע"א תוס' ד"ה גר: שם והונא חברין. קדושין מז ע"א:

**ליקוטי רש"י**

בא בע"ח וטרפה. והיא משובחת בזיבול וחרישה וזריעה [רשב"ם ב"ב קנז:].

**שֶׁנְּטָלוּהָ מַסִּיקִין** – if gentile **extortionists confiscated [the field]** because of the robber.[1] **בָּא נִגְזָל לִגְבּוֹת קֶרֶן** – **When the one from whom** the field **was stolen comes to collect** his lost **principal, גּוֹבֶה מִנְּכָסִים מְשׁוּעְבָּדִים** – **he collects from encumbered properties. בָּא נִגְזָל לִגְבּוֹת פֵּירוֹת** – **When the one from whom** the field **was stolen comes to collect the produce, גּוֹבֶה מִנְּכָסִים בְּנֵי חוֹרִין** – **he collects from properties free of encumberance.**

The Gemara explains why Rava and Rabbah offered differing explanations of the Baraisa:

**רָבָא לֹא אָמַר כְּרַבָּה בַּר רַב הוּנָא** – **Rava did not explain** the Baraisa **in accordance with** the explanation of **Rabbah bar Rav Huna** because **הֲרֵי הִיא יוֹצְאָה מִתַּחַת יָדוֹ** – the Baraisa's statement that [THE FIELD] LEAVES [THE ROBBER'S] POSSESSION **בְּדִינָא מַשְׁמַע** – **implies** that the field leaves **by legal means,** and not by illegal force, as through extortionists.[2] **וְרַבָּה בַּר רַב הוּנָא לֹא אָמַר כְּרָבָא** – **And Rabbah bar Rav Huna did not explain** the Baraisa **in accordance with** the explanation of **Rava** because **הֲרֵי הִיא יוֹצְאָה מִתַּחַת יָדוֹ** – the Baraisa's statement that [THE FIELD] LEAVES [THE ROBBER'S] POSSESSION **בְּעֵינָא מַשְׁמַע** – **implies** that the field leaves in its **original,** undamaged state, and not after depletion by digging.

A third explanation of the Baraisa, that does not refute Rav Nachman:

**רַב אַשִׁי אָמַר** – **Rav Ashi said: לִצְדָדִין קָתָנֵי** – **The Baraisa is teaching** independent rulings **for** two **separate** claimants:[3] **כְּגוֹן** – **For instance, שֶׁגָּזַל שָׂדֶה מֵחֲבֵירוֹ מְלֵאָה פֵּירוֹת** – **if one stole a produce-filled field from his fellow וְאָכַל אֶת הַפֵּירוֹת** – **and consumed the produce, וּמָכַר אֶת הַשָּׂדֶה** – **and sold the field,** and the field was then repossessed by its owner.[4] **בָּא לוֹקֵחַ לִגְבּוֹת קֶרֶן** – When **the purchaser comes to collect** his lost **principal** from the robber, **גּוֹבֶה מִנְּכָסִים מְשׁוּעְבָּדִים** – **he collects from encumbered properties. בָּא נִגְזָל לִגְבּוֹת פֵּירוֹת** – **When the one from whom** the field **was stolen comes to collect the produce** from the robber, **גּוֹבֶה מִנְּכָסִים בְּנֵי חוֹרִין** – **he collects from properties free of encumberance.**[5]

The Gemara analyzes the explanations of Rava and Rabbah: **בֵּין לְרָבָא בֵּין לְרַבָּה בַּר רַב הוּנָא** – **Both according to Rava and Rabbah bar Rav Huna,** who explained the Baraisa that the owner claims compensation for his lost principal from the robber, **מִלְוָה עַל פֶּה הוּא** – **it is an unrecorded obligation,**[6] **וּמִלְוָה עַל פֶּה אֵינוֹ גּוֹבֶה מִנְּכָסִים מְשׁוּעְבָּדִים** – **and one may not collect an unrecorded obligation from encumbered properties.**[7] If so, why does the Baraisa permit collection of the principal from the robber's encumbered property?

The Gemara answers:

**הָכָא בְּמַאי עַסְקִינַן** – **What are we discussing here? כְּשֶׁעָמַד בְּדִין** – **When [the robber] stood in judgment** concerning the stolen field and was found liable, **וְהָדַר זַבִּין** – **and subsequently sold** other property. Since the robber was obligated by the court, the obligation may be collected from any subsequently sold land.[8]

The Gemara challenges:

**אִי הָכִי** – **If so,** that the robber was obligated by the court, **פֵּירוֹת נַמִּי** – compensation for **the produce also** should be collected from sold property![9] Why does the Baraisa say it may be collected only from unsold property?

The Gemara answers:

**כְּשֶׁעָמַד בְּדִין עַל הַקֶּרֶן** – The Baraisa refers to a case **where [the robber] stood in judgment concerning the principal, וְלֹא עָמַד בְּדִין עַל הַפֵּירוֹת** – **but did not** yet **stand in judgment concerning the produce.** Therefore, only the principal amount may be collected from sold property.[10]

The Gemara objects:

**וּמַאי פַּסְקָא** – **And does [the Tanna of the Baraisa] presume** that one is ordinarily brought to justice only for the principal and not for the produce?[11]

NOTES

1. The robber was the cause of the field's confiscation by unprincipled government officials. For example: He was apprised that government agents were planning to confiscate some properties. The robber then pointed out the stolen field to them, saying, "Take this field" (*Bava Kamma* 116b). The Mishnah in *Bava Kamma* (ibid.) teaches that in such a case the robber must compensate the owner for his lost field.

According to this explanation, the Baraisa's statement that "[the field] leaves his possession" refers to the seizure of the land from the robber by the extortionists (*Rashi*).

2. Consequently, the "collection of principal from sold property" mentioned in the Baraisa must refer to compensation for depreciation due to the robber's digging (*Rashi*).

3. I.e. the ruling concerning the compensation for lost principal does not refer to the same claimant as the ruling for the compensation for lost produce.

4. According to this explanation, the Baraisa discusses a field which is legally collected from the purchaser in its original, undepleted state (*Rashi*). [Rav Ashi thus avoids the objections raised with the first two explanations.]

5. According to this explanation as well, since the Baraisa does not mention compensation to the purchaser by the seller for produce seized by the field's rightful owner, it does not contradict Rav Nachman's ruling which forbids such payment.

6. Literally: a loan by mouth. The robber's obligation to the owner for the loss of his property was obviously not recorded in a document by the robber and the owner.

7. An obligation which is recorded in a document carries an automatic lien on the debtor's property, which may be collected in payment of this obligation even if the property is subsequently sold. This is true only with a documented obligation, because such an obligation is generally public knowledge; it is therefore up to the buyer to protect himself with a thorough search before purchase to discover any liens on the property due to such obligations. An unrecorded obligation, on the other hand, is not well publicized, and a potential purchaser might not be aware of a lien on the property due to such an obligation. Therefore, these obligations do not carry a lien on the debtor's property, and the debt may be collected only from his unsold property (see *Rambam, Malveh V'loveh* 11:4; see *Bava Basra* 175a).

8. A ruling of the court generates as much publicity as a recorded debt. Consequently, anyone interested in purchasing a field from the robber would become aware of a lien on the robber's property resulting from such a ruling. Therefore, although it is not recorded in a document, this obligation creates a lien, and the owner can collect his principal from anyone who purchased land from the robber subsequent to the court's ruling (*Rashi*).

9. Since the robber's obligation for the produce is also well publicized as a result of the court's ruling.

10. When the seller is convicted of having stolen the field, the court orders him to return it (or its original value, where the seller had damaged it or caused it to be seized by government officials) to its rightful owner. Since the value of the field is known, potential buyers can protect their purchases up to that amount (see note 20 to 14b). On the other hand, since the court did not yet assign an amount to the robber's obligation for the produce he consumed, it is difficult for buyers to protect their purchases against seizure, because they do not know how much property the seller must retain to cover this debt. Therefore, the owner may not collect compensation for produce from land sold to buyers before the court assigned an amount for this compensation (see תוס׳ ד״ה כשעומד with explanation of *Maharam*).

11. I.e. can it be that the Baraisa states a law without qualifying it by stating that it applies only to the apparently rare case in which the robber was tried by the court only for stealing the property but not yet for the produce?

**discussing here?** כְּגוֹן שֶׁגָּזַל שָׂדֶה מֵחֲבֵירוֹ מְלֵאָה פֵּירוֹת – **For instance, if one stole a produce-filled**[35] **field from his fellow** וְאָכַל אֶת הַפֵּירוֹת – **and he consumed the produce,** וְחָפַר בָּהּ בּוֹרוֹת שִׁיחִין וּמְעָרוֹת – **and he** then **dug in it pits, ditches, and caves,** thereby depreciating the field. בָּא נִגְזָל לִגְבּוֹת קֶרֶן – **When the one from whom** the field **was stolen comes to collect** his lost **principal,**[36] גּוֹבֶה מִנְּכָסִים מְשׁוּעְבָּדִים – **he collects from** the robber's **encumbered properties** [i.e. from land which he sold after the robbery].[37] בָּא נִגְזָל לִגְבּוֹת פֵּירוֹת – **When the on**[e] **from whom** the field **was stolen comes to collect** compensatio[n] for **the produce,** גּוֹבֶה מִנְּכָסִים בְּנֵי חוֹרִין – **he collects fro**[m] **properties free of encumberance.**[38]

Another possible explanation of the Baraisa, according to whic[h] it does not refute Rav Nachman:

רַבָּה בַּר רַב הוּנָא אָמַר – **Rabbah bar Rav Huna said:** כְּגוֹן – **Fo**[r] **instance,**

NOTES

35. [The *Vilna Gaon* comments that these two words were incorrectly inserted into the text. Since the Baraisa states that compensation for produce may not be collected from sold properties, it follows that the produce was not fully grown at the time of the robbery. In such a case it is necessary to protect the rights of a subsequent purchaser who does not know how much produce will grow. However, if the produce was fully grown at the time of the theft, the obligation of the robber for the stolen produce is known, and there is no need to protect a subsequent purchaser. The owner should even be able to collect compensation for the produce from sold properties in such a case (see *Beur HaGra* to *Choshen Mishpat* 373:11).]

36. According to Rava's explanation, the phrase "and it [now] leaves his possession" in the Baraisa means that the rightful owner repossesses his field from the robber.

37. Ordinarily, recovery of the principal from the robber does not entai[l] collection of sold property, since all the owner need do is repossess hi[s] stolen field. Here, however, the robber dug pits in the field, depreciating its value. The Baraisa explains that the owner may seize sold property in order to recover the difference between the field's original value an[d] its current, depreciated value (*Rashi*).

38. Since the robber's obligation for the principal amount is known t[o] subsequent purchasers of the robber's property, the owner of the stole[n] field may collect the amount of the depreciation from them. However the amount of produce that will grow is not known to purchasers, an[d] the owner may thus not collect for the produce from them (see note 20).

יכול לחזור בו [א] משהחזיק בה אינו יכול לחזור בו דא"ל חייתא דקטרי סברת וקבלת מאימתי הויא חזקה [ב] מכי דייש אמצרי ואיכא דאמרי [ג] אפילו באחריות נמי דאמר ליה אחוי טרפך ואשלם לך איתמר המוכר שדה לחבירו ונמצאת שאינה שלו רב אמר יש לו מעות ויש לו שבח ושמואל אמר מעות יש לו שבח אין לו בעו מיניה מרב הונא פירש לו את השבח מהו טעמא דשמואל משום דלא פירש שבחא והכא הא פירש לה או דלמא טעמיה דשמואל כיון דלית ליה קרקע מחזי כרבית א"ל (א) אין ולאו ורפיא בידיה איתמר אמר רב נחמן אמר שמואל מעות יש לו שבח אין לו אע"פ שפירש לו את השבח מאי טעמא כיון דקרקע אין לו שכר מעותיו עומד ונוטל איתיביה רבא לרב נחמן (ב) [ד] אין מוציאין לאכילת פירות [ה] ולשבח קרקעות [ו] ולמזון האשה והבנות מנכסים משועבדים מפני תיקון העולם ממשעבדי הוא דלא מפקינן הא מבני חורין מפקינן וקתני מיהא לשבח קרקעות מאי לאו בלוקח מגזלן לא בבעל חוב אי בבעל חוב אימא רישא אין מוציאין לאכילת פירות ואי בבעל חוב בעל חוב מי אית ליה פירי (ג) והאמר שמואל [ז] בעל חוב גובה את השבח שבח אין [ח] אבל פירות לא אלא פשיטא בגוזל ונגזל ומדרישא בגוזל ונגזל סיפא נמי בגוזל ונגזל מידי אריא הא כדאיתא והא כדאיתא והא לא תני הכי (ד) לשבח קרקעות כיצד הרי שגזל שדה מחבירו והרי היא יוצאה מתחת ידו כשהוא גובה את הקרן מנכסים משועבדים ושבח גובה מנכסים בני חורין היכי דמי אילימא כדקתני גזלן ממאן גבי אלא לאו [ט] כגון שגזל שדה מחבירו ומכרה לאחר והשביחה א"ל לאו תרוצי קא מתרצת תריץ נמי בבעל חוב ת"ש לאכילת פירות כיצד הרי שגזל שדה מחבירו והרי היא יוצאה מתחת ידו כשהוא גובה את הקרן מנכסים משועבדים ופירות גובה מנכסים בני חורין היכי דמי אילימא כדקתני גזלן ממאן גבי אלא לאו [י] כגון שגזל שדה מחבירו ומכרה לאחר והשביחה אמר רבא הכא במאי עסקינן כגון שגזל שדה מחבירו [א] מלאה פירות ואכל את הפירות וחפר בה בורות שיחין ומערות [כ] בא נגזל לגבות קרן גובה מנכסים משועבדים בא נגזל לגבות פירות גובה מנכסים בני חורין רבה בר רב הונא אמר כגון

שנטלוה

## רש"י

יכול לחזור בו. ובשלא נתן מעות: אינו יכול לחזור בו. ואפילו לא נתן מעות שהקרקע נקנית בחזקה והמעות על זה מלוה: חייתא. שק מלא קשרים: מכי דייש אמצרי. מתקן גבולי השדה ומגביהם: איכא דאמרי אפי' באחריות נמי. אע"ג דסוף סוף עליה הדר אין יכול לחזור בו שהמוכר מעכב עליו ולא מצי אמר הוא הואיל וסופך לשלם לי מעותי השתא דבידי אעכבם: דאמר ליה אחוי טרפך ואשלם לך. כשיעמידוך (א) ויזכו בדין ויכתוב לך הדיין שטר טורף עלי שבדין טרפוה ממך בשבילי בא ואשלם לך וכל כמה דלא עמדת בדין איני ירא מהם: שאינה שלו. שלא היתה של מוכר שהיתה גזולה בידו והנגזל בא ומוציא מיד הלוקח: יש לו. ללוקח מן המוכר מעות: ויש לו שבח. אם זה השביח את הקרקע בזבל או בגדר קודם שהוציא נגזל מידו גובה לוקח מן המוכר שבח ואם תאמר הנגזל יתן השבח שהרי השיבו קרקע משובחת (ב) כגון שגזלה משובחת והכסיפה ביד הגזלן: שבח אין לו. לקמן מפרש טעמא: פירש לו את השבח. כשמכרה לו התנה אם יטרפוה מידך אשלם לך את השבח מהו: כיון דלית ליה קרקע. הואיל ואין קרקע זו שלו נמצא שאין כאן שום מכר והמעות מלוה אצלו וכשמשלם יותר ממה שנטל מחזי כרבית: אין ולאו. תחילה אמר אין וחזר ואמר לאו רפוי היה הדבר בידו שלא היה יודע טעמו של דבר יפה: לאכילת פירות כו'. מפרש להו לקמן: למזון האשה והבנות. תנאי כתובה שמקבל עליו את תהא יתבא בביתי ומיתזנא מנכסי וכן הבנות בנן נוקבן דיהוו ליכי מינאי אינון יהון יתבן בביתי ומיתזנן מנכסי עד דתלקחן לגוברין אין מוציאין לאחד מכל אלו מנכסים משועבדים: מפני תיקון העולם. שאם אתה אומר יטרפו לקוחות על כך אין לך אדם שלוקח שדה מחבירו דהא אין לך אדם שאין חוב זה מוטל עליו ודבר שאין לו קצבה היא ואכילת פירות ושבח קרקעות נמי דבר שאינו ידוע הוא ואין הלקוחות יודעין להזהר בכך: מאי לאו בלוקח שדה מגזלן. והשביחה ובא נגזל וטרפה חוזר לוקח וגובה קרן מן המוכר אפילו מנכסים משועבדים שמכר אחר מכירה זו דשטרו של זה קודם שכתב בו אחריות והשבח מנכסים בני חורין ולא ממשועבדים מפני תיקון העולם שהשבח לא היה קצוב בשעת מכירה כשקיבל עליו אחריות אלמא אית ליה ללוקח שבח מגזלן: לא בבעל חוב. שטרפה בעל חוב ממנו בשביל חובו ולא גזולה היתה דהשתא ודאי אית ליה שבחא דמכירה מעלייתא היא כל זמן שלא טרפה ממנו שאם פרע המוכר מעותיו לבע"ח הרי הוא מסולק מן הלקוחות הלכך כי משלם ליה יותר ממה שקיבל השתא הוא דהדר זבין מיניה קרקע המכורה לו ולא מחזי כשכר מעותיו: לאכילת פירות. ס"ד הא מיירי בשדה שטרפוה מליאה פירות מיד הלוקח וחוזר לוקח לגבות מן המוכר ואי בשטרפה בעל חוב מי אית ליה לבע"ח פירות גמורין המחוברין בקרקע ואין צריכין לקרקע כלום שיכול לטורפן: גובה את השבח. וכל הקרקע טורף מיד הלוקח כמו שהיא משובחת ע"י הלוקח: בגוזל ונגזל. וכגון שגזלה עם פירותיה ומכרה אי נמי גזלה בלא פירות ומכרה לאחר ועשה בה פירות וטוען נגזל ארעאי אשבח ומיהו היציאה שהוציא הלוקח ישלם לו הנגזל שהרי מתוך כך הושבחה יותר ואם אין השבח יותר אלא היציאה יתירה נותן לו יציאה שיעור שבח ודיו: הא כדאיתא כו'. רישא בנגזל וסיפא בבעל חוב ולקמיה מותיב לה מרישא: והא לא תני הכי. בברייתא עלה דהך מתניתין דאין מוציאין דתוקמה בבעל חוב: והרי היא יוצאה מתחת ידו. שבית דין מוציאין אותה מידו: כשהוא גובה. לקמיה מפרש לה: אילימא כדקתני. שלא מכרה גזלן ומידו היא יוצאה בדין: גזלן ממאן גבי. ממאן יש לו לגבות וכי מה נתן בה: והשביחה. והרי היא בדין יוצאה מתחת ידו של לוקח אלמא אית ליה שבחא ללוקח מגזלן: שגזל שדה מחבירו ומכרה לאחר והשביח. ונעשה פירות גמורין ונגזל לוקחה עם פירותיה ואינו נותן אלא יציאה דקאמר ארעאי אשבח וקתני דלוקח חוזר וגובה מגזלן מן המחוררין: אמר רבא כו'. האי כשהוא גובה לאו בלוקח קאמר דבשלא מכרה עסקינן וגובה את הקרן דקאמר בנגזל וא"ת קרן אמאי גובה מנכסים משועבדים הרי קרקע לפניו כגון שחפר בה בורות דאפחתה משוייה:

שנטלוה

## תוספות

ויש לו שבח. שהנגזל לוקח הקרקע עם השבח ואינו משלם ללוקח רק היציאה כדין יורד לתוך שדה חבירו שלא ברשות דאם השבח יתר על היציאה נותן לו את היציאה ואותו שבח היתר יקח הלוקח מן הגזלן ומיירי שנגזלה ריקנית: ושמואל אמר מעות יש לו. אפילו קנאה שלא באחריות כדפי' לעיל [ה] וכן משמע דמיירי דומיא דהכיר בה שאינה שלו דלקמן דמיירי על כרחך שלא באחריות כדקאמר שמואל מעות מתנה דאי באחריות אמאי מעות מתנה: סיפא נמי בגוזל כו'. מרישא עצמה היה יכול להקשות כדמקשה בסמוך אלא כמה שיכול להקשות משנה גופיה פריך: תריץ נמי בבעל חוב. בפרק מי שמת (ב"ב דף קנז: ושם ד"ה גובה) רצה להוכיח דאקני קנה ומכר משתעבד מהכא דגבי בעל חוב שבח שלא היה בעין בשעת הלואה ודחי ר"מ היא דאמר אדם מקנה דבר שלא בא לעולם וא"ת ולוכח משמואל דאמר בעל חוב גובה את השבח ושמואל גופיה הוא דבעי ליה התם דלא מצי למימר דשמואל נמי סבר כר"מ ומבעי ליה אליבא דרבנן דהא בפרק אע"פ (כתובות דף נט.) פסק שמואל כר' יוחנן הסנדלר דלית ליה אדם מקנה כו' וי"ל דהא דאמר שמואל בעל חוב גובה את השבח היינו לפי המסקנא דהתם דפשיט דאקני קנה ומכר משתעבד אף לרבנן ואם תאמר אדרבה לוכח מהכא דלא משתעבד מדלא טריף בע"ח ממשעבדי דטריף לוקח דאין לומר דאחר שטרף בע"ח קרקע מן הלוקח קנה המוכר קרקעות ומכרן דא"כ גם השבח יגבה מהנהו משעבדי דגם השבח היה קלוב כיון שכבר טרף הבעל חוב קודם שלקח זה הקרקע וי"ל דמיירי שזה הקרקע עשאו המוכר לבעל חוב אפותיקי ולכך גובה אותו בע"ח ואע"פ שיש שאר משעבדי אך קשה אמאי דחיק לדחויי בפרק מי שמת (ב"ב דף קנז: ושם) הא מני ר"מ היא יעמיד כשעשאו אפותיקי דאז בעל חוב גובה את השבח היתר על היציאה חנם כדין יורד לתוך שדה חבירו כדמשמע לקמן או יעמיד בלוקח מן הגזלן וכגון שיש לו קרקע או קנו מידו כדמתרך לקמן בשמעתין:

כשעמד

שהנגזל מוציאה בדין. כשהוא גובה. הלוקח חוזר על הגזלן שמכרה לו באחריות [ב"ק צה.]. מנכסים משועבדים. טורף לקוחות שלקחו אחריו מפני שהאחריות שכב בשטר מכירתו קודם למקחו [לקמן עב:]. שהוא קדם והוא כמלוה בשטר שהרי כתב לו בשטר המכירה שאם יטרפוה ממנו יחזור ויגבה מנכסיו [ב"ק צה:]. ושבח מנכסים בני חורין. ולא ממשועבדים מפני תיקון העולם
הלקוחות יכולין להזהר בדבר שאין לו קצבה כגון אחריות השבח והפירות דבשלמא בקרן נזהרין להניח מקום לגבות ממנו ואי לא נזהרו אפסידו אנפשייהו [לקמן עב:].

## עין משפט נר מצוה

קיז א ב ג מיי' פי"ט מהל' מכירה הל' ב סמג לאוין קט ועשין פב טוש"ע ח"מ סי' רכו סעיף ה:
קיח ד מיי' פי"ט מהל' גזילה ואבידה הל' ה ופכ"א מהל' מלוה ולוה הל' א סמג שם טוש"ע ח"מ סי' שעג סעיף ג:
קיט ה מיי' פי"ט מהל' גזלה ואבדה הל' ז ופכ"ו מהלכות מלוה ולוה הל' א סמג שם טוש"ע שם סעיף א וסי' קטו סעיף א:
קכ ו מיי' פכ"ח מהל' מלוה ולוה הל' א ופי"ח מהל' אישות הל' יג סמג עשין מח טוש"ע אה"ע סי' צג סעיף כח וסי' קיב סעיף ז:
קכא ז ח מיי' פכ"א מהל' מלוה ולוה הל' א סמג עשין צד טוש"ע ח"מ סי' קטו סעיף א:
קכב ט מיי' פ"ט מהל' גזלה ואבדה הל' ו ז סמג עשין עג טוש"ע ח"מ סי' שעג סעיף ב:
קכג י מיי' שם הל' ח טוש"ע שם סעיף ג:
קכד כ מיי' שם הל' ד סמג שם טוש"ע ח"מ סי' שעג סעיף א:

## רבינו חננאל

והחזיק בה אין יכול לחזור בו הלוקח ואפי' באחריות נמי אין יכול לחזור בו דיכול למימר ליה אחוי לי טירפא ואשלם לך הא דאמר אביי המוכר שדה לחבירו א) ויצאו עליה עסיקין וכו' הוי השמועה היא בפ' מי שהיה נשוי שתי נשים ובתחלת בבא קמא: איתמר המוכר שדה לחבירו ונמצאת שאינה שלו כלומר גזולה היתה בידו סוגיא דשמעתא בשבח דשבחא ארעא ממילא [פליגי] רב ושמואל הכא רב אמר יש לו מעות ויש לו שבח ושמואל אמר מעות יש לו שבח אין לו. ואמר רב נחמן אע"פ שפירש לו את השבח אין לו. מתיב רבא מהא דתנן בפ' הניזקין אין מוציאין לאכילת פירות ולשבח קרקעות ולמזון האשה והבנות מנכסים משועבדים מפני תיקון העולם הא מבני חרי מוציאין מאי לאו בלוקח מגזלן. ופריק רב נחמן תרויהו לאכילת ב) פירות ולשבח קרקעות בבעל חוב ופשוטה היא. רבא אמר כגון שגזל שדה מליאה פירות ואכל הפירות וחפר בשדה בורות שיחין ומערות ובא הנגזל להוציאה מידו כו'.

## חשק שלמה על ר"ח

א) אולי צ"ל זו השמועה היא וכו' או דצ"ל הא דאמר אביי ראובן שמכר שדה לשמעון באחריות וכו' זו השמועה היא וכו'. ב) לפנינו בגמ' דרישא דאין מוציאין לאכילת פירות בגזל ונגזל מיירי ואולי דרבינו היה לו גי' אחרת בגמ' וצ"ע.

## מסורת הש"ס

א) [שבת קיג., קדושין סה.], ב) גיטין מח:, ג) בבא קמא [לקמן טו., קיג., בכורות נב.], ד) לקמן עב:, ה) בתרא קנז: [ע"ש וכו' רשב"ם], ו) ע"ל ד' שבועות.

## הגהות הב"ח

(א) רש"י ד"ה דא אחוי וכו' כשיעמידוך בו ומזכו וכו' בשבילי בא ואשלם: (ב) ד"ה ויש וכו' קרקע משובחת לומר כגון שגזלה:

## הגהות הגר"א

[א] גמ' מלאה פירות. נ"ב הרמב"ם ל"ג (ועמ"ש רבינו בח"מ ס' שע"ג ס"ק י"א):

## ליקוטי רש"י

אין יכול לחזור בו. שהקרקע נקנה בחזקה א"ל לך חזק וקני ומשהחזיק בה נתנו המעות. חייתא. שק קטן. דקיטרי. קשרים [כתובות צג.]. סברת וקבלת. אפי' באחריות נמי. מכרה לו אינו יכול לחזור בו. אחוי טרפך. שטר טריפה שבדין טרפוה ממך ואשלם לך. אין ולאו. זימנין א"ל הן וזימנין א"ל לא [שבת קטו.]. ורפי בידיה. [קדושין סה.]. אין מוציאין לאכילת פירות ולשבח קרקעות. הנגזל [גיטין מח:]. גובה את השבח. [בכורות נב.]. והרי היא יוצאה מתחת ידו.

אֶלָּא – **Rather,** פְּשִׁיטָא בְּגוֹזֵל וְנִגְזַל – **it is obvious** that this first case of the Mishnah **refers to one who steals** land and sells it, **and** then **the one from whom it was stolen** seizes his land and its produce.[27]

The Gemara concludes its objection:

וּמִדְּרֵישָׁא בְּגוֹזֵל וְנִגְזַל – **Since the first case refers to** a sale of land by **a robber and** its subsequent seizure by **the one from whom it was stolen,** סֵיפָא נַמִּי בְּגוֹזֵל וְנִגְזַל – we may presume that **the latter case also refers to** a sale by **a robber and** the subsequent seizure of the land and its improvements by **the one from whom it was stolen.** Nevertheless, the Mishnah implies that the purchaser may be compensated by the robber for the seized improvements. This contradicts Rav Nachman's ruling. – ? –

The Gemara answers:

מִידֵי אִרְיָא – **Is this an argument?** The two cases do not refer to the same scenario! הָא כִּדְאִיתָא – **That** first case about compensation for produce **speaks about the circumstances that apply to it,** i.e. it refers to stolen land, seized by its rightful owner. וְהָא כִּדְאִיתָא – **And that** second case about compensation for improvements **speaks about the circumstances that apply to it,** i.e. it refers to non-stolen land, seized by a creditor. Rav Nachman's ruling concerning stolen property therefore stands, and the purchaser does not receive compensation for his improvements.

The Gemara challenges:

וְהָא לֹא תָּנֵי הָכִי – **But it was not so taught in a Baraisa** concerning that Mishnah: לְשֶׁבַח קַרְקָעוֹת כֵּיצַד – **WHAT IS** the case of compensation **FOR IMPROVEMENT OF LAND?** הֲרֵי שֶׁגָּזַל שָׂדֶה מֵחֲבֵירוֹ – **IF ONE STOLE A FIELD FROM HIS FELLOW** וַהֲרֵי הִיא יוֹצְאָה מִתַּחַת יָדוֹ – **AND IT** now **LEAVES HIS POSSESSION.** כְּשֶׁהוּא גּוֹבֶה – **WHEN HE COLLECTS** compensation for his loss,[28] גּוֹבֶה אֶת הַקֶּרֶן מִנְּכָסִים מְשׁוּעְבָּדִים – **HE COLLECTS** for **THE PRINCIPAL FROM ENCUMBERED PROPERTIES,** וְשֶׁבַח גּוֹבֶה מִנְּכָסִים בְּנֵי חוֹרִין – **AND HE COLLECTS** for **THE IMPROVEMENTS FROM PROPERTIES FREE OF ENCUMBERANCE.**

The Gemara explains:

הֵיכִי דָּמֵי – Now, **what is the case?** אִילֵימָא כִּדְקָתָנֵי – **If you say** that the case is precisely **as recorded in the Baraisa,** and the robber did not sell the stolen property,[29] גַּזְלָן מִמַּאן גָּבֵי – **from whom should the robber collect** compensation for the return of the stolen property? He never paid for it, and he loses nothing by its return! אֶלָּא – **Rather,** לַאו כְּגוֹן שֶׁגָּזַל שָׂדֶה מֵחֲבֵירוֹ – **is it not** referring to a case in which **for example, one stole a field from his fellow** וּמְכָרָהּ לְאַחֵר וְהִשְׁבִּיחָהּ – **and sold it to another who improved it?**[30] Although the field was stolen, the purchase may claim compensation from the seller for improvement confiscated by the rightful owner. This contradicts Rav Nach man's ruling that a purchaser is not compensated by the seller fo his improvements to stolen property. – ? –

The Gemara deflects the challenge:

אָמַר לֵיהּ – **[Rav Nachman] told [Rava]:** או תֵּרוּצֵי קָא מְתָרְצַת – **Have you not revised** the Baraisa yourself by inserting clause that the field was sold to another? תָּרֵיץ נַמִּי – If so, i **may also be revised** to read בְּבַעַל חוֹב – that **it refers t** non-stolen land which was sold and subsequently seized by th seller's **creditor.** Since the Baraisa is not accurate, it is not refutation of my ruling.[31]

The Gemara attempts a proof:

תָּא שְׁמַע – **Come, learn** a proof from a Baraisa which discusse the cited Mishnah: לַאֲכִילַת פֵּירוֹת כֵּיצַד – **WHAT IS** the case c compensation **FOR CONSUMPTION OF PRODUCE?** רי שֶׁגָּזַל שָׂדֶה מֵחֲבֵירוֹ – **IF ONE STOLE A FIELD FROM HIS FELLOW** הֲרֵי הִיא יוֹצְאָה מִתַּחַת יָדוֹ – **AND IT** now **LEAVES HIS POSSESSION,** שֶׁהוּא בֶה אֶת גּוֹבֶה – **WHEN HE COLLECTS** compensation for his loss[28] הַקֶּרֶן מִנְּכָסִים מְשׁוּעְבָּדִים – **HE COLLECTS** for **THE PRINCIPAL FRO ENCUMBERED PROPERTIES,** וּפֵירוֹת גּוֹבֶה מִנְּכָסִים בְּנֵי חוֹרִין – **AN HE COLLECTS** for **THE PRODUCE FROM PROPERTIES FREE O ENCUMBERANCE.**

The Gemara explains:

הֵיכִי דָּמֵי – **What is the case?** אִילֵימָא כִּדְקָתָנֵי – Now, **if you sa** that the case is precisely **as recorded in the Baraisa,** and th robber did not sell the stolen property, גַּזְלָן מִמַּאן גָּבֵי – **fron whom should the robber collect** compensation? He has not los anything! אֶלָּא – **Rather,** לַאו כְּגוֹן שֶׁגָּזַל שָׂדֶה מֵחֲבֵירוֹ – **is i not** referring to a case in which, **for example, one stole a fiel from his fellow,** וּמְכָרָהּ לְאַחֵר וְהִשְׁבִּיחָהּ – **and sold it t another who improved it** until the produce was ripe? Neverthe less, the purchaser may claim compensation from the seller fo the produce seized by the rightful owner together with his land.[32] Apparently, although the land was not the seller's, and the mone forwarded to the seller is viewed as a loan, the additional com pensation which he receives for the produce is not viewed a interest. This contradicts Rav Nachman's ruling.[33] – ? –

The Gemara answers that the Baraisa does not refer to a case o sold, stolen property, and it is therefore not a refutation of Ra Nachman:

אָמַר רָבָא – **Rava said:**[34] הָכָא בְּמַאי עַסְקִינָן – **What are w**

NOTES

27. Although the produce was grown by the purchaser, the rightful owner has a valid claim for the produce, since it grew on his land. However, he must compensate the purchaser for his expenses by paying him the lesser of his expenses or the value of the produce.

This ruling also applies where the land was stolen together with its produce, in which case the owner obviously has a valid claim for his stolen produce (see *Rashi*). [However, a creditor, who may only collect sold land but not other sold property, cannot claim the produce even if it was sold to the purchaser together with the land, since it is not considered as part of the land (see previous note).]

28. As recorded by the Gemara, the Baraisa is very difficult, for a robber is clearly not compensated when the stolen property is returned to its rightful owner. The Gemara below will explain this ruling.

29. According to this explanation, the phrase "and it [now] leaves his possession" in the Baraisa means that the court collects the field from the robber's possession (*Rashi*).

30. According to this explanation, the phrase "and it [now] leaves his possession" in the Baraisa means that the court collects the field from the purchaser's possession (*Rashi*).

31. The wording of a Baraisa is ordinarily assumed to be accurate. Consequently, an Amora whose position is challenged from a Baraisa may not deflect the challenge by simply revising the text of the Baraisa However, in our case, it is clear that the Baraisa needs correction since it cannot possibly be discussing compensation to the robber, as the Gemara explained. Rav Nachman now argues that once the Baraisa has been shown to contain errors in its wording, it cannot be considerec reliable, and can be emended further so that it does not refute his ruling

32. I.e. the owner need compensate him only for the lesser of his expenses or the improvement to the produce. If the improvements exceed his expenses, the purchaser collects the remainder from the unsold property of the seller.

The owner may claim compensation for the produce because it grew on his land (*Rashi,* see note 27).

33. The Gemara does not deflect this challenge by emending the Baraisa so that it discusses seizure by a creditor (as it did when challenged by the previous Baraisa). Since this Baraisa speaks of compensation for ripe produce seized from the purchaser, the Baraisa cannot be discussing seizure by a creditor, because a creditor may not seize ripe produce (as the Gemara noted earlier).

34. Although Rava originally questioned Rav Nachman's ruling, here he states that the Baraisa does not refute Rav Nachman (cf. *Tos. HaRosh*).

יכול לחזור בו [א]משהחזיק בה אינו יכול לחזור בו דא"ל חייתא דקטרי סברת וקבלת מאימתי הויא חזקה [ב]מכי דייש אמצרי ואיכא דאמרי [ג]אפילו באחריות נמי דאמר ליה אחוי טרפך ואשלם לך איתמר המוכר שדה לחבירו ונמצאת שאינה שלו רב אמר יש לו מעות ויש לו שבח ושמואל אמר מעות יש לו שבח אין לו בעו מיניה מרב הונא פירש לו את השבח מהו טעמא דשמואל משום דלא פירש שבחא והכא הא פירש לה או דלמא טעמיה דשמואל כיון דלית ליה קרקע מחזי כרבית א"ל (א) אין ולאו ורפיא בידיה איתמר אמר רב נחמן אמר שמואל מעות יש לו שבח אין לו אע"פ שפירש לו את השבח מאי טעמא כיון דקרקע אין לו שכר מעותיו עומד ונוטל איתיביה רבא לרב נחמן (ג) [ד]אין מוציאין לאכילת פירות [ה]ולשבח קרקעות [ו]ולמזון האשה והבנות מנכסים משועבדים מפני תיקון העולם ממשעבדי הוא דלא מפקינן הא מבני חורין מפקינן וקתני מיהא לשבח קרקעות מאי לאו בלוקח מגזלן לא בבעל חוב אי בבעל חוב אימא רישא אין מוציאין לאכילת פירות ואי בבעל חוב בעל חוב מי אית ליה פירי (ד) והאמר שמואל [ז]בעל חוב גובה את השבח שבח אין [ח]אבל פירות לא אלא פשיטא בגוזל ונגזל ומדרישא בגוזל ונגזל סיפא נמי בגוזל ונגזל מידי אריא הא כדאיתא והא כדאיתא והא לא תני הכי (ה) לשבח קרקעות כיצד הרי שגזל שדה מחבירו והרי היא יוצאה מתחת ידו כשהוא גובה גובה את הקרן מנכסים משועבדים ושבח גובה מנכסים בני חורין היכי דמי אילימא כדקתני גזלן ממאן גבי אלא לאו [ט]כגון שגזל שדה מחבירו ומכרה לאחר והשביחה א"ל לאו תרוצי קא מתרצת תריץ נמי בבעל חוב ת"ש לאכילת פירות כיצד הרי שגזל שדה מחבירו והרי היא יוצאה מתחת ידו כשהוא גובה גובה את הקרן מנכסים משועבדים ופירות גובה מנכסים בני חורין היכי דמי אילימא כדקתני גזלן ממאן גבי אלא לאו [י]כגון שגזל שדה מחבירו ומכרה לאחר והשביחה אמר רבא הכא במאי עסקינן כגון שגזל שדה מחבירו [א] מלאה פירות ואכל את הפירות וחפר בה בורות שיחין ומערות [כ]בא נגזל לגבות קרן גובה מנכסים משועבדים בא נגזל לגבות פירות גובה מנכסים בני חורין רבה בר רב הונא אמר כגון

שנטלוה

## רש"י

יכול לחזור בו. ובשלא נתן מעות: אינו יכול לחזור בו. ואפילו לא נתן מעות שהקרקע נקנית בחזקה והמעות על זה מלוה: חייתא. שק מלא קשרים: מכי דייש אמצרי. מתקן גבולי השדה ומגביהם: איכא דאמרי אפי' באחריות נמי. אע"ג דסוף סוף עליה הדר אין יכול לחזור בו שהמוכר מעכב עליו ולא מצי אמר הוא הואיל וסופך לשלם לי מעותי השתא דבידי אעכבם: דאמר ליה אחוי טרפך ואשלם לך. כשיעמידוך (א) ויזכו בדין ויכתוב לך הדיין שטר טורף עלי שבדין טרפוה ממך בשבילי בא ואשלם לך וכל כמה דלא עמדת בדין איני ירא מהם: שאינה שלו. שלא היתה של מוכר שהיתה גזולה בידו והנגזל בא ומוציא מיד הלוקח: יש לו. ללוקח מן המוכר מעות: ויש לו שבח. אם זה השביח את הקרקע בזבל או בגדר קודם שהוציא נגזל מידו גובה לוקח מן המוכר שבח ואם תאמר הנגזל יתן השבח שהרי השיבו קרקע משובחת (ב) כגון שגזלה משובחת והכסיפה ביד הגזלן: שבח אין לו. לקמן מפרש טעמא: פירש לו את השבח. כשמכרה לו התנה אם יטרפוה מידך אשלם לך את השבח מהו: כיון דלית ליה קרקע. הואיל ואין קרקע זו שלו נמצא שאין כאן שום מכר והמעות מלוה אצלו וכשמשלם יותר ממה שנטל מחזי כרבית: אין ולאו. תחילה אמר אין וחזר ואמר לאו רפוי היה הדבר בידו שלא היה יודע טעמו של דבר יפה: לאכילת פירות כו'. מפרש להו לקמן: למזון האשה והבנות. תנאי כתובה שמקבל עליו את תהא יתבא בביתי ומיתזנא מנכסי וכן הבנות בנן נוקבן דיהוו ליכי מינאי אינון יהון יתבן בביתי ומיתזנן מנכסי עד דתלקחן לגוברין אין מוציאין לאחד מכל אלו מנכסים משועבדים: מפני תיקון העולם. שאם אתה אומר יטרפו לקוחות על כך אין לך אדם שלוקח שדה מחבירו דהא אין לך אדם שאין חוב זה מוטל עליו ודבר שאין לו קצבה היא ואכילת פירות ושבח קרקעות נמי דבר שאינו ידוע הוא ואין הלקוחות יודעין להזהר בכך: מאי לאו בלוקח שדה מגזלן. והשביחה ובא נגזל וטרפה חוזר לוקח וגובה קרן מן המוכר אפילו מנכסים משועבדים שמכר אחר מכירה זו דשטרו של זה קודם שכתב בו אחריות והשבח מנכסים בני חורין ולא ממשועבדים מפני תיקון העולם שהשבח לא היה קצוב בשעת מכירה כשקיבל עליו אחריות אלמא אית ליה ללוקח שבח מגזלן: לא בבעל חוב. שטרפה בעל חוב ממנו בשביל חובו ולא גזולה היתה דההיא ודאי אית ליה שבחא דמכירה מעלייתא היא כל זמן שלא טרפה ממנו שאם פרע המוכר מעותיו לבע"ח הרי הוא מסולק מן הלקוחות הלכך כי משלם ליה יותר ממה שקיבל השתא הוא דהדר זבין מיניה קרקע המכורה לו ולא מחזי כשכר מעותיו: לאכילת פירות. ס"ד הא מיירי בשדה שטרפוה מליאה פירות מיד הלוקח וחוזר לוקח לגבות מן המוכר ואי בשטרפה בעל חוב מי אית ליה לבע"ח פירות גמורין המחוברין בקרקע ואינן צריכין לקרקע כלום שיכול לטורפן: גובה את השבח. וכל הקרקע טורף מיד הלוקח כמו שהיא משובחת ע"י הלוקח: בגוזל ונגזל. וכגון שגזלה עם פירותיה ומכרה אי נמי גזלה בלא פירות ומכרה לאחר ועשה בה פירות וטוען נגזל ארעאי אשבח ומיהו היציאה שהוציא הלוקח ישלם לו הנגזל שהרי מתוך כך הושבחה יותר ואם אין השבח יותר אלא היציאה יתירה נותן לו יציאה שיעור שבח ודיו: הא כדאיתא כו'. רישא בנגזל וסיפא בבעל חוב ולקמיה מותיב לה מרישא: והא לא תני הכי. בברייתא עלה דהך מתניתין דאין מוציאין דתוקמה בבעל חוב: והרי היא יוצאה מתחת ידו. שבית דין מוציאין אותה מידו: כשהוא גובה. לקמיה מפרש לה: אילימא כדקתני. שלא מכרה גזלן ומידו היא יוצאה בדין: גזלן ממאן גבי. ממאן יש לו לגבות וכי מה נתן בה: והשביחה. והרי היא בדין יוצאה מתחת ידו של לוקח אלמא אית ליה שבחא ללוקח מגזלן: שגזל שדה מחבירו ומכרה לאחר והשביח. ונעשה פירות גמורין ונגזל לוקחה עם פירותיה ואינו נותן אלא יציאה דקאמר ארעאי אשבח וקתני דלוקח חוזר וגובה מגזלן מן המחוררין: אמר רבא כו'. האי כשהוא גובה לאו בלוקח קאמר דבשלא מכרה עסקינן וגובה את הקרן דקאמר בנגזל וא"ת קרן אמאי גובה מנכסים משועבדים הרי קרקע לפניו כגון שחפר בה בורות דאפחתה משויה:

שנטלוה

## תוספות

ויש לו שבח. שהנגזל לוקח הקרקע עם השבח ואינו משלם ללוקח רק היציאה כדין יורד לתוך שדה חבירו שלא ברשות דאם השבח יתר על היציאה נותן לו את היציאה ואותו שבח היתר יקח הלוקח מן הגזלן ומיירי שנגזלה ריקנית: ושמואל אמר מעות יש לו. אפילו קנאה שלא באחריות כדפי' לעיל (ה) וכן משמע דמיירי דומיא דהכיר בה שאינה שלו דלקמן דמיירי על כרחך שלא באחריות כדקאמר שמואל מעות מתנה דאי באחריות אמאי מעות מתנה:

סיפא נמי בגוזל כו'. מרישא עצמה היה יכול להקשות כדמקשה בסמוך אלא כמה שיכול להקשות משבח גופיה פריך: תריץ נמי בבעל חוב. בפרק מי שמת (ב"ב דף קנז: ושם ד"ה גובה) רצה להוכיח דאקני קנה ומכר משתעבד מהכא דגבי בעל חוב שבח שלא היה בעין בשעת הלואה ודחי ר"מ היא דאמר אדם מקנה דבר שלא בא לעולם וא"ת ולוכח משמואל דאמר בעל חוב גובה את השבח ושמואל גופיה הוא דבעי ליה התם דלא מצי למימר דשמואל נמי סבר כר"מ ומבעי ליה אליבא דרבנן דהא בפרק אע"פ (כתובות דף נט.) פסק שמואל כר' יוחנן הסנדלר דלית ליה אדם מקנה כו' וי"ל דהא דאמר שמואל בעל חוב גובה את השבח היינו לפי המסקנא דהתם דפשיט דאקני קנה ומכר משתעבד אף לרבנן ואם תאמר אדרבה לוכח מהכא דלא משתעבד מדלא טריף בע"ח ממשעבדי דטריף לוקח דאין לומר דאחר שטרף בע"ח קרקע מן הלוקח קנה המוכר קרקעות ומכרן דא"כ גם השבח יגבה מהנהו משעבדי דגם השבח היה קצוב כיון שכבר טרף הבעל חוב קודם שלקח זה הקרקע וי"ל דמיירי שזה הקרקע עשאו המוכר לבעל חוב אפותיקי ולכך גובה אותו בע"ח ואע"פ שיש שאר משעבדי אך קשה אמאי דחיק לדחויי בפרק מי שמת (ב"ב דף קנז: ושם) הא מני ר"מ היא יעמיד כשעשאו אפותיקי דאז בעל חוב גובה את השבח היתר על היציאה חנם כדין יורד לתוך שדה חבירו כדמשמע לקמן או יעמיד בלוקח מן הגזלן וכגון שיש לו קרקע או קנו מידו כדמתרץ לקמן בשמעתין:

כשעמד



## עין משפט נר מצוה

קיז א ב ג מיי' פי"ט מהל' מכירה הל' ג סמג לאוין קט ועשין פב טוש"ע ח"מ סי' רכו סעיף ה:
קיח ד מיי' פ"ט מהל' גזלה ואבדה הל' ה ופכ"א מהל' מלוה ולוה הל' א סמג עשין עג לד טוש"ע ח"מ סי' שעג סעיף ב:
קיט ה מיי' פ"ט מהל' גזלה ואבדה הל' ז ופכ"א מהלכות מלוה ולוה הל' א סמג שם טוש"ע שם סעיף א וסי' קטו סעיף א:
קכ ו מיי' פכ"א מהל' מלוה ולוה הל' א ופי"ח מהל' אישות הל' יג סמג עשין מח טוש"ע אה"ע סי' לג סעיף כא וסי' קיב סעיף ז:
קכא ז ח מיי' פכ"א מהל' מלוה ולוה הל' א סמג עשין לד טוש"ע ח"מ סי' קטו סעיף א:
קכב ט מיי' פ"ט מהל' גזלה ואבדה הל' ו ז סמג עשין עג טוש"ע ח"מ סי' שעג סעיף א:
קכג י מיי' שם הל' ח טוש"ע שם סעיף ב:
קכד כ מיי' שם הל' ד סמג שם טוש"ע ח"מ סי' שעג סעיף א:

## רבינו חננאל

והחזיק בה אין יכול לחזור בו הלוקח ואפי' באחריות נמי אין יכול לחזור בו דיכול למימר ליה אחוי לי טירפא ואשלם לך הא דאמר אביי המוכר שדה לחבירו א) ויצאו עליה עסיקין וכו' הו השמועה היא בפ' מי שהיה נשוי שתי נשים ובתחלת בבא קמא: איתמר המוכר שדה לחבירו ונמצאת שאינה שלו כלומר גזולה היתה בידו סוגיא דשמעתא בשבח דשבחא ארעא ממילא [פליגי] רב ושמואל הכא רב אמר יש לו מעות ויש לו שבח ושמואל אמר מעות יש לו שבח אין לו. ואמר רב נחמן אע"פ שפירש לו את השבח אין לו. מתיב רבא מהא דתנן במס' גיטין פ' הניזקין אין מוציאין לאכילת פירות ולשבח קרקעות ולמזון האשה והבנות מנכסים משועבדים מפני תיקון העולם הא מבני חרי מוציאין מאי לאו בלוקח מגזלן. ופריק רב נחמן תרוייהו לאכילת ב) פירות ולשבח קרקעות בבעל חוב ופשוטה היא. רבא אמר כגון שגזל שדה מליאה פירות ואכל הפירות וחפר בשדה בורות שיחין ומערות ובא הנגזל להוציאה מידו כו'.

## מסורת הש"ס

א) [שבת קיג., קדושין סה.], ב) גי' מח., ג) בבא קמא [לקמן טו., קי., בכו' נב.], ד) לקמן עב:, בתרא קנז: [ע"ש ור רשב"ם], ה) ע"א שעבוד.

## הגהות הב"ח

(א) רש"י ד"ה דא אחוי וכו' כשיעמידוך ומזכו וכו' בשבילי א ואשלם: (ב) ד"ה ויש וכו' קרקע משובחת לומר כגון שגזלה:

## הגהות הגר"א

[א] גמ' מלאה פירו נ"ב הרמב"ם ל"ג (ועמ"ש רבינו בח"מ שע"ג ס"ק י"א):

## ליקוטי רש"י

אין יכול לחזור שהקרקע נקנה בחזקה א"ל לך חזק וקני שממחזיקין מיד ונו מעות לאחר ומשהחזיק בה נתח המעות. חייתא. קטן. דקיטרי. קשרים [כתובות צג.]. קשורה מלא רוח [ב"ק סברת וקבילת. בי חתיכות כסף כלו נתרלית לאבד מעו מספק. אפי' באחרי נמי. מכרה לו אינו לחזור בו מחמת עסי ולא אמרינן סוף סוף ע הדר ואטרוחי דייני ל לן [כתובות שם]. אפי' אחריות עליו דיי"ל הו וסופו לחזור עליו עכ נמי יחזור ויטלנה אפ אינו יכול לחזור בו. א טרפך. שכתבו לך שטר טירפא שבדין נ ממך ואשלם לך [ב"ק ש ואשלם לך. וכל שלא יצאה מידך לא א שהרבה עוררין שאין ז בדין [כתובות שם]. ולאו. זימנין א"ל זימנין א"ל לא [שבת קט לא היה מחזיק בדבריו לאיסור ולא להיתר פעו שאמר הן ופעמים שא לאו [קדושין סה.]. ורפ בידיה. רפויה הי התשובה בפיו אם לאו אם להתיר [שבת קיג.]. היתה מוחזקת הוראה בידו [קדושין שם]. מוציאין לאכי פירות ולש קרקעות. הגוזל ומכרה לאחר וחז ולמחה ועשתה פירות נגזל ונגלה עם פירוי מן הלוקח ואינו מ ללוקח כי אם היציאה הלוקח על המוכר ונ דמי קרקע מנכו משועבדים שמכרה באחריות וכתב לו מכירה והרי היא מ בשטר ואת הפי מנכסים בני חורין ממשועבדים וכו' לשבח קרקעות השביחה הלוקח בנטי אילנות או טייבה ודיירה [גיטין בע"ח גובה השבח. שהלוה לח מעות ומכר לוה הנכ והשביחום לקוחות ט בע"ח הגוף והש [בכורות נב.]. ואינו מח ללוקח כלום [ב"ק צ והרי היא יוצ מתחת ידו. של לו

**then** he reconsidered and said **no.**[13] **He was uncertain about the matter.**[14]

The Gemara cites a ruling by Shmuel in this matter:

**אִיתְּמַר – It was said: אָמַר רַב נַחְמָן אָמַר שְׁמוּאֵל – Rav Nachman said in the name of Shmuel: מָעוֹת יֵשׁ לוֹ – [The purchaser] has** the right to compensation for the **money** which he paid, **שְׁבָח אֵין לוֹ – but he does not have** the right to compensation for his **improvements, אַף עַל פִּי שֶׁפֵּירֵשׁ לוֹ אֶת הַשְּׁבָח – even though [the seller] explicitly told him** that he accepts responsibility for **the improvements. מַאי טַעְמָא – What is the reason? כֵּיוָן דְּקַרְקַע אֵין לוֹ – Since the land is not [the seller's], שְׂכַר מְעוֹתָיו עוֹמֵד וְנוֹטֵל –** it would appear as if **[the purchaser] collects a fee for** the use of **his money** [i.e. the loan to the seller] if he receives compensation for the improvements.[15]

The Gemara challenges:

**אֵיתִיבֵיהּ רָבָא לְרַב נַחְמָן – Rava challenged Rav Nachman** from a Mishnah:[16] **אֵין מוֹצִיאִין – WE DO NOT COLLECT לַאֲכִילַת פֵּירוֹת – FOR CONSUMPTION OF PRODUCE, וְלִשְׁבַח קַרְקָעוֹת – OR FOR IMPROVEMENT OF LAND,**[17] **וְלִמְזוֹן הָאִשָּׁה וְהַבָּנוֹת – OR FOR FOOD OF** a man's **WIFE AND DAUGHTERS**[18] **מִנְּכָסִים מְשׁוּעְבָּדִים – FROM ENCUMBERED PROPERTIES,**[19] **מִפְּנֵי תִּיקּוּן הָעוֹלָם – BECAUSE OF THE COMMON GOOD.**[20]

Rava explains his question:

**מִמְּשַׁעְבְּדֵי הוּא דְּלָא מַפְּקִינַן –** The Mishnah implies that it is **only from encumbered properties** that **we do not collect, הָא מִבְּנֵי חוֹרִין מַפְּקִינַן – but we** *do* **collect** these obligations **from properties free of encumberance. וְקָתָנֵי מִיהָא – And nevertheless the Mishnah taught** the case of collection **לִשְׁבַח קַרְקָעוֹת – for the improvement of land.**[21] **מַאי –** Now, **what** is the case referred to by the Mishnah? **לָאו בְּלוֹקֵחַ מִגַּזְלָן – Is it n[ot] referring to one who purchases** land **from a robber,** and clai[ms] compensation from the seller for his improvements that we[re] seized by the rightful owner?[22] Apparently, the Mishnah rul[es] that the purchaser of stolen property is compensated by the sell[er] for his improvements, which contradicts Rav Nachman. – ?

The Gemara answers:

**לֹא – No,** the Mishnah is not referring to one who purchases fro[m] a robber. **בְּבַעַל חוֹב –** Rather, **it refers to a** case in which pu[r]chased land is improved and then seized by the seller's **credito[r].** In such a case, it does not resemble interest if the purchaser [is] compensated by the seller for his improvements.[23] Rav Nac[h]man's ruling, that the purchaser of *stolen* property may not [be] compensated by the seller for improvements, stands.

The Gemara objects:

**אִי בְּבַעַל חוֹב – If** the Mishnah refers **to a** case in which land [is] seized by the seller's **creditor, אֵימָא רֵישָׁא – then explain t[he] first part** of the Mishnah, which states: **[אֵי]ן מוֹצִיאִין לַאֲכִילַת פֵּירוֹת – WE DO NOT COLLECT** from sold property **FOR CONSUM[P]TION OF PRODUCE. וְאִי בְּבַעַל חוֹב –** Now, **if it refers to t[he]** compensation of a purchaser for ripe produce[24] which was seiz[ed] **by a creditor** together with the purchased land,[25] **[בַּ]עַל חוֹב מִי אִית לֵיהּ פֵּירֵי – does a creditor have** a right to collect such **pr[o]duce** from a purchaser? **וְהָאָמַר שְׁמוּאֵל – But Shmuel sai[d]: בַּעַל חוֹב גּוֹבֶה אֶת הַשְּׁבָח –** The seller's **creditor collects the im[]provements** of the land from the purchaser. **שְׁבָח אֵין –** W[e] deduce from Shmuel's statement that he **indeed** collects the **im[]provements, אֲבָל פֵּירוֹת לֹא – but not** ripe **produce.**[26] Co[n]sequently, this case cannot refer to seizure by a creditor. – ?

NOTES

13. First, he said that the purchaser is compensated for his improvements in this case, even according to Shmuel. Later, he reconsidered and said that even in this case Shmuel rules that the purchaser is not compensated (*Rashi*).

14. Literally: It was loose in his hand. He was indecisive because he was unsure of the reason for Shmuel's ruling (*Rashi*).

15. I.e. it would appear as if the purchaser violated the prohibition against taking interest (see note 12).

16. *Gittin* 48b.

17. These rulings will be explained by the Gemara below.

18. Even if a man does not explicitly accept these obligations, it is a תְּנַאי כְּתוּבָּה, *an automatic feature of the marriage contract,* that he must provide for his wife's food during and after his lifetime until she remarries, and for his daughters' food after his death, until they are married or reach the age of twelve and a half (see *Rashi; Kesubos* 47b-48a, 53b).

19. Where the Gemara mentions 'encumbered property,' it refers to property sold by the debtor subsequent to incurring the debt. The debtor's unsold property — regardless of whether he owned it when he incurred the debt — is known as 'unencumbered property.'

20. When one borrows money or incurs some other financial obligations, all real property in his possession at that time becomes encumbered to the debt. Thus, if the debtor is unable to repay when the obligation becomes due, the creditor can collect that property even from a buyer who subsequently purchased it. Where the debtor sold several pieces of property, the creditor must collect the property sold *last.* If the value of that property is insufficient to satisfy the total debt, the creditor collects the property sold *next to last,* and so on (see *Bava Kamma* 8a).

Because of this law, a prudent buyer is able to protect his purchase against seizure by purchasing from a seller who retains enough property to cover his outstanding debts. This way, even if the seller should subsequently sell his other properties, the seller's creditors could not collect the land from the earlier buyer since they would be forced to seize the property sold last.

Now, if we permitted seizure of sold property to cover costs of support of a man's wife and daughters, a buyer could not possibly protect his purchase. Most sellers are subject to this obligation, and the sum of money needed to satisfy it is open-ended and cannot be predicted. The amounts needed to cover the consumption of produce and the improvements of land are also unpredictable (as we shall see below when the[se] cases are explained). Therefore, people might refrain from purchasi[ng] real property for fear of losing their investments to these creditors. T[o] preclude such hindrance to free trade, the Sages decreed that propert[y] could not be seized to satisfy these obligations (*Rashi*).

21. I.e. the Mishnah lists cases in which the Sages restricted seizure [of] sold property. One of these cases is that of a purchaser seeking compe[n]sation from the seller for seizure of improvements he made to the pu[r]chased property. Since the Mishnah states that the buyer may not colle[ct] from sold property, it is clear that he *may* collect from the seller's ow[n] property.

22. As the Mishnah teaches, the Sages restricted seizure of sold propert[y] where this might hinder free trade (see note 20). Here also, since a su[b]sequent purchaser of the seller's land could not estimate the amou[nt] which this previously sold property would appreciate before its seizur[e] he could not properly protect his purchase from subsequent seizure b[y] the first purchaser. Therefore, improvements may not be collected fro[m] sold property. The principal amount, however, may be collected fro[m] sold property, since the amount of the obligation is known to any subse[]quent purchaser (*Rashi*).

23. Since the land was owned by the seller, and since it may be retaine[d] by the purchaser if the creditor is paid directly by the seller, it is consi[d]ered an acquisition of the purchaser's until it is seized by the credito[r]. Consequently, the money forwarded from the purchaser to the seller i[s] a payment, not a loan. Therefore, when the purchaser claims compensa[]tion for the seized land and improvements, it appears as if he has resol[d] the property at a profit to the seller who then pays his debt with it; it doe[s] not appear as if the purchaser received interest on a loan (*Rashi*).

24. Although still connected to the ground, the produce was ready to b[e] harvested and did not require any additional nourishment from th[e] ground (*Rashi*).

25. The assumption is that the first two cases of the Mishnah discuss [a] like scenario. Thus, if the second case discusses collection by a credito[r] the earlier case must likewise discuss such collection.

26. Since the creditor has the right to collect the land, he may collect i[t] in its improved state (see *Rashi*). The ripe produce, however, is not con[]sidered part of the land, and may not be collected (see *Ramban* to 15a ד״ה שבח; cf. *Ritva*).

## גמרא

יכול לחזור בו א משהחזיק בה אינו יכול לחזור בו דא"ל חייתא דקטרי סברת וקבלת מאימתי הויא חזקה ב מכי דייש אמצרי ואיכא דאמרי ג אפילו באחריות נמי דאמר ליה אחוי טרפך ואשלם לך איתמר המוכר שדה לחבירו ונמצאת שאינה שלו רב אמר יש לו מעות ויש לו שבח ושמואל אמר מעות יש לו שבח אין לו בעו מיניה מרב הונא פירש לו את השבח מהו טעמא דשמואל משום דלא פירש שבחא והכא הא פירש לה או דלמא טעמיה דשמואל כיון דלית ליה קרקע מחזי כרבית א"ל (א) אין ולאו ורפיא בידיה איתמר אמר רב נחמן אמר שמואל מעות יש לו שבח אין לו אע"פ שפירש לו את השבח מאי טעמא כיון דקרקע אין לו שכר מעותיו עומד ונוטל איתיביה רבא לרב נחמן (ב) ד אין מוציאין לאכילת פירות ה ולשבח קרקעות ו ולמזון האשה והבנות מנכסים משועבדים מפני תיקון העולם ממשעבדי הוא דלא מפקינן הא מבני חורין מפקינן וקתני מיהא לשבח קרקעות מאי לאו בלוקח מגזלן לא בבעל חוב אי בבעל חוב אימא רישא אין מוציאין לאכילת פירות ואי בבעל חוב בעל חוב מי אית ליה פירי (ג) והאמר שמואל ז בעל חוב גובה את השבח שבח אין ח אבל פירות לא אלא פשיטא בגוזל ונגזל ומדרישא בגוזל ונגזל סיפא נמי בגוזל ונגזל מידי אריא הא כדאיתא והא כדאיתא והא לא תני הכי (ד) לשבח קרקעות כיצד הרי שגזל שדה מחבירו והרי היא יוצאה מתחת ידו כשהוא גובה גובה את הקרן מנכסים משועבדים ושבח גובה מנכסים בני חורין היכי דמי אילימא כדקתני גזלן ממאן גבי אלא לאו ט כגון שגזל שדה מחבירו ומכרה לאחר והשביחה א"ל לאו תרוצי קא מתרצת תריץ נמי בבעל חוב ת"ש לאכילת פירות כיצד הרי שגזל שדה מחבירו והרי היא יוצאה מתחת ידו כשהוא גובה גובה את הקרן מנכסים משועבדים ופירות גובה מנכסים בני חורין היכי דמי אילימא כדקתני גזלן ממאן גבי אלא לאו י כגון שגזל שדה מחבירו ומכרה לאחר והשביחה אמר רבא הכא במאי עסקינן כגון שגזל שדה מחבירו [א] מלאה פירות ואכל את הפירות וחפר בה בורות שיחין ומערות כ בא נגזל לגבות קרן גובה מנכסים משועבדים בא נגזל לגבות פירות גובה מנכסים בני חורין רבה בר רב הונא אמר כגון שנטלוה

## רש"י

יכול לחזור בו. ובשלא נתן מעות: אינו יכול לחזור בו. ואפילו לא נתן מעות שהקרקע נקנית בחזקה והמעות על זה מלוה: חייתא. שק מלא קשרים: מכי דייש אמצרי. מתקן גבולי השדה ומגביהם: איכא דאמרי אפי' באחריות נמי. אע"ג דסוף סוף עליה הדר אין יכול לחזור בו שהמוכר מעכב עליו ולא מצי אמר הוא הואיל וסופך לשלם לי מעותי השתא דבידי אעכבם: דאמר ליה אחוי טרפך ואשלם לך. כשיעמידוך (א) ויזכו בדין ויכתוב לך הדיין שטר טורף עלי שבדין טרפוה ממך בשבילי בא ואשלם לך וכל כמה דלא עמדת בדין איני ירא מהם: שאינה שלו. שלא היתה של מוכר שהיתה גזולה בידו והנגזל בא ומוציא מיד הלוקח: יש לו. ללוקח מן המוכר מעות: ויש לו שבח. אם זה השביח את הקרקע בזבל או בגדר קודם שהוציא נגזל מידו גובה לוקח מן המוכר שבח ואם תאמר הנגזל יתן השבח שהרי השיבו קרקע משובחת (ב) כגון שגזלה משובחת והכסיפה ביד הגזלן: שבח אין לו. לקמן מפרש טעמא: פירש לו את השבח. כשמכרה לו התנה אם יטרפוה מידך אשלם לך את השבח מהו: כיון דלית ליה קרקע. הואיל ואין קרקע זו שלו נמצא שאין כאן שום מכר והמעות מלוה אצלו וכשמשלם יותר ממה שנטל מחזי כרבית: אין ולאו. תחילה אמר אין וחזר ואמר לאו רפוי היה הדבר בידו שלא היה יודע טעמו של דבר יפה: לאכילת פירות כו'. מפרש להו לקמן: למזון האשה והבנות. תנאי כתובה שמקבל עליו את תהא יתבא בביתי ומיתזנא מנכסי וכן הבנות בנן נוקבן דיהוו ליכי מינאי אינון יהון יתבן בביתי ומיתזנן מנכסי עד דתלקחן לגוברין אין מוציאין לאחד מכל אלו מנכסים משועבדים: מפני תיקון העולם. שאם אתה אומר יטרפו לקוחות על כך אין לך אדם שלוקח שדה מחבירו דהא אין לך אדם שאין חוב זה מוטל עליו ודבר שאין לו קצבה היא ואכילת פירות ושבח קרקעות נמי דבר שאינו ידוע הוא ואין הלקוחות יודעין להזהר בכך: מאי לאו בלוקח שדה מגזלן. והשביחה ובא נגזל וטרפה חוזר לוקח וגובה קרן מן המוכר אפילו מנכסים משועבדים שמכר אחר מכירה זו דשטרו של זה קודם שכתב בו אחריות והשבח מנכסים בני חורין ולא ממשועבדים מפני תיקון העולם שהשבח לא היה קצוב בשעת מכירה כשקיבל עליו אחריות אלמא אית ליה ללוקח שבח מגזלן: לא בבעל חוב. שטרפה בעל חוב ממנו בשביל חובו ולא גזולה היתה דההיא ודאי אית ליה שבחא דמכירה מעלייתא היא כל זמן שלא טרפה ממנו שאם פרע המוכר מעותיו לבע"ח הרי הוא מסולק מן הלקוחות הלכך כי משלם ליה יותר ממה שקיבל השתא הוא דהדר זבין מיניה קרקע המכורה לו ולא מחזי כשכר מעותיו: לאכילת פירות. ס"ד הא מיירי בשדה שטרפוה מליאה פירות מיד הלוקח וחוזר לוקח לגבות מן המוכר ואי בשטרפה בעל חוב מי אית ליה לבע"ח פירות גמורין המחוברין בקרקע ואינן צריכין לקרקע כלום שיכול לטורפן: גובה את השבח. וכל הקרקע טורף מיד הלוקח כמו שהיא משובחת ע"י הלוקח: בגוזל ונגזל. וכגון שגזלה עם פירותיה ומכרה אי נמי גזלה בלא פירות ומכרה לאחר ועשה בה פירות וטוען נגזל ארעאי אשבח ומיהו היאלה שהוציא הלוקח ישלם לו הנגזל שהרי מתוך כך הושבחה יותר ואם אין השבח יותר אלא היאלה יתירה נותן לו יאלה שיעור שבח ודיו: הא כדאיתא כו'. רישא בנגזל וסיפא בבעל חוב ולקמיה מותיב לה מרישא: והא לא תני הכי. בברייתא עלה דהך מתניתין דאין מוציאין דתוקמה בבעל חוב: והרי היא יוצאה מתחת ידו. שבית דין מוציאין אותה מידו: כשהוא גובה. לקמיה מפרש לה: אילימא כדקתני. שלא מכרה גזלן ומידו היא יוצאה בדין: גזלן ממאן גבי. ממאן יש לו לגבות וכי מה נתן בה: והשביחה. והרי היא בדין יוצאה מתחת ידו של לוקח אלמא אית ליה שבחא ללוקח מגזלן: שגזל שדה מחבירו ומכרה לאחר והשביח. ונעשה פירות גמורין ונגזל לוקחה עם פירותיה ואינו נותן אלא יאלה דקאמר ארעאי אשבח וקתני דלוקח חוזר וגובה מגזלן מן המחוררין: אמר רבא כו'. האי כשהוא גובה לאו בלוקח קאמר דבשלא מכרה עסקינן וגובה את הקרן דקאמר בנגזל וא"ת קרן אמאי גובה מנכסים משועבדים הרי קרקע לפניו כגון שחפר בה בורות דאפחתה משויה: שנטלוה

## תוספות

ויש לו שבח. שהנגזל לוקח הקרקע עם השבח ואינו משלם ללוקח רק היציאה כדין יורד לתוך שדה חבירו שלא ברשות דאם השבח יתר על היציאה נותן לו את היציאה ואותו שבח היתר יקח הלוקח מן הגזלן ומיירי שנגזלה ריקנית: ושמואל אמר מעות יש לו. אפילו קנאה שלא באחריות כדפי' לעיל (ה) וכן משמע דמיירי דומיא דהכיר בה שאינה שלו דלקמן דמיירי על כרחך שלא באחריות כדקאמר שמואל מעות מתנה דאי באחריות אמאי מעות מתנה:

סיפא נמי בגזל כו'. מרישא עצמה היה יכול להקשות כדמקשה בסמוך אלא כמה שיכול להקשות משבח גופיה פריך: תריץ נמי בבעל חוב. בפרק מי שמת (ב"ב דף קנז: ושם ד"ה גובה) רצה להוכיח דאקני קנה ומכר משתעבד מהכא דגבי בעל חוב שבח שלא היה בעין בשעת הלואה ודחי ר"מ היא דאמר אדם מקנה דבר שלא בא לעולם וא"ת ולוכח משמואל דאמר בעל חוב גובה את השבח ושמואל גופיה הוא דבעי ליה התם דלא מצי למימר דשמואל נמי סבר כר"מ ומבעי ליה אליבא דרבנן דהא בפרק אע"פ (כתובות דף נט.) פסק שמואל כר' יוחנן הסנדלר דלית ליה אדם מקנה כו' וי"ל דהא דאמר שמואל בעל חוב גובה את השבח היינו לפי המסקנא דהתם דפשיט דאקני קנה ומכר משתעבד אף לרבנן ואם תאמר אדרבה לוכח מהכא דלא משתעבד מדלא טריף בע"ח ממשעבדי דטריף לוקח דאין לומר דאחר שטרף בע"ח קרקע מן הלוקח קנה המוכר קרקעות ומכרן דא"כ גם השבח יגבה מהנהו משעבדי דגם השבח היה קצוב כיון שכבר טרף הבעל חוב קודם שלקח זה הקרקע וי"ל דמיירי שזה הקרקע עשאו המוכר לבעל חוב אפותיקי ולכך גובה אותו בע"ח ואע"פ שיש שאר משעבדי אך קשה אמאי דחיק לדחויי בפרק מי שמת (ב"ב דף קנז: ושם) הא מני ר"מ היא יעמיד כשעשאו אפותיקי דאז בעל חוב גובה את השבח היתר על היציאה חנם כדין יורד לתוך שדה חבירו כדמשמע לקמן או יעמיד בלוקח מן הגזלן וכגון שיש לו קרקע או קנו מידו כדמתרך לקמן בשמעתין: כשעמד

## עין משפט נר מצוה

קיז א ב מיי' פ"ט מהל' מכירה הל' ג סמג לאוין קנו ועשין פב טוש"ע ח"מ סי' רכו סעיף ה:

קיח ד מיי' פ"ט מהל' גזלה ואבידה הל' ה ופכ"א מהל' מלוה ולוה הל' א סמג עשין עג טוש"ע ח"מ סי' שעג סעיף ב:

קיט ה מיי' פ"ט מהל' גזלה ואבידה הל' ז ופכ"א מהלכות מלוה ולוה הל' א סמג שם טוש"ע שם סעיף א וסי' קטו סעיף א:

קכ ו מיי' פכ"א מהל' מלוה ולוה הל' א ופי"ח מהל' אישות הל' יג סמג עשין מח טוש"ע אה"ע סי' צג סעיף כא וסי' קיב סעיף ז:

קכא ז ח מיי' פכ"א מהל' מלוה ולוה הל' א סמג עשין צד טוש"ע ח"מ סי' קטו סעיף א:

קכב ט מיי' פ"ט מהל' גזלה ואבידה הל' ו ז סמג עשין עג טוש"ע ח"מ סי' שעג סעיף א:

קכג י מיי' שם הל' ו טוש"ע שם סעיף ב:

קכד כ מיי' שם הל' ד סמג שם טוש"ע ח"מ סי' שעג סעיף א:

## רבינו חננאל

והחזיק בה אין יכול לחזור בו הלוקח ואפי' באחריות נמי אין יכול לחזור בו דיכול למימר ליה אחוי לי טירפא ואשלם לך הא דאמר אביי המוכר שדה לחבירו א) ויצא עליה עסיקין וכו' הוו השמועה היא בפ' מי שהיה נשוי שתי נשים ובתחלת בבא קמא: איתמר המוכר שדה לחבירו ונמצאת שאינה שלו כלומר גזולה היתה בידו סוגיא דשמעתא בשבח ארעא ממילא הכא [פליגי] רב ושמואל הכא רב אמר יש לו מעות ויש לו שבח ושמואל אמר מעות יש לו שבח אין לו. ואמר רב נחמן אע"פ שפירש לו את השבח אין לו. מתיב רבא מהא דתנן במס' גיטין פ' הניזקין אין מוציאין לאכילת פירות ולשבח קרקעות ולמזון האשה והבנות מנכסים משועבדים מפני תיקון העולם הא מבני חרי מוציאין מאי לאו בלוקח מגזלן. ת"ר נחמן תרוייהו לאכילת ב) פירות ולשבח קרקעות בבעל חוב ופשוטה היא. רבא אמר כגון שגזל שדה מליאה פירות ואכל הפירות וחפר בשדה בורות שיחין ומערות ובא הנגזל להוציא מידו כו'.

## חשק שלמה על ר"ח

א) אולי צ"ל זו השמועה היא וכו' או דצ"ל הא דאמר אביי ראובן שמכר שדה לשמעון באחריות וכו' הוו השמועה היא וכו'. ב) לפנינו בגמ' דרשב דאין מוציאין לאכילת פירות בגוזל ונגזל מיירי ואולי דרבינו היה לו גי' אחרת בגמ' וצ"ע.

## מסורת הש"ס

א) [שבת קיג, קדושין סה.], ב) ג' מח:, ג) בבא קמא [לקמן טו. קיג, כתו נג.], ד) לקמן קט: בתרא קנז [ע"ש ו רשב"ם], ה) ע"ח ז שעבוד.

## הגהות הב"ח

(א) רש"י ד"ה דאמר וכו' כשיעמידוך ויזכו וכו' בשבילי בא ואשלם: (ב) ד"ה ויש וכו' קרקע משובחת לומר כגון שגזלה:

## הגהות הגר"א

[א] גמ' מלאה פירות. נ"ב הרמב"ם ל"ג (ועמ"ש רבינו בח"מ סע"ג ס"ק י"א):

## ליקוטי רש"י

אין יכול לחזור שהקרקע נקנה בחזקה א"ל לך חזק וקני שמחזיקין מיד וגו' מעות לאחר ומשהחזיק בה נתח המעות. חייתא. קטן. דקיטרי. קשרים [כתובות צג.]. קשורה מלא רוח [ב"ק סברת וקבילת. חתיכות כסף כלו נתרלים לאבד מעו מספק. אפי' באחרי נמי. מכרה לו אינו לחזור בו מחמת עסי ולא אמרינן סוף סוף ע הדר ואטרוחי דייני ל לן [כתובות שם]. אפי' אחריות עליו די"ל הו וסופו לחזור עליו על נמי יחזור ויטלנה אפ אינו יכול לחזור בו. אח טרפך. שכתבו לך ב שטר טירפא שבדין נ ממך ואשלם לך [ב"ק ש ואשלם לך. וכל שלא יצאה מידך לא אפ שהרבה עוררין שאין ז בדין [כתובות שם]. ולאו. זימנין א"ל זימנין א"ל לא [שבת קט לא היה מחזיק בדבריו לאיסור ולא להיתר פעמ שאמר הן ופעמים שא לאו [קדושין סה.]. ורפ בידיה. רפויה הי התשובה בפיו אם לאס אם להתיר [שבת קיג.]. היתה מוחזקת הוראה בידו [קדושין שם]. מוציאין לאכילת פירות ולשבח קרקעות. הנגזל מוציא מנכסים משועבדים לקרקע ולשבח המוכר שאינו מטיל עליו בשעה שגזל מנכסים בני חורין. והשביחה הלוקח מעות ומכר לוה הנכסים והשביחום לקוחות בע"ח הגוף והש [בכורות נב.]. ואינו מח ללוקח כלום [ב"ק צה] והרי היא יוצא מתחת ידו. של לו שהנגזל מוציאה בדין. כשהוא גובה. הלוקח חוזר על הגזלן שהנגזל בא ונוטל שדהו כמות שהוא והלוקח חוזר על הגזלן שמכרה לו באחריות [ב"ק צה.]. מנכסים משועבדים. טורף לקוחות שלקחו אחריו מפני שהאחריות של בשטר מכירתו קודם למקחו [לקמן עב:]. שהוא קדם והויא כמלוה בשטר שהרי כתב לו בשטר המכירה שאם יטרפוה ממנו יחזור ויגבה מנכסיו [ב"ק צה:]. ושבח מנכסים בני חורין. ולא ממשועבדים מפני תקון העולם ד הלקוחות יכולין להזהר בדבר שאין לו קצבה כגון אחריות השבח והפירות דבשלמא בקרן נזהרין להניח מקום לגבות ממנו ואי לא נזהרו אפסידו אנפשייהו [לקמן עב:].

יָכוֹל לַחֲזוֹר בּוֹ – **he may withdraw** from the transaction and he need not proceed with payment for the field.[1] מִשֶּׁהֶחֱזִיק בָּהּ – However, **once he performed a proprietary act on [the field],** אֵינוֹ יָכוֹל לַחֲזוֹר בּוֹ – **he may not withdraw,** and must proceed with payment for the field.[2] דְּאָמַר לֵיהּ – **For [Reuven] may tell [Shimon]:** חַיִּיתָא דִּקְטָרֵי סְבָרַת וְקַבְּלַת – **"You knew** about **and accepted a bag** full **of knots";** i.e. you willingly purchased a field without insisting on a guarantee.[3]

The Gemara elaborates:

מֵאֵימָתַי הָוְיָא חֲזָקָה – **At what point is it** considered that Shimon has performed **a proprietary act** on the field? מִכִּי דַּיֵּישׁ אַמְּצְרֵי – **From when he walks along the borders** of the field.[4]

The Gemara presents an opinion that goes one step further:

וְאִיכָּא דְּאָמְרֵי – **And there are those who say** that this ruling applies אֲפִילּוּ בְּאַחֲרָיוּת נַמִּי – **even** if Reuven's sale to Shimon was **with a guarantee.** דְּאָמַר לֵיהּ – **For [Reuven] may tell [Shimon]:** אַחְוֵי טִרְפָּךְ – **"Show me your seizure receipt**[5] וַאֲשַׁלֵּם לָךְ – **and** then **I will pay you.**[6] In the meantime, however, you must pay me for the field."[7]

The Gemara now discusses the rights of a purchaser of stolen land:

אִיתְּמַר – **It was said:** הַמּוֹכֵר שָׂדֶה לַחֲבֵירוֹ – If **one sells a field to his fellow** וְנִמְצֵאת שֶׁאֵינָהּ שֶׁלּוֹ – **and it is discovered that [the field] was not his** to sell,[8] and the rightful owner repossesses his field, רַב אָמַר – **Rav says:** יֵשׁ לוֹ מָעוֹת – **[The purchaser] has** the right to compensation from the seller for the **money** that he paid for the field,[9] וְיֵשׁ לוֹ שְׁבָח – **and he has** right to compensation from the seller for his **improvements** to field.[10] וּשְׁמוּאֵל אָמַר – **But Shmuel says:** מָעוֹת יֵשׁ לוֹ – **He h** the right to compensation for the **money,** שְׁבָח אֵין לוֹ – **but does not have** the right to compensation for his **improvemen**

The Gemara analyzes Shmuel's opinion:

בָּעוּ מִינֵּיהּ מֵרַב הוּנָא – **They** [i.e. the scholars of the yeshivah] **quired of Rav Huna:** פֵּירַשׁ לוֹ אֶת הַשְּׁבָח מַהוּ – **What** is the l **where [the seller] explicitly stated to [the purchaser]** that would compensate him for **the improvements?** If the field w stolen property, does the purchaser collect compensation for improvements from the seller? מָא דִשְׁמוּאֵל מִשּׁוּם דְּלֹא פֵּירַשׁ שְׁבָחָא – **Is the reasoning of Shmuel** that he does not coll improvements from the seller **because [the seller] did not e plicitly accept** responsibility for **improvements** if the land w seized? וְהָכָא הָא פֵּירַשׁ לָהּ – **But here,** in this case, since **he e plicitly accepted [responsibility]** for them, he must compens the purchaser. אוֹ דִּלְמָא טַעֲמֵיהּ דִּשְׁמוּאֵל – **Or, perhaps, the re soning of Shmuel** is that כֵּיוָן דְּלֵית לֵיהּ קַרְקַע – **since the la is not [the seller's],** the money forwarded to him is not viewed payment, but as a loan.[11] מֶחְזֵי כְּרִיבִּית – Therefore, when t purchaser receives compensation for his improvements in ad tion to the return of the principal, **it appears as** if he receiv **interest** on the loan.[12] If so, even where the seller explicitly agre to compensate the purchaser for his improvements, it still rese bles interest and the purchaser may not be compensated. – ? אָמַר לְהוּ אֵין וְלָאו וְרַפְיָא בִּידֵיהּ – **[Rav Huna]** first **told them y**

NOTES

1. The Gemara discusses a case in which Shimon did not yet pay for the field [or perform an act of acquisition to it] (*Rashi*). Had he paid for the field, he would have acquired title even without having performed a proprietary act, and would then be unable to back out (see *Kiddushin* 26a).

Abaye teaches that Shimon's withdrawal is sanctioned by the Rabbis although they ordinarily frown upon one who backs out after a verbal commitment to make a purchase (*Shitah Mekubetzes*).

2. By performing a proprietary act [or any other act of acquisition] on the field, Shimon acquires title even if he has not yet paid for the field, and the unpaid purchase price is considered a loan. Thus, he may not back out of the purchase (*Rashi*, see *Kiddushin* 26a; see, however, *Tosafos* and *Rosh*).

Abaye's ruling applies only to an unguaranteed sale. However, if Reuven guaranteed the field, Shimon may back out of the sale even after performing a proprietary act. Since Shimon has not yet paid, and if he had, Reuven would eventually have to reimburse him for the collected land, there is no need for Shimon to pay for the field now and later receive a refund (see *Rashi* ד״ה איכא).

3. "A bag [full] of knots" is a colloquial expression denoting a risky transaction.

When someone purchases merchandise contained in a knotted bag, he cannot inspect the merchandise to determine its quality, and thus risks making a bad purchase. Similarly, Shimon purchased a field without a guarantee, thereby risking loss of his money if the field is seized (see *Rashash*).

4. By walking along the borders, Shimon compacts the ground, thereby shoring up the fence (see *Rashi* here and *Rashbam* to *Bava Basra* 100a ד״ה עד).

Making any physical improvement to a field constitutes a proprietary act and may be used to acquire title (see *Bava Basra* 42a). Thus, by repairing the boundary markers, Shimon acquires title and may not back out of the transaction; he must pay Reuven the purchase price agreed upon.

5. When the seller's creditor collects land, the court provides this document to the purchaser as evidence that his land was seized lawfully in payment of the seller's obligation (*Rashi*).

6. The seller denies the claims against the field and maintains that his ownership of the field will be upheld in court. Therefore, he argues that until the court decides otherwise, the sale is binding and the purchaser must pay (*Rashi*).

7. The purchaser may not retain the money in anticipation of its eve tual return (*Rashi;* see note 2).

8. I.e. the seller had stolen the land (*Rashi*).

9. Since it was discovered that the purchaser did not in fact purcha anything, he is entitled to a refund of his money (cf. *Rashbam* to *Ba Basra* 44b ד״ה נמצאת).

10. *Rashi* raises the objection that it is the owner of the field, rather th the seller, who should pay for at least a portion of the value of t improvements. This is based on the law that one who makes unauth rized improvements to a field has the right to demand from the own the lesser of his expenses or the increased value of the field due to t improvements (see below, 101a). Rashi therefore explains that o Gemara discusses a case in which the field depreciated while in t robber's possession and the purchaser improved it only to its value at t time of the theft. In this case, he cannot demand any payment from t owner, and must turn to the seller for the entire compensation (*Ras* as explained by *Pnei Yehoshua*).

Others disagree with *Rashi,* arguing that even in this case the pu chaser may demand payment from the owner, since he did improve t property. Rather, they explain that our Gemara discusses a case which the value of the improvements exceeds the purchaser's expense It is this excess amount which the purchaser demands from the sell (see *Tosafos, Shitah Mekubetzes*).

11. A transfer of money can be regarded as payment only where som thing was received in return for it. Since the property was not t seller's, he in fact did not give anything to the purchaser in return for h money. We are thus forced to regard the money forwarded to the sell as a loan from the purchaser (see *Rashi*).

12. Generally, whenever a lender collects an amount in excess of the su lent to the borrower, we regard the excess amount as compensation f the loan, and the lender violates the Torah's prohibition against takir interest (*Leviticus* 25:36, 37). Since we regard the money transferre from the purchaser to the seller as a loan, the refund of the purchaser money is viewed as the repayment of the loan. The excess amount r turned to the purchaser could, therefore, be regarded as interest.

In this case, however, the compensation is not for the loan, but f the loss of his improvements. Therefore, it is described by the Gema as having "the appearance of interest," but not being in fact actu interest.

יכול לחזור בו [א] משהחזיק בה אינו יכול לחזור בו דא"ל חייתא דקטרי סברת וקבלת מאימתי הויא חזקה [ב] מכי דייש אמצרי ואיכא דאמרי [ג] אפילו באחריות נמי דאמר ליה אחוי טרפך ואשלם לך איתמר המוכר שדה לחבירו ונמצאת שאינה שלו רב אמר יש לו מעות ויש לו שבח ושמואל אמר מעות יש לו שבח אין לו בעו מיניה מרב הונא פירש לו את השבח מהו טעמא דשמואל משום דלא פירש שבחא והכא הא פירש לה או דלמא טעמיה דשמואל כיון דלית ליה קרקע מחזי כרבית א"ל (א) אין ולאו ורפיא בידיה איתמר אמר רב נחמן אמר שמואל מעות יש לו שבח אין לו אע"פ שפירש לו את השבח מאי טעמא כיון דקרקע אין לו שכר מעותיו עומד ונוטל איתיביה רבא לרב נחמן (ג) [ד] אין מוציאין לאכילת פירות [ה] ולשבח קרקעות [ו] ולמזון האשה והבנות מנכסים משועבדים מפני תיקון העולם ממשעבדי הוא דלא מפקינן הא מבני חורין מפקינן וקתני מיהא לשבח קרקעות מאי לאו בלוקח מגזלן לא בבעל חוב אי בבעל חוב אימא רישא אין מוציאין לאכילת פירות ואי בבעל חוב בעל חוב מי אית ליה פירי (ג) והאמר שמואל [ז] בעל חוב גובה את השבח שבח אין [ח] אבל פירות לא אלא פשיטא בגוזל ונגזל ומדרישא בגוזל ונגזל סיפא נמי בגוזל ונגזל מידי אריא הא כדאיתא והא כדאיתא והא לא תני הכי (ד) לשבח קרקעות כיצד הרי שגזל שדה מחבירו והרי היא יוצאה מתחת ידו כשהוא גובה גובה את הקרן מנכסים משועבדים ושבח גובה מנכסים בני חורין היכי דמי אילימא כדקתני גזלן ממאן גבי אלא לאו [ט] כגון שגזל שדה מחבירו ומכרה לאחר והשביחה א"ל לאו תרוצי קא מתרצת תריץ נמי בבעל חוב ת"ש לאכילת פירות כיצד הרי שגזל שדה מחבירו והרי היא יוצאה מתחת ידו כשהוא גובה גובה את הקרן מנכסים משועבדים ופירות גובה מנכסים בני חורין היכי דמי אילימא כדקתני גזלן ממאן גבי אלא לאו [י] כגון שגזל שדה מחבירו ומכרה לאחר והשביחה אמר רבא הכא במאי עסקינן כגון שגזל שדה מחבירו [א] מלאה פירות ואכל את הפירות וחפר בה בורות שיחין ומערות [כ] בא נגזל לגבות קרן גובה מנכסים משועבדים בא נגזל לגבות פירות גובה מנכסים בני חורין רבה בר רב הונא אמר כגון

שנטלוה

**רש"י**

יכול לחזור בו. ובשלא נתן מעות: אינו יכול לחזור בו. ואפילו לא נתן מעות שהקרקע נקנית בחזקה והמעות על זה מלוה: חייתא. שק מלא קשרים: מכי דייש אמצרי. מתקן גבולי השדה ומגביהם: איכא דאמרי אפי' באחריות נמי. אע"ג דסוף סוף עליה הדר אין יכול לחזור בו שהמוכר מעכב עליו ולא מצי אמר הוא הואיל וסופך לשלם לי מעותי השתא דבידי אעכבם: דאמר ליה אחוי טרפך ואשלם לך. כשיעמידוך (א) ויזכו בדין ויכתוב לך הדיין שטר טורף עלי שבדין טרפוה ממך בשבילי בא ואשלם לך וכל כמה דלא עמדת בדין איני ירא מהם: שאינה שלו. שלא היתה של מוכר שהיתה גזולה בידו והנגזל בא ומוציא מיד הלוקח: יש לו. ללוקח מן המוכר מעות: ויש לו שבח. אם זה השביח את הקרקע בזבל או בגדר קודם שהוציא נגזל מידו גובה לוקח מן המוכר שבח ואם תאמר הנגזל יתן השבח שהרי השיבו קרקע משובחת (ב) כגון שגזלה משובחת והכסיפה ביד הגזלן: שבח אין לו. לקמן מפרש טעמא: פירש לו את השבח. כשמכרה לו התנה אם יטרפוה מידך אשלם לך את השבח מהו: כיון דלית ליה קרקע. הואיל ואין קרקע זו שלו נמצא שאין כאן שום מכר והמעות מלוה אצלו וכשמשלם יותר ממה שנטל מחזי כרבית: אין ולאו. תחילה אמר אין וחזר ואמר לאו רפוי היה הדבר בידו שלא היה יודע טעמו של דבר יפה: לאכילת פירות כו'. מפרש להו לקמן: למזון האשה והבנות. תנאי כתובה שמקבל עליו את תהא יתבא בביתי ומיתזנא מנכסי וכן הבנות בנן נוקבן דיהוו ליכי מינאי אינון יהון יתבן בביתי ומיתזנן מנכסי עד דתלקחן לגוברין אין מוציאין לאחד מכל אלו מנכסים משועבדים: מפני תיקון העולם. שאם אתה אומר יטרפו לקוחות על כך אין לך אדם שלוקח שדה מחבירו דהא אין לך אדם שאין חוב זה מוטל עליו ודבר שאין לו קצבה היא ואכילת פירות ושבח קרקעות נמי דבר שאינו ידוע הוא ואין הלקוחות יודעין להזהר בכך: מאי לאו בלוקח שדה מגזלן. והשביחה ובא נגזל וטרפה חוזר לוקח וגובה קרן מן המוכר אפילו מנכסים משועבדים שמכר אחר מכירה זו דשטרו של זה קודם שכתב בו אחריות והשבח מנכסים בני חורין ולא ממשועבדים מפני תיקון העולם שהשבח לא היה קצוב בשעת מכירה כשקיבל עליו אחריות אלמא אית ליה ללוקח שבח מגזלן: לא בבעל חוב. שטרפה בעל חוב ממנו בשביל חובו ולא גזולה היתה דההיא ודאי אית ליה שבחא דמכירה מעלייתא היא כל זמן שלא טרפה ממנו שאם פרע המוכר מעותיו לבע"ח הרי הוא מסולק מן הלקוחות הלכך כי משלם ליה יותר ממה שקיבל השתא הוא דהדר זבין מיניה קרקע המכורה לו ולא מחזי כשכר מעותיו: לאכילת פירות. ס"ד הא מיירי בשדה שטרפוה מליאה פירות מיד הלוקח וחוזר לוקח לגבות מן המוכר ואי בשטרפה בעל חוב מי אית ליה לבע"ח פירות גמורין המחוברין בקרקע ואינן צריכין לקרקע כלום שיכול לטורפן: גובה את השבח. וכל הקרקע טורף מיד הלוקח כמו שהיא משובחת ע"י הלוקח: בגוזל ונגזל. וכגון שגזלה עם פירותיה ומכרה אי נמי גזלה בלא פירות ומכרה לאחר ועשה בה פירות וטוען נגזל ארעאי אשבח ומיהו היציאה שהוציא הלוקח ישלם לו הנגזל שהרי מתוך כך הושבחה יותר ואם אין השבח יותר אלא היציאה יתירה נותן לו יציאה שיעור שבח ודיו: הא כדאיתא כו'. רישא בנגזל וסיפא בבעל חוב ולקמיה מותיב לה מרישא: והא לא תני הכי. בברייתא עלה דהך מתניתין דאין מוציאין דמוקמה בבעל חוב: והרי היא יוצאה מתחת ידו. שבית דין מוציאין אותה מידו: כשהוא גובה. לקמיה מפרש לה: אילימא כדקתני. שלא מכרה גזלן ומידו היא יוצאה בדין: גזלן ממאן גבי. ממאן יש לו לגבות וכי מה נתן בה: והשביחה. והרי היא בדין יוצאה מתחת ידו של לוקח אלמא אית ליה שבחא ללוקח מגזלן: שגזל שדה מחבירו ומכרה לאחר והשביח. ונעשה פירות גמורין ונגזל לוקחה עם פירותיה ואינו נותן אלא יציאה דקאמר ארעאי אשבח וקתני דלוקח חוזר וגובה מגזלן מן המחוררין: אמר רבא כו'. האי כשהוא גובה לאו בלוקח קאמר דבשלא מכרה עסקינן וגובה את הקרן דקאמר בנגזל וא"ת קרן אמאי גובה מנכסים משועבדים הרי קרקע לפניו כגון שחפר בה בורות דאפחתה משוייה:

שנטלוה

**תוספות**

ויש לו שבח. שהנגזל לוקח הקרקע עם השבח ואינו משלם ללוקח רק היציאה כדין יורד לתוך שדה חבירו שלא ברשות דאם השבח יתר על היציאה נותן לו את היציאה ואותו שבח היתר יקח הלוקח מן הגזלן ומיירי שנגזלה ריקנית: ושמואל אמר מעות יש לו. אפילו קנאה שלא באחריות כדפי' לעיל ה) וכן משמע דמיירי דומיא דהכיר בה שאינה שלו דלקמן דמיירי על כרחך שלא באחריות כדקאמר שמואל מעות מתנה דאי באחריות אמאי מעות מתנה:

סיפא נמי בגוזל כו'. מרישא עלמה היה יכול להקשות כדמקשה בסמוך אלא כמה שיכול להקשות מסתמא גופיה פריך: תריץ נמי בבעל חוב. בפרק מי שמת (ב"ב דף קנז: ושם ד"ה גובה) רלה להוכיח דאקני קנה ומכר משתעבד מהכא דגבי בעל חוב שבח שלא היה בעין בשעת הלואה ודאי ר"מ היא דאמר אדם מקנה דבר שלא בא לעולם וא"ת ולוכח משמואל דאמר בעל חוב גובה את השבח ושמואל גופיה הוא דבעי ליה התם דלא מצי למימר דשמואל נמי סבר כר"מ ומבעי ליה אליבא דרבנן דהא בפרק אע"פ (כתובות דף נט.) פסק שמואל כר' יוחנן הסנדלר דלית ליה אדם מקנה כו' וי"ל דהא דאמר שמואל בעל חוב גובה את השבח היינו לפי המסקנא דהתם דפשיט דאקני קנה ומכר משתעבד אף לרבנן ואם תאמר אדרבה לוכח מהכא דלא משתעבד מדלא טריף בע"ח ממשעבדי דטריף לוקח דאין לומר דאחר שטרף בע"ח קרקע מן הלוקח קנה המוכר קרקעות ומכרן דא"כ גם השבח יגבה מהנהו משעבדי דגם השבח היה קצוב כיון שכבר טרף הבעל חוב קודם שלקח זה הקרקע וי"ל דמיירי שזה הקרקע עשאו המוכר לבעל חוב אפותיקי ולכך גובה אותו בע"ח ואע"פ שיש שאר משעבדי אך קשה אמאי דחיק לדחויי בפרק מי שמת (ב"ב דף קמ: ושם) הא מני ר"מ היא יעמיד כשעשאו אפותיקי דאז בעל חוב גובה את השבח היתר על היציאה חנם כדין יורד לתוך שדה חבירו כדמשמע לקמן או יעמיד בלוקח מן הגזלן וכגון שיש לו קרקע או קנו מידו כדמתרך לקמן בשמעתין:

כשעמד

**מסורת הש"ס**

א) [שבת קיג., ק... קדושין סה.], ב) ג... מח:, ג) בבא קמא [לקמן טו., קי:, כת... נב.], ד) לקמן עב:, בתרא קמ: [ע"ש ו... רשב"ס], ה) ע"א ... שעבוד.

**הגהות הב"ח**

(א) רש"י ד"ה ד... אחוי וכו' כשיעמידוך ... ומזכו וכו' בשבילי או ואשלם: (ב) ד"ה ויש וכו' קרקע משובחת לומר כגון שגזלה:

**הגהות הגר"א**

[א] גמ' מלאה פיר... נ"ב הרמב"ם ל"ג (ועמ"ש רבינו בח"מ שע"ג ס"ק י"א):

**ליקוטי רש"י**

אין יכול לחזור. שהקרקע נקנה בחזקה א"ל לך חזק וקני שמחזיקין מיד ועו... מעות לאחר ומשהחזיק בה נתן המעות. חייתא. ... קטן. דקיטרי. ... קשרים [כתובות צג.]. קשורה מלא רום [ב"ק ... סברת וקבילת. ... חתיכות כסף כל ... נתרלים לאבד מעו... מספק. אפי' באחרי... נמי. מכרה לו אינו ... לחזור בו מחמת עס... ולא אמרינן סוף סוף ... הדר ולאטרוחי דייני ... לן [כתובות שם]. אפי' ... אחריות עליו דס"ל הו... וסופו לחזור עליו ע... נמי יחזור ויטלנה אם ... אינו יכול לחזור בו. א... טרפך. שכתבו לך ...

שהנגזל מוציאה בדין. כשהוא גובה. הלוקח חוזר על הגזלן שהנגזל בא ונוטל שדהו כמות שהוא והלוקח חוזר על הגזלן שמכרה לו באחריות [ב"ק צה.]. מנכסים משועבדים. טורף לקוחות שלקחו אחריו מפני שהאחריות ש... בשטר מכירתו קודם למקחו [לקמן עב:]. שהוא קדם והוא כמלוה בשטר שהרי כתב לו בשטר המכירה שאם יטרפוה ממנו יחזור ויגבה מנכסיו [ב"ק צה:]. ושבח מנכסים בני חורין. ולא ממשועבדים מפני תקון העולם ש... הלקוחות יכולין להזהר בדבר שאין לו קצבה כגון אחריות השבח והפירות דבשלמא בקרן נזהרין להניח מקום לגבות ממנו ואי לא נזהרו אפסידו אנפשייהו [לקמן עב:].

**עין משפט נר מצוה**

קיז א ב ג מיי' פי"ט מהל' מכירה הל' ג סמג לאוין קע ועשין פב טוש"ע ח"מ סי' רכו סעיף ה:

קיח ד מיי' פ"ט מהל' גזלה ואבידה הל' ה ופכ"א מהל' מלוה ולוה הל' א סמג עשין עג לד טוש"ע ח"מ סי' שעג סעיף ב:

קיט ה מיי' פ"ט מהל' גזלה ואבידה הל' ז ופכ"א מהלכות מלוה ולוה הל' א סמג שם טוש"ע שם סעיף א וסי' קטו סעיף א:

קכ ו מיי' פכ"א מהל' מלוה ולוה הל' א ופי"ח מהל' אישות הל' יג סמג עשין מח טוש"ע אה"ע סי' לג סעיף כא וסי' קיב סעיף ז:

קכא ז ח מיי' פכ"א מהל' מלוה ולוה הל' א סמג עשין לד טוש"ע ח"מ סי' קטו סעיף א:

קכב ט מיי' פ"ט מהל' גזלה ואבידה הל' ו ז סמג עשין עג טוש"ע ח"מ סי' שעג סעיף א:

קכג י מיי' שם הל' ח טוש"ע שם סעיף ב:

קכד כ מיי' שם הל' ד סמג שם טוש"ע ח"מ סי' שעב סעיף א:

**רבינו חננאל**

והחזיק בה אין יכול לחזור בו הלוקח ואפי' באחריות נמי אין יכול לחזור בו דיכול למימר ליה אחוי לי טירפא ואשלם לך הא דאמר אביי המוכר שדה לחבירו א) ויצאו עליה עסיקין וכו' וזו השמועה היא בפ' מי שהיה נשוי שתי נשים ובתחלת בבא קמא: איתמר המוכר שדה לחבירו ונמצאת שאינה שלו כלומר גזולה היתה בידו סוגיא דשמעתא בשבח דשבחא ארעא ממילא [פליגי] רב ושמואל הכא רב אמר יש לו מעות ויש לו שבח ושמואל אמר מעות יש לו שבח אין לו. ואמר רב נחמן אע"פ שפירש לו את השבח אין לו. מתיב רבא מהא דתנן במס' גיטין פ' הניזקין אין מוציאין לאכילת פירות ולשבח קרקעות ולמזון האשה והבנות מנכסים משועבדים מפני תיקון העולם הא מבני חרי מוציאין מאי לאו בלוקח מגזלן. ופריק רב נחמן תרוויהו לאכילת ב) פירות ולשבח קרקעות בבעל חוב ופשוטה היא. רבא אמר כגון שגזל שדה מליאה פירות ואכל הפירות וחפר בשדה בורות שיחין ומערות ובא הנגזל להוציאה מידו כו'.

**חשק שלמה על ר"ח**

א) אולי צ"ל זו השמועה היא וכו' או דצ"ל הא דאמר אביי ראובן שמכר שדה לשמעון באחריות וכו' חו השמועה היא וכו'. ב) לפנינו בגמ' דרישא דאין מוציאין לאכילת פירות בודאי בגזל ונגזל מיירי ואולי דרבינו היה לו גי' אחרת בגמ' וצ"ע.

חדא הוא דחד טעם הוא דמשום דקאמר רבי אלעזר מחלוקת בשאין חייב מודה הוא מתרץ הכי תיובתא דשמואל בתרתי חדא כרבי אלעזר דהא מוקי מתניתין בשאין חייב מודה והדא א) דאמר שמואל מצא שטר הקנאה בשוק יחזיר לבעלים ב) ולא חיישינן לפרעון תיובתא דקתני הכא אע"פ ששניהם מודים לא יחזיר לא לזה ולא לזה אלמא חיישינן לפרעון וכל שכן הכא דלא מודה לוה דחיישינן לפרעון אמר שמואל מ"ט דרבנן א סברי ג) אחריות טעות סופר הוא א"ל רבא בר איתי לרב אידי בר אבין ומי אמר שמואל הכי והאמר שמואל שבח שפר ושעבוד צריך לימלך לימא מאן דאמר הא לא אמר הא לא קשיא כאן בשטר הלואה דלא יהיב איניש זוזי בכדי כאן במקח וממכר דעביד איניש דזבין ארעא ליומיה כי ההיא דאבוה בר איהי זבין עליתא מאחתיה אתא בעל חוב טרפא מיניה אתא לקמיה דמר שמואל אמר ליה כתבה לך אחריות אמר ליה לא אמר ליה אם כן זיל לשלמא א"ל והא מר הוא דאמר אחריות טעות סופר הוא א"ל הני מילי בשטרי הלואה אבל בשטרי מקח וממכר לא דעביד איניש דזבין ארעא ליומיה ד) אמר אביי ראובן שמכר שדה לשמעון באחריות ובא בעל חוב דראובן וקא טריף ליה מיניה ב דינא הוא דאזיל ראובן ומשתעי דינא בהדיה ולא מצי א"ל לאו בעל דברים דידי את דא"ל דמפקת מיניה עלי דידי הדר איכא דאמרי ג אפי' שלא באחריות נמי דא"ל לא ניחא לי דליהוי לשמעון תרעומת עלי ואמר אביי ד ראובן שמכר שדה לשמעון שלא באחריות ויצאו עליה עסיקין עד שלא החזיק בה יכול

## רש"י

ומשני חדא הוא דחד טעמא הוא. טעם אחד הזקיקו לרבי אלעזר לומר את שתיהן דמשום דקאמר מחלוקת דמתניתין בשאין חייב מודה הוזקק לומר שאינו גובה אפילו מבני חורין וכיון דהולרך לסיים אבל כשחייב מודה דברי הכל יחזיר הוזקק לומר לא חיישינן לקנוניא: שטר הקנאה. דליכא למימר כתב ללות ולא לוה דהא אפילו לא לוה שעביד נפשיה: ולא חיישינן לפרעון. אפילו אין חייב מודה דאם איתא דפרעיה מקרע הוה קרע ליה והכא קתני אע"פ ששניהם מודים כו': וכ"ש בשאינו מודה. והא לא קשיא לר' אלעזר דהוא אמר בשאין חייב מודה לא יחזיר שום שטר הראוי לגבות דהאי דקאמר ר' מאיר יחזיר משום דלאו בר גבייה הוא: מאי טעמייהו דרבנן. דאמרי כי אין בו אחריות נכסים גובה אף מן המשועבדים: אחריות טעות סופר הוא. כשאינו כתוב בשטר סופר הוא שטעה אבל זה לא לוה לו מעותיו בלא אחריות נכסים דלא שדי איניש זוזי בכדי: שבח שפר ושעבוד צריך לימלך. הסופר צריך לימלך במוכר שדה לחבירו לישאל הימנו אם יקבל עליו לכתוב בשטר המכירה שהוא שיעבד לו נכסיו למכירה זו שאם יבא בעל חובו ויטרפנה מן הלוקח שיגבה לוקח זה הקרן והשבח שהשביח בה לפני טירפא משפר עידית שבנכסים ואם לא נמלך בו לא יכתוב שיש מוכר שאין מקבל עליו אחריות ואף אם קבל על הקרן לא קבל על השבח ואף אם קבל על שניהם לא קבל להגבותו מן העידית אלא מן הבינונית אלמא לאו טעות סופר הוא דאיכא למימר אמליך ביה ולא קבל עליה: לימא מאן דאמר הא. משמיה דשמואל: לא אמר הא. ואמוראי נינהו אליבא דשמואל: בשטרי הלואה. טעות סופר הוא כיון דלא אכיל פירות ולא מתהני מידי לא שדי זוזי בכדי לאוזפיה בלא אחריות וזה ימכור נכסיו וכשיבא לגבות לא ימצא כלום: עביד איניש דזבין ארעא ליומא. לספק יום אחד שמא לא יטרפוה ממנו ואם יטרפוה שמא לזמן מרובה ואוכל בתוך כך פירות הרבה: זיל לשלמא. אין כאן עוד דין שמחלת על הכל: באחריות. אם יטרפוה ממנו ישלם לו: לאשתעויי דינא בהדיה. דבע"ח ולסלקו מעל שמעון בכל טענה שיוכל לטעון ולומר פרעתיך כך וכך או כך וכך יש לי עליך תביעה ואני מעכב חוב זה תחתיו: ולא מצי. בע"ח למימר ליה לאו בעל דברים דידי את בדבר זה קרקע שמעון אני נוטל אם יש לך תביעה עלי העמידני בדין: דמפקת מיניה עלי הדר. מה שאתה מוציא משמעון יחזור עלי: עסיקין. עוררין כמו התעשקו עמו (בראשית כו):

## תוספות

מאי טעמייהו דרבנן. תימה אי שמואל ידע ברייתא דקתני אחד זה ואחד זה גובה מנכסים משועבדים א"כ היה לו לפרש המשנה כוותיה ולא הוה איתותב ואי לא ידע ברייתא מנליה דלרבנן אין בו אחריות וגבי ממשעבדי וי"ל דלא ידע הברייתא ומ"מ אית ליה מסברא כדפרישית לעיל (דף יג: ד"ה דברי) דאי לא גבי ממשעבדי לא גבי נמי מבני חרי כמו לר"מ: שעבוד צריך לימלך. בשטרי מקח ואי לא כתבו מבני חרי נמי לא גבי אי בעל חוב טרפה לה כדאמר בסמוך אפי' שלא באחריות דלא ניחא לי דלהוי תרעומת דשמעון עלי אלמא לא הדר עליה אבל אי נגזל טרפה חוזר על הגזלן אפילו בלא אחריות ואפילו ממשעבדי כיון דהוי מקח טעות הוי ליה שטר הלואה והשתא א"ש דלא קאמר הכא פירי דמיירי שבעל חוב טרפה ולית ליה פירי כדאמר לקמן (דף טו.) בעל חוב גובה את השבח שבח אין פירי לא והא ניחא נמי דלקמן (שם) אמר שמואל אמליך וכתוב שופרא ושבחא ופירי ולא קאמר שעבוד כדהכא משום דלקמן מיירי בנגזל שטרפה אף בלא כתיבת שעבוד חוזר עליו ואפי' ממשעבדי והיינו טעמא כדפרישית דכיון דיש לו שטר מקח והרי מקח בטל שגזולה היתה והוי ליה שטר הלואה דאמרינן ביה אחריות טעות סופר הוא והא דאמר שמואל בחזקת הבתים (ב"ב דף מג.) המוכר שדה שלא באחריות אין מעיד לו עליה מפני שמעמידה בפני בעל חובו הא לאו הכי מעיד לו עליה אפי' נמצאת שאינה שלו משמע דלא הדר עליה התם מיירי שפירש לו בשטר שלא באחריות אבל סתמא הדר עליה: דינא הוא דאתי ראובן. תימה מאי נפקא מינה דהא כל מה שיוכל לטעון ראובן טוען שמעון דטוענין ללוקח ואין לומר דנ"מ אם יש לבע"ח עדים שקרובים לראובן ורחוקים לשמעון דאי טעין נמי שמעון הם פסולים דכיון דאי מפסיד שמעון הדר על ראובן כדמוכח ספ"ק דמכות (דף ז.) גבי אלעא וטוביה קרובים דערבא הוו וקא מסיק דפסולים אף ללוה ולמלוה כיון דאי לית ליה ללוה אזיל בתר ערבא ומהאי טעמא נמי א"ל דנ"מ אם יש לשמעון עדים שהם קרובים לו ורחוקים לראובן דכי נמי טוען ראובן פסולים שעל פי עדותם ישאר הקרקע ביד שמעון שהוא קרובם וכל שכן כשקנה שלא באחריות שהם פסולים שאז מרויחים לו הקרקע לגמרי וי"ל דנ"מ אם אמר שמעון אין לי עדים ואין לי ראיה ואח"כ מצא עדים או ראיה שהוא אינו יכול להביא דאין הלכה כרשב"ג בראיה אחרונה (סנהדרין דף לא.) וראובן יביאם א"נ כגון שבעל חוב חייב שבועה דאורייתא לראובן והשתא יגלגל עליו שבועה שלא פרע אבל לשמעון לא ישבע אלא שבועה דרבנן ובפרק הכותב (כתובות דף פח.) אמר אי פקח הוא מייתי ליה לידי שבועה דאורייתא אלמא יש חומר בשבועה דאורייתא יותר משבועה דרבנן בנרות דולקות ונודות נפוחות כדמפרש בתשובת הגאונים ה) ועוד נפקא מינה כגון שראובן פקח ובעל דברים ועוד שאינו מעיז ברצון נגד ראובן לפי שידע שפרעו או אם יכול ראובן ללכת עמו לב"ד הגדול ושמעון אינו יכול [וע"ע תוס' כתובות לג: ד"ה דינא הוא וכו']: ויצאו עליה עסיקין. פי' עוררין ולא אנסין מדמפליג בין מכר באחריות ללא באחריות וכן מוכח פ' שבועת העדות (שבועות דף לא. ושם) ואשר לא טוב עשה וגו' זה הלוקח שדה שיש עליה עסיקין ואי אנסין תבא עליו ברכה: עד שלא החזיק בה כו'. תימה היכי מיירי אי גם לא נתן מעות פשיטא דיכול לחזור בו דאפילו מי שפרע ליכא ואי נתן המעות אמאי יכול לחזור בו והא קרקע נקנית בכסף אם לא נעמיד באתרא דלא קנו בכספא ועוד משהחזיק בה אינו יכול לחזור בו אבל באחריות יכול לחזור בו אמאי יכול לחזור בו כיון שנתן מעות והחזיק כמשפט ועוד חזקה דדייש אמגרי לא אשכחן בשום מקום ולמה הניח חזקה דתנן במתני' (ב"ב ד' מב.) דנעל גדר ופרץ ועוד מאי שנא הכא שנקט מאימתי הוי חזקה יותר מבשום מקום דבכמה מקומות מזכיר חזקה ולא בעי מאימת הוי חזקה ופירש ריב"א דמיירי כגון שקנאה בקנין גמור כגון בחליפין ולא נתן מעות וקאמר עד שלא החזיק בה חזקה דמפרש בתר הכי דייש אמגרי שלא הלך לארכה ולרחבה ולא סמכה דעתיה יכול לחזור בו משהחזיק בה שהלך לארכה ולרחבה אינו יכול לחזור בו אבל באחריות יכול לחזור בו כיון שלא נתן מעות ויש עוררים הואיל וסופו לשלם מעותיו עתה שהם בידו יעכבם וא"ש דדייש אמגרי אינה חזקה גמורה אלא לראותה אם היא מיושבת על לבו וא"ת כשהחזיק בה אמאי אינו יכול לחזור בו כיון שלא נתן מעות לימא ליה שקול ארעא בזוזך אפילו אית ליה זוזי מאי לסלק ליה לבע"ח בשאר דברים וגרסינן בהמוכר פירות (ב"ב ד' צב: ושם ד"ה אי) אי לתנהו להנהו זוזי כו' וי"ל דהכא מאי א"ל האי ארעא אינה שוה כפי מעותי לפי שיש עליה עוררים אבל שור שנגח כיון דלאייקר שוה מעותיו שפיר:

## עין משפט נר מצוה

קיד א מיי' פי"ח מהל' גזילה ואבידה הל' א ופי"ט מהל' מכירה הל' ג ופי"ח מהל' מלוה ולוה הל' ג ובסתם דלא פירש שאין לו עליו אחריות סמג עשין פב לד טוש"ע ח"מ סי' לט סעיף א וסי' קיא סעיף א וסי' רכה סעיף א:

קטו ב ג מיי' פי"ט מהל' מכירה הל' ט סמג לאוין קט ועשין פב טוש"ע ח"מ סי' רכו סעיף א:

קטז ד מיי' שם הל' ב טוש"ע שם סעיף ה:

## רבינו חננאל

והוא שמואל דאמר המוצא שטר הקנאה בשוק יחזירו לבעלים דלא חיישינן לפרעון מש"ה אמרי' תיובתא לשמואל בתרתי אבל ר' אלעזר לא שמעינן ליה דאמר בהדיא דברי הכל לא חיישינן לפרעון תיובתא עליה בחדא. וקי"ל כר' יוחנן דתניא כוותיה ונדחו דברי שמואל ור' אלעזר דהא איתותבו אבל תירוצא דרב אשי ודאביי לא נדחו דהא דר' יוחנן לא הוי להו תיובתא כדפרשינן לעילא. אמר שמואל מאי טעמייהו דרבנן דאמרי שטר שאין בו אחריות גבי אפי' ממשעבדי קסברי אחריות טעות סופר הוא. ומי אמר שמואל הכי והא אמר שמואל שפר שבח ושעבוד צריך לאימלוכי ביה לאו מכלל שאם לא נמלכו ביה אין כותבין ואי לא כתיב ליה א) לא שפר ולא שבח ולא שעבוד דהוא אחריות ואי אמרת אחריות טעות סופר הוא ואע"ג דלא כתב כמאן דכתב דמי אמאי לית ליה שעבוד. ופריק לא קשיא הא דאמר אחריות טעות סופר בשטרי הלואה ומתני' ומתניתא בשטרי הלואה אבל בשטרי מקנה לא אמרי' טעות סופר הוא דעביד מאן דזבין ארעא ליומיה כי הא דאיבות בר איהא זבן עיליתא מאחתיה וכו' ובהא אמר שמואל צריך לאימלוכי ולית הלכתא כשמואל אלא כדאסקינן לשמעתא והלכתא אחריות טעות סופר הוא בין בשטרי הלואה בין בשטרי מקח וממכר. המוכר שדה לחבירו ב) שלא באחריות

### חשק שלמה על ר"ח

א) אולי צ"ל ואם לא כתב ליה לית ליה לא שפר וכו'. ב) נראה דצ"ל שלא באחריות ויצאו עליה עסיקין והחזיק בה וכו'.

## מסורת הש"ס

… לקמן טו:, ב) [לעיל יג: …], ג) [לקמן טו:, … כתובות קד:, בבא בתרא … ט:], ד) בבא קמא ח: … כתובות לג: [ע"ש], [עיין ערוך ערך הסת].

## ליקוטי רש"י

… שטר הקנאה. שמקנה נכסיו מהיום בין ילוה … לא ילוה יגבה מהן … זמן מהיום [לעיל …]. אחריות טעות … סופר. שטר שאין בו … אחריות גובה מנכסים … משועבדים שלא הלוה זה … אלא באחריות … שעבוד נכסיו והסופר … [כתובות קד:]. … אחריות שלא נכתב בשטר … טעות סופר הוא וכמי … שנכתב בו דמי דלא שדי … איניש זוזי בכדי ולכך … מכוין המלוה שיכתוב … שטר אחריות אלא ששכח … הסופר וטעה ותפס שטר … אית ליה ולקוחות … דאפסידו אנפשייהו … קנו קרקע מן הלוה … הניחו לו בני חורין … לגבות מהן מלוה חובו … [רשב"ם ב"ב קנז.]. דאזיל … ראובן ומשתעי דינא … בהדיה. אם יש לו עליו … גלגול דברים לחשוב … כנגד חוב או אישתבע … דלא פרעתיך [כתובות …:]. לאו בעל דברים … דידי את. בקרקע זו … בר ילתה מרשותך ואנא … עבודי שקילנא [ב"ק ח:] … טורף ממך כלום … [כתובות שם]. עלי הדר. … שאתה מוציא משמעון … יחזור עלי שהרי קבלתי … אחריות [ב"ק שם]. … שלא באחריות נמי. … מכר ראובן לשמעון לא … אמר ליה בעל חוב … ראובן לאו בעל דברים … דידי את [כתובות שם]. … עסיקין. עוררין לומר … שלנו היא [ב"ק ט.]. כמו … (בראשית כו) כי התעשקו … עמו שמערערין על … המחזיק בה [שבועות לא.].

ccordance with Reuven's guarantee. Therefore, Reuven is considered a concerned party, and may personally argue the case with he creditor.

The Gemara presents an opinion that goes one step further:

אִיכָּא דְּאָמְרֵ – **There are those who say** that this ruling applies אֲפִילוּ שֶׁלֹּא בְּאַחֲרָיוּת נַמ – **even** if Reuven sold the field to Shimon **without a guarantee.** דְּאָמַר לֵיהּ – **For [Reuven] may tell [the creditor]:** לֹא נִיחָא לִי דְּלֶיהֱוֵי לְשִׁמְעוֹן תַּרְעוֹמֶת עֲלַי – **"I do not want Shimon to have a grievance against me."**[16] Reuven is therefore considered a concerned party, and may personally argue the case.[17]

Another law concerning a related matter:

וְאָמַר אַבַּיֵי – **And Abaye said:** רְאוּבֵן שֶׁמָּכַר שָׂדֶה לְשִׁמְעוֹן שֶׁלֹּא בְּאַחֲרָיוּת – **If Reuven sold a field to Shimon without a guarantee,** וְיָצְאוּ עָלֶיהָ עֲסִיקִין – **and protestors against** Reuven's ownership of **[the land] came forth,**[18] עַד שֶׁלֹּא הֶחֱזִיק בָּהּ – **as long as [Shimon] did not yet take possession of [the field],**

NOTES

6. If the creditor is successful in his bid to collect the property, Shimon annot recover his loss, because Reuven did not guarantee the land. himon would therefore be justified in being angry at Reuven for elling him an encumbered property.

7. The Gemara presumes that there are benefits which accrue to euven and Shimon by having Reuven argue the case. See *Tosafos* ד״ה דיו for suggestions as to some of these benefits.

[Among *Tosafos'* suggestions are: Reuven might be able to argue the ase more capably than Shimon. Additionally, if Reuven has already repaid the loan, the creditor might desist from pressing his false claim if that would entail brazenly confronting Reuven, who knows the truth. Shimon on the other hand, does not have first-hand knowledge of Reuven's repayment and he is therefore an easier target for the creditor's dishonest claim.]

18. They protest that the land belonged to them and not to Reuven. He therefore had no right to sell it to Shimon (*Rashi* to *Bava Kamma* 9a ד״ה עסיקין).

חדא הוא דחד טעם הוא דמשום דקאמר רבי אלעזר מחלוקת בשאין חייב מודה הוא מתרץ הכי תיובתא דשמואל בתרתי חדא כרבי אלעזר דהא מוקי מתניתין בשאין חייב מודה וחדא [א] דאמר שמואל מצא שטר הקנאה בשוק יחזיר לבעלים [ב] ולא חיישינן לפרעון תיובתא דקתני הכא אע"פ ששניהם מודים לא יחזיר לא לזה ולא לזה אלמא חיישינן לפרעון וכל שכן הכא דלא מודה לוה דחיישינן לפרעון אמר שמואל מ"ט דרבנן [א] סברי [ג] אחריות טעות סופר הוא א"ל רבא בר איתי לרב אידי בר אבין ומי אמר שמואל הכי והאמר שמואל שבח שפר ושעבוד צריך לימלך לימא מאן דאמר הא לא אמר הא לא קשיא כאן בשטר הלואה דלא יהיב איניש זוזי בכדי כאן במקח וממכר דעביד איניש דזבין ארעא ליומיה כי ההיא דאבוה בר איהי זבין עליתא מאחתיה אתא בעל חוב טרפא מיניה אתא לקמיה דמר שמואל אמר ליה כתבה לך אחריות אמר ליה לא אמר ליה אם כן זיל לשלמא א"ל והא מר הוא דאמר אחריות טעות סופר הוא א"ל הני מילי בשטרי הלואה אבל בשטרי מקח וממכר לא דעביד איניש דזבין ארעא ליומיה [ד] אמר אביי ראובן שמכר שדה לשמעון באחריות ובא בעל חוב דראובן וקא טריף ליה מיניה [ב] דינא הוא דאזיל ראובן ומשתעי דינא בהדיה ולא מצי א"ל לאו בעל דברים דידי את דא"ל דמפקת מיניה עלי דידי הדר איכא דאמרי [ג] אפי' שלא באחריות נמי דא"ל לא ניחא לי דליהוי לשמעון תרעומת עלי ואמר אביי [ד] ראובן שמכר שדה לשמעון שלא באחריות ויצאו עליה עסיקין עד שלא החזיק בה יכול

**רש"י**

ומשני חדא הוא דחד טעמא הוא. טעם אחד הזקיקו לרבי אלעזר לומר את שתיהן דמשום דקאמר מחלוקת דמתניתין בשאין חייב מודה הוזקק לומר שאינו גובה אפילו מבני חורין וכיון דהוצרך לסיים אבל כשחייב מודה דברי הכל יחזיר הוזקק לומר לא חיישינן לקנוניא: שטר הקנאה. דליכא למימר כתב ללות ולא לוה דהא אפילו לא לוה שעביד נפשיה: ולא חיישינן לפרעון. אפילו אין חייב מודה דאם איתא דפרעיה מקרע הוה קרע ליה והכא קתני אע"פ ששניהם מודים כו': וכ"ש בשאינו מודה. והא לא קשיא לר' אלעזר דהוא אמר בשאין חייב מודה לא יחזיר שום שטר הראוי לגבות דהאי דקאמר ר' מאיר יחזיר משום דלאו בר גבייה הוא: מאי טעמייהו דרבנן. דאמרי כי אין בו אחריות נכסים גובה אף מן המשועבדים: אחריות טעות סופר הוא. כשאינו כתוב בשטר סופר הוא שטעה אבל זה לא לוה לו מעותיו בלא אחריות נכסים דלא שדי איניש זוזי בכדי: שבח שפר ושעבוד צריך לימלך. הסופר צריך לימלך במוכר שדה לחבירו לישאל הימנו אם יקבל עליו לכתוב בשטר המכירה שהוא שיעבד לו נכסיו למכירה זו שאם יצא בעל חובו ויטרפנה מן הלוקח שיגבה לוקח זה הקרן והשבח שהשביח בה לפני טירפא מספר עידית שבנכסים ואם לא נמלך בו לא יכתוב שיש מוכר שאין מקבל עליו אחריות ואף אם קבל על הקרן לא קבל על השבח ואף אם קבל על שניהם לא קבל להגבותו מן העידית אלא מן הבינונית אלמא לאו טעות סופר הוא דאיכא למימר אמליך ביה ולא קבל עליה: לימא מאן דאמר הא. משמיה דשמואל: לא אמר הא. ואמוראי ניהו אליבא דשמואל: בשטרי הלואה. טעות סופר הוא כיון דלא אכיל פירות ולא מתהני מידי לא שדי זוזי בכדי לאוזפיה בלא אחריות וזה ימכור נכסיו וכשיבא לגבות לא ימצא כלום: עביד איניש דזבין ארעא ליומא. לספק יום אחד שמא לא יטרפוה ממנו ואם יטרפוה שמא לזמן מרובה ואוכל בתוך כך פירות הרבה: זיל לשלמא. אין כאן עוד דין שמחלת על הכל: באחריות. אם יטרפוה ממנו ישלם לו: לאשתעויי דינא בהדיה. דבע"ח ולסלקו מעל שמעון בכל טענה שיוכל לטעון ולומר פרעתיך כך וכך או כך וכך יש לי עליך תביעה ואני מעכב חוב זה תחתיו: ולא מצי. בע"ח למימר ליה לאו בעל דברים דידי את בדבר זה קרקע שמעון אני נוטל אם יש לך תביעה עלי העמידני בדין: דמפקת מיניה עלי הדר. מה שאתה מוציא משמעון יחזור עלי: עסיקין. עוררין כמו התעשקו עמו (בראשית כו):

**תוספות**

מאי טעמייהו דרבנן. תימה אי שמואל ידע ברייתא דקתני אחד זה ואחד זה גובה מנכסים משועבדים א"כ היה לו לפרש המשנה כוותיה ולא הוה איתותב ואי לא ידע ברייתא מנליה דלרבנן אין בו אחריות וגבי ממשעבדי וי"ל דלא ידע הברייתא ומ"מ אית ליה מסברא כדפרישית לעיל (דף יג: ד"ה דברי) דאי לא גבי ממשעבדי לא גבי נמי מבני חרי כמו לר"מ: שעבוד צריך לימלך. בשטרי מקח ואי לא כתבו מבני חרי נמי לא גבי אי בעל חוב טרפה לה כדאמר בסמוך אפי' שלא באחריות דלא ניחא לי דלהוי תרעומת דשמעון עלי אלמא לא הדר עליה אבל אי נגזל טרפה חוזר על הגזלן אפילו בלא אחריות ואפילו ממשעבדי כיון דהוי מקח טעות הוי ליה שטר הלואה והשתא א"ש דלא קאמר הכא פירי דמיירי שבעל חוב טרפה ולית ליה פירי כדאמר לקמן (דף טו.) בעל חוב גובה את השבח שבח אין פירי לא והא ניחא נמי דלקמן (שם) אמר שמואל אמליך וכתוב שופרא ושבחא ופירי ולא קאמר שעבוד כדהכא משום דלקמן מיירי בנגזל שטרפה אף בלא כתיבת שעבוד חוזר עליו ואפי' ממשעבדי והיינו טעמא כדפרישית דכיון דיש לו שטר מקח והרי מקח בטל שגזולה היתה והוי ליה שטר הלואה דאמרינן ביה אחריות טעות סופר הוא והא דאמר שמואל בחזקת הבתים (ב"ב דף מג.) המוכר שדה שלא באחריות אין מעיד לו עליה מפני שמעמידה בפני בעל חובו הא לאו הכי מעיד לו עליה אפי' נמצאת שאינה שלו משמע דלא הדר עליה התם מיירי שפירש לו בשטר שלא באחריות אבל סתמא הדר עליה: דינא הוא דאתי ראובן. תימה מאי נפקא מינה דהא כל מה שיוכל לטעון ראובן טוען שמעון דטוענין ללוקח ואין לומר דנ"מ אם יש לבע"ח עדים שקרובים לראובן ורחוקים לשמעון דאי טעין נמי שמעון הם פסולים דכיון דאי מפסיד שמעון הדר על ראובן כדמוכח ספ"ק דמכות (דף ז.) גבי אלעא וטוביה קרובים דערבא הוו וקא מסיק דפסולים אף ללוה ולמלוה כיון דאי לית ליה ללוה אזיל בתר ערבא ומהאי טעמא נמי א"ל דנ"מ אם יש לשמעון עדים שהם קרובים לו ורחוקים לראובן דכי נמי טוען ראובן פסולים שעל פי עדותם ישאר הקרקע ביד שמעון שהוא קרובם וכל שכן כשקנה שלא באחריות שהם פסולים שאז מרויחים לו הקרקע לגמרי וי"ל דנ"מ אם אמר שמעון אין לי עדים ואין לי ראיה ואח"כ מצא עדים או ראיה שהוא אינו יכול להביא דאין הלכה כרשב"ג בראיה אחרונה (סנהדרין דף לא.) וראובן יביאם א"נ כגון שבעל חוב חייב שבועה דאורייתא לראובן והשתא יגלגל עליו שבועה שלא פרע אבל לשמעון לא ישבע אלא שבועה דרבנן ובפרק הכותב (כתובות דף פח.) אמר אי פקח הוא מייתי ליה לידי שבועה דאורייתא אלמא יש חומר בשבועה דאורייתא יותר משבועה דרבנן בנרות דולקות ונודות נפוחות כדמפרש בתשובת הגאונים [ה] ועוד נפקא מינה כגון שראובן פקח ובעל דברים ועוד שאינו מעיז ברצון נגד ראובן לפי שידע שפרעו או אם יכול ראובן ללכת עמו לב"ד הגדול ושמעון אינו יכול [וע"ע תוס' כתובות לג: ד"ה דינא הוא וכו']: ויצאו עליה עסיקין. פי' עוררין ולא אנסין מדמפליג בין מכר באחריות ללא באחריות וכן מוכח פ' שבועת העדות (שבועות דף לא. ושם) ואשר לא טוב עשה וגו' זה הלוקח שדה שיש עליה עסיקין ואי אנסין תבא עליו ברכה: עד שלא החזיק בה כו'. תימה היכי מיירי אי גם לא נתן מעות פשיטא דיכול לחזור בו דאפילו מי שפרע ליכא ואי נתן המעות אמאי יכול לחזור בו והא קרקע נקנית בכסף אם לא נעמיד באתרא דלא קנו בכספא ועוד משהחזיק בה אינו יכול לחזור בו אבל באחריות יכול לחזור בו אמאי יכול לחזור בו כיון שנתן מעות והחזיק כמשפט ועוד חזקה דקיים אמגרי לא אשכחן בשום מקום ולמה הניח חזקה דתנן במתני' (ב"ב ד' מב.) דנעל גדר ופרץ ועוד מאי שנא הכא שנשאל מאימתי הוי חזקה יותר מבשום מקום דבכמה מקומות מזכיר חזקה ולא בעי מאימת הוי חזקה ופירש ריב"א דמיירי כגון שקנאה בקנין גמור כגון בחליפין ולא נתן מעות וקאמר עד שלא החזיק בה חזקה דמפרש בתר הכי דיים אמגרי שלא הלך לארכה ולרחבה ולא סמכה דעתיה יכול לחזור בו משהחזיק בה שהלך לארכה ולרחבה אינו יכול לחזור בו אבל באחריות יכול לחזור כיון שלא נתן מעות ויש עוררים הואיל וסופו לשלם מעותיו עתה שהם בידו יעכבם וא"ש דדיים אמגרי אינה חזקה גמורה אלא לראותה אם היא מיושבת על לבו וא"ת כשהחזיק בה אמאי אינו יכול לחזור בו כיון שלא נתן מעות לימא ליה שקול ארעא בזוזך אפילו אית ליה זוזי לפי המפרשים דאפילו אית ליה זוזי מצי לסלק ליה לבע"ח בשאר דברים וגרסינן בהמוכר פירות (ב"ב ד' לב: ושם ד"ה אי) אי לתנהו להנהו זוזי כו' וי"ל דהכא מצי א"ל האי ארעא אינה שוה כפי מעותי לפי שיש עליה עוררים אבל שור שנגח כיון דלאייקר שוה מעותיו שפיר:

**עין משפט נר מצוה**

קיד א מיי' פי"ח מהל' גזלה ואבידה הל' א ופי"ט מהל' מכירה הל' ג ופי"ח מהל' מלוה ולוה הל' ג ובכתם דלא פירש שאין לו עליו אחריות סמג עשין פב לד טוש"ע ח"מ סי' לט סעיף א וסי' קיא סעיף א וסי' רכה סעיף א:

קטו ב ג מיי' פי"ט מהל' מכירה הל' ט סמג לאוין קע ועשין פב טוש"ע ח"מ סי' רכו סעיף א:

קטז ד מיי' שם הל' ג טוש"ע שם סעיף ה:

**רבינו חננאל**

והוא שמואל דאמר המוצא שטר הקנאה בשוק יחזירו לבעלים דלא חיישינן לפרעון מש"ה אמרי' תיובתא לשמואל בתרתי אבל ר' אלעזר לא שמעינן ליה דאמר בהדיא דברי הכל לא חיישינן לפרעון תיובתא עליה בחדא. וקי"ל כר' יוחנן דתניא כוותיה ונדחו דברי שמואל ור' אלעזר דהא איתותבו אבל תירוצא דרב אשי ודאביי לא נדחו דהא דר' יוחנן לא הוי להו תיובתא כדפרשינן לעילא. אמר שמואל מאי טעמייהו דרבנן דאמרי שטר שאין בו אחריות גבי אפי' ממשעבדי קסברי אחריות טעות סופר הוא. ומי אמר שמואל הכי והא אמר שמואל שפר שבח ושעבוד צריך לאימלוכי ביה לאו מכלל שאם לא נמלכו ביה אין כותבין ואי לא כתיב ליה א) לא שפר ולא שבח ולא שעבוד דהוא אחריות ואי אמרת אחריות טעות סופר הוא ואע"ג דלא כתב כמאן דכתב דמי אמאי לית ליה שעבוד. ופריק לא קשיא הא דאמר אחריות טעות סופר בשטרי הלואה ומתני' ומתניתא בשטרי הלואה אבל בשטרי מקנה לא אמרי' טעות סופר הוא דעביד מאן דזבין ארעא ליומיה כי הא דאיבות בר איהא זבן עיליתא מאחתיה וכו' ובהא אמר שמואל צריך לאימלוכי ולית הלכתא כשמואל אלא כדאסקינן לשמעתא והלכתא אחריות טעות סופר הוא בין בשטרי הלואה בין בשטרי מקח וממכר. המוכר שדה לחבירו ב) שלא באחריות

**חשק שלמה על ר"ח**

א) אולי צ"ל ואם לא כתב ליה לית ליה לא שפר וכו'. ב) נראה דצ"ל שלא באחריות ויצאו עליה עסיקין והחזיק בה וכו'.

**מסורת הש"ס**

קמן טו:, ב) [לעיל יג:], ג) [לקמן טו:, ...ות קד:, בבא בתרא ...:], ד) בבא קמא ח: ...ות לג: [ע"ש], עיין ערוך ערך הסת].

**ליקוטי רש"י**

...ר הקנאה. שמקנה ...כסיו מהיום בין ילוה לא ילוה יגבה מהן ...ו זמן מהיום [לעיל ...]. אחריות טעות ...ר. שטר שאין בו ...יות גובה מנכסים עבדים שלא הלוה זה ...ת אלא באחריות ...בוד נכסיו והסופר ... [כתובות קד:]. ...יות שלא נכתב בשטר ...ת סופר הוא וכמי ...תב בו דמי דלא שדי ...ש זוזי בכדי ולכך ...ין המלוה שיכתוב ...ר אחריות אלא ששכח ...פר וטעה וכתם שטר ... אית ליה ולקוחות ... דאפסידו אנפשייהו ...חו קרקע מן הלוה ...הניחו לו בני חורין לגבות מהן מלוה חובו ...ב"ם ב"ב קנז.]. דאזיל ...ובן ומשתעי דינא ...דיה. אם יש לו עליו ... גלגול דברים לחשוב כנגד חוב או אישתבע דלא פרעתיך [כתובות ...]. לאו בעל דברים ...י את. בקרקע זו ...כר יצתה מרשותך ואנא ...כודי שקילנא [ב"ק ח:] ... טורף ממך כלום ...ובות שם]. עלי הדר. שאתה מוציא משמעון ...ר עלי שהרי קבלתי אחריות [ב"ק שם]. ...א באחריות נמי. ...ה ראובן לשמעון לא ...אמר ליה בעל חוב ...ובן לאו בעל דברים ... את [כתובות שם]. ...יקין. עוררין לומר ... היא [ב"ק ט.]. כמו ...אשית כו) כי התעשקו ... ושמערערין על ... מזיק בה [שבועות לא.].

The Gemara points out a contradiction to Shmuel's explanation from one of Shmuel's rulings:

אָמַר לֵיהּ רָבָא בַּר אִיתַי לְרַב אִידִי בַּר אָבִין — **Rava bar Ittei said to Rav Iddi bar Avin:** וּמִי אָמַר שְׁמוּאֵל הָכִי — **And did Shmuel** actually **say this,** i.e. that the absence of a guarantee in a document is presumed to be an oversight of the scribe? וְהָאָמַר שְׁמוּאֵל — **But Shmuel said:** שֶׁבַח שֶׁפֶר וְשִׁעְבּוּד — Regarding stipulations of compensation for **improvement,** that payment be rendered from **choice** properties, and provision for **a lien,**[8] צָרִיךְ לִימָּלֵךְ — if the scribe wants to insert these stipulations in a document recording the sale of land, **he must consult** the seller before inscribing them in the document.[9] Thus we see that provision for a lien must be stipulated in the document for a lien to be in effect, in contradiction to Shmuel's statement above that even in absence of such a stipulation a lien is still in effect. לֵימָא מַאן דְּאָמַר הָא — **Shall we say** then **that [the Sage] who relates this** statement in the name of Shmuel לָא אָמַר הָא — **does not relate this** other statement of Shmuel, i.e. will he reject it as not authentic? Are we faced with conflicting traditions about Shmuel's position in this matter?

The Gemara explains that there is no contradiction:

לָא קַשְׁיָא — **This is not a difficulty.** כָּאן בִּשְׁטַר הַלְוָאָה — **Here,** regarding Shmuel's explanation of the Rabbis' position, the reference is to **a loan document,** concerning which it is not necessary to stipulate a guarantee. דְּלָא יָהִיב אִינַשׁ זוּזֵי בְּכְדִי — Rather, the provision for a lien is implicit in the case of a loan, **for a person does not give away money for nothing.**[10] כָּאן בְּמִקָּח וּמִמְכָּר — But **here,** regarding Shmuel's other statement about "improvement, choice and lien," the reference is to a document of **buying and selling,** i.e. a contract of sale, concerning which it is necessary to stipulate a guarantee. דְּעָבֵיד אִינַשׁ דְּזָבִין אַרְעָא לְיוֹמֵי — In this case, a guarantee is not implied, **for it is conceivable for a person to buy** a piece of **land** even **for one day.**[11]

The Gemara finds corroboration for the distinction between loan documents and documents of sale in an episode that involved Shmuel himself:

כִּי הַהִיא דַּאֲבוּהַ בַּר אִיהִי — As related in **this** following episode, **in which Avuha bar Ihi** זְבִין עֲלִיתָא מֵאַחְתֵיהּ — **bought an upper story** of a house **from his sister.** אֲתָא בַּעַל חוֹב טַרְפָא מִינֵּיהּ — Then **a creditor** of the sister **came** and **seized [the second story] from him** in payment of a debt owed him by the sister. אֲתָא לְקַמֵּיהּ דְּמַר שְׁמוּאֵל — Avuha demanded that his sister recompense him, which she refused to do. So **he came before Shmuel** to sue his sister in court. אָמַר לֵיהּ כְּתְבָה לָךְ אַחֲרָיוּת — **[Shmuel] said to [Avuha], "Did she write for you** the stipulation of **a guarantee** in your document of sale?" אָמַר לֵיהּ לָא — **[Avuha] answered him, "No."** אָמַר לֵיהּ אִם כֵּן זִיל לִשְׁלָמָא — **[Shmuel]** then **said to [Avuha], "If so, go to peace."** I.e. you have no case. אָמַר לֵיהּ — **[Avuha] asked [Shmuel]:** וְהָא מַר הוּא דְּאָמַר אַחֲרָיוּת טָעוּת סוֹפֵר הוּא — **"But it is master who maintains that** the absence of **a guarantee** in a document **is an oversight of the scribe!** So I should have the right to a guarantee even if it was not spelled out in the document." אָמַר לֵיהּ — **[Shmuel] answered him:** הָנֵי מִילֵּי בִּשְׁטָרֵי הַלְוָאָה — **"That applies** only **in regard to loan documents;** אֲבָל בִּשְׁטָרֵי מִקָּח וּמִמְכָּר לָא — **but in regard to documents of buying and selling,** it does **not** apply. Rather, in sale documents, the guarantee must be spelled out, דְּעָבֵיד אִינַשׁ דְּזָבִין אַרְעָא לְיוֹמֵיהּ — **for it is conceivable for a person to buy** a piece of **land** even **for one day."**

The Gemara digresses to discuss a law relating to the sale of land with and without a guarantee:

אָמַר אַבַּיֵי — **Abaye said:** רְאוּבֵן שֶׁמָּכַר שָׂדֶה לְשִׁמְעוֹן בְּאַחֲרָיוּת — If **Reuven sold a field to Shimon with a guarantee,**[12] וּבָא בַּעַל חוֹב דִּרְאוּבֵן — **and Reuven's creditor comes** וְקָא טָרֵיף לֵיהּ מִינֵּיהּ — and attempts **to collect [the field] from [Shimon]** in payment of Reuven's obligation, דִּינָא הוּא — **the law is** דְּאָזִיל רְאוּבֵן וּמִשְׁתָּעֵי דִּינָא בַּהֲדֵיהּ — **that Reuven may go and argue the case with [the creditor]** to prevent him from collecting the field.[13] וְלָא מָצֵי אָמַר לֵיהּ — **And [the creditor] may not tell [Reuven]:** לָאו בַּעַל דְּבָרִים דִּידִי אַתְּ — **"You are not my legal opponent**[14] in this matter, and I need not respond to your arguments."[15] דְּאָמַר לֵיהּ — **For [Reuven] may respond to him:** דְּמַפַּקַתְּ מִינֵּיהּ עֲלֵי דִּידִי הָדַר — **"That land which you will remove from** the possession of **[Shimon] will in return** be demanded **from me,"** in

NOTES

8. If Reuven sells a field to Shimon and the field is later appropriated by Reuven's creditor who has a lien against the property, then if Shimon's sale document contains a stipulation that Reuven guarantees to recompense him for the loss of his field — both for the worth of the field and the improvements Shimon made in the field — Reuven is obligated to do so. Similarly, if Shimon stipulated that he have a lien for the guarantee against the real property Reuven possesses at the time of the sale, he may, in case of a default on Reuven's part, collect his guaranteed compensation from the properties Reuven sold after the sale to Shimon. Also, if Shimon stipulated that he be recompensed with choice land if the guarantee is paid with land, he has that right (*Rashi*).

9. If he did not receive permission from the seller to insert these stipulations, the scribe may not add them in on his own, for sometimes a seller may not want to obligate himself for any guarantee (i.e. even to recompense the buyer for the principal). Or even if he does accept an obligation to recompense the buyer for the field, he may not want to accept responsibility for the improvements. Similarly, even if he guaranteed the seller for both the principal and the improvements, the scribe may not insert a stipulation that the guarantee be paid from choice fields. Rather, in the absence of such an explicit stipulation, the buyer is entitled only to medium-grade land, like any other creditor (*Rashi*).

10. The lender receives no benefit from his loan, so it must be assumed that he at least wanted to guarantee his principal as much as possible and would certainly not lend the money if he felt that he had no lien against the borrower's real property. To lend without a lien is tantamount to giving away one's money for nothing, for the borrower may be insolvent when the creditor comes to collect the debt, and may have sold all of his properties in the interim (*Rashi*).

11. A person conceivably may buy a piece of land on a gamble [if the price is right], taking the chance that he may have to give the land up after one day, but that he may get to keep the land for a long time or even perpetually; it is possible that the seller's creditors will never get to appropriate the land [if the seller is able to pay from the property he retains for himself] or that they will not do so until a distant date. The buyer will then get to use the considerable amount of produce that will grow in the field during this long interval (*Rashi*).

12. I.e. Reuven agreed to refund Shimon's money in the event the field is collected by Reuven's creditor (*Rashi*).

13. Reuven may present his arguments for being absolved from his creditor's claim against him; e.g. that he already paid the creditor, or that the creditor owes *him* a sum of money as a result of a different obligation, which offsets this liability (*Rashi*).

14. Literally: master of words.

15. Ordinarily, a litigant need not respond to a third party, even one appointed as the representative of the other litigant (*Choshen Mishpat* 124; see *Beur HaGra* ad loc.). Accordingly, the creditor could claim that only Shimon may argue against him, for it is Shimon's land he desires to collect; as far as any claims that Reuven has against him, Reuven must initiate new proceedings, but may not block the collection of the land (*Rashi*). Therefore, unless Reuven is considered a concerned party, the creditor may refuse to respond to his arguments.

Others maintain that an appointed representative may argue the case for a litigant and they explain that Abaye discusses a case in which Shimon is out of town and therefore cannot appoint Reuven to represent him (*Tos. HaRosh;* also see *Ritva*).

חדא הוא דחד טעם הוא דמשום דקאמר רבי אלעזר מחלוקת בשאין חייב מודה הוא מתרץ הכי תיובתא דשמואל בתרתי חדא כרבי אלעזר דהא מוקי מתניתין בשאין חייב מודה וחדא דאמר שמואל מצא שטר הקנאה בשוק יחזיר לבעלים ולא חיישינן לפרעון תיובתא דקתני הכא אע"פ ששניהם מודים לא יחזיר לא לזה ולא לזה אלמא חיישינן לפרעון וכל שכן הכא דלא מודה לוה דחיישינן לפרעון אמר שמואל מ"ט דרבנן סברי אחריות טעות סופר הוא א"ל רבא בר איתי לרב אידי בר אבין ומי אמר שמואל הכי והאמר שמואל שבח שפר ושעבוד צריך לימלך לימא מאן דאמר הא לא אמר הא לא קשיא כאן בשטר הלואה דלא יהיב איניש זוזי בכדי כאן במקח וממכר דעביד איניש דזבין ארעא ליומיה כי ההיא דאבוה בר איהי זבין עליתא מאחתיה אתא בעל חוב טרפא מיניה אתא לקמיה דמר שמואל אמר ליה כתבה לך אחריות אמר ליה לא אמר ליה אם כן זיל לשלמא א"ל והא מר הוא דאמר אחריות טעות סופר הוא א"ל הני מילי בשטרי הלואה אבל בשטרי מקח וממכר לא דעביד איניש דזבין ארעא ליומיה אמר אביי ראובן שמכר שדה לשמעון באחריות ובא בעל חוב דראובן וקא טריף ליה מיניה דינא הוא דאזיל ראובן ומשתעי דינא בהדיה ולא מצי א"ל לאו בעל דברים דידי את דא"ל דמפקת מיניה עלי הדר איכא דאמרי אפי' שלא באחריות נמי דא"ל לא ניחא לי דליהוי לשמעון תרעומת עלי ואמר אביי ראובן שמכר שדה לשמעון שלא באחריות ויצאו עליה עסיקין עד שלא החזיק בה יכול

ומשני חדא הוא דחד טעמא הוא. טעם אחד הזקיקו לרבי אלעזר לומר את שתיהן דמשום דקאמר מחלוקת דמתניתין בשאין חייב מודה הוזקק לומר שאינו גובה אפילו מבני חורין וכיון דהולרך לסיים אבל כשחייב מודה דברי הכל יחזיר הוזקק לומר לא חיישינן לקנוניא: שטר הקנאה. דליכא למימר כתב ללות ולא לוה דהא אפילו לא לוה שעביד נפשיה: ולא חיישינן לפרעון. אפילו אין חייב מודה דאם איתא דפרעיה מקרע הוה קרע ליה והכא קתני אע"פ ששניהם מודים כו': וכ"ש בשאינו מודה. והא לא קשיא לר' אלעזר דהוא אמר בשאין חייב מודה לא יחזיר שום שטר הראוי לגבות דהאי דקאמר ר' מאיר יחזיר משום דלאו בר גבייה הוא: מאי טעמייהו דרבנן. דאמרי כי אין בו אחריות נכסים גובה אף מן המשועבדים: אחריות טעות סופר הוא. כשאינו כתוב בשטר סופר הוא שטעה אבל זה לא לוה לו מעותיו בלא אחריות נכסים דלא שדי איניש זוזי בכדי: שבח שפר ושעבוד צריך לימלך. הסופר לריך לימלך במוכר שדה לחבירו לישאל הימנו אם יקבל עליו לכתוב בשטר המכירה שהוא שיעבד לו נכסיו למכירה זו שאם יבא בעל חובו ויטרפנה מן הלוקח שיגבה לוקח זה הקרן והשבח שהשביח בה לפני טירפא משפר עידית שבנכסים ואם לא נמלך בו לא יכתוב שיש מוכר שאין מקבל עליו אחריות ואף אם קבל על הקרן לא קבל על השבח ואף אם קבל על שניהם לא קבל להגבותו מן העידית אלא מן הבינונית אלמא לאו טעות סופר הוא דאיכא למימר אמליך ביה ולא קבל עליה: לימא מאן דאמר הא. משמיה דשמואל: לא אמר הא. ואמוראי נינהו אליבא דשמואל: בשטרי הלואה. טעות סופר הוא כיון דלא אכיל פירות ולא מתהני מידי לא שדי זוזי בכדי לאוזפיה בלא אחריות וזה ימכור נכסיו וכשיבא לגבות לא ימצא כלום: עביד איניש דזבין ארעא ליומא. לספק יום אחד שמא לא יטרפוה ממנו ואם יטרפוה שמא לזמן מרובה ואוכל בתוך כך פירות הרבה: זיל לשלמא. אין כאן עוד דין שמחלת על הכל: באחריות. אם יטרפוה ממנו ישלם לו: לאשתעויי דינא בהדיה. דבע"ח ולסלקו מעל שמעון בכל טענה שיוכל לטעון ולומר פרעתיך כך וכך או כך וכך יש לי עליך תביעה ואני מעכב חוב זה תחתיו: ולא מצי. בע"ח למימר ליה לאו בעל דברים דידי את בדבר זה קרקע שמעון אני נוטל אם יש לך תביעה עלי העמידני בדין: דמפקת מיניה עלי הדר. מה שאתה מוליא משמעון יחזור עלי: עסיקין. עוררין כמו התעשקו עמו (בראשית כו): יכול

**מאי** טעמייהו דרבנן. תימה אי שמואל ידע ברייתא דקתני אחד זה ואחד זה גובה מנכסים משועבדים א"כ היה לו לפרש המשנה כוותיה ולא הוה איתותב ואי לא ידע ברייתא מנליה דלרבנן אין בו אחריות וגבי ממשעבדי וי"ל דלא ידע הברייתא ומ"מ אית ליה מסברא כדפרישית לעיל (דף יג: ד"ה דברי) דאי לא גבי ממשעבדי לא גבי נמי מבני חרי כמו לר"מ: **שעבוד** צריך לימלך. בשטרי מקח ואי לא כתבו מבני חרי נמי לא גבי אי בעל חוב טרפה לה כדאמר בסמוך אפי' שלא באחריות דלא ניחא לי דלהוי תרעומת דשמעון עלי אלמא לא הדר עליה אבל אי נגזל טרפה חוזר על הגזלן אפילו בלא אחריות ואפילו ממשעבדי כיון דהוי מקח טעות הוי ליה שטר הלואה והשתא א"ש דלא קאמר הכא פירי דמיירי שבעל חוב טרפה ולית ליה פירי כדאמר לקמן (דף טו.) בעל חוב גובה את השבח שבח אין פירי לא והא ניחא נמי דלקמן (שם) אמר שמואל אמליך וכתוב שופרא ושבחא ופירי ולא קאמר שעבוד כדהכא משום דלקמן מיירי בנגזל שטרפה אף בלא כתיבת שעבוד חוזר עליו ואפי' ממשעבדי והיינו טעמא כדפרישית דכיון דיש לו שטר מקח והרי מקח בטל שגזולה היתה והוי ליה שטר הלואה דאמרינן ביה אחריות טעות סופר הוא והא דאמר שמואל בחזקת הבתים (ב"ב דף מג.) המוכר שדה שלא באחריות אין מעיד לו עליה מפני שמעמידה בפני בעל חובו הא לאו הכי מעיד לו עליה אפי' נמלאת שאינה שלו משמע דלא הדר עליה התם מיירי שפירש לו בשטר שלא באחריות אבל סתמא הדר עליה: **דינא** הוא דאתי ראובן. תימה מאי נפקא מינה דהא כל מה שיוכל לטעון ראובן טוען שמעון דטוענין ללוקח ואין לומר דנ"מ אם יש לבע"ח עדים שקרובים לראובן ורחוקים לשמעון דאי טעין נמי שמעון הס פסולים דכיון דאי מפסיד שמעון הדר על ראובן כדמוכח ספ"ק דמכות (דף ז.) גבי אלעא וטוביה קרובים דערבא הוו וקא מסיק דפסולים אף ללוה ולמלוה כיון דאי לית ליה ללוה אזיל בתר ערבא ומהאי טעמא נמי א"ל דנ"מ אם יש לשמעון עדים שהם קרובים לו ורחוקים לראובן דכי נמי טוען ראובן פסולים שעל פי עדותם ישאר הקרקע ביד שמעון שהוא קרובם וכל שכן כשקנה שלא באחריות שהם פסולים שאז מרויחים לו הקרקע לגמרי וי"ל דנ"מ אם אמר שמעון אין לי עדים ואין לי ראיה ואח"כ מצא עדים או ראיה שהוא אינו יכול להביא דאין הלכה כרשב"ג בראיה אחרונה (סנהדרין דף לא.) וראובן יביאם א"נ כגון שבעל חוב חייב שבועה דאורייתא לראובן והשתא יגלגל עליו שבועה שלא פרע אבל לשמעון לא ישבע אלא שבועה דרבנן ובפרק הכותב (כתובות דף פח.) אמר אי פקח הוא מייתי ליה לידי שבועה דאורייתא אלמא יש חומר בשבועה דאורייתא יותר משבועה דרבנן בנרות דולקות ונודות נפוחות כדמפרש בתשובת הגאונים ועוד נפקא מינה כגון שראובן פקח ובעל דברים ועוד שאינו מעיז ברלון נגד ראובן לפי שידע שפרעו או אם יכול ראובן ללכת עמו לב"ד הגדול ושמעון אינו יכול [וע"ע תוס' כתובות לג: ד"ה דינא הוא וכו']: **ויצאו** עליה עסיקין. פי' עוררין ולא אנסין מדמפליג בין מכר באחריות ללא באחריות וכן מוכח פ' שבועת העדות (שבועות דף לא. ושם) ואשר לא טוב עשה וגו' זה הלוקח שדה שיש עליה עסיקין ואי אנסין תבא עליו ברכה: **עד** שלא החזיק בה כו'. תימה היכי מיירי אי גם לא נתן מעות פשיטא דיכול לחזור בו דאפילו מי שפרע ליכא ואי נתן המעות אמאי יכול לחזור בו והא קרקע נקנית בכסף אם לא נעמיד באתרא דלא קנו בכספא ועוד משהחזיק בה אינו יכול לחזור בו אבל באחריות יכול לחזור בו אמאי יכול לחזור בו כיון שנתן מעות והחזיק כמשפט ועוד חזקה דדייק אמגרי לא אשכחן בשום מקום ולמה הניח חזקה דתנן במתני' (ב"ב ד' מב.) דנעל גדר ופרץ ועוד מאי שנא הכא ששואל מאימתי הוי חזקה יותר מבשום מקום דבכמה מקומות מזכיר חזקה ולא בעי מאימת הוי חזקה ופירש ריב"א דמיירי כגון שקנאה בקנין גמור כגון בחליפין ולא נתן מעות וקאמר עד שלא החזיק בה חזקה דמפרש בתר הכי דייש אמגרי שלא הלך לארכה ולרחבה ולא סמכה דעתיה יכול לחזור בו משהחזיק בה שהלך לארכה ולרחבה אינו יכול לחזור בו אבל באחריות יכול לחזור כיון שלא נתן מעות ויש עוררים הואיל וסופו לשלם מעותיו עתה שהם בידו יעכבם וא"ש דדייש אמגרי אינה חזקה גמורה אלא לרצותה אם היא מיושבת על לבו וא"ת כשהחזיק בה אמאי אינו יכול לחזור בו כיון שלא נתן מעות לימא ליה שקול ארעא בזוזך אפילו אית ליה זוזי לפי המפרשים דאפילו אית ליה לבע"ח בשאר דברים וגרסינן בהמוכר פירות (ב"ב ד' צב: ושם ד"ה אי) אי לתנהו להנהו זוזי כו' וי"ל דהכא מצי א"ל האי ארעא אינה שוה כפי מעותי לפי שיש עליה עוררים אבל שור שנגח כיון דאייקר שוה מעותיו שפיר:

מסורת הש"ס

א) לקמן טז:, ב) [לעיל יג: יש"נ], ג) [לקמן טו:, כתובות קד:, בבא בתרא קסט:], ד) בבא קמא ח: כתובות לב: [ע"ש], ה) [עיין ערוך ערך הסת].

ליקוטי רש"י

שטר הקנאה. שמקנה לו נכסיו מהיום בין ילוה בין לא ילוה יגבה מהן מאותו זמן מהיום [לעיל יג.]. אחריות טעות סופר. שטר שאין בו אחריות גובה מנכסים משועבדים שלא הלוה זה מעות אלא באחריות שיעבוד נכסיו והסופר טעה [כתובות קד:]. אחריות שלא נכתב בשטר טעות סופר הוא וכמי שנכתב בו דמי דלא שדי איניש זוזי בכדי ולכך מכוין המלוה שיכתוב בשטר אחריות אלא שטעה הסופר וטעה וסתם שטר בלא אית ליה ולקוחות הוא דאפסידו אנפשייהו דלקחו קרקע מן הלוה דלא הניחו לו בני חורין די לגבות מהן מלוה חובו [רשב"ם ב"ב קנז.]. דאזיל ראובן ומשתעי דינא בהדיה. אם יש לו עליו שום גלגול דברים לחשוב חוב כנגד חוב או לישתבע דלא פרעתיך [כתובות לב:]. לאו בעל דברים דידי את. בקרקע זו כבר ילתה מרשותך ואנא יעבודי שקילנא [ב"ק ח:] אני טורף ממך כלום [כתובות שם]. עלי הדר. מה שאתה מוליא משמעון יחזור עלי שהרי קבלתי עלי אחריות [ב"ק שם]. שלא באחריות נמי. מכרה ראובן לשמעון לא מצי אמר ליה בעל חוב לראובן לאו בעל דברים דידי את [כתובות שם]. עסיקין. עוררין לומר שלנו היא [ב"ק ט.]. כמו (בראשית כו) כי התעשקו עמו שמערערין על המחזיק בה [שבועות לא.].

עין משפט
נר מצוה

קיד א מיי' פי"ח מהל' גזילה ואבידה הל' א ופי"ט מהל' מכירה הל' ג ופי"א מהל' מלוה ולוה הל' ג ובכסף דלא פירש שאין לו עליו אחריות סמג עשין פב לד טוש"ע ח"מ סי' לט סעיף א וסי' קיא סעיף א וסי' רכה סעיף א:
קטו ב ג מיי' פי"ט מהל' מכירה הל' ט סמג לאוין קט ועשין פב טוש"ע ח"מ סי' רכו סעיף א:
קטז ד מיי' שם הל' ב טוש"ע שם סעיף ה:

רבינו חננאל

והוא שמואל דאמר המוצא שטר הקנאה בשוק יחזירו לבעלים דלא חיישינן לפרעון מש"ה אמרי' תיובתא לשמואל בתרתי אבל ר' אלעזר לא שמעינן ליה דאמר בהדיא דברי הכל לא חיישינן לפרעון תיובתא עליה בחדא. וקי"ל כר' יוחנן דתניא כוותיה ונדחו דברי שמואל ור' אלעזר דהא איתותבו אבל תירוצא דרב אשי ודאביי לא נדחו דהא דר' יוחנן לא הוי להו תיובתא כדפרשינן לעילא. אמר שמואל מאי טעמייהו דרבנן דאמרי שטר שאין בו אחריות גבי אפי' ממשעבדי קסברי אחריות טעות סופר הוא. ומי אמר שמואל הכי והא אמר שמואל שפר שבח ושעבוד צריך לאימלוכי ביה לאו מכלל שאם לא נמלכו ביה אין כותבין ואי לא כתיב ליה א) לא שפר ולא שבח ולא שעבוד דהוא אחריות ואי אמרת אחריות טעות סופר הוא ואע"ג דלא כתב כמאן דכתב דמי אמאי לית ליה שעבוד. ופריק לא קשיא הא דאמר אחריות טעות סופר בשטרי הלואה ומתני' ומתניתא בשטרי הלואה אבל בשטרי מקנה לא אמרי' טעות סופר הוא דעביד מאן דזבין ארעא ליומיה כי הא דאיבות בר איהא זבן עיליתא מאחתיה וכו' ובהא אמר שמואל צריך לאימלוכי ולית הלכתא כשמואל אלא כדאסקינן לשמעתא והלכתא אחריות טעות סופר הוא בין בשטרי הלואה בין בשטרי מקח וממכר. המוכר שדה לחבירו ב) שלא באחריות

חשק שלמה על ר"ח

א) אולי צ"ל ואם לא כתב ליה לית ליה לא שפר וכו'. ב) נראה דל"ל שלא באחריות ויצאו עליה עסיקין והחזיק בה וכו'.

The Gemara clarifies the wording of the question:

חֲדָא הִ – Actually, **it is** only **one** point in which R' Elazar differs om the Baraisa, דְּחַד טַעַם הוּא – **for it is due to one reason** ıat R' Elazar's view diverges from the Baraisa's interpretation ı these two points.

The Gemara explains itself:

דְּמִשּׁוּם דְּקָאָמַר רַבִּי אֶלְעָ – **For it is because R' Elazar says** מַחְלוֹקֶת בְּשֶׁאֵין חַיָּיב מוֹדֶ – that **the disagreement** between R' [eir and the Sages **is** in a case **where the debtor does not admit** ıat he owes the debt הוּא מְתָרֵץ הָכִי – **that he interprets** the sagreement between R' Meir and the Sages **in this manner,** hich results in a twofold divergence from the Baraisa's interpre-tion.[1]

The Gemara now demonstrates the twofold refutation of hmuel's positions:

תְּיוּבְתָּא דִשְׁמוּאֵל בִּתְרֵ – The Gemara reiterates: **And** the araisa poses **a refutation of Shmuel's** view **on two** points. חֲדָא כְּרַבִּי אֶלְעָ – **On one** point, it is the same refutation **as** was osed to **R' Elazar;** דְּהָא מוּקֵי מַתְנִיתִין בְּשֶׁאֵין חַיָּיב מוֹדֶה – **for** hmuel], like R' Elazar, **interprets our Mishnah** as speaking oout a case **where the debtor does not admit** that the debt is ved,[2] which is contradicted by the Baraisa. וַחֲדָא – **And** the araisa **also** refutes Shmuel **on another** point. דְּאָמַר שְׁמוּאֵל – or **Shmuel said:** מָצָא שְׁטַר הַקְנָאָה בַּשּׁוּק – **If one found a note** acquisition in the marketplace, i.e. a loan document in which e borrower stipulates that he gives the person named as the nder a lien against his real property even in the event that the nder will not lend him the money, יַחֲזִיר לַבְּעָלִים – **he must** turn the note **to its owner,** וְלֹא חָיְישִׁינַן לְפֵרָעוֹן – **and we need not be concerned about payment.**[3]

The Gemara now points out how the Baraisa contradicts the view of Shmuel in regard to the concern about payment:[4]

תְּיוּבְתָּא – The Baraisa poses **a refutation** of Shmuel's view, דְּקָתָנֵי הָכָא – **for here the Baraisa teaches:** אַף עַל פִּי שֶׁשְּׁנֵיהֶם מוֹדִים – EVEN THOUGH BOTH the debtor and the creditor CONCUR that the notes were lost by the creditor, לֹא יַחֲזִיר לֹא לָזֶה וְלֹא לָזֶה – [THE FINDER] MAY NOT RETURN them TO EITHER [THE CREDITOR] OR TO [THE DEBTOR]. אַלְמָא חָיְישִׁינַן לְפֵרָעוֹן – **Thus,** we see from the Baraisa that **we need be concerned about payment** and collusion, even if the debtor admits that the debt is still owed, וְכָל שֶׁכֵּן הָכָא דְּלָא מוֹדֶה לֵיהּ – **and certainly where the borrower does not admit** that he owes the debt, but claims that he paid it, דְּחָיְישִׁינַן לְפֵרָעוֹן – **do we have to be concerned about payment.**[5] This contradicts Shmuel's ruling that even where the borrower does not admit that he owes the debt, the note is returned [if it is a note of acquisition] because, in his view, we need not be concerned about payment.

The Gemara cites Shmuel's explanation of the position of the Sages in our Mishnah:

אָמַר שְׁמוּאֵל – **Shmuel said:** מַאי טַעְמַיְיהוּ דְּרַבָּנַן – **What is the reason of the Rabbis** in our Mishnah, who say that even if a note of indebtedness does not make an explicit provision for a lien on real property, the creditor has the right to exact payment from the properties sold by the debtor after the loan was made?[6] סָבְרֵי אַחֲרָיוּת טָעוּת סוֹפֵר הוּא – **They maintain that** the absence of **a guarantee**[7] in a note **is** presumed to be **an oversight of the scribe,** and not an indication that such a guarantee is not implied.

NOTES

Because R' Elazar understands that the disagreement between R' eir and the Sages is in a case where the debtor does not admit that he ves the debt, he is forced to the conclusion that, according to R' Meir, e cannot collect even from the debtor with a note that has no lien; herwise, R' Meir would not allow the note to be returned in this case. ıe assumption that the disagreement between R' Meir and the Sages in a case where the debtor does not admit that he owes the debt also ıplies a second premise – that in a case where the debtor admits that owes the debt, R' Meir and the Sages concur that the finder must turn the note to the creditor, and we need not be concerned about llusion (*Rashi*).

[Above (13a), the Gemara cited Shmuel's opinion that we need not be ncerned about payment (see here, below), which raised the problem of w to interpret the Mishnah. He obviously cannot explain R' Meir's ling not to return the note that has a lien as due to the concern of yment and collusion, as Abaye does. The Gemara therefore postulated at Shmuel interprets the Mishnah as referring to a case where the btor does not admit that he owes the debt.]

The Gemara (there) also considered the possibility that Shmuel inter-ets the Mishnah as referring to a case where the debtor does admit at he owes the debt, but we are nevertheless concerned that perhaps e debtor drew up the note to borrow in the month of Nissan but did not tually borrow until Tishrei. This concern is based on the premise that such a scenario the lien does not take effect retroactively from Nissan, ntrary to Abaye's view. However, the Gemara here assumes that ımuel is in accord with Abaye, and is therefore constrained to interpret e Mishnah as referring to a case where the debtor does not admit that owes the debt (*Tosefos Shantz*, cited in *Shitah Mekubetzes*).

The finder must return the note to the creditor even if the debtor does t admit the debt. [The fact that the note is one of acquisition elimi-tes the concern that perhaps the note was drawn up but the loan was ver made.] We are not concerned that the debtor has already paid the bt and that the note is now his. Shmuel holds that we should assume at the loan was not paid, for the debtor would have torn up the note d he actually paid the debt as claimed (*Rashi*).

The contradiction regarding the point Shmuel shares with R' Elazar that the Mishnah refers to a case where the debtor does not admit at he owes the debt – does not need to be delineated here, since it has already been explained in regard to R' Elazar.

5. I.e. we have to be concerned that perhaps the debtor's claim that he repaid the debt is true.

6. In the Mishnah (above 12b), the Tanna Kamma [the Rabbis] ruled that even if there is no provision for a lien in the notes, they may not be returned because "the court will exact payment with them." Shmuel assumes that this means that the debt will be collected even from sold properties, just as is done when there is an explicit provision for a lien. What is the reason for this? (*Rashi*).

Actually, the Mishnah does not specify that according to the Rabbis one can exact payment with such a note from sold properties. Indeed, for the purpose of the Rabbis' ruling – not to return the note – it may be sufficient if one can exact payment from the debtor alone. [This is certainly so if one assumes that Shmuel concurs with Abaye, and is therefore constrained to interpret the Mishnah as referring to a case where the debtor denies that he owes the debt; see above, 13a.] Now, it is true that the Baraisa cited by the Gemara above (13b) clearly states that the Sages give a note without an explicit lien the same power as a note with one. But this Baraisa contradicts Shmuel on two points, as pointed out by the Gemara above, so he surely did not know of its existence [or considered it non-authoritative]. What, then, is the source for Shmuel's assumption?

*Tosafos* answer that Shmuel assumes that the Rabbis concede to R' Meir in principle that a note which records a debt for which one cannot exact payment from sold property is not a valid document (see above, 13a – 13b and note 3 there that this is how R' Meir is understood by Shmuel). If so, when the Sages rule that even a note without a lien may not be returned because "the court will exact payment with them," they cannot mean that the creditor will exact payment from only the debtor himself but not from his sold property, for then the note would be invalid, and could not be used even to collect from the debtor. The statement must then mean that they "will exact payment with them" even from sold property. Based on this premise, Shmuel concluded that the Sages merely maintain that the lack of an explicit stipulation providing for a lien does not preclude the existence of one. Therefore, Shmuel queried: "What is the reason of the Rabbis?"

7. I.e. a provision for a lien that guarantees the lender that he will be repaid even if the debtor sells his real property.

debtor and the creditor CONCUR that the notes were lost by the creditor, לֹא יַחֲזִיר לֹא לָזֶה וְלֹא לָזֶה – [THE FINDER] MAY NOT RETURN THEM EITHER TO [THE CREDITOR] OR TO [THE DEBTOR]. אַלְמָא חָיְישִׁינָן לִקְנוּנְיָא – **Thus,** we see that **we need be concerned about collusion,** contrary to R' Elazar's view. – **?** –

The Gemara digresses to discuss the wording of the refutati to R' Elazar's view:

וְהָא הָנֵי תַּרְתֵּי הוּא – **But these** contradictions to R' Elazar's vi **are two!**[17] Why does the questioner say that the Barai contradicts R' Elazar on only one point?

NOTES

Therefore, in the Sages' view, one may not return even a note that does not have an [explicit] lien, because of the concern for "payment and collusion" (*Rashi*).

17. 1) That, according to R' Meir, one cannot collect with a nc which has no lien even from the debtor; 2) that we need not be concern about collusion.

דאמר לא היו דברים מעולם אמר רבי אלעזר מחלוקת בשאין חייב מודה דרבי מאיר סבר שטר שאין בו אחריות נכסים אינו גובה לא ממשעבדי ולא מבני חרי ורבנן סברי [א] (ממשעבדי הוא דלא גבי מבני חרי) מגבא גבי אבל כשחייב מודה דברי הכל יחזיר [ג] ולא חיישינן לפרעון ולקנוניא ורבי יוחנן אמר מחלוקת כשחייב מודה דרבי מאיר סבר שטר שאין בו אחריות נכסים ממשעבדי הוא דלא גבי אבל מבני חרי מגבא גבי ורבנן סברי [א]ממשעבדי נמי גבי אבל כשאין חייב מודה דברי הכל לא יחזיר דחיישינן לפרעון תניא כוותיה דרבי יוחנן ותיובתא דרבי אלעזר בחדא ותיובתא דשמואל בתרתי מצא שטרי חוב ויש בהם אחריות נכסים אף על פי ששניהם מודים לא יחזיר לא לזה ולא לזה אין בהן אחריות נכסים בזמן שהלוה מודה יחזיר למלוה אין הלוה מודה לא יחזיר לא לזה ולא לזה דברי רבי מאיר שהיה רבי מאיר אומר שטרי (א) שיש בהם אחריות נכסים גובה מנכסים משועבדים ושאין בהם אחריות נכסים גובה מנכסים בני חורין וחכמים אומרים אחד זה ואחד זה גובה מנכסים משועבדים תיובתא דרבי אלעזר בחדא דאמר לרבי מאיר שטר שאין בו אחריות נכסים אינו גובה מנכסים משועבדים ולא מנכסים בני חורין וקאמר בין לר' מאיר בין לרבנן לא חיישינן לקנוניא ובריית' קתני שטר שאין בו אחריות נכסים ממשעבדי הוא דלא גבי הא מבני חורין מגבא גבי וקתני בין לר"מ בין לרבנן חיישינן לקנוניא דקתני אע"פ ששניהם מודים לא יחזיר לא לזה ולא לזה אלמא חיישינן לקנוניא והא הני תרתי הוא

חדא

אינו גובה לא מנכסים משועבדים ולא מבני חורין. אם אין הלוה מודה דשטרא דלא שעבד בה נכסים לאו שטרא הוא והוה כמלוה על פה ושאין עליה עדים: ורבנן סברי. להא מילתא הוי שטרא שתהא כמלוה על פה בעדים הלכך גבי מבני חרי והכי לא יחזיר דכיון דנפל אתרע ליה ואמרינן מזויף הוא כדקאמר לוה: ממשעבדי נמי גבי. כדמפרש לקמן אחריות טעות סופר הוא וחיישינן לפרעון ולקנוניא: אבל כשאין חייב מודה. ואפילו מודה שכתבו אלא שאמר פרעתיו: דברי הכל לא יחזיר. דחיישינן לפרעון כדקאמר: אף על פי ששניהם מודים כו'. חיישינן לקנוניא: בזמן שהלוה מודה. שהוא חייב לו: יחזיר למלוה. שאין כאן קנוניא דלא גבי ממשעבדי: גובה מנכסים משועבדים. ולא יחזיר ואפי' שניהם מודים דחיישינן לקנוניא: הני תרתי מילי הוי. ואת אמרת תיובתא דרבי אלעזר בחדא:

הא קאמר לא היו דברים מעולם. משמע שהלוה טוען שהוא מזויף דליכא למימר מה שטען לא היו דברים מעולם היינו שאומר פרעתי דא"כ נהדר ליה ללוה לגור ע"פ גלוסיתו ועוד דשמואל לא חייש לפרעון וקשה דאפילו יש בו אחריות אמאי לא יחזיר אם לא יקיימנו לא יגבה כלום ואם יקיימנו בדין יגבה ואין לומר דחיישינן שמא יוציאנו שלא בפניו או על הלקוחות ויתומים ולא נטעון להם מזויף משום דלא שכיח כמו שאין טוענין ליתמי נאנסו משום דלא שכיח כדאמרינן בהמוכר [את] הבית (ב"ב דף ע: ושם) וכיון דאין טוענין להו מזויף גם אין טוענין להם פרוע הוא אע"ג דשמואל סבר בפ' מי שמת (שם דף קנד: ושם) מודה בשטר שכתבו צריך לקיימו ונאמן לומר פרוע הוא במגו דאי בעי אמר מזויף מכל מקום ליתמי וללקוחות דלא טענינן מזויף לא טענינן פרוע הוא הא ליתא דאפילו לא נטעון להם מזויף הוא נטעון להם פרוע כדאמרי' בהמוכר [את] הבית (שם דף ע: ושם) גבי שטר כיס היוצא על היתומים דנשבע וגובה מחצה אבל בפלגא דפקדון טענינן להו החזרתי כמו אביהם שהיה נאמן לומר החזרתי במגו דאי בעי אמר נאנסו ולכך גם להם טענינן החזרתי אף על גב דלא טענינן להו נאנסו ועוד דעל כרחך טענינן להו מזויף או פרוע דאם לא כן לא שבקת חיי לכל בריה דיוכל כל אדם להוציא על היתומים ולקוחות ושלא בפניו שטר מלוה או שטר מכר שעשה כרצונו ולא נטעון להם וכן מוכח בפרק גט פשוט (שם דף קעד: ושם) דרב ושמואל דאמרי תרווייהו שכיב מרע שאמר מנה לפלוני בידי אמר תנו נותנין לא אמר תנו אין נותנין ומפרש התם דנקיט שטרא אמר תנו קיימיה לשטרא לא אמר תנו לא קיימיה לשטריה אלמא טענינן מזויף הוא בשביל יתומים דרב סבר בפ"ב דכתובות (דף יט.) מודה בשטר שכתבו אין צריך לקיימו ולא טענינן פרעתי א"כ אי לא קיימיה לשטריה טענינן מזויף וא"כ אמאי לא יחזיר ואין לומר כיון דנפל אתרע ליה הלכך אפילו יקיימנו יש לחוש שמא מזויף הוא ולכך קאמר לא יחזיר פן יטרוף כשתשתכח הנפילה דהא אמרינן לקמן (דף טז:) אמר שמואל מצא שטר הקנאה יחזיר דאי משום כתב ללות ולא לוה כו' משמע דאין הלוה בפניו שהוא מודה מדקאמר שמא כתב ללות ולא לוה ואמאי יחזיר ניחוש שמא מזויף הוא ואפילו אם מקיים אותו אינו מועיל וכן רב אסי דאמר לקמן (דף יז.) המוצא שטר שכתוב בו הנפק יחזיר אמאי יחזיר ניחוש שמא זייף חתימת הדיינין וי"ל דמילתא דשמואל ורב אסי מיירי שאין הלוה בפניו ולכך יחזיר ואין לחוש שמא מזויף הוא וכשירצה לגבות נטעון מזויף ואם יקיימנו יגבה ואפי' אם יצא אח"כ הלוה ויטעון מזויף הוא אין לחוש כיון שבא לידו בהיתר וכן משמע לעיל (דף ז:) דקאמר ואחר שמצא שטר שנפל ליד דיין כו' משמע אם המלוה מצאו גובה כיון שבא לידו בהיתר אבל הכא במתני' איירי שהלוה בפניו בשעת מציאה וטוען מזויף ולכך כיון דאיכא ריעותא דנפילה וגם טוען הלוה בודאי מזויף לא יחזיר כי יש לחוש שמא יגבה מיתומים ולקוחות או שלא בפניו ע"י קיום השטר והקיום אינו מועיל כי שמא טרח לזייף השטר בטוב עד שסבורים העדים שהיא חתימתן כי ההיא דגט פשוט (ב"ב דף קסז.): דמנח ידיה אזרנוקא וכתב שרבא בעצמו היה סבור שהיא חתימתו ומיהו מלוה עצמו יכול להיות שיגבה ע"י קיום לפי שהוא יודע באמת שהוא מזויף יטרח לסתור ראייתו [ג] וא"ת לעיל (דף ז:) דאמר רבי יוסי נפל ליד דיין הרי הוא בחזקתו ולא חיישינן לפרעון ואע"ג דמשמע שהלוה בפניו וטוען פרעתי דומיא דרישא דשנים אדוקין בשטר ואמאי לא יהא נאמן לומר פרעתי במגו דאי בעי אמר מזויף הוא דאז לא יחזיר פן יגבה מיתומים ולקוחות ואפילו מקויים לא מהני ליה כדפרישית וי"ל דאין זה מגו דטוב לו לומר פרעתי שלא יכחישנו שום אדם מלומר מזויף כי ירא פן יקיימנו ואע"ג שהקיום אינו מועיל לגבות בו מכל מקום אין טוען ברצון דבר שיכול להכחישו ואם נאמר שמן הלוה בעצמו הוא גובה ע"י קיום מלינו למימר דהרי הוא בחזקתו לא שיחזירנו למלוה שיש לחוש פן יוציאנו על יתומים ולקוחות אלא אם יקיימנו המלוה בעודו ביד המוצא יגבה מן הלוה ולא חיישינן לפרעון: דברי הכל יחזיר לפרעון ולקנוניא לא חיישינן. ולשמא כתב ללות בניסן כו' נמי לא חיישינן כדאביי ולקנוניא משום יש בו אחריות נקט דבשאין בו אחריות לא שייך קנוניא דלא גבי ממשעבדי דלא ידע ברייתא דבסמוך א"נ רבי אלעזר סבר דאין בו אחריות גבי ממשעבדי לרבנן דאחריות ט"ס הוא אע"ג דלא ידע ברייתא דבסמוך דסבר אי לאו טעות סופר הוא מבני חרי נמי לא גבי דכיון שמחל השעבוד מחל גם הקרן כמו לרבי מאיר וכן משמע קצת דקאמר מחלוקת כשאין חייב מודה דהיינו באין בו אחריות ועל זה קאמר בתר הכי אבל חייב מודה לפרעון ולקנוניא לא חיישינן משמע דאאין בו אחריות קאי: הא מבני חרי גבי. בלא דיוקא הוי מצי לאתויי דקתני בהדיא וגובה מנכסים בני חורין אלא שכן דרך הגמרא: אלמא חיישינן לקנוניא. ואע"ג דמצינו למימר טעמא דלא יחזיר משום דשמא כתב ללות בניסן מ"מ קשיא דר"א דאמר יחזיר ולא חייש: הני תרתי מילי נינהו חדא היא. וא"ת ואמאי חדא היא הלא לא הוצרך לומר ר"א אבל כשחייב מודה דברי הכל יחזיר לפרעון ולקנוניא לא חיישינן דהוה מצי למימר אבל כשחייב מודה דברי הכל יחזיר דהוה מצי למימר בין בשאינו מודה לרבי מאיר יחזיר באין בו אחריות דאינו גובה בו כלום ולרבנן לא יחזיר דגבי ממשעבדי וחיישינן לקנוניא וי"ל דהא דקאמר לפרעון ולקנוניא לא חיישינן מתניתין קשיתיה דתנן וכל מעשה ב"ד יחזיר אלמא לא חיישינן לקנוניא ולא יעמידנו בשטרי אלטאתא כדדחי לקמן (דף טז:) וכיון דמכח מתניתין קאמר לא חשיב לה אבל מה שמפרש דלר"מ אינו גובה כלום באין בו אחריות זה לא הזקיקה אותו המשנה לפרש ולכך קאמר חדא היא ולשמואל בתרתי משום דהא דקאמר לא חיישינן לפרעון ולקנוניא לא מכח מתניתין קאמר דהא בעלמא קאמר ליה מצא שטר הקנאה בשוק כו':

מאי

## עין משפט נר מצוה

קיג א מיי' פי"ח מהל' גזילה ואבידה הל' א ופי"ח מהל' מלוה ולוה הל' ג וע"ש ובלא פי' שאין לו אחריות כו' סמג עשין לד טוש"ע ח"מ סי' לט סעיף א:

## רבינו חננאל

אמר ר' אלעזר רישא דמתני' בשטרי דאית בהו אחריות דברי הכל לא יחזיר. ובשאין בהן אחריות מחלוקת שאין חייב מודה ר"מ אמר יחזיר דכל שטר שאין בו אחריות נכסין אינו גובה לא ממשעבדי ולא מבני חרי. ור' יוחנן אמר מחלוקת בשחייב מודה וכו'. תניא כוותיה דר' יוחנן מצא שטרי חוב אם יש בהן אחריות נכסים אע"פ ששניהן מודין לא יחזיר לא לזה ולא לזה אין בהן אחריות נכסים בזמן שמודה הלוה יחזיר למלוה אין הלוה מודה לא יחזיר לא לזה ולא לזה ששטר שאין בו אחריות נכסים אע"פ שאינו גובה ממשעבדי גובה מבני חרי דברי ר"מ. וחכ"א אחד זה ואחד זה גובה ממשעבדי. א) פי' בהא מתניתא בשטר שאין בו אחריות בזמן שהלוה מודה יחזיר דהא לא גבי אלא מבני חרי דברי ר"מ וחכ"א לא יחזיר שגם שטר שאין בו אחריות גובה ממשעבדי נמצאת חלוקתם בשחייב מודה תיובתא דשמואל ור"א דאמרי מחלוקת בשאין חייב מודה וכי ר"מ סבר כי שטר שאין בו אחריות נכסים אינו גובה לא ממשעבדי ולא מבני חרי ובהא מתניתא קתני כי שטר שאין בו אחריות נכסים גובה מבני חרי דברי ר"מ ובריש' דמתני' בשטרי שיש בהן אחריות לא דיבר ר"א כלום. שמואל דאמר כולה מתני' בשאין חייב [מודה] אבל בשחייב מודה דברי הכל יחזיר למלוה דלפרעון ולקנוניא לא חיישי רבנן ומתניתא דקתני אע"פ ששניהן מודין לא יחזיר מאי טעמא לא יחזיר לאו משום דחיישינן לפרעון ולקנוניא הלכך עוד הויא תיובת' למאן דתני בהדיא לא חיישינן לפרעון.

## חשק שלמה על ר"ח

א) נראה דצ"ל פי' דהא מתניתא ס"ל דשטר שאין בו וכו'.

## מסורת הש"ס

א) מהרש"ל מוחק ב) [לקמן יד., טז:], ג) בתוס' פרק מי שהיה דף לב: ד"ה ד מהרש"א.

## הגהות הב"ח

(א) גמ' שהיה ר"מ א שטרי חוב שיש:

The Gemara presents another interpretation of the dispute between the Sages and R' Meir:

וְרַבִּי יוֹחָנָן אָמַר – **And R' Yochanan says:** מַחְלוֹקֶת כְּשֶׁחַיָּיב מוֹדֶה – **The disagreement** between R' Meir and the Sages **is** in a case **where the debtor admits** that he owes the debt. Therefore, R' Meir holds that the note is returned to the creditor if it does not contain a provision for a lien. דְּרַבִּי מֵאִיר סָבַר – **For R' Meir holds** שְׁטָר שֶׁאֵין בּוֹ אַחֲרָיוּת נְכָסִים – that with **a note in which there is no** provision for a **lien on** real **property,** מִמְּשַׁעְבְּדֵי הוּא דְּלָא גָּבֵי – **it is only from encumbered property that [the creditor] cannot collect,** אֲבָל מִבְּנֵי חָרֵי מִגְבָּא גָּבֵי – **but from property free of encumbrance one can surely collect.** Thus, the possession of the note empowers the creditor only to collect from the properties still owned by the debtor but not from those that have been sold by the debtor. Therefore, there is no reason not to return the note to the creditor, since the debtor admits the debt. וְרַבָּנָן סָבְרֵי – **And the Rabbis hold** מִמְּשַׁעְבְּדֵי נַמִּי גָּבֵי – that with a note in which there is no lien, **one can collect** even **from encumbered property.**[10] Therefore the note may not be returned to the creditor, in spite of the debtor's admission, since the purchasers of the debtor's properties may be harmed thereby.[11]

R' Yochanan elaborates on the corollary that follows from his interpretation:

אֲבָל כְּשֶׁאֵין חַיָּיב מוֹדֶה – **But if the debtor does not admit** that he owes the debt, דִּבְרֵי הַכֹּל לֹא יַחֲזִיר – **all agree** that **[the finder] may not return** the note to the creditor, דְּחַיְישִׁינַן לְפֵרָעוֹן – **for** in this case **we must be concerned about** the possibility of **payment.**[12]

The Gemara cites a Baraisa that corroborates R' Yochanan's interepretation:

תַּנְיָא כְּוָותֵיהּ דְּרַבִּי יוֹחָנָן – **A Baraisa teaches that which corroborates R' Yochanan's** view, וּתְיוּבְתָּא דְּרַבִּי אֶלְעָזָר בַּחֲדָא – **and which** poses **a refutation of R' Elazar's** view **on one** point, וּתְיוּבְתָּא דִשְׁמוּאֵל בִּתַרְתֵּי – **and a refutation of Shmuel's** view[13] **on two** points.

The Gemara now cites the Baraisa:

מָצָא שְׁטָרֵי חוֹב – If ONE FOUND NOTES OF INDEBTEDNESS וְיֵשׁ בָּהֶם אַחֲרָיוּת נְכָסִים – AND THERE IS provision for A LIEN ON real PROPERTY IN THEM, אַף עַל פִּי שֶׁשְּׁנֵיהֶם מוֹדִים – then EVEN THOUGH BOTH the debtor and the creditor CONCUR that the notes were lost by the creditor, לֹא יַחֲזִיר לֹא לָזֶה וְלֹא לָזֶה – [THE FINDER] MAY NOT RETURN THEM EITHER TO [THE CREDITOR] OR TO [THE DEBTOR].[14] אֵין בָּהֶן אַחֲרָיוּת נְכָסִים – But IF THERE IS NO provision for A LIEN ON real PROPERTY IN [THE NOTES], בִּזְמַן שֶׁהַלֹּוֶה מוֹדֶה – then IF THE BORROWER ADMITS that the debt is still owed, יַחֲזִיר לַמַּלְוֶה – [THE FINDER] MUST return them **to the creditor.**[15] אֵין הַלֹּוֶה מוֹדֶה – IF THE BORROWER DOES NOT ADMIT that the debt is still owed, לֹא יַחֲזִיר לֹא לָזֶה וְלֹא לָזֶה – [THE FINDER] MAY NOT RETURN THEM EITHER TO [THE CREDITOR] OR TO [THE DEBTOR]. דִּבְרֵי רַבִּי מֵאִיר – These are THE WORDS OF R' MEIR. שֶׁהָיָה רַבִּי מֵאִיר אוֹמֵר – FOR R' MEIR WOULD SAY שְׁטָרֵי שֶׁיֵּשׁ בָּהֶם אַחֲרָיוּת נְכָסִים – that with NOTES of indebtedness IN WHICH THERE IS provision for A LIEN ON real PROPERTY, גּוֹבֶה מִנְּכָסִים מְשׁוּעְבָּדִים – [THE CREDITOR] CAN COLLECT even FROM ENCUMBERED PROPERTY, וְשֶׁאֵין בָּהֶם אַחֲרָיוּת נְכָסִים – but with THOSE notes IN WHICH THERE IS NO provision for a LIEN ON real PROPERTY, גּוֹבֶה מִנְּכָסִים בְּנֵי חוֹרִין – HE CAN COLLECT only FROM PROPERTY FREE OF ENCUMBRANCE. וַחֲכָמִים אוֹמְרִים – BUT THE SAGES SAY: אֶחָד זֶה וְאֶחָד זֶה – BOTH with [A NOTE IN WHICH THERE IS NO LIEN] OR with [ONE IN WHICH THERE IS A LIEN], גּוֹבֶה מִנְּכָסִים מְשׁוּעְבָּדִים – [THE CREDITOR] CAN COLLECT even FROM ENCUMBERED PROPERTY.[16] The Baraisa clearly delineates the positions of the Sages and R' Meir along the lines proposed by R' Yochanan.

The Gemara now explains how this Baraisa refutes the views of R' Elazar and Shmuel. The refutation of R' Elazar's view is focused on first:

תְּיוּבְתָּא דְּרַבִּי אֶלְעָזָר בַּחֲדָא – The Baraisa poses **a refutation of R' Elazar's** view **on one** point; דְּאָמַר לְרַבִּי מֵאִיר – **for he maintains that according to R' Meir,** שְׁטָר שֶׁאֵין בּוֹ אַחֲרָיוּת נְכָסִים – with **a note in which there is no** provision for a **lien on** real **property,** אֵינוֹ גּוֹבֶה מִנְּכָסִים מְשׁוּעְבָּדִים – **[the creditor] cannot collect from encumbered property,** לֹא מִנְּכָסִים בְּנֵי חוֹרִין – **or from property free of encumbrance.** וְאָמַר בֵּין לְר׳ מֵאִיר בֵּין לְרַבָּנָן – **And** [R' Elazar] also **says** that **both according to R' Meir and the Rabbis,** לֹא חַיְישִׁינַן לִקְנוּנְיָא – **we need not be concerned about collusion** between the debtor and the creditor to defraud the purchasers.

The Gemara now points out how the Baraisa contradicts these views of R' Elazar:

וּבָרַיְיתָא קָתָנֵי – **But the Baraisa teaches** R' Meir's view to be שְׁטָר שֶׁאֵין בּוֹ אַחֲרָיוּת נְכָסִים – that with **a note in which there is no** provision for a **lien on** real **property,** מִמְּשַׁעְבְּדֵי הוּא דְּלָא גָּבֵי – **it is only from encumbered property that [the creditor] cannot collect,** הָא מִבְּנֵי חוֹרִין מִגְבָּא גָּבֵי – **but from property free of encumbrance, he can surely collect.** קָתָנֵי בֵּין לְרַבִּי מֵאִיר בֵּין לְרַבָּנָן – **And [the Baraisa]** also **teaches** that **both according to R' Meir and the Rabbis** חַיְישִׁינַן לִקְנוּנְיָא – **we must be concerned about collusion** between the debtor and the creditor to defraud the purchasers. דְּקָתָנֵי – **For [the Baraisa] teaches:** אַף עַל פִּי שֶׁשְּׁנֵיהֶם מוֹדִים – EVEN THOUGH BOTH th

NOTES

concern that perhaps the debtor drew up the note to borrow in the month of Nissan but did not actually borrow until Tishrei and [the creditor] will thereby illegally appropriate the properties purchased from the debtor between Nissan and Tishrei (*Tosafos*).

10. As the Gemara will explain below (14a), the Rabbis maintain that it is always assumed that the creditor insists on a lien and that the debtor agrees to it. The absence in the note of an explicit provision for a lien is deemed to be the scribe's erroneous omission (*Rashi*).

11. For we must, according to R' Yochanan's view, be concerned about the possibility of payment and collusion (*Rashi*; see above, note 8). Thus, R' Yochanan's interpretation of R' Meir's position is identical with that advanced by the Gemara above (13a), according to Abaye; see above, note 2, interpretation 2.

12. I.e. even when the debtor admits that the note is authentic, but claims that he already paid the debt and it was he who lost the note (or in cases where the debtor is not present), we must be concerned about the possibility that the note is no longer valid; rather, the debt has been paid. Similarly, in a case where the debtor claims that the note was forged, we must be concerned that his claim is true (see *Rashi*).

13. The two points are: the interpretation of the Mishnah imputed to Shmuel above (13a), and another statement of Shmuel, which the Gemara will cite below (14a) as it delineates the refutation.

14. Because we must, according to the Baraisa (and R' Yochanan's view), be concerned about the possibility of payment and collusion (*Rashi*; see above, note 8).

15. Since, according to R' Meir, one can collect only from the debtor himself, there is no concern for conspiracy. The only person who can be harmed by the return of the note to the creditor is the debtor, and he admits that he still owes the debt (*Rashi*).

16. Thus, even in regard to a note that does not explicitly stipulate provision for a lien, the possibility of "payment and collusion" exist

דאמר לא היו דברים מעולם אמר רבי אלעזר מחלוקת בשאין חייב מודה דרבי מאיר סבר שטר שאין בו אחריות נכסים אינו גובה לא ממשעבדי ולא מבני חרי ורבנן סברי [א] (ממשעבדי הוא דלא גבי מבני חרי) מגבא גבי אבל כשחייב מודה דברי הכל יחזיר [ג] ולא חיישינן לפרעון ולקנוניא ורבי יוחנן אמר מחלוקת כשחייב מודה דרבי מאיר סבר שטר שאין בו אחריות נכסים ממשעבדי הוא דלא גבי אבל מבני חרי מגבא גבי ורבנן סברי [א] ממשעבדי נמי גבי אבל כשאין חייב מודה דברי הכל לא יחזיר דחיישינן לפרעון תניא כוותיה דרבי יוחנן ותיובתא דרבי אלעזר בחדא ותיובתא דשמואל בתרתי מצא שטרי חוב ויש בהם אחריות נכסים אף על פי ששניהם מודים לא יחזיר לא לזה ולא לזה אין בהן אחריות נכסים בזמן שהלוה מודה יחזיר למלוה אין הלוה מודה לא יחזיר לא לזה ולא לזה דברי רבי מאיר שהיה רבי מאיר אומר שטרי (א) שיש בהם אחריות נכסים גובה מנכסים משועבדים ושאין בהם אחריות נכסים גובה מנכסים בני חורין וחכמים אומרים אחד זה ואחד זה גובה מנכסים משועבדים תיובתא דרבי אלעזר בחדא דאמר לרבי מאיר שטר שאין בו אחריות נכסים אינו גובה מנכסים משועבדים ולא מנכסים בני חורין וקאמר בין לר' מאיר בין לרבנן לא חיישינן לקנוניא ובררייתא קתני שטר שאין בו אחריות נכסים ממשעבדי הוא דלא גבי הא מבני חורין מגבא גבי וקתני בין לר"מ בין לרבנן חיישינן לקנוניא דקתני אע"פ ששניהם מודים לא יחזיר לא לזה ולא לזה אלמא חיישינן לקנוניא והא הני תרתי הוא חדא

**רש"י**

אינו גובה לא מנכסים משועבדים ולא מבני חורין. אם אין הלוה מודה דשטרא דלא שעבד בה נכסים לאו שטרא הוא והוה כמלוה על פה ושאין עליה עדים: ורבנן סברי. להא מילתא הוי שטרא שתהא כמלוה על פה בעדים הלכך גבי מבני חרי ולהכי לא יחזיר דכיון דנפל אתרע ליה ואמרינן מזויף הוא כדקאמר לוה: ממשעבדי נמי גבי. כדמפרש לקמן אחריות טעות סופר הוא וחיישינן לפרעון ולקנוניא: אבל כשאין חייב מודה. ואפילו מודה שכתבו אלא שאמר פרעתיו: דברי הכל לא יחזיר. דחיישינן לפרעון כדקאמר: אף על פי ששניהם מודים כו'. חיישינן לקנוניא: בזמן שהלוה מודה. שהוא חייב לו: יחזיר למלוה. שאין כאן קנוניא דלא גבי ממשעבדי: גובה מנכסים משועבדים. ולא יחזיר ואפי' שניהם מודים דחיישינן לקנוניא: הני תרתי מילי הוי. ואת אמרת תיובתא דרבי אלעזר בחדא:

**תוספות**

**הא** קאמר לא היו דברים מעולם. משמע שהלוה טוען שהוא מזויף דליכא למימר מה שטען לא היו דברים מעולם היינו שאומר פרעתי דא"כ נהדר ליה ללוה לגור ע"פ לגוסיתו ועוד דשמואל לא חיש לפרעון וקשה דאפילו יש בו אחריות אמאי לא יחזיר אם לא יקיימנו לא יגבה כלום ואם יקיימנו בדין יגבה ואין לומר דחיישינן שמא יוציאנו שלא בפניו או על הלקוחות ויתומים ולא נטעון להם מזויף משום דלא שכיח כמו שאין טוענין ליתמי נאנסו משום דלא שכיח כדאמרינן בהמוכר [את] הבית (ב"ב דף ע: ושם) וכיון דאין טוענין להו מזויף גם אין טוענין להם פרוע הוא אע"ג דשמואל סבר בפ' מי שמת (שם דף קנד: ושם) מודה בשטר שכתבו צריך לקיימו ונאמן לומר פרוע הוא במגו דאי בעי אמר מזויף מכל מקום ליתמי וללקוחות דלא טענינן מזויף לא טענינן פרוע הוא הא ליתא דאפילו לא נטעון להם מזויף הוא נטעון להם פרוע כדאמרי' בהמוכר [את] הבית (שם דף ע: ושם) גבי שטר כים היוצא על היתומים דנשבע וגובה מחלה אבל בפלגא דפקדון טענינן להו החזרתי כמו אביהם שהיה נאמן לומר החזרתי במגו דאי בעי אמר נאנסו ולכך גם להם טענינן החזרתי אף על גב דלא טענינן להו נאנסו ועוד דעל כרחך טענינן להו מזויף או פרוע דאם לא כן לא שבקת חיי לכל בריה דיוכל כל אדם להוציא על היתומים ולקוחות ושלא בפניו שטר מלוה או שטר מכר שעשה כרצונו ולא נטעון להם וכן מוכח בפרק גט פשוט (שם דף קעד: ושם) דרב ושמואל דאמרי תרוייהו שכיב מרע שאמר מנה לפלוני בידי אמר תנו נותנין לא אמר תנו אין נותנין ומפרש התם דנקיט שטרא אמר תנו קיימיה לשטרא לא אמר תנו לא קיימיה לשטריה אלמא טענינן מזויף הוא בשביל יתומים דרב סבר בפ"ב דכתובות (דף יט.) מודה בשטר שכתבו אין צריך לקיימו ולא טענינן פרעתי א"כ אי לא קיימיה לשטריה טענינן מזויף וא"כ אמאי לא יחזיר ואין לומר כיון דנפל אתרע ליה הלכך אפילו יקיימנו יש לחוש שמא מזויף הוא ולכך קאמר לא יחזיר פן יטרוף כשתשכח הנפילה דהא אמרינן לקמן (דף טז:) אמר שמואל מצא שטר הקנאה יחזיר דאי משום כתב ללות ולא לוה כו' משמע דאין הלוה בפניו שהוא מודה מדקאמר שמא כתב ללות ולא לוה ואמאי יחזיר ניחוש שמא מזויף הוא ואפילו אם מקיים אותו אינו מועיל וכן רב אסי דאמר לקמן (דף יז.) המוצא שטר שכתוב בו הנפק יחזיר אמאי יחזיר ניחוש שמא זייף חתימת הדיינין וי"ל דמילתא דשמואל ורב אסי מיירי שאין הלוה בפניו ולכך יחזיר ואין לחוש שמא מזויף הוא וכשירצה לגבות נטעון מזויף ואם יקיימנו יגבה ואפי' אם יבא אח"כ הלוה ויטעון מזויף הוא אין לחוש כיון שבא לידו בהיתר וכן משמע לעיל (דף ז:) דקאמר ואחר שמצא שטר שנפל ליד דיין כו' משמע אם המלוה מצאו גובה כיון שבא לידו בהיתר אבל הכא במתני' איירי שהלוה בפניו בשעת מציאה וטוען מזויף ולכך כיון דאיכא ריעותא דנפילה וגם טוען הלוה בודאי מזויף לא יחזיר כי יש לחוש שמא יגבה מיתומים ולקוחות או שלא בפניו ע"י קיום השטר והקיום אינו מועיל כי שמא טרח לזייף השטר בטוב עד שסבורים העדים שהיא חתימתן כי ההיא דגט פשוט (ב"ב דף קסז.): דמנח ידיה אזרנוקא וכתב שרגא בעלמו היה סבור שהיא חתימתו ומיהו מלוה עצמו יכול להיות שיגבה ע"י קיום לפי שהוא יודע באמת שהוא מזויף יטרח לסתור ראייתו [ג] וא"ת לעיל (דף ז:) דאמר רבי יוסי נפל ליד דיין הרי הוא בחזקתו ולא חיישינן לפרעון ואע"ג דמשמע שהלוה בפניו וטוען פרעתי דומיא דרישא דשנים אדוקין בשטר ואמאי לא יהא נאמן לומר פרעתי במגו דאי בעי אמר מזויף הוא דאז לא יחזיר פן יגבה מיתומים ולקוחות ואפילו מקויים לא מהני ליה כדפרישית וי"ל דאין זה מגו דטוב לו לומר פרעתי שלא יכחישנו שום אדם מלומר מזויף כי ירא פן יקיימנו ואע"ג שהקיום אינו מועיל לגבות בו מכל מקום אין טוען ברצון דבר שיכול להכחישו ואם נאמר שמן הלוה בעצמו הוא גובה ע"י קיום מצינו למימר דהרי הוא בחזקתו לא שיחזירנו למלוה שיש לחוש פן יוציאנו על יתומים ולקוחות אלא אם יקיימנו המלוה בעודו ביד המוצא יגבה מן הלוה ולא חיישינן לפרעון: **דברי** הכל יחזיר לפרעון ולקנוניא לא חיישינן. ולשמא כתב ללות בניסן כו' נמי לא חיישינן כדאביי ולקנוניא משום יש בו אחריות נקט דבשאין בו אחריות לא שייך קנוניא דלא גבי ממשעבדי דלא ידע ברייתא דבסמוך א"נ רבי אלעזר סבר דאין בו אחריות גבי ממשעבדי לרבנן דאחריות ט"ס הוא אע"ג דלא ידע ברייתא דבסמוך דסבר אי לאו טעות סופר הוא מבני חרי נמי לא גבי דכיון שמחל השעבוד מחל גם הקרן כמו לרבי מאיר וכן משמע קצת דקאמר מחלוקת כשאין חייב מודה דהיינו באין בו אחריות ועל זה קאמר בתר הכי אבל חייב מודה לפרעון ולקנוניא לא חיישינן משמע דאאין בו אחריות קאי: **הא** מבני חרי גבי. בלא דיוקא הוי מצי לאתויי דקתני בהדיא וגובה מנכסים בני חורין אלא שכן דרך הגמרא: **אלמא** חיישינן לקנוניא. ואע"ג דמצינו למימר טעמא דלא יחזיר משום דשמא כתב ללות בניסן מ"מ קשיא דר"א דאמר יחזיר ולא חייש: **הני** תרתי מילי נינהו חדא היא. וא"ת ואמאי חדא היא הלא לא הוצרך לומר ר"א אבל כשחייב מודה דברי הכל יחזיר לפרעון ולקנוניא לא חיישינן דהוה"ל בין במודה בין באינו מודה לרבי מאיר יחזיר באין בו אחריות דאינו גובה בו כלום ולרבנן לא יחזיר דגבי ממשעבדי וחיישינן לקנוניא וי"ל דהא דקאמר לפרעון ולקנוניא לא חיישינן מתניתין קשיתיה דתנן וכל מעשה ב"ד יחזיר אלמא לא חיישינן לקנוניא ולא יעמידנו בשטרי חלטאתא כדדחי לקמן (דף טז:) וכיון דמכח מתניתין קאמר לא חשיב לה אבל מה שמפרש דלר"מ אינו גובה כלום באין בו אחריות זה לא הזקיקה אותו המשנה לפרש ולכך קאמר חדא היא ולשמואל בתרתי משום דהא דקאמר לא חיישינן לפרעון ולקנוניא לא מכח מתניתין קאמר דהא בעלמא קאמר ליה מצא שטר הקנאה בשוק כו':

מאי

**עין משפט נר מצוה**

קיג א מיי' פי"ח מהל' גזילה ואבידה הל' א ופי"ח מהל' מלוה ולוה הל' ג וע"ש ובלא פי' שאין לו אחריות כו' סמג עשין לד טוש"ע ח"מ סי' לט סעיף א:

**רבינו חננאל**

אמר ר' אלעזר רישא דמתני' בשטרי דאית בהו אחריות דברי הכל לא יחזיר. ובשאין בהן אחריות מחלוקת שאין חייב מודה ר"מ אמר יחזיר דכל שטר שאין בו אחריות נכסין אינו גובה לא ממשעבדי ולא מבני חרי. ור' יוחנן אמר מחלוקת בשחייב מודה וכו'. תניא כוותיה דר' יוחנן מצא שטרי חוב אם יש בהן אחריות נכסים אע"פ ששניהן מודין לא יחזיר לא לזה ולא לזה אין בהן אחריות נכסים בזמן שמודה הלוה יחזיר למלוה אין הלוה מודה לא יחזיר לא לזה ולא לזה ששטר שאין בו אחריות נכסים אע"פ שאינו גובה ממשעבדי גובה מבני חרי דברי ר"מ. וחכ"א אחד זה ואחד זה גובה ממשעבדי. א) פי' בהא מתניתא בשטר שאין בו אחריות בזמן שהלוה מודה יחזיר דהא לא גבי אלא מבני חרי דברי ר"מ וחכ"א לא יחזיר שגם שטר שאין בו אחריות גובה ממשעבדי נמצאת חלוקתם בשחייב מודה תיובתא דשמואל ור"א דאמרי מחלוקת בשאין חייב מודה וכי ר"מ סבר כי שטר שאין בו אחריות נכסים אינו גובה לא ממשעבדי ולא מבני חרי ובהא מתניתא קתני כי שטר שאין בו אחריות נכסים גובה מבני חרי דברי ר"מ וברישא דמתני' בשטרי שיש בהן אחריות לא דיבר ר"א כלום. שמואל דאמר כולה מתני' בשאין חייב [מודה] אבל בשחייב מודה דברי הכל יחזיר למלוה דלפרעון ולקנוניא לא חיישי רבנן ומתניתא דקתני אע"פ ששניהן מודין לא יחזיר מאי טעמא לא יחזיר לאו משום דחיישינן לפרעון ולקנוניא הלכך עוד הויא תיובת' למאן דתני בהדיא לא חיישינן לפרעון.

**חשק שלמה על ר"ח**

א) נראה דצ"ל פי' דהא מתניתא ס"ל דשטר שאין בו וכו'.

**מסורת הש"ס**

א) מהרש"ל מוחק ב) [לקמן יד., טז:], ג) בתוס' פרק מי שהיה דף לג: ד"ה מהרש"א.

**הגהות הב"ח**

(א) גמ' שהיה ר"מ שטרי חוב שיש:

**דְּאָמַר לֹא הָיוּ דְבָרִים מֵעוֹלָם – who claims that the whole matter never occurred.**[1] Since the debtor claims that he never drew up this note and that the note is forged, he surely has no claim that the note be given him "to wrap over his bottle"; the debtor has admitted, by his claim, that the paper of the note was never his.

The Gemara has now concluded its discussion of R' Meir's view.[2] It now presents various views on the issues that underlie the disagreement between the Sages and R' Meir:

**אָמַר רַבִּי אֶלְעָזָר – R' Elazar said: מַחְלוֹקֶת בְּשֶׁאֵין חַיָּיב מוֹדֶה – The disagreement** between R' Meir and the Sages **is** in a case **where the debtor does not admit** that he owes the debt. Nevertheless, R' Meir holds that the note is returned to the creditor if it does not contain a provision for a lien. **דְּרַבִּי מֵאִיר סָבַר – For R' Meir holds שְׁטָר שֶׁאֵין בּוֹ אַחֲרָיוּת נְכָסִים –** that with **a note in which there is no** provision for a **lien on** real **property, אֵינוֹ גּוֹבֶה לֹא מִמְּשַׁעְבְּדֵי – [the creditor] cannot collect either from encumbered property וְלֹא מִבְּנֵי חָרֵי – from property free of encumbrance.**[3] Since he cannot coll[ect] with this note, there is no reason not to return the note to [the] creditor, even if the debtor denies the debt.[4] **וְרַבָּנָן סָבְרֵי – B[ut] the Rabbis hold** (**מִמְּשַׁעְבְּדֵי הוּא דְּלָא גָּבֵי**) – that with a note t[hat] has no provision for a lien **(it is only from encumbered prope[rty] that [the creditor] cannot collect, מִבְּנֵי חָרֵי) מִגְבָּא גָּבֵי – [but] from property that is free of encumbrance), one can collec[t].** Since the debtor, who denies the validity of the note, can [be] harmed if it is returned to the creditor, it may not be returne[d].

R' Elazar elaborates on the corollary that follows from [his] interpretation:

**אֲבָל כְּשֶׁחַיָּיב מוֹדֶה – But if the debtor admits** that he owes t[he] debt, **דִּבְרֵי הַכֹּל יַחֲזִיר – all agree** that **[the finder] must retu[rn]** the note to the creditor,[7] **וְלָא חָיְישִׁינָן לְפֵרָעוֹן וְלִקְנוּנְיָא – for [we] need not be concerned about the possibility of payment a[nd] collusion.**[8] [9]

NOTES

1. I.e. the Mishnah, which presents R' Meir's ruling that the finder should return the note of indebtedness to the creditor if it does not provide for a lien on real property, refers to a case where the debtor claims that the loan was never made and that the note is forged. Therefore, the note is returned to the creditor, since the absence of a lien renders it invalid, and there is a consensus regarding the paper of the note that it belongs to the creditor (*Tosafos*). [Thus, if the debtor claims that the note is authentic but that he already paid the debt, R' Meir will concede that it may not be returned to the creditor.]

If however, the note provides for a lien, it may not be returned; we are concerned that the note may be forged, as the debtor claims. Even though the creditor must in any case first certify the note's signatures before collecting, the concern of forgery is not removed in this case, because the fact that the note was lost casts unusual suspicion upon it; we are concerned that the note may be forged in such a professional manner that the certifying witnesses will not discern the fraud (*Tosafos*).

2. The Gemara above, 13a, presented three explanations of R' Meir's position that the found note is returned to the creditor if it does not contain a lien, and is not returned if it does: 1) R' Meir speaks about a case where the debtor admits that he still owes the debt. Therefore, the note is returned if it does not contain a lien, since the matter concerns only the debtor. If the note does contain a lien, it may not be returned in spite of the debtor's admission, because of the concern that perhaps the debtor drew up the note in Nissan but did not borrow till Tishrei. 2) R' Meir speaks about a case where the debtor admits that he still owes the debt; therefore, a note without a lien is returned, as in explanation 1. If the note does contain a lien, it may not be returned, because of the concern that perhaps the debt was already paid and the debtor is conspiring with the creditor to defraud the buyers of the debtor's properties. 3) R' Meir speaks about a case where the debtor denies that he owes the debt; rather, he claims that the note was forged. Nevertheless a note without a lien is returned to the creditor, because – in R' Meir's view – a note that does not provide for a lien cannot be used to exact payment even from the debtor himself.

3. [As already stated above on 13a,] in R' Meir's view, a loan note without provision for a lien is not a valid document. Thus, one can collect the loan from the debtor only if the debtor admits the debt, for the loan recorded therein is in the category of an oral loan executed without the presence of witnesses [for the validity of the testimony of the witnesses signed on the loan document derives from the validity of the document] (*Rashi*). In *Kesubos* 20a (see *Tosafos* there ד״ה ורבי), the Gemara establishes that testimony is valid only when delivered by the witnesses orally in the court, not in writing. Legal documents [*shtaros*], however, are an exception to this rule. A loan document without a lien is not considered a *shtar* according to R' Meir, since it does not acquire anything. Therefore it is viewed as mere written testimony and is invalid, as is all written testimony other than *shtaros* (*Ramban, Rashba, Ran*).

4. The note is returned to the creditor "to wrap over the opening of his bottle," as explained on 13a. R' Elazar's explanation of R' Meir's position is the same as that advanced by the Gemara above (13a) to reconcile Shmuel with Abaye's view. See above, note 2, interpretation 3.

5. The Rabbis hold that the note is at least valid for establishing the f[act] that a loan took place (and, as a consequence, also proves – when [the] creditor produces it – that the loan was not paid). It is thus in [the] category of an oral loan to which there are witnesses. Thus, one m[ay] exact payment with this note at least from the debtor himself – fr[om] unencumbered property. Therefore, the note may not be returned to [the] creditor, for the fact that it was lost casts suspicion upon it, so that [we] are concerned that it may be forged as claimed by the debtor [i.e. [we] suspect that it was forged even if the creditor is able to certify it – [see] above, note 1] (*Rashi*).

[The Gemara below cites a Baraisa which states explicitly that, in t[he] Sages' view, one can collect from both encumbered and unencumber[ed] property even with a loan document that does not contain an expli[cit] provision for a lien. *Rashi's* commentary assumes that, at this point, [the] Gemara does not know of this Baraisa, and it is therefore possible th[at] in the Sages' view, one can collect only from unencumbered prope[rty] with a loan document that does not contain an explicit provision fo[r a] lien.

Actually, the position imputed to the Sages by *Rashi* is spelled out [in] the Gemara according to the version preserved in our texts (if one d[oes] not delete the words enclosed in parentheses). However, *Tosefos Sha[antz]* (cited in *Shitah Mekubetzes*) maintains that the words enclosed [in] parentheses are not part of the text proper and that they should [be] deleted (see also *Maharshal, Maharsha* and *Maharam Shif*, who poi[nt] out that *Tosafos* did not have these words in their texts). If one accep[ts] the emended version, it is possible that even at this point the Gemar[a's] interpretation of the Sages' view accords with that of the Barai[sa]. *Tosafos* (ד״ה דברי), in an alternative view, assert that this interpretati[on] is plausible. According to either version, the Sages' reason is the san[e]: Return of the document will harm someone, either the debtor (accordi[ng] to one version), or both the debtor and the buyers of his prope[rty] (according to the other version).]

6. Although the creditor must in any case first certify the not[e's] signatures before collecting, the concern of forgery still pertains in t[his] case, according to R' Elazar, as explained above, note 1.

7. The debtor's admission is valid even to collect from properties sold [by] him subsequent to the loan, if there is a lien; see Gemara above, 12b a[nd] note 25 there.

8. Above (13a), the Gemara had interpreted the Mishnah according [to] Abaye as referring to a case where the debtor does admit that he st[ill] owes the debt, and in spite of that the Mishnah rules not to return t[he] note if there is a lien. The Gemara there explained that we have to [be] concerned that the debt was actually paid, and the debtor's admission [to] the contrary is part of a conspiracy between the debtor and the credit[or] to defraud the owners of properties against which he has a lien, by on[ce] again collecting the debt – this time, from them. R' Elazar informs [us] that he does not share this view, and that one may return the note if t[he] debtor admits the debt.

9. R' Elazar also does not agree with the interpretation put forth by t[he] Gemara above according to Rav Assi, viz. that the Mishnah refers t[o a] case where the debtor admits that he still owes the debt, and t[he] Mishnah's ruling not to return the note (if there is a lien) is due to t[he]

דאמר לא היו דברים מעולם אמר רבי אלעזר מחלוקת בשאין חייב מודה דרבי מאיר סבר שטר שאין בו אחריות נכסים אינו גובה לא ממשעבדי ולא מבני חרי ורבנן סברי [א] (ממשעבדי הוא דלא גבי מבני חרי) מגבא גבי אבל כשחייב מודה דברי הכל יחזיר [ג] ולא חיישינן לפרעון ולקנוניא ורבי יוחנן אמר מחלוקת כשחייב מודה דרבי מאיר סבר שטר שאין בו אחריות נכסים ממשעבדי הוא דלא גבי אבל מבני חרי מגבא גבי ורבנן סברי [א]ממשעבדי נמי גבי אבל כשאין חייב מודה דברי הכל לא יחזיר דחיישינן לפרעון תניא כוותיה דרבי יוחנן ותיובתא דרבי אלעזר בחדא ותיובתא דשמואל בתרתי מצא שטרי חוב ויש בהם אחריות נכסים אף על פי ששניהם מודים לא יחזיר לא לזה ולא לזה אין בהן אחריות נכסים בזמן שהלוה מודה יחזיר למלוה אין הלוה מודה לא יחזיר לא לזה ולא לזה דברי רבי מאיר שהיה רבי מאיר אומר שטרי (א) שיש בהם אחריות נכסים גובה מנכסים משועבדים ושאין בהם אחריות נכסים גובה מנכסים בני חורין וחכמים אומרים אחד זה ואחד זה גובה מנכסים משועבדים תיובתא דרבי אלעזר בחדא דאמר לרבי מאיר שטר שאין בו אחריות נכסים אינו גובה מנכסים משועבדים ולא מנכסים בני חורין וקאמר בין לר' מאיר בין לרבנן לא חיישינן לקנוניא ובריתא קתני שטר שאין בו אחריות נכסים ממשעבדי הוא דלא גבי הא מבני חורין מגבא גבי וקתני בין לר"מ בין לרבנן חיישינן לקנוניא דקתני אע"פ ששניהם מודים לא יחזיר לא לזה ולא לזה אלמא חיישינן לקנוניא והא הני תרתי הוא חדא

אינו גובה לא מנכסים משועבדים ולא מבני חורין. אם אין הלוה מודה דשטרא דלא שעבד בה נכסים לאו שטרא הוא והוה כמלוה על פה ושאין עליה עדים: ורבנן סברי. לאו מילתא הוי שטרא שתהא כמלוה על פה בעדים הלכך גבי מבני חרי ולהכי לא יחזיר דכיון דנפל אתרע ליה ואמרינן מזויף הוא כדקאמר לזה: ממשעבדי נמי גבי. כדמפרש לקמן אחריות טעות סופר הוא וחיישינן לפרעון ולקנוניא: אבל כשאין חייב מודה. ואפילו מודה שכתבו אלא שאמר פרעתיו: דברי הכל לא יחזיר. דחיישינן לפרעון כדקאמר: אף על פי ששניהם מודים כו'. חיישינן לקנוניא: בזמן שהלוה מודה. שהוא חייב לו: יחזיר למלוה. שאין כאן קנוניא דלא גבי ממשעבדי: גובה מנכסים משועבדים. ולא יחזיר ואפי' שניהם מודים דחיישינן לקנוניא: הני תרתי מילי הוי. ואת אמרת תיובתא דרבי אלעזר בחדא:

הא קאמר לא היו דברים מעולם. משמע שהלוה טוען שהוא מזויף דליכא למימר מה שטען לא היו דברים מעולם היינו שאומר פרעתי דא"כ נהדר ליה ללוה לגור ע"פ צלוחיתו ועוד דשמואל לא חייש לפרעון וקשה דאפילו יש בו אחריות אמאי לא יחזיר אם לא יקיימנו לא יגבה כלום ואם יקיימנו בדין יגבה ואין לומר דחיישינן שמא יוציאנו שלא בפניו או על הלקוחות ויתומים ולא נטעון להם מזויף משום דלא שכיח כמו שאין טוענין ליתמי נאנסו משום דלא שכיח כדאמרינן בהמוכר [את] הבית (ב"ב דף ע: ושם) וכיון דאין טוענין להו מזויף גם אין טוענין להם פרוע הוא אע"ג דשמואל סבר בפ' מי שמת (שם דף קנד: ושם) מודה בשטר שכתבו צריך לקיימו ונאמן לומר פרוע הוא במגו דאי בעי אמר מזויף מכל מקום ליתמי וללקוחות דלא טענינן מזויף לא טענינן פרוע הוא הא ליתא דאפילו לא נטעון להם מזויף הוא נטעון להם פרוע כדאמרי' בהמוכר [את] הבית (שם דף ע: ושם) גבי שטר כיס היוצא על היתומים דנשבע וגובה מחצה אבל בפלגא דפקדון טענינן להו החזרתי כמו אביהם שהיה נאמן לומר החזרתי במגו דאי בעי אמר נאנסו ולכך גם להם טענינן החזרתי אף על גב דלא טענינן להו נאנסו ועוד דעל כרחך טענינן להו מזויף או פרוע דאם לא כן לא שבקת חיי לכל בריה דיוכל כל אדם להוציא על היתומים ולקוחות ושלא בפניו שטר מלוה או שטר מכר שעשה כרצונו ולא נטעון להם וכן מוכח בפרק גט פשוט (שם דף קעד: ושם) דרב ושמואל דאמרי תרוייהו שכיב מרע שאמר מנה לפלוני בידי אמר תנו נותנין לא אמר תנו אין נותנין ומפרש התם דנקיט שטרא אמר תנו קיימיה לשטרא לא אמר תנו לא קיימיה לשטריה אלמא טענינן מזויף הוא בשביל יתומים דרב סבר בפ"ב דכתובות (דף יט.) מודה בשטר שכתבו אין צריך לקיימו ולא טענינן פרעתי א"כ אי לא קיימיה לשטריה טענינן מזויף וא"כ אמאי לא יחזיר ואין לומר כיון דנפל אתרע ליה הלכך אפילו יקיימנו יש לחוש שמא מזויף הוא ולכך קאמר לא יחזיר פן יטרוף כשתשתכח הנפילה דהא אמרינן לקמן (דף טז:) אמר שמואל מצא שטר הקנאה יחזיר דאי משום כתב ללות ולא לוה כו' משמע דאין הלוה בפנינו שהוא מודה מדקאמר שמא כתב ללות ולא לוה ואמאי יחזיר ניחוש שמא מזויף הוא ואפילו אם מקיים אותו אינו מועיל וכן רב אסי דאמר לקמן (דף יז.) המוצא שטר שכתוב בו הנפק יחזיר אמאי יחזיר ניחוש שמא זייף חתימת הדיינין וי"ל דמילתא דשמואל ורב אסי מיירי שאין הלוה בפנינו ולכך יחזיר ואין לחוש שמא מזויף הוא וכשילוה לגבות נטעון מזויף ואם יקיימנו יגבה ואפי' אם יבא אח"כ הלוה ויטעון מזויף הוא אין לחוש כיון שבא לידו בהיתר וכן משמע לעיל (דף ז:) דקאמר ואחר שמצא שטר שנפל ליד דיין כו' משמע אם המלוה מצאו גובה כיון שבא לידו בהיתר אבל הכא במתני' איירי שהלוה בפנינו בשעת מציאה וטוען מזויף ולכך כיון דאיכא ריעותא דנפילה וגם טוען הלוה בודאי מזויף לא יחזיר כי יש לחוש שמא יגבה מיתומים ולקוחות או שלא בפניו ע"י קיום השטר והקיום אינו מועיל כי שמא טרח לזייף השטר בטוב עד שסבורים העדים שהיא חתימתן כי ההיא דגט פשוט (ב"ב דף קסז.): דמנח ידיה אזרנוקא וכתב שרגא בעלמו היה סבור שהיא חתימתו ומיהו מלוה עצמו יכול להיות שיגבה ע"י קיום לפי שהוא יודע באמת שהוא מזויף יטרח לסתור ראייתו [ג] וא"ת לעיל (דף ז:) דאמר רבי יוסי נפל ליד דיין הרי הוא בחזקתו ולא חיישינן לפרעון ואע"ג דמשמע שהלוה בפנינו וטוען פרעתי דומיא דרישא דשנים אדוקין בשטר ואמאי לא יהא נאמן לומר פרעתי במגו דאי בעי אמר מזויף הוא דאז לא יחזיר פן יגבה מיתומים ולקוחות ואפילו מקויים לא מהני ליה כדפרישית וי"ל דאין זה מגו דטוב לו לומר פרעתי שלא יכחישנו שום אדם מלומר מזויף כי ירא פן יקיימנו ואע"ג שהקיום אינו מועיל לגבות בו מכל מקום אין טוען ברצון דבר שיכול להכחישו ואם נאמר שמן הלוה בעצמו הוא גובה ע"י קיום מלינו למימר דהרי הוא בחזקתו לא שיחזירנו למלוה שיש לחוש פן יוציאנו על יתומים ולקוחות אלא אם יקיימנו המלוה בעודו ביד המוצא יגבה מן הלוה ולא חיישינן לפרעון: דברי הכל יחזיר לפרעון ולקנוניא לא חיישינן. ולשמא כתב ללות בניסן כו' נמי לא חיישינן כדאביי ולקנוניא משום יש בו אחריות נקט דבשאין בו אחריות לא שייך קנוניא דלא גבי ממשעבדי דלא ידע ברייתא דבסמוך א"נ רבי אלעזר סבר דאין בו אחריות גבי ממשעבדי לרבנן דאחריות ט"ס הוא אע"ג דלא ידע ברייתא דבסמוך דסבר אי לאו טעות סופר הוא מבני חרי נמי לא גבי דכיון שמחל השעבוד מחל גם הקרן כמו לרבי מאיר וכן משמע קצת דקאמר מחלוקת כשאין חייב מודה דהיינו באין בו אחריות ועל זה קאמר בתר הכי אבל חייב מודה לפרעון ולקנוניא לא חיישינן משמע דאאין בו אחריות קאי: הא מבני חרי גבי. בלא דיוקא הוי מצי לאתויי דקתני בהדיא וגובה מנכסים בני חורין אלא שכן דרך הגמרא: אלמא חיישינן לקנוניא. ואע"ג דמצינו למימר טעמא דלא יחזיר משום דשמא כתב ללות בניסן מ"מ קשיא דר"א דאמר יחזיר ולא חייש: הני תרתי מילי נינהו חדא היא. וא"ת ואמאי חדא היא הלא לא הוצרך לומר ר"א אבל כשחייב מודה דברי הכל יחזיר לפרעון ולקנוניא לא חיישינן דהומ"ל בין במודה בין באינו מודה לרבי מאיר יחזיר באין בו אחריות דאינו גובה בו כלום ולרבנן לא יחזיר דגבי ממשעבדי וחיישינן לקנוניא וי"ל דהא דקאמר לפרעון ולקנוניא לא חיישינן מתניתין קשיתיה דתנן וכל מעשה ב"ד יחזיר אלמא לא חיישינן לקנוניא ולא יעמידנו בשטרי חלטאתא כדדחי לקמן (דף טז:) וכיון דמכח מתניתין קאמר לא חשיב לה אבל מה שמפרש דלר"מ אינו גובה כלום באין בו אחריות זה לא הזקיקה אותו המשנה לפרש ולכך קאמר חדא היא ולשמואל בתרתי משום דהא דקאמר לא חיישינן לפרעון ולקנוניא לא מכח מתניתין קאמר דהא בעלמא קאמר ליה מצא שטר הקנאה בשוק כו':



עין משפט
נר מצוה

קיג א מיי' פי"ח מהל' גזילה ואבידה הל' א ופי"ח מהל' מלוה ולוה הל' ג וע"ש ובלא פי' שאין לו אחריות כו' סמג עשין לד טוש"ע ח"מ סי' לט סעיף א:

רבינו חננאל

אמר ר' אלעזר רישא דמתני' בשטרי דאית בהו אחריות דברי הכל לא יחזיר. ובשאין בהן אחריות מחלוקת שאין חייב מודה ר"מ אמר יחזיר דכל שטר שאין בו אחריות נכסין אינו גובה לא ממשעבדי ולא מבני חרי. ור' יוחנן אמר מחלוקת בשחייב מודה וכו'. תניא כוותיה דר' יוחנן מצא שטרי חוב אם יש בהן אחריות נכסים אע"פ ששניהן מודין לא יחזיר לא לזה ולא לזה אין בהן אחריות נכסים בזמן שמודה הלוה יחזיר למלוה אין הלוה מודה לא יחזיר לא לזה ולא לזה ששטר שאין בו אחריות נכסים אע"פ שאינו גובה ממשעבדי גובה מבני חרי דברי ר"מ. וחכ"א אחד זה ואחד זה גובה ממשעבדי. א) פי' בהא מתניתא בשטר שאין בו אחריות בזמן שהלוה מודה יחזיר דהא לא גבי אלא מבני חרי דברי ר"מ וחכ"א לא יחזיר שגם שטר שאין בו אחריות גובה ממשעבדי נמצאת חלוקתם בשחייב מודה תיובתא דשמואל ור"א דאמרי מחלוקת בשאין חייב מודה וכי ר"מ סבר כי שטר שאין בו אחריות נכסים אינו גובה לא ממשעבדי ולא מבני חרי ובהא מתניתא קתני כי שטר שאין בו אחריות נכסים גובה מבני חרי דברי ר"מ וברישא דמתני' בשטרי שיש בהן אחריות לא דיבר ר"א כלום. שמואל דאמר כולה מתני' בשאין חייב [מודה] אבל בשחייב מודה דברי הכל יחזיר למלוה דלפרעון ולקנוניא לא חיישי רבנן ומתניתא דקתני אע"פ ששניהן מודין לא יחזיר מאי טעמא לא יחזיר לאו משום דחיישינן לפרעון ולקנוניא הלכך עוד הויא תיובת' למאן דתני בהדיא לא חיישינן לפרעון.

חשק שלמה על ר"ח

א) נראה דצ"ל פי' דהא מתניתא ס"ל דשטר שאין בו וכו'.

מסורת הש"ס

א) מהרש"ל מוחק ב) [לקמן יד., טז:], ג) בתוס' פרק מי שהיה דף לב: ד"ה מהרש"א.

הגהות הב"ח

(א) גמ' שהיה ר"מ א' שטרי חוב שיש:

[א] בשטרי הקנאה דהא שעביד נפשיה אי הכי מתניתין דקתני אם יש בהן אחריות נכסים לא יחזיר ואוקימנא כשחייב מודה ומשום שמא כתב ללות בניסן ולא לוה עד תשרי ואתי למטרף לקוחות שלא כדין אמאי לא יחזיר נחזי אי בשטר הקנאה הא שעביד ליה נפשיה אי בשטר דלא הקנאה ליכא למיחש דהא אמרת כי ליכא מלוה בהדיה לא כתבינן א"ל רב אסי אע"ג דשטרי דלאו הקנאה כי ליכא מלוה בהדיה לא כתבינן מתניתין כיון דנפל אתרע ליה וחיישינן דלמא אקרי וכתוב (א) ° אביי אמר עדיו בחתומיו זכין לו ואפילו שטרי דלאו הקנאה משום דקשיא ליה כיון דאמרת בשטרי דלאו הקנאה כי ליתיה למלוה בהדיה לא כתבינן ליכא למיחש דאקרי וכתוב אלא הא דתנן [ג] מצא גיטי נשים ושחרורי עבדים דייתיקי מתנה ושוברים הרי זה לא יחזיר שמא כתובים היו ונמלך עליהם שלא ליתנם וכי נמלך עליהם מאי הוי והא אמרת עדיו בחתומיו זכין לו הני מילי היכא דקא מטו לידיה אבל היכא דלא מטו לידיה לא אמרינן אלא מתניתין דקתני מצא שטרי חוב אם יש בהם אחריות נכסים לא יחזיר ואוקימנא כשחייב מודה ומשום שמא כתב ללות בניסן ולא לוה עד תשרי בשלמא לרב אסי דאמר בשטרי אקנייתא מוקי לה בשטרי דלאו אקנייתא וכדאמרינן אלא לאביי דאמר עדיו בחתומיו זכין לו מאי איכא למימר אמר לך אביי מתני' היינו טעמא [ב] דחייש לפרעון ולקנוניא ולשמואל דאמר [ג] לא חיישינן לפרעון ולקנוניא מאי איכא למימר הניחא אי סבר לה כרב אסי דאמר בשטרי הקנאה מוקי (א) מתניתין בשטרי דלאו הקנאה אלא אי סבר כאביי דאמר עדיו בחתומיו זכין לו מאי איכא למימר שמואל מוקי למתניתין כשאין חייב מודה אי הכי כי אין בהן אחריות נכסים אמאי יחזיר נהי דלא גבי מן משעבדי מבני חרי מגבי גבי שמואל לטעמיה דאמר שמואל אומר היה רבי מאיר שטר חוב שאין בו אחריות נכסים אין גובה לא ממשעבדי ולא מבני חרי וכי מאחר שאינו גובה אמאי יחזיר אמר רבי נתן בר אושעיא [ד] לצור על פי צלוחיתו של מלוה ונהדריה להו ללוה לצור על פי צלוחיתו של לוה הוא דאמר

---

**בשטרי הקנאה.** שמקנה לו נכסיו מהיום בין לא ילוה יגבה מהן לאותו זמן מהיום: **אי הכי.** דבשטרי דלאו הקנאה לא עבידי דכתבי אלא אם כן ראו הלואת המעות מתני' דקתני כו': **כי ליכא מלוה בהדיה.** ונותן מעות בפניהם לא כתבינן: **אביי אמר.** הא דתנן כותבין שטר ללוה בלא מלוה אפילו בשטר דלאו הקנאה נמי ואי נמי אתי למיטרף מהאידנא והוא לא לוה עד תשרי לא שלא כדין הוא דעדיו בחתומיו זכין לו מיום שחתמוהו זכין לו השעבוד ואפילו לא הלוה המעות עד תשרי ולהכי מוקי ליה אביי בהאי טעמא משום דקשיא ליה כיון דאמרת כו' (ב) אבל השתא דתנן כותבין חיישינן דלמא כתב ללות ולא לוה ולקמיה פריך אמאי לא יחזיר הרי זכו ליה עדיו בחתומיו ושפיר טריף: **דייתיקי.** צוואת שכיב מרע ולשון דייתיקי דא תיקו זאת תיקום לדברי שכיב מרע ככתובין וכמסורין דמי: **מתנה.** מתנת בריא: **ושוברין.** פרעון שטר: **הני מילי היכא דמטא שטר לידיה.** ואפילו לאחר זמן זכו לו חותמיו לגבות מזמן הכתוב בו ואי קשיא הא דתנן (שביעית פ"י מ"ה) שטרי חוב המוקדמין פסולין והמאוחרין כשרין במאי מוקי לה אביי תריץ במוקדמת כתיבתן לחתימתן ולהכי פסולין שבא לטרוף משעת כתיבה א"נ שכתבו וחתמוהו בתשרי והם כתבו בתוכו ניסן שהוא ראש השנה לשטרות: **בשלמא לרב אסי.** דמוקי להאי דכותבין בשטרי אקנייתא: **מוקי.** מתניתין בדלאו אקנייתא ולהכי לא יחזיר כדקאמר איתרע ליה וחיישי' דלמא אקרי וכתב והוה ליה מוקדם ולכן הופקר להשליכו: **לפרעון ולקנוניא.** שמא פרעו ומן הלוה נפל והא דקא מודה לא פרעתי עצה היא ביניהם של רמאות לטרוף את הלקוחות שלקחו ממנו קרקע שלא באחריות ויחלקו ביניהם: **ולשמואל דאמר.** לקמן: **לא חיישינן לפרעון.** בשטר הנמצא ואפילו אין חייב מודה דאם איתא דפרעיה מקרע הוה קרע ליה דאמר שמואל לקמן (דף טז:) המוצא שטר הקנאה בשוק יחזיר לבעלים וכ"ש כשחייב מודה מהאי טעמא גופיה דמיום פריעתו הוא קורעו הלכך ליכא למיחש לאחר זמן לקנוניא מתני' במאי מוקי לה: **הניחא כו'.** ואי קשיא על כרחך לא סבירא ליה כאביי דאי כאביי ס"ל מאי איריא שטר הקנאה הא לאביי אין חילוק בין זה לזה דאפילו דלאו הקנאה נמי יחזיר הואיל ושמואל לא חייש לפרעון לאו פירכא הוא דמודה אביי בדלא מטא שטרא לידיה כדאמרן (ג) הלכך איכא למימר כתב ללות ולא לוה לגמרי ולא מטא לידיה מעולם: **שמואל מוקי לה כשאין חייב מודה.** בכתיבת השטר שאומר לוה לא כתבתי ומזויף הוא וא"ת יתקיים בחותמיו כיון שנפל אתרע ליה ואמרינן מפני שפסול היה לא נזהר והמניחו ליה להאי: אינו

---

**אביי** אמר עדיו בחתומיו זכין לו. מכאן קשה לרש"י דריש מסכת ראש השנה (דף ב. ושם ד"ה לשטרות) דתנן באחד בניסן ראש השנה למלכים ומפרש בגמרא דנפקא מינה לשטרי חוב המוקדמים ופרש"י שאם לא קבעו יום לתחלת שנת המלך אלא כל מלך לפי מה שעומד פעמים שאין להבחין כגון אם כתב בו בכסליו בשנת ג' למלך ובאו עדים ואמרו כשחתמנו בו לא ראינו שהלוהו אלא אמר הלוה לנו חתמו כאותה ששנינו כותבין שטר ללוה אע"פ שאין מלוה עמו אבל ראינו שהלוהו אותה מלוה בתמוז בשנת ג' למלך ואין אנו יודעים אם קודם לכן או אחרי כן שאין אנו יודעים מתי עמד המלך אם בין [ה] תמוז לכסליו של אחריו והוה ליה כסליו תחלה א"כ מוקדם הוא ופסול או בין כסליו לתמוז של אחריו והוה ליה מאוחר וכשר והשתא שקבעו ניסן ר"ה הוה ליה תמוז תחלה ושטר מאוחר הוא וכשר והשתא לאביי כה"ג לאו מוקדם הוא דעדיו בחתומיו זכין לו ולרב אסי נמי דלית ליה למה הוצרכו לעשות תקנה כיון דלית ליה כותבין שטר ללוה אלא בשטרי הקנאה ועוד וכי רגילות הוא שישכחו כל העולם והסופר וב"ד מתי עמד המלך שהוצרכו לעשות תקנה בשביל כך ועוד דהוה ליה למימר דנ"מ טובא בכל שטרות שלא ידעו מאימתי לגבות כיון דאין יודעים מתי מתחלת שנת המלך וע"ק יותר אך אין מקומו הנה ונראה לפרש דנ"מ לשטרי חוב המוקדמים היינו כגון שאם עמד המלך בכ"ט באדר כשיגיע כ"ט באדר בשנה של אחריו פעמים יטעה הסופר ביום אחד ויסבור שעמד המלך אשתקד באחד בניסן ויכתוב עתה בכ"ט באדר שנה ראשונה ונמצא שטר זה מוקדם שנה שלימה וזה פסול לכולי עלמא שכותב עתה שנה של אשתקד אבל כשקבעו ניסן ר"ה לא יטעה דמיום שני לעמידת המלך שהוא ראש חדש ניסן כתב הסופר שנה שניה ומשם ואילך עד ניסן הבא:

**משום** דקשיא ליה. לאביי תימה דבשביל כך לא הוצרך לומר עדיו בחתומיו זכין לו דאפילו יסבור דאין זכין כרב אסי ומתניתין שכותבין שטר ללוה בשטרי הקנאה ודלמא מיקרי וכתב לא אמרי' יעמיד משנתנו בשחייב מודה ולא יחזיר משום דחיישינן לפרעון ולקנוניא כדאמר בסמוך וי"ל משום דקשיא לאביי לא ניחא ליה שנויא דרב אסי ומילתא באפי נפשה היא ולא קאי אלדאמר אביי עדיו בחתומיו זכין לו: **היינו** טעמא דחיישינן לפרעון ולקנוניא. וסברי רבנן אחריות טעות סופר הוא ולכך לא יחזיר אפילו אין בו אחריות וכן לרב אסי תימה אמאי קאמר משום דחיישינן לקנוניא לימא משום דחיישינן שמא פרעו וכבר נמחל שעבודו ועתה רוצה לחזור וללות בו כדי להרויח פסיטי דספרא ומלוה נמי רוצה בדבר שיטרוף מזמן מוקדם וי"ל משום פסיטי דספרא לא יפסיד ללקוחות ממון מרובה אף על גב דרב אסי חייש לכתב ללות ולא לוה ועתה רוצה ללות ומפסיד ללקוחות משום פסיטי דספרא היינו משום שכבר נתן לסופר ואינו רוצה להפסיד ועוד שסובר המלוה שיצא הקול משעת כתיבה אבל כשלוה ופרע לא הפסיד פשוט שנתן לסופר ועוד שירא המלוה ששמעו הפריעה והלוואה שנית לא נכתב השטר:

הא

---

### עין משפט נר מצוה

קיא א מיי' פכ"ד מהל' מלוה ולוה הל' א ועיין מ"מ שהניח בצ"ע סמג עשין עד טוש"ע ח"מ סי' לט סעיף יג:

קיב ב מיי' פי"ח מהל' אבידה הל' א סמג עשין עד טוש"ע ח"מ סי' סה סעיף ו:

### גליון הש"ס

גמ' **אביי אמר עדיו בחתומיו.** עי' רשב"א בחידושי קדושין דף כז ע"א ד"ה ע"מ שתכתבו לו שטר:

### רבינו חננאל

מלוה עמו ניחוש שמא כתב ללות ולא לוה. ופריק רב אשי בשטרי הקנאה דהא שיעבד נפשיה בחליפין ולא חיישי' לנתינת המעות אלא נשתעבד מעידנא ההיא דקנו מיניה בחליפין. אביי אמר עדיו בחותמיו זכין לו פי' כיון שאמר לוה לעדים העידו עלי שיש לפלוני עלי כך וכך וכתבו שטר בזה וחתמו בו זכו למלוה ואע"ג דלא קנו מן הלוה והוא דנפיק שטרא מידא דמלוה אבל אי לא נפיק שטרא מתותי ידיה דמלוה חיישינן דלמא אכתי לא מטא לידיה דמלוה ומתני' דאוקימנא בשחייב מודה דהאי שטרא מטא לידיה דמלוה מההיא שעתא דנכתב ומיניה נפל. אמר לך אביי כי הא גוונא בדלא נקיט שטרא מתותי ידיה דמלוה חיישינן לקנוניא ומשום הכי לא הימנינן בהודאתו דלוה. ולא אשכחן פירכא לא להא דאביי ולא להא דרב אשי ותרוייהו בעינן דמטא שטרא בידא דמלוה. והא דר' יוחנן לא הוי להו תיובתא דיכול רב אשי למימר לא אמר ר' יוחנן אלא בשטרי דלאו אקנייאתא ולאביי נמי לא הויא תיובתא דהא לדבריו דר' יוחנן שייכי. מיהו סוגיא דשמעתין כר' יוחנן סלקא דאמר מחלוקת בשחייב מודה ר"מ דאמר יחזיר סבר שטר שאין בו אחריות נכסין לא גבי ממשעבדי מבני חרי הוא דגבי וכיון דמודה ליה ליכא למיחש הלכך יחזיר. ורבנן סברי גבי אפי' ממשעבדי הלכך לא יחזיר דחיישינן לקנוניא אבל בשאין חייב מודה דברי הכל לא יחזיר דחיישינן לפרעון ותניא בהדיא כוותיה. שמואל מוקי לה לכולה מתני' בשאין חייב מודה אבל בשחייב מודה דברי הכל יחזיר כי עדיו בחתומיו זכין לו א) (וכל) בשטרי הקנאה דהא שיעבד נפשיה. ובשטר שאין בו אחריות אע"פ שאין חייב מודה ב) ר"מ דאמר יחזיר למלוה לצור על פי צלוחיתו דכיון שאין בו אחריות נכסין אינו גובה לא ממשעבדי ולא מבני חרי.

### חשק שלמה על ר"ח

א) אולי צ"ל וכ"ש בשטרי הקנאה. ב) צ"ל אמר ר"מ דיחזיר למלוה וכו'.

---

### מסורת הש"ס

...מן [יט., כ.], לה:, ...מן יח., [גיטין כז.], ...קמן יד., טז:], ...עיל ז: וש"נ], ...רסת מהרש"א בין ... לתמוז שלפניו, ועי' מהרש"ל.

### הגהות הב"ח

...מ' מוקי לה למתני' ...א דלאו אקנייתא: ...יש"י ד"ה אביי אמר אבל השתא דתנן. נ"ב למאי דקס"ד השתא ...ס הכי פריך לקמיה ... לא יחזיר כו' אבל ... דמסיק הוה טעמיה ... משום דחיישינן ...ון ולקנוניא והוה ... שנמחל שעבודו: ...ה הניחא וכו' הלכך ... למימר. נ"ב פירוש ... שאין חייב מודה:

### ליקוטי רש"י

...טרי הקנאה. שקנו ... שאפי' לא ילוה ...ות שיעבד עצמו ...ס [לקמן טז:]. דליכא ...ר כתב ללות ולא לוה ... אפילו לא לוה שעביד ...ה [לקמן יד.]. עדיו ...תומיו. מיום שנחתם ... האדרכתא בב"ד ...פ שלא בא לידו [לקמן ...]. ומיום כתיבת השטר ...בד נפשיה [רשב"ם ...קעא:]. דייתיקי. דא ... למיקם שטר זה יהיה ... ולהיות בכל הכתוב ... לדברי שכיב מרע ...בין וכמסורין דמי ...[גיטין יט.]. לא יחזיר. ... לבעל ולא לאשה וכן ...יר וכן כולם [גיטין כז:].

e accepts Abaye's principle:
שְׁמוּאֵל מוֹקֵי לְמַתְנִיתִין כְּשֶׁאֵין חַיָּיב מ – **Shmuel can interpret** **Mishnah** as speaking about a case **where the debtor does** **admit** that the debt is owed.[20] Thus it is because of the btor's denial that the note may not be returned to the creditor t contains a lien.[21]

The Gemara questions this interpretation:

אִי – **If so,** כִּי אֵין בָּהֶן אַחֲרָיוּת נְכָסִים – then **if there is no** vision for **a lien on** real **property in [the notes],** אַמַּאי יַחֲזִיר – **why should [the finder] return them** to the creditor? נְהִי דְּלָא גָּבֵי מִן מְשַׁעְ – **Granted that [the creditor] cannot** lect with such a note, according to R' Meir, **from encumbered** operty, i.e. from real property which is no longer in the btor's possession and from which a creditor can collect only if has a lien against them, מִבְּנֵי חָרֵי מִגְבֵּי גָּבֵי – but **from** **encumbered property,** i.e. from real property that is still in debtor's possession, **[the creditor] can indeed collect.** How, n, can the finder be instructed to return a note to the creditor er the protest of the debtor that he will be unjustly harmed by s?[22]

The Gemara answers:

שְׁמוּאֵל לְטַעְ – **Shmuel is consistent with his own view,** דְּאָמַר שְׁמוּ – **for Shmuel said:** אוֹמֵר הָיָה רַבִּי מֵאִיר – **R' Meir** uld say שְׁטַר חוֹב שֶׁאֵין בּוֹ אַחֲרָיוּת נְכָסִים – that with **a note of** **indebtedness in which there is no** provision for **a lien on** real **property,** אֵין גּוֹבֶה לֹא מִמְּשַׁעְבְּדֵי – **[the creditor] cannot** collect **either from encumbered property** וְלֹא מִבְּנֵי חָרֵי – **or** **from property free of encumbrance.**[23] Since he cannot collect with this note, there is no reason not to return the note to the creditor, even if the debtor denies the debt. Thus, the author of the Mishnah's ruling to return the note without a lien – R' Meir – follows his own view regarding a note of indebtedness without a lien, viz. that it is a document without legal force. There is therefore no harm in returning it to the creditor.

The Gemara questions the interpretation:

וְכִי מֵאַחַר שֶׁאֵינוֹ גּוֹבֶה – **But since [the creditor] cannot collect** with this note, אַמַּאי יַחֲזִיר – **why should [the finder] return** it to him? Of what use is it to him?

The Gemara answers:

אָמַר רַבִּי נָתָן בַּר אוֹשַׁעְיָא – **Said R' Nassan bar Oshaya:** לָצוּר עַל פִּי צְלוֹחִיתוֹ שֶׁל מַלְוֶה – The note can be used **to wrap over the mouth of the creditor's bottle.**

The Gemara analyzes the above answer:

וְנַהַדְרֵיהּ לְהוּ לַלֹּוֶה – **Let us instead return [the note] to the debtor** לָצוּר עַל פִּי צְלוֹחִיתוֹ שֶׁל לֹוֶה – to use the note **to wrap over the mouth of the debtor's bottle.**

The Gemara answers:

לֹוֶה הוּא – But **it is the debtor**

NOTES

gular note of indebtedness does not effect a lien if the loan is never nsummated. Therefore, Shmuel implies that in contrast to a note of quisition, a regular note of indebtedness may not be returned, at least ere the debtor denies that he owes the debt, because of the concern at the loan was never consummated (*Rashi*, as understood by *Bach* d *Maharam Shif*).

. This is in contrast to the interpretations of Rav Assi and Abaye, ich follow the Gemara's original assumption (above, 12b) that the ishnah speaks about a case where the debtor admits that he still owes e debt.

. I.e. the debtor named in the note denies that he ever drew up the note d claims that the signatures are forged (*Rashi*). [*Rashi's* source for e assumption that in this interpretation the Mishnah speaks about a btor who claims that the note was forged is the Gemara below, which ates that the debtor claims "that the whole matter never occurred."] The Gemara's interpretation seems difficult. If the debtor's defense is erely that the note is forged, why is it not returned to the creditor even the note contains a lien? As long as the creditor does not certify the te, he cannot collect his debt anyway [either from the debtor or his yers] because of the concern that the note is forged. And if the creditor able to certify the note, then he has disproved the debtor's claim, and should be allowed to collect the debt (even from the buyers of the editor's properties). Thus, the debtor [and his buyers] have nothing to lose from the return of the note; and since everyone agrees that the note does not belong to the debtor (as explained by the Gemara below), why is it not given to the creditor in any case?

The answer is as follows: Although generally certification is sufficient to dispel the concern that a note is forged, in our case there are grounds for extra vigilance, since the fact that the note was lost leads us to consider that because the note was invalid its owner did not safeguard it and as a result lost it. Thus, in this case, if the debtor claims that the note was forged, even certification would not suffice to validate it, because we suspect that the note may have been forged in such a professional manner that the certifying witnesses will not discern the fraud (*Rashi*). Therefore the note is not returned, since return of the note will enable the creditor to certify the note and collect with it.

In Shmuel's case of a note of acquisition, however, we are not concerned that the note is forged (once it has been certified), because he is speaking about an instance where the debtor does not claim that the note is forged. Rather, in Shmuel's case, the debtor may either not be present, or he claims that he paid the debt (*Tosefos HaRosh*).

22. It was because of this difficulty that the Gemara rejected the possibility (above, 12b) that the Mishnah speaks about a case where the debtor denies that he still owes the debt. How, then, can Shmuel accept such an interpretation?

23. See below, 13b note 3, for an explanation of this view.

[א] בשטרי הקנאה דהא שעביד נפשיה אי הכי מתניתין דקתני אם יש בהן אחריות נכסים לא יחזיר ואוקימנא כשחייב מודה ומשום שמא כתב ללות בניסן ולא לוה עד תשרי ואתי למטרף לקוחות שלא כדין אמאי לא יחזיר נחזי אי בשטר הקנאה הא שעביד ליה נפשיה אי בשטר דלא הקנאה ליכא למיחש דהא אמרת כי ליכא מלוה בהדיה לא כתבינן א"ל רב אסי אע"ג דשטרי דלאו הקנאה כי ליכא מלוה בהדיה לא כתבינן מתניתין כיון דנפל אתרע ליה וחיישינן דלמא אקרי וכתוב (א) ° אביי אמר עדיו בחתומיו זכין לו ואפילו שטרי דלאו הקנאה משום דקשיא ליה כיון דאמרת בשטרי דלאו הקנאה כי ליתיה למלוה בהדיה לא כתבינן ליכא למיחש דאקרי וכתוב אלא הא דתנן (ג) מצא גיטי נשים ושחרורי עבדים דייתיקי מתנה ושוברים הרי זה לא יחזיר שמא כתובים היו ונמלך עליהם שלא ליתנם וכי נמלך עליהם מאי הוי והא אמרת עדיו בחתומיו זכין לו הני מילי היכא דקא מטו לידיה אבל היכא דלא מטו לידיה לא אמרינן אלא מתניתין דקתני מצא שטרי חוב אם יש בהם אחריות נכסים לא יחזיר ואוקימנא כשחייב מודה ומשום שמא כתב ללות בניסן ולא לוה עד תשרי בשלמא לרב אסי דאמר בשטרי אקנייתא מוקי לה בשטרי דלאו אקנייתא וכדאמרינן אלא לאביי דאמר עדיו בחתומיו זכין לו מאי איכא למימר אמר לך אביי מתני' היינו טעמא (ב) דחייש לפרעון ולקנוניא ולשמואל דאמר (ג) לא חיישינן לפרעון ולקנוניא מאי איכא למימר הניחא אי סבר לה כרב אסי דאמר בשטרי הקנאה מוקי (א) מתניתין בשטרי דלאו הקנאה אלא אי סבר כאביי דאמר עדיו בחתומיו זכין לו מאי איכא למימר שמואל מוקי למתניתין כשאין חייב מודה אי הכי כי אין בהן אחריות נכסים אמאי יחזיר נהי דלא גבי מן משעבדי מבני חרי מגבי גבי שמואל לטעמיה דאמר שמואל אומר היה רבי מאיר שטר חוב שאין בו אחריות נכסים אין גובה לא ממשעבדי ולא מבני חרי וכי מאחר שאינו גובה אמאי יחזיר אמר רבי נתן בר אושעיא (ד) לצור על פי צלוחיתו של מלוה ונהדריה להו ללוה לצור על פי צלוחיתו של לוה הוא

דאמר

**רש"י**

בשטרי הקנאה. שמקנה לו נכסיו מהיום בין ילוה בין לא ילוה יגבה מהן לאותו זמן מהיום: אי הכי. דבשטרי דלאו הקנאה לא עבידי דכתבי אלא אם כן ראו הלואת המעות מתני' דקתני כו': כי ליכא מלוה בהדיה. ונותן מעות בפניהם לא כתבינן: אביי אמר. הא דתנן כותבין שטר ללוה בלא מלוה אפילו בשטר דלאו הקנאה נמי ואי נמי אתי למיטרף מהאידנא והוא לא לוה עד תשרי לא שלא כדין הוא דעדיו בחתומיו זכין לו מיום שחתמוהו זכין לו השעבוד ואפילו לא הלוה המעות עד תשרי ולהכי מוקי ליה אביי בהאי טעמא משום דקשיא ליה כיון דאמרת כו' (ג) אבל השתא דתנן כותבין חיישינן דלמא כתב ללות ולא לוה ולקמיה פריך אמאי לא יחזיר הרי זכו ליה עדיו בחתומיו ושפיר טריף: דייתיקי. צוואת שכיב מרע ולשון דייתיקי דא תיקו זאת תיקום לדברי שכיב מרע ככתובין וכמסורין דמי: מתנה. מתנת בריא: ושוברין. פרעון שטר: הני מילי היכא דמטא שטר לידיה. ואפילו לאחר זמן זכו לו חותמיו לגבות מזמן הכתוב בו ואי קשיא הא דתנן (שביעית פ"י מ"ה) שטרי חוב המוקדמין פסולין והמאוחרין כשרין במאי מוקי לה אביי תריץ במוקדמת כתיבתן לחתימתן ולהכי פסולין שבא לטרוף משעת כתיבה א"נ שכתבו וחתמוהו בתשרי והם כתבו בתוכו ניסן שהוא ראש השנה לשטרות: בשלמא לרב אסי. דמוקי להאי דכותבין בשטרי אקנייתא: מוקי. מתניתין בדלאו אקנייתא ולהכי לא יחזיר כדקאמר איתרע ליה וחיישי' דלמא אקרי וכתב והוה ליה מוקדם ולכן הופקר להשליכו: לפרעון ולקנוניא. שמא פרעו ומן הלוה נפל והא דקא מודה לא פרעתי עצה היא ביניהם של רמאות לטרוף את הלקוחות שלקחו ממנו קרקע שלא באחריות ויחלקו ביניהם: ולשמואל דאמר. לקמן: לא חיישינן לפרעון. בשטר הנמצא ואפילו אין חייב מודה דאם איתא דפרעיה מקרע הוה קרע ליה דאמר שמואל לקמן (דף טז:) המוצא שטר הקנאה בשוק יחזיר לבעלים וכ"ש כשחייב מודה מהאי טעמא גופיה דמיום פריעתו הוא קורעו הלכך ליכא למיחש לאחר זמן לקנוניא מתני' במאי מוקי לה: הניחא כו'. ואי קשיא על כרחך לא סבירא ליה כאביי דאי כאביי ס"ל מאי איריא שטר הקנאה הא לאביי אין חילוק בין זה לזה דאפילו דלאו הקנאה נמי יחזיר הואיל ושמואל לא חייש לפרעון לאו פירכא הוא דמודה אביי בדלא מטא שטרא לידיה כדאמרן (ג) הלכך איכא למימר כתב ללות ולא לוה לגמרי ולא מטא לידיה מעולם: שמואל מוקי לה כשאין חייב מודה. בכתיבת השטר שאומר לוה לא כתבתי ומזויף הוא וא"ת יתקיים בחותמיו כיון שנפל אתרע ליה ואמרינן מפני שפסול היה לא נזהר והמנינן ליה להאי: אינו

**תוספות**

אביי אמר עדיו בחתומיו זכין לו. מכאן קשה לרש"י דפי' מסכת ראש השנה (דף ב. ושם ד"ה לשטרות) דתנן באחד בניסן ראש השנה למלכים ומפרש בגמרא דנפקא מינה לשטרי חוב המוקדמים ופרש"י שאם לא קבעו יום לתחלת שנת המלך אלא כל מלך לפי מה שעומד פעמים שאין להבחין כגון אם כתב בו בכסליו בשנת ג' למלך ובאו עדים ואמרו כשחתמנו בו לא ראינו שהלוהו אלא אמר הלוה לנו חתמו כאותה שנינו כותבין שטר ללוה אע"פ שאין מלוה עמו אבל ראינו שהלוהו אותה מלוה בתמוז בשנת ג' למלך ואין אנו יודעים אם קודם לכן או אחרי כן שאין אנו יודעים מתי עמד המלך אם בין (ה) תמוז לכסליו של אחריו והוה ליה כסליו תחלה א"כ מוקדם הוא ופסול או בין כסליו לתמוז של אחריו והוה ליה מאוחר וכשר והשתא שקבעו ניסן ר"ה הוה ליה תמוז תחלה ושטר מאוחר הוא וכשר והשתא לאביי כה"ג לאו מוקדם הוא דעדיו בחתומיו זכין לו ולרב אסי נמי דלית ליה למה הוצרכו לעשות תקנה כיון דלית ליה כותבין שטר ללוה אלא בשטרי הקנאה ועוד וכי רגילות הוא שישכחו כל העולם והסופר וב"ד מתי עמד המלך שהוצרכו לעשות תקנה בשביל כך ועוד דהוה ליה למימר דנ"מ טובא בכל שטרות שלא ידעו מאימתי לגבות כיון דאין יודעים מתי מתחלת שנת המלך וע"ק יותר אך אין מקומו הנה ונראה לפרש דנ"מ לשטרי חוב המוקדמים היינו כגון שאם עמד המלך בכ"ט באדר כשיגיע כ"ט באדר בשנה של אחריו פעמים יטעה הסופר ביום אחד ויסבור שעמד המלך אשתקד באחד בניסן ויכתוב עתה בכ"ט באדר שנה ראשונה ונמצא שטר זה מוקדם שנה שלימה וזה פסול לכולי עלמא שכותב עתה שנה של אשתקד אבל כשקבעו ניסן ר"ה לא יטעה דמיום שני לעמידת המלך שהוא ראש חדש ניסן כתב הסופר שנה שניה ומשם ואילך עד ניסן הבא:

משום דקשיא ליה. לאביי תימה דבשביל כך לא הוצרך לומר עדיו בחתומיו זכין לו דאפילו יסבור דאין זכין כרב אסי ומתניתין שכותבין שטר ללוה בשטרי הקנאה ודלמא מיקרי וכתב לא אמרי' יעמיד משנתנו בשחייב מודה ולא יחזיר משום דחיישינן לפרעון ולקנוניא כדאמר בסמוך וי"ל משום דקשיא לאביי לא ניחא ליה שנויא דרב אסי ומילתא באפי נפשה היא ולא קאי אדאמר אביי עדיו בחתומיו זכין לו: היינו טעמא דחיישינן לפרעון ולקנוניא. וסברי רבנן אחריות טעות סופר הוא ולכך לא יחזיר אפילו אין בו אחריות וכן לרב אסי תימה אמאי קאמר משום דחיישינן לקנוניא לימא משום דחיישינן שמא פרעו וכבר נמחל שעבודו ועתה רוצה לחזור וללות בו כדי להרויח פשיטי דספרא ומלוה נמי רוצה בדבר שיטרוף מזמן מוקדם וי"ל משום פשיטי דספרא לא יפסיד ללקוחות ממון מרובה אף על גב דרב אסי חייש לכתב ללות ולא לוה ועתה רוצה ללות ומפסיד ללקוחות משום פשיטי דספרא היינו משום שכבר נתן לסופר ואינו רוצה להפסיד ועוד שסובר המלוה שילא הקול משעת כתיבה אבל כשלוה ופרע לא הפסיד פשוט שנתן לסופר ועוד שירא המלוה ששמעו הפריעה והלוואה שנית לא נכתב השטר:

הא

**עין משפט נר מצוה**

קיא א מיי' פכ"ד מהל' מלוה ולוה הל' א ועיין מ"מ שהניח בצ"ע סמג עשין עד טוש"ע ח"מ סי' לט סעיף יג:

קיב ב מיי' פי"ח מהל' אבידה הל' א סמג עשין עד טוש"ע ח"מ סי' סה סעיף ו:

**גליון הש"ס**

גמ' אביי אמר עדיו בחתומיו. עי' רשב"א בחידושי קדושין דף כז ע"א ד"ה ע"מ שתכתבו לו שטר:

**רבינו חננאל**

מלוה עמו ניחוש שמא כתב ללות ולא לוה. ופריק רב אשי בשטרי הקנאה דהא שיעבד נפשיה בחליפין ולא חיישי' לנתינת המעות אלא נשתעבד מעידנא ההיא דקנו מיניה בחליפין. אביי אמר עדיו בחותמיו זכין לו פי' כיון שאמר לוה לעדים העידו עלי שיש לפלוני עלי כך וכך וכתבו שטר בזה וחתמו בו זכו למלוה ואע"ג דלא קנו מן הלוה והוא דנפיק שטרא מידא דמלוה אבל אי לא נפיק שטרא מתותי ידיה דמלוה חיישינן דלמא אכתי לא מטא לידיה דמלוה ומתני' דאוקימנא בשחייב מודה דהאי שטרא מטא לידיה דמלוה מההיא שעתא דנכתב ומיניה נפל. אמר לך אביי כי הא גוונא בדלא נקיט שטרא מתותי ידיה דמלוה חיישינן לקנוניא ומשום הכי לא הימנינן בהודאתו דלוה. ולא אשכחן פירכא לא להא דאביי ולא להא דרב אשי ותרוייהו בעינן דמטא שטרא בידא דמלוה. והא דר' יוחנן לא הוי להו תיובתא דיכול רב אשי למימר לא אמר ר' יוחנן אלא בשטרי דלאו אקנייאתא ולאביי נמי לא הויא תיובתא דהא לדבריו דר' יוחנן שייכי. מיהו סוגיא דשמעתין כר' יוחנן סלקא דאמר מחלוקת בשחייב מודה ר"מ דאמר יחזיר סבר שטר שאין בו אחריות נכסין לא גבי ממשעבדי מבני חרי הוא דגבי וכיון דמודה ליה ליכא למיחש הלכך יחזיר. ורבנן סברי גבי אפי' ממשעבדי הלכך לא יחזיר דחיישינן לקנוניא אבל בשאין חייב מודה דברי הכל לא יחזיר דחיישינן לפרעון ותניא בהדיא כוותיה. שמואל מוקי לה לכולה מתני' בשאין חייב מודה אבל בשחייב מודה דברי הכל יחזיר כי עדיו בחתומיו זכין לו א) (וכל) בשטרי הקנאה דהא שיעבד נפשיה. ובשטר שאין בו אחריות אע"פ שאין חייב מודה ב) ר"מ דאמר יחזיר למלוה לצור על פי צלוחיתו דכיון שאין בו אחריות נכסין אינו גובה לא ממשעבדי ולא מבני חרי.

**חשק שלמה על ר"ח**

א) אולי צ"ל וכ"ש בשטרי הקנאה. ב) צ"ל אמר ר"מ דיחזיר למלוה וכו'.

**מסורת הש"ס**

...מן [יט., כ.], לה:, ...מן יח. [גיטין כח.], ...קמן יד., טז:], ...עיל ז: וש"נ], ...יסת מהרש"א בין לתמוז שלפניו, ועי' מהרש"ל.

**הגהות הב"ח**

...מ' מוקי לה למתני' ...א דלאו אקנייתא: ...ש"י ד"ה אביי אמר ...אבל השתא דתנן. נ"ב ...מאי דקס"ד השתא ...ם הכי פריך לקמיה ...לא יחזיר כו' אבל ...דמסיק הוה טעמיה ...משום דחיישינן ...ון ולקנוניא והוה ...שנמחל שעבודו: ...ה הניחא וכו' הלכך ...למימר. נ"ב פירוש ...שאין חייב מודה:

**ליקוטי רש"י**

...טרי הקנאה. שקנו ...שאפי' לא ילוה ...ית שיעבד עצמו ...ם [לקמן טז:]. ליכא ...ר כתב ללות ולא לוה ...אפילו לא לוה שעביד ...ה [לקמן יד.]. עדיו ...תומיו. מיום שנחתם ...האדרכתא בב"ד ...פ שלא בא לידו [לקמן ...]. ומיום כתיבת השטר ...ד נפשיה [רשב"ם ...קעא:]. דייתיקי. לא ...למיקם שטר זה יהיה ...ולהיות בכל הכתוב ...לדברי שכיב מרע ...בין וכמסורין דמי ...ן יט.]. לא יחזיר. ...לבעל ולא לאשה וכן ...ור וכן כולם [גיטין כז.].

The Gemara now presents the problem that arises according to .baye's view:

אֶלָּא לְאַבַּיֵי דְּאָמַר עֵדָיו בַּחֲתוּמָיו זָכִין — **But according to Abaye, 'ho says that the [note's] witnesses by** their **signatures cquire,** מַאי אִיכָּא לְמֵימַר — **what is there to say?** In this view, ıe fear that perhaps the debtor drew up the note to borrow in the ıonth of Nissan but did not actually borrow the money until the ıonth of Tishrei should not be a cause for concern, since even if ıis were the case, the lien takes effect retroactively from Nissan s soon as the loan is made.[14] — ? —

The Gemara defends Abaye:

אָמַר לָךְ אַבַּ — **Abaye could answer you** as follows: מַתְנִיתִין הַיְינוּ טַעְמָא דְּחַיֵּישׁ לְפֵרָעוֹן וְלִקְנוּנְיָ — In **our Mishnah, this is the** eason not to return the note to the lender in spite of the orrower's admission: **For [R' Meir] is concerned about** the ossibility of **payment and collusion.** We are concerned that the ebt was actually paid up, and the debtor's admission to the ontrary is part of a conspiracy between the debtor and the reditor to defraud the owners of properties against which the reditor has a lien, by collecting the debt again — this time from ıese buyers of the properties.[15]

The Gemara examines whether Shmuel can accept Abaye's view:

וְלִשְׁמוּאֵל דְּאָמַר לֹא חָיְישִׁינַן לְפֵרָעוֹן וְלִקְנוּנְיָא — **And according to Shmuel, who maintains that we need not be concerned about payment and collusion,** מַאי אִיכָּא לְמֵימַר — **what is there to say?**[16] Shmuel cannot then explain that the reason of the Mishnah for not returning the note is because of the concern about conspiracy, as does Abaye. הָנִיחָא אִי סָבַר לָהּ כְּרַב אַסִּי — Now, **it is understandable if [Shmuel] holds the view of Rav Assi,** דְּאָמַר בִּשְׁטָרֵי הַקְנָאָה — **who says that [the Mishnah]** in *Bava Basra,* that permits having a loan document drawn up even if the lender is not present, speaks **about notes of acquisition,**[17] that our Mishnah presents no problem. מוֹקֵי מַתְנִיתִין בִּשְׁטָרֵי דְּלָאו הַקְנָאָה — **[Shmuel] will interpret [our Mishnah]** as speaking **about a note not of** the **acquisition** type, so that the lien takes effect only from the actual date of the loan.[18] אֶלָּא אִי סָבַר כְּאַבַּיֵי דְּאָמַר עֵדָיו בַּחֲתוּמָיו זָכִין לוֹ — **But if [Shmuel] holds the view of Abaye, who says that the [note's] witnesses by** their **signatures acquire,** מַאי אִיכָּא לְמֵימַר — **what is there to say?**[19]

The Gemara shows how Shmuel can explain the Mishnah even

NOTES

4. [We cannot answer that according to Abaye, we suspect that the note 'as pre-dated and invalid (see above, note 4), because as noted by the emara earlier, Abaye maintains that we need not be concerned that the ote was initially drawn in an invalid manner, even in regard to a lost ote.] We also are not concerned that the note was never given to the :editor (in which case Abaye would concede that the witnesses do not cquire, as explained by the Gemara above), for we now assume that the lishnah refers to an instance in which the debtor concedes that the :editor lost the note (*Ritva*).

5. That is, we are concerned that perhaps the loan was paid and the note eturned to the debtor, and that it was he who subsequently lost it. His resent admission that he still owes the debt cannot be relied on, for that dmission may be prompted by a desire to collude with the creditor in efrauding the buyers of the debtor's properties. The debtor may have old the properties without guaranteeing them against collection (see elow, 14a) so that if a creditor collects these properties in payment of a ebt, the buyer has no recourse to demand compensation from the ebtor. The debtor is therefore suspected of conspiring with the creditor allow him to fraudulently collect his debt again from such buyers, and divide the proceeds of the fraud with the creditor. It is because of the oncern about such a conspiracy that the Mishnah rules not to return ıe note to the creditor (*Rashi*).

6. Below (16b), the Gemara cites the following ruling of Shmuel: If one nds a note of acquisition [שְׁטַר הַקְנָאָה], he should return it to its owners - i.e. the creditor named therein (even if the debtor does not concede wing this debt; the Mishnah that rules not to return a found note of ıdebtedness refers only to a regular note of indebtedness). [The emara there explains that regarding a note of acquisition, we need not e concerned that the loan was never consummated, for the debtor has bligated himself to pay even if he ultimately does not borrow the ıoney. Also, we are not concerned about the possibility that the debtor ight have already repaid the loan, for if the debtor had repaid, he ould have received the note in return and promptly destroyed it.] hus, we see that Shmuel is never concerned that the loan recorded in n existing note was repaid; for he is of the opinion that the debtor is resumed to destroy the note as soon as he repays his debt. Therefore, ıere is no concern that some time subsequent to the repayment, the ebtor and creditor conspired to defraud the buyers, since the debtor is resumed to have destroyed the loan document immediately upon eceiving it (*Rashi*). [There is also no concern that the conspiracy was rranged at the time of the repayment, for if that were the case the reditor would have been careful not to lose the note (see 12b note 32). ur sole concern would be that the conspiracy is being arranged now ıat the paid note has been found. This concern does not exist, according Shmuel, who holds that the paid note would have been immediately estroyed, not lost.]

7. I.e. he holds, as does Rav Assi, that regular notes of indebtedness — ıose that are not of the acquisition type — may not be drawn without the lender's presence, because of the concern that the loan will not be made until later, and he therefore disagrees with Abaye and holds that the witnesses cannot acquire retroactively to the date of the note's signing; see Gemara above.

18. If Shmuel indeed accepts Rav Assi's view, then he has the option to interpret the Mishnah as it was interpreted according to Rav Assi: The Mishnah refers to a case where the debtor admits that he still owes the debt. Therefore, R' Meir rules that where there is no lien and the matter concerns only the debtor, the note may be returned to the creditor. Nevertheless, where the note contains a lien, the note may not be returned, because of the concern of "perhaps he wrote in Nissan but did not borrow until Tishrei." As the Gemara has already explained above, this interpretation is incompatible with Abaye's view.

19. As already explained by the Gemara, according to Abaye our Mishnah's ruling cannot be based on the concern that perhaps the debtor drew up the note to borrow in the month of Nissan but did not actually borrow until Tishrei. Rather, our Mishnah's ruling has its roots in another consideration; namely, the concern about "payment and collusion." But, as already explained earlier in the Gemara (see note 16), Shmuel holds that we need not be concerned about "payment and collusion," so that he cannot relate the Mishnah's ruling to this concern. How, then, will Shmuel explain the Mishnah, if we are to assume that he accepts Abaye's concept that the note's witnesses by their signatures acquire? Or must we conclude that he rejects Abaye's principle?

[*Rashi* raises the following question: How can the Gemara entertain the notion that Shmuel accepts Abaye's principle? According to Abaye, regular notes of indebtedness are equivalent to notes of acquisition, for in both cases the creditor acquires a lien from the moment of the note's signing. If so, why does Shmuel (on 16b; see above, note 16) differentiate between regular notes of indebtedness and notes of acquisition, ruling that the latter must be returned and thereby implying that the former may not be returned? Why is there this distinction between the two types of note?

The answer to this question is as follows: True, there should be no distinction between the two types of notes regarding the concern about writing in Nissan and borrowing in Tishrei or the concern about payment and collusion. Just as the former concern (writing in Nissan and borrowing in Tishrei) is not relevant to notes of acquisition, it also is not relevant to regular notes of indebtedness, if one accepts Abaye's principle. And just as the latter concern (payment and collusion) is not relevant to notes of indebtedness according to Shmuel, it also is not relevant to regular notes of indebtedness. There is, however, one matter that sets the two apart — the concern that perhaps the debtor drew up the note with the intent to borrow but never actually took the loan. This concern is obviously irrelevant to notes of acquisition which, by definition, effect an obligation even if no loan was made. However, this concern is relevant to regular notes, since the Gemara above demonstrates that even according to Abaye, the signing of the witnesses on a

[א] בשטרי הקנאה דהא שעביד נפשיה אי הכי מתניתין דקתני אם יש בהן אחריות נכסים לא יחזיר ואוקימנא כשחייב מודה ומשום שמא כתב ללות בניסן ולא לוה עד תשרי ואתי למטרף לקוחות שלא כדין אמאי לא יחזיר נחזי אי בשטר הקנאה הא שעביד ליה נפשיה אי בשטר דלא הקנאה ליכא למיחש דהא אמרת כי ליכא מלוה בהדיה לא כתבינן א"ל רב אסי אע"ג דשטרי דלאו הקנאה כי ליכא מלוה בהדיה לא כתבינן מתניתין כיון דנפל אתרע ליה וחיישינן דלמא אקרי וכתוב [ה] ° אביי אמר עדיו בחתומיו זכין לו ואפילו שטרי דלאו הקנאה משום דקשיא ליה כיון דאמרת בשטרי דלאו הקנאה כי ליתיה למלוה בהדיה לא כתבינן ליכא למיחש דאקרי וכתוב אלא הא דתנן [ג] מצא גיטי נשים ושחרורי עבדים דייתיקי מתנה ושוברים הרי זה לא יחזיר שמא כתובים היו ונמלך עליהם שלא ליתנם וכי נמלך עליהם מאי הוי והא אמרת עדיו בחתומיו זכין לו הני מילי היכא דקא מטו לידיה אבל היכא דלא מטו לידיה לא אמרינן אלא מתניתין דקתני מצא שטרי חוב אם יש בהם אחריות נכסים לא יחזיר ואוקימנא כשחייב מודה ומשום שמא כתב ללות בניסן ולא לוה עד תשרי בשלמא לרב אסי דאמר בשטרי אקנייתא מוקי לה בשטרי דלאו אקנייתא וכדאמרינן אלא לאביי דאמר עדיו בחתומיו זכין לו מאי איכא למימר אמר לך אביי מתני' היינו טעמא [ב] דחייש לפרעון ולקנוניא ולשמואל דאמר [ג] לא חיישינן לפרעון ולקנוניא מאי איכא למימר הניחא אי סבר לה כרב אסי דאמר בשטרי הקנאה מוקי (א) מתניתין בשטרי דלאו הקנאה אלא אי סבר כאביי דאמר עדיו בחתומיו זכין לו מאי איכא למימר שמואל מוקי למתניתין כשאין חייב מודה אי הכי כי אין בהן אחריות נכסים אמאי יחזיר נהי דלא גבי מן משעבדי מבני חרי מגבי גבי שמואל לטעמיה דאמר שמואל אומר היה רבי מאיר שטר חוב שאין בו אחריות נכסים אין גובה לא ממשעבדי ולא מבני חרי וכי מאחר שאינו גובה אמאי יחזיר אמר רבי נתן בר אושעיא [ד] לצור על פי צלוחיתו של מלוה ונהדריה להו ללוה לצור על פי צלוחיתו של לוה הוא דאמר

**רש"י**

בשטרי הקנאה. שמקנה לו נכסיו מהיום בין לא ילוה יגבה מהן לאותו זמן מהיום: אי הכי. דבשטרי דלאו הקנאה לא עבידי דכתבי אלא אם כן ראו הלואת המעות מתני' דקתני כו': כי ליכא מלוה בהדיה. ונותן מעות בפניהם לא כתבינן: אביי אמר. הא דתנן כותבין שטר ללוה בלא מלוה אפילו בשטר דלאו הקנאה נמי ואי נמי אתי למיטרף מהאידנא והוא לא לוה עד תשרי לא שלא כדין הוא דעדיו בחתומיו זכין לו מיום שחתמוהו וזכין לו השעבוד ואפילו לא הלוה המעות עד תשרי ולהכי מוקי ליה אביי בהאי טעמא משום דקשיא ליה כיון דאמרת כו' (ג) אבל השתא דתנן כותבין חיישינן דלמא כתב ללות ולא לוה ולקמיה פריך אמאי לא יחזיר הרי זכו ליה עדיו בחתומיו ושפיר טריף: דייתיקי. צואת שכיב מרע ולשון דייתיקי דא תיקו זאת תיקום לדברי שכיב מרע ככתובין וכמסורין דמי: מתנה. מתנת בריא: ושוברין. פרעון שטר: הני מילי היכא דמטא שטר לידיה. ואפילו לאחר זמן זכו לו חותמיו לגבות מזמן הכתוב בו ואי קשיא הא דתנן (שביעית פ"י מ"ה) שטרי חוב המוקדמין פסולין והמאוחרין כשרין במאי מוקי לה אביי תריץ במוקדמת כתיבתן לחתימתן ולהכי פסולין שבא לטרוף משעת כתיבה אע"ג שכתבו וחתמוהו בתשרי והם כתבו בתוכו ניסן שהוא ראש השנה לשטרות: בשלמא לרב אסי. דמוקי להאוא דכותבין בשטרי אקנייתא: מוקי. מתניתין בדלאו אקנייתא ולהכי לא יחזיר כדקאמר איתרע ליה וחיישי' דלמא אקרי וכתב והוה ליה מוקדם ולכן הופקר להשליכו: לפרעון ולקנוניא. שמא פרעו ומן הלוה נפל והא דקא מודה לא פרעתי עצה היא ביניהם של רמאות לטרוף את הלקוחות שלקחו ממנו קרקע שלא באחריות ויחלקו ביניהם: ולשמואל דאמר. לקמן: לא חיישינן לפרעון. בשטר הנמצא ואפילו אין חייב מודה דאם איתא דפרעיה מקרע הוה קרע ליה דאמר שמואל לקמן (דף טז:) המוצא שטר הקנאה בשוק יחזיר לבעלים וכ"ש כשחייב מודה מהאי טעמא גופיה דמיום פריעתו הוא קורעו הלכך ליכא למיחש לאחר זמן לקנוניא מתני' במאי מוקי לה: הניחא כו'. ואי קשיא על כרחך לא סבירא ליה כאביי דאי כאביי ס"ל מאי איריא שטר הקנאה הא לאביי אין חילוק בין זה לזה דאפילו דלאו הקנאה נמי יחזיר הואיל ושמואל לא חייש לפרעון לאו פירכא הוא דמודה אביי בדלא מטא שטרא לידיה כדאמרן (ג) הלכך איכא למימר כתב ללות ולא לוה לגמרי ולא מטא לידיה מעולם: שמואל מוקי לה בשאין חייב מודה. בכתיבת השטר שאומר לוה לא כתבתי ומזויף הוא וא"ת יתקיים בחותמיו כיון שנפל אתרע ליה ואמרינן מפני שפסול היה לא נזהר והמניחו ליה להאי: אינו

**תוספות**

אביי אמר עדיו בחתומיו זכין לו. מכאן קשה לרש"י דריש מסכת ראש השנה (דף ג. ושם ד"ה לשטרות) דתנן באחד בניסן ראש השנה למלכים ומפרש בגמרא דנפקא מינה לשטרי חוב המוקדמים ופרש"י שאם לא קבעו יום לתחלת שנת המלך אלא כל מלך לפי מה שעומד פעמים שאין להבחין כגון אם כתב בו בכסליו בשנת ג' למלך ובאו עדים ואמרו כשחתמנו בו לא ראינו שהלוהו אלא אמר הלוה לנו חתמו כאותה ששנינו כותבין שטר ללוה אע"פ שאין מלוה עמו אבל ראינו שהלוהו אותה מלוה בתמוז בשנת ג' למלך ואין אנו יודעים אם קודם לכן או אחרי כן שאין אנו יודעים מתי עמד המלך אם בין [ה] תמוז לכסליו של אחריו והוה ליה כסליו תחלה א"כ מוקדם הוא ופסול או בין כסליו לתמוז של אחריו והוה ליה מאוחר וכשר והשתא שקבעו ניסן ר"ה הוה ליה תמוז תחלה ושטר מאוחר הוא וכשר והשתא לאביי כה"ג לאו מוקדם הוא דעדיו בחתומיו זכין לו ולרב אסי נמי דלית ליה למה הוצרכו לעשות תקנה כיון דלית ליה כותבין שטר ללוה אלא בשטרי הקנאה ועוד וכי רגילות הוא שישכחו כל העולם והסופר וב"ד מתי עמד המלך שהוצרכו לעשות תקנה בשביל כך ועוד דהוה ליה למימר דנ"מ טובא בכל שטרות שלא ידעו מאימתי לגבות כיון דאין יודעים מתי מתחלת שנת המלך וע"ק יותר אך אין מקומו הנה ונראה לפרש דנ"מ לשטרי חוב המוקדמים היינו כגון שאם עמד המלך בכ"ט באדר כשיגיע כ"ט באדר בשנה של אחריו פעמים יטעה הסופר ביום אחד ויסבור שעמד המלך אשתקד באחד בניסן ויכתוב עתה בכ"ט באדר שנה ראשונה ונמצא שטר זה מוקדם שנה שלימה וזה פסול לכולי עלמא שכותב עתה שנה של אשתקד אבל כשקבעו ניסן ר"ה לא יטעה דמיום שני לעמידת המלך שהוא ראש חדש ניסן כתב הסופר שנה שניה ומשם ואילך עד ניסן הבא:

משום דקשיא ליה. לאביי תימה דבשביל כך לא הוצרך לומר עדיו בחתומיו זכין לו דאפילו יסבור דאין זכין כרב אסי ומתניתין שכותבין שטר ללוה בשטרי הקנאה ודלמא מיקרי וכתב לא אמרי' יעמיד משנתנו בשחייב מודה ולא יחזיר משום דחיישינן לפרעון ולקנוניא כדאמר בסמוך וי"ל משום דקשיא לאביי לא ניחא ליה שנויא דרב אסי ומילתא באפי נפשה היא ולא קאי אדאמר אביי עדיו בחתומיו זכין לו:

היינו טעמא דחיישינן לפרעון ולקנוניא. וסברי רבנן אחריות טעות סופר הוא ולכך לא יחזיר אפילו אין בו אחריות וכן לרב אסי תימה אמאי קאמר משום דחיישינן לקנוניא לימא משום דחיישינן שמא פרעו וכבר נמחל שעבודו ועתה רוצה לחזור וללות בו כדי להרויח פשיטי דספרא ומלוה נמי רוצה בדבר שיטרוף מזמן מוקדם וי"ל משום פשיטי דספרא לא יפסיד ללקוחות ממון מרובה אף על גב דרב אסי חייש לכתב ללות ולא לוה ועתה רוצה ללות ומפסיד ללקוחות משום פשיטי דספרא היינו משום שכבר נתן לסופר ואינו רוצה להפסיד ועוד שסובר המלוה שיצא הקול משעת כתיבה אבל כשלוה ופרע לא הפסיד פשוט שנתן לסופר ועוד שירא המלוה ששמעו הפריעה והלואה שניה לא נכתב השטר:

**עין משפט נר מצוה**

קיא א מיי' פכ"ד מהל' מלוה ולוה הל' א ועיין מ"מ שהניח בצ"ע סמג עשין עד טוש"ע ח"מ סי' לט סעיף יג:

קיב ב מיי' פי"ח מהל' אבידה הל' א סמג עשין עד טוש"ע ח"מ סי' סה סעיף ו:

**גליון הש"ס**

גמ' אביי אמר עדיו בחתומיו. עי' רשב"א בחידושי קדושין דף כז ע"א ד"ה ע"מ שתכתבו לו שטר:

**רבינו חננאל**

מלוה עמו ניחוש שמא כתב ללות ולא לוה. ופריק רב אשי בשטרי הקנאה דהא שיעבד נפשיה בחליפין ולא חיישי' לנתינת המעות אלא נשתעבד מעידנא ההיא דקנו מיניה בחליפין. אביי אמר עדיו בחותמיו זכין לו פי' כיון שאמר לוה לעדים העידו עלי שיש לפלוני עלי כך וכך וכתבו שטר בזה וחתמו בו זכו למלוה ואע"ג דלא קנו מן הלוה והוא דנפיק שטרא מידא דמלוה אבל אי לא נפיק שטרא מתותי ידיה דמלוה חיישינן דלמא אכתי לא מטא לידיה דמלוה ומתני' דאוקימנא בשחייב מודה דהאי שטרא מטא לידיה דמלוה מההיא שעתא דנכתב ומיניה נפל. אמר לך אביי כי הא גוונא בדלא נקיט שטרא מתותי ידיה דמלוה חיישינן לקנוניא ומשום הכי לא הימנינן בהודאתו דלוה. ולא אשכחן פירכא לא להא דאביי ולא להא דרב אשי ותרוייהו בעינן דמטא שטרא בידא דמלוה. והא דר' יוחנן לא הוי להו תיובתא דיכול רב אשי למימר לא אמר ר' יוחנן אלא בשטרי דלאו אקנייאתא ולאביי נמי לא הויא תיובתא דהא לדבריו דר' יוחנן שייכי. מיהו סוגיא דשמעתין כר' יוחנן סלקא דאמר מחלוקת בשחייב מודה ר"מ דאמר יחזיר סבר שטר שאין בו אחריות נכסין לא גבי ממשעבדי מבני חרי הוא דגבי וכיון דמודה ליה ליכא למיחש הלכך יחזיר. ורבנן סברי גבי אפי' ממשעבדי הלכך לא יחזיר דחיישינן לקנוניא אבל בשאין חייב מודה דברי הכל לא יחזיר דחיישינן לפרעון ותניא בהדיא כוותיה. שמואל מוקי לה לכולה מתני' בשאין חייב מודה אבל בשחייב מודה דברי הכל יחזיר כי עדיו בחתומיו זכין לו א) (וכל) בשטרי הקנאה דהא שיעבד נפשיה. ובשטר שאין בו אחריות אע"פ שאין חייב מודה ב) ר"מ דאמר יחזיר למלוה לצור על פי צלוחיתו דכיון שאין בו אחריות נכסין אינו גובה לא ממשעבדי ולא מבני חרי.

**חשק שלמה על ר"ח**

א) אולי צ"ל וכ"ש בשטרי הקנאה. ב) צ"ל אמר ר"מ דיחזיר למלוה וכו'.

**מסורת הש"ס**

לקמן [יט., כ.], לה:, קמן יח., [גיטין כח.], לקמן יד., טז:], לעיל ז: וש"נ], גירסת מהרש"א בין ...יו לתמוז שלפניו, ועי' מהרש"ל.

**הגהות הב"ח**

גמ' מוקי לה למתני' ...ורא דלאו אקנייתא: רש"י ד"ה אביי אמר אבל השתא דתנן. נ"ב למאי דקס"ד השתא ...וס הכי פריך לקמיה ...י לא יחזיר כו' אבל ...י דמסיק הוה טעמיה ...יי משום דחיישינן ...עון ולקנוניא והוה ...ר שנמחל שעבודו: ...ד"ה הניחא וכו' הלכך ...א למימר. נ"ב פירוש כשאין חייב מודה:

**ליקוטי רש"י**

...טרי הקנאה. שקנו ...ו שאפי' לא ילוה ...עות שיעבד עצמו ...מס [לקמן טז:]. דליכא ...מר כתב ללות ולא לוה ...א אפילו לא לוה שעביד ...יה [לקמן יד.]. עדיו ...תומיו. מיום שנחתם ...ר האדרכתא בב"ד ...פ שלא בא לידו [לקמן ...]. ומיום כתיבת השטר ...עבד נפשיה [רשב"ם ...: קעא:]. דייתיקי. דא ...א למיקם שטר זה יהיה ...ם ולהיות בכל הכתוב ...דדברי שכיב מרע ...תובין וכמסורין דמי ...מן יט.]. לא יחזיר. ...לבעל ולא לאשה וכן ...רור וכן כולם [גיטין כז.].

The Gemara cites a Mishnah which seems to contradict Abaye's iew that "the note's witnesses by their signatures acquire":

אֶלָּא הָא דִּתְ – **But** if so, that "the note's witnesses by their gnatures acquire," **that which we have learned in the** ɔllowing **Mishnah** is difficult:[6] מָצָא גִּיטֵּי נָשִׁים – IF ONE FOUND ILLS OF DIVORCE, וְשִׁחְרוּרֵי עֲבָדִים – OR bills of EMANCIPATION F SLAVES, דְּיַיתִּיקִי – OR sickbed WILLS,[7] מַתָּנָה – OR GIFT ocuments,[8] וְשׁוֹבְרִים – OR RECEIPTS of loan payments, הֲרֵי זֶה לֹא יַחֲזִי – [THE FINDER] MAY NOT RETURN THEM to the ecipients named in them. שֶׁמָּא כְּתוּבִים הָיוּ – We are concerned ıat PERHAPS [THE DOCUMENTS] HAD BEEN WRITTEN with the ıtent to give them, וְנִמְלַךְ עֲלֵיהֶם שֶׁלֹּא לִיתְּנָם – BUT subsequently HE AUTHOR] RECONSIDERED, and decided NOT TO GIVE THEM.[9]

The Gemara now explains how the Mishnah poses a difficulty to baye's view:

וְכִי נִמְלַךְ עֲלֵיהֶם מַאי הָ – But even **if the [authors of the docu-** ıents] **did reconsider regarding [these documents]** and ecided not to to give them, as suspected by the Mishnah, **what is** ıe problem that prevents the return of the document to the ecipient? וְהָא אָמְרַת עֵדָיו בַּחֲתוּמָיו זָכִין לוֹ – **But you say that the** locument's] **witnesses by** their **signatures acquire!** Thus, even the document was in fact not given over, the transaction is evertheless effective from the moment the witnesses signed it.[10] so, what harm is done by returning the document to its recipient, ven if it is true that it was in fact never given to him, as suspected y the Mishnah?

The Gemara answers:

הָנֵי מִיל הֵיכָא דְּקָא מָטוּ לִידֵי – **This** principle of Abaye **applies only where [the documents]** eventually **reach the [prospective recipient's] hand,** i.e. the author subsequently conveyed the ocument to the recipient, thereby executing the transaction ecorded therein.[11] אֲבָל הֵיכָא דְּלָא מָטוּ לִידֵיהּ לָא אָמְרִינַן – **But** here **[the documents] did not** eventually **reach the [prospective recipient's] hand,** i.e. the transaction was never executed, **we do not apply** this principle. Therefore the concern voiced in the Mishnah on 18a – that the author of the document might have reconsidered and decided not to give these documents – is a legitimate one, since in that case the transaction detailed in the document was never executed.

The Gemara now explores how Abaye understands our Mishnah, which speaks about the return of lost loan documents:

אֶלָּא מַתְנִיתִין דְּקָתָנֵי – **But** Abaye will apparently find difficulty with **our Mishnah, which states:** מָצָא שְׁטָרֵי חוֹב – IF ONE FOUND NOTES OF INDEBTEDNESS – אִם יֵשׁ בָּהֶם אַחֲרָיוּת נְכָסִים לֹא יַחֲזִיר – If THERE IS A LIEN ON PROPERTY IN [THE NOTES], [THE FINDER] MAY NOT RETURN THEM to the creditor, וְאוֹקִימְנָא כְּשֶׁחַיָּיב מוֹדֶה – **and** which **we have interpreted**[12] as referring to a case **where the debtor admits** that the debt is indeed owed, וּמִשּׁוּם שֶׁמָּא כָּתַב לִלְוֹת בְּנִיסָן וְלֹא לָוָה עַד תִּשְׁרֵי – **and** the reason the note is not to be returned is **because we are apprehensive that perhaps [the debtor] drew up** the note **to borrow in** the month of **Nissan** but did not actually borrow the money **until** the month of **Tishrei,** and [the creditor] will come to unlawfully seize real property from its purchasers.

The Gemara now presents the problem that arises according to Abaye's view, and prefaces this with a review of how the Mishnah is understood according to Rav Assi's view:

בִּשְׁלָמָא לְרַב אַסִּי – Now, the Mishnah **is understandable according to Rav Assi,** דְּאָמַר בִּשְׁטָרֵי אַקְנָיְיתָא – **who says that** the Mishnah in *Bava Basra,* which permits a loan document to be drawn up even if the lender is not present, speaks only **about notes of acquisition.** מוֹקֵי לָהּ בִּשְׁטָרֵי דְּלָאו אַקְנָיְיתָא – For **[Rav Assi] will interpret [our Mishnah]** as speaking **about a note not of** the **acquisition** type so that the lien takes effect only from the actual date of the loan, וְכִדְאָמְרִינַן – **as we have explained** above.[13]

NOTES

mple meaning of the Mishnah in *Bava Basra* is that we may draw up *ny* loan document for the borrower in the lender's absence, not only otes of acquisition, as Rav Assi asserts. Rav Assi's explanation limiting ıe permit of the Mishnah in *Bava Basra* specifically to notes of cquisition is forced, in Abaye's opinion.] However, Rav Assi's explanaon that our Mishnah was concerned that "perhaps he drew up the note Nissan" necessitates a rejection of Abaye's principle, for according to baye's principle that "the note's witnesses by their signatures cquire," a note drawn up in Nissan retroactively activates a lien against ıe borrower's properties from Nissan even if the loan is actually made nly in Tishrei. But Abaye insists that Rav Assi's interpretation does *not* erve to explain our Mishnah here, since even the fact that the note was st is not sufficient reason to suspect its writers of improperly writing in the lender's absence. Thus, once this obstacle to Abaye's view is emoved, Abaye is moved to accept the principle that the witnesses cquire with their signing, since, in his view, that is the reasonable nderstanding of the Mishnah in *Bava Basra.* As regards our Mishnah, nother explanation – one that does not contradict Abaye's principle – as to be sought, as elucidated in the Gemara below (*Tosefos Shantz* ted in *Shitah Mekubetzes, Ritva, Rashba* et al.).

Thus, our passage in the Gemara is to be interpreted as follows: *Abaye ys [in explanation of the Mishnah in Bava Basra]: The [note's] itnesses by [their] signatures acquire for [the lender] . . . because the llowing difficulty concerned him* . . . with Rav Assi's explanation of our lishnah *here.* Thus, since Rav Assi's explanation of the Mishnah in *ava Basra* does not really serve to explain our Mishnah here anyway, baye rejects that explanation of the Mishnah in *Bava Basra* in favor of is own.

. Below, 18a.

. A deathbed testament (*matnas shechiv mera*) is legally binding, ıbject to certain limitations; it does not take effect until the testator es, and if he recovers he has the right to void his testament. The ocument recording such a testament is known as a *daitiki* (see *Rashi*).

8. Documents regarding gifts given by a healthy person (*Rashi*).

9. There is therefore the concern that the transactions recorded in the documents were never executed.

10. The Gemara's challenge to Abaye is not from the Mishnah's concern regarding bills of divorce, for even Abaye would not apply his principle here and maintain that the divorce takes effect from the moment the witnesses sign the divorce bill (as stated in the Gemara below, 19a). For in order for the witnesses to acquire for the recipient of a document, the matter that is acquired must be an unmitigated benefit for the recipient (*zechus*); otherwise, the witnesses lack authorization to acquire (see Gemara there and *Tosafos* there 19a ד״ה וליחוש). Moreover, even regarding bills of emancipation, which are a *zechus* for the slave (according to the Sages in *Gittin* 11b), there is a question as to what extent the witnesses' acquisition through their signing is valid (*Tosafos* below, 20a ד״ה שובר, consider the possibility that it is effective only in regard to monetary issues, not those of a prohibitory nature). Rather, the Gemara's challenge is from the other documents listed in the Mishnah.

11. When the transaction is subsequently executed by the principal, then it is effective retroactive to the signing of the witnesses. [*Tosafos* to 20a ד״ה שובר consider it likely that the principle that the witnesses acquire with their signing is a Rabbinic enactment, not a Biblical law.]

12. Above, 12b.

13. Above, the Gemara explained that such a note may initially not be drawn without the presence of the creditor, precisely because of the concern that the borrower will not borrow on the date the note was drawn, i.e. perhaps he will draw up the note in Nissan but not borrow until Tishrei. Nevertheless, when a note of indebtedness is lost, the suspicion is raised that it was precisely because the note was flawed that it was discarded. Therefore, we must be concerned that, indeed, it so happened that he did (improperly) draw up the note in Nissan but did not borrow until Tishrei; it is because of this suspicion that the note is not returned to the creditor (*Rashi*).

**מסורת הש"ס**

לקמן [יט., כ.], לה:, לקמן יח., [גיטין כז.], לקמן יד., טז:], לעיל ז: וש"נ], גירסת מהרש"א בין ...יו לתמוז שלפניו, ועי' מהרש"ל.

**עין משפט נר מצוה**

קיא א מיי' פכ"ד מהל' מלוה ולוה הל' א ועיין מ"מ שהניח בצ"ע סמג עשין עד טוש"ע ח"מ סי' לט סעיף יג:

קיב ב מיי' פי"ח מהל' אבידה הל' א סמג עשין עד טוש"ע ח"מ סי' סה סעיף ו:

**גמרא**

א בשטרי הקנאה דהא שעביד נפשיה אי הכי מתניתין דקתני אם יש בהן אחריות נכסים לא יחזיר ואוקימנא כשחייב מודה ומשום שמא כתב ללות בניסן ולא לוה עד תשרי ואתי למטרף לקוחות שלא כדין אמאי לא יחזיר נחזי אי בשטר הקנאה הא שעביד ליה נפשיה אי בשטר דלא הקנאה ליכא למיחש דהא אמרת כי ליכא מלוה בהדיה לא כתבינן א"ל רב אסי אע"ג דשטרי דלאו הקנאה כי ליכא מלוה בהדיה לא כתבינן מתניתין כיון דנפל אתרע ליה וחיישינן דלמא אקרי וכתוב (א) ° אביי אמר עדיו בחתומיו זכין לו ואפילו שטרי דלאו הקנאה משום דקשיא ליה כיון דאמרת בשטרי דלאו הקנאה כי ליתיה למלוה בהדיה לא כתבינן ליכא למיחש דאקרי וכתוב אלא הא דתנן ג) מצא גיטי נשים ושחרורי עבדים דייתיקי מתנה ושוברים הרי זה לא יחזיר שמא כתובים היו ונמלך עליהם שלא ליתנם וכי נמלך עליהם מאי הוי והא אמרת עדיו בחתומיו זכין לו הני מילי היכא דקא מטו לידיה אבל היכא דלא מטו לידיה לא אמרינן אלא מתניתין דקתני מצא שטרי חוב אם יש בהם אחריות נכסים לא יחזיר ואוקימנא כשחייב מודה ומשום שמא כתב ללות בניסן ולא לוה עד תשרי בשלמא לרב אסי דאמר בשטרי אקנייתא מוקי לה בשטרי דלאו אקנייתא וכדאמרינן אלא לאביי דאמר עדיו בחתומיו זכין לו מאי איכא למימר אמר לך אביי מתני' היינו טעמא ב דחייש לפרעון ולקנוניא ולשמואל דאמר ג) לא חיישינן לפרעון ולקנוניא מאי איכא למימר הניחא אי סבר לה כרב אסי דאמר בשטרי הקנאה מוקי (א) מתניתין בשטרי דלאו הקנאה אלא אי סבר כאביי דאמר עדיו בחתומיו זכין לו מאי איכא למימר שמואל מוקי למתניתין כשאין חייב מודה אי הכי כי אין בהן אחריות נכסים אמאי יחזיר נהי דלא גבי מן משעבדי מבני חרי מגבי גבי שמואל לטעמיה דאמר שמואל אומר היה רבי מאיר שטר חוב שאין בו אחריות נכסים אין גובה לא ממשעבדי ולא מבני חרי וכי מאחר שאינו גובה אמאי יחזיר אמר רבי נתן בר אושעיא ד) לצור על פי צלוחיתו של מלוה ונהדריה להו ללוה לצור על פי צלוחיתו של לוה הוא דאמר

**רש"י**

בשטרי הקנאה. שמקנה לו נכסיו מהיום בין ילוה בין לא ילוה יגבה מהן לאותו זמן מהיום: אי הכי. דבשטרי דלאו הקנאה לא עבידי דכתבי אלא אם כן ראו הלואת המעות מתני' דקתני כו': כי ליכא מלוה בהדיה. ונותן מעות בפניהם לא כתבינן: אביי אמר. הא דתנן כותבין שטר ללוה בלא מלוה אפילו בשטר דלאו הקנאה נמי ואי נמי אתי למיטרף מהאידנא והוא לא לוה עד תשרי לא שלא כדין הוא דעדיו בחתומיו זכין לו מיום שחתמוהו זכין לו השעבוד ואפילו לא הלוה המעות עד תשרי ולהכי מוקי ליה אביי בהאי טעמא משום דקשיא ליה כיון דאמרת כו' (ב) אבל השתא דתנן כותבין חיישינן דלמא כתב ללות ולא לוה ולקמיה פריך אמאי לא יחזיר הרי זכו ליה עדיו בחתומיו ושפיר טריף: דייתיקי. לואת שכיב מרע ולשון דייתיקי דא תיקו זאת תיקום לדברי שכיב מרע ככתובין וכמסורין דמי: מתנה. מתנת בריא: ושוברין. פרעון שטר: הני מילי היכא דמטא שטר לידיה. ואפילו לאחר זמן זכו לו חותמיו לגבות מזמן הכתוב בו ואי קשיא הא דתנן (שביעית פ"י מ"ה) שטרי חוב המוקדמין פסולין והמאוחרין כשרין במאי מוקי לה אביי תריץ במוקדמת כתיבתן לחתימתן ולהכי פסולין שבא לטרוף משעת כתיבה א"נ שכתבו וחתמוהו בתשרי והם כתבו בתוכו ניסן שהוא ראש השנה לשטרות: בשלמא לרב אסי. דמוקי לההוא דכותבין בשטרי אקנייתא: מוקי. מתניתין בדלאו אקנייתא ולהכי לא יחזיר כדקאמר איתרע ליה וחיישי' דלמא אקרי וכתב והוה ליה מוקדם ולכן הופקר להשליכו: לפרעון ולקנוניא. שמא פרעו ומן הלוה נפל והא דקא מודה לא פרעתי עלה היא ביניהם של רמאות לטרוף את הלקוחות שלקחו ממנו קרקע שלא באחריות ויחלקו ביניהם: ולשמואל דאמר. לקמן: לא חיישינן לפרעון. בשטר הנמצא ואפילו אין חייב מודה דאם איתא דפרעיה מקרע הוה קרע ליה דאמר שמואל לקמן (דף טז:) המוצא שטר הקנאה בשוק יחזיר לבעלים וכ"ש כשחייב מודה מהאי טעמא גופיה דמיום פריעתו הוא קורעו הלכך ליכא למיחש לאחר זמן לקנוניא מתני' במאי מוקי לה: הניחא כו'. ואי קשיא על כרחך לא סבירא ליה כאביי דאי כאביי ס"ל מאי איריא שטר הקנאה הא לאביי אין חילוק בין זה לזה דאפילו דלאו הקנאה נמי יחזיר הואיל ושמואל לא חייש לפרעון לאו פירכא הוא דמודה אביי בדלא מטא שטרא לידיה כדאמרן (ג) הלכך איכא למימר כתב ללות ולא לוה לגמרי ולא מטא לידיה מעולם: שמואל מוקי לה כשאין חייב מודה. בכתיבת השטר שאומר לוה לא כתבתי ומזויף הוא וא"ת יתקיים בחותמיו כיון שנפל אתרע ליה ואמרינן מפני שפסול היה לא נזהר ומהמנינן ליה להאי: אינו

**תוספות**

אביי אמר עדיו בחתומיו זכין לו. מכאן קשה לרש"י דריש מסכת ראש השנה (דף ב. ושם ד"ה לשטרות) דתנן באחד בניסן ראש השנה למלכים ומפרש בגמרא דנפקא מינה לשטרי חוב המוקדמים ופרש"י שאם לא קבעו יום לתחלת שנת המלך אלא כל מלך לפי מה שעומד פעמים שאין להבחין כגון אם כתב בו בכסליו בשנת ג' למלך ובאו עדים ואמרו כשחתמנו בו לא ראינו שהלוהו אלא אמר הלוה לנו חתמו כאותה ששנינו כותבין שטר ללוה אע"פ שאין מלוה עמו אבל ראינו שהלוהו אותה מלוה בתמוז בשנת ג' למלך ואין אנו יודעים אם קודם לכן או אחרי כן שאין אנו יודעים מתי עמד המלך אם בין ה) תמוז לכסליו של אחריו והוה ליה כסליו תחלה א"כ מוקדם הוא ופסול או בין כסליו לתמוז של אחריו והוה ליה מאוחר וכשר והשתא שקבעו ניסן ר"ה הוה ליה תמוז תחלה ושטר מאוחר הוא וכשר והשתא לאביי כה"ג לאו מוקדם הוא דעדיו בחתומיו זכין לו ולרב אסי נמי דלית ליה למה הוצרכו לעשות תקנה כיון דלית ליה כותבין שטר ללוה אלא בשטרי הקנאה ועוד וכי רגילות הוא שישכחו כל העולם והסופר וב"ד מתי עמד המלך שהוצרכו לעשות תקנה בשביל כך ועוד דהוה ליה למימר דנ"מ טובא בכל שטרות שלא ידעו מאימתי לגבות כיון דאין יודעים מתי מתחלת שנת המלך וע"ק יותר אך אין מקומו הנה ונראה לפרש דנ"מ לשטרי חוב המוקדמים היינו כגון שאם עמד המלך בכ"ט באדר כשיגיע כ"ט באדר בשנה של אחריו פעמים יטעה הסופר ביום אחד ויסבור שעמד המלך אשתקד באחד בניסן ויכתוב עתה בכ"ט באדר שנה ראשונה ונמצא שטר זה מוקדם שנה שלימה וזה פסול לכולי עלמא שכותב עתה שנה של אשתקד אבל כשקבעו ניסן ר"ה לא יטעה דמיום שני לעמידת המלך שהוא ראש חדש ניסן כתב הסופר שנה שניה ומשם ואילך עד ניסן הבא:

משום דקשיא ליה. לאביי תימה דבשביל כך לא הוצרך לומר עדיו בחתומיו זכין לו דאפילו יסבור דאין זכין כרב אסי ומתניתין שכותבין שטר ללוה בשטרי הקנאה ודלמא מיקרי וכתב לא אמרי' יעמיד משנתנו בשחייב מודה ולא יחזיר משום דחיישינן לפרעון ולקנוניא כדאמר בסמוך וי"ל משום דקשיא לאביי לא ניחא ליה שנויא דרב אסי ומילתא באפי נפשה היא ולא קאי אדאמר אביי עדיו בחתומיו זכין לו:

היינו טעמא דחיישינן לפרעון ולקנוניא. וסברי רבנן אחריות טעות סופר הוא ולכך לא יחזיר אפילו אין בו אחריות וכן לרב אסי תימה אמאי קאמר משום דחיישינן לקנוניא לימא משום דחיישינן שמא פרעו וכבר נמחל שעבודו ועתה רוצה לחזור וללות בו כדי להרויח פשיטי דספרא ומלוה נמי רוצה בדבר שיטרוף מזמן מוקדם וי"ל משום פשיטי דספרא לא יפסיד ללקוחות ממון מרובה אף על גב דרב אסי חייש לכתב ללות ולא לוה ועתה רוצה ללות ומפסיד ללקוחות משום פשיטי דספרא היינו משום שכבר נתן לסופר ואינו רוצה להפסיד ועוד שסובר המלוה שיצא הקול משעת כתיבה אבל כשלוה ופרע לא הפסיד פשוט שנתן לסופר ועוד שירא המלוה ששמעו הפריעה והלוואה שנית לא נכתב השטר:

הא

**גליון הש"ס**

גמ' אביי אמר עדיו בחתומיו. עי' רשב"א בחידושי קדושין דף כז ע"א ד"ה ע"מ שתכתבו לו שטר:

**רבינו חננאל**

מלוה עמו ניחוש שמא כתב ללות ולא לוה. ופריק רב אשי בשטרי הקנאה דהא שיעבד נפשיה בחליפין ולא חיישי' לנתינת המעות אלא נשתעבד מעידנא ההיא דקנו מיניה בחליפין. אביי אמר עדיו בחותמיו זכין לו פי' כיון שאמר לוה לעדים העידו עלי שיש לפלוני עלי כך וכך וכתבו שטר בזה וחתמו בו זכו למלוה ואע"ג דלא קנו מן הלוה והוא דנפיק שטרא מידא דמלוה אבל אי לא נפיק שטרא מתותי ידיה דמלוה חיישינן דלמא אכתי לא מטא לידיה דמלוה ומתני' דאוקימנא בשחייב מודה דהאי שטרא מטא לידיה דמלוה מההיא שעתא דנכתב ומיניה נפל. אמר לך אביי כי הא גוונא בדלא נקיט שטרא מתותי ידיה דמלוה חיישינן לקנוניא ומשום הכי לא הימנינן בהודאתו דלוה. ולא אשכחן פירכא לא להא דאביי ולא להא דרב אשי ותרוייהו בעינן דמטא שטרא בידא דמלוה. והא דר' יוחנן לא הוי להו תיובתא דיכול רב אשי למימר לא אמר ר' יוחנן אלא בשטרי דלאו אקנייאתא ולאביי נמי לא הויא תיובתא דהא לדבריו דר' יוחנן שייכי. מיהו סוגיא דשמעתין כר' יוחנן סלקא דאמר מחלוקת בשחייב מודה ר"מ דאמר יחזיר סבר שטר שאין בו אחריות נכסין לא גבי ממשעבדי מבני חרי הוא דגבי וכיון דמודה ליה ליכא למיחש הלכך יחזיר. ורבנן סברי גבי אפי' ממשעבדי הלכך לא יחזיר דחיישינן לקנוניא אבל בשאין חייב מודה דברי הכל לא יחזיר דחיישינן לפרעון ותניא בהדיא כוותיה. שמואל מוקי לה לכולה מתני' בשאין חייב מודה אבל בשחייב מודה דברי הכל יחזיר כי עדיו בחתומיו זכין לו א) (וכל) בשטרי הקנאה דהא שיעבד נפשיה. ובשטר שאין בו אחריות אע"פ שאין חייב מודה ב) ר"מ דאמר יחזיר למלוה לצור על פי צלוחיתו דכיון שאין בו אחריות נכסין אינו גובה לא ממשעבדי ולא מבני חרי.

**חשק שלמה על ר"ח**

א) אולי צ"ל וכ"ש בשטרי הקנאה. ב) צ"ל אמר ר"מ דיחזיר למלוה וכו'.

**הגהות הב"ח**

(א) גמ' מוקי לה למתני' ...טרא דלאו אקנייתא: (ב) רש"י ד"ה אביי אמר ...' אבל השתא דתנן. נ"ב ... למאי דקס"ד השתא ...וס הכי פריך לקמיה ...אי לא יחזיר כו' אבל ...י דמסיק הוה טעמיה ...ביי משום דחיישינן ...רעון ולקנוניא והוה ...ר שנמחל שעבודו: (ג) ד"ה הניחא וכו' הלכך ...א למימר. נ"ב פירוש כשאין חייב מודה:

**ליקוטי רש"י**

...שטרי הקנאה. שקנו ...ו שאפי' לא ילוה ...עות שיעבד עצמו ...מס [לקמן טז:]. דליכא ...ימר כתב ללות ולא לוה ...א אפילו לא לוה שעביד ...יה [לקמן יד.]. עדיו ...תומיו. מיום שנחתם ...ר האדרכתא בב"ד ...פ שלא בא לידו [לקמן ...:]. ומיום כתיבת השטר ...עבד נפשיה [רשב"ם ...ב קעא:]. דייתיקי. דא ...א למיקם שטר זה יהיה ...ום ולהיות בכל הכתוב ... לדברי שכיב מרע ...תובין וכמסורין דמי ...קמן יט.]. לא יחזיר. ...לבעל ולא לאשה וכן ...רור וכן כולם [גיטין כז.].

בִּשְׁטָרֵי הַקְנָאָה – The Mishnah, that permits a note of indebtedness to be drawn up even if the lender is not present, speaks **about notes of acquisition,** i.e. loan documents which stipulate that the borrower gives the person named as the lender an immediate lien against his real property for the amount recorded as the loan, even in the event that the lender does not lend him the money. In this case, the apprehension that the loan did not take place on the date specified in the note is irrelevant, דְּהָא שַׁעְבֵּיד נַפְשֵׁיהּ – **for [the debtor] has obligated himself** to pay the sum stipulated in the note regardless of whether the loan is made or not.[1]

The Gemara challenges Rav Assi's solution:

אִי הָכִי – **If so,** that the only justification for drawing up a note of indebtedness without the lender's presence is in the case of a note of acquisition, מַתְנִיתִין דְּקָתָנֵי – then you will find difficulty with **our Mishnah, which teaches:** אִם יֵשׁ בָּהֶן אַחֲרָיוּת נְכָסִים לֹא יַחֲזִיר – IF THERE IS A LIEN ON PROPERTY IN [THE NOTES], [THE FINDER] MAY NOT RETURN THEM to the creditor, וְאוֹקִימְנָא בְּשֶׁחַיָּיב מוֹדֶה – **and we have interpreted** the Mishnah as referring to a case **where the debtor admits** that the debt is indeed owed, וּמִשּׁוּם שֶׁמָּא כָּתַב לִלְוֹת בְּנִיסָן וְלֹא לָוָה עַד תִּשְׁרֵי – **and** the reason the note may not be returned is **because** we are apprehensive that **perhaps [the debtor] drew up** the note **to borrow in** the month of **Nissan but did not** actually **borrow** the money **until** the month of **Tishrei,** וְאָתֵי לְמִטְרַף לְקוֹחוֹת שֶׁלֹּא כַּדִּין – **and [the creditor] will come to unlawfully seize** real property **from** its **purchasers.**

The Gemara now explains the difficulty:

אַמַּאי לֹא יַחֲזִיר – **Why should [the finder] not return** the note to the creditor? The possibility that the writing and dating of the note preceded the time of the loan should not concern us, as the following analysis will show: נֶחֱזֵי – **Let us see:** אִי בִּשְׁטַר הַקְנָאָה – **If** the found note was **a note of acquisition,** הָא שַׁעְבֵּיד לֵיהּ נַפְשֵׁיהּ – **then he [the borrower] has obligated himself** to pay the sum stipulated in the note based on the date appearing in the note, regardless of the actual time of the loan, thus rendering irrelevant the apprehension that the loan actually took place only later. אִי בִּשְׁטָר דְּלֹא הַקְנָאָה – And **if** the found note is **a note not of** the **acquisition** type, i.e. it was an ordinary loan document whereby a lien takes effect only from the date of the actual loan, לֵיכָּא לְמֵיחַשׁ – then **there is no** reason **to be apprehensive** that the date of the loan document precedes the time of the actual loan, דְּהָא אָמְרַת כִּי לֵיכָּא מַלְוֶה בַּהֲדֵיהּ לֹא כָּתְבִינַן – **for you** [Rav Assi] **say that when the lender is not present [with the borrower], we may not draw up** an ordinary loan document. In what case, then, does the Mishnah's ruling apply?

The Gemara answers:

אָמַר לָךְ רַב אַסִּי – **Rav Assi could answer you:**[2] אַף עַל גַּב דִּשְׁטָרֵי דְּלָאו הַקְנָאָה – **Even though** in the case of **notes** that are **not of** the **acquisition** type, i.e. ordinary loan documents, כִּי לֵיכָּא מַלְוֶה בַּהֲדֵיהּ לֹא כָּתְבִינַן – **when the lender is not present with [the borrower] we may not draw** them **up,** מַתְנִיתִין כֵּיוָן דְּנָפַל אִתְרַע לֵיהּ – nevertheless in the case of **our Mishnah, since [the note] was lost, it is flawed.** The fact that it was lost causes suspicion to be cast upon its genuineness,[3] וְחַיְישִׁינַן דִּלְמָא אִקְרִי וְכָתוּב – **and we are** therefore **apprehensive that perhaps it so happened that they did draw up** the note prior to the loan, although it was wrong for them to do so.

Abaye proposes another explanation for the law that a borrower may draw up a loan document without the lender being present:

אַבָּיֵי אָמַר – **Abaye says:** עֵדָיו בַּחֲתוּמָיו זָכִין לוֹ – **The [note's] witnesses by** their **signatures acquire** a lien **for [its recipient]** at the moment they sign the note. Thus, even if the actual loan transaction is made only at a later date, the lien has already taken effect earlier, at the time of the note's signing, וַאֲפִילּוּ שְׁטָרֵי דְּלָאו הַקְנָאָה – **even** in the case of **notes not of** the **acquisition** type, i.e. even regarding ordinary loan documents.[4] And why does Abaye advance this novel concept that the witnesses by their very signing of the note acquire the lien on behalf of the creditor? מִשּׁוּם דְּקַשְׁיָא לֵיהּ – He advanced this concept **because the following difficulty concerned him** regarding Rav Assi's explanation: כֵּיוָן דְּאָמְרַת בִּשְׁטָרֵי דְּלָאו הַקְנָאָה – **Since you** who follow Rav Assi's view **maintain regarding notes not of** the **acquisition** type, i.e. ordinary loan documents, כִּי לֵיתֵיהּ לְמַלְוֶה בַּהֲדֵיהּ לֹא כָּתְבִינַן – **that when the lender is not present [with the borrower], we do not draw up** the loan document, לֵיכָּא לְמֵיחַשׁ דְּאִקְרִי וְכָתוּב – **there is no** need **to be apprehensive that** perhaps **it so happened that they did** act improperly and **drew up** a note, prior to the date of the loan.[5]

NOTES

1. *Rashi;* see also *Rashi* to 16b ד״ה שטר הקנאה, cited in note 12 there. *Rosh* wonders why a person would draw up such a document. See *Teshuvos HaRivash* 161, cited in *Nesivos HaMishpat* 39:13, for a modification of *Rashi's* interpretation that removes this difficulty.

2. [Our texts have the abbreviation א״ל, which is usually deciphered as אָמַר לֵיהּ. In our context, however, this would mean that *he* [Rav Assi] *said to him* [the questioner], which does not fit, since the question was not posed by an identified scholar, but rather is part of the anonymous Gemara. Thus, it is clear that in our context, the abbreviation א״ל should be deciphered as אָמַר לָךְ (see *Dikdukei Sofrim*; see also *Ritva* and *Shitah Mekubetzes*).]

3. As explained in note 32 to 12b.

4. [The Gemara now understands that according to Abaye, there is no difference between notes of acquisition and regular notes of indebtedness; in both instances the obligation takes effect even if the borrower does not actually borrow the money, because "the witnesses acquire for him." The Gemara will later modify this.]

The Mishnah (*Sheviis* 10:5) rules that pre-dated loan documents are invalid. According to Abaye, this obviously does not refer to documents signed by witnesses prior to the actual loan. Rather, according to Abaye, pre-dated loan documents are invalid in two instances: 1) If the date on the document is the date of its writing but the witnesses signed it only on a subsequent date. Thus, although the witnesses acquire with their signatures, they do so only as per the date of their signing, whereas the document gives a prior date for the inception of the loan; or 2) if the date recorded on the document was earlier than the date of its actual writing (*Rashi* below, ד״ה הני מילי).

5. [Though it is somewhat curious that the note was lost, that is not a sufficient reason to suspect that those who drew up the note did so improperly.]

The Rishonim point out that the Gemara's linking of Abaye's rejection of Rav Assi's explanation of our Mishnah (the Mishnah is concerned that "perhaps he drew up in Nissan") to Abaye's acceptance of the principle that "the note's witnesses by their signatures acquire" is puzzling. Abaye's rejection of Rav Assi's explanation forces him only to seek another explanation – that R' Meir's ruling is based on a fear of "payment and collusion," as recorded by the Gemara below – an explanation that is equally compatible with Abaye's and Rav Assi's explanation of the Mishnah in *Bava Basra.* How, then, does Abaye's view that "the note's witnesses by their signatures acquire" follow from his rejection of Rav Assi's explanation of our Mishnah? [Though this passage: ... מִשּׁוּם דְּקַשְׁיָא לֵיהּ, *because the following difficulty concerned him . . .,* is absent from some Gemara texts (see *Ramban, Rashba,* and *Ritva*), it does appear in *Rashi's* text – see *Rashi* ד״ה אביי אמר. *Maharsha's* explanation is categorically rejected by *R' Akiva Eiger* in his *Derush VeChidush.*] How, then, are we to explain this puzzling passage?

Some Rishonim suggest the following explanation of this passage: Abaye subscribes to the principle that the witnesses acquire by their signing on the principle's own merits, not because it serves to answer any difficulties. [Perhaps, Abaye prefers this explanation because the

וְאָתֵי לְמִטְרַף לְקוֹחוֹת שֶׁלֹּא כַּדִּין – **thus, [the creditor,]** who will have been awarded custody of the note on the strength of the debtor's admission, **will come to unlawfully seize** the ostensibly mortaged property **from** its **purchasers.**[29]

The Gemara points out a difficulty that arises if one gives consideration to the apprehension that the drawing of the note preceded the actual debt:

אִי הָכִי – **If so,** that we are apprehensive that the drawing of the note preceded the actual debt, כָּל שְׁטָרֵי דְּאָתוּ לְקַמָּן – then regarding **all notes** of indebtedness **that come before us,** i.e. which are presented to a court of law, נֵיחוּשׁ לְהוּ הָכִי – **let us thus be apprehensive about them?** I.e. let us be concerned in the case of all notes of indebtedness containing the lien provision that the drawing of the note might have preceded the actual debt, and bar the creditor from satisfying his debt from encumbered property.[30] This is obviously not the case.[31] – ? –

The Gemara answers:

כָּל שְׁטָרֵי לֹא רִיעֵי – **All** ordinary **notes** of indebtedness **are not flawed,** i.e. there is no reason to suspect their genuineness. Therefore, since there is no reason to cast suspicion upon the note, we need not concern ourselves about the possibility that the drawing of the note preceded the actual debt. הָנֵי רִיעֵי – But **these** notes dealt with in the Mishnah **are flawed.** The fact th they were lost casts suspicion upon their genuineness.[32]

The Gemara finds yet another difficulty with the apprehensio that the drawing of the document preceded the actual debt:

אֶלָּא הָא דִּתְנַן – **But** how will you account for **that which we hav learned in a Mishnah:**[33] כּוֹתְבִין שְׁטָר לַלֹּוֶה – WE MAY DRAW U A debt DOCUMENT FOR THE BORROWER ף עַל פִּי שֶׁאֵין מַלְוֶה עִמּוֹ – EVEN THOUGH THE LENDER IS NOT WITH HIM. Since the lender not present, it is obvious that the witnesses who sign the no have not witnessed a loan. Nevertheless, we may draw up the no and the witnesses may sign it at the borrower's behest, since he the one whom the note will obligate.

The Gemara now presents its question:

לְכַתְּחִילָּה הֵיכִי כָּתְבִינַהוּ – **How may we draw up [the note initially?** נֵיחוּשׁ שֶׁמָּא כָּתַב לִלְוֹת בְּנִיסָן – **Let us be apprehensiv that perhaps [the debtor] drew up** the note **to borrow** th money **in** the month of **Nissan,** וְלֹא לָוָה עַד תִּשְׁרֵי – **but he di not** actually **borrow** the money **until** the month of **Tishre** וְאָתֵי לְמִטְרַף לְקוֹחוֹת שֶׁלֹּא כַּדִּין – **thus, [the creditor] will come t unlawfully seize** real property **from** its **purchasers.**[34] – ? -

The Gemara answers:

אָמַר רַב אַסִּי – **Rav Assi said:**

NOTES

the debt, the debtor admits that he still owes the debt (*Ritva;* cf. *Tosafos*).

[However, in the case of a note that does not have the lien provision, there is no potential for illegality even if the note *was* predated. For the creditor can collect only properties that are presently held by the debtor, who admits to still owing the loan. The date the loan was incurred is of no legal consequence.]

29. The properties that the debtor sold prior to Tishrei are certainly not mortgaged to the Tishrei loan. Thus, if the creditor were to collect these properties from the buyers based on his loan note that contains a Nissan date, it would certainly be an unlawful collection of the properties. Moreover, by Rabbinic decree, the predated note is invalid (see *Sheviis* 10:5), and cannot be used to collect even from properties that the debtor sold *after* Tishrei (see *Ritva*; see Gemara below, 72a).

30. Previously, it was assumed that the incidence of drawing up a note and loaning the money at a later date [and handing the note to the creditor] is very rare, and therefore one need not be concerned about it. But now that the Gemara has proposed that this is indeed a concern, we should be apprehensive about it even in the case of notes that were *not* lost (*Ritva*).

31. If we would always have to be concerned that the note was drawn at a date preceding the loan, the result would be that one could neve collect a debt from real property that had been sold by the debtor afte the date of the loan as recorded in the note. Obviously this is not so, sinc one *can* collect from such properties if the note contains the lie provision.

32. The fact that the note was lost casts doubt on its genuineness: Wer it a regular note that had been drawn and given to the creditor at th time of the loan, he would in all probability have been careful not to los it (*Rashi*). [The fact that it was lost gives rise to the suspicion that th debtor in fact had it drawn only in *anticipation* of a loan, which did nc materialize. As the note had no legal force, the "debtor" was careles with it and lost it. The "debtor" wishes to borrow the money *now* (i Tishrei, for example) and to avoid the cost and trouble of drawing up new note by having this found note (dated Nissan) returned to th creditor (see *Tosafos* ד״ה ולא לוה).

33. *Bava Basra* 167b.

34. Granted that post facto we do not suspect that a note produced by creditor was in fact drawn in advance of the loan [since there is n reason to suspect that it is anything but a normal note of indebtedness But how do we allow the debtor to draw up such a note initially, if it ca lead to the unlawful seizure of the buyer's property in case th anticipated loan is delayed? (*Ritva*).

עשו שאינו זוכה כזוכה מ"ט עניים גופייהו ניחא להו כי היכי דכי אגרו לדידהו נלקוט בנייהו בתרייהו ופליגא (א) דר' חייא בר אבא דאמר רבי חייא בר אבא אמר רבי יוחנן לא גדול גדול ממש ולא קטן קטן ממש אלא גדול וסמוך על שלחן אביו זהו קטן קטן ואינו סמוך על שלחן אביו זהו גדול: מציאת עבדו ושפחתו העברים הרי הוא של עצמן: אמאי לא יהא אלא פועל ותניא מציאת פועל לעצמו במה דברים אמורים בזמן שאמר לו נכש עמי היום עדור עמי היום אבל אמר לו עשה עמי מלאכה היום מציאתו לבעל הבית אמר רבי חייא בר אבא אמר רבי יוחנן הכא בעבד נוקב מרגליות עסקינן שאין רבו רוצה לשנותו למלאכה אחרת רבא אמר במגביה מציאה עם מלאכתו עסקינן רב פפא אמר כגון ששכרו ללקט מציאות והיכי דמי דאקפי אגמא בכוורי: האי שפחה היכי דמי אי דאייתי שתי שערות מאי בעיא גביה ואי דלא אייתי שתי שערות אי איתיה לאב דאבוה הויא ואי דליתיה לאב תיפוק במיתת האב דאמר ריש לקיש אמה העבריה קנה עצמה במיתת האב מרשות האדון מקל וחומר ולאו איתותב ריש לקיש נימא מהאי נמי תיהוי תיובתא לא לעולם דאיתיה לאב ומאי הרי הן שלהן לאפוקי דרבה: מציאת אשתו: גירשה פשיטא הכא במאי עסקינן במגורשת ואינה מגורשת דאמר רבי זירא אמר שמואל כל מקום שאמרו חכמים מגורשת ואינה מגורשת בעלה חייב במזונותיה טעמא מאי אמור רבנן מציאת אשה לבעלה כי היכי דלא תיהוי לה איבה הכא אית לה איבה ואיבה:

מתני' מצא שטרי חוב אם יש בהן אחריות נכסים לא יחזיר שבית דין נפרעין מהן אין בהן אחריות נכסים יחזיר שאין בית דין נפרעין מהן דברי רבי מאיר וחכמים אומרים בין כך ובין כך לא יחזיר מפני שבית דין נפרעין מהן: גמ' במאי עסקינן אילימא כשחייב מודה כי יש בהן אחריות נכסים אמאי לא יחזיר הא מודה ואי כשאין חייב מודה כי אין בהן אחריות נכסים אמאי יחזיר נהי דלא גבי ממשעבדי מבני חרי מגבא גבי לעולם כשחייב מודה והכא היינו טעמא דחיישינן שמא כתב ללות בניסן ולא לוה עד תשרי ואתי למטרף לקוחות שלא כדין אי הכי כל שטרי דאתו לקמן ניחוש להו הכי כל שטרי לא ריעי הני ריעי אלא הא דתנן כותבין שטר ללוה אף על פי שאין מלוה עמו לכתחילה היכי כתבינהו ניחוש שמא כתב ללות בניסן ולא לוה עד תשרי ואתי למטרף לקוחות שלא כדין אמר רב אסי

בשטרי

עשו את שאינו זוכה כזוכה. אע"פ שאין לקטן זכייה במקום אחר כאן עשאוהו כזוכה: מאי טעמא עניים גופייהו ניחא להו. בהאי תקנתא דכי אגרו להו לדידהו כו': ופליגא. דשמואל דפירש טעמא דמתני' משום דלית ליה זכייה: אדר' חייא בר אבא. דאמר אף גדול שיש לו זכייה אם סמוך הוא על שולחן אביו מציאתו לאביו משום איבה אבל אינו סמוך על שולחן אביו אפילו הוא קטן מציאתו שלו: לא יהא אלא פועל. לא יהא עבדו אלא שכיר בעלמא תניא דמציאתו לבעל הבית בזמן שלא פירש לו לאיזו מלאכה שכרו ועבד זה כשקנאו רבו לסתם מלאכה קנאו: שאין רבו רוצה לשנותו. הלכך לא ניחא ליה שיגביה לו מציאה דמציאה מעולה בדמיה משכר ביטול מלאכתו לא שכיחא הלכך אי אתרמי ואשכח שלו הוא וישלם לרבו שכר ביטולו: עם מלאכתו. שלא ביטל כלום הלכך לעצמו: רב פפא אמר. הא דתניא פועל מציאתו לבעל הבית: ששכרו ללקט מציאות. הרבה: והיכי דמי. דאתרמי: דאקפי אגמא בכוורי. שלף הנהר חוץ לגדותיו וצפו הדגים שם וכשיבשו המים היוצאים נמצאו שם דגים הרבה. דאקפי תרגום של הציף כדמתרגמינן ויצף הברזל וקפא ברזלא (מלכים ב ו): מאי בעיא גביה. הא תניא יוצאה בסימנין: דאבוה הויא. מציאתה דהא קטנה היא: ואי דליתיה לאב. מאי בעיא גבי האדון תיפוק מיניה במיתת האב: מקל וחומר. בפרק קמא דקדושין (דף טז.) מה סימנין שאין מוציאין מרשות האב מוציאין מרשות האדון כדילפינן ויצאה חנם אלו ימי בגרות אין כסף אלו ימי נערות מיתת האב שמוציאה מרשות האב שאינו מוריש לבניו מה שזכתה לו תורה בבתו שיהא מעשה ידיה לאחין כדילפינן (כתובות דף מג.) והתנחלתם אותם לבניכם ולא בנותיכם לבניכם אינו דין שמוציאה מרשות האדון: ולאו איתותב רבי שמעון בן לקיש. בקדושין (שם): לאפוקי דרבה. לאפוקי שאינו של רבה אלא של אביה וקרי ליה שלהן משום דלאב מינה קוזי: במגורשת ואינה מגורשת. כגון זרק לה גיטה ספק קרוב לה ספק קרוב לו ברה"ר: חייב במזונותיה. ומשום הכי אצטריך לאשמועינן דמציאתה שלה דטעמא מאי אמור רבנן מציאת האשה כו': מתני' אחריות נכסים. שעבוד קרקעות שיגבה מהן: יחזיר ולא יחזיר. טעמא בגמ' מפרש: גמ' כשחייב מודה. שהלוה מודה שהשטר אינו פרוע: אמאי לא יחזיר. אם לטרוף לקוחות בא בדין הוא טורפן: ממשעבדי. ממקרקעי שמכר אחרי כן: הני ריעי. הואיל ונפל אתרע דיש לומר אם היה כשר היה נזהר בו:

אביי

רבי יוחנן אמר לא גדול גדול ממש. [א] מפרש ר"ת כי היכי דפליגי הכא פליגי נמי גבי עירוב דתנן בפ' חלון (עירובין דף עט: ושם ד"ה ומזכה) ומזכה להם על ידי בנו ובתו (ב) ולשמואל דאמר הכא קטן ממש התם נמי גבי עירוב אינו זוכה דידו כיד אביו כיון דמציאתו לאביו ה"ה כל זכיותיו לאביו ואמה העבריה אע"פ שהיא קטנה זכיא בעירובה דמציאתה אינה לאדוניה אף על גב דשמואל אית ליה פרק התקבל (גיטין דף סד: ושם ד"ה אלא) קטן זוכה לעצמו ואינו זוכה לאחרים הא משני התם שאני שתופי מבואות דרבנן והא דאמר שמואל פרק מי שהוציאוהו (עירובין דף מט. ושם: ד"ה וקטן) דעירוב משום קנין ורבא אמר משום דירה ואמר איכא בינייהו קטן הא פר"ת התם דאית ליה בית לקטן קאמר ולא כפרש"י שפי' שאינו גובה העירוב לפי שאינו זוכה ולר"י דאמר לא גדול גדול ממש ה"ה דגבי עירוב נמי דקטן ואינו סמוך על שולחן אביו זוכה כאמה העבריה וגדול סמוך על שולחן אביו אינו זוכה וצריך ליזהר שלא לזכות העירוב ע"י בנו הגדול הסמוך לשולחנו דקי"ל כרבי יוחנן לגבי שמואל כדאמר פרק מי שהוציאוהו (שם מז:) ועבדו ושפחתו העברים אע"ג דסמוכין על שולחנו מציאתם לעצמם וכן זוכין בעירוב ולא הוי ידם כיד האדון דלא שייך איבה אלא בבנו שדרכו לזונו תמיד ואם לא יפרנסו אביו לא יפרנסו אחר אבל אדם אחר מעלמא סמוך על שולחן חבירו חנם כגון יתום וכיוצא בו אין סברא שתהא מציאתו לחבירו וכ"ש עבד ואמה שבשכר טרחם הם אוכלים ובתו אפילו נערה ואינה סמוכה על שולחן אביה מציאתה לאביה משום איבה דאי בעי מסר לה למנוול ומוכה שחין כדאמר בפרק נערה (כתובות דף מו ושם) ולא כרש"י שפירש משום דכתיב בנעוריה דההוא בהפרת נדרים הוא דכתיב כדאיתא בפרק קמא דקדושין (דף ג: ושם) ופרק נערה (שם מו:) ואשתו דזכיא בעירוב אף על גב דידה כיד בעלה מוקי לה בסוף נדרים (דף פח:) דאית לה בית באותו מבוי דמגו דזכיא לנפשה זכיא נמי לאחריני:

במגביה מציאה עם מלאכתו. וא"ת הא דתניא בפ"ק דקדושין (דף טז:) אמה העבריה מציאתה לאביה ושכר בטלה לרבה היכי מתוקמא אליבא דרבא דאם הגביהה עם מלאכתו ליכא שכר בטלה ואם לא הגביהה עם מלאכתו א"כ מציאתה לאדוניה וי"ל דהתם ודאי צריך להעמיד בנוקבת מרגליות:

ששכרו ללקט מציאות. [ב] וה"פ דברייתא בד"א בזמן שאמר ליה עשה עמי באותו ענין שהוא כמו נכש עמי היום אבל אמר ליה עשה עמי מלאכה של מציאות כו':

מאי בעיא גביה. דהיא נמי אינה יכולה למכור עצמה אחרי כן כדאיתא בספרי:

ולא לוה עד תשרי. פירוש ועתה רוצה ללות בו שיש לו טורח לכתוב שטר אחר וגם כדי להרויח פשיטי דספרא אבל אין לפרש שכבר לוה בו קודם שנפל דא"כ מאי משני הני ריעי לפי שנפל ויש הוכחה דמשום פסולו לא נזהר לשומרו והא לוה בו כבר ופשיטא שנזהר לשומרו:

כותבין שטר ללוה אף על פי שאין מלוה עמו. וליכא למיחש למחזי כשקרא כמו (יג) באשרתא דדייני דאם כתבו קודם דנחזי חתימת ידי סהדי (ג) פסולה דהכא כיון שהוא כותב חובתו לא שייך מחזי כשקרא:

אומרת עבד עברי גופו קנוי באה משנתנו להוציא מזה הטעם של רבא. מציאת אשה שגירשה אע"פ שלא נתן לה עדיין כתובתה מציאתה שלה. אוקימנא במגורשת ואינה מגורשת פי' בתלמוד א"י אדם שגירש את אשתו ולא נתן לה כתובתה חייב במזונותיה עד שיתן לה פרוטה אחרונה. אמר ר' יוסי מתני' אמרה כן אמר ר' אושעיא שלא תאמר הואיל וחייב במזונותיה עד שיפרע כתובתה תהא מציאתה שלו לפום כן תני מציאת אשה שגירשה לעצמה: מצא שטרי חוב אם יש בהן אחריות נכסים לא יחזיר. אוקימנא כשחייב מודה. ואמאי לא יחזיר דחיישינן שמא כתב ללות בניסן ולא לוה עד תשרי וטורף ללקוחות שלא כדין. אי הכי כל שטרי דעלמא נמי נימא הכי. ודחי' כל שטרי דעלמא לא ריעי הני כיון דנפלי ריעי. אלא הא דתנן כותבין שטר ללוה אע"פ שאין מלוה

דהתחיל בגירושין והוא שונא לה לא יחד לה קרקע למזונותיה כי בטורח יתן לה מזונות בגלגול כשיחייבוהו ב"ד. חייב במזונותיה. דלכתי אגידא ביה [רשב"ם ב"ב מז:]. יש בהן אחריות נכסים. שמשעבד לוה נכסיו לאותה מלוה לא יחזירנו מוצאו למלוה ואפי' הלוה מודה שהוא חייב לו ומפרש התם דחיישינן שמא פרעו ומן הלוה נפל וזה שהוא מודה עצת קנוניא היא ביניהם לטרוף לקוחות ויחלקו ביניהם [כתובות נא:]. אין בהן אחריות נכסים. שלא שיעבד לו לוה בשעת הלואה את נכסיו ולא כתב לו כל נכסי אחראין לך לפרוע מלוה זה. יחזיר שאין ב"ד נפרעין מהן. ואינו גובה מנכסים משועבדים ולא אמרינן אין לך אדם המלוה מעותיו בלא שעבוד נכסי לוה והסופר טעה ולא כתב בו אחריות אלא דוקא אזלינן בתר שטר [ב"ק צה.]. וחכמים אומרים כו'. דאחריות טעות סופר וטריף ממשעבדי ומפסדי לקוחות [שם ע"א]. כותבין שטר ללוה. להיות מזומן בידו לתת למלוה כשילוה לו מעות אע"פ שאין מלוה עמו ורשב"ם ב"ב קסז:].

עין משפט
נר מצוה

קד א מיי' פי"ז מהל' אבידה הל' יג סמג עשין עד טוש"ע ח"מ סי' ער סעיף ג:
קה ב ג מיי' פי"ט מהל' שכירות הל' יג סמג שם טוש"ע שם סעיף ג:
קו ד מיי' פי"ז מהל' אבידה הל' יג סמג עשין עד (טוש"ע ח"מ סי' ער סעיף ג):
קז ה מיי' שם סמג שם טוש"ע שם סעיף ג וטוש"ע אה"ע סי' פ:
קח ו מיי' פי"ח מהל' אישות הלכה כה טוש"ע אה"ע סי' עג סעיף ג:
קט ז ח מיי' פי"ח מהל' אבידה הלכה א סמג עשין עד טוש"ע ח"מ סי' סה סעיף ו:
קי ט מיי' פכ"ג מהל' מלוה ולוה הלכה ה ופכ"ד שם הל' א סמג עשין לד טוש"ע ח"מ סי' לט סעיף יג:

רבינו חננאל

ואסקה רבא עשו הקטן שאינו זוכה לעצמו מן התורה כזוכה מאי טעמא עניים גופייהו מחלי ליה דניחא להו דנלקטו בנייהו נמי בתרייהו דידהו ולפיכך אמר ר' יוסי בניו ואשתו מלקטין אחריו. פי' אינו זוכה כזוכה כדתנן פרק כל גט שנכתב שלא לשם אשה פסול. המלוה מעות את הכהן ואת הלוי ואת העני וכו' ואוקימנא אע"ג דלא אתו לידייהו כו'. ועולא אמר הא מני ר' יוסי היא דאמר עשו את שאינו זוכה כזוכה דתנן בבכורות כל שחליפין ביד כהן פטור מן המתנות וכו' עשו את שאינו זוכה כזוכה מאי טעמא עשאוה כשדה שהלכו בה הנמושות עניים גופייהו מסחו דעתייהו מההיא שדה אמרי בניו ואשתו דהאיך מלקטי בתריה פי' עשאוה כשדה שהלכו בה הנמושות כדתנינן מאימתי כל אדם מותרין בלקט ובשכחה ובפאה משהלכו בה הנמושות. ופליגא הא דר' יוחנן דאמר לא גדול גדול ממש ולא קטן קטן ממש אלא [גדול] וסמוך על שולחן אביו זהו קטן. קטן ואינו סמוך על שולחן אביו זהו גדול אדשמואל. מציאת עבדו ושפחתו העברים הרי אלו שלהם. ומקשי' והתניא בפועל אם שכרו עשה עמי מלאכה מציאתו לבעה"ב ולא יהיה העבד כפועל ומשני ר' יוחנן בקונה עבד נוקב מרגליות דאין רבו רוצה לשנותו למלאכה אחרת דלאו עשה עמי מלאכה הוא אלא במלאכה זו בלבד לפיכך לא נשתעבד לאותו אלא בזותה מלאכה בלבד. רבא אמר במגביה מציאה זו עם מלאכתו דלא בטל ממלאכת רבו. רב פפא אמר כי קתני בפועל מציאתו לבעה"ב כגון דאקפי אגמא בכוורי ושכרו ללקוט לו בכוורי. ושפחתו. הא שפחה היכי דמיא אי דאייתי ב' שערות וכו' עד אמר לך ריש לקיש לעולם דאיתיה לאב ומציאתה לאביה היא והאי דקתני במתני' הרי אלו שלהן לאפוקי דרבה פי' למעט את אדוניה ממציאתה. ויש אומר לאפוקי מהא דאמר רבא בפ' האשה נקנית זאת

מסורת הש"ס

א) גיטין נ., בכורות יח., ב) לעיל י., לקמן קיח., ג) גיטין סד:, ד) קדושין טז., ה) [קונה את עצמה כל"ן], ו) כתובות נז: ע"ש, גיטין עד. ע"ש, בבא בתרא מז: ע"ש, ז) כתובות נא., [לקמן יז., יט.], ח) [בבא בתרא קסז:], ט) עי' רש"י זבחים ו. ד"ה קופיא, י) ל"ל ורבה, יא) [אלו נערות מ:], יב) [וע"ע תוס' כתובות מז. ד"ה משום איבה], יג) [כתובות כא:].

הגהות הב"ח

(א) גמ' ופליגא אדר' חייא: (ב) תום' ד"ה ר' יוחנן וכו' בנו ובתו הגדולים לשמואל דאמר הכא: (ג) ד"ה כותבין וכו' ידי סהדי אחתימת ידייהו פסולה דהכא:

הגהות הגר"א

[א] תוס' ד"ה ר"י מפרש ר"ת כו'. נ"ב ורמב"ם חולק: [ב] שם ד"ה ששכרו וה"פ כו'. נ"ב והרמ"ה מפרש ששכרו סתם ומראה ללקט לו מציאות:

ליקוטי רש"י

עשו שאינו זוכה כזוכה. במקומות הרבה מפני התקנה עשו כן כרבי יוסי בהניזקין (לקמן דף נט:) עני המנקף בראש הזית ומצודות חיות ועופות ומציאת חרש ובבכורות (דף יח:) כל שחליפיו ביד כהן פטור מן המתנות ובגמרא דשנים אוחזין (ב"מ דף יב:) השוכר את הפועל ילקט בנו אחריו דאף על פי שאין זכיה לקטן עשאוהו כזוכה ובכולן י"ל מפני תקנה עשו [גיטין ל.]. אע"פ שלא זכה כהן בהאיך דהא לא מטא לידיה מעולם עשאוהו כאילו זכה בו הואיל ומעיקרא הוה שייכא ביה יד כהן דשמא דידיה הוא שויוה רבנן כמאן דמטא לידיה לשום בכורה [בכורות יח.]. נכש עמי היום. דלא נשכר עמו אלא לניכוש ועידור וכשהגביה המציאה אין זו ממלאכת בעה"ב וקנאה פועל והוא ינכה לו משכרו שכר פעולת ניכוש ועידור כל שעת הגבהה. אמר לו עשה עמי מלאכה היום. כל מלאכה שהוא עושה מלאכת בעה"ב היא וקנה בעה"ב וכו' [לעיל י.]. במיתת האב. אביה [קדושין טז.]. במגורשת ואינה מגורשת. ומן האירוסין ולא לאשמעינן דלא תמכור לכתובתה אלא בב"ד דהא מאלמנה מן האירוסין שמעינן לה אלא אגב אורחיה אשמעינן דמגורשת ואינה מגורשת כגון זרק לה גיטה ספק קרוב לה ספק קרוב לו ברה"ר אין לה מזונות מן היתומים אם מת [כתובות צז:]. כגון זרק לה גט ספק קרוב לה ספק קרוב לו דבעלה חייב במזונותיה עד דיהב לה גט ודאי כר' זירא ואיכא למימר כיון דמגורשת ואינה מגורשת אשתו היא וחייב במזונותיה והניח לה בעל קרקע זו בידה כדי שתיזון מפירותיה ולא הויא חזקה קמ"ל דהויא חזקה דכיון

הָכָא אִית לָהּ אֵיבָה וְאֵיבָה — But **here,** where the husband has already tried to divorce her, **there certainly is ill will** borne by her husband **towards her.** There is thus no longer any reason award her finds to him.

**Mishnah** The rest of the chapter deals with the finding of documents, which surely cannot be awarded to the finder and would not benefit him in any case. The document definitely belongs to one of the principals named in it. However, returning it to one of the principals will benefit him but harm the other.[16] The following Mishnahs will delineate when and to whom the documents should be returned.[17]

מָצָא שִׁטְרֵי חוֹב — If **one found notes of indebtedness,**[18] אִם יֵשׁ בָּהֶן אַחֲרָיוּת נְכָסִים— then **if there is** provision for **a lien on** real **property in [the notes],**[19] לֹא יַחֲזִיר— **[the finder] may not return them** to the creditor, שֶׁבֵּית דִּין נִפְרָעִין מֵהֶן— **for the court will exact payment from [the properties]** based on these notes. אֵין בָּהֶן אַחֲרָיוּת נְכָסִים— But **if there is no** provision for **a lien on** real **property in [the notes],** יַחֲזִיר— **[the finder] should return them** to the creditor, שֶׁאֵין בֵּית דִּין נִפְרָעִין מֵהֶן— **for the court will not exact payment from [the properties]** based on these notes,[20] דִּבְרֵי רַבִּי מֵאִיר— these are **the words of R' Meir.** וַחֲכָמִים אוֹמְרִים — **But the Sages say:** בֵּין כָּךְ וּבֵין כָּךְ— **In either case,** לֹא יַחֲזִיר— **[the finder] may not return them** to the creditor, מִפְּנֵי שֶׁבֵּית דִּין נִפְרָעִין מֵהֶן— **for the court will exact payment from [the properties]** based on these notes.[21]

**Gemara** The Gemara investigates the exact status of the debt in the found note:[22]

בְּמַאי עַסְקִינַן— **With what** case **are we dealing** in the Mishnah?[23] אִילֵימָא כְּשֶׁחַיָּיב מוֹדֶה— **If you say** that the Mishnah refers to a case **where the debtor admits** that the debt is indeed owed,[24] כִּי יֵשׁ בָּהֶן אַחֲרָיוּת נְכָסִים אַמַּאי לֹא יַחֲזִיר— then **when there is** provision for **a lien on** real **property in [the notes], why may [the finder] not return** them to the creditor? הָא מוֹדֶה— **Why, he admits** that he owes the debt![25] **— ? —**

The Gemara now considers whether the opposite circumstance is a viable possibility:

וְאִי כְּשֶׁאֵין חַיָּיב מוֹדֶה— **And if** the Mishnah refers to a case **where the debtor does not admit** that the debt is owed,[26] כִּי אֵין בָּהֶן אַחֲרָיוּת נְכָסִים אַמַּאי יַחֲזִיר — then **when there is no** provision for **a lien on** real **property in [the notes], why should [the finder] return them** to the creditor? נְהִי דְּלָא גָּבֵי מִמְּשַׁעְבְּדֵי — **Granted that [the creditor] will not** be able to use the note to **collect from encumbered properties** [i.e. from real properties that are no longer in the debtor's possession and from which the creditor can collect only if he has a lien against them], בְּנֵי חָרֵי מִגְבָּא גָּבֵי — but **from properties free of encumbran**[ces] [i.e. from properties which are still in the debtor's possession a[nd] from which the creditor can collect even without a lien], **[t**[he] **creditor] will indeed** be able to use the note to **collect.** Ho[w], then, can we instruct the finder to return a note to the credit[or] over the protest of the debtor that he will be unjustly harmed [by] this?[27]

The Gemara answers:

לְעוֹלָם כְּשֶׁחַיָּיב מוֹדֶה — **Actually,** the Mishnah refers to [a] case **where the debtor admits** that the debt is still owe[d]. וְהָכָא הַיְינוּ טַעְמָא — **And here,** in the case of a note that contai[ns] the lien provision, **the reason** for not returning the no[te] to the creditor **is** דְּחָיְישִׁינַן שֶׁמָּא כָּתַב לִלְווֹת בְּנִיסָן — **that w**[e] **are apprehensive that perhaps [the debtor] drew up t**[he] note **to borrow** the money **in** the month of **Nissan,** so that Niss[an] is the date that appears in the note as the date of t[he] loan, וְלֹא לָוָה עַד תִּשְׁרֵי — **but he did not** actually **borro**[w] the money **until** six months later in the month of **Tishrei;**[28]

NOTES

16. See below, note 23.

17. *Meiri.*

18. That is, notes that record a debt incurred by a debtor to his creditor. If the note is in the possesion of the creditor, he produces it as evidence that the debt has not yet been repaid. If the note is in the possession of the debtor, he produces it to prove that the debt was repaid (see below, note 23).

19. When the note contains such a provision, the creditor can collect from the mortgaged properties even if they have since been sold to another person — see 7b notes 37 and 38.

20. The Gemara will explain the Mishnah's reason for this distinction between these two types of notes (*Rashi*).

21. The Gemara (13b) will explain the Sages' position, and what their disagreement with R' Meir consists of.

22. Although the Gemara's discussion focuses on R' Meir's ruling, it also affects our understanding of the Sages' position, since they refer to the same circumstance as R' Meir. The Gemara discusses the Sages' view below, 13b.

23. When a debt is recorded in a note, the note is deposited with the creditor until the debt is satisfied. When this occurs, the note is returned to the debtor. Therefore, the creditor's possession of the note is generally regarded as proof that the debt has not yet been satisfied, for otherwise the debtor would have demanded that the note be returned to him. Thus, returning the note to the creditor is tantamount to empowering him to collect the debt, so that before returning it to the creditor, one has to first establish that the note is indeed genuine and that the debt is still outstanding. In our Mishnah, R' Meir differentiates between a note with a lien and one without. It is evident, then, that it refers to a situation in which the fact that the debt is outstanding can be established only in regard to the note without a lien, but not in rega[rd] to the one with a lien. What situation is this?

24. I.e. he admits that the debt has not yet been paid (*Rashi*) and th[at] the note was drawn properly (*Ritva*).

25. Even if the creditor now appropriates real estate sold by his debt[or] on the basis of his lien, he will be doing so lawfully, since the debt[or] admits that the debt is still owed (*Rashi*).

[It is not clear why the debtor's admission is given credence eve[n] regarding the buyers. See *Kovetz Shmuos* and references cited there; [see] *Ritva*.]

26. The debtor can deny the validity of the creditor's claim in any [of] three ways. The debtor can claim that: a) He already paid the debt, th[e] note was returned to him, and it was he who lost it; b) it was he who dre[w] up the note in anticipation of a loan but he did not yet borrow the mone[y] and it was he who lost the note; c) the note was fraudulently drawn u[p] by the creditor and the signatures of the witnesses affixed to it are fals[e] (*Ritva*).

27. Since the debtor denies that he owes the debt, there is no justificatio[n] to assume that he indeed owes it, so that in returning the note to th[e] creditor we would be empowering him to collect the debt illegally.

[See *Ritva* at length as to why the note is not returned in option "[b]" of the previous note, since the creditor will, presumably, have to certi[fy] the signatures before he can exact payment (see also *Tosafos* 13b ד"ה הא קאמר; see 13a note 21 at length).]

28. It is possible that the debtor drew up the note in Nissan i[n] *anticipation* of a loan but was not successful in obtaining it at th[at] time. Instead, the creditor loaned him the money six months later, i[n] Tishrei, and the debtor gave him the predated note at that time, whic[h] the creditor subsequently lost. Since it is true that he has not yet pa[id]

א) עשו שאינו זוכה כזוכה מ"ט עניים גופייהו ניחא להו כי היכי דכי אגרו לדידהו נלקוט בנייהו בתרייהו ופליגא (א) דר' חייא בר אבא דאמר רבי חייא בר אבא אמר רבי יוחנן א לא גדול גדול ממש ולא קטן קטן ממש אלא גדול וסמוך על שלחן אביו זהו קטן קטן ואינו סמוך על שלחן אביו זהו גדול: מציאת עבדו ושפחתו העברים הרי הוא של עצמן: אמאי לא יהא אלא פועל ב) ותניא ב מציאת פועל לעצמו במה דברים אמורים בזמן שאמר לו נכש עמי היום עדור עמי היום אבל אמר לו עשה עמי מלאכה היום מציאתו לבעל הבית אמר רבי חייא בר אבא אמר רבי יוחנן הכא בעבד נוקב מרגליות עסקינן שאין רבו רוצה לשנותו למלאכה אחרת רבא אמר במגביה מציאה עם מלאכתו עסקינן רב פפא אמר ג כגון ששכרו ללקט מציאות והיכי דמי דאקפי אגמא בכוורי: ג) האי שפחה היכי דמי אי דאייתי שתי שערות מאי בעיא גביה ואי דלא אייתי שתי שערות אי איתיה לאב ד דאבוה הויא ואי דליתיה לאב תיפוק במיתת האב ד) דאמר ריש לקיש אמה העבריה ה) קנה עצמה במיתת האב מרשות האדון מקל וחומר ולאו איתותב ריש לקיש נימא מהאי נמי תיהוי תיובתא לא לעולם דאיתיה לאב ומאי הרי הן שלהן לאפוקי דרבה: מציאת אשתו: גירשה פשיטא הכא במאי עסקינן ה במגורשת ואינה מגורשת ו) דאמר רבי זירא אמר שמואל ו כל מקום שאמרו חכמים מגורשת ואינה מגורשת בעלה חייב במזונותיה טעמא מאי אמור רבנן מציאת אשה לבעלה כי היכי דלא תיהוי לה איבה הכא אית לה איבה ואיבה: מתני' ז) מצא שטרי חוב אם יש בהן אחריות נכסים לא יחזיר שבית דין נפרעין מהן אין בהן אחריות נכסים יחזיר שאין בית דין נפרעין מהן דברי רבי מאיר וחכמים אומרים ז בין כך ובין כך לא יחזיר מפני שבית דין נפרעין מהן: גמ' במאי עסקינן אילימא כשחייב מודה כי יש בהן אחריות נכסים אמאי לא יחזיר הא מודה ואי כשאין חייב מודה כי אין בהן אחריות נכסים אמאי יחזיר נהי דלא גבי ממשעבדי מבני חרי מגבא גבי לעולם ח כשחייב מודה והכא היינו טעמא דחיישינן שמא כתב ללות בניסן ולא לוה עד תשרי ואתי למטרף לקוחות שלא כדין אי הכי כל שטרי דאתו לקמן ניחוש להו חכי כל שטרי לא ריעי הני ריעי אלא הא ח) דתנן ט כותבין שטר ללוה אף על פי שאין מלוה עמו לכתחילה היכי כתבינהו ניחוש שמא כתב ללות בניסן ולא לוה עד תשרי ואתי למטרף לקוחות שלא כדין אמר רב אסי

בשטרי

## רש"י

עשו את שאינו זוכה כזוכה. אע"פ שאין לקטן זכייה במקום אחר כאן עשאוהו כזוכה: מאי טעמא עניים גופייהו ניחא להו. בהאי תקנתא דכי אגרו להו לדידהו כו': ופליגא. דשמואל דפירש טעמא דמתני' משום דלית ליה זכייה: אדר' חייא בר אבא. דאמר אף גדול שיש לו זכייה אם סמוך הוא על שולחן אביו מציאתו לאביו משום איבה אבל אינו סמוך על שולחן אביו אפילו הוא קטן מציאתו שלו: לא יהא אלא פועל. לא יהא עבדו אלא שכיר בעלמא תניא דמציאתו לבעל הבית בזמן שלא פירש לו לאיזו מלאכה שכרו ועבד זה כשקנאו רבו לסתם מלאכה קנאו: שאין רבו רוצה לשנותו. הלכך לא ניחא ליה שיגביה לו מציאה דמציאה מעולה בדמיה משכר ביטול מלאכתו לא שכיחא הלכך אי אתרמי ואשכח שלו הוא וישלם לרבו שכר ביטולו: עם מלאכתו. שלא ביטל כלום הלכך לעצמו: רב פפא אמר. הא דתניא פועל מציאתו לבעל הבית: ששכרו ללקט מציאות. הרבה: והיכי דמי. דאתרמי: דאקפי אגמא בכוורי. שצף הנהר חוץ לגדותיו וצפו הדגים שם וכשיבשו המים היוצאים נמצאו שם דגים הרבה. דאקפי תרגום של הציף כדמתרגמינן ויצף הברזל וקפא ט) ברזלא (מלכים ב ו): מאי בעיא גביה. הא תניא יוצאה בסימנין: דאבוה הויא. מציאתה דהא קטנה היא: ואי דליתיה לאב. מאי בעיא גבי האדון תיפוק מיניה במיתת האב: מקל וחומר. בפרק קמא דקדושין (דף טז.) מה סימנין שאין מוציאין מרשות האב מוציאין מרשות האדון כדילפינן ויצאה חנם אלו ימי בגרות אין כסף אלו ימי נערות מיתת האב שמוציאה מרשות האב שאינו מוריש לבניו מה שזכתה לו תורה בבתו שיהא מעשה ידיה לאחין כדילפינן (כתובות דף מג.) והתנחלתם אותם לבניכם ולא בנותיכם לבניכם אינו דין שמוציאה מרשות האדון: ולאו איתותב רבי שמעון בן לקיש. בקדושין (שם): לאפוקי דרבה. לאפוקי שאינו של רבה אלא של אביה וקרי ליה שלהן משום דאב מינה קאתי: במגורשת ואינה מגורשת. כגון זרק לה גיטה ספק קרוב לה ספק קרוב לו ברה"ר: חייב במזונותיה. ומשום הכי אצטריך לאשמועינן דמציאתה שלה דטעמא מאי אמור רבנן מציאת האשה כו': מתני' אחריות נכסים. שעבוד קרקעות שיגבה מהן: יחזיר ולא יחזיר. טעמא בגמ' מפרש: גמ' כשחייב מודה. שהלוה מודה שהשטר אינו פרוע: אמאי לא יחזיר. אם לטרוף לקוחות בלא בדין הוא טורפן: ממשעבדי. ממקרקעי שמכר אחרי כן: הני ריעי. הואיל ונפל אתרע דיש לומר אם היה כשר היה נזהר בו:

בשטרי

## תוספות

רבי יוחנן אמר לא גדול גדול ממש. [א] מפרש ר"ת כי היכי דפליגי הכא פליגי נמי גבי עירוב דתנן בפ' חלון (עירובין דף עט: ושם ד"ה ומזכה) ומזכה להם על ידי בנו ובתו (ב) ולשמואל דאמר הכא קטן ממש התם נמי גבי עירוב אינו זוכה דידו כיד אביו כיון דמציאתו לאביו ה"ה כל זכיותיו לאביו ואמה העבריה אע"פ שהיא קטנה זכיא בעירובה דמציאתה אינה לאדוניה אף על גב דשמואל אית ליה פרק התקבל (גיטין דף סד: ושם ד"ה אלא) קטן זוכה לעצמו ואינו זוכה לאחרים הא משני התם שאני שתופי מבואות דרבנן והא דאמר שמואל פרק מי שהוציאוהו (עירובין דף מט. ושם: ד"ה וקטן) דעירוב משום קנין י) ורבא אמר משום דירה ואמר איכא בינייהו קטן הא פר"ת התם דאית ליה בית לקטן קאמר ולא כפרש"י שפי' שאינו גובה העירוב לפי שאינו זוכה ולר"י דאמר לא גדול גדול ממש ה"ה דגבי עירוב נמי דקטן ואינו סמוך על שולחן אביו זוכה כאמה העבריה וגדול סמוך על שולחן אביו אינו זוכה וצריך ליזהר שלא לזכות העירוב ע"י בנו הגדול הסמוך לשולחנו דקי"ל כרבי יוחנן לגבי שמואל כדאמר פרק מי שהוציאוהו (שם מז:) ועבדו ושפחתו העברים אע"ג דסמוכין על שולחנו מציאתם לעצמם וכן זוכין בעירוב ולא הוי ידם כיד האדון דלא שייך איבה אלא בבנו שדרכו לזונו תמיד ואם לא יפרנסו אביו לא יפרנסו אחר אבל אדם אחר מעלמא סמוך על שולחן חבירו חנם כגון יתום וכיוצא בו אין סברא שתהא מציאתו לחבירו וכ"ש עבד ואמה שבשכר טרחם הם אוכלים ובתו אפילו נערה ואינה סמוכה על שולחן אביה מציאתה לאביה משום איבה דאי בעי מסר לה למנוול ומוכה שחין כדאמר בפרק יא) נערה (כתובות דף מו ושם) יב) ודלא כרש"י שפירש משום דכתיב בנעוריה דההוא בהפרת נדרים הוא דכתיב כדאיתא בפרק קמא דקדושין (דף ג: ושם) ופרק נערה (שם מו:) ואשתו דזכיא בעירוב אף על גב דידה כיד בעלה מוקי לה בסוף נדרים (דף פח:) דאית לה בית באותו מבוי דמגו דזכיא לנפשה זכיא נמי לאחריני:

במגביה מציאה עם מלאכתו. וא"ת הא דתניא בפ"ק דקדושין (דף טז:) אמה העבריה מציאתה לאביה ושכר בטלה לרבה היכי מתוקמא אליבא דרבא דאם הגביהה עם מלאכתו ליכא שכר בטלה ואם לא הגביהה עם מלאכתו א"כ מציאתה לאדוניה וי"ל דהתם ודאי צריך להעמיד בנוקבת מרגליות:

ששכרו ללקט מציאות. [ב]וה"פ דברייתא בד"א בזמן שאמר ליה עשה עמי באותו ענין שהוא כמו נכש עמי היום אבל אמר ליה עשה עמי מלאכה של מציאות כו':

מאי בעיא גביה. דהיא נמי אינה יכולה למכור עצמה אחרי כן כדאיתא בספרי:

ולא לוה עד תשרי. פירוש ועתה רוצה ללות בו שיש לו טורח לכתוב שטר אחר וגם כדי להרויח פשיטי דספרא אבל אין לפרש שכבר לוה בו קודם שנפל דא"כ מאי משני הני ריעי לפי שנפל ויש הוכחה דמשום פסולו לא נזהר לשומרו והא לוה בו כבר ופשיטא שנזהר לשומרו:

כותבין שטר ללוה אף על פי שאין מלוה עמו. וליכא למיחש למחזי לשקרא כמו יג) באשרתא דדייני דאם כתבו קודם דנחזי חתימת ידי סהדי (ג) פסולה דהכא כיון שהוא כותב חובתו לא שייך מחזי כשקרא:

אביי

## עין משפט נר מצוה

קד א מיי' פי"ז מהל' אבידה הל' יג סמג עשין עד טוש"ע ח"מ סי' ער סעיף ג:
קה ב ג מיי' פי"ט מהל' שכירות הל' יא סמג שם טוש"ע שם סעיף ג:
קו ד מיי' פי"ז מהל' אבידה הל' יג סמג עשין עד (טוש"ע ח"מ סי' ער סעיף ג):
קז ה מיי' שם סמג שם טוש"ע ח"מ שם סעיף ג ועוש"ע אה"ע סי' פד:
קח ו מיי' פי"ח מהל' אישות הלכה כה טוש"ע אה"ע סי' לג סעיף ג:
קט ז ח מיי' פי"ח מהל' אבידה הלכה א סמג עשין עד טוש"ע ח"מ סי' סה סעיף ו:
קי ט מיי' פכ"ג מהל' מלוה ולוה הלכה ה ופכ"ד שם הל' א סמג עשין צד טוש"ע ח"מ סי' לט סעיף יג:

## רבינו חננאל

ואסקה רבא עשו הקטן שאינו זוכה לעצמו מן התורה כזוכה מאי טעמא עניים גופייהו מחלי ליה דניחא להו דנלקטו בנייהו נמי בתרייהו דידהו ולפיכך אמר ר' יוסי בניו ואשתו מלקטין אחריו. פי' אינו זוכה כזוכה כדתנן פרק כל גט שנכתב שלא לשם אשה פסול. המלוה מעות את הכהן ואת הלוי ואת העני וכו' ואוקימנא אע"ג דלא אתו לידייהו כו'. ועולא אמר הא מני ר' יוסי היא דאמר עשו את שאינו זוכה כזוכה דתנן בבכורות כל שחליפין ביד כהן פטור מן המתנות וכו' עשו את שאינו זוכה כזוכה מאי טעמא עשאוה כשדה שהלכו בה המנושות עניים גופייהו מסחו דעתייהו מההיא שדה אמרי בניו ואשתו דהאיך מלקטי בתריה פי' עשאוה כשדה שהלכו בה המנושות כדתנינן מאימתי כל אדם מותרין בלקט ובשכחה ובפאה משהלכו בה המנושות. ופליגא הא דר' יוחנן דאמר לא גדול גדול ממש ולא קטן קטן ממש אלא [גדול] וסמוך על שולחן אביו זהו קטן. קטן ואינו סמוך על שולחן אביו זהו גדול אדשמואל. מציאת עבדו ושפחתו העברים הרי אלו שלהם. ומקשי' והתניא בפועל אם שכרו עשה עמי מלאכה מציאתו לבעה"ב ולא יהיה העבד כפועל ומשני ר' יוחנן בקונה עבד נוקב מרגליות דאין רבו רוצה לשנותו למלאכה אחרת דלאו עשה עמי מלאכה הוא אלא במלאכה זו בלבד ליהירך לא נשתעבד לאדונו אלא באותה מלאכה בלבד. רבא אמר במגביה מציאה זו עם מלאכתו דלא בטל ממלאכת רבו. רב פפא אמר כי קתני בפועל מציאתו לבעה"ב כגון דאקפי אגמא בכוורי ושכרו ללקוט לו בכוורי. ושפחתו. הא שפחה היכי דמיא אי דאייתי ב' שערות וכו' עד אמר לך ריש לקיש לעולם דאיתיה לאב ומציאתה לאביה היא והאי דקתני במתני' הרי אלו שלהן לאפוקי דרבה פי' למעט את אדוניה ממציאתה. ויש אומר לאפוקי מהא דאמר רבא בפ' האשה נקנית זאת אומרת עבד עברי גופו קנוי באה משנתנו להוציא מזה הטעם של רבא. מציאת אשה שגירשה אע"פ שלא נתן לה עדיין כתובתה מציאתה שלה. אוקימנא במגורשת ואינה מגורשת פי' בתלמוד א"י אדם שגירש את אשתו ולא נתן לה כתובתה חייב במזונותיה עד שיתן לה פרוטה אחרונה. אמר ר' יוסי מתני' אמרה כן אמר ר' אושעיא שלא תאמר הואיל וחייב במזונותיה עד שיפרע כתובתה תהא מציאתה שלו לפום כן תני מציאת אשה שגירשה לעצמה: מצא שטרי חוב אם יש בהן אחריות נכסים לא יחזיר. אוקימנא כשחייב מודה. ואמאי לא יחזיר דחיישינן שמא כתב ללות בניסן ולא לוה עד תשרי וטורף ללקוחות שלא כדין. אי הכי כל שטרי דעלמא נמי נימא הכי. ודחי' כל שטרי דעלמא לא ריעי הני כיון דנפלי ריעי. אלא הא דתנן כותבין שטר ללוה אע"פ שאין מלוה

## מסורת הש"ס

א) גיטין ל. בכורות יח., ב) לעיל י., לקמן קיח., ג) גיטין סד:, ד) קדושין טז., ה) [קונה את עצמה כל"ג], ו) כתובות מז: ע"ש, גיטין עד. ע"ש, בבא בתרא מז: ע"ש, ז) כתובות מג., [לקמן יח., יט.], ח) [בבא בתרא קסז:], ט) עי' רש"י זבחים ו. ד"ה קופיא, י) צ"ל ורבה, יא) [אלו נערות מ:], יב) [וע"ע תוס' כתובות מז. ד"ה משום איבה], יג) [כתובות כא:].

## הגהות הב"ח

(א) גמ' ופליגא אדר' חייא: (ב) תוס' ד"ה ר' יוחנן וכו' בנו ובתו הגדולים ולשמואל דאמר הכא: (ג) ד"ה כותבין וכו' ידי סהדי אחתימת ידייהו פסולה דהכא:

## הגהות הגר"א

[א] תוס' ד"ה ר"י מפרש ר"ת כו'. נ"ב ורמב"ם חולק: [ב] שם ד"ה ששכרו וה"פ כו'. נ"ב והרמ"ה מפרש ששכרו סתם ומראה ללקט לו מציאות:

## ליקוטי רש"י

עשו שאינו זוכה כזוכה. במקומות הרבה מפני התקנה עשו כן כדברי יוסי הגלילי [לקמן דף נט:]: עני המנקף בראש הזית ומלגודות חיות ועופות ומלאת חרס ובבכורות (דף יח:) כל שחליפיו ביד כהן פטור מן המתנות ובגמרא דשניא חיזמן (ב"מ דף יב:) השוכר את הפועל ללקט בנו אחריו דאף על פי שאין זכיה לקטן עשאוהו כזוכה והכולן י"ל מפני תקנה עשו [גיטין ל.]. אע"פ שלא זכה כהן בהאליך דהא לא מטא לידיה מעולם עשאוהו כאילו זכה בו הואיל ומעיקרא הוה שייכא ביה יד כהן דשמא לידיה הוא שויה רבנן כמאן דמטא לידיה לשום בכורה [בכורות יח.]. נכש עמי היום. דלא נשכר עמו אלא לניכוש ועידור ובשהגביה המציאה אין זו ממלאכת בעה"ב וקנאה פועל והוא יכלה לו משכרו שכר פעולת ניכוש ועידור לכל שעת הגבהה. אמר לו עשה עמי מלאכה היום. כל מלאכה שהוא עושה מלאכת בעה"ב היא וקנה בעה"ב וכו' [לעיל י.]. במיתת האב. אביה [קדושין טז.]. במגורשת ואינה מגורשת. ומן הקירושין ולא לאשמעינן דלא מתכור לכתובתה אלא בב"ד דהא מלאמנה מן הקירושין שמעינן לה אלא אגב אורחיה לאשמעינן דמגורשת ואינה מגורשת כגון זרק לה גיטה ספק קרוב לה ספק קרוב לו כרה"ר אין לה מזונות מן היתומים אם מת [כתובות צז:]. כגון זרק לה גט ספק קרוב לו ספק קרוב לו דבעלה חייב במזונותיה עד דיהב לה גט ודאי כר' זירא ואיכא למימר כיון דמגורשת ואינה מגורשת אשתו היא וחייב במזונותיה והכניס לה בעל קרקע זו בידה כדי שתחיון מפירותיה ולא תהוא מוקה קמ"ל דהויא מוקה דכיון דהתחיל בגירושין והוא שונא לה לא יחד לה קרקע למזונותיה כי בטורח יתן לה מזונות בגלגול כשיתחייבו [כ"ב]. חייב במזונותיה. דאכתי אגידא ביה [רשב"ם ב"ב מז:]. יש בהן אחריות נכסים. שסיעבד לוה נכסיו לאותה מלוה לא יחזירנו מולאו למלוה ואפי' הלוה מודה שהוא חייב לו ומפרש התם בדחיישינן שמא פרעו ומן הלוה נפל וזה שהוא מודה עושה קנוניא היא ביניהם לטרוף לקוחות ויחלקו ביניהם [כתובות נא:]. אין בהן אחריות נכסים. שלא שיעבד לו לוה בשעת הלואה את נכסיו ולא כתב לו כל נכסי אחראין לך לפרוע מלוה זה. יחזיר שאין ב"ד נפרעין מהן. ואינו גובה מנכסים משועבדים ולא אמרינן אין לך אדם המלוה מעותיו בלא שעבוד נכסי לוה והסופר טעה ולא כתב בו אחריות אלא דוקא אזלינן בתר שטר [ב"ק צה.]. וחכמים אומרים כו'. דאחריות טעות סופר וטריף ממשעבדי ומפסדי לקוחות [שם ע"א]. כותבין שטר ללוה. להיות מזומן בידו לתת למלוה כשילוה לו מעות אע"פ שאין מלוה עמו [ורשב"ם ב"ב קסז:].

The Gemara continues to discuss the Mishnah. The Gemara raises a difficulty in regard to the ruling in our Mishnah that the find of a Hebrew maidservant belongs to her:

הַאי שִׁפְחָה הֵיכִי דָמֵי – **How is** the case of **this** Hebrew **maidservant** to be explained? אִי דְּאַיְיתִי שְׁתֵּי שְׂעָרוֹת – **If she has already produced two** pubic **hairs,** i.e. she has become a *naarah,*[7] מַאי בָּעֲיָא גַּבֵּיהּ – **then what is she doing in his possession,** i.e. why is she still a maidservant?[8] וְאִי דְּלָא אַיְיתִי שְׁתֵּי שְׂעָרוֹת – **And if she has not produced two** pubic **hairs, then:** אִי אִיתֵיהּ לְאָב – **If her father is alive,** דְּאָבוּהָ הָוְיָא – **her find belongs to her father,** since our Mishnah states that the find of a minor daughter belongs to her father;[9] וְאִי דְּלֵיתֵיהּ לְאָב – **and if the father is not alive,** תִּיפּוֹק בְּמִיתַת הָאָב – **then let her go free with her father's death,** דְּאָמַר רֵישׁ לָקִישׁ – **for Reish Lakish said:** אָמָה הָעִבְרִיָּה קָנָה עַצְמָהּ בְּמִיתַת הָאָב מֵרְשׁוּת הָאָדוֹן מִקַּל וָחוֹמֶר – It can be shown **from a** ***kal vachomer*** **that a Hebrew maidservant acquires herself from her master's jurisdiction through the death of [her] father.**[10] Given Reish Lakish's ruling that her father's death releases the maidservant from her master, there does not seem to be any case to which our Mishnah can apply. – ? –

The Gemara questions the difficulty:

וְלָאו אִיתּוֹתַב רֵישׁ לָקִישׁ – **But has Reish Lakish not been refuted?**[11]

The Gemara replies:

נֵימָא מֵהַאי נַמִי תֶּיהֱוֵי תְּיוּבְתָּא – Indeed, since Reish Lakish's ruling has been refuted, there is no difficulty in explaining our Mishnah. However, **let us say that this** Mishnah of ours **should also serve as a refutation** of Reish Lakish, since according to Reish Lakish there is no case in which a maidservant's find would belong to her.[12]

The Gemara concludes:

לֹא – **No;** our Mishnah furnishes no proof against Reish Lakish. לְעוֹלָם דְּאִיתֵיהּ לְאָב – **In fact,** the Mishnah may refer to a case **where the father is alive;** in such a case her find indeed belongs to her father. וּמַאי הֲרֵי הֵן שֶׁלָּהֶן – **And what does [the Mishnah] mean by** including a Hebrew maidservant among those whose finds **"belong to them"?** לְאַפּוּקֵי דְּרַבָּהּ – The Mishnah merely means **to exclude** the maidservant's find fro[m] **[the possession of] her master.** The Mishnah's intent was [to] explain that the find of a Hebrew maidservant does not belong [to] her master. However, the find is not actually hers, either, sin[ce] she is a minor, whose find belongs to her father.[13]

The Gemara discusses the next part of the Mishnah, whic[h] states:

מְצִיאַת אִשְׁתּוֹ – THE FIND OF ONE'S WIFE whom he divorced . [belongs to her].

The Gemara asks:

גֵּירְשָׁהּ – Does the Mishnah indeed refer to where **he divorce[d] her?** פְּשִׁיטָא – Then **it is obvious** that her find belongs to he[r] since she is no longer married! Why does the Mishnah have [to] teach us this?

The Gemara answers:

הָכָא בְּמַאי עָסְקִינַן – **With what** case **are we dealing here** in th[e] Mishnah? בִּמְגוֹרֶשֶׁת וְאֵינָהּ מְגוֹרֶשֶׁת – We are dealing with a cas[e] **in which the woman is divorced and yet not divorced,** i.e. he[r] divorce is questionable.[14] In such a case, I might think that th[e] husband would continue to be entitled to her finds, אָמַר רַבִּי זֵירָא אָמַר שְׁמוּאֵל – **for R' Zeira said in the name of Shmue[l]:** כָּל מָקוֹם שֶׁאָמְרוּ חֲכָמִים מְגוֹרֶשֶׁת וְאֵינָהּ מְגוֹרֶשֶׁת – **Wherever th[e] Sages used the expression "divorced and yet not divorced,"** i.e. in a case where the divorce is questionable, עָלָה חַיָּיב בִּמְזוֹנוֹתֶיהָ – **the husband** remains **obligated in her suppor[t],** i.e. to provide her with food. Since normally the husband i[s] entitled to his wife's finds and earnings in exchange for suppor[t]ing her, I might reason that even in a case where there is [a] possibility that she was divorced, the husband remains entitled t[o] her finds as long as he remains obligated to support he[r]. Therefore the Mishnah has to teach us that he is not entitled t[o] her finds, in this case, even though he is obligated in her support.

טַעְמָא מַאי אָמוּר רַבָּנַן מְצִיאַת אִשָּׁה לְבַעְלָהּ – For **why did th[e] Rabbis say that a wife's find belongs to her husband?** [כ]י הֵיכִי דְּלָא תֶּיהֱוֵי לָהּ אֵיבָה – **In order that there should not be any i[ll] will** borne by her husband **towards her,** out of resentment fo[r] having to support her without receiving anything in exchange.[15]

NOTES

to be interpreted as follows: "A worker's find belongs to him. When is this ruling said? When the [employer] said to him, 'Weed for me today,' [or] 'Dig for me today.' [I.e. he was hired for a job other than the specific task of collecting finds.] But if [the employer] said to him, 'Work for me today [at the task of collecting finds],' his find belongs to the employer" (see *Tosafos*). [Accordingly, a Hebrew servant, who was not employed specifically to collect finds, may keep his find for himself, as our Mishnah rules.]

7. A girl of twelve years who has two pubic hairs enters the first stage of her adulthood (see 12a note 7).

8. The Torah (*Exodus* 21:7) gives a father the right to sell his daughter as a maidservant. If she is not redeemed, and neither the master nor his son marries her, she must work until she becomes a *naarah,* at which time she goes free.

9. Although, as we have seen, Rav Yochanan taught in the Gemara above that the find of a minor son belongs to his father only if the father supports him financially, *Tosafos* (ד״ה ר׳ יוחנן) write that in the case of a minor daughter no such restriction applies (see *Tosafos* for the reason for this distinction). [Although *Tosafos* do not mention it, this distinction would seem to have support in this Gemara, which assumes that the find of a minor maidservant should belong to her father even though she is not supported financially by her father, but by her master.]

10. The *kal vachomer* argument runs as follows: The onset of puberty (i.e. when the daughter becomes a *naarah* – see 12a note 7) does not free a daughter from her father's possession; he retains the rights he has in her as a minor until she becomes a *bogeres* (see note loc. cit.) six months later. However, the advent of puberty does release a maidservant fro[m] her master's possession. Clearly, then, it is easier to effect release fro[m] the master's possession than from the father's. Now, the death of th[e] father releases his daughter from his possession, since he canno[t] bequeath his rights in her to his heirs. Accordingly, if the father's deat[h] releases the daughter from his possession, which is stronger than he[r] master's possession, is it not certain that the father's death shoul[d] release her from her master's possession? (*Rashi* from *Kiddushin* 16a)

11. The Gemara in *Kiddushin* (16b) refutes Reish Lakish's rulin[g] (*Rashi*). [Thus, the death of a maidservant's father does *not* release he[r] from her master. Accordingly, our Mishnah (which rules that a Hebre[w] maidservant may keep her own find) refers to a maidservant whos[e] father has died.]

12. Although Reish Lakish's ruling has in any case been refuted, th[e] Gemara is still interested in determining whether or not there i[s] additional evidence from our Mishnah against Reish Lakish's ruling

13. Nevertheless, the expression "belongs to them" in regard to the fin[d] of a Hebrew maidservant is appropriate; although the find in fac[t] belongs to her father, since the father acquires the find from hi[s] daughter, it is in a sense hers – that is, it is hers insofar as to make i[t] possible for the father to acquire the find from her (*Rashi*).

14. For instance, her husband threw her a *get* in a public domain and we are not certain if it fell closer to him or closer to her. The law states that the divorce is valid only if the *get* fell closer to her. Since we are not certain if that was the case, her status as a divorcee is in doubt.

15. That is why the Sages instituted that a wife's finds belong to her husband.

[א] עשו שאינו זוכה כזוכה מ"ט עניים גופייהו ניחא להו כי היכי דכי אגרו לדידהו נלקוט בנייהו בתרייהו ופליגא (א) דר' חייא בר אבא דאמר רבי חייא בר אבא אמר רבי יוחנן [א] לא גדול גדול ממש ולא קטן קטן ממש אלא גדול וסמוך על שלחן אביו זהו קטן קטן ואינו סמוך על שלחן אביו זהו גדול: מציאת עבדו ושפחתו העברים הרי הוא של עצמן: אמאי לא יהא אלא פועל [ב] ותניא [ב] מציאת פועל לעצמו במה דברים אמורים בזמן שאמר לו נכש עמי היום עדור עמי היום אבל אמר לו עשה עמי מלאכה היום מציאתו לבעל הבית אמר רבי חייא בר אבא אמר רבי יוחנן הכא בעבד נוקב מרגליות עסקינן שאין רבו רוצה לשנותו למלאכה אחרת רבא אמר במגביה מציאה עם מלאכתו עסקינן רב פפא אמר [ג] כגון ששכרו ללקט מציאות והיכי דמי דאקפי אגמא בכוורי: [ג] האי שפחה היכי דמי אי דאייתי שתי שערות מאי בעיא גביה ואי דלא אייתי שתי שערות אי איתיה לאב [ד] דאבוה הויא ואי דליתיה לאב תיפוק במיתת האב [ד] דאמר ריש לקיש אמה העבריה [ה] קנה עצמה במיתת האב מרשות האדון מקל וחומר ולאו איתותב ריש לקיש נימא מהאי נמי תיהוי תיובתא לא לעולם דאיתיה לאב ומאי הרי הן שלהן לאפוקי דרבה: מציאת אשתו: גירשה פשיטא הכא במאי עסקינן [ה] במגורשת ואינה מגורשת [ו] דאמר רבי זירא אמר שמואל [ו] כל מקום שאמרו חכמים מגורשת ואינה מגורשת בעלה חייב במזונותיה טעמא מאי אמור רבנן מציאת אשה לבעלה כי היכי דלא תיהוי לה איבה הכא אית לה איבה ואיבה:

מתני' [ז] מצא שטרי חוב אם יש בהן אחריות נכסים לא יחזיר שבית דין נפרעין מהן אין בהן אחריות נכסים יחזיר שאין בית דין נפרעין מהן דברי רבי מאיר וחכמים אומרים [ז] בין כך ובין כך לא יחזיר מפני שבית דין נפרעין מהן: גמ' במאי עסקינן אילימא כשחייב מודה כי יש בהן אחריות נכסים אמאי לא יחזיר הא מודה ואי כשאין חייב מודה כי אין בהן אחריות נכסים אמאי יחזיר נהי דלא גבי ממשעבדי מבני חרי מגבא גבי לעולם [ח] כשחייב מודה והכא היינו טעמא דחיישינן שמא כתב ללות בניסן ולא לוה עד תשרי ואתי למטרף לקוחות שלא כדין אי הכי כל שטרי דאתו לקמן ניחוש להו הכי כל שטרי לא ריעי הני ריעי אלא הא [ח] דתנן [ט] כותבין שטר ללוה אף על פי שאין מלוה עמו לכתחילה היכי כתבינהו ניחוש שמא כתב ללות בניסן ולא לוה עד תשרי ואתי למטרף לקוחות שלא כדין אמר רב אסי בשטרי

---

**רש"י**

עשו את שאינו זוכה כזוכה. אע"פ שאין לקטן זכייה במקום אחר כאן עשאוהו כזוכה: מאי טעמא עניים גופייהו ניחא להו. בהאי תקנתא דכי אגרו להו לדידהו כו': ופליגא. דשמואל דפירש טעמא דמתני' משום דלית ליה זכייה: אדר' חייא בר אבא. דאמר אף גדול שיש לו זכייה אם סמוך הוא על שולחן אביו מציאתו לאביו משום איבה אבל אינו סמוך על שולחן אביו אפילו הוא קטן מציאתו שלו: לא יהא אלא פועל. לא יהא עבדו אלא שכיר בעלמא תניא דמציאתו לבעל הבית בזמן שלא פירש לו לאיזו מלאכה שכרו ועבד זה כשקנאו רבו לסתם מלאכה קנאו: שאין רבו רוצה לשנותו. הלכך לא ניחא ליה שיגביה לו מציאה דמציאה מעולה בדמיה משכר ביטול מלאכתו לא שכיחא הלכך אי אתרמי ואשכח שלו הוא וישלם לרבו שכר ביטולו: עם מלאכתו. שלא ביטל כלום הלכך לעצמו: רב פפא אמר. הא דתניא פועל מציאתו לבעל הבית: ששכרו ללקט מציאות. הרבה: והיכי דמי. דאתרמי: דאקפי אגמא בכוורי. שלף הנהר חוץ לגדותיו וצפו הדגים שם וכשיבשו המים היוצאים נמצאו שם דגים הרבה. דאקפי תרגום של הציף כדמתרגמינן ויצף הברזל וקפא [ט] ברזלא (מלכים ב ו): מאי בעיא גביה. הא תניא יוצאה בסימנין: דאבוה הויא. מציאתה דהא קטנה היא: ואי דליתיה לאב. מאי בעיא גבי האדון תיפוק מיניה במיתת האב: מקל וחומר. בפרק קמא דקדושין (דף טז.) מה סימנין שאין מוציאין מרשות האב מוציאין מרשות האדון כדילפינן ויצאה חנם אלו ימי בגרות אין כסף אלו ימי נערות מיתת האב שמוציאה מרשות האב שאינו מוריש לבניו מה שזכתה לו תורה בבתו שיהא מעשה ידיה לאחין כדילפינן (כתובות דף מג.) והתנחלתם אותם לבניכם ולא בנותיכם לבניכם אינו דין שמוציאה מרשות האדון: ולאו איתותב רבי שמעון בן לקיש. בקדושין (שם): לאפוקי דרבה. לאפוקי שאינו של רבה אלא של אביה וקרי ליה שלהן משום דאב מינה קזכי: במגורשת ואינה מגורשת. כגון זרק לה גיטה ספק קרוב לה ספק קרוב לו ברה"ר: חייב במזונותיה. ומשום הכי אצטריך לאשמועינן דמציאתה שלה דטעמא מאי אמור רבנן מציאת האשה כו': מתני' אחריות נכסים. שעבוד קרקעות שיגבה מהן: יחזיר ולא יחזיר. טעמא בגמ' מפרש: גמ' כשחייב מודה. שהלוה מודה שהשטר אינו פרוע: אמאי לא יחזיר. אם לטרוף לקוחות בא בדין הוא טורפן: ממשעבדי. מקרקעי שמכר אחרי כן: הני ריעי. הואיל ונפל אתרע דיש לומר אם היה כשר היה נזהר בו:

**תוספות**

רבי יוחנן אמר לא גדול גדול ממש. [א] מפרש ר"ת כי היכי דפליגי הכא פליגי נמי גבי עירוב דתנן בפ' חלון (עירובין דף עט: ושם ד"ה ומזכה) ומזכה להם על ידי בנו ובתו (ב) ולשמואל דאמר הכא קטן ממש התם נמי גבי עירוב אינו זוכה דידו כיד אביו כיון דמציאתו לאביו ה"ה כל זכיותיו לאביו ואמה העבריה אע"פ שהיא קטנה זכיא בעירובה דמציאתה אינה לאדוניה אף על גב דשמואל אית ליה פרק התקבל (גיטין דף סד: ושם ד"ה אלא) קטן זוכה לעצמו ואינו זוכה לאחרים הא משני התם שאני שתופי מבואות דרבנן והא דאמר שמואל פרק מי שהוציאוהו (עירובין דף מט. ושם: ד"ה וקטן) דעירוב משום קנין [י] ורבא אמר משום דירה ואמר איכא בינייהו קטן הא פר"ח התם דאית ליה בית לקטן קאמר ולא כפרש"י שפי' שאינו גובה העירוב לפי שאינו זוכה ולר"י דאמר לא גדול גדול ממש ה"ה דגבי עירוב נמי דקטן ואינו סמוך על שולחן אביו זוכה כאמה העבריה וגדול סמוך על שולחן אביו אינו זוכה וצריך ליזהר שלא לזכות העירוב ע"י בנו הגדול הסמוך לשולחנו דקי"ל כרבי יוחנן לגבי שמואל כדאמר פרק מי שהוציאוהו (שם מז:) ועבדו ושפחתו העברים אע"ג דסמוכין על שולחנו מציאתם לעצמם וכן זוכין בעירוב ולא הוי ידם כיד האדון דלא שייך איבה אלא בבנו שדרכו לזונו תמיד ואם לא יפרנסו אביו לא יפרנסו אחר אבל אדם אחר מעלמא סמוך על שולחן חבירו חנם כגון יתום וכיוצא בו אין סברא שתהא מציאתו לחבירו וכ"ש עבד ואמה שבשכר טרחם הם אוכלים ובתו אפילו נערה ואינה סמוכה על שולחן אביה מציאתה לאביה משום איבה דאי בעי מסר לה למנוול ומוכה שחין כדאמר בפרק [יא] נערה (כתובות דף מו ושם) [יב] ולא כרש"י שפירש משום דכתיב בנעוריה דההוא בהפרת נדרים הוא דכתיב כדאיתא בפרק קמא דקדושין (דף ג: ושם) ופרק נערה (שם מו:) ואשתו דזכיא בעירוב אף על גב דידה כיד בעלה מוקי לה בסוף נדרים (דף פח:) דאית לה בית באותו מבוי דמגו דזכיא לנפשה זכיא נמי לאחריני:

במגביה מציאה עם מלאכתו. וא"ת הא דתניא בפ"ק דקדושין (דף טז:) אמה העבריה מציאתה לאביה ושכר בטלה לרבה היכי מתוקמא אליבא דרבא דאם הגביהה עם מלאכתו ליכא שכר בטלה ואם לא הגביהה עם מלאכתו א"כ מציאתה לאדוניה וי"ל דהתם ודאי צריך להעמיד בנוקבת תרגליות:

ששכרו ללקט מציאות. [ב] וה"פ דברייתא בד"א בזמן שאמר ליה עשה עמי באותו ענין שהוא כמו נכש עמי היום אבל אמר ליה עשה עמי מלאכה של מציאות כו':

מאי בעיא גביה. דהיא נמי אינה יכולה למכור עצמה אחרי כן כדאיתא בספרי:

ולא לוה עד תשרי. פירוש ועתה רוצה ללות בו שיש לו טורח לכתוב שטר אחר וגם כדי להרויח פשיטי דספרא אבל אין לפרש שכבר לוה בו קודם שנפל דא"כ מאי משני הני ריעי לפי שנפל ויש הוכחה דמשום פסולו לא נזהר לשומרו והא לוה בו כבר ופשיטא שנזהר לשומרו:

כותבין שטר ללוה אף על פי שאין מלוה עמו. וליכא למיחש למחזי כשקרא כמו [יג] באשרתא דדייני דאם כתבו קודם דנחזי חתימת ידי סהדי (ג) פסולה דהכא כיון שהוא כותב חובתו לא שייך מחזי כשקרא:

**עין משפט נר מצוה**

קד א מיי' פי"ז מהל' אבידה הל' יג סמג עשין עד טוש"ע ח"מ סי' ער סעיף ג:

קה ב ג מיי' פ"ט מהל' שכירות הל' יא סמג שם טוש"ע שם סעיף ג:

קו ד מיי' פי"ז מהל' אבידה הל' יג סמג עשין עד (טוש"ע ח"מ סי' ער סעיף ג):

קז ה מיי' שם סמג שם טוש"ע ח"מ שם סעיף ג וטוש"ע אה"ע סי' פד:

קח ו מיי' פי"ח מהל' אישות הלכה כה טוש"ע אה"ע סי' לג סעיף ג:

קט ז ח מיי' פי"ח מהל' אבידה הלכה א סמג עשין עד טוש"ע ח"מ סי' סה סעיף ו:

קי ט מיי' פכ"ג מהל' מלוה ולוה הלכה ה ופכ"ד שם הל' א סמג עשין לד טוש"ע ח"מ סי' לט סעיף יג:

**רבינו חננאל**

ואסקה רבא עשו הקטן שאינו זוכה לעצמו מן התורה כזוכה מאי טעמא עניים גופייהו מחלי ליה דניחא להו דנלקטו בנייהו נמי בתרייהו דידהו ולפיכך אמר ר' יוסי בניו ואשתו מלקטין אחריו. פי' אינו זוכה כזוכה כדתנן פרק כל גט שנכתב שלא לשם אשה פסול. המלוה מעות את הכהן ואת הלוי ואת העני וכו' ואוקימנא אע"ג דלא אתו לידייהו כו'. ועולא אמר הא מני ר' יוסי היא דאמר עשו את שאינו זוכה כזוכה דתנן בבכורות כל שחליפין ביד כהן פטור מן המתנות וכו' עשו את שאינו זוכה כזוכה מאי טעמא עשאוה כשדה שהלכו בה הנמושות עניים גופייהו מסחו דעתייהו מההיא שדה אמרי בניו ואשתו דהאיך מלקטי בתריה פי' עשאוה כשדה שהלכו בה הנמושות כדתנינן מאימתי כל אדם מותרין בלקט ובשכחה ובפאה משהלכו בה הנמושות. ופליגא הא דר' יוחנן דאמר לא גדול גדול ממש ולא קטן קטן ממש אלא [גדול] וסמוך על שולחן אביו זהו קטן. קטן ואינו סמוך על שולחן אביו זהו גדול אדשמואל. מציאת עבדו ושפחתו העברים הרי אלו שלהם. ומקשי' והתניא בפועל אם שכרו עשה עמי מלאכה מציאתו לבעה"ב ולא יהיה העבד כפועל ומשני ר' יוחנן בקונה עבד נוקב מרגליות דאין רבו רוצה לשנותו למלאכה אחרת דלאו עשה עמי מלאכה הוא אלא במלאכה זו בלבד לפיכך לא נשתעבד לאדונו אלא באותה מלאכה בלבד. רבא אמר במגביה מציאה זו עם מלאכתו דלא בטל ממלאכת רבו. רב פפא אמר כי קתני בפועל מציאתו לבעה"ב כגון דאקפי אגמא בכוורי ושכרו ללקוט לו בכוורי. ושפחתו. הא שפחה היכי דמיא אי דאייתי ב' שערות וכו' עד אמר לך ריש לקיש לעולם דאיתיה לאב ומציאתה לאביה היא והאי דקתני במתני' הרי אלו שלהן לאפוקי דרבה פי' למעט את אדוניה ממציאתה. ויש אומר לאפוקי מהא דאמר רבא בפ' האשה נקנית זאת אומרת עבד עברי גופו קנוי באה משנתנו להוציא מזה הטעם של רבא. מציאת אשה שגירשה אע"פ שלא נתן לה עדיין כתובתה מציאתה שלה. אוקימנא במגורשת ואינה מגורשת פי' בתלמוד א"י אדם שגירש את אשתו ולא נתן לה כתובתה חייב במזונותיה עד שיתן לה פרוטה אחרונה. אמר ר' יוסי מתני' אמרה כן אמר ר' אושעיא שלא תאמר הואיל וחייב במזונותיה עד שיתן לה כתובתה תהא מציאתה שלו קמ"ל דלא. מתני' מצא שטרי חוב אם יש בהן אחריות נכסים לא יחזיר. אוקימנא כשחייב מודה. ואמאי לא יחזיר דחיישינן שמא כתב ללוות בניסן ולא לוה עד תשרי וטורף ללקוחות שלא כדין. אי הכי כל שטרי דעלמא נמי נימא הכי. ודחי' כל שטרי דעלמא לא ריעי הני כיון דנפלי ריעי. אלא הא דתנן כותבין שטר ללוה אע"פ שאין מלוה

**מסורת הש"ס**

א) גיטין ל. בכורות יח., ב) לעיל י., לקמן קיח., ג) גיטין סד., ד) קדושין טז., ה) [קונה את עצמה כצ"ל], ו) כתובות מז: ע"ש, גיטין עד. ע"ש, בבא בתרא מז: ע"ש, ז) כתובות נא., [לקמן יח., יט.], ח) [בבא בתרא קסז:], ט) עי' רש"י וברש"י תוס' ו. ד"ה קופיא, י) צ"ל ורבה, יא) [אלו נערות מ:], יב) [וע"ע תוס' כתובות מז. ד"ה משום איבה], יג) [כתובות כא:].

**הגהות הב"ח**

(א) גמ' ופליגא אדר' חייא: (ב) תום' ד"ה ר' יוחנן וכו' בנו ובתו הגדולים לשמואל דאמר הכא: (ג) ד"ה כותבין וכו' ידי סהדי אחתימת ידייהו פסולה דהכא:

**הגהות הגר"א**

[א] תוס' ד"ה ר"י מפרש ר"ת כו'. נ"ב ורמב"ם חולק: [ב] שם ד"ה ששכרו וה"פ כו'. נ"ב והרמ"ה מפרש ששכרו סתם ומראה ללקט לו מציאות:

**ליקוטי רש"י**

עשו שאינו זוכה כזוכה. במקומות הרבה מפני התקנה עשו כן לרבי יוסי בהניזקין (לקמן דף נט:) עני המנקף בראש הזית ומלודות חיות ועופות ומציאת חרש ובבכורות (דף יח:) כל שחליפיו ביד כהן פטור מן המתנות ובגמרא דשנים אוחזין (ב"מ דף יב:) השוכר את הפועל ללקט בנו אחריו אע"פ שאין זכיה לקטן עשאוהו כזוכה ובכולן י"ל מפני תקנה עשו [גיטין ל.]. אע"פ שלא זכה כהן בהן מן התורה דלא אתו לידיה מעולם עשאוהו כאילו זכה בו הואיל ומעיקרא היה יכול למיהב ביה יד כהן דשמא ליה לא שויה רבנן כמאן דממטי לידיה לשם בכורה [בכורות יח.]. נכש עמי היום. דלא נשכר עמו אלא לניכוש ועידור והגבהת המציאה אין זו ממלאכת בעה"ב וקנאה פועל והוא יכול לנכות משכרו שכר פעולת ניכוש ועידור של אותה שעה. אמר לו עשה עמי מלאכה היום. כל מלאכה שהוא עושה מלאכת בעה"ב היא וכו' [לעיל י.]. במיתת האב. אביה [קדושין יח.]. במגורשת ואינה מגורשת. ומן האירוסין ולא לאשמועינן דלא תמכור לכתובתה אלא בב"ד מן האירוסין משמעינן לה אלא אגב אורחיה לאשמועינן דמגורשת ואינה מגורשת כגון זרק לה גיטה ספק קרוב לה ספק קרוב לו ברה"ר היתומים [כתובות צז:]. כגון זרק לה גט ספק קרוב לה ספק קרוב לו דבעלה חייב במזונותיה עד דיהיב לה גט ודאי כר' זירא וליכא למימר כיון דמגורשת היא ואינה מגורשת אשתו היא וחייב במזונותיה והכניס לה בעל קרקע זו בידה כדי שתזון מפירותיה ולא הויא מוקא דכיון

דהתחיל בגירושין והוא שונא לה לא יחד לה קרקע למזונותיה כי בשעת יחוד לה מזונות בגלגלות כשמחייבים ב"ד. חייב במזונותיה. דלאכי אגידא ביה [רשב"ם ב"ב קעה:]. יש בהן אחריות נכסים. שכתוב בו נכסיו בב"ד מלוה מוללה למלוה ולפני הלוה מודה שהוא חייב ומפרש בגמרא דחיישינן שמא פרעו ומן הלוה הוא שנפל וזה היא ביניים לטרוף לקוחות ולחלוק ביניים [כתובות נא.]. אין בהן אחריות נכסים. יחזיר שאין ב"ד נפרעין מהן. ואינו גובה מנכסים משועבדים [צה.]. וחכמים אומרים כו'. דאחריות טעות סופר ומפסידי לקוחות [שם ע"א]. כותבין שטר ללוה. להיות מזומן בידו לתת למלוה כשילוה לו מעות אע"פ שאין מלוה עמו [רשב"ם ב"ב קסז:].

עָשׂוּ שֶׁאֵינוֹ זוֹכֶה כְּזוֹכֶה – Although in general a minor cannot acquire an ownerless article on his own behalf, in this instance of *leket,* **[the Rabbis] made** the minor son, **who does not** normally **acquire** on his own behalf, **like [a person] who can acquire** on his own behalf.[1] מַאי טַעְמָא – **What is the reason** for this Rabbinic enactment? עֲנִיִּים גּוּפַיְיהוּ נִיחָא לְהוּ – Because the other **paupers themselves are agreeable** to have it so, since it is in their own interest to allow such an arrangement כִּי הֵיכִי דְּכִי אָגְרוּ לְדִידְהוּ – **in order that when people hire them** to harvest a crop in exchange for a share of the crop, נִלְקוּט בְּנַיְיהוּ בַּתְרַיְיהוּ – **their** own minor **sons should** be able to **collect** *leket* **behind them.**

The Gemara now returns to discuss the Mishnah:

וּפְלִיגָא דְּר׳ חִיָּיא בַּר אַבָּא – **And [Shmuel],** who explained that the reason for the Mishnah's ruling that a minor's find belongs to his father is because the son picks up the object on behalf of his father, **differs with R' Chiya bar Abba:** דְּאָמַר רַבִּי חִיָּיא בַּר אַבָּא אָמַר רַבִּי יוֹחָנָן – **For R' Chiya bar Abba said in the name of R' Yochanan** in explanation of our Mishnah: לֹא גָּדוֹל גָּדוֹל מַמָּשׁ – **The "son . . . who is of age"** mentioned in the Mishnah is **not literally "of age,"** וְלֹא קָטָן קָטָן מַמָּשׁ – **nor is the "minor son"** mentioned in the Mishnah **literally a minor.** אֶלָּא גָּדוֹל וְסָמוּךְ עַל שֻׁלְחַן אָבִיו זֶהוּ קָטָן – **Rather,** even **an adult who is dependent on his father's table,** i.e. he is supported by his father, **is** considered **a "minor"** in the context of our Mishnah; קָטָן וְאֵינוֹ סָמוּךְ עַל שֻׁלְחַן אָבִיו זֶהוּ גָּדוֹל – **and** even **a minor who is not dependent on his father's table is** considered **"of age"** in the context of our Mishnah.[2]

The Gemara now discusses that part of the Mishnah which states:

מְצִיאַת עַבְדּוֹ וְשִׁפְחָתוֹ הָעִבְרִים – THE FIND OF ONE'S HEBREW SERVANT OR MAIDSERVANT . . . הֲרֵי הוּא שֶׁל עַצְמָן – THESE BELONG TO THEM.

The Gemara questions the Mishnah's ruling:

אַמַּאי – **Why** should this be so? לֹא יְהֵא אֶלָּא פּוֹעֵל – **Let [the Hebrew servant] be** considered **no more than a laborer,** וְתַנְיָא – **and it was taught in a Baraisa:** מְצִיאַת פּוֹעֵל לְעַצְמוֹ – A WORKER'S FIND, i.e. an ownerless article that a hired worker picks up during his hours of employment, BELONGS TO HIM, not to his employer. בַּמֶּה דְּבָרִים אֲמוּרִים – WHEN IS THIS RULING SAID? בִּזְמַן שֶׁאָמַר לוֹ נַכֵּשׁ עִמִּי הַיּוֹם – WHEN [THE EMPLOYER] SAID TO HIM, "WEED FOR ME TODAY," עֲדוֹר עִמִּי הַיּוֹם – or "DIG FOR ME TODAY," i.e. he hired him for a specific task. אֲבָל אָמַר לוֹ עֲשֵׂה עִמִּי מְלָאכָה הַיּוֹם – IF, HOWEVER, [THE EMPLOYER] SAID TO HIM, "WORK FOR ME TODAY," without specifying a type of work, מְצִיאָתוֹ לְבַעַל הַבַּיִת – then HIS FIND BELONGS TO THE EMPLOYER.[3] Now, the master has acquired his Hebrew servant so that the servant should perform all manner of work for him. Thus, even if the servant was not actually owned by the master but merely a worker hired for all manner of work, his find would belong to the master. Why, then, does the Mishnah rule that the servant may keep his find for himself?

The Gemara offers several answers to this question:

אָמַר רַבִּי חִיָּיא בַּר אַבָּא אָמַר רַבִּי יוֹחָנָן – **R' Chiya bar Abba said in the name of R' Yochanan:** הָכָא בְּעֶבֶד נוֹקֵב מַרְגָּלִיּוֹת עַסְקִינָן – **Here** in the Mishnah **we are dealing with a servant who drills** holes in **pearls** (or is otherwise highly skilled), שֶׁאֵין רַבּוֹ רוֹצֶה לְשַׁנּוֹתוֹ לִמְלָאכָה אַחֶרֶת – **whose master does not wish to transfer him to any other work.** Since the servant is engaged in such a profitable labor, it would be unusual for it to be worthwhile for him to take off time to pick up a find. Our Mishnah deals with the unusual case in which the servant discovered a find whose value exceeded the value of the time necessary to acquire it. Since the master did not envisage such a happenstance, he never intended for the servant to acquire finds for him as part of his duties. The servant is therefore free to acquire the find for himself.[4]

A second answer:

רָבָא אָמַר – **Rava says:** בְּמַגְבִּיהַּ מְצִיאָה עִם מְלַאכְתּוֹ עַסְקִינָן – **We are dealing** in the Mishnah **with a case where [the servant] picks up a find while continuing to do his work** at the same time. Since he did not take off any time from his duties, he has discharged his duty to his master, and is free to acquire the find for himself.[5]

A third answer:

רַב פָּפָּא אָמַר – **Rav Pappa says:** כְּגוֹן שֶׁשְּׂכָרוֹ לְלַקֵּט מְצִיאוֹת – **[The Baraisa,]** which taught that the find of a laborer belongs to his employer, is dealing **with a case in which [the employer] hired him to collect finds?** וְהֵיכִי דָּמֵי – **And what is the case?** I.e. how could it happen that an employer would busy his workers with collecting finds? דְּאַקְפֵּי אַגְמָא בְּכַוְורֵי – This could happen **where,** for example, **the lake overflowed and beached fish** on the shore. In such a case an employer might hire workers specifically to collect the ownerless fish.[6]

NOTES

1. I.e. the Rabbis enacted that the sharecropper's minor son, who under Biblical law cannot make acquisition of the *leket* and then convey it to his father, should be as one who acquires the *leket* on his own behalf [and only then conveys it to the crop owner] (*Rashi*). In other words, though from the standpoint of Biblical law, it should be forbidden for the sharecropper's minor son to collect *leket* from this field, the Rabbis – using the authority vested in them by the Torah to legislate as they see fit in monetary matters – instituted that this should be permitted and the sharecropper should not be deemed to be in violation of the other paupers' rights.

2. R' Chiya bar Abba holds that the underlying rationale of the Mishnah is that whenever the father supports his child financially, the Sages awarded him the child's finds, regardless of the child's age, in order to prevent ill will; if the father's financial efforts on the child's behalf were unrequited by the child's finds accruing to the father, the father might become resentful. Where the child is not supported by the father, the Sages did not award the child's finds to the father. Accordingly, the term "minor" in the Mishnah refers to a son who is financially dependent on the father, and a "son who is of age" refers to a financially independent son. In contrast, according to Shmuel, who holds that the Mishnah's ruling is based on the observation that young children bring their finds to their fathers, the terms "minor" and "of age" in the Mishnah refer to actual chronological age (see *Rashi*).

3. The rationale for the distinction between a laborer who was hired to do work in general and one who was hired for a specific task is that in the first case the "work" of acquiring finds is also encompassed by the terms under which he was engaged, and the employer can, therefore, lay claim to the proceeds of that "work," whereas in the latter case the laborer was not engaged to do the "work" of acquiring finds, but only to do the specific task for which he was hired (see above, 10a notes 11 and 12).

4. The servant must, however, recompense the master for any time he takes off from drilling pearls in order to acquire the find (*Rashi;* see above, 10a).

5. [Although the servant is obligated to do all manner of work for his master, he is not obligated to do more than one task at a time. Thus, it is his *primary* task that is being done in the employ of his master; the secondary activity of picking up the ownerless article, which the servant does simultaneously with his primary task, is done on his own behalf.]

6. [Unlike the first two answers, Rav Pappa's answer qualifies the case of the Baraisa concerning the worker, rather than the case of our Mishnah concerning the servant.] According to Rav Pappa, a worker may keep his find even if he was hired to perform all manner of work for his employer. What the Baraisa means by "work for me today" is "work for me today *at the task of collecting finds.*" Accordingly, the Baraisa is

עשו שאינו זוכה כזוכה מ"ט עניים גופייהו ניחא להו כי היכי דכי אגרו לדידהו נלקוט בנייהו בתרייהו ופליגא (א) דר' חייא בר אבא דאמר רבי חייא בר אבא אמר רבי יוחנן לא גדול גדול ממש ולא קטן קטן ממש אלא גדול וסמוך על שלחן אביו זהו קטן קטן ואינו סמוך על שלחן אביו זהו גדול: מציאת עבדו ושפחתו העברים הרי הוא של עצמן: אמאי לא יהא אלא פועל ותניא מציאת פועל לעצמו במה דברים אמורים בזמן שאמר לו נכש עמי היום עדור עמי היום אבל אמר לו עשה עמי מלאכה היום מציאתו לבעל הבית אמר רבי חייא בר אבא אמר רבי יוחנן הכא בעבד נוקב מרגליות עסקינן שאין רבו רוצה לשנותו למלאכה אחרת רבא אמר במגביה מציאה עם מלאכתו עסקינן רב פפא אמר כגון ששכרו ללקט מציאות והיכי דמי דאקפי אגמא בכוורי: האי שפחה היכי דמי אי דאייתי שתי שערות מאי בעיא גביה ואי דלא אייתי שתי שערות אי איתיה לאב דאבוה הויא ואי דליתיה לאב תיפוק במיתת האב דאמר ריש לקיש אמה העבריה קנה עצמה במיתת האב מרשות האדון מקל וחומר ולאו איתותב ריש לקיש נימא מהאי נמי תיהוי תיובתא לא לעולם דאיתיה לאב ומאי הרי הן שלהן לאפוקי דרבה: מציאת אשתו: גירשה פשיטא הכא במאי עסקינן במגורשת ואינה מגורשת דאמר רבי זירא אמר שמואל כל מקום שאמרו חכמים מגורשת ואינה מגורשת בעלה חייב במזונותיה טעמא מאי אמור רבנן מציאת אשה לבעלה כי היכי דלא תיהוי לה איבה הכא אית לה איבה ואיבה:

מתני' מצא שטרי חוב אם יש בהן אחריות נכסים לא יחזיר שבית דין נפרעין מהן אין בהן אחריות נכסים יחזיר שאין בית דין נפרעין מהן דברי רבי מאיר וחכמים אומרים בין כך ובין כך לא יחזיר מפני שבית דין נפרעין מהן:

גמ' במאי עסקינן אילימא כשחייב מודה כי יש בהן אחריות נכסים אמאי לא יחזיר הא מודה ואי כשאין חייב מודה כי אין בהן אחריות נכסים אמאי יחזיר נהי דלא גבי ממשעבדי מבני חרי מגבא גבי לעולם כשחייב מודה והכא היינו טעמא דחיישינן שמא כתב ללות בניסן ולא לוה עד תשרי ואתי למטרף לקוחות שלא כדין אי הכי כל שטרי דאתו לקמן ניחוש להו הכי כל שטרי לא ריעי הני ריעי אלא הא דתנן כותבין שטר ללוה אף על פי שאין מלוה עמו לכתחילה היכי כתבינהו ניחוש שמא כתב ללות בניסן ולא לוה עד תשרי ואתי למטרף לקוחות שלא כדין אמר רב אסי

בשטרי

**רש"י**

עשו את שאינו זוכה כזוכה. אע"פ שאין לקטן זכייה במקום אחר כאן עשאוהו כזוכה: מאי טעמא עניים גופייהו ניחא להו. בהאי תקנתא דכי אגרו להו לדידהו כו': ופליגא. דשמואל דפירש טעמא דמתני' משום דלית ליה זכייה: אדר' חייא בר אבא. דאמר אף גדול שיש לו זכייה אם סמוך הוא על שולחן אביו מציאתו לאביו משום איבה אבל אינו סמוך על שולחן אביו אפילו הוא קטן מציאתו שלו: לא יהא אלא פועל. לא יהא עבדו אלא שכיר בעלמא תניא דמציאתו לבעל הבית בזמן שלא פירש לו לאיזו מלאכה שכרו ועבד זה כשקנאו רבו לסתם מלאכה קנאו: שאין רבו רוצה לשנותו. הלכך לא ניחא ליה שיגביה לו מציאה דמציאה מעולה בדמיה משכר ביטול מלאכתו לא שכיחא הלכך אי אתרמי ואשכח שלו הוא וישלם לרבו שכר ביטולו: עם מלאכתו. שלא ביטל כלום הלכך לעצמו: רב פפא אמר. הא דתניא פועל מציאתו לבעל הבית: ששכרו ללקט מציאות. הרבה: והיכי דמי. דאתרמי: דאקפי אגמא בכוורי. שצף הנהר חוץ לגדותיו וצפו הדגים שם וכשיבשו המים היוצאים נמצאו שם דגים הרבה. דאקפי תרגום של הציף כדמתרגמינן ויצף הברזל וקפא ברזלא (מלכים ב ו): מאי בעיא גביה. הא תניא יוצאה בסימנין: דאבוה הויא. מציאתה דהא קטנה היא: ואי דליתיה לאב. מאי בעיא גבי האדון תיפוק מיניה במיתת האב: מקל וחומר. בפרק קמא דקדושין (דף טז.) מה סימנין שאין מוציאין מרשות האב מוציאין מרשות האדון כדילפינן ויצאה חנם אלו ימי בגרות אין כסף אלו ימי נערות מיתת האב שמוציאה מרשות האב שאינו מוריש לבניו מה שזכתה לו תורה בבתו שיהא מעשה ידיה לאחין כדילפינן (כתובות דף מג.) והתנחלתם אותם לבניכם ולא בנותיכם לבניכם אינו דין שמוציאה מרשות האדון: ולאו איתותב רבי שמעון בן לקיש. בקדושין (שם): לאפוקי דרבה. לאפוקי שאינו של רבה אלא של אביה וקרי ליה שלהן משום דאב מינה קוזי: במגורשת ואינה מגורשת. כגון זרק לה גיטה ספק קרוב לה ספק קרוב לו ברה"ר: חייב במזונותיה. ומשום הכי אצטריך לאשמועינן דמציאתה שלה דטעמא מאי אמור רבנן מציאת האשה כו': מתני' אחריות נכסים. שעבוד קרקעות שיגבה מהן: יחזיר ולא יחזיר. טעמא בגמ' מפרש: גמ' כשחייב מודה. שהלוה מודה שהשטר אינו פרוע: אמאי לא יחזיר. אם לטרוף לקוחות בא בדין הוא טורפן: ממשעבדי. ממקרקעי שמכר אחרי כן: הני ריעי. הואיל ונפל אתרע דיש לומר אם היה כשר היה נזהר בו:

בשטרי

אביי

**תוספות**

רבי יוחנן אמר לא גדול גדול ממש. [א] מפרש ר"ת כי היכי דפליגי הכא פליגי נמי גבי עירוב דתנן בפ' חלון (עירובין דף עט: ושם ד"ה ומזכה) ומזכה להם על ידי בנו ובתו (ב) ולשמואל דאמר הכא קטן ממש התם נמי גבי עירוב אינו זוכה דידו כיד אביו כיון דמציאתו לאביו ה"ה כל זכיותיו לאביו ואמה העבריה אע"פ שהיא קטנה זכיא בעירובה דמציאתה אינה לאדוניה אף על גב דשמואל אית ליה פרק התקבל (גיטין דף סד: ושם ד"ה אלא) קטן זוכה לעצמו ואינו זוכה לאחרים הא משני התם שאני שתופי מבואות דרבנן והא דאמר שמואל פרק מי שהוציאוהו (עירובין דף מט. ושם: ד"ה וקטן) דעירוב משום קנין ורבא אמר משום דירה ואמר איכא בינייהו קטן הא פר"ת התם דאית ליה בית לקטן קאמר ולא כפרש"י שפי' שאינו גובה העירוב לפי שאינו זוכה ולר"י דאמר לא גדול גדול ממש ה"ה דגבי עירוב נמי דקטן ואינו סמוך על שולחן אביו זוכה כאמה העבריה וגדול סמוך על שולחן אביו אינו זוכה וצריך ליזהר שלא לזכות העירוב ע"י בנו הגדול הסמוך לשולחנו דקי"ל כרבי יוחנן לגבי שמואל כדאמר פרק מי שהוציאוהו (שם מז:) ועבדו ושפחתו העברים אע"ג דסמוכין על שולחנו מציאתם לעצמם וכן זוכין בעירוב ולא הוי ידם כיד האדון דלא שייך איבה אלא בבנו שדרכו לזונו תמיד ואם לא יפרנסו אביו לא יפרנסו אחר אבל אדם אחר מעלמא סמוך על שולחן חבירו חנם כגון יתום וכיוצא בו אין סברא שתהא מציאתו לחבירו וכ"ש עבד ואמה שבשכר טרחם הם אוכלים ובתו אפילו נערה ואינה סמוכה על שולחן אביה מציאתה לאביה משום איבה דאי בעי מסר לה למנוול ומוכה שחין כדאמר בפרק נערה (כתובות דף מו ושם) ולא כרש"י שפירש משום דכתיב בנעוריה דההוא בהפרת נדרים הוא דכתיב כדאיתא בפרק קמא דקדושין (דף ג: ושם) ופרק נערה (שם מו:) ואשתו דזכיא בעירוב אף על גב דידה כיד בעלה מוקי לה בסוף נדרים (דף פח:) דאית לה בית באותו מבוי דמגו דזכיא לנפשה זכיא נמי לאחריני: **במגביה** מציאה עם מלאכתו. וא"ת הא דתניא בפ"ק דקדושין (דף טז:) אמה העבריה מציאתה לאביה ושכר בטלה לרבה היכי מתוקמא אליבא דרבא דאם הגביהה עם מלאכתו ליכא שכר בטלה ואם לא הגביהה עם מלאכתו א"כ מציאתה לאדוניה וי"ל דהתם ודאי צריך להעמיד בנוקבת מרגליות: **ששכרו** ללקט מציאות. [ב] וה"פ דברייתא בד"א בזמן שאמר ליה עשה עמי באותו ענין שהוא כמו נכש עמי היום אבל אמר ליה עשה עמי מלאכה של מציאות כו': **מאי** בעיא גביה. דהיא נמי אינה יכולה למכור עצמה אחרי כן כדאיתא בספרי: **ולא** לוה עד תשרי. פירוש ועתה רוצה ללות בו שיש לו טורח לכתוב שטר אחר וגם כדי להרויח פשיטי דספרא אבל אין לפרש שכבר לוה בו קודם שנפל דא"כ מאי משני הני ריעי לפי שנפל ויש הוכחה דמשום פסולו לא נזהר לשומרו והא לוה בו כבר ופשיטא שנזהר לשומרו: **כותבין** שטר ללוה אף על פי שאין מלוה עמו. וליכא למיחש למחזי לשקרא כמו באשרתא דדייני דאם כתבו קודם דנחזי חתימת ידי סהדי (ג) פסולה דהכא כיון שהוא כותב חובתו לא שייך מחזי כשקרא:

**עין משפט נר מצוה**

קד א מיי' פי"ז מהל' אבידה הל' יג סמג עשין עד טוש"ע ח"מ סי' ער סעיף ג:
קה ב ג מיי' פ"ט מהל' שכירות הל' יא סמג שם טוש"ע שם סעיף ג:
קו ד מיי' פי"ז מהל' אבידה הל' יג סמג עשין עד (טוש"ע ח"מ סי' ער סעיף ב):
קז ה מיי' שם סמג שם טוש"ע ח"מ שם סעיף ב וטוש"ע אה"ע סי' פד:
קח ו מיי' פי"ח מהל' אישות הלכה כה טוש"ע אה"ע סי' לג סעיף ג:
קט ז ח מיי' פי"ח מהל' אבידה הלכה א סמג עשין עד טוש"ע ח"מ סי' סה סעיף ו:
קי ט מיי' פכ"ג מהל' מלוה ולוה הלכה ה ופכ"ד שם הל' א סמג עשין צד טוש"ע ח"מ סי' לט סעיף יג:

**רבינו חננאל**

ואסקה רבא עשו הקטן שאינו זוכה לעצמו מן התורה כזוכה מאי טעמא עניים גופייהו מחלי ליה דניחא להו דנלקטו בנייהו נמי בתרייהו דידהו ולפיכך אמר ר' יוסי בניו ואשתו מלקטין אחריו. פי' אינו זוכה כזוכה כדתנן פרק כל גט שנכתב שלא לשם אשה פסול. המלוה מעות את הכהן ואת הלוי ואת העני וכו' ואוקימנא אע"ג דלא אתו לידייהו כו'. ועולא אמר הא מני ר' יוסי היא דאמר עשו את שאינו זוכה כזוכה דתנן בבכורות כל שחליפין ביד כהן פטור מן המתנות וכו' עשו את שאינו זוכה כזוכה מאי טעמא עשאוה כשדה שהלכו בה הנמושות עניים גופייהו מסחו דעתייהו מההיא שדה אמרי בניו ואשתו דהאיך מלקטי בתריה פי' עשאוה כשדה שהלכו בה הנמושות כדתנינן מאימתי כל אדם מותרין בלקט ובשכחה ובפאה משהלכו בה הנמושות. ופליגא הא דר' יוחנן דאמר לא גדול גדול ממש ולא קטן קטן ממש אלא [גדול] וסמוך על שולחן אביו זהו קטן. קטן ואינו סמוך על שולחן אביו זהו גדול אדשמואל. מציאת עבדו ושפחתו העברים הרי אלו שלהם. ומקשי' והתניא בפועל אם שכרו עשה עמי מלאכה מציאתו לבעה"ב ולא יהיה העבד כפועל ומשני ר' יוחנן בקונה עבד נוקב מרגליות דאין רבו רוצה לשנותו למלאכה אחרת דלאו עשה עמי מלאכה הוא אלא במלאכה זו בלבד לפיכך ל"א נשתעבד לאדונו אלא באותה מלאכה בלבד. רבא אמר במגביה מציאה זו עם מלאכתו דלא בטל ממלאכת רבו. רב פפא אמר כי קתני בפועל מציאתו לבעה"ב כגון דאקפי אגמא בכוורי ושכרו ללקוט לו בכוורי. ושפחתו. הא שפחה היכי דמיא אי דאייתי ב' שערות וכו' עד אמר לך ריש לקיש לעולם דאיתיה לאב ומציאתה לאביה היא והאי דקתני במתני' הרי אלו שלהן לאפוקי דרבה פי' למעט את אדוניה ממציאתה. ויש אומר לאפוקי מהא דאמר רבא בפ' האשה נקנית זאת אומרת עבד עברי גופו קנוי באה משנתנו להוציא מזה הטעם של רבא. מציאת אשה שגירשה אע"פ שלא נתן לה עדיין כתובתה מציאתה שלה. אוקימנא במגורשת ואינה מגורשת פי' בתלמוד א"י אדם שגירש את אשתו ולא נתן לה כתובתה חייב במזונותיה עד שיתן לה פרוטה אחרונה. אמר ר' יוסי מתני' אמורה כן אמר ר' אושעיא שלא תאמר הואיל וחייב במזונותיה עד שיפרע כתובתה תהא מציאתה שלו לפום כן תני מציאת אשה שגירשה לעצמה: מצא שטרי חוב אם יש בהן אחריות נכסים לא יחזיר. אוקימנא כשחייב מודה. ואמאי לא יחזיר דחיישינן שמא כתב ללות בניסן ולא לוה עד תשרי וטורף ללקוחות שלא כדין. אי הכי כל שטרי נימא הכי. ודחי' כל שטרי דעלמא לא ריעי הני כיון דנפלי ריעי. אלא הא דתנן כותבין שטר ללוה אע"פ שאין מלוה

**מסורת הש"ס**

א) גיטין ל. בכורות יח., ב) לעיל י., לקמן קיח., ג) גיטין סד., ד) קדושין טז., ה) [קונה את עצמה כל"ל], ו) כתובות לז: ע"ש, גיטין עד. ע"ש, בבא בתרא מז: ע"ש, ז) כתובות נא., [לקמן יז., יט.], ח) [בבא בתרא קסז:], ט) עי' רש"י זבחים ו. ד"ה קופיה, י) ל"ל ורבה, יא) [אלו נערות מ:], יב) [וע"ע תוס' כתובות מז. ד"ה משום איבה], יג) [כתובות כא:].

**הגהות הב"ח**

(א) גמ' ופליגא אדר' חייא: (ב) תוס' ד"ה ר' יוחנן וכו' בנו ובתו הגדולים ולשמואל דאמר הכא: (ג) ד"ה כותבין וכו' ידי סהדי אחתימת ידייהו פסולה דהכא:

**הגהות הגר"א**

[א] תוס' ד"ה ר"י מפרש ר"ת כו'. נ"ב ורמב"ם חולק: [ב] שם ד"ה ששכרו וה"פ כו'. נ"ב והרמ"ה מפרש ששכרו סתם ומראה ללקט לו מציאות:

**ליקוטי רש"י**

עשו שאינו זוכה כזוכה. במקומות הרבה מפני התקנה עשו כן לרבי יוסי בהניזקין (לקמן דף נט:) עני המנקף בראש הזית ומלודות חיות ועופות ומציאת חרש ובבכורות (דף יח:) כל שחליפיו ביד כהן פטור מן המתנות ובגמרא דשנים אוחזין (ב"מ דף יב:) השוכר את הפועל ילקט בנו אחריו דאף על פי שאין זכיה לקטן עשאוהו כזוכה ובכולן י"ל מפני תקנה עשו [גיטין ל.]. אע"פ שלא זכה כהן בהאיך דהא לא מטא לידיה מעולם עשאוהו כאילו זכה בו הואיל ומעיקרא הוה שייכא ביה יד כהן דשמא דידיה הוא שויה רבנן כמאן דמטא לידיה לשום בכורה [בכורות יח.]. נכש עמי היום. דלא נשכר עמו אלא לניכוש ועידור וכשהגביה המציאה אין זו ממלאכת בעה"ב וקנאה פועל והוא ינכה לו משכרו שכר פעולת ניכוש ועידור כל שעת הגבהה. אמר לו עשה עמי מלאכה היום. כל מלאכה שהוא עושה מלאכת בעה"ב היא וקנה בעה"ב וכו' [לעיל י.]. במיתת האב. אביה [קדושין טז.]. במגורשת ואינה מגורשת. ומן האירוסין ולא לאשמעינן דלא תמכור לכתובתה אלא בב"ד דהא מאלמנה מן האירוסין שמעינן לה אלא אגב אורחיה אשמעינן דמגורשת ואינה מגורשת כגון זרק לה גיטה ספק קרוב לה ספק קרוב לו ברה"ר אין לה מזונות מן היתומים אם מת [כתובות צז:]. כגון זרק לה גט ספק קרוב לה ספק קרוב לו דבעלה חייב במזונותיה עד דיהיב לה גט ודאי כר' זירא ואיכא למימר כיון דמגורשת ואינה מגורשת אשתו היא וחייב במזונותיה והניח לה בעל קרקע זו בידה כדי שתזון מפירותיה ולא הויא חזקה קמ"ל דהויא חזקה דכיון דהתחיל בגירושין והוא שונא לה לא יחד לה קרקע למזונותיה כי בטורח יתן לה מזונות בגלגלום כשיתבעוהו ב"ד. חייב במזונותיה. דלאכתי אגידא ביה [רשב"ם ב"ב מז:]. יש בהן אחריות נכסים. ששיעבד לוה נכסיו לאותה מלוה לא יחזירנו מולאו למלוה ואפי' הלוה מודה שהוא חייב לו ומפרש התם בדחיישינן שמא פרעו ומן הלוה נפל חה שהוא מודה עלת קנוניא היא ביניהם לטרוף לקוחות ויחלקו ביניהם [כתובות נא:]. אין בהן אחריות נכסים. שלא שיעבד לו לוה בשעת הלואה את נכסיו ולא כתב לו כל נכסי אחראין לך לפרוע מלוה זה. יחזיר שאין ב"ד נפרעין מהן. ואינו גובה מנכסים משועבדים ולא אמרינן אין לך אדם המלוה מעותיו בלא שעבוד נכסי לוה והסופר טעה ולא כתב בו אחריות אלא דוקא אזלינן בתר שטר [ב"ק צה.]. וחכמים אומרים כו'. דאחריות טעות סופר וטריף ממשעבדי ומפסדי לקוחות [שם ע"א]. כותבין שטר ללוה. להיות מזומן בידו לתת למלוה כשילוה לו מעות אע"פ שאין מלוה עמו ורשב"ם ב"ב קסז:].

## גמרא

חצר איתרבאי משום יד ולא גרעה משליחות גבי גט דחוב הוא לה א) אין חבין לאדם אלא בפניו גבי מתנה דזכות הוא לו ב) זכין לאדם שלא בפניו גופא ראה אותן רצין אחר המציאה וכו' אמר רבי ירמיה אמר רבי יוחנן והוא שרץ אחריהן ומגיען בעי רבי ירמיה [א] במתנה היאך קבלה מיניה ר' אבא בר כהנא אע"פ שרץ אחריהן ואין מגיען ג) בעי רבא זרק ארנקי בפתח זה ויצא בפתח אחר מהו ו) אויר שאין סופו לנוח כמונח דמי או לא אמר ליה רב פפא לרבא ואמרי לה רב אדא בר מתנה לרבא ואמרי לה רבינא לרבא לאו היינו מתניתין ראה אותן רצין אחר המציאה ואמר רבי ירמיה אמר רבי יוחנן והוא שרץ אחריהן ומגיען ובעי רבי ירמיה במתנה היאך וקבלה מיניה רבי אבא בר כהנא במתנה אף על פי שרץ אחריהן ואין מגיען אמר ליה מתגלגל קאמרת שאני מתגלגל דכמונח דמי:

**מתני'** ד) מציאת בנו ובתו הקטנים מציאת עבדו ושפחתו הכנענים ה) מציאת אשתו הרי אלו שלו ו) מציאת בנו ובתו הגדולים מציאת עבדו ושפחתו העברים מציאת אשתו שגירשה אע"פ שלא נתן כתובה הרי אלו שלהן:

**גמ'** אמר שמואל מפני מה אמרו מציאת קטן לאביו שבשעה שמוצאה מריצה אצל אביו ואינו מאחר בידו למימרא דסבר שמואל קטן לית ליה זכייה לנפשיה מדאורייתא והתניא השוכר את הפועל ילקט בנו אחריו למחצה לשליש ולרביע לא ילקט בנו אחריו רבי יוסי אומר ז) בין כך ובין כך ילקט בנו ואשתו אחריו ואמר שמואל הלכה כרבי יוסי אי אמרת בשלמא קטן אית ליה זכייה לנפשיה (א) כי קא מלקט לנפשיה קא מלקט ואבוה מיניה קא זכי אלא אי אמרת קטן לית ליה זכייה לנפשיה כי קא מלקט לאביו קא מלקט (ב) אבוה עשיר הוא אמאי אשתו ובנו מלקט אחריו שמואל טעמא דתנא דידן קאמר וליה לא סבירא ליה וסבר רבי יוסי קטן אית ליה זכייה מדאורייתא ד) והתנן ח) מציאת חרש שוטה וקטן יש בהן משום גזל מפני דרכי שלום רבי יוסי אומר גזל גמור ואמר רב חסדא ט) גזל גמור מדבריהן נפקא מינה להוציאה בדיינין אלא אמר אביי עשאוה כמי שהלכו בה נמושות דעניים גופייהו מסחי דעתייהו סברי בריה דהיאך מלקטי ליה א"ל רב אדא בר מתנה לאביי ט) וכי מותר לאדם להרביץ ארי בתוך שדהו כדי שיראו עניים ויברחו אלא אמר רבא עשו

## רש"י

גבי מתנה דזכות הוא לו זכין לו לאדם שלא בפניו. ושלא מדעתו (ג) דאנן סהדי דניחא ליה שתהא שלוחו הלכך כי ליתיה בצד חצרו דליכא למהוי לידה דאינה סמוכה לה תיפוק לה זכייתה משליחותה כי היכי דשלוחו זוכה לו שלא בפניו חצרו נמי זוכה לו שלא בפניו ומיהו גבי מציאה כי ליתיה גבה דלא נפקא זכייתה משום יד ליכא לרבויי משליחות דגבי שליחות איכא דעת השולח או דעת שליח אבל חצר ליכא לא דעת שולח ולא דעת שליח הלכך בעינן י) דעת אחרת מקנה אותו: זרק ארנקי. והפקירו לכל הקודם: שאין סופו לנוח. בתוך האויר: כמונח דמי. וקנאו בעל הבית הראשון או לאו כמונח דמי להכי בעי אויר שאין סופו לנוח בתוך הבית כמונח דמי דאילו אויר שהיה סופו לנוח בתוך הבית פשיטא לן דאפילו קדם איש אחר וקלטה בתוך האויר לא קנה דמשנכנס לאויר קנאו בעל הבית דתנן במסכת גיטין (דף עט.) היתה עומדת בראש הגג וזרק לה גט כיון שנכנס לאויר הגג הרי זו מגורשת הוא למעלה והיא למטה כיון שיצא מרשות הגג נמחק או נשרף הרי זו מגורשת: ואינו מגיען. אלמא מתגלגלים ויוצאין הן ואין סופן לנוח וקאמר דקנה ליה שדהו: מתני' מציאת בנו ובתו הקטנים כו'. בנו קטן בגמרא מפרש מ"ט בתו הקטנה בכתובות (דף מו:) ילפינן לה מקראי דקטנה ואף נערה כל שבח נעוריה לאביה: מציאת עבדו ושפחתו הכנענים שלו. שהרי גופו קנוי לו עולמית כדכתיב (ויקרא כה) והתנחלתם וגו': מציאת אשתו. רבנן תקינו ליה משום איבה: מציאת עבדו ושפחתו העברים. בגמ' פריך לא יהא אלא פועל דאמרינן לעיל (דף י.) מציאתו לבעל הבית: גמ' מפני מה אמרו מציאת קטן לאביו. בשלמא בתו ואשתו טעמא מפרש להו במקומן בכתובות אלא בנו טעמא מאי: מריצה אצל אביו. הלכך כשמגביה לצורך אביו הגביהה: ילקט בנו אחריו. מותר לבנו של פועל אם עני הוא ללקוט אחר אביו את לקט הנושר אבל אם קבל הפועל את השדה למחצה לשליש ולרביע עשיר הוא והרי הוא כבעל הבית בשדה זה ולא ילקט בנו אחריו לפי שלקט בנו לאביו: בין כך ובין כך כו'. דאם האב עשיר הבן עני חוכה לעצמו: טעמא דתנא דידן קאמר. מפני מה אמרו מציאת קטן לאביו: וליה לא ס"ל. דמציאת קטן לאביו: מדבריהם. מפני דרכי שלום: ונפקא מינה. מדר' יוסי הא אתא לאשמועינן דהחמירו חכמים בתקנתן כגזל גמור להוציאו בדיינין וכיון דמדאורייתא לית ליה זכייה נמצא אביו גוזל את העניים: אלא אמר אביי. רבי יוסי נמי כתנא דידן ס"ל דקטן לית ליה זכייה וגבי לקט היינו טעם דכיון דיש לו לפועל זה בנים ואשה עניים עצמן מייאשי מלקט שלה לפיכך עשאוה כשדה שהלכו בו הנמושות דתנן (פאה פ"ח מ"א) מאימתי כל אדם מותרין בלקט משילכו בו הנמושות לקוטי בתר לקוטי דמההיא שעתא מסחו עניים דעתייהו מיניה והכא נמי מסחו דעתייהו כו':

עשו

## תוספות

**חצר** משום יד אתרבאי. ולכך כי הוי דומיא דיד דהיינו כשהוא בצד חצרו קונה אפילו בע"כ או אפילו קטנה י) בידה וכשאינה סמוכה לחצרה דלא הוי דומיא דיד לא תימא כי היכי דאין לו דין יד הכי נמי אין לו דין שליחות אלא לא גרע משליחות [ב] ובמידי דזכות כמו מתנה קנה ואפילו אינו עומד בצד חצרו ואפילו אינה משתמרת ובמציאה דאין דעת אחרת מקנה אותה בעינן משתמרת ובגט דחוב הוא לה אפילו במשתמרת אינה מתגרשת דלא עדיפא משליחות דאין חבין לאדם שלא בפניו:

**ויצא** בפתח אחר. ל"ג ואפקריה דהא חשיב ליה דעת אחרת מקנה אותו דמייתי ראיה ממתנה ואי אפקריה אם כן מיד כשיצא הארנקי מידו היה הפקר ובשעת זכייה ליכא דעת אחרת אלא ל"ג ואפקריה ולעולם היא שלו עד שיזכה בה אחר:

**ואמר** שמואל הלכה כרבי יוסי. תימה דבפ' כל הגט (גיטין דף ל. ושם ד"ה כיחידאה) לא בעי שמואל לאוקמי מתניתין דהמלוה מעות את הכהן ואת הלוי ח) [להיות מפריש עליהן מחלקן] כרבי יוסי דכיחידאה לא מוקמינן ט) והכא פסיק הלכה כמותו וי"ל דדוקא הכא גבי לקט פסיק כוותיה מהאי טעמא דמסתמא עניים גופייהו ניחא להו כו' והא דאוקמי בפרק כל הגט (שם) כרבי יוסי היינו רבי יוסי דפ' הלוקח עובר פרתו (בכורות דף יח. ושם ד"ה עשו) דאמר כל שחליפיו ביד כהן פטור מן המתנות ומפרש טעמא בגמ' משום דעשו את שאינו זוכה כזוכה דהוי דומיא דהמלוה מעות דהוו חליפין ביד כהן דהיינו מעות ועשו כאילו זכה במעשר עצמו והא דקרי ליה יחידאה אע"ג דבבכורות לא פליג אלא ר"מ מ"מ רבנן דפליגי עליה הכא גבי לקט כ"ש דפליגי עליה התם גבי מתנות:

**אי** אמרת בשלמא דאורייתא. תימה מנ"ל דלר' יוסי קטן זוכה מן התורה וכן בסמוך דפריך וסבר רבי יוסי מציאת קטן דאורייתא ומנ"ל ודלמא אינה אלא מדרבנן ואביו לא זכה מיניה כלל ולהכי מלקט אחריו וי"ל דמסתמא לא פליג ר' יוסי אכמה משניות דפרקין ודפרק חלון (עירובין דף עט: ושם) ודמסכת מעשר שני (פ"ד מ"ד) דמייתי בפרק התקבל (גיטין דף סה. ושם) דלכולהו משניות יד בן כיד אביו וא"ת ונימא לעולם זכי לנפשיה מדרבנן ובתר הכי זכי אבוה מיניה משום איבה ומשום הכי מלקט וי"ל דמדרבנן אין סברא שיתקנו שתי זכיות שיזכה הבן קודם ואח"כ יזכה האב ממנו אלא אי מדרבנן הוא בשעת זכיית הבן בא לו זכיית האב משום דבשעת הגבהה לוקחה להרילה לאביו אלא ודאי זכה לנפשיה מדאורייתא ואבוה זכה מיניה משום איבה שסמוך על שלחנו:

**ואבוה** עשיר הוא. לאו דוקא עשיר אלא כלומר כיון שיש לו חלק בשדה חייב בלקט כדדרשינן לר"א פ"ק דגיטין (דף יב. ושם) לא תלקט לעני להזהיר עני על שלו ולרבנן נמי או נפקא להו מקרא אחרינא או תרתי ש"מ:

**שמואל** טעמא דתנא דידן קאמר. וא"ת אמאי לא אוקמה בטעמא דידיה דסבר שמואל דזכי לנפשיה מדאורייתא ומדרבנן אבוה זכי מיניה משום איבה וכרבי יוסי וי"ל דקטן דקתני במתני' משמע ליה בקטן ממש ואע"פ שאינו סמוך על שלחנו ואילו היה זוכה לעצמו מן התורה לא היה להם לתקן שיזכה אביו כיון דליכא איבה שהרי אינו סמוך על שולחנו אלא ודאי לא זכי לנפשיה כלל אלא לאביו שבשעת הגבהה מגביה לצורך אביו:

רבי

## עין משפט נר מצוה

צו א ב מיי' פ"ה מהל' גירושין הלכה ג ופ"ד מהל' זכייה ומתנה הל' ג [רב אלפס כאן ובגיטין פ"ח דף קפד.]:

צז ג טוש"ע ח"מ סי' רמג סעיף כד:

צח ד מיי' פי"ז מהל' גזילה ואבידה הל' יג סמג עשין עד טוש"ע ח"מ סי' ער סעיף ב:

צט ה מיי' שם ופי"ב מהל' אישות הל' ג ופכ"א שם הל' א סמג שם וסי' מח טוש"ע שם וטוש"ע אה"ע סי' סט סעיף ג וסי' פד:

ק ו מיי' פי"ז מהלכות גזילה ואבידה הל' יג סמג עשין עד טוש"ע ח"מ סי' ער סעיף ב וטוש"ע אה"ע סי' פד:

קא ז מיי' פ"ד מהל' מתנות עניים הל' יא:

קב ח מיי' פי"ז מהל' גזילה ואבידה הל' יב סמג עשין עד טוש"ע ח"מ סי' ער סעיף א:

קג ט מיי' פ"ד מהלכות מתנות עניים הל' יג:

## רבינו חננאל

ופריק רב אשי חצר איתרבי משום יד ולא גרעה משליחות גבי גט דחוב הוא לה אינה מגורשת אם זרק לה גיטה בעלה בחצירה אא"כ עומדת בצד חצירה כדתנן אין חבין לאדם אלא בפניו. אבל מתנה דזכות הוא לו אע"פ שאינו עומד בצד שדהו קנה כדתנן זכין לאדם שלא בפניו. ואסקי' צבי שבור וכיוצא בו אם רץ אחריהן ומגיען ואמר זכתה לי שדי זכתה לו שדהו והוא שעומד בצד שדהו. ואם היו תרבות והקנה לו אחד במתנה אע"פ אם ירוץ אחריהן אין יכול להגיעם כיון שעברו בתוך שדהו קנאם הואיל ומתגלגלין וקי"ל מתגלגל כמונח דמי: מתני' מציאת בנו ובתו הקטנים הרי הם שלו. אמר שמואל מפני מה אמרו מציאת קטן לאביו שבשעה שמוצאה מריצה אצל אביו ואינה מאחרה בידו. למימרא דסבר שמואל דקטן לית ליה זכייה לנפשיה והתניא פועל ילקט בנו אחריו למחצה לשליש ולרביע לא ילקט בנו אחריו. פי' כיון שיש לו חלק בתבואת השדה אפי' א) הוה ליה עשיר. ותנן מי שיש לו מאתים זוז הרי זה לא יטול לקט שכחה ופאה ומעשר כו'. ר' יוסי אומר בין כך ובין כך אשתו ובניו מלקטין אחריו. ואמר שמואל הלכה כר' יוסי ואי אמרת לאביו הוא זוכה אביו עשיר הוא. ודחי' שמואל טעמיה דתנא דידן קאמר וליה לא ס"ל. ושקלינו וטרינו לאוקמא דר' יוסי סבר אית ליה זכיי' לנפשי' ולא איתוקמא אלא מדרבנן אית ליה זכייה לנפשיה.

## חשק שלמה על ר"ח

א) אולי צ"ל ואפילו עני הוה ליה כעשיר.

## מסורת הש"ס

[קדושין כג. וש"נ], [ב"ק קב.], ג) [זבחים ...], ד) גיטין עט:, ... עוש מא., ה) [גיטין ...], ו) פ"א חצר משתמרת, מהרש"ל ... ז) ל"ל כידה, ח) מהרש"ל.

## הגהות הב"ח

(א) גמ' אית ליה זכייה לנפשיה מדאורייתא כי קא מלקט: (ב) שם ואבוה עשיר: (ג) רש"י ד"ה גבי מתנה וכו' דאנן סהדי ... נ"ב אע"ג דקי"ל ... דף יג ע"ב ודף קלא ... דשגא מתנות ... היכא שמעצמו אומר ... אבל מסתמא אמרי' ... ליה ליקח במתנה וק"ל:

## הגהות הגר"א

[א] גמ' במתנה היאך קבלה כו'. נ"ב פי' ... מב"ס דוקא כה"ג אבל ... לבי רך לא וכ"ע ... מ"ש רבינו בח"מ ... רס"ח ס"ק י"ג: [ב] תוס' ד"ה חצר ... מידי דזכות כו'. נ"ב ... פפא ורמב"ם פסק כההוא מרבנן:

## גליון הש"ס

תוס' ד"ה ואמר וכו' והכא פסיק הלכה כמותו. עיין גיטין יג ע"א תוס' ד"ה והא:

## ליקוטי רש"י

אין חבין לאדם אלא בפניו. אין אדם יכול לעשות שלוחו שלא מדעתו לדבר שהוא חובה ... [קדושין כג.]. ... שלא בפניו כלומר שלא מדעתו [כתובות יא.]. זכין לאדם שלא בפניו. ... [גיטין יא:]. גזל גמור. ... זוכה ... [גיטין נט:]. מדבריהם. ... בדיינים ומיהו ... עליו בלאו [שם סא.].

ollecting all the *leket* in it."[27]

Rav Adda bar Masnah objects to Abaye's resolution:

**אָמַר לֵיהּ רַב אַדָּא בַּר מַתְנָה לְאַבַּ – Rav Adda bar Masnah said to baye: וְכִי מוּתָּר לְאָדָם לְהַרְבִּיץ אֲרִי בְּתוֹךְ שָׂדֵהוּ כְּדֵי שֶׁיִּרְאוּ עֲנִיִּים וְיִבְרְחוּ – Is it permissible for someone to set a lion down in his field in order that the paupers should see it and run away?**[28] Certainly not!

Rava resolves the contradiction in R' Yose's view differently: **אֶלָּא אָמַר רָבָא – Rather, said Rava,** the correct resolution is as follows:

NOTES

27. [I.e. though it should be forbidden for the sharecropper's minor son collect *leket* behind his father, the other paupers assume that the son ll do so anyway and preempt them. Consequently, they despair of llecting the *leket* of that field, which thereupon becomes absolutely vnerless. The sharecropper's son (or even the sharecropper himself, for that matter) is therefore permitted to take the *leket* for himself.]

28. [I.e. how is the sharecropper allowed to bring his minor son to the field and thereby cause the other paupers to despair of collecting its *leket*?]

חצר איתרבאי משום יד ולא גרעה משליחות גבי גט דחוב הוא לה [א] אין חבין לאדם אלא בפניו גבי מתנה דזכות הוא לו [ב] זכין לאדם שלא בפניו גופא ראה אותן רצין אחר המציאה וכו' אמר רבי ירמיה אמר רבי יוחנן והוא שרץ אחריהן ומגיען בעי רבי ירמיה [א] במתנה היאך קבלה מיניה ר' אבא בר כהנא אע"פ שרץ אחריהן ואין מגיען [ג] בעי רבא זרק ארנקי בפתח זה ויצא בפתח אחר מהו [ג] אויר שאין סופו לנוח כמונח דמי או לא אמר ליה רב פפא לרבא ואמרי לה רב אדא בר מתנה לרבא ואמרי לה רבינא לרבא לאו היינו מתניתין ראה אותן רצין אחר המציאה ואמר רבי ירמיה אמר רבי יוחנן והוא שרץ אחריהן ומגיען ובעי רבי ירמיה במתנה היאך וקבלה מיניה רבי אבא בר כהנא במתנה אף על פי שרץ אחריהן ואין מגיען אמר ליה מתגלגל קאמרת שאני מתגלגל דכמונח דמי:

**מתני'** [ד] מציאת בנו ובתו הקטנים מציאת עבדו ושפחתו הכנענים [ה] מציאת אשתו הרי אלו שלו [ו] מציאת בנו ובתו הגדולים מציאת עבדו ושפחתו העברים מציאת אשתו שגירשה אע"פ שלא נתן כתובה הרי אלו שלהן:

**גמ'** אמר שמואל מפני מה אמרו מציאת קטן לאביו שבשעה שמוצאה מריצה אצל אביו ואינו מאחר בידו למימרא דסבר שמואל קטן לית ליה זכייה לנפשיה מדאורייתא והתניא השוכר את הפועל ילקט בנו אחריו למחצה לשליש ולרביע לא ילקט בנו אחריו רבי יוסי אומר [ז] בין כך ובין כך ילקט בנו ואשתו אחריו ואמר שמואל הלכה כרבי יוסי אי אמרת בשלמא קטן אית ליה זכייה לנפשיה (א) כי קא מלקט לנפשיה קא מלקט ואבוה מיניה קא זכי אלא אי אמרת קטן לית ליה זכייה לנפשיה כי קא מלקט לאביו קא מלקט (ב) אבוה עשיר הוא אמאי אשתו ובנו מלקט אחריו שמואל טעמא דתנא דידן קאמר וליה לא סבירא ליה וסבר רבי יוסי קטן אית ליה זכייה מדאורייתא [ד] והתנן [ח] מציאת חרש שוטה וקטן יש בהן משום גזל מפני דרכי שלום רבי יוסי אומר גזל גמור ואמר רב חסדא [ט] גזל גמור מדבריהן נפקא מינה להוציאה בדיינין אלא אמר אביי עשאוה כמי שהלכו בה נמושות דעניים גופיהו מסחי דעתיהו סברי בריה דהיאך מלקטי ליה א"ל רב אדא בר מתנה לאביי [ט] וכי מותר לאדם להרביץ ארי בתוך שדהו כדי שיראו עניים ויברחו אלא אמר רבא

עשו

**רש"י**

גבי מתנה דזכות הוא לו זכין לו לאדם שלא בפניו. ושלא מדעתו (ג) דאנן סהדי דניחא ליה שתהא שלוחו הלכך כי ליתיה בצד חצרו דליכא לדמויי לידה דאינה סמוכה לה תיפוק לה זכייתה משליחותה כי היכי דשלוחו זוכה לו שלא בפניו חצרו נמי זוכה לו שלא בפניו ומיהו גבי מציאה כי ליתיה גבה דלא נפקא זכייתה משום יד ליכא לרבויי משליחות דגבי שליחות איכא דעת השולח או דעת שליח אבל חצר ליכא לא דעת שולח ולא דעת שליח הלכך בעינן [י] דעת אחרת מקנה אותו: זרק ארנקי. והפקירו לכל הקודם: שאין סופו לנוח. בתוך האויר: כמונח דמי. וקנאו בעל הבית הראשון או לאו כמונח דמי להכי בעי אויר שאין סופו לנוח בתוך הבית כמונח דמי דאילו אויר שהיה סופו לנוח בתוך הבית פשיטא לן דאפילו קדם איש אחר וקלטה בתוך האויר לא קנה דמשנכנס לאויר קנאו בעל הבית דתנן במסכת גיטין (דף עט.) היתה עומדת בראש הגג וזרק לה גט כיון שנכנס לאויר הגג הרי זו מגורשת הוא למעלה והיא למטה כיון שיצא מרשות הגג נמחק או נשרף הרי זו מגורשת: ואינו מגיען. אלמא מתגלגלים ויוצאין הן ואין סופן לנוח וקאמר דקנה ליה שדהו: **מתני'** מציאת בנו ובתו הקטנים כו'. בנו קטן בגמרא מפרש מ"ט בתו הקטנה בכתובות (דף מו:) ילפינן לה מקראי דקטנה ואף נערה כל שבח נעוריה לאביה: מציאת עבדו ושפחתו הכנענים שלו. שהרי גופו קנוי לו עולמית כדכתיב (ויקרא כה) והתנחלתם וגו': מציאת אשתו. רבנן תקינו ליה משום איבה: מציאת עבדו ושפחתו העברים. בגמ' פריך לא יהא אלא פועל דאמרינן לעיל (דף י.) מציאתו לבעל הבית: **גמ'** מפני מה אמרו מציאת קטן לאביו. בשלמא בתו ואשתו טעמא מפרש להו במקומן בכתובות אלא בנו טעמא מאי: מריצה אצל אביו. הלכך כשמגביה לצורך אביו הגביהה: ילקט בנו אחריו. מותר לבנו של פועל אם עני הוא ללקוט אחר אביו את לקט הנושר אבל אם קבל הפועל את השדה למחצה לשליש ולרביע עשיר הוא והרי הוא כבעל הבית בשדה זה ולא ילקט בנו אחריו לפי שלקט בנו לאביו: בין כך ובין כך כו'. דאם האב עשיר הבן עני חוכה לעצמו: טעמא דתנא דידן קאמר. מפני מה אמרו מציאת קטן לאביו: וליה לא ס"ל. דמציאת קטן לאביו: מדבריהם. מפני דרכי שלום: ונפקא מינה. מדר' יוסי הא אתא לאשמועינן דהחמירו חכמים בתקנתן כגזל גמור להוציאו בדיינין וכיון דמדאורייתא לית ליה זכייה נמצא אביו גוזל את העניים: אלא אמר אביי. רבי יוסי נמי כתנא דידן ס"ל דקטן לית ליה זכייה וגבי לקט היינו טעם דכיון דיש לו לפועל זה בנים ואשה עניים עלמן מייאשי מלקט שלה לפיכך עשאוה כשדה שהלכו בו הנמושות דתנן (פאה פ"ח מ"א) מאימתי כל אדם מותרין בלקט משילכו בו הנמושות לקוטי בתר לקוטי דמההיא שעתא מסחו עניים דעתייהו מיניה והכא נמי מסחו דעתייהו כו':

עשו

**תוספות**

**חצר** משום יד אתרבאי. ולכך כי הוי דומיא דיד דהיינו כשהוא בצד חצרו קונה אפילו בע"כ או אפילו קטנה [ז] בידה וכשאינה סמוכה לחצרה דלא הוי דומיא דיד לא תימא כי היכי דאין לו דין יד הכי נמי אין לו דין שליחות אלא לא גרע משליחות [ב] ובמידי דזכות כמו מתנה קנה ואפילו אינו עומד בצד חצרו ואפילו אינה משתמרת ובמציאה דאין דעת אחרת מקנה אותה בעינן משתמרת ובגט דחוב הוא לה אפילו במשתמרת אינה מתגרשת דלא עדיפא משליחות דאין חבין לאדם שלא בפניו:

**ויצא** בפתח אחר. ל"ג ואפקריה דהא חשיב ליה דעת אחרת מקנה אותו דמייתי ראיה ממתנה ואי אפקריה אם כן מיד כשיצא הארנקי מידו היה הפקר ובשעת זכייה ליכא דעת אחרת אלא ל"ג ואפקריה ולעולם היא שלו עד שיזכה בה אחר:

**ואמר** שמואל הלכה כרבי יוסי. תימה דבפ' כל הגט (גיטין דף ל. ושם ד"ה כיחידאה) לא בעי שמואל לאוקמי מתניתין דהמלוה מעות את הכהן ואת הלוי [ח] [להיות מפריש עליהן מחלקן] כרבי יוסי דכיחידאה לא מוקמינן ° והכא פסיק הלכה כמותו וי"ל דדוקא הכא גבי לקט פסיק כוותיה מהאי טעמא דמסתמא עניים גופייהו ניחא להו כו' והא דאוקמי בפרק כל הגט (שם) כרבי יוסי היינו רבי יוסי דפ' הלוקח עובר פרתו (בכורות דף יח. ושם ד"ה עשו) דאמר כל שחליפיו ביד כהן פטור מן המתנות ומפרש טעמא בגמ' משום דעשו את שאינו זוכה כזוכה דהוי דומיא דהמלוה מעות דהוו חליפין ביד כהן דהיינו מעות ועשו כאילו זכה במעשר עצמו והא דקרי ליה יחידאה אע"ג דבבכורות לא פליג אלא ר"מ מ"מ רבנן דפליגי עליה הכא גבי לקט כ"ש דפליגי עליה התם גבי מתנות:

**אי** אמרת בשלמא דאורייתא. תימה מנ"ל דלר' יוסי קטן זוכה מן התורה וכן בסמוך דפריך וסבר רבי יוסי מציאת קטן דאורייתא ומנ"ל ודלמא אינה אלא מדרבנן ואביו לא זכה מיניה כלל ולהכי מלקט אחריו וי"ל דמסתמא לא פליג ר' יוסי אכמה משניות דפרקין ודפרק חלון (עירובין דף עט: ושם) ודמסכת מעשר שני (פ"ד מ"ד) דמייתי בפרק התקבל (גיטין דף סה. ושם) דלכולהו משניות יד בן כיד אביו וא"ת ונימא לעולם זכי לנפשיה מדרבנן ובתר הכי זכי אבוה מיניה משום איבה ומשום הכי מלקט וי"ל דמדרבנן אין סברא שיתקנו שתי זכיות שיזכה הבן קודם ואח"כ יזכה האב ממנו אלא אי מדרבנן הוא בשעת זכיית הבן בא לו זכיית האב משום דבשעת הגבהה לוקחה להריצה לאביו אלא ודאי זכה לנפשיה מדאורייתא ואבוה זכה מיניה משום איבה שסמוך על שלחנו:

**ואבוה** עשיר הוא. לאו דוקא עשיר אלא כלומר כיון שיש לו חלק בשדה חייב בלקט כדדרשינן לר"א פ"ק דגיטין (דף יב. ושם) לא תלקט לעני להזהיר עני על שלו ולרבנן נמי או נפקא להו מקרא אחרינא או תרתי ש"מ:

**שמואל** טעמא דתנא דידן קאמר. וא"ת אמאי לא אוקמה בטעמא דידיה דסבר שמואל דזכי לנפשיה מדאורייתא ומדרבנן אבוה זכי מיניה משום איבה וכרבי יוסי וי"ל דקטן דקתני במתני' משמע ליה בקטן ממש ואע"פ שאינו סמוך על שלחנו ואילו היה זוכה לעצמו מן התורה לא היה להם לתקן שיזכה אביו כיון דליכא איבה שהרי אינו סמוך על שולחנו אלא ודאי לא זכי לנפשיה כלל אלא לאביו שבשעת הגבהה מגביה לצורך אביו:

רבי

**עין משפט נר מצוה**

צו א ב מיי' פ"ה מהל' גירושין הלכה ב ופ"ד מהל' זכייה ומתנה הל' ב [רב אלפס כאן ובגיטין פ"ח דף קפד.]:

צז ג טוש"ע ח"מ סי' רמג סעיף כד:

צח ד מיי' פי"ז מהל' גזלה ואבידה הל' יג סמג עשין עד טוש"ע ח"מ סי' ער סעיף ב:

צט ה מיי' שם ופי"ב מהל' אישות הל' ג ופכ"א שם הל' א סמג שם וסי' מח טוש"ע שם וטוש"ע אה"ע סי' סט סעיף ג וסי' פד:

ק ו מיי' פי"ז מהלכות גזלה ואבידה הל' יג סמג עשין עד טוש"ע ח"מ סי' ער סעיף ב וטוש"ע אה"ע סי' פד:

קא ז מיי' פ"ד מהל' מתנות עניים הל' יא:

קב ח מיי' פי"ז מהל' גזלה ואבידה הל' יג סמג עשין עד טוש"ע ח"מ סי' ער סעיף א:

קג ט מיי' פ"ד מהלכות מתנות עניים הל' יג:

**רבינו חננאל**

ופריק רב אשי חצר איתרבי משום יד ולא גרעה משליחות גבי גט דחוב הוא לה אינה מגורשת אם זרק לה גיטה בעלה בחצירה אא"כ עומדת בצד חצירה כדתנן אין חבין לאדם אלא בפניו. אבל מתנה דזכות הוא לו אע"פ שאינו עומד בצד שדהו קנה כדתנן זכין לאדם שלא בפניו. ואסקי' צבי שבור וכיוצא בו אם רץ אחריהן ומגיען ואמר זכתה לי שדי זכתה לו שדהו והוא שעומד בצד שדהו. ואם היו תרבות והקנה לו אחד במתנה אע"פ אם ירוץ אחריהן אין יכול להגיעם כיון שעברו בתוך שדהו קנאם הואיל ומתגלגלין וקי"ל מתגלגל כמונח דמי: מתני' מציאת בנו ובתו הקטנים הרי הם שלו. אמר שמואל מפני מה אמרו מציאת קטן לאביו שבשעה שמוצאה מריצה אצל אביו ואינה מאחרה בידו. למימרא דסבר שמואל דקטן לית ליה זכייה לנפשיה והתניא פועל ילקט בנו אחריו למחצה לשליש ולרביע לא ילקט בנו אחריו. פי' כיון שיש לו חלק בתבואת השדה אפי' א) הוה ליה עשיר. ותנן מי שיש לו מאתים זוז הרי זה לא יטול לקט שכחה ופאה ומעשר כו'. ר' יוסי אומר בין כך ובין כך אשתו ובניו מלקטין אחריו. ואמר שמואל הלכה כר' יוסי ואי אמרת לאביו הוא זוכה אביו עשיר הוא. ודחי' שמואל טעמיה דתנא דידן קאמר וליה לא ס"ל. ושקילנו וטרינו לאוקמא דר' יוסי סבר אית ליה זכי' לנפשי' ולא איתקמא אלא מדרבנן אית ליה זכייה לנפשיה.

**חשק שלמה על ר"ח**

א) אולי צ"ל ואפילו עני הוה ליה כעשיר.

**מסורת הש"ס**

קדושין כג. וש"נ], ...מן קב., ג) [זבחים ...], ד) גיטין נט:, ...ות מא., ה) [גיטין ...], ו) ס"א אגר ...תמרת, מהרש"ל ...ש"א, ז) צ"ל בידה, ח) מהרש"ל.

**הגהות הב"ח**

(א) גמ' אית ליה זכייה ...זיה מדאורייתא כי קא ...ט: (ב) שם ואבוה ...: (ג) רש"י ד"ה גבי ...ה וכו' דאנן סהדי ...א. נ"ב אע"ג דקי"ל ...ב דף יג ע"ב ודף קלא ...דשוא מתנות יחיה ...היכא שמעלמו אומר ...אבל מסתמא אמרי' ...א ליה ליקא במתנה וק"ל:

**הגהות הגר"א**

[א] גמ' במתנה היאך ...לה כו'. נ"ב פי' ...ב"ס דוקא כה"ג אבל ...פא לגבי רך לא וצ"ע ...י' מ"ש רבינו בח"מ ...רס"ח ס"ק י"ב): [ב] תוס' ד"ה חצר ...מידי דזכות כו'. נ"ב ...פפא ורמב"ם פסק כההוא מרבנן:

**גליון הש"ס**

...ס' ד"ה ואמר וכו' ...נא פסיק הלכה ...ותו. עיין גיטין יג ע"א תוס' ד"ה והא:

**ליקוטי רש"י**

...חבין לאדם אלא ...ניו. אין אדם יכול ...ות שלוחו שלא ...עתו לדבר שהוא חובה ...הפסד [קדושין כג.]. ...א בפניו כלומר שלא ...עתו [כתובות יא.]. זכין ...דם שלא בפניו. ...ה בהן השליח לצרכו ...ין יא:]. גזל גמור. ...' מפרש גזל גמור ...בריהם וטעמא דר' ...' בכולהו דקסבר עשו ...י דרכי שלום את ...ינו זוכה לקנות קנין ...ר כזוכה [גיטין נט:]. ...בריהם. אפי' לר' ...י לאו גזל דאורייתא ...א. להוציאו ...יינים. דלרבנן לא ...ק בדיינים ומיהו לר' ...י גזל מעליא לא הוי ...סל לעדות ולעבור עליו בלאו [שם סא.].

as independent acquisition; כִּי קָא מְלַקֵּט לְנַפְשֵׁיהּ קָא מְלַקֵּט – accordingly, when [the minor son] collects *leket*, he collects *leket* for himself and the father then acquires the *leket* as a gift from [the son].[14] אֶלָּא אִי אָמְרַתְּ קָטָן לֵית לֵיהּ זְכִיָּה לְנַפְשֵׁי – But if you say that a minor son does not have independent acquisition (rather, his acquisition of ownerless property automatically makes it the property of his father), then כִּי קָא מְלַקֵּט לְאָבִיו קָא מְלַקֵּט – when [the minor son] collects *leket*, it is on behalf of his father that he collects *leket*, אֲבוּהָ עָשִׁיר הוּא – and his father is a rich man,[15] who is not entitled to *leket*! אַמַּאי אִשְׁתּוֹ וּבְנוֹ מְלַקֵּט אַחֲרָיו – Why, then, can his wife and minor son collect behind him? The collecting of the minor son should be considered tantamount to the collecting of the father![16] – ? –

The Gemara resolves the contradiction:

שְׁמוּאֵל טַעֲמָא דְּתַנָּא דִּידָן קָאָמַ – Shmuel, when he said that a minor son always acquires on behalf of his father, was simply explaining the reasoning of the Tanna of our Mishnah, who says that the find of a minor son always belongs to his father. וְלֵיהּ לָא סְבִירָא לֵיהּ – But Shmuel himself is not of this opinion; rather, Shmuel himself holds the view of R' Yose that a minor son acquires on his own behalf.[17]

The Gemara points out a seeming contradiction in R' Yose's teachings:

וְסָבַר רַבִּי יוֹסֵי קָטָן אִית לֵיהּ זְכִיָּה מִדְּאוֹרַיְיתָא – And does R' Yose indeed hold that a minor son has independent acquisition under Biblical law?[18] וְהָתְנַן מְצִיאַת חֵרֵשׁ שׁוֹטֶה וְקָטָן יֵשׁ בָּהֶן מִשּׁוּם גָּזֵל מִפְּנֵי דַּרְכֵי שָׁלוֹם – But we have learned in a Mishnah:[19] THE FIND OF A DEAF-MUTE, OF A DERANGED PERSON OR OF A MINOR ARE SUBJECT TO the prohibition against THEFT, i.e. it is forbidden to take their find away from them, BECAUSE OF the principle that we must promote THE WAYS OF PEACE.[20] רַבִּי יוֹסֵי אוֹמֵר גָּזֵל גָּמוּר – R' YOSE SAYS: Taking a find away from them is UNEQUIVOCAL THEFT, not merely a breach in the ways of peace. וְאָמַר רַב חִסְדָּא גָּזֵל גָּמוּר מִדִּבְרֵיהֶן – And Rav Chisda said that R' Yose means that it is unequivocal theft by virtue of Rabbinic decree, not by Biblical law.[21]

The Gemara adds parenthetically:

נַפְקָא מִינָּהּ לְהוֹצִיאָהּ בְּדַיָּינִין – The practical difference between saying that stealing a find away from one of these legal incompetents is prohibited because we promote the ways of peace and saying that it is unequivocal theft by Rabbinic decree is whether it is possible to recover it through the courts.[22] At any rate, the two teachings of R' Yose seem to contradict each other.[23] – ? –

Abaye resolves the contradiction between R' Yose's views:

אֶלָּא אָמַר אַבָּיֵי – Rather, says Abaye,[24] the reason R' Yose permits the worker's minor son to collect in a field partly owned by his father is because עֲשָׂאוּהָ כְּמִי שֶׁהָלְכוּ בָּהּ נְמוּשׁוֹת – [the Rabbis] considered [the field] that the sharecropper harvests like [a field] that has already been traversed by the rummagers,[25] דַּעֲנִיִּים גּוּפַיְיהוּ מַסְּחֵי דַּעְתַּיְיהוּ – where the paupers themselves stop thinking about [the field].[26] סָבְרֵי בְּרֵיהּ דְּהֵיאָךְ מְלַקְּטֵי לֵיהּ – Similarly, in the Baraisa's case of a sharecropper, [the paupers] collectively, think: "That fellow's son is

NOTES

4. [The son does not own the crop in any way. Thus, as a poor person, e is entitled to collect the *leket*. It is then his prerogative to give away is *leket* to whomever he wishes – even to his father, the crop's owner. nd the father, too, is in no way enjoined from accepting *leket* that has een lawfully collected from his field (cf. *Tosafos*).]

[The Gemara assumes that this line of reasoning is valid only ccording to the position that the minor son acquires the *leket* for imself under Biblical law (*Ritva*; see below, note 21).]

5. I.e. a person who is ineligible to collect *leket* from this field. The vorker in this case is not actually rich; rather, he is a poor person who wns a share in the field. Therefore, he is like a rich man in that he is neligible to take the *leket* (see *Tosafos*).

6. [It would seem that the Gemara here finds difficulty only with ' Yose's allowing the minor son to collect, not with his allowing he wife to collect. The Gemara simply cites R' Yose's ruling in its ntirety.]

7. According to R' Yose, whose view Shmuel adopts, a minor son's find oes not belong to his father at all, unlike the ruling of our Mishnah *Rashi* ד״ה וליה לא סל; see *Pnei Yehoshua* and *Maharam Shif*).

8. See notes 14 and 21.

9. *Gittin* 59b.

0. This Tanna holds that under Biblical law, a deaf-mute, a deranged erson or a minor do not have the legal capacity to acquire an ownerless rticle. Thus, anyone would be legally permitted to take their find away rom them. Nevertheless, the Sages decreed that in the interests of ocial harmony, it is forbidden to "steal" a find that these legal ncompetents have taken.

1. Thus, as Rav Chisda explains, R' Yose holds that a minor does *not* ave the capacity to effect acquisition of an ownerless article (such as *eket*) under Biblical law. How, then, can R' Yose rule in the Baraisa hat a minor can collect *leket* from his father's field and then transfer he *leket* to his father? Since the *leket* that the minor has collected is not cquired under Biblical law, it remains uncollected *leket*, which the ather is prohibited from taking! (*Rashi*).

It cannot be that R' Yose's allowance of the minor to collect in his ather's field is based on the *Rabbinically* ordained capacity of the inor to acquire ownerless articles (it would not be "unequivocal theft y Rabbinic decree" were it not that there was this Rabbinically ordained capacity). The Rabbis granted a minor that capacity (in order to promote peace) only in regard to entirely ownerless articles, such as finds, since the Rabbinic institution does not then violate the rights of anyone else (the find is completely ownerless). However, the Rabbis did not institute this capacity in the case of *leket*, since such an institution would deprive the adult poor people of the rights that the Torah granted them to the *leket* (*Maharam Shif* in explanation of *Rashi*; cf. *Machazeh Avraham*, cited in *Otzar Mefarshei HaTalmud*; see *Tosafos* ד״ה אי אמרת בשלמא).

22. According to R' Yose, who considers theft from a legal incompetent to be "unequivocal theft" (albeit by Rabbinic decree), the court would take the stolen find away from the thief and return it to the deaf-mute, the deranged person or the minor, as the case may be. According to the Tanna Kamma, who holds that such theft is prohibited only so that strife not ensue, the court would not act to recover such a stolen article from the thief.

23. As explained in note 21.

24. [Abaye disagrees with the Gemara's previous understanding that R' Yose's ruling concerning *leket* precludes the view of our Tanna, that the find of a minor son belongs to his father.] According to Abaye, R' Yose indeed agrees with the Tanna of our Mishnah that the minor son's find belongs to his father. [And, as taught by Rav Chisda, a minor has no capacity to acquire ownerless articles under Biblical law.] Still, R' Yose allows the sharecropper's minor son to collect *leket* behind him for the reason Abaye will now advance (*Rashi*).

25. See next note.

26. The last paupers to collect *leket* in any given field were the old and weak, who would collect slowly and meticulously. The Mishnah in *Pe'ah* (8:11) rules that after these straggling paupers finish collecting *leket* from the field, all remaining grain is available to all – rich and poor alike. The reason for this rule is that people assume that the meticulous stragglers have left nothing of value in their wake. Accordingly, the poor people, collectively, despair of finding any more *leket* etc. in the field, in effect relinquishing their claim to whatever *leket* might in fact remain. Thus, whatever *leket* does remain is absolutely ownerless and may be taken by any person. Abaye asserts that the Rabbis applied this same principle to a field being harvested by a sharecropper, as he proceeds to explain.

חצר איתרבאי משום יד ולא גרעה משליחות גבי גט דחוב הוא לה (א) [א]אין חבין לאדם אלא בפניו גבי מתנה דזכות הוא לו [ב]זכין לאדם שלא בפניו גופא ראה אותן רצין אחר המציאה וכו' אמר רבי ירמיה אמר רבי יוחנן והוא שרץ אחריהן ומגיען בעי רבי ירמיה [א]במתנה היאך קבלה מיניה ר' אבא בר כהנא אע"פ שרץ אחריהן ואין מגיען (ב) [ג]בעי רבא זרק ארנקי בפתח זה ויצא בפתח אחר מהו (ג) אויר שאין סופו לנוח כמונח דמי או לא אמר ליה רב פפא לרבא ואמרי לה רב אדא בר מתנה לרבא ואמרי לה רבינא לרבא לאו היינו מתניתין ראה אותן רצין אחר המציאה ואמר רבי ירמיה אמר רבי יוחנן והוא שרץ אחריהן ומגיען ובעי רבי ירמיה במתנה היאך וקבלה מיניה רבי אבא בר כהנא במתנה אף על פי שרץ אחריהן ואין מגיען אמר ליה מתגלגל קאמרת שאני מתגלגל דכמונח דמי:

**מתני'** [ד]מציאת בנו ובתו הקטנים מציאת עבדו ושפחתו הכנענים [ה]מציאת אשתו הרי אלו שלו [ו]מציאת בנו ובתו הגדולים מציאת עבדו ושפחתו העברים מציאת אשתו שגירשה אע"פ שלא נתן כתובה הרי אלו שלהן:

**גמ'** אמר שמואל מפני מה אמרו מציאת קטן לאביו שבשעה שמוצאה מריצה אצל אביו ואינו מאחר בידו למימרא דסבר שמואל קטן לית ליה זכייה לנפשיה מדאורייתא והתניא השוכר את הפועל ילקט בנו אחריו למחצה לשליש ולרביע לא ילקט בנו אחריו רבי יוסי אומר [ז]בין כך ובין כך ילקט בנו ואשתו אחריו ואמר שמואל הלכה כרבי יוסי אי אמרת בשלמא קטן אית ליה זכייה לנפשיה (א) כי קא מלקט לנפשיה קא מלקט ואבוה מיניה קא זכי אלא אי אמרת קטן לית ליה זכייה לנפשיה כי קא מלקט לאביו קא מלקט (ב) אבוה עשיר הוא אמאי אשתו ובנו מלקט אחריו שמואל טעמא דתנא דידן קאמר וליה לא סבירא ליה וסבר רבי יוסי קטן אית ליה זכייה מדאורייתא (ד) והתנן [ח]מציאת חרש שוטה וקטן יש בהן משום גזל מפני דרכי שלום רבי יוסי אומר גזל גמור ואמר רב חסדא (ה) גזל גמור מדבריהן נפקא מינה להוציאה בדיינין אלא אמר אביי עשאוה כמי שהלכו בה נמושות דעניים גופייהו מסחי דעתייהו סברי בריה דהיאך מלקטי ליה א"ל רב אדא בר מתנה לאביי [ט]וכי מותר לאדם להרביץ ארי בתוך שדהו כדי שיראו עניים ויברחו אלא אמר רבא

עשו

**רש"י**

גבי מתנה דזכות הוא לו זכין לו לאדם שלא בפניו. ושלא מדעתו (ג) דאנן סהדי דניחא ליה שתהא שלוחו הלכך כי ליתיה בצד חצרו דליכא לדמויי לידה דאינה סמוכה לה תיפוק לה זכייתה משליחותה כי היכי דשלוחו זוכה לו שלא בפניו חצרו נמי זוכה לו שלא בפניו ומיהו גבי מציאה כי ליתיה גבה דלא נפקא זכייתה משום יד ליכא לרבויי משליחות דגבי שליחות איכא דעת השולח או דעת שליח אבל חצר ליכא לא דעת שולח ולא דעת שליח הלכך בעינן [י]דעת אחרת מקנה אותו: זרק ארנקי. והפקירו לכל הקודם: שאין סופו לנוח. בתוך האויר: כמונח דמי. וקנאו בעל הבית הראשון או לאו כמונח דמי להכי בעי אויר שאין סופו לנוח בתוך הבית כמונח דמי דאילו אויר שהיה סופו לנוח בתוך הבית פשיטא לן דאפילו קדם איש אחר וקלטה בתוך האויר לא קנה דמשנכנס לאויר קנאו בעל הבית דתנן במסכת גיטין (דף עט.) היתה עומדת בראש הגג וזרק לה גט כיון שנכנס לאויר הגג הרי זו מגורשת הוא למעלה והיא למטה כיון שיצא מרשות הגג נמחק או נשרף הרי זו מגורשת: ואינו מגיען. אלמא מתגלגלים ויוצאין הן ואין סופן לנוח וקאמר דקנה ליה שדהו: **מתני'** מציאת בנו ובתו הקטנים כו'. בנו קטן בגמרא מפרש מ"ט בתו הקטנה בכתובות (דף מו:) ילפינן לה מקראי דקטנה ואף נערה כל שבח נעוריה לאביה: מציאת עבדו ושפחתו הכנענים שלו. שהרי גופו קנוי לו עולמית כדכתיב (ויקרא כה) והתנחלתם וגו': מציאת אשתו. רבנן תקינו ליה משום איבה: מציאת עבדו ושפחתו העברים. בגמ' פריך לא יהא אלא פועל דאמרינן לעיל (דף י.) מציאתו לבעל הבית: **גמ'** מפני מה אמרו מציאת קטן לאביו. בשלמא בתו ואשתו טעמא מפרש להו במקומן בכתובות אלא בנו טעמא מאי: מריצה אצל אביו. הלכך כשמגביה לצורך אביו הגביהה: ילקט בנו אחריו. מותר לבנו של פועל אם עני הוא ללקוט אחר אביו את לקט הנושר אבל אם קבל הפועל את השדה למחצה לשליש ולרביע עשיר הוא והרי הוא כבעל הבית בשדה זה ולא ילקט בנו אחריו לפי שלקט בנו לאביו: בין כך ובין כך כו'. דאם האב עשיר הבן עני חוכה לעצמו: טעמא דתנא דידן קאמר. מפני מה אמרו מציאת קטן לאביו: וליה לא ס"ל. דמציאת קטן לאביו: מדבריהם. מפני דרכי שלום: ונפקא מינה. מדר' יוסי הא אתא לאשמועינן דהחמירו חכמים בתקנתן כגזל גמור להוציאו בדיינין וכיון דמדאורייתא לית ליה זכייה נמצא אביו גוזל את העניים: אלא אמר אביי. רבי יוסי נמי כתנא דידן ס"ל דקטן לית ליה זכייה וגבי לקט היינו טעם דכיון דיש לו לפועל זה בנים ואשה עניים עצמן מייאשי מלקט שלה לפיכך עשאוה כשדה שהלכו בו הנמושות דתנן (פאה פ"ח מ"א) מאימתי כל אדם מותרין בלקט משילכו בו הנמושות לקוטי בתר לקוטי דמההיא שעתא מסחו עניים דעתייהו מיניה והכא נמי מסחו דעתייהו כו':

**תוספות**

**חצר** משום יד אתרבאי. ולכך כי הוי דומיא דיד דהיינו כשהוא בצד חצרו קונה אפילו בע"כ או אפילו קטנה [י]בידה וכשאינה סמוכה לחצרה דלא הוי דומיא דיד לא תימא כי היכי דאין לו דין יד הכי נמי אין לו דין שליחות אלא לא גרע משליחות [ב]ובמידי דזכות כמו מתנה קנה ואפילו אינו עומד בצד חצרו ואפילו אינה משתמרת ובמציאה דאין דעת אחרת מקנה אותה בעינן משתמרת ובגט דחוב הוא לה אפילו במשתמרת אינה מתגרשת דלא עדיפא משליחות דאין חבין לאדם שלא בפניו:

**ויצא** בפתח אחר. ל"ג ואפקריה דהא חשיב ליה דעת אחרת מקנה אותו דמייתי ראיה ממתנה ואי אפקריה אם כן מיד כשיצא הארנקי מידו היה הפקר ובשעת זכייה ליכא דעת אחרת אלא ל"ג ואפקריה ולעולם היא שלו עד שיזכה בה אחר:

**ואמר** שמואל הלכה כרבי יוסי. תימה דבפ' כל הגט (גיטין דף ל. ושם ד"ה כיחידאה) לא בעי שמואל לאוקמי מתניתין דהמלוה מעות את הכהן ואת הלוי [כ][להיות מפריש עליהן מחלקן] כרבי יוסי דכיחידאה לא מוקמינן [ל]והכא פסיק הלכה כמותו וי"ל דדוקא הכא גבי לקט פסיק כוותיה מהאי טעמא דמסתמא עניים גופייהו ניחא להו כו' והא דאוקמי בפרק כל הגט (שם) כרבי יוסי היינו רבי יוסי דפ' הלוקח עובר פרתו (בכורות דף יח. ושם ד"ה עשו) דאמר כל שחליפיו ביד כהן פטור מן המתנות ומפרש טעמא בגמ' משום דעשו את שאינו זוכה כזוכה דהוי דומיא דהמלוה מעות דהוו חליפין ביד כהן דהיינו מעות ועשו כאילו זכה במעשר עצמו והא דקרי ליה יחידאה אע"ג דבבכורות לא פליג אלא ר"מ מ"מ רבנן דפליגי עליה הכא גבי לקט כ"ש דפליגי עליה התם גבי מתנות:

**אי** אמרת בשלמא דאורייתא. תימה מנ"ל דלר' יוסי קטן זוכה מן התורה וכן בסמוך דפריך וסבר רבי יוסי מציאת קטן דאורייתא ומנ"ל ודלמא אינה אלא מדרבנן ואביו לא זכה מיניה כלל ולהכי מלקט אחריו וי"ל דמסתמא לא פליג ר' יוסי אכמה משניות דפרקין ודפרק חלון (עירובין דף עט: ושם) ודמסכת מעשר שני (פ"ד מ"ד) דמייתי בפרק התקבל (גיטין דף סה. ושם) דלכולהו משניות יד בן כיד אביו וא"ת ונימא לעולם זכי לנפשיה מדרבנן ובתר הכי זכי אבוה מיניה משום איבה ומשום הכי מלקט וי"ל דמדרבנן אין סברא שיתקנו שתי זכיות שיזכה הבן קודם ואח"כ יזכה האב ממנו אלא אי מדרבנן הוא בשעת זכיית הבן בא לו זכיית האב משום דבשעת הגבהה לוקחה להריצה לאביו אלא ודאי זכה לנפשיה מדאורייתא ואבוה זכה מיניה משום איבה שסמוך על שלחנו: **ואבוה** עשיר הוא. לאו דוקא עשיר אלא כלומר כיון שיש לו חלק בשדה חייב בלקט כדדרשינן לר"א פ"ק דגיטין (דף יב. ושם) לא תלקט לעני להזהיר עני על שלו ולרבנן נמי או נפקא להו מקרא אחרינא או תרתי ש"מ: **שמואל** טעמא דתנא דידן קאמר. וא"ת אמאי לא אוקמה בטעמא דידיה דסבר שמואל דזכי לנפשיה מדאורייתא ומדרבנן אבוה זכי מיניה משום איבה וכרבי יוסי וי"ל דקטן דקתני במתני' משמע ליה בקטן ממש ואע"פ שאינו סמוך על שלחנו ואילו היה זוכה לעצמו מן התורה לא היה להם לתקן שיזכה אביו כיון דליכא איבה שהרי אינו סמוך על שולחנו אלא ודאי לא זכי לנפשיה כלל אלא לאביו שבשעת הגבהה מגביה לצורך אביו:

רבי

**עין משפט נר מצוה**

צו א ב מיי' פ"ה מהל' גירושין הלכה ג ופ"ד מהל' זכייה ומתנה הל' ג [רב אלפס כאן ובגיטין פ"ח דף קפד.]:
צז ג טוש"ע ח"מ סי' רמג סעיף כד:
צח ד מיי' פי"ז מהל' גזילה ואבידה הל' יג סמג עשין עד טוש"ע ח"מ סי' ער סעיף ג:
צט ה מיי' שם ופי"ג מהל' אישות הל' ג ופכ"א שם הל' א סמג שם וסי' מח טוש"ע שם וטוש"ע אה"ע סי' סט סעיף ג וסי' פד:
ק ו מיי' פי"ז מהלכות גזילה ואבידה הל' יג סמג עשין עד טוש"ע ח"מ סי' ער סעיף ב וטוש"ע אה"ע סי' פד:
קא ז מיי' פ"ד מהל' מתנות עניים הל' יא:
קב ח מיי' פי"ז מהל' גזילה ואבידה הל' יב סמג עשין עד טוש"ע ח"מ סי' ער סעיף א:
קג ט מיי' פ"ד מהלכות מתנות עניים הל' יג:

**רבינו חננאל**

ופריק רב אשי חצר איתרבי משום יד ולא גרעה משליחות גבי גט דחוב הוא לה אינה מגורשת אם זרק לה גיטה בעלה בחצירה אא"כ עומדת בצד חצירה כדתנן אין חבין לאדם אלא בפניו. אבל מתנה דזכות הוא לו אע"פ שאינו עומד בצד שדהו קנה כדתנן זכין לאדם שלא בפניו. ואסקי' צבי שבור וכיוצא בו אם רץ אחריהן ומגיען ואמר זכתה לי שדי זכתה לו שדהו והוא שעומד בצד שדהו. ואם היו תרבות והקנה לו אחד במתנה אע"פ אם ירוץ אחריהן אין יכול להגיעם כיון שעברו בתוך שדהו קנאם הואיל ומתגלגלין וקי"ל מתגלגל כמונח דמי: **מתני'** מציאת בנו ובתו הקטנים הרי הם שלו. אמר שמואל מפני מה אמרו מציאת קטן לאביו שבשעה שמוצאה מריצה אצל אביו ואינה מאחרה בידו. למימרא דסבר שמואל דקטן לית ליה זכייה לנפשיה והתניא פועל ילקט בנו אחריו למחצה לשליש ולרביע לא ילקט בנו אחריו. פי' כיון שיש לו חלק בתבואת השדה אפי' א) הוה ליה עשיר. ותנן מי שיש לו מאתים זוז הרי זה לא יטול לקט שכחה ופאה ומעשר כו'. ר' יוסי אומר בין כך ובין כך אשתו ובניו מלקטין אחריו. ואמר שמואל הלכה כר' יוסי ואי אמרת לאביו הוא זוכה אביו עשיר הוא. ודחי' שמואל טעמיה דתנא דידן קאמר וליה לא ס"ל. ושקלינו וטרינו לאוקומא דר' יוסי סבר אית ליה זכיי' לנפשי' ולא איתוקמא אלא מדרבנן אית ליה זכייה לנפשיה.

**חשק שלמה על ר"ח**

א) אולי צ"ל ואפילו עני הוה ליה כעשיר.

**מסורת הש"ס**

א) [קדושין כג. וש"נ], ב) לקמן קב., ג) [זבחים ב:], ד) גיטין נט:, בכורות מח., ה) [גיטין סא.], ו) ס"א חצר משתמרת, מהרש"ל מהרש"א, ז) נ"ל כידה, ח) מהרש"ל.

**הגהות הב"ח**

(א) גמ' אית ליה זכייה לנפשיה מדאורייתא כי קא מלקט: (ב) שם ואבוה עשיר: (ג) רש"י ד"ה גבי מתנה וכו' דאנן סהדי דניחא. נ"ב אע"ג דקי"ל בפ"ב דף יג ע"ב ודף קלא ע"א דשונא מתנות יחיה שאני היכא שמעצמו אומר לו אבל מסתמא אמרי' דניחא ליה ליקח במתנה וק"ל:

**הגהות הגר"א**

[א] גמ' במתנה היאך קבלה כו'. נ"ב פי' הרמב"ם דוקא כה"ג אבל בסיפא לגבי רץ לא ול"ע ועיי' מ"ש רבינו בח"מ סי' רס"ח ס"ק י"ב): [ב] תום' ד"ה חצר במידי דזכות כו'. נ"ב וכ"ב פפא ורמב"ם פסק כההוא מרבנן:

**גליון הש"ס**

תוס' ד"ה ואמר וכו' והכא פסיק הלכה כמותו. עיין גיטין יג ע"א תוס' ד"ה והא:

**ליקוטי רש"י**

אין חבין לאדם אלא בפניו. אין אדם יכול לעשות שלוחו שלא מדעתו לדבר שהוא חובה לו והפסד [קדושין כג.]. לא בפניו כלומר שלא מדעתו [כתובות יא.]. זכין לאדם שלא בפניו. כגה בהן השליח לצרכו [גיטין יא:]. גזל גמור. בגמ' מפרש גזל גמור מדבריהם וטעמא דר' יוסי כי בכולהו דקסבר עשו מפני דרכי שלום את שאינו זוכה לקנות קנין גמור כזוכה [גיטין נט:]. מדבריהם. אפי' לר' יוסי לאו גזל דאורייתא הוא. להוציאו בדיינים. לרבנן לא פיק בדיינים ומיהו לר' יוסי גזל מעליא לא הוי ופסל לעדות ולעבור עליו בלאו [שם סא.].

Rava, however, rejects the analogy of Rava's case to the case of ɪr Mishnah:

אָמַר לֵ – **[Rava] said to him:** מִתְגַּלְגֵּל קָאָמְרַתְּ – **You adduce** a proof from an object that is **rolling?** שָׁאנִי מִתְגַּלְגֵּל דִּכְמוּנָּח דָּמֵי – **A rolling object is different, because it is considered as if it were resting.**[6]

**Mishnah** מְצִיאַת בְּנוֹ וּבִתּוֹ הַקְּטַנִּים – **The find of one's minor son or daughter,**[7] מְצִיאַת עַבְדּוֹ וְשִׁפְחָתוֹ הַכְּנַעֲנִים – **the find of one's gentile slave, male or female,** מְצִיאַת אִשְׁתּוֹ – **and the find of one's wife:** הֲרֵי אֵלּוּ שֶׁלּוֹ – **These belong to him.**[8] מְצִיאַת בְּנוֹ וּבִתּוֹ הַגְּדוֹלִים – **The find of one's son or daughter who is of age,** מְצִיאַת עַבְדּוֹ וְשִׁפְחָתוֹ הָעִבְרִים – **the find of one's Hebrew servant or maidservant,** מְצִיאַת אִשְׁתּוֹ שֶׁגֵּירְשָׁהּ אַף עַל פִּי שֶׁלֹּא נָתַן כְּתוּבָּה – **and the find of one's wife whom he divorced, although he has not** yet **paid her** ***kesubah:*** הֲרֵי אֵלּוּ שֶׁלָּהֶן – **These belong to them.**

**Gemara** The Gemara discusses the first ruling of the Mishnah:

אָמַר שְׁמוּאֵל מִפְּנֵי מָה אָמְרוּ מְצִיאַת קָטָן לְאָ – **Shmuel said: Why d [the Rabbis of the Mishnah] say that the find of a minor** ɪn **belongs to his father?** שֶׁבְּשָׁעָה שֶׁמּוֹצְאָה מְרִיצָהּ אֵצֶל אָבִיו וְאֵינוֹ מְאַחֵר בָּ – **Because when [a minor son] finds something, he** ɪngs **it quickly to his father and does not let** it **tarry in his** ɪssession. Therefore, [it is presumed that] the minor son's ɪtent when picking up the find is to give it to his father; thus, the ɪther acquires the find.[9]

The Gemara points out a seeming contradiction in the teachɪgs of Shmuel:

לְמֵימְרָא דְּסָבַר שְׁמוּאֵל קָטָן לֵית לֵיהּ זְכִיָּיה לְנַפְשֵׁיהּ מִדְּאוֹרָיְיתָ – **Is this** ɪ **say that Shmuel holds that under Biblical law a minor** son ɪes **not have independent acquisition?**[10] וְהָתַנְיָא הַשּׂוֹכֵר אֶת הַפּוֹעֵל יְלַקֵּט בְּנוֹ אַחֲרָיו – **But it was taught in a Baraisa:** If ONE HIRED A poor WORKER to harvest his crop, THE [WORKER'S] SON MAY follow his father and COLLECT *LEKET* BEHIND HIM.[11] לְמֶחֱצָה לְשָׁלִישׁ וְלִרְבִיעַ לֹא יְלַקֵּט בְּנוֹ אַחֲרָיו – But if the worker receives a share of the crop – for example: A HALF, A THIRD OR A QUARTER of the crop – in exchange for his labor, then HIS SON CANNOT COLLECT *LEKET* BEHIND HIM.[12] רַבִּי יוֹסֵי אוֹמֵר בֵּין כָּךְ וּבֵין כָּךְ יְלַקֵּט בְּנוֹ וְאִשְׁתּוֹ אַחֲרָיו – R' YOSE SAYS: IN EITHER CASE, [THE WORKER'S] SON OR WIFE CAN COLLECT *LEKET* BEHIND HIM.[13] וְאָמַר שְׁמוּאֵל הֲלָכָה כְּרַבִּי יוֹסֵי – **And Shmuel said: The halachah follows R' Yose.**

The Gemara explains why these two rulings of Shmuel are seemingly contradictory:

אִי אָמְרַתְּ בִּשְׁלָמָא קָטָן אִית לֵיהּ זְכִיָּיה לְנַפְשֵׁיהּ – Now, **[R' Yose's ruling] is understandable if you say that a minor** son

NOTES

When an object is rolling [or running] through a field, it is making ɪntact with the ground. It is therefore possible that even though it does ɪt come to a halt in the field, it is as if it has come to rest and the field's ɪner can acquire it through *kinyan chatzeir.* But an object flying ɪrough the airspace of a property makes no contact with the ground; ɪnce, the property might not have the capacity to acquire it (unless it destined to come to rest there). Rava's inquiry is thus left unanswered.

A girl passes through two stages before becoming an adult. During the ɪst stage, which begins at birth, she is called a קְטַנָּה, *ketanah* (literally: small girl). During this stage she is legally a minor in every respect. ɪhen she reaches the age of twelve and, in addition, exhibits certain ɪns of puberty, she becomes a נַעֲרָה, *naarah* (literally: a maiden). ɪring this stage she is legally an adult, but the father still retains some ɪgal authority over her. Six months after becoming a *naarah* she ɪcomes a בּוֹגֶרֶת, *bogeres,* which is full adulthood, at which point the ɪther loses all legal authority over her.

The term "minor daughter" in our Mishnah applies both to a *ketanah* ɪd to a *naarah* (*Rashi*).

[Though it is the child, slave or wife who does the actual act of ɪquisition in the found article, it is the father, master or husband who the legal beneficiary of that acquisition.]

The Gemara will discuss why a minor son's find belongs to the father. In regard to the find of a minor daughter, *Rashi* writes that it belongs ɪer father by Biblical law. This is derived from a phrase in the section Scripture dealing with the absolution of vows: בִּנְעֻרֶיהָ בֵּית אָבִיהָ, *in her ɪaidenhood, in her father's house* (*Numbers* 30:17), which implies that long as she is a *naarah* (and certainly when she is a *ketanah*) she is ɪder her father's authority, and whatever benefits she produces belong him. [*Tosafos* (12b) disagree with *Rashi* on the grounds that the ɪemara itself (*Kiddushin* 3b) refutes this derivation, because of the ɪinciple that laws concerning monetary matters cannot be derived ɪm those related to prohibitory matters (such as vows).]

The find of a person's Canaanite slaves belongs to him, since he is the ɪrmanent owner of the slaves themselves (*Rashi*).

A wife's find belongs to her husband by Rabbinic fiat; the Rabbis ɪacted this law in order to remove a potential source of marital conflict *ɪashi*).

*Rashi.* [The act of acquisition (הַגְבָּהָה, *lifting*) that the minor performs the found article automatically makes it the property of his father.] Under Biblical law, a minor cannot acquire an ownerless article together [since there is no previous owner conveying the article to him (דַּעַת אַחֶרֶת מַקְנָה)]. However, in order to avoid the strife and contention that would arise from people trying to wrest a minor's finds away from him [דַּרְכֵי שָׁלוֹם], the Rabbis deemed it necessary to grant minors the legal capacity to take possession of a find. And since the minor means to take the find on behalf of his father, it was the minor's father whom the Rabbis designated as the beneficiary of the minor's act of acquisition (*Ritva* in explanation of *Rashi*; *Maharam Shif*; cf. *Be'ur* to *Maharam Shif* §4).

10. If Shmuel was of the opinion that under Biblical law a minor does have the capacity to acquire an ownerless article for himself, the Rabbis would never have instituted that it belongs automatically to his father simply because the son invariably rushes the article to him. Though the Torah does authorize the Rabbis to suspend its laws in monetary matters, Shmuel's reason is not sufficiently compelling for the Rabbis to do so here. Rather, we must assume that Shmuel takes the very capacity of the minor to acquire the ownerless article to be of Rabbinic origin. Thus, we can understand that the minor's presumed intent on behalf of his father prompted the Rabbis to make the father the beneficiary of the minor's Rabbinically ordained acquisition (see *Ritva*; *Maharam Shif*).

11. Scripture dictates that the stalks of grain which fall to the ground during the harvest be left for the poor (*Leviticus* 19:9; 23:22; see details in *Pe'ah* 4:10 and 6:5). These stalks are called לֶקֶט, *leket* (literally: collection). The owner of the field cannot collect the *leket* of his crop, even if he himself is a pauper and entitled to collect from other fields (*Tosafos* ד״ה ואבוה).

This Baraisa rules that a poor worker who receives a wage to harvest the field is not considered an owner of the crop and, therefore, as the worker harvests the field, his son [even if he is a minor, whose finds belong to his father] can follow behind him and collect the *leket* that falls to the ground.

12. Since the worker receives a share of the crop in exchange for his labor, he is considered a part owner of the crop. Accordingly, just as the sharecropper himself is not entitled to collect *leket* from this crop, his minor son may not do so either, since whatever *leket* the minor son collects accrues to his father; thus, it would be tantamount to the father collecting the *leket* himself (*Rashi, Ritva*). [The Gemara assumes that the Baraisa refers to the worker's *minor* son, whose finds belong to the father. For a poor son who has come of age and whose finds do not belong to the father is certainly entitled to collect *leket* from his father's field (see *Maharam Shif*).]

13. The Gemara will soon analyze R' Yose's reasoning.

חצר איתרבאי משום יד ולא גרעה משליחות גבי גט דחוב הוא לה (א) [א]אין חבין לאדם אלא בפניו גבי מתנה דזכות הוא לו [ב]זכין לאדם שלא בפניו גופא ראה אותן רצין אחר המציאה וכו' אמר רבי ירמיה אמר רבי יוחנן והוא שרץ אחריהן ומגיען בעי רבי ירמיה [א]במתנה היאך קבלה מיניה ר' אבא בר כהנא אע"פ שרץ אחריהן ואין מגיען (ב) [ג]בעי רבא זרק ארנקי בפתח זה ויצא בפתח אחר מהו (ג) אויר שאין סופו לנוח כמונח דמי או לא אמר ליה רב פפא לרבא ואמרי לה רב אדא בר מתנה לרבא ואמרי לה רבינא לרבא לאו היינו מתניתין ראה אותן רצין אחר המציאה ואמר רבי ירמיה אמר רבי יוחנן והוא שרץ אחריהן ומגיען ובעי רבי ירמיה במתנה היאך וקבלה מיניה רבי אבא בר כהנא במתנה אף על פי שרץ אחריהן ואין מגיען אמר ליה מתגלגל קאמרת שאני מתגלגל דכמונח דמי:

**מתני'** [ד]מציאת בנו ובתו הקטנים מציאת עבדו ושפחתו הכנענים [ה]מציאת אשתו הרי אלו שלו [ו]מציאת בנו ובתו הגדולים מציאת עבדו ושפחתו העברים מציאת אשתו שגירשה אע"פ שלא נתן כתובה הרי אלו שלהן:

**גמ'** אמר שמואל מפני מה אמרו מציאת קטן לאביו שבשעה שמוצאה מריצה אצל אביו ואינו מאחר בידו למימרא דסבר שמואל קטן לית ליה זכייה לנפשיה מדאורייתא והתניא השוכר את הפועל ילקט בנו אחריו למחצה לשליש ולרביע לא ילקט בנו אחריו רבי יוסי אומר [ז]בין כך ובין כך ילקט בנו ואשתו אחריו ואמר שמואל הלכה כרבי יוסי אי אמרת בשלמא קטן אית ליה זכייה לנפשיה (א) כי קא מלקט לנפשיה קא מלקט ואבוה מיניה קא זכי אלא אי אמרת קטן לית ליה זכייה לנפשיה כי קא מלקט לאביו קא מלקט (ב) אבוה עשיר הוא אמאי אשתו ובנו מלקט אחריו שמואל טעמא דתנא דידן קאמר וליה לא סבירא ליה וסבר רבי יוסי קטן אית ליה זכייה מדאורייתא (ד) והתנן [ח]מציאת חרש שוטה וקטן יש בהן משום גזל מפני דרכי שלום רבי יוסי אומר גזל גמור ואמר רב חסדא (ט) גזל גמור מדבריהן נפקא מינה להוציאה בדיינין אלא אמר אביי עשאוה כמי שהלכו בה נמושות דעניים גופייהו מסחי דעתייהו סברי בריה דהיאך מלקטי ליה א"ל רב אדא בר מתנה לאביי [ט]וכי מותר לאדם להרביץ ארי בתוך שדהו כדי שיראו עניים ויברחו אלא אמר רבא

עשו

---

גבי מתנה דזכות הוא לו זכין לו לאדם שלא בפניו. ושלא מדעתו (ג) דאנן סהדי דניחא ליה שתהא שלוחו הלכך כי ליתיה בצד חצרו דליכא לדמויי לידה דאינה סמוכה לה תיפוק לה זכייתה משליחותה כי היכי דשלוחו זוכה לו שלא בפניו חצרו נמי זוכה לו שלא בפניו ומיהו גבי מציאה כי ליתיה גבה דלא נפקא זכייתה משום יד ליכא לרבויי משליחות דגבי שליחות איכא דעת השולח או דעת שליח אבל חצר ליכא לא דעת שולח ולא דעת שליח הלכך בעינן (י) דעת אחרת מקנה אותו: זרק ארנקי. והפקירו לכל הקודם: שאין סופו לנוח. בתוך האויר: כמונח דמי. וקנאו בעל הבית הראשון או לאו כמונח דמי להכי בעי אויר שאין סופו לנוח בתוך הבית כמונח דמי דאילו אויר שהיה סופו לנוח בתוך הבית פשיטא לן דאפילו קדם איש אחר וקלטה בתוך האויר לא קנה דמשנכנס לאויר קנאו בעל הבית דתנן במסכת גיטין (דף עט.) היתה עומדת בראש הגג וזרק לה גט כיון שנכנס לאויר הגג הרי זו מגורשת הוא למעלה והיא למטה כיון שיצא מרשות הגג נמחק או נשרף הרי זו מגורשת: ואינו מגיען. אלמא מתגלגלים ויוצאין הן ואין סופן לנוח וקאמר דקנה ליה שדהו: **מתני'** מציאת בנו ובתו הקטנים כו'. בנו קטן בגמרא מפרש מ"ט בתו הקטנה בכתובות (דף מו:) ילפינן לה מקראי דקטנה ואף נערה כל שבח נעוריה לאביה: מציאת עבדו ושפחתו הכנענים שלו. שהרי גופו קנוי לו עולמית כדכתיב (ויקרא כה) והתנחלתם וגו': מציאת אשתו. רבנן תקינו ליה משום איבה: מציאת עבדו ושפחתו העברים. בגמ' פריך לא יהא אלא פועל דאמרינן לעיל (דף י.) מציאתו לבעל הבית: **גמ'** מפני מה אמרו מציאת קטן לאביו. בשלמא בתו ואשתו טעמא מפרש להו במקומן בכתובות אלא בנו טעמא מאי: מריצה אצל אביו. הלכך כשמגביה לצורך אביו הגביהה: ילקט בנו אחריו. מותר לבנו של פועל אם עני הוא ללקוט אחר אביו את לקט הנושר אבל אם קבל הפועל את השדה למחצה לשליש ולרביע עשיר הוא והרי הוא כבעל הבית בשדה זה ולא ילקט בנו אחריו לפי שלקט בנו לאביו: בין כך ובין כך כו'. דאם האב עשיר הבן עני חוכה לעצמו: טעמא דתנא דידן קאמר. מפני מה אמרו מציאת קטן לאביו: וליה לא ס"ל. דמציאת קטן לאביו: מדבריהם. מפני דרכי שלום: ונפקא מינה. מדר' יוסי הא אתא לאשמועינן דהחמירו חכמים בתקנתן כגזל גמור להוציאו בדיינין וכיון דמדאורייתא לית ליה זכייה נמצא אביו גוזל את העניים: אלא אמר אביי. רבי יוסי נמי כתנא דידן ס"ל דקטן לית ליה זכייה וגבי לקט היינו טעם דכיון דיש לו לפועל זה בנים ואשה עניים עצמן מייאשי מלקט שלה לפיכך עשאוה כשדה שהלכו בו הנמושות דתנן (פאה פ"ח מ"א) מאימתי כל אדם מותרין בלקט משילכו בו הנמושות לקוטי בתר לקוטי דמההיא שעתא מסחו עניים דעתייהו מיניה והכא נמי מסחו דעתייהו כו':

עשו

---

**חצר** משום יד אתרבאי. ולכך כי הוי דומיא דיד דהיינו כשהוא בצד חצרו קונה אפילו בע"כ או אפילו קטנה (ז) בידה וכשאינה סמוכה לחצרה דלא הוי דומיא דיד לא תימא כי היכי דאין לו דין יד הכי נמי אין לו דין שליחות אלא לא גרע משליחות [ב] ובמידי דזכות כמו מתנה קנה ואפילו אינו עומד בצד חצרו ואפילו אינה משתמרת ובמציאה דאין דעת אחרת מקנה אותה בעינן משתמרת ובגט דחוב הוא לה אפילו במשתמרת אינה מתגרשת דלא עדיפא משליחות דאין חבין לאדם שלא בפניו:

**ויצא** בפתח אחר. ל"ג והפקריה דהא חשיב ליה דעת אחרת מקנה אותו דמייתי ראיה ממתנה ואי אפקריה אם כן מיד כשיצא הארנקי מידו היה הפקר ובשעת זכייה ליכא דעת אחרת אלא ל"ג והפקריה ולעולם היא שלו עד שיזכה בה אחר:

**ואמר** שמואל הלכה כרבי יוסי. תימה דבפ' כל הגט (גיטין דף ל. ושם ד"ה כיחידאה) לא בעי שמואל לאוקמי מתניתין דהמלוה מעות את הכהן ואת הלוי (ח) [להיות מפריש עליהן מחלקן] כרבי יוסי כיחידאה לא מוקמינן (ט) והכא פסיק הלכה כמותו וי"ל דדוקא הכא גבי לקט פסיק כוותיה מהאי טעמא דמסתמא עניים גופייהו ניחא להו כו' והא דאוקמי בפרק כל הגט (שם) כרבי יוסי היינו רבי יוסי דפ' הלוקח עובר פרתו (בכורות דף יח. ושם ד"ה עשו) דאמר כל שחליפיו ביד כהן פטור מן המתנות ומפרש טעמא בגמ' משום דעשו את שאינו זוכה כזוכה דהוי דומיא דהמלוה מעות דהוו חליפין ביד כהן דהיינו מעות ועשו כאילו זכה במעשר עצמו והא דקרי ליה יחידאה אע"ג דבבכורות לא פליג אלא ר"מ מ"מ רבנן דפליגי עליה הכא גבי לקט כ"ש דפליגי עליה התם גבי מתנות:

**אי** אמרת בשלמא דאורייתא. תימה מנ"ל דלר' יוסי קטן זוכה מן התורה וכן בסמוך דפריך וסבר רבי יוסי מציאת קטן דאורייתא ומנ"ל ודלמא אינה אלא מדרבנן ואביו לא זכה מיניה כלל ולהכי מלקט אחריו וי"ל דמסתמא לא פליג ר' יוסי אכמה משניות דפרקין ודפרק חלון (עירובין דף עט: ושם) ודמסכת מעשר שני (פ"ד מ"ד) דמייתי בפרק התקבל (גיטין דף סה. ושם) דלכולהו משניות יד בן כיד אביו וא"ת ונימא לעולם זכי לנפשיה מדרבנן ובתר הכי זכי אבוה מיניה משום איבה ומשום הכי מלקט וי"ל דמדרבנן אין סברא שיתקנו שתי זכיות שיזכה הבן קודם ואח"כ יזכה האב ממנו אלא אי מדרבנן הוא בשעת זכיית הבן בא לו זכיית האב משום דבשעת הגבהה לוקחה להריצה לאביו אלא ודאי זכה לנפשיה מדאורייתא ואבוה זכה מיניה משום איבה שסמוך על שלחנו:

**ואבוה** עשיר הוא. לאו דוקא עשיר אלא כלומר כיון שיש לו חלק בשדה חייב בלקט כדדרשינן לר"א פ"ק דגיטין (דף יב. ושם) לא תלקט לעני להזהיר עני על שלו ולרבנן נמי או נפקא להו מקרא אחרינא או תרתי ש"מ:

**שמואל** טעמא דתנא דידן קאמר. וא"ת אמאי לא אוקמה בטעמא דידיה דסבר שמואל דזכי לנפשיה מדאורייתא ומדרבנן אבוה זכי מיניה משום איבה וכרבי יוסי וי"ל דקטן דקתני במתני' משמע ליה בקטן ממש ואע"פ שאינו סמוך על שלחנו ואילו היה זוכה לעצמו מן התורה לא היה להם לתקן שיזכה אביו כיון דליכא איבה שהרי אינו סמוך על שולחנו אלא ודאי לא זכי לנפשיה כלל אלא לאביו שבשעת הגבהה מגביה לצורך אביו:

רבי

---

עין משפט
נר מצוה

צו א ב מיי' פ"ה מהל' גירושין הלכה ג ופ"ד מהל' זכייה ומתנה הל' ג [רב אלפס כאן ובגיטין פ"ח דף קפד.]:

צז ג טוש"ע ח"מ סי' רמג סעיף כד:

צח ד מיי' פי"ז מהל' גזילה ואבידה הל' יג סמג עשין עד טוש"ע ח"מ סי' ער סעיף ב:

צט ה מיי' שם ופי"ב מהל' אישות הל' ג ופכ"א שם הל' א סמג שם וסי' מח טוש"ע שם וטוש"ע אה"ע סי' סט סעיף ג וסי' פד:

ק ו מיי' פי"ז מהלכות גזילה ואבידה הל' יג סמג עשין עד טוש"ע ח"מ סי' ער סעיף ב וטוש"ע אה"ע סי' פד:

קא ז מיי' פ"ד מהל' מתנות עניים הל' יא:

קב ח מיי' פי"ז מהל' גזילה ואבידה הל' יב סמג עשין עד טוש"ע ח"מ סי' ער סעיף א:

קג ט מיי' פ"ד מהלכות מתנות עניים הל' יג:

רבינו חננאל

ופריק רב אשי חצר איתרבי משום יד ולא גרעה משליחות גבי גט דחוב הוא לה אינה מגורשת אם זרק לה גיטה בעלה בחצירה אא"כ עומדת בצד חצירה כדתנן אין חבין לאדם אלא בפניו. אבל מתנה דזכות הוא לו אע"פ שאינו עומד בצד שדהו קנה כדתנן זכין לאדם שלא בפניו. ואסקי' צבי שבור וכיוצא בו אם רץ אחריהן ומגיען ואמר זכתה לי שדי זכתה לו שדהו והוא שעומד בצד שדהו. ואם היו תרבות והקנה לו אחד במתנה אע"פ אם ירוץ אחריהן אין יכול להגיעם כיון שעברו בתוך שדהו קנאם הואיל ומתגלגלין וקי"ל מתגלגל כמונח דמי: מתני' מציאת בנו ובתו הקטנים הרי הם שלו. אמר שמואל מפני מה אמרו מציאת קטן לאביו שבשעה שמוצאה מריצה אצל אביו ואינה מאחרה בידו. למימרא דסבר שמואל דקטן לית ליה זכייה לנפשיה והתניא פועל ילקט בנו אחריו למחצה לשליש ולרביע לא ילקט בנו אחריו. פי' כיון שיש לו חלק בתבואת השדה אפי' א) הוה ליה עשיר. ותנן מי שיש לו מאתים זוז הרי זה לא יטול לקט שכחה ופאה ומעשר כו'. ר' יוסי אומר בין כך ובין כך אשתו ובניו מלקטין אחריו. ואמר שמואל הלכה כר' יוסי ואי אמרת לאביו הוא זוכה אביו עשיר הוא. ודחי' שמואל טעמיה דתנא דידן קאמר וליה לא ס"ל. ושקלינו וטרינו לאוקומא דר' יוסי סבר אית ליה זכיי' לנפשי' ולא איתוקמא אלא מדרבנן אית ליה זכייה לנפשיה.

חשק שלמה על ר"ח
א) אולי צ"ל ואפילו עני הוה ליה כעשיר.

---

תורת הש"ם

א) [קידושין כג. וש"נ], ב) [גיטין קב.], ג) [זבחים ...], ד) גיטין נט:, ה) [גיטין מא.], ו) ס"א חצר ... מרת, מהרש"ל ...א, ז) נ"ל כידה, ח) מהרש"ל.

הגהות הב"ח

(א) גמ' אית ליה זכייה מדאורייתא כי קא ...: (ב) שם ואבוה ...: (ג) רש"י ד"ה גבי ... וכו' דאנן סהדי ... נ"ב אע"ג דקי"ל ... דף יג ע"ב ודף קלא ... דשולא מתנות יחיה ... היכא שמעצמו אומר ... בל מסתמא אמרי' ... ליה ליקח במתנה וק"ל:

הגהות הגר"א

[א] גמ' במתנה היאך ... ה כו'. נ"ב פי' ...ס דוקא כה"ג אבל ... לבי רץ לא וצ"ע ... מ"ש רבינו בח"מ ... רס"ח ס"ק י"ב): ... תוס' ד"ה חצר ... מידי דזכות כו'. נ"ב ... פפא ורמב"ם פסק ... כההוא מרבנן:

גליון הש"ס

... ד"ה ואמר וכו' ... א פסיק הלכה ... תו. עיין גיטין יג ע"א ... תוס' ד"ה והא:

ליקוטי רש"י

חבין לאדם אלא ... יו. אין אדם יכול ... ות שלוחו שלא ... תו לדבר שהוא מוכה ... הפסד [קידושין כג.]. ... בפניו כלומר שלא ... תו [כתובות יא.]. זכין ... ים שלא בפניו. ... בהן השליח לצרכו ... ין יא:]. גזל גמור. ... מפרש גזל גמור ... ריהם וטעמא דר' ... בכולהו דקבל עשו ... דרכי שלום את ... נו זוכה לקנות קנין ... כזוכה [גיטין נט:]. ... בריהם. אפי' לר' ... לאו גזל דאורייתא ... להוציאו ... דיינים. לדרבנן לא ... ן בדיינים ומיהו לר' ... גזל מעליא לא הוי ... אל לעדות ולעבור עליו ... בלאו [שם סא.].

חָצֵר אִיתְרַבַּאי מִשּׁוּם – Acquisition by means of one's **courtyard derived from** the capacity that one's **hand** has to acquire ›jects; וְלֹא גָּרְעָה מִשְּׁלִיחוּת – **but it is no worse than** the device agency.[1] גַּבֵּי גֵּט דְּחוֹב הוּא לָהּ – Hence, **with regard to a bill** divorce, which is possibly **disadvantageous to [the woman],** e must apply the principle: אֵין חָבִין לְאָדָם אֶלָּא בְּפָנָיו – **We may** ›t **disadvantage a person except in his presence.**[2] גַּבֵּי מַתָּנָה דִּזְכוּת הוּא – However, **with regard to a gift, which is** ›neficial to [the recipient], we apply the principle: זָכִין לְאָדָם שֶׁלֹּא בְּפָ – **We may benefit a person** even **in his absence.**[3]

The Gemara elaborates on a ruling cited earlier:

גּוּפָ – **The text** of a previously cited ruling is cited again. Our ishnah stated: רָאָה אוֹתָן רָצִין אַחַר הַמְּצִיאָה וכו׳ – If HE SAW EOPLE] RUNNING AFTER A FIND, a lame deer, or young pigeons .at never flew, **etc.,** the owner of the field acquires them by rtue of their presence in his field. אָמַר רַבִּי יִרְמְיָה אָמַר רַבִּי יוֹחָנָן In explanation, **R' Yirmiyah said in the name of R'** ›chanan: וְהוּא שֶׁרָץ אַחֲרֵיהֶן וּמַגִּיעָן – **Provided that [the field** ›wner] **can run after [the animals] and reach them** before they ave the field. בָּעֵי רַבִּי יִרְמְיָה – **R' Yirmiyah** then **inquired:** בְּמַתָּנָה הֵיא – **What is** the law **in** the case of **a gift?** Does the cipient have to be able to reach it before it leaves his field? קִבְּלָהּ מִינֵּיהּ ר׳ אַבָּא בַּר כַּהֲ – And **R' Abba bar Kahana accepted** .e distinction suggested **by [R' Yirmiyah],** אַף עַל פִּי שֶׁרָץ אַחֲרֵיהֶן וְאֵין מַגִּי – and the recipient acquires the animals as a ft **even if he could not reach them were he to run after them.**

The Gemara now makes an inquiry which will be analyzed in ;ht of the ruling just cited:

בָּעֵי רָבָא – **Rava inquired:** זָרַק אַרְנָקִי בְּפֶתַח זֶה וְיָצָא בְּפֶתַח אַחֵר – If **one threw a purse in this doorway and it went out another doorway,** מַהוּ – **what is [the law]?** Does the owner of the house acquire the purse?[4] אֲוִיר שֶׁאֵין סוֹפוֹ לָנוּחַ – **Is** an article that enters the **airspace** of a place **in which [the article] is not destined to come to rest** כְּמוּנָּח דָּמֵי אוֹ לֹא – **considered as if it is resting** in that place **or not?**[5]

The Gemara seeks to answer this inquiry:

אָמַר לֵיהּ רַב פָּפָּא לְרָבָא – **Rav Pappa responded to Rava;** וְאָמְרֵי לָהּ רַב אַדָּא בַּר מַתְנָה לְרָבָא – **and some say that** it was **Rav Adda bar Masnah** who **responded to Rava;** וְאָמְרֵי לָהּ רָבִינָא לְרָבָא – **and some say that** it was **Ravina** who **responded to Rava:** לַאו הַיְינוּ מַתְנִיתִין – **Is this not** the case of **our Mishnah?** רָאָה אוֹתָן רָצִין אַחַר הַמְּצִיאָה – The Mishnah stated: If HE SAW [PEOPLE] RUNNING AFTER A FIND, a lame deer, or young pigeons that never flew, etc. וְאָמַר רַבִּי יִרְמְיָה אָמַר רַבִּי יוֹחָנָן – **And,** in explanation, **R' Yirmiyah said in the name of R' Yochanan:** וְהוּא שֶׁרָץ אַחֲרֵיהֶן וּמַגִּיעָן – **Provided that [the field owner] can run after [the animals] and reach them** before they leave the field. וּבָעֵי רַבִּי יִרְמְיָה – Whereupon **R' Yirmiyah inquired:** בְּמַתָּנָה הֵיאַךְ – **What is** the law **in** the case of **a gift?** וְקִבְּלָהּ מִינֵּיהּ רַבִּי אַבָּא בַּר כַּהֲנָא – **And R' Abba bar Kahana accepted** the distinction suggested **by [R' Yirmiyah],** בְּמַתָּנָה אַף עַל פִּי שֶׁרָץ אַחֲרֵיהֶן וְאֵין מַגִּיעָן – and **in** the case of **a gift** the recipient would acquire the animals **even if he could not reach them were he to run after them.** At any rate, it is clear that the field can acquire the animals for its owner even though they will run through it without stopping to rest inside. Similarly, in Rava's case, the house would acquire the purse passing through its airspace.

NOTES

The Gemara concluded earlier [see above 10b] that a woman's capacity acquire her *get* through *kinyan chatzeir* is an extension of her capacity acquire it with her hand. [This extension of her hand is derived from ›pecial Scriptural source, as stated in a Baraisa on 10b.] However, even there were no special Scriptural source for *chatzeir,* a person's court-rd could function as his agent under the normal provisions of the law agency (see 10b note 28). Scripture had to grant the status of "hand" a woman's courtyard only for situations in which the courtyard could ›t function as her agent – i.e. if the woman being divorced is a minor nce there is no agency for a minor] or when the woman is being vorced against her will [since agency in disadvantageous matters re-ires the consent of the principal] (*Rashi* 11b, *Rashash*; see *Ritva*; see so *Maharsha* and *Maharam Shif*). Rav Ashi now shows how this dual pacity of *chatzeir* ("hand" and "agent") serves to resolve the diffi-lties raised above by Rav Simi.

A non-appointed agent cannot act on behalf of a principal unless the atter is clearly advantageous to the principal (see next note). Accord-gly, since the divorce may be disadvantageous to the woman, her prop-ty cannot acquire the *get* as her agent, but only as an extension of her ›nd. In order for the property to function as her hand, she must be anding there, for only then does the property bear a similarity to her ›nd (*Rashi* 11b). [When she is not standing there, however, the property nnot be construed as an extension of her hand even if it is guarded. ›us, in the case of divorce, even though the woman's property is ›arded and the husband is conveying the *get* to her, it cannot acquire e *get* on her behalf when she is not present.]

It can be assumed that a person wants to acquire a gift; hence, an agent n act to acquire the gift on the recipient's behalf without the recipi-›t's prior consent. Consequently, even if the recipient is not standing ›side his field [in which case the field cannot function as his hand to quire the gift], the field can still acquire the gift for him in the capacity his agent.

However, the normal case of acquisition by agency involves an *aware-ss* of the agent's acquisition – whether the awareness of the principal ›mself, who commissions the agent to acquire the article on his behalf, [at least] the awareness of the agent, who [by his own initiative] makes e acquisition. Now, when the agent is an inanimate *chatzeir,* the ele-›ent of awareness is lacking, unless the present owner of the article is conveying it to the recipient via the *chatzeir* (e.g. in the case of a gift, such as the gift of *maaser* that Rabban Gamliel made to his shipmates). But in the case of a found article in a field, where no one is conveying the article to the field's owner, the field cannot serve as his agent to acquire the article unless he is standing alongside [so that the field functions as his hand] (*Rashi*; see *Maharsha*; see also *Nachalas Moshe* at length). Also, if the *chatzeir* is guarded, then it can acquire for its owner an ownerless article even if he is not present and entirely unaware of the matter (*Tosafos*; *Rashi* as emended by *Maharsha*). [For when a *chatzeir* is guarded, it serves as the owner's hand to acquire the ownerless article on his behalf even though he is not present. Although in regard to *get,* the woman's *chatzeir* – even if guarded – cannot serve as her hand to acquire the *get* unless she is present, there is a fundamental difference between a beneficial article and a *get.* Instead of guarding a beneficial article in his hand, a person will often place it in his *guarded* property for safekeeping. Thus, since it is common for his guarded property to serve as his extended hand in this regard even in his absence, it can also serve as his extended hand in regard to acquisition of the beneficial article, even in the owner's absence. But as regards a *get,* which is considered disadvantageous, it is not the practice of the woman to place it in her guarded premises for safekeeping; on the contrary, it is common for her to seek to remove it from her property. Therefore, her premises – even if guarded – do not serve as her extended hand in regard to a *get* unless she is present (*Ran,* cited by *Nimukei Yosef*; cf. *Rosh, Tos. HaRosh,* and sources quoted in *Shitah Mekubetzes*).]

4. Before throwing his purse, the owner declared it ownerless in regard to whoever would take it first (*Rashi*; cf. *Tosafos, Nimukei Yosef*). The question is whether the owner of the house acquires the purse by means of *kinyan chatzeir,* even though the purse never lands in his house.

5. There is no question that a person's property acquires an article for him as soon as that article enters the airspace of the property, provided that the article is in the process of coming to rest in that property (see *Gittin* 79a). Hence, even if another person intercepts the object before it lands, the interceptor does not acquire it, for it is no longer ownerless (*Rashi*). Rava's uncertainty is whether the same is true of an object that has been thrown so hard that it will pass through and not land in the property. Is mere passage through a property's airspace sufficient for *kinyan chatzeir* to operate?

מְטַלְטְלִין אַגַּב מְקַרְקַע נְתִינָה אַלִּימְתָּא הִיא – whereas acquisition of **movable objects by dint of land, is a proper** way of **giving** *maaser* to its eligible recipients.[14]

Having successfully offered one defense of Ulla, the Gemara now suggests another:

רַב פָּפָּא אָמַר – **Rav Pappa says:** דַּעַת אַחֶרֶת מַקְנָה אוֹתָן שָׁאנִי – **It is different** when **another mind** [i.e. person] **transfers ownership of them** to the recipient. In that situation, the recipient need not stand beside his courtyard in order for it to make the acquisition.[15]

Rav Pappa now proves this distinction:

וּמְנָא תֵּימְרָא – **And from where do you** find evidence to **say** this distinction? דִּתְנַן – **For we learned in** our **Mishnah:** רָאָה אוֹתָן רָצִין אַחַר הַמְּצִיאָה כו׳ – IF **HE SAW [PEOPLE] RUNNING AFTER A FIND,** a lame deer, or young pigeons that never flew, **etc.,** the owner of the field acquires the ownerless articles by virtue of their presence in his field. וְאָמַר רַבִּי יִרְמְיָה אָמַר רַבִּי יוֹחָנָן – **And,** in explanation of this Mishnah, **R' Yirmiyah said in the name of R' Yochanan:** וְהוּא שֶׁרָץ אַחֲרֵיהֶן וּמַגִּיעָן – **Provided that [the field owner] can run after [the animals] and reach them** before they leave his field.[16] וּבָעֵי רַבִּי יִרְמְיָה – **Whereupon R' Yirmiyah inquired:** בְּמַתָּנָה הֵיאַךְ – **What is** the law **in** the case of **a gift?** Does the recipient have to be able to reach it before it leaves his field in order for his field to effect the acquisition?[17] קִבְּלָהּ מִינֵּיהּ רַבִּי אַבָּא בַּר כַּהֲנָא – **And R' Abba bar Kahana accepted** this distinction made **by [R' Yirmiyah],**[18] and the recipient acquires the animals as a gift אַף עַל פִּי שֶׁרָץ אַחֲרֵיהֶן וְאֵין מַגִּיעָן – **even if he could not reach them were he to run after them.** מַאי טַעְמָא – **What is the reason** for this distinction? לָאו מִשּׁוּם דְּדַעַת אַחֶרֶת מַקְנָה אוֹתָן שָׁאנִי – **Is it not because it is different** when **another mind transfers ownership** of **them?**[19]

The Gemara objects:

אָמַר לֵיהּ רַב שִׁימִי לְרַב פָּפָּא – **Rav Simi asked Rav Pappa:** י גֵּט – **But** in the case of **a bill of divorce,** עַת אַחֶרֶת מַקְנָה אוֹתָהּ – **where another mind** [i.e. the husband] **transfers ownersh** **of it** to his wife, the woman should not have to stand at h property's side to acquire it. מַר עוּלָּא וְהוּא שֶׁעוֹמֶדֶת בְּצַד בֵּיתָהּ אוֹ בְּצַד חֲצֵרָהּ – **Yet, Ulla ruled** that a woman can be divorced placing the bill of divorce in her house or courtyard, **provid** **that she is standing at the side of her house or at the side her courtyard!**[20] –?–

The Gemara answers:

שָׁאנִי גֵּט דְּאִיתֵיהּ בְּעַל כָּרְחָהּ – **A bill of divorce is differe because it is** effective even **against her will.**[21]

The Gemara refutes this answer:

מַתְקִיף לָהּ רַב שֵׁשֶׁת בְּרֵיהּ דְּרַב אִידִי – **Rav Sheishess the son of R Idi refuted** that answer with the following argument: וּ קַל וָחוֹמֶר הוּא – **Is it not a** ***kal vachomer*****?**[22] ה גֵּט דְּאִיתֵיהּ בְּעַל כָּרְחָהּ – **Now, if** in regard to **a bill of divorce, which is** effecti **against her will,** אִי עוֹמֶדֶת בְּצַד בֵּיתָהּ וּבְצַד חֲצֵרָהּ אִין – **if she standing at the side of her house or at the side of h courtyard – yes, she** becomes divorced, אִי לֹא לֹא – **but if n** she does **not** become divorced; מַתָּנָה דְּמִדַּעְתֵּיהּ – then, in rega to **a gift, which** is acquired only **with [the recipient's] conse** לֹא כָּל שֶׁכֵּן – **is it not certain** that the recipient must stand at t side of his courtyard in order for it to acquire on his behalf?

The Gemara resorts to a different defense of Rav Pappa:

אֶלָּא אָמַר רַב אַשִׁי – **Rather, Rav Ashi said:** A differe distinction can be drawn between acquiring a bill of divorce a acquiring a gift.

NOTES

*chalifin,* since it has the appearance of selling the *maaser* to the recipient (*Rashi*; cf. *Ketzos HaChoshen* 202:4).

14. *Rashi.* Although the land is being conveyed through a commercial transaction, nothing commercial is being done directly to the *maaser* that is being conveyed along with the land (see *Ritva*). The Gemara thus concludes that R' Abba's challenge to Ulla from the incident involving Rabban Gamliel was unfounded. For Rabban Gamliel might have leased the land to R' Yehoshua and R' Akiva in order to effect *kinyan agav,* not in order that the land should serve as their *chatzeir.*

15. An article that is being transferred by its owner to a recipient is more easily conveyed than an ownerless article that a person seeks to acquire on his own. A conveyed article can be acquired by means of the recipient's *chatzeir* even if he is not standing beside it. But an ownerless article cannot be acquired through the person's *chatzeir* unless he is standing beside it.

Accordingly, the Mishnah can be understood as originally proposed: R' Akiva and R' Yehoshua acquired their respective *maaser* portions through *kinyan chatzeir,* using the field that Rabban Gamliel had leased to them. Nevertheless, they were not required to stand at the field's side to effect the acquisition because the *maaser's* owner [Rabban Gamliel] was transferring the *maaser* to them (*Rashi*).

16. [For example, the deer must be sufficiently lame, and the field large enough, so that the owner of the field can catch the deer before it leaves his field. In such a case, the field is considered guarded and can effect the acquisition. But if the deer could escape before the field's owner reached it, his presence in the field would not render the field "secure."]

17. I.e. if someone owns a lame deer or newly hatched birds and wants to give them as a gift to another person by placing them in the recipient's field, is it necessary for the recipient to be capable of catching them before they can leave his field in order to acquire them through *kinyan chatzeir*? If he must, then his field cannot effect acquisition of the gift; the gift therefore remains the property of the donor, who can withdraw the offer [as long as the recipient has not performed a valid act of acquisition to the gift] (*Rashi*).

18. R' Yirmiyah's inquiry implies that there is a logical distinction between acquisition of a gift and acquisition of an ownerless article (*Rashi*).

19. When someone else is transferring ownership of the deer (e.g. in t case of a gift), the recipient does not have to be able to catch it in ord for his *chatzeir* to acquire it on his behalf. That requirement applies or when the person is acquiring the deer on his own (i.e. an ownerless dee Similarly, asserts Rav Pappa, the condition that the owner must sta beside his otherwise unguarded *chatzeir* applies only when he seeks acquire something on his own, not when an owner is transferring it him.

20. The Mishnah in *Gittin* states (77b) that a husband may place h wife's *get* into her house or courtyard to effect the divorce. Ulla adds th the woman must be standing at the side of her property for it to acqui the *get* for her (*Rashi*). But if a person can acquire a gift by means *kinyan chatzeir* without standing in the courtyard when someone else conveying ownership of the article, the same should be true of a wom receiving her *get.* She should not be required to stand in her courtya in order for it to acquire the *get* on her behalf, since someone else [h husband] is conveying it to her.

[Rav Pappa could have retorted that even Rav Simi must admit th something is different about the case of divorce, since we require that t wife stand beside her *chatzeir* even though it is a *guarded* property house or courtyard). In other cases, however, the requirement that t owner stand beside the property applies only when the property is ot erwise unguarded. Rav Pappa, however, simply responds by showir what is different about the case of divorce, without first observing th Rav Simi would be compelled to make that distinction as well (see *Rar ban, Rashba, Ritva, Tos. HaRosh*).]

21. Even if a woman does not want her marriage to be dissolved, sh becomes divorced when her husband gives her a *get* (*Rashi*). If, howeve someone does not wish to acquire a certain gift, he does not acquire against his will. Consequently, it stands to reason that although the *g* is being conveyed to her by another person, she does not acquire against her will unless she is standing beside the property into which is placed, even if the property is otherwise guarded (*Ritva*).

22. On the contrary, the fact that the Torah empowers a husband to d vorce his wife against her will should make it *easier* to convey the *get* her, not more difficult! (see *Rashi*).

ומקומו מושכר לו ועישור אחר שאני עתיד למוד נתון לעקיבא בן יוסף כדי שיזכה בו לעניים ומקומו מושכר לו וכי רבי יהושע ורבי עקיבא בצד שדהו של רבן גמליאל היו עומדין אמר ליה (א) דמי האי מרבנן כדלא גמרי אינשי שמעתא כי אתא לסורא אמר להו הכי אמר עולא והכי אותביתיה אמר ליה ההוא מרבנן רבן גמליאל מטלטלי אגב מקרקעי הקנה להם רבי זירא קבלה רבי אבא לא קבלה אמר רבא שפיר עביד דלא קבלה וכי לא היה להם סודר לקנות ממנו בחליפין אלא טובת הנאה אינה ממון לקנות ממנו בחליפין הכא נמי טובת הנאה אינה ממון לקנות על גבי קרקע ולא היא (ג) מתנות כהונה נתינה כתיבא בהו חליפין דרך מקח וממכר הוא מטלטלין אגב מקרקע נתינה אלימתא היא רב פפא אמר [א] דעת אחרת מקנה אותן שאני ומנא תימרא דתנן ראה אותן רצין אחר המציאה כו' ואמר רבי ירמיה אמר רבי יוחנן [ב] והוא שרץ אחריהן ומגיען ובעי רבי ירמיה במתנה היאך קבלה מיניה רבי אבא בר כהנא [ג] אע"פ שרץ אחריהן ואין מגיען מאי טעמא לאו משום דדעת אחרת מקנה אותן שאני אמר ליה רב שימי לרב פפא הרי גט דדעת אחרת מקנה אותה (ג) ואמר עולא [ד] והוא שעומדת בצד ביתה או בצד חצרה שאני גט [ה] דאיתיה בעל כרחה מתקיף לה רב ששת בריה דרב אידי ולאו קל וחומר הוא ומה גט דאיתיה בעל כרחה אי עומדת בצד ביתה ובצד חצרה אין אי לא לא מתנה דמדעתיה לא כל שכן אלא אמר רב אשי

ולתנם לבעלים וזה המעשה דר"ג תנן במסכת מעשר שני (פ"ה מ"ו) גבי ביעור דתנן התם ערב הפסח של רביעית ושל שביעית היה הביעור נותן תרומה ותרומת מעשר לכהן כו' מי שהיו פירותיו רחוק ממנו צריך לקרות להם שם פירוש שם הבעלים שיקנה אותם ללוי ולכהן ומעשה נמי בר"ג וזקנים כו' וא"ת ואמאי לא נתן תרומה גדולה כדתנן בהך דמע"ש נותן תרומה ותרומת מעשר לכהן שהרי ר"א בן עזריה היה עמו כדקתני סיפא עמד רבי יהושע ואמר תרומת מעשר שבו נתון לר"א בן עזריה וי"ל דתרומה גדולה טרם שנסע הפרישה ונתנה לפי שקלה היתה להפריש דחטה אחת פוטרת את הכרי וניטלת באומד ועוד שהתבואה היתה כבר ממורחת בביתו של ר"ג כדמוכח בירושלמי ותרומה גדולה מפרישה בשדה מיד אחר המרוח כדאמרינן בירושלמי דמעשר שני מלא פירות בשדה מפוזרין מותרין משום גזל וחייבין במעשר ופטורין מתרומה דא"א לגורן שתיעקר אא"כ נתרמה תרומה ממנה:

ד) **נתון** ליהושע. וא"ת והא קנסינהו עזרא וי"ל דס"ל כר"ע דאמר דקודם קנס דוקא ללוי ואחר קנסא לכהן וללוי כדאמר פ"ב דכתובות (דף כו. ושם ד"ה אין ה) ואם תאמר ר' יוחנן בן גודגדא שאמר לר' יהושע חזור בך שאתה מן המשוררים ואני מן המשוערין (ערכין דף יא:) משמע שהיו שניהם לוים ובשלהי החליל (סוכה דף נו:) אמרינן מגיפי דלתות שבמקדש היו נוטלין שכרן מלחם הפנים ולחם הפנים אינו מותר אלא לכהנים וי"ל בג' מקומות היו הכהנים שומרים בבהמ"ק כדאמרי' בריש מס' תמיד ואותן מגיפי דלתות היו נוטלין שכרן מלחם הפנים:

**מקומו** מושכר לו. בסיפא קתני שקבלו שכר זה מזה וא"ת אמאי קבלו שכר היה לו להשאיל להם או להשכיר בחליפין וי"ל דשאלה ושכירות אינה נקנית בחליפין ו): **וכי** בצד שדהו של ר"ג היו עומדין. וא"ת והלא התבואה היתה בביתו של ר"ג כדמוכח בירושלמי פרק ג' דמעשרות וביתו של רבן גמליאל היה משתמר ויש לומר דלגבי זקנים לא היה משתמר שלא היה הפסק בין תבואתו לתבואתן ואם תאמר שלהי השואל (לקמן דף קב.) גבי הזבל של בעל הבית מוקי לה בגמרא בתורי דאתו מעלמא ובחצר דמשכיר וכרבי יוסי בר' חנינא והשתא והלא השוכר משתמש בחצר ואם כן הזבל משתמר לדעת השוכר בחצר ואיך יזכה המשכיר בזבל תורי דאתו מעלמא ויש לומר שגם משכיר ביתו פתוח לאותו חצר ומקרי עומד בצד שדהו [וע"ע תוספות גיטין עט: ד"ה פנימית]:

חצר

ומקומו מושכר לו. וקבל ממנו שם שכר המקום דהכי קתני סיפא נתקבלו זה מזה שכר וכל כך למה כדי לקנות מעשר שתהא חצרו קונה לו לפי שהמטלטלין אין קונין אלא או במשיכה או חצרו תקנה לו: **נתון לעקיבא.** גבאי היה ואותה שנה שנת מעשר עני היתה: **כי אתא.** רבי אבא לסורא אמר להו כו': **מטלטלי אגב** מקרקעי **הקנה להם.** ולאו משום דתקני להם מקומם בתורת חצר שאפילו הקנה להן חצר אחרת שאינן בתוכה קנוי נמי כדתנן (קדושין דף כו.) נכסים שאין להן אחריות נקנין עם נכסים שיש להן אחריות בכסף משנתן הכסף בשביל הקרקע והמטלטלין או אפילו קרקע במכר ומטלטלין במתנה נקנין המטלטלין בקנין הקרקע בלא משיכה כדילפינן בקדושין (שם) מויתן להם אביהם מתנות רבות לכסף ולזהב עם ערים (א) בצורות אשר ביהודה: **קבלה.** להאי תירוצא: **וכי לא היה להן סודר** כו'. למה לו לקבל מהן מעות: **אלא.** סודר מאי טעמא לא דטובת הנאה שהיתה לו לרבן גמליאל במעשרות הללו: **אינה חשובה ממון.** דתהא נקנית בחליפין דליכא למימר כי קנה ליה ר"ג להאי סודר אקנייה חליפין דידיה בכל מקום שהן דכיון דאין לו בהן אלא טובת הנאה שבידו לתתו לכל מי שירצה אין זו חשובה ממון לחול על זו קנין חליפין: **הכא נמי.** גבי קנין קרקע: **אינה ממון לקנות על גבי קרקע.** בקנין שהקרקע נקנה בו אלא אפקורי בעלמא אפקר גבייהו וכי אוגר להו מקום קנתה לו חצרו בתורת חצר כשאר הפקר: **ולא היא.** מהאי דכי לא היה להן סודר לאו ראיה היא למילף מינה דאין טובת הנאה נקנית בחליפין ועל גבי קרקע דשפיר איכא למימר מטלטלי אגב קרקעי הקנה להן ודקשיא לך לקנינהו בחליפין:

**מתנות.** של כהונה ולויה ומעשר עני: **נתינה כתיבא בהו.** כדכתיב (דברים כו) ונתתה ללוי זה מעשר ראשון לגר ליתום ולאלמנה זה מעשר עני לפיכך אסור להקנותן בסודר דדרך מקח הוא שזה נותן לו כליו תחתיהן ונראה זה כמוכרן לו: **נתינה אלימתא היא.** מותר להקנות מתנות כהונה על גבי קרקע: **רב פפא אמר.** לעולם בתורת חצר קנאו ואפילו הכי לא תקשי לעולא דהא דלא בעינן הכא עומד בצד השדה משום דדעת אחרת מקנה אותן שרבן גמליאל הקנה להן מטלטלין שהיו לו בחצר שלהן ולא מהפקירא קנו ונוחה מתנה זו לקנות ואע"ג דאין עומד בצד השדה: **והוא שרץ אחריהן.** הצבי מהלך והגוזלות מדדין ומתניתין דקתני זכתה לו שדהו כגון שהיה יכול לרוץ אחריהן ומגיען קודם שיצאו משדהו: **ה"ג ובעי ר' ירמיה במתנה היאך.** אם היו צבי וגוזלות של אדם אחד והם בתוך שדה חבירו ונותנן בעליהן לבעל שדה במתנה היאך הדין מי בעינן והוא שרץ אחריהן ומגיען ואי לא לא קני ומאי נותן למיהדר ביה או לא: **קבלה מיניה רבי אבא.** להך בעיא מרבי ירמיה דשפיר דק שיש חילוק בין נותנם להפקר ובמתנה אע"ת כו': **ואמר עולא.** במסכת גיטין (דף עז:) גבי הזורק גט לאשתו בתוך ביתה או בתוך חצרה: **שאני גט דאיתיה בעל כרחה.** שהוא נותנו לה ולא ניחא לה למגרשה: **ולאו קל וחומר הוא.** מן הטעם הזה יש לדון דכ"ש לקנין אחר: **מה גט.** דכי איתה בצד חצרה ולא ניחא לה למקנייה אפילו הכי קנייה לה חצרה אמרינן דאי ליתה אין אי לא לא: **מתנה.** דליתה בע"כ דאי אמרה לא בעינא לא קניא: **לא כ"ש.** דכי אמרה בעינא צריכא שתהא בצד חצרה: **אלא אמר רב אשי.** לא תתלי טעמא משום דאיתה בעל כרחה אלא גבי מתנה היינו טעמא דלא בעינן עומד אצלה דכיון דמידה אתרבאי לא גרעה משלוחה להיטיב לה ואילו שלוחה שקיבל לה מתנה מי לא קני לה ואפילו אין עומדת בצדו חצרה נמי לא שנא הלכך גבי מתנה דזכות הוא לה אנן סהדי דניחא לה שתהא שלוחה וקנייא לה כשליח אבל גבי גט דחוב הוא לה לא ניחא לה שתהא שלוחה הלכך כי עומדת בצדה על כרחה ידה היא וידה קניא גבי גט על כרחה ואי לא לאו ידה הוא ולא שלוחה הוא טעמא דיש חילוק בין גט למתנה ואף על גב דתרווייהו דעת אחרת מקנה אותן משום דהך חצר אף על גב דאתרבאי משום יד כדאמרן לעיל (דף י:) לא גרעה משליחות דאי נמי לא אתרבאי מונתן בידה הוי נפקא לן חצר משליחות וכי אצטריך לרבויי משום יד משום קטן וקטנה דלתנהו בתורת שליחות אצטריך וכל היכא דאיתיה לשליחות איתיה לדין חצר הלכך גבי גט דחוב הוא לה אין חבין כו' כלומר אין אדם יכול לעשות שליח לחוב אדם שלא מדעתו וחצרו נמי לאו בתורת שליחות מלית לאתויי דתתגרש שלא מדעתה הלכך בגט לא תרבייה אלא משום יד ומה ידה דסמוכה לה אף חצירה בסמוכה לה:

גבי

### עין משפט נר מצוה

**צב א** מיי' פ"ד מהלכות זכייה ומתנה הל' ח ופי"ז מהל' גזילה ואבידה הל' יא סמג עשין פב טוש"ע ח"מ סי' רמג סעיף כ וסי' רסח סעיף ד:

**צג ב ג** מיי' פי"ז מהל' גזילה ואבידה הל' יא סמג עשין עד טוש"ע ח"מ סי' רסח סעיף ד:

**צד ד** מיי' פ"ה מהלכות גירושין הל' ב ועיין במ"מ סמג עשין נ טוש"ע אה"ע סי' קלט סעיף א ב:

**צה ה** מיי' שם פ"א הלכה ב סמג שם טוש"ע אה"ע סי' קיט סעיף ג בהג"ה וסעיף ו:

### רבינו חננאל

אמר רבן גמליאל עישור אחד שאני עתיד למוד נתון ליהושע (בן לוי) א) ומקומו מושכר לו זה מעשר ראשון. ועישור אחר שאני עתיד למוד זה מעשר עני נתון לעקיבא בן יוסף שהוא פרנס והוא יד לעניים ומקומו מושכר לו כדי שיזכה בו לעניים ונתקבלו שכר זה מזה וכי ר' יהושע ור"ע בצד שדהו של ר"ג היו עומדין. ופרקי' ר"ג מטלטלי אגב מקרקעי אקני להו ומכיון שקיבל ר"ג כסף שכירות הקרקע זכו הם בקרקע ובכל מה שבתוכו דקי"ל כשם שהקרקע נקנית בכסף ובשטר ובחזקה כך שכירות הקרקע נקנית בכסף ובשטר ובחזקה. ואמרי' אמאי לא אקני להו ר"ג האי מעשר אגב סודר. ואמרי' משום דעיקר המעשר ללוי הוא וכי מן השמים הקנוהו לו ואין לבעלים בו אלא טובת הנאה שהוא רשאי לתתו לאיזה לוי שירצה. וקי"ל דטובת הנאה אינה נקנית בחליפין ב) דחליפין דרך מקח וממכר הוא כלומר מקבל הסודר ומקנה לו חפץ אחד ומתנות כהונה כיון דבהדיא כתיבא בהו נתינה הקנאה אגב קרקע נתינה אלימתא היא. רב פפא פירק פירוק אחר דעת אחרת מקנה אותם שאני. כלומר אם אדם מקנה לחבירו כלום דבר והדבר ההוא נתון בתוך שדה מקבל המתנה קנאו ואע"ג דאינו עומד בצד שדהו. ומקשי' עליה והרי גט דדעת אחרת מקנה אותה וקי"ל והוא שעומדת בצד ביתה או בצד חצירה. ופריק

### חשק שלמה על ר"ח

א) נראה דל"ל שהיה לוי.
ב) נראה דחסר כאן ול"ל ה"נ אינה ממון לקנות ע"ג קרקע ולא היא חליפין דרך וכו' נתינה איתו יכול להקנות בחליפין אבל הקנאה אגב קרקע וכו'.

### מסורת הש"ס

א) [עירובין טו. ו... ב) [חולין קלד:], ג) ... עז:, ד) [שייך לע... ה) [וכן ביבמות ... ו) [וע"ע תוס' קדושי... ד"ה ומקומו, ועיין ערכין ל. בסוד"ה כט: ידענא].

### הגהות הב"ח

(א) רש"י ד"ה כי וכו' ערים מצורות א...

### ליקוטי רש"י

ומקומו מושכר ונתן לו רבי יהושע פ... בשכר המקום ו... מטלטלין נקנין הקרקע בכסף מסקנא דהך מילתא ... מעשר שני (פ"ה מ... ונתקבלו שכר זה ואע"פ שעדיין לא הו... קריית שם הוא ש... לשהות לחבריס דבר ... מתוקן ואפילו אכלו ... אין כאן חיוב מיתה ... טבל ומן המותר ... מעשרותיו. **לעקיבא בן יוסף.** מעשר עני היתה עקיבא גבאי עניים ובספינה היו שניהם [קידושין כז.]. **נת... כתיבא בהו.** ... ליתנן לכהן [חולין ק...

**וּמְקוֹמוֹ מוּשְׂכָּר לוֹ** – AND ITS PLACE, i.e. the place upon which the designated *maaser* rests, IS LEASED TO HIM.[1] **וְעִישּׂוּר אַחֵר שֶׁאֲנִי עָתִיד לָמוֹד** – AND ANOTHER TENTH of my produce THAT I WILL, IN THE FUTURE, MEASURE OUT as *maaser ani*,[2] **נָתוּן לַעֲקִיבָא בֶּן יוֹסֵף** – IS hereby GIVEN TO AKIVA BEN YOSEF, **כְּדֵי שֶׁיִּזְכֶּה בּוֹ לָעֲנִיִּים** – SO THAT HE WILL ACQUIRE IT ON BEHALF OF THE POOR;[3] **וּמְקוֹמוֹ מוּשְׂכָּר לוֹ** – AND ITS PLACE IS LEASED TO HIM.

Having cited this Mishnah, R' Abba now presents his challenge: **וְכִי רַבִּי יְהוֹשֻׁעַ וְרַבִּי עֲקִיבָא בְּצַד שָׂדֵהוּ שֶׁל רַבָּן גַּמְלִיאֵל הָיוּ עוֹמְדִין** – **Now, were R' Yehoshua and R' Akiva standing at the side of Rabban Gamliel's field?** Certainly not; they were at sea! Evidently then, a person need not stand at the side of his field in order to acquire the object within it.[4] – ? –

Ulla responds to his challenger: **אָמַר לֵיהּ** – **[Ulla] said to [R' Abba]:** **דָּמֵי הַאי מֵרַבָּנָן כִּדְלָא גָּמְרֵי אִינָשֵׁי שְׁמַעְתָּא** – **This Rabbi** [R' Abba] **seems like one to whom people never explained the law!**[5]

The Gemara continues: **כִּי אֲתָא לְסוּרָא** – **When [R' Abba] came to** the city of **Sura,** **אָמַר לְהוּ הָכִי אָמַר עוּלָּא וְהָכִי אוֹתְבִיתֵיהּ** – **he told [the Rabbis there]: This is what Ulla said, and this is how I challenged him.**[6] **אָמַר לֵיהּ הַהוּא מֵרַבָּנָן** – **One of the Rabbis said to [R' Abba]:** You can bring no proof from that case, since it is possible that **רַבָּן גַּמְלִיאֵל מִטַּלְטְלֵי אַגַּב מְקַרְקְעֵי הִקְנָה לָהֶם** – **Rabban Gamliel transferred ownership** of his **movable** *maaser* **[to R' Yehoshua a R' Akiva] by dint of** his **land** that he leased to them.[7]

The Gemara records: **רַבִּי זֵירָא קַבְּלָהּ** – **R' Zeira accepted it** [this rejection of R' Abb proof]; **רַבִּי אַבָּא לֹא קַבְּלָהּ** – but **R' Abba did not accept it.**

Rava sides with R' Abba: **אָמַר רָבָא** – **Rava said:** **שַׁפִּיר עָבִיד דְּלָא קַבְּלָהּ** – **[R' Abba] act correctly in not accepting it.** **לֹא הָיָה לָהֶם סוּדָר לִקְנוֹת מִמֶּנּוּ בַּחֲלִיפִין** – For, consider: **Did [R' Yehoshua and R' Akiva] n have a kerchief to acquire** the *maaser* **from [Rabban Gamli** directly **through *chalifin*?**[8] **אֶלָּא טוֹבַת הֲנָאָה** – **Rather,** it m be that **the** small **benefit of gratitude** that one can receive fr his *maaser* **אֵינָהּ מָמוֹן לִקְנוֹת מִמֶּנּוּ בַּחֲלִיפִין** – **is not** consider sufficient **equity** for it **to be acquired from [the owner] throu *chalifin*.**[9] **הָכָא נַמִּי טוֹבַת הֲנָאָה אֵינָהּ מָמוֹן לִקְנוֹת עַל גַּבֵּי קַרְקַע** – **S too, the** small **benefit of gratitude** that one can receive from *maaser* **is not** considered sufficient **equity** for it **to be acquired dint of the land.**[10]

The Gemara rejects Rava's reasoning: **וְלֹא הִיא** – **But it is not so.**[11] **מַתְּנוֹת כְּהוּנָּה נְתִינָה כְּתִיבָא בְּהוּ** – F with regard to **gifts for the Kohen,** as well as gifts for the Levi a for the poor, **"giving" is written** by Scripture.[12] **יפִין דֶּרֶךְ מֶקַח וּמִמְכָּר הוּא** – Therefore, ***chalifin*** cannot be used to acquire *maa* because **it is in the manner of business transactions,**

NOTES

1. R' Yehoshua gave Rabban Gamliel money to lease the place upon which the *maaser* was located. The Gemara now assumes that this rental was necessary so that R' Yehoshua could then acquire the *maaser* that was in his newly leased land by means of acquisition through *chatzeir* (*Rashi*). [A leased property can serve as the *chatzeir* of the lessee (renter). See *Choshen Mishpat* 313:3 and commentaries.]

2. As mentioned, this incident occurred in the third year of the *Shemittah* cycle, when the second tithe is *maasar ani* for the poor.

3. R' Akiva was a treasurer of funds for the poor [and it was in this capacity that he acquired the tithes for them] (*Rashi*).

4. The place that Rabban Gamliel rented to them was unguarded – see *Tosafos*.

5. Ulla dismissed R' Abba's challenge out of hand without explaining what flaw he saw in it. Apparently, Ulla meant the distinction that Rav Pappa makes below (*Shitah Mekubetzes* in the name of his teacher).

6. I.e. Ulla said that an otherwise unguarded field acquires on behalf of its owner only if he is standing there, and I (R' Abba) challenged him from the incident involving Rabban Gamliel.

7. Nothing about acquisition by *chatzeir* can be proven from the incident involving Rabban Gamliel, since it is not certain that R' Yehoshua and R' Akiva acquired their *maaser* through the law of *chatzeir*. For it is possible that Rabban Gamliel leased his property to R' Yehoshua and R' Akiva in order for them to acquire the produce by means of *kinyan agav* (literally: acquisition by dint of). With this method of acquisition, one acquires movable property along with the acquisition of real property, even if the movable property is not inside that real property. [Certainly, then, there is no reason for the recipient to stand at the side of the land to guard it; for the movable items do not have to be there at all] (*Rashi*, from *Kiddushin* 26a).

Hence, R' Yehoshua and R' Akiva might have acquired the *maaser* from Rabban Gamliel through *kinyan agav* by dint of their acquisition of the lease on his property. In that case, they certainly could acquire the *maaser* while they were on the ship, even though they were far away from the land upon which the *maaser* was located. Obviously, then, nothing can be inferred from this incident about the laws of acquisition by *chatzeir*.

8. *Chalifin* (lit. exchange) is a form of acquisition whereby an object is exchanged between two parties as a means of effecting a given transaction. This form of acquisition may be used to acquire either a purchased item or one received as a gift. In the case of a gift, the recipient hands one of his possessions [a kerchief is usually used] to his benefactor. Then, in exchange, the recipient obtains ownership of the gift, wherever it is located. Accordingly, Rava asks why R' Yehoshua and R' Akiva had to obtain their *maaser* from Rabban Gamliel by paying him [for his property, thereby acquiring the *maaser*]. They should have simply giv him a kerchief [to obtain the *maaser* directly through *chalifin*] ( *Rashi*).

9. The *maaser* that a person separates from his produce must be giv to eligible recipients and is no longer owned by him. He retains in t *maaser* that he has designated only the right to choose a *specific* rec ient and exercising this prerogative can yield a minimal financial g (see *Rashi* to *Pesachim* 46b). Rava now suggests that this right, wh Rabban Gamliel retained in his *maaser,* is not considered real equity the *maaser* so that he should be able to transfer ownership of the *maa* through a *kinyan,* such as *chalifin.* [A *kinyan* presumes that the ow conveys the article in his possession to the recipient; if the owner d not truly *own* the article, he cannot convey it to someone else] (*Rash*

10. *Kinyan agav,* too, serves to directly convey the movable article to t recipient by dint of the act of acquisition performed in the land. Si Rabban Gamliel did not truly own the *maaser,* he could not convey it R' Yehoshua and R' Akiva through *kinyan agav.* He could accompli this end only by leasing them the land on which the *maaser* was situat and then relinquishing any rights [of distribution] that he had in t *maaser* [הֶפְקֵר]. The abandoned *maaser* would then become the prope of the land's lessee through the law of *chatzeir* (*Rashi*).

Hence, R' Abba was correct in challenging Ulla from this Mishn because R' Yehoshua and R' Akiva apparently acquired their respect *maaser* portions through *chatzeir* even though they were on the ship, n standing at the side of the land they had leased from Rabban Gamli

11. It cannot be proved that Rabban Gamliel did not use *kinyan ag* from the fact that he did not use *kinyan chalifin.* For it is possible th the small benefit of choosing the recipient of one's *maaser* is conside sufficient equity in the *maaser* to allow the *maaser* to be convey through any type of *kinyan* – including *agav* and *chalifin.* Rabban Ga liel, however, used *agav* instead of *chalifin* for the reason that follo (*Rashi*; see *Shitah Mekubetzes*).

12. The main concern in this Gemara is the gifts for the Levi and for t poor, which Rabban Gamliel sought to transfer to R' Yehoshua and Akiva, respectively (see *Rashi*). [The Gemara mentions "gifts for t Kohen" because that is the expression used elsewhere in the Talmud see *Chullin* 134b.] Scripture states (*Deuteronomy* 26:12): תָּה לַלֵּוִי לַגֵּר לַיָּתוֹם וְלָאַלְמָנָה, *You shall "give" [the tithe] to the Levi, to the convert, to t orphan, and to the widow.* In this verse, the portion given to the Le refers to *maaser rishon*; the portion given to the convert etc. refers *maaser ani.* The Torah thus states that the respective *maaser* portio are to be *given* to the proper recipients, not *sold* to them.

13. *Chalifin* is a *kinyan* that is akin to sale, since it involves the symbo exchange of the kerchief (for example) for the article being acquire Therefore, it is forbidden to convey *maaser* to the recipient throu

ומקומו מושכר לו ועישור אחר שאני עתיד למוד נתון לעקיבא בן יוסף כדי שיזכה בו לעניים ומקומו מושכר לו וכי רבי יהושע ורבי עקיבא בצד שדהו של רבן גמליאל היו עומדין אמר ליה [א] דמי האי מרבנן כדלא גמרי אינשי שמעתא כי אתא לסורא אמר להו הכי אמר עולא והכי אותביתיה אמר ליה ההוא מרבנן רבן גמליאל מטלטלי אגב מקרקעי הקנה להם רבי זירא קבלה רבי אבא לא קבלה אמר רבא שפיר עביד דלא קבלה וכי לא היה להם סודר לקנות ממנו בחליפין אלא טובת הנאה אינה ממון לקנות ממנו בחליפין הכא נמי טובת הנאה אינה ממון לקנות על גבי קרקע ולא היא [ג] מתנות כהונה נתינה כתיבא בהו חליפין דרך מקח וממכר הוא מטלטלין אגב מקרקע נתינה אלימתא היא רב פפא אמר [א] דעת אחרת מקנה אותן שאני ומנא תימרא דתנן ראה אותן רצין אחר המציאה כו' ואמר רבי ירמיה אמר רבי יוחנן [ב] והוא שרץ אחריהן ומגיען ובעי רבי ירמיה במתנה היאך קבלה מיניה רבי אבא בר כהנא [ג] אע"פ שרץ אחריהן ואין מגיען מאי טעמא לאו משום דדעת אחרת מקנה אותן שאני אמר ליה רב שימי לרב פפא הרי גט דדעת אחרת מקנה אותה [ה] ואמר עולא [ד] והוא שעומדת בצד ביתה או בצד חצרה שאני גט [ה] דאיתיה בעל כרחה מתקיף לה רב ששת בריה דרב אידי ולאו קל וחומר הוא ומה גט דאיתיה בעל כרחה אי עומדת בצד ביתה ובצד חצרה אין אי לא לא מתנה דמדעתיה לא כל שכן אלא אמר רב אשי

ולתנם לבעלים חזה המעשה דר"ג תנן במסכת מעשר שני (פ"ה מ"ז) גבי ביעור דתנן התם ערב הפסח של רביעית ושל שביעית היה הביעור נותן תרומה ותרומת מעשר לכהן כו' מי שהיו פירותיו רחוק ממנו צריך לקרות להם שם הבעלים שיקנה אותם ללוי ולכהן ומעשה נמי בר"ג וזקנים כו' וא"ת ואמאי לא נתן תרומה גדולה כדתנן בכך דמעשר שני נותן תרומה ותרומת מעשר לכהן שהרי ר"א בן עזריה היה עמו כדקתני סיפא עמד רבי יהושע ואמר תרומת מעשר שבו נתון לר"א בן עזריה וי"ל דתרומה גדולה טרם שנסע הפרישה ונתנה לפי שקלה היתה להפריש דחטה אחת פוטרת את הכרי וניטלת באומד ועוד שהתבואה היתה כבר ממורחת בביתו של ר"ג כדמוכח בירושלמי ותרומה גדולה מפרישה בשדה מיד אחר המרוח כדאמרינן בירושלמי דמעשר שני מגלה פירות בשדה מפחדין מותרין משום גזל וחייבין במעשר ופטורין מתרומה דה"א לגורן שתיעקר אא"כ נתרמה תרומה ממנה:

[ד] **נתון** לרבי יהושע. וא"ת והא קנסינהו עזרא וי"ל דס"ל כר"ע דאמר דקודם קנס דוקא ללוי ואחר קנסא לכהן וללוי כדאמר פ"ב דכתובות (דף כו. ושם ד"ה אין [ד]) ואם תאמר ר' יוחנן בן גודגדא שאמר לר' יהושע חזור בך שאתה מן המשוררים ואני מן המשוערין (ערכין דף יא:) משמע שהיו שניהם לוים ובשלהי החליל (סוכה דף נו:) אמרינן מגיפי דלתות שבמקדש היו נוטלין שכרן מלחם הפנים ולחם הפנים אינו מותר אלא לכהנים וי"ל בג' מקומות היו הכהנים שומרים בבהמ"ק כדאמרי' בריש מס' תמיד ואותן מגיפי דלתות היו נוטלין שכרן מלחם הפנים:

**מקומו** מושכר לו. בסיפא קתני שקבלו שכר זה מזה וא"ת אמאי קבלו שכר היה לו להשאיל להם או להשכיר בחליפין וי"ל דשאלה ושכירות אינה נקנית בחליפין [י]: **וכי** בצד שדהו של ר"ג היו עומדין. וא"ת והלא התבואה היתה בביתו של ר"ג כדמוכח בירושלמי פרק ג' דמעשרות וביתו של רבן גמליאל היה משתמר ויש לומר דלגבי זקנים לא היה משתמר שלא היה הפסק בין תבואתו לתבואתן ואם תאמר שלהי השואל (לקמן דף קב.) גבי הזבל של בעל הבית מוקי לה בגמרא בתורי דלאו מעלמא ובחצר דמשכיר וכרבי יוסי בר' חנינא והשתא והלא השוכר משתמש בחצר ואם כן הזבל משתמר לדעת השוכר בחצר ואיך זוכה המשכיר בזבל תורי דלאו מעלמא ויש לומר שגם משכיר ביתו פתוח לאותו חצר ומקרי עומד בצד שדהו [וע"ע תוספות גיטין עט: ד"ה פנימית]:

חצר

ומקומו מושכר לו. וקבל ממנו שם שכר המקום דהכי קתני סיפא נתקבלו זה מזה שכר וכל כך למה כדי לקנות מעשר שהמחה חצרו קונה לו לפי שהמטלטלין אין קונין אלא או במשיכה או חצרו תקנה לו: **נתון לעקיבא.** גבאי היה ואותה שנה שנת מעשר עני היתה: **כי אתא.** רבי אבא לסורא אמר להו כו': **מטלטלי אגב מקרקעי הקנה להם.** ולאו משום דתקני להם מקומם בתורת חצר שאפילו הקנה להן חצר אחרת שאינן בתוכה קנו נמי כדתנן (קידושין דף כו.) נכסים שאין להן אחריות נקנין עם נכסים שיש להן אחריות בכסף משתתן הכסף בשביל הקרקע והמטלטלין או אפילו קרקע במכר ומטלטלין במתנה נקנין המטלטלין בקנין הקרקע בלא משיכה דילפינן בקידושין (שם) מויתן להם אביהם מתנות רבות לכסף ולזהב עם ערים [א] בצורות אשר ביהודה: **קבלה.** להאי פירוקא: **וכי לא היה להן סודר כו'.** למה לו לקבל מהן מעות: **אלא.** סודר מאי טעמא לא דטובת הנאה שהיתה לו לרבן גמליאל במעשרות הללו: **אינה חשובה ממון.** דתהא נקנית בחליפין דליכא למימר כי קנה ליה ר"ג להאי סודר אקנייה חליפין דידיה בכל מקום שהן דכיון דאין לו בהן אלא טובת הנאה שבידו ליתנו לכל מי שירצה אין זו חשובה ממון לחול על זו קנין חליפין: **הכא נמי.** גבי קנין קרקע: **אינה ממון לקנות על גבי קרקע.** בקנין שהקרקע נקנה בו אלא אפקורי בעלמא אפקר גביהו וכי אוגר להו מקום קנאה לו חצרו בתורת חצר כשאר הפקר: **ולא היא.** מהאי דכי לא היה להן סודר לאו ראיה היא למילף מינה דאין טובת הנאה נקנית בחליפין ועל גבי קרקע דשפיר איכא למימר מטלטלי אגב קרקעי הקנה להן ודקשיא לך לקנינהו בחליפין:

**מתנות.** של כהונה ולויה ומעשר עני: **נתינה כתיבא בהו.** כדכתיב (דברים כו) ונתתה ללוי זה מעשר ראשון לגר ליתום ולאלמנה זה מעשר עני ולפיכך אסור להקנותן בסודר דדרך מקח הוא שזה נותן לו כליו תחתיהן ונראה זה כמוכרן לו: **נתינה אלימתא היא.** מותר להקנות מתנות כהונה על גבי קרקע: **רב פפא אמר.** לעולם בתורת חצר קנאו ואפילו הכי לא מקשי לעולא דהא דלא בעינן הכא עומד בצד השדה משום דדעת אחרת מקנה אותן שרבן גמליאל הקנה להן מטלטלין שהיו לו בחצר שלהן ולא מהפקירא קנו ונותה מתנה זו לקנות ואע"ג דאין עומד בצד השדה: **והוא שרץ אחריהן.** הצבי מהלך והגוזלות מדדין ומתניתין דקתני זכתה לו שדהו כגון שהיה יכול לרוץ אחריהן ומגיען קודם שיצאו משדהו: **ה"ג ובעי ר' ירמיה במתנה היאך.** אם היו צבי וגוזלות של אדם אחד והם בתוך שדה חבירו ונותנן דוולהן לבעל שדה במתנה היאך הדין מי בעינן והוא שרץ אחריהן ומגיען או לא לא קני ומאי נותן למיהדר ביה או לא: **קבלה מיניה רבי אבא.** להך בעיא מרבי ירמיה דשפיר דק שיש חילוק בין מתנה להפקר ובמתנה אע"פ כו': **ואמר עולא.** במסכת גיטין (דף עז:) גבי הזורק גט לאשתו בתוך ביתה או בתוך חצרה: **שאני גט דאיתיה בעל כרחה.** שהוא נותנו לה ולא ניחא לה למגרשה: **ולאו קל וחומר הוא.** מן הטעם הזה יש לדון דכ"ש לקנין אחר: **מה גט.** דכי איתיה בצד חצרה ולא ניחא לה למקנייה אפילו הכי קנייה לה חצרה אמרינן דלאו איתיה אין אי לא לא: **מתנה.** דליתיה בע"כ דלאו אמרה לא בעינא לא קניא: **לא כ"ש.** דכי אמרה בעינא צריכא שתהא בצד חצרה: **אלא אמר רב אשי.** לא תתלי טעמא משום דליתיה בעל כרחה אלא גבי מתנה היינו טעמא דלא בעינן עומד אצלה דכיון דמידה אתרבאי לא גרעה משלוחה להיטיב לה ואילו שלוחה שקיבל לה מתנה מי לא קני לה ואפילו אין עומדת בצדו חצרה נמי לא שנא הלכך גבי מתנה זכות הוא לה שתהא שלוחה וקנייה לה כשליח אבל גבי גט דחוב הוא לה לא ניחא לה שתהא שלוחה הלכך כי עומדת בצדה על כרחה ידה היא וידה קניא גבי גט על כרחה ואי לאו לא ידה הוא ולא שלוחה הוא טעמא דיש חילוק בין גט למתנה ואף על גב דתרוייהו דעת אחרת מקנה אותן משום דהך חצר אף על גב דאתרבאי משום יד כדאמרן לעיל (דף י:) לא גרעה משליחות דלאו נמי לא אתרבאי מונתן בידה הוי נפקא לן חצר משליחות וכי אצטריך לרבויי משום יד משום קטן וקטנה דלתנהו בתורת שליחות אצטריך וכל היכא דליתיה לשליחות איתיה לידה לדין חצר הלכך גבי גט דחוב הוא לה אין חבין כו' כלומר אין אדם יכול לעשות שליח לחוב לאדם שלא מדעתו וחצרו נמי לאו בתורת שליחות מצית לאתויי דמתגרש שלא מדעתה הלכך בגט לא תרבייה אלא משום יד ומה ידה דסמוכה לה אף חצירה בסמוכה לה:

גבי

## עין משפט נר מצוה

צב א מיי' פ"ד מהלכות זכייה ומתנה הל' ח ופי"ז מהל' גזילה ואבידה הל' יא סמג עשין פב טוש"ע ח"מ סי' רמג סעיף כ וסי' רסח סעיף ד:

צג ב ג מיי' פי"ז מהל' גזילה ואבידה הל' יא סמג עשין עד טוש"ע ח"מ סי' רסח סעיף ד:

צד ד מיי' פ"ה מהלכות גירושין הל' ג ועיין במ"מ סמג עשין נ טוש"ע אה"ע סי' קלט סעיף א ב:

צה ה מיי' שם פ"ה הלכה ג סמג שם טוש"ע אה"ע סי' קיט סעיף ג בהגה"ה וסעיף ו:

## רבינו חננאל

אמר רבן גמליאל עישור אחד שאני עתיד למוד נתון ליהושע (בן לוי) [א] ומקומו מושכר לו זה מעשר ראשון. ועישור אחר שאני עתיד למוד זה מעשר עני נתון לעקיבא בן יוסף שהוא פרנס והוא יד לעניים ומקומו מושכר לו כדי שיזכה בו לעניים ונתקבלו שכר זה מזה וכי ר' יהושע ור"ע בצד שדהו של ר"ג היו עומדין. ופרקי' ר"ג מטלטלי אגב מקרקעי אקני להו ומכיון שקיבל ר"ג כסף שכירות הקרקע זכו הם בקרקע ובכל מה שבתוכו דקי"ל כשם שהקרקע נקנית בכסף ובשטר ובחזקה כך שכירות הקרקע נקנית בכסף ובשטר ובחזקה. ואמרי' אמאי לא אקני להו ר"ג האי מעשר אגב סודר. ואמרי' משום דעיקר המעשר ללוי הוא וכי מן השמים הקנוהו לו ואין לבעלים בו אלא טובת הנאה שהוא רשאי לתתו לאיזה לוי שירצה. וקי"ל דטובת הנאה אינה נקנית בחליפין [ב] דחליפין דרך מקח וממכר הוא כלומר מקבל הסודר ומקנה לו חפץ אחד ומתנות כהונה כיון דבהדיא כתיבא בהו נתינה הקנאה אגב קרקע נתינה אלימתא היא. רב פפא פירוק אחר דעת אחרת מקנה אותם שאני. כלומר אם אדם מקנה לחבירו כלום דבר הדבר ההוא נתון בתוך שדה מקבל המתנה קנאו ואע"ג דאינו עומד בצד שדהו. ומקשי' עליה והרי גט דדעת אחרת מקנה אותה וקי"ל והוא שעומדת בצד ביתה או בצד חצירה. ופריק

## חשק שלמה על ר"ח

א) נראה דצ"ל שהיה לוי. ב) נראה דחסר כאן וצ"ל ה"נ אינה ממון לקנות ע"ג קרקע ולא היא חליפין דרך וכו' נתינה אינו יכול להקנות בחליפין אבל הקנאה אגב קרקע וכו'.

## מסורת הש"ס

א) [עירובין עו. וש"... ב) [חולין קלד:], ג) ג... עז:, ד) [שייך לע"... ה) [וכן ביבמות פ... ו) [וע"ע תוס' קדושין ד"ה ומקומו, ועיין ... ערכין ל. בתוס' ד"ה כתו': ידענא].

## הגהות הב"ח

(א) רש"י ד"ה כי א... וכו' ערים מצורות א...

## ליקוטי רש"י

ומקומו מושכר ... ונתן לו רבי יהושע פרו... בשכר המקום ... מטלטלין נקנין ... הקרקע בכסף ... מסקנא דהך מילתא ב... מעשר שני (פ"ה מ"... ונתקבלו שכר זה ... ואע"פ שעדיין לא הוצ... קריית שם הוא שא... לשהות לחברים דבר ש... מתוקן ואפילו אכלו מ... אין כאן חיוב מיתה מ... טבל ומן המותר יפ... מעשרותיו. ... לעקיבא בן יוסף. ... מעשר עני היתה ... עקיבא גבאי עניים ... ובספינה היו שניהם ... [קידושין כז.]. נת... כתיבא בהו. ו... ליתנן לכהן [חולין קל...

ילפינן מציאה מגט ומר סבר לא ילפינן מציאה מגט ואיבעית אימא בקטנה כולי עלמא לא פליגי דילפינן מציאה מגט והכא בקטן קא מיפלגי מר סבר ילפינן קטן מקטנה ומר סבר [א]לא ילפינן קטן מקטנה ואיבעית אימא מר אמר חדא ומר אמר חדא ולא פליגי:

**מתני'** [ב]ראה אותן רצין אחר מציאה אחר צבי שבור אחר גוזלות שלא פרחו ואמר זכתה לי שדי זכתה לו היה צבי רץ כדרכו או שהיו גוזלות מפריחין ואמר זכתה לי שדי לא אמר כלום:

**גמ'** אמר רב יהודה אמר שמואל [ג]והוא שעומד בצד שדהו ותקני ליה שדהו א) דאמר ר' יוסי בר' חנינא [ד]חצרו של אדם קונה לו שלא מדעתו [ה]הני מילי בחצר המשתמרת אבל חצר שאינה משתמרת אי עומד בצד שדהו אין אי לא לא ומנא תימרא דחצר שאינה משתמרת אי עומד בצד שדהו אין אי לא לא דתניא היה עומד בעיר ואומר יודע אני שעומר שיש לי בשדה פועלים שכחוהו לא יהא שכחה יכול לא יהא שכחה תלמוד לומר א) ושכחת עומר בשדה ושכחת ולא בעיר הא גופא קשיא אמרת יכול לא יהא שכחה אלמא הוי שכחה ונסיב לה גמרא בשדה ושכחת ולא בעיר אלמא לא הוי שכחה אלא לאו הכי קאמר [ו]בשדה שכוח מעיקרו הוי שכחה זכור ולבסוף שכוח אין שכחה מאי טעמא דכיון דקאי גבה הויא ליה חצרו וזכתה ליה [ז]אבל בעיר אפילו זכור ולבסוף שכוח הויא שכחה מאי טעמא דליתיה גביה דלזכי ליה ממאי דלמא גזירת הכתוב היא דבשדה נהוי שכחה ובעיר לא נהוי שכחה אמר קרא א) לא תשוב לקחתו לרבות שכחת העיר האי מיבעי ליה ללאו אם כן נימא קרא לא תקחנו מאי לא תשוב לרבות שכחת העיר ואכתי מיבעי ליה לכדתנן ב) [ח]שלפניו אין שכחה שלאחריו יש שכחה שהוא בבל תשוב [ט]זה הכלל כל שהוא בבל תשוב שכחה כל שאינו בבל תשוב אינו שכחה אמר רב אשי אמר קרא א) יהיה לרבות שכחת העיר וכן אמר עולא והוא שעומד בצד שדהו וכן אמר רבה בר בר חנה והוא שעומד בצד שדהו איתיביה רבי אבא לעולא ג) מעשה ברבן גמליאל וזקנים שהיו באים בספינה אמר רבן גמליאל עישור שאני עתיד למוד נתון ליהושע

## רש"י

**ילפינן מציאה מגט.** כי היכי דגבי גט אית לה חצר לקטנה גבי מציאה נמי אית לה: **ומר סבר לא ילפינן.** ממונא מאיסורא וגבי ממונא חצר מאם המלא אתרבאי ואיכא למימר דשליחות הוא ° ומשום דאין שליח לדבר עבירה אצטריך למכתב התם: **והכא בקטן פליגי.** דלא אשכחן דרבי ביה חצר: **מר אמר חדא כו'.** ר"ש בן לקיש אמר לענין מציאה ורבי יוחנן לענין גט אי נמי מר אמר קטן ומר אמר קטנה: **מתני' אחר צבי שבור.** דהוא דומיא דמציאה שאינו יכול לרוץ ומשתמר בתוך השדה אם לא יטלוהו אחרים: **גמ' אי עומד בצד שדהו אין.** דעכשיו היא משתמרת על ידו: **עומר שיש לי בשדה.** שהנחתיו שם מדעתי וסמכתי על הפועלים שיביאוהו ופועלים שכחוהו: **לא יהא שכחה.** אם חזר ושכחו: **בשדה ושכחת.** אם שכחתו בעודך מן השדה הוי שכחה ולא ששכחתו משנכנסת לעיר: **אלא לאו הכי קאמר בשדה שכוח מעיקרו כו'.** בעוד האיש בשדה עומר השכוח מעיקרו ששכחו הוא תחילה לפועל הוי שכחה אבל זכור שהניחו שם מדעתו ולבסוף שכחו על ידי פועלים לא הוי שכחה: **אבל בעיר.** משנכנס לעיר אפילו זכור ולבסוף שכח הוי שכחה דליתיה גביה כו' והכי קא נסיב ליה תנא לתלמודיה יכול לא יהא שכחה ת"ל בשדה ושכחת בעודך בשדה הוא דבעינן דשכחתיה אתה ולא בעיר לא בעינן ושכחת שאף שכחת פועלים עושה אותה שכחה: **וממאי.** דקרא הכי מתרץ ומתני' הכי אמרה: **דלמא גזירת הכתוב היא.** דמשמע דבשדה יהא שכחה אבל משבא בעל הבית לעיר אין שכחתו ושכחת פועלים כלום והכי קאמר יכול יהא שכחה ת"ל כו': **שלפניו אין שכחה.** בשכחת הקוצר קאי יחיד שהתחיל לקצור מראש השורה ושכח לפניו ולאחריו שלאחריו הוי שכחה שלפניו לא הוי שכחה: **יהיה.** לגר ליתום ולאלמנה יהיה: **עישור שאני עתיד למוד.** נזכר שלא עישר מעשרותיו והוקשה לו ומיהר לעשרן באשר הוא שם: **נתון ליהושע.** לרבי יהושע בר חנניא שהיה עמו בספינה והוא לוי ונוטל מעשר ראשון כדאמרי' בערכין (דף יא:) מעשה ברבי יהושע שהלך לסייע את ר' יוחנן בן גודגדא בהגפת דלתות אמר לו חזור בך שאתה מן המשוררים ואני מן המשוערים ומשורר שסייע במיתה: ומקומו

## תוספות

**ילפינן מציאה מגט.** האי ילפינן הוי ° מדרבנן דמציאת קטן לא הוי אלא מדרבנן אפילו לרבי יוסי דאמר (לקמן דף יב.) גזל גמור היינו מדבריהם ולענין יד לא פליגי דילפינן אלא לענין חצר ד): **זכתה לו.** [א] נראה אע"ג דלא אמר זכתה לי דזכתה לו כדאמרי' לעיל (דף י.) אי תקון רבנן דלקני כי לא אמר מאי הוי ואין לומר דהתם היינו משום דנפל לו עליה דגלי בדעתיה שרוצה לקנות אבל הכא מי יימר דרוצה לקנות דאדרבה משמע לעיל דאי לא נפל קנה טפי ואע"ג דלא אמר אקני ועוד דאמר רבי יוסי בר' חנינא חצרו של אדם קונה לו שלא מדעתו אלמא אע"ג דלא אמר קני והכא נקט משום סיפא דאפילו אמר כיון דרץ כדרכו לא קני ה): **היה צבי רץ כדרכו.** ה"ה אפי' לצבי שבור אם רץ אחריו ואין מגיעו אלא אורחא דמילתא נקט דכשרץ כדרכו אין מגיעו: **ה"מ בחצר המשתמרת.** תימה דבפ' שור שנגח את הפרה (ב"ק דף מט: ושם ד"ה והלכתא) אמר משכונו של גר ביד ישראל ומת הגר כו' וזה קונה השאר כו' ופריך ותקני ליה חצרו דאמר ר' יוסי בר' חנינא כו' ומסיק דליתיה פי' למלוה בחצרו וקשה דהתם משמע דהוי בחצר המשתמרת מדמייתי עלה מרבי יוסי בר' חנינא דמיירי במשתמרת כדמוכח הכא ועוד דמסתמא ביתו ודאי משתמר הוא ששמר שם המשכון וא"כ כי ליתיה נמי לקני ועוד אדפריך ליה מדרבי יוסי בר' חנינא לפרוך ממתני' ומיהו זה נוכל לתרץ דמתני' הוי משום דנתכוין לזכות בה דאמר זכתה לי לכך מייתי מרבי יוסי בר' חנינא [ב] וי"ל דה"פ דליתיה למשכון בחצר אבל מלוה גם לפי המקשן מיירי דליתיה בחצר ולכך לא פריך ממתני' כ"א מרבי יוסי בר' חנינא וא"ת פרק הזורק (גיטין דף עז: ושם ד"ה והוא) דתנן זרק לתוך ביתה או לתוך חצרה מגורשת משמע דמשתמרת ואפילו הכי קאמר עולא והוא שעומדת בצד ביתה וי"ל דדוקא גבי גט דאיתיה בעל כרחה בעינן עומדת בצד ביתה כדאמר בשמעתין: **זכור ולבסוף שכוח.** פירוש זכור בשעה שהשכחה מתחלת שכבר שכחוהו פועלים ולבסוף שכח גם הוא ושכוח מעיקרו הוי כששכחו הפועלים שכח גם הוא אבל מה שהוא זכור בשעה שהפועלים זוכרין אין זה זכור ולבסוף שכוח דא"כ לא תמצא שכחה לעולם דכשדהו מלאה עומרין יאמר יזכה לי שדי: **דלמא גזירת הכתוב היא.** פרש"י ונגרוס יכול יהא שכחה ותימה לפי שרוצה לסתור ראייתו מגיה הברייתא ותו מה מתרץ לרבות שכחת העיר והלא בברייתא יליף דזכור ולבסוף שכוח לא הוי שכחה דקתני יודע אני שפועלים שכחוהו והכא דדריש לרבות שכחת העיר יעמיד בשכוח מעיקרא לכך י"ל שאינו סותר ראייתו אלא גמרא קשה לו על הברייתא מנ"ל למדרש מיעוטא על דיוקא דקרא דדריש בשדה ושכחת דהיינו שכוח מעיקרא אבל זכור ולבסוף שכוח לא הוי שכחה ועל זה קאי מיעוטא לומר דבעיר אפילו זכור ולבסוף שכוח הוי שכחה דלמא גזירת הכתוב היא דבשדה הוי שכחה שכוח מעיקרא ולא בעיר והכי מסתברא טפי לאוקמי מיעוט אגופיה דקרא בשדה ושכחת ולא בעיר והשתא משני שפיר לרבות שכחת העיר וע"כ לא מצי קאי אפשטיה דקרא: **זה הכלל.** לאתויי קרן זוית: **עישור שאני עתיד למוד.** פרש"י פרק קמא דקידושין (דף כו: ושם ד"ה מעשה) שהיה ירא פן יסמכו עליו בני ביתו שעישר ויאכלו טבל לחזקה על חבר שאינו מוציא מתחת ידו דבר שאינו מתוקן וקשה דהיינו דוקא בחבר שמת או בהולך ואין בדעתו לשוב עד ימים רבים ועוד למה נתנם לרבי יהושע ולרבי עקיבא יקרא להם שם ולא יותר ועוד דאין זה קריאת שם דלא אמר עשרה יהא מעשר אלא אמר מעשר ראשון יהא נתון ליהושע ופר"ת דשנת הביעור היתה וכבר הפריש והיה צריך להוציאם מתחת ידו ולתנם

## מסורת הש"ס

בבא קמא מט:, לקמן ..., קיח., חולין קמא:, פאה פרק ו משנה ד, מעשר שני פרק ה ... נה ט, קדושין כו:, [וע"ע תוס' יבמות יט: ... ה גמרינן], ה) [וע"ע ... ' בעירובין מט: ד"ה ואמר].

## הגהות הגר"א

[א] תוס' ד"ה זכתה ... נראה כו'. נ"ב אבל ... מב"ס מחלק בין ד' ... ות וחצר המשתמרת ... ר שא"מ (ועמ"ש ... ע בח"מ סי' רס"מ ... ק י"א): [ב] שם ... ה ה"מ כו' וי"ל ... ה"פ כו'. נ"ב וכן פי' ... י"ף בפ"ג דכ"ב והרמב"ם:

## גליון הש"ס

... ד"ה ומר סבר ... ומשום דאין ... ליה לדבר עבירה. ... ה לי דאם מסברא לא ... ינא דבחצר לא מקרי ... ר עבירה מהנך טעמים ... ל דלאו בר חיובא או ... ם אי בעי עביד מנ"ל ... מת דלמא גם בגניבה ... רבאי חצר משום ידו ... יך באמת דוקא בעומד ... ' אצירו ול"ע: תוס' ... ה ילפינן כו' ... דרבנן. עיין תוס' ... ות יט ע"ב ד"ה גמרינן:

## תורה אור השלם

א) כִּי תִקְצֹר קְצִירְךָ ... דֶךָ וְשָׁכַחְתָּ עֹמֶר ... דֶה לֹא תָשׁוּב ... חְתּוֹ לַגֵּר לַיָּתוֹם ... אַלְמָנָה יִהְיֶה לְמַעַן ... רֶכְךָ יְיָ אֱלֹהֶיךָ בְּכֹל מַעֲשֵׂה יָדֶיךָ: [דברים כד, יט]

## ליקוטי רש"י

... היו באים בספינה. ... ולא נתן רשות לתרום ... ושין כו:]. נתון ... יהושע. רבי יהושע בן ... יא כדאמר במס' ערכין ... יא:) מעשה ברבי ... שע ברבי חנניא שהלך ... יע את ר' יוחנן בן ... גדא בהגפת דלתות ... ר לו חזור בך שאתה מן ... שוררים ואני מן ... שוערים [קידושין כו.].

## עין משפט נר מצוה

פז א מיי' פי"ז מהלכות אבידה הל' י ופ"ד מהל' זכייה ומתנה הל' ט ועי' בהשגות ובמ"מ סמג עשין עד טוש"ע ח"מ סי' רסח סעיף ה וסי' רמג סעיף כג:

פח ב ג מיי' פי"ז מהל' אבידה הל' יא סמג עשין עד טוש"ע ח"מ סי' רסח סעיף ד:

פט ד ה מיי' שם הל' ח ופט"ז שם הלכה ח ופ"א מהל' זכייה ומתנה הלכה ד ועי' בהשגות ובמ"מ ופ"ד שם הל' ט סמג עשין עד פג טוש"ע ח"מ סי' רמג סעיף כ כא וסי' רסח סעיף ג וסי' ערה סעיף כח וסי' שיג סעיף ג:

צ ו ז מיי' פ"ה מהלכות מתנות עניים הל' ב:

צא ח ט מיי' שם הל' י:

## רבינו חננאל

כי פליגי במציאה ר"י סבר ילפינן מציאה מגט ור"ל סבר לא ילפינן. איבעי תימא [בקטנה] כ"ע ילפינן מציאה מגט וכי פליגי בקטן ר"י יליף לקטן מקטנה כשם שזוכה חצירה של קטנה לקטנה כך זוכה חצר של קטן לקטן. ור"ל [ס"ל] ריבתה התורה החצר כיד לאשה ואפי' קטנה אבל לקטן לא. איבעי תימא כ"ע לא ילפי קטן מקטנה ור' יוחנן וריש לקיש לא פליגי אלא ר' יוחנן הורה בקטנה דיש לה חצר ויש לה ד' אמות וריש לקיש הורה בקטן דאין חצירו זוכה לו ולא ד' אמות שלו כך מסקנא דשמעתא: **פיסקא** ראה אותן רצין אחר המציאה וכו' עד זכתה לי שדי זכתה לו שדהו: גמ' והוא שעומד בצד שדהו. ואמרי' אמאי צריך להיות עומד בצד שדהו ותקני ליה שדהו כר' יוסי בר חנינא דאמר חצירו של אדם קונה לו שלא מדעתו ודחי' הני מילי בחצר המשתמרת אבל שדה שאינה משתמרת אי עומד בצד שדהו זכתה לו שדהו ואם אינו עומד שם לא זכתה לו שדהו. מנא הני מילי דתניא היה עומד בעיר ואומר יודע אני כי העומר שיש לי בשדה פועלים שכחוהו לא יהא שכחה יכול לא יהא שכחה ת"ל ושכחת עומר בשדה. בשדה ושכחת ולא בעיר. ופרישנא בשדה שכוח מעיקרו הוי שכחה זכור ולבסוף שכוח לא הוי שכחה מאי טעמא כיון דכי קאי בשדה וזכור לו זכתה לו שדהו ואע"ג דבתר הכי שכחו אינה שכחה שכבר זכתה לו שדהו וכאילו נטלו מאותה העת אבל בעיר אפי' זכור ולבסוף שכחו הוי שכחה מאי טעמא דהא ליתיה גביה בשדה דליזכי ליה שדהו ש"מ דאי עומד בצד שדהו זכתה לו שדהו ואי אינו עומד בצד שדהו לא זכתה לו שדהו. ואמרי' וממאי דמשום דלא הוה קאי בצד שדהו נעשה שכחה דלמא גזירת הכתוב היא א) דבשדה לא ניהוי שכחה. ובעיר כי האי גוונא זכור ולבסוף שכוח ליהוי שכחה מדכתיב לא תשוב לקחתו גמרינן מינה לרבות שכחת העיר. ונדחו הדברים האלו ואסקה רב אשי יהיה לרבות שכחת העיר. ולא נתברר כי אם עומד בצד שדהו זכתה לו שדהו ואי לא לא. וכן אמר עולא והוא שעומד בצד שדהו. איתיביה רבא מעשה ברבן גמליאל וזקנים שהיו באין בספינה.

חשק שלמה על ר"ח א) הדבר מבואר דרבינו היה גורס בגמ' דבשדה לא נהוי שכחה ובעיר נהוי שכחה דלאמר קרא וכו' וכן דלאמר קרא הכל מן הקושיא היא ועי' בש"מ שהביא ג"כ לד' רבינו וגרסתו ע"ש.

וְכֵן אָמַר עוּ – And so did Ulla say regarding our Mishnah: וְהוּא שֶׁעוֹמֵד בְּצַד שָׂדֵהוּ – Provided that [the owner] is standing at the side of his field. וְכֵן אָמַר רַבָּה בַּר בַּר חָנָה – And so did Rabbah bar bar Chana say: וְהוּא שֶׁעוֹמֵד בְּצַד שָׂדֵהוּ – Provided that [the owner] is standing at the side of his field.

The Gemara challenges the ruling that the owner must be present at his otherwise unguarded courtyard in order for it to acquire an object on his behalf:

אֵיתִיבֵיהּ רַבִּי אַבָּא לְעוּלָּא – R' Abba challenged Ulla from a Mishnah:[30] מַעֲשֶׂה בְּרַבָּן גַּמְלִיאֵל וּזְקֵנִים – THERE WAS AN INCIDENT INVOLVING RABBAN GAMLIEL AND THE ELDERS, שֶׁהָיוּ בָּאִים בִּסְפִינָה – WHO WERE TRAVELING ON A SHIP.[31] אָמַר רַבָּן גַּמְלִיאֵל – RABBAN GAMLIEL DECLARED: עִישּׂוּר שֶׁאֲנִי עָתִיד לָמוֹד נָתוּן לִיהוֹשֻׁעַ – THE TENTH of my produce THAT I WILL, IN THE FUTURE, MEASURE OUT as *maaser rishon*[32] IS hereby GIVEN TO YEHOSHUA,[33]

NOTES

30. *Maaser Sheni* 5:9.

31. Rabban Gamliel remembered that he had left untithed produce at home; consequently, the produce was prohibited to consume in its untithed state. He was therefore apprehensive that people in his household might eat the produce on the assumption that he had surely not left his produce untithed, so he hurried to separate the tithes while he was still at sea (see *Rashi* and *Tosafos*).

32. Every year except for *Shemittah* (the seventh year of the seven-year cycle), a person is required to separate two tithes from his harvest. The first tithe (known as *maaser rishon*) is given to a Levi (see *Numbers* 18:21), while the assignment of the second tithe varies from year to year. This incident occurred in either the third or the sixth year of the cycle, when the second tithe is given to the poor [*maasar ani*]. Until all tithes are separated the produce is prohibited for consumption.

In order to remove the prohibition, it is not necessary to *physically* separate the *maaser* from the rest of the produce. It is sufficient to merely *designate* part of the produce as *maaser*; the physical removal of that designated *maaser* from the rest of the produce can be done later. Thus, by dint of Rabban Gamliel's declaration, the designated produce attained *maaser* status, thereby removing the prohibition from the rest of the produce. Rabban Gamliel was also certain that [the produce would not be consumed in its entirety before his return so that] he would be able to physically separate the *maaser* from the remainder (*Rashi* to *Kiddushin* 27a).

33. R' Yehoshua bar Chananya was one of the Sages accompanying Rabban Gamliel on this voyage. Since R' Yehoshua was a Levi [see *Arachin* 11b], he was eligible to receive the first tithe (*Rashi*).

The prohibition is removed from produce as soon as its *maaser* has been designated, and even before it has been given to a Levi. Nevertheless, Rabban Gamliel now took the additional step of giving the *maaser* to a Levi to fulfill that mitzvah as soon as possible. This was in line with the principle: זְרִיזִין מַקְדִּימִין לְמִצְוֹת, *Those who are punctilious are early to [perform] mitzvos,* as stated in *Pesachim* 4a (*Pnei Yehoshua* to *Kiddushin* 26b).

ילפינן מציאה מגט ומר סבר לא ילפינן מציאה מגט ואיבעית אימא בקטנה כולי עלמא לא פליגי דילפינן מציאה מגט והכא בקטן קא מיפלגי מר סבר ילפינן קטן מקטנה ומר סבר א) לא ילפינן קטן מקטנה ואיבעית אימא מר אמר חדא ומר אמר חדא ולא פליגי:

**מתני'** ב) ראה אותן רצין אחר מציאה אחר צבי שבור אחר גוזלות שלא פרחו ואמר זכתה לי שדי זכתה לו היה צבי רץ כדרכו או שהיו גוזלות מפריחין ואמר זכתה לי שדי לא אמר כלום:

**גמ'** אמר רב יהודה אמר שמואל ג) והוא שעומד בצד שדהו ותקני ליה שדהו א) דאמר ר' יוסי בר' חנינא ד) חצרו של אדם קונה לו שלא מדעתו ה) הני מילי בחצר המשתמרת אבל חצר שאינה משתמרת אי עומד בצד שדהו אין אי לא לא ומנא תימרא דחצר שאינה משתמרת אי עומד בצד שדהו אין אי לא לא דתניא היה עומד בעיר ואומר יודע אני שעומר שיש לי בשדה פועלים שכחוהו לא יהא שכחה יכול לא יהא שכחה תלמוד לומר א) ושכחת עומר בשדה בשדה ושכחת ולא בעיר הא גופא קשיא אמרת יכול לא יהא שכחה אלמא הוי שכחה ונסיב לה גמרא בשדה ושכחת ולא בעיר אלמא לא הוי שכחה אלא לאו הכי קאמר ו) בשדה שכוח מעיקרו הוי שכחה זכור ולבסוף שכוח אין שכחה מאי טעמא דכיון דקאי גבה הויא ליה חצרו וזכתה ליה ז) אבל בעיר אפילו זכור ולבסוף שכוח הויא שכחה מאי טעמא דליתיה גביה דלזכי ליה ממאי דלמא גזירת הכתוב היא דבשדה נהוי שכחה ובעיר לא נהוי שכחה אמר קרא א) לא תשוב לקחתו לרבות שכחת העיר האי מיבעי ליה ללאו אם כן נימא קרא לא תקחנו מאי לא תשוב לרבות שכחת העיר ואכתי מיבעי ליה לכדתנן ג) ח) שלפניו אין שכחה שלאחריו יש שכחה שהוא בבל תשוב ט) זה הכלל כל שהוא בבל תשוב שכחה כל שאינו בבל תשוב אינו שכחה אמר רב אשי אמר קרא א) יהיה לרבות שכחת העיר וכן אמר עולא והוא שעומד בצד שדהו וכן אמר רבה בר בר חנה והוא שעומד בצד שדהו איתיביה רבי אבא לעולא ג) מעשה ברבן גמליאל וזקנים שהיו באים בספינה אמר רבן גמליאל עישור שאני עתיד למוד נתון ליהושע ומקומו

---

**רש"י**

ילפינן מציאה מגט. כי היכי דגבי גט אית לה חצר לקטנה גבי מציאה נמי אית לה: ומר סבר לא ילפינן. ממונא מאיסורא וגבי ממונא חצר מאם המלא אתרבאי ואיכא למימר דשליחות הוא ° ומשום דאין שליח לדבר עבירה אצטריך למכתב התם: והכא בקטן פליגי. דלא אשכחן דרבי ביה חצר: מר אמר חדא כו'. ר"ש בן לקיש אמר לענין מציאה ורבי יוחנן לענין גט אי נמי מר אמר קטן ומר אמר קטנה: **מתני'** אחר צבי שבור. דהוא דומיא דמציאה שאינו יכול לרוץ ומשתמר בתוך השדה אם לא יטלוהו אחרים: **גמ'** אי עומד בצד שדהו אין. דעכשיו היא משתמרת על ידו: עומר שיש לי בשדה. שהנחתיו שם מדעתי וסמכתי על הפועלים שיביאוהו ופועלים שכחוהו: לא יהא שכחה. אם חזר ושכחו: בשדה ושכחת. אם שכחתו בעודך מן השדה הוי שכחה ולא ששכחתו משנכנסת לעיר: אלא לאו הכי קאמר בשדה שכוח מעיקרו כו'. בעוד האיש בשדה עומר השכוח מעיקרו ששכחו הוא תחילה לפועל הוי שכחה אבל זכור שהניחו שם מדעתו ולבסוף שכחו על ידי פועלים לא הוי שכחה: אבל בעיר. משנכנס לעיר אפילו זכור ולבסוף שכח הוי שכחה דליתיה גביה כו' והכי קא נסיב ליה תנא לתלמודיה יכול לא יהא שכחה ת"ל בשדה ושכחת בעודך בשדה הוא דבעינן דשכחתיה אתה ולא בעיר לא בעינן ושכחת שלך שכחת פועלים עושה אותה שכחה: וממאי. דקרא הכי מתרך ומתני' הכי אמרה: דלמא גזירת הכתוב היא. דמשמע דבשדה יהא שכחה אבל משבא בעל הבית לעיר אין שכחתו ושכחת פועלים כלום והכי קאמר יכול יהא שכחה ת"ל כו': שלפניו אין שכחה. בשכחת הקוצר קאי יחיד שהתחיל לקצור מראש השורה ושכח לפניו ולאחריו שלאחריו הוי שכחה שלפניו לא הוי שכחה: יהיה. לגר ליתום ולאלמנה יהיה: עישור שאני עתיד למוד. נזכר שלא עישר מעשרותיו והוקשה לו ומיהר לעשרן באשר הוא שם: נתון ליהושע. לרבי יהושע בר חנניא שהיה עמו בספינה והוא לוי ונוטל מעשר ראשון כדאמרי' בערכין (דף יא:) מעשה ברבי יהושע שהלך לסייע את ר' יוחנן בן גודגדא בהגפת דלתות אמר לו חזור בך שאתה מן המשוררים ואני מן המשוערים ומשורר שסיער במיתה:

**תוספות**

ילפינן מציאה מגט. האי ילפינן הוי ° מדרבנן דמציאת קטן לא הוי אלא מדרבנן אפילו לרבי יוסי דאמר (לקמן דף יב.) גזל גמור היינו מדבריהם ולענין יד לא פליגי דילפינן אלא לענין חצר ד):

זכתה לו. [א] נראה אע"ג דלא אמר זכתה לי דזכתה לו כדאמרי' לעיל (דף י.) אי תקון רבנן דלקני כי לא אמר מאי הוי ואין לומר דהתם היינו משום דנפל לו עליה דגלי בדעתיה שרוצה לקנות אבל הכא מי יימר דרוצה לקנות דאדרבה משמע לעיל דאי לא נפל קנה טפי ואע"ג דלא אמר אקני ועוד דאמר רבי יוסי בר' חנינא חצרו של אדם קונה לו שלא מדעתו אלמא אע"ג דלא אמר קני והכא נקט משום סיפא דאפילו אמר כיון דרץ כדרכו לא קני ה):

היה צבי רץ כדרכו. ה"ה אפי' צבי שבור אם רץ אחריו ואין מגיעו אלא אורחא דמילתא נקט דכשרץ כדרכו אין מגיעו:

ה"מ בחצר המשתמרת. תימה דבפ' שור שנגח את הפרה (ב"ק דף מט: ושם ד"ה והלכתא) אמר משכונו של גר ביד ישראל ומת הגר כו' וזה קונה השאר כו' ופריך ותקני ליה חצרו דאמר ר' יוסי בר' חנינא כו' ומסיק דליתיה פי' למלוה בחצרו וקשה דהתם משמע דהוי בחצר המשתמרת מדמייתי עלה מרבי יוסי בר' חנינא דמיירי במשתמרת כדמוכח הכא ועוד דמסתמא ביתו ודאי משתמר הוא ששמר שם המשכון וא"כ כי ליתיה נמי לקני ועוד אדפריך ליה מדרבי יוסי בר' חנינא לפרוך ממתני' ומיהו זה נוכל לתרץ דמתני' הוי משום דנתכוין לזכות בה דאמר זכתה לי לכך מייתי מרבי יוסי בר' חנינא [ב] וי"ל דה"פ דליתיה למשכון בחצר אבל מלוה גם לפי המקשן מיירי דליתיה בחצר ולכך לא פריך ממתני' כ"א מרבי יוסי בר' חנינא וא"ת פרק הזורק (גיטין דף עז: ושם ד"ה והוא) דתנן זרק לתוך ביתה או לתוך חצרה מגורשת משמע דמשתמרת ואפילו הכי קאמר עולא והוא שעומדת בצד ביתה וי"ל דדוקא גבי גט דאיתיה בעל כרחה בעינן עומדת בצד ביתה כדאמר בשמעתין:

זכור ולבסוף שכוח. פירוש זכור בשעה שהשכחה מתחלת שכבר שכחוהו פועלים ולבסוף שכח גם הוא ושכוח מעיקרו הוי כששכחו הפועלים שכח גם הוא אבל מה שהוא זכור בשעה שהפועלים זוכרין אין זה זכור ולבסוף שכוח דא"כ לא תמצא שכחה לעולם דכשסדהו מלאה עומרין יאמר יזכה לי שדי:

דלמא גזירת הכתוב היא. פרש"י ונגרוס יכול יהא שכחה ותימה לפי שרוצה לסתור ראייתו מגיה הברייתא ותו מה מתרך לרבות שכחת העיר והלא בברייתא יליף דזכור ולבסוף שכוח לא הוי שכחה דקתני יודע אני שפועלים שכחוהו והכא דדריש לרבות שכחת העיר יעמיד בשכוח מעיקרא לכך י"ל שאינו סותר ראייתו אלא גמרא קשה לו על הברייתא מנ"ל למדרש מיעוטא על דיוקא דקרא דדריש בשדה ושכחת דהיינו שכוח מעיקרא אבל זכור ולבסוף שכוח לא הוי שכחה ועל זה קאי מיעוטא לומר דבעיר אפילו זכור ולבסוף שכוח הוי שכחה דלמא גזירת הכתוב היא דבשדה הוי שכחה שכוח מעיקרא ולא בעיר והכי מסתברא טפי לאוקמי מיעוט אגופיה דקרא בשדה ושכחת ולא בעיר והשתא משני שפיר לרבות שכחת העיר וע"כ לא מצי קאי אפשטיה דקרא:

זה הכלל. לאתויי קרן זוית:

עישור שאני עתיד למוד. פרש"י פרק קמא דקידושין (דף כו: ושם ד"ה מעשה) שהיה ירא פן יסמכו עליו בני ביתו שעישר ויאכלו טבל דחזקה על חבר שאינו מוציא מתחת ידו דבר שאינו מתוקן וקשה דהיינו דוקא בחבר שמת או בהולך ואין בדעתו לשוב עד ימים רבים ועוד למה נתנם לרבי יהושע ולרבי עקיבא יקרא להם שם ולא יותר ועוד דאין זה קריאת שם דלא אמר עשרה יהא מעשר אלא אמר מעשר ראשון יהא נתון ליהושע ופר"ת דשנת הביעור היתה וכבר הפליגו והיה צריך להוציאם מתחת ידו ולתנם

---

**עין משפט נר מצוה**

פז א מיי' פי"ז מהלכות אבידה הל' י ופ"ד מהל' זכייה ומתנה הל' ט ועי' בהשגות ובמ"מ סמג עשין עד טוש"ע ח"מ סי' רסח סעיף ה וסי' רמג סעיף כג:

פח ב ג מיי' פי"ז מהל' אבידה הל' יא סמג עשין עד טוש"ע ח"מ סי' רסח סעיף ד:

פט ד ה מיי' שם הל' ח ופט"ז שם הלכה ח ופ"א מהל' זכייה ומתנה הלכה ד ועי' בהשגות ובמ"מ ופ"ד שם הל' ט סמג עשין עד פב טוש"ע ח"מ סי' רמג סעיף כ כא וסי' רסח סעיף ג וסי' ערה סעיף כח וסי' שיג סעיף ג:

צ ו ז מיי' פ"ה מהלכות מתנות עניים הל' ג:

צא ח ט מיי' שם הל' י:

**רבינו חננאל**

כי פליגי במציאה ר"י סבר ילפינן מציאה מגט ור"ל סבר לא ילפינן. איבעי תימא [בקטנה] כ"ע ילפינן מציאה מגט וכי פליגי בקטן ר"י יליף לקטן מקטנה כשם שזוכה חצירה של קטנה לקטנה כך זוכה חצר של קטן לקטן. ור"ל [ס"ל] ריבתה התורה החצר כיד לאשה ואפי' קטנה אבל לקטן לא. איבעי תימא כ"ע לא ילפי קטן מקטנה ור' יוחנן וריש לקיש לא פליגי אלא ר' יוחנן הורה בקטנה דיש לה חצר ויש לה ד' אמות וריש לקיש הורה בקטן דאין חצירו זוכה לו ולא ד' אמות שלו כך מסקנא דשמעתא: פיסקא ראה אותן רצין אחר המציאה וכו' עד זכתה לי שדי זכתה לו שדהו: גמ' והוא שעומד בצד שדהו. ואמרי' אמאי צריך להיות עומד בצד שדהו ותקני ליה שדהו כר' יוסי בר חנינא דאמר חצירו של אדם קונה לו שלא מדעתו ודחי' הני מילי בחצר המשתמרת אבל שדה שאינה משתמרת אי עומד בצד שדהו זכתה לו שדהו ואם אינו עומד שם לא זכתה לו שדהו. מנא הני מילי דתניא היה עומד בעיר ואומר יודע אני כי העומר שיש לי בשדה פועלים שכחוהו לא יהא שכחה יכול לא יהא שכחה ת"ל ושכחת עומר בשדה. בשדה ושכחת ולא בעיר. ופרישנא בשדה שכוח מעיקרו הוי שכחה זכור ולבסוף שכוח לא הוי שכחה מאי טעמא כיון דכי קאי בשדה וזכור לו זכתה לו שדהו ואע"ג דבתר הכי שכחו אינה שכחה שכבר זכתה לו שדהו וכאילו נטלו מאותה העת אבל בעיר אפי' זכור ולבסוף שכחו הוי שכחה מאי טעמא דהא ליתיה גביה בשדה דליזכי ליה שדהו ש"מ דאי עומד בצד שדהו זכתה לו שדהו ואי אינו עומד בצד שדהו לא זכתה לו שדהו. ואמרי' וממאי דמשום דלא הוה קאי בצד שדהו נעשה שכחה דלמא גזירת הכתוב היא א) דבשדה לא ניהוי שכחה. ובעיר כי האי גוונא זכור ולבסוף שכוח ליהוי שכחה מדכתיב לא תשוב לקחתו גמרינן מינה לרבות שכחת העיר. ונדחו הדברים האלו ואסקה רב אשי יהיה לרבות שכחת העיר. ולא נתברר כי אם עומד בצד שדהו זכתה לו שדהו ואי לא לא. וכן אמר עולא והוא שעומד בצד שדהו. איתיביה רבא מעשה ברבן גמליאל וזקנים שהיו באין בספינה.

**מסורת הש"ס**

א) ב"ק קמא מט:, לקמן קיח., חולין קמא:, ב) פאה פרק ו משנה ד, ג) מעשר שני פרק ה ... ט, קדושין כו:, ד) ע"ע תוס' יבמות יט: גמרינן], ה) [וע"ע בעירובין מט: ד"ה ואמר].

**הגהות הגר"א**

[א] תום' ד"ה זכתה ... נראה כו'. נ"ב אבל ... ב"ס מחלק בין ד' ... וחצר המשתמרת ... שא"מ (ועמ"ש ... בח"מ סי' רס"ח ... י"א): [ב] שם ... ה"מ כו' וי"ל ... פ כו'. נ"ב וכן פי' ... ף בפ"ג דב"ב והרמב"ם:

**גליון הש"ס**

... ד"ה ומר סבר ... ומשום דאין ... שליח לדבר עבירה. ... לי דאם מסברא לא ... נא דבחצר לא מקרי ... עבירה מהנך טעמים ... ל דלאו בר חיובא או ... ם אי בעי עביד מנ"ל ... ת דלמא גם בגניבה ... רבאי חצר משום ידו ... ר באמת דוקא בעומד ... אצירו וצ"ע: תוס' ... ילפינן כו' ... רבנן. עיין תוס' ... ות יט ע"ב ד"ה גמרינן:

**תורה אור השלם**

א) כִּי תִקְצֹר קְצִירְךָ ... דֶךָ וְשָׁכַחְתָּ עֹמֶר ... דֶה לֹא תָשׁוּב ... חְתּוֹ לַגֵּר לַיָּתוֹם ... לְמָנָה יִהְיֶה לְמַעַן ... כְךָ יְיָ אֱלֹהֶיךָ בְּכֹל מַעֲשֵׂה יָדֶיךָ: [דברים כד, יט]

**ליקוטי רש"י**

... היו באים בספינה. ... ולא נתן רשות לתרום ... ושין כו:]. נתון ... יהושע. רבי יהושע בן ... יא כדאמר במס' ערכין ... יא:) מעשה ברבי ... שע ברבי חנניא שהלך ... יע את ר' יוחנן בן ... גדא בהגפת דלתות ... ר לו חזור בך שאתה מן ... שוררים ואני מן ... שוערים [קידושין כז.].

---

חשק שלמה על ר"ח א) הדבר מבואר לרבינו היה גורס בגמ' דבשדה לא נהוי שכחה ובעיר נהוי שכחה והך דאמר קרא לא תשוב וכו' והך דאמר קרא יהיה וכו' הכל מן הקושיא היא ועי' בש"מ שהביא ג"כ לד' רבינו וגרסתו ע"ש.

eason that the sheaf becomes *shich'chah* in this case? דְּלֵיתֵיהּ גַּבֵּיהּ דְּלִזְכֵּי לֵיהּ – **Because [the owner] is not in [the field] for it** o **acquire** the sheaf **for him.**[20] If this is the correct interpreta-.on of the Baraisa, we see from the Baraisa that an open field can cquire on behalf of its owner only if he is present to guard it.[21]

The Gemara suggests another interpretation of the Baraisa, hereby refuting the proof that the capacity of an open property to cquire on behalf of its owner depends on whether or not he is resent:

מִמַּאי – **How** do you know that the foregoing is what the Baraisa neans? דִּלְמָא גְּזֵירַת הַכָּתוּב הִיא – **Perhaps it is a Scriptural** ecree דְּבַשָּׂדֶה הָוֵי שִׁכְחָה – **that** when the owner is **in the field,** a forgotten sheaf] **can become** ***shich'chah*****;** וּבָעִיר לֹא הָוֵי שִׁכְחָה – **but** when the owner is **in the city, it cannot become** *hich'chah!*[22] – ? –

The Gemara answers that it is impossible to say that the *hich'chah* laws apply only when the owner is still in his field:

אָמַר קְרָא לֹא תָשׁוּב לְקַחְתּוֹ – For **the verse states:**[23] ***you shall not*** ***urn back to take it;*** לְרַבּוֹת שִׁכְחַת הָעִיר – these words come **to** nclude in the *shich'chah* laws the sheaf **forgotten** by the owner vhen he is **in the city.**[24]

The Gemara objects:

הַאי מִיבְּעֵי לֵיהּ לְלָאו – **That** verse **is needed to** add **a prohibition** o the commandment of *shich'chah,* not to extend the *shich'chah* aws to a case in which the owner is in the city.[25] – ? –

The Gemara answers:

אִם כֵּן נֵימָא קְרָא לֹא תִקָּחֶנּוּ – **If** it is **so** that Scripture meant only to add a prohibition to the *shich'chah* laws, **let the verse state** simply: **"Do not take it."** מַאי לֹא תָשׁוּב – **Why** does it add: ***you shall not "turn back"*** *to take it*? לְרַבּוֹת שִׁכְחַת הָעִיר – It must mean **to include** in the *shich'chah* laws the sheaf **forgotten** by the owner when he is **in the city.**[26]

The Gemara still objects:

וְאַכַּתִּי מִיבְּעֵי לֵיהּ לִכְדִתְנַן – **But [the verse] is still needed to** teach **that which we learned in a Mishnah:** שֶׁלְּפָנָיו אֵין שִׁכְחָה – WHAT IS IN FRONT OF HIM IS NOT *SHICH'CHAH;* שֶׁלְּאַחֲרָיו יֵשׁ שִׁכְחָה שֶׁהוּא בְּבַל תָּשׁוּב – BUT WHAT IS BEHIND HIM IS *SHICH'CHAH,* BECAUSE IT IS included IN the prohibition NOT TO TURN BACK.[27] זֶה הַכְּלָל – THIS IS THE RULE; כָּל שֶׁהוּא בְּבַל תָּשׁוּב שִׁכְחָה – ANYTHING THAT IS GOVERNED BY the prohibition NOT TO TURN BACK IS *SHICH'CHAH;* כָּל שֶׁאֵינוֹ בְּבַל תָּשׁוּב אֵינוֹ שִׁכְחָה – ANYTHING THAT IS NOT GOVERNED BY the prohibition NOT TO TURN BACK IS NOT *SHICH'CHAH.* At any rate, the verse is needed to teach this distinction between sheaves he must "turn back" for and those that he can still retrieve without "turning back." There is now no verse available to extend the mitzvah of *shich'chah* to cases when the owner is in the city. – ? –

The Gemara answers:

אָמַר רַב אָשֵׁי – **Rav Ashi said:** אָמַר קְרָא: ,,יִהְיֶה" – **The verse states:**[28] *[The forgotten sheaf]* ***shall be;*** this expression comes לְרַבּוֹת שִׁכְחַת הָעִיר – **to include** the sheaf **forgotten** by the owner when he is **in the city.**[29]

The Gemara cites supporting views to Rav Yehudah's earlier qualification of our Mishnah:

NOTES

0. Since the owner is not at the side of his field when the workers forget he sheaf, his unguarded field cannot acquire the sheaf in its emi-*shich'chah* stage [even if he declares his intent that it should do o]. Hence, when he eventually forgets about the sheaf, it becomes bona de *shich'chah,* having been forgotten by both the owner and his orkers (*Rashi,* as explained by *Ri Abohab* in *Shitah Mekubetzes*).

Accordingly, the Baraisa's Scriptural exposition is to be interpreted in he following manner: בַּשָּׂדֶה וְשָׁכַחְתָּ – "Only in the field is it necessary or you, the owner, to forget the sheaf" [before the workers forget about ] in order for it to become *shich'chah*; וְלֹא בָּעִיר – "but not when you re in the city," for in that case it can become *shich'chah* even if the wner's workers forgot about it [first] (*Rashi*).

1. The Baraisa refers to a field, which is not normally fenced in. evertheless, if the owner is standing in his field it is then considered uarded and can acquire objects for him, but not if he is absent (i.e. in he city).

2. [The foregoing interpretation understood that when the owner is in he field, a sheaf is less susceptible to becoming *shich'chah* than when e is in the city. The Gemara now asks that a strict interpretation of the erse's words: "and you forget a sheaf *in the field*" would yield the pposite result: Forgetting the sheaf renders it *shich'chah* when the wner is in the field, but not when the owner is in the city!] Rather than dopt a forced interpretation of the verse (which the earlier understand-ng of the Baraisa must accept), it is better to emend the Baraisa to read: יָכוֹל יְהֵא שִׁכְחָה, *It would be possible [to think] that it does become hich'chah.* Accordingly, the Baraisa teaches simply that *shich'chah* pplies only if the owner is in the field when he forgets the sheaf. But if he owner does not forget the sheaf until he arrives in the city [even hough the workers in the field have forgotten it], the Torah decrees that he sheaf does *not* become *shich'chah* (*Rashi* as elaborated by *Ritva*). ccording to this interpretation, the Baraisa does not deal at all with cquisition by *chatzeir,* and has no bearing on the question of whether he owner must be standing beside his otherwise unguarded *chatzeir* in rder for it to acquire on his behalf.

3. *Deuteronomy* 24:19. [This verse was quoted in note 15 above.]

4. Scripture could have left out these words and stated simply: כִּי תִקְצֹר קְצִירְךָ בְשָׂדֶךָ וְשָׁכַחְתָּ עֹמֶר בַּשָּׂדֶה . . . לַגֵּר לַיָּתוֹם וְלָאַלְמָנָה יִהְיֶה, *When you reap your arvest in your field and you forget a sheaf in the field . . . for the convert, or the orphan, and for the widow shall it be.* By adding the words: לֹא תָשׁוּב לְקַחְתּוֹ, *you shall not turn back to take it,* Scripture must be adding that even if the owner is no longer in the field, the produce becomes *shich'chah* and he may no longer take it. Therefore, since a person's produce can become *shich'chah* even when he has left his field, the Baraisa must be interpreted as first suggested: When the owner is in his field, it is *less* susceptible to *shich'chah*, since the field can acquire the sheaf for him and prevent it from becoming *shich'chah.*

25. In addition to the positive commandment to leave the forgotten sheaf for the poor (לַגֵּר לַיָּתוֹם וְלָאַלְמָנָה יִהְיֶה, *for the convert, for the orphan, and for the widow shall it be*), Scripture adds a prohibition (לֹא תָשׁוּב לְקַחְתּוֹ, *you shall not turn back to take it*), with its attendant liability.

26. ["Turning back" can be construed to mean turning back *to the field* after one has already left it.] Accordingly, the clause לֹא תָשׁוּב לְקַחְתּוֹ, *you shall not turn back to take it*, performs two functions: It adds a prohibition and it extends the *shich'chah* laws to a case in which the owner has left the field and gone to the city.

27. *Pe'ah* 6:4. This Mishnah refers to a lone worker who started harvesting [i.e. collecting sheaves for removal to the threshing floor] at the beginning of a row [of sheaves]. He forgot some sheaves in front of him and behind him (see further in this note). Those behind him are *shich'chah,* whereas those in front of him are not (*Rashi*). [*Rash* to that Mishnah elaborates that the sheaf collector skipped over some sheaves ("behind him") and stopped short of collecting some at the end of the row ("in front of him"), turning his attention instead to a new row. Those left at the end of the row can be construed as part of another row running perpendicular to the one he is presently collecting. These sheaves "forgotten in front of him" are not deemed *shich'chah,* since he need not "return to them" – he has not *bypassed* them, and further-more, they can be construed as part of a row whose collection he has not yet begun (see *Yad Avraham* to that Mishnah at length).]

28. *Deuteronomy* 24:19. [See note 15 above for the verse in context.]

29. Here, Scripture implies that a sheaf becomes *shich'chah wherever* the owner is when he forgets it.

Now that it is clear that *shich'chah* applies even when the owner has left his field, the previously cited Baraisa, which took into account the location of the owner, must have based its rulings on the capacity of the owner to acquire the sheaf when he stands at the side of his field, as first suggested by the Gemara above. The Gemara has thus successfully proven that an otherwise unguarded courtyard acquires objects for its owner when he is standing at its side, but not when he is absent.

ילפינן מציאה מגט ומר סבר לא ילפינן מציאה מגט ואיבעית אימא בקטנה כולי עלמא לא פליגי דילפינן מציאה מגט והכא בקטן קא מיפלגי מר סבר ילפינן קטן מקטנה ומר סבר א לא ילפינן קטן מקטנה ואיבעית אימא מר אמר חדא ומר אמר חדא ולא פליגי:

מתני׳ ב ראה אותן רצין אחר מציאה אחר צבי שבור אחר גוזלות שלא פרחו ואמר זכתה לי שדי זכתה לו היה צבי רץ כדרכו או שהיו גוזלות מפריחין ואמר זכתה לי שדי לא אמר כלום: גמ׳ אמר רב יהודה אמר שמואל ג והוא שעומד בצד שדהו ותקני ליה שדהו א) דאמר ר׳ יוסי בר׳ חנינא ד חצרו של אדם קונה לו שלא מדעתו ה הני מילי בחצר המשתמרת אבל חצר שאינה משתמרת אי עומד בצד שדהו אין אי לא לא ומנא תימרא דחצר שאינה משתמרת אי עומד בצד שדהו אין אי לא לא דתניא היה עומד בעיר ואומר יודע אני שעומר שיש לי בשדה פועלים שכחוהו לא יהא שכחה יכול לא יהא שכחה תלמוד לומר א) ושכחת עומר בשדה בשדה ושכחת ולא בעיר הא גופא קשיא אמרת יכול לא יהא שכחה אלמא הוי שכחה והדר תני בשדה ושכחת ולא בעיר אלמא לא הוי שכחה אלא לאו הכי קאמר ו בשדה שכוח מעיקרו הוי שכחה זכור ולבסוף שכוח אין שכחה מאי טעמא דכיון דקאי גבה הויא ליה חצרו וזכתה ליה ז אבל בעיר אפילו זכור ולבסוף שכוח הויא שכחה מאי טעמא דליתיה גביה דלזכי ליה ממאי דלמא גזירת הכתוב היא דבשדה נהוי שכחה ובעיר לא נהוי שכחה אמר קרא א) לא תשוב לקחתו לרבות שכחת העיר האי מיבעי ליה ללאו אם כן נימא קרא לא תקחנו מאי לא תשוב לרבות שכחת העיר ואכתי מיבעי ליה לכדתנן ג) ח שלפניו אין שכחה שלאחריו יש שכחה שהוא בבל תשוב ט זה הכלל כל שהוא בבל תשוב שכחה כל שאינו בבל תשוב אינו שכחה אמר רב אשי אמר קרא א) יהיה לרבות שכחת העיר וכן אמר עולא והוא שעומד בצד שדהו וכן אמר רבה בר בר חנה והוא שעומד בצד שדהו איתיביה רבי אבא לעולא ג) מעשה ברבן גמליאל וזקנים שהיו באים בספינה אמר רבן גמליאל עישור שאני עתיד למוד נתון ליהושע ומקומו

ילפינן מציאה מגט. כי היכי דגבי גט אית לה חצר לקטנה גבי מציאה נמי אית לה: ומר סבר לא ילפינן. ממונא חצר מאם המלא אתרבאי ואיכא למימר דשליחות הוא ° ומשום דאין שליח לדבר עבירה אצטריך למכתב התם: והכא בקטן פליגי. דלא אשכחן דרבי ביה חצר: מר אמר חדא כו׳. ר"ש בן לקיש אמר לענין מציאה ורבי יוחנן לענין גט אי נמי מר אמר קטן ומר אמר קטנה: מתני׳ אחר צבי שבור. דהוא דומיא דמציאה שאינו יכול לרוץ ומשתמר בתוך השדה אם לא יטלוהו אחרים: גמ׳ אי עומד בצד שדהו אין. דעכשיו היא משתמרת על ידו: עומר שיש לי בשדה. שהנחתיו שם מדעתי וסמכתי על הפועלים שיביאוהו ופועלים שכחוהו: לא יהא שכחה. אם חזר ושכחו: בשדה ושכחת. אם שכחתו בעודך מן השדה הוי שכחה ולא ששכחתו משנכנסת לעיר: אלא לאו הכי קאמר בשדה שכוח מעיקרו כו׳. בעוד האיש בשדה עומר השכוח מעיקרו ששכחו הוא תחילה לפועל הוי שכחה אבל זכור שהניחו שם מדעתו ולבסוף שכחו על ידי פועלים לא הוי שכחה: אבל בעיר. משנכנס לעיר אפילו זכור ולבסוף שכח הוי שכחה דליתיה גביה כו׳ והכי קא נסיב ליה תנא לתלמודיה יכול לא יהא שכחה ת"ל בשדה ושכחת בעודך בשדה הוא דבעינן דשכחתיה אתה ולא בעיר לא בעינן ושכחת שאף שכחת פועלים עושה אותה שכחה: וממאי. דקרא הכי מתרץ ומתני׳ הכי אמרה: דלמא גזירת הכתוב היא. דמשמע דבשדה יהא שכחה אבל משבא בעל הבית לעיר אין שכחתו ושכחת פועלים כלום והכי קאמר יכול יהא שכחה ת"ל כו׳: שלפניו אין שכחה. בשכחת הקוצר קאי יחיד שהתחיל לקצור מראש השורה ושכח לפניו ולאחריו שלאחריו הוי שכחה שלפניו לא הוי שכחה: יהיה. לגר ליתום ולאלמנה יהיה: עישור שאני עתיד למוד. נזכר שלא עישר מעשרותיו והוקשה לו ומיהר לעשרן באשר הוא שם: נתון ליהושע. לרבי יהושע בר חנניא שהיה עמו בספינה והוא לוי ונוטל מעשר ראשון כדאמרי׳ בערכין (דף יא:) מעשה ברבי יהושע שהלך לסייע את ר׳ יוחנן בן גודגדא בהגפת דלתות אמר לו חזור בך שאתה מן המשוררים ואני מן המשוערים ומשורר שסיעי במיתה:

ילפינן מציאה מגט. האי ילפינן הוי ° מדרבנן דמציאת קטן לא הוי אלא מדרבנן אפילו לרבי יוסי דאמר (לקמן דף יב.) גזל גמור היינו מדבריהם ולענין יד לא פליגי דילפינן אלא לענין חצר ד): זכתה לו. [א] נראה אע"ג דלא אמר זכתה לי דזכתה לו כדאמרי׳ לעיל (דף י.) אי תקון רבנן דלקני כי לא אמר מאי הוי ואין לומר דהתם היינו משום דנפל לו עליה דגלי בדעתיה שרוצה לקנות אבל הכא מי יימר דרוצה לקנות דאדרבה משמע לעיל דאי לא נפל קנה טפי ואע"ג דלא אמר אקני ועוד דאמר רבי יוסי בר׳ חנינא חצרו של אדם קונה לו שלא מדעתו אלמא אע"ג דלא אמר קני והכא נקט משום סיפא דאפילו אמר כיון דרך כדרכו לא קני ה): היה צבי רץ כדרכו. ה"ה אפי׳ צבי שבור אם רץ אחריו ואין מגיעו אלא אורחא דמילתא נקט דכשרץ כדרכו אין מגיעו: ה"מ בחצר המשתמרת. תימה דבפ׳ שור שנגח את הפרה (ב"ק דף מט: ושם ד"ה והלכתא) אמר משכונו של גר ביד ישראל ומת הגר כו׳ וזה קונה השאר כו׳ ופריך ותקני ליה חצרו דאמר ר׳ יוסי בר׳ חנינא כו׳ ומסיק דליתיה פי׳ למלוה בחצרו וקשה דהתם משמע דהוי בחצר המשתמרת מדמייתי עלה מרבי יוסי בר׳ חנינא דמיירי במשתמרת כדמוכח הכא ועוד דמסתמא ביתו ודאי משתמר הוא ששמר שם המשכון וא"כ כי ליתיה נמי לקני ועוד אדפריך ליה מדרבי יוסי בר׳ חנינא לפרוך ממתני׳ ומיהו זה נוכל לתרץ דמתני׳ הוי משום דנתכוין לזכות בה דאמר זכתה לי לכך מייתי מרבי יוסי בר׳ חנינא [ב] וי"ל דה"פ דליתיה למשכון בחצר אבל מלוה גם לפי המקשן מיירי דליתיה בחצר ולכך לא פריך ממתני׳ כ"א מרבי יוסי בר׳ חנינא וא"ת פרק הזורק (גיטין דף עז: ושם ד"ה והוא) דתנן זרק לתוך ביתה או לתוך חצרה מגורשת משמע דמשתמרת ואפילו הכי קאמר עולא והוא שעומדת בצד ביתה וי"ל דדוקא גבי גט דאיתיה בעל כרחה בעינן עומדת בצד ביתה כדאמר בשמעתין: זכור ולבסוף שכוח. פירוש זכור בשעה שהשכחה מתחלת שכבר שכחוהו פועלים ולבסוף שכח גם הוא ושכוח מעיקרו הוי כששכחו הפועלים שכח גם הוא אבל מה שהוא זכור בשעה שהפועלים זוכרין אין זה זכור ולבסוף שכוח דאל"כ לא תמצא שכחה לעולם דכששדהו מלאה עומרין יאמר יזכה לי שדי: דלמא גזירת הכתוב היא. פרש"י ונגרוס יכול יהא שכחה ותימה לפי שרוצה לסתור ראייתו מגיה הברייתא ותו מה מתרץ לרבות שכחת העיר והלא בברייתא יליף דזכור ולבסוף שכוח לא הוי שכחה דקתני יודע אני שפועלים שכחוהו והכא דדריש לרבות שכחת העיר יעמיד בשכוח מעיקרא לכך י"ל שאינו סותר ראייתו אלא גמרא קשה לו על הברייתא מנ"ל למדרש מיעוטא על דיוקא דקרא דדריש בשדה ושכחת דהיינו שכוח מעיקרא אבל זכור ולבסוף שכוח לא הוי שכחה ועל זה קאי מיעוטא לומר דבעיר אפילו זכור ולבסוף שכוח הוי שכחה דלמא גזירת הכתוב היא דבשדה הוי שכחה שכוח מעיקרא ולא בעיר והכי מסתברא טפי לאוקמי מיעוט אגופיה דקרא בשדה ושכחת ולא בעיר והשתא משני שפיר לרבות שכחת העיר וע"כ לא מצי קאי אפשטיה דקרא: זה הכלל. לאתויי קרן זוית: עישור שאני עתיד למוד. פרש"י פרק קמא דקידושין (דף כו: ושם ד"ה מעשה) שהיה ירא פן יסמכו עליו בני ביתו שעישר ויאכלו טבל דחזקה על חבר שאינו מוציא מתחת ידו דבר שאינו מתוקן וקשה דהיינו דוקא בחבר שמת או בהולך ואין בדעתו לשוב עד ימים רבים ועוד למה נתנם לרבי יהושע ולרבי עקיבא יקרא להם שם ולא יותר ועוד דאין זה קריאת שם דלא אמר עשרה יהא מעשר אלא אמר מעשר ראשון יהא נתון ליהושע ופר"ת דשנת הביעור היתה וכבר הפריש והיה צריך להוציאם מתחת ידו ולתנם

עין משפט
נר מצוה

פז א מיי׳ פי"ז מהלכות אבידה הל׳ י ופ"ד מהל׳ זכייה ומתנה הל׳ ט ועי׳ בהשגות ובמ"מ סמג עשין עד טוש"ע ח"מ סי׳ רסח סעיף ה וסי׳ רמג סעיף כג:
פח ב ג מיי׳ פי"ז מהל׳ אבידה הל׳ יא סמג עשין עד טוש"ע ח"מ סי׳ רסח סעיף ד:
פט ד ה מיי׳ שם הל׳ ח ופט"ז שם הלכה ח ופ"א מהל׳ זכייה ומתנה הלכה ד ועי׳ בהשגות ובמ"מ ופ"ד שם הל׳ ט סמג עשין עד פב טוש"ע ח"מ סי׳ רמג סעיף כ כא וסי׳ רסח סעיף ג וסי׳ ערה סעיף כח וסי׳ שיג סעיף ג:
צ ו ז מיי׳ פ"ה מהלכות מתנות עניים הל׳ ג:
צא ח ט מיי׳ שם הל׳ י:

רבינו חננאל

כי פליגי במציאה ר"י סבר ילפינן מציאה מגט ור"ל סבר לא ילפינן. איבעי תימא [בקטנה] כ"ע ילפינן מציאה מגט וכי פליגי בקטן ר"י יליף לקטן מקטנה כשם שזוכה חצירה של קטנה לקטנה כך זוכה חצר של קטן לקטן. ור"ל [ס"ל] ריבתה התורה החצר כיד לאשה ואפי׳ קטנה אבל לקטן לא. איבעי תימא כ"ע לא ילפי קטן מקטנה ור׳ יוחנן וריש לקיש לא פליגי אלא ר׳ יוחנן הורה בקטנה דיש לה חצר ויש לה ד׳ אמות וריש לקיש הורה בקטן דאין חצירו זוכה לו ולא ד׳ אמות שלו כך מסקנא דשמעתא: פיסקא ראה אותן רצין אחר המציאה וכו׳ עד זכתה לי שדי זכתה לו שדהו: גמ׳ והוא שעומד בצד שדהו. ואמרי׳ אמאי צריך להיות עומד בצד שדהו ותקני ליה שדהו כר׳ יוסי בר חנינא דאמר חצירו של אדם קונה לו שלא מדעתו ודחי׳ הני מילי בחצר המשתמרת אבל שדה שאינה משתמרת אי עומד בצד שדהו זכתה לו שדהו ואם אינו עומד שם לא זכתה לו שדהו. מנא הני מילי דתניא היה עומד בעיר ואומר יודע אני כי העומר שיש לי בשדה פועלים שכחוהו לא יהא שכחה יכול לא יהא שכחה ת"ל ושכחת עומר בשדה. בשדה ושכחת ולא בעיר. ופרישנא בשדה שכוח מעיקרו הוי שכחה זכור ולבסוף שכוח לא הוי שכחה מאי טעמא כיון דכי קאי בשדה וזכור לו זכתה לו שדהו ואע"ג דבתר הכי שכחו אינה שכחה שכבר זכתה לו שדהו וכאילו נטלו מאותה העת אבל בעיר אפי׳ זכור ולבסוף שכחו הוי שכחה מאי טעמא דהא ליתיה גביה בשדה דליזכי ליה שדהו ש"מ דאי עומד בצד שדהו זכתה לו שדהו ואי אינו עומד בצד שדהו לא זכתה לו שדהו. ואמרי׳ וממאי דמשום דלא הוה קאי בצד שדהו נעשה שכחה דלמא גזירת הכתוב היא א) דבשדה לא ניהוי שכחה. ובעיר כי האי גוונא זכור ולבסוף שכוח ליהוי שכחה מדכתיב לא תשוב לקחתו גמרינן מינה לרבות שכחת העיר. ונדחו הדברים האלו ואסקה רב אשי יהיה לרבות שכחת העיר. ולא נתברר כי אם עומד בצד שדהו זכתה לו שדהו ואי לא לא. וכן אמר עולא והוא שעומד בצד שדהו. איתיביה רבא מעשה ברבן גמליאל וזקנים שהיו באין בספינה.

חשק שלמה על ר"ח א) הדבר מבואר דרבינו היה גורס בגמ׳ דבשדה לא נהוי שכחה ובעיר נהוי שכחה דלאמר קרא וכו׳ והן דלאמר קרא הכל מן הקושיא היא ועי׳ בש"מ דהביא ג"כ לד׳ רבינו וגרסתו ע"ש.

מסורת הש"ס

...א קמא מט:, לקמן ...קיח., חולין קמא:, ...אה פרק ו משנה ד, ...עשר שני פרק ה ... ט, קדושין כו:, ...ע"ע תוס׳ יבמות יט: ...גמרינן, ה) [וע"ע ...בעירובין מט: ד"ה ...ואמר].

הגהות הגר"א

...תוס׳ ד"ה זכתה ...ראה כו׳. נ"ב אבל ...ב"ס מחלק בין ד׳ ...ת וחצר המשתמרת ... שא"מ (ועמ"ש ... בח"מ סי׳ רס"ח ...י"א): [ב] שם ... ה"מ כו׳ וי"ל ...יפ כו׳. נ"ב וכן פי׳ ...ף בפ"ג דב"ב ...והרמב"ס:

גליון הש"ס

...י ד"ה ומר סבר ...ומשום דאין ...יח לדבר עבירה. ... לי דאם מסברא לא ...א דבחצר לא מקרי ... עבירה מהנך טעמים ...ל דלאו בר חיובא או ...ם אי בעי עביד מנ"ל ...ת דלמא גם בגניבה ...בלאי חצר משום ידו ... באמת דוקא בעומד ... חצירו ול"ע: תוס׳ ...א ילפינן כו׳ ...רבנן. עיין תוס׳ ...ות יט ע"ב ד"ה ...גמרינן:

תורה אור השלם

...כִּי תִקְצֹר קְצִירְךָ ...דֶךָ וְשָׁכַחְתָּ עֹמֶר ...דֶה לֹא תָשׁוּב ...חְתּוֹ לַגֵּר לַיָּתוֹם ...אַלְמָנָה יִהְיֶה לְמַעַן ...רֶכְךָ יְיָ אֱלֹהֶיךָ בְּכֹל מַעֲשֵׂה יָדֶיךָ: [דברים כד, יט]

ליקוטי רש"י

...יו באים בספינה. ...ם ולא נתן רשות לתרום ...רשין כו:]. נתון ...הושע. רבי יהושע בן ...יא כדאמר במס׳ ערכין ...יא:) מעשה ברבי ...שע ברבי חנניא שהלך ...יע את ר׳ יוחנן בן ...גדא בהגפת דלתות ...ר לו חזור בך שאתה מן ...שוררים ואני מן ...שוערים [קידושין כו.].

is not standing there! דְּאָמַר ר׳ יוֹסֵי בְּר׳ חֲנִינָא – **For R' Yose** **e son of R' Chanina said:** חֲצֵרוֹ שֶׁל אָדָם קוֹנָה לוֹ שֶׁלֹּא מִדַּעְתּוֹ – **e courtyard of a person acquires** objects **for him** even **ithout his knowledge.**[11] – ? –

The Gemara answers:

הָנֵי מִילֵּי בְּחָצֵר הַמִּשְׁתַּמֶּרֶת – **This ruling** of R' Yose the son of R' anina applies only **with** regard to **a guarded courtyard;** אֲבָל חָצֵר שֶׁאֵינָהּ מִשְׁתַּמֶּרֶת – **but** with regard to **a courtyard that is not arded** – אִי עוֹמֵד בְּצַד שָׂדֵהוּ אִין – **if [the owner] stands at e side of** his **field – yes,** it makes the acquisition on his behalf; אִי לֹא ל – but **if** he does **not** stand there, it does **not** make the quisition on his behalf.[12]

The Gemara supports its contention:

וּמְנָא תֵּימְרָ – **And from where do you say** דְּחָצֵר שֶׁאֵינָהּ מִשְׁתַּמֶּרֶת – **that** with regard to **a courtyard that is not guard-** – אִי עוֹמֵד בְּצַד שָׂדֵהוּ אִין – **if [the owner] stands at the side the field – yes,** it makes the acquisition; אִי לֹא לֹא – but **if** ot, **not?** דְּתַנְיָא – **For** the following case **was taught in a araisa:**[13] הָיָה עוֹמֵד בָּעִיר – If [THE OWNER] had left his field d WAS STANDING IN THE CITY, וְאוֹמֵר יוֹדֵעַ אֲנִי שֶׁעוֹמֶר שֶׁיֵּשׁ לִי בַּשָּׂדֶה פּוֹעֲלִים שְׁכָחוּהוּ – AND HE DECLARES, "I KNOW THAT THE ORKERS FORGOT A SHEAF THAT I HAVE IN THE FIELD; לֹא יְהֵא שִׁכְחָה – IT SHALL NOT BECOME *SHICH'CHAH* even if I, too, entually forget about it."[14] יָכוֹל לֹא יְהֵא שִׁכְחָה – IT WOULD BE SSIBLE to THINK THAT IT DOES NOT BECOME *SHICH'CHAH* even if e owner, too, subsequently forgets it. תַּלְמוּד לוֹמַר: "וְשָׁכַחְתָּ עֹמֶר בַּשָּׂדֶה" – THE TORAH THEREFORE TEACHES:[15] *AND YOU RGET A SHEAF IN THE FIELD.* This implies: בַּשָּׂדֶה וְשָׁכַחְתָּ – hen you are IN THE FIELD AND YOU FORGET the sheaf, it is *shich'chah;* וְלֹא בָּעִיר – BUT NOT when you forget while IN THE CITY.[16]

The Gemara first seeks to clarify the meaning of the Baraisa: הָא גּוּפָא קַשְׁיָא – **This** Baraisa is apparently **self-contradictory:** אָמַרְתָּ יָכוֹל לֹא יְהֵא שִׁכְחָה – First, **you said:** IT WOULD BE POSSIBLE to think that IT DOES *NOT* BECOME *SHICH'CHAH.* אַלְמָא הָוֵי שִׁכְחָה – **Thus,** we see that **[the sheaf] becomes *shich'chah*** when the owner forgets it after arriving in the city.[17] וְנָסֵיב לָהּ גְּמָרָא בַּשָּׂדֶה וְשָׁכַחְתָּ וְלֹא בָּעִיר – **Then, [the Baraisa] cites the exposition:** When you are IN THE FIELD AND YOU FORGET THE SHEAF, it is *shich'chah*; BUT NOT when you forget while IN THE CITY. אַלְמָא לֹא הָוֵי שִׁכְחָה – **Thus,** we see that **it does not become *shich'chah*** in such a case! אֶלָּא לָאו הָכִי קָאָמַר – **Rather,** are we **not** forced to say that **the following is what [the Baraisa] means?** בַּשָּׂדֶה – While the owner is still **in the field,** שָׁכוּחַ מֵעִיקָּרוֹ הָוֵי שִׁכְחָה – if **[the sheaf] was initially forgotten** by the owner [i.e. the owner forgot it first and then the workers], **it becomes *shich'chah*;** זָכוּר וּלְבַסּוֹף שָׁכוּחַ אֵין שִׁכְחָה – but if **it was** initially **remembered** by the owner **and eventually forgotten** [i.e. the workers forgot it first and then the owner], **it is not *shich'chah.***[18] מַאי טַעְמָא – **What is the reason** that the sheaf does not become *shich'chah* in that second case? דְּכֵיוָן דְּקָאֵי גַּבָּהּ הָוְיָא לֵיהּ חֲצֵרוֹ וְזָכְתָה לֵיהּ – **Because since [the owner] is standing in [the field], it serves as his courtyard and acquires** the sheaf **for him.**[19] אֲבָל בָּעִיר אֲפִילּוּ זָכוּר וּלְבַסּוֹף שָׁכוּחַ הָוְיָא שִׁכְחָה – **But,** the Baraisa rules, if the owner is already **in the city** when he makes his declaration, **even if [the sheaf] was** initially **remembered** by the owner **and** only **eventually forgotten, it** nevertheless **becomes *shich'chah.*** מַאי טַעְמָא – **What is the**

NOTES

. It is assumed that R' Yose the son of R' Chanina refers even to a case which the owner is not standing beside his field, since one who stands side his field is ordinarily aware of what is in it; if he is aware, then s field is not acquiring "without his knowledge" (*Ein Yehoseif*; cf. *ishash*).

. The Gemara answers that Rav Yehudah's additional condition that e field's owner stand at its side was in order that the field become arded, for a person's courtyard cannot effect an acquisition unless it guarded from outside intruders [even if the object is of a type that uld remain secure in the yard if no one else entered and took it]. This quirement is fulfilled in one of two ways: Either the courtyard is nced in – it is in such a courtyard that R' Yose the son of R' Chanina es not require the owner to stand at its side; or, in the case of an open ld – the case discussed by Rav Yehudah – its owner stands at its side personally guard it (see *Rashi*; *Shitah Mekubetzes*).

. This Baraisa deals with the law of *shich'chah* [forgotten sheaves]. As entioned above (10a note 27), the Torah obligates a grower in Eretz srael to leave for the poor any sheaves forgotten in the field during the moval to the threshing floor (as well as standing produce overlooked the harvester).

As stated in the Mishnah *Pe'ah* 5:7, a sheaf is not deemed to be orgotten" until it is forgotten by both the owner *and* by his workers at are harvesting the field. However, if only one of them has forgotten e sheaf, it is not yet *shich'chah,* and the poor may not take it (see *Ritva* d *Maharam Schif*).

. The field's owner has come to the city still mindful of a particular eaf that he has purposely not moved to the threshing floor with the her sheaves. Although the workers have forgotten about that sheaf, e owner has not; thus, it is not yet *shich'chah.* The owner seeks to sure that the sheaf does not become *shich'chah* even if he, too, bsequently forgets about it (see *Rashi*).

. *Deuteronomy* 24:19. The verse states: כִּי תִקְצֹר קְצִירְךָ בְשָׂדֶךָ וְשָׁכַחְתָּ עֹמֶר בַּשָּׂדֶה לֹא תָשׁוּב לְקַחְתּוֹ לַגֵּר לַיָּתוֹם וְלָאַלְמָנָה יִהְ, *When you reap your harvest your field and you forget a sheaf in the field, you shall not turn back take it; for the convert, for the orphan, and for the widow shall it be.*

. The sheaf becomes *shich'chah* only if the owner forgot it immediately on leaving the field, but not if he forgot it later, when he had already rived in the city (*Rashi*).

The Gemara will immediately ask that the Baraisa was seeking to prove that the owner's declaration is ineffective, and the sheaf becomes *shich'chah* even if the owner forgets it while he is in the city; yet the Baraisa apparently expounds the verse to indicate that the sheaf does *not* become *shich'chah* if the owner forgets it while he is in the city!

17. Whenever the expression "it would be possible [to think]" is used, the meaning is that one might think so were it not that a verse teaches otherwise. Thus, if the Baraisa states that it would be possible to think that a sheaf is not *shich'chah* if the owner forgets it while he is in the city, the meaning is that a verse teaches otherwise and the sheaf is indeed *shich'chah* even in that case.

18. *Rashi* as explained by *Ri Abohab* in *Shitah Mekubetzes*; see also *Ritva*; cf. *Dibros Moshe.* [The Baraisa is distinguishing between where the owner forgets the sheaf while he is still in the field and where he forgets it after he arrives in the city.]

19. The rationale for this law is the following: As stated in note 13, a sheaf is not *shich'chah* unless it is forgotten by both the owner and the workers that are harvesting the field. Once the workers forget the sheaf, the process of *shich'chah* begins, but is not complete until the owner forgets it as well. At this point of semi-*shich'chah* the owner can declare that he wishes his field to acquire the incomplete *shich'chah* for him; this acquisition serves to restore the sheaf as his property, which can no longer become *shich'chah* even if he subsequently forgets it as well. [If the owner does *not* declare this, however, his field does not automatically acquire the sheaf on his behalf, despite the general rule that one's *chatzeir* acquires for him without his knowledge. For without the owner's explicit indication that he wishes to acquire the semi-forgotten sheaf, it is presumed that he is content to allow the *shich'chah* process to run its course should he, too, forget the sheaf. And though one's *chatzeir* acquires without his knowledge, it does not acquire against his will (see *Ritva*; cf. *Ran*).] However, if neither the owner nor the workers have forgotten the sheaf, the owner's acquisition of the sheaf accomplishes nothing, since the process of *shich'chah* has not yet begun; the sheaf is still his absolute property and it is at this stage of ownership that the Torah decrees that the sheaf be left for the poor if forgotten (*Ritva* in explanation of *Rashi*; see also *Ramban* and *Ran*).

## גמרא

ילפינן מציאה מגט ומר סבר לא ילפינן מציאה מגט ואיבעית אימא בקטנה כולי עלמא לא פליגי דילפינן מציאה מגט והכא בקטן קא מיפלגי מר סבר ילפינן קטן מקטנה ומר סבר [א]לא ילפינן קטן מקטנה ואיבעית אימא מר אמר חדא ומר אמר חדא ולא פליגי:

**מתני'** [ב]ראה אותן רצין אחר מציאה אחר צבי שבור אחר גוזלות שלא פרחו ואמר זכתה לי שדי זכתה לו היה צבי רץ כדרכו או שהיו גוזלות מפריחין ואמר זכתה לי שדי לא אמר כלום:

**גמ'** אמר רב יהודה אמר שמואל [ג]והוא שעומד בצד שדהו ותקני ליה שדהו (א) דאמר ר' יוסי בר' חנינא [ד]חצרו של אדם קונה לו שלא מדעתו [ה]הני מילי בחצר המשתמרת אבל חצר שאינה משתמרת אי עומד בצד שדהו אין אי לא לא ומנא תימרא דחצר שאינה משתמרת אי עומד בצד שדהו אין אי לא לא דתניא היה עומד בעיר ואומר יודע אני שעומר שיש לי בשדה פועלים שכחוהו לא יהא שכחה יכול לא יהא שכחה תלמוד לומר (א) ושכחת עומר בשדה בשדה ושכחת ולא בעיר הא גופא קשיא אמרת יכול לא יהא שכחה אלמא הוי שכחה ונסיב לה גמרא בשדה ושכחת ולא בעיר אלמא לא הוי שכחה אלא לאו הכי קאמר [ו]בשדה שכוח מעיקרו הוי שכחה זכור ולבסוף שכוח אין שכחה מאי טעמא דכיון דקאי גבה הויא ליה חצרו וזכתה ליה [ז]אבל בעיר אפילו זכור ולבסוף שכוח הויא שכחה מאי טעמא דליתיה גביה דלזכי ליה ממאי דלמא גזירת הכתוב היא דבשדה נהוי שכחה ובעיר לא נהוי שכחה אמר קרא (א) לא תשוב לקחתו לרבות שכחת העיר האי מיבעי ליה ללאו אם כן נימא קרא לא תקחנו מאי לא תשוב לרבות שכחת העיר ואכתי מיבעי ליה לכדתנן (ג) [ח]שלפניו אין שכחה שלאחריו יש שכחה שהוא בבל תשוב [ט]זה הכלל כל שהוא בבל תשוב שכחה כל שאינו בבל תשוב אינו שכחה אמר רב אשי אמר קרא (א) יהיה לרבות שכחת העיר וכן אמר עולא והוא שעומד בצד שדהו וכן אמר רבה בר בר חנה והוא שעומד בצד שדהו איתיביה רבי אבא לעולא (ג) מעשה ברבן גמליאל וזקנים שהיו באים בספינה אמר רבן גמליאל עישור שאני עתיד למוד נתון ליהושע

## רש"י

ילפינן מציאה מגט. כי היכי דגבי גט אית לה חצר לקטנה גבי מציאה נמי אית לה: ומר סבר לא ילפינן. ממונא מאיסורא וגבי ממונא חצר מאס המנא אתרבאי ואיכא למימר דשליחות הוא ° ומשום דאין שליח לדבר עבירה אצטריך למכתב התם: והכא בקטן פליגי. דלא אשכחן דרבי ביה חצר: מר אמר חדא כו'. ר"ש בן לקיש אמר לענין מציאה ורבי יוחנן לענין גט אי נמי מר אמר קטן ומר אמר קטנה: **מתני'** אחר צבי שבור. דהוא דומיא דמציאה שאינו יכול לרוץ ומשתמר בתוך השדה אם לא יטלוהו אחרים: **גמ'** אי עומד בצד שדהו אין. דעכשיו היא משתמרת על ידו: עומר שיש לי בשדה. שהנחתיו שם מדעתי וסמכתי על הפועלים שיביאוהו ופועלים שכחוהו: לא יהא שכחה. אם חזר ושכחו: בשדה ושכחת. אם שכחתו בעודך מן השדה הוי שכחה ולא ששכחתו משנכנסת לעיר: אלא לאו הכי קאמר בשדה שכוח מעיקרו כו'. בעוד האיש בשדה עומר השכוח מעיקרו ששכחו הוא תחילה לפועל הוי שכחה אבל זכור שהניחו שם מדעתו ולבסוף שכחו על ידי פועלים לא הוי שכחה: אבל בעיר. משנכנס לעיר אפילו זכור ולבסוף שכח הוי שכחה דליתיה גביה כו' והכי קא נסיב ליה תנא לתלמודיה יכול לא יהא שכחה ת"ל בשדה ושכחת בעודך בשדה הוא דבעינן דשכחתיה אתה ולא בעיר לא בעינן ושכחת שאף שכחת פועלים עושה אותה שכחה: וממאי. דקרא הכי מתרץ ומתני' הכי אמרה: דלמא גזירת הכתוב היא. דמשמע דבשדה יהא שכחה אבל משבא בעל הבית לעיר אין שכחתו ושכחת פועלים כלום והכי קאמר יכול יהא שכחה ת"ל כו': שלפניו אין שכחה. בשכחת הקולר קאי יחיד שהתחיל לקצור מראש השורה ושכח לפניו ולאחריו שלאחריו הוי שכחה שלפניו לא הוי שכחה: יהיה. לגר ליתום ולאלמנה יהיה: עישור שאני עתיד למוד. נזכר שלא עישר מעשרותיו והוקשה לו ומיהר לעשרן באשר הוא שם: נתון ליהושע. לרבי יהושע בר חנניא שהיה עמו בספינה והוא לוי ונוטל מעשר ראשון כדאמרי' בערכין (דף יא:) מעשה ברבי יהושע שהלך לסייע את ר' יוחנן בן גודגדא בהגפת דלתות אמר לו חזור בך שאתה מן המשוררים ואני מן המשוערים ומשורר שסייער במיתה:

ומקומו

## תוספות

**ילפינן** מציאה מגט. האי ילפינן הוי ° מדרבנן דמציאת קטן לא הוי אלא מדרבנן אפילו לרבי יוסי דאמר (לקמן דף יב.) גזל גמור היינו מדבריהם ולענין יד לא פליגי דילפינן אלא לענין חצר ד):

**זכתה** לו. [א] נראה אע"ג דלא אמר זכתה לי דזכתה לו כדאמרי' לעיל (דף י.) אי תקון רבנן דלקני כי לא אמר מאי הוי ואין לומר דהתם היינו משום דנפל לו עליה דגלי בדעתיה שרוצה לקנות אבל הכא מי יימר דרוצה לקנות דאדרבה משמע לעיל דאי לא נפל קנה טפי ואע"ג דלא אמר אקני ועוד דאמר רבי יוסי בר' חנינא חצרו של אדם קונה לו שלא מדעתו אלמא אע"ג דלא אמר קני והכא נקט משום סיפא דאפילו אמר כיון דרץ כדרכו לא קני ה):

**היה** צבי רץ כדרכו. ה"ה אפי' צבי שבור אם רץ אחריו ואין מגיעו אלא אורחא דמילתא נקט דכשרץ כדרכו אין מגיעו:

**ה"מ** בחצר המשתמרת. תימה דבפ' שור שנגח את הפרה (ב"ק דף מט: ושם ד"ה והלכתא) אמר משכונו של גר ביד ישראל ומת הגר כו' וזה קונה השאר כו' ופריך ותקני ליה חצרו דאמר ר' יוסי בר' חנינא כו' ומסיק דליתיה פי' למלוה בחצרו וקשה דהתם משמע דהוי בחצר המשתמרת מדמייתי עלה מרבי יוסי בר' חנינא דמיירי במשתמרת כדמוכח הכא ועוד דמסתמא ביתו ודאי משתמר הוא שמשר שם המשכון וא"כ כי ליתיה נמי לקני ועוד אדפריך ליה מדרבי יוסי בר' חנינא לפרוך ממתני' ומיהו זה נוכל לתרץ דמתני' הוי משום דנתכוין לזכות בה דאמר זכתה לי לכך מייתי מרבי יוסי בר' חנינא [ב] וי"ל דה"פ דליתיה למשכון בחצר אבל מלוה גם לפי המקשן מיירי דליתיה בחצר ולכך לא פריך ממתני' כ"א מרבי יוסי בר' חנינא וא"ת פרק הזורק (גיטין דף עז: ושם ד"ה והוא) דתנן זרק לתוך ביתה או לתוך חצרה מגורשת משמע דמשתמרת ואפילו הכי קאמר עולא והוא שעומדת בצד ביתה וי"ל דדוקא גבי גט דאיתיה בעל כרחה בעינן עומדת בצד ביתה כדאמר בשמעתין:

**זכור** ולבסוף שכוח. פירוש זכור בשעה ששכחה מתחלת שכבר שכחוהו פועלים ולבסוף שכח גם הוא ושכוח מעיקרו הוי כששכחו הפועלים שכח גם הוא אבל מה שהוא זכור בשעה שהפועלים זוכרין אין זה זכור ולבסוף שכוח דאל"כ לא תמצא שכחה לעולם דכשדהו מלאה עומרין יאמר יזכה לי שדי:

**דלמא** גזירת הכתוב היא. פרש"י ונגרוס יכול יהא שכחה ותימה לפי שרוצה לסתור ראייתו מגיה הברייתא ותו מה מתרץ לרבות שכחת העיר והלא בברייתא יליף דזכור ולבסוף שכוח לא הוי שכחה דקתני יודע אני שפועלים שכחוהו והכא דדריש לרבות שכחת העיר יעמיד בשכוח מעיקרא לכך י"ל שאינו סותר ראייתו אלא גמרא קשה לו על הברייתא מנ"ל למדרש מיעוטא על דיוקא דקרא דדריש בשדה ושכחת דהיינו שכוח מעיקרא אבל זכור ולבסוף שכוח לא הוי שכחה ועל זה קאי מיעוטא לומר דבעיר אפילו זכור ולבסוף שכוח הוי שכחה דלמא גזירת הכתוב היא דבשדה הוי שכחה שכוח מעיקרא ולא בעיר והכי מסתברא טפי לאוקמי מיעוט אגופיה דקרא בשדה ושכחת ולא בעיר והשתא משני שפיר לרבות שכחת העיר וע"כ לא מני קאי אפשטיה דקרא:

**זה** הכלל. לאתויי קרן זוית:

**עישור** שאני עתיד למוד. פרש"י פרק קמא דקידושין (דף כו: ושם ד"ה מעשה) שהיה ירא פן יסמכו עליו בני ביתו שעישר ויאכלו טבל דחזקה על חבר שאינו מוציא מתחת ידו דבר שאינו מתוקן וקשה דהיינו דוקא בחבר שמת או בהולך ואין בדעתו לשוב עד ימים רבים ועוד למה נתנם לרבי יהושע ולרבי עקיבא יקרא להם שם ולא יותר ועוד דאין זה קריאת שם דלא אמר עשרה יהא מעשר אלא אמר מעשר ראשון יהא נתון ליהושע ופר"ת דשנת הביעור היתה וכבר הפריסם והיה צריך להוציאם מתחת ידו ולתנם

## עין משפט נר מצוה

פז א מיי' פי"ז מהלכות אבידה הל' י ופ"ד מהל' זכייה ומתנה הל' ט ועי' בהשגות ובמ"מ סמג עשין עד טוש"ע ח"מ סי' רסח סעיף ה וסי' רמג סעיף כג:

פח ב ג מיי' פי"ז מהל' אבידה הל' יא סמג עשין עד טוש"ע ח"מ סי' רסח סעיף ד:

פט ד ה מיי' שם הל' ח ופט"ז שם הלכה ח ופ"א מהל' זכייה ומתנה הלכה ד ועי' בהשגות ובמ"מ ופ"ד שם הל' ט סמג עשין עד פב טוש"ע ח"מ סי' רמג סעיף כ לא וסי' רסח סעיף ג וסי' ערה סעיף כח וסי' שיג סעיף ג:

צ ו ז מיי' פ"ה מהלכות מתנות עניים הל' ג:

צא ח ט מיי' שם הל' י:

## רבינו חננאל

כי פליגי במציאה ר"י סבר ילפינן מציאה מגט ור"ל סבר לא ילפינן. איבעי תימא [בקטנה] כ"ע ילפינן מציאה מגט וכי פליגי בקטן ר"י יליף לקטן מקטנה כשם שזוכה חצירה של קטנה לקטנה כך זוכה חצר של קטן לקטן. ור"ל [ס"ל] ריבתה התורה החצר כיד לאשה ואפי' קטנה אבל לקטן לא. איבעי תימא כ"ע לא ילפי קטן מקטנה ור' יוחנן וריש לקיש לא פליגי אלא ר' יוחנן הורה בקטנה דיש לה חצר ויש לה ד' אמות וריש לקיש הורה בקטן דאין חצירו זוכה לו ולא ד' אמות שלו כך מסקנא דשמעתא: **פיסקא** ראה אותן רצין אחר המציאה וכו' עד זכתה לי שדי זכתה לו שדהו: **גמ'** והוא שעומד בצד שדהו. ואמרי' אמאי צריך להיות עומד בצד שדהו ותקני ליה שדהו כר' יוסי בר חנינא דאמר חצירו של אדם קונה לו שלא מדעתו ודחי' הני מילי בחצר המשתמרת אבל שדה שאינה משתמרת אי עומד בצד שדהו זכתה לו שדהו ואם אינו עומד שם לא זכתה לו שדהו. מנא הני מילי דתניא היה עומד בעיר ואומר יודע אני כי העומר שיש לי בשדה פועלים שכחוהו לא יהא שכחה יכול לא יהא שכחה ת"ל ושכחת עומר בשדה. בשדה ושכחת ולא בעיר. ופרישנא בשדה שכוח מעיקרו הוי שכחה זכור ולבסוף שכוח לא הוי שכחה מאי טעמא כיון דכי קאי בשדה וזכור לו זכתה לו שדהו ואע"ג דבתר הכי שכחו אינה שכחה שכבר זכתה לו שדהו וכאילו נטלו מאותה העת אבל בעיר אפי' זכור ולבסוף שכחו הוי שכחה מאי טעמא דהא ליתיה גביה דליזכי ליה שדהו ש"מ דאי עומד בצד שדהו זכתה לו שדהו ואי אינו עומד בצד שדהו לא זכתה לו שדהו. ואמרי' וממאי דמשום דלא הוה קאי בצד שדהו נעשה שכחה דלמא גזירת הכתוב היא (א) דבשדה לא ניהוי שכחה. ובעיר כי האי גוונא זכור ולבסוף שכוח ליהוי שכחה מדכתיב לא תשוב לקחתו גמרינן מינה לרבות שכחת העיר. ונדחו הדברים האלו ואסקה רב אשי יהיה לרבות שכחת העיר. ולא נתברר כי אם עומד בצד שדהו זכתה לו שדהו ואי לא לא. וכן אמר עולא והוא שעומד בצד שדהו. איתיביה רבא מעשה ברבן גמליאל וזקנים שהיו באין בספינה.

## מסורת הש"ס

בא קמא מט:, לקמן קיח., חולין קמא:, אה פרק ו משנה ד, עשר שני פרק ה ה ט, קדושין כו:, וע"ע תוס' יבמות יט: גמרינן], ה) [וע"ע בעירובין מט: ד"ה ואמר].

## הגהות הגר"א

תוס' ד"ה זכתה ראה כו'. נ"ב אבל ב"ס מחלק בין ד' וחצר המשתמרת שא"מ (ועמ"ש בח"מ סי' רס"ח י"א): [ב] שם ה"מ כו' וי"ל "פ כו'. נ"ב וכן פי' "ף בפ"ג דב"ב והרמב"ם:

## גליון הש"ס

י ד"ה ומר סבר ' ומשום דאין יח לדבר עבירה. ה לי דאם מסברא לא ינא דבחצר לא מקרי ר עבירה מהך טעמים ל דלאו בר חיובא או ם אי בעי עביד מנ"ל ת דלמא גם בגניבה רבאי חצר משום ידו ך באמת דוקא בעומד אצירו וצ"ע: תוס' ה ילפינן כו' רבנן. עיין תוס' ות יט ע"ב ד"ה גמרינן:

## תורה אור השלם

כִּי תִקְצֹר קְצִירְךָ [בְשָׂ]דֶךָ וְשָׁכַחְתָּ עֹמֶר [בַּשָּׂ]דֶה לֹא תָשׁוּב [לְקַ]חְתּוֹ לַגֵּר לַיָּתוֹם [וְלָ]אַלְמָנָה יִהְיֶה לְמַעַן [יְבָרֶ]כְךָ יְיָ אֱלֹהֶיךָ בְּכֹל מַעֲשֵׂה יָדֶיךָ: [דברים כד, יט]

## ליקוטי רש"י

היו באים בספינה. ם ולא נתן רשות לתרום יושין כו:]. נתון הושע. רבי יהושע בן וי לכהן במ"מ ערכין יא:) מעשה ברבי שע בן חנניה שהלך ייע את ר' יוחנן בן דגדא בהגפת דלתות מר לו חזור בך שאתה מן משוררים ואני מן משוערים [קידושין כו:].

חשק שלמה על ר"ח (א) הדבר מבואר דרבינו היה גורס בגמ' דבשדה לא נהוי שכחה ובעיר נהוי שכחה דלאמר קרא וכו' והן דלאמר קרא הכל מן הקושיא היא ועי' בש"מ דהביא ג"כ לד' רבינו וגרסתו ע"ש.

יַלְפִינַן מְצִיאָה מִ – **we derive** the laws of **a found article from** the laws of **divorce.**[1] וּמַר סָבַר לָא יַלְפִינַן מְצִיאָה מִגֵּט – **And one master** [Reish Lakish] **holds that we do not derive** the laws of **a found article from** the laws of **a bill of divorce.**[2]

The Gemara offers another explanation of the dispute between R' Yochanan and Reish Lakish:

וְאִיבָּעֵית אֵימָא – **And if you prefer, say that** בִּקְטַנָּה כּוּלֵי עָלְמָא לָא פְּלִיגֵי דִּילְפִינַן מְצִיאָה מִגֵּט – **with** regard to **a minor girl, everyone agrees that we derive** the laws of **a found article from** the laws of **a bill of divorce.**[3] וְהָכָא בְּקָטָן קָא מִיפַּלְגֵי – **And here they disagree about a minor boy.** מַר סָבַר יַלְפִינַן קָטָן מִקְּטַנָּה – **One master** [R' Yochanan] **holds that we derive** the laws of **a minor boy from** those of **a minor girl** to enable his courtyard to acquire an ownerless article for him. וּמַר סָבַר לָא יַלְפִינַן קָטָן מִקְּטַנָּה – **And** one **master** [Reish Lakish] **holds that we do not derive** the laws of **a minor boy from** those of **a minor girl;** consequently, his courtyard cannot acquire an ownerless article for him.[4]

The Gemara offers yet another understanding of the rulings set down by R' Yochanan and Reish Lakish:

וְאִיבָּעֵית אֵימָא – **And if you prefer, say that** מַר אָמַר חֲדָא וּמַר אָמַר חֲדָא וְלָא פְּלִיגֵי – one **master said** his ruling in **one** case, **whereas** the other **master said** his ruling in **another** case, **and they do not disagree** at all.[5]

**Mishnah** This Mishnah discusses a situation of acquisition by courtyard: רָאָה אוֹתָן רָצִין אַחַר מְצִיאָה – **If one saw [people] running after a find,**[6] אַחַר צְבִי שָׁבוּר – **after a lame deer,**[7] אַחַר גּוֹזָלוֹת שֶׁלֹּא פָּרְחוּ – or **after young pigeons that cannot** yet **fly,** וְאָמַר זָכְתָה לִי שָׂדִי – **and he said, "My field has acquired** it **for me,"** זָכְתָה לוֹ – **it has** indeed **acquired** it **for him.**[8] הָיָה צְבִי רָץ כְּדַרְכּוֹ – **If the deer was running normally,** אוֹ שֶׁהָיוּ גּוֹזָלוֹת מַפְרִיחִין – **or the young pigeons were flying,** וְאָמַר זָכְתָה לִי שָׂדִי – **and he said, "My field has acquired** it **for me,"** לֹא אָמַר כְּלוּם – **he** has **said nothing.**[9]

**Gemara** The Gemara elaborates on the first section of the Mishnah, which states that one's field can acquire ownerless articles on his behalf:

אָמַר רַב יְהוּדָה אָמַר שְׁמוּאֵל – **Rav Yehudah said in the name of Shmuel:** וְהוּא שֶׁעוֹמֵד בְּצַד שָׂדֵהוּ – **Provided that [the owner] is standing at the side of his field.**[10]

The Gemara objects:

וְתִקְנֵי לֵיהּ שָׂדֵהוּ – **But let his field acquire** objects **for him** even if

NOTES

According to R' Yochanan, just as we find that a minor's courtyard can function as her "hand" in regard to acquiring her bill of divorce, so too it can function as her "hand" in regard to acquiring for her a lost article (Rashi; see *Tosafos*).

Reish Lakish holds that monetary law cannot be derived from prohibitory law (such as the law of divorce). Therefore, the fact that the Torah allows a minor's courtyard to function as her *hand* in regard to receiving her bill of divorce does not indicate that the courtyard can serve the minor in the same capacity in regard to *monetary* acquisition (e.g. acquiring a find). Rather, in regard to monetary acquisition, a courtyard functions as the owner's *agent*; and since a minor does not have the capacity to commission an agent [see 10b note 14], her courtyard cannot make a monetary acquisition on her behalf (*Rashi*).

[Now, both in a prohibitory and monetary context, the Torah provides a special Scriptural source to teach the law of acquisition by *chatzeir* – one source in the context of divorce (see 10b and note 28 there) and one source in the context of theft (see 10b and notes 15-17 there). However, in regard to divorce, the meaning of the source is that a woman's *chatzeir* can serve as her "hand." In regard to financial law, the meaning of the source is that a person's *chatzeir* serves as his "agent." Although no special source should be necessary to teach the capacity of *chatzeir* to serve as one's agent (see 10b note 28), the Torah had to provide a source in the context of theft, because the principles of agency would not otherwise operate there since it is a case of agency for an act of transgression (*Rashi*, as explained by *Maharsha* here and *Maharam* to 10b; *Nimukei Yosef* to 10b; cf. *Rashash*). Though the Gemara on 10b distinguishes between ordinary agency for an act of transgression and the agency of the non-commanded, non-independent *chatzeir*, those distinctions are not naturally indicated, but compelled by the special Scriptural source which indicates that theft can indeed be accomplished via one's *chatzeir* (*Ramban* to 10b; cf. *R' Akiva Eiger* in *Gilyon HaShas*).]

Thus, all agree that a minor girl's *chatzeir* can acquire an ownerless object on her behalf, just as the *chatzeir* can acquire for her a bill of divorce.

It is in the context of a woman receiving her bill of divorce that the Torah provides that a *chatzeir* can acquire on behalf of its owner. Since the laws of divorce apply even to a minor girl, the Torah's provision of *chatzeir* apply to her as well. But we do not find anywhere that the Torah provides for a minor *boy* to have his *chatzeir* acquire on his behalf. Therefore, in the absence of such a source, Reish Lakish holds that a minor boy's *chatzeir* indeed does not acquire anything on his behalf (Rashi; see *Nachalas David*).

Both R' Yochanan and Reish Lakish agree that a minor's *chatzeir* can acquire for her a bill of divorce, but not an ownerless article. Reish Lakish, who said that a minor girl has no *chatzeir*, referred to its capacity to acquire an ownerless article. R' Yochanan, who said that a minor girl does have a *chatzeir*, referred to its capacity to acquire her bill of divorce (*Rashi*). [Both agree that we do not derive monetary law from prohibitory law.]

Alternatively, both R' Yochanan and Reish Lakish agree that a minor girl has a *chatzeir* but a minor boy does not [we do not learn the laws of a minor boy from those of a minor girl]. R' Yochanan was referring to a minor girl, whereas Reish Lakish was referring to a minor boy (*Rashi*). Although Reish Lakish states explicitly, "A minor *girl* has no *chatzeir*," he means that she has no *chatzeir whose law can be extended to a minor boy* (*Ritva*).

6. A person sees people running through his field in order to acquire a find that was lying there. The find is an inanimate article, which will remain lying in the field unless someone takes it out.

7. Since it cannot run away, it is similar to the inanimate find mentioned first in the Mishnah, which is secure in a person's field as long as other people do not take it (*Rashi*). The same applies to the young birds mentioned next in the Mishnah – since they cannot fly away, they too are secure in one's field.

8. An object found in a person's property becomes his by means of acquisition through *chatzeir*, as we have seen previously (see 9b note 11). Our Mishnah adds that this method of acquisition applies only to objects that remain secure in the property.

Although the Mishnah describes a case in which the owner stated his desire that his property make the acquisition, it does not necessarily mean that a declaration is required to effect acquisition. *Tosafos* explain that the Mishnah stated a case in which the owner declared his intention only in order to contrast it with the next case in the Mishnah, where the owner does not acquire the object even though he declared his intention to do so (cf. *Ran* cited in *Shitah Mekubetzes*).

9. Since these animals will not remain secure in the field, the field cannot effect acquisition on behalf of its owner.

*Tosafos* write that this ruling would be true even of a lame deer, if the owner could not catch the deer before it ran out of the yard. The Mishnah, however, chose the case of a healthy deer because that is the usual case in which the owner cannot reach it before it runs out of his field.

10. The Mishnah stated that a person can acquire objects that are in his field only if they are secure inside. Rav Yehudah now adds that the field's owner must be standing at the side of his field in order to acquire the objects.

*Ritva* asserts that Rav Yehudah does not require the owner to stand inside the field proper; rather, it is sufficient if he stands outside the confines of the field, but next to the border, in order to guard it.

acquisition by courtyard is *not* derived from the law of agency.[28] – ? –

The Gemara must therefore revise its understanding of the dispute between Reish Lakish and R' Yochanan:

לְעִנְיַן גֵּט כּוּלֵּי עָלְמָא לֹא פְּלִיגֵי – **With regard to a bill of divorce, all agree** דְּחָצֵר מִשּׁוּם יָדָהּ אִיתְרַבַּאי – **that** a wife's acquisition of a bill of divorce by means of her **courtyard is derived from** her acquisition by means of **her hand.** כִּי פְּלִיגֵי – **In** regard to **what do they argue?** לְעִנְיַן מְצִיאָה – **With regard to a found article.**[29] מַר סָבַר – **One master** [R' Yochanan] **holds th**

NOTES

28. For the law of agency is derived by a Baraisa (*Kiddushin* 41a) from the *next* word in the verse: וְשִׁלְּחָהּ, *and he shall send her away* (see there). Had courtyard been a derivative of agency, the Baraisa here should have derived courtyard from this latter word. Since the Baraisa instead finds it necessary to derive courtyard from the first part of the verse, we see that the Baraisa understands courtyard to be a derivative of "hand" rather than of "agency" (*Rashi*). [The Rishonim understand *Rashi* to mean that a special Scriptural source to include acquisition through one's "courtyard" is necessary only if the courtyard must function as the person's "hand." But if the courtyard is assumed to function as his *agent,* then no special Scriptural source is needed to include "courtyard" in the law of agency; rather, once the Torah makes provision for the law of agency, a person's courtyard automatically included, since it is no worse than any other ager (*Ramban* et al.; see *Ritva*; see also *Rashi* to 11b ד״ה אלא אמר רב אשי; c *Rashash* to 11a ד״ה בא״ד וגבי ממונא).]

The Amora Reish Lakish would certainly not dispute an unconteste Baraisa. Therefore, he must agree that "courtyard" is a derivative "hand." Why, then, does he rule that a minor girl cannot be divorce by placement of the bill in her courtyard?

29. That is, R' Yochanan and Reish Lakish disagree as to whether minor can acquire a lost article if it is in the minor's courtyard or if it within four *amos* of the minor.

רב פפא אמר כי תקינו ליה רבנן ארבע אמות [א] בעלמא בשדה דבעל הבית לא תקינו ליה רבנן ואע"ג דזכה ליה רחמנא בגוה כי זכה ליה רחמנא להלוכי בה ולנקוטי פיאה למיהוי חצירו לא זכה ליה רחמנא אמר רבא מותיב ר' יעקב בר אידי נזיקין ראה את המציאה ונפל לו עליה ובא אחר והחזיק בה זה שהחזיק בה זכה בה ואי אמרת ארבע אמות של אדם קונות לו בכל מקום נקנו ליה ארבע אמות דידיה הכא במאי עסקינן דלא אמר אקני ואי תקון רבנן כי לא אמר מאי הוי כיון דנפל עליה גלי דעתיה דבנפילה ניחא ליה דנקני בארבע אמות לא ניחא ליה דנקני רב ששת אמר כי תקינו רבנן בסמטא דלא דחקי רבים ברשות הרבים דקא דחקי רבים לא תקינו רבנן והא בכל מקום קאמר כל מקום לאתויי צידי רשות הרבים ואמר ריש לקיש משום אבא כהן ברדלא קטנה אין לה חצר ואין לה ארבע אמות ור' יוחנן משום ר' ינאי אמר יש לה חצר ויש לה ארבע אמות במאי קמיפלגי מר סבר חצר משום ידה איתרבאי כי היכי דאית לה יד חצר נמי אית לה ומר סבר חצר משום שליחות איתרבאי וכי היכי דשליחות לית לה חצר נמי לית לה מי איכא מאן דאמר חצר משום שליחות איתרבאי והתניא בידו אין לי אלא ידו גגו חצירו וקרפיפו מנין ת"ל המצא תמצא מכל מקום ואי סלקא דעתך חצר משום שליחות איתרבאי אם כן מצינו שליח לדבר עבירה וקיימא לן אין שליח לדבר עבירה אמר רבינא היכא אמרינן דאין שליח לדבר עבירה היכא דשליח בר חיובא הוא אבל בחצר דלאו בר חיובא הוא מיחייב שולחו אלא מעתה האומר לאשה ועבד צאו גנבו לי דלאו בני חיובא נינהו הכי נמי דמיחייב שולחן אמרת אשה ועבד בני חיובא נינהו והשתא מיהא לית להו לשלומי דתנן נתגרשה האשה נשתחרר העבד חייבין לשלם רב סמא אמר היכא אמרינן אין שליח לדבר עבירה היכא דאי בעי עביד ואי בעי לא עביד אבל חצר דבעל כרחיה מותיב בה מיחייב שולחו מאי בינייהו איכא בינייהו כהן דאמר ליה לישראל צא וקדש לי אשה גרושה אי נמי איש דאמר לה לאשה אקפי לי קטן להך לישנא דאמר כל היכא דאי בעי עביד אי בעי לא עביד לא מיחייב שולחו ה"נ אי בעי עביד אי בעי לא עביד לא מיחייב שולחן להך לישנא דאמרת כל היכא דשליח לאו בר חיובא מיחייב שולחו הני נמי כיון דלאו בני חיובא נינהו מיחייב שולחן ומי איכא למ"ד חצר לאו משום ידה איתרבאי והתניא ידה אין לי אלא ידה גגה חצירה וקרפיפה מנין ת"ל ונתן מכל מקום לענין גט כולי עלמא לא פליגי דחצר משום ידה איתרבאי כי פליגי לענין מציאה מ"ס

## רש"י

ה"ג כי תקון ליה רבנן בעלמא. כגון בסמטא שהוא רשות לכל אדם או ברה"ר או בצידי רשות הרבים והיא הפקר לרבים למשוך לתוכה הצריכין לצאת מן הדחק: לא תקון ליה רבנן. שהרי אין לאדם שם ד' אמות מיוחדות שהרבה חברים יש לו בתוכה עומדים אצלו: קטנה אין לה חצר. אם זרק לה בעלה גט לתוך חצרה לא קנתה לה חצרה להתגרש בו וכן אם היתה עומדת ברה"ר וזרקו לה גט בארבע אמותיה ואע"ג דגדולה מיגרשה כדתנן (גיטין דף עח.) הזורק גט לאשתו בתוך ביתה כו' היתה עומדת ברה"ר וזרקו לה קרוב לה מגורשת כו': משום ידה אתרבאי. דכתיב ונתן בידה וידה רשותה משמע כדכתיב (במדבר כא) ויקח את כל ארצו מידו: כי היכי דאית לה יד. דמשיודעת לשמור את גיטה מגורשת דלא מיעט רחמנא אלא שוטה דמשלחה והיא חוזרת: משום שליחות איתרבאי. מדרבי רחמנא שליחות לאדם כדתניא (קידושין דף מא.) ושלח מלמד שהאיש עושה שליח ושלחה מלמד שהאשה עושה שליח אתרבאי נמי חצרה דהויא לה כשלוחה: וכי היכי דשליחות לית לה. דתנן שאין הקטן עושה שליח דכי כתיב שליחות בין בגיטין בין בפסח איש כתיב בענין: ידו. אם המצא תמצא בידו: גגו חצרו וקרפיפו מנין. שאם נכנסה שם ונעל בפניה לגונבה שהוא חייב: א"כ מצינו תורת שליחות לדבר עבירה. לומר שלוחו כמותו וחייב השולח במעשה השליח: וקי"ל. בקידושין בפ"ב (דף מב:): בר חיובא הוא. שאף הוא מוזהר על הדבר התם פטור השולח דאמרינן ליה דברי הרב ודברי התלמיד דברי מי שומעין ולא היה לו לעשות: דלאו בני חיובא נינהו. לשלם כדתנן הם שחבלו באחרים פטורין (ב"ק פז.): דאי בעי עביד. את השליחות: וקדש לי אשה גרושה. ומשעת קידושין עובר משום לא יקחו: אשה אינה באזהרת לא תקיפו לפי שאינה בבל תשחית פאת זקנך כדאמר בקידושין (ד' לה:) והמקיף את הקטן חייב שהמקיף באזהרה כניקף דכתיב לא תקיפו אחד הניקף ואחד המקיף במשמע במס' [נזיר] (דף נז:) וקטן דנקט משום דסתמא גדול לא שביק לאקופי נפשיה: תלמוד לומר ונתן מכל מקום. מדלא כתיב ובידה יתנהו דרוש ונתן אוכתב לה ונתן אלמא משום ידה אתרבאי דאי משום שליחות הא כבר כתיבא הכא כדתניא (ושלח) [ושלחה] מלמד שהאשה עושה שליח בקידושין בפרק ב' (דף מא.): ילפינן

## תוספות

רבי יוחנן אמר יש לה ד' אמות. תימה דלקמן מסיק משום דיליף מציאה מגט אלמא שייך קנין ד' אמות בגט ובפרק הזורק (גיטין דף עח: ושם ד"ה ר"י) קאמר ר"י קרוב לה אפילו מאה אמה ויכולה לשמרו הוי גט וי"ל דבד' אמות שלה אפילו יכול לשמור כמוה מגורשת וחוץ לד' אמות צריך שתוכל היא לשמרו: ת"ל המצא תמצא מ"מ. וא"ת וניהא המצא תמצא כלל בידו פרט וכלל ופרט אין בכלל אלא מה שבפרט וי"ל שדי ידו בין המצא תמצא וה"ל כלל ופרט וכלל כדאמרינן במרובה (ב"ק דף סד: ושם) כל מקום שאתה מוצא שני כללות הסמוכין זה לזה הטל פרט ביניהם וכן בסמוך גבי גט דמרבה גגה מונתן בידה י"ל ושלחה חזר וכלל: ואי משום שליחות א"כ מצינו שליח לדבר עבירה. וא"ת מה צריך להוכיח מכח דאין שליח כו' אמאי לא מוכיח מדאתרבאי חצר מקרא דידו כדבסמוך גבי גט מוכיח דחצר משום ידה איתרבאי מדאתרבאי מקרא דידה ולא עביד שום הוכחה וי"ל דבסמוך מכח התנא מוכיח דמרבה גגה וחצרה כידה להתגרש אפילו בעל כרחה או אפילו היא קטנה ואי מטעם שליחות לא היתה מתגרשת בעל כרחה ולא קטנה אבל הכא אי אפשר להוכיח מכח זה דאפילו בידו אינו קונה הגניבה בעל כרחו ולא אם הוא קטן: אין שליח לדבר עבירה. בפ' האיש מקדש (קדושין דף מג.) איכא דיליף משחוטי חוץ דכתיב הוא ולא שלוחו ואיכא דיליף משום דהוה ליה מעילה וטביחה שני כתובים הבאים כאחד דיש שליח ואין מלמדין: אשה ועבד בני חיובא נינהו. ואם תאמר והתנן פרק הכונס (ב"ק דף נט:) השולח את הבערה ביד חרש שוטה וקטן פטור ואמאי והא לאו בני חיובא נינהו וי"ל דהתם משום דלאו בני שליחות נינהו: אי בעי לא עביד. וא"ת והא דתנן (ב"ק דף עט. ושם) היה מושכו ויוצא [ומת ברשות בעלים] פטור הגביהו [או הוציאו מרשות בעלים ומת] חייב ופרש"י בלשון אחד שאמר גנב לשומר שור אחד יש לי בבית פלוני קחנו ותהא עליו שומר חנם הוציאו השומר מרשות בעלים ומת חייב הגנב במשיכת השומר ואמאי והא אי בעי לא עביד וי"ל כיון שאין השומר יודע שהוא גנוב הוה ליה כחצר דבעל כרחו מותיב ביה: דאמר לישראל קדש לי אשה גרושה. וא"ת ואפי' אמר לכהן נמי וי"ל דכהן מקרי בר חיובא הואיל ואם מקדשה לעצמו חייב אבל ישראל אע"ג דעובר משום לפני עור לא תתן מכשול כשמקדשה לכהן כיון דאי מקדשה לעצמו לא מיחייב לא מקרי בר חיובא וא"ת מאי נ"מ בין למ"ד אי בעי עביד ובין למ"ד שליח בר חיובא לא לקי על הקדושין לרבא דאמר בעשרה יוחסין (קדושין דף עח.) קידש אינו לוקה בעל לוקה וי"ל דכי בעל אח"כ לוקה אף על הקדושין כדמוכח בריש תמורה (דף ה: ושם) א"נ י"ל דאף לרבא נפקא מינה דאי יש שליחות חלין הקדושין ואי אין שליחות אין חלין הקדושין: אקפי לי קטן. וה"ה דהוה מצי למימר אקפי לי גדול אלא שהגדול לא יניח עצמו להקיף כדאמר פרק אלו הן הלוקין (מכות דף כ:) דאחד הניקף ואחד המקיף חייב ואע"ג דמוקי לה התם כי ניקף מסייע ליה בהדיה היינו משום דבענין אחר לא לקי דהוה לאו שאין בו מעשה אבל הלאו עובר לעולם [ועיין תוס' שבועות ג. ד"ה ועל הזקן ותוספות נזיר נז: ד"ה ורב אדא]:

## עין משפט נר מצוה

פא א ב ג מיי' פי"ז מהל' אבידה הל' ט ופ"ד מהל' זכייה ומתנה הל' ט סמג עשין עד טוש"ע ח"מ סי' רסח סעיף ב:

פב ד מיי' פי"ז מהל' אבידה הל' י ופ"ד מהל' זכייה ומתנה הל' ט ועי' בהשגות ובמ"מ סמג שם טוש"ע שם סעיף ה וסי' רמג סעיף כג:

פג ה מיי' פי"ז מהלכות אבידה הלכה י:

פד ו מיי' פ"ז מהלכות מעילה הל' ב טוש"ע ח"מ סי' תי סעיף ח וסי' קפב סעיף א בהגה"ה:

פה ז מיי' פ"ד מהלכות חובל ומזיק הל' כא סמג עשין ע טוש"ע ח"מ סי' תכד סעיף ט:

פו ח מיי' פ"ה מהל' גירושין הל' א סמג עשין נ טוש"ע אה"ע סי' קלט סעיף א:

## תורה אור השלם

א) אִם הִמָּצֵא תִמָּצֵא בְיָדוֹ הַגְּנֵבָה מִשּׁוֹר עַד חֲמוֹר עַד שֶׂה חַיִּים שְׁנַיִם יְשַׁלֵּם: [שמות כב, ג]

א) כִּי יִקַּח אִישׁ אִשָּׁה וּבְעָלָהּ וְהָיָה אִם לֹא תִמְצָא חֵן בְּעֵינָיו כִּי מָצָא בָהּ עֶרְוַת דָּבָר וְכָתַב לָהּ סֵפֶר כְּרִיתֻת וְנָתַן בְּיָדָהּ וְשִׁלְּחָהּ מִבֵּיתוֹ: [דברים כד, א]

## רבינו חננאל

אמר ריש לקיש משום אבא כהן ברדלא קטנה אין לה חצר ואין לה ד' אמות. ור' יוחנן משום ר' ינאי אמר יש לה פי' האי דאמרי רבנן חצירו של אדם המשתמרת קונה לו שלא מדעתו וכן ד' אמות של אדם קונות לו בכל מקום הני מילי גדול תקינו ליה רבנן אבל לא לקטנה. ור' יוחנן אמר אפי' קטנה יש לה. ר' יוחנן אמר חצירה מכח ידה איתרבי כשם שיש לה יד וכל מה שיגיע לידה זכתה בו כך כל המגיע לחצירה זכתה בו. וריש לקיש אמר חצירה משום שליחות איתרבי כשם שאין שליחות לקטנה כך אין לה זכייה בחצר. איני והתניא אם המצא תמצא בידו אין לי אלא שנמצאת בידו ממש נמצאת בחצירו או בגגו או בקרפיפו מנין שחייב כאילו בידו ממש נמצאת ת"ל המצא תמצא מכל מקום הנה חצירו משום ידו איתרבי קשיא ליה לריש לקיש ואם תאמר גם משום שליחות נתרבה הא קי"ל אין שליח לדבר עבירה. פי' אע"ג דאמרי' שלוחו של אדם כמותו וכל מה שעשה השליח כאילו שולחו עשאו הני מילי בזולתי דבר עבירה אבל בדבר עבירה השליח חייב ולא השולחו וכיון שהחצר שליח בעלה הוא והוא שנמצאת הגניבה בה אמאי מיחייב בעלה שהוא השולח. ופריק רבינא אליבא דריש לקיש היכא אמרי' השולח פטור היכא דהשליח בר חיובא הוא אבל חצר דלאו בת חיובא היא מיחייב שולחה והוא בעל החצר. ואקשי' אי הכי האומר לעבד ולאשת איש צאו וגנבו דלאו בני חיובא נינהו כדתנן בפ' החובל לחבירו העבד והאשה פגיעתן רעה החובל בהן חייב הן שחבלו באחרים פטורין הכי נמי דמיחייב שולחן. ופרקי' הני נמי בני חיובא נינהו דתנן נתגרשה האשה ונשתחרר העבד חייבין לשלם. בא רב סמא ופירק פירוק אחר ואמר כי אמרי' אין שליח לדבר עבירה כל היכא דאי בעי השליח עביד אי בעי לא עביד אבל חצר דעל כורחה עבדה מיחייב שולחה. מאי איכא בין רבינא לרב סמא איכא בינייהו כהן שאמר לישראל לך קדש לי אשה גרושה או איש שאמר לאשה אקיף לי ראשו של קטן לרבינא כיון דהני לאו בני חיובא נינהו דאין ישראל מוזהר על הגרושה ולא אשה בהקפת הראש מיחייב שולחה. לרב סמא כיון דאי בעו עבדי אי בעו לא עבדי לא מיחייב שולחם. ומתמהינן מי איכא מאן דאמר חצר לאו משום ידה איתרבי והתניא וכתב לה ספר כריתות ונתן בידה. בידה אין לי אלא בידה ממש גגה חצירה וקרפיפה מנין שהנותן גט בהן כנותנו בידה הוא ת"ל ונתן מכל מקום. ואמרי' לענין גט כ"ע לא פליגי דחצר משום ידה איתרבי דהא קרא בהדיא כתיב.

## מסורת הש"ס

א) מהרש"ל כה..., ב) [גיטין עז:], ג) ... קמא סד:, לקמן נו:, ג... עז., ד) [קדושין מ... וש"נ], ה) בבא קמא ... ו) [גיטין עז.].

## הגהות הגר"א

[א] בעלמא. נ"ב הרי"ף בשדה דעלמא

## גליון הש"ס

גמ' רב סמא ... רקתא קמי' דרבי ... משמי' דר' חי... בריה דר' אויא אמ... כ"ה בר"ן: תוס' ד"ה ר"י וכו' אלמא שי... קנין ד' אמות בגט. זכיתי להבין דאמן ילפי' דחצר הוי כיד. אבל ... נקרא חצר לא שייך למ... דמה שהקנו לו חכמים חצירו ובגט הקנו לה אמה ובממון הקנו לה ד' אמות ולע"ג:

## ליקוטי רש"י

בסמטא. קרן ז... הסמוכה לרה"ר ובני ... העושין סחורה זה עם ... בשוק ורוצים ל... דבריהם בנחת וי... הדעת מסתלקין ... [כתובות פד:]. וסימ... אית דאמר שביל יחידים ואני שמעתי כני... בולטת מרה"ר ויש רש... לבני אדם להעמיד ... חפצים שלהם כ... השותפים דאינו ע... להילוך בני רשות הרב... [רשב"ם ב"ב פד:]. צי... רשות הרבים. ס... לבתים שנותנין להלן הבתים אבנים ומכשו... להרחיק חיכוך העגל... ומאותן חיפופי ולפ... קרי צידי רה"ר [כתוב... לא:]. סמוך לכתלים ש... דרך בני אדם לעבור ... ולהתחכך בכותלים [... פו:]. אין לי. שיתח... כפל. אלא. בזמן שלק... בידו [לקמן נו:]. ג... חצרו וקרפיפו מני... שאם נכנסה שם ונ... בפניה לגנבה מנין שקנ... לו חצרו ומתחייב כ... [שם]. קרפיפו. הי... גדול חוץ לעיר להכניס ... עצים לאוצר [עירובין יח...]. אין שליח. חשוב של... לדבר עבירה שיתחי... שולחו אלא הרי ה... כעושה מאליו [קדוש... מב:]. וסברא הוא דאמו... ליה דברי הרב וד... התלמיד דברי מי שומ... [ב"ק נא.]. נתגרש... האשה וכו'. ו... נכסים. חייבין לשל... שהרי מתחלה הן חיי... אלא שאין להם מה לש... שנכסי מלוג של א... משועבדים לבעל לפיר... ולירושה [ב"ק פז.]. ת"... ונתן מ"מ. ודרשי' ... באנפי נפשיה מדלא כת... ובידה יתננו משמע נתינה כל דהוא וי... דכתב רחמנא דבע... דומיא דידה דמשתמ... לדעתה כו' [גיטין עז.]

The Gemara answers:

**אָמְרַת – You can say:** **אִשָּׁה וְעֶבֶד בְּנֵי חִיּוּבָא נִינְהוּ – A** married **woman and a slave are** actually **responsible parties;** **וְהַשְׁתָּא מִיהָא לֵית לְהוּ לְשַׁלּוּמֵי** – it is **only** that **now, however, they do not have** any means **to pay** compensation. **דִּתְנַן – As we learned in a Mishnah:** **נִתְגָּרְשָׁה הָאִשָּׁה נִשְׁתַּחְרֵר הָעֶבֶד** – If THE WOMAN BECAME DIVORCED and THE SLAVE WAS FREED, **חַיָּיבִין לְשַׁלֵּם** – THEY ARE LIABLE TO PAY for the damages that they inflicted while married or while enslaved.[21]

An alternative reason why theft through the agency of one's courtyard does not violate the principle that there is no agency for an act of transgression:

**רַב סָמָא אָמַר – Rav Samma says:** **הֵיכָא אַמְרִינַן אֵין שָׁלִיחַ לִדְבַר עֲבֵירָה – Where do we say that there can be no agent for an act of transgression?** **הֵיכָא דְּאִי בָּעֵי עָבִיד וְאִי בָּעֵי לָא עָבִיד – Where [the agent]** can exercise a choice: **If he wishes he can execute** his commission **and if he wishes he does not** have to **execute** his commission. **אֲבָל חָצֵר דִּבְעַל כָּרְחֵיהּ מוֹתִיב בָּהּ – But a courtyard, in which** something **is placed without** the courtyard's **consent,** **מִיחַיֵּיב שׁוֹלְחוֹ – its "sender"** [the owner] **is liable.**[22]

The Gemara shows the practical differences between the two reasons:

**מַאי בֵּינַיְיהוּ – What** practical **difference is there between [the two reasons]?** **אִיכָּא בֵּינַיְיהוּ כֹּהֵן דְּאָמַר לֵיהּ לְיִשְׂרָאֵל צֵא וְקַדֵּשׁ לִי אִשָּׁה גְּרוּשָׁה – There is a** practical **difference between them** in a case where **a Kohen instructed an ordinary Jew, "Go, betroth for me a divorced woman";**[23] **אִי נַמִּי אִישׁ דְּאָמַר לָהּ לְאִשָּׁה – or** where **a man instructed a woman,** **אַקְפִי לִי קָטָן – "Round for me** the corners of **a minor."**[24] **לְהָךְ לִישָּׁנָא דְּאָמַר כָּל הֵיכָא דְּאִי בָּעֵי עָבִיד אִי בָּעֵי לָא עָבִיד לָא מִיחַיֵּיב שׁוֹלְחוֹ – According to that version which says** that **wherever [the agent]** can exercise a choice – **he wishes he can execute** his commission **and if he wishes** does not have to **execute** his commission – **his sender is n** **liable,** **הָכָא נַמִּי – here also,** in these two cases, the agent c exercise a choice – **אִי בָּעֵי עָבִיד אִי בָּעֵי לָא עָבִיד – if he wishes** **can execute** his commission **and if he wishes he does not ha** to **execute** his commission. **לָא מִיחַיֵּיב שׁוֹלְחָן** – Therefore, both cases **their sender is not liable.** **ךְ לִישָּׁנָא דְּאָמְרַת כָּל הֵיכָא דְּשָׁלִיחַ לָאו בַּר חִיּוּבָא מִיחַיֵּיב שׁוֹלְחוֹ – But according to th version in which you say** that **wherever the agent is not responsible party his sender is liable,** **הָנֵי נַמִּי** – then in t cases of **these** people [the ordinary Jew or the woman] **as we** **כֵּיוָן דְּלָאו בְּנֵי חִיּוּבָא נִינְהוּ – since [the agents] are not responsib parties,** **מִיחַיֵּיב שׁוֹלְחָן – their sender is liable** for the a committed by his agents.[25]

Having deflected one challenge to the premise that Rei Lakish considers a courtyard the agent of its owner, the Gema presents another challenge to that premise:

**וּמִי אִיכָּא לְמַאן דְּאָמַר חָצֵר לָאו מִשּׁוּם יָדָהּ אִיתְרַבַּאי – Is the anyone who can say that** a wife's acquisition of a bill of divor by means of her **courtyard is not derived from** her acquisiti by means of **her hand?** **וְהָתַנְיָא – But it was taught in Baraisa:** **,,יָדָהּ'' –** The Torah states that the husband plac the bill of divorce in *HER HAND.*[26] **אֵין לִי אֶלָּא יָדָהּ – I KNO ONLY** that she is divorced if it is placed in HER HAND; **ה** **חֲצֵירָהּ וְקַרְפֵּיפָהּ מִנַּיִן – FROM WHERE** do I know that she is d vorced if it is placed in HER ROOF, HER COURTYARD, OR HI ENCLOSURE? **תַּלְמוּד לוֹמַר ,,וְנָתַן'' מִכָּל מָקוֹם –** Therefore, TI TORAH STATES in that verse: *HE PLACES,* which implies: AN WHERE in her possession.[27] Thus, this Baraisa indicates th

NOTES

note), if someone steals through the agency of a married woman or a slave (who is not a responsible party), he should be held responsible for the act even though he did not personally commit the theft! [Yet, it was well known to the Gemara that the principal is exempt from liability even in that case (*Ein Yehoseif* cited in *Otzar Mefarshei HaTalmud*).]

[*R' Akiva Eiger* and *Rashash* (as well as many other Acharonim) are puzzled by the Gemara's question, since married women and slaves – though not liable, perhaps, to *pay* for their theft – are certainly prohibited to commit the sin of theft just as men are. Consequently, they are, in fact, responsible parties who should not have listened to the principal. See the Acharonim for various solutions.]

21. *Bava Kamma* ibid. It is thus clear from the Mishnah that both a married woman and a slave are actually liable to pay for their actions. However, as long as the woman is married, she is unable to fulfill that monetary obligation, since all of her assets are in her husband's possession. Similarly, as long as the slave is in bondage, all of his assets belong to his master. But both married women and slaves are liable for their thefts and, hence, are not considered legal agents if they steal for their principal.

22. According to Rav Samma, even when the agent is not a responsible party (i.e. not subject to the prohibition that is violated by his act – see Gemara below), the principal can argue that the agent should not have been party to an act of transgression. Thus, there is no agency for an act of transgression unless the agent had no choice but to execute the directive of the principal (*Mishneh LaMelech, Hil. Malveh VeLoveh* 5:14).

23. A Kohen who betroths a divorced woman violates a Biblical law (*Rashi*). An ordinary Jew, however, is permitted to betroth a divorcee. Hence, the agent in this case, although able to exercise free choice, is not personally prohibited from the act of marrying a divorcee.

24. The Torah commands (*Leviticus* 19:27): *You shall not round the corners of your head;* that is, do not cut the hair on the temples so as to make the hairline even all around from the forehead to behind the ears (*Rashi* ad loc.). The prohibition encompasses both allowing one's ov head to be rounded, as well as rounding someone else's head (see *Naz* 57b). A woman, however, is not included in this prohibition, as deriv in *Kiddushin* 35b. Hence, the agent in this case, although she is able exercise free choice, is not personally prohibited from the act rounding the corners of the male child's head (*Rashi*).

[The same law would apply if the woman was commissioned to rour the head of an adult male.] The Gemara chooses the case of a minc because an adult male would generally not allow anyone to round h head (*Rashi*).

25. However, if the Kohen would commission another Kohen to betro a divorcee on his behalf, the agent *would* be considered a responsib party and the law of agency would not be in effect. Even though th Kohanite agent still does not personally violate the divorcee proh bition by betrothing her on behalf of his fellow Kohen, he is co sidered a responsible party. For since he is bound by the divorc prohibition, it is more serious in his eyes than in the eyes of non-Kohen. Therefore, the principal can argue that he did not thir the Kohanite agent would follow his directive to participate in th sinful act of betrothing a divorcee to a Kohen (*Tos. HaRosh*; see als *Tosafos*).

26. *Deuteronomy* 24:3, which details the divorce procedure, states: וְכָתַב לָהּ סֵפֶר כְּרִיתֻת וְנָתַן בְּיָדָהּ, *and he [the husband] writes for her a document* *severance and places [it] in her hand.*

27. The verse does not mention "hand" before "placement" and stat וְכָתַב לָהּ סֵפֶר כְּרִיתֻת וּבְיָדָהּ יִתְּנֶנּוּ, *and he writes for her a document* *severance and in her hand places it* [which would have made inescapably clear that placement *in her hand* is the fundament requirement]. Rather, the verse mentions "placement" before "hand. This is taken to indicate that we should expound the juxtaposition the words: וְכָתַב לָהּ ... וְנָתַן, *and he writes for her ... and places,* an derive that the fundamental requirement is *placement* of the documer anywhere in her possession; "in her hand" is specified to indicate th the place where the document is placed must be analogous to her han in that it is under her control (see *Rashi* here and to *Gittin* 77a; c *Ritva*).

רב פפא אמר [א] כי תקינו ליה רבנן ארבע אמות [א] בעלמא בשדה דבעל הבית לא תקינו ליה רבנן ואע"ג דזכה ליה רחמנא בגוה כי זכה ליה רחמנא להלוכי בה ולנקוטי פיאה למיהוי חצירו לא זכה ליה רחמנא אמר רבא מותיב ר' יעקב בר אידי נזיקין ראה את המציאה ונפל לו עליה ובא אחר והחזיק בה זה שהחזיק בה זכה בה ואי אמרת ארבע אמות של אדם קונות לו בכל מקום נקנו ליה ארבע אמות דידיה הכא במאי עסקינן דלא אמר אקני ואי תקון רבנן כי לא אמר מאי הוי כיון דנפל עליה גלי דעתיה דבנפילה ניחא ליה דנקני בארבע אמות לא ניחא ליה דנקני רב ששת אמר [ב] כי תקינו רבנן בסמטא דלא דחקי רבים ברשות הרבים דקא דחקי רבים לא תקינו רבנן והא בכל מקום קאמר כל מקום [ג] לאתויי צידי רשות הרבים ואמר ריש לקיש משום אבא [א] כהן ברדלא קטנה אין לה חצר ואין לה ארבע אמות ור' יוחנן משום ר' ינאי אמר [ד] יש לה חצר ויש לה ארבע אמות במאי קמיפלגי מר סבר [ב] חצר [ה] משום ידה איתרבאי כי היכי דאית לה יד חצר נמי אית לה ומר סבר חצר משום שליחות איתרבאי וכי היכי דשליחות לית לה חצר נמי לית לה מי איכא מאן דאמר חצר משום שליחות איתרבאי [ג] והתניא [א] בידו אין לי אלא ידו גגו חצירו וקרפיפו מנין ת"ל [א] המצא תמצא מכל מקום ואי סלקא דעתך חצר משום שליחות איתרבאי אם כן מצינו שליח לדבר עבירה [ד] [ו] וקיימא לן אין שליח לדבר עבירה אמר רבינא היכא אמרינן דאין שליח לדבר עבירה היכא דשליח בר חיובא הוא אבל בחצר דלאו בר חיובא הוא מיחייב שולחו אלא מעתה האומר לאשה ועבד צאו גנבו לי דלאו בני חיובא נינהו הכי נמי דמיחייב שולחן אמרת אשה ועבד בני חיובא נינהו והשתא מיהא לית להו לשלומי [ה] דתנן [ז] נתגרשה האשה נשתחרר העבד חייבין לשלם [ו] רב סמא אמר היכא אמרינן אין שליח לדבר עבירה היכא דאי בעי עביד ואי בעי לא עביד אבל חצר דבעל כרחיה מותיב בה מיחייב שולחו מאי בינייהו איכא בינייהו כהן דאמר ליה לישראל צא וקדש לי אשה גרושה אי נמי איש דאמר לה לאשה אקפי לי קטן להך לישנא דאמר כל היכא דאי בעי עביד אי בעי לא עביד לא מיחייב שולחו ה"נ אי בעי עביד אי בעי לא עביד לא מיחייב שולחן להך לישנא דאמרת כל היכא דשליח לאו בר חיובא מיחייב שולחו הני נמי כיון דלאו בני חיובא נינהו מיחייב שולחן ומי איכא למ"ד חצר לאו משום ידה איתרבאי והתניא [ו] [ב] ידה אין לי אלא ידה גגה חצירה וקרפיפה מנין ת"ל ונתן [ח] מכל מקום לענין גט כולי עלמא לא פליגי דחצר משום ידה איתרבאי כי פליגי לענין מציאה מ"ס

## רש"י

ה"ג כי תקון ליה רבנן בעלמא. כגון בסמטא שהוא רשות לכל אדם או ברה"ר או בצידי רשות הרבים והיא הפקר לרבים למשוך לתוכה הצריכין לצאת מן הדחק: לא תקון ליה רבנן. שהרי אין לאדם שם ד' אמות מיוחדות שהרבה חברים יש לו בתוכה עומדים אצלו: קטנה אין לה חצר. אם זרק לה בעלה גט לתוך חצרה לא קנתה לה חצרה להתגרש בו וכן אם היתה עומדת ברה"ר וזרקו לה גט בארבע אמותיה ואע"ג דגדולה מיגרשה כדתנן (גיטין דף עח.) הזורק גט לאשתו בתוך ביתה כו' היתה עומדת ברה"ר וזרקו לה קרוב לה מגורשת כו': משום ידה אתרבאי. דכתיב ונתן בידה וידה רשותה משמע כדכתיב (במדבר כא) ויקח את כל ארצו מידו: כי היכי דאית לה יד. דמשיודעת לשמור את גיטה מגורשת דלא מיעט רחמנא אלא שוטה דמשלחה והיא חוזרת: משום שליחות איתרבאי. מדרבי רחמנא שליחות לאדם כדתניא (קידושין דף מא.) ושלח מלמד שהאיש עושה שליח ושלחה מלמד שהאשה עושה שליח אתרבאי נמי חצרה דהויא לה כשלוחה: וכי היכי דשליחות לית לה. דתנן שאין הקטן עושה שליח דכי כתיב שליחות בין בגיטין בין בפסח איש כתיב בענין: ידו. אם המצא תמצא בידו: גגו חצרו וקרפיפו מנין. שאם נכנסה שם ונעל בפניה לגונבה שהוא חייב: א"כ מצינו תורת שליחות לדבר עבירה. לומר שלוחו כמותו וחייב השולח במעשה השליח: וקי"ל. בקידושין בפ"ב (דף מג:): בר חיובא הוא. שאף הוא מוזהר על הדבר התם פטור השולח דאמרינן ליה דברי הרב ודברי התלמיד דברי מי שומעין ולא היה לו לעשות: דלאו בני חיובא נינהו. לשלם כדתנן הם שחבלו באחרים פטורין (ב"ק פז.): דאי בעי עביד. את השליחות: וקדש לי אשה גרושה. ומשעת קידושין עובר משום לא יקחו: אשה אינה באזהרת לא תקיפו לפי שאינה בבל תשחית פאת זקנך כדאמר בקדושין (ד' לה:) והמקיף את הקטן חייב שהמקיף באזהרה כניקף דכתיב לא תקיפו אחד הניקף ואחד המקיף במשמע במס' [נזיר] (דף נז:) וקטן דנקט משום דסתמא גדול לא שביק לאקופי נפשיה: תלמוד לומר ונתן מכל מקום. מדלא כתיב ובידה יתנהו דרוש ונתן אוכתב לה ונתן אלמא משום ידה אתרבאי דאי משום שליחות הא הדר רבינהו הכא כדתניא (ושלח) [ושלחה] מלמד שהאשה עושה שליח בקדושין בפרק ב' (דף מא.): ילפינן

## תוספות

רבי יוחנן אמר יש לה ד' אמות. תימה דלקמן מסיק משום דיליף מציאה מגט [ט] אלמא שייך קנין ד' אמות בגט ובפרק הזורק (גיטין דף עח: ושם ד"ה ר"י) קאמר ר"י קרוב לה אפילו מאה אמה ויכולה לשמרו הוי גט וי"ל דבד' אמות שלה אפילו יכול לשמור כמוה מגורשת וחוץ לד' אמות צריך שתוכל היא לשמרו: ת"ל המצא תמצא מ"מ. וא"ת ונימא המצא תמצא כלל בידו פרט וכלל ופרט אין בכלל אלא מה שבפרט וי"ל שדי ידו בין המצא תמצא וה"ל כלל ופרט וכלל כדאמרינן במרובה (ב"ק דף סד: ושם) כל מקום שאתה מוצא שני כללות הסמוכין זה לזה הטל פרט ביניהם וכן בסמוך גבי גט דמרבה גגה מונתן בידה י"ל ושלחה חזר וכלל: ואי משום שליחות א"כ מצינו שליח לדבר עבירה. וא"ת מה צריך להוכיח מכח דאין שליח כו' אמאי לא מוכיח מדאתרבאי חצר מקרא דידו כדבסמוך גבי גט מוכיח דחצר משום ידה איתרבאי מדאתרבאי מקרא דידה ולא עביד שום הוכחה וי"ל דבסמוך מכח התנא מוכיח דמרבה גגה וחצרה כידה להתגרש אפילו בעל כרחה או אפילו היא קטנה ואי מטעם שליחות לא היתה מתגרשת בעל כרחה ולא קטנה אבל הכא אי אפשר להוכיח מכח זה דאפילו בידו אינו קונה הגניבה בעל כרחו ולא אם הוא קטן: אין שליח לדבר עבירה. בפ' האיש מקדש (קידושין דף מג.) איכא דיליף משחוטי חוץ דכתיב הוא ולא שלוחו ואיכא דיליף משום דהוה ליה מעילה וטביחה שני כתובים הבאים כאחד דיש שליח ואין מלמדין: אשה ועבד בני חיובא נינהו. ואם תאמר והתנן פרק הכונס (ב"ק דף נט:) השולח את הבערה ביד חרש שוטה וקטן פטור ואמאי והא לאו בני חיובא נינהו וי"ל דהתם משום דלאו בני שליחות נינהו: אי בעי לא עביד. וא"ת והא דתנן (ב"ק דף עט. ושם) היה מושכו ויוצא [ומת ברשות בעלים] פטור הגביהו [או הוציאו מרשות בעלים ומת] חייב ופרש"י בלשון אחד שאמר גנב לשומר שור אחד יש לי בבית פלוני קחנו ותהא עליו שומר חנם הוציאו השומר מרשות בעלים ומת חייב הגנב במשיכת השומר ואמאי והא אי בעי לא עביד וי"ל כיון שאין השומר יודע שהוא גנוב הוה ליה כחצר דבעל כרחו מותיב ביה: דאמר לישראל קדש לי אשה גרושה. וא"ת ואפי' אמר לכהן נמי וי"ל דכהן מקרי בר חיובא הואיל ואם מקדשה לעצמו חייב אבל ישראל אע"ג דעובר משום לפני עור לא תתן מכשול כשמקדשה לכהן כיון דאי מקדשה לעצמו לא מיחייב לא מקרי בר חיובא וא"ת מאי נ"מ בין למ"ד אי בעי עביד ובין למ"ד שליח בר חיובא לא לקי על הקדושין לרבא דאמר בעשרה יוחסין (קדושין דף עח.) קידש אינו לוקה בעל לוקה וי"ל דכי בעל אח"כ לוקה אף על הקדושין כדמוכח בריש תמורה (דף ה: ושם) א"נ י"ל דאף לרבא נפקא מינה דאי יש שליחות חלין הקדושין ואי אין שליחות אין חלין הקדושין: אקפי לי קטן. וה"ה דהוה מצי למימר אקפי לי גדול אלא שהגדול לא יניח עצמו להקיף כדאמר פרק אלו הן הלוקין (מכות דף כ:) דאחד הניקף ואחד המקיף חייב ואע"ג דמוקי לה התם כי ניקף מסייע ליה בהדיה היינו משום דבענין אחר לא לקי דהוה לאו שאין בו מעשה אבל הלאו עובר לעולם [ועיין תוס' שבועות ג. ד"ה ועל הזקן ותוספות נזיר נז: ד"ה ורב אדא]:

## רבינו חננאל

אמר ריש לקיש משום אבא כהן ברדלא קטנה אין לה חצר ואין לה ד' אמות. ור' יוחנן משום ר' ינאי אמר יש לה פי' האי דאמרי רבנן חצירו של אדם המשתמרת קונה לו שלא מדעתו וכן ד' אמות של אדם קונות לו בכל מקום הני מילי גדול תקינו ליה רבנן אבל לא לקטנה. ור' יוחנן אמר אפי' קטנה יש לה. ר' יוחנן אמר חצירה מכח ידה איתרבי כשם שיש לה יד וכל מה שיגיע לידה זכתה בו כך כל המגיע לחצירה זכתה בו. וריש לקיש אמר חצירה משום שליחות איתרבי כשם שאין שליחות לקטנה כך אין לה זכייה בחצר. איני והתניא אם המצא תמצא בידו אין לי אלא שנמצאת בידו ממש נמצאת בחצירו או בגגו או בקרפיפו מנין שחייב כאילו בידו ממש נמצאת ת"ל המצא תמצא מכל מקום הנה חצירו משום ידו איתרבי קשיא ליה לריש לקיש ואם תאמר גם משום שליחות נתרבה הא קי"ל אין שליח לדבר עבירה. פי' אע"ג דאמרי' שלוחו של אדם כמותו וכל מה שעשה השליח כאילו שולחו עשאו הני מילי בזולתי דבר עבירה אבל בדבר עבירה השליח חייב ולא השולחו וכיון שהחצר שליח בעלה הוא והוא שנמצאת הגניבה בה אמאי מיחייב בעלה שהוא השולח. ופריק רבינא אליבא דריש לקיש היכא אמרי' השולח פטור היכא דהשליח בר חיובא הוא אבל חצר דלאו בת חיובא היא מיחייב שולחה והוא בעל החצר. ואקשי' אי הכי האומר לעבד ולאשת איש צאו וגנבו דלאו בני חיובא נינהו כדתנן בפ' החובל לחבירו העבד והאשה פגיעתן רעה החובל בהן חייב הן שחבלו באחרים פטורין הכי נמי דמיחייב שולחן. ופרקי' הני נמי בני חיובא נינהו דתנן נתגרשה האשה ונשתחרר העבד חייבין לשלם. בא רב סמא ופירק פירוק אחר ואמר כי אמרי' אין שליח לדבר עבירה כל היכא דאי בעי השליח עביד אי בעי לא עביד אבל חצר דעל כורחה עבדה מיחייב שולחה. מאי איכא בין רבינא לרב סמא איכא בינייהו כהן שאמר לישראל לך קדש לי אשה גרושה או איש שאמר לאשה אקיף לי ראשו של קטן דהני לאו בני חיובא נינהו דאין ישראל מוזהר על הגרושה ולא אשה בהקפת הראש מיחייב שולחה. לרב סמא כיון דאי בעו לא בעו עבדי אי בעו לא עבדי לא מיחייב שולחם. ומתמהינן מי איכא מאן דאמר חצר לאו משום ידה איתרבי והתניא וכתב לה ספר כריתות ונתן בידה. בידה אין לי אלא בידה ממש גגה חצירה וקרפיפה מנין שהנותן גט בהן כנותנו בידה הוא ת"ל ונתן מכל מקום. ואמרי' לענין גט כ"ע לא פליגי דחצר משום ידה איתרבי דהא קרא בהדיא כתיב.

## עין משפט נר מצוה

פא א ב ג מיי' פי"ז מהל' אבידה הל' ט ופ"ד מהל' זכייה ומתנה הל' ט סמג עשין עד טוש"ע ח"מ סי' רסח סעיף ג:
פב ד מיי' פי"ז מהל' אבידה הל' י ופ"ד מהל' זכייה ומתנה הל' ט ועי' בהשגות ובמ"מ סמג שם טוש"ע שם סעיף ה וסי' רמג סעיף כג:
פג ה מיי' פי"ז מהלכות אבידה הלכה י:
פד ו מיי' פ"ז מהלכות מעילה הל' ב טוש"ע ח"מ סי' תי סעיף ח וסי' קפב סעיף א בהגה"ה:
פה ז מיי' פ"ד מהלכות חובל ומזיק הל' כא סמג עשין ע טוש"ע ח"מ סי' תכד סעיף ט:
פו ח מיי' פ"ה מהל' גירושין הל' א סמג עשין נ טוש"ע אה"ע סי' קלט סעיף א:

## תורה אור השלם

א) אִם הִמָּצֵא תִמָּצֵא בְיָדוֹ הַגְּנֵבָה מִשּׁוֹר עַד חֲמוֹר עַד שֶׂה חַיִּים שְׁנַיִם יְשַׁלֵּם: [שמות כב, ג]
א) כִּי יִקַּח אִישׁ אִשָּׁה וּבְעָלָהּ וְהָיָה אִם לֹא תִמְצָא חֵן בְּעֵינָיו כִּי מָצָא בָהּ עֶרְוַת דָּבָר וְכָתַב לָהּ סֵפֶר כְּרִיתֻת וְנָתַן בְּיָדָהּ וְשִׁלְּחָהּ מִבֵּיתוֹ: [דברים כד, א]

## מסורת הש"ס

א) מהרש"ל כהנא ב) [גיטין עז:], ג) בב[א] קמא סד:, לקמן נו:, גיט[ין] עז., ד) [קדושין מב: וש"נ], ה) בבא קמא פז., ו) [גיטין עז.].

## הגהות הגר"א

[א] בעלמא. נ"ב ג[י'] הרי"ף בשדה דעלמא:

## גליון הש"ס

גמ' רב סמא בו[רקתא] קמי' דרבינ[א] משמי' דר' חיי[א] בריה דר' אויא אמר כ"ה בר"ן: תוס' ד"ה ר"י וכו' אלמא שייך קנין ד' אמות בגט. ל[א] זכיתי להבין דאכן ילפי' ר[...] דחצר הוי כיד. אבל מ[...] נקרא חצר לא שייך למיל[...] דמה שהקנו לו חכמים ה[...] חצירו ובגט הקנו לה כ[...] אמה ובממון הקנו לה ר[...] ד' אמות ולע"ג:

## ליקוטי רש"י

בסמטא. קרן זוי[ת] הסמוכה לרה"ר ובני אד[ם] העושין סחורה זה עם ז[ה] בשוק ורוצים לדב[ר] דבריהם בנחת ויש[ו]ב הדעת מסתלקין ש[ם] [כתובות פד:]. וסימט[א] איכא דאמר שביל ש[ל] יחידים ואני שמעתי כניס[ה] בולטת מרה"ר ויש רשו[ת] לבני אדם להעמיד ש[ם] חפצים שלהם כמ[ו] השותפים דאינו ע[שוי] להילוך בני רשות הרבי[ם] [רשב"ם ב"ב פד:]. ציד[י] רשות הרבים. סמו[כים] לבתים שנותנין להלן [מן] הבתים אבנים ומכשול להרחיק חיכוך העגלו[ת] ומאותן חיפופי ולפני[ם] קרי צידי רה"ר [כתובו[ת] לא:]. סמוך לכתלים שא[ין] דרך בני אדם לעבור ש[ם] ולהתחכך בכותלים [ש[ם] פו:]. אין לי. שיתחיי[ב] כפל. אלא. בזמן שלקח בידו [לקמן נו:]. ג[גו] חצרו וקרפיפו מני[ן] שאם נכנסה שם ונע[ל] בפניה לגנבה מנין שקנא[ה] לו חצרו ומתחייב כפ[ל] [שם]. קרפיפו. היק[ף] גדול חוץ לעיר להכניס ש[ם] עצים לאוצר [עירובין יח.]. אין שליח. חשוב שלי[ח] לדבר עבירה שיתחיי[ב] שולחו אלא הרי הו[א] כעושה מאליו [קדוש[ין] מב:]. וסברא הוא דאמר ליה דברי הרב ודב[רי] התלמיד דברי מי שומע [ב"ק נא.]. נתגרש האשה וכו'. וק[...] נכסים. חייבין לשל[ם] שהרי מתחלה הן חייב[ין] אלא שאין להם מה לשל[ם] שנכסי מלוג של אש[ה] משועבדים לבעל לפירו[ת] ולירושה [ב"ק פז.]. ת"[ל] ונתן מ"מ. ודרשי' [...] באנפי נפשיה מדלא כת[יב] ובידה יתננו משמע נתינה כל דהוא ויד[ה] דכתב רחמנא דבעי[נן] דומיא דידה דמשתמר[ת] [לעצמה כו' [גיטין עז.]

**courtyard is derived from** her acquisition by means of **her hand.**[11] כִּי הֵיכִי דְּאִית לָהּ יָד – Therefore, **just as [a minor girl] has** the capacity to become divorced by placement of the document in her **hand,** חָצֵר נַמִּי אִית לָהּ – **she also has** the capacity to become divorced by placement of the document in her **courtyard.**[12] וּמָר סָבַר חָצֵר מִשּׁוּם שְׁלִיחוּת אִיתְרַבַּאי – **And the** other **master** [Reish Lakish] **holds that** acquisition by means of one's **courtyard is derived from** the law of **agency.**[13] וְכִי הֵיכִי דִּשְׁלִיחוּת לֵית לָהּ – **Therefore, just as [a minor] does not have** the capacity to utilize the device of **agency,** חָצֵר נַמִּי לֵית לָהּ – **she also does not have** the capacity to acquire by means of her **courtyard.**[14]

The Gemara objects to that understanding of the dispute:

מִי אִיכָּא מַאן דְּאָמַר חָצֵר מִשּׁוּם שְׁלִיחוּת אִיתְרַבַּאי – **Can there be someone who holds that** acquisition by **courtyard is derived from** the law of **agency?** וְהָתַנְיָא – **But it was taught in a Baraisa** that discusses the law of a thief: ,,בְּיָדוֹ״ – The verse states:[15] *If the stolen article will be found* IN HIS HAND. אֵין לִי אֶלָּא יָדוֹ – From this alone, I WOULD KNOW ONLY that a thief is liable to make a twofold payment if he steals with HIS HAND; גַּגּוֹ חֲצֵירוֹ וְקַרְפֵּיפוֹ מִנַּיִן – FROM WHERE would I know that he is liable if he steals with HIS ROOF, HIS COURTYARD, OR HIS ENCLOSURE?[16] תַּלְמוּד לוֹמַר: ,,הִמָּצֵא תִמָּצֵא״ מִכָּל מָקוֹם – Therefore, THE TORAH STATES: *IF FINDING IT WILL BE FOUND* which implies: ANYWHERE in his possession.[17] וְאִי סָלְקָא דַּעְתָּךְ חָצֵר מִשּׁוּם שְׁלִיחוּת אִיתְרַבַּאי – **Now, if you think that** acquisition by **courtyard is derived fro**m the law of **agency,** אִם כֵּן מָצִינוּ שָׁלִיחַ לִדְבַר עֲבֵירָה – **if so, we wi**ll **have found** that there can be **an agent for an act of transgre**s**sion.** וְקַיְימָא לָן אֵין שָׁלִיחַ לִדְבַר עֲבֵירָה – **Yet, we hold** the **estab**lished principle that **there can be no agent for an act of tran**s**gression.**[18] – ? –

The Gemara answers:

אָמַר רָבִינָא – **Ravina said:** הֵיכָא אָמְרִינַן דְּאֵין שָׁלִיחַ לִדְבַר עֲבֵירָה – **Where do we say that there can be no agent for an act of tran**s**gression?** הֵיכָא דִּשְׁלִיחַ בַּר חִיּוּבָא הוּא – **Where the agent is responsible party,** i.e. he is subject to the Torah's injunctio[n] against committing that act of transgression. בָל בְּחָצֵר דְּלָאו בַּר חִיּוּבָא הוּא – **But with regard to a courtyard, which is not responsible party,** מִיחַיֵּיב שׁוֹלְחוֹ – **its "sender"** [i.e the cour[t]yard owner] **is liable.**[19]

The Gemara objects:

אֶלָּא מֵעַתָּה – **But now,** if you say that the principal is liable for h[is] agent's act where the agent himself is not a responsible part[y], הָאוֹמֵר לְאִשָּׁה וְעֶבֶד צְאוּ גִּנְבוּ לִי – then if **someone says to a** marrie[d] **woman or slave, "Go, steal for me,"** דְּלָאו בְּנֵי חִיּוּבָא נִינְהוּ – **since they are not responsible parties,** כִי נַמִּי דְּמִיחַיֵּיב שׁוֹלְחָן – **it is also so that their sender is liable?**[20]

NOTES

11. The Torah (*Deuteronomy* 24:3) states that divorce is effected when וְנָתַן בְּיָדָהּ, *he [the husband] places [the bill of divorce] in her hand.* However, we find elsewhere in Scripture that the term "hand" has the broader meaning of "possession" or "control," as in *Numbers* 21:26 (which describes the conquest of Moabite lands by Sichon, king of the Amorites): וַיִּקַּח אֶת־כָּל־אַרְצוֹ מִיָּדוֹ, *and he took all his [Moab's] land from his "hand."* Accordingly, R' Yochanan holds that the requirement to place the bill of divorce in the wife's "hand" is fulfilled by placing the bill in an area over which she has legal control, such as her courtyard (*Rashi; see Pnei Yehoshua*).

12. A minor girl (that is, a girl who is under the legal age of majority) who is mature enough to guard her *get* [i.e. to appreciate its implications – see *Gittin* 64b] has the capacity to be divorced (*Rashi* from *Gittin* 64b). [This is evident from the fact that Scripture (as expounded by the Gemara *Yevamos* 113b) deprives only an imbecile of the capacity to be divorced, since she would continuously return to her husband; thus, the requirement that the husband "send her away" cannot be fulfilled. We infer, then, that an intelligent minor, who will not return if sent away, can be divorced (*Rashi*)].

[If a minor girl can be divorced, this means – at the very minimum – that the basic Torah procedure of placing the *get* in her hand is effective.]

13. [The law of agency states that a principal may appoint an agent to carry out a particular act and the agent's execution of this act is attributed to the principal.] The Gemara in *Kiddushin* (41a) derives that one may appoint an agent to present or receive a *get* on his or her behalf, or to offer the Pesach sacrifice in his stead [as well as to perform other acts for the principal]. Our Gemara now posits that Reish Lakish holds that a courtyard can acquire an object for its owner because it is viewed as his agent (*Rashi*).

14. A minor cannot appoint an agent [see Mishnah in *Gittin* 65a] because the Biblical references to agency specify an adult as the one who can appoint the agent. Therefore, Reish Lakish holds that a minor girl cannot be divorced if the *get* is thrown into her courtyard because she cannot have the courtyard serve as her agent (*Rashi*).

The same dispute between Reish Lakish and R' Yochanan applies to a minor girl's acquisition by means of the four *amos* surrounding her, since that Rabbinic institution is patterned after the Biblical law of acquisition by courtyard; thus, acquisition by four *amos* is effective only where acquisition by courtyard would be (*Pnei Yehoshua*).

15. *Exodus* 22:3. The verse in its entirety states: אִם־הִמָּצֵא תִמָּצֵא בְיָדוֹ הַגְּנֵבָה מִשּׁוֹר עַד־חֲמוֹר עַד־שֶׂה חַיִּים שְׁנַיִם יְשַׁלֵּם, *If the stolen article will surely be found in his [the thief's] hand, from an ox to a mule to a sheep – alive – he shall pay twofold.* [Though the Torah speaks of where the stolen object is *found,* the ensuing exposition takes the main point to be how the object was *stolen* – i.e. where the object is found at the moment [of] theft (see *Ritva*).]

16. That is, if someone else's animal entered one of these properties an[d] the property owner locked the animal inside in order to steal it, he [is] liable to pay the twofold penalty to the animal's owner [just as if ha[d] stolen the animal by taking hold of it with his hands] (*Rashi*).

17. Instead of simply stating אִם תִּמָּצֵא בְיָדוֹ הַגְּנֵבָה, *if the stolen article wi[ll] be found in his hand,* Scripture uses repetitive language: הִמָּצֵא תִמָּצֵא [literally: finding it will be found] to indicate that *wherever* the stole[n] article is found at the moment of theft, the thief must pay double th[e] value to his victim. This indicates that one can accomplish theft b[y] stealing the article by means of his property.

18. The Gemara in *Kiddushin* (42b) states that the device of com[missioning] an agent to carry out a particular act is not applicable to a[n] act of transgression; that is, the agent's execution of the act [of] transgression is not legally attributed to the person who commissione[d] him. For example, if someone commissions an agent to steal for him, [it] is the agent who is responsible to repay the theft, not the one wh[o] commissioned the agent. Our Gemara therefore asks that if a person['s] courtyard acquires an article for him as a corollary of the agency law[s] a person should not be liable if his courtyard "steals" an animal for hi[m].

19. The reason there is no agency for an act of transgression is that a[n] agent commissioned to do so should not have executed his commissio[n]. For we say to him, "If you have a choice of following the order of th[e] Master [i.e. God, Who commands you not to do the sin] or the order [of] the disciple [your principal, who commissions you to do the sin], whos[e] order shall you follow?" Obviously, the agent should follow God's orde[r] and not execute his commission. Therefore, the principal is not liable fo[r] the sin committed by his agent (*Rashi* from *Kiddushin* ibid.), for th[e] principal can argue that he thought the agent would not listen to hi[m] and disobey the Master (*Tos. Shantz*; *Tos. HaRosh* below, ד״ה הני נמי; *Sma* 182:2; see *Chidushei R' Akiva Eiger*). It is thus as if the agent acte[d] on his own [and the principal bears only *moral* but not *lega[l]* responsibility for the transgression – see *Kiddushin* 43a].

This logic applies when the agent is a responsible party. However, i[n] the case of one who steals an article by means of his courtyard, th[e] courtyard cannot be commanded to disobey the principal's orde[r]. Therefore, the courtyard is indeed deemed the principal's agent and th[e] principal is liable for the theft.

20. The Mishnah in *Bava Kamma* (87a) states that married women o[r] slaves who damage persons or property are not liable to pay compensa[-]tion (since they have no assets of their own with which to pay). Similarly they are not liable to pay if they stole from another person. Therefore according to the assertion that the law of agency is suspended in case of transgression only when the agent is a responsible party (see previou[s]

רב פפא אמר [א] כי תקינו ליה רבנן ארבע אמות [א] בעלמא בשדה דבעל הבית לא תקינו ליה רבנן ואע"ג דזכה ליה רחמנא בגוה כי זכה ליה רחמנא להלוכי בה ולנקוטי פיאה למיהוי חצירו לא זכה ליה רחמנא אמר רבא מותיב ר' יעקב בר אידי נזיקין ראה את המציאה ונפל לו עליה ובא אחר והחזיק בה זה שהחזיק בה זכה בה ואי אמרת ארבע אמות של אדם קונות לו בכל מקום נקנו ליה ארבע אמות דידיה הכא במאי עסקינן דלא אמר אקני ואי תקון רבנן כי לא אמר מאי הוי כיון דנפל עליה גלי דעתיה דבנפילה ניחא ליה דנקני בארבע אמות לא ניחא ליה דנקני רב ששת אמר [ב] כי תקינו רבנן בסמטא דלא דחקי רבים ברשות הרבים דקא דחקי רבים לא תקינו רבנן והא בכל מקום קאמר כל מקום [ג] לאתויי צידי רשות הרבים ואמר ריש לקיש משום אבא [א] כהן ברדלא קטנה אין לה חצר ואין לה ארבע אמות ור' יוחנן משום ר' ינאי אמר [ד] יש לה חצר ויש לה ארבע אמות במאי קמיפלגי מר סבר [ג] חצר [ה] משום ידה איתרבאי כי היכי דאית לה יד חצר נמי אית לה ומר סבר חצר משום שליחות איתרבאי וכי היכי דשליחות לית לה חצר נמי לית לה מי איכא מאן דאמר חצר משום שליחות איתרבאי [ג] והתניא [א] בידו אין לי אלא ידו גגו חצירו וקרפיפו מנין ת"ל [א] המצא תמצא מכל מקום ואי סלקא דעתך חצר משום שליחות איתרבאי אם כן מצינו שליח לדבר עבירה [ד] [ו] וקיימא לן אין שליח לדבר עבירה אמר רבינא היכא אמרינן דאין שליח לדבר עבירה היכא דשליח בר חיובא הוא אבל בחצר דלאו בר חיובא הוא מיחייב שולחו אלא מעתה האומר לאשה ועבד צאו גנבו לי דלאו בני חיובא נינהו הכי נמי דמיחייב שולחן אמרת אשה ועבד בני חיובא נינהו והשתא מיהא לית להו לשלומי [ה] דתנן [ז] נתגרשה האשה נשתחרר העבד חייבין לשלם [ו] רב סמא אמר היכא אמרינן אין שליח לדבר עבירה היכא דאי בעי עביד ואי בעי לא עביד אבל חצר דבעל כרחיה מותיב בה מיחייב שולחו מאי בינייהו איכא בינייהו כהן דאמר ליה לישראל צא וקדש לי אשה גרושה אי נמי איש דאמר לה לאשה אקפי לי קטן להך לישנא דאמר כל היכא דאי בעי עביד אי בעי לא עביד לא מיחייב שולחו ה"נ אי בעי עביד אי בעי לא עביד לא מיחייב שולחן להך לישנא דאמרת כל היכא דשליח לאו בר חיובא מיחייב שולחו הני נמי כיון דלאו בני חיובא נינהו מיחייב שולחן ומי איכא למ"ד חצר לאו משום ידה איתרבאי והתניא [ו] [ב] ידה אין לי אלא ידה גגה חצירה וקרפיפה מנין ת"ל ונתן [ח] מכל מקום לענין גט כולי עלמא לא פליגי דחצר משום ידה איתרבאי כי פליגי לענין מציאה מ"ם

**רש"י**

ה"ג כי תקון ליה רבנן בעלמא. כגון בסמטא שהוא רשות לכל אדם או ברה"ר או בצידי רשות הרבים והיא הפקר לרבים למשוך לתוכה הצריכין לצאת מן הדחק: לא תקון ליה רבנן. שהרי אין לאדם שם ד' אמות מיוחדות שהרבה חברים יש לו בתוכה עומדים אצלו: קטנה אין לה חצר. אם זרק לה בעלה גט לתוך חצרה לא קנתה לה חצרה להתגרש בו וכן אם היתה עומדת ברה"ר וזרקו לה גט בארבע אמותיה ואע"ג דגדולה מיגרשה כדתנן (גיטין דף עח.) הזורק גט לאשתו בתוך ביתה כו' היתה עומדת ברה"ר וזרקו לה קרוב לה מגורשת כו': משום ידה אתרבאי. דכתיב ונתן בידה וידה רשותה משמע כדכתיב (במדבר כא) ויקח את כל ארצו מידו: כי היכי דאית לה יד. דמשיודעת לשמור את גיטה מגורשת דלא מיעט רחמנא אלא שוטה דמשלחה והיא חוזרת: משום שליחות איתרבאי. מדרבי רחמנא שליחות לאדם כדתניא (קידושין דף מא.) ושלח מלמד שהאיש עושה שליח ושלחה מלמד שהאשה עושה שליח אתרבאי נמי חצרה דהויא לה כשלוחה: וכי היכי דשליחות לית לה. דתנן שאין הקטן עושה שליח דכי כתיב שליחות בין בגיטין בין בפסח איש כתיב בענין: ידו. אם המצא תמצא בידו: גגו חצרו וקרפיפו מנין. שאם נכנסה שם ונעל בפניה לגונבה שהוא חייב: א"כ מצינו תורת שליחות לדבר עבירה. לומר שלוחו כמותו וחייב השולח במעשה השליח: וקי"ל. בקידושין בפ"ב (דף מב:): בר חיובא הוא. שאף הוא מוזהר על הדבר התם פטור השולח דאמרינן ליה דברי הרב ודברי התלמיד דברי מי שומעין ולא היה לו לעשות: דלאו בני חיובא נינהו. לשלם כדתנן הם שחבלו באחרים פטורין (ב"ק פז.): דאי בעי עביד. את השליחות: וקדש לי אשה גרושה. ומשעת קידושין עובר משום לא יקחו: אשה אינה באזהרת לא תקיפו לפי שאינה בבל תשחית פאת זקנך כדאמר בקידושין (ד' לה:) והמקיף את הקטן חייב שהמקיף באזהרה כניקף דכתיב לא תקיפו אחד הניקף ואחד המקיף במשמע במס' [נזיר] (דף נז:) וקטן דנקט משום דסתמא גדול לא שביק לאקופי נפשיה: תלמוד לומר ונתן מכל מקום. מדלא כתיב ובידה יתנהו דרוש ונתן אוכתב לה ונתן אלמא משום ידה אתרבאי דאי משום שליחות הא כבר כתיבא הכא כדתניא (ושלח) [ושלחה] מלמד שהאשה עושה שליח בקידושין בפרק ב' (דף מא.) ילפינן

**תוספות**

רבי יוחנן אמר יש לה ד' אמות. תימה דלקמן מסיק משום דיליף מגיטה מגט [ט] אלמא שייך קנין ד' אמות בגט ובפרק הזורק (גיטין דף עח: ושם ד"ה ר"י) קאמר ר"י קרוב לה אפילו מאה אמה ויכולה לשמרו הוי גט וי"ל דבד' אמות שלה אפילו יכול לשמור כמוה מגורשת וחוץ לד' אמות צריך שתוכל היא לשמרו: ת"ל המצא תמצא מ"מ. וא"ת ונימא המצא תמצא כלל בידו פרט וכלל ופרט אין בכלל אלא מה שבפרט וי"ל שדי ידו בין המצא תמצא וה"ל כלל ופרט וכלל כדאמרינן במרובה (ב"ק דף סד: ושם) כל מקום שאתה מוצא שני כללות הסמוכין זה לזה הטל פרט ביניהם וכן בסמוך גבי גט דמרבה גגה מונתן בידה י"ל ושלחה חזר וכלל: ואי משום שליחות א"כ מצינו שליח לדבר עבירה. וא"ת מה צריך להוכיח מכח דאין שליח כו' אמאי לא מוכיח מדאתרבאי חצר מקרא דידו כדבסמוך גבי גט מוכיח דחצר משום ידה איתרבאי מדאתרבאי מקרא דידה ולא עביד שום הוכחה וי"ל דבסמוך מכח התנא מוכיח דמרבה גגה וחצרה כידה להתגרש אפילו בעל כרחה או אפילו היא קטנה ואי מטעם שליחות לא היתה מתגרשת בעל כרחה ולא קטנה אבל הכא אי אפשר להוכיח מכח זה דאפילו בידו אינו קונה הגניבה בעל כרחו ולא אם הוא קטן: אין שליח לדבר עבירה. בפ' האיש מקדש (קדושין דף מג.) איכא דיליף משחוטי חוץ דכתיב הוא ולא שלוחו ואיכא דיליף משום דהוה ליה מעילה וטביחה שני כתובים הבאים כאחד דיש שליח ואין מלמדין: אשה ועבד בני חיובא נינהו. ואם תאמר והתנן פרק הכונס (ב"ק דף נט:) השולח את הבערה ביד חרש שוטה וקטן פטור ואמאי והא לאו בני חיובא נינהו וי"ל דהתם משום דלאו בני שליחות נינהו: אי בעי לא עביד. וא"ת והא דתנן (ב"ק דף עט. ושם) היה מושכו ויוצא [ומת ברשות בעלים] פטור הגביהו [או הוציאו מרשות בעלים ומת] חייב ופרש"י בלשון אחד שאמר גנב לשומר שור אחד יש לי בבית פלוני קחנו ותהא עליו שומר חנם הוציאו השומר מרשות בעלים ומת חייב הגנב במשיכת השומר ואמאי והא אי בעי לא עביד וי"ל כיון שאין השומר יודע שהוא גנוב הוה ליה כחצר דבעל כרחו מותיב ביה: דאמר לישראל קדש לי אשה גרושה. וא"ת ואפי' אמר לכהן נמי וי"ל דכהן מקרי בר חיובא הואיל ואם מקדשה לעצמו חייב אבל ישראל אע"ג דעובר משום לפני עור לא תתן מכשול כשמקדשה לכהן כיון דאי מקדשה לעצמו לא מיחייב לא מקרי בר חיובא וא"ת מאי נ"מ בין למ"ד אי בעי עביד ובין למ"ד שליח בר חיובא לא לקי על הקדושין לרבא דאמר בעשרה יוחסין (קדושין דף עח.) קידש אינו לוקה בעל לוקה וי"ל דכי בעל אח"כ לוקה אף על הקדושין כדמוכח בריש תמורה (דף ה: ושם) א"נ י"ל דאף לרבא נפקא מינה דאי יש שליחות חלין הקדושין ואי אין שליחות אין חלין הקדושין: אקפי לי קטן. וה"ה דהוה מצי למימר אקפי לי גדול אלא שהגדול לא יניח עצמו להקיף כדאמר פרק אלו הן הלוקין (מכות דף כ:) דאחד הניקף ואחד המקיף חייב ואע"ג דמוקי לה התם כי ניקף מסייע ליה בהדיה היינו משום דבענין אחר לא לקי דהוה לאו שאין בו מעשה אבל הלאו עובר לעולם [ועיין תוס' שבועות ג. ד"ה ועל הזקן ותוספות נזיר נז: ד"ה ורב אדא]:

**עין משפט נר מצוה**

פא א ב ג מיי' פי"ז מהל' אבידה הל' ט ופ"ד מהל' זכייה ומתנה הל' ט סמג עשין עד טוש"ע ח"מ סי' רסח סעיף ג:
פב ד מיי' פי"ז מהל' אבידה הל' י ופ"ד מהל' זכייה ומתנה הל' ט ועי' בהשגות ובמ"מ סמג שם טוש"ע שם סעיף ה וסי' רמג סעיף כג:
פג ה מיי' פי"ז מהלכות אבידה הלכה י:
פד ו מיי' פ"ז מהלכות מעילה הל' ב טוש"ע ח"מ סי' תי סעיף ח וסי' קפב סעיף א בהגה"ה:
פה ז מיי' פ"ד מהלכות חובל ומזיק הל' כא סמג עשין ע טוש"ע ח"מ סי' תכד סעיף ט:
פו ח מיי' פ"ה מהל' גירושין הל' א סמג עשין כ טוש"ע אה"ע סי' קלט סעיף א:

**תורה אור השלם**

א) אִם הִמָּצֵא תִמָּצֵא בְיָדוֹ הַגְּנֵבָה מִשּׁוֹר עַד חֲמוֹר עַד שֶׂה חַיִּים שְׁנַיִם יְשַׁלֵּם: [שמות כב, ג]
א) כִּי יִקַּח אִישׁ אִשָּׁה וּבְעָלָהּ וְהָיָה אִם לֹא תִמְצָא חֵן בְּעֵינָיו כִּי מָצָא בָהּ עֶרְוַת דָּבָר וְכָתַב לָהּ סֵפֶר כְּרִיתֻת וְנָתַן בְּיָדָהּ וְשִׁלְּחָהּ מִבֵּיתוֹ: [דברים כד, א]

**רבינו חננאל**

אמר ריש לקיש משום אבא כהן ברדלא קטנה אין לה חצר ואין לה ד' אמות. ור' יוחנן משום ר' ינאי אמר יש לה פי' האי דאמרי רבנן חצירו של אדם המשתמרת קונה לו שלא מדעתו וכן ד' אמות של אדם קונות לו בכל מקום הני מילי גדול תקינו ליה רבנן אבל לא לקטנה. ור' יוחנן אמר אפי' קטנה יש לה. ר' יוחנן אמר חצירה מכח ידה איתרבי כשם שיש לה יד וכל מה שיגיע לידה זכתה בו כך כל המגיע לחצירה זכתה בו. וריש לקיש אמר חצירה משום שליחות איתרבי כשם שאין שליחות לקטנה כך אין לה זכייה בחצר. איני והתניא אם המצא תמצא בידו אין לי אלא שנמצאת בידו ממש נמצאת בחצירו או בגגו או בקרפיפו מנין שחייב כאילו בידו ממש נמצאת ת"ל המצא תמצא מכל מקום הנה חצירו משום ידו איתרבי קשיא ליה לריש לקיש ואם תזומר גם משום שליחות נתרבה הא קי"ל אין שליח לדבר עבירה. פי' אע"ג דאמרי' שלוחו של אדם כמותו וכל מה שעשה השליח כאילו שולחו עשאו הני מילי בזולתי דבר עבירה אבל בדבר עבירה השליח חייב ולא השולחו וכיון שהחצר שליח בעלה הוא והוא שנמצאת הגניבה בה אמאי מיחייב בעלה שהוא השולח. ופריק רבינא אליבא דריש לקיש היכא אמרי' השולח פטור היכא דהשליח בר חיובא הוא אבל חצר דלאו בת חיובא היא מיחייב שולחה והוא בעל החצר. ואקשי' אי הכי האומר לעבד ולאשת איש צאו וגנבו דלאו בני חיובא נינהו כדתנן בפ' החובל לחבירו העבד והאשה פגיעתן רעה החובל בהן חייב הן שחבלו באחרים פטורין הכי נמי דמיחייב שולחן. ופרקי' הני נמי בני חיובא נינהו דתנן נתגרשה האשה ונשתחרר העבד חייבין לשלם. בא רב סמא ופירק פירוק אחר ואמר כי אמרי' אין שליח לדבר עבירה כל היכא דאי בעי השליח עביד אי בעי לא עביד אבל חצר דעל כורחה עבדה מיחייב שולחה. מאי איכא בין רבינא לרב סמא איכא בינייהו כהן שאמר לישראל לך קדש לי אשה גרושה או איש שאמר לאשה אקיף לי ראשו של קטן לרבינא כיון דהני לאו בני חיובא נינהו דאין ישראל מוזהר על הגרושה ולא אשה בהקפת הראש מיחייב שולחה. לרב סמא כיון דאי בעו לא עבדי אי בעו עבדי לא מיחייב שולחם. ומתמהינן מי איכא מאן דאמר חצר לאו משום ידה איתרבי והתניא וכתב לה ספר כריתות ונתן בידה. בידה אין לי אלא בידה ממש גגה חצירה וקרפיפה מנין שהנותן גט בהן כנותנו בידה הוא ת"ל ונתן מכל מקום. ואמרי' לענין גט כ"ע לא פליגי דחצר משום ידה איתרבי דהא קרא בהדיא כתיב.

**מסורת הש"ס**

א) מהרש"ל כהנא ב) [גיטין עז:], ג) ב"ק סד:, לקמן נו:, גיטין עז., ד) [קדושין מב: וש"נ], ה) בבא קמא פז., ו) [גיטין עז.].

**הגהות הגר"א**

[א] בעלמא. נ"ב גי' הרי"ף בשדה דעלמא:

**גליון הש"ס**

גמ' רב סמא ב[ריה] דרב רקתא קמי' דרבינא משמי' דר' חייא בריה דר' אויא אמר כ"ה בר"ן: תוס' ד"ה ר"י וכו' אלמא שייך קנין ד' אמות בגט. [illegible] זכיתי להבין דאכן ילפי' [illegible] דחצר הוי כיד. אבל [illegible] נקרא חצר לא שייך למיל[illegible] דמה שהקנו לו חכמים [illegible] אצירו ובגט הקנו לה [illegible] אמה ובממון הקנו לה [illegible] ד' אמות ולע"ג:

**ליקוטי רש"י**

בסמטא. קרן זוית הסמוכה לרה"ר ובני אדם העושין סחורה זה עם זה בשוק ורוצים לדבר דבריהם בנחת ויש[ו] הדעת מסתלקין [illegible] [כתובות פד:]. וסימט[א] אית דאמר שביל [illegible] יחידים ואני שמעתי כנים בולטות מרה"ר ויש רשו[ת] לבני אדם להעמיד [illegible] חפצים שלהם כמו השותפים דאינו [illegible] להילוך בני רשות הרבים [רשב"ם ב"ב פד:]. צידי רשות הרבים. סמו[ך] לבתים שנותנין להן [illegible] הבתים אבנים ומכשול להרחיק חיכוך העגלו[ת] ומאותן חיפופי ולפני קרי לידי רה"ר [כתובות לא:]. סמוך לכתלים שא[ין] דרך בני אדם לעבור [illegible] ולהתחכך בכותלים [illegible] אין לי. שיתחייב כפל. אלא. בזמן שנמצא בידו [לקמן נו:]. גגו חצרו וקרפיפו מנין [illegible]

The Gemara offers an alternative defense of Reish Lakish:

רַב פָּפָּא אָמַר – **Rav Pappa says:** כִּי תַּקִּינוּ לֵיהּ רַבָּנָן אַרְבַּע אַמּוֹת בְּעָלְמָא – **When did the Rabbis institute [for a person]** acquisition by his **four *amos*?** When he is **in** areas belonging to the **general** public.[1] בְּשָׂדֶה דְּבַעַל הַבַּיִת לֹא תַּקִּינוּ לֵיהּ רַבָּנָן – **But in a private person's field, the Rabbis did not institute this** method of acquisition.[2] וְאַף עַל גַּב דְּזָכָה לֵיהּ רַחֲמָנָא בְּגַוָּהּ – **And even though the Merciful One granted [a poor man] rights in [the field],** כִּי זָכָה לֵיהּ רַחֲמָנָא לְהַלּוּכֵי בָּהּ וּלְנַקּוּטֵי פֵּיאָה – **the Merciful One granted him rights only to walk in it and to take *pe'ah*;** לְמֶיהֱוֵי חֲצֵירוֹ לֹא זָכָה לֵיהּ רַחֲמָנָא – **but for it to be his courtyard, the Merciful One did not grant him** such **rights.**[3]

The Gemara now elaborates R' Yaakov bar Idi's objection (mentioned on 10a) to Reish Lakish's ruling:

אָמַר רָבָא – **Rava said:** מוֹתִיב ר' יַעֲקֹב בַּר אִידִי נְזִיקִין – **R' Yaakov bar Idi challenged** Reish Lakish **from** our Mishnah in ***Nezikin*:** רָאָה אֶת הַמְּצִיאָה וְנָפַל לוֹ עָלֶיהָ – IF ONE SAW A LOST ARTICLE AND FELL UPON IT וּבָא אַחֵר וְהֶחֱזִיק בָּהּ – AND ANOTHER CAME AND SEIZED IT, זֶה שֶׁהֶחֱזִיק בָּהּ זָכָה בָּהּ – THE ONE WHO SEIZED IT HAS ACQUIRED IT. וְאִי אָמְרַתְּ אַרְבַּע אַמּוֹת שֶׁל אָדָם קוֹנוֹת לוֹ בְּכָל מָקוֹם – **Now, if you say** that **the four *amos* of a person acquire** an object **for him in any location,** נִקְנוּ לֵיהּ אַרְבַּע אַמּוֹת דִּידֵיהּ – **let [the first person's] four *amos* acquire** the lost object **for him!**[4] – ? –

The Gemara answers:

הָכָא בְּמַאי עָסְקִינַן דְּלָא אָמַר אֶקְנֵי – **With what** case **are we dealing here?** With a case **where he did not say, "I wish to acquire** the lost object through the institution of four *amos*."

The Gemara objects:

וְאִי תַּקּוּן רַבָּנָן – **But if the Rabbis instituted** that a person acquires an object that is within his four *amos*, כִּי לֹא אָמַר מַאי הָוֵי – then even **when he did not say** that he wanted to acquire the object, **what is** lacking to effect the acquisition?[5]

The Gemara answers:

כֵּיוָן דְּנָפַל עָלֶיהָ – **Since he fell upon [the lost object],** גַּלֵּי דַּעְתֵּיהּ דִּבְנְפִילָה נִיחָא לֵיהּ דְּנִקְנֵי – **he has revealed his intention that he wants to acquire** the object **through** his act of **falling** on בְּאַרְבַּע אַמּוֹת לֹא נִיחָא לֵיהּ דְּנִקְנֵי – but **he does not want to acqui** it **by** virtue of it being within his **four *amos*.**[6]

The Gemara offers an alternative defense of Reish Lakish:

רַב שֵׁשֶׁת אָמַר – **Rav Sheishess says:** כִּי תַּקִּינוּ רַבָּנָן בְּסִמְטָא – **When did the Rabbis institute** acquisition by four *amos*? On when the person is **in a recessed area,**[7] דְּלָא דָּחֲקֵי רַבִּים – **where the public does not crowd.** שׁוּת הָרַבִּים דְּקָא דָּחֲקֵי רַבִּים – But **in a public thoroughfare, where the public crowd** לֹא תַּקִּינוּ רַבָּנָן – **the Rabbis did not institute** this method acquisition.[8]

The Gemara objects:

וְהָא בְּכָל מָקוֹם קָאָמַר – **But [Reish Lakish] states** that four *am* **acquire in *any* location!** Is not the word "any" meant to inclu even a public thoroughfare?

The Gemara answers:

כָּל מָקוֹם לְאֲתוּיֵי צִידֵּי רְשׁוּת הָרַבִּים – No. The phrase **"any place"** meant **to include the shoulders of the public thoroughfar** not the thoroughfare itself.[9]

The Gemara cites another ruling that Reish Lakish stated the name of Abba Kohen Bardela:

וְאָמַר רֵישׁ לָקִישׁ מִשּׁוּם אַבָּא כֹּהֵן בַּרְדְּלָא – **And Reish Lakish state in the name of Abba Kohen Bardela:** קְטַנָּה אֵין לָהּ חָצֵר – **minor girl does not have** the capacity for her **courtyard** acquire on her behalf, וְאֵין לָהּ אַרְבַּע אַמּוֹת – **nor does she hav** the capacity for her **four *amos*** to acquire on her behalf.[10]

The Gemara presents a dissenting opinion:

וְר' יוֹחָנָן מִשּׁוּם ר' יַנַּאי אָמַר – **But R' Yochanan states in the nam of R' Yannai:** יֵשׁ לָהּ חָצֵר – **[A minor girl] has** the capacity f her **courtyard** to acquire on her behalf, וְיֵשׁ לָהּ אַרְבַּע אַמּוֹת – **and she has** the capacity for her **four *amos*** to acquire on h behalf.

The Gemara explains the source of the dispute:

בְּמַאי קָמִיפַּלְגֵי – **In what** underlying principle **do they disagre** מַר סָבַר חָצֵר מִשּׁוּם יָדָהּ אִיתְרַבַּאי – **One master** [R' Yochana **holds that** a wife's acquisition of a bill of divorce by means of h

NOTES

1. For example, in a recessed area off the market [which is in the public domain]; or in a public thoroughfare; or on the shoulders of a public thoroughfare [which are available to anyone who wants to escape the crowded conditions of the thoroughfare] (*Rashi*; see note 6 below).

2. [The Sages did not grant a person four *amos* in another person's domain, since that would interfere with the owner's rights to that area. (*Rashi's* comments in ד״ה לא תקון ליה רבנן do not refer to this Gemara but to the Gemara below.)]

Therefore, a poor person collecting *pe'ah* in a private person's field does not acquire the produce simply by walking to within four *amos* of it; rather, he must perform a valid act of acquisition to the produce.

3. At first glance, the Torah grants a poor person in a private field rights with regard to *pe'ah* that are similar to every person's rights in a public domain. Consequently, the Rabbis could have applied their institution of acquisition by four *amos* to a poor person in a private field. Therefore, the Gemara explains that the Torah grants the poor person only the right to walk in the field and collect its *pe'ah,* but the field is not his for him to stay there and use. Thus, the Sages could not grant him ownership of four *amos* in the field without violating the owner's rights (see *Ritva*).

4. Since he fell on the object, he obviously was within four *amos* of it. Hence, why does he not acquire the object by virtue of that fact?

5. See 10a note 29.

6. See 10a note 30.

7. A *simta* is a quiet, recessed area close to the public thoroughfare, to which people who must discuss transactions with clear thought withdraw to escape the hubbub and commotion of the thoroughfare (*Rashi* to *Kesubos* 84b).

8. The Rabbis did not grant a person four *amos* in the often crowde public thoroughfare, since he invariably shares those four *am* simultaneously with other people (*Rashi*). [Rather, the institutio of four *amos* was limited to the less populated areas of the publ domain, where it is common for people to have four *amos* to then selves.]

[*Shitah Mekubetzes* notes that according to *Rashi,* Rav Pappa abov (who does not mention any difference between crowded and uncrowde areas of the public domain) apparently disagrees with Rav Sheishe (who makes this distinction). For in *Rashi's* comments to Rav Pappa view (ד״ה ה״ג כי תקון, cited in note 1), *Rashi* lists the public thoroughfa itself among the areas in which the Rabbinic institution of four *am* operates.]

9. [Even though these shoulders carry the overflow of the mai thoroughfare during hours of peak traffic, the Rabbis allowed the institution of four *amos* to operate there (see *Kesubos* 31b).]

10. The Gemara now assumes that this statement refers primarily t divorce law. In order to be divorced, a woman must receive a bill divorce (*get*) from her husband, acquiring it through a method acquisition generally effective for documents. One such method "acquisition by courtyard" (קִנְיַן חָצֵר), whereby the husband places th bill of divorce in his wife's courtyard (or other property). Similarly, if th wife is in a public area and the husband throws the bill of divorce int the four *amos* surrounding her (which, by Rabbinic enactment, a deemed to be her "domain"), it is as if the bill has been placed in h property and she is divorced. However, Reish Lakish teaches that minor girl cannot be divorced by placing the bill in her "courtyard" in her "four *amos*" (*Rashi*; see *Pnei Yehoshua*). Rather, the bill must b placed into her hand.

רב פפא אמר א כי תקינו ליה רבנן ארבע אמות [א] בעלמא בשדה דבעל הבית לא תקינו ליה רבנן ואע"ג דזכה ליה רחמנא בגוה כי זכה ליה רחמנא להלוכי בה ולנקוטי פיאה למיהוי חצירו לא זכה ליה רחמנא אמר רבא מותיב ר' יעקב בר אידי נזיקן ראה את המציאה ונפל לו עליה ובא אחר והחזיק בה זה שהחזיק בה זכה בה ואי אמרת ארבע אמות של אדם קונות לו בכל מקום נקנו ליה ארבע אמות דידיה הכא במאי עסקינן דלא אמר אקני ואי תקון רבנן כי לא אמר מאי הוי כיון דנפל עליה גלי דעתיה דבנפילה ניחא ליה דנקני בארבע אמות לא ניחא ליה דנקני רב ששת אמר ב כי תקינו רבנן בסמטא דלא דחקי רבים ברשות הרבים דקא דחקי רבים לא תקינו רבנן והא בכל מקום קאמר כל מקום ג לאתויי צידי רשות הרבים ואמר ריש לקיש משום אבא ה) כהן ברדלא קטנה אין לה חצר ואין לה ארבע אמות ור' יוחנן משום ר' ינאי אמר ד יש לה חצר ויש לה ארבע אמות במאי קמיפלגי מר סבר ג) חצר ה משום ידה איתרבאי כי היכי דאית לה יד חצר נמי אית לה ומר סבר חצר משום שליחות איתרבאי וכי היכי דשליחות לית לה חצר נמי לית לה מי איכא מאן דאמר חצר משום שליחות איתרבאי ג) והתניא א) בידו אין לי אלא ידו גגו חצירו וקרפיפו מנין ת"ל א) המצא תמצא מכל מקום ואי סלקא דעתך חצר משום שליחות איתרבאי אם כן מצינו שליח לדבר עבירה ד) ו וקיימא לן אין שליח לדבר עבירה אמר רבינא היכא אמרינן דאין שליח לדבר עבירה היכא דשליח בר חיובא הוא אבל בחצר דלאו בר חיובא הוא מיחייב שולחו אלא מעתה האומר לאשה ועבד צאו גנבו לי דלאו בני חיובא נינהו הכי נמי דמיחייב שולחן אמרת אשה ועבד בני חיובא נינהו והשתא מיהא לית להו לשלומי ה) דתנן ז נתגרשה האשה נשתחרר העבד חייבין לשלם ° רב סמא אמר היכא אמרינן אין שליח לדבר עבירה היכא דאי בעי עביד ואי בעי לא עביד אבל חצר דבעל כרחיה מותיב בה מיחייב שולחו מאי בינייהו איכא בינייהו כהן דאמר ליה לישראל צא וקדש לי אשה גרושה אי נמי איש דאמר לה לאשה אקפי לי קטן להך לישנא דאמר כל היכא דאי בעי עביד אי בעי לא עביד לא מיחייב שולחו ה"נ אי בעי עביד אי בעי לא עביד לא מיחייב שולחן להך לישנא דאמרת כל היכא דשליח לאו בר חיובא מיחייב שולחו הני נמי כיון דלאו בני חיובא נינהו מיחייב שולחן ומי איכא למ"ד חצר לאו משום ידה איתרבאי והתניא י) ב ידה אין לי אלא ידה גגה חצירה וקרפיפה מנין ת"ל ונתן ח מכל מקום לענין גט כולי עלמא לא פליגי דחצר משום ידה איתרבאי כי פליגי לענין מציאה מ"ם

## רש"י

ה"ג כי תקון ליה רבנן בעלמא. כגון בסמטא שהוא רשות לכל אדם או ברה"ר או בצידי רשות הרבים והיא הפקר לרבים למשוך לתוכה הצריכין לצאת מן הדחק: לא תקון ליה רבנן. שהרי אין לאדם שם ד' אמות מיוחדות שהרבה חברים יש לו בתוכה עומדים אצלו: קטנה אין לה חצר. אם זרק לה בעלה גט לתוך חצרה לא קנתה לה חצרה להתגרש בו וכן אם היתה עומדת ברה"ר וזרקו לה גט בארבע אמותיה ואע"ג דגדולה מיגרשה כדתנן (גיטין דף עח.) הזורק גט לאשתו בתוך ביתה כו' היתה עומדת ברה"ר וזרקו לה קרוב לה מגורשת כו': משום ידה אתרבאי. דכתיב ונתן בידה וידה רשותה משמע כדכתיב (במדבר כא) ויקח את כל ארצו מידו: כי היכי דאית לה יד. דמשיודעת לשמור את גיטה מגורשת דלא מיעט רחמנא אלא שוטה דמשלחה והיא חוזרת: משום שליחות איתרבאי. מדרבי רחמנא שליחות לאדם כדתניא (קידושין דף מא.) ושלח מלמד שהאיש עושה שליח ושלחה מלמד שהאשה עושה שליח אתרבאי נמי חצרה דהויא לה כשלוחה: וכי היכי דשליחות לית לה. דתנן שאין הקטן עושה שליח דכי כתיב שליחות בין בגיטין בין בפסח איש כתיב בענין: ידו. אם המצא תמצא בידו: גגו חצרו וקרפיפו מנין. שאם נכנסה שם ונעל בפניה לגונבה שהוא חייב: א"כ מצינו תורת שליחות לדבר עבירה. לומר שלוחו כמותו וחייב השולח במעשה השליח: וקיי"ל. בקידושין בפ"ב (דף מב:): בר חיובא הוא. שאף הוא מוזהר על הדבר התם פטור השולח דאמרינן ליה דברי הרב ודברי התלמיד דברי מי שומעין ולא היה לו לעשות: דלאו בני חיובא נינהו. לשלם כדתנן הם שחבלו באחרים פטורין (ב"ק פז.): דאי בעי עביד. את השליחות: וקדש לי אשה גרושה. ומשעת קידושין עובר משום לא יקחו: אשה אינה באזהרת לא תקיפו לפי שאינה בבל תשחית פאת זקנך כדאמר בקדושין (ד' לה:) והמקיף את הקטן חייב שהמקיף באזהרה כניקף דכתיב לא תקיפו אחד הניקף ואחד המקיף במשמע במס' [נזיר] (דף נז:) וקטן דנקט משום דסתמא גדול לא שביק לאקופי נפשיה: תלמוד לומר ונתן מכל מקום. מדלא כתיב ובידה יתנהו דרוש ונתן אוכתב לה ונתן אלמא משום ידה אתרבאי דאי משום שליחות הא כבר כתיבא הכא כדתניא (ושלח) [ושלחה] מלמד שהאשה עושה שליח בקדושין בפרק ב' (דף מא.): ילפינן

## תוספות

רבי יוחנן אמר יש לה ד' אמות. תימה דלקמן מסיק משום דיליף מציאה מגט ° אלמא שייך קנין ד' אמות בגט ובפרק הזורק (גיטין דף עח: ושם ד"ה ר"י) קאמר ר"י קרוב לה אפילו מאה אמה ויכולה לשמרו הוי גט וי"ל דבד' אמות שלה אפילו יכול לשמור כמוה מגורשת וחוץ לד' אמות צריך שתוכל היא לשמרו: ת"ל המצא תמצא מ"מ. וא"ת ונימא המצא תמצא כלל בידו פרט וכלל ופרט אין בכלל אלא מה שבפרט וי"ל שדי ידו בין המצא תמצא וה"ל כלל ופרט וכלל כדאמרינן במרובה (ב"ק דף סד: ושם) כל מקום שאתה מוצא שני כללות הסמוכין זה לזה הטל פרט ביניהם וכן בסמוך גבי גט דמרבה גגה מונתן בידה י"ל ושלחה חזר וכלל: ואי משום שליחות א"כ מצינו שליח לדבר עבירה. וא"ת מה צריך להוכיח מכח דאין שליח כו' אמאי לא מוכיח מדאתרבאי חצר מקרא דידו כדבסמוך גבי גט מוכיח דחצר משום ידה איתרבאי מדאתרבאי מקרא דידה ולא עביד שום הוכחה וי"ל דבסמוך מכח התנא מוכיח דמרבה גגה וחצרה כידה להתגרש אפילו בעל כרחה או אפילו היא קטנה ואי מטעם שליחות לא היתה מתגרשת בעל כרחה ולא קטנה אבל הכא אי אפשר להוכיח מכח זה דאפילו בידו אינו קונה הגניבה בעל כרחו ולא אם הוא קטן: אין שליח לדבר עבירה. בפ' האיש מקדש (קדושין דף מג.) איכא דיליף משחוטי חוץ דכתיב הוא ולא שלוחו ואיכא דיליף משום דהוה ליה מעילה וטביחה שני כתובים הבאים כאחד דיש שליח ואין מלמדין: אשה ועבד בני חיובא נינהו. ואם תאמר והתנן פרק הכונס (ב"ק דף נט:) השולח את הבערה ביד חרש שוטה וקטן פטור ואמאי והא לאו בני חיובא נינהו וי"ל דהתם משום דלאו בני שליחות נינהו: אי בעי לא עביד. וא"ת והא דתנן (ב"ק דף עט. ושם) היה מושכו ויוצא [ומת ברשות בעלים] פטור הגביהו [או הוציאו מרשות בעלים ומת] חייב ופרש"י בלשון אחד שאמר גנב לשומר שור אחד יש לי בבית פלוני קחנו ותהא עליו שומר חנם הוציאו השומר מרשות בעלים ומת חייב הגנב במשיכת השומר ואמאי והא אי בעי לא עביד וי"ל כיון שאין השומר יודע שהוא גנוב הוה ליה כחצר דבעל כרחו מותיב ביה: דאמר לישראל קדש לי אשה גרושה. וא"ת ואפי' אמר לכהן נמי וי"ל דכהן מקרי בר חיובא הואיל ואם מקדשה לעצמו חייב אבל ישראל אע"ג דעובר משום לפני עור לא תתן מכשול כשמקדשה לכהן כיון דאי מקדשה לעצמו לא מיחייב לא מקרי בר חיובא וא"ת מאי נ"מ בין למ"ד אי בעי עביד ובין למ"ד שליח בר חיובא לא לקי על הקדושין לרבא דאמר בעשרה יוחסין (קדושין דף עח.) קידש אינו לוקה בעל לוקה וי"ל דכי בעל את"כ לוקה אף על הקדושין כדמוכח בריש תמורה (דף ה: ושם) א"נ י"ל דאף לרבא נפקא מינה דאי יש שליחות חלין הקדושין ואי אין שליחות אין חלין הקדושין: אקפי לי קטן. וה"ה דהוה מצי למימר אקפי לי גדול אלא שהגדול לא יניח עצמו להקיף כדאמר פרק אלו הן הלוקין (מכות דף כ:) דאחד הניקף ואחד המקיף חייב ואע"ג דמוקי לה התם כי ניקף מסייע ליה בהדיה היינו משום דבענין אחר לא לקי דהוה לאו שאין בו מעשה אבל הלאו עובר לעולם [ועיין תוס' שבועות ג. ד"ה ועל הזקן ותוספות נזיר נז: ד"ה ורב אדא]:

## עין משפט נר מצוה

פא א ב ג מיי' פי"ז מהל' אבידה הל' ט ופ"ד מהל' זכייה ומתנה הל' ט סמג עשין עד טוש"ע ח"מ סי' רסח סעיף ב:

פב ד מיי' פי"ז מהל' אבידה הל' י ופ"ד מהל' זכייה ומתנה הל' ט ועי' בהשגות ובמ"מ סמג שם טוש"ע שם סעיף ה וסי' רמג סעיף כג:

פג ה מיי' פי"ז מהלכות אבידה הלכה י:

פד ו מיי' פ"ז מהלכות מעילה הל' ב טוש"ע ח"מ סי' תי סעיף ח וסי' קפב סעיף א בהגה"ה:

פה ז מיי' פ"ד מהלכות חובל ומזיק הל' כא סמג עשין ע טוש"ע ח"מ סי' תכד סעיף ט:

פו ח מיי' פ"ה מהל' גירושין הל' א סמג עשין נ טוש"ע אה"ע סי' קלט סעיף א:

## תורה אור השלם

א) אִם הִמָּצֵא תִמָּצֵא בְיָדוֹ הַגְּנֵבָה מִשּׁוֹר עַד חֲמוֹר עַד שֶׂה חַיִּים שְׁנַיִם יְשַׁלֵּם: [שמות כב, ג]

א) כִּי יִקַּח אִישׁ אִשָּׁה וּבְעָלָהּ וְהָיָה אִם לֹא תִמְצָא חֵן בְּעֵינָיו כִּי מָצָא בָהּ עֶרְוַת דָּבָר וְכָתַב לָהּ סֵפֶר כְּרִיתֻת וְנָתַן בְּיָדָהּ וְשִׁלְּחָהּ מִבֵּיתוֹ: [דברים כד, א]

## רבינו חננאל

אמר ריש לקיש משום אבא כהן ברדלא קטנה אין לה חצר ואין לה ד' אמות. ור' יוחנן משום ר' ינאי אמר יש לה פי' האי דאמרי רבנן חצירו של אדם המשתמרת קונה לו שלא מדעתו וכן ד' אמות של אדם קונות לו בכל מקום הני מילי גדול תקינו ליה רבנן אבל לא לקטנה. ור' יוחנן אמר אפי' קטנה יש לה. ר' יוחנן אמר חצירה מכח ידה איתרבי כשם שיש לה יד וכל מה שיגיע לידה זכתה בו כך כל המגיע לחצירה זכתה בו. וריש לקיש אמר חצירה משום שליחות איתרבי כשם שאין שליחות לקטנה כך אין לה זכייה בחצר. איני והתניא אם המצא תמצא בידו אין לי אלא שנמצאת בידו ממש נמצאת בחצירו או בגגו או בקרפיפו מנין שחייב כאילו בידו ממש נמצאת ת"ל המצא תמצא מכל מקום הנה חצירו משום ידו איתרבי קשיא ליה לריש לקיש ואם תאמר גם משום שליחות נתרבה הא קי"ל אין שליח לדבר עבירה. פי' אע"ג דאמרי' שלוחו של אדם כמותו וכל מה שעשה השליח כאילו שולחו עשאו הני מילי בזולתי דבר עבירה אבל בדבר עבירה השליח חייב ולא השולחו וכיון שהחצר שליח בעלה הוא והוא שנמצאת הגניבה בה אמאי מיחייב בעלה שהוא השולח. ופריק רבינא אליבא דריש לקיש היכא אמרי' השולח פטור היכא דהשליח בר חיובא הוא אבל חצר דלאו בת חיובא היא מיחייב שולחה והוא בעל החצר. ואקשי' אי הכי האומר לעבד ולאשת איש צאו וגנבו דלאו בני חיובא נינהו כדתנן בפ' החובל לחבירו העבד והאשה פגיעתן רעה החובל בהן חייב הן שחבלו באחרים פטורין הכי נמי דמיחייב שולחן. ופרקי' הני נמי בני חיובא נינהו דתנן נתגרשה האשה ונשתחרר העבד חייבין לשלם. בא רב סמא ופירק פירוק אחר ואמר כי אמרי' אין שליח לדבר עבירה כל היכא דאי בעי השליח עביד אי בעי לא עביד אבל חצר דעל כורחה עבדה מיחייב שולחה. מאי איכא בין רבינא לרב סמא איכא בינייהו כהן שאמר לישראל לך קדש לי אשה גרושה או איש שאמר לאשה אקיף לי ראשו של קטן לרבינא כיון דהני לאו בני חיובא נינהו דאין ישראל מוזהר על הגרושה ולא אשה בהקפת הראש מיחייב שולחה. לרב סמא כיון דאי בעו עבדי אי בעו לא עבדי לא מיחייב שולחם. ומתמהינן מי איכא מאן דאמר חצר לאו משום ידה איתרבי והתניא וכתב לה ספר כריתות ונתן בידה. בידה אין לי אלא בידה ממש גגה חצירה וקרפיפה מנין שהנותן גט בהן כנותנו בידה הוא ת"ל ונתן מכל מקום. ואמרי' לענין גט כ"ע לא פליגי דחצר משום ידה איתרבי דהא קרא בהדיא כתיב.

## מסורת הש"ס

א) מהרש"ל כהנא, ב) [גיטין עז:], ג) בבא קמא סד:, לקמן יא:, גיטין עז., ד) [קדושין מב: וש"נ], ה) בבא קמא פז., ו) [גיטין עז.].

## הגהות הגר"א

[א] בעלמא. נ"ב גי' הרי"ף בשדה דעלמא:

## גליון הש"ס

גמ' רב סמא בר רקתא קמי' דרבינא משמי' דר' חייא בריה דר' אויא אמר. כ"ה בר"ן: תוס' ד"ה ר"י וכו' אלמא שייך קנין ד' אמות בגט. לא זכיתי להבין דאמן ילפי' רק דאמר הוי כיד. אבל מה נקרא חצר לא שייך למילף דמה שהקנו לו חכמים הוי חצירו ובגט הקנו לה ק' אמה ובממון הקנו לה רק ד' אמות ולע"ג:

## ליקוטי רש"י

בסמטא. קרן זוית הסמוכה לרה"ר ובני אדם העושין סחורה זה עם זה בשוק ורוצים לדבר דבריהם בנחת וישוב הדעת מסתלקין שם [כתובות פד:]. וסימטא אית דאמר שביל של יחידים ואני שמעתי כניסה בולטת מרה"ר ויש רשות לבני אדם להעמיד שם חפצים שלהם כחצר השותפים דאינו עשוי להילוך בני רשות הרבים [רשב"ם ב"ב פד:]. צידי רשות הרבים. סמוך לבתים שנותנין להלן מן הבתים אבנים ומכשולין להרחיק מיכון העגלות ומאותן חיפופי ולפנים קרי לידי רה"ר [כתובות לא:]. סמוך לכתלים שאין דרך בני אדם לעבור שם ולהתחכך בכותלים [שם פו:]. אין לי. שיתחייב כפל. אלא. בזמן שקנאה בידו [לקמן נו:]. גגו חצרו וקרפיפו מנין. שאם נכנסה שם ונעל בפניה לגנבה מנין שקנאתה לו חצרו ומתחייב כפל [שם]. קרפיפו. היקף גדול חוץ לעיר להכניס שם עצים לאוצר [עירובין יח.]. אין שליח. חשוב שליח לדבר עבירה שיתחייב שולחו אלא הרי הוא כעושה מאליו [קידושין מב:]. וסברא הוא דאמרי' ליה דברי הרב ודברי התלמיד דברי מי שומעין [ב"ק נא.]. נתגרשה האשה וכו'. וקנו נכסים. חייבין לשלם. אלא שאין להם מה לשלם שנכסי מלוג של אשה משועבדים לבעל לפירות ולירושה [ב"ק פז.]. ת"ל ונתן מ"מ. ודרשי' [illegible] ונתן [illegible] דכתב רחמנא [illegible] לעתשתמרת לדעתה כו' [גיטין עז.].

מתניתין מני רבנן היא אלא אי אמרת בעשיר ועני מחלוקת אבל מעני לעני דברי הכל זכה לו הא מני לא רבנן ולא ר' אליעזר אמר ליה מתני' דאמר תחילה הכי נמי מסתברא דקתני סיפא אם משנתנה לו אמר אני זכיתי בה תחילה לא אמר כלום תחילה בסיפא למה לי פשיטא אע"ג דלא אמר תחילה תחילה קאמר אלא לאו הא קמ"ל רישא דאמר תחילה ואידך תנא סיפא לגלויי (א) רישא סיפא דאמר תחילה רישא דלא אמר תחילה רב נחמן ורב חסדא דאמרי תרוייהו א) המגביה מציאה לחבירו לא קנה חבירו מאי טעמא הוי תופס לבעל חוב במקום שחב לאחרים ב) א והתופס לבעל חוב במקום שחב לאחרים לא קנה איתיביה רבא לרב נחמן ג) ב מציאת פועל לעצמו במה דברים אמורים בזמן שאמר לו בעל הבית נכש עמי היום עדור עמי היום אבל אמר לו עשה עמי מלאכה היום מציאתו של בעל הבית הוא א"ל שאני פועל דידו כיד בעל הבית הוא ד) והאמר רב ג פועל יכול לחזור בו אפי' בחצי היום אמר ליה כל כמה דלא הדר ביה כיד בעל הבית הוא כי הדר ביה ד טעמא אחרינא הוא דכתיב א) כי לי בני ישראל עבדים ה) עבדי הם ולא עבדים לעבדים אמר ר' חייא בר אבא אמר ר' יוחנן ו) המגביה מציאה לחבירו קנה חבירו ואם תאמר משנתינו ה דאמר תנה לי ולא אמר זכה לי:

מתני' ו ראה את המציאה ונפל עליה ובא אחר והחזיק בה זה שהחזיק בה זכה בה:

גמ' אמר ריש לקיש משום אבא ז) כהן ברדלא ז ארבע אמות של אדם קונות לו בכל מקום ח) [מאי טעמא] תקינו רבנן דלא (ב) אתי לאנצויי אמר אביי מותיב ר' חייא בר יוסף פיאה אמר רבא מותיב ר' יעקב בר אידי נזיקין אמר אביי מותיב ר' חייא בר יוסף פיאה ט) ח נטל מקצת פיאה וזרק על השאר אין לו בה כלום נפל לו עליה פרס טליתו עליה מעבירין אותו הימנה וכן בעומר שכחה ואי אמרת ארבע אמות של אדם קונות לו בכל מקום נקנו ליה ארבע אמות דידיה הכא במאי עסקינן דלא אמר אקני ואי תקון רבנן כי לא אמר מאי הוי ° כיון דנפל גלי דעתיה דבנפילה ניחא ליה דנקני בארבע אמות לא ניחא ליה דנקני

רב

## רש"י

מתני' רבנן היא. ואשמועינן רישא דהיכא דזכי ביה איהו אמרינן מגו וסיפא אשמועינן דהיכא דלא זכי ביה איהו מגו דאי בעי זכי לא אמרי': הא. מתני' דהכא מני: דאמר תחילה. האי אני זכיתי בה דקאמר תחילה קאמר ליה מתחילה הגבהתיה לצורכי ולא לצרכך ולעולם המגביה מציאה לחבירו קנה חבירו דומיא דמעני לעני: הכי נמי מסתברא. דזכיתי תחילה משעת הגבהה קאמר מתני': מדקתני סיפא כו'. ואי תחילה דסיפא לאו משעת הגבהה קאמר אלא אני זכיתי תחילה קודם שנתתיה לך נתכוונתי לזכות בה: למה לי. למיתנא בה תחילה פשיטא דאפי' לא אמר תחילה בפירוש מסתמא תחילה קאמר דמי מצי למימר אני זוכה בה עכשיו והלא אינה בידו: אלא לאו הא קמ"ל. דרישא דמתני' דקתני זכה בה בדאמר תחילה ואשמועינן סיפא דאם משנתנה לו טען לו אותה טענה ואמר אני הגבהתיה מתחילה לצורכי לא אמר כלום דגלי דעתיה כשנתנה לו דאדעתיה דהאי אגבהה: ואידך. רב נחמן אמר לך דתנא סיפא תחילה: לגלויי רישא. למימר דוקא קתני מדסיפא תחילה קתני ורישא לא תנא דוקא הוא: סיפא. דלא אפשר בלא תחילה אמר אני זכיתי תחילה קודם שנתתיה לך לא אמר כלום דגלי דעתיה כשנתנה לו דאדעתא דהאי אגבהה ורישא דלא אמר תחילה ואפ"ה זכה בה: הוי תופס לבעל חוב במקום שחב לאחרים. כאדם הבא מאליו ותופס ממון חבירו בשביל חוב שיש לאחר עליו ובא לקדם עד שלא יתפסנו בעל חוב אחר ונמצא תופס זה חב בתפיסתו זאת את הנושים האחרים: חב לאחרים. מפסיד את האחרים כמו אין חבין לאדם (כתובות דף יא.): לא קנה. כדאמר בכתובות דלאו כל כמיניה להיות קופץ מאליו וחב לאלו מאחר שלא עשאו אותו הנושה שליח לתפוס: נכש עמי היום. דלא נשכר עמו אלא לניכוש ועידור וכשהגביה המציאה אין זו ממלאכת בעל הבית וקנאה פועל והוא ינכה לו משכרו שכר פעולת ניכוש ועידור כל שעת הגבהה: אמר לו עשה עמי מלאכה היום. כל מלאכה שהוא עושה מלאכת בעל הבית היא וקנה בעל הבית אלמא המגביה מציאה לחבירו קנה חבירו: כי הדר ביה טעמא אחרינא הוא. הא דאמר דכי הדר ביה הרשות בידו לאו משום דעד השתא לאו כיד בעל הבית הוא אלא טעמא אחרינא הוא שאינו שלו כעבד שאם בא לעזוב לו שכרו מכאן ואילך ולחזור בו יחזור בו: ואם תאמר משנתינו. דקתני אני זכיתי בה זכה בה ומשמע לן אני זוכה בה עכשיו זכה בה ואע"פ שהגביה לצורך חבירו היינו טעמא משום דקתני ואמר לחבירו תנה לי ולא אמר זכה אתה לי בהגבהתך נמצא שלא עשאו שליח להקנות בהגבהתו עד שעת נתינה והרי קודם נתינה הדר בו זה משליחותו: קונות לו. אם יש סביבותיו דבר הפקר אין אחר רשאי לתופסו: אמר אביי מותיב ר' חייא. עלה תיובתא ממתני' דמסכת פיאה: ואמר רבא מותיב ר' יעקב. עלה ממתני' דסדר נזיקין: נטל. אחד מן העניים: מקצת פיאה. שליקט כבר: וזרק (לה) על השאר. כדי לקנות: ליקנו ליה. גבי נפל לו עליה ארבע אמות דתקון ליה רבנן: בנפילה ניחא ליה דנקני. לא נתכוין לקנות בתורת תקנת חכמים כסבור שנפילתו יפה לו:

## תוספות

רב נחמן ורב חסדא כו'. תימה דבשלהי משילין (ביצה דף לט. ושם: ד"ה הכא) אמר מילא מים ונתן לחבירו רב ששת אמר כרגלי הממלא ור"נ אמר כרגלי מי שנתמלאו לו ומסיק דבמגביה מציאה לחבירו פליגי דמר סבר קנה ומר סבר לא קנה ומשמע דלרב נחמן קנה חבירו ולכך הוי כרגלי מי שנתמלאו לו ורש"י גרס התם מ"ס קני ומר סבר לא קני ול"ג חבירו וכולהו סברי דלא קני חבירו אלא רב נחמן סבר דמגביה נמי לא קני ולכך כשלקח חבירו ממנו קנאו י) [מן ההפקר שמתכוין לקנות אבל המגביה לא הגביה לקנות] ורב ששת סבר דקנה הממלא דכיון דלא קנה חבירו הוא קנה ולכך הוי כרגליו ור"ת פי' דהתם רב נחמן מודה דקנה חבירו דאינו חב לאחרים שיש הרבה מים בבור ועוד אומר ר"ת דשפיר גרסינן חבירו וסבר ר"נ לא קנה חבירו כי הכא וגם הממלא לא קנה ולכך כשנתנם לו קנאם והוי כרגליו ורב ששת סבר קני חבירו מטעם מגו דזכי לנפשיה וכיון דלא קנה חבירו אלא מטעם דזכי לנפשיה ואי הוה זכי לנפשיה הוי כרגליו והשתא נמי דזכי לחבריה הוי כרגליו ולא עדיף מיניה לענין תחומין והוי כאילו זכי לנפשיה:

תופס לבע"ח במקום שחב לאחרים לא קני. מה שפרש"י משום דלא עשאו שליח אין נראה דבפ' הכותב (כתובות דף פד: ושם ד"ה אף) משמע גבי עובדא דיימר בר חשו דתופס לבע"ח במקום שחב לאחרים לא קני אפילו עשאו שליח:

איתיביה רבא לרב נחמן. אע"ג דלעיל (ד' ח.) דחי רבא דיוקיה דרמי בר חמא משמע דסבר לא קנה חבירו שמא קבלה הכא מר"נ:

יכול לחזור בו אפי' בחצי היום. וא"ת ומאי קמ"ל והלא בפרק האומנין (לקמן דף עז.) לא פליגי רבי דוסא ורבנן אלא דר' דוסא סבר דיד פועל על התחתונה ורבנן סברי דידו על העליונה אבל לכולהו יכול לחזור בו וי"ל דקמ"ל דיכול לחזור בו וידו על העליונה כרבנן אפילו אם נתייקרו פועלים בחצי היום לאחר שחזר בו לא יפחתו לו מחצי שכרו ולכך מייתי מילתיה דרב דכיון דידו על העליונה א"כ אין ידו כיד בעל הבית וכן מוכיח בפרק האומנין (שם) דסובר כרבנן בשכיר יום ולא בקבלנות:

כי לי בני ישראל עבדים. [א] נ"ל דמ"מ מותר אדם להשכיר עצמו דדוקא עבד עברי שאינו יכול לחזור בו ואינו יוצא קודם זמנו אלא בשטר שחרור עובר משום עבדי הם:

א"ר יוחנן המגביה מציאה לחבירו קנה חבירו. ואע"ג דאית ליה לרבי יוחנן בפרק הכותב (כתובות דף פד: ושם ד"ה ואמר) ובפ"ק דגיטין (דף יא: ושם ד"ה התופס) תופס לבע"ח לא קני היינו דוקא היכא דלא שייך מגו דזכי לנפשיה דאין הלוה חייב כלום לתופס אבל במציאה דאיכא מגו קנה:

ולא אמר זכי לי. וא"ת דבפ"ק דגיטין (שם) קאמר ר' יוחנן כל האומר תנו כאומר זכו וי"ל דשאני התם דדעת אחרת מקנה אותו:

ארבע אמות קונות לו בכל מקום. וא"ת באלו נערות (כתובות דף לא: ושם ד"ה אי) דאמר גבי גונב כיס בשבת היה מגרר ויוצא פטור דאיסור שבת ואיסור גניבה באין כאחד וקאמר אי דאפקיה לרה"ר איסור שבת איכא איסור גניבה ליכא ואמאי הא ארבע אמות קונות לו וי"ל דבגניבה לא תקינו רבנן דקני אלא במציאה דלא ליתי לאנצויי ובגט משום עיגונא ולרב ששת דאמר בסמוך דברה"ר לא תקינו ארבע אמות אתי שפיר:

מעבירין אותו הימנה. [ב] אפי' רשע לא מיקרי ואע"ג דעני המהפך בחררה ובא אחר ונטלו נקרא רשע (קדושין דף נט. ושם ד"ה עני) היינו משום דאפשר ליה למיטרח ולמיזבן ארעא אחריתי אבל במציאה או בהפקר דליכא למימר הכי אפילו רשע לא מיקרי [וע"ע תוספות בבא בתרא דף כא: ד"ה מרחיקין]:

רבי

## עין משפט נר מצוה

עד א מיי' פ"כ מהל' מלוה ולוה הל' ב סמג עשין צד טוש"ע ח"מ סי' קה סעיף א:

עה ב מיי' פ"ט מהל' שכירות הלכה יא ופי"ז מהל' גזילה ואבידה הל' יג סמג עשין עד טוש"ע ח"מ סי' ער סעיף ג ואפי' אמר לו עשה עמי מלאכה היום וע"ש:

עו ג ד מיי' פ"ט מהל' שכירות הל' ד סמג עשין פט טוש"ע ח"מ סי' שלג סעיף ג:

עז ה מיי' פי"ז מהלכות גזילה ואבידה הל' ב סמג עשין עד טוש"ע ח"מ סי' רסט סעיף ו:

עח ו מיי' שם הלכה א סמג שם טוש"ע שם סי' רסח סעיף א:

עט ז מיי' שם הל' ח ופ"ד מהל' זכייה ומתנה הל' ט סמג עשין עב טוש"ע ח"מ סי' רסח סעיף ב וסי' רמג סעיף כב:

פ ח מיי' פ"ב מהלכות מתנות עניים הל' יח סמג לאוין רפד:

## רבינו חננאל

מתני' דקתני זכה בה לעצמו המגביהה רבנן היא דאמרי לא קנה מי שליקטה לו אלא יתננה לעני הנמצא ראשון אלא אי אמרת מחלוקת מעשיר לעני אבל עני לעני דברי הכל זכה בה מי שנתלקטה לו מתני' מני לא רבנן ולא ר' אליעזר. ופרקי' דאמר תחילה פי' קודם שיגביהנה אמר לעצמי אני מגביהה כדי שאזכה בה אני. ודייקינן מדקתני סיפא אם משנתנה לו אמר אני זכיתי בה תחילה לא אמר כלום. פי' רישא וסיפא דאמר תחלה מיהו רישא פירש מקודם שיגביהנה אמר כי לעצמי אני מגביהה כדי שאזכה בה אני. וסיפא הגביה סתם ונתנה לו וטוען עכשיו כי אני אמרתי מתחילה כי לעצמי אני מגביהה לא אמר כלום. ואידך תנא סיפא תחילה לגלויי רישא [דלא אמר תחילה] רב נחמן ורב חסדא דאמרי תרויהו המגביה מציאה לחבירו לא קנה חבירו מאי טעמא הוי תופס לבעל חוב במקום שחב לאחרים דלא קנה. ומותיב רבא לרב נחמן מציאת פועל לעצמו בד"א בזמן שאמר לו נכש עמי היום. אבל אמר לו עשה עמי מלאכה היום מציאתו לבעל הבית. ופריק רב נחמן שאני פועל דכל זמן דלא הדר ביה כיד בעה"ב דמי. א) והדר ביה רב נחמן דגרסי' בסוף מס' יו"ט איתמר מילא מים ונתן לחבירו [כו'] ר' נחמן [אמר] כרגלי מי שנתמלאו לו. ופריש בה רב נחמן סבר המגביה מציאה לחבירו קנה חבירו. ורב ששת אמר לא קנה חבירו. אמר רב חייא בר אבא א"ר יוחנן המגביה מציאה לחבירו קנה חבירו והוא דאמר ליה זכה לי. ואם תאמר משנתנו דלא אמר ליה זכה לי אלא תנה לי וקי"ל כר' יוחנן. ופי' רב פפא בהלכה דבתר הא דתניא פועל מציאתו לבעה"ב בששכרו ללקט לו מציאות היכי דמי דאקפי אגמא בכוורי וקי"ל כוותיה: מתני' ראה את המציאה ונפל עליה ובא אחר והחזיק בה זכה המחזיק בה. ואוקימנא ברה"ר דקא דחקי רבים לא תקנו ליה רבנן דליקנן ליה ד' אמות דידיה כי תקינו ליה רבנן ד' אמות בשדה דעלמא ובסימטא ובצידי רה"ר וכדומה להן דלא ליתו לאינצויי.

חשק שלמה על ר"ח א) דברי רבינו ז"ל אלו הובא גם בש"מ כאן בשם הרמב"ן ז"ל שכתב דרבינו כתב דהדר ביה ר"נ ע"ש ועי' בתוס' כאן ד"ה ר"נ.

## מסורת הש"ס

א) [כה"ג ביצה לט:], ב) כתובות פד:, גיטין יא:, ג) [לקמן יב:, קיח.], ד) בבא קמא קטז:, לקמן עז, ה) [בבא קמא קטז:, קדושין כג:], ו) לעיל ח., ז) נ"א כהנא, ח) מהרש"ל, ט) פיאה פרק ד' משנה ג, י) ס"א.

## הגהות הב"ח

(א) גמ' סיפא לגלויי ארישא: (ב) שם דלא ליתי לאנצויי:

## הגהות הגר"א

[א] תוס' ד"ה כי. נ"ל כו'. נ"ב והגמ"ר אוסר ביותר משלש (ועמ"ש רבינו בח"מ סי' שלג ס"ק י"ב): [ב] שם ד"ה מעבירין. אפי' כו'. נ"ב ורש"י בקדושין (נט ע"א) חולק:

## גליון הש"ס

גמ' כיון דנפל גלי דעתיה. עיין נדרים לד ע"ב בר"ן ד"ה אמר רבא:

## תורה אור השלם

א) כִּי לִי בְנֵי יִשְׂרָאֵל עֲבָדִים עֲבָדַי הֵם אֲשֶׁר הוֹצֵאתִי אוֹתָם מֵאֶרֶץ מִצְרָיִם אֲנִי יְיָ אֱלֹהֵיכֶם: [ויקרא כה, נה]

## ליקוטי רש"י

התופס לבעל חוב. שלא התופס מטלטלין של לוה לצורך בעל חוב [כתובות פד:]. אדם מן השוק שתופס מטלטלי בנכסי ראובן לצורך שמעון שהוא בעל חוב [גיטין יא:]. במקום שחב לאחרים. שמפסיד בע"ח אחרים בתפיסתו [כתובות שם]. במקום שחב התופס הזה בתפיסתו זאת ללוי דהו"ל נמי בע"ח דראובן ותופס זה שקדם ותפס לצורך שמעון מפסיד את לוי [גיטין שם]. לא קנה. דלאו כל כמיניה לחוב זה כדי לזכות את זה [כתובות פה.]. עשה עמי מלאכה היום וכו'. בזמן שלא פירש לו לאיזו מלאכה שכרו [לקמן יב:]. שאני פועל וכו'. דפועל לאו בכלל המגביה מציאה לחבירו הוא אלא כיד בעה"ב הוא וקנייה בעה"ב בהגבהה דפועל וכו' [לקמן קיח.]. כי לי בני ישראל עבדים. שטרי קודם [ויקרא כה, נה].

The Gemara elaborates R' Chiya bar Yosef's challenge:

**אָמַר אַבַּיֵי – Abaye said: מוֹתִיב ר׳ חִיָּיא בַּר יוֹסֵף פֵּיאָה – R' Chiya bar Yosef challenged** Reish Lakish's statement **from a Mishnah** in tractate ***Pe'ah***, which states:[23] נָטַל מִקְצָת פֵּיאָה וְזָרַק עַל הַשְּׁאָר – IF SOMEONE TOOK SOME *PE'AH* AND THREW IT OVER THE REST,[24] אֵין לוֹ בָּהּ כְּלוּם – HE DOES NOT HAVE rights IN IT AT ALL.[25] נָפַל לוֹ עָלֶיהָ – If HE FELL UPON IT, פָּרַס טַלִּיתוֹ עָלֶיהָ – or if HE SPREAD HIS CLOAK OVER IT, מַעֲבִירִין אוֹתוֹ הֵימֶנָּה – THEY MAY REMOVE HIM FROM IT.[26] וְכֵן בְּעוֹמֶר שִׁכְחָה – AND THE SAME applies WITH regard to A FORGOTTEN SHEAF.[27] וְאִי אָמְרַת אַרְבַּע אַמּוֹת שֶׁל אָדָם קוֹנוֹת לוֹ בְּכָל מָקוֹם – **Now, if you say that the four *amos* of a person acquire** an object **for him in any location,** נִקְנוּ לֵיהּ אַרְבַּע אַמּוֹת דִּידֵיהּ – then **let his four *amos* acquire** the *pe'ah* **for him!**[28] – ? –

The Gemara answers:

**הָכָא בְּמַאי עַסְקִינָן דְּלֹא אָמַר אִקְנֵי – With what** case **are we dealing here?** With a case **where he did not say, "I wish to acquire** the produce through the institution of four *amos.*"

The Gemara objects:

**וְאִי תַּקּוּן רַבָּנַן – But if the Rabbis instituted** that a person acquires an object that is within four *amos* of him, כִּי לֹא אָמַר מַאי הָוֵי – then even **when he did not say** that he wanted to acquire the *pe'ah,* **what is** lacking to effect the acquisition?[29]

The Gemara answers:

**כֵּיוָן דְּנָפַל – Since he fell** upon the produce, גַּלֵּי דַּעְתֵּיהּ דִּבְנְפִילָה נִיחָא לֵיהּ דְּנִקְנֵי – **he has revealed his intention that he wants to acquire** the *pe'ah* **through** his act of **falling** on it; בְּאַרְבַּע אַמּוֹת לֹא נִיחָא לֵיהּ דְּנִקְנֵי – but **he does not want to acquire** it **by** virtue of it being within **four *amos*** of him.[30]

NOTES

23. *Pe'ah* 4:3.

24. As mentioned above (9b note 27), the Torah (*Leviticus* 19:9-10; 23:22) commands growers in Eretz Yisrael to leave a portion of their crops called *pe'ah* (literally: corner)] for the poor to harvest for themselves. In the case of this Mishnah, a poor person reaped and collected some *pe'ah,* and then threw it over other *pe'ah* that was still attached to the ground in the mistaken] belief that such an act was a valid way of acquiring the standing *pe'ah* (*Rashi*).

25. I.e. not only does he fail to acquire the standing *pe'ah* by throwing other *pe'ah* on it, but he also loses his rights to the *pe'ah* that he had collected legitimately and then threw (*Rashba, Ritva*; cf. *Shitah Mekubetzes*).

[This loss of legally acquired *pe'ah* is a Rabbinic penalty, intended to discourage this potentially provocative behavior. For the Rabbis feared that if one poor person were to pile his collected *pe'ah* on the standing *pe'ah* that is near his competitor, the latter might become enraged and violent (ibid.).]

26. I.e. the other poor people may remove him from the produce and take it for themselves (see *Shitah Mekubetzes, Tosafos*). [Falling on the produce or spreading one's cloak over it does not effect any acquisition.]

27. *Shich'chah* (literally: forgotten) is another portion of the harvest that the Torah grants to the poor. It refers to sheaves forgotten in the field during the removal to the threshing floor (as well as to standing produce that the harvester overlooked).

28. In the second case of the Mishnah, where the person threw himself on the produce, he obviously came within four *amos* of it. Yet, the Mishnah rules that others can remove him from it. Why has he not acquired it through the Rabbinic institution that a person gains ownership of any ownerless object within four *amos* of him (*Rashi*)?

29. The standard methods of acquisition are effective even if the acquirer does not announce beforehand his intention to acquire the object through that method. Therefore, if Reish Lakish is correct in his assertion that by Rabbinic enactment a person acquires an object that is within four *amos* of him, why must the person announce that he wishes to take advantage of that enactment? He should acquire the produce as soon as he comes within four *amos* of it.

30. Since he fell on top of the produce, we can assume that he did not intend to acquire the produce by taking advantage of the Rabbinic enactment; rather, he thought that he could acquire the produce by falling upon it (*Rashi*). Thus, he is likened to one who declares, "I do not wish the Rabbinic enactment [for my benefit] to be effective for me," in which case the enactment is indeed ineffective for him (*Ran*). [See *Ran* and *Shitah Mekubetzes* for a discussion as to whether a person can forfeit his rights to a Biblical method of acquisition as well.]

## מסורת הש"ס

א) [כס"ג ביצה לט:], ב) כתובות פד., גיטין יא., ג) [לקמן יב:, קיח.], ד) בבא קמא קטז:, לקמן עז., ה) [בבא קמא קטז:, קדושין כב:], ו) לעיל ח., ז) נ"א כהנא, ח) מהרש"ל, ט) פיאה פרק ד' משנה ג, י) ס"א.

## הגהות הב"ח

(א) גמ' סיפא לגלויי ארישא: (ב) שם דלא ליתי לאנצויי:

## הגהות הגר"א

[א] תוס' ד"ה כי. נ"ל כו'. נ"ב והגמ"א אוסר ביותר משלש (ועמ"ש רבינו בח"מ סי' שלג ס"ק י"ג): [ב] שם ד"ה מעבירין. אפי' כו'. נ"ב ורש"י בקדושין (נט ע"א) חולק:

## גליון הש"ס

גמ' כיון דנפל גלי דעתיה. עיין נדרים לד ע"ב בר"ן ד"ה אמר רבא:

## תורה אור השלם

א) כִּי לִי בְנֵי יִשְׂרָאֵל עֲבָדִים עֲבָדַי הֵם אֲשֶׁר הוֹצֵאתִי אוֹתָם מֵאֶרֶץ מִצְרָיִם אֲנִי יְיָ אֱלֹהֵיכֶם: [ויקרא כה, נה]

## ליקוטי רש"י

התופס לבעל חוב. שלית התופס מטלטלין של לוה לצורך בעל חוב [כתובות פד:]. אדם מן השוק שתופס מטלטלי בנכסי ראובן לצורך שמעון שהוא בעל חוב [גיטין יא:]. במקום שחב לאחרים. שמפסיד בע"ח אחרים בתפיסתו [כתובות שם]. במקום שחב התופס הזה בתפיסתו זאת ללוי דהו"ל נמי בע"ח דראובן ותופס זה שקדם ותפס לצורך שמעון מפסיד את לוי [גיטין שם]. לא קנה. דלאו כל כמיניה לחוב זה כדי לזכות את זה [כתובות פד.]. עשה עמי מלאכה היום וכו'. [לקמן יב:]. שאני פועל וכו'. דפועל לאו בכלל המגביה לחבירו הוא אלא כיד בעה"ב הוא וקנייה בעה"ב בהגבהה דפועל [לקמן קיח.]. כי לי בני ישראל עבדים. שטרי קודם [ויקרא כה, נה].

## גמרא

מתניתין מני רבנן היא אלא אי אמרת בעשיר ועני מחלוקת אבל מעני לעני דברי הכל זכה לו הא מני לא רבנן ולא ר' אליעזר אמר ליה מתני' דאמר תחילה הכי נמי מסתברא דקתני סיפא אם משנתנה לו אמר אני זכיתי בה תחילה לא אמר כלום תחילה בסיפא למה לי פשיטא אע"ג דלא אמר תחילה תחילה קאמר אלא לאו הא קמ"ל רישא דאמר תחילה ואידך תנא סיפא לגלויי (א) רישא סיפא דאמר תחילה רישא דלא אמר תחילה רב נחמן ורב חסדא דאמרי תרוייהו המגביה מציאה לחבירו לא קנה חבירו מאי טעמא הוי תופס לבעל חוב במקום שחב לאחרים ג) והתופס לבעל חוב במקום שחב לאחרים לא קנה איתיביה רבא לרב נחמן ג) מציאת פועל לעצמו במה דברים אמורים בזמן שאמר לו בעל הבית נכש עמי היום עדור עמי היום אבל אמר לו עשה עמי מלאכה היום מציאתו של בעל הבית הוא א"ל שאני פועל דידו כיד בעל הבית הוא ד) והאמר רב פועל יכול לחזור בו אפי' בחצי היום אמר ליה כל כמה דלא הדר ביה כיד בעל הבית הוא כי הדר ביה טעמא אחרינא הוא דכתיב א) כי לי בני ישראל עבדים ה) עבדי הם ולא עבדים לעבדים אמר ר' חייא בר אבא אמר ר' יוחנן ו) המגביה מציאה לחבירו קנה חבירו ואם תאמר משנתינו דאמר תנה לי ולא אמר זכה לי:

**מתני'** ראה את המציאה ונפל עליה ובא אחר והחזיק בה זה שהחזיק בה זכה בה:

**גמ'** אמר ריש לקיש משום אבא ז) כהן ברדלא ארבע אמות של אדם קונות לו בכל מקום ח) [מאי טעמא] תקינו רבנן דלא (ב) אתי לאנצויי אמר אביי מותיב ר' חייא בר יוסף פיאה אמר רבא מותיב ר' יעקב בר אידי נזיקין אמר אביי מותיב ר' חייא בר יוסף פיאה ט) נטל מקצת פיאה וזרק על השאר אין לו בה כלום נפל לו עליה פרס טליתו עליה מעבירין אותו הימנה וכן בעומר שכחה ואי אמרת ארבע אמות של אדם קונות לו בכל מקום נקנו ליה ארבע אמות דידיה הכא במאי עסקינן דלא אמר אקני ואי תקון רבנן כי לא אמר מאי הוי כיון דנפל גלי דעתיה דבנפילה ניחא ליה דנקני בארבע אמות לא ניחא ליה דנקני

רב

## רש"י

מתני' רבנן היא. ואשמועינן רישא דהיכא דזכי ביה איהו אמרינן מגו וסיפא אשמועינן דהיכא דלא זכי ביה איהו מגו דאי בעי זכי לא אמרי': הא. מתני' דהכא מני: דאמר תחילה. האי אני זכיתי בה דקאמר תחילה קאמר ליה מתחילה הגבהתיה לצורכי ולא לצרכך ולעולם המגביה מציאה לחבירו קנה חבירו דומיא דמעני לעני: הכי נמי מסתברא. דזכיתי תחילה משעת הגבהה קאמר מתני': מדקתני סיפא כו'. ואי תחילה דסיפא לאו משעת הגבהה קאמר אלא אני זכיתי תחילה קודם שנתתיה לך נתכוונתי לזכות בה: למה לי. למיתנא בה תחילה פשיטא דאפי' לא אמר תחילה בפירוש מסתמא תחילה קאמר דמי מצי למימר אני זוכה בה עכשיו והלא אינה בידו: אלא לאו הא קמ"ל. דרישא דמתני' דקתני זכה בה בדאמר תחילה ואשמועינן סיפא דאם משנתנה לו טען לו אותה טענה ואמר אני הגבהתיה מתחילה לצורכי לא אמר כלום דגלי דעתיה כשנתנה לו דאדעתיה דהאי אגבהה: ואידך. רב נחמן אמר לך דתנא סיפא תחילה: לגלויי רישא. למימר דוקא קתני מדסיפא תחילה קתני ורישא לא תנא דוקא הוא: סיפא. דלא אפשר בלא תחילה אמר אני זכיתי תחילה קודם שנתתיה לך לא אמר כלום דגלי דעתיה כשנתנה לו דאדעתא דהאי אגבהה ורישא דלא אמר תחילה ואפ"ה זכה בה: הוי תופס לבעל חוב במקום שחב לאחרים. כאדם הבא מאליו ותופס ממון חבירו בשביל חוב שיש לאחר עליו ובא לקדם עד שלא יתפסנו בעל חוב אחר ונמצא תופס זה חב בתפיסתו זאת את הנושים האחרים: חב לאחרים. מפסיד את האחרים כמו אין חבין לאדם (כתובות דף יא.): לא קנה. כדאמר בכתובות דלאו כל כמיניה להיות קופץ מאליו וחב לאלו מאחר שלא עשאו אותו הנושה שליח לתפוס: נכש עמי היום. דלא נשכר עמו אלא לניכוש ועידור וכשהגביה המציאה אין זו ממלאכת בעל הבית וקנאה פועל והוא ינכה לו משכרו שכר פעולת ניכוש ועידור כל שעת הגבהה: אמר לו עשה עמי מלאכה היום. כל מלאכה שהוא עושה מלאכת בעל הבית היא וקנה בעל הבית אלמא המגביה מציאה לחבירו קנה חבירו: כי הדר ביה טעמא אחרינא הוא. הא דאמר דכי הדר ביה הרשות בידו לאו משום דעד השתא לאו כיד בעל הבית הוא אלא טעמא אחרינא הוא שאינו שלו כעבד שאם בא לעזוב לו שכרו מכאן ואילך ולחזור בו יחזור בו: ואם תאמר משנתינו. דקתני אני זכיתי בה זכה בה ומשמע לן אני זוכה בה עכשיו זכה בה ואע"פ שהגביה לצורך חבירו היינו טעמא משום דקתני ואמר לחבירו תנה לי ולא אמר זכה אתה לי בהגבהתך נמצא שלא עשאו שליח להקנות בהגבהתה עד שעת נתינה והרי קודם נתינה הדר בו זה משליחותו: קונות לו. אם יש סביבותיו דבר הפקר אין אחר רשאי לתופסו: אמר אביי מותיב ר' חייא. עלה תיובתא ממתני' דמסכת פיאה: ואמר רבא מותיב ר' יעקב. עלה ממתני' דסדר נזיקין: נטל. אחד מן העניים: מקצת פיאה. שליקט כבר: וזרק (לה) על השאר. כדי לקנות: ליקנו ליה. גבי נפל לו עליה ארבע אמות דתקון ליה רבנן: בנפילה ניחא ליה דנקני. לא נתכוין לקנות בתורת תקנת חכמים כסבור שנפילתו יפה לו:

ה"ג

## תוספות

**רב** נחמן ורב חסדא כו'. תימה דבשלהי משילין (ביצה דף לט. ושם: ד"ה הכא) אמר מילא מיא ונתן לחבירו רב ששת אמר כרגלי הממלא ור"נ אמר כרגלי מי שנתמלאו לו ומסיק דבמגביה מציאה לחבירו פליגי דמר סבר קנה ומר סבר לא קנה ומשמע דלרב נחמן קנה חבירו ולכך הוי כרגלי מי שנתמלאו לו ורש"י גרס התם מ"ס קני ומר סבר לא קני ול"ג חבירו וכולהו סברי דלא קני חבירו אלא רב נחמן סבר דמגביה נמי לא קני ולכך כשלקח חבירו ממנו קנאו י) [מן ההפקר שמתכוין לקנות אבל המגביה לא הגביה לקנות] ורב ששת סבר דקנה הממלא דכיון דלא קנה חבירו הוא קנה ולכך הוי כרגליו ור"ת פי' דהתם רב נחמן מודה דקנה חבירו דאינו חב לאחרים שיש הרבה מים בבור ועוד אומר ר"ת דשפיר גרסינן חבירו וסבר ר"נ לא קנה חבירו כי הכא וגם הממלא לא קנה ולכך כשנתנם לו קנאם והוי כרגליו ורב ששת סבר קני חבירו מטעם מגו דזכי לנפשיה וכיון דלא קנה חבירו אלא מטעם דזכי לנפשיה ואי הוה זכי לנפשיה הוי כרגליו והשתא נמי דזכי לחבריה הוי כרגליו ולא עדיף מיניה לענין תחומין והוי כאילו זכי לנפשיה:

**תופס** לבע"ח במקום שחב לאחרים לא קני. מה שפרש"י משום דלא עשאו שליח אין נראה דבפ' הכותב (כתובות דף פד: ושם ד"ה את) משמע גבי עובדא דיימר בר חשו דתופס לבע"ח במקום שחב לאחרים לא קני אפילו עשאו שליח:

**איתיביה** רבא לרב נחמן. אע"ג דלעיל (ד' ח.) דחי רבא דיוקיה דרמי בר חמא משמע דסבר לא קנה חבירו שמא קבלה הכא מר"נ:

**יכול** לחזור בו אפי' בחצי היום. וא"ת ומאי קמ"ל והלא בפרק האומנין (לקמן דף עז.) לא פליגי רבי דוסא ורבנן אלא דר' דוסא סבר דיד פועל על התחתונה ורבנן סברי דידו על העליונה אבל לכולהו יכול לחזור בו וי"ל דקמ"ל דיכול לחזור בו וידו על העליונה כרבנן אפילו אם נתייקרו פועלים בחצי היום לאחר שחזר בו לא יפחתו לו מחצי שכרו ולכך מייתי מילתיה דרב דכיון דידו על העליונה א"כ אין ידו כיד בעל הבית וכן מוכיח בפרק האומנין (שם) דסובר כרבנן בשכיר יום ולא בקבלנות:

**כי** לי בני ישראל עבדים. [א] נ"ל דמ"מ מותר אדם להשכיר עצמו דדוקא עבד עברי שאינו יכול לחזור בו ואינו יוצא קודם זמנו אלא בשטר שחרור עובר משום עבדי הם:

**א"ר** יוחנן המגביה מציאה לחבירו קנה חבירו. ואע"ג דאית ליה לרבי יוחנן בפרק הכותב (כתובות דף פד: ושם ד"ה ואמר) ובפ"ק דגיטין (דף יא: ושם ד"ה התופס) תופס לבע"ח לא קני היינו דוקא היכא דלא שייך מגו דזכי לנפשיה דאין הלוה חייב כלום לתופס אבל במציאה דאיכא מגו קנה:

**ולא** אמר זכי לי. וא"ת דבפ"ק דגיטין (שם) קאמר ר' יוחנן כל האומר תנו כאומר זכו וי"ל דשאני התם דדעת אחרת מקנה אותו:

**ארבע** אמות קונות לו בכל מקום. וא"ת באלו נערות (כתובות דף לא: ושם ד"ה אי) דאמר גבי גונב כיס בשבת היה מגרר ויוצא פטור דאיסור שבת ואיסור גניבה באין כאחד וקאמר אי דאפקיה לרה"ר איסור שבת איכא איסור גניבה ליכא ואמאי הא ארבע אמות קונות לו וי"ל דבגניבה לא תקינו רבנן דקני אלא במציאה דלא ליתי לאנצויי ובגט משום עיגונא ולרב ששת דאמר בסמוך דברה"ר לא תקינו ארבע אמות אתי שפיר:

**מעבירין** אותו הימנה. [ב] אפי' רשע לא מיקרי ואע"ג דעני המהפך בחררה ובא אחר ונטלו נקרא רשע (קדושין דף נט. ושם ד"ה עני) היינו משום דאפשר ליה למיטרח ולמיזבן ארעא אחריתי אבל במציאה או בהפקר דליכא למימר הכי אפילו רשע לא מיקרי [וע"ע תוספות בבא בתרא דף כא: ד"ה מרחיקין]:

רבי

## עין משפט נר מצוה

עד א מיי' פ"כ מהל' מלוה ולוה הל' ב סמג עשין צד טוש"ע ח"מ סי' קה סעיף א:

עה ב מיי' פ"ט מהל' שכירות הלכה יא ופי"ז מהל' גזילה ואבידה הל' יג סמג עשין עד טוש"ע ח"מ סי' ער סעיף ג ואפי' אמר לו עשה עמי מלאכה היום וע"ש:

עו ג ד מיי' פ"ט מהל' שכירות הל' ד סמג עשין פט טוש"ע ח"מ סי' שלג סעיף ג:

עז ה מיי' פי"ז מהלכות גזילה ואבידה הל' ג סמג עשין עד טוש"ע ח"מ סי' רסט סעיף ו:

עח ו מיי' שם הלכה א סמג שם טוש"ע שם סי' רסא סעיף א:

עט ז מיי' שם הל' ח ופ"ד מהל' זכייה ומתנה הל' ט סמג עשין עב טוש"ע ח"מ סי' רסח סעיף ב וסי' רמג סעיף כב:

פ ח מיי' פ"ב מהלכות מתנות עניים הל' יח סמג לאוין רפד:

## רבינו חננאל

מתני' דקתני זכה בה לעצמו המגביהה רבנן היא דאמרי לא קנה מי שליקטה לו אלא יתננה לעני הנמצא ראשון אלא אי אמרת מחלוקת מעשיר לעני אבל עני לעני דברי הכל זכה בה מי שנתלקטה לו מתני' מני לא רבנן ולא ר' אליעזר. ופרקי' דאמר תחילה פי' קודם שיגביהנה אמר לעצמי אני מגביהה כדי שאזכה בה אני. ודייקינן מדקתני סיפא אם משנתנה לו אמר אני זכיתי בה תחלה לא אמר כלום. פי' רישא וסיפא דאמר תחלה מיהו רישא פירש מקודם שיגביהנה אמר כי לעצמי אני מגביהה כדי שאזכה בה אני. וסיפא הגביה סתם ונתנה לו וטוען עכשיו כי אני אמרתי מתחילה כי לעצמי אני מגביהה לא אמר כלום. ואידך תנא סיפא תחילה לגלויי רישא [דלא אמר תחילה] רב נחמן ורב חסדא דאמרי תרוייהו המגביה מציאה לחבירו לא קנה חבירו מאי טעמא הוי תופס לבעל חוב במקום שחב לאחרים דלא קנה. ומותיב רבא לרב נחמן מציאת פועל לעצמו בד"א בזמן שאמר לו נכש עמי היום. אבל אמר לו עשה עמי מלאכה היום מציאתו לבעל הבית. ופריק רב נחמן שאני פועל דכל זמן דלא הדר ביה כיד בעה"ב דמי. א) והדר ביה רב נחמן דגרסי' בסוף מס' יו"ט איתמר מילא מים ונתן לחבירו [כו'] ר' נחמן [אמר] כרגלי מי שנתמלאו לו. ופריש בה רב נחמן סבר המגביה מציאה לחבירו קנה חבירו. ורב ששת אמר לא קנה חבירו. אמר רב חייא בר אבא א"ר יוחנן המגביה מציאה לחבירו קנה חבירו והוא דאמר ליה זכה לי. ואם תאמר משנתנו דלא אמר ליה זכה לי אלא תנה לי וקי"ל כר' יוחנן. ופי' רב פפא בהלכה דבתר הא דתניא פועל מציאתו לבעה"ב בששכרו ללקט לו מציאות היכי דמי דאקפי אגמא בכוורי וקי"ל כוותיה: **מתני'** ראה את המציאה ונפל עליה ובא אחר והחזיק בה זכה המחזיק בה. ואוקימנא ברה"ר דקא דחקי רבים לא תקינו ליה רבנן דליקנון ליה ד' אמות דידיה כי תקינו ליה רבנן ד' אמות בשדה דעלמא ובסימטא ובצידי רה"ר וכדומה להן דלא ליתו לאינצויי.

חשק שלמה על ר"ח א) דברי רבינו ז"ל אלו הובא גם בש"מ כאן בשם הרמב"ן ז"ל שכתב דרבינו כתב דהדר ביה ר"נ ע"ש ועי' בתוס' כאן ד"ה ר"נ.

Rava counters:

**וְהָאָמַר ר — But surely Rav said:** **פּוֹעֵל יָכוֹל לַחֲזוֹר בּוֹ אֲפִילּוּ בַּחֲצִי יוֹם — A worker can withdraw** from his employment **even in** **the middle of the** working **day.**[14] How then can you contend that he is "owned" by his employer?

Rav Nachman replies:

**אָמַר לֵיהּ – [Rav Nachman] said to him:** **כָּל כַּמָּה דְּלָא הָדַר בֵּיהּ – As long as [the worker] has not withdrawn,** **כְּיַד בַּעַל הַבַּיִת הוּא – he** is "owned" by the employer, and his hand **is like the employer's hand.** **כִּי הָדַר בֵּיהּ – However, when [the worker] withdraws** from his employment, his action is valid – not because he has not been "owned" until this point, but rather **טַעֲמָא אַחֲרִינָא הוּא דִּכְתִיב – for a different reason; for it is written:**[15] **"כִּי־לִי בְנֵי־יִשְׂרָאֵל עֲבָדִים" – *For the children of Israel are slaves unto Me.*** **עֲבָדַי הֵם – In effect, God says, They are *My* slaves,** **וְלֹא עֲבָדִים לַעֲבָדִים – and not slaves to other slaves!"** No Jew can be forced to work for someone else against his will.[16]

The Gemara presents a conflicting opinion regarding acquisition of an ownerless article on behalf of someone else:

**אָמַר ר׳ חִיָּיא בַּר אַבָּא אָמַר ר׳ יוֹחָנָן – R' Chiya bar Abba said in the name of R' Yochanan:** **הַמַּגְבִּיהַּ מְצִיאָה לַחֲבֵירוֹ – If someone picks up a find on behalf of his fellow,** **קָנָה חֲבֵירוֹ – his fellow** *has* **acquired** it by that act. **וְאִם תֹּאמַר מִשְׁנָתֵינוּ – And if you will object: "What about our Mishnah?"** which seems to rule otherwise,[17] I will explain to you that our Mishnah refers to **דְּאָמַר תְּנָה לִי – where [the rider] said** to the pedestrian, **"*Give* it to me,"** **וְלֹא אָמַר זְכֵה לִי – and he did not say, "*Acquire* it for me."** The rider never instructed the pedestrian to *acquire* the find on his behalf. Rather, he instructed the pedestrian to simply lift the find from the ground and deliver it into his hand.[18]

**Mishnah** **רָאָה אֶת הַמְּצִיאָה וְנָפַל עָלֶיהָ – If someone saw a find,** i.e. an ownerless article, **and fell upon it** **וּבָא אַחֵר וְהֶחֱזִיק בָּהּ – and another came and seized it,** **זֶה שֶׁהֶחֱזִיק בָּהּ זָכָה בָהּ – the one who seized it has acquired it.**[19]

**Gemara** The Gemara cites a ruling, which will be found to be related to our Mishnah:

**אָמַר רֵישׁ לָקִישׁ מִשּׁוּם אַבָּא כֹּהֵן בַּרְדְּלָא – Reish Lakish stated in the name of Abba Kohen Bardela:** **אַרְבַּע אַמּוֹת שֶׁל אָדָם קוֹנוֹת לוֹ בְּכָל מָקוֹם – A person's four *amos* acquire** an object **for him in any location.**[20] **מַאי טַעְמָא – What is the reason?** **תַּקִּינוּ רַבָּנָן דְּלָא אָתֵי לְאִנְצוּיֵי – The Rabbis instituted** this method of acquisition **so that [people] would not come to quarrel** with one another.[21]

The Gemara introduces two objections to Reish Lakish's ruling:

**אָמַר אַבַּיֵי – Abaye said:** **מוֹתִיב ר׳ חִיָּיא בַּר יוֹסֵף פֵּיאָה – R' Chiya bar Yosef challenged** Reish Lakish's statement **from a Mishnah** in Tractate *Pe'ah.* **אָמַר רָבָא – Rava said:** **מוֹתִיב ר׳ יַעֲקֹב בַּר אִידִי נְזִיקִין – R' Yaakov bar Idi challenged** Reish Lakish's statement **from a Mishnah** in *Seder Nezikin.*[22]

NOTES

14. [He must, of course, give his employer notice of his withdrawal or at least declare before witnesses that he is henceforth no longer in the employ of his employer. Furthermore, there are regulations regarding the circumstances under which an employee is liable for any loss incurred by his employer as a result of his early withdrawal.]

15. *Leviticus* 25:55.

16. [Unless he has legally been sold into actual slavery.] An employee *is* owned by his employer for the term of his employment. A special Scriptural directive, however, grants the employee the right to withdraw from his employer's service at any time (see *Rashi* and *Ritva*).

17. I.e. you will insist (as Rav Nachman does above) that the Mishnah's omission of the word "first" in the first clause is intentional – for in the first clause, the pedestrian may keep the find even if he did *not* initially pick it up in order to acquire it for himself [see above, note 8]. Thus, you will seek to prove from this Mishnah that one cannot acquire an ownerless article on behalf of someone else, and though the pedestrian picked it up for the rider, the rider does not automatically acquire it (see *Rashba* and *Ritva*).

18. The pedestrian was asked simply to perform the mechanical task of delivering the find into the rider's hand, rather than to legally acquire the find on the rider's behalf. It is therefore assumed that the pedestrian did precisely what he was instructed to do: He picked up the find in order to *deliver* it to the rider, not to acquire it on the rider's behalf. Accordingly, until the rider actually receives the find, the pedestrian can terminate his agency and decide to keep the find for himself (see *Rashi* and *Rashba*). [But had the pedestrian indeed picked up the find in order to acquire it on behalf of the rider, it would automatically belong to the rider, and the pedestrian could not change his mind even if he has not yet delivered the find into the rider's hand.]

Though R' Yochanan rules here that one can acquire an ownerless article on behalf of someone else, he also subscribes to the principle that one cannot seize property for one creditor at the expense of other creditors (as his view is recorded in *Gittin* 11b). How are these two rulings of R' Yochanan to be reconciled?

*Tosafos* explain that R' Yochanan does not consider acquisition of an ownerless article to be in the category of "to the detriment of others," since the one performing the act of acquisition could, if he wanted to, acquire the article for *himself* [the single "since" argument mentioned in 9b]. A non-creditor, on the other hand, has no such potential to take the debtor's property for himself. [It follows, then, that one creditor can seize a debtor's property on behalf of another creditor even where this disadvantages others, since the one seizing the property could, if he wished, seize it for himself (*Rosh*).]

Other Rishonim (see *Ramban* et al.) explain that in R' Yochanan's opinion, taking an ownerless article is not considered to be at the expense of others altogether. By missing an opportunity to acquire an ownerless article, no one suffers a *loss,* only the potential of gaining a windfall. This is in contrast to the actual loss incurred by other creditors who are not able to collect assets that are actually due them.

19. Falling on an article is not a valid act of acquisition. Therefore, the first person has not gained possession of the article; rather, the second person (who is the first to perform a valid act of acquisition to the article) becomes its owner.

[As stated in the Gemara above (9a), merely seizing an article without lifting it is not a valid act of acquisition either. Thus, the Mishnah here must mean that the second person seized *and* lifted the article (see *Tur, Choshen Mishpat* 268 and *Shitah Mekubetzes*).]

20. The Rabbis instituted that a person who comes within four *amos* of an ownerless article shall have the exclusive right to acquire the article and no one else may grab it away (*Rashi*). Moreover the four *amos* surrounding the person serve as his "courtyard" [see 9b notes 11-12] through which he can acquire the ownerless article (*Ran* to *Gittin* 78a; see *Avnei Miluim* 30:5).

The Gemara below (10b) will explain what Reish Lakish meant by the phrase "in any location."

21. That is, to prevent quarrels [that would ensue from people competing for ownerless objects], the Sages enacted that a person may not encroach upon an ownerless object that is already within four *amos* of another person (*Beis Aharon,* in explanation of *Rashi*).

Although the reason for this Rabbinic institution applies only to acquiring ownerless objects, the Rabbis extended their enactment to include all types of acquisition, including commercial transactions and gift transfers; all can use "four *amos*" as the method of acquisition (*Ritva*, *Nimukei Yosef; cf. Meiri*).

22. *Nezikin* is the fourth *seder* [order] of the Mishnah. Our tractate, *Bava Metzia,* is included in that *seder*, and it is from our Mishnah in *Bava Metzia* that R' Yaakov bar Idi challenged Reish Lakish (*Rashi; Rashash*).

מתניתין מני רבנן היא אלא אי אמרת בעשיר ועני מחלוקת אבל מעני לעני דברי הכל זכה לו הא מני לא רבנן ולא ר' אליעזר אמר ליה מתני' דאמר תחילה הכי נמי מסתברא דקתני סיפא אם משנתנה לו אמר אני זכיתי בה תחילה לא אמר כלום תחילה בסיפא למה לי פשיטא אע"ג דלא אמר תחילה תחילה קאמר אלא לאו הא קמ"ל רישא דאמר תחילה ואידך תנא סיפא לגלויי (א) רישא סיפא דאמר תחילה רישא דלא אמר תחילה רב נחמן ורב חסדא דאמרי תרוייהו [א] המגביה מציאה לחבירו לא קנה חבירו מאי טעמא הוי תופס לבעל חוב במקום שחב לאחרים [ג] א והתופס לבעל חוב במקום שחב לאחרים לא קנה איתיביה רבא לרב נחמן [ג] ב מציאת פועל לעצמו במה דברים אמורים בזמן שאמר לו בעל הבית נכש עמי היום עדור עמי היום אבל אמר לו עשה עמי מלאכה היום מציאתו של בעל הבית הוא א"ל שאני פועל דידו כיד בעל הבית הוא [ד] והאמר רב ג פועל יכול לחזור בו אפי' בחצי היום אמר ליה כל כמה דלא הדר ביה כיד בעל הבית הוא כי הדר ביה ד טעמא אחרינא הוא דכתיב [א] כי לי בני ישראל עבדים [ה] עבדי הם ולא עבדים לעבדים אמר ר' חייא בר אבא אמר ר' יוחנן [ו] המגביה מציאה לחבירו קנה חבירו ואם תאמר משנתינו ה דאמר תנה לי ולא אמר זכה לי:

מתני' ו ראה את המציאה ונפל עליה ובא אחר והחזיק בה זה שהחזיק בה זכה בה:

גמ' אמר ריש לקיש משום אבא [ז] כהן ברדלא ז ארבע אמות של אדם קונות לו בכל מקום [ח] [מאי טעמא] תקינו רבנן דלא (ג) אתי לאנצויי אמר אביי מותיב ר' חייא בר יוסף פיאה אמר רבא מותיב ר' יעקב בר אידי נזיקין אמר אביי מותיב ר' חייא בר יוסף פיאה [ט] ח נטל מקצת פיאה וזרק על השאר אין לו בה כלום נפל לו עליה פרס טליתו עליה מעבירין אותו הימנה וכן בעומר שכחה ואי אמרת ארבע אמות של אדם קונות לו בכל מקום נקנו ליה ארבע אמות דידיה הכא במאי עסקינן דלא אמר אקני ואי תקון רבנן כי לא אמר מאי הוי [ס] כיון דנפל גלי דעתיה דבנפילה ניחא ליה דנקני בארבע אמות לא ניחא ליה דנקני רב

## רש"י

מתני' רבנן היא. ואשמועינן רישא דהיכא דזכי ביה איהו אמרינן מגו וסיפא אשמועינן דהיכא דלא זכי ביה איהו מגו דאי בעי זכי לא אמרי': הא. מתני' דהכא מני: דאמר תחילה. הא אני זכיתי בה דקאמר תחילה קאמר ליה מתחילה הגבהתיה לצורכי ולא לצרכך ולעולם המגביה מציאה לחבירו קנה חבירו דומיא דמעני לעני: הכי נמי מסתברא. דזכיתי תחילה משעת הגבהה קאמר מתני': מדקתני סיפא כו'. ואי תחילה דסיפא לאו משעת הגבהה קאמר אלא אני זכיתי תחילה קודם שנתתיה לך נתכוונתי לזכות בה: למה לי. למיתנא בה תחילה פשיטא דאפי' לא אמר תחילה בפירוש מסתמא תחילה קאמר דמי מצי למימר אני זוכה בה עכשיו והלא אינה בידו: אלא לאו הא קמ"ל. דרישא דמתני' דקתני זכה בה בדאמר תחילה ואשמועינן סיפא דאם משנתנה לו טוען לו אותה טענה ואמר אני הגבהתיה מתחילה לצורכי לא אמר כלום דגלי דעתיה כשנתנה לו דלאדעתיה דהאי אגבהה: ואידך. רב נחמן אמר לך דתנא סיפא תחילה: לגלויי רישא. למימר דוקא קתני מדסיפא תחילה קתני ורישא לא תנא דוקא הוא: סיפא. דלא אפשר בלא תחילה אמר אני זכיתי תחילה קודם שנתתיה לך לא אמר כלום דגלי דעתיה כשנתנה לו דלאדעתיה דהאי אגבהה ורישא דלא אמר תחילה ואפ"ה זכה בה: הוי תופס לבעל חוב במקום שחב לאחרים. כאדם הבא מאליו ותופס ממון חבירו בשביל חוב שיש לאחר עליו ובא לקדם עד שלא יתפסנו בעל חוב אחר ונמצא תופס זה חב בתפיסתו זאת את הנושים האחרים: חב לאחרים. מפסיד את האחרים כמו אין חבין לאדם (כתובות דף יא.): לא קנה. כדאמר בכתובות דלאו כל כמיניה להיות קופץ מאליו וחב לאלו מאחר שלא עשאו אותו הנושה שליח לתפוס: נכש עמי היום. דלא נשכר עמו אלא לניכוש ועידור וכשהגביה המציאה אין זו ממלאכת בעל הבית וקנאה פועל והוא ינכה לו משכרו שכר פעולת ניכוש ועידור כל שעת הגבהה: אמר לו עשה עמי מלאכה היום. כל מלאכה שהוא עושה מלאכת בעל הבית היא וקנה בעל הבית אלמא המגביה מציאה לחבירו קנה חבירו: כי הדר ביה טעמא אחרינא הוא. הא דאמר דכי הדר ביה הרשות בידו לאו משום דעד השתא לאו כיד בעל הבית הוא אלא טעמא אחרינא הוא שאינו שלו כעבד שאם בא לעזוב לו שכרו מכאן ואילך ולחזור בו יחזור בו: ואם תאמר משנתינו. דקתני אני זכיתי בה זכה בה ומשמע לן אני זוכה בה עכשיו זכה בה ואע"פ שהגביה לצורך חבירו היינו טעמא משום דקתני ואמר לחבירו תנה לי ולא אמר זכה אתה לי בהגבהתך נמצא שלא עשאו שליח להקנות בהגבהתה עד שעת נתינה והרי קודם נתינה הדר בו זה משליחותו: קונות לו. אם יש סביבותיו דבר הפקר אין אחר רשאי לתופסו: אמר אביי מותיב ר' חייא. עלה מיובתא ממתני' דמסכת פיאה: ואמר רבא מותיב ר' יעקב. עלה ממתני' דסדר נזיקין: נטל. אחד מן העניים: מקצת פיאה. שליקט כבר: וזרק (לה) על השאר. כדי לקנות: ליקנו ליה. גבי נפל לו עליה ארבע אמות דתקון ליה רבנן: בנפילה ניחא ליה דנקני. לא נתכוין לקנות בתורת תקנת חכמים כסבור שנפילתו יפה לו:

## תוספות

רב נחמן ורב חסדא כו'. תימה דבשלהי מסלין (גיטין דף נט. ושם ד"ה הכא) אמר מילא מיס ונתן לחבירו רב ששת אמר כרגלי הממלא ור"נ אמר כרגלי מי שנתמלאו לו ומסיק דמגביה מציאה לחבירו פליגי דמר סבר קנה ומר סבר לא קנה ומשמע דלרב נחמן קנה חבירו ולכך הוי כרגלי מי שנתמלאו לו ור"ח גרס התם מ"ס קני ומר סבר לא קני ול"ג חבירו וכולהו סברי דלא קני חבירו אלא רב נחמן סבר דמגביה נמי לא קני ולכך כשלקח חבירו ממנו קנאו [ומן ההפקר שמתכוין לקנות אבל המגביה לא הגביה לקנות] ורב ששת סבר דקנה הממלא דכיון דלא קנה חבירו הוא קנה ולכך הוי כרגליו ור"ת פי' דהתם רב נחמן מודה דקנה חבירו דלאו חב לאחרים שיש הרבה מים בבור ועוד אומר ר"ת דשפיר גרסינן חבירו וסבר ר"נ לא קנה חבירו כי הכא וגם הממלא לא קנה ולכך כשנתנם לו קנאם והוי כרגליו ורב ששת סבר קני חבירו מטעם מגו דזכי לנפשיה וכיון דלא קנה חבירו אלא מטעם דזכי לנפשיה ואי הוה זכי לנפשיה הוי כרגליו והשתא נמי דזכי לחבריה הוי כרגליו ולא עדיף מיניה לענין תחומין והוי כאילו זכי לנפשיה:

**תופס** לבע"ח במקום שחב לאחרים לא קני. מה שפרש"י משום דלא עשאו שליח אין נראה דבפ' הכותב (כתובות דף פד: ושם ד"ה אם) משמע גבי עובדא דיימר בר חשו דתופס לבע"ח במקום שחב לאחרים לא קני אפילו עשאו שליח:

**איתיביה** רבא לרב נחמן. אע"ג דלעיל (דף ח.) דחי רבא דיוקיה דרמי בר חמא משמע דסבר לא קנה חבירו שמא קבלה הכא מר"נ:

**יכול** לחזור בו אפי' בחצי היום. וא"ת ומאי קמ"ל והלא בפרק האומנין (לקמן דף עז.) לא פליגי רבי דוסא ורבנן אלא דר' דוסא סבר דיד פועל על התחתונה ורבנן סברי דידו על העליונה אבל לכולהו יכול לחזור בו וי"ל דקמ"ל דיכול לחזור בו וידו על העליונה כרבנן אפילו אם נתייקרו פועלים בחצי היום לאחר שחזר בו לא יפחתו לו מחצי שכרו ולכך מייתי מילתיה דרב דכיון דידו על העליונה א"כ אין ידו כיד בעל הבית וכן מוכח בפרק האומנין (שם) דסובר כרבנן בשכיר יום ולא בקבלנות:

**כי** לי בני ישראל עבדים. [אן נ"ל דמ"מ מותר אדם להשכיר עצמו לדווקא עבד עברי שאינו יכול לחזור בו ואינו יוצא קודם זמנו אלא בשטר שחרור עובר משום עבדי הם:

**א"ר** יוחנן המגביה מציאה לחבירו קנה חבירו. ואע"ג דאית ליה לרבי יוחנן בפרק הכותב (כתובות דף פד: ושם ד"ה ולאמר) ובפ"ק דגיטין (דף יא: ושם ד"ה התופס) תופס לבע"ח לא קני היינו דוקא היכא דלא שייך מגו דזכי לנפשיה דלאין הלוה חייב כלום לתופס אבל במציאה דהיכא מגו קנה:

**ולא** אמר זכי לי. וא"ת דבפ' דגיטין (שם) קאמר ר' יוחנן כל האומר תנו כאומר זכו דמי וי"ל דשאני התם דלדעת אחרת מקנה אותו:

**ארבע** אמות קונות לו בכל מקום. וא"ת באלו נערות (כתובות דף לא: ושם ד"ה אי) דאמר גבי גונב כיס בשבת היה מגרר ויוצא פטור דאיסור שבת ואיסור גניבה באין כאחד ואמאי לא דאפקיה לרה"ר איסור שבת איכא איסור גניבה ליכא ואמאי הא ארבע אמות קונות לו וי"ל דבגניבה לא תקינו רבנן דקני אלא במציאה דלא ליתי לאנצויי ובגט משום עיגונא ולרב ששת דאמר בסמוך דברה"ר לא תקינו ארבע אמות אתי שפיר:

**מעבירין** אותו הימנה. [בן אפי' רשע לא מיקרי ואע"ג דעני המהפך בחררה ובא אחר ונטלו נקרא רשע (קדושין דף נט. ושם ד"ה עני) היינו משום דאפשר ליה למיטרח ולמיזבן אבל במציאה או בהפקר דליכא למימר הכי אפילו רשע לא מיקרי [וע"ע תוספות בבא בתרא דף כא: ד"ה מרקיקין]:

רבי

## מסורת הש"ס

[סה"ג גולה לט:], כתובות פד:, גיטין יא:, [לקמן יב:, קיח.], בבא קמא קטו:, לקמן ה) [בבא קמא קטו:, ו) לעיל ושם כב:], ז"ל בהגא, מהרש"ל, ט) פיאה פרק ד' משנה ג, י) פ"א.

## עין משפט נר מצוה

עד א מיי' פ"כ מהל' מלוה ולוה הל' ג סמג עשין צד טוש"ע ח"מ סי' קה סעיף א:

עה ב מיי' פ"ט מהל' שכירות הלכה יא ופי"ז מהל' גזילה ואבידה הל' יג סמג עשין עד טוש"ע ח"מ סי' ער סעיף ג ואפי' אמר לו עשה עמי מלאכה היום וע"ש:

עו ג ד מיי' פ"ט מהל' שכירות הל' ד סמג עשין פט טוש"ע ח"מ סי' שלג סעיף ג:

עז ה מיי' פי"ז מהלכות גזילה ואבידה הל' ג סמג עשין עד טוש"ע ח"מ סי' רסט סעיף ו:

עח ו מיי' שם הלכה ח סמג שם טוש"ע שם סי' רסח סעיף א:

עט ז מיי' שם הל' ט ופ"ד מהל' זכיה ומתנה הל' ט סמג עשין עב טוש"ע ח"מ סי' רסח סעיף ב וסי' רמג סעיף ג:

פ ח מיי' פ"ב מהלכות מתנות עניים הל' יח סמג לאוין רפד:

## רבינו חננאל

מתני' דקתני זכה בה לעצמו המגביהה רבנן היא דאמרי לא קנה מי שליקטה לו אלא יתננה לעני המוצא ראשון שלא אי אמרת מחלוקת מעשיר לעני אבל עני לעני דברי הכל זכה בה מי שנתלקטה לו הא מתני' לא רבנן ולא ר' אליעזר. ופריק' דאמר תחילה פי' קודם שיגביהנה אמר לעצמי אני מגביהה כדי שאזכה בה אני. ודייקינן מדקתני סיפא אם משנתנה לו אמר אני זכיתי בה תחילה לא אמר כלום. פי' רישא וסיפא דאמר תחלה מיהו רישא פירש מקודם שיגביהנה אמר כי לעצמי אני מגביהה כדי שאזכה בה אני. וסיפא הגביה סתם ונתנה לו וטוען עכשיו כי אני אמרתי מתחילה כי לעצמי אני מגביהה לא אמר כלום. ואידך תנא סיפא תחילה לגלויי רישא [דלא אמר תחילה] רב נחמן ורב חסדא דאמרי תרווייהו המגביה מציאה לחבירו לא קנה חבירו מאי טעמא הוי תופס לבעל חוב במקום שחב לאחרים דלא קנה. ומותיב רבא לרב נחמן מציאת פועל לעצמו בד"א בזמן שאמר לו נכש עמי היום. אבל אמר לו עשה עמי מלאכה היום מציאתו לבעל הבית. ופריק רב נחמן שאני פועל דכל זמן דלא הדר ביה כיד בעה"ב דמי. [א] והדר ביה רב נחמן דגרסי' בסוף מס' יו"ט איתמר מילא מים ונתן לחבירו [כר'] ר' נחמן [אמר] כרגלי מי שנתמלאו לו. ופריש בה רב נחמן סבר המגביה מציאה לחבירו קנה חבירו. ורב ששת סבר לא קנה חבירו. אמר רב חייא בר אבא א"ר יוחנן המגביה מציאה לחבירו קנה חבירו והוא דאמר ליה זכה לי. ואם תאמר משנתנו דלא אמר ליה זכה לי אלא תנה לי וקי"ל כר' יוחנן. ופי' רב פפא בהלכה דבתר הא דתניא פועל מציאתו לבעה"ב בששכרו ללקט לו מציאות היכי דמי דאפקי אגמא בכוורי וקי"ל כוותיה: מתני' ראה את המציאה ונפל

## הגהות הב"ח

(א) גמ' סיפא לגלויי רישא: (ב) שם דלא ליתי לאנצויי:

## הגהות הגר"א

[א] תוס' ד"ה כי. נ"ל א'. נ"ב והגמ"ר אוסר ותר משלם (ועמ"ש רבינו ח"מ סי' שלג ס"ק ג): [ב] שם ד"ה מעבירין. אפי' כו'. נ"ב ע"ש בקדושין (נט ע"א) תולק:

## גליון הש"ס

גמ' כיון דנפל גלי דעתיה. עיין נדרים לד ע"ב בר"ן ד"ה אמר רבא:

## תורה אור השלם

א) כי לי בני ישראל עבדים עבדי הם אשר הוצאתי אותם מארץ מצרים אני יי אלהיכם: (ויקרא כה, נה)

## ליקוטי רש"י

תופס לבעל חוב. אלים ותופס מטלטלין של לוה לצורך בעל חוב [כתובות פד:]. אדם מן השוק שתופס מטלטלי דבר לאחרון לצורך ממון שהוא בעל חוב [גיטין יא:]. במקום שחב לאחרים. שמפסיד לאחרים [כתובות שם]. במקום שחב לאחרים כגון זה בתפיסתו זאת את האחרים. לא קנה. דלאו כל כמיניה לזכות שלא מדעת [כתובות פד.]. עשה עמי מלאכה היום. כל מלאכה שהוא עושה מלאכת בעל הבית [לקמן יב:]. שאני פועל וכו'. המגביה מציאה לחבירו הוא אלא כיד בעה"ב הוא וקנייה בעה"ב בהגבהה דפועל [לקמן קיח.]. כי לי בני ישראל עבדים. שטרי קודם [ויקרא כה, נה].

עליה ובא אחר והחזיק בה זכה המחזיק בה. ואוקימנא ברה"ר דקא דחקי רבים לא תקינו ליה רבנן דליקנון ליה ד' אמות דידיה כי תקינו ליה רבנן ד' אמות בשדה דעלמא ובסימטא ובצידי רה"ר וכדומה להן דלא ליתו לאינצויי.

חשק שלמה על ר"ח א) דברי רבינו ז"ל אלו הובא גם בנ"מ כאן בשם הרמב"ן ז"ל שכתב דרבינו כתב דהדר ביה ר"נ ע"ש וע"ע נמוקי כאן ד"ה ר"ש.

The Gemara answers:

תָּנָא סֵיפָא – Rav Nachman will explain that **[the Mishnah] states** the word "first" in **the latter clause** לְגַלּוּיֵי רֵישָׁא – **to reveal** the meaning of **the first clause** – סֵיפָא דְּאָמַר תְּחִילָּה – **the *latter*** clause concerns a case **where [the pedestrian] says "first"** as part of his claim, רֵישָׁא דְּלֹא אָמַר תְּחִילָּה – which indicates that the **first clause** concerns a case **where he did *not* say "first";** rather, he claims that he means to acquire the find for himself now.[8]

The discussion concerning acquisition of an ownerless article on behalf of someone else continues:

רַב נַחְמָן וְרַב חִסְדָּא דְּאָמְרֵי תַּרְוַויְיהוּ – **Rav Nachman and Rav Chisda both say:** הַמַּגְבִּיהַּ מְצִיאָה לַחֲבֵירוֹ – **If someone picks up a find** (i.e. an ownerless article) **on behalf of his fellow,** לֹא קָנָה חֲבֵירוֹ – **his fellow has not acquired** it through that act, and the article remains ownerless. מַאי טַעְמָא – **What is the reason?** הָוֵי תּוֹפֵס לְבַעַל חוֹב בִּמְקוֹם שֶׁחָב לַאֲחֵרִים – **It is** as if **[the one picking up the find] is seizing** a debtor's property **on behalf of a creditor in a situation where he** thereby **disadvantages other [creditors];**[9] וְהַתּוֹפֵס לְבַעַל חוֹב בִּמְקוֹם שֶׁחָב לַאֲחֵרִים – **and** the law is that if **someone seizes** a debtor's property **on behalf of a creditor in a situation where he** thereby **disadvantages other [creditors],** לֹא קָנָה – **[that creditor] has not acquired** it, and all creditors still have equal rights to it. Similarly, a person cannot acquire an ownerless article on behalf of someone else, because it is at the expense of other potential finders.[10]

An objection is raised to the above ruling:

אֵיתִיבֵיהּ רָבָא לְרַב נַחְמָן – **Rava raised an objection against Rav Nachman** from the following Baraisa: מְצִיאַת פּוֹעֵל לְעַצְמוֹ – **A WORKER'S FIND,** i.e. an ownerless article that a hired worker picks up during his hours of employment, **BELONGS TO HIM,** and his employer has no claim to it. בַּמֶּה דְּבָרִים אֲמוּרִים – **WHEN IS THIS RULING SAID?** בִּזְמַן שֶׁאָמַר לוֹ בַּעַל הַבַּיִת – **WHEN THE EMPLOYER** employed him for a specific task; for example, he **SAID TO HIM,** נַכֵּשׁ עִמִּי הַיּוֹם עֲדוֹר עִמִּי הַיּוֹם – **"WEED FOR ME TODAY,"** or **"DIG FOR ME TODAY."**[11] אֲבָל אָמַר לוֹ עֲשֵׂה עִמִּי מְלָאכָה הַיּוֹם – **IF, HOWEVER, [THE EMPLOYER] SAID TO HIM** simply, **"WORK FOR ME TODAY,"** without specifying a type of work, מְצִיאָתוֹ שֶׁל בַּעַל הַבַּיִת הוּא – then **HIS FIND BELONGS TO THE EMPLOYER.**[12] We see in this Baraisa that a worker *does* effect acquisition of an ownerless article on behalf of his employer – contrary to Rav Nachman's view that no one can effect acquisition of ownerless articles on behalf of someone else. – ? –

Rav Nachman replies to Rava:

אָמַר לֵיהּ – **[Rav Nachman] said to him:** שָׁאנֵי פּוֹעֵל – **A worker is different,** דְּיָדוֹ כְּיַד בַּעַל הַבַּיִת הוּא – **because his hand is like** an extension of **the employer's hand.**[13] Therefore, when the worker picks up a find, it is as if the employer himself picked it up and acquired it on his own behalf. But generally, one person *cannot* effect acquisition of an ownerless article on behalf of someone else.

NOTES

8. Rav Nachman maintains his original assertion, that by "first," the pedestrian means only that he intended to acquire it for himself before handing it to the rider. (What the pedestrian had in mind when he picked it up, or even subsequently, is of no consequence – the rider cannot acquire the find until it enters his hand.) Now, as the Gemara has noted, it is indeed obvious in this case that he means "first" and it did not have to be stated explicitly. Nevertheless, the Mishnah attributes the word "first" to the pedestrian in the latter clause to indicate that this is *not* what he says in the first clause; for the Mishnah's omission of the word "first" in the first clause was intentional. In the first clause, where the pedestrian states his claim while the find is still in his hand, he need not say that he meant to acquire it for himself *first.* Rather, he can claim that he means to acquire the find for himself *at this very moment.* Even if he initially picked up the find on behalf of the rider and did not change his mind until just before handing it to him, the pedestrian can take the find for himself. For, as Rav Nachman explains, our Mishnah follows the view that a person cannot acquire an ownerless article on behalf of another person (see *Rashi* and *Ritva*; see also *Maharam*).

[Even according to Rav Nachman, the pedestrian's claim in both cases is the same – he meant to acquire the find for himself at some point prior to handing the find to the rider. The difference between the *wording* of the claim in the two clauses results from the time at which he *states* his claim. In the first clause, he states his claim at the very moment he intends to acquire it for himself; therefore, he omits the word "first." In the latter clause, he does not state this claim until after he hands the find to the rider; therefore, he says that he actually acquired it for himself *first* – before handing it to the rider.]

9. A creditor has a right to seize the movable property of a debtor that defaults on his uncontested loan. A third party can also seize the property on behalf of a particular creditor, providing there are enough assets remaining to satisfy the debtor's other creditors. The moment the third party seizes, the creditor acquires the property although he is totally unaware of the whole matter. This is in accordance with the principle of זְכִיָּה, *zechiyah,* which states: זָכִין לְאָדָם שֶׁלֹּא בְּפָנָיו, *one may benefit a person even in his absence* [see 9b note 28].

However, in a situation where the debtor's assets are insufficient to satisfy all his creditors, a third party cannot seize them for one particular creditor's sake. The third party does not have the authority to give preference to one creditor at the expense of others who will be left with no assets from which to claim their debt. Such a case is known as תּוֹפֵס לְבַעַל חוֹב בִּמְקוֹם שֶׁחָב לַאֲחֵר, *seizing on behalf of a creditor when it is at the expense of others* [see also 9b note 31].

Of course, the creditor *himself* can seize a debtor's property without regard to the effect this has on other creditors. "The expense of others" is a consideration only when a third party wishes to involve himself through the mechanism of *zechiyah.*

[In *Rashi's* opinion, an agent *appointed* by a creditor has the same right of seizure as the creditor himself. *Tosafos* and other Rishonim, however, dissent, arguing that a duly appointed agent has no more right to intervene than an independent third party.]

10. Obviously, however, anyone can pick up an ownerless article for himself and then give it to someone else as a gift. The point here is that a person cannot effect acquisition of the article *directly* on behalf of someone else through the mechanism of *zechiyah.* Accordingly, the one who picks it up still has the option to change his mind and keep the article for himself, as long he has not yet given it to anyone.

[Above, Rav Nachman explained the opinion of the Sages in *Pe'ah* to be that one cannot acquire an ownerless article on behalf of someone else, even if the one performing the act of acquisition could acquire the article for himself if he so desired. The Gemara here notes that Rav Nachman indeed accepts this view as the halachah (since he ascribes it to the majority view of the Sages).]

11. The worker has been hired for the specific task, which does not include the task of picking up finds. Thus, the find belongs to the worker [even if he found it in the process of weeding or digging (*Mishpat HaAveidah*)], since his act of picking it up is done as an independent, not as a hired worker. The employer can, however, deduct from the worker's wages the time he spent procuring the find, since the worker was absent during that time from the job he was hired to do (*Rashi*).

[Clearly, we are dealing here with a case in which the premises on which the article is found cannot serve as the employer's *chatzeir* to effect acquisition of the article for him (e.g. the premises were not protected). Otherwise, the employer, through his *chatzeir,* would precede the worker in acquiring the find.]

12. Since the terms of the worker's employment do not specify a particular type of work, his job is construed to be whatever work he engages in during his hours of employment. Thus, even the work of picking up a find is being done in the employ of his employer, and the find therefore belongs to the employer (*Rashi*).

13. I.e. for the duration of his employment, a worker is in a sense owned by the employer. More than a mere agent, one owned by his master is like a legal extension of the master (see *Ritva* ד״ה והא אמר רב).

מתניתין מני רבנן היא אלא אי אמרת בעשיר ועני מחלוקת אבל מעני לעני דברי הכל זכה לו הא מני לא רבנן ולא ר' אליעזר אמר ליה מתני' דאמר תחילה הכי נמי מסתברא דקתני סיפא אם משנתנה לו אמר אני זכיתי בה תחילה לא אמר כלום תחילה בסיפא למה לי פשיטא אע"ג דלא אמר תחילה תחילה קאמר אלא לאו הא קמ"ל רישא דאמר תחילה ואידך תנא סיפא לגלויי (א) רישא סיפא דאמר תחילה רישא דלא אמר תחילה רב נחמן ורב חסדא דאמרי תרווייהו [א] המגביה מציאה לחבירו לא קנה חבירו מאי טעמא הוי תופס לבעל חוב במקום שחב לאחרים [ב] א והתופס לבעל חוב במקום שחב לאחרים לא קנה איתיביה רבא לרב נחמן [ג] ב מציאת פועל לעצמו במה דברים אמורים בזמן שאמר לו בעל הבית נכש עמי היום עדור עמי היום אבל אמר לו עשה עמי מלאכה היום מציאתו של בעל הבית הוא א"ל שאני פועל דידו כיד בעל הבית הוא [ד] והאמר רב ג פועל יכול לחזור בו אפי' בחצי היום אמר ליה כל כמה דלא הדר ביה כיד בעל הבית הוא כי הדר ביה ד טעמא אחרינא הוא דכתיב (א) כי לי בני ישראל עבדים [ה] עבדי הם ולא עבדים לעבדים אמר ר' חייא בר אבא אמר ר' יוחנן [ו] המגביה מציאה לחבירו קנה חבירו ואם תאמר משנתינו ה דאמר תנה לי ולא אמר זכה לי:

מתני' ו ראה את המציאה ונפל עליה ובא אחר והחזיק בה זה שהחזיק בה זכה בה:

גמ' אמר ריש לקיש משום אבא [ז] כהן ברדלא ז ארבע אמות של אדם קונות לו בכל מקום [ח] [מאי טעמא] תקינו רבנן דלא (ב) אתי לאנצויי אמר אביי מותיב ר' חייא בר יוסף פיאה אמר רבא מותיב ר' יעקב בר אידי נזיקין אמר אביי מותיב ר' חייא בר יוסף פיאה [ט] ח נטל מקצת פיאה וזרק על השאר אין לו בה כלום נפל לו עליה פרס טליתו עליה מעבירין אותו הימנה וכן בעומר שכחה ואי אמרת ארבע אמות של אדם קונות לו בכל מקום נקנו ליה ארבע אמות דידיה הכא במאי עסקינן דלא אמר אקני ואי תקון רבנן כי לא אמר מאי הוי ° כיון דנפל גלי דעתיה דבנפילה ניחא ליה דנקני בארבע אמות לא ניחא ליה דנקני

רב

רש"י

מתני' רבנן היא. ואשמועינן רישא דהיכא דזכי ביה איהו אמרינן מגו וסיפא אשמועינן דהיכא דלא זכי ביה איהו מגו דאי בעי זכי לא אמרי': הא. מתני' דהכא מני: דאמר תחילה. האי אני זכיתי בה דקאמר תחילה קאמר ליה מתחילה הגבהתיה לצורכי ולא לצרכך ולעולם המגביה מציאה לחבירו קנה חבירו דומיא דמעני לעני: הכי נמי מסתברא. דזכיתי תחילה משעת הגבהה קאמר מתני': מדקתני סיפא כו'. ואי תחילה דסיפא לאו משעת הגבהה קאמר אלא אני זכיתי תחילה קודם שנתתיה לך נתכוונתי לזכות בה: למה לי. למיתנא בה תחילה פשיטא דאפי' לא אמר תחילה בפירוש מסתמא תחילה קאמר דמי מצי למימר אני זוכה בה עכשיו והלא אינה בידו: אלא לאו הא קמ"ל. דרישא דמתני' דקתני זכה בה בדאמר תחילה ואשמועינן סיפא דאם משנתנה לו טען לו אותה טענה ואמר אני הגבהתיה מתחילה לצורכי לא אמר כלום דגלי דעתיה כשנתנה לו דאדעתיה דהאי אגבהה: ואידך. רב נחמן אמר לך דתנא סיפא תחילה: לגלויי רישא. למימר דוקא קתני מדסיפא תחילה קתני ורישא לא תנא דוקא הוא: סיפא. דלא אפשר בלא תחילה אמר אני זכיתי תחילה קודם שנתתיה לך לא אמר כלום דגלי דעתיה כשנתנה לו דאדעתא דהאי אגבהה ורישא דלא אמר תחילה ואפ"ה זכה בה: הוי תופס לבעל חוב במקום שחב לאחרים. כאדם הבא מאליו ותופס ממון חבירו בשביל חוב שיש לאחר עליו ובא לקדם עד שלא יתפסנו בעל חוב אחר ונמצא תופס זה חב בתפיסתו זאת את הנושים האחרים: חב לאחרים. מפסיד את האחרים כמו אין חבין לאדם (כתובות דף יא.): לא קנה. כדאמר בכתובות דלאו כל כמיניה להיות קופץ מאליו וחב לאלו מאחר שלא עשאו אותו הנושה שליח לתפוס: נכש עמי היום. דלא נשכר עמו אלא לניכוש ועידור וכשהגביה המציאה אין זו ממלאכת בעל הבית וקנאה פועל והוא ינכה לו משכרו שכר פעולת ניכוש ועידור כל שעת הגבהה: אמר לו עשה עמי מלאכה היום. כל מלאכה שהוא עושה מלאכת בעל הבית היא וקנה בעל הבית אלמא המגביה מציאה לחבירו קנה חבירו: כי הדר ביה טעמא אחרינא הוא. הא דאמר דכי הדר ביה הרשות בידו לאו משום דעד השתא לאו כיד בעל הבית הוא אלא טעמא אחרינא הוא שאינו שלו כעבד שאם בא לעזוב לו שכרו מכאן ואילך ולחזור בו יחזור בו: ואם תאמר משנתינו. דקתני אני זכיתי בה זכה בה ומשמע לן אני זוכה בה עכשיו זכה בה ואע"פ שהגביה לצורך חבירו היינו טעמא משום דקתני ואמר לחבירו תנה לי ולא אמר זכה אתה לי בהגבהתך נמצא שלא עשאו שליח להקנות בהגבהתה עד שעת נתינה והרי קודם נתינה הדר בו זה משליחותו: קונות לו. אם יש סביבותיו דבר הפקר אין אחר רשאי לתופסו: אמר אביי מותיב ר' חייא. עלה תיובתא ממתני' דמסכת פיאה: ואמר רבא מותיב ר' יעקב. עלה ממתני' דסדר נזיקין: נטל. אחד מן העניים: מקצת פיאה. שליקט כבר: וזרק (לה) על השאר. כדי לקנות: ליקנו ליה. גבי נפל לו עליה ארבע אמות דתקון ליה רבנן: בנפילה ניחא ליה דנקני. לא נתכוין לקנות בתורת תקנת חכמים כסבור שנפילתו יפה לו:

ה"ג

תוספות

רב נחמן ורב חסדא כו'. תימה דבשלהי משילין (ביצה דף לט. ושם: ד"ה הכא) אמר מילא מים ונתן לחבירו רב ששת אמר כרגלי הממלא ור"נ אמר כרגלי מי שנתמלאו לו ומסיק דבמגביה מציאה לחבירו פליגי דמר סבר קנה ומר סבר לא קנה ומשמע דלרב נחמן קנה חבירו ולכך הוי כרגלי מי שנתמלאו לו ורש"י גרס התם מ"ס קני ומר סבר לא קני ול"ג חבירו וכולהו סברי דלא קני חבירו אלא רב נחמן סבר דמגביה נמי לא קני ולכך כשלקח חבירו ממנו קנאו [י] [מן ההפקר שמתכוין לקנות אבל המגביה לא הגביה לקנות] ורב ששת סבר דקנה הממלא דכיון דלא קנה חבירו הוא קנה ולכך הוי כרגליו ור"ת פי' דהתם רב נחמן מודה דקנה חבירו דאינו חב לאחרים שיש הרבה מים בבור ועוד אומר ר"ת דשפיר גרסינן חבירו וסבר ר"נ לא קנה חבירו כי הכא וגם הממלא לא קנה ולכך כשנתנם לו קנאם והוי כרגליו ורב ששת סבר קני חבירו מטעם מגו דזכי לנפשיה וכיון דלא קנה חבירו אלא מטעם דזכי לנפשיה ואי הוה זכי לנפשיה הוי כרגליו והשתא נמי דזכי לחבריה הוי כרגליו ולא עדיף מיניה לענין תחומין והוי כאילו זכי לנפשיה:

תופס לבע"ח במקום שחב לאחרים לא קני. מה שפרש"י משום דלא עשאו שליח אין נראה דבפ' הכותב (כתובות דף פד: ושם ד"ה את) משמע גבי עובדא דיימר בר חשו דתופס לבע"ח במקום שחב לאחרים לא קני אפילו עשאו שליח:

איתיביה רבא לרב נחמן. אע"ג דלעיל (ד' ח.) דחי רבא דיוקיה דרמי בר חמא משמע דסבר לא קנה חבירו שמא קבלה הכא מר"נ:

יכול לחזור בו אפי' בחצי היום. וא"ת ומאי קמ"ל והלא בפרק האומנין (לקמן דף עז.) לא פליגי רבי דוסא ורבנן אלא דר' דוסא סבר דיד פועל על התחתונה ורבנן סברי דידו על העליונה אבל לכולהו יכול לחזור בו וי"ל דקמ"ל דיכול לחזור בו וידו על העליונה כרבנן אפילו אם נתייקרו פועלים בחצי היום לאחר שחזר בו לא יפחתו לו מחצי שכרו ולכך מייתי מילתיה דרב דכיון דידו על העליונה א"כ אין ידו כיד בעל הבית וכן מוכח בפרק האומנין (שם) דסובר כרבנן בשכיר יום ולא בקבלנות:

כי לי בני ישראל עבדים. [א] נ"ל דמ"מ מותר אדם להשכיר עצמו דדוקא עבד עברי שאינו יכול לחזור בו ואינו יוצא קודם זמנו אלא בשטר שחרור עובר משום עבדי הם:

א"ר יוחנן המגביה מציאה לחבירו קנה חבירו. ואע"ג דאית ליה לרבי יוחנן בפרק הכותב (כתובות דף פד: ושם ד"ה ואמר) ובפ"ק דגיטין (דף יא: ושם ד"ה התופס) תופס לבע"ח לא קני היינו דוקא היכא דלא שייך מגו דזכי לנפשיה דאין הלוה חייב כלום לתופס אבל במציאה דאיכא מגו קנה:

ולא אמר זכי לי. וא"ת דבפ"ק דגיטין (שם) קאמר ר' יוחנן כל האומר תנו כאומר זכו וי"ל דשאני התם דדעת אחרת מקנה אותו:

ארבע אמות קונות לו בכל מקום. וא"ת באלו נערות (כתובות דף לא: ושם ד"ה אי) דאמר גבי גונב כיס בשבת היה מגרר ויוצא פטור דאיסור שבת ואיסור גניבה באין כאחד וקאמר אי דאפקיה לרה"ר איסור שבת איכא איסור גניבה ליכא ואמאי הא ארבע אמות קונות לו וי"ל דבגניבה לא תקינו רבנן דקני אלא במציאה דלא ליתי לאנצויי ובגט משום עיגונא ולרב ששת דאמר בסמוך דברה"ר לא תקינו ארבע אמות אתי שפיר:

מעבירין אותו הימנה. [ב] אפי' רשע לא מיקרי ואע"ג דעני המהפך בחררה ובא אחר ונטלו נקרא רשע (קדושין דף נט. ושם ד"ה עני) היינו משום דאפשר ליה למיטרח ולמיזבן ארעא אחריתי אבל במציאה או בהפקר דליכא למימר הכי אפילו רשע לא מיקרי [וע"ע תוספות בבא בתרא דף כא: ד"ה מרחיקין]:

רבי

עין משפט נר מצוה

עד א מיי' פ"כ מהל' מלוה ולוה הל' ב סמג עשין לד טוש"ע ח"מ סי' קה סעיף א:

עה ב מיי' פ"ט מהל' שכירות הלכה יא ופי"ז מהל' גזילה ואבידה הל' יג סמג עשין עד טוש"ע ח"מ סי' ער סעיף ג ואפי' אמר לו עשה עמי מלאכה היום וע"ש:

עו ג ד מיי' פ"ט מהל' שכירות הל' ד סמג עשין פט טוש"ע ח"מ סי' שלג סעיף ג:

עז ה מיי' פי"ז מהלכות גזילה ואבידה הל' ב סמג עשין עד טוש"ע ח"מ סי' רסט סעיף ו:

עח ו מיי' שם הלכה א סמג שם טוש"ע שם סי' רסח סעיף א:

עט ז מיי' שם הל' ח ופ"ד מהל' זכייה ומתנה הל' ט סמג עשין עב טוש"ע ח"מ סי' רסח סעיף ב וסי' רמג סעיף כב:

פ ח מיי' פ"ב מהלכות מתנות עניים הל' יח סמג לאוין רפד:

רבינו חננאל

מתני' דקתני זכה בה לעצמו המגביהה רבנן היא דאמרי לא קנה מי שליקטה לו אלא יתננה לעני הנמצא ראשון אלא אי אמרת מחלוקת מעשיר לעני אבל עני לעני דברי הכל זכה בה מי שנתלקטה לו מתני' מני לא רבנן ולא ר' אליעזר. ופרקי' דאמר תחילה פי' קודם שיגביהנה אמר לעצמי אני מגביהה כדי שאזכה בה אני. ודייקינן מדקתני סיפא אם משנתנה לו אמר אני זכיתי בה תחילה לא אמר כלום. פי' רישא וסיפא דאמר תחלה מיהו רישא פירש מקודם שיגביהנה אמר כי לעצמי אני מגביהה כדי שאזכה בה אני. וסיפא הגביה סתם ונתנה לו וטוען עכשיו כי אני אמרתי מתחילה כי לעצמי אני מגביהה לא אמר כלום. ואידך תנא סיפא תחילה לגלויי רישא [דלא אמר תחילה] רב נחמן ורב חסדא דאמרי תרווייהו המגביה מציאה לחבירו לא קנה חבירו מאי טעמא הוי תופס לבעל חוב במקום שחב לאחרים דלא קנה. ומותיב רבא לרב נחמן מציאת פועל לעצמו בד"א בזמן שאמר לו נכש עמי היום. אבל אמר לו עשה עמי מלאכה היום מציאתו לבעל הבית. ופריק רב נחמן שאני פועל דכל זמן דלא הדר ביה כיד בעה"ב דמי. א) והדר ביה רב נחמן דגרסי' בסוף מס' יו"ט איתמר מילא מים ונתן לחבירו [כו'] ר' נחמן [אמר] כרגלי מי שנתמלאו לו. ופריש בה רב נחמן סבר המגביה מציאה לחבירו קנה חבירו. ורב ששת אמר לא קנה חבירו. אמר רב חייא בר אבא א"ר יוחנן המגביה מציאה לחבירו קנה חבירו והוא דאמר ליה זכה לי. ואם תאמר משנתנו דלא אמר ליה זכה לי אלא תנה לי וקי"ל כר' יוחנן. ופי' רב פפא בהלכה דבתר הא דתניא פועל מציאתו לבעה"ב בששכרו ללקט לו מציאות היכי דמי דאקפי אגמא בכוורי וקי"ל כוותיה: מתני' ראה את המציאה ונפל עליה ובא אחר והחזיק בה זכה המחזיק בה. ואוקימנא ברה"ר דקא דחקי רבים לא תקינו ליה רבנן דליקנון ליה ד' אמות דידיה כי תקינו ליה רבנן ד' אמות בשדה דעלמא ובסימטא ובצידי רה"ר וכדומה להן דלא ליתו לאינצויי.



מסורת הש"ס

א) [ס"ג ביצה לט:], ב) כתובות פד:, גיטין יא:, ג) [לקמן יב:, קיח.], ד) בבא קמא קטז:, לקמן עז., ה) [בבא קמא קטז:, קדושין כב:], ו) לעיל ח., ז) נ"א כהנא, ח) מהרש"ל, ט) פיאה פרק ד' משנה ג, י) ס"א.

הגהות הב"ח

(א) גמ' סיפא לגלויי רישא: (ב) שם דלא ליתי לאנצויי:

הגהות הגר"א

[א] תוס' ד"ה כי. נ"ל כו'. נ"ב והגמ"ר אוסר יותר משלש (ועמ"ש רבינו ח"מ סי' שלג ס"ק ג): [ב] שם ד"ה מעבירין. אפי' כו'. נ"ב רש"י בקדושין (נט ע"א) חולק:

גליון הש"ס

גמ' כיון דנפל גלי דעתיה. עיין נדרים לד ע"ב בר"ן ד"ה אמר רבא:

תורה אור השלם

א) כִּי לִי בְנֵי יִשְׂרָאֵל עֲבָדִים עֲבָדַי הֵם אֲשֶׁר הוֹצֵאתִי אוֹתָם מֵאֶרֶץ מִצְרָיִם אֲנִי יְיָ אֱלֹהֵיכֶם: [ויקרא כה, נה]

ליקוטי רש"י

התופס לבעל חוב. אלים התופס מטלטלין של זה לצורך בעל חוב [כתובות פד:]. אדם מן השוק שתופס מטלטלי נכסי ראובן לצורך שמעון שהוא בעל חוב [גיטין יא:]. במקום שחב לאחרים. שמפסיד בע"ח אחרים בתפיסתו [כתובות שם]. במקום שחב התופס הזה בתפיסתו זאת ללוי דהו"ל נמי בע"ח דראובן ותופס זה שקדם תפס לצורך שמעון מפסיד את לוי [גיטין שם]. לא קנה. דלאו כל כמיניה לחוב זה כדי לזכות את זה [כתובות פה.]. עשה עמי מלאכה היום וכו'. בזמן שלא פירש לו לאיזו מלאכה שכרו [לקמן יב:]. שאני פועל וכו'. דפועל לאו בכלל המגביה מציאה לחבירו הוא אלא כיד בעה"ב הוא וקנייה בעה"ב בהגבהה דפועל וכו' [לקמן קיח.]. כי לי בני ישראל עבדים. שטרי קודם [ויקרא כה, נה].

מַתְנִיתִין מַ – for our Mishnah then follows whose opinion? רַבָּנַן הִי – It follows the opinion of the Sages of the Mishnah in *Pe'ah.*[1] אֶלָּא אִי אָמְרַת בְּעָשִׁיר וְעָנִי מַחְלוֹקֶת – But if, on the other hand, you say that the dispute of the Mishnah in *Pe'ah* concerns a case of a rich man and a poor man, as you, Ulla, assert, אֲבָל מֵעָנִי לְעָנִי דִּבְרֵי הַכֹּל זָכָה לוֹ – but if the *pe'ah* is collected by a poor man for a poor man, everyone would agree that [the collector] has effectively acquired it for [the other's] sake, הָא מַנִּי – then whose opinion does this Mishnah of ours follow? לֹא רַבָּנַן וְלֹא ר׳ אֱלִיעֶזֶר – It follows neither the opinion of the Sages nor of R' Eliezer![2] – ? –

Ulla rebuts this proof:[3]

אָמַר לֵיהּ – [Ulla] said to him: מַתְנִיתִין דְּאָמַר תְּחִילָּה – Our Mishnah refers to a case where [the pedestrian] says, "I acquired it for myself *first.*" I.e. he claims that he never intended to acquire the article on behalf of the rider, but that he *initially* picked it up to acquire it for himself.[4]

The Gemara finds support for Ulla's interpretation in the Mishnah itself:

הָכִי נַמִּי מִסְתַּבְּרָא – This interpretation is, in fact, more reasonable. דְּקָתָנֵי סֵיפָא – For the latter part of the Mishnah states: אִם מִשֶּׁנְּתָנָהּ לוֹ – IF, however, AFTER HE HAD GIVEN IT TO [THE RIDER], אָמַר אֲנִי זָכִיתִי בָּהּ תְּחִילָּה – HE SAID, "I ACQUIRED IT FIRST," לֹא אָמַר כְּלוּם – HE HAS SAID NOTHING. Now, if the sole issue is (as Rav Nachman maintains) whether the pedestrian meant to acquire the find for himself before handing it to the rider, תְּחִילָּה בְּסֵיפָא לָמָּה לִי – then why is it necessary for the Mishnah in this latter clause to explicitly state the word "first" in the pedestrian's claim? פְּשִׁיטָא – It is self-understood! אַף עַל גַּב דְּלֹא אָמַר תְּחִילָּה – Even if he does not explicitly say, "I acquired it *first,*" but says simply, "I acquired it," תְּחִילָּה קָאָמַר – he obviously means that he acquired it "first."[5] אֶלָּא לָאו הָא קָא מַשְׁמַע לָן – Rather, does the [Mishnah] not inform us by mentioning the word "first" explicitly in the latter clause רֵישָׁא דְּאָמַר תְּחִילָּה – that in the case of the first clause as well, [the pedestrian] claims that he acquired the find for himself *first,* i.e. initially upon picking it up?[6] Only in such a case is the pedestrian entitled to keep the article – precisely as Ulla interpreted the Mishnah.

The Gemara asks:

וְאִידָךְ – And how does the other one [Rav Nachman] account for the apparently unnecessary word "first"?[7]

NOTES

Our Mishnah, which apparently rules that the pedestrian cannot acquire an ownerless object directly on behalf of the rider, would follow the view of the Sages in *Pe'ah* that even a single "since" argument [since he could acquire it for himself, he can acquire it for someone else] does not empower a person to perform *zechiyah* for one person where it is to the detriment of others. [In the case of our Mishnah, acquiring the ownerless article for one person is to the detriment of everyone else, who would potentially acquire the ownerless article for themselves.]

[Accordingly, the previous Mishnah (2a) teaches that a person can make acquisition of an ownerless article on behalf of his fellow when he is at the same time performing that act of acquisition for *himself* [i.e. he intends that *both* should acquire the article]. (In the Gemara above [8a], Rami bar Chama demonstrates this law from the words of the previous Mishnah.) The present Mishnah then teaches that where the one performing the act of acquisition is *not* acquiring the ownerless article for himself as well, then his act is not effective for the other person either (*Rashi*).]

For in the case of our Mishnah, a single "since" argument suffices to establish the pedestrian's rights to the ownerless article, yet the Mishnah apparently rules that he cannot acquire it on behalf of the rider. But Ulla asserts that even the Sages agree that a single "since" argument can establish such rights. Accordingly, our Mishnah follows neither the Sages (who allow one "since" argument) nor R' Eliezer (who allows two), which is an inadmissible supposition. [Had there been another Tannaic view in addition to those of R' Eliezer and the Sages, presumably the Mishnah in *Pe'ah* would have mentioned it.]

Rav Nachman's proof was based on the assumption that the pedestrian initially picked up the article on behalf of the rider. Ulla will now show that the Mishnah bears a different interpretation.

[Even though the claim "first" is not explicitly attributed to the pedestrian in the first part of the Mishnah, that is what his claim really means.] Although the rider brought the article to his notice, the pedestrian claims that he never intended to pick it up on the rider's behalf. [He is believed in this assertion since he has not yet given the article over to the rider.] If, however, he had indeed picked it up on the rider's behalf, the rider would have acquired it immediately [in accordance with both the views of R' Eliezer and the Sages as explained by Ulla] (*Rashi*).

The two interpretations of our Mishnah actually hinge on how we are to interpret the critical word תְּחִילָּה, *first,* which the Mishnah attributes to the pedestrian in the second case. Ulla interprets that the pedestrian claims to have *initially* picked up the article for himself, not for the rider. But if the pedestrian would admit that he initially picked it up for the rider, then it would be the property of the rider even if the pedestrian changed his mind *before* handing it to him (since picking up an ownerless article on behalf of another person automatically makes the article the property of that other person). Still, the Mishnah rules that if the pedestrian states his claim (of initially picking up the find for himself) only *after* handing the find to the rider, his claim is of no consequence.

Rav Nachman, on the other hand, explains that by "first," the pedestrian means simply that he acquired the find for himself *before* handing it to the rider. (What the pedestrian had in mind when he picked up the article is immaterial – the find cannot become the property of the rider until it is actually handed to him. The sole consideration is whether the pedestrian acquired it for himself before handing it to the rider or not.)

Thus, according to Ulla, "first" means: "at the moment I picked it up." According to Rav Nachman, "first" means: "before I gave it to you."

Accordingly, the Gemara now argues that Rav Nachman's view cannot account for the word "first" explicitly attributed to the pedestrian in the Mishnah's latter case (where the claim is stated after he hands the article to the rider). For according to Rav Nachman's view, it is self-understood that the pedestrian means that he acquired it "first" (before handing it to the rider) – how could he possible acquire it *after* it is in the rider's hand?! Why, then, did the Mishnah find it necessary to state the word "first"? (see *Rashi* and *Ritva*).

6. We can account for the word "first" mentioned in the latter clause of the Mishnah only if we understand "first" as Ulla understands it – that the pedestrian claims to have *initially* picked up the find for himself, not for the rider. Accordingly, the Mishnah *must* teach us that the pedestrian claims to have acquired it "first," i.e. initially, upon picking it up. Only then can he possibly lay any claim to the find. But had he not intended to acquire it for himself until after he had picked it up on behalf of the rider, the find would already belong to the rider even if the pedestrian changed his mind before handing the find to the rider.

Accordingly, the word "first" found in the latter clause indicates that this is the claim in the first clause as well. For what the latter clause really means is: If the claim recorded in the first clause is not stated until *after* the find is handed to the rider, the pedestrian's claim amounts to nothing. [The claims in both clauses, though worded differently, are assumed to be identical; the only real difference between the clauses is that in the first case, the pedestrian states his claim *before* giving the find to the rider; in the latter case, he states his claim *afterwards.*] When stated afterwards, the claim amounts to nothing, because the pedestrian's actions belie his words. He has tacitly carried out the rider's instructions to pick up the find and deliver it to him, thereby indicating that he indeed picked up the find for the rider, not for himself (see *Rashi*). [The Mishnah did not deem it necessary to state "first" explicitly in the first clause, since it indicates in the latter clause that this is indeed the case.]

7. Unless Rav Nachman finds a different way to account for the word "first" in the Mishnah, he will have to accept the Gemara's contention that the appearance of that word in the Mishnah supports Ulla's view.

**Mishnah:** הָיָה רוֹכֵב עַל גַּבֵּי בְהֵמָה – If SOMEONE WAS RIDING ON AN ANIMAL וְרָאָה אֶת הַמְּצִיאָה – AND HE SIGHTED A FIND, וְאָמַר לַחֲבֵירוֹ – AND HE SAID TO HIS FELLOW, תְּנָה לִי – "GIVE IT TO ME"; נְטָלָהּ – and [THAT OTHER PERSON] TOOK IT וְאָמַר אֲנִי זָכִיתִי בָהּ – AND then SAID, "I HAVE ACQUIRED IT for myself," זָכָה בָהּ – HE HAS indeed ACQUIRED IT for himself. Apparently, the Mishnah is discussing a case in which the pedestrian initially picked up the find on behalf of the rider and only afterwards reconsidered and decided to keep the find f himself. Nevertheless, the Mishnah rules that the initial act acquisition on behalf of the rider was *not* effective and t pedestrian can keep the find for himself. אִי אָמְרַתְּ בִּשְׁלָמָא Now, **[the Mishnah's ruling] is understandable if you s** מֵעָנִי לְעָנִי מַחֲלוֹקֶת – **that the dispute** in the Mishnah in *Pe'ah* **is** regard to *pe'ah* collected **by a poor man for a poor man,** as I, R Nachman, maintain,

NOTES

*pe'ah* for himself and *then* give it to the poor man of his choice as a gift. The issue being considered here, however, is whether the poor collector can perform an act of acquisition to the *pe'ah* that is *directly* effective for the second poor man – an act that would immediately render the *pe'c* the property of the second poor person, which even the collector hims could not then decide to keep for himself.]

ואי רשות הרבים הוא [א]קני ואי אדם חשוב הוא קני ואי אשה היא קניא ואי איניש זילא הוא קני בעי ר' אלעזר האומר לחבירו משוך בהמה זו לקנות כלים שעליה מהו ב לקנות מי אמר ליה קני אלא משוך בהמה זו וקני כלים שעליה מהו מי מהניא משיכה דבהמה לאקנויי כלים ג או לא אמר רבא אי אמר ליה קני בהמה וקני כלים מי קני כלים ד חצר מהלכת היא וחצר מהלכת לא קנה וכי תימא כשעמדה והא א) כל ה שאילו מהלך לא קנה עומד ויושב לא קנה ° ו והלכתא בכפותה אמרו ליה רב פפא ורב הונא בריה דרב יהושע לרבא אלא מעתה היה מהלך בספינה וקפצו דגים ונפלו לתוך הספינה הכי נמי דחצר מהלכת היא ולא קני אמר ליה ז ספינה מינח נייחא ומיא הוא דקא ממטו לה א"ל רבינא לרב אשי אלא מעתה היתה מהלכת ברשות הרבים וזרק לה גט לתוך חיקה או לתוך קלתה הכא נמי דלא מגרשה א"ל ח קלתה מינח נייחא ואיהי דקא מסגיא מתותה:

מתני' ט היה רוכב על גבי בהמה וראה את המציאה ואמר לחבירו תנה לי נטלה ואמר אני זכיתי בה זכה בה אם משנתנה לו אמר אני זכיתי בה תחלה לא אמר כלום: גמ' ב) תנן התם מי שליקט את הפאה ואמר הרי זו לפלוני עני ר' אליעזר אומר זכה לו וחכמים אומרים י יתננה לעני הנמצא ראשון אמר עולא אמר ר' יהושע בן לוי מחלוקת מעשיר לעני דר' אליעזר סבר ג) מגו דאי בעי מפקר נכסיה והוי עני וחזי ליה השתא נמי חזי ליה ד) ומגו דזכי לנפשיה זכי נמי לחבריה ורבנן סברי ה) כ חד מגו אמרינן תרי מגו לא אמרינן אבל מעני לעני דברי הכל זכה לו דמגו דזכי לנפשיה זכי נמי לחבריה אמר ליה רב נחמן לעולא ולימא מר מעני לעני מחלוקת דהא מציאה הכל עניים אצלה ותנן היה רוכב על גבי בהמה וראה את המציאה ואמר לחבירו תנה לי נטלה ואמר אני זכיתי בה זכה בה אי אמרת בשלמא מעני לעני מחלוקת

---

**תוספות**

משוך בהמה זו וקני כלים שעליה כו'. מבעיא ליה כיון דמשיכת הבהמה שהולכת מעצמה לא שייכא בכלים לא יקנה הכלים אבל אם אמר משוך קופה וקני כלים שבתוכה פשיטא ליה דקני ואם תאמר תפשוט מברייתא דהמוכר את הספינה (ב"ב דף פה: ושם) דקתני משך חמרין ופועלין לתוך ביתו שניהם יכולין לחזור אלמא דלא קני פירות במשיכת הבהמה וי"ל דהתם לא אמר ליה קני לכך לא קני ו) [א"נ התם כשמשך החמרין ולא משך את החמור] והא דקתני בין פסק כו' ה"ה אפי' פסק ומדד יכולין לחזור אלא משום דסיפא מפליג בין פסק עד שלא מדד ובין מדד עד שלא פסק נקט נמי ברישא האי לישנא וכן צריך לתרץ בסיפא דקתני פרקן והכניסן לתוך ביתו פסק עד שלא מדד אין יכולין לחזור ובעי למפשט מינה התם דכלי של מוכר ברשות לוקח לא קני המוכר שהמקח קיים אלמא הכלי מתבטל אצל הרשות משמע מטעם משיכה אינה קונה לפי שהוא בכליו של מוכר וכי משני התם ומוקי לה שספקן מכליו של מוכר או במתכלי דתומי משמע שאם היה בכליו של מוכר לא היה קונה אף על פי שהכניסן לתוך ביתו דהיינו משיכה ואמאי והא פשיטא לן במשוך קופה זו וקני כלים שבתוכה קני אלא התם י"ל משום דלא אמר ליה קני ואינו רוצה שיקנה אלא במשיכת פירות עצמן ועוד מצינו למימר דהתם משמע ליה שלא פסק עד אחר המשיכה ולכך לא קניא במשיכה וא"ת אמאי נקט משוך בהמה זו ולא נקיט קני אי משום דבקני פשיטא ליה דקני מטעם חצר אע"פ שהיא מהלכת א"כ במשוך נמי אמאי מספקא ליה כיון שהשאילה לו הרי היא כאילו היא שלו עד לאחר הקנין ויקנה מטעם חצר וי"ל דכשא"ל משוך לא השאיל לו הבהמה לקנות הכלים מטעם חצר אלא במשיכת הבהמה אי נמי אי הוי בעי קני בהמה וכלים והוה מהדר ליה דקני לא היה יכול לידע מזה שבמשיכת הבהמה יקנה הכלים כי שמא מטעם חצר קני ובכפותה ולכך איבעי ליה במשוך:

ספינה מינח נייחא ומיא הוא דקא ממטו לה. אע"ג דבפ"ק דקדושין (דף לג:) אמרינן דתלמיד חכם רכוב כמהלך דמי הכא חצר משום יד אתרבאי והוה שפיר ° דומיא דיד דמינח נייח וממטו לה עם גופיה וכן בפ"ק דשבת (דף ה: ושם ד"ה אגוז) אגוז לף ע"ג מים לא הוי הנחה אגוז בכלי וכלי לף על גבי מים מהו התם חשוב דדומיא דמלאכת המשכן בעינן ולא היו מצניעין חפצים בדבר שהיה מתנענע ומתנדנד אבל גבי קנייה כיון שהוא דומיא דידו קני: ה"נ דלא מגרשה. פרש"י הא דתנן זרק לתוך קלתה מגורשת ותימה לוקמה בכפותה ושמא נ"ל דוחק א"נ הכא מסברא פריך כדפריך מספינה ולא מכח משנה:

ולימא מר מעני לעני מחלוקת. ויחלקו בתופס לב"ח במקום שחב לאחרים ולא מטעם מגו דהא רב חסדא דקאמר כמו רב נחמן בסמוך המגביה מציאה לחבירו לא קנה חבירו אית ליה פרק קמא דגיטין (דף יא: ושם) דפליגי בתופס לבעל חוב ולא מטעם מגו עד דדחי ליה רב פפא דלמא במגו פליגי:

רב

---

**רש"י**

ואי רשות הרבים הוא קני. בעיר דדרך לרכוב שם ולא להנהיג פן יפסקו עוברי דרכים בינו לבין בהמתו: ואי אדם חשוב הוא. אין דרכו להנהיג בהמה ברגליו ודרך כבוד לרכוב עליה אף בסמטא שאין בני אדם שם וכן אשה שאין בה כח לאחוז הבהמה פן תינתק הימנה: ואי איניש זילא הוא קני. שדרכו לרכוב לפני כל אף בלא דוחק לפי שאינו נגוע אבל אדם בינוני כגון שאינו חשוב בעושר ואינו בוש להוליך בהמה ברגליו אין דרכו לרכוב בסמטא בעיר משום צניעות: משוך בהמה זו על מנת לקנות כלים שעליה. במקח וממכר ומוכר לו את הכלים ולא את הבהמה: לקנות מי קאמר ליה קני. לקנות משמע אתה התכוין לקנות אני איני מקנה לך: מי קני כלים. במשיכה דבהמה עם הבהמה דמדקא מבעיא לך במוכר כלים בלא בהמה מכלל דבמוכר שניהם פשיטא לך (א) דמקני בהמה קני כלים משום תורת חצר דקיימא לן חצרו של אדם קונה לו ובהמתו כחצרו והא חצר מהלכת היא וחצר מהלכת לא שמעינן דתקני דכי אתרבאי (גיטין דף עז.) מאם המצא תמצא בידו גגו חצרו וקרפיפו אתרבאי דלא נייד והוי משתמר: וכי תימא כשעמדה. לאחר שעקרה ידה ורגלה ונקנית לו הבהמה במשיכה עמדה ולא הלכה ונקנו כלים בעמידתה דקנה לו חצרו: כל שאילו מהלך לא קנה כו'. כלומר כיון דראויה היא לילך לאו דומיא דחצר היא ואין קונה בתורת חצר: והלכתא. האי דפשיטא ליה דכי אמר ליה קני בהמה וקני כלים קני: בכפותה. היא דפשיטא ליה (ב) דדומיא דחצר הוא קני וכל היכא דאמרינן בגמרא והאמר רבא כל שאילו מהלך לא קני כו' מהכא קאמרי ליה: קלתה. סל שעל ראשה שנותנת בה כלי מלאכתה וטווי שלה: ה"נ דלא הוי גיטא. והאנן תנן במס' גיטין (דף עז.) זרק לה גיטה לתוך חיקה או לתוך קלתה הרי זו מגורשת: מתני' לא אמר כלום. דאפילו אמרי' המגביה מציאה לחבירו לא קנה חבירו כיון דיהבה ליה קנייה ממה נפשך אי קנייה קמא דלא מתכוין להקנות לחבירו הא יהבה ניהליה במתנה ואי לא קנייה קמא משום דלא היה מתכוין לקנות הויא ליה הפקר עד דמטא לידיה דהאי וקנייה האי במאי דעקרה מידיה דקמא לשם קנייה: גמ' מי שליקט את הפאה. אדם בעלמא שאינו בעל שדה דאי בבעל שדה לא אמר ר' אליעזר זכה דליכא למימר מיגו דזכי לנפשיה דאפילו הוא עני מוזהר הוא שלא ללקט פאה משדה שלו כדאמר בשחיטת חולין (דף קלא:) לא תלקט לעני להזהיר עני על שלו: מעשיר לעני. שעשיר הוא שליקטה לצורך העני: מגו דזכי לנפשיה. דאי בעי הוה זכי לנפשיה אם הגביה לעצמו: חד מגו. מעני לעני: ולימא מר דאפילו מעני לעני. אמרי רבנן דלא זכה לו: דהא מציאה הכל עניים אצלה. כלומר הכל כשרים לזכות בה כעניים בפאה: ותנן. המגביה מציאה לחבירו לא קנה חבירו ולא אמרינן מגו דאי הוה בעי הוה זכי לנפשיה זכי נמי לחבריה כי מגבה לה כולה לשם חבירו דתנן היה רוכב כו': ואמר אני זכיתי בה. קס"ד אני רוצה לזכות בה עכשיו קאמר ומודה הוא שמתחילה הגביה לשם חבירו וקתני זכה בה אלמא לא קנה חבירו: אי אמרת בשלמא מעני לעני מחלוקת. דאמרי רבנן לא אמרינן מגו דזכי לנפשיה זכי נמי לחבריה אלא היכא דהגביה לדעת שניהם כגון שנים שהגביהו מציאה דאמר בה לעיל (דף ח.) גבי בזמן שהם מודים חולקים בלא שבועה דטעמא משום מגו דזכי בהגבהה זו לנפשיה זכי נמי לחבריה אבל מגו דאי בעי הוה זכי לנפשיה זכי לחבריה לא אמרינן:

מתני'

---

**עין משפט נר מצוה**

סו א מיי' פ"ב מהל' מכירה הל' י סמג עשין פב טוש"ע ח"מ סי' קצז סעיף ה:

סז ב מיי' שם הלכה ח ועי' פי' במ"מ טוש"ע שם סעיף ו:

סח ג מיי' פ"ג מהל' מכירה הל' יג סמג עשין פב טוש"ע ח"מ סי' רב סעיף יד:

סט ד ה ו מיי' שם הל' יג יד סמג שם טוש"ע שם סעיף יג וטוש"ע אה"ע סי' קלט סעיף טז:

ע ז מיי' פ"א מהלכות זכיה ומתנה הל' ה סמג עשין עג טוש"ע ח"מ סי' רעג סעיף טו:

עא ח מיי' פ"ה מהלכות גירושין הל' ח וע"ש סמג עשין נ טוש"ע אה"ע סי' קלט סעיף י:

עב ט מיי' פי"ז מהל' גזילה ואבידה הל' ב סמג עשין עד טוש"ע ח"מ סי' רסט סעיף ו:

עג י כ מיי' פ"ב מהל' מתנות עניים הל' יט:

**רבינו חננאל**

וכן אם הוא אדם חשוב שאין דרכו להלך רגלי קנה ברכיבה. וכן האשה. וכן אי גברא זילא הוא קני. בעי ר"א האומר לחבירו משוך בהמה זו וקני כלים שעליה מהו אמר רבא אי אמר ליה קני בהמה וקני כלים שעליה מי קנו כלים במשיכה דבהמה אמאי חצר מהלכת היא ואסקי' והלכתא בכפותה. וכן ספינה דקפצו דגים בתוכה קנאם בעל הספינה דספינה מינח נייחא ומיא הוא דממטו לה. ואסיקו רב אשי ורבינא באשה מהלכת ברה"ר וזרק לה בעלה גיטא בתוך קלתה נתגרשה מאי טעמא קלתה מינח נייחא ואיהי מסגיא תות' הני כולהי לאו חצר מהלכת נינהו וכן הלכה: ירושלמי אמר רב הונא בשם רבנן [תני] תמן אשה שהיתה רוכבת על גבי בהמה ושנים מנהיגין אותה היא אומרת אלו עבדיי והבהמה והמשוי שלי וזה אומר זו אשתי וזה עבדי וזו חבילתי א) צריכה גט משניהן והיא משחררת את שניהן ושניהן משחררין זה את זה ובבהמה ובמשוי שלשתן שוין: פיסקא מתני' היה רוכב על גבי בהמה וכו' תנן התם בפאה פ"ד מי שליקט [את הפאה] ואמר הרי זו לאיש פלוני עני ר"א אומר זכה לו וחכ"א יתננה לעני הנמצא ראשון. ואמר מחלוקת מעשיר לעני וכו' ולימא מר מעני לעני מחלוקת דהא מציאה הכל כעניים הן אצלה. ותנן ראה את המציאה ואמר לחבירו תנה לי נטלה ואמר אני זכיתי בה זכה בה לעצמו אי אמרת בשלמא מחלוקת מעני לעני

**חשק שלמה על ר"ח**

א) וזה אומר זו אשתי וזה עבדי וזו חבילתי צריכה גט וכו' [ועי' בקדושין ס"ה ע"ב ובפרש"י שם וי"ל].

---

**מסורת הש"ס**

א) בבא קמא יב., גיטין עח., ב) פאה פרק ד' מ"ט, גיטין יא:, ג) [ב"מ מז. וש"נ], ד) [לעיל נדרים פח:], ה) [תו' יא:], ו) מהרש"ל.

**הגהות הב"ח**

(א) רש"י ד"ה מי וכו', פשיטא לך דמ... בהמה: (ב) ד"ה וכו' האי וכו' דפשיטא ליה ... דדומיא:

**הגהות הגר"א**

[א] גמ' קני ואי. ... קו על מלת קני ועל ה... ממלת ואי ונ"ב הר... ל"ג זה אבל הרמב"ם ... כגירסא שלנו:

**גליון הש"ס**

גמ' והלכתא בכפותה. כעין זה ע... ז. והלכתא דיתבי: ... ד"ה ספינה ... דומיא דיד דמי תמוה לי דא"כ ... עלמא מקרי מהלך ול... מהני נותן גט על רא... גם אמאי בנתן גט עבדה מקרי חצר מה... הא היד מינח. אלא דיד והגוף חד הוא דאמרי' מה ידה ... מהלך היינו דאינו ... מהקונה דבכ"מ ... מהלך שם הוא ה... משא"כ חצר דמה מהקונה ולע"ג:

**ליקוטי רש"י**

וחצר מהלכת קנה. דכי אמור רבנן ... של אדם קונה לו לאו ... מהלכת אמור ד... מקרקעי דניידי ממתר דלא נייד [גיטין כא.]. ... קונה לבעליה כלום ... חצר היא ... והלכתא בכפותה שאינו ואי לילך ... לתלך [ב"ק יב.]. שליקט את הפאה בעה"ב עשיר שליקט הפאה וכו' [גיטין י...] ומגו דזכי לנפשיה עיין לעיל דף ח ע"...

עָנִי – AND SAID, "BEHOLD THIS IS FOR THIS-AND-THIS POOR MAN" – ר׳ אֱלִיעֶזֶר אוֹמֵר זָכָה לוֹ – R' ELIEZER SAYS: HE HAS ACQUIRED IT FOR [THAT POOR MAN], and he may not give it to anyone else.[28] וַחֲכָמִים אוֹמְרִים יִתְּנֶנָּה לֶעָנִי הַנִּמְצָא רִאשׁוֹן – BUT THE SAGES SAY: HE SHOULD GIVE IT TO THE FIRST AVAILABLE POOR MAN.[29]

Ulla expounds that Mishnah:

אָמַר עוּלָּא אָמַר ר׳ יְהוֹשֻׁעַ בֶּן לֵוִי – **Ulla said in the name of R' Yehoshua ben Levi:** מַחְלוֹקֶת מֵעָשִׁיר לֶעָנִי – **The dispute** of the Tannaim in the above Mishnah **concerns** specifically the case of *pe'ah* collected **by a rich man** (who is not eligible himself to acquire *pe'ah*) **for** the sake of **a poor man.** Only in that case is there a dispute, דְּר׳ אֱלִיעֶזֶר סָבַר – **for R' Eliezer holds** that מִגּוֹ דְּאִי בָּעֵי מַפְקַר נִכְסֵיהּ – **since [the rich man], if he wants to, can renounce** ownership of **his possessions** וְהָוֵי עָנִי וְחָזֵי לֵיהּ – **and** thereby **become a poor man, for whom [*pe'ah*] is appropriate,** הַשְׁתָּא נַמִּי חָזֵי לֵיהּ – **now, too,** while he is still in possession of his wealth, **[the *pe'ah*] is** also regarded as **appropriate for him,** וּמִגּוֹ דְּזָכֵי לְנַפְשֵׁיהּ – **and since he can acquire** it **for himself,** זָכֵי נַמִּי לְחַבְרֵיהּ – **he can also acquire** it **for** the sake of **his fellow,** the poor man. By a combination of these two "since" arguments, R' Eliezer maintains that the rich man's acquisition of the *pe'ah* on behalf of the poor recipient is effective.[30] וְרַבָּנָן סָבְרֵי – **Whereas the Sages hold** חַד מִגּוֹ אָמְרִינַן – **that we can say one "since"** argument, תְּרֵי מִגּוֹ לֹא אָמְרִינַן – **but cannot say two "since"** arguments.[31] [32]

Ulla continues his exposition:

אֲבָל מֵעָנִי לֶעָנִי – **However,** in the case of *pe'ah* collected **by a poor man for** the sake of **a** different **poor man,** דִּבְרֵי הַכֹּל זָכָה לוֹ – **all** [even the Sages] would **agree that [the poor collector] acquires** the *pe'ah* **for [the specified poor person].** מִגּוֹ דְּזָכֵי לְנַפְשֵׁיהּ – **For** in that case, **since [the poor collector] can acquire** the *pe'ah* **for himself,** זָכֵי נַמִּי לְחַבְרֵיהּ – **he can also acquire it for** the sake of **his fellow.**[33] This is Ulla's explanation of the Mishnah in *Pe'ah*.

Rav Nachman challenges Ulla's explanation:

אָמַר לֵיהּ רַב נַחְמָן לְעוּלָּא – **Rav Nachman said to Ulla:** מָא מַר מֵעָנִי לֶעָנִי מַחְלוֹקֶת – **Let Master say** instead that **the dispute** in that Mishnah **is** in regard to *pe'ah* collected **by a poor man for** a different **poor man.** I.e. say that even in that case, where the collector requires only *one* "since" argument to establish his right to the *pe'ah,* the Sages rule that he cannot acquire it on behalf of another poor person.[34]

Rav Nachman now attempts to prove his interpretation of the Mishnah in *Pe'ah*:

דְּהָא מְצִיאָה הַכֹּל עֲנִיִּים אֶצְלָהּ – **For surely, all are considered "poor" in regard to a find,** i.e. any person in the world is entitled to acquire ownerless property for himself, just as a poor man is entitled to take *pe'ah,* וּתְנַן – **yet we have learned in o**

NOTES

28. The act of picking up the produce is a formal mode of acquisition (הַגְבָּהָה, *lifting*). In R' Eliezer's opinion, when someone picks up the *pe'ah* with the express intention that it should thereby become the property of a specific poor man, the intended recipient automatically acquires it, although he is unaware of the whole matter. This is in accordance with the rule of זְכִיָּה, *zechiyah,* which states: זָכִין לְאָדָם שֶׁלֹּא בְּפָנָיו, *we may benefit a person [even] in his absence,* i.e. one can act as a person's agent in a legal proceeding without the person's prior knowledge or consent if the proceeding is clearly advantageous to the beneficiary; the beneficiary's consent to the agency is then assumed.

[R' Eliezer's ruling applies only if the collector is not the field's owner (*Rashi*) – see below, note 32.]

29. In the opinion of the Sages, the specified poor man has not acquired the *pe'ah* through the act of the collector, and the *pe'ah* should therefore be given to the first available eligible poor man that comes by.

30. See next note.

31. [In the case of this Mishnah, the normally operative principle of *zechiyah* must be considered in light of the fact that it is חַב לַאֲחֵרִים, *to the detriment of others.* That is, by acquiring the *pe'ah* on behalf of one poor person, the collector thereby deprives other poor people of their potential claim to the *pe'ah.* In situations of detriment to others, *zechiyah* is effective only if the one performing the act of acquisition is entitled to acquire the item for himself. Since he could exercise his right to take the item for himself and thereby deprive the other claimants of their potential claim, he has, by the same token, the power to acquire it on behalf of some other eligible party even though it is to the detriment of the other claimants. This is known as מִגּוֹ דְּזָכֵי לְנַפְשֵׁיהּ זָכֵי נַמִּי לְחַבְרֵיהּ, *since he can acquire [it] for himself, he can also acquire* [it] *on behalf of his fellow* (see below, 10a; *Gittin* 12a).

R' Eliezer argues that the rich man has it in his power to deprive the other poor people of their claim to this *pe'ah* by declaring his property ownerless and then taking this *pe'ah* for himself. Even though this power is two steps removed from being exercised (i.e. the rich person would have to abandon his property and also take the *pe'ah* for *himself* – neither of which he is actually doing), R' Eliezer rules that this potential is sufficient to allow him to perform *zechiyah* on behalf of the poor recipient. Thus, R' Eliezer allows combining two "since he could have" arguments to establish the collector's right to deprive other poor people of their claim to *pe'ah* and perform *zechiyah* in it for a specific poor person.

Now, according to Ulla, the Sages also agree that one *poor* person can acquire *pe'ah* on behalf of another one because the first person anyway had the *potential* to deprive the other claimants of this *pe'ah* by taking it for himself ("we say one 'since' argument"). Nevertheless, th[e Sages] rule that this potential is sufficient because it is only *one* step remov[ed] from being exercised (i.e. he can take it for himself instead of for h[is] friend). But they rule that the *zechiyah* of a *rich* person in *pe'ah* [on] behalf of his poor friend is ineffective, because the rich man's potent[ial] rights to the *pe'ah* are *two* steps removed (i.e. the rich person wou[ld] have to abandon his property and *also* take the *pe'ah* for *himself*). Th[ey] thus consider this potential too remote to enable him to perfor[m] *zechiyah* in *pe'ah* for a poor person and thereby deprive other po[or] people of their claim to it. In other words, the Sages do not allo[w] combining two "since" arguments to allow a *zechiyah* that is to t[he] detriment of others.]

32. There is a law recorded in *Chullin* 131b and *Gittin* 12a that a po[or] farmer is forbidden to take for himself the *pe'ah* of his own field, ev[en] though he is entitled to take *pe'ah* from other fields. Accordingly, *Ras[hi]* here (ד״ה מי שליקט) maintains that the Mishnah cannot refer to a case [in] which the field's *owner* collects *pe'ah* for a specific poor person, sin[ce] the field's owner can never be regarded as entitled to the *pe'ah* of h[is] field. Therefore, even R' Eliezer would not rule that the collect[or] acquires the *pe'ah* on behalf of the specified poor man.

[Other Rishonim (see *Tos. HaRosh*; *Rash* and *Rosh* to Mishnah *Pe'a[h]* ad loc.), however, argue that the Mishnah could indeed refer even to th[e] field's owner. For R' Eliezer's ruling is predicated on the collector['s] ability to declare his property ownerless, in which eventuality he wou[ld] cease to be the field's owner!

In defense of *Rashi, Ritva* explains that the Scriptural directi[ve] against the owner taking the *pe'ah* of his own field prohibits the own[er] of the field *at the time of the harvest* from ever taking that harvest['s] *pe'ah*. Accordingly, the owner can never become eligible for his *pe'ah* even if he were to subsequently declare his field ownerless. H[is] subsequent abandonment of his field would not retroactively chang[e] the fact that he was the field's owner at the time of the harvest (see als[o] *Tos. R' Akiva* to Mishnah *Pe'ah* ad loc.).]

33. In this case, the collector (who is himself poor and entitled to tak[e] the *pe'ah*) requires only one "since" argument to establish his ability t[o] deprive the other poor people of their rights to this *pe'ah*. In such a cas[e] even the Sages agree that he can perform *zechiyah* on behalf of on[e] person though it is to the detriment of others.

34. That is, perhaps the Sages' view is that we do not even apply th[e] simple argument of מִגּוֹ דְּזָכֵי לְנַפְשֵׁיהּ זָכֵי נַמִּי לְחַבְרֵיהּ, *since he can acquire* [it] *for himself, he can also acquire* [it] *on behalf of his fellow,* where th[e] *zechiyah* for one person will be to the detriment of others.

[Clearly, the first poor man (the collector) can actually acquire th

[א] ואי רשות הרבים הוא [א] קני ואי אדם חשוב הוא קני ואי אשה היא קניא ואי איניש זילא הוא קני בעי ר' אלעזר האומר לחבירו משוך בהמה זו לקנות כלים שעליה מהו [ב] לקנות מי אמר ליה קני אלא משוך בהמה זו וקני כלים שעליה מהו מי מהניא משיכה דבהמה לאקנויי כלים [ג] או לא אמר רבא אי אמר ליה קני בהמה וקני כלים מי קני כלים [ד] חצר מהלכת היא וחצר מהלכת לא קנה וכי תימא כשעמדה והא (א) כל [ה] שאילו מהלך לא קנה עומד ויושב לא קנה ° [ו] והלכתא בכפותה אמרו ליה רב פפא ורב הונא בריה דרב יהושע לרבא אלא מעתה היה מהלך בספינה וקפצו דגים ונפלו לתוך הספינה הכי נמי דחצר מהלכת היא ולא קני אמר ליה [ז] ספינה מינח נייחא ומיא הוא דקא ממטו לה א"ל רבינא לרב אשי אלא מעתה היתה מהלכת ברשות הרבים וזרק לה גט לתוך חיקה או לתוך קלתה הכא נמי דלא מגרשה א"ל [ח] קלתה מינח נייחא ואיהי דקא מסגיא מתותה:

**מתני'** [ט] היה רוכב על גבי בהמה וראה את המציאה ואמר לחבירו תנה לי נטלה ואמר אני זכיתי בה זכה בה אם משנתנה לו אמר אני זכיתי בה תחלה לא אמר כלום:

**גמ'** (ב) [י] תנן התם מי שליקט את הפאה ואמר הרי זו לפלוני עני ר' אליעזר אומר זכה לו וחכמים אומרים [כ] יתננה לעני הנמצא ראשון אמר עולא אמר ר' יהושע בן לוי מחלוקת מעשיר לעני דר' אליעזר סבר (ג) מגו דאי בעי מפקר נכסיה והוי עני וחזי ליה השתא נמי חזי ליה (ד) ומגו דזכי לנפשיה זכי נמי לחבריה ורבנן סברי (ה) [כ] חד מגו אמרינן תרי מגו לא אמרינן אבל מעני לעני דברי הכל זכה לו דמגו דזכי לנפשיה זכי נמי לחבריה אמר ליה רב נחמן לעולא ולימא מר מעני לעני מחלוקת דהא מציאה הכל עניים אצלה ותנן היה רוכב על גבי בהמה וראה את המציאה ואמר לחבירו תנה לי נטלה ואמר אני זכיתי בה זכה בה אי אמרת בשלמא מעני לעני מחלוקת

---

**ואי רשות הרבים הוא קני.** בעיר דדרך לרכוב שם ולא להנהיג פן יפסקו עוברי דרכים בינו לבין בהמתו: **ואי אדם חשוב הוא.** אין דרכו להנהיג בהמה ברגליו ודרך כבוד לרכוב עליה אף בסמטא שאין בני אדם שם וכן אשה שאין בה כח לאחוז הבהמה פן תינתק הימנה: **ואי איניש זילא הוא קני.** שדרכו לרכוב לפני כל אף בלא דוחק לפי שאינו נגוע אבל אדם בינוני כגון שאינו חשוב בעושר ואינו בוש להוליך בהמה ברגליו אין דרכו לרכוב בסמטא בעיר משום צניעות: **משוך בהמה זו על מנת לקנות כלים שעליה.** במקח וממכר ומוכר לו את הכלים ולא את הבהמה: **לקנות מי קאמר ליה קני.** לקנות משמע אתה התכוין לקנות אני איני מקנה לך: **מי קני כלים.** במשיכה דבהמה עם הבהמה דמדקא מבעיא לך במוכר כלים בלא בהמה מכלל דבמוכר שניהם פשיטא לך (א) דמקני בהמה קני כלים משום תורת חצר דקיימא לן חצרו של אדם קונה לו ובהמתו כחצרו והא חצר מהלכת היא וחצר מהלכת לא שמעינן דתקני דכי אתרבאי (גיטין דף עז.) מאם המצא תמצא בידו גגו חצרו וקרפיפו אתרבאי דלא נייד והוי משתמר: **וכי תימא כשעמדה.** לאחר שעקרה ידה ורגלה ונקנית לו הבהמה במשיכה עמדה ולא הלכה ונקנו כלים בעמידתה דקנה לו חצרו: **כל שאילו מהלך לא קנה כו'.** כלומר כיון דראויה היא לילך לאו דומיא דחצר היא ואין קונה בתורת חצר: **והלכתא.** האי דפשיטא ליה דכי אמר ליה קני בהמה וקני כלים קני: **בכפותה.** היא דפשיטא ליה (ב) דדומיא דחצר הוא קני וכל היכא דאמרינן בגמרא והאמר רבא כל שאילו מהלך לא קני כו' מהכא קאמרי ליה: **קלתה.** סל שעל ראשה שנותנת בה כלי מלאכתה וטווי שלה: **ה"נ דלא הוי גיטא.** והאנן תנן במס' גיטין (דף עז.) זרק לה גיטה לתוך חיקה או לתוך קלתה הרי זו מגורשת: **מתני' לא אמר כלום.** דאפילו אמרי' המגביה מציאה לחבירו לא קנה חבירו כיון דיהבה ליה קנייה ממה נפשך אי קנייה קמא דלא מתכוין להקנות לחבירו הא יהבה ניהליה במתנה ואי לא קנייה קמא משום דלא היה מתכוין לקנות הויא ליה הפקר עד דמטא לידיה דהאי וקנייה האי במאי דעקרה מידיה דקמא לשם קנייה: **גמ' מי שליקט את הפאה.** אדם בעלמא שאינו בעל שדה דאי בבעל שדה לא אמר ר' אליעזר זכה דליכא למימר מיגו דזכי לנפשיה דאפילו הוא עני מוזהר הוא שלא ללקט פאה משדה שלו כדאמר בשחיטת חולין (דף קלא:) לא תלקט לעני להזהיר עני על שלו: **מעשיר לעני.** שעשיר הוא שליקטה לצורך העני: **מגו דזכי לנפשיה.** דאי בעי הוה זכי לנפשיה אם הגביה לעצמו: **חד מגו.** מעני לעני: **ולימא מר דאפילו מעני לעני.** אמרי רבנן דלא זכה לו: **דהא מציאה הכל עניים אצלה.** כלומר הכל כשרים לזכות בה כעניים בפאה: **ותנן.** המגביה מציאה לחבירו לא קנה חבירו ולא אמרינן מגו דאי הוה בעי הוה זכי לנפשיה זכי נמי לחבריה כי מגבה לה כולה לשם חבירו דתנן היה רוכב כו': **ואמר אני זכיתי בה.** קס"ד אני רוצה לזכות בה עכשיו קאמר ומודה הוא שמתחילה הגביה לשם חבירו וקתני זכה בה אלמא לא קנה חבירו: **אי אמרת בשלמא מעני לעני מחלוקת.** דאמרי רבנן לא אמרינן מגו דזכי לנפשיה זכי נמי לחבריה אלא היכא דהגביה לדעת שניהם כגון שנים שהגביהו מציאה דאמר בה לעיל (דף ח.) גבי בזמן שהם מודים חולקים בלא שבועה דטעמא משום מגו דזכי בהגבהה זו לנפשיה זכי נמי לחבריה אבל מגו דאי בעי הוה זכי לנפשיה זכי לחבריה לא אמרינן:

מתני'

---

**משוך** בהמה זו וקני כלים שעליה כו'. מבעיא ליה כיון דמשיכת הבהמה שהולכת מעצמה לא שייכא בכלים לא יקנה הכלים אבל אם אמר משוך קופה וקני כלים שבתוכה פשיטא ליה דקני ואם תאמר תפשוט מברייתא דהמוכר את הספינה (ב"ב דף פה: ושם) דקתני משך חמרין ופועלין לתוך ביתו שניהם יכולין לחזור אלמא דלא קני פירות במשיכת הבהמה וי"ל דהתם לא אמר ליה קני לכך לא קני [י] [א"נ התם כשמשך החמרין ולא משך את החמור] והא דקתני בין פסק כו' ה"ה אפי' פסק ומדד יכולין לחזור אלא משום דסיפא מפליג בין פסק עד שלא מדד ובין מדד עד שלא פסק נקט נמי ברישא האי לישנא וכן צריך לתרץ בסיפא דקתני פרקן והכניסן לתוך ביתו פסק עד שלא מדד אין יכולין לחזור ובעי למפשט מינה התם דכלי של מוכר ברשות לוקח לא קני המוכר שהמקח קיים אלמא הכלי מתבטל אגב הרשות משמע מטעם משיכה אינה קונה לפי שהוא בכליו של מוכר וכי משני התם ומוקי לה שספקן מכליו של מוכר או במתבלי דתומי משמע שאם היה בכליו של מוכר לא היה קונה אף על פי שהכניסן לתוך ביתו דהיינו משיכה ואמאי והא פשיטא לן במשוך קופה זו וקני כלים שבתוכה קני אלא התם י"ל משום דלא אמר ליה קני ואינו רוצה שיקנה אלא במשיכת פירות עצמן ועוד מצינו למימר דהתם משמע ליה שלא פסק עד אחר המשיכה ולכך לא קניא במשיכה וא"ת אמאי נקט משוך בהמה זו ולא נקיט קני אי משום דבקני פשיטא ליה דקני מטעם חצר אע"פ שהיא מהלכת א"כ במשוך נמי אמאי מספקא ליה כיון שהשאילה לו הרי היא כאילו היא שלו עד לאחר הקנין ויקנה מטעם חצר וי"ל דכשא"ל משוך לא השאיל לו הבהמה לקנות הכלים מטעם חצר אלא במשיכת הבהמה אי נמי אי הוי בעי קני בהמה וכלים והוה מהדר ליה דקני לא היה יכול לידע מזה שבמשיכת הבהמה יקנה הכלים כי שמא מטעם חצר קני ובכפותה ולכך איבעי ליה במשוך:

**ספינה** מינח נייחא ומיא הוא דקא ממטו לה. אע"ג דבפ"ק דקדושין (דף כג:) אמרינן דתלמיד חכם רכוב כמהלך דמי הכא חצר משום יד אתרבאי והוה שפיר ° דומיא דיד דמינח נייח וממטו לה עם גופיה וכן בפ"ק דשבת (דף ה: ושם ד"ה אגוד) אגוד לף ע"ג מים לא הוי הנחה אגוד בכלי וכלי לף על גבי מים מהו התם משום דדומיא למלאכת המשכן בעינן ולא היו מניחין חפצים בדבר שהיה מתנענע ומתנדנד אבל גבי קנייה כיון שהוא דומיא דידו קני: **ה"נ** דלא מגרשה. פרש"י הא דתנן זרק לתוך קלתה מגורשת ותימה לוקמה בכפותה ושמא נ"ל דוחק א"נ הכא מסברא פריך כדפריך מספינה ולא מכח משנה:

**ולימא** מר מעני לעני מחלוקת. ויחלקו בתופס לב"ח במקום שחב לאחרים ולא מטעם מגו דהא רב חסדא דקאמר כמו רב נחמן בסמוך המגביה מציאה לחבירו לא קנה חבירו אית ליה פרק קמא דגיטין (דף יא: ושם) דפליגי בתופס לבעל חוב ולא מטעם מגו עד דדחי ליה רב פפא דלמא במגו פליגי:

רב

---



סו א מיי' פ"ג מהל' מכירה הל' י סמג עשין פב טוש"ע ח"מ סי' קצז סעיף ה:
סז ב מיי' שם הלכה ח ועי' פי' במ"מ טוש"ע שם סעיף ו:
סח ג מיי' פ"ג מהל' מכירה הל' יג סמג עשין פב טוש"ע ח"מ סי' רב סעיף יד:
סט ד ה ו מיי' שם הל' יג יד סמג שם טוש"ע שם סעיף יג וטוש"ע אה"ע סי' קלט סעיף טו:
ע ז מיי' פ"א מהלכות זכיה ומתנה הל' ה סמג עשין עג טוש"ע ח"מ סי' רעג סעיף טו:
עא ח מיי' פ"ה מהלכות גירושין הל' ח וע"ש סמג עשין נ טוש"ע אה"ע סי' קלט סעיף י:
עב ט מיי' פי"ז מהל' גזילה ואבידה הל' ב סמג עשין עד טוש"ע ח"מ סי' רסט סעיף ו:
עג י כ מיי' פ"ב מהל' מתנות עניים הל' יט:

### רבינו חננאל

וכן אם הוא אדם חשוב שאין דרכו להלך רגלי קנה ברכיבה. וכן האשה. וכן אי גברא זילא הוא קני. **בעי ר"א האומר** לחבירו משוך בהמה זו וקני כלים שעליה מהו אמר רבא אי אמר ליה קני בהמה וקני כלים שעליה מי קנו כלים במשיכה דבהמה אמאי חצר מהלכת היא ואסקי' והלכתא בכפותה. וכן ספינה דקפצו דגים בתוכה קנאם בעל הספינה דספינה מינח נייחא ומיא הוא דממטו לה. ואסיקו רב אשי ורבינא באשה מהלכת ברה"ר וזרק לה בעלה גיטא בתוך קלתה נתגרשה מאי טעמא קלתה מינח נייחא ואיהי מסגיא תות' הני כולהי לאו חצר מהלכת נינהו וכן הלכה: **ירושלמי** אמר רב הונא בשם רבנן [תני] תמן אשה שהיתה רוכבת על גבי בהמה ושנים מנהיגין אותה היא אומרת אלו עבדיי והבהמה והמשוי שלי וזה אומר זו אשתי וזה עבדי וזו חבילתי (א) צריכה גט משניהן והיא משחררת את שניהן ושניהן משחררין זה את זה ובבהמה ובמשוי שלשתן שוין: **פיסקא** מתני' היה רוכב על גבי בהמה וכו' תנן התם בפאה פ"ד מי שליקט [את הפאה] ואמר הרי זו לאיש פלוני עני ר"א אומר זכה לו וחכ"א יתננה לעני הנמצא ראשון. **ואמר** מחלוקת מעשיר לעני וכו' ולימא מר מעני לעני מחלוקת דהא מציאה הכל כעניים הן אצלה. ותנן ראה את המציאה ואמר לחבירו תנה לי נטלה ואמר אני זכיתי בה זכה בה לעצמו אי אמרת בשלמא מחלוקת מעני לעני

### חשק שלמה על ר"ח

א) הה אומר זו אשתי הה עבדי הו חבילתי צריכה גט וכו' [ועי' בקדושין ס"ה ע"ב ובפרש"י שם וי"ל].

---



א) בבא קמא יב., גיטין כ... עח., ב) פאה פרק ד' מ... ט', גיטין יא:, ג) [ברכ... מז. וש"נ], ד) [לעיל... נדרים פט:], ה) [תמו... יא:], ו) מהרש"ל.

### הגהות הב"ח

(א) רש"י ד"ה מי ... וכו', פשיטא לך דמד... בהמה: (ב) ד"ה והלכ... האי וכו' דפשיטא ליה ד... דדומיא:

### הגהות הגר"א

[א] גמ' קני ואי. ר... קו על מלת קני ועל הו... ממלת ואי וכ"כ הרא... ל"ג זה אבל הרמב"ם ג... כגירסא שלנו:

### גליון הש"ס

גמ' והלכ... בכפותה. כעין זה ער... ז. והלכתא דיתבי: ת... ד"ה ספינה ו... דומיא דיד דמינ... תמוה לי דא"כ ה... עצמה מקרי מהלך ואו... מהני נותן גט על רא... גם אמאי בנתן גט... עבדה מקרי חצר מהל... הא היד מינח. אלא ע... דיד והגוף חד הוא ... דאמרי' מה ידה ש... מהלך היינו דאינו מ... מהקונה דבכ"מ ש... מהלך שם הוא הק... משא"כ חצר דמהו... מהקונה ולע"ג:

### ליקוטי רש"י

**וחצר מהלכת** קנה. דכי אמור רבנן ח... של אדם קונה לו לאו ב... מהלכת אמור ד... מקרקעי דניידי ממקר... דלא ניידי [גיטין כא.]. ... קונה לבעליה כלום ד... חצר היא במהל... **והלכתא בכפו...** שאינו ראוי לילך ד... לחצר [ב"ק יב.]. **שליקט את הפא...** בעה"ב עשיר שליקט הפאה וכו' [גיטין י... **ומגו דזכי לנפש...** עיין לעיל דף ח ע"...

you will say in reply, כְּשֶׁעָמְדָה – that the animal serves as the buyer's courtyard **when it stands still,**[13] וְהָא כָּל שֶׁאִילּוּ מְהַלֵּךְ לֹא קָנָה – but **surely** the rule is that **whatever cannot** serve as a courtyard to **effect acquisition while it is traveling** עוֹמֵד וְיוֹשֵׁב לֹא קָנָה – **cannot effect acquisition while it is standing or sitting** still either.[14] – ? –

The Gemara arrives at its final understanding of R' Elazar's case:

וְהִלְכְתָא בִּכְפוּתָה – **The point of law** about which R' Elazar inquired[15] concerns a case **where [the animal] is bound.**[16] In this case, the animal can indeed serve as a "courtyard," since it does not have the capacity to travel. Therefore, R' Elazar had to make his inquiry in a case where the animal itself is not being acquired and thus cannot serve as a courtyard to acquire the utensils.

The Gemara inquires further into situations of a traveling courtyard:

אָמְרוּ לֵיהּ רַב פָּפָּא וְרַב הוּנָא בְּרֵיהּ דְּרַב יְהוֹשֻׁעַ לְרָבָא – **Rav Pappa and Rav Huna the son of Rav Yehoshua said to Rava:** אֶלָּא מֵעַתָּה – **But now** that you have ruled that a traveling courtyard does not effect acquisition, הָיָה מְהַלֵּךְ בִּסְפִינָה – then if **someone was traveling in [his] boat** וְקָפְצוּ דָּגִים וְנָפְלוּ לְתוֹךְ הַסְּפִינָה – **and** some **fish jumped** out of the water **and fell into the boat,**[17] הָכִי נַמִי דְּחָצֵר מְהַלֶּכֶת הִיא וְלֹא קָנֵי – would you maintain **that so, to [the boat] is a traveling courtyard and it can** therefore **n**[ot] **effect acquisition?**[18]

Rava replies:

אָמַר (ליה) [לְהוּ] – **He said to them:** סְפִינָה מֵינָח נַיְיחָא – **A bo**[at] **is at rest** וּמַיָּא הוּא דְּקָא מְמַטוּ לָהּ – **and it is the water th**[at] **moves it.** Since a boat is not self-propelling, it is not considered [a] traveling courtyard and the owner does acquire the fish.[19]

A further inquiry into an apparent situation of a traveli[ng] courtyard:

אָמַר לֵיהּ רָבִינָא לְרַב אַשִׁי – **Ravina said to Rav Ashi:** [אֶ]לָּא מֵעַתָּה – **But now** that it has been ruled that a traveling courtyard do[es] not effect acquisition, הָיְתָה מְהַלֶּכֶת בִּרְשׁוּת הָרַבִּים – then if [a] **woman] was walking in a public domain** וְזָרַק לָהּ גֵּט – **an**[d] **[her husband] threw her a bill of divorce** [לְ]תוֹךְ חֵיקָהּ אוֹ לְתוֹךְ קַלְתָּהּ – **into her lap or into her basket,** which she carried on h[er] head,[20] הָכָא נַמִי דְּלֹא מְגָרְשָׁה – would you maintain that **he**[re] **too** the basket constitutes a traveling courtyard and **she** therefore **not divorced?**[21]

Rav Ashi replies:

אָמַר לֵיהּ – **He said to him:** קַלְתָּהּ מֵינָח נַיְיחָא – **Her basket is** [at] **rest** וְאִיהִי דְּקָא מְסַגְיָא מִתּוּתָהּ – **and it is she that is walkin**[g] **beneath it.** Therefore, the basket is not a traveling courtyard an[d] it can effect acquisition of the bill of divorce.

**Mishnah** הָיָה רוֹכֵב עַל גַּבֵּי בְהֵמָה – **If someone was riding on an animal** וְרָאָה אֶת הַמְּצִיאָה – **and he sighted a find,** i.e. an ownerless article,[22] וְאָמַר לַחֲבֵירוֹ – **and he said to his fellow,** who was standing nearby, תְּנָה לִי – **"Give it to me";** נְטָלָהּ – **and [that other person] took it**[23] וְאָמַר אֲנִי זָכִיתִי בָהּ – **and** then **said, "I have acquired it** for myself," זָכָה בָהּ – he has indeed **acquired it** for himself.[24] אִם מִשֶּׁנְּתָנָהּ לוֹ – **If,** however, **after he had given it to [the rider],** אָמַר אֲנִי זָכִיתִי בָהּ תְּחִלָּה – **he said, "I acquired it first,"**[25] לֹא אָמַר כְּלוּם – **he has said nothing,** i.e. his claim is dismissed and the rider may keep it.[26]

**Gemara** The Gemara introduces a Mishnah in tractate *Pe'ah* (4:9), which has a bearing on our Mishnah: תְּנַן הָתָם – **We have learned there in a Mishnah:** [מִ]י שֶׁלִּיקֵּט אֶת הַפֵּאָה – SOMEONE WHO GATHERED *PE'AH*[27] [וְאָ]מַר הֲרֵי זוֹ לִפְלוֹנִי

NOTES

Torah states specifically in terms of "hand," only such properties that are similar to one's hand in that they are stationary (relative to the person) and protected by him are included. But an animal, which travels, is not a property that can serve as a *chatzeir* to effect acquisition (see *Rashi, Tosafos* and *Tos. HaRosh*; *Rosh* to *Gittin* 8:5; cf. *Divrei Mishpat* 200:2 and *Meiri* to *Bava Kamma* 12a ד״ה הקנה לו).

13. Thus, R' Elazar saw no need to inquire about a case in which the animal, too, was being sold, since the utensils in that case would be acquired by the buyer as soon as the animal stopped walking (see *Rashi*).

14. The fact that it is presently standing or sitting does not alter its status of a traveling *chatzeir*. It still differs from the standard *chatzeir* [derived from the context of "hand"] in that it has the *potential* to travel (*Rashi*).

15. [Translation follows *Ritva*.]

16. I.e. R' Elazar inquired whether the *meshichah* of even an animal bound so that it cannot walk is effective to acquire the utensils that are on it [see above, note 8] (see *Rosh* and *Nemukei Yosef*; cf. *Hagahos MeAlfas Yashan*).

17. The fish are ownerless and belong to the first person to legally acquire them. A boat constitutes a *chatzeir* and can acquire its contents for its owner.

18. Since the boat moves in the water, it should be classed as a traveling *chatzeir*.

19. The exclusion of a traveling property as a viable *chatzeir* applies only to a property that is self-propelled, such as an animal.

20. [Women used to carry on their heads baskets containing their implements and their weave (*Rashi*).]

As mentioned above in note 12, the Torah's requirement that the bill of divorce be placed in the wife's hand is fulfilled by placing it in her *chatzeir*. Since the wife is in a public domain, the ground on which she stands cannot function as her *chatzeir*, but the basket on her head can.

21. Yet, a Mishnah (*Gittin* 77a) teaches explicitly that if a husba[nd] throws a bill of divorce into his wife's basket, she *is* divorced (*Rashi*). [Presumably, the basket of the Mishnah was being carried on her hea[d] as was the usual custom.] Does this Mishnah not disprove the assertio[n] that a traveling property cannot serve as a *chatzeir*?

22. Which belongs to the first one to legally acquire it.

23. The act of picking it up is a formal mode of acquisition (הַגְבָּהָה, *lif[t]ing*).

24. Although he picked it up at the rider's bidding, he is neverthele[ss] entitled to keep it for himself. The act of picking it up at the rider's bi[d]ding does not automatically effect acquisition for the rider. The Gema[ra] will elaborate on this point.

25. I.e. the pedestrian who picked up the find claims that he actual[ly] intended to acquire it for himself and that he gave it to the rider just t[o] show it to him or so that he should hold it for him (*Meiri*).

26. Even if we assume the position that the pedestrian's picking u[p] of the article for the rider does not automatically acquire it for th[e] rider (see Gemara), the rider acquires the article when the pedestria[n] hands it over to him, in any event: If the pedestrian meant to acquire [it] for himself, he has in effect given it as a gift to the rider by handin[g] it to him. And if the pedestrian did not intend to acquire it f[or] himself, then the rider acquires the still ownerless article as soon a[s] he receives it in his hand (*Rashi*). [Since the pedestrian does n[ot] claim that he really meant to keep the article for himself (and gave it t[o] the rider simply to hold for him) until after the rider has physical posse[s]sion of it, he is not believed to remove the article from the rider's posse[s]sion.]

27. The Torah (*Leviticus* 19:9-10; 23:22) commands growers in Eret[z] Yisrael to leave a portion of their crops [called *pe'ah* (literally: corner)] for the poor to harvest for themselves. Only a poor man is entitled t[o] acquire it.

ואי רשות הרבים הוא [א]קני ואי אדם חשוב הוא קני ואי אשה היא קניא ואי איניש זילא הוא קני בעי ר' אלעזר האומר לחבירו משוך בהמה זו לקנות כלים שעליה מהו לקנות מי אמר ליה קני אלא משוך בהמה זו וקני כלים שעליה מהו מי מהניא משיכה דבהמה לאקנויי כלים או לא אמר רבא אי אמר ליה קני בהמה וקני כלים מי קני כלים חצר מהלכת היא וחצר מהלכת לא קנה וכי תימא כשעמדה והא כל שאילו מהלך לא קנה עומד ויושב לא קנה והלכתא בכפותה אמרו ליה רב פפא ורב הונא בריה דרב יהושע לרבא אלא מעתה היה מהלך בספינה וקפצו דגים ונפלו לתוך הספינה הכי נמי דחצר מהלכת היא ולא קני אמר ליה ספינה מינח נייחא ומיא הוא דקא ממטו לה א"ל רבינא לרב אשי אלא מעתה היתה מהלכת ברשות הרבים וזרק לה גט לתוך חיקה או לתוך קלתה הכא נמי דלא מגרשה א"ל קלתה מינח נייחא ואיהי דקא מסגיא מתותה:

מתני' היה רוכב על גבי בהמה וראה את המציאה ואמר לחבירו תנה לי נטלה ואמר אני זכיתי בה זכה בה אם משנתנה לו אמר אני זכיתי בה תחלה לא אמר כלום:

גמ' תנן התם מי שליקט את הפאה ואמר הרי זו לפלוני עני ר' אליעזר אומר זכה לו וחכמים אומרים יתננה לעני הנמצא ראשון אמר עולא אמר ר' יהושע בן לוי מחלוקת מעשיר לעני דר' אליעזר סבר מגו דאי בעי מפקר נכסיה והוי עני וחזי ליה השתא נמי חזי ליה ומגו דזכי לנפשיה זכי נמי לחבריה ורבנן סברי חד מגו אמרינן תרי מגו לא אמרינן אבל מעני לעני דברי הכל זכה לו דמגו דזכי לנפשיה זכי נמי לחבריה אמר ליה רב נחמן לעולא ולימא מר מעני לעני מחלוקת דהא מציאה הכל עניים אצלה ותנן היה רוכב על גבי בהמה וראה את המציאה ואמר לחבירו תנה לי נטלה ואמר אני זכיתי בה זכה בה אי אמרת בשלמא מעני לעני מחלוקת

רב

**רש"י**

ואי רשות הרבים הוא קני. בעיר לדרך לרכוב שם ולא להנהיג פן יפסקו עוברי דרכים בינו לבין בהמתו: ואי אדם חשוב הוא. אין דרכו להנהיג בהמה ברגליו ודרך כבוד לרכוב עליה אף בסמטא שאין בני אדם שם וכן אשה שאין בה כח לנחות הבהמה פן תינתק הימנה: ואי איניש זילא הוא קני. שדרכו לרכוב לפני כל אף בלא דוחק לפי שאינו נגוע אצל אדם בינוני כגון שאינו חשוב בעושר ואינו בוש להוליך בהמה ברגליו אין דרכו לרכוב בסמטא בעיר משום גניעות: משוך בהמה זו על מנת לקנות כלים שעליה. במקח וממכר ומוכר לו את הכלים ולא את הבהמה: לקנות מי קאמר ליה קני. לקנות משמע אתה התכוין לקנות אני איני מקנה לך: מי קני כלים. במשיכה דבהמה עם הבהמה דמדקא מבעיא לך במוכר כלים בלא בהמה מכלל דבמוכר שניהם פשיטא לך (א) דמקני בהמה קני כלים משום תורת חצר דקיימא לן חצרו של אדם קונה לו ובהמתו כחצרו והא חצר מהלכת היא וחצר מהלכת לא שמעינן דתקני דכי אתרבאי (גיטין דף עז.) מאם המצא תמצא בידו גגו חצרו וקרפיפו אתרבאי דלא נייד והוי משתמר: וכי תימא כשעמדה. לאחר שעקרה ידה ורגלה ונקנית לו הבהמה במשיכה עמדה ולא הלכה ונקנו כלים בעמידתה קקנה לו חצרו: כל שאילו מהלך לא קנה כו'. כלומר כיון דלהויה היא לילך לאו דומיא דחצר היא ואין קונה בתורת חצר: והלכתא. האי דפשיטא ליה דכי אמר ליה קני בהמה וקני כלים קני: בכפותה. היא דפשיטא ליה (ב) דדומיא דחצר הוא קני וכל היכא דאמרינן בגמרא והאמר רבא כל שאילו מהלך לא קני כו' מהכא קאמרי ליה: קלתה. סל שעל ראשה שנותנת בה כלי מלאכתה וטווי שלה: ה"נ דלא הוי גיטא. והאנן תנן במס' גיטין (דף עז.) זרק לה גיטה לתוך חיקה או לתוך קלתה הרי זו מגורשת: מתני' לא אמר כלום. דאפילו אמרי' המגביה מציאה לחבירו לא קנה חבירו כיון דיהבה ליה קנייה ממה נפשך אי קנייה קמא דלא מתכוין להקנות לחבירו הא יהבה ניהליה במתנה ואי לא קנייה קמא משום דלא היה מתכוין לקנות הויא ליה הפקר עד דמטא לידיה דהאי וקנייה האי במאי דעקרה מידיה דקמא לשם קנייה: גמ' מי שליקט את הפאה. אדם בעלמא שאינו בעל שדה דאי בבעל שדה לא אמר ר' אליעזר זכה דליכא למימר מיגו דזכי לנפשיה דאפילו הוא עני מוזהר הוא שלא ללקט פאה משדה שלו כדאמר בשחיטת חולין (דף קלא:) לא תלקט לעני להזהיר עני על שלו: מעשיר לעני. שעשיר הוא שליקטום לצורך העני: מגו דזכי לנפשיה. דאי בעי הוה זכי לנפשיה אם הגביה לעצמו: חד מגו. מעני לעני: ולימא מר דאפילו מעני לעני. אמרי רבנן דלא זכה לו: דהא מציאה הכל עניים אצלה. כלומר הכל כשרים לזכות בה כעניים בפאה: ותנן. המגביה מציאה לחבירו לא קנה חבירו ולא אמרינן מגו דאי הוה בעי הוה זכי לנפשיה זכי נמי לחבריה כי מגבה לה כולה לשם חבירו דתנן היה רוכב כו': ואמר אני זכיתי בה. קס"ד אני רוצה לזכות בה עכשיו קאמר ומודה הוא שמתחילה הגביה לשם חבירו וקתני זכה בה אלמא לא קנה חבירו: אי אמרת בשלמא מעני לעני מחלוקת. דאמרי רבנן לא אמרינן מגו דזכי לנפשיה זכי נמי לחבריה אלא היכא דהגביה לדעת שניהם כגון שנים שהגביהו מציאה דאמר בה לעיל (דף ח.) גבי זמן שהם מודים חולקים בלא שבועה דטעמא משום מגו דזכי בהגבהה זו לנפשיה זכי נמי לחבריה אבל מגו דאי בעי הוה זכי לנפשיה זכי לחבריה לא אמרינן:

מתני'

**תוספות**

משוך בהמה זו וקני כלים שעליה כו'. מבעיא ליה כיון דמשיכת הבהמה שהולכת מעצמה לא שייכא בכלים לא יקנה הכלים אבל אם אמר משוך קופה וקני כלים שבתוכה פשיטא ליה דקני ואם תאמר תפשוט מברייתא דהמוכר את הספינה (ב"ב דף פה: ושם) דקתני משך חמרין ופועלין לתוך ביתו שניהם יכולין לחזור אלמא דלא קני פירות במשיכת הבהמה וי"ל דהתם לא אמר ליה קני לכך לא קני [א"נ התם כשמשך החמרין ולא משך את החמור] והא דקתני בין פסק כו' ה"ה אפי' פסק ומדד יכולין לחזור אלא משום דסיפא מפליג בין פסק עד שלא מדד ובין מדד עד שלא פסק נקט נמי ברישא האי לישנא וכן צריך לתרץ בסיפא דקתני פרקן והכניסן לתוך ביתו פסק עד שלא מדד אין יכולין לחזור ובעי למפשט מינה התם דכלי של מוכר ברשות לוקח לא קני המוכר שהסמקת קיים אלמא הכלי מתבטל אגב הרשות משמע מטעם משיכה אינה קונה לפי שהוא בכליו של מוכר וכי משני התם ומוקי לה שספקן מכליו של מוכר או במתכלי דלוקח משמע שאם היה בכליו של מוכר לא היה קונה אף על פי שהכניסן לתוך ביתו דהיינו משיכה ואמאי והא פשיטא לן במשוך קופה זו וקני כלים שבתוכה קני אלא התם י"ל משום דלא אמר ליה קני ואינו רוצה שיקנה אלא במשיכת פירות עצמן ועוד מצינו למימר דהתם משמע ליה שלא פסק עד אחר המשיכה ולכך לא קניא במשיכה וא"ת אמאי נקט משוך בהמה זו ולא נקט קני אי משום דבקני פשיטא ליה דקני מטעם חצר אע"פ שהיא מהלכת א"כ במשוך נמי אמאי מספקא ליה כיון שהשאילה לו הרי היא כאילו היא שלו עד לאחר הקנין ויקנה מטעם חצר וי"ל דכשא"ל משוך לא השאיל לו הבהמה לקנות הכלים מטעם חצר אלא במשיכת הבהמה אי נמי אי הוי בעי קני בהמה וכלים והוה מהדר ליה דקני לא היה יכול לידע מזה שבמשיכת הבהמה יקנה הכלים כי שמא מטעם חצר קני ובכפותה ולכך איבעי ליה במשוך:

ספינה מינח נייחא ומיא הוא דקא ממטו לה. אע"ג דבפ"ק דקדושין (דף כג:) אמרינן דתלמיד חכם רכוב כמהלך דמי הכא חצר משום יד אתרבאי והוה שפיר דומיא דיד דמינח נייח וממטו לה עם גופיה וכן בפ"ק דשבת (דף ה: ושם ד"ה אגוז) אגוז לך ע"ג מים לא הוי הנחה אגוז בכלי והלך לך על גבי מים מהו התם משום דדומיא למלאכת המשכן בעינן ולא היו מניחין חפצים בדבר שהיה מתנענע ומתגלגל אבל גבי קנייה כיון שהוא דומיא דידו קני: ה"נ דלא מגרשה. פרש"י הא דתנן זרק לתוך קלתה מגורשת ומיהו לוקמה בכפותה ושמא נ"ל דוחק א"נ הכא מסברא פריך כדפריך מספינה ולא מכח משנה:

ולימא מר מעני לעני מחלוקת. ויחלקו בתופס לב"ח במקום שחב לאחרים ולא מטעם מגו דהא רב חסדא דקאמר כמו רב נחמן בסמוך המגביה מציאה לחבירו לא קנה חבירו אית ליה פרק קמא דגיטין (דף יא: ושם) דפליגי בתופס לבעל חוב ולא מטעם מגו עד דדחי ליה רב פפא דלמא במגו פליגי:

**עין משפט נר מצוה**

סו א מיי' פ"ב מהל' מכירה הל' י סמג עשין פב טוש"ע ח"מ סי' קצז סעיף ה:
סז ב מיי' שם הלכה ח ועי' פי' במ"מ טוש"ע שם סעיף ו:
סח ג מיי' פ"ג מהל' מכירה הל' יג סמג עשין פב טוש"ע ח"מ סי' רכ סעיף יד:
סט ד ה ו מיי' שם הל' יג יד סמג שם טוש"ע שם סעיף יג וטוש"ע אה"ע סי' קלט סעיף טז:
ע ז מיי' פ"א מהלכות זכיה ומתנה הל' ה סמג עשין עג טוש"ע ח"מ סי' רעג סעיף טו:
עא ח מיי' פ"ה מהלכות גירושין הל' ח וע"ש סמג עשין נ טוש"ע אה"ע סי' קלט סעיף י:
עב ט מיי' פי"ז מהל' גזילה ואבידה הל' ג סמג עשין עד טוש"ע ח"מ סי' רסט סעיף ו:
עג י כ מיי' פ"ב מהל' מתנות עניים הל' יט:

**רבינו חננאל**

וכן אם הוא אדם חשוב שאין דרכו להלך רגלי קנה ברכיבה. וכן האשה. וכן אי גברא זילא הוא קני. בעי ר"א האומר לחבירו משוך בהמה זו וקני כלים שעליה מהו אמר רבא אי אמר ליה קני בהמה וקני כלים שעליה מי קנו כלים במשיכה דבהמה אמאי חצר מהלכת היא ואסקי' והלכתא בכפותה. וכן ספינה דקפצו דגים בתוכה קנאם בעל הספינה דספינה מינח נייחא ומיא הוא דממטו לה. ואסיקו רב אשי ורבינא באשה מהלכת ברה"ר וזרק לה בעלה גיטא בתוך קלתה נתגרשה מאי טעמא קלתה מינח נייחא ואיהי מסגיא תות' הני כולהי לאו חצר מהלכת נינהו וכן הלכה: ירושלמי אמר רב הונא בשם רבנן [תני] תמן אשה שהיתה רוכבת על גבי בהמה ושנים מנהיגין אותה היא אומרת אלו עבדיי והבהמה והמשוי שלי וזה אומר זו אשתי וזה עבדי וזו חבילתי א) צריכה גט משניהן והיא משחררת את שניהן ושניהן משחררין זה את זה ובבהמה ובמשוי שלשתן שוין: פיסקא מתני' היה רוכב על גבי בהמה וכו' תנן התם בפאה פ"ד מי שליקט [את הפאה] ואמר הרי זו לאיש פלוני עני ר"א אומר זכה לו וחכ"א יתננה לעני הנמצא ראשון. ואמר מחלוקת מעשיר לעני וכו' ולימא מר מעני לעני מחלוקת דהא מציאה הכל כעניים הן אצלה. ותנן ראה את המציאה ואמר לחבירו תנה לי נטלה ואמר אני זכיתי בה זכה בה לעצמו אי אמרת בשלמא מחלוקת מעני לעני

**חשק שלמה על ר"ח**

א) וזה אומר זו אשתי וזה עבדי וזו חבילתי צריכה גט וכו' [ועי' בקדושין ס"ה ע"ב ובפרש"י שם וי"ל].

**מסורת הש"ס**

א) בבא קמא יג., גיטין עח., ב) פאה פרק ד' מ"ט, גיטין יא:, ג) [בכ מז. וש"נ], ד) [לעיל נדרים פח:], ה) [תמ יא:], ו) מהרש"ל.

**הגהות הב"ח**

(א) רש"י ד"ה מי וכו', פשיטא לך דמ בהמה: (ב) ד"ה והל האי וכו' דפשיטא ליה ד דדומיא:

**הגהות הגר"א**

[א] גמ' קני ואי. ר קו על מלת קני ועל הו ממלת ואי ונ"ב הרי ל"ג זה אבל הרמב"ם ג כגירסא שלנו:

**גליון הש"ס**

גמ' והלכ בכפותה. כעין זה ע ז. והלכתא דיתבי: ח ד"ה ספינה דומיא דיד דמי תמוה לי דא"כ ה עצמה מקרי מהלך ול מהני נותן גט על ר גם אמאי בנתן גט עבדה מקרי חצר מה הא היד מינח. אלא דיד והגוף חד הוא דאמרי' מה ידה מהלך היינו דאינו מ מהקונה דבכ"מ מהלך שם הוא הכ משא"כ חצר דמה מהקונה ולע"ג:

**ליקוטי רש"י**

וחצר מהלכת קנה. דכי אמור רבנן של אדם קונה לו לאו מהלכת אמור ד מקרקעי דניידי ממקר דלא נייד [גיטין כא.]. קונה לבעליה כלום חצר היא במהו והלכתא בכפו שאינו ראוי לילך ד לחצר [ב"ק יב.]. שליקט את הפא בעה"ב עשיר שליקט הפאה וכו' [גיטין ומגו דזכי לנפש עיין לעיל דף ח ע"

The Gemara adds a number of qualifications to the law that a rider does not acquire in a town:

וְאִי רְשׁוּת הָרַבִּים הוּא – **But if it is** in **a public domain** in the town that he rides the animal, i.e. on a street, קָנֵי – **he does acquire** the animal;[1] וְאִי אָדָם חָשׁוּב הוּא – **and if [the buyer] is a distinguished person** for whom it is customary to ride even in a town,[2] קָנֵי – **he does acquire** the animal; וְאִי אִשָּׁה הִיא – **and if [the buyer] is a woman** for whom it is likewise customary to ride even in a town,[3] קָנְיָא – **she does acquire** the animal; וְאִי אִינִישׁ זִילָא הוּא – **and if [the buyer] is a base person**[4] who is wont to flout convention and rides even in a town, קָנֵי – **he does acquire** the animal.

R' Elazar poses a query:[5]

בָּעֵי ר' אֶלְעָזָר – **R' Elazar inquired:** הָאוֹמֵר לַחֲבֵירוֹ – **If [a seller] says to his fellow** [a buyer]: מְשׁוֹךְ בְּהֵמָה זוּ לִקְנוֹת כֵּלִים שֶׁעָלֶיהָ – **"Draw this animal near in order to acquire the utensils that are on it,"**[6] מַהוּ – **what is [the law]?** Is the act of drawing near performed to the animal effective for acquiring the utensils?

The Gemara questions the query as presented:

לִקְנוֹת – Do you really mean that the seller said, "Draw this animal near **in order to acquire** the utensils"? מִי אָמַר לֵיהּ קְנֵי – But in that case, **did he ever tell him, "Acquire** the utensils"? Since the seller did not explicitly tell the buyer to acquire them, the buyer certainly does not acquire them![7] – ? –

The Gemara rephrases R' Elazar's inquiry:

אֶלָּא – **Rather,** R' Elazar inquired: מְשׁוֹךְ בְּהֵמָה זוּ – If a sel[ler] says to a buyer, **"Draw this animal near** וּקְנֵי כֵּלִים שֶׁעָלֶיהָ – a[nd] **acquire the utensils on it,"** מַהוּ – **what is [the law]?**

The Gemara explains the essence of R' Elazar's query:

מִי מְהַנְיָא מְשִׁיכָה דִבְהֵמָה – **Is the drawing near of the anim[al] effective** לְאַקְנוּיֵי כֵּלִים – **to acquire the utensils** אוֹ לֹא – **or not?**[8] The Gemara leaves R' Elazar's query unanswered.[9]

R' Elazar, in his inquiry, referred specifically to a case in whi[ch] only the utensils on the animal are being sold, not the anim[al] itself.[10] This implies that where both the animal and the utens[ils] are being sold, there is no doubt in R' Elazar's mind that drawi[ng] the animal near serves to acquire the utensils as well. It is t[he] assumption implicit in R' Elazar's query that Rava now ch[al]lenges:

אָמַר רָבָא – **Rava said:** אִי אָמַר לֵיהּ – **If [the seller] said to [t]he buyer],** קְנֵי בְּהֵמָה וּקְנֵי כֵּלִים – **"Acquire the animal a[nd] acquire the utensils** on it," מִי קָנֵי כֵּלִים – **would he th[en] acquire the utensils**, as implied by R' Elazar's query? Pr[e]sumably, this assumes that the animal would serve as the buye[r's] "courtyard."[11] חָצֵר מְהַלֶּכֶת הִיא – But surely **it is a traveli[ng] courtyard** וְחָצֵר מְהַלֶּכֶת לֹא קָנָה – **and a traveling courtya[rd] cannot effect acquisition** for its owner![12] וְכִי תֵּימָא – **And**

NOTES

1. It is customary to ride in a street where there is traffic, even in a town, and not to merely lead on foot, because of the apprehension that one may be separated from his animal by the throng (*Rashi*). The rule that riding is not a valid *kinyan* in a town refers only to places where traffic is not dense, as in a *simta* [alley].

2. It is more dignified for him to ride, instead of leading on foot, even in the areas of the town where there is no human traffic (*Rashi*).

3. A woman is not usually strong enough to keep the animal in check when leading it on foot. Therefore, it is customary for her to ride on the animal even where there is no traffic because of the apprehension that the animal will get away from her (*Rashi*).

4. However, an average person, who carries no special dignity, i.e. he is not a rich man [or otherwise dignified], and is not ashamed to lead an animal on foot, will not ride in a traffic-free area of the town (i.e. a *simta*); it is to such average persons that the Baraisa's rule refers (*Rashi*).

5. R' Elazar's query concerns acquisition by means of "drawing near" (מְשִׁיכָה). *Meshichah* [mentioned above on 8a-b] is a formal mode of acquisition for items too heavy to be lifted. The buyer of such an article legally takes possession of it when he pulls it or moves it out of its place. In the case of animals, it is not necessary to actually pull the animal; it is enough that the buyer call out to or strike the animal, causing it to move a foreleg and hindleg from their place.

6. In this case, the seller wished to sell only the utensils on the animal, not the animal itself (*Rashi*).

7. An act of acquisition effects transfer of ownership only if the seller first indicates his willingness to transfer ownership of the article, e.g. by explicitly telling the buyer, "Acquire it." Simply instructing the buyer to perform an act of acquisition is insufficient, since the seller is merely instructing the buyer as to what *he* should do, but not indicating his *own* intent in the matter. Therefore, if the seller instructs the buyer, "Draw the article near in order to acquire," the buyer does not acquire anything, since "in order to acquire" merely describes the intent the buyer should have when he draws the article. The seller, however, has still not said that the buyer should acquire anything with his action (*Rashi*, see *Rosh*).

8. "Drawing near" is certainly an effective way to acquire utensils [even if one draws them near by pulling a larger receptacle that contains them]. However, the *meshichah* that normally effects the acquisition of utensils is the pulling of the utensils. The drawing near that normally effects acquisition of animals is the act of making the animal move itself. Since animals and utensils are thus governed by two different rules of *meshichah,* R' Elazar is uncertain whether the *meshichah* of an animal is effective to acquire utensils (*Tosafos*). [An animal can be acquir[ed] through *meshichah* even if the person drags a bound animal that cann[ot] move. Yet, as emerges from the Gemara below, R' Elazar is uncerta[in] whether the *meshichah* of even such an animal can serve to acquire t[he] utensils on it. Although in that case, the *meshichah* of the animal [is] identical to the *meshichah* of utensils, it might still be considered [a] different mechanism of *meshichah,* since the *primary* means [of] performing *meshichah* to an animal is by making it walk (*Rosh*).]

9. Thus, the law remains in doubt. Hence, in accordance with the gener[al] principle that in cases of doubtful transfer, the article remains in t[he] possession of the last undisputed owner (חֲזָקַת מָרָא קַמָּא), the seller in [R'] Elazar's case retains legal possession of the utensils on the anim[al] (*Rosh*).

10. *Rashi,* cited above in note 6.

11. R' Elazar's inquiry considers the possibility that the *meshichah* of [a]n animal is *not* an effective *meshichah* for the utensils that are on it (s[ee] note 8). Now, as far as the *meshichah* of the utensils is concerned, [it] makes no difference whether the act of drawing the animal near actual[ly] acquires the animal; the utensils still have not undergone t[he] *meshichah* of utensils. If R' Elazar nevertheless assumes with certain[ty] that when the animal is acquired, the utensils on it are acquired as we[ll,] he cannot assume that they are acquired through the mechanism [of] *meshichah,* but rather through the mechanism of "courtyard." That i[s,] once the *meshichah* of the animal makes it the property of the buyer, t[he] utensils on the animal are acquired by the buyer by virtue of the[ir] presence in his property (the animal). For the law of acquisition b[y] *chatzeir* [literally: courtyard] states that a person's courtyard or oth[er] property has the capacity to acquire articles found in its confines o[n] behalf of its owner.

12. The Torah source for acquisition by *chatzeir* is found in the conte[xt] of theft, where the Torah considers a thief liable if the stolen artic[le] "found will be found in his hand" (*Exodus* 22:3), i.e. if he steals t[he] article *with his hand.* A Baraisa interprets the redundant expressio[n] "found will be found" to extend the definition of theft to include not on[ly] theft with one's physical hand, but theft with his *domain* in genera[l,] such as his roof, courtyard or enclosure [see *Rashi* to 10b ד"ה משום ידה]. Thus, if an article enters a person's domain and he restricts it there wit[h] intent to steal it, he is liable as a thief (below, 10b; *Gittin* 77a). [A simila[r] exposition is found in connection with the law of divorce, where t[he] Torah ordains that the husband place the bill of divorce in his wife['s] "hand," a requirement which is expanded by exegesis to include h[er] domain in general (ibid.).]

Now, since the law of *chatzeir* is an expansion of the law which t[he]

א ואי רשות הרבים הוא [א] קני ואי אדם חשוב הוא קני ואי אשה היא קניא ואי איניש זילא הוא קני בעי ר' אלעזר האומר לחבירו משוך בהמה זו לקנות כלים שעליה מהו ב לקנות מי אמר ליה קני אלא משוך בהמה זו וקני כלים שעליה מהו מי מהניא משיכה דבהמה לאקנויי כלים ג או לא אמר רבא אי אמר ליה קני בהמה וקני כלים מי קני כלים ד חצר מהלכת היא וחצר מהלכת לא קנה וכי תימא כשעמדה והא א) כל ה שאילו מהלך לא קנה עומד ויושב לא קנה ° ו והלכתא בכפותה אמרו ליה רב פפא ורב הונא בריה דרב יהושע לרבא אלא מעתה היה מהלך בספינה וקפצו דגים ונפלו לתוך הספינה הכי נמי דחצר מהלכת היא ולא קני אמר ליה ז ספינה מינח נייחא ומיא הוא דקא ממטו לה א"ל רבינא לרב אשי אלא מעתה היתה מהלכת ברשות הרבים וזרק לה גט לתוך חיקה או לתוך קלתה הכא נמי דלא מגרשה א"ל ח קלתה מינח נייחא ואיהי דקא מסגיא מתותה:

**מתני'** ט היה רוכב על גבי בהמה וראה את המציאה ואמר לחבירו תנה לי נטלה ואמר אני זכיתי בה זכה בה אם משנתנה לו אמר אני זכיתי בה תחלה לא אמר כלום: **גמ'** ב) תנן התם מי שליקט את הפאה ואמר הרי זו לפלוני עני ר' אליעזר אומר זכה לו וחכמים אומרים י יתננה לעני הנמצא ראשון אמר עולא אמר ר' יהושע בן לוי מחלוקת מעשיר לעני דר' אליעזר סבר ג) מגו דאי בעי מפקר נכסיה והוי עני וחזי ליה השתא נמי חזי ליה ד) ומגו דזכי לנפשיה זכי נמי לחבריה ורבנן סברי ה) כ חד מגו אמרינן תרי מגו לא אמרינן אבל מעני לעני דברי הכל זכה לו דמגו דזכי לנפשיה זכי נמי לחבריה אמר ליה רב נחמן לעולא ולימא מר מעני לעני מחלוקת דהא מציאה הכל עניים אצלה ותנן היה רוכב על גבי בהמה וראה את המציאה ואמר לחבירו תנה לי נטלה ואמר אני זכיתי בה זכה בה אי אמרת בשלמא מעני לעני מחלוקת

**רש"י**

ואי רשות הרבים הוא קני. בעיר דדרך לרכוב שם ולא להנהיג פן יפסקו עוברי דרכים בינו לבין בהמתו: ואי אדם חשוב הוא. אין דרכו להנהיג בהמה ברגליו ודרך כבוד לרכוב עליה אף בסמטא שאין בני אדם שם וכן אשה שאין בה כח לאחוז הבהמה פן תינתק הימנה: ואי איניש זילא הוא קני. שדרכו לרכוב לפני כל אף בלא דוחק לפי שאינו נגוע אבל אדם בינוני כגון שאינו חשוב בעושר ואינו בוש להוליך בהמה ברגליו אין דרכו לרכוב בסמטא בעיר משום צניעות: משוך בהמה זו על מנת לקנות כלים שעליה. במקח וממכר ומוכר לו את הכלים ולא את הבהמה: לקנות מי קאמר ליה קני. לקנות משמע אתה התכוין לקנות אני איני מקנה לך: מי קני כלים. במשיכה דבהמה עם הבהמה דמדקא מבעיא לך במוכר כלים בלא בהמה מכלל דבמוכר שניהם פשיטא לך (א) דמקני בהמה קני כלים משום תורת חצר דקיימא לן חצרו של אדם קונה לו ובהמתו כחצרו והא חצר מהלכת היא וחצר מהלכת לא שמעינן דתקני דכי אתרבאי (גיטין דף עז.) מאם המצא תמצא בידו גגו חצרו וקרפיפו אתרבאי דלא נייד והוי משתמר: וכי תימא כשעמדה. לאחר שעקרה ידה ורגלה ונקנית לו הבהמה במשיכה עמדה ולא הלכה ונקנו כלים בעמידתה דקנה לו חצרו: כל שאילו מהלך לא קנה כו'. כלומר כיון דראויה היא לילך לאו דומיא דחצר היא ואין קונה בתורת חצר: והלכתא. הא דפשיטא ליה דכי אמר ליה קני בהמה וקני כלים קני: בכפותה. היא דפשיטא ליה (ב) דדומיא דחצר הוא קני וכל היכא דאמרינן בגמרא והאמר רבא כל שאילו מהלך לא קני כו' מהכא קאמרי ליה: קלתה. סל שעל ראשה שנותנת בה כלי מלאכתה וטווי שלה: ה"נ דלא הוי גיטא. והאנן תנן במס' גיטין (דף עז.) זרק לה גיטה לתוך חיקה או לתוך קלתה הרי זו מגורשת: **מתני'** לא אמר כלום. דאפילו אמרי' המגביה מציאה לחבירו לא קנה חבירו כיון דיהבה ליה קנייה ממה נפשך אי קנייה קמא דלא מתכוין להקנות לחבירו הא יהבה ניהליה במתנה ואי לא קנייה קמא משום דלא היה מתכוין לקנות הויא ליה הפקר עד דמטא לידיה דהאי וקנייה האי במאי דעקרה מידיה דקמא לשם קנייה: **גמ'** מי שליקט את הפאה. אדם בעלמא שאינו בעל שדה דאי בבעל שדה לא אמר ר' אליעזר זכה דליכא למימר מיגו דזכי לנפשיה דאפילו הוא עני מוזהר הוא שלא ללקט פאה משדה שלו כדאמר בשחיטת חולין (דף קלא:) לא תלקט לעני להזהיר עני על שלו: מעשיר לעני. שעשיר הוא שליקטה לצורך העני: מגו דזכי לנפשיה. דאי בעי הוה זכי לנפשיה אם הגביה לעצמו: חד מגו. מעני לעני: ולימא מר דאפילו מעני לעני. אמרי רבנן דלא זכה לו: דהא מציאה הכל עניים אצלה. כלומר הכל כשרים לזכות בה כעניים בפאה: ותנן. המגביה מציאה לחבירו לא קנה חבירו ולא אמרינן מגו דאי הוה בעי הוה זכי לנפשיה זכי נמי לחבריה כי מגבה לה כולה לשם חבירו דתנן היה רוכב כו': ואמר אני זכיתי בה. קס"ד אני רוצה לזכות בה עכשיו קאמר ומודה הוא שמתחילה הגביה לשם חבירו וקתני זכה בה אלמא לא קנה חבירו: אי אמרת בשלמא מעני לעני מחלוקת. דאמרי רבנן לא אמרינן מגו דזכי לנפשיה זכי נמי לחבריה אלא היכא דהגביה לדעת שניהם כגון שנים שהגביהו מציאה דאמר בה לעיל (דף ח.) גבי בזמן שהם מודים חולקים בלא שבועה דטעמא משום מגו דזכי בהגבהה זו לנפשיה זכי נמי לחבריה אבל מגו דאי בעי הוה זכי לנפשיה זכי לחבריה לא אמרינן:

מתני'

**תוספות**

**משוך** בהמה זו וקני כלים שעליה כו'. מבעיא ליה כיון דמשיכת הבהמה שהולכת מעצמה לא שייכא בכלים לא יקנה הכלים אבל אם אמר משוך קופה וקני כלים שבתוכה פשיטא ליה דקני ואם תאמר תפשוט מברייתא דהמוכר את הספינה (ב"ב דף פה: ושם) דקתני משך חמרין ופועלין לתוך ביתו שניהם יכולין לחזור אלמא דלא קני פירות במשיכת הבהמה וי"ל דהתם לא אמר ליה קני לכך לא קני [א"נ התם כשמשך החמרין ולא משך את החמור] והא דקתני בין פסק כו' ה"ה אפי' פסק ומדד יכולין לחזור אלא משום דסיפא מפליג בין פסק עד שלא מדד ובין מדד עד שלא פסק נקט נמי ברישא האי לישנא וכן צריך לתרץ בסיפא דקתני פרקן והכניסן לתוך ביתו פסק עד שלא מדד אין יכולין לחזור ובעי למפשט מינה התם דכלי של מוכר ברשות לוקח לא קני המוכר שהמקח קיים אלמא הכלי מתבטל אגב הרשות משמע מטעם משיכה אינה קונה לפי שהוא בכליו של מוכר וכי משני התם ומוקי לה ששפכן מכליו של מוכר או במתכלי דתומי משמע שאם היה בכליו של מוכר לא היה קונה אף על פי שהכניסן לתוך ביתו דהיינו משיכה ואמאי והא פשיטא לן במשוך קופה זו וקני כלים שבתוכה קני אלא התם י"ל משום דלא אמר ליה קני ואינו רוצה שיקנה אלא במשיכת פירות עצמן ועוד מצינו למימר דהתם משמע ליה שלא פסק עד אחר המשיכה ולכך לא קניא במשיכה וא"ת אמאי נקט משוך בהמה זו ולא נקיט קני אי משום דבקני פשיטא ליה דקני מטעם חצר אע"פ שהיא מהלכת א"כ במשוך נמי אמאי מספקא ליה כיון שהשאילה לו הרי היא כאילו היא שלו עד לאחר הקנין ויקנה מטעם חצר וי"ל דכשא"ל משוך לא השאיל לו הבהמה לקנות הכלים מטעם חצר אלא במשיכת הבהמה אי נמי אי הוי בעי קני בהמה וכלים והוה מהדר ליה דקני לא היה יכול לידע מזה שבמשיכת הבהמה יקנה הכלים כי שמא מטעם חצר קני ובכפותה ולכך איבעי ליה במשוך:

**ספינה** מינח נייחא ומיא הוא דקא ממטו לה. אע"ג דבפ"ק דקדושין (דף כג:) אמרינן דתלמיד חכם רכוב כמהלך דמי הכא חצר משום יד אתרבאי והוה שפיר ° דומיא דיד דמינח נייח וממטו לה עם גופיה וכן בפ"ק דשבת (דף ה: ושם ד"ה אגוז) אגוז לף ע"ג מים לא הוי הנחה אגוז בכלי וכלי לף על גבי מיים חהו התם משום דדומיא דמלאכת המשכן בעינן ולא היו מצניעין חפצים בדבר שהיה מתנענע ומתנדנד אבל גבי קנייה כיון שהוא דומיא דידו קני: **ה"נ** דלא מגרשה. פרש"י הא דתנן זרק לתוך קלתה מגורשת ותימה לוקמה בכפותה ושמא נ"ל דוחק א"נ הכא מסברא פריך כדפריך מספינה ולא מכח משנה:

**ולימא** מר מעני לעני מחלוקת. ויחלקו בתופס לב"ח במקום שחב לאחרים ולא מטעם מגו דהא רב חסדא דקאמר כמו רב נחמן בסמוך המגביה מציאה לחבירו לא קנה חבירו אית ליה פרק קמא דגיטין (דף יא: ושם) דפליגי בתופס לבעל חוב ולא מטעם מגו עד דדחי ליה רב פפא דלמא במגו פליגי:

רב

**עין משפט נר מצוה**

סו א מיי' פ"ב מהל' מכירה הל' י סמג עשין פב טוש"ע ח"מ סי' קלז סעיף ה:

סז ב מיי' שם הלכה ח ועי' פי' במ"מ טוש"ע שם סעיף ו:

סח ג מיי' פ"ג מהל' מכירה הל' יג סמג עשין פב טוש"ע ח"מ סי' רב סעיף יד:

סט ד ה ו מיי' שם הל' יג יד סמג שם טוש"ע שם סעיף יג וטוש"ע אה"ע סי' קלט סעיף טז:

ע ז מיי' פ"א מהלכות זכיה ומתנה הל' ה סמג עשין עג טוש"ע ח"מ סי' רעג סעיף טו:

עא ח מיי' פ"ה מהלכות גירושין הל' ח וע"ש סמג עשין נ טוש"ע אה"ע סי' קלט סעיף י:

עב ט מיי' פי"ז מהל' גזילה ואבידה הל' ג סמג עשין עד טוש"ע ח"מ סי' רסט סעיף ו:

עג י כ מיי' פ"ב מהל' מתנות עניים הל' יט:

**רבינו חננאל**

וכן אם הוא אדם חשוב שאין דרכו להלך רגלי קנה ברכיבה. וכן האשה. וכן אי גברא זילא הוא קני. **בעי ר"א** האומר לחבירו משוך בהמה זו וקני כלים שעליה מהו אמר רבא אי אמר ליה קני בהמה וקני כלים שעליה מי קנו כלים במשיכה דבהמה אמאי חצר מהלכת היא ואסקי' והלכתא בכפותה. וכן ספינה דקפצו דגים בתוכה קנאם בעל הספינה דספינה מינח נייחא ומיא הוא דממטו לה. ואסיקו רב אשי ורבינא באשה מהלכת ברה"ר וזרק לה בעלה גיטא בתוך קלתה נתגרשה מאי טעמא קלתה מינח נייחא ואיהי מסגיא תות' הני כולהי לאו חצר מהלכת נינהו וכן הלכה: **ירושלמי** אמר רב הונא בשם רבנן [תני] תמן אשה שהיתה רוכבת על גבי בהמה ושנים מנהיגין אותה היא אומרת אלו עבדיי והבהמה והמשוי שלי וזה אומר זו אשתי וזה עבדי וזו חבילתי א) צריכה גט משניהן והיא משחררת את שניהן ושניהן משחררין זה את זה ובבהמה ובמשוי שלשתן שוין: **פיסקא** מתני' היה רוכב על גבי בהמה וכו' תנן התם בפאה פ"ד מי שליקט [את הפאה] ואמר הרי זו לאיש פלוני עני ר"א אומר זכה לו וחכ"א יתננה לעני הנמצא ראשון. ואומר מחלוקת מעשיר לעני וכו' ולימא מר מעני לעני מחלוקת דהא מציאה הכל כעניים הן אצלה. ותנן ראה את המציאה ואמר לחבירו תנה לי נטלה ואמר אני זכיתי בה זכה בה לעצמו אי אמרת בשלמא מחלוקת מעני לעני

**חשק שלמה על ר"ח**

א) הא אומר זו אשתי הא עבדי הוו חבילתי צריכה גט וכו' [ועי' בקדושין ס"ה ע"ב ובפרש"י שם ד"ה].

**מסורת הש"ס**

א) בבא קמא יב., גיטין עח., ב) פאה פרק ד' מ"ט, גיטין יא., ג) [ב"מ מז. וש"נ], ד) [לעיל ח.], נדרים פח:], ה) [תוס' גיטין יא:], ו) מהרש"ל

**הגהות הב"ח**

(א) רש"י ד"ה מי קני וכו', פשיטא לך דמקני בהמה: (ב) ד"ה והלכתא וכו' דפשיטא ליה דדומיא:

**הגהות הגר"א**

[א] גמ' קני ואי. קו על מלת קני ועל ה ממלא ואי וכ"ב הר"ן ל"ג זה אבל הרמב"ם כגירסא שלנו:

**גליון הש"ס**

גמ' והלכתא בכפותה. כעין זה ... ז. והלכתא דיתבי: ... ד"ה ספינה דומיא דיד דמי ... תמוה לי דא"כ ... עצמה מקרי מהלך ... מהני נותן גט על ... גם אמאי בנתן גט ... עבדה מקרי חצר מה ... הא היד מינח. אלא ... דיד והגוף חד הוא ... דאמרי' מה ידה ... מהלך היינו דאינו ... מהקונה דבכ"מ ... מהלך שם הוא ... משא"כ חצר דמ... מהקונה ולע"ג:

**ליקוטי רש"י**

וחצר מהלכת קנה. דכי אמור רבנן של אדם קונה לו לאו מהלכת אמור ... מקרקעי דניידי ממק... דלא ניידי [גיטין כא.]. קונה לבעליה כלום ... חצר היא במה... והלכתא בכפו... שאינו ראוי לילך ... לחצר [ב"ק יב.]. שליקט את הפ... בעה"ב עשיר שליק... הפאה וכו' [גיטין ... ומגו דזכי לנפש... עיין לעיל דף ח ע...

במדה זאת קנו ר' יהודה אומר לעולם לא קנה עד שתהא משיכה בגמל והנהגה בחמור קתני מיהת או שהיה אחד מושך ואחד מנהיג מושך ומנהיג אין אבל רכוב לא הוא הדין דאפילו רכוב והא דקתני מושך ומנהיג לאפוקי מדר' יהודה דאמר עד שתהא משיכה בגמל והנהגה בחמור קמשמע לן דאפילו איפכא נמי קני אי הכי ליערבינהו וליתנינהו שנים שהיו מושכין ומנהיגין בין בגמל בין בחמור איכא חד צד דלא קני איכא דאמרי משיכה בחמור ואיכא דאמרי [א]הנהגה בגמל ואית דמותיב מסיפא במדה זו קנה במדה זו למעוטי מאי לאו למעוטי רכוב לא למעוטי איפכא אי הכי היינו ר' יהודה איכא בינייהו צד אחד דלא קנה אית דאמרי משיכה בחמור ואיכא דאמרי הנהגה בגמל ת"ש [ב]אחד רכוב חמור ואחד תפוס במוסירה זה קנה חמור וזה קנה מוסירה שמע מינה רכוב קני הכא נמי במנהיג ברגליו אי הכי נקני נמי רכוב במוסירה אימא זה קנה חמור וחצי מוסירה וזה קנה חצי מוסירה בשלמא רכוב קני דקמגבה ליה בן דעת אלא תפוס במוסירה במאי קני אימא זה קנה חמור וכוליה מוסירה וזה קני מה שתפוס בידו [ה] האי מאי אם תימצי לומר המגביה מציאה לחבירו קנה חבירו הני מילי היכא דקא מגבה ליה אדעתא דחבריה האי אדעתא דידיה קא מגבה ליה איהו לא קני לאחריני מקני אמר רב אשי [ג]זה קנה חמור ובית פגיה וזה קנה מה שתפוס בידו והשאר לא קנה לא זה ולא זה רבי אבהו אמר לעולם כדקתני הואיל ויכול לנתקה ולהביאה אצלו [ד] והא דר' אבהו [ו] ברותא [ז] היא דאי לא תימא הכי [ה]טלית שהיא מונחת חציה על גבי קרקע וחציה על גבי עמוד ובא אחד והגביה חציה מעל גבי קרקע ובא אחר והגביה חציה מעל גבי עמוד הכי נמי דקמא קני ובתרא לא קני הואיל ויכול לנתק ולהביא אצלו אלא הא דר' אבהו ברותא היא ת"ש ר' אליעזר אומר [ו]רכוב בשדה ומנהיג בעיר קנה הכא נמי מנהיג ברגליו אי הכי היינו מנהיג תרי גווני מנהיג אי הכי רכוב בעיר מאי טעמא לא קני אמר רב כהנא לפי שאין דרכן של בני אדם לרכוב בעיר אמר ליה רב אשי לרב כהנא אלא מעתה הגביה ארנקי בשבת שאין דרכן של בני אדם להגביה ארנקי בשבת הכי נמי דלא קני אלא מאי דעבד עבד וקני הכא נמי מאי דעבד עבד וקני אלא [ז]במקח וממכר עסקינן דאמר ליה קני כדרך שבני אדם קונין

ואי

**רש"י**

**במדה זו.** לקמיה מפרש למעוטי מאי: **אי הכי.** דלתנא קמא איפכא קני אמאי קתני משיכה בגמל והנהגה בחמור ליערבינהו וכו' מושכין ומנהיגין: **איכא חד צד דלא קני.** להכי לא מצי למתני בתרוייהו משיכה והנהגה ותנא הכי מושכין בגמל ומנהיגין בחמור או שהיה אחד מושך ואחד מנהיג באחד מהן אותו שדרכו בשניהם: **במדה הזאת.** קס"ד במשיכה או בהנהגה בין בגמל בין בחמור: **אחד תפוס במוסירה.** ואינו מנהיג: **ש"מ רכוב קני.** שלא במקום מנהיג וכיון דשלא במקום מנהיג קני כוליה במקום מנהיג פלגי: **נקני נמי רכוב במוסירה.** שבראש החמור שהוא תכשיט החמור וכחמור דמי: **בשלמא רכוב.** מצית למימר דקנה בהגבהת חבירו שהגביה ראשו השני מן הקרקע דקא מגבה לה בן דעת: **אלא תפוס במוסירה במאי קני.** פלגא והלא ראשה השני מונח במקומו והגבהת הפקר לא קניא עד דעקר לכוליה: **האי מאי.** דקא אמרת הגבהת תופס במוסירה לא הויא הגבהה לדידיה והויא הגבהה לאחריני אפילו אם תימצי לומר כו': **ובית פגיה.** קיבצי"ל בלע"ז מה שבראש החמור וכחמור דמי: **מה שתפוס בידו.** דמה שבתוך ידו הוי מגביה לגמרי: **לא זה ולא זה.** והבא לחוטפו יחטוף: **כדקתני.** זה קנה חמור וזה קנה מוסירה אפי' בית פגיה של חמור: **הואיל ויכול.** התפוס במוסירה למושכו בכח וינתק מראש החמור ויביאנו אצלו דהואיל וראש החמור גבוה נוח להביאה אצלו בנתיקה אחת: **ברותא היא.** דאע"ג דיכול לנתק לאו הגבהה היא: **חציה על גב העמוד.** דכיון דמקום גבוה הוא האוחזה בראשה השני נוח לו לנתק ולהביאה אצלו דלא מחסר הגבהה: **הכי נמי דקמא קני.** דמכי אגבהה קניא כולה משום דיכול לנתקה אם כן יש חילוק בשנים שהגביהו מציאה זה מכאן וזה מכאן בין מקום גבוה למקום נמוך דהיכא דשני ראשיה מונחים בקרקע אין הגבהת של ראשון קונה כולה שאין יכול לנתקו ולהביאו אצלו מתוך שהוא ארוך ומונח בקרקע כל מה שהוא נותקו ומושכו אחריו נגרר הוא על גבי קרקע והיכא דלאחד מראשיה גבוה כגון בראש החמור או על גבי עמוד המגביה תחלה ראש שעל גבי קרקע קונה כולה ואנן לא אשכחן תנא דמפליג: **רכוב בשדה.** בהמה של מציאה קונה אבל לא בעיר וטעמא מפרש לקמיה ומנהיג אף בעיר קנה וכ"ש בשדה ש"מ רכוב לחודיה קני כו': **אין דרכן.** משום לניעותא:

ואי

**תוספות**

**מושך** ומנהיג אין אבל רכוב לא. תימה מנ"ל דלמא כ"ש רכוב דתפיס ביה ואי משום דשייר אטו בכל דוכתי תנא כולהו קניינין וי"ל דממשנה יתיר' קדייק דליערבינהו ולתנינהו שנים שהיו מושכין או מנהיגים בין בגמל בין בחמור ותו לא מדקתני בלישנא יתירא ש"מ דלמעוטי רכוב אתא והיינו דפריך בתר הכי וליערבינהו ולתנינהו וא"ת לעולם מנ"ל למעוטי רכוב דלמא הא דלא ערבינהו כדי לאשמועינן דמשיכה אורחא בגמל והנהגה בחמור ואפ"ה אחד מושך ואחד מנהיג בגמל לא מבטל משיכה דאורחא בגמל את ההנהגה דלאו אורחא וכן בחמור איפכא ולכך תנא בתר הכי אחד מושך ואחד מנהיג ולא למעוטי רכוב וי"ל כיון שישמיענו שמשיכה והנהגה שניהם קנו בגמל ובחמור פשיטא שאין אחד מבטל חבירו משום דהאי אורחיה והאי לאו אורחיה אבל במתני' משמיענו שפיר שאין מבטל רכוב ומנהיג ברגליו את מנהיג לחודיה לפי שיש ברכוב כל מה שיש במנהיג ועוד דתפיס בה: **אי** הכי ליערבינהו ולתנינהו. לפי מאי דס"ד דרכוב קני ומשיכה והנהגה בין בגמל בין בחמור במדה זו קנה אתא למעוטי שום קנין אחר או רכוב במקום מנהיג: **אי** הכי היינו ר' יהודה. הוה מצי לאקשויי מגופה דקתני או שהיה אחד מושך ואחד מנהיג ש"מ דבחד לא קני: **ונקני** נמי רכוב במוסירה. אי גרסינן אי הכי ה"פ אי אמרת בשלמא כשאין מנהיג ברגליו ורכוב קני הבהמה משום דתפיס בה א"ש דלא קני מוסירה דבמטלטלין לא שייך קנין של מוסירה אלא בהגבהה או משיכה אבל אי מיירי במנהיג ברגליו לקני נמי מוסירה במשיכת הבהמה אי אמרינן משוך בהמה זו וקני כלים שעליה קני דלקמן מיבעיא לן אי קני אי לא קני ליפשוט מהכא דלא מהני: **והשאר** לא קנה לא זה ולא זה. ואפילו אי אמרינן משוך בהמה וקני כלים שעליה קני הכא כיון דתפיס במוסירה לא קני רכוב נמי לא קני כדאמרינן אדעתא דידיה אגבהה איהו לא קני כו': **דאי** לא תימא הכי טלית שחציה כו'. קצת קשה מנ"ל שלא יחלוק רבי אבהו אף בזה: **הואיל** ויכול לנתקו ולהביאו אצלו. תימה דמשמע דאם נתקה שהוא קונה כו' משום שעל ידו הוגבהה למעלה משלש ומאי שנא מעני המנקף בראש הזית (גיטין דף נט:) שאין בו גזל אלא מפני דרכי שלום וכן פרק הגוזל קמא (ב"ק דף לח. ושם ד"ה והני מילי) הזורק סלע של חבירו ליס פטור ומוקי לה בדאדיי' אדויי אלמא לא חשיב מה שהוגבהה על ידו הואיל וסופו ליפול וי"ל דשאני הכא שתופס בידו אחד מן הראש א"נ הכא איירי כשניתק מן העמוד אינו ארוך כ"כ שיגיע ראש השני לארץ ושלהי שילוח הקן (חולין דף קמא:) דקאמר זיל טרוף אקן דלגבהינהו ולקנינהו התם נמי הוגבהו על ידו יותר ממה שהיה תחילה שהרי קצת מפריחים למעלה לכך [ד] קני: **אי** הכי רכוב בעיר מאי טעמא לא קני. אי גרסינן א"ה ה"פ אי אמרת בשלמא לא מיירי במנהיג ברגליו לכך בעיר לא קני דלא אזלא ממתתיה לפי שיש בני אדם שמדברים יחד ויש כמה דברים באמצע הדרכים אלא אי אמרינן במנהיג ברגליו א"כ אזלא ממתתיה טובא ואמאי לא קני:

משוך

**עין משפט נר מצוה**

סב א מיי' פי"ז מהל' אבידה הל' ה ועי' בהשגות ובמ"מ סמג עשין עד טוש"ע ח"מ סי' רעא סעיף א:

סג ב ג מיי' שם הל' ז טוש"ע שם סעיף ג:

סד ד ה טוש"ע ח"מ סי' רסט סעיף ה וע"ש:

סה ו ז מיי' פ"ב מהל' מכירה הל' י ועיין במ"מ סמג עשין פב טוש"ע ח"מ סי' קצז סעיף ה:

**רבינו חננאל**

פי' איכא חד צד דלא קני יש מי שאומר משיכה בחמור לא קני אבל בגמל בין במשיכה בין בהנהגה קני. ויש מי שאומר הנהגה בגמל לא קנה אבל חמור בין במשיכה בין בהנהגה קני. פי' פגיה רצועות של מוסירה הנתונות על לחייה ועל פדחתה. סוגיא דשמעתא טלית מונחת על גבי קרקע וחציה על גבי עמוד בא אחד והגביה חציה מעל גבי קרקע ובא אחר והגביה חציה שעל גבי עמוד א). רכוב אי קני אי לא קני ת"ש ר"א אומר רכוב בשדה קנה וכו' ודחי' התם במנהיג ברגליו אי הכי היינו מנהיג. ופרקי' תרי גווני מנהיג. ואסקי' במקח וממכר אי אמר ליה קני כדרך שבני אדם קונין אי ברשות הרבים רכוב קנה.

**חשק שלמה על ר"ח**

א) חסר פה בהעתקה ונראה דצ"ל קנו תרוייהו.

**מסורת הש"ס**

[לע]יל ח.], ב) פ"א תא [ועיין פסחים יא. ...ן מהרי"ב], ג) [פי' ...וס שטעו חכמים ולא ... כהלכה לא רצה ...זס ולומר טעו אלא ...ו ברותא היא כלומר מילונית היא, ערוך ...בר ד'], ד) [ועיין עוד כתובות ל: ד"ה ואי דלא מצי].

**ליקוטי רש"י**

תימצי לומר. ...ר אפי' אם תמצא ... המגביה מציאה ...רו כו' [לעיל ח.]. ...ת פגיה. קיבצי"ל ... ראשה ולחייה [שבת ... לשון חבישה. ...דידור"א בית ראש של ...ר קורין כן [סוטה מה.].

**לעזי רש"י**

...ציי"ל. פירוש בית ...יה ולחייה (רש"י שבת ...נא ע"ב ד"ה בפגי ...זלא), בית ראש של ...ר (רש"י סוטה דף ...ע"א ד"ה אבי פאגי), ...נות של מוסרה ...ונות על לחיה ועל ...תה (רבינו חננאל ...ערוך ערך פג ה').

The Gemara cites a Baraisa to prove that a rider in fact quires, thus refuting Rav Yehudah's position.

תָּא שְׁ – **Come, learn** that a rider does acquire **from the llowing Baraisa:** רִ׳ אֱלִיעֶזֶר אוֹמֵר – R' ELIEZER SAYS: רָכוּב בַּשָּׂ – ONE WHO RIDES a found animal[26] IN THE FIELDS וּמַנְהִיג בָּעִ – OR ONE WHO LEADS it even IN THE CITY קָנָה – ACQUIRES. This proves that a rider alone does acquire, at least in the lds.

The Gemara rejects this proof as well:

הָכָא נַמִּי מַנְהִיג בְּרַגְ – **Here too,** as in the Mishnah and the raisa cited earlier, the term "rider" refers to one **who "leads,"** . spurs the animal, **with his feet.** Since spurring the animal til it moves constitutes a form of "leading," the rider acquires. is does not prove, however, that mere riding constitutes a valid *iyan.*

The Gemara challenges this interpretation:

אִי הָ – **If** it is **so** that the rider also "leads" the animal, הַיְינוּ מַנְ – then such riding is **identical to "leading"!** It is thus dundant to teach that both riding and leading acquire.[27] – **?** –

The Gemara answers:

תְּרֵי גַּוְונֵי מַנְ – There are **two types of leader,** one that prods or lls the animal, and another that spurs it with his feet. The raisa informs us that even the latter type of leading constitutes *inyan.*

The Gemara challenges the above assertion that the rider in the raisa's case spurred the animal:

אִי הָכִי רָכוּב בָּעִיר מַאי טַעְמָא לֹא – **If so, what is the reason at one riding in the city does not acquire?**[28]

The Gemara answers:

אָמַר רַב כַּהֲנָא – **Rav Kahana said:** לְפִי שֶׁאֵין דַּרְכָּן שֶׁל בְּנֵי אָדָם לִרְכּוֹב בָּעִיר – **Because it is not customary for people to ride in the city;** that is why he does not acquire through riding.[29]

The Gemara rejects Rav Kahana's principle:[30]

אָמַר לֵיהּ רַב אַשִׁי לְרַב כַּהֲנָא – **Rav Ashi asked Rav Kahana:** אֶלָּא מֵעַתָּה הִגְבִּיהַּ אַרְנָקִי בְּשַׁבָּת – **But now,** if you assume this to be true, then **if one lifted a** lost money **pouch on the Sabbath,** שֶׁאֵין דַּרְכָּן שֶׁל בְּנֵי אָדָם לְהַגְבִּיהַּ אַרְנָקִי בְּשַׁבָּת – **since it is not customary for people to lift** such **a pouch on the Sabbath,**[31] הָכִי נַמִּי דְּלֹא קָנֵי – is the law **also so that he does not acquire** it? Certainly not! אֶלָּא מַאי דְּעָבַד עָבַד וְקָנֵי – **Rather,** we say that **whatever he has done he has done,** i.e. although he transgressed the laws of the Sabbath when he lifted the pouch, still his act constitutes a *kinyan* **and he acquires** the pouch. הָכָא נַמִּי מַאי דְּעָבַד עָבַד וְקָנֵי – **Here too,** if someone rides an animal in the city, **what he has done he has done,** i.e. although he violated convention, still his act should constitute a *kinyan* **and he** should thus **acquire** the animal.

Having rejected Rav Kahana's explanation of the Baraisa, Rav Ashi presents another:

אֶלָּא בְּמִקָּח וּמִמְכָּר עַסְקִינַן – **Rather,** the Baraisa that disqualifies riding as a *kinyan* in the city **speaks** exclusively **about** a case of **buying and selling,** דְּאָמַר לֵיהּ קְנֵי כְּדֶרֶךְ שֶׁבְּנֵי אָדָם קוֹנִין – **where [the animal's seller] said to the [buyer], "Acquire the animal in the manner that people acquire."** Since the seller stipulated that the buyer perform a conventional *kinyan,* he cannot acquire through riding in the city, for that is unconventional.[32]

NOTES

The Gemara initially makes two assumptions: that the Baraisa cusses ways to acquire a found animal and that it is easier to acquire e in the fields than in the city. [The Gemara will explain its second sumption later.] Therefore, it interprets the Baraisa's rulings as lows. Riding (an animal) constitutes a valid *kinyan* in the fields but in the city. Leading one, on the other hand, constitutes a valid *iyan* even in the city and surely in the fields (*Rashi*).

. *Rosh* (cited in *Shitah Mekubetzes*) notes that the answer to this estion is obvious: The Baraisa taught that unlike other leaders, a rider at "leads with his feet" acquires only in the field. *Rosh* therefore etes the section of Gemara from "If so" to "two types of leader."

As explained in note 5, when a question begins אִי הָכִי, *if so*, it usually empts to refute the Gemara's last statement and to justify its initial umption. Now our Gemara just stated that the rider in the Baraisa's se spurred the animal, reversing its initial assumption that he did not. cordingly, *if so,* would mean as follows: If the rider in the Baraisa's se spurred the animal, then why does he not acquire in the city? If he not, though, then the ruling is understandable. The Gemara is, wever, difficult to understand. Why is the ruling understandable in e case while it is not in the other?

To understand the answer to this question, we must first understand e difference between riding in the fields and riding in the city. cording to *Tosafos* the questioner understood the difference as lows: When a rider mounts an animal in the fields, he definitely uses the animal to move instinctively (see 8b notes 6 and 9) and thus quires the animal. Not so if he mounts in the city. There, if the animal ves when he mounts it, the movement might be attributable to other muli, e.g. the sound of people conversing, rather than to his mounting. us, he does not acquire.

Now this distinction is understandable as long as the rider did not ur the animal. If he spurred it, though, causing the animal to move a ostantial distance, then it is irrelevant where he mounted the animal; that movement is certainly attributable to the rider. He should thus acquire the animal even if he mounted it in the city. [The above explanation follows *Tosafos'* view, that even if the rider did not spur, the animal still instinctively moves slightly, and not that of *Rashi* (see 8b notes 2 and 6). *Shitah Mekubetzes* cites other explanations of the phrase, "If so," notably that of *Raavad*. He also notes, though, that the words "if so" are missing from some texts (see also *Ritva* and *Dikdukei Sofrim*). They were apparently missing from *Rashi's* text as well (see above, note 26).]

29. Rav Kahana extends the principle put forth by the Baraisa cited earlier (9b), that camels and donkeys can be acquired only with the type of *meshichah* customary for each species. According to the Baraisa, there is a basic premise that a *kinyan* is effective only if it is done in a "usual manner" (see also *Bava Basra* 86a). For example, if people usually move a certain species of animal by leading it, one cannot acquire one of that species through pulling it. However, the Baraisa states only that the manner of *kinyan* must be usual for the animal that is being acquired. Rav Kahana extends this principle, asserting that the site of the *kinyan* is also a factor. That is, although people generally ride animals, an animal still cannot be acquired at a site where it is unusual to ride, i.e. in a city.

30. Certainly the Gemara agrees with the above-cited Baraisa's general principle that a *kinyan* must be done in a usual manner. It challenges only Rav Kahana's extension of it (see previous note).

31. A money pouch is *muktzeh* on the Sabbath. Since it is thus forbidden to move it, people refrain from lifting it on the Sabbath (*Tosefos HaRosh*).

32. If the seller made no such stipulation [and surely with regard to acquiring a found animal] riding in the city does constitute a valid *kinyan*. (The Gemara's text follows *Rambam Hilchos Mechirah* 2:10; cf. *Sma, Choshen Mishpat* 197:12.)

במדה זאת קנו ר' יהודה אומר לעולם לא קנה עד שתהא משיכה בגמל והנהגה בחמור קתני מידת או שהיה אחד מושך ואחד מנהיג מושך ומנהיג אין אבל רכוב לא הוא הדין דאפילו רכוב והא דקתני מושך ומנהיג לאפוקי מדר' יהודה דאמר עד שתהא משיכה בגמל והנהגה בחמור קמשמע לן דאפילו איפכא נמי קני אי הכי ליערבינהו וליתנינהו שנים שהיו מושכין ומנהיגין בין בגמל בין בחמור איכא חד צד דלא קני איכא דאמרי משיכה בחמור ואיכא דאמרי [א]הנהגה בגמל ואית דמותיב מסיפא במדה זו קנה במדה זו למעוטי מאי לאו למעוטי רכוב לא למעוטי איפכא אי הכי היינו ר' יהודה איכא בינייהו צד אחד דלא קנה אית דאמרי משיכה בחמור ואיכא דאמרי הנהגה בגמל ת"ש [ב]אחד רכוב חמור ואחד תפוס במוסירה זה קנה חמור וזה קנה מוסירה שמע מינה רכוב קני הכא נמי במנהיג ברגליו אי הכי נקני נמי רכוב במוסירה אימא זה קנה חמור וחצי מוסירה וזה קנה חצי מוסירה בשלמא רכוב קני דקמגבה ליה בן דעת אלא תפוס במוסירה במאי קני אימא זה קנה חמור וכוליה מוסירה וזה קני מה שתפוס בידו [א] האי מאי אם תימצי לומר המגביה מציאה לחבירו קנה חבירו הני מילי היכא דקא מגבה ליה אדעתא דחבריה האי אדעתא דידיה קא מגבה ליה איהו לא קני לאחריני מקני אמר רב אשי [ג]זה קנה חמור ובית פגיה וזה קנה מה שתפוס בידו והשאר לא קנה לא זה ולא זה רבי אבהו אמר לעולם כדקתני הואיל ויכול לנתקה ולהביאה אצלו [ד] והא דר' אבהו [ב] ברותא [ג] היא דאי לא תימא הכי [ה]טלית שהיא מונחת חציה על גבי קרקע וחציה על גבי עמוד ובא אחד והגביה חציה מעל גבי קרקע ובא אחר והגביה חציה מעל גבי עמוד הכי נמי דקמא קני ובתרא לא קני הואיל ויכול לנתק ולהביא אצלו אלא הא דר' אבהו ברותא היא ת"ש ר' אליעזר אומר [ו]רכוב בשדה ומנהיג בעיר קנה הכא נמי מנהיג ברגליו אי הכי היינו מנהיג תרי גווני מנהיג אי הכי רכוב בעיר מאי טעמא לא קני אמר רב כהנא לפי שאין דרכן של בני אדם לרכוב בעיר אמר ליה רב אשי לרב כהנא אלא מעתה הגביה ארנקי בשבת שאין דרכן של בני אדם להגביה ארנקי בשבת הכי נמי דלא קני אלא מאי דעבד עבד וקני הכא נמי מאי דעבד עבד וקני אלא [ז]במקח וממכר עסקינן דאמר ליה קני כדרך שבני אדם קונין ואי

במדה זו. לקמיה מפרש למעוטי מאי: אי הכי. דלתנא קמא איפכא קני אמאי קתני משיכה בגמל והנהגה בחמור ליערבינהו וכו' מושכין ומנהיגין: איכא חד צד דלא קני. להכי לא מצי למתני בתרוייהו משיכה והנהגה ותנא הכי מושכין בגמל ומנהיגין בחמור או שהיה אחד מושך ואחד מנהיג באחד מהן אותו שדרכו בשניהם: במדה הזאת. קס"ד במשיכה או בהנהגה בין בגמל בין בחמור: אחד תפוס במוסירה. ואינו מנהיג: ש"מ רכוב קני. שלא במקום מנהיג וכיון דשלא במקום מנהיג קני כוליה במקום מנהיג פלגי: נקני נמי רכוב במוסירה. שבראש החמור שהוא תכשיט החמור וכחמור דמי: בשלמא רכוב. מצית למימר דקנה בהגבהת חבירו שהגביה ראשו השני מן הקרקע דקא מגבה לה בן דעת: אלא תפוס במוסירה במאי קני. פלגא והלא ראשה השני מונח במקומו והגבהת הפקר לא קניא עד דעקר לכוליה: האי מאי. דקא אמרת הגבהת תופס במוסירה לא הויא הגבהה לדידיה והויא הגבהה לאחריני אפילו אם תימצי לומר כו': ובית פגיה. קיבלי"ל בלע"ז מה שבראש החמור וכחמור דמי: מה שתפוס בידו. דמה שבתוך ידו הוי מגביה לגמרי: לא זה ולא זה. והבא לחוטפו יחטוף: כדקתני. זה קנה חמור וזה קנה מוסירה אפי' בית פגיה של חמור: הואיל ויכול. התפוס במוסירה למושכו בכח וינתק מראש החמור ויביאנו אצלו דהואיל וראש החמור גבוה נוח להביאה אצלו בנתיקה אחת: ברותא היא. דאע"ג דיכול לנתק לאו הגבהה היא: חציה על גב העמוד. דכיון דבמקום גבוה הוא האוחזה בראשה השני נוח לו לנתק ולהביאה אצלו דלא מחסר הגבהה: הכי נמי דקמא קני. דמכי אגבהה קניא כולה משום דיכול לנתקה אם כן יש חילוק בשנים שהגביהו מציאה זה מכאן וזה מכאן בין מקום גבוה למקום נמוך דהיכא דשני ראשיה מונחים בקרקע אין הגבהת של ראשון קונה כולה שאין יכול לנתקו ולהביאו אצלו מתוך שהוא ארוך ומונח בקרקע כל מה שהוא נותקו ומושכו אחריו נגרר הוא על גבי קרקע והיכא דאחד מראשיה גבוה כגון בראש החמור או על גבי עמוד המגביה תחלה ראש שעל גבי קרקע קונה כולה ואנן לא אשכחן תנא דמפליג: רכוב בשדה. בהמה של מציאה קונה אבל לא בעיר וטעמא מפרש לקמיה ומנהיג אף בעיר קנה וכ"ש בשדה ש"מ רכוב לחודיה קני כו': אין דרכן. משום צניעותא: ואי

מושך ומנהיג אין אבל רכוב לא. תימה מנ"ל דלמא כ"ש רכוב דתפיס ביה ואי משום דשייר אטו בכל דוכתי תנא כולהו קניינין וי"ל דממשנה יתיר' קדייק דליערבינהו ולתנינהו שנים שהיו מושכין או מנהיגים בין בגמל בין בחמור ותו לא מדקתני בלישנא יתירא ש"מ דלמעוטי רכוב אתא והיינו דפריך בתר הכי וליערבינהו ולתנינהו וא"ת לעולם מנ"ל למעוטי רכוב דלמא הא דלא ערבינהו כדי לאשמועינן דמשיכה אורחא בגמל והנהגה בחמור ואפ"ה אחד מושך ואחד מנהיג בגמל לא מבטל משיכה דאורחא בגמל את ההנהגה דלאו אורחא וכן בחמור איפכא ולכך תנא בתר הכי אחד מושך ואחד מנהיג ולא למעוטי רכוב וי"ל כיון שישמיענו שמשיכה והנהגה שניהם קנו בגמל ובחמור פשיטא שאין אחד מבטל חבירו משום דהאי אורחיה והאי לאו אורחיה אבל במתני' משמיענו שפיר שאין מבטל רכוב ומנהיג ברגליו את מנהיג לחודיה לפי שיש ברכוב כל מה שיש במנהיג ועוד דתפיס בה: אי הכי ליערבינהו ולתנינהו. לפי מאי דס"ד דרכוב קני ומשיכה והנהגה בין בגמל בין בחמור במדה זו קנה אתא למעוטי שום קנין אחר או רכוב במקום מנהיג: אי הכי היינו ר' יהודה. הוה מצי לאקשויי מגופה דקתני או שהיה אחד מושך ואחד מנהיג ש"מ דבחד לד קני: ונקני נמי רכוב במוסירה. אי גרסינן אי הכי ה"פ אי אמרת בשלמא כשאין מנהיג ברגליו ורכוב קני הבהמה משום דתפיס בה א"ש דלא קני מוסירה דבמטלטלין לא שייך קנין של מוסירה אלא בהגבהה או משיכה אבל אי מיירי במנהיג ברגליו לקני נמי מוסירה במשיכת הבהמה אי אמרינן משוך בהמה זו וקני כלים שעליה קני דלקמן מיבעיא לן אי קני אי לא קני ליפשוט מהכא דלא מהני:

והשאר לא קנה לא זה ולא זה. ואפילו אי אמרינן משוך בהמה וקני כלים שעליה קני הכא כיון דתפיס במוסירה לא קני רכוב נמי לא קני כדאמרינן אדעתא דידיה אגבהה איהו לא קני כו':

דאי לא תימא הכי טלית שחציה כו'. קצת קשה מנ"ל שלא יחלוק רבי אבהו אף בזה:

הואיל ויכול לנתקו ולהביאו אצלו. תימה דמשמע דאם נתקה שהוא קונה כו' משום שעל ידו הוגבהה למעלה משלש ומאי שנא מעני המנקף בראש הזית (גיטין דף נט:) שאין בו גזל אלא מפני דרכי שלום וכן פרק הגוזל קמא (ב"ק דף לח. ושם ד"ה והני מילי) הזורק סלע של חבירו לים פטור ומוקי לה בדאדיי' אדויי אלמא לא חשיב מה שהוגבהה על ידו הואיל וסופו ליפול וי"ל דשאני הכא שתופס בידו אחד מן הראש א"נ הכא איירי כשניתק מן העמוד אינו ארוך כ"כ שיגיע ראש השני לארץ ושאני שילוח הקן (חולין דף קמא:) דקאמר זיל טרוף אקן לגבהינהו ולקנינהו התם נמי הוגבהו על ידו יותר ממה שהיה תחילה שהרי קצת מפריחים למעלה לכך [ד] קני: אי הכי רכוב בעיר מאי טעמא לא קני. אי גרסינן א"ה ה"פ אי אמרת בשלמא לא מיירי במנהיג ברגליו לכך בעיר לא קני דלא אזלא מחמתיה לפי שיש בני אדם שמדברים יחד ויש כמה דברים באמצע הדרכים אלא אי אמרינן במנהיג ברגליו א"כ אזלא מחמתיה טובא ואמאי לא קני:

מסוך

עין משפט
נר מצוה

סב א מיי' פי"ז מהל' אבידה הל' ה ועי' בהשגות ובמ"מ סמג עשין עד טוש"ע ח"מ סי' רעא סעיף א:
סג ב ג מיי' שם הל' ז טוש"ע שם סעיף ג:
סד ד ה טוש"ע ח"מ סי' רסט סעיף ה וע"ש:
סה ו ז מיי' פ"ב מהל' מכירה הל' י ועיין במ"מ סמג עשין פב טוש"ע ח"מ סי' קצז סעיף ה:

רבינו חננאל

פי' איכא חד צד דלא קני יש מי שאומר משיכה בחמור לא קני אבל בגמל בין במשיכה בין בהנהגה קני. ויש מי שאומר הנהגה בגמל לא קנה אבל חמור בין במשיכה בין בהנהגה קני. פי' פגיה רצועות של מוסירה הנתונות על לחייה ועל פדחתה. סוגיא דשמעתא טלית מונחת על גבי קרקע וחציה על גבי עמוד בא אחד והגביה חציה מעל גבי קרקע ובא אחר והגביה חציה שעל גבי עמוד א). רכוב אי קני אי לא קני ת"ש ר"א אומר רכוב בשדה קנה וכו' ודחי' התם במנהיג ברגליו אי הכי היינו מנהיג. ופרקי' תרי גווני מנהיג. ואסקי' במקח וממכר אי אמר ליה קני כדרך שבני אדם קונין אי ברשות הרבים רכוב קנה.

חשק שלמה על ר"ח

א) חסר פה בהעתקה ונראה דצ"ל קנו תרוייהו.

[ת]ורת הש"ם

[...]יל ח.], ב) ס"א א [ועיין פסחים יא. מהרי"ב], ג) [פי' שטעו חכמים ולא כהלכה לא רצה ולומר טעו אלא ברותא היא כלומר [ב]ילונית היא, ערוך [...]ר ד'], ד) [ועיין עוד [כ]תובות ל: ד"ה ואי דלא מצי].

[ל]קוטי רש"י

תימצי לומר. אפי' אם תמצא המגביה מציאה כו' [לעיל ח.]. [...] פגיה. קיבליי"ל [...]אשה ולחייה [שבת [...] לשון חבישה. [...]דור"א בית ראש של [...] קורין כן [סוטה מה.].

[ל]עזי רש"י

[...]יי"ל. פירוש בית [...] ולחייה (רש"י שבת [...] ע"ב ד"ה בפגי [...]א), בית ראש של [...] (רש"י סוטה דף [...]"א ד"ה אבי פאגי), [...] של מוסרה [...]ם על לחיה ועל [...]ה (רבינו חננאל [...]וך ערך פג ה').

le's headstall.[17] – ? –

he Gemara emends the Baraisa again:

אֵימָא זֶה קָנָה חֲמוֹר וְכוּלֵּיהּ מוֹ – **Say,** i.e. emend the Baraisa, **as** **ows:** THIS ONE ACQUIRES THE DONKEY AND THE WHOLE DLE,[18] וְזֶה קָנֵי מַה שֶּׁתָּפוּס בְּיָדוֹ – AND THE OTHER ONE UIRES only [THE PART OF THE BRIDLE] THAT HE GRASPS IN HIS D.[19]

he Gemara objects to the emendation:

הַאי – **What** sort of reasoning **is this?** אִם תִּימְצֵי לוֹמַר הַמַּגְבִּיהַּ מְצִיאָה לַחֲבֵירוֹ קָנָה חֲ – **Even if you assume** that if **one** **ks up a found object** intending to acquire it just **for his** **ow, his fellow does acquire** it, הָנֵי מִילֵּי הֵיכָא דְּקָא מַגְבַּהּ לֵיהּ אַדַּעְתָּא דְּחַבְ – still **this is** so only **where one lifts [the object]** **h the intent that his fellow** acquire it. הַאי אַדַּעְתָּא דִּידֵיהּ קָא מַגְבַּהּ – But **this** one holding the bridle **is lifting it** primarily **h the intent that he himself** acquire it. אִיהוּ לֹא קָנֵי – **He** self **does not acquire** a portion of the bridle, לְאַחֲרִינֵי מַקְנֵי – **does he** intend to **acquire** it **for others?** Of course not! Since thus never intended to acquire for the rider, the latter should acquire.[20] – ? –

he Gemara suggests a final emendation:

אָמַר רַב – **Rav Ashi said:** Emend the Baraisa as follows: זֶה קָנָה חֲמוֹר וּבֵית – THIS ONE ACQUIRES THE DONKEY AND ITS ADSTALL,[21] וְזֶה קָנָה מַה שֶּׁתָּפוּס בְּיָדוֹ – AND THE OTHER ONE UIRES [THE PART OF THE BRIDLE] THAT HE HOLDS IN HIS HAND. וְהַשְּׁאָר לֹא קָנָה לֹא זֶה וְלֹא – **But the rest of** the bridle – **ther this one nor the other acquires** it.

After emending the Baraisa in response to its question, the Gemara attempts to defend the original version of the Baraisa: ר׳ אַבָּהוּ אָמַר – **R' Abahu said:** לְעוֹלָם כִּדְקָתָנֵי – **Really,** the Baraisa was correct **as it was taught** originally, i.e. the one holding the bridle acquires it even though the entire bridle was not actually lifted. The reason for this is that הוֹאִיל וְיָכוֹל לְנַתְּקָהּ וְלַהֲבִיאָהּ אֶצְלוֹ – **"since" he is able to yank [the bridle]** off the animal **and bring it to himself,** he acquires it even without actually doing so.[22]

The Gemara rejects R' Abahu's principle of "since":

וְהָא דְּר׳ אַבָּהוּ בְּרוּתָא הִיא – **But R' Abahu's** principle **is an outside view,**[23] i.e. it is not an accepted, mainstream view. דְּאִי לֹא תֵּימָא הָכִי – **For if you do not say so** that R' Abahu's principle is unacceptable, this presents the following difficulty: טַלִּית שֶׁהִיא מוּנַחַת חֶצְיָהּ עַל גַּבֵּי קַרְקַע – **If half a cloak is lying** on the ground וְחֶצְיָהּ עַל גַּבֵּי עַמּוּד – **and half of it upon a pillar** וּבָא אֶחָד וְהִגְבִּיהַּ חֶצְיָהּ מֵעַל גַּבֵּי קַרְקַע – **and one** person **came** and **lifted half of it from the ground,** leaving the other half on the pillar,[24] וּבָא אַחֵר וְהִגְבִּיהַּ חֶצְיָהּ מֵעַל גַּבֵּי עַמּוּד – **and** then **another came** afterwards **and lifted up the** other **half from atop the pillar,** הָכִי נַמֵּי דְּקַמָּא קָנֵי וּבַתְרָא לֹא קָנֵי – **so too,** will you say **that the first person** already **acquired** the entire cloak **and** therefore **the latter does not acquire** any part of it, הוֹאִיל וְיָכוֹל לְנַתֵּק וּלְהָבִיא אֶצְלוֹ – **since [the first] was able to yank [the cloak]** off the pillar **and bring it to himself?** Of course not.[25] אֶלָּא הָא דְּר׳ אַבָּהוּ בְּרוּתָא הִיא – **Rather, this** principle of "since" **that R' Abahu** proposed **is an outside view.**

NOTES

I.e. the part of the bridle that fits over the donkey's head. Since part he bridle was never lifted, the one holding the bridle should acquire part of it at all.

he Gemara's position, at this point, is very difficult to understand. If t of the bridle was never lifted, why does the Gemara understand at point that the rider acquires any part of the bridle but finds it diffi- to understand the acquisition of the one holding the bridle? As men- ed in note 16, the Gemara assumes that the litigants in the Baraisa's e performed a *kinyan hagbahah* upon the bridle. For this to be effec- , the entire bridle must have been lifted on behalf of both. Why does Gemara understand, then, that the rider acquires a portion of the dle? Just as the bridle's headstall was never lifted at all in regard to holder of the bridle, it was also not lifted for the rider! See *Mahari z* cited in *Shitah Mekubetzes;* see also note 20 for a fuller discussion his point.

This respondent also mistakenly believes that according to the ques- ner, the rider can acquire more of the bridle than just the headstall *tva;* see also note 15).

For he has lifted that part of the bridle (*Rashi*). [Legally, the part of bridle in his grasp is considered separate from the rest of the bridle. us, he acquires it because when he lifts it he has lifted the entire object e above, 7a, with *Ritva*).]

Because the rider can acquire through *kinyan hagbahah* only if the ire bridle was lifted on his behalf.

The implication of the Gemara seems to be that indeed the rider has de a *hagbahah* upon his part of the bridle, and that he lacks the par- pation of the holder of the bridle only to complete his *kinyan.* But this ery difficult to understand. Who has performed a valid *hagbahah* for rider? Surely, the fact that part of the bridle is lifted by the donkey nnot be considered a valid *hagbahah* for its rider, just as it is not for holder of the bridle. Now if we were to assume that the rider's *kinyan meshichah* (see above, note 16) this problem is resolved, but a new blem arises: Why does the rider need the holder's assistance to com- te his *kinyan?* His *meshichah* is complete without assistance from yone.

*Tosefos HaRosh* (cited by *Shitah Mekubetzes*) advances a novel con- t to resolve the difficulty. Indeed, spurring the animal can constitute alid *kinyan meshichah* upon the whole bridle. In the Baraisa's case, wever, the *kinyan meshichah* is ineffective because the person holding other part of the bridle objects to the rider's performing the *kinyan*: is cancels his *kinyan meshichah* on the bridle. Accordingly, the rider can acquire it only if the other's *kinyan hagbahah* is effective and he lifted the object intending that they both acquire. In the Baraisa's case, though, where this was not the other person's intent, the rider should not acquire any part of the bridle. *Shitah Mekubetzes* 8a ascribes this premise to *Tosfei HaRosh* as well. *Rashba* there also seems to agree with this principle; see *Chidushei R' Shimon Yehudah HaKohen* ch. 8, and *Ketzos HaChoshen* 269:2.

21. Finally, Rav Ashi reveals the true nature of the above question, "If so, let the rider acquire part of the bridle as well." What the questioner meant was that the rider should acquire the donkey's headstall, which is legally "part" of the donkey (see note 14); he admittedly acquires no more of the bridle, however, because the other litigant never intended to acquire it for him. The questioner actually meant this from the begin- ning of the discussion. He was consistently misunderstood, however, by the Gemara's respondents (*Ritva*).

22. Since the donkey's head is high above the ground, the one holding the bridle can easily bring it to himself with one yank (*Rashi*); he would then hold it in the air for an instant. This, like lifting, is a form of *kinyan hag- bahah.* R' Abahu therefore asserts : Since he *can* take hold of the entire bridle, he acquires the entire bridle as if he actually did so.

23. Not wishing to denigrate the Amora that put forth this view, the Gemara uses this term as a euphemism for a mistaken view (*Aruch*).

24. Having lifted only one end of the garment, he presumably did not ac- quire it. See 8a note 5.

25. For if the first person did acquire it, the following illogical distinction would emerge: If the entire found cloak lay on level ground and someone lifted part of it, he certainly does not acquire it because he cannot bring it to himself with one yank; it would just drag on the ground. If, however, part of the cloak lay upon a pillar or high ground and someone lifted the other part of it from the ground, he would acquire it since he *can* bring it to himself with a yank. However, no Tanna ever suggested that such a distinction exists (*Rashi*). [In our Mishnah's case, for example, each litigant claims to have found the cloak first. According to R' Abahu, if one of the litigants proved that he lifted his end first, the law should depend upon whether the entire cloak lay on level ground or not. Nevertheless, the Mishnah suggests no such distinction (see *Raavad* in *Shitah Meku- betzes*). Hence, we must conclude that in either case, the first person to lift part of the cloak does not acquire it. Accordingly, if another person then lifts the rest of the cloak, this is tantamount to two people having lifted it simultaneously: Each acquires an equal portion of the cloak, as stated above on 8a.]

במדה זאת קנו ר' יהודה אומר לעולם לא קנה עד שתהא משיכה בגמל והנהגה בחמור קתני מיהת או שהיה אחד מושך ואחד מנהיג מושך ומנהיג אין אבל רכוב לא הוא הדין דאפילו רכוב והא דקתני מושך ומנהיג לאפוקי מדר' יהודה דאמר עד שתהא משיכה בגמל והנהגה בחמור קמשמע לן דאפילו איפכא נמי קני אי הכי ליערבינהו וליתנינהו שנים שהיו מושכין ומנהיגין בין בגמל בין בחמור איכא חד צד דלא קני איכא דאמרי משיכה בחמור ואיכא דאמרי [א]הנהגה בגמל ואית דמותיב מסיפא במדה זו קנה במדה זו למעוטי מאי לאו למעוטי רכוב לא למעוטי איפכא אי הכי היינו ר' יהודה איכא בינייהו צד אחד דלא קנה אית דאמרי משיכה בחמור ואיכא דאמרי הנהגה בגמל ת"ש [ב]אחד רכוב חמור ואחד תפוס במוסירה זה קנה חמור וזה קנה מוסירה שמע מינה רכוב קני הכא נמי במנהיג ברגליו אי הכי נקני נמי רכוב במוסירה אימא זה קנה חמור וחצי מוסירה וזה קנה חצי מוסירה בשלמא רכוב קני דקמגבה ליה בן דעת אלא תפוס במוסירה במאי קני אימא זה קנה חמור וכוליה מוסירה וזה קני מה שתפוס בידו [א] האי מאי אם תימצי לומר המגביה מציאה לחבירו קנה חבירו הני מילי היכא דקא מגבה ליה אדעתא דחבריה האי אדעתא דידיה קא מגבה ליה איהו לא קני לאחריני מקני אמר רב אשי [ג]זה קנה חמור ובית פגיה וזה קנה מה שתפוס בידו והשאר לא קנה לא זה ולא זה רבי אבהו אמר לעולם כדקתני הואיל ויכול לנתקה ולהביאה אצלו [ד]והא דר' אבהו [ב]ברותא היא דאי לא תימא הכי [ה]טלית שהיא מונחת חציה על גבי קרקע וחציה על גבי עמוד ובא אחד והגביה חציה מעל גבי קרקע ובא אחר והגביה חציה מעל גבי עמוד הכי נמי דקמא קני ובתרא לא קני הואיל ויכול לנתק ולהביא אצלו אלא הא דר' אבהו ברותא היא ת"ש ר' אליעזר אומר [ו]רכוב בשדה ומנהיג בעיר קנה הכא נמי מנהיג ברגליו אי הכי היינו מנהיג תרי גווני מנהיג אי הכי רכוב בעיר מאי טעמא לא קני אמר רב כהנא לפי שאין דרכן של בני אדם לרכוב בעיר אמר ליה רב אשי לרב כהנא אלא מעתה הגביה ארנקי בשבת שאין דרכן של בני אדם להגביה ארנקי בשבת הכי נמי דלא קני אלא מאי דעבד עבד וקני הכא נמי מאי דעבד עבד וקני אלא [ז]במקח וממכר עסקינן דאמר ליה קני כדרך שבני אדם קונין ואי

---

**רש"י**

במדה זו. לקמיה מפרש למעוטי מאי: אי הכי. דלתנא קמא איפכא קני אמאי קתני משיכה בגמל והנהגה בחמור ליערבינהו וכו' מושכין ומנהיגין: איכא חד צד דלא קני. להכי לא מצי למתני בתרוייהו משיכה והנהגה ותנא הכי מושכין בגמל ומנהיגין בחמור או שהיה אחד מושך ואחד מנהיג באחד מהן אותו שדרכו בשניהם: במדה הזאת. קס"ד במשיכה או בהנהגה בין בגמל בין בחמור: אחד תפוס במוסירה. ואינו מנהיג: ש"מ רכוב קני. שלא במקום מנהיג וכיון דשלא במקום מנהיג קני כוליה במקום מנהיג פלגי: נקני נמי רכוב במוסירה. שבראש החמור שהוא תכשיט החמור וכחמור דמי: בשלמא רכוב. מצית למימר דקנה בהגבהת חבירו שהגביה ראשו השני מן הקרקע דקא מגבה לה בן דעת: אלא תפוס במוסירה במאי קני. פלגא והלא ראשה השני מונח במקומו והגבהת הפקר לא קניא עד דעקר לכוליה: האי מאי. דקא אמרת הגבהת תופס במוסירה לא הויא הגבהה לדידיה והויא הגבהה לאחריני אפילו אם תימצי לומר כו': ובית פגיה. קיבצויי"ל בלע"ז מה שבראש החמור וכחמור דמי: מה שתפוס בידו. דמה שבתוך ידו הוי מגביה לגמרי: לא זה ולא זה. והבא לחוטפו יחטוף: כדקתני. זה קנה חמור וזה קנה מוסירה אפי' בית פגיה של חמור: הואיל ויכול. התפוס במוסירה למושכו בכח וינתק מראש החמור ויביאנו אצלו דהואיל וראש החמור גבוה נוח להביאה אצלו בנתיקה אחת: ברותא היא. דאע"ג דיכול לנתק לאו הגבהה היא: חציה על גב העמוד. דכיון דמקום גבוה הוא האוחזה בראשה השני נוח לו לנתק ולהביאה אצלו דלא מחסר הגבהה: הכי נמי דקמא קני. דמכי אגבהה קניא כולה משום דיכול לנתקה אם כן יש חילוק בשנים שהגביהו מציאה זה מכאן וזה מכאן בין מקום גבוה למקום נמוך דהיכא דשני ראשיה מונחים בקרקע אין הגבהת של ראשון קונה כולה שאין יכול לנתקו ולהביאו אצלו מתוך שהוא ארוך ומונח בקרקע כל מה שהוא נותקו ומושכו אחריו נגרר הוא על גבי קרקע והיכא דאחד מראשיה גבוה כגון בראש החמור או על גבי עמוד המגביה תחלה ראש שעל גבי קרקע קונה כולה ואנן לא אשכחן תנא דמפליג: רכוב בשדה. בהמה של מציאה קונה אבל לא בעיר וטעמא מפרש לקמיה ומנהיג אף בעיר קנה וכ"ש בשדה ש"מ רכוב לחודיה קני כו': אין דרכן. משום לניעותא: ואי

---

**תוספות**

מושך ומנהיג אין אבל רכוב לא. תימה מנ"ל דלמא כ"ש רכוב דתפיס ביה ואי משום דשייה אטו בכל דוכתי תנא כולהו קניינין וי"ל דממשנה יתיר' קדייק דליערבינהו ולתנינהו שנים שהיו מושכין או מנהיגים בין בגמל בין בחמור ותו לא מדקתני בלישנא יתירא ש"מ דלמעוטי רכוב אתא והיינו דפריך בתר הכי וליערבינהו ולתניינהו וא"ת לעולם מנ"ל למעוטי רכוב דלמא הא דלא ערבינהו כדי לאשמועינן דמשיכה אורחא בגמל והנהגה בחמור ואפ"ה אחד מושך ואחד מנהיג בגמל לא מבטל משיכה דאורחא בגמל את ההנהגה דלאו אורחא וכן בחמור איפכא ולכך תנא בתר הכי אחד מושך ואחד מנהיג ולא למעוטי רכוב וי"ל כיון שישמיענו שמשיכה והנהגה שניהם קנו בגמל ובחמור פשיטא שאין אחד מבטל חבירו משום דהאי אורחיה והאי לאו אורחיה אבל במתני' משמיענו שפיר שאין מבטל רכוב ומנהיג ברגליו את מנהיג לחודיה לפי שיש ברכוב כל מה שיש במנהיג ועוד דתפיס בה: אי הכי ליערבינהו ולתנינהו. לפי מאי דס"ד דרכוב קני ומשיכה והנהגה בין בגמל בין בחמור במדה זו קנה אתא למעוטי שום קנין אחר או רכוב במקום מנהיג: אי הכי היינו ר' יהודה. הוה מצי לאקשויי מגופה דקתני או שהיה אחד מושך ואחד מנהיג ש"מ דבחד לא קני: ונקני נמי רכוב במוסירה. אי גרסינן אי הכי ה"פ אי אמרת בשלמא כשאין מנהיג ברגליו ורכוב קני הבהמה משום דתפיס בה א"ש דלא קני מוסירה דבמטלטלין לא שייך קנין של מוסירה אלא בהגבהה או משיכה אבל אי מיירי במנהיג ברגליו לקני נמי מוסירה במשיכת הבהמה אי אמרינן משוך בהמה זו וקני כלים שעליה קני דלקמן מיבעיא לן אי קני אי לא קני ליפשוט מהכא דלא מהני:

והשאר לא קנה לא זה ולא זה. ואפילו אי אמרינן משוך בהמה וקני כלים שעליה קני הכא כיון דתפיס במוסירה לא קני רכוב נמי לא קני כדאמרינן אדעתא דידיה אגבהה איהו לא קני כו':

דאי לא תימא הכי טלית שחציה כו'. קצת קשה מנ"ל שלא יחלוק רבי אבהו אף בזה:

הואיל ויכול לנתקו ולהביאו אצלו. תימה דמשמע דאם נתקה שהוא קונה כו' משום שעל ידו הוגבהה למעלה משלש ומאי שנא מעני המנקף בראש הזית (גיטין דף נט:) שאין בו גזל אלא מפני דרכי שלום וכן פרק הגוזל קמא (ב"ק דף לח. ושם ד"ה והני מילי) הזורק סלע של חבירו לים פטור ומוקי לה בדאדיי' אדויי אלמא לא חשיב מה שהוגבהה על ידו הואיל וסופו ליפול וי"ל דשאני הכא שתופס בידו אחד מן הראש א"נ הכא איירי כשניתק מן העמוד אינו ארוך כ"כ שיגיע ראש השני לארץ ושאני שילוח הקן (חולין דף קמא:) דקאמר זיל טרוף אקן דלגבהינהו ולקנינהו התם נמי הוגבהו על ידו יותר ממה שהיה תחילה שהרי קצת מפריחים למעלה לכך [ד]קני: אי הכי רכוב בעיר מאי טעמא לא קני. אי גרסינן א"ה ה"פ אי אמרת בשלמא לא מיירי במנהיג ברגליו לכך בעיר לא קני דלא אזלא מחמתיה לפי שיש בני אדם שמדברים יחד ויש כמה דברים באמצע הדרכים אלא אי אמרינן במנהיג ברגליו א"כ אזלא מחמתיה טובא ואמאי לא קני:

משוך

---

**עין משפט נר מצוה**

סב א מיי' פי"ז מהל' אבידה הל' ה ועי' בהשגות ובמ"מ סמג עשין עד טוש"ע ח"מ סי' רעא סעיף א:

סג ב ג מיי' שם הל' ז טוש"ע שם סעיף ג:

סד ד ה טוש"ע ח"מ סי' רסט סעיף ה וע"ש:

סה ו ז מיי' פ"ב מהל' מכירה הל' י ועיין במ"מ סמג עשין פב טוש"ע ח"מ סי' קצז סעיף ה:

**רבינו חננאל**

פי' איכא חד צד דלא קני יש מי שאומר משיכה בחמור לא קני אבל בגמל בין במשיכה בין בהנהגה קני. ויש מי שאומר הנהגה בגמל לא קנה אבל חמור בין במשיכה בין בהנהגה קני. פי' פגיה רצועות של מוסירה הנתונות על לחייה ועל פדחתה. סוגיא דשמעתא טלית מונחת על גבי קרקע וחציה על גבי עמוד בא אחד והגביה חציה מעל גבי קרקע ובא אחר והגביה חציה שעל גבי עמוד א). רכוב אי קני אי לא קני ת"ש ר"א אומר רכוב בשדה קנה וכו' ודחי' התם במנהיג ברגליו אי הכי היינו מנהיג. ופרקי' תרי גווני מנהיג. ואסקי' במקח וממכר אי אמר ליה קני כדרך שבני אדם קונין אי ברשות הרבים רכוב קנה.

**חשק שלמה על ר"ח**

א) חסר פה בהעתקה ונראה דצ"ל קנו תרוייהו.

**מסורת הש"ס**

...ח.], ב) ס"א [ועיין פסחים יא. ...מהרי"ב], ג) [פי' ...שטעו חכמים ולא ...הלכה לא רלה ...ולומר טעו אלא ...ברותא היא כלומר ...שונית היא, ערוך ...ד'], ד) [ועיין עוד ...תוספות לו: ד"ה ואי דלא מצי].

**...קוטי רש"י**

...תימצי לומר. ...אפי' אם תמצא ...המגביה מציאה ...כו' [לעיל ח.]. ...פגיה. קיבצויי"ל ...אשה ולחייה [שבת ...לשון חבישה. ...ור"א בית ראש של ...קורין כן [סוטה מה.].

**...עזי רש"י**

...י"ל. פירוש בית ...ולחייה (רש"י שבת ...ע"ב ד"ה בפגי ...), בית ראש של ...(רש"י סוטה דף ...א ד"ה אבי פאגי), ...של מוסרה ...על לחיה ועל ...(רבינו חננאל ...ערך פג ה').

The Gemara responds that even according to the rebuttal, the vo views in fact differ:

אִיכָּא בֵּינַיְיהוּ צַד אֶחָד דְּלֹא קָנָ – **There is** in fact a difference **etween them** with regard to the **one combination that does ot acquire** the animal according to R' Yehudah, but does acquire ccording to the Tanna Kamma.[10]

The Gemara cites two views concerning which combination the anna Kamma invalidates:

אִית דְּאָמְרֵי מְשִׁיכָה בַּחֲמוֹ – **Some say** that it is **pulling a donkey** וְאִיכָּא דְּאָמְרֵי הַנְהָגָה בְּגָמָ – **And some say** that it is **leading a amel.**

The Gemara cites another Baraisa to resolve the question of hether a rider acquires:

תָּא שְׁמַ – **Come, learn** the resolution from the following araisa: אֶחָד רָכוּב חֲמוֹר – If two litigants appear in court, ONE IDING A DONKEY וְאֶחָד תָּפוּס בְּמוֹסֵירָה – AND ONE HOLDING ON O THE BRIDLE,[11] זֶה קָנָה חֲמוֹר – then THIS ONE ACQUIRES THE ONKEY וְזֶה קָנָה מוֹסֵירָה – AND THE OTHER ONE ACQUIRES THE RIDLE. שְׁמַע מִינָּהּ רָכוּב קָנֵי – Since the Baraisa clearly states at the rider acquires the donkey, **learn from this that a rider cquires!**[12]

The Gemara refutes the proof:

הָכָא נַמִּי בְּמַנְהִיג בְּרַגְלָיו – **Here too,** as in our Mishnah, the Baraisa **refers** only **to** one **who "leads,"** i.e. spurs the animal **with his feet.**[13] Perhaps it agrees with Rav Yehudah, though, that if someone merely rides the animal, he does not acquire it.

The Gemara questions this interpretation of the Baraisa:

אִי הָכִי נִקְנֵי נַמִּי רָכוּב בְּמוֹסֵירָה – **If** it is **so** that the rider "led" the donkey with his feet, **let him acquire** a portion **of the bridle as well!**[14] Why, then, does the Baraisa imply that the entire bridle is awarded to the one holding it and not to the rider?

The Gemara emends the Baraisa:

אֵימָא זֶה קָנָה חֲמוֹר וַחֲצִי מוֹסֵירָה – **Say,** i.e. emend the ruling of the Baraisa, as follows: THIS ONE ACQUIRES THE DONKEY AND HALF OF THE BRIDLE, וְזֶה קָנָה חֲצִי מוֹסֵירָה – AND THE OTHER ONE ACQUIRES HALF OF THE BRIDLE.[15]

The Gemara analyzes the emendation:

בִּשְׁלָמָא רָכוּב קָנֵי – **It is understandable** that **the rider acquires** a portion of the bridle without having lifted it completely, דְּקָמַגְבַּהּ לֵיהּ בֶּן דַּעַת – **for a mentally competent** person **has lifted** his end of the bridle on behalf of the rider.[16] אֶלָּא תָּפוּס בְּמוֹסֵירָה בְּמַאי קָנֵי – **But the one holding on to the bridle – how does he acquire** a portion of the bridle? Nobody ever lifted the

NOTES

). The Tanna Kamma in fact disputes R' Yehudah concerning one ombination, maintaining that it constitutes a valid *kinyan*. He agrees ith R' Yehudah, though, that another combination is invalid, as the ebuttal maintained.

. I.e. he only holds the bridle but does not *lead* the animal (*Rashi*).

2. I.e. if he rides alone without anyone leading the animal (*Rashi*). This oes not explicitly resolve the question of whether a rider acquires "in e presence of a leader," however, because the second party only held e bridle but never *led* the animal. *Rashi* adds, though, that if a rider one acquires the entire animal, this implies that a rider "in the resence of a leader" acquires half. This assertion puzzles the com-entators: How does *Rashi's* conclusion follow from his premise? erhaps a rider acquires the entire animal if he is alone but acquires othing "in the presence of" a leader (see Gemara above 8b). See *Shitah ekubetzes, Maharsha* et al.

3. When a rider spurs the animal until it moves, he performs a bona fide *inyan meshichah*, thereby acquiring the animal. See above, end of 8b.

4. *Rashi* explains the Gemara's question as follows: If someone erforms a *kinyan* upon an animal wearing an adornment, he acquires e adornment as well, for it is considered a part of the animal. If so, let e rider in the Baraisa's case acquire the bridle's headstall (i.e. the part the bridle that fits over the donkey's head) since this is an adornment."

Now according to this interpretation, the Gemara's question is nrelated to its previous discussion of whether in the Baraisa, the rider led" with his feet; either way, the Gemara asks, he should acquire the eadstall along with the donkey. This is apparently contradicted, owever, by the question's introductory phrase אִי הָכִי, *if so*, which dicates that the question does in fact relate to the previous discussion. Rashi's defense, *Ritva* notes that many texts omit this phrase and sserts that *Rashi's* did as well.

Additionally, he suggests an alternative explanation of the Gemara's uestion that in fact relates it to the previous discussion. Initially, the emara "proved" that simply riding (i.e. sitting upon) an animal allows person to acquire it. Since a bridle does not help a person sit on an nimal, when someone acquires an animal through "riding" he might ave no intention of acquiring the bridle since it does not assist him in erforming the *kinyan*. Without intent, he does not acquire it. However, bridle does help a person drive his animal. Thus, if a rider must drive is animal to acquire it, as the Gemara now maintains, he presumably tends to acquire the bridle along with the animal. Why, then, asks the emara, does he not acquire the headstall when he acquires the donkey, nce it is in fact in the category of an adornment for the animal?

5. The respondent's emendation is difficult to understand. Why did he ssume that the rider acquires a full half of the bridle? Even the uestioner asserted only that the rider should acquire the headstall (see *Rashi's* interpretation cited in the previous note).

*Ritva* explains that the respondent misunderstood the questioner, supposing that the questioner believed the rider to be entitled to half the bridle. The respondent then acknowledged his readiness to accept this position without challenging its premise. In fact, however, the questioner meant only that the rider should acquire the headstall (see below, note 20). The Gemara now tests the validity of the respondent's assumptions until it concludes (in Rav Ashi's explanation below) that indeed all the questioner had meant to assert was that the rider should acquire the headstall (see also *Rashba*).

16. It seems that the Gemara's question assumes, as per the above respondent's misunderstanding of the questioner's position, that in the Baraisa's case, the litigants acquire the bridle through *kinyan hagbahah*, i.e. by lifting it. The *kinyan hagbahah* is valid, however, only if the entire bridle was lifted on behalf of the prospective owner; otherwise, the *kinyan* is void and nothing at all is acquired. Generally, when two people perform a *kinyan* simultaneously, each intends to lift it for his fellow as well as for himself so that his own *kinyan* will be valid (see 8a note 5). Here too, since the person holding the bridle presumably lifted it for the rider as well as for himself, the rider seemingly acquires half of it.

*Ritva* notes, however, that the rider cannot actually acquire half of the bridle: If the one holding the bridle does not acquire it himself, as the Gemara maintains he does not, then he would not acquire it for the rider either (see 8a notes 9 and 15 and Gemara below). Thus, the questioner must mean as follows. We understand that the rider would theoretically acquire if the one holding the bridle acquired as well. How, though, can the one holding the bridle acquire?

Alternatively, the Gemara's question [on the misunderstood position of the above questioner] assumes that the rider of the donkey and the one who holds the bridle acquire parts of the bridle with different *kinyanim*. The one who holds the bridle acquires his part through *hagbahah*, since he lifts one end of the bridle off the ground. The rider of the donkey, however, acquires through *meshichah*. Their understanding of the above question, "If so, let him acquire a part of the bridle as well," was as follows: If a rider acquires just by taking hold of the animal, as the Gemara initially assumed, then he obviously cannot acquire the bridle with this *kinyan*, for he has not taken hold of the bridle, so that no *kinyan* was performed with it. If, on the other hand, the rider must actually cause the animal [and the bridle] to move, as the Gemara now maintains, he performs a bona fide *kinyan meshichah* upon the bridle as well when he does so, for the bridle, too, is caused to move by his action. Why, then, does he not acquire the bridle as well? (Based on *Tosafos*, as explained by *Ritzbash* in *Shitah Mekubetzes*. See *Nachalas David*, who attempts to reconcile this interpretation with the view [see above, 8b note 6] that riding an animal causes it to move somewhat when he mounts it.)

במדה זאת קנו ר' יהודה אומר לעולם לא קנה עד שתהא משיכה בגמל והנהגה בחמור קתני מיהת או שהיה אחד מושך ואחד מנהיג מושך ומנהיג אין אבל רכוב לא הוא הדין דאפילו רכוב והא דקתני מושך ומנהיג לאפוקי מדר' יהודה דאמר עד שתהא משיכה בגמל והנהגה בחמור קמשמע לן דאפילו איפכא נמי קני אי הכי ליערבינהו וליתנינהו שנים שהיו מושכין ומנהיגין בין בגמל בין בחמור איכא חד צד דלא קני איכא דאמרי משיכה בחמור ואיכא דאמרי [א]הנהגה בגמל ואית דמותיב מסיפא במדה זו קנה במדה זו למעוטי מאי לאו למעוטי רכוב לא למעוטי איפכא אי הכי היינו ר' יהודה איכא בינייהו צד אחד דלא קנה אית דאמרי משיכה בחמור ואיכא דאמרי הנהגה בגמל ת"ש [ב]אחד רכוב חמור ואחד תפוס במוסירה זה קנה חמור וזה קנה מוסירה שמע מינה רכוב קני הכא נמי במנהיג ברגליו אי הכי נקני נמי רכוב במוסירה אימא זה קנה חמור וחצי מוסירה וזה קנה חצי מוסירה בשלמא רכוב קני דקמגבה ליה בן דעת אלא תפוס במוסירה במאי קני אימא זה קנה חמור וכוליה מוסירה וזה קני מה שתפוס בידו [א] האי מאי אם תימצי לומר המגביה מציאה לחבירו קנה חבירו הני מילי היכא דקא מגבה ליה אדעתא דחבריה האי אדעתא דידיה קא מגבה ליה איהו לא קני לאחריני מקני אמר רב אשי [ג]זה קנה חמור ובית פגיה וזה קנה מה שתפוס בידו והשאר לא קנה לא זה ולא זה רבי אבהו אמר לעולם כדקתני הואיל ויכול לנתקה ולהביאה אצלו [ד] והא דר' אבהו [ב] ברותא [ג] היא דאי לא תימא הכי [ה]טלית שהיא מונחת חציה על גבי קרקע וחציה על גבי עמוד ובא אחד והגביה חציה מעל גבי קרקע ובא אחר והגביה חציה מעל גבי עמוד הכי נמי דקמא קני ובתרא לא קני הואיל ויכול לנתק ולהביא אצלו אלא הא דר' אבהו ברותא היא ת"ש ר' אליעזר אומר [ו]רכוב בשדה ומנהיג בעיר קנה הכא נמי מנהיג ברגליו אי הכי היינו מנהיג תרי גווני מנהיג אי הכי רכוב בעיר מאי טעמא לא קני אמר רב כהנא לפי שאין דרכן של בני אדם לרכוב בעיר אמר ליה רב אשי לרב כהנא אלא מעתה הגביה ארנקי בשבת שאין דרכן של בני אדם להגביה ארנקי בשבת הכי נמי דלא קני אלא מאי דעבד עבד וקני הכא נמי מאי דעבד עבד וקני אלא [ז]במקח וממכר עסקינן דאמר ליה קני כדרך שבני אדם קונין ואי

## רש"י

במדה זו. לקמיה מפרש למעוטי מאי: אי הכי. דלתנא קמא איפכא קני אמאי קתני משיכה בגמל והנהגה בחמור ליערבינהו וכו' מושכין ומנהיגין: איכא חד צד דלא קני. להכי לא מצי למתני בתרוייהו משיכה והנהגה ותנא הכי מושכין בגמל ומנהיגין בחמור או שהיה אחד מושך ואחד מנהיג באחד מהן אותו שדרכו בשניהם: במדה הזאת. קס"ד במשיכה או בהנהגה בין בגמל בין בחמור: אחד תפוס במוסירה. ואינו מנהיג: ש"מ רכוב קני. שלא במקום מנהיג וכיון דשלא במקום מנהיג קני כוליה במקום מנהיג פלגי: נקני נמי רכוב במוסירה. שבראש החמור שהוא תכשיט החמור וכחמור דמי: בשלמא רכוב. מצית למימר דקנה בהגבהת חבירו שהגביה ראשו השני מן הקרקע דקא מגבה לה בן דעת: אלא תפוס במוסירה במאי קני. פלגא והלא ראשה השני מונח במקומו והגבהת הפקר לא קניא עד דעקר לכוליה: האי מאי. דקא אמרת הגבהת תופס במוסירה לא הויא הגבהה לדידיה והויא הגבהה לאחריני אפילו אם תימצי לומר כו': ובית פגיה. קיבצי"ל בלע"ז מה שבראש החמור וכחמור דמי: מה שתפוס בידו. דמה שבתוך ידו הוי מגביה לגמרי: לא זה ולא זה. והבא לחוטפו יחטוף: כדקתני. זה קנה חמור וזה קנה מוסירה אפי' בית פגיה של חמור: הואיל ויכול. התפוס במוסירה למושכו בכח וינתק מראש החמור ויביאנו אצלו דהואיל וראש החמור גבוה נוח להביאה אצלו בנתיקה אחת: ברותא היא. דאע"ג דיכול לנתק לאו הגבהה היא: חציה על גב העמוד. דכיון דבמקום גבוה הוא האוחזה בראשה השני נוח לו לנתק ולהביאה אצלו דלא מחסר הגבהה: הכי נמי דקמא קני. דמכי אגבהה קניא כולה משום דיכול לנתקה אם כן יש חילוק בשנים שהגביהו מציאה זה מכאן וזה מכאן בין מקום גבוה למקום נמוך דהיכא דשני ראשיה מונחים בקרקע אין הגבהת של ראשון קונה כולה שאין יכול לנתקו ולהביאו אצלו מתוך שהוא ארוך ומונח בקרקע כל מה שהוא נותקו ומושכו אחריו נגרר הוא על גבי קרקע והיכא דלאחד מראשיה גבוה כגון בראש החמור או על גבי עמוד המגביה תחלה ראש שעל גבי קרקע קונה כולה ואנן לא אשכחן תנא דמפליג: רכוב בשדה. בהמה של מציאה קונה אבל לא בעיר וטעמא מפרש לקמיה ומנהיג אף בעיר קנה וכ"ש בשדה ש"מ רכוב לחודיה קני כו': אין דרכן. משום צניעותא: ואי

## תוספות

מושך ומנהיג אין אבל רכוב לא. תימה מנ"ל דלמא כ"ש רכוב דתפיס ביה ואי משום דשייה אטו בכל דוכתי תנא כולהו קניינין וי"ל דממשנה יתיר' קדייק דליערבינהו ולתנינהו שנים שהיו מושכין או מנהיגים בין בגמל בין בחמור ותו לא מדקתני בלישנא יתירא ש"מ דלמעוטי רכוב אתא והיינו דפריך בתר הכי וליערבינהו ולתניינהו וא"ת לעולם מנ"ל למעוטי רכוב דלמא הא דלא ערבינהו כדי לאשמועינן דמשיכה אורחא בגמל והנהגה בחמור ואפ"ה אחד מושך ואחד מנהיג בגמל לא מבטל משיכה דאורחא בגמל את ההנהגה דלאו אורחא וכן בחמור איפכא ולכך תנא בתר הכי אחד מושך ואחד מנהיג ולא למעוטי רכוב וי"ל כיון שישמיענו שמשיכה והנהגה שניהם קנו בגמל ובחמור פשיטא שאין אחד מבטל חבירו משום דהאי אורחיה והאי לאו אורחיה אבל במתני' משמיענו שפיר שאין מבטל רכוב ומנהיג ברגליו את מנהיג לחודיה לפי שיש ברכוב כל מה שיש במנהיג ועוד דתפיס בה: אי הכי ליערבינהו ולתנינהו. לפי מאי דס"ד דרכוב קני ומשיכה והנהגה בין בגמל בין בחמור במדה זו קנה אתא למעוטי שום קנין אחר או רכוב במקום מנהיג: אי הכי היינו ר' יהודה. הוה מצי לאקשויי מגופה דקתני או שהיה אחד מושך ואחד מנהיג ש"מ דבחד לד קני: ונקני נמי רכוב במוסירה. אי גרסינן אי הכי ה"פ אי אמרת בשלמא כשאין מנהיג ברגליו ורכוב קני הבהמה משום דתפיס בה א"ש דלא קני מוסירה דבמטלטלין לא שייך קנין של מוסירה אלא בהגבהה או משיכה אבל אי מיירי במנהיג ברגליו לקני נמי מוסירה במשיכת הבהמה אי אמרינן משוך בהמה זו וקני כלים שעליה קני דלקמן מיבעיא לן אי קני אי לא קני ליפשוט מהכא דלא מהני:

והשאר לא קנה לא זה ולא זה. ואפילו אי אמרינן משוך בהמה וקני כלים שעליה קני הכא כיון דתפיס במוסירה לא קני רכוב נמי לא קני כדאמרינן אדעתא דידיה אגבהה איהו לא קני כו':

דאי לא תימא הכי טלית שחציה כו'. קצת קשה מנ"ל שלא יחלוק רבי אבהו אף בזה:

הואיל ויכול לנתקו ולהביאו אצלו. תימה דמשמע דאם נתקה שהוא קונה כו' משום שעל ידו הוגבהה למעלה משלש ומאי שנא מעני המנקף בראש הזית (גיטין דף נט:) שאין בו גזל אלא מפני דרכי שלום וכן פרק הגוזל קמא (ב"ק דף לח. ושם ד"ה והני מילי) הזורק סלע של חבירו לים פטור ומוקי לה בדאדיי' אדויי אלמא לא חשיב מה שהוגבהה על ידו הואיל וסופו ליפול וי"ל דשאני הכא שתופס בידו אחד מן הראש א"נ הכא איירי כשניתק מן העמוד אינו ארוך כ"כ שיגיע ראש השני לארץ ושאני שילוח הקן (חולין דף קמא:) דקאמר זיל טרוף אקן דלגבהינהו ולקנינהו התם נמי הוגבהו על ידו יותר ממה שהיה תחילה שהרי קצת מפריחים למעלה לכך [ד] קני: אי הכי רכוב בעיר מאי טעמא לא קני. אי גרסינן א"ה ה"פ אי אמרת בשלמא לא מיירי במנהיג ברגליו לכך בעיר לא קני דלא אזלא מחמתיה לפי שיש בני אדם שמדברים יחד ויש כמה דברים באמצע הדרכים אלא אי אמרינן במנהיג ברגליו א"כ אזלא מחמתיה טובא ואמאי לא קני:

משוך

## עין משפט נר מצוה

סב א מיי' פי"ז מהל' אבידה הל' ה ועי' בהשגות ובמ"מ סמג עשין עד טוש"ע ח"מ סי' רעא סעיף א:

סג ב ג מיי' שם הל' ז טוש"ע שם סעיף ג:

סד ד ה טוש"ע ח"מ סי' רסט סעיף ה וע"ש:

סה ו ז מיי' פ"ב מהל' מכירה הל' י ועיין במ"מ סמג עשין פב טוש"ע ח"מ סי' קנו סעיף ה:

## רבינו חננאל

פי' איכא חד צד דלא קני יש מי שאומר משיכה בחמור לא קני אבל בגמל בין במשיכה בין בהנהגה קני. ויש מי שאומר הנהגה בגמל לא קנה אבל חמור בין במשיכה בין בהנהגה קני. פי' פגיה רצועות של מוסירה הנתונות על לחייה ועל פדחתה. סוגיא דשמעתא טלית מונחת על גבי קרקע וחציה על גבי עמוד בא אחד והגביה חציה מעל גבי קרקע ובא אחר והגביה חציה שעל גבי עמוד א). רכוב אי קני אי לא קני ת"ש ר"א אומר רכוב בשדה קנה וכו' ודחי' התם במנהיג ברגליו אי הכי היינו מנהיג. ופרקי' תרי גווני מנהיג. ואסקי' במקח וממכר אי אמר ליה קני כדרך שבני אדם קונין אי ברשות הרבים רכוב קנה.

## חשק שלמה על ר"ח

א) חסר פה בהעתקה ונראה דצ"ל קנו תרוייהו.

## מסורת הש"ס

[ל]עיל ח.], ב) ס"א [ב]רותא [ועיין פסחים יא. ...]ין מהרי"ב], ג) [פי' ...]קום שטעו חכמים ולא [...]ו כהלכה לא רצה [...]תם ולומר טעו אלא [...]ו ברותא היא כלומר [...] חילונית היא, ערוך [...] בר ד'], ד) [ועיין עוד [...]' כתובות ל: ד"ה ואי דלא מלי].

## ליקוטי רש"י

[...] תימצי לומר. [...]מר אפי' אם תמצא [...]ר המגביה מציאה [...]ירו כו' [לעיל ח.]. [...]ת פגיה. קיבצי"ל [...] ראשה ולחייה [שבת ...]. לשון חבישה. [...]ודידור"א בית ראש של [...]ר קורין כן [סוטה מה.].

## לעזי רש"י

[קי]בצי"ל. פירוש בית [ראש ...]ה ולחייה (רש"י שבת [...]א ע"ב ד"ה בפני [...]ולא), בית ראש של [...]ר (רש"י סוטה דף [...] ע"א ד"ה אבי פאגי), [...]עות של מוסרה [...]ונות על לחיה ועל [...]תה (רבינו חננאל [...]ערוך ערך פג ה').

ְ בְּמִדָּה זֹאת — if the *kinyan* is performed IN THIS MANNER,[1] EY ACQUIRE the animal. ר׳ יְהוּדָה אוֹמֵר — R' YEHUDAH SAYS: לְעוֹלָם לֹא קָנָה עַד שֶׁתְּהֵא מְשִׁיכָה בְּגָמָ — ONE CAN ACQUIRE A CAMEL NLY THROUGH PULLING וְהַנְהָגָה בַּחֲמוֹר — AND A DONKEY ONLY IROUGH LEADING.[2]

The Gemara now presents its proof:

קָתָנֵי מִיהָ — **At any rate, [the Tanna Kamma] teaches,** אוֹ שֶׁהָיָה אֶחָד מוֹשֵׁךְ וְאֶחָד מַנְהִ — OR if ONE WAS PULLING AND THE HER LEADING an animal, they acquire it. מוֹשֵׁךְ וּמַנְהִיג אִין — ne Baraisa which lists the effective types of *meshichah* but omits ding, thus teaches that if **one** was **pulling or leading,** then, es," he does acquire. This implies אֲבָל רָכוּב לֹא — **but if one** ere **riding,** then, **"no,"** he would not acquire. This corroborates av Yehudah's[3] position that even riding alone does not consti- te a valid *kinyan*.[4]

The Gemara rebuts the proof:

הוּא הַדִּין דַּאֲפִילּוּ רָכוּ — It is possible that **the same law** applies en to a rider, i.e. he acquires. וְהָא דְּקָתָנֵי מוֹשֵׁךְ וּמַנְהִיג — owever, the reason [the Tanna Kamma] teaches only that ne who pulls or one who leads acquires לְאַפּוּקֵי מִדְּרַבִּי יְהוּדָה is **to counter the position of R' Yehudah,** דְּאָמַר עַד שֶׁתְּהֵא מְשִׁיכָה בְּגָמָל וְהַנְהָגָה בַּחֲמוֹר — **who maintains** that ONE CAN QUIRE A CAMEL ONLY THROUGH PULLING AND A DONKEY ONLY IROUGH LEADING. קָמַשְׁמַע לָן דַּאֲפִילּוּ אִיפְּכָא נַמִּי קָנֵי — [The nna Kamma] therefore **teaches us that even** if one performs a nyan in **the opposite** manner from that mentioned, i.e. if he ads a camel or pulls a donkey, **he acquires as well.** Accordingly, camel or donkey can be acquired in one of two ways: by pulling or by leading it.

The Gemara questions this interpretation of the Tanna amma:

אִי הָכִי לִיעָרְבִינְהוּ וְלִתְנִינְ — **If** it is **so** that according to the Tanna amma, a *kinyan* performed in the opposite manner is valid,[5] **let he Tanna Kamma] simply merge [the two manners of inyan] and teach them** as one: שְׁנַיִם שֶׁהָיוּ מוֹשְׁכִין וּמַנְהִיגִין בֵּין בְּגָמָל בֵּין בַּחֲמוֹר — If TWO persons WERE PULLING OR LEADING an animal, BE IT A CAMEL OR A DONKEY, they acquire it. — ? —

The Gemara explains why such a formulation would be misleading:

אִיכָּא חַד צַד דְּלָא קָנֵי — According to the Tanna Kamma, **there is one combination that does not acquire** the animal.[6] The suggested formulation of the Baraisa would not reflect this and thus cannot be used.

The Gemara cites two views concerning which combination does not acquire:

אִיכָּא דְּאָמְרֵי מְשִׁיכָה בַּחֲמוֹר — **Some say** that it is **pulling a donkey.** וְאִיכָּא דְּאָמְרֵי הַנְהָגָה בְּגָמָל — **And some say** that it is **leading a camel.**

In the previous exchange, the Gemara presented its proof from the beginning of the Baraisa. The Gemara now cites a different version of the proof:

וְאִית דְּמוֹתִיב מְסֵיפָא — **And some responded** that the question[7] is resolved **from the final clause** of the Tanna Kamma's statement.

בְּמִדָּה זוֹ קָנָה — The Baraisa states: If the *kinyan* is performed IN THIS MANNER,THEY ACQUIRE the animal. בְּמִדָּה זוֹ לְמַעוּטֵי מַאי — Now **what** type of *kinyan* **does** the expression IN THIS MANNER come **to exclude?**[8] לָאו לְמַעוּטֵי רָכוּב — Does it **not** come **to exclude** the *kinyan* of **a rider,** i.e. to teach that he does not acquire? This corroborates Rav Yehudah's position that even riding alone does not constitute a valid *kinyan*.

The Gemara rebuts the proof:

לֹא לְמַעוּטֵי אִיפְּכָא — **No!** He used the expression **to exclude** a *kinyan* performed in the **opposite** manner from that mentioned in the Baraisa's initial clause; such a *kinyan* is invalid. Riding alone, though, may indeed constitute a valid *kinyan*.

The Gemara questions the rebuttal:

אִי הָכִי הַיְינוּ ר׳ יְהוּדָה — **If** it is **so** that the *kinyan* must be performed in the prescribed manner, **[the Tanna Kamma's view] is** then identical with that of **R' Yehudah!**[9] — ? —

NOTES

The Gemara below will explain what this phrase excludes [i.e. which anner of *kinyan* act the Baraisa invalidates] (*Rashi*).

R' Yehudah holds that *meshichah* is effective only if it is performed in e manner customary for the animal being acquired. Hence, various rms of *meshichah* are effective only for certain species of animals.

This refers to *Rav* Yehudah mentioned on 8b, not to be confused with Yehudah cited in the Baraisa above.

This reflects both the view of *Tosafos* (see *Tosafos* ד״ה אי הכי ליערבינהו re, ד״ה או דילמא on 8b and *Maharam Shif*) and the simple meaning of e Gemara's wording. Some, however, maintain that the Gemara oves only that a rider does not acquire "in the presence of a leader" e *Maharsha, Maharam Shif*).

*Rashi*. When a question begins אִי הָכִי, *if so*, it usually points out a fficulty arising out of a new position taken by the Gemara, which ould otherwise not be problematic. In our case, for example, the emara just explained the Tanna Kamma's omission of riding with the emise that one may acquire either a camel or donkey through one of o methods: pulling or leading. The Gemara's question, which begins אִי הָ, *if so*, should thus be viewed as an attempt to disprove the premise. is, however, seems impossible. The Tanna Kamma rules explicitly in e Baraisa's second clause that one animal can be acquired through her method. If, however, the question does not attempt to refute the emara's previous premise, but is merely a difficulty which must be dressed by every one, why does it begin with אִי הָכִי, *if so? Pnei hoshua* makes an admittedly forced attempt to resolve this problem. owever *Tosafos* below, 93a ד״ה אי הכי, asserts that many times, the emara poses a question beginning with אִי הָכִי, *if so*, even when it is not ecifically directed at the Gemara's last statement. Our Gemara may be e example of such usage. See also *R' Yosef Caro, Klallei HaGemara, Halichos Olam, Shaar* 2, beginning of chapter 2.

If the Baraisa had merged the two *kinyanim* in one clause as proposed, this would imply that all four combinations of *kinyan* and animal are effective: One can acquire a camel through either pulling or leading it and one can acquire a donkey through either pulling or leading it. This, the Gemara notes, does not reflect the Tanna Kamma's actual opinion. According to the Tanna Kamma, one of these combinations is ineffective, i.e. one of the animals mentioned can be acquired through only one of the *kinyanim*. It was therefore necessary for the Baraisa to teach the two *kinyanim* separately. The Gemara will soon discuss which combination is ineffective.

The Baraisa's second clause, however, does indicate that both *kinyanim* are effective for *one* animal, stating that "even if one was pulling and another leading [the same animal], in this manner they acquire it." Obviously, this clause refers to the animal that can be acquired through either *kinyan* (*Rashi*).

7. [I.e. of whether riding alone constitutes a valid *kinyan*; see above, 8b.]

Literally, the term מוֹתִיב means *he returned*. In the context of a discussion, it is generally used to mean *he countered* or *he challenged* (literally: he returned an argument). In our case, though, where the Gemara attempts to resolve its question (of whether riding constitutes a *kinyan*), it means: he responded to the question by citing the Tanna Kamma's final clause (*Talmid* of *R' Peretz* cited in *Shitah Mekubetzes;* see *R' Yosef Caro, Klallei HaGemara,* in *Halichos Olam, Shaar* 2, beginning of chapter 1, for more examples of this usage).

8. I.e. to teach that a certain *kinyan* is ineffective for acquiring animals.

9. Actually, the Gemara could have raised a more basic objection. The Tanna Kamma himself ruled (in the second clause) that if one was pulling and another leading [the same animal], both acquire it. Since the two performed different *kinyanim* upon the same animal, one of them perforce performed his *kinyan* in the "opposite" manner. Hence, the Tanna Kamma himself has stated that a *kinyan* "performed in the opposite manner" is valid (*Tosafos*).

Having shown that taking hold of a found animal's bridle does not constitute a *kinyan,* the Gemara digresses to explain Rav Huna's distinction between acquiring a found animal and one belonging to someone else. The Gemara begins by analyzing the word *mosseirah,* the Hebrew term for bridle:

**מַאי לְשׁוֹן מוֹסֵירָה – What is the etymology of** the word ***mosseirah*** (the Hebrew equivalent of bridle)? **אָמַר רָבָא – Rava answered: אִידִי אַסְבְּרָא לִי – Iddi explained this to me: כְּאָדָם הַמּוֹסֵר דָּבָר לַחֲבֵירוֹ** – To transfer an animal to a purchaser, the seller hands him the bridle **just as** when **a person transfers [*mosseir*] an object to his fellow,** he hands him the object itself.[21]

The Gemara shows how this explains Rav Huna's distinction: **בִּשְׁלָמָא מֵחֲבֵירוֹ קָנֵי – Now it is understandable** that **from one's fellow one acquires** an animal when he takes hold of its bridle, **דְּקָא מָסַר לֵיהּ חַבְרֵיהּ – for his fellow transfers** (*mosser*) the animal **to him** when he hands him the bridle. **אֶלָּא בִּמְצִיאָה וּבְנִכְסֵי הַגֵּר – But regarding a found [animal] or the possessions of a** dead **proselyte, מַאן קָא מָסַר לֵיהּ דְּלִיקְנֵי – who transfers** the animal **to him** so **that he can acquire** it?[22] Obviously nobody. Consequently, if a person takes hold of a found animal's bridle, he does not acquire it.

The Gemara challenges Rav Yehudah's conclusion that even a lone rider does not acquire:

**מֵיתִיבֵי – They challenged** Rav Yehudah's conclusion from our Mishnah:[23] **הָיוּ שְׁנַיִם רוֹכְבִין עַל גַּבֵּי בְהֵמָה וכו׳ – If TWO** litigants come before the court **RIDING ON AN ANIMAL ETC.**, each claiming that it is his, they must divide the animal. The Mishnah's ruling clearly indicates that riding an animal is an effective *kinyan*.

Before posing its challenge, the Gemara determines the authorship of the Mishnah:

**מַנִּי – Whose view** does the Mishnah reflect? **אִילֵימָא רַבִּי מֵאִיר – If you say** it is that of **R' Meir,**[24] this presents a difficulty. **הַשְׁתָּא יוֹשֵׁב קָנֵי – Now** if even **one that sits** in a wagon **acquires,** as R' Meir maintains, **רָכוּב מִיבַּעְיָא – is there** then **any question** that **a rider** acquires as well? He obviously does![25] If the Mishnah reflects R' Meir's view, then, this clause is redundant; R' Meir already taught that a rider acquires.[26] – ? –

The Gemara poses its challenge:

**אֶלָּא לָאו רַבָּנָן – Rather, does** the Mishnah **not reflect** the view **the Rabbis** that one cannot acquire through merely sitting on a wagon? **וּשְׁמַע מִינָּהּ רָכוּב קָנֵי – So learn from [this Mishnah]** that **a rider acquires** even though someone sitting in a wagon does not. This refutes Rav Yehudah's conclusion.[27] – ? –

The Gemara deflects the challenge:

**הָכָא בְּמַאי עַסְקִינַן – Here** in our Mishnah, **with what are we dealing? בְּמַנְהִיג בְּרַגְלָיו – With** a rider **that drives** the animal **with his feet.**[28] Thus, the Mishnah indeed concedes that riding (i.e. sitting upon) an animal is comparable to sitting in a wagon. Neither constitutes a valid *kinyan.* In our Mishnah's case, the rider acquires the animal only because he drove it.

The Gemara challenges this interpretation:

**אִי הָכִי – If** it is **so** that in our Mishnah's case, the rider drove the animal, **הַיְינוּ מַנְהִיג – this** constitutes **leading!** Why, then, does the Mishnah state, "One was riding and one was leading"? Let it simply state that both litigants were leading. – ? –

The Gemara answers:

**תְּרֵי גַּוְונֵי מַנְהִיג – There are two types of leading:** leading the animal by its bridle, and driving it with one's feet. The Mishnah thus means that one litigant "led" by means of driving the animal with his legs and the other led by different means.[29]

The Gemara explains why it was necessary to mention both types of leading:

**מַהוּ דְּתֵימָא רָכוּב עָדִיף – You could have said that a rider** that also leads is **superior** to **someone that just leads, דְּהָא מַנְהִיג וְתָפִיס בָּהּ – since [the former] "leads"** the animal **and** also **holds it.**[30] **קָא מַשְׁמַע לָן – [The Mishnah]** therefore **teaches us** that this is not so.[31]

In summary, the Gemara upholds Rav Yehudah's assertion that riding does not constitute a valid *kinyan.*

The Gemara cites a Baraisa to support Rav Yehudah's position: **תָּא שְׁמַע – Come** and **hear** a Baraisa: **שְׁנַיִם שֶׁהָיוּ מוֹשְׁכִין בְּגָמָל** – If **TWO** persons **WERE PULLING A CAMEL, וּמַנְהִיגִין בַּחֲמוֹר – OR THEY WERE LEADING A DONKEY,**[32] **אוֹ שֶׁהָיָה אֶחָד מוֹשֵׁךְ – OR ONE WAS PULLING** the animal **וְאֶחָד מַנְהִיג – AND THE OTHER LEADING** it,

NOTES

inherits his estate (see *Bava Kamma* 109a, Mishnah *Bava Basra* 115a, Gemara there 115b).

21. Thus, the bridle is called *mosseirah* because it is through it that a seller transfers [*mosseir*] his animal to the buyer (*Rashi*).

22. Not all *kinyanim* are governed by the same principle. For example, the underlying concept of *mesirah* (transfer), as the name implies, is that the seller transfers the animal to the buyer's possession. Hence, one cannot acquire a found animal through such a *kinyan,* for there is nobody to transfer it. The underlying concept of *meshichah,* however, is that the acquiring party brings the object into his possession. Thus, one can acquire even an ownerless object through *meshichah.*

23. Rav Yehudah had concluded, because of his analogy between a rider and a person sitting in a wagon, that just as the latter's action is legally insignificant, so, also, is a rider's. Consequently, Rav Yehudah concluded that a rider does not acquire.

24. I.e. Shmuel's version of R' Meir. According to Shmuel's version, R' Meir holds that one sitting in a wagon attached to *kilayim* receives lashes. It follows from this, Rav Yehudah maintained, that if one sits in a wagon, he acquires the animal attached to it.

25. For according to Rav Yehudah, there is no legal difference between sitting in a wagon and riding an animal (see note 15).

26. Moreover, the Mishnah's initial clause already taught that disputed objects are divided between the litigants. What, then, would this clause teach?

27. *Rashi*. The Mishnah does not necessarily contradict Shmuel himself; he may hold only that a rider cannot acquire in the presence of a leader but admit that both a rider and a leader can acquire independently. Rav Yehudah, however, asserted that Shmuel equates sitting in a wagon with riding an animal (see note 15). Our Mishnah apparently contradicts this view (*Shitah Mekubetzes,* citing his teacher; see also above, note 7).

28. I.e. he spurs the animal until it moves, as horse riders do. Having caused the animal to move, he acquires it through *meshichah* (*Rashi*; see note 2).

29. Had the Mishnah stated that both litigants led the animal, we would have assumed that it refers to a case in which both litigants led it by the bridle (*Rashi*).

30. According to this argument, if two litigants appeared in court, one riding and spurring the animal and the other merely leading, we would consider the rider more in possession of the animal than the leader. We would therefore award him the entire animal (see *Tosafos*).

31. For the term "riding" that appears in the Mishnah refers to "leading (i.e. driving) the animal while riding." Thus, when the Mishnah rules that a rider and leader divide the animal, this teaches that "riding" is in fact no different than mere leading.

32. Usually, a donkey is "led" and a camel is "pulled" (*Rashi*). "Pulling" the animal means to forcibly move it, either by pulling its bridle or any other manner. "Leading" refers either to calling the animal or prodding it with a stick. (It probably also includes walking in front of it while holding its reins loosely.)

## גמרא

שמעית מיניה דמר שמואל תרתי ° רכוב ומנהיג חד קני וחד לא קני ולא ידענא הי מינייהו היכי דמי אילימא רכוב לחודיה ומנהיג לחודיה מנהיג לחודיה מי איכא מאן דאמר לא קני אלא אי איכא למימר דלא קני רכוב הוא דאיכא למימר אלא רכוב במקום מנהיג איבעיא ליה מאי רכוב עדיף דהא תפיס בה או דלמא מנהיג עדיף דאזלא מחמתיה אמר רב יוסף אמר לי רב יהודה נחזי אנן [א] דתנן [א] המנהיג סופג את הארבעים והיושב בקרון סופג את הארבעים ר"מ פוטר [ב] את היושב בקרון ומדאפיך שמואל ותני וחכמים פוטרין את היושב בקרון שמע מינה רכוב לחודיה לא קני וכל שכן רכוב במקום מנהיג אמר ליה אביי לרב יוסף הא זמנין סגיאין אמרת לן נחזי אנן ולא אמרת לן משמיה דרב יהודה א"ל אברא ודכרנן נמי דאמרי ליה היכי פשיט מר רכוב מיושב יושב לא תפיס במוסירה רכוב תפיס במוסירה ואמר לי רב ושמואל דאמרי תרוייהו [ב] מוסירה לא קני איכא דאמרי א"ל אביי לרב יוסף היכי פשיט מר רכוב מיושב יושב לא תפיס במוסירה רכוב תפיס במוסירה א"ל הכי תנא אידי מוסירה לא קני אתמר נמי אמר רבי חלבו אמר רב הונא [ג] מוסירה מחבירו קנה [ג] במציאה ובנכסי הגר לא קני מאי לשון מוסירה אמר רבא אידי אסברא לי כאדם המוסר דבר לחבירו בשלמא מחבירו קני דקא מסר ליה חבריה אלא במציאה ובנכסי הגר מאן קא מסר ליה דליקני מיתיבי [ד] היו שנים רוכבין על גבי בהמה וכו' מני אילימא רבי מאיר השתא יושב קני רכוב מיבעי אלא לאו רבנן ושמע מינה [ד] רכוב קני הכא במאי עסקינן במנהיג ברגליו אי הכי היינו מנהיג תרי גווני מנהיג מהו דתימא רכוב עדיף דהא מנהיג ותפיס בה קמ"ל ת"ש [ה] שנים שהיו מושכין בגמל ומנהיגין בחמור או שהיה אחד מושך ואחד מנהיג

במדה

## תוספות

**מנהיג** לחודיה מי איכא מאן דאמר לא קנה. אע"ג דלר"ש אית ליה בפ"ק דקדושין (דף כה: ושם) דבהמה [בין דקה בין גסה] אינה נקנית אלא בהגבהה ° מ"מ פריך מכח סתם מתניתין דהא תנן אחד רכוב ואחד מנהיג כו' והא דתנן בפ"ק דקדושין (שם) [ה] בהמה גסה נקנית במסירה דברי ר"מ ור"א אף במסירה קאמר וכ"ש במשיכה וכן התם בגמ' דהיכא דמזכיר מסירה הוי פי' אף במסירה ובמקום שמזכיר משיכה דוקא ולא מסירה ובלאו הכי צריך לומר כן התם:

**רכוב** הוא דלא קני. ומתני' דאחד רכוב דחי לקמן במנהיג ברגליו:

**רכוב** עדיף דתפיס בה. ° אין לפרש דתפיס ברגליו או במה שיושב עליה דהאי לא מיקרי תפיס בה אלא במה שהוא תפוס במוסירה קרי תפיס בה דהא בסמוך נקט האי לישנא וצריך לומר דתפיס בה ואזלא נמי מעט מחמתיה או דלמא מנהיג עדיף דאזלא מחמתיה טובא דאי לא מיבעיא ליה ברכוב אלא משום דתפיס בה גרידא א"כ מה פושט בסמוך מיושב דפטור והכי נמי דרכוב לא קני והלא לענין כלאים אינו תלוי כלל בתפיסה אלא באזלא מחמתיה ולענין קנין אינו תלוי כי אם בתפיס בה ולא באזלא מחמתיה:

**או** דלמא מנהיג עדיף כו'. תימה לפשוט ממתני' דמנהיג קונה במקום רכוב ואי רכוב איירי במנהיג ברגליו כ"ש דמנהיג עדיף דאפילו במקום רכוב ומנהיג ברגליו קני כ"ש במקום רכוב לחודיה וי"ל דמן המשנה אין להוכיח דקני מנהיג במקום רכוב דאפילו לא קני מיקרי מוחזק דכיון דמנהיג לחודיה שלא במקום רכוב קני מקרי מוחזק אפי' במקום רכוב ומ"מ לקמן מוכיח שפיר ממתניתין דרכוב לחודיה קני מאחר שקרוי מוחזק דאי אפילו לחודיה לא קני סברא הוא דאפי' מוחזק נמי לא הוי וכן לעיל דקאמר אילימא מהא שנים אוחזין האי אמר כולה אגבהתי' אבל שנים שהגביהו לא קנו התם נמי אע"ג דכמו שהם שניהם תפוסים לא קנו מקרי מוחזק כיון דאם היה מגביה לחודיה אילו לא היה חבירו תפוס בצד השני היה קונה לכך איקרי מוחזק אפילו עם חבירו ° ומסיפא אין להוכיח דרכוב ומנהיג קנו שניהם זה במקום זה דקתני אם היו שניהם מודים יחלוקו דאין שניהם מודים שכך קנו אותה ביחד זה ברכיבה וזה בהנהגה אלא שניהם בהנהגה או בקנין אחר:

**רכוב** לחודיה לא קני. נראה דרב יהודה היה מסופק אם שמע משמואל ברכוב לחודיה ומנהיג לחודיה ואז פשיט ליה דרכוב הוא דלא קני או אם שמיע ליה ברכוב במקום מנהיג ואז מספקא ליה הי נינייהו קני דאי לא מתפקא ליה אלא שמע משמואל ברכוב במקום מנהיג ותו לא א"כ ס"ל לשמואל דרכוב לחודיה קני והשתא פשיט רב יהודה דאפילו לחודיה לא קני:

**מהו** דתימא רכוב עדיף. פי' חזקתו עדיף ויבטל את חזקת המנהיג קמ"ל דשניהם מוחזקים ויחלוקו אבל אין לפרש מהו דתימא דרכוב עדיף ויבטל את קנין המנהיג קמ"ל דשניהם קנו כדפרישית לעיל דאפילו לא הוי קני במקום רכוב מקרי מוחזק כיון דמנהיג לחודיה קני וא"ת לעיל כי פריך השתא יושב קני רכוב מיבעיא ליבני דקא משמע לן דלא מבטל חזקת רכוב דתפיס בה ואזלא מחמתיה את חזקת המנהיג וי"ל דאין צריך להשמיענו דפשיטא דרכוב לחודיה בלא מנהיג ברגליו לא חשיב לבטל את חזקת המנהיג דאי משום דתפיס בה מנהיג נמי אזלא מחמתיה טפי מרכוב אבל השתא דמיירי במנהיג ברגליו דכיון דכל מה שיש במנהיג יש ברכוב ועוד דתפיס בה יבטל את חזקת המנהיג קא משמע לן ולפי מאי דאוקימנא השתא במנהיג ברגליו אתיא כרבנן וכל שכן כרבי מאיר:

## רש"י

שמעית מיניה דמר שמואל תרתי. שמעתי ממנו שני דברים דין רכוב ודין מנהיג בחד אמר לי קני ובחד אמר לי לא קני ולא ידענא כו': אי נימא רכוב לחודיה. שאין אחר מנהיג עמו ובא אחד מן השוק וחוטפו ממנו בפניו ומושכה לקנותה וכן מנהיג ואין רכוב עמו ובא אחד וחוטפו ממנו בפניו לקנותה וקאמר שמואל בחד מינייהו דלא קני ומאן דחטף שפיר חטף ומבעיא ליה לרב יהודה בהי מינייהו: מנהיג לחודיה מי איכא למאן דאמר דלא קני. הא משיכה היא זו ובהמה נקנית במשיכה ומאי תיבעי ליה לרב יהודה אי ודאי אמר שמואל בחד מינייהו דלא קני ברכוב הוא דקאמר דקסבר משיכה בעינן שתעקור יד ורגל כדאמרינן בקדושין (דף כב:): אלא רכוב במקום מנהיג. שניהם באים לפנינו זה רכוב וזה מנהיג זה אומר כולה שלי וזה אומר כולה שלי אמר שמואל חד קני ומבעיא ליה לרב יהודה היכא דאיתנהו לתרוייהו הי עדיף רכוב עדיף דהא תפיס בה וכי אמרינן משיכה קני היכא דליכא רכוב אבל במקום רכוב לא: או דלמא מנהיג עדיף דקאזלא מחמתיה. והיא הגדולה בקנין: למאן אי לר"מ כו' עד לרבנן. לא גרס: נחזי אנן. אית לן למפשט משמעתא דמר שמואל בהי מינייהו אמר: המנהיג. בשור וחמור: פוטר. קסבר לאו מידי עביד: ומדאפיך שמואל כו'. ש"מ סבירא לשמואל רכוב לאו מידי מעשה עביד ומשום דיחיד ורבים הלכה כרבים אפכה למתני' לאוקמה פטורא כרבנן: הכי גרסינן שמע מינה ס"ל לשמואל רכוב לחודיה לא קני ולא גרס לרבנן: והא זמנין סגיאין אמרת. להא שמעתין נחזי אנן: ולא אמרת לן. אלא משמך למפשט ספיקו דרב יהודה: אברא. אמת הוא אמר לי נחזי אנן וזכור אני שאמרתי לו היכי תפשוט מר רכוב מיושב בקרון: מוסירה. קבישטר"א: מוסירה אינה קונה. במציאה עד שיוליכנה ותעקור יד ורגל ואע"ג דבמכירה קני כדתנן (קדושין דף כה:) בהמה גסה נקנית במסירה לגבי מציאה לא קני כדאמרינן טעמא לקמן בשמעתין: איכא דאמרי. רב יוסף משמיה דנפשיה קאמר נחזי אנן וא"ל אביי היכי תפשוט רכוב כו': אידי. שם חכם: מחבירו. מקח וממכר: בנכסי הגר. שמת ואין לו יורשין וכל הקודם בנכסיו זכה בהן: ומהו לשון מוסירה. שמוסרין אותו בו ללוקח: אי נימא ר"מ. דאמר היושב בקרון סופג את הארבעים ומתני' יחידאה היא ולית הלכתא כוותיה: השתא לר"מ יושב קני. דקאמר היושב בקרון סופג את הארבעים: רכוב מיבעיא. ולמה לי לאשמועינן בתרתי: אלא לאו רבנן. ואשמועינן דיושב הוא דפטור אבל רכוב לא ותיובתא לרב יהודה דפשט רוכב מיושב: במנהיג ברגליו. דקנייה במשיכה שבועט בה ברגליו והולכת מחמתו כדרך רוכבי סוסים: היינו מנהיג. והו"ל למיתני או שהיו שניהם מנהיגים: תרי גווני מנהיג. דאי אשמועינן בשני מנהיגים דיחלוקו לא היינו יודעים להאי מהו דתימא כו': חמור דרכו בהנהגה וגמל דרכו במשיכה:

במדה

מוסך

## עין משפט נר מצוה

נז א מיי' פ"ט מהלכות כלאים הלכה ט סמג לאוין רפב טוש"ע י"ד סי' רצז סעיף יג:
נח ב ש"ע ח"מ סי' קצז סעיף א וע"ש בטור וב"י:
נט ג מיי' פי"ז מהלכות אבידה הל' ו סמג עשין עד טוש"ע ח"מ סי' רעא סעיף ב:
ס ד מיי' פי"ז מהלכות אבידה הלכה ז ופ"ב מהל' מכירה הל' ו ופ"ט מהל' טוען ונטען הל' ז סמג עשין עד וסי' פב וסי' לה טוש"ע ח"מ סי' קלח סעיף א וסי' קצז סעיף ה וסי' רעא סעיף ג:
סא ה מיי' פי"ז מהל' אבידה הל' ה ועי' בהשגות ובמ"מ ובכ"מ סמג עשין עד טוש"ע ח"מ סי' רעא סעיף א:

## רבינו חננאל

הא דאמרן רוכב ומנהיג חד קני וחד לא קני ואמר רב יהודה נחזי אנן מדתנן בפ' כלאי הכרם המנהיג סופג מ' וכו'. פי' המנהיג בשור (או) ובחמור ודש או חרש סופג מ' והיושב בקרון סופג מ' ר"מ פוטר את היושב בקרון. שמואל מפיך ותני היושב בקרון סופג מ' דברי ר' מאיר וחכמים פוטרין את היושב בקרון הנה היושב בקרון כמו רוכב הוא וכיון דפטרי ליה רבנן שמעינן מינה דלא א) הוא מנהיג הבהמה שרוכב עליה ולא מתעבידא מכחו ולא חרישה ולא דישה לפיכך הוא פטור הלכך רוכב לחודיה לא קני וכ"ש רוכב במקום מנהיג ודברים פשוטין הן. פי' מוסירה כגון פרומביא ואפסר כל בהמה בראוי לה. התופס במוסירה לא קני לא במציאה ולא בנכסי הגר דהא לא מסר ליה אחרינא אבל מוסירה מחבירו קני דהא מסר ליה חבריה. מיתיבי היו שנים רוכבין על גבי בהמה וכו'. ופרקי' במנהיג הבהמה שרוכב עליה (בקרקע) [ברגליו].

## חשק שלמה על ר"ח

א) אולי צ"ל דלא הוי כמנהיג הבהמה כשרוכב עליה דלא איתעבידא מכחו ולא הוי כחרישה ודישה לפיכך וכו'.

## מסורת הש"ס

א) כלאים פרק ח' משנה ... ב) [במשנה שם ליתא ... ג' תיבות את היו... בקרון], ג) [עיין ... בבא בתרא עה: ... אחזה], ד) [לעיל ...] ה) עיין מהרש"א.

## גליון הש"ס

גמ' רכוב. עי' תוי"ט ... משנה ג' דנדרים ד... אביה ובעלה: תוס' ד"ה מנהיג וכו' מ"מ פר... מכח סתם מתני'. כ... זה בכתובות דף לה ע... ומי איכא למ"ד מ... מיתות שוגגי' ... ובתוס' שם: שם ד"ה רכוב וכו' אין לפר... עיין תשובת מהר"ס ... בוטון סי' ס"ג: שם ד"ה או וכו' ומסיפא א... להוכיח. קשה לי ... דאמרי' לעיל ע"א ... מסיפא בזמן שהן מו... כו' וש"מ המגביה מצי... לחבירו מנ"ל דהן מו... קאי אהגביהו מצי... ומודים שהגביהו ... ונוכיח מזה דהמגב... מציאה לחבירו קנה חב... דלמא קאי על אחד ר... ואחד מנהיג דמודים ש... יחד בזה ונוכיח מזה דר... במקום מנהיג קנה:

## ליקוטי רש"י

מוסירה. אפסר [ש... נב.]. היו שנ... רוכבין. עיין ... עמוד א.

## לעזי רש"י

קבישטר"א. פי' אפסר (רש"י שבת נב ע"א ד"ה במוסר חבל שקשורה בו הבה... ונמשכת (ערוך ... מסר ג').

רַבִּי מֵאִיר פּוֹטֵר אֶת הַיּוֹשֵׁב בַּקָּרוֹן – R' MEIR EXEMPTS THE ONE SITTING IN A WAGON.[13]

Rav Yehudah now quotes Shmuel's revision of the Mishnah to prove how he ruled on the original question:

וּמִדְּאַפִּיךְ שְׁמוּאֵל – **And from** the fact **that Shmuel switched** the statements of the Tanna Kamma and R' Meir, וְתָנֵי – **and taught the Mishnah** as follows: וַחֲכָמִים פּוֹטְרִין אֶת הַיּוֹשֵׁב בַּקָּרוֹן – BUT THE SAGES EXEMPT THE ONE SITTING IN A WAGON,[14] שְׁמַע מִינָּהּ – you can **learn from this,** that according to Shmuel, רָכוּב לְחוּדֵיהּ לֹא קָנֵי – even **someone riding alone** without a leader **does not acquire,**[15] וְכָל שֶׁכֵּן רָכוּב בִּמְקוֹם מַנְהִיג – **and surely** not **a rider in the presence of a leader.** Accordingly, Rav Yehudah argues that Shmuel must have ruled that even riding alone does not constitute a valid *kinyan* but leading does.[16]

Abaye questions Rav Yosef's presentation of the above proof:

אֲמַר לֵיהּ אַבַּיֵי לְרַב יוֹסֵף – **Abaye said to Rav Yosef:** הָא זִמְנִין סַגִּיאִין אָמְרַתְּ לָן נֶחֱזֵי אֲנַן – **But many times you have taught us** this proof beginning with the words **"We shall see,"** וְלָא אָמְרַתְּ לָן מִשְּׁמֵיהּ דְּרַב יְהוּדָה – **and you did not report it to us in the name of Rav Yehudah!**

Rav Yosef responds:

אָמַר לֵיהּ – **[Rav Yosef] answered [Abaye]:** אִבְרָא – But it is **true** that Rav Yehudah himself adduced this proof. וּדְכִרְנָן נַמִּי דַּאֲמְרִי לֵיהּ – **And** now **I remember also that I responded to [Rav Yehudah]** with the following argument: הֵיכִי פָּשִׁיט מָר רָכוּב מִיּוֹשֵׁב – **How can master derive** the law regarding **a rider from** that regarding **one sitting** in a wagon? These two cases differ! יוֹשֵׁב לֹא תָּפִיס בְּמוֹסֵירָה – **Someone sitting** in a wagon **does not hold the** animal's **bridle;** therefore, it is understandable that he cannot acquire. רָכוּב תָּפִיס בְּמוֹסֵירָה – But the **rider does hold the** animal's **bridle.** Therefore, perhaps a rider does acquire even though a person sitting in a wagon does not.[17] וְאָמַר לִי – **And [Rav Yehudah] answered me:** רַב וּשְׁמוּאֵל דְּאָמְרֵי תַּרְוַיְיהוּ – **Rav and Shmuel both say:** מוֹסֵירָה לֹא קָנֵי – A person taking hold a found animal's **bridle does not acquire** the animal through h action.[18] Holding a found animal's bridle, then, does n strengthen the rider's position; he thus has the same rights as o sitting in a wagon. Accordingly, if sitting in the wagon does n constitute a *kinyan* as the Mishnah in *Kilayim* implies, neith does riding a found animal.

The Gemara presents a different version of the above e change:[19]

אִיכָּא דְּאָמְרֵי – **Some say** that the exchange between Rav Yosef ar Abaye was as follows: אֲמַר לֵיהּ אַבַּיֵי לְרַב יוֹסֵף – **Abaye said Rav Yosef:** הֵיכִי פָּשִׁיט מָר רָכוּב מִיּוֹשֵׁב – **How can Master deriv** the law regarding **a rider from** that regarding **one sitting** in wagon? These two cases differ! יוֹשֵׁב לֹא תָּפִיס בְּמוֹסֵירָה – **Someone sitting** in a wagon **does not take hold of the** animal **bridle;** therefore, it is understandable that he cannot acquire th animal. רָכוּב תָּפִיס בְּמוֹסֵירָה – But the **rider does take hold the** animal's **bridle.** Therefore, perhaps a rider does acquire eve though a person sitting in a wagon does not. אָמַר לֵיהּ – **[Ra Yosef] answered [Abaye]:** הָכִי תָּנָא אִידִי – **This is what Id taught from a Baraisa:** מוֹסֵירָה לֹא קָנֵי – A person taking ho of a found animal's BRIDLE DOES NOT ACQUIRE the animal throug his action. There is thus no legal distinction between riding on a animal and sitting in a wagon; neither constitutes a valid *kinyan*

The Gemara cites another Amoraic statement proving th taking hold of a found animal's bridle does not constitute a *kinyan*

אִתְּמַר נַמִּי – **It has also been said:** אָמַר רַבִּי חֶלְבּוֹ אָמַר רַב הוּנָא – **R' Chelbo said in the name of Rav Huna:** מוֹסֵירָה – Concer ing someone that takes hold of an animal's **bridle,** מֵחֲבֵירוֹ קָנָה – if he does so to acquire the animal **from his fellow, he do acquire it,** בִּמְצִיאָה וּבְנִכְסֵי הַגֵּר לֹא קָנֵי – but if he does so acquire **a found object or the possessions of a** dead **proselyt** who left no heirs,[20] **he does not acquire.**

NOTES

be viewed as having moved because of the person sitting upon the wagon, so that he has performed "work" with *kilayim* (*Rashba*, *Rash* to *Kilayim* 8:3).

13. When a person sits down in the wagon, although the animals move slightly [and thus pull the wagon], this movement is not attributed to the person because he is not in control of it; rather, it is viewed as if the animals moved on their own volition. Consequently, according to this opinion, he has not transgressed the prohibition against working with *kilayim* (*Ramban*).

14. Generally, halachah is in accordance with the majority view. Now according to the original version of the Mishnah, the majority view (i.e. the Tanna Kamma) holds that if one sits in the wagon, he receives lashes, while the ruling that exempts him from lashes is attributed to an individual Tanna, R' Meir. Shmuel, however, switched the attribution of the rulings so that the majority view exempts him from lashes; this, then, implies that according to Shmuel, the halachah accords with this opinion (*Rashi*). [It may have been that Shmuel had conflicting traditions as to the attribution of these rulings. Shmuel would thus have assumed that the majority opinion concurs with the view that he saw as most reasonable.]

15. Our Gemara assumes that if someone sitting in the wagon is exempt from lashes, it follows that riding alone does not constitute a *kinyan.* This reasoning rests upon two assumptions: first, that there is no legal difference between riding an animal and sitting in a wagon attached to one; and second, that the laws of *kilayim* are analogous to those of acquisition. Now, according to Shmuel's version of the Mishnah, the Sages maintain that if a man sits in the wagon, he is exempt from lashes. Sitting in the wagon, then, has no legal significance regarding the laws of *kilayim* (and by analogy, to the laws of acquisition). This proves that even if someone rides alone without a leader, still he does not acquire.

16. This conclusion seems to contradict the Gemara's previous interpretation of Rav Yehudah (i.e. that riding certainly constitutes a valid *kinyan;* it is doubtful only whether a rider acquires an animal if anoth simultaneously leads it – see note 7). In fact, however, there is r contradiction, for the previous Gemara meant only as follows: Ra Yehudah could not have *known* initially that Shmuel's ruling about *rider* concerned someone riding alone; had he known this, he could hav deduced how Shmuel ruled in these two cases (see Gemara above However, Rav Yehudah might have been uncertain as to wheth Shmuel ruled on someone riding alone or on someone riding in th presence of a leader. Now Rav Yehudah proves that he in fact discusse someone riding alone, ruling that such a person does not acquire th animal (*Tosafos*).

17. I.e. you equated the legal significance of riding an animal with th of sitting in a wagon (see previous note). In fact, however, they are ver different: A rider takes hold of the animal's bridle, whereas one sittin in a wagon does not. Now the Mishnah in *Kiddushin* (25b) states th taking hold of an animal's bridle constitutes a valid *kinyan.* It thu follows that riding an animal might constitute a valid *kinyan* eve though sitting in a wagon does not.

18. Indeed a purchaser [or gift recipient] does acquire an animal when h takes hold of its bridle, as the Mishnah states in *Kiddushin* (25b Nevertheless, one cannot acquire a found animal by this means; he mus perform *meshichah,* i.e. move the animal. The Gemara below wi explain the reason for this distinction (*Rashi*).

19. This version attributes the above arguments and the ruling about bridle to different people than the last does. The arguments and th rulings themselves, however, are the same.

20. The laws of inheritance contain a provision applying to proselyte which is inapplicable to Jews by birth. When a gentile converts, h severs all ties with his gentile family (see *Yevamos* 97b). If he die without issue, then, he leaves no heirs. Since his estate is thus ownerles [*hefker*], anyone may acquire it. When a Jew by birth dies, on the othe hand, his nearest living relative (no matter how remote the kinshi

שמעית מיניה דמר שמואל תרתי ° רכוב ומנהיג חד קני וחד לא קני ולא ידענא הי מינייהו היכי דמי אילימא רכוב לחודיה ומנהיג לחודיה מנהיג לחודיה מי איכא מאן דאמר לא קני אלא אי איכא למימר דלא קני רכוב הוא דאיכא למימר אלא רכוב במקום מנהיג איבעיא ליה מאי רכוב עדיף דהא תפיס בה או דלמא מנהיג עדיף דאזלא מחמתיה אמר רב יוסף אמר לי רב יהודה נחזי אנן [א] דתנן [א] המנהיג סופג את הארבעים והיושב בקרון סופג את הארבעים ר"מ פוטר [ב] את היושב בקרון ומדאפיך שמואל ותני וחכמים פוטרין את היושב בקרון שמע מינה רכוב לחודיה לא קני וכל שכן רכוב במקום מנהיג אמר ליה אביי לרב יוסף הא זמנין סגיאין אמרת לן נחזי אנן ולא אמרת לן משמיה דרב יהודה א"ל אברא ודכרנן נמי דאמרי ליה היכי פשיט מר רכוב מיושב יושב לא תפיס במוסירה רכוב תפיס במוסירה ואמר לי רב ושמואל דאמרי תרוייהו [ב] מוסירה לא קני איכא דאמרי א"ל אביי לרב יוסף היכי פשיט מר רכוב מיושב יושב לא תפיס במוסירה רכוב תפים במוסירה א"ל הכי תנא אידי מוסירה לא קני אתמר נמי אמר רבי חלבו אמר רב הונא [ג] מוסירה מחבירו קנה [ג] במציאה ובנכסי הגר לא קני מאי לשון מוסירה אמר רבא אידי אסברא לי כאדם המוסר דבר לחבירו בשלמא מחבירו קני דקא מסר ליה חבריה אלא במציאה ובנכסי הגר מאן קא מסר ליה דליקני מיתיבי [ד] היו שנים רוכבין על גבי בהמה וכו' מני אילימא רבי מאיר השתא יושב קני רכוב מיבעי אלא לאו רבנן ושמע מינה [ד] רכוב קני הכא במאי עסקינן במנהיג ברגליו אי הכי היינו מנהיג תרי גווני מנהיג מהו דתימא רכוב עדיף דהא מנהיג ותפיס בה קמ"ל ת"ש [ה] שנים שהיו מושכין בגמל ומנהיגין בחמור או שהיה אחד מושך ואחד מנהיג

במדה

---

שמעית מיניה דמר שמואל תרתי. שמעתי ממנו שני דברים דין רכוב ודין מנהיג בחד אמר לי קני ובחד אמר לי לא קני ולא ידענא כו': אי נימא רכוב לחודיה. שאין אחר מנהיג עמו ובא אחד מן השוק וחוטפו ממנו בפניו ומושכה לקנותה וכן מנהיג ואין רכוב עמו ובא אחד וחוטפו ממנו בפניו לקנותה וקאמר שמואל בחד מינייהו דלא קני ומאן דחטף שפיר חטף ומבעיא ליה לרב יהודה בהי מינייהו: מנהיג לחודיה מי איכא למאן דאמר דלא קני. הא משיכה היא זו ובהמה נקנית במשיכה ומאי תיבעי ליה לרב יהודה אי ודאי אמר שמואל בחד מינייהו דלא קני ברכוב הוא דקאמר דקסבר משיכה בעינן שתעקור יד ורגל כדאמרינן בקדושין (דף כב:): אלא רכוב במקום מנהיג. שניהם באים לפנינו זה רכוב וזה מנהיג זה אומר כולה שלי וזה אומר כולה שלי אמר שמואל חד קני ומבעיא ליה לרב יהודה היכא דאיתנהו לתרוייהו הי עדיף רכוב עדיף דהא תפיס בה וכי אמרינן משיכה קני היכא דליכא רכוב אבל במקום רכוב לא: או דלמא מנהיג עדיף דקאזלא מחמתיה. והיא הגדולה בקנין: למאן אי לר"מ כו' עד לרבנן. לא גרס: נחזי אנן. אית לן למפשט משמעתא דמר שמואל בהי מינייהו אמר: המנהיג. בשור וחמור: פוטר. קסבר לאו מידי עביד: ומדאפיך שמואל כו'. ש"מ סבירא לשמואל רכוב לאו מידי מעשה עביד ומשום דיחיד ורבים הלכה כרבים אפכה למתני' לאוקמה פטורא כרבנן: הכי גרסינן שמע מינה ס"ל לשמואל רכוב לחודיה לא קני ולא גרס לרבנן: והא זמנין סגיאין אמרת. להא שמעתין נחזי אנן: ולא אמרת לן. אלא משמך למפשט ספיקו דרב יהודה: אברא. אמת הוא אמר לי נחזי אנן וזכור אני שאמרתי לו היכי תפשוט מר רכוב מיושב בקרון: מוסירה. קבישטר"א: מוסירה אינה קונה. במציאה עד שיוליכנה ותעקור יד ורגל ואע"ג דבמכירה קני כדתנן (קדושין דף כה:) בהמה גסה נקנית במסירה לגבי מציאה לא קני כדאמרינן טעמא לקמן בשמעתין: איכא דאמרי. רב יוסף משמיה דנפשיה קאמר נחזי אנן וא"ל אביי היכי תפשוט רכוב כו': אידי. שם חכם: מחבירו. מקח וממכר: בנכסי הגר. שמת ואין לו יורשין וכל הקודם בנכסיו זכה בהן: ומהו לשון מוסירה. שמוסרין אותו בו ללוקח: אי נימא ר"מ. דאמר היושב בקרון סופג את הארבעים ומתני' יחידאה היא ולית הלכתא כוותיה: השתא לר"מ יושב קני. דקאמר היושב בקרון סופג את הארבעים: רכוב מיבעיא. ולמה לי לאשמועינן בתרתי: אלא לאו רבנן. ואשמועינן דיושב הוא דפטור אבל רכוב לא ותיובתא לרב יהודה דפשט רוכב מיושב: במנהיג ברגליו. דקנייה במשיכה שבועט בה ברגליו והולכת מחמתו כדרך רוכבי סוסים: היינו מנהיג. והו"ל למיתני או שהיו שניהם מנהיגים: תרי גווני מנהיג. דאי אשמועינן בשני מנהיגים דיחלוקו לא היינו יודעים להאי מהו דתימא כו': חמור דרכו בהנהגה וגמל דרכו במשיכה:

במדה

---

**מנהיג** לחודיה מי איכא מאן דאמר לא קנה. אע"ג דלר"ש אית ליה בפ"ק דקדושין (דף כה: ושם) דבהמה [בין דקה בין גסה] אינה נקנית אלא בהגבהה ° מ"מ פריך מכח סתם מתניתין דהא תנן אחד רכוב ואחד מנהיג כו' והא דתנן בפ"ק דקדושין (שם) [ה] בהמה גסה נקנית במסירה דברי ר"מ ור"א אף במסירה קאמר וכ"ש במשיכה וכן התם בגמ' דהיכא דמזכיר מסירה הוי פי' אף במסירה ובמקום שמזכיר משיכה דוקא ולא מסירה ובלאו הכי צריך לומר כן התם:

**רכוב** הוא דלא קני. ומתני' דאחד רכוב דחי לקמן במנהיג ברגליו:

**רכוב** עדיף דתפיס בה. ° אין לפרש דתפיס ברגליו או במה שיושב עליה דהאי לא מיקרי תפיס בה אלא במה שהוא תפוס במוסירה קרי תפיס בה דהא בסמוך נקט האי לישנא וצריך לומר דתפיס בה ואזלא נמי מעט מחמתיה או דלמא מנהיג עדיף דאזלא מחמתיה טובא דאי לא מיבעיא ליה ברכוב אלא משום דתפיס בה גרידא א"כ מה פושט בסמוך מיושב דפטור והכי נמי דרכוב לא קני והלא לענין כלאים אינו תלוי כלל בתפיסה אלא באזלא מחמתיה ולענין קנין אינו תלוי כי אם בתפיס בה ולא באזלא מחמתיה:

**או** דלמא מנהיג עדיף כו'. תימה דלפשוט ממתני' דמנהיג קונה במקום רכוב ואי רכוב איירי במנהיג ברגליו כ"ש דמנהיג עדיף דאפילו במקום רכוב ומנהיג ברגליו קני כ"ש במקום רכוב לחודיה וי"ל דמן המשנה אין להוכיח דקני מנהיג במקום רכוב דאפילו לא קני מיקרי מוחזק דכיון דמנהיג לחודיה שלא במקום רכוב קני מקרי מוחזק אפי' במקום רכוב ומ"מ לקמן מוכיח שפיר ממתניתין דרכוב לחודיה קני מאחר שקרוי מוחזק דאי אפילו לחודיה לא קני סברא הוא דאפי' מוחזק נמי לא הוי וכן לעיל דקאמר אילימא מהא שנים אוחזין האי אמר כולה אגבהתי' אבל שנים שהגביהו לא קנו התם נמי אע"ג דכמו שהם שניהם תפוסים לא קנו מקרי מוחזק כיון דאם היה מגביה לחודיה אילו לא היה חבירו תפוס בצד השני היה קונה לכך איקרי מוחזק אפילו עם חבירו ° ומסיפא אין להוכיח דרכוב ומנהיג קנו שניהם זה במקום זה דקתני אם היו שניהם מודים יחלוקו דאין שניהם מודים שכך קנו אותה ביחד זה ברכיבה וזה בהנהגה אלא שניהם בהנהגה או בקנין אחר:

**רכוב** לחודיה לא קני. נראה דרב יהודה היה מסופק אם שמע משמואל ברכוב לחודיה ומנהיג לחודיה ואז פשיט ליה דרכוב הוא דלא קני או אם שמיע ליה ברכוב במקום מנהיג ואז מספקא ליה הי מינייהו קני דאי לא מספקא ליה אלא שמע משמואל ברכוב במקום מנהיג ותו לא א"כ ס"ל לשמואל דרכוב לחודיה קני והשתא פשיט רב יהודה דאפילו לחודיה לא קני:

**מהו** דתימא רכוב עדיף. פי' חזקתו עדיף ויבטל את חזקת המנהיג קמ"ל דשניהם מוחזקים ויחלוקו אבל אין לפרש מהו דתימא דרכוב עדיף ויבטל את קנין המנהיג קמ"ל דשניהם קנו כדפרישית לעיל דאפילו לא הוי קני במקום רכוב מקרי מוחזק כיון דמנהיג לחודיה קני וא"ת לעיל כי פריך השתא יושב קני רכוב מיבעיא ליפני דקא משמע לן דלא מבטל חזקת רכוב דתפיס בה ואזלא מחמתיה את חזקת המנהיג וי"ל דאין צריך להשמיענו דפשיטא דרכוב לחודיה בלא מנהיג ברגליו לא חשיב לבטל את חזקת המנהיג דאי משום דתפיס בה מנהיג נמי אזלא מחמתיה טפי מרכוב אבל השתא דמיירי במנהיג ברגליו דכיון דכל מה שיש במנהיג יש ברכוב ועוד דתפיס בה יבטל את חזקת המנהיג קא משמע לן ולפי מאי דאוקימנא השתא במנהיג ברגליו אתיא כרבנן וכל שכן כרבי מאיר:

מושך

---

עין משפט
נר מצוה

נז א מיי' פ"ט מהלכות כלאים הלכה ט סמג לאוין רפב טוש"ע י"ד סי' רצז סעיף יב:

נח ב ש"ע ח"מ סי' קצז סעיף א וע"ש בטור וב"י:

נט ג מיי' פי"ז מהלכות אבידה הל' ו סמג עשין עד טוש"ע ח"מ סי' רעא סעיף ב:

ס ד מיי' פי"ז מהלכות אבידה הלכה ז ופ"ב מהל' מכירה הל' ו ופ"ט מהל' טוען ונטען הל' ז סמג עשין עד וסי' פב וסי' צה טוש"ע ח"מ סי' קלח סעיף א וסי' קצז סעיף ה וסי' רעא סעיף ג:

סא ה מיי' פי"ז מהל' אבידה הל' ה ועי' בהשגות ובמ"מ ובכ"מ סמג עשין עד טוש"ע ח"מ סי' רעא סעיף א:

רבינו חננאל

הא דאמרן רוכב ומנהיג חד קני וחד לא קני ואמר רב יהודה נחזי אנן מדתנן בפ' כלאי הכרם המנהיג סופג מ' וכו'. פי' המנהיג בשור (או) ובחמור ודש או חרש סופג מ' והיושב בקרון סופג מ' ר"מ פוטר את היושב בקרון. שמואל מפיך ותני היושב בקרון סופג מ' דברי ר' מאיר וחכמים פוטרין את היושב בקרון הנה היושב בקרון כמו רוכב הוא וכיון דפטרי ליה רבנן שמעינן מינה דלא [א] הוא מנהיג הבהמה שרוכב עליה ולא מתעבידא מכחו ולא חרישה ולא דישה לפיכך הוא פטור הלכך רוכב לחודיה לא קני וכ"ש רוכב במקום מנהיג ודברים פשוטין הן. פי' מוסירה כגון פרומביא ואפסר כל בהמה בראוי לה. התופס במוסירה לא קני לא במציאה ולא בנכסי הגר דהא לא מסר ליה אחרינא אבל מוסירה מחבירו קני דהא מסר ליה חבריה. מיתיבי היו שנים רוכבין על גבי בהמה וכו'. ופרקי' במנהיג הבהמה שרוכב עליה (בקרקע) [ברגליו].

חשק שלמה על ר"ח

א) אולי צ"ל דלא הוי כמנהיג הבהמה כשרוכב עליה דלא איתעבידא מכחו ולא הוי כחרישה ודישה לפיכך וכו'.

---

מסורת הש"ס

א) כלאים פרק ח' משנה ג [במשנה שם ליתא לה ג' תיבות את היושב בקרון], ג) [עיין תוס' בבא בתרא עה: ד"ה אחזה], ד) [לעיל ג.], ה) עיין מהרש"א.

גליון הש"ס

גמ' רכוב. עי' תוי"ט פ"ח משנה ג' דנדרים ד"ה אביה ובעלה: תוס' ד"ה מנהיג וכו' מ"מ פריך מכח סתם מתני'. כעין זה בכתובות דף לה ע"א ומי איכא למ"ד חייבי מיתות שוגגי' חייבי' ובתוס' שם: שם ד"ה רכוב וכו' אין לפרש עיין תשובת מהר"ם בוטון סי' ס"ג: שם ד"ה או וכו' ומסיפא אין להוכיח. קשה לי כמו דאמרי' לעיל ע"א אי מסיפא בזמן שהן מודים כו' וש"מ המגביה מציאה לחבירו מנ"ל דהן מודים קאי אהגביהו מציאה ומודים שהגביהו יחד ונוכיח מזה דהמגביה מציאה לחבירו קנה חבירו דלמא קאי על אחד רוכב ואחד מנהיג דמודים שקנו יחד בזה ונוכיח מזה דרכוב במקום מנהיג קנה:

ליקוטי רש"י

מוסירה. אפסר [שבת נב.]. היו שנים רוכבין. עיין לעיל עמוד א.

לעזי רש"י

קבישטר"א. פירוש אפסר (רש"י שבת נב ע"א ד"ה במוסרה. חבל שקשורה בו הבהמה ונמשכת (ערוך ערך מסר ג').

שְׁמָעִית מִינֵּיהּ דְּמָר שְׁמוּאֵל תַּרְתֵּי – **I have heard from Master Shmuel**[1] **two** diverse rulings: רָכוּב וּמַנְהִיג – One with regard to **a rider**[2] **and** one with regard to **a leader,** i.e. a person leading an animal:[3] חַד קָנֵי – **One** of the two **does acquire** וְחַד לֹא קָנֵי – **and** the other **one does not acquire,** וְלֹא יָדַעְנָא הֵי מִינַּיְיהוּ – **but I do not know which of them** acquires and which does not.

Rav Yehudah quoted Shmuel's rulings without explaining the cases that he ruled on. The Gemara therefore ponders:

הֵיכִי דָּמֵי – **What are the circumstances** of the case? אִילֵימָא רָכוּב לְחוּדֵיהּ – **If you say** that Shmuel ruled on two different cases: on **a rider alone,** i.e. without a leader, וּמַנְהִיג לְחוּדֵיהּ – **and** on **a leader alone,** without a rider,[4] this is untenable! מַנְהִיג לְחוּדֵיהּ מִי אִיכָּא מַאן דְּאָמַר לֹא קָנֵי – If the **leader** was **alone** without a rider – **is there anyone who maintains that he does not acquire?** Impossible! If a person leads a found animal, he certainly acquires it through his action;[5] Rav Yehudah undoubtedly knew this as well.

The Gemara concludes the argument:

אֶלָּא אִי אִיכָּא לְמֵימַר דְּלֹא קָנֵי – **Rather, if it is possible to maintain that [either of these two]** – a rider or a leader – **does not acquire,** רָכוּב הוּא דְּאִיכָּא לְמֵימַר – **it is** only regarding **a rider that we can maintain this.**[6] Rav Yehudah should thus have realized that a leader does acquire whereas a rider does not. – ?

Having rejected its first interpretation of Rav Yehudah statement, the Gemara now presents its definitive one:

אֶלָּא רָכוּב בִּמְקוֹם מַנְהִיג אִיבַּעְיָא לֵיהּ – **Rather [Rav Yehudah] w in doubt about** whether **a rider** can acquire **in the presence of leader.**[7]

The Gemara explains Rav Yehudah's uncertainty:

מַאי – **What** is the law in this case? Does the leader acquire, does the rider? רָכוּב עָדִיף דְּהָא תָּפִיס בָּהּ – Does **the rider** have **superior** right to the animal **since he holds it?**[8] דִּלְמָא מַנְהִיג עָדִיף דְּאָזְלָא מֵחֲמָתֵיהּ – **Or perhaps the leader** has **a superi** right **since [the animal] moves because of him?**[9]

The Gemara records Rav Yehudah's own attempt to resolve t uncertainty:

אָמַר רַב יוֹסֵף אָמַר לִי רַב יְהוּדָה – **Rav Yosef related: Rav Yehuda said to me,** נֶחֱזֵי אֲנַן – **"Let us see** if we can determine ho Shmuel ruled from a different statement of his. דִּתְנַן – **For w have learned in a Mishnah:**[10] הַמַּנְהִיג סוֹפֵג אֶת הָאַרְבָּעִים – ONE LEADS a team of animals consisting of *kilayim,*[11] H RECEIVES FORTY [LASHES] for transgressing a Scriptural prohib tion. וְהַיּוֹשֵׁב בַּקָּרוֹן סוֹפֵג אֶת הָאַרְבָּעִים – AND IF ONE SITS IN WAGON attached to *kilayim,* HE RECEIVES FORTY [LASHES].[

NOTES

1. Shmuel, the well-known Amora and colleague of Rav, was one of Rav Yehudah's mentors.

2. I.e. a person sitting on an animal without causing it to move (see *Rashi* ד״ה מנהיג לחודיה and above, 8a ד״ה רכוב קני). If he does cause the animal to move, however, he certainly acquires it, for he has thereby performed a *kinyan meshichah* [lit. pulling]; see *Kiddushin* 22b.

Others contend that in order to acquire, the rider must cause the animal to move at least slightly (see *Tosafos*). Some maintain that Rashi concedes this point as well; see further, notes 6,7,15.

3. In this context, "leading" means causing the animal to move. There are several ways for one to do so: walking either behind the animal or in front of it, prodding it with a stick or even calling it (see *Kiddushin* 22b).

4. That is, Shmuel ruled someone can acquire a found animal if he performed either of the following acts: riding while nobody was leading or leading while nobody was riding. The practical difference as to whether or not he acquires through such an act emerges in a case where he performed such an act and then another grabbed the animal from him. If the first person indeed acquired the animal, the second person must return it. If not, then the second person was justified in grabbing it and may thus keep it (*Rashi*).

5. According to a Baraisa cited in *Kiddushin* 22b, if someone causes an animal to move [at least] its foreleg and hind leg, this constitutes a valid *kinyan meshichah* (literally: pulling). Obviously, then, a person can acquire an animal through leading it (see *Rashi*).

6. According to *Rashi,* the legal distinction between riding an animal (as defined in the context of this discussion; see note 2) and leading it is that the latter action causes the animal to move whereas the former does not. Leading, then, certainly constitutes a *kinyan meshichah* (see note 5). Accordingly, if Rav Yehudah knew that Shmuel held only one of these actions to be a valid *kinyan,* he should have inferred that it was leading rather than riding (*Rashi*).

As mentioned earlier, others maintain that whenever a rider mounts an animal, the animal moves instinctively (see *Tosafos* and *Toras Chaim*). Nevertheless, although the rider thus causes the animal to move, still he does not control movement. For this reason, the Gemara now believes that merely mounting an animal does not constitute a *kinyan* (*Rashba;* see *Toras Chaim*). *Imrei Binah* (*Choshen Mishpat* p. 234b) asserts that Rashi subscribes to this view as well; for a full discussion of this interpretation, see there.

7. The Gemara now reverses its previous position, assuming that according to Shmuel a person can acquire an animal either through riding it or through leading it. [Thus, although the Baraisa in *Kiddushin* states that to acquire through *kinyan meshichah* one must cause the animal to move, riding is an exception to the rule; a rider acquires even if the animal does not move (see *Rashi*).] According to this interpretation, Shmuel discusses a case in which two litigants appear in court, one riding an animal and the other leading it. Each claims to have acquired tl animal through his respective actions; yet they both agree that th acted simultaneously. Rav Yehudah's question, then, was whether ri ing or leading is the superior *kinyan.* (Obviously, the litigant who pe formed the superior *kinyan* acquired the animal.) Rav Yehudah forgc however, how Shmuel had ruled (*Rashi,* according to *Pnei Yehoshua*

Now, our Mishnah discussed a similar case, ruling that if two litigan appear in court, one riding an animal and the other leading it, they d vide it equally. The Mishnah does not refute Shmuel's ruling (that on one litigant acquires), though, for its case differs from Shmuel's in or important respect. In the Mishnah's case, each litigant claims to hav performed his *kinyan* before the other. Since a corollary of these clain is that each owns the entire animal, they divide. Not so in Shmuel's cas In that case, the litigants agree that they acted simultaneously (*Pn Yehoshua;* see *Tosafos,* cf. *Ritva*).

8. The underlying assumption of this argument is that if a person act ally takes possession of an article when he performs a *kinyan,* such *kinyan* is superior to others. Thus, riding should be superior to leadir (*Nachalas David* in explanation of *Rashi's* view). See following note fo an explanation of *Tosafos'* position.

9. Actually, according to *Tosafos,* mounting an animal causes it to mov as well (see above, notes 2 and 6). Nevertheless, since only the leade *controls* the animal's movement, his *kinyan* is superior (*Ramban;* *Rashba*).

10. *Kilayim* 8:3.

Earlier, it has been noted, that according to *Rashi,* mounting an an mal does not cause it to move at all (see above, notes 2 and 6). Howeve *Tosafos* (ד״ה רכוב עדיף) points out that the Gemara's forthcoming ana ogy to the laws of *kilayim* is extremely difficult to understand accordir to *Rashi's* interpretation of "riding." We will therefore present the di cussion according to *Tosafos'* interpretation of riding.

11. I.e. a team of animals consisting of different species. The Tora (*Deuteronomy* 22:10) states: *You may not plow with ox and donkey t gether.* Now the verse mentions only plowing with *kilayim;* neverth less, it is forbidden to lead or perform any other work with them as we (*Sifri* ad loc.). Thus, if a person leads *kilayim,* he certainly violates tl prohibition and is punished with lashes.

12. The Mishnah does not discuss a single case in which one person le *kilayim* that had been harnessed to a wagon and another sat in tl wagon. If it did, it would have combined its two rulings as follows: *someone leads kilayim and another sits in a wagon attached to ther each receives forty lashes.* Rather, it discusses two separate cases: one i which a person led *kilayim* and another in which a person sat upon wagon attached to *kilayim* (*Maharsha* in *Mahadura Basra*).

The reason that the person sitting in the wagon receives lashes is a follows: Animals harnessed to a wagon sense when someone sits down i it. They then move, thereby pulling the wagon slightly. Thus, they ma

שמעית מיניה דמר שמואל תרתי ° רכוב ומנהיג חד קני וחד לא קני ולא ידענא הי מינייהו היכי דמי אילימא רכוב לחודיה ומנהיג לחודיה מנהיג לחודיה מי איכא מאן דאמר לא קני אלא אי איכא למימר דלא קני רכוב הוא דאיכא למימר אלא רכוב במקום מנהיג איבעיא ליה מאי רכוב עדיף דהא תפיס בה או דלמא מנהיג עדיף דאזלא מחמתיה אמר רב יוסף אמר לי רב יהודה נחזי אנן א) דתנן א המנהיג סופג את הארבעים והיושב בקרון סופג את הארבעים ר"מ פוטר ב) את היושב בקרון ומדאפיך שמואל ותני וחכמים פוטרין את היושב בקרון שמע מינה רכוב לחודיה לא קני וכל שכן רכוב במקום מנהיג אמר ליה אביי לרב יוסף הא זמנין סגיאין אמרת לן נחזי אנן ולא אמרת לן משמיה דרב יהודה א"ל אברא ודכרנן נמי דאמרי ליה היכי פשיט מר רכוב מיושב יושב לא תפיס במוסירה רכוב תפיס במוסירה ואמר לי רב ושמואל דאמרי תרוייהו ב מוסירה לא קני איכא דאמרי א"ל אביי לרב יוסף היכי פשיט מר רכוב מיושב יושב לא תפיס במוסירה רכוב תפיס במוסירה א"ל הכי תנא אידי מוסירה לא קני אתמר נמי אמר רבי חלבו אמר רב הונא ג) מוסירה מחבירו קנה ג במציאה ובנכסי הגר לא קני מאי לשון מוסירה אמר רבא אידי אסברא לי כאדם המוסר דבר לחבירו בשלמא מחבירו קני דקא מסר ליה חבריה אלא במציאה ובנכסי הגר מאן קא מסר ליה דליקני מיתיבי ד) היו שנים רוכבין על גבי בהמה וכו' מני אילימא רבי מאיר השתא יושב קני רכוב מיבעי אלא לאו רבנן ושמע מינה ד רכוב קני הכא במאי עסקינן במנהיג ברגליו אי הכי היינו מנהיג תרי גווני מנהיג מהו דתימא רכוב עדיף דהא מנהיג ותפיס בה קמ"ל ת"ש ה שנים שהיו מושכין בגמל ומנהיגין בחמור או שהיה אחד מושך ואחד מנהיג

במדה

## רש"י

שמעית מיניה דמר שמואל תרתי. שמעתי ממנו שני דברים דין רכוב ודין מנהיג בחד אמר לי קני ובחד אמר לי לא קני ולא ידענא כו': אי נימא רכוב לחודיה. שאין אחר מנהיג עמו ובא אחד מן השוק וחוטפו ממנו בפניו ומושכה לקנותה וכן מנהיג ואין רכוב עמו ובא אחד וחוטפו ממנו בפניו לקנותה וקאמר שמואל בחד מינייהו דלא קני ומאן דחטף שפיר חטף ומבעיא ליה לרב יהודה בהי מינייהו: מנהיג לחודיה מי איכא למאן דאמר דלא קני. הא משיכה היא זו ובהמה נקנית במשיכה ומאי תיבעי ליה לרב יהודה אי ודאי אמר שמואל בחד מינייהו דלא קני ברכוב הוא דקאמר דקסבר משיכה בעינן שתעקור יד ורגל כדאמרינן בקדושין (דף כב:): אלא רכוב במקום מנהיג. שניהם באים לפנינו זה רכוב וזה מנהיג זה אומר כולה שלי וזה אומר כולה שלי אמר שמואל חד קני ומבעיא ליה לרב יהודה היכא דאיתנהו לתרוייהו הי עדיף רכוב עדיף דהא תפיס בה וכי אמרינן משיכה קני היכא דליכא רכוב אבל במקום רכוב לא: או דלמא מנהיג עדיף דקאזלא מחמתיה. והיא הגדולה בקנין: למאן אי לר"מ כו' עד לרבנן. לא גרס: נחזי אנן. אית לן למפשט משמעתא דמר שמואל בהי מינייהו אמר: המנהיג. בשור וחמור: פוטר. קסבר לאו מידי עביד: ומדאפיך שמואל כו'. ש"מ סבירא לשמואל רכוב לאו מידי מעשה עביד ומשום דיחיד ורבים הלכה כרבים אפכה למתני' לאוקמה פטורא כרבנן: הכי גרסינן שמע מינה ס"ל לשמואל רכוב לחודיה לא קני ולא גרס לרבנן: והא זמנין סגיאין אמרת. להא שמעתין נחזי אנן: ולא אמרת לן. אלא משמך למפשט ספיקו דרב יהודה: אברא. אמת הוא אמר לי נחזי אנן וזכור אני שאמרתי לו היכי תפשוט מר רכוב מיושב בקרון: מוסירה. קבישטר"א: מוסירה אינה קונה. במליאה עד שיוליכנה ותעקור יד ורגל ואע"ג דבמכירה קני כדתנן (קדושין דף כה:) בהמה גסה נקנית במסירה לגבי מליאה לא קני כדאמרינן טעמא לקמן בשמעתין: איכא דאמרי. רב יוסף משמיה דנפשיה קאמר נחזי אנן וא"ל אביי היכי תפשוט רכוב כו': אידי. שם חכם: מחבירו. מקח וממכר: בנכסי הגר. שמת ואין לו יורשין וכל הקודם בנכסיו זכה בהן: ומהו לשון מוסירה. שמוסרין אותו בו ללוקח: אי נימא ר"מ. דאמר היושב בקרון סופג את הארבעים ומתני' יחידאה היא ולית הלכתא כוותיה: השתא לר"מ יושב קני. דקאמר היושב בקרון סופג את הארבעים: רכוב מיבעיא. ולנוס לי לאשמועינן בתרתי: אלא לאו רבנן. ואשמועינן דיושב הוא דפטור אבל רכוב לא ותיובתא לרב יהודה דפשט רוכב מיושב: במנהיג ברגליו. דקנייה במשיכה שבועט בה ברגליו והולכת מחמתו כדרך רוכבי סוסים: היינו מנהיג. והו"ל למיתני או שהיו שניהם מנהיגים: תרי גווני מנהיג. דאי אשמועינן בשני מנהיגים דיחלוקו לא היינו יודעים להאי מהו דתימא כו': חמור דרכו בהנהגה וגמל דרכו במשיכה:

במדה

## תוספות

**מנהיג** לחודיה מי איכא מאן דאמר לא קנה. אע"ג דלר"ש אית ליה בפ"ק דקדושין (דף כה: ושם) דבהמה [בין דקה בין גסה] אינה נקנית אלא בהגבהה ° מ"מ פריך מכח סתם מתניתין דהא תנן אחד רכוב ואחד מנהיג כו' והא דתנן בפ"ק דקדושין (שם) ה) בהמה גסה נקנית במסירה דברי ר"מ ור"א אף במסירה קאמר וכ"ש במשיכה וכן התם בגמ' דהיכא דמזכיר מסירה הוי פי' אף במסירה ובמקום שמזכיר משיכה דוקא ולא מסירה ובלאו הכי צריך לומר כן התם:

**רכוב** הוא דלא קני. ומתני' דאחד רכוב דחי לקמן במנהיג ברגליו:

**רכוב** עדיף דתפיס בה. ° אין לפרש דתפיס ברגליו או במה שיושב עליה דהאי לא מיקרי תפיס בה אלא במה שהוא תפוס במוסירה קרי תפיס בה דהא בסמוך נקט האי לישנא וצריך לומר דתפיס בה ואזלא נמי מעט מחמתיה או דלמא מנהיג עדיף דאזלא מחמתיה טובא דאי לא מיבעיא ליה ברכוב אלא משום דתפיס בה גרידא א"כ מה פושט בסמוך מיושב דפטור והכי נמי דרכוב לא קני והלא לענין כלאים אינו תלוי כלל בתפיסה אלא באזלא מחמתיה ולענין קנין אינו תלוי כי אם בתפיס בה ולא באזלא מחמתיה:

**או** דלמא מנהיג עדיף כו'. תימה דלפשוט ממתני' דמנהיג קונה במקום רכוב ואי רכוב איירי במנהיג ברגליו כ"ש דמנהיג עדיף דאפילו במקום רכוב ומנהיג ברגליו קני כ"ש במקום רכוב לחודיה וי"ל דמן המשנה אין להוכיח דקני מנהיג במקום רכוב דאפילו לא קני מיקרי מוחזק דכיון דמנהיג לחודיה שלא במקום רכוב קני מקרי מוחזק אפי' במקום רכוב ומ"מ לקמן מוכיח שפיר ממתניתין דרכוב לחודיה קני מאחר שקרוי מוחזק דאי אפילו לחודיה לא קני סברא הוא דאפי' מוחזק נמי לא הוי וכן לעיל דקאמר אילימא מהא שנים אוחזין האי אמר כולה אגבהתי' אבל שנים שהגביהו לא קנו התם נמי אע"ג דכמו שהם שניהם תפוסים לא קנו מקרי מוחזק כיון דאם היה מגביה לחודיה אילו לא היה חבירו תפוס בלד השני היה קונה לכך איקרי מוחזק אפילו עם חבירו ° ומסיפא אין להוכיח דרכוב ומנהיג קנו שניהם זה במקום זה דקתני אם היו שניהם מודים יחלוקו דאין שניהם מודים שכך קנו אותה ביחד זה ברכיבה וזה בהנהגה אלא שניהם בהנהגה או בקנין אחר:

**רכוב** לחודיה לא קני. נראה דרב יהודה היה מסופק אם שמע משמואל ברכוב לחודיה ומנהיג לחודיה ואז פשיט ליה דרכוב הוא דלא קני או אם שמיע ליה ברכוב במקום מנהיג ואז מספקא ליה הי מינייהו קני דאי לא מספקא ליה אלא שמע משמואל ברכוב במקום מנהיג ותו לא א"כ ס"ל לשמואל דרכוב לחודיה קני והשתא פשיט רב יהודה דאפילו לחודיה לא קני:

**מהו** דתימא רכוב עדיף. פי' חזקתו עדיף ויבטל את חזקת המנהיג קמ"ל דשניהם מוחזקים ויחלוקו אבל אין לפרש מהו דתימא דרכוב עדיף ויבטל את קנין המנהיג קמ"ל דשניהם קנו כדפרישית לעיל דאפילו לא הוי קני במקום רכוב מקרי מוחזק כיון דמנהיג לחודיה קני וא"ת לעיל כי פריך השתא יושב קני רכוב מיבעיא לישני דקא משמע לן דלא מבטל חזקת רכוב דתפיס בה ואזלא מחמתיה את חזקת המנהיג וי"ל דאין צריך להשמיענו דפשיטא דרכוב לחודיה בלא מנהיג ברגליו לא חשיב לבטל את חזקת המנהיג דאי משום דתפיס בה מנהיג נמי אזלא מחמתיה טפי מרכוב אבל השתא דמיירי במנהיג ברגליו דכיון דכל מה שיש במנהיג יש ברכוב ועוד דתפיס בה יבטל את חזקת המנהיג קא משמע לן ולפי מאי דאוקימנא השתא במנהיג ברגליו אתיא כרבנן וכל שכן כרבי מאיר:

מושך

## עין משפט נר מצוה

נז א מיי' פ"ט מהלכות כלאים הלכה ט סמג לאוין רפב טוש"ע י"ד סי' רצז סעיף יג:

נח ב ש"ע ח"מ סי' קצז סעיף א וע"ש בטור וב"י:

נט ג מיי' פי"ז מהלכות אבידה הל' ו סמג עשין עד טוש"ע ח"מ סי' רעא סעיף ג:

ס ד מיי' פי"ז מהלכות אבידה הלכה ז ופ"ב מהל' מכירה הל' ו ופ"ט מהל' טוען ונטען הל' ז סמג עשין עד וסי' פב וסי' לה טוש"ע ח"מ סי' קלח סעיף א וסי' קצז סעיף ה וסי' רעא סעיף ג:

סא ה מיי' פי"ז מהל' אבידה הל' ה ועי' בהשגות ובמ"מ ובכ"מ סמג עשין עד טוש"ע ח"מ סי' רעא סעיף א:

## רבינו חננאל

הא דאמרן רוכב ומנהיג חד קני וחד לא קני ואמר רב יהודה נחזי אנן מדתנן בפ' כלאי הכרם המנהיג סופג מ' וכו'. פי' המנהיג בשור (או) ובחמור ודש או חרש סופג מ' והיושב בקרון סופג מ' ר"מ פוטר את היושב בקרון. שמואל מפיך ותני היושב בקרון סופג מ' דברי ר' מאיר וחכמים פוטרין את היושב בקרון הנה היושב בקרון כמו רוכב הוא וכיון דפטרי ליה רבנן שמעינן מינה דלא א) הוא מנהיג הבהמה שרוכב עליה ולא מתעבידא מכחו ולא חרישה ולא דישה לפיכך הוא פטור הלכך רוכב לחודיה לא קני וכ"ש רוכב במקום מנהיג ודברים פשוטין הן. פי' מוסירה כגון פרומביא ואפסר כל בהמה בראוי לה. התופס במוסירה לא קני לא במציאה ולא בנכסי הגר דהא לא מסר ליה אחרינא אבל מוסירה מחבירו קני דהא מסר ליה חבריה. מיתיבי היו שנים רוכבין על גבי בהמה וכו'. ופרקי' במנהיג הבהמה שרוכב עליה (בקרקע) [ברגליו].

## חשק שלמה על ר"ח

א) אולי צ"ל דלא הוי כמנהיג הבהמה כשרוכב עליה דלא איתעבידא מכחו ולא הוי כחרישה ודישה לפיכך וכו'.

## מסורת הש"ס

א) כלאים פרק ח' משנה ... ב) [במשנה שם ליתא ... ג' תיבות את היוש... בקרון], ג) [עיין ... בבא בתרא עה: ... אחזה], ד) [לעיל ...] ה) עיין מהרש"א.

## גליון הש"ס

גמ' רכוב. עי' תוי"ט ... משנה ג' דנדרים ד... אביה ובעלה: תוס' ד"ה מנהיג וכו' מ"מ פר... מכח סתם מתני'. כ... זה בכתובות דף לה ע... ומי איכא למ"ד חי... מיתות שוגגי' חי... ובתוס' שם: שם ד"ה רכוב וכו' אין לפר... עיין תשובת מהר"ס בוטון סי' ס"ג: שם ד"ה או וכו' ומסיפא א... להוכיח. קשה לי ב... דאמרי' לעיל ע"א ... מסיפא בזמן שהן מו... כו' וש"מ המגביה מלי... לחבירו מנ"ל דהן מו... קאי אהגביהו מלי... ומודים שהגביהו ... ונוכיח מזה דהמגב... מליאה לחבירו קנה חבי... דלמא קאי על אחד ר... ואחד מנהיג דמודים ש... יחד בזה ונוכיח מזה דר... במקום מנהיג קנה:

## ליקוטי רש"י

מוסירה. אפסר [ש... נב.]. היו שנ... רוכבין. עיין ל... עמוד א.

## לעזי רש"י

קבישטר"א. פי... אפסר (רש"י שבת נב ע"א ד"ה במוסר... חבל שקשורה בו הבה... ונמשכת (ערוך ט... מסר ג').

דחזיא לקטנים והא דאמר רבא (א) אם היתה טלית מוזהבת חולקין ה"נ דפלגי לה הא אפסדוה הא לא קשיא דחזיא לבני מלכים והא דתנן (ב) היו שנים רוכבין על גבי בהמה וכו' הכי נמי דפלגי לה הא אפסדוה בשלמא טהורה חזיא לבשר אלא טמאה הא אפסדוה א אלא לדמי הכא נמי לדמי אמר רמי בר חמא זאת אומרת (ג) ב המגביה מציאה לחבירו קנה חבירו דאי סלקא דעתך לא קנה חבירו תיעשה זו כמי שמונחת על גבי קרקע וזו כמי שמונחת על גבי קרקע ולא יקנה לא זה ולא זה אלא לאו ש"מ המגביה מציאה לחבירו קנה חבירו (ה) אמר רבא לעולם אימא לך המגביה מציאה לחבירו לא קנה חבירו והכא היינו טעמא (ד) מגו דזכי לנפשיה זכי נמי לחבריה תדע שאילו אמר לשלוחו צא וגנוב לי וגנב פטור (ה) ג ושותפין שגנבו חייבין מאי טעמא לאו משום דאמרינן מגו דזכי לנפשיה זכי נמי לחבריה ש"מ אמר רבא השתא דאמרת (א) אמרינן מגו חרש ופקח שהגביהו מציאה מתוך שקנה חרש קנה פקח בשלמא חרש קנה דקא מגבה ליה בן דעת אלא פקח במאי קנה אלא אימא חרש קנה פקח לא קנה ומאי מגו מגו דשני חרשין בעלמא קנו האי נמי קני (ו) האי מאי אם תמצא לומר המגביה מציאה לחבירו קנה חבירו הני מילי היכא דקא מגבה ליה אדעתא דחבריה האי אדעתא דידיה קא מגבה ליה איהו לא קני לאחריני מקני אלא אימא ד מתוך שלא קנה פקח לא קנה חרש וכי תימא מאי שנא משני חרשין דעלמא התם ה תקינו להו רבנן דלא (ז) אתי לאנצויי הכא מימר אמר פקח לא קני אנא אקני אמר ליה רב אחא בריה דרב אדא לרב אשי דיוקיה דרמי בר חמא מהיכא אי נימא מרישא שנים אוחזין בטלית התם האי קאמר כולה שלי ואנא אגבהתה כולה והאי אמר כולה שלי ואנא אגבהתה כולה אלא מהא דקתני זה אומר כולה שלי וזה אומר כולה שלי הא תו למה לי אלא ממשנה יתירה שמע מינה המגביה מציאה לחבירו קנה חבירו והא אוקימנא (ח) רישא במציאה וסיפא במקח וממכר אלא מסיפא זה אומר כולה שלי וזה אומר חציה שלי הא תו למה לי אלא ממשנה יתירה שמע מינה המגביה מציאה לחבירו קנה חבירו וממאי דבמציאה דלמא במקח וממכר וכי תימא אי במקח וממכר מאי למימרא איצטריך סלקא דעתך אמינא האי דקאמר חציה שלי להוי כמשיב אבידה וליפטר קמשמע לן דהאי (ט) איערומי קא מערים סבר אי אמינא כולה שלי בעינא אשתבועי אימא הכי דאהוי כמשיב אבידה ואיפטר אלא מהא היו שנים רוכבין על גבי בהמה הא תו למה לי אלא ממשנה יתירה שמע מינה המגביה מציאה לחבירו קנה חבירו ודלמא הא קמשמע לן דרוכב נמי קני אלא מסיפא בזמן שהן מודין או שיש להן עדים חולקין בלא שבועה במאי אי במקח וממכר צריכא למימר אלא לאו במציאה ושמע מינה המגביה מציאה לחבירו קנה חבירו ורבא אמר לך מגו דזכי לנפשיה זכי נמי לחבריה: היו שנים רוכבין: אמר רב יוסף אמר לי רב יהודה

שמעית

**רש"י**

דחזיא לבני מלכים. לבנים קטנים: זאת אומרת. מתני' דקתני שנים שהגביהו מציאה קנאוה ויחלוקו וכשמגביה מגביה לדעת שיקנה בה חבירו חציה ש"מ המגביה מציאה כו' ולקמיה פריך דיוקא דרמי בר חמא מהיכא מאיזו בבא ממשנתנו הוא למד כן: ולא יקנה לא זה ולא זה. וכל הרוצה יחטפנה מידם: לעולם אימא לך לא קנה חבירו. היכא דמגביה לא נתכוין לקנות בה כלום וטעמא אמר לקמן (דף י.) דהוי תופס לבעל חוב במקום כו': והכא. דקתני במתני' שנים שהגביהו מציאה קנו מגו דזכי לנפשיה זכי נמי לחבריה: תדע. דאפי' אמר לא קנה חבירו היכא דהגביה כולה לדעת חבירו הכא דהגביה לעצמו ולחבירו קני משום מגו: פטור. המשלח פטור מלשלם כפל דקי"ל אין שליח לדבר עבירה להתחייב שולחו אלא שליח דדברי הרב ודברי התלמיד דברי מי שומעין ואילו שותפין שגנבו. והאחד הוציאה מרשות בעלים לדעתו ולדעת חבירו אמרינן בבבא קמא (דף עח:) דחייבין: השתא דאמרת מגו. דזכי לנפשיה כו' חרש ופקח שהגביהו מציאה קנאוה אע"פ שהגבהה של חרש אינה הגבהה לקנות אלא מפני דרכי שלום כדתנן (גיטין דף נט:) חרש שוטה וקטן יש בהן גזל מפני דרכי שלום אפילו הכי אמר מגו דזכי לנפשיה כו': בשלמא חרש קני דקא מגבה לה בן דעת. לראשה השני לצורך שניהם וראשו של צד חרש לגבי חרש מיהא הויא הגבהה כדתקון ליה מפני דרכי שלום אלא פקח במאי קני לגבי פקח הוי ראשה שהגביה החרש כמונח על גבי קרקע דהגבהה דחרש לא קניא אלא מדרכי שלום בעלמא: ומאי מגו. איכא למימר הכא דקאמר השתא דאמרת מגו אמרינן מגו וחרש אמאי קני הא לא זכי פקח לנפשיה דנימא דזכי נמי לחבריה ולא הויא הגבהה דפקח הגבהה: אם תמצא לומר. כלומר אפי' אם תמצא לומר המגביה מציאה לחבירו כו': הכא אדעתא דידיה קא מגבה ליה. האי פיקח: דלא ליתי לאינצויי. עם החוטפים מהם: מהיכא. מאיזו בבא ממשנתנו קא דייק לומר זאת אומרת: הא קאמר כולה שלי ואנא אגבהתיה. והיאך נאמר לא יקנה לא זה ולא זה ויבא אחר ויטלנה והלא כל אחד טוען אני הגבהתיה ואין כאן מגביה מציאה לחבירו ומה יש לו להשיב בשלמא האי שכנגדו המוחזק בה כמוהו אמר לא הגבהת אתה כי אם אני אבל אחר מן השוק מה יטעון: ממשנה יתירה. אמרינן דהמגביה מציאה כו' ומשום הכי אמרינן יחלוקו דאמרינן שניהם הגביהוה והוה ליה כל אחד מגביה מציאה לו ולחבירו וקני דאי משום דלא ידעינן הי מינייהו משקר והוה ליה ממון המוטל בספק וחולקין בשבועה משום שלא יהא כל אחד ואחד הולך ותוקף כדאמרי' לעיל (דף ג.) הא שמענא ליה מרישא: דאהוי כמשיב אבידה. מדהוה מצי למימר כולה שלי ואמר חציה שלי: וליפטר. משבועה: ממשנה יתירה כו'. כדפרישית: דרכוב קני. ואע"ג דלא משיכה היא שאינה זזה ממקומה שאין מנהיגה ברגליו: צריכא למימר. דהיכא דלקוחה בין שניהם שיחלקוה בלא שבועה: אלא לאו במציאה. ואיצטריך לאשמועינן שאין אחר יכול לחוטפה דמגביה מציאה לחבירו קנה חבירו: ורבא אמר לך. בעלמא היכא דלא נתכוון המגביה לזכות בה לא קנה חבירו ומשנה יתירה דמתני' אשמועינן המגביה מציאה לו ולחבירו קנה אף חבירו דמגו דזכי לנפשיה זכי נמי לחבריה:

שמעית

**תוספות**

דחזיא לקטנים. ופריך דטלית מוזהבת לא עבדי לקטנים ול"ג דחזיא לתרוייהו דא"כ מאי פריך מטלית מוזהבת: ושותפין שגנבו. פי' בקונטרס שהוציא לדעתו ולדעת חבירו כדאיתא בב"ק (דף עח:) ואין נראה דהתם בטביחה איירי וטביחה אפי' אמר לא וטבח לי חייב דדרשינן (שם דף עא.) תחת לרבות השליח אלא שותפין שגנבו שהגביהו שניהם:

ומאי מגו מגו דשני חרשין. תימה מנלן דלמא תרי מגו לא אמרי' דב' חרשין דקנו היינו מטעם מגו דזכי לנפשיה זכי נמי לחבריה:

אלא מסיפא זה אומר כולה שלי וזה אומר חציה שלי. אית דל"ג הכא הא תו למה לי דממשנה גופה קא דייק דקאמר חציה שלי והיינו שהגביה עם חבירו ולפי דבריו לא יטול כלום אלא ודאי מגביה מציאה לחבירו זכה ופריך ממאי דבמציאה דלמא במקח וממכר והוא הדין דהוה מצי למדחי דהא דאמר חציה שלי כגון דאמר תפסתיה חציה בידי או הגבהתיה כולה לקנות חציה אבל עדיין היה מדקדק מיתורא דמתני' לכך דחי ליה דאפי' מיתורא אינו יכול לדקדק ולספרים דגרסי הא תו למה לי י"ל דמשום דמגופא דמתני' לא מצי למידק כדפרישית אך קשה אמאי קאמר דלמא במקח וממכר אפילו מיירי במציאה מצי לדחויי כדדחי וי"ל בדוחק ממאי דבמציאה דלהכי לא מוקמת במקח וממכר משום דלא משכחת חידוש אלא במגביה מציאה לחבירו כי נמי איירי במקח וממכר יש חידוש דלא נימא משיב אבידה הוא וה"ה אם מיירי במציאה לא יוכל להוכיח כלום:

מנהיג

**עין משפט נר מצוה**

נג א מיי' פ"ט מהלכות טוען ונטען הל' י סמג עשין לה טוש"ע ח"מ סי' קלח סעיף ד:

נד ב מיי' פי"ז מהלכות אבידה הל' ג סמג עשין עד טוש"ע ח"מ סי' רסט סעיף א:

נה ג מיי' פ"ב מהל' גניבה הל' יד סמג עשין עא טוש"מ סי' שנ:

נו ד ה מיי' פי"ז מהל' גזילה ואבידה הל' ד סמג עשין עד טוש"ע ח"מ סי' רסט סעיף ד:

**רבינו חננאל**

כיון שהעמיד רב פפא משנתנו דקתני יחלוקו בתפסי לה בכרכשתא דקדק רמי בר חמא ואמר זאת אומרת המגביה מציאה לחבירו קנה חבירו. רבא אמר לעולם לא קנה ומתני' היינו טעמא מגו דזכי לנפשיה זכי נמי לחבריה. תדע דאילו האומר לחבירו צא וגנוב לי פטור המשלח דקי"ל אין שליח לדבר עבירה ואילו שותפין שגנבו חייבין ושקלי' וטרי' בה ואסיקנא דוקיא דרמי בר חמא מסיפא דמתני' בזמן שהן מודין או שיש להן עדים כי שניהם ביחד מצאוה ושניהן אגב' אגבהוה בכרכשתא חולקין בלא שבועה ש"מ המגביה מציאה לחבירו קנה חבירו דהא תרוייהו מסייעי להדדי בעידנא דמגבהי לה. ורבא אמר לך שאני הכא מגו דזכי לנפשיה זכי נמי לחבריה. וקי"ל כרמי בר חמא והוא דאמר ליה זכי לי דהא ר' יוחנן קאי כוותיה ואמר המגביה מציאה לחבירו קנה חבירו ואם יקשה לך הא דתנן היה רוכב על גבי בהמה וכו' התם באומר תנה לי ולא אמר זכה לי. היו שניהם רוכבין על גבי בהמה וכו'.

**מסורת הש"ס**

לעיל ז.], ב) [לעיל ב.], לקמן י.], ד) [לקמן נדרים פח:], ה) [שבת, עיין שם, בבא קמא :], ו) [לקמן ט.], צ"ל ליתי], ח) [לעיל ב.], ט) [לעיל ד:].

**הגהות הב"ח**

גמ' השתא דאמרי דאמרי' מגו:

**גליון הש"ס**

אמר רבא לעולם. לקמן דף י ע"א תוס' איתיביה ובנדרים דף ע"ב בר"ן ד"ה אמר רבא:

**ליקוטי רש"י**

היתה טלית זהבת. כלומר אפילו מוזהבת חולקים [לעיל ז.]. היו שנים כבין. לאשמועינן אתא וכב ומנהיג שניהם שוין ות בהמה מן ההפקר [לעיל ב.]. מיגו דזכי פשיה וכו'. דאי בעי זכי לנפשיה אם ביה לעצמו [לקמן ט:]. יפא במקח וממכר. ימיה מיד פלוני וכו' [לעיל ב.]. איערומי קא ברים. דליחזקיה בנאמן [לעיל ד:].

The Gemara rejects this as well:

וְדִלְמָא הָא קָמַשְׁמַע לָן – But perhaps the Mishnah teaches us this following principle: דְּרוֹכֵב נַמִּי קָנֵי – that a rider too acquires.[33] Hence, since this clause is not superfluous either, it does not prove Rami bar Chama's rule.

The Gemara now presents the actual source of Rami bar Chama's inference:

אֶלָּא מִסֵּיפָא – Rather, Rami inferred his ruling from the final clause of the Mishnah, which states:

בִּזְמַן שֶׁהֵן מוֹדִים – WHENEVER THEY both AGREE to having acquired the article simultaneously אוֹ שֶׁיֵּשׁ לָהֶן עֵדִים – OR IF THEY HAVE WITNESSES to that effect, חוֹלְקִין בְּלֹא שְׁבוּעָה – THEY DIVIDE it WITHOUT AN OATH. בְּמַאי – Now regarding what does the Mishnah make its statement? אִי בְּמִקָּח וּמִמְכָּר – If it is regarding buying and selling, צְרִיכָא לְמֵימַר – does [the Mishnah] need to state this clause? Of course not! If they concede to having acquired the article simultaneously or if witnesses testify that they did, obviously they must divide it.

The Gemara concludes:

אֶלָּא לָאו בִּמְצִיאָה – Rather, is the Mishnah not speaking about a found object? וּשְׁמַע מִינָּהּ – And infer from [this clause of the Mishnah] הַמַּגְבִּיהַּ מְצִיאָה לַחֲבֵירוֹ קָנָה חֲבֵירוֹ – that if one lifts a found object intending to acquire it entirely for his fellow, his fellow acquires it.[34]

The Gemara now restates Rava's objection to Rami's inference:

וְרָבָא אָמַר לָךְ – But Rava will contend to you that this is no proof. Indeed, the Mishnah teaches that if two people simultaneously lift an object, each lifting it for himself and his fellow, they both acquire it because מִגּוֹ דְּזָכֵי לְנַפְשֵׁיהּ – "since" each acquires for himself, זָכֵי נַמִּי לְחַבְרֵיהּ – he acquires for his fellow as well. If someone lifts an object entirely for his fellow, however, the fellow does not acquire it.

The Gemara cites and comments upon a segment of our Mishnah:

הָיוּ שְׁנַיִם רוֹכְבִין – If TWO litigants come before the court RIDING on an animal, each claiming that the animal is his, they must divide the animal. אָמַר רַב יוֹסֵף אָמַר לִי רַב יְהוּדָה – Rav Yosef said: Rav Yehudah told me,

NOTES

33. The Mishnah in *Kiddushin* 25b discusses acquiring an animal through *kinyan meshichah,* i.e. causing it to move, or *mesirah,* i.e. handing over its reins; it never discusses acquiring it through riding (i.e. sitting upon it without causing it to move). It can be proven from our Mishnah's ruling (i.e. that two riders divide the animal), however, that riding indeed constitutes a valid *kinyan.*

How does the Mishnah's ruling prove that a rider acquires? It is possible that in the Mishnah's case each of the litigants claims that he acquired the animal with a valid *kinyan* other than riding and later appeared in the court riding upon the animal. So how does the Mishnah's ruling prove that riding is a valid *kinyan?* The answer to this question is as follows: According to law, litigants must share legal possession (*muchzak*) of disputed property in order to divide it. When our Mishnah rules that the riders divide, then this is tantamount to acknowledging that a rider has legal possession of the animal. Now legal possession is defined as exercising control over something in a way that could constitute a *kinyan*. Hence, since riding grants a person legal possession of an animal, it follows that it constitutes a valid *kinyan* as well (*Tosafos* 8b ד״ה או).

34. Once we determine that the concluding clause of the Mishnah refers to a found object, regarding which the Mishnah rules that when they both agree they divide, we can establish that when two people pick up a found object simultaneously, the law is that both acquire. It was from this law, implicit in the Mishnah, that Rami inferred that if one lifts an object entirely for his fellow, then the fellow acquires it.

דחזיא לקטנים והא דאמר רבא [א] אם היתה טלית מוזהבת חולקין ה״נ דפלגי לה הא אפסדוה הא לא קשיא דחזיא לבני מלכים והא דתנן [ב] היו שנים רוכבין על גבי בהמה וכו׳ הכי נמי דפלגי לה הא אפסדוה בשלמא טהורה חזיא לבשר אלא טמאה הא אפסדוה [א] אלא לדמי הכא נמי לדמי אמר רמי בר חמא זאת אומרת [ג] [ב] המגביה מציאה לחבירו קנה חבירו דאי סלקא דעתך לא קנה חבירו תיעשה זו כמי שמונחת על גבי קרקע וזו כמי שמונחת על גבי קרקע ולא יקנה לא זה ולא זה אלא לאו ש״מ המגביה מציאה לחבירו קנה חבירו [ה] אמר רבא לעולם אימא לך המגביה מציאה לחבירו לא קנה חבירו והכא היינו טעמא [ד] מגו דזכי לנפשיה זכי נמי לחבריה תדע שאילו אמר לשלוחו צא וגנוב לי וגנב פטור [ה] [ג] ושותפין שגנבו חייבין מאי טעמא לאו משום דאמרינן מגו דזכי לנפשיה זכי נמי לחבריה ש״מ אמר רבא השתא דאמרת (א) אמרינן מגו חרש ופקח שהגביהו מציאה מתוך שקנה חרש קנה פקח בשלמא חרש קנה דקא מגבה ליה בן דעת אלא פקח במאי קנה אלא אימא חרש קנה פקח לא קנה ומאי מגו מגו דשני חרשין בעלמא קנו האי נמי קני [ו] האי מאי אם תמצא לומר המגביה מציאה לחבירו קנה חבירו הני מילי היכא דקא מגבה ליה אדעתא דחבריה האי אדעתא דידיה קא מגבה ליה איהו לא קני לאחריני מקני אלא אימא [ד] מתוך שלא קנה פקח לא קנה חרש וכי תימא מאי שנא משני חרשין דעלמא התם [ה] תקינו להו רבנן דלא [ז] אתי לאנצויי הכא מימר אמר פקח לא קני אנא אקני אמר ליה רב אחא בריה דרב אדא לרב אשי דיוקיה דרמי בר חמא מהיכא אי נימא מרישא שנים אוחזין בטלית התם האי קאמר כולה שלי ואנא אגבהתה כולה והאי אמר כולה שלי ואנא אגבהתה כולה אלא מהא דקתני זה אומר כולה שלי וזה אומר כולה שלי הא תו למה לי אלא ממשנה יתירה שמע מינה המגביה מציאה לחבירו קנה חבירו והא אוקימנא [ח] רישא במציאה וסיפא במקח וממכר אלא מסיפא זה אומר כולה שלי וזה אומר חציה שלי הא תו למה לי אלא ממשנה יתירה שמע מינה המגביה מציאה לחבירו קנה חבירו וממאי דבמציאה דלמא במקח וממכר וכי תימא אי במקח וממכר מאי למימרא איצטריך סלקא דעתך אמינא האי דקאמר חציה שלי להוי כמשיב אבידה וליפטר קמשמע לן דהאי [ט] איערומי קא מערים סבר אי אמינא כולה שלי בעינא אשתבועי אימא הכי דאהוי כמשיב אבידה ואיפטר אלא מהא היו שנים רוכבין על גבי בהמה הא תו למה לי אלא ממשנה יתירה שמע מינה המגביה מציאה לחבירו קנה חבירו ודלמא הא קמשמע לן דרוכב נמי קני אלא מסיפא בזמן שהן מודין או שיש להן עדים חולקין בלא שבועה במאי אי במקח וממכר צריכא למימר אלא לאו במציאה ושמע מינה המגביה מציאה לחבירו קנה חבירו ורבא אמר לך מגו דזכי לנפשיה זכי נמי לחבריה: היו שנים רוכבין: אמר רב יוסף אמר לי רב יהודה

שמעית

## רש״י

דחזיא לבני מלכים. לבנים קטנים: זאת אומרת. מתני׳ דקתני שנים שהגביהו מציאה קנאוה ויחלוקו וכשמגביה מגביה לדעת שיקנה בה חבירו חציה ש״מ המגביה מציאה כו׳ ולקמיה פריך דיוקא דרמי בר חמא מהיכא מאיזו בבא ממשנתנו הוא למד כן: ולא יקנה לא זה ולא זה. וכל הרוצה יחטפנה מידם: לעולם אימא לך לא קנה חבירו. היכא דמגביה לא נתכוין לקנות בה כלום וטעמא אמר לקמן (דף י.) דהוי תופס לבעל חוב במקום כו׳: והכא. דקתני במתני׳ שנים שהגביהו מציאה קנו מגו דזכי לנפשיה זכי נמי לחבריה: תדע. דאפי׳ אמר לא קנה חבירו היכא דהגביה כולה לדעת חבירו הכא דהגביה לעצמו ולחבירו קני משום מגו: פטור. המשלח פטור מלשלם כפל דקי״ל אין שליח לדבר עבירה להתחייב שולחו אלא שליח דדברי הרב ודברי התלמיד דברי מי שומעין ואילו שותפין שגנבו. והאחד הוציאה מרשות בעלים לדעתו ולדעת חבירו אמרינן בבבא קמא (דף עח:) דחייבין: השתא דאמרת מגו. דזכי לנפשיה כו׳ חרש ופקח שהגביהו מציאה קנאוה אע״פ שהגבהה של חרש אינה הגבהה לקנות אלא מפני דרכי שלום כדתנן (גיטין דף נט:) חרש שוטה וקטן יש בהן גזל מפני דרכי שלום אפילו הכי אמר מגו דזכי לנפשיה כו׳: בשלמא חרש קני דקא מגבה לה בן דעת. לראשה השני לצורך שניהם וראשו של זה חרש לגבי חרש מיהא הויא הגבהה כדתקון ליה מפני דרכי שלום אלא פקח במאי קני לגבי פקח הוי ראשה שהגביה החרש כמונח על גבי קרקע דהגבהה דחרש לא קניא אלא מדרכי שלום בעלמא: ומאי מגו. איכא למימר הכא דקאמר השתא דאמרת מגו אמרינן מגו וחרש אמאי קני הא לא זכי פקח לנפשיה דנימא דזכי נמי לחבריה ולא הויא הגבהה דפקח הגבהה: אם תמצא לומר. כלומר אפי׳ אם תמצא לומר המגביה מציאה לחבירו כו׳: הכא אדעתא דידיה קא מגבה ליה. האי פיקח: דלא ליתי לאינצויי. עם החוטפים מהם: מהיכא. מאיזו בבא ממשנתנו קא דייק לומר זאת אומרת: הא קאמר כולה שלי ואנא אגבהתיה. והיאך נאמר לא יקנה לא זה ולא זה ויבא אחר ויטלנה והלא כל אחד טוען אני הגבהתיה ואין כאן מגביה מציאה לחבירו ומה יש לו להשיב בשלמא האי שכנגדו המוחזק בה כמוהו אמר לא הגבהת אתה כי אם אני אבל אחר מן השוק מה יטעון: ממשנה יתירה. אמרינן דהמגביה מציאה כו׳ ומשום הכי אמרינן יחלוקו דאמרינן שניהם הגביהוה והוה ליה כל אחד מגביה מציאה לו ולחבירו וקני דאי משום דלא ידעינן הי מינייהו משקר והוה ליה ממון המוטל בספק וחולקין בשבועה משום שלא יהא כל אחד ואחד הולך ותוקף כדאמרי׳ לעיל (דף ג.) הא שמענא ליה מרישא: דאהוי כמשיב אבידה. מדהוה מצי למימר כולה שלי ואמר חציה שלי: וליפטר. משבועה: ממשנה יתירה כו׳. כדפרישית: דרכוב קני. ואע״ג דלא משיכה היא שאינה זזה ממקומה שאין מנהיגה ברגליו: צריכא למימר. דהיכא דלקוחה בין שניהם שיחלקוה בלא שבועה: אלא לאו במציאה. ואיצטריך לאשמועינן שאין אחר יכול לחוטפה דמגביה מציאה לחבירו קנה חבירו: ורבא אמר לך. בעלמא היכא דלא נתכוין המגביה לזכות בה לא קנה חבירו ומשנה יתירה דמתני׳ אשמועינן המגביה מציאה לו ולחבירו קנה אף חבירו דמגו דזכי לנפשיה זכי נמי לחבריה:

שמעית

## תוספות

דחזיא לקטנים. ופריך דטלית מוזהבת לא עבדי לקטנים ול״ג דחזיא לתרוייהו דא״כ מאי פריך מטלית מוזהבת: ושותפין שגנבו. פי׳ בקונטרס שהוציא לדעתו ולדעת חבירו כדאיתא בב״ק (דף עח:) ואין נראה דהתם בטביחה איירי וטביחה אפי׳ אמר לא וטבח לי חייב דדרשינן (שם דף עא.) תחת לרבות השליח אלא שותפין שגנבו שהגביהו שניהם:

ומאי מגו מגו דשני חרשין. תימה מנלן דלמא תרי מגו לא אמרי׳ דב׳ חרשין דקנו היינו מטעם מגו דזכי לנפשיה זכי נמי לחבריה:

אלא מסיפא זה אומר כולה שלי וזה אומר חציה שלי. אית דל״ג הכא הא תו למה לי דממשנה גופה קא דייק דקאמר חציה שלי והיינו שהגביה עם חבירו ולפי דבריו לא יטול כלום אלא ודאי מגביה מציאה לחבירו זכה ופריך ממאי דבמציאה דלמא במקח וממכר והוא הדין דהוה מצי למדחי דהא דאמר חציה שלי כגון דאמר תפסתיה חציה בידי או הגבהתיה כולה לקנות חציה אבל עדיין היה מדקדק מיתורא דמתני׳ לכך דחי ליה דאפי׳ מיתורא אינו יכול לדקדק ולספרים דגרסי הא תו למה לי י״ל דמשום דמגופא דמתני׳ לא מצי למידק כדפרישית אך קשה אמאי קאמר דלמא במקח וממכר אפילו מיירי במציאה מצי לדחויי כדדחי וי״ל בדוחק ממאי דבמציאה דלהכי לא מוקמת במקח וממכר משום דלא משכחת חידוש אלא במגביה מציאה לחבירו כי נמי איירי במקח וממכר יש חידוש דלא נימא משיב אבידה הוא וה״ה אם מיירי במציאה לא יוכל להוכיח כלום:

מנהיג

## עין משפט נר מצוה

נג א מיי׳ פ״ט מהלכות טוען ונטען הל׳ י סמג עשין לה טוש״ע ח״מ סי׳ קלח סעיף ד:

נד ב מיי׳ פי״ז מהלכות אבידה הל׳ ג סמג עשין עד טוש״ע ח״מ סי׳ רסט סעיף א:

נה ג מיי׳ פ״ב מהל׳ גניבה הל׳ יד סמג עשין עא טוש״מ סי׳ שנ:

נו ד ה מיי׳ פי״ז מהל׳ גזילה ואבידה הל׳ ד סמג עשין עד טוש״ע ח״מ סי׳ רסט סעיף ד:

## רבינו חננאל

כיון שהעמיד רב פפא משנתנו דקתני יחלוקו בתפסי לה בכרכשתא דקדק רמי בר חמא ואמר זאת אומרת המגביה מציאה לחבירו קנה חבירו. רבא אמר לעולם לא קנה ומתני׳ היינו טעמא מגו דזכי לנפשיה זכי נמי לחבריה. תדע דאילו האומר לחבירו צא וגנוב לי פטור המשלח דקי״ל אין שליח לדבר עבירה ואילו שותפין שגנבו חייבין ושקלי׳ וטרי׳ בה ואסיקנא דוקיא דרמי בר חמא מסיפא דמתני׳ בזמן שהן מודין או שיש להן עדים כי שניהם ביחד מצאוה ושניהן אגב׳ אגבהוה בכרכשתא חולקין בלא שבועה ש״מ המגביה מציאה לחבירו קנה חבירו דהא תרוייהו מסייעי להדדי בעידנא דמגבהי לה. ורבא אמר לך שאני הכא מגו דזכי לנפשיה זכי נמי לחבריה. וקי״ל כרמי בר חמא והוא דאמר ליה זכי לי דהא ר׳ יוחנן קאי כוותיה ואמר המגביה מציאה לחבירו קנה חבירו ואם יקשה לך הא דתנן היה רוכב על גבי בהמה וכו׳ התם באומר תנה לי ולא אמר זכה לי. היו שניהם רוכבין על גבי בהמה וכו׳.

## מסורת הש״ס

[לעיל ז.], ג) [לעיל ב.], [לקמן י.], ד) [לקמן נדרים פח:], ה) [שבת עיין שם, בבא קמא], ו) [לקמן ט.], [צ״ל ליתי], ח) [לעיל ב.], ט) [לעיל ד:].

## הגהות הב״ח

גמ׳ השתא דאמרי דאמרי׳ מגו:

## גליון הש״ס

אמר רבא לעולם. לקמן דף י ע״א תוס׳ איתיביה ובנדרים דף ע״ב בר״ן ד״ה אמר רבא:

## ליקוטי רש״י

היתה טלית מוזהבת. כלומר אפילו מוזהבת חולקים [לעיל ז.]. היו שנים רוכבין. לאשמועינן אחד רוכב ומנהיג שניהם שוין בהמה מן ההפקר [לעיל ב.]. מיגו דזכי לנפשיה וכו׳. דאי בעי זכי לנפשיה אם זכיה לעצמו [לקמן ט:]. סיפא במקח וממכר. מיד פלוני וכו׳ [לעיל ב.]. איערומי קא מערים. דליחזקיה בנאמן [לעיל ד:].

The Gemara suggests that the inference is from the Mishnah's ext phrase:

אֶלָּא מֵהָא דְּקָתָנֵ – **Rather,** Rami inferred his rule **from this** hrase, **which teaches:** זֶה אוֹמֵר כּוּלָּהּ שֶׁלִּי – IF THIS ONE SAYS, "IT IS ALL MINE," וְזֶה אוֹמֵר כּוּלָּהּ שֶׁלִּי – AND THIS ONE SAYS, "IT IS LL MINE," they divide the cloak. הָא תּוּ לָמָּה לִי – **Why do I need** he litigant to state **this** claim **too?** He already implied this when e declared, "I found it." אֶלָּא – **Rather,** מִמִּשְׁנָה יְתֵירָה שְׁמַע מִינָּ – **from the superfluous** phrase in the **Mishnah one can nfer** הַמַּגְבִּיהַּ מְצִיאָה לַחֲבֵירוֹ קָנָה חֲבֵירוֹ – that **if one lifts a found bject** intending to acquire it entirely **for his fellow, his fellow cquires** the object.[26]

The Gemara rejects this as well:

וְהָא אוֹקִימְנָ – **But we have already interpreted** רֵישָׁא בִּמְצִיאָה - that **the** Mishnah's **initial phrase concerns a found object,** וְסֵיפָא בְּמִקָּח וּמִמְכָּ – **whereas** its **concluding phrase concerns uying and selling.**[27] Thus, the concluding phrase cannot teach ami bar Chama's rule, because it already teaches another.

The Gemara suggests that the inference is from the Mishnah's ext clause:

אֶלָּא מִסֵּיפָ – **Rather,** Rami's source is **from a concluding clause** f the Mishnah: זֶה אוֹמֵר כּוּלָּהּ שֶׁלִּי – THIS ONE SAYS, "IT IS ALL INE," וְזֶה אוֹמֵר חֶצְיָהּ שֶׁלִּי – AND THIS ONE SAYS, "HALF OF IT IS INE." הָא תּוּ לָמָּה לִי – **Why do I need this** clause **too?** The lishnah's initial clause already taught that objects whose ownerhip is disputed are divided.[28] אֶלָּא – **Rather,** מִמִּשְׁנָה יְתֵירָה שְׁמַע מִינָּ – **from the superfluous** clause in the **Mishnah one an infer** הַמַּגְבִּיהַּ מְצִיאָה לַחֲבֵירוֹ קָנָה חֲבֵירוֹ – that **if one lifts a ound object** intending to acquire it entirely **for his fellow, his ellow acquires** it.

The Gemara rejects this as well:

וּמִמַּאי דְּבִמְצִיאָ – **And from where** do you know **that** this clause **efers to a found object** whose ownership is disputed? דִּלְמָא בְּמִקָּח וּמִמְכָּ – **Perhaps** it refers only to a dispute **concerning uying and selling** and not to one concerning a lost object. Hence, ami bar Chama cannot prove his rule from this clause.[29]

The Gemara raises an objection to its suggestion that this clause might discuss "buying and selling."

וְכִי תֵּימָא – **And if you will argue** אִי בְּמִקָּח וּמִמְכָּר – that **if** the Mishnah **refers to buying and selling** an object, מַאי לְמֵימְרָא – **why** is it necessary for the Mishnah **to state** this clause? The previous clause already taught that a disputed purchase is also divided.[30]

The Gemara defends its suggestion:

אִיצְטְרִיךְ – **It is** indeed **necessary** for the Mishnah to state this clause. סַלְקָא דַּעְתָּךְ אֲמִינָא – Without the clause **it could enter your mind** to say as follows: הַאי דְּקָאָמַר חֶצְיָהּ שֶׁלִּי – **This [litigant] that says, "Half of it is mine,"** לֶהֱוֵי כִּמְשִׁיב אֲבֵידָה – **should be** considered **as one who returns a lost object** וְלִיפָּטַר – **and** he should thus **be exempt** from taking an oath.[31] קָמַשְׁמַע לָן – Therefore **[the Mishnah] teaches us** that he must nevertheless take an oath, דְּהַאי אִיעֲרוּמֵי קָא מַעֲרִים – **for this [litigant]** may be **resorting to deception.** סָבַר – **He** might **reason,** אִי אֲמִינָא כּוּלָּהּ שֶׁלִּי בְּעֵינָא אִשְׁתַּבּוּעֵי – **"If I contend, 'It is all mine,' I will have to swear.** אֵימָא הָכִי – **Therefore I will contend thus,** 'Half of it is mine,' דְּאֶהֱוֵי כִּמְשִׁיב אֲבֵידָה – **so that I will be** considered **as one who returns a lost object,** וְאִיפָּטַר – **and I will** thus **be exempt** taking an oath." Accordingly, since the Mishnah's ruling may refer to a disputed purchase, it does not prove Rami bar Chama's ruling.

The Gemara suggests that the inference is from the Mishnah's next clause:

אֶלָּא מֵהָא – **Rather,** Rami's inference is **from this** clause: הָיוּ שְׁנַיִם רוֹכְבִין עַל גַּבֵּי בְהֵמָה – IF TWO litigants come before the court RIDING ON AN ANIMAL, each claiming that the animal is his, they must divide the animal. הָא תּוּ לָמָּה לִי – **Why do I need this** clause **too?** It merely applies the Mishnah's first ruling to a dispute involving an animal. אֶלָּא – **Rather,** מִמִּשְׁנָה יְתֵירָה שְׁמַע מִינָּהּ – **from the superfluous** clause in the **Mishnah one can infer** הַמַּגְבִּיהַּ מְצִיאָה לַחֲבֵירוֹ קָנָה חֲבֵירוֹ – that **if one lifts a found object** intending to acquire it entirely **for his fellow, his fellow acquires** it.[32]

NOTES

6. The Mishnah's ruling can be explained in one of two ways. Without ie superfluity, we would have explained that when the ownership of roperty is disputed, we divide it between the litigants and require each take an oath, as explained above on 3a. As the Gemara noted, owever, the Mishnah does contain a superfluous phrase. Therefore ami bar Chama infers from the superfluity of the phrase that in such case, we divide only if it is at least remotely possible that the claims of oth litigants are true; if one claim must be false, the property is not ivided. In the Mishnah's case, for example, where they both claim to wn a cloak, they would divide it only if it were possible that they cquired it simultaneously. Since this is possible only if each can acquire r his fellow as well as for himself (see note 5), it must be that each can fact do so. Rami bar Chama therefore argues that just as someone can cquire for his fellow and himself together, so can he acquire just for his llow (*Rashi*, according to *Ramban* et al.; see *Rashi* to 2a and Gemara a).

7. The Gemara above (2b) explains why it is necessary to teach that the lishnah's ruling applies both to found objects and purchases.

8. In this case, both litigants agree that one owns half the cloak; they spute only the ownership of the second half. Hence, this ruling (that ich litigant substantiates half his claim with an oath and they divide ie disputed second half) is simply an application of the Mishnah's itial ruling. Why, then, was it necessary to teach this ruling? (For a ller explanation of this ruling, see *Rashi* 2a.)

9. The question of whether Rami bar Chama's ruling is correct timately hinges on the following question: Can someone acquire a und object for his fellow even though such an acquisition represents a otential loss to others [that is, other prospective finders lose the iance to acquire the lost object for free] or can he not (see above, note ? This question is obviously irrelevant to a purchase, where the buyer pays for the object: A person can certainly buy something for his fellow. If this clause discusses a disputed purchase, then, it obviously teaches nothing about whether one can acquire a found object for his fellow.

30. Let us then assume that this clause does not refer to "buying and selling" but rather simply repeats the Mishnah's first ruling (that a found object whose ownership is disputed is divided). The superfluity thus teaches that one can acquire a found object for his fellow (see note 25).

31. I.e. if the litigant had claimed the entire cloak, we would have awarded him half. Conceding one half of it to the other litigant is thus tantamount to returning a lost object (*Rashi*). The Mishnah (*Gittin* 48b) states that one who returns a lost object need not take an oath if the loser claims that only part of the lost object was returned. A Baraisa (ibid. 51b) extends this rule to any case where a defendant concedes what is, in effect, lost property. E.g. if Reuven approaches Shimon and tells him: I owed your father a *maneh,* but I repaid half of it, his obligation to take an oath is waived.

32. It is unclear how Rami bar Chama proves his rule (i.e. that one can acquire a lost object on behalf of his fellow) from this clause, for it discusses a case in which the litigants neither lifted the found animal nor claimed to have done so. *Ritva* explains the proof as follows. Since the clause is superfluous, this indicates that we divide something whose ownership is disputed only if both litigants might actually have acquired it (see above, note 25). (In our case, this is indeed possible if the two leaped upon the animal simultaneously.) Now the Mishnah's first clause states that a cloak whose ownership is disputed is divided between the litigants. Given the above, this implies that the litigants could have acquired it simultaneously. This proves that one can lift a lost object on behalf of his fellow (see note 5).

**דחזיא** לקטנים והא דאמר רבא [א] אם היתה טלית מוזהבת חולקין ה"נ דפלגי לה הא אפסדוה הא לא קשיא דחזיא לבני מלכים והא דתנן [ב] היו שנים רוכבין על גבי בהמה וכו' הכי נמי דפלגי לה הא אפסדוה בשלמא טהורה חזיא לבשר אלא טמאה הא אפסדוה [א] אלא לדמי הכא נמי לדמי אמר רמי בר חמא זאת אומרת [ג] [ב] המגביה מציאה לחבירו קנה חבירו דאי סלקא דעתך לא קנה חבירו תיעשה זו כמי שמונחת על גבי קרקע וזו כמי שמונחת על גבי קרקע ולא יקנה לא זה ולא זה אלא לאו ש"מ המגביה מציאה לחבירו קנה חבירו [ד] אמר רבא לעולם אימא לך המגביה מציאה לחבירו לא קנה חבירו והכא היינו טעמא [ד] מגו דזכי לנפשיה זכי נמי לחבריה תדע שאילו אמר לשלוחו צא וגנוב לי וגנב פטור [ה] [ג] ושותפין שגנבו חייבין מאי טעמא לאו משום דאמרינן מגו דזכי לנפשיה זכי נמי לחבריה ש"מ אמר רבא השתא דאמרת [א] אמרינן מגו חרש ופקח שהגביהו מציאה מתוך שקנה חרש קנה פקח בשלמא חרש קנה דקא מגבה ליה בן דעת אלא פקח במאי קנה אלא אימא חרש קנה פקח לא קנה ומאי מגו מגו דשני חרשין בעלמא קנו האי נמי קני [ו] האי מאי אם תמצא לומר המגביה מציאה לחבירו קנה חבירו הני מילי היכא דקא מגבה ליה אדעתא דחבריה האי אדעתא דידיה קא מגבה ליה איהו לא קני לאחריני מקני אלא אימא [ד] מתוך שלא קנה פקח לא קנה חרש וכי תימא מאי שנא משני חרשין דעלמא התם [ה] תקינו להו רבנן דלא [ז] אתי לאנצויי הכא מימר אמר פקח לא קני אנא אקני אמר ליה רב אחא בריה דרב אדא לרב אשי דיוקיה דרמי בר חמא מהיכא אי נימא מרישא שנים אוחזין בטלית התם האי קאמר כולה שלי ואנא אגבהתה כולה והאי אמר כולה שלי ואנא אגבהתה כולה אלא מהא דקתני זה אומר כולה שלי וזה אומר כולה שלי הא תו למה לי אלא ממשנה יתירה שמע מינה המגביה מציאה לחבירו קנה חבירו והא אוקימנא [ח] רישא במציאה וסיפא במקח וממכר אלא מסיפא זה אומר כולה שלי וזה אומר חציה שלי הא תו למה לי אלא ממשנה יתירה שמע מינה המגביה מציאה לחבירו קנה חבירו ומאי דבמציאה דלמא במקח וממכר וכי תימא אי במקח וממכר מאי למימרא איצטריך סלקא דעתך אמינא האי דקאמר חציה שלי להוי כמשיב אבידה וליפטר קמשמע לן דהאי [ט] איערומי קא מערים סבר אי אמינא כולה שלי בעינא אשתבועי אימא הכי דאהוי כמשיב אבידה ואיפטר אלא מהא היו שנים רוכבין על גבי בהמה הא תו למה לי אלא ממשנה יתירה שמע מינה המגביה מציאה לחבירו קנה חבירו ודלמא הא קמשמע לן דרוכב נמי קני אלא מסיפא בזמן שהן מודין או שיש להן עדים חולקין בלא שבועה במאי אי במקח וממכר צריכא למימר אלא לאו במציאה ושמע מינה המגביה מציאה לחבירו קנה חבירו ורבא אמר לך מגו דזכי לנפשיה זכי נמי לחבריה: היו שנים רוכבין: אמר רב יוסף אמר לי רב יהודה

שמעית

**רש"י**

דחזיא לבני מלכים. לבנים קטנים: זאת אומרת. מתני' דקתני שנים שהגביהו מציאה קנאוה ויחלוקו וכשמגביה מגביה לדעת שיקנה בה חבירו עמיה ש"מ המגביה מציאה כו' ולקמיה פריך דיוקא דרמי בר חמא מהיכא מאיזו בבא ממשנתנו הוא למד כן: ולא יקנה לא זה ולא זה. וכל הרוצה יחטפנה מידם: לעולם אימא לך לא קנה חבירו. היכא דמגביה לא נתכוין לקנות בה כלום וטעמא אמר לקמן (דף י.) דהוי תופס לבעל חוב במקום כו': והכא. דקתני במתני' שנים שהגביהו מציאה קנו מגו דזכי לנפשיה זכי נמי לחבריה: תדע. דאפי' אמר לא קנה חבירו היכא דהגביה כולה לדעת חבירו הכא דהגביה לעצמו ולחבירו קני משום מגו: פטור. המשלח פטור מלשלם כפל דקי"ל אין שליח לדבר עבירה להתחייב שולחו אלא שליח לדברי הרב ודברי התלמיד דברי מי שומעין ואילו שותפין שגנבו. והאחד הוציאה מרשות בעלים לדעתו ולדעת חבירו אמרינן בבבא קמא (דף עח:) דחייבין: השתא דאמרת מגו. דזכי לנפשיה כו' חרש ופקח שהגביהו מציאה קנאוה אע"פ שהגבהה של חרש אינה הגבהה לקנות אלא מפני דרכי שלום כדתנן (גיטין דף נט:) חרש שוטה וקטן יש בהן גזל מפני דרכי שלום אפילו הכי אמר מגו דזכי לנפשיה כו': בשלמא חרש קני דקא מגבה לה בן דעת. לראשה השני לצורך שניהם וראשו של צד חרש לגבי חרש מיהא הויא הגבהה כדתקון ליה מפני דרכי שלום אלא פקח במאי קני לגבי פקח הוי ראשה שהגביה החרש כמונח על גבי קרקע דהגבהה דחרש לא קניא אלא מדרכי שלום בעלמא: ומאי מגו. איכא למימר הכא דקאמר השתא דאמרת מגו אמרינן מגו וחרש אמאי קני הא לא זכי פקח לנפשיה דנימא דזכי נמי לחבריה ולא הויא הגבהה דפקח הגבהה: אם תמצא לומר. כלומר אפי' אם תמצא לומר המגביה מציאה לחבירו כו': הכא אדעתא דידיה קא מגבה ליה. האי פיקח: דלא ליתי לאינצויי. עם החוטפים מהם: מהיכא. מאיזו בבא ממשנתנו קא דייק לומר זאת אומרת: הא קאמר כולה שלי ואנא אגבהתיה. והיאך נאמר לא יקנה לא זה ולא זה ויבא אחר ויטלנה והלא כל אחד טוען אני הגבהתיה ואין כאן מגביה מציאה לחבירו ומה יש לו להשיב בשלמא האי שכנגדו המוחזק בה כמוהו אמר לא הגבהת אתה כי אם אני אבל אחר מן השוק מה יטעון: ממשנה יתירה. אמרינן דהמגביה מציאה כו' ומשום הכי אמרינן יחלוקו דאמרינן שניהם הגביהוה והוה ליה כל אחד מגביה מציאה לו ולחבירו וקני דאי משום דלא ידעינן הי מינייהו משקר והוה ליה ממון המוטל בספק וחולקין בשבועה משום שלא יהא כל אחד ואחד הולך ותוקף כדאמרי' לעיל (דף ג.) הא שמענא ליה מרישא: דאהוי כמשיב אבידה. מדהוה מצי למימר כולה שלי ואמר חציה שלי: וליפטר. משבועה: ממשנה יתירה כו'. כדפרישית: דרוכב קני. ואע"ג דלא משיכה היא שאינה זזה ממקומה שאין מנהיגה ברגליו: צריכא למימר. דהיכא דלקוחה בין שניהם שיחלקוה בלא שבועה: אלא לאו במציאה. ואיצטריך לאשמועינן שאין אחר יכול לחוטפה דמגביה מציאה לחבירו קנה חבירו: ורבא אמר לך. בעלמא היכא דלא נתכוין המגביה לזכות בה לא קנה חבירו ומשנה יתירה דמתני' אשמועינן המגביה מציאה לו ולחבירו קנה אף חבירו דמגו דזכי לנפשיה זכי נמי לחבריה:

שמעית

**תוספות**

**דחזיא** לקטנים. ופריך דטלית מוזהבת לא עבדי לקטנים ול"ג דחזיא לתרוייהו דא"כ מאי פריך מטלית מוזהבת:

**ושותפין** שגנבו. פי' בקונטרס שהוציא לדעתו ולדעת חבירו כדאיתא בב"ק (דף עח:) ואין נראה דהתם בטביחה איירי וטביחה אפי' אמר לא וטבח לי חייב דדרשינן (שם דף עא.) תחת לרבות השליח אלא שותפין שגנבו שהגביהו שניהם:

**ומאי** מגו מגו דשני חרשין. תימה מנלן דלמא תרי מגו לא אמרי' דב' חרשין דקנו היינו מטעם מגו דזכי לנפשיה זכי נמי לחבריה:

**אלא** מסיפא זה אומר כולה שלי וזה אומר חציה שלי. אית דל"ג הכא הא תו למה לי דממשנה גופה קא דייק דקאמר חציה שלי והיינו שהגביה עם חבירו ולפי דבריו לא יטול כלום אלא ודאי מגביה מציאה לחבירו זכה ופריך ממאי דבמציאה דלמא במקח וממכר והוא הדין דהוה מצי למדחי דהא דאמר חציה שלי כגון דאמר תפסתיה חציה בידי או הגבהתיה כולה לקנות חציה אבל עדיין היה מדקדק מיתורא דמתני' לכך דחי ליה דאפי' מיתורא אינו יכול לדקדק ולספרים דגרסי הא תו למה לי י"ל דמשום דמגופא דמתני' לא מצי למידק כדפרישית אך קשה אמאי קאמר דלמא במקח וממכר אפילו מיירי במציאה מצי לדחויי כדדחי וי"ל בדוחק ממאי דבמציאה דלהכי לא מוקמת במקח וממכר משום דלא משכחת חידוש אלא במגביה מציאה לחבירו כי נמי איירי במקח וממכר יש חידוש דלא נימא משיב אבידה הוא וה"ה אם מיירי במציאה לא יוכל להוכיח כלום:

מנהיג

**עין משפט נר מצוה**

נג א מיי' פ"ט מהלכות טוען ונטען הל' י סמג עשין לה טוש"ע ח"מ סי' קלח סעיף ד:

נד ב מיי' פי"ז מהלכות אבידה הל' ג סמג עשין עד טוש"ע ח"מ סי' רסט סעיף א:

נה ג מיי' פ"ב מהל' גניבה הל' יד סמג עשין עא טוח"מ סי' שנ:

נו ד ה מיי' פי"ז מהל' גזילה ואבידה הל' ד סמג עשין עד טוש"ע ח"מ סי' רסט סעיף ד:

**רבינו חננאל**

כיון שהעמיד רב פפא משנתנו דקתני יחלוקו בתפסי לה בכרכשתא דקדק רמי בר חמא ואמר זאת אומרת המגביה מציאה לחבירו קנה חבירו. רבא אמר לעולם לא קנה ומתני' היינו טעמא מגו דזכי לנפשיה זכי נמי לחבריה. תדע דאילו האומר לחבירו צא וגנוב לי פטור המשלח דקי"ל אין שליח לדבר עבירה ואילו שותפין שגנבו חייבין ושקלי' וטרי' בה ואסיקנא דוקיא דרמי בר חמא מסיפא דמתני' בזמן שהן מודין או שיש להן עדים כי שניהם ביחד מצאוה ושניהן אגב' אגבהוה בכרכשתא חולקין בלא שבועה ש"מ המגביה מציאה לחבירו קנה חבירו דהא תרוייהו מסייעי להדדי בעידנא דמגבהי לה. ורבא אמר לך שאני הכא מגו דזכי לנפשיה זכי נמי לחבריה. וקי"ל כרמי בר חמא והוא דאמר ליה זכי לי דהא ר' יוחנן קאי כוותיה ואמר המגביה מציאה לחבירו קנה חבירו ואם יקשה לך הא דתנן היה רוכב על גבי בהמה וכו' התם באומר תנה לי ולא אמר זכה לי. היו שניהם רוכבין על גבי בהמה וכו'.

**מסורת הש"ס**

[לעיל ז.], ג) [לעיל ב.], [לקמן י.], ד) [לקמן ...], נדרים פח:], ה) [שבת ...:, עיין שם, בבא קמא ...:], ו) [לקמן ט.], [נ"ל ליתי], ח) [לעיל ב.], ט) [לעיל ד:].

**הגהות הב"ח**

(א) גמ' השתא דאמרי דאמרי' מגו:

**גליון הש"ס**

גמ' אמר רבא לעולם. עיין לקמן דף י ע"א תוס' ד"ה איתיביה ובנדרים דף ... ע"ב בר"ן ד"ה אמר רבא:

**ליקוטי רש"י**

אם היתה טלית מוזהבת. כלומר אפילו טלית מוזהבת חולקים [לעיל ז.]. היו שנים רוכבין. לאשמועינן אתא רוכב ומנהיג שניהם שוין לקנות בהמה מן ההפקר [לעיל ב.]. מיגו דזכי לנפשיה וכו'. דאי בעי ... זכי לנפשיה אם הגביה לעצמו [לקמן ט:]. וסיפא במקח וממכר. ... ימיה מיד פלוני וכו' [לעיל ב.]. איערומי קא מערים. דליחזקיה כנאמן [לעיל ד:].

since" principle that enables the deaf-mute to acquire?[19]

The Gemara answers:

מגו דשני חרשין בעלמא ק – "**Since" two deaf-mutes generally** acquire a found object if they lift it simultaneously, האי נמי קני – **this** deaf-mute **also acquires** a found object when he lifts it together with a competent person.[20]

The Gemara objects to this interpretation of Rava's statement:

האי מ – **What** kind of ruling **is this?** It is untenable! אם תמצא לומר המגביה מציאה לחבירו קנה חבי – Even **if you assume** that **when one lifts a found object** intending to acquire it entirely for **his fellow** and not for himself, **his fellow does acquire** it, הני מי – still **this is** so only היכא דקא מגבה ליה אדעתא דחבריה **where he lifted [the object] with the intent that his fellow** acquire it; that is why the fellow acquires it. האי אדעתא דידיה קא מגבה לי – But **this** competent person **lifted [the object]** primarily **with the intent that he himself** acquire it. איהו לא קני – **He** himself **does not acquire** a portion of it, לאחריני מקני – **does he** intend to **acquire** it **for others?** Of course not! Accordingly, since the competent person never intended to acquire for the deaf-mute, the latter should not acquire.[21] – ? –

Having rejected the previous emendation of Rava's statement, the Gemara suggests another:

אלא אימ – **Rather, say:** מתוך שלא קנה פקח – **Because the competent person did not acquire** the object, לא קנה חרש – **the deaf-mute did not acquire** it either.[22]

The Gemara questions this emendation:

וכי תימ – **And if you ask:** מאי שנא משני חרשין דעלמא – **Why is this different than two deaf-mutes in general,** who acquire a found object if they lift it simultaneously?[23]

The Gemara answers:

התם – **There,** in the case of the two deaf-mutes, תקינו להו רבנן – **the Rabbis enacted** a special provision **for [deaf-mutes]** enabling them to acquire under Rabbinic law דלא אתי לאנצוויי – so **that [deaf people] should not come to quarrel** when told that their acquisitions are meaningless.[24] הכא – **Here** in Rava's case, however, the deaf-mute will not quarrel if his acquisition is taken from him, because מימר אמר – **he will reason,** פקח לא קני – **"The competent person did not acquire** a share in the object; אנא אקני – **I should acquire?"** Seeing no reason to enact a special provision, the Sages did not do so. Since the deaf-mute is thus subject to Biblical law, he cannot acquire.

Earlier, Rami bar Chamah inferred from our Mishnah that if someone lifted an object, intending to acquire it entirely for his fellow, the fellow acquires it. The Gemara now asks:

אמר ליה רב אחא בריה דרב אדא לרב אשי – **Rav Acha son of Rav Adda asked Rav Ashi:** דיוקיה דרמי בר חמא מהיכא – **The inference of Rami bar Chama – from where** in our Mishnah is it derived? אי נימא מרישא – **If you say** that it is derived **from the initial clause** of the Mishnah, viz. שנים אוחזין בטלית – if TWO litigants come before the court HOLDING ON TO A CLOAK and each claims, "I have found it"... they must divide it, that is impossible! That clause does not support Rami bar Chamah's inference at all! התם האי קאמר – **There, this** litigant means to **claim,** כולה שלי – **"It is all mine,** ואנא אגבהתה כולה – **and I lifted the *entire*** [**object**] for myself." והאי אמר – **And that** litigant means to **claim,** כולה שלי – **"It is all mine,** ואנא אגבהתה כולה – **and I lifted the *entire*** [**object**] for myself"; neither claims to have lifted the object for the other. How, then, does Rami bar Chamah infer his ruling from this section of the Mishnah?[25]

NOTES

19. According to the Gemara's emendation, Rava's statement reads as follows: Now that we have established the principle of "since," we may state that if a deaf-mute and competent person lift an object simultaneously, the deaf-mute acquires but the competent person does not. How, though, does Rava's ruling follow from having established the "since" principle? "Since" would allow the competent person to acquire for the deaf-mute as long as he acquires for himself as well. According to Rava, though, he never does acquire for himself; his act on behalf of the deaf-mute should thus also be void (*Rashi*).

20. True, the competent person does not acquire for himself, but this is only because the deaf-mute lacks the capacity to acquire for him (see note 18). This would change if the competent person was a deaf-mute himself. In such a case, the other deaf-mute would have the capacity to acquire for him, because Rabbinic law recognizes a deaf-mute's acquisition for other deaf-mutes.

Given this, the Gemara apparently employs two applications of the "since" principle to explain how the deaf-mute acquires. First, "since" if the competent person had been a deaf-mute he could have acquired, we regard him as having acquired for the purpose of acquiring for others. Second, "since" the competent person is regarded as having acquired for himself, he can acquire for his fellow (i.e. the deaf-mute) as well (see *Tosafos,* cf. *Ritva*).

21. The principle of "since" cannot be applied to a case where the competent person has no intent to acquire for the deaf-mute. This principle can only remove the legal impediments that render a *kinyan* invalid. It cannot however supply intent – an essential requirement for the effectiveness of a *kinyan*. I.e. it cannot be said that "since" one would have intended to acquire for one's fellow in one situation, therefore his *kinyan* is also valid for his fellow even when he does not intend to acquire for him.

22. In conclusion, Rava's statement is to be construed as follows: We have established that a competent person can acquire for another only while acquiring for himself as well; i.e. in order for him to acquire, an application of the "since" principle is necessary. Accordingly, if a deaf-mute and a competent person lifted a lost object simultaneously, neither acquires it because the "since" principle does not apply. I.e. since the competent person cannot acquire and the "since" principle cannot be applied, therefore the deaf-mute can also not acquire (*Ritva*; see also *Maharsha* in *Mahadura Basra,* cf. *Maharsha, Shitah Mekubetzes*).

23. Actually, this question is difficult to understand; the Gemara has just explained the difference between this case and that of two deaf-mutes. In the case of two deaf-mutes, if each intends to acquire not only for himself but for the other as well, they both acquire half; each therefore lifts it for the other as well as for himself. In Rava's case, however, where the competent person cannot acquire for himself, he certainly does not intend to acquire for the other. *Ritva* therefore explains the Gemara's question as follows: Under Biblical law, a deaf-mute's *kinyan* is invalid. Thus, if two deaf-mutes lift an object simultaneously, they acquire only by dint of a Rabbinic decree in the interest of peace (see note 16). Why did the Sages not decree, then, that a deaf-mute can also acquire together with a competent person, in the interest of peace? (*Ritva;* cf. *Maharsha, Shitah Mekubetzes*).

24. If anyone took a lost object from the deaf-mutes' grasps, they would surely quarrel (*Rashi*).

25. Rami bar Chama argued that if two people lift a found object simultaneously, they acquire it only if we assume that a person has the legal capacity to acquire for his fellow; only then do we say that if each lifted the object for himself and for his fellow they both acquire (see notes 5 and 6). If this were not the case, though, the object would remain ownerless, allowing anyone to seize it and thus acquire it. Hence, our Mishnah's ruling (that the two split the object in such a case) implies that a person can acquire for his fellow.

The Gemara now ponders which of our Mishnah's rulings implies this. It certainly cannot be the Mishnah's first ruling, asserts the Gemara, because that ruling discusses a case in which nobody even claimed to have lifted the object for his fellow. On the contrary, in that ruling, each litigant claimed the entire object. Accordingly, the object is divided not because they both acquired it, but rather because we cannot determine who acquired it first. This clause, then, has no relevance to Rami bar Chama's teaching (*Rashi*).

דחזיא לקטנים והא דאמר רבא [א] אם היתה טלית מוזהבת חולקין ה"נ דפלגי לה הא אפסדוה הא לא קשיא דחזיא לבני מלכים והא דתנן [ב] היו שנים רוכבין על גבי בהמה וכו' הכי נמי דפלגי לה הא אפסדוה בשלמא טהורה חזיא לבשר אלא טמאה הא אפסדוה [א] אלא לדמי הכא נמי לדמי אמר רמי בר חמא זאת אומרת [ג] [ב] המגביה מציאה לחבירו קנה חבירו דאי סלקא דעתך לא קנה חבירו תיעשה זו כמי שמונחת על גבי קרקע וזו כמי שמונחת על גבי קרקע ולא יקנה לא זה ולא זה אלא לאו ש"מ המגביה מציאה לחבירו קנה חבירו [ה] אמר רבא לעולם אימא לך המגביה מציאה לחבירו לא קנה חבירו והכא היינו טעמא [ד] מגו דזכי לנפשיה זכי נמי לחבריה תדע שאילו אמר לשלוחו צא וגנוב לי וגנב פטור [ה] [ג] ושותפין שגנבו חייבין מאי טעמא לאו משום דאמרינן מגו דזכי לנפשיה זכי נמי לחבריה ש"מ אמר רבא השתא דאמרת (א) אמרינן מגו חרש ופקח שהגביהו מציאה מתוך שקנה חרש קנה פקח בשלמא חרש קנה דקא מגבה ליה בן דעת אלא פקח במאי קנה אלא אימא חרש קנה פקח לא קנה ומאי מגו מגו דשני חרשין בעלמא קנו האי נמי קני [ו] האי מאי אם תמצא לומר המגביה מציאה לחבירו קנה חבירו הני מילי היכא דקא מגבה ליה אדעתא דחבריה האי אדעתא דידיה קא מגבה ליה איהו לא קני לאחריני מקני אלא אימא [ד] מתוך שלא קנה פקח לא קנה חרש וכי תימא מאי שנא משני חרשין דעלמא התם [ה] תקינו להו רבנן דלא [ז] אתי לאנצויי הכא מימר אמר פקח לא קני אנא אקני אמר ליה רב אחא בריה דרב אדא לרב אשי דיוקיה דרמי בר חמא מהיכא אי נימא מרישא שנים אוחזין בטלית התם האי קאמר כולה שלי ואנא אגבהתה כולה והאי אמר כולה שלי ואנא אגבהתה כולה אלא מהא דקתני זה אומר כולה שלי וזה אומר כולה שלי הא תו למה לי אלא ממשנה יתירה שמע מינה המגביה מציאה לחבירו קנה חבירו והא אוקימנא [ח] רישא במציאה וסיפא במקח וממכר אלא מסיפא זה אומר כולה שלי וזה אומר חציה שלי הא תו למה לי אלא ממשנה יתירה שמע מינה המגביה מציאה לחבירו קנה חבירו וממאי דבמציאה דלמא במקח וממכר וכי תימא אי במקח וממכר מאי למימרא איצטריך סלקא דעתך אמינא האי דקאמר חציה שלי להוי כמשיב אבידה וליפטר קמשמע לן דהאי [ט] איערומי קא מערים סבר אי אמינא כולה שלי בעינא אשתבועי אימא הכי דאהוי כמשיב אבידה ואיפטר אלא מהא היו שנים רוכבין על גבי בהמה הא תו למה לי אלא ממשנה יתירה שמע מינה המגביה מציאה לחבירו קנה חבירו ודלמא הא קמשמע לן דרוכב נמי קני אלא מסיפא בזמן שהן מודין או שיש להן עדים חולקין בלא שבועה במאי אי במקח וממכר צריכא למימר אלא לאו במציאה ושמע מינה המגביה מציאה לחבירו קנה חבירו ורבא אמר לך מגו דזכי לנפשיה זכי נמי לחבריה: היו שנים רוכבין: אמר רב יוסף אמר לי רב יהודה

שמעית

**רש"י**

דחזיא לבני מלכים. לבנים קטנים: זאת אומרת. מתני' דקתני שנים שהגביהו מציאה קנאוה ויחלוקו וכשמגביה מגביה לדעת שיקנה בה חבירו חציה ש"מ המגביה מציאה כו' ולקמיה פריך דיוקא דרמי בר חמא מהיכא מאיזו בבא ממשנתנו הוא למד כן: ולא יקנה לא זה ולא זה. וכל הרוצה יחטפנה מידם: לעולם אימא לך לא קנה חבירו. היכא דמגביה לא נתכוין לקנות בה כלום וטעמא אמר לקמן (דף י.) דהוי תופס לבעל חוב במקום כו': והכא. דקתני במתני' שנים שהגביהו מציאה קנו מגו דזכי לנפשיה זכי נמי לחבריה: תדע. דלפי' אמר לא קנה חבירו היכא דהגביה כולה לדעת חבירו הכא דהגביה לעצמו ולחבירו קני משום מגו: פטור. המשלח פטור מלשלם כפל דקי"ל אין שליח לדבר עבירה להתחייב שולחו אלא שליח דדברי הרב ודברי התלמיד דברי מי שומעין ואילו שותפין שגנבו. והאחד הוציאה מרשות בעלים לדעתו ולדעת חבירו אמרינן בבבא קמא (דף עח:) דחייבין: השתא דאמרת מגו. דזכי לנפשיה כו' חרש ופקח שהגביהו מציאה קנאוה אע"פ שהגבהה של חרש אינה הגבהה לקנות אלא מפני דרכי שלום כדתנן (גיטין דף נט:) חרש שוטה וקטן יש בהן גזל מפני דרכי שלום אפילו הכי אמר מגו דזכי לנפשיה כו': בשלמא חרש קני דקא מגבה לה בן דעת. לראשה השני לאורך שניהם וראשו של זה חרש לגבי חרש מיהא הויא הגבהה כדתקון ליה מפני דרכי שלום אלא פקח במאי קני לגבי פקח הוי ראשה שהגביה החרש כמונח על גבי קרקע דהגבהה דחרש לא קניא אלא מדרכי שלום בעלמא: ומאי מגו. איכא למימר הכא דקאמר השתא דאמרת מגו אמרינן מגו וחרש אמאי קני הא לא זכי פקח לנפשיה דנימא דזכי נמי לחבריה ולא הויא הגבהה דפקח הגבהה: אם תמצא לומר. כלומר אפי' אם תמצא לומר המגביה מציאה לחבירו כו': הכא אדעתא דידיה קא מגבה ליה. האי פיקח: דלא ליתי לאינצויי. עם החוטפים מהם: מהיכא. מאיזו בבא ממשנתנו קא דייק לומר זאת אומרת: הא קאמר כולה שלי ואנא אגבהתיה. והיאך נאמר לא יקנה לא זה ולא זה ויבא אחר ויטלנה והלא כל אחד טוען אני הגבהתיה ואין כאן מגביה מציאה לחבירו ומה יש לו להשיב בשלמא האי שכנגדו המוחזק בה כמוהו אמר לא הגבהת אתה כי אם אני אבל אחר מן השוק מה יטעון: ממשנה יתירה. אמרינן דהמגביה מציאה כו' ומשום הכי אמרינן יחלוקו דאמרינן שניהם הגביהוה והוה ליה כל אחד מגביה מציאה לו ולחבירו וקני דאי משום דלא ידעינן הי מינייהו משקר והוה ליה ממון המוטל בספק וחולקין בשבועה משום שלא יהא כל אחד ואחד הולך ותוקף כדאמרי' לעיל (דף ג.) הא שמעתא ליה מרישא: דאהוי כמשיב אבידה. מדהוה מצי למימר כולה שלי ואמר חציה שלי: וליפטר. משבועה: ממשנה יתירה כו'. כדפרישית: דרכוב קני. ואע"ג דלא משיכה היא שאינה זזה ממקומה שאין מנהיגה ברגליו: צריכא למימר. דהיכא דלקוחה בין שניהם שיחלקוה בלא שבועה: אלא לאו במציאה. ואיצטריך לאשמועינן שאין אחר יכול לחוטפה דמגביה מציאה לחבירו קנה חבירו: ורבא אמר לך. בעלמא היכא דלא נתכוון המגביה לזכות בה לא קנה חבירו ומשנה יתירה דמתני' אשמועינן המגביה מציאה לו ולחבירו קנה אף חבירו דמגו דזכי לנפשיה זכי נמי לחבריה:

שמעית

**תוספות**

דחזיא לקטנים. ופריך דטלית מוזהבת לא עבדי לקטנים ול"ג דחזיא לתרוייהו דא"כ מאי פריך מטלית מוזהבת:

ושותפין שגנבו. פי' בקונטרס שהוציא לדעתו ולדעת חבירו כדאיתא בב"ק (דף עח:) ואין נראה דהתם בטביחה איירי וטביחה אפי' אמר לא וטבח לי חייב דדרשינן (שם דף עא.) תחת לרבות השליח אלא שותפין שגנבו שהגביהו שניהם:

ומאי מגו מגו דשני חרשין. תימה מנלן דלמא תרי מגו לא אמרי' דב' חרשין דקנו היינו מטעם מגו דזכי לנפשיה זכי נמי לחבריה:

אלא מסיפא זה אומר כולה שלי וזה אומר חציה שלי. לית דל"ג הכא הא תו למה לי דממשנה גופה קא דייק דקאמר חציה שלי והיינו שהגביה עם חבירו ולפי דבריו לא יטול כלום אלא ודאי מגביה מציאה לחבירו זכה ופריך ממאי דבמציאה דלמא במקח וממכר והוא הדין דהוה מצי למדחי דהא דאמר חציה שלי כגון דאמר תפסתיה חציה בידי או הגבהתיה כולה לקנות חציה אבל עדיין היה מדקדק מיתורא דמתני' לכך דחי ליה דלפי' מיתורא אינו יכול לדקדק ולספרים דגרסי הא תו למה לי י"ל דמשום דמגופא דמתני' לא מצי למידק כדפרישית אך קשה אמאי קאמר דלמא במקח וממכר אפילו מיירי במציאה מצי לדחויי כדדחי וי"ל בדוחק ממאי דבמציאה דלהכי לא מוקמת במקח וממכר משום דלא משכחת חידוש אלא במגביה מציאה לחבירו כי נמי איירי במקח וממכר יש חידוש דלא נימא משיב אבידה הוא וה"ה אם מיירי במציאה לא יוכל להוכיח כלום:

מנהיג

מסורת הש"ס

א) [לעיל ז.], ב) [לעיל ב.], ג) [לקמן י.], ד) [לקמן ... נדרים פח:], ה) [שבת ... עיין שם, בבא קמא ...], ו) [לקמן ט.], ... נ"ל ליתי], ח) [לעיל ב.], ט) [לעיל ד:].

**הגהות הב"ח**

(א) גמ' השתא דאמרי דאמרי' מגו:

**גליון הש"ס**

... אמר רבא לעולם. ... לקמן דף י ע"א תוס' ... איתיביה ובנדרים דף ... ע"ב בר"ן ד"ה אמר רבא:

**ליקוטי רש"י**

... היתה טלית ... זהבת. כלומר אפילו ... מוזהבת חולקים ... [לעיל ז.]. היו שנים ... רוכבין. לאשמועינן אתא ... וכב ומנהיג שניהם שוין ... ות בהמה מן ההפקר ... [לעיל ב.]. מיגו דזכי ... לנפשיה וכו'. דאי בעי ... זכי לנפשיה אם ... כיה לעצמו [לקמן ט:]. ... סיפא במקח וממכר. ... ימיה מיד פלוני וכו' ... [לעיל ב.]. איערומי קא ... מערים. דליחזקיה בנאמן [לעיל ד:].

**עין משפט נר מצוה**

נג א מיי' פ"ט מהלכות טוען ונטען הל' י סמג עשין צה טוש"ע ח"מ סי' קלח סעיף ד:

נד ב מיי' פי"ז מהלכות אבידה הל' ג סמג עשין עד טוש"ע ח"מ סי' רסט סעיף א:

נה ג מיי' פ"ב מהל' גניבה הל' יד סמג עשין עא טוח"מ סי' שנ:

נו ד ה מיי' פי"ז מהל' גזילה ואבידה הל' ד סמג עשין עד טוש"ע ח"מ סי' רסט סעיף ד:

**רבינו חננאל**

כיון שהעמיד רב פפא משנתנו דקתני יחלוקו בתפסי לה בכרכשתא דקדק רמי בר חמא ואמר זאת אומרת המגביה מציאה לחבירו קנה חבירו. רבא אמר לעולם לא קנה ומתני' היינו טעמא מגו דזכי לנפשיה זכי נמי לחבריה. תדע דאילו האומר לחבירו צא וגנוב לי פטור המשלח דקי"ל אין שליח לדבר עבירה ואילו שותפין שגנבו חייבין ושקלי' וטרי' בה ואסיקנא דוקיא דרמי בר חמא מסיפא דמתני' בזמן שהן מודין או שיש להן עדים כי שניהם ביחד מצאוה ושניהן אגב' אגבהוה בכרכשתא חולקין בלא שבועה ש"מ המגביה מציאה לחבירו קנה חבירו דהא תרוייהו מסייעי להדדי בעידנא דמגבהי לה. ורבא אמר לך שאני הכא מגו דזכי לנפשיה זכי נמי לחבריה. וקי"ל כרמי בר חמא והוא דאמר ליה זכי לי דהא ר' יוחנן קאי כוותיה ואמר המגביה מציאה לחבירו קנה חבירו ואם יקשה לך הא דתנן היה רוכב על גבי בהמה וכו' התם באומר תנה לי ולא אמר זכה לי. היו שניהם רוכבין על גבי בהמה וכו'.

Iishnah's case,[8] **the reason** that each acquires half the object **is** he following principle: מִגּוֹ דְּזָכֵי לְנַפְשֵׁיהּ – **"Since" [the person** ifting the object] **acquires for himself,** זָכֵי נַמִּי לְחַבְרֵיהּ – **he** icquires for his fellow as well.[9]

Rava presents a logical argument to prove that "since" is a alid legal principle:

תֵּדַע – **Know** that this is so, שֶׁאִילּוּ אָמַר לִשְׁלוּחוֹ – **For if one** aid to his agent, צֵא וּגְנוֹב לִי – **"Go out and steal** something n my behalf," וְגָנַב – **and** the agent **stole** it, פָּטוּר – **then** the sender] is not liable for the agent's theft.[10] וְשׁוּתָּפִין שֶׁגָּנְבוּ – **But if** one of two **partners stole,** חַיָּיבִין – **they are** both iable.[11]

Rava concludes his argument:

מַאי טַעְמָא – **What is the reason** that the principal is exempt in he former case, yet both partners are liable in the latter case?[12] לָאו מִשּׁוּם דְּאָמְרִינַן – **Is it not because** in the latter case, **we apply** he "since" principle: מִגּוֹ דְּזָכֵי לְנַפְשֵׁיהּ – **"Since" [one partner] acquires** the stolen object **for himself,**[13] זָכֵי נַמִּי לְחַבְרֵיהּ – **e acquires** it **for his fellow as well.** שְׁמַע מִינָּהּ – Indeed, **earn from this** that "since" is a valid legal principle. This, then, efutes Rami bar Chama's deduction.[14]

Rava applies the "since" principle to another case:

אָמַר רָבָא – **Rava said:** הַשְׁתָּא דְּאָמְרַתְּ אָמְרִינַן מִגּוֹ – **Now that it has been established that we apply** the **"since"** principle, we may state the following: חֵרֵשׁ וּפִקֵּחַ שֶׁהִגְבִּיהוּ מְצִיאָה – **If a deaf-mute**[15] **and a competent person lifted a found object** simultaneously, each intending to acquire half of it, מִתּוֹךְ שֶׁקָּנָה חֵרֵשׁ – then **"since" the deaf-mute acquires** a portion of the object, קָנָה פִּקֵּחַ – **the competent person acquires** a portion as well.[16]

The Gemara challenges Rava's application of the "since" principle to this case:

בִּשְׁלָמָא חֵרֵשׁ קָנָה – **It is understandable** that **the deaf-mute acquires,** דְּקָא מַגְבַּהּ לֵיהּ בֶּן דַּעַת – **for** the **competent person lifted** it intending to acquire it **for him.**[17] אֶלָּא פִּקֵּחַ בְּמַאי קָנָה – **But the competent person – how can he acquire?** Surely the deaf-mute cannot acquire the object for the competent one![18]

To deflect the challenge, the Gemara emends Rava's statement:

אֶלָּא אֵימָא – **Rather, say:** חֵרֵשׁ קָנָה – **The deaf-mute acquires** פִּקֵּחַ לֹא קָנָה – but **the competent person does not acquire.**

The Gemara attempts to refute the emendation:

וּמַאי מִגּוֹ – **Now** if this was indeed Rava's ruling, **what** is the

NOTES

. I.e. where two people lifted an object simultaneously, and each one's ct of lifting it is effective not only for himself but for the other as ell.

. When two people perform a *kinyan hagbahah,* lifting an object ogether to acquire it, there are two aspects to each person's *kinyan:* the cquisition on the person's own behalf and that on behalf of his fellow. ow according to Rava, neither person has authority to perform a *inyan* on behalf of his fellow. Still, since one aspect of each person's act valid on its own merit (i.e. the acquisition on his own behalf), we onsider the entire act valid. According to Rava, then, although one erson cannot perform a *kinyan* just for his fellow, he can nevertheless erform a *kinyan* for his fellow and himself.

). I.e. the sender is exempt from paying *keifel,* the twofold payment a hief pays as punishment for his transgression. Instead, the agent imself must pay it. (If the stolen goods become damaged and cannot be eturned, there is some question as to the extent of the sender's xemption: Is he free from paying only the punitive *keifel* payment ut liable for the basic value of the goods or is he exempt from paying anything? See *Nesivos HaMishpat* 182:1 for a discussion of the atter.)

The reason for the sender's exemption is as follows. Torah law ecognizes *shelichus* (agency) – the concept that a principal is liable for ctions his agent performs in fulfillment of his charge. According to the emara in *Kiddushin* (42b), however, a principal is not liable if his gent sins, because the agent should have heeded the words of his aster [i.e. the Almighty] rather than the words of the disciple [i.e. the rincipal] (*Rashi*). Thus, if an agent steals for his principal, the latter is xempt from paying *keifel.*

. [If two people conspired to steal and then] one of them actually took he object from its owner's possession, intending to acquire it for imself and his partner, they are both liable. The source of this ruling a Baraisa cited in *Bava Kamma* (78b) (*Rashi*).

. The Gemara reasons as follows. It seems illogical to hold two artners (i.e. co-conspirators) responsible for a theft if only one actually ole; nevertheless, the Baraisa does just that. The Baraisa is underandable, however, if we assume that a principal is liable for his gent's theft. If this is the case, both partners are liable, because the hief also acted as his co-conspirator's agent. Having thus proven that a rincipal is liable for his agent's theft, the Gemara notes that this ontradicts the rule that one is not liable for his agent's theft.

. I.e. when he lifts the object, he steals it for himself.

. For in the Mishnah's case, each person intends to acquire the lost bject for himself and for his fellow simultaneously. Thus, since he cquires for himself, he acquires for his fellow as well. However, this oes not support Rami bar Chama's contention that one can acquire a st object just for his fellow.

. Literally, the term חֵרֵשׁ means *deaf* person (see *Chagigah* 2b). In the Mishnah and Talmud, however, it usually refers to a deaf-mute, whom halachah considers legally incompetent because of mental deficiency (see Mishnah, *Terumos* 1:2).

16. Under Biblical law, a deaf-mute's *kinyan* (act of acquisition) is invalid because halachah considers him mentally incompetent. [In practice, however, a deaf-mute would surely fight to retain his acquisitions.] Therefore, in the interest of peace, the Sages recognized a deaf-mute's acquisitions, declaring that taking something from a deaf-mute constitutes theft (Mishnah *Gittin* 59b). [Under Rabbinic law, then, a deaf-mute can acquire for himself but not for other competent people.]

Given this, if a competent person and a deaf-mute performed a *kinyan hagbahah* together, lifting an object simultaneously, the *kinyan* should be void for the following reason. Two people can acquire a lost object together only if each lifts it not only for himself but for the other as well (see note 5). In our case, then, since the deaf-mute cannot acquire for the competent person, the latter apparently would not acquire the object. Rava now argues, however, that the competent person does in fact acquire it through the principle of "since" (*Rashi*).

17. A *kinyan hagbahah* transfers ownership only if the *kinyan* was performed upon the whole of the object. Thus, if two people lift an object simultaneously, either one acquires ownership only if he performs a *kinyan* with intent to acquire it himself and the other does so with intent that both acquire it (see note 5). Now in Rava's case, the deaf-mute met both requirements: He performed a Rabbinic *kinyan* on his own behalf (see previous note) and the competent person performed a Biblically valid *kinyan* on behalf of both. It thus follows that the deaf-mute should "acquire" the object (*Rashi*).

[*Ritva* somewhat qualifies *Rashi's* interpretation. He notes that according to Rava, the competent person cannot perform a valid *kinyan* on behalf of the deaf-mute unless he himself actually acquires (see note 9). Now it seems illogical for the Gemara to argue that the deaf-mute's *kinyan* takes effect while maintaining that the competent person's does not. Accordingly, the Gemara cannot mean that the deaf-mute actually acquires; rather, it means that the competent person's *kinyan* is not an impediment to the deaf-mute's acquiring.]

18. As noted above, a *kinyan hagbahah* transfers ownership only if the *kinyan* was performed upon the whole of the object. Under Biblical law a deaf-mute's *kinyan* is invalid; he may keep his acquisitions only by Rabbinic decree in the interest of peace. [If he cannot perform a bona fide *kinyan* even on his own behalf, he certainly cannot perform one on behalf of the competent person (see note 9).] His *kinyan,* then, is totally meaningless as far as the competent person is concerned; it is as if one part of the object remained on the ground. Accordingly, the competent person should not acquire the lost object (*Rashi;* see above, note 5).

דחזיא לקטנים והא דאמר רבא (א) אם היתה טלית מוזהבת חולקין ה"נ דפלגי לה הא אפסדוה הא לא קשיא דחזיא לבני מלכים והא דתנן (ב) היו שנים רוכבין על גבי בהמה וכו' הכי נמי דפלגי לה הא אפסדוה בשלמא טהורה חזיא לבשר אלא טמאה הא אפסדוה [א]אלא לדמי הכא נמי לדמי אמר רמי בר חמא זאת אומרת (ג) [ב]המגביה מציאה לחבירו קנה חבירו דאי סלקא דעתך לא קנה חבירו תיעשה זו כמי שמונחת על גבי קרקע וזו כמי שמונחת על גבי קרקע ולא יקנה לא זה ולא זה אלא לאו ש"מ המגביה מציאה לחבירו קנה חבירו (ט) אמר רבא לעולם אימא לך המגביה מציאה לחבירו לא קנה חבירו והכא היינו טעמא (ד) מגו דזכי לנפשיה זכי נמי לחבריה תדע שאילו אמר לשלוחו צא וגנוב לי וגנב פטור (ה) [ג]ושותפין שגנבו חייבין מאי טעמא לאו משום דאמרינן מגו דזכי לנפשיה זכי נמי לחבריה ש"מ אמר רבא השתא דאמרת (א) אמרינן מגו חרש ופקח שהגביהו מציאה מתוך שקנה חרש קנה פקח בשלמא חרש קנה דקא מגבה ליה בן דעת אלא פקח במאי קנה אלא אימא חרש קנה פקח לא קנה ומאי מגו דשני חרשין בעלמא קנו האי נמי קני (י) האי מאי אם תמצא לומר המגביה מציאה לחבירו קנה חבירו הני מילי היכא דקא מגבה ליה אדעתא דחבריה האי אדעתא דידיה קא מגבה ליה איהו לא קני לאחריני מקני אלא אימא [ד]מתוך שלא קנה פקח לא קנה חרש וכי תימא מאי שנא משני חרשין דעלמא התם [ה]תקינו להו רבנן דלא (ז) אתי לאנצויי הכא מימר אמר פקח לא קני אנא אקני אמר ליה רב אחא בריה דרב אדא לרב אשי דיוקיה דרמי בר חמא מהיכא אי נימא מרישא שנים אוחזין בטלית התם האי קאמר כולה שלי ואנא אגבהתה כולה והאי אמר כולה שלי ואנא אגבהתה כולה אלא מהא דקתני זה אומר כולה שלי וזה אומר כולה שלי הא תו למה לי אלא ממשנה יתירה שמע מינה המגביה מציאה לחבירו קנה חבירו והא אוקימנא (ח) רישא במציאה וסיפא במקח וממכר אלא מסיפא זה אומר כולה שלי וזה אומר חציה שלי הא תו למה לי אלא ממשנה יתירה שמע מינה המגביה מציאה לחבירו קנה חבירו וממאי דבמציאה דלמא במקח וממכר וכי תימא אי במקח וממכר מאי למימרא איצטריך סלקא דעתך אמינא האי דקאמר חציה שלי להוי כמשיב אבידה וליפטר קמשמע לן דהאי (ט) איערומי קא מערים סבר אי אמינא כולה שלי בעינא אשתבועי אימא הכי דאהוי כמשיב אבידה ואיפטר אלא מהא היו שנים רוכבין על גבי בהמה הא תו למה לי אלא ממשנה יתירה שמע מינה המגביה מציאה לחבירו קנה חבירו ודלמא הא קמשמע לן דרוכב נמי קני אלא מסיפא בזמן שהן מודין או שיש להן עדים חולקין בלא שבועה במאי אי במקח וממכר צריכא למימר אלא לאו במציאה ושמע מינה המגביה מציאה לחבירו קנה חבירו ורבא אמר לך מגו דזכי לנפשיה זכי נמי לחבריה: היו שנים רוכבין: אמר רב יוסף אמר לי רב יהודה

שמעית

---

**רש"י**

דחזיא לבני מלכים. לבניס קטניס: זאת אומרת. מתני' דקתני שניס שהגביהו מליאה קנאוה ויחלוקו וכשמגביה מגביה לדעת שיקנה בה חבירו חליה ש"מ המגביה מליאה כו' ולקמיה פריך דיוקא דרמי בר חמא מהיכא מאיזו בבא ממשנתנו הוא למד כן: ולא יקנה לא זה ולא זה. וכל הרוצה יחטפנה מידס:

לעולם אימא לך לא קנה חבירו. היכא דמגביה לא נתכוין לקנות בה כלוס וטעמא אמר לקמן (דף י.) דהוי תופס לבעל חוב במקוס כו': והכא. דקתני במתני' שניס שהגביהו מליאה קנו מגו דזכי לנפשיה זכי נמי לחבריה: תדע. דאפי' אמר לא קנה חבירו היכא דהגביה כולה לדעת חבירו הכא דהגביה לעלמו ולחבירו קני משוס מגו: פטור. המשלח מלשלס כפל דקי"ל אין שליח לדבר עבירה להתחייב שולחו אלא שליח דדברי הרב ודברי התלמיד דברי מי שומעין ואילו שותפין שגנבו. והאחד הוליאה מרשות בעליס לדעתו ולדעת חבירו אמרינן בבבא קמא (דף עח:) דחייבין: השתא דאמרת מגו. דזכי לנפשיה כו' חרש ופקח שהגביהו מליאה קנאוה אע"פ שהגבהה של חרש אינה הגבהה לקנות אלא מפני דרכי שלוס כדתנן (גיטין דף נט:) חרש שוטה וקטן יש בהן גזל מפני דרכי שלוס אפילו הכי אמר מגו דזכי לנפשיה כו': בשלמא חרש קני דקא מגבה לה בן דעת. לראשה השני לאורך שניהס וראשו של לד חרש לגבי חרש מיהא הויא הגבהה כדתקון ליה מפני דרכי שלוס אלא פקח במאי קני לגבי פקח הוי ראשה שהגביה החרש כמונח על גבי קרקע דהגבהה דחרש לא קניא אלא מדרכי שלוס בעלמא: ומאי מגו. איכא למימר הכא דקאמר השתא דאמרת מגו אמרינן מגו וחרש אמאי קני הא לא זכי פקח לנפשיה דנימא דזכי נמי לחבריה ולא הויא הגבהה דפקח הגבהה: אם תמצא לומר. כלומר אפי' אם תמלא לומר המגביה מליאה לחבירו כו': הכא אדעתא דידיה קא מגבה ליה. האי פיקח: דלא ליתי לאינצויי. עס החוטפיס מהס: מהיכא. מאיזו בבא ממשנתנו קא דייק לומר זאת אומרת: הא קאמר כולה שלי ואנא אגבהתיה. והיאך נאמר לא יקנה לא זה ולא זה ויבא אחר ויטלנה והלא כל אחד טוען אני הגבהתיה ואין כאן מגביה מליאה לחבירו ומה יש לו להשיב בשלמא האי שכנגדו המוחזק בה כמוהו אמר לא הגבהת אתה כי אס אני אבל אחר מן השוק מה יטעון: ממשנה יתירה. אמרינן דהמגביה מליאה כו' ומשוס הכי אמרינן יחלוקו דאמרינן שניהס הגביהוה והוה ליה כל אחד מגביה מליאה לו ולחבירו וקני דאי משוס דלא ידעינן הי מינייהו משקר והוה ליה ממון המוטל בספק וחולקין בשבועה משוס שלא יהא כל אחד ואחד הולך ותוקף כדאמרי' לעיל (דף ג.) הא שמענא ליה מרישא: דאהוי כמשיב אבידה. מדהוה מלי למימר כולה שלי ואמר חליה שלי: וליפטר. משבועה: ממשנה יתירה כו'. כדפרישית: דרכוב קני. ואע"ג דלא משיכה היא שאינה זזה ממקומה שאין מנהיגה ברגליו: צריכא למימר. דהיכא דלקוחה בין שניהס שיחלקוה בלא שבועה: אלא לאו במציאה. ואיצטריך לאשמועינן שאין אחר יכול לחוטפה דמגביה מליאה לחבירו קנה חבירו: ורבא אמר לך. בעלמא היכא דלא נתכוין המגביה לזכות בה לא קנה חבירו ומשנה יתירה דמתני' אשמועינן המגביה מליאה לו ולחבירו קנה אף חבירו דמגו דזכי לנפשיה זכי נמי לחבריה:

שמעית

---

**תוספות**

**דחזיא** לקטניס. ופריך דטלית מוזהבת לא עבדי לקטניס ול"ג דחזיא לתרוייהו דא"כ מאי פריך מטלית מוזהבת:

**ושותפין** שגנבו. פי' בקונטרס שהוליא לדעתו ולדעת חבירו כדאיתא בב"ק (דף עח:) ואין נראה דהתס בטביחה איירי וטביחה אפי' אמר לא וטבח לי חייב דדרשינן (שס דף עא.) תחת לרבות השליח אלא שותפין שגנבו שהגביהו שניהס:

**ומאי** מגו מגו דשני חרשין. תימה מנלן דלמא תרי מגו לא אמרי' דב' חרשין דקנו היינו מטעס מגו דזכי לנפשיה זכי נמי לחבריה:

**אלא** מסיפא זה אומר כולה שלי וזה אומר חציה שלי. אית דל"ג הכא הא תו למה לי דממשנה גופה קא דייק דקאמר חליה שלי והיינו שהגביה עס חבירו ולפי דבריו לא יטול כלוס אלא ודאי מגביה מליאה לחבירו זכה ופריך ממאי דבמליאה דלמא במקח וממכר והוא הדין דהוה מלי למדחי דהא דאמר חליה שלי כגון דאמר תפסתיה חליה בידי או הגבהתיה כולה לקנות חליה אבל עדיין היה מדקדק מיתורא דמתני' לכך דחי ליה דאפי' מיתורא אינו יכול לדקדק ולספרים דגרסי הא תו למה לי י"ל דמשוס דמגופא דמתני' לא מלי למידק כדפרישית אך קשה אמאי קאמר דלמא במקח וממכר אפילו מיירי במליאה מלי לדחויי כדדחי וי"ל בדוחק ממאי דבמליאה דלהכי לא מוקמת במקח וממכר משוס דלא משכחת חידוש אלא במגביה מליאה לחבירו כי נמי איירי במקח וממכר יש חידוש דלא נימא משיב אבידה הוא וה"ה אס מיירי במליאה לא יוכל להוכיח כלוס:

מנהיג

---

**עין משפט נר מצוה**

נג א מיי' פ"ט מהלכות טוען ונטען הל' י סמג עשין לה טוש"ע ח"מ סי' קלח סעיף ד:

נד ב מיי' פי"ז מהלכות אבידה הל' ג סמג עשין עד טוש"ע ח"מ סי' רסט סעיף א:

נה ג מיי' פ"ב מהל' גניבה הל' יד סמג עשין עא טוש"מ סי' שנ:

נו ד ה מיי' פי"ז מהל' גזילה ואבידה הל' ד סמג עשין עד טוש"ע ח"מ סי' רסט סעיף ד:

**רבינו חננאל**

כיון שהעמיד רב פפא משנתנו דקתני יחלוקו בתפסי לה בכרכשתא דקדק רמי בר חמא ואמר זאת אומרת המגביה מציאה לחבירו קנה חבירו. רבא אמר לעולם לא קנה ומתני' היינו טעמא מגו דזכי לנפשיה זכי נמי לחבריה. תדע דאילו האומר לחבירו צא וגנוב לי פטור המשלח דקי"ל אין שליח לדבר עבירה ואילו שותפין שגנבו חייבין ושקלי' וטרי' בה ואסיקנא דוקיא דרמי בר חמא מסיפא דמתני' בזמן שהן מודין או שיש להן עדים כי שניהם ביחד מצאוה ושניהן אגב' אגבהוה בכרכשתא חולקין בלא שבועה ש"מ המגביה מציאה לחבירו קנה חבירו דהא תרוייהו מסייעי להדדי בעידנא דמגבהי לה. ורבא אמר לך שאני הכא מגו דזכי לנפשיה זכי נמי לחבריה. וקי"ל כרמי בר חמא והוא דאמר ליה זכי לי דהא ר' יוחנן קאי כוותיה ואמר המגביה מציאה לחבירו קנה חבירו ואם יקשה לך הא דתנן היה רוכב על גבי בהמה וכו' התם באומר תנה לי ולא אמר זכה לי. היו שניהם רוכבין על גבי בהמה וכו'.

**מסורת הש"ם**

[לעיל ז.], ג) [לעיל ב.], ...לקמן י.], ד) [לקמן נדרים פח:], ה) [שבת ... עיין שם, בבא קמא ...], ו) [לקמן ט.], ...ל ליתין], ח) [לעיל ב.], ט) [לעיל ד:].

**הגהות הב"ח**

גמ' השתא דאמרי דאמרי' מגו:

**גליון הש"ם**

אמר רבא לעולם. ...לקמן דף י ע"א תוס' ...ה איתיביה ובנדרים דף ...ע"ב בר"ן ד"ה אמר רבא:

**ליקוטי רש"י**

...היתה טלית ...והבת. כלומר אפילו ...מוזהבת חולקים ...יל ז.]. היו שנים ...בין. לאשמועינן אתא ...כב ומנהיג שניהם שוין ...ות בהמה מן ההפקר ...יל ב.]. מיגו דזכי ...פשיה וכו'. דאי בעי ...זכי לנפשיה אם ...ביה לעצמו [לקמן ט:]. ...יפא במקח וממכר. ...חיה מיד פלוני וכו' ...יל ב.]. איערומי קא ...רים. לאחזוקיה בגאמן [לעיל ד:].

דְּחַזְיָא לְקְטַנֵּי – Dividing a cloak does not ruin it, **for [half a cloak] fit for children.** Thus, the Mishnah may indeed mean that the oak is actually divided; it does not prove that the court divides :cording to value.

The Gemara now cites an Amoraic statement to support its ssertion:

וְהָא דְּאָמַר רָבָ – **And** regarding **that which Rava said:** אִם הָיְתָה טַלִּית מוּזְהֶבֶ – Even **if [the disputed object] was a gilded cloak** חוֹלְק – **they divide** it,[1] הָכִי נַמִּי דְּפָלְגֵי לָהּ – **is it also so** as ou contend **that they split [the cloak]** in two? הָא אַפְסְדוּהָ – they do so **in this** case, **they damage [the cloak]!**[2] Surely, then, hen Rava said *divide,* he meant "to divide according to value"; it us follows that the term *divide* always connotes this type of vision.

The Gemara rejects the proof:

הָא לָא קַשְׁיָ – **That is not a difficulty.** דְּחַזְיָא לִבְנֵי מְלָכִים – **Because** even half a gilded cloak **is fit for young princes.** hus, Rava may have meant that they split the cloak in vo.

The Gemara now cites a Mishnah to support its assertion:

וְהָא דְּתְ – **And** regarding **that which we have learned in our** ishnah: הָיוּ שְׁנַיִם רוֹכְבִין עַל גַּבֵּי בְהֵמָה וכו׳ – If TWO litigants me before the court RIDING UPON AN ANIMAL etc., each contend-g that the animal is his, then they divide the animal, הָכִי נַמִּי דְּפָלְגֵי לָ – **is it also so** as you contend **that they split [the nimal]** in two, i.e. that they actually slaughter the animal and vide the carcass? הָא אַפְסְדוּהָ – But if they do so **in this** case, ey **damage it!**

The Gemara explains the proof:

בִּשְׁלָמָא טְהוֹרָ – Now **it is understandable** that **a *kosher***, edible nimal is not totally ruined if they split it in two, חַזְיָא לְבָשָׂר – r **it is** still **fit** to use **as meat,** i.e. they may slaughter the animal and then divide it in two. אֶלָּא טְמֵאָה – **But regarding a non-*kosher* animal,** הָא אַפְסְדוּהָ – if they actually split it in half **in this** case, **they** totally **ruin it!** Obviously, then, such an animal is not split in two. אֶלָּא לִדְמֵי – **Rather,** it must be divided **according to value.** הָכָא נַמִּי לִדְמֵי – **Here too** (in Rabban Shimon's ruling), then, the document is divided **according to value.**

The Gemara returns to discuss an implicit ruling of our Mishnah on 2a, viz. if two people pick up a found object simultaneously, each acquires half the object.[3]

The Gemara deduces:

אָמַר רָמִי בַּר חָמָא – **Rami bar Chama said:** זֹאת אוֹמֶרֶת – **This teaches** that הַמַּגְבִּיהַּ מְצִיאָה לַחֲבֵירוֹ – if **one lifts a found object** intending to acquire it entirely **for his fellow,** קָנָה חֲבֵירוֹ – then **his fellow acquires** it.[4] דְּאִי סָלְקָא דַּעְתָּךְ לֹא קָנָה חֲבֵירוֹ – **For if it should enter your mind** that **his fellow does not acquire** it, תֵּיעָשֶׂה זוֹ כְּמִי שֶׁמּוּנַּחַת עַל גַּבֵּי קַרְקַע – then in the Mishnah's case, **let this** end of the object **be considered as if it were lying on the ground,** וְזוֹ כְּמִי שֶׁמּוּנַּחַת עַל גַּבֵּי קַרְקַע – **and this** other end of the object be considered **as if it were lying on the ground,**[5] וְלֹא יִקְנֶה לֹא זֶה וְלֹא זֶה – **and** thus **neither this [litigant] nor that [litigant] should acquire** the object.[6] אֶלָּא לָאו שְׁמַע מִינָּהּ – **Rather, infer from this** ruling in the Mishnah that הַמַּגְבִּיהַּ מְצִיאָה לַחֲבֵירוֹ – **if one picks up a found object,** intending to acquire it entirely **for his fellow,** קָנָה חֲבֵירוֹ – then **his fellow acquires the object.**

Rava distinguishes between Rami bar Chama's case and that of our Mishnah, thereby refuting the deduction:

אָמַר רָבָא – **Rava said:** לְעוֹלָם אֵימָא לָךְ – **Really I can maintain** הַמַּגְבִּיהַּ מְצִיאָה לַחֲבֵירוֹ – that if **one lifts a found object** intending to acquire it entirely **for his fellow,** לֹא קָנָה חֲבֵירוֹ – then **his fellow does not acquire** it.[7] וְהָכָא הַיְינוּ טַעְמָא – **But here** in our

NOTES

The Gemara above (7a) explains the novelty of Rava's ruling.

The Gemara assumes that its previous rebuttal, i.e. that half a cloak fit for children, does not apply to a gilded cloak, because children nerally do not wear such expensive cloaks.

Later, the Gemara will determine which section of the Mishnah iplies this ruling (*Rashi*).

[In order to legally acquire an object, a *kinyan* (formal act of quisition) must be performed for the prospective owner. One such nyan is the *kinyan* of *hagbahah,* lifting the object off the ground (or rface upon which it rests). Now the prospective owner may either rform the *kinyan* himself or appoint an agent (*sheliach*) to perform e *kinyan* for him. Moreover, if the acquisition is a *zechus*, an nqualified benefit, for the prospective owner, e.g. the acquisition of a esent, the principle of *zechiyah* allows even someone who has not been pointed as an agent to perform the *kinyan* for him. Rami bar Chama's ling applies this ruling to the acquisition of a found object. The novelty the ruling will be explained below in note 7.

A *kinyan hagbahah* is valid only if the entire object was lifted off the ound on behalf of the prospective owner; if only part was lifted for him, e *kinyan* is void and nothing at all is acquired. Now if two people lifted object (e.g. a cloak) together and then one let go of his end, that end ould obviously fall to the ground; each person is thus lifting only part the cloak. (Admittedly, certain objects would remain suspended in the r even if one person let go of his end. *Rashba* explains why even in such case, each person in effect lifts only part of the object; cf. *Raavad* cited loc.). Accordingly, if each of the two intended to acquire the object rough *kinyan hagbahah*, the *kinyan* should be void because only part the object was lifted for each person.

This, however, would change if we assume that a person has the legal pacity to acquire an object for his fellow. If that were true, then it ould be possible for the entire object to be lifted on both persons' half: Each could then lift it not only for himself but for the other as ell. Given this, if two people lifted a found object simultaneously, each presumably realizes that his *kinyan* is void unless he lifts it for his fellow as well as for himself. Therefore, they would both do so, thereby acquiring the object jointly.

To prove that a person indeed has the legal capacity to acquire a found object for his fellow, Rami bar Chama cites our Mishnah's ruling that if two people lift a found object simultaneously, they acquire it jointly (see note 3). This proves, Rami bar Chama asserts, that if someone lifts a found object entirely on behalf of his fellow, the fellow acquires it as well (see *Rashi*).

6. A lost object is ownerless until someone acquires it. In the Mishnah's case, then, if neither fellow acquires the object, anyone should then have the right to grab it and thereby acquire it for himself. In fact, however, our Mishnah rules that they divide the object equally – implying that the two acquired the object jointly. This proves Rami bar Chama's rule.

7. I.e. unless the person lifting the object intends to acquire part of it for himself as well, he does not acquire any part of it at all. The Gemara on 10a explains Rava's opinion as follows. It is logical to assume that one cannot acquire something for his fellow if the acquisition represents a potential loss to others. Given this, one should not have the legal capacity to acquire a lost object on behalf of another since this deprives other prospective owners of the opportunity to acquire it (*Rashi*).

Rami bar Chama responds with the following argument. Although such an acquisition indeed represents a potential loss to others, still it is not actually detrimental to them. Rami bar Chama would agree, for example, that if someone is indebted to several creditors, a third party cannot seize the debtor's property on behalf of a particular creditor since in doing so, he preempts the other creditors; the seizure actually cancels whatever chance the other creditors had of collecting the property. In our case, on the other hand, nobody ever had preexisting rights to the lost object. Therefore, Rami bar Chama argues, a person should be able to acquire a lost object for his fellow (*Ramban* to 10a; see there for other explanations).

– who maintains that **this one takes the** document's **form** וְזֶה נוֹטֵל תּוֹרֶף – **and this one takes the** document's **essence,**[33] לָמָּה לֵיהּ – **what is the purpose** of giving a portion of the document **to [the debtor]?** וְכִי לָצוּר עַל פִּי צְלוֹחִיתוֹ הוּא צָרִיךְ – **Does he need it to wrap it over the opening of his flask?!**[34]

In response, Ravina clarifies R' Elazar's ruling:

אָמַר לֵיהּ – **[Ravina] answered [Rav Acha]:** לְדָמֵי – The document is divided **according to its value.**[35] דְּאָמַר הָכִי – **That is, [the litigant holding the document's essence] can claim** the following: שְׁטָרָא דְּאִית בֵּיהּ זְמַן – **A document that has a date** – e.g. the *toref* – כַּמָּה שָׁוֵי – **how much is it worth?** וּדְלֵית בֵּיהּ זְמַן – **And one that has no date** – e.g. the *tofes* – כַּמָּה שָׁוֵי – **how much is it worth?**[36] בִּשְׁטָרָא דְּאִית בֵּיהּ זְמַן גָּבֵי מִמְּשַׁעְבְּדֵי – **With a document that has a date one can collect from encumbered property,**[37] וְאִידָךְ לָא גָּבֵי מִמְּשַׁעְבְּדֵי – **but with the other** type of document, i.e. one without a date, **one cannot collect from encumbered property.**[38] Obviously, then, the document's essence, which is dated, is worth more than its form, which is not. יָהִיב לֵיהּ הֵיאךְ דְּבֵינֵי בֵּינֵי – Therefore, **[whoever holds the document's form] must give [his adversary] the difference** between its value and that of the document's essence.[39]

The Gemara applies this concept to yet another area of law:

וְיַחֲלוֹקוּ נַמִּי דְּאָמְרָן – **And** Rabban Shimon ben Gamliel's ruling, **"They shall divide," which has been stated** regarding a case in which two litigants are holding the same section of a document, **also** means לְדָמֵי – they shall divide, **according to value.**

The Gemara cites our Mishnah to support its assertion:

דְּאִי לָא תֵּימָא הָכִי – **For if you do not say so** but argue instead that the ruling requires them to split the article in two, שְׁנַיִם אוֹחֲזִין בְּטַלִּית – then in a case in which **two are holding on to a cloak,** where the Mishnah requires them to "divide" it, הָכִי נַמִּי דְּפָלְגֵי – **is it** then **also so that they split** the cloak in two? הָא אַפְסְדוּהָ – But if they do so **in this** case **they will damage it!** Obviously, then, the Mishnah means for them to divide according to value. Presumably, this is what Rabban Shimon ben Gamliel meant as well.

The Gemara rejects the proof:

הָא לָא קַשְׁיָא – **That is not a difficulty.**

NOTES

33. Actually, even R' Yochanan agrees with this ruling, as the Gemara above explained. The Gemara attributes the ruling to R' Elazar only because he stated the rule explicitly (*Ritva*).

34. The Gemara now assumes that there is no point in awarding the debtor a section of debt document unless this somehow prevents the creditor from collecting his debt. (He obviously does not need the document just to serve as a cork.) To collect a loan from the debtor though, the creditor need only possess a section of the document containing the names of the principals and the amount of the loan; both the *tofes* and *toref* contain this information. What, then, is accomplished by awarding one of these sections to the debtor if the other is awarded to the creditor? (*Rashi,* according to *Ramban* et al.).

Actually, the Gemara below indicates that awarding the *toref* to the debtor does accomplish something: It prevents the creditor from collecting encumbered property held by third parties. This is because the creditor must hold a dated document in order to collect his debt from encumbered property. Since a document's date appears only in its *toref*, the creditor must hold this section of the document to collect such property. (For a definition of encumbered property, see note 37.) Accordingly, the Gemara must mean to ask as follows: The debtor himself gains nothing if he precludes the creditor from collecting encumbered property. What benefit does the debtor himself receive, then, if he is awarded the *toref* section of a debt document?

According to some Rishonim (*Ramban* et al.), the Gemara's text actually reads: טוֹפֵס לָמָּה לֵיהּ, *What is the purpose* of giving *the* ***tofes*** [to the debtor]? According to this version, the Gemara indeed understands the purpose of awarding the *toref* to the debtor: It precludes the creditor from collecting encumbered property. It questions only the purpose of awarding him the *tofes.*

35. R' Elazar never meant that we actually rip the document in two and give one section to each principal. Rather, we allow the creditor to collect the value of his section and the debtor to keep the value of his. The Gemara elaborates.

36. It may seem that the *tofes* should be worth no less than the *toref*. The last line of the *tofes* actually summarizes all the significant information contained in the *toref* except for the document's date. Moreover, the *tofes'* version of the information is considered the more authoritative. Still, the *toref* is worth more because it empowers the creditor to collect encumbered property (see note 34).

Actually, the *tofes* does contain one element that the *toref* lacks: the witnesses' signatures. Generally, then, the *tofes* should be more valuable than the *toref* because to certify a document it is necessary to verify the signatures. This is not true, however, in the case that R' Elazar discusses (i.e. a case in which the debtor concedes the document's authenticity) for the following reason. In Rabban Shimon ben Gamliel's view, which R' Elazar accepts, a document need not be certified if the debtor concedes its authenticity (see Gemara 7a). In such a case, then, the signatures add no value to the *tofes (Rashi*). [See *Tosafos* and other Rishonim, who raise several objections to *Rashi's* commentary and therefore propose several alternative interpretations.]

37. נְכָסִים מְשׁוּעְבָּדִים, *encumbered property*, is land owned by a debtor at the time he incurred a debt, but which he later sold to a third party. Such land is *encumbered* by the debt; for the creditor can collect it from the buyer to satisfy the debt if the debtor defaults.

38. A debt document's date allows us to compare the date that the debtor borrowed money with the date on which he sold a given property. If the property was sold after the loan took place, the creditor can collect it from the purchaser because it is encumbered by the loan; otherwise, he cannot. Consequently, a creditor cannot collect sold property with an undated debt document, because it does not prove that the property is encumbered by his loan.

39. The difference between an undated and a dated document is assessed and awarded to the creditor, if it is he who has the *toref* in his hand. The remainder of the debt is divided equally between the parties (*Ramban* et al.).

מאי שנא ליד דיין אמר רבא הכי קאמר [א] ואחר שמצא שטר שנפל ליד דיין והיכי דמי (א) דכתב ביה הנפק לא יוציאו עולמית ולא מיבעיא לא כתב ביה הנפק דאיכא למימר כתב ללות ולא לוה אלא אפי' כתב ביה הנפק דמקוים לא יחזיר דחיישינן לפירעון ורבי יוסי אומר הרי הוא בחזקתו ולא חיישינן לפירעון ולא חייש ר' יוסי לפירעון והתניא מצא שטר כתובה בשוק בזמן שהבעל מודה יחזיר לאשה אין הבעל מודה [ב] לא יחזיר לא לזה ולא [א] לזה רבי יוסי אומר עודה תחת בעלה יחזיר לאשה נתארמלה או נתגרשה לא יחזיר לא לזה ולא לזה איפוך נפל ליד דיין לא יוציאו עולמית דברי רבי יוסי וחכ"א הרי הוא בחזקתו אי הכי קשיא דרבנן אדרבנן שטר כתובה כולה רבי יוסי וחסורי מחסרא והכי קתני אין הבעל מודה לא יחזיר לא לזה ולא לזה בד"א שנתארמלה או שנתגרשה אבל עודה תחת בעלה יחזיר לאשה (ב) שר"י אומר עודה תחת בעלה יחזיר לאשה נתארמלה או שנתגרשה לא יחזיר לא לזה ולא לזה רב פפא אמר לעולם לא תיפוך רבי יוסי לדבריהם דרבנן קאמר להו לדידי אפילו נתארמלה או נתגרשה נמי לא חיישינן לפירעון לדידכו אודו לי מיהת בעודה תחת בעלה דיחזיר לאשה דלאו בת פירעון היא ואמרו ליה רבנן אימור צררי אתפסה רבינא אמר לעולם איפוך קמייתא וטעמא דרבנן הכא משום דחיישינן לשתי כתובות ורבי יוסי לשתי כתובות לא חייש אמר רבי אלעזר [ג] מחלוקת בששניהם אדוקים בטופס ושניהם בתורף [ג] אבל אחד אדוק בטופס ואחד אדוק בתורף זה נוטל טופס וזה נוטל תורף ור' יוחנן אמר לעולם חולקין ואפילו אחד אדוק בטופס ואחד אדוק בתורף והתניא זה נוטל עד מקום שידו מגעת לא צריכא דקאי תורף בי מצעי אי הכי מאי למימרא לא צריכא דמקרב לגבי דחד [ג] מהו דתימא א"ל פלוג הכי קמ"ל דא"ל מאי חזית דפלגת הכי פלוג הכי א"ל רב אחא מדפתי לרבינא לרבי אלעזר דאמר זה נוטל טופס וזה נוטל תורף למה ליה [ד] וכי לצור ע"פ צלוחיתו הוא צריך א"ל [ד] לדמי דאמר הכי שטרא דאית ביה זמן כמה שוי ודלית ביה זמן כמה שוי בשטרא דאית ביה זמן גבי ממשעבדי ואידך לא גבי ממשעבדי יהיב ליה היאך דביני ביני ויחלוקו נמי דאמרן לדמי דאי לא תימא הכי שנים אוחזין בטלית הכי נמי דפלגי הא אפסדוה הא לא קשיא

דחזיא

---

מאי שנא ליד דיין. מאיש אחר: הכי קאמר ואחר. שאינו לא לוה ולא מלוה: שמצא שטר שנפל. כבר ליד הדיין ומאי ניהו הך נפילה דכתיב ביה הנפק: לא יוציאוהו מידו. לא לוה ולא מלוה עד שיבא אליהו או עדים שראו מיד מי נפל: לפירעון. שמא אמת טוען הלוה שפרעו: ורבי יוסי לא חייש לפירעון. דמאן דמהדרי ליה שטר פרוע לאלתר זהיר ביה לקורעו ולא משהי ליה: שהבעל מודה. שלא נתן לה כתובתה: אין הבעל מודה. שאמר פרעתי ומידי נפל: עודה תחת בעלה. שלא גרשה: יחזיר לאשה. דלא עביד איניש ליתן כתובה קודם גירושין: צררי אתפסה. מעות צרורות או כספים מסר לה ליחוד כתובתה כשנשאה או לאחר מכאן שלא יטריחוה יורשים אם תתאלמן: לעולם איפוך קמייתא. ודקשיא לך דרבנן אדרבנן לא תיקשי דטעמייהו דרבנן בכתובה לאו משום דחיישינן לפירעון דמאן דפרע ואהדר ליה שטרא לאלתר קרע ליה אלא משום דחיישינן לשתי כתובות שמא חזר וכתב לה כתובה אחרת שניה לאחר שנפלה זאת מידה ואין הבעל מודה דקתני לאו באומר פרעתי אלא באומר אל תחזרו לה שיש בידה אחרת ותוליא על יורשי שטר אחר שטר: מחלוקת. האי יחלוקו דקאמר ר"ש [ב"ג] דמשמע חולקין בשוה כך שמעתי משום ר' יצחק ב"ר מנחם ונראה בעיני: ושניהם אדוקים בתורף. כלומר או שניהם אדוקין בתורף ותורף גילוי של שטר מקום הלוה והמלוה והמעות והזמן טופס שאר כל לשון השטר: זה נוטל כו'. דמאי דתפיס דידיה הוא כדקתני לעיל זה נוטל עד מקום שידו מגעת כו' ולקמן מפרש למאי מיבעי ליה: ואפי' אחד אדוק כו'. בתמיה: והא תניא עד מקום שידו מגעת. שלו: דקאי תורף בי מצעי. ומר אמר חדא ומר אמר חדא ולא פליגי: לדמי. מעלין בדמים כמה תורף יפה מן הטופס: שטרא דאית ביה זמן כמה שוה. דתורף עדיף מטופס דאית ביה מקום הזמן דאילו שם המלוה והלוה והמעות כתובין אף בטופס שצריך לחזור מעניינו של שטר בשיטה אחרונה והוא עיקר כדתנן (ב"ב דף קסה:) כתוב בו [מלמעלה מנה ולמטה מאתים] מלמעלה מאתים ולמטה מנה הכל הולך אחר התחתון אבל זמן לא מיהדר ואי משום חתימת עדים דהוא תחת הטופס הא אית ליה לרשב"ג מודה בשטר שכתבו אין צריך לקיימו והאי מודה שכתבו הוא:

דחזיא

---

מאי שנא ליד דיין. לספרים דגרסי בשניא והיכי דמי כגון דכתוב ביה הנפק השתא לא ידע דנפל ליד דיין דהיינו הנפק אלא סבור דהיינו שהדיין מצאו ולכך בעי מאי שנא דיין מאיש אחר ולספרים דלא גרסי בתר הכי והיכי דמי כגון דכתוב ביה הנפק ידע שפיר השתא דנפל ליד דיין היינו שכתוב בו הנפק ומיבעיא ליה מאי שנא כתוב בו הנפק דלא יוציאו לעולם הלא אם אין כתוב בו הנפק נראה דכ"ש הוא שלא יוציאו עולמית דאיכא למימר שמא כתב ללות ולא לוה ומשני דלא מיבעיא קאמר:

בזמן שהבעל מודה יחזיר לאשה. דלא חיישינן לקנוניא וליכא למיחש לשמא כתב בניסן ולא נשא עד תשרי [ה] דמנה ומאתים משתעבדי מן האירוסין אף בלא כתובה דאירוסין קלא אית להו ולקודם אירוסין ליכא למיחש דכתב לה ותוספת נמי לאביי דאמר עדיו בחתומיו זכין לו א"ש ור' אסי יעמיד כשהקנה לה:

דחיישינן לשתי כתובות. ובלאו איפוך לא מצי לאוקמא דרבי יוסי חיים לשתי כתובות דא"כ עודה תחת בעלה אמאי יחזיר לאשה כשאין הבעל מודה:

מחלוקת. פרש"י דהיינו יחלוקו דקאמר רשב"ג והדין עמו שלא רצה לפרש פלוגתא דרבי ורשב"ג משום דהיכי קאמר אבל אחד אדוק בטופס כו' משמע דהתם לא פליגי וזה אינו דגם שם אם אינו מקוים לא שקיל לרבי מידי:

דאית ביה זמן כמה שוה. פרש"י דמעות ולוה ומלוה לא שיימינן דכתיבי נמי בשיטה אחרונה בטופס והוא עיקר דתנן (ב"ב דף קסה:) כתוב [בו] מלמעלה מנה כו' ותימה הא אין למידין משיטה אחרונה ולכך עושין חזרת השטר ומתני' דכתוב למעלה מנה לא מיירי בשיטה אחרונה וגם פי' דבעדים לא שיימינן דרשב"ג אית ליה מודה בשטר שכתבו אין צריך לקיימו ופירושו תימה דאם חשב אותו שאינו תופס עדים כאילו יש לו שטר בלא עדים א"כ לרשב"ג נמי לא א"ש דנהי דסבר דאין צריך לקיימו מ"מ כשאין כלל עדי חתימה פסול ועוד במה עדיף תורף מטופס כך השטר פסול בלא טופס כמו בלא תורף דאם נמחק אפי' שיטה אחת מן השטר הוא פסול אלא ודאי יש לומר דבמה שהשטר נפסל אין שמין דכך שוה כשתופס שיטה אחת מן הטופס כמו תופס לוה ומלוה ומעות ועדים והשטר אינו כשר בלא זה כמו בלא זה אבל זמן שהשטר כשר בלא זמנו שמין כמה שוה ובירושלמי איכא א"ר אלעזר הכל הולך אחר מי שתפוס עדים ופליג אגמ' שלנו דמזכיר זמן וסובר דעדי מסירה כרתי והשטר כשר בלא עדי חתימה ושמין כמה שוה שאין צריך לחזור אחר עדי מסירה ולית ליה ההוא לישנא דג"פ (ב"ב דף קע.) דסבר רשב"ג עדי חתימה כרתי:

ויחלוקו נמי לדמי. ואין חולקין את החוב כמו שכתוב בשטר אלא כמו ששוה לו למכור מזה יפרע החצי דאי לא תימא הכי אלא חצי החוב ממש גבי טלית מי חולקין ממש הא אפסדוה ולא גרסי' לא דפסקינן לשטרא דא"כ מה מביא מטלית אדרבה בטלית אם יחתכנו לשנים אין פסידא כל כך ואם יחתוך השטר לא ישוה לכלום ועוד דפשיטא הוא דלא יחלוקו השטר לשנים דאוקימנא לעיל פלוגתא דרבי ורבי שמעון בן גמליאל במודה בשטר שכתבו אלא כדפרישית:

דחזיא

---

עין משפט נר מצוה

נ א מיי' פי"ח מהלכות גזילה ואבידה הל' יג סמג עשין עד טוש"ע ח"מ סי' סה סעיף ו וסעיף ז:

נא ב מיי' שם הל' יג ואף אם שניהם מודים דחיישינן לקנוניא וע"ש במ"מ:

נב ג ד טוש"ע ח"מ סי' סה סעיף טו:

רבינו חננאל

לקיימו יחלוקו דמודה בשטר שכתבו א"צ לקיימו ואין הלכה כמותו. אדם שמצא שטר שכתוב בו קיום ב"ד לא יוציאו עולמית חיישינן שמא פרוע הוא דברי א) ר' יוסי וחכ"א הרי [הוא] בחזקתו וכ"ש המוצא שטר שאין בו קיום שלא יוציאו עולמית דחיישינן שמא כתב ללות ולא לוה: אמר ר"א מחלוקת בשניהן אדוקין בתופס ובתורף וכו' ור' יוחנן אמר לעולם חולקין והאי דקאי תורף בינייהו ואע"ג דמקרב לגבי דחד לא חיישינן אלא חולקים. פי' תורף כדתנן בפרק כל גט שנכתב שלא לשם אשה כו' הכותב תופסי גיטין צריך שיניח מקום שם האיש והאשה ומקום הזמן שטרי מלוה צריך שיניח מקום המלוה ומקום הלוה ומקום המעות ומקום הזמן זהו תורף והשאר תופס וזה שאמרו חולקין בשטר לא שיחתכוהו כי זה הפסד הוא אלא דמיו חולקין ושקלינן וטרינן בה טובא ואסיקנא הכי מהא דתנן היו רוכבין על גבי בהמה או א' רוכב וא' מנהיג וכו' עד ויחלוקו הכי נמי דפלגי לה ממש בשלמא בהמה טהורה חזיא לבישרא אלא בהמה טמא' אפסדוה אלא לדמי וכן הלכה. ואם היו שנים אדוקין בשטר זה בתורף וזה בתופס ב). בשלמא שם המלוה והלוה והמעות יתכן לעמוד בהן עכשיו ואחר כך אם אבד השטר אין חוששין לו אלא הזמן שרוצה להיות בידו לטרוף ממשעבדי שמין כמה שוה שטר שיש בו זמן ויש לו לגבות ממשעבדי דבאין ללוה נכסים בני חורין ויש בו זמן טריף ממשעבדי ואם אין בו זמן אבד ממונו ומה שעולה בה השומא שקיל מי שהתורף בידו וכן הדין. ור' יוחנן לא חלק אלא בזמן שהתורף באמצע אבל בזמן שזה תופס בתורף וזה בתופס לא חלק שדמי כל הזוזי למי שבידו התורף והדין כאשר פירשנו ולדברי הכל כל דבר שאם יחלק יפסד שמין אותו בדמים וחולקין בדמים כדתנן בפ' השותפין אין חולקין את החצר עד שיהא בה כדי לזה וכדי לזה וכו' ואסיק התם בגמ' ת"ש זה הכלל כל שאילו יחלק ושמו עליו חולקין אותו ואם לאו מעלין אותו בדמים. ר' יוסי אומר הרי הוא בחזקתו. ומקשי' וכי ר' יוסי לא חייש לפירעון והתניא מצא כתובת אשה בשוק בזמן שהבעל מודה יחזיר לאשה אין הבעל מודה לא יחזיר לא לזה ולא לזה. ור' יוסי [אומר] עודה תחת בעלה יחזיר לאשה נתארמלה או נתגרשה לא יחזיר לא לזה ולא לזה. ופריק רבינא דהוא בתרא אפוך ואימא הכי נפל ליד הדיין כגון שכתוב בו קיום ב"ד לא יוציאו עולמית דברי ר' יוסי וחכ"א הרי הוא בחזקתו וטעמא דרבנן התם דאמרו לא יחזיר לא לזה ולא לזה לאו משום דחיישי לפירעון אלא משום דחיישי לשתי כתובות. ור' יוסי לשתי כתובות לא חייש.

כיון

---

מסורת הש"ס

א) [נ"ל לזון], ב) [... בתוס' חגיגה ו: ... שאין להם], ג) [... קז.], ד) [לקמן יג., ... קמא מט:, בבא ... עו:].

הגהות הב"ח

(א) גמ' והיכי דמי ... דכתב ביה הנפק ... (ב) שם יחזיר ... דברי ר' יוסי שר' ... אומר:

גליון הש"ס

תוס' ד"ה בזמן ... דמנה ומאר ... משתעבדי. עי' לקמ... ע"א תד"ה הטוען

ליקוטי רש"י

וכי לצור על צלוחיתו. וכי לצור פי צלוחיתו קנאו זה סברא היא דמשום ג... חוב הכתוב בו קונין [רשב"ם ב"ב עו:].

---

חשק שלמה על ר"ח א) בגמ' איתא להיפך ואולי דרבינו העתיק כאן כפי המסקנא לקמן בסמוך. ב) נראה דצ"ל זה נוטל טופס וזה נוטל תורף ומסקינן דנ"מ משום הזמן דבשלמא וכו'.

Rabban Shimon ben Gamliel's ruling:[23] אָמַר רַבִּי אֶלְעָזָר – **R' Elazar said:** מַחֲלוֹקֶת – Rabban Shimon's ruling, which prescribes equal **division,**[24] בְּשֶׁשְּׁנֵיהֶם אֲדוּקִים בְּטוֹפֶס – refers only to a case **in which** either **both** [the creditor and the debtor] **are holding on to the** document's **form** וּשְׁנֵיהֶם בְּתוֹרֶף – **or both are holding on to the** document's **essence;**[25] only in such cases does Rabban Shimon rule, "They shall divide it equally." אֲבָל אֶחָד אָדוּק בְּטוֹפֶס – **But if one** of the principals **is holding on to the** document's **form** וְאֶחָד אָדוּק בְּתוֹרֶף – **and** the other **one is holding on to the** document's **essence,** זֶה נוֹטֵל טוֹפֶס – then **this one takes the** document's **form** וְזֶה נוֹטֵל תּוֹרֶף – **and that one takes the** document's **essence,** i.e. each is awarded the section of document already in his possession.[26] וְר' יוֹחָנָן אָמַר – **But R' Yochanan says:** לְעוֹלָם חוֹלְקִין – **They always divide** it equally.[27]

The Gemara challenges R' Yochanan from a Baraisa:

וַאֲפִילוּ אֶחָד אָדוּק בְּטוֹפֶס וְאֶחָד אָדוּק בְּתוֹרֶף – **Now** does R' Yochanan mean that they divide **even if one** of the principals **is holding on to the** document's **form and the other** is holding on **to the** document's **essence?** וְהָתַנְיָא – **But it was taught in a Baraisa:** זֶה נוֹטֵל עַד מְקוֹם שֶׁיָּדוֹ מַגַּעַת – THIS ONE TAKES the portion of the garment that extends AS FAR AS HIS HAND REACHES.[28] The Baraisa states clearly that a litigant is awarded any portion of an article in his possession. This supports R' Elazar's ruling and contradicts that of R' Yochanan. – ? –

To deflect the challenge, the Gemara limits R' Yochanan's ruling to a specific case:

לֹא צְרִיכָא – R' Yochanan's ruling **applies only** to a case דְּקָאֵי תּוֹרֶף בֵּי מִצְעֵי – **in which the** document's **essence is situated** in **the middle** so that neither principal is holding it; only in such case do they divide the document. In the Baraisa's case, howev[er,] where each principal holds a different section of the document, [R'] Yochanan agrees with R' Elazar that each is awarded the secti[on] in his possession.[29]

The Gemara challenges this interpretation of R' Yochanan's statement:

אִי הָכִי מַאי לְמֵימְרָא – **If so, why** was it necessary for R' Yochan[an] **to state** his ruling? If neither principal holds the documen[t's] essence, they obviously must divide the document. – ? –

**The Gemara answers:**

לֹא צְרִיכָא – **[The statement] is necessary** for a case קָרֵב לְגַבֵּי דְּחַד – **in which [the document's essence] is closer to o[ne]** of the principals than to the other.[30] מַהוּ דְּתֵימָא אָמַר לֵיהּ פְּלוֹג הָכִי – **You might argue that** the principal closer to t[he] document's essence **can tell [his adversary], "Divide** t[he] document **this way,"** so that the document's entire essence w[ill] be allocated to me.[31] קָא מַשְׁמַע לָן – **[R' Yochanan's sta[te]ment]** therefore **informs us** דְּאָמַר לֵיהּ – **that [the adversar[y]] can tell him:** מַאי חָזֵית דְּפָלְגַת הָכִי – **What** reason **do you s[ee]** **for dividing** it **this way** so that your portion will be worth mo[re] than mine? פְּלוֹג הָכִי – Let us rather **divide** it **that way** so th[at] our portions will be of equal value![32]

The Gemara clarifies R' Elazar's ruling:

אָמַר לֵיהּ רַב אַחָא מִדִּפְתִּי לְרָבִינָא – **Rav Acha of Difti asked Ra[vi]na:** לְרַבִּי אֶלְעָזָר – **According to R' Elazar,** [א]מַר זֶה נוֹטֵל טוֹפֶס

NOTES

23. The Gemara expounds Rabban Shimon's explicit ruling of יַחֲלוֹקוּ, they shall divide. Rebbi also agrees, however, that if the disputed document were certified, the principals would divide it (see Gemara 7a). Thus, although the Gemara directs its discussion at Rabban Shimon's explicit ruling, it concerns Rebbi's view as well.

24. מַחֲלוֹקֶת (*division*) is the noun form of the expression יַחֲלוֹקוּ (*they shall divide*), which Rabban Shimon used in his ruling. The root of these words (חלק) connotes an equal division (*Rashi*).

In Talmudic usage, the term מַחֲלוֹקֶת usually means *disagreement,* rather than *division*. If that were R' Elazar's intent, his statement would read: *The disagreement* between Rabban Shimon and Rebbi *concerns* only a case *in which both* of the principals *hold on to the* document's *form...* Our commentary follows *Rashi's* interpretation; see *Tosafos,* who explain why *Rashi* interpreted the Gemara as he did.

25. The document's essence – the *toref* – [is written at the beginning of the document and] specifies the document's date, the names of the principals, and the amount of the loan. The document's form – the *tofes* – contains the rest of the document's text (*Rashi*).

26. Because anything that a man grasps in his hand is assumed to be his.

The Tannaic source for this rule is a Baraisa on 7a, which states that if two disputants are holding on to a cloak, each is awarded the portion of the cloak that he is grasping in his hand; the rest is divided equally. Similarly, in our case, if each disputant is holding a different section of the document, each is awarded the section he is grasping. The Gemara below will explain why a portion of a document is worth anything (*Rashi*).

27. Initially, the Gemara assumes that R' Yochanan disputes R' Elazar's ruling, maintaining that even if one of the principals holds the *toref* and the other the *tofes,* they still must "divide the document." The Gemara will soon disprove this assumption.

28. The Baraisa discusses a case in which two people are holding on to a cloak, each claiming to own it. See Gemara (7a) which cites the Baraisa's full text.

29. Hence, there is no dispute between R' Elazar and R' Yochanan: Both agree that if the two litigants hold different sections of the document, each is awarded the section in his hand; whereas if they both hold one section, they divide the document equally (*Rashi*; cf. *Rambam, Hilchos Malveh V'Loveh* 14:14 and *Maggid Mishneh* ad loc.).

30. I.e. both principals hold only the blank margins of the document, b[ut] the *toref* is closer to one than to the other.

31. The *toref* is closer to the beginning of the document; the *tofes* is clos[er] to the end. Hence, the principal holding the top of the document is clos[er] to the *toref* than the other. That principal may thus request that t[he] document be divided according to width so that the entire *toref* will [be] allocated to him (see diagram).

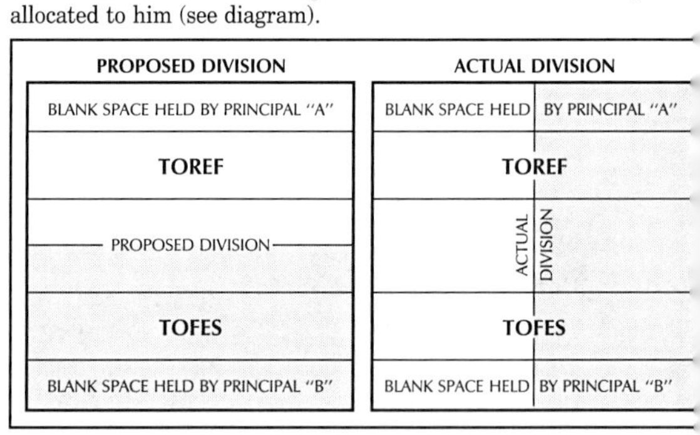


32. Having proven that R' Yochanan agreed with R' Elazar's ruling, [R'] Yochanan's own ruling seemed difficult to understand. R' Elazar rul[ed] that if the litigants are both holding either the *tofes* or *toref,* they divi[de] equally; but if one holds the *tofes* and the other the *toref*, each is award[ed] the section that he is holding. If R' Yochanan agrees to this, what do[es] he teach when he states: לְעוֹלָם, they *always* divide?

In response, our Gemara explains that R' Yochanan teaches [as] follows: Even if the *toref* is closer to one of the principals, they still divi[de] equally. [If one is actually holding the *tofes*, though, he is certain[ly]] awarded that section. Seemingly, then, the Gemara here interpre[ts] לְעוֹלָם to mean not that we always divide but rather that in all cas[es] where we do divide, the division must be completely equal qualitatively as well as quantitatively. (Not only must each litiga[nt] receive a portion of equal size, but each must also receive a portion [of] equal value.) Hence, the court will not heed one litigant's plea that he [be] awarded the entire *toref*, for he would then receive a portion of great[er] value than his adversary. Instead, it will honor his adversary's reque[st] and divide the *toref* between them.

מאי שנא ליד דיין אמר רבא הכי קאמר [א]ואחר שמצא שטר שנפל ליד דיין והיכי דמי (א) דכתב ביה הנפק לא יוציאו עולמית ולא מיבעיא לא כתב ביה הנפק דאיכא למימר כתב ללות ולא לוה אלא אפי' כתב ביה הנפק דמקוים לא יחזיר דחיישינן לפירעון ורבי יוסי אומר הרי הוא בחזקתו ולא חיישינן לפירעון ולא חייש ר' יוסי לפירעון והתניא מצא שטר כתובה בשוק בזמן שהבעל מודה יחזיר לאשה אין הבעל מודה [ב]לא יחזיר לא לזה ולא [א]לזה רבי יוסי אומר עודה תחת בעלה יחזיר לאשה נתארמלה או נתגרשה לא יחזיר לא לזה ולא לזה איפוך נפל ליד דיין לא יוציאו עולמית דברי רבי יוסי וחכ"א הרי הוא בחזקתו אי הכי קשיא דרבנן אדרבנן שטר כתובה כולה רבי יוסי וחסורי מחסרא והכי קתני אין הבעל מודה לא יחזיר לא לזה ולא לזה בד"א שנתארמלה או שנתגרשה אבל עודה תחת בעלה יחזיר לאשה (ב) שר"י אומר עודה תחת בעלה יחזיר לאשה נתארמלה או שנתגרשה לא יחזיר לא לזה ולא לזה רב פפא אמר לעולם לא תיפוך רבי יוסי לדבריהם דרבנן קאמר להו לדידי אפילו נתארמלה או נתגרשה נמי לא חיישינן לפירעון לדידכו אודו לי מיהת בעודה תחת בעלה דיחזיר לאשה דלאו בת פירעון היא ואמרו ליה רבנן אימור צררי אתפסה רבינא אמר לעולם איפוך קמייתא וטעמא דרבנן הכא משום דחיישינן לשתי כתובות ורבי יוסי לשתי כתובות לא חייש אמר רבי אלעזר [ג]מחלוקת בששניהם אדוקים בטופס ושניהם בתורף [ג]אבל אחד אדוק בטופס ואחד אדוק בתורף זה נוטל טופס וזה נוטל תורף ור' יוחנן אמר לעולם חולקין ואפילו אחד אדוק בטופס ואחד אדוק בתורף והתניא זה נוטל עד מקום שידו מגעת לא צריכא דקאי תורף בי מצעי אי הכי מאי למימרא לא צריכא דמקרב לגבי דחד [ג]מהו דתימא א"ל פלוג הכי קמ"ל דא"ל מאי חזית דפלגת הכי פלוג הכי א"ל רב אחא מדפתי לרבינא לרבי אלעזר דאמר זה נוטל טופס וזה נוטל תורף למה ליה [ד]וכי לצור ע"פ צלוחיתו הוא צריך א"ל [ד]לדמי דאמר הכי שטרא דאית ביה זמן כמה שוי ודלית ביה זמן כמה שוי בשטרא דאית ביה זמן גבי ממשעבדי ואידך לא גבי ממשעבדי יהיב ליה היאך דביני ביני ויחלוקו נמי דאמרן לדמי דאי לא תימא הכי שנים אוחזין בטלית הכי נמי דפלגי הא אפסדוה הא לא קשיא

דחזיא

## רש"י

מאי שנא ליד דיין. מאיש אחר: הכי קאמר ואחר. שאינו לא לוה ולא מלוה: שמצא שטר שנפל. כבר ליד הדיין ומאי ניהו הך נפילה דכתיב ביה הנפק: לא יוציאוהו מידו. לא לוה ולא מלוה עד שיבאו אליהו או עדים שראו מיד מי נפל: לפירעון. שמא אמת טוען הלוה שפרעו: ורבי יוסי לא חייש לפירעון. דמאן דמהדרי ליה שטר פרוע לאלתר זהיר ביה לקורעו ולא משהי ליה: שהבעל מודה. שלא נתן לה כתובתה: אין הבעל מודה. שאמר פרעתי ומידי נפל: עודה תחת בעלה. שלא גרשה: יחזיר לאשה. דלא עביד איניש ליתן כתובה קודם גירושין: צררי אתפסה. מעות צרורות או כספים מסר לה ליחוד כתובתה כשנשאה או לאחר מכאן שלא יטריחוה יורשים אם תתאלמן: לעולם איפוך קמייתא. ודקשיא לך דרבנן אדרבנן לא תיקשי דטעמייהו דרבנן בכתובה לאו משום דחיישינן לפירעון דמאן דפרע ואהדר ליה שטרא לאלתר קרע ליה אלא משום דחיישינן לשתי כתובות שמא חזר וכתב לה כתובה אחרת שניה לאחר שנפלה זאת מידה ואין הבעל מודה דקתני לאו באומר פרעתי אלא באומר אל תחזרו לה שיש בידה אחרת ותוציא על יורשי שטר אחר שטר: מחלוקת. האי יחלוקו דקאמר ר"ש [ב"ג] דמשמע חולקין בשוה כך שמעתי משום ר' יצחק ב"ר מנחם ונראה בעיני: ושניהם אדוקים בתורף. כלומר או שניהם אדוקין בתורף ותורף גילוי של שטר מקום הלוה והמלוה והמעות והזמן טופס שאר כל לשון השטר: זה נוטל כו'. דמאי דתפיס דידיה הוא כדקתני לעיל זה נוטל עד מקום שידו מגעת כו' ולקמן מפרש למאי מיבעי ליה: ואפי' אחד אדוק כו'. בתמיה: והא תניא עד מקום שידו מגעת. שלו: דקאי תורף בי מצעי. ומר אמר חדא ומר אמר חדא ולא פליגי: לדמי. מעלין בדמים כמה תורף יפה מן הטופס: שטרא דאית ביה זמן כמה שוה. דתורף עדיף מטופס דאית ביה מקום הזמן דאילו שם המלוה והלוה והמעות כתובין אף בטופס שצריך לחזור מעניינו של שטר בשיטה אחרונה והוא עיקר כדתנן (ב"ב דף קסה:) כתוב בו [מלמעלה מנה ולמטה מאתים] מלמעלה מאתים ולמטה מנה הכל הולך אחר התחתון אבל זמן לא מיהדר ואי משום חתימת עדים דהוא תחת הטופס הא אית ליה לרשב"ג מודה בשטר שכתבו אין צריך לקיימו והאי מודה שכתבו הוא:

דחזיא

## תוספות

**מאי** שנא ליד דיין. לספרים דגרסי בשנויא והיכי דמי כגון דכתוב ביה הנפק השתא לא ידע דנפל ליד דיין דהיינו הנפק אלא סבור דהיינו שהדיין מצאו ולכך בעי מאי שנא דיין מאיש אחר ולספרים דלא גרסי בתר הכי והיכי דמי כגון דכתוב ביה הנפק ידע שפיר השתא דנפל ליד דיין היינו שכתוב בו הנפק ומיבעיא ליה מאי שנא כתוב בו הנפק דלא יוציאו לעולם הלא אם אין כתוב בו הנפק נראה דכ"ש הוא שלא יוציאו עולמית דאיכא למימר שמא כתב ללות ולא לוה ומשני דלא מיבעיא קאמר:

**בזמן** שהבעל מודה יחזיר לאשה. דלא חיישינן לקנויא וליכא למיחש לשמא כתב בניסן ולא נשא עד תשרי [ה]דמנה ומאתים משתעבדי מן האירוסין אף בלא כתובה דאירוסין קלא אית להו ולקודם אירוסין ליכא למיחש דכתב לה ותוספת נמי לאביי דאמר עדיו בחתומיו זכין לו א"ש ור' אסי יעמיד כשהקנה לה:

**דחיישינן** לשתי כתובות. ובלאו איפוך לא מצי לאוקמא דרבי יוסי חייש לשתי כתובות דא"כ עודה תחת בעלה אמאי יחזיר לאשה כשאין הבעל מודה:

**מחלוקת.** פרש"י דהיינו יחלוקו דקאמר רשב"ג והדין עמו שלא רצה לפרש פלוגתא דרבי ורשב"ג משום דהיכי קאמר אבל אחד אדוק בטופס כו' משמע דהתם לא פליגי חה אינו דגם שם אם אינו מקוים לא שקיל לרבי מידי:

**דאית** ביה זמן כמה שוה. פרש"י דמעות ולוה ומלוה לא שיימינן דכתיבי נמי בשיטה אחרונה בטופס והוא עיקר דתנן (ב"ב דף קסה:) כתוב [בו] מלמעלה מנה כו' ותימה הא אין למידין משיטה אחרונה ולכך עושין חזרת השטר ומתני' דכתוב למעלה מנה לא איירי בשיטה אחרונה וגם פי' דבעדים לא שיימינן דרשב"ג אית ליה מודה בשטר שכתבו אין צריך לקיימו ופירושו תימה דאם חשב אותו שאינו תופס עדים כאילו יש לו שטר בלא עדים א"כ לרשב"ג נמי לא א"ש דנהי דסבר דאין צריך לקיימו מ"מ כשאין כלל עדי חתימה פסול ועוד במה עדיף תורף מטופס כך השטר פסול בלא טופס כמו בלא תורף דאם נמחק אפי' שיטה אחת מן השטר הוא פסול אלא ודאי יש לומר דבמה שהשטר נפסל אין שמין דכך שוה כשתופס שיטה אחת מן הטופס כמו תופס לוה ומלוה ומעות ועדים והשטר אינו כשר בלא זה כמו בלא זה אבל זמן שהשטר כשר בלא זמנו שמין כמה שוה ובירושלמי איכא א"ר אלעזר הכל הולך אחר מי שתפוס עדים ופליג אגמ' שלנו דמזכיר זמן וסובר דעדי מסירה כרתי והשטר כשר בלא עדי חתימה ושמין כמה שוה שאין צריך לחזור אחר עדי מסירה ולית ליה ההוא לישנא דג"פ (ב"ב דף קע.) דסבר רשב"ג עדי חתימה כרתי: **ויחלוקו** נמי לדמי. ואין חולקין את החוב כמו שכתוב בשטר אלא כמו ששוה לו למכור מזה יפרע החלי דאי לא תימא הכי אלא חצי החוב ממש גבי טלית מי חולקין ממש הא אפסדוה ולא גרסי' לא דפסקינן לשטרא דא"כ מה מביא מטלית אדרבה בטלית אם יחתכנו לשנים אין פסידא כל כך ואם יחתוך השטר לא ישוה לכלום ועוד דפשיטא הוא דלא יחלוקו השטר לשנים דאוקימנא לעיל פלוגתא דרבי ורבי שמעון בן גמליאל במודה בשטר שכתבו אלא כדפרישית:

דחזיא

## עין משפט נר מצוה

נ א מיי' פי"ח מהלכות גזלה ואבידה הל' יג סמג עשין עד טוש"ע ח"מ סי' סה סעיף ו וסעיף ז:

נא ב מיי' שם הל' יג ואף אם שניהם מודים דחיישינן לקנויא וע"ש במ"מ:

נב ג ד טוש"ע ח"מ סי' סה סעיף טו:

## רבינו חננאל

לקיימו יחלוקו דמודה בשטר שכתבו א"צ לקיימו ואין הלכה כמותו. אדם שמצא שטר שכתוב בו קיום ב"ד לא יוציאו עולמית חיישינן שמא פרוע הוא דברי א) ר' יוסי וחכ"א הרי [הוא] בחזקתו וכ"ש המוצא שטר שאין בו קיום שלא יוציאו עולמית דחיישינן שמא כתב ללות ולא לוה: **אמר ר"א מחלוקת בשניהן אדוקין בתופס ובתורף וכו' ור' יוחנן אמר לעולם** חולקין והאי דקאי תורף בינייהו ואע"ג דמקרב לגבי דחד לא חיישינן אלא חולקים. פי' תורף כדתנן בפרק כל גט שנכתב שלא לשם אשה כו' הכותב תופסי גיטין צריך שיניח מקום שם האיש והאשה ומקום הזמן שטרי מלוה צריך שיניח מקום המלוה ומקום הלוה ומקום המעות ומקום הזמן זהו תורף והשאר תופס וזה שאמרו חולקין בשטר לא שיחתכוהו כי זה הפסד הוא אלא דמיו חולקין ושקלינן וטרינן בה טובא ואסיקנא הכי מהא דתנן היו רוכבין על גבי בהמה או א' רוכב וא' מנהיג וכו' עד ויחלוקו הכי נמי דפלגי לה ממש בשלמא בהמה טהורה חזיא לבישרא אלא בהמה טמא' אפסדוה אלא לדמי וכן הלכה. ואם היו שנים אדוקין בשטר זה בתורף וזה בתופס ב). בשלמא שם המלוה והלוה והמעות יתכן לעמוד בהן עכשיו ואחר כך אם אבד השטר אין חוששין לו אלא הזמן שרוצה להיות בידו לטרוף ממשעבדי שמין כמה שוה שטר שיש בו זמן ויש לו לגבות ממשעבדי דבאין ללוה נכסים בני חורין ויש בו זמן טריף ממשעבדי ואם אין בו זמן אבד ממונו ומה שעולה בה השומא שקיל מי שהתורף בידו וכן הדין. ור' יוחנן לא חלק אלא בזמן שהתורף באמצע אבל בזמן שזה תופס בתורף וזה בתופס לא חלק שו' פל השטר למי שבידו התורף והדין כאשר פירשנו ולדברי הכל כל דבר שאם יחלק יפסד שמין אותו בדמים וחולקין בדמים כדתנן בפ' השותפין אין חולקין את החצר עד שיהא בה כדי לזה וכדי לזה וכו' ואסיק התם בגמ' ת"ש זה הכלל כל שאילו יחלק ושמו עליו חולקין אותו ואם לאו מעלין אותו בדמים. ר' יוסי אומר הרי הוא בחזקתו. ומקשי' וכי ר' יוסי לא חייש לפירעון והתניא מצא כתובת אשה בשוק בזמן שהבעל מודה יחזיר לאשה אין הבעל מודה לא יחזיר לא לזה ולא לזה. ור' יוסי [אומר] עודה תחת בעלה יחזיר לאשה נתארמלה או נתגרשה לא יחזיר לא לזה ולא לזה. ופריק רבינא דהוא בתרא אפוך ואימא הכי נפל ליד הדיין כגון שכתוב בו קיום ב"ד לא יוציאו עולמית דברי ר' יוסי וחכ"א הרי הוא בחזקתו וטעמא דרבנן התם דאמרו לא יחזיר לא לזה ולא לזה לאו משום דחיישי לפירעון אלא משום דחיישי לשתי כתובות. ור' יוסי לשתי כתובות לא חייש.

כיון

**חשק שלמה על ר"ח** א) בגמ' איתא להיפך ואולי דרבינו העתיק כאן כפי המסקנא לקמן בסמוך. ב) נראה דל"ל זה נוטל טופס וזה נוטל תורף ומסקינן דנ"מ משום הזמן דבשלמא וכו'.

## מסורת הש"ס

א) [נ"ל לזו], ב) בתוס' חגיגה ו: שאין להם], ג) [... קז.], ד) [לקמן יג., קמא מט:, בבא ב... עו:].

## הגהות הב"ח

(א) גמ' והיכי דמי דכתב ביה הנ... (ב) שם יחזיר ל... דברי ר' יוסי שר' אומר:

## גליון הש"ס

תוס' ד"ה בזמן דמנה ומאו... משתעבדי. ע' לקו... ע"א תד"ה הטוע...

## ליקוטי רש"י

וכי לצור על צלוחיתו. וכי לצור פי צלוחיתו קנאו זה סברא היא דמשום ג... חוב הכתוב בו קונין [רשב"ם ב"ב עו:].

Tanna Kamma) in the second Baraisa, i.e. that the finder may not return the document.[12] – ? –

To defend its answer, the Gemara reinterprets the second Baraisa:

**שְׁטַר כְּתוּבָּה** – The Baraisa that discusses the ***kesubah* document**, i.e. the second Baraisa, **כּוּלָּהּ רַבִּי יוֹסֵי** – **is in its entirety** a reflection of the view of **R' Yose. וְחַסּוּרֵי מִחַסְּרָא וְהָכִי קָתָנֵי** – **And it is as if [the Baraisa] is deficient and this is how it should read: אֵין הַבַּעַל מוֹדֶה** – IF THE HUSBAND DOES NOT CONCEDE that the *kesubah* obligation is unpaid, **לֹא יַחֲזִיר לֹא לָזֶה וְלֹא לָזֶה** – then [THE FINDER] MAY NOT RETURN [THE *KESUBAH* DOCUMENT] TO EITHER THIS party OR TO THAT party. **בַּמֶּה דְּבָרִים אֲמוּרִים** – TO WHAT instance DOES THIS RULING REFER? **שֶׁנִּתְאַרְמְלָה אוֹ שֶׁנִּתְגָּרְשָׁה** – To an instance IN WHICH [the wife] HAD BEEN WIDOWED OR DIVORCED at the time the document was found. **אֲבָל עוֹדָהּ תַּחַת בַּעְלָהּ** – But IF SHE WAS STILL UNDER the jurisdiction of HER HUSBAND, i.e. she was still married when the document was found, **יַחֲזִיר לָאִשָּׁה** – [THE FINDER] MUST RETURN it TO THE WIFE. **שֶׁרַבִּי יוֹסֵי אוֹמֵר** – FOR R' YOSE SAYS: **עוֹדָהּ תַּחַת בַּעְלָהּ** – IF SHE IS still UNDER the jurisdiction of HER HUSBAND, **יַחֲזִיר לָאִשָּׁה** – [THE FINDER] MUST RETURN the document TO THE WIFE, **נִתְאַרְמְלָה אוֹ שֶׁנִּתְגָּרְשָׁה** – but IF SHE HAD BEEN WIDOWED OR DIVORCED, **לֹא יַחֲזִיר לֹא לָזֶה וְלֹא לָזֶה** – [THE FINDER] MAY NOT RETURN it EITHER TO THIS party, i.e. the husband, OR TO THAT party. Never having mentioned the Sages' view, this Baraisa obviously does not contradict any ruling attributed to them.[13]

Earlier, the Gemara presented Baraisos that attribute contradictory rulings to R' Yose; to resolve the contradiction, it switched the statements of R' Yose and the Sages in the first Baraisa. The Gemara now proposes another solution:

**רַב פָּפָּא אָמַר לְעוֹלָם לֹא תֵּיפוֹךְ** – **Rav Pappa said: Actually you** need **not switch** the statements; R' Yose indeed rules that if a debt document is found, we are not concerned about payment. This does not contradict his statement quoted in the second Baraisa, however, because there, **רַבִּי יוֹסֵי לְדִבְרֵיהֶם דְּרַבָּנָן קָאָמַר לְהוּ** – **R' Yose was** responding to the words of the Sages **on their own terms.**[14] He thus meant as follows: **לְדִידִי** – **According to me, אֲפִילּוּ נִתְאַרְמְלָה אוֹ נִתְגָּרְשָׁה** – **even if [a woman] was widowed or divorced** when her *kesubah* document was found, **נַמִּי לֹא חַיְישִׁינַן לְפֵירָעוֹן** – **still we are not concerned about payment**;[15] the finder may thus return the document to her. **לְדִידְכוּ** – However, even **according to your premise,** i.e. that we must be concerned about payment, **אוֹדוּ לִי מִיהַת** – **concede me at least בְּעוֹדָהּ תַּחַת בַּעְלָהּ** – that **if [the woman] is st under** the jurisdiction of **her husband** when her *kesub* document is found **דְּיַחֲזִיר לָאִשָּׁה** – **that [the finder] mu return** it **to the woman דְּלָאו בַּת פֵּירָעוֹן הִיא** – because married woman] **is not [someone to whom]** a *kesubah* **payme** is due.[16] Why, then, do the Sages maintain that the finder mu keep the *kesubah* document unless the husband concedes that t *kesubah* obligation is unpaid? **וְאָמְרוּ לֵיהּ רַבָּנָן** – **But t Rabbis,** i.e. the Sages, **retorted to him: אֵימוּר צְרָרֵי אַתְפַּסָה** **Say** that perhaps **[the husband]** had previously[17] **deposit "bundles"** of valuables **with [the woman],** designating t deposit as payment for the *kesubah*.[18] Therefore, if the husba objects to the finder's returning the *kesubah* to the wife,[19] must keep it.

Earlier, after switching the attribution in the first Baraisa, t Gemara first asserted that such a change creates a contradicti between the Sages' rulings in the two Baraisos.[20] Havi previously suggested one resolution to the contradiction, t Gemara now suggests another:

**רָבִינָא אָמַר** – **Ravina said: לְעוֹלָם אֵיפוֹךְ קַמַּיְיתָא** – **Actually, y should switch** the statements of R' Yose and the Sages in the fi Baraisa: Thus, the Sages in fact are not concerned about payme Nevertheless, the apparent contradiction is not difficult, **וְטַעְמָא דְּרַבָּנָן הָכָא** – **and the reasoning of the Rabbis** here (i.e. t Sages cited in the second Baraisa, who require the finder to ke the *kesubah* document) is **מִשּׁוּם דְּחַיְישִׁינַן לִשְׁתֵּי כְתוּבּוֹת** **because we are concerned about** the possibility that t husband may have written **two *kesubah* documents.**[21] To avc the woman's defrauding her husband with a second *kesubah*, t finder must keep the found document.

The Gemara questions the reasoning of the Sages' disputar

**וְרַבִּי יוֹסֵי** – **But R' Yose!** Why does he permit a finder to return t found *kesubah* document to the wife?

The Gemara answers:

**לִשְׁתֵּי כְתוּבּוֹת לֹא חָיֵישׁ** – **He is not concerned about** t possibility that the husband wrote **two *kesubah* documents.**

The Baraisa on 7a presents a dispute concerning a case in whi two litigants are holding on to an uncertified debt document, ea claiming to have lost it: Rebbi rules that the creditor cann collect anything, whereas Rabban Shimon ben Gamliel rules th they "divide" it. The Gemara now cites two interpretations

NOTES

12. Because we are "concerned about payment."

13. According to this interpretation, the second Baraisa's opening statement is actually a formulation of R' Yose's opinion and not that of an anonymous disputant. Hence, since the Baraisa never mentions the Sages' view, it obviously does not contradict the ruling attributed to them in the first Baraisa.

14. Since R' Yose's statement in the second Baraisa does not represent his own opinion, it does not contradict his ruling in the first Baraisa.

15. For according to R' Yose himself, the mere existence of a *kesubah* document creates a presumption that the husband never paid (see note 8 above).

16. For *kesubah* payments become due only upon termination of the marriage. Hence, if a married woman's *kesubah* is found, we should assume that it is still unpaid and thus fell from the woman. Why, then, do the Sages require the finder to keep it "until Elijah comes"?

17. I.e. when he married her or at some later time (*Rashi;* cf. *Rashba* and *Ritva*).

18. Perhaps he did so to save his wife the trouble of collecting from his heirs when he dies (*Rashi*).

19. See *Mayenei HaChochmah*, who explains the husband's objection.

20. Thus far, the Gemara had assumed that the Sages (i.e. the Tan Kamma) of the second Baraisa are concerned about payment, where the Sages of the first Baraisa (after the switching of views) are n concerned about payment. To resolve the contradiction, the Gema now explains the second Baraisa differently (*Rashi*).

21. I.e. when the woman lost her *kesubah* document, the husband m have drafted another, as required by law.

Now if a woman possesses two documents recording the same *kesubc* obligation, this affords her the opportunity to defraud her husband: S can take each document to a different court and thus collect her *kesubc* twice. Hence, if a *kesubah* document is found, the husband can argu "Do not return this document to my wife, for doing so will enable her defraud me." According to this interpretation, when the Barai requires the finder to keep the document "if the husband does n concede," it means that he claimed to have written a second *kesubah* ar not (as previously assumed) that he claimed to have paid his *kesubc* obligation (*Rashi*).

22. R' Yose maintains that if the husband had drafted a second *kesubc* document, he would have done so publicly in *beis din*. Thus, if the pub is unaware of a second *kesubah*, we dismiss the possibility that one m exist (*Ritva*).

מאי שנא ליד דיין אמר רבא הכי קאמר [א]ואחר שמצא שטר שנפל ליד דיין והיכי דמי (א) דכתב ביה הנפק לא יוציאו עולמית ולא מיבעיא לא כתב ביה הנפק דאיכא למימר כתב ללות ולא לוה אלא אפי' כתב ביה הנפק דמקוים לא יחזיר דחיישינן לפירעון ורבי יוסי אומר הרי הוא בחזקתו ולא חיישינן לפירעון ולא חייש ר' יוסי לפירעון והתניא מצא שטר כתובה בשוק בזמן שהבעל מודה יחזיר לאשה אין הבעל מודה [ב]לא יחזיר לא לזה ולא (א) לזה רבי יוסי אומר עודה תחת בעלה יחזיר לאשה נתארמלה או נתגרשה לא יחזיר לא לזה ולא לזה איפוך נפל ליד דיין לא יוציאו עולמית דברי רבי יוסי וחכ"א הרי הוא בחזקתו אי הכי קשיא דרבנן אדרבנן שטר כתובה כולה רבי יוסי וחסורי מחסרא והכי קתני אין הבעל מודה לא יחזיר לא לזה ולא לזה בד"א שנתארמלה או שנתגרשה אבל עודה תחת בעלה יחזיר לאשה (ב) שר"י אומר עודה תחת בעלה יחזיר לאשה נתארמלה או שנתגרשה לא יחזיר לא לזה ולא לזה רב פפא אמר לעולם לא תיפוך רבי יוסי לדבריהם דרבנן קאמר להו לדידי אפילו נתארמלה או נתגרשה נמי לא חיישינן לפירעון לדידכו אודו לי מיהת בעודה תחת בעלה דיחזיר לאשה דלאו בת פירעון היא ואמרו ליה רבנן אימור צררי אתפסה רבינא אמר לעולם איפוך קמייתא וטעמא דרבנן הכא משום דחיישינן לשתי כתובות ורבי יוסי לשתי כתובות לא חייש אמר רבי אלעזר [ג]מחלוקת בששניהם אדוקים בטופס ושניהם בתורף [ג]אבל אחד אדוק בטופס ואחד אדוק בתורף זה נוטל טופס וזה נוטל תורף ור' יוחנן אמר לעולם חולקין ואפילו אחד אדוק בטופס ואחד אדוק בתורף והתניא זה נוטל עד מקום שידו מגעת לא צריכא דקאי תורף בי מצעי אי הכי מאי למימרא לא צריכא דמקרב לגבי דחד [ג]מהו דתימא א"ל פלוג הכי קמ"ל דא"ל מאי חזית דפלגת הכי פלוג הכי א"ל רב אחא מדפתי לרבינא לרבי אלעזר דאמר זה נוטל טופס וזה נוטל תורף למה ליה [ד]וכי לצור ע"פ צלוחיתו הוא צריך א"ל [ד]לדמי דאמר הכי שטרא דאית ביה זמן כמה שוי ודלית ביה זמן כמה שוי בשטרא דאית ביה זמן גבי ממשעבדי ואידך לא גבי ממשעבדי יהיב ליה היאך דביני ביני ויחלוקו נמי דאמרן לדמי דאי לא תימא הכי שנים אוחזין בטלית הכי נמי דפלגי הא אפסדוה הא לא קשיא

דחזיא

**רש"י**

מאי שנא ליד דיין. מאיש אחר: הכי קאמר ואחר. שאינו לא לוה ולא מלוה: שמצא שטר שנפל. כבר ליד הדיין ומאי ניהו הך נפילה דכתיב ביה הנפק: לא יוציאוהו מידו. לא לוה ולא מלוה עד שיבא אליהו או עדים שראו מיד מי נפל: לפירעון. שמא אמת טוען הלוה שפרעו: ורבי יוסי לא חייש לפירעון. דמאן דמהדרי ליה שטר פרוע לאלתר זהיר ביה לקורעו ולא משהי ליה: שהבעל מודה. שלא נתן לה כתובתה: אין הבעל מודה. שאמר פרעתי ומידי נפל: עודה תחת בעלה. שלא גרשה: יחזיר לאשה. דלא עביד איניש ליתן כתובה קודם גירושין: צררי אתפסה. מעות צרורות או כספים מסר לה ליחוד כתובתה כשנשאה או לאחר מכאן שלא יטריחוה יורשים אם תתאלמן: לעולם איפוך קמייתא. ודקשיא לך דרבנן אדרבנן לא תיקשי דטעמייהו דרבנן בכתובה לאו משום דחיישינן לפירעון דמאן דפרע ואהדר ליה שטרא לאלתר קרע ליה אלא משום דחיישינן לשתי כתובות שמא חזר וכתב לה כתובה אחרת שניה לאחר שנפלה זאת מידה ואין הבעל מודה דקתני לאו באומר פרעתי אלא באומר אל תחזרו לה שיש בידה אחרת ותוליא על יורשי שטר אחר שטר: מחלוקת. הא' יחלוקו דקאמר ר"ש [ב"ג] דמשמע חולקין בשוה כך שמעתי משום ר' יצחק ב"ר מנחם ונראה בעיני: ושניהם אדוקים בתורף. כלומר או שניהם אדוקין בתורף ותורף גילוי של שטר מקום הלוה והמלוה והמעות והזמן טופס שאר כל לשון השטר: זה נוטל כו'. דמאי דתפיס דידיה הוא כדקתני לעיל זה נוטל עד מקום שידו מגעת כו' ולקמן מפרש למאי מיבעי ליה: ואפי' אחד אדוק כו'. בתמיה: והא תניא עד מקום שידו מגעת. שלו: דקאי תורף בי מצעי. ומר אמר חדא ומר אמר חדא ולא פליגי: לדמי. מעלין בדמים כמה תורף יפה מן הטופס: שטרא דאית ביה זמן כמה שוה. דתורף עדיף מטופס דאית ביה מקום הזמן דאילו שם המלוה והלוה והמעות כתובין אף בטופס שצריך לחזור מעניינו של שטר בשיטה אחרונה והוא עיקר כדתנן (ב"ב דף קסה:) כתוב בו [מלמעלה מנה ולמטה מאתים] מלמעלה מאתים ולמטה מנה הכל הולך אחר התחתון אבל זמן לא מיהדר ואי משום חתימת עדים דהוא תחת הטופס הא אית ליה לרשב"ג מודה בשטר שכתבו אין צריך לקיימו והאי מודה שכתבו הוא:

דחזיא

**תוספות**

מאי שנא ליד דיין. לספרים דגרסי בשנויא והיכי דמי כגון דכתוב ביה הנפק השתא לא ידע דנפל ליד דיין דהיינו הנפק אלא סבור דהיינו שהדיין מצאו ולכך בעי מאי שנא דיין מאיש אחר ולספרים דלא גרסי בתר הכי והיכי דמי כגון דכתוב ביה הנפק ידע שפיר השתא דנפל ליד דיין היינו שכתוב בו הנפק ומיבעיא ליה מאי שנא כתוב בו הנפק דלא יוציאו לעולם הלא אם אין כתוב בו הנפק נראה דכ"ש הוא שלא יוציאו עולמית דאיכא למימר שמא כתב ללות ולא לוה ומשני דלא מיבעיא קאמר:

בזמן שהבעל מודה יחזיר לאשה. דלא חיישינן לקנוניא וליכא למיחש לשמא כתב בניסן ולא נשא עד תשרי [ה]דמנה ומאתים משתעבדי מן האירוסין אף בלא כתובה דאירוסין קלא אית להו ולקודם אירוסין ליכא למיחש דכתב לה ותוספת נמי לאביי דאמר עדיו בחתומיו זכין לו א"ש ור' אסי יעמיד כשהקנה לה:

דחיישינן לשתי כתובות. ובלאו איפוך לא מצי לאוקמא דרבי יוסי חייש לשתי כתובות דא"כ עודה תחת בעלה אמאי יחזיר לאשה כשאין הבעל מודה:

מחלוקת. פרש"י דהיינו יחלוקו דקאמר רשב"ג והדין עמו שלא רצה לפרש פלוגתא דרבי ורשב"ג משום דהיכי קאמר אבל אחד אדוק בטופס כו' משמע דהתם לא פליגי וזה אינו דגם שם אם אינו מקוים לא שקיל לרבי מידי:

דאית ביה זמן כמה שוה. פרש"י דמעות ולוה ומלוה לא סיימין דכתיבי נמי בשיטה אחרונה בטופס והוא עיקר דתנן (ב"ב דף קסה:) כתוב [בו] מלמעלה מנה כו' ותימה הא אין למידין משיטה אחרונה ולכך עושין חזרת השטר ומתני' דכתוב למעלה מנה לא מיירי בשיטה אחרונה וגם פי' דבעדים לא סיימין דרשב"ג אית ליה מודה בשטר שכתבו אין צריך לקיימו ופירושו תימה דאם חשב אותו שאינו תופס עדים כאילו יש לו שטר בלא עדים א"כ לרשב"ג נמי לא א"ש דנהי דסבר דאין צריך לקיימו מ"מ כשאין כלל עדי חתימה פסול ועוד במה עדיף תורף מטופס כך השטר פסול בלא טופס כמו בלא תורף דאם נמחק אפי' שיטה אחת מן השטר הוא פסול אלא ודאי יש לומר דבמה שהשטר נפסל אין שמין דכך שוה כשתופס שיטה אחת מן הטופס כמו תופס לוה ומלוה ומעות ועדים והשטר אינו כשר בלא זה כמו בלא זה אבל זמן שהשטר כשר בלא זמנו שמין כמה שוה ובירושלמי איכא א"ר אלעזר הכל הולך אחר מי שתפוס עדים ופליג אגמ' שלנו דמזכיר זמן וסובר דעדי מסירה כרתי והשטר כשר בלא עדי חתימה ושמין כמה שוה שאין צריך לחזור אחר עדי מסירה ולית ליה ההוא לישנא דג"פ (ב"ב דף קע.) דסבר רשב"ג עדי חתימה כרתי:

ויחלוקו נמי לדמי. ואין חולקין את החוב כמו שכתוב בשטר אלא כמו ששוה לו למכור מזה יפרע האי דאי לא תימא הכי אלא חאי החוב ממש גבי טלית מי חולקין ממש הא אפסדוה ולא גרסי' לא דפסקינן לשטרא דא"כ מה מביא מטלית אדרבה בטלית אם יחתכנו לשנים אין פסידא כל כך ואם יחתוך השטר לא ישוה לכלום ועוד דפשיטא הוא דלא יחלוקו השטר לשנים דאוקימנא לעיל פלוגתא דרבי ורבי שמעון בן גמליאל במודה בשטר שכתבו אלא כדפרישית:

דחזיא

**עין משפט נר מצוה**

נ א מיי' פי"ח מהלכות גזילה ואבידה הל' יג סמג עשין עד טוש"ע ח"מ סי' סה סעיף ו וסעיף ז:

נא ב מיי' שם הל' יב ואף אם שניהם מודים דחיישינן לקנוניא וע"ש במ"מ:

נב ג ד טוש"ע ח"מ סי' סה סעיף טו:

**רבינו חננאל**

לקיימו יחלוקו דמודה בשטר שכתבו א"צ לקיימו ואין הלכה כמותו. אדם שמצא שטר שכתוב בו קיום ב"ד לא יוציאו עולמית חיישינן שמא פרוע הוא דברי א) ר' יוסי וחכ"א הרי [הוא] בחזקתו וכ"ש המוצא שטר שאין בו קיום שלא יוציאו עולמית דחיישינן שמא כתב ללות ולא לוה: אמר ר"א מחלוקת בשניהן אדוקין בתופס ובתורף וכו' ור' יוחנן אמר לעולם חולקין והאי דקאי תורף בינייהו ואע"ג דמקרב לגבי דחד לא חיישינן אלא חולקים. פי' תורף כדתנן בפרק כל גט שנכתב שלא לשם אשה כו' הכותב תופסי גיטין צריך שיניח מקום שם האיש והאשה ומקום הזמן שטרי מלוה צריך שיניח מקום המלוה ומקום הלוה ומקום המעות ומקום הזמן זהו תורף והשאר תופס וזה שאמרו חולקין בשטר לא שיחתכוהו כי זה הפסד הוא אלא דמיו חולקין ושקלינן וטרינן בה טובא ואסיקנא הכי מהא דתנן היו רוכבין על גבי בהמה או א' רוכב וא' מנהיג וכו' עד ויחלוקו הכי נמי דפלגי לה ממש בשלמא בהמה טהורה חזיא לבישרא אלא בהמה טמא' אפסדוה אלא לדמי וכן הלכה. ואם היו שנים אדוקין בשטר זה בתורף וזה בתופס ב). בשלמא שם המלוה והלוה והמעות יתכן לעמוד בהן עכשיו ואחר כך אם אבד השטר אין חוששין לו אלא הזמן שרוצה להיות בידו לטרוף ממשעבדי שמין כמה שוה שטר שיש בו זמן ויש לו לגבות ממשעבדי דבאין ללוה נכסים בני חורין ויש בו זמן טריף ממשעבדי ואם אין בו זמן אבד ממונו ומה שעולה בה השומא שקיל מי שהתורף בידו וכן הדין. ור' יוחנן לא חלק אלא בזמן שהתורף באמצע אבל בזמן שזה תופס בתורף וזה בתופס לא וה"ק שדמי כל הזיזור למי שבידו התורף והדין כאשר פירשנו ולדברי הכל כל דבר שאם יחלק יפסד שמין אותו בדמים וחולקין בדמים כדתנן בפ' השותפין אין חולקין את החצר עד שיהא בה כדי לזה וכדי לזה וכו' ואסיק התם בגמ' ת"ש זה הכלל כל שאילו יחלק ושמו עליו חולקין אותו ואם לאו מעלין אותו בדמים. ר' יוסי אומר הרי הוא בחזקתו. ומקשי' וכי ר' יוסי לא חייש לפירעון והתניא מצא כתובת אשה בשוק בזמן שהבעל מודה יחזיר לאשה אין הבעל מודה לא יחזיר לא לזה ולא לזה. ור' יוסי [אומר] עודה תחת בעלה יחזיר לאשה נתארמלה או נתגרשה לא יחזיר לא לזה ולא לזה. ופריק רבינא דהוא בתרא אפוך ואימא הכי נפל ליד הדיין כגון שכתוב בו קיום ב"ד לא יוציאו עולמית דברי ר' יוסי וחכ"א הרי הוא בחזקתו וטעמא דרבנן התם דאמרו לא יחזיר לא לזה ולא לזה לאו משום דחיישי לפירעון אלא משום דחיישי לשתי כתובות. ור' יוסי לשתי כתובות לא חייש.

כיון

**מסורת הש"ס**

א) [נ"ל לזו], ב) כתוס' חגיגה ו: שאין להם, ג) [ קז.], ד) [לקמן יג., קמא מט:, בבא ב עו:].

**הגהות הב"ח**

(א) גמ' והיכי דמי דכתב ביה הנפק (ב) שם יחזיר לאשה דברי ר' יוסי שר' אומר:

**גליון הש"ס**

תוס' ד"ה בזמן דמנה ומא' משתעבדי. עי' לק' ע"א תד"ה הטוע

**ליקוטי רש"י**

וכי לצור על צלוחיתו. וכי לצור פי צלוחיתו קנאו זה סברא היא דמשום חוב הכתוב בו קונין [רשב"ם ב"ב עו:].

חשק שלמה על ר"ח א) בגמ' איתא להיפך ואולי דרבינו העתיק כאן כפי המסקנא לקמן בסמוך. ב) נראה דל"ל זה נוטל טופס וזה נוטל תורף ומסקינן דנ"מ משום הזמן דבשלמא וכו'.

Initially, the Gemara interprets the expression *into the hand of a judge* literally. It therefore asks:

**מַאי שְׁנָא לְיַד דַּיָּין – Why is** the law **different** if it fell **into the hand of a judge** than if it fell into the hands of a layman?[1]

In response to the question, the Gemara reinterprets the Baraisa's statement:

**אָמַר רָבָא – Rava said: הָכִי קָאָמַר – This is what [the statement] means: וְאַחֵר שֶׁמָּצָא שְׁטָר שֶׁנָּפַל לְיַד דַּיָּין – But** if **another** person (i.e. other than the debtor or creditor) **found a document that had** previously **fallen into the hand of a judge – וְהֵיכִי דָמֵי – and what does this mean? דִּכְתַב בֵּיהּ הֶנְפֵּק –** It means **that** a judge **had** already **written a formula of certification on [the found document].**[2] **לֹא יוֹצִיאוּ עוֹלָמִית –** If such a document is found, **the [principals] cannot ever retrieve** it from the finder.[3]

The Gemara now explains why the Baraisa specifies that the document has already been certified:[4]

**וְלֹא מִיבָּעְיָא לֹא כָּתַב בֵּיהּ הֶנְפֵּק – And needless to say, if a formula of certification had not been written on [the document]** then the finder may not return it to the creditor, **דְּאִיכָּא לְמֵימַר כָּתַב לִלְוֹת וְלֹא לָוָה – for** in such a case, **it is possible to say that [a prospective debtor] drafted** the document intending **to borrow but did not** actually **borrow.**[5] Obviously, then, a finder may not return an uncertified document to the creditor. **אֶלָּא אֲפִילוּ כָּתַב בֵּיהּ הֶנְפֵּק דִּמְקוּיָּים – But even if a formula of certification is written on [the document] so that it is certified,** thus proving that the creditor actually advanced the loan,[6] **לֹא יַחֲזִיר –** still **[the finder] may not return** the document to him, **דְּחָיְישִׁינַן לְפֵירָעוֹן – for we are concerned about payment,** i.e. we entertain the thought that the debtor may have repaid the loan.[7]

The Gemara cites and explains R' Yose's dissenting opinion:

**וְרַבִּי יוֹסֵי אוֹמֵר הֲרֵי הוּא בְּחֶזְקָתוֹ – BUT R' YOSE SAYS: [THE DEBT DOCUMENT] RETAINS ITS STATUS** as a valid document **וְלֹא חָיְישִׁינַן לְפֵירָעוֹן – and we are not concerned about payment;** the mere existence of the document proves that the debt was not paid.[8]

The Gemara questions R' Yose's ruling:

**וְלֹא חָיֵישׁ ר׳ יוֹסֵי לְפֵירָעוֹן – Now is R' Yose** in fact **not co[n]cerned about payment? וְהָתַנְיָא – But it was taught in** a **Baraisa: מָצָא שְׁטַר כְּתוּבָּה בַּשּׁוּק – IF ONE FOUND A *KESUB[AH]* DOCUMENT IN THE STREET, בִּזְמַן שֶׁהַבַּעַל מוֹדֶה – IF THE HUSBA[ND] CONCEDES** that the *kesubah* obligation is still unpaid, **[יַחֲז]יר לְאִשָּׁה –** the finder **MUST RETURN** the document **TO THE WI[FE]. אֵין הַבַּעַל מוֹדֶה –** However, **IF THE HUSBAND DOES NOT CONCE[DE]** this, i.e. he maintains that he has already paid the *kesub[ah]* obligation, **לֹא יַחֲזִיר לֹא לָזֶה וְלֹא לָזֶה –** then **[THE FINDER] M[AY] NOT RETURN [THE DOCUMENT] TO EITHER THIS** party, i.e. t[he] husband, **OR TO THAT** party, i.e. the wife.[9] **רַבִּי יוֹסֵי אוֹמֵר – [R'] YOSE SAYS: עוֹדָהּ תַּחַת בַּעְלָהּ – IF SHE IS STILL UNDER** t[he] jurisdiction of **HER HUSBAND,** i.e. if she is still married when t[he] document is found, **יַחֲזִיר לְאִשָּׁה – [THE FINDER] MUST RETURN TO THE WIFE,**[10] **נִתְאַרְמְלָה אוֹ נִתְגָּרְשָׁה –** but **IF SHE W[AS] WIDOWED OR DIVORCED** at the time, **לֹא יַחֲזִיר לֹא לָזֶה וְלֹא לָזֶה [THE FINDER] MAY NOT RETURN IT EITHER TO THIS** party, i.e. t[he] husband, **OR TO THAT** party, i.e. the wife, because we do not kn[ow] whether the *kesubah* was already paid. R' Yose's latter rul[ing] proves that he is concerned about payment; this contradicts t[he] view attributed to him in the first Baraisa. – ? –

The Gemara answers:

**אֵיפוֹךְ – Switch** the statement of R' Yose and the Sages quoted [in] the first Baraisa. The Baraisa then reads as follows: **[בְּ]לְיַד דַּיָּין לֹא יוֹצִיאוּ עוֹלָמִית – IF [THE DOCUMENT] FELL INTO THE HAND OF [A] JUDGE, [THE PRINCIPALS] CANNOT EVER RETRIEVE [IT]** because [w]e are concerned about payment; **דִּבְרֵי רַבִּי יוֹסֵי – these are TH[E] WORDS OF R' YOSE. וַחֲכָמִים אוֹמְרִים – BUT THE SAGES SAY: [הֲרֵ]י הוּא בְּחֶזְקָתוֹ – [THE DOCUMENT] RETAINS ITS PRESUMPTION** [of] validity. Both Baraisos agree, then, that according to R' Yose, [w]e are concerned about payment.

The Gemara challenges the answer:

**אִי הָכִי – If** it is **so** that the statements of R' Yose and the Sages a[re] to be inverted, **קַשְׁיָא דְּרַבָּנַן אַדְּרַבָּנַן –** then the statement **of t[he] Sages** in the first Baraisa, i.e. that a found document retains i[ts] presumption of validity,[11] **contradicts that of the Sages** (i.e. t[he]

NOTES

1. Since we cannot determine who lost the document, even a layman that found it should be obligated to keep it "until Elijah comes." See Mishnah 12b.

2. See 7a note 32.

3. Regardless of who found the document, the finder must keep it "until Elijah comes"; he may not return it to either debtor or creditor unless witnesses testify from whom it fell (*Rashi*). Thus, the phrase "if it fell into the hand of the judge" means only that *beis din* had certified the document and not that a judge found it.

4. According to Rava, the Baraisa states that a third party must keep a found debt document "until Elijah comes" if it was certified, apparently implying that if it was uncertified, he should return it. This, however, is illogical: If the document was uncertified, it too should not be returned to the creditor, out of concern that the creditor may then certify it. The Gemara therefore concludes that indeed, whenever a third party finds a debt document (whether certified or not), he may not return it. It will now explain why the Baraisa specifically mentions a certified document.

5. Anticipating a loan, a person may draft a debt document without consulting his prospective creditor. It is thus possible that the debt document exists even though the creditor never actually advanced the loan. See Mishnah *Bava Basra* 167b and Gemara below 12b-13a.

6. A certified document provides the following proof that the loan took place. Generally, the debtor drafts a debt document and keeps it until the creditor actually advances the loan. Now, certifying the debt document enables the creditor to collect with it. Since this is against the debtor's interest, only the creditor would ever certify it. Thus, if a debt document is certified, this proves that the creditor actually advanced the loan, received the document and had it certified.

7. Thus, we cannot know who lost the document. If the debtor had in fa[ct] paid his debt, then the creditor would have returned the debt docume[nt] to him at the time; the document then would have fallen from t[he] debtor. We cannot know, however, that the debtor paid. If he did n[ot] then the document would have fallen from the creditor. Since it is th[us] unclear who actually lost the document, the finder must keep it "un[til] Elijah comes."

8. For had the debt actually been paid and the document returned to t[he] debtor, he would have destroyed it immediately (*Rashi*); the document['s] existence thus proves that the debt is still unpaid. Accordingly, t[he] finder must therefore return it to the creditor.

9. A *kesubah* document represents a man's obligation to pay his wife [a] set sum when their marriage is terminated. When a man marries, [he] drafts a *kesubah* document and gives it to his wife; she returns it aft[er] he or his heirs pay the obligation recorded therein.

According to the Tanna Kamma, whenever a *kesubah* document [is] found, we are concerned about payment, i.e. we suppose that t[he] husband may have already paid the *kesubah* obligation, received t[he] *kesubah* document in return and then lost it. If we knew this to be tru[e] then the finder could simply return the document to the husband. Sin[ce] we do not know who actually lost the *kesubah* document, however, t[he] finder must hold it "until Elijah comes."

10. R' Yose notes that a husband usually pays his wife's *kesubah* on[ly] after divorcing her. Therefore, if a *kesubah* document is found while t[he] principals are still married, we assume that the husband did not yet pa[y] the *kesubah* obligation (*Rashi*); the finder thus returns the *kesub[ah]* document to the wife.

11. I.e. and we thus are not "concerned about payment."

מאי שנא ליד דיין אמר רבא הכי קאמר [א]ואחר שמצא שטר שנפל ליד דיין והיכי דמי (א) דכתב ביה הנפק לא יוציאו עולמית ולא מיבעיא לא כתב ביה הנפק דאיכא למימר כתב ללות ולא לוה אלא אפי' כתב ביה הנפק דמקוים לא יחזיר דחיישינן לפירעון ורבי יוסי אומר הרי הוא בחזקתו ולא חיישינן לפירעון ולא חייש ר' יוסי לפירעון והתניא מצא שטר כתובה בשוק בזמן שהבעל מודה יחזיר לאשה אין הבעל מודה [ב]לא יחזיר לא לזה ולא [א]לזה רבי יוסי אומר עודה תחת בעלה יחזיר לאשה נתארמלה או נתגרשה לא יחזיר לא לזה ולא לזה איפוך נפל ליד דיין לא יוציאו עולמית דברי רבי יוסי וחכ"א הרי הוא בחזקתו אי הכי קשיא דרבנן אדרבנן שטר כתובה כולה רבי יוסי וחסורי מחסרא והכי קתני אין הבעל מודה לא יחזיר לא לזה ולא לזה בד"א שנתארמלה או שנתגרשה אבל עודה תחת בעלה יחזיר לאשה (ב) שר"י אומר עודה תחת בעלה יחזיר לאשה נתארמלה או שנתגרשה לא יחזיר לא לזה ולא לזה רב פפא אמר לעולם לא תיפוך רבי יוסי לדבריהם דרבנן קאמר להו לדידי אפילו נתארמלה או נתגרשה נמי לא חיישינן לפירעון לדידכו אודו לי מיהת בעודה תחת בעלה דיחזיר לאשה דלאו בת פירעון היא ואמרו ליה רבנן אימור צררי אתפסה רבינא אמר לעולם איפוך קמייתא וטעמא דרבנן הכא משום דחיישינן לשתי כתובות ורבי יוסי לשתי כתובות לא חייש אמר רבי אלעזר [ג]מחלוקת בששניהם אדוקים בטופס ושניהם בתורף [ג]אבל אחד אדוק בטופס ואחד אדוק בתורף זה נוטל טופס וזה נוטל תורף ור' יוחנן אמר לעולם חולקין ואפילו אחד אדוק בטופס ואחד אדוק בתורף והתניא זה נוטל עד מקום שידו מגעת לא צריכא דקאי תורף בי מצעי אי הכי מאי למימרא לא צריכא דמקרב לגבי דחד [ג]מהו דתימא א"ל פלוג הכי קמ"ל דא"ל מאי חזית דפלגת הכי פלוג הכי א"ל רב אחא מדפתי לרבינא לרבי אלעזר דאמר זה נוטל טופס וזה נוטל תורף למה ליה [ד]וכי לצור ע"פ צלוחיתו הוא צריך א"ל [ד]לדמי דאמר הכי שטרא דאית ביה זמן כמה שוי ודלית ביה זמן כמה שוי בשטרא דאית ביה זמן גבי ממשעבדי ואידך לא גבי ממשעבדי יהיב ליה היאך דביני ביני ויחלוקו נמי דאמרן לדמי דאי לא תימא הכי שנים אוחזין בטלית הכי נמי דפלגי הא אפסדוה הא לא קשיא

דחזיא

**רש"י**

**מאי** שנא ליד דיין. לספרים דגרסי בשנויא והיכי דמי כגון דכתוב ביה הנפק השתא לא ידע דנפל ליד דיין דהיינו הנפק אלא סבור דהיינו שהדיין מצאו ולכך בעי מאי שנא דיין מאיש אחר ולספרים דלא גרסי בתר הכי והיכי דמי כגון דכתוב ביה הנפק ידע שפיר השתא דנפל ליד דיין היינו שכתוב בו הנפק ומיבעיא ליה מאי שנא כתוב בו הנפק דלא יוציאו לעולם הלא אם אין כתוב בו הנפק נראה דכ"ש הוא שלא יוציאו עולמית דאיכא למימר שמא כתב ללות ולא לוה ומשני דלא מיבעיא קאמר: **בזמן** שהבעל מודה יחזיר לאשה. דלא חיישינן לקנוניא וליכא למיחש לשמא כתב בניסן ולא נשא עד תשרי [°]דמנה ומאתים משתעבדי מן האירוסין אף בלא כתובה דאירוסין קלא אית להו ולקודם אירוסין ליכא למיחש דכתב לה ותוספת נמי לאביי דאמר עדיו בחתומיו זכין לו א"ש ור' אסי יעמיד כשהקנה לה: **דחיישינן** לשתי כתובות. ובלאו איפוך לא מצי לאוקמא דרבי יוסי חייש לשתי כתובות דא"כ עודה תחת בעלה אמאי יחזיר לאשה כשאין הבעל מודה: **מחלוקת.** פרש"י דהיינו יחלוקו דקאמר רשב"ג והדין עמו שלא רצה לפרש פלוגתא דרבי ורשב"ג משום דהיכי קאמר אבל אחד אדוק בטופס כו' משמע דהתם לא פליגי וזה אינו דגם שם אם אינו מקוים לא שקיל לרבי מידי: **דאית** ביה זמן כמה שוה. פרש"י דמעות ולוה ומלוה לא שיימינן דכתיבי נמי בשיטה אחרונה בטופס והוא עיקר דתנן (ב"ב דף קסה:) כתוב [בו] מלמעלה מנה כו' ותימה הא אין למידין משיטה אחרונה ולכך עושין חזרת השטר ומתני' דכתוב למעלה מנה לא איירי בשיטה אחרונה וגם פי' דבעדים לא שיימינן דרשב"ג אית ליה מודה בשטר שכתבו אין צריך לקיימו ופירושו תימה דאם חשב אותו שאינו תופס עדים כאילו יש לו שטר בלא עדים א"כ לרשב"ג נמי לא א"ש דנהי דסבר דאין צריך לקיימו מ"מ כשאין כלל עדי חתימה פסול ועוד במה עדיף תורף מטופס כך השטר פסול בלא טופס כמו בלא תורף דאם נמחק אפי' שיטה אחת מן השטר הוא פסול אלא ודאי יש לומר דבמה שהשטר נפסל אין שמין דכך שוה כשתופס שיטה אחת מן הטופס כמו תופס לוה ומלוה ומעות ועדים והשטר אינו כשר בלא זה כמו בלא זה אבל זמן שהשטר כשר בלא זמנו שמין כמה שוה ובירושלמי איכא א"ר אלעזר הכל הולך אחר מי שתפוס עדים ופליג אגמ' שלנו דמזכיר זמן וסובר דעדי מסירה כרתי והשטר כשר בלא עדי חתימה ושמין כמה שוה שאין צריך לחזור אחר עדי מסירה ולית ליה ההוא לישנא דג"פ (ב"ב דף קע.) דסבר רשב"ג עדי חתימה כרתי: **ויחלוקו** נמי לדמי. ואין חולקין את החוב כמו שכתוב בשטר אלא כמו ששוה לו למכור מזה יפרע החלי דאי לא תימא הכי אלא חלי החוב ממש גבי טלית מי חולקין ממש הא אפסדוה ולא גרסי' לא דפסקינן לשטרא דא"כ מה מביא מטלית אדרבה בטלית אם יחתכנו לשנים אין פסידא כל כך ואם יחתוך השטר לא ישוה לכלום ועוד דפשיטא הוא דלא יחלוקו השטר לשנים דאוקימנא לעיל פלוגתא דרבי ורבי שמעון בן גמליאל במודה בשטר שכתבו אלא כדפרישית:

דחזיא

**תוספות**

מאי שנא ליד דיין. מאיש אחר: הכי קאמר ואחר. שאינו לא לוה ולא מלוה: שמצא שטר שנפל. כבר ליד הדיין ומאי ניהו הך נפילה דכתיב ביה הנפק: לא יוציאוהו מידו. לא לוה ולא מלוה עד שיבא אליהו או עדים שראו מיד מי נפל: לפירעון. שמא אמת טוען הלוה שפרעו: ורבי יוסי לא חייש לפירעון. דמאן דמהדרי ליה שטר פרוע לאלתר זהיר ביה לקורעו ולא משהי ליה: שהבעל מודה. שלא נתן לה כתובתה: אין הבעל מודה. שאמר פרעתי ומידי נפל: עודה תחת בעלה. שלא גרשה: יחזיר לאשה. דלא עביד איניש ליתן כתובה קודם גירושין: צררי אתפסה. מעות צרורות או כספים מסר לה ליחוד כתובתה כשנשאה או לאחר מכאן שלא יטריחוה יורשים אם תתאלמן: לעולם איפוך קמייתא. ודקשיא לך דרבנן אדרבנן לא תיקשי דטעמייהו דרבנן בכתובה לאו משום דחיישינן לפירעון דמאן דפרע והדר ליה שטרא לאלתר קרע ליה אלא משום דחיישינן לשתי כתובות שמא חזר וכתב לה כתובה אחרת שניה לאחר שנפלה זאת מידה ואין הבעל מודה דקתני לאו באומר פרעתי אלא באומר אל תחזרו לה שיש בידה אחרת ותוציא על יורשי שטר אחר שטר: מחלוקת. האי יחלוקו דקאמר ר"ש [ב"ג] דמשמע חולקין בשוה כך שמעתי משום ר' יצחק ב"ר מנחם ונראה בעיני: ושניהם אדוקים בתורף. כלומר או שניהם אדוקין בתורף ותורף גילוי של שטר מקום הלוה והמלוה והמעות והזמן טופס שאר כל לשון השטר: זה נוטל כו'. דמאי דתפיס דידיה הוא כדקתני לעיל זה נוטל עד מקום שידו מגעת כו' ולקמן מפרש למאי מיבעי ליה: ואפי' אחד אדוק כו'. בתמיה: והא תניא עד מקום שידו מגעת. שלו: דקאי תורף בי מצעי. ומר אמר חדא ומר אמר חדא ולא פליגי: לדמי. מעלין בדמים כמה תורף יפה מן הטופס: שטרא דאית ביה זמן כמה שוה. דתורף עדיף מטופס דאית ביה מקום הזמן דאילו שם המלוה והלוה והמעות כתובין אף בטופס שצריך לחזור מענייני של שטר בשיטה אחרונה והוא עיקר כדתנן (ב"ב דף קסה:) כתוב בו [מלמעלה מנה ומלמטה מאתים] מלמעלה מאתים ומלמטה מנה הכל הולך אחר התחתון אבל זמן לא מיהדר ואי משום חתימת עדים דהוא תחת הטופס הא אית ליה לרשב"ג מודה בשטר שכתבו אין צריך לקיימו והאי מודה שכתבו הוא:

דחזיא

**עין משפט נר מצוה**

נ א מיי' פי"ח מהלכות גזילה ואבידה הל' יג סמג עשין עד טוש"ע ח"מ סי' סה סעיף ו וסעיף ז:

נא ב מיי' שם הל' יב ואף אם שניהם מודים דחיישינן לקנוניא וע"ש במ"מ:

נב ג ד טוש"ע ח"מ סי' סה סעיף טו:

**רבינו חננאל**

לקיימו יחלוקו דמודה בשטר שכתבו א"צ לקיימו ואין הלכה כמותו. אדם שמצא שטר שכתוב בו קיום ב"ד לא יוציאו עולמית חיישינן שמא פרוע הוא דברי א) ר' יוסי וחכ"א הרי [הוא] בחזקתו וכ"ש המוצא שטר שאין בו קיום שלא יוציאו עולמית דחיישינן שמא כתב ללות ולא לוה: **אמר ר"א מחלוקת בשניהן אדוקין בתופס ובתורף וכו' ור' יוחנן אמר לעולם** חולקין והאי דקאי תורף בינייהו ואע"ג דמקרב לגבי דחד לא חיישינן אלא חולקים. פי' תורף כדתנן בפרק כל גט שנכתב שלא לשם אשה כו' הכותב תופסי גיטין צריך שיניח מקום שם האיש והאשה ומקום הזמן שטרי מלוה צריך שיניח מקום המלוה ומקום הלוה ומקום המעות ומקום הזמן זהו תורף והשאר תופס וזה שאמרו חולקין בשטר לא שיחתכוהו כי זה הפסד הוא אלא דמיו חולקין ושקלינן וטרינן בה טובא ואסיקנא הכי מהא דתנן היו רוכבין על גבי בהמה או א' רוכב וא' מנהיג וכו' עד ויחלוקו הכי נמי דפלגי לה ממש בשלמא בהמה טהורה חזיא לבישרא אלא בהמה טמא' אפסדוה אלא לדמי וכן הלכה. ואם היו שנים אדוקין בשטר זה בתורף וזה בתופס ב). בשלמא שם המלוה והלוה והמעות יתכן לעמוד בהן עכשיו ואחר כך אם אבד השטר אין חוששין לו אלא הזמן שרוצה להיות בידו לטרוף ממשעבדי שמין כמה שוה שטר שיש בו זמן ויש לו לגבות ממשעבדי דבאין ללוה נכסים בני חורין ויש בו זמן טריף ממשעבדי ואם אין בו זמן אבד ממונו ומה שעולה בה השומא שקיל מי שהתורף בידו וכן הדין. ור' יוחנן לא חלק אלא בזמן שהתורף באמצע אבל בזמן שזה תופס בתורף וזה בתופס לא חלק שדמי כל השטר למי שבידו התורף והדין כאשר פירשנו ולדברי הכל כל דבר שאם יחלק יפסד שמין אותו בדמים וחולקין בדמים כדתנן בפ' השותפין אין חולקין את החצר עד שיהא בה כדי לזה וכדי לזה וכו' ואסיק התם בגמ' ת"ש זה הכלל כל שאילו יחלק ושמו עליו חולקין אותו ואם לאו מעלין אותו בדמים. ר' יוסי אומר הרי הוא בחזקתו. ומקשי' וכי ר' יוסי לא חייש לפירעון והתניא מצא כתובת אשה בשוק בזמן שהבעל מודה יחזיר לאשה אין הבעל מודה לא יחזיר לא לזה ולא לזה. ור' יוסי [אומר] עודה תחת בעלה יחזיר לאשה נתארמלה או נתגרשה לא יחזיר לא לזה ולא לזה. ופרק רבינא דהוא בתרא אפוך ואימא הכי נפל ליד הדיין כגון שכתוב בו קיום ב"ד לא יוציאו עולמית דברי ר' יוסי וחכ"א הרי הוא בחזקתו וטעמא דרבנן התם דאמרו לא יחזיר לא לזה ולא לזה לאו משום דחיישי לפירעון אלא משום דחיישי לשתי כתובות. ור' יוסי לשתי כתובות לא חייש.

כיון

**מסורת הש"ס**

א) [צ"ל לזו], ב) בתוס' חגיגה ו: שאין להם, ג) [קז.], ד) [לקמן יג., קמא מט:, בבא ... עו:].

**הגהות הב"ח**

(א) גמ' והיכי דמי דכתב ביה ה... (ב) שם יחזיר ... דברי ר' יוסי שר' אומר:

**גליון הש"ס**

תוס' ד"ה בזמן דמנה ומא משתעבדי. עי' לק ע"א תד"ה הטוע

**ליקוטי רש"י**

וכי לצור על צלוחיתו. וכי לצור פי צלוחיתו קנאו זה סברא היא דמשום ... חוב הכתוב בו קונין [רשב"ם ב"ב עו:].

**חשק שלמה על ר"ח** א) נגמ' איתא להיפך ואולי דרבינו העתיק כאן כפי המסקנא לקמן בסמוך. ב) נראה דצ"ל זה נוטל טופס וזה נוטל תורף ומסקינן דנ"מ משום הזמן דבשלמא וכו'.

אלא מאי אית לך למימר (א) עשירי ודאי אמר רחמנא ולא עשירי ספק הכא נמי עשירי ודאי אמר רחמנא ולא עשירי ספק א"ל רב אחא מדפתי לרבינא מאי ספיקות אילימא ספק בכורות (א) יהיה קדש אמר רחמנא ולא שכבר קדוש אלא ספק פדיון פטר חמור וכדרב נחמן (ג) דאמר רב נחמן אמר רבה בר אבוה (א) ישראל שיש לו עשרה ספק פטרי חמור בתוך ביתו מפריש עליהן עשרה שיין ומעשרן והן שלו מאי הוי עלה דמסותא ת"ש דא"ר חייא בר אבין הוה עובדא בי רב חסדא ורב חסדא בי רב הונא ופשטה מהא דאמר רב נחמן כל ממון שאין יכול להוציאו בדיינין הקדישו אינו קדוש הא יכול להוציאו בדיינין הקדישו קדוש אע"ג דלא אפקיה (ג) והאמר ר' יוחנן (ב) גזל ולא נתייאשו הבעלים שניהם אינם יכולין להקדישו זה לפי שאינה שלו וזה לפי שאינה ברשותו מי סברת במסותא מטלטלין עסקינן (ג) (ס) במסותא מקרקעי עסקינן דכי יכול להוציאה בדיינין ברשותיה קיימא תני רב תחליפא בר מערבא קמיה דר' אבהו (ד) שנים אדוקים בטלית זה נוטל עד מקום שידו מגעת וזה נוטל עד מקום שידו מגעת והשאר חולקין בשוה מחוי ליה רבי אבהו (ה) ובשבועה אלא מתניתין דקתני דפלגי בהדדי ולא קתני זה נוטל עד מקום שידו מגעת היכי משכחת לה אמר רב פפא (ו) דתפיסי בכרכשתא אמר רב משרשיא ש"מ (ז) האי סודרא כיון דתפיס ביה שלש על שלש קרינן ביה (ב) ונתן לרעהו דכמאן דפסיק דמי וקני ומאי שנא מדרב חסדא (ד) דאמר רב חסדא (ח) גט בידה ומשיחה בידו אם יכול לנתקו ולהביאו אצלו אינה מגורשת ואם לאו מגורשת (ס) התם כריתות בעינן וליכא הכא נתינה בעינן והא איכא אמר רבא (ה) (ט) אם היתה טלית מוזהבת חולקין פשיטא לא צריכא דקאי דהבא בי מצעי הא נמי פשיטא לא צריכא דמיקרב לגבי דחד מהו דתימא (ו) דא"ל פלוג הכי קמ"ל (י) דא"ל מאי חזית דפלגת הכי פלוג הכי: ת"ר (ז) שנים אדוקין בשטר מלוה אומר שלי הוא ונפל ממני ומצאתיו ולוה אמר (ח) שלך הוא ופרעתיו לך יתקיים השטר בחותמיו דברי רבי רשב"ג אומר יחלוקו נפל ליד דיין לא יוציאו עולמית ר' יוסי אומר הרי הוא בחזקתו אמר מר יתקיים השטר בחותמיו וגבי ליה מלוה כוליה ולית ליה מתני' שנים אוחזין כו' אמר רבא אמר רב נחמן (כ) במקוים דברי הכל יחלוקו כי פליגי בשאינו מקוים רבי סבר (ט) (ל) מודה בשטר שכתבו צריך לקיימו ואי מקיים ליה פליג ואי לא מקיים ליה לא פליג מאי טעמא חספא בעלמא הוא מאן קא משוי ליה להאי שטרא לוה הא קאמר דפריע ורבי שמעון בן גמליאל סבר מודה בשטר שכתבו אין צריך לקיימו ואע"ג דלא מקיים ליה יחלוקו נפל ליד דיין לא יוציאו עולמית מאי

## רש"י

**אלא מאי אית לך למימר.** למה לא חייבוהו לעשר ממה נפשך: **עשירי ודאי.** הצריך הכתוב לעשר ולא הצריך לעשר את הספק וכל עשירי שבכאן ספק הן שאפי' יצא הפטור בחמישי שוב אין העשירי קרוי עשירי אלא תשיעי שהפטור אינו מן המנין: **מאי ספיקות.** דאמרן לעיל הספיקות נכנסין לדיר להתעשר: **ספק פדיון פטר חמור.** טלה שהופרש על ספק פטר חמור שאפילו הוא פטר חמור ודאי אין בטלה זה של פדיון משום קדושה: **עשרה שיין.** לאפקועי איסורייהו למשרי להו בעבודה: **עובדא הוה בי רב חסדא ורב חסדא בי רב הונא.** מעשה היה ובא לפני רב חסדא ורב חסדא הביאו לפני רב הונא: **שאינו יכול להוציאו כו'.** והאי נמי דחזינן ליה דאין יכול להוציאו בדיינין שאין לו ראיה בדבר אין הקדישו קדוש: **הא יכול להוציאו כו'.** בתמיה: **שאינה ברשותו.** והא סתם גזילה יכולין להוציאו בדיינין הוא: **במסותא מטלטלין.** כגון גיגית: **מקרקעי.** דכל היכא דאיתיה ברשות מרי' קיימא דקרקע אינה נגזלת ושפיר פשיטנא מהא דאי הוה ליה ראיה עלה הקדישו הקדש: **בר מערבא.** מארץ ישראל: **מחוי ליה.** מראה באצבעותיו כלפי מעלה: **בכרכשתא.** בגרדין שבשני ראשין שקורין ברניי"ש: **ש"מ.** מדקתני עד מקום שידו מגעת קנוי לו: **האי סודרא.** של קונה שקונין בו קנין: **כיון דתפיס ביה.** מקנה שלש על שלש קרינא ביה ושלף איש נעלו ונתן לרעהו: **דכמאן דפסיק דמי.** וקנייה מקנה והמכר נקנה בו ללוקח ודוקא נקט שלש על שלש (ס) דכלי בעינן דכתיב (רות ד) נעלו ובציר משלש אצבעות לאו בגד הוא כדאשכחן גבי טומאה: **גט בידה.** שנתנו לה: **ומשיחה.** שקשור בה בידו אם יש כח באותו חוט שיכול לנתקו לגט מידה ולהביאו אצלו: **אינה מגורשת.** אלמא לאו נתינה היא: **כריתות.** הבדלה שיהיו מובדלים זה מזה והרי אגודים הם בחוט זה: **אם היתה טלית מוזהבת.** כלומר אפילו היא מוזהבת חולקים: **פלוג הכי.** לרוחבה ויהא הזהב לאחד מהם: **קא משמע לן דא"ל כו' פלוג.** לאורכה: **שנים אדוקים בשטר.** המלוה והלוה: **שלך הוא ופרעתיו לך.** והחזרת לי וממני נפל: **יתקיים השטר בחותמיו.** קס"ד דהכי קאמר אם השטר כשר שיקיימוהו חותמיו לומר כתב ידינו הוא הרי הוא בחזקתו: **נפל השטר ליד הדיין.** משמע דהכי קאמר אם מצאו דיין לא יוציאו אותו עולמית מיד דיין ולקמן פריך מאי שנא דיין מאינשי דעלמא: **וגבי ליה מלוה כוליה.** בתמיה: **במקוים.** שכתוב בו הנפק שילא כבר בב"ד והעידו עדים על חתימת ידן וכותבין הדיינין בו שטרא דנן נפק קדמנא ואסהידו פלוני ופלוני על חתימת ידייהו ואשרנוהו וקיימנוהו כדחזי: **כולי עלמא** ל"פ דיחלוקו. דכי אמרינן דיתקיים השטר בחותמיו לא למגבי מלוה כולו קאמר אלא למגבי פלגיה ופלוגתייהו כשאינו מקוים רבי סבר אף על פי שהלוה מודה ליה שכתב שטר זה ולוה לו מעות צריך המלוה לקיימו בחותמיו ואפילו השטר בידו נאמן הלוה לומר פרעתיך דכל זמן שאינו מקוים מאן קמשוי ליה שטרא לוה שמודה לו שכתבו הא אמר דפריע אבל משהשטר מוחזק על פי עדיו אין הלוה נאמן לומר פרעתי הלכך זה שניהם מוחזקים אי מקיים ליה מלוה בעדות ומשוי ליה שטר מעליא אין הלוה נאמן באמירתו אלא על ידי חזקה זה שאדוק בו והרי הוא כשאר מציאה ופליג: **ואי לא לא פליג.** שאפילו כולו ביד המלוה נאמן הלוה לומר פרעתי:

## תוספות

**ולא** עשירי ספק. אין להקשות איצטריך קרא למעוטי ספיקא (י) כדפריך במסכת חולין (דף כב: ד"ה איצטריך):

**מפריש** עליהן עשרה שיין. תימה דבפ"ק דבכורות (דף ט. (יא) ושם) אמרי' דשה אחד פוטר כמה פטרי חמורים ומה צריך עשרה שיים ותו מאי קא משמע לן מתני' היא הספיקות נכנסים לדיר להתעשר ותו כיון דאמר מעשרן מה צריך להשמיענו דהן שלו פשיטא כיון דמעשרן דהן שלו דאילו היו של כהן לא היה מעשרן דהוו להו כלקוח דתנן (שם דף נה:) הלקוח והניתן לו במתנה פטור ואי קמ"ל דאע"ג דמעשרן עדיין הם שלו פשיטא דמעשר בהמה של בעלים הוא:

**מחוי** ר' אבהו והשאר בשבועה. [א] נראה דלא גרסי' והשאר דאף במה שידו מגעת ישבע כיון דנתקנה השבועה שלא יהא אדם הולך ותוקף מטעם זה ישבע אף במה שהוא תופס ומכל מקום שפיר מוכח בסמוך דבקנין מאי דתפיס כמאן דפסיק דמי כיון דהכא לאחר שבועה נוטל כל מה שהוא תופס אפילו יותר ממחצה והשבועה היא בשביל הטענה ומפני התקנה:

**אם** יכול לנתקו. נראה דאם היתה ידה פתוחה בשעת שנתן גט לידה ונשארה המשיחה בידו וקפלה ידה בחוזק שאם מושך המשיחה לא יוכל להביאו אצלו שאינה מגורשת שהרי כשנתן בידה קודם שקפלה ידה היה יכול להביאו אצלו והקפילה לא עשה הוא אלא היא והוה כטלי גיטך מעל גבי קרקע דאינה מגורשת דלא קרינן ביה ונתן בידה והכא דקאמר אם אינו יכול להביאו אצלו דמגורשת כגון שהיתה ידה קפוצה והוא תחב בידה כל כך בחוזק שאם ימשוך המשיחה לא יביא הגט אצלו ור"ת (יב) (נמי) פירש אם הגט כבד כל כך שאם רוצה למשוך הגט אליו תנתק המשיחה מגורשת ומיירי בידה פתוחה ולא קפלה ולא עשתה שום דבר: מאי

## עין משפט נר מצוה

מא א מיי' פי"ב מהל' בכורים הלכה כג סמג עשין קמו:

מב ב מיי' פ"ו מהל' ערכין הל' כד סמג עשין קלג טוש"ע ח"מ סי' שנד סעיף ו וטוש"ע י"ד סי' רנח סעיף ז:

מג ג מיי' שם הל' כג סמג שם טוש"ע י"ד שם [רב אלפס כאן ובב"ק פ"ד דף כ.]:

מד ד ה ו מיי' פ"ט מהל' טוען ונטען הל' ט י סמג עשין צה טוש"ע ח"מ סי' קלח סעיף ג:

מה ז מיי' פ"ה מהלכות מכירה הל' ז סמג עשין פב טוש"ע ח"מ סי' קצה סעיף ד:

מו ח מיי' פ"ה מהלכות גירושין הל' טו סמג עשין נ טוש"ע אה"ע סי' קלט סעיף ב:

מז ט י מיי' פ"ט מהל' טוען ונטען הל' י סמג עשין צה טוש"ע ח"מ סי' קלח סעיף ג:

מח כ מיי' פי"ד מהל' מלוה ולוה הל' יד סמג עשין צד טוש"ע ח"מ סי' סה סעיף טו:

מט ל מיי' שם וסמג שם טוש"ע ח"מ סי' פב סעיף א:

## רבינו חננאל

מאי הוי עלה דמסותא ת"ש מהא דאמר רב [נחמן] כל ממון שאינו יכול להוציאו בדיינין הקדישו אינו קדוש. הא יכול להוציאו אע"פ שלא הוציאו קדוש. ומקשי' עלה והאמר ר' יוחנן גזל ולא נתייאשו הבעלי' שניהן אינן יכולין להקדישו זה לפי שאינו שלו וזה לפי שאינו ברשותו. וקי"ל דלא מקשינן לא ממשנה ולא מברייתא ולא ממימרא אלא אם היא הלכה. ועוד לא דחאוה להא דר' יוחנן אלא פירקו על דבריו ואמר מי סברת מסותא מטלטלא היא וקשיא עליה הא דר' יוחנן לא כי קאמר רב [נחמן] כל ממון שאינו יכול להוציאו בדיינין וכו' האי ממון קרקע הוא וכיוצא בו האי מסותא מקרקעא הוא דקי"ל קרקע אינה נגזלת ולעולם ברשותיה דמרא קיימא הלכך אם יכול להוציאה בדיינין ברשותיה קיימא ושפיר קא מקדיש. האי דקתני שנים אדוקין בטלית זה נוטל עד מקום שידו מגעת וזה נוטל עד מקום שידו מגעת והשאר חולקין בשוה ובשבועה אוקימנא בשאדוקין בטלית עצמו ומתני' דקתני חולקין הטלית שני חצאין ונוטל כל אחד חציה בשאדוקין בנימין שבקצותיה והן הנקראים כרכשתא. ופשוטה היא. דייק רב (אשי) [משרשיא] מינה מדקתני זה נוטל עד מקום שידו מגעת ש"מ דהאי סודרא כיון דתפיס ביה ג' אצבעות על ג' אצבעות הרי הוא קנין לתופסן ואע"ג דלא פסיק כמאן דפסיק דמי ולא אמרי' עד דמשיך ליה כוליה לא קני ליה אלא אע"ג דלא משיך ליה לכוליה קני להוא דתפס וכן הלכה. אמר רבא אם היתה טלית מוזהבת והזהב קרוב לגבי חד ברחבה של טלית ואם יחלקוה לרחבה לשני חצאין יבא הזהב בחלקו של אחד יכול האחד לומר זה שבינינו לאורכה נחלקה כדי שנחלק בטלית ובזהב והדין עמו: ת"ר שנים אדוקין בשטר כו' אסיק' בשטר מקוים דברי הכל יחלוקו. ושאינו מקוים ומלוה אמר שלי הוא ונפל ממני ומצאתיו ולוה אמר שלך היה ופרעתיך ונתתי לך [וממני נפל] אם נתקיים בחותמיו יחלוקו דברי ר' דרבי קסבר מודה בשטר שכתבו צריך לקיימו וקי"ל כרבי. רשב"ג אומר אע"פ שאין יכול

## מסורת הש"ס

[בכורות נח:], ב) שם, ג) בבא קמא סח:, ע., קדושין נב., גיטין עח:, ה) לקמן ח., [לקמן קז.], ז) בבא בתרא קע., ח) [של' וכן הא בהרי"ף והרא"ש, רש"י שאגל האלפסי הא שלך היה פרעתיו לך], ט) בבא בתרא קע., ודף קנד., כתובות יט., שבת עח: [לקמן עב:], י) [נ"ל] פרישים, יא) [ועיין תוס' שם ד: ד"ה ופודה עוד היטב תוס' יל. ד"ה שהיו], יב) מהר"ס מוחק זה.

## הגהות הגר"א

[א] תוס' ד"ה מחוי ר"א כו'. נ"ב והרמב"ם כתב כן אלא ע"י גלגול וכל רא"ש הוכיח כדברי תוס' ע"ש:

## גליון הש"ס

גמ' במסותא מקרקעי. קשה לי הא מאי קא הסילוק בין מטלטלי למקרקעי דמטלטלין ניזלין וקם ליה ברשותיה וגזלן מקרי אינו ברשותו דנגזל אבל קרקע אינה נגזלת ולא קם ברשותיה דגזלן. א"כ במטלטלין וגזל אם קנין דלא קם ברשותיה דהנגזל אינו חייב באחריותו דאימא בב"ק עט ע"א מתני' הוי כקרקע דמנחי ברשותיה דהנגזל. וא"כ לא במסותא דהגזילה לא דאמר דידי הוא יכול קנין להקדישו וצ"ע: שם התם כריתות בעינן. עיין כתובות נ ע"ב תוס' ד"ה ואי וצ"ע: רש"י ד"ה דכמאן וכו' דכלי בעינן. עיין לקמן מז ע"א ובתוס' ד"ה לאפוקי:

## תורה אור השלם

א) וְכָל מַעְשַׂר בָּקָר וָצֹאן כֹּל אֲשֶׁר יַעֲבֹר תַּחַת הַשָּׁבֶט הָעֲשִׂירִי יִהְיֶה קֹּדֶשׁ לַייָ: [ויקרא כז, לב]

ב) וְזֹאת לְפָנִים בְּיִשְׂרָאֵל עַל הַגְּאוּלָּה וְעַל הַתְּמוּרָה לְקַיֵּם כָּל דָּבָר שָׁלַף אִישׁ נַעֲלוֹ וְנָתַן לְרֵעֵהוּ וְזֹאת הַתְּעוּדָה בְּיִשְׂרָאֵל: [רות ד, ז]

## לעזי רש"י

ברניי"ש. פירוש חוטין המשתיירין בסוף בגד אותכין מן הבגד לאחר אריגתו (ערוך ערך גרד ועיין רש"י סוכה דף ט ע"א ד"ה מן הגרדין ובכורות דף ח ע"ב ד"ה כרוכו לי).

## ליקוטי רש"י

**עשירי ודאי.** משום עשירי ודאי אמר רחמנא יהיה קודש ולא ספק [בכורות נח:]. **ספק פטרי חמור.** כגון שהיה לו עשר חמורות וילדו כולן זכר נקבה שמפריש עליהן עשרה שיין לאפקועי לאיסורייהו. **ומעשרן והן שלו.** ומעשרן לשיין כשאר בהמות חולין והן שלו המעשר קרב שלמים והוא אוכלו כדין שאר מעשר בהמה. **כרכשתא.** פריינ"ש שתולין בסוף הטלית מותר האריגה [סוכה ט.]. **גט בידה.** שנתנו לה וראש המשיחה עדיין בידו [בכורות יא.]. **ומשיחה.** חוט שהגט קשור בו לינ"ל בלע"ז [גיטין עח:]. **חספא.** חרס [עי' סוכה נג:]. **מודה.** לוה בשטר שכתבו ואינו מזוייף אלא שטוען פרעתיו או שכ"מ הייתי או שטר אמנה או שטר פסים הוא [רשב"ם ב"ב קנד.]. **צריך לקיימו.** ולומר לא פרעתי וכל כמה דלא אמר הכי לאו שטרא הוא אי לאו משכח סהדי להכיר החתימה דמאן קא משוי ליה שטרא לוה דאמר כתבתיו לוה נמי הא קאמר פרעתי הפה שאסר הוא הפה שהתיר [שבת עח:]. **אין צריך לקיימו.** בעדים החתומים בו שאין הלוה שוב נאמן לומר פרעתיו ולא אמרינן בהאי הפה שאסר הוא הפה שהתיר דמכיון שאמר כשר היה הרי הוחזק השטר וכי אמר פרעתיו לא מהימן שהרי ביד המלוה הוא [כתובות יט.]. דסתם שטרות הרי הם כשרים ובשטרות לא נימא הפה שאסר הוא הפה שהתיר לפסלו [רשב"ם ב"ב קנד.]. דלא דמי לשאר דינים שהפה שאסר הוא הפה שהתיר שאפילו אם היה זה מערער ואומר לא כתבתיו לא היה לנו לחשוד את זה הלוקח בכך שלא נחשדו ישראל לעשות שטרות מזוייפים אלא שהחמירו חכמים להצטרך קיום היכא דמערערי עליה הלכך כי אמר כתבתיו נהמניה למי שהשטר בידו [שם קע.].

Nachman: בִּמְקוּיָּם דִּבְרֵי הַכֹּל יַחֲלוֹקוּ – With regard to a certified document,[32] everyone (i.e. both Rebbi and Rabban Shimon ben Gamliel) agrees that [the litigants] divide the document in accordance with the Mishnah's ruling. כִּי פְּלִיגֵי בְּשֶׁאֵינוֹ מְקוּיָּם – With regard to what, then, do they disagree? With regard to an uncertified document.

The Gemara explains the dispute:

רַבִּי סָבַר – Rebbi holds מוֹדֶה בִּשְׁטָר שֶׁכְּתָבוֹ צָרִיךְ לְקַיְּימוֹ – that even if [a debtor] concedes that he drafted a document, still [the creditor] must have it certified in order to collect anything with it.[33] וְאִי מְקַיֵּים לֵיהּ פָּלֵיג – And therefore, if [the creditor] has [the document] certified, he divides it with the debtor in accordance with our Mishnah's ruling, i.e. he collects half the sum recorded in the document. וְאִי לֹא מְקַיֵּים לֵיהּ לֹא פָּלֵיג – But if he does not have it certified, he does not divide it, i.e. he collects nothing.[34]

The Gemara examines Rebbi's position:

מַאי טַעְמָא – What is the reason that even if a debtor authenticates the document, still the creditor must have it certified?[35]

The Gemara explains:

חַסְפָּא בְּעָלְמָא הוּא – [An uncertified document] per se is a mere shard, i.e. it cannot be used to collect a debt until its authenticity is established. מַאן קָא מַשְׁוֵי לֵיהּ לְהַאי שְׁטָרָא לְוָה – Who, then, transforms this [uncertified document] into a valid document? The debtor, when he authenticates it. הָא קָאָמַר דִּפְרִיעַ – But in Rebbi's case, [the debtor] himself maintains that [the debt recorded in the document] has been satisfied. Since the debtor denies the document's validity, the creditor cannot collect with it until he has it certified.[36]

The Gemara now explains Rabban Shimon ben Gamliel's ruling:

וְרַבִּי שִׁמְעוֹן בֶּן גַּמְלִיאֵל סָבַר – But Rabban Shimon ben Gamliel holds מוֹדֶה בִּשְׁטָר שֶׁכְּתָבוֹ אֵין צָרִיךְ לְקַיְּימוֹ – that if [a debtor] concedes that he drafted a document, [the creditor] need not have it certified before collecting the debt. וְאַף עַל גַּב דְּלֹא מְקַיֵּים לֵיהּ – And therefore, even though [the creditor] does not have [the document] certified, יַחֲלוֹקוּ – still they must divide it equally.[37]

The Gemara quotes and explains the last clause of the Baraisa:

נָפַל לְיַד דַּיָּין לֹא יוֹצִיאוּ עוֹלָמִית – IF [THE DOCUMENT] FELL INTO THE HAND OF A JUDGE, [THE PRINCIPALS] CANNOT EVER RETRIEVE [THE DOCUMENT].

NOTES

[3]2. To certify a document, *beis din* appends a statement of certification [h]enpeik) to it stating that they examined it and heard witnesses [co]nfirm the authenticity of the signatures that appear on it. In the [B]araisa's case, where the signatories verified their own signatures, its [w]ording is as follows: "When this document came before us, the [fo]llowing signatories [the signatories' names are inserted here] con[fir]med the authenticity of their signatures. We then strengthened and [ce]rtified [the document], as it is proper to do" (*Rashi*).

[33]. I.e. if a debtor concedes the document's authenticity but claims that [he] repaid the debt, the creditor can collect only after the signatories [ce]rtify the document. The Gemara will soon explain Rebbi's reasoning.

[34]. Accordingly, the dispute between Rebbi and Rabban Shimon ben [G]amliel is as follows. Rebbi insists that the creditor can collect nothing [wi]th an uncertified document, whereas Rabban Shimon ben Gamliel [al]lows him to collect half the sum with it (*Rashi*).

[35]. When a note of indebtedness is certified, this proves only that it is [au]thentic (i.e. that the debtor in fact drafted the document and incurred [th]e debt recorded therein) and not that the debt is still unpaid; only the [cr]editor's possession of an authentic document proves this point. Once [a d]ebtor concedes a document's authenticity, then, there should be no [po]int in certifying it. Why, then, does Rebbi in fact require certification?

[36]. An uncertified note of indebtedness may be invalid for one of two [re]asons: It may be forged or it may represent a loan that has already [be]en repaid. If the debtor claims that the document is forged, he is [de]finitely believed. Now in Rebbi's case, he did not claim that; he [co]nceded the document's authenticity, claiming only to have repaid the [de]bt. Nevertheless, since we would have accepted a stronger plea (i.e. [th]at the document was forged), we accept the weaker plea (that the debt [wa]s repaid) as well (see *Tosafos* to *Kesubos* 19a ד״ה מודה).

This reasoning holds true only as long as it is the debtor who [au]thenticates the document. Once the signatories certify it, however, the debtor's plea is rejected, and he must "divide" with the creditor (i.e. the creditor collects half the debt) in accordance with our Mishnah's ruling (*Rashi*).

The principle that a weaker plea is accepted in place of a stronger one is called *migo* (lit: since); it is generally explained as follows. A dishonest litigant would prefer to enter a stronger plea rather than a weaker one. If a litigant enters the weaker plea, then, this creates a presumption that he is telling the truth. In Rebbi's case for example, a dishonest debtor would have entered his strongest possible plea: The document is forged. Since the debtor in fact conceded its authenticity and claimed only to have repaid it, he is assumed to be telling the truth. Thus, although the creditor's possession of the document creates the presumption of non-payment, still the debtor's *migo* outweighs the presumption (see *Bava Basra* 170a and note 10 below. See also *Even HaAzel* to *Hilchos Malveh U'Loveh* 10:14 for a somewhat different interpretation of Rebbi's reasoning).

37. If a creditor has an authentic note of indebtedness in his possession, this creates a presumption of non-payment (see note 1); he can thus use it to collect his debt. According to Rabban Shimon ben Gamliel, this is true even if the debtor conceded the document's authenticity but claimed to have repaid the debt; he rejects Rebbi's *migo* for the following reason. Granted the debtor could have entered a stronger plea (that the document was forged) rather than a weaker one (that the debt was repaid). This does not create a presumption that he is telling the truth (i.e. a *migo*), though, because the stronger plea may have been refuted by witnesses; the debtor may thus have chosen the weaker plea (i.e. that he repaid the debt) not because he is telling the truth but because that plea is irrefutable (see *Tosafos* to *Kesubos* 19a ד״ה מודה). Now when the debtor authenticates the document in the creditor's possession, this creates a presumption of non-payment (see note 1). Since there is no *migo* to outweigh this presumption, the creditor can collect with the document.

**אלא מאי אית לך למימר.** למה לא חייבוהו לעשר ממה נפשך: **עשירי ודאי.** הצריך הכתוב לעשר ולא הצריך לעשר את הספק וכל עשירי שבכאן ספק הן שאפי' יצא הפטור בחמישי שוב אין העשירי קרוי עשירי אלא תשיעי שהפטור אינו מן המנין: **מאי ספיקות.** דאמרן לעיל הספיקות נכנסין לדיר להתעשר: **ספק פדיון פטר חמור.** טלה שהופרש על ספק פטר חמור שאפילו הוא פטר חמור ודאי אין בטלה זה של פדיון משום קדושה: **עשרה שיין.** לאפקועי איסורייהו למשרי להו בעבודה: **עובדא הוה בי רב חסדא ורב חסדא בי רב הונא.** מעשה היה ובא לפני רב חסדא ורב חסדא הביאו לפני רב הונא: **שאינו יכול להוציאו כו'.** והאי נמי דחזינן ליה דאין יכול להוציאו בדיינין שאין לו ראיה בדבר אין הקדישו קדוש: **הא יכול להוציאו כו'.** בתמיה: **שאינה ברשותו.** והא סתם גזילה יכולין להוציאו בדיינין הוא: **במסותא מטלטלין.** כגון גיגית: **מקרקעי.** דכל היכא דאיתיה ברשות מרי' קיימא דקרקע אינה נגזלת ושפיר פשיטנא מהא דאי הוה ליה ראיה עלה הקדישו הקדש: **בר מערבא.** מארץ ישראל: **מחוי ליה.** מראה באצבעותיו כלפי מעלה: **בכרבשתא.** בגרדין שבשני ראשין שקורין ברניי"ש: **ש"מ.** מדקתני עד מקום שידו מגעת קנוי לו: **האי סודרא.** של קונה שקונין בו קנין: **כיון דתפיס ביה.** מקנה שלש על שלש קרינא ביה ושלף איש נעלו ונתן לרעהו: **דכמאן דפסיק דמי.** וקנייה מקנה והמכר נקנה בו ללוקח ודוקא נקט שלש על שלש ° דכלי בעינן דכתיב (רות ד) נעלו ובציר משלש אצבעות לאו בגד הוא כדאשכחן גבי טומאה: **גט בידה.** שנתנו לה: **ומשיחה.** שקשור בה בידו אם יש כח באותו חוט שיכול לנתקו לגט מידה ולהביאו אצלו: **אינה מגורשת.** אלמא לאו נתינה היא: **כריתות.** הבדלה שיהיו מובדלים זה מזה והרי אגודים הם בחוט זה: **אם היתה טלית מוזהבת.** כלומר אפילו היא מוזהבת חולקים: **פלוג הכי.** לרוחבה ויהא הזהב לאחד מהם: **קא משמע לן דא"ל כו' פלוג.** לאורכה: **שנים אדוקים בשטר.** המלוה והלוה: **שלך הוא ופרעתיו לך.** והחזרת לי וממני נפל: **יתקיים השטר בחותמיו.** קס"ד דהכי קאמר אם השטר כשר שיקיימוהו חותמיו לומר כתב ידינו הוא הרי הוא בחזקתו: **נפל השטר ליד הדיין.** משמע דהכי קאמר אם מלאו דיין לא יוציאו אותו עולמית מיד דיין ולקמן פריך מאי שנא דיין מאינשי דעלמא: **וגבי ליה מלוה כוליה.** בתמיה: **במקוים.** שכתוב בו הנפק שילא כבר בב"ד והעידו עדים על חתימת ידן וכותבין הדיינין בו שטרא דנן נפק קדמנא ואסהידו פלוני ופלוני על חתימת ידייהו ואשרנוהו וקיימנוהו כדחזי: **כולי עלמא ל"פ דיחלוקו.** דכי אמרינן דיתקיים השטר בחותמיו לא למגבי מלוה כולו קאמר אלא למגבי פלגיה ופלוגתייהו כשאינו מקוים רבי סבר אף על פי שהלוה מודה ליה שכתב שטר זה ולוה לו מעות צריך המלוה לקיימו בחותמיו ואפילו השטר בידו נאמן הלוה לומר פרעתיך דכל זמן שאינו מקוים מאן קמשוי ליה שטרא לוה שמודה לו שכתבו הא אמר דפריע אבל משהשטר מוחזק על פי עדיו אין הלוה נאמן לומר פרעתי הלכך זה ששניהם מוחזקים אי מקיים ליה מלוה בעדות ומשוי ליה שטר מעליא אין הלוה נאמן באמירתו אלא על ידי חזקה זה שאדוק בו והרי הוא כשאר מציאה ופליג: **ואי לא לא פליג.** שאפילו כולו ביד המלוה נאמן הלוה לומר פרעתי:

אלא מאי אית לך למימר [א] עשירי ודאי אמר רחמנא ולא עשירי ספק הכא נמי עשירי ודאי אמר רחמנא ולא עשירי ספק א"ל רב אחא מדפתי לרבינא מאי ספיקות אילימא ספק בכורות [א] יהיה קדש אמר רחמנא ולא שכבר קדוש אלא ספק פדיון פטר חמור וכדרב נחמן [ב] דאמר רב נחמן אמר רבה בר אבוה [א] ישראל שיש לו עשרה ספק פטרי חמור בתוך ביתו מפריש עליהן עשרה שיין ומעשרן והן שלו מאי הוי עלה דמסותא ת"ש דא"ר חייא בר אבין הוה עובדא בי רב חסדא ורב חסדא בי רב הונא ופשטה מהא דאמר רב נחמן כל ממון שאין יכול להוציאו בדיינין הקדישו אינו קדוש הא יכול להוציאו בדיינין הקדישו קדוש אע"ג דלא אפקיה [ג] והאמר ר' יוחנן [ב] גזל ולא נתייאשו הבעלים שניהם אינם יכולין להקדישו זה לפי שאינה שלו וזה לפי שאינה ברשותו מי סברת במסותא מטלטלין עסקינן [ג] ° במסותא מקרקעי עסקינן דכי יכול להוציאה בדיינין ברשותיה קיימא תני רב תחליפא בר מערבא קמיה דר' אבהו [ד] שנים אדוקים בטלית זה נוטל עד מקום שידו מגעת וזה נוטל עד מקום שידו מגעת והשאר חולקין בשוה מחוי ליה רבי אבהו [ה] ובשבועה אלא מתניתין דקתני דפלגי בהדדי ולא קתני זה נוטל עד מקום שידו מגעת היכי משכחת לה אמר רב פפא [ו] דתפיסי בכרכשתא אמר רב משרשיא ש"מ [ז] האי סודרא כיון דתפיס ביה שלש על שלש קרינן ביה [ב] ונתן לרעהו דכמאן דפסיק דמי וקני ומאי שנא מדרב חסדא [ד] דאמר רב חסדא [ח] גט בידה ומשיחה בידו אם יכול לנתקו ולהביאו אצלו אינה מגורשת ואם לאו מגורשת ° התם כריתות בעינן וליכא הכא נתינה בעינן והא איכא אמר רבא [ה] [ט] אם היתה טלית מוזהבת חולקין פשיטא לא צריכא דקאי דהבא בי מצעי הא נמי פשיטא לא צריכא דמיקרב לגבי דחד מהו דתימא [י] דא"ל פלוג הכי קמ"ל [י] דא"ל מאי חזית דפלגת הכי פלוג הכי: ת"ר [ז] שנים אדוקין בשטר מלוה אומר שלי הוא ונפל ממני ומצאתיו ולוה אמר [ח] שלך הוא ופרעתיו לך יתקיים השטר בחותמיו דברי רבי רשב"ג אומר יחלוקו נפל ליד דיין לא יוציאו עולמית ר' יוסי אומר הרי הוא בחזקתו אמר מר יתקיים השטר בחותמיו וגבי ליה מלוה כוליה ולית ליה מתני' שנים אוחזין כו' אמר רבא אמר רב נחמן [כ] במקוים דברי הכל יחלוקו כי פליגי בשאינו מקוים רבי סבר [ט] [ל] מודה בשטר שכתבו צריך לקיימו ואי מקיים ליה פליג ואי לא מקיים ליה לא פליג מאי טעמא חספא בעלמא הוא מאן קא משוי ליה להאי שטרא לוה הא קאמר דפריע ורבי שמעון בן גמליאל סבר מודה בשטר שכתבו אין צריך לקיימו ואע"ג דלא מקיים ליה יחלוקו נפל ליד דיין לא יוציאו עולמית
מאי

**ולא** עשירי ספק. אין להקשות איצטריך קרא למעוטי ספיקא [י] כדפריך במסכת חולין (דף כב: ד"ה איצטריך): **מפריש** עליהן עשרה שיין. תימה דבפ"ק דבכורות (דף ט. [יא] ושם) אמרי' דשה אחד פוטר כמה פטרי חמורים ומה צריך עשרה שיים ותו מאי קא משמע לן מתני' היא הספיקות נכנסים לדיר להתעשר ותו כיון דאמר מעשרן מה צריך להשמיענו דהן שלו פשיטא כיון דמעשרן דהן שלו דאילו היו של כהן לא היה מעשרן דהוו להו כלקוח דתנן (שם דף נה:) הלקוח והניתן לו במתנה פטור ואי קמ"ל דאע"ג דמעשרן עדיין הם שלו פשיטא דמעשר בהמה של בעלים הוא: **מחוי** ר' אבהו והשאר בשבועה. [א] נראה דלא גרסי' והשאר דאף במה שידו מגעת ישבע כיון דנתקנה השבועה שלא יהא אדם הולך ותוקף מטעם זה ישבע אף במה שהוא תופס ומכל מקום שפיר מוכח בסמוך דבקנין מאי דתפיס כמאן דפסיק דמי כיון דהכא לאחר שבועה נוטל כל מה שהוא תופס אפילו יותר ממחצה והשבועה היא בשביל הטענה ומפני התקנה: **אם** יכול לנתקו. נראה דאם היתה ידה פתוחה בשעת שנתן גט לידה ונשארה המשיחה בידו וקפלה ידה בחוזק שאם מושך המשיחה לא יוכל להביאו אצלו שאינה מגורשת שהרי כשנתן בידה קודם שקפלה ידה היה יכול להביאו אצלו והקפילה לא עשה הוא אלא היא והוה כטלי גיטך מעל גבי קרקע דאינה מגורשת דלא קרינן ביה ונתן בידה והכא דקאמר אם אינו יכול להביאו אצלו דמגורשת כגון שהיתה ידה קפולה והוא תחב בידה כל כך בחוזק שאם ימשוך המשיחה לא יביא הגט אצלו ור"ת [יב] (נמי) פירש אם הגט כבד כל כך שאם רוצה למשוך הגט אליו תנתק המשיחה מגורשת ומיירי בידה פתוחה ולא קפלה ולא עשתה שום דבר:
מאי



**עשירי ודאי.** משום דעשירי ודאי אמר רחמנא דיהיה קודש ולא ספק [בכורות נח:]. **ספק פטרי חמור.** כגון שהיה לו עשר חמורות וילדו כולן זכר ונקבה שמפריש עליהן עשרה שיין לאפקועי לאיסורייהו. ומעשרן והן שלו. ומעשרן לשיין כשאר בהמות חולין והן שלו והמעשר קרב שלמים והוא אוכלו כדין שאר מעשר בהמה. **כרבשתא.** פריינ"ש שתולין בסוף הטלית מותר האריגה [סוכה ט.]. **גט בידה.** שנתנו לה ורלאש המשיחה עדיין בידו [בכורות יא.]. **ומשיחה.** חוט שהגט קשור בו ליי"ל בלע"ז [גיטין עח:]. **חספא.** חרס [עי' סוכה נג:]. **מודה.** לוה בשטר שכתבו ואינו מזייף אלא שטוען פרעתיו או שכ"מ הייתי או שטר אמנה או שטר פסים הוא [רשב"ם ב"ב קנד.]. **צריך לקיימו.** ולומר לא פרעתי וכל כמה דלא אמר הכי לאו שטרא הוא אי לאו משכח סהדי להכיר החתימה דמאן קא משוי ליה שטרא לוה דאמר כתבתיו לוה נמי הא קאמר פרעתי הפה שאסר הוא הפה שהתיר [שבת עח:]. **אין צריך לקיימו.** בעדים החתומים בו שאין הלוה שוב נאמן לומר פרעתיו ולא אמרינן בהאי הפה שאסר הוא הפה שהתיר דמכיון שאמר כשר היה הרי הוחזק השטר וכי אמר פרעתיו לא מהימן שהרי ביד המלוה הוא [כתובות יט.]. דסתם שטרות הרי הם כשרים ובשטרות לא נימא הפה שאסר הוא הפה שהתיר לפסלו [רשב"ם ב"ב קנד.]. דלא דמי לשאר דינים שהפה שאסר הוא הפה שהתיר שאפילו אם היה זה מערער ואומר לא כתבתיו לא היה לנו לחשוד את זה הלוקח בכך שלא נחשדו ישראל לעשות שטרות מזוייפים אלא שהחמירו חכמים להצטרך קיום היכא דמערערי עליה הלכך כי אמר כתבתיו נהמניה למי שהשטר בידו [שם קע.].

מסורת הש"ס

א) [בכורות נח:], ב) שם יא., ג) בבא קמא סח., סט., ע., קדושין נב., ד) גיטין עח., ה) לקמן ח., ו) [לקמן קז.], ז) בבא בתרא קע., ח) [שלי וכן איתא בהרי"ף והרא"ש, וברש"י שאצל האלפסי איתא שלך היה ופרעתיו לך], ט) בבא בתרא קע., ודף קנד., כתובות יט., שבת עח: [לקמן עב:], י) [צ"ל כדפריטית], יא) [ועיין בתוס' שם ד: ד"ה ופודה ועיין עוד היטב תוס' יא. ד"ה שהיו], יב) מהרש"ם מוחק זה.

הגהות הגר"א

[א] תוס' ד"ה מחוי נראה כו'. נ"ב והרמב"ם לא כתב כן אלא ע"י גלגול אבל רא"ש הוכיח כדברי תוס' ע"ש:

גליון הש"ס

גמ' במסותא מקרקעי. קשה לי הא עיקר החילוק בין מטלטלי למקרקעי דמטלטלין נגזלין וקם ליה ברשותיה דגזלן מקרי אינו ברשותו דהנגזל אבל קרקע אינה נגזלת ולא קם ברשותיה דגזלן. א"כ במטלטלין וגזל בלא קנין דלא קם ברשותיה דהגזל ואינו חייב באחריותו וכדאיתא בב"ק עט ע"א במתני' הוי כקרקע דמנחי ברשותיה דהנגזל. וא"כ הכא במסותא דהגזילה במה דאמר דידי הוא וליכא קנין יכול להקדישו וצ"ע: שם התם כריתות בעינן. עיין כתובות נ ע"ב תוס' ד"ה ואי וצ"ע: רש"י ד"ה דכמאן וכו' דכלי בעינן. עיין לקמן מז ע"א ד"ה ובתוס' ד"ה לאפוקי:

תורה אור השלם

א) וְכָל מַעְשַׂר בָּקָר וָצֹאן כֹּל אֲשֶׁר יַעֲבֹר תַּחַת הַשָּׁבֶט הָעֲשִׂירִי יִהְיֶה קֹּדֶשׁ לַייָ: [ויקרא כז, לב]

ב) וְזֹאת לְפָנִים בְּיִשְׂרָאֵל עַל הַגְּאוּלָּה וְעַל הַתְּמוּרָה לְקַיֵּם כָּל דָּבָר שָׁלַף אִישׁ נַעֲלוֹ וְנָתַן לְרֵעֵהוּ וְזֹאת הַתְּעוּדָה בְּיִשְׂרָאֵל: [רות ד, ז]

לעזי רש"י

ברנייי"ש. פירוש פוזין (שמתפרדין בסוף בגד שמוציאין מן הבגד לאחר אריגתו) (ערוך ערך גרד ד' ועיין רש"י סוכה דף ט ע"א ד"ה מן הגרדין ובכורות דף מ ע"ב ד"ה כרכום לך).

עין משפט נר מצוה

מא א מיי' פ"ב מהל' בכורים הלכה כג סמג עשין קמו:
מב ב מיי' פ"ו מהל' ערכין הל' כד סמג עשין קלב טוש"ע ח"מ סי' שנד סעיף ו וטוש"ע י"ד סי' רנח סעיף ז:
מג ג מיי' שם הל' כג סמג שם טוש"ע י"ד שם [רב אלפס כאן ובב"ק פ"ד דף כ.]:
מד ד ה ו מיי' פ"ט מהל' טוען ונטען הל' ט י סמג עשין צה טוש"ע ח"מ סי' קלח סעיף ג:
מה ז מיי' פ"ה מהלכות מכירה הל' ז סמג עשין פב טוש"ע ח"מ סי' קצה סעיף ד:
מו ח מיי' פ"ה מהלכות גירושין הל' טו סמג עשין נ טוש"ע אה"ע סי' קלט סעיף ב:
מז ט י מיי' פ"ט מהל' טוען ונטען הל' י סמג עשין צה טוש"ע ח"מ סי' קלח סעיף ג:
מח כ מיי' פי"ד מהל' מלוה ולוה הל' יד סמג עשין צד טוש"ע ח"מ סי' סה סעיף טו:
מט ל מיי' שם וסמג שם טוש"ע ח"מ סי' פב סעיף א:

רבינו חננאל

מאי הוי עלה דמסותא ת"ש מהא דאמר רב [נחמן] כל ממון שאינו יכול להוציאו בדיינין הקדישו אינו קדוש. הא יכול להוציאו אע"פ שלא הוציאו קדוש. ומקשי' עלה והאמר ר' יוחנן גזל ולא נתייאשו הבעלי' שניהן אינן יכולין להקדישו זה לפי שאינו שלו וזה לפי שאינו ברשותו. וקי"ל דלא מקשינן לא ממשנה ולא מברייתא ולא ממימרא אלא אם היא הלכה. ועוד לא דחאוה להא דר' יוחנן אלא פירקו על דבריו ואמר מי סברת במסותא מטלטלא היא וקשיא עליה הא דר' יוחנן לא כי קאמר רב [נחמן] כל ממון שאינו יכול להוציאו בדיינין וכו' האי ממון קרקע הוא וכיוצא בו כהאי מסותא דקי"ל קרקע אינה נגזלת ולעולם ברשותיה דמרא קיימא הלכך אם יכול להוציאה בדיינין ברשותיה קיימא ושפיר קא מקדיש. האי דקתני שנים אדוקין בטלית זה נוטל עד מקום שידו מגעת וזה נוטל עד מקום שידו מגעת והשאר חולקין בשוה ובשבועה אוקימנא בשאדוקין בטלית עצמו ומתני' דקתני חולקין הטלית שני חצאין ונוטל כל אחד חצאין בנימין שבקצותיה והן הנקראים כרכשתא. ופשוטה היא. דייק רב (אשי) [משרשיא] מינה מדקתני זה נוטל עד מקום שידו מגעת ש"מ דהאי סודרא כיון דתפיס ביה ג' אצבעות על ג' אצבעות הרי הוא קנין לתופסן ואע"ג דלא פסיק כמאן דפסיק דמי ולא אמרי' עד דמשיך ליה כוליה לא קני ליה אלא אע"ג דלא משיך ליה לכוליה קני לההוא דתפס וכן הלכה. אמר רבא אם היתה טלית מוזהבת והזהב קרוב לגבי חד ברחבה של טלית ואם יחלקו לרחבה לשני חצאין יבא הזהב בחלקו של אחד יכול האחד לומר זה שבינינו לאורכה נחלקה כדי שנחלק בטלית ובזהב והדין עמו: ת"ר שנים אדוקין בשטר כו' אסיק' בשטר מקוים דברי הכל יחלוקו. ושאינו מקוים ומלוה אמר שלי הוא ונפל ממני ומצאתיו ולוה אמר שלך היה ופרעתיך ונתתי לך [וממני נפל] אם נתקיים בחותמיו יחלוקו דברי ר' דרבי קסבר מודה בשטר שכתבו צריך לקיימו וקי"ל כרבי. רשב"ג אומר אע"פ שאין יכול

**uire** only that the buyer perform an act of **"giving,"** וְהָא א – **and there is** such giving even where he is still holding on he kerchief.[21]

'he Gemara discusses another rule pertaining to the case of litigants who enter the court holding on to a cloak:

אָמַר רָ – **Rava said:** אִם הָיְתָה טַלִּית מוּזְהֶבֶת חוֹלְקִין – Even **if cloak was** made of **gold** thread, **it is divided.**

The Gemara asks:

פְּשִׁי – **This is obvious!** The material of the cloak is surely not etermining factor. – ? –

'he Gemara answers:

– Rava's ruling is **not** obvious. צְרִיכָא דְּקָאֵי דַּהֲבָא בֵּי מִצְעֵי – **is required** in a case **where there is** a strip of **gold in the ddle** of the cloak.

The Gemara is not satisfied with this answer:

הָא נַמִּי פְּשִׁי – In **that** case **too** it **is obvious** that the cloak is ided equally. – ? –

The Gemara answers:

– Rava's ruling is **not** obvious. צְרִיכָא דְּמִיקְּרַב לְגַבֵּי דְּחַד – **It required** in a case where **[the gold strip] is closer to one** of disputants. מַהוּ דְּתֵימָא – **One might have thought** דְּאָמַר – that **he** [the disputant closer to the strip] **may say to [the ıer],** פְּלוֹג הָכִי – **"Divide** it **this way** [i.e. along a line that ıs parallel to the sides of the cloak held by the disputants]." us, only one of them receives the gold strip. קָא מַשְׁמַע לָן – **ava]** therefore **teaches us** דְּאָמַר לֵיהּ – **that [the other rty] may respond to him:** מַאי חָזֵית דְּפָלְגַּת הָכִי – **"Why do u see fit to divide** the cloak **that way?** פְּלוֹג הָכִי – Instead, let **divide** the cloak **this way** [i.e along a line that runs rpendicular to the sides held by the disputants]." And thus the d strip is divided equally.

The Gemara now discusses a dispute between two litigants over o last had possession of a lost document:[22]

תָּנוּ רַ – **The Rabbis taught in a Baraisa:** שְׁנַיִם אֲדוּקִין בִּשְׁטָר – If TWO persons, i.e. a creditor and his debtor, appear in the *beis din* HOLDING ON TO A NOTE OF INDEBTEDNESS מַלְוֶה אוֹמֵר שֶׁלִּי הוּא וְנָפַל מִמֶּנִּי וּמְצָאתִיו – and THE CREDITOR SAYS, "IT IS MINE: IT FELL FROM ME AND I subsequently FOUND IT." וְלֹוֶה אָמַר שֶׁלְּךָ הוּא וּפְרַעְתִּיו לְךָ – BUT THE DEBTOR SAYS, "IT WAS indeed YOURS; HOWEVER I REPAID [THE DEBT recorded in the document] TO YOU,"[23] יִתְקַיֵּים הַשְּׁטָר בְּחוֹתְמָיו – then THE DOCUMENT MUST BE CERTIFIED THROUGH ITS SIGNERS, i.e. the witnesses whose names appear on the document must certify that the signatures are indeed authentic.[24] דִּבְרֵי רַבִּי – These are THE WORDS OF REBBI. רַבָּן שִׁמְעוֹן בֶּן גַּמְלִיאֵל אוֹמֵר – RABBAN SHIMON BEN GAMLIEL SAYS: יַחֲלוֹקוּ – THEY SHOULD DIVIDE it equally.[25]

The Baraisa now rules on a case in which the document is held by a third party:

נָפַל לְיַד דַּיָּין – IF [THE DOCUMENT] FELL INTO THE HAND OF A JUDGE לֹא יוֹצִיאוּ עוֹלָמִית – [THE PRINCIPALS] CANNOT EVER RETRIEVE [THE DOCUMENT] from him.[26] ר׳ יוֹסֵי אוֹמֵר – R' YOSE SAYS: הֲרֵי הוּא בְּחֶזְקָתוֹ – [THE DOCUMENT] RETAINS ITS STATUS as a valid document.[27]

The Gemara cites Rebbi's ruling and challenges its implication:

אָמַר מַר – **Master said:** יִתְקַיֵּים הַשְּׁטָר בְּחוֹתְמָיו – THE DOCUMENT SHOULD BE CERTIFIED BY ITS SIGNATORIES. וְגָבֵי לֵיהּ מַלְוֶה כּוּלֵּיהּ – **Now** does this mean that if the document is certified, **the creditor can** then **collect [the full sum mentioned in the document]?**[28] וְלֵית לֵיהּ מַתְנִיתִין שְׁנַיִם אוֹחֲזִין כו׳ – **Does [Rebbi]** then **not hold** the rule expressed in **our Mishnah,** viz. IF TWO persons ARE HOLDING ON TO A GARMENT **etc.** they divide it?[29] The Mishnah records no debate concerning its ruling; surely Rebbi accepts it. Why, in the Baraisa's case, then, does he assign the entire disputed sum to the creditor? Let the debtor and creditor divide the sum[30] in accordance with the Mishnah's ruling. – ? –

To deflect the challenge, the Gemara retracts its initial interpretation of Rebbi's ruling[31] and suggests another:

אָמַר רָבָא אָמַר רַב נַחְמָן – **Rava stated in the name of Rav**

NOTES

The legal device of כְּמַאן דִּפְסִיק דָּמֵי, *it is [viewed] as if it were cut off,* fices for נְתִינָה, *giving,* but not for כְּרִיתַת, *severance,* where actual, as posed to legal, separation is required.

To collect a debt, a creditor must prove not only that he advanced the ın but also that it was never repaid. Showing that he possesses the n document [or that he was the last to possess it before it was lost] ıstitutes such proof for the following reason: When a debt is recorded a document, the document is deposited in the creditor's possession til the debt is repaid; at that time, the debtor may demand that the cument be returned to him. Hence, as long as the document is in the editor's possession, it serves as proof that the debt has not yet been ɔaid. If, on the other hand, it is not in the creditor's possession (and ely if it is in the debtor's possession), the debtor can maintain that he s already satisfied the debt. The Gemara will now discuss a case in ıich both the debtor and creditor claim to have possessed the cument before it was lost.

[I.e. the debtor and creditor both agree that the document is thentic; they disagree only over whether the debt recorded therein s been repaid. The creditor claims, "The document was in my ssession until I lost it; I never returned it to the debtor." A corollary the claim is that the debt was never repaid.] The debtor responds, 'rue, I incurred a debt and deposited the document in the creditor's ssession. However, the creditor subsequently returned the debt cument to me because I repaid the debt; it thus fell from me" (*Rashi*).

Initially, the Gemara interprets Rebbi's ruling as follows. If the editor and debtor are holding on to a found debt document, we do not tomatically assume that it is valid; the creditor must first have *beis* ı authenticate the signatures and certify the document. Once the cument is certified, however, it is presumed valid; the creditor may en collect the entire debt.

Actually, there are two ways for *beis din* to authenticate the signatures. One, which the Baraisa mentions, is to have the signatories themselves affirm that they signed. Another equally valid method is to find other pairs of witnesses that recognize the signatories' handwriting and to have them authenticate the signatures (see *Shitah Mekubetzes*).

25. According to the Gemara's conclusion on 7b, this means that the creditor collects half the debt.

26. Our translation reflects the Gemara's initial interpretation of the Baraisa. According to this interpretation, the Baraisa's ruling applies only if the document was found by a judge and not by a layman. Later, the Gemara will challenge this distinction (*Rashi*).

27. Since the creditor can thus use the document to collect the debt, it is returned to him.

28. Actually, Rebbi stated only that the creditor must have his document certified before collecting anything; he never ruled that once certified, the creditor can collect the full sum. Nevertheless, the Gemara infers that Rebbi indeed holds this to be true because it assumes his stated ruling to be axiomatic: No one would dispute his ruling that a document must be certified before collecting with it. If so, when Rabban Shimon ben Gamliel allowed the creditor to collect half the debt with his document he must have referred only to collecting with a certified document. Now having presented Rebbi's ruling (that the creditor need only certify the document to collect) immediately before that of Rabban Shimon ben Gamliel, the Baraisa obviously indicates that the two disagree. Thus, since Rabban Shimon ben Gamliel allows the creditor to collect only half the debt with a certified document, it follows that Rebbi allows him to collect the entire debt.

29. See full text of the Mishnah on 2a.

30. I.e. let the creditor collect only half.

31. I.e. that according to Rebbi, the creditor can collect the entire disputed sum once the document is certified.

אלא מאי אית לך למימר [א] עשירי ודאי אמר רחמנא ולא עשירי ספק הכא נמי עשירי ודאי אמר רחמנא ולא עשירי ספק א"ל רב אחא מדפתי לרבינא מאי ספיקות אילימא ספק בבכורות [א] יהיה קדש אמר רחמנא ולא שכבר קדוש אלא ספק פדיון פטר חמור וכדרב נחמן [ב] דאמר רב נחמן אמר רבה בר אבוה [א] ישראל שיש לו עשרה ספק פטרי חמור בתוך ביתו מפריש עליהן עשרה שיין ומעשרן והן שלו מאי הוי עלה דמסותא ת"ש דא"ר חייא בר אבין הוה עובדא בי רב חסדא ורב חסדא בי רב הונא ופשטה מהא דאמר רב נחמן כל ממון שאין יכול להוציאו בדיינין הקדישו אינו קדוש הא יכול להוציאו בדיינין הקדישו קדוש אע"ג דלא אפקיה [ג] והאמר ר' יוחנן [ב] גזל ולא נתייאשו הבעלים שניהם אינם יכולין להקדישו זה לפי שאינה שלו וזה לפי שאינה ברשותו מי סברת במסותא מטלטלין עסקינן [ג] במסותא מקרקעי עסקינן דכי יכול להוציאה בדיינין ברשותיה קיימא תני רב תחליפא בר מערבא קמיה דר' אבהו [ד] שנים אדוקים בטלית זה נוטל עד מקום שידו מגעת וזה נוטל עד מקום שידו מגעת והשאר חולקין בשוה מחוי ליה רבי אבהו [ה] ובשבועה אלא מתניתין דקתני דפלגי בהדדי ולא קתני זה נוטל עד מקום שידו מגעת היכי משכחת לה אמר רב פפא [ו] דתפיסי בכרכשתא אמר רב משרשיא ש"מ [ז] האי סודרא כיון דתפיס ביה שלש על שלש קרינן ביה [ב] ונתן לרעהו דכמאן דפסיק דמי וקני ומאי שנא מדרב חסדא [ד] דאמר רב חסדא [ח] גט בידה ומשיחה בידו אם יכול לנתקו ולהביאו אצלו אינה מגורשת ואם לאו מגורשת [ה] התם כריתות בעינן וליכא הכא נתינה בעינן והא איכא אמר רבא [ו] [ט] אם היתה טלית מוזהבת חולקין פשיטא לא צריכא דקאי דהבא בי מצעי הא נמי פשיטא לא צריכא דמיקרב לגבי דחד מהו דתימא [י] דא"ל פלוג הכי קמ"ל [י] דא"ל מאי חזית דפלגת הכי פלוג הכי: ת"ר [ז] שנים אדוקין בשטר מלוה אומר שלי הוא ונפל ממני ומצאתיו ולוה אמר [ח] שלך הוא ופרעתיו לך יתקיים השטר בחותמיו דברי רבי רשב"ג אומר יחלוקו נפל ליד דיין לא יוציאו עולמית ר' יוסי אומר הרי הוא בחזקתו אמר מר יתקיים השטר בחותמיו וגבי ליה מלוה כוליה ולית ליה מתני' שנים אוחזין כו' אמר רבא אמר רב נחמן [כ] במקוים דברי הכל יחלוקו כי פליגי בשאינו מקוים רבי סבר [ט] [ל] מודה בשטר שכתבו צריך לקיימו ואי מקיים ליה פליג ואי לא מקיים ליה לא פליג מאי טעמא חספא בעלמא הוא מאן קא משוי ליה להאי שטרא לוה הא קאמר דפריע ורבי שמעון בן גמליאל סבר מודה בשטר שכתבו אין צריך לקיימו ואע"ג דלא מקיים ליה יחלוקו נפל ליד דיין לא יוציאו עולמית מאי

**רש"י**

אלא מאי אית לך למימר. למה לא חייבוהו לעשר ממה נפשך: עשירי ודאי. הצריך הכתוב לעשר ולא הצריך לעשר את הספק וכל עשירי שבכאן ספק הן שאפי' יצא הפטור בחמישי שוב אין העשירי קרוי עשירי אלא תשיעי שהפטור אינו מן המנין: מאי ספיקות. דאמרן לעיל הספיקות נכנסין לדיר להתעשר: ספק פדיון פטר חמור. טלה שהופרש על ספק פטר חמור שאפילו הוא פטר חמור ודאי אין בטלה זה של פדיון משום קדושה: עשרה שיין. לאפקועי איסורייהו למשרי להו בעבודה: עובדא הוה בי רב חסדא ורב חסדא בי רב הונא. מעשה היה ובא לפני רב חסדא ורב חסדא הביאו לפני רב הונא: שאינו יכול להוציאו כו'. והאי נמי דחזינן ליה דאין יכול להוציאו בדיינין שאין לו ראיה בדבר אין הקדישו קדוש: הא יכול להוציאו כו'. בתמיה: שאינה ברשותו. והא סתם גזילה יכולין להוציאו בדיינין הוא: במסותא מטלטלין. כגון גיגית: מקרקעי. דכל היכא דאיתיה ברשות מרי' קיימא דקרקע אינה נגזלת ושפיר פשיטנא מהא דאי הוה ליה ראיה עלה הקדישו הקדש: בר מערבא. מארץ ישראל: מחוי ליה. מראה באצבעותיו כלפי מעלה: בכרכשתא. בגדין שבשני ראשין שקורין ברניי"ש: ש"מ. מדקתני עד מקום שידו מגעת קנוי לו: האי סודרא. של קונה שקונין בו קנין: כיון דתפיס ביה. מקנה שלש על שלש קרינא ביה ושלף איש נעלו ונתן לרעהו: דכמאן דפסיק דמי. וקנייה מקנה והמכר נקנה בו ללוקח ודוקא נקט שלש על שלש [ס] דכלי בעינן דכתיב (רות ד) נעלו ובציר משלש אצבעות לאו בגד הוא כדאשכחן גבי טומאה: גט בידה. שנתנו לה: ומשיחה. שקשור בה בידו אם יש כח באותו חוט שיכול לנתקו לגט מידה ולהביאו אצלו: אינה מגורשת. אלמא לאו נתינה היא: כריתות. הבדלה שיהיו מובדלים זה מזה והרי אגודים הם בחוט זה: אם היתה טלית מוזהבת. כלומר אפילו היא מוזהבת חולקים: פלוג הכי. לרוחבה ויהא הזהב לאחד מהם: קא משמע לן דא"ל כו' פלוג. לאורכה: שנים אדוקים בשטר. המלוה והלוה: שלך הוא ופרעתיו לך. והחזרת לי וממני נפל: יתקיים השטר בחותמיו. קס"ד דהכי קאמר אם השטר כשר שיקיימוהו חותמיו לומר כתב ידינו הוא הרי הוא בחזקתו: נפל השטר ליד הדיין. משמע דהכי קאמר אם מלאו דיין לא יוציאו אותו עולמית מיד דיין ולקמן פריך מאי שנא דיין מאינשי דעלמא: וגבי ליה מלוה כוליה. בתמיה: במקוים. שכתוב בו הנפק שילא כבר בב"ד והעידו עדים על חתימת ידן וכותבין הדיינין בו שטרא דנן נפק קדמנא ואסהידו פלוני ופלוני על חתימת ידייהו ואשרנוהו וקיימנוהו כדחזי: כולי עלמא ל"פ דיחלוקו. דכי אמרינן דיתקיים השטר בחותמיו לא למגבי מלוה כולו קאמר אלא למגבי פלגיה ופלוגתייהו כשאינו מקוים רבי סבר אף על פי שהלוה מודה ליה שכתב שטר זה ולוה לו מעות צריך המלוה לקיימו בחותמיו ואפילו השטר בידו נאמן הלוה לומר פרעתיך דכל זמן שאינו מקוים מאן קמשוי ליה שטרא לוה שמודה לו שכתבו הא אמר דפריע אבל משהשטר מוחזק על פי עדיו אין הלוה נאמן לומר פרעתי הלכך זה שניהם מוחזקים אי מקיים ליה מלוה בעדות ומשוי ליה שטר מעליא אין הלוה נאמן באמירתו אלא על ידי חזקה זה שאדוק בו והרי הוא כשאר מציאה ופליג: ואי לא לא פליג. שאפילו כולו ביד המלוה נאמן הלוה לומר פרעתי:

**תוספות**

ולא עשירי ספק. אין להקשות איצטריך קרא למעוטי ספיקא [י] כדפריך במסכת חולין (דף כב: ד"ה איצטריך):

מפריש עליהן עשרה שיין. תימה דבפ"ק דבכורות (דף ט. [יא] וסם) אמרי' דשה אחד פוטר כמה פטרי חמורים ומה צריך עשרה שיים ותו מאי קא משמע לן מתני' היא הספיקות נכנסים לדיר להתעשר ותו כיון דאמר מעשרן מה צריך להשמיענו דהן שלו פשיטא כיון דמעשרן דהן שלו דאילו היו של כהן לא היה מעשרן דהוו להו כלקוח דתנן (שם דף נה:) הלקוח והניתן לו במתנה פטור ואי קמ"ל דאע"ג דמעשרן עדיין הם שלו פשיטא דמעשר בהמה של בעלים הוא:

מחוי ר' אבהו והשאר בשבועה. [א] נראה דלא גרסי' והשאר דאף במה שידו מגעת ישבע כיון דנתקנה השבועה שלא יהא אדם הולך ותוקף מטעם זה ישבע אף במה שהוא תופס ומכל מקום שפיר מוכח בסמוך דקנין מאי דתפיס כמאן דפסיק דמי כיון דהכא לאחר שבועה נוטל כל מה שהוא תופס אפילו יותר ממחצה והשבועה היא בשביל הטענה ומפני התקנה:

אם יכול לנתקו. נראה דאם היתה ידה פתוחה בשעת שנתן גט לידה ונשארה המשיחה בידו וקפלה ידה בחוזק שאם מושך המשיחה לא יוכל להביאו אצלו שאינה מגורשת שהרי כשנתן בידה קודם שקפלה ידה היה יכול להביאו אצלו והקפילה לא עשה הוא אלא היא והוה כטלי גיטך מעל גבי קרקע דאינה מגורשת דלא קרינן ביה ונתן בידה והכא דקאמר אם אינו יכול להביאו אצלו דמגורשת כגון שהיתה ידה קפולה והוא תחב בידה כל כך בחוזק שאם ימשוך המשיחה לא יביא הגט אצלו ור"ת [יב] (נמי) פירש אם הגט כבד כל כך שאם רוצה למשוך הגט אליו תנתק המשיחה מגורשת ומיירי בידה פתוחה ולא קפלה ולא עשתה שום דבר:

**עין משפט נר מצוה**

מא א מיי' פי"ב מהל' בכורים הלכה כג סמג עשין קמו:

מב ב מיי' פ"ו מהל' ערכין הל' כד סמג עשין קלב טוש"ע ח"מ סי' שנד סעיף ו וטוש"ע י"ד סי' רנח סעיף ז:

מג ג מיי' שם הל' כג סמג שם טוש"ע י"ד שם [רב אלפס כאן ובב"ק פ"ד דף כ.]:

מד ד ה ו מיי' פ"ט מהל' טוען ונטען הל' ט י סמג עשין צה טוש"ע ח"מ סי' קלח סעיף ג:

מה ז מיי' פ"ה מהלכות מכירה הל' ז סמג עשין פב טוש"ע ח"מ סי' קצה סעיף ד:

מו ח מיי' פ"ה מהלכות גירושין הל' טו סמג עשין נ טוש"ע אה"ע סי' קלט סעיף ב:

מז ט י מיי' פ"ט מהל' טוען ונטען הל' י סמג עשין צה טוש"ע ח"מ סי' קלח סעיף ג:

מח כ מיי' פי"ד מהל' מלוה ולוה הל' יד סמג עשין צד טוש"ע ח"מ סי' סה סעיף טו:

מט ל מיי' שם וסמג שם טוש"ע ח"מ סי' פב סעיף א:

**רבינו חננאל**

מאי הוי עלה דמסותא ת"ש מהא דאמר רב [נחמן] כל ממון שאינו יכול להוציאו בדיינין הקדישו אינו קדוש. הא יכול להוציאו אע"פ שלא הוציאו קדוש. ומקשי' עלה והאמר ר' יוחנן גזל ולא נתייאשו הבעלי' שניהן אינן יכולין להקדישו זה לפי שאינו שלו וזה לפי שאינו ברשותו. וקי"ל דלא מקשינן לא ממשנה ולא מברייתא ולא ממימרא אלא אם היא הלכה. ועוד לא דחאוה להא דר' יוחנן אלא פירקו על דבריו ואמר מי סברת מסותא מטלטלא היא וקשיא עליה הא דר' יוחנן לא כי קאמר רב [נחמן] כל ממון שאינו יכול להוציאו בדיינין וכו' האי ממון קרקע הוא וכיוצא בו האי מסותא מקרקעא הוא דקי"ל קרקע אינה נגזלת ולעולם ברשותיה דמרא קיימא הלכך אם יכול להוציאה בדיינין ברשותיה קיימא ושפיר קא מקדיש. האי דקתני **שנים אדוקין בטלית זה נוטל עד מקום שידו מגעת וזה נוטל עד מקום שידו מגעת והשאר** חולקין בשוה ובשבועה אוקימנא בשאדוקין בטלית עצמו ומתני' דקתני חולקין הטלית שני חצאין ונוטל כל אחד חציה בשאדוקין בנימין שבקצותיה והן הנקראים כרכשתא. ופשוטה היא. דייק רב (אשי) [משרשיא] מינה מדקתני זה נוטל עד מקום שידו מגעת ש"מ דהאי סודרא כיון דתפיס ביה ג' אצבעות על ג' אצבעות הרי הוא קנין לתופסן ואע"ג דלא פסיק כמאן דפסיק דמי ולא אמרי' עד דמשיך ליה כוליה לא קני ליה אלא אע"ג דלא משיך ליה לכוליה קני לההוא דתפס וכן הלכה. אמר רבא אם היתה טלית מוזהבת והזהב קרוב לגבי חד ברחבה של טלית ואם יחלקוה לרחבה לשני חצאין יבא הזהב בחלקו של אחד יכול האחד לומר זה שבינינו לאורכה נחלקה כדי שנחלק בטלית ובזהב והדין עמו: ת"ר שנים אדוקין בשטר כו' אסיק' בשטר מקוים דברי הכל יחלוקו. ושאינו מקוים ומלוה אמר שלי הוא ונפל ממני ומצאתיו ולוה אמר שלך היה ופרעתיך ונתתי לך [וממני נפל] אם נתקיים בחותמיו יחלוקו דברי ר' דרבי קסבר מודה בשטר שכתבו צריך לקיימו וקי"ל כרבי. רשב"ג אומר אע"פ שאין יכול

**מסורת הש"ס**

[א] בכורות נח:], ב) שם ..., ג) בבא קמא סח., ... ע., קדושין נב., ... גיטין עח., ה) לקמן ח., ... לקמן קז., ז) בבא ... קע., ח) [שלי וכן ... בהרי"ף והרא"ש, ... שאלל האלפסי ... שלך היה ... פרעתיו לך], ט) בבא ... קע., ודף קנד., ... יט., שבת עח: ... עב:], י) [צ"ל ... ישית], יא) [ועיין ... שם ד: ד"ה ופודה ... עוד היטב תוס' יא. ... שהיו], יב) מהר"ם ... מוחק זה.

**הגהות הגר"א**

[א] תוס' ד"ה מחוי ... כו'. נ"ב והרמב"ם ... כתב כן אלא ע"י גלגול ... רא"ש הוכיח כדברי תוס' ע"ש:

**גליון הש"ס**

במסותא ... מקרקעי. קשה לי הא ... החילוק בין מטלטלי ... מקרקעי דמטלטלין ... וקם ליה ברשותיה ... מקרי אינו ברשותו ... וגזל אבל קרקע אינה ... ולא קם ברשותיה ... א"כ במטלטלין וגזל ... קנין דלא קם ... ברשותיה דהנגזל ... חייב באחריותו ... דאיתא בב"ק עט ע"א ... מתני' הוי כקרקע דמנחי ... ברשותיה דהנגזל. וא"כ ... במסותא דהגזילה ... דאמר דידי הוא ... קנין יכול ... הקדישו וצ"ע: שם ... התם כריתות בעינן. ... כתובות נ ע"ב תוס' ... ואי וצ"ע: רש"י ... ד"ה דכמאן וכו' דכלי ... בעינן. עיין לקמן מז ... ובתוס' ד"ה לאפוקי:

**תורה אור השלם**

א) וְכָל מַעְשַׂר בָּקָר וָצֹאן כֹּל אֲשֶׁר יַעֲבֹר תַּחַת הַשָּׁבֶט הָעֲשִׂירִי יִהְיֶה קֹּדֶשׁ לַיְיָ: [ויקרא כז, לב]

ב) וְזֹאת לְפָנִים בְּיִשְׂרָאֵל עַל הַגְּאוּלָּה וְעַל הַתְּמוּרָה לְקַיֵּם כָּל דָּבָר שָׁלַף אִישׁ נַעֲלוֹ וְנָתַן לְרֵעֵהוּ וְזֹאת הַתְּעוּדָה בְּיִשְׂרָאֵל: [רות ד, ז]

**לעזי רש"י**

ברניי"ש. פירוש חוטין שמשתיירין בסוף בגד שמותכין מן הבגד לאחר אריגתו (ערוך ערך גרד ... ועיין רש"י סוכה דף ט ע"א ד"ה מן הגרדין בכורות דף ח ע"ב ד"ה כרוכו לי).

**ליקוטי רש"י**

עשירי ודאי. משום דעשירי ודאי אמר רחמנא יהיה קודש ולא ספק [בכורות נח:]. ספק פטרי חמור. כגון שהיה לו עשר חמורות וילדו כולן זכר ונקבה שמפריש עליהן עשרה שיין לאפקועי לאיסורייהו. ומעשרן לשיין כשאר בהמות חולין והן שלו והמעשר קרב שלמים והוא אוכלו כדין שאר מעשר בהמה. כרכשתא. פרייו"ש שתולין בסוף הטלית מותר האריגה [סוכה ט.]. גט בידה. שנתנו לה ולאש המשיחה עדיין בידו [בכורות יא.]. ומשיחה. חוט שהגט קשור בו לילי"ל בלע"ז [גיטין עח:]. חספא. חרס [עי' סוכה נג:]. מודה. לוה בשטר שכתבו ואינו מזייף אלא שטוען פרעתיו או שכ"מ הייתי או שטר אמנה או שטר פסים הוא [רשב"ם ב"ב קנד.]. צריך לקיימו. ולומר לא פרעתי וכל כמה דלא אמר הכי לאו שטרא הוא אי לאו משכח סהדי להכיר החתימה דמאן קא משוי ליה שטרא לוה דאמר כתבתיו לוה נמי הא קאמר פרעתי הפה שאסר הוא הפה שהתיר [שבת עח:]. אין צריך לקיימו. בעדים החתומים בו שאין הלוה שוב נאמן לומר פרעתיו ולא אמרינן בהאי הפה שאסר הוא הפה שהתיר למכון שאמר כשר היה הרי הוחזק השטר וכי אמר פרעתיו לא מהימן שהרי ביד המלוה הוא [כתובות יט.]. דסתם שטרות הרי הם כשרים ובשטרות לא נימא הפה שאסר הוא הפה שהתיר לפסלו [רשב"ם ב"ב קנד.]. דלא דמי לשאר דינים שהפה שאסר הוא הפה שהתיר שאפילו אם היה זה מערער ואומר לא כתבתיו לא היה לנו לחשוד את זה הלוקח בכך שלא נחשדו ישראל לעשות שטרות מזוייפים אלא שהחמירו חכמים להצריך קיום היכא דמערערי עליה הלכך כי אמר כתבתיו נהמניה למי שהשטר בידו [שם קע.].

The Gemara answers:
מִי סָבְרַת בְּמְסוּתָא מִטַּלְטְלִין עָסְק – Do you think that the bath we are dealing with here is movable property (i.e. a bathtub)?! בְּמְסוּתָא מְקַרְקְעֵי עָסְק – We are dealing with a bath that is real property (i.e. a pool), דְּכִי יָכוֹל לְהוֹצִיאָהּ בְּדַיָּינִין – which, if [the claimant] can exact it through legal proceedings, בִּרְשׁוּתֵיהּ קָיְיכָ – in effect remained in his possession throughout, for real property cannot be removed from the possession of its true owner.[13]

The Gemara discusses a variation of our Mishnah's case where two people enter the court holding on to a cloak:
תָּנֵי רַב תַּחְלִיפָא בַּר מַעַרְבָא קַמֵּיהּ דר׳ אַבָּ – Rav Tachlifa from the West [Eretz Yisrael] taught the following Baraisa before R' Abahu: שְׁנַיִם אֲדוּקִים בְּטַלִּית – If TWO litigants enter the court CLUTCHING A CLOAK, it is divided as follows: זֶה נוֹטֵל עַד מָקוֹם שֶׁיָּדוֹ מַגַּעַ – THIS ONE TAKES AS FAR AS HIS HAND EXTENDS וְזֶה נוֹטֵל עַד מָקוֹם שֶׁיָּדוֹ מַגַּעַ – AND THE OTHER TAKES AS FAR AS HIS HAND EXTENDS וְהַשְּׁאָר חוֹלְקִין בְּשָׁוֶה – AND THE REST of the cloak IS DIVIDED EQUALLY between them.[14] מַחְוֵי לֵיהּ רַבִּי אַבָּהוּ – R' Abahu gestured to [Rav Tachlifa]. He pointed heavenward, thereby imparting the message: וּבִשְׁבוּעָה – "But only with an oath!"[15]

The Gemara asks:
אֶלָּא מַתְנִיתִ – But then our Mishnah, דְּקָתָנֵי דְּפָלְגֵי בַּהֲדָדֵי – which teaches only that [the litigants] divide the cloak between themselves, וְלֹא קָתָנֵי זֶה נוֹטֵל עַד מָקוֹם שֶׁיָּדוֹ מַגַּעַת – and does not teach that [each] takes as far as his hand extends, הֵיכִי מַשְׁכַּחַת לָהּ – under what circumstances does it apply? Surely they are holding on to the cloak with their hands! – ? –

The Gemara answers:
אָמַר רַב פַּפָּ – Rav Pappa said: דְּתָפִיסֵי בִּכְרַכַּשְׁתָּא – The Mishnah speaks of a case where they are holding the fringes at the edges of the cloak.[16]

A law is inferred from the Baraisa's ruling that each disputant takes what is in his hand:
אָמַר רַב מְשַׁרְשִׁיָּא – Rav Mesharshiya said: שְׁמַע מִינָּהּ – One can learn the following law from [the Baraisa]: הַאי סוּדָרָא – Regarding this kerchief (i.e. a kerchief that is used to effect *chalifin*),[17] כֵּיוָן דְּתָפִיס בֵּיהּ שָׁלֹשׁ עַל שָׁלֹשׁ – as soon as [the seller] grasps a portion of it that measures three by three fingerbreadths, קָרֵינַן בֵּיהּ: ,,וְנָתַן לְרֵעֵהוּ״ – we apply to it the verse, *and he gave it to his fellow,*[18] דִּכְמַאן דְּפָסִיק דָּמֵי – because it [the portion in his hand] is viewed as if it were cut off from the rest of the kerchief, וְקָנֵי – and thus the transaction is effected.[19]

The Gemara asks:
וּמַאי שְׁנָא מִדְּרַב חִסְדָּא – But how is this different from [the ruling] taught by Rav Chisda? דְּאָמַר רַב חִסְדָּא – For Rav Chisda said: Concerning a man who gives his wife a bill of divorce to which a string is attached, גֵּט בְּיָדָהּ וּמְשִׁיחָה בְּיָדוֹ – and the bill of divorce is in her hand and the string is in his hand, the law is determined according to the following distinction: אִם יָכוֹל לְנַתְּקוֹ וְלַהֲבִיאוֹ אֶצְלוֹ – If the string is so strong that he could pull [the bill of divorce] and bring it towards himself, אֵינָהּ מְגוֹרֶשֶׁת – she is not divorced. וְאִם לָאו – But if the string is not that strong, מְגוֹרֶשֶׁת – she is divorced. This contradicts the previous teaching that whatever is in a person's hand is considered "given" to him. – ? –

The Gemara answers:
הָתָם כְּרִיתוּת בְּעִינַן – There, with regard to divorce, we require that he give her a document of "severance"[20] and he must therefore give it to her in a way that severs the connection between them, וְלֵיכָּא – and there is no such severance where he continues to hold on to the document by means of a string. הָכָא נְתִינָה בְּעִינַן – Here, however, with regard to *chalifin*, we

NOTES

13. **Summary:** The Gemara discussed (1) the seizure and (2) the consecration of disputed objects:

*Cloak*: With regard to the case of two people holding on to a cloak, the issue of seizure was not resolved (see 6b note 11). The issue of consecration was resolved with R' Yochanan's ruling that a person cannot consecrate even his own property unless it is in his possession (see previous note).

*Bath*: The issue of seizure was not discussed in relation to this case (see 6b note 2). The issue of consecration was resolved with Rav Nachman's teaching that one cannot consecrate property unless one has the evidence required to exact it through legal proceedings. [This is the law as it applies to real property, which never leaves the owner's possession. With regard to movable property, the law is that even if one can exact it through legal proceedings, one cannot consecrate it unless it is in one's possession] (Gemara above).

*Bechor*: If a Kohen seizes a questionable *bechor* from a Yisrael, he must return it. This is derived from the Mishnah: *[Animals] of questionable status enter the pen to be tithed.* Nevertheless, a questionable *bechor* is sacred (out of doubt) from birth, for this sanctity is acquired automatically (Gemara 6b).

14. The portion of the cloak that is in a disputant's hand is considered to be held only by him. The portion *between* their hands is held by both parties.

15. Each party swears not only with regard to the portion that is divided but also with regard to the portion in his hand. Since the oath was instituted to deter one from taking hold of an object in the hands of another and then claiming it as one's own, it applies to the portions in the disputants' hands as well (*Tosafos, Rosh*)

Alternatively: The text of the Gemara reads: וְהַשְּׁאָר בִּשְׁבוּעָה, *and the rest with an oath.* According to this version of the text, the oath concerns only the portion that is divided. [Once someone is taking this oath, however, his opponent may require him to add mention of the portion in his hands, in accordance with the law of גִּלְגּוּל שְׁבוּעָה, *a devolved oath*] (*Rambam Hil. To'ein V' Nitan* 9:9).

16. [The fringes are of no value in themselves. However, since they are part of the cloak, one who holds the fringes is considered to be holding the cloak.]

17. חֲלִיפִין, *chalifin* [acquisition by] exchange: A token object is exchanged between two parties as a means of effecting a given transaction. It was traditional to use a kerchief for this purpose. (Hence, this method of acquisition is commonly referred to as קִנְיַן סוּדָר, *acquisition by kerchief.*) It is a matter of dispute whether the token object is passed from the buyer to the seller or vice versa. *Rashi* here follows the former view.

18. The source for *chalifin* is *Ruth* 4:7-8 where it is written that Boaz acquired an estate with the exchange of a shoe. In reference to that transaction, Scripture states (ibid. v. 7): שָׁלַף אִישׁ נַעֲלוֹ וְנָתַן לְרֵעֵהוּ, *a man took off his shoe and gave it to his fellow.*

19. The verse teaches that to effect *chalifin* the token object must be "given." This means that it must not only enter the possession of the seller but also leave the possession of the buyer. Therefore, if the buyer is still holding on to the object, the transaction is not effected. Rav Mesharshiya deduces from the Baraisa, however, that where an item such as a kerchief is used, the transaction is effected even if the buyer is still holding on to it. For the Baraisa rules that the portion of the cloak in a disputant's hands is considered exclusively his, and his opponent is not deemed to be holding that portion at all. Evidently, that portion is viewed as if it were "cut off" from the rest of the cloak (see *Rashi* ד״ה אינה; cf. *Ritva*; see *Ohr Same'ach* to *Hil. To'ein V'Nitan* ch. 9).

The portion in the seller's hand must measure at least three by three fingerbreadths, because a smaller piece of cloth is not classified as a כְּלִי, *utensil*. From the verse's mention of a shoe, it is derived that the only items valid for *chalifin* are those which, like a shoe, fall under the category of utensils (see *Rashi*).

20. Scripture (*Deuteronomy* 24:1,3) refers to a bill of divorce as a סֵפֶר כְּרִיתֻת, *document of severance.*

**מסורת הש"ס**

א) [בכורות נח:], ב) שם ..., ג) בבא קמא סח., ... ע., קדושין נב., ... גיטין עח:, ה) לקמן ח., ... [לקמן קז.], ז) בבא ... קע., ח) [שלי וכן ... בהרי"ף והרא"ש, ... שאלו האלפסי ... שלך היה ... פרעתיו לך], ט) בבא ... קע., ודף קנד., ... יט., שבת עח:, ... לקמן עב:], י) [נ"ל ... פרשים], יא) [ועיין ... שם ד: ד"ה ופודה ... עוד היטב תוס' יא. ... שסין], יב) מהר"ם מוחק זה.

**הגהות הגר"א**

[א] תוס' ד"ה מחוי ... כו'. נ"ב והרמב"ם ... כתב כן אלא ע"י גלגול ... הרא"ש הוכיח כדברי תוס' ע"ש:

**גליון הש"ס**

... במסותא מקרקעי. קשה לי הא ... עיקר החילוק בין מטלטלי למקרקעי דמטלטלין ... גזלן וקם ליה ברשותיה ... גזלן מקרי אינו ברשותו ... הנגזל אבל קרקע אינה נגזלת ולא קם ברשותיה ... גזלן. א"כ במטלטלין וגזל ... לא קנין דלא קם ... ברשותיה דהנגזל ... אינו חייב באחריותו ... דאיתא בב"ק עט ע"א ... מתני' הוי כקרקע דמנחי ... ברשותיה דהנגזל. וא"כ ... הכא במסותא דהגזילה ... מה דאמר דידי הוא ... ליכא קנין יכול ... להקדישו וצ"ע: שם ... התם כריתות בעינן. ... עיין כתובות כ ע"ב תוס' ... ואי ולע"ע: רש"י ... דכמאן וכו' דפסיק ... בעינן. עיין לקמן מז ... ע"א ... ד"ה ... לאפוקי:

**תורה אור השלם**

א) וְכָל מַעְשַׂר בָּקָר וָצֹאן כֹּל אֲשֶׁר יַעֲבֹר תַּחַת הַשָּׁבֶט הָעֲשִׂירִי יִהְיֶה קֹּדֶשׁ לַיי: [ויקרא כז, לב]
ב) וְזֹאת לְפָנִים בְּיִשְׂרָאֵל עַל הַגְּאוּלָּה וְעַל הַתְּמוּרָה לְקַיֵּם כָּל דָּבָר שָׁלַף אִישׁ נַעֲלוֹ וְנָתַן לְרֵעֵהוּ וְזֹאת הַתְּעוּדָה בְּיִשְׂרָאֵל: [רות ד, ז]

**לעזי רש"י**

ברנייש. פירוש חוטין שמשיירין בסוף בגד ומתוכסין מן הבגד לאחר אריגתו (ערוך ערך גרד) * ועיין רש"י סוכה דף ט ע"א ד"ה מן הגרדין ... בכורות דף ... כרוכו לי).

**ליקוטי רש"י**

עשירי ודאי. משום עשירי ודאי אמר רחמנא יהיה קודש ולא ספק [בכורות נח:]. ספק פטרי חמור. כגון שהיו לו עשר חמורות וילדו כולן זכר ...

---

**גמרא**

אלא מאי אית לך למימר [א] עשירי ודאי אמר רחמנא ולא עשירי ספק הכא נמי עשירי ודאי אמר רחמנא ולא עשירי ספק א"ל רב אחא מדפתי לרבינא מאי ספיקות אילימא ספק בכורות [א] יהיה קדש אמר רחמנא ולא שכבר קדוש אלא ספק פדיון פטר חמור וכדרב נחמן [ג] דאמר רב נחמן אמר רבה בר אבוה [א] ישראל שיש לו עשרה ספק פטרי חמור בתוך ביתו מפריש עליהן עשרה שיין ומעשרן והן שלו מאי הוי עלה דמסותא ת"ש דא"ר חייא בר אבין הוה עובדא בי רב חסדא ורב חסדא בי רב הונא ופשטה מהא דאמר רב נחמן כל ממון שאין יכול להוציאו בדיינין הקדישו אינו קדוש הא יכול להוציאו בדיינין הקדישו קדוש אע"ג דלא אפקיה [ד] והאמר ר' יוחנן [ב] גזל ולא נתייאשו הבעלים שניהם אינם יכולין להקדישו זה לפי שאינה שלו וזה לפי שאינה ברשותו מי סברת במסותא מטלטלין עסקינן [ג] במסותא מקרקעי עסקינן דכי יכול להוציאה בדיינין ברשותיה קיימא תני רב תחליפא בר מערבא קמיה דר' אבהו [ד] שנים אדוקים בטלית זה נוטל עד מקום שידו מגעת וזה נוטל עד מקום שידו מגעת והשאר חולקין בשוה מחוי ליה רבי אבהו [ה] ובשבועה אלא מתניתין דקתני דפלגי בהדדי ולא קתני זה נוטל עד מקום שידו מגעת היכי משכחת לה אמר רב פפא [ו] דתפיסי בכרכשתא אמר רב משרשיא ש"מ [ז] האי סודרא כיון דתפיס ביה שלש על שלש קרינן ביה [ב] ונתן לרעהו דכמאן דפסיק דמי וקני ומאי שנא מדרב חסדא [ז] דאמר רב חסדא [ח] גט בידה ומשיחה בידו אם יכול לנתקו ולהביאו אצלו אינה מגורשת ואם לאו מגורשת [°] התם כריתות בעינן וליכא הכא נתינה בעינן והא איכא אמר רבא [ח] [ט] אם היתה טלית מוזהבת חולקין פשיטא לא צריכא דקאי דהבא בי מצעי הא נמי פשיטא לא צריכא דמיקרב לגבי דחד מהו דתימא [י] דא"ל פלוג הכי קמ"ל [י] דא"ל מאי חזית דפלגת הכי פלוג הכי: ת"ר [ז] שנים אדוקין בשטר מלוה אומר שלי הוא ונפל ממני ומצאתיו ולוה אמר [ח] שלך הוא ופרעתיו לך יתקיים השטר בחותמיו דברי רבי רשב"ג אומר יחלוקו נפל ליד דיין לא יוציאו עולמית ר' יוסי אומר הרי הוא בחזקתו אמר מר יתקיים השטר בחותמיו וגבי ליה מלוה כוליה ולית ליה מתני' שנים אוחזין כו' אמר רבא אמר רב נחמן [כ] במקוים דברי הכל יחלוקו כי פליגי בשאינו מקוים רבי סבר [ט] [ל] מודה בשטר שכתבו צריך לקיימו ואי מקיים ליה פליג ואי לא מקיים ליה לא פליג מאי טעמא חספא בעלמא הוא מאן קא משוי ליה להאי שטרא לוה הא קאמר דפריע ורבי שמעון בן גמליאל סבר מודה בשטר שכתבו אין צריך לקיימו ואע"ג דלא מקיים ליה יחלוקו נפל ליד דיין לא יוציאו עולמית מאי

**רש"י**

אלא מאי אית לך למימר. למה לא חייבוהו לעשר ממה נפשך: עשירי ודאי. הצריך הכתוב לעשר ולא הצריך לעשר את הספק וכל עשירי שבכאן ספק הן שאפי' יצא הפטור בחמישי שוב אין העשירי קרוי עשירי אלא תשיעי שהפטור אינו מן המנין: מאי ספיקות. דאמרן לעיל הספיקות נכנסין לדיר להתעשר: ספק פדיון פטר חמור. טלה שהופרש על ספק פטר חמור שאפילו הוא פטר חמור ודאי אין בטלה זה של פדיון משום קדושה: עשרה שיין. לאפקועי איסורייהו למשרי להו בעבודה: עובדא הוה בי רב חסדא ורב חסדא בי רב הונא. מעשה היה ובא לפני רב חסדא ורב חסדא הביאו לפני רב הונא: שאינו יכול להוציאו כו'. והאי נמי דחזינן ליה דאין יכול להוציאו בדיינין שאין לו ראיה בדבר אין הקדישו קדוש: הא יכול להוציאו כו'. בתמיה: שאינה ברשותו. והא סתם גזילה יכולין להוציאו בדיינין הוא: במסותא מטלטלין. כגון גיגית: מקרקעי. דכל היכא דאיתיה ברשות מרי' קיימא דקרקע אינה נגזלת ושפיר פשיטנא מהא דאי הוה ליה ראיה עלה הקדישו הקדש: בר מערבא. מארץ ישראל: מחוי ליה. מראה באצבעותיו כלפי מעלה: בכרכשתא. בגרדין שבשני ראשין שקורין ברניי"ש: ש"מ. מדקתני עד מקום שידו מגעת קנוי לו: האי סודרא. של קונה שקונין בו קנין: כיון דתפיס ביה. מקנה שלש על שלש קרינא ביה ושלף איש נעלו ונתן לרעהו: דכמאן דפסיק דמי. וקנייה מקנה והמכר נקנה בו ללוקח ודוקא נקט שלש על שלש ° דכלי בעינן דכתיב (רות ד) נעלו ובציר משלש אצבעות לאו בגד הוא כדאשכחן גבי טומאה: גט בידה. שנתנו לה: ומשיחה. שקשור בה בידו אם יש כח באותו חוט שיכול לנתקו לגט מידה ולהביאו אצלו: אינה מגורשת. אלמא לאו נתינה היא: כריתות. הבדלה שיהיו מובדלים זה מזה והרי אגודים הם בחוט זה: אם היתה טלית מוזהבת. כלומר אפילו היא מוזהבת חולקים: פלוג הכי. לרוחבה ויהא הזהב לאחד מהם: קא משמע לן דא"ל כו' פלוג. לאורכה: שנים אדוקים בשטר. המלוה והלוה: שלך הוא ופרעתיו לך. והחזרת לי וממני נפל: יתקיים השטר בחותמיו. קס"ד דהכי קאמר אם השטר כשר שיקיימוהו חותמיו לומר כתב ידינו הוא הרי הוא בחזקתו: נפל השטר ליד הדיין. משמע דהכי קאמר אם מלאו דיין לא יוציאו אותו עולמית מיד דיין ולקמן פריך מאי שנא דיין מאינשי דעלמא: וגבי ליה מלוה כוליה. בתמיה: במקוים. שכתוב בו הנפק שילא כבר בב"ד והעידו עדים על חתימת ידן וכותבין הדיינין בו שטרא דנן נפק קדמנא ואסהידו פלוני ופלוני על חתימת ידייהו ואשרנוהו וקיימנוהו כדחזי: כולי עלמא ל"פ דיחלוקו. דכי אמרינן דיתקיים השטר בחותמיו לא למגבי מלוה כולו קאמר אלא למגבי פלגיה ופלוגתייהו כשאינו מקוים רבי סבר אף על פי שהלוה מודה ליה שכתב שטר זה ולוה לו מעות צריך המלוה לקיימו בחותמיו ואפילו השטר בידו נאמן הלוה לומר פרעתיך דכל זמן שאינו מקוים מאן קמשוי ליה שטרא לוה שמודה לו שכתבו הא אמר דפריע אבל משהשטר מוחזק על פי עדיו אין הלוה נאמן לומר פרעתי הלכך זה שניהם מוחזקים אי מקיים ליה מלוה בעדות ומשוי ליה שטר מעליא אין הלוה נאמן באמירתו אלא על ידי חזקה זה שאדוק בו והרי הוא כשאר מציאה ופליג: ואי לא לא פליג. שאפילו כולו ביד המלוה נאמן הלוה לומר פרעתי:

**תוספות**

ולא עשירי ספק. אין להקשות איצטריך קרא למעוטי ספיקא [י] כדפריך במסכת חולין (דף כב: ד"ה איצטריך): מפריש עליהן עשרה שיין. תימה דבפ"ק דבכורות (דף ט. [יא] ושם) אמרי' דשה אחד פוטר כמה פטרי חמורים ומה צריך עשרה שיים ותו מאי קא משמע לן מתני' היא הספיקות נכנסים לדיר להתעשר ותו כיון דאמר מעשרן מה צריך להשמיענו דהן שלו פשיטא כיון דמעשרן דהן שלו דאילו היו של כהן לא היה מעשרן דהוו להו כלקוח דתנן (שם דף נה:) הלקוח והניתן לו במתנה פטור ואי קמ"ל דאע"ג דמעשרן עדיין הם שלו פשיטא דמעשר בהמה של בעלים הוא:

מחוי ר' אבהו והשאר בשבועה. [א] נראה דלא גרסי' והשאר דאף במה שידו מגעת ישבע כיון דנתקנה השבועה שלא יהא אדם הולך ותוקף מטעם זה ישבע אף במה שהוא תופס ומכל מקום שפיר מוכח בסמוך דקנין מאי דתפיס כמאן דפסיק דמי כיון דהכא לאחר שבועה נוטל כל מה שהוא תופס אפילו יותר ממחצה והשבועה היא בשביל הטענה ומפני התקנה:

אם יכול לנתקו. נראה דאם היתה ידה פתוחה בשעת שנתן גט לידה ונשארה המשיחה בידו וקפלה ידה בחוזק שאם מושך המשיחה לא יוכל להביאו אצלו שאינה מגורשת שהרי כשנתן בידה קודם שקפלה ידה היה יכול להביאו אצלו והקפילה לא עשה הוא אלא היא והוה כטלי גיטך מעל גבי קרקע דאינה מגורשת דלא קרינן ביה ונתן בידה והכא דקאמר אם אינו יכול להביאו אצלו דמגורשת כגון שהיתה ידה קפולה והוא תחב בידה כל כך בחוזק שאם ימשוך המשיחה לא יביא הגט אצלו ור"ת [יב] (נמי) פירש אם הגט כבד כל כך שאם רוצה למשוך הגט אליו תנתק המשיחה מגורשת ומיירי בידה פתוחה ולא קפלה ולא עשתה שום דבר:

**עין משפט נר מצוה**

מא א מיי' פי"ב מהל' בכורים הלכה כג סמג עשין קמו:

מב ב מיי' פ"ו מהל' ערכין הל' כד סמג עשין קלב טוש"ע ח"מ סי' שנד סעיף ו וטוש"ע י"ד סי' רנח סעיף ז:

מג ג מיי' שם הל' כג סמג שם טוש"ע י"ד שם [רב אלפס כאן ובב"ק פ"ד דף כ.]:

מד ד ה ו מיי' פ"ט מהל' טוען ונטען הל' ט י סמג עשין צה טוש"ע ח"מ סי' קלח סעיף ג:

מה ז מיי' פ"ה מהלכות מכירה הל' ז סמג עשין פב טוש"ע ח"מ סי' קצה סעיף ד:

מו ח מיי' פ"ה מהלכות גירושין הל' טו סמג עשין נ טוש"ע אה"ע סי' קלט סעיף ב:

מז ט י מיי' פ"ט מהל' טוען ונטען הל' י סמג עשין צה טוש"ע ח"מ סי' קלח סעיף ג:

מח כ מיי' פי"ד מהל' מלוה ולוה הל' יד סמג עשין צד טוש"ע ח"מ סי' סה סעיף טו:

מט ל מיי' שם וסמג שם טוש"ע ח"מ סי' פב סעיף א:

**רבינו חננאל**

מאי הוי עלה דמסותא ת"ש מהא דאמר רב [נחמן] כל ממון שאינו יכול להוציאו בדיינין הקדישו אינו קדוש. הא יכול להוציאו אע"פ שלא הוציאו קדוש. ומקשי' עלה והאמר ר' יוחנן גזל ולא נתייאשו הבעלי' שניהן אינן יכולין להקדישו זה לפי שאינו שלו וזה לפי שאינו ברשותו. וקי"ל דלא מקשינן לא ממשנה ולא מברייתא ולא ממימרא אלא אם היא הלכה. ועוד לא דחאוה להא דר' יוחנן אלא פירקו על דבריו ואמר מי סברת מסותא מטלטלא היא וקשיא עליה הא דר' יוחנן לא כי קאמר רב [נחמן] כל ממון שאינו יכול להוציאו בדיינין וכו' האי ממון קרקע הוא וכיוצא בו האי מסותא מקרקעא הוא דקי"ל קרקע אינה נגזלת ולעולם ברשותיה דמרא קיימא הלכך אם יכול להוציאה בדיינין ברשותיה קיימא ושפיר קא מקדיש. האי דקתני **שנים אדוקין בטלית זה נוטל עד מקום שידו מגעת וזה נוטל עד מקום שידו מגעת והשאר חולקין בשוה ובשבועה** אוקימנא בשאדוקין בטלית עצמו ומתני' דקתני חולקין הטלית שני חצאין ונוטל כל אחד חציה בשאדוקין בנימין שבקצותיה והן הנקראים כרכשתא. ופשוטה היא. דייק רב (אשי) [משרשיא] מינה מדקתני זה נוטל עד מקום שידו מגעת ש"מ דהאי סודרא כיון דתפיס ביה ג' אצבעות על ג' אצבעות הרי הוא קנין לתופסן ואע"ג דלא פסיק כמאן דפסיק דמי ולא אמרי' עד דמשיך ליה כוליה לא קני ליה אלא אע"ג דלא משיך ליה לכוליה קני לההוא דתפס וכן הלכה. אמר רבא אם היתה טלית מוזהבת והזהב קרוב לגבי חד ברחבה של טלית ואם יחלקוה לרחבה לשני חצאין יבא הזהב בחלקו של אחד יכול האחד לומר זה שבינינו לאורכה נחלקה כדי שנחלק בטלית ובזהב והדין עמו: ת"ר שנים אדוקין בשטר כו' אסיק' בשטר מקוים דברי הכל יחלוקו. ושאינו מקוים ומלוה אומר שלי הוא ונפל ממני ומצאתיו ולוה אמר שלך היה ופרעתיך ונתתי לך [וממני נפל] אם נתקיים בחותמיו יחלוקו דברי ר' דרבי קסבר מודה בשטר שכתבו צריך לקיימו וקי"ל כרבי. רשב"ג אומר אע"פ שאין יכול

---

... שיין לאפקועי לאיסורייהו. ומעשרן לשיין כשאר בהמות חולין והן שלו ... אוכלו כדין שאר מעשר בהמה. כרכשתא. פריי"ש שתולין בסוף הטלית מותר האריגה ... נתנו לה ולא המשיחה עדיין בידו [בכורות יא.]. ומשיחה. חוט שהגט קשור בו לינ"ל בלע"ז ... [עי' סוכה נג:]. מודה. לוה בשטר שכתבו ואינו מזייף אלא שטוען פרעתיו או שכ"מ הייתי או ... הוא [רשב"ם ב"ב קנד.]. צריך לקיימו. ולומר לא פרעתי וכל כמה דלא אמר הכי לאו שטרא ... הכיל החתימה דמאן קא משוי ליה שטרא לוה דאמר כתבתיו לוה נמי הא קאמר פרעתי הפה שאמר הוא הפה שהתיר [שבת עח:]. אין צריך לקיימו. בעדים החתומים בו שאין הלוה שוב נאמן לומר פרעתיו ולא אמרינן בהאי הפה שאמר כשר היה הרי הוא מוחזק השטר וכי אמר פרעתיו לא מהימן שהרי ביד המלוה הוא [כתובות יט.]. דסתם שטרות הרי הם כשרים ובשטרות לא נימא הפה שאמר הוא הפה שהתיר לפטלו [רשב"ם ב"ב קנד.]. דלא דמי לשאר דינים שהפה ... אפילו אם היה זה מערער ואומר לא כתבתיו לא היה לנו לחשוד את זה הלוקח בכך שלא נחשדו ישראל לעשות שטרות מזוייפים אלא שהחמירו חכמים להצטרך קיום היכא דמערערי עליה הלכך כי אמר כתבתיו נהמניה למי שהשטר בידו [שם קע.].

אֶלָּא מַאי אִית לָךְ לְמֵימַ – So what can you say? Why is the owner ot required to continue tithing his animals if one that had al- eady been counted became mixed with them? The reason must be he following: עֲשִׂירִי וַדַּאי אָמַר רַחֲמָנָא – The Merciful One tated in His Torah that one is required to tithe only where the nimal that will be counted as tenth is of definite status,[1] וְלֹא עֲשִׂירִי סָפֵ – and not where the animal that will be counted as enth is of questionable status. Therefore, where an animal ımped back after it had been counted, since every tenth animal to e counted would be of questionable status,[2] he is not required to ontinue tithing.

Abaye concludes:

הָכָא נַ – So here too, with regard to the questionable redemp- on lambs, if they are subject to tithing only out of doubt, the wner would not be required to tithe them, עֲשִׂירִי וַדַּאי אָמַר רַחֲמָנָ – for the Merciful One stated that one is required to tithe nly where the animal that will be counted as tenth is of definite tatus, וְלֹא עֲשִׂירִי סָפֵק – and not where the animal that will be ounted as tenth is of doubtful status. Therefore, since the law is ıat one must tithe the questionable redemption lambs, evidently, ıeir status with regard to tithing is not in doubt. This corrobo- ates Rabbah's viewpoint that a Kohen is not empowered to seize ıch an animal.[3]

It has been assumed thus far that the Tannaic statement[4] uoted above, הַסְפֵיקוֹת נִכְנָסִין לַדִּיר לְהִתְעַשֵּׂר, *[Animals] of question- ble status enter the pen to be tithed,* refers to questionable edemption lambs. The Gemara now proves that this is so:

אָמַר לֵיהּ רַב אַחָא מִדִּפְתִּי לְרָבִינָ – Rav Acha from Difti said to avina: מַאי סְפֵיקוֹת – What is meant by "[ANIMALS] OF UESTIONABLE STATUS"? אִילֵימָא סְפֵק בְּכוֹרוֹת – If you say that signifies questionable *bechors* of kosher livestock,[5] the llowing difficulty arises: A *bechor* of kosher livestock is not ıbject to tithing, "יִהְיֶה־קֹּדֶשׁ" אָמַר רַחֲמָנָא – for the Merciful ne stated in reference to the animal designated as the tithe, *it all be holy,*[6] to teach that only an animal that acquires nctity through its designation as the tithe is subject to tithing, וְלֹא שֶׁכְּבָר קָדוֹ – and not [an animal] such as a *bechor* of kosher vestock, that is already sanctified.[7] אֶלָּא סְפֵק פִּדְיוֹן פֶּטֶר חֲמוֹר – Rather, the reference must be to a redemption [lamb] of a uestionable *bechor* of a donkey, for redemption lambs are not ready sanctified.[8] וּכְדְרַב נַחְמָן – And this accords with [a aching] of Rav Nachman to the effect that questionable redemption lambs are subject to tithing. דְּאָמַר רַב נַחְמָן אָמַר רַבָּה בַּר אֲבוּהָ – For Rav Nachman said in the name of Rabbah bar Avuha: יִשְׂרָאֵל שֶׁיֵּשׁ לוֹ עֲשָׂרָה סְפֵק פִּטְרֵי חֲמוֹר בְּתוֹךְ בֵּיתוֹ – If a Yisrael has ten questionable donkey *bechors* in his posses- sion, מַפְרִישׁ עֲלֵיהֶן עֲשָׂרָה שֶׂיִין – he sets aside ten lambs for them (i.e. for their redemption).[9] וּמְעַשְּׂרָן וְהֵן שֶׁלּוֹ – He then tithes [the lambs], and they are his.[10]

The Gemara reports the following discussion about the disputed bath that was consecrated by one of the parties laying claim to it: מַאי הָוֵי עֲלָהּ דִּמְסוּתָא – What is [the ruling] with regard to the bath? Is it consecrated or not? תָּא שְׁמַע – Come, hear the following proof: דְּאָמַר רַבִּי חִיָּיא בַּר אָבִין – R' Chiya bar Avin said: הֲוָה עוּבְדָא בֵּי רַב חִסְדָּא – An analogous case came before Rav Chisda, וְרַב חִסְדָּא בֵּי רַב הוּנָא – and Rav Chisda brought it before Rav Huna, וּפְשַׁטָה מֵהָא דְּאָמַר רַב נַחְמָן – [who] resolved it from that which Rav Nachman said: כָּל מָמוֹן שֶׁאֵין יָכוֹל לְהוֹצִיאוֹ בְּדַיָּינִין – Regarding any property [whose claimant] is unable to exact it through legal proceedings, הִקְדִּישׁוֹ אֵינוֹ קָדוֹשׁ – if he consecrated it, it is not consecrated. Hence, in the case of the bath, where it is clear that the one who consecrated it lacked the evidence required to exact it through legal proceedings, the consecration is not valid.

Rav Huna ruled that the bath is not consecrated *because* the one who consecrated it lacked adequate evidence. The implication of this decision was then questioned:

הָא יָכוֹל לְהוֹצִיאוֹ בְּדַיָּינִין – But this decision implies that if he [the one who consecrated the bath] could exact it through legal proceedings, הִקְדִּישׁוֹ קָדוֹשׁ – he could consecrate it אַף עַל גַּב דְּלֹא אַפְקֵיהּ – even though he did not exact it. Is this so? וְהָאָמַר רַבִּי יוֹחָנָן – But R' Yochanan has said: גָּזַל וְלֹא נִתְיָיאֲשׁוּ הַבְּעָלִים – If [a thief] stole some property and the owner did not yet despair of recovering it, שְׁנֵיהֶם אֵינָם יְכוֹלִין לְהַקְדִּישׁוֹ – neither of them [the thief or the owner] can consecrate it. זֶה לְפִי שֶׁאֵינָהּ שֶׁלּוֹ – This one [the thief] cannot consecrate it because it is not his,[11] וְזֶה לְפִי שֶׁאֵינָהּ בִּרְשׁוּתוֹ – and the other one [the owner] cannot consecrate it because it is not in his possession.[12] Now stolen property can usually be exacted from a thief through legal proceedings and yet R' Yochanan rules that the owner cannot consecrate it because it is not currently in his possession. Rav Huna's decision, however, implied that the owner of the bath could consecrate it (provided that he had sufficient evidence) even *without* bringing it into his possession. – ? –

NOTES

This is derived from the verse (*Leviticus* 27:32): וְכָל־מַעְשַׂר בָּקָר וָצֹאן כֹּל אֲשֶׁר־יַעֲבֹר תַּחַת הַשָּׁבֶט הָעֲשִׂירִי יִהְיֶה־קֹּדֶשׁ לַ, *Any tithe of the herd or the flock, ıy that passes under the staff, the tenth one shall be holy to HASHEM.* The ord "tenth" is interpreted as meaning *definitely* tenth.

The "tenth" is of doubtful status for (1) it might be the exempted ıimal; or (2) the exempted animal might be among the previous nine, which case the "tenth" is not really the tenth but the ninth (for the ːempted animal is not included in the true count) (see *Rashi*).

An owner is liable to tithe only those animals that are *definitely* his ɔr otherwise they are excluded from the obligation by the Scriptural rivation "a tenth of definite status and not a tenth of doubtful atus"). Therefore, from the Mishnah's ruling that one is required to :he questionable redemption lambs, it is evident that such animals are ewed as *definitely* belonging to the owner. This proves that a Kohen is ɔt empowered to seize them (see 6a note 18, 6b note 17).

See 6b note 13.

See 6b note 3.

See above, note 1.

A *bechor* of kosher livestock is sacred from birth (see 6b note 3).

A redemption lamb, even of a donkey that is definitely a *bechor,* is not .bued with any sanctity (*Rashi*).

9. It is forbidden to use a donkey *bechor* for work. Therefore, since these animals are possibly donkey *bechors*, the owner redeems them so that they will become permitted (*Rashi*).

10. Since the questionable redemption lambs are in the possession of the Yisrael, the burden of proof rests upon the Kohen.

11. As is evident from R' Yochanan's statement, this applies only before the owner has given up hope of recovering the stolen property. After that point, the thief *can* consecrate it (see *Bava Kamma* 67a).

12. An apparent difficulty: Here, the Gemara takes as given R' Yochanan's ruling that one cannot consecrate property that is not in one's possession, whereas the Gemara above raised an inquiry as to this very point!

See *Shitah Mekubetzes* for various resolutions to this problem. [According to the approach we have been following, perhaps the answer is as follows: Initially, the Gemara did not know whether R' Yochanan's ruling applies to disputed property (perhaps it is relevant only to *stolen* property, which is "acquired" by the thief – see 40b note 23). The question recorded here, וְהָאָמַר רַבִּי יוֹחָנָן, *But R' Yochanan has said*... is part of a discussion held in an earlier generation about the case of the bath. From the fact that the participants in this discussion applied R' Yochanan's ruling to this case, the Gemara deduces that his ruling *is* relevant to the original inquiry. (See *Ketzos HaChoshen* 211:3.)]

required to tithe questionable redemption lambs – it is evident that a Kohen is not empowered to seize such animals.[21]

Abaye proves that the animal-tithe obligation does not apply in cases of doubt:

דִּתְנַן – **For we learned in a Mishnah:**[22] קָפַץ אֶחָד מִן הַמְּנוּיִין לְתוֹכָן – If ONE OF [THE ANIMALS] THAT HAD already BEEN COUNTED JUMPED back INTO THE MIDST OF [THE ANIMALS IN THE PEN],[23] and its identity cannot be ascertained, כּוּלָּן פְּטוּרִין – ALL [THE ANIMALS], both those that have been counted and those that are still inside the pen, ARE EXEMPT from tithing.[24] וְאִי סָלְקָא דַּעְתָּךְ סְפֵיקָא בָּעֵי עִשּׂוּרֵי – **Now if you should think that [an animal] of questionable status must be tithed,** לְעַשֵּׂר מִמָּה נַּפְשָׁךְ – **let him tithe** the animals inside the pen, for **however you want** to view the situation, the outcome will be acceptable, and possibly desirable: דְּאִי בַּר חִיּוּבָא הוּא – **If it** [the anim designated as the tithe] **is subject** to tithing (for the group of t in which it was counted does not include the previously count one), שַׁפִּיר מְעַשֵּׂר – **he is properly designating** it as **the tith** וְאִי לָאו בַּר חִיּוּבָא הוּא – **And if it** [the animal designated as t tithe] **is not subject** to tithing (for the group of ten animals which it was counted *does* include the previously counted one), has done no wrong, נִפְטַר בְּמִנְיָן הָרָאוּי – because **[each anim in the group] is** permanently **exempted** from tithing once it w included **in a count that was fit** to reach the requisite number ten.[25] דְּאָמַר רָבָא – **For Rava said:**[26] מִנְיָן הָרָאוּי פּוֹטֵר – T fact that an animal was included in **a count that was fit** to rea ten **exempts** that animal from tithing, even if the count did n subsequently reach ten.

NOTES

21. For such lambs are viewed as definitely belonging to the Yisrael – see note 17.

22. *Bechoros* 58b.

23. The animals were being counted, one at a time, as they left the pen. Before the owner had counted ten animals, one of those that had already been counted jumped back into the pen (*Rashi*).

24. The animals that have already left the pen are exempt for the following reason: If an animal is counted when there are still enough animals left inside the pen for the count to reach ten, it is permanently exempt. (For example, if the owner had ten newborn lambs and after he counted five of them, a lamb inside the pen died, he is not required to combine the five lambs that have been counted with lambs born later and tithe them all at the next tithing season.) This law is derived from the verse (*Leviticus* 27:32): אֲשֶׁר־יַעֲבֹר, [he takes the tithe from those] *that "will" pass*, which indicates that the tithe is taken only from tho animals that have yet to be counted and not from those that have alrea been counted.

The animals inside the pen are exempt for the following reason: Sin the animal that has already been counted cannot be identified, each the animals in the pen is exempt for it might be the previously count one (*Rashi*).

25. I.e when it was counted there was a sufficient number of animals st inside the pen so that the count could reach ten. Once an animal h been included in such a count it is permanently exempt from tithing ar one is not required to combine it with animals born later and tithe the all at the next season (*Rashi*, see note 24; see *Raavad* cited by *Shita Mekubetzes* ד״ה הדר ).

26. Rava's statement is recorded in *Bechoros* 59a (*Rashi*).

א) מסותא דהוו מנצו עלה בי תרי האי אמר דידי הוא והאי אמר דידי הוא קם חד מינייהו אקדשה פרשי מינה רב חנניה ורב אושעיא וכולהו רבנן וא"ל רב אושעיא לרבה כי אזלת קמיה דרב חסדא לכפרי בעי מיניה כי אתא לסורא א"ל רב המנונא מתני' היא ג) ספק בכורות אחד א בכור אדם ואחד ב בכור בהמה בין טהורים בין טמאים ס) המוציא מחבירו עליו הראיה ותני עלה ג אסורים בגיזה ובעבודה והא הכא דאמר תקפו כהן ד אין מוציאין אותו מידו דקתני המע"ה וכי לא תקפו אסורין בגיזה ובעבודה אמר ליה רבה קדושת בכור קאמרת לעולם אימא לך תקפו כהן מוציאין אותו מידו ואפילו הכי אסורים בגיזה ובעבודה דקדושה הבאה מאליה שאני אמר ליה רב חנניה לרבה תניא דמסייע לך ג) הספיקות נכנסין לדיר להתעשר ואי ס"ד תקפו כהן אין מוציאין אותו מידו אמאי נכנסין לדיר נמצא זה פוטר ממונו בממונו של כהן אמר ליה אביי אי משום הא לא תסייעיה למר הכא במאי עסקינן כגון דלית ליה אלא תשעה והוא דמה נפשך אי בר חיובא הוא שפיר קא מעשר אי לאו בר חיובא הוא תשעה לאו בר עשורי נינהו הדר אמר אביי לאו מילתא היא דאמרי דספיקא לאו בר עשורי היא ז) דתנן ה קפץ אחד מן המנויין לתוכן כולן פטורין ואי ס"ד ספיקא בעי עשורי לעשר ממה נפשך דאי בר חיובא הוא שפיר מעשר ואי לאו בר חיובא הוא נפטר במנין הראוי ס) דאמר (א) רבא ו מנין הראוי פוטר
אלא

**רש"י**

מסותא. מרחץ: פרשי מינה. מלרחוץ בה: ואמר ליה רב אושעיא לרבה גרסינן: לכפרי. שם מקום: כי אתא לסורא. כשהיה עובר דרך סורא לילך לכפרי: ספק בכורות. כגון בהמה שילדה ואין ידוע אם בכרה כבר אם לא: אחד בכור אדם. כגון שהפילה אמו לפניו ספק דבר הפוטר בבכורה ספק רוח הפילה והבא אחריו בכור: בין טמאין. כגון פטר חמור: המוציא מחבירו כו'. קס"ד אם ביד ישראל הן הוי כהן מוציא מחבירו עליו הראיה ואם תקפה כהן ושתיק ישראל והדר לווח הוי ישראל מוציא מחבירו: אסורין בגיזה ועבודה. מספק שמא קדשים הם: דקתני המוציא. משמע בין כהן בין ישראל: וכי לא תקפו. חמור כח הקדש לאוסרן בגיזה ועבודה ש"מ דאת"ל תקפו אין מוציאין אותו מידו הקדישה מקודשת: לעולם אימא לך. גבי בכור דאפי' תקפו כהן מוציאין אותו מידו מסתמא בחזקת ישראל הן ולעולם הכהן קרוי מוציא מחבירו וטעמא דגיזה ועבודה לאו משום דיהא לכהן שום כח בהן דתפשוט מינה להיכא דאי תקפו אין מוציאין מידו הקדישה הוי הקדש אלא הכא משום איסור ספק גיזת קדשים וקדושה הבאה מאליה שאני שאם בכור הוא מאליו קדוש ואיכא לספוקי בהכי אבל גבי מסותא דאין קדושה באה אלא על פיו של זה אימא לך דאפי' אם תמצי לומר תקפה אין מוציאין הקדישה בלא תקפה לא הוי הקדש דאין יכול להקדיש דבר שאינו ברשותו: דמסייע לך. דגבי ספק בכורות אם תקפה כהן מוציאין מידו: הספיקות. לקמן מפרש בספק פדיון פטר חמור דמפריש עליו טלה לאפקועי איסורא והוא לעצמו שאין צריך ליתנו לכהן שהמוציא מחבירו עליו הראיה ופדיון פטר חמור בר עשורי הוא אם יש לכהן י' פטרי חמורים שנפלו לו מבית אבי אמו ישראל מפריש עליהם עשרה שיין ומעשרן והן שלו הלכך ספק פדיון פטר חמור ביד ישראל נכנס לדיר עם שאר טלאים שלו להתעשר ואי נפקא בעשירי ליפוק: ואי ס"ד. יש לכהן צד זכייה בו נמצא זה אם יצא בעשירי פוטר ממונו בממונו של כהן: למר. רבה שהוא רבו: אם בר חיובא הוא. אי האי גברא בר חיובא הוא לעשורי שפדיון זה לאו פדיון פטר חמור שלו הוא הרי יש לו י' טלאים וחייב לעשרן שפיר קמעשר: אי לאו בר חיובא הוא. שפדיון זה של כהן לא פטר ליה מידי דתשעה לאו בני עשורי נינהו: לאו מילתא היא דאמרי. דודאי סייעתא היא למר דאי הוה צד זכייה לכהן ביה מספק ואשתכח דכל הני טלאים ספק חייבים במעשר ספק אין חייבים מספיקא לא הוי צריך לעשורינהו י) כדקאמרת לעשורי ממה נפשך דכל ספק חייב ספק פטור לאו בני עשורי נינהו ואפילו היכא דאיכא למימר ממה נפשך: קפץ אחד מן המנויין כו'. היה מעשר טלאים והתחיל למנות כשהיו יוצאים בפתח הדיר ועד שלא הגיע לעשרה קפץ אחד מן המנויין לתוך הדיר ואינו מכירו: כולן פטורין. בין אותן שיצאו בין אותן שבתוך הדיר ואפילו הן אלף שיצאו עשורין ה) (שוטט) מנין הראוי שכשמנאן היה המנין ראוי להשלים ולבא לכלל מעשר ואמרינן בבכורות והכי מייתינן לה מנין הראוי פוטר ואותן שבתוך הדיר פטורין משום זה המעורב דכל אשר יעבור תחת השבט אמר רחמנא ולא שעבר כבר וכל חד מינייהו ספק כבר עבר הוא: ואי ס"ד ספיקא. דאיכא למימר ממה נפשך בעי לעשורי שמא יעשה כתורה וכמלוה נעשרינהו להנך דבתוך הדיר ממה נפשך כל י' שיוצאין אם מעשר שלהן בר חיוב וכראוי הוא כגון שלא יצא אותו הקופץ לתוכן שפיר קא מעשר: ואי לאו בר חיובא. כגון אותן עשרה שיצא זה לתוכן ואין עשירי שלהן מעשר: נפטרו. מן המעשר: במנין הראוי. שכשמנה א' ב' ג' היו בדיר טלאים הרבה שהיו ראוין להשלים ופוטרין מנייתו: דאמר רבא. בבכורות (דף נט.): מנין הראוי פוטר. היה לו י' טלאים ומנה חמש ומת אחד מן שאינן מנוין המנוין פטורין ושאינן מנוין מצטרפין לגורן אחר שיולדו לו טלאים עד שיגיע זמן הגורן ויצטרפם עם אלו אבל המנוין פטורין במנין הראוי ויליף לה מאשר יעבור ולא שכבר עבר דמשעבר תחת השבט ולא עלה בידו לעשר שוב אינו מעבירו פעם אחרת כשיולדו לו טלאים לצרף עמהם:
אלא

**תוספות**

תקפה כהן אין מוציאין ולכך אפי' לא תקפה אסורין בגיזה ועבודה מספק משום דשמא יש לכהן חלק בו ולכך יכול לתופסה אלמא אפי' לא תקפה חשיב כאילו תקפה כבר והקדישה בעודה בידו ודמי רבה דהתם אם תקפה כהן מוציאין מידו ואע"פ שאין לכהן בו כלום דאפי' כבר תקפה מוציאין מידו ואפי' הכי אסורין בגיזה ועבודה ועל כרחך משום דקדושה הבאה מאליה שאני וא"ת אמאי אין מוציאין מידו והלא הבעלים יאמרו ליתן לכהן אחר וי"ל במכירי כהונה ° א"נ אינו יכול לתובעו רק טובת הנאה שיש לו בו למ"ד טובת הנאה ממון ומפרק הזרוע (חולין דף קלא.) דאמר בן לוי דחטף מתנתא פרילותא הוא משמע דאינו חייב לשלם אין ראיה דשמא מיירי כשאכלו כדאמרינן התם (דף קל:) המזיק מתנות כהונה או אכלן פטור:

פוטר ממונו בממון כהן. [א] וכן הוא מסקנא דאם תקפה כהן מוציאין מידו תימה דבפ' השואל (לקמן דף קב: ושם) ובפרק בית כור (ב"ב דף קה. ושם ד"ה אבל) גבי אחד ששכר מרחץ מוקי שמואל הא דיחלוקו בבא באמצע החדש אבל בבא בסוף החדש כולו לשוכר והא מסיק הכא דמוציאין מידו וי"ל דהתם נכנס בהיתר לכך מהניא תפיסתו אבל הכא לא בהיתר תפס כי אם בספק והא דאמרי' בפ"ב דכתובות (דף כ. ושם ד"ה ואוקי) שנים החתומים על השטר ובאו אחרים ואמרו אנוסים היו כו' אין נאמנים ומסיק דאוקי תרי בהדי תרי ואוקי ממונא בחזקת מריה ואין נאמנין דקאמר פרש"י דאם תפס המלוה לא מפקינן מיניה נ"ל שתפס קודם שבאו עדים לפסול השטר דהיינו קודם שנולד הספק ועי"ל דאין נאמנין דלא מקרעינן ליה ולא מגבינן ביה ולא לענין תפיסה:

ותשעה לאו בר עשורי נינהו. דאין צריך לצרפו לגורן אחר דלא באו לעולם לכלל חיוב ודאי ודוקא היכא דהוו עשרה מתחלה הוא דאיצטריך לצרפו לגורן אחר:

קפיץ כולן פטורין. תימה דלבטל ברובא וליחייבו כולהו במעשר דהא דדבר שבמנין לא בטיל היינו מדרבנן וקבוע נמי אין שייך אלא בדבר שהאיסור וההיתר ניכרין וידועין ולא ידע מאיזה לקח כגון ק) ט' חנויות ובריה נמי לא הוי כדפרי' בחולין (דף נה ט) ואין לומר שלא נשאר בעדר רק אחד דליכא רובא דלשון לתוכן לא משמע הכי:

לפטרו במנין הראוי. תימה דהכא לא שייך מנין הראוי דלא שייך אלא היכא דאין כי אם עשרה והתחיל למנות ומת אחד מהן ואין כאן י' אפ"ה פטורים אותן שיצאו ולא יצטרפו לגורן אחר כיון שתחילת יציאתן היה ראוי להשלים המנין אבל הכא שיש בעדר הרבה ישלים המנין ויהא עשירי וי"א קודש ויקרא לשניהם עשירי מספק אם יש מנוי ביניהם אם לאו וכן יעשה בכל אחד עשר ובאחרונה שלא ישאר עשרה יצטרפו לגורן אחר:
ולא

**עין משפט נר מצוה**

לה א מיי' פי"א מהל' בכורות הלכה יט סמג עשין קמד טוש"ע י"ד סי' שה סעיף יג וסעיף כ וסעיף כה:
לו ב מיי' שם פי"ב הל' כג ועי' בהשגות ובכ"מ ופ"ד מהל' בכורות הל' ז ופ"ה שם הל' ג סמג שם וסי' ריא טוש"ע י"ד סי' שכא סעיף י וסעיף יג יד טו טז וסי' שטו סעיף א:
לז ג מיי' פ"א מהלכות מעילה הל' ח סמג לאוין שמ טוש"ע י"ד סי' שטו סעיף א:
לח ד מיי' פ"ה מהל' בכורות הל' ג סמג עשין ריא טוש"ע י"ד סי' שטו סעיף א וע"ש בהגה"ה:
לט ה מיי' פ"ח שם הלכה יד סמג עשין ריב:
מ ו מיי' שם הל' ח והל"י סמג עשין שם:

**רבינו חננאל**

מסותא דהוו מינצו עליה בי תרי כל חד אמר דידי הוא קם חד מינייהו אקדשה והוו פרשי מיניה רב חנינא ורב הושעיא וכולהו רבנן. ופשיט רב המנונא מהא דתנן ספק בכורות אחד בכור אדם ואחד בכור בהמה בין טהורין בין טמאין המע"ה. ותני עלה אסורין בגיזה ובעבודה. והא הכא אילו תקפו כהן אין מוציאין אותה מידו דקתני המע"ה ואע"ג דלא תקפן אסורין בגיזה ועבודה ש"מ דכל היכא דאילו תקפן אין מוציאין אותה מידו הקדישה בלא תקפה מקודשת. ודחי לה רב' ואמר לעולם אימא לך אפי' תקפן כהן (אין) מוציאין אותה מידו ואפ"ה אסורין בגיזה ועבודה דקדושת בכור קדושה הבאה מאליה היא ושאני מקדושה דמקדישין לה במילי. אמר ליה רב חנינא לרב' תניא דמסייעא לך שאם תקפן כהן מוציאין אותו מידו דתניא הספיקות נכנסין לדיר להתעשר וכו' ואמר ליה אביי הא לא מסייעא ליה הכא במאי עסקינן בדלית ליה אלא ט' וזה הספק דמה נפשך אי לא בכור הוא שפיר קא מעשר ואי בכור הוא בני ט' נינהו וט' לאו בני עשורי נינהו. ופשטינן לקמן דהני ספיקות לאו ספק בכורות הוא אלא ספק פטרי חמורים הן וכדרב נחמן דאמר בבכורות פ"א [דף יא] ישראל שיש לו י' פטרי חמורים מעשרן והן שלו ושם פירשנו שמועה זו. והדר ביה אביי ואמר לאו [מילתא] היא דאמרי דכל ספק לאו בר עשורי הוא מדתנן קפץ א' מן המנוין לתוכן כולן פטורין פי' כיצד מעשרן מכניס צאנו לדיר ומוציאן אחד אחד במנין כדתנן כיצד מעשרן כונסן לדיר ועושה להן פתח קטן כדי שלא יוכלו שנים לצאת באחד ומונה בשבט א' ב' ג' ד' ה' ו' ז' ח' ט' והיוצא עשירי סוקרו בסיקרא ואומר ה"ז מעשר. ואם קפץ מאותן שהן חוץ לדיר ונכנס לדיר ונתערב בצאן שבדיר שעדיין לא נתעשרו ואינם יודעים איזהו. נעשו אותן ספק ונפטרו כולן ואם נאמר כי דין הספיקות להתעשר ממה נפשך אמאי אין מעשרין גם (לאו) [להון] ממה נפשך נעשרינהו ואם יצא עשירי זולתי זה שקפץ מן המנין שפיר ואם זה שיצא עשירי הוא זה שקפץ שהוא פטור ואין הפטור פוטר את החייב נפטרו במנין הראוי פי' מנין הראוי כגון שיש לו עשר צאן בדיר ורצה לעשרן ופתח להם הפתח שיצאו ועשירי יסקרהו בסיקרא והתחיל לצאת אחד אחד והוא מונה מי שיצא בתחלה קורא אחד והיוצא אחריו מנאו שני ואחריו שלישי וכן כולן עד שיצאו התשעה אלו התשעה כולן המנין פטרן שאין אחד מהן נקרא עליו שם עשירי והיוצא עשירי הוא הקדוש וכיון שכל אחד שיצא מן הדיר נשאר בדיר הראוי להיות א) בדיר נפטר היוצא מיד ואע"פ שקודם יסקרו בסיקרא קפץ מתוך הדיר ויצא לחרץ ונתערב עם המנוין התשעה נפטרו במנין הראוי למעשר אע"פ שלא יצא אחריהן עשירי הואיל ובשעה שיצאו במניינם היה בדיר מי שיעבור עשירי תחת השבט היוצא ראשון ראשון נפטר. ובהדיא בבכורות פרק אחרון אמר רבא מנין הראוי פוטר.

**מסורת הש"ס**

א) [עי' תוס' מנחות ... ד"ה ומתירין], ב) [... פרק ד' משנה יב, יט.], ג) [עיקרו ... בכורות ט. ולדך לקצר כמו שכתבו סוכה ד. ד"ה ...], ד) בכורות נח:, ה) שם ..., ו) נ"א ... מהרש"ל, ז) נ"ל ... מהרש"ל, ח) [ועיין חולין לה. ד"ה ...], ט) [נו. ד"ה מ"ט ...]

**הגהות הב"ח**

(א) גמ' דאמר רבה הראוי:

**הגהות הגר"א**

[א] תוס' ד"ה ... וכ"ה מסקנא כו'. וכ"ד ש"פ אבל הרב חולק וכתב הרב דלמסקנא דמפרש ספק ספק פ"ח אין דבפ"ח לא זכה כהן כבר אתחזק בה הבעלים (ועמ"ש רבינו ביו"ד סט"ו ס"ק ב'):

**גליון הש"ס**

גמ' המוציא מחב... עיין נדה כה ע"א ד"ה גבי: תוס' והא כו' א"נ לתובעו. נראה שכן רש"י בב"ק סו ע"א עד שלבעו:

**ליקוטי רש"י**

מסותא. מרחץ מסחוחה וירחץ מתר... ואסחי [סנהדרין ...] ספק בכורות. דבעי לאפוקי מיניה להביא ראיה שהן בכ... שלא הפילה נפל קודם ואי תפס להו כהן ... הבעלים להביא ראיה ... בכור הוא [נדרים ...] קפץ אחד המנויין. מאותן ש... עברו בפתח תחת ה... אע"פ שאין ... מעושרין וכגון שמנה ... אחד מהן וקפץ ... הדיר להמנויין ... פטורין במנין ה... כדמפרש בגמ' ומ... דאין ידוע איזה הפ... לכך מה שבדיר פט... [בכורות נח:]. ... הראוי פוטר. כש... תשעה בפתח היה ... מנין הראוי לעשר ש... היה עשירי קיים ש... ראוי לצאת אחר ... ולפוטרן וכיון דראוי ל... דמי כמאן דיצא כבר ו... את המנין וכו' אבל ... גופיה מיהא לא ... קדוש עד שיצא [שם ...

חשק שלמה על ר"ח א) אולי צ"ל הראוי להיות מעשר נפטר היוצא וכו'.

וַאֲפִילּוּ הָכִי אֲסוּרִים בְּגִיזָּה וּבַעֲבוֹדָה – **and nevertheless it is forbidden with regard to shearing** its wool **and** using it for **work.** Why is it consecrated even though the Kohen cannot bring it into his possession? דִּקְדוּשָּׁה הַבָּאָה מֵאֵלֶיהָ שָׁאנֵי – **Because sanctity that is acquired automatically is different** than sanctity that is effected by human intervention. The sanctity of a *bechor* is acquired automatically at birth regardless of the Kohen's ownership of the *bechor*. Hence, a *bechor* is not comparable to an object (such as a bath) the sanctity of which is effected by a person's declaration and is therefore dependent upon that person's degree of ownership in it.[12]

The Gemara cites support for Rabbah's contention that if a Kohen were to seize a questionable *bechor,* the court removes it from him:

אָמַר לֵיהּ רַב חֲנַנְיָה לְרַבָּה – **Rav Chananyah said to Rabbah:** תַּנְיָא דִּמְסַיֵּיעַ לָךְ – **[A ruling] has been taught** in a Mishnah **which supports** the position advanced by **you.** The Mishnah states:[13] הַסְּפֵיקוֹת נִכְנָסִין לַדִּיר לְהִתְעַשֵּׂר – [ANIMALS] OF QUESTIONABLE STATUS (i.e. lambs that have been used to redeem questionable firstborns of a donkey)[14] ENTER THE PEN TO BE TITHED.[15] וְאִי סָלְקָא דַּעְתָּךְ – **Now should you think** תְּקָפוֹ כֹּהֵן אֵין מוֹצִיאִין אוֹתוֹ מִיָּדוֹ – that if **a Kohen seized [a questionable *bechor*]** the law is that **we do not take it away from him,** אַמַּאי נִכְנָסִין לַדִּיר – **why do [these lambs] enter the pen** to be tithed? If one of these lambs is designated as the tithe, נִמְצָא זֶה פּוֹטֵר מָמוֹנוֹ בְּמָמוֹנוֹ שֶׁל כֹּהֵן – **it transpires that [the owner] is exempting his property** from the animal-tithe obligation **with the property of a Kohen.**[16] Hence it is evident that, as Rabbah proposed, a Kohen is not empowered to seize a questionable *bechor.*[17]

This support for Rabbah's position is rejected:

אָמַר לֵיהּ אַבַּיֵּי – **Abaye said to [Rav Chananyah]:** אִי מִשּׁוּם הָא – **On the basis of this** Mishnah, לָא תְּסַיְּיעֵיהּ לְמָר – **you cannot support** the position of **master** [Rabbah].[18] It could be argued that, contrary to Rabbah's position, a Kohen *is* empowered to seize a questionable *bechor*. Nevertheless, the Mishnah rules that a Yisrael tithes his questionable redemption lamb together with his other animals, and there is no concern that this might result in the Yisrael exempting his property from the animal-tithe obligation with the property of a Kohen, דְּלֵית לֵיהּ אֶלָּא ... בְּמַאי עָסְקִינַן – for **what are we dealing with here?** תִּשְׁעָה וְהוּא – We are dealing with a case **where [the Yisrael]** has **only nine** newborn lambs **and this one** [the questionable redemption lamb]. דְּמָה נַפְשָׁךְ – In such a case, he tithes the questionable redemption with his other lambs, **because however you want** to view the situation – whether the disputed lamb belongs to him or not – it will not transpire that he exempts his property from the animal-tithe obligation with the property of a Kohen: אִי בַּר חִיּוּבָא הוּא – **If he is obligated** to tithe the lambs (for all ten, including the disputed one, belong to him), ...יר קָא מְעַשֵּׂר – **he is tithing properly.** אִי לָאו בַּר חִיּוּבָא הוּא – And if **he is not obligated** to tithe the lambs (for the disputed lamb belongs to the Kohen), he has not exempted his property from the animal-tithe obligation, תִּשְׁעָה לָאו בַּר עִשּׂוּרֵי נִינְהוּ – because **nine** animals **are not subject to tithing.**[19]

Abaye then retracted his rejection of Rav Chananyah's support for Rabbah's position:

הֲדַר אָמַר אַבַּיֵּי – **Abaye then said:** לָאו מִילְּתָא הִיא דַּאֲמָרִי – **What I said is not valid.** If, as I suggested, a Kohen is empowered to seize a questionable redemption lamb, it follows that such a lamb is subject to tithing only out of doubt.[20] The Mishnah therefore would not have ruled that one must tithe such animals, דִּסְפֵיקָא לָאו בַּר עִשּׂוּרֵי הִיא – for the law is that **[an animal]** which is **of doubtful status** with regard to tithing **is not subject** to **tithing** at all. Hence, from the Mishnah's ruling – viz. one

NOTES

silent and then protest), the court would remove it from him (*Avi Ezri* ibid.; see also 6a note 18).

[However, this does not *necessarily* mean that in the case of the two litigants holding on to a cloak if one were to seize it and the other were to be silent and then protest, the court would remove it from the one who seized it (see *Ran*). Since he was holding on to the cloak even before he seized it, the law might be different than in the case of the questionable *bechor* where prior to his seizure of the animal, the Kohen was not holding on to it at all.]

12. According to this approach, it is possible that in the case of the bath the law is that if one of the disputants were to take possession of it, he would be allowed to keep it, and yet if he were to declare it sacred (without seizing it), his declaration would not be effective because the bath is not currently in his possession (*Rashi*).

13. The following is an abbreviated form of the Mishnah, *Bechoros* 9a (marginal gloss to *Vilna Shas*).

14. [The Gemara below, 7a, proves that this is what the Baraisa means.] If a doubt exists as to whether a donkey is a *bechor*, one must still set aside a lamb as a redemption in order to remove the possible sanctity of the donkey. But the lamb is kept by the owner. This ruling is based on the principle: הַמּוֹצִיא מֵחֲבֵירוֹ עָלָיו הָרְאָיָה, *the burden of proof is on the one who seeks to exact property from the possession of another.* Since the lamb is in the possession of the Yisrael, the Kohen is required to show proof that this donkey is a *bechor*, and that the redemption lamb, therefore, belongs to him (*Rashi*).

15. This refers to the obligation of מַעֲשַׂר בְּהֵמָה, *maaser beheimah* (the animal tithe). It is a Biblical command to set aside one-tenth *(maaser)* of the kosher animals (specifically: cattle, sheep and goats) born to one's herds and flocks each year. The newborn animals are gathered into a pen and made to pass through the gate, one at a time. Every tenth animal to pass through the gate is designated as *maaser*. It is brought as an offering in the Temple, and is eaten by the owner in Jerusalem. Animals that are sold or given away are not subject to tithing; inherited animals, however, are subject to tithing. The Rabbis established three periods of the years as "tithing seasons," when one is supposed to tithe all the animals born since the last "season." (*Leviticus* 27:32, *Bechoros* ch. 9.)

The fact that a lamb was used to redeem the *bechor* of a donkey does not exempt it from tithing (for example, if a Kohen inherited firstborn donkeys from his mother's father, who was a Yisrael, and he redeemed them with lambs of his own, he must tithe the lambs). Therefore, in our case where the lambs are treated as the property of the Yisrael (see previous note), he is obligated to include them with his other newborn animals in the tithing procedure, and if one is designated as the tenth animal, it is *maaser* (*Rashi*; see *Maharsha*).

16. If a Kohen is empowered to seize the disputed lambs, evidently the law is that the lamb is viewed as possibly belonging to him (see above note 8, and 6a note 18).

[The Gemara's point can be illustrated with the following example. A Yisrael who has fifteen newborn lambs (including the disputed lambs) is liable to designate one of his lambs as *maaser.* If the lamb that he designates as *maaser* is a disputed lamb, it transpires that instead of designating one of his *own* lambs as *maaser*, he has designated a lamb that possibly belongs to someone else.]

17. [Since the disputed animal is in the possession of the Yisrael, the court views it as definitely belonging to him. Therefore, if the Kohen were to seize it, he would have to return it (even if the Yisrael was silent when the animal was seized and did not protest until afterwards) (see 6a note 18).]

18. Rabbah was [Abaye's] teacher (*Rashi*).

19. He is not required to combine his nine lambs with lambs that are born later and tithe them all together at the next tithing season. Since at the current season, there were less than ten newborn lambs in his flock, they are permanently exempt from tithing (*Tosafos*).

20. For it might not belong to the owner – see note 16.

(א) מסותא דהוו מנצו עלה בי תרי האי אמר דידי הוא והאי אמר דידי הוא קם חד מינייהו אקדשה פרשי מינה רב חנניה ורב אושעיא וכולהו רבנן וא"ל רב אושעיא לרבה כי אזלת קמיה דרב חסדא לכפרי בעי מיניה כי אתא לסורא א"ל רב המנונא מתני' היא (ג) ספק בכורות אחד [א] בכור אדם ואחד [ב] בכור בהמה בין טהורים בין טמאים (ה) המוציא מחבירו עליו הראיה ותני עלה [ג] אסורים בגיזה ובעבודה והא הכא דאמר תקפו כהן [ד] אין מוציאין אותו מידו דקתני המע"ה וכי לא תקפו אסורין בגיזה ובעבודה אמר ליה רבה קדושת בכור קאמרת לעולם אימא לך תקפו כהן מוציאין אותו מידו ואפילו הכי אסורים בגיזה ובעבודה דקדושה הבאה מאליה שאני אמר ליה רב חנניה לרבה תניא דמסייע לך (ו) הספיקות נכנסין לדיר להתעשר ואי ס"ד תקפו כהן אין מוציאין אותו מידו אמאי נכנסין לדיר נמצא זה פוטר ממונו בממונו של כהן אמר ליה אביי אי משום הא לא תסייעיה למר הכא במאי עסקינן כגון דלית ליה אלא תשעה והוא דמה נפשך אי בר חיובא הוא שפיר קא מעשר אי לאו בר חיובא הוא תשעה לאו בר עשורי נינהו הדר אמר אביי לאו מילתא היא דאמרי דספיקא לאו בר עשורי היא (ז) דתנן [ה] קפץ אחד מן המנויין לתוכן כולן פטורין ואי ס"ד ספיקא בעי עשורי לעשר ממה נפשך דאי בר חיובא הוא שפיר מעשר ואי לאו בר חיובא הוא נפטר במנין הראוי (ח) דאמר (א) רבא [ו] מנין הראוי פוטר

אלא

## רש"י

מסותא. מרחץ: פרשי מינה. מלרחוץ בה: ואמר ליה רב אושעיא לרבה גרסינן: לכפרי. שם מקום: כי אתא לסורא. כשהיה עובר דרך סורא לילך לכפרי: ספק בכורות. כגון בהמה שילדה ואין ידוע אם בכרה כבר אם לא: אחד בכור אדם. כגון שהפילה אמו לפניו ספק דבר הפוטר בבכורה ספק רוח הפילה והבא אחריו בכור: בין טמאין. כגון פטר חמור: המוציא מחבירו כו'. קס"ד אם ביד ישראל הן הוי כהן מוציא מחבירו עליו הראיה ואם תקפה כהן ושתיק ישראל והדר לוות הוי ישראל מוציא מחבירו: אסורין בגיזה ועבודה. מספק שמא קדשים הם: דקתני המוציא. משמע בין כהן בין ישראל: וכי לא תקפו. חמור כח הקדש לאוסרן בגיזה ועבודה ש"מ דאת"ל תקפו אין מוציאין אותו מידו הקדישה מקודשת: לעולם אימא לך. גבי בכור דאפי' תקפו כהן מוציאין אותו מידו מסתמא בחזקת ישראל הן ולעולם הכהן קרוי מוציא מחבירו וטעמא דגיזה ועבודה לאו משום דיהא לכהן שום כח בהן דתפשוט מינה להיכא דאי תקפו אין מוציאין מידו הקדישה הוי הקדש אלא הכא משום איסור ספק גיזת קדשים וקדושה הבא מאליה שאני שאם בכור הוא מאליו קדוש ואיכא לספוקי בהכי אבל גבי מסותא דאין קדושה באה אלא על פיו של זה אימא לך דאפי' אם תמצי לומר תקפה אין מוציאין הקדישה בלא תקפה לא הוי הקדש דאין יכול להקדיש דבר שאינו ברשותו: דמסייע לך. דגבי ספק בכורות אם תקפה כהן מוציאין מידו: הספיקות. לקמן מפרש בספק פדיון פטר חמור דמפריש עליו טלה לאפקועי איסורא והוא לעצמו שאין צריך ליתנו לכהן שהמוציא מחבירו עליו הראיה ופדיון פטר חמור בר עשורי הוא אם יש לכהן י' פטרי חמורים שנפלו לו מבית אבי אמו ישראל מפריש עליהם עשרה שיין ומעשרן והן שלו הלכך ספק פדיון פטר חמור ביד ישראל נכנס לדיר עם שאר טלאים שלו להתעשר ואי נפקא בעשירי ליפוק: ואי ס"ד. יש לכהן צד זכייה בו נמצא זה אם יצא בעשירי פוטר ממונו בממונו של כהן: למר. רבה שהוא רבו: אם בר חיובא הוא. אי האי גברא בר חיובא הוא לעשורי שפדיון זה לאו פדיון פטר חמור שלו הוא הרי יש לו י' טלאים וחייב לעשרן שפיר קמעשר: אי לאו בר חיובא הוא. שפדיון זה של כהן לא פטר ליה מידי דתשעה לאו בני עשורי נינהו: לאו מילתא היא דאמרי. דודאי סייעתא היא למר דאי הוה צד זכייה לכהן ביה מספק ואשתכח דכל הני טלאים ספק חייבים במעשר ספק אין חייבים מספיקא לא הוי צריך לעשורינהו (י) כדקאמרת לעשורי ממה נפשך דכל ספק חייב ספק פטור לאו בני עשורי נינהו ואפילו היכא דאיכא למימר ממה נפשך: קפץ אחד מן המנויין כו'. היה מעשר טלאים והתחיל למנות כשהיו יוצאים בפתח הדיר ועד שלא הגיע לעשרה קפץ אחד מן המנויין לתוך הדיר ואינו מכירו: כולן פטורין. בין אותן שיצאו בין אותן שבתוך הדיר ואפילו הן אלף שיצאו פטורין (י) (שהם) מנין הראוי שכשמנאן היה המנין ראוי להשלים ולבא לכלל מעשר ואמרינן בבכורות והכי מייתינן לה מנין הראוי פוטר ואותן שבתוך הדיר פטורין משום זה המעורב דכל אשר יעבור תחת השבט אמר רחמנא ולא שעבר כבר וכל חד מינייהו ספק כבר עבר הוא: ואי ס"ד ספיקא. דאיכא למימר ממה נפשך בעי לעשורי שמא יעשה כתורה וכמלוה נעשרינהו להנך דבתוך הדיר ממה נפשך כל י' שיוצאין אם מעשר שלהן בר חיוב וכראוי הוא כגון שלא יצא אותו הקופץ לתוכן שפיר קא מעשר: ואי לאו בר חיובא. כגון אותן עשרה שיצא זה לתוכן ואין עשירי שלהן מעשר: נפטרו. מן המעשר: במנין הראוי. שכשמנה א' ב' ג' היו בדיר טלאים הרבה שהיו ראוין להשלים ופוטרין מניינו: דאמר רבא. בבכורות (דף נט.): מנין הראוי פוטר. היה לו י' טלאים ומנה חמש ומת אחד מן שאינן מנוין המנוין פטורין ושאינן מנוין מצטרפין לגורן אחר שיולדו לו טלאים עד שיגיע זמן הגורן ויצטרפו עם אלו אבל המנוין פטורין במנין הראוי ויליף לה מאשר יעבור ולא שכבר עבר דמשעבר תחת השבט ולא עלה בידו לעשר שוב אינו מעבירו פעם אחרת כשיולדו לו טלאים לצרף עמהם:

אלא

## תוספות

תקפה כהן אין מוציאין ולכך אפי' לא תקפה אסורין בגיזה ועבודה מספק משום דשמא יש לכהן חלק בו ולכך יכול לתופסה אלמא אפי' לא תקפה חשיב כאילו תקפה כבר והקדישה בעודה בידו ודחי רבה דהתם אם תקפה כהן מוציאין מידו ואע"פ שאין לכהן בו כלום דאפי' כבר תקפה מוציאין מידו ואפי' הכי אסורין בגיזה ועבודה ועל כרחך משום דקדושה הבאה מאליה שאני וא"ת אמאי אין מוציאין מידו והלא הבעלים יאמרו ליתן לכהן אחר וי"ל במכירי כהונה (ה) א"נ אינו יכול לתובעו רק טובת הנאה שיש לו בו למ"ד טובת הנאה ממון ומפרק הזרוע (חולין דף קלא.) דאמר בן לוי דחטף מתנתא פרילותא הוא משמע דאינו חייב לשלם אין ראיה דשמא איירי כשאכלו כדאמרינן התם (דף קל:) המזיק מתנות כהונה או אכלן פטור:

**פוטר** ממונו בממון כהן. [א] וכן הוא מסקנא דאם תקפה כהן מוציאין מידו תימה דבפ' השואל (לקמן דף קב: ושם) ובפרק בית כור (ב"ב דף קה. ושם ד"ה אבל) גבי אחד שכר מרחץ מוקי שמואל הא דיחלוקו בבא באמצע החדש אבל בבא בסוף החדש כולו לשוכר והא מסיק הכא דמוציאין מידו וי"ל דהתם נכנס בהיתר לכך מהניא תפיסתו אבל הכא לא בהיתר תפס כי אם בספק והא דאמרי' בפ"ב דכתובות (דף כ. ושם ד"ה ואוקי) שנים החתומים על השטר ובאו אחרים ואמרו אנוסים היו כו' אין נאמנים ומסיק דאוקי תרי בהדי תרי ואוקי ממונא בחזקת מריה ואין נאמנין דקאמר פרש"י דאם תפס המלוה לא מפקינן מיניה נ"ל שתפס קודם שבאו עדים לפסול השטר דהיינו קודם שנולד הספק ועי"ל דאין נאמנין דלא מקרעינן ליה ולא מגבינן ביה ולא לענין תפיסה:

**ותשעה** לאו בר עשורי נינהו. דאין צריך לצרפו לגורן אחר דלא באו לעולם לכלל חיוב ודאי ודוקא היכא דהוו עשרה מתחלה הוא דאיצטריך לצרפו לגורן אחר:

**קפץ** כולן פטורין. תימה דלבטל ברובא וליחייבו כולהו במעשר דהא דדבר שבמנין לא בטיל היינו מדרבנן וקבוע נמי אין שייך אלא בדבר שהאיסור וההיתר ניכרין וידועין ולא ידע מאיזה לקח כגון (ח) ט' חנויות ובריה נמי לא הוי כדפרי' בחולין (דף לה (ט)) ואין לומר שלא נשאר בעדר רק אחד דליכא רובא דלשון לתוכן לא משמע הכי:

**לפטרו** במנין הראוי. תימה דהכא לא שייך מנין הראוי דלא שייך אלא היכא דאין כי אם עשרה והתחיל למנות ומת אחד מהן ואין כאן י' אפ"ה פטורים אותן שיצאו ולא יצטרפו לגורן אחר כיון שתחילת יציאתן היה ראוי להשלים המנין אבל הכא שיש בעדר הרבה ישלים המנין ויהא עשירי וי"א קודש ויקרא לשניהם עשירי מספק אם יש מנוי ביניהם אם לאו וכן יעשה בכל אחד עשר ובאחרונה שלא ישאר עשרה יצטרפו לגורן אחר:

ולא

## עין משפט נר מצוה

לה א מיי' פ"א מהל' בכורות הלכה יט סמג עשין קמד טוש"ע י"ד סי' שה סעיף יג וסעיף כ וסעיף כה:

לו ב מיי' שם פי"ב הל' כג ועי' בהשגות ובכ"מ ופ"ד מהל' בכורות הל' ז ופ"ה שם הל' ב סמג שם וסי' ריא טוש"ע י"ד סי' שכא סעיף י וסעיף יג יד טו טז וסי' שטו סעיף א:

לז ג מיי' פ"א מהלכות מעילה הל' ח סמג לאוין שמ טוש"ע י"ד סי' שטו סעיף א:

לח ד מיי' פ"ה מהל' בכורות הל' ג סמג עשין ריא טוש"ע י"ד סי' שטו סעיף א וע"ש בהגה"ה:

לט ה מיי' פ"ח שם הלכה יד סמג עשין ריב:

מ ו מיי' שם הל' ח והל"י סמג עשין שם:

## רבינו חננאל

מסותא דהוו מינצו עליה בי תרי כל חד אמר דידי הוא קם חד מינייהו אקדשה והוו פרשי מיניה רב חנינא ורב הושעיא וכולהו רבנן. ופשיט רב המנונא מהא דתנן ספק בכורות אחד בכור אדם ואחד בכור בהמה בין טהורין בין טמאין המע"ה. ותני עלה אסורין בגיזה ובעבודה. והא הכא אילו תקפו כהן אין מוציאין אותה מידו דקתני המע"ה ואע"ג דלא תקפן אסורין בגיזה ועבודה ש"מ דכל היכא דאילו תקפן אין מוציאין אותה מידו הקדישה בלא תקפה מקודשת. ודחי לה רב' ואמר לעולם אימא לך אפי' תקפן כהן (אין) מוציאין אותו מידו ואפ"ה אסורין בגיזה ועבודה דקדושת בכור קדושה הבאה מאליה היא ושאני ממקדיש דמקדישין לה במילו. אמר ליה רב חנינא לרבה תניא דמסייעא לך שאם תקפן כהן מוציאין אותו מידו דתניא הספיקות נכנסין לדיר להתעשר וכו' ואמר ליה אביי הא לא מסייעא ליה הכא במאי עסקינן כגון דלית ליה אלא ט' וזה הספק דמה נפשך אי לא בכור הוא פטור ואי לאו בכור הוא בני ט' נינהו וט' לאו בני עשורי נינהו. ופשטינן לקמן דהני ספיקות לאו ספק בכורות הוא אלא ספק פטרי חמורים הן וכדרב נחמן דאמר בבכורות פ"א [דף יא] ישראל שיש לו י' פיטרי חמורים מעשרן הן שלו ושם פירשנו שמועה זו. והדר ביה אביי ואמר לאו [מילתא] היא דאמרי דכל ספק לאו בר עשורי הוא מדתנן קפץ א' מן המנוין לתוכן כולן פטורין פי' כיצד מעשרן מכניס צאנו לדיר ומוציאן אחד אחד במנין כדתנן כיצד מעשרן כונסן לדיר ועושה להן פתח קטן כדי שלא יוכלו שנים לצאת באחד ומונה בשבט א' ב' ג' ד' ה' ו' ז' ח' ט' והיוצא עשירי סוקרו בסיקרא ואומר ה"ז מעשר. ואם קפץ מאותן שהן חרץ לדיר ונכנס לדיר ונתערב בצאן שבדיר שעדיין לא נתעשרו ואינם ידועים איזהו. נעשו אותן ספק ונפטרו כולן ואם נאמר כי דין הספיקות להתעשר ממה נפשך אמאי אין מעשרין גם (לאו) [להון] ממה נפשך נעשרינהו ואם יצא עשירי זולתי זה שקפץ מן המנין שפיר ואם זה שיצא עשירי הוא זה שקפץ שהוא פטור ואין הפטור פוטר את החייב נפטרו במנין הראוי פי' מנין הראוי כגון שיש לו עשר צאן בדיר ורצה לעשרן ופתח להם הפתח שיצאו ועשירי יסקרהו בסיקרא והתחיל לצאת אחד אחד והוא מונה מי שיצא בתחלה קורא אחד והיוצא אחריו מנאו שני ואחריו שלישי וכן כולן עד שיצאו התשעה אלו התשעה כולן המנין פטרן שאין אחד מהן נקרא עליו שם עשירי והיוצא עשירי הוא הקדוש וכיון שכל אחד שיצא מן הדיר נשאר בדיר הראוי להיות (א) בדיר נפטר היוצא מיד ואע"פ שקודם יסקרו בסיקרא קפץ מתוך הדיר ויצא לחרץ ונתערב עם המנוין התשעה נפטרו במנין הראוי למעשר אע"פ שלא יצא אחריהן עשירי הואיל ובשעה שיצאו במניינם היה בדיר מי שיעבור עשירי תחת השבט היוצא ראשון ראשון נפטר. וההדיא בבכורות פרק אחרון אמר רבא מנין הראוי פוטר.

חשק שלמה על ר"ח (א) אולי צ"ל הראוי להיות מעשר נפטר היוצא וכו'.

## מסורת הש"ס

א) [ע' תוס' מנחות ... ד"ה ומחירין], ב) [טה פרק ד' משנה יב, נד יט.], ג) [עיקרו במ' בכורות ט. ולקמן ... כמו שכתבו ... סוכה ד. ד"ה ...], ד) בכורות נח:, ה) שם ..., ו) ג"ח דקלק מהרש"ל, ז) צ"ל ... מהרש"ל, ח) [ועיין חולין לה. ד"ה ספיו], ט) [ע. ד"ה מ"ט ...

## הגהות הב"ח

(א) גמ' דאמר רבה כו' הראוי:

## הגהות הגר"א

[א] תוס' ד"ה פו... וכ"ה מסקנא כו'. וכ"ה ס"פ אלו ... הרמב"ם חולק וכתב ... למסקנא דמספק ספיו ספק פ"ח אין ... דכפ"ח לא זכה כהן ... כבר אתחזק בה הבעלים (ועמ"ש רבינו ביו"ד סט"ו ס"ק ב'):

## גליון הש"ס

גמ' המוציא מחבי... עיין נדה כה ע"ב ... ד"ה גבי. תוס' ד"ה ... א"נ א... לתובעו. נראה שכן ... רש"י בכ"ק סו ע"ב ... עד שלבעו:

## ליקוטי רש"י

מסותא. מרחץ ... ספק בבכורות. ... דבעי לאפוקי מיניה ... להביא ראיה שהן בכור ... שלא הפילה נפל קודם ... ואי תפס להו כהן ... הבעלים להביא ראיה ... בכור הוא [נדרים ...]. קפץ אחד המנויין. מאותן ש... עברו בפתח תחת ה... אע"פ שאינן ... מעושרין ובנגון ... אחד מהן וקפץ ... לדיר דהמנויין ... פטורין במנין הר... ... דאין ידוע איזה הוא ... לכך מה שדבר פט... [בכורות נח:]. ... הראוי פוטר. ... תשעה בפתח היה ... מנין הראוי לעשר ... היה עשירי קיים ... ראוי לצאת אחרי ... ולפוטרן וכיון דראוי ... דמי כמאן דיצא כבר ... את המנין וכו' אבל ... קדוש עד שיצא [שם ...].

מְסוּתָא – bath דַּהֲווּ מִנְצוּ עֲלָהּ בֵּי תְרֵי – over which two people were quarreling. הַאי אָמַר דִּידִי הוּא – This one said, "It is mine," וְהַאי אָמַר דִּידִי הוּא – and the other one said, "It is mine." קָם חַד מִינַּיְיהוּ אַקְדְּשָׁהּ – One of them arose and consecrated it. פָּרְשֵׁי מִינָּהּ רַב חֲנַנְיָה וְרַב אוֹשַׁעְיָא וְכוּלְּהוּ רַבָּנָן – Rav Chananyah, Rav Oshaya and all the other Rabbis refrained from washing themselves in it out of concern that it might be consecrated.[1] וְאָמַר לֵיהּ רַב אוֹשַׁעְיָא לְרַבָּה – And Rav Oshaya said to Rabbah, כִּי אָזְלַתְּ קַמֵּיהּ דְּרַב חִסְדָּא לְכַפְרֵי – "When you go to Rav Chisda in Kafrei, בְּעֵי מִינֵּיהּ – ask him whether the bath is consecrated."[2] כִּי אָתָא לְסוּרָא – When [Rabbah] came to Sura on his way to Kafrei, אָמַר לֵיהּ רַב הַמְנוּנָא – Rav Hamnuna said to him: מַתְנִיתִין הִיא – [This case] is analogous to that of the following Mishnah:[3] סָפֵק בְּכוֹרוֹת – Concerning A *BECHOR* OF DOUBTFUL STATUS,[4] אֶחָד בְּכוֹר אָדָם – WHETHER IT IS A *BECHOR* OF A PERSON[5] וְאֶחָד בְּכוֹר בְּהֵמָה בֵּין טְהוֹרִים בֵּין טְמֵאִים – OR A *BECHOR* OF AN ANIMAL, EITHER KOSHER OR NON-KOSHER,[6] the law is: הַמּוֹצִיא מֵחֲבֵירוֹ עָלָיו הָרְאָיָה – THE burden of PROOF IS ON THE ONE WHO [SEEKS TO] EXACT property FROM the possession of ANOTHER.

Rav Hamnuna understands this as meaning that while the questionable *bechor* is still in the possession of the Yisrael (who claims to own it), the burden of proof is upon the Kohen. But if the Kohen seized the questionable *bechor,*[7] thereby bringing it into his possession, the burden of proof shifts to the Yisrael.[8]

Rav Hamnuna continues:

וְתָנֵי עֲלָהּ – And a Baraisa taught in reference to [this Mishnah]: אֲסוּרִים בְּגִיזָּה וּבַעֲבוֹדָה – IT [a questionable *bechor* of kosher livestock] IS FORBIDDEN WITH REGARD TO SHEARING i wool AND using it for WORK.[9]

Rav Hamnuna concludes his proof:

וְהָא הָכָא דְּאָמַר – Now here (in the Mishnah from *Bechoros*) says תָּקְפוֹ כֹּהֵן אֵין מוֹצִיאִין אוֹתוֹ מִיָּדוֹ – that if a Kohen seized questionable *bechor*] we do not take it away from hi דְּקָתָנֵי הַמּוֹצִיא מֵחֲבֵירוֹ עָלָיו הָרְאָיָה – for such is evident from th which the Mishnah teaches: "THE burden of PROOF IS ON TI ONE WHO [SEEKS TO] EXACT property FROM the possession ANOTHER," which seemingly applies to either the Kohen or t Yisrael, whoever is seeking to exact the questionable *bechor*. B the Kohen must first seize the questionable *bechor* for it to l treated as his, וְכִי לֹא תְּקָפוֹ – and yet, even if he did not sei it, it is consecrated, for the Baraisa teaches: סוּרִין בְּגִיזָּה וּבַעֲבוֹדָה – IT IS FORBIDDEN WITH REGARD TO SHEARING its wo AND using it for WORK. Thus, it is evident that in a situation whe the taking of a disputed object into one's possession cannot l reversed by the court, one can consecrate it even without taking into one's possession. Therefore, the law with regard to the bath that it *is* consecrated.[10]

Rav Hamnuna's proof is rejected:

אָמַר לֵיהּ רַבָּה – [Rabbah] responded to [Rav Hamnuna קְדוּשַּׁת בְּכוֹר קָאָמְרַתְּ – You adduce a proof that is derived fro a case involving the sanctity of a *bechor?!* Your proof is n valid, לְעוֹלָם אֵימָא לָךְ – for, in fact, I could say to you קָפוֹ כֹּהֵן מוֹצִיאִין אוֹתוֹ מִיָּדוֹ – that if a Kohen seized [a questio able *bechor*], the law is that we do take it away from him,[

NOTES

1. It is forbidden to make personal use of Temple property. This transgression is known as מְעִילָה, *me'ilah* (see 43a note 17).

2. [It is assumed that were one of the disputants to seize the disputed object (the bath) the court would not remove it from him (see *Rashi* סד"ה לעולם, *Tosafos* ד"ה והא). Therefore, the inquiry raised here resembles the Gemara's inquiry above: In a case where seizing the disputed object is effective, can either of the parties consecrate it even without seizing it?]

3. *Taharos* 4:12. This Mishnah discusses the laws of a *bechor* (firstborn). There are three types of *bechor:*

(1) *Bechor* of a person – a male firstborn child, both of whose parents are Yisraelim. The father of the child is obligated to redeem him from a Kohen [פִּדְיוֹן הַבֵּן, *redemption of the son*] by paying five *selaim* (*Numbers* 18:16).

(2) *Bechor* of kosher livestock – a firstborn male of a cow, sheep or goat. From birth, such a *bechor* is the sacred property of the Kohanim. One may not use it for work or shear its wool. The owner must give it over to a Kohen, and (if it is unblemished) the Kohen brings it as an offering in the Temple (*Deuteronomy* 15:19-23).

(3) *Bechor* of a donkey – a male firstborn donkey that is owned by a Yisrael. It acquires sanctity at birth. The owner is forbidden to derive any benefit from it until he redeems it with a sheep or goat, which is then given to a Kohen (*Exodus* 13:13).

4. It is not known whether or not this offspring is the firstborn of its mother (*Rashi*).

5. A firstborn male child is not deemed a *bechor* if its birth was preceded by the miscarriage of a fetus that falls under the category of פֶּטֶר רֶחֶם, *that which opens the womb* (see *Bechoros* 46a-47b). Thus, a case of doubt arises where a woman miscarried during her first pregnancy and it is not clear whether the ejected fetus is classified as *"that which opens the womb"* (see *Rashi*).

6. I.e. a donkey (see note 3).

7. And the Yisrael was silent at first and then protested (*Rashi).* [This must be the case to which the Mishnah refers. For if the Yisrael would have protested immediately, the court would remove the animal from the possession of the Kohen. And if the Yisrael would have remained silent throughout, he would not be able to exact the animal from the Kohen even if he were to furnish proof (see 6a note 21).]

Many commentators disagree with *Rashi*. In their view, it makes no difference whether the Yisrael was silent or protested. Since no or knows whether or not this animal is a *bechor*, the Yisrael's silenc cannot be construed as an admission (see *Rashba, Ritva, Pnei Yehoshu* et al.).

Evidently, according to *Rashi*, the Baraisa speaks of a case where th Yisrael *knew* that the animal was not a *bechor* (*Maamar Mordechai*; se other explanations cited by *Otzar Meforshei HaTalmud*).

8. Rav Hamnuna holds that where a genuine doubt exists as to th ownership of an object, the court does not view it as *definitely* belongin to the one who is in possession of it. Rather, they leave it in h possession in accordance with the principle, מִסְפֵּיקָא לֹא מַפְקִינַן מָמוֹנָא, *u do not remove property* [from someone's possession] *out of doub* Therefore, if the Kohen seizes it from the Yisrael [who is silent at leas temporarily – see previous note], he is allowed to keep it (*Avi Ezri*, *Hi Bechoros* 5:3; see 6a note 18).

9. For it might be consecrated (*Rashi*; see note 3).

10. Rav Hamnuna holds that the sanctity of a *bechor* stems from it status as Kohanite property (see *Ritva*, *Shitah Mekubetzes* in the nam of *Ritzbash*, *Avi Ezri* ibid.). A *bechor* is imbued with sanctity to th extent that the Kohanim own it, and could – if it were privat property – consecrate it themselves. Hence, Rav Hamnun reasons, since the disputed *bechor* is sacred even though no Kohe seized it, the law must be that a person can consecrate a disputed objec even without seizing it (provided that if he were to seize it and hi adversary would be silent at least temporarily, he would be allowed t keep it).

This resolves the inquiry regarding the case of two people holding o to a cloak: Just as a Kohen can "consecrate" a questionable *bechor* eve though it is in the possession of the Yisrael, so too, one of the litigant holding on to the cloak can consecrate the opposite half even though i is in the possession of his opponent.

11. According to this approach, the Mishnah's ruling, "The burden c proof is on the one etc.," applies only to the Kohen. Regardless c whether the animal happens to be in the physical possession of th Yisrael or the physical possession of the Kohen, the burden of proof i upon the Kohen (see *Rashi*).

Rabbah holds that even in cases of genuine doubt, the court views th disputed object as *definitely* belonging to the one who is in possession o it. Hence, if his adversary were to seize it (and the possessor were to b

א) מסותא דהוו מנצו עלה בי תרי האי אמר דידי הוא והאי אמר דידי הוא קם חד מינייהו אקדשה פרשי מינה רב חנניה ורב אושעיא וכולהו רבנן וא"ל רב אושעיא לרבה כי אזלת קמיה דרב חסדא לכפרי בעי מיניה כי אתא לסורא א"ל רב המנונא מתני' היא ג) ספק בכורות אחד א בכור אדם ואחד ב בכור בהמה בין טהורים בין טמאים ° המוציא מחבירו עליו הראיה ותני עלה ג אסורים בגיזה ובעבודה והא הכא דאמר תקפו כהן ד אין מוציאין אותו מידו דקתני המע"ה וכי לא תקפו אסורין בגיזה ובעבודה אמר ליה רבה קדושת בכור קאמרת לעולם אימא לך תקפו כהן מוציאין אותו מידו ואפילו הכי אסורים בגיזה ובעבודה דקדושה הבאה מאליה שאני אמר ליה רב חנניה לרבה תניא דמסייע לך ג) הספיקות נכנסין לדיר להתעשר ואי ס"ד תקפו כהן אין מוציאין אותו מידו אמאי נכנסין לדיר נמצא זה פוטר ממונו בממונו של כהן אמר ליה אביי אי משום הא לא תסייעיה למר הכא במאי עסקינן כגון דלית ליה אלא תשעה והוא דמה נפשך אי בר חיובא הוא שפיר קא מעשר אי לאו בר חיובא הוא תשעה לאו בר עשורי נינהו הדר אמר אביי לאו מילתא היא דאמרי דספיקא לאו בר עשורי היא ד) דתנן ה קפץ אחד מן המנויין לתוכן כולן פטורין ואי ס"ד ספיקא בעי עשורי לעשר ממה נפשך דאי בר חיובא הוא שפיר מעשר ואי לאו בר חיובא הוא נפטר במנין הראוי ה) דאמר (א) רבא ו מנין הראוי פוטר

אלא

מסותא. מרחץ: פרשי מינה. מלרחוץ בה: ואמר ליה רב אושעיא לרבה גרסינן: לכפרי. שם מקום: כי אתא לסורא. כשהיה עובר דרך סורא לילך לכפרי: ספק בכורות. כגון בהמה שילדה ואין ידוע אם בכרה כבר אם לא: אחד בכור אדם. כגון שהפילה אמו לפניו ספק דבר הפוטר בבכורה ספק רוח הפילה והבא אחריו בכור: בין טמאין. כגון פטר חמור: המוציא מחבירו כו'. קס"ד אם ביד ישראל הן הוי כהן מוציא מחבירו עליו הראיה ואם תקפה כהן ושתיק ישראל והדר לווח הוי ישראל מוציא מחבירו: אסורין בגיזה ועבודה. מספק שמא קדשים הם: דקתני המוציא. משמע בין כהן בין ישראל: וכי לא תקפו. אמור כאן הקדש לאוסרן בגיזה ועבודה ש"מ דאת"ל תקפו אין מוציאין אותו מידו הקדישה מקודשת: לעולם אימא לך. גבי בכור דאפי' תקפו כהן מוציאין אותו מידו מסתמא בחזקת ישראל הן ולעולם הכהן קרוי מוציא מחבירו וטעמא דגיזה ועבודה לאו משום דיהא לכהן שום כח בהן דתפשוט מינה להיכא דאי תקפו אין מוציאין מידו הקדישה הוי הקדש אלא הכא משום איסור ספק גיזת קדשים וקדושה הבאה מאליה שאני שאם בכור הוא מאליו קדוש ואיכא לספוקי בהכי אבל גבי מסותא דאין קדושה באה אלא על פיו של זה אימא לך דאפי' אם תמצי לומר תקפה אין מוציאין הקדישה בלא תקפה לא הוי הקדש דאין יכול להקדיש דבר שאינו ברשותו: דמסייע לך. דגבי ספק בכורות אם תקפה כהן מוציאין מידו: הספיקות. לקמן מפרש בספק פדיון פטר חמור דמפריש עליו טלה לאפקועי איסורא והוא לעצמו שאין צריך ליתנו לכהן שהמוציא מחבירו עליו הראיה ופדיון פטר חמור בר עשורי הוא אם יש לכהן י' פטרי חמורים שנפלו לו מבית אבי אמו ישראל מפריש עליהם עשרה שיין ומעשרן והן שלו הלכך ספק פדיון פטר חמור ביד ישראל נכנס לדיר עם שאר טלאים שלו להתעשר ואי נפקא בעשירי ליפוק: ואי ס"ד. יש לכהן צד זכייה בו נמצא זה אם יצא בעשירי פוטר ממונו בממונו של כהן: למר. רבה שהוא רבו: אם בר חיובא הוא. אי האי גברא בר חיובא הוא לעשורי שפדיון זה לאו פדיון פטר חמור שלו הוא הרי יש לו י' טלאים וחייב לעשרן שפיר קמעשר: אי לאו בר חיובא הוא. שפדיון זה של כהן לא פטר ליה מידי דתשעה לאו בני עשורי נינהו: לאו מילתא היא דאמרי. דודאי סייעתא היא למר דאי הוה צד זכייה לכהן ביה מספק ואשתכח דכל הני טלאים ספק חייבים במעשר ספק אין חייבים מספיקא לא הוי צריך לעשורינהו ו) כדקאמרת לעשורי ממה נפשך דכל ספק חייב ספק פטור לאו בני עשורי נינהו ואפילו היכא דאיכא למימר ממה נפשך: קפץ אחד מן המנויין כו'. היה מעשר טלאים והתחיל למנות כשהיו יוצאים בפתח הדיר ועד שלא הגיע לעשרה קפץ אחד מן המנויין לתוך הדיר ואינו מכירו. כולן פטורין. בין אותן שיצאו בין אותן שבתוך הדיר ואפילו הן אלף שיצאו פטורין ז) (שהם) מנין הראוי שכשמנאן היה המנין ראוי להשלים ולבא לכלל מעשר ואמרינן בבכורות והכי מייתינן לה מנין הראוי פוטר ואותן שבתוך הדיר פטורין משום זה המעורב דכל אשר יעבור תחת השבט אמר רחמנא ולא שעבר כבר וכל חד מינייהו ספק כבר עבר הוא: ואי ס"ד ספיקא. דאיכא למימר ממה נפשך בעי לעשורי שמא יעשה כתורה וכמלוה נעשרינהו להנך דבתוך הדיר ממה נפשך כל י' שיוצאין אם מעשר שלהן בר חיוב וכראוי הוא כגון שלא יצא אותו הקופץ לתוכן שפיר קא מעשר: ואי לאו בר חיובא. כגון אותן עשרה שיצא זה לתוכן ואין עשירי שלהן מעשר: נפטרו. מן המעשר: במנין הראוי. שכשמנה א' ב' ג' היו בדיר טלאים הרבה שהיו ראוין להשלים ופוטרין מנייהו: דאמר רבא. בבכורות (דף נט.): מנין הראוי פוטר. היה לו י' טלאים ומנה חמש ומת אחד מן שאינן מנוין המנוין פטורין ושאינן מנוין מצטרפין לגורן אחר שיולדו לו טלאים עד שיגיע זמן הגורן ויצטרפס עם אלו אבל המנוין פטורין במנין הראוי ויליף לה מאשר יעבור ולא שכבר עבר דמשעבר תחת השבט ולא עלה בידו לעשר שוב אינו מעבירו פעם אחרת כשיולדו לו טלאים לצרף עמהם:

אלא

תקפה כהן אין מוציאין ולכך אפי' לא תקפה אסורין בגיזה ועבודה מספק משום דשמא יש לכהן חלק בו ולכך יכול לתופסה אלמא אפי' לא תקפה חשיב כאילו תקפה כבר והקדישה בעודה בידו ודחי רבה דהתם אם תקפה כהן מוציאין מידו ואע"פ שאין לכהן בו כלום דאפי' כבר תקפה מוציאין מידו ואפי' הכי אסורין בגיזה ועבודה ועל כרחך משום דקדושה הבאה מאליה שאני וא"ת אמאי אין מוציאין מידו והלא הבעלים יאמרו ליתן לכהן אחר וי"ל במכירי כהונה ° א"נ אינו יכול לתובעו רק טובת הנאה שיש לו בו למ"ד טובת הנאה ממון ומפרק הזרוע (חולין דף קלא.) דאמר בן לוי דחטף מתנתא פרילותא הוא משמע דאינו חייב לשלם אין ראיה דשמא איירי כשאכלו כדאמרינן התם (דף קל:) המזיק מתנות כהונה או אכלן פטור:

**פוטר** ממונו בממון כהן. [א] וכן הוא מסקנא דאם תקפה כהן מוציאין מידו תימה דבפ' השואל (לקמן דף קב: ושם) ובפרק בית כור (ב"ב דף קה. ושם ד"ה אבל) גבי אחד ששכר מרחץ מוקי שמואל הא דיחלוקו בבא באמצע החדש אבל בבא בסוף החדש כולו לשוכר והא מסיק הכא דמוציאין מידו וי"ל דהתם נכנס בהיתר לכך מהניא תפיסתו אבל הכא לא בהיתר תפס כי אם בספק והא דאמרי' בפ"ב דכתובות (דף כ. ושם ד"ה ואוקי) שנים החתומים על השטר ובאו אחרים ואמרו אנוסים היו כו' אין נאמנים ומסיק דאוקי תרי בהדי תרי ואוקי ממונא בחזקת מריה ואין נאמנין דקאמר פרש"י דאם תפס המלוה לא מפקינן מיניה צ"ל שתפס קודם שבאו עדים לפסול השטר דהיינו קודם שנולד הספק ועי"ל דאין נאמנין דלא מקרעינן ליה ולא מגבינן ביה ולא לענין תפיסה: **ותשעה** לאו בר עשורי נינהו. דאין צריך לצרפו לגורן אחר דלא באו לעולם לכלל חיוב ודאי ודוקא היכא דהוו עשרה מתחלה הוא דאיצטריך לצרפו לגורן אחר: **קפץ** כולן פטורין. תימה דלבטל ברובא וליחייבו כולהו במעשר דהא לדבר שבמנין לא בטיל היינו מדרבנן וקבוע נמי אין שייך אלא בדבר שהאיסור וההיתר ניכרין וידועין ולא ידע מאיזה לקח כגון ח) ט' חנויות ובריה נמי לא הוי כדפרי' בחולין (דף צה ט) ואין לומר שלא נשאר בעדר רק אחד דליכא רובא דלשון לתוכן לא משמע הכי: **לפטרו** במנין הראוי. תימה דהכא לא שייך מנין הראוי דלא שייך אלא היכא דאין כי אם עשרה והתחיל למנות ומת אחד מהן ואין כאן י' אפ"ה פטורים אותן שיצאו ולא יצטרפו לגורן אחר כיון שתחילת יציאתן היה ראוי להשלים המנין אבל הכא שיש בעדר הרבה ישלים המנין ויהא עשירי וי"א קודש ויקרא לשניהם עשירי מספק אם יש מנוי ביניהם אם לאו וכן יעשה בכל אחד עשר ובאחרונה שלא ישאר עשרה יצטרפו לגורן אחר:

ולא

## עין משפט נר מצוה

לה א מיי' פי"א מהל' בכורות הלכה יט סמג עשין קמד טוש"ע י"ד סי' שה סעיף יג וסעיף כ וסעיף כה:

לו ב מיי' שם פי"ב הל' כג ועי' בהשגות ובכ"מ ופ"ד מהל' בכורות הל' ז ופ"ה שם הל' ג סמג שם וסי' ריא טוש"ע י"ד סי' שכא סעיף י וסעיף יג יד טו טז וסי' שטו סעיף א:

לז ג מיי' פ"א מהלכות מעילה הל' ח סמג לאוין שמ טוש"ע י"ד סי' שטו סעיף א:

לח ד מיי' פ"ה מהל' בכורות הל' ג סמג עשין ריא טוש"ע י"ד סי' שטו סעיף א וע"ש בהגה"ה:

לט ה מיי' פ"ח שם הלכה יד סמג עשין ריב:

מ ו מיי' שם הל' ח והל"י סמג עשין שם:

## רבינו חננאל

מסותא דהוו מינצו עליה בי תרי כל חד אמר דידי הוא קם חד מינייהו אקדשה והוו פרשי מיניה רב חנינא ורב הושעיא וכולהו רבנן. ופשיט רב המנונא מהא דתנן ספק בכורות אחד בכור אדם ואחד בכור בהמה בין טהורין בין טמאין המע"ה. ותני עלה אסורין בגיזה ובעבודה. והא הכא אילו תקפו כהן אין מוציאין אותה מידו דקתני המע"ה ואע"ג דלא תקפן אסורין בגיזה ועבודה ש"מ דכל היכא דאילו תקפן אין מוציאין אותה מידו הקדישה בלא תקפה מקודשת. ודחי לה רב' ואמר לעולם אימא לך אפי' תקפן כהן (אין) מוציאין אותה מידו ואפ"ה אסורין בגיזה ועבודה דקדושת בכור קדושה הבאה מאליה היא ושאני מקדושה דמקדישין לה במילי. אמר ליה רב חנינא לרב' תניא דמסייעא לך שאם תקפן כהן מוציאין אותו מידו דתניא הספיקות נכנסין לדיר להתעשר וכו' ואמר ליה אביי הא לא מסייעא ליה הכא במאי עסקינן בדלית ליה אלא ט' וזה הספק דמה נפשך אי לא בכור הוא שפיר קא מעשר ואי בכור הוא בני ט' נינהו וט' לאו בני עשורי נינהו. ופשטינן לקמן דהני ספיקות לאו ספק בכורות הוא אלא ספק פטרי חמורים הן וכדרב נחמן דאמר בבכורות פ"א [דף יא] ישראל שיש לו י' פטרי חמורים מעשרן והן שלו ושם פירשנו שמועה זו. והדר ביה אביי ואמר לאו [מילתא] היא דאמרי דכל ספק לאו בר עשורי הוא מדתנן קפץ א' מן המנוין לתוכן כולן פטורין פי' כיצד מעשרן מכניס צאנו לדיר ומוציאן אחד אחד במנין כדתנן כיצד מעשרן כונסן לדיר ועושה להן פתח קטן כדי שלא יוכלו שנים לצאת באחד ומונה בשבט א' ב' ג' ד' ה' ו' ז' ח' ט' והיוצא עשירי סוקרו בסיקרא ואומר ה"ז מעשר. ואם קפץ מאותן שהן חוץ לדיר ונכנס לדיר ונתערב בצאן שבדיר שעדיין לא נתעשרו ואינם יודעים איזהו. נעשו אותן ספק ונפטרו כולן ואם נאמר כי דין הספיקות להתעשר ממה נפשך אמאי אין מעשרין גם (לאו) [להון] ממה נפשך נעשרינהו ואם יצא עשירי זולתי זה שקפץ מן המנין שפיר ואם זה שיצא עשירי הוא זה שקפץ שהוא פטור ואין הפטור פוטר את החייב נפטרו במנין הראוי פי' מנין הראוי כגון שיש לו עשר צאן בדיר ורצה לעשרן ופתח להם הפתח שיצאו ועשירי יסקרהו בסיקרא והתחיל לצאת אחד אחד והוא מונה מי שיצא בתחלה קורא אחד והיוצא אחריו מנאו שני ואחריו שלישי וכן כולן עד שיצאו התשעה אלו התשעה כולן המנין פטרן שאין אחד מהן נקרא עליו שם עשירי והיוצא עשירי הוא הקדוש וכיון שכל אחד שיצא מן הדיר נפטר היוצא מיד ואע"פ שקודם יסקרו בסיקרא קפץ מתוך הדיר ויצא לחוץ ונתערב עם המנוין התשעה נפטרו במנין הראוי למעשר אע"פ שלא יצא אחריהן עשירי הואיל ובשעה שיצאו במניינם היה בדיר מי שיעבור עשירי תחת השבט היוצא ראשון ראשון נפטר. ובהדיא בבכורות פרק אחרון אמר רבא מנין הראוי פוטר.

חשק שלמה על ר"ח א) אולי צ"ל הראוי להיות מעשר נפטר היוצא וכו'.

## מסורת הש"ס

א) [עי' תוס' מנחות ד"ה ומתירין], ב) [... פרק ד' משנה יב, יט.], ג) [עיקרו בכורות ט. ודלך לקלר כמו שכתבו סוכה ז. ד"ה], ד) בכורות נח:, ה) ..., ו) כ"א ... מהרש"ל, ז) צ"ל ... מהרש"ל, ח) [ועיין חולין לה. ד"ה ...], ט) [לו. ד"ה מ"ט ...]

## הגהות הב"ח

(א) גמ' דאמר רבה הראוי:

## הגהות הגר"א

[א] תוס' ד"ה ... וכ"ה מסקנא כו'. וכ"ד ש"פ אבל הר... חולק וכתב הר... דלמסקנא דמפרש ... ספק פ"ח אין ... דבפ"ח לא זכה כהן כבר אתחזק בה הבעל... (ועמ"ש רבינו ביו"ד סט"ו ס"ק ב')

## גליון הש"ס

גמ' המוציא מחב... עיין נדה כה ע"א ד"ה גבי: תוס' והא כו' א"נ לתובעו. נראה שכן רש"י בב"ק סו ע"א עד שלבעו:

## ליקוטי רש"י

מסותא. מרחץ מסחותא ורחץ מתר... ואסמי [סנהדרין ...]. ספק בכורות. דבעי לאפוקי מיניה להביא ראיה שהן ב... שלא הפילה נפל קודם... ואי תפס להו כהן הבעלים להביא ראיה בכור הוא [נדרים ...]. קפץ אחד המנויין. מאותן ש... עברו בפתח תחת ה... אע"פ שאינן ... מעושרין וכגון שמנה אחד מהן וקפץ הדיר להמנויין פטורין במנין ה... כדמפרש בגמ' ו... דאין ידוע איזה ה... לכך מה שבדיר פ... [בכורות נח:]. ... הראוי פוטר. כ... תשעה בפתח היה מנין הראוי לעשר ש... היה עשירי קיים ... ראוי לצאת אחר... ולפוטרן וכיון דראוי ... דמי כמאן דיצא כבר ו... את המנין וכו' אבל ... גופיה מיהא לא קדוש עד שיצא [שם ...]

ואלא הא [א] דאמר רב נחמן משביעין אותו שבועת היסת נימא מיגו דחשיד אממונא חשיד אשבועתא ותו הא [ב] דתני רבי חייא שניהם נשבעין ונוטלין מבעה״ב נימא מיגו דחשיד אממונא חשיד אשבועתא ותו הא [ג] דאמר רב ששת [א] שלש שבועות משביעין אותו שבועה שלא פשעתי בה שבועה שלא שלחתי בה יד שבועה שאינה ברשותי נימא מיגו דחשיד אממונא חשיד אשבועתא אלא לא אמרינן מיגו דחשיד אממונא חשיד אשבועתא אביי אמר חיישינן שמא מלוה ישנה יש לו עליו אי הכי נשקול בלא שבועה [ב] אלא חיישינן שמא ספק מלוה ישנה יש לו עליו ולאו אמרינן תפיס ממונא מספיקא משתבע נמי מספק אמר רב ששת בריה דרב אידי פרשי אינשי מספק שבועה ולא פרשי מספק ממונא מאי טעמא ממון איתיה בחזרה שבועה ליתיה בחזרה: בעי ר׳ זירא תקפה אחד בפנינו מהו היכי דמי אי דשתיק אודויי אודי ליה ואי דקא צווח מאי הוה ליה למעבד לא צריכא דשתיק מעיקרא והדר צווח מאי מדאשתיק אודויי אודי ליה או דלמא כיון דקא צווח השתא איגלאי מילתא דהאי דשתיק מעיקרא סבר הא קא חזו ליה רבנן אמר רב נחמן ת״ש [ג] בד״א ששניהם אדוקין בה אבל היתה טלית יוצאת מתחת ידו של אחד מהן המוציא מחבירו עליו הראיה היכי דמי אי נימא כדקתני פשיטא [א] אלא שתקפה אחד בפנינו לא הכא במאי עסקינן [ד] כגון דאתו לקמן כדתפיסו לה תרוייהו ואמרינן להו זילו פלוגו ונפקו והדר אתו כי תפיס לה חד מינייהו האי אמר אודויי אודי לי והאי אמר בדמי אגרתי ניהליה דאמרינן ליה עד השתא חשדת ליה בגזלן והשתא מוגרת ליה בלא סהדי ואיבעית אימא כדקתני דאתו לקמן כי תפיס לה חד מינייהו ואידך מסרך בה סרוכי ואפילו [ד] לסומכוס דאמר ממון המוטל בספק חולקין בלא שבועה מודה סומכוס [ה] דסרכא לאו כלום היא אם תמצי לומר תקפה אחד בפנינו מוציאין אותה מידו הקדישה אינה מקודשת אם תמצי לומר תקפה אחד בפנינו [ו] אין מוציאין אותה מידו הקדישה בלא תקפה מהו כיון [ה] דאמר מר [ז] אמירתו לגבוה כמסירתו להדיוט דמי כמאן דתקפה דמי או דלמא השתא מיהא הא לא תקפה וכתיב [א] ואיש כי יקדיש את ביתו קדש וגו׳ [ו] מה ביתו ברשותו [ח] אף כל ברשותו לאפוקי האי דלא ברשותו ת״ש דההיא

**רש״י**

משביעין אותו. לשאינו מודה במקצת: נימא מיגו. דמעיז פניו לכפור הכל לאו לאשתמוטי בעי וחשוד אשבועה: שניהם נשבעים. גבי חנוני על פנקסו וקשה לי אמאי שבקה למתני׳ דשבועות ומייתי לה מברייתא: נימא מיגו. כיון דחד מינייהו ודאי חשיד אממונא: שלש שבועות משביעין אותו. לשומר חנם שטוען נגנבה: שלא שלחתי בה יד. לעשות מלאכתי דאי שלח בה יד הוי גזלן עליה ומיחייב באונסיה ואפילו נאנסה ברשותיה היא קיימא ודידיה היא: נימא. גבי שבועה שאינה ברשותי מיגו דחשיד אממונא שמא ברשותיה הוא וכופר בה חשיד נמי אשבועתא: אביי אמר. טעמא דמתני׳ לאו כדר׳ יוחנן דאי הוה חשיד לן אהולך ותוקף בטלית חבירו חנם הוה לן חשוד אשבועה אלא חיישינן שמא מלוה ישנה יש לו עליו על זה ומכיר בו ששכחה ויכפור בו והולך ותוקף בטליתו ונשבע שיש לו בה דמי חציה וטלית זו שלו דהא אפי׳ גלימא דעל כתפיה שעביד ליה: אי הכי. אמאי רמו עליה שבועה כיון דאי לא הוי עליה לא הוי תפיס בה: נשקלה בלא שבועה. לגבות מלוה שלו: ולא פרשי מספק ממונא. אבל מודאי דממונא פרשי ומאן דלא פריש חשיד נמי אשבועתא: תקפה אחד. הוציאה מיד חבירו בחזקה והרי כולה בידו קודם שנשבעו: יוצאה מתחת ידו של אחד מהם. יוצאה (לבדו) לפני ב״ד מתחת יד האחד שהוא לבדו אחוז בה ולא חבירו: הראיה. בעדים: כדקתני. שזה לבדו אחוז בה וזה: אלא לאו כו׳. וכדאוקמינן דשתיק ולבסוף צווח: אפי׳ לסומכוס כו׳. כלומר ואליבא דסומכוס דמיקל בחלוקה ולא מצריך אפי׳ שבועה איצטריך לאשמועינן דבכה״ג מודי סומכוס דאפי׳ בשבועה לא שקיל דהא לאו ממון המוטל בספק הוא: דסרכא לאו כלום היא. ואין שור שחוט לפניך ולא דמי לנמצאת עוברה בלדה (ב״ק דף מו.): ואת״ל. בשאילתנו לפשוט דמוציאין אותה מידו ויחלוקו: הקדישה. בלא תקפה: אינה מקודשת. דלא אלים הקדישה מתקפה: הא לא תקפה. ואין יכול להקדישה:
מסותא

**תוספות**

**אלא** הא דאמר רב נחמן. תימה הא הכא נמי משתמיט וי״ל דרב נחמן מחייב שבועת היסת אפי׳ היכא שתובעו ואמר זה החפץ שהוא בידך שלי הוא דלא שייך אישתמוטי וכן פי׳ רב האי גאון שמשביעין שבועת היסת אקרקעות אע״ג דלא שייך בהו אישתמוטי וקשה דבפ׳ שבועת הדיינים (דף מ: ושם ד״ה אישתמוטי) משמע דלא מחייב שבועת היסת אלא משום אישתמוטי דקא פריך אדרבה אין אדם מעיז ומשני דמשתמיט וי״ל כיון דבשאינו בעין משתמיט אף כשהוא בעין לא פלוג רבנן אי נמי אקושיא דר׳ חייא סמיך: **דתני** ר׳ חייא. הקשה רש״י אמאי לא מייתי מתני׳ דשבועות וי״ל דע״י ר׳ חייא שנאה רבי כדמוכח התם (דף מז:): **שבועה** שלא שלחתי בה יד. פרש״י דאם שלח בה יד אפילו נאנסה חייב ואף על פי דמשהחזירה פטור כדקתני בהמפקיד (לקמן דף [ז] לד) מ״מ שמא נאנסה קודם שהחזירה אבל קשה משלהי האומנין (לקמן דף פג.) דקאמר ונשבר או נשבה אין רואה הא יש רואה יביא ראיה ויפטר והא שמא שלח בה יד וי״ל שיפטר משבועה שנאנסה אך ישבע שלא שלח בה יד אי נמי שלא שלחתי בה יד אינו נשבע אלא ע״י גלגול שבועה שלא פשעתי בה וכשיש רואה שנאנסה פטור לגמרי ור״ת מפרש אפי׳ ע״י גלגול לא ישבע היכא שהיא מתה בפנינו דאין מגלגלין אלא בדבר הדומה דלמה י״ל ששלח בו יד דדוקא בשותפין שחלקו ונתחייב שבועה ממקום אחר מגלגלין משום דמורי היתרא ושבועה שלא שלחתי בה יד מפרש ר״ת שלא אכלה דאינו בכלל שבועה שלא פשע בה ושאינה ברשותו: **ספק** מלוה ישנה יש לו עליו. וההיא דמשביעין אותו ג׳ שבועות ודשניהם נשבעין ונוטלין נמי חיישינן שמא מלוה ישנה יש לו עליו ולכך אין לפוטרו בלא שבועה וגם לא יטול בלא שבועה אבל בגזלן ודאי וכופר בפקדון אין להכשיר מטעם שמא ספק מלוה ישנה יש לו עליו: **ממון** אפשר בחזרה. אם לא יזכור יחזיר ולא יעכבנו מספק אבל אין לפרש אם יזכור שאינו חייב לו יחזיר אבל אם לא יזכור יעכבנו אע״פ שיודע שלא יזכור עוד דא״כ גם מספק שבועה לא יפרוש: **אגרת** ליה בלא סהדי. ואינו נאמן במיגו דאי בעי אמר תקפה ממני דמיגו במקום עדים הוא: **הקדישה** בלא תקפה מהו. ומיירי נמי כגון ששתק בשעה שהקדיש ולבסוף כששאלה הגזבר צווח ומבעיא ליה כיון דאמירתו לגבוה כו׳ הוה הקדש כתקפה דכיון ששתק אודויי אודי ליה והוה הקדש ולא דמי לגזל ולא נתייאשו הבעלים דשניהם אין יכולין להקדיש זה לפי שאינו שלו וזה לפי שאינו ברשותו דכיון דלאודי ליה הוי כפקדון שיש לו ביד אחרים דיכול להקדיש כדמוכח בהמוכר את הספינה (ב״ב דף פח.) גבי ההוא דאייתי קרי כו׳ דאי לא קיי״ל דמייהו הוי קדושות או דלמא הקדש לא הוי כתקיפה דלמה יצווח בשביל דבריו ומייתי מההיא מסותא דהקדיש חד ושתק אידך ומסקנא דלא הוי הקדש אלמא שתיקתו אינו כהודאה: [ט] **והא** הכא דכי תקפה כהן כו׳. נראה דהכי מיבעי ליה במסותא כיון דמקרקעי היא והוה דינא כל דאלים גבר וכיון דאם תקפה האחד והקדישה כשהיא בידו מסתמא תו לא פקע אפי׳ חזר חבירו ותקפה ממנו כי הקדישה בלא תקפה נמי הוי הקדש או דלמא כיון דאפי׳ גבר האחד אם יכול השני לחזור ולתוקפה ממנו זוכה ה״ה הקדיש בלא תקפה לא יחול הקדש כלל כיון דחבירו אם תקפה היה זוכה דלא אליס הקדש מתקיפה והשתא אייתי והא הכא אם
תקפה

**עין משפט נר מצוה**

כח א מיי׳ פ״ו מהל׳ שאלה ופקדון הלכה א סמג עשין פח טוש״ע ח״מ סי׳ (רלו סעיף א וסי׳) רלה סעיף ב:
כט ב טוש״ע ח״מ סי׳ לב סעיף ג:
ל ג ד מיי׳ פ״ט מהל׳ טוען ונטען הלכה יג ועי׳ בהשגות ובמ״מ טור ש״ע ח״מ סי׳ קלא סעי׳ ח:
לא ה מיי׳ שם הל׳ יב טוש״ע שם סעיף ה:
לב ו מיי׳ שם הל׳ יא טוש״ע שם סעיף ז:
לג ז מיי׳ פ״ט מהלכות מכירה הל׳ א סמג עשין פב טוש״ע י״ד סי׳ רנח סעיף יג:
לד ח מיי׳ פ״ו מהל׳ ערכין הל׳ כב סמג עשין קלב טוש״ע שם סעיף ז:

**רבינו חננאל**

והא דאמר רב נחמן ג׳ שבועות משביעין אותו כו׳ הוא בפ׳ הגוזל קמא. ואסקי׳ פרשי אינשי מספק שבועה ולא פרשי מספק ממונא מאי טעמא ממון אפשר בחזרה. שבוע׳ לא אפשר בחזרה. **בעי** ר׳ זירא תקפה א׳ בפנינו מהו כו׳ ת״ש בד״א בששניהם אדוקין בה אבל אם היה יוצא מתחת ידי אחד המע״ה. ופשיטנא הכא במאי עסקינן דאתו לקמן שניהן אדוקין בה ואמרי׳ להו דינא הוא דפלגיתו לה ואזלו והדרי כי תפיס לה חד מנהון וטעין דאודי לי ואמר לי שקלא דידך היא. ואידך טעין אוגרתה ליה דאמרי׳ ליה עד השתא חשדת ליה בגזלן וטענת כולה דידי הוא ואתא הוא ותפיס בהדאי וטעין בה והשתא אמרת אוגרתה ליה בלא סהדי שקרא אנת. אי בעית תימא לעולם דאתו לקמן כי תפיס לה חד ואידך מסרך סרוכי דאמרי׳ אפילו סומכוס דאמר ממון המוטל בספק חולקין בלא שבועה מודה סומכוס דסרכא לאו כלום היא. אם תמצא לומר תקפה א׳ בפנינו מרציאין אותו מידו הקדישה אינה מקודשת. ואם תמצא לומר אין מוציאין אותה מידו הקדישה מקודשת. הקדישה בלא תקפה מהו מי אמרי׳ כיון דאמר מר אמירתו לגבוה כמסירתו להדיוט דמי כמאן דתקפה דמי או דלמא השתא מיהא הא לא תקפה. ת״ש דההיא

**מסורת הש״ס**

...עות מ: [לעיל ה.], ...עות מז., ג) בבא ...קז., עיין שם, ...ל ב: וש״נ], ...דה זרה סג., בבא ...קלג., קדושין כח., ...כט., תמורה כט., ...תא קידושין פרק א׳, ...תא בבא קמא פרק ...ופפתא ערכין פרק ...ע״ז סג., [ב״ק סח: ...סט., חולין קלט., ...ה ט., כט., ערכין ...ז) [אולי צ״ל דף מ: ...בפלוגתא של ר׳ ...אל ור״ע], ח) [שייך לע״ב].

**הגהות הגר״א**

...גמ׳ אלא שתקפה ...בפנינו. נ״ב וכה״ג ...שתיק לא מהני ראיה. ...״א וטור. (ועמ״ש ...בח״מ סי׳ קל״ח ...ט״ו דלא כמ״ש ...שם בדעת הטור):

**תורה אור השלם**

...איש כִּי יַקְדִּשׁ אֶת ...קֹדֶשׁ לַייָ וְהֶעֱרִיכוֹ ...ן בֵּין טוֹב וּבֵין רָע ...שֶׁר יַעֲרִיךְ אֹתוֹ הַכֹּהֵן כֵּן יָקוּם: [ויקרא כז, יד]

**ליקוטי רש״י**

...ועת היסת. שבועה ...יתו חכמים לכך ...יתו להודות. וטעמא ...ים בשבועות (דף מ:) ...ה אין אדם טוען אא״כ ...לו בידו [לעיל ה.]. לשון ...לא ששמו חכמים עליו ...עה כמו (שמואל א כו) ...ה׳ הסיתך בי [שבועות ...]. שניהם נשבעין ...טלין מבעל הבית. ...מר ליה פועלים לא ...ימנו לי בשבועה את ...מנתינהו דלא אמרת לי ...הדי הב להו וכן פועלין ...רי ליה לא מהימן לן ...י בשבועה [שבועות ...]. שלא פשעתי. ...מירתו כשנגנבה דאי ...ע בה חייב דכתיב על כל ...ר פשע. שלא שלחתי ...ה יד. ליהנות בה קודם ...דאם שלח בה יד קמה ...ברשותיה דנעשה גזלן ...יה ומיחייב באונסין ...״ש בגניבה ואבידה [ב״ק ...]. אמירתו לגבוה ...מסירתו להדיוט. ...כתיב (ויקרא כז) ואיש ...יקדיש וגו׳ (דברים כג) ...לא שפתיך תשמור וגו׳ ...שב״ם ב״ב קלג:]. ולא מלי ...ויהדר כאילו מסרתו להדיוט [תמורה כט:].

itigants **snatched [the cloak]** from the other **before us** (and the ther party was silent at first and then protested) the law is מוֹצִיאִין אוֹתָהּ מִיָּד – that **we remove it from his possession,** הִקְדִּישָׁהּ אֵינָהּ מְקוּדֶּשֶׁ – if **[one of the litigants] consecrated it,** t **is** certainly **not consecrated.**[27]

אִם תִּמְצֵי לוֹמַר תְּקָפָהּ אֶחָד בְּפָנֵינ – **Assuming,** however, that where ne of the litigants **snatched [the cloak] before us** (and the ther party was silent and then protested) the law is אֵין מוֹצִיאִין אוֹתָהּ מִיָּד – that **we do not remove it from his possession,** הִקְדִּישָׁהּ בְּלֹא תְּקָפָהּ מַה – if **[one of the litigants] consecrated it, without snatching it, what is [the law]?** Does the consecration ake effect?[28]

The Gemara explains the two sides of this question:

כֵּיוָן דְּאָמַר מַ – Perhaps we say: **Since a master has taught** that אֲמִירָתוֹ לַגָּבוֹהַּ כִּמְסִירָתוֹ לַהֶדְיוֹט דָּמֵ – "ONE'S DECLARATION onsecrating an object TO THE HOLY DOMAIN IS as effective a ransaction AS ONE'S HANDING it OVER TO A PRIVATE PERSON,"[29] כְּמַאן דְּתַקְפָהּ דָּמֵי – were one of the litigants to declare the cloak sacred **it is** the same **as if he snatched it.**[30] אוֹ דִּלְמָא – **Or perhaps** we say: הַשְׁתָּא מִיהָא הָא לֹא תְּקָפָהּ – **Now** (i.e. when he declared the cloak sacred), since **he has not seized it,** it is not in his possession, and therefore the following teaching applies: וּכְתִיב: ,,וְאִישׁ כִּי־יַקְדִּשׁ אֶת־בֵּיתוֹ קֹדֶשׁ וגו׳ – **It is written:**[31] ***If a man consecrates his house to be holy etc.*** With regard to consecration, the Torah specifically mentions a person's house to teach מַה בֵּיתוֹ בִּרְשׁוּתוֹ – that **just as his house is in his possession,** אַף כָּל בִּרְשׁוּתוֹ – so **too, anything** that is to be consecrated must be **in his possession** לְאַפּוּקֵי הַאי דְּלֹא רְשׁוּתוֹ – **to the exclusion of** a case such as **this** one, **where** the object to be consecrated [the cloak] is **not in his possession.**[32]

The Gemara attempts to decide this issue:

תָּא שְׁמַע – **Come, hear** the following proof: דְּהַהִיא – **There was this**

NOTES

7. For verbal consecration of an object is not *more* effective than hysically seizing it (*Rashi*). Thus, in a situation where seizing would be neffective, consecration would likewise be ineffective.

[If, as proposed above (note 18), *Rashi* takes the approach of *Ran,* this omment was made only in reference to the present position of the emara – viz. the disputed object definitely does not belong to the one who is attempting to consecrate it.]

[*Rashi* specifies that the Gemara refers to a case where the one who eclared the cloak sacred did so without seizing it. This seems to imply hat were he to seize it and then declare it sacred, the cloak would indeed ecome consecrated. Many commentators argue, however, that this annot be what *Rashi* means. Since the cloak stands to be removed from im by the court, his current possession of it is of no significance (see *Maharam Shif*).]

8. The Gemara's inquiry applies to the half of the cloak attributed to his dversary. As far as his half is concerned, it is very possible that he can onsecrate it, even if the law is that he cannot consecrate the other half see *Meiri*, *Terumas HaKri* §138).

9. *Kiddushin* 28b.

0. And the cloak is consecrated. [According to *Ran,* the consecration akes effect out of doubt – see note 32.]

1. *Leviticus* 27:14.

2. Thus, he cannot consecrate the cloak (*Rashi*).

An apparent difficulty: Why does the Gemara connect this inquiry whether one can consecrate an article that is not in one's possession) to he previous one which is seemingly about the unrelated issue of whether silence followed by a protest is considered an admission?

The Rishonim offer various approaches (see *Tosafos, Ramban, Rashba, Ritva* et al.; see also *Ketzuos HaChoshen* 211:3). *Chasam Sofer* suggests that *Rashi* takes the approach of *Ran.*

As explained above, according to *Ran,* the previous inquiry was not about the status of a temporary silence as an admission. The Gemara took as given that a silence which is followed by a protest is possibly an admission. Rather, the previous inquiry was whether each party is considered as *definitely* owning his half of the cloak or as *possibly* owning the entire cloak (see note 25).

In this light, the present passage of Gemara is understood as follows: אִם תִּימְצֵי לוֹמַר תְּקָפָהּ אֶחָד בְּפָנֵינוּ מוֹצִיאִין אוֹתָהּ מִיָּדוֹ – *Assuming that where one snatched [the cloak] before us we remove it from his possession etc.* If the law is that the one who seized the cloak is not allowed to keep it even where there was possibly an admission (on the part of his opponent) that the cloak is his, it is evident that the other half of the cloak definitely does not belong to him. Therefore, he certainly cannot consecrate that half of the cloak.

אִם תִּימְצֵי לוֹמַר תְּקָפָהּ אֶחָד בְּפָנֵינוּ אֵין מוֹצִיאִין אוֹתָהּ מִיָּדוֹ – *Assuming that where one snatched [the cloak] before us we do not remove it from his possession etc.* But if the answer to the previous inquiry is that the one who seized the cloak may keep it, evidently, each litigant is viewed as possibly owning the entire cloak. Assuming this to be so, the Gemara now asks whether either one of the parties can consecrate the cloak (even without seizing it, and even if his opponent protested immediately). On the one hand, since the entire cloak is possibly his, were he to declare it sacred it should become sacred out of doubt. On the other hand, since the other half is not in his physical possession, perhaps he cannot consecrate that half at all.

ואלא הא [א] דאמר רב נחמן משביעין אותו שבועת היסת נימא מיגו דחשיד אממונא חשיד אשבועתא ותו הא [ב] דתני רבי חייא שניהם נשבעין ונוטלין מבעה"ב נימא מיגו דחשיד אממונא חשיד אשבועתא ותו הא [ג] דאמר רב ששת [א] שלש שבועות משביעין אותו שבועה שלא פשעתי בה שבועה שלא שלחתי בה יד שבועה שאינה ברשותי נימא מיגו דחשיד אממונא חשיד אשבועתא אלא לא אמרינן מיגו דחשיד אממונא חשיד אשבועתא אביי אמר חיישינן שמא מלוה ישנה יש לו עליו אי הכי נשקול בלא שבועה [ב] אלא חיישינן שמא ספק מלוה ישנה יש לו עליו ולאו אמרינן תפיס ממונא מספיקא משתבע נמי מספק אמר רב ששת בריה דרב אידי פרשי אינשי מספק שבועה ולא פרשי מספק ממונא מאי טעמא ממון איתיה בחזרה שבועה ליתיה בחזרה: בעי ר' זירא תקפה אחד בפנינו מהו היכי דמי אי דשתיק אודויי אודי ליה ואי דקא צווח מאי הוה ליה למעבד לא צריכא דשתיק מעיקרא והדר צווח מאי מדאשתיק אודויי אודי ליה או דלמא כיון דקא צווח השתא איגלאי מילתא דהאי דשתיק מעיקרא סבר הא קא חזו ליה רבנן אמר רב נחמן ת"ש [ג] בד"א ששניהם אדוקין בה אבל היתה טלית יוצאת מתחת ידו של אחד מהן המוציא מחבירו עליו הראיה היכי דמי אי נימא כדקתני פשיטא [א] אלא שתקפה אחד בפנינו לא הכא במאי עסקינן [ד] כגון דאתו לקמן כדתפיסו לה תרוייהו ואמרינן להו זילו פלוגו ונפקו והדר אתו כי תפיס לה חד מינייהו האי אמר אודויי אודי לי והאי אמר בדמי אגרתי ניהליה דאמרינן ליה עד השתא חשדת ליה בגזלן והשתא מוגרת ליה בלא סהדי ואיבעית אימא כדקתני דאתו לקמן כי תפיס לה חד מינייהו ואידך מסרך בה סרוכי ואפילו [ד] לסומכוס דאמר ממון המוטל בספק חולקין בלא שבועה מודה סומכוס [ה] דסרכא לאו כלום היא אם תמצי לומר תקפה אחד בפנינו מוציאין אותה מידו הקדישה אינה מקודשת אם תמצי לומר תקפה אחד בפנינו [ו] אין מוציאין אותה מידו הקדישה בלא תקפה מהו כיון [ה] דאמר מר [ז] אמירתו לגבוה כמסירתו להדיוט דמי כמאן דתקפה דמי או דלמא השתא מיהא הא לא תקפה וכתיב [א] ואיש כי יקדיש את ביתו קדש וגו' [ו] מה ביתו ברשותו [ח] אף כל ברשותו לאפוקי האי דלא ברשותו ת"ש דההיא

**רש"י**

משביעין אותו. לשאינו מודה במקלת: נימא מיגו. דמעיז פניו לכפור הכל לאו לאשתמוטי בעי וחשוד אשבועה: שניהם נשבעים. גבי חנוני על פנקסו וקשה לי אמאי שבקה למתני' דשבועות ומייתי לה מברייתא: נימא מיגו. כיון דחד מינייהו ודאי חשיד אממונא: שלש שבועות משביעין אותו. לשומר חנם שטוען נגנבה: שלא שלחתי בה יד. לעשות מלאכתי דאי שלח בה יד הוי גזלן עליה ומיחייב באונסיה ואפילו נאנסה ברשותיה היא קיימא ודידיה היא: נימא. גבי שבועה שאינה ברשותי מיגו דחשיד אממונא שמא ברשותיה הוא וכופר בה חשיד נמי אשבועתא: אביי אמר. טעמא דמתני' לאו כדר' יוחנן דאי הוה חשיד לן אהולך ותוקף בטלית חבירו חמס הוה לן חשוד אשבועה אלא חיישינן שמא מלוה ישנה יש לו עליו על זה ומכיר בו ששכחה ויכפור בו והולך ותוקף בטליתו ונשבע שיש לו בה דמי חליה וטלית זו שלו דהא אפי' גלימא דעל כתפיה שעביד ליה: אי הכי. אמאי רמו עליה שבועה כיון דאי לא הוי עליה לא הוי תפיס בה: נשקלה בלא שבועה. לגבות מלוה שלו: ולא פרשי מספק ממונא. אבל מודאי דממונא פרשי ומאן דלא פריש חשיד נמי אשבועתא: תקפה אחד. הוציאה מיד חבירו בחזקה והרי כולה בידו קודם שנשבעו: יוצאה מתחת ידו של אחד מהם. יוצאה (לבדו) לפני ב"ד מתחת יד האחד שהוא לבדו אחוז בה ולא חבירו: הראיה. בעדים: כדקתני. שזה לבדו אחוז בה וכו': אלא לאו כו'. וכדאוקמינן דשתיק ולבסוף צווח: אפי' לסומכוס כו'. כלומר ואליבא דסומכוס דמיקל בחלוקה ולא מצריך אפי' שבועה איצטריך לאשמועינן דבכה"ג מודי סומכוס דאפי' בשבועה לא שקיל דהא לאו ממון המוטל בספק הוא: דסרכא לאו כלום היא. ואין שור שחוט לפניך ולא דמי לנמצא עוברה בלדה (ב"ק דף מו.): ואת"ל. בשאילתנו לפשוט דמוציאין אותה מידו ויחלוקו: הקדישה. בלא תקפה: אינה מקודשת. דלא אלים הקדישה מתקפה: הא לא תקפה. ואין יכול להקדישה: מסותא

**תוספות**

**אלא** הא דאמר רב נחמן. תימה הא הכא נמי משתמיט וי"ל דרב נחמן מחייב שבועת היסת אפי' היכא שתובעו ואמר זה החפץ שהוא בידך שלי הוא דלא שייך אישתמוטי וכן פי' רב האי גאון שמשביעין שבועת היסת אקרקעות אע"ג דלא שייך בהו אישתמוטי וקשה דבפ' שבועת הדיינים (דף מ: ושם ד"ה אישתמוטי) משמע דלא מחייב שבועת היסת אלא משום אישתמוטי דקא פריך אדרבה אין אדם מעיז ומשני דמשתמיט וי"ל כיון דבשאינו בעין משתמיט אף כשהוא בעין לא פלוג רבנן אי נמי אקושיא דר' חייא סמיך: **דתני** ר' חייא. הקשה רש"י אמאי לא מייתי מתני' דשבועות וי"ל דע"י ר' חייא שנאה רבי כדמוכח התם (דף מז:):

**שבועה** שלא שלחתי בה יד. פרש"י דאם שלח בה יד אפילו נאנסה חייב ואף על פי דמשהחזירה פטור כדקתני בהמפקיד (לקמן דף [י] לד) מ"מ שמא נאנסה קודם שהחזירה אבל קשה משלהי האומנין (לקמן דף פג.) דקאמר ונשבר או נשבה אין רואה הא יש רואה יביא ראיה ויפטר והא שמא שלח בה יד וי"ל שיפטר משבועה שנאנסה אך ישבע שלא שלח בה יד אי נמי שלא שלחתי בה יד אינו נשבע אלא ע"י גלגול שבועה שלא פשעתי בה וכשיש רואה שנאנסה פטור לגמרי ור"ת מפרש אפי' ע"י גלגול לא ישבע היכא שהיא מתה בפנינו דאין מגלגלין אלא בדבר הדומה דלמה י"ל ששלח בו יד דדוקא בשותפין שחלקו ונתחייב שבועה ממקום אחר מגלגלין משום דמורי היתרא ושבועה שלא שלחתי בה יד מפרש ר"ת שלא אכלה דאינו בכלל שבועה שלא פשע בה ושאינה ברשותו:

**ספק** מלוה ישנה יש לו עליו. והכא דמשביעין אותו ג' שבועות ודשניהם נשבעין ונוטלין נמי חיישינן שמא מלוה ישנה יש לו עליו ולכך אין לפוטרו בלא שבועה וגם לא יטול בלא שבועה אבל בגזלן ודאי וכופר בפקדון אין להכשיר מטעם שמא ספק מלוה ישנה יש לו עליו:

**ממון** אפשר בחזרה. אם לא יזכור יחזיר ולא יעכבנו מספק אבל אין לפרש אם יזכור שאינו חייב לו יחזיר אבל אם לא יזכור יעכבנו אע"פ שיודע שלא יזכור עוד דא"כ גם מספק שבועה לא יפרוש:

**אגרת** ליה בלא סהדי. ואינו נאמן במיגו דאי בעי אמר תקפה ממני דמיגו במקום עדים הוא:

**הקדישה** בלא תקפה מהו. ומיירי נמי כגון ששתק בשעה שהקדיש ולבסוף כששאלה הגזבר צווח ומבעיא ליה כיון דאמירתו לגבוה כו' הוה הקדש כתקפה דכיון ששתק אודויי אודי ליה והוה הקדש ולא דמי לגזל ולא נתייאשו הבעלים דשניהם אין יכולין להקדיש זה לפי שאינו שלו וזה לפי שאינו ברשותו דכיון דאודי ליה הוי כפקדון שיש לו ביד אחרים דיכול להקדיש כדמוכח בהמוכר את הספינה (ב"ב דף פח.) גבי ההוא דאייתי קרי כו' דאי לא קיילי דמייהו הוי קדושות או דלמא הקדש לא הוי כתקיפה דלמה יצווח בשביל דבריו ומייתי מההיא מסותא דהקדיש חד ושתק אידך ומסקנא דלא הוי הקדש אלמא שתיקתו אינו כהודאה: [ט] **והא** הכא דבי תקפה בכהן כו'. נראה דהכי מיבעי ליה במסותא כיון דמקרקעי היא והוה דינא כל דאלים גבר וכיון דאם תקפה האחד והקדישה כשהיא בידו מסתמא תו לא פקע אפי' חזר חבירו ותקפה ממנו כי הקדישה בלא תקפה נמי הוי הקדש או דלמא כיון דאפי' גבר האחד אם יכול השני לחזור ולתוקפה ממנו זוכה ה"ה הקדיש בלא תקפה לא יחול הקדש כלל כיון דלחבירו אם תקפה היה זוכה דלא אלים הקדש מתקיפה והשתא אייתי והא הכא אם תקפה

**עין משפט נר מצוה**

כח א מיי' פ"ו מהל' שאלה ופקדון הלכה א סמג עשין פח טוש"ע ח"מ סי' (רצו סעיף א וסי') רצה סעיף ב:
כט ב טוש"ע ח"מ סי' צב סעיף ג:
ל ג ד מיי' פ"ט מהל' טוען ונטען הלכה יג ועי' בהשגות ובמ"מ טור ש"ע ח"מ סי' קלח סעי' א:
לא ה מיי' שם הל' יב טוש"ע שם סעיף ה:
לב ו מיי' שם הל' יא טוש"ע שם סעיף ז:
לג ז מיי' פ"ט מהלכות מכירה הל' א סמג עשין פב טוש"ע י"ד סי' רנא סעיף יג:
לד ח מיי' פ"ו מהל' ערכין הל' כב סמג עשין קלב טוש"ע שם סעיף ז:

**רבינו חננאל**

והא דאמר רב נחמן ג' שבועות משביעין אותו כו' הוא בפ' הגוזל קמא. ואסקי' פרשי אינשי מספק שבועה ולא פרשי מספק ממונא מאי טעמא ממון אפשר בחזרה. שבוע' לא אפשר בחזרה. **בעי** ר' זירא תקפה א' בפנינו מהו כו' ת"ש בד"א בששניהם אדוקין בה אבל אם היה יוצא מתחת ידי אחד המע"ה. ופשיטנא הכא במאי עסקינן דאתו לקמן שניהן אדוקין בה ואמרי' להו דינא הוא דפלגיתו לה ואזלו והדרי כי תפיס לה חד מנהון וטעין דאודי לי ואמר לי שקלא דידך היא. ואידך טעין אוגרתה ליה דאמרי' ליה עד השתא חשדת ליה בגזלן וטענת כולה דידי הוא ואתא הוא ותפיס בהדאי וטעין בה והשתא אמרת אוגרתה ליה בלא סהדי שקרא אנת. אי בעית תימא לעולם דאתו לקמן כי תפיס לה חד ואידך מסרך סרוכי דאמרי' אפילו סומכוס דאמר ממון המוטל בספק חולקין בלא שבועה מודה סומכוס דסרכא לאו כלום היא. אם תמצא לומר תקפה א' בפנינו מרציאין אותו מידו הקדישה אינה מקודשת. ואם תמצא לומר אין מוציאין אותה מידו הקדישה מקודשת. הקדישה בלא תקפה מהו מי אמרי' כיון דאמר מר אמירתו לגבוה כמסירתו להדיוט דמי כמאן דתקפה דמי או דלמא השתא מיהא הא לא תקפה. ת"ש דההיא

**מסורת הש"ם**

א) שבועות מ: [לעיל ה.], ב) שבועות מז:, ג) בבא בתרא קז:, עיין שם, [לעיל ב: וש"נ], ד) עבודה זרה סג., בבא בתרא קלג:, קדושין כח:, נדרים כט:, תמורה כט:, תוספתא קידושין פרק א', תוספתא בבא קמא פרק ..., תוספתא ערכין פרק ..., ו) ע"ז סג., [ב"ק סח:], ...ש, סט:, חולין קלט., תמורה ט., כט:, ערכין ...], ז) [אולי צ"ל דף מ: ... אינו בפלוגתא של ר' ... מעאל ור"ע], ח) [שייך לע"ב].

**הגהות הגר"א**

[א] גמ' אלא שתקפה אחד בפנינו. נ"ב וכה"ג ... בשתיק לא מהני ראיה. ...טב"א וטור. (ועמ"ש ...ינו בח"מ סי' קל"ח ...ק ט"ו דלא כמ"ש ...ש"ך שם בדעת הטור):

**תורה אור השלם**

א) וְאִישׁ כִּי יַקְדִּשׁ אֶת בֵּיתוֹ קֹדֶשׁ לַייָ וְהֶעֱרִיכוֹ הַכֹּהֵן בֵּין טוֹב וּבֵין רָע כַּאֲשֶׁר יַעֲרִיךְ אֹתוֹ הַכֹּהֵן כֵּן יָקוּם: [ויקרא כז, יד]

**ליקוטי רש"י**

שבועת היסת. שבועה שהסיתו חכמים לכך שהסיתו להודות. וטעמא מפרש בשבועות (דף מ:) ...קה אין אדם טוען אא"כ ...א לו בידו [לעיל ה.]. לשון ...ומא ששמו חכמים עליו ...בועה כמו (שמואל א כו) ...ם ה' הסיתך בי [שבועות ...:]. שניהם נשבעין ...נוטלין מבעל הבית. ...אמר ליה פועלים לא ...הימנו לי בשבועה את ...אמנתיהו דלא אמרת לי ...סהדי הב להו וכן פועלין ...מרי ליה לא מהימן לן ...ווי בשבועה [שבועות ...ז:]. שלא פשעתי. ...שמירתו כשנגנבה דאי ...פשע בה חייב דכתיב על כל ...דבר פשע. שלא שלחתי ...בה יד. ליהנות בה קודם ...כן דאם שלח בה יד קמה ...ליה ברשותיה דנעשה גזלן ...עליה ומיחייב באונסין ...כ"ש בגניבה ואבידה [ב"ק ...ז:]. אמירתו לגבוה ...כמסירתו להדיוט. ...דכתיב (ויקרא כז) ואיש ...כי יקדיש ...

אָמַר רַב נַ – Rav Nachman said: תָּא שְׁמַע – Come, learn om the following Baraisa, which qualifies our Mishnah's ruling at the cloak is divided: בַּמֶּה דְּבָרִים אֲמוּרִים – IN WHAT RCUMSTANCES DOES [THIS RULING] APPLY? שֶׁשְּׁנֵיהֶם אֲדוּקִין בָּהּ It applies WHERE BOTH [LITIGANTS] ARE HOLDING ON TO [THE OAK]. אֲבָל הָיְתָה טַלִּית יוֹצֵאת מִתַּחַת יָדוֹ שֶׁל אֶחָד מֵהֶן – BUT if E CLOAK IS IN THE POSSESSION[19] OF only ONE OF THEM, the llowing principle applies: הַמּוֹצִיא מֵחֲבֵירוֹ עָלָיו הָרְאָיָה – THE rden of PROOF RESTS ON THE ONE WHO SEEKS TO EXACT operty FROM the possession of HIS FELLOW; i.e. the cloak is kept the one who is holding it, unless the other party furnishes oof[20] that the cloak is his.

Rav Nachman demonstrates how this Baraisa answers R' ira's inquiry:

הֵיכִי דָ – What are the exact circumstances of the case scussed in the Baraisa? אִי נֵימָא כִּדְקָתָנֵי – If we say that the araisa should be understood as it is taught, i.e. when the igants entered the court only one of them was holding the cloak, פְּשִׁיטָ – then its ruling is obvious! There is no question that in ıch a case the cloak is regarded as the property of the one who is olding it and the burden of proof rests on the other. אֶלָּא שֶׁתְּקָפָה אֶחָד בְּפָנֵי – Rather, the case must be that both were olding on to the cloak when they entered the court and then one them snatched it from the other before us [the judges], and e other was silent at first and then he protested.[21] Hence, this araisa, which rules that the court does not remove the cloak om the one who seized it, resolves R' Zeira's inquiry.

The Gemara rejects the proof:

ל – That is not necessarily the case to which the Baraisa refers. הָכָא בְּמַאי עָסְקִי – For what might we be dealing with here? כְּגוֹן דְּאָתוּ לְקַמָּן כִּדְתְפִיסוּ לָהּ תַּרְוַיְיהוּ – The Baraisa possibly refers ) a case where both of them were holding on to [the cloak] hen they came before us [the judges], וְאַמְרִינַן לְהוּ – and we aid to them: זִילוּ פַּלּוּגוּ – Go and divide the cloak between yourselves, וְנָפְקוּ – and they went out to divide the cloak, וְהָדַר אָתוּ כִּי תָּפֵיס לָהּ חַד מִינַּיְיהוּ – but when they came back only one of them was holding it. הַאי אָמַר – This one [the one holding it] says: אוֹדוּיֵי אוֹדִי לִי – "He admitted to me that the cloak is mine." וְהַאי אָמַר – And the other one says: בִּדְמֵי אֲגַרְתֵּיהּ נִיהֲלֵיהּ – "He is holding it because I rented it to him for payment, but really the cloak is mine." The Baraisa teaches that in such a case the cloak is considered the property of the one holding it, דְּאַמְרִינַן לֵיהּ – because we say to [the other]: עַד הַשְׁתָּא חֲשַׁדְתְּ לֵיהּ בְּגַזְלָן – Until now you suspected [your opponent] of being a thief,[22] וְהַשְׁתָּא מוֹגְרַת לֵיהּ בְּלֹא סַהֲדֵי – and now you rent it to him without witnesses to the arrangement! Your claim is patently absurd. Therefore, we assume that your opponent's claim is the valid one.[23]

The Gemara suggests yet another explanation of the Baraisa: וְאִיבָּעֵית אֵימָא כִּדְקָתָנֵי – And if you prefer, say that the Baraisa should be understood as it is taught; דְּאָתוּ לְקַמָּן כִּי תָּפֵיס לָהּ חַד מִינַּיְיהוּ – i.e. it speaks of a case where only one of [the litigants] was holding on to [the cloak] when they came before us. וְאִידָךְ מִסְרָךְ בָּהּ סְרוּכֵי – However, the other was in the act of wresting it[24] from him. The Baraisa teaches that in such a case the cloak is considered the exclusive property of the one who is holding it. וַאֲפִילּוּ לְסוּמְכוֹס – And this is so even according to Sumchos, דְּאָמַר מָמוֹן הַמּוּטָּל בְּסָפֵק חוֹלְקִין בְּלֹא שְׁבוּעָה – who says that money whose ownership is in doubt is divided between the litigants even without their having to take an oath, מוֹדֶה סוּמְכוֹס דְּסִרְכָא לָאו כְּלוּם הִיא – because Sumchos concedes that the act of wresting the cloak is not a demonstration of possession at all.[25]

In the light of R' Zeira's inquiry, the Gemara now discusses what the law would be if two disputants entered the court holding on to a cloak and one of them verbally dedicated it to the Temple treasury:[26]

אִם תִּמְצֵי לוֹמַר תְּקָפָה אֶחָד בְּפָנֵינוּ – Assuming that where one of the

NOTES

at what this one holds is his and what this one holds is his.) Therefore, ıe one who seized the cloak must relinquish it.

(2) The court views each litigant as *possibly* owning the entire cloak. herefore, the one who seized the cloak is allowed to keep it.

[The reason why *Ran* takes this approach will become evident below - see note 32.]

9. Literally: comes out from under his hand.

0. [Such as] witnesses (*Rashi*).

1. An apparent difficulty: How does Rav Nachman know that the Baraisa speaks of a case where the one from whom the cloak was taken was silent at first and then protested? Perhaps it refers to a case where e remained silent, and that is why the burden of proof is upon him.

The answer is that if he remained silent, his silence is taken as an dmission, and therefore even if he were to furnish proof (e.g. witnesses) hat the cloak is his, the court would not rule in his favor. An admission arries more weight than the testimony of witnesses, as expressed by the 'almudic formula, הוֹדָאַת בַּעַל דִּין כְּמֵאָה עֵדִים דָּמֵי, *Admission on the part of litigant is equivalent to* [the testimony of] *a hundred witnesses*.

However, where he was silent at first and then protested, even if this s regarded as an admission, it is possible to counter it with witnesses. 'or in such a case the testimony of witnesses does not supersede the dmission; rather, it proves that there never was an admission. The estimony indicates that he was silent not because the cloak belonged to he other but because he relied upon the judges' intervention ("the abbis see what he is doing") (*Pnei Yehoshua* in the name of *Bach*). According to *Ran's* approach (see note 18), a temporary silence is not aken as a definite admission in the first place. Therefore, the testimony of witnesses is certainly effective against it.]

22. You said that you picked up the cloak first and then your opponent grabbed on to it claiming it as his.

23. An apparent difficulty: The Gemara implies that if the one who is not holding the cloak would have claimed that the other party *snatched* it from him, he would be believed. This contradicts the principle that if an article is in the possession of someone, the court presumes that he owns it and the previous owner cannot claim that it was stolen.

The answer is that this principle is based on the assumption that a person would not have something in his possession unless he acquired it lawfully. In this case, however, where both parties were fighting over the cloak, each one claiming it as his, this assumption is not valid, for it is very possible that one party unlawfully snatched it from the other (*Rosh* §11, *Tosafos;* cf. *Rambam;* see *Pnei Yehoshua*).

24. Literally: clinging. One was holding the entire cloak and the other was fighting with him and hanging onto the cloak (*Rambam Hil. To'ein V'nitan* 9:11; see *Tur Choshen Mishpat* 138).

25. Generally, Sumchos is more inclined to rule that disputed property should be divided than the Rabbis are. This is evidenced by Sumchos' ruling that in the case of our Mishnah the cloak is divided between the disputants without their having to take an oath. According to the present interpretation of the Baraisa, it teaches that in this case, however, Sumchos concedes that the cloak is not divided (even if the one trying to seize it were to take an oath), because it is not regarded as property whose ownership is in doubt. Sumchos disagrees with the Rabbis only in clear cases of doubt such as that recorded in the Mishnah, *Bava Kamma* 46a, where after a cow was gored, a newborn calf was found dead at its side and it is not known whether the calf was born before or after the goring [or the case of our Mishnah, where two litigants enter the court holding on to a cloak] (*Rashi;* see *Nachalas Moshe*).

26. The Mishnah, *Kiddushin* 28b, states: אֲמִירָתוֹ לַגָּבוֹהַּ כִּמְסִירָתוֹ לַהֶדְיוֹט, *One's declaration* [consecrating an object] *to the holy domain is* [as effective a transaction] *as one's handing* [it] *over to a private person*. This means that it is possible to transfer one's property to the Temple's ownership merely by saying, "This article is consecrated," or some similar formula.

## גמרא

ואלא הא [א] דאמר רב נחמן משביעין אותו שבועת היסת נימא מיגו דחשיד אממונא חשיד אשבועתא ותו הא [ב] דתני רבי חייא שניהם נשבעין ונוטלין מבעה"ב נימא מיגו דחשיד אממונא חשיד אשבועתא ותו הא [ג] דאמר רב ששת [א] שלש שבועות משביעין אותו שבועה שלא פשעתי בה שבועה שלא שלחתי בה יד שבועה שאינה ברשותי נימא מיגו דחשיד אממונא חשיד אשבועתא אלא לא אמרינן מיגו דחשיד אממונא חשיד אשבועתא אביי אמר חיישינן שמא מלוה ישנה יש לו עליו אי הכי נשקול בלא שבועה [ב] אלא חיישינן שמא ספק מלוה ישנה יש לו עליו ולאו אמרינן תפים ממונא מספיקא משתבע נמי מספק אמר רב ששת בריה דרב אידי פרשי אינשי מספק שבועה ולא פרשי מספק ממונא מאי טעמא ממון איתיה בחזרה שבועה ליתיה בחזרה: בעי ר' זירא תקפה אחד בפנינו מהו היכי דמי אי דשתיק אודויי אודי ליה ואי דקא צווח מאי הוה ליה למעבד לא צריכא דשתיק מעיקרא והדר צווח מאי מדאשתיק אודויי אודי ליה או דלמא כיון דקא צווח השתא איגלאי מילתא דהאי דשתיק מעיקרא סבר הא קא חזו ליה רבנן אמר רב נחמן ת"ש [ג] בד"א ששניהם אדוקין בה אבל היתה טלית יוצאת מתחת ידו של אחד מהן המוציא מחבירו עליו הראיה היכי דמי אי נימא כדקתני פשיטא [א] אלא שתקפה אחד בפנינו לא הכא במאי עסקינן [ד] כגון דאתו לקמן כדתפיסו לה תרוייהו ואמרינן להו זילו פלוגו ונפקו והדר אתו כי תפים לה חד מינייהו האי אמר אודויי אודי לי והאי אמר בדמי אגרתי ניהליה דאמרינן ליה עד השתא חשדת ליה בגזלן והשתא מוגרת ליה בלא סהדי ואיבעית אימא כדקתני דאתו לקמן כי תפים לה חד מינייהו ואידך מסרך בה סרוכי ואפילו [ד] לסומכוס דאמר ממון המוטל בספק חולקין בלא שבועה מודה סומכוס [ה] דסרכא לאו כלום היא אם תמצי לומר תקפה אחד בפנינו מוציאין אותה מידו הקדישה אינה מקודשת אם תמצי לומר תקפה אחד בפנינו [ו] אין מוציאין אותה מידו הקדישה בלא תקפה מהו כיון [ה] דאמר מר [ז] אמירתו לגבוה כמסירתו להדיוט דמי כמאן דתקפה דמי או דלמא השתא מיהא הא לא תקפה וכתיב [א] ואיש כי יקדיש את ביתו קדש וגו' [ו] מה ביתו ברשותו [ח] אף כל ברשותו לאפוקי האי דלא ברשותו ת"ש דההיא

## רש"י

משביעין אותו. לשאינו מודה במקלת: נימא מיגו. דמעיז פניו לכפור הכל לאו לאשתמוטי בעי וחשוד אשבועה: שניהם נשבעים. גבי חנוני על פנקסו וקשה לי אמאי שבקה למתני' דשבועות ומייתי לה מברייתא: נימא מיגו. כיון דחד מינייהו ודאי חשיד אממונא: שלש שבועות משביעין אותו. לשומר חנם שטוען נגנבה: שלא שלחתי בה יד. לעשות מלאכתי דאי שלח בה יד הוי גזלן עליה ומיחייב באונסיה ואפילו נאנסה ברשותיה היא קיימא ודידיה היא: נימא. גבי שבועה שאינה ברשותי מיגו דחשיד אממונא שמא ברשותיה הוא וכופר בה חשיד נמי אשבועתא: אביי אמר. טעמא דמתני' לאו כדר' יוחנן דאי הוה חשיד לן אהולך ותוקף בטלית חבירו חנם הוה לן חשוד אשבועה אלא חיישינן שמא מלוה ישנה יש לו עליו על זה ומכיר בו ששכחה ויכפור בו והולך ותוקף בטליתו ונשבע שיש לו בה דמי חליה וטלית זו שלו דהא אפי' גלימא דעל כתפיה שעביד ליה: אי הכי. אמאי רמו עליה שבועה כיון דאי לא הוי עליה לא הוי תפים בה: נשקלה בלא שבועה. לגבות מלוה שלו: ולא פרשי מספק ממונא. אבל מודאי דממונא פרשי ומאן דלא פריש חשיד נמי אשבועתא: תקפה אחד. הוציאה מיד חבירו בחזקה והרי כולה בידו קודם שנשבעו: יוצאה מתחת ידו של אחד מהם. יוצאה (לבדו) לפני ב"ד מתחת יד האחד שהוא לבדו אחוז בה ולא חבירו: הראיה. בעדים: כדקתני. שזה לבדו אחוז בה ובא: אלא לאו כו'. וכדאוקמינן דשתיק ולבסוף צווח: אפי' לסומכוס כו'. כלומר ואליבא דסומכוס דמיקל בחלוקה ולא מצריך אפי' שבועה איצטריך לאשמועינן דבכה"ג מודי סומכוס דאפי' בשבועה לא שקיל דהא לאו ממון המוטל בספק הוא: דסרכא לאו כלום היא. ואין שור שחוט לפניך ולא דמי לנמלא עוברה בלדה (ב"ק דף מו.): ואת"ל. בשאילתנו לפשוט דמוליאין אותה מידו ויחלוקו: הקדישה. בלא תקפה: אינה מקודשת. דלא אלים הקדישה מתקפה: הא לא תקפה. ואין יכול להקדישה: מסותא

## תוספות

**אלא** הא דאמר רב נחמן. תימה הא הכא נמי משתמיט וי"ל דרב נחמן מחייב שבועת היסת אפי' היכא שתובעו ואמר זה החפץ שהוא בידך שלי הוא דלא שייך אישתמוטי וכן פי' רב האי גאון שמשביעין שבועת היסת אקרקעות אע"ג דלא שייך בהו אישתמוטי וקשה דבפ' שבועת הדיינים (דף מ: ושם ד"ה אישתמוטי) משמע דלא מחייב שבועת היסת אלא משום אישתמוטי דקא פריך אדרבה אין אדם מעיז ומשני דמשתמיט וי"ל כיון דבשאינו בעין משתמיט אף כשהוא בעין לא פלוג רבנן אי נמי אקושיא דר' חייא סמיך: **דתני** ר' חייא. הקשה רש"י אמאי לא מייתי מתני' דשבועות וי"ל דע"י ר' חייא שנאה רבי כדמוכח התם (דף מז:):

**שבועה** שלא שלחתי בה יד. פרש"י דאם שלח בה יד אפילו נאנסה חייב ואף על פי דמשהחזירה פטור כדקתני בהמפקיד (לקמן דף [ז] לד) מ"מ שמא נאנסה קודם שהחזירה אבל קשה משלהי האומנין (לקמן דף פג.) דקאמר ונשבר או נשבה אין רואה הא יש רואה יביא ראיה ויפטר והא שמא שלח בה יד וי"ל שיפטר משבועה שנאנסה אך ישבע שלא שלח בה יד אי נמי שלא שלחתי בה יד אינו נשבע אלא ע"י גלגול שבועה שלא פשעתי בה וכשיש רואה שנאנסה פטור לגמרי ור"ת מפרש אפי' ע"י גלגול לא ישבע היכא שהיא מתה בפנינו דאין מגלגלין אלא בדבר הדומה דלמה י"ל ששלח בו יד דדוקא בשותפין שחלקו ונתחייב שבועה ממקום אחר מגלגלין משום דמורי היתרא ושבועה שלא שלחתי בה יד מפרש ר"ת שלא אכלה דאינו בכלל שבועה שלא פשע בה ושאינה ברשותו:

**ספק** מלוה ישנה יש לו עליו. והיא דמשביעין אותו ג' שבועות ודשניהם נשבעין ונוטלין נמי חיישינן שמא מלוה ישנה יש לו עליו ולכך אין לפוטרו בלא שבועה וגם לא יטול בלא שבועה אבל בגזלן ודאי וכופר בפקדון אין להכשיר מטעם שמא ספק מלוה ישנה יש לו עליו:

**ממון** אפשר בחזרה. אם לא יזכור יחזיר ולא יעכבנו מספק אבל אין לפרש אם יזכור שאינו חייב לו יחזיר אבל אם לא יזכור יעכבנו אע"פ שיודע שלא יזכור עוד דא"כ גם מספק שבועה לא יפרוש:

**אגרת** ליה בלא סהדי. ואינו נאמן במיגו דאי בעי אמר תקפה ממני דמיגו במקום עדים הוא:

**הקדישה** בלא תקפה מהו. ומיירי נמי כגון ששתק בשעה שהקדיש ולבסוף כששאלה הגזבר צווח ומבעיא ליה כיון דאמירתו לגבוה כו' הוה הקדש כתקפה דכיון ששתק אודויי אודי ליה והוה הקדש ולא דמי לגזל ולא נתייאשו הבעלים דשניהם אין יכולין להקדיש זה לפי שאינו שלו וזה לפי שאינו ברשותו דכיון דאודי ליה הוי כפקדון שיש לו ביד אחרים דיכול להקדיש כדמוכח בהמוכר את הספינה (ב"ב דף פח.) גבי ההוא דאייתי קרי כו' דאי לא קיי"ל דמייהו הוי קדושות או דלמא הקדש לא הוי כתקיפה דלמה יצווח בשביל דבריו ומייתי מההיא מסותא דהקדיש חד ושתק אידך ומסקנא דלא הוי הקדש אלמא שתיקתו אינו כהודאה: [ט] **והא** הכא דכי תקפה כהן כו'. נראה דהכי מיבעי ליה במסותא כיון דמקרקעי היא והוה דינא כל דאלים גבר וכיון דאם תקפה האחד והקדישה כשהיא בידו מסתמא תו לא פקע אפי' חזר חבירו ותקפה ממנו כי הקדישה בלא תקפה נמי הוי הקדש או דלמא כיון דאפי' גבר האחד אם יכול השני לחזור ולתוקפה ממנו זוכה ה"ה הקדיש בלא תקפה לא יחול הקדש כלל כיון דחבירו אם תקפה היה זוכה דלא אלים הקדש מתקיפה והשתא אייתי והא הכא אם תקפה

## עין משפט נר מצוה

כח א מיי' פ"ו מהל' שאלה ופקדון הלכה א סמג עשין פח טוש"ע ח"מ סי' (רלו סעיף א וסי') רלה סעיף ב:

כט ב טוש"ע ח"מ סי' לב סעיף ג:

ל ג ד מיי' פ"ט מהל' טוען ונטען הלכה יג ועי' בהשגות וכמ"מ טור ש"ע ח"מ סי' קלח סעי' ח:

לא ה מיי' שם הל' יב טוש"ע שם סעיף ה:

לב ו מיי' שם הל' יא טוש"ע שם סעיף ז:

לג ז מיי' פ"ט מהלכות מכירה הל' א סמג עשין פב טוש"ע י"ד סי' רנח סעיף יג:

לד ח מיי' פ"ו מהל' ערכין הל' כב סמג עשין קלב טוש"ע שם סעיף ז:

## רבינו חננאל

והא דאמר רב נחמן ג' שבועות משביעין אותו כו' הוא בפ' הגוזל קמא. ואסקי' פרשי אינשי מספק שבועה ולא פרשי מספק ממונא מאי טעמא ממון אפשר בחזרה. שבוע' לא אפשר בחזרה. **בעי** ר' זירא תקפה א' בפנינו מהו כו' ת"ש בד"א בששניהם אדוקין בה אבל אם היה יוצא מתחת ידי אחד המע"ה. ופשיטנא הכא במאי עסקינן דאתו לקמן שניהן אדוקין בה ואמרי' להו דינא הוא דפלגיתו לה ואזלו והדרי כי תפיס לה חד מנהון וטעין דאודי לי ואמר לי שקלא דידך היא. ואידך טעין אוגרתה ליה דאמרי' ליה עד השתא חשדת ליה בגזלן וטענת כולה דידי הוא ואתא הוא ותפיס בהדאי וטעין בה והשתא אמרת אוגרתה ליה בלא סהדי שקרא אנת. אי בעית תימא לעולם דאתו לקמן כי תפיס לה חד ואידך מסרך סרוכי דאמרי' אפילו סומכוס דאמר ממון המוטל בספק חולקין בלא שבועה מודה סומכוס דסרכא לאו כלום היא. אם תמצא לומר תקפה א' בפנינו מוציאין אותו מידו הקדישה אינה מקודשת. ואם תמצא לומר אין מוציאין אותה מידו הקדישה מקודשת. הקדישה בלא תקפה מהו מי אמרי' כיון דאמר מר אמירתו לגבוה כמסירתו להדיוט דמי כמאן דתקפה דמי או דלמא השתא מיהא הא לא תקפה. ת"ש דההיא

## תורה אור השלם

...ואיש כי יקדש את ...ו קדש ליי והעריכו ...הן בין טוב ובין רע ...שר יעריך אתו הכהן כן יקום: [ויקרא כז, יד]

## הגהות הגר"א

גמ' אלא שתקפה ...בפנינו. נ"ב וכה"ג ...בשמיק לא מהני ראיה. ...ה"א וטור. (ועמ"ש ...בח"מ סי' קל"ח ...ט"ו דלא כמ"ש ...ך שם בדעת הטור):

## מסורת הש"ס

...ועות מ: [לעיל ה.], ...ועות מז:, ג) בבא ...קז:, עיין שם, ...גיל ב: וש"נ], ...ודה זרה סג., בבא ...קלג:, קדושין כח:, ...כט:, תמורה כט:, ...פתא קידושין פרק א', ...תא בבא קמא פרק ...תוספתא ערכין פרק ...) ע"ז סג., [ב"ק סח: ...סט:, חולין קלט., ...ה ע., כט:, ערכין ...ז) [אולי צ"ל דף מ: ...ו בפלוגתא של ר' ...אל ור"ע], ח) [שייך ...לע"ב].

## ליקוטי רש"י

...בועת היסת. שבועה ...סימו חכמים לכך ...ימו להודות. וטעמא ...רש בשבועות (דף מ:) ...קה אין אדם טוען אא"כ ...לו בידו [לעיל ה.]. לשון ...לא ששמו חכמים עליו ...עה כמו (שמואל א כו) ...ה' הסיתך בי [שבועות ...]. שניהם נשבעין ...טלין מבעל הבית. ...מר ליה פועלים לא ...ימנו לי בשבועה את ...מנתינהו דלא אמרת לי ...הדי הב להו וכן פועלין ...רי ליה לא מהימן לן ...ני בשבועה [שבועות ...:]. שלא פשעתי. ...מירתו כשנגנבה דאי ...ע בה חייב דכתיב על כל ...ר פשע. שלא שלחתי ...יד. ליהנות בה קודם ...ן דאם שלח בה יד קמה ...ברשותיה דנעשה גזלן ...יה ומחייב באונסין ...ש בגניבה ואבידה [ב"ק ...:]. אמירתו לגבוה ...מסירתו להדיוט. ...דכתיב (ויקרא ס) ואיש ...יקדיש וגו' (דברים כג) ...לא שפתיך תשמור וגו' ...שב"ם ב"ב קלג:]. ולא מלי ...יהדר כאילו מסרתו ...להדיוט [תמורה כט:].

The Gemara therefore explains:

אֶלָּא חָיְישִׁינָן שֶׁמָּא סָפֵק מִלְוֶה יְשָׁנָה יֵשׁ לוֹ עָלָיו – **Rather, we are concerned for the possibility that [one litigant] has a *questionable* old loan against [the cloak's owner].**[11] A person certainly has no right to forcibly collect a questionable debt; therefore, we impose an oath upon him so that he should halt his collection of that debt.

The Gemara asks:

וְלֹא אָמְרִינַן תָּפִיס מָמוֹנָא מִסְפֵּיקָא מִשְׁתַּבַּע נַמִּי מִסָּפֵק – **But do we not say that one who will grab money based on** a claim about which he is himself in **doubt will also swear based on** that **doubt?** He is aware that the money might not be owed to him, yet he is willing to take it forcibly and thereby risk being guilty of theft. Will he not, by the same token, be willing to risk being guilty of swearing falsely?[12]

The Gemara answers:

אָמַר רַב שֵׁשֶׁת בְּרֵיהּ דְּרַב אִידִי – **Rav Sheishess the son of Rav Iddi said:** פָּרְשֵׁי אִינָשֵׁי מִסְּפֵק שְׁבוּעָה וְלֹא פָּרְשֵׁי מִסְּפֵק מָמוֹנָא – There are **people** who **will withdraw from** taking **a doubtful oath but will not withdraw from** taking **doubtful money.** מַאי טַעְמָא – **What is the reason** for this difference in attitude? מָמוֹן אִיתֵיהּ בַּחֲזָרָה – **Money** taken improperly **can be returned,** שְׁבוּעָה לֵיתֵיהּ בַּחֲזָרָה – but **an oath** once uttered **cannot be recalled.**[13]

The Gemara discusses a development of our Mishnah's case where two litigants come before the court holding on to a cloak: בָּעֵי ר׳ זֵירָא – **R' Zeira asked:** תְּקָפָה אֶחָד בְּפָנֵינוּ – If **one** of them **snatched [the cloak]** from the other **before us** [the judges], so that only he is holding it, מַהוּ – **what is [the law]?** Do we allow him to keep the whole cloak, or do we take it from him for division between the litigants?[14]

The Gemara asks why this is a question:

הֵיכִי דָּמֵי – **What are the circumstances** in which this would be a question? אִי דְּשָׁתִיק – **If he** [the one from whom the cloak was taken] **was silent,** i.e. he did not protest, אוֹדוּיֵי אוֹדֵי לֵיהּ – **he has,** in effect, **admitted to [the other]** that the cloak is his.[15] וְאִי דְּקָא צָוַוח – **And if he exclaimed** in protest, מַאי הֲוָה לֵיהּ לְמֶעֱבַד – **what** more **should he have done?**[16] Thus, either way – whether he was silent or whether he protested – the answer to R' Zeira's inquiry is obvious. – ? –

The Gemara answers:

לֹא – R' Zeira's inquiry is **not** redundant. צְרִיכָא דְּשָׁתִיק מֵעִיקָּרָא וְהָדַר צָוַוח – **It is warranted** in a case **where he** [the one from whom the cloak was taken] **was silent** at first **and then he exclaimed** in protest.[17] מַאי – **What** is the law in such a case? מִדְּאִשְׁתִּיק אוֹדוּיֵי אוֹדֵי לֵיהּ – Do we say that **since he was silent** when the cloak was taken from him **he has admitted to [the other]** that the cloak is his? אוֹ דִּלְמָא כֵּיוָן דְּקָא צָוַוח הַשְׁתָּא – **Or perhaps** we say that **since now he is exclaiming** in protest, אִיגַּלַּאי מִילְּתָא דְּהַאי דִּשְׁתִיק מֵעִיקָּרָא סָבַר – **it is evident that [the reason] he was silent in the first place is that he thought:** הָא קָא חָזוּ לֵיהּ רַבָּנָן – **But the rabbis see** what **[my opponent]** is doing, so there is no need for me to protest![18]

The Gemara attempts to answer this inquiry:

NOTES

11. I.e. the "lender" himself is unsure whether the cloak's owner really owes him any money.

12. [We are now discussing the view of Abaye, who asserts that a person suspect in monetary matters is also suspect in regard to swearing falsely.]

13. But a person who is suspect to take money to which he *certainly* has no claim is suspect to swear falsely as well, according to Abaye (*Rashi*).

The Gemara above adduced three rulings to prove that a person suspect in monetary matters is *not* suspect in regard to swearing falsely. There, too, Abaye will explain that our concern is not that the defendant is an outright thief, but rather that he seeks to take the money in collection of a questionable debt that the plaintiff has forgotten about. Nevertheless, a convicted thief [גַּזְלָן] or a custodian who has clearly denied owing a deposit [כּוֹפֵר בְּפִקָּדוֹן] is disqualified from testifying or swearing. Though it is possible in those cases, too, that the convicted person was only trying to collect a forgotten debt, that *possibility* cannot alter the *definite* status of disqualification that emerges from his conviction as a thief. The possibility of a forgotten debt only serves to allow a mere *suspect* to swear, since the suspect has not yet been legally *disqualified* from swearing, but only suspected of a willingness to swear falsely (see *Ramban* and *Ri Migash* cited in *Shitah Mekubetzes*).

14. He snatched the cloak before they took the oath ["not less than half of it is mine" – see Mishnah 2a] (*Rashi*). [After the oath is taken, each party definitely owns his half of the cloak, and thus snatching it from him is blatant theft (based on *Ran,* see below, note 18; cf. *Ketzos HaChoshen* 138:2).]

15. Silence on the part of a litigant, where a protest would have been expected, is regarded as an admission that the other party's claim is valid. This is expressed by the Talmudic formula, שְׁתִיקָה כְּהוֹדָאָה, *silence is tantamount to admission* (see below, 37b).

16. [He is not expected to resist physically in court, where he can rely upon the judges to correct any wrongdoing.]

17. That is, he was silent while the cloak was being tugged from him, and he protested as soon as it left his hands (*Ritva;* see *Chasam Sofer*).

Alternatively: He remained silent even after the cloak left his hands; he protested when he was about to leave the court [and realized that the judges were not going to remove the cloak from the one who had snatched it] (*Rashba, Nimukei Yosef*).

18. Many Rishonim (*Rosh, Tosafos* et al.) understand the Gemara to be asking whether this temporary silence should be construed as an admission or not.

*Ran,* however, explains the inquiry as follows: According to both sides, it is uncertain whether silence followed by a protest is considered an admission. Rather, the inquiry is based on the question of how the ownership of the disputed cloak is viewed, as follows:

**The role of legal possession in deciding ownership:** In cases of doubtful ownership that are *created* by the disputant's claims (i.e. were it not for their claims, the court would not consider the object's ownership to be in question), it is assumed that the disputed object *definitely* belongs to the one who has it in his possession. But where the court itself is in doubt as to the ownership of an object (e.g. our case, where two people enter the court holding on to a cloak) there are two possible approaches:

(1) Even in such cases, the court assumes that the object *definitely* belongs to whoever is in possession of it.

(2) In such cases, the possession of the object plays no role in the deciding of its ownership. The court rules that the object remains with the one who has it in his possession, not on the assumption that it *definitely* belongs to him, but because it *possibly* belongs to him and מִסְפֵּיקָא לֹא מַפְּקִינָן מָמוֹנָא, *we do not remove property* [from someone's possession] *out of doubt.*

According to either of these approaches, if the party that is not in possession of the object were to seize it, and the possessor reacts by protesting, the object would have to be returned. The difference between the approaches involves a case where the other party seized the object from the possessor, and the possessor was silent at first and then protested. According to the first approach, since it is assumed that the object *definitely* belongs to the possessor, the court would remove the object from the one who seized it (even though the possessor's temporary silence can possibly be construed as an admission). According to the second approach, the court would *not* remove the disputed object from the one who seized it. Since the court's original ruling was not based on a definite assumption, and now the possessor has possibly admitted that the object is not his, the court leaves the object with the one that seized it.

Thus, the two sides of the Gemara's inquiry – which involves the case where one snatches the cloak from the other who is silent at first and then protests – are as follows:

(1) The court views each litigant as *definitely* owning the half of the cloak that is in his legal possession. (The Gemara, 3a, expresses it thus: אֲנַן סָהֲדֵי דְּמַאי דְּתָפִיס הַאי דִּידֵיהּ הוּא וּמַאי דְּתָפִיס הַאי דִּידֵיהּ הוּא, *We are witnesses*

ואלא הא [א] דאמר רב נחמן משביעין אותו שבועת היסת נימא מיגו דחשיד אממונא חשיד אשבועתא ותו הא [ב] דתני רבי חייא שניהם נשבעין ונוטלין מבעה"ב נימא מיגו דחשיד אממונא חשיד אשבועתא ותו הא [ג] דאמר רב ששת [א] שלש שבועות משביעין אותו שבועה שלא פשעתי בה שבועה שלא שלחתי בה יד שבועה שאינה ברשותי נימא מיגו דחשיד אממונא חשיד אשבועתא אלא לא אמרינן מיגו דחשיד אממונא חשיד אשבועתא אביי אמר חיישינן שמא מלוה ישנה יש לו עליו אי הכי נשקול בלא שבועה [ב] אלא חיישינן שמא ספק מלוה ישנה יש לו עליו ולאו אמרינן תפיס ממונא מספיקא משתבע נמי מספק אמר רב ששת בריה דרב אידי אינשי פרשי מספק שבועה ולא פרשי מספק ממונא מאי טעמא ממון איתיה בחזרה שבועה ליתיה בחזרה: בעי ר' זירא תקפה אחד בפנינו מהו היכי דמי אי דשתיק אודויי אודי ליה ואי דקא צווח מאי הוה ליה למעבד לא צריכא דשתיק מעיקרא והדר צווח מאי מדאשתיק אודויי אודי ליה או דלמא כיון דקא צווח השתא איגלאי מילתא דהאי דשתיק מעיקרא סבר הא קא חזו ליה רבנן אמר רב נחמן ת"ש [ג] בד"א ששניהם אדוקין בה אבל היתה טלית יוצאת מתחת ידו של אחד מהן המוציא מחבירו עליו הראיה היכי דמי אי נימא כדקתני פשיטא [א] אלא שתקפה אחד בפנינו לא הכא במאי עסקינן [ד] כגון דאתו לקמן כדתפיסו לה תרוייהו ואמרינן להו זילו פלוגו ונפקו והדר אתו כי תפיס לה חד מינייהו האי אמר אודויי אודי לי והאי אמר בדמי אגרתי ניהליה דאמרינן ליה עד השתא חשדת ליה בגזלן והשתא מוגרת ליה בלא סהדי ואיבעית אימא כדקתני דאתו לקמן כי תפיס לה חד מינייהו ואידך מסרך בה סרוכי ואפילו [ד] לסומכוס דאמר ממון המוטל בספק חולקין בלא שבועה מודה סומכוס [ה] דסרכא לאו כלום היא אם תמצי לומר תקפה אחד בפנינו מוציאין אותה מידו הקדישה אינה מקודשת אם תמצי לומר תקפה אחד בפנינו [ו] אין מוציאין אותה מידו הקדישה בלא תקפה מהו כיון [ה] דאמר מר [ז] אמירתו לגבוה כמסירתו להדיוט דמי כמאן דתקפה דמי או דלמא השתא מיהא הא לא תקפה וכתיב [א] ואיש כי יקדיש את ביתו קדש וגו' [ו] מה ביתו ברשותו [ח] אף כל ברשותו לאפוקי האי דלא ברשותו ת"ש דההיא

**רש"י**

משביעין אותו. לשאינו מודה במקלת: נימא מיגו. דמעיז פניו לכפור הכל לאו לאשתמוטי בעי וחשוד אשבועה: שניהם נשבעים. גבי חנוני על פנקסו וקשה לי אמאי שבקה למתני' דשבועות ומייתי לה מברייתא: נימא מיגו. כיון דחד מינייהו ודאי חשיד אממונא: שלש שבועות משביעין אותו. לשומר חנם שטוען נגנבה: שלא שלחתי בה יד. לעשות מלאכתי דאי שלח בה יד הוי גזלן עליה ומיחייב באונסיה ואפילו נאנסה ברשותיה היא קיימא ודידיה היא: נימא. גבי שבועה שאינה ברשותי מיגו דחשיד אממונא שמא ברשותיה הוא וכופר בה חשיד נמי אשבועתא: אביי אמר. טעמא דמתני' לאו כדר' יוחנן דאי הוה חשיד לן אהולך ותוקף בטלית חבירו חנם הוה לן חשוד אשבועה אלא חיישינן שמא מלוה ישנה יש לו עליו על זה ומכיר בו ששכחה ויכפור בו והולך ותוקף בטליתו ונשבע שיש לו בה דמי חליה וטלית זו שלו דהא אפי' גלימא דעל כתפיה שעביד ליה: אי הכי. אמאי רמו עליה שבועה כיון דאי לא הוי עליה לא הוי תפיס בה: נשקלה בלא שבועה. לגבות מלוה שלו: ולא פרשי מספק ממונא. אבל מודאי דממונא פרשי ומאן דלא פריש חשיד נמי אשבועתא: תקפה אחד. הוציאה מיד חבירו בחזקה והרי כולה בידו קודם שנשבעו: יוצאה מתחת ידו של אחד מהם. יוצאה (לבדו) לפני ב"ד מתחת יד האחד שהוא לבדו אחוז בה ולא חבירו: הראיה. בעדים: כדקתני. שזה לבדו אחוז בה וכו': אלא לאו כו'. וכדאוקמינן דשתיק ולבסוף צווח: אפי' לסומכוס כו'. כלומר ואליבא דסומכוס דמיקל בחלוקה ולא מצריך אפי' שבועה איצטריך לאשמועינן דבכה"ג מודי סומכוס דאפי' בשבועה לא שקיל דהא לאו ממון המוטל בספק הוא: דסרכא לאו כלום היא. ואין שור שחוט לפניך ולא דמי לנמצא עוברה בלדה (ב"ק דף מו.): ואת"ל. בשאילתנו לפשוט דמוליאין אותה מידו ויחלוקו: הקדישה. בלא תקפה: אינה מקודשת. דלא אלים הקדישה מתקפה: הא לא תקפה. ואין יכול להקדישה:

**תוספות**

**אלא** הא דאמר רב נחמן. תימה הא הכא נמי משתמיט וי"ל דרב נחמן מחייב שבועת היסת אפי' היכא שתובעו ואמר זה החפץ שהוא בידך שלי הוא דלא שייך אישתמוטי וכן פי' רב האי גאון שמשביעין שבועת היסת אקרקעות אע"ג דלא שייך בהו אישתמוטי וקשה דבפ' שבועת הדיינים (דף מ: ושם ד"ה אישתמוטי) משמע דלא מחייב שבועת היסת אלא משום אישתמוטי דקא פריך אדרבה אין אדם מעיז ומשני דמשתמיט וי"ל כיון דבשאינו בעין משתמיט אף כשהוא בעין לא פלוג רבנן אי נמי אקושיא דר' חייא סמיך: **דתני** ר' חייא. הקשה רש"י אמאי לא מייתי מתני' דשבועות וי"ל דע"י ר' חייא שנאה רבי כדמוכח התם (דף מז:):

**שבועה** שלא שלחתי בה יד. פרש"י דאם שלח בה יד אפילו נאנסה חייב ואף על פי דמשהחזירה פטור כדקתני בהמפקיד (לקמן דף לד) מ"מ שמא נאנסה קודם שהחזירה אבל קשה מאלהי האומנין (לקמן דף פג.) דקאמר ונשבר או נשבה אין רואה הא יש רואה יביא ראיה ויפטר והא שמא שלח בה יד וי"ל שיפטר משבועה שנאנסה אך ישבע שלא שלח בה יד אי נמי שלא שלחתי בה יד אינו נשבע אלא ע"י גלגול שבועה שלא פשעתי בה וכשיש רואה שנאנסה פטור לגמרי ור"ת מפרש אפי' ע"י גלגול לא ישבע היכא שהיא מתה בפנינו דאין מגלגלין אלא בדבר הדומה דלמה י"ל ששלח בו יד דדוקא בשותפין שחלקו ונתחייב שבועה ממקום אחר מגלגלין משום דמורי היתרא ושבועה שלא שלחתי בה יד מפרש ר"ת שלא אכלה דאינו בכלל שבועה שלא פשע בה ושאינה ברשותו:

**ספק** מלוה ישנה יש לו עליו. והיא דמשביעין אותו ג' שבועות ודשניהם נשבעין ונוטלין נמי חיישינן שמא מלוה ישנה יש לו עליו ולכך אין לפוטרו בלא שבועה וגם לא יטול בלא שבועה אבל בגזלן ודאי וכופר בפקדון אין להכשיר מטעם שמא ספק מלוה ישנה יש לו עליו:

**ממון** אפשר בחזרה. אם לא יזכור יחזיר ולא יעכבנו מספק אבל אין לפרש אם יזכור שאינו חייב לו יחזיר אבל אם לא יזכור יעכבנו אע"פ שיודע שלא יזכור עוד דא"כ גם מספק שבועה לא יפרוש:

**אגרת** ליה בלא סהדי. ואינו נאמן במיגו דאי בעי אמר תקפה ממני דמיגו במקום עדים הוא:

**הקדישה** בלא תקפה מהו. ומיירי נמי כגון ששתק בשעה שהקדיש ולבסוף כששאלה הגזבר צווח ומבעיא ליה כיון דאמירתו לגבוה כו' הוה הקדש כתקפה דכיון ששתק אודויי אודי ליה והוה הקדש ולא דמי לגזל ולא נתייאשו הבעלים דשניהם אין יכולין להקדיש זה לפי שאינו שלו וזה לפי שאינו ברשותו דכיון דאודי ליה הוי כפקדון שיש לו ביד אחרים דיכול להקדיש כדמוכח בהמוכר את הספינה (ב"ב דף פח.) גבי ההוא דאייתי קרי כו' דאי לא קיי"ל דמייתו הוי קדושות או דלמא הקדש לא הוי כתקיפה דלמה יצווח בשביל דבריו ומייתי מההיא מסותא דהקדיש חד ושתק אידך ומסקנא דלא הוי הקדש אלמא שתיקתו אינו כהודאה: [ט] **והא** הכא דכי תקפה כהן כו'. נראה דהכי מיבעי ליה במסותא כיון דמקרקעי היא והוה דינא כל דאלים גבר וכיון דאם תקפה האחד והקדישה כשהיא בידו מסתמא תו לא פקע אפי' חזר חבירו ותקפה ממנו כי הקדישה בלא תקפה נמי הוי הקדש או דלמא כיון דאפי' גבר האחד אם יכול השני לחזור ולתוקפה ממנו זוכה ה"ה הקדיש בלא תקפה לא יחול הקדש כלל כיון דלחבירו אם תקפה היה זוכה דלא אלים הקדש מתקיפה והשתא אייתי והא הכא אם תקפה

מסותא

---

**עין משפט נר מצוה**

כח א מיי' פ"ו מהל' שאלה ופקדון הלכה א סמג עשין פח טוש"ע ח"מ סי' (רצו סעיף ח וסי') רצה סעיף ג:

כט ב טוש"ע ח"מ סי' לב סעיף ג:

ל ג ד מיי' פ"ט מהל' טוען ונטען הלכה יג ועי' בהשגות ובמ"מ טור ש"ע ח"מ סי' קלח סעי' ח:

לא ה מיי' שם הל' יב טוש"ע שם סעיף ה:

לב ו מיי' שם הל' יא טוש"ע שם סעיף ז:

לג ז מיי' פ"ט מהלכות מכירה הל' א סמג עשין פב טוש"ע י"ד סי' רנח סעיף יג:

לד ח מיי' פ"ו מהל' ערכין הל' כב סמג עשין קלב טוש"ע שם סעיף ז:

**רבינו חננאל**

והא דאמר רב נחמן ג' שבועות משביעין אותו כו' הוא בפ' הגוזל קמא. ואסקי' פרשי אינשי מספק שבועה ולא פרשי מספק ממונא מאי טעמא ממון אפשר בחזרה. שבוע' לא אפשר בחזרה. בעי ר' זירא תקפה א' בפנינו מהו כו' ת"ש בד"א בששניהם אדוקין בה אבל אם היה יוצא מתחת ידי אחד המע"ה. ופשיטנא הכא במאי עסקינן דאתו לקמן שניהן אדוקין בה ואמרי' להו דינא הוא דפלגיתו לה ואזלו והדרי כי תפיס לה חד מנהון וטעין דאודי לי ואמר לי שקלא דידך היא. ואידך טעין אוגרתה ליה דאמרי' ליה עד השתא חשדת ליה בגזלן וטענת כולה דידי הוא ואתא הוא ותפיס בהדאי וטעין בה והשתא אמרת אוגרתה ליה בלא סהדי שקרא אנת. אי בעית תימא לעולם דאתו לקמן כי תפיס לה חד ואידך מסרך סרוכי דאמרי' אפילו סומכוס דאמר ממון המוטל בספק חולקין בלא שבועה מודה סומכוס דסרכא לאו כלום היא. אם תמצא לומר תקפה א' בפנינו מוציאין אותו מידו הקדישה אינה מקודשת. ואם תמצא לומר אין מוציאין אותה מידו הקדישה מקודשת. הקדישה בלא תקפה מהו מי אמרי' כיון דאמר מר אמירתו לגבוה כמסירתו להדיוט דמי כמאן דתקפה דמי או דלמא השתא מיהא הא לא תקפה. ת"ש דההיא

**מסורת הש"ס**

א) שבועות מ: [לעיל ה.], ב) שבועות מז., ג) בבא קמא קז., עיין שם, ד) [לעיל ג: וש"נ], ה) עבודה זרה סג., בבא בתרא קלג., קדושין כח., נדרים כט., תמורה כט., תוספתא קידושין פרק א', תוספתא בבא קמא פרק ז', תוספתא ערכין פרק ד'], ו) ע"ז סג., [ב"ק סח: ב"ש, סט., חולין קלט., תמורה ט., כט., ערכין כא.], ז) [אולי צ"ל דף מ: דהיינו בפלוגתא של ר' ישמעאל ור"ע], ח) [שייך לע"ב].

**הגהות הגר"א**

[א] גמ' אלא שתקפה אחד בפנינו. נ"ב וכה"ג אי בשתיק לא מהני ראיה. יטב"א וטור. (ועמ"ש ביתו בח"מ סי' קל"ח ס"ק ט"ו דלא כמ"ש הש"ך שם בדעת הטור):

**תורה אור השלם**

א) וְאִישׁ כִּי יַקְדִּשׁ אֶת בֵּיתוֹ קֹדֶשׁ לַייָ וְהֶעֱרִיכוֹ הַכֹּהֵן בֵּין טוֹב וּבֵין רָע כַּאֲשֶׁר יַעֲרִיךְ אֹתוֹ הַכֹּהֵן כֵּן יָקוּם: [ויקרא כז, יד]

**ליקוטי רש"י**

שבועת היסת. שבועה הסיתו חכמים לכך הסיתו להודות. וטעמא פרש בשבועות (דף מ:) ...זקה אין אדם טוען אא"כ ...ש לו בידו [לעיל ה.]. לשון ...ומא ששמו חכמים עליו ...שבועה כמו (שמואל א כו) ...ם ה' הסיתך בי [שבועות ...:]. שניהם נשבעין ...ונוטלין מבעל הבית. ...אמר ליה פועלים לא ...הימנו לי בשבועה את ...אמנתינהו דלא אמרת לי ...שהדי הב להו וכן פועלין ...אמרי ליה לא מהימן לן ...חנוני בשבועה [שבועות ...:]. שלא פשעתי. ...אמירתו כשנגנבה דאי ...פשע בה חייב דכתיב על כל ...דבר פשע. שלא שלחתי ...בה יד. ליהנות בה קודם ...דאם שלח בה יד קמה ...ה ברשותיה דנעשה גזלן ...עליה ומיחייב באונסין ...ש בגניבה ואבידה [ב"ק ...:]. אמירתו לגבוה ...כמסירתו להדיוט. ...דכתיב (ויקרא כז) ואיש ...יקדיש וגו' (דברים כג) ...לא תאחר לשלמו וגו' ...לא שפתיך תשמור וגו' [ב"ב קלג:]. ולא מלי ...יזהר כלום מסרתו להדיוט [תמורה כט:].

The Gemara now questions from a series of sources the ssumption that one who is suspect in monetary matters is also spect with regard to swearing falsely:

וְאֶלָּא הָא דְּאָמַר רַב נַחְ – But how will you account for that which av Nachman said: מַשְׁבִּיעִין אוֹתוֹ שְׁבוּעַת הֶיסֵּת – Although a efendant who denies entirely the plaintiff's claim against him is iblically exempt from swearing, by Rabbinic enactment we npose upon him an oath of "incitement" to elicit a confession om him.[1] נֵימָא מִיגּוֹ דְּחָשִׁיד אַמָּמוֹנָא חָשִׁיד אַשְּׁבוּעֲתָא – But if we spect him of dishonesty, then let us say that since he is spect in monetary matters, he is also suspect in regard to vearing falsely![2] – ? –

וְ – And furthermore, הָא דְּתָנֵי רַבִּי חִיָּיא – how will you count for that Baraisa which R' Chiya taught: שְׁנֵיהֶם נִשְׁבָּעִין וְנוֹטְלִין מִבַּעַל הַבַּ – THEY BOTH SWEAR AND COLLECT FROM THE MPLOYER?[3] Now, one of them is certainly lying and seeking to ctort money from the employer. How, then, can we impose an ath? נֵימָא מִיגּוֹ דְּחָשִׁיד אַמָּמוֹנָא חָשִׁיד אַשְּׁבוּעֲתָא – Let us say that nce he is suspect in monetary matters, he is also suspect ith regard to swearing falsely! – ? –

וְ – And furthermore, הָא דְּאָמַר רַב שֵׁשֶׁת – you will not be ole to account for that which Rav Sheishess taught: שָׁלֹשׁ שְׁבוּעוֹת מַשְׁבִּיעִין אוֹ – We obligate [the unpaid custodian] who claims that he is exempt from liability because the deposit ntrusted to his care was stolen) to swear three oaths: שְׁבוּעָה שֶׁלֹּא פָּשַׁעְתִּי בָּ – First he must state, "I swear that I was not egligent in my care of [the deposit]";[4] שְׁבוּעָה שֶׁלֹּא שָׁלַחְתִּי בָּהּ יָד – second, he must state, "I swear that I did not misappropriate it";[5] שְׁבוּעָה שֶׁאֵינָהּ בִּרְשׁוּתִי – and third, he must state, "I swear that it is not in my possession."[6] Now, if we are concerned that the custodian might be an outright thief who is withholding the deposit for himself, נֵימָא מִיגּוֹ דְּחָשִׁיד אַמָּמוֹנָא חָשִׁיד אַשְּׁבוּעֲתָא – then let us say that since he is suspect in monetary matters, he is also suspect with regard to swearing falsely![7] – ? –

The Gemara therefore concludes:

אֶלָּא לָא אָמְרִינַן מִיגּוֹ דְּחָשִׁיד אַמָּמוֹנָא חָשִׁיד אַשְּׁבוּעֲתָא – Rather, as indicated by these rulings just cited, we must conclude that we do *not* say that since one is suspect in monetary matters, he is also suspect with regard to swearing falsely. Accordingly, we can impose an oath even upon one who is suspect in monetary matters, and there is no longer any objection to R' Yochanan's explanation for the oath imposed by our Mishnah.[8]

Abaye, however, rejects R' Yochanan's explanation, insisting that a person suspect in monetary matters is indeed suspect to swear falsely and thereby ineligible to take an oath. Rather:

אַבַּיֵי אָמַר – Abaye says that the following is the reason for the oath in our Mishnah: חָיְישִׁינַן שֶׁמָּא מִלְוָה יְשָׁנָה יֵשׁ לוֹ עָלָיו – We are concerned for the possibility that [one litigant] has the outstanding claim of an old loan against [the cloak's owner].[9]

The Gemara immediately objects:

אִי הָכִי נִשְׁקוֹל בְּלָא שְׁבוּעָה – If so, let him take half the cloak without first swearing an oath![10] – ? –

NOTES

See above, 5a note 26.

Although we accept the notion that a person might deny his loan bligation in order to buy time and he is therefore not necessarily an tright thief, that does not apply to one who falsely denies his loan bligation *entirely;* for a borrower who wished to buy time with his nial would not be so brazen as to deny the entire obligation to his nder (see end of 3a and beginning of 3b). Rather, if the defendant indeed lying when he denies owing anything to the plaintiff, it must assumed that the defendant has no intention of ever repaying his nder. Thus, he is suspect in monetary matters; how, then, can we npose upon him the Rabbinic oath of incitement? (see *Rashi*; cf. *osafos*).

[Literally: the householder.] This Baraisa (found in *Shevuos* 47b) fers to the case of "the shopkeeper concerning his ledger" (see 2b note ), in which a shopkeeper is instructed by an employer to pay his nployee. Subsequently, the shopkeeper insists that he paid; the nployee insists that he did not. This Baraisa rules that both the opkeeper and the employee state their claims under oath and receive yment from the employer. (*Rashi* questions why the Gemara here es this ruling from a Baraisa rather than from the Mishnah *Shevuos* a. See *Tosafos.*)

I.e. it was not stolen because of any negligence on my part.

I.e. I did not make any personal use of the deposit prior to its theft. For a custodian makes personal use of a deposit entrusted to his care hich he was not given permission to do), then it is as if he has stolen As a thief, he is liable even if the article is subsequently lost as a result an unavoidable occurrence for which he would otherwise *not* have en liable (*Rashi*; see Gemara below, 41a). [The rationale for this bsequent liability is that upon the custodian's "theft" of the deposit, e deposit "enters his possession in regard to liability for all occurnces." That is, he becomes obligated to return intact what he has olen. Until such return, he can no longer be exempt on the basis of avoidable accident, since in the final analysis he has not returned the olen article intact (see *Rashi*).]

For we are concerned that the custodian fabricated the whole story d the article was not stolen altogether. Rather, the custodian seeks to ep it for himself.

Since the oath of "it is not in my possession" *is* imposed, we see that person suspect in monetary matters is *not* necessarily suspect to swear sely (see *Rashi*).

[Of the three oaths imposed by Rav Sheishess, only the oath of "it is not in my possession" furnishes proof that one suspect in monetary matters is not suspect to swear falsely. However, no proof can be adduced from the oath of "I was not negligent," since negligence is not tantamount to theft. And even the oath of "I did not misappropriate it" does not prove anything, because there are mild forms of misappropriation that are not tantamount to outright theft, though they do cause the custodian to become liable for all accidents [see below, 41a] (*Ritva* in explanation of *Rashi*).]

8. On 5b, R' Yochanan had explained that the oath in our Mishnah was imposed out of concern that one of the litigants simply grabbed the other fellow's cloak in order to steal it. The Gemara there had objected that if that were indeed our concern, then the litigant would be suspect in monetary matters and would not be allowed to swear. The Gemara here overrules that objection by demonstrating that someone suspect in monetary matters is indeed allowed to swear, for it is not likely that he will violate the severe prohibition against swearing falsely (see 5b note 17).

9. According to Abaye, our concern is not that one of the litigants is an outright thief. Rather, the concern is that one of the litigants has a loan outstanding against the cloak's true owner, which he realizes that the cloak's owner has forgotten and will deny. [Unable to prove that the loan is owed to him] the lender grabs the borrower's cloak and claims it as his own. Since a borrower, when he takes a loan, obligates himself to repay "even the cloak on his shoulder," the lender can truthfully swear that he owns at least half of the cloak (*Rashi*). [The oath does not contain any statement about the *basis* of the litigant's claim to the cloak – see *Maharam Shif* at length.]

[The Gemara will immediately object that there is then no purpose to the oath.]

10. If what prompts us to impose the oath is the concern that one of the litigants is not really the owner but is seeking to collect it in payment for a loan due him, then why make him swear altogether? If the loan is indeed due him, let him collect it without first taking an oath! (*Rashi*). [See *Maharam Shif* who explains why the Gemara did not simply ask: What would imposition of the oath accomplish? If he is indeed owed the money, he will take the oath!]

[See *Baal HaMaor* and *Milchamos* as to whether a creditor who has an unprovable claim against his debtor is indeed allowed to grab an article of the debtor and claim it as his own.]

Does the Torah's imposition of an oath in this case not prove that a suspected thief *is* allowed to swear?

The Gemara answers:

**הָתָם נַמִּי אִשְׁתַּמּוּטֵי קָא מִשְׁתַּמֵּיט – There, too,** it is possible that **he is** simply **evading** the depositor, **סָבַר מַשְׁכַּחְנָא לְגַנָּב וְתָפִיסְנָא לֵיהּ – thinking: "I will find the thief and seize [the stolen animal]** from him," **אִי נַמִּי מַשְׁכַּחְנָא לֵיהּ בָּאֲגַם וּמַיְיתִינָא לֵיהּ – or: "I will find [the lost animal] in the meadow and bring it** to the owner."[25]

The Gemara has thus considered the possibility of temporary evasion even in the case of one who denies a deposit. Accordingly, the Gemara asks:

**אִי הָכִי הַכּוֹפֵר בְּפִקָּדוֹן אַמַּאי פָּסוּל לְעֵדוּת – If so, why is one who denies a deposit disqualified from being a witness?**[26] **נֵימָא אִשְׁתַּמּוּטֵי קָא מִשְׁתַּמֵּיט – Let us say that** he lost the deposit and **he is** simply **evading [the depositor],** **סָבַר עַד דְּבָחֲשְׁנָא וּמַשְׁכַּחְנָא לֵיהּ – thinking:** "I will try to gain time **until I** am able to **search for and find [the deposit]."** – ? –

The Gemara concedes this point and therefore qualifies Rav Chisda's ruling that one who falsely denies a deposit is disqualified from being a witness:

**כִּי אָמְרִינַן הַכּוֹפֵר בְּפִקָּדוֹן פָּסוּל לְעֵדוּת – When do we say that one who denies a deposit is disqualified from being a witness?** **כְּגוֹן דְּאָתוּ סַהֲדֵי – In a case where witnesses came** before the court **וְאַסְהִידוּ בֵּיהּ – and testified against [the custodian]** **דְּהַהִיא שַׁעְתָּא אִיתֵיהּ לְפִקָּדוֹן בְּבֵיתֵיהּ וַהֲוָה יָדַע – that at the very moment** that he denied having received it, **he was aware that the deposit was in his house.** **אִי נַמִּי דַּהֲוָה נָקִיט לֵיהּ בִּידֵיהּ – Alternatively,** they testified **that** at the time of his denial **he had it on his person.**[27] Thus, it is clear that his denial of the deposit was an attempt to steal it, and he is disqualified from serving as a witness. However, when witnesses do not rule out the possibility of temporary evasion, one who falsely denies a deposit remains qualified to serve as a witness.

Thus, we remain with our original assumption that one who suspected of being a thief is not allowed to swear.

However, the Gemara challenges this assumption from anoth source:

**אֶלָּא הָא דְּאָמַר רַב הוּנָא – But** you must account for **that whic Rav Huna said** regarding a custodian who prefers to pay rath than swear:[28] **מַשְׁבִּיעִין אוֹתוֹ שְׁבוּעָה שֶׁאֵינָהּ בִּרְשׁוּתוֹ – "We mal him swear that [the deposit] is not in his possession."** For v are concerned that he has the deposit and wishes to pay and kee it for himself. Now, if that is the concern, **מִּא מִיגּוֹ דְּחָשִׁיד אַמָּמוֹנָא חָשִׁיד אַשְּׁבוּעֲתָא – let us say: Since he is suspect monetary matters,**[29] **he is also suspect in regard to swearin** Yet, Rav Huna rules that he must swear! – ? –

The Gemara answers:

**הָתָם נַמִּי מוֹרֶה וְאָמַר דָּמֵי קָא יָהֵבְנָא לֵיהּ – There, too, [th custodian]** is not considered to be suspect in monetary matter for he **rationalizes** his actions **and says: "**After all, **I** am willir to **give him money** for what I am taking from him."[30]

The Gemara asks:

**אָמַר לֵיהּ רַב אַחָא מִדִּיפְתִּי לְרָבִינָא – Rav Acha of Difti said Ravina:** **וְהָא קָא עָבַר עַל לָאו דְּלֹא תַחְמֹד – But [the custodia** thereby knowingly **transgresses the prohibition of "do n covet** your fellow's property." He should be suspect in moneta matters on that basis![31] – ? –

The Gemara answers:

**לֹא תַחְמֹד לְאִינְשֵׁי בְּלָא דָּמֵי מַשְׁמַע לְהוּ –** Many **people** wrong **assume that** even the prohibition **"do not covet" applies** on **where no money** is given in exchange for the coveted object.[ Therefore, the custodian who pays the depositor for the article th custodian wishes to keep for himself is not considered an outrigl thief. Accordingly, he can be made to swear the oath imposed b Rav Huna's ruling.

---

NOTES

upon him. Does this not prove that one who is suspected of theft is *not* suspected of being prepared to swear falsely? (see *Rashi*).

[This *modeh bemiktzas* is not the only oath imposed on the custodian. He also must swear the specific "custodian's oath" that the third cow indeed met its fate through an occurrence for which he is not liable (e.g. the custodian claims that the third cow died as a result of an unavoidable accident). The Gemara, however, could prove nothing from this oath in regard to the question of allowing a suspected thief to swear. For this oath is not prompted by the suspicion that the custodian is a thief. Rather, it is possible that the custodian was negligent in caring for the third cow and the accident resulted from this negligence. The custodian might be planning to pay for his negligence, but claims "unavoidable accident" as a delaying tactic so that he has time to obtain the necessary funds. Neither his negligence nor his playing for time makes him a thief who might be disqualified from swearing (*Rashi*).]

[Actually, there are two additional oaths that the custodian must swear (see 6a). What bearing these oaths have on the question of whether a suspected thief is also suspect in regard to swearing falsely will be discussed on 6a (see note 7 there.]

25. That is, although the custodian denies ever having received the second cow (or claims to have already returned it), it is possible that the second cow was in fact stolen or lost from him. Rather than pay for the theft or loss [e.g. he is a paid custodian, who is liable for such occurrences], he feels that, given time, he will be able to retrieve it and restore it to the rightful owner. Therefore, he denies liability entirely in order to play for time, but he does not mean to deprive the depositor of what is rightfully his (see *Rashi* and *Ritva*). [The Torah, however, imposed an oath upon him so that he should admit his liability immediately.]

26. As Rav Chisda ruled earlier on this *amud.*

27. [Literally: he was holding it in his hand.]

28. Rav Huna's ruling is found below, 34b, concerning a custodian wl asserts his exemption from liability, yet prefers to pay rather than clai his exemption under oath. For example, an unpaid custodian claims th the deposit was stolen from him. The law is that he states his clai under oath and is exempt from liability. The custodian, however, insis that he prefers to pay rather than exempt himself by taking the oath. I is possible that he is motivated by the desire to voluntarily compensa the depositor, or by the religious fear of taking any kind of oath, or – we shall soon see – by some other consideration.]

29. Even a person who compensates the owner for what he is stealir from him is considered a thief (see below).

30. Although that rationalization is without legal merit, it does mal him something less than an outright thief and we have no reason suspect that such a person will swear falsely.

31. The custodian may be under the impression that "stealing" refe only to taking someone else's property without compensating him for But he apparently realizes that even in such a case, taking the proper is a violation of "you shall not covet" (*Exodus* 20:14), since he ha coveted the depositor's property and obtained it for himself (se *Rambam, Hil. Gezeilah* 1:9 and *Ravad* ad loc.). Accordingly, what diffe ence does it make whether the custodian is suspected of stealing or coveting? Either way, he is suspected of knowingly violating prohibition concerning monetary matters and should be suspect swear falsely as well (*Rashi*).

32. [Accordingly, these people think that "do not covet" comes add a second prohibition to the already prohibited act of theft (se *Tosafos*).]

[א] ותקנתא לתקנתא לא עבדינן ותיפוק ליה דהוה ליה רועה [ב] ואמר רב יהודה [א] סתם רועה פסול לא קשיא [ב] הא דידיה הא דעלמא דאי לא תימא הכי אנן חיותא לרועה היכי מסרינן והא כתיב [א] לפני עור לא תתן מכשול אלא [ג] חזקה אין אדם חוטא ולא לו: זה ישבע שאין לו בה פחות מחציה [וכו']: על דאית ליה משתבע או על דלית ליה משתבע אמר רב הונא [ג] דאמר שבועה שיש לי בה ואין לי בה פחות מחציה ונימא שבועה שכולה שלי ומי יהבינן ליה כולה ונימא שבועה שחציה שלי מרע ליה לדיבוריה השתא נמי מרע ליה לדיבוריה דאמר כולה שלי ולדבריכם שבועה שיש לי בה ואין לי בה פחות מחציה וכי מאחר שזה תפוס ועומד וזה תפוס ועומד שבועה זו למה [ד] אמר ר' יוחנן שבועה זו תקנת חכמים היא שלא יהא כל אחד ואחד הולך ותוקף בטליתו של חבירו ואומר שלי הוא ונימא מיגו דחשיד אממונא חשיד נמי אשבועתא [ד] לא אמרינן מיגו דחשיד אממונא חשיד אשבועתא דאי לא תימא הכי האי דאמר רחמנא מודה מקצת הטענה ישבע נימא מיגו דחשיד אממונא חשיד אשבועתא התם אשתמוטי קא משתמיט ליה [ה] כדרבה תדע [ו] דאמר רב אידי בר אבין אמר רב חסדא הכופר במלוה כשר לעדות בפקדון פסול לעדות אלא הא [ז] דתני רמי בר חמא ארבעה שומרין צריכין כפירה במקצת והודאה במקצת שומר חנם והשואל נושא שכר והשוכר נימא מיגו דחשיד אממונא חשיד אשבועתא התם נמי אשתמוטי קא משתמיט סבר משכחנא לגנב ותפיסנא ליה א"נ משכחנא ליה באגם ומייתינא ליה אי הכי הכופר בפקדון אמאי פסול לעדות נימא אשתמוטי קא משתמיט סבר עד דבחשנא ומשכחנא ליה [ה] כי אמרינן הכופר בפקדון פסול לעדות כגון דאתו סהדי ואסהידו ביה דההיא שעתא איתיה לפקדון בביתיה והוה ידע א"נ דהוה נקיט ליה בידיה אלא הא [ח] דאמר רב הונא משביעין אותו שבועה שאינה ברשותו נימא מיגו דחשיד אממונא חשיד אשבועתא התם נמי מורה ואמר דמי קא יהבנא ליה אמר ליה רב אחא מדיפתי לרבינא והא קא עבר על לאו [ב] דלא תחמוד [ו] ולא תחמוד לאינשי [ט] בלא דמי משמע להו

ואלא

**רש"י**

ותקנתא. דכשכנגדו ישבע ויטול דהויא נמי תקנתא דמן התורה מי שעליו לשלם הוא ישבע ויפטר מן התשלומין ואין נשבע ונוטל מן התורה ואותן המנויין בשבועות (דף מד:) תקנת חכמים הן ולשבועה דאורייתא עבוד רבנן תקנתא אבל תקנתא לתקנתא לא עבדינן: ותיפוק ליה דהוה ליה רועה. אדאביי קא מתמה דקשיא ליה והא גזלן הוא ותיפוק ליה דבלאו הך גזילה פסול לשבועה: דאמר רב יהודה סתם רועה. אפילו לא הועד עליו שגזל: פסול. לעדות דסתמיה גזלן הוא שמרעה בהמותיו בשדות של אחרים: דידיה. רועה בהמות שלו פסול דבשביל הנאתו רועה אותן בשדות אחרות אבל רועה בהמות העיר בשכר בשביל הנאת אחרים אינו חוטא להרעות עד שיגיע למרעה המופקר לכל: דאי לא תימא הכי. דלא אמרינן על רועה בהמות דעלמא שהוא גזלן אנן חיותא לרועה היכי מסרינן: על דאית ליה משתבע או על דלית ליה משתבע. הבא לישבע וליטול חציה צריך הוא לישבע שיש לו בה חציה או לישבע שאין לו בה פחות מחציה שמא אין לו בה כלום וכי משתבע שאין לו בה פחות מחציה באמת הוא נשבע שהרי אין לו כלום דבשלמא אם היה לו בה שליש או רביע והוא נשבע שאין לו בה פחות מחציה נשבע בשקר שהרי יש לו בה שליש שהוא פחות מחציה ואין לו בה חציה אבל כשאין לו בה כלום נשבע הוא באמת: שבועה שיש לי בה. ואם תאמרו שמא שליש או רביע שבועה שאין לי חלק בה פחות מחציה: מי יהבינן ליה כולה. הרי חבירו תופס בה ואם ישביעוהו על כולה הרי לעז לב"ד מאחר שכולה שלו והם אמרו יחלוקו: מרע ליה לדיבוריה. דאמר ברישא כולה שלי והשתא אמר בהדיא חציה שלי: דאמר כולה שלי. תירוצא הוא: ולדבריכם. שאין אתם מאמינים לי בכולה שבועה שיש לי בה ואין לי בה פחות מחציה: ונימא מגו דחשיד אממונא חשיד כו'. אדרבי יוחנן פריך דאמר חשדוהו רבנן שמא ילך ותוקף בטליתו של חבירו ואומר שלי הוא אם חשוד הוא בכך חשוד הוא נמי לישבע: לא אמרינן כו'. דחמיר הוא לאינשי איסור שבועה מאיסור גזילה: אשתמוטי משתמיט ליה. ולא חשיד אממונא: כדרבה. דאמר לעיל מפני מה אמרה תורה כו': תדע. דלאו הגזלן חשדינן ליה אלא באשתמוטי בעלמא: דאמר רב אידי בר אבין הכופר במלוה. שבאו עדים והחזיקוהו בכפרן שהעידוהו שהוא חייב לו: כשר לעדות. אלמא לאו דעתיה למגזליה דנימא אל תשת עד חמס אלא לאשתמוטי עביד: בפקדון פסול לעדות. דמאי אשתמוטי איכא הרי לא ניתן להוצאה ובעין הוא ואם אבד יטעון שאבד ויפטר: ולימא מיגו דחשיד אממונא. דההוא דאמר לא היו דברים מעולם כופר בפקדון הוא וליכא למימר משתמיט: חשיד נמי אשבועה דידה. דבשלמא אשבועת שומרין דההוא דקטעין נאנסה דחייביה רחמנא שבועה איכא למימר דלא חשיד אממונא אלא שמא פשע בשמירתה וחייב לשלם אונסיה וסבר עד דהוי לי זוזי ופרענא ליה אלא ההיא דכפירה הא ודאי כופר בפקדון הוא ומשקר והיכי משבעינן ליה עלה: התם נמי אשתמוטי משתמיט. שאבדה ממנו וסבר משכחנא לגנב כו': אי הכי. בפקדון איכא למימר משתמיט: דבחשנא. אחפש: ה"ג דההיא שעתא הוה גביה. ולא גרס ההיא שעתא דאשתבע: דאמר רב הונא. לקמן בהמפקיד גבי שילם ולא רצה לישבע אמר רב הונא אם בא לשלם משביעין אותו שבועה שאינה ברשותו חיישינן שמא עיניו נתן בה: התם. לא חשיד אממונא דמורי היתירא למימר דמי בעינא למיתב: הא קא עבר בלא תחמוד. מה לי חשוד על לא תחמוד מה לי חשוד על לא תגזול נימא מיגו דחשיד עליה חשיד אשבועתא:

משביעין

**תוספות**

ותקנתא לתקנתא. ומתוך שאינו יכול לישבע משלם לא שייך הכא כדפרישית [ו]: על דאית ליה משתבע כו'. ואע"ג דעל דעת ב"ד משביעין אותו מ"מ לא הו"ל לתקן שבועה בלשון דלא משתמע שחציה שלו: ונימא שבועה שכולה שלי. לרבנן דבן ננס פריך דלא חיישי לשבועת שוא: כולה שלי ולדבריכם כו'. אף על גב דקאמר כולה שלי לא משתבע שחציה שלו שמרע לדיבוריה: דחשיד אממונא לא חשיד אשבועתא. נראה דהיינו טעמא משום דשבועה חמורה כדאיתא ביומא (דף פו.) ובשבועות (דף לט.) שהעולם נזדעזע על לא תשא וא"ת א"כ אמאי גזלן פסול לשבועה דאמר שכנגדו נשבע ונוטל וי"ל דגזלן לא פסול לשבועה אלא מדרבנן ולעדות הוא דפסול מדאורייתא משום אל תשת רשע עד וי"מ בשם ה"ר יהודה חסיד הא דחשיד אממונא כשר לשבועה משום דשמא ע"י שבועה יפרוש מגזל אבל גזלן ודאי כמו שממון אינו פורש ה"ה משבועה ולא קשה מההוא רעיא דאסהידו ביה דאכל (א) מינייהו אמאי פסול דבהנך תרי דאכל צריך לשלם ומהשאר יפרוש על ידי שבועה דמה שהוא משלם על ידי עדים אין זה השבה מעליא דעל כרחו משלם והיינו טעמא דכופר בפקדון פסול לעדות: ההיא שעתא דאיתיה בביתיה. ל"ג דאשתבע דאי איכא סהדי דנשבע לשקר במלוה נמי פסול וכן משמע בהגוזל קמא (ב"ק דף קה:) דמיירי בלא שבועה: בלא דמי משמע להו. וא"ת תיפוק ליה מלא תגזול וי"ל לעבור עליו בשני לאוין וא"ת והא כי יהיב דמי נמי חמסן הוה כדמוכח שלהי הכונס (שם דף סב. ושם) וחמסן פסול לעדות כדכתיב אל תשת ידך עם רשע להיות עד חמס והפסול לעדות פסול לשבועה דכל הנהו דחשיב בפסולי עדות בפרק זה בורר (סנהדרין דף כה: ושם) פוסל להו לשבועה בפרק כל הנשבעין (שבועות דף מה.) וי"ל דחמסן לא פסול לעדות אלא מדרבנן מדתני בפרק זה בורר הוסיפו עליהם החמסנין ולא פריך חמסן דאורייתא הוא כדפריך אגזלן וחמסן דקרא דלא יהיב דמי ושלהי הגוזל (ב"ק דף קיט.) דמייתי קרא דמחמס בני יהודה אפי' אי יהיב דמי אסמכתא בעלמא הוא ואע"ג דהוסיפו עליהם החמסנין לפסול לעדות וה"ה שפסול לשבועה היינו חמסן שחטוף לחטוף מיד ליד בידיעת הבעלים אבל הכא לא חניף אלא מעלים חמסנותו ואמר שנאבדה לו לא פסיל:

אלא

**עין משפט נר מצוה**

כג א ב מיי' פ"י מהל' עדות הל' ד סמג לאוין ריד טוש"ע ח"מ סי' לד סי"ג [רב אלפס סנהדרין פ"ג דף רסא]:
כד ג טוש"ע ח"מ סי' קלח סעיף א:
כה ד טוש"ע ח"מ סי' לג ס"ג וע"ש [דהיינו אם אין עדים שלקח ממון חבירו]:
כו ה טוש"ע שם ס"ד:
כז ו שם בהג"ה:

**רבינו חננאל**

עבדינן. ש"מ דאפילו היכא דליכא דררא דממונא בינייהו היה לך בידי ופרעתיך א) מחייב רב נחמן שבועת היסת. הא דאמר רב יהודה סתם רועה פסול ברועה בהמות שלו משום דמרעה אותן בשדות בני אדם אבל רועה בהמות אחרים חזקה אין אדם חוטא ולא לו. ואע"ג דאמר ר' זירא אי איתא לדר' חייא קמייתא לית לן למימר דדחאי לגמרי דהא אשכחן כי האי גוונא בתחלת פ' המדיר את אשתו שאמרו ואם איתא לדרב הונא אמר רב דאמר יכולה אשה שתאמר לבעלה איני ניזונת ואיני עושה וכו' שמראין הדברים שדחאה. וכבר מצינו בפ' שני דייני גזילות והיל' כרב הונא אמר רב דאמר יכולה אשה שתאמר איני ניזונת ואיני עושה שמעינן מיניה דכי האי גוונא אינה נדחת הילכך הלכתא כר' חייא בקמייתא: פיסקא זה ישבע שאין לו בה פחות מחציה וכו'. אוקימנא באומר כולה שלי ולדבריכם דלא יהביתו לי כולה שבועה שיש לי בה ואין לי בה פחות מחציה. אמר ר' יוחנן שבועה זו תקנת חכמים היא שלא יהא כל אחד תופס בטלית חבירו ואומר שלי הוא. ואסקי' לא אמרי' מגו דחשיד אממונא חשיד נמי אשבועתא והאי דאמר הכופר בפקדון פסול לעדות שנינן בדאיכא סהדי דההיא שעתא דכפר בה בב"ד הוה נקיט ליה ב) אי הוה ידע היכא איתיה ברשותיה. הא דאמר רב הונא משביעין אותו שבועה שאינה ברשותו בתחלת פ' המפקיד.

**חשק שלמה על ר"ח**

א) ור"ל דאפילו בטוען אין לך בידי ג"כ חייב היסת וכו' דרב נחמן בשבועות מ'. ב) נראה דל"ל הוה נקיט ליה בידיה או הוה ידע וכו'.

**תורה אור השלם**

א) לֹא תְקַלֵּל חֵרֵשׁ וְלִפְנֵי עִוֵּר לֹא תִתֵּן מִכְשֹׁל וְיָרֵאתָ מֵּאֱלֹהֶיךָ אֲנִי יְיָ: [ויקרא יט, יד]
ב) לֹא תַחְמֹד בֵּית רֵעֶךָ לֹא תַחְמֹד אֵשֶׁת רֵעֶךָ וְעַבְדּוֹ וַאֲמָתוֹ וְשׁוֹרוֹ וַחֲמֹרוֹ וְכֹל אֲשֶׁר לְרֵעֶךָ: [שמות כ, יד]

**מסורת הש"ס**

א) [שבועות מא., מו.] ב) [סנהדרין כה:] ג) [קידושין סג:, שבועות מב:, ערכין כג.], ד) לעיל ג., ה) [לעיל ג. וש"נ], ו) [לעיל ד., בבא קמא קה:, שבועות מ:], ז) [לקמן לה., בבא קמא קז.], ח) לקמן לד:, ט) [עיין תוספות סנהדרין כה: ד"ה מעיקרא], י) [ע"א ד"ה שכנגדו].

**הגהות הב"ח**

(א) תום' ד"ה דחשיד וכו' דאכל תרתי מינייהו אמאי פסול:

**ליקוטי רש"י**

סתם רועה. דאכתי ל חזינן דעיילו בהמותי בשדות אחרות [סנהדרי כה:]. לפני עור ל תתן מכשול. לפ הסומא בדבר לא תתן על שאינה הוגנת לו [ויקרא יט, יד]. אין אדם חוטא ולא לו. בדבר שאינו נהנ ממנו [קידושין סג:]. להרוי בשביל אחר לא יחט [ערכין כג.]. ותוקף. או [לעיל ג.]. הכופר במלוה. בין על כולה ב על מקצת ובאו עדי והעידוהו עד שלא נשב כשר לעדות. ול אמרינן גזלן הוא והתור אמרה (שמות כג) אל תש רשע עד דכיון דמלו להוצאה ניתנה דלמא לב להוציאה וסבר עד דהוה זוזי ופרענא ליה ו מודינא ליה השתא יתבע מיד. בפקדון פסו לעדות. אבל הכופ בפקדון אפי' על מקצ ובאו עדים והעידוהו פס לעדות דמאי הוה ליה ג פקדון לאשתמוטי נפש וכו' [לעיל ד.]. ואפי' נשבע דמשעה דכ איחשיד ליה אממו [שבועות מ:]. ארבע שומרים וכו'. ראה לע בעמוד א.

to state my original claim under oath, שְׁבוּעָה שֶׁיֵּשׁ לִי בָּהּ וְאֵין לִי בָּהּ פָּחוֹת מֵחֶצְיָהּ – **"I swear that I own** something **of [this cloak] and I do not own less than half of it."**[13]

The Gemara now offers R' Yochanan's reason for the oath imposed in our Mishnah:

וְכִי מֵאַחַר שֶׁזֶּה תָּפוּס וְעוֹמֵד וְזֶה תָּפוּס וְעוֹמֵד – **But now that this** litigant **already holds** the cloak **and this** litigant **already holds** the cloak, שְׁבוּעָה זוּ לָמָּה – **why this oath?**[14] אָמַר ר׳ יוֹחָנָן – **Said R' Yochanan:** שְׁבוּעָה זוּ תַּקָּנַת חֲכָמִים הִיא – **This oath is a Rabbinic measure** decreed שֶׁלֹּא יְהֵא כָּל אֶחָד וְאֶחָד הוֹלֵךְ וְתוֹקֵף בְּטַלִּיתוֹ שֶׁל חֲבֵירוֹ וְאוֹמֵר שֶׁלִּי הוּא – **so that each and every person should not** be able to **go and seize his fellow's cloak and** then **claim** in court, **"It is mine!"**[15] Though a person might be willing to steal someone else's cloak, he is still likely to refrain from swearing falsely. Hence, the Rabbis obligated the litigants to swear.

The Gemara asks:

וְנֵימָא מִיגּוֹ דְּחָשִׁיד אַמָּמוֹנָא חָשִׁיד נַמִּי אַשְּׁבוּעֲתָא – **But let us say: Since he is suspect in monetary matters, he is also suspect in regard to swearing,** i.e. if he is prepared to steal to achieve his aim, he will also swear falsely if necessary. Accordingly, how can we impose an oath on the litigants? [16]

The Gemara answers:

לֹא אָמְרִינַן מִיגּוֹ דְּחָשִׁיד אַמָּמוֹנָא חָשִׁיד אַשְּׁבוּעֲתָא – **We do *not* say: Since he is suspect in monetary matters, he is also suspect in regard to swearing.** Although a person might steal to achieve his aim, he is not likely to swear falsely.[17] Hence, we impose an oath upon the litigants.

The Gemara proves that we do not suspect a thief of a willingness to swear falsely as well:

דְּאִי לֹא תֵּימָא הָכִי – **For if you do not say this** distinction between theft and swearing falsely, הַאי דְּאָמַר רַחֲמָנָא מוֹדֶה מִקְצָת הַטַּעֲנָה יִשָּׁבַע – then how can you understand **that which the Merciful One says** in the Torah that **one who admits part of a claim must swear?**[18] Obviously, the Torah imposes this oath on the defendant because we suspect him of falsely denying the second part of the claim. נֵימָא מִיגּוֹ דְּחָשִׁיד אַמָּמוֹנָא חָשִׁיד אַשְּׁבוּעֲתָא – Accordingly, **let us say** that **since he is suspect in monetary matters, he is also suspect in regard to swearing,** and he should not be allowed to swear! Since the Torah *does* impose an oath upon him, it is apparently proven that a thief is not suspect to swear falsely.

The Gemara rejects this proof:

הָתָם אִשְׁתַּמּוֹטֵי קָא מִשְׁתַּמֵּיט לֵיהּ כִּדְרַבָּה – **There,** in the case of one who admits part of a claim, it is possible that **he is** simply **evading [the creditor], as Rabbah** previously explained.[19]

The Gemara supports its assertion that one who denies part of a claim against him is not viewed as an outright thief:

תֵּדַע – **Know** that this is so, דְּאָמַר רַב אִידִי בַּר אָבִין אָמַר רַב חִסְדָּא – **for Rav Idi bar Avin said in the name of Rav Chisda:** הַכּוֹפֵר בְּמִלְוָה כָּשֵׁר לְעֵדוּת – **One who** falsely **denies a loan** obligation **remains qualified to be a witness;**[20] בְּפִקָּדוֹן פָּסוּל לְעֵדוּת – **but one who falsely denies** even part of **a deposit** obligation **is disqualified from being a witness.**[21] We see, then, that in the classic *modeh bemiktzas* case of one who admits part of a loan obligation, the defendant upon whom the oath obligation is imposed is *not* suspected of being a thief. Thus, we remain with our original assumption that one who is suspected of being a thief is also suspected of being prepared to swear falsely:

The Gemara, however, challenges this assumption from another source:

אֶלָּא הָא דְּתָנֵי רָמֵי בַּר חָמָא – **But** how will you account for the ruling in **that Baraisa which Rami bar Chama taught:**[22] אַרְבָּעָה שׁוֹמְרִין צְרִיכִין כְּפִירָה בְּמִקְצָת וְהוֹדָאָה בְּמִקְצָת – The **FOUR CUSTODIANS REQUIRE PARTIAL DENIAL AND PARTIAL ADMISSION** as a condition for the custodian's oath imposed on them by the Torah. They are: שׁוֹמֵר חִנָּם וְהַשּׁוֹאֵל נוֹשֵׂא שָׂכָר וְהַשּׂוֹכֵר – **THE UNPAID CUSTODIAN, THE BORROWER, THE PAID CUSTODIAN, AND THE RENTER?**[23] נֵימָא מִיגּוֹ דְּחָשִׁיד אַמָּמוֹנָא חָשִׁיד אַשְּׁבוּעֲתָא – **Let us say** that **since he is suspect in monetary matters, he is also suspect in regard to swearing,** and he should not be allowed to swear![24]

NOTES

13. [The oath that he owns not less than half does not *contradict* his original claim of the entire cloak; it simply fails to corroborate that claim. Therefore, the disclaimer that he is restricting his oath because of the limits imposed upon him by the court is sufficient to remove the appearance of retraction. But if he were to swear, "Half the cloak is mine," the appearance of retraction would remain despite his disclaimer, since the oath as stated contradicts the original claim.]

14. [This is not an actual question of the Gemara (which has already discussed the reason for the oath above – see 2b), but rather R' Yochanan's own introductory question to the reason he is about to offer. It is as if the words "said R' Yochanan" actually precede the question that he asks (*Ritva*; *Ran* to 2b).] If the presumptive evidence of each one having physical possession of half the cloak already indicates the final settlement awarding each one half, why impose an oath on the litigants altogether?

15. See above, 3a note 3.

16. The only reason we make the litigants swear is that we suspect one of them of trying to steal the other one's cloak. But if we suspect him of a willingness to violate the injunction against stealing, then we should have to suspect him of a willingness to violate the injunction against swearing falsely as well! How, then, can we impose an oath on such a person, since by doing so we are likely causing him to sin? (*Ritva*).

17. For people – even sinners – consider swearing falsely to be a graver sin than stealing (*Rashi*; see *Tosafos*).

18. This refers to the standard Biblical oath of *modeh bemiktzas* (see 3a note 27).

19. Above, 3a-b; see 3b note 2.

20. I.e. even if witnesses attest that he indeed owes the money and he is thus confirmed to be a liar. The ruling that this confirmed liar remains qualified to serve as a witness proves that he is not viewed as an outright thief, who is disqualified from serving as a witness, as the Torah states (*Exodus* 23:1): אַל־תָּשֶׁת ... עֵד חָמָס, *Do not place . . . a thieving witness* (*Rashi*; see 4a note 13).

21. There is no way to extenuate a custodian's false denial of a deposit entrusted to his care. If it has been lost, then he should say so and he will be exempt from liability [in the case of an unpaid custodian]. If he spent the deposit and is playing for time to obtain the money necessary to repay the plaintiff, then he is a thief by virtue of his initial spending of the deposit, which was entrusted to him to guard, not to spend (*Rashi*; see 4a note 13).

22. This Baraisa has been cited and explained on 5a; see notes 7 and 8 there.

23. As explained in note 8 to 5a, this Baraisa teaches that the Torah does not impose the custodian's oaths unless there are *three* elements to the depositor's claim – one part that the custodian categorically denies, a second part that he categorically admits, and a third part whose basis he admits but about which he claims exemption from liability. For example, the depositor demands the return of three cows that he claims to have entrusted to an unpaid custodian. The custodian returns one cow (partial admission), denies ever having received the second cow or claims to have already returned it (partial *absolute* denial), and claims that the third cow was stolen. In this case, one of the oaths the custodian must swear is the *modeh bemiktzas* oath generated by his admission of the first cow and denial of the second one. It is regarding this oath that the Gemara asks its next question (see *Rashi*).

24. I.e. the *modeh bemiktzas* oath that the depositor's claim of the second cow has no basis. The only reason for making him swear this oath is that we suspect him of trying to illegally retain the second cow for himself – something for which he could have no excuse. But if we suspect him of theft, we should also suspect him of being prepared to swear falsely and we should not allow him to swear. Yet the Torah *does* impose an oath

(א) ותקנתא לתקנתא לא עבדינן ותיפוק ליה דהוה ליה רועה (ג) ואמר רב יהודה אסתם רועה פסול לא קשיא בהא דידיה הא דעלמא דאי לא תימא הכי אנן חיותא לרועה היכי מסרינן והא כתיב א) לפני עור לא תתן מכשול אלא (ג) חזקה אין אדם חוטא ולא לו: זה ישבע שאין לו בה פחות מחציה [וכו']: על דאית ליה משתבע או על דלית ליה משתבע אמר רב הונא גדאמר שבועה שיש לי בה ואין לי בה פחות מחציה ונימא שבועה שכולה שלי ומי יהבינן ליה כולה ונימא שבועה שחציה שלי מרע ליה לדיבוריה השתא נמי מרע ליה לדיבוריה דאמר כולה שלי ולדבריכם שבועה שיש לי בה ואין לי בה פחות מחציה וכי מאחר שזה תפוס ועומד וזה תפוס ועומד שבועה זו למה (ד) אמר ר' יוחנן שבועה זו תקנת חכמים היא שלא יהא כל אחד ואחד הולך ותוקף בטליתו של חבירו ואומר שלי הוא ונימא מיגו דחשיד אממונא חשיד נמי אשבועתא דלא אמרינן מיגו דחשיד אממונא חשיד אשבועתא דאי לא תימא הכי האי דאמר רחמנא מודה מקצת הטענה ישבע נימא מיגו דחשיד אממונא חשיד אשבועתא התם אשתמוטי קא משתמיט ליה (ה) כדרבה תדע (ו) דאמר רב אידי בר אבין אמר רב חסדא הכופר במלוה כשר לעדות בפקדון פסול לעדות אלא הא (ז) דתני רמי בר חמא ארבעה שומרין צריכין כפירה במקצת והודאה במקצת שומר חנם והשואל נושא שכר והשוכר נימא מיגו דחשיד אממונא חשיד אשבועתא התם נמי אשתמוטי קא משתמיט סבר משכחנא לגנב ותפיסנא ליה א"נ משכחנא ליה באגם ומייתינא ליה אי הכי הכופר בפקדון אמאי פסול לעדות נימא אשתמוטי קא משתמיט סבר עד דבחשנא ומשכחנא ליה הכי אמרינן הכופר בפקדון פסול לעדות כגון דאתו סהדי ואסהידו ביה דההיא שעתא איתיה לפקדון בביתיה והוה ידע א"נ דהוה נקיט ליה בידיה אלא הא (ח) דאמר רב הונא משביעין אותו שבועה שאינה ברשותו נימא מיגו דחשיד אממונא חשיד אשבועתא התם נמי מורה ואמר דמי קא יהבנא ליה אמר ליה רב אחא מדיפתי לרבינא והא קא עבר על לאו ב) דלא תחמוד (י) ולא תחמוד לאינשי (ט) בלא דמי משמע להו

ואלא

**רש"י**

ותקנתא. דכשכנגדו ישבע ויטול דהויא נמי תקנתא דמן התורה מי שעליו לשלם הוא ישבע ויפטר מן התשלומין ואין נשבע ונוטל מן התורה ואותן המנויין בשבועות (דף מד:) תקנת חכמים הן ולשבועה דאורייתא עבוד רבנן תקנתא אבל תקנתא לתקנתא לא עבדינן: ותיפוק ליה דהוה ליה רועה. אדאביי קא מתמה דקשיא ליה והא גזלן הוא ותיפוק ליה דבלאו הך גזילה פסול לשבועה: דאמר רב יהודה סתם רועה. אפילו לא הועד עליו שגזל: פסול. לעדות דסתמיה גזלן הוא שמרעה בהמותיו בשדות של אחרים: דידיה. רועה בהמות שלו פסול דבשביל הנאתו רועה אותן בשדות אחרות אבל רועה בהמות העיר בשכר בשביל הנאת אחרים אינו חוטא להרעות עד שיגיע למרעה המופקר לכל: דאי לא תימא הכי. דלא אמרינן על רועה בהמות דעלמא שהוא גזלן אנן חיותא לרועה היכי מסרינן: על דאית ליה משתבע או על דלית ליה משתבע. הבא לישבע וליטול חציה צריך הוא לישבע שיש לו בה חציה או לישבע שאין לו בה פחות מחציה שמא אין לו בה כלום וכי משתבע שאין לו בה פחות מחציה באמת הוא נשבע שהרי אין לו כלום דבשלמא אם היה לו בה שליש או רביע והוא נשבע שאין לו בה פחות מחציה נשבע בשקר שהרי יש לו בה שליש שהוא פחות מחציה ואין לו בה חציה אבל כשאין לו בה כלום נשבע הוא באמת: שבועה שיש לי בה. ואם תאמרו שמא שליש או רביע שבועה שאין לי חלק בה פחות מחציה: מי יהבינן ליה כולה. הרי חבירו תופס בה ואם ישביעוהו על כולה הרי לעז לב"ד מאחר שכולה שלו והם אמרו יחלוקו: מרע ליה לדיבוריה. דאמר ברישא כולה שלי והשתא אמר בהדיא חציה שלי: דאמר כולה שלי. תירוצא הוא: ולדבריכם. שאין אתם מאמינים לי בכולה שבועה שיש לי בה ואין לי בה פחות מחציה: ונימא מגו דחשיד אממונא חשיד כו'. אדרבי יוחנן פריך דאמר חשדוהו רבנן שמא ילך ותוקף בטליתו של חבירו ואומר שלי הוא אם חשוד הוא בכך חשוד הוא נמי לישבע: לא אמרינן כו'. דחמיר הוא לאינשי איסור שבועה מאיסור גזילה: אשתמוטי משתמיט ליה. ולא חשיד אממונא: כדרבה. דאמר לעיל מפני מה אמרה תורה כו': תדע. דלאו הגזלן תחדינן ליה אלא באשתמוטי בעלמא: דאמר רב אידי בר אבין הכופר במלוה. שבאו עדים והחזיקוהו בכפרן שהעידוהו שהוא חייב לו: כשר לעדות. אלמא לאו דעתיה למגזליה דנימא אל תשת עד חמס אלא לאשתמוטי עביד: בפקדון פסול לעדות. דמאי אשתמוטי איכא הרי לא ניתן להוצאה ובעין הוא ואם אבד יטעון שאבד ויפטר: ולימא מיגו דחשיד אממונא. דההוא דאמר לא היו דברים מעולם כופר בפקדון הוא וליכא למימר משתמיט: חשיד נמי אשבועה דידה. דבשלמא אשבועת שומרין דההוא דקטעין נאנסה דחייביה רחמנא שבועה איכא למימר דלא חשיד אממונא אלא שמא פשע בשמירתה וחייב לשלם אונסיה וסבר עד דהוי לי זוזי ופרענא ליה אלא ההיא דכפירה הא ודאי כופר בפקדון הוא ומשקר והיכי משבעינן ליה עלה: התם נמי אשתמוטי משתמיט. שאבדה ממנו וסבר משכחנא לגנב כו': אי הכי. בפקדון איכא למימר משתמיט: דבחשנא. אחפש: ה"ג דההיא שעתא הוה גביה. ולא גרס ההיא שעתא דאשתבע: דאמר רב הונא. לקמן בהמפקיד גבי שילם ולא רצה לישבע אמר רב הונא אם בא לשלם משביעין אותו שבועה שאינה ברשותו חיישינן שמא עיניו נתן בה: התם. לא חשיד אממונא דמורי היתירא למימר דמי בעינא למיתב: הא קא עבר בלא תחמוד. מה לי חשוד על לא תחמוד מה לי חשוד על לא תגזול נימא מיגו דחשיד עליה חשיד אשבועתא:

משביעין

**תוספות**

ותקנתא לתקנתא. ומתוך שאינו יכול לישבע משלם לא שייך הכא כדפרישית (ו): על דאית ליה משתבע כו'. ואע"ג דעל דעת ב"ד משביעין אותו מ"מ לא הו"ל לתקן שבועה בלשון דלא משתמע שחציה שלו: ונימא שבועה שכולה שלי. לרבנן דבן ננס פריך דלא חיישי לשבועת שוא: כולה שלי ולדבריכם כו'. אף על גב דקאמר כולה שלי לא משתבע שחציה שלו שמרע לדיבוריה: דחשיד אממונא לא חשיד אשבועתא. נראה דהיינו טעמא משום דשבועה חמורה כדאיתא ביומא (דף פו.) ובשבועות (דף לט.) שהעולם נזדעזע על לא תשא וא"ת א"כ אמאי גזלן פסול לשבועה דאמר שכנגדו נשבע ונוטל וי"ל דגזלן לא פסול לשבועה אלא מדרבנן ולעדות הוא דפסול מדאורייתא משום אל תשת רשע עד וי"מ בשם ה"ר יהודה חסיד הא דחשיד אממונא כשר לשבועה משום דשמא ע"י שבועה יפרוש מגזל אבל גזלן ודאי כמו שממון אינו פורש ה"ה משבועה ולא קשה מההוא רעיא דאסהידו ביה דאכל (א) מינייהו אמאי פסול דבהנך תרי דאכל נריך לשלם ומהשאר יפרוש על ידי שבועה דמה שהוא משלם על ידי עדים אין זה השבה מעליא דעל כרחו משלם והיינו טעמא דכופר בפקדון פסול לעדות: ההיא שעתא דאיתיה בביתיה. ל"ג דאשתבע דאי איכא סהדי דנשבע לשקר במלוה נמי פסול וכן משמע בהגוזל קמא (ב"ק דף קה:) דמיירי בלא שבועה: בלא דמי משמע להו. וא"ת תיפוק ליה מלא תגזול וי"ל לעבור עליו בשני לאוין וא"ת והא כי יהיב דמי נמי חמסן הוה כדמוכח שלהי הכונס (שם דף סב. ושם) וחמסן פסול לעדות כדכתיב אל תשת ידך עם רשע להיות עד חמס והפסול לעדות פסול לשבועה דכל הנהו דחשיב בפסולי עדות בפרק זה בורר (סנהדרין דף כה: ושם) פוסל להו לשבועה בפרק כל הנשבעין (שבועות דף מה.) וי"ל דחמסן לא פסול לעדות אלא מדרבנן מדתני בפרק זה בורר הוסיפו עליהם החמסנין ולא פריך חמסן דאורייתא הוא כדפריך אגזלן וחמסן דקרא דלא יהיב דמי ושלהי הגוזל (ב"ק דף קיט.) דמייתי קרא דמחמס בני יהודה אפי' אי יהיב דמי אסמכתא בעלמא הוא ואע"ג דהוסיפו עליהם החמסנין לפסול לעדות וה"ה שפסול לשבועה היינו חמסן שחטוף לחטוף מיד ליד בידיעת הבעלים אבל הכא לא חטיף אלא מעליס חמסנותו ואמר שנאבדה לו לא פסיל:

אלא

**עין משפט נר מצוה**

כג א ב מיי' פ"י מהל' עדות הל' ד סמג לאוין ריד טוש"ע ח"מ סי' לד סי"ג [רב אלפס סנהדרין פ"ג דף רסא]:
כד ג טוש"ע ח"מ סי' קלח סעיף א:
כה ד טוש"ע ח"מ סי' לב ס"ג וע"ש [דהיינו אם אין עדים שלקח ממון חבירו]:
כו ה טוש"ע שם ס"ד:
כז ו שם בהג"ה:

**רבינו חננאל**

עבדינן. ש"מ דאפילו היכא דליכא דררא דממונא בינייהו היה לך בידי ופרעתיך א) מחייב רב נחמן שבועת היסת. הא דאמר רב יהודה סתם רועה פסול ברועה בהמות שלו משום דמרעה אותן בשדות בני אדם אבל רועה בהמות אחרים חזקה אין אדם חוטא ולא לו. ואע"ג דאמר ר' זירא אי איתא לדר' חייא קמייתא לית לן למימר דדחאי לגמרי דהא אשכחן כי האי גוונא בתחלת פ' המדיר את אשתו שאמרו ואם איתא לדרב הונא אמר רב דאמר יכולה אשה שתאמר לבעלה איני ניזונת ואיני עושה וכו' שמראין הדברים שדחאה. וכבר מצינו בפ' שני דייני גזילות והיל' כרב הונא אמר רב דאמר יכולה אשה שתאמר איני ניזונת ואיני עושה שמעינן מיניה דכי האי גוונא אינה נדחת הילכך הלכתא כר' חייא בקמייתא: **פיסקא זה ישבע שאין לו בה פחות מחציה וכו'.** אוקימנא באומר כולה שלי ולדבריכם דלא יהביתו לי כולה שבועה שיש לי בה ואין לי בה פחות מחציה. אמר ר' יוחנן שבועה זו תקנת חכמים היא שלא יהא כל אחד תופס בטלית חבירו ואומר שלי הוא. ואסקי' לא אמרי' מגו דחשיד אממונא חשיד נמי אשבועתא והאי דאמר הכופר בפקדון פסול לעדות שנינן בדאיכא סהדי דההיא שעתא דכפר בה בב"ד הוה נקיט ליה ב) אי הוה ידע היכא איתיה ברשותיה. הא דאמר רב הונא משביעין אותו שבועה שאינה ברשותו בתחלת פ' המפקיד.

**חשק שלמה על ר"ח**

א) וי"ל דאפילו בטוען אין לך בידי ג"כ חייב היסת ודלי"ק דרב נחמן בשבועות מ'.
ב) נראה דצ"ל הוה נקיט ליה בידיה או הוה ידע וכו'.

**תורה אור השלם**

א) לֹא תְקַלֵּל חֵרֵשׁ וְלִפְנֵי עִוֵּר לֹא תִתֵּן מִכְשֹׁל וְיָרֵאתָ מֵּאֱלֹהֶיךָ אֲנִי יְיָ: [ויקרא יט, יד]
ב) לֹא תַחְמֹד בֵּית רֵעֶךָ לֹא תַחְמֹד אֵשֶׁת רֵעֶךָ וְעַבְדּוֹ וַאֲמָתוֹ וְשׁוֹרוֹ וַחֲמֹרוֹ וְכֹל אֲשֶׁר לְרֵעֶךָ: [שמות כ, יד]

**מסורת הש"ס**

א) [שבועות מא., מ... ב) [סנהדרין כה... ג) [קידושין סג:, שבו... מב:, ערכין כג.], ד) ל... ג., ה) [לעיל ג. וש"... ו) [לעיל ד., ב"ק ק... קס:, שבועות מ... ז) [לקמן לה., ב"ק ק... קז.], ח) לקמן לד:, ט) [... תוספות סנהדרין כה: ד... מעיקרא], י) [ע"א ד... שכנגדו].

**הגהות הב"ח**

(א) תוס' ד"ה דחשיד דאכל תרתי מינייהו א... פסול:

**ליקוטי רש"י**

סתם רועה. דאכתי חזקן דעיילו בהמ... בשדות אחרות [סנה... כה:]. לפני עור תתן מכשול. ... הסומא בדבר לא תתן ... שאינה הוגנת לו [ויקרא יט, יד]. אין אדם חוטא ולא לו. בדבר שאינו נ... ממנו [קידושין סג:]. ... בשביל אחר לא ... [ערכין כג.]. ותוקף. ... [לעיל ג.]. הכו... במלוה. בין על כולה על מקצת ובאו ע... והעידוהו עד שלא נש... כשר לעדות. ... אמרינן גזלן הוא והת... אמרה [שמות כג] אל ... רשע עד דכיון ד... להוצאה ניתנה דלמא ... להוציאה וסבר עד דהו... זוזי ופרענא ליה ... מודינא ליה השתא יתב... מיד. בפקדון פ... לעדות. אבל הכ... בפקדון אפי' על מ... ובאו עדים והעידוהו פ... לעדות דמאי הוה ליה ... פקדון לאשתמוטי נפ... וכו' [לעיל ד.]. ואפי' נשבע למשעה ד... איחשיד ליה אמו... [שבועות מ:]. ארבע שומרים וכו'. ראה ... בעמוד א.

**וְתַקַּנְתָּא לְתַקַּנְתָּא לֹא עָבְדִינַן – And we do not apply one enactment to another enactment,** i.e. we do not superimpose one Rabbinic enactment upon another.[1] Hence, only if we adopt R' Chiya's first ruling (according to which the shepherd becomes obligated in the Biblical oath of *modeh bemiktzas*) will the oath be shifted to the townspeople.

The Gemara now asks why Abaye objected to R' Zeira that this particular shepherd could not swear because of his confirmed status as a thief. Even had he not been a confirmed thief, he should be disqualified from swearing:[2]

**וְתִיפּוֹק לֵיהּ דַּהֲוָה לֵיהּ רוֹעֶה – But let it emerge** that the shepherd is disqualified from swearing from the very fact **that he is a shepherd, וְאָמַר רַב יְהוּדָה – and** that **Rav Yehudah said: סְתָם רוֹעֶה פָּסוּל – An ordinary shepherd is disqualified** from serving as a witness.[3]

The Gemara answers:

**לֹא קַשְׁיָא – This is not a difficulty. הָא דִּידֵיהּ – This** ruling that an ordinary shepherd is disqualified applies when the animals he grazes are **his own. הָא דְּעָלְמָא – In this** case of R' Zeira, the shepherd in question grazes animals **of the general** public. This type of shepherd is not automatically disqualified.[4]

The Gemara proves this distinction:

**דְּאִי לֹא תֵּימָא הָכִי – For if you do not say this** distinction between the private shepherd and the public shepherd, rather we assume all shepherds to be thieves, **אֲנַן חֵיוָתָא לְרוֹעֶה הֵיכִי מַסְרִינַן – then how do we** allow ourselves to **entrust** our **animals to a** public **shepherd? וְהָא כְּתִיב: ,,לִפְנֵי עִוֵּר לֹא תִתֵּן מִכְשֹׁל" – But it is written** in the Torah: ***Do not place a stumbling block before the blind.***[5] **אֶלָּא חֲזָקָה אֵין אָדָם חוֹטֵא וְלֹא לוֹ – Rather, there is a presumption that a person does not sin if no** benefit accrues **to him** from the sin.[6] Therefore, a public shepherd is not presumed to be a thief.

The Mishnah ruled regarding the two litigants holding the disputed cloak:

**זֶה יִשָּׁבַע שֶׁאֵין לוֹ בָּהּ פָּחוֹת מֵחֶצְיָהּ [וכו'] – THIS ONE MUST SWEAR THAT HE DOES NOT OWN LESS THAN HALF OF IT [etc.].**

The Gemara questions why the oath was worded in this way:

**עַל דְּאִית לֵיהּ מִשְׁתַּבַּע אוֹ עַל דְּלֵית לֵיהּ מִשְׁתַּבַּע – Should h swear concerning what he owns** (i.e. "I own half the cloak **or should he swear concerning what he does not own** (a the oath is, in fact, formulated in the Mishnah)? Would it n have been better to require him to swear directly that he own half?[7]

The Gemara answers:

**אָמַר רַב הוּנָא – Rav Huna said:** The Mishnah is to be understo as follows: **דְּאָמַר שְׁבוּעָה שֶׁיֵּשׁ לִי בָּהּ – [Each litigant] says, " swear that I own** something **of [this cloak], ...ין לִי בָּהּ פָּחוֹת מֵחֶצְיָהּ – and I do not own less than half of it.**"[8]

The Gemara asks:

**וְנֵימָא שְׁבוּעָה שֶׁכּוּלָּהּ שֶׁלִּי – But let each one say, "I swear that is all mine,"** as each initially claimed. Why does the oath impos on the litigant not fully reflect his stated claim to the enti cloak?[9]

The Gemara answers:

**וּמִי יָהֲבִינַן לֵיהּ כּוּלָּהּ – Do we** indeed **award him all of it?** Certain not, since the other litigant is also holding the disputed cloa Therefore, the oath is formulated to reflect the final division th follows the oath.[10]

The Gemara asks:

**וְנֵימָא שְׁבוּעָה שֶׁחֶצְיָהּ שֶׁלִּי – But let each say** simply, **"I swear th half of it is mine."** Why the circumlocution: "I do not own le than half of it"?

The Gemara answers:

**מֵרַע לֵיהּ לְדִיבּוּרֵיהּ –** If he were to swear that he owns half, h **would** thereby **undermine his** original **declaration** that he own the entire cloak.[11]

The Gemara asks:

**הַשְׁתָּא נַמִּי מֵרַע לֵיהּ לְדִיבּוּרֵיהּ – Even now** according to Rav Huna formulation of the oath, **he undermines his original declar tion.**[12] **– ? –**

The Gemara answers:

**דְּאָמַר כּוּלָּהּ שֶׁלִּי –** In fact, **[each litigant]** prefaces his oath ar **says** to the court: **"It is all mine,"** as I claimed originall **וּלְדִבְרֵיכֶם – But according to your opinion** that my claim to th *entire* cloak is not to be believed and you therefore do not allow m

NOTES

1. Shifting the oath obligation from the disqualified defendant to the plaintiff is but a Rabbinic enactment, which therefore does not apply where the initial oath is itself of Rabbinic origin (*Rashi*).

2. *Rashi*. See, however, *Rabbeinu Peretz* cited in *Shitah Mekubetzes*.

3. I.e. a shepherd is disqualified as a witness even if there is no specific evidence that he is a thief, since shepherds are assumed to allow their animals to graze in the fields of others, which constitutes theft (*Rashi*).

4. In general, a person will not sin unless he stands to gain something from his crime (see Gemara below). Thus, a shepherd is suspected of grazing his animals in private fields only when he stands to profit from such theft. Now, a flock owner profits by allowing his animals to graze in private fields [since he saves himself the time it would take to lead his flock out to the public pastures]. However, a public shepherd [who is paid for whatever time he cares for the animals entrusted to him] gains nothing by using the private fields that are close by. Thus, the public shepherd is not disqualified unless there is specific evidence that he is a thief (see *Rashi*).

5. *Leviticus* 19:14. This injunction includes the prohibition against creating a situation in which the morally blind will stumble and sin (see *Pesachim* 22b; see also *Rambam, Sefer HaMitzvos, Prohibitions* §299, *Hil. Rotzeiach* 12:14, and *Sefer HaChinuch* §232). Thus, if all shepherds were presumed to graze their animals in private fields, we would not be allowed to entrust animals to a public shepherd, for by doing so we would be creating a situation in which he will steal.

6. See note 4 above.

7. The way the oath is formulated in the Mishnah ("I do not own less than half"), it is possible for a false claimant to take the oath and rationalize that – notwithstanding how the court construes his inte – he is not swearing falsely. For if he owns *nothing*, it is technicall true that he does not own "less than half." Apparently, it would ha been better to make each litigant swear simply, "I own half." In th way, a false claimant could not maintain his fraud without taking patently false oath, and the oath would function more fully as tl deterrent it was meant to be (*Rashi*; *Maharam Shif*; see also *Tosaf* ד"ה על).

8. I.e. the Mishnah did not state the actual formula of the oath, for ( the Gemara has pointed out) an oath formulated in that way contains loophole. Rather, the litigants must actually swear a two-part oath: own a portion of this cloak and that portion is not less than half of it (s *Chochmas Manoach*).

9. [The Gemara asks this question according to the view of the Sag that dispute Ben Nanas (see above, 2b, and notes 11 and 12 there) ar allow adversaries in a dispute to take oaths that are mutually exclusiv even though one of them will necessarily be swearing falsely (*Tosafos*)

10. If the court were to impose an oath that reflects the claims rath than the final settlement, the stature of the court might be compr mised in people's eyes: The litigant swears that he owns the enti cloak, yet the court does not award it to him! (*Rashi*).

11. The oath "I own half" implies that he does not own more than ha which is not what he originally claimed (*Rashi*). [And we do not ma a person take an oath that implies a retraction of his original claim

12. By limiting his oath to the less ambitious assertion that he owns least half, he also seems to be backing away from his original claim th he owns the entire cloak.

[א] ותקנתא לתקנתא לא עבדינן ותיפוק ליה דהוה ליה רועה [ב] ואמר רב יהודה [א]סתם רועה פסול לא קשיא [ג]הא דידיה הא דעלמא דאי לא תימא הכי אנן חיותא לרועה היכי מסרינן והא כתיב [א] לפני עור לא תתן מכשול אלא [ג] חזקה אין אדם חוטא ולא לו: זה ישבע שאין לו בה פחות מחציה [וכו']: על דאית ליה משתבע או על דלית ליה משתבע אמר רב הונא [ג]דאמר שבועה שיש לי בה ואין לי בה פחות מחציה ונימא שבועה שכולה שלי ומי יהבינן ליה כולה ונימא שבועה שחציה שלי מרע ליה לדיבוריה השתא נמי מרע ליה לדיבוריה דאמר כולה שלי ולדבריכם שבועה שיש לי בה ואין לי בה פחות מחציה וכי מאחר שזה תפוס ועומד וזה תפוס ועומד שבועה זו למה [ד]אמר ר' יוחנן שבועה זו תקנת חכמים היא שלא יהא כל אחד ואחד הולך ותוקף בטליתו של חבירו ואומר שלי הוא ונימא מיגו דחשיד אממונא חשיד נמי אשבועתא [ד]לא אמרינן מיגו דחשיד אממונא חשיד אשבועתא דאי לא תימא הכי האי דאמר רחמנא מודה מקצת הטענה ישבע נימא מיגו דחשיד אממונא חשיד אשבועתא התם אשתמוטי קא משתמיט ליה [ה] כדרבה תדע [ו]דאמר רב אידי בר אבין אמר רב חסדא הכופר במלוה כשר לעדות בפקדון פסול לעדות אלא הא [ז]דתני רמי בר חמא ארבעה שומרין צריכין כפירה במקצת והודאה במקצת שומר חנם והשואל נושא שכר והשוכר נימא מיגו דחשיד אממונא חשיד אשבועתא התם נמי אשתמוטי קא משתמיט סבר משכחנא לגנב ותפיסנא ליה א"נ משכחנא ליה באגם ומייתינא ליה אי הכי הכופר בפקדון אמאי פסול לעדות נימא אשתמוטי קא משתמיט סבר עד דבחשנא ומשכחנא ליה [ה]כי אמרינן הכופר בפקדון פסול לעדות כגון דאתו סהדי ואסהידו ביה דההיא שעתא איתיה לפקדון בביתיה והוה ידע א"נ דהוה נקיט ליה בידיה אלא הא [ח] דאמר רב הונא משביעין אותו שבועה שאינה ברשותו נימא מיגו דחשיד אממונא חשיד אשבועתא התם נמי מורה ואמר דמי קא יהבנא ליה אמר ליה רב אחא מדיפתי לרבינא והא קא עבר על לאו [ב] דלא תחמוד [י]לא תחמוד לאינשי [ט]בלא דמי משמע להו ואלא

רש"י

ותקנתא. דכשכנגדו ישבע ויטול דהויא נמי תקנתא דמן התורה מי שעליו לשלם הוא ישבע ויפטר מן התשלומין ואין נשבע ונוטל מן התורה ואותן המנויין בשבועות (דף מה:) תקנת חכמים הן ולשבועה דאורייתא עבוד רבנן תקנתא אבל תקנתא לתקנתא לא עבדינן: ותיפוק ליה דהוה ליה רועה. אלאביי קא מתמה דקשיא ליה והא גזלן הוא ותיפוק ליה דבלאו הך גזילה פסול לשבועה: דאמר רב יהודה סתם רועה. אפילו לא הועד עליו שגזל: פסול. לעדות דסתמיה גזלן הוא שמרעה בהמותיו בשדות של אחרים: דידיה. רועה בהמות שלו פסול דבשביל הנאתו רועה אותן בשדות אחרות אבל רועה בהמות העיר בשכר בשביל הנאת אחרים אינו חוטא להרעות עד שיגיע למרעה המופקר לכל: דאי לא תימא הכי. דלא אמרינן על רועה בהמות דעלמא שהוא גזלן אנן חיותא לרועה היכי מסרינן: על דאית ליה משתבע או על דלית ליה משתבע. הכא לישבע וליטול חציה צריך הוא לישבע שיש לו בה חציה או לישבע שאין לו בה פחות מחציה שמא אין לו בה כלום וכי משתבע שאין לו בה פחות מחציה באמת הוא נשבע שהרי אין לו כלום דבשלמא אם היה לו בה שליש או רביע והוא נשבע שאין לו בה פחות מחציה נשבע בשקר שהרי יש לו בה שליש שהוא פחות מחציה ואין לו בה חציה אבל כשאין לו בה כלום נשבע הוא באמת: שבועה שיש לי בה. ואם תאמרו שמא שליש או רביע שבועה שאין לי חלק בה פחות מחציה: מי יהבינן ליה כולה. הרי חבירו תופס בה ואם ישביעוהו על כולה הרי לעז לב"ד מאחר שכולה שלו והם אמרו יחלוקו: מרע ליה לדיבוריה. דאמר ברישא כולה שלי והשתא אמר בהדיא חציה שלי: דאמר כולה שלי. תירוצא הוא: ולדבריכם. שאין אתם מאמינים לי בכולה שבועה שיש לי בה ואין לי בה פחות מחציה: ונימא מגו דחשיד אממונא חשיד כו'. אדרבי יוחנן פריך דאמר חשדוהו רבנן שמא ילך ותוקף בטליתו של חבירו ואומר שלי הוא אם חשוד הוא בכך חשוד הוא נמי לישבע: לא אמרינן כו'. דחמיר הוא לאינשי איסור שבועה מאיסור גזילה: אשתמוטי משתמיט ליה. ולא חשיד אממונא: כדרבה. דאמר לעיל מפני מה אמרה תורה כו': תדע. דלאו בגזלן חשדינן ליה אלא באשתמוטי בעלמא: דאמר רב אידי בר אבין הכופר במלוה. שבאו עדים והחזיקוהו בכפרן שהעידוהו שהוא חייב לו: כשר לעדות. אלמא לאו דעתיה למגזליה דנימא אל תשת עד חמס אלא לאשתמוטי עביד: בפקדון פסול לעדות. דמאי אשתמוטי איכא הרי לא ניתן להוצאה ובעין הוא ואם אבד יטעון שאבד ויפטר: ולימא מיגו דחשיד אממונא. דההוא דאמר לא היו דברים מעולם כופר בפקדון הוא וליכא למימר משתמיט: חשיד נמי אשבועה דידה. דבשלמא אשבועת שומרין דההוא דקטעין נאנסה דחייביה רחמנא שבועה איכא למימר דלא חשיד אממונא אלא שמא פשע בשמירתה וחייב לשלם אונסיה וסבר עד דהוי לי זוזי ופרענא ליה אלא ההיא דכפירה הא ודאי כופר בפקדון הוא ומשקר והיכי משבעינן ליה עלה: התם נמי אשתמוטי משתמיט. שאבדה ממנו וסבר משכחנא לגנב כו': אי הכי. בפקדון איכא למימר משתמיט: דבחשנא. אחפש: ה"ג דההיא שעתא הוה גביה. ולא גרס ההיא שעתא דאשתבע: דאמר רב הונא. לקמן בהמפקיד גבי שילם ולא רצה לישבע אמר רב הונא אם בא לשלם משביעין אותו שבועה שאינה ברשותו חיישינן שמא עיניו נתן בה: התם. לא חשיד אממונא דמורי היתרא למימר דמי בעינא למיתב: הא קא עבר בלא תחמוד. מה לי חשוד על לא תחמוד מה לי חשוד על לא תגזול נימא מיגו דחשיד עליה חשיד אשבועתא:

משביעין

תוספות

ותקנתא לתקנתא. וממוך שאינו יכול לישבע משלם לא שייך הכא כדפרישית [י]: על דאית ליה משתבע כו'. ואע"ג דעל דעת ב"ד משביעין אותו מ"מ לא הו"ל לתקן שבועה בלשון דלא משתמע שחציה שלו: ונימא שבועה שכולה שלי. לרבנן דכן נמי פריך דלא חיישי לשבועת שוא: כולה שלי ולדבריכם כו'. אף על גב דקאמר כולה שלי לא משתבע שחציה שלו שמרע לדיבוריה: דחשיד אממונא לא חשיד אשבועתא. נראה דהיינו טעמא משום דשבועה חמורה כדאיתא ביומא (דף פו.) ובשבועות (דף לט.) שהעולם נזדעזע על לא תשא וא"ת א"כ אמאי גזלן פסול לשבועה דאמר שכנגדו נשבע ונוטל וי"ל דגזלן לא פסול לשבועה אלא מדרבנן ולעדות הוא דפסול מדאורייתא משום אל תשת רשע עד וי"מ בשם ה"ר יהודה חסיד הא דחשיד אממונא כשר לשבועה משום דשמא ע"י שבועה יפרוש מגזל אבל גזלן ודאי כמו שממון אינו פורש ה"ה משבועה ולא קשה מההוא רעיא דאסהידו ביה דאכל (א) מינייהו אמאי פסול דבהנך תרי דאכל צריך לשלם ומהשאר יפרוש על ידי שבועה דמה שהוא משלם על ידי עדים אין זה השבה מעליא דעל כרחו משלם והיינו טעמא דכופר בפקדון פסול לעדות: ההיא שעתא דאיתיה בביתיה. ל"ג דאשתבע דאי איכא סהדי דנשבע לשקר במלוה נמי פסול וכן משמע בהגוזל קמא (ב"ק דף קה:) דמיירי בלא שבועה: בלא דמי משמע להו. וא"ת תיפוק ליה מלא תגזול וי"ל לעבור עליו בשני לאוין וא"ת והא כי יהיב דמי נמי חמסן הוה כדמוכח שלהי הכונס (שם דף סב. ושם) וחמסן פסול לעדות כדכתיב אל תשת ידך עם רשע להיות עד חמס והפסול לעדות פסול לשבועה דכל הנהו דחשיב בפסולי עדות בפרק זה בורר (סנהדרין דף כה: ושם) פוסל להו לשבועה בפרק כל הנשבעין (שבועות דף מה.) וי"ל דחמסן לא פסול לעדות אלא מדרבנן מדתני בפרק זה בורר הוסיפו עליהם החמסנין ולא פריך חמסן דאורייתא הוא כדפריך אגזלן וחמסן דקרא דלא יהיב דמי ושלהי הגוזל (ב"ק דף קיט.) דמייתי קרא דמחמס בני יהודה אפי' אי יהיב דמי אסמכתא בעלמא הוא ואע"ג דהוסיפו עליהם החמסנין לפסול לעדות וה"ה שפסול לשבועה היינו חמסן שחטף להוציא מיד ליד בידיעת הבעלים אבל הכא לא חטף אלא מעלים חמסנותו ואמר שנאבדה לו לא פסיל:

אלא

עין משפט נר מצוה

כג א ב מיי' פ"י מהל' עדות הל' ד סמג לאוין ריד טוש"ע ח"מ סי' לד סי"ג [רב אלפס סנהדרין פ"ג דף רסא]:

כד ג טוש"ע ח"מ סי' קלח סעיף א:

כה ד טוש"ע ח"מ סי' לג ס"ג וע"ש [דסיינו אם אין עדים שלקח ממון חבירו]:

כו ה טוש"ע שם ס"ד:

כז ו שם בהג"ה:

רבינו חננאל

עבדינן. ש"מ דאפילו היכא דליכא דררא דממונא בינייהו היה לך בידי ופרעתיך (א) מחייב רב נחמן שבועת היסת. הא דאמר רב יהודה סתם רועה פסול ברועה בהמות שלו משום דמרעה אותן בשדות בני אדם אבל רועה בהמות אחרים חזקה אין אדם חוטא ולא לו. ואע"ג דאמר ר' זירא אי איתא לדר' חייא קמייתא לית לן למימר דדחאי לגמרי דהא אשכחן כי האי גוונא בתחלת פ' המדיר את אשתו שאמרו ואם איתא לדרב הונא אמר רב דאמר יכולה אשה שתאמר לבעלה איני ניזונת ואיני עושה וכו' שמראין הדברים שדחאה. וכבר מצינו בפ' שני דייני גזילות והיל' כרב הונא אמר רב דאמר יכולה אשה שתאמר איני ניזונת ואיני עושה שמעינן מיניה דכי האי גוונא אינה נדחת הילכך הלכתא כר' חייא בקמייתא: פיסקא זה ישבע שאין לו בה פחות מחציה וכו'. אוקימנא באומר כולה שלי ולדבריכם דלא יהביתו לי כולה שבועה שיש לי בה ואין לי בה פחות מחציה. אמר ר' יוחנן שבועה זו תקנת חכמים היא שלא יהא כל אחד תופס בטלית חבירו ואומר שלי הוא. ואסקי' לא אמרי' מגו דחשיד אממונא חשיד נמי אשבועתא והאי דאמר הכופר בפקדון פסול לעדות שנינן בדאיכא סהדי דההיא שעתא דכפר בה בב"ד הוה נקיט ליה (ב) אי הוה ידע היכא איתיה ברשותיה. הא דאמר רב הונא משביעין אותו שבועה שאינה ברשותו בתחלת פ' המפקיד.

חשק שלמה על ר"ח

(א) ור"ל דאפילו בטוען אין לך בידי וכו' מחייב היסת וכו' דרב נחמן בשבועות מ'. (ב) נראה דל"ל הוה נקיט ליה בידיה או הוה ידע וכו'.

תורה אור השלם

א) לֹא תְקַלֵּל חֵרֵשׁ וְלִפְנֵי עִוֵּר לֹא תִתֵּן מִכְשֹׁל וְיָרֵאתָ מֵּאֱלֹהֶיךָ אֲנִי יְיָ: [ויקרא יט, יד]

ב) לֹא תַחְמֹד בֵּית רֵעֶךָ לֹא תַחְמֹד אֵשֶׁת רֵעֶךָ וְעַבְדּוֹ וַאֲמָתוֹ וְשׁוֹרוֹ וַחֲמֹרוֹ וְכֹל אֲשֶׁר לְרֵעֶךָ: [שמות כ, יד]

מסורת הש"ס

א) [שבועות מא., מו.] ב) [סנהדרין כה:] ג) [קידושין סג., שבועות מב:, ערכין כג.], ד) [לעיל ג., ה) [לעיל ג. וש"נ] ו) [לעיל ד., בבא קמא קה:, שבועות מ:] ז) [לקמן לה., בבא קמא קז.], ח) לקמן לד:, ט) [עי' תוספות סנהדרין כה: ד"ה מעיקרא], י) [ע"א ד"ה שכנגדו].

הגהות הב"ח

(א) תוס' ד"ה דחשיד וכו' דאכל תרתי מינייהו אמאי פסול:

ליקוטי רש"י

סתם רועה. דאכתי חזינן דעיילו בהמות בשדות אחרות [סנהדרין כה:]. לפני עור לא תתן מכשול. לפני הסומא בדבר לא תתן עצה שאינה הוגנת לו [ויקרא יט, יד]. אין אדם חוטא ולא לו. בדבר שאינו נהנה ממנו [קידושין סג:]. להרויח בשביל אחר לא יחטא [ערכין כג.]. ותוקף. או [לעיל ג.]. הכופר במלוה. בין על כולה בין על מקצת ובאו עדים והעידוהו על שלא נשבע כשר לעדות. ולא אמרינן גזלן הוא והתורה אמרה (שמות כג) אל תשת רשע עד דכיון דמלוה להוצאה ניתנה דלמא לא להוציאה וסבר עד דהוו לי זוזי ופרענא ליה ולא מודינא ליה השתא יתבענו מיד. בפקדון פסול לעדות. אבל הכופר בפקדון אפי' על מקצת ובאו עדים והעידוהו פסול לעדות דמאי הוה ליה בפקדון לאשתמוטי נפשיה וכו' [לעיל ד.]. ואפי' נשבע דמשעה דכפר איחשיד ליה אממונא [שבועות מ:]. ארבעה שומרים וכו'. ראה לעיל בעמוד א.

ולמאן דאמר הילך פטור אמאי איצטריך קרא למעוטי קרקע משבועה הא כל קרקע הילך הוא אמר לך איצטריך קרא היכא דחפר בה בורות שיחין ומערות א"נ [א] היכא דטענו כלים וקרקעות והודה בכלים וכפר בקרקעות ת"ש [א] דתני רמי בר חמא ארבעה שומרין צריכין כפירה במקצת והודאה במקצת שומר חנם והשואל נושא שכר והשוכר היכי דמי לאו דא"ל הילך לא דאמר ליה ג' פרות מסרתי לך ומתו כולהו בפשיעה וא"ל איהו חדא לא היו דברים מעולם וחדא מתה באונס וחדא מתה בפשיעה דבעינא שלומי לך דלאו הילך הוא ת"ש דתני אבוה דרבי אפטוריקי לדרבי חייא קמייתא מנה לי בידך והלה אומר אין לך בידי כלום והעדים מעידים אותו שיש בידו חמשים זוז יכול ישבע על השאר ת"ל [א] על כל אבדה אשר יאמר כי הוא זה על הודאת פיו אתה מחייבו ואי אתה מחייבו על העדאת עדים מתניתא קא רמית עליה דר' חייא ר' חייא תנא הוא ופליג והא קרא קאמר ההוא [ג] למודה מקצת הטענה ואבוה דר' אפטוריקי אמר לך כתיב הוא וכתיב זה חד למודה מקצת הטענה וחד להעדאת עדים דפטור ואידך חד למודה מקצת הטענה וחד [א] למודה ממין הטענה ואידך מודה ממין הטענה לית ליה (א) [א] וסבר ליה כר"ג דתנן [ג] [ב] טענו חטין והודה לו בשעורין פטור ור"ג מחייב: ההוא רעיא דהוו מסרי ליה כל יומא חיותא בסהדי יומא חד מסרו ליה בלא סהדי לסוף אמר להו לא היו דברים מעולם אתו סהדי אסהידו ביה דאכל תרתי מינייהו א"ר זירא אם איתא לדר' חייא קמייתא משתבע אשארא אמר ליה אביי אם איתא משתבע והא גזלן הוא א"ל שכנגדו קאמינא השתא נמי דליתא לדר' חייא נחייביה מדרב נחמן דתנן [ד] מנה לי בידך אין לך בידי פטור [ה] ואמר רב נחמן [ג] משביעין אותו שבועת היסת דרב נחמן תקנתא היא ותקנתא

ותקנתא

## רש"י

למאי איצטריך קרא למעוטי קרקע משבועה. דילפינן לה מכלל ופרט בשבועות (דף מב:) ולקמן בפרק הזהב (דף נז:): וחפר בה בורות שיחין ומערות. דלאו הילך הוא שהרי קלקלה: אי נמי. להיכן דהודה בכלים דלאו הילך הוא ואשמועינן דאינו נשבע אכפירת [י] (שעבוד) קרקעות: ד' שומרין. שבועה האמורה בהן בשומר חנם שנגנבה הימנו ושומר שכר שנאנסה ובשואל שמתה מחמת מלאכה: צריכין כפירה במקצת והודאה במקצת. כפירה לא הויא אלא בכופר ממש או לא היו דברים מעולם או החזרתי לך הודאה לא הויא אא"כ הודה ממש שיש לו בידו שחייב להחזיר לו נמצא שאין חיוב שבועת השומרים באה אלא אם כן טען שלש פרות באחת כפר לו ובאחת הודה לו שישנה בידו והשלישית אומר לו נאנסה או אם שומר חנם הוא אומר לו בשלישית נגנבה דחייב עליה שבועה האמורה בפרשה (שמות כב) שלא שלח ידו במלאכת רעהו דאילו שבועה דכפירה אין זו שבועה האמורה בשומרים ובלא כפירה נמי לא תחייביה שבועת שומרים דכתיב בשומר חנם כי הוא זה דמינה נפקא לן (שבועות לט:) שמודה במקצת וכפר במקצת ולאפוקי ממ"ד בבבא קמא בהגוזל [קמא] (דף קז.) עירוב פרשיות כתוב כאן וכי כתיב כי הוא זה לאו אשומר חנם דכתיב גביה קאי אלא אאם כסף תלוה ואשמועינן האי תנא דבשומרים נמי בעינן כפירה והודאה והשבועה האמורה בפרשה על פרה שלישית: היכי דמי. פרה של הודאה: לאו. דקיימא קמן ואמר ליה קחנה בכל מקום שהיא דהיינו הילך: אידך מתה לה באונס. ועליה הוא נשבע שבועת שומרין: וחדא מתה לה בפשיעה. היא של הודאה ולאו הילך הוא: ת"ש דתני אבוה דרבי אפטוריקי. ת"ש מינה תיובתא: לרבי חייא קמייתא. כלומר ת"ש לדרבי חייא קמייתא דאמר לעיל שלא תהא הודאת פיו גדולה מהעדאת עדים כו': אשר יאמר וגו'. מודה לו במקצת מכלל דכופר במקצת וכתב בההוא לעיל מיניה ונקרב בעל הבית אל האלהים ודרשינן לקמן (דף מא:) ונקרב לשבועה: ההוא. מיבעי ליה להודאת מקצת דמחייבא עליה שבועה ואתיא העדאת עדים מינה בקל וחומר כדלעיל דליכא קרא יתירא לתדרוש מינה מיעוטא: וחד להעדאת עדים. למעוטה: וחד להודאה ממין הטענה. דבעינן שתהא הודאה ממין טענת כפירה שאם טענו סאה של חטים והודה לו בשעורים פטור: אם איתא לדרבי חייא. אם הלכה כמותו: אמר ליה אביי ואם איתא לדרבי חייא משתבע האי. בתמיה: והא גזלן הוא. וכי אמר רבי חייא במלוה אי נמי בפקדון שלא שלח בו יד ואבד ממנו דאיכא למימר אשתמוטי משתמיט: לשכנגדו קאמינא. אם שבועה מוטלת עליו נשבע שכנגדו ונוטל כדאמרינן בשבועות (דף מד:) שהחשוד על השבועה תקנו חכמים שכנגדו נשבע: השתא נמי. כי ליתא לדר' חייא ואין כאן הודאה במקצת: נחייביה. שבועת היסת מדרב נחמן וישבע שכנגדו ויטול: היסת. שבועה שהסיתו חכמים לכך להסיתו להודות וטעמא מפרש בשבועות (דף מ:) חזקה אין אדם טוען אא"כ יש לו בידו: דר"נ תקנתא היא. דהא מדאורייתא לא רמי שבועה עליה:

## תוספות

למ"ד הילך פטור קרא אמאי איצטריך כו'. תימה גם למ"ד הילך חייב אמאי איצטריך קרא למעוטי הא בקרקע לא שייך משתמיט וכן [ז] [פר"י] לקמן דכי כופר במקצת קרקע פטור הוא דנאמן הוא מטעם דאין אדם מעיז כיון דלא שייך הכא אשתמוטי קא משתמיט ושמא גם בקרקע שייך קצת אשתמוטי קא משתמיט כי שמא משכנה וסבר עד דהוה לי זוזי ופרענא ליה: אמאי איצטריך קרא למעוטי. תימה הא ליכא קרא מיותר למעוטי קרקעות אלא מכלל ופרט וכלל ממעטינן להו וכלל ופרט וכלל אצטריך למעוטי שטרות וי"ל דקשיא ליה אמאי אצטריך תנא למילף קרקעות מכלל ופרט כיון דהילך פטור וא"ת לימא דאיצטריך למעוטי משבועה דעד אחד מיהו י"ל משום דמתני' דאין נשבעין על הקרקעות איירי בשבועה דמודה במקצת: א"נ דטענו כלים וקרקעות. מהכא משמע דטענו חטין ושעורים והודה באחד מהן דחייב דדוקא כלים וקרקעות פטור הא חטין ושעורים חייב וכן סברי שמואל ורבי יוחנן לחד לישנא פרק שבועת הדיינין (שבועות דף מ.): שומר חנם. פטור מכל חוץ מפשיעה ושואל חייב בכל חוץ ממתה מחמת מלאכה ונושא שכר והשוכר במקצת חייב ובמקצת פטור ולכך תנא להו כסדר זה ולא שנאם כסדר כתיבתם וא"ת ואמאי לא מקשה מכמה משניות [ח] דזה אומר עד הזיז וזה אומר עד החלון ועשרה גפנים דשבועות (דף מב:) ומתניתין דהשואל (לקמן דף צז: ושם) דזה אומר שאולה וזה אומר שכורה דמיירי בפקדון הא הילך הוא וי"ל דניחא ליה לאקשויי מכל ד' שומרין: רבי חייא תנא הוא ופליג. אי גרס לעיל (ג.) ° א"ר חייא א"ש ואפילו אי גרסינן תני ר' חייא י"ל דהכי קאמר דאפילו לא הוה ברייתא תנא הוא ופליג: והודה בשעורים פטור. אף מן השעורים כדמוכח שלהי המניח (ב"ק דף לה: ושם ד"ה לימא): מסרי ליה בסהדי. ומיירי דאמרי ליה אל תחזיר אלא בעדים דאל"כ הא קי"ל (כתובות יח.) המלוה את חבירו בעדים א"צ לפרעו בעדים: אי איתא לדרבי חייא. נראה ° דהלכה כרבי חייא דהא לעיל מוקי לה כרבנן דר"ג דהלכה כוותייהו כדפריך שלהי המניח (ב"ק שם) מאי קמ"ל תנינא וכן בפ' השואל (לקמן ק. ושם) פריך אמאי טענו חטין והודה לו בשעורים הוא וכן סברי רב ושמואל בפ' שבועת הדיינין (שבועות דף מ. ושם) אע"ג דקאמר הכא אם איתא הכי נמי אשכחנא פ' [ט] (אע"פ) (כתובות דף נט) דקאמר אם איתא לדרב הונא דאמר יכולה אשה שתאמר לבעלה איני ניזונת וכו' ובפרק שני דייני גזירות (שם דף קז:) פסיק כרב הונא [י] תימה אפי' אי איתא לדרבי חייא לא משתבע הכא דאסהידו עליה דאכל תרי מינייהו דמה להנך השוה שבהן שכן לא הוחזק כפרן תאמר הכא דהוחזק כפרן כדפריך לעיל (ד.) והכא לא שייך משתמיט ושמא י"ל אחרי שלמד שיש שבועה בהעדאת עדים במלוה מעתה אין לחלק בין מלוה לפקדון: שכנגדו קאמינא. ° וא"ת מאי שנא דבחשוד על השבועה שכנגדו נשבע ונוטל אמאי לא אמרינן מתוך שא"י לישבע משלם כדאמר גבי חמשין ידענא וחמשין לא ידענא (לקמן דף לח.) ובנסכא דר' אבא (שבועות דף [כ]) וי"ל הכא אי אמרי' משלם לא שבקת ליה חיי דכל העולם יביאוהו לידי שבועה ויטלו כל אשר לו ועוד דהתם אמר ליה שבועה דאורייתא אית לי עליך או תשבע או תשלם אבל הכא הוא ברצון ישבע אם ניזוקו ולכך לא ישלם: אין לך בידי פטור וא"ר נחמן. מהכא משמע דהלכה כלישנא קמא דפ' שבועת הדיינים (שם דף מא. ושם ד"ה מאן) דלא בעי דררא דממונא אלא אפי' כופר הכל חייב שבועת היסת מדלא מייתי הכא סיפא דנתתיו לך פטור וכן פירש בשערים דרב האי ואי טוען איני יודע בכל ישבע שאינו יודע:

ותקנתא

## מסורת הש"ס

א) לקמן נח., בבא קמא קז., ב) [שבועות לט:], ג) לקמן ק:, בבא קמא לה:, שבועות לח:, מ., (כתובות קח:), ד) שבועות לח:, ה) [שם מ:, לקמן ו.], ו) רש"ל מ"ז, ז) מהרש"ל, ח) עיין נמוקי יוסף כאן ובגמרא שם, ט) צ"ל המדיר דף ע:, י) [ועיין עוד תוס' שבועות מו. ד"ה בטוענו], כ) [לג:, מז. ובבא בתרא לג:].

## הגהות הב"ח

(א) גמ' דסבר ליה כרבן גמליאל:

## גליון הש"ס

תוס' ד"ה רבי חייא וכו' אר"ח א"ש. עיין נדה דף כו ע"א ברש"י ד"ה אמר אביי: ד"ה אי וכו' דהלכה כר"ח. עיין שבועות דף מו ע"א תוס' ד"ה בטוענו: ד"ה שכנגדו. וא"ת מ"ש. יש לעיין איך תלי הקושיא כאן הא דין זה ערוך במתני' רפ"ז דשבועות דשכנגדו חשוד נשבע ונוטל והו"מ להקשות שם במקומו:

## ליקוטי רש"י

בורות שיחין ומערות. בור עגול הוא שיח ארוכה וקצרה מערה מרובעת ומכוסה בקרוי אלא שיש לה פה [ב"ק נ:]. ארבעה שומרים כו'. בשבועות האמורות בהן כגון ש"ח לישבע שנגנבה וש"ש לישבע שנאנסה ושואל לישבע שמתה ממלאכה [לקמן צח.]. צריכין כפירה במקצת והודאה במקצת. קודם שיתחייבו שבועה ואם נשבעו בלא כפירה והודאה אין שבועתו של ש"ח כלום ולא מחייבתו כפל [ב"ק קז:]. על כל אבדה אשר יאמר. ורבותינו ז"ל דרשו כי הוא זה ללמד שאין מחייבין אותו שבועה אלא אם כן הודה במקצת לומר כך וכך אני חייב לך והמותר נגנב ממני [שמות כב, ח]. ההוא למודה מקצת הטענה. זה מיבעי ליה דאין שבועה אלא בהודאה במקצת כלומר את זה אני מודה [שבועות לט:]. והודה לו בשעורים פטור. דבעינן הודאה ממין הטענה עצמה [לקמן ק:]. ור"ג מחייב. דלא בעי הודאה ממין הטענה [שבועות מ.]. חיותא. בהמות [לקמן צג.]. אין לך בידי פטור. שאין כאן הודאה [שבועות לח:]. משביעין אותו וכו'. לשאינו מודה במקצת [לקמן ו.]. שבועת היסת. לשון שומא ששמו חכמים עליו שבועה כמו (שמואל א כו ח) אם ה' הסיתך בי [שבועות מ:]. תקנתא היא וכו'. שבועה עצמה של היסת תקנתא היא ותקנתא שיהא מועב נשבע ונוטל לתקנתא היסת שבועה שלא באה עליו אלא בתקנת חכמים לא עבדינן [שבועות מא.].

## עין משפט נר מצוה

[א] [רב אלפס כאן ובשבועות פ"ו דף שה]:

כ א מיי' פ"ג מהל' טוען ונטען ה"א סמג עשין לה טוש"ע ח"מ סי' פח סעיף ז:

כא ב מיי' שם הלכה ח ופ"א שם הל' ג ופ"ט מהל' ג"מ הלכה יא סמג שם טוש"ע שם סי"ב וסי' ת ס"ד:

כב ג מיי' פ"א מהלכות טוען ונטען ה"ג סמג שם טוש"ע שם סי' עה ס"ז וסי' פז סעיף א:

## הגהות הגר"א

[א] גמ' (וס"ל כר"ג דתנן טענו חטין והודה לו בשעורין פטור ור"ג מחייב) תא"מ:

## תורה אור השלם

א) עַל כָּל דְּבַר פֶּשַׁע עַל שׁוֹר עַל חֲמוֹר עַל שֶׂה עַל שַׂלְמָה עַל כָּל אֲבֵדָה אֲשֶׁר יֹאמַר כִּי הוּא זֶה עַד הָאֱלֹהִים יָבֹא דְּבַר שְׁנֵיהֶם אֲשֶׁר יַרְשִׁיעֻן אֱלֹהִים יְשַׁלֵּם שְׁנַיִם לְרֵעֵהוּ: [שמות כב, ח]

## רבינו חננאל

ומקשי' על רב ששת מהא דתני רמי בר חמא בהגוזל קמא הלכ' נתן לו את הקרן. ד' שומרין צריכין כפירה במקצת והודאה במקצת ואלו הן שומר חנם והשואל נושא שכר והשוכר והא בהאי דקא מודה ליה הילך וקתני דחייב. ודחי רב ששת לא לעולם הילך פטור והאי כגון דטעין ליה ג' בהמות מסרתי לך ומתו להו כולהו בפשיעותך וחייב אתה בשלשתן ואמר לו השומר חדא לא היו דברים מעולם זו היא כפירה במקצת. וחדא פשעתי בה ומתה ואני חייב לשלמה לך זו היא הודאה במקצת ואינו הילך דהא ליתא בעינא אלא אני חייב לשלם קאמר ליה. וחדא מתה לה באונס וסבר רמי דהאי דחייבה תורה לשומר שבועה בטענת אונסין מדכת' כי יתן אל רעהו חמור או שור או שה וכל בהמה לשמור וטען השומר מת באונס או נשבר או נשבה שבועת ה' תהיה בין שניהם. צריכה כפירה והודאה במקצת כשאר כל חייבי שבועה שבתור' כדכתיב אשר יאמר כי הוא זה ופירושו אשר יאמר הנתבע כי הוא שאתה טועני אינו כולו אמת אלא זהו בלבד שנמצאת כפירה במקצת והודאה במקצת ואי אתה מוצא כפירה במקצת והודאה במקצת ושבועה באונסין אלא בטוען ג' פרות מסרתי לך כמו שפירשנו למעלה אבל אם יטעון עליו בשתים והלה טוען חדא לא היה דברים מעולם וחדא מתה באונס כפירה איכא הודאה ליכא ואי טעין חדא מתה בפשיעה וחדא באונס הודאה איכא כפירה ליכא הלכך לא משכחת כפירה במקצת והודאה במקצת וחיוב שבועה באונסין אלא בטוען ג' פרות מסרתי לך כו'. ואע"ג דפריק רבי חייא כל קושיא דאקשן עליה וסוגייא כוותיה רהטא כרב ששת קיימא לן דהוא בתרא ותוב מדקתני לה בפ' השואל היו לו עבדים ומכר אחד הלוקח טוען הגדול קניתי והמוכר אמר הקטן מכרתי ישבע המוכר שהקטן מכר ואמרי' אמאי ישבע מה שטענו לא הודה לו כי בגדול טענו והוא לא הודה לו בגדול אמאי ישבע ועוד הילך הוא ועוד אין נשבעין על העבדים ש"מ מדתני לה גבי הלכת' פסיקתא הילך נמי הלכת' הוא דפטור. ומקשי' תוב אקמייתא דר' חייא מהא דתני אבוה דר' אפטוריקי מנה לי בידך והלה אומר אין לך בידי כלום והעדים מעידים עליו בנ' יכול ישבע על השאר וכו'. ופרקי' ר' חייא נמי תנא הוא ופליג על התנאים. והאי קרא דגמיר מיניה אבוה דר' אפטוריקי דריש ליה ר' חייא הכי אשר יאמר כי הוא [זה] מכאן דבעינן הודאה ממין הטענה ומקצת הטענה. אבל אבוה דר' אפטוריקי הני תרי קראי חד ש"מ דאין נשבעין בהעדאת עדים וחד למקצת הטענה אבל ממין הטענה לא בעי. וקיימא לן בהא כר' חייא. ההוא רעיא דהוו מסרי ליה כל יומא חיותא בסהדי יומא חד מסרו ליה בלא סהדי אמר לא היה דברים מעולם אתו סהדי אסהידו דאכל תרי מינייהו אמר רבי זירא אי איתא לדר' חייא כלומר אילו נתברר לי דהלכתא כר' חייא בהא הייתי דן אותו לשלם השנים שאכל ולישבע על השאר שבועה דאורייתא דכיון שהוא גזלן ישבע שכנגדו ויטול. ומקשה לר' זירא אפי' הכי אי ליתא לר' חייא נחייביה מדתנן מנה לי בידך והלה אומר אין לך בידי כלום פטור. ואמר רב נחמן ומשביעין אותו שבועת היסת מדרבנן. ופריק לה דרב נחמן תקנתא היא מדרבנן ותקנתא לתקנתא לא עבדינן כלומר נעשה עוד תקנה על זו דרב נחמן להישבע כנגדו ויטול כולי האי תקנת' לתקנתא לא עבדינן

Accordingly, the Gemara asks:

וְאִי – And from where does the other authority (the author of e Baraisa) derive this condition (that the admission must relate the type of item claimed)?[17]

The Gemara answers:

מוֹדֶה מִמִּין הַטַּעֲנָה לֵית לֵ – In fact, he does not hold that [the fendant] must admit something of the type that was aimed; וְסָבַר לֵיהּ כְּרַבָּן גַּמְלִיאֵל – rather, he holds the view ' Rabban Gamliel. דִּתְנַן – As we learned in a Mishnah: טְעָנוֹ חִטִּין וְהוֹדָה לוֹ בִּשְׂעוֹרִין פָּטַ – If [THE PLAINTIFF] CLAIMED HEAT FROM HIM, BUT [THE DEFENDANT] ADMITTED owing HIM ARLEY, HE IS EXEMPT from swearing the oath of *modeh bemikzas*; וְרַבָּן גַּמְלִיאֵל מְחַיֵּיב – BUT RABBAN GAMLIEL REQUIRES him swear it.[18]

The Gemara applies R' Chiya's first law (that partial substantiion by witnesses creates a *modeh bemiktzas* situation) to an tual case:

הַהוּא רָעֲ – A certain shepherd דַּהֲווּ מַסְרֵי לֵיהּ כָּל יוֹמָא חֵיוָתָא בְּסָהֲ – to whom [the townspeople] – in the presence of itnesses – would deliver their animals each day to shepherd r them.[19] יוֹמָא חַד מַסְרוּ לֵיהּ בְּלֹא סָהֲדֵי – One day, they livered their animals to him without witnesses being esent. לְסוֹף אָמַר לְהוּ – Eventually, i.e. at the end of the day, hen the owners came to retrieve their animals, he said to them, לֹא הָיוּ דְּבָרִים מֵעוֹ – "The matter never happened," i.e. I did ot receive any animals from you today. אָתוּ סָהֲדֵי אַסְהִידוּ בֵּיהּ – owever, witnesses came and testified against him דְּאָכַל תַּרְתֵּי מִינַּיְ – that he in fact ate two of [the animals] that day, ereby establishing that he had received at least two of the animals claimed by the townspeople.[20] אָמַר רַבִּי זֵירָא – R' Zeira said about this case: אִם אִיתָא לִדְר' חִיָּיא קַמַּיְיתָא – If R' Chiya's first law is indeed accepted as halachah,[21] מִשְׁתַּבַּע אַשְּׁאָרָא – then he must swear the *modeh bemiktzas* oath regarding the remaining animals.[22]

Abaye objects:

אָמַר לֵיהּ אַבַּיֵי – Abaye said to [R' Zeira]: אִם אִיתָא מִשְׁתַּבַּע – If [R' Chiya's first law] is accepted, [the shepherd] swears? How can this be? וְהָא גַּזְלָן הוּא – But he is a confirmed thief and is thereby disqualified from taking an oath![23]

R' Zeira clarifies his statement:

אָמַר לֵיהּ – [R' Zeira] said to [Abaye]: שֶׁכְּנֶגְדוֹ קָאָמִינָא – I meant that his opponent swears.[24]

The Gemara questions R' Zeira's need to resort to R' Chiya's law in order to impose an oath in this case:

הַשְׁתָּא נַמִּי דְּלֵיתָא לִדְר' חִיָּיא – But even if R' Chiya's first law is not accepted as the halachah, נְחַיְּיבֵיהּ מִדְּרַב נַחְמָן – let us obligate him to swear because of R' Nachman's ruling. דִּתְנַן – For we learned in a Mishnah: מָנֶה לִי בְּיָדְךָ – If a plaintiff claims: "YOU OWE ME A *MANEH*," and the defendant replies: אֵין לְךָ בְּיָדִי – "I DO NOT OWE YOU anything," פָּטוּר – HE IS EXEMPT from swearing.[25] וְאָמַר רַב נַחְמָן – But Rav Nachman said: מַשְׁבִּיעִין אוֹתוֹ שְׁבוּעַת הֶיסֵּת – Nevertheless, by Rabbinic enactment, we impose upon him an oath of "incitement"[26] to elicit a confession from him. Thus, even if we do not accept R' Chiya's first law, an oath should be imposed in the case of the shepherd because of Rav Nachman's rule.[27] – ? –

The Gemara answers:

דְּרַב נַחְמָן תַּקַּנְתָּא הִיא – The oath ordained by the rule of Rav Nachman is but a Rabbinical enactment,

NOTES

rse is not intended to limit the oath to situations of personal mission, but rather to limit the oath to situations in which the mission relates to the type of item claimed.

[*Rashi* adds that the admission must also relate to the type of item nied. *Rashi* apparently alludes to yet another Tannaic view recorded *Shevuos* (loc. cit.), that the *modeh bemiktzas* oath does not apply less the claim, admission *and* denial all relate to the same type. Thus, the plaintiff claims wheat *and* barley and the defendant admits only e barley (for example), the *modeh bemiktzas* oath does not apply, cording to this view, since the admission and denial do not relate to the me type of item. *Rashash* writes that he is at a loss to explain what mpelled *Rashi* to introduce this view in our Gemara.]

. He cannot derive it from the superfluous expression in the verse (as Chiya does), since he uses that superfluous expression to teach a fferent law.

. [*Shevuos* 38b.] Thus, Rabban Gamliel does not consider admission of e type claimed to be a condition of the *modeh bemiktzas* oath.

. In this way, the shepherd could not deny having received the animals d would be forced to return them at day's end.

. Thus, the situation is one in which the defendant [the shepherd] has nied the entire claim against him, yet that claim is partially bstantiated by witnesses.

. [As mentioned earlier on this *amud,* the Baraisa taught by R' toriki's father disagrees with R' Chiya's first law. Thus, R' Zeira nnot take it for granted that R' Chiya's first law is the halachah. (See so *Tosafos.*)]

. Apparently, R' Zeira means that the shepherd must assert his ntinued denial of the remaining animals under oath, since part of the aim against him has been substantiated by witnesses.

. The shepherd's wanton theft of at least two of the animals has been tablished by witnesses who saw him eating them. Therefore, the epherd should be disqualified from swearing.

Although every case of R' Chiya's first law involves a defendant whose nial of the claim against him has been partially contradicted by tnesses, the Gemara above (4a) has explained that R' Chiya's law applies only when the denial does not constitute outright theft. For example, the defendant has denied a debt, but witnesses testify that he owes at least half. It is possible that he did not mean to evade the debt altogether, but was merely stalling for time until he could obtain the funds necessary to repay it. Similarly, if a defendant denies ever having received an object for safekeeping, but witnesses testify that he received at least part of what is claimed, his denial does not necessarily constitute outright theft. For it is possible that the object was lost in a manner for which he is liable, and he is stalling for time so that he can obtain the funds to pay the owner. But in the present case of the shepherd, he is certainly an outright thief, since witnesses testify that he has misappropriated two animals entrusted to his care (*Rashi*).

24. When a situation calls for an oath, and the defendant is unable to swear (e.g. he is suspected of being willing to swear falsely), the Rabbis instituted that the oath obligation be shifted to his opponent – the plaintiff. Thus, the plaintiff must swear that the obligation is due him and only then can he collect it (*Rashi*, from *Shevuos* 44b).

25. *Shevuos* 38b. This is the Biblical law that a defendant who denies the *entire* claim against him is not obligated to assert his denial under oath (see above, 3a note 23).

26. I.e. though the defendant who denies the entire claim against him is Biblically exempt from swearing, the post-Mishnaic Rabbis obligated him to swear to "incite" him to admit the claim against him if it is true (see *Rashi*; cf. *Rashi* to *Shevuos* 40b).

The Rabbis imposed this special oath, because it is presumed that the plaintiff would not make a totally frivolous claim. Thus, the claim itself creates the suspicion that the defendant might be lying. To offset this suspicion, the Rabbis made the defendant take an oath. This will either induce the defendant to admit his debt rather than swear falsely, or establish the credibility of his denial if he indeed swears the oath (see *Rashi* from *Shevuos* 40b).

27. That is, since the shepherd cannot swear the Rabbinic oath in our case, that oath obligation should be shifted to the claimants, who should have to swear that they delivered the animals to the shepherd, and then collect from him (*Rashi*).

ולמאן דאמר הילך פטור אמאי איצטריך קרא למעוטי קרקע משבועה הא כל קרקע הילך הוא אמר לך איצטריך קרא היכא דחפר בה בורות שיחין ומערות א"נ [א] היכא דטענו כלים וקרקעות והודה בכלים וכפר בקרקעות ת"ש [א] דתני רמי בר חמא ארבעה שומרין צריכין כפירה במקצת והודאה במקצת שומר חנם והשואל נושא שכר והשוכר היכי דמי לאו דא"ל הילך לא דאמר ליה ג' פרות מסרתי לך ומתו כולהו בפשיעה וא"ל איהו חדא לא היו דברים מעולם וחדא מתה באונס וחדא מתה בפשיעה דבעינא שלומי לך דלאו הילך הוא ת"ש דתני אבוה דרבי אפטוריקי לדרבי חייא קמייתא מנה לי בידך והלה אומר אין לך בידי כלום והעדים מעידים אותו שיש בידו חמשים זוז יכול ישבע על השאר ת"ל א) על כל אבדה אשר יאמר כי הוא זה על הודאת פיו אתה מחייבו ואי אתה מחייבו על העדאת עדים מתניתא קא רמית עליה דר' חייא ר' חייא תנא הוא ופליג והא קרא קאמר ההוא ג) למודה מקצת הטענה ואבוה דר' אפטוריקי אמר לך כתיב הוא וכתיב זה חד למודה מקצת הטענה וחד להעדאת עדים דפטור ואידך חד למודה מקצת הטענה וחד א למודה ממין הטענה ואידך מודה ממין הטענה לית ליה (א) [א] וסבר ליה כר"ג דתנן ג) ב טענו חטין והודה לו בשעורין פטור ור"ג מחייב: ההוא רעיא דהוו מסרי ליה כל יומא חיותא בסהדי יומא חד מסרו ליה בלא סהדי לסוף אמר להו לא היו דברים מעולם אתו סהדי אסהידו ביה דאכל תרתי מינייהו א"ר זירא אם איתא לדר' חייא קמייתא משתבע אשארא אמר ליה אביי אם איתא משתבע והא גזלן הוא א"ל שכנגדו קאמינא השתא נמי דליתא לדר' חייא נחייביה מדרב נחמן דתנן ד) מנה לי בידך אין לך בידי פטור ה) ואמר רב נחמן ג משביעין אותו שבועת היסת דרב נחמן תקנתא היא ותקנתא

**רש"י**

למאי איצטריך קרא למעוטי קרקע משבועה. דילפינן לה מכלל ופרט בשבועות (דף מג:) ולקמן בפרק הזהב (דף מז:): וחפר בה בורות שיחין ומערות. דלאו הילך הוא שהרי קלקלה: אי נמי. להיכן דהודה בכלים דלאו הילך הוא ואשמועינן דאינו נשבע אכפירת י) (שעבוד) קרקעות: ד' שומרין. שבועה האמורה בהן בשומר חנם שנגנבה הימנו ושומר שכר שנאנסה ובשואל שמתה מחמת מלאכה: צריכין כפירה במקצת והודאה במקצת. כפירה לא הויא אלא בכופר ממש או לא היו דברים מעולם או החזרתי לך הודאה לא הויא אא"כ הודה ממש שיש לו בידו שחייב להחזיר לו נמצא שאין חיוב שבועת השומרים בא אלא אם כן טוען שלש פרות באחת כפר לו ובאחת הודה לו שישנה בידו והשלישית אומר לו נאנסה או אם שומר חנם הוא אומר לו בשלישית נגנבה דחייב עליה שבועה האמורה בפרשה (שמות כב) שלא שלח ידו במלאכת רעהו דאילו שבועה דכפירה אין זו שבועה האמורה בשומרים ובלאו כפירה נמי לא תחייביה שבועת שומרים דכתיב בשומר חנם כי הוא זה דמינה נפקא לן (שבועות לט:) שמודה במקצת וכפר במקצת ולאפוקי ממ"ד בבבא קמא בהגוזל [קמא] (דף קז.) עירוב פרשיות כתוב כאן וכי כתיב כי הוא זה לאו אשומר חנם דכתיב גביה קאי אלא אאם כסף תלוה ואשמועינן האי תנא דבשומרים נמי בעינן כפירה והודאה והשבועה האמורה בפרשה על פרה שלישית: היכי דמי. פרה של הודאה: לאו. דקיימא קמן ואמר ליה קחנה בכל מקום שהיא דהיינו הילך: אידך מתה לה באונס. ועליה הוא נשבע שבועת שומרין: וחדא מתה לה בפשיעה. היא של הודאה ולאו הילך הוא: ת"ש דתני אבוה דרבי אפטוריקי. ת"ש מינה תיובתא: לרבי חייא קמייתא. כלומר ת"ש לדרבי חייא קמייתא דאמר לעיל שלא תהא הודאת פיו גדולה מהעדאת עדים כו': אשר יאמר וגו'. מודה לו במקצת מכלל דכופר במקצת וכתב בההוא לעיל מיניה ונקרב בעל הבית אל האלהים ודרשינן לקמן (דף מא:) ונקרב לשבועה: ההוא. מיבעי ליה להודאת מקצת דמחייבא עליה שבועה ואתיא העדאת עדים מינה בקל וחומר כדלעיל דליכא קרא יתירא לתדרוש מינה מיעוטא: וחד להעדאת עדים. למעוטה: וחד להודאה ממין הטענה. דבעינן שתהא הודאה ממין טענת כפירה שאם טענו סאה של חטים והודה לו בשעורים פטור: אם איתא לדרבי חייא. אם הלכה כמותו: אמר ליה אביי ואם איתא לדרבי חייא משתבע האי. בתמיה: והא גזלן הוא. וכי אמר רבי חייא במלוה אי נמי בפקדון שלא שלח בו יד ואבד ממנו דאיכא למימר אשתמוטי משתמיט: לשכנגדו קאמינא. אם שבועה מוטלת עליו נשבע שכנגדו ונוטל כדאמרינן בשבועות (דף מד:) שהחשוד על השבועה תקנו חכמים שכנגדו נשבע: השתא נמי. כי ליתא לדר' חייא ואין כאן הודאה במקצת: נחייביה. שבועת היסת מדרב נחמן וישבע שכנגדו ויטול: היסת. שבועה שהסיתו חכמים לכך להסיתו להודות וטעמא מפרש בשבועות (דף מ:) חזקה אין אדם טוען אא"כ יש לו בידו: דר"נ תקנתא היא. דהא מדאורייתא לא רמי שבועה עליה:

ותקנתא

**תוספות**

למ"ד הילך פטור קרא אמאי איצטריך כו'. תימה גם למ"ד הילך חייב אמאי איצטריך קרא למעוטי הא בקרקע לא שייך משתמיט וכן י) [פר"י] לקמן דכי כופר במקצת קרקע פטור הוא דנאמן הוא מטעם דאין אדם מעיז כיון דלא שייך הכא אשתמוטי קא משתמיט ושמא גם בקרקע שייך קצת אשתמוטי קא משתמיט כי שמא משכנה וסבר עד דהוה לי זוזי ופרענא ליה: אמאי איצטריך קרא למעוטי. תימה הא ליכא קרא מיותר למעוטי קרקעות אלא מכלל ופרט וכלל ממעטינן להו וכלל ופרט וכלל אצטריך למעוטי שטרות וי"ל דקשיא ליה אמאי איצטריך תנא למילף קרקעות מכלל ופרט כיון דהילך פטור וא"ת לימא דאיצטריך למעוטי משבועה דעד אחד מיהו י"ל משום דמתני' דאין נשבעין על הקרקעות איירי בשבועה דמודה במקצת: א"נ דטענו כלים וקרקעות. מהכא משמע דטענו חטין ושעורים והודה באחד מהן דחייב דדוקא כלים וקרקעות פטור הא חטין ושעורים חייב וכן סברי שמואל ורבי יוחנן לחד לישנא פרק שבועת הדיינין (שבועות דף מ.): שומר חנם. פטור מכל חוץ מפשיעה ושואל חייב בכל חוץ ממתה מחמת מלאכה ונושא שכר והשוכר במקצת חייב ובמקצת פטור ולכך תנא להו כסדר זה ולא שנאם כסדר כתיבתם וא"ת ואמאי לא מקשה מכמה משניות ח) דזה אומר עד הזיז וזה אומר עד החלון ועשרה גפנים דשבועות (דף מב:) ומתניתין דהשואל (לקמן דף צז: ושם) דזה אומר שאולה וזה אומר שכורה דמיירי בפקדון הא הילך הוא וי"ל דניחא ליה לאקשויי מכל ד' שומרין: רבי חייא תנא הוא ופליג. אי גרס לעיל (ג.) ° א"ר חייא א"ש ואפילו אי גרסינן תני ר' חייא י"ל דהכי קאמר דאפילו לא הוה ברייתא תנא הוא ופליג: והודה בשעורים פטור. אף מן השעורים כדמוכח שלהי המניח (ב"ק דף לה: ושם ד"ה לימא): מסרי ליה בסהדי. ומיירי דאמרי ליה אל תחזיר אלא בעדים דאל"כ הא קי"ל (כתובות יח.) המלוה את חבירו בעדים א"צ לפרעו בעדים: אי איתא לדרבי חייא. נראה ° דהלכה כרבי חייא דהא לעיל מוקי לה כרבנן דר"ג דהלכה כוותייהו כדפריך שלהי המניח (ב"ק שם) מאי קמ"ל תנינא וכן בפ' השואל (לקמן ק. ושם) פריך אמאי טענו חטין והודה לו בשעורים הוא וכן סברי רב ושמואל בפ' שבועת הדיינין (שבועות דף מ. ושם) אע"ג דקאמר הכא אם איתא הכי נמי אשכחנא פ' ט) (אע"פ) (כתובות דף נט) דקאמר אם איתא לדרב הונא דאמר יכולה אשה שתאמר לבעלה איני ניזונת וכו' ובפרק שני דייני גזירות (שם דף קז:) פסיק כרב הונא י) תימה אפי' אי איתא לדרבי חייא לא משתבע הכא דאסהידו עליה דאכל תרי מינייהו דמה להצד השוה שבהן שכן לא הוחזק כפרן תאמר הכא דהוחזק כפרן כדפריך לעיל (ד.) והכא לא שייך משתמיט ושמא י"ל אחרי שלמד שיש שבועה בהעדאת עדים במלוה מעתה אין לחלק בין מלוה לפקדון: שכנגדו קאמינא. ° וא"ת מאי שנא דבחשוד על השבועה שכנגדו נשבע ונוטל אמאי לא אמרינן מתוך שא"י לישבע משלם כדאמר גבי חמשין ידענא וחמשין לא ידענא (לקמן דף לח.) ובנסכא דר' אבא (שבועות דף ל) וי"ל הכא אי אמרי' משלם לא שבקת ליה חיי דכל העולם יביאוהו לידי שבועה ויטלו כל אשר לו ועוד דהתם אמר ליה שבועה דאורייתא אית לי עליך או תשבע או תשלם אבל הכא הוא ברצון ישבע אם ניחא ולכך לא ישלם: אין לך בידי פטור וא"ר נחמן. מהכא משמע דהלכה כלישנא קמא דפ' שבועת הדיינים (שם דף מא. ושם ד"ה מאן) דלא בעי דררא דממונא אלא אפי' כופר הכל חייב שבועת היסת מדלא מייתי הכא סיפא דנתתיו לך פטור וכן פירש בשערים דרב האי ואי טוען איני יודע בכל ישבע שאינו יודע:

ותקנתא

**עין משפט נר מצוה**

[א] [רב אלפס כאן ובשבועות פ"ו דף שה]:

כ א מיי' פ"ג מהל' טוען ונטען ה"ח סמג עשין לה טוש"ע ח"מ סי' פח סעיף ז:

כא ב מיי' שם הלכה ח ופ"א שם הל' ג ופ"ט מהל' כ"מ הלכה יא סמג שם טוש"ע שם סי"ג וסי' ח ס"ד:

כב ג מיי' פ"א מהלכות טוען ונטען ה"ג סמג שם טוש"ע שם סי' עה ס"ז וסי' פז סעיף א:

**הגהות הגר"א**

[א] גמ' (וס"ל כר"ג דתנן טענו חטין והודה לו בשעורין פטור ור"ג מחייב) תא"מ:

**תורה אור השלם**

א) עַל כָּל דְּבַר פֶּשַׁע עַל שׁוֹר עַל חֲמוֹר עַל שֶׂה עַל שַׂלְמָה עַל כָּל אֲבֵדָה אֲשֶׁר יֹאמַר כִּי הוּא זֶה עַד הָאֱלֹהִים יָבֹא דְּבַר שְׁנֵיהֶם אֲשֶׁר יַרְשִׁיעֻן אֱלֹהִים יְשַׁלֵּם שְׁנַיִם לְרֵעֵהוּ: [שמות כב, ח]

**רבינו חננאל**

ומקשי' על רב ששת מהא דתני רמי בר חמא בהגוזל קמא הלכ' נתן לו את הקרן. ד' שומרין צריכין כפירה במקצת והודאה במקצת ואלו הן שומר חנם והשואל נושא שכר והשוכר והא בהאי דקא מודה ליה הילך וקתני דחייב. ודחי רב ששת לא לעולם הילך פטור והאי כגון דטעין ליה ג' בהמות מסרתי לך ומתו להו כולהו בפשיעותך וחייב אתה בשלשתן ואמר לו השומר חדא לא היו דברים מעולם זו היא כפירה במקצת. וחדא פשעתי בה ומתה ואני חייב לשלמה לך זו היא הודאה במקצת ואינו הילך דהא ליתא בעינא אלא אני חייב לשלם קאמר ליה. וחדא מתה לה באונס וסבר רמי דהאי דחייבה תורה לשומר שבועה בטענת אונסין מדכת' כי יתן אל רעהו חמור או שור או שה וכל בהמה לשמור וטען השומר מת באונס או נשבר או נשבה שבועת ה' תהיה בין שניהם. צריכה כפירה והודאה במקצת כשאר כל חייבי שבועה שבתור' כדכתיב אשר יאמר כי הוא זה ופירושו אשר יאמר הנתבע כי הוא שאתה טועני אינו כולו אמת אלא זהו בלבד שנמצאת כפירה במקצת והודאה במקצת ואי אתה מוצא כפירה במקצת והודאה במקצת ושבועה באונסין אלא בטוען ג' פרות מסרתי לך כמו שפירשנו למעלה אבל אם יטעון עליו בשתים והלה טוען חדא לא היה דברים מעולם וחדא מתה באונס כפירה איכא הודאה ליכא ואי טעין חדא מתה בפשיעה וחדא באונס הודאה איכא כפירה ליכא הלכך לא משכחת כפירה במקצת והודאה במקצת וחיוב שבועה באונסין אלא בטוען ג' פרות מסרתי לך כו'. ואע"ג דפריק רבי חייא כל קושיא דאקשן עליה וסוגייא כוותיה רהטא כרב ששת קיימא לן דהוא בתרא ותוב מדקתני לה בפ' השואל היו לו עבדים ומכר אחד הלוקח טוען הגדול קניתי והמוכר אמר הקטן מכרתי ישבע המוכר שהקטן מכר ואמרי' אמאי ישבע מה שטענו לא הודה לו כי בגדול טענו והוא לא הודה לו בגדול אמאי ישבע ועוד הילך הוא ועוד אין נשבעין על העבדים ש"מ מדתני לה גבי הלכת' פסיקתא הילך נמי הלכת' הוא דפטור. ומקשי' תוב אקמייתא דר' חייא מהא דתני אבוה דר' אפטוריקי מנה לי בידך והלה אומר אין לך בידי כלום והעדים מעידים עליו בנ' יכול ישבע על השאר וכו'. ופרקי' ר' חייא נמי תנא הוא ופליג על התנאים. והאי קרא דגמיר מיניה אבוה דר' אפטוריקי דריש ליה ר' חייא הכי אשר יאמר כי הוא [זה] מכאן דבעינן הודאה ממין הטענה ומקצת הטענה. אבל אבוה דר' אפטוריקי הני תרי קראי חד ש"מ דאין נשבעין בהעדאת עדים וחד למקצת הטענה אבל ממין הטענה לא בעי. וקיימא לן בהא כר' חייא. ההוא רעיא דהוו מסרי ליה כל יומא חיותא בסהדי יומא חד מסרו ליה בלא סהדי אמר לא היה דברים מעולם אתו סהדי אסהידו דאכל תרי מינייהו אמר רבי זירא אי איתא לדר' חייא כלומר אילו נתברר לי דהלכתא כר' חייא בהא הייתי דן אותו לשלם השנים שאכל ולישבע על השאר שבועה דאורייתא דכיון שהוא גזלן ישבע שכנגדו ויטול. ומקשה לר' זירא אפי' הכי אי ליתא לר' חייא נחייביה מדתנן מנה לי בידך והלה אומר אין לך בידי כלום פטור. ואמר רב נחמן ומשביעין אותו שבועת היסת מדרבנן. ופריק לה דרב נחמן תקנתא היא מדרבנן ותקנתא לתקנתא לא עבדינן כלומר נעשה עוד תקנה על זו דרב נחמן להישבע כנגדו ויטול כולי האי תקנת' לתקנתא לא עבדינן

**מסורת הש"ס**

א) לקמן לח., בבא קמא קו., ב) [שבועות לט:], ג) לקמן ק:, בבא קמא לה:, שבועות לח:, מ., (כתובות קח:), ד) שבועות לח:, ה) [שם מ:, לקמן ו.], ו) רש"ל מ"ז, ז) מהרש"ל, ח) עיין נמוקי יוסף כאן ובגמרא שם, ט) צ"ל המדיר דף ע:, י) [ועיין עוד תוס' שבועות מו. ד"ה בטוענו], כ) [לב:, מז. ובבא בתרא לג:].

**הגהות הב"ח**

(א) גמ' דסבר ליה כרבן גמליאל:

**גליון הש"ס**

תוס' ד"ה רבי חייא וכו' אר"ח א"ש. עיין נדה דף כו ע"א ברש"י ד"ה אמר אביי: ד"ה אי וכו' דהלכה כר"ח. עיין שבועות דף מו ע"א תוס' ד"ה בטוענו: ד"ה שכנגדו. וא"ת מ"ש. יש לעיין איך תלי הקושיא כאן הא דין זה ערוך במתני' רפ"ז דשבועות דשכנגדו חשוד נשבע ונוטל והו"מ להקשות שם במקומו:

**ליקוטי רש"י**

בורות שיחין ומערות. בור עגול הוא שיח ארוכה וקצרה מערה מרובעת ומכוסה בקרוי אלא שיש לה פה [ב"ק נ:]. ארבעה שומרים כו'. בשבועות האמורות בהן כגון ש"ח לישבע שנגנבה וש"ש לישבע שנאנסה ושואל לישבע שמתה ממלאכה [לקמן צח.]. צריכין כפירה במקצת והודאה במקצת. קודם שיתחייבו שבועה ואם נשבעו בלא כפירה והודאה אין שבועתו של ש"ח כלום ולא מחייבתו כפל [ב"ק קז:]. על כל אבדה אשר יאמר. ורבותינו ז"ל דרשו כי הוא זה ללמד שאין מחייבין אותו שבועה אלא אם כן הודה במקצת לומר כך וכך אני חייב לך והמותר נגנב ממני [שמות כב, ח]. ההוא למודה מקצת הטענה. זה מיבעי ליה דאין שבועה אלא בהודאה במקצת כלומר את זה אני מודה [שבועות לט:]. והודה לו בשעורים פטור. דבעינן הודאה ממין הטענה עצמה [לקמן ק:]. ור"ג מחייב. דלא בעי הודאה ממין הטענה [שבועות מ.]. חיותא. בהמות [לקמן צג.]. אין לך בידי פטור. שאין כאן הודאה [שבועות לח:]. משביעין אותו וכו'. לשאינו מודה במקצת [לקמן ו.]. שבועת היסת. לשון שומא ששמו חכמים עליו שבועה כמו (שמואל א כו ח) אם ה' הסיתך בי [שבועות מ:]. תקנתא היא וכו'. שבועה עצמה של היסת תקנתא היא ותקנתא שיהא תובע נשבע ונוטל לתקנתא היסת שבועה שלא באה עליו אלא בתקנת חכמים לא עבדינן [שבועות מא.].

ours," regarding the article that he admits having in his cus- ody?[8] This apparently proves that the oath of *modeh bemiktzas* pplies even in situations of "here, it is yours." – ? –

The Gemara refutes this proof:

ל׳ – **No,** this might not be the Baraisa's case. Rather, the Baraisa night refer to דְּאָמַר לֵיהּ ג׳ פָּרוֹת מָסַרְתִּי לְךָ – **where [the laintiff] said to [the custodian]: – I handed over to you hree cows** for safekeeping וּמֵתוּ כּוּלְּהוּ בִּפְשִׁיעָה – **and all of hem died as a result of** your **negligence.** Thus, you are obligated ) pay for them. וְאָמַר לֵיהּ אִיהוּ – **But [the custodian] replies:** חֲדָא לֹא הָיוּ דְבָרִים מֵעוֹלָ – Regarding **one** of the cows – **the natter never happened;** you never gave me a third cow to watch, nly two. וַחֲדָא מֵתָה בְּאוֹנֶס – **And one died through an un- voidable accident,** for which I am not liable, וַחֲדָא מֵתָה בִּפְשִׁיעָה · **and one** indeed **died** – as you say – **through** my **negligence,** דִּבְעֵינָא שַׁלּוֹמֵי לָ – **for which I must pay you.** דְּלָאו הֵילָךְ הוּא – **hus, [the case] is not one of "here, it is yours."**[9]

The Gemara now returns to consider a proof offered against R' hiya's first law, that partial substantiation through witnesses lso establishes a *modeh bemiktzas* situation:

תָּא שְׁמַע דְּתָנֵי אֲבוּהּ דְּרַבִּי אַפְטוֹרִיקִי לְדְרַבִּי חִיָּיא קַמַּיְיתָ – **Come, earn** a refutation **to the first** ruling **of R' Chiya from the llowing Baraisa that the father of R' Aftoriki taught:** מָנֶה לִי בְּיָדְךָ – If a plaintiff claims: "YOU OWE ME A *MANEH*," וְהַלָּה אוֹמֵר אֵין לְךָ בְּיָדִי כְּלוּ – AND THIS ONE [the defendant] REPLIES: OWE YOU NOTHING," וְהָעֵדִים מְעִידִים אוֹתוֹ שֶׁיֵּשׁ בְּיָדוֹ חֲמִשִּׁים זוּז · BUT WITNESSES TESTIFY ON [THE PLAINTIFF'S] BEHALF THAT E IS indeed OWED FIFTY *ZUZ* by the defendant,[10] יָכוֹל יִשָּׁבַע עַל הַשְּׁאָ – IT COULD BE thought that [THE DEFENDANT] SHOULD WEAR the *modeh bemiktzas* oath CONCERNING THE REMAINDER hat he continues to deny.[11] תַּלְמוּד לוֹמַר – Therefore THE ORAH STATES that the oath of *modeh bemiktzas* applies: ,,עַל כָּל־אֲבֵדָה אֲשֶׁר יֹאמַר כִּי־הוּא זֶ – *REGARDING ANY LOSS – WHEN IE SAYS" THAT IT IS THIS* [that I owe you, but not more].[12] This eaches that עַל הוֹדָאַת פִּיו אַתָּה מְחַיְּיבוֹ – based ON THE DMISSION OF HIS own MOUTH CAN YOU OBLIGATE HIM to swear the *modeh bemiktzas* oath, וְאִי אַתָּה מְחַיְּיבוֹ עַל הַעֲדָאַת עֵדִים – BUT YOU CANNOT OBLIGATE HIM to swear the oath based ON THE TESTIMONY OF WITNESSES. This Baraisa directly contradicts R' Chiya's first ruling! – ? –

The Gemara replies:

מַתְנִיתָא קָא רָמֵית עֲלֵיהּ דְּר׳ חִיָּיא – **Are you presenting a Baraisa** as proof **against R' Chiya?** ר׳ חִיָּיא תַּנָּא הוּא וּפָלִיג – **R' Chiya is** ranked as **a Tanna and can dispute** the ruling of a Tannaic source, such as a Baraisa.[13]

Still, the Gemara asks:

וְהָא קְרָא קָאָמַר – **But [the Baraisa] adduces a verse** in support of its ruling. How, then, can R' Chiya disagree?

The Gemara answers:

הַהוּא לְמוֹדֶה מִקְצָת הַטַּעֲנָה – According to R' Chiya, the purpose of **that** verse is **to** teach the basic law of **one who admits part of the claim** against him.[14]

Accordingly, the Gemara asks:

וַאֲבוּהּ דְּר׳ אַפְטוֹרִיקִי – **And** what would the author of the Baraisa cited by **the father of R' Aftoriki** reply to R' Chiya's rejoinder?

The Gemara answers:

אָמַר לָךְ – **He would say to you:** כְּתִיב ,,הוּא" וּכְתִיב ,,זֶה" – The word ***it* is written** in the verse **and** the word ***this* is written** there.[15] חַד לְמוֹדֶה מִקְצָת הַטַּעֲנָה – **One** of these words is needed **to** teach the basic law of one **who admits part of the claim** וְחַד לְהַעֲדָאַת עֵדִים דְּפָטוּר – **and** the other **one** is understood **to** indicate that when the partial substantiation of the claim results from **the testimony of witnesses, then [the defendant] is exempt** from swearing.

Accordingly, the Gemara asks:

וְאִידָךְ – **And** how does **the other** authority (R' Chiya) account for the superfluous expression in this verse?

The Gemara answers:

חַד לְמוֹדֶה מִקְצָת הַטַּעֲנָה וְחַד לְמוֹדֶה מִמִּין הַטַּעֲנָה – R' Chiya explains that **one** expression is needed **to** teach the basic law of **one who admits part of the claim, and one** expression is needed **to** teach that **he must admit** something **of the type that was claimed** in order for the *modeh bemiktzas* oath to apply.[16]

NOTES

As explained in the previous note, this Baraisa requires that the claim ntain three elements in order for the custodian's oath to apply. Two the elements are necessary in order to create a situation of *modeh miktzas* – the admission to owing the first cow and the denial of ever ving received the second (or the claim that he already returned it). ne Gemara now assumes that the cow which the custodian admits ving is alive and well [see *Pnei Yehoshua,* who explains the basis for is assumption]. Thus, the situation is one of "here, it is yours": The stodian concedes that the cow belongs to the plaintiff and the plaintiff ready has legal possession of it (*Rashi*). Nevertheless, the Baraisa is of e opinion that the situation still qualifies as a case of *modeh bemiktzas.* oes this not prove, then, that *modeh bemiktzas* applies even in uations of "here, it is yours"?

Since the cow that the custodian admits owing is dead, the situation not one of "here, it is yours." For although the custodian concedes ving the plaintiff compensation for that cow, the compensation is not t in the possession of the plaintiff.

. This is the identical case addressed by R' Chiya's first ruling (above, ). However, unlike R' Chiya, this Baraisa concludes shortly that the fendant does *not* swear the *modeh bemiktzas* oath in this case.

. [As R' Chiya, in fact, ruled.]

. *Exodus* 22:8. As explained above in note 7, this is the verse that aches the oath of *modeh bemiktzas.* And the verse speaks specifically a case in which the defendant *himself* admits partial liability.

. The Baraisa taught by the father of R' Aftoriki indeed contradicts R' iiya's first ruling. However, R' Chiya has the license to dispute the araisa's ruling, since he is himself ranked as a Tanna. [R' Chiya longed to the transitional generation that followed Rebbi, the redactor of the Mishnah. Some members of that new generation, though not recorded in the Mishnah, are nevertheless ranked as Tannaim and can dispute the views of earlier Tannaim (based on *Meiri, Preface to Avos*).]

14. That verse contains no superfluous expression that might be construed as *limiting* the oath obligation to cases of personal admission. Rather, the verse states the law in the case of personal admission, and R' Chiya employs standard principles of legal argument to derive that the same law applies in the case of partial substantiation by witnesses (see *Rashi*).

15. [The author of the Baraisa contends that there *is* indeed an element of superfluity contained in the verse. For the verse could have stated simply that the oath is required when he says כִּי הוּא (which would translate as: *that it is [so]*) or כִּי זֶה (which would translate as: *that this [is so]*). Either expression by itself would serve to teach the basic law of *modeh bemiktzas.* The double expression (כִּי הוּא זֶה), then, is taken to limit the law specifically to the case of *personal* admission discussed by the verse, as the Gemara proceeds to explain.

16. In order to account for the superfluous expression in the verse, R' Chiya must subscribe to the Tannaic opinion that the *modeh bemiktzas* oath does not apply unless the item admitted by the defendant is of the type claimed by the plaintiff (e.g. the plaintiff claims one hundred bushels of *wheat* and the defendant admits owing him fifty bushels of *wheat*). However, if the defendant admits something other than what was claimed by the plaintiff (e.g. the plaintiff claims one hundred bushels of *wheat* and the defendant admits owing him fifty bushels of *barley*), the *modeh bemiktzas* oath does not apply. (This condition of the oath is the subject of a Tannaic dispute in *Shevuos* 38b and will be cited shortly by the Gemara.)

Accordingly, R' Chiya asserts that the superfluous expression in the

ולמאן דאמר הילך פטור אמאי איצטריך קרא למעוטי קרקע משבועה הא כל קרקע הילך הוא אמר לך איצטריך קרא היכא דחפר בה בורות שיחין ומערות א"נ [א] היכא דטענו כלים וקרקעות והודה בכלים וכפר בקרקעות ת"ש [א] דתני רמי בר חמא ארבעה שומרין צריכין כפירה במקצת והודאה במקצת שומר חנם והשואל נושא שכר והשוכר היכי דמי לאו דא"ל הילך לא דאמר ליה ג' פרות מסרתי לך ומתו כולהו בפשיעה וא"ל איהו חדא לא היו דברים מעולם וחדא מתה באונס וחדא מתה בפשיעה דבעינא שלומי לך דלאו הילך הוא ת"ש דתני אבוה דרבי אפטוריקי לדרבי חייא קמייתא מנה לי בידך והלה אומר אין לך בידי כלום והעדים מעידים אותו שיש בידו חמשים זוז יכול ישבע על השאר ת"ל א) על כל אבדה אשר יאמר כי הוא זה על הודאת פיו אתה מחייבו ואי אתה מחייבו על העדאת עדים מתניתא קא רמית עליה דר' חייא ר' חייא תנא הוא ופליג והא קרא קאמר ההוא [ב] למודה מקצת הטענה ואבוה דר' אפטוריקי אמר לך כתיב הוא וכתיב זה חד למודה מקצת הטענה וחד להעדאת עדים דפטור ואידך חד למודה מקצת הטענה וחד א למודה ממין הטענה ואידך מודה ממין הטענה לית ליה (א) [א] וסבר ליה כר"ג דתנן [ג] ב טענו חטין והודה לו בשעורין פטור ור"ג מחייב: ההוא רעיא דהוו מסרי ליה כל יומא חיותא בסהדי יומא חד מסרו ליה בלא סהדי לסוף אמר להו לא היו דברים מעולם אתו סהדי אסהידו ביה דאכל תרתי מינייהו א"ר זירא אם איתא לדר' חייא קמייתא משתבע אשארא אמר ליה אביי אם איתא משתבע והא גזלן הוא א"ל שכנגדו קאמינא השתא נמי דליתא לדר' חייא נחייביה מדרב נחמן דתנן [ד] מנה לי בידך והלה אומר אין לך בידי פטור [ה] ואמר רב נחמן ג משביעין אותו שבועת היסת דרב נחמן תקנתא היא ותקנתא

**רש"י**

למאי איצטריך קרא למעוטי קרקע משבועה. דילפינן לה מכלל ופרט בשבועות (דף מב:) ולקמן בפרק הזהב (דף נז:): וחפר בה בורות שיחין ומערות. דלאו הילך הוא שהרי קלקלה: אי נמי. לטיכן דהודה בכלים דלאו הילך הוא ואשמועינן דאינו נשבע אכפירת [י] (שעבוד) קרקעות: ד' שומרין. שבועה האמורה בהן בשומר חנם שנגנבה הימנו ושומר שכר שנאנסה ובשואל שמתה מחמת מלאכה: צריכין כפירה במקצת והודאה במקצת. כפירה לא הויא אלא בכופר ממש או לא היו דברים מעולם או החזרתי לך הודאה לא הויא אא"כ הודה ממש שיש לו בידו שחייב להחזיר לו נמצא שאין חיוב שבועת השומרים בהא אלא אם כן טען שלש פרות באחת כפר לו ובאחת הודה לו שישנה בידו והשלישית אומר לו נאנסה או אם שומר חנם הוא אומר לו בשלישית נגנבה דחייב עליה שבועה האמורה בפרשה (שמות כב) שלא שלח ידו במלאכת רעהו דאילו שבועה דכפירה אין זו שבועה האמורה בשומרים ובלאו כפירה נמי לא מחייביה שבועת שומרים דכתיב בשומר חנם כי הוא זה דמינה נפקא לן (שבועות לט:) שמודה במקצת וכפר במקצת ולאפוקי ממ"ד בבבא קמא בהגוזל [קמא] (דף קז.) עירוב פרשיות כתוב כאן וכי כתיב כי הוא זה לאו אשומר חנם דכתיב גביה קאי אלא אאם כסף תלוה ואשמועינן האי תנא דבשומרים נמי בעינן כפירה והודאה והשבועה האמורה בפרשה על פרה שלישית: היכי דמי. פרה של הודאה: לאו. דקיימא קמן ואמר ליה קחנה בכל מקום שהיא דהיינו הילך: אידך מתה לה באונס. ועליה הוא נשבע שבועת שומרין: וחדא מתה לה בפשיעה. היא של הודאה ולאו הילך הוא: ת"ש דתני אבוה דרבי אפטוריקי. ת"ש מינה תיובתא: לרבי חייא קמייתא. כלומר ת"ש לדרבי חייא קמייתא דאמר לעיל שלא תהא הודאת פיו גדולה מהעדאת עדים כו': אשר יאמר וגו'. מודה לו במקצת מכלל דכופר במקצת וכתב בההוא לעיל מיניה ונקרב בעל הבית אל האלהים ודרשינן לקמן (דף מא:) ונקרב לשבועה: ההוא. מיבעי ליה להודאת מקצת דמחייבא עליה שבועה ואתיא העדאת עדים מינה בקל וחומר כדלעיל דליכא קרא יתירא דתדרוש מינה מיעוטא: וחד להעדאת עדים. למעוטה: וחד להודאה ממין הטענה. דבעינן שתהא הודאה ממין טענת כפירה שאם טענו סאה של חטים והודה לו בשעורים פטור: אם איתא לדרבי חייא. אם הלכה כמותו: אמר ליה אביי ואם איתא לדרבי חייא משתבע האי. בתמיה: והא גזלן הוא. וכי אמר רבי חייא במלוה אי נמי בפקדון שלא שלח בו יד ואבד ממנו דאיכא למימר אשתמוטי משתמיט: לשכנגדו קאמינא. אם שבועה מוטלת עליו נשבע שכנגדו ונוטל כדאמרינן בשבועות (דף מד:) שהחשוד על השבועה תקנו חכמים שכנגדו נשבע: השתא נמי. כי ליתא לדר' חייא ואין כאן הודאה במקצת: נחייביה. שבועת היסת מדרב נחמן וישבע שכנגדו ויטול: היסת. שבועה שהסיתו חכמים לכך להסיתו להודות וטעמא מפרש בשבועות (דף מ:) חזקה אין אדם טוען אא"כ יש לו בידו: דר"נ תקנתא היא. דהא מדאורייתא לא רמי שבועה עליה:

ותקנתא

**תוספות**

למ"ד הילך פטור קרא אמאי איצטריך כו'. תימה גם למ"ד הילך חייב אמאי איצטריך קרא למעוטי הא בקרקע לא שייך משתמיט וכן [י] [פר"י] לקמן דכי כופר במקצת קרקע פטור הוא דנאמן הוא מטעם דאין אדם מעיז כיון דלא שייך הכא אשתמוטי קא משתמיט ושמא גם בקרקע שייך קצת אשתמוטי קא משתמיט כי שמא משכנה וסבר עד דהוה לי זוזי ופרענא ליה: אמאי איצטריך קרא למעוטי. תימה הא ליכא קרא מיותר למעוטי קרקעות אלא מכלל ופרט וכלל ממעטינן להו וכלל ופרט וכלל אצטריך למעוטי שטרות וי"ל דקשיא ליה אמאי איצטריך תנא למילף קרקעות מכלל ופרט כיון דהילך פטור וא"ת לימא דאיצטריך למעוטי משבועה דעד אחד מיהו י"ל משום דמתני' דאין נשבעין על הקרקעות איירי בשבועה דמודה במקצת: א"נ דטענו כלים וקרקעות. מהכא משמע דטענו חטין ושעורים והודה באחד מהן דחייב דדוקא כלים וקרקעות פטור הא חטין ושעורים חייב וכן סברי שמואל ורבי יוחנן לחד לישנא פרק שבועת הדיינין (שבועות דף מ.): שומר חנם. פטור מכל חוץ מפשיעה ושואל חייב בכל חוץ ממתה מחמת מלאכה ונושא שכר והשוכר במקצת חייב ובמקצת פטור ולכך תנא להו כסדר זה ולא שנאם כסדר כתיבתם וא"ת ואמאי לא מקשה מכמה משניות [ח] דזה אומר עד הזיז וזה אומר עד החלון ועשרה גפנים דשבועות (דף מב:) ומתניתין דהשואל (לקמן דף צז: ושם) דזה אומר שאולה וזה אומר שכורה דמיירי בפקדון הא הילך הוא וי"ל דניחא ליה לאקשויי מכל ד' שומרין: רבי חייא תנא הוא ופליג. אי גרס לעיל (ג.) ° א"ר חייא א"ש ואפילו אי גרסינן תני ר' חייא י"ל דהכי קאמר דאפילו לא הוה ברייתא תנא הוא ופליג: והודה בשעורים פטור. אף מן השעורים כדמוכח בשלהי המניח (ב"ק דף לה: ושם ד"ה לימא): מסרי ליה בסהדי. ומיירי דאמרי ליה אל תחזיר אלא בעדים דאל"כ הא קי"ל (כתובות יח.) המלוה את חבירו בעדים א"צ לפרעו בעדים: אי איתא לדרבי חייא. נראה ° דהלכה כרבי חייא דהא לעיל מוקי לה כרבנן דר"ג דהלכה כוותייהו כדפריך בשלהי המניח (ב"ק שם) מאי קמ"ל תנינא וכן בפ' השואל (לקמן ק. ושם) פריך אמאי טענו חטין והודה לו בשעורים הוא וכן סברי רב ושמואל בפ' שבועת הדיינין (שבועות דף מ. ושם) אע"ג דקאמר הכא אם איתא הכי נמי אשכחנא פ' [ט] (אע"פ) (כתובות דף נט) דקאמר אם איתא לדרב הונא דאמר יכולה אשה שתאמר לבעלה איני ניזונת וכו' ובפרק שני דייני גזירות (שם דף קז:) פסיק כרב הונא [י] תימה אפי' אי איתא לדרבי חייא לא משתבע הכא דאסהידו עליה דאכל תרי מינייהו דמה להצד השוה שבהן שכן לא הוחזק כפרן תאמר הכא דהוחזק כפרן כדפריך לעיל (ד.) והכא לא שייך משתמיט ושמא י"ל אחרי שלמד שיש שבועה בהעדאת עדים במלוה מעתה אין לחלק בין מלוה לפקדון: שכנגדו קאמינא. ° וא"ת מאי שנא דבחשוד על השבועה שכנגדו נשבע ונוטל אמאי לא אמרינן מתוך שא"י לישבע משלם כדאמר גבי חמשין ידענא וחמשין לא ידענא (לקמן דף לח.) ונסכא דר' אבא (שבועות דף [כ]) וי"ל הכא אי אמרי' משלם לא שבקת ליה חיי דכל העולם יביאוהו לידי שבועה ויטלו כל אשר לו ועוד דהתם אמר ליה שבועה דאורייתא אית לי עליך או תשבע או תשלם אבל הכא הוא ברצון ישבע אם נייחו ולכך לא ישלם: אין לך בידי פטור וא"ר נחמן. מהכא משמע דהלכה כלישנא קמא דפ' שבועת הדיינים (שם דף מא. ושם ד"ה מאן) דלא בעי דררא דממונא אלא אפי' כופר הכל חייב שבועת היסת מדלא מייתי הכא סיפא דנתתיו לך פטור וכן פירש בשערים דרב האי ואי טעין איני יודע בכל ישבע שאינו יודע:

ותקנתא

**מסורת הש"ס**

א) לקמן לח., בבא קמא קז., ב) [שבועות לט:], ג) לקמן ק., בבא קמא לה:, שבועות לח:, מ., (כתובות קח:), ד) שבועות לח:, ה) [שם מ:, לקמן ו.], ו) רש"ל מ"ז, ז) מהרש"ל, ח) עיין נמוקי יוסף כאן ובגמרא שם, ט) צ"ל המדיר דף ע:, י) [ועיין עוד תוס' שבועות מו. ד"ה בטוענו], כ) [לב: מז. ובבא בתרא לג:].

**הגהות הב"ח**

(א) גמ' דסבר ליה כרבן גמליאל:

**גליון הש"ס**

תוס' ד"ה רבי חייא וכו' אר"ח א"ש. עיין נדה דף כו ע"א ברש"י ד"ה אמר אביי: ד"ה אי וכו' דהלכה כר"ח. עיין שבועות דף מו ע"א תוס' ד"ה בטוענו: ד"ה שכנגדו. ואת מ"ש. יש לעיין איך תלי הקושיא כאן הא דין זה ערוך במתני' רפ"ז דשבועות דשכנגדו חשוד נשבע ונוטל והו"מ להקשות שם במקומו:

**ליקוטי רש"י**

בורות שיחין ומערות. בור עגול הוא שיח ארוכה וקצרה מערה מרובעת ומכוסה בקירוי אלא שיש לה פה [ב"ק נ:]. ארבעה שומרים כו'. בשבועות האמורות בהן כגון ש"ח לישבע שנגנבה וש"ש לישבע שנאנסה ושואל לישבע שמתה ממלאכה [לקמן צח.]. צריכין כפירה במקצת והודאה במקצת. קודם שיתחייבו שבועה ואם נשבעו בלא כפירה והודאה אין שבועתו של ש"ח כלום ולא מחייבתו כפל [ב"ק קז:]. על כל אבדה אשר יאמר. ורבותינו ז"ל דרשו כי הוא זה ללמד שאין מחייבין אותו שבועה אלא אם כן הודה במקצת לומר כך וכך אני חייב לך והמותר נגנב ממני [שמות כב, ח]. ההוא למודה מקצת הטענה. זה מיבעי ליה דאין שבועה אלא בהודאה במקצת כלומר את זה אני מודה [שבועות לט:]. והודה לו בשעורים פטור. דבעינן הודאה ממין הטענה עצמה [לקמן ק:]. ור"ג מחייב. דלא בעי הודאה ממין הטענה [שבועות מ.]. חיותא. בהמות [לקמן צג.]. אין לך בידי פטור. שאין כאן הודאה [שבועות לח:]. משביעין אותו וכו'. לשאינו מודה במקצת [לקמן ו.]. שבועת היסת. לשון שומא ששמו חכמים עליו שבועה כמו (שמואל א כו ח) אם ה' הסיתך בי [שבועות מ:]. תקנתא היא וכו'. שבועה עצמה של היסת תקנתא היא ותקנתא שיהא תובע נשבע ונוטל לתקנתא היסת שבועה שלא באה עליו אלא בתקנת חכמים לא עבדינן [שבועות מא.].

**עין משפט נר מצוה**

[א] [רב אלפס כאן ובשבועות פ"ו דף שם]:
כ א מיי' פ"ג מהל' טוען ונטען ה"ח סמג עשין צה טוש"ע ח"מ סי' פח סעיף ז:
כא ב מיי' שם הלכה ח ופ"א שם הל' ג ופ"ט מהל' נ"מ הלכה יא סמג שם טוש"ע שם סי' ע"ב וסי' פח ס"ד:
כב ג מיי' פ"א מהלכות טוען ונטען ה"ג סמג שם טוש"ע שם סי' עה ס"ז וסי' פז סעיף א:

**הגהות הגר"א**

[א] גמ' (וס"ל כר"ג דתנן טענו חטין והודה לו בשעורין פטור ור"ג מחייב) תא"מ:

**תורה אור השלם**

א) עַל כָּל דְּבַר פֶּשַׁע עַל שׁוֹר עַל חֲמוֹר עַל שֶׂה עַל שַׂלְמָה עַל כָּל אֲבֵדָה אֲשֶׁר יֹאמַר כִּי הוּא זֶה עַד הָאֱלֹהִים יָבֹא דְּבַר שְׁנֵיהֶם אֲשֶׁר יַרְשִׁיעֻן אֱלֹהִים יְשַׁלֵּם שְׁנַיִם לְרֵעֵהוּ: [שמות כב, ח]

**רבינו חננאל**

ומקשי' על רב ששת מהא דתני רמי בר חמא בהגוזל קמא הלכ' נתן לו את הקרן. ד' שומרין צריכין כפירה במקצת והודאה במקצת ואלו הן שומר חנם והשואל נושא שכר והשוכר והא בהאי דקא מודה ליה הילך וקתני דחייב. ודחי רב ששת לא לעולם הילך פטור והאי כגון דטעין ליה ג' בהמות מסרתי לך ומתו להו כולהו בפשיעותך וחייב אתה בשלשתן ואמר לו השומר חדא לא היו דברים מעולם זו היא כפירה במקצת. וחדא פשעתי בה ומתה ואני חייב לשלמה לך זו היא הודאה במקצת ואינו הילך דהא ליתא בעינא אלא אני חייב לשלם קאמר ליה. וחדא מתה לה באונס וסבר רמי דהאי דחייבה תורה לשומר שבועה בטענת אונסין מדכת' כי יתן אל רעהו חמור או שור או שה וכל בהמה לשמור וטוען השומר מת באונס או נשבר או נשבה שבועת ה' תהיה בין שניהם. צריכה כפירה והודאה במקצת כשאר כל חייבי שבועה שבתור' כדכתיב אשר יאמר כי הוא זה ופירושו אשר יאמר הנתבע כי הוא שאתה טוענני אינו כולו אמת אלא זהו בלבד שנמצאת כפירה במקצת והודאה במקצת ואי אתה מוצא כפירה במקצת והודאה במקצת ושבועה באונסין אלא בטוען ג' פרות מסרתי לך כמו שפירשנו למעלה אבל אם יטעון עליו בשתים והלה טוען חדא לא היה דברים מעולם וחדא מתה באונס כפירה איכא הודאה ליכא ואי טעין חדא מתה בפשיעה וחדא באונס הודאה איכא כפירה ליכא הלכך לא משכחת כפירה במקצת והודאה במקצת וחיוב שבועה באונסין אלא בטוען ג' פרות מסרתי לך כו'. ואע"ג דפריק רבי חייא כל קושיא דאקשן עליה וסוגייא כוותיה רהטא כרב ששת קיימא לן דהוא בתרא ותוב מדקתני לה בפ' השואל היו לו עבדים ומכר אחד הלוקח טוען הגדול קניתי והמוכר אמר הקטן מכרתי ישבע המוכר שהקטן מכר ואמרי' אמאי ישבע מה שטענו לא הודה לו כי בגדול טענו והוא לא הודה לו בגדול אמאי ישבע ועוד הילך הוא ועוד אין נשבעין על העבדים ש"מ מדתני לה גבי הלכת' פסיקתא הילך נמי הלכת' הוא דפטור. ומקשי' תוב אקמייתא דר' חייא מהא דתני אבוה דר' אפטוריקי מנה לי בידך והלה אומר אין לך בידי כלום והעדים מעידים עליו בנ' יכול ישבע על השאר וכו'. ופרקי' ר' חייא נמי תנא הוא ופליג על התנאים. והאי קרא דגמיר מיניה אבוה דר' אפטוריקי דריש ליה ר' חייא הכי אשר יאמר כי הוא [זה] מכאן דבעינן הודאה ממין הטענה ומקצת הטענה. אבל אבוה דר' אפטוריקי הני תרי קראי חד ש"מ דאין נשבעין בהעדאת עדים וחד למקצת הטענה אבל ממין הטענה לא בעי. וקיימא לן בהא כר' חייא. ההוא רעיא דהוו מסרי ליה כל יומא חיותא בסהדי יומא חד מסרו ליה בלא סהדי אמר לא היה דברים מעולם אתו סהדי אסהידו דאכל תרי מינייהו אמר רבי זירא אי איתא לדר' חייא כלומר אילו נתברר לי דהלכתא כר' חייא בהא הייתי דן אותו לשלם השנים שאכל ולישבע על השאר שבועה דאורייתא דכיון שהוא גזלן ישבע שכנגדו ויטול. ומקשה לר' זירא אפי' הכי אי ליתא לר' חייא נחייביה מדתנן מנה לי בידך והלה אומר אין לך בידי כלום פטור. ואמר רב נחמן ומשביעין אותו שבועת היסת מדרבנן. ופריק לה דרב נחמן תקנתא היא מדרבנן ותקנתא לתקנתא לא עבדינן כלומר נעשה עוד תקנה על זו דרב נחמן להישבע כנגדו ויטול כולי האי תקנת' לתקנתא לא עבדינן

The Gemara now presents a challenge to Rav Sheishess' view, hat saying "here, it is yours" about the admitted part of the laim exempts the defendant from swearing. The Gemara asks: **וּלְמַאן דְּאָמַר הֵילָךְ פָּטוּר – But according to the one who says hat** a defendant who says, **"Here, it is yours,"** about the part he dmits **is exempt** from swearing, **אַמַּאי אִיצְטְרִיךְ קְרָא לְמַעוּטֵי קַרְקַע מִשְּׁבוּעָה – why is a verse needed to exclude land** claims rom being subject to the law of **oath?**[1] **הָא כָּל קַרְקַע הֵילָךְ הוּא – Why, every** case concerning **land is** a situation of **"here, it is ours"!**[2] **– ? –**

The Gemara answers:

**אָמַר לָךְ – He** [Rav Sheishess] **will answer you: אִיצְטְרִיךְ קְרָא הֵיכָא דְּחָפַר בָּהּ בּוֹרוֹת שִׁיחִין וּמְעָרוֹת – [The verse] is needed where the defendant] dug pits, ditches, or caverns in [the land]** that e admits owing to the plaintiff.[3] Since the situation is thus not ne of "here, it is yours," the defendant would have been bligated to swear the *modeh bemiktzas* oath were it not that the erse specifically excludes cases of land litigation from the laws of ath.

An alternative answer:

**אִי נַמִּי – Alternatively,** the verse is needed for **הֵיכָא דְּטָעֲנוֹ כֵּלִים וְקַרְקָעוֹת – where [the plaintiff] claimed** from **[the defendant] utensils and land, וְהוֹדָה בַּכֵּלִים וְכָפַר בַּקַּרְקָעוֹת – and [the defendant] admitted** owing **the utensils but denied** owing **the land.**[4] Though this situation, which is not a case of "here, it is yours," would ordinarily warrant the oath of *modeh bemiktzas,* the verse teaches that no oath applies, since the denial concerns land.[5]

The Gemara considers whether the law concerning *heilach* can be proven from the following Baraisa:

**תָּא שְׁמַע – Come, learn** a proof from the following: **דְּתָנֵי רָמִי בַּר חָמָא – For Rami bar Chama taught a Baraisa,** which states: **אַרְבָּעָה שׁוֹמְרִין צְרִיכִין כְּפִירָה בְּמִקְצָת וְהוֹדָאָה בְּמִקְצָת** – The FOUR CUSTODIANS REQUIRE PARTIAL DENIAL AND PARTIAL ADMISSION as a condition for the custodian's oath imposed on them by the Torah. They are: **שׁוֹמֵר חִנָּם וְהַשּׁוֹאֵל נוֹשֵׂא שָׂכָר וְהַשּׂוֹכֵר** – THE UNPAID CUSTODIAN, THE BORROWER, THE PAID CUSTODIAN, AND THE RENTER.[6] [7]

The Gemara now develops its proof:

**הֵיכִי דָּמֵי – What is the** Baraisa's **case? לָאו דְּאָמַר לֵיהּ הֵילָךְ – Is it not that [the custodian] said to [the plaintiff]: "Here, it is**

NOTES

[As mentioned above (4b note 12)] the Gemara in *Shevuos* (42a-b; also elow, 57b) derives from Scripture that the Torah's oath obligations do ot apply to claims concerning land (*Rashi*).

. Whenever a defendant admits owing land but denies the rest of the aim, the situation is one of "here, it is yours," since the land that he dmits is already in the legal possession of the plaintiff. Thus, according ) Rav Sheishess, the Gemara (below, 57b and in *Shevuos* 42b) should ot require a special Scriptural source to suspend the *modeh bemiktzas* ath in such cases of land litigation, since that oath is suspended anyway ecause the situation is one of "here, it is yours"! (See *Tosafos* ד״ה אמאי).

In this case, the defendant has damaged the land he admits owing and e is obligated to restore it to its original state or to pay the difference. ince the defendant has not yet made this restoration, the plaintiff does ot yet possess in full what the defendant admits owing to him. Thus, e situation is not one of "here, it is yours" (*Rashi* as understood by *itva, Ran* and *Nimukei Yosef*; cf. *Shach, Choshen Mishpat* 95:18).

And the situation is not one of "here, it is yours" – e.g the utensils at he admits owing are no longer intact or they are not with him in urt (see 4b note 27).

[As explained above (4b note 12), the verse exempts the defendant om swearing if either his admission or denial is limited to land.]

In *Exodus* 22:6-14, the Torah details three levels of responsibility for amage or loss to an item entrusted to a custodian. An unpaid custodian responsible only if the damage or loss results from his negligence. The id custodian and the renter are responsible even if the article is lost or olen (since better safeguards might have prevented these occurnces), but they are not liable for unavoidable accidents, such as death, tural breakage, or forced seizure. The borrower is responsible even in e event of these unavoidable accidents, and exempt from liability only the article broke as a result of the normal use for which he had rrowed it. (This follows the view of R' Yehudah, that a renter is uated with a paid custodian. R' Meir, however, holds that a renter is uated with an unpaid custodian. See below, 80b.)

When a custodian claims that the article entrusted to his care was lost damaged through an occurrence for which he is not liable (e.g. the paid custodian claims that it was stolen; the paid custodian claims at it died; the borrower claims that it broke in the normal course of e), the Torah requires that he take the custodian's oath asserting his emption from liability (v. 7; see Gemara below, 6a: *Three oaths are posed upon him. . .*).

Now, the very next verse also states the oath of מוֹדֶה בְּמִקְצָת, *partial mission*; for the verse states that an oath be taken: אֲשֶׁר יֹאמַר כִּי־הוּא זֶה, *en he [the custodian] says that it is this* [that I owe you, but not *more*]; . the custodian admits that part of the deposit remains in his possesn, but claims that the rest was lost (see above, 3a note 27). There is ispute in the Gemara (*Bava Kamma* 106b) whether this verse means make partial admission a precondition for the oath obligation even *in this context* of the custodian's oath, or whether the verse means to make it a precondition for oath only in another context – viz. the context of a loan obligation [עִירוּב פָּרָשִׁיּוֹת]. According to the first view, the custodian's oath is not mandated unless the custodian has admitted partial liability. Thus, if (for example) an unpaid custodian is sued for the return of a single cow, which he admits receiving for safekeeping, but claims that it was stolen, he does not swear the custodian's oath to confirm his claim, since he has not admitted any liability. According to the second view, however, the custodian's oath is mandated in this case; the condition of partial admission, although stated here in the context of custodians, is a precondition for oath only in the case of loan litigations [i.e. the standard case of *modeh bemiktzas* described above, 3a note 23] (*Rashi* ad loc.; cf. *Tosafos* there).

Rami bar Chama's Baraisa, which states: "four custodians require partial denial and partial admission," certainly advocates the first view, that the verse of *modeh bemiktzas* is to be understood as establishing a precondition for oath even in its own context – the context of custodian (*Rashi*). [Although the verse states this requirement only in the case of the unpaid custodian, we derive the laws of other custodians from there as well; hence, the Baraisa stresses that all *four* custodians have this requirement.]

Furthermore, the Baraisa is of the opinion that the custodian's denial of *liability* does not qualify as the partial denial needed for the oath. For example, if the unpaid custodian admits receiving two cows for safekeeping and returns one but claims that the other was stolen, there is still no custodian's oath required (even though he has admitted owing one cow and denied owing the second). Rather, the denial needed as a precondition for the custodian's oath is an *absolute* denial of any obligation regarding part of the claim. Thus, the custodian's oath applies only if there are *three* elements to the claim – one part that is categorically denied, a second part that is categorically admitted, and a third part whose basis is admitted but about which the custodian claims exemption from liability. For example, the plaintiff demands the return of three cows that he claims to have entrusted to an unpaid custodian. The custodian returns one cow (partial admission), denies ever having received the second cow or claims to have already returned it (partial *absolute* denial), and claims that the third cow was stolen. The first two elements create the situation of *modeh bemiktzas* (partial admission and partial denial). The third element (the cow that has allegedly been stolen) is the element about which the custodian must swear the custodian's oath (*Rashi*). [Had denial of *liability* been sufficient to fulfill the *modeh bemiktzas* condition (the "two cow" case described above), the Baraisa would have stated simply: "The four custodians require partial admission," and no more. It would have been self-evident that the case *also* involves a denial of liability for damage or loss, since that is the only claim the custodian's oath ever addresses! Rather, the Baraisa's statement that the four custodians require "partial denial" indicates that a denial is required *in addition to* the denial of liability for loss addressed by the custodian's oath (*Rashi* to the Gemara below, 98a).]

– [MOVABLE PROPERTY] CAN SUBJECT REAL PROPERTY[31] to the requirement THAT ONE TAKE AN OATH REGARDING IT.[32]

The Gemara answers:

הָכָא עִיקָּר – **Here** [the Mishnah in *Shevuos*] **is the** law's **primar** place. הָתָם אַגַּב גְּרָרָא נְסָבָהּ – **There** [in the Mishnah i *Kiddushin*] **it cites [the law] incidentally.**[33]

NOTES

31. Literally: "Properties that do not provide a guarantee can subject properties that do provide a guarantee . . ." As explained above in note 5, a borrower's real property (land and its fixtures) becomes mortgaged to the lender. Should the borrower default on his obligation, the lender can seize the buyer's real property to satisfy the debt, even if that property has since been sold to a third party. For this reason, real property is called property that "guarantees" the debt. Unlike movable property, real property will always be there for collection; the lender therefore relies on such property for surety when he lends money (*Rashi* to Mishnah ad loc.). The fact that movable property does not provide a guarantee and real property does is not pertinent to the point of law discussed here. The terms "property that provides a guarantee" and "property that does not provide a guarantee" are merely the Mishnah's idiom for "real property" and "movables" – a way of referring to th two types of property by their legal differences.

32. I.e. though an oath is generally not imposed in litigations involvir land, once an oath is imposed because of the non-land aspect of th dispute, that obligation can be extended to cover the land aspect of th dispute as well.

33. The primary topic of Tractate *Shevuos* is the laws of oath; th Mishnah in *Kiddushin* deals primarily with laws of acquisition. Thu the primary place for the law of subjection is *Shevuos*. That law is cite again in *Kiddushin* only because it is similar to another law in th tractate, which states that movables can be acquired together with re property by dint of an act of acquisition in the real property (*Rashi*

סלעים דינרין מלוה אומר חמש ולוה אומר שלש ר"ש בן אלעזר אומר הואיל והודה מקצת הטענה ישבע [א] ר"ע אומר [א] אינו אלא כמשיב אבידה ופטור קתני מיהת רשב"א אומר הואיל והודה מקצת הטענה ישבע טעמא דאמר שלש הא שתים פטור והאי שטר דקמודי ביה הילך הוא וש"מ הילך פטור לא לעולם אימא לך שתים חייב והאי דקתני שלש לאפוקי מדר' עקיבא דאמר משיב אבידה הוי ופטור קמ"ל דמודה מקצת הטענה הוי וחייב אי הכי רשב"א אומר הואיל והודה מקצת הטענה ישבע אף זה ישבע מבעי ליה אלא לעולם שתים פטור והילך חייב ושאני הכא דקא מסייע ליה שטרא אי נמי [ג] משום דהוה ליה שטר שעבוד קרקעות [ג] [ב] ואין נשבעין על כפירת שעבוד קרקעות איכא דמותיב מסיפא ר"ע אומר אינו אלא כמשיב אבידה ופטור טעמא דאמר שלש הא שתים חייב והא שטר ([ד] כיון) דקא מודי ביה כהילך דמי ש"מ הילך חייב לא לעולם אימא לך שתים נמי פטור והאי דקתני שלש לאפוקי מדרשב"א דאמר מודה מקצת הטענה הוי וחייב קמ"ל דמשיב אבידה הוי ופטור הכי נמי מסתברא דאי סלקא דעתך שתים חייב בשלש היכי פטר ליה ר"ע [ה] האי אערומי קא מערים סבר אי אמינא שתים בעינא אשתבועי אימא שלש דאהוי כמשיב אבידה ואיפטר אלא ש"מ [ג] שתים נמי פטור אלא קשיא לרבי חייא שאני התם דקא מסייע ליה שטרא א"נ משום דהוה ליה שטר שעבוד קרקעות ואין נשבעין על כפירת שעבוד קרקעות מתיב מר זוטרא בריה דרב נחמן [ו] [ד] טענו כלים וקרקעות הודה בכלים וכפר בקרקעות הודה בקרקעות וכפר בכלים פטור הודה מקצת קרקעות פטור [ה] מקצת כלים חייב טעמא דכלים וקרקעות דקרקע לאו בת שבועה היא הא כלים וכלים דומיא דכלים וקרקעות חייב היכי דמי לאו דאמר ליה הילך וש"מ הילך חייב לא לעולם אימא לך כלים וכלים נמי פטור והא דקתני כלים וקרקעות הא קמ"ל הודה במקצת כלים חייב אף על הקרקעות מאי קמ"ל זוקקין [ז] תנינא [ו] זוקקין הנכסים שאין להן אחריות את הנכסים שיש להן אחריות לישבע עליהם הכא עיקר התם אגב גררא נסבה ולמאן

סלעים דינרין. שטר שכתוב בו פלוני לוה מפלוני סלעין ולא פירש כמה וכן שטר שכתוב בו דינרין סתם: אינו אלא כמשיב אבידה. מדהוה ליה למימר שתים והשטר מסייעו דכיון דלא פירש ניכרים הדברים ששנים היו לכך לא הוצרך לפרש דמיעוט סלעים ב' וכיון דאמר ג' משיב אבידה הוא וחכמים פטרו את משיב אבידה מן השבועה דתנן המוצא את המציאה לא ישבע וכו' (גיטין דף מח:): טעמא דאמר שלש. קס"ד השתא דמייתי תיובתא מדנקט פלוגתייהו בשלש וחמש ולא נקט ולוה אמר שתים ש"מ בשתים לא מחייב ליה רשב"א וכדמפרש ואזיל דכיון דכל הודאתו בשטר כתובה דשטר נמי שתים משמע וכל משמעות השטר הילך הוא שהרי הקרקעות משועבדים על כך אבל כי אמר שלש סלעים שלישי מלוה ע"פ הוא דלאו בשטר כתובה ואין הקרקעות משועבדים ולאו הילך הוא: ה"ג ושטרא דקמודה הילך הוא ול"ג כיון דקמודה ביה דבלאו הודאתו נמי כל שטרי הילך הוא וה"פ ומאי דקמודה ביה דכתוב בשטר הילך הוא: לאפוקי מדר"ע כו'. דאי תנא שתים לא הוה פליג ר"ע: א"ה. דבשתים נמי חייב אמאי תנא הואיל והודה מקצת הטענה ישבע רשב"א אומר אף זה ישבע מבעיא ליה ושמעינן דלא משיב אבידה חשיב ליה ומדנקט הואיל משמע דחיובא משום דגרס לעצמו שהודה במקצת דהשתא הוא דהויא הודאה משום דסלע שלישי לאו הילך הוא אבל שתים לא הוי הודאה משום הילך: אלא לעולם כו'. אלא אי אית לך לתרולי תריץ הכי לעולם כדקאמרת הא שתים פטור וטעמא לאו משום הילך דהילך בעלמא חייב: ושאני הכא דקא מסייע ליה שטרא. העדים החתומים על השטר מעידין כדבריו שלא היו אלא שתים ולכך לא פירשו מניינן הלכך א"צ שבועה: א"נ. להכי לא הוו שתים הודאה לחייבו שבועה לפי שהשטר אומר כן ושטר הוי שעבוד קרקעות וכשם שאין נשבעין על כפירת קרקעות כך הודאתן אינה מביאה לידי שבועה דקרקעות אמעוט מתורת שבועה במס' שבועות פ' שבועת הדיינין (מב:) אבל כי אמר מלוה חמש ולוה שלש איכא כפירה והודאה במה שאין כתוב בשטר: הא שתים. דליכא משיב אבידה: חייב. מדלא תנא פטור בשתים ונימא טעמא משום הילך: מודה מקצת הוי. ואינו משיב אבידה דאיערומי קמערים דלחזקיה בנאמן: קמ"ל. כיון דבשתים נמי פטור ליכא למימר איערומי מערים אלא משיב אבידה הוי: הכי נמי מסתברא. דבשתים פטור: ואלא קשיא לרבי חייא. דהא איכא למידק מינה דשתים פטור כדאמרינן לאי ס"ד כו': שאני הכא. האי דקאמר שתים פטור טעמא לאו משום הילך אלא דקא מסייע ליה שטרא: טענו. חבירו בב"ד כלים וקרקעות: פטור. דלא כפירתו ולא הודאתו מביאתו לידי שבועה: חייב. אף על הקרקעות לישבע כדאמרינן לקמן שהנכסים שאין להן אחריות זוקקין את הקרקעות לישבע עליהן משנתחייב לישבע על המטלטלין זוקקין ומגלגלין עמהם שבועת קרקע: דומיא דכלים וקרקעות. שכלים שהודה עליהם מונחים לפניו וא"ל הילך: זוקקין. המטלטלין זוקקין הקרקעות לישבע ע"י גלגול: תנינא. בקדושין (דף כו.) הנכסים שאין להן אחריות זוקקין את הנכסים שיש להן אחריות לישבע עליהם: הכא עיקר. שמשנה זו שנויה במסכת שבועות (דף לח.): התם. בקדושין: אגב גררא נסבה. דאיירי התם נכסים שאין להם אחריות נקנין עם נכסים שיש להן אחריות בכסף בשטר ובחזקה ואגב דאיירי דנקנין עמהם תנא בהדה זוקקין אותן לישבע עליהם:
למאי

לעולם שתים חייב. ואע"ג דשתים חייב חשיב ליה רבי עקיבא משיב אבידה דכשאמר שתים נראה יותר נאמן לפי שהשטר מסייעו: לעולם שתים פטור והילך חייב. וא"ת כיון דהילך חייב כי אמר נמי שתים אינו כופר הכל וכי אמר שלש יהא נאמן במיגו דאי בעי אמר שתים ומאי טעמא דרשב"א וי"ל דס"ל דמה שהשטר מסייעו אינו טוען ברצון לפי שנראה שמחמת השטר מודה ואם לא היה השטר היה כופר הכל: אין נשבעין על כפירת שעבוד קרקעות. וא"ת למ"ד בפרק גט פשוט (ב"ב דף קעה:) שעבודא דאורייתא מודה מקצת הטענה למה נשבע הא כופר שעבוד קרקעות וי"ל שמחל לו השעבוד או שאין לו כלל קרקעות אפי' משעבדי אבל לרבי יוחנן דאמר בפ' שבועת הפקדון (שבועות דף לז: ושם ד"ה ואין) כופר בממון שיש עליו עדים חייב קרבן שיש עליו שטר פטור משום דכופר שעבוד קרקעות דבעדים לא חשיב כופר שעבוד קרקעות אע"ג דסבר ר' יוחנן שעבודא דאורייתא היינו משום כיון שהפקיעו חכמים השעבוד במלוה ע"פ משום פסידא דלקוחות חשיב כאילו מחל לו השעבוד ומיירי דאית ליה משעבדי ולית ליה בני חרי דאי אית ליה בני חרי אפי' יש עליו עדים פטור ואי לית ליה אפי' משועבדים אפילו יש עליו שטר חייב: אין נשבעין על כפירת כו'. לספרים דגרסי בברייתא ר"ע אין להקשות הא ר"ע דריש ריבויי ומיעוטי פ"ק דשבועות (דף ד: ושם ד"ה רבי) ובפרק ג' מינים (נזיר לה. ושם) ומאן דדריש ריבויי ומיעוטי אינו ממעט קרקעות כ"א שטרות כדמוכח בפרק הגוזל בתרא (ב"ק דף קיז:) והיכי קאמר הכא אין נשבעין על כפירת שעבוד קרקעות וי"ל שיש לו שום מיעוט למעט קרקעות וכן צ"ל לקמן בפ' השואל (דף ק: ושם ד"ה ר"מ) אליבא דר"מ דאית ליה נשבעין אעבדים ולא אקרקעות ואע"ג דעבדים הוקשו לקרקעות לכ"ע דמהאי טעמא עבד נקנה בכסף בפ"ק דקדושין (דף כב:) אלא דר"מ דריש ריבויי ומיעוטי להוציא שטרות ויש לו שום מיעוט למעט קרקעות ובאותו מיעוט אין למעט עבדים אע"ג דהוקשו לקרקעות כדמוכח במרובה (ב"ק סג. ושם ד"ה וחד) דמאן דדריש בריבה ומיעט וריבה צריך שני מיעוטי לקרקעות ועבדים ואע"ג דרשב"א היה תלמידו של ר"ע אין לחוש מה שחולק עמו [ט] והוזכר [ח] קודם דכעין זה מצינו לקמן (דף ז.) גבי שנים אדוקים בשטר דפליג רבי עם רשב"ג אביו ויש ספרים דגרסי הכא ר' יעקב: הא כלים וכלים חייב. הוה מצי לשנויי בחפר בה בורות שיחין ומערות כדבסמוך: [הודה במקצת כלים חייב. וא"ת יהא נאמן במיגו דאי בעי כפר בכלים והיה מודה במקצת קרקעות וי"ל שמא חפץ בקרקעות יותר] ס"א: למ"ד



טז א מיי' פ"ד מהל' טוען ונטען הל' ה סמג עשין לה טוש"ע ח"מ סי' פח סעיף לג:
יז ב מיי' שם פ"ה הל' א סמג שם טוש"ע ח"מ סי' לה ס"א:
יח ג (מיי' פ"ד שם הל' ה) סמג שם טוש"ע ח"מ סי' פח סעיף לג:
יט ד ה ו מיי' פ"ה שם הל' ג סמג שם טוש"ע ח"מ סי' לה סעיף ה:

רבינו חננאל

מודה מקצת הטענה הוא ומתני' תקנת חכמים היא וכר' יוחנן. מיתיבי סלעין דינרים וכו'. פי' שטר שכתוב בו סתם פלוני חייב לפלוני סלעים או דינרין. מלוה אמר ה' סלעים חייב לי ולוה אמר ג' ר' שמעון בן אלעזר אומר הואיל והודה מקצת הטענה ישבע. ודייקי' טעמא דהודה בג' הא הודה בב' פטור מאי טעמא דשטר כיון דמודה במלוה בשטר כי הילך דמי דקיימא לן מלוה בשטר תורתו כקרקע והמודה בקרקע הילך הוא ודייקי' דבשתים פטור קשיא לר' חייא. ופריק לא ואפילו הודה בשתים חייב והאי דקתני ג' לאפוקי מדר' עקיבא דאמר הודאתו בשלישית משיב אבידה הוי מיגו דאי בעי אמר תרתי כדכתיב בשטר סלעים ואמר ג' משיב אבידה הוא ופטור משבועה. ואקשי' אי הכי דר' שמעון אפילו בשתים מחייב והוא הדין לג' אף זה חייב לישבע היה לו לומר. ופרקי' לעולם שתים פטור ושאני הכא משום דמסייע ליה דכתיב בה סלעין וסתם סלעין שתים הן. אי נמי משום דהוי שטר שיעבוד קרקעות ואין נשבעין על כפירת שעבוד קרקעות. פי' נמצא המלוה טוענו ה' סלעין ועדי השטר מעידין שחייב לו סלעים לא פחות משתים לדברי ר' חייא דאמר מנה לי בידך והלה אומר אין לך בידי כלום ועדים מעידים אותן נ' אותן נ' נותן לו ונשבע על השאר וכל שכן בשמודה לו במקצת היה מן הדין לחייבו שבועה גם בשמודה בשתים ואמר לך ר' חייא כי קאמינא במלוה על פה אבל במלוה בשטר דשעבודיה על הקרקע כאילו קרקע בה' סלעין הוא דטעין ומודה לו במקצת מן הקרקע ובשאר כופר בו. ותנן אין נשבעין על הקרקעות וכשם שאם ישען עליו שדה זו רידך שלי הוא והלה כופר בו אין חייב שבועה עליה כך הטוען על חבירו בשעבוד קרקעות והלה כופר בו אין חייב שבועה על כפירתו. ור' שמעון סבר הא דטעין עליה בה' סלעין תרתי מינהון בשטרא ותלת מינהון על פה כפר בתלת פטור כדתנן מנה לי בידך והלה אומר אין לך בידי כלום פטור. הודה אחת מן השלש חייב. ומותבינן תוב מדברי ר' עקיבא דפטר בג' וכל שכן בב' והנה דפריש להו שטרא הילך הוא וקתני פטור [א] קשיא לרבי חייא. ופריק שאני הכא דקא מסייע ליה שטרא. אי נמי משום דהוי ליה שטר שעבוד קרקעות כו'. כדפרשינן לזה לעילא. ש"מ דדברי הכל הודה בשתים פטור כי פליגי בשמודה בג'. ר' עקיבא סבר מיגו דאי בעי אמר שתים ואמר ג' משיב אבידה הוי ופטור דכי אמרה תורה כי הוא זה דשמעינן מיניה מודה מקצת הטענה חייב הא פריש רבה טעמא דקרא דאמר מפני מה אמרה תורה מודה מקצת הטענה ישבע חזקה אין אדם מעיז פניו בפני בעל חובו והאי בכוליה בעי דליכפריה וכו' והאי כיון דאית ליה עליה שטרא לא יכול לכפור בכל לית עליה הדין דינא הלכך פטור הוא. ור' שמעון סבר לא שנא אלא הרי הוא ככל טענתא דעלמא הכופר בכל פטור והמודה במקצת חייב. תוב אקשינן מהא טענו כלים וקרקעות וכו'. ופשוטה היא. פי' הכא עיקר התם אגב גררא נסבה. הכא בשבועות דקתני הודה במקצת כלים מיגו דנתחייב שבועה בכלים נשבע גם על הקרקע בזקיקה זה מקום עיקרו. והתם בקידושין פ"א דקתני זוקקין את הנכסים שיש להם אחריות לישבע עליהם [אגב] גררא נסבה.
ומקשי'



א) [בבא בתרא קכח...], ב) [שבועות דף לז...], ג) [כתובות פז:], ד) ו... בס' ת"ח שמקיים הספרים, ה) [לקמן ...], ו) שבועות לח:, ז) לקמן ק:, קידושין ..., שבועות לח:, מב:, ח) [... תוס' סוטה ז. ד"ה עוזי].

גליון הש"ס

תוס' ד"ה אין ו... והוזכר קודם. ... תוי"ט פ"ג משנה דבכורים:

ליקוטי רש"י

כמשיב אבדה. ופט... משבועה דסלעין משמע טפי משנ... דתפסת מרובה לא תפס... ויד בעל השטר התחתונה ועל השלי... שהודה הוה משיב אב... ותנן המוצא מציאה ... ישבע מפני תיקון העו... [רשב"ם ב"ב קכח...]. משום דהוה ליה. ... שטר ממון שהקרקע משועבדים לו והכופר ככופר בקרקעות וקי... דאין נשבעין על הקרקע [שבועות לז:]. כל שטר שיעבוד קרקעות הן ו... נשבעין על הקרקע כדאמרינן בשבוע... ובהזהב [כתובות פז...]. הודה מקצת קרקעו... פטור. שאין נשבעין ... הקרקעות כדילפינן לק... בפירקין ואף הודאתן אי... מביאה לידי שבוע... מקצת כלים חיי... שבועה אף על הקרקע ע"י גלגול דשבועה מק... כלים [שבועות מ...]. זוקקים וכו' לישב... עליהם. אע"ג ד... נשבעין על הקרקעות לג... כדנפקא לן בשבועות (... מב:) היכא דטענו כל... וקרקעות ונתחייב ליש... על המטלטלין זוקק... המטלטלין את הקרקע... לישבע עליהן [קידושין כו...]. הכא עיקר. דכו... מסכת בהלכות שבו... [שבועות שם].

חשק שלמה על ר"ח א) לפנינו הגי' הא שתים חייב וש"מ דהילך חייב ואמנם רבינו נראה דגרים וכ"ש בשתים וד' רבינו ז"ל הובא בש"מ כאן בשמו ע"ש.

**Rather,** we must **learn from this** [ruling of R' Akiva] **that** a borrower who admits only **two is also exempt** from swearing.[17]

This analysis has proved that a borrower who admits only two *selaim* is exempt from swearing, as Rav Sheishess ruled. Accordingly, the question arises:
**אֶלָּא קַשְׁיָא לְרַבִּי חִיָּיא – Rather, [this Baraisa] poses difficulty for R' Chiya,** who rules that one who admits partial liability is obligated to swear even in situations of "here, it is yours."[18] – ? –

The Gemara answers, explaining that there are reasons other than *heilach* for exempting one who admits only two *selaim* from swearing:
**שָׁאנֵי הָתָם דְּקָא מְסַיַּיע לֵיהּ שְׁטָרָא – It is different there** [where the borrower admits only two *selaim*], **for the** wording of the **note** (which uses only the non-specific plural term "*selaim*") **supports him** in his assertion that he borrowed only two.[19]

An alternative explanation:
**אִי נַמִּי מִשּׁוּם דַּהֲוָה לֵיהּ שְׁטָר שִׁעְבּוּד קַרְקָעוֹת – Alternatively,** one who admits only two *selaim* does not swear, **because the note represents a lien on land, וְאֵין נִשְׁבָּעִין עַל כְּפִירַת שִׁעְבּוּד קַרְקָעוֹת – and** there is a rule that **one does not swear concerning** his **denial of a lien on land,** or – by the same token – because of his *admission* of a lien on land.[20]

Another challenge to Rav Sheishess' view is presented:
**מְתִיב מַר זוּטְרָא בְּרֵיהּ דְּרַב נַחְמָן – Mar Zutra the son of Rav Nachman challenged** Rav Sheishess' view from **a Mishnah,** which considers the law in the following case:[21] **טְעָנוֹ כֵּלִים וְקַרְקָעוֹת – [THE PLAINTIFF] CLAIMED** in court that the defendant owes **HIM UTENSILS AND LAND.**[22] **הוֹדָה בַּכֵּלִים וְכָפַר בַּקַּרְקָעוֹת – If [THE DEFENDANT] ADMITTED** owing **THE UTENSILS BUT DENIED** owing **THE LAND, הוֹדָה בַּקַּרְקָעוֹת וְכָפַר בַּכֵּלִים – or if HE ADMITTED** owing **THE LAND BUT DENIED** owing **THE UTENSILS, פָּטוּר – HE IS EXEMPT** from swearing, since the *modeh bemiktzas* oath does not apply if either the admission or the denial concerns land.[23] **הוֹדָה מִקְצָת קַרְקָעוֹת פָּטוּר –** Similarly, if **HE ADMITTED** owing **PART OF THE LAND** but denied owing the rest of the land as well as the utensils, **HE IS EXEMPT** from swearing.[24] **מִקְצָת כֵּלִים חַיָּיב – B**ut if he admits owing **PART OF THE UTENSILS** and denies the rest, **HE IS OBLIGATED** to swear the *modeh bemiktzas* oath.[25]

The Gemara considers the implications of this Mishnah:
**טַעְמָא דְּכֵלִים וְקַרְקָעוֹת – The reason** the Mishnah exempts him from swearing in the first two cases **is that** the dispute concerns **utensils *and* land, דְּקַרְקַע לָאו בַּת שְׁבוּעָה הִיא – for** a claim concerning **land is not subject to an oath. כֵּלִים וְכֵלִים דּוּמְיָא דְּכֵלִים וְקַרְקָעוֹת חַיָּיב – But** had the case involved the admission of **utensils and** the denial of **utensils** in a situation **analogous** to the Mishnah's actual case of **utensils and land, [the defendant] would be obligated** to swear.[26] **הֵיכִי דָּמֵי – How is it?** What is this analogous case? **לָאו דְּאָמַר לֵיהּ הֵילָךְ – Is it not** a case where **[the defendant] said to [the plaintiff], "Here, it is yours"?** Yet, as we have inferred, the defendant would be obligated to swear in this case! **וּשְׁמַע מִינָּהּ הֵילָךְ חַיָּיב – Thus, learn from here that** one who admits partial liability and states, **"Here, it is yours," is obligated** to swear. – ? –

The Gemara rebuts:
**לֹא – No.** Your proof is not conclusive. **לְעוֹלָם אֵימָא לָךְ כֵּלִים וְכֵלִים נַמִּי פָּטוּר – For I can tell you that, in fact, even** in the analogous case of **utensils and utensils, [the defendant] is also exempt** from swearing, because it is a situation of "here, it is yours." **וְהָא דְּקָתָנֵי כֵּלִים וְקַרְקָעוֹת – And the reason the Mishnah states** a case of **utensils and land קָא מַשְׁמַע לָן הוֹדָה בְּמִקְצָת כֵּלִים חַיָּיב אַף עַל הַקַּרְקָעוֹת – is to inform us** that if **[the defendant] admitted** to owing **part of the utensils, he is obligated** to swear **even regarding the land** that he denies.[28]

The Gemara asks:
**מַאי קָא מַשְׁמַע לָן זוֹקְקִין – Accordingly, what is [the Mishnah] teaching us?** The law of **"subjection."**[29] **תְּנֵינָא – But we learned** that law already **in a** previous **Mishnah:**[30] **זוֹקְקִין נְכָסִים שֶׁאֵין לָהֶן אַחֲרָיוּת אֶת הַנְּכָסִים שֶׁיֵּשׁ לָהֶן אַחֲרָיוּת לִישָּׁבַע עֲלֵיהֶם**

NOTES

17. Only then can we understand R' Akiva's view that one who admits three is granted the dispensation of a returner of lost property.

18. As assumed initially by the first analysis above, this analysis also initially assumes that the reason one who admits only the two *selaim* attested to by the note is exempt from swearing is that the lender already has possession of them, since they are secured by the borrower's land. Thus, the situation is one of "here, it is yours" and the exemption proves that there is no *modeh bemiktzas* oath in situations of "here, it is yours."

19. See above, note 10.

20. See above, note 12.

21. This Mishnah is found in *Shevuos* 38b.

22. E.g. the plaintiff claims that the defendant borrowed utensils and land from him and the plaintiff now demands their return.

23. As explained above in note 12.

24. Since his admission concerns only land.

25. Since his admission and denial both concern movables (i.e. the utensils). [The fact that his denial *also* concerns land is of no consequence. The involvement of land is not an obstacle to swearing. It is only that the factors generating the oath obligation must pertain to non-land.]

As evident from the Mishnah there, its ruling that one who admits part of the utensils is obligated to swear means that he is obligated to swear concerning *everything* that he denies – even the land. For (as cited also in the Gemara below) once an oath obligation has been generated by a non-land claim, that obligation can be extended to cover the land portion of the claim as well (*Rashi*). [This extension of the oath is known as גִּלְגּוּל שְׁבוּעָה, *the devolvement of oath*; see 4a note 2.]

26. Our Gemara assumes that the Mishnah in *Shevuos* did not list this case of utensils and land merely to teach that there is no oath of *modeh bemiktzas* when either the admission or denial concerns land. For this rule is already implicit in another Mishnah in *Shevuos* (42b): "And these are the things concerning which one does swear – slaves, documents, land . . ." Rather, the Mishnah must have stated the case of utensils and land in order to imply that in an analagous case involving utensils *exclusively,* the *modeh bemiktzas* oath *does* apply (*Tos. HaRosh* cited also in *Shitah Mekubetzes*; see alternative explanations cited there).

The Gemara will now explain what the analogous situation is.

27. [A fundamental feature of land is that it invariably remains in the legal domain of its true owner (unlike movables, which can be destroyed or removed to a different legal domain through theft and the like). Thus land will invariably represent a situation of "here, it is yours," since whenever the defendant concedes that the land belongs to the plaintiff the land is already in the plaintiff's possession.] Thus, the analogous situation involving utensils exclusively would be that the defendant denies owing some utensils but admits owing others, which he produces in court, saying to the plaintiff: "Here, it is yours" (see *Rashi*).

[*Ritva* questions why *Rashi* had to explain that the admitted utensils were present with the defendant in court, since they are in the legal possession of the plaintiff no matter where they are. See also *Rashi* to 4a ד״ה והילך. (Perhaps, *Rashi's* words מונחים לפנינו do not mean that the utensils are present *in court,* but rather that they are *intact* wherever they may be. See a similar usage in *Rashi* to 5a ד״ה לאו.)]

28. See above, end of note 25.

29. The law of "subjection" is explained in the Mishnah that will now be cited, as well as in the Mishnah of *Shevuos* that is the subject of our discussion.

30. *Kiddushin* 26a.

סלעים דינרין מלוה אומר חמש ולוה אומר שלש ר"ש בן אלעזר אומר הואיל והודה מקצת הטענה ישבע [א] ר"ע אומר א אינו אלא כמשיב אבידה ופטור קתני מיהת רשב"א אומר הואיל והודה מקצת הטענה ישבע טעמא דאמר שלש הא שתים פטור והאי שטר דקמודי ביה הילך הוא וש"מ הילך פטור לא לעולם אימא לך שתים חייב והאי דקתני שלש לאפוקי מדר' עקיבא דאמר משיב אבידה הוי ופטור קמ"ל דמודה מקצת הטענה הוי וחייב אי הכי רשב"א אומר הואיל והודה מקצת הטענה ישבע אף זה ישבע מבעי ליה אלא לעולם שתים פטור והילך חייב ושאני הכא דקא מסייע ליה שטרא אי נמי [ג] משום דהוה ליה שטר שעבוד קרקעות [ג] ב ואין נשבעין על כפירת שעבוד קרקעות איכא דמותיב מסיפא ר"ע אומר אינו אלא כמשיב אבידה ופטור טעמא דאמר שלש הא שתים חייב והא שטר ([ד] כיון) דקא מודי ביה כהילך דמי ש"מ הילך חייב לא לעולם אימא לך שתים נמי פטור והאי דקתני שלש לאפוקי מדרשב"א דאמר מודה מקצת הטענה הוי וחייב קמ"ל דמשיב אבידה הוי ופטור הכי נמי מסתברא דאי סלקא דעתך שתים חייב בשלש היכי פטר ליה ר"ע [ה] האי ארעומי קא מערים סבר אי אמינא שתים בעינא אשתבועי אימא שלש דאהוי כמשיב אבידה ואיפטר אלא ש"מ ג שתים נמי פטור אלא קשיא לרבי חייא שאני התם דקא מסייע ליה שטרא א"נ משום דהוה ליה שטר שעבוד קרקעות ואין נשבעין על כפירת שעבוד קרקעות מתיב מר זוטרא בריה דרב נחמן [ו] ד טענו כלים וקרקעות הודה בכלים וכפר בקרקעות הודה בקרקעות וכפר בכלים פטור הודה מקצת קרקעות פטור ה מקצת כלים חייב טעמא דכלים וקרקעות דקרקע לאו בת שבועה היא הא כלים וכלים דומיא דכלים וקרקעות חייב היכי דמי לאו דאמר ליה הילך וש"מ הילך חייב לא לעולם אימא לך כלים וכלים נמי פטור והא דקתני כלים וקרקעות הא קמ"ל הודה במקצת כלים חייב אף על הקרקעות מאי קמ"ל זוקקין [ז] תנינא ו זוקקין הנכסים שאין להן אחריות את הנכסים שיש להן אחריות לישבע עליהם הכא עיקר התם אגב גררא נסבה ולמאן

**רש"י**

**סלעים דינרין.** שטר שכתוב בו פלוני לוה מפלוני סלעין ולא פירש כמה וכן שטר שכתוב בו דינרין סתם: **אינו אלא כמשיב אבידה.** מדהוה ליה למימר שתים והשטר מסייעו דכיון דלא פירש ניכרים הדברים ששנים היו לכך לא הוצרך לפרש דמיעוט סלעים ב' וכיון דאמר ג' משיב אבידה הוא וחכמים פטרו את משיב אבידה מן השבועה דתנן המוצא את המציאה לא ישבע וכו' (גיטין דף מח:): **טעמא דאמר שלש.** קס"ד השתא דמייתי תיובתא מדנקט פלוגתייהו בשלש וחמש ולא נקט ולוה אמר שתים ש"מ בשתים לא מחייב ליה רשב"א וכדמפרש ואזיל דכיון דכל הודאתו בשטר כתובה דשטר נמי שתים משמע וכל משמעות השטר הילך הוא שהרי הקרקעות משועבדים על כך אבל כי אמר שלש סלעים שלישי מלוה ע"פ הוא דלאו בשטר כתובה ואין הקרקעות משועבדים ולאו הילך הוא: ה"ג ושטרא דקמודה הילך הוא ול"ג כיון דקמודה ביה דבלאו הודאתו נמי כל שטרי הילך הוא וה"פ ומאי דקמודה ביה דכתוב בשטר הילך הוא: **לאפוקי מדר"ע כו'.** דאי תנא שתים לא הוה פליג ר"ע: **א"ה.** דבשתים נמי חייב אמאי תנא הואיל והודה מקצת הטענה ישבע רשב"א אומר אף זה ישבע מבעיא ליה ושמעינן דלא משיב אבידה חשיב ליה ומדנקט הואיל משמע דחיובא משום דגרם לעצמו שהודה במקצת דהשתא הוא דהויא הודאה משום דסלע שלישי לאו הילך הוא אבל שתים לא הוי הודאה משום הילך: **אלא לעולם כו'.** אלא אי אית לך לתרוצי תריץ הכי לעולם כדקאמרת הא שתים פטור וטעמא לאו משום הילך דהילך בעלמא חייב: **ושאני הכא דקא מסייע ליה שטרא.** העדים החתומים על השטר מעידין כדבריו שלא היו אלא שתים ולכך לא פירשו מניין הלכך א"צ שבועה: **א"נ.** להכי לא הוו שתים הודאה לחייבו שבועה לפי שהשטר אומר כן ושטר הוי שעבוד קרקעות וכשם שאין נשבעין על כפירת קרקעות כך הודאתן אינה מביאה לידי שבועה דקרקעות אמעוט מתורת שבועה במס' שבועות פ' שבועת הדיינין (מג:) אבל כי אמר מלוה חמש ולוה שלש איכא כפירה והודאה במה שאין כתוב בשטר: **הא שתים.** דליכא משיב אבידה: **חייב.** מדלא תנא פטור בשתים ונימא טעמא משום הילך: **מודה מקצת הוי.** ואינו משיב אבידה דאיערומי קמערים דלחזקיה בנאמן: **קמ"ל.** כיון דבשתים נמי פטור ליכא למימר איערומי מערים אלא משיב אבידה הוי: **הכי נמי מסתברא.** דבשתים פטור: **ואלא** קשיא לרבי חייא. דהא איכא למידק מינה דשתים פטור כדאמרינן לאי ס"ד כו': **שאני הכא.** האי דקאמר שתים פטור טעמא לאו משום הילך אלא דקא מסייע ליה שטרא: **טענו.** חבירו בב"ד כלים וקרקעות: **פטור.** דלא כפירתו ולא הודאתו מביאתו לידי שבועה: **חייב.** אף על הקרקעות לישבע כדאמרינן לקמן שהנכסים שאין להן אחריות זוקקין את הקרקעות לישבע עליהן משנתחייב לישבע על המטלטלין זוקקין ומגלגלין עמהם שבועת קרקע: **דומיא דכלים וקרקעות.** שכלים שהודה עליהם מונחים לפניו וא"ל הילך: **זוקקין.** המטלטלין זוקקין הקרקעות לישבע ע"י גלגול: **תנינא.** בקדושין (דף כו.) הנכסים שאין להן אחריות זוקקין את הנכסים שיש להן אחריות לישבע עליהם: **הכא עיקר.** שמשנה זו שנויה במסכת שבועות (דף לח:): **התם.** בקדושין: **אגב גררא נסבה.** דאיירי התם נכסים שאין להם אחריות נקנין עם נכסים שיש להן אחריות בכסף בשטר ובחזקה ואגב דאיירי דנקנין עמהם תנא בהדה זוקקין אותן לישבע עליהם:

למאי

**תוספות**

**לעולם** שתים חייב. ואע"ג דשתים חייב חשיב ליה רבי עקיבא משיב אבידה דכשאמר שתים נראה יותר נאמן לפי שהשטר מסייעו: **לעולם** שתים פטור והילך חייב. וא"ת כיון דהילך חייב כי אמר נמי שתים אינו כופר הכל וכי אמר שלש יהא נאמן במיגו דאי בעי אמר שתים ומאי טעמא דרשב"א וי"ל דס"ל דמה שהשטר מסייעו אינו טוען ברצון לפי שנראה שמחמת השטר מודה ואם לא היה השטר היה כופר הכל: **אין** נשבעין על כפירת שעבוד קרקעות. וא"ת למ"ד בפרק גט פשוט (ב"ב דף קעה:) שעבודא דאורייתא מודה מקצת הטענה למה נשבע הא כופר שעבוד קרקעות וי"ל שמחל לו השעבוד או שאין לו כלל קרקעות אפי' משעבדי אבל לרבי יוחנן דאמר בפ' שבועת הפקדון (שבועות דף לז: ושם ד"ה ואין) כופר בממון שיש עליו עדים חייב קרבן שיש עליו שטר פטור משום דכופר שעבוד קרקעות דבעדים לא חשיב כופר שעבוד קרקעות אע"ג דסבר ר' יוחנן שעבודא דאורייתא היינו משום כיון שהפקיעו חכמים השעבוד במלוה ע"פ משום פסידא דלקוחות חשיב כאילו מחל לו השעבוד ומיירי דאית ליה משעבדי ולית ליה בני חרי דאי אית ליה בני חרי אפי' יש עליו עדים פטור ואי לית ליה אפי' משועבדים אפילו יש עליו שטר חייב: **אין** נשבעין על כפירת כו'. לספרים דגרסי בברייתא ר"ע אין להקשות הא ר"ע דריש ריבויי ומיעוטי פ"ק דשבועות (דף ד: ושם ד"ה רבי) ובפרק ג' מינים (נזיר לה. ושם) ומאן דדריש ריבויי ומיעוטי אינו ממעט קרקעות כ"א שטרות כדמוכח בפרק הגוזל בתרא (ב"ק דף קיז:) והיכי קאמר הכא אין נשבעין על כפירת שעבוד קרקעות וי"ל שיש לו שום מיעוט למעט קרקעות וכן צ"ל לקמן בפ' השואל (דף ק: ושם ד"ה ר"מ) אליבא דר"מ דאית ליה נשבעין אעבדים ולא אקרקעות ואע"ג דעבדים הוקשו לקרקעות לכ"ע דמהאי טעמא עבד נקנה בכסף בפ"ק דקדושין (דף כב:) אלא דר"מ דריש ריבויי ומיעוטי להוציא שטרות ויש לו שום מיעוט למעט קרקעות ובאותו מיעוט אין למעט עבדים אע"ג דהוקשו לקרקעות כדמוכח במרובה (ב"ק סג. ושם ד"ה וחד) דמאן דדריש בריבה ומיעט וריבה צריך שני מיעוטי לקרקעות ועבדים ואע"ג דרשב"א היה תלמידו של ר"ע אין לחוש מה שחולק עמו [ט] והוזכר [ח] קודם דכעין זה מצינו לקמן (דף ז.) גבי שנים אדוקים בשטר דפליג רבי עם רשב"ג אביו ויש ספרים דגרסי הכא ר' יעקב: **הא** כלים וכלים חייב. הוה מצי לשנויי בחפר בה בורות שיחין ומערות כדבסמוך: [**הודה** במקצת כלים חייב. וא"ת יהא נאמן במיגו דאי בעי כפר בכלים והיה מודה במקצת קרקעות וי"ל שמא חפץ בקרקעות יותר] ס"א:

למ"ד

**מסורת הש"ס**

א) [בבא בתרא קכח:] ב) [שבועות דף לז:] ג) [כתובות פז:], ד) ועי' בס' ת"ח שמקיים גי' הספרים, ה) [לקמן ח.] ו) שבועות לח:, מ. ז) לקמן ק:, קידושין כו. שבועות לח:, מ:, ח) [עי' תוס' סוטה ד. ד"ה ב עוזאי].

**גליון הש"ס**

תוס' ד"ה אין וכו' והוזכר קודם. עי' תוי"ט פ"ג משנה דבכורים:

**ליקוטי רש"י**

**כמשיב אבדה.** ופטור משבועה דסלעין לא משמע טפי משנים דתפסת מרובה לא תפסת ויד בעל השטר על התחתונה ועל השלישי שהודה הוה משיב אבדה ותנן המוצא מציאה לא ישבע מפני תיקון העולם [רשב"ם ב"ב קכח:]. **משום דהוה ליה.** הא שטר ממון שהקרקעות משועבדים לו והכופר בו ככופר בקרקעות וקי"ל דאין נשבעין על הקרקעות [שבועות לז:]. כל שטרות שיעבוד קרקעות הן ואין נשבעין על הקרקעות כדאמרינן בשבועות ובהזהב [כתובות פז:]. **הודה מקצת קרקעות פטור.** שאין נשבעין על הקרקעות כדילפינן לקמן בפירקין ואף הודאתן אינה מביאה לידי שבועה. **מקצת כלים חייב** שבועה אף על הקרקעות ע"י גלגול דשבועה מקצת כלים [שבועות מ:]. **זוקקים וכו' לישבע עליהם.** אע"ג דלא נשבעין על הקרקעות לבד כדנפקא לן בשבועות (דף מב:) היכא דטענו כלים וקרקעות ונתחייב לישבע על המטלטלין זוקקין המטלטלין את הקרקעות לישבע עליהן [קידושין כו.]. **הכא עיקר.** דכולה מסכת בהלכות שבועה [שבועות שם].

**עין משפט נר מצוה**

טז א מיי' פ"ד מהל' טוען ונטען הל' ה סמג עשין צה טוש"ע ח"מ סי' פח סעיף לב:

יז ב מיי' שם פ"ה הל' א סמג שם טוש"ע ח"מ סי' צה ס"א:

יח ג (מיי' פ"ד שם הל' ה) סמג שם טוש"ע ח"מ סי' פח סעיף לב:

יט ד ה ו מיי' פ"ה שם הל' ג סמג שם טוש"ע ח"מ סי' צה סעיף ה:

**רבינו חננאל**

מודה מקצת הטענה הוא ומתני' תקנת חכמים היא וכר' יוחנן. מיתיבי סלעין דינרים וכו'. פי' שטר שכתוב בו סתם פלוני חייב לפלוני סלעים או דינרין. מלוה אמר ה' סלעים חייב לי ולוה אמר ג' ר' שמעון בן אלעזר אומר הואיל והודה מקצת הטענה ישבע. ודייקי' טעמא דהודה בג' הא הודה בב' פטור מאי טעמא דשטר כיון דמודה במלוה בשטר כי הילך דמי דקיימא לן מלוה בשטר תורתו כקרקע והמודה בקרקע הילך הוא ודייקי' דבשתים פטור קשיא לר' חייא. ופריק לא ואפילו הודה בשתים חייב והאי דקתני ג' לאפוקי מדר' עקיבא דאמר הודאתו בשלישית משיב אבידה הוי מיגו דאי בעי אמר תרתי כדכתיב בשטר סלעים ואמר ג' משיב אבידה הוא ופטור משבועה. ואקשי' אי הכי דר' שמעון אפילו בשתים מחייב והוא הדין לג' אף זה חייב לישבע היה לו לומר. ופרקי' לעולם שתים פטור ושאני הכא משום דמסייע ליה דכתיב בה סלעין וסתם סלעין שתים הן. אי נמי משום דהוי שטר שיעבוד קרקעות ואין נשבעין על כפירת שעבוד קרקעות. פי' נמצא המלוה טוענו ה' סלעין ועדי השטר מעידין שחייב לו סלעים לא פחות משתים לדברי ר' חייא דאמר מנה לי בידך והלה אומר אין לך בידי כלום ועדים מעידים אותן נ' אותן נ' נותן לו ונשבע על השאר וכל שכן בשמודה לו במקצת היה מן הדין לחייבו שבועה גם בשמודה בשתים ואמר לך ר' חייא כי קאמינא במלוה על פה אבל במלוה בשטר דשעבודיה על הקרקע כאילו קרקע בה' סלעין הוא דטעין ומודה לו במקצת מן הקרקע ובשאר כופר בו. ותנן אין נשבעין על הקרקעות וכשם שאם יטען עליו שדה זו בידך שלי הוא והלה כופר בו אין חייב שבועה עליה כך הטוען על חבירו בשעבוד קרקעות והלה כופר בו אין חייב שבועה על כפירתו. ור' שמעון סבר הא דטעין עליה בה' סלעין תרתי מינהון בשטרא ותלת מינהון על פה כפר בתלת פטור כדתנן מנה לי בידך והלה אומר אין לך בידי כלום פטור. הודה אחת מן השלש חייב. ומותבינן תוב מדברי ר' עקיבא דפטר בג' וכל שכן בב' והנה דפריש להו שטרא הילך הוא וקתני פטור א) קשיא לרבי חייא. ופריק שאני הכא דקא מסייע ליה שטרא. אי נמי משום דהוי ליה שטר שעבוד קרקעות כו'. כדפרשינן לזה לעילא. ש"מ דדברי הכל הודה בשתים פטור כי פליגי בשמודה בג'. ר' עקיבא סבר מיגו דאי בעי אמר שתים ואמר ג' משיב אבידה הוי ופטור דכי אמרה תורה כי הוא זה דשמעינן מיניה מודה מקצת הטענה חייב הא פריש רבה טעמא דקרא דאמר מפני מה אמרה תורה מודה מקצת הטענה ישבע חזקה אין אדם מעיז פניו בפני בעל חובו והאי בכוליה בעי דליכפריה וכו' והאי כיון דאית ליה עליה שטרא לא יכול לכפור בכל לית עליה הדין דינא הלכך פטור הוא. ור' שמעון סבר לא שנא אלא הרי הוא ככל טענתא דעלמא הכופר בכל פטור והמודה במקצת חייב. תוב אקשינן מהא טענו כלים וקרקעות וכו'. ופשוטה היא. פי' הכא עיקר התם אגב גררא נסבה. הכא בשבועות דקתני הודה במקצת כלים מיגו דנתחייב שבועה בכלים נשבע גם על הקרקע בזקיקה זה מקום עיקרו. והתם בקידושין פ"א דקתני זוקקין את הנכסים שיש להם אחריות לישבע עליהם [אגב] גררא נסבה.

ומקשי'

חשק שלמה על ר"ח א) לפנינו הגי' הא שתים חייב וש"מ דהילך חייב ולמגס רבינו נראה דגרים וכ"ש בשתים וד' רבינו ז"ל הובא בש"מ כאן בשמו ע"ש.

swearing – apparently because there is no oath of *modeh bemiktzas* in situations of *heilach.* – ? –

The Gemara concedes that R' Shimon ben Elazar would not obligate an oath if the borrower admits only two *selaim,* but provides a different defense of R' Chiya's view:

אֶלָּא לְעוֹלָם שְׁתַּיִם פָּטוּר – **Rather,** though we must say that **indeed** the Baraisa means that the borrower who admits only **two** *selaim* **is exempt** from swearing, as demonstrated by the language of R' Shimon ben Elazar's ruling, וְהֵילָךְ חַיָּיב – it is **still** possible that, ordinarily, even in situations of **"here, it is yours"** the borrower **is obligated** to swear, as R' Chiya rules. וְשָׁאנֵי הָכָא דְּקָא מְסַיַּיע לֵיהּ שְׁטָרָא – **And it is different here** in the case of the Baraisa, **for** the wording of **the note supports [the borrower]** who insists that he borrowed only two *selaim.*[10] It is for this reason that the borrower who admits only two *selaim* would be exempt from swearing, and not because the situation is one of "here, it is yours."

The Gemara offers an alternative reason why an admission of only two *selaim* would not generate an oath obligation, even assuming that the *modeh bemiktzas* oath obligation is not affected by a situation of *heilach*:

אִי נַמִּי – **Alternatively,** the borrower who admits only two *selaim* does not swear מִשּׁוּם דַּהֲוָה לֵיהּ שְׁטָר שִׁעְבּוּד קַרְקָעוֹת – **because the note represents a lien on land**[11] וְאֵין נִשְׁבָּעִין עַל כְּפִירַת שִׁעְבּוּד קַרְקָעוֹת – **and** there is a rule that **one does not swear concerning** his **denial of a lien on land,** or – by the same token – because of his *admission* of a lien on land.[12]

The Gemara cites an alternative analysis that was made of this Baraisa and its bearing on the question of whether the *modeh bemiktzas* oath is imposed in situations of "here, it is yours." This analysis initially challenges the view of Rav Sheishess (that no oath is imposed in situations of "here, it is yours"):

אִיכָּא דְּמוֹתִיב מְסֵיפָא – **There are those who** issue a **challenge from the latter part of the Baraisa,** which states: רַבִּי עֲקִיבָא אוֹמֵר אֵינוֹ אֶלָּא כְּמֵשִׁיב אֲבֵידָה וּפָטוּר – **R' AKIVA SAYS: [THE DEFENDANT] IS NOTHING BUT A RETURNER OF LOST PROPERTY, AND IS** therefore **EXEMPT** from swearing.[13] ...מָא דְּאָמַר שָׁלֹשׁ הָא שְׁתַּיִם חַיָּיב – We can infer that **the reason** R' Akiva exempts t... defendant from swearing **is that** he admitted owing **three** *selai...* **But** had he admitted only **two, he would be obligated** ... swear.[14] וְהָא שְׁטָר (כיון) דְּקָא מוֹדֵי בֵּיהּ כְּהֵילָךְ דָּמֵי – **But** t... **note**-recorded amount of two *selaim* **that he admits is** in the ca... egory of **"here, it is yours,"**[15] yet he is obligated to swear. ...עַ מִינָּהּ הֵילָךְ חַיָּיב – **Learn from here that** one who admits parti... liability but states, **"Here, it is yours," is obligated** to swear t... oath of *modeh bemiktzas,* unlike Rav Sheishess' ruling. – ? –

The Gemara answers:

לֹא – **No.** Your proof is not conclusive. ...עוֹלָם אֵימָא לָךְ שְׁתַּיִם נַמִּי פָּטוּר – **I can tell you that, in fact, even** if the borrower admi... **two** *selaim,* **he is exempt** from swearing, as Rav Sheishess rule... וְהַאי דְּקָתָנֵי שָׁלֹשׁ – **And that which [R' Akiva] states** his ruling ... a case of the borrower admitting **three** *selaim* rather than two לְאַפּוּקֵי מִדְּרַבִּי שִׁמְעוֹן בֶּן אֶלְעָזָר – **to exclude** the view of **R' Shim... ben Elazar,** דְּאָמַר מוֹדֶה מִקְצָת הַטַּעֲנָה הֲוֵי וְחַיָּיב – **who says** (... the beginning of the Baraisa) **that [the borrower]** who admi... three *selaim* **is** still **one who admits part of the claim and obligated** to swear. קָא מַשְׁמַע לָן דְּמֵשִׁיב אֲבֵידָה הֲוֵי וּפָטוּר – Therefore, **[R' Akiva] informs us that [the borrower]** wh... admits owing three *selaim* **is, in fact, a returner of lost proper... and is** therefore **exempt** from swearing.

The Gemara adds:

הָכִי נַמִּי מִסְתַּבְּרָא – **This** latter explanation **is indeed** mo... **logical.** דְּאִי סָלְקָא דַּעְתָּךְ שְׁתַּיִם חַיָּיב – **For if you were to thin... that** a borrower who admits only **two** *selaim* **is obligated** ... swear (as this analysis sought to infer initially), שָׁלֹשׁ הֵיכִי פָּטַר לֵיהּ רַבִּי עֲקִיבָא – then **how could R' Akiva exempt him** fro... swearing **when** he admits **three?** ...הַאי אַעֲרוּמֵי קָא מַעֲרִים – Perhaps **this** fellow **is scheming,** סָבַר – **reasoning:** ...אֵמִינָא שְׁתַּיִם בְּעֵינָא אִשְׁתַּבּוּעֵי – **If I say** that I owe **two** *selaim,* **I will hav... to swear** the oath of *modeh bemiktzas.* אֵימָא שָׁלֹשׁ – **I wi...** therefore **say** that I owe **three** דְּאֶהֱוֵי כְּמֵשִׁיב אֲבֵידָה וְאִיפְּטַר – s... **that I will be considered a returner of lost property and wi... be exempt** from swearing.[16] ...אֶלָּא שְׁמַע מִינָּהּ שְׁתַּיִם נַמִּי פָּטוּר –

NOTES

have been: "*Even* this [one who admits three *selaim*] must swear." This phraseology would have indicated that not only one who admits two *selaim* must swear (as a classic *modeh bemiktzas*) but even one who admits three *selaim* (and thus might be construed as a returner of lost property) must swear nonetheless. The expression R' Shimon ben Elazar does use, however – "*since* he admitted part of the claim" – indicates that it is because he admitted *three* that he is considered a *modeh bemiktzas*; had he admitted only two *selaim,* he would have been exempt from swearing – apparently because there is no oath of *modeh bemiktzas* in a situation of "here, it is yours" (see *Rashi*; see also *Ritva*).

10. Barring evidence to the contrary (e.g. the borrower's admission that more is owed), the plural but non-specific term "*selaim*" mentioned in the note must be taken to mean "two" *selaim* and no more (see note 3 above). Now, a note signed by witnesses has the force of witnesses that the information contained therein is true. And, as stated on 4a, witnesses who support a defendant's denial of half the claim against him exempt him from the *modeh bemiktzas* oath. Accordingly, in the case of the Baraisa, if the borrower admits only two *selaim,* the non-specific term "*selaim*" used in the note (which is signed by witnesses) in effect constitutes testimony supporting his assertion that he borrowed *only* two *selaim.* It is for this reason that he is exempt from swearing, not because the two *selaim* that he admits are viewed as *heilach* (see *Rashi*).

11. See note 5 above.

12. A defendant's obligation to deny the claim against him *under oath* does not apply if it is land that he denies (as derived by the Gemara in *Shevuos* 42b-43a). Thus, for example, if a plaintiff claims that the defendant owes him a group of properties but the defendant denie... owing him the land that is among those properties, the defendant doe... not swear the oath of *modeh bemiktzas.* Moreover, the underlyin... principle of this exemption is that land cannot be a factor *at all* i... creating an oath obligation. Thus, in the case of *modeh bemiktza...* (which requires both admission and denial of the claim), there is n... oath imposed if either the denial or the admission concerns land.

Now, the same exemption from oath applies to a denial or admissio... that relates to a *lien* on land, since that, too, in effect relates to lan... Accordingly, in the case of our Baraisa, the borrower does not swear ... he admits only the two *selaim* attested to by the note, since he ha... admitted only the portion of the claim for which there is a lien on lan... However, if he admits owing three *selaim,* then he does indeed swea... (according to R' Shimon ben Elazar), since there is no lien on land fo... the third *sela,* which is not attested to by the note. In that case, h... admits non-land (the third *sela*) and denies non-land (the fourth an... fifth *selaim* claimed by the lender), creating a classic situation of *mode... bemiktzas* (*Rashi*).

Thus, the borrower is exempt from swearing if he admits only tw... *selaim* not because the two *selaim* are *heilach,* but because those tw... *selaim* are secured by the borrower's land.

13. See above, note 3.

14. The borrower has no choice but to admit owing two *selaim,* whic... are attested to by the note. Thus, he is considered a returner of los... property only if he admits an additional amount not stated in the not...

15. See above, note 5.

16. [It is worth the defendant's while to pay the extra *sela* and thereb... avoid having to swear regarding the remaining two.]

סלעים דינרין מלוה אומר חמש ולוה אומר שלש ר"ש בן אלעזר אומר הואיל והודה מקצת הטענה ישבע (א) ר"ע אומר [א] אינו אלא כמשיב אבידה ופטור קתני מיהת רשב"א אומר הואיל והודה מקצת הטענה ישבע טעמא דאמר שלש הא שתים פטור והאי שטר דקמודי ביה הילך הוא וש"מ הילך פטור לא לעולם אימא לך שתים חייב והאי דקתני שלש לאפוקי מדר' עקיבא דאמר משיב אבידה הוי ופטור קמ"ל דמודה מקצת הטענה הוי וחייב אי הכי רשב"א אומר הואיל והודה מקצת הטענה ישבע אף זה ישבע מבעי ליה אלא לעולם שתים פטור והילך חייב ושאני הכא דקא מסייע ליה שטרא אי נמי (ג) משום דהוה ליה שטר שעבוד קרקעות (ג) [ב] ואין נשבעין על כפירת שעבוד קרקעות איכא דמותיב מסיפא ר"ע אומר אינו אלא כמשיב אבידה ופטור טעמא דאמר שלש הא שתים חייב והא שטר (ד) (כיון) דקא מודי ביה כהילך דמי ש"מ הילך חייב לא לעולם אימא לך שתים נמי פטור והאי דקתני שלש לאפוקי מדרשב"א דאמר מודה מקצת הטענה הוי וחייב קמ"ל דמשיב אבידה הוי ופטור הכי נמי מסתברא דאי סלקא דעתך שתים חייב בשלש היכי פטר ליה ר"ע (ה) האי אערומי קא מערים סבר אי אמינא שתים בעינא אשתבועי אימא שלש דאהוי כמשיב אבידה ואיפטר אלא ש"מ [ג] שתים נמי פטור אלא קשיא לרבי חייא שאני התם דקא מסייע ליה שטרא א"נ משום דהוה ליה שטר שעבוד קרקעות ואין נשבעין על כפירת שעבוד קרקעות מתיב מר זוטרא בריה דרב נחמן (ו) [ד] טענו כלים וקרקעות הודה בכלים וכפר בקרקעות הודה בקרקעות וכפר בכלים פטור הודה מקצת קרקעות פטור [ה] מקצת כלים חייב טעמא דכלים וקרקעות דקרקע לאו בת שבועה היא הא כלים וכלים דומיא דכלים וקרקעות חייב היכי דמי לאו דאמר ליה הילך וש"מ הילך חייב לא לעולם אימא לך כלים וכלים נמי פטור והא דקתני כלים וקרקעות הא קמ"ל הודה במקצת כלים חייב אף על הקרקעות מאי קמ"ל זוקקין (ז) תנינא [ו] זוקקין הנכסים שאין להן אחריות את הנכסים שיש להן אחריות לישבע עליהם הכא עיקר התם אגב גררא נסבה ולמאן

**רש"י**

סלעים דינרין. שטר שכתוב בו פלוני לוה מפלוני סלעין ולא פירש כמה וכן שטר שכתוב בו דינרין סתם: אינו אלא כמשיב אבידה. מדהוה ליה למימר שתים והשטר מסייעו דכיון דלא פירש ניכרים הדברים ששנים היו לכך לא הוצרך לפרש דמיעוט סלעים ב' וכיון דאמר ג' משיב אבידה הוא וחכמים פטרו את משיב אבידה מן השבועה דתנן המוצא את המציאה לא ישבע וכו' (גיטין דף מח:): טעמא דאמר שלש. קס"ד השתא דמייתי תיובתא מדנקט פלוגתייהו בשלש וחמש ולא נקט ולוה אמר שתים ש"מ בשתים לא מחייב ליה רשב"א וכדמפרש ואזיל דכיון דכל הודאתו בשטר כתובה דשטר נמי שתים משמע וכל משמעות השטר הילך הוא שהרי הקרקעות משועבדים על כך אבל כי אמר שלש סלעים שלישי מלוה ע"פ הוא דלאו בשטר כתובה ואין הקרקעות משועבדים ולאו הילך הוא: ה"ג ושטרא דקמודה הילך הוא ול"ג כיון דקמודה ביה דבלאו הודאתו נמי כל שטרי הילך הוא וה"פ ומאי דקמודה ביה דכתוב בשטר הילך הוא: לאפוקי מדר"ע כו'. דאי תנא שתים לא הוה פליג ר"ע: א"ה. דבשתים נמי חייב אמאי תנא הואיל והודה מקצת הטענה ישבע רשב"א אומר אף זה ישבע מבעיא ליה ושמעינן דלא משיב אבידה חשיב ליה ומדנקט הואיל משמע דחיובא משום דגרס לעצמו שהודה במקצת דהשתא הוא דהויא הודאה משום דסלע שלישי לאו הילך הוא אבל שתים לא הוי הודאה משום הילך: אלא לעולם כו'. אלא אי אית לך לתרוצי תריץ הכי לעולם כדקאמרת הא שתים פטור וטעמא לאו משום הילך דהילך בעלמא חייב: ושאני הכא דקא מסייע ליה שטרא. העדים החתומים על השטר מעידין כדבריו שלא היו אלא שתים ולכך לא פירשו מניין הלכך א"צ שבועה: א"נ. להכי לא הוו שתים הודאה לחייבו שבועה לפי שהשטר אומר כן ושטר הוי שעבוד קרקעות וכשם שאין נשבעין על כפירת קרקעות כך הודאתן אינה מביאה לידי שבועה דקרקעות אמעוט מתורת שבועה במס' שבועות פ' שבועת הדיינין (מב:) אבל כי אמר מלוה חמש ולוה שלש איכא כפירה והודאה במה שאין כתוב בשטר: הא שתים. דליכא משיב אבידה: חייב. מדלא תנא פטור בשתים ונימא טעמא משום הילך: מודה מקצת הוי. ואינו משיב אבידה דאיערומי קמערים דלחזקיה בנאמן: קמ"ל. כיון דבשתים נמי פטור ליכא למימר איערומי מיירים אלא משיב אבידה הוי: הכי נמי מסתברא. דבשתים פטור: ואלא קשיא לרבי חייא. דהא איכא למידק מינה דשתים פטור כדאמרינן דאי ס"ד כו': שאני הכא. הא דקאמר שתים פטור טעמא לאו משום הילך אלא דקא מסייע ליה שטרא: טענו. חבירו בב"ד כלים וקרקעות: פטור. דלא כפירתו ולא הודאתו מביאתו לידי שבועה: חייב. אף על הקרקעות לישבע כדאמרינן לקמן שהנכסים שאין להן אחריות זוקקין את הקרקעות לישבע עליהן משנתחייב לישבע על המטלטלין זוקקין ומגלגלין עמהם שבועת קרקע: דומיא דכלים וקרקעות. שכלים שהודה עליהם מונחים לפניו וא"ל הילך: זוקקין. המטלטלין זוקקין הקרקעות לישבע ע"י גלגול: תנינא. בקדושין (דף כו.) הנכסים שאין להן אחריות זוקקין את הנכסים שיש להן אחריות לישבע עליהם: הכא עיקר. שמשנה זו שנויה במסכת שבועות (דף לח.): התם. בקדושין: אגב גררא נסבה. דאיירי התם נכסים שאין להם אחריות נקנין עם נכסים שיש להן אחריות בכסף בשטר ובחזקה ואגב דאיירי דנקנין עמהם תנא בהדה זוקקין אותן לישבע עליהם:

למאי

**תוספות**

לעולם שתים חייב. ואע"ג דשתים חשיב ליה רבי עקיבא משיב אבידה דכשאמר שתים נראה יותר נאמן לפי שהשטר מסייעו: לעולם שתים פטור והילך חייב. וא"ת כיון דהילך חייב כי אמר נמי שתים אינו כופר הכל וכי אמר שלש יהא נאמן במיגו דאי בעי אמר שתים ומאי טעמא דרשב"א וי"ל דס"ל דמה שהשטר מסייעו אינו טוען ברצון לפי שנראה שמחמת השטר מודה ואם לא היה השטר היה כופר הכל: אין נשבעין על כפירת שעבוד קרקעות. וא"ת למ"ד בפרק גט פשוט (ב"ב דף קעה:) שעבודא דאורייתא מודה מקצת הטענה למה נשבע הא כופר שעבוד קרקעות וי"ל שמחל לו השעבוד או שאין לו כלל קרקעות אפי' משעבדי אבל לרבי יוחנן דאמר בפ' שבועת הפקדון (שבועות דף לז: ושם ד"ה ואין) כופר בממון שיש עליו עדים חייב קרבן שיש עליו שטר פטור משום דכופר שעבוד קרקעות דבעדים לא חשיב כופר שעבוד קרקעות אע"ג דסבר ר' יוחנן שעבודא דאורייתא היינו משום כיון שהפקיעו חכמים השעבוד במלוה ע"פ משום פסידא דלקוחות חשיב כאילו מחל לו השעבוד ומיירי דאית ליה משעבדי ולית ליה בני חרי דאי אית ליה בני חרי אפי' יש עליו עדים פטור ואי לית ליה אפי' משועבדים אפילו יש עליו שטר חייב: אין נשבעין על כפירת כו'. לספרים דגרסי בברייתא ר"ע אין להקשות הא ר"ע דריש ריבויי ומיעוטי פ"ק דשבועות (דף ד: ושם ד"ה רבי) ובפרק ג' מינים (נזיר לה. ושם) ומאן דדריש ריבויי ומיעוטי אינו ממעט קרקעות כ"א שטרות כדמוכח בפרק הגוזל בתרא (ב"ק דף קיז:) והיכי קאמר הכא אין נשבעין על כפירת שעבוד קרקעות וי"ל שיש לו שום מיעוט למעט קרקעות וכן צ"ל לקמן בפ' השואל (דף ק: ושם ד"ה ר"מ) אליבא דר"מ דאית ליה נשבעין אעבדים ולא אקרקעות ואע"ג דעבדים הוקשו לקרקעות לכ"ע דמהאי טעמא עבד נקנה בכסף בפ"ק דקדושין (דף כב:) אלא דר"מ דריש ריבויי ומיעוטי להוציא שטרות ויש לו שום מיעוט למעט קרקעות ובאותו מיעוט אין למעט עבדים אע"ג דהוקשו לקרקעות כדמוכח במרובה (ב"ק סג. ושם ד"ה וחד) דמאן דדריש בריבה ומיעט וריבה צריך שני מיעוטי לקרקעות ועבדים ואע"ג דרשב"א היה תלמידו של ר"ע אין לחוש מה שחולק עמו (ט) והוזכר (ח) קודם דרוין זה מליו לקמן (דף ז.) גבי שנים אדוקים בשטר דפליג רבי עם רשב"ג אביו ויש ספרים דגרסי הכא ר' יעקב: הא כלים וכלים חייב. הוה מצי לשנויי בחפר בה בורות שיחין ומערות כדבסמוך: [הודה במקצת כלים חייב. וא"ת יהא נאמן במיגו דאי בעי כפר בכלים והיה מודה במקצת קרקעות וי"ל שמא חפץ בקרקעות יותר] ס"א:

למ"ד



טז א מיי' פ"ד מהל' טוען ונטען הל' ה סמג עשין צה טוש"ע ח"מ סי' פח סעיף לב:
יז ב מיי' שם פ"ה הל' א סמג שם טוש"ע ח"מ סי' צה סעיף א:
יח ג (מיי' פ"ד שם הל' ה) סמג שם טוש"ע ח"מ סי' פח סעיף לב:
יט ד ה ו מיי' פ"ה שם הל' ג סמג שם טוש"ע ח"מ סי' צה סעיף ה:

**רבינו חננאל**

מודה מקצת הטענה הוא ומתני' תקנת חכמים היא וכר' יוחנן. מיתיבי סלעין דינרים וכו'. פי' שטר שכתוב בו סתם פלוני חייב לפלוני סלעים או דינרין. מלוה אמר ה' סלעים חייב לי ולוה אמר ג' ר' שמעון בן אלעזר אומר הואיל והודה מקצת הטענה ישבע. ודייקי' טעמא דהודה בג' הא הודה בב' פטור מאי טעמא דשטר כיון דמודה במלוה בשטר כי הילך דמי דקיימא לן מלוה בשטר תורתו כקרקע והמודה בקרקע הילך הוא ודייקי' דבשתים פטור קשיא לר' חייא. ופריק לא ואפילו הודה בשתים חייב והאי דקתני ג' לאפוקי מדר' עקיבא דאמר הודאתו בשלישית משיב אבידה הוי מיגו דאי בעי אמר תרתי כדכתיב בשטר סלעים ואמר ג' משיב אבידה הוא ופטור משבועה. ואקשי' אי הכי דר' שמעון אפילו בשתים מחייב והוא הדין לג' אף זה חייב לישבע היה לו לומר. ופרקי' לעולם שתים פטור ושאני הכא משום דמסייע ליה דכתיב בה סלעין וסתם סלעין שתים הן. אי נמי משום דהוי שטר שיעבוד קרקעות ואין נשבעין על כפירת שעבוד קרקעות. פי' נמצא המלוה טוענו ה' סלעין ועדי השטר מעידין שחייב לו סלעים לא פחות משתים לדברי ר' חייא דאמר מנה לי בידך והלה אומר אין לך בידי כלום ועדים מעידים אותן ג' אותן נ' נותן לו ונשבע על השאר וכל שכן בשמודה לו במקצת היה מן הדין שחייב שבועה גם בשמודה בשתים ואמר לך ר' חייא כי קאמינא במלוה על פה אבל במלוה בשטר שעבודיה על הקרקע כאילו קרקע בה' סלעין הוא דטעין ומודה לו במקצת מן הקרקע ובשאר כופר בו. ותנן אין נשבעין על הקרקעות וכשם שאם יטען עליו שדה זו בידך שלי הוא והלה כופר בו אין חייב שבועה עליה כך הטוען על חבירו בשעבוד קרקעות והלה כופר בו אין חייב שבועה על כפירתו. ור' שמעון סבר הא דטעין עליה בה' סלעין תרתי מינהון בשטרא ותלת מינהון על פה כפר בתלת פטור כדתנן מנה לי בידך והלה אומר אין לך בידי כלום פטור. הודה אחת מן השלש חייב. ומותבינן תוב מדברי ר' עקיבא דפטר בג' וכל שכן בב' והנה דפריש להו שטרא הילך הוא וקתני פטור א) קשיא לרבי חייא. ופריק שאני הכא דקא מסייע ליה שטרא. אי נמי משום דהוי ליה שטר שעבוד קרקעות כו'. כדפרשינן לזה לעילא. ש"מ דדברי הכל הודה בשתים פטור כי פליגי בשמודה בג'. ר' עקיבא סבר מיגו דאי בעי אמר שתים ואמר ג' משיב אבידה הוי ופטור דכי אמרה תורה כי הוא זה דשמעינן מיניה מודה מקצת הטענה חייב הא פריש רבה טעמא דקרא דאמר מפני מה אמרה תורה מודה מקצת הטענה ישבע חזקה אין אדם מעיז פניו בפני בעל חובו והאי בכוליה בעי דליכפריה וכו' והאי כיון דאית ליה עליה שטרא לא יכול לכפור בכל לית עליה הדין דינא הלכך פטור הוא. ור' שמעון סבר לא שנא אלא הרי הוא ככל טענתא דעלמא הכופר בכל פטור והמודה במקצת חייב. תוב אקשינן מהא טענו כלים וקרקעות וכו'. ופשוטה היא. פי' הכא עיקר התם אגב גררא נסבה. הכא בשבועות דקתני הודה במקצת כלים מיגו דנתחייב שבועה בכלים נשבע גם על הקרקע בזקיקה זה מקום עיקרו. והתם בקידושין פ"א דקתני זוקקין את הנכסים שיש להם אחריות לישבע עליהם [אגב] גררא נסבה.

ומקשי'

חשק שלמה על ר"ח א) לפנינו הגי' הא שתים חייב וש"מ דהילך חייב ואמנם רבינו נראה דגרים וכ"ש בשתים וד' רבינו ז"ל הובא בש"מ כאן בשמו ע"ש.



א) [נבא בתרא קכח:], ב) [שבועות דף לז:], ג) [כתובות פז:], ד) ועי' בס' ש"מ שמקשים ג"כ הספרים, ה) [לקמן ח.], ו) שבועות לח:, מ., ז) לקמן ק: קידושין כו: שבועות לח: מ: מ, ח) [עי' תוס' סוטה ד. ד"ה בן עזאי].

**גליון הש"ס**

תוס' ד"ה אין וכו' והוזכר קודם. עי' תוי"ט פ"ג משנה דבכורים.

**ליקוטי רש"י**

כמשיב אבדה. ופטור משבועה דסלעין לא משמע טפי משתים דתפסת מרובה לא תפסת ויד בעל השטר על התחתונה ועל השלישי שהודה הוא משיב אבדה ותנן המוצא מציאה לא ישבע מפני תיקון העולם [רשב"ב קכח:]. משום דהוה ליה. הא שטר ממון שהקרקעות משועבדים לו והכופר בו ככופר בקרקעות וקי"ל דאין נשבעין על הקרקעות [שבועות לז:]. כל שטרות שיעבוד קרקעות הן ואין נשבעין על הקרקעות כדאמרינן בשבועות ובהזהב [כתובות פז:]. הודה מקצת קרקעות פטור. שאין נשבעין על הקרקעות כדלפינן לקמן בפירקין ואף הודאתן אינה מביאה לידי שבועה. מקצת כלים חייב. שבועה אף על הקרקעות ע"י גלגול שבועה [שבועות מ:]. זוקקים וכו' לישבע עליהם. אע"פ שאין נשבעין על הקרקעות לבד כדנפקא לן בשבועות (מב:) היכא דטענו כלים וקרקעות ונתחייב לישבע על המטלטלין זוקקין המטלטלין את הקרקעות לישבע עליהן [קידושין כו.]. הכא עיקר. דכולה מסכת בהלכות שבועות [שבועות שם].

סְלָעִים דִּינָרִין – A note of indebtedness [debenture] states that the borrower owes **SELAIM** or **DINARIM**[1] without specifying an amount. מַלְוֶה אוֹמֵר חָמֵשׁ – **THE LENDER SAYS** that **FIVE** *selaim* or *dinarim* is the amount of the loan referred to in the note, וְלֹוֶה אוֹמֵר שָׁלֹשׁ – **WHEREAS THE BORROWER SAYS** that only **THREE** *selaim* or *dinarim* are meant. רַבִּי שִׁמְעוֹן בֶּן אֶלְעָזָר אוֹמֵר הוֹאִיל וְהוֹדָה מִקְצָת הַטַּעֲנָה יִשָּׁבַע – **R' SHIMON BEN ELAZAR SAYS: SINCE HE ADMITTED PART OF THE CLAIM** against him, **HE MUST SWEAR** that he does not owe the rest.[2] רַבִּי עֲקִיבָא אוֹמֵר אֵינוֹ אֶלָּא כְּמֵשִׁיב אֲבֵידָה וּפָטוּר – But **R' AKIVA SAYS: [THE DEFENDANT] IS NOTHING BUT A RETURNER OF LOST PROPERTY, AND IS** therefore **EXEMPT** from swearing.[3]

The Gemara now examines the implications of the Baraisa just cited:

קָתָנֵי מִיהַת – **At any rate, the Baraisa states:** רַבִּי שִׁמְעוֹן בֶּן אֶלְעָזָר אוֹמֵר הוֹאִיל וְהוֹדָה מִקְצָת הַטַּעֲנָה יִשָּׁבַע – **R' SHIMON BEN ELAZAR SAYS: SINCE HE ADMITTED PART OF THE CLAIM, HE MUST SWEAR.** טַעְמָא דְּאָמַר שָׁלֹשׁ הָא שְׁתַּיִם פָּטוּר – We can infer that **the reason** the defendant must swear **is that he admits three** *selaim;* **but** if he would have admitted only **two, he would have been exempt** from taking the oath.[4] וְהַאי שְׁטָר דְּקָמוֹדֵי בֵּיהּ הֵילָךְ הוּא – The reason the borrower is exempt when he admits only two *selaim* must be that **this note**-recorded amount **that he admits is** in the category of **"here, it is yours."**[5] וּשְׁמַע מִינָּהּ הֵילָךְ פָּטוּר – **Thus, learn from here that** one who admits partia[l] liability but states, **"Here, it is yours," is exempt** from the oat[h] of *modeh bemiktzas.*[6] – ? –

The Gemara answers:

לֹא – **No.** Your proof is not conclusive. [ל]עוֹלָם אֵימָא לָךְ שְׁתַּיִם חַיָּיב – **I can tell you that, in fact,** even if the borrower admits on[ly] two *selaim,* **he is obligated** to swear. וְהַאי דְּקָתָנֵי שָׁלֹשׁ – **An[d] that which the Baraisa states** a case of the borrower admittin[g] **three** *selaim* rather than two is [ל]אַפּוּקֵי מִדְּר׳ עֲקִיבָא דְּאָמַר מֵשִׁיב אֲבֵידָה הָוֵי וּפָטוּר – **to exclude** the view of **R' Akiva, who says tha[t] he is a returner of lost property and exempt** from swearing.[7] קָא מַשְׁמַע לָן דְּמוֹדֶה מִקְצָת הַטַּעֲנָה הָוֵי וְחַיָּיב – Therefore, **[th]e Baraisa] informs us that** in the view of R' Shimon ben Elaza[r] even **[the borrower]** who admits three *selaim* **is** judged as **on[e] who admits partial liability**[8] and is obligated to swear.

The Gemara rejects this answer, by observing:

אִי הָכִי – **If so,** that R' Shimon ben Elazar obligates the borrowe[r] to swear even if he admits only two *selaim,* is it proper for th[e] Baraisa to state: [ר]בִּי שִׁמְעוֹן בֶּן אֶלְעָזָר אוֹמֵר הוֹאִיל וְהוֹדָה מִקְצָת הַטַּעֲנָה יִשָּׁבַע – **R' SHIMON BEN ELAZAR SAYS: SINCE HE ADMITTE[D] PART OF THE CLAIM, HE MUST SWEAR,** אַף זֶה יִשָּׁבַע מִבְּעֵי לֵיהּ – **[The Baraisa] should** rather **have stated: "Even this borrowe[r] must swear"!**[9] R' Shimon ben Elazar's choice of words indicate[s] that if the borrower admits only two *selaim,* he is exempt fro[m]

NOTES

1. *Sela* (pl. *selaim*) and *dinar* (pl. *dinarim*) are monetary units.

2. According to R' Shimon ben Elazar, this situation is a classic case of *modeh bemiktzas.* The defendant has admitted borrowing three of the five *selaim* claimed by the plaintiff; thus, the defendant must swear that he does not owe the remaining two.

3. The classic case of "a returner of lost property" deals with a person who finds, for example, a lost purse and returns it to its owner only to have the owner assert that the purse had contained more money than is presently found in it. The owner claims that the finder has stolen the missing money; the finder insists that he found no more than what is now in the purse. In essence, the finder is a *modeh bemiktzas* – he admits a portion of the claim against him and denies the rest. According to Biblical law, then, he should have to swear that he did not take the additional amount claimed by the owner. However, for the common good [מִפְּנֵי תִּקּוּן הָעוֹלָם], the Rabbis legislated that the finder should not have to swear, so that the prospect of becoming liable to swear should not dissuade people from returning lost objects to their owners (*Gittin* 48b). [The Torah empowers the Rabbis to legislate as they see fit in financial matters (הֶפְקֵר בֵּית דִּין הֶפְקֵר).]

Accordingly, R' Akiva argues that the borrower in the Baraisa's case is a returner of lost property, since he could have claimed that he owes only two *selaim* – the minimum that could be meant by the plural but non-specific "*selaim*" mentioned in the note. Since he voluntarily admits owing a third *sela,* he is no different from the classic "returner of lost property," who has also extended himself in order to restore property to its rightful owner. Accordingly, the borrower who admits three *selaim* is granted the same Rabbinic dispensation from oath granted to the returner of lost property.

Now, it is true that in a regular case of *modeh bemiktzas,* the borrower – though he voluntarily admits part of the claim against him – is not deemed a returner of lost property; for his admission is not truly voluntary, since (as Rabbah explains on 3a) he could not be so bold as to deny his creditor's claim against him altogether. Rather, he felt compelled to make some concession to his creditor. Similarly, one could argue that in the Baraisa's case, the borrower who admits owing three *selaim* is not a returner of lost property, since he felt compelled to make some concession to his creditor. (Admitting only two *selaim* is not a concession, since two *selaim* is the unavoidable minimum attested to by the note.) However, this is not quite so. For in the Baraisa's case, the borrower could have been bold enough to insist that he owes only two *selaim,* since that assertion would have been backed by the simple meaning of the note; had more been borrowed, it is unlikely that the note would have failed to state the specific amount. Nevertheless, the borrower has voluntarily admitted owing a third *sela.* Therefore, argues R' Akiva, he is deemed a returner of lost property (see *Rashi* and *Ramban*).

4. [The simplest example] the Baraisa could have chosen for its case i[s] that the borrower claims that the plural but non-specific "*selaim*" means "two *selaim.*" Since the Baraisa instead chooses the case i[n] which the borrower claims that "*selaim*" means "three *selaim,*" it mus[t] be that R' Shimon ben Elazar would not require an oath where th[e] borrower admitted only two (*Rashi*).

5. When a loan is duly recorded in a note, the lender has a lien on th[e] borrower's land. Should the borrower default on his loan, the lender ca[n] collect from the borrower's land even if it has since been sold to a thir[d] party. Therefore, a debt recorded in a note always represents a situatio[n] of "here, it is yours," since it is considered as if the lender is already i[n] possession of the property on which he has a lien.

Now, when a note of indebtedness states simply that a non-specif[ic] number of "*selaim*" is owed, the note records only a loan of two *selai[m]* (the minimum that can be meant by the plural term) even if the loan wa[s] in fact larger. No more than two *selaim* is *clearly* meant by the not[e;] whatever additional amount might have been loaned is considered [a] mere oral loan, since the note furnishes no proof for that addition[al] amount. A borrower is certainly duty bound to repay even an oral loa[n] but his properties are not encumbered by it. Thus, regardless of ho[w] large the loan actually was, a note that records the amount of the loa[n] simply as "*selaim*" provides the lender with a lien of only two *selaim* o[n] the borrower's land.

Accordingly, if the borrower admits owing only two of the five *selai[m]* claimed by the lender, the amount he admits is already "possessed" b[y] the lender, who has a lien in that amount on the borrower's propert[y;] hence, the situation is one of "here, it is yours" (see *Rashi*).

6. At this point, the Gemara knows of no reason other than *heilach* fo[r] why one who admits only two of the five *selaim* claimed by the lende[r] should be exempt from the oath of *modeh bemiktzas.*

7. R' Akiva agrees that the borrower must swear if he admits only tw[o] *selaim,* since he is not then a returner of lost property – he had n[o] choice but to admit the minimum of two *selaim* documented by the not[e.] Had the Baraisa cited R' Shimon ben Elazar's ruling in a case in whic[h] the borrower admits only two of the five *selaim* claimed by the lende[r,] it would not have emerged that R' Shimon ben Elazar disagrees with R[']
Akiva and requires the borrower to swear even if he admits three *selai[m]* – one more than the minimum documented by the note.

8. I.e. he is not granted the dispensation granted the one who return[s] lost property.

9. If R' Shimon ben Elazar held that a two-*sela* admission also obligate[s] an oath, but used the example of a three-*sela* admission only to dispel th[e] notion that the borrower in that case is a returner of lost property an[d] exempt from swearing, then the logical way to phrase his ruling woul[d]

סלעים דינרין מלוה אומר חמש ולוה אומר שלש ר"ש בן אלעזר אומר הואיל והודה מקצת הטענה ישבע [א] ר"ע אומר [א] אינו אלא כמשיב אבידה ופטור קתני מיהת רשב"א אומר הואיל והודה מקצת הטענה ישבע טעמא דאמר שלש הא שתים פטור והאי שטר דקמודי ביה הילך הוא וש"מ הילך פטור לא לעולם אימא לך שתים חייב והאי דקתני שלש לאפוקי מדר' עקיבא דאמר משיב אבידה הוי ופטור קמ"ל דמודה מקצת הטענה הוי וחייב אי הכי רשב"א אומר הואיל והודה מקצת הטענה ישבע אף זה ישבע מבעי ליה אלא לעולם שתים פטור והילך חייב ושאני הכא דקא מסייע ליה שטרא אי נמי [ג] משום דהוה ליה שטר שעבוד קרקעות [ג] [ב] ואין נשבעין על כפירת שעבוד קרקעות איכא דמותיב מסיפא ר"ע אומר אינו אלא כמשיב אבידה ופטור טעמא דאמר שלש הא שתים חייב והא שטר ([ד] כיון) דקא מודי ביה כהילך דמי ש"מ הילך חייב לא לעולם אימא לך שתים נמי פטור והאי דקתני שלש לאפוקי מדרשב"א דאמר מודה מקצת הטענה הוי וחייב קמ"ל דמשיב אבידה הוי ופטור הכי נמי מסתברא דאי סלקא דעתך שתים חייב בשלש היכי פטר ליה ר"ע [ה] האי אערומי קא מערים סבר אי אמינא שתים בעינא אשתבועי אימא שלש דאהוי כמשיב אבידה ואיפטר אלא ש"מ [ג] שתים נמי פטור אלא קשיא לרבי חייא שאני התם דקא מסייע ליה שטרא א"נ משום דהוה ליה שטר שעבוד קרקעות ואין נשבעין על כפירת שעבוד קרקעות מתיב מר זוטרא בריה דרב נחמן [ו] [ד] טענו כלים וקרקעות הודה בכלים וכפר בקרקעות הודה בקרקעות וכפר בכלים פטור הודה מקצת קרקעות פטור [ה] מקצת כלים חייב טעמא דכלים וקרקעות דקרקע לאו בת שבועה היא הא כלים וכלים דומיא דכלים וקרקעות חייב היכי דמי לאו דאמר ליה הילך וש"מ הילך חייב לא לעולם אימא לך כלים וכלים נמי פטור והא דקתני כלים וקרקעות הא קמ"ל הודה במקצת כלים חייב אף על הקרקעות מאי קמ"ל זוקקין [ז] תנינא [ו] זוקקין הנכסים שאין להן אחריות את הנכסים שיש להן אחריות לישבע עליהם הכא עיקר התם אגב גררא נסבה ולמאן

## רש"י

סלעים דינרין. שטר שכתוב בו פלוני לוה מפלוני סלעין ולא פירש כמה וכן שטר שכתוב בו דינרין סתם: **אינו אלא כמשיב אבידה.** מדהוה ליה למימר שתים והשטר מסייעו דכיון דלא פירש ניכרים הדברים ששנים היו לכך לא הוצרך לפרש דמיעוט סלעים ב' וכיון דאמר ג' משיב אבידה הוא וחכמים פטרו את משיב אבידה מן השבועה דתנן המוצא את המציאה לא ישבע וכו' (גיטין דף מח:): **טעמא דאמר** שלש. קס"ד השתא דמייתי תיובתא מדנקט פלוגתייהו בשלש וחמש ולא נקט ולוה אמר שתים ש"מ בשתים לא מחייב ליה רשב"א וכדמפרש ואזיל דכיון דכל הודאתו בשטר כתובה דשטר נמי שתים משמע וכל משמעות השטר הילך הוא שהרי הקרקעות משועבדים על כך אבל כי אמר שלש סלעים שלישי מלוה ע"פ הוא דלאו בשטר כתובה ואין הקרקעות משועבדים ולאו הילך הוא: ה"ג ושטרא דקמודה הילך הוא ול"ג כיון דקמודה ביה דבלאו הודאתו נמי כל שטרי הילך הוא וה"פ ומאי דקמודה ביה דכתוב בשטר הילך הוא: **לאפוקי** מדר"ע כו'. דאי תנא שתים לא הוה פליג ר"ע: **א"ה.** דבשתים נמי חייב אמאי תנא הואיל והודה מקצת הטענה ישבע רשב"א אומר אף זה ישבע מבעיא ליה ושמעינן דלא משיב אבידה חשיב ליה ומדנקט הואיל משמע דחיובא משום דגרס לעצמו שהודה במקצת דהשתא הוא דהויא הודאה משום דסלע שלישי לאו הילך הוא אבל שתים לא הוי הודאה משום הילך: **אלא לעולם כו'.** אלא אי אית לך לתרוצי תריץ הכי לעולם כדקאמרת הא שתים פטור וטעמא לאו משום הילך דהילך בעלמא חייב: **ושאני הכא דקא מסייע ליה שטרא.** העדים החתומים על השטר מעידין כדבריו שלא היו אלא שתים ולכך לא פירשו מניין הלכך א"צ שבועה: **א"נ.** להכי לא הוו שתים הודאה לחייבו שבועה לפי שהשטר אומר כן ושטר הוי שעבוד קרקעות וכשם שאין נשבעין על כפירת קרקעות כך הודאתן אינה מביאה לידי שבועה דקרקעות אמעוט מתורת שבועה במס' שבועות פ' שבועת הדיינין (מב:) אבל כי אמר מלוה חמש ולוה שלש איכא כפירה והודאה במה שאין כתוב בשטר: **הא שתים.** דליכא משיב אבידה: **חייב.** מדלא תנא פטור בשתים ונימא טעמא משום הילך: **מודה מקצת הוי.** ואינו משיב אבידה דלאיערומי קמערים דלחזקיה בנאמן: **קמ"ל.** כיון דבשתים נמי פטור ליכא למימר איערומי מערים אלא משיב אבידה הוי: **הכי נמי מסתברא.** דבשתים פטור: **ואלא קשיא לרבי חייא.** דהא איכא למידק מינה דשתים פטור כדאמרינן דאי ס"ד כו': **שאני הכא.** האי דקאמר שתים פטור טעמא לאו משום הילך אלא דקא מסייע ליה שטרא: **טענו.** חבירו בב"ד כלים וקרקעות: **פטור.** דלא כפירתו ולא הודאתו מביאתו לידי שבועה: **חייב.** אף על הקרקעות לישבע כדאמרינן לקמן שהנכסים שאין להן אחריות זוקקין את הקרקעות לישבע עליהן משנתחייב לישבע על המטלטלין זוקקין ומגלגלין עמהם שבועת קרקע: **דומיא דכלים וקרקעות.** שכלים שהודה עליהם מונחים לפניו וא"ל הילך: **זוקקין.** המטלטלין זוקקין הקרקעות לישבע ע"י גלגול: **תנינא.** בקדושין (דף כו.) הנכסים שאין להן אחריות זוקקין את הנכסים שיש להן אחריות לישבע עליהם: **הכא עיקר.** שמשנה זו שנויה במסכת שבועות (דף לח:): **התם.** בקדושין: **אגב גררא נסבה.** דאיירי התם נכסים שאין להם אחריות נקנין עם נכסים שיש להן אחריות בכסף בשטר ובחזקה ואגב דאיירי דנקנין עמהם תנא בהדה זוקקין אותן לישבע עליהם:

למאי

## תוספות

**לעולם** שתים חייב. ואע"ג דשתים חייב חשיב ליה רבי עקיבא משיב אבידה דכשאמר שתים נראה יותר נאמן לפי שהשטר מסייעו: **לעולם** שתים פטור והילך חייב. וא"ת כיון דהילך חייב כי אמר נמי שתים אינו כופר הכל וכי אמר שלש יהא נאמן במיגו דאי בעי אמר שתים ומאי טעמא דרשב"א וי"ל דס"ל דמה שהשטר מסייעו אינו טוען ברצון לפי שנראה שמחמת השטר מודה ואם לא היה השטר היה כופר הכל: **אין** נשבעין על כפירת שעבוד קרקעות. וא"ת למ"ד בפרק גט פשוט (ב"ב דף קעה:) שעבודא דאורייתא מודה מקצת הטענה למה נשבע הא כופר שעבוד קרקעות וי"ל שמחל לו השעבוד או שאין לו כלל קרקעות אפי' משעבדי אבל לרבי יוחנן דאמר בפ' שבועת הפקדון (שבועות דף לז: ושם ד"ה ואין) כופר בממון שיש עליו עדים חייב קרבן שיש עליו שטר פטור משום דכופר שעבוד קרקעות דבעדים לא חשיב כופר שעבוד קרקעות אע"ג דסבר ר' יוחנן שעבודא דאורייתא היינו משום כיון שהפקיעו חכמים השעבוד במלוה ע"פ משום פסידא דלקוחות חשיב כאילו מחל לו השעבוד ומיירי דאית ליה משעבדי ולית ליה בני חרי דאי אית ליה בני חרי אפי' יש עליו עדים פטור ואי לית ליה אפי' משועבדים אפילו יש עליו שטר חייב: **אין** נשבעין על כפירת כו'. לספרים דגרסי בברייתא ר"ע אין להקשות הא ר"ע דריש ריבויי ומיעוטי פ"ק דשבועות (דף ד: ושם ד"ה רבי) ובפרק ג' מינים (נזיר לה. ושם) ומאן דדריש ריבויי ומיעוטי אינו ממעט קרקעות כ"א שטרות כדמוכח בפרק הגוזל בתרא (ב"ק דף קיז:) והיכי קאמר הכא אין נשבעין על כפירת שעבוד קרקעות וי"ל שיש לו שום מיעוט למעט קרקעות וכן צ"ל לקמן בפ' השואל (דף ק: ושם ד"ה ר"מ) אליבא דר"מ דאית ליה נשבעין אעבדים ולא אקרקעות ואע"ג דעבדים הוקשו לקרקעות לכ"ע דמהאי טעמא עבד נקנה בכסף בפ"ק דקדושין (דף כב:) אלא דר"מ דריש ריבויי ומיעוטי להוציא שטרות ויש לו שום מיעוט למעט קרקעות ובאותו מיעוט אין למעט עבדים אע"ג דהוקשו לקרקעות כדמוכח במרובה (ב"ק סג. ושם ד"ה וחד) דמאן דדריש בריבה ומיעט וריבה צריך שני מיעוטי לקרקעות ועבדים ואע"ג דרשב"א היה תלמידו של ר"ע אין לחוש מה שחולק עמו [ט] והוזכר [ח] קודם דכעין זה מצינו לקמן (דף ז.) גבי שנים אדוקים בשטר דפליג רבי עם רשב"ג אביו ויש ספרים דגרסי הכא ר' יעקב: **הא** כלים וכלים חייב. הוה מצי לשנויי בחפר בה בורות שיחין ומערות כדבסמוך: [**הודה** במקצת כלים חייב. וא"ת יהא נאמן במיגו דאי בעי כפר בכלים והיה מודה במקצת קרקעות וי"ל שמא חפץ בקרקעות יותר] ס"א:

למ"ד

## עין משפט נר מצוה

טז א מיי' פ"ד מהל' טוען ונטען הל' ה סמג עשין צה טוש"ע ח"מ סי' פח סעיף לג:
יז ב מיי' שם פ"ה הל' א סמג שם טוש"ע ח"מ סי' צה ס"א:
יח ג (מיי' פ"ד שם הל' ה) סמג שם טוש"ע ח"מ סי' פח סעיף לג:
יט ד ה ו מיי' פ"ה שם הל' ג סמג שם טוש"ע ח"מ סי' צה סעיף ה:

## רבינו חננאל

מודה מקצת הטענה הוא ומתני' תקנת חכמים היא וכר' יוחנן. **מיתיבי סלעין דינרים וכו'.** פי' שטר שכתוב בו סתם פלוני חייב לפלוני סלעים או דינרין. מלוה אמר ה' סלעים חייב לי ולוה אמר ג' ר' שמעון בן אלעזר אומר הואיל והודה מקצת הטענה ישבע. ודייקי' טעמא דהודה בג' הא הודה בב' פטור מאי טעמא דשטר כיון דמודה במלוה בשטר כי הילך דמי דקיימא לן מלוה בשטר תורתו כקרקע והמודה בקרקע הילך הוא ודייקי' דבשתים פטור קשיא לר' חייא. ופריק לא ואפילו הודה בשתים חייב והאי דקתני ג' לאפוקי מדר' עקיבא דאמר הודאתו בשלישית משיב אבידה הוי מיגו דאי בעי אמר תרתי כדכתיב בשטר סלעים ואמר ג' משיב אבידה הוא ופטור משבועה. ואקשי' אי הכי דר' שמעון אפילו בשתים מחייב והוא הדין לג' אף זה חייב לישבע היה לו לומר. ופרקי' לעולם שתים פטור ושאני הכא משום דמסייע ליה דכתיב בה סלעין וסתם סלעין שתים הן. אי נמי משום דהוי שטר שיעבוד קרקעות ואין נשבעין על כפירת שעבוד קרקעות. פי' נמצא המלוה טוענו ה' סלעין ועדי השטר מעידין שחייב לו סלעים לא פחות משתים לדברי ר' חייא דאמר מנה לי בידך והלה אומר אין לך בידי כלום ועדים מעידים אותן נ' אותן נ' נותן לו ונשבע על השאר וכל שכן בשמודה לו במקצת היה מן הדין לחייבו שבועה גם בשמודה בשתים ואמר לך ר' חייא כי קאמינא במלוה על פה אבל במלוה בשטר דשעבודיה על הקרקע כאילו קרקע בה' סלעין הוא דטעין ומודה לו במקצת מן הקרקע ובשאר כופר בו. ותנן אין נשבעין על הקרקעות וכשם שאם יטען עליו שדה זו בידך שלי הוא והלה כופר בו אין חייב שבועה עליה כך הטוען על חבירו בשעבוד קרקעות והלה כופר בו אין חייב שבועה על כפירתו. ור' שמעון סבר הא דטעין עליה בה' סלעין תרתי מינהון בשטרא ותלת מינהון על פה כפר בתלת פטור כדתנן מנה לי בידך והלה אומר אין לך בידי כלום פטור. הודה אחת מן השלש חייב. ומותבינן תוב מדברי ר' עקיבא דפטר בג' וכל שכן בב' והנה דפריש להו שטרא הילך הוא וקתני פטור [א] קשיא לרבי חייא. ופריק שאני הכא דקא מסייע ליה שטרא. אי נמי משום דהוי ליה שטר שעבוד קרקעות כו'. כדפרשינן לזה לעילא. ש"מ דדברי הכל הודה בשתים פטור כי פליגי בשמודה בג'. ר' עקיבא סבר מיגו דאי בעי אמר שתים ואמר ג' משיב אבידה הוי ופטור דכי אמרה תורה כי הוא זה דשמעינן מיניה מודה מקצת הטענה חייב הא פריש רבה טעמא דקרא דאמר מפני מה אמרה תורה מודה מקצת הטענה ישבע חזקה אין אדם מעיז פניו בפני בעל חובו והאי בכוליה בעי דליכפריה וכו' והאי כיון דאית ליה עליה שטרא לא יכול לכפור בכל לית עליה הדין דינא הלכך פטור הוא. ור' שמעון סבר לא שנא אלא הרי הוא ככל טענתא דעלמא הכופר בכל פטור והמודה במקצת חייב. תוב אקשינן מהא טענו כלים וקרקעות וכו'. ופשוטה היא. פי' הכא עיקר התם אגב גרא נסבה. הכא בשבועות דקתני הודה במקצת כלים מיגו דנתחייב שבועה בכלים נשבע גם על הקרקע בזקיקה זה מקום עיקרו. והתם בקידושין פ"א דקתני זוקקין את הנכסים שיש להם אחריות לישבע עליהם [אגב] גרא נסבה.

ומקשי'

חשק שלמה על ר"ח א) לפנינו הגי' הא שתים חייב וש"מ הילך חייב ולאמת רבינו נראה דגרים בשתים פטור כמו שהיה לפני רבינו ז"ל הוכא בש"מ כאן נגמו ע"ש.

## מסורת הש"ס

א) [בבא בתרא קמ.] ב) [שבועות דף לז:] ג) [כתובות פז:], ד) וע' בס' ש"מ שמקיים ג' הספרים, ה) [לקמן דף ז.] ו) שבועות לח., ז) לקמן ק., קידושין כו. שבועות לח, מג, מ; ח) [ג' תוס' סוטה ז. ד"ה עולין].

## גליון הש"ס

תוס' ד"ה אין וכו' והוזכר קודם. ע' תוי"ט פ"ג משנה דבכורים.

## ליקוטי רש"י

כמשיב אבדה. ופטור משבועה דסלעין משמע טפי משני דתפסת מרובה לא תפסת ויד בעל השטר התחתונה ועל השלישי שהודה הוא משיב אבדה ותקנו המוצא מציאה לא ישבע מפני תיקון העולם [רשב"ם ב"ב קכח:]. משום דהוה ליה שטר ממון שהקרקע משועבדים לו והכופר ככופר בקרקעות וקי"ל דאין נשבעין על קרקע [שבועות לז:]. כל שטר שיעבוד קרקעות הן ואין נשבעין על הקרקע כדאמרינן בשבועות [כתובות פז.]. הודה מקצת קרקעות פטור. שאין נשבעין כפירתן ואף הודאתן מביאה לידי שבועה. מקצת כלים חייב. שבועה אף על קרקעות ע"י גלגול [שבועות לח:]. כלים זוקקים וכו' לישבע עליהם. ואע"ג דלא נשבעין על הקרקעות כדתנינן לן בשבועות (מג:) הילכך דטענו כלים וקרקעות ונתחייב לישבע על המטלטלין זוקק המטלטלין את הקרקע לישבע עליו [קידושין כו.]. הכא עיקר. דכך מסכת בהלכות שבועות [שבועות שם].

תאמר בעדים שעל מה שכפר הוא נשבע אלא אמר רב פפא אתי מגלגול שבועה דעד אחד מה לגלגול שבועה דעד אחד שכן שבועה גוררת שבועה תאמר בעדים דממון קא מחייבי פיו יוכיח מה לפיו שכן אינו בהכחשה עד אחד יוכיח שישנו בהכחשה ומחייבו שבועה מה לעד אחד שכן על מה שמעיד הוא נשבע תאמר בעדים שעל מה שכפר הוא נשבע פיו יוכיח [א] וחזר הדין לא ראי זה כראי זה ולא ראי זה כראי זה הצד השוה שבהן שעל ידי טענה וכפירה הן באין ונשבע אף אני אביא עדים שעל ידי טענה וכפירה הם באין ונשבע מה להצד השוה שבהן שכן לא הוחזק כפרן תאמר בעדים שכן הוחזק כפרן ובעדים מי הוחזק כפרן [ב] והאמר רב אידי בר אבין אמר רב חסדא [א] הכופר במלוה כשר לעדות בפקדון פסול לעדות אלא פריך הכי מה להצד השוה שבהן שכן אינן בתורת הזמה תאמר בעדים שישנן בתורת הזמה הא לא קשיא רבי חייא תורת הזמה לא פריך אלא דקאמר ותנא תונא מי דמי התם למלוה אית ליה סהדי ללוה לית ליה סהדי דלא מסיק ליה ולא מידי דאי הוו ליה סהדי ללוה דלא מסיק ליה ולא מידי לא בעי רבי חייא לאשתבועי הכא כי היכי דאנן סהדי (א) בהאי אנן סהדי בהאי ואפילו הכי משתבעי אלא כי איתמר ותנא תונא אאידך דרבי חייא איתמר דאמר ר' חייא מנה לי בידך והלה אומר אין לך בידי אלא נ' זוז והילך חייב מאי טעמא הילך נמי כמודה מקצת הטענה דמי ותנא תונא שנים אוחזין בטלית והא הכא כיון דתפים [ג] [אנן סהדי דמאי דתפים] הילך הוא וקתני ישבע ורב ששת אמר [ב] הילך פטור מ"ט כיון דאמר ליה הילך הני זוזי דקא מודי בגוייהו כמאן דנקיט להו מלוה דמי באינך חמשים הא לא מודי הלכך ליכא הודאת מקצת הטענה ולרב ששת קשיא מתניתין אמר לך רב ששת מתניתין תקנת חכמים היא ואידך אין תקנת חכמים היא ומיהו אי אמרת בשלמא מדאורייתא הילך חייב מתקני רבנן שבועה כעין דאורייתא אלא אי אמרת מדאורייתא הילך פטור מתקני רבנן שבועה דליתא דכוותה בדאורייתא מיתיבי

סלעים

## רש"י

תאמר. בשבועה דעדים שאינו נשבע על מה שלא העידו ועל כפירתו הוא נשבע ולא אהעדאתן ומנין לך להחמיר כל כך: מגלגול שבועה דעד אחד. אם נתחייב לו שבועה על ידי עד אחד כדאמרינן והיתה עליו טענה אחרת שלא היתה מוטלת עליו שבועה מגלגלין אותה עם שבועה זאת ונשבע על שניהן דגלגול שבועה דאורייתא היא דילפינן לה בקדושין (דף כז:) מואמרה האשה אמן אמן הרי שעל מה שלא העיד העד הוא משביעו: שכן שבועה גוררת שבועה. עד לא חייבו שבועה אלא על מה שהעיד והשבועה גוררת שבועה תאמר בעדים הללו שהחמשים שהעידוהו הם מחייבין אותו לשלם ואין כאן שבועה לגרור על ידה שבועה על השאר: פיו יוכיח. מודה מקצת הטענה שעל מה שכופר ופיו לא הודה הוא נשבע: טענה וכפירה. זה טוען וזה כופר הן באין לדין: לא הוחזק כפרן. על מה שכפר אינו מוחזק כפרן שמא לא כיחש שהעד אינו נאמן להכחישו ולהחזיקו כפרן: תאמר בעדים. שמאחר שכפר הכל והם העידו על החמשים הוחזק כפרן ולא נאמר נאמניהו על השבועה: הכופר במלוה. בין על כולה בין על מקצת ובאו עדים והעידוהו עד שלא נשבע: כשר לעדות. ולא אמרינן גזלן הוא והתורה אמרה (שמות כג) אל תשת רשע עד דכיון דמלוה להוצאה נתנה דלמא צריך להוציאה וסבר עד דהוה לי [זוזי] ופרענא ליה ואי מודינא ליה השתא יתבעני מיד אבל הכופר בפקדון אפי' על מקצת ובאו עדים והעידוהו פסול לעדות דמאי הוה ליה גבי פקדון לאשתמוטי נפשיה ושמא תאמר אבד ממנו ואשתמיט ליה עד דמשכח ליה לקמן בפירקין (דף ה:) מוקמינן בדאתו סהדי ואמרי ההיא שעתא בידיה נקיט ליה: בתורת הזמה. לשלם קנס דכאשר זמם דעד אחד שהוזם פטור ופיו גבי הודאה כל שכן דלא שייכא הזמה כלל: תאמר בעדים. אם הוזמו בחמשים שהעידו משלמין ממון: תורת הזמה לא פריך. אינה חשובה לו פירכא דכיון דעד אחד ישנו בהזמה ליבטל עדותו [ד] בעדות שני עדים אם הוה לן למימר בעדים משום דישנן בהזמה לא יחייבוהו שבועה הוה לן למימר נמי בעד אחד לא יחייבהו שבועה דהא ישנו בהזמה ליבטל עדותו ואי משום דאין משלם קנס אין בזו יפוי כח להאמין עדותו: אלא דקאמר ותנא תונא. אלא אם יש לך להשיב על דברי רבי חייא כך יש לך להשיב דקאמר ותנא תונא והביא ראיה לדבריו ממשנתינו מי דמי: התם. בדרבי חייא: למלוה אית ליה סהדי. דמסיק ביה חמשים: ללוה לית ליה סהדי. באינך חמשים שאינו חייב לו עליה: אי הוה ליה כו'. כגון אילו העידו העדים חמשים חייב וחמשים פרע בכה"ג לא הוה אמר ר' חייא דצריך לישבע על השאר: מתני' כי היכי דאנן סהדי להאי. דחציה שלו: אנן סהדי להאי. דחציה שלו ולמה הצריכוהו חכמים שבועה ש"מ טעמא לאו משום מודה מקצת הטענה הוא כר' חייא ואינה שבועה דאורייתא אלא תקנת חכמים שלא יהא כל אחד הולך כו': והילך. לא [או] הוצאתים והן שלך בכ"מ שהם: חייב. לישבע על השאר ולא אמרינן הני דקמודי ליה בגוייהו הואיל ואיתנהו בעינייהו כמאן דנקיט להו דמי אלא כשאר מודה במקצת הוא וחייב: ותנא תונא כו'. קס"ד דלר' חייא טעמא דמתני' משום דאנן סהדי דמאי דתפיס דיליה הוא והוי כמנה לי בידך והלה אמר אין לך בידי כלום והעדים מעידים אותו שיש לו חמשים וכי אידך דרבי חייא דמחייב ליה שבועה דאורייתא: והא הכא. דהך העדאת עדים אנן סהדי דמאי דתפיס האי הילך הוא שהרי בפניו הוא: וקתני. דמחייב שבועה אשארא וה"ה להודאה במקצת: תקנת חכמים היא. ולא משום העדאת עדים וכדפרכינן לעיל כי היכי דאנן סהדי להאי אנן סהדי להאי: אי אמרת בשלמא הילך מדאורייתא חייב. כלומר גבי שבועה דאורייתא כגון בהודאה במקצת:

סלעים

## תוספות

עד אחד יוכיח שישנו בהכחשה ובהזמה. שפיר גרס הכא ובהזמה כיון שע"י הזמה דבורו בטל ואין להקשות מה לפיו שכן אינו משלם בהזמה תאמר בעדים שמשלמין בהזמה ואז לא יכול לומר עד אחד יוכיח [ה] שמשלם כי מה שהעד אינו משלם כשהוא מוזם אינו חומרא אלא לפי שבעדותו אינו מחייבו ממון לכך הואיל ודיבורו בטל חשיב ישנו בהזמה ובסמוך על מה הלד פרכינן ליה משום דעל מה הלד פרכינן פירכא כל דהו ורבי חייא אפי' על מה הלד לא פריך ליה משום דמה שאינו משלם העד כשמוזם זהו גריעותו לפי שלא היה כח בעדותו לחייב ממון:

הצד השוה [שבהן] שע"י טענה כו'. וא"ת [ו] כופר הכל יוכיח שע"י טענה וכפירה פטור וי"ל דבהלד השוה שבהן יש טענה חשובה דכשמודה מקצת או עד מכחישו נראה דמשקר ולכך יש שבועה:

ותנא תונא אאידך דר' חייא. אנן סהדי דמאי דתפיס האי כו' פרש"י כיון דהוי כהעדאת עדים משתבע מדרבי חייא קמייתא וקשה כיון דלא מצי לאוקומי הך ברייתא דהילך אלא מכח קמייתא לימא ותנא תונא אקמייתא לכך י"ל דאנן סהדי לאו דוקא דמאי דתפיס מחשבינן ליה השתא טפי מהעדאת עדים וחשיב כאילו מודה ליה דדידיה הוא אך [ב] קשה דמ"מ איכא למיפרך דמתני' כי היכי דהאי מודה להאי האי נמי מודה להאי ואפ"ה קמשתבעי כדפריך אקמייתא ומאי תיקן וי"ל דהשתא נמי מוכח מכח טעמא דבסמוך אי הילך פטור לא הוי מתקני רבנן שבועה דליכא כוותה באורייתא אבל לרבי חייא קמייתא כי נמי בהעדאת עדים פטור מתקני רבנן שבועה במתני' דחשיב הודאה במאי דתפיס חבריה ודוחק דלפ"ז הא דלא קאמר ותנא תונא אקמייתא משום דמאי דתפיס חשיב כהודאה וזו לא היתה פירכתו למעלה אלא מטעם כי היכי דאנן סהדי להאי כו': ורב ששת אמר הילך פטור. נראה שהלכה כרב ששת דבפ' השואל (לקמן דף ק.) גבי עבד קטן פריך ועוד הילך הוא אך בספר חפץ משמע דהילך חייב [וע' תוס' ב"ב קכח: ד"ה הלכתא]:

[ז] וש"מ דהילך פטור. וא"ת יהא נאמן בשלש דמיגו דבעי אמר שתים וי"ל כיון דהילך פטור אם יאמר שתים הו"ל כופר הכל ואין אדם מעיז ולר"ע לא הוי עזות דמסייע ליה שטרא:

לעולם

## עין משפט נר מצוה

יד א (מיי' פ"ב מהל' טוען ונטען הל' ג) טוש"ע ח"מ סימן לב ס"ד ועי' בב"י:

טו ב מיי' שם פ"א הל' ג סמג עשין לה טוש"ע ח"מ סי' פז סעיף א וסי' עה סעיף ו [רב אלפס כאן ופ"ו דשבועות דף לט]:

## רבינו חננאל

אלא תיתי מגלגול שבועה דעד אחד ונדחה גם זה. ואתינן לרביה מפיו ועד אחד. ואמרי' הכי מה פיו שאין מחייבו קנס מחייבו שבועה עדים שמחייבין אותו קנס לא כל שכן. ופרכינן מה לפיו שכן אינו בהכחשה כמו שפירשנו למעלה. עד אחד יוכיח שכן ישנו בהכחשה ומחייבו שבועה. מה לעד אחד שכן על מה שהעיד עליו הוא נשבע תאמר בעדים שעל מה שכפר הוא נשבע פיו יוכיח שמשלם במה שהודה ונשבע על מה שכפר וחזר הדין וכו'. ופרכי' (מי) [מה] להצד השוה שבהן שכן לא הוחזק כפרן פי' אם כפר הלוה והעיד עליו עד אחד לא הוחזק כפרן שנאמר לא יקום עד אחד באיש וגו'. וכן אם כפר וחזר והודה לא הוחזק כפרן כדרבא דאמר רבא אדם קרוב אצל עצמו ואין אדם משים עצמו רשע תאמר בעדים שאם כפר ובאו עדים והעידו עליו [שחייב] שהוחזק כפרן ונפסל. ודחי' לה הכי וכי מי שכפר במלוה נפסל והאמר רב חסדא הכופר במלוה כשר לעדות והא דר' חייא מלוה היא ונדחית זו הפירכא. וחזרנו לפרך פירכא אחרת. מה להצד השוה שבהן שכן אינו בתורת הזמה א) פיו כדאמרן למעלה. עד אחד אינו בתורת הזמה שהתורה אמרה ועשיתם לו כאשר וגו' וכיון שאין עדות עד אחד אלא לשבועה ואי אפשר להשביע העד זו השבועה נדחת תורת הזמה מעליו שאין אתה יכול לקיים ועשיתם לו כאשר זמם וגו' וכדתנן [בריש מכות] מעידים אנו באיש פלו' שהוא בן גרושה וכו' ולעולם אין תורת הזמה אלא בשנים ועד שיזומו שניהם. בוא וראה כיון דאמר רב [שם ג ע"א] עד זומם משלם לפי חלקו מקשי' עליה והתניא אין משלמין ממון עד שיזומו שניהן ותריצנא להא דרב באומר העדנו והוזמנו בבית דינו של פלו' ונתחייבנו ממון כי האי גוונא משלם אבל כשיוזם עד אחד אין שם תשלומין. ותנן נמי ור' שמעון אומר מה שנים אין נהרגין עד שיזומו שניהן אף שלשה עד שיזומו שלשתן. ופרקי' דלמא רבי חייא תורת הזמה לא פריך כלומר אין זו פירכא. פי' ר' חייא תורת הזמה לא פריך אמר לך רבי חייא לא נדחת תורת הזמה מעד אחד מפני כחו של עד אחד אלא מפני שעד אחד אינו בא אלא לשבועה וכשיוזם אינו יכול להשביעו השבועה שזמם לעשות לאחיו וכיוצא בו נדחית תורת הזמה בשני עדים שהעידו על כהן שהוא בן גרושה וכו'. ואתינן ג) לאוקמה לדר' חייא כמתניתין ולא דמיא דהא מתני' כי היכי דאנן סהדי להאי דכל מה דתפיס בהאי טלית דידיה הוא הכי [נמי] אנן סהדי לאידך. ג) ותוב מתני' במאי דמסהדי (שהרי) [סהדי] דהוא דיליה עליה נשבע ותופס. לאפוקי דר' חייא דעל מה שכופר הוא נשבע. אלא אי איתמר והתנא שנאה על אידך דר' חייא דאמר מנה לי בידך והלה אומר אין לך בידי אלא נ' והילך חייב מאי טעמא דאע"ג דאמר ליה הילך כיון דעדיין לא נתן מודה מקצת הטענה הוא ותנא תונא שנים אוחזין בטלית וקתני ישבע והא אנן סהדי דבמאי דתפיס הילך הוא וקתני ישבע ש"מ דאפי' אמר ליה הילך מודה מקצת הטענה הוא וחייב. ורב ששת אמר הילך פטור דכיון דאמר ליה הילך כמאן דפרע להו דמי ובשאר הא לא מודה ליה ולא מידי הלכך לאו

חשק שלמה על ר"ח א) עי' בש"מ כאן שהעתיק לדברי רבינו בזה באריכות יותר. ב) נראה דל"ל ואתינן לדחויי להא דאוקמא לעיל לדברי חייא כמתני' דלא דמיא וכו'. ג) מדברי רבינו אלו נראה מוכח דהי' לו גי' אחרת בסוגין דדחי דלא דמי למתני' נמי בזה דהכא במאי דמסהדי סהדי הוא נשבע וכו'.

## מסורת הש"ס

קדושין ה:, כח. וש"נ], לקמן ה:], בבא קמא [עיין שם] [שבועות ג) מהרש"ל, ד) [נ"ל ...ים], ה) ס"א שאין ...שלם, ו) שייך לע"ב.

## הגהות הב"ח

גמ' דאנן סהדי להאי סהדי להאי ואפילו:

## גליון הש"ס

...' ד"ה הצד וכו' ...ר הכל יוכיח. עיין ...בות מהריב"ל ח"א כלל ...ף טו ע"א ובתשובות ...מלירות ח"ב סימן קסט:

## הגהות הגר"א

רש"י ד"ה והילך הוצאתים כו'. נ"ב הר"ן חולק ע"ז וכתב ...מלוה להוצאה ניתנה ...א בפקדון הדין כן ...מ"ש רבינו בח"מ סי' ...ס"ק י"ו): [ב] תוס' ...ה ותנא כו' אך ...ה כו'. נ"ב והרז"ה ...ים דלאו משום הודאה ...יע ליה ממתני' דודאי ...' אין בה הודאה כלל ...דרב ששת דפוטר ...לך ס"ל דמזומנים בידו ...אן דנקיט להו כאילו כבר ...' והא מתני' דבידם ...מנין לחלוק ליחזי כאילו ...חלקו ואין כאן שבועה ...תע"ה וע"ל ו' א' ודלא ...י"י ד"ה והילך שכתב ...מקום כו' דדוקא ...קדון הדין כן (ועמ"ש ...שם בס"ק י"א):

## ליקוטי רש"י

...ופר במלוה. שבאו ...ם והחזיקוהו בכפרן ...עידוהו שהוא חייב לו ...מן ה:]. ולא נשבע ...ו עדים [ב"ק קה:]. ...ר לעדות. דמלוה ...לא ניתנה ואינה ...ו בידו ורוצה ...ומו עד שתשיג ידו ...ק שם]. ולא אמרן ...יד אמונה הוא אלא ...תמוטי ליה [שבועות ...]. בפקדון פסול ...דות. דמאי ...תמוטי איכא הרי לא ...להוצאה ועין הוא ...[לקמן שם]. ...קמינן לה כגון שנים ...י) כגון דאמרי ...די דהסיא שעתא ...פר ליה נקיט בידיה ...פסול אע"ג דלא ...מבעה דאי לאשתבועי ...לי מלוה מה לי ...ון [ב"ק שם]. ואפי' ...נשבע במשבעה דכפר ...שיד ליה אמונה ...[שבועות שם].

shnah) **enact an oath that has no counterpart in Biblical v?**[35]

The Gemara presents a challenge to R' Chiya's view:

**מֵיתִיבֵי – They challenged** R' Chiya from the following Baraisa:

NOTES

5. [If there is no oath of *modeh bemiktzas* in a situation of *heilach,* en the case of our Mishnah does not resemble even remotely a uation of *modeh bemiktzas.*]

Thus, when R' Chiya said that our Mishnah has taught his law, he eant that the Rabbinic oath imposed by our Mishnah makes sense ly if we assume that in a true situation of *modeh bemiktzas,* a efendant who says regarding the admitted portion, "Here, it is yours," mains obligated to swear.

This proves only R' Chiya's second law, but not his first. For even if e testimony of witnesses does *not* obligate a *modeh bemiktzas* oath, e case of our Mishnah can be said to resemble a situation of *modeh miktzas,* since each litigant must concede to the other litigant half his aim. But if there were no *modeh bemiktzas* oath in situations of *eilach,* then there would be no situation of Biblical oath after which to attern a Rabbinic oath in the *heilach* situation of our Mishnah. herefore, the Gemara above had to shift to R' Chiya's second law in der to sustain R' Chiya's assertion that our Mishnah teaches his law ee *Ritva* and *Chidushei HaRan*).

[Furthermore, in order to resolve the problem raised in note 29 above, *Ritva* explains that the respective discussions of R' Chiya's two laws and whether they can be proven from our Mishnah were propounded independently and did not form one extended discussion. One discussion proceeded from the premise that R' Chiya meant to prove his first law; the second discussion proceeded from the premise that he meant to prove the second. The first discussion concluded that the first law could not be proven from the Mishnah (because the same "witnesses" that substantiate half the claim substantiate the defendant's denial of the other half). The second discussion *could* have used this argument to reach its conclusion that R' Chiya never meant that our Mishnah was an *actual* case of *modeh bemiktzas,* but – unaware of the first discussion – arrived at this conclusion by different means. When the Gemara at the end of the first discussion stated that R' Chiya must have meant to prove his second law rather than his first, the Gemara was referring to the proof that emerges at the *conclusion* of the second discussion (which concedes that the oath in our Mishnah is but a Rabbinic enactment). Nevertheless, the Gemara proceeded to record the second discussion in its entirety as originally propounded.]

## גמרא

תאמר בעדים שעל מה שכפר הוא נשבע אלא אמר רב פפא אתי מגלגול שבועה דעד אחד מה לגלגול שבועה דעד אחד שכן שבועה גוררת שבועה תאמר בעדים דממון קא מחייבי פיו יוכיח מה לפיו שכן אינו בהכחשה עד אחד יוכיח שישנו בהכחשה ומחייבו שבועה מה לעד אחד שכן על מה שמעיד הוא נשבע תאמר בעדים שעל מה שכפר הוא נשבע פיו יוכיח [א] וחזר הדין לא ראי זה כראי זה ולא ראי זה כראי זה הצד השוה שבהן שעל ידי טענה וכפירה הן באין ונשבע אף אני אביא עדים שעל ידי טענה וכפירה הם באין ונשבע מה להצד השוה שבהן שכן לא הוחזק כפרן תאמר בעדים שכן הוחזק כפרן ובעדים מי הוחזק כפרן [ג] והאמר רב אידי בר אבין אמר רב חסדא [א] הכופר במלוה כשר לעדות בפקדון פסול לעדות אלא פריך הכי מה להצד השוה שבהן שכן אינן בתורת הזמה תאמר בעדים שישנן בתורת הזמה הא לא קשיא רבי חייא תורת הזמה לא פריך אלא דקאמר ותנא תונא מי דמי התם למלוה אית ליה סהדי ללוה לית ליה סהדי דלא מסיק ליה ולא מידי דאי הוו ליה סהדי ללוה דלא מסיק ליה ולא מידי לא בעי רבי חייא לאשתבועי הכא כי היכי דאנן סהדי [א] בהאי אנן סהדי בהאי ואפילו הכי משתבעי אלא כי איתמר ותנא תונא אאידך דרבי חייא איתמר דאמר ר' חייא מנה לי בידך והלה אומר אין לך בידי אלא נ' זוז והילך חייב מאי טעמא הילך נמי כמודה מקצת הטענה דמי ותנא תונא שנים אוחזין בטלית והא הכא כיון דתפיס [ג] [אנן סהדי דמאי דתפיס] הילך הוא וקתני ישבע ורב ששת אמר [ב] הילך פטור מ"ט כיון דאמר ליה הילך הני זוזי דקא מודי בגוייהו כמאן דנקיט להו מלוה דמי באינך חמשים הא לא מודי הלכך ליכא הודאת מקצת הטענה ולרב ששת קשיא מתניתין אמר לך רב ששת מתניתין תקנת חכמים היא ואידך אין תקנת חכמים היא ומיהו אי אמרת בשלמא מדאורייתא הילך חייב מתקני רבנן שבועה כעין דאורייתא אלא אי אמרת מדאורייתא הילך פטור מתקני רבנן שבועה דליתא דכוותה בדאורייתא מיתיבי

סלעים

## רש"י

תאמר. בשבועה דעדים שאינו נשבע על מה שלא העידו ועל כפירתו הוא נשבע ולא אהעדאתן ומנין לך להחמיר כל כך: מגלגל שבועה דעד אחד. אם נתחייב לו שבועה על ידי עד אחד כדאמרינן והיתה עליו טענה אחרת שלא היתה מוטלת עליו שבועה מגלגלין אותה עם שבועה זאת ונשבע על שניהן דגלגול שבועה דאורייתא היא דילפינן לה בקדושין (דף כז:) מואמרה האשה אמן אמן הרי שעל מה שלא העיד העד הוא משביעו: שכן שבועה גוררת שבועה. עד לא חייבו שבועה אלא על מה שהעיד והשבועה גוררת שבועה תאמר בעדים הללו שהחמשים שהעידוהו הם מחייבין אותו לשלם ואין כאן שבועה לגרור על ידה שבועה על השאר: פיו יוכיח. מודה מקצת הטענה שעל מה שכופר ופיו לא הודה הוא נשבע: טענה וכפירה. זה טוען וזה כופר הן באין לדין: לא הוחזק כפרן. על מה שכפר אינו מוחזק כפרן שמא לא כיחש שהעד אינו נאמן להכחישו ולהחזיקו כפרן: תאמר בעדים. שמאחר שכפר הכל והם העידו על החמשים הוחזק כפרן ולא נאמר נאמינהו על השבועה: הכופר במלוה. בין על כולה בין על מקצת ובאו עדים והעידוהו עד שלא נשבע: כשר לעדות. ולא אמרינן גזלן הוא והתורה אמרה (שמות כג) אל תשת רשע עד דכיון דמלוה להוצאה נתנה דלמא צריך להוציאה וסבר עד דהוו לי [זוזי] ופרענא ליה ואי מודינא ליה השתא יתבעני מיד אבל הכופר בפקדון אפי' על מקצת ובאו עדים והעידוהו פסול לעדות דמאי הוה ליה גבי פקדון לאשתמוטי נפשיה ושמא תאמר אבד ממנו ואשתמיט ליה עד דמשכח ליה לקמן בפירקין (דף ה:) מוקמינן בדאתו סהדי ואמרי ההיא שעתא בידיה נקיט ליה: בתורת הזמה. לשלם קנס דכאשר זמם דעד אחד שהוזם פטור ופיו גבי הודאה כל שכן דלא שייכא הזמה כלל: תאמר בעדים. אם הוזמו בחמשים שהעידו משלמין ממון: תורת הזמה לא פריך. אינה חשובה לו פירכא דכיון דעד אחד ישנו בהזמה ליבטל עדותו [ד] בעדות שני עדים אם הוה לן למימר בעדים משום דישנן בהזמה לא יחייבוהו שבועה הוה לן למימר נמי בעד אחד לא יחייבהו שבועה דהא ישנו בהזמה ליבטל עדותו ואי משום דאין משלם קנס אין בזו יפוי כח להאמין עדותו: אלא דקאמר ותנא תונא. אלא אם יש לך להשיב על דברי רבי חייא כך יש לך להשיב דקאמר ותנא תונא והביא ראיה לדבריו ממשנתינו מי דמי: התם. בדרבי חייא: למלוה אית ליה סהדי. דמסיק ביה חמשים: ללוה לית ליה סהדי. באינך חמשים שאינו חייב לו עליה: אי הוה ליה כו'. כגון אילו העידו העדים חמשים חייב וחמשים פרע בכה"ג לא הוה אמר ר' חייא דלריך לישבע על השאר: מתני' כי היכי דאנן סהדי להאי. דאליה שלו: אנן סהדי להאי. דאליה שלו ולמה הצריכוהו חכמים שבועה ש"מ טעמא לאו משום מודה מקצת הטענה הוא כר' חייא ואינה שבועה דאורייתא אלא תקנת חכמים שלא יהא כל אחד הולך כו': והילך. לא [א] הוצאתים והן שלך בכ"מ שהם: חייב. לישבע על השאר ולא אמרינן הני דקמודי ליה בגוייהו הואיל ואיתנהו בעינייהו כמאן דנקיט להו דמי אלא כשאר מודה במקצת הוא וחייב: ותנא תונא כו'. קס"ד דלר' חייא טעמא דמתני' משום דאנן סהדי דמאי דתפיס דיליה הוא והוי כמנה לי בידך והלה אמר אין לך בידי כלום והעדים מעידים אותו שיש לו חמשים וכי אידך דרבי חייא דמחייב ליה שבועה דאורייתא: והא הכא. דהך העדאת עדים אנן סהדי דמאי דתפיס האי הילך הוא שהרי בפניו הוא: וקתני. דמחייב שבועה אשארא וה"ה להודאה במקצת: תקנת חכמים היא. ולא משום העדאת עדים ודפרכינן לעיל כי היכי דאנן סהדי להאי אנן סהדי להאי: אי אמרת בשלמא הילך מדאורייתא חייב. כלומר גבי שבועה דאורייתא כגון בהודאה במקצת:

סלעים

## תוספות

עד אחד יוכיח שישנו בהכחשה ובהזמה. שפיר גרס הכא ובהזמה כיון שע"י הזמה דבורו בטל ואין להקשות מה לפיו שכן אינו משלם בהזמה תאמר בעדים שמשלמין בהזמה ואז לא יכול לומר עד אחד יוכיח [ה] שמשלם כי מה שהעד אינו משלם כשהוא מוזם אינו חומרא אלא לפי שבעדותו אינו מחייבו ממון לכך הואיל ודיבורו בטל חשיב ישנו בהזמה ובסמוך על מה הלד פרכינן ליה משום דעל מה הלד פרכינן פירכא כל דהו ורבי חייא אפי' על מה הלד לא פריך ליה משום דמה שאינו משלם העד כשמוזם זהו גריעותו לפי שלא היה כח בעדותו לחייב ממון:

הצד השוה [שבהן] שע"י טענה כו'. וא"ת [ו] כופר הכל יוכיח שע"י טענה וכפירה פטור ויש לומר דבהלד השוה שבהן יש טענה חשובה דכשמודה מקצת או עד מכחישו נראה דמשקר ולכך יש שבועה:

ותנא תונא אאידך דר' חייא. אנן סהדי דמאי דתפיס האי כו'. פרש"י כיון דהוי כהעדאת עדים משתבע מדרבי חייא קמייתא וקשה כיון דלא מצי לאוכוחי הך ברייתא דהילך אלא מכח קמייתא לימא ותנא תונא אקמייתא לכך י"ל דאנן סהדי לאו דוקא דמאי דתפיס מחשבינן ליה השתא טפי מהעדאת עדים וחשיב כאילו מודה ליה דדידיה הוא אך [ב] קשה דמ"מ איכא למיפרך דמתני' כי היכי דהאי מודה להאי האי נמי מודה להאי ואפ"ה קמשתבעי כדפריך אקמייתא ומאי תיקן וי"ל דהשתא נמי מוכח מכח טעמא דבסמוך אי הילך פטור לא הוי מתקני רבנן שבועה דליכא דכוותה באורייתא אבל לרבי חייא קמייתא כי נמי בהעדאת עדים פטור מתקני רבנן שבועה במתני' דחשיב הודאה במאי דתפיס חבריה ודוחק דלפ"ז הא דלא קאמר ותנא תונא אקמייתא משום דמאי דתפיס חשיב כהודאה וזו לא היתה פירכתו למעלה אלא מטעם כי היכי דאנן סהדי להאי כו':

ורב ששת אמר הילך פטור. נראה שהלכה כרב ששת דבפ' השואל (לקמן דף ק.) גבי עבד קטן פריך ועוד הילך הוא אך בספר חפץ משמע דהילך חייב [וע' תוס' ב"ב קכח: ד"ה הלכתא]:

[ו] וש"מ דהילך פטור. וא"ת יהא נאמן בשלם דמיגו דבעי אמר שתים וי"ל כיון דהילך פטור אם יאמר שתים הו"ל כופר הכל ואין אדם מעיז ולר"ע לא הוי עזות דמסייע ליה שטרא:

לעולם

## עין משפט נר מצוה

יד א (מיי' פ"ב מהל' טוען ונטען הל' ג) טוש"ע ח"מ סימן לב ס"ד ועי' בב"י:

טו ב מיי' שם פ"א הל' ג סמג עשין צה טוש"ע ח"מ סי' פז סעיף א וסי' עה סעיף ו [רב אלפס כאן ופ"ו דשבועות דף כט]:

## רבינו חננאל

אלא תיתי מגלגול שבועה דעד אחד ונדחה גם זה. ואתינן לרבויה מפיו ועד אחד. ואמרי' הכי מה פיו שאין מחייבו קנס מחייבו שבועה עדים שמחייבין אותו קנס לא כל שכן. ופרכינן מה לפיו שכן אינו בהכחשה כמו שפירשנו למעלה. עד אחד יוכיח שכן ישנו בהכחשה ומחייבו שבועה. מה לעד אחד שכן על מה שהעיד עליו הוא נשבע תאמר בעדים שעל מה שכפר הוא נשבע פיו יוכיח שמשלם במה שהודה ונשבע על מה שכפר וחזר הדין וכו'. ופרכי' (מי) [מה] להצד השוה שבהן שכן לא הוחזק כפרן פי' אם כפר הלוה והעיד עליו עד אחד לא הוחזק כפרן שנאמר לא יקום עד אחד באיש וגו'. וכן אם כפר וחזר והודה לא הוחזק כפרן כדרבא דאמר רבא אדם קרוב אצל עצמו ואין אדם משים עצמו רשע תאמר בעדים שאם כפר ובאו עדים והעידו עליו [שחייב] שהוחזק כפרן ונפסל. ודחי' לה הכי וכי מי שכפר במלוה נפסל והאמר רב חסדא הכופר במלוה כשר לעדות והא דר' חייא מלוה היא ונדחית זו הפירכא. וחזרנו לפרך פירכא אחרת. מה להצד השוה שבהן שכן אינו בתורת הזמה [א] פיו כדאמרן למעלה. עד אחד אינו בתורת הזמה שהתורה אמרה ועשיתם לו כאשר וגו' וכיון שאין עדות עד אחד אלא לשבועה ואי אפשר להשביע העד זו השבועה נדחת תורת הזמה מעליו שאין אתה יכול לקיים ועשיתם לו כאשר זמם וגו' וכדתנן [בריש מכות] מעידים אנו באיש פלו' שהוא בן גרושה וכו' ולעולם אין תורת הזמה אלא בשנים ועד שיזומו שניהם. בוא וראה כיון דאמר רב [שם ג ע"א] עד זומם משלם לפי חלקו מקשי' עליה והתניא אין משלמין ממון עד שיזומו שניהן ותריצנא להא דרב באומר העדנו והוזמנו בבית דינו של פלו' ונתחייבנו ממון כי האי גוונא משלם אבל כשיוזם עד אחד אין שם תשלומין. ותנן נמי ור' שמעון אומר מה שנים אין נהרגין עד שיזומו שניהן אף שלשה עד שיזומו שלשתן. ופרקי' דלמא רבי חייא תורת הזמה לא פריך כלומר אין זו פירכא. פי' ר' חייא תורת הזמה לא פריך אמר לך רבי חייא לא נדחת תורת הזמה מעד אחד מפני כחו של עד אחד אלא מפני שעד אחד אינו בא אלא לשבועה וכשיוזם אינו יכול להשביעו השבועה שזמם לעשות לאחיו וכיוצא בו נדחית תורת הזמה בשני עדים שהעידו על כהן שהוא בן גרושה וכו'. ואתינן [ב] לאוקמה לדר' חייא כמתניתין ולא דמיא דהא מתני' כי היכי דאנן סהדי להאי דכל מה דתפיס בהאי טלית דידיה הוא הכי [נמי] אנן סהדי לאידך. [ג] ותוב מתני' במאי דמסהדי (שהרי) [סהדין] דהוא דיליה עליה נשבע ותופס. לאפוקי דר' חייא דעל מה שכופר הוא נשבע. אלא אי איתמר והתנא שנאה על אידך דר' חייא דאמר מנה לי בידך והלה אומר אין לך בידי אלא נ' והילך חייב מאי טעמא דאע"ג דאמר ליה הילך כיון דעדיין לא נתן מודה מקצת הטענה הוא ותנא תונא שנים אוחזין בטלית וקתני ישבע והא אנן סהדי דבמאי דתפיס הילך הוא וקתני ישבע ש"מ דאפי' אמר ליה הילך מודה מקצת הטענה הוא וחייב. ורב ששת אמר הילך פטור דכיון דאמר ליה הילך מודה מקצת הטענה הוא וחייב. ורב ששת אמר הילך פטור דכיון דאמר ליה הילך כמאן דפרע להו דמי ובשאר הא לא מודה ליה ולא מידי הלכך לאו

**חשק שלמה על ר"ח** א) עי' בש"מ כאן שהעתיק לדברי רבינו בזה בארוכות יותר. ב) נראה דצ"ל ואתינן לחויי להא דאוקמא לעיל לדברי ר' חייא כמתני' דלא דמיא וכו'. ג) מדברי רבינו אלו נראה מוכח דס"ל גי' אחרת בסוגיין דדחי דלא דמי למתני' נמי בזה דהתם במאי דמסהדי סהדי הוא נשבע וכו'.

## מסורת הש"ס

[קדושין ה:, כח. וש"נ], [לקמן ה:], בבא קמא [עיין שם] [שבועות ...], ג) מהרש"ל, ד) [צ"ל ...], ה) פ"א שאין ... שלם, ו) שייך לע"ב.

## הגהות הב"ח

(א) גמ' דאנן סהדי להאי סהדי להאי ואפילו:

## גליון הש"ס

תוס' ד"ה הצד וכו' כופר הכל יוכיח. עיין תשובות מהריב"ל ח"א כלל ... סי' טו ע"א ובתשובות מאירות ח"ב סימן קסט:

## הגהות הגר"א

[א] רש"י ד"ה והילך הוצאתים כו'. נ"ב ... הר"ן חולק ע"ז וכתב ... מלוה להוצאה ניתנה ... בפקדון הדין כן ... מ"ש רבינו בח"מ סי' ... ס"ק י"ז): [ב] תוס' ד"ה ותנא כו' אך ... ה כו'. נ"ב והרא"ה ... דלאו משום הודאה ... ליה ממתני' דודאי ... אין בה הודאה כלל ... דרב ששת דפוטר ... ס"ל דמזומנים בידו ... דנקיט להו כאילו כבר ... והא מתני' דבידם ... מנין לחלוק ליחזי כאילו ... חלקו ואין כאן שבועה ... ע"ש וע"ל ו' א' ודלא ... רש"י ד"ה והילך שכתב ... מקום כו' דדוקא ... פקדון הדין כן (ועמ"ש ... שם בס"ק י"א):

## ליקוטי רש"י

הכופר במלוה. שבאו עדים והחזיקוהו בכפרן ... עידוהו שהוא חייב לו [לקמן ה:]. ולא נשבע ... באו עדים [ב"ק קה:]. כשר לעדות. דמלוה להוצאה ניתנה ואינה ... שיו בידו ורוצה ... אותו עד שתשיג ידו [ב"ק שם]. ולא אמרן ... עד אמוגא הוא אלא ... לאשתמוטי ליה [שבועות ...]. בפקדון פסול לעדות. דמאי ... לאשתמוטי איכא הרי לא ... נתן להוצאה ובעין הוא ... [לקמן שם]. ... מוקמינן לה בריש שנים אוחזין (ה:) כגון דאמרי ... בידיה ... דלא ... משתבע ... לי ... ואפי' ... דכפר ... אמונא [שבועות שם].

es that **[each litigant] must swear.** This apparently supports Chiya's contention that the oath of *modeh bemiktzas* applies n when the admitted portion is in the legal possession of the intiff.[29]

The Gemara cites a dissenting view:

ורב ששת אמר הילך פ – **But Rav Sheishess says** that a endant who admits part of a claim and says regarding that t, **"Here, it is yours," is exempt** from the oath obligation *modeh bemiktzas.* מאי טעמא – **What is the reason?** כיון דאמר ליה הי – **Since he says to [the plaintiff], "Here, it yours,"** הני זוזי דקא מודי בגווייהו כמאן דנקיט להו מלוה דמי – se fifty ***zuz*** **that he admits** owing to the lender **are** viewed **if the lender is holding them** in his hand; thus, they are t considered part of the lender's claim. באינך חמשים הא לא מ – **Regarding the other fifty** still claimed by the lender, **e borrower] does not admit** anything. הלכך ליכא הודאת מקצת הטע – **Therefore, there is no admission to part of the im** and the borrower does not swear the oath of *modeh niktzas.*[30] [31]

The Gemara asks:

ולרב ששת קשיא מתניו – **But our Mishnah poses a difficulty Rav Sheishess,** since it was previously shown to support R' iya's ruling that "here, it is yours" does *not* remove that money from the claim; rather, the situation remains one of *modeh bemiktzas.* – ? –

The Gemara answers:

אמר לך רב ששת – **Rav Sheishess will say to you** in his defense: מתניתין תקנת חכמים היא – The oath in the case of **our Mishnah is a Rabbinic measure** and has nothing to do with the Biblically ordained oath of *modeh bemiktzas.*[32]

The Gemara continues:

ואידך – **And the other one** [R' Chiya] will reply: אין תקנת חכמים היא – **True, it** [the oath in our Mishnah] **is a Rabbinic measure** and not a real case of *modeh bemiktzas.*[33] ומיהו אי אמרת בשלמא מדאורייתא הילך חייב – **However,** our Mishnah **is understandable** only **if you say that in** the case of **a Biblical** oath of *modeh bemiktzas,* a defendant who says, **"Here, it is yours,"** about the substantiated portion of the claim against him **is obligated** to swear. מתקני רבנן שבועה כעין דאורייתא – In the case of our Mishnah, then, **the Rabbis** could **enact an oath that mimics the Biblical law.**[34] אלא אי אמרת מדאורייתא הילך פטור – **But if you say that in** the case of **a Biblical** oath of *modeh bemiktzas,* a defendant who says, **"Here, it is yours,"** about the substantiated portion of the claim against him **is exempt** from swearing, מתקני רבנן שבועה דליתא דכוותה בדאורייתא – **would the Rabbis** (in the case of our

NOTES

. The Gemara again reverts to its previous understanding that the h in our Mishnah is the oath of *modeh bemiktzas,* in which each gant becomes obligated because the other one's possession of half cloak is tantamount to witnesses supporting half his claim (see ove, note 20). Thus, according to R' Chiya's first law (that a *modeh niktzas* oath is generated even when the claim is partially substanti- d not by personal admission but by witnesses), each litigant must ear the oath of *modeh bemiktzas.*

However, the Gemara now considers the additional factor that the bstantiated part of each claim is already in the possession of the spective plaintiffs. Now, if the portion of the claim already possessed not regarded as part of the claim, then it is as if the claim of each igant is limited to that half of the cloak which he does *not* possess — laim that is neither admitted by the other litigant nor substantiated witnesses or their equivalent. Accordingly, there should be no oath of *deh bemiktzas* in our Mishnah. The fact that the Mishnah rules that e litigants *do* swear supports R' Chiya's position that "here, it is urs" does *not* remove that portion from being considered part of the im (*Rashi*).

The Rishonim point out an obvious problem: The Mishnah can be an plication of R' Chiya's second law [the oath of *modeh bemiktzas* plies even in situations of *heilach*] only if it is first and foremost an plication of his first law [partial substantiation through witnesses (or ysical possession) also generates a *modeh bemiktzas* oath]. But the evious Gemara has just rejected the notion that our Mishnah is an plication of R' Chiya's first law, since the same "witnesses" which stify that half the cloak belongs to one litigant also testify that the her half belongs to the other litigant. What, then, has the Gemara complished by explaining our Mishnah to be an application of R' iya's first and second laws? (*Ritva*; see also *Tosafos, Baal HaMaor d Chidushei HaRan*; see below, note 35, for *Ritva's* resolution).

. Since he is deemed to be "one who denies the whole" [כופר הכל] – e above, note 27.

. Above (see note 26), it was explained that a situation of *heilach* exists hen a borrower says that the part of the loan he admits to has not been ent and belongs to the lender wherever it is. Many Rishonim, however, spute this, arguing that since a loan is given to be spent [מלוה להוצאה נת – see above, note 15], the original coins – even if they have not en spent – do not belong to the lender until the borrower actually turns them to him. Thus, it cannot be said that saying "here, it is urs" is tantamount to the lender already owning it. Rather, these shonim assert that *heilach* generally applies only in a case of stodianship [פקדון]; viz. the plaintiff claims that he entrusted one ndred *zuz* to the defendant for safekeeping, but the defendant admits ceiving only fifty and says that he has not spent it and it belongs to the claimant wherever it is (*Rashba*; *Ran* to *Shevuos* 38b, cited here in *Hagahos HaGra*).

Our version of the Gemara here [הני זוזי דקא מודי בגווייהו כמאן דנקיט להו "מלוה" דמי, *these zuz that he admits to are as if the "lender" is holding them*] supports the former view, that the Gemara deals here with a case of loan, not custodianship. In other Gemara texts, however, the key word מלוה, *lender,* is absent; thus, the Gemara might indeed refer here to a case of custodianship (ibid.).

Alternatively, these Rishonim explain that the essence of *heilach* is not necessarily (as *Rashi* asserts) that the claimant *already* has legal possession of the admitted portion of the claim. Rather, *heilach* also applies when the defendant has with him the money he admits owing and is prepared to pay it immediately ("here, it is yours"). This imminent payment is sufficient to remove that money from being deemed part of the claim, even though the lender is not yet in possession of the money. If *heilach* is understood in this way, our Gemara can indeed refer to a case of loan litigation.

32. As explained by the Gemara on 3a, this Rabbinic measure is designed to discourage frivolous claims. The oath in the Mishnah *cannot* be the *modeh bemiktzas* oath, however, since the same "witnesses" (i.e. the presumptive evidence of possession) which testify that half the cloak belongs to one litigant also testify that the other half belongs to the other litigant [as noted in the Gemara above – see note 22] (*Rashi*).

33. [R' Chiya *must* agree that the oath in the Mishnah is not the Biblical oath of *modeh bemiktzas,* as demonstrated in the Gemara above (see previous note).]

34. As a rule, Rabbinic enactments must be patterned after some analogous Biblical law. Accordingly, R' Chiya argues that the Rabbinic oath of our Mishnah could have been enacted only if the Mishnah's situation resembles one in which the Biblical oath of *modeh bemiktzas* would be required. The Rabbis could then enact an oath obligation, since the situation looks – at least superficially – like a situation of *modeh bemiktzas.* It must be, then, that our Mishnah's case has all the earmarks of a true case of *modeh bemiktzas.* The possession of half the cloak is tantamount to witnesses who testify that the holder is the owner (partial substantiation by witnesses) and an oath obligation is therefore in order even though the claimant already has possession of that portion of the claim (*heilach*). The Gemara's earlier argument against likening the Mishnah's case to one of *modeh bemiktzas* (since the same evidence that subtantiates part of the claim refutes the rest of it) showed only that the Mishnah was not a *true* case of *modeh bemiktzas.* However, the Mishnah's case still bears sufficient similarity to the case of *modeh bemiktzas* to justify the enactment of a Rabbinic oath that can be said to be patterned after the Biblical law of *modeh bemiktzas* prevailing even in situations of *heilach* (see *Chidushei HaRan*).

תאמר בעדים שעל מה שכפר הוא נשבע אלא אמר רב פפא אתי מגלגול שבועה דעד אחד מה לגלגול שבועה דעד אחד שכן שבועה גוררת שבועה תאמר בעדים דממון קא מחייבי פיו יוכיח מה לפיו שכן אינו בהכחשה עד אחד יוכיח שישנו בהכחשה ומחייבו שבועה מה לעד אחד שכן על מה שמעיד הוא נשבע תאמר בעדים שעל מה שכפר הוא נשבע פיו יוכיח [א] וחזר הדין לא ראי זה כראי זה ולא ראי זה כראי זה הצד השוה שבהן שעל ידי טענה וכפירה הן באין ונשבע אף אני אביא עדים שעל ידי טענה וכפירה הם באין ונשבע מה להצד השוה שבהן שכן לא הוחזק כפרן תאמר בעדים שכן הוחזק כפרן ובעדים מי הוחזק כפרן [ג] והאמר רב אידי בר אבין אמר רב חסדא א הכופר במלוה כשר לעדות בפקדון פסול לעדות אלא פריך הכי מה להצד השוה שבהן שכן אינן בתורת הזמה תאמר בעדים שישנן בתורת הזמה הא לא קשיא רבי חייא תורת הזמה לא פריך אלא דקאמר ותנא תונא מי דמי התם למלוה אית ליה סהדי ללוה לית ליה סהדי דלא מסיק ליה ולא מידי דאי הוו ליה סהדי ללוה דלא מסיק ליה ולא מידי לא בעי רבי חייא לאשתבועי הכא כי היכי דאנן סהדי (א) בהאי אנן סהדי בהאי ואפילו הכי משתבעי אלא כי איתמר ותנא תונא אאידך דרבי חייא איתמר דאמר ר' חייא מנה לי בידך והלה אומר אין לך בידי אלא נ' זוז והילך חייב מאי טעמא הילך נמי כמודה מקצת הטענה דמי ותנא תונא שנים אוחזין בטלית והא הכא כיון דתפיס [ג] [אנן סהדי דמאי דתפיס] הילך הוא וקתני ישבע ורב ששת אמר [ב] הילך פטור מ"ט כיון דאמר ליה הילך הני זוזי דקא מודי בגוייהו כמאן דנקיט להו מלוה דמי באינך חמשים הא לא מודי הלכך ליכא הודאת מקצת הטענה ולרב ששת קשיא מתניתין אמר לך רב ששת מתניתין תקנת חכמים היא ואידך אין תקנת חכמים היא ומיהו אי אמרת בשלמא מדאורייתא הילך חייב מתקני רבנן שבועה כעין דאורייתא אלא אי אמרת מדאורייתא הילך פטור מתקני רבנן שבועה דליתא דכוותה בדאורייתא מיתיבי

סלעים

**רש"י**

**תאמר.** בשבועה דעדים שאינו נשבע על מה שהעידו אלא על מה שלא העידו ועל כפירתו הוא נשבע ולא אהעדאתן ומנין לך להחמיר כל כך: **מגלגול שבועה דעד אחד.** אם נתחייב לו שבועה על ידי עד אחד כדאמרינן והיתה עליו טענה אחרת שלא היתה מוטלת עליו שבועה מגלגלין אותה עם שבועה זאת ונשבע על שתיהן דגלגול שבועה דאורייתא היא דילפינן לה בקדושין (דף מ:) מואמרה האשה אמן אמן הרי שעל מה שלא העיד העד הוא משביעו: **שכן שבועה גוררת שבועה.** עד לא חייבו שבועה אלא על מה שהעיד והשבועה גוררת שבועה תאמר בעדים הללו שהחמשים שהעידוהו הם מחייבין אותו לשלם ואין כאן שבועה לגרור על ידה שבועה על השאר: **פיו יוכיח.** מודה מקצת הטענה שעל מה שכופר ופיו לא הודה הוא נשבע: **טענה וכפירה.** זה טוען וזה כופר הן באין לדין: **לא הוחזק כפרן.** על מה שכפר אינו מוחזק כפרן שמא לא כיחש שהעד אינו נאמן להכחישו ולהחזיקו כפרן: **תאמר בעדים.** שמאחר שכפר הכל והם העידו על החמשים הוחזק כפרן ולא נאמר נאמינהו על השבועה: **הכופר במלוה.** בין על כולה בין על מקצת ובאו עדים והעידוהו עד שלא נשבע: **כשר לעדות.** ולא אמרינן גזלן הוא והתורה אמרה (שמות כג) אל תשת רשע עד דכיון דמלוה להוצאה נתנה דלמא צריך להוציאה וסבר עד דהוה לי [זוזי] ופרענא ליה ואי מודינא ליה השתא יתבעני מיד אבל הכופר בפקדון אפי' על מקצת ובאו עדים והעידוהו פסול לעדות דמאי הוה ליה גבי פקדון לאשתמוטי נפשיה ושמא תאמר אבד ממנו ואשתמיט ליה עד דמשכח ליה לקמן בפירקין (דף ה:) מוקמינן בדאתו סהדי ואמרי ההיא שעתא בידיה נקיט ליה: **בתורת הזמה.** לשלם קנס דכאשר זמם דעד אחד שהוזם פטור ופיו גבי הודאה כל שכן דלא שייכא הזמה כלל: **תאמר בעדים.** אם הוזמו בחמשים שהעידו משלמין ממון: **תורת הזמה לא פריך.** אינה חשובה לו פירכא דכיון דעד אחד ישנו בהזמה ליבטל עדותו [ד] בעדות שני עדים אם הוה לן למימר בעדים משום דישנן בהזמה לא יחייבוהו שבועה הוה לן למימר נמי בעד אחד לא יחייבהו שבועה דהא ישנו בהזמה ליבטל עדותו ואי משום דאין משלם קנס אין בזו יפוי כח להאמין עדותו: **אלא דקאמר ותנא תונא.** אלא אם יש לך להשיב על דברי רבי חייא כך יש לך להשיב דקאמר ותנא תונא והביא ראיה לדבריו ממשנתינו מי דמי: **התם.** בדרבי חייא: **למלוה אית ליה סהדי.** דמסיק ביה חמשים: **ללוה לית ליה סהדי.** באינך חמשים שאינו חייב לו עליה: **אי הוה ליה כו'.** כגון אילו העידו העדים חמשים חייב וחמשים פרע בכה"ג לא הוה אמר ר' חייא דצריך לישבע על השאר: **מתני' כי היכי דאנן סהדי להאי.** דחציה שלו: **אנן סהדי להאי.** דחציה שלו ולמה הצריכוהו חכמים שבועה ש"מ טעמא לאו משום מודה מקצת הטענה הוא כר' חייא ואינה שבועה דאורייתא אלא תקנת חכמים שלא יהא כל אחד הולך כו': **והילך.** לא [א] הוצאתים והן שלך בכ"מ שהם: **חייב.** לישבע על השאר ולא אמרינן הני דקמודי ליה בגווייהו הוציל ואיתנהו בעינייהו כמאן דנקיט להו דמי אלא כשאר מודה במקצת הוא וחייב: **ותנא תונא כו'.** קס"ד לר' חייא טעמא דמתני' משום דאנן סהדי דמאי דתפיס דיליה הוא והוי כמנה לי בידך והלה אמר אין לך בידי כלום והעדים מעידים אותו שיש לו חמשים וכי אידך דרבי חייא דמחייב ליה שבועה דאורייתא: **והא הכא.** דהך העדאת עדים אנן סהדי דמאי דתפיס האי הילך הוא שהרי בפניו הוא: **וקתני.** דמחייב שבועה אשארא וה"ה להודאה במקצת: **תקנת חכמים היא.** ולא משום העדאת עדים וכדפרכינן לעיל כי היכי דאנן סהדי להאי אנן סהדי להאי: **אי אמרת בשלמא הילך מדאורייתא חייב.** כלומר גבי שבועה דאורייתא כגון בהודאה במקצת:

סלעים

**תוספות**

**עד** אחד יוכיח שישנו בהכחשה ובהזמה. שפיר גרס הכא ובהזמה כיון שע"י הזמה דבורו בטל ואין להקשות מה לפיו שכן אינו משלם בהזמה תאמר בעדים שמשלמין בהזמה ואז לא יכול לומר עד אחד יוכיח [ה] שמשלם כי מה שהעד אינו משלם כשהוא מוזם אינו חומרא אלא לפי שבעדותו אינו מחייבו ממון לכך הואיל ודיבורו בטל חשיב ישנו בהזמה ובסמוך על מה הצד פרכינן ליה משום דעל מה הצד פרכינן פירכא כל דהו ורבי חייא אפי' על מה הצד לא פריך ליה משום דמה שאינו משלם העד כשמוזם זהו גריעותו לפי שלא היה כח בעדותו לחייב ממון:

**הצד** השוה [שבהן] שע"י טענה כו'. וא"ת [ו] כופר הכל יוכיח שע"י טענה וכפירה פטור ויש לומר דבהצד השוה שבהן יש טענה חשובה דכשמודה מקצת או עד מכחישו נראה דמשקר ולכך יש שבועה:

**ותנא** תונא אאידך דר' חייא. אנן סהדי דמאי דתפיס האי כו' פרש"י כיון דהוי כהעדאת עדים משתבע מדרבי חייא קמייתא וקשה כיון דלא מצי לאוכוחי הך ברייתא דהילך אלא מכח קמייתא לימא ותנא תונא אקמייתא לכך י"ל דאנן סהדי לאו דוקא דמאי דתפיס מחשבינן ליה השתא טפי מהעדאת עדים וחשיב כאילו מודה ליה דדידיה הוא אך [ב] וקשה דמ"מ איכא למיפרך דמתני' כי היכי דהאי מודה להאי האי נמי מודה להאי ואפ"ה קמשתבעי כדפריך אקמייתא ומאי תיקן וי"ל דהשתא נמי מוכח מכח טעמא דבסמוך אי הילך פטור לא הוי מתקני רבנן שבועה דליכא דכוותה בדאורייתא אבל לרבי חייא קמייתא כי נמי בהעדאת עדים פטור מתקני רבנן שבועה במתני' דחשיב הודאה במאי דתפיס חבריה ודוחק דלפ"ז הא דלא קאמר ותנא תונא אקמייתא משום דמאי דתפיס חשיב כהודאה וזו לא היתה פירכתו למעלה אלא מטעם כי היכי דאנן סהדי להאי כו':

**ורב** ששת אמר הילך פטור. נראה שהלכה כרב ששת דבפ' השואל (לקמן דף ק.) גבי עבד קטן פריך ועוד הילך הוא אך בספר חפץ משמע דהילך חייב [וע' תוס' ב"ב קכח: ד"ה הלכתא]:

[ז] **וש"מ** דהילך פטור. וא"ת יהא נאמן בשלש דמיגו דבעי אמר שתים וי"ל כיון דהילך פטור אם יאמר שתים הו"ל כופר הכל ואין אדם מעיז ולר"ע לא הוי עזות דמסייע ליה שטרא:

לעולם

**רבינו חננאל**

אלא תיתי מגלגול שבועה דעד אחד ונדחה גם זה. ואתינן לרבויה מפיו ועד אחד. ואמרי' הכי מה פיו שאין מחייבו קנס מחייבו שבועה עדים שמחייבין אותו קנס לא כל שכן. ופרכינן מה לפיו שכן אינו בהכחשה כמו שפירשנו למעלה. עד אחד יוכיח שכן ישנו בהכחשה ומחייבו שבועה. מה לעד אחד שכן על מה שהעיד עליו הוא נשבע תאמר בעדים שעל מה שכפר הוא נשבע פיו יוכיח שמשלם במה שהודה ונשבע על מה שכפר וחזר הדין וכו'. ופרכי' (מי) [מה] להצד השוה שבהן שכן לא הוחזק כפרן פי' אם כפר הלוה והעיד עליו עד אחד לא הוחזק כפרן שנאמר לא יקום עד אחד באיש וגו'. וכן אם כפר וחזר והודה לא הוחזק כפרן כדרבא דאמר רבא אדם קרוב אצל עצמו ואין אדם משים עצמו רשע תאמר בעדים שאם כפר ובאו עדים והעידו עליו [שחייב] שהוחזק כפרן ונפסל. ודחי' לה הכי וכי מי שכפר במלוה נפסל והאמר רב חסדא הכופר במלוה כשר לעדות והא דר' חייא מלוה היא ונדחית זו הפירכא. וחזרנו לפרך פירכא אחרת. מה להצד השוה שבהן שכן אינו בתורת הזמה [א] פיו כדאמרן למעלה. עד אחד אינו בתורת הזמה שהתורה אמרה ועשיתם לו כאשר וגו' וכיון שאין עדות עד אחד אלא לשבועה ואי אפשר להשביע העד זו השבועה נדחת תורת הזמה מעליו שאין אתה יכול לקיים ועשיתם לו כאשר זמם וגו' וכדתנן [בריש מכות] מעידים אנו באיש פלו' שהוא בן גרושה וכו' ולעולם אין תורת הזמה אלא בשנים ועד שיזומו שניהם. בוא וראה כיון דאמר רב [שם ג ע"א] עד זומם משלם לפי חלקו מקשי' עליה והתניא אין משלמין ממון עד שיזומו שניהן ותריצנא להא דרב באומר העדנו והוזמנו בבית דינו של פלו' ונתחייבנו ממון כי האי גוונא משלם אבל כשיוזם עד אחד אין שם תשלומין. ותנן נמי ור' שמעון אומר מה שנים אין נהרגין עד שיזומו שניהן אף שלשה עד שיזומו שלשתן. ופרקי' דלמא רבי חייא תורת הזמה לא פריך כלומר אין זו פירכא. פי' ר' חייא תורת הזמה לא פריך אמר לך רבי חייא לא נדחת תורת הזמה מעד אחד מפני כחו של עד אחד אלא מפני שעד אחד אינו בא אלא לשבועה וכשיזום אינו יכול להשביעו השבועה שזמם לעשות לאחיו וכיוצא בו נדחית תורת הזמה בשני עדים שהעידו על כהן שהוא בן גרושה וכו'. ואתינן [ג] לאוקמה לדר' חייא כמתניתין ולא דמיא דהא מתני' כי היכי דאנן סהדי להאי דכל מה דתפיס בהאי טלית דידיה הוא הכי [נמי] אנן סהדי לאידך. [ג] ותוב מתני' במאי דמסהדי (שהרי) [סהדי] דהוא דיליה עליה נשבע ותופס. לאפוקי דר' חייא דעל מה שכופר הוא נשבע. אלא אי איתמר והתנא שנאה על אידך דר' חייא דאמר מנה לי בידך והלה אומר אין לך בידי אלא נ' והילך חייב מאי טעמא דאע"ג דאמר ליה הילך כיון דעדיין לא נתן מודה מקצת הטענה הוא ותנא תונא שנים אוחזין בטלית וקתני ישבע והא אנן סהדי דבמאי דתפיס הילך הוא וקתני ישבע ש"מ דאפי' אמר ליה הילך מודה מקצת הטענה הוא וחייב. ורב ששת אמר הילך פטור דכיון דאמר ליה הילך כמאן דפרע להו דמי ובשאר הא לא מודה ליה ולא מידי הלכך לאו

**חשק שלמה על ר"ח** [א] עי' בש"מ כאן שהעתיק לדברי רבינו בזה באריכות יותר. [ב] נראה דל"ל ואתינן לדחויי להא דאוקמא לעיל לדברי חייא כמתני' דלא דמיא וכו'. [ג] מדברי רבינו אלו נראה מוכח דס"ל לו גי' אחרת בסוגיין דדחי דלא דמי למתני' נמי בזה דהתם במאי דמסהדי סהדי הוא נשבע וכו'.

**עין משפט נר מצוה**

יד א (מיי' פ"ב מהל' טוען ונטען הל' ג) טוש"ע ח"מ סימן לב ס"ד ועי' בב"י:

טו ב מיי' שם פ"א הל' ג סמג עשין צה טוש"ע ח"מ סי' פז סעיף א וסי' עה סעיף ו [רב אלפס כאן ופ"ו דשבועות דף דש]:

**מסורת הש"ס**

**הגהות הב"ח**

**גליון הש"ס**

**הגהות הגר"א**

**ליקוטי רש"י**

generate an oath obligation).[19]

The Gemara has arrived at the conclusion that R' Chiya correctly derived his law from the common characteristics exhibited by personal admission and a solitary witness. However, the Gemara now challenges R' Chiya's additional assertion (above 3a) that his law is reflected in our Mishnah:

אֶלָּא דְּקָאָמַר וְתַנָּא תּוּנָא – **Rather,** we can object to **that which [R' Chiya] says, "And our Tanna has taught [this law]** in our **Mishnah."**[20] מִי דָּמֵי – **Are [the two cases]** truly **analogous?** הָתָם לַמַּלְוֶה אִית לֵיהּ סַהֲדֵי – **There,** in the case of R' Chiya's law, **the lender has witnesses** who support part of his claim, לַלֹּוֶה לֵית לֵיהּ סַהֲדֵי דְּלֹא מַסִּיק לֵיהּ וְלֹא מִידֵּי – whereas **the borrower has no witnesses** to support his assertion **that [the lender] has no** further **claim against him;** דְּאִי הֲווּ לֵיהּ סַהֲדֵי לַלֹּוֶה דְּלֹא מַסִּיק לֵיהּ וְלֹא מִידֵּי לֹא בָּעֵי רַבִּי חִיָּיא לְאִשְׁתַּבּוּעֵי – **for if the borrower did have witnesses** to support his assertion **that [the lender] has no** further **claim against him, then R' Chiya would not require** the borrower **to swear.**[21] הָכָא כִּי הֵיכִי דַּאֲנַן סַהֲדֵי בְּהַאי אֲנַן סַהֲדֵי בְּהַאי – **Here** in the case of the Mishnah, however, **just as we are witnesses regarding this** half of the cloak that it belongs to the litigant holding it, **we are witnesses regarding the other** half of the cloak that it *does* belong to him;[22] וַאֲפִילּוּ הָכִי מִשְׁתַּבְּעֵי – **yet,** the Mishnah rules that **[the litigants] must swear** in support of their claims. This proves, then, that the oath required by our Mishnah has nothing to do with R' Chiya's law that a Biblical oath of *modeh bemiktzas* is required when witnesses support half a plaintiff's claim.[23] – ? –

In response to this objection, the Gemara revises its understanding of R' Chiya's statement that "our Tanna has taught it":

אֶלָּא כִּי אִיתְּמַר וְתַנָּא תּוּנָא אַאִידָךְ דְּרַבִּי חִיָּיא אִיתְּמַר – **Rather, regarding what was it said** by R' Chiya, **"And our Tanna has taught it"? Regarding the** following **other** ruling **of R' Chiya.**[24] דְּאָמַר ר׳ חִיָּיא מָנֶה לִי בְּיָדְךָ וְהַלָּה אוֹמֵר אֵין לְךָ בְּיָדִי אֶלָּא נ׳ זוּז וְהֵילָךְ – **For R' Chiya said:** If a plaintiff claims to a defendant, **"You owe me a *maneh*,"**[25] **and the other one** [the defendant] **says, "I owe you only fifty *zuz* and here, it is yours,"**[26] חַיָּיב – **[the defendant] is obligated** to swear the oath of *modeh bemiktzas* like any other defendant who admits partial liability. מַאי טַעְמָא – **What is the reason?** הֵילָךְ נַמִּי כְּמוֹדֶה מִקְצַת הַטַּעֲנָה דָּמֵי – Because **even** in a case of **"here, it is yours," it is considered that [the defendant] admits part of the claim.**[27] וְתַנָּא תּוּנָא – It was regarding this law that R' Chiya observed: **"And our Tanna has taught it."** For our Tanna states: שְׁנַיִם אוֹחֲזִין בְּטַלִּית – **TWO** litigants **ARE HOLDING ON TO A CLOAK** etc. Our Tanna rules that each litigant is required to swear. וְהָא הָכָא כֵּיוָן דְּתָפִיס אֲנַן סַהֲדֵי דְּמַאי דְּתָפִיס הֵילָךְ הוּא – **Now, here** in this case, **since he** [each litigant] **is holding** the cloak, it is as if **we are witnesses that what he holds is** already his, as if the other litigant had said, **"Here, it is yours."**[28] וְקָתָנֵי יִשָּׁבַע – **Yet the Mishnah**

NOTES

19. The solitary witness' exemption from the law of *hazamah* is not the result of any strength granted to his testimony. On the contrary, the exemption results from the weakness of his testimony in that (unlike the testimony of two witnesses) it is incapable of imposing any penalty on the defendant (see note 17). As far as the capacity of *hazamah* to *disprove* testimony is concerned, the testimony of a solitary witness is certainly as much subject to disproof through *hazamah* as is the testimony of two witnesses.

Now, if we are to argue that the testimony of witnesses might not have the capacity to obligate an oath because such testimony has the weakness of being subject to *hazamah,* it is certainly only the "disproof" aspect of *hazamah* that indicates any degree of weakness. But if so, we would have to reject on the same grounds the ability of a solitary witness to generate an oath obligation, since his testimony, too, is subject to disproof through *hazamah* (*Rashi*). [And since the Torah does indeed grant a solitary witness the power to create an oath obligation, we see that immunity from disproof through *hazamah* is not a prerequisite for being able to create an oath obligation. Thus, the derivation of the testimony of two witnesses from the common characteristic is restored.]

20. Above (3a), R' Chiya asserted that our Mishnah's imposition of oaths on the litigants holding the cloak reflects his law that the partial substantiation of a claim by witnesses obligates the defendant to swear regarding the part of the claim he still denies. For in the case of the Mishnah, each litigant's physical possession of half the cloak is tantamount to the testimony of witnesses that he owns that half. Thus, each litigant must swear the oath of *modeh bemiktzas* that he indeed owns that half of the cloak *not* held by the other one (see 3a note 30 at length).

21. For example, if in addition to testifying that the borrower owes half the claim, the witnesses would also testify that he does *not* owe the other half, R' Chiya would certainly not require the defendant to take the oath of *modeh bemiktzas* to corroborate the second half of the witnesses' testimony (*Rashi*).

22. Above (3a), R' Chiya's proof to his law from our Mishnah was based on the premise that the presumption of ownership inherent in each litigant's physical possession of half the cloak is tantamount to the testimony of witnesses that the half he is holding belongs to him. Accordingly, his claim to the other half of the cloak must be denied under the oath of *modeh bemiktzas* by the other litigant. The Gemara now objects, however, that there is no place here for the oath of *modeh bemiktzas,* since the same presumption of ownership which indicates that half the cloak belongs to one litigant also indicates that the other half belongs to the other litigant.

23. Rather, the oath in the case of our Mishnah is a Rabbinic measure designed to discourage people from grabbing someone else's cloak and then claiming that it belongs to them [as explained above (3a) by R' Yochanan] (*Rashi*).

24. [That is, R' Chiya adduced support from our Mishnah to a different ruling of his. It was the Gemara above which mistakenly thought that the proof had been adduced regarding his ruling that the testimony of witnesses generates a *modeh bemiktzas* oath obligation.]

25. [Literally: there is a *maneh* belonging to me in your hand (i.e. possession).] A *maneh* is one hundred *zuz.*

26. הֵילָךְ, *heilach,* literally: behold [it is] for you (see *Genesis* 47:23). In the present case, the defendant means by "here, it is yours" that he has not spent the fifty *zuz* lent to him and they are already in the plaintiff's legal possession wherever they are (*Rashi,* as explained by *Ritva*; see below, note 31).

27. R' Chiya means to reject the view (held by Rav Sheishess below) that a case of "here, it is yours" does not qualify as a case of *modeh bemiktzas.* The proponents of that view reason that when the plaintiff already has legal possession of the portion of the claim admitted by the defendant, the admitted portion cannot be deemed part of the claim. For the plaintiff is not really "claiming" that portion at all – his rights to it are unchallenged and he already has legal possession of it. Therefore, only the unadmitted portion is viewed as the plaintiff's claim – a claim that the defendant denies in its entirety. Thus, the defendant is deemed "one who denies the whole" [כופר הכל] and is not subject to any Biblical oath (see 3a note 23).

R' Chiya, however, rejects that reasoning and insists that the plaintiff's legal possession of the admitted portion does not remove it from being viewed as part of the larger claim. Thus, R' Chiya states that even when a defendant who admits part of a claim states, "Here, the portion I admit is yours," it is considered a bona fide case of *modeh bemiktzas,* in which the defendant must make his continued denial of the rest of the claim under oath.

28. [Actually, neither litigant is willing to concede that half the cloak belongs to the other one. However, the essence of *heilach* is not that the defendant actually states, "Here, it is yours," but rather that the plaintiff already has legal possession of what the defendant admits (or is forced to concede because of witnesses). This is indeed the case in the situation described by the Mishnah, in which each litigant already has possession of half the cloak, which the other litigant is thus forced to concede to him (see *Rashi*). See following note.]

תאמר בעדים שעל מה שכפר הוא נשבע אלא אמר רב פפא אתי מגלגול שבועה דעד אחד מה לגלגול שבועה דעד אחד שכן שבועה גוררת שבועה תאמר בעדים דממון קא מחייבי פיו יוכיח מה לפיו שכן אינו בהכחשה עד אחד יוכיח שישנו בהכחשה ומחייבו שבועה מה לעד אחד שכן על מה שמעיד הוא נשבע תאמר בעדים שעל מה שכפר הוא נשבע פיו יוכיח (א) וחזר הדין לא ראי זה כראי זה ולא ראי זה כראי זה הצד השוה שבהן שעל ידי טענה וכפירה הן באין ונשבע אף אני אביא עדים שעל ידי טענה וכפירה הם באין ונשבע מה להצד השוה שבהן שכן לא הוחזק כפרן תאמר בעדים שכן הוחזק כפרן ובעדים מי הוחזק כפרן ג) והאמר רב אידי בר אבין אמר רב חסדא א הכופר במלוה כשר לעדות בפקדון פסול לעדות אלא פריך הכי מה להצד השוה שבהן שכן אינן בתורת הזמה תאמר בעדים שישנן בתורת הזמה הא לא קשיא רבי חייא תורת הזמה לא פריך אלא דקאמר ותנא תונא מי דמי התם למלוה אית ליה סהדי ללוה לית ליה סהדי דלא מסיק ליה ולא מידי דאי הוו ליה סהדי ללוה דלא מסיק ליה ולא מידי לא בעי רבי חייא לאשתבועי הכא כי היכי דאנן סהדי (א) בהאי אנן סהדי בהאי ואפילו הכי משתבעי אלא כי איתמר ותנא תונא אאידך דרבי חייא איתמר דאמר ר' חייא מנה לי בידך והלה אומר אין לך בידי אלא נ' זוז והילך חייב מאי טעמא הילך נמי כמודה מקצת הטענה דמי ותנא תונא שנים אוחזין בטלית והא הכא כיון דתפיס ג) [אנן סהדי דמאי דתפיס] הילך הוא וקתני ישבע ורב ששת אמר ב הילך פטור מ"ט כיון דאמר ליה הילך הני זוזי דקא מודי בגוייהו כמאן דנקיט להו מלוה דמי באינך חמשים הא לא מודי הלכך ליכא הודאת מקצת הטענה ולרב ששת קשיא מתניתין אמר לך רב ששת מתניתין תקנת חכמים היא ואידך אין תקנת חכמים היא ומיהו אי אמרת בשלמא מדאורייתא הילך חייב מתקני רבנן שבועה כעין דאורייתא אלא אי אמרת מדאורייתא הילך פטור מתקני רבנן שבועה דליתא דכוותה בדאורייתא מיתיבי

סלעים

**רש"י**

תאמר. בשבועה דעדים שאינו נשבע על מה שהעידו אלא על מה שלא העידו ועל כפירתו הוא נשבע ולא אהעדאתן ומנין לך להחמיר כל כך: מגלגול שבועה דעד אחד. אם נתחייב לו שבועה על ידי עד אחד כדאמרינן והיתה עליו טענה אחרת שלא היתה מוטלת עליו שבועה מגלגלין אותה עם שבועה זאת ונשבע על שתיהן דגלגול שבועה דאורייתא היא דילפינן לה בקדושין (דף כז:) מואמרה האשה אמן אמן הרי שעל מה שלא העיד העד הוא משביעו: שכן שבועה גוררת שבועה. עד לא חייבו שבועה אלא על מה שהעיד והשבועה גוררת שבועה תאמר בעדים הללו שהחמשים שהעידוהו הם מחייבין אותו לשלם ואין כאן שבועה לגרור על ידה שבועה על השאר: פיו יוכיח. מודה מקצת הטענה שעל מה שכופר ופיו לא הודה הוא נשבע: טענה וכפירה. זה טוען וזה כופר הן באין לדין: לא הוחזק כפרן. על מה שכפר אינו מוחזק כפרן שמא לא כיחש שהעד אינו נאמן להכחישו ולהחזיקו כפרן: תאמר בעדים. שמאחר שכפר הכל והם העידו על החמשים הוחזק כפרן ולא נאמר נאמניהו על השבועה: הכופר במלוה. בין על כולה בין על מקצת ובאו עדים והעידוהו עד שלא נשבע: כשר לעדות. ולא אמרינן גזלן הוא והתורה אמרה (שמות כג) אל תשת רשע עד דכיון דמלוה להוצאה נתנה דלמא צריך להוציאה וסבר עד דהוה לי [זוזי] ופרענא ליה ואי מודינא ליה השתא יתבעני מיד אבל הכופר בפקדון אפי' על מקצת ובאו עדים והעידוהו פסול לעדות דמאי הוה ליה גבי פקדון לאשתמוטי נפשיה ושמא תאמר אבד ממנו ואשתמיט ליה עד דמשכח ליה לקמן בפירקין (דף ה:) מוקמינן בדאתו סהדי ואמרי ההיא שעתא בידיה נקיט ליה: בתורת הזמה. לשלם קנס דכאשר זמם דעד אחד שהוזם פטור ופיו גבי הודאה כל שכן דלא שייכא הזמה כלל: תאמר בעדים. אם הוזמו בחמשים שהעידו משלמין ממון: תורת הזמה לא פריך. אינה תשובה לו פירכא דכיון דעד אחד ישנו בהזמה ליבטל עדותו ד) בעדות שני עדים אם הוה לן למימר בעדים משום דישנן בהזמה לא יחייבוהו שבועה הוה לן למימר נמי בעד אחד לא יחייבהו שבועה דהא ישנו בהזמה ליבטל עדותו ואי משום דאין משלם קנס אין בזו יפוי כח להאמין עדותו: אלא דקאמר ותנא תונא. אלא אם יש לך להשיב על דברי רבי חייא כך יש לך להשיב דקאמר ותנא תונא והביא ראיה לדבריו ממשנתינו מי דמי: התם. בדרבי חייא: למלוה אית ליה סהדי. דמסיק ביה חמשים: ללוה לית ליה סהדי. באינך חמשים שאינו חייב לו עליה: אי הוה ליה כו'. כגון אילו העידו העדים חמשים חייב וחמשים פרע בכה"ג לא הוה אמר ר' חייא דצריך לישבע על השאר: מתני' כי היכי דאנן סהדי להאי. דחציה שלו: אנן סהדי להאי. דחציה שלו ולמה הצריכוהו חכמים שבועה ש"מ טעמא לאו משום מודה מקצת הטענה הוא כר' חייא ואינה שבועה דאורייתא אלא תקנת חכמים שלא יהא כל אחד הולך כו': והילך. לא [א] הוצאתים והן שלך בכ"מ שהם: חייב. לישבע על השאר ולא אמרינן הני דקמודי ליה בגוייהו הואיל ואיתנהו בעינייהו כמאן דנקיט להו דמי אלא כשאר מודה במקצת הוא וחייב: ותנא תונא כו'. קס"ד דלר' חייא טעמא דמתני' משום דאנן סהדי דמאי דתפיס דיליה הוא והוי כמנה לי בידך והלה אמר אין לך בידי כלום והעדים מעידים אותו שיש לו חמשים וכי אידך דרבי חייא דמחייב ליה שבועה דאורייתא: והא הכא. דהך העדאת עדים אנן סהדי דמאי דתפיס האי הילך הוא שהרי בפניו הוא: וקתני. דמחייב שבועה אשארא וה"ה להודאה במקצת: תקנת חכמים היא. ולא משום העדאת עדים ודפרכינן לעיל כי היכי דאנן סהדי להאי אנן סהדי להאי: אי אמרת בשלמא הילך מדאורייתא חייב. כלומר גבי שבועה דאורייתא כגון בהודאה במקצת:

**תוספות**

עד אחד יוכיח שישנו בהכחשה ובהזמה. שפיר גרס הכא ובהזמה כיון שע"י הזמה דבורו בטל ואין להקשות מה לפיו שכן אינו משלם בהזמה תאמר בעדים שמשלמין בהזמה ואז לא יכול לומר עד אחד יוכיח ה) שמשלם כי מה שהעד אינו משלם כשהוא מוזם אינו חומרא אלא לפי שבעדותו אינו מחייבו ממון לכך הואיל ודיבורו בטל חשיב ישנו בהזמה ובסמוך על מה הצד פרכינן ליה משום דעל מה הצד פרכינן פירכא כל דהו ורבי חייא אפי' על מה הצד לא פריך ליה משום דמה שאינו משלם העד כשמוזם זהו גריעותו לפי שלא היה כח בעדותו לחייב ממון:

הצד השוה [שבהן] שע"י טענה כו'. וא"ת ו) כופר הכל יוכיח שע"י טענה וכפירה פטור ויש לומר דבהצד השוה שבהן יש טענה חשובה דכשמודה מקצת או עד מכחישו נראה דמשקר ולכך יש שבועה:

ותנא תונא אאידך דר' חייא. אנן סהדי דמאי דתפיס האי כו'. פרש"י כיון דהוי כהעדאת עדים משתבע מדרבי חייא קמייתא וקשה כיון דלא מצי לאוכוחי הך ברייתא דהילך אלא מכח קמייתא לימא ותנא תונא אקמייתא לכך י"ל דאנן סהדי לאו דוקא דמאי דתפיס מחשבינן ליה השתא טפי מהעדאת עדים וחשיב כאילו מודה ליה דדידיה הוא אך [ב] וקשה דמ"מ איכא למיפרך דמתני' כי היכי דהאי מודה להאי האי נמי מודה להאי ואפ"ה קמשתבעי כדפריך אקמייתא ומאי תיקן וי"ל דהשתא נמי מוכח מכח טעמא דבסמוך אי הילך פטור לא הוי מתקני רבנן שבועה דליכא דכוותה באורייתא אבל לרבי חייא קמייתא כי נמי בהעדאת עדים פטור מתקני רבנן שבועה במתני' דחשיב הודאה במאי דתפיס חבריה ודוחק דלפ"ז הא דלא קאמר ותנא תונא אקמייתא משום דמאי דתפיס חשיב כהודאה וזו לא היתה פירכתו למעלה אלא מטעם כי היכי דאנן סהדי להאי כו':

ורב ששת אמר הילך פטור. נראה שהלכה כרב ששת דבפ' השואל (לקמן דף ק.) גבי עבד קטן פריך ועוד הילך הוא אך בספר חפץ משמע דהילך חייב [וע' תוס' ב"ב קכח: ד"ה הלכתא]:

ז) וש"מ דהילך פטור. וא"ת יהא נאמן בשלש דמיגו דבעי אמר שתים וי"ל כיון דהילך פטור אם יאמר שתים הו"ל כופר הכל ואין אדם מעיז ולר"ע לא הוי עזות דמסייע ליה שטרא:

לעולם

**רבינו חננאל**

אלא אתיא מגלגול שבועה דעד אחד ונדחה גם זה. ואתינן לרבריה מפיו ועד אחד. ואמרי' הכי מה פיו שאין מחייבו קנס מחייבו שבועה עדים שמחייבין אותו קנס לא כל שכן. ופרכינן מה לפיו שכן אינו בהכחשה כמו שפירשנו למעלה. עד אחד יוכיח שכן ישנו בהכחשה ומחייבו שבועה. מה לעד אחד שכן על מה שהעיד עליו הוא נשבע תאמר בעדים שעל מה שכפר הוא נשבע פיו יוכיח שמשלם במה שהודה ונשבע על מה שכפר וחזר הדין וכו'. ופרכי' (מי) [מה] להצד השוה שבהן שכן לא הוחזק כפרן פי' אם כפר הלוה והעיד עליו עד אחד לא הוחזק כפרן שנאמר לא יקום עד אחד באיש וגו'. וכן אם כפר חזור והודה לא הוחזק כפרן כדרבא דאמר רבא אדם קרוב אצל עצמו ואין אדם משים עצמו רשע תאמר בעדים שאם כפר ובאו עדים והעידו עליו [שחייב] שהוחזק כפרן ונפסל. ודחי' לה הכי וכי מי שכפר במלוה נפסל והאמר רב חסדא הכופר במלוה כשר לעדות והא דר' חייא מלוה היא ונדחית זו הפירכא. וחזרנו לפרך פירכא אחרת. מה להצד השוה שבהן שכן אינו בתורת הזמה לו פיו כדאמרן למעלה. עד אחד אינו בתורת הזמה שהתורה אמרה ועשיתם לו כאשר זמם וגו' וכיון שאין עדות עד אחד אלא לשבועה ואי אפשר להשביע העד זו השבועה נדחית תורת הזמה מעליו שאין אתה יכול לקיים ועשיתם לו כאשר זמם וגו' וכדתנן [בריש מכות] מעידים אנו באיש פלו' שהוא בן גרושה וכו' ולעולם אין תורת הזמה אלא בשנים ועד שיזומו שניהם. בוא וראה כיון דאמר רב [שם ג ע"א] עד זומם משלם לפי חלקו מקשי' עליה והתניא אין משלמין ממון עד שיזומו שניהן ותריצנא להא דרב באומר העדנו והוזמנו בבית דינו של פלו' ונתחייבנו ממון כי האי גוונא משלם אבל כשיזום עד אחד אין שם תשלומין. ותנן נמי ור' שמעון אומר מה שנים אין נהרגין עד שיזומו שניהן אף שלשה עד שיזומו שלשתן. ופרקי' דלמא רבי חייא תורת הזמה לא פריך כלומר אין זו פירכא. פי' ר' חייא תורת הזמה לא פריך אמר לך רבי חייא לא נדחת תורת הזמה מעד אחד מפני כחו של עד אחד אלא מפני שעד אחד אינו בא אלא לשבועה וכשיזום אינו יכול להשביעו השבועה שזמם לעשות לאחיו וכיוצא בו נדחית תורת הזמה בשני עדים שהעידו על כהן שהוא בן גרושה וכו'. ואתינן ג) לאוקמה לדר' חייא כמתניתין ולא דמיא דהא מתני' כי היכי דאנן סהדי להאי דכל מה דתפיס בהאי טלית דידיה הוא הכי [נמי] אנן סהדי לאידך. ג) ותוב מתני' במאי דמסהדי (שהרי) [סהדי] דהוא דיליה עליה נשבע ותופס. לאפוקי דר' חייא דעל מה שכופר הוא נשבע. אלא אי איתמר והתנא שנאה על אידך דר' חייא דאמר מנה לי בידך והלה אומר אין לך בידי אלא נ' והילך חייב מאי טעמא דאע"ג דאמר ליה הילך כיון דעדיין לא נתן מודה מקצת הטענה הוא ותנא תונא שנים אוחזין בטלית וקתני ישבע והא אנן סהדי דבמאי דתפיס הילך הוא וקתני ישבע ש"מ דאפי' אמר ליה הילך מודה מקצת הטענה הוא וחייב. ורב ששת אמר הילך פטור דכיון דאמר ליה הילך כמאן דפרע להו דמי ובשאר הא לא מודה ליה ולא מידי הלכך לאו

**עין משפט נר מצוה**

יד א (מיי' פ"ב מהל' טוען ונטען הל' ג) טוש"ע ח"מ סימן נג ס"ד ועי' בב"י.

טו ב מיי' שם פ"א הל' ג סמג עשין לה טוש"ע ח"מ סי' פז סעיף א וסי' עה סעיף ז [רב אלפס כאן ופ"ו דשבועות דף דש]:

**מסורת הש"ס**

[קדושין ה:, כח. וש"נ], [לקמן ה:, בבא קמא ה:] [עיין שם] [שבועות ג:], ג) מכות ה:, ד) [נ"ע בגדות], ה) ס"א שאין משלם, ו) שייך לע"ב.

**הגהות הב"ח**

(א) גמ' דאנן סהדי להאי אנן סהדי להאי ואפילו:

**גליון הש"ס**

תוס' ד"ה הצד וכו' כופר הכל יוכיח. עיין תשובות מהרי"ט ח"א כלל דף טו ע"א ובתשובות גנת ורדים ח"מ כלל ב סימן קטע:

**הגהות הגר"א**

[א] רש"י ד"ה והילך לא הוצאתים כו'. נ"ב כל הר"ן חולק ע"ז וכתב דה מלוה להוצאה ניתנה ודוקא בפקדון הדין כן ע"ש: [ב] תוס' ד"ה ותנא כו' אך קשה כו'. נ"ב והרח"ה פרש דלאו משום הודאה חייב ליה מתמתני' דלמאי דנמי אין כח הודאה כלל לנ' דכל שאת דפטור דהילך ש"מ דמזומנים הוא ממאן דנקיט להו כאילו כבר דו ודה מתני' לדידה דומנין לממלוך ליומי כאילו בר מלקי ואין כאן שבועה מצע"ש וא"ל ד' א' דלא רש"י ד"ה והילך שכתב כל מקום כו' דלוקא בפקדון הדין כן (ועמ"ש בס כב"ק י"א).

**ליקוטי רש"י**

כופר במלוה. שבאו עדים והחזיקוהו בכפרן והעידו שהוא חייב לו [לקמן ה:]. ולא נשבע [ב"ק קה:]. כשר לעדות. דמלוה להוצאה ניתנה ואינה בידו ויש לומר דעתו שלתו עד שתשיג ידו [ב"ק שם]. בפקדון פסול. שיד ממונה הוא אלא שמשתמטי איכא ליה [שבועות מ:]. בפקדון פסול לעדות. דמאי להשתמוטי איכא הרי לא להוצאה ועבין הוא [לקמן שם]. כגון בריש שנים אוחזין (ה:) כגון דאמרי דהכל ההיא שעתא בידיה נקיט ליה ואפילו הכי נשבע דלא משתבע דלאו כפירה לי מלוה מה לי פקדון [ב"ק שם]. ואפי' נשבע למעשה דכפר יחשיד ליה אמוונה [שבועות שם].

**חשק שלמה על ר"ח** א) עי' בס"מ כאן שהעתיק לדברי רבינו בזה באריכות יותר. ב) נראה דל"ל ואתינן לדחוי להא דאוקמא לעיל לדברי חייא כמתני' דלא דמיא וכו'. ג) מדברי רבינו אלו נראה מוכח דהס' לו גי' אחרת בסוגיין דדחי דלא דמי למתני' נמי בזה דהתם במאי דמסהדי סהדי הוא נשבע וכו'.

**is as a result of** supported **claim and denial that [the litigants] come** before the court, **and [the defendant] swears.** אַף אֲנִי אָבִיא עֵדִים שֶׁעַל יְדֵי טַעֲנָה וּכְפִירָה הֵם בָּאִין וְנִשְׁבָּע – **So, too, do I present** the case of **witnesses, in which [the litigants] come** before the court **as a result of** supported **claim and denial, and** I derive that **[the defendant] swears.**[11]

However, this derivation from the common characteristic is challenged as well:

מָה לְהַצַּד הַשָּׁוֶה שֶׁבָּהֶן שֶׁכֵּן לֹא הוּחְזַק כַּפְרָן – **What** can you prove **from the common characteristic, when** in both cases **[the defendant] has not been established** to be **a denier** of his debt?[12] It is reasonable, therefore, to impose an oath on the defendant in those cases. תֹּאמַר בְּעֵדִים שֶׁכֵּן הוּחְזַק כַּפְרָן – **Can you say** the same **with regard to** the case of two **witnesses, where [the defendant] has been established** to be **a denier** of his debt?[13]

The Gemara answers by challenging the questioner's premise:

וּבְעֵדִים מִי הוּחְזַק כַּפְרָן – **And has [the defendant] been established to be a denier** of his debt **by witnesses** who contradict his denial? וְהָאָמַר רַב אִידִי בַּר אָבִין אָמַר רַב חִסְדָּא – **But Rav Idi bar Avin said in the name of Rav Chisda:** הַכּוֹפֵר בְּמִלְוֶה כָּשֵׁר לְעֵדוּת – **One who** falsely **denies a loan** obligation[14] **remains qualified to be a witness;** בְּפִקָּדוֹן פָּסוּל לְעֵדוּת – but one who falsely denies even part of **a deposit** obligation **is disqualified from being a witness.**[15] Thus, we see that one who falsely denies a loan obligation is not deemed an outright thief, and there is no reason, therefore, to refrain from imposing an oath obligation on him.[16]

Still, the Gemara objects:

אֶלָּא פָּרִיךְ הָכִי – **Rather, challenge** R' Chiya's law **thus:** מַה לְהַצַּד הַשָּׁוֶה שֶׁבָּהֶן שֶׁכֵּן אֵינָן בְּתוֹרַת הֲזָמָה – **What** can you prove **from the common characteristic** shared by personal admission and a solitary witness, **when they are not subject to the law of** ***hazamah*****?**[17] תֹּאמַר בְּעֵדִים שֶׁיֶּשְׁנָן בְּתוֹרַת הֲזָמָה – **Can you say** the same **with regard to** two **witnesses, who are subject to the law of** ***hazamah*****?**[18] How, then, can you derive the law of witnesses from the source laws of personal admission and a solitary witness?

The Gemara answers that this is not a valid objection to R' Chiya's law:

הָא לָא קַשְׁיָא רבי חייא תורת הֲזָמָה לֹא פָּרִיךְ – **This is not a difficulty,** for **R' Chiya does not see any objection** to his derivation on the basis of **the law of** ***hazamah*** (since the implementation of that law has no bearing on the ability of testimony to

NOTES

one . . ." introduces the derivation of צַד הַשָּׁוֶה, *the common characteristic.* This derivation presumes that a law found in two contexts results from characteristics common to both rather than from characteristics unique to each. Therefore, once we isolate the characteristics common to the two contexts, we can conclude that any other context possessing these characteristics is also subject to the common law, even if this third context differs from the first two in regard to their *unique* features.

Thus, the Gemara will proceed to isolate the characteristics common to the two contexts in which an oath is imposed on the defendant – the cases of personal admission and the testimony of a solitary witness.

11. The oath obligated by personal admission of part of the claim is not related to the unassailability of personal admission, since the assailable testimony of a solitary witness also obligates an oath. Neither can the oath obligated by a solitary witness be conceptually restricted to the portion of the claim about which he testifies, since no such restriction exists in the case of personal admission. The essential features of the contexts in which oaths are imposed, then, are that the defendant denies a claim which is supported to some degree (e.g. by personal admission or by a solitary witness). Since this same situation prevails in the case of witnesses who substantiate part of a plaintiff's claim, an oath obligation is generated there as well.

However, no oath obligation exists on a Biblical level when the defendant denies the claim in its entirety (see 3a note 23). Though the issue in that case as well is one of claim and denial, the claim in that case has not been supported at all. When the Gemara here speaks of "claim and denial," the reference is to a *supported* claim (*Tosafos*).

12. In the case of personal admission, it is simply the plaintiff's word against the defendant's. And even in the case of a solitary witness who supports the plaintiff's claim, it has not been *proven* that the defendant has falsely denied the debt, since the testimony of a solitary witness is not conclusive evidence.

13. In R' Chiya's case of two witnesses who substantiate half the claim that the defendant denies, their testimony is conclusive evidence that the defendant has lied at least in regard to half the claim. How, then, can we derive that an oath is imposed on an established denier of his debt from the law that an oath is imposed on persons who have never been proven to be liars? The established denier of his debt is one who has been willing to steal money from his creditor and his oath cannot be trusted! (*Rashi*; see also 3b note 1).

14. I.e. he denies owing a loan, but witnesses testify that he indeed owes it.

15. One who seeks to withhold for himself something owned by or owed to another person is no different than a thief and is Biblically disqualified from being a witness in any legal proceeding (see *Sanhedrin* 27a). However, Rav Chisda teaches that one who falsely denies owing a loan is not automatically considered a thief. For it is quite possible that he intends to repay the loan at some later date but does not have the wherewithal to do so at present. He therefore denies the loan in order to play for time. (Though it is wrong to deny a loan even as a delaying tactic, one who does so cannot be deemed a thief.) But there is no way to extenuate a custodian's false denial of a deposit entrusted to his care. His false denial can only be construed as an attempt to withhold it for himself; thus, he is deemed a thief and is subsequently disqualified from being a witness (*Rashi*).

[It is indeed possible for an honest custodian to lose a deposit and play for time so that he can locate it. Therefore, the Gemara below (5b) explains that Rav Chisda refers to a case in which witnesses testify that at the time the custodian denied the deposit, it was in his possession and its location was known to him (*Rashi*). In an analogous loan situation, however, the borrower would remain qualified to be a witness. Even if witnesses testify that the borrowed money was still in the borrower's possession at the time he denied the loan, his denial does not render him a thief. For the loaned money, which is meant to be spent by the borrower, immediately becomes the property of the borrower. The actual coins no longer belong to the lender, who now has only a debt owed to him (מִלְוָה לְהוֹצָאָה נִתְּנָה). Thus, it is possible that the borrower needs the money now and is playing for time. He is not thereby deemed a thief, since he is not withholding the creditor's actual money but merely trying to delay repayment of the debt (ibid.).]

16. Thus, the derivation from the common characteristic is restored. The fact that the defendant has been proven to be a liar in R' Chiya's case (which is not the situation in the cases of personal admission and a solitary witness) is not a reason to argue that no oath should be imposed. For R' Chiya speaks of a defendant who denies a *loan* obligation, and falsely denying a loan obligation does not undermine the person's credibility regarding testimony or oath.

17. As explained above [3b note 23], a defendant's personal admission cannot be discredited by witnesses who testify otherwise, even if they testify that the person was elsewhere at the time he claims to have incurred the obligation in a certain place [הֲזָמָה, *hazamah*]. And though the testimony of a solitary witness can be *discredited* through *hazamah,* he is not subject to the *law* of *hazamah,* which stipulates that a reciprocal penalty be imposed on the false witnesses [i.e. whatever penalty the false witnesses intended to impose on the defendant is imposed on them – see *Deuteronomy* 19:19] (*Rashi*). [Since the testimony of a solitary witness is insufficient to impose any penalty on the defendant (see 3b note 24), there is no intended penalty that can be reciprocally imposed on the witness. Thus, a solitary witness is not subject to the law of *hazamah* (see *Ketzos HaChoshen* 38:5)].

18. E.g. if the witnesses testify that the defendant owes fifty of the hundred *zuz* that he denies and their testimony is disproven through *hazamah,* the false witnesses must pay the defendant the fifty *zuz* that they sought to have him pay (*Rashi*).

תאמר בעדים שעל מה שכפר הוא נשבע אלא אמר רב פפא אתי מגלגול שבועה דעד אחד מה לגלגול שבועה דעד אחד שכן שבועה גוררת שבועה תאמר בעדים דממון קא מחייבי פיו יוכיח מה לפיו שכן אינו בהכחשה עד אחד יוכיח שישנו בהכחשה ומחייבו שבועה מה לעד אחד שכן על מה שמעיד הוא נשבע תאמר בעדים שעל מה שכפר הוא נשבע פיו יוכיח (א) וחזר הדין לא ראי זה כראי זה ולא ראי זה כראי זה הצד השוה שבהן שעל ידי טענה וכפירה הן באין ונשבע אף אני אביא עדים שעל ידי טענה וכפירה הם באין ונשבע מה להצד השוה שבהן שכן לא הוחזק כפרן תאמר בעדים שכן הוחזק כפרן ובעדים מי הוחזק כפרן (ב) והאמר רב אידי בר אבין אמר רב חסדא [א] הכופר במלוה כשר לעדות בפקדון פסול לעדות אלא פריך הכי מה להצד השוה שבהן שכן אינן בתורת הזמה תאמר בעדים שישנן בתורת הזמה הא לא קשיא רבי חייא תורת הזמה לא פריך אלא דקאמר ותנא תונא מי דמי התם למלוה אית ליה סהדי ללוה לית ליה סהדי דלא מסיק ליה ולא מידי דאי הוו ליה סהדי ללוה דלא מסיק ליה ולא מידי לא בעי רבי חייא לאשתבועי הכא כי היכי דאנן סהדי (א) בהאי אנן סהדי בהאי ואפילו הכי משתבעי אלא כי איתמר ותנא תונא אאידך דרבי חייא איתמר דאמר ר' חייא מנה לי בידך והלה אומר אין לך בידי אלא נ' זוז והילך חייב מאי טעמא הילך נמי כמודה מקצת הטענה דמי ותנא תונא שנים אוחזין בטלית והא הכא כיון דתפיס (ג) [אנן סהדי דמאי דתפיס] הילך הוא וקתני ישבע ורב ששת אמר [ב] הילך פטור מ"ט כיון דאמר ליה הילך הני זוזי דקא מודי בגוייהו כמאן דנקיט להו מלוה דמי באינך חמשים הא לא מודי הלכך ליכא הודאת מקצת הטענה ולרב ששת קשיא מתניתין אמר לך רב ששת מתניתין תקנת חכמים היא ואידך אין תקנת חכמים היא ומיהו אי אמרת בשלמא מדאורייתא הילך חייב מתקני רבנן שבועה כעין דאורייתא אלא אי אמרת מדאורייתא הילך פטור מתקני רבנן שבועה דליתא דכוותה בדאורייתא מיתיבי

סלעים

## רש"י

תאמר. בשבועה דעדים שאינו נשבע על מה שלא העידו ועל כפירתו הוא נשבע ולא אהעדאתן ומנין לך להחמיר כל כך: מגלגול שבועה דעד אחד. אם נתחייב לו שבועה על ידי עד אחד כדאמרינן והיתה עליו טענה אחרת שלא היתה מוטלת עליו שבועה מגלגלין אותה עם שבועה זאת ונשבע על שניהן דגלגול שבועה דאורייתא היא דילפינן לה בקדושין (דף כז:) מואמרה האשה אמן אמן הרי שעל מה שלא העיד העד הוא משביעו: שכן שבועה גוררת שבועה. עד לא חייבו שבועה אלא על מה שהעיד והשבועה גוררת שבועה תאמר בעדים הללו שהחמשים שהעידוהו הם מחייבין אותו לשלם ואין כאן שבועה לגרור על ידה שבועה על השאר: פיו יוכיח. מודה מקצת הטענה שעל מה שכופר ופיו לא הודה הוא נשבע: טענה וכפירה. זה טוען וזה כופר הן באין לדין: לא הוחזק כפרן. על מה שכפר אינו מוחזק כפרן שמא לא כיחש שהעד אינו נאמן להכחישו ולהחזיקו כפרן: תאמר בעדים. שמאחר שכפר הכל והם העידו על החמשים הוחזק כפרן ולא נאמר נאמניהו על השבועה: הכופר במלוה. בין על כולה בין על מקצת ובאו עדים והעידוהו עד שלא נשבע: כשר לעדות. ולא אמרינן גזלן הוא והתורה אמרה (שמות כג) אל תשת רשע עד דכיון דמלוה להוצאה נתנה דלמא צריך להוציאה וסבר עד דהוה לי [זוזי] ופרענא ליה ואי מודינא ליה השתא יתבעני מיד אבל הכופר בפקדון אפי' על מקצת ובאו עדים והעידוהו פסול לעדות דמאי הוה ליה גבי פקדון לאשתמוטי נפשיה ושמא תאמר אבד ממנו ואשתמיט ליה עד דמשכח ליה לקמן בפירקין (דף ה:) מוקמינן בדאתו סהדי ואמרי ההיא שעתא בידיה נקיט ליה: בתורת הזמה. לשלם קנס דכאשר זמם דעד אחד שהוזם פטור ופיו גבי הודאה כל שכן דלא שייכא הזמה כלל: תאמר בעדים. אם הוזמו בחמשים שהעידו משלמין ממון: תורת הזמה לא פריך. אינה חשובה לו פירכא דכיון דעד אחד ישנו בהזמה ליבטל עדותו (ד) בעדות שני עדים אם הוה לן למימר בעדים משום דישנן בהזמה לא יחייבוהו שבועה הוה לן למימר נמי בעד אחד לא יחייבהו שבועה דהא ישנו בהזמה ליבטל עדותו ואי משום דאין משלם קנס אין בזו יפוי כח להאמין עדותו: אלא דקאמר ותנא תונא. אלא אם יש לך להשיב על דברי רבי חייא כך יש לך להשיב דקאמר ותנא תונא והביא ראיה לדבריו ממשנתינו מי דמי: התם. בדרבי חייא: למלוה אית ליה סהדי. דמסיק ביה חמשים: ללוה לית ליה סהדי. באינך חמשים שאינו חייב לו עליה: אי הוה ליה כו'. כגון אילו העידו העדים חמשים חייב וחמשים פרע בכה"ג לא הוה אמר ר' חייא דצריך לישבע על השאר: מתני' כי היכי דאנן סהדי להאי. דחליה שלו: אנן סהדי להאי. דחליה שלו ולמה הצריכוהו חכמים שבועה ש"מ טעמא לאו משום מודה מקצת הטענה הוא כר' חייא ואינה שבועה דאורייתא אלא תקנת חכמים שלא יהא כל אחד הולך כו': והילך. לא [א] הוצאתים והן שלך בכ"מ שהם: חייב. לישבע על השאר ולא אמרינן הני דקמודי ליה בגוייהו הואיל ואיתנהו בעינייהו כמאן דנקיט להו דמי אלא כשאר מודה במקצת הוא וחייב: ותנא תונא כו'. קס"ד דלר' חייא טעמא דמתני' משום דאנן סהדי דמאי דתפיס דיליה הוא והוי כמנה לי בידך והלה אמר אין לך בידי כלום והעדים מעידים אותו שיש לו חמשים וכי אידך דרבי חייא דמחייב ליה שבועה דאורייתא: והא הכא. דהך העדאת עדים אנן סהדי דמאי דתפיס האי הילך הוא שהרי בפניו הוא: וקתני. דמחייב שבועה אשארא וה"ה להודאה במקצת: תקנת חכמים היא. ולא משום העדאת עדים ודפרכינן לעיל כי היכי דאנן סהדי להאי אנן סהדי להאי: אי אמרת בשלמא הילך מדאורייתא חייב. כלומר גבי שבועה דאורייתא כגון בהודאה במקצת:

## תוספות

**עד** אחד יוכיח שישנו בהכחשה ובהזמה. שפיר גרס הכא ובהזמה כיון שע"י הזמה דבורו בטל ואין להקשות מה לפיו שכן אינו משלם בהזמה תאמר בעדים שמשלמין בהזמה ואז לא יכול לומר עד אחד יוכיח (ה) שמשלם כי מה שהעד אינו משלם כשהוא מוזם אינו חומרא אלא לפי שבעדותו אינו מחייבו ממון לכך הואיל ודיבורו בטל חשיב ישנו בהזמה ובסמוך על מה הלד פרכינן ליה משום דעל מה הלד פרכינן פירכא כל דהו ורבי חייא אפי' על מה הלד לא פריך ליה משום דמה שאינו משלם העד כשמוזם זהו גריעותו לפי שלא היה כח בעדותו לחייב ממון:

**הצד** השוה [שבהן] שע"י טענה כו'. וא"ת (ו) כופר הכל יוכיח שע"י טענה וכפירה פטור ויש לומר דבהלד השוה שבהן יש טענה חשובה דכשמודה מקצת או עד מכחישו נראה דמשקר ולכך יש שבועה:

**ותנא** תונא אאידך דר' חייא. אנן סהדי דמאי דתפיס האי כו' פרש"י כיון דהוי כהעדאת עדים משתבע מדרבי חייא קמייתא וקשה כיון דלא מצי לאוכוחי הך ברייתא דהילך אלא מכח קמייתא לימא ותנא תונא אקמייתא לכך י"ל דאנן סהדי לאו דוקא דמאי דתפיס מחשבינן ליה השתא טפי מהעדאת עדים וחשיב כאילו מודה ליה דדידיה הוא אך [ב] קשה דמ"מ איכא למיפרך דמתני' כי היכי דהאי מודה להאי האי נמי מודה להאי ואפ"ה קמשתבעי כדפריך אקמייתא ומאי תיקן וי"ל דהשתא נמי מוכח מכח טעמא דבסמוך אי הילך פטור לא הוי מתקני רבנן שבועה דליכא דכוותה באורייתא אבל לרבי חייא קמייתא כי נמי בהעדאת עדים פטור מתקני רבנן שבועה במתני' דחשיב הודאה במאי דתפיס חבריה ודוחק דלפ"ז הא דלא קאמר ותנא תונא אקמייתא משום דמאי דתפיס חשיב כהודאה וזו לא היתה פירכתו למעלה אלא מטעם כי היכי דאנן סהדי להאי כו':

**ורב** ששת אמר הילך פטור. נראה שהלכה כרב ששת דבפ' השואל (לקמן דף ק.) גבי עבד קטן פריך ועוד הילך הוא אך בספר חפץ משמע דהילך חייב [וע' תוס' ב"ב קכח: ד"ה הלכתא]:

(ו) **וש"מ** דהילך פטור. וא"ת יהא נאמן בשלש דמיגו דבעי אמר שתים וי"ל כיון דהילך פטור אם יאמר שתים הו"ל כופר הכל ואין אדם מעיז ולר"ע לא הוי עזות דמסייע ליה שטרא:

לעולם

## רבינו חננאל

אלא תיתי מגלגול שבועה דעד אחד ונדחה גם זה. ואתינן לרבויה מפיו ועד אחד. ואמרי' הכי מה פיו שאין מחייבו קנס מחייבו שבועה עדים שמחייבין אותו קנס לא כל שכן. ופרכינן מה לפיו שכן אינו בהכחשה כמו שפירשנו למעלה. עד אחד יוכיח שכן ישנו בהכחשה ומחייבו שבועה. מה לעד אחד שכן על מה שהעיד עליו הוא נשבע תאמר בעדים שעל מה שכפר הוא נשבע פיו יוכיח שמשלם במה שהודה ונשבע על מה שכפר וחזר הדין וכו'. ופרכי' (מי) [מה] להצד השוה שבהן שכן לא הוחזק כפרן פי' אם כפר הלוה והעיד עליו עד אחד לא הוחזק כפרן שנאמר לא יקום עד אחד באיש וגו'. וכן אם כפר וחזר והודה לא הוחזק כפרן כדרבא דאמר רבא אדם קרוב אצל עצמו ואין אדם משים עצמו רשע תאמר בעדים שאם כפר ובאו עדים והעידו עליו [שחייב] שהוחזק כפרן ונפסל. ודחי' לה הכי וכי מי שכפר במלוה נפסל והאמר רב חסדא הכופר במלוה כשר לעדות והא דר' חייא מלוה היא ונדחית זו הפירכא. וחזרנו לפרך פירכא אחרת. מה להצד השוה שבהן שכן אינו בתורת הזמה א) פיו כדאמרן למעלה. עד אחד אינו בתורת הזמה שהתורה אמרה ועשיתם לו כאשר וגו' וכיון שאין עדות עד אחד אלא לשבועה ואי אפשר להשביע העד זו השבועה נדחת תורת הזמה מעליו שאין אתה יכול לקיים ועשיתם לו כאשר זמם וגו' וכדתנן [בריש מכות] מעידים אנו באיש פלו' שהוא בן גרושה וכו' ולעולם אין תורת הזמה אלא בשנים ועד שיזומו שניהם. בוא וראה כיון דאמר רב [שם ג ע"א] עד זומם משלם לפי חלקו מקשי' עליה והתניא אין משלמין ממון עד שיזומו שניהן ותריצנא להא דרב באומר העדנו והוזמנו בבית דינו של פלו' ונתחייבנו ממון כי האי גוונא משלם אבל כשיזום עד אחד אין שם תשלומין. ותנן נמי ור' שמעון אומר מה שנים אין נהרגין עד שיזומו שניהן אף שלשה עד שיזומו שלשתן. ופרקי' דלמא רבי חייא תורת הזמה לא פריך כלומר אין זו פירכא. פי' ר' חייא תורת הזמה לא פריך אמר לך רבי חייא לא נדחת תורת הזמה מעד אחד מפני כחו של עד אחד אלא מפני שעד אחד אינו בא אלא לשבועה וכשיזום אינו יכול להשביעו השבועה שזמם לעשות לאחיו וכיוצא בו נדחית תורת הזמה בשני עדים שהעידו על כהן שהוא בן גרושה וכו'. ואתינן ג) לאוקמה לדר' חייא כמתניתין ולא דמיא דהא מתני' כי היכי דאנן סהדי להאי דכל מה דתפיס בהאי טלית דידיה הוא הכי [נמי] אנן סהדי לאידך. ג) ותוב מתני' במאי דמסהדי (שהרי) [סהדין] דהוא דיליה עליה נשבע ותופס. לאפוקי דר' חייא דעל מה שכופר הוא נשבע. אלא אי איתמר והתנא שנאה על אידך דר' חייא דאמר מנה לי בידך והלה אומר אין לך בידי אלא נ' והילך חייב מאי טעמא דאע"ג דאמר ליה הילך כיון דעדיין לא נתן מודה מקצת הטענה הוא ותנא תונא שנים אוחזין בטלית וקתני ישבע והא אנן סהדי דבמאי דתפיס הילך הוא וקתני ישבע ש"מ דאפי' אמר ליה הילך מודה מקצת הטענה הוא וחייב. ורב ששת אמר הילך פטור דכיון דאמר ליה הילך כמאן דפרע להו דמי ובשאר הא לא מודה ליה ולא מידי הלכך לאו

## עין משפט נר מצוה

יד א (מיי' פ"ב מהל' טוען ונטען הל' ג) טוש"ע ח"מ סימן לב ס"ד ועי' בב"י:

טו ב מיי' שם פ"א הל' ג סמג עשין לה טוש"ע ח"מ סי' פז סעיף א וסי' עה סעיף ו [רב אלפס כאן ופ"ו דשבועות דף לח]:

## מסורת הש"ס

[קדושין כז:, כח. וש"נ], [לקמן ה:], בבא קמא ה: [עיין שם] [שבועות :], ג) מהרש"ל, ד) [צ"ל גדות], ה) ס"א שאין משלם, ו) שייך לע"ב.

## הגהות הב"ח

(א) גמ' דאנן סהדי להאי אנן סהדי להאי ואפילו:

## גליון הש"ס

תוס' ד"ה הצד וכו' ופר הכל יוכיח. עיין שובות מהריב"ל ח"א כלל דף טו ע"א ובתשובות ניס מאירות ח"ב סימן קסט:

## הגהות הגר"א

[א] רש"י ד"ה והילך א הוצאתים כו'. נ"ב כל הר"ן חולק ע"ז וכתב הא מלוה להוצאה ניתנה יוקא בפקדון הדין כן יעמ"ש רבינו בח"מ סי' "ז ס"ק י"ז): [ב] תוס' "ה ותנא כו' אך שה כו'. נ"ב והרז"ה פרש דלאו משום הודאה סייע ליה ממתני' דודאי תני' אין בה הודאה כלל לא דרב ששת דפוטר הילך ס"ל דמזומנים בידו מאן דנקיט להו כאילו כבר ידו והא מתני' דבידים מזומנין לחלוק ליחזי כאילו בר חלקו ואין כאן שבועה המע"ה וע"ל ו' א' ודלא רש"י ד"ה והילך שכתב כל מקום כו' דדוקא פקדון הדין כן (ועמ"ש שם בס"ק י"א):

## ליקוטי רש"י

הכופר במלוה. שבאו עדים והחזיקוהו בכפרן שהעידוהו שהוא חייב לו [לקמן ה:]. ולא נשבע באו עדים [ב"ק קה:]. כשר לעדות. דמלוה להוצאה ניתנה ואינה נכסיו בידו ורוצה לדחותו עד שתשיג ידו [ב"ק שם]. ולא אמרן חשיד אממונא הוא אלא אשתמוטי ליה [שבועות מ:]. בפקדון פסול לעדות. דמאי אישתמוטי איכא הרי לא ניתן להוצאה ובעין הוא כו' [לקמן שם]. מוקמינן לה בריש שנים אוחזין (ה:) כגון דאמרי סהדי דההיא שעתא דכפר ליה נקיט בידיה מפסיל אע"ג דלא אישתבע דאי באישתבע מה לי מלוה מה לי פקדון [ב"ק שם]. ואפי' לא נשבע דמשעה דכפר איחשיד ליה אממונא [שבועות שם].

---

חשק שלמה על ר"ח א) עי' בש"מ כאן שהעתיק לדברי רבינו בזה באריכות יותר. ב) נראה דצ"ל ואתינן לאחוי להא דאוקמא לעיל לדברי חייא כמתני' דלא דמיא וכו'. ג) מדברי רבינו אלו נראה מוכח דהי' לו גי' אחרת בסוגיין דדחי דלא דמי למתני' נמי בזה דהתם במאי דמסהדי סהדי הוא נשבע וכו'.

תֹּאמַר בְּעֵדִים שֶׁעַל מַה שֶּׁכָּפַר הוּא נִשְׁבָּ – **Can you say** the same **of** vo **witnesses,** in whose case you seek to prove **that [the** efendant] **must swear regarding that which he denied?** How ın the obligation of one form of oath be derived from the ɔligation of a different form?[1]

The Gemara concedes this point and must therefore modify its revious answer:

אֶלָּא אָמַר רַב פָּפָּ – **Rather, Rav Pappa said,** אָתֵי מִגִּלְגּוּל שְׁבוּעָה דְּעֵד אֶ – **[R' Chiya's law] is derived** through a *kal vachomer* om **the devolved oath** generated by the testimony **of a solitary** itness.[2] If the testimony of a solitary witness (which cannot ɔligate the payment of money) can create (through devolvement) ıe obligation to take an oath denying an unsubstantiated claim, ıen certainly the testimony of witnesses (which *can* obligate the ayment of money) can create the obligation to take an oath enying an unsubstantiated claim.[3]

The Gemara challenges this derivation as well:

מַה לְּגִלְגּוּל שְׁבוּעָה דְּעֵד אֶחָד שֶׁכֵּן שְׁבוּעָה גּוֹרֶרֶת שְׁבוּעָ – **What** can ɔu prove **from the devolved oath of a solitary witness, where** ıe **oath draws another oath?** תֹּאמַר בְּעֵדִים דְּמָמוֹן קָא מְחַיְּיבֵי – **an you say** the same **about** two **witnesses, who** initially **bligate** the payment of **money** and not an oath?[4]

The Gemara is forced to concede that Rav Pappa's shift to eriving his law from the devolved oath of a solitary witness does ɔt improve matters. However, we can return to the original proof rawn from the basic oath generated by the solitary witness.[5] nd as regards the previous objection, that the solitary witness enerates an oath regarding what he testifies, whereas R' Chiya ishes to derive the greater ability of witnesses to generate an ıth regarding that which they did *not* testify, we can answer:

פִּיו יוֹכִ – **Let** the oath generated by the admission of **his own** ıouth **demonstrate** that the portion of the claim the oath involves is not an essential factor. For one's own admission indeed creates an oath obligation in regard to the portion of the claim that he has *not* admitted.[6]

Now, one could object, as above:

מַה לְּפִיו שֶׁכֵּן אֵינוֹ בְּהַכְחָשָׁה – **What** can you prove **from** the admission of **his own mouth, which is not subject to contradiction** by witnesses? Perhaps it is that unassailable quality of admission – not shared by the testimony of witnesses – that enables admission to generate an oath obligation.[7] – ? –

To this we would say:

עֵד אֶחָד יוֹכִיחַ שֶׁיֶּשְׁנוֹ בְּהַכְחָשָׁה וּמְחַיְּיבוֹ שְׁבוּעָה – **Let** the case of **the solitary witness demonstrate** that the unassailability of admission is not essential to creating the oath obligation; **for [the testimony of the solitary witness] is subject to contradiction** by other witnesses, **yet it obligates [the defendant] to take an oath** countering it.

Now, if you object, as above:

מַה לְּעֵד אֶחָד שֶׁכֵּן עַל מַה שֶּׁמֵּעִיד הוּא נִשְׁבָּע – **What** can you prove from the case **of the solitary witness, where [the defendant] must swear regarding that which [the solitary witness] testifies?** תֹּאמַר בְּעֵדִים שֶׁעַל מַה שֶּׁכָּפַר הוּא נִשְׁבָּע – **Can you say** the same **of** two **witnesses,** in whose case you seek to prove **that [the defendant] must swear regarding that which he denied?**[8]

Again we would counter:

פִּיו יוֹכִיחַ – **Let** the oath generated by the admission of **his own mouth demonstrate** that the portion of the claim the oath involves is not an essential factor (as explained above), וְחָזַר הַדִּין – **but the argument would repeat** itself.[9]

In the final analysis:

לֹא רְאִי זֶה כִּרְאִי זֶה וְלֹא רְאִי זֶה כִּרְאִי זֶה – **The nature of this** case **is not like the nature of that** case, **and the nature of that** case **is not like the nature of this** case.[10] הַצַּד הַשָּׁוֶה שֶׁבָּהֶן שֶׁעַל יְדֵי טַעֲנָה וּכְפִירָה הֵן בָּאִין וְנִשְׁבָּע – **Their common characteristic is that it**

NOTES

In the case of the solitary witness, the witness has offered testimony erifying a claim against the defendant. Mere denial by the defendant is sufficient; the denial of the witness-supported claim must now be ade under oath. However, in the case of witnesses who verify half a aintiff's claim, the second half of that claim has not been verified at all. ow can R' Chiya derive the more stringent law that the defendant ust deny under oath the *unsupported* second half of a claim? A *kal chomer* can prove only that a law found in the lenient case must *also* ɔply in the stringent case. But a *kal vachomer* cannot prove that a law und in the lenient case must apply *in a more stringent form* in the ringent case [דַּיּוֹ לַבָּא מִן הַדִּין לִהְיוֹת כַּנִּדּוֹן] (*Ritva* based on *Rashi*).

The rule of "devolvement of oath" states that once an obligation to vear is established in regard to a specific claim, the defendant can be ade to swear in regard to other claims the plaintiff has against him as ell, even if those other claims would not in themselves create an ɔligation for the defendant to swear. [The Gemara in *Kiddushin* (27b) erives this Biblical rule from Scripture.]

For example, a plaintiff presents two claims against a defendant, one aim unsupported and the other claim supported by the testimony of a litary witness. Since the testimony of the solitary witness obligates the efendant to swear in denial of that claim [as explained above], the efendant can be made to swear in denial of the unsupported claim as ell (*Rashi*).

Viz. in R' Chiya's case, where witnesses confirm half the claim that ıe defendant denies entirely. Their substantiation of half the claim ɔligates the defendant to take the *modeh bemiktzas* oath regarding the ısubstantiated second half.

The testimony of a solitary witness never generates an oath obligation regard to an unsupported claim. The solitary witness merely creates ı oath obligation in regard to the *supported* claim, and it is that oath ligation which thereupon extends to encompass the unsupported aim. We cannot, therefore, derive that two witnesses who support half claim generate an oath obligation in regard to the unsupported second half of that claim. For their testimony never imposed an oath obligation regarding the first half of the claim, but rather actual payment. Thus, there is no oath obligation generated by witnesses that can be extended to claims beyond what they testify (*Rashi*).

5. This is how the Gemara must apparently be explained according to our versions of the text below. See *Ritva* at length.

6. Earlier the Gemara had rejected the possibility of deriving R' Chiya's law from the law of a solitary witness, since a solitary witness creates an oath obligation only in regard to what he has confirmed. The Gemara now counters that this should not be considered an essential feature of the requirement to swear, since one's own admission, which also creates the obligation to swear, indeed does so in regard to the portion of the claim that has *not* been confirmed by the admission.

Thus, we revert to deriving R' Chiya's law by *kal vachomer* from the law of a solitary witness. As to the objection that a solitary witness obligates an oath only in regard to what he confirms, the law that one's own admission obligates the oath of *modeh bemiktzas* demonstrates that this is not a critical factor.

7. This is the same objection raised by the Gemara above (3b) against the first *kal vachomer* adduced to prove R' Chiya's law.

8. See above, note 1.

9. I.e. you could object again that personal admission is not subject to contradiction and thereby begin the same cycle of arguments and counter-arguments all over. Thus, we have not succeeded in our efforts to derive R' Chiya's law from either personal admission or from the testimony of a solitary witness. For each case has a feature not shared by the case of witnesses, and those respective features might be related to the capacity to create an oath obligation.

10. I.e. the special feature of personal admission (that it is not subject to contradiction) differs from the special feature of a solitary witness (that his testimony obligates an oath in regard to what he has testified) and vice versa.

The expression "the nature of this one is not like the nature of that has the strength **that it is not subject to** being impugned **by** the **contradiction** of witnesses[22] **or by *hazamah?***[23] **תֹּאמַר בְּעֵדִים שֶׁיֶּשְׁנָן בְּהַכְחָשָׁה וּבַהֲזָמָה – Can you say** the same **of witnesses, who are subject to** being impugned **by** the **contradiction** of other witnesses **or by *hazamah?*** In this respect, the strength of personal admission exceeds that of witnesses. How, then, can you adduce a *kal vachomer?*

The Gemara is forced to concede the validity of this objection and must resort to a different argument to prove R' Chiya's law that the partial corroboration of a claim by witnesses requires the defendant to state his continued denial of the remainder of the claim under oath:

**אֶלָּא אָתְיָא מֵעֵד אֶחָד – Rather, [R' Chiya's law] emerges** throu[g] a *kal vachomer* **from** the law of **a solitary witness:** [מ]ה עֵד אֶחָד שֶׁאֵין מְחַיְּיבוֹ מָמוֹן מְחַיְּיבוֹ שְׁבוּעָה – **If a solitary witness, wh**[o] **cannot obligate him** to pay **money, can obligate him** to take a[n] **oath,**[24] עֵדִים שֶׁמְּחַיְּיבִין אוֹתוֹ מָמוֹן אֵינוֹ דִין שֶׁמְּחַיְּיבִין אוֹתוֹ שְׁבוּעָה then two **witnesses, who can obligate him** to pay **money,**[25] **is** [it] **not certain that they obligate him** to take **an oath,** i.e. wh[en] they substantiate part of the claim that he denies?

The Gemara challenges this new *kal vachomer* as well: **מַה לְּעֵד אֶחָד שֶׁכֵּן עַל מַה שֶּׁהוּא מֵעִיד הוּא נִשְׁבָּע – What** can you pro[ve] from the case of **a solitary witness, where [the defendant] mu**[st] **swear regarding that which [the solitary witness] testifies?**[26]

NOTES

22. If a person has confessed to owing a debt, he is obligated to pay that debt even if witnesses testify that his confession was untrue. For the confession of a person in monetary matters is like the testimony of a hundred witnesses (*Rashi*; see above, note 7). That is, a person's confession *even when it contradicts witnesses* is like the *uncontested* testimony of one hundred witnesses (*Ritva*).

23. *Hazamah* is the discrediting of a pair of witnesses by the testimony of a second pair that places the first pair elsewhere at the time of the alleged incident. Unlike simple contradiction by a second pair (in which case we cannot determine which pair tells the truth, and the two testimonies neutralize each other), the Torah decrees in the case of *hazamah* that the testimony of the discrediting witnesses prevail over the denial of the first pair (see *Makkos* chapter 1).

A defendant's confession, however, cannot be negated through *hazamah*. Thus, if a person confesses to having incurred a debt in a specific place on a specific date, he is obligated to pay that debt even if witnesses testify that he was elsewhere at the time of the alleged incurrence of debt (*R' Chananel;* cf. *Shitah Mekubetzes*).

24. The testimony of a solitary witness cannot obligate a defendant t[o] pay, but it does Biblically obligate him to support his denial with an oat[h]. Thus, if a plaintiff claims that the defendant owes him a sum of mone[y] and produces a solitary witness who supports that claim, the defendan[t] must contradict the solitary witness with an oath in order to avoi[d] paying the claim. This law of a solitary witness is indicated in the vers[e] (*Deuteronomy* 19:15): לֹא־יָקוּם עֵד אֶחָד בְּאִישׁ לְכָל־עָוֺן וּלְכָל־חַטָּאת, *A solitar*[*y*] *witness shall not stand against a man for any crime or for any sin* [i.e. the testimony of a solitary witness shall be insufficient to impose an[y] bodily or monetary punishment for any type of crime or obligation (se[e] *Rashi* ad loc.)]. The Gemara infers: *It is for any crime or for any sin* th[at] a solitary witness not stand, but he does stand to require denial unde[r] oath (*Rashi* from *Shevuos* 40a).

25. [As the verse (ibid.) concludes: *by the word of two witnesses . . . sha*[*ll*] *a matter stand.*]

26. As noted above, the contradicting testimony of a solitary wi[t]ness obligates the defendant to take an oath denying the witnes[s'] assertion.

עין משפט
נר מצוה

יא א מיי׳ פ״ו מהלכות טוען ונטען הל׳ ג טוש״ע ח״מ סימן פא סעיף ח:
יב ב מיי׳ פ״א מהלכות גניבה הל׳ ה ופ״ג שם הל׳ ז ופ״א מהלכות טוען ונטען הל׳ טו יז טוש״ע ח״מ סי׳ פז סעיף כו:
יג ג מיי׳ פ״ג מהלכות שגגות הלכה א סמג עשין ריג:

והאי בכוליה בעי דלודי ליה והאי דלא אודי אשתמוטי הוא דקא מישתמט מיניה סבר עד דהוו לי זוזי ופרענא ליה ואמר רחמנא רמי שבועה עליה כי היכי דלודי ליה בכוליה אבל העדאת עדים דליכא למימר הכי אימא לא קמ״ל ק״ו ומאי ק״ו ומה פיו שאין מחייבו ממון מחייבו שבועה עדים שמחייבין אותו ממון אינו דין שמחייבין אותו שבועה ופיו אין מחייבו ממון והא (א) [א]הודאת בעל דין כמאה עדים דמי מאי ממון קנס ומה פיו [ב]שאין מחייבו קנס מחייבו שבועה עדים שמחייבין אותו קנס אינו דין שמחייבין אותו שבועה מה לפיו שכן מחייבו קרבן תאמר בעדים שאין מחייבין אותו קרבן הא לא קשיא רבי חייא כרבי מאיר סבירא ליה דאמר עדים מחייבין אותו קרבן מק״ו [ג]דתנן אמרו לו שנים אכלת חלב והוא אומר לא אכלתי רבי מאיר מחייב וחכמים [ג]פוטרים אמר רבי מאיר אם הביאוהו שנים לידי מיתה חמורה לא יביאוהו לידי קרבן הקל אמרו לו מה אם ירצה לומר מזיד הייתי יפטר אלא מה לפיו שכן מחייבו אשם היינו קרבן אלא מה לפיו שכן מחייבו חומש הא לא קשיא רבי חייא כרבי מאיר סבירא ליה כי היכי דמחייב ליה קרבן מק״ו מחייב ליה חומש מקל וחומר אלא מה לפיו שכן אינו בהכחשה ובהזמה תאמר בעדים שישנן בהכחשה ובהזמה אלא אתיא מעד אחד ומה עד אחד שאין מחייבו ממון מחייבו שבועה עדים שמחייבין אותו ממון אינו דין שמחייבין אותו שבועה מה לעד אחד שכן על מה שהוא מעיד הוא נשבע

**רש״י**

והאי בכוליה בעי דלודי כו׳. וכ״ת מגו דחשיד אממונא חשיד אשבועתא ולא נרמי עליה שבועתא לא חשיד אממונא לפי שברצונו היה מודה בכולו אלא שאין בידו לפרוע וסבר עד דהוי לי [זוזי] ופרענא ליה: דליכא למימר הכי. שהרי כפר בכולו ונימא מגו דחשיד אממונא חשיד אשבועתא: פיו שאינו מחייבו ממון. בהודאתו ולקמיה מפרש לה: מחייבו שבועה. על השאר: עדים שמחייבין [אותו] ממון. במה שהעידו: אינו דין שיחייבוהו שבועה. על השאר: הודאת בעל דין כמאה עדים. ברייתא היא בתוספתא דבבא מליעא בפ׳ ראשון: פיו אינו מחייבו קנס. דילפינן (ב״ק דף עה.) מקראי דמודה בקנס פטור אשר ירשיעון אלהים פרט למרשיע את עצמו: פיו מחייבו קרבן. דכתיב והתודה אשר חטא והביא (ויקרא ה): עדים אין מחייבין אותו קרבן. אם (א) [ג]מכחישין אותו דכתיב (שם ד) או הודע אליו ולא שיודיעוהו אחרים: אמרו לו שנים אכלת חלב. שוגג: והוא אומר לא [אכלתי]. פטור שהיה יכול לומר מזיד הייתי ויפטר מן הקרבן אף כשאמר לא אכלתי פטור דמה לו לשקר: חומש ואשם. אם נשבע וכפר ממון והודה כתיב או מכל אשר ישבע עליו לשקר וגו׳ (שם ה): אינו בהכחשה ובהזמה. אם הודה לו במנה ובאו עדים והכחישוהו לומר אינך חייב לו כלום אינו נפטר בכך דהודאת בעל דין כמאה עדים: שישנן בהכחשה ובהזמה. שאם באו שנים עדים והכחישום או הזימום אין זה משלם ממון על פיהם: מחייבו שבועה. טענו חבירו מנה לי בידך והוא אומר אין לך בידי כלום ועד אחד מעידו שהוא חייב לו הרי זה נשבע להכחיש את העד דכתיב (דברים יט) לא יקום עד אחד באיש וגו׳ לכל עון ולכל חטאת הוא דאינו קם אבל לשבועה קם (שבועות דף מ.): מה לעד אחד. כלומר היכי ילפת שבועה דשנים משבועה דעד אחד מה לעד אחד שכן על מה שהעד מעיד הוא נשבע להכחישו:
תאמר

**תוספות**

בכוליה בעי דלודי ליה. מה שפירש רש״י כיון דחשיד אממונא היכי נשבע נימא מגו דחשיד אממונא חשיד אשבועתא ומשני דמשתמיט ולא חשיד ועל זה תימה דהא מסיק לקמן (דף ו.) דחשיד אממונא לא חשיד אשבועתא ואין לומר דהיינו מדרבנן לפי שראו שהיתה שבועה חמורה עליהם אבל מדאורייתא חשוד לזה דהא לקמן מייתי מרב נחמן דמשביעין אותו שלש שבועות ואחד מהן שלא שלחתי בו יד ומשמע בהגוזל קמא (ב״ק דף קו: ושם) דהוי דאורייתא וכן בנסכא דר׳ אבא (שבועות דף לב:) משמע דאי אמר לא חטפתי היה נשבע להכחיש את העד שבועה דאורייתא מדאמר מתוך שאינו יכול לישבע משלם דאשבועה דרבנן לא אמר הכי לכן י״ל ובכוליה בעי דלודי ליה כלומר מאחר דאין מעיז א״כ אמת הוא שאין חייב לו יותר ולמה ישבע יהא נאמן במגו דאי בעי כופר הכל ומשני דאין זה העזה דאשתמוטי קמשתמיט ואם תאמר כופר הכל נמי אשתמוטי קא משתמיט ואינו העזה כדאמרי׳ בפ׳ שבועת הדיינין (שבועות דף מ:) אמר רב נחמן כופר הכל משביעין אותו שבועת היסת משום חזקה דאין אדם תובע אלא א״כ יש לו עליו ופריך אדרבה אין אדם מעיז פניו בפני ב״ח ומשני אשתמוטי קא משתמיט וי״ל דמ״מ העזה יש יותר בכופר הכל מבכופר חצי וליכא מגו: אבל העדאת עדים דליכא למימר. כל כך משתמיט כיון שכפר הכל אימא כיון דחשוד הוא לגזול חשוד נמי אשבועתא קמ״ל ק״ו דלא הוי גזלן בהכי דאשתמוטי קא משתמיט דהכופר במלוה כשר לעדות ואע״ג דאמרי׳ לקמן (דף ו.) דלא אמרינן מגו דחשיד כו׳ מ״מ גם התנא אשמעינן דלא אמרינן מק״ו מפיו ועד אחד ואם תאמר אמאי אצטריך לטעמא דאשתמוטי לימא אי לאו ק״ו ה״א הודאת פיו גדולה מהעדאת עדים משום שכן אינו בהכחשה ובהזמה כדפריך לקמן ולקמן נמי הוה ליה למפרך מה לפיו שכן משתמיט וי״ל דהכא דאתא לפרושי דהודאת פיו גדולה מהעדאת עדים ניחא ליה למינקט טעמא דמשתמיט דסברא הוא דמטעם זה ישבע בהודאת פיו ולא בהעדאת עדים וחומר שאינו בהכחשה והזמה ניחא ליה למנקט לקמן לסתור ק״ו שכן דרך הגמרא למפרך פירכא על קל וחומר ולא מסברא לכך לא מייתי לקמן סברא דמשתמיט: מה לפיו שכן מחייבו קרבן תאמר בעדים כו׳. פי׳ שכן מחייבו קרבן אפילו העדים מכחישין אותו ואומרים לאו חלב הוה אלא שומן דאי אין העדים מכחישין אותו היכי קאמר תאמר בעדים כו׳ עדים נמי מחייבין אותו קרבן אם אינו מכחישן ואפילו עד אחד אם אינו מכחישו מחייבו קרבן וחדא הסוגיא סוברת כלישנא דפרק אמרו לו (כריתות דף יב. ושם) דמפרש טעמייהו דרבנן דלקמן דאמרו לו אכלת חלב והוא אומר לא אכלתי דפטור משום דאדם נאמן על עצמו יותר ממאה איש ולכך פיו מחייבו קרבן אפילו עדים מכחישין אותו ועדים אין מחייבין אותו קרבן אם מכחישן דלאידך לישנא דמפרש טעמייהו דרבנן דמתרץ דיבוריה ואמר דלא אכלתי שוגג אלא מזיד ומיירי דכשאמר לא אכלתי לא בדקנו אותו היאך היה דעתו אבל להכחיש העדים אינו נאמן א״כ חשיבי עדים מפיו שכן חייבוהו קרבן אפי׳ מכחישן והוא לא מחייב עצמו קרבן אם היו מכחישין אותו ואתי רבי חייא אפילו כרבנן: רבי חייא כר״מ סבירא ליה. וא״ת א״כ נימא ק״ו דר״מ אם הביאוהו לידי מיתה לא יביאוהו לידי שבועה הקלה וי״ל דאיכא למפרך דמה למיתה שכן על מה שהן מעידין הוא מת תאמר גבי שבועה שעל מה שהוא כופר הוא נשבע כדאמרי׳ לקמן: מה אם ירצה לומר מזיד הייתי. ללישנא דאדם נאמן על עצמו יותר מק׳ עדים האי אם ירצה לומר לדבריו דר״מ קאמרי (כדתניא) [כדאיתא] [ד] בפרק אמרו לו (שם דף יב. ושם) דלאידך לישנא טעמא דנפשייהו קאמרי ואין לפרש ומה אם ירצה לומר כו׳ שיהא נאמן לומר לא אכלתי מגו דאי בעי אמר מזיד הייתי דהא מגו במקום עדים הוא אלא כלומר אף מה שאמר לא אכלתי יכול לתרץ דבריו ולומר לא אכלתי שוגג אלא מזיד ומיירי דכשאמר לא אכלתי לא בדקו אותו איך היה דעתו ולבסוף אומר שמזיד היה וסברי רבנן דמה שאמר לא אכלתי כך היה דעתו שלא אכל שוגג אלא מזיד ולר״מ אע״פ שלבסוף אמר מזיד הייתי אין בכך כלום דהכי אמר (בתורת כהנים) אמר רבי מאיר אם בתחלה אמר מזיד הייתי שומעין לו אם היה דן עמו כל היום ובאחרונה אמר מזיד הייתי אין שומעין לו ואם תאמר והיאך נאמן לומר מזיד הייתי הא אין אדם משים עצמו רשע כדאמר בפ״ק דסנהדרין (דף ט: ושם) גבי פלוני רבעני לרצוני וי״ל דאין נאמן לפסול עצמו אבל הכא עושה תשובה ואינו רוצה להביא חולין לעזרה:

אשם היינו קרבן. דלרבי מאיר עדים מחייבין אותו אשם תימה דבמתני׳ דד׳ שומרין (שבועות דף מט. ושם) תנן היכן שורי נגנב משביעך אני ואמר אמן והעדים מעידים אותו שאכלו משלם כפל הודה מעצמו משלם קרן וחומש ואשם אבל על פי עדים אין משלם חומש ואשם וכן תנן בפרק הגוזל קמא (ב״ק דף קח.) ומוקי לה בפרק הגוזל קמא [ה] כר״מ וי״ל דסוגיא דהכא דלרבי מאיר עדים מחייבין אותו אשם לא יעמיד ההיא משנה כר״מ אלא כדבעי לאוקמה התם כשאכלו טריפה וההיא סוגיא דהתם דסבר דלרבי מאיר עדים לא מחייבי אשם משום דגבי אשם כתיב והתודה לא סבר כסוגיא דהכא דאשם היינו קרבן וליף במה הצד מפיו ועד אחד כדמסיק הכא:
עד

**רבינו חננאל**

והיאך זו חמורה מזו דהא אע״פ שהודאת פיו מחייבתו ממון דקי״ל הודאת בע״ד כק׳ עדים דמי אינה מחייבתו קנס דקי״ל מודה בקנס פטור הודאתו במקצת הטענה מחייבתו שבוע׳ העדאת עדים שמחייבתו קנס אינו דין שיחייבוהו שבועה במקצת. ופרכינן מה לפיו שכן מחייבתו קרבן. שנאמר והיה כי יאשם לאחת מאלה והתודה אשר חטא עליה והביא את אשמו לה׳ וגו׳. תאמר בעדים [שמעידין] עליו שחטא אין מחייבין אותו קרבן למה שאם ירצה אמר מזיד הייתי ואין קרבן למזיד ואם יודה להם כי שוגג הייתי בהודאתו מתחייב ולא בעדות העדים. ודחי׳ הא לא קשיא דר׳ חייא כר״מ ס״ל דאמר עדים מחייבין אותו קרבן דתנן בכריתות (פ׳ ד׳ מחוסרי כפרה) אמרו לו שנים אכלת חלב והוא אומר לא אכלתי ר״מ מחייב א״ר מאיר אם הביאוהו ב׳ לידי מיתה חמורה לא יביאוהו לידי קרבן הקל אמרו לו ומה אם ירצה לומר מזיד הייתי כלומר מה תועיל עדותם אם ירצה לומר מזיד הייתי וכו׳ וחזר לפרק פירכא אחריתי מה לפיו שכן אינו בהכחשה ובהזמה כלומר אם יודה שלויתי מפלוני מנה ביום פלוני במקום פלוני ויבואו עדים ויעידו כי שם היינו עמך בו ביום באותו מקום שאמרת ולא לויתה אתה ממנו כלום אחר הוא שלוה או אם יאמרו לו אותו היום היית עמנו במקום פלוני רחוק מזה המקום יותר ממהלך יום והוא מכחישם דכל כי האי גוונא אמרי׳ הודאת בע״ד כמאה עדים ואין העדים יכולין להכחישו ולא להזימו ולפיכך כשמודה מקצת הטענה חייב תאמר בעדים שישנן בהכחשה ובהזמה נמצא כח העדים פחות מהודאת פיו כך בחיוב שבועה כח העדים פחות הוא מהודאת פיו. ונדחה זה הק״ו וחזרנו לפרק דרך אחרת. ומה עד א׳ שאין מחייבו ממון מחייבו שבועה שנאמר לא יקום עד אחד באיש לכל עון וגו׳ ודרשינן ליה לכל עון ולכל חטאת הוא דאינו קם אבל קם הוא לשבועה עדים שמחייבין אותו ממון אינו דין שיחייבוהו שבועה. ודחי׳ מה לעד א׳ שכן על מה שהעיד הוא נשבע וכו׳.

**מסורת הש״ס**

א) [תוספתא פרק קידושין סה:, גיטין סד.], ב) יבמות ... כריתות יא:, ג) [מכ... אותן, כל״ל], ד) מהר... ועיין מהרש״א, ה) דף ...

**הגהות הב״ח**

(א) רש״י ד״ה עדים ... אם מכחישין דכתיב ... הודע, כל״ל, ותיבת א... נמחק:

**ליקוטי רש״י**

בכוליה בעי דל... וכו׳. וכי תימא ... נשבעים אשארא ד... דחשוד אממונא חשוד אשבועתא אממונא חשוד מדלא כפ... בכוליה דהאי כי א... בפלגא בכוליה נמי ... דלודי והאי דלא אודי ... לאו דדעתו למיגזליה ... אישתמוטי אישתמ... לדחויי השתא [גיטין נ... הודאת בעל ... כמאה עדים ד... דכתיב אשר יאמר כי ... זה הרי שסמך על מ... הודאתו [קדושין ס... עבד וכן מקבל מתנה ... דאמר לא קבלתי נ... ויכול זה לחזור ולזכות ... אם ירלה דאמרינן ... כסבור שקבלה זה ... [גיטין מ:]. ממון דאיתי... למחילה שאם מחלו ... [שם סד.]. אכלת חל... בשוגג וחייב אתה ק... [קידושין סה:]. ... הביאוהו שנים ל... מיתה חמורה. כגון העידו בו שהרג ... הנפש. אם ירצה לו... מזיד הייתי. אם ... רולה לפטור עלמו ב... היה יכול לומר מזיד ... ומזיד פטור [כריתות י... הרי זה נאמן לפטור ... מקרבן דאין עדים ... להכחישו בהא הילכך ... אמר נמי לא אכלתי נ... [יבמות פז:]. מחי... שבועה. על ממון ש... היו שנים היה מ... עכשיו ישבע שהעד מ... [כתובות פז:].

stronger than testimony in this respect, how can we make a *kal vachomer* predicated on testimony having the greater strength?

The Gemara answers:

**הָא לֹא קַשְׁיָא – This is not difficult.** רַבִּי חִיָּיא כְּרַבִּי מֵאִיר סְבִירָא לֵיהּ – We can say that **R' Chiya,** who propounds the *kal vachomer,* **holds the view of R' Meir,** דְּאָמַר עֵדִים מְחַיְּיבִין אוֹתוֹ קָרְבָּן מִקַּל וָחוֹמֶר – **who says that witnesses** indeed **obligate a person** to bring **a** *chatas* **offering by force of a *kal vachomer.*** דִּתְנַן – **For we learned in a Mishnah:**[11] אָמְרוּ לוֹ שְׁנַיִם אָכַלְתָּ חֵלֶב – IF TWO witnesses SAY TO [A PERSON], "YOU ATE *CHEILEV* inadvertently," and you are thus liable to bring a *chatas,* וְהוּא אוֹמֵר לֹא אָכַלְתִּי – AND HE SAYS, "I DID NOT EAT it," רַבִּי מֵאִיר מְחַיֵּיב וַחֲכָמִים פּוֹטְרִים – R' MEIR OBLIGATES him to bring a *chatas,* BUT THE SAGES EXEMPT him from that obligation. אָמַר רַבִּי מֵאִיר – R' MEIR SAID to the Sages: אִם הֱבִיאוּהוּ שְׁנַיִם לִידֵי מִיתָה חֲמוּרָה לֹא יְבִיאוּהוּ לִידֵי קָרְבָּן הַקַּל – It is a *kal vachomer*: IF WITNESSES CAN IMPOSE UPON HIM THE SEVERE punishment of DEATH,[12] SHOULD THEY NOT certainly be able to IMPOSE UPON HIM THE relatively LENIENT requirement of a *chatas* OFFERING?[13] אָמְרוּ לוֹ מַה אִם יִרְצֶה לוֹמַר מֵזִיד הָיִיתִי יִפָּטֵר – [THE SAGES] REPLIED TO HIM: WHAT IF HE WOULD WISH TO SAY, "I TRANSGRESSED DELIBERATELY"? HE WOULD then BE EXEMPT from a *chatas* even according to you![14] Therefore, he is believed over the witnesses even if he altogether denies having transgressed.[15]

Thus, the Mishnah records R' Meir's view that witnesses can indeed impose a *chatas* obligation on a person. If R' Chiya subscribes to R' Meir's position in this matter, then *chatas* is not an instance in which one's personal admission is superior to witnesses, and R' Chiya's *kal vachomer* is restored.

The Gemara raises another objection to R' Chiya's *kal vachomer:*

אֶלָּא מַה לְּפִיו שֶׁכֵּן מְחַיְּיבוֹ אָשָׁם – **Rather,** we can object: **What** can you prove from the admission **of his** own **mouth, which** has t[he] strength that it **obligates him** to bring **an *asham*** offering?[16] T[he] testimony of witnesses, however, which does not obligate him [to bring] the *asham,* is thus weaker in this respect.[17] – ? –

The Gemara answers:

אָשָׁם הַיְינוּ קָרְבָּן – The law regarding ***asham* is the same as** th[e law] regarding a *chatas* **offering.** R' Meir (followed by R' Chiya), w[ho] holds that witnesses certainly obligate a person to bring a *chat[as]* despite the person's protestations of innocence, will also hold th[at] witnesses obligate a person to bring an *asham.*[18]

The Gemara modifies its challenge:

אֶלָּא מַה לְּפִיו שֶׁכֵּן מְחַיְּיבוֹ חוֹמֶשׁ – **Rather,** we can object: **What** c[an] you prove from the admission **of his** own **mouth, which** has t[he] strength that it **obligates him** to pay **a fifth** in addition to t[he] principal (when the defendant admits perjury)? If, howev[er,] witnesses testify that he has perjured himself, no penalty of a fif[th] is added; thus, the testimony of witnesses is weaker in th[is] respect.[19] – ? –

The Gemara responds:

הָא לֹא קַשְׁיָא – **This is not difficult.** For, as stated above, [רַבִּי] חִיָּיא כְּרַבִּי מֵאִיר סְבִירָא לֵיהּ – **R' Chiya holds the view of R' Me[ir]** in the matter of witnesses obligating a person to bring a *chata[s].* Accordingly: כִּי הֵיכִי דִּמְחַיֵּיב לֵיהּ קָרְבָּן מִקַּל וָחוֹמֶר – **Just as he** [R' Meir, followed by R' Chiya] **obligates [a person]** in a *chat[as]* **offering** on the basis of witnesses **by means of a *kal v[a]chomer,***[20] מְחַיֵּיב לֵיהּ חוֹמֶשׁ מִקַּל וָחוֹמֶר – **so, too, does [he] obligate [a person]** in the additional payment of **a fifth** on t[he] basis of witnesses **by means of the** very same ***kal vachomer.***

The Gemara presents its final objection to R' Chiya's *k[al] vachomer*:

אֶלָּא מַה לְּפִיו שֶׁכֵּן אֵינוֹ בְּהַכְחָשָׁה וּבַהֲזָמָה – **Rather,** we can obje[ct:] **What** can you prove from the admission **of his** own **mouth, whic[h]**

NOTES

but he contradicts them; in this case, the sin remains unknown to him. However, if he does not contradict the witnesses, then he is obligated to bring a *chatas* for the sin that has become known to him through witnesses (see *Ritva*).]

11. *Kereisos* 11b.

12. If witnesses testify that a person has committed a capital offense, the person can be executed on the basis of their testimony even if he protests his innocence (*R' Gershom* to *Kereisos* ad loc.).

13. The obligation to bring a *chatas* is undoubtedly a more lenient "penalty" than capital punishment. Certainly, then, the testimony of witnesses, which can cause the death penalty, should make a person liable to a *chatas* even if he protests his innocence.

14. A *chatas* obligation (for transgressing a prohibition that carries the *kares* penalty) is incurred only if the transgression was inadvertent (e.g. the person was unaware that the fat he was eating was *cheilev* or that it is forbidden to eat *cheilev*). But if the person transgresses deliberately, then no *chatas* is brought.

Now, witnesses are not in a position to know with certainty what the person was thinking when he ate *cheilev.* Thus, even when witnesses testify that a person ate *cheilev,* he can avoid the *chatas* obligation generated by their testimony by averring that he ate the *cheilev* deliberately. [When the witnesses testified initially that he ate the *cheilev accidentally,* they could testify only that *circumstances indicated* that the transgression was accidental (see *Shitah Mekubetzes* ד"ה ר"מ מחייב). The circumstantial evidence can be relied upon to assume that the transgression was indeed accidental. However, if the person declares that he transgressed *knowingly,* his personal testimony about his intent at the time of the transgression must be accepted over the circumstantial indications to the contrary.]

15. From *Rashi* it would seem that the person is believed over witnesses in this case because he has a *migo* [see 3a note 32]; that is, had he wished to lie in order to avoid the *chatas* obligation, he could have fabricated a better lie and asserted that his transgression was deliberate. [This latter claim would have had the advantage that he does not undermine h[is] general credibility by contradicting witnesses (see *Aruch LaNer Kereisos* 12a).] Therefore, the person's failure to opt for a better [lie] indicates that he indeed tells the truth.

*Tos. HaRosh* (see also *Tosafos*), however, object to *Rashi's* explan[a]tion on grounds of the general rule that a *migo* is of no avail in the fa[ce] of the testimony of witnesses to the contrary. [*Migo* lends credibility [to] the person's actual claim. But no degree of credibility can enable [a] person's claim to prevail over the testimony of witnesses, to which th[e] Torah accords the status of legal fact.] Moreover, the defendant in th[is] case does not have a true *migo,* since he might not want to claim that [he] transgressed deliberately and thereby condemn himself as a delibera[te] sinner. See *Tosafos* for an alternative explanation. See also *Ramba[n].*

16. If a defendant denies under oath a monetary claim against him an[d] then admits that he perjured himself, he must pay the debt plus a fif[th] to the plaintiff and offer an *asham* sacrifice (*Leviticus* 5:20-26; *Numbe[rs]* 5:5-8; see *Rambam, Hil. Shegagos* 9:7). [This *asham* is known as אָשָׁם גְּזֵלוֹת, *asham gezeilos* (*asham of theft*).]

17. Regarding *asham gezeilos,* the Torah states (*Numbers* 5:7): וְהִתְוַדּוּ אֶת־חַטָּאתָם אֲשֶׁר עָשׂוּ, *and they [the violators] shall confess their sin th[at] they committed.* This indicates that the *asham* obligation and penalty [of] a fifth are incurred only if the defendant's perjury is established [by] personal confession, but not if it is established by the testimony [of] witnesses (see *Rashi* to *Numbers* 5:6).

18. [R' Meir's *kal vachomer* proving the power of witnesses to impose th[e] obligation to bring an offering applies equally to a *chatas* and an *asha[m] gezeilos.* The term קָרְבָּן, *offering,* used by R' Meir covers both types [of] offering.]

19. See above, notes 16 and 17.

20. This *kal vachomer* is detailed above in note 13.

21. If witnesses can make a person liable to the death penalty, is it n[ot] certain that they can make him liable to pay an additional fifth f[or] perjury?

והאי בבוליה בעי דלודי ליה והאי דלא אודי אשתמוטי הוא דקא מישתמט מיניה סבר עד דהוו לי זוזי ופרענא ליה ואמר רחמנא רמי שבועה עליה כי היכי דלודי ליה בבוליה אבל העדאת עדים דליכא למימר הכי אימא לא קמ"ל ק"ו ומאי ק"ו ומה פיו שאין מחייבו ממון מחייבו שבועה עדים שמחייבין אותו ממון אינו דין שמחייבין אותו שבועה ופיו אין מחייבו ממון והא (א) [א]הודאת בעל דין כמאה עדים דמי מאי ממון קנס ומה פיו [ב]שאין מחייבו קנס מחייבו שבועה עדים שמחייבין אותו קנס אינו דין שמחייבין אותו שבועה מה לפיו שכן מחייבו קרבן תאמר בעדים שאין מחייבין אותו קרבן הא לא קשיא רבי חייא כרבי מאיר סבירא ליה דאמר עדים מחייבין אותו קרבן מק"ו (ג) דתנן אמרו לו שנים אכלת חלב והוא אומר לא אכלתי רבי מאיר מחייב וחכמים [ג]פוטרים אמר רבי מאיר אם הביאוהו שנים לידי מיתה חמורה לא יביאוהו לידי קרבן הקל אמרו לו מה אם ירצה לומר מזיד הייתי יפטר אלא מה לפיו שכן מחייבו אשם אשם היינו קרבן אלא מה לפיו שכן מחייבו חומש הא לא קשיא רבי חייא כרבי מאיר סבירא ליה כי היכי דמחייב ליה קרבן מק"ו מחייב ליה חומש מקל וחומר אלא מה לפיו שכן אינו בהכחשה ובהזמה תאמר בעדים שישנן בהכחשה ובהזמה אלא אתיא מעד אחד ומה עד אחד שאין מחייבו ממון מחייבו שבועה עדים שמחייבין אותו ממון אינו דין שמחייבין אותו שבועה מה לעד אחד שכן על מה שהוא מעיד הוא נשבע

## רש"י

והאי בבוליה בעי דלודי כו'. וכ"ת מגו דחשיד אממונא חשיד אשבועתא ולא נרמי עליה שבועתא לא חשיד אממונא לפי שברצונו היה מודה בכולו אלא שאין בידו לפרוע וסבר עד דהוי לי [זוזי] ופרענא ליה: דליכא למימר הכי. שהרי כפר בכולו ונימא מגו דחשיד אממונא חשיד אשבועתא: פיו שאינו מחייבו ממון. בהודאתו ולקמיה מפרש לה: מחייבו שבועה. על השאר: עדים שמחייבין [אותו] ממון. במה שהעידו: אינו דין שיחייבוהו שבועה. על השאר: הודאת בעל דין כמאה עדים. ברייתא היא בתוספתא דבבא מציעא בפ' ראשון: פיו אינו מחייבו קנס. דילפינן (ב"ק דף עה.) מקראי דמודה בקנס פטור אשר ירשיעון אלהים פרט למרשיע את עצמו: פיו מחייבו קרבן. דכתיב והתודה אשר חטא והביא (ויקרא ה): עדים אין מחייבין אותו קרבן. אם (א) [ג]מכחישן אותו דכתיב (שם ד) או הודע אליו ולא שיודיעוהו אחרים: אמרו לו שנים אכלת חלב. שוגג: והוא אומר לא [אכלתי]. פטור שהיה יכול לומר מזיד הייתי ויפטר מן הקרבן אף כשאמר לא אכלתי פטור דמה לו לשקר: חומש ואשם. אם נשבע וכפר ממון והודה כתיב או מכל אשר ישבע עליו לשקר וגו' (שם ה): אינו בהכחשה ובהזמה. אם הודה לו במנה ובאו עדים והכחישוהו לומר אינך חייב לו כלום אינו נפטר בכך דהודאת בעל דין כמאה עדים: שישנן בהכחשה ובהזמה. שאם באו שנים עדים והכחישום או הזימום אין זה משלם ממון על פיהם: מחייבו שבועה. טענו חבירו מנה לי בידך והוא אומר אין לך בידי כלום ועד אחד מעידו שהוא חייב לו הרי זה נשבע להכחיש את העד דכתיב (דברים יט) לא יקום עד אחד באיש וגו' לכל עון ולכל חטאת הוא דאינו קם אבל לשבועה קם (שבועות דף מ.): מה לעד אחד. כלומר היכי ילפת שבועה דשנים משבועה דעד אחד מה לעד אחד שכן על מה שהעד מעיד הוא נשבע להכחישו:

תאמר

## תוספות

בבוליה בעי דלודי ליה. מה שפירש רש"י כיון דחשיד אממונא היכי נשבע נימא מגו דחשיד אממונא חשיד אשבועתא ומשני דמשתמיט ולא חשיד ועל זה תימה דהא מסיק לקמן (דף ו.) דחשיד אממונא לא חשיד אשבועתא ואין לומר דהיינו מדרבנן לפי שראו שהיתה שבועה חמורה עליהם אבל מדאורייתא חשוד לזה חשוד לזה דהא לקמן מייתי מרב נחמן דמשביעין אותו שלש שבועות ואחד מהן שלא שלחתי בו יד ומשמע בהגוזל קמא (ב"ק דף קו: ושם) דהוי דאורייתא וכן בנסכא דר' אבא (שבועות דף לב:) משמע דאי אמר לא חטפתי היה נשבע להכחיש את העד שבועה דאורייתא מדאמר מתוך שאינו יכול לישבע משלם דאשבועה דרבנן לא אמר הכי לכן י"ל ובבוליה בעי דלודי ליה כלומר מאחר דאין מעיז א"כ אמת הוא שאין חייב לו יותר ולמה ישבע יהא נאמן במגו דאי בעי כופר הכל ומשני דאין זה העזה דאשתמוטי קמשתמיט ואם תאמר כופר הכל נמי אשתמוטי קא משתמיט ואינו העזה כדאמרי' בפ' שבועת הדיינין (שבועות דף מ:) אמר רב נחמן כופר הכל משביעין אותו שבועת היסת משום חזקה דאין אדם תובע אלא א"כ יש לו עליו ופריך אדרבה אין אדם מעיז פניו בפני ב"ח ומשני אשתמוטי קא משתמיט וי"ל דמ"מ העזה יש יותר בכופר הכל מבכופר אלי וליכא מגו: אבל העדאת עדים דליכא למימר. כל כך משתמיט כיון שכפר הכל אימא כיון דחשוד הוא לגזול חשוד נמי אשבועתא קמ"ל ק"ו דלא הוי גזלן בהכי דאשתמוטי קא משתמיט דהכופר במלוה כשר לעדות ואע"ג דאמרי' לקמן (דף ו.) דלא אמרינן מגו דחשיד כו' מ"מ גם התנא אשמעינן דלא אמרינן מק"ו מפיו ועד אחד ואם תאמר אמאי אצטריך לטעמא דאשתמוטי לימא אי לאו ק"ו ה"א הודאת פיו גדולה מהעדאת עדים משום שכן אינו בהכחשה ובהזמה כדפריך לקמן ולקמן נמי הוה ליה למפרך מה לפיו שכן משתמיט וי"ל דהכא דאתא לפרושי דהודאת פיו גדולה מהעדאת עדים ניחא ליה למינקט טעמא דמשתמיט דסברא הוא דמטעם זה ישבע בהודאת פיו ולא בהעדאת עדים וחומר שאינו בהכחשה ובהזמה ניחא ליה למנקט לקמן לסתור ק"ו שכן דרך הגמרא למפרך פירכא על קל וחומר ולא מסברא לכך לא מייתי לקמן סברא דמשתמיט: מה לפיו שכן מחייבו קרבן תאמר בעדים כו'. פי' שכן מחייבו קרבן אפילו העדים מכחישין אותו ואומרים לאו חלב הוה אלא שומן דאי אין העדים מכחישין אותו היכי קאמר תאמר בעדים כו' עדים נמי מחייבין אותו קרבן אם אינו מכחישן ואפילו עד אחד אם אינו מכחישו מחייבו קרבן ואת הסוגיא סוברת כלישנא דפרק אמרו לו (כריתות דף יב. ושם) דמפרש טעמייהו דרבנן דלקמן דאמרו לו אכלת חלב והוא אומר לא אכלתי דפטור משום דאדם נאמן על עצמו יותר ממאה איש ולכך פיו מחייבו קרבן אפילו עדים מכחישין אותו ועדים אין מחייבין אותו קרבן אם מכחישן דלאידך לישנא דמפרש טעמייהו דרבנן דמתרץ דיבוריה ואמר דלא אכלתי שוגג אלא מזיד ומיירי דכשאמר לא אכלתי לא בדקנו אותו היאך היה דעתו אבל להכחיש העדים אינו נאמן א"כ חשיבי עדים מפיו שכן חייבוהו קרבן אפי' מכחישן והוא לא מחייב עצמו קרבן אם היו מכחישין אותו ואתי רבי חייא אפילו כרבנן: רבי חייא כר"מ סבירא ליה. וא"ת א"כ נימא ק"ו דר"מ אם הביאוהו לידי מיתה לא יביאוהו לידי שבועה הקלה וי"ל דליכא למפרך דמה למיתה שכן על מה שהן מעידין הוא מת תאמר גבי שבועה שעל מה שהוא כופר הוא נשבע כדאמרי' לקמן: מה אם ירצה לומר מזיד הייתי. ללישנא דאדם נאמן על עצמו יותר מק' עדים האי אם ירצה לומר לדבריו דר"מ קאמרי (כדתניא) [ד][כדאיתא] בפרק אמרו לו (שם דף יב. ושם) דלאידך לישנא טעמא דנפשייהו קאמרי ואין לפרש ומה אם ירצה לומר כו' שיהא נאמן לומר לא אכלתי מגו דאי בעי אמר מזיד הייתי דהא מגו במקום עדים הוא אלא כלומר אף מה שאמר לא אכלתי יכול לתרץ דבריו ולומר לא אכלתי שוגג אלא מזיד ומיירי דכשאמר לא אכלתי לא בדקו אותו איך היה דעתו ולבסוף אומר שמזיד היה וסברי רבנן דמה שאמר לא אכלתי כך היה דעתו שלא אכל שוגג אלא מזיד ולר"מ אע"פ שלבסוף אמר מזיד הייתי אין בכך כלום דהכי אמר (בתורת כהנים) אמר רבי מאיר אם בתחלה אמר מזיד הייתי שומעין לו אם היה דן עמו כל היום ובאחרונה אמר מזיד הייתי אין שומעין לו ואם תאמר והיאך נאמן לומר מזיד הייתי הא אין אדם משים עצמו רשע כדאמר בפ"ק דסנהדרין (דף ט: ושם) גבי פלוני רבעני לרצוני וי"ל דאין נאמן לפסול עצמו אבל הכא עושה תשובה ואינו רוצה להביא חולין לעזרה:

אשם היינו קרבן. לרבי מאיר עדים מחייבין אותו אשם תימה דבמתני' דד' שומרין (שבועות דף מט. ושם) תנן היכן שורי נגנב משביעך אני ואמר אמן והעדים מעידים אותו שאכלו משלם כפל הודה מעצמו משלם קרן וחומש ואשם אבל על פי עדים אין משלם חומש ואשם וכן תנן בפרק הגוזל קמא (ב"ק דף קח.) ומוקי לה בפרק הגוזל קמא [ה] כר"מ וי"ל דסוגיא דהכא דלרבי מאיר עדים מחייבין אותו אשם לא יעמיד ההיא משנה כר"מ אלא כדבעי לאוקמה התם כשאכלו טריפה וההיא סוגיא דהתם דסבר דלרבי מאיר עדים לא מחייבי אשם משום דגבי אשם כתיב והתודה לא סבר כסוגיא דהכא דאשם היינו קרבן וילף במה הצד מפיו ועד אחד כדמסיק הכא:

עד

## עין משפט נר מצוה

יא א מיי' פ"ו מהלכות טוען ונטען הל' ג טוש"ע ח"מ סימן פח סעיף ח:

יב ב מיי' פ"א מהלכות גניבה הל' ה ופ"ג שם הל' ז ופ"א מהלכות טוען ונטען הל' טו יז טוש"ע ח"מ סי' פז סעיף כו:

יג ג מיי' פ"ג מהלכות שגגות הלכה א סמג עשין ריג:

## רבינו חננאל

והיאך זו חמורה מזו דהא אע"פ שהודאת פיו מחייבתו ממון דקי"ל הודאת בע"ד כק' עדים דמי אינה מחייבתו קנס דקי"ל מודה בקנס פטור הודאתו במקצת הטענה מחייבתו שבוע' העדאת עדים שמחייבתו קנס אינו דין שיחייבוהו שבועה במקצת. ופרכינן מה לפיו שכן מחייבתו קרבן. שנאמר והיה כי יאשם לאחת מאלה והתודה אשר חטא עליה והביא את אשמו לה' וגו'. תאמר בעדים [שמעידין] עליו שחטא אין מחייבין אותו קרבן למה שאם ירצה אמר מזיד הייתי ואין קרבן למזיד ואם יודה להם כי שוגג הייתי בהודאתו מתחייב ולא בעדות העדים. ודחי' הא לא קשיא דר' חייא כר"מ ס"ל דאמר עדים מחייבין אותו קרבן דתנן בכריתות (פ' ד' מחוסרי כפרה) אמרו לו שנים אכלת חלב והוא אומר לא אכלתי ר"מ מחייב א"ר מאיר אם הביאוהו ב' לידי מיתה חמורה לא יביאוהו לידי קרבן הקל אמרו לו ומה אם ירצה לומר מזיד הייתי כלומר מה תועיל עדותם אם ירצה לומר מזיד הייתי וכו' וחזר לפרך פירכא אחריתי מה לפיו שכן אינו בהכחשה ובהזמה כלומר אם יודה שלויתי מפלוני מנה ביום פלוני במקום פלוני ויבואו עדים ויעידו כי שם היינו עמך בו ביום באותו מקום שאמרת ולא לויתה אתה ממנו כלום אחר הוא שלוה או אם יאמרו לו אותו היום היית עמנו במקום פלוני רחוק מזה המקום יותר ממהלך יום והוא מכחישם דכל כי האי גוונא אמרי' הודאת בע"ד כמאה עדים ואין העדים יכולין להכחישו ולא להזימו ולפיכך כשמודה מקצת הטענה חייב תאמר בעדים שישנן בהכחשה ובהזמה נמצא כח העדים פחות מהודאת פיו רך רחיוב שבועה כח העדים פחות הוא מהודאת פיו. ונדחה זה הק"ו וחזרנו לפרק דרך אחרת. ומה עד א' שאין מחייבו ממון מחייבו שבועה שנאמר לא יקום עד אחד באיש לכל עון וגו' ודרשינן ליה לכל עון ולכל חטאת הוא דאינו קם אבל קם הוא לשבועה עדים שמחייבין אותו ממון אינו דין שיחייבוהו שבועה. ודחי' מה לעד א' שכן על מה שהעיד הוא נשבע וכו'.

## מסורת הש"ס

א) [תוספתא פרק א, קידושין סה:, גיטין מ: סד.], ב) יבמות פז:, כריתות יא:, ג) [מכחיש אותו, כצ"ל], ד) מהרש"ל, ה) ועיין מהרש"א, ה) דף קו:.

## הגהות הב"ח

(א) רש"י ד"ה עדים וכו' אם מכחישן דכתיב או הודע, כצ"ל, ותיבת אותו נמחק:

## ליקוטי רש"י

בבוליה בעי דלודי וכו'. וכי תימא לא נשבעיה אשארא דמיגו דחשוד אממונא חשוד נמי אשבועתא אממונא לא חשוד מדלא כפריה בכוליה דהאי כי אודי בפלגא בכוליה נמי בעי דלודי והאי דלא אודי ליה לאו דדעתו למיגזליה אלא אישתמוטי אישתמיט לדחויי השתא [גיטין נא:]. הודאת בעל דין כמאה עדים דמי. דכתיב אשר יאמר כי הוא זה הרי שסמך על מקלא הודאתו [קידושין סה:]. עבד וכן מקבל מתנה כיון דאמר לא קבלתי נאמן ויכול זה לחזור ולזכות בו אם ירצה דאמרינן טעם כסבור שקבלה זה מיד [גיטין מ:]. ממון דאיתיהיב למחילה שאם מחלו מחול [שם סד.]. אכלת חלב. בשוגג וחייב אתה קרבן [קידושין סה:]. אם הביאוהו שנים לידי מיתה חמורה. כגון אם העידו בו שהרג את הנפש. אם ירצה לומר מזיד הייתי. אם היה רוצה לפטור עצמו בשקר היה יכול לומר מזיד הייתי ומזיד פטור [כריתות יא:]. הרי זה נאמן לפטור עצמו מקרבן דאין אדם עדים אל להכחישו בהא הילכך אמר כאן לא אכלתי פטור [יבמות פז:]. מחייב שבועה. על ממון שאלו היו שנים היה משלם עכשיו ישבע שהעד מכחו [כתובות פז:].

Rabbah continues:[1]

וְהַאי בְּכוּלֵּיהּ בָּעֵי דְּלוֹדֵי לֵיהּ – **And** really, **this** defendant **would want to admit [the claim] in its entirety.** וְהַאי דְּלָא אוֹדֵי – **And the reason he did not admit** the entire claim is that אִשְׁתַּמּוּטֵי הוּא דְּקָא מִישְׁתַּמֵּט מִינֵּיהּ – **he is** simply **evading [the creditor],** סָבַר עַד דַּהֲווּ לִי זוּזֵי וּפָרַעְנָא לֵיהּ – **thinking,** "I will put him off **until I have money and** then **I will pay him.**"[2] וְאָמַר רַחֲמָנָא רְמֵי שְׁבוּעָה עֲלֵיהּ כִּי הֵיכִי דְּלוֹדֵי לֵיהּ בְּכוּלֵּיהּ – **Therefore, the Merciful One said: Impose an oath on him so that he will admit [the claim] in its entirety** rather than swear falsely. And if he indeed denies the rest under oath, then we can accept that sworn denial as the truth.

Based on Rabbah's analysis, the Gemara reasons: אֲבָל הַעֲדָאַת עֵדִים דְּלֵיכָּא לְמֵימַר הָכִי אֵימָא לֹא – **But** where the partial liability is established by **the testimony of witnesses, where this** analysis **cannot be said,** since the defendant has in fact denied the entire claim, **I would say** that he does **not** swear.[3] קָא מַשְׁמַע לָן קַל וָחוֹמֶר – Therefore, we need **the *kal vachomer*,** which **informs us** that the defendant must swear even if the plaintiff's claim is partially substantiated not by admission but by witnesses.[4]

The Gemara now presents R' Chiya's *kal vachomer:* וּמַאי קַל וָחוֹמֶר – **And what is the *kal vachomer*** meant by R' Chiya? וּמָה פִּיו שֶׁאֵין מְחַיְּיבוֹ מָמוֹן מְחַיְּיבוֹ שְׁבוּעָה – **If** the admission of **his own mouth, which cannot obligate him** to pay **money,**[5] nevertheless **obligates him** to take **an oath,** i.e. where he admits part of a claim, עֵדִים שֶׁמְּחַיְּיבִין אוֹתוֹ מָמוֹן אֵינוֹ דִּין שֶׁמְּחַיְּיבִין אוֹתוֹ שְׁבוּעָה – then **witnesses, who can obligate him** to pay **money,**[6] **is it not certain that they obligate him** to take **an oath,** i.e. where they substantiate part of the claim that he denies?

The Gemara challenges the premise on which the *kal vachomer* is based:

וּפִיו אֵין מְחַיְּיבוֹ מָמוֹן – **But does** the admission of **his** own **mouth not obligate him** to pay **money?** וְהָא הוֹדָאַת בַּעַל דִּין כְּמֵאָה עֵדִים דָּמֵי – **Why,** we have a rule that **the admission of a litigant is like** the testimony of **one hundred witnesses!**[7] What do you mean, then, when you say that one's admission cannot obligate him to pay money?

The Gemara answers:

מַאי מָמוֹן קְנָס – **What "money"** is meant here? **Penalty** money.[8] Accordingly, the *kal vachomer* argument runs: מָה פִּיו שֶׁאֵין מְחַיְּיבוֹ קְנָס מְחַיְּיבוֹ שְׁבוּעָה – **If** the admission of **his** own **mouth, which cannot obligate him** to pay **a penalty,** nevertheless **obligates him** to take **an oath,** i.e. where he admits part of a claim, עֵדִים שֶׁמְּחַיְּיבִין אוֹתוֹ קְנָס אֵינוֹ דִּין שֶׁמְּחַיְּיבִין אוֹתוֹ שְׁבוּעָה – then two **witnesses, who can obligate him** to pay **a penalty, is it not certain that they obligate him** to take **an oath,** i.e. when they substantiate part of the claim that he denies?

The Gemara challenges the *kal vachomer:*

מָה לְפִיו שֶׁכֵּן מְחַיְּיבוֹ קָרְבָּן – **What** can you prove from the admission **of his** own **mouth, which** has the strength that it **obligates him** to bring **a** *chatas* **offering?**[9] תֹּאמַר בְּעֵדִים שֶׁאֵין מְחַיְּיבִין אוֹתוֹ קָרְבָּן – **Can you say** the same **of witnesses, who do not obligate him** to bring **a** *chatas* **offering** when they are contradicted by his own account of the incident?[10] Since personal admission is

NOTES

1. *Rashi* explains that Rabbah is now addressing the following difficulty: Obviously, the Torah's imposition of an oath on the defendant who admits part of the claim stems from the concern that he is lying when he denies the remainder. But if the defendant is lying about the remainder, then he is in effect trying to steal that remainder from the plaintiff. Accordingly, how can we impose an oath on him? Just as he is prepared to steal, he is prepared to swear falsely! (Cf. *Tosafos*). Thus, by imposing an oath on him, we will likely be guilty of causing him to sin by swearing falsely (*Ritva* to 5b ד״ה א״ר יוחנן).

2. Thus, the oath of *modeh bemiktzas* is not directed at an outright thief. It is rather directed at the defendant who would really like to admit his entire debt to the plaintiff, but is seeking to buy time with his partial denial so that he can obtain the necessary funds. Such a defendant will not resort to swearing falsely in order to achieve his aim.

3. Since the defendant in this case has not exhibited a degree of honesty by admitting part of the claim (and his integrity has indeed been discredited by witnesses who testify that he lies, at any rate, about part of the claim!), I would say that he is an outright thief who will even swear falsely in order to achieve his aim. Accordingly, although the claim of the plaintiff has been partially substantiated by the witnesses, I would say that the defendant is ineligible to swear the oath of *modeh bemiktzas* (*Rashi*; see *Ritva*).

4. If not for the *kal vachomer,* we would have argued that the law of partial admission does not naturally extend to the case of partial substantiation by witnesses, since there is less reason to assume in the latter case that the defendant is basically honest. However, the *kal vachomer* militates for extending the law to the case of witnesses as well, and is a stronger argument than the reason advanced above for limiting the law to partial substantiation by admission. Therefore, we must preserve the *kal vachomer* by reasoning that even in the case of witnesses, the defendant (who presumably knew that witnesses could contradict him) might have merely been trying to buy time with his denial until he would be able to obtain funds to repay his debt (see *Ritva* and *Nachalas David*).

5. The Gemara below will explain this assertion.

6. If witnesses testify that a person is subject to a monetary obligation, the court imposes that obligation on him.

7. I.e. a defendant's personal admission to a claim made against him is deemed valid legal proof of his liability (see *Rashi* to *Kiddushin* 65b, who notes the Biblical source of this rule; see also *Ketzos HaChoshen* 34:4 at length).

[There is no legal advantage to the testimony of numerous witnesses over the testimony of two witnesses. The Gemara uses the expression "one hundred witnesses" only to emphasize the absolute acceptance of a defendant's admission to the monetary claim against him (see *Shevuos* 42a).]

8. [קְנָס, *kenass,* refers to punitive rather than compensatory awards levied by the court. For example, the Torah states that a thief must pay double what he stole [כֶּפֶל] (*Exodus* 22:3,6,8). The second portion of the payment is a punitive *kenass,* since it is in excess of the loss actually caused to the victim.] The law is that a *kenass* penalty is imposed only when the crime is established through witnesses, but not when it is established through confession. For Scripture imposes the double penalty on *the one whom the "judges" convict* (*Exodus* 22:8), which is expounded to exclude one who convicts *himself* (*Rashi* from *Bava Kamma* 75a).

9. [A *chatas* is an offering that one must bring for the inadvertent violation of a prohibition whose willful violation incurs the *kares* penalty, or for violating one of four less serious transgressions enumerated in *Leviticus* 5:1-4. In the case of these latter four violations the *chatas* obligation incurred is that of the variable *chatas* offering (קָרְבָּן עוֹלֶה וְיוֹרֵד; this offering varies according to what the violator can afford).

In regard to a *chatas* offering, the Torah states (*Leviticus* 5:5-6) that if the violator *shall confess what he has sinned . . . then he shall bring his guilt offering to HASHEM.* This implies that one's own confession obligates him to bring a *chatas* (*Rashi*) even if witnesses contradict that confession and assert that he did *not* commit the transgression (*Tosafos, Ritva* in explanation of *Rashi*). [This verse is stated in regard to the variable *chatas* offering, but the law applies to all *chataos* – see *Ritva*.

10. For example, two witnesses testify that a person inadvertently ate *cheilev* [forbidden fats; the willful consumption of *cheilev* incurs the *kares* penalty], but he contradicts them and insists that he did not eat it. Since he contradicts their testimony, he does not bring a *chatas*.

This [exception to the general principle of the court's absolute reliance on witnesses] is derived from the Torah's statement (*Leviticus* 4:23) that one incurs a *chatas* obligation if *the sin that he committed becomes known to him* – but not if others inform him of the sin (*Rashi*). [This exposition excludes the case in which others inform him of the si

והאי בכוליה בעי דלודי ליה והאי דלא אודי אשתמוטי הוא דקא מישתמט מיניה סבר עד דהוו לי זוזי ופרענא ליה ואמר רחמנא רמי שבועה עליה כי היכי דלודי ליה בכוליה אבל העדאת עדים דליכא למימר הכי אימא לא קמ"ל ק"ו ומאי ק"ו ומה פיו שאין מחייבו ממון מחייבו שבועה עדים שמחייבין אותו ממון אינו דין שמחייבין אותו שבועה ופיו אין מחייבו ממון והא (א) א הודאת בעל דין כמאה עדים דמי מאי ממון קנס ומה פיו ב שאין מחייבו קנס מחייבו שבועה עדים שמחייבין אותו קנס אינו דין שמחייבין אותו שבועה מה לפיו שכן מחייבו קרבן תאמר בעדים שאין מחייבין אותו קרבן הא לא קשיא רבי חייא כרבי מאיר סבירא ליה דאמר עדים מחייבין אותו קרבן מק"ו ג דתנן אמרו לו שנים אכלת חלב והוא אומר לא אכלתי רבי מאיר מחייב וחכמים ד פוטרים אמר רבי מאיר אם הביאוהו שנים לידי מיתה חמורה לא יביאוהו לידי קרבן הקל אמרו לו מה אם ירצה לומר מזיד הייתי יפטר אלא מה לפיו שכן מחייבו אשם היינו קרבן אלא מה לפיו שכן מחייבו חומש הא לא קשיא רבי חייא כרבי מאיר סבירא ליה כי היכי דמחייב ליה קרבן מק"ו מחייב ליה חומש מקל וחומר אלא מה לפיו שכן אינו בהכחשה ובהזמה תאמר בעדים שישנן בהכחשה ובהזמה אלא אתיא מעד אחד ומה עד אחד שאין מחייבו ממון מחייבו שבועה עדים שמחייבין אותו ממון אינו דין שמחייבין אותו שבועה מה לעד אחד שכן על מה שהוא מעיד הוא נשבע

**והאי בכוליה בעי דלודי כו'.** וכ"ת מגו דחשיד אממונא חשיד אשבועתא ולא נרמי עליה שבועתא לא חשיד אממונא לפי שברצונו היה מודה בכולו אלא שאין בידו לפרוע וסבר עד דהוי לי [זוזי] ופרענא ליה: **דליכא למימר הכי.** שהרי כפר בכולו ונימא מגו דחשיד אממונא חשיד אשבועתא: **פיו שאינו מחייבו ממון.** בהודאתו ולקמיה מפרש לה: **מחייבו שבועה.** על השאר: **עדים שמחייבין [אותו] ממון.** במה שהעידו: **אינו דין שיחייבוהו שבועה.** על השאר: **הודאת בעל דין כמאה עדים.** ברייתא היא בתוספתא דבבא מציעא בפ' ראשון: **פיו אינו מחייבו קנס.** דילפינן (ב"ק דף עה.) מקראי דמודה בקנס פטור אשר ירשיעון אלהים פרט למרשיע את עצמו: **פיו מחייבו קרבן.** דכתיב והתודה אשר חטא והביא (ויקרא ה): **עדים אין מחייבין אותו קרבן.** אם (א) ג מכחישין אותו דכתיב (שם ד) או הודע אליו ולא שיודיעוהו אחרים: **אמרו לו שנים אכלת חלב.** שוגג: **והוא אומר לא [אכלתי].** פטור שהיה יכול לומר מזיד הייתי ויפטר מן הקרבן אף כשאמר לא אכלתי פטור דמה לו לשקר: **חומש ואשם.** אם נשבע וכפר ממון והודה כתיב או מכל אשר ישבע עליו לשקר וגו' (שם ה): **אינו בהכחשה ובהזמה.** אם הודה לו במנה ובאו עדים והכחישוהו לומר אינך חייב לו כלום אינו נפטר בכך דהודאת בעל דין כמאה עדים: **שישנן בהכחשה ובהזמה.** שאם באו שנים עדים והכחישום או הזימום אין זה משלם ממון על פיהם: **מחייבו שבועה.** טענו חבירו מנה לי בידך והוא אומר אין לך בידי כלום ועד אחד מעידו שהוא חייב לו הרי זה נשבע להכחיש את העד דכתיב (דברים יט) לא יקום עד אחד באיש וגו' לכל עון ולכל חטאת הוא דאינו קם אבל לשבועה קם (שבועות דף מ.): **מה לעד אחד.** כלומר היכי ילפת שבועה דשנים משבועה דעד אחד מה לעד אחד שכן על מה שהעד מעיד הוא נשבע להכחישו:

**בכוליה בעי דלודי ליה.** מה שפירש רש"י כיון דחשיד אממונא היכי נשבע נימא מגו דחשיד אממונא חשיד אשבועתא ומשני דמשתמיט ולא חשיד ועל זה תימה דהא מסיק לקמן (דף ו.) דחשיד אממונא לא חשיד אשבועתא ואין לומר דהיינו מדרבנן לפי שראו שהיתה שבועה חמורה עליהם אבל מדאורייתא חשוד לזה חשוד לזה דהא לקמן מייתי מרב נחמן דמשביעין אותו שלש שבועות ואחד מהן שלא שלחתי בו יד ומשמע בהגוזל קמא (ב"ק דף קו: ושם) דהוי דאורייתא וכן בנסכא דר' אבא (שבועות דף לג:) משמע דאי אמר לא חטפתי היה נשבע להכחיש את העד שבועה דאורייתא מדאמר מתוך שאינו יכול לישבע משלם דאשבועה דרבנן לא אמר הכי לכן י"ל ובכוליה בעי דלודי ליה כלומר מאחר דאין מעיז א"כ אמת הוא שאין חייב לו יותר ולמה ישבע יהא נאמן במגו דאי בעי כופר הכל ומשני דאין זה העזה דאשתמוטי קמשתמיט ואם תאמר כופר הכל נמי אשתמוטי קא משתמיט ואינו העזה כדאמרי' בפ' שבועת הדיינין (שבועות דף מ:) אמר רב נחמן כופר הכל משביעין אותו שבועת היסת משום חזקה דאין אדם תובע אלא א"כ יש לו עליו ופריך אדרבה אין אדם מעיז פניו בפני ב"ח ומשני אשתמוטי קא משתמיט וי"ל דמ"מ העזה יש יותר בכופר הכל מבכופר חצי וליכא מגו: **אבל העדאת עדים דליכא למימר.** כל כך משתמיט כיון שכפר הכל אימא כיון דחשוד הוא לגזול חשוד נמי אשבועתא קמ"ל ק"ו דלא הוי גזלן בהכי דאשתמוטי קא משתמיט דהכופר במלוה כשר לעדות ואע"ג דאמרי' לקמן (דף ו.) דלא אמרינן מגו דחשיד כו' מ"מ גם התנא אשמעינן דלא אמרינן מק"ו מפיו ועד אחד ואם תאמר אמאי אצטריך לטעמא דאשתמוטי לימא אי לאו ק"ו ה"א הודאת פיו גדולה מהעדאת עדים משום שכן אינו בהכחשה ובהזמה כדפריך לקמן ולקמן נמי הוה ליה למפרך מה לפיו שכן משתמיט וי"ל דהכא דאתא לפרושי דהודאת פיו גדולה מהעדאת עדים ניחא ליה למינקט טעמא דמשתמיט דסברא הוא דמטעם זה ישבע בהודאת פיו ולא בהעדאת עדים וחומר שאינו בהכחשה ובהזמה ניחא ליה למנקט לקמן לסתור ק"ו שכן דרך הגמרא למפרך פירכא על קל וחומר ולא מסברא לכך לא מייתי לקמן סברא דמשתמיט: **מה לפיו שכן מחייבו קרבן תאמר בעדים כו'.** פי' שכן מחייבו קרבן אפילו העדים מכחישין אותו ואומרים לאו חלב הוה אלא שומן דאי אין העדים מכחישין אותו היכי קאמר תאמר בעדים כו' עדים נמי מחייבין אותו קרבן אם אינו מכחישן ואפילו עד אחד אם אינו מכחישו מחייבו קרבן וזאת הסוגיא סוברת כלישנא דפרק אמרו לו (כריתות דף יב. ושם) דמפרש טעמייהו דרבנן דלקמן דאמרו לו אכלת חלב והוא אומר לא אכלתי דפטור משום דאדם נאמן על עצמו יותר ממאה איש ולכך פיו מחייבו קרבן אפילו עדים מכחישין אותו ועדים אין מחייבין אותו קרבן אם מכחישן דלאידך לישנא דמפרש טעמייהו דרבנן דמתרץ דיבוריה ואמר דלא אכלתי שוגג אלא מזיד ומיירי דכשאמר לא אכלתי לא בדקנו אותו היאך היה דעתו אבל להכחיש העדים אינו נאמן א"כ חשיבי עדים מפיו שכן חייבוהו קרבן אפי' מכחישן והוא לא מחייב עצמו קרבן אם היו מכחישין אותו ואתי רבי חייא אפילו כרבנן: **רבי חייא כר"מ סבירא ליה.** וא"ת א"כ נימא ק"ו דר"מ אם הביאוהו לידי מיתה לא יביאוהו לידי שבועה הקלה וי"ל דליכא למפרך דמה למיתה שכן על מה שהן מעידין הוא מת תאמר גבי שבועה שעל מה שהוא כופר הוא נשבע כדאמרי' לקמן: **מה אם ירצה לומר מזיד הייתי.** ללישנא דאדם נאמן על עצמו יותר מק' עדים האי אם ירצה לומר לדבריו דר"מ קאמרי (כדתניא) ד [כדאיתא] בפרק אמרו לו (שם דף יב. ושם) דלאידך לישנא טעמא דנפשייהו קאמרי ואין לפרש ומה אם ירצה לומר כו' שיהא נאמן לומר לא אכלתי מגו דאי בעי אמר מזיד הייתי דהא מגו במקום עדים הוא אלא כלומר אף מה שאמר לא אכלתי יכול לתרץ דבריו ולומר לא אכלתי שוגג אלא מזיד ומיירי דכשאמר לא אכלתי לא בדקו אותו איך היה דעתו ולבסוף אומר שמזיד היה וסברי רבנן דמה שאמר לא אכלתי כך היה דעתו שלא אכל שוגג אלא מזיד ולר"מ אע"פ שלבסוף אמר מזיד הייתי אין בכך כלום דהכי אמר (בתורת כהנים) אמר רבי מאיר אם בתחלה אמר מזיד הייתי שומעין לו אם היה דן עמו כל היום ובאחרונה אמר מזיד הייתי אין שומעין לו ואם תאמר והיאך נאמן לומר מזיד הייתי הא אין אדם משים עצמו רשע כדאמר בפ"ק דסנהדרין (דף ט: ושם) גבי פלוני רבעני לרצוני וי"ל דאין נאמן לפסול עצמו אבל הכא עושה תשובה ואינו רוצה להביא חולין לעזרה:

**אשם היינו קרבן.** דלרבי מאיר עדים מחייבין אותו אשם תימה דבמתני' דד' שומרין (שבועות דף מט. ושם) תנן היכן שורי נגנב משביעך אני ואמר אמן והעדים מעידים אותו שאכלו משלם כפל הודה מעצמו משלם קרן וחומש ואשם אבל על פי עדים אין משלם חומש ואשם וכן תנן בפרק הגוזל קמא (ב"ק דף קח.) ומוקי לה בפרק הגוזל קמא ה כר"מ וי"ל דסוגיא דהכא דלרבי מאיר עדים מחייבין אותו אשם לא יעמיד ההיא משנה כר"מ אלא כדבעי לאוקמה התם כשאכלו טריפה וההיא סוגיא דהתם דסבר דלרבי מאיר עדים לא מחייבי אשם משום דגבי אשם כתיב והתודה לא סבר כסוגיא דהכא דאשם היינו קרבן ויליף במה הצד מפיו ועד אחד כדמסיק הכא:

עד

### עין משפט נר מצוה

יא א מיי' פ"ו מהלכות טוען ונטען הל' ג טוש"ע ח"מ סימן פא סעיף ח:

יב ב מיי' פ"א מהלכות גניבה הל' ה ופ"ג שם הל' ז ופ"א מהלכות טוען ונטען הל' טז יז טוש"ע ח"מ סי' פז סעיף כו:

יג ג מיי' פ"ג מהלכות שגגות הלכה א סמג עשין ריג:

### רבינו חננאל

והיאך זו חמורה מזו דהא אע"פ שהודאת פיו מחייבתו ממון דקי"ל הודאת בע"ד כק' עדים דמי אינה מחייבתו קנס דקי"ל מודה בקנס פטור הודאתו במקצת הטענה מחייבתו שבוע' העדאת עדים שמחייבתו קנס אינו דין שיחייבוהו שבועה במקצת. ופרכינן מה לפיו שכן מחייבתו קרבן. שנאמר והיה כי יאשם לאחת מאלה והתודה אשר חטא עליה והביא את אשמו לה' וגו'. תאמר בעדים [שמעידין] עליו שחטא אין מחייבין אותו קרבן למה שאם ירצה אמר מזיד הייתי ואין קרבן למזיד ואם יודה להם כי שוגג הייתי בהודאתו מתחייב ולא בעדות העדים. ודחי' הא לא קשיא דר' חייא כר"מ ס"ל דאמר עדים מחייבין אותו קרבן דתנן בכריתות (פ' ד' מחוסרי כפרה) אמרו לו שנים אכלת חלב והוא אומר לא אכלתי ר"מ מחייב א"ר מאיר אם הביאוהו ב' לידי מיתה חמורה לא יביאוהו לידי קרבן הקל אמרו לו ומה אם ירצה לומר מזיד הייתי כלומר מה תועיל עדותם אם ירצה לומר מזיד הייתי וכו' וחזר לפרך פירכא אחריתי מה לפיו שכן אינו בהכחשה ובהזמה כלומר אם יודה שלויתי מפלוני מנה ביום פלוני במקום פלוני ויבואו עדים ויעידו כי שם היינו עמך בו ביום באותו מקום שאמרת ולא לויתה אתה ממנו כלום אחר הוא שלוה או אם יאמרו לו אותו היום היית עמנו במקום פלוני רחוק מזה המקום יותר ממהלך יום והוא מכחישם דכל כי האי גוונא אמרי' הודאת בע"ד כמאה עדים ואין העדים יכולין להכחישו ולא להזימו ולפיכך כשמודה מקצת הטענה חייב תאמר בעדים שישנן בהכחשה ובהזמה נמצא כח העדים פחות מהודאת פיו כך בחיוב שבועה כח העדים פחות הוא מהודאת פיו. ונדחה זה הק"ו וחזרנו לפרק דרך אחרת. ומה עד א' שאין מחייבו ממון מחייבו שבועה שנאמר לא יקום עד אחד באיש לכל עון וגו' ודרשינן ליה לכל עון ולכל חטאת הוא דאינו קם אבל קם הוא לשבועה עדים שמחייבין אותו ממון אינו דין שיחייבוהו שבועה. ודחי' מה לעד א' שכן על מה שהעיד הוא נשבע וכו'.

### מסורת הש"ס

א) [תוספתא פרק ... קידושין סה:, גיטין ... סד.], ב) יבמות פ... כריתות יא:, ג) [מכת... אותן, כצ"ל], ד) מהר"... ועיין מהרש"א, ה) דף ק...

### הגהות הב"ח

(א) רש"י ד"ה עדים ו... אם מכחישן דכתיב ... הודע, כצ"ל, ותיבת או... נמחק:

### ליקוטי רש"י

בכוליה בעי דלו... וכו'. וכי תימא ... נשבעיה אשארא דמי... דחשוד אממונא חשוד ... אשבועתא אממונא חשוד מדלא כפר בכוליה דהאי כי א... בפלגא בכוליה נמי ב... לאודי והאי דלא אודי ... לאו דדעתו למיגזליה א... אישתמוטי אישתמ... לדחויי השתא [גיטין נא... הודאת בעל ד... כמאה עדים ד... דכתיב אשר יאמר כי ה... זה הרי שסמך על מק... הודאתו [קדושין סה... עבד וכן מקבל מתנה ... דאמר לא קבלתי נ... ויכול זה לחזור ולזכות אם ירצה דאמרינן ט... כסבור שקבלה זה מ... [גיטין מ:]. ממון דאיתי... למחילה שאם מחלו מ... [שם סד.]. אכלת חל... בשוגג וחייב אתה ק... [קידושין סה:]. ... הביאוהו שנים ל... מיתה חמורה. כגון העידו בו שהרג הנפש. אם ירצה לו... מזיד הייתי. אם ... רוצה לפטור עצמו בש... היה יכול לומר מזיד ... ומזיד פטור [כריתות יא... הרי זה נאמן לפטור ע... מקרבן דאין עדים ... להכחישו בהא הילכך אמר נמי לא אכלתי נ... [יבמות פז:]. מחיי... שבועה. על ממון ש... היו שנים היה מ... עכשיו ישבע שהעד מכ... [כתובות פז:].

ואיכא למימר כולה למר ואיכא למימר כולה למר אמר סומכוס ממון המוטל בספק חולקין בלא שבועה הכא דליכא דררא דממונא דאיכא למימר דתרוייהו היא לא כ"ש אפילו תימא סומכוס שבועה זו מדרבנן היא כדרבי יוחנן דאמר ר' יוחנן (א) [א] שבועה זו תקנת חכמים היא שלא יהא כל אחד ואחד הולך ותוקף בטליתו של חבירו ואומר שלי הוא לימא מתניתין דלא כרבי יוסי דאי כרבי יוסי הא אמר (ב) א"כ מה הפסיד רמאי אלא הכל יהא מונח עד שיבא אליהו אלא מאי רבנן כיון דאמרי רבנן השאר יהא מונח עד שיבא אליהו הא נמי כשאר דמי דספיקא היא האי מאי אי אמרת בשלמא רבנן התם דודאי האי מנה דחד מינייהו הוא אמרי רבנן יהא מונח עד שיבא אליהו הכא דאיכא למימר דתרוייהו הוא אמרי רבנן פלגי בשבועה אלא אי אמרת ר' יוסי היא השתא ומה התם דבודאי איכא מנה למר ואיכא מנה למר אמר ר' יוסי יהא מונח עד שיבא אליהו הכא דאיכא למימר דחד מינייהו הוא לא כ"ש אפי' תימא ר' יוסי התם ודאי איכא רמאי הכא מי יימר דאיכא רמאי אימא תרוייהו בהדי הדדי אגבהוה אי נמי התם קניס ליה רבי יוסי לרמאי כי היכי דלודי הכא מאי פסידא אית ליה דלודי תינח מציאה מקח וממכר מאי איכא למימר (ה) אלא מחוורתא כדשנין מעיקרא בין לרבנן ובין לר' יוסי התם (ג) גבי חנוני על פנקסו דקתני [ב] זה נשבע ונוטל וזה נשבע ונוטל מ"ש דלא אמרינן נפקיה לממונא מבעה"ב ויהא מונח עד שיבא אליהו דהא בודאי איכא רמאי אמרי התם היינו טעמא דאמר ליה חנוני לבעה"ב אנא שליחותא דידך קא עבדינא מאי אית לי גבי שכיר אע"ג דקא משתבע לי לא מהימן לי בשבועה את האמנתיה דלא אמרת לי בסהדי הב ליה ושכיר נמי א"ל לבעה"ב אנא עבדי עבידתא גבך מאי אית לי גבי חנוני אע"ג דמשתבע לי לא מהימן לי הלכך תרוייהו משתבעי ושקלי מבעל הבית: (ד) תני רבי חייא [ג] מנה לי בידך והלה אומר אין לך בידי כלום והעדים מעידים אותו שיש לו חמשים זוז נותן לו חמשים זוז (ה) וישבע על השאר שלא תהא הודאת פיו גדולה מהעדאת עדים מק"ו ותנא תונא שנים אוחזין בטלית זה אומר אני מצאתיה וכו' והא הכא כיון דתפיס אנן סהדי דמאי דתפיס האי דידיה הוא ומאי דתפיס האי דידיה הוא וקתני ישבע מאי שלא תהא הודאת פיו גדולה מהעדאת עדי' מק"ו שלא תאמר הודאת פיו הוא דרמיא רחמנא שבועה עליה כדרבה (ו) דאמר רבה מפני מה אמרה תורה [ד] מודה מקצת הטענה ישבע חזקה אין אדם מעיז פניו בפני בע"ח והאי בכוליה בעי דנכפריה והא דלא כפריה משום דאין אדם מעיז פניו

**רש"י**

ואיכא למימר כוליה דמר. ועוד על כרחך או כוליה דמר או כוליה דמר אפילו הכי חולקין בלא שבועה: הכא דליכא דררא דממונא. ועוד דאיכא למימר דתרוייהו בהדי הדדי אגבהוה: לא כ"ש. דחולקין בלא שבועה: ותוקף. אוחז: דר' יוסי. לקמן בהמפקיד (דף לז.) שנים שהפקידו אצל אחד זה מנה וזה מאתים זה אומר מאתים שלי וזה אומר מאתים שלי וקאמר ת"ק נותן לזה מנה ולזה מנה והשאר יהא מונח עד שיבא אליהו אמר ר' יוסי א"כ מה הפסיד הרמאי ולמה יודה הרי קיבל את שלו אלא הכל יהא מונח ויפסיד הרמאי וה"נ יהא מונח: הא נמי כשאר דמיא. דהתם על מנה השני הם דנין ואלו דנין על הטלית כולה: דחד מינייהו הוא. ואין לומר יחלוקו: הכא דאיכא למימר דחד מינייהו הוא. ואין לחבירו חלק בה לא כ"ש דלית ליה יחלוקו: מאי פסידא אית ליה. למי שאין לו חלק בה אם תהא מונחת: דלודי. שאין לו חלק בה כשיודה מה יטול: מקח וממכר מאי איכא למימר. הא אוקימנא דקיבל דמים מתרוייהו ואי הוה אמרינן יהא הטלית והדמים מונחים אית ליה פסידא לרמאי ויודה על האמת קודם שיפסיד: התם היינו טעמא. דשניהם נשבעין ונוטלין דחנוני אומר לבעל הבית אנא שליחותא דידך עבדי ונתתי לפועלך ממון שצויתני: מאי אית לי גבי שכיר. לערער: לא מהימן לי. איני מאמינו בשבועה אני אומר שהוא רשע ואין לי להאמין אדם בשבועה על כרחי אלא אם כן האמנתיו מתחילה להפקיד אצלו או להתנות עמו: את הימנתיה. ואתה הוא שקלקלת ואין לי להפסיד בקלקולך שיהיו מעותי מונחין עד שיבא אליהו: וישבע על השאר. כדין מודה מקצת הטענה שאמרה תורה ישבע כדילפינן בשבועות (דף לט:) מכי הוא זה ואע"ג דזה לא הודה הרי יש עדים במקצת ולא תהא הודאת פיו גדולה לחייבו על השאר שבועה מהעדאת עדים: מק"ו. לקמן מפרש מאי ק"ו: ותנא תונא. ותנא דידן סייעתא לדידי: זה אומר כו'. וקתני שניהם ישבעו: אנן סהדי דמה דתפס האי. היינו פלגא: דידיה הוא. שהרי מוחזק הוא בפנינו והרי הוא תובע את כולה וחבירו כופר את כולה שאומר כולה שלי ואף מה שאתה תפוס בידך ואנו מעידין אותו שיש לו בה מקצת ומחייבים את חבירו שבועה על השאר דהיינו חצי שעיכב לעצמו: מאי לא תהא הודאת פיו גדולה מהעדאת עדים. מהיכי תיתי לן למידק דתיסק אדעתין דתהא הודאת פיו גדולה מהעדאת עדים דאיצטריך לתנא למילף מק"ו דלא תהא הודאת פיו גדולה: מפני מה אמרה תורה כו'. ולא חשבו כמשיב אבידה לפוטרו שלא כפר בכולו:

**תוספות**

**התם** ודאי איכא רמאי. לכך קניס ליה גם במה שהוא שלו בודאי אבל הכא איכא למימר תרוייהו בהדי הדדי אגבהוה דליכא רמאי דכל חד סבור שהוא הגביה קודם: **אי** נמי התם קניס כי היכי דלודי. אבל הכא אפילו איכא ודאי רמאי כגון שזה אומר אני מצאתיה היום וזה אומר אני מצאתיה אתמול מודה דיחלוקו ולא אמרינן יהא מונח עד שיבא אליהו דבשביל כך לא יפרוש דהא אינו מפסיד כלום:

**אלא** מחוורתא כדשנין מעיקרא. נוכל לומר (ז) דהדר ביה ולא סגי בטעמא דמפסיד הרמאי לבד דלא קניס ר' יוסי אלא היכא דאיכא ודאי רמאי ואית ליה פסידא אבל היכא דאיכא רמאי וליכא פסידא לא יקנוס כדמשמע לישנא דא"כ מה הפסיד הרמאי מיהו לשון אלא משמע דהדר לגמרי וכן בסמוך דפריך בין לרבנן בין לרבי יוסי נימא יהא מונח אף על גב דהתם לית ליה פסידא לרמאי:

**גבי** חנוני נמי יהא מונח. לר"ע דאמר (יבמות דף קיח:) בלקח מחמשה ואינו יודע מאיזה מהם לקח נותן לכאו"א לא פריך אמאי נותן לכאו"א יהא מונח דהתם הוה ליה למדכר ואיהו דאפסיד אנפשיה:

**ולא** אמרת לי הב ליה בסהדי. תימה לימא ליה בעל הבית לתקוני שדרתיך ולא לעוותי אע"ג דלא אמר ליה הב ליה בסהדי היה לו מעצמו להשים על לב כדאמרינן בפ' הכותב (כתובות דף פה.) גבי אבימי דהוי מסקי ביה זוזי בי חוזאי ושדרינהו ביד (ח) רבא ופרענהו ואמר להו הב לי שטרא ואמרו ליה הנך סטראי נינהו ומסיק התם דלא שנא א"ל שקול שטרא והב להו זוזי ולא שנא הב זוזי ושקול שטרא מחייב השליח משום דאמר ליה לתקוני שדרתיך ולא לעוותי וי"ל דהתם כיון דהזכיר לקיחת השטר כאילו אומר עשה באותו ענין שיבא השטר לידך אבל הכא לא הזכיר עדים כלל:

**מפני** מה אמרה תורה כו'. פי' יהא נאמן במגו דאי בעי כופר הכל או נילף מהכא דלא נימא מגו בעלמא ומשני דאין זה מגו דאין אדם מעיז פניו לכפור הכל הואיל וחבירו מכיר בשקרו אבל במקום שיכול להעיז כגון בבנו ואמר מנה לאביך בידי והאכלתיו פרס נאמן במגו דאי בעי כפר הכל כדאיתא פ"ב דכתובות (דף יח. ושם) ובפרק שבועת הדיינים (שבועות דף מב.) וא"ת כופר הכל מנלן דפטור ואין לומר מטעם חזקה דאין אדם מעיז דהא אפי' במקום שיכול להעיז פטור כגון בבנו ואפילו מודה מקצת פטור התם מגו דאי בעי כפר הכל ואין לומר דילפינן מדאיצטריך למכתב שעד אחד מחייבו שבועה ואי כופר הכל חייב מאי נפקא מינה מעד אחד הא בלאו הכי חייב דהא איצטריך במקום שהוא אינו תובע כלום ואינו יודע והעד מעיד שהוא גנב או שאביו הלוה לו וי"ל (ט) דמכי הוא זה משמע דגזירת הכתוב הוא דדוקא מודה מקצת הטענה חייב ולא כופר הכל (י):

בכוליה

**עין משפט נר מצוה**

ז א מיי' פ"ט מהלכות טוען ונטען הלכה ז סמג עשין לה:

ח ב מיי' פט"ז מהלכות מלוה ולוה הלכה ה סמג עשין לד טוש"ע ח"מ סי' לא סעיף א:

ט ג מיי' פ"ד מהל' טוען ונטען הלכה י סמג עשין לה טוש"ע ח"מ סי' עה סעיף ד:

י ד מיי' פ"א שם הל' א סמג עשין שם טוש"ע ח"מ סי' פז סעיף א:

**רבינו חננאל**

ואסקי' לשמעתי' אפי' תימא סומכוס שבועה זו דקתני במתני' מדרבנן היא דאמר ר' יוחנן שבועה זו תקנת חכמים היא. סוגיא דשמעתין בגמרא דשור שנגח את הפרה כסומכוס. תוב אמר לימא מתני' דלא כר' יוסי דאמר בפ' המפקיד א"כ מה הפסיד הרמאי אלא הכל יהא מונח עד שיבוא אליהו ויאמר למי הם. ושנינן אפי' תימא ר' יוסי התם ודאי איכא רמאי אבל הכא די"ל תרוייהו בהדי הדדי אגבהוה וכו' ואקשי' תוב לר' יוסי ולרבנן הא דתנן גבי חנוני על פנקסו שחנוני אמר נתתי והפועל אמר לא לקחתי ושנינו שניהן נשבעין ונוטלין מבעה"ב והא הכא דודאי איכא רמאי ולא אמרו הכל יהא מונח עד שיבוא אליהו. ודחינן התם היינו טעמא משום דיכול פועל למימר אנא לך עבדי עבידתא הב לי אגראי מאי אית לי גבי חנוני. חנוני אמר ליה לבעה"ב אנא שליחותך עבדי וכו'. **תני** ר' חייא מנה לי בידך והלה אומר אין לך בידי כלום והעדים מעידין אותו חמשים נותן לו חמשים וחייב שבועה על השאר שלא תהא הודאת פיו גדולה מהעדאת עדים מק"ו. ותנא תונא. פירושו והתנא שנאה. כלומר שנינו במשנתינו כשמעתיה דר' חייא דתנן שנים אוחזין בטלית וכו'. [מאי] שלא תהא הודאת פיו גדול' מהעדאת עדים וכו' אמרה תורה מודה מקצת הטענה ישבע שנאמר אשר יאמר כי הוא זה. ודרשינן לזה אשר יאמר כי הוא הוא שאתה טוענני (זה בלבד) יש לך אצלי זה בלבד שנמצא מודה במקצת הלכך ישבע. הנה בהודאת פיו במקצת שהיא קלה חייב שבועה העדאת עדים שהיא חמורה ממנה לא כ"ש שיהיה חייב.

**מסורת הש"ס**

א) [לקמן ה:], ב) לקמן ..., ג) [שבועות מה.], ד) [עיין תוס' לקמן ה. ד"ה ר' חייא], ה) עיין תוס' שבועות לד: ד"ה ... ו) כתובות יח., גיטין נא:, בבא קמא קז., ח) שבועות מב: [לקמן ה:], ... ס"א דלא הדר ביה ... אמרי אלא דלא סגי, ... ל"ל חמת, ט) [לקמן ...], י) ועיין עוד אריכות זה בתוס' בבא קמא קז. ד"ה עירוב.

**גליון הש"ס**

גמ' אלא מחוורתא. ... שיא הא תוס' ד"ה ולמזי ... כו' כתבו ומיהו הו"מ ... שנוי דליתא קמן דנשיילית ... ס כן איך ההכרעה ... דשנין מעיקרא דלמא ... ו"מ מיירי בנקט זוזי מחד ... ליתא קמן דנשיילית ... ליך ביה טעמא כי היכי דלודי:

**ליקוטי רש"י**

מה הפסיד רמאי. א"כ לא יודה לעולם על האמת [לקמן לז.]. מחוורתא. דבר ברור הוא כמו (נזיר דף סג) במחוורת עליו [מעילה טו.]. חנוני על פנקסו. על מה שכתוב בפנקסו שהוא כותב עליה הקפות שהוא מקיף. זה נשבע ונוטל וזה נשבע ונוטל. שתיקנו להם חכמים לישבע וליטול [שבועות מד:]. ותנא תונא. תנא דידן כמו תונא אתונא [יבמות נו:]. תנא דמתניתין דפרקין מסייע ליה. תונא כמו תנא דידן [חולין מד.]. אין אדם מעיז פניו בפני בע"ח. זה שעושה לו טובה הילכך היכא דכפר כל פטור משבועה דלאו קושטא בהדיה לא הוה מצי למכפר ביה והיכא דמודה מקצת בכוליה בעי למכפריה והא דלא כפריה משום דאין אדם מעיז [ב"ק קז.]. חזקה אין אדם מעיז פניו לכפור את הכל הלכך בשביל הודאת המקצת אינו נאמן על השאר דהאי בכוליה בעי דלכפריה וכו' [גיטין נא:].

ach.[29] וְקָתָנֵי יִשָּׁבַע – **And the Mishnah states** that **each must swear!** R' Chiya maintains that this proves his contention that the testimony of witnesses in support of half a claim obligates an oath regarding the other half.[30]

The Gemara analyzes R' Chiya's teaching:

מַאי שֶׁלֹּא תְּהֵא הוֹדָאַת פִּיו גְּדוֹלָה מֵהַעֲדָאַת עֵדִים מִקַּל וָחוֹמֶר – **What is** behind R' Chiya's statement: **"For the admission of his own mouth shall not be greater than the testimony of witnesses,** as can be demonstrated **from a *kal vachomer*"?** Why is a *kal vachomer* needed?[31]

The Gemara explains:

שֶׁלֹּא תֹּאמַר הוֹדָאַת פִּיו הוּא דְּרַמְיָא רַחֲמָנָא שְׁבוּעָה עֲלֵיהּ כִּדְרַבָּה – A *kal vachomer* is needed **so that you should not argue: It is only in** the case of **[the defendant's] own admission** to part of the claim **that the Merciful One imposed an oath upon him, as** one might think based on what **Rabbah said.** דְּאָמַר רַבָּה מִפְּנֵי מָה אָמְרָה תּוֹרָה מוֹדֶה מִקְצַת הַטַּעֲנָה יִשָּׁבַע – **For Rabbah said: Because of what** reason **did the Torah say that one who admits part of the claim must swear** that his denial of the other is the truth?[32] חֲזָקָה אֵין אָדָם מֵעִיז פָּנָיו בִּפְנֵי בַּעַל חוֹבוֹ – Because **it is presumed that a person is not** so **brazen** as to deny his obligation **to the face of his creditor.**[33] וְהַאי בְּכוּלֵּיהּ בָּעֵי דְּנִכְפְּרֵיהּ – **Thus,** it is possible that **this** defendant **would want to deny the entire [claim],** וְהָא דְּלָא כָּפְרֵיהּ מִשּׁוּם דְּאֵין אָדָם מֵעִיז פָּנָיו – **and that which he did not deny it** entirely **is because a person cannot** bring himself to **be** so **brazen.**[34]

NOTES

29. The Gemara now understands that since both hold the entire cloak (see 2a note 1, 2b notes 18 and 21), it is as if each has exclusive possession of half. The prima facie evidence coming before the court, then, is that each one owns half the cloak (see *Ritva*).

30. [Unlike Rav Pappa and R' Yochanan above,] R' Chiya understands that the oath in the case of our Mishnah is Biblically mandated and not a Rabbinic enactment (*Ritva*). Now, on what basis is a Biblical oath required in the case of our Mishnah? It must be on the basis that each litigant denies a claim that is partially supported by witnesses or their equivalent. For in the case of our Mishnah, each litigant claims the entire cloak; and though the other litigant denies the claim entirely, there is the presumptive evidence of possession to support half the claim. According to R' Chiya's law, then, each litigant must take the Biblical oath of *modeh bemiktzas* to support his denial of the other half of the claim against him. [That is, by swearing that he owns at least half the cloak, he denies the other litigant's claim to that half.] Does the Mishnah's requirement of an oath not prove, then, R' Chiya's contention that the oath of *modeh bemiktzas* is required not only when part of the claim is admitted by the defendant, but even when it is attested to by witnesses or their equivalent?

[The Gemara below (4a) will object that in the case of our Mishnah, the same presumptive evidence that supports half one litigant's claim also supports his opponent's denial of the other half.]

31. This statement of R' Chiya implies that were it not for the *kal vachomer,* one would have said that the oath of *modeh bemiktzas* is required only when the plaintiff's claim is partially supported by the defendant's admission, but not when it is partially supported by witnesses. Accordingly, the Gemara asks why such a distinction would have been made. What difference does it make whether half the claim is supported by the defendant's admission or by witnesses? (*Rashi*). [As explained above (note 23), the basis for the oath is that the claim has been strengthened by its partial corroboration. What difference does it make whether that partial corroboration was accomplished by admission or by witnesses? (see *Nachalas David*).]

32. Rabbah is *not* inquiring about the Torah's reason for imposing an oath on a defendant who admits part of the plaintiff's claim in contradistinction to one who denies it entirely (*Tos. HaRosh*; see also *Rashi* and *Tosafos*; cf. *Ramban* here and *Rashi* to *Bava Kamma* 107a). Rather, he is pointing out the following apparent anomaly in that law: Had the defendant who admits part of the claim wished to lie, he could have opted for the better lie of denying the obligation *entirely* [thereby avoiding partial payment as well as an oath]. Does his willingness to admit part of the claim, therefore, not indicate that he is indeed telling the truth? Why, then, does the Torah require him to substantiate his denial with an oath? (*Tosafos*). [The credibility of a claim based on the fact that a liar would have chosen a better lie is known as מִיגּוֹ, *migo* (literally: since; that is, believe his present claim *since* he could have presented a stronger claim had he wished to lie).]

Thus, Rabbah asks that the defendant's *migo* should absolve him from the oath of *modeh bemiktzas*. Alternatively, we should learn from the law of *modeh bemiktzas* that the concept of *migo* (used throughout the Talmud) is flawed (*Tosafos*).

[*Rashi* explains Rabbah's question in terms of "one who returns a lost object." This is a reference to the case of one who returns a lost object to its owner (e.g. a purse containing a sum of money), whereupon the owner claims that part is missing and that the returner might have kept that part for himself. The law is that the returner need not deny the owner's claim under oath (see *Gittin* 48b). Similarly, any defendant who admits part of the plaintiff's claim should be adjudged "a returner" (who is absolved from an oath), since he could have denied the claim entirely. *Ritva* apparently understands *Rashi* to be using the case of "one who returns a lost object" as another way of expressing the concept of *migo* (i.e. had the returner wished to steal, he did not have to return the lost object altogether). See also *Talmid HaRaf* cited in *Shitah Mekubetzes*. Cf. *Ramban, Ran* and *Nachalas David.* See Schottentstein edition to *Gittin* 51b and *Shevuos* 42b for a different explanation of *Rashi's* view.]

33. Because the creditor knows full well that he is lying (*Tosafos*) or because the creditor has done him a favor by lending him money (*Rashi* to *Bava Kamma* 107a; cf. *Tosafos* to *Kesubos* 18a ד״ה חזקה).

34. Thus, it cannot be argued that the defendant's partial admission of the claim proves that he speaks the truth. For it is possible that he could not bring himself to lie so brazenly to his creditor and deny the entire obligation (*Tosafos*).

**התם ודאי איכא רמאי.** לכך קנים ליה גם במה שהוא שלו בודאי אבל הכא איכא למימר תרוייהו בהדי הדדי אגבהוה דליכא רמאי דכל חד סבור שהוא הגביה קודם: **אי** נמי התם קנים כי היכי דלודי. אבל הכא אפילו איכא ודאי רמאי כגון שזה אומר אני מלאתיה היום וזה אומר אני מלאתיה אתמול מודה דיחלוקו ולא אמרינן יהא מונח עד שיבא אליהו דבשביל כך לא יפרוש דהא אינו מפסיד כלום:

**ואיכא למימר כוליה דמר.** ועוד על כרחך או כוליה דמר או כוליה דמר אפילו הכי חולקין בלא שבועה: **הכא דליכא דררא דממונא.** ועוד דאיכא למימר דתרוייהו בהדי הדדי אגבהוה: **לא כ"ש.** דחולקין בלא שבועה: **ותוקף.** אוחז: **דר' יוסי.** לקמן בהמפקיד (דף לז.) שנים שהפקידו אצל אחד זה מנה וזה מאתים זה אומר מאתים שלי וזה אומר מאתים שלי וקאמר ת"ק נותן לזה מנה ולזה מנה והשאר יהא מונח עד שיבא אליהו אמר ר' יוסי א"כ מה הפסיד הרמאי ולמה יודה הרי קיבל את שלו אלא הכל יהא מונח ויפסיד הרמאי וה"נ יהא מונח: **הא נמי כשאר דמיא.** דהתם על מנה השני הם דנין ואלו דנין על הטלית כולה: **דחד מינייהו הוא.** ואין לומר יחלוקו: **הכא דאיכא למימר דחד מינייהו הוא.** ואין לחבירו חלק בה לא כ"ש דלית ליה יחלוקו: **מאי פסידא אית ליה.** למי שאין לו חלק בה אם תהא מונחת: **דלודי.** שאין לו חלק בה כשיודה מה יטול: **מקח וממכר מאי איכא למימר.** הא אוקימנא דקיבל דמים מתרוייהו ואי הוה אמרינן יהא הטלית והדמים מונחים אית ליה פסידא לרמאי ויודה על האמת קודם שיפסיד: **התם היינו טעמא.** דשניהם נשבעין ונוטלין דחנוני אומר לבעל הבית אנא שליחותא דידך עבדי ונתתי לפועלך ממון שלויתני: **מאי אית לי גבי שכיר.** לערער: **לא מהימן לי.** איני מאמינו בשבועה אני אומר שהוא רשע ואין לי להאמין אדם בשבועה על כרחי אלא אם כן האמנתיו מתחילה להפקיד אצלו או להתנות עמו: **את הימנתיה.** ואתה הוא שקלקלת ואין לי להפסיד בקלקולך שיהיו מעותי מונחין עד שיבא אליהו: **וישבע על השאר.** כדין מודה מקצת הטענה שאמרה תורה ישבע כדילפינן בשבועות (דף לט:) מכי הוא זה ואע"ג דזה לא הודה הרי יש עדים במקצת ולא תהא הודאת פיו גדולה לחייבו על השאר שבועה מהעדאת עדים: **מקל וחומר.** לקמן מפרש מאי ק"ו: **ותנא תונא.** ותנא דידן סייעתא לדידי: **זה אומר כו'.** וקתני שניהם ישבעו: **אנן סהדי דמה דתפס האי. היינו פלגא: דידיה הוא.** שהרי מוחזק הוא בפנינו והרי הוא תובע את כולה וחבירו כופר את כולה שאומר כולה שלי ואף מה שאתה תפוס בידך ואנו מעידין אותו שיש לו בה מקצת ומחייבים את חבירו שבועה על השאר דהיינו חצי שעיכב לעצמו: **מאי לא תהא הודאת פיו גדולה מהעדאת עדים.** מהיכי תיתי לן למידק דתיסק אדעתין דתהא הודאת פיו גדולה מהעדאת עדים דאיצטריך לתנא למילף מק"ו דלא תהא הודאת פיו גדולה: **מפני מה אמרה תורה כו'.** ולא חשבו כמשיב אבידה לפטרו שלא כפר בכולו:

ואיכא למימר כולה למר ואיכא למימר כולה למר אמר סומכוס ממון המוטל בספק חולקין בלא שבועה הכא דליכא דררא דממונא דאיכא למימר דתרוייהו היא לא כ"ש אפילו תימא סומכוס שבועה זו מדרבנן היא כדרבי יוחנן דאמר ר' יוחנן [א] שבועה זו תקנת חכמים היא שלא יהא כל אחד ואחד הולך ותוקף בטליתו של חבירו ואומר שלי הוא לימא מתניתין דלא כרבי יוסי דאי כרבי יוסי הא אמר [ב] א"כ מה הפסיד רמאי אלא הכל יהא מונח עד שיבא אליהו אלא מאי רבנן כיון דאמרי רבנן השאר יהא מונח עד שיבא אליהו הא נמי כשאר דמי דספיקא היא האי מאי אי אמרת בשלמא רבנן התם דודאי האי מנה דחד מינייהו הוא אמרי רבנן יהא מונח עד שיבא אליהו הכא דאיכא למימר דתרוייהו הוא אמרי רבנן פלגי בשבועה אלא אי אמרת ר' יוסי היא השתא ומה התם דבודאי איכא מנה למר ואיכא מנה למר אמר ר' יוסי יהא מונח עד שיבא אליהו הכא דאיכא למימר דחד מינייהו הוא לא כ"ש אפי' תימא ר' יוסי התם ודאי איכא רמאי הכא מי יימר דאיכא רמאי אימא תרוייהו בהדי הדדי אגבהוה אי נמי התם קניס ליה רבי יוסי לרמאי כי היכי דלודי הכא מאי פסידא אית ליה דלודי תינח מציאה מקח וממכר מאי איכא למימר * אלא מחוורתא כדשנין מעיקרא בין לרבנן ובין לר' יוסי התם [ג] גבי חנוני על פנקסו דקתני [ב] זה נשבע ונוטל וזה נשבע ונוטל מ"ש דלא אמרינן נפקיה לממונא מבעה"ב ויהא מונח עד שיבא אליהו דהא בודאי איכא רמאי אמרי התם היינו טעמא דאמר ליה חנוני לבעה"ב אנא שליחותא דידך קא עבדינא מאי אית לי גבי שכיר אע"ג דקא משתבע לי לא מהימן לי בשבועה את האמנתיה דלא אמרת לי בסהדי הב ליה ושכיר נמי א"ל לבעה"ב אנא עבדי עבידתא גבך מאי אית לי גבי חנוני אע"ג דמשתבע לי לא מהימן לי הלכך תרוייהו משתבעי ושקלי מבעל הבית: [ד] תני רבי חייא [ג] מנה לי בידך והלה אומר אין לך בידי כלום והעדים מעידים אותו שיש לו חמשים זוז נותן לו חמשים זוז [ה] וישבע על השאר שלא תהא הודאת פיו גדולה מהעדאת עדים מק"ו ותנא תונא שנים אוחזין בטלית זה אומר אני מצאתיה וכו' והא הכא כיון דתפיס אנן סהדי דמאי דתפיס האי דידיה הוא ומאי דתפיס האי דידיה הוא וקתני ישבע מאי שלא תהא הודאת פיו גדולה מהעדא' עדי' מק"ו שלא תאמר הודאת פיו הוא דרמיא רחמנא שבועה עליה כדרבה [ו] דאמר רבה מפני מה אמרה תורה [ד] מודה מקצת הטענה ישבע חזקה אין אדם מעיז פניו בפני בע"ח והאי בכוליה בעי דנכפריה והא דלא כפריה משום דאין אדם מעיז פניו

**אלא** מחוורתא כדשנין מעיקרא. נוכל לומר [ז] דהדר ביה ולא סגי בטעמא דמפסיד הרמאי לבד דלא קניס ר' יוסי אלא היכא דאיכא ודאי רמאי ואית ליה פסידא אבל היכא דאיכא רמאי וליכא פסידא לא יקנוס כדמשמע לישנא דא"כ מה הפסיד הרמאי מיהו לשון אלא משמע דהדר לגמרי וכן בסמוך דפריך בין לרבנן בין לרבי יוסי נימא יהא מונח אף על גב דהתם לית ליה פסידא לרמאי:

**גבי** חנוני נמי יהא מונח. לר"ע דאמר (יבמות דף קיח:) בלקח מחמשה ואינו יודע מאיזה מהם לקח נותן לכאו"א לא פריך אמאי נותן לכאו"א יהא מונח דהתם הוה ליה למדכר ואיהו דאפסיד אנפשיה:

**ולא** אמרת לי הב ליה בסהדי. תימה לימא ליה בעל הבית לתקוני שדרתיך ולא לעוותי אע"ג דלא אמר ליה הב ליה בסהדי היה לו מעצמו להשים על לב כדאמרינן בפ' הכותב (כתובות דף פה.) גבי אבימי דהוי מסקי ביה זוזי בי חוזאי ושדרינהו ביד ([ח] רבא) ופרענהו ואמר להו הב לי שטרא ואמרו ליה הנך סטראי ניהו ומסיק התם דלא שנא א"ל שקול שטרא והב להו זוזי ולא שנא הב זוזי ושקול שטרא מחייב השליח משום דאמר ליה לתקוני שדרתיך ולא לעוותי וי"ל דהתם כיון דהזכיר לקיחת השטר כאילו אומר עשה באותו ענין שיבא השטר לידך אבל הכא לא הזכיר עדים כלל:

**מפני** מה אמרה תורה כו'. פי' יהא נאמן במגו דאי בעי כופר הכל או נילף מהכא דלא נימא מגו בעלמא ומשני דאין זה מגו דאין אדם מעיז פניו לכפור הכל הואיל וחבירו מכיר בשקרו אבל במקום שיכול להעיז כגון בבנו ואמר מנה לאביך בידי והאכלתיו פרס נאמן במגו דאי בעי כפר הכל כדאיתא פ"ב דכתובות (דף יח. ושם) ובפרק שבועת הדיינים (שבועות דף מב.) וא"ת כופר הכל מנלן דפטור ואין לומר מטעם חזקה דאין אדם מעיז דהא אפי' במקום שיכול להעיז פטור כגון בבנו ואפילו מודה מקצת פטור התם מגו דאי בעי כפר הכל ואין לומר דילפינן מדאיצטריך למכתב שעד אחד מחייבו שבועה ואי כופר הכל חייב מאי נפקא מינה מעד אחד הא בלאו הכי חייב דהא איצטריך במקום שהוא אינו תובע כלום ואינו יודע והעד מעיד שהוא גנב או שאביו הלוה לו וי"ל [ט] דמכי הוא זה משמע דגזירת הכתוב הוא דדוקא מודה מקצת הטענה חייב ולא כופר הכל [י]:

בכוליה

---

**עין משפט נר מצוה**

ז א מיי' פ"ט מהלכות טוען ונטען הלכה ז סמג עשין לה:

ח ב מיי' פט"ז מהלכות מלוה ולוה הלכה ה סמג עשין לד טוש"ע ח"מ סי' לא סעיף א:

ט ג מיי' פ"ד מהל' טוען ונטען הלכה י סמג עשין לה טוש"ע ח"מ סי' עה סעיף ד:

י ד מיי' פ"א שם הל' א סמג עשין שם טוש"ע ח"מ סי' פז סעיף א:

**רבינו חננאל**

ואסקי' לשמעתי' אפי' תימא סומכוס שבועה זו דקתני במתני' מדרבנן היא דאמר ר' יוחנן שבועה זו תקנת חכמים היא. סוגיא דשמעתין בגמרא דשור שנגח את הפרה כסומכוס. תוב אמר לימא מתני' דלא כר' יוסי דאמר בפ' המפקיד א"כ מה הפסיד הרמאי אלא הכל יהא מונח עד שיבוא אליהו ויאמר למי הם. ושנינן אפי' תימא ר' יוסי התם ודאי איכא רמאי אבל הכא די"ל תרוייהו בהדי הדדי אגבהוה וכו' ואקשי' תוב לר' יוסי ולרבנן הא דתנן גבי חנוני על פנקסו שחנוני אמר נתתי והפועל אמר לא לקחתי ושנינו שניהן נשבעין ונוטלין מבעה"ב והא הכא דודאי איכא רמאי ולא אמרו הכל יהא מונח עד שיבוא אליהו. ודחינן התם היינו טעמא משום דיכול פועל למימר אנא לך עבדי עבידתא הב לי אגראי מאי אית לי גבי חנוני. חנוני אמר ליה לבעה"ב אנא שליחותך עבדי וכו'. **תני** ר' חייא מנה לי בידך והלה אומר אין לך בידי כלום והעדים מעידין אותו חמשים נותן לו חמשים וחייב שבועה על השאר שלא תהא הודאת פיו גדולה מהעדאת עדים מק"ו. ותנא תונא. פירושו והתנא שנאה. כלומר שנינו במשנתינו כשמעתיה דר' חייא דתנן שנים אוחזין בטלית וכו'. [מאי] שלא תהא הודאת פיו גדול' מהעדאת עדים וכו' אמרה תורה מודה מקצת הטענה ישבע שנאמר אשר יאמר כי הוא זה. ודרשינן לזה אשר יאמר כי הוא הוא שאתה טועני (זה בלבד) יש לך אצלי זה בלבד שנמצא מודה במקצת הלכך ישבע. הנה בהודאת פיו במקצת שהיא קלה חייב שבועה העדאת עדים שהיא חמורה ממנה לא כ"ש שיהיה חייב.

**מסורת הש"ס**

[לקמן ה:], ב) לקמן ..., ג) [שבועות מה.], [עיין תוס' לקמן ה. ד"ה ר' חייא], ה) עיין ... שבועות לד: ד"ה ..., ו) כתובות יח., גיטין ..., בבא קמא קז., ... שבועות מב: [לקמן ה:], ... מ"א דלא הדר ביה ... אלא דלא סגי, ... ל"ל חמא, ט) [לקמן ...], י) ועיין עוד אריכות ... בתוס' בבא קמא קז. ד"ה עירוב.

**גליון הש"ס**

... אלא מחוורתא. ... הא תוס' ד"ה ולמזי ... כתבו ומיהו הו"מ ... גוי דליתא קמן דנשיילה ... כן איך ההכרעה ... שנין מעיקרא דלמא ... מ"מ מיירי בנקט זוזי מחד ... קמן דנשיילה ... ך ביה טעמא כי היכי דלודי:

**ליקוטי רש"י**

... הפסיד רמאי. א"כ ... יודה לעולם על האמת [לקמן לז.]. **מחוורתא.** ... ברור הוא כמו (נזיר ... סג) במחוורת עליו [... עילה טו.]. **חנוני על פנקסו.** על מה שכתוב פנקסו שהוא כותב עליה ... קפות שהוא מקיף. **זה נשבע ונוטל וזה נשבע ונוטל.** שתיקנו ... חכמים לישבע וליטול [שבועות מד:]. **ותנא תונא.** תנא דידן כמו ... תונא אחונא [יבמות נז:] ... דמתניתין דפרקין ... סייע ליה. תונא כמו תנא ... [חולין מד.]. **אין אדם מעיז פניו בפני בע"ח.** זה שעשה לו ... טובה הילכך היכא דכפר ... כל פטור משבועה דאי ... קושטא בהדיה לא ... מאי למכפר ביה ... היכא דמודה מקצת ... כוליה בעי למכפריה והא ... לא כפריה משום דאין ... אדם מעיז [ב"ק קז.]. ... אין אדם מעיז פניו ... לפטור את הכל הלכך ... בשביל הודאת המקצת ... נו נאמן על השאר דהאי ... כוליה בעי דלכפריה וכו' [גיטין נא:].

The Gemara answers:
אָמְ – They say: הָתָם הַיְינוּ טַעֲמָא – There in the case of the opkeeper, this is the reason each litigant collects his claim: דְּאָמַר לֵיהּ חֶנְוָנִי לְבַעַל הַבַּ – For the shopkeeper says to the meowner [i.e. the employer], אֲנָא שְׁלִיחוּתָא דִּידָךְ קָא עֲבַדִינָא – did your bidding and paid the employee. מַאי אִית לִי גַּבֵּי שָׂכִיר What have I now to do with the employee and his denial? אַף עַל גַּב דְּקָא מִשְׁתַּבַּע לִי לָא מְהֵימַן לִי בִּשְׁבוּ – Even if he swears me that I never paid him, I do not consider him trustworthy en under oath.[20] אַתְּ הֶאֱמַנְתֵּיהּ דְּלָא אָמְרַת לִי בְּסַהֲדֵי הַב לֵיהּ – ather, it is you [the employer] who trusted him by not telling e to give him his wages in the presence of witnesses, who could bsequently confirm that payment was made."[21]

The Gemara now explains why the employee collects his claim: וְשָׂכִיר נַמִּי אָמַר לֵיהּ לְבַעַל הַבַּ – And the employee, too, says to e homeowner [i.e. the employer], אֲנָא עַבְדִי עֲבִידְתָּא גַּבָּךְ – "I d work for you, for which I am entitled to payment. מַאי אִית לִי גַּבֵּי חֶנְ – What have I to do with the shopkeeper and his sertion? אַף עַל גַּב דְּמִשְׁתַּבַּע לִי לָא מְהֵימַן לִי – Even if he vears to me, I do not consider him trustworthy."[22] הִלְכָּךְ תַּרְוַיְיהוּ מִשְׁתַּבְּעֵי וְשָׁקְלֵי מִבַּעַל הַבַּ – Therefore, both of them vear and collect from the homeowner.

The Torah mandates that a defendant who admits part of the aintiff's claim but denies the rest must support his denial with oath. (This is known as the oath of מוֹדֶה בְמִקְצָת, *modeh miktzas; one who admits part [of the claim].*)[23] The Gemara w considers a variation of this law, which it seeks to support om the case of our Mishnah:

תָּנֵי רַבִּי חִיָּיא – R' Chiya taught the law in the following case:[24]

מָנֶה לִי בְּיָדְךָ – A plaintiff claims: "You owe me a *maneh*,"[25] וְהַלָּה אוֹמֵר אֵין לְךָ בְּיָדִי כְּלוּם – and this one [the defendant] replies: "I owe you nothing."[26] וְהָעֵדִים מְעִידִים אוֹתוֹ שֶׁיֵּשׁ לוֹ חֲמִשִּׁים זוּז – But witnesses testify on [the plaintiff's] behalf that he is indeed owed fifty *zuz* by the defendant. The law is: נוֹתֵן לוֹ חֲמִשִּׁים זוּז וְיִשָּׁבַע עַל הַשְּׁאָר – [The defendant] gives [the plaintiff] the fifty *zuz* owed, as attested by the witnesses, and he must swear to [the plaintiff] regarding the rest that he does not owe it to him. שֶׁלֹּא תְּהֵא הוֹדָאַת פִּיו גְּדוֹלָה מֵהַעֲדָאַת עֵדִים מִקַּל וָחוֹמֶר – For the admission of his own mouth shall not be greater than the testimony of witnesses,[27] as can be demonstrated from a *kal vachomer.*[28]

Before demonstrating the *kal vachomer,* the Gemara records what R' Chiya said in support of his teaching:

וְתַנָּא תּוּנָא – "And our Tanna has taught it." I.e. the Tanna of our Mishnah supports my teaching, for our Tanna states: שְׁנַיִם אוֹחֲזִין בְּטַלִּית זֶה אוֹמֵר אֲנִי מְצָאתִיהָ וכו׳ – TWO litigants ARE HOLDING ON TO A CLOAK. THIS ONE SAYS, "I FOUND IT, first," etc. וְהָא הָכָא כֵּיוָן דְּתָפֵיס – Now, here in this case, since he [each litigant] is holding the cloak, אֲנַן סַהֲדֵי דְּמַאי דְּתָפֵיס הַאי דִּידֵיהּ הוּא וּמַאי דְּתָפֵיס הַאי דִּידֵיהּ הוּא – it is as if we are witnesses that what this one holds is his and what this one holds is his. I.e. the presumption made by the court is that an object belongs to the one who has physical possession of it; since each litigant is legally in possession of half the cloak, the presumption – equivalent in force to the testimony of witnesses – is that half belongs to

NOTES

. As far as I, the shopkeeper, am concerned, the employee is a liar and hief, whose oath is meaningless to me. And a claimant is not bound to cept [in lieu of payment that is due him] the oath of another person less the claimant initially accepted upon himself the trustworthiness that person (see *Rashi*).

. The shopkeeper argues that it was not his responsibility to have tnesses present when he paid the employee. Rather, it was the ployer who should have stipulated this condition, and his failure to so is what has caused the current predicament. It is not fair that his ne shopkeeper's] money should be permanently set aside as a result of e employer's negligence. [Rather, the employer should have to imburse him, even if this will mean that the employer has to pay ice – once to him and once to the employee] (*Rashi,* see *Ritva*; see so *Shitah Mekubetzes,* who explains the need for the various elements the shopkeeper's argument).

Reduced to its essentials, the argument of the shopkeeper is that his aim against the homeowner is completely independent of the ployee's conflicting claim, which he is not bound to contend with. ne homeowner trusted him to disburse funds, which he did, and he w seeks reimbursement from the homeowner (*Ritva*). [This is in ntrast to the case of the three *manehs,* where the conflicting claims e part of a single lawsuit. Therefore, the claim of each litigant is unterbalanced by the claim of the other.]

. [The employee's argument is essentially the same as the shopeper's: His claim against his employer is completely independent of e shopkeeper's conflicting claim, and there is no reason for him to ntend with the shopkeeper. The employer owed him wages and has no oof that they were ever paid (see *Ritva*).]

. Under Biblical law, a defendant who altogether denies the monetary aim of a plaintiff [כּוֹפֵר הַכֹּל, *one who denies the whole*] does not have to pport his denial with an oath. One who admits part of the claim, wever, must support his denial of the rest with a Biblical oath (see te 27 for the Scriptural source). [The rationale for this distinction is at an unsubstantiated denial is an adequate response to an substantiated claim. However, where the claim has been somewhat bstantiated (e.g. the defendant has admitted that it is partly true and t entirely baseless), simple denial is not adequate. Rather, the Torah quires that the defendant substantiate his denial with an oath (see *tva* ד״ה דאמר רבה and *Tosafos* to 4a ד״ה הצד השוה).]

To illustrate: A plaintiff claims that the defendant owes him one hundred *zuz* (a monetary unit). If the defendant asserts that he owes the plaintiff absolutely nothing, the defendant need not assert his denial under oath. But if the defendant admits that he owes, say, fifty *zuz,* then he must swear that he owes no more than that amount.

[In the times of the Gemara, however, the Rabbis imposed a Rabbinic oath (שְׁבוּעַת הֶיסֵּת, *an oath of incitement,* i.e. imposed to induce confession) even on one who categorically denies the plaintiff's claim – see below, 5a, 6a.]

24. [Actually, the words תָּנֵי רַבִּי חִיָּיא are more literally translated as: R' Chiya taught *a Baraisa* (see *Rashi* to *Niddah* 26a [cited in *Gilyon HaShas*] and *Tosafos* to 5a [cited in margin]). However, *Rashi* (ד״ה ותנא תונא) seems to have understood this teaching to be that of R' Chiya himself, and *Tosafos* (loc. cit.) indeed cite a version of our Gemara that reads: אָמַר רַבִּי חִיָּיא, *R' Chiya said.*]

25. [Literally: there is a *maneh* belonging to me in your hand (i.e. possession).] A *maneh* is one hundred *zuz.*

26. [Literally: there is nothing belonging to you in my hand.]

27. As expounded by the Gemara (*Shevuos* 39b, *Bava Kamma* 106b), the Torah (*Exodus* 22:8) requires a defendant to swear when his own admission partially substantiates the claim against him. The verse there discusses the case of a custodian who, when asked to return the article entrusted to him, claims that it was stolen – an occurrence for which he is not liable. The verse states the custodian must swear that his claim is true: אֲשֶׁר יֹאמַר כִּי־הוּא זֶה, *when he [the custodian] says that it is this* [that I owe you, but not more]; i.e. the custodian admits that part of the deposit remains in his possession, but claims that the *rest* was stolen (see Gemara below, 5a; see also *Rashi* to that verse, who explains the verse's simple meaning). R' Chiya teaches that the same Biblical oath applies when the plaintiff's claim is partially substantiated not by the defendant's own admission but by witnesses.

28. [*Kal vachomer* – an a fortiori argument from minor to major premise (see glossary).] A *kal vachomer* (detailed in the Gemara below) demonstrates that the testimony of witnesses is stronger than a person's own admission. Consequently, if a person's own admission to half the claim obligates him to assert his denial of the other half under oath, then the testimony of witnesses to half the claim certainly obligates him in an oath.

ואיכא למימר כולה למר ואיכא למימר כולה למר אמר סומכוס ממון המוטל בספק חולקין בלא שבועה הכא דליכא דררא דממונא דאיכא למימר דתרווייהו היא לא כ"ש אפילו תימא סומכוס שבועה זו מדרבנן היא כדרבי יוחנן דאמר ר' יוחנן [א] שבועה זו תקנת חכמים היא שלא יהא כל אחד ואחד הולך ותוקף בטליתו של חבירו ואומר שלי הוא לימא מתניתין דלא כרבי יוסי דאי כרבי יוסי הא אמר [ב] א"כ מה הפסיד רמאי אלא הכל יהא מונח עד שיבא אליהו אלא מאי רבנן כיון דאמרי רבנן השאר יהא מונח עד שיבא אליהו הא נמי כשאר דמי דספיקא היא האי מאי אי אמרת בשלמא רבנן התם דודאי האי מנה דחד מינייהו הוא אמרי רבנן יהא מונח עד שיבא אליהו הכא דאיכא למימר דתרווייהו הוא אמרי רבנן פלגי בשבועה אלא אי אמרת ר' יוסי היא השתא ומה התם דבודאי איכא מנה למר ואיכא מנה למר אמר ר' יוסי יהא מונח עד שיבא אליהו הכא דאיכא למימר דחד מינייהו הוא לא כ"ש אפי' תימא ר' יוסי התם ודאי איכא רמאי הכא מי יימר דאיכא רמאי אימא תרווייהו בהדי הדדי אגבהוה אי נמי התם קניס ליה רבי יוסי לרמאי כי היכי דלודי הכא מאי פסידא אית ליה דלודי תינח מציאה מקח וממכר מאי איכא למימר ° אלא מחוורתא כדשנין מעיקרא בין לרבנן ובין לר' יוסי התם [ג] גבי חנוני על פנקסו דקתני [ב] זה נשבע ונוטל וזה נשבע ונוטל מ"ש דלא אמרינן נפקיה לממונא מבעה"ב ויהא מונח עד שיבא אליהו דהא בודאי איכא רמאי אמרי התם היינו טעמא דאמר ליה חנוני לבעה"ב אנא שליחותא דידך קא עבדינא מאי אית לי גבי שכיר אע"ג דקא משתבע לי לא מהימן לי בשבועה את האמנתיה דלא אמרת לי בסהדי הב ליה ושכיר נמי א"ל לבעה"ב אנא עבדי עבידתא גבך מאי אית לי גבי חנוני אע"ג דמשתבע לי לא מהימן לי הלכך תרווייהו משתבעי ושקלי מבעל הבית: [ד] תני רבי חייא [ג] מנה לי בידך והלה אומר אין לך בידי כלום והעדים מעידים אותו שיש לו חמשים זוז נותן לו חמשים זוז [ה] וישבע על השאר שלא תהא הודאת פיו גדולה מהעדאת עדים מק"ו ותנא תונא שנים אוחזין בטלית זה אומר אני מצאתיה וכו' והא הכא כיון דתפיס אנן סהדי דמאי דתפיס האי דידיה הוא ומאי דתפיס האי דידיה הוא וקתני ישבע מאי שלא תהא הודאת פיו גדולה מהעדאת עדי' מק"ו שלא תאמר הודאת פיו הוא דרמיא רחמנא שבועה עליה כדרבה [ו] דאמר רבה מפני מה אמרה תורה [ד] מודה מקצת הטענה ישבע חזקה אין אדם מעיז פניו בפני בע"ח והאי בכוליה בעי דנכפריה והא דלא כפריה משום דאין אדם מעיז פניו

---

ואיכא למימר כוליה דמר. ועוד על כרחך או כוליה דמר או כוליה דמר אפילו הכי חולקין בלא שבועה: הכא דליכא דררא דממונא. ועוד דאיכא למימר דתרוייהו בהדי הדדי אגבהוה: לא כ"ש. דחולקין בלא שבועה: ותוקף. אוחז: דר' יוסי. לקמן בהמפקיד (דף לז.) שנים שהפקידו אצל אחד זה מנה וזה מאתים זה אומר מאתים שלי וזה אומר מאתים שלי וקאמר ת"ק נותן לזה מנה ולזה מנה והשאר יהא מונח עד שיבא אליהו אמר ר' יוסי א"כ מה הפסיד הרמאי ולמה יודה הרי קיבל את שלו אלא הכל יהא מונח ויפסיד הרמאי וה"נ יהא מונח: הא נמי כשאר דמיא. דהתם על מנה השני הם דנין ואלו דנין על הטלית כולה: דחד מינייהו הוא. ואין לומר יחלוקו: הכא דאיכא למימר דחד מינייהו הוא. ואין לחבירו חלק בה לא כ"ש דלית ליה יחלוקו: מאי פסידא אית ליה. למי שאין לו חלק בה אם תהא מונחת: דלודי. שאין לו חלק בה כשיודה מה יטול: מקח וממכר מאי איכא למימר. הא אוקימנא דקיבל דמים מתרווייהו ואי הוה אמרינן יהא הטלית והדמים מונחים אית ליה פסידא לרמאי ויודה על האמת קודם שיפסיד: התם היינו טעמא. דשניהם נשבעין ונוטלין דחנוני אומר לבעל הבית אנא שליחותא דידך עבדי ונתתי לפועלך ממון שצויתני: מאי אית לי גבי שכיר. לערער: לא מהימן לי. איני מאמינו בשבועה אני אומר שהוא רשע ואין לי להאמין אדם בשבועה על כרחי אלא אם כן האמנתיו מתחילה להפקיד אצלו או להתנות עמו: את הימנתיה. ואתה הוא שקילקלת ואין לי להפסיד בקלקולך שיהיו מעותי מונחין עד שיבא אליהו: וישבע על השאר. כדין מודה מקצת הטענה שאמרה תורה ישבע כדילפינן בשבועות (דף לט:) מכי הוא זה ואע"ג דזה לא הודה הרי יש עדים במקצת ולא תהא הודאת פיו גדולה לחייבו על השאר שבועה מהעדאת עדים: מקל וחומר. לקמן מפרש מאי ק"ו: ותנא תונא. ותנא דידן סייעתא לדידי: זה אומר כו'. וקתני שניהם ישבעו: אנן סהדי דמה דתפס האי. היינו פלגא: דידיה הוא. שהרי מוחזק הוא בפנינו והרי הוא תובע את כולה וחבירו כופר את כולה שאומר כולה שלי ואף מה שאתה תפוס בידך ואנו מעידין אותו שיש לו בה מקצת ומחייבים את חבירו שבועה על השאר דהיינו חצי שעיכב לעצמו: מאי לא תהא הודאת פיו גדולה מהעדאת עדים. מהיכי תיתי לן למידק דתיסק אדעתין דתהא הודאת פיו גדולה מהעדאת עדים דאיצטריך לתנא למילף מק"ו דלא תהא הודאת פיו גדולה: מפני מה אמרה תורה כו'. ולא חשבו כמשיב אבידה לפטרו שלא כפר בכולו:

---

**התם** ודאי איכא רמאי. לכך קניס ליה גם במה שהוא שלו בודאי אבל הכא איכא למימר תרווייהו בהדי הדדי אגבהוה דליכא רמאי דכל חד סבור שהוא הגביה קודם: **אי** נמי התם קניס כי היכי דלודי. אבל הכא אפילו איכא ודאי רמאי כגון שזה אומר אני מצאתיה היום וזה אומר אני מצאתיה אתמול מודה דיחלוקו ולא אמרינן יהא מונח עד שיבא אליהו דבשביל כך לא יפרוש דהא אינו מפסיד כלום:

**אלא** מחוורתא כדשנין מעיקרא. נוכל לומר [ז] דהדר ביה ולא סגי בטעמא דמפסיד הרמאי לבד דלא קניס ר' יוסי אלא היכא דאיכא ודאי רמאי ואית ליה פסידא אבל היכא דאיכא רמאי וליכא פסידא לא יקנוס כדמשמע לישנא דא"כ מה הפסיד הרמאי מיהו לשון אלא משמע דהדר לגמרי וכן בסמוך דפריך בין לרבנן בין לרבי יוסי נימא יהא מונח אף על גב דהתם לית ליה פסידא לרמאי:

**גבי** חנוני נמי יהא מונח. לר"ע דאמר (יבמות דף קיח:) בלקח מחמשה ואינו יודע מאיזה מהם לקח נותן לכאו"א לא פריך אמאי נותן לכאו"א יהא מונח דהתם הוה ליה למדכר ואיהו דאפסיד אנפשיה:

**ולא** אמרת לי הב ליה בסהדי. תימה לימא ליה בעל הבית לתקוני שדרתיך ולא לעוותי אע"ג דלא אמר ליה הב ליה בסהדי היה לו מעצמו להשים על לב כדאמרינן בפ' הכותב (כתובות דף פה.) גבי אבימי דהוי מסקי ביה זוזי בי חוזאי ושדרינהו ביד ([ח] רבא) ופרענהו ואמר להו הב לי שטרא ואמרו ליה הנך סטראי נינהו ומסיק התם דלא שנא א"ל שקול שטרא והב להו זוזי ולא שנא הב זוזי ושקול שטרא מחייב השליח משום דאמר ליה לתקוני שדרתיך ולא לעוותי וי"ל דהתם כיון דהזכיר לקיחת השטר כאילו אומר עשה באותו ענין שיבא השטר לידך אבל הכא לא הזכיר עדים כלל:

**מפני** מה אמרה תורה כו'. פי' יהא נאמן במגו דאי בעי כופר הכל או נילף מהכא דלא נימא מגו בעלמא ומשני דאין זה מגו דאין אדם מעיז פניו לכפור הכל הואיל וחבירו מכיר בשקרו אבל במקום שיכול להעיז כגון בבנו ואמר מנה לאביך בידי והאכלתיו פרס נאמן במגו דאי בעי כפר הכל כדאיתא פ"ב דכתובות (דף יח. ושם) ובפרק שבועת הדיינים (שבועות דף מב.) וא"ת כופר הכל מנלן דפטור ואין לומר מטעם חזקה דאין אדם מעיז דהא אפי' במקום שיכול להעיז פטור כגון בבנו ואפילו מודה מקצת פטור התם מגו דאי בעי כפר הכל ואין לומר דילפינן מדאיצטריך למכתב שעד אחד מחייבו שבועה ואי כופר הכל חייב מאי נפקא מינה מעד אחד הא בלאו הכי חייב דהא איצטריך במקום שהוא אינו תובע כלום ואינו יודע והעד מעיד שהוא גנב או שאביו הלוה לו וי"ל [ט] דמכי הוא זה משמע דגזירת הכתוב הוא דדוקא מודה מקצת הטענה חייב ולא כופר הכל [י]:

בכוליה

---

## עין משפט נר מצוה

ז א מיי' פ"ט מהלכות טוען ונטען הלכה ז סמג עשין לה:

ח ב מיי' פט"ז מהלכות מלוה ולוה הלכה ה סמג עשין לד טוש"ע ח"מ סי' לא סעיף א:

ט ג מיי' פ"ד מהל' טוען ונטען הלכה י סמג עשין לה טוש"ע ח"מ סי' עה סעיף ד:

י ד מיי' פ"א שם הל' א סמג עשין שם טוש"ע ח"מ סי' פז סעיף א:

## רבינו חננאל

ואסקי' לשמעתי' אפי' תימא סומכוס שבועה זו דקתני במתני' מדרבנן היא דאמר ר' יוחנן שבועה זו תקנת חכמים היא. סוגיא דשמעתין בגמרא דשור שנגח את הפרה כסומכוס. תוב אמר לימא מתני' דלא כר' יוסי דאמר בפ' המפקיד א"כ מה הפסיד הרמאי אלא הכל יהא מונח עד שיבוא אליהו ויאמר למי הם. ושנינן אפי' תימא ר' יוסי התם ודאי איכא רמאי אבל הכא די"ל תרוייהו בהדי הדדי אגבהוה וכו' ואקשי' תוב לר' יוסי ולרבנן הא דתנן גבי חנוני על פנקסו שחנוני אמר נתתי והפועל אמר לא לקחתי ושנינו שניהן נשבעין ונוטלין מבעה"ב והא הכא דודאי איכא רמאי ולא אמרו הכל יהא מונח עד שיבוא אליהו. ודחינן התם היינו טעמא משום דיכול פועל למימר אנא לך עבדי עבידתא הב לי אגראי מאי אית לי גבי חנוני. חנוני אמר ליה לבעה"ב אנא שליחותך עבדי וכו'. **תני** ר' חייא מנה לי בידך והלה אומר אין לך בידי כלום והעדים מעידין אותו חמשים נותן לו חמשים וחייב שבועה על השאר שלא תהא הודאת פיו גדולה מהעדאת עדים מק"ו. ותנא תונא. פירושו והתנא שנאה. כלומר שנינו במשנתינו כשמעתיה דר' חייא דתנן שנים אוחזין בטלית וכו'. [מאי] שלא תהא הודאת פיו גדול' מהעדאת עדים וכו' אמרה תורה מודה מקצת הטענה ישבע שנאמר אשר יאמר כי הוא זה. ודרשינן לזה אשר יאמר כי הוא הוא שאתה טועני (זה בלבד) יש לך אצלי זה בלבד שנמצא מודה במקצת הלכך ישבע. הנה בהודאת פיו במקצת שהיא קלה חייב שבועה העדאת עדים שהיא חמורה ממנה לא כ"ש שיהיה חייב.

## מסורת הש"ס

לקמן ה:], ב) לקמן ג) [שבועות מה.], עיין תוס' לקמן ה. ר' חייא], ה) עיין שבועות לד: ד"ה ו) כתובות יח., גיטין בבא קמא קז., ...ת מב: [לקמן ה:], ...א דלא הדר ביה ...אלא דלא סגי, ...ל חמא, ט) [לקמן י) ועיין עוד אריכות בתוס' בבא קמא קז. ד"ה עירוב.

## גליון הש"ס

אלא מחוורתא. הא תוס' ד"ה ולחזי כתבו ומיהו הו"מ ...י דליתא קמן דנשייליה ...כן איך ההכרעה ...ין מעיקרא דלמא ...מיירי בנקט זוזי מחד ...קמן דנשייליה ביה טעמא כי היכי דלודי:

## ליקוטי רש"י

הפסיד רמאי. א"כ ...דה לעולם על האמת ...[לז.]. מחוורתא. ברור הוא כמו (מזיר סג) במחוורת עליו ...[לה טו.]. חנוני על ...סו. על מה שכתוב ...קסו שהוא כותב עליה ...ות שהוא מקיף. זה ...נשבע ונוטל וזה ...נשבע ונוטל. שתיקנו חכמים לישבע וליטול ...[שבועות מד:]. ותנא ...א. תנא דידן כמו ...א אחונא [יבמות נו:]. דמתניתין דפרקין ...ע ליה. תונא כמו תנא [חולין מד.]. אין ...ם מעיז פניו בפני ...ח. זה שעושה לו ...הילכך היכא דכפר פטור משבועה דאי קושטא בהדיה לא מצי למכפר ביה ...א דמודה מקצת ...יה בעי למכפריה והא ...כפריה משום דאין ...מעיז [ב"ק קז.]. ...ה אין אדם מעיז פניו ...ר את הכל הלכך ...יל הודאת המקצת נאמן על השאר דהאי ...יה בעי דלכפריה וכו' [גיטין נא:].

ijah comes.[7] הָכָא דְּאִיכָּא לְמֵימַר דִּתַרְוַיְיהוּ הוּא – Here in our ishnah, on the other hand, **where it is possible to say that [the oak] belongs to both** litigants, since they might have picked it ) simultaneously, אָמְרֵי רַבָּנַן פָּלְגֵי בִּשְׁבוּעָה – **the Rabbis say** at they divide it under oath.[8]

אֶלָּא אִי אָמְרַת ר׳ יוֹסֵי ה – **But if you say that [our Mishnah]** consistent with the view of **R' Yose,** you are faced with the llowing difficulty: הַשְׁתָּא וּמָה הָתָם דִּבְוַדַּאי אִיכָּא מָנֶה לְמַר וְאִיכָּא מָנֶה לְ – **Now, if there** in the case of the three *manehs,* **where** ere **is definitely a *maneh*** belonging **to this one and a** *aneh* belonging **to that one,** still אָמַר ר׳ יוֹסֵי יְהֵא מוּנָּח עַד שֶׁיָּבֹא אֵלִיָּ – **R' Yose said that it should be set aside until** ijah comes – even those two *manehs* whose ownership is finitely known; הָכָא דְּאִיכָּא לְמֵימַר דְּחַד מִינַּיְיהוּ הוּא לֹא כָּל שֶׁ – then, **here** in the case of our Mishnah, **where it is** ossible to say that [the cloak] is the property **of** only **one of** em, **is it not certain** that R' Yose would advocate putting the oak aside until Elijah comes?![9]

The Gemara replies:

אֲפִילוּ תֵּימָא ר׳ יוֹ – **You can even say** that our Mishnah is consistent with the view of **R' Yose.** הָתָם וַדַּאי אִיכָּא רַמַּאי – **There** the case of the three *manehs*, **there is definitely a deceiver.**[10] הָכָא מִי יֵימַר דְּאִיכָּא רַמַּ – **Here** in the case of our Mishnah, **who** to say that there is a deceiver? אֵימָא תַּרְוַיְיהוּ בַּהֲדֵי הֲדָדֵי אַגְבַּה – **I could say that they both picked up [the cloak]** gether.[11] Since the case of our Mishnah does not necessarily volve a deceiver, it is possible that R' Yose would agree that viding the cloak is preferable to setting it aside.[12]

An alternative resolution:

אִי נ – **Alternatively,** you can reconcile our Mishnah with R' se in the following way: הָתָם קָנֵיס לֵיהּ רַבִּי יוֹסֵי לְרַמַּאי כִּי הֵיכִי דְּלוֹ – **There** in the case of the three *manehs,* **R' Yose penalizes** e **deceiver so that he should** be induced to **admit** his fraud.[13] הָכָא מַאי פְּסֵידָא אִית לֵיהּ דְּלוֹדֵי – **Here** in the case of our Mishnah, **what loss does he have that he should** be induced to **admit?** If the found cloak is not his, he has nothing to lose, and withholding it from him does not induce him to admit his fraud. Therefore, R' Yose would agree that the cloak is divided.[14]

The Gemara rejects this alternative resolution:

תֵּינַח מְצִיאָה – **This** alternative resolution **settles** the case of **a found object.** There, indeed, withholding the cloak will not induce the deceiver to admit, and R' Yose would therefore agree that the cloak is divided. מִקָּח וּמִמְכָּר מַאי אִיכָּא לְמֵימַר – But **what is there to say about** the Mishnah's second case – the case of **buying and selling?** In that case, withholding the cloak and the monies that each litigant paid the seller would induce the deceiver to admit his fraud![15] – ? –

The Gemara concedes this point:

אֶלָּא מְחַוַּורְתָּא כִּדְשַׁנִּין מֵעִיקָּרָא – **Rather, the clear [resolution] is the one we originally advanced;** namely, that according to R' Yose, dividing or withholding depends on whether or not there is a definite deceiver.[16]

The Gemara asks:

בֵּין לְרַבָּנַן וּבֵין לְר׳ יוֹסֵי – **Both according to the Rabbis and according to R' Yose,** who ruled in the case of the three *manehs,* הָתָם גַּבֵּי חֶנְוָנִי עַל פִּנְקָסוֹ – **there, regarding "the shopkeeper concerning his ledger,"** דְּקָתָנֵי זֶה נִשְׁבָּע וְנוֹטֵל וְזֶה נִשְׁבָּע וְנוֹטֵל – **where the Mishnah**[17] **states that this one swears and collects, and this one swears and collects,** i.e. each litigant is paid in full after swearing to his claim, מַאי שְׁנָא דְּלָא אָמְרִינַן נַפְּקֵיהּ לְמָמוֹנָא מִבַּעַל הַבַּיִת וִיהֵא מוּנָּח עַד שֶׁיָּבֹא אֵלִיָּהוּ – **what is different** about that case **that we do not say** there, **"Let us take the money from the homeowner** [i.e. the employer], **and let it be set aside until Elijah comes"?**[18] דְּהָא בְּוַדַּאי אִיכָּא רַמַּאי – **Why,** in that case, too, **there is definitely a deceiver!**[19] – ? –

NOTES

Since it is an undisputed fact that one depositor deposited two *manehs* d the other deposited only one, they certainly do not both own the ird *maneh.* Consequently, the court cannot divide the third *maneh* tween them, since doing so necessarily constitutes the wrongful ard of half the amount. Therefore, the Rabbis rule that the third *aneh* must be set aside (see *Ritva*).

Where it is possible that division is actually the true distribution of the sputed amount, the Rabbis would agree that division is preferable to tting it aside until the coming of Elijah.

[Thus, nothing was lacking in our initial understanding of our shnah, which is fully compatible with the view of the Rabbis.]

[From R' Yose's ruling in the case of the three *manehs,* we see that his iority in cases of doubt is thwarting the deceiver, even though this tails depriving the deceiver and his opponent of money that is finitely theirs. Certainly, then, R' Yose would rule in the case of our shnah that we thwart the deceiver by withholding from him what ay not be his at all, in order to prevent him from profiting by his fraud. us, R' Yose would rule that the entire cloak be set aside until the ming of Elijah, so that the deceiver not profit by his fraud.]

. Only one of the litigants deposited the disputed *maneh,* yet both are iming it. There is no room for honest error; the false claimant lfully seeks to perpetrate a fraud.

. In the case of our Mishnah, it is possible that neither means to ceive. They may have picked up the cloak at approximately the same ne, and each may honestly believe that he picked it up first (*Tosafos*). milarly, in the case of a bought cloak, both may have sought to buy the m from the seller and each may honestly believe that the seller ended to sell it to him (*Ritva*).

. [R' Yose might agree that division is the preferred way to settle the estion of disputed ownership. It is only that in his view, thwarting the ceiver takes precedence over fair distribution of the monies. But varting the deceiver has priority only when one of the litigants is finitely a deceiver. However, when neither necessarily intends to deceive, fair distribution of the monies is paramount.]

According to this resolution, which understands the essential difference between the two cases to be the presence of a definite deceiver, the found cloak would indeed be withheld from both litigants if one of them was definitely a deceiver – e.g. one claims to have found it today and the other claims to have found it yesterday (see *Tosafos* ד״ה אי נמי).

13. Withholding all three *manehs* induces the deceiver to admit his fraud so that he can recover the *maneh* that is actually his.

14. According to this resolution, our Mishnah would rule that they divide the cloak even if one of them was definitely a deceiver [e.g. one claims to have found it today and the other claims to have found it yesterday], since withholding the cloak from both would not achieve the desired aim of inducing the deceiver to admit his fraud (*Tosafos* ד״ה אי נמי). Cf. end of note 12.

15. As stated at the beginning of 2b, our Mishnah also discusses the case of a bought cloak, in which the seller received payment for the cloak from *both* litigants. In that case, withholding the cloak and the monies will induce the deceiver to admit his fraud so that he can at least recover the payment that he forced upon the seller (*Rashi*).

16. Accordingly, R' Yose rules that we withhold whatever is necessary to thwart the deceiver, provided that one of the litigants is definitely a deceiver (see *Tosafos* ד״ה אלא מחוורתא).

17. *Shevuos* 44b-45a. This case has been explained in note 11 to 2b.

18. Both according to the Rabbis and R' Yose, the Mishnah in *Shevuos* should rule that the employer need only deposit the disputed wages with the court and that the money will be withheld from the litigants until the truth is ascertained. Why does the Mishnah rule instead that the employer must pay twice – once to the shopkeeper and once to the employee?

19. Either the shopkeeper or the employee is certainly lying when he claims that the homeowner owes him the money. Why, then, is the money in question not simply deposited with the court until the truth is ascertained, as is done in the case of the three *manehs*?

ואיכא למימר כולה למר ואיכא למימר כולה למר אמר סומכוס ממון המוטל בספק חולקין בלא שבועה הכא דליכא דררא דממונא דאיכא למימר דתרוייהו היא לא כ"ש אפילו תימא סומכוס שבועה זו מדרבנן היא כדרבי יוחנן דאמר ר' יוחנן [א] א שבועה זו תקנת חכמים היא שלא יהא כל אחד ואחד הולך ותוקף בטליתו של חבירו ואומר שלי הוא לימא מתניתין דלא כרבי יוסי דאי כרבי יוסי הא אמר [ב] א"כ מה הפסיד רמאי אלא הכל יהא מונח עד שיבא אליהו אלא מאי רבנן כיון דאמרי רבנן השאר יהא מונח עד שיבא אליהו הא נמי כשאר דמי דספיקא היא האי מאי אי אמרת בשלמא רבנן התם דודאי האי מנה דחד מינייהו הוא אמרי רבנן יהא מונח עד שיבא אליהו הכא דאיכא למימר דתרוייהו הוא אמרי רבנן פלגי בשבועה אלא אי אמרת ר' יוסי היא השתא ומה התם דבודאי איכא מנה למר ואיכא מנה למר אמר ר' יוסי יהא מונח עד שיבא אליהו הכא דאיכא למימר דחד מינייהו הוא לא כ"ש אפי' תימא ר' יוסי התם ודאי איכא רמאי הכא מי יימר דאיכא רמאי אימא תרוייהו בהדי הדדי אגבהוה אי נמי התם קניס ליה רבי יוסי לרמאי כי היכי דלודי הכא מאי פסידא אית ליה דלודי תינח מציאה מקח וממכר מאי איכא למימר ° אלא מחוורתא כדשנין מעיקרא בין לרבנן ובין לר' יוסי התם [ג] גבי חנוני על פנקסו דקתני ב זה נשבע ונוטל וזה נשבע ונוטל מ"ש דלא אמרינן נפקיה לממונא מבעה"ב ויהא מונח עד שיבא אליהו דהא בודאי איכא רמאי אמרי התם היינו טעמא דאמר ליה חנוני לבעה"ב אנא שליחותא דידך קא עבדינא מאי אית לי גבי שכיר אע"ג דקא משתבע לי לא מהימן לי בשבועה את האמנתיה דלא אמרת לי בסהדי הב ליה ושכיר נמי א"ל לבעה"ב אנא עבדי עבידתא גבך מאי אית לי גבי חנוני אע"ג דמשתבע לי לא מהימן לי הלכך תרוייהו משתבעי ושקלי מבעל הבית: [ד] תני רבי חייא ג מנה לי בידך והלה אומר אין לך בידי כלום והעדים מעידים אותו שיש לו חמשים זוז נותן לו חמשים זוז [ה] וישבע על השאר שלא תהא הודאת פיו גדולה מהעדאת עדים מק"ו ותנא תונא שנים אוחזין בטלית זה אומר אני מצאתיה וכו' והא הכא כיון דתפיס אנן סהדי דמאי דתפיס האי דידיה הוא ומאי דתפיס האי דידיה הוא וקתני ישבע מאי שלא תהא הודאת פיו גדולה מהעדאת עדי' מק"ו שלא תאמר הודאת פיו הוא דרמיא רחמנא שבועה עליה כדרבה [ו] דאמר רבה מפני מה אמרה תורה ד מודה מקצת הטענה ישבע חזקה אין אדם מעיז פניו בפני בע"ח והאי בכוליה בעי דנכפריה והא דלא כפריה משום דאין אדם מעיז פניו

---

ואיכא למימר כוליה דמר. ועוד על כרחך או כוליה דמר או כוליה דמר אפילו הכי חולקין בלא שבועה: הכא דליכא דררא דממונא. ועוד דאיכא למימר דתרוייהו בהדי הדדי אגבהוה: לא כ"ש. דחולקין בלא שבועה: ותוקף. אוחז: דר' יוסי. לקמן בהמפקיד (דף לז.) שנים שהפקידו אצל אחד זה מנה וזה מאתים זה אומר מאתים שלי וזה אומר מאתים שלי וקאמר ת"ק נותן לזה מנה ולזה מנה והשאר יהא מונח עד שיבא אליהו אמר ר' יוסי א"כ מה הפסיד הרמאי ולמה יודה הרי קיבל את שלו אלא הכל יהא מונח ויפסיד הרמאי וה"נ יהא מונח: הא נמי כשאר דמיא. דהתם על מנה השני הם דנין ואלו דנין על הטלית כולה: דחד מינייהו הוא. ואין לומר יחלוקו: הכא דאיכא למימר דחד מינייהו הוא. ואין לחבירו חלק בה לא כ"ש דלית ליה יחלוקו: מאי פסידא אית ליה. למי שאין לו חלק בה אם תהא מונחת: דלודי. שאין לו חלק בה כשיודה מה יטול: מקח וממכר מאי איכא למימר. הא אוקימנא דקיבל דמים מתרוייהו ואי הוה אמרינן יהא הטלית והדמים מונחים אית ליה פסידא לרמאי ויודה על האמת קודם שיפסיד: התם היינו טעמא. דשניהם נשבעין ונוטלין דחנוני אומר לבעל הבית אנא שליחותא דידך עבדי ונתתי לפועלך ממון שצויתני: מאי אית לי גבי שכיר. לערער: לא מהימן לי. איני מאמינו בשבועה אני אומר שהוא רשע ואין לי להאמין אדם בשבועה על כרחי אלא אם כן האמנתיו מתחילה להפקיד אצלו או להתנות עמו: את הימנתיה. ואתה הוא שקילקלת ואין לי להפסיד בקלקולך שיהיו מעותי מונחין עד שיבא אליהו: וישבע על השאר. כדין מודה מקצת הטענה שאמרה תורה ישבע כדילפינן בשבועות (דף לט:) מכי הוא זה ואע"ג דזה לא הודה הרי יש עדים במקצת ולא תהא הודאת פיו גדולה לחייבו על השאר שבועה מהעדאת עדים: מקל וחומר. לקמן מפרש מאי ק"ו: ותנא תונא. ותנא דידן סייעתא לדידי: זה אומר כו'. וקתני שניהם ישבעו: אנן סהדי דמה דתפס האי. היינו פלגא: דידיה הוא. שהרי מוחזק הוא בפנינו והרי הוא תובע את כולה וחבירו כופר את כולה שאומר כולה שלי ואף מה שאתה תפוס בידך ואנו מעידין אותו שיש לו בה מקצת ומחייבים את חבירו שבועה על השאר דהיינו חצי שעיכב לעצמו: מאי לא תהא הודאת פיו גדולה מהעדאת עדים. מהיכי תיתי לן למידק דתיסק אדעתין דתהא הודאת פיו גדולה מהעדאת עדים דאיצטריך לתנא למילף מק"ו דלא תהא הודאת פיו גדולה: מפני מה אמרה תורה כו'. ולא חשבו כמשיב אבידה לפטרו שלא כפר בכולו:

---

**התם** ודאי איכא רמאי. לכך קניס ליה גם במה שהוא שלו בודאי אבל הכא אימור תרוייהו בהדי הדדי אגבהוה דליכא רמאי דכל חד סבור שהוא הגביה קודם: **אי** נמי התם קניס כי היכי דלודי. אבל הכא אפילו איכא ודאי רמאי כגון שזה אומר אני מלאתיה היום וזה אומר אני מלאתיה אתמול מודה דיחלוקו ולא אמרינן יהא מונח עד שיבא אליהו דבשביל כך לא יפרוש דהא אינו מפסיד כלום:

**אלא** מחוורתא כדשנין מעיקרא. נוכל לומר [ז] דהדר ביה ולא סגי בטעמא דמפסיד הרמאי לבד דלא קניס ר' יוסי אלא היכא דאיכא ודאי רמאי ואית ליה פסידא אבל היכא דאיכא רמאי וליכא פסידא לא יקנוס כדמשמע לישנא דא"כ מה הפסיד הרמאי מיהו לשון אלא משמע דהדר לגמרי וכן בסמוך דפריך בין לרבנן בין לרבי יוסי נימא יהא מונח אף על גב דהתם לית ליה פסידא לרמאי:

**גבי** חנוני נמי יהא מונח. לר"ע דאמר (יבמות דף קיח:) בלקח מחמשה ואינו יודע מאיזה מהם לקח נותן לכאו"א לא פריך אמאי נותן לכאו"א יהא מונח דהתם הוה ליה למדכר ואיהו דאפסיד אנפשיה:

**ולא** אמרת לי הב ליה בסהדי. תימה לימא ליה בעל הבית לתקוני שדרתיך ולא לעוותי אע"ג דלא אמר ליה הב ליה בסהדי היה לו מעצמו להשים על לב כדאמרינן בפ' הכותב (כתובות דף פה.) גבי אבימי דהוי מסקי ביה זוזי בי חוזאי ושדרינהו ביד ([ח] רבא) ופרענהו ואמר להו הב לי שטרא ואמרו ליה הנך סטראי נינהו ומסיק התם דלא שנא א"ל שקול שטרא והב להו זוזי ולא שנא הב זוזי ושקול שטרא מחייב השליח משום דאמר ליה לתקוני שדרתיך ולא לעוותי וי"ל דהתם כיון דהזכיר לקיחת השטר כאילו אומר עשה באותו ענין שיבא השטר לידך אבל הכא לא הזכיר עדים כלל:

**מפני** מה אמרה תורה כו'. פי' יהא נאמן במגו דאי בעי כופר הכל או נילף מהכא דלא נימא מגו בעלמא ומשני דאין זה מגו דאין אדם מעיז פניו לכפור הכל הואיל וחבירו מכיר בשקרו אבל במקום שיכול להעיז כגון בבנו ואמר מנה לאביך בידי והאכלתיו פרס נאמן במגו דאי בעי כפר הכל כדאיתא פ"ב דכתובות (דף יח. ושם) ובפרק שבועת הדיינים (שבועות דף מב.) וא"ת כופר הכל מנלן דפטור ואין לומר מטעם חזקה דאין אדם מעיז דהא אפי' במקום שיכול להעיז פטור כגון בבנו ואפילו מודה מקצת פטור התם מגו דאי בעי כפר הכל ואין לומר דילפינן מדאיצטריך למכתב שעד אחד מחייבו שבועה ואי כופר הכל חייב מאי נפקא מינה מעד אחד הא בלאו הכי חייב דהא איצטריך במקום שהוא אינו תובע כלום ואינו יודע והעד מעיד שהוא גנב או שאביו הלוה לו וי"ל [ט] דמכי הוא זה משמע דגזירת הכתוב הוא דדוקא מודה מקצת הטענה חייב ולא כופר הכל [י]:
בכוליה

---

עין משפט
נר מצוה

ז א מיי' פ"ט מהלכות טוען ונטען הלכה ז סמג עשין לה:
ח ב מיי' פט"ז מהלכות מלוה ולוה הלכה ה סמג עשין לד טוש"ע ח"מ סי' לא סעיף א:
ט ג מיי' פ"ד מהל' טוען ונטען הלכה י סמג עשין לה טוש"ע ח"מ סי' עה סעיף ד:
י ד מיי' פ"א שם הל' א סמג עשין שם טוש"ע ח"מ סי' פז סעיף א:

רבינו חננאל

ואסקי' לשמעתי' אפי' תימא סומכוס שבועה זו דקתני במתני' מדרבנן היא דאמר ר' יוחנן שבועה זו תקנת חכמים היא. סוגיא דשמעתין בגמרא דשור שנגח את הפרה כסומכוס. תוב אמר לימא מתני' דלא כר' יוסי דאמר בפ' המפקיד א"כ מה הפסיד הרמאי אלא הכל יהא מונח עד שיבוא אליהו ויאמר למי הם. ושנינן אפי' תימא ר' יוסי התם ודאי איכא רמאי אבל הכא די"ל תרוייהו בהדי הדדי אגבהוה וכו' ואקשי' תוב לר' יוסי ולרבנן הא דתנן גבי חנוני על פנקסו שחנוני אמר נתתי והפועל אמר לא לקחתי ושנינו שניהן נשבעין ונוטלין מבעה"ב והא הכא דודאי איכא רמאי ולא אמרו הכל יהא מונח עד שיבוא אליהו. ודחינן התם היינו טעמא משום דיכול פועל למימר אנא לך עבדי עבידתא הב לי אגראי מאי אית לי גבי חנוני. חנוני אמר ליה לבעה"ב אנא שליחותך עבדי וכו'. תני ר' חייא מנה לי בידך והלה אומר אין לך בידי כלום והעדים מעידין אותו חמשים נותן לו חמשים וחייב שבועה על השאר שלא תהא הודאת פיו גדולה מהעדאת עדים מק"ו. ותנא תונא. פירושו והתנא שנאה. כלומר שנינו במשנתינו כשמעתיה דר' חייא דתנן שנים אוחזין בטלית וכו'. [מאי] שלא תהא הודאת פיו גדול' מהעדאת עדים כו' פי' תורה מודה מקצת הטענה ישבע שנאמר אשר יאמר כי הוא זה. ודרשינן לזה אשר יאמר כי הוא הוא שאתה טוענו (זה בלבד) יש לך אצלי זה בלבד שנמצא מודה במקצת הלכך ישבע. הנה בהודאת פיו במקצת שהיא קלה חייב שבועה העדאת עדים שהיא חמורה ממנה לא כ"ש שיהיה חייב.

מסורת הש"ס

[א] לקמן ה:], ב) לקמן ג) [שבועות מה.], עיין תוס' לקמן ה. ר' חייא], ה) עיין שבועות לד: ד"ה ו) כתובות יח., גיטין בבא קמא קז., שבועות מב: [לקמן ה:], א דלא הדר ביה אלא דלא סגי, ל חמא, ט) [לקמן י) ועיין עוד אריכות בתוס' בבא קמא קז. ד"ה עירוב.

גליון הש"ס

אלא מחוורתא. הא תוס' ד"ה ולחזי כתבו ומיהו הו"מ דליתא קמן דנשייליה כן איך ההכרעה ינן מעיקרא דלמא מיירי בנקט זוזי מחד קמן דנשייליה ביה טעמא כי היכי דלודי:

ליקוטי רש"י

הפסיד רמאי. א"כ ידה לעולם על האמת [לז.]. מחוורתא. ברור הוא כמו (נזיר סג) במחוורת עליו [לה טו.]. חנוני על פנקסו. על מה שכתוב בפנקסו שהוא כותב עליה הקפות שהוא מקיף. זה נשבע ונוטל וזה נשבע ונוטל. שתיקנו חכמים לישבע וליטול [שבועות מד:]. ותנא תונא. תנא דידן כמו תנא אחונא [יבמות נו:]. דמתניתין דפרקין סייע ליה. תונא כמו תנא [חולין מד.]. אין אדם מעיז פניו בפני בע"ח. זה שעושה לו טובה הילכך היכא דכפר פטור משבועה דאי קושטא בהדיה לא מצי למכפר ביה א דמודה מקצת יה בעי למכפריה והא כפריה משום דאין מעיז [ב"ק קז.]. אין אדם מעיז פניו את הכל הלכך הודאת המקצת נאמן על השאר דהאי יה בעי דלכפריה וכו' [גיטין נא:].

וְאִיכָּא לְמֵימַר כּוּלָּה לְמַר וְאִיכָּא לְמֵימַר כּוּלָּה לְמ – **And** furthermore, **can be argued that it belongs entirely to one or entirely to e other,** i.e. the money in question (the monetary value of the tus) certainly belongs entirely to one of the litigants. אָמַר סוּמְכוֹס מָמוֹן הַמּוּטָל בְּסָפֵק חוֹלְקִין בְּלֹא שְׁבוּ – Still, **Sumchos said** that case **that money in doubt is divided without an oath.**[1] הָכָא דְּלֵיכָּא דְּרָרָא דְּמָמוֹ – Accordingly, **here** in our Mishnah, here **there is no loss of money** involved, דְּאִיכָּא לְמֵימַר דְּתַרְוַיְיהוּ ה – and furthermore, **it is possible to say [the cloak]** tually **belongs to both,** since they may have picked it up simultaneously, לֹא כָּל שֶׁכֵּן – **is it not certain** that the cloak should divided *without* swearing?![2]

The Gemara replies:

אֲפִילּוּ תֵּימָא סוּמְכ – **You can even say** that our Mishnah follows e view of **Sumchos,** who does not require swearing as a ndition for dividing the money in doubt. However, שְׁבוּעָה זוּ מִדְּרַבָּנָן הִיא כִּדְרַבִּי יוֹחָ – **this oath** that our Mishnah imposes **is a** ecial **Rabbinic** measure, **as R' Yochanan** taught. דְּאָמַר ר׳ יוֹחָ – **For R' Yochanan said:** שְׁבוּעָה זוּ תַּקָּנַת חֲכָמִים הִיא – **This** th that our Mishnah imposes **is a Rabbinic measure** decreed שֶׁלֹּא יְהֵא כָּל אֶחָד וְאֶחָד הוֹלֵךְ וְתוֹקֵף בְּטַלִּיתוֹ שֶׁל חֲבֵירוֹ וְאוֹמֵר שֶׁלִּי ה – **that each and every person should not** be able to **go and ize his fellow's cloak and** then **claim** in court, **"It is mine!"**[3] r this reason, even Sumchos would agree in the case of our ishnah that an oath is a condition for dividing.

The Gemara now considers whether our Mishnah is consistent th a ruling of R' Yose:

The Gemara asks:

לֵימָא מַתְנִיתִין דְּלֹא כְּרַבִּי יוֹ – **Shall we say that** the ruling of **our Mishnah is not in accordance with** the view of **R' Yose?** דְּאִי כְּרַבִּי יוֹסֵי הָא אָמַר אִם כֵּן מָה הִפְסִיד רַמַּאי אֶלָּא הַכֹּל יְהֵא מוּנָּח עַד שֶׁיָּבֹא אֵלִיָּהוּ – **For were it in accordance with the view of R' Yose – why, he says, "If so, what does the deceiver** stand to **lose? Rather, it should all be set aside until Elijah** the prophet **comes!"**[4] Similarly, in the case of our Mishnah R' Yose would apparently rule that the cloak is not divided at all. Rather, it is withheld entirely from both disputants and set aside until the coming of Elijah.

The Gemara counters:

אֶלָּא מַאי רַבָּנָן – **What then?** Does the Mishnah rather follow the view of **the Rabbis** that dispute R' Yose? כֵּיוָן דְּאָמְרֵי רַבָּנָן הַשְּׁאָר יְהֵא מוּנָּח עַד שֶׁיָּבֹא אֵלִיָּהוּ – But **since the Rabbis say that the remainder should be set aside until Elijah comes,** הָא נַמִּי כִּשְׁאָר דָּמֵי דִּסְפֵיקָא הִיא – they would apparently oppose division in the case of our Mishnah, since **this** cloak **is analogous to the remainder** in the case of three *manehs,* **for its** ownership is in **doubt.**[5] Apparently, then, our Mishnah follows neither the Rabbis nor R' Yose![6]

The Gemara rejects the contention that our Mishnah is equally incompatible with the view of the Rabbis:

הָאי מַאי – **What** kind of argument **is this?** אִי אָמְרַתְּ בִּשְׁלָמָא רַבָּנָן – **It is understandable if you say** that our Mishnah is consistent with the view of **the Rabbis,** for their ruling in the case of three *manehs* does not, in fact, conflict with our Mishnah: הָתָם – **There** in the case of the three *manehs,* דְּוַדַּאי הַאי מָנֶה דְּחַד מִינַּיְיהוּ הוּא – **where this** third ***maneh*** **certainly is the property of** only **one of them,** אָמְרֵי רַבָּנָן יְהֵא מוּנָּח עַד שֶׁיָּבֹא אֵלִיָּהוּ – **the Rabbis say it should be set aside until**

NOTES

[The Gemara is analyzing Sumchos's ruling in the case of the gored w according to the view that he ruled so even in a case of "certainly" d "certainly." That is, even if the cow's owner claims to have seen the cause the cow to abort and the ox's owner claims to have seen the cow ort spontaneously, Sumchos rules that they divide the disputed ıount without an oath.] The fact that division causes an actual loss to e true owner argues for making that verdict contingent on the igants swearing to their claims [in the hope that the liar will retract s fraudulent claim rather than swear falsely to it]. Moreover, the fact at the disputed amount belongs to either one or the other but not to th argues against the verdict of division altogether, since division nnot possibly fully satisfy the claims of the true owner. Yet, despite ese two factors militating against dividing without an oath, Sumchos les that the respective claims of the litigants are sufficient reason to ride the monies without an oath (*Ritva* in explanation of *Rashi*).

If Sumchos ruled that disputed money is divided without an oath even ere there are two factors militating against that verdict (see preling note), then is it not certain that he rules this way in the case of r Mishnah, where those two factors are *not* present? For in the case of r Mishnah, the true owner does not stand to suffer an actual loss so at we should insist on the litigants swearing. Moreover, it is indeed ssible that the cloak belongs equally to both and the verdict of division ıs fully satisfies the claims of the true owner. Is it not certain, then, at Sumchos would rule in our case that the cloak is divided without an h? (ibid.).

Unlike Rav Pappa above (2b), who explained that the oath in our shnah is directed at a person who might rationalize his fraudulent ion in case of a found object or of a sale, R' Yochanan explains that the h is directed even against a person who would simply approach neone else, grab his cloak, and then lay claim to it in court. To courage such anarchy, the Rabbis enacted that the litigants state eir claims under oath (*Ritva* in explanation of *Rashi*; see also *Ran* to .

Even according to the view of Rav Pappa, that the oath of our Mishnah plies only in situations where the false claimant can rationalize his ud, the oath of our Mishnah is a special Rabbinic measure enacted to courage such fraud. Accordingly, the Gemara did not have to resort R' Yochanan's reason in order to reconcile our Mishnah with Sumchos, but could have said that the oath in our Mishnah is a special Rabbinic measure as *Rav Pappa* taught. Nevertheless, the Gemara introduced R' Yochanan's reason, since R' Yochanan states *explicitly* that the oath is a "Rabbinic measure" instituted to prevent anarchy (*Rashba*; see also *Ritva* and *Rashash*). [There was no need to institute this oath in Sumchos' case, since the situation of doubt created by the unwitnessed goring of a pregnant cow is an uncommon occurrence (*Tos. HaRosh*).]

4. R' Yose ruled in the following case of the Mishnah below (37a): Two people deposited money for safekeeping with a third party. One person deposited a *maneh* [one hundred *zuz*] and the other deposited two *manehs.* When reclaiming their deposits, each depositor claims to be the owner of the two-*maneh* deposit. The Rabbis rule that the custodian returns a *maneh* to each depositor, since the ownership of these two *manehs* is not in dispute; the third *maneh*, which is in dispute, is withheld until its ownership can be ascertained ("it is set aside until the coming of Elijah"). R' Yose there rejects this ruling, because it does not penalize the deceiver. [The Gemara will discuss shortly the rationale for penalizing the deceiver.] Rather, R' Yose rules that the entire three *manehs* should be set aside until the coming of Elijah; in this way, the deceiver is penalized by depriving him even of the *maneh* that is indisputably his.

[Regarding "setting aside," *Rashi* (37b ד״ה ואם נטל) explains that the money is left with the depositary (the watchman to whom it was originally entrusted). *Tosafos* (*Bava Kamma* 103a ד״ה אבל), however, explain that it is held by the court.]

5. R' Yose and the Rabbis disagree only about the disposition of the monies whose ownership is known. But they agree that the disputed monies are set aside until their ownership is ascertained. Now, in the case of our Mishnah, it is the entire cloak that is in dispute. Accordingly, even the Rabbis should agree that the cloak is not divided, but set aside.

6. The same argument that you use to show that our Mishnah does not follow R' Yose shows that it cannot follow his disputants, the Rabbis, either. But this is an untenable position, since the Mishnah must reflect one of the two views (see 2b note 19). Consequently, our understanding of the Mishnah must be deficient and, pending its clarification, we can draw no inferences as to whose view the Mishnah reflects.

**under oath.**[21]

אֶלָּא אִי אָמְרַתְּ סוּמְכוֹס – **But if you say** that our Mishnah is consistent with **Sumchos,** you are faced with the following difficulty: הַשְׁתָּא וּמַה הָתָם דְּלָא תָּפְסֵי תַּרְוַיְיהוּ – **Now if there** in the case of the gored cow, **where both** litigants **are not in physical possession** of the money in doubt, rather the owner of the ox has sole possession of it, חוֹלְקִין בְּלֹא שְׁבוּעָה – Sumchos nevertheless rules that **they divide it without an oath,** and the owner of the cow exacts partial payment for the fetus without swearing to substantiate his claim, הָכָא דְּתַרְוַיְיהוּ תָּפְסֵי לָהּ לֹא כָּל שֶׁכֵּן – then **here** in the case of our Mishnah, **where both [litigants] are in physical possession** of the disputed cloak, **is it not certain** that no oath is required in order to divide the cloak?[22] The ruling of Sumchos is therefore seemingly irreconcilable with the ruling of our Mishnah! – **?** –

The Gemara replies:

אֲפִילּוּ תֵּימָא סוּמְכוֹס – **You can even say** that our Mishnah is consistent with the ruling of **Sumchos.** כִּי אָמַר סוּמְכוֹס שֶׁמָּא וְשֶׁמָּא – **When did Sumchos say** that money in doubt is divided without an oath? Only when the litigants claim **"perhaps" and "perhaps,"** i.e. when neither litigant is certain about his claim to the money, such as in the case of the gored cow, where neither claims to know the true sequence of events.[23] אֲבָל בָּרִי וּבָרִי לֹא אָמַר – **But** when the litigants claim **"certainly" and "certainly,"** Sumchos did **not say** his ruling. I.e. when each litigant asserts his claim with certainty (such as in the case of our Mishnah, where each one claims with certainty to have taken possession of the cloak first), even Sumchos would agree that the cloak is divided only if each litigant swears in order to substantiate his claim, as our Mishnah rules.[24]

The Gemara asks:

וּלְרַבָּה בַּר רַב הוּנָא דְּאָמַר – **But according to Rabbah bar R Huna, who says** אָמַר סוּמְכוֹס אֲפִילּוּ בָּרִי וּבָרִי – that **Sumch said** his rule that money in doubt is divided without an oath **ev** in a case of **"certainly" and "certainly,"**[25] מַאי אִיכָּא לְמֵימַר **what is there to say?** I.e. what reason could possibly be advanc to explain why our Mishnah requires them to swear before th divide? Is it not proven, then, that our Mishnah does not refle the view of Sumchos (as his view is understood by Rabbah bar R Huna)?

The Gemara replies:

אֲפִילּוּ תֵּימָא סוּמְכוֹס – **You can even say** that our Mishnah consistent with the ruling of **Sumchos,** even assuming th Sumchos said his rule in the case of positive claims. אָמַר סוּמְכוֹס הֵיכָא דְּאִיכָּא דְּרָרָא דְּמָמוֹנָא – **When did Sumchos say** h **rule** that no oath is required? **Only where there is a** true **loss money** involved, such as in the case of the gored cow.[26] לֹ הֵיכָא דְּלֵיכָּא דְּרָרָא דְּמָמוֹנָא לֹא – **But where there is no** true **loss money** involved, such as in the case of our Mishnah,[27] Sumch did **not** rule that an oath is unnecessary.[28]

The Gemara rejects this reasoning:

וְלָאו קַל וָחוֹמֶר הוּא – **But is it not,** rather, demonstrable by mea of a ***kal vachomer*** that Sumchos does not require an oath in t case of our Mishnah?[29] ה הָתָם דְּאִיכָּא דְּרָרָא דְּמָמוֹנָא לְמַר וְאִיכָּא דְּרָרָא דְּמָמוֹנָא לְמַר – **Now, there** in the case of the gored co **there is a loss of money for this one and a loss of money f that one,** i.e. regardless of which one is the true owner, he is losi money by the court-imposed division of the amount in dispu

NOTES

21. Since both litigants are holding the disputed cloak, both are considered to be in physical possession of the entire cloak and awarding part of it to each does not entail exacting payment from the physical possession of another [but rather leaving it in the possession of its present holder]. Therefore, the claims do not require the absolute corroboration of witnesses. Nevertheless, since neither litigant holds the cloak exclusively, for it is held by his antagonist as well, there is a certain element of exaction involved in awarding each litigant half the cloak. The Rabbis would not allow this lesser form of exaction to occur without any substantiation whatever, and in place of the absolute corroboration of witnesses required the lesser corroboration of an oath (*Rashi*).

[Thus, nothing was lacking in our initial understanding of our Mishnah, which has now been shown to be fully compatible with the view of the Rabbis.]

22. [Unlike Rav Pappa's explanation above, that oaths were specially imposed in the case of our Mishnah to discourage rationalized fraud, the Gemara at this point understands that our Mishnah requires an oath as a basic condition of division; i.e. that division is not warranted unless some degree of proof, such as an oath, is furnished to the claim, albeit a lesser degree of proof than witnesses (see previous note). Thus, if Sumchos does not require the corroborative proof of swearing in order to *exact* payment, he certainly would not require the corroborative proof of swearing in order to be awarded payment that need *not* be exacted (see *Rashba* to 3a ד״ה אפי׳ תימא סומכוס).]

23. Neither litigant claims to have witnessed the goring. Rather, the plaintiff argues that *perhaps* the ox caused the cow to abort, whereas the defendant counters that *perhaps* the cow aborted spontaneously before the goring. Obviously, we cannot require that the litigants support their possible claims by swearing about events of which they know nothing.

24. The Gemara now understands that Sumchos requires the corroborative evidence of an oath to divide disputed money, unless the uncertain nature of the claim renders imposition of an oath inappropriate (s above, note 22).

25. See below, 100a, and *Bava Kamma* 35b.

26. [This is how *Rashi* understands the term דְּרָרָא דְּמָמוֹנָא. Cf. *Tosafi Ramban* et al.] In the case of the gored cow whose dead fetus is fou alongside her, awarding the money for the fetus to either litigant ru the risk of causing the other litigant a loss. For if we make the ox's own pay for the fetus, and the cow in fact aborted spontaneously, then we w have caused the ox's owner an unwarranted loss. On the other hand, we absolve the ox's owner from payment for the fetus, and his ox in fa caused the fetus's death, then we will have caused the cow's owner unwarranted loss (*Rashi*). [Consequently, no oath is needed in order justify the compromise award of division, since such compromise inherently indicated as the only logical way to reduce the degree of los

27. In the case of our Mishnah, neither litigant stands to suffer a tr monetary loss, since the found cloak was a windfall to the find Similarly, in the case of a bought cloak (which is also the subject of o Mishnah, as the Gemara above has explained), neither litigant stands suffer a true monetary loss; for if one is awarded the cloak, the sel refunds the other his money (see *Ritva*).

28. [Rather, since there is no *true* loss involved, we are not compelled minimize the degree of loss; therefore, the compromise of division is n inherently indicated (see note 26). In this case, Sumchos agrees that do not divide the disputed article unless each litigant swears to the tru of his claim, thereby bolstering the claims sufficiently to call division.]

29. [*Kal vachomer* – an a fortiori argument from minor to maj premise (see glossary).] The Gemara now proceeds to demonstrate th on the contrary, if Sumchos does not require an oath in the case of t gored cow, where a loss of money is involved, then he certainly shou not require an oath in the case of our Mishnah, where no loss of mon is involved.

דאי תנא מציאה הוה אמינא מציאה הוא דרמו רבנן שבועה עליה משום דמורי ואמר חבראי לאו מידי חסר בה איזל אתפיס ואתפליג בהדיה אבל מקח וממכר דליכא למימר הכי אימא לא ואי תנא מקח וממכר (א) הוא דרמו רבנן שבועה עליה משום דמורי ואמר חבראי דמי קא יהיב ואנא דמי קא יהיבנא השתא דצריכא לדידי אשקליה אנא וחבראי ליזיל לטרח ליזבן אבל מציאה דליכא למימר הכי אימא לא צריכא מקח וממכר [א] ולחזי זוזי ממאן נקט לא צריכא [א] דנקט מתרוייהו מחד מדעתיה ומחד בע"כ ולא ידענא מי הוא מדעתיה ומי הוא בעל כורחיה לימא מתני' דלא כבן ננס דאי בן ננס האמר [ב] כיצד אלו ואלו באין לידי שבועת שוא אפילו תימא בן ננס התם ודאי איכא שבועת שוא הכא איכא למימר דליכא שבועת שוא אימור דתרוייהו בהדי הדדי אגבהוה לימא מתני' דלא כסומכוס דאי כסומכוס האמר [ג] ממון המוטל בספק חולקין בלא שבועה ואלא מאי רבנן הא אמרי המע"ה האי מאי אא"ב רבנן התם דלא תפסי תרוייהו אמרו רבנן המוציא מחבירו עליו הראיה הכא דתרוייהו תפסי [פלגי] לה בשבועה אלא אי אמרת סומכוס השתא ומה התם דלא תפסי תרוייהו חולקין בלא שבועה הכא דתרוייהו תפסי לה לא כ"ש אפי' תימא סומכוס כי אמר סומכוס שמא ושמא אבל ברי וברי לא אמר [ד] ולרבה בר רב הונא דאמר אמר סומכוס אפילו ברי וברי מאי איכא למימר אפי' תימא סומכוס כי אמר סומכוס היכא דאיכא דררא דממונא אבל היכא דליכא דררא דממונא לא ולאו קל וחומר הוא ומה התם דאיכא דררא דממונא למר ואיכא דררא דממונא למר
ואיכא

**אי** תנא מציאה. משום דמורה ואמר חבראי לאו מידי חסר לכך תפיס אע"ג שיודע שחבירו מצאה ורמו רבנן שבועה עליה כדי שיפרוש אבל מקח וממכר דליכא למימר הכי שאם יודע שחבירו קנאה לא הוי תפיס ומדתפיס בה סבור שלו הוא ונתרצה המוכר כדמסיק לקמן דנקיט זוזי מתרוייהו אימא לא ישבע דמשום שבועה לא יפרוש שהרי סבור הוא לומר אמת קמ"ל דאפ"ה ישבע והיכא שודאי אינו סבור לומר אמת כגון דקא טעין כל אחד אני ארגתיה שאחד מהן טוען שקר במזיד או כגון שנים אדוקין בשטר דלקמן (דף ז.) התם פשיטא דיחלוקו בשבועה דע"י שבועה ודאי יפרוש דחשיד אממונא לא חשיד אשבועתא:

**ולחזי** זוזי ממאן נקט. פרש"י נשאל למוכר ואע"ג דאין המוכר נאמן כשאין מקחו בידו כדאי' בעשרה יוחסין (קדושין דף עג: ושם ד"ה בד"א) ה"מ בדנקיט מתרוייהו אבל בדנקיט מחד נאמן אפילו אין מקחו בידו וגרסינן בתר הכי ולא ידעינן ובחנם דחק לפרש כן דהכא פריך שפיר דאע"ג דאין מקחו בידו נאמן הוא כעד אחד ואמאי שניהם נשבעין אותו שהמוכר מסייעו יפטר משבועה ואידך ישבע שבועה דאורייתא והשתא גרס שפיר ולא ידע דאי ידע הוה נאמן כעד אחד ומיהו ה"מ לשנויי דליתיה קמן דנשייליה ור"י מפרש דנשאל להם ממי קבל המוכר המעות שאין אנו חושדין אותן לשקר בזה לומר נתתי והוא לא נתן וגם הם אינם חלוקים אלא למי נתרצה המוכר אבל בנתינת המעות אינם חלוקין:

**לימא** מתני' דלא כבן ננס. מלינו למימר דידע שפיר דמתני' אפשר דתרוייהו בהדי הדדי אגבהוה ומ"מ פריך שיחלוקו בלא שבועה אחרי שאפשר לבא לידי שבועת שוא ומשני התם ודאי איכא שבועת שוא:

**התם** דלא תפסי תרוייהו. כ"א האחד ואע"ג דאפי' בעומדת באגם אית להו לרבנן המוציא מחבירו עליו הראיה מ"מ מיקרי האחד תפיס מחמת חזקת מריה קמא ואית דגרס התם דחד מינייהו הוא:

**היכא** דאיכא דררא דממונא. פירוש שבלא טענותיהם יש ספק לב"ד דיש לאחד תביעה על חבירו בלא טענותם כגון בשור שנגח את הפרה (ב"ק דף מו.) ומחליף פרה בחמור [ה] אחרי שהספק נולד מעצמו דין הוא שיחלוקו אפילו בלא שבועה:

**ומה** התם דאיכא דררא דממונא. ואיכא למימר כולה דמר. לא פריך אלא אי סומכוס ס"ל כרבנן דבן ננס דלא חיישי לשבועת שוא דלבן ננס אדרבה היכא דאיכא למימר כולה דמר פלגי בלא שבועה משום דאיכא בודאי שבועת שוא:

**ומה** התם דאיכא דררא דממונא. בפרק ח"ה (ב"ב דף לה. ושם) גבי ארבא דאמר רב נחמן כל דאלים גבר פריך מהמחליף פרה בחמור דיחלוקו ומשני התם איכא דררא דממונא ולא פריך ומה התם דאיכא דררא דממונא ואיכא למימר כולה דמר יחלוקו גבי ארבא דאיכא למימר דתרווייהו הוא ואין חולקין אלא כל דאלים גבר כדפריך הכא היינו משום דלענין חלוקה סברת דררא דממונא היא טובה מאחר שספק גמור הוא בלא טענותם דין שיחלוקו אבל ארבא אע"ג דאפשר דתרווייהו היא כיון דליכא דררא דממונא ואין אוחזין הוי דינא כל דאלים גבר אבל לענין שבועה אין מועיל סברת דררא דממונא לחלוק בלא שבועה אחרי שהוא בודאי של אחד מהם סברא הוא שיחלוקו בשבועה אולי יודה אחד מהם:
התם

דמורה ואמר. מורה היתר לעצמו לאחוז בה בלא משפט: **לאו מידי** חסר. אינו מפסיד כלום בחנם באה לו ואף בלא טורח: **אבל מקח** וממכר דליכא למימר הכי. ואע"ג שזה גם הוא נתן את המעות למוכר כדאוקמינן לקמן דנקט מתרוייהו חד מדעתיה וחד בע"כ וכשיחלוקו יטול זה חצי מעותיו וזה חצי מעותיו אפ"ה חסרון הוא אצלו דאי לא הוה צריך לה לא הוה מהדר אבתרה למזבנה וזה שבא לחלוק וליתן חצי דמים שלא כדין מחסרו: **דמי קא** יהיבנא. דמים אני רוצה ליתן: **אבל** מציאה **דליכא** למימר. חברי ילך וימצא אחרת זה ודאי מחסרו ממון: **ולחזי** זוזי ממאן נקט. נשאל את המוכר ממי קיבל דמיה דתניא בקדושין (דף עג:) נאמן בעל המקח לומר לזה מכרתי ולזה לא מכרתי ואע"ג דמסיים בד"א שמקחו בידו אבל אין מקחו בידו אינו נאמן שלא נתן לב לדבר כל כך להיות זכור מאחר ששניהם חזרו אחריו בפיסוק דמיה הא אוקימנא התם בדנקט זוזי מתרוייהו מחד מדעתיה ומחד בע"כ דכיון דלא עליה רמיא לאסהודי לא דק כולי האי להיות נזהר משהלכו מלפניו הי מדעתיה והי בע"כ אבל היכא דלא קיבל דמים אלא מחד מידכר דכיר ליה: **לא צריכא** דנקט זוזי מתרוייהו. ה"ג ולא ידעינן מהי מדעתיה ומהי בעל כורחיה ולא גרסי' ולא ידע דאפי' ידע בזו אין המוכר נאמן משהלכו כדמוקי התם: **מתני'**. דמשבע לתרוייהו וחד משתבע לשיקרא: **דלא** כבן ננס. במסכת שבועות (דף מה.) גבי חנוני על פנקסו אלו ואלו באין לב"ד על מנת לישבע אחד מהם לשוא אמר בעל הבית לחנוני תן לבני חטים בדינר ועלי לשלם או לפועלים בסלע מעות שאני חייב בשכרם ועלי ליתן סלע הוא אומר נתתי והוא אומר לא נטלתי ושניהם תובעין את בעה"ב שניהם נשבעין ונוטלין מבעל הבית אמר בן ננס כיצד אלו ואלו באין לידי שבועת שוא אלא שניהם נוטלין בלא שבועה: **אימור** בהדי הדדי אגבהוה. למציאה וכל אחד ואחד סבור אני הגבהתיה תחילה וכולה שלי וכי משתבע על חציה קושטא משתבע ולענין מקח וממכר נמי שמא לשניהם נתרצה: **כסומכוס**. בבבא קמא גבי שור שנגח את הפרה ונמצא עוברה בצדה (דף מו.): **עליו הראיה**. בעדים ואי לא לא גבי מידי והכא חולקין [בשבועה]: ה"ג אי אמרת בשלמא רבנן התם דלא תפסי תרוייהו אמור רבנן כו' הכא דתפסי תרוייהו פלגי בשבועה אלא אי אמרת סומכוס ומה התם דלא תפסי תרוייהו אמר סומכוס פלגי בלא שבועה הכא דתפסי תרוייהו לא כל שכן: **תרוייהו תפסי**. ואין כאן מוציא מחבירו: **בשבועה פלגי לה**. כיון דמחסר גויינא במה שחבירו תופס דהאי תפיס בכולה והאי תפיס [בכולה] לא קים להו לרבנן להוציא ממון מחזקתו בכדי כדאמרי' התם לרבנן דבעי ראיה הצריכום שבועה: **שמא ושמא**. כי התם דקתני נמצא עוברה בצדה ואין ידוע אם עד שלא ילדה נגחה אם משילדה נגחה ולא מת הולד מחמת הנגיחה אלא מאליו וכיון דכל חד שמא טעין ליכא למרמי עלייהו שבועה: **דרבה בר רב הונא**. בפרק השואל לקמן (דף ק.): **דררא דממונא**. חסרון ממון שאם יפרע זה שלא כדין הוי חסרון ממון ואם נפטרנו שלא כדין נמצא זה חסר ולד פרתו: **ומה התם דאיכא דררא דממונא** כו'. איזה מהן שמפסיד החצי שלא כדין אתה מחסרו ממון:
ואיכא

עין משפט
נר מצוה

ו א מיי' פ"כ מהלכות מכירה הלכה ד ועיין בהשגות ובמ"מ סמג עשין פב טוש"ע ח"מ סי' רכב סעיף א:

רבינו חננאל

ואמרי אי הכי נשאל למוכר למי מהן מכר וממי קבל דמיה ושנינן באומר לא ידעתי ואמר ששניהן תבעוה ממני לקנותה ואמרתי להן מי שיתן לי דמיה הרי היא מכורה לו ונתן לי א' מהן דמים והא' השליך המעות לפני ולקחו הטלית ואיני יודע מי מהן שנתן ומי שהשליך כגון זה שנינו שניהן נשבעין וחולקין. וכיון שא' הוא שקנה והא' טוען בשקר ותני תנא שניהן נשבעין ונוטלין מכלל דהאי תנא לא חייש לשבועת שוא של אחד מהן. **מתני'** דלא כבן ננס דאי בן ננס הא חייש וקתני שניהן נוטלין בלא שבועה. דברי בן ננס הן בשבועות פרק כל הנשבעין שבתורה הלכה וחנוני על פנקסו. ודחינן אפי' תימא בן ננס [הכא] איכא למימר דלמא תרוייהו בחדא אגבהוה וה"ה בקנייתא שניהן כא' קנאוה ואין ביניהן שבועת שוא. תוב אמרי' לימא מתני' דלא כסומכוס דאמר ממון המוטל בספק חולקין בלא שבועה דתנן שור שנגח את הפרה ונמצאת עוברה בצדה וכו'. ואמרי' בגמ' אר"י אמר שמואל זו דברי סומכוס אבל חכמים אומרים זה כלל [גדול] בדין המוציא מחבירו עליו הראיה. תניא נמי הכי שור שנגח את הפרה ונמצא עוברה בצידה ואינו יודע אם עד שלא נגחה ילדה ואם משנגחה ילדה משלם ח"נ לפרה ורביע נזק לולד דברי סומכוס וחכ"א המע"ה. ואמרי' אלא מאי מתני' אינה כסומכוס אלא כרבנן אמאי נשבעין והא המוציא מחבירו עליו הראיה אמרי. ופרקי היכא דתפיס חד ואידך טעין עליה אמור רבנן המע"ה. הכא דתרוייהו תפסי לה אמרי רבנן חולקין בשבועה. אלא אי אמרת סומכוס השתא ומה התם דלא תפסי תרוייהו וכו'. דברי רבה בר [רב] הונא דאמר אמר סומכוס אפי' ברי וברי בהמחליף פרה בחמור בפ' השואל את הפרה ודברי ר' חייא בר אבא אמר סומכוס אפי' ברי וברי כרבה בר [רב] הונא בסוף פ' המניח את הכד.

מסורת הש"ס

א) קידושין עג., ב) שב[ועות] מה., ג) [בבא קמא מו. וש"נ], ד) שם לה: [...] (ודף מו.) לקמן ק[...] וע"ב, ה) [לקמן ק...]

הגהות הב"ח

(א) גמ' ואי תנא ומקח וממכר. ה"א התם דרמו:

ליקוטי רש"י

ולחזי זוזי. קא שלא קיבל מעות מאחד מהם הא מדכיר דכיר זוזי [...] קביל. **ולא ידענא**. ידוע לנו [קדושין...] **כיצד אלו** [...] **באין**. לב"ד ל[...] שבועת שוא מכי דלית בהו דאינו מ[...] [שבועות מה.]. [...] **סומכוס אפילו** **וברי**. דשניהם טו[ענים] טוענת ברי ואפי' דנתבע טוען ברי שאיני חייב ואפי' כיון דלבי דינא מס[...] מאן קאמר קו[...] חולקין [ב"ק לה:]

**oath?"**[11] Our Mishnah, then, which rules that each litigant swears to the truth of half his claim, would seem to be inconsistent with the view of Ben Nanas, who rules that the court does not impose conflicting oaths on two litigants, since a false oath will result if both indeed swear.

The Gemara replies:

**אֲפִילּוּ תֵּימָא בֶּן נַנָּס – You can even say** that the Mishnah is consistent with the ruling of **Ben Nanas. הָתָם וַדַּאי אִיכָּא שְׁבוּעַת שָׁוְא – There** in Ben Nanas's case, **there is definitely a false oath** involved.[12] **הָכָא אִיכָּא לְמֵימַר דְּלֵיכָּא שְׁבוּעַת שָׁוְא** – Here in the case of our Mishnah, however, **it is possible**[13] **that there is no false oath** involved. **אֵימוּר דְּתַרְוַייהוּ בַּהֲדֵי הֲדָדֵי אַגְבְּהוּהָ – For it is possible**[14] **that both picked it up simultaneously** and neither is swearing falsely.[15]

The Gemara now considers whether the ruling of our Mishnah is consistent with the view of the Tanna Sumchos:

**לֵימָא מַתְנִיתִין דְּלָא כְּסוּמְכוֹס – Shall we say that** the ruling of **our Mishnah is not in accordance with** the view of **Sumchos? דְּאִי כְּסוּמְכוֹס הָאָמַר מָמוֹן הַמּוּטָל בְּסָפֵק חוֹלְקִין בְּלֹא שְׁבוּעָה – For were it in accordance with** the view of **Sumchos – why, he says** that **money** whose ownership is **in doubt is divided** by the litigants **without an oath.**[16] This seems to conflict with our Mishnah, which stipulates that each litigant must swear before the money in doubt (i.e. the cloak) is divided.

The Gemara counters:

**וְאֶלָּא מַאי רַבָּנָן – But what** then? Does the Mishnah, rath follow the view of the **Rabbis** that dispute Sumchos? **אָמְרִי הַמּוֹצִיא מֵחֲבֵירוֹ עָלָיו הָרְאָיָה – But [the Rabbis] say** that t burden of **proof rests on the one who seeks to exact** payme **from his fellow.**[17] Their ruling, too, seems to conflict with c Mishnah, which awards each litigant half the disputed cloak h equally by the other, even though neither substantiates his cla with witnesses.[18] Apparently, then, our Mishnah follows neith the Rabbis nor Sumchos![19]

The Gemara rejects the contention that our Mishnah is equa incompatible with the view of the Rabbis:

**הַאי מַאי – What** kind of argument **is this? אָמְרַת בִּשְׁלָמָא רַבָּנָן – All is well if you say** that the Mishnah follows **the Rabb** for their ruling in the case of the gored cow does not, in fa conflict with our Mishnah: **הָתָם דְּלָא תָּפְסֵי תַּרְוַייהוּ – There** the case of the gored cow, **where both** litigants **are not physical possession of the money in doubt,** rather the own of the ox has possession of it,[20] **רו רַבָּנָן הַמּוֹצִיא מֵחֲבֵירוֹ עָלָיו הָרְאָיָה – the Rabbis said** that **the** burden of **proof res on the one who seeks to exact** money **from his fellow.** Th the owner of the cow can exact nothing for the fetus unless proves his claim conclusively. **הָכָא דְּתַרְוַייהוּ תָּפְסֵי – But he** in our Mishnah, **where both** litigants **are in physical possessi** of the cloak, the Rabbis would indeed rule – as our Mishn does – that **פָּלְגֵי לָהּ בִּשְׁבוּעָה – they** [the litigants] **divide**

NOTES

11. [Translation follows *Rashi* here and to *Shevuos* 45a.] Ben Nanas' statement is recorded in the Mishnah *Shevuos* 45a, regarding the case of חֶנְוָנִי עַל פִּנְקָסוֹ, *the shopkeeper concerning his ledger.* The case concerns a man who instructs a shopkeeper to disburse funds to the man's employees (or other payees) and to place the sum on his account. Subsequently, the shopkeeper claims that he disbursed the funds as instructed, but the payees deny ever receiving them. Both now demand payment from the man – the storekeeper demands reimbursement and the employees demand their wages. The Tanna Kamma there rules that both claimants swear and receive payment. The shopkeeper swears that he disbursed the funds and the employees swear that they never received them; both then collect from the man. Ben Nanas, however, objects that according to this ruling, if both litigants follow the court's directive to swear, one of them will necessarily swear falsely. How can the court issue instructions that directly lead to the swearing of a false oath!? Rather, rules Ben Nanas, both collect from the man *without* swearing to the truth of their claims.

12. I.e. if both claimants follow the court's directive to swear, one of them will necessarily swear falsely.

13. Literally: it can be said.

14. Literally: say.

15. In the case of our Mishnah, the court is not necessarily issuing directives that will lead to false swearing. For in the case of a found cloak, it is possible that what actually occurred was that both picked it up simultaneously (though each thinks that he picked it up slightly before the other one did). If that is indeed what happened, then no false oath will be caused by instructing each litigant to swear that he owns not less than half, for the truth is indeed that each owns half (*Rashi*). Similarly, in the Mishnah's case of a sold cloak, it is possible that the seller in fact intended to sell the cloak to both of them, and indeed they both own half (ibid.).

16. Sumchos ruled in the case of the Mishnah *Bava Kamma* 46a, in which an ox gores a cow and the cow's fetus is found dead next to her. It is not known whether the ox gored the cow while she was still carrying the fetus, causing her to abort (in which case the owner of the ox would be liable for the fetus as well), or whether the cow had aborted spontaneously before being gored (in which case the owner of the ox need not pay anything for the fetus). The owner of the cow maintains the position that the ox caused the cow to abort, whereas the owner of the ox maintains the position that the cow aborted spontaneously. The Mishnah there rules that the owner of the ox must pay in compensation for the dead fetus half of what he would pay had it been certain that ox caused its death. The Gemara there observes that this ruling refle the view of Sumchos, that money whose ownership is in doubt divided. (Indeed, the Gemara there [46b] cites a Baraisa that explici attributes the Mishnah's ruling to Sumchos.) Applying Sumchos' ru to the case of the Mishnah there, it emerges that since it is uncerta whether the owner of the ox must pay for the dead fetus, he pays h the money in question. Since no mention of an oath is found Sumchos' ruling, the Gemara here cites Sumchos' ruling as: Money doubt is divided *without an oath.*

17. That is, payment cannot be exacted unless the plaintiff's cla is substantiated by actual witnesses (*Rashi*). The Gemara and Barai in *Bava Kamma* (ibid.) state that the Rabbis dispute Sumchos and ru in the case of the gored cow that the owner of the ox pays nothi for the dead fetus. For in that case, the disputed money is the payme for the dead fetus that the cow's owner seeks to recover from the own of the ox. That payment is currently in the exclusive possession of t owner of the ox. The Rabbis rule that we cannot remove anythi from the possession of the ox's owner unless the cow's own substantiates his claim by producing witnesses who saw the ox cau the cow to abort.

18. Since both litigants are holding the cloak, both are considered to in physical possession of the entire cloak. Consequently, dividing t cloak on the basis of an oath alone would seem to constitute r moving half the cloak from the possession of the other without t compelling evidence of witnesses (see *Ritzbash* cited in *Shitah Mek betzes*).

19. [Since the Gemara in *Bava Kamma* mentions only the views Sumchos and the Rabbis regarding the disposition of disputed monie it is assumed that all authorities must subscribe to one of the two view Since our Mishnah seems not to conform to either view, we must lacking a crucial element in the understanding of our Mishnah, whi – if properly understood – would reconcile our Mishnah with at lea one of the two views. Thus, to the assertion above that our Mishna does not seem to accord with the view of Sumchos, the Gemara he counters with the observation that by the same token it does not see to accord with the view of the Rabbis, either. Consequently, o understanding of the Mishnah must be deficient, and pending i clarification we can draw no inferences as to whose view the Mishna reflects. (Cf. *Ritva*.)]

20. As explained in note 17.

דאי תנא מציאה הוה אמינא מציאה הוא דרמו רבנן שבועה עליה משום דמורי ואמר חבראי לאו מידי חסר בה איזל אתפים ואתפליג בהדיה אבל מקח וממכר דליכא למימר הכי אימא לא ואי תנא מקח וממכר (א) הוא דרמו רבנן שבועה עליה משום דמורי ואמר חבראי דמי קא יהיב ואנא דמי קא יהיבנא השתא דצריכא לדידי אשקליה אנא וחבראי ליזיל לטרח ליזבן אבל מציאה דליכא למימר הכי אימא לא צריכא מקח וממכר [א] ולחזי זוזי ממאן נקט לא צריכא [א] דנקט מתרוייהו מחד מדעתיה ומחד בע"כ ולא ידענא מי הוא מדעתיה ומי הוא בעל כורחיה לימא מתני' דלא כבן ננס דאי בן ננס האמר [ג] כיצד אלו ואלו באין לידי שבועת שוא אפילו תימא בן ננס התם ודאי איכא שבועת שוא הכא איכא למימר דליכא שבועת שוא אימור דתרוייהו בהדי הדדי אגבהוה לימא מתני' דלא כסומכוס דאי כסומכוס האמר [ג] ממון המוטל בספק חולקין בלא שבועה ואלא מאי רבנן הא אמרי המע"ה האי מאי אא"ב רבנן התם דלא תפסי תרוייהו אמרו רבנן המוציא מחבירו עליו הראיה הכא דתרוייהו תפסי [פלגי] לה בשבועה אלא אי אמרת סומכוס השתא ומה התם דלא תפסי תרוייהו חולקין בלא שבועה הכא דתרוייהו תפסי לה לא כ"ש אפי' תימא סומכוס כי אמר סומכוס שמא ושמא אבל ברי וברי לא אמר [ד] ולרבה בר רב הונא דאמר אמר סומכוס אפילו ברי וברי מאי איכא למימר אפי' תימא סומכוס כי אמר סומכוס היכא דאיכא דררא דממונא אבל היכא דליכא דררא דממונא לא ולאו קל וחומר הוא ומה התם דאיכא דררא דממונא למר ואיכא דררא דממונא למר ואיכא

**רש"י**

דמורה ואמר. מורה היתר לעצמו לאחוז בה בלא משפט: **לאו מידי חסר.** אינו מפסיד כלום בחנם באה לו ואף בלא טורח: **אבל מקח וממכר דליכא למימר הכי.** ואע"ג שזה גם הוא נתן את המעות למוכר כדאוקמינן לקמן דנקט מתרוייהו חד מדעתיה וחד בע"כ וכשיחלוקו יטול זה חצי מעותיו וזה חצי מעותיו אפ"ה חסרון הוא אצלו דאי לא הוה צריך לה לא הוה מהדר אבתרה למזבנה וזה שבא לחלוק וליתן חצי דמים שלא כדין מחסרו: **דמי קא יהיבנא.** דמים אני רוצה ליתן: **אבל מציאה דליכא למימר.** חברי ילך וימצא אחרת זה ודאי מחסרו ממון: **ולחזי זוזי ממאן נקט.** נשאל את המוכר ממי קיבל דמיה דתניא בקדושין (דף עג:) נאמן בעל המקח לומר לזה מכרתי ולזה לא מכרתי ואע"ג דמסיים בד"א שמקחו בידו אבל אין מקחו בידו אינו נאמן שלא נתן לב לדבר כל כך להיות זכור מאחר ששניהם חזרו אחריו בפיסוק דמיה הא אוקימנא התם בדנקט זוזי מתרוייהו מחד מדעתיה ומחד בע"כ דכיון דלא עליה רמיא לאסהודי לא דק כולי האי להיות נזהר משהלכו מלפניו הי מדעתיה והי בע"כ אבל היכא דלא קיבל דמים אלא מאחד מידכר דכיר ליה: **לא צריכא דנקט זוזי מתרוייהו.** ה"ג ולא ידעינן מהי מדעתיה ומהי בעל כורחיה ולא גרסי' ולא ידע דאפי' ידע בזו אין המוכר נאמן משהלכו כדמוקי התם: **מתני'.** דמשבע לתרוייהו וחד משתבע לשיקרא: **דלא כבן ננס.** במסכת שבועות (דף מה.) גבי חנוני על פנקסו אלו ואלו באין לב"ד על מנת לישבע אחד מהם לשוא אמר בעל הבית לחנוני תן לבני חטים בדינר ועלי לשלם או לפועלים בסלע מעות שאני חייב בשכרם ועלי ליתן סלע הוא אומר נתתי והוא אומר לא נטלתי ושניהם תובעין את בעה"ב שניהם נשבעין ונוטלין מבעל הבית אמר בן ננס כיצד אלו ואלו באין לידי שבועת שוא אלא שניהם נוטלין בלא שבועה: **אימור בהדי הדדי אגבהוה.** למציאה וכל אחד ואחד סבור אני הגבהתיה תחילה וכולה שלי וכי משתבע על חציה קושטא משתבע ולענין מקח וממכר נמי שמא לשניהם נתרצה: **כסומכוס.** בבבא קמא גבי שור שנגח את הפרה ונמצא עוברה בלדה (דף מו.): **עליו הראיה.** בעדים ואי לא לא גבי מידי והכא חולקין [בשבועה]: ה"ג אי אמרת בשלמא רבנן התם דלא תפסי תרוייהו אמור רבנן כו' הכא דתפסי תרוייהו פלגי בשבועה אלא אי אמרת סומכוס ומה התם דלא תפסי תרוייהו אמר סומכוס פלגי בלא שבועה הכא דתפסי תרוייהו לא כל שכן: **תרוייהו תפסי.** ואין כאן מוציא מחבירו: **בשבועה פלגי לה.** כיון דמחסר גויינא במה שחבירו תופס דהאי תפיס בכולה והאי תפיס [בכולה] לא קים להו לרבנן להוציא ממון מחזקתו בכדי כדאמרי' התם לרבנן דבעי ראיה הצריכום שבועה: **שמא ושמא.** כי התם דקתני נמצא עוברה בלדה ואין ידוע אם עד שלא ילדה נגחה אם משילדה נגחה ולא מת הולד מחמת הנגיחה אלא מאליו וכיון דלכל חד שמא טענין ליכא למרמי עלייהו שבועה: **דרבה בר רב הונא.** בפרק השואל לקמן (דף ק.): **דררא דממונא.** חסרון ממון שאם יפרע זה שלא כדין הוי חסרון ממון ואם נפטרו שלא כדין נמצא זה חסר ולד פרתו: **ומה התם דאיכא דררא דממונא כו'.** איזה מהן שמפסיד החצי שלא כדין אתה מחסרו ממון: ואיכא

**תוספות**

**אי** תנא מציאה. משום דמורה ואמר חבראי לאו מידי חסר לכך תפיס אע"ג שיודע שחבירו מצאה ורמו רבנן שבועה עליה כדי שיפרוש אבל מקח וממכר דליכא למימר הכי שאם יודע שחבירו קנאה לא הוי תפיס ומדתפיס בה סבור שלו הוא ונתרצה המוכר כדמסיק לקמן דנקיט זוזי מתרוייהו אימא לא ישבע דמשום שבועה לא יפרוש שהרי סבור הוא לומר אמת קמ"ל דאפ"ה ישבע והיכא שודאי אינו סבור לומר אמת כגון דקא טעין כל אחד אני ארגתיה שאחד מהן טוען שקר במזיד או כגון שנים אדוקין בשטר דלקמן (דף ז.) התם פשיטא דיחלוקו בשבועה דע"י שבועה ודאי יפרוש דחשיד אממונא לא חשיד אשבועתא:

**ולחזי** זוזי ממאן נקט. פרש"י נשאל למוכר ואע"ג דאין המוכר נאמן כשאין מקחו בידו כדאי' בעשרה יוחסין (קדושין דף עג: ושם ד"ה בד"א) ה"מ בדנקיט מתרוייהו אבל בדנקיט מחד נאמן אפילו אין מקחו בידו וגרסינן בתר הכי ולא ידעינן ובחנם דחק לפרש כן דהכא פריך שפיר דאע"ג דאין מקחו בידו נאמן הוא כעד אחד ואמאי שניהם נשבעין אותו שהמוכר מסייעו יפטר משבועה ואידך ישבע שבועה דאורייתא והשתא גרס שפיר ולא ידע דאי ידע הוה נאמן כעד אחד ומיהו ה"מ לשנויי דליתיה קמן דנשייליה ור"י מפרש דנשאל להם ממי קבל המוכר המעות שאין אנו חושדין אותן לשקר בזה לומר נתתי והוא לא נתן וגם הם אינם חלוקים אלא למי נתרצה המוכר אבל בנתינת המעות אינם חלוקין:

**לימא** מתני' דלא כבן ננס. מצינו למימר דידע שפיר דמתני' אפשר דתרוייהו בהדי הדדי אגבהוה ומ"מ פריך שיחלוקו בלא שבועה אחרי שאפשר לבא לידי שבועת שוא ומשני התם ודאי איכא שבועת שוא:

**התם** דלא תפסי תרוייהו. כ"א האחד ואע"ג דאפי' בעומדת באגם אית להו לרבנן המוציא מחבירו עליו הראיה מ"מ מיקרי האחד תפיס מחמת חזקת מריה קמא ואית דגרס התם דחד מינייהו הוא:

**היכא** דאיכא דררא דממונא. פירוש שבלא טענותיהם יש ספק לב"ד דיש לאחד תביעה על חבירו בלא טענותם כגון בשור שנגח את הפרה (ב"ק דף מו.) ומחליף פרה בחמור [ה] אחרי שהספק נולד מעצמו דין הוא שיחלוקו אפילו בלא שבועה:

**ומה** התם דאיכא דררא דממונא. ואיכא למימר כולה דמר. לא פריך אלא אי סומכוס ס"ל כרבנן דבן ננס דלא חיישי לשבועת שוא דלבן ננס אדרבה היכא דאיכא למימר כולה דמר פלגי בלא שבועה משום דליכא בודאי שבועת שוא:

**ומה** התם דאיכא דררא דממונא. בפרק ח"ה (ב"ב דף לה. ושם) גבי ארבא דאמר רב נחמן כל דאלים גבר פריך מהמחליף פרה בחמור דיחלוקו ומשני התם איכא דררא דממונא ולא פריך ומה התם דליכא דררא דממונא ואיכא למימר כולה דמר יחלוקו גבי ארבא דאיכא למימר דתרוייהו הוא ואין חולקין אלא כל דאלים גבר כדפריך הכא היינו משום דלענין חלוקה סברת דררא דממונא היא טובה מאחר שספק גמור הוא בלא טענותם דין שיחלוקו אבל ארבא אע"ג דאפשר דתרוייהו היא כיון דליכא דררא דממונא ואין אוחזין הוי דינא כל דאלים גבר אבל לענין שבועה אין מועיל סברת דררא דממונא לחלוק בלא שבועה אחרי שהוא בודאי של אחד מהם סברא הוא שיחלוקו בשבועה אולי יודה אחד מהם:

התם

**עין משפט נר מצוה**

ו א מיי' פ"כ מהלכות מכירה הלכה ד ועיין בהשגות ובמ"מ סמג עשין פב טוש"ע ח"מ סי' רכב סעיף א:

**רבינו חננאל**

ואמרי אי הכי נשאל למוכר למי מהן מכר וממי קבל דמיה ושנינן באומר לא ידעתי ואמר ששניהן תבעוה ממני לקנותה ואמרתי להן מי שיתן לי דמיה הרי היא מכורה לו ונתן לי א' מהן דמים והא' השליך המעות לפני ולקחו הטלית ואיני יודע מי מהן שנתן ומי שהשליך כגון זה שנינו שניהן נשבעין וחולקין. וכיון שא' הוא שקנה והא' טוען בשקר ותני תנא שניהן נשבעין ונוטלין מכלל דהאי תנא לא חייש לשבועת שוא של אחד מהן. **מתני'** דלא כבן ננס דאי בן ננס הא חייש וקתני שניהן נוטלין בלא שבועה. דברי בן ננס הן בשבועות פרק כל הנשבעין שבתורה הלכה וחנוני על פנקסו. ודחינן אפי' תימא בן ננס [הכא] איכא למימר דלמא תרוייהו בחדא אגבהוה וה"ה בקנייתא שניהן כא' קנאוה ואין ביניהן שבועת שוא. תוב אמרי' לימא מתני' דלא כסומכוס דאמר ממון המוטל בספק חולקין בלא שבועה דתנן שור שנגח את הפרה ונמצאת עוברה בצדה וכו'. ואמרי' בגמ' אר"י אמר שמואל זו דברי סומכוס אבל חכמים אומרים זה כלל [גדול] בדין המוציא מחבירו עליו הראיה. תניא נמי הכי שור שנגח את הפרה ונמצא עוברה בצידה ואינו יודע אם עד שלא נגחה ילדה ואם משנגחה ילדה משלם ח"נ לפרה ורביע נזק לולד דברי סומכוס וחכ"א המע"ה. ואמרי' אלא מאי מתני' אינה כסומכוס אלא כרבנן אמאי נשבעין והא המוציא מחבירו עליו הראיה אמרי. ופרקי' היכא דתפיס חד ואידך טעין עליה אמור רבנן המע"ה. הכא דתרוייהו תפסי לה אמרי רבנן חולקין בשבועה. אלא אי אמרת סומכוס השתא ומה התם דלא תפסי תרוייהו וכו'. דברי רבה בר [רב] הונא דאמר אמר סומכוס אפי' ברי וברי בהמחליף פרה בחמור בפ' השואל את הפרה ו[ב]ו' ר' חייא בר אבא אמר סומכוס אפי' ברי וברי כרבה בר [רב] הונא בסוף פ' המניח את הכד.

**מסורת הש"ס**

א) קידושין עג., ג) שבועות מה., ג) [בבא קמא לו וש"נ], ד) שם לה: [ע"ש (ודף מו.) לקמן ק ע' וע"ב, ה) [לקמן ק.].

**הגהות הב"ח**

(א) גמ' ואי תנא מקח וממכר. ה"א התם ה דרמו:

**ליקוטי רש"י**

ולחזי זוזי. קא ס' שלא קיבל מעות א מאחד מהם הא וד מדכיר דכיר זוזי דמ קביל. ולא ידענא. ל ידוע לנו [קדושין עד כיצד אלו וא באין. לב"ד לישב שבועת שוא מביני דלית בהו דאינו משב [שבועות מה.]. אפ סומכוס אפילו בו וברי. דשניהם טוענ טענת ברי ואפי' הי דנתבע טוען ברי שאיני חייב ואפי' ה כיון דלבי דינא מספו מאן קאמר קושט חולקין [ב"ק לה:].

**דְאִי תְּנָא מְצִיאָה — For if the Mishnah had stated** only the case of **a found object,** **הֲוָה אָמִינָא מְצִיאָה הוּא דְּרָמוּ רַבָּנָן שְׁבוּעָה עֲלֵיהּ — I might have said** that **only** in the case of **a found object did the Rabbis impose an oath upon him** [each litigant] **מִשּׁוּם דְּמוֹרֵי וְאָמַר חַבְרָאִי לָאו מִידֵי חָסֵר בָּהּ — because** it is possible that **one** of them **rationalizes and says** to himself: **"This fellow is not losing anything because of it. אֵיזִיל אֶתְפּוֹס וְאֶתְפְּלִיג בַּהֲדֵיהּ — I will** therefore **go and take hold** of the cloak he has found **and divide it with him!** To discourage such a false claim, the Rabbis made the litigants swear to the truth of their claims.[1] **אֲבָל מִקָּח וּמִמְכָּר דְּלֵיכָּא לְמֵימַר הָכִי — But** in the case of **buying and selling, where this** justification **cannot be said,**[2] **אֵימָא לֹא — I would say** that **no** oath can be imposed.[3] **וְאִי תְּנָא מִקָּח וּמִמְכָּר — And if the Mishnah had stated** only the case of **buying and selling,** **הוּא דְּרָמוּ רַבָּנָן שְׁבוּעָה עֲלֵיהּ —** I might have said that **only in that case did the Rabbis impose an oath upon him** [each litigant], **מִשּׁוּם דְּמוֹרֵי וְאָמַר — because he rationalizes and says** to himself: **חַבְרָאִי דְּמֵי קָא יָהֵיב — "This fellow is giving money** to the seller **וַאֲנָא דְּמֵי קָא יָהֵיבְנָא — and I, too, am** planning on **giving money** to the seller.[4] **הַשְׁתָּא דִּצְרִיכָא לְדִידִי — Now that I need [the cloak] for myself,** **אֶשְׁקְלֵיהּ אֲנָא— I will take it;** **וְחַבְרָאִי לֵיזִיל לִטְרַח לִיזְבַּן — and** as for **this fellow — let him go to the trouble of buying** a different cloak.[5] **אֲבָל מְצִיאָה דְּלֵיכָּא לְמֵימַר הָכִי— However,** in the case of **a found object, where this** rationalization **cannot be said,**[6] **אֵימָא לֹא — I would say** that **no** oath can be imposed.[7] **צְרִיכָא — It is** therefore **necessary** for the Mishnah to state its ruling that they divide under oath both in the case of a found object and in the case of sold object.[8]

The Gemara asks:

**מִקָּח וּמִמְכָּר —** Can the Mishnah be discussing a case of **buying an selling?** Why would the Mishnah's ruling apply in that cas **וְלֶחֱזֵי זוּזֵי מִמַּאן נְקַט — Let us** simply **see from whom** [the selle **took the money!**[9] **— ? —**

The Gemara answers:

**לֹא צְרִיכָא — No. [The Mishnah's ruling] is needed** in a case sale **דִּנְקַט מִתַּרְוַיְיהוּ — where** [the seller] **accepted** payme **from both** [litigants] **— מֵחַד מִדַּעְתֵּיהּ — from one** of them h accepted the payment **willingly,** **וּמֵחַד בְּעַל כּוֹרְחֵיהּ — and fro the other** he accepted the payment **unwillingly,** i.e. one of th two forced the money upon him. **וְלָא יָדְעִינָא מִי הוּא מִדַּעְתֵּיהּ וּמִי הוּא בְּעַל כּוֹרְחֵיהּ — And we do not know who is the one fro** whom he **willingly** accepted **and who is the one** from whom h **unwillingly** accepted.[10] Since we have no way of determinin which of the two is telling the truth, they divide the cloak und oath.

The Gemara now considers whether the ruling of our Mishna is consistent with the view of the Tanna Ben Nanas:

**לֵימָא מַתְנִיתִין דְּלָא כְּבֶן נַנָּס — Shall we say that** the ruling of **ou Mishnah is not in accordance with** the view of **Ben Nanas?** **אִי בֶּן נַנָּס הָאָמַר כֵּיצַד אֵלּוּ וָאֵלּוּ בָּאִין לִידֵי שְׁבוּעַת שָׁוְא — For were it i accordance with** the view of **Ben Nanas — why, he says, "Ho can both come to** court for a judgment that entails **a fals**

NOTES

1. The fact that both litigants state diametrically opposite claims does not show that one of them intends to be an outright thief. Rather, it is possible that the false claimant rationalizes that what he seeks to do is not actual theft, since the true finder expended neither money nor effort in obtaining the cloak but it came to him as a complete windfall. In this way, the liar justifies his decision to lay false claim to the cloak in order to end up dividing it with the finder. However, this type of thief will not swear a false oath, which cannot be justified in any way. Thus, it is possible that the Rabbis instituted an oath in this case in order to discourage the spurious claim of this type of thief [see 2a note 7].

2. [The analogous case of sale would be one in which the false claimant sees someone buying a cloak and decides that he would like to have it. He, too, pays the seller and seizes the cloak, claiming later in court that it was *he* who bought the cloak, not the other fellow.] Now, it is true that in this case as well, the true buyer does not lose any money if half the cloak is awarded to the false claimant, since he still owns half the cloak and the seller refunds each litigant half the value of the cloak. [As the Gemara below explains, the seller received full payment from both litigants.] Nevertheless, even the false claimant realizes that the buyer would not have gone to the trouble of buying the cloak if he did not really need it. Therefore, he cannot rationalize his attempt to deprive the buyer of his rightful purchase (*Rashi*). [Rather, his false claim indicates that he is an outright thief.]

3. I would think that an outright thief, who is willing to blatantly violate the sin of theft in order to achieve his end, will also commit the sin of swearing falsely, if necessary. Therefore, it is pointless to impose an oath, since this will only cause the liar to compound the sin of theft with the sin of swearing falsely (*Rashba* and *Ritva* in explanation of *Rashi*; see there at length). Rather, in absence of an oath, the law would be that the disputed cloak must be withheld from both litigants until definite ownership can be established (ibid., based on *Rashi* 2a ד״ה במקח וממכר).

4. *Rashi*. [*Rashi* apparently understands that the Gemara here is describing the false claimant's initial thoughts in deciding to interrupt the sale and attempt to buy the cloak for himself.]

5. In the case of a sale, the false claimant might rationalize that his actions do not cause the true buyer to suffer any monetary loss, but only the trouble of finding another cloak to buy. Such a claimant will be deterred by the prospect of swearing falsely, a sin that he cannot rationalize.

6. I.e. the false claimant cannot rationalize that the true finder wi find another lost cloak to replace this one. Thus, the false clain ant clearly intends to cause the finder actual monetary los (*Rashi*). Such a thief will not be deterred by the prospect of swearin falsely.

7. As explained in note 3.

8. The Mishnah teaches that there is room for rationalization in eithe case, and therefore the Rabbis imposed an oath in both cases to induc the false claimant to retract his claim.

It emerges, then, that in cases where there is no room fc rationalization (e.g. both claim to have actually woven the cloak), we d not impose an oath. Rather, the cloak must be withheld from bot litigants until definite ownership can be established (*Ritva* in explana tion of *Rashi*; see *Rashi* 2a ד״ה במקח וממכר).

9. [Literally: from whom he took the *zuzim; zuz* was the standard un of currency in Talmudic times.] I.e. let us ask the seller which one of th litigants paid him for the cloak and that will show us who the true buye is. For, as taught by a Baraisa in *Kiddushin* (73b), the court does rely o the unassisted testimony of a seller who testifies as to which of tw litigants really bought an article from him (*Rashi*). [This credibilit granted a seller is an exception to the normal rules of evidence, whicl prevent the court from relying on the testimony of a lone witness (se *Nachalas David*).]

Accordingly, the Gemara here asks why the Mishnah would rule i the case of dispute over a bought cloak that the litigants swear an divide. Why not simply ask the seller which one bought the cloak fron him and award it to that person?

10. As the Gemara in *Kiddushin* (ibid.) explains, when a seller receive money from two parties and no longer has the sold object in hi possession, the court cannot rely on his testimony as to which of the tw he really meant to sell the item, even if the seller asserts that h remembers the matter clearly. The special reliance on the seller' testimony regarding a cloak that he no longer has (see previous note) i limited to where he received money from only one of the parties. Onl then do we assume that he has a clear recollection of the matte (*Rashi*). [However, if the seller still has the disputed item in hi possession, we rely on his recollection even when he has received mone from both parties, since the seller — realizing that it will be his duty t testify about the status of the disputed item in his possession — make sure to keep the facts clearly in mind (ibid.).]

דאי תנא מציאה הוה אמינא מציאה הוא דרמו רבנן שבועה עליה משום דמורי ואמר חבראי לאו מידי חסר בה איזל אתפים ואתפליג בהדיה אבל מקח וממכר דליכא למימר הכי אימא לא ואי תנא מקח וממכר (א) הוא דרמו רבנן שבועה עליה משום דמורי ואמר חבראי דמי קא יהיב ואנא דמי קא יהיבנא השתא דצריכא לדידי אשקליה אנא וחבראי ליזיל לטרח ליזבן אבל מציאה דליכא למימר הכי אימא לא צריכא מקח וממכר [א] ולחזי זוזי ממאן נקט לא צריכא [א] דנקט מתרווייהו מחד מדעתיה ומחד בע"כ ולא ידענא מי הוא מדעתיה ומי הוא בעל כורחיה לימא מתני' דלא כבן ננס דאי בן ננס האמר [ב] כיצד אלו ואלו באין לידי שבועת שוא אפילו תימא בן ננס התם ודאי איכא שבועת שוא הכא איכא למימר דליכא שבועת שוא אימור דתרווייהו בהדי הדדי אגבהוה לימא מתני' דלא כסומכוס דאי כסומכוס האמר [ג] ממון המוטל בספק חולקין בלא שבועה ואלא מאי רבנן הא אמרי המע"ה האי מאי אא"ב רבנן התם דלא תפסי תרוייהו אמרו רבנן המוציא מחבירו עליו הראיה הכא דתרווייהו תפסי [פלגי] לה בשבועה אלא אי אמרת סומכוס השתא ומה התם דלא תפסי תרווייהו חולקין בלא שבועה הכא דתרווייהו תפסי לה לא כ"ש אפי' תימא סומכוס כי אמר סומכוס שמא ושמא אבל ברי וברי לא אמר [ד] ולרבה בר רב הונא דאמר אמר סומכוס אפילו ברי וברי מאי איכא למימר אפי' תימא סומכוס כי אמר סומכוס היכא דאיכא דררא דממונא אבל היכא דליכא דררא דממונא לא ולאו קל וחומר הוא ומה התם דאיכא דררא דממונא למר ואיכא דררא דממונא למר

ואיכא

דמורה ואמר. מורה היתר לעצמו לאחוז בה בלא משפט: לאו מידי חסר. אינו מפסיד כלום בחנם בזה לו ואף בלא טורח: אבל מקח וממכר דליכא למימר הכי. ואע"ג שזה גם הוא נתן את המעות למוכר כדאוקמינן לקמן דנקט מתרווייהו חד מדעתיה וחד בע"כ וכשיחלוקו יטול זה חצי מעותיו וזה חצי מעותיו אפ"ה חסרון הוא אצלו דאי לא הוה צריך לה לא הוה מהדר אבתרה למזבנה וזה שבא לחלוק וליתן חצי דמים שלא כדין מחסרו: דמי קא יהיבנא. דמים אני רוצה ליתן: אבל מציאה דליכא למימר. חברי ילך וימצא אחרת זה ודאי מחסרו ממון: ולחזי זוזי ממאן נקט. נשאל את המוכר ממי קיבל דמיה דתניא בקדושין (דף עג:) נאמן בעל המקח לומר לזה מכרתי ולזה לא מכרתי ואע"ג דמסיים בד"א שמקחו בידו אבל אין מקחו בידו אינו נאמן שלא נתן לב לדבר כל כך להיות זכור מאחר שניהם חזרו אחריו בפיסוק דמיה הא אוקימנא התם בדנקט זוזי מתרווייהו מחד מדעתיה ומחד בע"כ דכיון דלא עליה רמיא לאסהודי לא דק כולי האי להיות נזהר משהלכו מלפניו הי מדעתיה והי בע"כ אבל היכא דלא קיבל דמים אלא מחד מידכר דכיר ליה: לא צריכא דנקט זוזי מתרווייהו. ה"ג ולא ידעינן מהי מדעתיה ומהי בעל כורחיה ולא גרסי' ולא ידע דאפי' ידע בזו אין המוכר נאמן משהלכו כדמוקי התם: מתני'. דמשבע לתרווייהו וחד משתבע לשיקרא: דלא כבן ננס. במסכת שבועות (דף מה.) גבי חנוני על פנקסו אלו ואלו באין לב"ד על מנת לישבע אחד מהם לשוא אמר בעל הבית לחנוני תן לבני חטים בדינר ועלי לשלם או לפועלים בסלע מעות שאני חייב בשכרם ועלי ליתן סלע הוא אומר נתתי והוא אומר לא נטלתי ושניהם תובעין את בעה"ב שניהם נשבעין ונוטלין מבעל הבית אמר בן ננס כיצד אלו ואלו באין לידי שבועת שוא אלא שניהם נוטלין בלא שבועה: אימור בהדי הדדי אגבהוה. למציאה וכל אחד ואחד סבור אני הגבהתיה תחילה וכולה שלי וכי משתבע על חציה קושטא משתבע ולענין מקח וממכר נמי שמא לשניהם נתרצה: כסומכוס. בבבא קמא גבי שור שנגח את הפרה ונמצא עוברה בלדה (דף מו.): עליו הראיה. בעדים ואי לא לא גבי מידי והכא חולקין [בשבועה]: ה"ג אי אמרת בשלמא רבנן התם דלא תפסי תרוייהו אמור רבנן כו' הכא דתפסי תרוייהו פלגי בשבועה אלא אי אמרת סומכוס ומה התם דלא תפסי תרוייהו אמר סומכוס פלגי בלא שבועה הכא דתפסי תרוייהו לא כל שכן: תרווידהו תפסי. ואין כאן מוציא מחבירו: בשבועה פלגי לה. כיון דמחסר גויינא במה שחבירו תופס דהאי תפיס בכולה והאי תפיס [בכולה] לא קים להו לרבנן להוציא ממון מחזקתו בכדי כדאמרי' התם לרבנן דבעי ראיה הצריכום שבועה: שמא ושמא. כי התם דקתני נמצא עוברה בלדה ואין ידוע אם עד שלא ילדה נגחה אם משילדה נגחה ולא מת הולד מחמת הנגיחה אלא מאליו וכיון דכל חד שמא טעין ליכא למרמי עלייהו שבועה: דרבה בר רב הונא. בפרק השואל לקמן (דף ק.): דררא דממונא. חסרון ממון שאם יפרע זה שלא כדין הוי חסרון ממון ואם נפטרנו שלא כדין נמצא זה חסר ולד פרתו: ומה התם דאיכא דררא דממונא כו'. איזה מהן שמפסיד החצי שלא כדין אתה מחסרו ממון:

ואיכא

אי תנא מציאה. משום דמורה ואמר חבראי לאו מידי חסר לכך תפיס אע"ג שיודע שחבירו מצאה ורמו רבנן שבועה עליה כדי שיפרוש אבל מקח וממכר דליכא למימר הכי שאם יודע שחבירו קנאה לא הוי תפיס ומדתפיס בה סבור שלו הוא ונתרצה המוכר כדמסיק לקמן דנקיט זוזי מתרווייהו אימא לא ישבע דמשום שבועה לא יפרוש שהרי סבור הוא לומר אמת קמ"ל דאפ"ה ישבע והיכא שודאי אינו סבור לומר אמת כגון דקא טוען כל אחד אני ארגתיה שאחד מהן טוען שקר במזיד או כגון שנים אדוקין בשטר דלקמן (דף ז.) התם פשיטא דיחלוקו בשבועה דע"י שבועה ודאי יפרוש דחשיד אממונא לא חשיד אשבועתא: ולחזי זוזי ממאן נקט. פרש"י נשאל למוכר ואע"ג דאין המוכר נאמן כשאין מקחו בידו כדאי' בעשרה יוחסין (קדושין דף עג: ושם ד"ה בד"א) ה"מ בדנקיט מתרווייהו אבל בדנקיט מחד נאמן אפילו אין מקחו בידו וגרסינן בתר הכי ולא ידעינן ובחנם דחק לפרש כן דהכא פריך שפיר דאע"ג דאין מקחו בידו נאמן הוא כעד אחד ואמאי שניהם נשבעין אותו שהמוכר מסייעו יפטר משבועה ואידך ישבע שבועה דאורייתא והשתא גרס שפיר ולא ידע דאי ידע הוה נאמן כעד אחד ומיהו ה"מ לשנויי דליתיה קמן דנשייליה ור"י מפרש דנשאל להם ממי קבל המוכר המעות שאין אנו חושדין אותן לשקר בזה לומר נתתי והוא לא נתן וגם הם אינם חלוקים אלא למי נתרצה המוכר אבל בנתינת המעות אינם חלוקין: לימא מתני' דלא כבן ננס. מצינו למימר דידע שפיר דמתני' אפשר דתרווייהו בהדי הדדי אגבהוה ומ"מ פריך שיחלוקו בלא שבועה אחרי שאפשר לבא לידי שבועת שוא ומשני התם ודאי איכא שבועת שוא: התם דלא תפסי תרווידהו. כ"א האחד ואע"ג דאפי' בעומדת באגם אית להו לרבנן המוציא מחבירו עליו הראיה מ"מ מיקרי האחד תפיס מחמת חזקת מריה קמא ואית דגרס התם דחד מינייהו הוא: היכא דאיכא דררא דממונא. פירוש שבלא טענותיהם יש ספק לב"ד דיש לאחד תביעה על חבירו בלא טענותם כגון בשור שנגח את הפרה (ב"ק דף מו.) ומחליף פרה בחמור [ה] אחרי שהספק נולד מעצמו דין הוא שיחלוקו אפילו בלא שבועה: ומה התם דאיכא דררא דממונא. ואיכא למימר כולה דמר. לא פריך אלא אי סומכוס ס"ל כרבנן דבן ננס דלא חיישי לשבועת שוא דלבן ננס אדרבה היכא דאיכא למימר כולה דמר פלגי בלא שבועה משום דאיכא בודאי שבועת שוא: ומה התם דאיכא דררא דממונא. בפרק ח"ה (ב"ב דף לה. ושם) גבי ארבא דאמר רב נחמן כל דאלים גבר פריך מהמחליף פרה בחמור דיחלוקו ומשני התם איכא דררא דממונא ולא פריך ומה התם דאיכא דררא דממונא ואיכא למימר כולה דמר יחלוקו גבי ארבא דאיכא למימר דתרווייהו הוא ואין חולקין אלא כל דאלים גבר כדפריך הכא היינו משום דלענין חלוקה סברת דררא דממונא היא טובה מאחר שספק גמור הוא בלא טענותם דין שיחלוקו אבל ארבא אע"ג דאפשר דתרווייהו היא כיון דליכא דררא דממונא ואין אוחזין הוי דינא כל דאלים גבר אבל לענין שבועה אין מועיל סברת דררא דממונא לחלוק בלא שבועה אחרי שהוא בודאי של אחד מהם סברא הוא שיחלוקו בשבועה אולי יודה אחד מהם:

התם

עין משפט
נר מצוה

ו א מיי' פ"כ מהלכות מכירה הלכה ד ועיין בהשגות ובמ"מ סמג עשין פב טוש"ע ח"מ סי' רכב סעיף א:

## רבינו חננאל

ואמרי אי הכי נשאל למוכר למי מהן מכר וממי קבל דמיה ושנינן באומר לא ידעתי ואמר ששניהן תבעוה ממני לקנותה ואמרתי להן מי שיתן לי דמיה הרי היא מכורה לו ונתן לי א' מהן דמים והא' השליך המעות לפני ולקחו הטלית ואיני יודע מי מהן שנתן ומי שהשליך כגון זה שנינו שניהן נשבעין וחולקין. וכיון שא' הוא שקנה והא' טוען בשקר ותני תנא שניהן נשבעין ונוטלין מכלל דהאי תנא לא חייש לשבועת שוא של אחד מהן. **מתני' דלא כבן ננס** דאי בן ננס הא חייש וקתני שניהן נוטלין בלא שבועה. דברי בן ננס הן בשבועות פרק כל הנשבעין שבתורה הלכה וחנוני על פנקסו. ודחינן אפי' תימא בן ננס [הכא] איכא למימר דלמא תרווייהו בחדא אגבהוה וה"ה בקנייתא שניהן כא' קנאוה ואין ביניהן שבועת שוא. תוב אמרי' לימא מתני' דלא כסומכוס דאמר ממון המוטל בספק חולקין בלא שבועה דתנן שור שנגח את הפרה ונמצאת עוברה בצדה וכו'. ואמרי' בגמ' אר"י אמר שמואל זו דברי סומכוס אבל חכמים אומרים זה כלל [גדול] בדין המוציא מחבירו עליו הראיה. תניא נמי הכי שור שנגח את הפרה ונמצא עוברה בצידה ואינו יודע אם עד שלא נגחה ילדה ואם משנגחה ילדה משלם ח"נ לפרה ורביע נזק לולד דברי סומכוס וחכ"א המע"ה. ואמרי' אלא מאי מתני' אינה כסומכוס אלא כרבנן אמאי נשבעין והא המוציא מחבירו עליו הראיה אמרי. ופרקי היכא דתפיס חד ואידך טעין עליה אמור רבנן המע"ה. הכא דתרווייהו תפסי לה אמרי רבנן חולקין בשבועה. אלא אי אמרת סומכוס השתא ומה התם דלא תפסי תרוייהו וכו'. דברי רבה בר [רב] הונא דאמר אמר סומכוס אפי' ברי וברי בהמחליף פרה בחמור בפ' השואל את הפרה ודברי ר' חייא בר אבא אמר סומכוס אפי' ברי וברי כרבה בר [רב] הונא בסוף פ' המניח את הכד.

## מסורת הש"ס

א) קידושין עג., ב) שבו[עות] מה., ג) [בבא קמא ... וש"נ], ד) שם לה: [ע' ... ודף מו.) לקמן ק ... וע"ב, ה) [לקמן ק.]

## הגהות הב"ח

(א) גמ' ואי תנא מ[קח] וממכר. ה"א התם ... דרמו:

## ליקוטי רש"י

ולחזי זוזי. קא ... שלא קיבל מעות ... מאחד מהם הא ... מדכיר דכיר זוזי ד... קביל. ולא ידענא. ... ידוע לנו [קדושין ע...]. כיצד אלו וא[לו] באין. לב"ד ליש[בע] שבועת שוא מביני ... דלית בהו דאינו מש... [שבועות מה.]. א[פילו] סומכוס אפילו ב[רי] וברי. דשניהם טוע[נים] טענת ברי ואפי' ה... דנתבע טוען ברי שאיני חייב ואפי' ... כיון דלגבי דינא מספ[קא] מאן קאמר קוש[טא] חולקין [ב"ק לה:].

## שנים

א) אאוחזין בטלית זה אומר אני מצאתיה וזה אומר אני מצאתיה זה אומר כולה שלי וזה אומר כולה שלי זה ישבע שאין לו בה פחות מחציה וזה ישבע שאין לו בה פחות מחציה ויחלוקו בזה אומר כולה שלי וזה אומר חציה שלי האומר כולה שלי ישבע שאין לו בה פחות משלשה חלקים והאומר חציה שלי ישבע שאין לו בה פחות מרביע זה נוטל שלשה חלקים וזה נוטל רביע ב) גהיו שנים רוכבין על גבי בהמה או שהיה אחד רוכב ואחד מנהיג זה אומר כולה שלי וזה אומר כולה שלי זה ישבע שאין לו בה פחות מחציה וזה ישבע שאין לו בה פחות מחציה ויחלוקו בזמן שהם מודים או שיש להן עדים חולקין בלא שבועה: גמ' למה לי למתנא זה אומר אני מצאתיה וזה אומר אני מצאתיה זה אומר כולה שלי וזה אומר כולה שלי ליתני חדא חדא קתני זה אומר אני מצאתיה וכולה שלי וזה אומר אני מצאתיה וכולה שלי וליתני אני מצאתיה ואנא ידענא דכולה שלי אי תנא אני מצאתיה הוה אמינא מאי מצאתיה ראיתיה אע"ג דלא אתאי לידיה בראיה בעלמא קני תנא כולה שלי דבראיה לא קני ומי מצית אמרת מאי מצאתיה ראיתיה ג) והא אמר ד) רבנאי א) ומצאתה דאתאי לידיה משמע אין ומצאתה דקרא דאתא לידיה משמע ומיהו תנא לישנא דעלמא נקט ומדחזי ליה אמר אנא אשכחית ואע"ג דלא אתאי לידיה בראיה בעלמא קני תני כולה שלי דדבראיה בעלמא לא קני לה וליתני כולה שלי ולא בעי אני מצאתיה אי תני כולה שלי הוה אמינא בעלמא דקתני מצאתיה בראיה בעלמא קני תנא אני מצאתיה והדר תנא כולה שלי דממשנה יתירה אשמעינן דראיה לא קני ומי מצית אמרת חדא קתני והא זה וזה קתני זה אומר אני מצאתיה וזה אומר אני מצאתיה זה אומר כולה שלי וכו' אמר רב פפא ואיתימא רב שימי בר אשי ואמרי לה ט) כדי י) רישא במציאה הוסיפא במקח וממכר וצריכא דאי

### רש"י

שנים אוחזין בטלית. דוקא אוחזין דשניהם מוחזקים בה ואין לזה כח בה יותר מזה שאילו היתה ביד אחד לבדו הוי אידך המוציא מחבירו ועליו להביא ראיה בעדים שהיא שלו ואינו נאמן זה ליטול בשבועה: זה אומר כולה שלי. בגמרא מפרש למאי תנא תרתי: זה ישבע. מפרש בגמרא (דף ג.) שבועה זו למה: שאין לו בה פחות מחציה. בגמרא (דף ה:) מפ' אמאי תקון כי האי לישנא בהך שבועה: וזה אומר חציה שלי. מודה הוא שהחצי של חבירו ואין דנין אלא על חציה הלכך זה האומר כולה שלי ישבע כו' כמשפט הראשון מה שהן דנין עליו נשבעין שניהם שאין לכל אחד בו פחות מחציו ונוטל כל אחד חציו: היו שנים רוכבין כו'. לאשמועינן אתא (א) דרכוב ומנהיג שניהם שוין לקנות בהמה מן ההפקר: בזמן שהן מודין. בגמרא (דף ח.) מפרש [דבהאי] אשמעינן דהמגביה מציאה לחבירו קנה חבירו: גמ' ראיתיה. קודס ז) שהגבהת אותה: בראיה קני. מדקתני יחלוקו: תנא כולה שלי. בחזקה גמורה שהגבהתי תחילה ואתה תפסת מידי משזכיתי בה: והאמר רבנאי. בבבא קמא בהגוזל ומאכיל ח): ומצאתה דאתא לידיה משמע. ואפי' הכי אחיך ולא עובד כוכבים ולא תימא כי מיעט רחמנא עובד כוכבים היכא דלא אתאי לידיה דישראל לא מיחייב למטרח עלה ולאהדורה אבל אתא לידיה מיחייב להחזירה דאבידתו אסורה: תנא לישנא דעלמא נקט. אי לא הדר תנא כולה שלי הוה אמינא מאי מצאתיה דקתני תנא לשון בני אדם אחז במשנתנו ולא לשון המקרא והרבה בני אדם קורין לה מציאה משעת ראיה: בעלמא דקתני מצאתיה. בכ"מ ששנינו שהמוצא מציאה קנאה הוה אמינא דמציאה קני לה משעת ראיה דלא אשמעינן שום תנא דלא קני לה אלא בהגבהה להכי אשמעינן הכא ממשנה יתירה: והא זה וזה קתני. גבי מצאתיה תנא זה אומר וגבי כולה שלי קתני זה אומר ואי חדא הוא הכי אבעי ליה למתני זה אומר מצאתיה וכולה שלי: במקח וממכר. קניתיה מיד פלוני ודוקא מקח וממכר הוא דאמרינן יחלוקו בשבועה דאיכא למימר שניהם קנאוה ולשניהם נתרצה המוכר אבל זה אומר אני ארגתיה וזה אומר אני ארגתיה לא יחלוקו דודאי חד מינייהו רמאי הוא ותהא מונחת עד שיבא אליהו: דמורה

### תוספות

שנים אוחזין בטלית. איידי דאיירי בהגוזל בתרא (ב"ק דף קיט.) מחלוקת נסורת נגר ובעל הבית דקתני במעצד הרי אלו שלו ובכשיל הרי אלו של בעל הבית תני הכא נמי דיני חלוקות ואע"ג דבתרי מסכתא אין סדר למשנה ט) ואיכא מ"ד כולה נזיקין לאו חדא מסכתא הוא ה"מ לענין מחלוקת ואח"כ סתם לפי שרבי לא היה לומד כסדר אלא כמו שהיו חפצים התלמידים אבל כשחברם על הסדר חברם וצריך בכל מסכתא טעם למה נשנית אחר שלפניה כלדייק בריש מסכת שבועות (דף ב:) מכדי תנא ממכות קסליק כו' וכן בסוטה (דף ב.):

ויחלוקו. תימה דמאי שנא מההיא דארבא דאמר כל דאלים גבר פרק חזקת הבתים (ב"ב דף לד: ושם) וי"ל דאוחזין שאני דחשיב כאילו כל אחד יש לו בה בודאי החצי דאנן סהדי דמאי דתפיס האי דידיה הוא וכן במנה שלישי דמדמי בגמרא לטלית חשיב ההוא שהנפקד תופס בחזקת שניהם כאילו הם עצמם מוחזקים בו לכך משני דהתם ודאי דחד מינייהו הוא ואין החלוקה יכולה להיות אמת ולכך יהא מונח אבל טלית דאיכא למימר דתרוייהו הוא יחלוקו וכן שנים אדוקים בשטר דמדמי לקמן (דף ז.) למתני' משום דשניהם אדוקים בו דהחלוקה יכולה להיות אמת דאפשר שפרע לו החצי ובמנה אין דרך שיקנה לו החצי אחרי שהוא ביד חבירו אבל בארבא אע"ג דאפשר שהיא של שניהם כיון דאין מוחזקין בו הוי דינא כל דאלים גבר ולסומכוס אע"ג דאין מוחזקין בו ואין החלוקה יכולה להיות אמת היכא דאיכא דררא דממונא פירוש שבלא טענותיהם יש ספק לבית דין יחלוקו:

וזה נוטל רביע. וא"ת יהא נאמן דחציו שלו מיגו דאי בעי אמר כולה שלי כדאמרי' בגמ' (לקמן דף ח.) האי מיגו גופיה לפטרו משבועה אי לא משום דאיערומי קמערים ומפרש ריב"ס דמיגו להוציא לא אמרי' דבחציו השני מוחזק זה כמו זה והיא דחזקת הבתים (ב"ב דף לג: ושם ל) דגאין ולחיש ליה לרבה אין שטרא זייפא הוא ומיהו שטרא מעליא הוה לי בידי ואבד והימניה רבה להוציא במיגו דאי בעי אמר שטרא מעליא הוא ° התם היינו טעמא משום דאפי' הוה שתיק רק שלא היה מודה שהוא מזויף היה נאמן כי החתימה היתה נכרת לעומדים שם ורב יוסף אית ליה דאפילו מיגו לא הוה כיון שטענה ראשונה שהוא טוען בהאי שטרא הוא שקר ואין לומר מיגו אלא היכא שטענתו ראשונה היא אמת מיגו שהיה טוען אחרת ולכך אינו מיגו אפילו להחזיק כגון בעובדא קמייתא וא"ת ונימא דאין ספק מוציא מידי ודאי דהאומר כולה שלי יש לו בודאי חציה והאומר חציה שלי ספק אם יש לו בה כלום כדאמרינן בפרק החולץ (יבמות דף לח.) ספק ויבם שבאו לחלוק בנכסי סבא ספק אמר אנא בר מתנא אנא ואית לי פלגא ויבם אמר את ברא דידי ולית לך ולא מידי הוה ליה יבם ודאי וספק ספק ואין ספק מוציא מידי ודאי וי"ל דהתם יבם שהוא ודאי יורשו ולא יוציא הספק מספק ממונו אבל הכא אין סברא מה שהוא ודאי בחציו שיועיל לו לחציו השני:

בראיה בעלמא קנה. אע"ג דקתני במתני' (לקמן דף ט:) ראה את המציאה ואמר לחבירו תנה לי דלא קנה בראיה וכן ראה את המציאה ונפל עליה (לקמן דף י.) קתני נמי דלא קני מאי למדאי כיון דאמר תנה לי או שנפל עליה גלי דעתיה דלא ניחא ליה למקני עד שיגיע לידו:

דבראיה בעלמא לא קני. והא דאמרי' בפרק הבית והעלייה (לקמן דף קיח. ושם) הבטה בהפקר קני היינו שעשה מעשה כל דהו כגון שגדר גדר קטן:

והא זה וזה קתני. איכא דוכתי דפריך כי האי גוונא ואיכא דוכתי דלא פריך: [עי' תוס' בכורות דף לא: ד"ה א"כ]: אי



א א מיי' פ"ט מהלכות טוען ונטען הל' ז סמג עשין לה טוש"ע ח"מ סי' קלח סעיף א:
ב ב מיי' שם הלכה ח טוש"ע שם סעיף ב:
ג ג מיי' שם הלכה ז טוש"ע שם סעיף א:
ד ד מיי' פי"ז מהלכות גזילה ואבידה הל' א סמג עשין עד טוש"ע ח"מ סי' רסח סעיף א:
ה ה מיי' פ"כ מהלכות מכירה הל' ד ועיין בהשגות ובמ"מ סמג עשין פב טוש"ע ח"מ סי' רכב סעיף א:

### רבינו חננאל

שנים אוחזין בטלית זה אומר אני מצאתיה וכו'. ואקשי' עלה למה לי למתנא תוב זה אומר כולה שלי הלא באומרו אני מצאתיה משמע דכולה שלי היא. ופרקי הא אתא לאשמועי' דבראיה בעלמא לא קני לה למציאה. הא לא מיבעיא דהא אמר רבינא ומצאתה דאתאי לידיה משמע. דברי רבינא בהגוזל בתרא הל' אין פורטין מתיבת המוכסין ופשוטה היא. ואוקימנא למתני' רישא במציאה וסיפא דקתני זה אומר כולה שלי בקנייתא בשטוען אני קניתיה ונתתי דמיה לבעליה



בבא בתרא קע., לקמן ח.], ג) לקמן ח., קמא קיג:, רבינא, מהרש"ל, עיין מהרש"ל], לקמן ח.], ז) שהגבהתי, רש"א, ח) [דף קיג:], בבא קמא קב.], י) [ד"ה אמאי].

### הגהות הב"ח

(א) רש"י ד"ה היו וכו' אתא דרוכב ומנהיג:

### גליון הש"ס

תוס' ד"ה וזה כו' התם וכו'. עיין לקמן דף ע"א תוס' ד"ה והא:

### תורה אור השלם

וְכֵן תַּעֲשֶׂה לַחֲמֹרוֹ וְכֵן תַּעֲשֶׂה לְשִׂמְלָתוֹ וְכֵן תַּעֲשֶׂה לְכָל אֲבֵדַת אָחִיךָ אֲשֶׁר תֹּאבַד מִמֶּנּוּ וּמְצָאתָהּ לֹא תוּכַל לְהִתְעַלֵּם: [דברים כב, ג]

### ליקוטי רש"י

כדי. שם תכס [גיטין פה:].

ome say it was **Rav Simi bar Ashi** who said it, **וְאָמְרֵי לָהּ כְּדִי** – nd **some say** it was **Kedi:**[20] **רֵישָׁא בִּמְצִיאָה** – **The first part** of he Mishnah ["This one says, 'I found it,'. . ."] **refers to** the case f **a found object,** **וְסֵיפָא בְּמִקָּח וּמִמְכָּר** – **whereas the latter part** of the Mishnah ["This one says, 'It is all mine'. . ."] **refers to** the case of **buying and selling.**[21] **וּצְרִיכָא** – **And it was necessary** for the Mishnah to state its ruling in regard to both cases of dispute:

NOTES

ne says, "I found it and it is all mine," and this one says, "I found it and ; is all mine" (*Rashi*).

0. The rendering of the word כְּדִי as the name of a sage is based on *Rashi* ɔ *Gittin* 85b ד״ה ולורכיה. Alternatively, כְּדִי means: *without attribution*, e. some say that the explanation attributed to Rav Pappa or to Rav Simi ar Ashi is actually *without* definite *attribution* (*Rabbeinu Chananel* rinted on *Horayos* 10b line 8; see also *Be'er Sheva* to *Horayos* 8a; *'hochmas Shlomo* to the present Gemara and the notes of *Maharatz Chayes*; *Yuchasin HaShalem* p. 160 ד״ה כדי and *Seder HaDoros, Tannaim Va'Amoraim* p. 253 ד״ה כדי).

21. That is, the Mishnah indeed refers to two distinct cases. The first case deals with a dispute over a found cloak, in which each litigant claims, "I found it." The second case deals with a dispute over a bought cloak, in which each litigant claims, "It is all mine," i.e. the seller sold the cloak to *me*. It is in regard to both cases that the Mishnah concludes that each swears to half his claim and they divide the cloak.

**שנים** אוחזין בטלית זה אומר אני מצאתיה וזה אומר אני מצאתיה זה אומר כולה שלי וזה אומר כולה שלי זה ישבע שאין לו בה פחות מחציה וזה ישבע שאין לו בה פחות מחציה ויחלוקו ב זה אומר כולה שלי וזה אומר חציה שלי האומר כולה שלי ישבע שאין לו בה פחות משלשה חלקים והאומר חציה שלי ישבע שאין לו בה פחות מרביע זה נוטל שלשה חלקים וזה נוטל רביע ג היו שנים רוכבין על גבי בהמה או שהיה אחד רוכב ואחד מנהיג זה אומר כולה שלי וזה אומר כולה שלי זה ישבע שאין לו בה פחות מחציה וזה ישבע שאין לו בה פחות מחציה ויחלוקו בזמן שהם מודים או שיש להן עדים חולקין בלא שבועה: גמ' למה לי למתנא זה אומר אני מצאתיה וזה אומר אני מצאתיה זה אומר כולה שלי וזה אומר כולה שלי ליתני חדא חדא קתני זה אומר אני מצאתיה וכולה שלי וזה אומר אני מצאתיה וכולה שלי וליתני אני מצאתיה ואנא ידענא דכולה שלי אי תנא אני מצאתיה הוה אמינא מאי מצאתיה ראיתיה אע"ג דלא אתאי לידיה בראיה בעלמא קני תנא כולה שלי דבראיה לא קני ומי מצית אמרת מאי מצאתיה ראיתיה ג) והא אמר ד) רבנאי א) ומצאתה דאתאי לידיה משמע אין ומצאתה דקרא דאתא לידיה משמע ומיהו תנא לישנא דעלמא נקט ומדחזי ליה אמר אנא אשכחית ואע"ג דלא אתאי לידיה בראיה בעלמא קני תני כולה שלי ד דבראיה בעלמא לא קני לה וליתני כולה שלי ולא בעי אני מצאתיה אי תני כולה שלי הוה אמינא בעלמא דקתני מצאתיה בראיה קני תנא אני מצאתיה והדר תנא כולה שלי דממשנה יתירה אשמעינן דראיה לא קני ומי מצית אמרת חדא קתני והא זה וזה קתני זה אומר אני מצאתיה וזה אומר אני מצאתיה זה אומר כולה שלי וכו' אמר רב פפא ואיתימא רב שימי בר אשי ואמרי לה ה) כדי ו) רישא במציאה ה וסיפא במקח וממכר וצריכא דאי

**רש"י**

**שנים** אוחזין בטלית. דוקא אוחזין דשניהם מוחזקים בה ואין לזה כח בה יותר מזה שאילו היתה ביד אחד לבדו הוי אידך המוציא מחבירו ועליו להביא ראיה בעדים שהיא שלו ואינו נאמן זה ליטול בשבועה: זה אומר כולה שלי. בגמרא מפרש למאי תנא תרתי: זה ישבע. מפרש בגמרא (דף ג.) שבועה זו למה: שאין לו בה פחות מחציה. בגמרא (דף ה:) מפ' אמאי תקון כי האי לישנא בהך שבועה: וזה אומר חציה שלי. מודה הוא שהחצי של חבירו ואין דנין אלא על חציה הלכך זה האומר כולה שלי ישבע כו' כמשפט הראשון מה שהן דנין עליו נשבעין שניהם שאין לכל אחד בו פחות מחציו ונוטל כל אחד חציו: היו שנים רוכבין כו'. לאשמועינן אתא (א) דרוכב ומנהיג שניהם שוין לקנות בהמה מן ההפקר: בזמן שהן מודין. בגמרא (דף ח.) מפרש [דבהאי] אשמעינן דהמגביה מציאה לחבירו קנה חבירו: גמ' ראיתיה. קודם ז) שהגבהת אותה: בראיה קני. מדקתני יחלוקו: תנא כולה שלי. בחזקה גמורה שהגבהתי תחילה ואתה תפסת מידי משזכיתי בה: והאמר רבנאי. בבבא קמא בהגוזל ומאכיל ח): ומצאתה דאתא לידיה משמע. ואפי' הכי אחיך ולא עובד כוכבים ולא תימא כי מיעט רחמנא עובד כוכבים היכא דלא אתאי לידיה דישראל לא מיחייב למטרח עלה ולאהדורה אבל אתא לידיה מיחייב להחזירה דאבידתו אסורה: תנא לישנא דעלמא נקט. אי לא הדר תנא כולה שלי הוה אמינא מאי מצאתיה דקתני תנא לשון בני אדם אחז במשנתו ולא לשון המקרא והרבה בני אדם קורין לה מציאה משעת ראיה: בעלמא דקתני מצאתיה. בכ"מ ששנינו שהמוצא מציאה קנאה הוה אמינא דמציאה קני לה משעת ראיה דלא אשמעינן שום תנא דלא קני לה אלא בהגבהה להכי אשמעינן הכא ממשנה יתירה: והא זה וזה קתני. גבי מצאתיה תנא זה אומר וגבי כולה שלי קתני זה אומר ואי חדא הוא הכי אבעי ליה למתני זה אומר מצאתיה וכולה שלי: במקח וממכר. קניתיה מיד פלוני ודוקא מקח וממכר הוא דאמרינן יחלוקו בשבועה דאיכא למימר שניהם קנאוה ולשניהם נתרצה המוכר אבל זה אומר אני ארגתיה וזה אומר אני ארגתיה לא יחלוקו דודאי חד מינייהו רמאי הוא ותהא מונחת עד שיבא אליהו:

דמורה

**תוספות**

**שנים** אוחזין בטלית. איידי דאיירי בהגוזל בתרא (ב"ק דף קיט.) מחלוקת נסורת נגר ובעל הבית דקתני במעצד הרי אלו שלו ובכשיל הרי אלו של בעל הבית תני הכא נמי דיני חלוקות ואע"ג דבתרי מסכתא אין סדר למשנה ט) ואיכא מ"ד כולה נזיקין לאו חדא מסכתא הוא ה"מ לענין מחלוקת ואח"כ סתם לפי שרבי לא היה לומד כסדר אלא כמו שהיו חפצים התלמידים אבל כשחברם על הסדר חברם וצריך בכל מסכתא טעם למה נשנית אחר שלפניה כדדייק בריש מסכת שבועות (דף ב:) מכדי תנא ממכות קסליק כו' וכן בסוטה (דף ב.):

**ויחלוקו.** תימה דמאי שנא מההיא דארבא דאמר כל דאלים גבר פרק חזקת הבתים (ב"ב דף לד: ושם) וי"ל דאוחזין שאני דחשיב כאילו כל אחד יש לו בה בודאי החצי דאנן סהדי דמאי דתפיס האי דידיה הוא וכן במנה שלישי דמדמי בגמרא לטלית חשיב ההוא שהנפקד תופס בחזקת שניהם כאילו הם עצמם מוחזקים בו לכך משני דהתם ודאי דחד מינייהו הוא ואין החלוקה יכולה להיות אמת ולכך יהא מונח אבל טלית דאיכא למימר דתרוייהו הוא יחלוקו וכן שנים אדוקים בשטר דמדמי לקמן (דף ז.) למתני' משום דשניהם אדוקים בו דהחלוקה יכולה להיות אמת דאפשר שפרע לו החצי ובמנה אין דרך שיקנה לו החצי אחרי שהוא ביד חבירו אבל בארבא אע"ג דאפשר שהיא של שניהם כיון דאין מוחזקין בו הוי דינא כל דאלים גבר ולסומכוס אע"ג דאין מוחזקין בו ואין החלוקה יכולה להיות אמת היכא דאיכא דררא דממונא פירוש שבלא טענותיהם יש ספק לבית דין יחלוקו:

**וזה** נוטל רביע. וא"ת יהא נאמן דחציו שלו מיגו דאי בעי אמר כולה שלי כדאמרי' בגמ' (לקמן דף ח.) האי מיגו גופיה לפטרו משבועה אי לא משום דאיערומי קמערים ומפרש ריב"ם דמיגו להוציא לא אמרי' דבחציו השני מוחזק זה כמו זה והיא דחזקת הבתים (ב"ב דף לב: ושם ל) דגחין ולחיש ליה לרבה אין שטרא זייפא הוא ומיהו שטרא מעליא הוה לי בידי ואבד והימניה רבה להוציא במיגו דאי בעי אמר שטרא מעליא הוא ○ התם היינו טעמא משום דאפי' הוה שתיק רק שלא היה מודה שהוא מזוייף היה נאמן כי החתימה היתה נכרת לעומדים שם ורב יוסף אית ליה דאפילו מיגו לא הוה כיון שטענה ראשונה שהוא טוען בהאי שטרא הוא שקר ואין לומר מיגו אלא היכא שטענתו ראשונה היא אמת מיגו שהיה טוען אחרת ולכך אינו מיגו אפילו להחזיק כגון בעובדא קמייתא וא"ת ונימא דאין ספק מוציא מידי ודאי דהאומר כולה שלי יש לו בודאי חציה והאומר חציה שלי ספק אם יש לו בה כלום כדאמרינן בפרק החולץ (יבמות דף לח.) ספק ויבם שבאו לחלוק בנכסי סבא ספק אמר אנא בר מתנא אנא ואית לי פלגא ויבם אמר את ברא דידי ולית לך ולא מידי הוה ליה יבם ודאי וספק ספק ואין ספק מוציא מידי ודאי וי"ל דהתם יבם שהוא בנו של סבא הוי ודאי יורשו ולא יוציא הספק מספק ממונו אבל הכא אין סברא מה שהוא ודאי בחציו שיועיל לו לחציו השני: **בראיה** בעלמא קנה. אע"ג דקתני במתני' (לקמן דף ט:) ראה את המציאה ואמר לחבירו תנה לי דלא קנה בראיה וכן ראה את המציאה ונפל עליה (לקמן דף י.) קתני נמי דלא קני מצי למדחי כיון דאמר תנה לי או שנפל עליה גלי דעתיה דלא ניחא ליה למקני עד שיגיע לידו: **דבראיה** בעלמא לא קני. והא דאמרי' בפרק הבית והעלייה (לקמן דף קיח. ושם) הבטה בהפקר קני היינו שעשה מעשה כל דהו כגון שגדר גדר קטן: **והא** זה וזה קתני. איכא דוכתי דפריך כי האי גוונא ואיכא דוכתי דלא פריך: [עי' תוס' בכורות דף לא: ד"ה א"כ]:

אי

**עין משפט נר מצוה**

א א מיי' פ"ט מהלכות טוען ונטען הל' ז סמג עשין לה טוש"ע ח"מ סי' קלח סעיף א:

ב ב מיי' שם הלכה ח טוש"ע שם סעיף ב:

ג ג מיי' שם הלכה ז טוש"ע שם סעיף א:

ד ד מיי' פי"ז מהלכות גזילה ואבידה הל' א סמג עשין עד טוש"ע ח"מ סי' רסח סעיף א:

ה ה מיי' פ"כ מהלכות מכירה הל' ד ועיין בהשגות ובמ"מ סמג עשין פב טוש"ע ח"מ סי' רכב סעיף א:

**רבינו חננאל**

שנים אוחזין בטלית זה אומר אני מצאתיה וכו'. ואקשי' עלה למה לי למתנא תוב זה אומר כולה שלי הלא באומרו אני מצאתיה משמע דכולה שלי היא. ופרקי' הא אתא לאשמועי' דבראיה בעלמא לא קני לה למציאה. הא לא מיבעיא דהא אמר רבינא ומצאתה דאתאי לידיה משמע. דברי רבינא בהגוזל בתרא הל' אין פורטין מתיבת המוכסין ופשוטה היא. ואוקימנא למתני' רישא במציאה וסיפא דקתני זה אומר כולה שלי בקנייתא בשטוען אני קניתיה ונתתי דמיה לבעליה

**מסורת הש"ס**

בבא בתרא קע., [לקמן ח.], ג) לקמן ח., ...קמא קיג:, רבינא, מהרש"ל, [עיין מהרש"ל], [לקמן ח.], ז) שהגבהתי, ...רש"א, ח) [דף קיג:], [בבא קמא קב.], י) [ד"ה אמאי].

**הגהות הב"ח**

...) רש"י ד"ה היו וכו' אתא דרוכב ומנהיג:

**גליון הש"ס**

...ס' ד"ה וזה כו' התם ...ט וכו'. עיין לקמן דף ...ז ע"א תוס' ד"ה והא:

**תורה אור השלם**

...וְכֵן תַּעֲשֶׂה לַחֲמֹרוֹ ...ן תַּעֲשֶׂה לְשִׂמְלָתוֹ ...ן תַּעֲשֶׂה לְכָל אֲבֵדַת ...חִיךָ אֲשֶׁר תֹּאבַד ...מֶּנּוּ וּמְצָאתָהּ לֹא תוּכַל לְהִתְעַלֵּם: [דברים כב, ג]

**ליקוטי רש"י**

כדי. שם חכם [גיטין פה:].

ne says, "I found it *and* it is all mine," וְזֶה אוֹמֵר אֲנִי מְצָאתִיהָ וְכוּלָּהּ שֶׁלִּ – and this one says, "I found it *and* it is all nine."

The Gemara asks:

וְלִיתְנֵי אֲנִי מְצָאתִי – But let [the Mishnah] state that each itigant claims only, "I found it," וַאֲנָא יָדַעְנָא דְּכוּלָּהּ שֶׁלִּי – and would already know that he means, therefore, to claim, "It is ll mine." Why does the Mishnah attribute to him this second laim explicitly if it is already implicit in his first claim "I found ?"?

The Gemara answers:

אִי תָּנָ – If [the Mishnah] had stated only the claim of אֲנִי מְצָאתִי – "I found it," הֲוָה אָמֵינָא – I might have said: מַאי מְצָאתִיהָ רְאִיתִי – What does "I found it" mean? It means: "I aw it." That is, each litigant lays claim to the cloak on the basis hat he *saw* it first. אַף עַל גַּב דְּלָא אֲתָאי לִידֵיהּ – And even hough it did not yet come into his hands, בִּרְאִיָּה בְּעָלְמָא קָנֵי – e acquires the lost object with the mere act of looking upon t.[13] תָּנָא כּוּלָּהּ שֶׁלִּי – Therefore, [the Mishnah] stated the laim of "It is all mine" דִּבְרְאִיָּה לֹא קָנֵי – to teach that by nerely looking upon it he does not acquire it.[14]

The Gemara asks:

וּמִי מָצֵית אָמְרַ – But could you have thought to say that מַאי מְצָאתִי – what is the meaning of "I found it" – רְאִיתִיהָ – "I saw it"? וְהָא אָמַר רַבְּנַאי – but Rabbenai said: "וּמְצָאתָהּ" – The Biblical expression *and you find it* דַּאֲתַאי לִידֵיהּ מַשְׁמַע – onnotes that it has come into his hand.[15] – ? –

The Gemara answers:

אִי – True, "וּמְצָאתָהּ" דִּקְרָא דַּאֲתָא לִידֵיהּ מַשְׁמַע – the criptural expression *and you "find" it* indeed connotes that it as come into his hand. וּמִיהוּ – However, תַּנָּא לִישָּׁנָא דְּעָלְמָא נָקַ – I might have thought that the Tanna in this Aishnah followed the common usage of language; וּמִדְּחָזֵי לֵיהּ אָמַר אֲנָא אַשְׁכַּחְתּ – and in common usage, as soon as one sees a lost object], he says, "I found it." וְאַף עַל גַּב דְּלָא אֲתַאי לִידֵיהּ בִּרְאִיָּה בְּעָלְמָא קָנ – And therefore I might have thought that even though it did not come into his hand, he acquires the lost object by the mere act of looking upon it, as explained above. תָּנֵי כּוּלָּהּ שֶׁלִּי – Therefore [the Mishnah] states also the claim of "it is all mine" דִּבְרְאִיָּה בְּעָלְמָא לֹא קָנֵי לָהּ – to teach that by the mere act of looking upon it he cannot acquire it.[16]

Still, the Gemara asks:

וְלִיתְנֵי כּוּלָּהּ שֶׁלִּי – Accordingly, let [the Mishnah] state only the claim of "it is all mine" וְלֹא בָּעֵי אֲנִי מְצָאתִיהָ – and it would not need to also state the claim of "I found it."[17] – ? –

The Gemara answers:

אִי תָּנֵי כּוּלָּהּ שֶׁלִּי – If [the Mishnah] had stated only the claim of "it is all mine," הֲוָה אָמֵינָא בְּעָלְמָא דְּקָתָנֵי מְצָאתִיהָ – I might have said that generally when the Mishnah elsewhere states a case of "I found it," בִּרְאִיָּה בְּעָלְמָא קָנֵי – the intent is that by the mere act of looking upon the lost object, [the finder] acquires it. תָּנָא אֲנִי מְצָאתִיהָ וְהָדַר תָּנָא כּוּלָּהּ שֶׁלִּי – Therefore, [the Mishnah] here states the claim of "I found it" and continues to state the claim of "it is all mine," דְּמִמִּשְׁנָה יְתֵירָה – so that from the otherwise superfluous expression of the Mishnah אַשְׁמְעִינַן דִּרְאִיָּה לֹא קָנֵי – [the Tanna] teaches us that merely looking upon a lost article does not suffice to acquire it.[18]

Thus, the Gemara has explained that the Mishnah indeed refers to a single set of claims regarding a lost article. However, this explanation is now rejected:

וּמִי מָצֵית אָמְרַת – But can you really say חֲדָא קָתָנֵי – that the Mishnah refers to one set of claims? וְהָא זֶה וְזֶה קָתָנֵי – But [the Mishnah] states: "THIS ONE..." and again "THIS ONE...," as the Gemara proceeds to cite: זֶה אוֹמֵר אֲנִי מְצָאתִיהָ וְזֶה אוֹמֵר אֲנִי מְצָאתִיהָ – THIS ONE SAYS, "I FOUND IT," AND THIS ONE SAYS, "I FOUND IT." זֶה אוֹמֵר כּוּלָּהּ שֶׁלִּי וכו׳ – THIS ONE SAYS, "IT IS ALL MINE," etc. Surely, this indicates that we are dealing with two distinct cases![19] – ? –

The Gemara therefore explains:

אָמַר רַב פַּפָּא – Rav Pappa said, וְאִיתֵּימָא רַב שִׁימִי בַּר אַשִׁי – and

NOTES

3. If each claimant means only that the cloak belongs to him because e *saw* it first, then the Mishnah's ruling that they divide the cloak vould confirm the notion that mere *seeing* is sufficient to acquire a lost r otherwise ownerless object (*Rashi*).

It is only in the case of an ownerless object that one could have ntertained the notion that looking upon the object alone without erforming an actual *kinyan* [formal act of acquisition] suffices to cquire it (*Ritva*; see also *Otzar Mefarshei HaTalmud* pp. 62-63).

4. By definition, the expression כּוּלָּהּ שֶׁלִּי, *it is all mine,* connotes hysically taking hold of the object (*Ritva;* cf. *Ravad* cited in *Shitah Aekubetzes;* see also *Otzar Mefarshei HaTalmud* p. 63 note 415). The 'anna attributes this claim to the litigants in order to indicate hat even in regard to found or otherwise ownerless items, the general ules of acquisition prevail and an actual *kinyan* [formal act of cquisition] must be performed in order to acquire the lost object [e.g. icking it up].

5. Rabbenai refers to the verse in *Deuteronomy* 22:3 that commands he return of lost objects to their owner: וְכֵן תַּעֲשֶׂה לְכָל־אֲבֵדַת אָחִיךָ אֲשֶׁר־תֹּאבַד מִמֶּנּוּ וּמְצָאתָ, *and so shall you do with regard to any lost object f your brother that might be lost from him and you find it.* The Gemara n *Bava Kamma* (113b) explains that the expression "your brother" imits the command of returning lost objects to those objects lost by our *Jewish* brethren, but there is no commandment to return the lost bject of an idolater. The Gemara there considers the possibility that he limitation might be only in regard to *retrieving* and returning a lost bject; that is, there is no obligation to go to the trouble of retrieving omeone else's lost object unless that someone is a Jew. But once the inder has already gone through the trouble of retrieving the lost object, e might be commanded to return it to its original owner even if the wner is an idolater. To this, Rabbenai responds (ibid.) that the limitation is written in regard to a lost object that "you find," which connotes that you have already taken it in hand. Even in that case, the command to return the object does not apply to the lost object of an idolater (*Rashi*; see *Bava Kamma* 113b. Schottenstein ed., note 22).

Thus, we see that the expression "find" connotes physical possession of the lost object. How, then, can the Gemara above maintain that had the Mishnah stated only "I found it," one might have said that the claimant means only that he *saw* it but not that he took hold of it?

16. As explained above, the expression כּוּלָּהּ שֶׁלִּי, *it is all mine,* connotes physical possession (see note 14).

17. If the Mishnah had stated only the claim of "it is all mine," which connotes physical possession, there would be no basis for the mistaken notion that mere looking suffices to acquire a lost object. Why, then, did the Mishnah have to also state the first claim of "I found it"?

18. Thus, the Gemara answers that indeed there was no need for the Mishnah to state both claims in this particular case. The claim "it is all mine" would have sufficed to indicate that the case is one in which each litigant claims that he actually picked up the lost object first, not that he *saw* it first. However, in other instances, where the law does indeed speak of "finding" a lost object, one might have thought that the intent is that the finder acquires the lost object simply by looking upon it. Therefore, the Tanna here took the opportunity to teach that an actual *kinyan* is required. He teaches this by using the apparently redundant set of claims to indicate that "finding" in the Mishnah means taking actual physical possession of the lost article.

19. If the Mishnah had been referring to a single case in which each litigant claims, "I found it and it is all mine," it should not have stated the second claim separately, prefacing that claim as well with the words "this one says." Rather, the Mishnah should have stated simply: This

# שנים

א) ^א^ אוחזין בטלית זה אומר אני מצאתיה וזה אומר אני מצאתיה זה אומר כולה שלי וזה אומר כולה שלי זה ישבע שאין לו בה פחות מחציה וזה ישבע שאין לו בה פחות מחציה ויחלוקו ^ב^ זה אומר כולה שלי וזה אומר חציה שלי האומר כולה שלי ישבע שאין לו בה פחות משלשה חלקים והאומר חציה שלי ישבע שאין לו בה פחות מרביע זה נוטל שלשה חלקים וזה נוטל רביע ב) ^ג^ היו שנים רוכבין על גבי בהמה או שהיה אחד רוכב ואחד מנהיג זה אומר כולה שלי וזה אומר כולה שלי זה ישבע שאין לו בה פחות מחציה וזה ישבע שאין לו בה פחות מחציה ויחלוקו בזמן שהם מודים או שיש להן עדים חולקין בלא שבועה: גמ' למה לי למתנא זה אומר אני מצאתיה וזה אומר אני מצאתיה זה אומר כולה שלי וזה אומר כולה שלי ליתני חדא חדא קתני זה אומר אני מצאתיה וכולה שלי וזה אומר אני מצאתיה וכולה שלי וליתני אני מצאתיה ואנא ידענא דכולה שלי אי תנא אני מצאתיה הוה אמינא מאי מצאתיה ראיתיה אע"ג דלא אתאי לידיה בראיה בעלמא קני תנא כולה שלי דבראיה לא קני ומי מצית אמרת מאי מצאתיה ראיתיה ג) והא אמר ד) רבנאי א) ומצאתה דאתאי לידיה משמע אין ומצאתה דקרא דאתא לידיה משמע ומיהו תנא לישנא דעלמא נקט ומדחזי ליה אמר אנא אשכחית ואע"ג דלא אתאי לידיה בראיה בעלמא קני תני כולה שלי ^ד^ דבראיה בעלמא לא קני לה וליתני כולה שלי ולא בעי אני מצאתיה אי תני כולה שלי הוה אמינא בעלמא דקתני מצאתיה בראיה בעלמא קני תנא אני מצאתיה והדר תנא כולה שלי דממשנה יתירה אשמעינן דראיה לא קני ומי מצית אמרת חדא קתני והא זה וזה קתני זה אומר אני מצאתיה וזה אומר אני מצאתיה זה אומר כולה שלי וכו' אמר רב פפא ואיתימא רב שימי בר אשי ואמרי לה ה) כדי ו) רישא במציאה ^ה^ וסיפא במקח וממכר וצריכא דאי

**רש"י**

**שנים** אוחזין בטלית. דוקא אוחזין דשניהם מוחזקים בה ואין לזה כח בה יותר מזה שאילו היתה ביד אחד לבדו הוי אידך המוציא מחבירו ועליו להביא ראיה בעדים שהיא שלו ואינו נאמן זה ליטול בשבועה: זה אומר כולה שלי. בגמרא מפרש למאי תנא תרתי: זה ישבע. מפרש בגמרא (דף ג.) שבועה זו למה: שאין לו בה פחות מחציה. בגמרא (דף ה:) מפ' אמאי תקון כי האי לישנא בהך שבועה: וזה אומר חציה שלי. מודה הוא שהחצי של חבירו ואין דנין אלא על חציה הלכך זה האומר כולה שלי ישבע כו' כמשפט הראשון מה שהן דנין עליו נשבעין שניהם שאין לכל אחד בו פחות מחציו ונוטל כל אחד חציו: היו שנים רוכבין כו'. לאשמועינן אתא (א) דרכוב ומנהיג שניהם שוין לקנות בהמה מן ההפקר: בזמן שהן מודין. בגמרא (דף ח.) מפרש [דבהאי] אשמעינן דהמגביה מציאה לחבירו קנה חבירו: גמ' ראיתיה. קודם ז) שהגבהת אותה: בראיה קני. מדקתני יחלוקו: תנא כולה שלי. בחזקה גמורה שהגבהתי תחילה ואתה תפסת מידי משזכיתי בה: והאמר רבנאי. בבבא קמא בהגוזל ומאכיל ח): ומצאתה דאתא לידיה משמע. ואפי' הכי אחיך ולא עובד כוכבים ולא תימא כי מיעט רחמנא עובד כוכבים היכא דלא אתאי לידיה דישראל לא מחייב למטרח עלה ולאהדורה אבל אתא לידיה מחייב להחזירה דאבידתו אסורה: תנא לישנא דעלמא נקט. אי לא הדר תנא כולה שלי הוה אמינא מאי מצאתיה דקתני תנא לשון בני אדם אחז במשנתנו ולא לשון המקרא והרבה בני אדם קורין לה מציאה משעת ראיה: בעלמא דקתני מצאתיה. בכ"מ ששנינו שהמוצא מציאה קנאה הוה אמינא דמציאה קני לה משעת ראיה דלא אשמעינן שום תנא דלא קני לה אלא בהגבהה להכי אשמעינן הכא ממשנה יתירה: והא זה וזה קתני. גבי מצאתיה תנא זה אומר וגבי כולה שלי קתני זה אומר ואי חדא הוא הכי אבעי ליה למתני זה אומר מצאתיה וכולה שלי: במקח וממכר. קניתיה מיד פלוני ודוקא מקח וממכר הוא דאמרינן יחלוקו בשבועה דאיכא למימר שניהם קנאוה ולשניהם נתרצה המוכר אבל זה אומר אני ארגתיה וזה אומר אני ארגתיה לא יחלוקו דודאי חד מינייהו רמאי הוא ותהא מונחת עד שיבא אליהו: דמורה

**תוספות**

**שנים** אוחזין בטלית. איידי דאיירי בהגוזל בתרא (ב"ק דף קיט.) מחלוקת נסורת נגר ובעל הבית דקתני במעצד הרי אלו שלו ובכשיל הרי אלו של בעל הבית תני הכא נמי דיני חלוקות ואע"ג דבתרי מסכתא אין סדר למשנה ט) ואיכא מ"ד כולה נזיקין לאו חדא מסכתא הוא ה"מ לענין מחלוקת ואח"כ סתם לפי שרבי לא היה לומד כסדר אלא כמו שהיו חפצים התלמידים אבל כשחברם על הסדר חברם וצריך בכל מסכתא טעם למה נשנית אחר שלפניה כדדייק בריש מסכת שבועות (דף ב:) מכדי תנא ממכות קסליק כו' וכן בסוטה (דף ב.):

**ויחלוקו.** תימה דמאי שנא מההיא דארבא דאמר כל דאלים גבר פרק חזקת הבתים (ב"ב דף לד: ושם) וי"ל דאוחזין שאני דחשיב כאילו כל אחד יש לו בה בודאי החצי דאנן סהדי דמאי דתפיס האי דידיה הוא וכן במנה שלישי דמדמי בגמרא לטלית חשיב ההוא שהנפקד תופס בחזקת שניהם כאילו הם עצמם מוחזקים בו לכך משני דהתם ודאי דחד מינייהו הוא ואין החלוקה יכולה להיות אמת ולכך יהא מונח אבל טלית דאיכא למימר דתרוייהו הוא יחלוקו וכן שנים אדוקים בשטר דמדמי לקמן (דף ז.) למתני' משום דשניהם אדוקים בו דהחלוקה יכולה להיות אמת דאפשר שפרע לו החצי ובמנה אין דרך שיקנה לו החצי אחרי שהוא ביד חבירו אבל בארבא אע"ג דאפשר שהיא של שניהם כיון דאין מוחזקין בו הוי דינא כל דאלים גבר ולסומכוס אע"ג דאין מוחזקין בו ואין החלוקה יכולה להיות אמת היכא דאיכא דררא דממונא פירוש שבלא טענותיהם יש ספק לבית דין יחלוקו:

**וזה** נוטל רביע. וא"ת יהא נאמן דחציו שלו מיגו דאי בעי אמר כולה שלי כדאמרי' בגמ' (לקמן דף ח.) האי מיגו גופיה לפטרו משבועה אי לא משום דאיערומי קמערים ומפרש ריב"ם דמיגו להוציא לא אמרי' דבחציו השני מוחזק זה כמו זה וההיא דחזקת הבתים (ב"ב דף לב: ושם י) דגחין ולחיש ליה לרבה אין שטרא זייפא הוא ומיהו שטרא מעליא הוה לי בידי ואבד והימניה רבה להוציא במיגו דאי בעי אמר שטרא מעליא הוא ° התם היינו טעמא משום דאפי' הוה שתיק רק שלא היה מודה שהוא מזויף היה נאמן כי החתימה היתה נכרת לעומדים שם ורב יוסף אית ליה דאפילו מיגו לא הוה כיון שטענה ראשונה שהוא טוען בהאי שטרא הוא שקר ואין לומר מיגו אלא היכא שטענתו ראשונה היא אמת מיגו שהיה טוען אחרת ולכך אינו מיגו אפילו להחזיק כגון בעובדא קמייתא וא"ת ונימא דאין ספק מוציא מידי ודאי דהאומר כולה שלי יש לו בודאי חציה והאומר חציה שלי ספק אם יש לו בה כלום כדאמרינן בפרק החולץ (יבמות דף לח.) ספק ויבם שבאו לחלוק בנכסי סבא ספק אמר אנא בר מתנא אנא ואית לי פלגא ויבם אמר את ברא דידי ולית לך ולא מידי הוה ליה יבם ודאי וספק ספק ואין ספק מוציא מידי ודאי וי"ל דהתם יבם שהוא בנו של סבא הוי ודאי יורשו ולא יוציא הספק מספק ממונו אבל הכא אין סברא מה שהוא ודאי בחציו שיועיל לו לחציו השני: **בראיה** בעלמא קנה. אע"ג דקתני במתני' (לקמן דף ט:) ראה את המציאה ואמר לחבירו תנה לי דלא קנה בראיה וכן ראה את המציאה ונפל עליה (לקמן דף י.) קתני נמי דלא קני מאי למדחי כיון דאמר תנה לי או שנפל עליה גלי דעתיה דלא ניחא ליה למקני עד שיגיע לידו: **דבראיה** בעלמא לא קני. והא דאמרי' בפרק הבית והעלייה (לקמן דף קיח. ושם) הבטה בהפקר קני היינו שעשה מעשה כל דהו כגון שגדר גדר קטן: **והא** זה וזה קתני. איכא דוכתי דפריך כי האי גוונא ואיכא דוכתי דלא פריך: [עי' תוס' בכורות דף לג: ד"ה א"כ]: אי

**עין משפט נר מצוה**

א א מיי' פ"ט מהלכות טוען ונטען הל' ז סמג עשין צה טוש"ע ח"מ סי' קלח סעיף א:
ב ב מיי' שם הלכה ח טוש"ע שם סעיף ב:
ג ג מיי' שם הלכה ז טוש"ע שם סעיף א:
ד ד מיי' פי"ז מהלכות גזילה ואבידה הל' א סמג עשין עד טוש"ע ח"מ סי' רסח סעיף א:
ה ה מיי' פ"כ מהלכות מכירה הל' ד ועיין בהשגות ובמ"מ סמג עשין פב טוש"ע ח"מ סי' רכב סעיף א:

**רבינו חננאל**

שנים אוחזין בטלית זה אומר אני מצאתיה וכו'. ואקשי' עלה למה לי למתנא תוב זה אומר כולה שלי הלא באומרו אני מצאתיה משמע דכולה שלי היא. ופרקי הא אתא לאשמועי' דבראיה בעלמא לא קני לה למציאה. הא לא מיבעיא דהא אמר רבינא ומצאתה דאתאי לידיה משמע. דברי רבינא בהגוזל בתרא הל' אין פורטין מתיבת המוכסין ופשוטה היא. ואוקימנא למתני' רישא במציאה וסיפא דקתני זה אומר כולה שלי בקנייתא בשטוען אני קניתיה ונתתי דמיה לבעליה

**מסורת הש"ס**

בבא בתרא קע., [לקמן ח.], ג) לקמן ח., [בבא] קמא קיג., רבינא, מהרש"ל, [עיין מהרש"ל], [לקמן ח.], ז) שהגבהתי, מהרש"א, ח) [דף קיג:], [בבא קמא קג.], י) [ד"ה אמאי].

**הגהות הב"ח**

(א) רש"י ד"ה היו וכו' אתא דרוכב ומנהיג:

**גליון הש"ס**

תוס' ד"ה וזה כו' התם היינו טעמא וכו'. עיין לקמן דף ... ע"א תוס' ד"ה והא:

**תורה אור השלם**

א) וְכֵן תַּעֲשֶׂה לַחֲמֹרוֹ וְכֵן תַּעֲשֶׂה לְשִׂמְלָתוֹ וְכֵן תַּעֲשֶׂה לְכָל אֲבֵדַת אָחִיךָ אֲשֶׁר תֹּאבַד מִמֶּנּוּ וּמְצָאתָהּ לֹא תוּכַל לְהִתְעַלֵּם: [דברים כב, ג]

**ליקוטי רש"י**

בדי. שם חכם [גיטין פה:].

# Chapter One

**Mishnah** The Mishnah considers the law in the following case:

שְׁנַיִם אוֹחֲזִין בְּטַלִּית – Two litigants come before the court **holding on to a cloak.**[1] זֶה אוֹמֵר אֲנִי מְצָאתִיהָ – **This one says, "I found it** first," וְזֶה אוֹמֵר אֲנִי מְצָאתִיהָ – **and this one says, "I found it** first"; זֶה אוֹמֵר כּוּלָּהּ שֶׁלִּי – **this one says, "It is all mine,"** וְזֶה אוֹמֵר כּוּלָּהּ שֶׁלִּי – **and this one says, "It is all mine."** The law is: זֶה יִשָּׁבַע שֶׁאֵין לוֹ בָּהּ פָּחוֹת מֵחֶצְיָהּ – **This one must swear that he owns not less than half of it**[2] וְזֶה יִשָּׁבַע שֶׁאֵין לוֹ בָּהּ פָּחוֹת מֵחֶצְיָהּ – **and this one must swear that he owns not less than half of it,** וְיַחֲלוֹקוּ – **and they** then **divide** the cloak.[3] [4]

The Mishnah considers the law in a variation of the first case:

זֶה אוֹמֵר כּוּלָּהּ שֶׁלִּי – Again, both litigants are holding the cloak. However, **this one says, "It is all mine,"** claiming that he took hold of it first, וְזֶה אוֹמֵר חֶצְיָהּ שֶׁלִּי – **and this one says, "Half of it is mine,"** claiming that both took hold of it simultaneously.[5] The law is: הָאוֹמֵר כּוּלָּהּ שֶׁלִּי יִשָּׁבַע שֶׁאֵין לוֹ בָּהּ פָּחוֹת מִשְּׁלֹשָׁה חֲלָקִים – **The one who says, "It is all mine," must swear that he owns not less than three parts** [fourths] of the cloak, וְהָאוֹמֵר חֶצְיָהּ שֶׁלִּי יִשָּׁבַע שֶׁאֵין לוֹ בָּהּ פָּחוֹת מֵרְבִיעַ – **and the one who says, "Half of it is mine," must swear that he owns not less than one-fourth** of the cloak; זֶה נוֹטֵל שְׁלֹשָׁה חֲלָקִים וְזֶה נוֹטֵל רְבִיעַ – **this** first **one takes three parts** [fourths] of the cloak, in accordance with his oath, **and this** second **one takes one-fourth.**[6] [7]

The Mishnah discusses an analogous situation:

הָיוּ שְׁנַיִם רוֹכְבִין עַל גַּבֵּי בְהֵמָה – **Two** litigants come before the court **riding on an animal,** אוֹ שֶׁהָיָה אֶחָד רוֹכֵב וְאֶחָד מַנְהִיג – **or one was riding** the animal **and one was leading** it. זֶה אוֹמֵר כּוּלָּהּ שֶׁלִּי וְזֶה אוֹמֵר כּוּלָּהּ שֶׁלִּי – **This one says, "It is all mine," and this one says, "It is all mine."** Each one claims to have found and taken possession of the ownerless animal first – either by riding it or leading it.[8] זֶה יִשָּׁבַע שֶׁאֵין לוֹ בָּהּ פָּחוֹת מֵחֶצְיָהּ – **This one must swear that he owns not less than half of it** [the animal], וְזֶה יִשָּׁבַע שֶׁאֵין לוֹ בָּהּ פָּחוֹת מֵחֶצְיָהּ – **and this one must swear that he owns not less than half of it,** וְיַחֲלוֹקוּ – **and they** then **divide** the animal.[9]

The Mishnah closes with a ruling that pertains to all the above cases:

בִּזְמַן שֶׁהֵם מוֹדִים – **Whenever they** both **agree** that they acquired the article simultaneously אוֹ שֶׁיֵּשׁ לָהֶן עֵדִים – **or they have witnesses** that this was the case,[10] חוֹלְקִין בְּלֹא שְׁבוּעָה – **they divide it without an oath.**[11]

**Gemara** The Gemara asks:

לָמָּה לִי לְמִתְנָא – **Why do I need** the Mishnah **to state:** זֶה אוֹמֵר אֲנִי מְצָאתִיהָ וְזֶה אוֹמֵר אֲנִי מְצָאתִיהָ – THIS ONE SAYS, "I FOUND IT," AND THIS ONE SAYS, "I FOUND IT," as well as זֶה אוֹמֵר כּוּלָּהּ שֶׁלִּי וְזֶה אוֹמֵר כּוּלָּהּ שֶׁלִּי – THIS ONE SAYS, "IT IS ALL MINE," AND THIS ONE SAYS, "IT IS ALL MINE"? לִיתְנֵי חֲדָא – **Let [the Mishnah] state** only **one** case![12] – ? –

The Gemara answers:

חֲדָא קָתָנֵי – Indeed, **[the Mishnah] states** only **one** case, which should be understood as: זֶה אוֹמֵר אֲנִי מְצָאתִיהָ וְכוּלָּהּ שֶׁלִּי – **This**

NOTES

1. As explained in the Gemara, the two litigants are grasping the fringes at opposite ends of the cloak and thereby both are considered to be holding the entire cloak (see below, 7a; *Rashi* to 2b ד"ה בשבועה פלגי לה).

2. The Gemara (below, 5b) will explain why the oath must be worded in this way.

3. If the cloak itself can be physically divided so that each half retains half the original value, then it is physically divided. Otherwise, the cloak is sold and the litigants divide the proceeds (see Gemara below, 7b-8a; *Choshen Mishpat* 138:4 and *Sema*; cf. *Baer Heiteiv* and *Nesivos* ad loc.).

[Obviously, the Mishnah deals with a cloak found under circumstances that do not obligate the finder to return the cloak to the person who lost it – see *Rosh*.]

4. The Mishnah rules that they divide it under oath only when both are holding the cloak. However, if only one of them would be holding the cloak, then he would be awarded the entire cloak since the other litigant would then be seeking to exact it from the first one's exclusive physical possession. The rule in such cases is that the plaintiff cannot exact anything from the possession of the defendant unless witnesses corroborate the plaintiff's claim; mere swearing is insufficient (*Rashi*).

5. *Meiri*.

6. In this case, both agree that half the cloak belongs to the first litigant; their dispute relates only to the second half. Consequently, as in the Mishnah's first case, each takes an oath substantiating half his claim to the disputed article and they then divide it. Accordingly, the first litigant takes three-fourths [half the cloak, which was never in dispute, plus half the disputed second half]; the second litigant takes one-fourth [half the disputed second half] (*Rashi*).

7. By rights, the first litigant should not have to swear that the first half of the cloak is his since ownership of that first half was never in dispute. Nevertheless the Mishnah requires the first litigant to mention that undisputed half in his oath ("I own not less than three-fourths"). The reason the Mishnah requires this is that the purpose of an oath is to discourage spurious claims. [People generally regard the sin of swearing falsely as more serious than that of theft. Therefore, though a false claimant is not deterred by the prospect of theft, he might retract his claim rather than swear falsely to it (see Gemara 5b).] Now, it is possible that the first litigant is lying when he says that he owns the entire cloak, for he knows that he in fact took hold of it simultaneously with his disputant. If that is the case, making him swear that he owns not less than half of the disputed portion does not pressure him so strongly to retract. For he might be tempted to take that oath and assuage his conscience by rationalizing that regardless of how the court understands that oath, *he* means that he owns not less than half the *entire* cloak, which is indeed true. To forestall this rationalized perjury, we make him swear that he owns not less than three-fourths of the entire cloak, a formula that inescapably includes half the *disputed* portion (*Rosh*; see *Shitah Mekubetzes* at length).

8. *Meiri* to 8a; see also *Rashi*.

9. [See above, note 3.] This section of the Mishnah teaches that riding or leading an ownerless animal are equally valid methods of acquiring it (*Rashi*). [Thus, if in fact one of them began riding the animal at the same time that the other began leading it, they are deemed to have acquired it simultaneously.] Additionally, this section of the Mishnah teaches that both riding and leading an animal are considered physical possession of it, analogous to the Mishnah's first case of two people holding a cloak (*Meiri* to 8a; see also *Maharam Shif* ד"ה מאי מצאתיה ראיתיה and *Nachalas David*).

10. *Meiri* to 8a; cf. *Rashash*.

11. The Gemara (8a) explains that [this seemingly obvious ruling] teaches a special law (see *Rashi*).

12. [The Mishnah seems to be referring to two different cases – one in which each litigant claims, "I found it," and another in which each claims, "It is all mine." Why does the Mishnah have to teach its ruling in two different cases? (cf. *Ritva*).]

# Chapter One

# Introduction

This chapter deals primarily with laws pertaining to found articles, litigation concerning the ownership of found article (under circumstances that it need not be returned to its original owner) and the methods through whic the found article can be acquired. The chapter also delineates which people are the beneficiaries of their dependent' acquisition of found articles, as well as rules for determining to which of two possible owners certain found article should be returned.

Pursuant to this chapter's treatment of litigation surrounding ownership of a found item, the Gemara discusses th laws of oaths and the situations in which oaths are administered.

Pursuant to its treatment of the methods through which found articles can be acquired, the Gemara in this chapte deals extensively with acquisition by means of an article's presence in one's property. The Gemara details th conditions necessary for such acquisition, considering factors such as the owner's physical proximity to the propert the security the property affords the article that is within in its confines, the nature of the article being acquired, an the legal status of the property's owner.

Pursuant to its discussion concerning the return of found documents to one of the parties listed therein, the Gemar in this chapter deals with many aspects of documents, their ability to effect transactions, and the legal advantages the confer on their holders.

**TERMS RELEVANT TO THIS CHAPTER**

חָצֵר, *chatzeir* – literally: courtyard; the prototypical property used when referring to a person' acquisition of an article through its presence in his property.

נְכָסִים מְשֻׁעְבָּדִים – encumbered property; land owned by a debtor at the time he incurred a debt, bu which he later sold or gave to a third party. Such land is encumbered by the debt for if the debtor defaults, the creditor can collect the encumbered land from th current owner to satisfy the debt.

קִנְיָן, *kinyan* – a formal act of acquisition, necessary for acquiring articles and for effecting othe legal procedures.

מִגּוֹ, *migo* – literally: since; a rule of procedure. If a litigant asserts a certain claim that woul not ordinarily be believed by the court, that claim is nonetheless accepted "since" had the person wished to tell an untruth, he could have chosen a different clain that would have been believed.

קָטָן, minor – a boy under the age of thirteen or a girl under the age of twelve. Even upon reachin these ages, the minors are not deemed to be legal adults unless they exhibit certai signs of puberty.

מוֹדֶה בְּמִקְצָת, *modeh bemiktzas* – the Biblical oath imposed on a defendant who admits part of the plaintiff's clain against him; the defendant must assert his denial of the rest of that claim unde oath.

זְכִיָּה, *zechiyah* – the rule which states that one can act as a person's agent without the person's prio knowledge or consent, in matters that are clearly advantageous to the beneficiary the beneficiary's consent to the agency is then assumed.

# מסכת בבא מציעא / Bava Metzia

# General Introduction

*Bava Metzia,* literally, the middle gate, is the second tractate in the fourth order of the Mishnah, known as *Nezikin,* literally, torts or damages. It is also the second part of a threefold sub-group of tractates within this order that is also called *Nezikin,* and which is comprised of *Bava Kamma*, *Bava Metzia* and *Bava Basra,* i.e. the first, middle and last parts of *Nezikin.* According to the Amora Rav Yosef, these three tractates are not separate tractates but merely three subdivisions, each consisting of ten chapters, of the large tractate *Nezikin* (*Avodah Zarah* 7a with *Rashi*; see *Ramban* to *Shevuos* 2a). *Bava Metzia,* however, does not deal primarily with the laws of torts, but with other areas of civil law, such as the disposal of found items, the definition of custodial obligations (*shomrim*), sales and acquisitions, the prohibition against taking interest for a loan, hiring of artisans, workers and animals etc., loans of objects for use, sharecroppers, rental of apartments and various related topics.

**מוּחְזָק, Muchzak** One of the more basic principles relevant to most civil litigation is the concept of *muchzak,* possession. The general rule is that in cases of doubt, הַמּוֹצִיא מֵחֲבֵרוֹ עָלָיו הָרְאָיָה, *the burden of proof is on the one who seeks to exact property from his fellow.* The Gemara (*Bava Kamma* 46b) holds this principle to be so logically self-evident that no Scriptural basis for it is necessary. Nevertheless, the Tannaim disagree as to the parameters of this rule, with Sumchos holding that in some cases the disputed property is divided among the litigants even if the plaintiff has no proof to corroborate his claim against the one presently in possession of the disputed article (see *Bava Kamma* 46a, *Bava Metzia 2b*). The principle does not, however, establish a presumption of ownership on the part of the person in possession of the object; rather, it delineates the rules of evidence and predicates that whenever the evidence is insufficient to establish the facts, the object is granted to the person who is in prior possession of the object (see *Kuntres Hasfeikos* 1:5). Acccording to some, there is also a presumption that whatever is in one's possession is his (see *Tosafos* 2a ד״ה ויחלוקו).

**קִנְיָן, Kinyan** Another basic principle of civil law is that the transfer of ownership (save in the case of inheritance) must be accomplished through a formal mode of acquisition. The method of *kinyan* necessary to accomplish the transfer varies according to the article being transferred and the place in which the transfer is taking place.

**הֶפְקֵר בֵּית דִּין, Declared Ownerless by the Court** The Torah authorizes the Sages to declare property ownerless and to assign it to whomever they wish. This authorization is the main basis for the Sages' power to legislate financial laws that differ from those prescribed by the Torah. For even if one of the litigants is entitled to the disputed property under Biblical law, that same Biblical law empowers the Sages to declare that property ownerless and assign it to the other litigant.

**Rules of Evidence** As is true in most other areas of Torah law, monetary obligations can be imposed only on the basis of the testimony of two valid witnesses. However, although the testimony of a solitary witness cannot impose a monetary obligation, it can require that the defendant against whom the solitary witness testifies take an oath denying the charge that the witness corroborates.

# מסכת בבא מציעא
# TRACTATE BAVA METZIA

Loyal friends who have been instrumental in the success of our work and to whom we owe a debt of gratitude are, in alphabetical order:

Our very dear friends: RABBI RAPAHEL B. BUTLER, founder of the Afikim Foundation, a laboratory to create innovative Torah programs; RABBI ALAN CINER, whose warmth and erudition will draw Jews closer to Judaism in his new position in Palm Beach, Florida. RABBIS BUTLER and CINER were instrumental in moving this edition of the Talmud from dream to reality in its formative stage; REUVEN DESSLER, a good friend and respected leader who adds luster to a distinguished family lineage; ABRAHAM FRUCHTHANDLER, who has placed support for Torah institutions on a new plateau; LOUIS GLICK, who sponsored the ArtScroll Mishnah Series with the *Yad Avraham* commentary; SHIMMIE HORN, patron of the HORN EDITION OF SEDER MOED, a self-effacing gentleman to whom support of Torah is a priority; MOSHE REICHMANN, whose name is synonymous with visionary magnanimity for Torah study; DAVID RUBIN, dedicator of the RUBIN EDITION OF THE PROPHETS, whose visionary generosity is a vital force in his community and beyond; SHLOMO SEGEV of Bank Leumi, who has been a responsible and effective friend; HESHE SEIF, patron of the SEIF EDITION TRANSLITERATED PRAYER BOOKS, who has added our work to his long list of important causes; NATHAN SILBERMAN, who makes his skills and judgment available in too many ways to mention; A. JOSEPH STERN, patron of the SEFARD ARTSCROLL MACHZORIM and of tractates in this Talmud edition, whose warmth and concern for people and causes are justly legendary; ELLIOT TANNENBAUM, a warm and gracious patron of several volumes, whose example has motivated many others; STEVEN WEISZ, whose infectious zeal for our work has brought many others under its banner; and HIRSCH WOLF, a valued friend from our very beginning, and an energetic, effective leader in many causes.

We are grateful, as well, to many other friends who have come forward when their help was needed most: DR. YISRAEL BLUMENFRUCHT, YERUCHAM LAX, YEHUDAH LEVI, RABBI ARTHUR SCHICK, FRED SCHULMAN, and MENDY YARMISH.

We thank RABBI YEHOSHUA LEIFER, head of KOLLEL OZ VEHADAR, for permission to reproduce the folios from their new edition of the classic Vilna Talmud. Newly typeset and with many additions and enhancements, it establishes a new standard in Talmud publishing.

We conclude with gratitude to *Hashem Yisbarach* for His infinite blessings and for the privilege of being the vehicle to disseminate His word. May this work continue so that all who thirst for His word may find what they seek in the refreshing words of the Torah.

Rabbi Nosson Scherman / Rabbi Meir Zlotowitz

*Rosh Chodesh Cheshvan 5761*
*October, 2000*

# ACKNOWLEDGMENTS

We are grateful to the distinguished *roshei hayeshivah* and rabbinic leaders שליט״א in Israel and the United States whose guidance and encouragement have been indispensable to the success of this Talmud, from its inception. Their letters of approbation appear earlier in this volume.

A huge investment of time and resources was required to make this edition of the Talmud a reality. Only through the generous support of many people is it possible not only to undertake and sustain such a huge and ambitious undertaking, but to keep the price of the volumes within reach of the average family and student. We are grateful to them all.

The Trustees and Governors of the MESORAH HERITAGE FOUNDATION saw the need to support the scholarship and production of this and other outstanding works of Torah literature. Their names are listed on an earlier page.

JAY SCHOTTENSTEIN is chairman of the Board of Governors and has enlisted many others in support of this monumental project. In addition, he and his wife JEANIE have dedicated the HEBREW ELUCIDATION OF THE SCHOTTENSTEIN EDITION OF THE TALMUD and the DAF YOMI EDITION OF THE TALMUD in honor of their parents. But those are only formal identifications. The Schottensteins are deeply involved in a host of causes and their generosity is beyond description. Most recently they have undertaken sponsorship of the SCHOTTENSTEIN INTERLINEAR SERIES, which is bringing a new and innovative dimension of understanding to tefillah. Nevertheless, this Talmud is their *liebling*. They surpass every commitment to assure its continuity and it has justly become synonymous with their name.

HAGAON RAV DAVID FEINSTEIN שליט״א has been a guide, mentor, and friend since the first day of the ArtScroll Series. We are honored that, though complex halachic matters come to the Rosh Yeshivah from across the world, he regards our work as an important contribution to *harbatzas haTorah* and that he has graciously consented to be a trustee of the Foundation.

In addition, we are grateful to:

LAURENCE A. TISCH, JAMES S. TISCH and THOMAS J. TISCH, who have been more than gracious on numerous occasions; JOEL L. FLEISHMAN, Founding Trustee of the Foundation, whose sage advice and active intervention was a turning point in our work; ELLIS A. SAFDEYE, the dedicator of the SAFDEYE EDITION OF SEDER NASHIM, a legendary supporter of worthy causes and a warm, treasured friend; BENJAMIN C. FISHOFF, patron of several volumes of the Talmud, and a sensitive, visionary friend who has brought many people under the banner of this project; ZVI RYZMAN, patron of the HEBREW RYZMAN EDITION OF THE MISHNAH and of tractates in this Talmud edition, a dynamic and imaginative force for Torah life and scholarship, and a loyal, devoted friend; SOLI SPIRA, patron of Talmud volumes, who is respected on three continents for his learning and magnanimity; RABBI MEYER H. MAY, a man who devotes his considerable acumen and prestige to the service of Torah. He has been a proven and invaluable friend at many junctures; ABRAHAM BIDERMAN, a Trustee, whose achievement for Torah and community, here and abroad, are astounding; JUDAH SEPTIMUS, a Trustee, whose acumen and resources are devoted to numerous Torah causes; and RABBI SHLOMO GERTZULIN, whose competence and vision are invaluable assets to Klal Yisrael.

# פטרוני התלמוד

| | |
|---|---|
| KESUBOS I: | **Ben Fishoff and Family** (New York) |
| KESUBOS II: | **Jacob and Esther Gold** (New York) |
| KESUBOS III: | **David and Roslyn Lowy** (Forest Hills) |
| NEDARIM I: | **Soli and Vera Spira** (New York / Jerusalem) |
| NEDARIM II: | **Mr. and Mrs. Yehudah Klein   Mr. and Mrs. Moshe Klein** |
| NAZIR: | **Shlomo and Esther Ben Arosh** (Jerusalem) |
| SOTAH: | **Motty and Malka Klein** (New York) |
| GITTIN I: | **Mrs. Kate Tannenbaum;**<br>**Elliot and Debra Tannenbaum; Edward and Linda Zizmor** |
| GITTIN II: | **Mordchai Aron and Dvorah Gombo** (New York) |
| KIDDUSHIN I: | **Dr. Allan and Dr. Chaikie Novetsky** (Jerusalem) |
| KIDDUSHIN II: | **Jacqui and Patty Oltuski** (Savyon) |
| BAVA KAMMA I: | **Lloyd and Hadassah Keilson** (New York) |
| BAVA KAMMA II: | **Faivel and Roiza Weinreich** (New York) |
| BAVA KAMMA III: | **David and Fanny Malek** |
| BAVA METZIA I: | **Joseph and Rachel Leah Neumann** (Monsey) |
| BAVA METZIA II: | **Shlomo and Tirzah Eisenberg** (Bnei Brak) |
| BAVA METZIA III: | **A. George and Stephanie Saks** (New York) |
| BAVA BASRA I: | **Ezra and Debbie Beyman** (New York) |
| BAVA BASRA II: | **Ezra and Debbie Beyman** (New York) |
| BAVA BASRA III: | **Ezra and Debbie Beyman** (New York) |
| SANHEDRIN I: | **Martin and Rivka Rapaport** (Jerusalem) |
| SANHEDRIN II: | **Aryeh and Faige Lebovic   Avrom and Susie Lebovic** (Toronto) |
| SANHEDRIN III: | In honor of **Joseph and Anita Wolf** (Tel Aviv) |
| MAKKOS: | **Hirsch and Raquel Wolf** (New York) |
| SHEVUOS: | **Jacques and Miriam Monderer** (Antwerp) |
| AVODAH ZARAH I: | **Mr. and Mrs. Eli Kaufman** (Petach Tikva) |
| AVODAH ZARAH II: | **Mr. and Mrs. Chaim Schweid** (New York) |
| HORAYOS-EDUYOS: | **Woli and Chaja Stern, Jacques and Ariane Stern** (Sao Paulo, Brazil) |
| ZEVACHIM I: | **Mr. and Mrs. Eli Kaufman** (Petach Tikva) |
| ZEVACHIM II: | **Mr. and Mrs. Eli Kaufman** (Petach Tikva) |
| ZEVACHIM III: | **Mr. and Mrs. Eli Kaufman** (Petach Tikva) |
| MENACHOS I: | **Yaakov and Beatrice Herzog and family** (Toronto) |
| MENACHOS II: | **Yaakov and Beatrice Herzog and family** (Toronto) |
| MENACHOS III: | **Yaakov and Beatrice Herzog and family** (Toronto) |
| CHULLIN I: | **The Pluczenik Families** (Antwerp) |
| CHULLIN II: | **Avrohom David and Chaya Baila Klein** (Monsey) |
| CHULLIN III: | **Avrohom David and Chaya Baila Klein** (Monsey) |
| CHULLIN IV: | **The Frankel Family** (New York) |
| BECHOROS I: | **Mordchai Aron and Dvorah Gombo** (New York) |
| BECHOROS II: | **Howard and Chaya Balter** (New York) |
| ARACHIN: | **Mr. and Mrs. Eli Kaufman** (Petach Tikva) |
| TEMURAH: | **Abraham and Bayla Fluk** (Tel Aviv) |
| KEREISOS: | **Mr. and Mrs. Eli Kaufman** (Petach Tikva) |
| ME'ILAH, TAMID, MIDDOS KINNIM: | In memory of **ר׳ אליהו אלעזר ב״ר יוסף ברוך ז״ל** |
| NIDDAH I: | **Daniel and Margaret, Allan and Brocha, and David and Elky Retter and Families** |
| NIDDAH II: | **Jay and Jeanie Schottenstein** (Columbus, Ohio) |

# פטרוני התלמוד

We express our appreciation to the distinguished patrons
who have dedicated volumes in the

**HEBREW ELUCIDATION OF THE SCHOTTENSTEIN EDITION OF THE TALMUD**

מהדורת שוטנשטין

# תלמוד בבלי

Dedicated by

**JAY AND JEANIE SCHOTTENSTEIN**

and their children

**Joseph Aaron and Lindsay Brooke, Jonathan Richard and Nicole Lauren, Jeffrey Adam and Ariella**

**Jacob Meir Jonah Philip Emma Blake Winnie Simone Teddi Isabella Allegra Giselle**

| | |
|---|---|
| **SEDER ZERA'IM:** | **Mrs. Margot Guez and Family**<br>**Paul Vivianne Michelle Hubert Monique Gerard Aline Yves** |
| **SEDER MOED:** | **Jacob M. M. and Pnina (Rand) Graff** (Los Angeles)<br>**Malka Ita and Aaron Rubenstein Chaya Rivka Graff Meira and Elie Portnoy**<br>**Joy and Adam Kushnir Meir Reuven Yekusiel and Itta Graff**<br>**Ahuva Esther and Yehuda Levin and Families** |
| **SEDER NASHIM:** | **Geoffrey and Mimi Rochwarger** (Bet Shemesh)<br>**Tehila Rivka Naftali Zvi Atara Kaila Aryeh Shalom Dalia Eliana** |
| **SEDER NEZIKIN:** | **Yisrael and Gittie Ury and Family** (Los Angeles) |
| **SEDER KODASHIM:** | **Yaakov and Beatrice Herzog and Family** (Toronto) |
| INTRODUCTION TO THE TALMUD: | **Robin and Warren Shimoff** |
| BERACHOS I: | **Jay and Jeanie Schottenstein** (Columbus, Ohio) |
| BERACHOS II: | **Zvi and Betty Ryzman** (Los Angeles) |
| SHABBOS I: | **Moshe and Hessie Neiman** (New York) |
| SHABBOS II: | **David and Elky Retter and Family** (New York) |
| SHABBOS III: | **Mendy and Itta Klein** (Cleveland) |
| SHABBOS IV: | **Mayer and Shavy Gross** (New York) |
| ERUVIN I: | **The Schottenstein Family** (Columbus, Ohio) |
| ERUVIN II: | **The Schottenstein Family** (Columbus, Ohio) |
| PESACHIM I: | **Serge and Nina Muller** (Antwerp) |
| PESACHIM II: | **The Cohen Family** |
| PESACHIM III: | **Morris and Devora Smith** (New York / Jerusalem) |
| SHEKALIM: | **The Rieder, Wiesen and Karasick Families** |
| YOMA I: | **Peretz and Frieda Friedberg** (Toronto) |
| YOMA II: | **Mr. and Mrs. Avrohom Noach Klein** (New York) |
| SUCCAH I: | **The Pruwer Family** (Jerusalem) |
| SUCCAH II: | **The Pruwer Family** (Jerusalem) |
| BEITZAH: | **Chaim and Chava Fink** (Tel Aviv) |
| ROSH HASHANAH: | **Avi and Meira Schnur** (Savyon) |
| TAANIS: | **Mendy and Itta Klein** (Cleveland) |
| MEGILLAH: | **In memory of Jerome Schottenstein ז"ל** |
| MOED KATTAN: | **Yisroel and Shoshana Lefkowitz** (New York) |
| CHAGIGAH: | **Steven and Hadassah Weisz** (New York) |
| YEVAMOS I: | **Phillip and Ruth Wojdyslawski** (Sao Paulo, Brazil) |
| YEVAMOS II: | **Phillip and Ruth Wojdyslawski** (Sao Paulo, Brazil) |
| YEVAMOS III: | **Phillip and Ruth Wojdyslawski** (Sao Paulo, Brazil) |

# In Memoriam — לזכרון עולם

Dedicated by the Talmud Associates
to those who forged eternal links

❖

Nissel — שלמה מאיר בן הרב חיים לייב עזריאל ז״ל
Paneth — אלטע חיה שרה ע״ה בת ר׳ פנחס שיחי׳ לאוי״ט
Parnes — אריה לייבש בן יוסף יצחק ועטיא בת אשר ראובן ע״ה
Parnes — הרב אברהם זאב ב״ר ישכר ע״ה
Parsons — משה זלמן בן אהרן דוב ע״ה
Perlman — יוסף ב״ר נפתלי בנימין ז״ל ורעכל לאה בת ר׳ שלמה ע״ה
Perlowitz — הרב משה ב״ר אליעזר הלל ע״ה
Pinczower — אפרים ב״ר ישראל חיים ופיגלא בת ר׳ יעקב ע״ה
Rabin — ישראל בן נחום ע״ה
Reiff — לוי יצחק ב״ר עזריאל ז״ל ויהודית בת ר׳ יצחק אייזיק ע״ה
Rennert — שרה בת יצחק יעקב ע״ה
Rennert — יונה מנחם בן אהרן ע״ה
Rosenberg — חיים נחמן ב״ר דוד ולאה בת יוסף ע״ה
Sam and Leah Rosenbloom ע״ה
Roth — ר׳ צבי יהודה ז״ל ב״ר אברהם יצחק שיחי׳ לאוי״ט
Roth — משה ב״ר יעקב הכהן ע״ה Weisner — יצחק ב״ר זאב ע״ה
In memory of the Sanz-Klausenburger Rebbe זצוק״ל
כ״ק אדמו״ר אבדק״ק צאנז־קלויזענבורג זי״ע
מרן הרהגה״צ ר׳ יקותיאל יהודה בהרהגה״צ ר׳ צבי זצוק״ל
נלב״ע ש״ק פ׳ חקת, ט׳ תמוז תשנ״ד
William Shachat ע״ה and Israel Ira Shachat ע״ה
Scharf — אליהו ב״ר משה יעקב ושרה בת אלכסנדר זיסקינד ע״ה
Scherman — ר׳ אברהם דוב ב״ר שמואל נטע ע״ה
Scherman — ליבא בת ר׳ זאב וואלף ע״ה
Schneerson — כ״ק אדמו״ר יוסף יצחק בן כ״ק אדמו״ר שלום דובער זצ״ל
Schneerson — חי׳ מושקא בת כ״ק אדמו״ר יוסף יצחק ע״ה
Schneerson — כ״ק אדמו״ר מנחם מענדל בן הרב לוי יצחק זצ״ל
Schnur — אברהם יצחק בן אהרן הי״ד וחנה בת חיים יעקב ע״ה
Schonbrun — שרגא פייבל ב״ר יעקב הכהן ז״ל
Schonbrun — מאטל אסתר בת מרדכי הלוי ע״ה
Schron — אליעזר דוב בן חיים משה ע״ה
Schron — חוה בת שמעון ע״ה
Schulman — חיים חייקל בן ר׳ שמואל ע״ה
Schulman — חיה בת הרב ישראל יהודה ע״ה
Schwebel — אברהם זכריה מנחם בן יוסף ז״ל
Schwebel — מחלה בת ישראל מרדכי ע״ה
Scherman — חיים שמואל ב״ר אברהם דוב ע״ה
Scherman — הילד אברהם דוב ע״ה ב״ר זאב יוסף שיחי׳
Sol Scheiner — שלמה טוביה בן יהושע מנחם הלוי ע״ה
Rose Schwartz — רייזל בת הרה״ג ר׳ אברהם יצחק ע״ה
Shafran — ר׳ יהושע ב״ר אברהם ע״ה
Shayovich — משה יעקב ב״ר נחום ועטיא פייגא בת מרדכי ע״ה

Shimoff — ר׳ ישראל דוב ב״ר אהרן יעקב ז״ל
Shimoff — חיה רבקה לאה בת ר׳ אליעזר יהודה ע״ה
Shubow — יוסף שלום בן משה ע״ה
Silberman — ר׳ צבי ב״ר זאב הלוי ע״ה
Silberman — דבורה אסתר בת ישראל ע״ה
Silbermintz — יהושע ב״ר יוסף שמריהו ע״ה
Singer — צבי בן ר׳ חיים ע״ה
Singer — הינדי בת ר׳ שלמה ע״ה
Soclof — אברהם אבא ב״ר שמריהו ע״ה
Soclof — חיה ברכה בת צבי הירש הלוי ע״ה
Smouha — הרב אליהו בן מאיר הלוי ע״ה
Steir — משה בן מיכאל ע״ה
Steinberg – יצחק גדליה בן יהודה לייב ע״ה
Steinberg – מלכה בת מאיר לוי ע״ה
Stern — ר׳ חיים מאיר ב״ר שמחה ז״ל ובינה בת ר׳ יוסף מרדכי ע״ה
Tabak — שיינא רחל בת יוסף מרדכי ע״ה
Taub — ר׳ יעקב ב״ר יהודה אריה ע״ה נפ׳ ד׳ מנחם אב תשל״ט
Taub — אליעזר יוסף בן מענדל ע״ה
Taub — מענדל בן אליעזר יוסף חיה בת הירש ע״ה
Taub — רויזא בת ר׳ משה ע״ה
Wealcatch — חיים דוב ב״ר זאב ואסתר בת ר׳ יוסף אייזיק ע״ה
Weiss — צבי בן יואל ע״ה
Weiss — גיטל בת ישראל ע״ה
Werdiger — ר׳ שלמה אלימלך ב״ר ישראל יצחק ע״ה
Westreich — הרב יהושע בן הרב יוסף יאסקא ז״ל
Leo Werter ע״ה
Wiesner — הרב שמעיה בן הרב זאב ע״ה
Wiesner — שרה לאה בת ר׳ צבי אריה ע״ה
Zakheim-Brecher — בתיה רחל ע״ה בת ר׳ משה יוסף שיחי׳ לאוי״ט
Zalstain — שמעון בן מרדכי יוסף הלוי ע״ה
Zimmer — ר׳ אברהם יעקב בן אהרן אליעזר ע״ה
הרב אהרן ב״ר מאיר יעקב ע״ה
הרבנית פרומא בת ר׳ חיים צבי ע״ה
Zinn — צבי יהודה בן שמעון ע״ה
Zinn — דבורה בת יחיאל מרדכי ע״ה
Leslie Zukor — ר׳ יצחק חיים ב״ר יוסף ע״ה
Zlatow — ר׳ שמואל דוד ב״ר מאיר יעקב ז״ל
הרב אהרן ב״ר מאיר יעקב זצ״ל
הרבנית פרומא בת ר׳ חיים צבי ע״ה
צבי יהודה ז״ל בן אברהם יצחק לאוי״ט
חיים מאיר בן שמחה ז״ל ובינה בת יוסף מרדכי הכהן ע״ה
אליעזר ב״ר אברהם ברוך ז״ל וגולדה זהבה בת משה הלוי ע״ה

# In Memoriam — לזכרון עולם

Dedicated by the Talmud Associates
to those who forged eternal links

❖

Abraham — שמחה בן ר׳ יהודה לייב הכהן ע״ה
דוד חי ב״ר שלום הכהן ע״ה וחנה בת ר׳ עזרא ע״ה
אהרן בן חיים זאב ע״ה גאלדע בת ר׳ דוד ע״ה
Ashkenazy — ר׳ שלמה ב״ר יצחק זצ״ל ורעיתו עלי׳ מינדעל בת ר׳ יעקב ע״
Sarah T. Belz — שרה בת אהרן צבי הלוי ע״ה
Ben-Ari — אליעזר בן מרדכי ע״ה ושרה בת ר׳ אברהם ע״ה
Ben-Ari — מרדכי בן אליעזר ע״ה
Berber — משה ורחל
Menashe Bernath — ר׳ מנשה בן שמואל שמעלקא ז״ל
Hency Bernath — הענצה רייזעל בת אברהם ארי׳ ע״ה
Biegeleisen — שמעון דוד ז״ל ב״ר יעקב שלמה שיחי׳ לאוי״ט
Blitz — דוב מאיר ב״ר דוד הכהן ע״ה
Freddy Bradfield — יעקב בן צבי ע״ה
אהרן ב״ר דוד הכהן ז״ל
Elihu Brodsky — אליהו ב״ר חיים ע״ה
Vera (Greif) Brodsky — יונה בת ר׳ פינחס ע״ה
Cooperberg — שימה רייזל בת ר׳ אהרן שלמה ע״ה
Cooperberg — אברהם אשר בן ר׳ מאיר ע״ה
Cumsky — דוב בער בן אברהם יששכר ע״ה ופעשא מאטלא בת יוסף ע״
צבי טעביל בן ישראל ע״ה וליבע בת דוד ע״ה
Diamant — אשר ב״ר יהושע מרדכי הכהן ע״ה
Diamant — שרה בת ר׳ אריה ע״ה
Diamant — ר׳ דוב ב״ר משה ע״ה ורייזל בת ר׳ אברהם ע״ה
Diamond — דר. ר׳ יצחק ב״ר ברוך בענדיט ע״ה
Dicker — מרדכי צבי ב״ר יעקב ע״ה
Dicker — קיילא בת ר׳ משה ע״ה
Djmal — טופיק טוביה בן משה ושושנה ע״ה
Paul and Jeannette Dubin ע״ה
Mollie Dubinsky ע״ה
Abram B. Efroymson ע״ה
Sylvia Spira Efroymson ע״ה
Ehrenberg — אברהם בן עמנואל ע״ה ויוכבד בת ר׳ אלימלך ע״ה
Einhorn — משה בן ברוך ז״ל ורבקה נעכא בת חיים צבי ע״ה
Eshaghian — אברהם בן דוד ע״ה
Esrig — דוד בן שלמה ע״ה וחיה אייגא בת שלום ע״ה
Feiden — ישראל בן אהרן ע״ה
Feinerman — אליעזר בן יוסף ע״ה ולאה בת ישראל יצחק ע״ה
יוסף בן צבי יחזקאל ע״ה ושרה בת ר׳ משה ע״ה
Feinstein — הרה״ג ר׳ דוד בן הרה״ג ר׳ משה זצ״ל
Freier — ישעיה צבי ב״ר חיים אלכסנדר יוסף ע״ה
Freier — שיינדל בת ר׳ משה הלוי ע״ה
Freilich — הרב יצחק דוב ב״ר אברהם יעקב ז״ל
Frenkel — גרשון בן יחיאל דוד ע״ה Rottenstreich — דוד בן עקיבא ע״
Friedman — ר׳ אהרן ב״ר יעקב מאיר ע״ה
Friedman — ר׳ אברהם ב״ר אלטר יצחק אייזיק ע״ה
Frishman — מרים בת ר׳ יוסף מרדכי ע״ה
Frishman — יצחק אריה ב״ר יהודה ע״ה ומרים לאה בת ר׳ יצחק ע״ה
Furmanovich — לע״נ שרה הניה בת פסח הלוי ע״ה
Furmanovich — לע״נ גדליה דב בן אברהם יואל ז״ל
Goldman — אביו, צבי יעקב בן חיים ז״ל
Goldman — אמו, שפרה בת ר׳ קלונימוס קלמן ע״ה
Goldberger — אברהם צבי בן מתתיהו ע״ה
Gugenheim — החבר אפרים בן רפאל ע״ה
Gugenheim — בריינדל בת החבר נתן הכהן ע״ה
Hanz — חיים בן מרדכי הי״ד
Henzel — אברהם בן ר׳ מנחם זאב ע״ה
Hirtz — אליעזר בן ישעיה ז״ל ולאה בת יוסף הלוי ע״ה
Horowitz — שלמה יהודה ב״ר זלמן יוסף הלוי ז״ל ומרים בת אברהם הכהן ע״ה
Imanuel — מרדכי בן רחמים ז״ל
Kahn — ר׳ ישראל אריה ב״ר שמואל הכהן ז״ל
Kahn — גיטל בת נתן ע״ה
Katzef — פרומה באדענה בת אלחנן ע״ה
Kleinbart — משה ב״ר אריה לייב ע״ה
Kleinbart — בתיה בת ר׳ משה אברהם ע״ה
Kriegel — רויזא מינצא בת הרב ישראל יהודה ע״ה
Kulefsky — הילד יהודה לייב ע״ה בן נתן נטע לאי״ט
Langer — משה בן יצחק הי״ד
Landowne — שלמה בן יוסף ע״ה
Lasry — שאול ב״ר אברהם ע״ה וזהרה אסתר בת משה ע״ה
Lazar — אליעזר שאול בן זאב מאיר ע״ה
Lefkovich — ר׳ זאב וועלוול ב״ר יצחק אייזיק ע״ה
Lemberger — יצחק בן אריה ע״ה
Leibel — יחזקאל שרגא ב״ר חיים ע״ה
Leibel — רויזא בת ר׳ אברהם משה ע״ה
Levi — הרב חיים מאיר בן ר׳ מנחם ע״ה
Levi — שושנה טייבא רייזל בת ר׳ יחזקאל גרשון ע״ה
Light — משה גבריאל בן אברהם אליהו ז״ל וחנה בת נתן ע״ה
Lowy — מרדכי אריה ב״ר רפאל הלוי ז״ל ומינדל בת ר׳ שלמה זלמן ע״ה
May — ר׳ יוסף בן הרב יהודה אריה ע״ה
Meizner — מרדכי חיים ב״ר זבולן יצחק חייא ז״ל
Miller — אלטער משה יוסף ב״ר צבי אריה ז״ל
Moskowitz — אליעזר ב״ר אברהם ברוך ז״ל וזהבה בת ר׳ משה ע״ה
Neuman — ר׳ יצחק אייזיק צבי בן מאיר אהרן ז״ל
Dr. Moshe Neuman — ר׳ משה ב״ר יצחק אייזיק ז״ל
Bobi Neuman — פייגא יכט בת שרגא פייבל ע״ה
Rochel Neuman — רחל בת משה הכהן ע״ה

תנצב״ה

# The Talmud Associates*

A fellowship of benefactors dedicated to
the dissemination of the Talmud

Robby and Judy Neuman and Family
לזכות בניהם היקרים שיחיו:
אברהם לייב ושרה מאטיל, מרדכי שרגא וזיסל,
שמואל שמעלקא ונחמה, רחל ברכה וישראל זכריהו,
מנשה ברוך וחיה רחל

RoAnna and Moshe Pascher
לזכות בניהם היקרים שיחיו:
נח צבי, דוד ישראל, אילנה שירה בתיה

Naftali Binyomin and Zypora Perlman

Kenneth Ephraim and Julie Pinczower
לרפו״ש ישראל חיים בן פייגלא שיחי׳

Dr. Douglas and Vivian Rabin

Michael G. Reiff

Ingeborg and Ira Leon Rennert

Alan Jay and Hindy Rosenberg

Aviva and Oscar Rosenberg

John and Sue Rossler Family

Mr. and Mrs. David Rubin and Family

Dinah Rubinoff and Family

Ms. Ruth Russ

Mr. and Mrs. Alexander Scharf

Mark and Chani Scheiner

Avi and Michou Schnur

Rubin and Marta Schron

Rivie and Leba Schwebel and Family

Shlomo Segev (Smouha)

Bernard and Chaya Shafran
לזכות בניהם היקרים שיחיו:
דבורה, יעקב חיים, דוד זאב, אסתר מנוחה

Jeffrey and Catherine Shachat
in honor of Rabbeim Howard Zack and Judah Dardik

Steven J. Shaer

Joel and Malka Shafran
לזכות בניהם היקרים שיחיו:
אשר נחמן, טובה חיה, תמר פעסיל, שרה חוה

Robin and Warren Shimoff

Nathan B. and Malka Silberman

The Soclof Family

Dr. Edward L. and Judith Steinberg

Avrohom Chaim and Elisa Taub
Hadassah, Yaakov Yehuda Aryeh, Shifra, Faige,
Devorah Raizel, and Golda Leah

Max Taub
and his son Yitzchak

Jay and Sari Tepper

Walter and Adele Wasser

Melvin, Armond and Larry Waxman

William and Noémie Wealcatch

The Wegbreit Family

Robert and Rachel Weinstein and Family

Dr. Zelig and Evelyn (Gutwein) Weinstein
Yaakov, Daniella, Aliza and Zev

Erwin and Myra Weiss

Morry and Judy Weiss

Shlomo and Esther Werdiger

Leslie M. and Shira Westreich

Willie and Blimie Wiesner

The Yad Velvel Foundation

Moshe and Venezia Zakheim

Dr. Harry and Holly Zinn

Mrs. Edith Zukor and Family

*In formation

# The Talmud Associates*

A fellowship of benefactors dedicated to
the dissemination of the Talmud

Audrey and Sargent Aborn and Family

Dr. Mark and Dr. Barbara Bell,
Bentzion Yosef and Mordechai Yehudah

The Belz Family

Richard Bookstaber and Janice Horowitz
In memory of his son
Michael and Bettina Bradfield
Gabrielle and Matthew
(London)

Nachi and Zippi Brown,
Jessica, Daniella, Shachar and Mindy
in honor of their parents and grandparents

Columbus Jewish Foundation

Milton Cooper and Family

Dr. and Mrs. David Diamond

Nahum and Feige Hinde Dicker and Family

Sophia, Alberto and Rose Djmal

Dr. Richard Dubin

Kenneth and Cochava Dubin

Dr. Martin and Esther Ehrenberg

David and Simone Eshaghian

Rabbi Judah and Ruth Feinerman

In honor of
Mr. and Mrs. Yehoshua Chaim Fischman
by their children

Mayer and Ruthy Friedman
Ari, Yitzy, Suri, Dovi

Dr. Michael and Susan Friedman
לזכות בניהם, כלתם, ונכדם; בנותיהם, וחתניהם שיחי׳

Yeshaya and Perel Friedman

Julius Frishman

David and Sally Frenkel
לזכות בניהם וכלתם היקרים שיחיו:
דניאל שמואל ומאשה שושנה, אורי גבריאל, רונית פרימיט

Daniel and Ruth Furmanovich

Sander and Tracy Gerber
לזכות בניהם היקרים יעקב עקיבא, אסתר פערל, טליה גולדו
חנה טובה, רותי רבקה, שרה אורה, ושושנה חוה שיחי׳
שיתעלו בתורה ויראת שמים

Leon and Agi Goldenberg
in honor of the marriage of their children
Mendy and Estie Blau

Robert and Rita Gluck
לרפו״ש טויבא רחל בת פריידא שתחי׳

Shari and Jay Gold and Family

Dr. Martin and Shera Goldman and Family

Esther Henzel

Hirtz, Adler and Zupnick Families

Hashi and Miriam Herzka

Norman and Sandy Nissel Horowitz

Mrs. Farokh Imanuel, Kamram Imanuel
Dr. Mehran and Sepideh Imanuel
Eli and Fariba Maghen

David and Trudy Justin and Family
in honor of their parents
Zoltan and Kitty Justin

Nosson Shmuel and Ann Kahn and Family
ולזכות בניהם היקרים שיחיו:
חיים דוד, צבי מנחם, אברהם יצחק, ומשפחתם

David J. and Dora Kleinbart

In honor of
Mr. and Mrs. Label Kutoff
by their children

The Landowne Family

Ezriel and Miriam Langer

Mr. and Mrs. Chaim Leibel

Yehuda and Rasie Levi

Donald Light

Rudolph and Esther Lowy

Raphael and Blimie Manela
לזכות בניהם היקרים שיחיו:
מתתיהו, ישראל, ישעיהו, חיים משה, ושמעון

Howard and Debra Margolin and Family

Mendy and Phyllis Mendlowitz

formation

# Community Guardians of the Talmud

A community is more than a collection of individuals. It is a new entity that is a living expression of support of Torah and dedication to the heritage of Klal Yisrael.

In honor of

**Rabbi Reuven Fink** and the *maggidei shiur* of **Young Israel of New Rochelle**

**Dr. Joey and Lisa Bernstein**
in memory of
שרה אלטע בת אברהם ע״ה
Mrs. Sondra Goldman ע״ה

**Stanley and Vivian Bernstein** and children
in honor of their parents and grandparents
Jules and Adele Bernstein
Andrew and Renee Weiss

**Aaron and Carol Greenwald**
in honor of their children and grandchildren
Ira and Jamie Gurvitch and children
Shlomo and Tobi Greenwald and children

**Meyer and Ellen Koplow**
in honor of their children
Tovah and Michael Koplow,
Jonathan, and Aliza

**Dr. Ronald and Susan Moskovich**
in honor of their children
Adam Moshe, Leah Rivka, and David
״עשה תורתך קבע״

**Karen and Michael Raskas and Family**

**Stanley and Sheri Raskas**
in memory of his parents
ראובן ב״ר חיים שבתי לייב ע״ה וחנה בת הרב טוביה ע״ה
Ralph and Annette Raskas ז״ל

**Drs. Arthur and Rochelle Turetsky**
in honor of their children and grandson
Avi and Melissa, Jonathan and Nili, Yehuda
Shmuel Chaim

**Mark and Anne Wasserman**
in honor of their children
Joseph, Bailey, Erin, Rebeccah
and Jordyn

**Stanley and Ellen Wasserman**
in memory of
חיה פיגא בת שמריהו — Viola Charles ע״ה
רות גולדה בת שמריהו — Ruth Schreiber ע״ה
לאה בת יוסף — Lee Salzberg ע״ה

**Gerald and Judith Ziering**
in memory of
יחיאל מיכל בן אפרים פישל ז״ל וזלטא בת נחמן ע״ה
Jesse and Laurette Ziering ז״ל

**Daf Yomi shiur**
in honor of their wives

**Lakewood Links**
in honor of
Rabbi Abish Zelishovsky

## The Community of Great Neck, New York

**YOUNG ISRAEL OF GREAT NECK**
**Rabbi Yaacov Lerner**
**Rabbi Eric Goldstein**
**Dr. Leeber Cohen**
**Professor Lawrence Schiffman**

**GREAT NECK SYNAGOGUE**
**Rabbi Ephraim R. Wolf ז״ל**
**Rabbi Dale Polakoff**
**Rabbi Shalom Axelrod**
**Rabbi Yoel Aryeh**
**Rabbi Yossi Singer**

**In Memoriam**
**Rabbi Ephraim R. Wolf ז״ל,**
a pioneer of *harbotzas Torah*, a *kiruv* visionary, and a gifted spiritual leader. His legacy is the flourishing Torah community of Great Neck, New York.

## The Community of Columbus, Ohio

In memory of **Jerome Schottenstein** Of Blessed Memory
and in honor of **Geraldine Schottenstein and Family**

**Jay And Jeanie Schottenstein**
**Joseph, Jonathan, Jeffrey**
**Ann And Ari Deshe**
**Elie, David, Dara, Daniel**
**Susie And Jon Diamond**
**Jillian, Joshua, Jacob**
**Lori Schottenstein**
**Saul And Sonia Schottenstein**

**Sarah and Edward Arndt & Family**
**Irwin and Beverly Bain**
**Daniela & Yoram Benary**
**Liron & Alexandra, Oron, Doreen**
**Deborah & Michael Broidy**
**Michelle & Daniel**
**Families of Columbus Kollel**
**Naomi & Reuven Dessler**
**Sylvia & Murray Ebner & Family**

**Tod and Cherie Friedman**
**Rachel, Ross & Kara**
**Jim & Angie Gesler**
**Gerald & Karon Greenfield**
**Ben & Tracy Kraner & Family**
**Mike, Heidi, Brian, Deena & Leah Levey**
**Helene & Michael Lehv**
**Gary Narin**
**Ira & Laura Nutis & Family**

**Lea & Thomas Schottenstein & Family**
**Jeff & Amy Swanson**
**Jon**
**Marcy, Mark, Sam, & Adam Ungar**
**Drs. Philip & Julia Weinerman**
**Michael & Channa Weisz & Family**
**Dr. Daniel & Chaya Wuensch & Family**
**Main Street Synagogue**
**Howard Zack, Rabbi**

# Guardians of the Talmud*

A society of visionary people who recognize the primacy of the Jewish people's commitment to intellect, ethics, integrity, law, and religion — and pursue it by presenting the treasures of the eternal Talmud in the language of today . . . for the generations of tomorrow.

**Rona and Edward Jutkowitz**

In honor of our family's continuing commitment to Torah learning and Klal Yisrael.
We dedicate this volume to our daughters, **Rebecca and Mollie,**
who are the light of our lives and our blessings, and always fill our hearts with nachas;
and to their zeide, **Mr. Herman Jutkowitz**, who is a constant source of guidance and inspiration;
and in memory of our beloved parents
משה בן מאניס ז״ל ורחל בת אברהם הכהן ע״ה — Martin W. and Ruth Trencher ז״ל
ברכה בת שניאור זלמן ע״ה — Bernice Jutkowitz ע״ה
May our daughters have the honor to teach the value of Torah to their own children,
and may Torah be the guiding light for all of Klal Yisrael.

לעילוי נשמת

**הבחור מרדכי גדליהו ז״ל בן משה ואסתר שיחי׳ — Franky Ehrenberg**

June 22, 2003 / נפ׳ כ״ג סיון תשס״ג

With a life of Torah study and service to Klal Yisrael ahead of him,
our beloved son, brother, and uncle was plucked from this life at only twenty-three.

כי **מרדכי** . . . דרש טוב לעמו ודבר שלום לכל זרעו

**Dr. Martin and Esther Ehrenberg**

**Scott Leon** **Dr. Judy and Hillel Olshin**

**Yonatan Eliezer** **Sara Elisheva** **Shmuel Abba**

**Richard Bookstaber and Janice Horowitz**

In memory of his son

May his memory be a blessing
to all those whose lives he touched.

**Michael and Patricia Schiff**

**Sophia, Juliette and Stefan**

in memory and appreciation of

**Jerome Schottenstein ז״ל**

and in honor of beloved parents and grandparents

**Shirlie and Milton Levitin** **Solange and Joseph Fretas** **Judy and Robert Schiff**

and Torah scholars

**Rabbi Mordechai Schiff ז״ל** and **Rabbi Ephraim Schiff ז״ל**

May we all bring honor to Hashem

ı formation

# Guardians of the Talmud*

A society of visionary people who recognize the primacy of the Jewish people's commitment to intellect, ethics, integrity, law, and religion — and pursue it by presenting the treasures of the eternal Talmud in the language of today . . . for the generations of tomorrow.

**Milton and Rita Kramer**

in honor of their 50th wedding anniversary and Milton's 80th birthday (April 1999),
in honor of the marriage of Ellen to George Gross (September 18, 2000),
and in honor of their children and grandchildren

**Daniel and Gina Kramer and Children** **Jonathan and Marian Kramer and Children**

**Ellen K. and George Gross and their Children**

and in everlasting memory of their beloved parents and grandparents
חיים שניאור זלמן הלוי (חזק) ופייגע דינה ע״ה — Hyman S. and Fannie D. Kramer ע״ה
חיים אלטער ושרה חנה ע״ה — Adolph H. and Sadie A. Gross ע״ה
משה אליעזר הלוי ורחל עלקא ע״ה — Morris L. and Rachel E. Kramer ע״ה
דוב בער הכהן ודבורה ע״ה — Barney and Dvorah Cohen ע״ה
משולם צבי ולאה ע״ה — Herman M. and Leah Gross ע״ה
פסח אלכסנדר וחנה ע״ה — Peisach and Hannah Neustadter ע״ה

**Helene and Moshe Talansky** **Ida Bobrowsky** **Irene and Kalman Talansky** **Shoshana Silbert**

in honor of

**Rebecca Talansky's 100th birthday עמו״ש**

and in memory of
הרב דוד בן הרב אברהם חיים ז״ל — Rabbi David Talansky ז״ל
בלומא בת ר׳ שלמה הלוי ע״ה — Blanche Moshel ע״ה
ר׳ אברהם חיים בן הרב דוד ז״ל — Abraham R. Talansky ז״ל
הרב יעקב בן ר׳ אברהם ז״ל — Rabbi Jacob Bobrowsky ז״ל
תמר בת הרב יעקב ע״ה — Tema Bobrowsky ע״ה
ר׳ משה בן ר׳ לייב ז״ל — ברײנה בת ר׳ זלמן ע״ה — Rebecca and Morris Weisinger ז״ל
הרב אברהם בן ר׳ נחמיה ז״ל — Rabbi Avraham Silbert ז״ל
ר׳ מרדכי בן ר׳ שאול ז״ל — שפרה רייזל בת ר׳ צבי ע״ה — Ruth and Marek Stromer ז״ל
ר׳ אהרון בן ר׳ שלמה אריה ז״ל — רחל בת ר׳ יהושע אהרון ע״ה — Rose and Aaron Lerer ז״ל

**Thomas R. and Janet F. Ketteler**

in memory of his mentor

**Jerome Schottenstein ע״ה**

**Alan and Myrna Cohen**

in honor of

their children

Alison and Matthew

*In formation

*The Written Word is Forever*

## Guardians of the Talmud*

A society of visionary people who recognize the primacy of the Jewish people's commitment to intellect, ethics, integrity, law, and religion — and pursue it by presenting the treasures of the eternal Talmud in the language of today . . . for the generations of tomorrow.

**David and Jean Bernstein**
**Matthew Bernstein**
**Scott and Andrea Bernstein**

in memory of
Mr. and Mrs. Harry Bernstein ע״ה
Mr. and Mrs. Joseph Furman ע״ה

The publishers pay tribute to the memory of a couple that embodied Torah knowledge and service to our people

**Rabbi Yitzchok Filler ז״ל – הרב יצחק בן ר׳ שמואל ז״ל**
נפטר ל״ג בעומר תש״ל

**Mrs. Dorothy Filler ע״ה – הרבנית דבורה בת ר׳ אברהם בצלאל ע״ה**
נפטרה כ״א מרחשון תשס״ג

and the memory of a man of integrity and sensitivity

**George May ז״ל – ר׳ יוסף בן הרב יהודה אריה ז״ל**
נפטר כ״ז שבט תש״ס

**תנצב״ה**

We also honor a matriarch and role model

**Mrs. Sylvia May תחי׳**

**Stephen L. and Terri Geifman and children**
**Leonard and Linda Comess and children**
**Alan and Cherie Weiss and children**

in loving memory of
Morris M. Geifman – משה מרדכי בן יחיאל מיכאל ז״ל
and in honor of
Geraldine G. Geifman

**Elliot and Debbie Gibber**
**Daniel and Amy Gibber and family, Jacob and Jennifer Gibber and family,**
**Marc, Michael, Mindy, and David**

in memory of our parents and grandparents
Charles Goldner ז״ל – אלימלך חיים בן ירמיה הלוי ז״ל
נפ׳ כ׳ חשון תשס״ב
who completed Shas many times
Kate Ettlinger Goldner ע״ה – מינדל בת משולם ע״ה
נפ׳ כ״א תמוז תשכ״ח

formation

TEMURAH: **Dr. and Mrs. Walter Silver**
Shlomo, Chani, and Avi Cohen
Sheri, Terri, Jennifer and Michelle Kraut
Evan and Alison Silver
in memory of our parents, and great grandparents
צבי יצחק ב״ר שמואל ע״ה — Harry Silver ע״ה
שרה פיגא בת מענדל ע״ה — Sarah Silver ע״ה
אברהם משה בן הרב שלמה זאלי ע״ה — Morris Bienenfeld ע״ה
גוטקה טובה בת אברהם דוד ע״ה — Gertrude Bienenfeld ע״ה

KEREISOS: **Mouky and Charlotte Landau** (Antwerp)
in honor of their children
**Natalie and Chemi Friedman** **Yanky and Miriam Landau**
**Steve and Nechama Landau**
and in beloved memory of their parents
חיים יעקב ב״ר יהושע ז״ל — Chaim Yaakov Landau ז״ל
אסתר בת ר׳ יעקב קאפל הכהן ע״ה — Esther Landau ע״ה
בן ציון ב״ר יצחק צבי ז״ל — Benzion Gottlob ז״ל
צילה בת ר׳ שמואל יהודה לייב ע״ה — Cila Herskovic ע״ה
and in beloved memory of our partner
מורנו הרב ר׳ יוסף יצחק בן מורנו ורבנו הרה״ג ר׳ מרדכי רוטנברג זצ״ל אבדק״ק אנטווערפן

ME'ILAH, TAMID, MIDDOS, KINNIM: **Steven and Renée Adelsberg**
**Sarita and Rubin Gober** **Israel Joseph and Menachem Yechezkel**
**David and Joclyn** **Sammy** **Avi**
in loving memory of
שמואל שמעלקא ב״ר גדליה ז״ל — Samuel Adelsberg ז״ל
and in honor of
Helen Adelsberg Weinberg שתחי׳
and
Chaim and Rose Fraiman שיחי׳

NIDDAH I: In memory of
**Joseph and Eva Hurwitz ע״ה**
**יוסף ב״ר מרדכי הלוי וחוה פיגא ב״ר אליעזר הלוי ע״ה**
and
**Lorraine Hurwitz Greenblott — לאה בילא חיה בת ר׳ יוסף ע״ה**
by
Marc and Rachel Hurwitz,
Elisheva Ruchama, Michal, and Nechama Leah;

Martin and Geraldine Schottenstein Hoffman,
Jay and Jeanie Schottenstein, Ann and Ari Deshe,
Susan and Jon Diamond, and Lori Schottenstein;

and Pam and Neil Lazaroff, Frank Millman, and Dawn Petel

NIDDAH II: In memory of
**Jerome Schottenstein ע״ה**
**יעקב מאיר חיים בן אפרים אליעזר הכהן ע״ה**

ZEVACHIM III: **Friends of Value City Department Stores**
In memory of
יעקב מאיר חיים בן אפרים אליעזר הכהן ע״ה — Jerome Schottenstein ע״ה

MENACHOS I: **Terumah Foundation**

MENACHOS II: **Terumah Foundation**

MENACHOS III: **Terumah Foundation**

CHULLIN I: **The Kassin Family**
in memory of
הרב יעקב שאול קצין זצ״ל — Rabbi Dr. Jacob Saul Kassin זצ״ל
The late Chief Rabbi of the Syrian-Sephardic Community
and in honor of
הרב שאול יעקב קצין שליט״א — Rabbi Saul Jacob Kassin שליט״א
Chief Rabbi of the Syrian-Sephardic Community

CHULLIN II: **Marty Silverman**
in memory of
Joseph and Fannie Silverman ע״ה and Dorothy Silverman ע״ה

CHULLIN III: **Harold and Ann Platt**
in memory of their beloved parents
אליעזר ושרה פיגא ע״ה — Eliezer and Sarah Feiga (Olshak) Platkowski ע״ה of Malkinia, Poland
ברוך ולאה ע״ה — Baruch and Laura Bienstock ע״ה of Lwow, Poland
and in memory of their entire families who perished in the Holocaust

CHULLIN IV: **Terumah Foundation**

BECHOROS I: **Howard Tzvi and Chaya Friedman**
**Gabrielle and Noam Charnowitz Aryeh Yerachmiel Alexander and Daniella**
in memory of their father and grandfather
הרב ירחמיאל ברוך בן הרה״ח ר׳ אלעזר ז״ל — Yerachmiel Friedman ז״ל

BECHOROS II: **Howard and Chaya Balter**
**Nachum and Perri Augenbaum Gavriel Shmuel, Rachel**
**Naftali and Perele Balter Aryeh Leib Akiva**
in memory of our parents and grandparents
דוד זאב בן ר׳ שלמה ז״ל, נפ׳ ז׳ תמוז תשס״ח — **David Balter** ז״ל
רחל בת ר׳ חיים ע״ה, נפ׳ ז׳ שבט תשנ״ט — **Ruth L. Balter** ע״ה
and in honor of their parents and grandparents שיחי׳
**Noah and Shirley Schall**
and in beloved memory of their grandparents and great grandparents
ר׳ שלמה ב״ר דוד ז״ל אדעל בת ר׳ זאב ע״ה — Balter
ר׳ חיים ב״ר לייב ז״ל פערל בת ר׳ בייניש הערש ע״ה — Lelling
ר׳ דוב בער ב״ר אליעזר ז״ל ליבה בת ר׳ ישראל ע״ה — Zabrowsky
ר׳ נפתלי ב״ר יעקב שלמה ז״ל שרה בת ר׳ רפאל ע״ה — Schall

ARACHIN: **Chanoch and Hadassah Weisz and Family**
in memory of his father:
לעי״נ אביו ר׳ צבי ב״ר שמחה הלוי ע״ה, נפ׳ כ״ז מנחם אב תשמ״ה — Weisz
his maternal grandfather:
לעי״נ ר׳ שלמה ב״ר יצחק ע״ה, נפ׳ ה׳ סיון תש״א — Grunwald
his maternal grandmother and their children who perished in the Holocaust:
לעי״נ מרת גנדל בת ר׳ חנוך העניך ע״ה, שנהרגה עקה״ש כ״ז סיון תש״ד הי״ד — Grunwald
ולעי״נ בניהם משה ב״ר שלמה, יעקב ב״ר שלמה, יצחק ב״ר שלמה, בנימין ב״ר שלמה,
שנהרגו עקה״ש כ״ז סיון תש״ד הי״ד

and in memory of her grandparents:
לעי״נ ר׳ חייא בן חכם ר׳ רפאל ע״ה, נפ׳ כ״ד מנחם אב תשל״ה — Aryeh
וזוגתו מרת מלכה בת ר׳ אליהו ע״ה, נפ׳ י״ח טבת תשל״ד

SANHEDRIN I: **Mortimer and Barbara Klaus** **Lester and Esther Klaus**
**Arthur and Vivian Klaus**
in memory of their beloved parents
ר׳ שמשון ב״ר יעקב ע״ה באשא בת ר׳ מרדכי נתן ע״ה
**Samuel and Bessie Klaus** ע״ה
and in memory of their sister
דייזל בת ר׳ שמשון ע״ה — **Rosalie Klaus Sohn**

SANHEDRIN II: Dedicated by a fellowship of people who revere the Talmud, its sanctity and wisdom, who foster its study, and who join in helping bring its treasures to future generations, the world over.

SANHEDRIN III: **Joseph and Adina Russak**
**Dr. Leonard and Bobbee Feiner**
**Larry and Rochelle Russak**
in memory of
צבי הירש ורחל רוסק ע״ה — Mr. and Mrs. Harry Russak ע״ה
אליעזר ובריינדל דייטש ע״ה — Mr. and Mrs. Eliezer Deutsch ע״ה
יעקב ורבקה לאה פיינר ע״ה — Mr. and Mrs. Jacob Feiner ע״ה

MAKKOS: **Mr. and Mrs. Marcos Katz**
in honor of הרב אפרים לייבוש בן הרב מרדכי דוד הכהן כ״ץ שליט״א
Rabbi Ephraim Leibush Katz שליט״א

SHEVUOS: Dedicated by
**Michael and Danielle Gross**
(London)

AVODAH ZARAH I: **The Kuhl Family**
in memory of
יחיאל ב״ר יצחק אייזיק ע״ה Dr. Julius Kuhl ע״ה
פרומט בת ר׳ שמואל הלוי ע״ה Mrs. Yvonne Kuhl ע״ה
שמואל ב״ר יחיאל ע״ה Sydney Kuhl ע״ה

AVODAH ZARAH II: In memory of
**Jerome Schottenstein** ע״ה
**יעקב מאיר חיים בן אפרים אליעזר הכהן ע״ה**

HORAYOS-EDUYOS: **Woli and Chaja Stern** (Sao Paulo, Brazil)
in memory of his parents
ר׳ צבי בן ר׳ חיים הלוי ומרת מרים ז״ל – Stern
מרת דאכא בת ר׳ פרץ ומרת ברכה ע״ה — Tager
and in memory of her parents
ר׳ דוד אריה בן ר׳ יעקב ומרת שיינדל ז״ל – Brenner
מרת איטלה בת ר׳ חיים ומרת מדל ע״ה — Stern
and in memory of their mechutanim
ר׳ ישראל מרדכי ב״ר צבי יוסף סג״ל ז״ל – Landau
ר׳ יששכר טוביה ב״ר יוסף ז״ל — Weitman
ר׳ שמואל עקיבא ב״ר שלמה צבי ז״ל — Kierszenbaum
and in memory of their brother and sister-in-law
ר׳ אריה בן ר׳ צבי הלוי ומרת דאכא ע״ה – Stern
מרת זלטה פסל בת ר׳ אברהם יעקב ומרת חנה גיטל ע״ה – Stern
and in honor of their children
Jacques and Ariane Stern Jaime and Ariela Landau Michaël and Annete Kierszenbaum

ZEVACHIM I: **Mr. and Mrs. Samson Bitensky**

ZEVACHIM II: **Victor Posner**

BAVA KAMMA II: **William and Esther Bein, and**
**Joseph Hillel, Abraham Chaim Zev, and Bella Leah**
In memory of parents and grandparents
מנחם מענדל ב״ר שמואל יצחק הכהן ע״ה — Edward (Mendus) Bein ע״ה
לאה בת חיים זאב הכהן ע״ה — Ilus Hartstein Bein ע״ה
מרדכי בן יוסף ע״ה — Mordochej Szer ע״ה
בילה בת אברהם ע״ה — Baila Silber Szer ע״ה
שמואל יצחק הכהן ושרהביין ע״ה – חיים זאב הכהן ושרה הרטשטיין ע״ה
יוסף ויענטה שער ע״ה – אברהם ואסתר זילבר ע״ה

BAVA KAMMA III: **Dedicated to Klal Yisrael,**
**and particularly to the Six Million.**
הקב״ה שוכן בתוך בני ישראל והוא חד עם כנסת ישראל
*"The Holy One Blessed is He dwells among the children of Israel;*
*He and the congregation of Israel are one."* — *Tzidkas Hatzaddik* 179

BAVA METZIA I: **Drs. Robert and Susan Schulman**
**Howard and Tzila Schulman Fred and Cindy Schulman**
**and Families**
in memory of
מיכאל בן צבי הירש ע״ה ומלכה בת ר׳ יוסף ע״ה — Milton and Molly Schulman ע״ה

BAVA METZIA II: **Donald E. and Eydie R. Garlikov, and Jennifer**
in memory of beloved son and brother
צבי שלמה בן דן ע״ה — Kenneth Scott Garlikov ע״ה
and in memory of parents and grandparents
עזריאל וועלוויל ב״ר אנשיל ע״ה טשארנא בת ר׳ אריה לייב ע״ה
Irve W. and Cecelia (Kiki) Garlikov ע״ה
and in honor of parents and grandparents, brother and uncle
מרדכי ואסתר פריידל ריטטער — Marcus and Elfrieda Ritter
נפתלי חיים ריטטער — Dr. Nathaniel Ritter

BAVA METZIA III: **The David H. Gluck Foundation**
in memory of
**The Gluck Family**
זאב בן דוד צבי ע״ה ואסתר בת אשר זעליג ע״ה — Zev and Esther Gluck ע״ה
ליבא, אשר זעליג, דוד צבי, שמואל, מנשה, יחזקאל שרגא ע״ה —
Lee, George, David H., Samuel C., Emanuel M., Henry ע״ה, and
יעקב יצחק בן זאב ע״ה ומיימי בת זאב ע״ה — Dr. Jack I. and Mrs. Mae Saks ע״ה
and in memory of
זאב בן חיים דוד וחיה ביילע בת יצחק יעקב ע״ה — Wolf and Chaye Beilah Saks ע״ה
יחיאל בן משה ע״ה — Elie Neustadter ע״ה

BAVA BASRA I: In memory of
**מנחם מענדל בן אלימלך יהושע העשל ע״ה**
**חיה בת יהושע הכהן ע״ה**

BAVA BASRA II: **Paul and Beth Guez and Family**
in memory of
Felix (Mazal) Guez ע״ה

BAVA BASRA III: **Irving and Frances Schottenstein**
in honor of their beloved parents
מאיר בן יהושע הכהן ע״ה ליבא בת הרב יצחק משה ע״ה — Meyer and Libbie Schottenstein
טוביה ע״ה ויבדל״ח שיינדל תחי׳ — Tobias ע״ה and Jennie Polster תחי׳
**Melvin ע״ה and Lenore תחי׳ Schottenstein**
in honor of their beloved parents
אברהם יוסף בן יהושע הכהן ע״ה ויבדל״ח בליה זילפה בת יצחק תחי׳
Abe J. ע״ה and Bessie (Stone) תחי׳ Schottenstein
יצחק ע״ה ויבדל״ח שרה תחי׳ — Isadore J. ע״ה and Sophie תחי׳ Green

NAZIR II: **Alan and Myrna Cohen, Alison and Matthew**
in memory of
Harry and Kate Cohen ע״ה Harry and Pauline Katkin ע״ה

SOTAH: **Motty and Malka Klein**
for the merit of their children שיחי׳
Esther and Chaim Baruch Fogel Dovid and Chavie Binyomin Zvi ז״ל
Elana Leah and Natan Goldstein Moshe Yosef and Rikki Yaakov Eliyahu and Tammy
In honor of his mother שתחי׳
Mrs. Suri Klein לאוי״ט
In memory of his father
ר׳ יהודה ב״ר דוד הלוי ז״ל נפ׳ כ״ז אדר ב׳ תשס״ג – Yidel Klein
In memory of her parents
ר׳ אשר אנשיל ב״ר משה יוסף ז״ל נפ׳ ג׳ שבט תשנ״ט – Anchel Gross
שרה בת ר׳ חיים אליהו ע״ה נפ׳ כ״ד סיון תשס״א – Suri Gross
And in memory of their grandparents who perished על קידוש השם in the Holocaust
ר׳ דוד ב״ר יעקב הלוי ע״ה ופערל בת ר׳ צבי ע״ה הי״ד – Klein
ר׳ מרדכי ב״ר דוד הלוי ע״ה ולאה בת ר׳ יעקב הלוי ע״ה הי״ד – Klein
ר׳ משה יוסף ב״ר בנימין צבי ע״ה ומלכה בת ר׳ יחיאל מיכל ע״ה הי״ד – Gross
ר׳ חיים אליהו ב״ר מרדכי ע״ה ויוטא בת ר׳ שלמה אליעזר ע״ה הי״ד – Gartenberg

GITTIN I: **Mrs. Kate Tannenbaum**
**Elliot and Debra Tannenbaum Edward and Linda Zizmor**
**and Families**
commemorating the first yahrzeit of beloved husband, father and grandfather
ר׳ נפתלי ב״ר יהודה אריה ע״ה — Fred Tannenbaum ע״ה
נפטר ח׳ ניסן תשנ״ב

GITTIN II: **Richard and Bonnie Golding**
in honor of Julian and Frances Golding Lawrence Cohen and Helen Lee Cohen
and in memory of Vivian Cohen ע״ה
**Irving and Ethel Tromberg Clarence and Jean Permut**
in memory of
Benjamin and Sara Tromberg ע״ה Harry and Lena Brown ע״ה
Molly and Julius Permut ע״ה Lizzie and Meyer Moscovitz ע״ה

KIDDUSHIN I: **Ellis A. and Altoon Safdeye**
in memory of their beloved parents
המנוח יהודה אצלאן ומרת צלחה ויקטוריא ע״ה — Aslan and Victoria Safdeye ע״ה
המנוח יהודה ומרת מרגלית ע״ה — Judah and Margie Sultan ע״ה
and in memory of his brother יוסף ע״ה — Joseph Safdeye ע״ה

KIDDUSHIN II: **Mr. and Mrs. Ben Heller**
in memory of his father
יואל נתן ב״ר חיים הלוי ע״ה — Joseph Heller ע״ה
and in honor of his mother
צפורה שתחי׳ לאוי״ט בת ר׳ בנימין ע״ה — Fanya Gottesfeld-Heller שתחי׳

BAVA KAMMA I: **Yitzchok and Shoshana Ganger**
**and Children**
in memory of
ר׳ יצחק ישעיהו ב״ר שלמה זלמן ע״ה–רויזא גיטל בת ר׳ משה ע״ה — Ganger
מיכאל ב״ר אברהם מרדכי ע״ה–מרים יוכבד בת ר׳ בנימין ע״ה — Ferber
ר׳ משה דוד ב״ר יצחק זעליג מקוצק ע״ה–פיגא בת ר׳ אברהם מרדכי ע״ה — Morgenstern
ר׳ מתתיהו ב״ר שמואל דוב ע״ה–אסתר מלכה בת ר׳ אריה ליב ע״ה — Newman

YEVAMOS II: **Phillip and Ruth Wojdyslawski and Family**
In memory of her beloved mother
Chaya (Cytryn) Valt ע״ה
חיה צירל בת ר׳ שלמה זלמן ע״ה

YEVAMOS III: **Phillip and Ruth Wojdyslawski and Family**
In honor of
Benjamin C. Fishoff לאוי״ט
To the public he is a leader with vision and dedication.
To us he has always been a role model, a father,
and a constant inspiration.

KESUBOS I: **The Fishoff Families**
in memory of their beloved mother
מינדל בת ר׳ ישראל ע״ה — Mrs. Mindl Fishoff ע״ה
נפ׳ כד תשרי תשמ״ט
and in memory of their dear grandparents
Fishoff — ר׳ דוב ב״ר מנחם אשר ע״ה   מרת מירל בת ר׳ מנחם מענדל ע״ה
Neider — ר׳ ישראל ב״ר אברהם ע״ה   מרת חיה זיסא בת ר׳ שרגא פייוועל ע״ה

KESUBOS II **Arthur A. and Carla Rand**
in memory of their parents
ר׳ ישראל ב״ר צבי Rand ומרת ליבא מלכה ב״ר יהודה Marcus ע״ה
ר׳ שלמה ב״ר מרדכי יהודה Ratzersdorfer ומרת חוה ב״ר חיים Finkelstein ע״ה
and in honor of their children
Lydia M. and Lionel S. Zuckier — ר׳ אריה יהושע ב״ר אליהו דוב ומרת ליבא מלכה שיחי׳
Gigi A. and Joel A. Baum — ר׳ יואל אשר ב״ר חיים שלמה ומרת גנענדל חנה שיחי׳
Jay J. and Cyndi G. Finkel-Rand — ר׳ ישראל יהודה ומרת צפורה געלא ב״ר יצחק חיים שיחי׳
and grandchildren
דניאל יעקב, נפתלי צבי, חוה, בנימין, צפורה מרים, רחל, בתשבע Baum שיחי׳
שלמה יצחק, שירה חיה, צבי, שפרה לאה, בן ציון Zuckier שיחי׳
אליהו אריה לייב, יעקב שלמה, צבי, חסיה ליבא, מתתיהו דוד Rand שיחי׳

KESUBOS III **ישימך אלהים כשרה רבקה רחל ולאה**
**May God make you like Sarah, Rebecca, Rachel and Leah**

NEDARIM I: **Mrs. Goldy Golombeck**
**Hyman P. and Elaine Golombeck**   **Blanche B. Lerer**
**Moishe Zvi and Sara Leifer**   **Avrohom Chaim and Renee Fruchthandler**
In memory of
Morris J. Golombeck ע״ה – ר׳ משה יוסף ב״ר חיים פנחס ע״ה
and by Moishe Zvi and Sara Leifer in memory of
הרב ברוך יוסף ב״ר משה צבי ע״ה – האשה הצנועה מרים יוטא בת ר׳ לוי יצחק ע״ה
Mr. and Mrs. Baruch Leifer ע״ה

NEDARIM II: **The Rothstein Family**
In loving memory of
Warren Rothstein ע״ה – וועלוועל ב״ר יוסף ע״ה
David and Esther Rothstein ע״ה   Max and Gussie Gottlieb ע״ה
and in honor of
Howard and Beatrice Rothstein

NAZIR I: **Albert and Gail Nassi**
**Garrett A. Nassi**
**Jessica Lea Nassi**
in memory of
Samuel Nassi ע״ה
Albert and Leona Nassi ע״ה
Benjamin and Adell Eisenberg ע״ה
Arthur and Sarah Dector ע״ה

**Daniel and Susan Kane**
**Jessica, Adam and Stacey**
in memory of
Abraham and Rose Kanofsky ע״ה
Benjamin and Sophie Gornstein ע״ה
Elie and Irma Darsa ע״ה
Mack and Naomi Mann ע״ה

SUCCAH I: [continued] **Arthur and Randi Luxenberg**
in honor of their parents
Irwin and Joan Luxenberg שיחי׳ Bernard and Evelyn Beeber שיחי׳
their children Elizabeth Jewel and Jacqueline Paige שיחי׳
in memory of his grandparents
ר׳ אברהם בן אהרן מרדכי ז״ל ורחל בת ר׳ משה ע״ה — Abraham and Rose Luxenberg ע״ה
ישעיהו צבי בן הרב טוביה ז״ל ושרה צירל בת ר׳ יעקב ע״ה — Jesse and Celia Aronson ע״ה

SUCCAH II: **Thomas and Lea Schottenstein William and Amy Schottenstein**
in memory of
אריה ליב בן אפרים אליעזר הכהן ע״ה — Leon Schottenstein ע״ה
מאיר אבנר בן דוד הלוי ע״ה — Meir Avner Levy ע״ה
and in honor of
Mrs. Jean S. Schottenstein שתחי׳ Bertram and Corinne Natelson שיחי׳
Mrs. Flory Levy שתחי׳

BEITZAH: **Paul and Suzanne Peyser Irwin and Bea Peyser**
in memory of
דוד בן פינחס ע״ה פריידע רייזעל בת יהושע ע״ה — David and Rose Peyser ע״ה

ROSH HASHANAH: **Steve and Genie Savitsky David and Roslyn Savitsky**
In memory of
יואל בן אברהם ע״ה — Jerry J. Savitsky ע״ה
ישראל בן מנחם מאנעס ע״ה — Irving Tennenbaum ע״ה
שמואל בן יצחק ע״ה — George Hillelsohn ע״ה
רחל בת דוד הלוי ע״ה — Ruth Hillelsohn ע״ה
אהרן בן יהודה אריה ע״ה — Aaron Seif ע״ה

TAANIS: **David and Jean Bernstein**
**Matthew Bernstein, Owen and Kei**
**Scott and Andrea Bernstein, Samara, Jonah, and Jesse**
**Albert and Gail Nassi, Jessica and Garrett**
in memory of
Annna and Harry Bernstein ע״ה Sarah and Joseph Furman ע״ה
Mr. Samuel Nassi ע״ה

MEGILLAH: Special Commemorative Edition published in conjunction with the Sh'loshim of the patron of this edition of the Talmud
**Jerome Schottenstein ע״ה**
**יעקב מאיר חיים בן אפרים אליעזר הכהן ע״ה**

MOED KATAN: **Solomon T. and Leah Scharf**
and their children
**David and Tzipi Diamond Alexander and Naomi Scharf**
**Joseph and Lisa Scharf Dovid and Chani Scharf**
לזכרון עולם
ר׳ אליהו בן משה יעקב ע״ה — R' Eliyahu Scharf ע״ה
שרה בת אלכסנדר זיסקינד ע״ה — Sara Scharf ע״ה
ר׳ יוסף בן צבי הירש ע״ה — R' Joseph Felder ע״ה
עטיל בת מוה״ר שמעון ע״ה — Mrs. Ettel Felder-Hollander ע״ה

CHAGIGAH: **The Alvin E. Schottenstein Family**
In memory of
חיים אברהם יונה בן אפרים אליעזר הכהן ז״ל — Alvin E. Schottenstein ז״ל
יצחק אייזיק בן עקיבא הכהן ז״ל — Irving Altman ז״ל
הדס בת אברהם אביש ע״ה — Helen Altman ע״ה
שרגא פייוול בן יצחק אייזיק הכהן ז״ל — Frank Altman ז״ל

YEVAMOS I: **Phillip and Ruth Wojdyslawski and Family**
In memory of his beloved parents
Abraham Michel and Ora Wojdyslawski ע״ה
ר׳ אברהם מיכאל ב״ר פינחס ע״ה
אורה בת ר׳ צבי הירש ע״ה

PESACHIM I: **Vera and Soli Spira and Family**
in memory of
ברוך בן חיים ע״ה — Baruch Spira ע״ה
בילה בת נתן שלום ע״ה — Bella Spira ע״ה
שמואל בן אברהם ע״ה — Shmuel Lebovits ע״ה
and their respective families הי״ד who perished in the Holocaust
and in honor of
שפרה בת משה — Caroline Lebovits תחי׳

PESACHIM II: **Vera and Soli Spira and Family**
in memory of an uncle who was like a father
and a cousin who was like a brother
ישראל בן נתן שלום ע״ה — Israel Stern ע״ה
נתן שלום בן ישראל ע״ה — Noussi Stern ע״ה

PESACHIM III: **Lorraine and Mordy Sohn** **Ann and Pinky Sohn**
in memory of
ר׳ צבי ב״ר אלעזר ע״ה — Dr. Harry Sohn ע״ה
מרת הענדיל דבורה ב״ר אברהם שלמה ע״ה — Dora F. Sohn ע״ה
ר׳ יחזקאל ב״ר אליקים חנוך הלוי ע״ה — Harold Levine ע״ה
רבקה הענא בת שמעון הלוי ע״ה — Ruth Levine ע״ה
רייזל ב״ר שמשון ע״ה — Rosalie Sohn ע״ה

SHEKALIM: In loving memory of
**Mr. Maurice Lowinger ז״ל**
**ר׳ מאיר משה ב״ר בן ציון הלוי ז״ל**
נפ׳ כ״ז אדר תשס״א

YOMA I: **A. Joseph and Rochelle Stern**
**Moshe Dov, Zev, Shani, Esty, and Shaye**
in honor of their parents and grandparents
Eli and Frieda Stern שיחיו
Frida Weiss שתחי׳
and in memory of
ר׳ ישעי׳ בן ר׳ ישראל שמואל ווייס ז״ל

YOMA II: **A. Leibish and Edith Elbogen**
**and Family**
לזכר נשמות
מוה״ר אהרן בן מוה״ר יעקב קאפל עלבוגן ז״ל
וזו׳ אלטע חנה חיה מלכה בת מוה״ר חיים יצחק מאיר ע״ה
אחותי פערל עם בעלה ושבע בנים ובנות
ושלשה אחי: חיים יצחק מאיר, משה יוסף, יעקב קאפל הי״ד
בני אהרן עלבוגן שנהרגו עקד״ה
מוה״ר נתן פייטל בן מוה״ר אברהם וואלד ז״ל
וזו׳ ברכה בת מוה״ר דוד יהודה הי״ד שנאספה עקד״ה באושוויץ

SUCCAH I: **Howard and Roslyn Zuckerman** **Steven and Shellie Zuckerman**
**Leo and Rochelle Goldberg**
in memory of their parents
ר׳ פסח יהודה ב״ר יצחק אייזיק ע״ה וחוה בת ר׳ יהודה לייב ע״ה — Philip and Evelyn Zuckerman ע״ה

in honor of their children
Yisroel and Shoshana Pesi Zuckerman שיחי׳
Pesach Yehudah and Asher Anshel שיחי׳
Michael (Ezra) and Lauren Zuckerman שיחי׳
Adrianne & Shawn Meller, Elliot, & Joshua Goldberg שיחי׳

in honor of their children
Glenn and Heidi, Jamie Elle, Benjamin,
Brett and Robin, Brandon Noah, Ross and T.J. שיחי׳
and in honor of their parents
Marilyn and Aaron Feinerman שיחי׳

in memory of
ר׳ ישראל צבי ב״ר ברוך ע״ה ושיינדל בת ר׳ ישראל ע״ה — Israel and Shaindel Ray ע״ה
and in memory of Mrs. Rose Ray (Glass) ע״ה

# PATRONS OF THE TALMUD ❖ FULL-SIZE EDITION

SHABBOS II: **David and Bonnie Anfang** **Chaim and Ruthie Anfang**
**Rachel, Julie and Elliot** **Ariella Hope** **Michael Brett**
In loving memory of
Leib Anfang ע״ה — ר׳ אריה ליב ב״ר דוד אביגדור ע״ה
Barbara Anfang ע״ה — בשה לאה בת ר׳ אלימלך דוב ע״ה

**Mimi Rosenbaum** **Joseph and Sharon Prawer** **Alan and Louisa Prawer**
**Stacey and Danny** **Dovid and Natalie White** **Ruben Pinchas**
**Shlomo Haim, Sarah Meira, Yishai Shalom**
**Dena and Adam Ballew, Shlomo Gavriel, Ariella Shira, Daniella Elise**
**Alana and Meir Popowitz** **Naomi White**
In loving memory of
Pinkus and Genia Prawer ע״ה, and — ר׳ פנחס ב״ר יוסף ברוך הלוי ע״ה גילה בת אשר יונה ע״ה
Sarah Cukierman ע״ה — שרה בת שמעון ליב ע״ה

**Rabbi Eliyahu and Yehudit Fishman**
**Rivka and Zvi Silberstein and Leah** **Akiva Yitzchak Fishman**
**Rabbi Yechiel Meir and Chagit Fishman** **Rabbi Yosef and Aliza Fishman**
**Talia Chanah, Ariel Yishai and Daniel**
In loving memory of
Yosef and Rude Rivka Fishman ע״ה — ר׳ יוסף ב״ר טוביה ע״ה רודע רבקה בת ר׳ הירש מאיר ע״ה
and their children Yechiel Meir, Leah and Chanah הי״ד who perished in the Holocaust

SHABBOS III: **Stanley and Ellen Wasserman**
and their children
**Alan and Svetlana Wasserman** **Mark and Anne Wasserman**
**Neil and Yael Wasserman** **Stuart and Rivka Berger**
and families
In loving memory of
Joseph and Bess Wasserman ע״ה, and — יוסף בן דוב בער ע״ה בילא בת יעקב ע״ה
Sascha and Regina (Czaczkes) Charles ע״ה — שמריהו בן משה ע״ה רבקה בת הרב יוסף הכהן ע״ה

SHABBOS IV: לעילוי נשמות
הורינו היקרים **ר׳ לוי ב״ר יהודה הלוי ע״ה וצירל בת ר׳ מרדכי ע״ה לוינגר**
זקנינו היקרים **ר׳ יהודה ב״ר אליעזר צבי הלוי ע״ה וטלצא בת פרומט ע״ה לוינגר**
**ר׳ מרדכי ב״ר שמואל ע״ה ומלכה בת ר׳ נתן ע״ה אדלר**
אחינו **שמואל הלוי ע״ה יהודה הלוי ע״ה יהונתן הלוי הי״ד**
אחותנו **לאה בת ר׳ לוי סג״ל ע״ה ובעלה ר׳ טוביה ע״ה**
גיסינו **ר׳ מיכאל ב״ר ברוך שמואל ע״ה שוויצר ר׳ שמואל ב״ר יעקב ע״ה מיכל**
ולעילוי נשמות דודינו ודודותינו ויוצאי חלוציהם שנפטרו ושנהרגו על קידוש השם הי״ד
Dedicated by **Louis and Morris Lowinger**
**Teri Schweitzer** **Kato Michel** **Margit Baldinger** **Eva Lowinger**

ERUVIN: [two volumes] **Jerome and Geraldine Schottenstein** **Saul and Sonia Schottenstein**
**Jay and Jeanie Schottenstein** **Ann and Ari Deshe**
**Susan and Jon Diamond** **Lori Schottenstein**
in memory of
Ephraim Schottenstein ע״ה — אפרים אליעזר בן יהושע הכהן ע״ה
Anna Schottenstein ע״ה — חנה בת צבי הירש ע״ה

The Edmond J. Safra Edition of the Talmud Bavli in French,
adapted from the Schottenstein Edition, is now in progress.

**The Edmond J. Safra Edition**
is dedicated by
**Lily Safra**
in memory of her beloved husband
**Edmond J. Safra רפאל אדמון עזרא בן אסתר ע״ה**

His desire is in the Torah of HASHEM, and in His Torah he meditates day and night.
He shall be like a tree deeply rooted alongside brooks of water;
that yields its fruit in due season, and whose leaf never withers,
and everything that he does will succeed (Psalms 1:2-3).

# PATRONS OF THE TALMUD ❖ FULL-SIZE EDITION

With generosity, vision, and devotion to the perpetuation of Torah study,
the following patrons have dedicated individual volumes of the Talmud

INTRODUCTION TO THE TALMUD: **Robin and Warren Shimoff**
In honor of **Kollel Yisroel V'Shimshon** of the West Side
In memory of our parents
Lynn and Irving Shimoff
ישראל דוב בן אהרן יעקב ז״ל   חיה רבקה לאה בת אליעזר יהודה ע״ה

BERACHOS I: In memory of
**Jerome Schottenstein ע״ה**
**יעקב מאיר חיים בן אפרים אליעזר הכהן ע״ה**

BERACHOS II: **Zvi and Betty Ryzman**
**Mickey and Shelly Fenig — Aliza, Yissachar David, Batsheva, Aharon Yakov and Elazar**
**Elie and Adina Ryzman — Leora, Yonatan, Ari and Shai**
**Avi and Zahava Ryzman — Sarah Chloe and Eliana Shayna**
**Rafi and Elimor Ryzman — Ora and Nava**
In memory of
הרב יהושע השיל ב״ר חיים ז״ל נפ׳ י׳ טבת, תשס״ט — Rabbi Yehoshua Heschel Ryzman ז״ל
מרת הלינה שיינדל בת ר׳ צבי ע״ה נפ׳ ה׳ מנחם אב, תשנ״ז — Halina Shaindel Ryzman ע״ה
and in honor of Mrs. Mila Kornwasser שתחי׳
and in memory of
הרב אהרן יעקב ב״ר אליעזר ז״ל נפ׳ ז׳ תמוז, תשס״ב — Rabbi Aharon Yaakov Kornwasser ז״ל

**Malcolm and Joy Lyons**
in honour of their parents שיחי׳
Eve Lyons
Cecil and Mona Jacobs
and in memory of his father
יהודה בן גרשון ע״ה נפ׳ כ״ב שבט תשס״ג — Leopold Lyons ע״ה

SHABBOS I: **Nachshon and Bruria Minucha [Nuchi] Draiman and Family**
in memory of
הר״ר יהודה ליב מנדלקורן זצ״ל בן הר״ר צבי הי״ו
Rabbi Yehuda Leib Mandelcorn **זצ״ל** — נפטר כ׳ תמוז, תשנ״ג

---

A Hebrew edition of the Talmud Bavli is now in progress.
The Hebrew edition is dedicated by

**Jay and Jeanie Schottenstein**

and their children

**Joseph Aaron and Lindsay Brooke, Jonathan Richard, and Jeffrey Adam**

— in honor of their cherished loved ones who have left indelible marks on their own lives and the lives of countless others, as models of inspiration, generosity, integrity, and devotion to the noblest causes in Jewish life:
his parents **JEROME ז״ל AND GERALDINE SCHOTTENSTEIN**,
her parents **LEONARD AND HEDDY RABE**
and **SAUL AND SONIA SCHOTTENSTEIN**

**JAY AND JEANIE SCHOTTENSTEIN**
have a perspective that transcends time and community.
Through their dedication of these editions of the Talmud, they spread Torah study around the globe and across generations.
Multitudes yet unborn will be indebted to them for their vision and generosity.

# PATRONS OF THE SEDARIM

## THE DAVIDOWITZ FAMILY
## RENOV STAHLER ROSENWALD PERLYSKY EDITION OF SEDER NEZIKIN

is lovingly dedicated to

**Rozi and Morty Davis-Davidowitz**

builders of this dynasty

by their children and grandchildren

**Esti and Ushi Stahler**

Jamie, Danny, Duvi, Lisi, Avi, Eli, Malka and Loni

**Rivki and Lindsay Rosenwald**

Doni, Joshy, Demi, Davey and Tamar Rina

**Ruki and Kal Renov**

Tova, Tani, Eli, Ari, Yoni, Yael, Emi and Benji

**Laya and Dov Perlysky**

Ayala Malka, Tova Batsheva, Naftali Yonatan, Atara Yael, Eitan Moshe, Shira Avital, Akiva Yair, Avigail and Gavriel Yehuda

and is lovingly dedicated to the memory of our grandparents

**Emily and Nathan Selengut ע״ה**

**נפתלי ב״ר יעקב ע״ה ומלכה בת ר׳ אלתר חיים ע״ה**

## THE SCHWARTZ EDITION OF SEDER KODASHIM

is lovingly dedicated by

**Avrohom Yeshaya and Sally Schwartz**

and their children

**Ari and Daniella, Moshe, Dani, and Dovi**

in memory of their beloved parents and grandparents

**Isaac and Rebecca Jarnicki ז״ל — ר׳ יצחק ב״ר אשר ז״ל וחיה רבקה בת הרב בצלאל הירש ז״ל**

נפ׳ יג׳ תמוז תשנ״ז    נפ׳ ג׳ אדר תשס״ד

and their beloved grandmother

**Mrs. Pearl Septytor ע״ה — פערל בת ר׳ מרדכי ע״ה**

and in honor of יבלח״ט their parents and grandparents

**Rabbi and Mrs. Gedalia Dov Schwartz שליט״א**

and in memory of our grandparents

**Rabbi Eliezer and Pesha Chaya Poupko ז״ל    Abraham Schwartz ז״ל**

**Betzalel Hersh and Hendel Berliner ז״ל    Asher and Gittel Jarnicki ז״ל**

# PATRONS OF THE SEDARIM

Recognizing the need for the holy legacy of the Talmud
to be available to its heirs in their own language,
these generous and visionary patrons have each dedicated
one of the six Sedarim/Orders of the Talmud.

## THE FORMAN EDITION OF SEDER ZERAIM

is lovingly dedicated by

**Mr. and Mrs. Sam Forman, Brett and Wendy**

in memory of their beloved parents and grandparents

**Mr. and Mrs. George Forman ע״ה** **Dr. and Mrs. Morey Chapman ע״ה**

## THE HORN EDITION OF SEDER MOED

is lovingly dedicated to the memory of

**ר׳ משה מניס ב״ר יעקב יצחק ע״ה — Moishe Horn ע״ה**

נפטר ב׳ מנחם אב תשנ״ד

by his wife **Malkie**

his parents **Jacob ע״ה and Genia Horn ע״ה**

and his children

**Shimmie and Alissa**
Ari Shana Michal Tali

**Devorah and Dov Elias**
Moishe Ariella Eli Chaviva Tehilla Tova

**Shandi and Sruli Glaser**
Ruthi Jack Miri Rachelli

## THE ELLIS A. SAFDEYE EDITION OF SEDER NASHIM

is reverently dedicated to the memory of

**המנוח יהודה אצלאן ומרת צלחה ויקטוריא ע״ה**

**Aslan and Victoria Safdeye ע״ה**

and

**המנוח יהודה ומרת מרגלית ע״ה**

**Judah and Margie Sultan ע״ה**

by their children

**Ellis A. and Altoon Safdeye**

and grandchildren

**Alan Judah and Rachel Safdeye** **Joseph and Rochelle Safdeye**
**Ezra and Victoria Esses** **Michael and Bobbi Safdeye**

THE SCHOTTENSTEIN EDITION

# TALMUD BAVLI

is reverently dedicated to the memory of
the patron of this Talmud
and of countless other noble causes in Jewish life

**יעקב מאיר חיים בן אפרים אליעזר הכהן ע״ה**

נפטר ה׳ אדר ב׳ תשנ״ב

**Jerome Schottenstein ע״ה**

and to the memory of his parents

**אפרים אליעזר בן יהושע הכהן ע״ה** — נפטר ב׳ אייר תשט״ז

**חנה בת צבי הירש ע״ה** — נפטרה ט״ו מנחם אב תשט״ו

**Ephraim and Anna Schottenstein ע״ה**

by

**Geraldine Schottenstein**

**Saul and Sonia Schottenstein**

and

**Jay and Jeanie Schottenstein**

and their children

Joseph Aaron and Lindsay Brooke, Jacob Meir, Jonah Philip, Emma Blake
Jonathan Richard and Nicole Lauren, Winnie Simone, Teddi Isabella, and Allegra Giselle
Jeffrey Adam and Ariella

**Ann and Ari Deshe**

and their children

Elie Michael, David Scott, Dara Lauren, Daniel Matthew

**Susan and Jon Diamond**

and their children

Jillian Leigh, Joshua Louis, Jacob Meyer

and

**Lori Schottenstein**

# The Schottenstein Edition of the Talmud

*They never surrendered the principles of Judaism or the love of Torah that they had absorbed in Lithuania.*

This pioneering elucidation of the entire Talmud was named THE SCHOTTENSTEIN EDITION in memory of EPHRAIM AND ANNA SCHOTTENSTEIN ז"ל, of Columbus, Ohio. Mr. and Mrs. Schottenstein came to the United States as children, but they never surrendered the principles of Judaism or the love of Torah that they had absorbed in their native Lithuania. Tenacious was their devotion to the Sabbath, kashruth, and halachah; their support of needy Jews in a private, sensitive manner; their generosity to Torah institutions; and their refusal to speak ill of others.

This noble and historic gesture of dedication was made by their sons and daughters-in-law JEROME ז"ל AND GERALDINE SCHOTTENSTEIN and SAUL AND SONIA SCHOTTENSTEIN.

*Jerome left numerous memorials of accomplishment and generosity, but surely the Schottenstein Edition of the Talmud – spanning centuries – will be the most enduring.*

**With the untimely passing of JEROME SCHOTTENSTEIN ז"ל, it became our sad privilege to rededicate THE SCHOTTENSTEIN EDITION to his memory, in addition to that of his parents.**

Jerome Schottenstein ז"ל was a dear friend and inspirational patron. He saw the world through the lens of eternity, and devoted his mind, heart and resources to the task of assuring that the Torah would never be forgotten by its people. He left numerous memorials of accomplishment and generosity, but surely the SCHOTTENSTEIN EDITION OF THE TALMUD – spanning centuries – will be the most enduring.

*The Schottensteins are worthy heirs to the traditions and principles of Jerome and his parents. Gracious and generous, kind and caring, they have opened their hearts to countless causes and people.*

The Schottensteins are worthy heirs to the traditions and principles of Jerome and his parents. Gracious and generous, kind and caring, they have opened their hearts to countless causes and people. Quietly and considerately, they elevate the dignity and self-respect of those they help; they make their beneficiaries feel like benefactors; they imbue institutions with a new sense of mission to be worthy of the trust placed in them.

THE MESORAH HERITAGE FOUNDATION is proud and grateful to be joined with the Schottenstein family as partners in this monumental endeavor.

We pray that this great undertaking will be a source of merit for the continued health and success of the entire Schottenstein family, including the children and grandchildren:

JAY **and** JEANIE SCHOTTENSTEIN and their children, Joseph Aaron and Lindsay Brooke, Jonathan Richard, and Jeffrey Adam; ANN **and** ARI DESHE and their children, Elie Michael, David Scott, Dara Lauren, and Daniel Matthew; SUSAN **and** JON DIAMOND and their children, Jillian Leigh, Joshua Louis, and Jacob Meyer; and LORI SCHOTTENSTEIN.

The Schottensteins will be remembered with gratitude for as long as English-speaking Jews are nourished by the eternity of the Talmud's wisdom, for, thanks to them, millions of Jews over the generations will become closer to their heritage.

A Jew can accomplish nothing more meaningful or lasting in his sojourn on earth.

# PATRONS OF THE TALMUD ❖ DAF YOMI EDITION

BECHOROS II: **Hilda and Yitz Applbaum**
in honor of their children Aaron Jacob Ariel Tsvi Miriam Gabriella Zahava
and in memory of their deceased parents
אהרן ב״ר יהודה לייב ז״ל ומרים בת ר׳ מנחם מענדל ע״ה — Aaron and Miriam Goetz ז״ל
הרב יהושע בן הרב מנחם צבי ז״ל וטובה גיטל בת ר׳ אברהם יהושע העשיל ע״ה
Rabbi Sidney and Tovah Gertrude Applbaum ז״ל

ARACHIN: **The Brown Family**
in memory of
בעריש דוב בן מרדכי אליהו ז״ל וטובא בת אברהם ע״ה — Bernard and Tillie Tublin ז״ל
אברהם בן בעריש דוב ז״ל ומייטא בת ישראל ע״ה — Abraham and Mae Tublin ז״ל
נחום בן אברהם ז״ל — Neil Tublin ז״ל
Harry and Molly Brown ז״ל
Beatrice Geller ע״ה
Sophie Noble Scherr ע״ה

TEMURAH: **Dr. Tommy and Bernice (Hornblass) Kohn** and children
**The Kohn, Gunsburg, Eisenberger, Hornblass and Dushey Families**
**Dr. Allan and Susan Seidenfeld** and their children
**Mordechai and Shaindy Aaron and Dassi Dov and Chanala Yosef and Ahuva**
**Josh and Ahuva Eli and Esti**
in memory of
דניאל בן מרדכי ז״ל (נפ׳ י״ט אב תשס״ח) — Daniel Rubinstein ז״ל
מינדל בת חיים ע״ה (נפ׳ כ״ה אדר ב׳ תשס״ג) — Vera Rubinstein ע״ה
ר׳ שמחה ב״ר שלמה ז״ל (נפ׳ ביום שב״ק ב׳ אדר תשע״ב) — Salomon Seidenfeld ז״ל
חיה מירל בת אברהם ע״ה (נפ׳ כ״ה מרחשון תש״ס) — Margit Seidenfeld ע״ה
ר׳ שלמה יהודה בן ר׳ משה הכהן ז״ל (נפ׳ י״א אייר תשע״ה) — Eugene Kohn ז״ל
ליבא בת אשר אנשל ע״ה (נפ׳ ה׳ ניסן תשע״ח) — Eva Kohn ע״ה
בלימה רבקה אדל בת דניאל ע״ה (נפ׳ ז׳ ניסן תשס״ז) — Annie Kohn ע״ה

KEREISOS: לעילוי נשמת מיסד ורוח החיים של רעיון הדף יומי
**הגאון הרב ר׳ מאיר ב״ר יעקב שמשון שפירא זצ״ל** נפ׳ ז׳ חשון תרצ״ד
In memory of **Rabbi Meir Shapiro זצ״ל, the Lubliner Rav**
whose revolutionary Daf Yomi initiative grows day by day.

ME'ILAH, TAMID, MIDDOS, KINNIM: **Steven and Renée Adelsberg**
**Sarita and Rubin Gober** **Israel Joseph and Menachem Yechezkel**
**David and Joclyn Sammy Avi**
in loving memory of
שמואל שמעלקא ב״ר גדליה ז״ל — Samuel Adelsberg ז״ל
and יבלח״ט in honor of
Helen Adelsberg Weinberg שתחי׳
and Chaim and Rose Fraiman שיחי׳

NIDDAH I: In memory of
**Joseph and Eva Hurwitz ע״ה**
**יוסף ב״ר מרדכי הלוי וחוה פיגא ב״ר אליעזר הלוי ע״ה**
and **Lorraine Hurwitz Greenblott — לאה בילא חיה בת ר׳ יוסף ע״ה**
by Marc and Rachel Hurwitz,
Elisheva Ruchama, Michal, and Nechama Leah;
Martin and Geraldine Schottenstein Hoffman,
Jay and Jeanie Schottenstein, Ann and Ari Deshe,
Susan and Jon Diamond, and Lori Schottenstein;
and Pam and Neil Lazaroff, Frank Millman, and Dawn and Avi Petel

NIDDAH II: In memory of
**Jerome Schottenstein ע״ה**
**יעקב מאיר חיים בן אפרים אליעזר הכהן ע״ה**

---

**Malcolm and Joy Lyons**
in loving memory of her father זיסל בן אברהם דוד ז״ל — Cecil Jacobs ז״ל
and in honor of their parents שיחי׳ — Leo and Eve Lyons Mona Jacobs

ZEVACHIM II: **Abbie Spetner**

**Ari and Chaya** **Sara and Dovi Nussbaum** **Chanoch** **Moshe**
**Rivkah Dinah** **Moshe Yosef**
in honor of their father and grandfather
Kenneth Spetner שיחי׳ לאוי״ט
and in memory of their mother and grandmother
רבקה דינה בת ר׳ משה יעקב ע״ה — Rita Spetner ע״ה
נפ׳ ד׳ ניסן תשס״ב

ZEVACHIM III: **Yaakov and Yona Spinner**

**Dovi** **Elisheva** **Yitzy** **Shiri** **Leora** **Gavriel**
in memory of their father and grandfather
אפרים יצחק ב״ר אברהם ז״ל — Ephraim Spinner ז״ל
נפ׳ י״ז שבט תשנ״ז
and in memory of their grandparents and great-grandparents
משה יודה בן דוד ע״ה רחל בת חיים דוד יהודה הכהן ע״ה
אברהם בן יוסף משה ע״ה צירל בת אברהם אליהו ע״ה
משה שלמה בן יעקב ע״ה רבקה בת משה ע״ה

MENACHOS I: **Terumah Foundation**

MENACHOS II: **Terumah Foundation**

MENACHOS III: **Terumah Foundation**

CHULLIN I: **Rabbi Heshie and Rookie Billet**

in honor of our children Dassi and Daniel Jacobson David and Anouche Billet
Avraham and Chana Billet Shira and Steven Exler Moshe and Rebecca Billet
Nava and Daniel Teger
our grandchildren Miriam Tehila, Aharon Ariel, Yehuda Akiva, Netanel Yedidya, Noam Ezra, and Elichai Yonah Jacobson Ora Zisl, Ellie Haya, Yonina Talya, and Nava Peninah Billet
Aliza Miriam, Yehuda Yaakov, Yael Tamar, Yonatan Michael, Temima Perel, and Menachem Billet
Ilan Shmuel and Talya Adirah Exler
and in memory of our parents
ר׳ אהרן ב״ר יצחק הכהן כ״ץ ז״ל — Arthur Katz ז״ל
פיגא בת דוד יעקב ע״ה — Phyllis Katz ע״ה
ר׳ יהודה יעקב ב״ר אברהם ז״ל — Jack Billet ז״ל
פעריל מינדעל בת אלחנן חנא ע״ה — Pearl Billet ע״ה
their daughter מרים רות ע״ה — Miriam Rus ע״ה
their granddaughter אליענה שרה ע״ה — Eliana Sara ע״ה

CHULLIN II: **The Kleinman Family**

לעילוי נשמות their parents and grandparents
ר׳ אברהם אייזיק ב״ר אלכסנדר ז״ל — Avrohom Kleinman ז״ל
מרת עטיא בת הר׳ אלימלך ע״ה — Ethel Kleinman ע״ה
ר׳ אלכסנדר ב״ר צבי אריה הי״ד
ומרת סימא לאה בת ר׳ אברהם ע״ה – הי״ד
הרב אלימלך ב״ר ישראל הי״ד
ומרת יוטא ברכה בת ר׳ אברהם ע״ה – הי״ד
ר׳ מנחם דוד ב״ר מרדכי שמואל ז״ל

CHULLIN III: **Members of the International Board of Governors of the Mesorah Heritage Foundation**

as a source of merit for all our brethren wherever they are

CHULLIN IV: **Terumah Foundation**

BECHOROS I: **Jeff and Leslie Gould** **Jody and Sheldon Hirst**

**Rachel** **Jacob** **Marci** **Tracy**
in memory of their father
ראובן בן יוסף ע״ה — Rubin Gould ע״ה

SANHEDRIN I: **Martin and Rivka Rapaport**
and their children
**Mordechai Ezriel Yehuda Aryeh Miriam Dreizel Shimshon**
**Leah Penina Eliyahu Meir Bracha**
in memory of
ר׳ יהודה אריה ב״ר מרדכי הכהן ז״ל — Leo Rapaport ז״ל

SANHEDRIN II: **Martin and Rivka Rapaport**
and their children
**Mordechai Ezriel Yehuda Aryeh Miriam Dreizel Shimshon**
**Leah Penina Eliyahu Meir Bracha**
in memory of
ר׳ ישראל דוב ב״ר מרדכי ז״ל — Albert Berger ז״ל
חנה גיטל בת ר׳ עזריאל ע״ה — Chana Gittel Berger ע״ה

SANHEDRIN III: **Marvin and Roz Samuels**
in memory of
ר׳ צבי יוסף ב״ר יצחק ז״ל — Joseph Samuels ז״ל
רחל בת ר׳ זכריה מנחם ע״ה — Rose Samuels ע״ה
of Scranton, PA
בנימין נח ב״ר ישראל הלוי ז״ל — Norman Newman ז״ל
אלטאביילא ראשקה בת נחמן הלוי ע״ה — Ruth Newman ע״ה

SHEVUOS: **Michael and Danielle Gross** (Herzlia and London)
in loving memory of their parents
Paul Gross — פסח בן צבי הלוי ע״ה
Marta Gross — מרים בת גרשון ע״ה
David Beissah — דוד בן נתן ע״ה
and in honor of
Edith Beissah

MAKKOS: **The Tepper Families**
**Beth and Yisroel Rabinowitz Jay and Sari Tepper**
**Hope and Moshe Abramson Neil and Leah Tepper**
and children
in honor of their parents
**David and Joan Tepper**
and in memory of their grandparents
ר׳ מנחם מענדל ב״ר יעקב ז״ל ומרת מינדל בת ר׳ אריה ליב ע״ה — Tepper
ר׳ ראובן ב״ר נחמיה ז״ל ומרת עטיל בת ר׳ ישראל נתן נטע ע״ה — Gralla

AVODAH ZARAH I: **The Kuhl Family**
in memory of
יחיאל ב״ר יצחק אייזיק ע״ה Dr. Julius Kuhl ע״ה
פרומט בת ר׳ שמואל הלוי ע״ה Mrs. Yvonne Kuhl ע״ה
שמואל ב״ר יחיאל ע״ה Sydney Kuhl ע״ה

AVODAH ZARAH II: In memory of
**Jerome Schottenstein ע״ה**
**יעקב מאיר חיים בן אפרים אליעזר הכהן ע״ה**

HORAYOS-EDUYOS: **Woli and Chaja Stern** (Sao Paulo, Brazil)
in honor of their children
Jacques and Ariane Stern Jaime and Ariela Landau Michäel and Annete Kierszenbaum

ZEVACHIM I: **Robin and Warren Shimoff**
in memory of his parents
ישראל דוב ב״ר אהרן יעקב ז״ל — Irving Shimoff ז״ל
חיה רבקה לאה בת ר׳ אליעזר יהודה ע״ה — Lynn Shimoff ע״ה
and יבלח״ט in honor of their children שיחיו
Lael and Jonathan Seplowitz Atara and David Kramer Alexander Ariana

BAVA KAMMA III: **Robert and Malka Friedlander** (Sao Paulo, Brazil)
**Debby, David and Daniel**
in memory of their fathers and grandfathers
הרב ישראל יעקב ב״ר יצחק מאיר ז״ל — Rabbi Israel Jacob Weisberger ז״ל
הרב נפתלי צבי נח ב״ר יהודה ז״ל — Rabbi Bela Friedlander ז״ל

BAVA METZIA I: **Drs. Robert and Susan Schulman** **Howard and Tzila Schulman**
**Fred and Cindy Schulman**
dedicated to our beloved parents
**Milton ז״ל and Molly ע״ה Schulman**
**Stanley and Ruth Beck שיחי׳**
**Albert ז״ל and Sylvia תחי׳ Kuhr**
**Naftali שיחי׳ and Berta ע״ה Rendel**

BAVA METZIA II: **Suzy and Yussie Ostreicher**
**Ilana and Menachem Ostreicher** **Miriam and Dovid Ostreicher**
**Shayna and Yitzchok Steg** **Ricki and Michoel Lopiansky**
in memory of our parents and grandparents
**Michael and Rose Pollack ע״ה**
**Hershi Ostreicher ז״ל**
and יבלח״ט in honor of our mother and grandmother
**Helly Ostreicher שתחי׳**

BAVA METZIA III: **Stephanie and George Saks**
in memory of
**The Gluck Family**
זאב בן דוד צבי ע״ה ואסתר בת אשר זעליג ע״ה – Zev and Esther Gluck ע״ה
ליבא, אשר זעליג, דוד צבי, שמואל, מנשה, יחזקאל שרגא ע״ה –
Lee, George, David H., Samuel C., Emanuel M., Henry ע״ה, and
in memory of their parents and grandparents
פייוועל בן אליה ע״ה ומלכה בת אברהם ע״ה – Philip and Mildred Pines ע״ה
יעקב יצחק בן זאב ע״ה ומיימי בת זאב ע״ה – Dr. Jack I. and Mrs. Mae Saks ע״ה
זאב בן חיים דוד ע״ה וחיה ביילע בת יצחק יעקב ע״ה – Wolf and Chaye Beilah Saks ע״ה
and in memory of
יחיאל בן משה ע״ה – Elie Neustadter ע״ה

BAVA BASRA I: **Nachum and Malkie Silberman**
in memory of his parents
ר׳ צבי ב״ר זאב הלוי ז״ל דבורה אסתר בת ר׳ ישראל ע״ה — Silberman
his paternal grandparents and their children who perished על קידוש השם in the Holocaust
ר׳ זאב ב״ר משה הלוי ז״ל הי״ד גיטל בת ר׳ אפרים אלימלך הכהן ע״ה הי״ד — Silberman
ובנותיהם רחל, לאה, ומרים ע״ה הי״ד
and his maternal grandparents
ר׳ ישראל ב״ר לוי משה ז״ל שיינדל רחל בת ר׳ יעקב ע״ה — Weitman

BAVA BASRA II: **Roger and Caroline Markfield**
and their children
**Eric** and **Maxine**
in memory of his parents
מרדכי ב״ר נתנאל ואודל בת ר׳ מאיר דוד ז״ל — Max and Eileen Markfield ז״ל
and his sister
זיסל ע״ה — Lynn Herzel ע״ה

BAVA BASRA III: **Jaime and Marilyn Sohacheski**
in honor of their children and grandchildren
**Jasmine and Dovid Brafman**
**Melisa and Jonathan Beck**
**Lindsay and Steven Turk**
**Benyamin and Suri Sohacheski**

SOTAH: **Motty and Malka Klein and Family**
In memory of
ר׳ ישעי׳ נפתלי הירץ ב״ר אהרן ז״ל – Norman Newman

GITTIN I: **Mrs. Kate Tannenbaum**
**Elliot and Debra Tannenbaum Edward and Linda Zizmor**
**and Families**
in memory of beloved husband, father and grandfather
ר׳ נפתלי ב״ר יהודה אריה ע״ה — Fred Tannenbaum ע״ה
נפטר ח׳ ניסן תשנ״ב

GITTIN II: **Mrs. Kate Tannenbaum**
**Elliot and Debra Tannenbaum Edward and Linda Zizmor**
**and Families**
in memory of beloved husband, father and grandfather
ר׳ נפתלי ב״ר יהודה אריה ע״ה — Fred Tannenbaum ע״ה
נפטר ח׳ ניסן תשנ״ב

KIDDUSHIN I: **Leslie and Shira Westreich**
and our children
**Adam and Dayna Westreich Ezra and Rayna Rosenzweig Daniel and Dina Lieberman**
**Joshua and Julie**
in honor of our Rosh Yeshiva
HaGaon Harav Shmuel Kamenetsky שליט״א
and in memory of our parents and grandparents
הרב יהושע בן מו״ר הרה״ג יוסף יאסקא ז״ל — Rabbi Yehoshua and Gerda Westreich ז״ל
מרת גיטל בת זאב וואלף ע״ה
ר׳ יצחק בן משה ז״ל
מו״ר הרה״ג רב יוסף יאסקא בן בן ציון יצחק אב״ד קאנטשוגא ז״ל הי״ד
מרת סרקא בת הרה״ג אלעזר אב״ד היבניו ע״ה הי״ד
ר׳ זאב וואלף בן ר׳ יונה ז״ל
מרת איטא הענע בת ר׳ אריה לייב ע״ה

KIDDUSHIN II: In honor of our dear parents
**Rav Berish and Hannah Fuchs**
and in memory of our grandmother and great-grandmother
**"Bobby" Serena (Molly) Fuchs**
by their children
**Dovy and Devory Freund — Sury, Chavy, Shmuly, Ruchy, Lippy, and Leiby**
**Shabse and Tova Fuchs — Goldie Tehila, Miriam Yehudis, Yehuda Boruch, and Risi**
**Gadi and Aliza Fuchs — Shmuel, Fay Fay, Mimi, and Ariella**
**Dovid and Miriam Ostreicher — Yocheved, Shabsi, Shmuel, Raizy, Rikki, and Sarah**
**Yoily and Shaindy Edelstein — Miri, Aryeh, Shmuli, Raizy, and Yaakov**

BAVA KAMMA I: **Yitzchok and Shoshana Ganger**
in honor of their children and grandchildren
Aviva and Moshe Sigler — Aliza Saul Chani Ari Perri
Ilana and Menachem Ostreicher — Dov Ber Miriam Binyomin Paltiel Raizy Aryeh Leib Esti
Dovid and Penina Ganger — Yosef Yaakov Gavriel Moshe Ettie Aryeh Leib Tzipora Baila Eliyahu
Daniella — Batsheva Esther
and in memory of their parents
ר׳ יוסף יעקב ב״ר יצחק ישעיהו ע״ה — Joseph Ganger ע״ה
נפטר ט״ז כסלו תשנ״ז
הרב אריה ליב ב״ר מתתיהו ע״ה — Rabbi Aria Leib Newman ע״ה
נפטר כ״ח ניסן תשס״ד
אסתר פערל בת הרב משה דוד ע״ה — Pearl Newman ע״ה
נפטר ט״ו שבט תש״ע

BAVA KAMMA II: **The Magid Families** (Sao Paulo, Brazil)
לעילוי נשמת — in memory of their dear husband and father
ר׳ אברהם יהודה אביר בן ר׳ יהושע ז״ל — R' Abir Magid ז״ל
נלב״ע כ״ו אדר תשמ״ב
ולעילוי נשמות — and in memory of
ר׳ יהושע ב״ר צבי חיים ז״ל וזוגתו מרת שרה פייגא בת ר׳ ישׂשכר דוב ע״ה
ר׳ יעקב ישראל ב״ר מרדכי ז״ל וזוגתו מרת אסתר פרומה בת ר׳ חיים ע״ה

YEVAMOS II: **Phillip and Ruth Wojdyslawski and Family**
In memory of her beloved mother
Chaya (Cytryn) Valt ע״ה
חיה צירל בת ר׳ שלמה זלמן ע״ה

YEVAMOS III: **Phillip and Ruth Wojdyslawski and Family**
In honor of
Benjamin C. Fishoff לאוי״ט
To the public he is a leader with vision and dedication.
To us he has always been a role model, a father,
and a constant inspiration.

KESUBOS I: **The Fishoff Families**
in memory of their beloved mother
מינדל בת ר׳ ישראל ע״ה — Mrs. Mindl Fishoff ע״ה
נפ׳ כד תשרי תשמ״ט
and in memory of their dear grandparents
Fishoff — ר׳ דוב ב״ר מנחם אשר ע״ה מרת מירל בת ר׳ מנחם מענדל ע״ה
Neider — ר׳ ישראל ב״ר אברהם ע״ה מרת חיה זיסא בת ר׳ שרגא פייוועל ע״ה

KESUBOS II: **Moise & Angie Hendeles Hayim & Miriam Hendeles Jerry & Cecille Cohen**
and their families
in memory of their beloved parents and grandparents
אליעזר ב״ר משה ז״ל — Lazare Hendeles ז״ל
נפ׳ כ׳ ניסן ד׳ חוה״מ פסח תשס״א
מזל־טוב בת שלמה פינחס הכהן ע״ה — Moselle Hendeles ע״ה
נפ׳ ט״ו כסלו תשע״ח

KESUBOS III: **Brenda and Isaac Gozdzik**
**Tova Chava Tzeryl Leah**
in memory of their beloved parents and grandparents
שרגא פייוועל בן משה הענדעלעס ז״ל — Fred Hendeles ז״ל
נפ׳ ה׳ אלול תשס״ג
ביילע בת אליהו הלוי פערשלייסער ע״ה — Betty Hendeles ע״ה
נפ׳ כ״ו בניסן תשנ״ט

NEDARIM I: **Fradie Rapp**
**Raizy, Menachem, Shimshon, Bashie, Tzvi**
in memory of their beloved husband and father
הרב ישראל בן יעקב ז״ל — David Rapp ז״ל
נפ׳ כ׳ מרחשון תשס״ד

NEDARIM II: In memory of
**Laurence A. Tisch**
לייבל בן אברהם ע״ה

NAZIR I: **Andrew and Nancy Neff**
**Abby and Adi Isaacs — Nesanel Simcha, Daniel Yisrael, Baruch, and Miriam Esther Isaacs**
**Esther and Jonah Mermelstein Barnet and Devora Neff Philip**
in memory of our mother and grandmother
לאה מרים בת ישראל ע״ה — Lucy Rabin ע״ה
נפ׳ י״ד סיון תשס״ז
and in honor of our parents and grandparents
Alan and Joyce Neff
Sidney Rabin

NAZIR II: **Andrew and Nancy Neff**
**Abby and Adi Isaacs — Nesanel Simcha, Daniel Yisrael, Baruch, and Miriam Esther Isaacs**
**Esther and Jonah Mermelstein Barnet and Devora Neff Philip**
in honor of our brothers and sisters
Garth and Valerie Heald
Lauren Neff
Douglas and Vivian Rabin
Andrew and Liat Rabin

YOMA I: **Mrs. Ann Makovsky**
**Shmulie and Daryle Spero and children**
**Reuven and Dvora Makovsky and children**
**Leslie and Linda Spero and children**
in memory of
משה דוד בן אברהם אשר ז״ל – Morris Makovsky ז״ל
אברהם אשר בן משה דוד ז״ל ופרומא דבורה בת אלחנן דוב ע״ה – Abraham Osher and Fanny Makovsky ז״ל
גמליאל בן שלמה ז״ל ורבקה בת אברהם חיים ע״ה – Meyer and Riva Nissen ז״ל

YOMA II: **Trudy and David Justin**
and their children
**Daniel, Brandel, Nina, Adam and Ayala Justin**
in honor of their parents and grandparents
Malka Karp תחי׳
Kitty and Zoltan Justin שיחיו
and in loving memory of
צבי בן דוב ז״ל – Hersh Karp ז״ל

SUCCAH II: **Reuven and Ruth Fasman and Family**
**Rudolph and Esther Lowy and Family**
**Allan and Ettie Lowy and Family**
in memory of their parents
מרדכי אריה בן ר׳ רפאל הלוי ז״ל – Marcus Lowy ז״ל
מינדל בת ר׳ שלמה זלמן ע״ה – Mina Lowy ע״ה

TAANIS: **David and Jean Bernstein**
**Matthew Bernstein, Owen and Kei**
**Scott and Andrea Bernstein, Samara, Jonah, and Jesse**
**Albert and Gail Nassi, Jessica and Garrett**
in memory of
Annna and Harry Bernstein ע״ה   Sarah and Joseph Furman ע״ה
Mr. Samuel Nassi ע״ה

MEGILLAH: In memory of
**Jerome Schottenstein ע״ה**
**יעקב מאיר חיים בן אפרים אליעזר הכהן ע״ה**

MOED KATAN: In honor of our beloved parents
**Jochanan שיחי׳ לאוי״ט and Barbara ע״ה Klein** (Sao Paulo, Brazil)
by their children
**Leon and Olga Klein   Allen and Sylvia Klein   Daniel and Esther Ollech and Families**

CHAGIGAH: **Benzi and Esther Dunner**
in memory of their grandparents
החבר ר׳ אורי יהודה ז״ל ב״ר אברהם אריה הכהן הי״ד – Reb Uri Cohen ז״ל
נפ׳ באמשטרדם כג כסלו תשס״א
מרת רבקה ע״ה בת ר׳ יצחק הי״ד – Mrs. Rivka Cohen ע״ה
נפ׳ באמשטרדם יב מרחשון תשס״א
הרה״צ ר׳ משה ב״ר שרגא פייבעל הי״ד – Reb Moshe Stempel הי״ד
נהרג על קדה״ש ד׳ מנחם אב תש״ב

YEVAMOS I: **Phillip and Ruth Wojdyslawski and Family**
In memory of his beloved parents
Abraham Michel and Ora Wojdyslawski ע״ה
ר׳ אברהם מיכאל ב״ר פינחס ע״ה
אורה בת ר׳ צבי הירש ע״ה

# PATRONS OF THE TALMUD ❖ DAF YOMI EDITION

PESACHIM I: **Tommy and Judy Rosenthal**
**Yitzchok and Tamar** **Dani and Michali** **Michal and Avi Orzel** and their children
in memory of our parents
Yitzchok and Magda Rosenthal ז"ל — ר' יצחק ב"ר יעקב קאפיל ז"ל מחלה בת אשר זעליג ע"ה
Moshe Yaakov Jakabovits ז"ל — ר' משה יעקב בן ר' אברהם יצחק הכהן ז"ל
and in honor of our mother יבלח"ט
Beila Jakabovits שתחי' עמו"ש

PESACHIM II: **Yisroel and Rochi Zlotowitz**
**Gitty, Aaron and Sori**
in memory of their beloved grandparents and great grandparents
Zlotowitz — הרב אהרן ב"ר מאיר יעקב זצ"ל והרבנית פרומא בת ר' חיים צבי ע"ה
Schulman — ר' חיים חייקל ב"ר שמואל ז"ל וחיה בת הרב ישראל יהודה ע"ה
Maybloom — הרב משה יהודה ב"ר יצחק צבי ז"ל ושרה בת הרב שבתי ע"ה
Goldman — החבר שלום בן שבתי ז"ל וגיטל בת החבר פינחס צבי ע"ה

PESACHIM III: **Lorraine and Mordy Sohn** **Ann and Pinky Sohn**
in memory of
Dr. Harry Sohn ע"ה — ר' צבי ב"ר אלעזר ע"ה
Dora F. Sohn ע"ה — מרת הענדיל דבורה ב"ר אברהם שלמה ע"ה
Harold Levine ע"ה — ר' יחזקאל ב"ר אליקים חנוך הלוי ע"ה
Ruth Levine ע"ה — רבקה הענא בת שמעון הלוי ע"ה
Rosalie Sohn ע"ה — רייזל ב"ר שמשון ע"ה

SHEKALIM: **Laibish and Tanya Kamenetsky**
in memory of his parents
Max and Brenda Kamenetsky ז"ל — מרדכי בן משה צבי הלוי ז"ל ובראנשע בת צבי הערש ע"ה
in memory of her father
David Gottesman ז"ל — דוד פישל בן יחיאל מאיר ז"ל
and in memory of their grandparents
Kamenetsky — משה צבי בן מרדכי הלוי ז"ל וצירל בת זעליג ע"ה
Berman — צבי הערש ז"ל וחיה לאה בת לייביש אליהו ע"ה
Bolag — משה בן ישראל ז"ל ורעכיל בת משה בונם ע"ה
Gottesman — יחיאל מאיר בן שמואל ושרה בת יהודה דוב ע"ה

BEITZAH: **Eric and Joyce Austein**
and their children
**Ilana and Avi Tobias** **Michael and Aliza**
**Jonathan and Ilana Miriam** **Adam and Sara** **Eytan and Elizabeth**
in honor of their parents and grandparents שיחי'
Morris ע"ה and Susi Austein שתחי'
Leo and Shirley Schachter

ROSH HASHANAH: **Steve and Genie Savitsky**
and their children and families
**Julie and Shabsi Schreier** **Avi and Cheryl Savitsky**
**Penina and Zvi Wiener** **Yehuda and Estie Berman**
In honor of their mothers and grandmothers
Mrs. Hilda Savitsky שתחי' Mrs. Amelia Seif שתחי'
And in honor of their grandparents
Mrs. Faye Raitzik שתחי' Max and Edith Grunfeld שתחי'
לעילוי נשמות — And in loving memory of their grandparents
Shabsi Raitzik ע"ה — ר' שבתי בן ר' מיכאל הלוי ע"ה
Sigmund and Regina Schreier ע"ה — ר' אשר זעליג בן ר' יהושע הלוי ע"ה רבקה בת ר' משה נתן ע"ה
Irving and Goldie Stein ע"ה — ר' ישראל יצחק בן ר' אלימלך הכהן ע"ה גולדה בת ר' דוד לייב ע"ה
Sam and Rose Gottlieb ע"ה — ר' שמואל סנדר בן ר' אליעזר ליפא ע"ה ריזל זלדה בת ר' שלום קלמן ע"ה
Harry and Goldie Wiener ע"ה — ר' צבי הירש בן ר' נחום ע"ה חיה שרה גאלדא בת ר' יוסף ע"ה
And in loving memory of Cheryl Savitsky's father
Dr. Steven F. Stein ע"ה — ר' שמעון פייביש בן ר' ישראל יצחק הכהן ע"ה

# PATRONS OF THE TALMUD ✧ DAF YOMI EDITION

With generosity, vision, and devotion to the perpetuation of Torah study,
the following patrons have dedicated individual volumes of the Daf Yomi Edition of the Talmud

INTRODUCTION TO THE TALMUD: **Robin and Warren Shimoff**
In honor of **Kollel Yisroel V'Shimshon** of the West Side
In memory of our parents Lynn and Irving Shimoff
ישראל דוב בן אהרן יעקב ז״ל   חיה רבקה לאה בת אליעזר יהודה ע״ה

BERACHOS I: In memory of **Jerome Schottenstein ע״ה**
**יעקב מאיר חיים בן אפרים אליעזר הכהן ע״ה**

BERACHOS II: **Zvi and Betty Ryzman**
and their children
**Mickey and Shelly Fenig — Aliza, Yissachar David, Batsheva, Aharon Yakov and Elazar**
**Elie and Adina Ryzman — Leora, Yonatan, Ari and Shai**
**Avi and Zahava Ryzman — Sarah Chloe and Eliana Shayna**
**Rafi and Elimor Ryzman — Ora and Nava**
In memory of
**Hagaon Harav Meir Shapiro זצ״ל**, the unforgettable Rav of Lublin,
and in honor of
**Chief Rabbi Hagaon Harav Yisrael Meir Lau שליט״א**

SHABBOS I: **Dr. Paul and Esther Rosenstock**   **Jake and Dr. Helaine Harman**
**Mrs. Faigy Harman**
and their children and grandchildren
**Nechama   Mordechai   Binyamin**   **Michelle   Marc**
**Yonina and Dov Wisnicki, Avi and Leora**
**Shira and Shlomie Rosenberg**
in memory of our father, husband, and grandfather
מרדכי ב״ר אברהם ע״ה — Mordechai (Mottel) Harman

SHABBOS II: **Stanley and Ellen Wasserman**
and their children
**Alan and Svetlana Wasserman   Mark and Anne Wasserman**
**Neil and Yael Wasserman   Stuart and Rivka Berger**
and families
In loving memory of
יוסף בן דוב בער ע״ה   בילא בת יעקב ע״ה — Joseph and Bess Wasserman ע״ה, and
שמריהו בן משה ע״ה   רבקה בת הרב יוסף הכהן ע״ה — Sascha and Regina (Czaczkes) Charles ע״ה

SHABBOS III: **Stanley and Ellen Wasserman**
and their children
**Alan and Svetlana Wasserman   Mark and Anne Wasserman**
**Neil and Yael Wasserman   Stuart and Rivka Berger**
and families
in loving memory of
יוסף בן דוב בער ע״ה   בילא בת יעקב ע״ה — Joseph and Bess Wasserman ע״ה, and
שמריהו בן משה ע״ה   רבקה בת הרב יוסף הכהן ע״ה — Sascha and Regina (Czaczkes) Charles ע״ה

SHABBOS IV: **Malkie and Nachum Silberman**
**Leonard and Cassia Friedlander**
**Elkie Friedlander**
in memory of their parents
ר׳ סיני ב״ר אריה לייב ורבקה גיטל בת ר׳ יוסף דוד ז״ל — Sidney and Gussie Friedlander ז״ל
and in memory of their grandparents
ר׳ יוסף דוד ב״ר משה ז״ל וזיסל בת ר׳ ישעיהו ע״ה — Joseph and Jennie Trattner ז״ל

ERUVIN: [two volumes] **Jerome and Geraldine Schottenstein   Saul and Sonia Schottenstein**
**Jay and Jeanie Schottenstein   Ann and Ari Deshe**
**Susan and Jon Diamond   Lori Schottenstein**
in memory of
אפרים אליעזר בן יהושע הכהן ע״ה — Ephraim Schottenstein ע״ה
חנה בת צבי הירש ע״ה — Anna Schottenstein ע״ה

THE SCHOTTENSTEIN DAF YOMI EDITION

# TALMUD BAVLI

This edition — in a convenient new size
to serve the growing number of people
who are making the Talmud an indispensable part of their lives —
is dedicated by

**Jay and Jeanie Schottenstein**

and their children

**Joseph Aaron and Lindsay Brooke**

**Jacob Meir, Jonah Philip, and Emma Blake**

**Jonathan Richard and Nicole Lauren**

**Winnie Simone, Teddi Isabella, and Allegra Giselle**

**Jeffrey Adam and Ariella**

They dedicate it in honor of their cherished loved ones
who have left indelible marks on their own lives
and the lives of countless others,
as models of inspiration, generosity, integrity,
and devotion to the noblest causes of Jewish life.

They are:
his parents

**Jerome ע״ה and Geraldine Schottenstein**

her parents

**Leonard and Heddy Rabe**

and their uncle and aunt

**Saul and Sonia Schottenstein**

**Jay and Jeanie Schottenstein**

have a perspective that transcends time and community.
Their names have become synonymous with
imaginative and effective initiatives
to bring Torah study and Jewish tradition to the masses of our people.

Through their magnanimous support of the various editions of

**The Schottenstein Talmud**

— this Daf Yomi Edition, the Hebrew Edition,
and the original full-size English Edition —
they spread Torah study around the globe and across generations.
Few people have ever had such a positive impact on Jewish life.
Myriads yet unborn will be indebted to them
for their vision and generosity.

The publishers pay tribute to
the memory of the unforgettable

**Jerome Schottenstein ז״ל**

whose wisdom, warmth, vision, and generosity wrote new chapters
of Jewish life and learning in America and around the world.
Generations from now, he will be remembered as the one
whose enlightened support made the Talmud accessible
to English-speaking Jews everywhere;

**Geraldine Schottenstein תחי׳**

who wears her mantle with unusual grace
and firm adherence to the values with which she set
the strong foundation of her family.
She sets a powerful and principled example
for her children and grandchildren.
We are grateful for her support and that of her children:

**Jay and Jeanie Schottenstein,**
**Ann and Ari Deshe,**
**Susan and Jon Diamond,**
and **Lori Schottenstein,**

friends from the start,
as staunch supporters who have been instrumental
in the ten years of the Talmud's success.
They bring energy, devotion, magnanimity, and graciousness
to a host of vital causes
in their native Columbus and throughout the world.

*Dedication of the*

DAF YOMI EDITION

This volume is dedicated to
our beloved parents

**Milton ז״ל and Molly ע״ה Schulman**
**Stanley and Ruth Beck שיחי׳**
**Albert ז״ל and Sylvia תחי׳ Kuhr**
**Naftali שיחי׳ and Berta ע״ה Rendel**

Their values, integrity, and dedication
guarantee the survival of the Torah nation.

Whatever we are,
it is because of their example, vision, and sacrifice,
and if we and our children have succeeded
in repaying them with a modicum of nachas,
it is but a small installment of a debt
that can never be fully repaid.

May the countless hours of Torah study
that will radiate from this volume
be a constant source of merit for them,
and for their adoring children,
grandchildren and great-grandchildren.

**Robert and Susan Schulman**
**Howard and Tzila Schulman**
**Fred and Cindy Schulman**
**and Families**

*Dedication of the*

## FULL-SIZE EDITION

This Volume is dedicated to the memory of

# Milton and Mollie Schulman ז״ל

## מיכאל בן צבי הירש ז״ל

נפטר י״א כסלו תשנ״ב

## מלכה בת יוסף ע״ה

נפטרה י׳ אייר תשס״ג

מצוה גדולה להיות בשמחה תמיד
It is a great mitzvah to be joyous, always

They were a model couple — a shining example
of love and marriage and a life well lived.

They were totally devoted to their family and one another,
always together in thought and deed.
They weathered adversity with humor and dignity,
always looking forward, generously forgiving and forgetting.
They energetically pursued chessed and continuous growth in Torah and mitzvos. They lived a life of modesty, honesty, and integrity.

For the joy of having each other, their family, and their abundant nachas,
they were always grateful to Hashem.

And we are grateful that their legacy continues to inspire us.

**תנצב״ה**

**Robert and Susan Schulman**

**Joshua and Tzipora Wolff**
Yaakov Michoel, Meira, Adina and Tzvi

**Shalom and Tamar Rosner**
Yehoshua, Avigayil Bracha, Avraham Yitzchak, Naama Ora, Michoel, Eliyahu Yehuda and Chananya Dovid

**Ariel Yosef and Andrea Schulman**
Eitan and Noam Michael

**Howard and Tzila Schulman**

**Jonathan and Aliza Hollander**
Gavriel

**Yossie and Elisheva Schulman**
Racheli, Michoel, Adina, Moshe, Mali and Riki

**Sulky and Shira Reischer**
Yechiel, Michoel, Yael Golda and Charlie

**Isaac and Alana Schulman**
Ruth, Oliver, Millie and Davis

**Elie and Andrea Schulman**
Goldie, Leah and Malkie

**Shanie and Dovid Warman**
Nachman Dov, Tzvi Yehudah and Sheva Rachel

**Fred and Cindy Schulman**

**Eitan and Naomi Aghbashoff**
Malka, Yehuda Dovid, Shira and Devora

**Michal and Shmuel Carrey**

**Joshua**

**Dovid and Miriam Schulman**
Malka Leeba and Tzvi

**Mark**

A PROJECT OF THE

Mesorah Heritage Foundation

We gratefully acknowledge the outstanding
Torah scholars who contributed to this volume:
**Rabbi Mordechai Kuber** and
**Rabbis Avraham Berman, Yehezkel Danziger,
Hillel Danziger, Yosef Davis, David Fohrman, Eliezer Herzka,
Nesanel Kasnett, Henoch Morris, Abba Zvi Naiman,
Israel Schneider, Feivel Wahl, Chaim Weinfeld,**
together with
**Rabbis Chanany Greenwald, Tzvi Horowitz
Eliyahu Shulman,** and **Yosaif Asher Weiss**
**Rabbi Hersh Goldwurm** and **Rabbi Yisroel Simcha Schorr**
reviewed and commented on the entire manuscript.
**Rabbi Yehezkel Danziger**
is the Editorial Director of this project.

FULL-SIZE EDITION
*First Impression . . . September 1992*
DAF YOMI EDITION
*First Impression . . . January 2005*
SECOND EDITION
*Twelve Impressions . . . October 2000 — April 2016*
THIRD EDITION
*Eight Impressions . . . July 2016 — October 2022*

*Published and Distributed by*
**MESORAH PUBLICATIONS, Ltd.**
313 Regina Avenue / Rahway, N.J. 07065

*Distributed in Europe by*
**LEHMANNS**
Unit E, Viking Business Park
Rolling Mill Road
Jarrow, Tyne & Wear NE32 3DP
England

*Distributed in Israel by*
**SIFRIATI / A. GITLER — BOOKS**
POB 2351
Bnei Brak 51122

*Distributed in Australia & New Zealand by*
**GOLDS WORLD OF JUDAICA**
3-13 William Street
Balaclava, Melbourne 3183
Victoria Australia

*Distributed in South Africa by*
**KOLLEL BOOKSHOP**
Northfield Centre, 17 Northfield Avenue
Glenhazel 2192, Johannesburg, South Africa

**THE ARTSCROLL® SERIES / SCHOTTENSTEIN DAF YOMI EDITION**
**TALMUD BAVLI / TRACTATE BAVA METZIA VOL. I**


ITEM CODE: DTBM1
ISBN 10: 1-57819-637-X
ISBN 13: 978-1-57819-637-1

*Typography by Compuscribe at* ArtScroll Studios, Ltd.
Custom bound by **Sefercraft, Inc.**, Rahway, NJ

# The Schottenstein Daf Yomi Edition

# TALMUD

**THE GEMARA:** THE CLASSIC VILNA EDITION,
WITH AN ANNOTATED, INTERPRETIVE ELUCIDATION,
AS AN AID TO TALMUD STUDY

The Hebrew folios are reproduced from
the newly typeset and enhanced
OZ VEHADAR Edition of the Classic Vilna Talmud

Published by
Mesorah Publications, ltd

# תלמוד בבלי

## מהדורת דף היומי

# BAVLI

THE DAVIDOWITZ FAMILY
RENOV STAHLER ROSENWALD PERLYSKY EDITION OF SEDER NEZIKIN

# מסכת בבא מציעא
# TRACTATE BAVA METZIA

VOLUME I

Elucidated and edited by a team of scholars
under the General Editorship of
Rabbi Hersh Goldwurm זצ"ל

# THE SCHOTTENSTEIN DAF YOMI EDITION

# תלמוד בבלי

# TALMUD BAVLI

## מהדורת דף היומי

The ArtScroll Series®

THE DAVIDOWITZ FAMILY
RENOV STAHLER ROSENWALD PERLYSKY EDITION OF SEDER NEZIKIN

## מסכת בבא מציעא

## TRACTATE BAVA METZIA

TALMUD BAVLI
תלמוד בבלי